The National Hockey League

Official Guide & Record Book 2002

HOCKEY FIGHTS CANCER

NHL HockeyRules

SALT LAKE 2002

THE NATIONAL HOCKEY LEAGUE
Official Guide & Record Book/2002

Compiled by the NHL Public Relations Department and the 30 NHL Club Public Relations Directors.

Printed in Canada.

Published in Canada by:
Dan Diamond and Associates, Inc, 194 Dovercourt Road, Toronto, Ontario M6J 3C8 Canada
ISBN in Canada 0-920445-75-6

Published in the United States by:
Total Sports Publishing Inc., 100 Enterprise Drive, Kingston, NY 12401
ISBN in USA 1-930844-34-4

Staff

For the NHL: Dave McCarthy, Denise Gomez; Supervising Editor: Greg Inglis; Statistician: Benny Ercolani; Editorial Staff: David Keon, Jackie Rinaldi, Kelley Rosset, Chris Tredree, Julie Young.

Managing Editor: Ralph Dinger
Photo Editor: Eric Zweig
Assistant Editors: Paul Bontje, Jonathan Zweig
Player Register Editor: James Duplacey
Production Editors: John Pasternak, Alex Dubiel
European Statistical Consultant: Patrick Houda

Contributors: Ken Anderson, Mark Bartschat (CIAU), Heiko Behrens, Steven M. Black, Bob Borgen, Paul R. Carroll Jr., Steve Cherwonak (WPHL), Diana Danforth (ECHL), Michael deMaine (WCHL), Denis Demers (QMJHL), Bob Duff, Gene Dupras, Peter Fillman, Ernie Fitzsimmons, Mel Foster, Pierre Genest, Dan Gognavic, Steve Hagwell (ECAC), Lloyd Hamshaw (WHL), Hockey Hall of Fame, Mary Hutchinson (WCHL), Seppo Kittila, Len Kotylo, Sean Kraback (IHL), Dana Lapierre, Eric Lavigne, Eric Leblanc, Roger Leblond, Manon Gagnon Leroux (QMJHL); Dave Lord (CHL), John MacKinnon (CHA), Al Mason, Kathy McAdam (Vancouver), Christopher McDonald, Penny McEwen, Herb Morell (OHL), NHL Broadcasters' Association, NHL Central Registry, NHL Players' Association, Joseph Nieforth, John Norlin, Nicole Norris (IHL), John D. Painter (NCAA), Becky Pasternak, Brenda Pasternak, Stephanie Pasternak, John Paton, Gary J. Pearce, Amy Pickett (CentralHL), Valentina Riazanova, Ron Rumball, Minako Saki, Robert Schultz, Sherry Skalko (CCHA), Ralph Slate, Noah Smith (Hockey East), Doug Spencer (WCHA), David Stewart-Candy, Bret Stothart (AHL), Andrew Szabo, U.S. Hockey Hall of Fame, Laurie Wheeler (Calgary), William Wolper (UHL).

Publisher: Dan Diamond

Data Management and Typesetting: Caledon Data Management, Hillsburgh, Ontario
Film Output and Scanning: Stafford Graphics, Toronto, Ontario
Printing: vistainfo, Scarborough, Ontario
Production Management: Dan Diamond and Associates, Inc., Toronto Ontario

Photo Credits

NHL Images: Anita Cechowski.

Photographers: Graig Abel, Toronto; Marc Archambault, Montreal; Scott Audette, Tampa Bay; Steve Babineau; Greg Bartram/Better Image, Columbus; Bruce Bennett Studios; Andrew D. Bernstein/Andrew Bernstein Associates, Los Angeles; David Bier; Joe Black; Mark Buckner, St. Louis; J. Bushey, Vancouver; Scott Cunningham, Atlanta; Gregg Forwerck, Carolina; Barry Gossage, Phoenix; Jon Hayt, Tampa Bay; J. Henson Photographics, Mark A. Hicks/Action Image, Detroit; Hockey Hall of Fame Collections; Glenn James, Dallas; Bruck Kluckhohn, Minnesota; Robert Laberge, Montreal; Mitchell Layton, Washington; Jim Leary; Richard C. Lewis, Florida; V.J. Lovero, San Jose; D. MacMillan, Calgary; Silvia Pecota; Andre Pichette, Montreal; Mike Polk, Pittsburgh; Len Redkoles, Philadelphia; Debora Robinson, Anaheim and San Jose; John Russell, Nashville; Robert Shaver, Slapshot Photo, Chicago; Don Smith, San Jose; Diane Sobolewski; Teckles/McElligott Sports Focus Imaging, Ottawa; Sandra Tenuto, Phoenix; Gerry Thomas, Calgary and Edmonton; Jim Turner, Jeff Vinnick, Vancouver; Bill Wippert, Buffalo, Dale Zanine, Atlanta.

Distribution

Trade sales and distribution in Canada by:
North 49 Books, 35 Prince Andrew Drive, Toronto, Ontario M3C 2H2
416/449-4000; FAX 416/449-9924

Dan Diamond and Associates, Inc., 194 Dovercourt Road, Toronto, Ontario M6J 3C8
416/531-6535; FAX 416/531-3939 e-mail: dda.nhl@sympatico.ca

Trade sales and distribution in the United States by:
Publishers Group West, 1700 Fourth Street, Berkeley, CA 94710

International representatives:
Barkers Worldwide Publications, Unit 6/7 The Elms Centre, Glaziers Lane, Normandy, Guildford, Surrey GU3 2DF England
Tel: 011/441/483/811-971 and FAX: 011/441/483/811-972 e-mail: sales@bwpu.demon.co.uk website: www.bwpu.demon.co.uk

Dan Diamond and Associates books may be purchased for educational, business or sales promotional use.
For information please write to: Dan Diamond and Associates, 194 Dovercourt Road, Toronto, Ontario M6J 3C8 Canada
e-mail: dda.nhl@sympatico.ca

The National Hockey League
1251 Avenue of the Americas, 47th Floor, New York, New York 10020-1198
1800 McGill College Ave., Suite 2600, Montreal, Quebec H3A 3J6
50 Bay Street, 11th Floor, Toronto, Ontario M5J 2X8

Table of Contents

Table of Contents *continued*

(2001-02 NHL Schedule begins inside front cover)

Introduction

WELCOME TO *THE NHL OFFICIAL GUIDE & RECORD BOOK 2002.* This is the 70th edition of a book that traces its roots back to a 140-page vest-pocket sized edition that cost twenty-five cents and had the grand title *National Hockey Guide and Record Book Containing Rules and Records of All Leagues 1932-33*. The book's editor was Jim Hendy who would later be inducted into the Hockey Hall of Fame for his statistical innovations and for his efforts as an executive in minor professional hockey. The NHL published its first *Press and Radio Guide* in 1947-48 under the editorship of Ken McKenzie who was also the founder of "The Hockey News." Hendy's work was combined with the official NHL edition beginning in 1951-52 when the first player register was published by the NHL. This edition was 208 pages in length and sold for one dollar. Over the next 30 years, the book grew to accomodate the increasing number of teams and players in the NHL. The first color photo on the cover appeared in 1969-70 and showed the Bruins and Canadiens. The book's editor was statistician Ron Andrews who had taken on the task in 1963-64. Computerization of statistics was first introduced in 1970, improving accuracy and speed. As the NHL grew to 21 teams in 1979-80, the *NHL Guide* kept getting thicker, topping out at 872 pages in 1980-81. For ease of use, the publication was split into two volumes in 1982-83, but this proved to be confusing to reporters, broadcasters and scouts who used the books every day.

A major redesign took place in 1984-85 when today's big-page format was introduced. The first "big Guide" (properly titled the *NHL Official Guide & Record Book*) spanned 352 pages and incorporated everything that was contained in earlier volumes plus 300 photographs. The NHL began another cycle of expansion when the San Jose Sharks began play in 1991-92, so the book began to grow to accommodate new teams, players from Eastern Europe and additional features. New statistical categories and a small photo of every NHL player and goaltender were added in 1999-2000 when the book surpassed 600 pages for the first time. Today we are at 640 pages. A combination of upgraded statistical tracking, e-mail correspondents throughout the hockey world and internet research enable us to obtain more information all the time. After 70 seasons in the big leagues, *The NHL Official Guide & Record Book*'s task remains unchanged: to provide comprehensive statistical coverage of the National Hockey League, its players and top prospects in minor pro, European, junior or college leagues and conferences. Thank you for your support through the years.

The 2002 edition contains two special features. Men's and women's 2002 Olympic hockey schedules are found on page 13. The Olympic experience of every active NHL player and goaltender is listed along with the results and medal counts from all previous Games. The career of superstar defenseman and 2001 Stanley Cup winner Raymond Bourque is saluted on page 229.

Records, rosters and management for each NHL club begin on page 19. Readers will note a change in how team data is presented: overtime losses are included in each club's Year-By-Year Record and All-Time Record vs. Other Clubs. Overtime Losses (abbreviated OL or, if space permits, OTL) are no longer included in a team's loss total. Therefore W+L+T+OTL=GP. In 1999-2000, the first season in which a loser in overtime received a point in the standings, this was not the case. Beginning with this edition, the 1999-2000 standings (page 159) have been modified to incorporate today's standard. Also note that overtime losses are only reflected in team statistics. Goaltender and coaching statistics do not include OTLs.

This edition's Player Register begins on page 275 with a Prospect Register made up of active forwards and defensemen who have yet to play in the NHL. Players in the Prospect Register either have been recently drafted, signed as free agents or invited to training camp by NHL clubs.

The NHL Player Register begins on page 338. It includes active forwards and defensemen who have appeared in an NHL regular-season or playoff game at any time. We continue to include the following new statistical categories, listed from left to right as they appear in a player's panel: power-play goals (PP), shorthand goals (SH), game-winning goals (GW), shots on goal (S), percentage of shots that score (%), plus-minus rating (+/–), total faceoffs taken (TF*), faceoff winning percentage (F%*), hits (H*), shots blocked (SB*) and average time-on-ice per game played (Min*). Categories marked with an asterisk (*) are NHL Real-Time statistics gathered by teams of trained spotters who, working with laptop computers and custom software, record hits, shots blocked, faceoff wins, etc. "on-the-fly" at each game. These statistics were kept officially for the first time in 1998-99, so no player in this year's *NHL Guide* has more than three years of Real-Time statistics.

New enhancements to player panels include notes for all NHLers who missed more than 41 games due to injury and for those players who terminated their college hockey careers to turn pro. As well, major junior trades completed since the 2000 Memorial Cup have been added.

The order of the Registers is as follows: Prospect, NHL Player, Goaltender (page 575), Retired Player (601) and Retired Goaltender (633).

A key to the abbreviations and symbols used in individual player and goaltender data panels, along with useful information on how to use the Registers, is found on page 337. Late additions to the Registers are found on page 274 along with a list of abbreviations used for league names . Each NHL club's minor-pro affiliates are found on page 18.

As always, our thanks to readers, correspondents and members of the media who take the time to comment on the *Guide & Record Book*. Thanks as well to the people working in the communications departments of the NHL's member clubs and to their counterparts in minor pro, junior, college and European hockey.

Best wishes for an enjoyable 2001-02 NHL season.

ACCURACY REMAINS THE *GUIDE & RECORD BOOK*'S TOP PRIORITY.

We appreciate comments and clarification from our readers. Please direct these to:

- James Duplacey — Player Register Editor, 194 Dovercourt Road, Toronto, Ontario M6J 3C8. e-mail: jj.nhl@sympatico.ca.
- Greg Inglis — 47th floor, 1251 Avenue of the Americas, New York, New York 10020-1198 . . . or . . .
- David Keon — 50 Bay Street, 11th Floor, Toronto, Ontario, M5J 2X8

Your involvement makes a better book.

NATIONAL HOCKEY LEAGUE

Established November 22, 1917

New York, 1251 Avenue of the Americas, 47th Floor, New York, NY 10020-1198, 212/789-2000, Fax: 212/789-2020, PR Fax: 212/789-2080
Montréal, 1800 McGill College Avenue, Suite 2600, Montréal, Québec, H3A 3J6, 514/841-9220, Fax: 514/841-1070
Toronto, 50 Bay Street, 11th Floor, Toronto, Ontario, M5J 2X8, 416/981-2777, Fax: 416/981-2779
NHL Enterprises, L.P. — 1251 Avenue of the Americas, 47th Floor, New York, NY 10020-1198, (212) 789-2000, Fax: (212) 789-2020
NHL Enterprises Canada, L.P. — 50 Bay Street, 11th Floor, Toronto, Ontario, M5J 2X8, 416/981-2777, Fax: 416/981-2779
NHL Productions — 183 Oak Tree Road, Tappan, NY 10983-2809, 845/365-6701, Fax: 845/365-6010

Executive

Commissioner	Gary B. Bettman
Executive Vice President & Chief Legal Officer	William Daly
Executive Vice President & Director of Hockey Operations	Colin Campbell
Executive Vice President & Chief Operating Officer	Jon Litner
Executive Vice President & Chief Financial Officer	Craig Harnett
Director, Administration & Executive Assistant to the Commissioner	Debbie Jordan

Administration

Director of Administration	Debbie Jordan
Director, Human Resources	Janet Meyers
Director, Offices & Facilities	Andrew Crawford
Manager, Human Resources	Patrice Distler

Broadcasting/Scheduling

Vice President, Broadcasting & Programming	Adam Acone
Director, Television Production & Technology	Onnie Bose
Director, NHL Radio	Brian G. Hamilton
Manager, Business & Special Events	Phyllis DeCongilio
Manager, Television Production & Operations	Stacie Watkins
Vice President, Scheduling, Operations & Research (Montreal)	Steve Hatze Petros
Director, Research & Scheduling	Mark Erlichson
Manager, Scheduling & Operations	William Bredin

NHL Productions

Executive Producer	Ken Rosen
Vice President	Patti Fallick
Coordinating Producer	Darryl Lepik
Executive Director	Ben Nygaard
Director, Operations/Footage	Peg Walsh
Producers	Janice Arbour, Michele Giordano-Moore, Gary Waksman
Associate Producers	Robert Lekhwani, Warren Rogan
Senior Editors	Chip Swain, Nick Mascolo
Senior Production Manager	Christine Cortez
Manager, Video Services	Chris Cesa

NHL Images

Director	Anita Cechowski

Communications

Group Vice President, Communications	Bernadette Mansur
Vice President, Media Relations	Frank Brown
Vice President, Public Relations & Media Services (Toronto)	Gary Meagher
Chief Statistician (Toronto)	Benny Ercolani
Director, Communications	Jamey Horan
Director, Community Relations	Ken Martin
Director, Media Relations	Amy Early
Director, News Services	Greg Inglis
Senior Manager, Player Publicity	Sandra Carreon
Manager, Corporate Communications	Brian Walker
Manager, Community Relations	Ann Marie Lynch
Manager, Diversity Task Force	Nirva Milord
Manager, News Services	Adam Schwartz
Managers, Public Relations (Toronto)	David Keon, Chris Tredree
Associate, Public Relations (Toronto)	Julie Young

Events and Entertainment

Group Vice President	Frank Supovitz
Senior Director	Ken Chin
Directors	Sammy Choi, Bill Miller
Senior Manager	Susan Aglietti
Managers	Danny Frank, Kimberly Guarachi, Dean Matsuzaki, Greta Palmer, Chie Sakuma

Finance

Executive Vice President & Chief Financial Officer	Craig Harnett
Senior Vice President, Finance	Joseph DeSousa
Vice President, Finance and Office Manager (Montreal)	Olivia Pietrantonio
Director, Financial Systems	Belinda Haeberlein
Director, Finance	Lowell Heit
Corporate Controller	Kenneth Cartisano

Hockey Operations

Executive Vice President & Director of Hockey Operations	Colin Campbell
Senior Vice President, Hockey Operations (Toronto)	Jim Gregory
Vice President, Hockey Operations (Toronto)	Mike Murphy
Hockey Operations Manager	Claude Loiselle
Vice President & Managing Director, Central Registry (Toronto)	Stephen Pellegrini
Assistant Director, Central Registry (Montreal)	Madeleine Supino
Project Manager, Central Registry (Toronto)	Sean MacLeod
Director, Central Scouting (Toronto)	Frank Bonello
Director of Officiating (Toronto)	Andy VanHellemond
Director of Alumni Relations (Toronto)	Patrick Flatley
Video Director	Damian Echevarrieta
Video Coordinator (Toronto)	Paul Brighty
Ice Consultant	Dan Craig
Consultant	Dave Dryden

Information Technology

Vice President, Information Technology	Peter DelGiacco
Assistant Director (Montreal)	Luc Coulombe
Director, Network Services	Patrick Powers
Director, Technical Services	John Ho
Manager, RTSS Support	Dan O'Neill

Legal

Executive Vice President & Chief Legal Officer	William Daly
Senior Vice President, General Counsel	David Zimmerman
Deputy General Counsel	Julie Grand
Associate Counsel	Daniel Ages
Contract Administrator	Magdale L. Labbe

Pension

Vice President and Managing Director, Pension (Montreal)	Yvon Chamberland
Controller, Pension (Montreal)	Mary Skiadopoulos
Manager, Pension (Montreal)	Lise de Jocas

Security

Vice President, Security	Dennis Cunningham
Director, Security	Joseph Caporicci

Television and Media Ventures

Senior Vice President, Television and Media Ventures	Doug Perlman
Vice President, Television & Business Affairs	Leslie Gittess
Director, Team Television & Business Affairs	John Tortora
Director, NHL Center Ice & Program Development	Ken Gelman
Manager, NHL Center Ice & Media Ventures	Peter Aquilone

NHL Interactive CyberEnterprises (NHL ICE)

President, NHL ICE & Senior Vice President, New Business Development	Keith Ritter
Vice President, Editorial & Production	Richard Libero
Vice President, Revenue & Administration	Ken Nova
Director, Technology & Operations	Grant Nodine

NHL Enterprises

President, NHL Enterprises	Ed Horne

Consumer Products Marketing

Group Vice President, Consumer Products Marketing	Brian Jennings
Vice President, Consumer Products Marketing (Toronto)	Glenn Wakefield
Senior Director, Consumer Products Marketing	James Haskins
Director, Retail Sales, Canada (Toronto)	Barry Monahan
Director, Center Ice Program and Sporting Goods	Lloyd Haymes
Director, Consumer Products Marketing, Canada (Toronto)	Karen Hanson
Director, Entertainment Products	Dave McCarthy
Director, Non-Apparel	Judith Salsberg
Director, Retail Sales	Cathy Groves
Manager, Youth Licensing	Rachel Podradchik

Club Marketing

Vice President, Club Marketing	Scott Carmichael
Manager	Maryann Thorgrimson
Coordinator	Tammy Levine

Corporate Marketing

Vice President, Corporate Marketing	Andrew Judelson
Directors	Ian Lasher, Susan Rosenfeld
Director, Canada (Toronto)	Laurie Kepron
Managers	Jean Marie Cesare, Eustace King, David Levy, Chris Long, Chris Petrie
Manager, Canada (Toronto)	Mark Leno

Creative Services

Associate Director, Creative Services	Kathy Drew

Fan Development

Vice President, Fan Development	Alysse Soll
Director, Off-Ice Programs	Brian Mullen
Managers	Roy Edmondson, Felicia Sass, Suzanne Sherman

Finance

Vice President, Finance, NHL Enterprises	Mary McCarthy
Director, Finance	Scott Weinfeld
Director, Accounting Operations	Deborah Corletta

International

Group Vice President & Managing Director, NHL International	Ken Yaffe
Senior Director, International Business Operations	Frank Nakano
Director, International Marketing	Kamini Sharma
Director, International Broadcasting	Susanna Mandel-Mantello
Director, International Licensing & Special Projects	Lynn White
Manager, International Marketing & Olympic Planning	Michael Rolnick

NHLE Legal and Business Affairs

Executive Vice President & General Counsel	Richard Zahnd
Vice President & Associate General Counsel	Mary Sotis
Vice President, Licensing and Trademark Compliance	Ruth Gruhin
Vice President & Corporate Counsel	Robert Hawkins
Senior Counsels	Tom Prochnow, Yvette Quinson
Associate Counsel	Matthew Kline
Staff Attorneys	Jason Camhi, Michael Gold
Director, Contract Administration	Heather Atria
Director, Quality Control	Catherine O'Brien
Intellectual Property Administrator	Alison Nunez

Strategic Development

Vice President, Strategic Development	Susan Cohig

BOARD OF GOVERNORS

Chairman of the Board – Harley N. Hotchkiss

Mighty Ducks of Anaheim

Tony Tavares .... Governor
Michael D. Eisner .... Alternate Governor
Pierre Gauthier .... Alternate Governor
Rick Schlesinger .... Alternate Governor

Atlanta Thrashers

Stan Kasten .... Governor
Don Waddell .... Alternate Governor

Boston Bruins

Jeremy M. Jacobs .... Governor
Louis Jacobs .... Alternate Governor
Harry J. Sinden .... Alternate Governor
Jeremy M. Jacobs, Jr. .... Alternate Governor
Charles M. Jacobs .... Alternate Governor
Mike O'Connell .... Alternate Governor

Buffalo Sabres

John J. Rigas .... Governor
Timothy J. Rigas .... Alternate Governor
Michael J. Rigas .... Alternate Governor
James P. Rigas .... Alternate Governor
Ed Hartman .... Alternate Governor
Darcy Regier .... Alternate Governor
Kevin Billet .... Alternate Governor

Calgary Flames

Harley N. Hotchkiss .... Governor
Byron J. Seaman .... Alternate Governor
Ken King .... Alternate Governor
N. Murray Edwards .... Alternate Governor
Grant A. Bartlett .... Alternate Governor

Carolina Hurricanes

Peter Karmanos, Jr. .... Governor
Jim Rutherford .... Alternate Governor
Jason Karmanos .... Alternate Governor
Jim Cain .... Alternate Governor

Chicago Blackhawks

William W. Wirtz .... Governor
John A. Ziegler, Jr. .... Alternate Governor
Robert J. Pulford .... Alternate Governor
Peter R. Wirtz .... Alternate Governor

Colorado Avalanche

E. Stanley Kroenke .... Governor
Donald M. Elliman, Jr. .... Alternate Governor
Pierre Lacroix .... Alternate Governor

Columbus Blue Jackets

John H. McConnell .... Governor
John P. McConnell .... Alternate Governor
John S. Christie .... Alternate Governor
Doug MacLean .... Alternate Governor

Dallas Stars

Thomas O. Hicks .... Governor
James R. Lites .... Alternate Governor
Robert Gainey .... Alternate Governor

Detroit Red Wings

Michael Ilitch .... Governor
Jay A. Bielfield .... Alternate Governor
Jim Devellano .... Alternate Governor
Atanas Ilitch .... Alternate Governor
Christopher Ilitch .... Alternate Governor
Denise Ilitch .... Alternate Governor
Ken Holland .... Alternate Governor

Edmonton Oilers

Cal Nichols .... Governor
Kevin Lowe .... Alternate Governor
Gordon Buchanan .... Alternate Governor
Patrick R. LaForge .... Alternate Governor

Florida Panthers

William A. Torrey .... Governor
Alan Cohen .... Alternate Governor
David Epstein .... Alternate Governor

Los Angeles Kings

Timothy J. Leiweke .... Governor
Philip F. Anschutz .... Alternate Governor
David Taylor .... Alternate Governor

Minnesota Wild

Robert O. Naegele, Jr. .... Governor
Jac Sperling .... Alternate Governor

Montréal Canadiens

George N. Gillett, Jr. .... Governor
Pierre Boivin .... Alternate Governor
Fred Steer .... Alternate Governor

Nashville Predators

Craig Leipold .... Governor
David Poile .... Alternate Governor
Jack Diller .... Alternate Governor
Terry London .... Alternate Governor

New Jersey Devils

Lou Lamoriello .... Governor
Harvey Schiller .... Alternate Governor
Michael Gilfillan .... Alternate Governor

New York Islanders

Charles B. Wang .... Governor
Sanjay Kumar .... Alternate Governor
Michael J. Picker .... Alternate Governor
Roy E. Reichbach .... Alternate Governor
William M. Skehan .... Alternate Governor

New York Rangers

James L. Dolan .... Governor
Kenneth W. Munoz .... Alternate Governor
Glen Sather .... Alternate Governor

Ottawa Senators

Roderick M. Bryden .... Governor
Roy Mlakar .... Alternate Governor

Philadelphia Flyers

Edward M. Snider .... Governor
Bob Clarke .... Alternate Governor
Ronald K. Ryan .... Alternate Governor
Philip I. Weinberg .... Alternate Governor

Phoenix Coyotes

Steve Ellman .... Governor
Wayne Gretzky .... Alternate Governor
Shawn Hunter .... Alternate Governor

Pittsburgh Penguins

Kenneth Sawyer .... Governor
Craig Patrick .... Alternate Governor
Thomas J. Rooney .... Alternate Governor
Ronald Burkle .... Alternate Governor
Anthony Liberati .... Alternate Governor

St. Louis Blues

William J. Laurie .... Governor
Richard C. Thomas .... Alternate Governor
Mark Sauer .... Alternate Governor
Larry Pleau .... Alternate Governor
Brent P. Karasiuk .... Alternate Governor

San Jose Sharks

George Gund III .... Governor
Gordon Gund .... Alternate Governor
Irvin A. Leonard .... Alternate Governor
Greg Jamison .... Alternate Governor
Dean Lombardi .... Alternate Governor

Tampa Bay Lightning

Thomas S. Wilson .... Governor
Ronald J. Campbell .... Alternate Governor
Jay H. Feaster .... Alternate Governor

Toronto Maple Leafs

Steve A. Stavro .... Governor
Brian P. Bellmore .... Alternate Governor
Ken Dryden .... Alternate Governor
Richard Peddie .... Alternate Governor

Vancouver Canucks

John E. McCaw, Jr. .... Governor
Stanley B. McCammon .... Alternate Governor
Brian P. Burke .... Alternate Governor
David M. Nonis .... Alternate Governor
David Cobb .... Alternate Governor

Washington Capitals

Richard M. Patrick .... Governor
Ted Leonsis .... Alternate Governor
Jonathan Ledecky .... Alternate Governor
George McPhee .... Alternate Governor

Commissioner and League Presidents

Gary B. Bettman

Gary B. Bettman took office as the NHL's first Commissioner on February 1, 1993. Since the League was formed in 1917, there have been five League Presidents.

NHL President	Years in Office
Frank Calder	1917-1943
Mervyn "Red" Dutton	1943-1946
Clarence Campbell	1946-1977
John A. Ziegler, Jr.	1977-1992
Gil Stein	1992-1993

Hockey Hall of Fame

BCE Place
30 Yonge Street
Toronto, Ontario M5E 1X8
Phone: 416/360-7735
Executive Fax: 416/360-1501
Resource Center Fax: 416/360-1316
www.hhof.com

Bill Hay – Chairman and Chief Executive Officer
Jeff Denomme – President, Chief Operating Officer and Treasurer
Craig Baines – Director, Marketing and Facility Services
Ron Ellis – Director, Public Affairs and Assistant to the President
Ray Paquet – Creative Director, Exhibit Development
Phil Pritchard – Director, Hockey Operations and Curator
Craig Campbell – Manager, Resource Center and Archives
Peter Jagla – Producer, New Media and E-Business
Jan Barrina – Manager, Special Events and Hospitality
Kelly Massé – Manager, Corporate and Media Relations
Tim McWilliams – Manager, Retail Services
Craig Beckim – Manager, Merchandising
Jackie Boughazale – Manager, Attractions Services and Group Sales
Anthony Fusco – Manager, Information Systems
Sandra Walters – Controller and Office Manager
Pearl Rajwanth – Executive Assistant, President

National Hockey League Players' Association

777 Bay Street, Suite 2400
Toronto, Ontario M5G 2C8
Phone: 416/313-2300
Fax: 416/313-2301
www.nhlpa.com

Robert W. Goodenow – Executive Director and General Counsel
Ted Saskin – Senior Director, Business Affairs and Licensing
Mike Gartner – Director, Business Relations
Kenneth Kim – Director, Marketing
Ian Pulver, Ian Penny, Roland Lee – Associate Counsels
Mike Ouellet – Associate Counsel, Licensing
Eric Weisz – Manager, Licensing and International Business
Greg Dick – Senior Manager, Finance and Business Administration
Kim Murdoch – Manager, Pensions and Benefits
Devin Smith – Program Manager, Goals & Dreams Fund
Dave Tredgett – Executive Producer-Television
Jonathan Weatherdon – Media Relations

NHL On-Ice Officials

Total NHL Games and 2000-01 Games columns count regular-season games only.

Referees

#	Name	Birthplace	Birthdate	First NHL Game	Total NHL Games	2000-01 Games
9	Blaine Angus	Shawville, Que.	9/25/1961	10/17/1992	247	73
28	Stephane Auger	Montreal, Que.	12/9/1970	4/1/2000	27	26
5	Bernard DeGrace	Lameque, N.B.	5/1/1967	10/15/1991	*315	70
10	Paul Devorski	Guelph, Ont.	8/18/1958	10/14/1989	677	74
44	Harry Dumas	Mount Laurel, N.J.	7/7/1973	12/27/2000	1	1
11	Mark Faucette	Springfield, MA	6/9/1958	12/23/1987	774	72
2	Kerry Fraser	Sarnia, Ont.	5/30/1952	4/6/1975	1335	72
39	Eric Furlatt	Cap de la Madelaine, Que.	12/2/1971			0
4	Terry Gregson	Erin, Ont.	11/7/1953	12/19/1981	1218	71
30	Mike Hasenfratz	Regina, Sask.	7/19/1966	10/21/2000	34	34
17	Shane Heyer	Summerland, B.C.	2/7/1964	**10/1/1999	*882	68
8	Dave Jackson	Montreal, Que.	11/28/1964	12/23/1990	538	72
25	Marc Joannette	Verdun, Que.	11/3/1968	10/27/1999	72	69
18	Greg Kimmerly	Toronto, Ont.	12/8/1964	11/30/1996	160	71
12	Don Koharski	Halifax, N.S.	12/2/1955	10/14/1977	*1362	69
32	Tom Kowal	Vernon, B.C.	11/2/1967	10/29/1999	71	66
37	Bob Langdon	Woodstock, Ont.	3/11/1971			0
14	Dennis LaRue	Savannah, GA	7/14/1959	3/26/1991	362	73
49	Chris Lee	Saint John, N.B.	7/7/1970	4/2/2000	5	4
3	Mike Leggo	North Bay, Ont.	10/7/1964	3/3/1998	154	73
6	Dan Marouelli	Edmonton, Alta.	7/16/1955	11/2/1984	1061	70
26	Rob Martell	Winnipeg, Man.	10/21/1963	3/14/1984	*77	43
7	Bill McCreary	Guelph, Ont.	11/17/1955	11/3/1984	1088	72
19	Mick McGeough	Regina, Sask.	6/20/1957	1/19/1989	665	73
34	Brad Meier	Dayton, OH	4/11/1967	10/23/1999	77	68
36	Dean Morton	Peterborough, Ont.	2/27/1968	11/11/2000	1	1
15	Dan O'Halloran	Essex, Ont.	3/25/1964	10/14/1995	230	74
42	Dan O'Rourke	Calgary, Alta.	8/31/1972	10/2/1999	*120	66
20	Tim Peel	Toronto, Ont.	4/27/1966	10/21/1999	81	71
33	Kevin Pollock	Kincardine, Ont.	2/7/1970	3/28/2000	77	76
43	Chris Rooney	Boston, MA	5/26/1974	11/22/2000	13	13
40	Jay Sharrers	Jamaica, West Indies	7/3/1967	**4/3/2001	*643	1
16	Rob Shick	Port Alberni, B.C.	12/4/1957	4/6/1986	858	73
31	Kelly Sutherland	Victoria, B.C.	4/18/1971	12/19/2000		0
22	Paul Stewart	Boston, MA	3/21/1955	3/27/1987	877	73
21	Don Van Massenhoven	London, Ont.	7/17/1960	11/11/1993	476	74
24	Stephen Walkom	North Bay, Ont.	8/8/1963	10/18/1992	476	73
45	Ian Walsh	Philadelphia, PA	5/9/1972	10/14/2000		0
35	Dean Warren	Toronto, Ont.	7/22/1963	10/8/1999	77	71
23	Brad Watson	Regina, Sask.	10/4/1961	2/5/1994	179	68
29	Scott Zelkin	Wilmette, IL	9/12/1968	4/13/1997	164	74

* Includes some games worked as a linesman. ** First game as an NHL referee. Previously worked as a linesman.

Linesmen

#	Name	Birthplace	Birthdate	First NHL Game	Total NHL Games	2000-01 Games
75	Derek Amell	Port Colborne, Ont.	9/16/1968	10/13/1997	215	70
59	Steve Barton	Ottawa, Ont.	12/27/1971	11/1/2000	23	23
94	Wayne Bonney	Ottawa, Ont.	5/27/1953	10/10/1979	1527	71
96	David Brisebois	Sudbury, Ont.	4/14/1976	10/11/1999	70	25
55	Gord Broseker	Baltimore, MD	7/8/1950	1/14/1975	1842	51
74	Lonnie Cameron	Victoria, B.C.	7/15/1964	10/5/1996	330	71
67	Pierre Champoux	Ville St-Pierre, Que.	4/18/1963	10/8/1988	832	62
50	Kevin Collins	Springfield, MA	12/15/1950	10/13/1977	1828	70
88	Mike Cvik	Calgary, Alta.	7/6/1962	10/8/1987	927	76
83	Angelo D'Amico	Etobicoke, Ont.	5/29/1974	11/27/2000	8	8
60	Pat Dapuzzo	Hoboken, NJ	12/29/1958	12/5/1984	1199	57
54	Greg Devorski	Guelph, Ont.	8/3/1969	10/9/1993	503	72
68	Scott Driscoll	Seaforth, Ont.	5/2/1968	10/10/1992	573	80
63	Gerard Gauthier	Montreal, Que.	9/5/1948	10/16/1971	2206	68
66	Darren Gibbs	Edmonton, Alta.	9/30/1966	10/1/1997	230	68
91	Don Henderson	Calgary, Alta.	9/23/1968	3/10/1995	322	74
71	Brad Kovachik	Woodstock, Ont.	3/7/1971	10/10/1996	305	74
86	Brad Lazarowich	Vancouver, B.C.	8/4/1962	10/9/1986	1013	60
78	Brian Mach	Little Falls, MN	4/15/1974	10/7/2000	63	63
51	Dan McCourt	Falconbridge, Ont.	8/14/1954	12/27/1980	1414	73
90	Andy McElman	Chicago Heights, IL	8/4/1961	10/7/1993	505	70
89	Steve Miller	Stratford, Ont.	6/22/1972	10/7/2000	65	65
98	Randy Mitton	Fredericton, N.B.	9/22/1950	2/2/1974	1899	67
97	Jean Morin	Sorel, Que.	8/10/1963	10/5/1991	629	68
93	Brian Murphy	Dover, NH	12/13/1964	10/7/1988	*802	59
95	Jonny Murray	Beauport, Que.	8/10/1974	10/7/2000	66	66
80	Thor Nelson	Westminister, CA	1/6/1968	2/16/1995	239	65
77	Tim Nowak	Buffalo, NY	9/6/1967	10/8/1993	515	71
79	Mark Paré	Windsor, Ont.	7/26/1957	10/11/1979	1610	72
72	Stephane Provost	Montreal, Que.	5/5/1967	1/25/1995	483	76
65	Pierre Racicot	Verdun, Que.	2/15/1967	10/12/1993	540	74
73	Vaughan Rody	Winnipeg, Man.	12/13/1968	10/8/2000	70	70
81	Troy Sartison	Swift Current, Sask.	2/25/1970	10/6/1999	123	64
53	Ray Scapinello	Guelph, Ont.	11/5/1946	10/17/1971	2292	68
61	Lyle Seitz	Brooks, Alta.	1/22/1969	10/6/1992	*244	65
52	Dan Schachte	Madison, WI	7/13/1958	10/6/1982	1324	71
84	Anthony Sericolo	Troy, NY	7/17/1968	10/21/1998	161	70
56	Mark Wheler	North Battleford, Sask.	9/20/1965	10/10/1992	595	80

* Includes some games worked as a referee.

NHL History

1917 — National Hockey League organized November 22 in Montreal following suspension of operations by the National Hockey Association of Canada Limited (NHA). Montreal Canadiens, Montreal Wanderers, Ottawa Senators and Quebec Bulldogs attended founding meeting. Delegates decided to use NHA rules.

Toronto Arenas were later admitted as fifth team; Quebec decided not to operate during the first season. Quebec players allocated to remaining four teams.

Frank Calder elected president and secretary-treasurer.

First NHL games played December 19, with Toronto only arena with artificial ice. Clubs played 22-game split schedule.

1918 — Emergency meeting held January 3 due to destruction by fire of Montreal Arena which was home ice for both Canadiens and Wanderers.

Wanderers withdrew, reducing the NHL to three teams; Canadiens played remaining home games at 3,250-seat Jubilee rink.

Quebec franchise sold to P.J. Quinn of Toronto on October 18 on the condition that the team operate in Quebec City for 1918-19 season. Quinn did not attend the November League meeting and Quebec did not play in 1918-19.

1919-20 — NHL reactivated Quebec Bulldogs franchise. Former Quebec players returned to the club. New Mount Royal Arena became home of Canadiens. Toronto Arenas changed name to St. Patricks. Clubs played 24-game split schedule.

1920-21 — H.P. Thompson of Hamilton, Ontario made application for the purchase of an NHL franchise. Quebec franchise shifted to Hamilton with other NHL teams providing players to strengthen the club.

1921-22 — Split schedule abandoned. First and second place teams at the end of full schedule to play for championship.

1922-23 — Clubs agreed that players could not be sold or traded to clubs in any other league without first being offered to all other clubs in the NHL. In March, Foster Hewitt broadcasts radio's first hockey game.

1923-24 — Ottawa's new 10,000-seat arena opened. First U.S. franchise granted to Boston for following season.

Dr. Cecil Hart Trophy donated to NHL to be awarded to the player judged most useful to his team.

1924-25 — Canadian Arena Company of Montreal granted a franchise to operate Montreal Maroons. NHL now six team league with two clubs in Montreal. Inaugural game in new Montreal Forum played November 29, 1924 as Canadiens defeated Toronto 7-1. Forum was home rink for the Maroons, but no ice was available in the Canadiens arena November 29, resulting in shift to Forum.

Hamilton finished first in the standings, receiving a bye into the finals. But Hamilton players, demanding $200 each for additional games in the playoffs, went on strike. The NHL suspended all players, fining them $200 each. Stanley Cup finalist to be the winner of NHL semi-final between Toronto and Canadiens.

Prince of Wales and Lady Byng trophies donated to NHL.

Clubs played 30-game schedule.

1925-26 — Hamilton club dropped from NHL. Players signed by new New York Americans franchise. Pittsburgh Pirates granted franchise.

Clubs played 36-game schedule.

1926-27 — New York Rangers granted franchise May 15, 1926. Chicago Black Hawks and Detroit Cougars granted franchises September 25, 1926. NHL now ten-team league with an American and a Canadian Division.

Stanley Cup came under the control of NHL. In previous seasons, winners of the now-defunct Western or Pacific Coast leagues would play NHL champion in Cup finals.

Toronto franchise sold to a new company controlled by Hugh Aird and Conn Smythe. Name changed from St. Patricks to Maple Leafs.

Clubs played 44-game schedule.

The Montreal Canadiens donated the Vezina Trophy to be awarded to the team allowing the fewest goals-against in regular season play. The winning team would, in turn, present the trophy to the goaltender playing in the greatest number of games during the season.

1930-31 — Detroit franchise changed name from Cougars to Falcons. Pittsburgh transferred to Philadelphia for one season. Pirates changed name to Philadelphia Quakers. Trading deadline for teams set at February 15 of each year. NHL approved operation of farm teams by Rangers, Americans, Falcons and Bruins. Four-sided electric arena clock first demonstrated.

1931-32 — Philadelphia dropped out. Ottawa withdrew for one season. New Maple Leaf Gardens completed.

Clubs played 48-game schedule

1932-33 — Detroit franchise changed name from Falcons to Red Wings. Franchise application received from St. Louis but refused because of additional travel costs. Ottawa team resumed play.

1933-34 — First All-Star Game played as a benefit for injured player Ace Bailey. Leafs defeated All-Stars 7-3 in Toronto.

1934-35 — Ottawa franchise transferred to St. Louis. Team called St. Louis Eagles and consisted largely of Ottawa's players.

1935-36 — Ottawa-St. Louis franchise terminated. Montreal Canadiens finished season with very poor record. To strengthen the club, NHL gave Canadiens first call on the services of all French-Canadian players for three seasons.

1937-38 — Second benefit All-Star game staged November 2 in Montreal in aid of the family of the late Canadiens star Howie Morenz.

Montreal Maroons withdrew from the NHL on June 22, 1938, leaving seven clubs in the League.

1938-39 — Expenses for each club regulated at $5 per man per day for meals and $2.50 per man per day for accommodation.

1939-40 — Benefit All-Star Game played October 29, 1939 in Montreal for the children of the late Albert (Babe) Siebert.

1940-41 — Ross-Tyer puck adopted as the official puck of the NHL. Early in the season it was apparent that this puck was too soft. The Spalding puck was adopted in its place.

On May 16, 1941, Arthur Ross, NHL governor from Boston, donated a perpetual trophy to be awarded annually to the player voted outstanding in the league. Due to wartime restrictions, the trophy was never awarded.

1941-42 — New York Americans changed name to Brooklyn Americans.

1942-43 — Brooklyn Americans withdrew from NHL, leaving six teams: Boston, Chicago, Detroit, Montreal, New York and Toronto. Playoff format saw first-place team play third-place team and second play fourth.

Clubs played 50-game schedule.

Frank Calder, president of the NHL since its inception, died in Montreal. Meryn "Red" Dutton, former manager of the New York Americans, became president. The NHL commissioned the Calder Memorial Trophy to be awarded to the League's outstanding rookie each year.

1945-46 — Philadelphia, Los Angeles and San Francisco applied for NHL franchises.

The Philadelphia Arena Company of the American Hockey League applied for an injunction to prevent the possible operation of an NHL franchise in that city.

1946-47 — Mervyn Dutton retired as president of the NHL prior to the start of the season. He was succeeded by Clarence S. Campbell.

Individual trophy winners and all-star team members to receive $1,000 awards.

Playoff guarantees for players introduced.

Clubs played 60-game schedule.

1947-48 — The first annual All-Star Game for the benefit of the players' pension fund was played when the All-Stars defeated the Stanley Cup Champion Toronto Maple Leafs 4-3 in Toronto on October 13, 1947.

Criteria for awarding Art Ross Trophy changed. Now awarded to top scorer. Elmer Lach was its first winner.

Philadelphia and Los Angeles franchise applications refused.

National Hockey League Pension Society formed.

1949-50 — Clubs played 70-game schedule.

First intra-league draft held April 30, 1950. Clubs allowed to protect 30 players. Remaining players available for $25,000 each.

1951-52 — Referees included in the League's pension plan.

1952-53 — In May of 1952, City of Cleveland applied for NHL franchise. Application denied. In March of 1953, the Cleveland Barons of the AHL challenged the NHL champions for the Stanley Cup. The NHL governors did not accept this challenge.

1953-54 — The James Norris Memorial Trophy presented to the NHL for annual presentation to the League's best defenseman.

Intra-league draft rules amended to allow teams to protect 18 skaters and two goaltenders, claiming price reduced to $15,000.

1954-55 — Each arena to operate an "out-of-town" scoreboard. Referees and linesmen to wear shirts of black and white vertical stripes.

1956-57 — Standardized signals for referees and linesmen introduced.

1960-61 — Canadian National Exhibition, City of Toronto and NHL reach agreement for the construction of a Hockey Hall of Fame on the CNE grounds. Hall opens on August 26, 1961.

1963-64 — Player development league established with clubs operated by NHL franchises located in Minneapolis, St. Paul, Indianapolis, Omaha and, beginning in 1964-65, Tulsa. First universal amateur draft took place. All players of qualifying age (17) unaffected by sponsorship of junior teams available to be drafted.

1964-65 — Conn Smythe Trophy presented to the NHL to be awarded annually to the outstanding player in the Stanley Cup playoffs.

Minimum age of players subject to amateur draft changed to 18.

1965-66 — NHL announced expansion plans for a second six-team division to begin play in 1967-68.

1966-67 — Fourteen applications for NHL franchises received.

Lester Patrick Trophy presented to the NHL to be awarded annually for outstanding service to hockey in the United States.

NHL sponsorship of junior teams ceased, making all players of qualifying age not already on NHL-sponsored lists eligible for the amateur draft.

1967-68 — Six new teams added: California Seals, Los Angeles Kings, Minnesota North Stars, Philadelphia Flyers, Pittsburgh Penguins, St. Louis Blues. New teams to play in West Division. Remaining six teams to play in East Division.

Minimum age of players subject to amateur draft changed to 20.

Clubs played 74-game schedule.

Clarence S. Campbell Trophy awarded to team finishing the regular season in first place in West Division.

California Seals change name to Oakland Seals on December 8, 1967.

1968-69 — Clubs played 76-game schedule.

Amateur draft expanded to cover any amateur player of qualifying age throughout the world.

1970-71 — Two new teams added: Buffalo Sabres and Vancouver Canucks. These teams joined East Division: Chicago switched to West Division. Oakland Seals change name to California Golden Seals prior to season.

Clubs played 78-game schedule.

1971-72 — Playoff format amended. In each division, first to play fourth; second to play third.

1972-73 — Soviet Nationals and Canadian NHL stars play eight-game pre-season series. Canadians win 4-3-1.

Two new teams added. Atlanta Flames join West Division; New York Islanders join East Division.

1974-75 — Two new teams added: Kansas City Scouts and Washington Capitals. Teams realigned into two nine-team conferences, the Prince of Wales made up of the Norris and Adams Divisions, and the Clarence Campbell made up of the Smythe and Patrick Divisions.

Clubs played 80-game schedule.

1976-77 — California franchise transferred to Cleveland. Team named Cleveland Barons. Kansas City franchise transferred to Denver. Team named Colorado Rockies.

1977-78 — Clarence S. Campbell retires as NHL president. Succeeded by John A. Ziegler, Jr.

1978-79 — Cleveland and Minnesota franchises merge, leaving NHL with 17 teams. Merged team placed in Adams Division, playing home games in Minnesota.

Minimum age of players subject to amateur draft changed to 19.

1979-80 — Four new teams added: Edmonton Oilers, Hartford Whalers, Quebec Nordiques and Winnipeg Jets.

Minimum age of players subject to entry draft changed to 18.

1980-81 — Atlanta franchise shifted to Calgary, retaining "Flames" name.

1981-82 — Teams realigned within existing divisions. New groupings based on geographical areas. Unbalanced schedule adopted.

1982-83 — Colorado Rockies franchise shifted to East Rutherford, New Jersey. Team named New Jersey Devils. Franchise moved to Patrick Division from Smythe; Winnipeg moved to Smythe Division from Norris.

NHL History — *continued*

1991-92 — San Jose Sharks added, making the NHL a 22-team league. NHL celebrates 75th Anniversary Season. The 1991-92 regular season suspended due to a strike by members of the NHL Players' Association on April 1, 1992. Play resumed April 12, 1992.

1992-93 — Gil Stein named NHL president (October, 1992). Gary Bettman named first NHL Commissioner (February, 1993). Ottawa Senators and Tampa Bay Lightning added, making the NHL a 24-team league. NHL celebrates Stanley Cup Centennial. Clubs played 84-game schedule.

1993-94 — Mighty Ducks of Anaheim and Florida Panthers added, making the NHL a 26-team league. Minnesota franchise shifted to Dallas, team named Dallas Stars. Prince of Wales and Clarence Campbell Conferences renamed Eastern and Western. Adams, Patrick, Norris and Smythe Divisions renamed Northeast, Atlantic, Central and Pacific. Winnipeg moved to Central Division from Pacific; Tampa Bay moved to Atlantic Division from Central; Pittsburgh moved to Northeast Division from Atlantic.

1994-95 — A labor disruption forced the cancellation of 468 games from October 1, 1994 to January 19, 1995. Clubs played a 48-game schedule that began January 20, 1995 and ended May 3, 1995. No inter-conference games were played.

1995-96 — Quebec franchise transferred to Denver. Team named Colorado Avalanche and placed in Pacific Division of Western Conference. Clubs to play 82-game schedule.

1996-97 — Winnipeg franchise transferred to Phoenix. Team named Phoenix Coyotes and placed in Central Division of Western Conference.

1997-98 — Hartford franchise transferred to Raleigh. Team named Carolina Hurricanes and remains in Northeast Division of Eastern Conference.

1998-99 — The addition of the Nashville Predators made the NHL a 27-team league and brought about the creation of two new divisions and a League-wide realignment in preparation for further expansion to 30 teams by 2000-2001. Nashville was added to the Central Division of the Western Conference, while Toronto moved into the Northeast Division of the Eastern Conference. Pittsburgh was shifted from the Northeast to the Atlantic, while Carolina left the Northeast for the newly created Southeast Division of the Eastern Conference. Florida, Tampa Bay and Washington also joined the Southeast. In the Western Conference, Calgary, Colorado, Edmonton and Vancouver make up the new Northwest Division. Dallas and Phoenix moved from the Central to the Pacific Division.

The NHL retired uniform number 99 in honor of all-time scoring leader Wayne Gretzky who retired at the end of the season.

1999-2000 — Atlanta Thrashers added, making the NHL a 28-team league.

2000-01 — Columbus Blue Jackets and Minnesota Wild added, making the NHL a 30-team league.

NHL Attendance

Season	Regular Season Games	Regular Season Attendance	Playoffs Games	Playoffs Attendance	Total Attendance
1960-61	210	2,317,142	17	242,000	2,559,142
1961-62	210	2,435,424	18	277,000	2,712,424
1962-63	210	2,590,574	16	220,906	2,811,480
1963-64	210	2,732,642	21	309,149	3,041,791
1964-65	210	2,822,635	20	303,859	3,126,494
1965-66	210	2,941,164	16	249,000	3,190,184
1966-67	210	3,084,759	16	248,336	3,333,095
1967-68[1]	444	4,938,043	40	495,089	5,433,132
1968-69	456	5,550,613	33	431,739	5,982,352
1969-70	456	5,992,065	34	461,694	6,453,759
1970-71[2]	546	7,257,677	43	707,633	7,965,310
1971-72	546	7,609,368	36	582,666	8,192,034
1972-73[3]	624	8,575,651	38	624,637	9,200,288
1973-74	624	8,640,978	38	600,442	9,241,420
1974-75[4]	720	9,521,536	51	784,181	10,305,717
1975-76	720	9,103,761	48	726,279	9,830,040
1976-77	720	8,563,890	44	646,279	9,210,169
1977-78	720	8,526,564	45	686,634	9,213,198
1978-79	680	7,758,053	45	694,521	8,452,574
1979-80[5]	840	10,533,623	63	976,699	11,510,322
1980-81	840	10,726,198	68	966,390	11,692,588
1981-82	840	10,710,894	71	1,058,948	11,769,842
1982-83	840	11,020,610	66	1,088,222	12,028,832
1983-84	840	11,359,386	70	1,107,400	12,466,786
1984-85	840	11,633,730	70	1,107,500	12,741,230
1985-86	840	11,621,000	72	1,152,503	12,773,503
1986-87	840	11,855,880	87	1,383,967	13,239,847
1987-88	840	12,117,512	83	1,336,901	13,454,413
1988-89	840	12,417,969	83	1,327,214	13,745,183
1989-90	840	12,579,651	85	1,355,593	13,935,244
1990-91	840	12,343,897	92	1,442,203	13,786,100
1991-92[6]	880	12,769,676	86	1,327,920	14,097,596
1992-93[7]	1,008	14,158,177[8]	83	1,346,034	15,504,211
1993-94[9]	1,092	16,105,604[10]	90	1,440,095	17,545,699
1994-95	624[11]	9,233,884	81	1,329,130	10,563,014
1995-96	1,066	17,041,614	86	1,540,140	18,581,754
1996-97	1,066	17,640,529	82	1,494,878	19,135,407
1997-98	1,066	17,264,678	82	1,507,416	18,772,094
1998-99[12]	1,107	18,001,741	86	1,509,411	19,511,152
1999-2000[13]	1,148	18,800,139	83	1,524,629	20,324,768
2000-01[14]	1,230	20,373,379	86	1,584,011	21,957,390

[1] First expansion: Los Angeles, Pittsburgh, California (Cleveland),Philadelphia, St. Louis and Minnesota (Dallas)
[2] Second expansion: Buffalo and Vancouver
[3] Third expansion: Atlanta (Calgary) and New York Islanders
[4] Fourth expansion: Kansas City (Colorado, New Jersey) and Washington
[5] Fifth expansion: Edmonton, Hartford, Quebec (Colorado) and Winnipeg
[6] Sixth expansion: San Jose
[7] Seventh expansion: Ottawa and Tampa Bay
[8] Includes 24 neutral site games
[9] Eighth expansion: Anaheim and Florida
[10] Includes 26 neutral site games
[11] Lockout resulted in the cancellation of 468 regular-season games.
[12] Ninth expansion: Nashville
[13] Tenth expansion: Atlanta
[14] Eleventh expansion: Columbus and Minnesota

Major Rule Changes

1910-11 — Game changed from two 30-minute periods to three 20-minute periods.

1911-12 — National Hockey Association (forerunner of the NHL) originated six-man hockey, replacing seven-man game.

1917-18 — Goalies permitted to fall to the ice to make saves. Previously a goaltender was penalized for dropping to the ice.

1918-19 — Penalty rules amended. For minor fouls, substitutes not allowed until penalized player had served three minutes. For major fouls, no substitutes for five minutes. For match fouls, no substitutes allowed for the remainder of the game.

With the addition of two lines painted on the ice twenty feet from center, three playing zones were created, producing a forty-foot neutral center ice area in which forward passing was permitted. Kicking the puck was permitted in this neutral zone.

Tabulation of assists began.

1921-22 — Goaltenders allowed to pass the puck forward up to their own blue line.

Overtime limited to twenty minutes.

Minor penalties changed from three minutes to two minutes.

1923-24 — Match foul defined as actions deliberately injuring or disabling an opponent. For such actions, a player was fined not less than $50 and ruled off the ice for the balance of the game. A player assessed a match penalty may be replaced by a substitute at the end of 20 minutes. Match penalty recipients must meet with the League president who can assess additional punishment.

1925-26 — Delayed penalty rules introduced. Each team must have a minimum of four players on the ice at all times.

Two rules were amended to encourage offense: No more than two defensemen permitted to remain inside a team's own blue line when the puck has left the defensive zone. A faceoff to be called for ragging the puck unless short-handed.

Team captains only players allowed to talk to referees.

Goaltender's leg pads limited to 12-inch width.

Timekeeper's gong to mark end of periods rather than referee's whistle. Teams to dress a maximum of 12 players for each game from a roster of no more than 14 players.

1926-27 — Blue lines repositioned to sixty feet from each goal-line, thereby enlarging the neutral zone and standardizing distance from blueline to goal.

Uniform goal nets adopted throughout NHL with goal posts securely fastened to the ice.

1927-28 — To further encourage offense, forward passes allowed in defending and neutral zones and goaltender's pads reduced in width from 12 to 10 inches.

Game standardized at three twenty-minute periods of stop-time separated by ten-minute intermissions.

Teams to change ends after each period.

Ten minutes of sudden-death overtime to be played if the score is tied after regulation time.

Minor penalty to be assessed to any player other than a goaltender for deliberately picking up the puck while it is in play. Minor penalty to be assessed for deliberately shooting the puck out of play.

The Art Ross goal net adopted as the official net of the NHL.

Maximum length of hockey sticks limited to 53 inches measured from heel of blade to end of handle. No minimum length stipulated.

Home teams given choice of end to defend at start of game.

1928-29 — Forward passing permitted in defensive and neutral zones and into attacking zone if pass receiver is in neutral zone when pass is made. No forward passing allowed inside attacking zone.

Minor penalty to be assessed to any player who delays the game by passing the puck back into his defensive zone.

Ten-minute overtime without sudden-death provision to be played in games tied after regulation time. Games tied after this overtime period declared a draw.

Exclusive of goaltenders, team to dress at least 8 and no more than 12 skaters.

Major Rule Changes — *continued*

1929-30 — Forward passing permitted inside all three zones but not permitted across either blue line.

Kicking the puck allowed, but a goal cannot be scored by kicking the puck in.

No more than three players including the goaltender may remain in their defensive zone when the puck has gone up ice. Minor penalties to be assessed for the first two violations of this rule in a game; major penalties thereafter.

Goaltenders forbidden to hold the puck. Pucks caught must be cleared immediately. For infringement of this rule, a faceoff to be taken ten feet in front of the goal with no player except the goaltender standing between the faceoff spot and the goal-line.

Highsticking penalties introduced.

Maximum number of players in uniform increased from 12 to 15.

December 21, 1929 — Forward passing rules instituted at the beginning of the 1929-30 season more than doubled number of goals scored. Partway through the season, these rules were further amended to read, "No attacking player allowed to precede the play when entering the opposing defensive zone." This is similar to modern offside rule.

1930-31 — A player without a complete stick ruled out of play and forbidden from taking part in further action until a new stick is obtained. A player who has broken his stick must obtain a replacement at his bench.

A further refinement of the offside rule stated that the puck must first be propelled into the attacking zone before any player of the attacking side can enter that zone; for infringement of this rule a faceoff to take place at the spot where the infraction took place.

1931-32 — Though there is no record of a team attempting to play with two goaltenders on the ice, a rule was instituted which stated that each team was allowed only one goaltender on the ice at one time.

Attacking players forbidden to impede the movement or obstruct the vision of opposing goaltenders.

Defending players with the exception of the goaltender forbidden from falling on the puck within 10 feet of the net.

1932-33 — Each team to have captain on the ice at all times.

If the goaltender is removed from the ice to serve a penalty, the manager of the club to appoint a substitute.

Match penalty with substitution after five minutes instituted for kicking another player.

1933-34 — Number of players permitted to stand in defensive zone restricted to three including goaltender.

Visible time clocks required in each rink.

Two referees replace one referee and one linesman.

1934-35 — Penalty shot awarded when a player is tripped and thus prevented from having a clear shot on goal, having no player to pass to other than the offending player. Shot taken from inside a 10-foot circle located 38 feet from the goal. The goaltender must not advance more than one foot from his goal-line when the shot is taken.

1937-38 — Rules introduced governing icing the puck.

Penalty shot awarded when a player other than a goaltender falls on the puck within 10 feet of the goal.

1938-39 — Penalty shot modified to allow puck carrier to skate in before shooting.

One referee and one linesman replace two referee system.

Blue line widened to 12 inches.

Maximum number of players in uniform increased from 14 to 15.

1939-40 — A substitute replacing a goaltender removed from ice to serve a penalty may use a goaltender's stick and gloves but no other goaltending equipment.

1940-41 — Flooding ice surface between periods made obligatory.

1941-42 — Penalty shots classified as minor and major. Minor shot to be taken from a line 28 feet from the goal. Major shot, awarded when a player is tripped with only the goaltender to beat, permits the player taking the penalty shot to skate right into the goalkeeper and shoot from point-blank range.

One referee and two linesmen employed to officiate games.

For playoffs, standby minor league goaltenders employed by NHL as emergency substitutes.

1942-43 — Because of wartime restrictions on train scheduling, regular-season overtime was discontinued on November 21, 1942.

Player limit reduced from 15 to 14. Minimum of 12 men in uniform abolished.

1943-44 — Red line at center ice introduced to speed up the game and reduce offside calls. This rule is considered to mark the beginning of the modern era in the NHL.

1945-46 — Goal indicator lights synchronized with official time clock required at all rinks.

1946-47 — System of signals by officials to indicate infractions introduced.

Linesmen from neutral cities employed for all games.

1947-48 — Goal awarded when a player with the puck has an open net to shoot at and a thrown stick prevents the shot on goal. Major penalty to any player who throws his stick in any zone other than defending zone. If a stick is thrown by a player in his defending zone but the thrown stick is not considered to have prevented a goal, a penalty shot is awarded.

All playoff games played until a winner determined, with 20-minute sudden-death overtime periods separated by 10-minute intermissions.

1949-50 — Ice surface painted white.

Clubs allowed to dress 17 players exclusive of goaltenders.

Major penalties incurred by goaltenders served by a member of the goaltender's team instead of resulting in a penalty shot.

1950-51 — Each team required to provide an emergency goaltender in attendance with full equipment at each game for use by either team in the event of illness or injury to a regular goaltender.

1951-52 — Home teams to wear basic white uniforms; visiting teams basic colored uniforms.

Goal crease enlarged from 3 × 7 feet to 4 × 8 feet.

Number of players in uniform reduced to 15 plus goaltenders.

Faceoff circles enlarged from 10-foot to 15-foot radius.

1952-53 — Teams permitted to dress 15 skaters on the road and 16 at home.

1953-54 — Number of players in uniform set at 16 plus goaltenders.

1954-55 — Number of players in uniform set at 18 plus goaltenders up to December 1 and 16 plus goaltenders thereafter. Teams agree to wear colored uniforms at home and white uniforms on the road.

1956-57 — Player serving a minor penalty allowed to return to ice when a goal is scored by opposing team.

1959-60 — Players prevented from leaving their benches to enter into an altercation. Substitutions permitted providing substitutes do not enter into altercation.

1960-61 — Number of players in uniform set at 16 plus goaltenders.

1961-62 — Penalty shots to be taken by the player against whom the foul was committed. In the event of a penalty shot called in a situation where a particular player hasn't been fouled, the penalty shot to be taken by any player on the ice when the foul was committed.

1964-65 — No bodily contact on faceoffs.

In playoff games, each team to have its substitute goaltender dressed in his regular uniform except for leg pads and body protector. All previous rules governing standby goaltenders terminated.

1965-66 — Teams required to dress two goaltenders for each regular-season game. Maximum stick length increased to 55 inches.

1966-67 — Substitution allowed on coincidental major penalties.

Between-periods intermissions fixed at 15 minutes.

1967-68 — If a penalty incurred by a goaltender is a co-incident major, the penalty to be served by a player of the goaltender's team on the ice at the time the penalty was called. Limit of curvature of hockey stick blade set at 1-1/2 inches.

1969-70 — Limit of curvature of hockey stick blade set at 1 inch.

1970-71 — Home teams to wear basic white uniforms; visiting teams basic colored uniforms.

Limit of curvature of hockey stick blade set at 1/2 inch.

Minor penalty for deliberately shooting the puck out of the playing area.

1971-72 — Number of players in uniform set at 17 plus 2 goaltenders.

Third man to enter an altercation assessed an automatic game misconduct penalty.

1972-73 — Minimum width of stick blade reduced to 2 inches from 2-1/2 inches.

1974-75 — Bench minor penalty imposed if a penalized player does not proceed directly and immediately to the penalty box.

1976-77 — Rule dealing with fighting amended to provide a major and game misconduct penalty for any player who is clearly the instigator of a fight.

1977-78 — Teams requesting a stick measurement to be assessed a minor penalty in the event that the measured stick does not violate the rules.

1979-80 — Wearing of helmets made mandatory for players entering the NHL.

1980-81 — Maximum stick length increased to 58 inches.

1981-82 — If both of a team's listed goaltenders are incapacitated, the team can dress and play any eligible goaltender who is available.

1982-83 — Number of players in uniform set at 18 plus 2 goaltenders.

1983-84 — Five-minute sudden-death overtime to be played in regular-season games that are tied at the end of regulation time.

1985-86 — Substitutions allowed in the event of co-incidental minor penalties. Maximum stick length increased to 60 inches.

1986-87 — Delayed off-side is no longer in effect once the players of the offending team have cleared the opponents' defensive zone.

1990-91 — The goal lines, blue lines, defensive zone face-off circles and markings all moved one foot out from the end boards, creating 11 feet of room behind the nets and shrinking the neutral zone from 60 to 58 feet.

1991-92 — Video replays employed to assist referees in goal/no goal situations. Size of goal crease increased. Crease changed to semi-circular configuration. Time clock to record tenths of a second in last minute of each period and overtime. Major and game misconduct penalty for checking from behind into boards. Penalties added for crease infringement and unnecessary contact with goaltender. Goal disallowed if puck enters net while a player of the attacking team is standing on the goal crease line, is in the goal crease or places his stick in the goal crease.

1992-93 — No substitutions allowed in the event of coincidental minor penalties called when both teams are at full strength. Wearing of helmets made optional for forwards and defensemen. Minor penalty for attempting to draw a penalty ("diving"). Major and game misconduct penalty for checking from behind into goal frame. Game misconduct penalty for instigating a fight. Highsticking redefined to include any use of the stick above waist-height. Previous rule stipulated shoulder-height.

1993-94 — High sticking redefined to allow goals scored with a high stick below the height of the crossbar of the goal frame.

1996-97 — Maximum stick length increased to 63 inches.

1998-99 — The league instituted a two-referee system with each team to play 20 regular-season games with two referees and a pair of linesmen. Also, the goal lines, blue lines, defensive zone face-off circles and markings all moved two feet closer to center, creating 13 feet of room behind the nets and cutting the neutral zone from 58 to 54 feet. The goal crease was altered so that it extends only one foot beyond each goal post (eight feet across in total) and has square sides for the first 4'6". Only the top of the crease remains rounded.

1999-2000 — Each team to play 25 home and 25 road games using the two-referee system. Crease rule revised to implement a "no harm, no foul, no video review" standard. An attacking player's position, whether inside or outside the crease, does not, in itself, determine whether a goal should be allowed or disallowed. The on-ice judgement of the referee(s) — instead of video review — will determine if a goal is "good" or not. Also, regular-season games tied at the end of three periods will result in each team being awarded one point in the standings. As before, there will be a five-minute sudden death overtime when the score is tied after three periods, but each team will play "four on four," with four skaters and a goalkeeper. In the event that penalties dictate that one team has a two-man advantage, the penalized team plays with three skaters while the team with the two-man advantage adds a fifth skater. A team that scores a goal in regular-season overtime is credited with a win and earns two points in the standings. A team scored upon in regular-season overtime is credited with an overtime loss and earns one point in the standings.

2000-01 — All games to be played using the two-referee system.

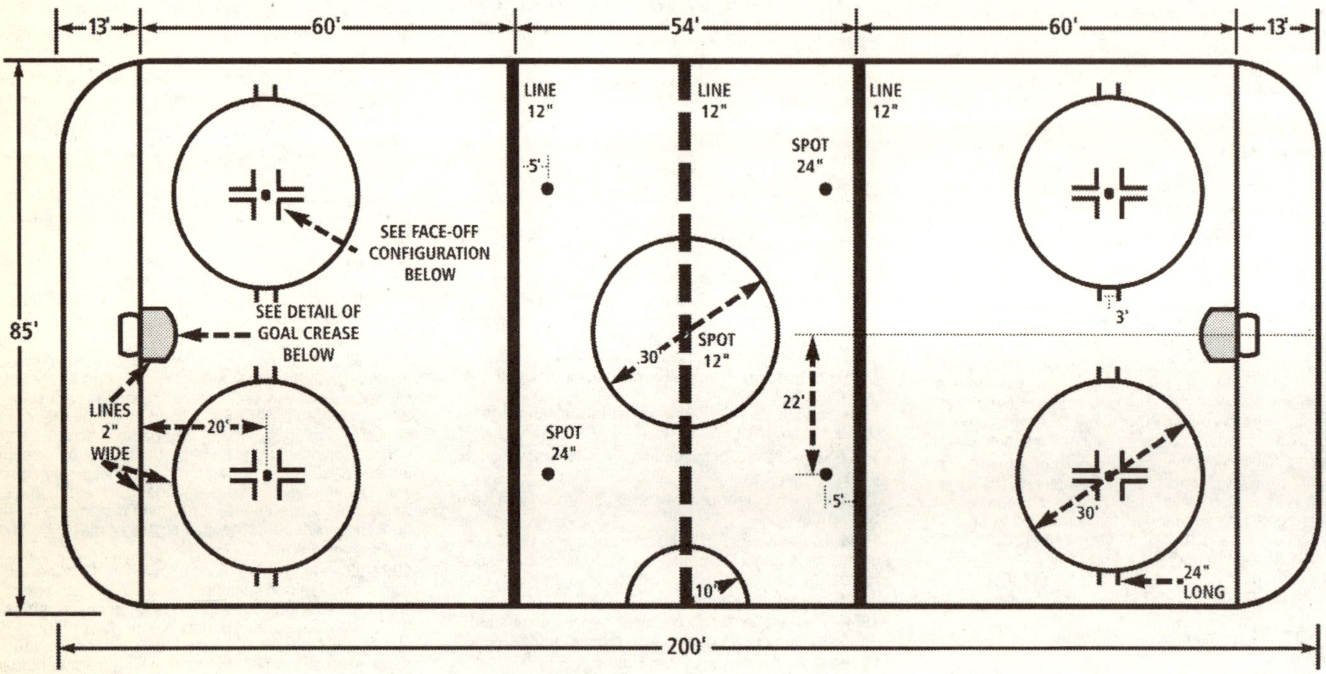

NHL RINK DIMENSIONS

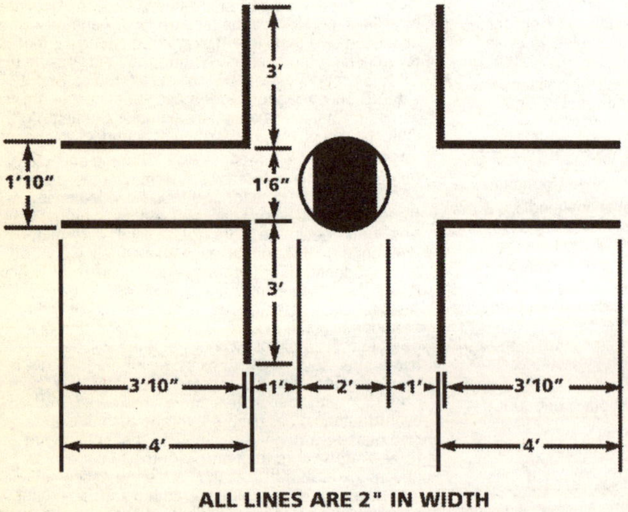

FACEOFF CONFIGURATION

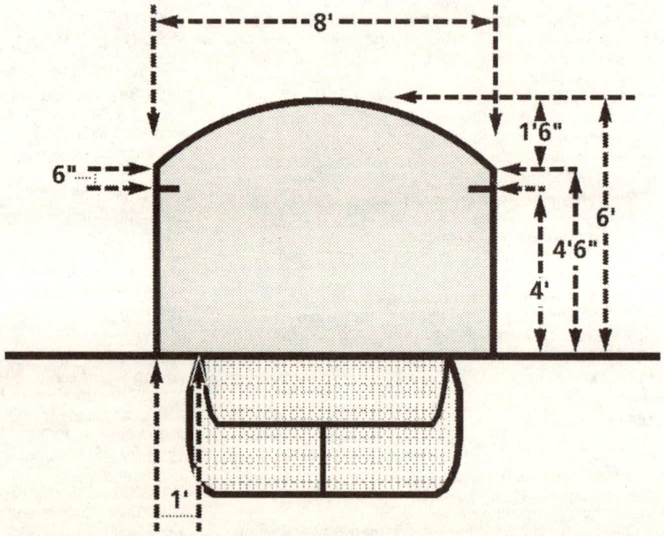

CREASE DIMENSIONS

NHL Players at the 2002 Olympic Winter Games

As in 1997-98, the NHL's 2001-02 regular season will be interrupted in order to allow the League's players to represent their countries at the Olympic Winter Games in Salt Lake City, Utah.

Once again, the Olympic tournament will be played in two phases: a preliminary round and a final round. From Feb. 9 to Feb. 13, eight national teams will play three games each (one against each of the other teams in their group). Slovakia, Austria Latvia and Germany will compete in Group A, while Group B will consist of Switzerland, Belarus, Ukraine and France. The winners of Group A and Group B will advance to the final round where one qualifier will be grouped with the Czech Republic, Canada and Sweden and the other will be grouped with Russia, Finland and the United States.

Beginning on February 15, the eight teams in the final round will play three games (one against each of the other teams in their group) to determine the seedings for the quarterfinals. Single-game playoffs will then determine the winner of the quarterfinals, the semifinals, the bronze medal game and the gold medal game.

2002 Men's Olympic Hockey Schedule

(Start times listed in Mountain Standard Time)

Preliminary Round (round robin)

Feb. 9	Belarus	vs.	Ukraine	2:00 pm
Feb. 9	Slovakia	vs.	Germany	4:00 pm
Feb. 9	Austria	vs.	Latvia	7:00 pm
Feb. 9	Switzerland	vs.	France	9:00 pm
Feb. 10	Austria	vs.	Germany	4:00 pm
Feb. 10	Latvia	vs.	Slovakia	7:00 pm
Feb. 11	Ukraine	vs.	Switzerland	4:00 pm
Feb. 11	Belarus	vs.	France	7:00 pm
Feb. 12	Slovakia	vs.	Austria	4:00 pm
Feb. 12	Germany	vs.	Latvia	7:00 pm
Feb. 13	Switzerland	vs.	Belarus	4:00 pm
Feb. 13	France	vs.	Ukraine	7:00 pm
Feb. 14	11th place game			3:00 pm
Feb. 14	9th place game			8:00 pm
Feb. 14	13th place game			9:00 pm

Final Round (round robin)

Feb. 15	Russia	vs.	Qualifier 1	11:00 am
Feb. 15	Canada	vs.	Sweden	4:00 pm
Feb. 15	Czech Republic	vs.	Qualifier 2	7:00 pm
Feb. 15	Finland	vs.	United States	8:45 pm
Feb. 16	Finland	vs.	Qualifier 1	4:45 pm
Feb. 16	United States	vs.	Russia	9:30 pm
Feb. 17	Sweden	vs.	Czech Republic	4:00 pm
Feb. 17	Canada	vs.	Qualifier 2	6:00 pm
Feb. 18	Qualifier 1	vs.	United States	11:00 am
Feb. 18	Russia	vs.	Finland	1:30 pm
Feb. 18	Czech Republic	vs.	Canada	4:00 pm
Feb. 18	Qualifier 2	vs.	Sweden	7:00 pm

Playoff Round (single elimination)

Feb. 20	Quarterfinals	11:00 am
Feb. 20	Quarterfinals	1:30 pm
Feb. 20	Quarterfinals	4:00 pm
Feb. 20	Quarterfinals	8:15 pm
Feb. 22	Semifinals	12:00 pm
Feb. 22	Semifinals	4:15 pm
Feb. 23	Bronze Medal Game	12:15 pm
Feb. 24	Gold Medal Game	1:00 pm

2002 Women's Olympic Hockey Schedule

(Start times listed in Mountain Standard Time)

Feb. 11	Canada	vs.	Kazakhstan	11:00 am
Feb. 11	Sweden	vs.	Russia	2:00 pm
Feb. 12	United States	vs.	Germany	11:00 am
Feb. 12	Finland	vs.	China	2:00 pm
Feb. 13	Russia	vs.	Canada	11:00 am
Feb. 13	Sweden	vs.	Kazakhstan	2:00 pm
Feb. 14	Finland	vs.	Germany	11:00 am
Feb. 14	China	vs.	United States	4:00 pm
Feb. 15	Kazakhstan	vs.	Russia	2:00 pm
Feb. 16	United States	vs.	Finland	11:00 am
Feb. 16	Germany	vs.	China	2:00 pm
Feb. 16	Canada	vs.	Sweden	7:00 pm
Feb. 17	Classification Game A3 vs. B4			2:00 pm
Feb. 17	Classification Game B3 vs. A4			9:00 pm
Feb. 19	Semifinal			11:00 am
Feb. 19	7th place game			2:00 pm
Feb. 19	Semifinal			4:30 pm
Feb. 19	5th place game			7:00 pm
Feb. 21	Bronze Medal Game			12:00 pm
Feb. 21	Gold Medal Game			5:00 pm

Cumulative Medal Standings, Women's Olympic Hockey, 1998

	G	S	B	Total	Last Medal
1. USA	1	0	0	1	Gold 98
2. Canada	0	1	0	1	Silver 98
3. Finland	0	0	1	1	Bronze 98

Cumulative Medal Standings, Men's Olympic Hockey, 1924-1998

	G	S	B	Total	Last Medal
1. USSR/Russia*	8	2	1	11	Silver 98
2. Canada	5	4	2	11	Silver 94
3. USA	2	5	1	8	Gold 80
4. Sweden	1	2	4	7	Gold 94
5. Czechoslovakia/ Czech Republic	1	4	3	8	Gold 98
6. Great Britain	1	0	1	2	Gold 36
7. Finland	0	1	2	3	Bronze 98
8. W. Germany	0	0	2	2	Bronze 76
9. Switzerland	0	0	2	2	Bronze 48

* *Soviet Union/Russia played as the Unified Team in 1992.*

Nagano, Japan • 1998

Men

Preliminary Round

Group A

Team	GP	W	L	T	GF	GA	Pts
Kazakhstan	3	2	0	1	14	11	5
Slovakia	3	1	1	1	9	9	3
Italy	3	1	2	0	11	11	2
Austria	3	0	1	2	9	12	2

Group B

Team	GP	W	L	T	GF	GA	Pts
Belarus	3	2	0	1	14	4	5
Germany	3	2	1	0	7	9	4
France	3	1	2	0	5	8	2
Japan	3	0	2	1	5	10	1

Final Round

Group A

Team	GP	W	L	T	GF	GA	Pts
Canada	3	3	0	0	12	3	6
Sweden	3	2	1	0	11	7	4
USA	3	1	2	0	8	10	2
Belarus	3	0	3	0	4	15	0

Group B

Team	GP	W	L	T	GF	GA	Pts
Russia	3	3	0	0	15	6	6
Czech Rep.	3	2	1	0	12	4	4
Finland	3	1	2	0	11	9	2
Kazakhstan	3	0	3	0	6	25	0

Quarterfinals

Canada	4	Kazakhstan	1
Czech Republic	4	USA	1
Finland	2	Sweden	1
Russia	4	Belarus	1

Semifinals

Czech Republic	2	Canada	1
Russia	7	Finland	4

Bronze Medal game

Finland	3	Canada	2

Gold Medal game

Czech Republic	1	Russia	0

1998 Final Rankings, Men

1	Czech Republic
2	Russia
3	Finland
4	Canada
5–8	USA
5–8	Sweden
5–8	Belarus
5–8	Kazakhstan
9	Germany
10	Slovakia
11	France
12	Italy
13	Japan
14	Austria

1998 Scoring Leaders

Player	Team	GP	G	A	PTS	PIM
Teemu Selanne	Finland	5	4	6	10	8
Saku Koivu	Finland	6	2	8	10	4
Pavel Bure	Russia	6	9	0	9	2
Alex. Koreshkov	Kazakhstan	7	3	6	9	2
Phillipe Bozon	France	4	5	2	7	4
K. Shafranov	Kazakhstan	7	4	3	7	6
Dominik Lavoie	Austria	4	5	1	6	8
Jere Lehtinen	Finland	6	4	2	6	2
Alexei Yashin	Russia	6	3	3	6	0
Serge Poudrier	France	6	2	4	6	4
Sergei Fedorov	Russia	6	1	5	6	8

Lillehammer, Norway • 1994

Group A

Team	GP	W	L	T	GF	GA	PTS
Finland	5	5	0	0	25	4	10
Germany	5	3	2	0	11	14	6
Czech Rep.	5	3	2	0	16	11	6
Russia	5	3	2	0	20	14	6
Austria	5	1	4	0	13	28	2
Norway	5	0	5	0	5	19	0

Group B

Team	GP	W	L	T	GF	GA	PTS
Slovakia	5	3	0	2	26	14	8
Canada	5	3	1	1	17	11	7
Sweden	5	3	1	1	23	13	7
USA	5	1	1	3	21	17	5
Italy	5	1	4	0	15	31	2
France	5	0	4	1	11	27	1

Quarterfinals

Canada	3	Czech Rep.	2
Finland	6	USA	1
Sweden	3	Germany	0
Russia	3	Slovakia	2

Semifinals

Canada	5	Finland	3
Sweden	4	Russia	3

Bronze Medal Game

Finland	4	Russia	0

Gold Medal Game

Sweden	3	Canada	2

1994 Final Standings

1. Sweden
2. Canada
3. Finland
4. Russia
5. Czech Republic
6. Slovakia
7. Germany
8. USA
9. Italy
10. France
11. Norway
12. Austria

1994 Scoring Leaders

Player	Team	GP	G	A	PTS	PIM
Ziggy Palffy	Slovakia	8	3	7	10	8
Miroslav Satan	Slovakia	8	9	0	9	0
Peter Stastny	Slovakia	8	5	4	9	9
Hakan Loob	Sweden	8	4	5	9	2
Gates Orlando	Italy	7	3	6	9	41
Patrik Juhlin	Sweden	8	7	1	8	16
Jiri Kucera	Czech Rep.	8	6	2	8	4
Marty Dallman	Austria	7	4	4	8	8
Mika Nieminen	Finland	8	3	5	8	0
David Sacco	USA	8	3	5	8	12
Peter Forsberg	Sweden	8	2	6	8	6

Albertville, France • 1992

Group A

Team	GP	W	L	T	GF	GA	PTS
USA	5	4	0	1	18	7	9
Sweden	5	3	0	2	22	11	8
Finland	5	3	0	1	22	11	7
Germany	5	2	3	0	11	12	4
Italy	5	1	4	0	18	24	2
Poland	5	0	5	0	4	30	0

Group B

Team	GP	W	L	T	GF	GA	PTS
Canada	5	4	1	0	28	9	8
Unified Team*	5	4	1	0	32	10	8
Czechoslovakia	5	4	1	0	25	15	8
France	5	2	3	0	14	22	4
Switzerland	5	1	4	0	13	25	2
Norway	5	0	5	0	7	38	0

* Soviet Union/Russia played as Unified Team in 1992.

Medal Round

Canada	4	Germany	3
Czechoslovakia	3	Sweden	1
USA	4	France	1
Unified Team	6	Finland	1

Semifinals

Canada	4	Czechoslovakia	2
Unified Team	5	USA	2

Bronze Medal Game

Czechoslovakia	6	USA	1

Gold Medal Game

Unified Team	3	Canada	1

1992 Final Rankings

1. Unified Team
2. Canada
3. Czechoslovakia
4. USA
5. Sweden
6. Germany
7. Finland
8. France
9. Norway
10. Switzerland
11. Poland
12. Italy

1992 Scoring Leaders

Player	Team	GP	G	A	PTS	PIM
Joe Juneau	Canada	8	6	9	15	5
Andrei Khomutov	Unified	8	7	7	14	2
Robert Lang	Czech.	8	5	8	13	8
Teemu Selanne	Finland	8	7	4	11	6
Eric Lindros	Canada	8	5	6	11	5
H. Jarvenpaa	Finland	8	5	6	11	14
V. Bykov	Unified	8	4	7	11	2
Yuri Khmylev	Unified	8	4	6	10	4
Mika Nieminen	Finland	8	4	6	10	6
N. Borschevsky	Unified	8	7	2	9	0

Calgary, Canada • 1988

Group A

Team	GP	W	L	T	GF	GA	PTS
Finland	5	3	1	1	22	8	7
Sweden	5	2	0	3	23	10	7
Canada	5	3	1	1	17	12	7
Switzerland	5	3	2	0	19	10	6
Poland	5	0	4	1	3	13	1
France	5	1	4	0	10	41	0

Group B

Team	GP	W	L	T	GF	GA	PTS
Soviet Union	5	5	0	0	32	10	10
W. Germany	5	4	1	0	19	12	8
Czech.	5	3	2	0	23	14	6
USA	5	2	3	0	27	27	4
Austria	5	0	4	1	12	29	1
Norway	5	0	4	1	11	32	1

Final Round

Team	GP	W	L	T	GF	GA	PTS
Soviet Union	5	4	1	0	25	7	8
Finland	5	3	1	1	18	10	7
Sweden	5	2	1	2	15	16	6
Canada	5	2	2	1	17	14	5
W. Germany	5	1	4	0	8	26	2
Czech.	5	1	4	0	12	22	2

1988 Final Rankings

1. Soviet Union
2. Finland
3. Sweden
4. Canada
5. W. Germany
6. Czechoslovakia
7. USA
8. Switzerland
9. Austria
10. Poland
11. France
12. Norway

1988 Scoring Leaders

Player	Team	GP	G	A	PTS	PIM
Vladimir Krutov	Soviet Union	8	6	9	15	0
Igor Larionov	Soviet Union	8	4	9	13	4
V. Fetisov	Soviet Union	8	4	9	13	6
Corey Millen	USA	6	6	5	11	4
Dusan Pasek	Czech.	8	6	5	11	8
Sergei Makarov	Soviet Union	8	3	8	11	10
Erkki Lehtonen	Finland	8	4	6	10	2
Anders Eldebrink	Sweden	8	4	6	10	4
Igor Liba	Czech.	8	4	6	10	8
Gerd Truntschka	W. Germany	8	3	7	10	10
Raimo Helminen	Finland	7	2	8	10	4

Sarajevo, Yugoslavia • 1984

Group A

Team	GP	W	L	T	GF	GA	PTS
Soviet Union	5	5	0	0	42	5	10
Sweden	5	3	1	1	34	15	7
W. Germany	5	3	1	1	27	17	7
Poland	5	1	4	0	16	37	2
Italy	5	1	4	0	15	31	2
Yugoslavia	5	1	4	0	8	37	2

Group B

Team	GP	W	L	T	GF	GA	PTS
Czech.	5	5	0	0	38	7	10
Canada	5	4	1	0	24	10	8
Finland	5	2	2	1	27	19	5
USA	5	1	2	2	16	17	4
Austria	5	1	4	0	13	37	2
Norway	5	0	4	1	15	43	1

Final Round

Team	GP	W	L	T	GF	GA	PTS
Soviet Union	3	3	0	0	16	1	6
Czech.	3	2	1	0	6	2	4
Sweden	3	1	2	0	3	12	2
Canada	3	0	3	0	0	10	0

Consolation Round

Team	GP	W	L	T	GF	GA	PTS
W. Germany	1	1	0	0	7	4	2
USA	1	1	0	0	7	4	2
Finland	1	0	1	0	4	7	0
Poland	1	0	1	0	4	7	0

1984 Final Rankings

1. Soviet Union
2. Czechoslovakia
3. Sweden
4. Canada
5. W. Germany
6. Finland
7. USA
8. Poland

1984 Scoring Leaders

Player	Team	GP	G	A	PTS	PIM
Erich Kuhnhackl	W. Germany	6	8	6	14	12
Peter Gradin	Sweden	7	9	4	13	6
N. Drozdetski	Soviet Union	7	10	2	12	2
V. Fetisov	Soviet Union	7	3	8	11	8
Petri Skriko	Finland	6	6	4	10	8
Vladimir Ruzicka	Czech.	7	4	6	10	0
R. Summanen	Finland	6	4	6	10	4
Darius Rusnak	Czech.	7	4	6	10	6
Jiri Hrdina	Czech.	7	4	6	10	10
Vincent Lukac	Czech.	7	4	5	9	2
Viktor Tjumenev	Soviet Union	6	0	9	9	2

Lake Placid, New York, USA • 1980

Red Division

Team	GP	W	L	T	GF	GA	PTS
Soviet Union	5	5	0	0	51	11	10
Finland	5	3	2	0	26	18	6
Canada	5	3	2	0	28	12	6
Poland	5	2	3	0	15	23	4
Holland	5	1	3	1	16	43	3
Japan	5	0	4	1	7	36	1

Blue Division

Team	GP	W	L	T	GF	GA	PTS
Sweden	5	4	0	1	26	7	9
USA	5	4	0	1	25	10	9
Czech.	5	3	2	0	34	16	6
Romania	5	1	3	1	13	29	3
W. Germany	5	1	4	0	21	30	2
Norway	5	0	4	1	9	36	1

Final Round

Team	GP	W	L	T	GF	GA	PTS
USA	3	2	0	1	10	7	5
Soviet Union	3	2	1	0	16	8	4
Sweden	3	0	1	2	7	14	2
Finland	3	0	2	1	7	11	1

1980 Final Rankings

1. USA
2. Soviet Union
3. Sweden
4. Finland
5. Czechoslovakia
6. Canada
7. Poland
8. Holland
9. Romania
10. W. Germany
11. Norway
12. Japan

1980 Scoring Leaders

Player	Team	GP	G	A	PTS	PIM
Milan Novy	Czech.	6	7	8	15	0
Peter Stastny	Czech.	6	7	7	14	6
Jaroslav Pouzar	Czech.	6	8	5	13	8
Alexander Golikov	Soviet Union	7	7	6	13	6
Jukka Porvari	Finland	7	7	4	11	4
Boris Mikhailov	Soviet Union	7	6	5	11	2
Vladimir Krutov	Soviet Union	7	6	5	11	4
Sergei Makarov	Soviet Union	7	5	6	11	2
Marian Stastny	Czech.	6	5	6	11	4
Mark Johnson	USA	7	5	6	11	6

Innsbruck, Austria • 1976

Group A

Team	GP	W	L	T	GF	GA	PTS
Soviet Union	5	5	0	0	40	11	10
Czech.	5	3	2	0	17	10	6
W. Germany	5	2	3	0	21	24	4
Finland	5	2	3	0	19	18	4
USA	5	2	3	0	15	21	4
Poland	5	0	5	0	9	37	0

Group B

Team	GP	W	L	T	GF	GA	PTS
Romania	5	4	1	0	23	15	8
Austria	5	3	2	0	18	14	6
Japan	5	3	2	0	20	18	6
Yugoslavia	5	3	2	0	22	19	6
Switzerland	5	2	3	0	24	22	4
Bulgaria	5	0	5	0	19	38	0

1976 Final Rankings

1. Soviet Union
2. Czechoslovakia
3. W. Germany
4. Finland
5. USA
6. Poland
7. Romania
8. Austria
9. Japan
10. Yugoslavia
11. Switzerland
12. Bulgaria

1976 Scoring Leaders

Player	Team	GP	G	A	PTS	PIM
Vladimir Shadrin	Soviet Union	5	6	4	10	0
Alexander Maltsev	Soviet Union	5	5	5	10	0
Victor Shalimov	Soviet Union	5	5	5	10	2
Erich Kuhnhackl	W. Germany	5	5	5	10	10
Valeri Kharlamov	Soviet Union	5	3	6	9	6
Ernst Kopf	W. Germany	5	3	5	8	2
Vladimir Petrov	Soviet Union	5	4	3	7	8
A. Yakushev	Soviet Union	5	3	4	7	2
Bob Dobek	USA	5	3	4	7	4
Lorenz Funk	W. Germany	5	2	5	7	4
Victor Zhluktov	Soviet Union	5	1	6	7	2

Sapporo, Japan • 1972

Group A

Team	GP	W	L	T	GF	GA	PTS
Soviet Union	5	4	0	1	33	13	9
USA	5	3	2	0	18	15	6
Czech.	5	3	2	0	26	13	6
Sweden	5	2	2	1	17	13	5
Finland	5	2	3	0	14	24	4
Poland	5	0	5	0	9	39	0

Group B

Team	GP	W	L	T	GF	GA	PTS
W. Germany	4	3	1	0	22	10	6
Norway	4	3	1	0	16	14	6
Japan	4	2	1	1	17	16	5
Switzerland	4	0	2	2	9	16	2
Yugoslavia	4	0	3	1	9	17	1

1972 Final Rankings

1. Soviet Union
2. USA
3. Czechoslovakia
4. Sweden
5. Finland
6. Poland
7. W. Germany
8. Norway
9. Japan
10. Switzerland
11. Yugoslavia

1972 Scoring Leaders

Player	Team	GP	G	A	PTS	PIM
Valeri Kharlamov	Soviet Union	5	9	6	15	2
V. Nedomansky	Czech.	5	6	3	9	0
Vladimir Vikulov	Soviet Union	5	5	4	9	0
Craig Sarner	USA	5	4	5	9	0
Kevin Ahearn	USA	5	4	3	7	0
Alexander Maltsev	Soviet Union	5	4	3	7	0
Anatoli Firsov	Soviet Union	5	2	5	7	0
Yuri Blinov	Soviet Union	5	3	3	6	0
Jiri Kochta	Czech.	5	3	3	6	0
Richard Farda	Czech.	5	1	5	6	0

Grenoble, France • 1968

Group A

Team	GP	W	L	T	GF	GA	PTS
Soviet Union	7	6	1	0	48	10	12
Czech.	7	5	1	1	33	17	11
Canada	7	5	2	0	28	15	10
Sweden	7	4	2	1	23	18	9
Finland	7	3	3	1	17	23	7
USA	7	2	4	1	23	28	5
W. Germany	7	1	6	0	13	39	2
E. Germany	7	0	7	0	13	48	0

Group B

Team	GP	W	L	T	GF	GA	PTS
Yugoslavia	5	5	0	0	33	9	10
Japan	5	4	1	0	27	12	8
Norway	5	3	2	0	15	15	6
Romania	5	2	3	0	22	23	4
Austria	5	1	4	0	12	27	2
France	5	0	5	0	9	32	0

1968 Final Rankings

1. Soviet Union
2. Czechoslovakia
3. Canada
4. Sweden
5. Finland
6. USA
7. W. Germany
8. E. Germany
9. Yugoslavia
10. Japan
11. Norway
12. Romania
13. Austria
14. France

1968 Scoring Leaders

Player	Team	GP	G	A	PTS	PIM
Anatoli Firsov	Soviet Union	7	12	4	16	4
Vladimir Vikulov	Soviet Union	7	2	10	12	2
Vyatch. Starshinov	Soviet Union	7	6	6	12	2
Victor Populanov	Soviet Union	7	6	6	12	10
Josef Golonka	Czech.	7	4	6	10	8
Jan Hrbaty	Czech.	7	2	7	9	2
Fran Huck	Canada	7	4	5	9	10
Marshall Johnston	Canada	7	2	6	8	4
Jack Morrison	USA	7	2	6	8	10
V. Nedomansky	Czech.	7	5	2	7	4

Innsbruck, Austria • 1964

Group A

Team	GP	W	L	T	GF	GA	PTS
Soviet Union	7	7	0	0	54	10	14
Sweden	7	5	2	0	47	16	10
Czech.	7	5	2	0	38	19	10
Canada	7	5	2	0	32	17	10
USA	7	2	5	0	29	33	4
Finland	7	2	5	0	10	31	4
W. Germany	7	2	5	0	13	49	4
Switzerland	7	0	7	0	9	57	0

Group B

Team	GP	W	L	T	GF	GA	PTS
Poland	7	6	1	0	40	13	12
Norway	7	5	2	0	40	19	10
Japan	7	4	2	1	35	31	9
Romania	7	3	3	1	31	28	7
Austria	7	3	3	1	24	28	7
Yugoslavia	7	3	3	1	29	37	7
Italy	7	2	5	0	24	42	4
Hungary	7	0	7	0	14	39	0

1964 Final Rankings

1. Soviet Union
2. Sweden
3. Czechoslovakia
4. Canada
5. USA
6. Finland
7. W. Germany
8. Switzerland
9. Poland
10. Norway
11. Japan
12. Romania
13. Austria
14. Yugoslavia
15. Italy
16. Hungary

1964 Scoring Leaders

Player	Team	GP	G	A	PTS	PIM
Sven Tumba	Sweden	7	8	3	11	0
Ulf Sterner	Sweden	7	6	5	11	0
Victor Yakushev	Soviet Union	7	7	3	10	0
Boris Mayorov	Soviet Union	7	7	3	10	0
Jiri Dolana	Czech.	7	7	3	10	0
Vy. Starshinov	Soviet Union	7	7	3	10	6
Josef Cerny	Czech.	7	5	5	10	2
A. Andersson	Sweden	7	7	2	9	8
K. Loktev	Soviet Union	7	4	5	9	8
Gary Dineen	Canada	7	3	6	9	10

Squaw Valley, California, USA • 1960

Group A

Team	GP	W	L	T	GF	GA	PTS
Canada	2	2	0	0	24	3	4
Sweden	2	1	1	0	21	5	2
Japan	2	0	2	0	1	38	0

Group B

Team	GP	W	L	T	GF	GA	PTS
Soviet Union	2	2	0	0	16	4	4
W. Germany	2	1	1	0	4	9	2
Finland	2	0	2	0	5	12	0

Group C

Team	GP	W	L	T	GF	GA	PTS
USA	2	2	0	0	19	6	4
Czech.	2	1	1	0	23	6	2
Austria	2	0	2	0	2	30	0

Final Round

Team	GP	W	L	T	GF	GA	PTS
USA	5	5	0	0	29	11	10
Canada	5	4	1	0	31	12	8
Soviet Union	5	2	2	1	24	19	5
Czech.	5	2	3	0	21	23	4
Sweden	5	1	3	1	19	19	3
W. Germany	5	0	5	0	5	45	0

Consolation Round

Team	GP	W	L	T	GF	GA	PTS
Finland	4	3	0	1	50	11	7
Japan	4	2	1	1	32	22	5
Austria	4	0	4	0	8	57	0

1960 Final Rankings

1. USA
2. Canada
3. Soviet Union
4. Czechoslovakia
5. Sweden
6. W. Germany
7. Finland
8. Japan
9. Austria

1960 Scoring Leaders

Player	Team	GP	G	A	PTS	PIM
Fred Etcher	Canada	7	9	12	21	0
Bobby Attersley	Canada	7	6	12	18	4
Bill Cleary	USA	7	7	7	14	2
Bill Christian	USA	7	2	11	13	2
G. Samolenko	Canada	7	8	4	12	0
Lars E. Lundvall	Sweden	7	8	4	12	2
Vaclav Panucek	Czech.	7	7	5	12	0
John Mayasich	USA	7	7	5	12	2
Nisse Nilsson	Sweden	7	7	5	12	4
V. Alexandrov	Soviet Union	7	7	5	12	8
Butch Martin	Canada	7	6	6	12	14
Ronald Petersson	Sweden	7	4	8	12	2

Cortina d'Ampezzo, Italy • 1956

Group A

Team	GP	W	L	T	GF	GA	PTS
Canada	3	3	0	0	30	1	6
W. Germany	3	1	1	1	9	6	3
Italy	3	0	1	2	5	7	2
Austria	3	0	2	1	2	32	1

Group B

Team	GP	W	L	T	GF	GA	PTS
Czech.	2	2	0	0	12	6	4
USA	2	1	1	0	7	4	2
Poland	2	0	2	0	3	12	0

Group C

Team	GP	W	L	T	GF	GA	PTS
Soviet Union	2	2	0	0	15	4	4
Sweden	2	1	1	0	7	10	2
Switzerland	2	0	2	0	8	16	0

Final Round

Team	GP	W	L	T	GF	GA	PTS
Soviet Union	5	5	0	0	25	5	10
USA	5	4	1	0	26	12	8
Canada	5	3	2	0	23	11	6
Sweden	5	1	3	1	10	17	3
Czech.	5	1	4	0	20	30	2
W. Germany	5	0	4	1	6	35	1

Consolation Round

Team	GP	W	L	T	GF	GA	PTS
Italy	3	3	0	0	21	7	6
Poland	3	2	1	0	12	10	4
Switzerland	3	1	2	0	12	8	2
Austria	3	0	3	0	9	19	0

1956 Final Rankings

1. Soviet Union
2. USA
3. Canada
4. Sweden
5. Czechoslovakia
6. W. Germany
7. Italy
8. Poland
9. Switzerland
10. Austria

1956 Scoring Leaders

Player	Team	GP	G	A	PTS	PIM
Jim Logan	Canada	8	7	5	12	2
Paul Knox	Canada	8	7	5	12	2
Vsevolod Bobrov	Soviet Union	7	9	2	11	4
Gerry Theberge	Canada	8	9	2	11	8
Jack McKenzie	Canada	8	7	4	11	4
John Mayasich	USA	7	7	3	10	2
Alexei Guryshev	Soviet Union	7	7	2	9	0
Vlastimil Bubnik	Czech.	7	5	4	9	14
George Scholes	Canada	8	5	3	8	2

Oslo, Norway • 1952

Team	GP	W	L	T	GF	GA	PTS
Canada	8	7	0	1	71	1	15
USA	8	6	1	1	43	21	13
Sweden	8	6	2	0	48	19	12
Czech.	8	6	2	0	47	18	12
Switzerland	8	4	4	0	40	40	8
Poland	8	2	5	1	21	56	5
Finland	8	2	6	0	21	60	4
W. Germany	8	1	6	1	21	53	3
Norway	8	0	8	0	15	46	0

1952 Final Rankings

1. Canada
2. USA
3. Sweden
4. Czechoslovakia
5. Switzerland
6. Poland
7. Finland
8. W. Germany
9. Norway

St. Moritz, Switzerland • 1948

Team	GP	W	L	T	GF	GA	PTS
Canada	7	6	0	1	57	2	13
Czech.	7	6	0	1	76	15	13
Switzerland	7	5	2	0	62	17	10
Sweden	7	4	3	0	53	23	8
Great Britain	7	3	4	0	36	43	6
Poland	7	2	5	0	25	74	4
Austria	7	1	6	0	31	64	2
Italy	7	0	7	0	23	125	0

** USA also competed as an unofficial entry.*

1948 Final Rankings

1. Canada
2. Czechoslovakia
3. Switzerland
4. Sweden
5. Great Britain
6. Poland
7. Austria
8. Italy

Garmisch-Partenkirchen, Germany • 1936

Group A

Team	GP	W	L	T	GF	GA	PTS
Canada	3	3	0	0	24	3	6
Austria	3	2	1	0	11	7	4
Poland	3	1	2	0	11	12	2
Latvia	3	0	0	3	3	27	0

Group B

Team	GP	W	L	T	GF	GA	PTS
Germany	3	2	1	0	5	1	4
USA	3	2	1	0	5	2	4
Italy	3	1	2	0	2	5	2
Switzerland	3	1	2	0	1	5	2

Group C

Team	GP	W	L	T	GF	GA	PTS
Czech.	3	3	0	0	10	0	6
Hungary	3	2	1	0	14	5	4
France	3	1	2	0	4	7	2
Belgium	3	0	3	0	4	20	6

Group D

Team	GP	W	L	T	GF	GA	PTS
Great Britain	2	2	0	0	4	0	4
Sweden	2	1	1	0	2	1	2
Japan	2	0	2	0	0	5	0

Group A Semifinal Round

Team	GP	W	L	T	GF	GA	PTS
Great Britain	3	2	0	1	8	3	5
Canada	3	2	1	0	22	4	4
Germany	3	1	1	1	5	8	3
Hungary	3	0	0	3	2	22	0

Group B Semifinal Round

Team	GP	W	L	T	GF	GA	PTS
USA	3	3	0	0	5	1	6
Czech.	3	2	1	0	6	4	4
Sweden	3	1	2	0	3	6	2
Austria	3	0	3	0	1	4	0

Final Round

Team	GP	W	L	T	GF	GA	PTS
Great Britain	3	2	0	1	7	1	5
Canada	3	2	1	0	9	2	4
USA	3	1	1	1	2	1	3
Czech.	3	0	3	0	0	14	0

1936 Final Rankings

1. Great Britain
2. Canada
3. USA
4. Czechoslovakia
5. Germany
5. Sweden
7. Hungary
7. Austria

Lake Placid, New York, USA • 1932

Team	GP	W	L	T	GF	GA	PTS
Canada	6	5	0	1	32	4	11
USA	6	4	1	1	27	5	9
Germany	6	2	4	0	7	26	4
Poland	6	0	6	0	3	34	0

1932 Final Rankings

1. Canada
2. USA
3. Germany
4. Poland

St. Moritz, Switzerland • 1928

Group A

Team	GP	W	L	T	GF	GA	PTS
Great Britain	3	2	1	0	10	6	4
France	3	2	1	0	6	5	4
Belgium	3	2	1	0	9	10	4
Hungary	3	0	3	0	2	6	0

Group B

Team	GP	W	L	T	GF	GA	PTS
Sweden	2	1	0	1	5	2	3
Czech.	2	1	1	0	3	5	2
Poland	2	0	0	1	4	5	1

Group C

Team	GP	W	L	T	GF	GA	PTS
Switzerland	2	1	0	1	5	4	3
Austria	2	0	0	2	4	4	2
Germany	2	0	0	1	0	1	1

Final Round

Team	GP	W	L	T	GF	GA	PTS
Canada	3	3	0	0	38	0	6
Sweden	3	2	1	0	7	12	4
Switzerland	3	1	2	0	4	17	2
Great Britain	3	0	3	0	1	21	0

1928 Final Rankings

1. Canada
2. Sweden
3. Switzerland
4. Great Britain
5. France
5. Czechoslovakia
5. Austria
8. Belgium
8. Poland
8. Germany
11. Hungary

Chamonix, France • 1924

Group A

Team	GP	W	L	T	GF	GA	PTS
Canada	3	3	0	0	85	0	6
Sweden	3	2	1	0	18	25	4
Czech.	3	1	2	0	14	41	2
Switzerland	3	0	3	0	2	53	0

Group B

Team	GP	W	L	T	GF	GA	PTS
USA	3	3	0	0	52	0	6
Great Britain	3	2	1	0	34	16	4
France	3	1	2	0	9	42	2
Belgium	3	0	3	0	8	35	0

Final Round

Team	GP	W	L	T	GF	GA	PTS
Canada	3	3	0	0	47	3	6
USA	3	2	1	0	32	6	4
Great Britain	3	1	2	0	6	33	2
Sweden	3	0	3	0	3	46	0

1924 Final Rankings

1. Canada
2. USA
3. Great Britain
4. Sweden
5. Czechoslovakia
5. France
7. Switzerland
7. Belgium

Antwerp, Belgium • 1920

(unofficial)

Hockey was played at the 1920 Summer Olympics in Antwerp, Belgium. This tournament is not counted in cumulative Winter Olympic Hockey statistics. The IIHF has declared it the first World Championship.

1920 Final Rankings

1. Canada
2. USA
3. Czechoslovakia
4. Sweden
5. Switzerland

Olympic Results, Active NHL Players

Medal	Name	Year	Team	GP	G	A	Pts	PIM	2000-01 Club
B	Alatalo, Mika	1994	FIN	7	2	1	3	2	PHX
	Albelin, Tommy	1998	SWE	3	0	0	0	4	CGY
	Alfredsson, Daniel	1998	SWE	4	2	3	5	2	OTT
	Amonte, Tony	1998	USA	4	0	1	1	4	CHI
S	Aucoin, Adrian	1994	CAN	4	0	0	0	2	VAN-TB
	Benda, Jan	1994	GER	8	0	1	1	6	(Finland)
	Benda, Jan	1998	GER	4	3	0	3	8	(Finland)
G	Beranek, Josef	1998	CZE	6	1	0	1	4	PIT
	Berezin, Sergei	1994	RUS	8	3	2	5	2	TOR
B	Berg, Aki	1998	FIN	6	0	0	0	6	LA-TOR
	Blake, Rob	1998	CAN	6	1	1	2	2	LA-COL
	Bondra, Peter	1998	SVK	2	1	0	1	25	WSH
	Brind'Amour, Rod	1998	CAN	6	1	2	3	0	CAR
S	Bure, Pavel	1998	RUS	6	9	0	9	2	FLA
S	Bure, Valeri	1998	RUS	6	1	0	1	0	CGY
G	Caloun, Jan	1998	CZE	3	0	0	0	6	CBJ
	Campbell, Jim	1994	USA	8	0	0	0	6	MTL
	Carney, Keith	1998	USA	4	0	0	0	2	PHX
	Chelios, Chris	1984	USA	6	0	4	4	8	DET
	Chelios, Chris	1998	USA	4	2	0	2	2	DET
	Ciger, Zdeno	1998	SVK	4	1	1	2	4	(Slovakia)
	Corson, Shayne	1998	CAN	6	1	1	2	2	TOR
	Czerkawski, Mariusz	1992	POL	5	0	1	1	4	NYI
G	Dackell, Andreas	1994	SWE	4	0	0	0	0	OTT
	Dahl, Kevin	1992	CAN	8	2	0	2	6	CBJ
	Dahlen, Ulf	1998	SWE	4	1	0	1	2	WSH
	Daigneault, J.J.	1984	CAN	7	1	1	2	0	MIN
	Deadmarsh, Adam	1998	USA	4	1	0	1	2	COL-LA
	Desjardins, Eric	1998	CAN	6	0	0	0	2	PHI
	Dineen, Kevin	1984	CAN	7	0	0	0	8	COL
	Donato, Ted	1992	USA	8	4	3	7	8	DAL
	Drury, Ted	1992	USA	7	1	1	2	0	CBJ
	Drury, Ted	1994	USA	7	1	2	3	2	CBJ

Medal	Name	Year	Team	GP	G	A	Pts	PIM	2000-01 Club
	Emma, David	1992	USA	6	0	1	1	6	FLA
S	Fedorov, Sergei	1998	RUS	6	1	5	6	8	DET
	Ferraro, Peter	1994	USA	8	6	0	6	6	(AHL)
	Fleury, Theoren	1998	CAN	6	1	3	4	2	NYR
	Foote, Adam	1998	CAN	6	0	1	1	4	COL
G	Forsberg, Peter	1994	SWE	8	2	6	8	6	COL
	Forsberg, Peter	1998	SWE	4	1	4	5	6	COL
S	Gonchar, Sergei	1998	RUS	6	0	2	2	0	WSH
	Granato, Tony	1988	USA	6	1	7	8	4	SJ
	Guerin, Bill	1998	USA	4	0	3	3	2	EDM-BOS
G	Gusarov, Alexei	1988	USSR	8	1	3	4	6	COL-NYR-STL
S	Gusarov, Alexei	1998	RUS	6	0	1	1	8	COL-NYR-STL
	Gusmanov, Ravil	1994	RUS	8	3	1	4	0	Europe
G	Hamrlik, Roman	1998	CZE	6	1	0	1	2	NYI
S	Harlock, David	1994	CAN	8	0	0	0	8	ATL
	Hatcher, Derian	1998	USA	4	0	0	0	0	DAL
	Hatcher, Kevin	1998	USA	3	0	2	2	0	CAR
	Hauer, Brett	1994	USA	8	0	0	0	10	(IHL)
	Hecht, Jochen	1998	GER	4	1	0	1	6	STL
	Hedican, Bret	1992	USA	8	0	0	0	4	FLA
	Heinze, Steve	1992	USA	8	1	3	4	8	CBJ-BUF
G	Hejduk, Milan	1998	CZE	4	0	0	0	2	COL
	Hendrickson, Darby	1994	USA	8	0	0	0	6	MIN
	Hill, Sean	1992	USA	8	2	0	2	6	STL
	Hull, Brett	1998	USA	4	2	1	3	0	DAL
G	Jagr, Jaromir	1998	CZE	6	1	4	5	2	PIT
	Johansson, Calle	1998	SWE	4	0	0	0	2	WSH
	Johnson, Craig	1994	USA	8	0	4	4	4	LA
S	Johnson, Greg	1994	CAN	8	0	3	3	0	NSH
G	Jonsson, Kenny	1994	SWE	3	1	0	1	0	NYI
G	Juhlin, Patrik	1994	SWE	8	7	1	8	16	(Finland)
	Juneau, Joe	1992	CAN	8	6	9	15	4	PHX
G	Kamensky, Valeri	1988	USSR	8	4	2	6	4	NYR

Medal	Name	Year	Team	GP	G	A	Pts	PIM	2000-01 Club
S	Kamensky, Valeri	1998	RUS	6	1	2	3	0	NYR
B	Kapanen, Sami	1994	FIN	8	1	0	1	2	CAR
B	Kapanen, Sami	1998	FIN	6	0	1	1	0	CAR
S	Kariya, Paul	1994	CAN	8	3	4	7	2	ANA
S	Kasparaitis, Darius	1998	RUS	6	0	2	2	6	PIT
B	Kiprusoff, Marko	1994	FIN	8	3	3	6	4	(Finland)
G	Kjellberk, Patrik	1994	SWE	8	0	1	1	2	NSH
	Knutsen, Espen	1994	NOR	7	1	3	4	2	CBJ
B	Koivu, Saku	1994	FIN	8	4	3	7	12	MTL
B	Koivu, Saku	1998	FIN	6	2	8	10	4	MTL
G	Kovalenko, Andrei	1992	RUS	8	1	1	2	2	BOS
S	Kovalenko, Andrei	1998	RUS	6	4	1	5	14	BOS
G	Kovalev, Alexei	1992	RUS	8	1	2	3	14	PIT
G	Kravchuk, Igor	1988	USSR	6	1	0	1	0	OTT-CGY
G	Kravchuk, Igor	1992	RUS	8	3	2	5	6	OTT-CGY
S	Kravchuk, Igor	1998	RUS	6	0	2	2	2	OTT-CGY
S	Krivokrasov, Sergei	1998	RUS	6	0	0	0	4	MIN
G	Kucera, Frantisek	1998	CZE	6	0	0	0	0	PIT
	Lachance, Scott	1992	USA	8	0	1	1	6	VAN
B	Lang, Robert	1992	CZE	8	5	8	13	8	PIT
G	Lang, Robert	1998	CZE	6	0	3	3	0	PIT
	Langenbrunner, Jamie	1998	USA	3	0	0	0	4	DAL
G	Larionov, Igor	1984	USSR	6	1	4	5	6	FLA-DET
G	Larionov, Igor	1988	USSR	8	4	9	13	4	FLA-DET
	Laukkanen, Janne	1992	FIN	8	0	1	1	6	PIT
B	Laukkanen, Janne	1994	FIN	8	0	2	2	12	PIT
B	Laukkanen, Janne	1998	FIN	6	0	0	0	4	PIT
	LeClair, John	1998	USA	4	0	1	1	0	PHI
	Leetch, Brian	1988	USA	6	1	5	6	4	NYR
	Leetch, Brian	1998	USA	4	1	1	2	0	NYR
B	Lehtinen, Jere	1994	FIN	8	3	0	3	0	DAL
B	Lehtinen, Jere	1998	FIN	6	4	2	6	2	DAL
	Lidstrom, Nicklas	1998	SWE	4	1	1	2	2	DET
B	Lind, Juha	1998	FIN	6	0	1	1	6	MTL
	Linden, Trevor	1998	CAN	6	1	0	1	10	MTL-WSH
	Lindgren, Mats	1998	SWE	4	0	0	0	2	NHI
S	Lindros, Eric	1992	CAN	8	5	6	11	5	(did not play)
	Lindros, Eric	1998	CAN	6	2	3	5	2	(did not play)
	Lumme, Jyrki	1988	FIN	6	0	1	1	2	PHX
B	Lumme, Jyrki	1998	FIN	6	1	0	1	16	PHX
	MacInnis, Al	1998	CAN	6	2	0	2	2	STL
G	Malakhov, Vladimir	1992	RUS	8	3	0	3	4	NYR
S	Manderville, Kent	1992	CAN	8	1	2	3	0	PHI
	Marchant, Todd	1994	USA	8	1	1	2	6	EDM
	McEachern, Shawn	1992	USA	8	1	0	1	10	OTT
	McInnis, Marty	1992	USA	8	5	2	7	4	ANA
S	Mironov, Boris	1998	RUS	6	0	2	2	2	CHI
G	Mironov, Dmitri	1992	RUS	8	3	1	4	6	WSH
S	Mironov, Dmitri	1998	RUS	6	0	3	3	0	WSH
	Modano, Mike	1998	USA	4	2	0	2	0	DAL
G	Mogilny, Alexander	1988	USSR	6	3	2	5	2	NJ
S	Morozov, Aleksey	1998	RUS	6	2	2	4	0	PIT
	Muller, Kirk	1984	CAN	6	2	1	3	0	DAL
S	Nedved, Petr	1994	CAN	8	5	1	6	6	NYR
S	Nemchinov, Sergei	1998	RUS	6	1	0	1	0	NJ
	Nieuwendyk, Joe	1998	CAN	6	2	3	5	2	DAL
B	Niinimaa, Janne	1998	FIN	6	0	3	3	8	EDM
	Nikolishin, Andrei	1994	RUS	8	2	5	7	6	WSH
	Norstrom, Mattias	1998	SWE	4	0	1	1	2	LA
	Norton, Jeff	1988	USA	6	0	4	4	4	PIT-SJ
	Numminen, Teppo	1988	FIN	6	1	4	5	0	PHX
B	Numminen, Teppo	1998	FIN	6	1	1	2	2	PHX
	Nylander, Michael	1998	SWE	4	0	0	0	6	CHI
	Ohlund, Mattias	1998	SWE	4	0	1	1	4	VAN
	Palffy, Ziggy	1994	SVK	8	3	7	10	8	LA
	Patrick, James	1984	CAN	7	0	3	3	4	BUF
B	Peltonen, Ville	1994	FIN	8	4	3	7	0	NSH
B	Peltonen, Ville	1998	FIN	6	2	1	3	6	NSH
	Petrovicky, Robert	1994	SVK	8	1	6	7	18	NYI
	Petrovicky, Robert	1998	SVK	4	2	1	3	0	NYI
	Primeau, Keith	1998	CAN	6	2	1	3	4	PHI
	Pronger, Chris	1998	CAN	6	0	0	0	4	STL
	Recchi, Mark	1998	CAN	5	0	2	2	0	PHI
G	Reichel, Robert	1998	CZE	6	3	0	3	0	(Czech.)
	Renberg, Mikael	1998	SWE	4	1	2	3	4	(Sweden)
	Richards, Travis	1994	USA	8	0	0	0	2	(IHL)
	Richter, Barry	1994	USA	8	0	3	3	4	MTL
	Roenick, Jeremy	1998	USA	4	0	1	1	6	PHX
	Rolston, Brian	1994	USA	8	7	0	7	8	BOS
G	Rucinsky, Martin	1998	CZE	6	3	1	4	4	MTL
	Sacco, Joe	1992	USA	8	0	2	2	0	WSH
	Sakic, Joe	1998	CAN	4	1	2	3	4	COL
	Salei, Ruslan	1998	BLR	7	1	0	1	4	ANA
	Satan, Miroslav	1994	SVK	8	9	0	9	0	BUF
S	Savage, Brian	1994	CAN	8	2	2	4	6	MTL
	Schneider, Mathieu	1998	USA	4	0	0	0	6	LA
	Selanne, Teemu	1992	FIN	8	7	4	11	6	ANA-SJ
B	Selanne, Teemu	1998	FIN	5	4	6	10	8	ANA-SJ
	Shanahan, Brendan	1998	CAN	6	2	0	2	0	DET
B	Slegr, Jiri	1992	CZE	8	1	1	2	14	ATL
G	Slegr, Jiri	1998	CZE	6	1	0	1	8	ATL
B	Smehlik, Richard	1992	CZE	8	0	1	1	2	BUF
G	Smehlik, Richard	1998	CZE	6	0	1	1	4	BUF
	Stevens, Kevin	1988	USA	5	1	3	4	2	PHI-PIT
	Stevens, Scott	1998	CAN	6	0	0	0	2	NJ
G	Straka, Martin	1998	CZE	6	1	2	3	0	PIT
	Sturm, Marco	1998	GER	2	0	0	0	0	SJ
	Sundin, Mats	1998	SWE	4	3	0	3	4	TOR
	Sundstrom, Niklas	1998	SWE	4	1	1	2	2	SJ
	Suter, Gary	1998	USA	4	0	0	0	2	SJ
B	Svehla, Robert	1992	CZE	8	2	1	3	8	FLA
	Svehla, Robert	1994	SVK	8	2	4	6	26	FLA
	Svehla, Robert	1998	SVK	2	0	1	1	0	FLA
G	Svoboda, Petr	1998	CZE	6	1	1	2	39	TB
S	Therien, Chris	1994	CAN	4	0	0	0	4	PHI
B	Timonen, Kimmo	1998	FIN	6	0	1	1	2	NSH
S	Titov, German	1998	RUS	6	1	0	1	6	ANA
	Tkachuk, Keith	1992	USA	8	1	1	2	12	PHX-STL
	Tkachuk, Keith	1998	USA	4	0	2	2	6	PHX-STL
	Tsyplakov, Vladimir	1998	BLR	5	1	1	2	2	BUF
S	Warriner, Todd	1994	CAN	4	1	1	2	0	TB
	Weight, Doug	1998	USA	4	0	2	2	2	EDM
	Weinrich, Eric	1988	USA	3	0	0	0	0	MTL-BOS
S	Werenka, Brad	1994	CAN	8	2	2	4	8	CGY
S	Woolley, Jason	1992	CAN	8	0	5	5	4	BUF
S	Yashin, Alexei	1998	RUS	6	3	3	6	0	OTT
B	Ylonen, Juha	1998	FIN	6	0	0	0	8	PHX
	Young, Scott	1988	USA	6	2	6	8	4	STL
	Young, Scott	1992	USA	8	2	1	3	2	STL
G	Yushkevich, Dmitry	1992	RUS	8	1	2	3	4	TOR
S	Yushkevich, Dmitry	1998	RUS	6	0	0	0	2	TOR
	Yzerman, Steve	1998	CAN	6	1	1	2	10	DET
	Zamuner, Rob	1998	CAN	6	1	0	1	8	OTT
S	Zelepukin, Valeri	1998	RUS	6	1	2	3	0	CHI
G	Zhamnov, Alexei	1992	RUS	8	0	3	3	8	CHI
S	Zhamnov, Alexei	1998	RUS	6	2	1	3	2	CHI
G	Zhitnik, Alexei	1992	RUS	8	1	0	1	0	BUF
S	Zhitnik, Alexei	1998	RUS	6	0	2	2	2	BUF
G	Zubov, Sergei	1992	RUS	8	0	1	1	0	DAL

Olympic Results, Active NHL Goaltenders

Medal	Name	Year	Team	GPI	W	L	T	Mins	GA	SO	Avg	2000-01 Club
	Brodeur, Martin	1998	CAN	Did not play – backup goaltender								NJ
	Burke, Sean	1988	CAN	4	1	2	1	238	12	0	3.02	PHX
S	Burke, Sean	1992	CAN	7	5	2	0	429	17	0	2.37	PHX
G	Cechmanek, Roman	1998	CZE	Did not play – backup goaltender								PHI
	Dunham, Mike	1992	USA	Did not play – backup goaltender								NSH
	Dunham, Mike	1994	USA	3	0	1	2	180	15	0	5.00	NSH
	Hasek, Dominik	1988	CZE	5	3	2	0	217	18	1	4.98	BUF
G	Hasek, Dominik	1998	CZE	6	5	1	0	369	6	2	0.97	BUF
	Hedberg, Johan	1998	SWE	Did not play – backup goaltender								PIT
S	Hirsch, Corey	1994	CAN	8	5	2	1	495	18	0	2.18	WSH
G	Hnilicka, Milan	1998	CZE	Did not play – backup goaltender								ATL
	Joseph, Curtis	1998	CAN	Did not play – backup goaltender								TOR
G	Khabibulin, Nikolai	1992	RUS	Did not play – backup goaltender								TB
S	Kidd, Trevor	1992	CAN	1	1	0	0	60	0	1	0.00	FLA
	Kolzig, Olaf	1998	GER	2	2	0	0	120	2	1	1.00	WSH
S	Legace, Manny	1994	CAN	Did not play – backup goaltender								DET
	Richter, Mike	1988	USA	4	2	2	0	230	15	0	3.91	NYR
	Richter, Mike	1998	USA	4	1	3	0	237	14	0	3.55	NYR
	Roy, Patrick	1998	CAN	6	4	2	0	369	9	1	1.46	COL
G	Salo, Tommy	1994	SWE	6	5	1	0	370	13	1	2.11	EDM
	Salo, Tommy	1998	SWE	4	2	2	0	238	9	0	2.27	EDM
G	Shtalenkov, Mikhail	1992	RUS	8	7	1	0	440	12	1	1.64	(Russia)
S	Shtalenkov, Mikhail	1998	RUS	5	4	1	0	290	8	0	1.65	(Russia)
	Snow, Garth	1994	USA	5	1	3	1	299	17	0	3.41	PIT
	Terreri, Chris	1988	USA	3	1	1	0	127	14	0	6.58	NJ-NYI
	Turek, Roman	1994	CZE	2	2	0	0	120	3	0	1.50	STL
	Vanbiesbrouck, John	1998	USA	1	0	0	0	1	0	0	0.00	NYI-NJ
	Yeremeyev, Vitali	1998	KAZ	7	1	3	1	292	28	0	5.76	NYR

NHL Clubs' Minor-League Affiliations, 2001-02

NHL Club	Minor-League Affiliate
Anaheim	Cincinnati Mighty Ducks (AHL)
Atlanta	Chicago Wolves (AHL) Greenville Grrrowl (ECHL)
Boston	Providence Bruins (AHL) Greenville Grrrowl (ECHL)
Buffalo	Rochester Americans (AHL) South Carolina Stingrays (ECHL)
Calgary	Saint John Flames (AHL)
Carolina	Lowell Lock Monsters (AHL) Florida Everblades (ECHL)
Chicago	Norfolk Admirals (AHL)
Colorado	Hershey Bears (AHL)
Columbus	Syracuse Crunch (AHL) Dayton Bombers (ECHL) Elmira Jackals (UHL)
Dallas	Utah Grizzlies (AHL)
Detroit	Cincinnati Mighty Ducks (AHL) Toledo Storm (ECHL)
Edmonton	Hamilton Bulldogs (AHL) Columbus Cottonmouths (ECHL)
Florida	– none –
Los Angeles	Manchester Monarchs (AHL) Reading Royals (ECHL)
Minnesota	Houston Aeros (AHL) Louisiana IceGators (ECHL)

NHL Club	Minor-League Affiliate
Montreal	Citadelles de Québec (AHL) Mississippi Sea Wolves (ECHL) New Mexico Scorpions (CHL)
Nashville	Milwaukee Admirals (AHL) Cincinnati Cyclones (ECHL)
New Jersey	Albany River Rats (AHL)
NY Islanders	Bridgeport Sound Tigers (AHL) Trenton Titans (ECHL)
NY Rangers	Hartford Wolf Pack (AHL)
Ottawa	Grand Rapids Griffins (AHL) Mobile Mysticks (ECHL)
Philadelphia	Philadelphia Phantoms (AHL) Trenton Titans (ECHL)
Phoenix	Springfield Falcons (AHL) Mississippi Sea Wolves (ECHL)
Pittsburgh	Wilkes-Barre/Scranton Penguins (AHL) Wheeling Nailers (ECHL)
St. Louis	Worcester IceCats (AHL) Peoria Rivermen (ECHL)
San Jose	Cleveland Barons (AHL) Richmond Renegades (ECHL) Dayton Bombers (ECHL)
Tampa Bay	Springfield Falcons (AHL)) Pensacola Ice Pilots (ECHL)
Toronto	St. John's Maple Leafs (AHL)
Vancouver	Manitoba Moose (AHL)
Washington	Portland Pirates (AHL) Richmond Renagades (ECHL) Quad City Mallards (UHL)

HockeyRules
SALT LAKE 2002

Mighty Ducks of Anaheim

2000-01 Results: 25W-41L-11T-5OTL 66PTS. Fifth, Pacific Division

Year-by-Year Record

		Home				Road				Overall								
Season	GP	W	L	T	OL	W	L	T	OL	W	L	T	OL	GF	GA	Pts.	Finished	Playoff Result
2000-01	82	15	20	4	2	10	21	7	3	25	41	11	5	188	245	66	5th, Pacific Div.	Out of Playoffs
1999-2000	82	19	13	7	2	15	20	5	1	34	33	12	3	217	227	83	5th, Pacific Div.	Out of Playoffs
1998-99	82	21	14	6	...	14	20	7	...	35	34	13	...	215	206	83	3rd, Pacific Div.	Lost Conf. Quarter-Final
1997-98	82	12	23	6	...	14	20	7	...	26	43	13	...	205	261	65	6th, Pacific Div.	Out of Playoffs
1996-97	82	23	12	6	...	13	21	7	...	36	33	13	...	245	233	85	2nd, Pacific Div.	Lost Conf. Semi-Final
1995-96	82	22	15	4	...	13	24	4	...	35	39	8	...	234	247	78	4th, Pacific Div.	Out of Playoffs
1994-95	48	11	9	4	...	5	18	1	...	16	27	5	...	125	164	37	6th, Pacific Div.	Out of Playoffs
1993-94	84	14	26	2	...	19	20	3	...	33	46	5	...	229	251	71	4th, Pacific Div.	Out of Playoffs

2001-02 Schedule

Month	Day	Date	Opponent
Oct.	Thu.	4	at Boston
	Sat.	6	at Pittsburgh
	Mon.	8	at Toronto
	Tue.	9	at Montreal
	Fri.	12	Washington
	Sun.	14	Tampa Bay*
	Wed.	17	Boston
	Thu.	18	at Los Angeles
	Sun.	21	Vancouver*
	Wed.	24	at Phoenix
	Sun.	28	Colorado*
	Wed.	31	San Jose
Nov.	Fri.	2	Chicago
	Sun.	4	Atlanta*
	Wed.	7	Calgary
	Fri.	9	Detroit
	Sun.	11	Dallas*
	Wed.	14	San Jose
	Fri.	16	at Columbus
	Sat.	17	at Washington
	Tue.	20	at Tampa Bay
	Wed.	21	at Florida
	Sat.	24	at NY Islanders
	Sun.	25	at NY Rangers*
	Wed.	28	Edmonton
	Fri.	30	San Jose
Dec.	Sun.	2	Nashville*
	Wed.	5	at Edmonton
	Thu.	6	at Vancouver
	Sat.	8	at Calgary
	Mon.	10	at Colorado
	Wed.	12	Vancouver
	Fri.	14	Columbus
	Sun.	16	Los Angeles*
	Tue.	18	at Minnesota
	Wed.	19	at Colorado
	Fri.	21	Phoenix
	Sun.	23	at Phoenix*
	Wed.	26	at San Jose
	Thu.	27	at Los Angeles
	Sun.	30	at Chicago
	Mon.	31	at Columbus
Jan.	Wed.	2	at Detroit
	Fri.	4	Florida
	Wed.	9	St. Louis
	Fri.	11	at Minnesota
	Sat.	12	at Nashville
	Mon.	14	Nashville
	Wed.	16	Buffalo
	Fri.	18	at Edmonton
	Sat.	19	at Calgary
	Mon.	21	Los Angeles
	Wed.	23	Minnesota
	Fri.	25	at Dallas
	Sat.	26	at Nashville
	Mon.	28	at St. Louis
	Wed.	30	Columbus
Feb.	Wed.	6	Philadelphia
	Fri.	8	Carolina
	Sun.	10	Dallas*
	Wed.	13	Calgary
	Wed.	27	Minnesota
Mar.	Sun.	3	at Chicago*
	Wed.	6	at Atlanta
	Fri.	8	New Jersey
	Sun.	10	Ottawa*
	Wed.	13	Pittsburgh
	Fri.	15	Chicago
	Sun.	17	St. Louis*
	Tue.	19	at Detroit
	Thu.	21	at Philadelphia
	Fri.	22	at St. Louis
	Sun.	24	at Dallas*
	Wed.	27	Phoenix
	Thu.	28	at Phoenix
	Sat.	30	at Vancouver
Apr.	Tue.	2	at San Jose
	Wed.	3	Detroit
	Fri.	5	Edmonton
	Sun.	7	Dallas*
	Fri.	12	Colorado
	Sun.	14	at Los Angeles*

* Denotes afternoon game.

After more than six seasons in a Sharks uniform, Jeff Friesen was acquired by Anaheim (with goalie Steve Shields) when the Mighty Ducks dealt Teemu Selanne to San Jose last season. Friesen was the 11th player taken in the 1994 Entry Draft.

Franchise date: June 15, 1993

PACIFIC DIVISION

9th NHL Season

2001-02 Player Personnel

FORWARDS	HT	WT	S	Place of Birth	Date	2000-01 Club
BALMOCHNYKH, Maxim	6-1	180	L	Lipetsk, USSR	3/7/79	Cincinnati (AHL)
BYLSMA, Dan	6-2	212	L	Grand Haven, MI	9/19/70	Anaheim
CHOUINARD, Marc	6-5	206	R	Charlesbourg, Que.	5/6/77	Anaheim-Cin (AHL)
CULLEN, Matt	6-1	204	L	Virginia, MN	11/2/76	Anaheim
CUMMINS, Jim	6-2	212	R	Dearborn, MI	5/17/70	Anaheim
DiROBERTO, Torrey	5-11	186	L	Utica, NY	4/17/78	Baton Rouge-Cin (AHL)
FRIESEN, Jeff	6-0	215	L	Meadow Lake, Sask.	8/5/76	San Jose-Anaheim
KARIYA, Paul	5-10	173	L	Vancouver, B.C.	10/16/74	Anaheim
LAMBERT, Denny	5-10	215	L	Wawa, Ont.	1/7/70	Atlanta
LECLERC, Mike	6-2	204	L	Winnipeg, Man.	11/10/76	Anaheim
LEGAULT, Jay	6-4	214	L	Peterborough, Ont.	5/15/79	Baton Rouge-Cin (AHL)
McDONALD, Andy	5-10	173	L	Strathroy, Ont.	8/25/77	Anaheim-Cin (AHL)
McINNIS, Marty	5-11	187	R	Weymouth, MA	6/2/70	Anaheim
PAHLSSON, Sami	5-11	190	L	Ornskoldsvik, Sweden	12/17/77	Boston-Anaheim
PARSSINEN, Timo	5-10	176	L	Lohjan mlk., Finland	1/19/77	HPK Hameenlinna
RONNQVIST, Jonas	6-2	200	R	Kalix, Sweden	8/22/73	Anaheim-Cin (AHL)
RUCCHIN, Steve	6-3	212	L	Thunder Bay, Ont.	7/4/71	Anaheim
SAWYER, Kevin	6-2	205	L	Christina Lake, B.C.	2/21/74	Anaheim-Cin (AHL)
SMIRNOV, Alexei	6-3	207	L	Tver, USSR	1/28/82	Dynamo Moscow
SMITH, Jarrett	6-2	201	L	Edmonton, Alta.	6/15/79	Cin (AHL)-Baton Rouge
STEPP, Joel	6-0	185	L	Estevan, Sask.	2/11/83	Red Deer
TENKRAT, Petr	5-11	207	R	Kladno, Czech.	5/31/77	Anaheim-Cin (AHL)
TITOV, German	6-1	205	L	Moscow, USSR	10/16/65	Anaheim
DEFENSEMEN						
BANNISTER, Drew	6-2	200	R	Belleville, Ont.	9/4/74	NY Rangers-Hartford
BRIMANIS, Aris	6-3	210	R	Cleveland, OH	3/14/72	NY Islanders-Chi (IHL)
CARNEY, Keith	6-2	214	L	Providence, RI	2/3/70	Phoenix
HAVELID, Niclas	5-11	196	L	Stockholm, Sweden	4/12/73	Anaheim
NIEMI, Antti-Jussi	6-1	193	L	Vantaa, Finland	9/22/77	Anaheim-Cin (AHL)
PODHRADSKY, Peter	6-2	182	R	Bratislava, Czech.	12/10/79	Cincinnati (AHL)
POPOVIC, Mark	6-1	194	L	Stoney Creek, Ont.	10/11/82	St. Michael's
SALEI, Ruslan	6-1	207	L	Minsk, USSR	11/2/74	Anaheim
TRNKA, Pavel	6-2	200	L	Plzen, Czech.	7/27/76	Anaheim
TVERDOVSKY, Oleg	6-1	204	L	Donetsk, USSR	5/18/76	Anaheim
VISHNEVSKI, Vitaly	6-2	206	L	Kharkov, USSR	3/18/80	Anaheim
WHITE, Brian	6-1	195	R	Winchester, MA	2/7/76	Hershey
YORK, Jason	6-1	200	R	Nepean, Ont.	5/20/70	Ottawa

GOALTENDERS	HT	WT	C	Place of Birth	Date	2000-01 Club
BRYZGALOV, Ilja	6-3	196	L	Togliatti, USSR	6/22/80	Lada Togliatti
GIGUERE, Jean-Sebastien	6-1	175	L	Montreal, Que.	5/16/77	Anaheim-Cin (AHL)
NAUMENKO, Gregg	6-1	201	L	Chicago, IL	3/30/77	Anaheim-Cin (AHL)
SHIELDS, Steve	6-3	215	L	Toronto, Ont.	7/19/72	San Jose

2000-01 Scoring

* – rookie

Regular Season

Pos	#	Player	Team	GP	G	A	Pts	+/–	PIM	PP	SH	GW	GT	S	%
L	9	Paul Kariya	ANA	66	33	34	67	–9	20	18	3	3	0	230	14.3
D	10	Oleg Tverdovsky	ANA	82	14	39	53	–11	32	8	0	3	2	188	7.4
L	11	Jeff Friesen	S.J.	64	12	24	36	7	56	2	0	1	0	120	10.0
			ANA	15	2	10	12	–2	10	2	0	0	0	29	6.9
			TOTAL	79	14	34	48	5	66	4	0	1	0	149	9.4
L	16	Marty McInnis	ANA	75	20	22	42	–21	40	10	0	1	0	136	14.7
C	17	Matt Cullen	ANA	82	10	30	40	–23	38	4	0	1	0	159	6.3
C	15	Tony Hrkac	ANA	80	13	25	38	0	29	0	0	1	0	88	14.8
L	12	Mike Leclerc	ANA	54	15	20	35	–1	26	3	0	3	2	130	11.5
C	13	German Titov	ANA	71	9	11	20	–21	61	1	0	0	0	78	11.5
L	18 *	Petr Tenkrat	ANA	46	5	9	14	–11	16	0	0	2	1	79	6.3
D	28	Niclas Havelid	ANA	47	4	10	14	–6	34	2	0	1	0	69	5.8
R	19	Jim Cummins	ANA	79	5	6	11	–11	167	0	0	1	0	45	11.1
D	25	Mike Crowley	ANA	39	1	10	11	–16	20	0	0	1	0	45	2.2
D	5	Vitaly Vishnevski	ANA	76	1	10	11	–1	99	0	0	0	0	49	2.0
D	27	Pascal Trepanier	ANA	57	6	4	10	–12	73	3	0	0	1	86	7.0
L	21	Dan Bylsma	ANA	82	1	9	10	–12	22	0	0	0	0	50	2.0
C	26 *	Samuel Pahlsson	BOS	17	1	1	2	–5	6	0	0	0	0	13	7.7
			ANA	59	3	4	7	–9	14	1	1	1	0	46	6.5
			TOTAL	76	4	5	9	–14	20	1	1	1	0	59	6.8
C	20	Steve Rucchin	ANA	16	3	5	8	–5	0	2	0	0	0	19	15.8
D	7	Pavel Trnka	ANA	59	1	7	8	–12	42	0	0	0	0	59	1.7
C	32 *	Marc Chouinard	ANA	44	3	4	7	–5	12	0	0	1	0	26	11.5
D	24	Ruslan Salei	ANA	50	1	5	6	–14	70	0	0	0	0	73	1.4
C	22	Jonas Ronnqvist	ANA	38	0	4	4	–7	14	0	0	0	0	30	0.0
C	14	Antti Aalto	ANA	12	1	1	2	1	2	0	0	0	0	18	5.6
D	40 *	Antti-Jussi Niemi	ANA	28	1	1	2	–6	22	0	0	0	0	18	5.6
G	35	J-S Giguere	ANA	34	0	2	2	0	8	0	0	0	0	0	0.0
C	11 *	Andy McDonald	ANA	16	1	0	1	0	6	0	0	0	0	21	4.8
L	46	Kevin Sawyer	ANA	9	0	1	1	–1	27	0	0	0	0	6	0.0
L	37 *	Bob Wren	ANA	1	0	0	0	–1	0	0	0	0	0	0	0.0
G	1 *	Gregg Naumenko	ANA	2	0	0	0	0	2	0	0	0	0	0	0.0

Goaltending

No.	Goaltender	GPI	Mins	Avg	W	L	T	EN	SO	GA	SA	S%
35	J-S Giguere	34	2031	2.57	11	17	5	3	4	87	976	.911
30	Dominic Roussel	13	653	2.85	2	5	2	2	0	31	295	.895
31	Guy Hebert	41	2215	3.12	12	23	4	0	2	115	1112	.897
1	* Gregg Naumenko	2	70	6.00	0	1	0	0	0	7	29	.759
	Totals	**82**	**4995**	**2.94**	**25**	**46**	**11**	**5**	**6**	**245**	**2417**	**.899**

Originally Anaheim's first choice, second overall, in the 1994 Entry Draft, Oleg Tverdovsky was reacquired by the team in 1999 and has been the club's top-scoring defenseman in each of the last two seasons.

President and General Manager

GAUTHIER, PIERRE
President and General Manager, Mighty Ducks of Anaheim.
Born in Montreal, Que., May 28, 1953.

Pierre Gauthier enters his fourth season as president and general manager of the Mighty Ducks. He is responsible for the overall hockey and front office operations of the club. Gauthier rejoined the Mighty Ducks on July 16, 1998.

An original member of Anaheim's management team in 1993, Gauthier spent two-and-a-half seasons as general manager of the Ottawa Senators from 1995 to 1998. He has earned a reputation as one of the most astute judges of hockey talent in the NHL during his 20 years in the league. Gauthier joined Ottawa as the team's general manager in December of 1995. Just 17 months later, the club had earned its first-ever playoff berth.

Gauthier served as assistant general manager of the Mighty Ducks from 1993 to 1995 before joining the Senators. He was a key part of management in starting up the Anaheim franchise in 1993.

Prior to his first stint with the Mighty Ducks, Gauthier had spent 12 seasons in the scouting department with the Quebec Nordiques. He had joined the club as a scout in 1983 and worked in that capacity for three seasons before being named assistant director of scouting in 1986. Gauthier was promoted to chief scout in 1988, serving at that capacity until he joined Anaheim in 1993.

Gauthier received a master's degree in sports administration in 1983 from the University of Minnesota, where he also served as a teaching associate in physical education. He is also a graduate of Syracuse University, where he earned a bachelor of science degree in physical education.

Club Records

Team

(Figures in brackets for season records are games played; records for fewest points, wins, ties, losses, goals, goals against are for 70 or more games)

Most Points 85 1996-97 (82)
Most Wins 36 1996-97 (82)
Most Ties 13 1996-97 (82); 1997-98 (82); 1998-99 (82)
Most Losses 46 1993-94 (84)
Most Goals 245 1996-97 (82)
Most Goals Against 261 1997-98 (82)
Fewest Points 65 1997-98 (82)
Fewest Wins 25 2000-01 (82)
Fewest Ties 5 1993-94 (84)
Fewest Losses 33 1996-97 (82)
Fewest Goals 188 2000-01 (82)
Fewest Goals Against 206 1998-99 (82)
Longest Winning Streak
Overall .... 7 Feb. 20-Mar. 7/99
Home .... 5 Oct. 22-Nov. 5/95; Mar. 8-Apr. 3/96
Away .... 5 Nov. 26-Dec. 26/99
Longest Undefeated Streak
Overall .... 12 Feb. 22-Mar. 19/97 (7 wins, 5 ties)
Home .... 14 Feb. 12-Apr. 9/97 (10 wins, 4 ties)
Away .... 5 Five times
Longest Losing Streak
Overall .... 8 Oct. 12-30/96
Home .... 6 Feb. 7-Mar. 11/98
Away .... 6 Three times
Longest Winless Streak
Overall .... 9 Twice
Home .... 6 Twice
Away .... 10 Mar. 26-Oct. 11/95 (9 losses, 1 tie)
Most Shutouts, Season 7 1998-99 (82)
Most PIM, Season 1,843 1997-98 (82)
Most Goals, Game .... 8 Jan. 21/98 (Ana. 8, Fla. 3)

Individual

Most Seasons .... 8 Guy Hebert
Most Games .... 441 Guy Hebert
Most Goals, Career .... 243 Paul Kariya
Most Assists, Career .... 288 Paul Kariya
Most Points, Career .... 531 Paul Kariya (243G, 288A)
Most PIM, Career .... 788 Dave Karpa
Most Shutouts, Career .... 27 Guy Hebert
Longest Consecutive Games Streak .... 159 Bobby Dollas (Oct. 9/95-Mar. 30/97)
Most Goals, Season .... 52 Teemu Selanne (1997-98)
Most Assists, Season .... 62 Paul Kariya (1998-99)
Most Points, Season .... 109 Teemu Selanne (1996-97; 51G, 58A)
Most PIM, Season .... 285 Todd Ewen (1995-96)
Most Points, Defenseman, Season .... 56 Fredrik Olausson (1998-99; 16G, 40A)
Most Points, Center, Season .... 67 Steve Rucchin (1996-97; 19G, 48A)
Most Points, Right Wing, Season .... 109 Teemu Selanne (1996-97; 51G, 58A)
Most Points, Left Wing, Season .... 108 Paul Kariya (1995-96; 50G, 58A)
Most Points, Rookie, Season .... 39 Paul Kariya (1994-95; 18G, 21A)
Most Shutouts, Season .... 6 Guy Hebert (1998-99)
Most Goals, Game .... 3 Thirteen times
Most Assists, Game .... 5 Dmitri Mironov (Dec. 12/97)
Most Points, Game .... 5 Six times

General Managers' History

Jack Ferreira, 1993-94 to 1997-98; Pierre Gauthier, 1998-99 to date.

Coaching History

Ron Wilson, 1993-94 to 1996-97; Pierre Page, 1997-98; Craig Hartsburg, 1998-99, 1999-2000; Craig Hartsburg and Guy Charron, 2000-01; Bryan Murray, 2001-02.

Captains' History

Troy Loney, 1993-94; Randy Ladouceur, 1994-95, 1995-96; Paul Kariya, 1996-97; Paul Kariya and Teemu Selanne, 1997-98; Paul Kariya, 1998-99 to date.

All-time Record vs. Other Clubs

Regular Season

	At Home								On Road								Total							
	GP	W	L	T	OL	GF	GA	PTS	GP	W	L	T	OL	GF	GA	PTS	GP	W	L	T	OL	GF	GA	PTS
Atlanta	2	1	1	0	0	6	5	2	1	1	0	0	0	5	2	2	3	2	1	0	0	11	7	4
Boston	7	2	3	1	1	13	18	6	6	3	3	0	0	18	18	6	13	5	6	1	1	31	36	12
Buffalo	7	2	5	0	0	12	22	4	7	2	2	3	0	18	16	7	14	4	7	3	0	30	38	11
Calgary	20	9	7	4	0	65	53	22	19	7	11	1	0	46	56	15	39	16	18	5	0	111	109	37
Carolina	6	3	2	1	0	23	19	7	7	1	5	1	0	12	22	3	13	4	7	2	0	35	41	10
Chicago	16	8	7	1	0	39	36	17	18	7	9	2	0	42	52	16	34	15	16	3	0	81	88	33
Colorado	15	4	8	3	0	34	38	11	15	4	8	3	0	41	52	11	30	8	16	6	0	75	90	22
Columbus	2	1	1	0	0	7	9	2	2	0	2	0	0	3	7	0	4	1	3	0	0	10	16	2
Dallas	19	8	11	0	0	44	50	16	19	2	15	1	1	33	80	6	38	10	26	1	1	77	130	22
Detroit	16	5	9	2	0	35	50	12	16	1	11	3	1	39	63	6	32	6	20	5	1	74	113	18
Edmonton	20	13	5	2	0	62	52	28	19	8	11	0	0	42	42	16	39	21	16	2	0	104	94	44
Florida	7	3	4	0	0	22	24	6	5	1	1	2	1	13	13	5	12	4	5	2	1	35	37	11
Los Angeles	22	11	4	5	2	73	51	29	22	8	11	3	0	59	65	19	44	19	15	8	2	132	116	48
Minnesota	2	1	1	0	0	3	6	2	2	1	1	0	0	3	3	2	4	2	2	0	0	6	9	4
Montreal	6	2	4	0	0	20	21	4	6	2	3	1	0	16	19	5	12	4	7	1	0	36	40	9
Nashville	6	5	1	0	0	14	7	10	6	2	2	2	0	16	14	6	12	7	3	2	0	30	21	16
New Jersey	7	3	4	0	0	20	19	6	7	1	6	0	0	12	28	2	14	4	10	0	0	32	47	8
NY Islanders	7	2	3	2	0	15	19	6	6	3	2	1	0	19	15	7	13	5	5	3	0	34	34	13
NY Rangers	7	6	0	0	1	30	19	13	6	3	2	1	0	18	17	7	13	9	2	1	1	48	36	20
Ottawa	6	3	1	2	0	16	9	8	7	3	3	1	0	18	21	7	13	6	4	3	0	34	30	15
Philadelphia	6	2	2	2	0	21	20	6	7	2	2	3	0	16	20	7	13	4	4	5	0	37	40	13
Phoenix	19	10	7	2	0	54	52	22	18	9	8	1	0	58	58	19	37	19	15	3	0	112	110	41
Pittsburgh	6	3	3	0	0	20	22	6	7	1	4	2	0	22	25	4	13	4	7	2	0	42	47	10
St. Louis	16	4	11	1	0	38	52	9	16	5	8	3	0	44	53	13	32	9	19	4	0	82	105	22
San Jose	22	9	11	2	0	60	72	20	22	10	9	2	1	66	67	23	44	19	20	4	1	126	139	43
Tampa Bay	7	4	2	1	0	22	17	9	6	4	2	0	0	19	12	8	13	8	4	1	0	41	29	17
Toronto	10	4	5	1	0	29	27	9	13	2	7	4	0	27	39	8	23	6	12	5	0	56	66	17
Vancouver	19	5	8	6	0	48	62	16	20	6	13	1	0	47	73	13	39	11	21	7	0	95	135	29
Washington	7	4	2	1	0	24	21	9	7	4	3	0	0	17	10	8	14	8	5	1	0	41	31	17
Totals	**312**	**137**	**132**	**39**	**4**	**869**	**872**	**317**	**312**	**103**	**164**	**41**	**4**	**789**	**962**	**251**	**624**	**240**	**296**	**80**	**8**	**1658**	**1834**	**568**

Playoffs

	Series	W	L	GP	W	L	T	GF	GA	Last Mtg.	Round	Result
Detroit	2	0	2	8	0	8	0	14	30	1999	CQF	L 0-4
Phoenix	1	1	0	7	4	3	0	17	17	1997	CQF	W 4-3
Totals	**3**	**1**	**2**	**15**	**4**	**11**	**0**	**31**	**47**			

Carolina totals include Hartford, 1993-94 to 1996-97.
Colorado totals include Quebec, 1993-94 to 1994-95.
Phoenix totals include Winnipeg, 1993-94 to 1995-96.

Playoff Results 2001-1997

Year	Round	Opponent	Result	GF	GA
1999	CQF	Detroit	L 0-4	6	17
1997	CSF	Detroit	L 0-4	8	13
	CQF	Phoenix	W 4-3	17	17

Abbreviations: Round: CSF – conference semi-final; **CQF** – conference quarter-final

2000-01 Results

Oct.	6	Minnesota	3-1	**Jan.**	3	Florida	3-2*
	8	St. Louis	1-5		5	Calgary	4-4
	11	Boston	2-3*		10	St. Louis	2-4
	14	at New Jersey	2-4		12	Buffalo	0-4
	16	at NY Rangers	4-3		14	at Carolina	0-4
	17	at NY Islanders	4-3		15	at Pittsburgh	2-3
	20	at Buffalo	2-2		17	at Atlanta	5-2
	21	at Philadelphia	4-3		19	Phoenix	3-4
	23	Los Angeles	4-5*		21	Colorado	2-4
	25	at Los Angeles	2-6		24	Minnesota	0-5
	27	Edmonton	3-2		26	at Detroit	2-3
	29	at Calgary	6-3		27	at Columbus	1-2
	30	at Edmonton	3-5		31	Nashville	0-3
Nov.	1	Phoenix	1-1	**Feb.**	1	at Phoenix	4-2
	4	at Nashville	3-3		7	Chicago	2-3
	5	at Chicago	2-4		9	Washington	3-4
	8	Vancouver	2-7		11	Carolina	2-2
	11	at Colorado	1-3		14	Edmonton	3-3
	12	Detroit	2-3		16	at Dallas	2-3*
	15	Colorado	0-3		19	Calgary	6-2
	18	at Phoenix	6-2		21	San Jose	1-0
	19	NY Islanders	2-1		23	at San Jose	1-3
	22	New Jersey	2-5		25	Columbus	2-5
	24	at Calgary	2-2		28	Detroit	1-3
	25	at Edmonton	2-3	**Mar.**	2	Dallas	2-5
	28	at Vancouver	1-4		4	Los Angeles	4-0
	30	at San Jose	2-3*		7	Montreal	4-2
Dec.	3	Los Angeles	4-0		9	Chicago	3-1
	5	at St. Louis	0-1		11	Nashville	1-0*
	6	at Columbus	2-5		13	at Washington	2-0
	8	at Minnesota	1-0*		14	at Toronto	2-3
	10	Dallas	0-1		16	at Ottawa	1-4
	13	Columbus	5-4*		18	at Chicago	4-1
	15	NY Rangers	6-4		21	at Dallas	0-8
	17	Tampa Bay	3-1		24	at Los Angeles	3-3
	20	Atlanta	2-4		29	at San Jose	4-7
	22	at Detroit	1-2*		30	at Vancouver	2-2
	23	at St. Louis	2-5	**Apr.**	1	Vancouver	2-1
	27	at Dallas	1-3		4	at Colorado	1-1
	28	at Nashville	2-2		6	Phoenix	2-5
	31	at Minnesota	2-3		8	San Jose	1-4

* – Overtime

Entry Draft Selections 2001-1993

2001
Pick
5 Stanislav Chistov
35 Mark Popovic
69 Joel Stepp
102 Timo Parssinen
105 Vladimir Korsunov
118 Brandon Rogers
137 Joel Perreault
170 Jan Tabacek
224 Tony Martensson
232 Martin Gerber
264 Pierre Parenteau

2000
Pick
12 Alexei Smirnov
44 Ilja Bryzgalov
98 Jonas Ronnqvist
134 Peter Podhradsky
153 Bill Cass

1999
Pick
44 Jordan Leopold
83 Niclas Havelid
105 Alexandr Chagodayev
141 Maxim Rybin
173 Jan Sandstrom
230 Petr Tenkrat
258 Brian Gornick

1998
Pick
5 Vitaly Vishnevski
32 Stephen Peat
112 Viktor Wallin
150 Trent Hunter
178 Jesse Fibiger
205 David Bernier
233 Pelle Prestberg
245 Andreas Andersson

1997
Pick
18 Mikael Holmqvist
45 Maxim Balmochnykh
72 Jay Legault
125 Luc Vaillancourt
178 Tony Mohagen
181 Mat Snesrud
209 Rene Stussi
235 Tommi Degerman

1996
Pick
9 Ruslan Salei
35 Matt Cullen
117 Brendan Buckley
149 Blaine Russell
172 Timo Ahmaoja
198 Kevin Kellett
224 Tobias Johansson

1995
Pick
4 Chad Kilger
29 Brian Wesenberg
55 Mike Leclerc
107 Igor Nikulin
133 Peter LeBoutillier
159 Mike LaPlante
185 Igor Karpenko

1994
Pick
2 Oleg Tverdovsky
28 Johan Davidsson
67 Craig Reichert
80 Byron Briske
106 Pavel Trnka
132 Bates Battaglia
158 Rocky Welsing
184 Brad Englehart
236 Tommi Miettinen
262 Jeremy Stevenson

1993
Pick
4 Paul Kariya
30 Nikolai Tsulygin
56 Valeri Karpov
82 Joel Gagnon
108 Mikhail Shtalenkov
134 Antti Aalto
160 Matt Peterson
186 Tom Askey
212 Vitali Kozel
238 Anatoli Fedotov
264 David Penney

Coach

MURRAY, BRYAN CLARENCE
Coach, Mighty Ducks of Anaheim.
Born in Shawville, Que., December 5, 1942.

The Mighty Ducks of Anaheim announced Bryan Murray as the club's head coach on May 25, 2001. Murray was most recently with the Florida Panthers as vice president and general manager from 1994 to 2001. He also assumed head coaching duties with Florida during the 1997-98 season, prior to naming his brother Terry Murray as head coach before the 1998-99 season. Bryan joined the Panthers on August 1, 1994 and assembled a team that went to the Stanley Cup Finals in just its third year of existence (1996).

Prior to joining the Panthers, Murray was the general manager of the Detroit Red Wings from 1990 to 1994, also taking on head coaching duties for the first three seasons. He earned his first NHL head coaching job with the Washington Capitals, taking over on November 11, 1981. He spent the next eight and a half seasons with the Capitals, winning the Jack Adams Award as coach of the year in 1983-84. Murray led Washington to the postseason seven times during his tenure, including the club's first division title in 1988-89.

A graduate of McGill University, Murray spent four years as the athletic director and coach at the school. He left that post to become the coach of the Regina Pats (WHL) in 1979-80. Murray took over as coach of the Hershey Bears (AHL) the next season and was named the Minor League Coach of the Year by *The Hockey News* after leading Hershey to its best mark in 40 years.

NHL Coaching Record

		Regular Season				Playoffs		
Season	Team	Games	W	L	T	Games	W	L
1981-82	Washington	66	25	28	13	....	....	....
1982-83	Washington	80	39	25	16	4	1	3
1983-84	Washington	80	48	27	5	8	4	4
1984-85	Washington	80	46	25	9	5	2	3
1985-86	Washington	80	50	23	7	9	5	4
1986-87	Washington	80	38	32	10	7	3	4
1987-88	Washington	80	38	33	9	14	7	7
1988-89	Washington	80	41	29	10	6	2	4
1989-90	Washington	46	18	24	4	....	....	....
1990-91	Detroit	80	34	38	8	7	3	4
1991-92	Detroit	80	43	25	12	11	4	7
1992-93	Detroit	84	47	28	9	7	3	4
1997-98	Florida	59	17	31	11	....	....	....
	NHL Totals	**975**	**484**	**368**	**123**	**78**	**34**	**44**

Club Directory

Arrowhead Pond of Anaheim

Mighty Ducks of Anaheim
Arrowhead Pond of Anaheim
2695 Katella Ave.
Anaheim, CA 92806
Phone **714/940-2900**
FAX 714/940-2953
Ticket Information 714/704-2701
www.mightyducks.com
Capacity: 17,174

Executive Management
Chairman and Governor . . . Tony Tavares
President and General Manager . . . Pierre Gauthier
Assistant General Manager . . . David McNab
Vice President, Finance and Administration . . . Andy Roundtree
Vice President, Advertising Sales and Broadcasting . . . John Covarrubias
Vice President, Communications . . . Tim Mead
Vice President, Business and Legal Affairs . . . Rick Schlesinger
Vice President, Sales and Marketing . . . Lawrence Cohen
Administrative Assistant to Tony Tavares . . . Meta Maynard
Administrative Assistant to Pierre Gauthier . . . Maureen Nyeholt
Administrative Assistant to Andy Roundtree . . . Monica Campanis
Administrative Assistant to John Covarrubias . . . Janine Schunk
Sr. Paralegal . . . Tia Wood
Administrative Assistant, Communications . . . Lisa Parris
Administrative Assistant, Sales . . . Pat Navarro

Coaches
Head Coach . . . Bryan Murray
Assistant Coaches . . . Guy Charron, Tom Watt
Goaltending Consultant . . . François Allaire

Hockey Club Operations
Director of Scouting . . . Alain Chainey
Scouting Coordinator . . . Greg Carvel
Pro Scout . . . Lucien DeBlois
Amateur Scouts . . . Jan-Åke Danielson, Richard Green, Mark Odnokon
Scouting Staff . . . Ross Ainsworth, Donald Marier, Konstantin Krylov, Al MacPherson, Mike McGraw, Tomas Prucha
Head Athletic Trainer . . . Chris Phillips
Assistant Athletic Trainer . . . Greg Thayer
Equipment Manager . . . Mark O'Neill
Assistant Equipment Manager . . . John Allaway
Cincinnati Mighty Ducks (AHL) Head Coach . . . Mike Babcock
Cincinnati Assistant Coach . . . Kevin Kaminski
Team Physicians . . . Dr. Ronald Glousman, Dr. Craig Milhouse
Oral Surgeon . . . Dr. Jeff Pulver
Visiting Team Equipment Attendant . . . Chris Kincaid

Communications
Communications and Team Services Manager . . . Alex Gilchrist
Publications Manager . . . Doug Ward
Media Relations Representative . . . Merit Tully
Community Development Representative . . . Renee Zidan
Website Editor . . . Terry Crowley
Team Photographer . . . V.J. Lovero (Lovero Group)

Finance and Administration
Director, Finance . . . Molly Taylor
Sr. Financial Analyst . . . Amy Langdale
Manager, Human Resources . . . Jenny Price
Manager, Information Services . . . Al Castro
Sr. Network Engineer . . . Neil Fariss
Sr. End User Analyst . . . Phil Alger
Desktop Support Analyst . . . David Yun
Assistant Controller . . . Melody Martin
Accountant . . . Rosanna Sitzman
Accounting Assistants . . . Linda Chubak, Rob Dumlao
Administrative Assistant, Human Resources . . . Cindy Williams
Human Resources Assistant . . . Alex Oftelie
Director, Ballpark Operations . . . John Drum
Assistant Operations Manager . . . Sam Maida
Administrative Assistant, Operations . . . Leslie Flammini
Sr. Travel Consultant . . . Chantelle Ball
General Manager, Disney ICE . . . Art Trottier
Receptionists . . . Jeannette Bryan, Vivian Swope

Sales and Marketing
Director, Ticket Sales & Customer Service . . . Bill Chapin
Director, Marketing and Promotions . . . Robert Alvarado
Premium Ticket Services Manager . . . Anne McNiff-Gaeta
Marketing Associate . . . Jared Rice
Marketing Representative . . . Joel Hobson
Telemarketing Supervisor . . . Ari Rubinstein
Account Executives . . . Ron Campbell, Tom Ledbetter, Bob Ruiz, Matt Traverse
Group Sales Account Executives . . . Ken Bamberg, Frank Tullo, Derek Wilson
Ticketing Supervisor . . . Jonas Calicdan

Ticketing
Ticketing Operations Manager . . . Christa Richards
Ticketing Representative . . . Lisa Yamamoto

Advertising Sales and Broadcasting
Director, Advertising Sales & Broadcasting . . . Richard McClemmy
Director, Entertainment . . . Rod Murray
Sponsorship Services Manager . . . Beke Lubeach
Broadcast Services Manager . . . Benjie Bautista
Advertising Sales Managers . . . Jeff Cova, Neil Johnson, Bill Pedigo, Sam Piccione, Bob Welch
Administrative Assistant, Advertising and Broadcast Sales . . . Jacklyn Perkins
Telecast Director . . . Aaron Teats
Producer, Video & Scoreboard Operations . . . Robert Castillo
Associate Producer, Video & Scoreboard Operations . . . David Tsuruda
Television . . . KCAL (Ch. 9) & Fox Sports West 2 (Cable) Chris Madsen, Brian Hayward
Radio . . . XTRA Sports (690 AM) and Mighty Ducks Radio Network – Steve Carroll
Practice Facilities . . . Disney ICE (300 W. Lincoln Ave.) and Arrowhead Pond (2695 Katella Ave.)

Atlanta Thrashers

2000-01 Results: 23W-45L-12T-2OTL 60PTS. Fourth, Southeast Division

Year-by-Year Record

		Home				Road				Overall								
Season	GP	W	L	T	OL	W	L	T	OL	W	L	T	OL	GF	GA	Pts.	Finished	Playoff Result
2000-01	82	10	23	6	2	13	22	6	0	23	45	12	2	211	289	60	4th, Southeast Div.	Out of Playoffs
1999-2000	82	9	26	3	3	5	31	4	1	14	57	7	4	170	313	39	5th, Southeast Div.	Out of Playoffs

2001-02 Schedule

Oct.	Thu.	4	at Buffalo
	Sat.	6	at Boston
	Sat.	13	Carolina
	Tue.	16	Philadelphia
	Fri.	19	NY Rangers
	Sat.	20	at Carolina
	Tue.	23	Pittsburgh
	Fri.	26	Washington
	Sat.	27	Tampa Bay
	Tue.	30	Ottawa
Nov.	Thu.	1	at San Jose
	Sat.	3	at Los Angeles*
	Sun.	4	at Anaheim*
	Wed.	7	at New Jersey
	Thu.	8	at Buffalo
	Sat.	10	at Washington
	Tue.	13	at Minnesota
	Fri.	16	Nashville
	Sun.	18	at NY Rangers
	Mon.	19	Buffalo
	Thu.	22	Montreal
	Sat.	24	at Ottawa*
	Tue.	27	at Montreal
	Thu.	29	at Tampa Bay
Dec.	Sat.	1	at Florida*
	Tue.	4	Boston
	Thu.	6	Washington
	Sat.	8	at Pittsburgh
	Mon.	10	Philadelphia
	Wed.	12	Montreal
	Fri.	14	Chicago
	Sat.	15	at Washington
	Tue.	18	at Boston
	Wed.	19	San Jose
	Fri.	21	at Carolina
	Sun.	23	Dallas
	Wed.	26	Florida
	Fri.	28	Toronto
	Mon.	31	at Florida*
Jan.	Wed.	2	at Dallas
	Thu.	3	at Phoenix
	Sun.	6	NY Islanders
	Tue.	8	at Philadelphia
	Wed.	9	Ottawa
	Fri.	11	Calgary
	Sun.	13	Tampa Bay
	Tue.	15	at Toronto
	Thu.	17	at Philadelphia
	Sat.	19	at Florida
	Tue.	22	Washington
	Thu.	24	New Jersey
	Sat.	26	at Pittsburgh*
	Mon.	28	Phoenix
	Wed.	30	Toronto
Feb.	Tue.	5	Edmonton
	Thu.	7	at New Jersey
	Fri.	8	NY Rangers
	Mon.	11	at Toronto
	Tue.	12	at St. Louis
	Tue.	26	Buffalo
Mar.	Fri.	1	NY Islanders
	Sat.	2	at NY Islanders
	Mon.	4	at Montreal
	Wed.	6	Anaheim
	Fri.	8	Boston
	Sun.	10	at NY Islanders*
	Tue.	12	Tampa Bay
	Thu.	14	Colorado
	Sat.	16	Vancouver
	Mon.	18	Pittsburgh
	Wed.	20	at Tampa Bay
	Fri.	22	at NY Rangers
	Sat.	23	at Ottawa
	Wed.	27	Minnesota
	Sat.	30	at Detroit
Apr.	Tue.	2	at Calgary
	Wed.	3	at Colorado
	Fri.	5	New Jersey
	Sun.	7	at Carolina*
	Wed.	10	Florida
	Fri.	12	at Columbus
	Sun.	14	Carolina*

* Denotes afternoon game.

Chris Tamer (top, left) and Jiri Slegr (top, right) anchored a defense that provided improved protection for netminders like Milan Hnilicka (right) in 2000-01. The Thrashers cut their goals against by 24 and recorded a much-improved 23 wins.

Franchise date: June 25, 1997

EASTERN CONFERENCE

SOUTHEAST DIVISION

3rd NHL Season

2001-02 Player Personnel

FORWARDS	HT	WT	S	Place of Birth	Date	2000-01 Club
ADAMS, Bryan	6-0	185	L	Fort St. James, B.C.	3/20/77	Atlanta-Orlando
BARTECKO, Lubos	6-1	200	L	Kezmarok, Czech.	7/14/76	St. Louis
BLATNY, Zdenek	6-1	195	L	Brno, Czech.	1/14/81	Kootenay
CORKUM, Bob	6-2	225	R	Salisbury, MA	12/18/67	Los Angeles-New Jersey
DOMENICHELLI, Hnat	6-0	195	L	Edmonton, Alta.	2/17/76	Atlanta
DONOVAN, Shean	6-3	210	R	Timmins, Ont.	1/22/75	Atlanta
FERRARO, Ray	5-9	200	L	Trail, B.C.	8/23/64	Atlanta
HEATLEY, Dany	6-2	210	L	Freiburg, West Germany	1/21/81	U. of Wisconsin
HORDICHUK, Darcy	6-1	215	L	Kamsack, Sask.	8/10/80	Atlanta-Orlando
HRKAC, Tony	5-11	190	L	Thunder Bay, Ont.	7/7/66	Anaheim
KACZOWKA, David	6-2	205	L	Regina, Sask.	7/5/81	Regina
KALLIO, Tomi	6-0	190	L	Turku, Finland	1/27/77	Atlanta
KARLSSON, Andreas	6-3	210	L	Ludvika, Sweden	8/19/75	Atlanta
KOVALCHUK, Ilya	6-2	202	R	Tver, USSR	4/15/83	Krylja Sovetov
MacKENZIE, Derek	5-11	180	L	Sudbury, Ont.	6/11/81	Sudbury
ODGERS, Jeff	6-0	200	R	Spy Hill, Sask.	5/31/69	Atlanta
PIROS, Kamil	6-1	195	L	Most, Czech.	11/20/78	CHZ Litvinov
SIMON, Ben	6-0	195	L	Shaker Heights, OH	6/14/78	Orlando
SKALDE, Jarrod	6-0	185	L	Niagara Falls, Ont.	2/26/71	Atlanta-Orlando
SNYDER, Dan	6-0	185	L	Elmira, Ont.	2/23/78	Atlanta-Orlando
STEFAN, Patrik	6-3	205	L	Pribram, Czech.	9/16/80	Atlanta
SVARTVADET, Per	6-1	195	L	Solleftea, Sweden	5/17/75	Atlanta
TAPPER, Brad	6-0	185	R	Scarborough, Ont.	4/28/78	Atlanta-Orlando
VIGIER, Jean-Pierre	6-0	195	R	Notre Dame de Lourdes, Man.	9/11/76	Atlanta-Orlando
VLASENKOV, Dmitri	6-1	200	L	Safonovo, USSR	1/1/78	Orlando
DEFENSEMEN						
BURT, Adam	6-2	205	L	Detroit, MI	1/15/69	Atlanta
BUZEK, Petr	6-0	210	L	Jihlava, Czech.	4/26/77	Atlanta
CLARK, Brett	6-0	185	L	Wapella, Sask.	12/23/76	Atlanta-Orlando
DESSNER, Jeff	6-2	195	L	Skokie, IL	4/16/77	U. of Wisconsin
EXELBY, Garnet	6-1	200	L	Craik, Sask.	8/16/81	Saskatoon-Regina
HARLOCK, David	6-2	215	L	Toronto, Ont.	3/16/71	Atlanta
KABERLE, Frantisek	6-0	185	L	Kladno, Czech.	11/8/73	Atlanta
POTHIER, Brian	6-0	195	R	New Bedford, MA	4/15/77	Atlanta-Orlando
REIRDEN, Todd	6-5	225	L	Deerfield, IL	6/25/71	St. Louis-Worcester
SELLARS, Luke	6-1	195	L	Toronto, Ont.	5/21/81	Ottawa 67's
SLEGR, Jiri	6-0	216	L	Jihlava, Czech.	5/30/71	Pittsburgh-Atlanta
TAMER, Chris	6-2	205	L	Dearborn, MI	11/17/70	Atlanta
TJARNQVIST, Daniel	6-2	195	L	Umea, Sweden	10/14/76	Djurgardens IF
TREMBLAY, Yannick	6-2	195	R	Pointe-aux-Trembles, Que.	11/15/75	Atlanta
USTRNUL, Libor	6-4	220	L	Steruberk, Czech.	2/20/82	Plymouth Whalers
WEAVER, Mike	5-9	185	R	Bramalea, Ont.	5/2/78	Orlando

GOALTENDERS	HT	WT	C	Place of Birth	Date	2000-01 Club
FANKHOUSER, Scott	6-2	205	L	Bismark, ND	7/1/75	Atlanta-Orlando
HNILICKA, Milan	6-1	195	L	Kladno, Czech.	6/25/73	Atlanta
MARACLE, Norm	5-9	190	L	Belleville, Ont.	10/2/74	Atlanta-Orlando
NURMINEN, Pasi	5-10	189	L	Lahti, Finland	12/17/75	Jokerit Helsinki
RHODES, Damian	5-11	195	L	St. Paul, MN	5/28/69	Atlanta

General Managers' History

Don Waddell, 1999-2000 to date.

General Manager

WADDELL, DON
General Manager, Atlanta Thrashers. Born in Detroit, MI, August 19, 1958.

Don Waddell serves as vice president and general manager of the Atlanta Thrashers. He came to the Thrashers on June 23, 1998, — almost a year to the day after the NHL granted Atlanta a franchise — bringing with him more than 20 years experience in professional hockey as a player, coach and general manager. He brings extensive organizational skills to the Thrashers having previously built two professional hockey franchises, the San Diego Gulls and the Orlando Solar Bears of the International Hockey League. He's also no stranger to winning through his role as assistant general manager for the NHL's Stanley Cup champion Detroit Red Wings during the 1997-98 season.

Prior to Detroit, Waddell was vice president of RDV Sports, where he served on the Executive Committee which oversaw operations of the National Basketball Association's Orlando Magic, the International Hockey League's Orlando Solar Bears, Magic Fanattics (retail) and Magic Carpet Aviation. While at RDV Sports, Waddell was vice president and general manager of the IHL's Orlando Solar Bears from 1995 to 1997. Prior to the Solar Bears, he held the same role with the IHL's San Diego Gulls from 1990 to 1995. He also served as the club's head coach for the 1991-92 season, guiding the team to the franchise's first playoff berth. He spent two seasons with the IHL's Flint Spirits where he served as head coach and general manager in 1988-89, and general manager in 1989-90.

Waddell's playing experience includes being player/coach for the Flint Spirits from 1986 to 1988, and the Goaldiggers Hockey Club in Toledo, Ohio for the 1985-86 season. He was drafted by the NHL's Los Angeles Kings back in 1978, and spent three years with the organization from 1980 to 1983. He was a member of the 1983 U.S. National Team and had been a member of the 1980 gold medal Olympic hockey team, but was injured prior to play.

Waddell played Division I hockey at Northern Michigan University from 1976 to 1980, where he majored in business management. He was inducted into the Northern Michigan University Sports Hall of Fame in 1992.

2000-01 Scoring

* - rookie

Regular Season

Pos	#	Player	Team	GP	G	A	Pts	+/–	PIM	PP	SH	GW	GT	S	%
C	21	Ray Ferraro	ATL	81	29	47	76	–11	91	11	0	2	0	172	16.9
L	15	Andrew Brunette	ATL	77	15	44	59	–5	26	6	0	4	1	104	14.4
D	71	Jiri Slegr	PIT	42	5	10	15	–9	60	0	1	1	0	67	7.5
			ATL	33	3	16	19	–1	36	2	0	0	0	78	3.8
			TOTAL	75	8	26	34	–10	96	2	1	1	0	145	5.5
C	13	Patrik Stefan	ATL	66	10	21	31	–3	22	0	0	1	0	93	10.8
C	12	Stephen Guolla	ATL	63	12	16	28	–6	23	2	0	3	1	96	12.5
L	9	Hnat Domenichelli	ATL	63	15	12	27	–9	18	4	0	1	0	150	10.0
L	14 *	Tomi Kallio	ATL	56	14	13	27	–3	22	2	0	2	0	115	12.2
R	22	Shean Donovan	ATL	63	12	11	23	–14	47	1	3	1	0	93	12.9
R	25	Steve Staios	ATL	70	9	13	22	–23	137	4	0	0	2	156	5.8
C	39	Per Svartvadet	ATL	69	10	11	21	–6	20	0	2	1	0	98	10.2
D	4	Chris Tamer	ATL	82	4	13	17	–1	128	0	1	1	0	90	4.4
C	24	Andreas Karlsson	ATL	60	5	11	16	–2	16	0	1	0	0	83	6.0
D	8	Frantisek Kaberle	ATL	51	4	11	15	11	18	1	0	1	0	99	4.0
R	17	Ladislav Kohn	ANA	51	4	3	7	–15	42	0	1	0	0	86	4.7
			ATL	26	3	4	7	–12	44	0	1	0	0	43	7.0
			TOTAL	77	7	7	14	–27	86	0	2	0	0	129	5.4
D	5	Gord Murphy	ATL	27	3	11	14	–11	12	2	0	0	0	44	6.8
R	20	Jeff Odgers	ATL	82	6	7	13	–8	226	0	0	1	0	67	9.0
D	38	Yannick Tremblay	ATL	46	4	8	12	–6	30	1	0	1	0	102	3.9
R	11	Dean Sylvester	ATL	43	5	6	11	–16	8	1	0	0	1	82	6.1
L	32	Yves Sarault	ATL	20	5	4	9	–9	26	2	0	0	1	44	11.4
R	37 *	Herbert Vasiljevs	ATL	21	4	5	9	–11	14	2	0	1	0	41	9.8
L	27	Denny Lambert	ATL	67	1	7	8	–5	215	0	0	0	0	44	2.3
R	19 *	Brad Tapper	ATL	16	2	3	5	1	6	0	0	0	0	21	9.5
D	3	Chris Joseph	PHX	24	1	1	2	–4	16	0	1	0	0	33	3.0
			ATL	19	0	3	3	–7	20	0	0	0	0	25	0.0
			TOTAL	43	1	4	5	–11	36	0	1	0	0	58	1.7
D	41	Andrei Skopintsev	ATL	17	1	3	4	–7	16	0	0	1	0	10	10.0
C	18	Jarrod Skalde	ATL	19	1	2	3	–8	20	0	0	0	0	24	4.2
D	3 *	Sergei Vyshedkevich	ATL	23	1	2	3	–7	14	0	0	0	0	28	3.6
D	23	Brett Clark	ATL	28	1	2	3	–12	14	0	0	0	0	35	2.9
D	7	Adam Burt	ATL	27	0	2	2	2	27	0	0	0	0	18	0.0
L	26 *	Bryan Adams	ATL	9	0	1	1	–4	2	0	0	0	0	3	0.0
D	6	David Harlock	ATL	65	0	1	1	–28	62	0	0	0	0	26	0.0
C	26 *	Dan Snyder	ATL	2	0	0	0	0	0	0	0	0	0	2	0.0
R	29 *	Jean-Pierre Vigier	ATL	2	0	0	0	–2	0	0	0	0	0	1	0.0
D	29 *	Brian Pothier	ATL	3	0	0	0	4	2	0	0	0	0	0	0.0
D	2	Petr Buzek	ATL	5	0	0	0	2	8	0	0	0	0	11	0.0
G	30 *	Scott Fankhouser	ATL	7	0	0	0	0	2	0	0	0	0	0	0.0
L	10 *	Darcy Hordichuk	ATL	11	0	0	0	–3	38	0	0	0	0	6	0.0
G	34	Norm Maracle	ATL	13	0	0	0	0	0	0	0	0	0	0	0.0
G	33	Milan Hnilicka	ATL	36	0	0	0	0	4	0	0	0	0	0	0.0
G	1	Damian Rhodes	ATL	38	0	0	0	0	16	0	0	0	0	0	0.0

Goaltending

No.	Goaltender	GPI	Mins	Avg	W	L	T	EN	SO	GA	SA	S%
33	Milan Hnilicka	36	1879	3.35	12	19	2	1	2	105	951	.890
1	Damian Rhodes	38	2072	3.36	7	19	7	5	0	116	1129	.897
34	Norm Maracle	13	753	3.43	2	8	3	3	0	43	406	.894
30	* Scott Fankhouser	7	260	3.69	2	1	0	0	0	16	160	.900
	Totals	**82**	**4983**	**3.48**	**23**	**47**	**12**	**9**	**2**	**289**	**2655**	**.891**

Captains' History

Kelly Buchberger, 1999-2000; Steve Staios, 2000-01.

Coaching History

Curt Fraser, 1999-2000 to date.

Club Records

Team

(Figures in brackets for season records are games played.)

Most Points	**60**	2000-01 (82)
Most Wins	**23**	2000-01 (82)
Most Ties	**12**	2000-01 (82)
Most Losses	**61**	1999-2000 (82)
Most Goals	**211**	2000-01 (82)
Most Goals Against	**313**	1999-2000 (82)
Fewest Points	**39**	1999-2000 (82)
Fewest Wins	**14**	1999-2000 (82)
Fewest Ties	**7**	1999-2000 (82)
Fewest Losses	**45**	2000-01 (82)
Fewest Goals	**170**	1999-2000 (82)
Fewest Goals Against	**289**	2000-01 (82)
Longest Winning Streak		
Overall	**3**	Dec. 1-4/00
Home	**2**	Three times
Away	**2**	Dec. 2-9/00, Dec. 19-20/00
Longest Undefeated Streak		
Overall	**4**	Oct. 21-28/00 (1 win, 3 ties)
Home	**3**	Feb. 13-Mar. 3/01 (1 win, 2 ties)
Away	**7**	Oct. 21-Nov. 13/00 (3 wins, 4 ties)
Longest Losing Streak		
Overall	**12**	Jan. 24-Feb. 20/00
Home	***11**	Jan. 24-Mar. 16/00
Away	**8**	Oct. 17-Nov. 27/99
Longest Winless Streak		
Overall	**16**	Jan. 16-Feb. 20/00 (2 ties, 14 losses)
Home	***17**	Jan. 19-Mar. 29/00 (2 ties, 15 losses)
Away	**9**	Oct. 16-Nov. 27/99 (1 tie, 8 losses), Jan. 8-Feb. 20/00 (1 tie, 8 losses)
Most Shutouts, Season	**2**	1999-2000 (82)
Most PIM, Season	**1,422**	1999-2000 (82)
Most Goals, Game	**6**	Nov. 22/99 (Van. 3 at Atl. 6), Dec. 26/99 (T.B. 3 at Atl. 6)

Individual

Most Seasons	**2**	Many players
Most Games	**162**	Ray Ferraro
Most Goals, Career	**48**	Ray Ferraro
Most Assists, Career	**72**	Ray Ferraro
Most Points, Career	**120**	Ray Ferraro (48G, 72A)
Most PIM, Career	**434**	Denny Lambert
Most Shutouts, Career	**2**	Milan Hnilicka
Most Goals, Season	**32**	Donald Audette (2000-01)
Most Assists, Season	**47**	Ray Ferraro (2000-01)
Most Points, Season	**76**	Ray Ferraro (2000-01; 29G, 47A)
Most PIM, Season	**226**	Jeff Odgers (2000-01)
Most Points, Defenseman, Season	**31**	Yannick Tremblay (1999-2000; 10G, 21A)
Most Points, Center, Season	**76**	Ray Ferraro (2000-01; 29G, 47A)
Most Points, Right Wing, Season	**71**	Donald Audette (2000-01; 32G, 39A)
Most Points, Left Wing, Season	**59**	Andrew Brunette (2000-01; 15G, 44A)
Most Points, Rookie, Season	**27**	Tomi Kallio (2000-01; 14G, 13A)
Most Shutouts, Season	**2**	Milan Hnilicka (2000-01)
Most Goals, Game	**3**	Seven times
Most Assists, Game	**4**	Twice
Most Points, Game	**4**	Five times

* NHL Record.

Ray Ferraro's 29 goals last season were the most he's had since scoring 40 in 1991-92. His 47 assists tied a career high established back in 1985-86.

All-time Record vs. Other Clubs

Regular Season

	At Home								On Road								Total							
	GP	W	L	T	OL	GF	GA	PTS	GP	W	L	T	OL	GF	GA	PTS	GP	W	L	T	OL	GF	GA	PTS
Anaheim	1	0	1	0	0	2	5	0	2	1	1	0	0	5	6	2	3	1	2	0	0	7	11	2
Boston	4	2	2	0	0	14	12	4	4	2	1	1	0	20	15	5	8	4	3	1	0	34	27	9
Buffalo	4	1	2	1	0	10	17	3	4	1	3	0	0	9	15	2	8	2	5	1	0	19	32	5
Calgary	2	1	0	1	0	5	4	3	1	0	1	0	0	2	5	0	3	1	1	1	0	7	9	3
Carolina	5	0	4	1	0	10	17	1	5	0	5	0	0	9	20	0	10	0	9	1	0	19	37	1
Chicago	2	1	1	0	0	6	5	2	1	0	1	0	0	0	1	0	3	1	2	0	0	6	6	2
Colorado	2	0	1	0	1	4	7	1	2	1	1	0	0	6	8	2	4	1	2	0	1	10	15	3
Columbus	1	0	1	0	0	0	3	0	1	1	0	0	0	2	1	2	2	1	1	0	0	2	4	2
Dallas	2	0	2	0	0	4	7	0	1	0	1	0	0	1	2	0	3	0	3	0	0	5	9	0
Detroit	2	0	2	0	0	5	13	0	2	0	1	0	1	2	7	1	4	0	3	0	1	7	20	1
Edmonton	1	0	1	0	0	0	3	0	2	1	1	0	0	7	6	2	3	1	2	0	0	7	9	2
Florida	5	2	1	2	0	14	16	6	5	2	2	1	0	12	14	5	10	4	3	3	0	26	30	11
Los Angeles	2	0	2	0	0	3	9	0	2	1	1	0	0	7	10	2	4	1	3	0	0	10	19	2
Minnesota	0	0	0	0	0	0	0	0	1	0	0	1	0	1	1	1	1	0	0	1	0	1	1	1
Montreal	4	0	3	1	0	2	15	1	4	1	3	0	0	9	12	2	8	1	6	1	0	11	27	3
Nashville	2	1	0	0	1	4	4	3	2	0	2	0	0	3	10	0	4	1	2	0	1	7	14	3
New Jersey	4	0	3	1	0	6	20	1	4	0	4	0	0	3	18	0	8	0	7	1	0	9	38	1
NY Islanders	4	1	2	1	0	14	17	3	4	3	1	0	0	13	10	6	8	4	3	1	0	27	27	9
NY Rangers	4	0	4	0	0	9	18	0	4	2	2	0	0	15	13	4	8	2	6	0	0	24	31	4
Ottawa	4	1	3	0	0	14	17	2	4	0	3	1	0	10	24	1	8	1	6	1	0	24	41	3
Philadelphia	4	1	2	0	1	10	14	3	4	0	2	2	0	8	14	2	8	1	4	2	1	18	28	5
Phoenix	1	0	1	0	0	2	3	0	2	0	2	0	0	3	9	0	3	0	3	0	0	5	12	0
Pittsburgh	4	0	3	0	1	10	18	1	4	0	4	0	0	5	17	0	8	0	7	0	1	15	35	1
St. Louis	2	0	2	0	0	5	11	0	1	0	1	0	0	1	4	0	3	0	3	0	0	6	15	0
San Jose	1	0	1	0	0	0	3	0	2	0	1	1	0	3	6	1	3	0	2	1	0	3	9	1
Tampa Bay	5	4	1	0	0	23	15	8	5	1	3	1	0	11	19	3	10	5	4	1	0	34	34	11
Toronto	3	1	1	0	1	6	9	3	3	1	2	0	0	5	12	2	6	2	3	0	1	11	21	5
Vancouver	2	1	1	0	0	9	8	2	1	0	0	1	0	1	1	1	3	1	1	1	0	10	9	3
Washington	5	2	2	1	0	10	14	5	5	0	4	1	0	7	18	1	10	2	6	2	0	17	32	6
Totals	**82**	**19**	**49**	**9**	**5**	**201**	**304**	**52**	**82**	**18**	**53**	**10**	**1**	**180**	**298**	**47**	**164**	**37**	**102**	**19**	**6**	**381**	**602**	**99**

2000-01 Results

Oct.	7	NY Rangers	1-2		10	Dallas	2-3
	11	Washington	3-3		12	Montreal	0-3
	15	at Tampa Bay	2-5		13	at Washington	1-4
	17	New Jersey	3-3		17	Anaheim	2-5
	20	NY Islanders	3-5		20	at New Jersey	2-3
	21	at Ottawa	6-6		21	NY Islanders	4-4
	25	at Edmonton	3-1		23	at Nashville	3-4
	27	at Vancouver	1-1		25	Toronto	1-2*
	28	at San Jose	2-2		27	at Pittsburgh	1-5
Nov.	2	Los Angeles	2-5		29	at NY Rangers	7-2
	4	at Boston	8-3		30	Pittsburgh	3-6
	6	Ottawa	2-3	**Feb.**	1	Carolina	1-3
	12	at Washington	2-2		7	at Toronto	1-7
	13	at Florida	4-1		9	Boston	5-1
	15	Nashville	1-0		10	Florida	3-7
	17	Philadelphia	2-3*		13	Buffalo	5-4
	18	at Pittsburgh	1-3		15	at Buffalo	1-3
	22	at Tampa Bay	2-8		17	at Philadelphia	1-5
	23	Montreal	0-6		21	at Carolina	3-6
	25	Washington	2-1		23	at Chicago	0-1
	27	at Montreal	2-3		25	at Colorado	2-5
	29	Detroit	4-6		27	Carolina	1-1
Dec.	1	Tampa Bay	5-3	**Mar.**	2	at Florida	4-3
	2	at Columbus	2-1		3	Florida	2-2
	4	Boston	5-4		6	Colorado	2-4
	6	Carolina	3-5		8	Pittsburgh	3-5
	8	Florida	4-3*		10	at Boston	7-5
	9	at NY Islanders	5-2		11	Calgary	3-3
	11	at New Jersey	0-4		14	at Ottawa	1-8
	13	Chicago	3-1		16	Columbus	0-3
	15	St. Louis	3-6		18	Vancouver	3-5
	19	at Los Angeles	7-6*		21	Tampa Bay	3-4
	20	at Anaheim	4-2		22	at Tampa Bay	2-0
	22	at Phoenix	1-5		24	at Montreal	3-2
	26	Toronto	5-3		26	Buffalo	0-4
	28	at NY Rangers	4-1		28	New Jersey	2-4
	29	at NY Islanders	2-5		30	at Buffalo	0-4
Jan.	1	at Washington	2-4	**Apr.**	1	NY Rangers	2-4
	3	at Minnesota	1-1		3	Ottawa	5-2
	5	Philadelphia	4-6		5	at Detroit	0-4
	6	at Philadelphia	2-2		6	at Carolina	2-3

* – Overtime

Entry Draft Selections 2001-1999

2001 Pick		2000 Pick		1999 Pick	
1	Ilya Kovalchuk	2	Dany Heatley	1	Patrik Stefan
80	Michael Garnett	31	Ilja Nikulin	30	Luke Sellars
100	Brian Sipotz	42	Libor Ustrnul	68	Zdenek Blatny
112	Milan Gajic	107	Carl Mallette	98	David Kaczowka
135	Colin Stuart	108	Blake Robson	99	Rob Zepp
189	Pasi Nurminen	147	Matt McRae	128	Derek MacKenzie
199	Matt Suderman	168	Zdenek Smid	159	Yuri Dobryshkin
201	Colin Fitzrandolph	178	Jeff Dwyer	188	Stephan Baby
262	Mario Cartelli	180	Darcy Hordichuk	217	Garnet Exelby
		230	Samu Isosalo	245	Tommi Santala
		242	Evan Nielsen	246	Raymond DiLauro
		244	Eric Bowen		
		288	Mark McRae		
		290	Simon Gamache		

Originally drafted by Colorado in 1995, Tomi Kallio was acquired by Atlanta in the 1999 Expansion Draft and ranked among the top rookie scorers last season.

Coach

FRASER, CURT
Coach, Atlanta Thrashers. Born in Cincinnati, OH, January 12, 1958.

Curt Fraser became the first head coach in the history of the Atlanta Thrashers on July 14, 1999. Fraser had spent the previous four seasons as the head coach of the IHL's Orlando Solar Bears, where he worked with Thrashers g.m. Don Waddell from 1995 to 1997.

During Fraser's four years with Orlando, the Solar Bears posted a 192-111-25 record with four consecutive playoff appearances, including reaching the Eastern Conference Finals on three occasions and two Turner Cup Finals (1995-96 and 1998-99). He won eight of 12 playoff rounds and posted a 17-4 record in playoff elimination games during that span.

In 1996-97, Fraser led the club to its second consecutive 50-plus win season and eclipsed the 100-point plateau for the second time with Orlando and the third time in his IHL career. He led the club to a 16-game winning streak, the third longest in professional hockey history. He was also named as co-coach for the Eastern Conference at the 1997 IHL All-Star Game for the second consecutive season (with Orlando) and for the third time in his IHL career. He also represented Milwaukee in 1993.

During their 1995-96 inaugural season, the Solar Bears clinched the Central Division championship and became the first Eastern Conference expansion team to reach the Turner Cup Finals in the history of the IHL.

Fraser came to Orlando in 1995 after 12 years as a player in the NHL and five years as a coach in the professional ranks. He spent the 1994-95 season as an associate coach with the AHL's Syracuse Crunch, the top affiliate for the Vancouver Canucks. Before joining Syracuse, Fraser served as an assistant coach and later head coach of the IHL's Milwaukee Admirals.

Prior to reaching the coaching ranks, Fraser was a highly respected left winger in the NHL with Vancouver, Chicago and Minnesota. In 704 career games, he scored 193 goals, notched 433 points and amassed 1,306 penalty minutes. Originally a second round pick of Vancouver in 1978, Fraser established himself as a hard working and fearless player, who combined toughness with the ability to score.

Coaching Record

		Regular Season				Playoffs		
Season	Team	Games	W	L	T	Games	W	L
1992-93	Milwaukee (IHL)	82	49	23	10	6	2	4
1993-94	Milwaukee (IHL)	81	40	24	17	4	0	4
1995-96	Orlando (IHL)	82	52	24	6	23	11	12
1996-97	Orlando (IHL)	82	53	24	5	10	4	6
1997-98	Orlando (IHL)	82	42	30	10	17	9	8
1998-99	Orlando (IHL)	82	45	33	4	17	10	7
1999-2000	**Atlanta (NHL)**	**82**	**14**	**61**	**7**	....	....	....
2000-01	**Atlanta (NHL)**	**82**	**23**	**47**	**12**	....	....	....
	NHL Totals	**164**	**37**	**102**	**19**	....	....	....

Club Directory

Philips Arena

Atlanta Thrashers
One CNN Center
12 South
Atlanta, GA 30303
Phone **404/827-5300**
FAX 404/827-5769
www.atlantathrashers.com
Capacity: 18,545

Executive Management
President and Governor . . . . . Stan Kasten
VP & Gen. Manager (Alt. Governor) . . . . . Don Waddell
VP of Sales and Marketing . . . . . Derek Schiller
Senior Vice President of Public Relations . . . . . Greg Hughes
Team Counsel . . . . . John Cooper

Hockey Operations
Dir. of Player Personnel . . . . . Jack Ferreira
Dir. of Player Development & Evaluation . . . . . Bob Owen
Head Coach . . . . . Curt Fraser
Assistant Coaches . . . . . Tim Bothwell and Steve Weeks
Chief Scout . . . . . Dan Marr
Professional Scouts . . . . . Mark Dobson and Peter Mahovlich
Amateur Scouts . . . . . Bernd Freimuller, John Perpich, Normand Poisson, Marcel Comeau
Part-Time Scouts . . . . . Evgeny Bogdanovich, Terry Brennan, Pat Carmichael, Pentti Katainen, Jan Lindegren
Dir. of Team Services . . . . . Michele Zarzaca
Manager of Hockey Administration . . . . . Larry Simmons
Coordinator of Scouting/Video . . . . . Jon Barkan
Strength and Conditioning Coach . . . . . TBA
Head Athletic Trainer . . . . . Scott Green
Assistant Athletic Trainer . . . . . Craig Brewer
Massage Therapist . . . . . Inar Treiguts
Head Equipment Manager . . . . . Bobby Stewart
Assistant Equipment Managers . . . . . Joe Guilmet and Rob Thomson
Team Physician . . . . . Dr. Scott Gillogly
Team Internist . . . . . Dr. William Whaley
Team Dentists . . . . . Dr. Gary Saban, Dr. Lawrence Saltzman, Dr. Brett Silverman
Hockey Operations Coordinator . . . . . Tony Borgford

Administration
Assistant to Stan Kasten . . . . . Tracey Hammeran
Assistant to Derek Schiller . . . . . Farrah Downing
Receptionist . . . . . Kayla Denson

Corporate Sales
(Philips Arena Sports Marketing)
V.P. of Broadcast and Corp. Sales . . . . . Tracy White
Dir. of Broadcast and Corp. Sales . . . . . Terri Scalcucci, Bill Abercrombie
Dir. of Sponsor Services . . . . . Joan Lanier-Heath
Mgr. of Broadcast and Corp. Sales . . . . . Stewart Tanner, Arden Robbins
Account Executive . . . . . Chris Beaudin
Mgr. of Broadcast Operations . . . . . Diana Corbin
Sponsor Services Coord. . . . . . Chris Carter, Robin Halliburton, Amanda E. McCullin, Cari Pawlicki
Broadcast and Corp. Sales Assistant . . . . . Doug Armistead
Broadcast Operations Assistant . . . . . Burnquetta Lomax
Executive Assistant . . . . . Catherine Lawrence

Finance/Accounting
Controller . . . . . David Kane
Senior Financial Analyst . . . . . TBA
Manager of Accounting . . . . . Darius Nixon
Financial Analyst . . . . . Stephanie Tooke
Staff Accountants . . . . . Raiford Hodges and Julia Wu

Marketing
Director of Marketing . . . . . Jim Pfeifer
Senior Manager of Marketing . . . . . Rob Preiditsch
Manager of Community Relations . . . . . Terri Hickman
Senior Manager of Game Presentation and Special Events . . . . . Peter Sorckoff
Manager of Special Events . . . . . Connie Zaleski
Community Relations Coordinator . . . . . Cameron Brent
Mascot Coordinator . . . . . Javier Presas
Marketing Coordinator . . . . . Ralph Humphlett
Fan Development Coordinator . . . . . David Porter
Fan Development Assistant . . . . . Lauren Shrensky
Sales & Marketing Administrator . . . . . Farrah Downing

Media Relations
Director of Media Relations . . . . . Tom Hughes
Manager of Media Relations . . . . . Rob Koch
Manager of Publications . . . . . Matt Musgrove
Multimedia Specialist . . . . . John Heid
Junior Publicist . . . . . Susan Sanderman

Television/Radio Broadcasting
Coordinating Television Producer . . . . . Tim Kiely
Television Producer . . . . . Scott Cockerill
Television Director . . . . . Dan Reagan
Assistant Director . . . . . Jim Allen
Director of Radio Operations/ Radio Play by Play Broadcaster . . . . . Dan Kamal
Radio Analyst . . . . . Billy Jaffe
Broadcast Operations Associate . . . . . Mary Moran
TV Broadcasters . . . . . Matt McConnell and Darren Eliot

Ticket Sales
Director of Ticket Sales . . . . . Dan Froehlich
New Account Sales, Sr. Manager . . . . . Keith Brennan
Ticket Operations Director . . . . . Wendell Byrne
Client Services Managers . . . . . Annette Dancausse, Grady Landis, Jenny Powers
Group Sales Managers . . . . . Evan Kellner, Travis Pelleymounter
New Account Sales Managers . . . . . John Farrell, David Forrest, Tracy Frank, John Morgan
Ticket Operations Assistant . . . . . Scott Squillance

Boston Bruins

2000-01 Results: 36W-30L-8T-8OTL 88PTS. Fourth, Northeast Division

After his trade from the Oilers last year, Bill Guerin wound up playing in 85 games. He had 40 goals on the season but, with 12 for Edmonton and 28 in Boston, Joe Thornton actually led the Bruins with 37.

2001-02 Schedule

Month	Day	Date	Opponent
Oct.	Thu.	4	Anaheim
	Sat.	6	Atlanta
	Mon.	8	Washington*
	Wed.	10	at Minnesota
	Sat.	13	at San Jose
	Tue.	16	at Phoenix
	Wed.	17	at Anaheim
	Sat.	20	at Nashville
	Tue.	23	at Toronto
	Thu.	25	Toronto
	Sat.	27	NY Rangers
	Sun.	28	at Chicago
	Tue.	30	New Jersey
Nov.	Sat.	3	at New Jersey*
	Tue.	6	Edmonton
	Thu.	8	Minnesota
	Sat.	10	Columbus
	Tue.	13	Montreal
	Thu.	15	New Jersey
	Sat.	17	Buffalo
	Tue.	20	at Montreal
	Fri.	23	Vancouver*
	Sat.	24	at Toronto
	Tue.	27	Tampa Bay
	Thu.	29	at Philadelphia
Dec.	Sat.	1	at Ottawa
	Tue.	4	at Atlanta
	Thu.	6	Pittsburgh
	Sat.	8	Buffalo
	Wed.	12	at Pittsburgh
	Thu.	13	at Washington
	Sat.	15	Philadelphia
	Tue.	18	Atlanta
	Thu.	20	Montreal
	Sat.	22	at NY Islanders
	Wed.	26	Ottawa
	Fri.	28	at Florida
	Sat.	29	at Tampa Bay
	Mon.	31	at Dallas
Jan.	Wed.	2	at Carolina
	Thu.	3	Toronto
	Sat.	5	Washington*
	Tue.	8	at Pittsburgh
	Thu.	10	Los Angeles
	Sat.	12	NY Islanders
	Mon.	14	at Washington
	Thu.	17	Ottawa
	Sat.	19	at St. Louis
	Mon.	21	St. Louis*
	Wed.	23	at NY Rangers
	Thu.	24	at Ottawa
	Sat.	26	Florida
	Mon.	28	Chicago
	Wed.	30	at Montreal
Feb.	Mon.	4	at Columbus
	Tue.	5	Buffalo
	Sat.	9	Florida*
	Mon.	11	at Colorado
	Tue.	12	at Vancouver
	Tue.	26	at NY Islanders
	Thu.	28	Carolina
Mar.	Fri.	1	at Buffalo
	Mon.	4	Philadelphia
	Wed.	6	at Montreal
	Fri.	8	at Atlanta
	Sat.	9	Calgary
	Wed.	13	at NY Rangers
	Thu.	14	Toronto
	Sat.	16	Detroit*
	Tue.	19	Phoenix
	Thu.	21	at Buffalo
	Sat.	23	at Florida
	Sun.	24	at Tampa Bay
	Tue.	26	at Carolina
	Sat.	30	Carolina*
Apr.	Tue.	2	at Philadelphia
	Thu.	4	NY Islanders
	Sat.	6	NY Rangers*
	Sun.	7	at New Jersey*
	Tue.	9	Tampa Bay
	Thu.	11	at Ottawa
	Sat.	13	Pittsburgh

* Denotes afternoon game.

Franchise date: November 1, 1924

EASTERN CONFERENCE

NORTHEAST DIVISION

78th NHL Season

Year-by-Year Record

		Home				Road				Overall								
Season	**GP**	**W**	**L**	**T**	**OL**	**W**	**L**	**T**	**OL**	**W**	**L**	**T**	**OL**	**GF**	**GA**	**Pts.**	**Finished**	**Playoff Result**
2000-01	82	21	12	5	3	15	18	3	5	36	30	8	8	227	249	88	4th, Northeast Div.	Out of Playoffs
1999-2000	82	12	17	11	1	12	16	8	5	24	33	19	6	210	248	73	5th, Northeast Div.	Out of Playoffs
1998-99	82	22	10	9	...	17	20	4	...	39	30	13	...	214	181	91	3rd, Northeast Div.	Lost Conf. Semi-Final
1997-98	82	19	16	6	...	20	14	7	...	39	30	13	...	221	194	91	2nd, Northeast Div.	Lost Conf. Quarter-Final
1996-97	82	14	20	7	...	12	27	2	...	26	47	9	...	234	300	61	6th, Northeast Div.	Out of Playoffs
1995-96	82	22	14	5	...	18	17	6	...	40	31	11	...	282	269	91	2nd, Northeast Div.	Lost Conf. Quarter-Final
1994-95	48	15	7	2	...	12	11	1	...	27	18	3	...	150	127	57	3rd, Northeast Div.	Lost Conf. Quarter-Final
1993-94	84	20	14	8	...	22	15	5	...	42	29	13	...	289	252	97	2nd, Northeast Div.	Lost Conf. Semi-Final
1992-93	84	29	10	3	...	22	16	4	...	51	26	7	...	332	268	109	1st, Adams Div.	Lost Div. Semi-Final
1991-92	80	23	11	6	...	13	21	6	...	36	32	12	...	270	275	84	2nd, Adams Div.	Lost Conf. Championship
1990-91	80	26	9	5	...	18	15	7	...	44	24	12	...	299	264	100	1st, Adams Div.	Lost Conf. Championship
1989-90	80	23	13	4	...	23	12	5	...	46	25	9	...	289	232	101	1st, Adams Div.	Lost Final
1988-89	80	17	15	8	...	20	14	6	...	37	29	14	...	289	256	88	2nd, Adams Div.	Lost Div. Final
1987-88	80	24	13	3	...	20	17	3	...	44	30	6	...	300	251	94	2nd, Adams Div.	Lost Final
1986-87	80	25	11	4	...	14	23	3	...	39	34	7	...	301	276	85	3rd, Adams Div.	Lost Div. Semi-Final
1985-86	80	24	9	7	...	13	22	5	...	37	31	12	...	311	288	86	3rd, Adams Div.	Lost Div. Semi-Final
1984-85	80	21	15	4	...	15	19	6	...	36	34	10	...	303	287	82	4th, Adams Div.	Lost Div. Semi-Final
1983-84	80	25	12	3	...	24	13	3	...	49	25	6	...	336	261	104	1st, Adams Div.	Lost Div. Semi-Final
1982-83	80	28	6	6	...	22	14	4	...	50	20	10	...	327	228	110	1st, Adams Div.	Lost Conf. Championship
1981-82	80	24	12	4	...	19	15	6	...	43	27	10	...	323	285	96	2nd, Adams Div.	Lost Div. Final
1980-81	80	26	10	4	...	11	20	9	...	37	30	13	...	316	272	87	2nd, Adams Div.	Lost Prelim. Round
1979-80	80	27	9	4	...	19	12	9	...	46	21	13	...	310	234	105	2nd, Adams Div.	Lost Quarter-Final
1978-79	80	25	10	5	...	18	13	9	...	43	23	14	...	316	270	100	1st, Adams Div.	Lost Semi-Final
1977-78	80	29	6	5	...	22	12	6	...	51	18	11	...	333	218	113	1st, Adams Div.	Lost Final
1976-77	80	27	7	6	...	22	16	2	...	49	23	8	...	312	240	106	1st, Adams Div.	Lost Final
1975-76	80	27	5	8	...	21	10	9	...	48	15	17	...	313	237	113	1st, Adams Div.	Lost Semi-Final
1974-75	80	29	5	6	...	11	21	8	...	40	26	14	...	345	245	94	2nd, Adams Div.	Lost Prelim. Round
1973-74	78	33	4	2	...	19	13	7	...	52	17	9	...	349	221	113	1st, East Div.	Lost Final
1972-73	78	27	10	2	...	24	12	3	...	51	22	5	...	330	235	107	2nd, East Div.	Lost Quarter-Final
1971-72	**78**	**28**	**4**	**7**	**...**	**26**	**9**	**4**	**...**	**54**	**13**	**11**	**...**	**330**	**204**	**119**	**1st, East Div.**	**Won Stanley Cup**
1970-71	78	33	4	2	...	24	10	5	...	57	14	7	...	399	207	121	1st, East Div.	Lost Quarter-Final
1969-70	**76**	**27**	**3**	**8**	**...**	**13**	**14**	**11**	**...**	**40**	**17**	**19**	**...**	**277**	**216**	**99**	**2nd, East Div.**	**Won Stanley Cup**
1968-69	76	29	3	6	...	13	15	10	...	42	18	16	...	303	221	100	2nd, East Div.	Lost Semi-Final
1967-68	74	22	9	6	...	15	18	4	...	37	27	10	...	259	216	84	3rd, East Div.	Lost Quarter-Final
1966-67	70	10	21	4	...	7	22	6	...	17	43	10	...	182	253	44	6th,	Out of Playoffs
1965-66	70	15	17	3	...	6	26	3	...	21	43	6	...	174	275	48	5th,	Out of Playoffs
1964-65	70	12	17	6	...	9	26	0	...	21	43	6	...	166	253	48	6th,	Out of Playoffs
1963-64	70	13	15	7	...	5	25	5	...	18	40	12	...	170	212	48	6th,	Out of Playoffs
1962-63	70	7	18	10	...	7	21	7	...	14	39	17	...	198	281	45	6th,	Out of Playoffs
1961-62	70	9	22	4	...	6	25	4	...	15	47	8	...	177	306	38	6th,	Out of Playoffs
1960-61	70	13	17	5	...	2	25	8	...	15	42	13	...	176	254	43	6th,	Out of Playoffs
1959-60	70	21	11	3	...	7	23	5	...	28	34	8	...	220	241	64	5th,	Out of Playoffs
1958-59	70	21	11	3	...	11	18	6	...	32	29	9	...	205	215	73	2nd,	Lost Semi-Final
1957-58	70	15	14	6	...	12	14	9	...	27	28	15	...	199	194	69	4th,	Lost Final
1956-57	70	20	9	6	...	14	15	6	...	34	24	12	...	195	174	80	3rd,	Lost Final
1955-56	70	14	14	7	...	9	20	6	...	23	34	13	...	147	185	59	5th,	Out of Playoffs
1954-55	70	16	10	9	...	7	16	12	...	23	26	21	...	169	188	67	4th,	Lost Semi-Final
1953-54	70	22	8	5	...	10	20	5	...	32	28	10	...	177	181	74	4th,	Lost Semi-Final
1952-53	70	19	10	6	...	9	19	7	...	28	29	13	...	152	172	69	3rd,	Lost Final
1951-52	70	15	12	8	...	10	17	8	...	25	29	16	...	162	176	66	4th,	Lost Semi-Final
1950-51	70	13	12	10	...	9	18	8	...	22	30	18	...	178	197	62	4th,	Lost Semi-Final
1949-50	70	15	12	8	...	7	20	8	...	22	32	16	...	198	228	60	5th,	Out of Playoffs
1948-49	60	18	10	2	...	11	13	6	...	29	23	8	...	178	163	66	2nd,	Lost Semi-Final
1947-48	60	12	8	10	...	11	16	3	...	23	24	13	...	167	168	59	3rd,	Lost Semi-Final
1946-47	60	18	7	5	...	8	16	6	...	26	23	11	...	190	175	63	3rd,	Lost Semi-Final
1945-46	50	11	5	4	...	13	13	4	...	24	18	8	...	167	156	56	2nd,	Lost Final
1944-45	50	11	12	2	...	5	18	2	...	16	30	4	...	179	219	36	4th,	Lost Semi-Final
1943-44	50	15	8	2	...	4	18	3	...	19	26	5	...	223	268	43	5th,	Out of Playoffs
1942-43	50	17	3	5	...	7	14	4	...	24	17	9	...	195	176	57	2nd,	Lost Final
1941-42	48	17	4	3	...	8	13	3	...	25	17	6	...	160	118	56	3rd,	Lost Semi-Final
1940-41	**48**	**15**	**4**	**5**	**...**	**12**	**4**	**8**	**...**	**27**	**8**	**13**	**...**	**168**	**102**	**67**	**1st,**	**Won Stanley Cup**
1939-40	48	20	3	1	...	11	9	4	...	31	12	5	...	170	98	67	1st,	Lost Semi-Final
1938-39	**48**	**20**	**2**	**2**	**...**	**16**	**8**	**0**	**...**	**36**	**10**	**2**	**...**	**156**	**76**	**74**	**1st,**	**Won Stanley Cup**
1937-38	48	18	3	3	...	12	8	4	...	30	11	7	...	142	89	67	1st, Amn. Div.	Lost Semi-Final
1936-37	48	9	11	4	...	14	7	3	...	23	18	7	...	120	110	53	2nd, Amn. Div.	Lost Quarter-Final
1935-36	48	15	8	1	...	7	12	5	...	22	20	6	...	92	83	50	2nd, Amn. Div.	Lost Quarter-Final
1934-35	48	17	7	0	...	9	9	6	...	26	16	6	...	129	112	58	1st, Amn. Div.	Lost Semi-Final
1933-34	48	11	11	2	...	7	14	3	...	18	25	5	...	111	130	41	4th, Amn. Div.	Out of Playoffs
1932-33	48	19	2	3	...	6	13	5	...	25	15	8	...	124	88	58	1st, Amn. Div.	Lost Semi-Final
1931-32	48	11	10	3	...	4	11	9	...	15	21	12	...	122	117	42	4th, Amn. Div.	Out of Playoffs
1930-31	44	16	1	5	...	12	9	1	...	28	10	6	...	143	90	62	1st, Amn. Div.	Lost Semi-Final
1929-30	44	21	1	0	...	17	4	1	...	38	5	1	...	179	98	77	1st, Amn. Div.	Lost Final
1928-29	**44**	**15**	**6**	**1**	**...**	**11**	**7**	**4**	**...**	**26**	**13**	**5**	**...**	**89**	**52**	**57**	**1st, Amn. Div.**	**Won Stanley Cup**
1927-28	44	13	4	5	...	7	9	6	...	20	13	11	...	77	70	51	1st, Amn. Div.	Lost Semi-Final
1926-27	44	15	7	0	...	6	13	3	...	21	20	3	...	97	89	45	2nd, Amn. Div.	Lost Final
1925-26	36	10	7	1	...	7	8	3	...	17	15	4	...	92	85	38	4th,	Out of Playoffs
1924-25	30	3	12	0	...	3	12	0	...	6	24	0	...	49	119	12	6th,	Out of Playoffs

2001-02 Player Personnel

FORWARDS	HT	WT	S	Place of Birth	Date	2000-01 Club
ALLISON, Jason	6-3	215	R	North York, Ont.	5/29/75	Boston
AXELSSON, P.J.	6-1	175	L	Kungalv, Sweden	2/26/75	Boston
CORAZZINI, Carl	5-9	170	R	Framingham, MA	4/21/79	Boston University
CROZIER, Greg	6-3	200	L	Calgary, Alta.	7/6/76	Pittsburgh-Wilkes-Barre
ELORANTA, Mikko	6-0	190	L	Turku, Finland	8/24/72	Boston
EMMONS, John	6-1	203	L	San Jose, CA	8/17/74	Ott.-Grand Rapids-T.B.
GELLARD, Mike	6-1	193	L	Markham, Ont.	10/10/78	St. Lawrence
GOREN, Lee	6-3	205	R	Winnipeg, Man.	12/26/77	Boston-Prov (AHL)
GUERIN, Bill	6-2	210	R	Worcester, MA	11/9/70	Edmonton-Boston
HENDERSON, Jay	5-11	190	L	Edmonton, Alta.	9/17/7	Boston-Prov (AHL)
HILBERT, Andy	5-11	190	L	Howell, MI	2/6/81	U. of Michigan
HUML, Ivan	6-2	195	L	Kladno, Czech.	9/6/81	Providence (AHL)
KARLIN, Mattias	5-11	183	L	Domsjo, Sweden	7/4/79	Providence (AHL)
KNUBLE, Mike	6-3	208	R	Toronto, Ont.	7/4/72	Boston
LAPOINTE, Martin	5-11	200	R	Ville St-Pierre, Que.	9/12/73	Detroit
MANLOW, Eric	6-0	190	L	Belleville, Ont.	4/7/75	Boston-Prov (AHL)
NAZAROV, Andrei	6-5	230	R	Chelyabinsk, USSR	5/22/74	Anaheim-Boston
PELLERIN, Scott	5-11	190	L	Shediac, N.B.	1/9/70	Minnesota-Carolina
ROLSTON, Brian	6-2	205	L	Flint, MI	2/21/73	Boston
SAMSONOV, Sergei	5-8	180	R	Moscow, USSR	10/27/78	Boston
THORNTON, Joe	6-4	215	L	London, Ont.	7/2/79	Boston
TUZZOLINO, Tony	6-2	208	R	Buffalo, NY	10/9/75	Hartford-NY Rangers
ZAMUNER, Rob	6-3	203	L	Oakville, Ont.	9/17/69	Ottawa
ZEHR, Jeff	6-3	195	L	Woodstock, Ont.	12/10/78	Greenville
DEFENSEMEN						
ALLEN, Bobby	6-1	205	L	Braintree, MA	11/14/78	Boston College
BOYNTON, Nick	6-2	210	R	Nobleton, Ont.	1/14/79	Boston-Prov (AHL)
CECH, Vratislav	6-3	196	L	Tabor, Czech.	1/28/79	Greenville-Prov (AHL)
GILL, Hal	6-7	230	L	Concord, MA	4/6/75	Boston
GIRARD, Jonathan	5-11	192	R	Joliette, Que.	5/27/80	Boston-Prov (AHL)
JACKMAN, Richard	6-2	192	R	Toronto, Ont.	6/28/78	Dallas-Utah
KELLEHER, Chris	6-1	210	L	Cambridge, MA	3/23/75	Wilkes-Barre
KOLARIK, Pavel	6-1	207	L	Vyskov, Czech.	10/24/72	Boston-Prov (AHL)
KULTANEN, Jarno	6-2	198	L	Luumaki, Finland	1/8/73	Boston
KUTLAK, Zdenek	6-3	207	L	Budejovice, Czech.	2/13/80	Boston-Prov (AHL)
McLAREN, Kyle	6-4	230	L	Humboldt, Sask.	6/18/77	Boston
O'DONNELL, Sean	6-3	230	L	Ottawa, Ont.	10/13/71	Minnesota-New Jersey
SWEENEY, Don	5-10	185	L	St. Stephen, N.B.	8/17/66	Boston
VAN ACKER, Eric	6-5	246	L	St-Jean, Que.	3/1/79	Greenville

GOALTENDERS	HT	WT	C	Place of Birth	Date	2000-01 Club
DAFOE, Byron	5-11	200	L	Sussex, England	2/25/71	Boston
GRAHAME, John	6-2	214	L	Denver, CO	8/31/75	Boston-Prov (AHL)
MAUND, Jeff	6-0	174	L	Belleville, Ont.	4/8/76	Norfolk
RAYCROFT, Andrew	6-0	174	L	Belleville, Ont.	5/4/80	Boston-Prov (AHL)

Coach

FTOREK, ROBBIE
Coach, Boston Bruins. Born in Needham, MA, January 2, 1952.

Robbie Ftorek was named the head coach of the Bruins on May 9, 2001. Ftorek began his coaching career as head coach of the Los Angeles Kings' American Hockey League affiliate in New Haven in 1985 and was named as the head coach in Los Angeles on December 9, 1987. In 1989-90 he joined the Quebec Nordiques organization when he was named head coach of their AHL affiliate in Halifax. After 48 games, he was called to Quebec as an assistant coach through the 1990-91 season.

Ftorek went on to spend 10 seasons in the New Jersey Devils organization. He won a Calder Cup championship with Albany in 1994-95 and was named the AHL's outstanding coach in both 1994-95 and 1995-96. He moved up to New Jersey as an assistant coach in 1996-97 before being named the club's head coach in 1998.

A native of Needham, Massachusetts, Ftorek was a schoolboy standout in both hockey and soccer and is still regarded as the top high school hockey player in state history. He joined the U.S. National Team in 1971 and won a silver medal with the 1972 U.S. Olympic Team in Japan before signing with the Detroit Red Wings. Ftorek later starred in the WHA from 1974-75 to 1978-79 before returning to the NHL for six more seasons. Ftorek was honored with induction into the U. S. Hockey Hall of Fame in 1991.

Coaching Record

		Regular Season				Playoffs		
Season	Team	Games	W	L	T	Games	W	L
1985-86	New Haven (AHL)	80	36	37	7	5	1	4
1986-87	New Haven (AHL)	80	44	25	11	7	3	4
1987-88	New Haven (AHL)	27	16	8	3	....	....	....
	Los Angeles (NHL)	**52**	**23**	**25**	**4**	**5**	**1**	**4**
1988-89	**Los Angeles (NHL)**	**80**	**42**	**31**	**7**	**11**	**4**	**7**
1989-90	Halifax (AHL)	48	25	19	4	....	....	....
1992-93	Utica (AHL)	80	33	36	11	5	1	4
1993-94	Albany (AHL)	80	38	34	8	5	1	4
1994-95	Albany (AHL)	80	46	17	17	14	12	2
1995-96	Albany (AHL)	80	54	19	17	4	1	3
1998-99	**New Jersey (NHL)**	**82**	**47**	**24**	**11**	**7**	**3**	**4**
1999-2000	**New Jersey (NHL)**	**74**	**41**	**25**	**8**	....	....	....
	NHL Totals	**288**	**153**	**105**	**30**	**23**	**8**	**15**

2000-01 Scoring

* - rookie

Regular Season

Pos	#	Player	Team	GP	G	A	Pts	+/–	PIM	PP	SH	GW	GT	S	%
C	41	Jason Allison	BOS	82	36	59	95	–8	85	11	3	6	0	185	19.5
R	13	Bill Guerin	EDM	21	12	10	22	11	18	4	0	1	0	64	18.8
			BOS	64	28	35	63	–4	122	7	1	4	0	225	12.4
			TOTAL	85	40	45	85	7	140	11	1	5	0	289	13.8
L	14	Sergei Samsonov	BOS	82	29	46	75	6	18	3	0	3	2	215	13.5
C	19	Joe Thornton	BOS	72	37	34	71	–4	107	19	1	5	0	181	20.4
R	12	Brian Rolston	BOS	77	19	39	58	6	28	5	0	4	0	286	6.6
R	51	Andrei Kovalenko	BOS	76	16	21	37	–14	27	7	1	3	1	119	13.4
D	27	Eric Weinrich	MTL	60	6	19	25	–1	34	2	0	1	1	81	7.4
			BOS	22	1	5	6	–8	10	1	0	1	0	28	3.6
			TOTAL	82	7	24	31	–9	44	3	0	2	1	109	6.4
C	22	Mikko Eloranta	BOS	62	12	11	23	2	38	1	1	2	0	89	13.5
L	11	P.J. Axelsson	BOS	81	8	15	23	–12	27	0	0	2	0	146	5.5
R	26	Mike Knuble	BOS	82	7	13	20	0	37	0	1	1	1	92	7.6
R	29	Dixon Ward	BOS	63	5	13	18	–1	65	0	0	0	0	88	5.7
D	18	Kyle McLaren	BOS	58	5	12	17	–5	53	2	0	0	1	91	5.5
D	55	* Jonathan Girard	BOS	31	3	13	16	2	14	2	0	1	0	42	7.1
D	20	Darren Van Impe	BOS	31	3	10	13	–9	41	2	0	0	0	40	7.5
D	32	Don Sweeney	BOS	72	2	10	12	–1	26	1	0	1	0	60	3.3
D	25	Hal Gill	BOS	80	1	10	11	–2	71	0	0	0	0	79	1.3
D	64	Jarno Kultanen	BOS	62	2	8	10	–3	26	0	0	1	0	76	2.6
D	23	Peter Popovic	BOS	60	1	6	7	–5	48	0	0	0	0	34	2.9
L	62	Andrei Nazarov	ANA	16	1	0	1	–9	29	0	0	0	0	13	7.7
			BOS	63	1	4	5	–14	200	0	0	0	0	50	2.0
			TOTAL	79	2	4	6	–23	229	0	0	0	0	63	3.2
C	17	Shawn Bates	BOS	45	2	3	5	–12	26	0	0	0	0	59	3.4
L	16	Ken Belanger	BOS	40	2	2	4	–6	121	0	0	1	0	35	5.7
R	10	Cameron Mann	BOS	15	1	3	4	0	6	0	0	0	0	17	5.9
D	44	Paul Coffey	BOS	18	0	4	4	–6	30	0	0	0	0	28	0.0
R	37	* Lee Goren	BOS	21	2	0	2	–3	7	1	0	0	0	9	22.2
D	39	* Zdenek Kutlak	BOS	10	0	2	2	–3	4	0	0	0	0	7	0.0
G	34	Byron Dafoe	BOS	45	0	2	2	0	6	0	0	0	0	0	0.0
D	53	Brandon Smith	BOS	3	1	0	1	–1	0	1	0	0	0	2	50.0
C	57	* Eric Manlow	BOS	8	0	1	1	0	2	0	0	0	0	3	0.0
C	61	Marquis Mathieu	BOS	1	0	0	0	0	2	0	0	0	0	0	0.0
D	44	* Nick Boynton	BOS	1	0	0	0	–1	0	0	0	0	0	1	0.0
C	28	Andre Savage	BOS	1	0	0	0	0	0	0	0	0	0	1	0.0
G	31	Kay Whitmore	BOS	5	0	0	0	0	0	0	0	0	0	0	0.0
L	48	Joe Hulbig	BOS	7	0	0	0	–3	4	0	0	0	0	0	0.0
R	21	* Eric Nickulas	BOS	7	0	0	0	–2	4	0	0	0	0	6	0.0
G	47	* John Grahame	BOS	10	0	0	0	0	2	0	0	0	0	0	0.0
D	72	Pavel Kolarik	BOS	10	0	0	0	–2	4	0	0	0	0	1	0.0
L	38	* Jay Henderson	BOS	13	0	0	0	–1	26	0	0	0	0	12	0.0
G	1	* Andrew Raycroft	BOS	15	0	0	0	0	0	0	0	0	0	0	0.0
G	35	Peter Skudra	BUF	1	0	0	0	0	0	0	0	0	0	0	0.0
			BOS	25	0	0	0	0	0	0	0	0	0	0	0.0
			TOTAL	26	0	0	0	0	0	0	0	0	0	0	0.0

Goaltending

No.	Goaltender	GPI	Mins	Avg	W	L	T	EN	SO	GA	SA	S%
34	Byron Dafoe	45	2536	2.39	22	14	7	1	2	101	1076	.906
1	* Andrew Raycroft	15	649	2.96	4	6	0	3	0	32	291	.890
35	Peter Skudra	25	1116	3.33	6	12	1	1	0	62	511	.879
47	* John Grahame	10	471	3.57	3	4	0	3	0	28	211	.867
31	Kay Whitmore	5	203	5.32	1	2	0	0	0	18	94	.809
	Totals	**82**	**4991**	**2.99**	**36**	**38**	**8**	**8**	**2**	**249**	**2191**	**.886**

Coaching History

Art Ross, 1924-25 to 1927-28; Cy Denneny, 1928-29; Art Ross, 1929-30 to 1933-34; Frank Patrick, 1934-35, 1935-36; Art Ross, 1936-37 to 1938-39; Cooney Weiland, 1939-40, 1940-41; Art Ross, 1941-42 to 1944-45; Dit Clapper, 1945-46 to 1948-49; George Boucher, 1949-50; Lynn Patrick, 1950-51 to 1953-54; Lynn Patrick and Milt Schmidt, 1954-55; Milt Schmidt, 1955-56 to 1960-61; Phil Watson, 1961-62; Phil Watson and Milt Schmidt, 1962-63; Milt Schmidt, 1963-64 to 1965-66; Harry Sinden, 1966-67 to 1969-70; Tom Johnson, 1970-71, 1971-72; Tom Johnson and Bep Guidolin, 1972-73; Bep Guidolin, 1973-74; Don Cherry, 1974-75 to 1978-79; Fred Creighton and Harry Sinden, 1979-80; Gerry Cheevers, 1980-81 to 1983-84; Gerry Cheevers and Harry Sinden, 1984-85; Butch Goring, 1985-86; Butch Goring and Terry O'Reilly, 1986-87; Terry O'Reilly, 1987-88, 1988-89; Mike Milbury, 1989-90, 1990-91; Rick Bowness, 1991-92; Brian Sutter, 1992-93 to 1994-95; Steve Kasper, 1995-96, 1996-97; Pat Burns, 1997-98 to 1999-2000; Pat Burns and Mike Keenan, 2000-01; Robbie Ftorek, 2001-02.

Club Records

Team

(Figures in brackets for season records are games played; records for fewest points, wins, ties, losses, goals, goals against are for 70 or more games)

Most Points **121** 1970-71 (78)
Most Wins **57** 1970-71 (78)
Most Ties **21** 1954-55 (70)
Most Losses **47** 1961-62 (70), 1996-97 (82)
Most Goals **399** 1970-71 (78)
Most Goals Against **306** 1961-62 (70)
Fewest Points **38** 1961-62 (70)
Fewest Wins **14** 1962-63 (70)
Fewest Ties **5** 1972-73 (78)
Fewest Losses **13** 1971-72 (78)
Fewest Goals **147** 1955-56 (70)
Fewest Goals Against **172** 1952-53 (70)
Longest Winning Streak
Overall . . . . **14** Dec. 3/29-Jan. 9/30
Home . . . . ***20** Dec. 3/29-Mar. 18/30
Away . . . . **8** Feb. 17-Mar. 8/72, Mar. 15-Apr. 14/93
Longest Undefeated Streak
Overall . . . . **23** Dec. 22/40-Feb. 23/41 (15 wins, 8 ties)
Home . . . . **27** Nov. 22/70-Mar. 20/71 (26 wins, 1 tie)
Away . . . . **15** Dec. 22/40-Mar. 16/41 (9 wins, 6 ties)
Longest Losing Streak
Overall . . . . **11** Dec. 3/24-Jan. 5/25
Home . . . . ***11** Dec. 8/24-Feb. 17/25
Away . . . . **14** Dec. 27/64-Feb. 21/65
Longest Winless Streak
Overall . . . . **20** Jan. 28-Mar. 11/62 (16 losses, 4 ties)
Home . . . . **11** Dec. 8/24-Feb. 17/25 (11 losses)
Away . . . . **14** Three times
Most Shutouts, Season **15** 1927-28 (44)
Most PIM, Season **2,443** 1987-88 (80)
Most Goals, Game . . . . **14** Jan. 21/45 (NYR 3 at Bos. 14)

Individual

Most Seasons . . . . **21** John Bucyk, Raymond Bourque
Most Games . . . . **1,518** Raymond Bourque
Most Goals, Career . . . . **545** John Bucyk
Most Assists, Career . . . . **1,111** Raymond Bourque
Most Points, Career . . . . **1,506** Raymond Bourque (395G, 1,111A)
Most PIM, Career . . . . **2,095** Terry O'Reilly
Most Shutouts, Career . . . . **74** Tiny Thompson
Longest Consecutive Games Streak . . . . **418** John Bucyk (Jan. 23/69-Mar. 2/75)
Most Goals, Season . . . . **76** Phil Esposito (1970-71)
Most Assists, Season . . . . **102** Bobby Orr (1970-71)
Most Points, Season . . . . **152** Phil Esposito (1970-71; 76G, 76A)
Most PIM, Season . . . . **302** Jay Miller (1987-88)
Most Points, Defenseman, Season . . . . ***139** Bobby Orr (1970-71; 37G, 102A)
Most Points, Center, Season . . . . **152** Phil Esposito (1970-71; 76G, 76A)
Most Points, Right Wing, Season . . . . **105** Ken Hodge (1970-71; 43G, 62A), (1973-74; 50G, 55A), Rick Middleton (1983-84; 47G, 58A)
Most Points, Left Wing, Season . . . . **116** John Bucyk (1970-71; 51G, 65A)
Most Points, Rookie, Season . . . . **102** Joe Juneau (1992-93; 32G, 70A)
Most Shutouts, Season . . . . **15** Hal Winkler (1927-28)
Most Goals, Game . . . . **4** Twenty times
Most Assists, Game . . . . **6** Ken Hodge (Feb. 9/71), Bobby Orr (Jan. 1/73)
Most Points, Game . . . . **7** Bobby Orr (Nov. 15/73; 3G, 4A), Phil Esposito (Dec. 19/74; 3G, 4A), Barry Pederson (Apr. 4/82; 3G, 4A), Cam Neely (Oct. 16/88; 3G, 4A)

* NHL Record.

Retired Numbers

2	Eddie Shore	1926-1940
3	Lionel Hitchman	1925-1934
4	Bobby Orr	1966-1976
5	Dit Clapper	1927-1947
7	Phil Esposito	1967-1975
9	John Bucyk	1957-1978
15	Milt Schmidt	1936-1955

All-time Record vs. Other Clubs

Regular Season

	At Home								On Road								Total							
	GP	W	L	T	OL	GF	GA	PTS	GP	W	L	T	OL	GF	GA	PTS	GP	W	L	T	OL	GF	GA	PTS
Anaheim	6	3	3	0	0	18	18	6	7	4	2	1	0	18	13	9	13	7	5	1	0	36	31	15
Atlanta	4	1	2	1	0	15	20	3	4	2	2	0	0	12	14	4	8	3	4	1	0	27	34	7
Buffalo	99	55	31	13	0	370	292	123	100	35	49	15	1	299	366	86	199	90	80	28	1	669	658	209
Calgary	44	26	11	6	1	155	121	59	43	22	18	3	0	151	157	47	87	48	29	9	1	306	278	106
Carolina	72	45	20	7	0	266	190	97	70	32	31	7	0	243	239	71	142	77	51	14	0	509	429	168
Chicago	282	160	88	34	0	1020	804	354	283	94	144	44	1	758	913	233	565	254	232	78	1	1778	1717	587
Colorado	61	31	21	9	0	238	189	71	63	34	23	6	0	263	227	74	124	65	44	15	0	501	416	145
Columbus	0	0	0	0	0	0	0	0	1	0	0	0	1	2	3	1	1	0	0	0	1	2	3	1
Dallas	58	40	9	9	0	249	140	89	59	29	16	13	1	217	173	72	117	69	25	22	1	466	313	161
Detroit	285	152	89	43	1	1003	759	348	283	78	153	52	0	716	950	208	568	230	242	95	1	1719	1709	556
Edmonton	27	18	6	3	0	115	76	39	28	14	11	3	0	93	95	31	55	32	17	6	0	208	171	70
Florida	16	5	8	3	0	40	46	13	15	7	7	0	1	40	45	15	31	12	15	3	1	80	91	28
Los Angeles	60	43	11	6	0	282	169	92	59	31	21	7	0	216	204	69	119	74	32	13	0	498	373	161
Minnesota	1	0	1	0	0	1	6	0	0	0	0	0	0	0	0	0	1	0	1	0	0	1	6	0
Montreal	327	150	121	56	0	963	886	356	326	95	185	46	0	774	1101	236	653	245	306	102	0	1737	1987	592
Nashville	3	1	1	1	0	11	6	3	3	2	0	0	1	10	5	5	6	3	1	1	1	21	11	8
New Jersey	50	29	13	7	1	201	151	66	47	24	12	10	1	157	128	59	97	53	25	17	2	358	279	125
NY Islanders	53	29	14	10	0	202	151	68	55	26	23	6	0	182	183	58	108	55	37	16	0	384	334	126
NY Rangers	292	157	93	42	0	1059	818	356	296	113	128	55	0	835	902	281	588	270	221	97	0	1894	1720	637
Ottawa	25	15	7	3	0	98	73	33	23	14	4	3	2	79	52	33	48	29	11	6	2	177	125	66
Philadelphia	70	44	16	10	0	273	196	98	67	28	31	8	0	194	227	64	137	72	47	18	0	467	423	162
Phoenix	28	21	4	3	0	129	87	45	28	14	12	2	0	100	98	30	56	35	16	5	0	229	185	75
Pittsburgh	72	53	13	6	0	325	204	112	74	28	31	15	0	264	260	71	146	81	44	21	0	589	464	183
St. Louis	57	35	13	9	0	244	153	79	57	23	24	9	1	194	182	56	114	58	37	18	1	438	335	135
San Jose	8	6	0	2	0	29	19	14	9	5	2	2	0	34	24	12	17	11	2	4	0	63	43	26
Tampa Bay	17	13	1	3	0	65	35	29	17	8	6	3	0	50	44	19	34	21	7	6	0	115	79	48
Toronto	290	157	85	47	1	951	766	362	291	89	151	51	0	754	987	229	581	246	236	98	1	1705	1753	591
Vancouver	49	36	6	7	0	208	115	79	49	25	16	8	0	201	162	58	98	61	22	15	0	409	277	137
Washington	50	28	15	7	0	184	135	63	49	24	13	12	0	172	138	60	99	52	28	19	0	356	273	123
Defunct Clubs	164	112	39	13	0	525	306	237	164	79	67	18	0	496	440	176	328	191	106	31	0	1021	746	413
Totals	**2570**	**1465**	**741**	**360**	**4**	**9239**	**6931**	**3294**	**2570**	**979**	**1182**	**399**	**10**	**7524**	**8332**	**2367**	**5140**	**2444**	**1923**	**759**	**14**	**16763**	**15263**	**5661**

Playoffs

	Series	W	L	GP	W	L	T	GF	GA	Last Mtg.	Round	Result
Buffalo	7	5	2	39	21	18	0	139	130	1999	CSF	L 2-4
Carolina	3	3	0	19	12	7	0	63	48	1999	CQF	W 4-2
Chicago	6	5	1	22	16	5	1	97	63	1978	QF	W 4-0
Colorado	2	1	1	11	6	5	0	37	36	1983	DSF	W 3-1
Dallas	1	0	1	3	0	3	0	13	20	1981	PR	L 0-3
Detroit	7	4	3	33	19	14	0	96	98	1957	SF	W 4-1
Edmonton	2	0	2	9	1	8	0	20	41	1990	F	L 1-4
Florida	1	0	1	5	1	4	0	16	22	1996	CQF	L 1-4
Los Angeles	2	2	0	13	8	5	0	56	38	1977	QF	W 4-2
Montreal	28	7	21	139	52	87	0	339	430	1994	CQF	W 4-3
New Jersey	3	1	2	18	7	11	0	52	55	1995	CQF	L 1-4
NY Islanders	2	0	2	11	3	8	0	35	49	1983	CF	L 2-4
NY Rangers	9	6	3	42	22	18	2	114	104	1973	QF	L 1-4
Philadelphia	4	2	2	20	11	9	0	60	57	1978	SF	W 4-1
Pittsburgh	4	2	2	19	9	10	0	62	67	1992	CF	L 0-4
St. Louis	2	2	0	8	8	0	0	48	15	1972	SF	W 4-0
Toronto	13	5	8	62	30	31	1	153	150	1974	QF	W 4-0
Washington	2	1	1	10	6	4	0	28	21	1998	CQF	L 2-4
Defunct Clubs	3	1	2	11	4	5	2	20	20			
Totals	**101**	**47**	**54**	**494**	**236**	**252**	**6**	**1448**	**1464**			

Playoff Results 2001-1997

Year	Round	Opponent	Result	GF	GA
1999	CSF	Buffalo	L 2-4	14	17
	CQF	Carolina	W 4-2	16	10
1998	CQF	Washington	L 2-4	13	15

Abbreviations: Round: F – Final; **CF** – conference final; **CSF** – conference semi-final; **CQF** – conference quarter-final; **DSF** – division semi-final; **SF** – semi-final; **QF** – quarter-final; **PR** – preliminary round.

Calgary totals include Atlanta Flames, 1972-73 to 1979-80. Carolina totals include Hartford, 1979-80 to 1996-97.
Colorado totals include Quebec, 1979-80 to 1994-95. Dallas totals include Minnesota North Stars, 1967-68 to 1992-93.
New Jersey totals include Kansas City, 1974-75 to 1975-76, and Colorado Rockies, 1976-77 to 1981-82.
Phoenix totals include Winnipeg, 1979-80 to 1995-96.

2000-01 Results

Oct.	5	Ottawa	4-4
	7	at Philadelphia	5-1
	9	Florida	4-2
	11	at Anaheim	3-2*
	13	at Los Angeles	0-5
	14	at San Jose	2-5
	17	at Edmonton	1-6
	20	at Calgary	2-3
	26	Washington	4-1
	28	Toronto	1-2*
	29	at NY Rangers	1-5
	31	at NY Islanders	2-4
Nov.	2	Chicago	5-4
	4	Atlanta	3-8
	5	at Toronto	1-7
	9	Ottawa	2-1
	11	Nashville	2-2
	16	New Jersey	2-3*
	18	Minnesota	1-6
	21	at Ottawa	1-2
	22	at Detroit	5-4
	24	Carolina	1-3
	26	Los Angeles	4-4
	28	Pittsburgh	3-1
Dec.	1	at Washington	2-3
	2	Washington	0-2
	4	at Atlanta	4-5
	6	at Pittsburgh	3-2
	8	at Columbus	2-3*
	9	NY Rangers	6-4
	12	Buffalo	0-3
	16	Carolina	4-1
	19	Philadelphia	4-4
	21	Toronto	4-0
	23	Detroit	1-2*
	27	at NY Islanders	5-2
	29	at Florida	0-3
	30	at Tampa Bay	1-1
Jan.	1	at Buffalo	4-3
	5	at Washington	1-1
	6	Dallas	0-4
	9	Pittsburgh	5-2
	10	at Montreal	2-1
	13	NY Rangers	4-1
	16	at New Jersey	5-4
	18	at Carolina	2-4
	19	at Nashville	0-1*
	22	Florida	2-3
	24	at Toronto	2-1
	26	at Buffalo	2-1
	27	New Jersey	4-3*
	30	St. Louis	5-1
Feb.	1	Montreal	0-3
	6	Philadelphia	4-3
	9	at Atlanta	1-5
	10	Tampa Bay	6-2
	15	at Tampa Bay	6-3
	16	at Florida	1-2
	18	at Carolina	4-5
	21	at Colorado	2-8
	23	at Dallas	4-5*
	24	at St. Louis	2-3*
	27	Phoenix	7-4
Mar.	1	Tampa Bay	3-1
	3	San Jose	3-2
	5	at Philadelphia	4-6
	6	Buffalo	1-3
	8	Ottawa	3-5
	10	Atlanta	5-7
	15	Vancouver	2-2
	17	at Montreal	3-2
	20	at Pittsburgh	2-2
	22	Montreal	3-2*
	24	Colorado	2-4
	25	at NY Rangers	3-2
	28	at Toronto	3-0
	30	at Ottawa	4-5*
	31	NY Islanders	4-2
Apr.	2	Montreal	3-2*
	4	at Buffalo	3-2
	6	at New Jersey	2-5
	7	NY Islanders	4-2

* – Overtime

Entry Draft Selections 2001-1987

2001

Pick	
19	Shaone Morrisonn
77	Darren McLachlan
111	Matti Kaltiainen
147	Jiri Jakes
179	Andrew Alberts
209	Jordan Sigalet
241	Milan Jurcina
282	Marcel Rodman

2000

Pick	
7	Lars Jonsson
27	Martin Samuelsson
37	Andy Hilbert
59	Ivan Huml
66	Tuukka Makela
73	Sergei Zinovjev
102	Brett Nowak
174	Jarno Kultanen
204	Chris Berti
237	Zdenek Kutlak
268	Pavel Kolarik
279	Andreas Lindstrom

1999

Pick	
21	Nick Boynton
56	Matt Zultek
89	Kyle Wanvig
118	Jaakko Harikkala
147	Seamus Kotyk
179	Donald Choukalos
207	Greg Barber
236	John Cronin
247	Mikko Eloranta
264	Georgy Pujacs

1998

Pick	
48	Jonathan Girard
52	Bobby Allen
78	Peter Nordstrom
135	Andrew Raycroft
165	Ryan Milanovic

1997

Pick	
1	Joe Thornton
8	Sergei Samsonov
27	Ben Clymer
54	Mattias Karlin
63	Lee Goren
81	Karol Bartanus
135	Denis Timofeev
162	Joel Trottier
180	Jim Baxter
191	Antti Laaksonen
218	Eric Van Acker
246	Jay Henderson

1996

Pick	
8	Johnathan Aitken
45	Henry Kuster
53	Eric Naud
80	Jason Doyle
100	Trent Whitfield
132	Elias Abrahamsson
155	Chris Lane
182	Thomas Brown
208	Bob Prier
234	Anders Soderberg

1995

Pick	
9	Kyle McLaren
21	Sean Brown
47	Paxton Schafer
73	Bill McCauley
99	Cameron Mann
151	Yevgeny Shaldybin
177	P.J. Axelsson
203	Sergei Zhukov
229	Jonathon Murphy

1994

Pick	
21	Evgeni Ryabchikov
47	Daniel Goneau
99	Eric Nickulas
125	Darren Wright
151	Andre Roy
177	Jeremy Schaefer
229	John Grahame
255	Neil Savary
281	Andrei Yakhanov

1993

Pick	
25	Kevyn Adams
51	Matt Alvey
88	Charles Paquette
103	Shawn Bates
129	Andrei Sapozhnikov
155	Milt Mastad
181	Ryan Golden
207	Hal Gill
233	Joel Prpic
259	Joakim Persson

1992

Pick	
16	Dmitri Kvartalnov
55	Sergei Zholtok
112	Scott Bailey
133	Jiri Dopita
136	Grigori Panteleev
184	Kurt Seher
208	Mattias Timander
232	Chris Crombie
256	Denis Chervyakov
257	Evgeny Pavlov

1991

Pick	
18	Glen Murray
40	Jozef Stumpel
62	Marcel Cousineau
84	Brad Tiley
106	Mariusz Czerkawski
150	Gary Golczewski
172	Jay Moser
194	Daniel Hodge
216	Steve Norton
238	Stephen Lombardi
260	Torsten Kienass

1990

Pick	
21	Bryan Smolinski
63	Cam Stewart
84	Jerome Buckley
105	Mike Bales
126	Mark Woolf
147	Jim Mackey
168	John Gruden
189	Darren Wetherill
210	Dean Capuano
231	Andy Bezeau
252	Ted Miskolczi

1989

Pick	
17	Shayne Stevenson
38	Mike Parson
57	Wes Walz
80	Jackson Penney
101	Mark Montanari
122	Stephen Foster
143	Otto Hascak
164	Rick Allain
185	James Lavish
206	Geoff Simpson
227	David Franzosa

1988

Pick	
18	Rob Cimetta
60	Steve Heinze
81	Joe Juneau
102	Daniel Murphy
123	Derek Geary
165	Mark Krys
186	Jon Rohloff
228	Eric Reisman
249	Doug Jones

1987

Pick	
3	Glen Wesley
14	Stephane Quintal
56	Todd Lalonde
67	Darwin McPherson
77	Matt DelGuidice
98	Ted Donato
119	Matt Glennon
140	Rob Cheevers
161	Chris Winnes
182	Paul Ohman
203	Casey Jones
224	Eric Lemarque
245	Sean Gorman

General Manager

O'CONNELL, MIKE
General Manager, Boston Bruins. Born in Chicago, IL, November 25, 1955.

Mike O'Connell was named the general manager of the Boston Bruins on November 1, 2000, becoming just the sixth man in club history to hold that position. He was involved in all aspects of the on-ice operation of the hockey team over the previous six seasons as the team's assistant general manager and was instrumental in bringing much of the young talent into the organization.

O'Connell's experience as both a player and assistant coach in the National Hockey League, and as a head coach in both the American and International Hockey Leagues, dates back to the 1977-78 season. Raised in Cohasset, MA, he played two years of high school hockey at Archbishop Williams High School in Braintree, MA. He then made what at the time was an unusual move for an American player, jumping to the Ontario Hockey League to play Canadian major junior hockey at the suggestion of Harry Sinden and Tom Johnson. The move proved beneficial as, after two seasons with Kingston of the OHL, he was drafted by Chicago 43rd overall in the 1975 NHL Amateur Draft.

He turned professional with the Blackhawks organization in 1975 and played five-plus seasons with Chicago and their Central Hockey League affiliate in Dallas before coming to Boston on December 18, 1980, in a trade for Al Secord. He enjoyed his best NHL seasons during his six years in a Bruins uniform, recording 50+ point campaigns for three straight years from 1982 to 1985 and representing the team in the 1984 NHL All-Star Game in New Jersey. He was traded to Detroit for Reed Larson on March 10, 1986 and concluded his playing career with the Red Wings at the end of the 1989-90 season.

O'Connell then moved into the coaching ranks, assuming the head coaching position for the IHL's San Diego Gulls in 1990-91. He then moved into the NHL, returning to Boston as an assistant coach. On June 12, 1992, he was named as the head coach of Boston's American Hockey League affiliate in Providence. Working with many players who also wore a Boston uniform during his tenure, he compiled a 74-71-15 record over a two-year span and won a Northern Division title in 1992-93. He then returned to Boston when he was named the club's assistant general manager on July 5, 1994. He was named as a vice president of the team in 1998.

Club Directory

FleetCenter

Boston Bruins
One FleetCenter, Suite 250
Boston, MA 02114-1303
Phone **617/624-1900**
FAX 617/523-7184
www.bostonbruins.com
Capacity: 17,565

Executive

Owner and Governor	Jeremy M. Jacobs
Alternate Governor	Louis Jacobs
President and Alternate Governor	Harry Sinden
Senior Assistant to the President	Nate Greenberg
Vice President, General Manager and Alternate Governor	Mike O'Connell
Assistant General Manager	Jeff Gorton
Executive Vice President	Richard A. Krezwick
Chief Legal Officer	Michael Wall
Director of Administration	Dale Hamilton-Powers
Assistant to the President	Joe Curnane
Team Travel Coordinator/Administrative Assistant	Carol Gould
Receptionist	Karen Ondo

Coaching Staff

Head Coach	Robbie Ftorek
Assistant Coaches	Wayne Cashman, Jim Hughes
Goaltending Consultant	Brian Daccord
Video Coordinator	Nickolai Bobrov
Coach, Providence Bruins	Bill Armstrong
Coach, Greenville Grrrowl	John Marks

Scouting Staff

Director of Pro Scouting & Player Development	Sean Coady
Director of Amateur Scouting	Scott Bradley
Scouting Staff	Adam Creighton, Gerry Cheevers, Daniel Dore, Yuri Karmanov, Don Matheson, David McNamara, Tom McVie, Don Saatzer, Tom Songin, Svenake Svensson

Medical & Training Staff

Strength and Conditioning Coach	John Whitesides
Athletic Trainer	Don DelNegro
Physical Therapist	Scott Waugh
Equipment Manager	Peter Henderson
Assistant Equipment Managers	Chris "Muggsy" Aldrich, Keith Robinson
Team Physicians	Dr. Bertram Zarins, Dr. Ashby Moncure, Dr. James Dineen, Dr. Tom Gill, Dr. Arthur Boland
Team Dentists	Dr. Edwin Riley, DMD; Dr. Bruce Donoff, DMD; Dr. Robert Amato, DMD
Team Opthalmic Consultant	Dr. Bradford Shingleton
Team Psychologist	Dr. Fred Neff

Communications & Marketing Staff

Director of Media Relations	Heidi Holland
Media Relations Manager	Mark Awdycki
Director of Marketing & Community Relations	Sue Byrne
Promotions Manager	Dave Murray
Community Relations Coordinator	Heather Riva
Game Presentation and Marketing Coordinator	Mike Burns
Director of Alumni Community Relations	John Bucyk
Administrative Assistant, Alumni Office	Mal Viola

Ticketing & Finance Staff

Director of Ticket Operations	Matt Brennan
Assistant Director of Ticket Operations	Jim Foley
Ticket Office Receptionist	Jo-Ann Connolly-White
Controller	Rick McGlinchey
Payroll Manager	TBA
Accounts Payable	Linda Bartlett

Television & Radio

TV Outlets	New England Sports Network (NESN) & UPN38-WSBK
Radio Station	WBZ (1030 AM) and Bruins Radio Network
Television Broadcasters	Dave Shea & Dale Arnold (Play-by-Play); Gord Kluzak, Andy Brickley & Gerry Cheevers (Color)
Radio Broadcasters	Dave Goucher (Play-by-Play) & Bob Beers (Color)

Miscellaneous

Club Colors	Gold, Black & White
Ice Surface	200 feet by 85 feet

General Managers' History

Art Ross, 1924-25 to 1953-54; Lynn Patrick, 1954-55 to 1964-65; Hap Emms, 1965-66, 1966-67; Milt Schmidt, 1967-68 to 1971-72; Harry Sinden, 1972-73 to 1999-2000; Harry Sinden and Mike O'Connell, 2000-01; Mike O'Connell, 2001-02.

Captains' History

No captain, 1924-25 to 1926-27; Lionel Hitchman, 1927-28 to 1930-31; George Owen, 1931-32; Dit Clapper, 1932-33 to 1937-38; Cooney Weiland, 1938-39; Dit Clapper, 1939-40 to 1945-46; Dit Clapper and John Crawford, 1946-47; John Crawford 1947-48 to 1949-50; Milt Schmidt, 1950-51 to 1953-54; Milt Schmidt, Ed Sanford, 1954-55; Fern Flaman, 1955-56 to 1960-61; Don McKenney, 1961-62, 1962-63; Leo Boivin, 1963-64 to 1965-66; John Bucyk, 1966-67; no captain, 1967-68 to 1972-73; John Bucyk, 1973-74 to 1976-77; Wayne Cashman, 1977-78 to 1982-83; Terry O'Reilly, 1983-84, 1984-85; Raymond Bourque, Rick Middleton (co-captains) 1985-86 to 1987-88; Raymond Bourque, 1988-89 to 1999-2000; Jason Allison, 2000-01 to date.

Buffalo Sabres

2000-01 Results: 46W-30L-5T-1OTL 98PTS. Second, Northeast Division

2001-02 Schedule

Month	Day	Date	Opponent
Oct.	Thu.	4	Atlanta
	Sat.	6	Ottawa
	Sun.	7	at NY Rangers
	Wed.	10	Philadelphia
	Fri.	12	at Detroit
	Sun.	14	Pittsburgh*
	Tue.	16	Nashville
	Fri.	19	Columbus
	Sat.	20	at Montreal
	Tue.	23	San Jose
	Fri.	26	Montreal
	Sat.	27	at New Jersey
	Tue.	30	Phoenix
Nov.	Fri.	2	Tampa Bay
	Sat.	3	at Ottawa
	Thu.	8	Atlanta
	Sat.	10	NY Rangers
	Mon.	12	at Florida
	Tue.	13	at Nashville
	Fri.	16	Florida
	Sat.	17	at Boston
	Mon.	19	at Atlanta
	Wed.	21	Toronto
	Fri.	23	Calgary
	Sat.	24	at Pittsburgh
	Tue.	27	NY Rangers
	Wed.	28	at Washington
Dec.	Sat.	1	at NY Islanders
	Tue.	4	at Carolina
	Fri.	7	Colorado
	Sat.	8	at Boston
	Wed.	12	at Dallas
	Fri.	14	Carolina
	Sat.	15	at NY Rangers
	Wed.	19	Chicago
	Fri.	21	Toronto
	Sat.	22	at Toronto
	Wed.	26	Montreal
	Sat.	29	at Columbus
	Mon.	31	Carolina
Jan.	Thu.	3	at Calgary
	Sun.	6	at Minnesota*
	Tue.	8	Vancouver
	Thu.	10	Pittsburgh
	Sat.	12	New Jersey
	Wed.	16	at Anaheim
	Thu.	17	at Los Angeles
	Sat.	19	at Phoenix
	Mon.	21	at Colorado
	Wed.	23	St. Louis
	Fri.	25	Tampa Bay
	Sun.	27	at Washington*
	Tue.	29	at Carolina
Feb.	Tue.	5	at Boston
	Fri.	8	Ottawa
	Sun.	10	at New Jersey
	Tue.	12	New Jersey
	Tue.	26	at Atlanta
Mar.	Fri.	1	Boston
	Sat.	2	at Toronto
	Mon.	4	Edmonton
	Thu.	7	at NY Islanders
	Fri.	8	Montreal
	Sun.	10	Detroit*
	Tue.	12	NY Islanders
	Thu.	14	at Philadelphia
	Fri.	15	at Florida
	Sun.	17	at Tampa Bay*
	Tue.	19	Ottawa
	Thu.	21	Boston
	Sat.	23	at Toronto
	Sun.	24	at Ottawa*
	Tue.	26	Washington
	Thu.	28	at St. Louis
	Sat.	30	at Philadelphia*
Apr.	Mon.	1	Philadelphia
	Wed.	3	NY Islanders
	Fri.	5	Florida
	Sun.	7	at Tampa Bay*
	Wed.	10	at Pittsburgh
	Fri.	12	Washington
	Sat.	13	at Montreal

* Denotes afternoon game.

Left wing Miroslav Satan scored eight goals on the power-play and four game winners during the 2000-01 regular season. He was Buffalo's leading scorer in the 2001 playoffs, recording 13 points (3G, 10A) in 13 playoff games for the Sabres.

Franchise date: May 22, 1970

EASTERN NHL CONFERENCE

NORTHEAST DIVISION

32nd NHL Season

Year-by-Year Record

		Home				Road				Overall								
Season	**GP**	**W**	**L**	**T**	**OL**	**W**	**L**	**T**	**OL**	**W**	**L**	**T**	**OL**	**GF**	**GA**	**Pts.**	**Finished**	**Playoff Result**
2000-01	82	26	12	3	0	20	18	2	1	46	30	5	1	218	184	98	2nd, Northeast Div.	Lost Conf. Semi-Final
1999-2000	82	21	14	5	1	14	18	6	3	35	32	11	4	213	204	85	3rd, Northeast Div.	Lost Conf. Quarter-Final
1998-99	82	23	12	6	...	14	16	11	...	37	28	17	...	207	175	91	4th, Northeast Div.	Lost Final
1997-98	82	20	13	8	...	16	16	9	...	36	29	17	...	211	187	89	3rd, Northeast Div.	Lost Conf. Final
1996-97	82	24	11	6	...	16	19	6	...	40	30	12	...	237	208	92	1st, Northeast Div.	Lost Conf. Semi-Final
1995-96	82	19	17	5	...	14	25	2	...	33	42	7	...	247	262	73	5th, Northeast Div.	Out of Playoffs
1994-95	48	15	8	1	...	7	11	6	...	22	19	7	...	130	119	51	4th, Northeast Div.	Lost Conf. Quarter-Final
1993-94	84	22	17	3	...	21	15	6	...	43	32	9	...	282	218	95	4th, Northeast Div.	Lost Conf. Quarter-Final
1992-93	84	25	15	2	...	13	21	8	...	38	36	10	...	335	297	86	4th, Adams Div.	Lost Div. Final
1991-92	80	22	13	5	...	9	24	7	...	31	37	12	...	289	299	74	3rd, Adams Div.	Lost Div. Semi-Final
1990-91	80	15	13	12	...	16	17	7	...	31	30	19	...	292	278	81	3rd, Adams Div.	Lost Div. Semi-Final
1989-90	80	27	11	2		18	16	6		45	27	8		286	248	98	2nd, Adams Div.	Lost Div. Semi-Final
1988-89	80	25	12	3	...	13	23	4	...	38	35	7	...	291	299	83	3rd, Adams Div.	Lost Div. Semi-Final
1987-88	80	19	14	7	...	18	18	4	...	37	32	11	...	283	305	85	3rd, Adams Div.	Lost Div. Semi-Final
1986-87	80	18	18	4	...	10	26	4	...	28	44	8	...	280	308	64	5th, Adams Div.	Out of Playoffs
1985-86	80	23	16	1	...	14	21	5	...	37	37	6	...	296	291	80	5th, Adams Div.	Out of Playoffs
1984-85	80	23	10	7	...	15	18	7	...	38	28	14	...	290	237	90	3rd, Adams Div.	Lost Div. Semi-Final
1983-84	80	25	9	6	...	23	16	1	...	48	25	7	...	315	257	103	2nd, Adams Div.	Lost Div. Semi-Final
1982-83	80	25	7	8	...	13	22	5	...	38	29	13	...	318	285	89	3rd, Adams Div.	Lost Div. Final
1981-82	80	23	8	9	...	16	18	6	...	39	26	15	...	307	273	93	3rd, Adams Div.	Lost Div. Semi-Final
1980-81	80	21	7	12	...	18	13	9	...	39	20	21	...	327	250	99	1st, Adams Div.	Lost Quarter-Final
1979-80	80	27	5	8	...	20	12	8	...	47	17	16	...	318	201	110	1st, Adams Div.	Lost Semi-Final
1978-79	80	19	13	8	...	17	15	8	...	36	28	16	...	280	263	88	2nd, Adams Div.	Lost Prelim. Round
1977-78	80	25	7	8	...	19	12	9	...	44	19	17	...	288	215	105	2nd, Adams Div.	Lost Quarter-Final
1976-77	80	27	8	5	...	21	16	3	...	48	24	8	...	301	220	104	2nd, Adams Div.	Lost Quarter-Final
1975-76	80	28	7	5	...	18	14	8	...	46	21	13	...	339	240	105	2nd, Adams Div.	Lost Quarter-Final
1974-75	80	28	6	6	...	21	10	9	...	49	16	15	...	354	240	113	1st, Adams Div.	Lost Final
1973-74	78	23	10	6	...	9	24	6	...	32	34	12	...	242	250	76	5th, East Div.	Out of Playoffs
1972-73	78	30	6	3	...	7	21	11	...	37	27	14	...	257	219	88	4th, East Div.	Lost Quarter-Final
1971-72	78	11	19	9	...	5	24	10	...	16	43	19	...	203	289	51	6th, East Div.	Out of Playoffs
1970-71	78	16	13	10	...	8	26	5	...	24	39	15	...	217	291	63	5th, East Div.	Out of Playoffs

2001-02 Player Personnel

FORWARDS	HT	WT	S	Place of Birth	Date	2000-01 Club
ADDUONO, Jeremy	6-0	183	R	Thunder Bay, Ont.	8/4/78	Rochester
AFINOGENOV, Maxim	6-0	195	L	Moscow, USSR	9/4/79	Buffalo
BARNES, Stu	5-11	180	R	Spruce Grove, Alta.	12/25/70	Buffalo
BARTOVIC, Milan	6-0	194	L	Trencin, Czech.	4/9/81	Brandon-Rochester
BOULTON, Eric	6-1	215	L	Halifax, N.S.	8/17/76	Buffalo
BROWN, Curtis	6-0	196	L	Unity, Sask.	2/12/76	Buffalo
CONNOLLY, Tim	6-0	186	R	Syracuse, NY	5/7/81	NY Islanders
DUMONT, J.P.	6-2	202	L	Montreal, Que.	4/1/78	Buffalo
GRATTON, Chris	6-4	226	L	Brantford, Ont.	7/5/75	Buffalo
HAMEL, Denis	6-2	200	L	Lachute, Que.	5/10/77	Buffalo
KOTALIK, Ales	6-1	198	R	Jindrichuv Hradec, Czech.	12/23/78	HC Budejovice
KOZLOV, Vyacheslav	5-10	180	L	Voskresensk, USSR	5/3/72	Detroit
KRISTEK, Jaroslav	6-2	190	L	Zlin, Czech.	3/16/80	Rochester
MATTE, Christian	6-0	190	R	Hull, Que.	1/20/75	Minnesota-Cleveland
METHOT, Francois	6-0	184	R	Montreal, Que.	4/26/78	Rochester
MILLEY, Norman	6-0	200	R	Toronto, Ont.	2/14/80	Rochester
MORAVEC, David	6-0	180	L	Vitkovice, Czech.	3/24/73	HC Vitkovice
PETERS, Andrew	6-4	213	L	St. Catharines, Ont.	5/5/80	Rochester
PYATT, Taylor	6-4	220	L	Thunder Bay, Ont.	8/19/81	NY Islanders
RASMUSSEN, Erik	6-3	208	L	Minneapolis, MN	3/28/77	Buffalo
RAY, Rob	6-0	216	L	Stirling, Ont.	6/8/68	Buffalo
SATAN, Miroslav	6-3	192	L	Topolcany, Czech.	10/22/74	Buffalo
TAYLOR, Chris	6-2	195	L	Stratford, Ont.	3/6/72	Buffalo-Rochester
VAN OENE, Darren	6-4	216	L	Edmonton, Alta.	1/18/78	Rochester
VARADA, Vaclav	6-0	214	L	Vsetin, Czech.	4/26/76	Buffalo
DEFENSEMEN						
CAMPBELL, Brian	6-0	190	L	Strathroy, Ont.	5/23/79	Buffalo-Rochester
FITZPATRICK, Rory	6-2	208	R	Rochester, NY	1/11/75	Nsh-Milw-Hamilton
HOUDA, Doug	6-2	209	R	Blairmore, Alta.	6/3/66	Rochester
KALININ, Dmitri	6-2	206	L	Chelyabinsk, USSR	7/22/80	Buffalo
LAROCQUE, Mario	6-2	182	L	Montreal, Que.	4/24/78	Detroit (IHL)
McKEE, Jay	6-4	201	L	Kingston, Ont.	9/8/77	Buffalo
PATRICK, James	6-3	201	R	Winnipeg, Man.	6/14/63	Buffalo
SMEHLIK, Richard	6-4	222	L	Ostrava, Czech.	1/23/70	Buffalo
WARRENER, Rhett	6-1	206	R	Shaunavon, Sask.	1/27/76	Buffalo
WOOLLEY, Jason	6-0	200	L	Toronto, Ont.	7/27/69	Buffalo
ZHITNIK, Alexei	5-11	215	L	Kiev, USSR	10/10/72	Buffalo

GOALTENDERS	HT	WT	C	Place of Birth	Date	2000-01 Club
ASKEY, Tom	6-2	185	L	Kenmore, NY	10/4/74	Rochester
BIRON, Martin	6-2	163	L	Lac St-Charles, Que.	8/15/77	Buffalo-Rochester
ESSENSA, Bob	6-0	190	L	Toronto, Ont.	1/14/65	Vancouver
NORONEN, Mika	6-1	206	L	Tampere, Finland	6/17/79	Buffalo-Rochester

Coaching History

Punch Imlach, 1970-71; Punch Imlach, Floyd Smith and Joe Crozier, 1971-72; Joe Crozier, 1972-73, 1973-74; Floyd Smith, 1974-75 to 1976-77; Marcel Pronovost, 1977-78; Marcel Pronovost and Billy Inglis, 1978-79; Scotty Bowman, 1979-80; Roger Neilson, 1980-81; Jim Roberts and Scotty Bowman, 1981-82; Scotty Bowman 1982-83 to 1984-85; Jim Schoenfeld and Scotty Bowman, 1985-86; Scotty Bowman, Craig Ramsay and Ted Sator, 1986-87; Ted Sator, 1987-88, 1988-89; Rick Dudley, 1989-90, 1990-91; Rick Dudley and John Muckler, 1991-92; John Muckler, 1992-93 to 1994-95; Ted Nolan, 1995-96, 1996-97; Lindy Ruff, 1997-98 to date.

Head Coach

RUFF, LINDY
Head Coach, Buffalo Sabres. Born in Warburg, Alta., February, 17, 1960.

A former captain of the Sabres, Lindy Ruff was appointed as the club's 15th head coach on July 21, 1997. In 1999, he led the Sabres to the Stanley Cup Finals for just the second time in club history. As a player, Ruff was drafted 32nd overall by the Sabres in the 1979 Entry Draft. He played both defense and left wing in an NHL career that spanned 12 seasons including 608 regular-season games with Buffalo. He became a playing assistant coach with Rochester of the AHL in 1991-92 and San Diego of the IHL in 1992-93. Ruff's San Diego club set a pro hockey record with 62 wins. In 1993-94 he became an NHL assistant coach with the Florida Panthers.

Coaching Record

		Regular Season				Playoffs		
Season	Team	Games	W	L	T	Games	W	L
1997-98	Buffalo (NHL)	82	36	29	17	15	10	5
1998-99	Buffalo (NHL)	82	37	28	17	21	14	7
1999-2000	Buffalo (NHL)	82	35	36	11	5	1	4
2000-01	Buffalo (NHL)	82	46	31	5	13	7	6
	NHL Totals	328	154	124	50	54	32	22

2000-01 Scoring

* - rookie

Regular Season

Pos	#	Player	Team	GP	G	A	Pts	+/–	PIM	PP	SH	GW	GT	S	%
R	28	Donald Audette	ATL	64	32	39	71	–3	64	13	1	2	2	187	17.1
			BUF	12	2	6	8	1	12	1	0	1	0	38	5.3
			TOTAL	76	34	45	79	–2	76	14	1	3	2	225	15.1
L	81	Miroslav Satan	BUF	82	29	33	62	5	36	8	2	4	1	206	14.1
R	57	Steve Heinze	CBJ	65	22	20	42	–19	38	14	0	3	0	125	17.6
			BUF	14	5	7	12	6	8	1	0	1	0	19	26.3
			TOTAL	79	27	27	54	–13	46	15	0	4	0	144	18.8
R	17	Jean-Pierre Dumont	BUF	79	23	28	51	1	54	9	0	5	0	156	14.7
C	41	Stu Barnes	BUF	75	19	24	43	–2	26	3	2	5	0	160	11.9
C	77	Chris Gratton	BUF	82	19	21	40	0	102	5	0	5	1	156	12.2
C	93	Doug Gilmour	BUF	71	7	31	38	3	70	4	0	0	0	91	7.7
D	44	Alexei Zhitnik	BUF	78	8	29	37	–3	75	5	0	1	1	149	5.4
R	61	Maxim Afinogenov	BUF	78	14	22	36	1	40	3	0	5	0	190	7.4
L	52	Dave Andreychuk	BUF	74	20	13	33	0	32	8	0	4	0	119	16.8
C	37	Curtis Brown	BUF	70	10	22	32	15	34	2	1	0	0	105	9.5
C	9	Erik Rasmussen	BUF	82	12	19	31	0	51	1	0	3	0	95	12.6
R	25	Vaclav Varada	BUF	75	10	21	31	–2	81	2	0	2	0	112	8.9
D	5	Jason Woolley	BUF	67	5	18	23	0	46	4	0	3	0	92	5.4
D	45 *	Dimitri Kalinin	BUF	79	4	18	22	–2	38	2	0	0	0	88	4.5
D	4	Rhett Warrener	BUF	77	3	16	19	10	78	0	0	2	0	103	2.9
D	42	Richard Smehlik	BUF	56	3	12	15	6	4	0	0	1	0	40	7.5
L	29	Vladimir Tsyplakov	BUF	36	7	7	14	2	10	0	0	0	0	39	17.9
D	3	James Patrick	BUF	54	4	9	13	9	12	1	0	0	0	48	8.3
L	55 *	Denis Hamel	BUF	41	8	3	11	–2	22	1	1	3	0	55	14.5
D	74	Jay McKee	BUF	74	1	10	11	9	76	0	0	0	0	62	1.6
R	32	Rob Ray	BUF	63	4	6	10	2	210	0	0	1	0	33	12.1
L	26 *	Eric Boulton	BUF	35	1	2	3	–1	94	0	0	0	0	20	5.0
G	39	Dominik Hasek	BUF	67	0	3	3	0	22	0	0	0	0	0	0.0
C	16	Chris Taylor	BUF	14	0	2	2	1	6	0	0	0	0	21	0.0
G	35 *	Mika Noronen	BUF	2	0	0	0	0	0	0	0	0	0	0	0.0
D	51 *	Brian Campbell	BUF	8	0	0	0	–2	2	0	0	0	0	7	0.0
G	43	Martin Biron	BUF	18	0	0	0	0	0	0	0	0	0	0	0.0

Goaltending

No.	Goaltender	GPI	Mins	Avg	W	L	T	EN	SO	GA	SA	S%
35	Peter Skudra	1	0	0.00	0	0	0	0	0	0	0	.000
39	Dominik Hasek	67	3904	2.11	37	24	4	2	11	137	1726	.921
43	Martin Biron	18	918	2.55	7	7	1	1	2	39	427	.909
35	* Mika Noronen	2	108	2.78	2	0	0	0	0	5	39	.872
	Totals	**82**	**4956**	**2.23**	**46**	**31**	**5**	**3**	**13**	**184**	**2195**	**.916**

Playoffs

Pos	#	Player	Team	GP	G	A	Pts	+/–	PIM	PP	SH	GW	GT	S	%
L	81	Miroslav Satan	BUF	13	3	10	13	4	8	1	0	0	0	40	7.5
C	77	Chris Gratton	BUF	13	6	4	10	0	14	2	0	1	0	22	27.3
R	28	Donald Audette	BUF	13	3	6	9	–1	4	0	0	0	0	32	9.4
C	41	Stu Barnes	BUF	13	4	4	8	0	2	2	0	2	1	21	19.0
R	17	Jean-Pierre Dumont	BUF	13	4	3	7	4	8	0	0	0	0	23	17.4
R	57	Steve Heinze	BUF	13	3	4	7	0	10	3	0	0	0	21	14.3
D	44	Alexei Zhitnik	BUF	13	1	6	7	–3	12	0	0	0	0	18	5.6
C	93	Doug Gilmour	BUF	13	2	4	6	–1	12	1	0	1	0	17	11.8
D	5	Jason Woolley	BUF	8	1	5	6	1	2	0	0	1	0	10	10.0
C	37	Curtis Brown	BUF	13	5	0	5	4	8	0	2	1	1	29	17.2
R	61	Maxim Afinogenov	BUF	11	2	3	5	1	4	0	0	0	0	19	10.5
R	25	Vaclav Varada	BUF	13	0	4	4	2	8	0	0	0	0	22	0.0
L	52	Dave Andreychuk	BUF	13	1	2	3	0	4	1	0	0	0	17	5.9
D	3	James Patrick	BUF	13	1	2	3	0	2	0	0	0	0	16	6.3
D	4	Rhett Warrener	BUF	13	0	2	2	5	4	0	0	0	0	12	0.0
D	45 *	Dimitri Kalinin	BUF	13	0	2	2	5	4	0	0	0	0	16	0.0
D	74	Jay McKee	BUF	8	1	0	1	3	6	0	0	1	1	5	20.0
L	29	Vladimir Tsyplakov	BUF	9	1	0	1	1	4	0	0	0	0	10	10.0
C	9	Erik Rasmussen	BUF	3	0	1	1	2	0	0	0	0	0	8	0.0
D	42	Richard Smehlik	BUF	10	0	1	1	3	4	0	0	0	0	7	0.0
R	32	Rob Ray	BUF	3	0	0	0	0	2	0	0	0	0	0	0.0
G	39	Dominik Hasek	BUF	13	0	0	0	0	14	0	0	0	0	0	0.0

Goaltending

No.	Goaltender	GPI	Mins	Avg	W	L	EN	SO	GA	SA	S%
39	Dominik Hasek	13	833	2.09	7	6	1	1	29	347	.916
	Totals	**13**	**837**	**2.15**	**7**	**6**	**1**	**1**	**30**	**348**	**.914**

Captains' History

Floyd Smith, 1970-71; Gerry Meehan, 1971-72 to 1973-74; Gerry Meehan and Jim Schoenfeld, 1974-75; Jim Schoenfeld, 1975-76, 1976-77; Danny Gare, 1977-78 to 1980-81; Danny Gare and Gilbert Perreault, 1981-82; Gilbert Perreault, 1982-83 to 1985-86; Gilbert Perreault and Lindy Ruff, 1986-87; Lindy Ruff, 1987-88; Lindy Ruff and Mike Foligno, 1988-89; Mike Foligno, 1989-90; Mike Foligno and Mike Ramsey, 1990-91; Mike Ramsey, 1991-92; Mike Ramsey and Pat LaFontaine, 1992-93; Pat LaFontaine and Alexander Mogilny, 1993-94; Pat LaFontaine, 1994-95 to 1996-97; Donald Audette and Michael Peca, 1997-98; Michael Peca, 1998-99, 1999-2000; no captain, 2000-01.

Club Records

Team

(Figures in brackets for season records are games played; records for fewest points, wins, ties, losses, goals, goals against are for 70 or more games)

Most Points	**113**	1974-75 (80)
Most Wins	**49**	1974-75 (80)
Most Ties	**21**	1980-81 (80)
Most Losses	**44**	1986-87 (80)
Most Goals	**354**	1974-75 (80)
Most Goals Against	**308**	1986-87 (80)
Fewest Points	**51**	1971-72 (78)
Fewest Wins	**16**	1971-72 (78)
Fewest Ties	**6**	1985-86 (80)
Fewest Losses	**16**	1974-75 (80)
Fewest Goals	**203**	1971-72 (78)
Fewest Goals Against	**175**	1998-99 (82)
Longest Winning Streak		
Overall	**10**	Jan. 4-23/84
Home	**12**	Nov. 12/72-Jan. 7/73, Oct. 13-Dec. 10/89
Away	***10**	Dec. 10/83-Jan. 23/84
Longest Undefeated Streak		
Overall	**14**	Mar. 6-Apr. 6/80 (8 wins, 6 ties)
Home	**21**	Oct. 8/72-Jan. 7/73 (18 wins, 3 ties)
Away	**10**	Dec. 10/83-Jan. 23/84 (10 wins)
Longest Losing Streak		
Overall	**7**	Oct. 25-Nov. 8/70, Apr. 3-15/93, Oct. 9-22/93
Home	**6**	Oct. 10-Nov. 10/93, Mar. 3-Apr. 3/96
Away	**7**	Oct. 14-Nov. 7/70, Feb. 6-27/71, Jan. 10-Feb. 3/96
Longest Winless Streak		
Overall	**12**	Nov. 23-Dec. 20/91 (8 losses, 4 ties)
Home	**12**	Jan. 27-Mar. 10/91 (7 losses, 5 ties)
Away	**23**	Oct. 30/71-Feb. 19/72 (15 losses, 8 ties)
Most Shutouts, Season	**13**	1997-98 (82)
Most PIM, Season	***2,713**	1991-92 (80)
Most Goals, Game	**14**	Jan. 21/75 (Wsh. 2 at Buf. 14), Mar. 19/81 (Tor. 4 at Buf. 14)

Individual

Most Seasons	**17**	Gilbert Perreault
Most Games	**1,191**	Gilbert Perreault
Most Goals, Career	**512**	Gilbert Perreault
Most Assists, Career	**814**	Gilbert Perreault
Most Points, Career	**1,326**	Gilbert Perreault (512G, 814A)
Most PIM, Career	**2,897**	Rob Ray
Most Shutouts, Career	**55**	Dominik Hasek
Longest Consecutive Games Streak	**776**	Craig Ramsay (Mar. 27/73-Feb. 10/83)
Most Goals, Season	**76**	Alexander Mogilny (1992-93)
Most Assists, Season	**95**	Pat LaFontaine (1992-93)
Most Points, Season	**148**	Pat LaFontaine (1992-93; 53G, 95A)
Most PIM, Season	**354**	Rob Ray (1991-92)
Most Points, Defenseman, Season	**81**	Phil Housley (1989-90; 21G, 60A)
Most Points, Center, Season	**148**	Pat LaFontaine (1992-93; 53G, 95A)
Most Points, Right Wing, Season	**127**	Alexander Mogilny (1992-93; 76G, 51A)
Most Points, Left Wing, Season	**95**	Rick Martin (1974-75; 52G, 43A)
Most Points, Rookie, Season	**74**	Rick Martin (1971-72; 44G, 30A)
Most Shutouts, Season	**13**	Dominik Hasek (1997-98)
Most Goals, Game	**5**	Dave Andreychuk (Feb. 6/86)
Most Assists, Game	**5**	Gilbert Perreault (Feb. 1/76, Mar. 9/80, Jan. 4/84), Dale Hawerchuk (Jan. 15/92), Pat LaFontaine (Dec. 31/92, Feb. 10/93)
Most Points, Game	**7**	Gilbert Perreault (Feb. 1/76; 2G, 5A)

* NHL Record.

Retired Numbers

2	Tim Horton	1972-1974
7	Rick Martin	1971-1981
11	Gilbert Perreault	1970-1987
14	Rene Robert	1971-1979

All-time Record vs. Other Clubs

Regular Season

	At Home								On Road								Total							
	GP	W	L	T	OL	GF	GA	PTS	GP	W	L	T	OL	GF	GA	PTS	GP	W	L	T	OL	GF	GA	PTS
Anaheim	7	2	2	3	0	16	18	7	7	5	2	0	0	22	12	10	14	7	4	3	0	38	30	17
Atlanta	4	3	1	0	0	15	9	6	4	2	1	1	0	17	10	5	8	5	2	1	0	32	19	11
Boston	100	50	35	15	0	366	299	115	99	31	55	13	0	292	370	75	199	81	90	28	0	658	669	190
Calgary	44	26	13	5	0	184	129	57	43	17	15	11	0	143	146	45	87	43	28	16	0	327	275	102
Carolina	71	42	22	7	0	286	212	91	72	32	30	10	0	216	216	74	143	74	52	17	0	502	428	165
Chicago	51	32	13	6	0	193	131	70	49	17	26	6	0	136	159	40	100	49	39	12	0	329	290	110
Colorado	61	35	17	9	0	242	197	79	62	21	30	11	0	192	223	53	123	56	47	20	0	434	420	132
Columbus	1	0	1	0	0	1	2	0	0	0	0	0	0	0	0	0	1	0	1	0	0	1	2	0
Dallas	50	26	13	11	0	179	133	63	52	21	25	6	0	153	166	48	102	47	38	17	0	332	299	111
Detroit	50	32	10	8	0	219	145	72	53	18	29	5	1	155	195	42	103	50	39	13	1	374	340	114
Edmonton	29	10	12	7	0	109	109	27	27	5	20	2	0	72	115	12	56	15	32	9	0	181	224	39
Florida	17	12	3	2	0	54	26	26	15	7	8	0	0	47	46	14	32	19	11	2	0	101	72	40
Los Angeles	51	27	15	9	0	208	150	63	52	22	21	9	0	180	180	53	103	49	36	18	0	388	330	116
Minnesota	1	1	0	0	0	3	1	2	0	0	0	0	0	0	0	0	1	1	0	0	0	3	1	2
Montreal	94	47	28	19	0	295	257	113	95	30	53	12	0	285	370	72	189	77	81	31	0	580	627	185
Nashville	2	0	2	0	0	5	8	0	3	3	0	0	0	7	2	6	5	3	2	0	0	12	10	6
New Jersey	48	30	13	5	0	202	151	65	48	26	13	9	0	168	135	61	96	56	26	14	0	370	286	126
NY Islanders	55	31	16	8	0	189	148	70	55	23	23	9	0	152	157	55	110	54	39	17	0	341	305	125
NY Rangers	62	37	17	8	0	262	194	82	60	20	25	15	0	163	197	55	122	57	42	23	0	425	391	137
Ottawa	23	16	5	2	0	75	29	34	25	13	6	6	0	73	53	32	48	29	11	8	0	148	82	66
Philadelphia	57	27	23	7	0	190	168	61	61	13	35	12	1	153	217	39	118	40	58	19	1	343	385	100
Phoenix	28	20	3	5	0	121	71	45	27	12	13	2	0	88	86	26	55	32	16	7	0	209	157	71
Pittsburgh	65	32	16	16	1	263	180	81	65	17	32	16	0	205	245	50	130	49	48	32	1	468	425	131
St. Louis	49	29	14	6	0	195	151	64	48	14	27	7	0	123	174	35	97	43	41	13	0	318	325	99
San Jose	9	9	0	0	0	46	25	18	9	1	4	3	1	31	34	6	18	10	4	3	1	77	59	24
Tampa Bay	17	10	6	1	0	47	50	21	17	12	4	1	0	56	37	25	34	22	10	2	0	103	87	46
Toronto	61	39	17	5	0	252	163	83	59	25	23	10	1	206	181	61	120	64	40	15	1	458	344	144
Vancouver	50	25	17	8	0	181	146	58	50	16	24	10	0	160	186	42	100	41	41	18	0	341	332	100
Washington	50	32	12	6	0	195	131	70	50	28	13	9	0	174	128	65	100	60	25	15	0	369	259	135
Defunct Clubs	23	13	5	5	0	94	63	31	23	12	8	3	0	97	76	27	46	25	13	8	0	191	139	58
Totals	**1230**	**695**	**351**	**183**	**1**	**4687**	**3496**	**1574**	**1230**	**463**	**565**	**198**	**4**	**3766**	**4116**	**1128**	**2460**	**1158**	**916**	**381**	**5**	**8453**	**7612**	**2702**

Playoffs

	Series	W	L	GP	W	L	T	GF	GA	Last Mtg.	Round	Result
Boston	7	2	5	39	18	21	0	130	139	1999	CSF	W 4-2
Chicago	2	2	0	9	8	1	0	36	17	1980	QF	W 4-0
Colorado	2	0	2	8	2	6	0	27	35	1985	DSF	L 2-3
Dallas	3	1	2	13	5	8	0	37	39	1999	F	L 2-4
Montreal	7	3	4	35	17	18	0	111	124	1998	CSF	W 4-0
New Jersey	1	0	1	7	3	4	0	14	14	1994	CQF	L 3-4
NY Islanders	3	0	3	16	4	12	0	45	59	1980	SF	L 2-4
NY Rangers	1	1	0	3	2	1	0	11	6	1978	PR	W 2-1
Ottawa	2	2	0	11	8	3	0	26	19	1999	CQF	W 4-0
Philadelphia	6	2	5	37	23	14	0	96	110	2001	CQF	W 4-2
Pittsburgh	2	0	2	10	4	6	0	26	26	2001	CSF	L 3-4
St. Louis	1	1	0	3	2	1	0	7	8	1976	PR	W 2-1
Toronto	1	1	0	5	4	1	0	21	16	1999	CF	W 4-1
Vancouver	2	2	0	7	6	1	0	28	14	1981	PR	W 3-0
Washington	1	0	1	6	2	4	0	11	13	1998	CF	L 2-4
Totals	**42**	**17**	**25**	**209**	**99**	**110**	**0**	**626**	**639**			

Playoff Results 2001-1997

Year	Round	Opponent	Result	GF	GA
2001	CSF	Pittsburgh	L 3-4	17	17
	CQF	Philadelphia	W 4-2	21	13
2000	CQF	Philadelphia	L 1-4	8	14
1999	F	Dallas	L 2-4	9	13
	CF	Toronto	W 4-1	21	16
	CSF	Boston	W 4-2	17	14
	CQF	Ottawa	W 4-0	12	6
1998	CF	Washington	L 2-4	11	13
	CSF	Montreal	W 4-0	17	10
	CQF	Philadelphia	W 4-1	18	9
1997	CSF	Philadelphia	L 1-4	13	21
	CQF	Ottawa	W 4-3	14	13

Abbreviations: Round: F – final; **CF** – conference final; **CSF** – conference semi-final; **CQF** – conference quarter-final; **DSF** – division semi-final; **SF** – semi-final; **QF** – quarter-final; **PR** – preliminary round.

Calgary totals include Atlanta Flames, 1972-73 to 1979-80.
Colorado totals include Quebec, 1979-80 to 1994-95.
Carolina totals include Hartford, 1979-80 to 1996-97.
Dallas totals include Minnesota North Stars, 1970-71 to 1992-93.
New Jersey totals include Kansas City, 1974-75 to 1975-76, and Colorado Rockies, 1976-77 to 1981-82.
Phoenix totals include Winnipeg, 1979-80 to 1995-96.

2000-01 Results

Oct.	5	Chicago	4-2
	7	Los Angeles	5-3
	13	at Edmonton	2-3
	14	at Vancouver	0-4
	17	at Montreal	3-4
	20	Anaheim	2-2
	21	at Detroit	4-5*
	25	Carolina	4-1
	27	Toronto	2-1
	28	at Chicago	3-1
Nov.	3	Montreal	5-4
	4	at Philadelphia	0-3
	9	NY Islanders	3-0
	11	at New Jersey	4-0
	13	Calgary	3-2*
	15	Dallas	2-2
	17	Minnesota	3-1
	18	at St. Louis	1-4
	22	Philadelphia	1-3
	24	NY Rangers	3-2
	25	at Montreal	5-3
	28	at Ottawa	1-3
Dec.	1	Pittsburgh	4-6
	2	at Pittsburgh	3-2
	5	at Montreal	3-2
	7	New Jersey	5-2
	8	at NY Rangers	2-5
	12	at Boston	3-0
	15	at Carolina	3-5
	16	Florida	3-2
	20	at Washington	2-2
	21	Washington	1-3
	23	San Jose	5-2
	26	Pittsburgh	3-5
	29	Ottawa	2-0
	30	at NY Islanders	2-0
Jan.	1	Boston	3-4
	3	at Toronto	1-1
	5	Toronto	3-3
	6	at Nashville	2-0
	9	at San Jose	1-2
	11	at Los Angeles	2-3
	12	at Anaheim	4-0
	16	Tampa Bay	3-1
	19	Florida	1-0
	20	at Toronto	0-2
	23	Columbus	1-2
	26	Boston	1-2
	27	at NY Islanders	2-1
	31	at Florida	2-5
Feb.	1	at Tampa Bay	2-4
	6	at NY Rangers	6-3
	7	NY Islanders	2-1*
	10	at Ottawa	2-1*
	11	Montreal	3-4
	13	at Atlanta	4-5
	15	Atlanta	3-1
	17	New Jersey	5-1
	19	Ottawa	2-0
	22	at New Jersey	1-0
	23	Phoenix	3-7
	25	Tampa Bay	5-4
	27	at Ottawa	4-1
Mar.	1	at Philadelphia	0-2
	3	at Colorado	3-2*
	4	at Dallas	1-4
	6	at Boston	3-1
	9	Edmonton	0-4
	14	NY Rangers	6-3
	16	Vancouver	4-2
	17	at Washington	3-2
	20	Toronto	3-0
	21	at Carolina	0-1
	24	Carolina	3-1
	26	at Atlanta	4-0
	27	at Pittsburgh	1-4
	30	Atlanta	4-0
Apr.	1	at Tampa Bay	4-2
	2	at Florida	5-3
	4	Boston	2-3
	6	Washington	2-1
	8	Philadelphia	1-2

* – Overtime

Entry Draft Selections 2001-1987

2001

Pick	
22	Jiri Novotny
32	Derek Roy
50	Chris Thorburn
55	Jason Pominville
155	Michal Vondrka
234	Calle Aslund
247	Marek Dubec
279	Ryan Jorde

2000

Pick	
15	Artem Kryukov
48	Gerard Dicaire
111	Ghyslain Rousseau
149	Denis Denisov
213	Vasili Bizyayev
220	Paul Gaustad
258	Sean McMorrow
277	Ryan Courtney

1999

Pick	
20	Barrett Heisten
35	Milan Bartovic
55	Doug Janik
64	Michael Zigomanis
73	Tim Preston
117	Karel Mosovsky
138	Ryan Miller
146	Matt Kinch
178	Seneque Hyacinthe
206	Bret DeCecco
235	Brad Self
263	Craig Brunel

1998

Pick	
18	Dmitri Kalinin
34	Andrew Peters
47	Norman Milley
50	Jaroslav Kristek
77	Mike Pandolfo
137	Aaron Goldade
164	Ales Kotalik
191	Brad Moran
218	David Moravec
249	Edo Terglav

1997

Pick	
21	Mika Noronen
48	Henrik Tallinder
69	Maxim Afinogenov
75	Jeff Martin
101	Luc Theoret
128	Torrey DiRoberto
156	Brian Campbell
184	Jeremy Adduono
212	Kamil Piros
238	Dylan Kemp

1996

Pick	
7	Erik Rasmussen
27	Cory Sarich
33	Darren Van Oene
54	Francois Methot
87	Kurt Walsh
106	Mike Martone
115	Alexei Tezikov
142	Ryan Davis
161	Darren Mortier
222	Scott Buhler

1995

Pick	
14	Jay McKee
16	Martin Biron
42	Mark Dutiaume
68	Mathieu Sunderland
94	Matt Davidson
111	Marian Menhart
119	Kevin Popp
123	Daniel Bienvenue
172	Brian Scott
198	Mike Zanutto
224	Rob Skrlac

1994

Pick	
17	Wayne Primeau
43	Curtis Brown
69	Rumun Ndur
121	Sergei Klimentiev
147	Cal Benazic
168	Steve Plouffe
173	Shane Hnidy
176	Steve Webb
199	Bob Westerby
225	Craig Millar
251	Mark Polak
277	Shayne Wright

1993

Pick	
38	Denis Tsygurov
64	Ethan Philpott
116	Richard Safarik
142	Kevin Pozzo
168	Sergei Petrenko
194	Mike Barrie
220	Barrie Moore
246	Chris Davis
272	Scott Nichol

1992

Pick	
11	David Cooper
35	Jozef Cierny
59	Ondrej Steiner
80	Dean Melanson
83	Matthew Barnaby
107	Markus Ketterer
108	Yuri Khmylev
131	Paul Rushforth
179	Dean Tiltgen
203	Todd Simon
227	Rick Kowalsky
251	Chris Clancy

1991

Pick	
13	Philippe Boucher
35	Jason Dawe
57	Jason Young
72	Peter Ambroziak
101	Steve Shields
123	Sean O'Donnell
124	Brian Holzinger
145	Chris Snell
162	Jiri Kuntos
189	Tony Iob
211	Spencer Meany
233	Mikhail Volkov
255	Michael Smith

1990

Pick	
14	Brad May
82	Brian McCarthy
97	Richard Smehlik
100	Todd Bojcun
103	Brad Pascall
142	Viktor Gordiouk
166	Milan Nedoma
187	Jason Winch
208	Sylvain Naud
229	Kenneth Martin
250	Brad Rubachuk

1989

Pick	
14	Kevin Haller
56	Scott Thomas
77	Doug MacDonald
98	Ken Sutton
107	Bill Pye
119	Mike Barkley
161	Derek Plante
183	Donald Audette
194	Mark Astley
203	John Nelson
224	Todd Henderson
245	Michael Bavis

1988

Pick	
13	Joel Savage
55	Darcy Loewen
76	Keith Carney
89	Alexander Mogilny
97	Rob Ray
106	David Di Vita
118	Mike McLaughlin
139	Mike Griffith
160	Daniel Ruoho
181	Wade Flaherty
223	Thomas Nieman
243	Michael Pohl

1987

Pick	
1	Pierre Turgeon
22	Brad Miller
53	Andrew MacVicar
84	John Bradley
85	David Pergola
106	Chris Marshall
127	Paul Flanagan
148	Sean Dooley
153	Tim Roberts
169	Grant Tkachuk
190	Ian Herbers
211	David Littman
232	Allan MacIsaac

General Managers' History

Punch Imlach, 1970-71 to 1977-78; John Anderson, 1978-79; Scotty Bowman, 1979-80 to 1985-86; Scotty Bowman and Gerry Meehan, 1986-87; Gerry Meehan, 1987-88 to 1992-93; John Muckler, 1993-94 to 1996-97; Darcy Regier, 1997-98 to date.

General Manager

REGIER, DARCY
General Manager, Buffalo Sabres. Born in Swift Current, Sask., Nov. 27, 1957.

Darcy Regier became the sixth general manager of the Buffalo Sabres on June 11, 1997 after a lengthy management apprenticeship in the New York Islanders organization. As a player, Regier played eight pro seasons, including part of the 1977-78 season with the Cleveland Barons and parts of the 1982-83 and 1983-84 campaigns with the New York Islanders.

He began his career as an administrator with the Islanders in 1984-85 and went on to serve in a variety of capacities including director of administration, assistant director of hockey operations, assistant coach and assistant general manager. He also served as an assistant coach with Hartford in 1991-92.

While with the Islanders, Regier benefitted from working with talented managers and coaches including Bill Torrey and Al Arbour. As a minor pro player with Indianapolis of the CHL he became associated with another important influence on his hockey career, current Detroit Red Wing executive Jim Devellano.

Club Directory

HSBC Arena

Buffalo Sabres
HSBC Arena
One Seymour H. Knox III Plaza
Buffalo, NY 14203
Phone **716/855-4100**
Fax 716/855-4110
Tickets, U.S.: 716/223-6000
Tickets, Canada: 888/669-GOAL
Capacity: 18,690

Board of Patmos Inc.
Chairman of the Board . . . . . John J. Rigas
Chief Executive Officer . . . . . Timothy J. Rigas
Directors . . . . . Michael J. Rigas, James P. Rigas

Executive
Executive Vice President/Administration . . . . . Ron Bertovich
Executive Vice President/Finance & Business Development . . . . . Ed Hartman
Executive Vice President/Integrated Marketing . . . . . John Cimperman
Senior Vice President/ Sales . . . . . Kerry Atkinson
Senior Vice President/Legal & Business Affairs . . . . . Kevin Billet
Senior Vice President/Marketing . . . . . Christye Peterson
Vice President/Communications . . . . . Michael Gilbert
Vice President/Corporate Relations . . . . . Seymour H. Knox, IV
Vice President/Ticket Sales & Operations . . . . . John Sinclair
Senior Director of Sports & Arena Planning . . . . . Chris Schoepflin
Special Consultant . . . . . Joe Crozier
Executive Assistants . . . . . Eleanore MacKenzie, Donna Webb-Smith

Hockey Department
General Manager . . . . . Darcy Regier
Assistant to the General Manager . . . . . Larry Carriere
Director of Player Personnel . . . . . Don Luce
Executive Assistant . . . . . Elaine Burzynski
On-Site Travel Coordinator . . . . . Kim Christiano
Professional Scouts . . . . . Kevin Devine, Terry Martin
Scouting Staff . . . . . Don Barrie, Jim Benning, Bo Berglund, Iouri Khmylev, Paul Merritt, Rudy Migay, Darryl Plandowski, Mike Racicot, David Volek
Head Coach . . . . . Lindy Ruff
Associate Coach . . . . . Don Lever
Assistant Coach . . . . . Brian McCutcheon
Strength & Conditioning Coach . . . . . Doug McKenney
Assistant Strength Coach . . . . . Dennis Cole
Goaltender Coach . . . . . Jim Corsi
Administrative Assistant, Coaches . . . . . Jeff Holbrook
Head Trainer/Massage Therapist . . . . . Jim Pizzutelli
Head Equipment Manager . . . . . Rip Simonick
Assistant Equipment Manager . . . . . George Babcock
Equipment Assistant . . . . . Encil "Porky" Palmer

Medical
Club Doctor . . . . . Les Bisson, M.D.
Doctors . . . . . Nicholas Aquino, M.D., William Hartrich, M.D.
Oral Surgeon . . . . . Steven Jenson, DDS
Club Dentist . . . . . Daniel Yustin, DDS, M.S.
Physical Therapist . . . . . Joe Aquino
Club Doctor Emeritus . . . . . John L. Butsch, M.D.

Legal
Associate Counsel . . . . . Richard Mugel

Administration
Human Resources Coordinator . . . . . Vanessa Roberts

Broadcast Production
Senior Director of Broadcast & Production Services . Joe Guarnieri
Producer . . . . . Lowell MacDonald
Director . . . . . Phil Mollica
Broadcast Team . . . Rick Jeanneret (play-by-play), Jim Lorentz (color commentary), Danny Gare (reporter)

Merchandise
Director of Merchandise . . . . . Mike Kaminska
Store Manager . . . . . Tammy Preteroti

Communications
Director of Communications . . . . . Gregg Huller
Communications Coordinator – Buffalo Sabres . . . . Kevin Wiles
Team Photographer . . . . . Bill Wippert
Director of Alumni Relations . . . . . Larry Playfair
Corporate & Community Relations Liaison . . . . . Gilbert Perreault

Empire Sports Sales
General Sales Manager . . . . . Dan Rozanski
National Sales Manager . . . . . Mark Kennedy
Radio General Sales Manager . . . . . Steve Cuccia

Finance
Controller . . . . . John Marsh
Accounting Manager – Buffalo Sabres . . . . . Christine Ivansitz

Marketing
Director of Advertising and Promotions . . . . . Robert Kopacz
Director of Game Presentation & Special Events . . . TBA

Community Development
Director of Community Development . . . . . Peter Hassen

Canadian Sales & Marketing
Director of Canadian Sales & Marketing . . . . . Steve Katzman

Ticket Sales & Operations
Ticket Sales Manager . . . . . Dan Carroll
Box Office Manager . . . . . Michael Tout

HSBC Arena
Senior Director of Facilities Management . . . . . Stan Makowski
Director of Event Booking . . . . . Jennifer Stich
Director of Event Services . . . . . John Faso
Director of Premium Sales . . . . . Nick Turano
Director of Suite Services . . . . . Natalie DeSilva

General Information
Practice Site . . . . . Pepsi Center, Amherst, NY
TV Station . . . . . Empire Sports Network
Radio Flagship Station . . . . . WNSA FM 107.7

Calgary Flames

2000-01 Results: 27W-36L-15T-4OTL 73PTS. Fourth, Northwest Division

2001-02 Schedule

Month	Day	Date	Opponent	Month	Day	Date	Opponent
Oct.	Wed.	3	Edmonton		Sat.	5	Montreal*
	Sat.	6	Chicago		Tue.	8	at NY Islanders
	Mon.	8	Phoenix		Wed.	9	at New Jersey
	Wed.	10	at Detroit		Fri.	11	at Atlanta
	Thu.	11	at Nashville		Tue.	15	NY Islanders
	Sat.	13	at Dallas		Thu.	17	Pittsburgh
	Thu.	18	Florida		Sat.	19	Anaheim
	Sat.	20	Toronto*		Tue.	22	Toronto
	Mon.	22	at St. Louis		Thu.	24	Colorado
	Tue.	23	at Chicago		Sat.	26	Vancouver
	Thu.	25	Nashville		Mon.	28	at Minnesota
	Sat.	27	Minnesota		Wed.	30	Detroit
Nov.	Thu.	1	Columbus	Feb.	Wed.	6	at San Jose
	Sat.	3	Montreal*		Fri.	8	Vancouver
	Wed.	7	at Anaheim		Sat.	9	at Vancouver
	Thu.	8	at Los Angeles		Tue.	12	at Phoenix
	Sat.	10	Colorado		Wed.	13	at Anaheim
	Thu.	15	Chicago		Tue.	26	at Colorado
	Sat.	17	St. Louis		Thu.	28	St. Louis
	Tue.	20	Los Angeles	Mar.	Sat.	2	Nashville
	Thu.	22	at Ottawa		Mon.	4	at NY Rangers
	Fri.	23	at Buffalo		Wed.	6	at Washington
	Sun.	25	at Columbus*		Thu.	7	at Philadelphia
	Tue.	27	at Detroit		Sat.	9	at Boston
	Thu.	29	Dallas		Mon.	11	at Carolina
Dec.	Sat.	1	Colorado		Wed.	13	at Florida
	Mon.	3	at Los Angeles		Thu.	14	at Tampa Bay
	Tue.	4	at San Jose		Sat.	16	at Columbus
	Thu.	6	San Jose		Mon.	18	at Minnesota
	Sat.	8	Anaheim		Thu.	21	San Jose
	Mon.	10	Detroit		Sat.	23	at Edmonton
	Wed.	12	Tampa Bay		Mon.	25	Columbus
	Fri.	14	at Dallas		Thu.	28	Dallas
	Sat.	15	at St. Louis		Sat.	30	Los Angeles
	Wed.	19	at Phoenix	Apr.	Tue.	2	Atlanta
	Fri.	21	at Colorado		Thu.	4	Minnesota
	Wed.	26	at Edmonton		Sat.	6	at Nashville
	Thu.	27	at Vancouver		Sun.	7	at Chicago
	Sat.	29	Minnesota		Tue.	9	Phoenix
	Mon.	31	Edmonton		Fri.	12	at Edmonton
Jan.	Thu.	3	Buffalo		Sat.	13	Vancouver

* Denotes afternoon game.

Franchise date: June 6, 1972
Transferred from Atlanta to Calgary, June 24, 1980.

NORTHWEST DIVISION

30th NHL Season

Signed as a free agent by the Flames prior to the 2000-01 season, 16-year NHL veteran Dave Lowry assumed the captaincy in Calgary following the retirement of Steve Smith.

Year-by-Year Record

		Home				Road				Overall								
Season	GP	W	L	T	OL	W	L	T	OL	W	L	T	OL	GF	GA	Pts.	Finished	Playoff Result
2000-01	82	12	18	9	2	15	18	6	2	27	36	15	4	197	236	73	4th, Northwest Div.	Out of Playoffs
1999-2000	82	20	14	6	1	11	22	4	4	31	36	10	5	211	256	77	4th, Northwest Div.	Out of Playoffs
1998-99	82	15	20	6	...	15	20	6	...	30	40	12	...	211	234	72	3rd, Northwest Div.	Out of Playoffs
1997-98	82	18	17	6	...	8	24	9	...	26	41	15	...	217	252	67	5th, Pacific Div.	Out of Playoffs
1996-97	82	21	18	2	...	11	23	7	...	32	41	9	...	214	239	73	5th, Pacific Div.	Out of Playoffs
1995-96	82	18	18	5	...	16	19	6	...	34	37	11	...	241	240	79	2nd, Pacific Div.	Lost Conf. Quarter-Final
1994-95	48	15	7	2	...	9	10	5	...	24	17	7	...	163	135	55	1st, Pacific Div.	Lost Conf. Quarter-Final
1993-94	84	25	12	5	...	17	17	8	...	42	29	13	...	302	256	97	1st, Pacific Div.	Lost Conf. Quarter-Final
1992-93	84	23	14	5	...	20	16	6	...	43	30	11	...	322	282	97	2nd, Smythe Div.	Lost Div. Semi-Final
1991-92	80	19	14	7	...	12	23	5	...	31	37	12	...	296	305	74	5th, Smythe Div.	Out of Playoffs
1990-91	80	29	8	3	...	17	18	5	...	46	26	8	...	344	263	100	2nd, Smythe Div.	Lost Div. Semi-Final
1989-90	80	28	7	5	...	14	16	10	...	42	23	15	...	348	265	99	1st, Smythe Div.	Lost Div. Semi-Final
1988-89	**80**	**32**	**4**	**4**	**...**	**22**	**13**	**5**	**...**	**54**	**17**	**9**	**...**	**354**	**226**	**117**	**1st, Smythe Div.**	**Won Stanley Cup**
1987-88	80	26	11	3	...	22	12	6	...	48	23	9	...	397	305	105	1st, Smythe Div.	Lost Div. Final
1986-87	80	25	13	2	...	21	18	1	...	46	31	3	...	318	289	95	2nd, Smythe Div.	Lost Div. Semi-Final
1985-86	80	23	11	6	...	17	20	3	...	40	31	9	...	354	315	89	2nd, Smythe Div.	Lost Final
1984-85	80	23	11	6	...	18	16	6	...	41	27	12	...	363	302	94	3rd, Smythe Div.	Lost Div. Semi-Final
1983-84	80	22	11	7	...	12	21	7	...	34	32	14	...	311	314	82	2nd, Smythe Div.	Lost Div. Final
1982-83	80	21	12	7	...	11	22	7	...	32	34	14	...	321	317	78	2nd, Smythe Div.	Lost Div. Final
1981-82	80	20	11	9	...	9	23	8	...	29	34	17	...	334	345	75	3rd, Smythe Div.	Lost Div. Semi-Final
1980-81	80	25	5	10	...	14	22	4	...	39	27	14	...	329	298	92	3rd, Patrick Div.	Lost Semi-Final
1979-80*	80	18	15	7	...	17	17	6	...	35	32	13	...	282	269	83	4th, Patrick Div.	Lost Prelim. Round
1978-79*	80	25	11	4	...	16	20	4	...	41	31	8	...	327	280	90	4th, Patrick Div.	Lost Prelim. Round
1977-78*	80	20	13	7	...	14	14	12	...	34	27	19	...	274	252	87	3rd, Patrick Div.	Lost Prelim. Round
1976-77*	80	22	11	7	...	12	23	5	...	34	34	12	...	264	265	80	3rd, Patrick Div.	Lost Prelim. Round
1975-76*	80	19	14	7	...	16	19	5	...	35	33	12	...	262	237	82	3rd, Patrick Div.	Lost Prelim. Round
1974-75*	80	24	9	7	...	10	22	8	...	34	31	15	...	243	233	83	4th, Patrick Div.	Out of Playoffs
1973-74*	78	17	15	7	...	13	19	7	...	30	34	14	...	214	238	74	4th, West Div.	Lost Quarter-Final
1972-73*	78	16	16	7	...	9	22	8	...	25	38	15	...	191	239	65	7th, West Div.	Out of Playoffs

* Atlanta Flames

2001-02 Player Personnel

FORWARDS	HT	WT	S	Place of Birth	Date	2000-01 Club
BEGIN, Steve	5-11	190	L	Trois-Rivieres, Que.	6/14/78	Calgary-Saint John
BETTS, Blair	6-1	200	L	Edmonton, Alta.	2/16/80	Saint John
CHRISTIE, Ryan	6-3	200	L	Beamsville, Ont.	7/3/78	Utah
CLARK, Chris	6-0	200	R	Manchester, CT	3/8/76	Calgary-Saint John
CONROY, Craig	6-2	197	R	Potsdam, NY	9/4/71	St. Louis-Calgary
COWAN, Jeff	6-2	195	L	Scarborough, Ont.	9/27/76	Calgary
ELOMO, Miika	6-0	200	L	Turku, Finland	4/21/77	Saint John
FATA, Rico	5-11	200	L	Sault Ste. Marie, Ont.	2/12/80	Calgary-Saint John
HAY, Dwayne	6-1	203	L	London, Ont.	2/11/77	Calgary
HENTUNEN, Jukka	5-10	194	R	Joroinen, Finland	5/3/74	Jokerit Helsinki
IGINLA, Jarome	6-1	200	R	Edmonton, Alta.	7/1/77	Calgary
LOWRY, Dave	6-1	200	L	Sudbury, Ont.	2/14/65	Calgary
McAMMOND, Dean	5-11	200	L	Grand Cache, Alta.	6/15/73	Chicago-Philadelphia
MURRAY, Rob	6-1	180	R	Toronto, Ont.	4/4/67	Philadelphia (AHL)-Springfield
NICHOL, Scott	5-8	160	R	Edmonton, Alta.	12/31/74	Detroit (IHL)
NIEDERMAYER, Rob	6-2	204	L	Cassiar, B.C.	12/28/74	Florida
PETROVICKY, Ronald	5-11	190	R	Zilina, Czech.	2/15/77	Calgary
SAPRYKIN, Oleg	6-0	195	L	Moscow, USSR	2/12/81	Calgary
SAVARD, Marc	5-10	185	L	Ottawa, Ont.	7/17/77	Calgary
SHANTZ, Jeff	6-0	195	R	Duchess, Alta.	10/10/73	Calgary
WILM, Clarke	6-0	202	L	Central Butte, Sask.	10/24/76	Calgary
WRIGHT, Jamie	6-0	195	L	Kitchener, Ont.	5/13/76	Dallas-Utah
DEFENSEMEN						
BOUGHNER, Bob	6-0	203	R	Windsor, Ont.	3/8/71	Pittsburgh
DuPONT, Micki	5-9	180	R	Calgary, Alta.	4/15/80	Saint John
EAKINS, Dallas	6-2	195	L	Dade City, FL	2/27/67	Calgary-Chicago (IHL)
GAUTHIER, Denis	6-2	210	L	Montreal, Que.	10/1/76	Calgary
HOUSLEY, Phil	5-10	185	L	St. Paul, MN	3/9/64	Calgary
KRAVCHUK, Igor	6-1	218	L	Ufa, USSR	9/13/66	Ottawa-Calgary
LYDMAN, Toni	6-1	200	L	Lahti, Finland	9/25/77	Calgary
MARTIN, Mike	6-2	205	R	Stratford, Ont.	10/27/76	Saint John
MORRIS, Derek	5-11	200	R	Edmonton, Alta.	8/24/78	Calgary-Saint John
REGEHR, Robyn	6-2	210	L	Recife, Brazil	4/19/80	Calgary
WERENKA, Brad	6-1	225	L	Two Hills, Alta.	2/12/69	Calgary

GOALTENDERS	HT	WT	C	Place of Birth	Date	2000-01 Club
SZUPER, Levente	5-11	180	L	Budapest, Hungary	6/11/80	Saint John
TUREK, Roman	6-3	215	R	Strakonice, Czech.	5/21/70	St. Louis
VERNON, Mike	5-9	180	L	Calgary, Alta.	2/24/63	Calgary
WHITMORE, Kay	5-11	175	L	Sudbury, Ont.	4/10/67	Boston-Prov (AHL)

Marc Savard continues to improve in Calgary, scoring 23 goals and leading the club with 42 assists last season.

General Manager

BUTTON, CRAIG
Vice President/General Manager, Calgary Flames.
Born in Montreal, Que., January 3, 1963.

Craig Button is entering his second season with the Calgary Flames having been named vice president and general manager of the team on June 6, 2000. Button spent the previous 12 seasons with the Dallas Stars organization, serving as the director of player personnel for the last two seasons after spending six years as the director of scouting. Button oversaw the Stars' top minor league team in Kalamazoo, aiding in the evaluation and development of the Stars' minor league prospects. His other responsibilities included the management and development of the Stars' amateur and professional scouting program, the evaluation of players as it relates to movement within the organization, including the Entry Draft, trades and free agent signings, and the player development program for their amateur prospects.

A native of Montreal, Button graduated from Concordia University in Montreal in 1987 with a BA in Economics with an emphasis in international finance.

Button's family has a long history in hockey. His late father, Jack, was a former NHL general manager and a highly respected 34-year veteran of NHL management. His mother, Bridget, worked for Punch Imlach and the Toronto Maple Leafs, and his brother Tod is a pro scout with the Flames.

2000-01 Scoring

* - rookie

Regular Season

Pos	#	Player	Team	GP	G	A	Pts	+/–	PIM	PP	SH	GW	GT	S	%
R	12	Jarome Iginla	CGY	77	31	40	71	–2	62	10	0	4	3	229	13.5
C	27	Marc Savard	CGY	77	23	42	65	–12	46	10	1	5	2	197	11.7
R	8	Valeri Bure	CGY	78	27	28	55	–21	26	16	0	2	0	276	9.8
L	10	Dave Lowry	CGY	79	18	17	35	–2	47	5	0	5	0	108	16.7
D	6	Phil Housley	CGY	69	4	30	34	–15	24	0	0	0	0	115	3.5
C	22	Craig Conroy	STL	69	11	14	25	2	46	0	3	2	0	101	10.9
			CGY	14	3	4	7	0	14	0	1	0	0	32	9.4
			TOTAL	83	14	18	32	2	60	0	4	2	0	133	10.5
D	53	Derek Morris	CGY	51	5	23	28	–15	56	3	1	4	0	142	3.5
C	19	* Oleg Saprykin	CGY	59	9	14	23	4	43	2	0	0	0	95	9.5
C	11	Jeff Shantz	CGY	73	5	15	20	–7	58	0	0	0	0	88	5.7
D	5	Tommy Albelin	CGY	77	1	19	20	2	22	1	0	0	0	69	1.4
D	32	* Toni Lydman	CGY	62	3	16	19	–7	30	1	0	0	0	80	3.8
C	24	Jason Wiemer	CGY	65	10	5	15	–15	177	3	0	1	1	76	13.2
C	23	Clarke Wilm	CGY	81	7	8	15	–11	69	2	0	0	0	85	8.2
D	25	Igor Kravchuk	OTT	15	1	5	6	4	14	0	0	1	0	13	7.7
			CGY	37	0	8	8	–12	4	0	0	0	0	54	0.0
			TOTAL	52	1	13	14	–8	18	0	0	1	0	67	1.5
L	38	* Jeff Cowan	CGY	51	9	4	13	–8	74	2	0	1	0	48	18.8
C	18	* Daniel Tkaczuk	CGY	19	4	7	11	1	14	1	0	0	0	34	11.8
R	36	* Ronald Petrovicky	CGY	30	4	5	9	0	54	1	0	1	0	30	13.3
D	3	Denis Gauthier	CGY	62	2	6	8	3	78	0	0	0	0	33	6.1
R	17	* Chris Clark	CGY	29	5	1	6	0	38	1	0	0	0	43	11.6
D	2	Brad Werenka	CGY	33	1	4	5	–3	16	0	0	0	0	23	4.3
C	39	Benoit Gratton	CGY	14	1	3	4	0	14	0	0	0	1	13	7.7
C	20	Ron Sutter	CGY	21	1	3	4	4	12	0	0	0	0	16	6.3
L	21	Dwayne Hay	CGY	49	1	3	4	–4	16	0	0	0	0	39	2.6
D	28	Robyn Regehr	CGY	71	1	3	4	–7	70	0	0	0	0	62	1.6
D	55	Steve Smith	CGY	13	0	2	2	–2	17	0	0	0	0	3	0.0
L	25	Niklas Andersson	CGY	11	0	1	1	0	4	0	0	0	0	8	0.0
D	4	Dallas Eakins	CGY	17	0	1	1	–1	11	0	0	0	0	4	0.0
G	29	Mike Vernon	CGY	41	0	1	1	0	16	0	0	0	0	0	0.0
G	40	Fred Brathwaite	CGY	49	0	1	1	0	2	0	0	0	0	0	0.0
C	26	* Steve Begin	CGY	4	0	0	0	0	21	0	0	0	0	3	0.0
R	15	* Rico Fata	CGY	5	0	0	0	–3	6	0	0	0	0	6	0.0
C	20	* Marty Murray	CGY	7	0	0	0	–2	0	0	0	0	0	6	0.0

Goaltending

No.	Goaltender	GPI	Mins	Avg	W	L	T	EN	SO	GA	SA	S%
40	Fred Brathwaite	49	2742	2.32	15	17	10	6	5	106	1181	.910
29	Mike Vernon	41	2246	3.23	12	23	5	3	3	121	1034	.883
	Totals	**82**	**5009**	**2.83**	**27**	**40**	**15**	**9**	**8**	**236**	**2224**	**.894**

Captains' History

Keith McCreary, 1972-73 to 1974-75; Pat Quinn, 1975-76, 1976-77; Tom Lysiak, 1977-78, 1978-79; Jean Pronovost, 1979-80; Brad Marsh, 1980-81; Phil Russell, 1981-82, 1982-83; Lanny McDonald, Doug Risebrough (co-captains), 1983-84; Lanny McDonald, Doug Risebrough, Jim Peplinski (tri-captains), 1984-85 to 1986-87; Lanny McDonald, Jim Peplinski (co-captains), 1987-88; Lanny McDonald, Jim Peplinski, Tim Hunter (tri-captains), 1988-89; Brad McCrimmon, 1989-90; alternating captains, 1990-91; Joe Nieuwendyk, 1991-92 to 1994-95; Theoren Fleury, 1995-96, 1996-97; Todd Simpson, 1997-98, 1998-99; Steve Smith, 1999-2000; Steve Smith and Dave Lowry, 2000-01.

General Managers' History

Cliff Fletcher, 1972-73 to 1990-91; Doug Risebrough, 1991-92 to 1994-95; Doug Risebrough and Al Coates, 1995-96; Al Coates, 1996-97 to 1999-2000; Craig Button, 2000-01 to date.

Coaching History

Bernie Geoffrion, 1972-73, 1973-74; Bernie Geoffrion and Fred Creighton, 1974-75; Fred Creighton, 1975-76 to 1978-79; Al MacNeil, 1979-80 to 1981-82; Bob Johnson, 1982-83 to 1986-87; Terry Crisp, 1987-88 to 1989-90; Doug Risebrough, 1990-91; Doug Risebrough and Guy Charron, 1991-92; Dave King, 1992-93 to 1994-95; Pierre Page, 1995-96, 1996-97; Brian Sutter, 1997-98 to 1999-2000; Don Hay and Greg Gilbert, 2000-01; Greg Gilbert, 2001-02.

Club Records

Team

(Figures in brackets for season records are games played; records for fewest points, wins, ties, losses, goals, goals against are for 70 or more games)

Most Points **117** 1988-89 (80)
Most Wins **54** 1988-89 (80)
Most Ties **19** 1977-78 (80)
Most Losses **41** 1996-97 (82), 1997-98 (82), 1999-2000 (82)
Most Goals **397** 1987-88 (80)
Most Goals Against **345** 1981-82 (80)
Fewest Points **65** 1972-73 (78)
Fewest Wins **25** 1972-73 (78)
Fewest Ties **3** 1986-87 (80)
Fewest Losses **17** 1988-89 (80)
Fewest Goals **191** 1972-73 (78)
Fewest Goals Against **226** 1988-89 (80)
Longest Winning Streak
Overall .... **10** Oct. 14-Nov. 3/78
Home .... **9** Oct. 17-Nov. 15/78, Jan. 3-Feb. 5/89, Mar. 3-Apr. 1/90, Feb. 21-Mar. 14/91
Away .... **7** Nov. 10-Dec. 4/88
Longest Undefeated Streak
Overall .... **13** Nov. 10-Dec. 8/88 (12 wins, 1 tie)
Home .... **18** Dec. 29/90-Mar. 14/91 (17 wins, 1 tie)
Away .... **9** Feb. 20-Mar. 21/88 (6 wins, 3 ties), Nov. 11-Dec. 16/90 (6 wins, 3 ties)
Longest Losing Streak
Overall .... **11** Dec. 14/85-Jan. 7/86
Home .... **6** Dec. 5-31/98
Away .... **9** Dec. 1/85-Jan. 12/86
Longest Winless Streak
Overall .... **11** Dec. 14/85-Jan. 7/86 (11 losses), Jan. 5-26/93 (9 losses, 2 ties)
Home .... **10** Oct. 21-Dec. 4/00 (6 losses, 4 ties)
Away .... **13** Feb. 3-Mar. 29/73 (10 losses, 3 ties)
Most Shutouts, Season **8** 1974-75 (80), 2000-01 (82)
Most PIM, Season **2,643** 1991-92 (80)
Most Goals, Game .... **13** Feb. 10/93 (S.J. 1 at Cgy. 13)

Individual

Most Seasons .... **13** Al MacInnis
Most Games .... **803** Al MacInnis
Most Goals, Career .... **364** Theoren Fleury
Most Assists, Career .... **609** Al MacInnis
Most Points, Career .... **830** Theoren Fleury (364G, 466A)
Most PIM, Career .... **2,405** Tim Hunter
Most Shutouts, Career .... **20** Dan Bouchard
Longest Consecutive Games Streak .... **257** Brad Marsh (Oct. 11/78-Nov. 10/81)
Most Goals, Season .... **66** Lanny McDonald (1982-83)
Most Assists, Season .... **82** Kent Nilsson (1980-81)
Most Points, Season .... **131** Kent Nilsson (1980-81) (49G, 82A)
Most PIM, Season .... **375** Tim Hunter (1988-89)
Most Points, Defenseman, Season .... **103** Al MacInnis (1990-91; 28G, 75A)
Most Points, Center, Season .... **131** Kent Nilsson (1980-81; 49G, 82A)
Most Points, Right Wing, Season .... **110** Joe Mullen (1988-89; 51G, 59A)
Most Points, Left Wing, Season .... **90** Gary Roberts (1991-92; 53G, 37A)
Most Points, Rookie, Season .... **92** Joe Nieuwendyk (1987-88; 51G, 41A)
Most Shutouts, Season .... **5** Dan Bouchard (1973-74), Phil Myre (1974-75), Fred Brathwaite (1999-2000, 2000-01)
Most Goals, Game .... **5** Joe Nieuwendyk (Jan. 11/89)
Most Assists, Game .... **6** Guy Chouinard (Feb. 25/81), Gary Suter (Apr. 4/86)
Most Points, Game .... **7** Sergei Makarov (Feb. 25/90; 2G, 5A)

Records include Atlanta Flames, 1972-73 through 1979-80.

Retired Numbers

9 Lanny McDonald 1981-1989

All-time Record vs. Other Clubs

Regular Season

	At Home								On Road								Total							
	GP	W	L	T	OL	GF	GA	PTS	GP	W	L	T	OL	GF	GA	PTS	GP	W	L	T	OL	GF	GA	PTS
Anaheim	19	11	7	1	0	56	46	23	20	7	8	4	1	53	65	19	39	18	15	5	1	109	111	42
Atlanta	1	1	0	0	0	5	2	2	2	0	1	1	0	4	5	1	3	1	1	1	0	9	7	3
Boston	43	18	22	3	0	157	151	39	44	12	26	6	0	121	155	30	87	30	48	9	0	278	306	69
Buffalo	43	15	17	11	0	146	143	41	44	13	25	5	1	129	184	32	87	28	42	16	1	275	327	73
Carolina	27	20	5	2	0	136	88	42	27	13	10	4	0	100	88	30	54	33	15	6	0	236	176	72
Chicago	57	26	20	11	0	185	177	63	55	19	23	13	0	160	180	51	112	45	43	24	0	345	357	114
Colorado	39	19	14	6	0	144	121	44	39	14	15	9	1	131	149	38	78	33	29	15	1	275	270	82
Columbus	2	1	1	0	0	5	3	2	2	0	2	0	0	4	9	0	4	1	3	0	0	9	12	2
Dallas	56	32	12	12	0	199	139	76	56	19	27	10	0	182	208	48	112	51	39	22	0	381	347	124
Detroit	54	31	17	6	0	217	165	68	53	16	27	10	0	161	198	42	107	47	44	16	0	378	363	110
Edmonton	73	39	27	7	0	310	260	85	73	24	39	10	0	245	291	58	146	63	66	17	0	555	551	143
Florida	6	2	3	1	0	14	17	5	7	4	2	1	0	19	15	9	13	6	5	2	0	33	32	14
Los Angeles	88	51	27	10	0	392	294	112	85	32	43	9	1	301	325	74	173	83	70	19	1	693	619	186
Minnesota	2	0	0	1	1	3	4	2	3	1	1	1	0	3	4	3	5	1	1	2	1	6	8	5
Montreal	45	14	25	6	0	135	156	34	44	12	24	8	0	109	155	32	89	26	49	14	0	244	311	66
Nashville	6	4	1	1	0	18	13	9	7	3	4	0	0	15	23	6	13	7	5	1	0	33	36	15
New Jersey	41	27	6	8	0	179	107	62	42	26	13	3	0	157	118	55	83	53	19	11	0	336	225	117
NY Islanders	48	24	13	11	0	171	142	59	48	14	25	9	0	131	185	37	96	38	38	20	0	302	327	96
NY Rangers	48	27	10	10	1	215	146	65	49	21	22	5	1	174	174	48	97	48	32	15	2	389	320	113
Ottawa	9	5	3	1	0	34	22	11	8	2	4	2	0	19	21	6	17	7	7	3	0	53	43	17
Philadelphia	51	25	17	9	0	204	167	59	49	13	33	3	0	130	195	29	100	38	50	12	0	334	362	88
Phoenix	65	36	20	9	0	284	212	81	64	22	31	11	0	219	247	55	129	58	51	20	0	503	459	136
Pittsburgh	44	26	10	8	0	194	133	60	43	10	23	10	0	133	165	30	87	36	33	18	0	327	298	90
St. Louis	56	27	23	5	1	191	169	60	58	21	28	9	0	180	209	51	114	48	51	14	1	371	378	111
San Jose	26	15	8	3	0	102	72	33	28	17	8	3	0	93	81	37	54	32	16	6	0	195	153	70
Tampa Bay	7	5	2	0	0	25	14	10	9	4	4	1	0	30	28	9	16	9	6	1	0	55	42	19
Toronto	56	31	20	5	0	224	179	67	51	18	26	7	0	186	195	43	107	49	46	12	0	410	374	110
Vancouver	90	57	20	13	0	383	259	127	91	40	33	17	1	305	315	98	181	97	53	30	1	688	574	225
Washington	37	24	6	7	0	156	89	55	38	14	19	5	0	132	143	33	75	38	25	12	0	288	232	88
Defunct Clubs	13	8	4	1	0	51	34	17	13	7	3	3	0	43	33	17	26	15	7	4	0	94	67	34
Totals	**1152**	**621**	**360**	**168**	**3**	**4535**	**3524**	**1413**	**1152**	**418**	**549**	**179**	**6**	**3669**	**4163**	**1021**	**2304**	**1039**	**909**	**347**	**9**	**8204**	**7687**	**2434**

Playoffs

	Series	W	L	GP	W	L	T	GF	GA	Last Mtg.	Round	Result
Chicago	3	2	1	12	7	5	0	37	33	1996	CQF	L 0-4
Dallas	1	0	1	6	2	4	0	18	25	1981	SF	L 2-4
Detroit	1	0	1	2	0	2	0	5	8	1978	PR	L 0-2
Edmonton	5	1	4	30	11	19	0	96	132	1991	DSF	L 3-4
Los Angeles	6	2	4	26	13	13	0	102	105	1993	DSF	L 2-4
Montreal	2	1	1	11	5	6	0	32	31	1989	F	W 4-2
NY Rangers	1	0	1	4	1	3	0	8	14	1980	PR	L 1-3
Philadelphia	2	1	1	11	4	7	0	28	43	1981	QF	W 4-3
St. Louis	1	1	0	7	4	3	0	28	22	1986	CF	W 4-3
San Jose	1	0	1	7	3	4	0	35	26	1995	CQF	L 3-4
Toronto	1	0	1	2	0	2	0	5	9	1979	PR	L 0-2
Vancouver	5	3	2	25	13	12	0	82	80	1994	CQF	L 3-4
Winnipeg	3	1	2	13	6	7	0	43	45	1987	DSF	L 2-4
Totals	**32**	**12**	**20**	**156**	**69**	**87**	**0**	**529**	**590**			

Carolina totals include Hartford, 1979-80 to 1996-97.
Colorado totals include Quebec, 1979-80 to 1994-95.
Dallas totals include Minnesota North Stars, 1972-73 to 1992-93.
New Jersey totals include Kansas City, 1974-75 to 1975-76, and Colorado Rockies, 1976-77 to 1981-82.
Phoenix totals include Winnipeg, 1979-80 to 1995-96.

Playoff Results 2001-1997

Year	Round	Opponent	Result	GF	GA

(Last playoff appearance: 1996)

Abbreviations: Round: F – Final; **CF** – conference final; **CQF** – conference quarter-final; **DSF** – division semi-final; **SF** – semi-final; **QF** – quarter-final; **PR** – preliminary round.

2000-01 Results

Oct.	5	Detroit	3-4		6	at Los Angeles	0-5
	10	Colorado	1-3		11	Nashville	2-1
	12	Columbus	2-3		13	Ottawa	2-5
	14	at NY Islanders	2-0		14	at Vancouver	1-5
	15	at Detroit	4-2		17	at San Jose	4-4
	18	at Vancouver	1-4		21	Detroit	4-2
	20	Boston	3-2		23	Phoenix	2-4
	21	Toronto	1-2		25	at Los Angeles	3-0
	24	Phoenix	2-2		27	Vancouver	3-5
	26	at St. Louis	3-4		30	Edmonton	3-5
	27	at Minnesota	1-3	**Feb.**	1	Chicago	5-3
	29	Anaheim	3-6		6	San Jose	1-1
Nov.	1	at Edmonton	2-3		9	at Colorado	5-3
	4	Pittsburgh	1-1		10	at Vancouver	4-1
	5	Minnesota	2-3*		13	Washington	4-4
	8	at Minnesota	1-0		15	at St. Louis	1-4
	10	at Florida	3-3		18	at Phoenix	4-1
	11	at Tampa Bay	4-3		19	at Anaheim	2-6
	13	at Buffalo	2-3*		22	Los Angeles	0-2
	16	Chicago	2-5		24	Edmonton	1-3
	18	NY Rangers	4-5*		26	Dallas	3-2
	19	at Edmonton	0-2	**Mar.**	1	Minnesota	1-1
	22	at Minnesota	1-1		3	St. Louis	3-2*
	24	Anaheim	2-2		6	Toronto	1-3
	25	at Colorado	2-3*		8	at Philadelphia	2-5
	28	at Nashville	1-6		10	at Pittsburgh	3-6
	29	at Dallas	4-3		11	at Atlanta	3-3
Dec.	2	Montreal	1-1		14	at Columbus	0-3
	4	San Jose	0-8		15	at Detroit	2-5
	7	Nashville	3-0		17	St. Louis	2-2
	9	Carolina	7-2		19	New Jersey	2-4
	13	at Montreal	3-1		22	Philadelphia	3-1
	14	at Ottawa	2-4		24	at Columbus	4-6
	16	at Toronto	6-5*		25	at Chicago	3-1
	19	at Colorado	3-0		27	Columbus	3-0
	20	at Phoenix	2-4		29	Colorado	0-1
	22	Edmonton	1-1		31	Dallas	0-2
	29	Vancouver	5-0	**Apr.**	2	at Dallas	4-4
	31	Montreal	5-4*		4	at Chicago	5-2
Jan.	3	at San Jose	1-0		5	at Nashville	0-4
	5	at Anaheim	4-4		7	Los Angeles	2-3

* – Overtime

Entry Draft Selections 2001-1987

2001
Pick
14 Chuck Kobasew
41 Andrei Taratukhin
56 Andrei Medvedev
108 Tomi Maki
124 Yegor Shastin
145 James Hakewill
164 Yuri Trubachev
207 Garrett Bembridge
220 David Moss
233 Joe Campbell
251 Ville Hamalainen

2000
Pick
9 Brent Krahn
40 Kurtis Foster
46 Jarret Stoll
116 Levente Szuper
141 Wade Davis
155 Travis Moen
176 Jukka Hentunen
239 David Hajek
270 Micki DuPont

1999
Pick
11 Oleg Saprykin
38 Dan Cavanaugh
77 Craig Andersson
106 Rail Rozakov
135 Matt Doman
153 Jesse Cook
166 Cory Pecker
170 Matt Underhill
190 Blair Stayzer
252 Dmitri Kirilenko

1998
Pick
6 Rico Fata
33 Blair Betts
62 Paul Manning
102 Shaun Sutter
108 Dany Sabourin
120 Brent Gauvreau
192 Radek Duda
206 Jonas Frogren
234 Kevin Mitchell

1997
Pick
6 Daniel Tkaczuk
32 Evan Lindsay
42 John Tripp
51 Dimitri Kokorev
60 Derek Schutz
70 Erik Andersson
92 Chris St. Croix
100 Ryan Ready
113 Martin Moise
140 Ilja Demidov
167 Jeremy Rondeau
223 Dustin Paul

1996
Pick
13 Derek Morris
39 Travis Brigley
40 Steve Begin
73 Dmitri Vlasenkov
89 Toni Lydman
94 Christian Lefebvre
122 Josef Straka
202 Ryan Wade
228 Ronald Petrovicky

1995
Pick
20 Denis Gauthier
46 Pavel Smirnov
72 Rocky Thompson
98 Jan Labraaten
150 Clarke Wilm
176 Ryan Gillis
233 Steve Shirreffs

1994
Pick
19 Chris Dingman
45 Dmitri Ryabykin
77 Chris Clark
91 Ryan Duthie
97 Johan Finnstrom
107 Nils Ekman
123 Frank Appel
149 Patrick Haltia
175 Ladislav Kohn
201 Keith McCambridge
227 Jorgen Jonsson
253 Mike Peluso
279 Pavel Torgaev

1993
Pick
18 Jesper Mattsson
44 Jamie Allison
70 Dan Tompkins
95 Jason Smith
96 Marty Murray
121 Darryl Lafrance
122 John Emmons
148 Andreas Karlsson
200 Derek Sylvester
252 German Titov
278 Burke Murphy

1992
Pick
6 Cory Stillman
30 Chris O'Sullivan
54 Mathias Johansson
78 Robert Svehla
102 Sami Helenius
126 Ravil Yakubov
129 Joel Bouchard
150 Pavel Rajnoha
174 Ryan Mulhern
198 Brandon Carper
222 Jonas Hoglund
246 Andrei Potaichuk

1991
Pick
19 Niklas Sundblad
41 Francois Groleau
52 Sandy McCarthy
63 Brian Caruso
85 Steven Magnusson
107 Jerome Butler
129 Bobby Marshall
140 Matt Hoffman
151 Kelly Harper
173 David St. Pierre
195 David Struch
217 Sergei Zolotov
239 Marko Jantunen
261 Andrei Trefilov

1990
Pick
11 Trevor Kidd
26 Nicolas Perreault
32 Vesa Viitakoski
41 Etienne Belzile
62 Glen Mears
83 Paul Kruse
125 Chris Tschupp
146 Dimitri Frolov
167 Shawn Murray
188 Mike Murray
209 Rob Sumner
230 invalid claim
251 Leo Gudas

1989
Pick
24 Kent Manderville
42 Ted Drury
50 Veli-Pekka Kautonen
63 Corey Lyons
70 Robert Reichel
84 Ryan O'Leary
105 Toby Kearney
147 Alex Nikolic
168 Kevin Wortman
189 Sergei Gomolyako
210 Dan Sawyer
231 Alexander Yudin
252 Kenneth Kennholt

1988
Pick
21 Jason Muzzatti
42 Todd Harkins
84 Gary Socha
85 Tomas Forslund
90 Scott Matusovich
126 Jonas Bergqvist
168 Troy Kennedy
189 Brett Peterson
210 Guy Darveau
231 Dave Tretowicz
252 Sergei Priakin

1987
Pick
19 Bryan Deasley
25 Stephane Matteau
40 Kevin Grant
61 Scott Mahoney
70 Tim Harris
103 Tim Corkery
124 Joe Aloi
145 Peter Ciavaglia
166 Theoren Fleury
187 Mark Osiecki
208 William Sedergren
229 Peter Hasselblad
250 Magnus Svensson

Coach

GILBERT, GREG
Coach, Calgary Flames. Born in Mississauga, Ont., January 22, 1962.

Greg Gilbert joined the Calgary Flames as an assistant coach on August 11, 2000 and assumed the head coaching duties on March 14, 2001. He was formally announced as the club's new head coach on May 1, 2001.

Before joining the Flames, Gilbert spent four seasons as the bench boss of the St. Louis Blues' American Hockey League affiliate in Worcester, Massachusetts. In his first season as head coach of the IceCats, Gilbert guided the 1996-97 club to a first place finish in the New England Division. He was subsequently named the AHL Coach of the Year and *The Sporting News* Minor League Coach of the Year. Under Gilbert's direction, the IceCats made the playoffs every season.

Gilbert began coaching immediately following a successful 15-year National Hockey League playing career with the New York Islanders, Chicago Blackhawks, New York Rangers and St. Louis Blues. Drafted 80th overall by the Islanders in the 1980 NHL Entry Draft, the 1981-82 season was to be the first of his three Stanley Cup championships. Gilbert was also a member of the Islanders' Stanley Cup team the following season and celebrated his third and final Cup win with the Rangers in 1994. Statistically, his finest season was the 1983-84 campaign with the Islanders when he scored 31 goals and added 35 assists. In 837 career games, Gilbert recorded 150 goals and 228 assists for 378 points. He retired after the 1995-96 season.

Coaching Record

		Regular Season				Playoffs		
Season	**Team**	**Games**	**W**	**L**	**T**	**Games**	**W**	**L**
1996-97	Worcester (AHL)	80	43	23	14	5	2	3
1997-98	Worcester (AHL)	80	34	31	15	11	6	5
1998-99	Worcester (AHL)	80	34	36	10	4	1	3
1999-2000	Worcester (AHL)	80	34	41	15	9	4	5
2000-01	**Calgary (NHL)**	**14**	**4**	**8**	**2**	....	....	....
	NHL Total	**14**	**4**	**8**	**2**	....	....	....

Club Directory

Pengrowth Saddledome

Calgary Flames
Pengrowth Saddledome
P.O. Box 1540 Station M
Calgary, Alberta T2P 3B9
Phone **403/777-2177**
FAX 403/777-2199
www.calgaryflames.com
Capacity: 17,158

Owners: N. Murray Edwards, Harley N. Hotchkiss, Alvin G. Libin, Allan P. Markin, J.R. (Bud) McCaig, Byron J. Seaman, Daryl K. Seaman

Executive
President & Chief Executive Officer . . . . Ken King
Vice-President/General Manager . . . . Craig Button
Vice President, Finance & Administration. . . . . Michael Holditch
Vice President, Marketing & Sales . . . . Garry McKenzie

Hockey Club Personnel
Vice-President/General Manager . . . . Craig Button
Assistant to the General Manager . . . . Dan Stuchal
Head Coach . . . . Greg Gilbert
Assistant Coaches . . . . Brad McCrimmon, Brian Skrudland, Rob Cookson
Development Coach . . . . Jamie Hislop
Goaltending Consultants. Wendell Young, Grant Fuhr
Director, Hockey Administration . . . . Mike Burke
Director ofScouting . . . . Tod Button
Chief Amateur Scout. . . . . Mike Sands
Scouts. . . . . Bob Atrill, Jeff Crisp, Tomas Jelinek, Larry Johnston, Pertii Hasahen, Bob Richardson, Sergei Samoilov, Al Tuer, Steve Graves
Team Services Manager. . . . . Kelly Chesla
Saint John Flames Head Coach . . . . Jim Playfair
Saint John Flames Asst. Coach . . . . Ron Wilson
Exec. Asst. to President/CEO . . . . Yvette Mutcheson
Exec. Asst. to GM and Hockey Operations. . . . . . . Brenda Koyich
Exec. Asst. to VP, Finance & Corporate Development . . . . Gita Nayak

Medical/Training Staff
Athletic Therapist . . . . Morris Boyer
Assistant Athletic Therapist . . . . Terence "TC" Forss
Equipment Manager . . . . Gus Thorson
Strength & Conditioning . . . . Rich Hesketh
Assistant Equipment Manager. . . . . Les Jarvis
Head Physicians. . . . . Dr. William Meeuwisse, Dr. Nicholas Mohtadi
Internal Medicine . . . . Dr. Terry Groves
Team Dentist. . . . . Dr. Bill Blair
Dressing Room Attendant . . . . Jules Carriere

Communications
Director, Communications. . . . . Peter Hanlon
Manager, Media Relations. . . . . Sean O'Brien
Administrative Assistant, Communications . . . . Bernie Hargrave

Community Relations
Director, Community Relations . . . . Holly Brown
Community Relations Ambassador . . . . Jim "Bearcat" Murray

Administration/Human Resources
Controller . . . . Jackie Manwaring
Assistant Controller. . . . . Karen Kingham
Director, Human Resources . . . . Eleanor Culver

Marketing
Director of Marketing . . . . Al Molnar
Director, Retail/FanAttic. Dean Borle
Director, Advertising and Publishing . . . . Pat Halls
Director, Executive Suites . . . . Bob White
Business Development Manager . . . . Kevin Gross
Director, Game Presentation . . . . Dave Imbach

Sales/Customer Relations
Director, Sales & Customer Care . . . . Dave Sclanders

Pengrowth Saddledome
GM, Building Operations. Libby Raines
Operations Manager . . . . George Greenwood
Food Services Manager . . . . Art Hernandez
Concessions Manager . . . . Sheila Parisien
Security/Parking Superintendent . . . . Bob Godun

Mascot . . . . Harvey the Hound

Calgary Hitmen
General Manager . . . . Kelly Kisio
Asst. General Manager . . . . Blaine Forsythe
Head Coach . . . . Richard Kromm
Assistant Coach . . . . Jeff Maher

Broadcasting
Radio Affiliate . . . . The Team 920 (920 AM)
TV Affiliate . . . . Sportsnet, CBC

Carolina Hurricanes

2000-01 Results: 38W-32L-9T-3OTL 88PTS. Second, Southeast Division

Year-by-Year Record

Season	GP	Home W	Home L	Home T	Home OL	Road W	Road L	Road T	Road OL	Overall W	Overall L	Overall T	Overall OL	GF	GA	Pts.	Finished	Playoff Result
2000-01	82	23	15	3	0	15	17	6	3	38	32	9	3	212	225	88	2nd, Southeast Div.	Lost Conf. Quarter-Final
1999-2000	82	20	16	5	0	17	19	5	0	37	35	10	0	217	216	84	3rd, Southeast Div.	Out of Playoffs
1998-99	82	20	12	9	...	14	18	9	...	34	30	18	...	210	202	86	1st, Southeast Div.	Lost Conf. Quarter-Final
1997-98	82	16	18	7	...	17	23	1	...	33	41	8	...	200	219	74	6th, Northeast Div.	Out of Playoffs
1996-97*	82	23	15	3	...	9	24	8	...	32	39	11	...	226	256	75	5th, Northeast Div.	Out of Playoffs
1995-96*	82	22	15	4	...	12	24	5	...	34	39	9	...	237	259	77	4th, Northeast Div.	Out of Playoffs
1994-95*	48	12	10	2	...	7	14	3	...	19	24	5	...	127	141	43	5th, Northeast Div.	Out of Playoffs
1993-94*	84	14	22	6	...	13	26	3	...	27	48	9	...	227	288	63	6th, Northeast Div.	Out of Playoffs
1992-93*	84	12	25	5	...	14	27	1	...	26	52	6	...	284	369	58	5th, Adams Div.	Out of Playoffs
1991-92*	80	13	17	10	...	13	24	3	...	26	41	13	...	247	283	65	4th, Adams Div.	Lost Div. Semi-Final
1990-91*	80	18	16	6	...	13	22	5	...	31	38	11	...	238	276	73	4th, Adams Div.	Lost Div. Semi-Final
1989-90*	80	17	18	5	...	21	15	4	...	38	33	9	...	275	268	85	4th, Adams Div.	Lost Div. Semi-Final
1988-89*	80	21	17	2	...	16	21	3	...	37	38	5	...	299	290	79	4th, Adams Div.	Lost Div. Semi-Final
1987-88*	80	21	14	5	...	14	24	2	...	35	38	7	...	249	267	77	4th, Adams Div.	Lost Div. Semi-Final
1986-87*	80	26	9	5	...	17	21	2	...	43	30	7	...	287	270	93	1st, Adams Div.	Lost Div. Semi-Final
1985-86*	80	21	17	2	...	19	19	2	...	40	36	4	...	332	302	84	4th, Adams Div.	Lost Div. Final
1984-85*	80	17	18	5	...	13	23	4	...	30	41	9	...	268	318	69	5th, Adams Div.	Out of Playoffs
1983-84*	80	19	16	5	...	9	26	5	...	28	42	10	...	288	320	66	5th, Adams Div.	Out of Playoffs
1982-83*	80	13	22	5	...	6	32	2	...	19	54	7	...	261	403	45	5th, Adams Div.	Out of Playoffs
1981-82*	80	13	17	10	...	8	24	8	...	21	41	18	...	264	351	60	5th, Adams Div.	Out of Playoffs
1980-81*	80	14	17	9	...	7	24	9	...	21	41	18	...	292	372	60	4th, Norris Div.	Out of Playoffs
1979-80*	80	22	12	6	...	5	22	13	...	27	34	19	...	303	312	73	4th, Norris Div.	Lost Prelim. Round

* Hartford Whalers

2001-02 Schedule

Oct.	Fri.	5	NY Rangers
	Sun.	7	Dallas*
	Tue.	9	Ottawa
	Thu.	11	Toronto
	Sat.	13	at Atlanta
	Wed.	17	NY Islanders
	Thu.	18	at NY Islanders
	Sat.	20	Atlanta
	Tue.	23	at Colorado
	Wed.	24	at Minnesota
	Fri.	26	NY Islanders
	Sun.	28	Los Angeles*
	Tue.	30	Detroit
Nov.	Thu.	1	at St. Louis
	Fri.	2	NY Rangers
	Sun.	4	Phoenix*
	Tue.	6	Pittsburgh
	Thu.	8	at Washington
	Fri.	9	San Jose
	Sun.	11	Edmonton*
	Tue.	13	at Detroit
	Thu.	15	at Ottawa
	Sat.	17	at Tampa Bay
	Mon.	19	Columbus
	Wed.	21	at Dallas
	Sun.	25	Tampa Bay*
	Tue.	27	at Toronto
	Thu.	29	at NY Rangers
	Fri.	30	at Washington
Dec.	Sun.	2	Washington*
	Tue.	4	Buffalo
	Sat.	8	at Florida
	Mon.	10	at NY Rangers
	Wed.	12	Florida
	Fri.	14	at Buffalo
	Sun.	16	at Pittsburgh*
	Tue.	18	Ottawa
	Fri.	21	Atlanta
	Sat.	22	at Philadelphia
	Wed.	26	Toronto
	Thu.	27	at Tampa Bay
	Sun.	30	at Washington*
	Mon.	31	at Buffalo
Jan.	Wed.	2	Boston
	Sat.	5	New Jersey
	Sun.	6	Philadelphia*
	Thu.	10	at Edmonton
	Sat.	12	at Vancouver
	Tue.	15	Minnesota
	Thu.	17	Montreal
	Sat.	19	at New Jersey*
	Mon.	21	Vancouver
	Wed.	23	Nashville
	Fri.	25	Florida
	Sat.	26	at Philadelphia
	Tue.	29	Buffalo
	Wed.	30	at Tampa Bay
Feb.	Tue.	5	Pittsburgh
	Thu.	7	at Los Angeles
	Fri.	8	at Anaheim
	Sun.	10	at San Jose*
	Tue.	26	at Toronto
	Thu.	28	at Boston
Mar.	Sat.	2	at Montreal
	Tue.	5	at Chicago
	Thu.	7	at Pittsburgh
	Fri.	8	Washington
	Mon.	11	Calgary
	Sat.	16	at Montreal
	Mon.	18	Montreal
	Thu.	21	Florida
	Sat.	23	at New Jersey*
	Tue.	26	Boston
	Thu.	28	Philadelphia
	Sat.	30	at Boston*
Apr.	Tue.	2	at Ottawa
	Wed.	3	New Jersey
	Sun.	7	Atlanta*
	Mon.	8	at NY Islanders
	Wed.	10	Tampa Bay
	Fri.	12	at Florida
	Sun.	14	at Atlanta*

* Denotes afternoon game.

Franchise date: June 22, 1979
Transferred from Hartford to Carolina, June 25, 1997.

SOUTHEAST DIVISION

23rd NHL Season

A product of the University of Wisconsin and the U.S. National Team Development Program, David Tanabe was Carolina's first pick in the 1999 Entry Draft. Only Sandis Ozolinsh had more points among Hurricanes blueliners last season.

2001-02 Player Personnel

FORWARDS	HT	WT	S	Place of Birth	Date	2000-01 Club
ADAMS, Craig	6-0	200	R	Brunei, Borneo	4/26/77	Carolina-Cin (IHL)
BATTAGLIA, Bates	6-2	205	L	Chicago, IL	12/13/75	Carolina
BRIND'AMOUR, Rod	6-1	202	L	Ottawa, Ont.	8/9/70	Carolina
COLE, Erik	6-1	200	L	Oswego, NY	11/6/78	Cincinnati (IHL)
DANIELS, Jeff	6-1	200	L	Oshawa, Ont.	6/24/68	Carolina
DINGMAN, Chris	6-4	245	L	Edmonton, Alta.	7/6/76	Colorado
FRANCIS, Ron	6-3	200	L	Sault Ste. Marie, Ont.	3/1/63	Carolina
GELINAS, Martin	5-11	195	L	Shawinigan, Que.	6/5/70	Carolina
KAPANEN, Sami	5-10	195	L	Vantaa, Finland	6/14/73	Carolina
KOEHLER, Greg	6-2	195	L	Scarborough, Ont.	2/27/75	Cin (IHL)-Carolina
LANGDON, Darren	6-1	205	L	Deer Lake, Nfld.	1/8/71	Carolina
MacDONALD, Craig	6-2	195	L	Antigonish, N.S.	4/7/77	Cincinnati (IHL)
MacNEIL, Ian	6-2	190	L	Halifax, N.S.	4/27/77	Cincinnati (IHL)
O'NEILL, Jeff	6-1	190	R	Richmond Hill, Ont.	2/23/76	Carolina
RITCHIE, Byron	5-10	185	L	Burnaby, B.C.	4/24/77	Cincinnati (IHL)
SVOBODA, Jaroslav	6-2	190	L	Cervenka, Czech.	6/1/80	Cincinnati (IHL)
VASICEK, Josef	6-4	200	L	Havlickuv Brod, Czech.	9/12/80	Carolina-Cin (IHL)
WESTLUND, Tommy	6-0	210	R	Fors, Sweden	12/29/74	Carolina
WILLIS, Shane	6-0	185	R	Edmonton, Alta.	6/13/77	Carolina
DEFENSEMEN						
HALKO, Steven	6-1	200	R	Etobicoke, Ont.	3/8/74	Carolina
KNYAZEV, Igor	6-0	191	L	Elektrostal, USSR	1/27/83	Krylja Sovetov
KUZNIK, Greg	6-0	185	L	Prince George, B.C.	6/12/78	Carolina-Cin (IHL)
MALIK, Marek	6-5	215	L	Ostrava, Czech.	6/24/75	Carolina
McCARTHY, Jeremiah	6-0	210	L	Boston, MA	3/1/76	Cincinnati (IHL)
OZOLINSH, Sandis	6-3	205	L	Riga, Latvia	8/3/72	Carolina
RUCINSKI, Mike	5-11	179	L	Trenton, MI	3/30/75	Carolina-Cin (IHL)
TANABE, David	6-1	190	R	Minneapolis, MN	7/19/80	Carolina
TSELIOS, Nikos	6-5	210	L	Oak Park, IL	1/20/79	Cincinnati (IHL)
WALLIN, Niclas	6-3	220	L	Boden, Sweden	2/20/75	Carolina-Cin (IHL)
WARD, Aaron	6-2	200	R	Windsor, Ont.	1/17/73	Detroit
WESLEY, Glen	6-1	205	L	Red Deer, Alta.	10/2/68	Carolina

GOALTENDERS	HT	WT	C	Place of Birth	Date	2000-01 Club
BARRASSO, Tom	6-3	210	R	Boston, MA	3/31/65	DID NOT PLAY
IRBE, Arturs	5-8	190	L	Riga, Latvia	2/2/67	Carolina
MOSS, Tyler	6-0	185	R	Ottawa, Ont.	6/29/75	Carolina-Cin (IHL)
PELLETIER, Jean-Marc	6-3	200	L	Atlanta, GA	3/4/78	Cincinnati (IHL)
PETRUK, Randy	5-9	175	R	Cranbrook, B.C.	4/23/78	Cin (IHL)-Florida (ECHL)

Coach

MAURICE, PAUL
Coach, Carolina Hurricanes. Born in Sault Ste. Marie, Ont., January 30, 1967.

Paul Maurice is entering his seventh year as the franchise's head coach and is the only head coach of the Carolina Hurricanes. Maurice became the tenth coach in the history of the franchise on November 6, 1995, just 12 games into the 1995-96 season. Maurice stepped in as the youngest coach in the National Hockey League and remains the youngest head coach in the NHL despite ranking in the top five in tenure among NHL head coaches. In franchise history, Maurice ranks first in all-time wins (203) and games coached (480). In the 1996-97 season, Maurice was chosen to coach in the 1997 NHL All-Star Game.

Maurice joined the Whalers in June of 1995 as an assistant coach after serving as the head coach of the Detroit Junior Red Wings for two seasons. The Junior Wings won the OHL Western Division regular season title and played for the 1995 Memorial Cup by winning the OHL playoffs. The Wings lost in the Cup finals to Kamloops. For his efforts, Maurice was the runner-up for OHL coach of the year honors in 1995. In the 1993-94 season, Maurice's squad won the OHL Hap Emms Division title and advanced to the finals of the OHL playoffs before losing in seven games to North Bay.

Maurice began his coaching career in 1986 as an assistant coach for the Detroit Junior Red Wings after an eye injury ended his junior playing career. He served six seasons in that capacity before taking over the head coaching responsibilities in the 1993-94 season.

Coaching Record

		Regular Season				Playoffs		
Season	Team	Games	W	L	T	Games	W	L
1993-94	Detroit (OHL)	66	42	20	4	17	11	6
1994-95	Detroit (OHL)	66	44	18	4	21	16	5
1995-96	**Hartford (NHL)**	**70**	**29**	**33**	**8**	....	....	....
1996-97	**Hartford (NHL)**	**82**	**32**	**39**	**11**	....	....	....
1997-98	**Carolina (NHL)**	**82**	**33**	**41**	**8**	....	....	....
1998-99	**Carolina (NHL)**	**82**	**34**	**30**	**18**	**6**	**2**	**4**
1999-2000	**Carolina (NHL)**	**82**	**37**	**35**	**10**	....	....	....
2000-01	**Carolina (NHL)**	**82**	**38**	**35**	**9**	**6**	**2**	**4**
	NHL Totals	**480**	**203**	**213**	**64**	**12**	**4**	**8**

2000-01 Scoring

* - rookie

Regular Season

Pos	#	Player	Team	GP	G	A	Pts	+/–	PIM	PP	SH	GW	GT	S	%
C	92	Jeff O'Neill	CAR	82	41	26	67	–18	106	17	0	5	2	242	16.9
C	10	Ron Francis	CAR	82	15	50	65	–15	32	7	0	4	0	130	11.5
R	24	Sami Kapanen	CAR	82	20	37	57	–12	24	7	0	4	0	223	9.0
C	17	Rod Brind'Amour	CAR	79	20	36	56	–7	47	5	1	5	0	163	12.3
L	23	Martin Gelinas	CAR	79	23	29	52	–4	59	6	1	4	0	170	13.5
R	25 *	Shane Willis	CAR	73	20	24	44	–6	45	9	0	6	0	172	11.6
D	8	Sandis Ozolinsh	CAR	72	12	32	44	–25	71	4	2	2	0	145	8.3
L	38	Scott Pellerin	MIN	58	11	28	39	6	45	2	2	2	0	117	9.4
			CAR	19	0	5	5	–4	6	0	0	0	0	21	0.0
			TOTAL	77	11	33	44	2	51	2	2	2	0	138	8.0
D	45	David Tanabe	CAR	74	7	22	29	–9	42	5	0	1	0	130	5.4
L	13	Bates Battaglia	CAR	80	12	15	27	–14	76	2	0	3	0	133	9.0
L	19	Rob DiMaio	CAR	74	6	18	24	–14	54	0	2	1	0	99	6.1
C	63 *	Josef Vasicek	CAR	76	8	13	21	–8	53	1	0	0	0	103	7.8
D	2	Glen Wesley	CAR	71	5	16	21	–2	42	3	0	0	0	92	5.4
D	5	Marek Malik	CAR	61	6	14	20	–4	34	1	0	1	0	72	8.3
D	4	Kevin Hatcher	CAR	57	4	14	18	2	38	3	0	1	0	98	4.1
D	33	Dave Karpa	CAR	80	4	6	10	–19	159	2	0	0	0	69	5.8
L	16	Tommy Westlund	CAR	79	5	3	8	–9	23	0	0	1	0	47	10.6
D	7 *	Niclas Wallin	CAR	37	2	3	5	–11	21	0	0	0	0	19	10.5
L	11	Jeff Daniels	CAR	67	1	1	2	–3	15	0	0	0	0	42	2.4
L	20	Darren Langdon	CAR	54	0	2	2	–4	94	0	0	0	0	6	0.0
G	1	Arturs Irbe	CAR	77	0	2	2	0	6	0	0	0	0	0	0.0
R	27 *	Craig Adams	CAR	44	1	0	1	–7	20	0	0	0	0	15	6.7
D	14	Steven Halko	CAR	48	0	1	1	–10	6	0	0	0	0	24	0.0
D	53 *	Greg Kuznik	CAR	1	0	0	0	0	0	0	0	0	0	0	0.0
C	36 *	Greg Koehler	CAR	1	0	0	0	0	0	0	0	0	0	0	0.0
D	18	Mike Rucinski	CAR	2	0	0	0	0	0	0	0	0	0	2	0.0
G	31	Tyler Moss	CAR	12	0	0	0	0	0	0	0	0	0	0	0.0

Goaltending

No.	Goaltender	GPI	Mins	Avg	W	L	T	EN	SO	GA	SA	S%
1	Arturs Irbe	77	4406	2.45	37	29	9	7	6	180	1947	.908
31	Tyler Moss	12	557	3.99	1	6	0	1	0	37	251	.853
	Totals	**82**	**4986**	**2.71**	**38**	**35**	**9**	**8**	**6**	**225**	**2206**	**.898**

Playoffs

Pos	#	Player	Team	GP	G	A	Pts	+/–	PIM	PP	SH	GW	GT	S	%
R	24	Sami Kapanen	CAR	6	2	3	5	–7	0	1	0	0	0	16	12.5
C	17	Rod Brind'Amour	CAR	6	1	3	4	–7	6	0	0	1	1	7	14.3
C	92	Jeff O'Neill	CAR	6	1	2	3	–3	10	0	0	1	0	13	7.7
C	63 *	Josef Vasicek	CAR	6	2	0	2	–1	0	0	0	0	0	9	22.2
D	45	David Tanabe	CAR	6	2	0	2	–4	12	2	0	0	0	10	20.0
L	11	Jeff Daniels	CAR	6	0	2	2	–1	2	0	0	0	0	3	0.0
D	8	Sandis Ozolinsh	CAR	6	0	2	2	–2	5	0	0	0	0	4	0.0
L	13	Bates Battaglia	CAR	6	0	2	2	–3	2	0	0	0	0	6	0.0
L	23	Martin Gelinas	CAR	6	0	1	1	–4	6	0	0	0	0	4	0.0
R	25 *	Shane Willis	CAR	2	0	0	0	–1	0	0	0	0	0	2	0.0
C	10	Ron Francis	CAR	3	0	0	0	–2	0	0	0	0	0	5	0.0
D	5	Marek Malik	CAR	3	0	0	0	–3	6	0	0	0	0	1	0.0
R	27 *	Craig Adams	CAR	3	0	0	0	0	0	0	0	0	0	1	0.0
D	7 *	Niclas Wallin	CAR	3	0	0	0	–2	2	0	0	0	0	0	0.0
L	20	Darren Langdon	CAR	4	0	0	0	0	12	0	0	0	0	2	0.0
L	19	Rob DiMaio	CAR	6	0	0	0	–5	4	0	0	0	0	7	0.0
D	4	Kevin Hatcher	CAR	6	0	0	0	–6	6	0	0	0	0	6	0.0
D	2	Glen Wesley	CAR	6	0	0	0	–6	0	0	0	0	0	4	0.0
G	1	Arturs Irbe	CAR	6	0	0	0	0	4	0	0	0	0	0	0.0
L	38	Scott Pellerin	CAR	6	0	0	0	–3	4	0	0	0	0	8	0.0
D	33	Dave Karpa	CAR	6	0	0	0	–3	17	0	0	0	0	5	0.0
L	16	Tommy Westlund	CAR	6	0	0	0	–2	17	0	0	0	0	1	0.0

Goaltending

No.	Goaltender	GPI	Mins	Avg	W	L	EN	SO	GA	SA	S%
1	Arturs Irbe	6	360	3.33	2	4	0	0	20	201	.900
	Totals	**6**	**361**	**3.32**	**2**	**4**	**0**	**0**	**20**	**201**	**.900**

General Managers' History

Jack Kelly, 1979-80, 1980-81; Larry Pleau, 1981-82, 1982-83; Emile Francis, 1983-84 to 1988-89; Ed Johnston, 1989-90 to 1991-92; Brian Burke, 1992-93; Paul Holmgren, 1993-94; Jim Rutherford, 1994-95 to date.

Coaching History

Don Blackburn, 1979-80; Don Blackburn and Larry Pleau, 1980-81; Larry Pleau, 1981-82; Larry Kish, Larry Pleau and John Cuniff, 1982- 83; Jack Evans, 1983-84 to 1986-87; Jack Evans and Larry Pleau, 1987-88; Larry Pleau, 1988-89; Rick Ley, 1989-90, 1990-91; Jim Roberts, 1991-92; Paul Holmgren, 1992-93; Paul Holmgren and Pierre Maguire, 1993-94; Paul Holmgren, 1994-95; Paul Holmgren and Paul Maurice, 1995-96; Paul Maurice, 1996-97 to date.

Captains' History

Rick Ley, 1979-80; Rick Ley and Mike Rogers, 1980-81; Dave Keon, 1981-82; Russ Anderson, 1982-83; Mark Johnson, 1983-84; Mark Johnson and Ron Francis, 1984-85; Ron Francis, 1985-86 to 1990-91; Randy Ladouceur, 1991-92; Pat Verbeek, 1992-93 to 1994-95; Brendan Shanahan, 1995-96; Kevin Dineen, 1996-97, 1997-98; Keith Primeau, 1998-99; Keith Primeau and Ron Francis, 1999-2000; Ron Francis, 2000-01 to date.

Club Records

Team

(Figures in brackets for season records are games played; records for fewest points, wins, ties, losses, goals, goals against are for 70 or more games)

Most Points	**93**	1986-87 (80)
Most Wins	**43**	1986-87 (80)
Most Ties	**19**	1979-80 (80)
Most Losses	**54**	1982-83 (80)
Most Goals	**332**	1985-86 (80)
Most Goals Against	**403**	1982-83 (80)
Fewest Points	**45**	1982-83 (80)
Fewest Wins	**19**	1982-83 (80)
Fewest Ties	**4**	1985-86 (80)
Fewest Losses	**30**	1986-87 (80); 1998-99 (82)
Fewest Goals	**200**	1997-98 (82)
Fewest Goals Against	**202**	1998-99 (82)
Longest Winning Streak		
Overall	**7**	Mar. 16-29/85
Home	**5**	Mar. 17-29/85
Away	**6**	Nov. 10-Dec. 7/90
Longest Undefeated Streak		
Overall	**10**	Jan. 20-Feb. 10/82 (6 wins, 4 ties)
Home	**9**	Dec. 15/00-Jan. 18/01 (8 wins, 1 tie)
Away	**8**	Nov. 11-Dec. 5/96 (4 wins, 4 ties)
Longest Losing Streak		
Overall	**9**	Feb. 19-Mar. 8/83
Home	**6**	Feb. 19-Mar. 12/83, Feb. 10-Mar. 3/85
Away	**13**	Dec. 18/82-Feb. 5/83
Longest Winless Streak		
Overall	**14**	Jan. 4-Feb. 9/92 (8 losses, 6 ties)
Home	**13**	Jan. 15-Mar. 10/85 (11 losses, 2 ties)
Away	**15**	Nov. 11/79-Jan. 9/80 (11 losses, 4 ties)
Most Shutouts, Season	**8**	1998-99 (82)
Most PIM, Season	**2,354**	1992-93 (84)
Most Goals, Game	**11**	Feb. 12/84 (Edm. 0 at Hfd. 11), Oct. 19/85 (Mtl. 6 at Hfd. 11), Jan. 17/86 (Que. 6 at Hfd. 11), Mar. 15/86 (Chi. 4 at Hfd. 11)

Individual

Most Seasons	**13**	Ron Francis
Most Games	**956**	Ron Francis
Most Goals, Career	**323**	Ron Francis
Most Assists, Career	**688**	Ron Francis
Most Points, Career	**1,011**	Ron Francis (323G, 688A)
Most PIM, Career	**1,439**	Kevin Dineen
Most Shutouts, Career	**17**	Arturs Irbe
Longest Consecutive Games Streak	**419**	Dave Tippett (Mar. 3/84-Oct. 7/89)
Most Goals, Season	**56**	Blaine Stoughton (1979-80)
Most Assists, Season	**69**	Ron Francis (1989-90)
Most Points, Season	**105**	Mike Rogers (1979-80; 44G, 61A), (1980-81; 40G, 65A)
Most PIM, Season	**358**	Torrie Robertson (1985-86)
Most Points, Defenseman, Season	**69**	Dave Babych (1985-86; 14G, 55A)
Most Points, Center, Season	**105**	Mike Rogers (1979-80; 44G, 61A), (1980-81; 40G, 65A)
Most Points, Right Wing, Season	**100**	Blaine Stoughton (1979-80; 56G, 44A)
Most Points, Left Wing, Season	**89**	Geoff Sanderson (1992-93; 46G, 43A)
Most Points, Rookie, Season	**72**	Sylvain Turgeon (1983-84; 40G, 32A)
Most Shutouts, Season	**6**	Arturs Irbe (1998-99, 2000-01)
Most Goals, Game	**4**	Jordy Douglas (Feb. 3/80), Ron Francis (Feb. 12/84)
Most Assists, Game	**6**	Ron Francis (Mar. 5/87)
Most Points, Game	**6**	Paul Lawless (Jan. 4/87; 2G, 4A), Ron Francis (Mar. 5/87; 6A), (Oct. 8/89; 3G, 3A)

Records include Hartford Whalers, 1979-80 through 1996-97.

All-time Record vs. Other Clubs

Regular Season

	At Home								On Road								Total							
	GP	W	L	T	OL	GF	GA	PTS	GP	W	L	T	OL	GF	GA	PTS	GP	W	L	T	OL	GF	GA	PTS
Anaheim	7	5	1	1	0	22	12	11	6	2	3	1	0	19	23	5	13	7	4	2	0	41	35	16
Atlanta	5	5	0	0	0	20	9	10	5	4	0	1	0	17	10	9	10	9	0	1	0	37	19	19
Boston	70	31	32	7	0	239	243	69	72	20	45	7	0	190	266	47	142	51	77	14	0	429	509	116
Buffalo	72	30	32	10	0	216	216	70	71	22	42	7	0	212	286	51	143	52	74	17	0	428	502	121
Calgary	27	10	13	4	0	88	100	24	27	5	20	2	0	88	136	12	54	15	33	6	0	176	236	36
Chicago	29	14	12	3	0	94	90	31	27	8	16	3	0	78	114	19	56	22	28	6	0	172	204	50
Colorado	61	24	25	12	0	201	211	60	63	17	37	9	0	189	266	43	124	41	62	21	0	390	477	103
Columbus	1	1	0	0	0	2	1	2	1	0	1	0	0	1	3	0	2	1	1	0	0	3	4	2
Dallas	29	11	14	4	0	96	107	26	27	10	16	1	0	81	109	21	56	21	30	5	0	177	216	47
Detroit	27	16	10	1	0	95	73	33	29	7	15	6	1	79	111	21	56	23	25	7	1	174	184	54
Edmonton	28	11	11	6	0	111	97	28	28	5	18	5	0	84	114	15	56	16	29	11	0	195	211	43
Florida	17	8	8	1	0	54	51	17	18	5	6	7	0	36	48	17	35	13	14	8	0	90	99	34
Los Angeles	28	13	11	4	0	108	111	30	28	10	15	3	0	110	119	23	56	23	26	7	0	218	230	53
Minnesota	0	0	0	0	0	0	0	0	1	0	0	1	0	1	1	1	1	0	0	1	0	1	1	1
Montreal	72	28	35	9	0	217	258	65	69	16	46	7	0	196	291	39	141	44	81	16	0	413	549	104
Nashville	3	2	1	0	0	11	9	4	3	0	3	0	0	5	8	0	6	2	4	0	0	16	17	4
New Jersey	38	17	13	8	0	128	118	42	39	13	22	3	1	126	142	30	77	30	35	11	1	254	260	72
NY Islanders	39	20	14	5	0	139	128	45	38	16	18	4	0	109	123	36	77	36	32	9	0	248	251	81
NY Rangers	37	20	14	3	0	129	123	43	39	13	23	3	0	106	150	29	76	33	37	6	0	235	273	72
Ottawa	21	16	3	2	0	66	39	34	23	12	8	3	0	67	59	27	44	28	11	5	0	133	98	61
Philadelphia	38	12	19	7	0	127	144	31	37	9	24	3	1	91	139	22	75	21	43	10	1	218	283	53
Phoenix	27	12	9	6	0	99	84	30	30	15	13	2	0	110	106	32	57	27	22	8	0	209	190	62
Pittsburgh	42	19	20	3	0	164	164	41	40	14	21	5	0	150	176	33	82	33	41	8	0	314	340	74
St. Louis	29	11	16	2	0	87	92	24	29	9	17	3	0	90	113	21	58	20	33	5	0	177	205	45
San Jose	9	4	5	0	0	28	21	8	9	4	5	0	0	29	40	8	18	8	10	0	0	57	61	16
Tampa Bay	19	14	2	3	0	70	49	31	18	6	9	3	0	47	50	15	37	20	11	6	0	117	99	46
Toronto	31	17	9	5	0	131	103	39	30	15	10	5	0	112	105	35	61	32	19	10	0	243	208	74
Vancouver	27	12	10	5	0	87	90	29	28	10	12	6	0	79	96	26	55	22	22	11	0	166	186	55
Washington	41	14	19	8	0	111	129	36	39	12	24	3	0	101	131	27	80	26	43	11	0	212	260	63
Totals	**874**	**397**	**358**	**119**	**0**	**2940**	**2872**	**913**	**874**	**279**	**489**	**103**	**3**	**2603**	**3335**	**664**	**1748**	**676**	**847**	**222**	**3**	**5543**	**6207**	**1577**

Playoffs

	Series	W	L	GP	W	L	T	GF	GA	Last Mtg.	Round	Result
Boston	3	0	3	19	7	12	0	48	63	1999	CQF	L 2-4
Colorado	2	1	1	9	5	4	0	35	34	1987	DSF	L 2-4
Montreal	5	0	5	27	8	19	0	70	96	1992	DSF	L 3-4
New Jersey	1	0	1	6	2	4	0	8	20	2001	CQF	L 2-4
Totals	**11**	**1**	**10**	**61**	**22**	**39**	**0**	**161**	**213**			

Playoff Results 2001-1997

Year	Round	Opponent	Result	GF	GA
2001	CQF	New Jersey	L 2-4	8	20
1999	CQF	Boston	L 2-4	10	16

Abbreviations: Round: CQF – conference quarter-final; **DSF** – division semi-final.

Calgary totals include Atlanta Flames, 1979-80.
Dallas totals include Minnesota North Stars, 1979-80 to 1992-93.
Phoenix totals include Winnipeg, 1979-80 to 1995-96.
Colorado totals include Quebec, 1979-80 to 1994-95.
New Jersey totals include Colorado Rockies, 1979-80 to 1981-82.

2000-01 Results

Oct.	7	Washington	3-3
	10	Dallas	5-2
	13	at Florida	2-2
	14	at Nashville	1-2
	18	at Pittsburgh	3-2
	21	at Montreal	2-5
	24	San Jose	2-3
	25	at Buffalo	1-4
	27	New Jersey	3-3
	29	St. Louis	1-4
	31	Tampa Bay	6-5*
Nov.	3	at Colorado	3-5
	4	at San Jose	1-4
	8	at Toronto	0-5
	10	Toronto	3-1
	12	Ottawa	4-0
	15	Florida	1-4
	16	at Ottawa	1-0
	18	at New Jersey	2-3*
	22	at Pittsburgh	3-1
	24	at Boston	3-1
	26	Nashville	4-7
	29	at Florida	2-1*
	30	Philadelphia	2-0
Dec.	3	Ottawa	0-2
	6	at Atlanta	5-3
	9	at Calgary	2-7
	13	at Minnesota	1-1
	15	Buffalo	5-3
	16	at Boston	1-4
	19	at NY Islanders	1-2
	23	at Philadelphia	1-2*
	26	at Tampa Bay	2-3
	27	NY Rangers	4-3
	29	at Columbus	1-3
	31	Chicago	2-1
Jan.	3	Tampa Bay	3-2
	6	Colorado	2-2
	7	NY Islanders	5-2
	9	Florida	7-3
	12	at Florida	2-2
	14	Anaheim	4-0
	16	at Montreal	3-2*
	18	Boston	4-2
	20	Los Angeles	3-6
	22	NY Rangers	2-5
	24	at NY Rangers	3-2
	27	Philadelphia	3-4
	29	Tampa Bay	5-2
	31	Toronto	3-4
Feb.	1	at Atlanta	3-1
	7	at Phoenix	2-1*
	8	at Los Angeles	2-4
	11	at Anaheim	2-2
	14	at Detroit	3-4*
	16	Phoenix	0-2
	18	Boston	5-4
	19	at Philadelphia	0-4
	21	Atlanta	6-3
	23	New Jersey	3-2
	24	Washington	1-2
	27	at Atlanta	1-1
Mar.	1	at NY Islanders	3-1
	2	at New Jersey	3-7
	4	at Chicago	6-3
	7	Columbus	2-1
	8	at Tampa Bay	0-1
	11	Edmonton	2-3
	14	Montreal	3-6
	15	at Washington	3-0
	18	NY Islanders	2-1
	21	Buffalo	1-0
	23	Pittsburgh	5-3
	24	at Buffalo	1-3
	26	Montreal	2-4
	28	at Washington	0-7
	30	Washington	4-3*
Apr.	1	at Ottawa	3-2*
	3	at St. Louis	2-2
	4	at NY Rangers	3-1
	6	Atlanta	3-2
	8	Pittsburgh	4-6

* – Overtime

Entry Draft Selections 2001-1987

2001
Pick
15 Igor Knyazev
46 Michael Zigomanis
91 Kevin Estrada
110 Rob Zepp
181 Daniel Boisclair
211 Sean Curry
244 Carter Trevisani
274 Peter Reynolds

2000
Pick
32 Tomas Kurka
80 Ryan Bayda
97 Niclas Wallin
110 Jared Newman
181 J.D. Forrest
212 Magnus Kahnberg
235 Craig Kowalski
276 Troy Ferguson

1999
Pick
16 David Tanabe
49 Brett Lysak
84 Brad Fast
113 Ryan Murphy
174 Damian Surma
202 Jim Baxter
231 David Evans
237 Antti Jokela
259 Yevgeny Kurilin

1998
Pick
11 Jeff Heerema
70 Kevin Holdridge
71 Erik Cole
91 Josef Vasicek
93 Tommy Westlund
97 Chris Madden
184 Don Smith
208 Jaroslav Svoboda
211 Mark Kosick
239 Brent McDonald

1997
Pick
22 Nikos Tselios
28 Brad DeFauw
80 Francis Lessard
88 Shane Willis
142 Kyle Dafoe
169 Andrew Merrick
195 Niklas Nordgren
199 Randy Fitzgerald
225 Kent McDonell

1996
Pick
34 Trevor Wasyluk
61 Andrei Petrunin
88 Craig MacDonald
104 Steve Wasylko
116 Mark McMahon
143 Aaron Baker
171 Greg Kuznik
197 Kevin Marsh
223 Craig Adams
231 Ashkat Rakhmatullin

1995
Pick
13 Jean-Sebastien Giguere
35 Sergei Fedotov
85 Ian MacNeil
87 Sami Kapanen
113 Hugh Hamilton
165 Byron Ritchie
191 Milan Kostolny
217 Mike Rucinski

1994
Pick
5 Jeff O'Neill
83 Hnat Domenichelli
109 Ryan Risidore
187 Tom Buckley
213 Ashlin Halfnight
230 Matt Ball
239 Brian Regan
265 Steve Nimigon

1993
Pick
2 Chris Pronger
72 Marek Malik
84 Trevor Roenick
115 Nolan Pratt
188 Manny Legace
214 Dmitri Gorenko
240 Wes Swinson
266 Igor Chibirev

1992
Pick
9 Robert Petrovicky
47 Andrei Nikolishin
57 Jan Vopat
79 Kevin Smyth
81 Jason McBain
143 Jarrett Reid
153 Ken Belanger
177 Konstantin Korotkov
201 Greg Zwakman
225 Steven Halko
249 Joacim Esbjors

1991
Pick
9 Patrick Poulin
31 Martin Hamrlik
53 Todd Hall
59 Michael Nylander
75 Jim Storm
119 Mike Harding
141 Brian Mueller
163 Steve Yule
185 Chris Belanger
207 Jason Currie
229 Mike Santonelli
251 Rob Peters

1990
Pick
15 Mark Greig
36 Geoff Sanderson
57 Mike Lenarduzzi
78 Chris Bright
120 Cory Keenan
141 Jergus Baca
162 Martin D'Orsonnens
183 Corey Osmak
204 Espen Knutsen
225 Tommie Eriksen
246 Denis Chalifoux

1989
Pick
10 Bobby Holik
52 Blair Atcheynum
73 Jim McKenzie
94 James Black
115 Jerome Bechard
136 Scott Daniels
157 Raymond Saumier
178 Michel Picard
199 Trevor Buchanan
220 John Battice
241 Peter Kasowski

1988
Pick
11 Chris Govedaris
32 Barry Richter
74 Dean Dyer
95 Scott Morrow
116 Corey Beaulieu
137 Kerry Russell
158 Jim Burke
179 Mark Hirth
200 Wayde Bucsis
221 Rob White
242 Dan Slatalla

1987
Pick
18 Jody Hull
39 Adam Burt
81 Terry Yake
102 Marc Rousseau
123 Jeff St. Cyr
144 Greg Wolf
165 John Moore
186 Joe Day
228 Kevin Sullivan
249 Steve Laurin

Club Directory

Entertainment and Sports Arena

Carolina Hurricanes
1400 Edwards Mill Rd.
Raleigh, NC 27607
Phone **919/467-7825**
FAX 919/462-0123
www.carolinahurricanes.com
Capacity: 18,730

Directory

Owner/Governor . . . . Peter Karmanos, Jr.
Chief Executive Officer/GM . . . . Jim Rutherford
President/Chief Operating Officer . . . . Jim Cain
Vice President/Asst. GM . . . . Jason Karmanos
Chief Financial Officer . . . . Mike Amendola
Executive VP, Business Operations . . . . Doug Piper
Director of Amateur Scouting . . . . Sheldon Ferguson
Head Coach . . . . Paul Maurice
Assistant Coaches . . . . Randy Ladouceur, Kevin McCarthy
Goaltending Advisor . . . . Don Edwards
Strength & Conditioning Coach . . . . Peter Friesen
Team Services Manager . . . . Brian Tatum
Head Athletic Therapist . . . . Peter Friesen
Associate Athletic Trainer . . . . Stu Lempke
Massage Therapist . . . . Dave Duffy
Team Physicians . . . . Jay Stevens, MD; Hadley Callaway, MD; Gabriel Rich, DDS
Equipment Managers . . . . Wally Tatomir, Skip Cunningham, Bob Gorman
Director of Public/Media Relations . . . . Jerry Higgins
Media Relations Manager . . . . Mike Sundheim
Events Coordination for Hockey Ops. . . . . Kelly Kirwin
Director of Administration . . . . Debbie Shannon
Television . . . . Comcast SportsNet, Fox Sports South, Fox-50
Radio Flagship . . . . WRBZ-850 AM
Practice Facility . . . . Reczone
912 Hodges St.
Raleigh, NC 27608

A first-round draft choice in 1994 when the club was still based in Hartford, Jeff O'Neill shattered his previous career best when he scored 41 goals last season. O'Neill also led the team with 67 points.

President and General Manager

RUTHERFORD, JIM
President and General Manager, Carolina Hurricanes.
Born in Beeton, Ont., February 17, 1949.

Jim Rutherford, a former NHL goaltender, is the franchise's seventh general manager and the first general manager of the Carolina Hurricanes. Named to his position on June 28, 1994, Rutherford has taken an aggressive approach towards improving the fortunes of the franchise through trades and the NHL draft.

A veteran of 13 NHL seasons, Rutherford began his professional goaltending career in 1969 as a first-round selection of the Detroit Red Wings. While playing for Detroit, Pittsburgh, Toronto and Los Angeles, Rutherford collected 14 career shutouts. For five seasons he also served as the Red Wings' player representative. Rutherford also played for Team Canada in the IIHF World Championships in Vienna in 1977 and Moscow in 1979.

After his playing days with the Red Wings, Rutherford joined Compuware to serve as the director of hockey operations for Compuware Sports Corporation. Rutherford gained a wealth of experience in youth hockey and junior programs. As a former player, coach, and general manager, his ability to develop players and produce winning programs is widely respected throughout the hockey community.

He started his management career by guiding Compuware Sports Corporation's purchase of the Windsor Spitfires of the Ontario Hockey League in April of 1984. During the next four years, Rutherford acted as general manager of the Spitfires. After the Spitfires advanced to the 1988 Memorial Cup finals, Rutherford led Compuware's efforts to bring the first American-based OHL franchise to Detroit on December 11, 1989. Rutherford was voted the 1987 executive of the year in both the OHL and the Canadian Hockey League and won the OHL executive of the year award again in 1988.

Chicago Blackhawks

2000-01 Results: 29W-40L-8T-5OTL 71PTS. Fourth, Central Division

Although his 34 goals were one less than Tony Amonte, Steve Sullivan's 75 points made him the first player other than Amonte to lead the Blackhawks in scoring since the 1995-96 season.

2001-02 Schedule

Oct.	Thu.	4	at Vancouver		Sun.	30	Anaheim
	Sat.	6	at Calgary		Mon.	31	at Ottawa
	Tue.	9	at Edmonton	**Jan.**	Fri.	4	Tampa Bay
	Thu.	11	Phoenix		Sun.	6	Pittsburgh
	Fri.	12	at Minnesota		Wed.	9	at Colorado
	Sun.	14	Columbus		Thu.	10	Columbus
	Thu.	18	at Nashville		Sat.	12	at Columbus
	Sat.	20	at Dallas		Mon.	14	Edmonton
	Sun.	21	Colorado		Wed.	16	at Florida
	Tue.	23	Calgary		Fri.	18	at Tampa Bay
	Thu.	25	San Jose		Sun.	20	Dallas
	Sun.	28	Boston		Wed.	23	Phoenix
	Tue.	30	Los Angeles		Fri.	25	St. Louis
Nov.	Thu.	1	at Los Angeles		Mon.	28	at Boston
	Fri.	2	at Anaheim		Wed.	30	at New Jersey
	Sun.	4	Detroit	**Feb.**	Wed.	6	at Phoenix
	Tue.	6	Philadelphia		Fri.	8	at San Jose
	Fri.	9	Vancouver		Sat.	9	at Colorado
	Sun.	11	San Jose		Wed.	13	Florida
	Tue.	13	at Vancouver		Tue.	26	at Philadelphia
	Thu.	15	at Calgary		Wed.	27	Montreal
	Fri.	16	at Edmonton	**Mar.**	Sun.	3	Anaheim*
	Wed.	21	at Nashville		Tue.	5	Carolina
	Fri.	23	at Columbus		Thu.	7	NY Rangers
	Sun.	25	at Detroit		Mon.	11	at Los Angeles
	Wed.	28	Vancouver		Tue.	12	at Phoenix
	Fri.	30	Toronto		Fri.	15	at Anaheim
Dec.	Sat.	1	at Toronto		Sat.	16	at San Jose
	Mon.	3	at Montreal		Mon.	18	Dallas
	Wed.	5	Minnesota		Wed.	20	New Jersey
	Fri.	7	NY Islanders		Sun.	24	St. Louis*
	Sun.	9	Los Angeles		Wed.	27	Nashville
	Wed.	12	St. Louis		Fri.	29	at Minnesota
	Fri.	14	at Atlanta		Sun.	31	Minnesota*
	Sat.	15	at Nashville	**Apr.**	Wed.	3	Nashville
	Mon.	17	at Detroit		Fri.	5	at St. Louis
	Wed.	19	at Buffalo		Sun.	7	Calgary
	Fri.	21	Edmonton		Tue.	9	at Washington
	Sun.	23	Detroit		Wed.	10	at Detroit
	Wed.	26	at St. Louis		Fri.	12	at Dallas
	Thu.	27	Colorado		Sun.	14	Columbus*

* Denotes afternoon game.

Franchise date: September 25, 1926

CENTRAL DIVISION

76th NHL Season

Year-by-Year Record

		Home				Road				Overall								
Season	**GP**	**W**	**L**	**T**	**OL**	**W**	**L**	**T**	**OL**	**W**	**L**	**T**	**OL**	**GF**	**GA**	**Pts.**	**Finished**	**Playoff Result**
2000-01	82	14	21	4	2	15	19	4	3	29	40	8	5	210	246	71	4th, Central Div.	Out of Playoffs
1999-2000	82	16	19	5	1	17	18	5	1	33	37	10	2	242	245	78	3rd, Central Div.	Out of Playoffs
1998-99	82	20	17	4	...	9	24	8	...	29	41	12	...	202	248	70	3rd, Central Div.	Out of Playoffs
1997-98	82	14	19	8	...	16	20	5	...	30	39	13	...	192	199	73	5th, Central Div.	Out of Playoffs
1996-97	82	16	21	4	...	18	14	9	...	34	35	13	...	223	210	81	5th, Central Div.	Lost Conf. Quarter-Final
1995-96	82	22	13	6	...	18	15	8	...	40	28	14	...	273	220	94	2nd, Central Div.	Lost Conf. Semi-Final
1994-95	48	11	10	3	...	13	9	2	...	24	19	5	...	156	115	53	3rd, Central Div.	Lost Conf. Championship
1993-94	84	21	16	5	...	18	20	4	...	39	36	9	...	254	240	87	5th, Central Div.	Lost Conf. Quarter-Final
1992-93	84	25	11	6	...	22	14	6	...	47	25	12	...	279	230	106	1st, Norris Div.	Lost Div. Semi-Final
1991-92	80	23	9	8	...	13	20	7	...	36	29	15	...	257	236	87	2nd, Norris Div.	Lost Final
1990-91	80	28	8	4	...	21	15	4	...	49	23	8	...	284	211	106	1st, Norris Div.	Lost Div. Semi-Final
1989-90	80	25	13	2	...	16	20	4	...	41	33	6	...	316	294	88	1st, Norris Div.	Lost Conf. Championship
1988-89	80	16	14	10	...	11	27	2	...	27	41	12	...	297	335	66	4th, Norris Div.	Lost Conf. Championship
1987-88	80	21	17	2	...	9	24	7	...	30	41	9	...	284	328	69	3rd, Norris Div.	Lost Div. Semi-Final
1986-87	80	18	13	9	...	11	24	5	...	29	37	14	...	290	310	72	3rd, Norris Div.	Lost Div. Semi-Final
1985-86	80	23	12	5	...	16	21	3	...	39	33	8	...	351	349	86	1st, Norris Div.	Lost Div. Semi-Final
1984-85	80	22	16	2	...	16	19	5	...	38	35	7	...	309	299	83	2nd, Norris Div.	Lost Conf. Championship
1983-84	80	25	13	2	...	5	29	6	...	30	42	8	...	277	311	68	4th, Norris Div.	Lost Div. Semi-Final
1982-83	80	29	8	3	...	18	15	7	...	47	23	10	...	338	268	104	1st, Norris Div.	Lost Conf. Championship
1981-82	80	20	13	7	...	10	25	5	...	30	38	12	...	332	363	72	4th, Norris Div.	Lost Conf. Championship
1980-81	80	21	11	8	...	10	22	8	...	31	33	16	...	304	315	78	2nd, Smythe Div.	Lost Prelim. Round
1979-80	80	21	12	7	...	13	15	12	...	34	27	19	...	241	250	87	1st, Smythe Div.	Lost Quarter-Final
1978-79	80	18	12	10	...	11	24	5	...	29	36	15	...	244	277	73	1st, Smythe Div.	Lost Quarter-Final
1977-78	80	20	9	11	...	12	20	8	...	32	29	19	...	230	220	83	1st, Smythe Div.	Lost Quarter-Final
1976-77	80	19	16	5	...	7	27	6	...	26	43	11	...	240	298	63	3rd, Smythe Div.	Lost Prelim. Round
1975-76	80	17	15	8	...	15	15	10	...	32	30	18	...	254	261	82	1st, Smythe Div.	Lost Quarter-Final
1974-75	80	24	12	4	...	13	23	4	...	37	35	8	...	268	241	82	3rd, Smythe Div.	Lost Quarter-Final
1973-74	78	20	6	13	...	21	8	10	...	41	14	23	...	272	164	105	2nd, West Div.	Lost Semi-Final
1972-73	78	26	9	4	...	16	18	5	...	42	27	9	...	284	225	93	1st, West Div.	Lost Final
1971-72	78	28	3	8	...	18	14	7	...	46	17	15	...	256	166	107	1st, West Div.	Lost Semi-Final
1970-71	78	30	6	3	...	19	14	6	...	49	20	9	...	277	184	107	1st, West Div.	Lost Final
1969-70	76	26	7	5	...	19	15	4	...	45	22	9	...	250	170	99	1st, East Div.	Lost Semi-Final
1968-69	76	20	14	4	...	14	19	5	...	34	33	9	...	280	246	77	6th, East Div.	Out of Playoffs
1967-68	74	20	13	4	...	12	13	12	...	32	26	16	...	212	222	80	4th, East Div.	Lost Semi-Final
1966-67	70	24	5	6	...	17	12	6	...	41	17	12	...	264	170	94	1st,	Lost Semi-Final
1965-66	70	21	8	6	...	16	17	2	...	37	25	8	...	240	187	82	2nd,	Lost Semi-Final
1964-65	70	20	13	2	...	14	15	6	...	34	28	8	...	224	176	76	3rd,	Lost Final
1963-64	70	26	4	5	...	10	18	7	...	36	22	12	...	218	169	84	2nd,	Lost Semi-Final
1962-63	70	17	9	9	...	15	12	8	...	32	21	17	...	194	178	81	2nd,	Lost Semi-Final
1961-62	70	20	10	5	...	11	16	8	...	31	26	13	...	217	186	75	3rd,	Lost Final
1960-61	**70**	**20**	**6**	**9**	**...**	**9**	**18**	**8**	**...**	**29**	**24**	**17**	**...**	**198**	**180**	**75**	**3rd,**	**Won Stanley Cup**
1959-60	70	18	11	6	...	10	18	7	...	28	29	13	...	191	180	69	3rd,	Lost Semi-Final
1958-59	70	14	12	9	...	14	17	4	...	28	29	13	...	197	208	69	3rd,	Lost Semi-Final
1957-58	70	15	17	3	...	9	22	4	...	24	39	7	...	163	202	55	5th,	Out of Playoffs
1956-57	70	12	15	8	...	4	24	7	...	16	39	15	...	169	225	47	6th,	Out of Playoffs
1955-56	70	9	19	7	...	10	20	5	...	19	39	12	...	155	216	50	6th,	Out of Playoffs
1954-55	70	6	21	8	...	7	19	9	...	13	40	17	...	161	235	43	6th,	Out of Playoffs
1953-54	70	8	21	6	...	4	30	1	...	12	51	7	...	133	242	31	6th,	Out of Playoffs
1952-53	70	14	11	10	...	13	17	5	...	27	28	15	...	169	175	69	4th,	Lost Semi-Final
1951-52	70	9	19	7	...	8	25	2	...	17	44	9	...	158	241	43	6th,	Out of Playoffs
1950-51	70	8	22	5	...	5	25	5	...	13	47	10	...	171	280	36	6th,	Out of Playoffs
1949-50	70	13	18	4	...	9	20	6	...	22	38	10	...	203	244	54	6th,	Out of Playoffs
1948-49	60	13	12	5	...	8	19	3	...	21	31	8	...	173	211	50	5th,	Out of Playoffs
1947-48	60	10	17	3	...	10	17	3	...	20	34	6	...	195	225	46	6th,	Out of Playoffs
1946-47	60	10	17	3	...	9	20	1	...	19	37	4	...	193	274	42	6th,	Out of Playoffs
1945-46	50	15	5	5	...	8	15	2	...	23	20	7	...	200	178	53	3rd,	Lost Semi-Final
1944-45	50	9	14	2	...	4	16	5	...	13	30	7	...	141	194	33	5th,	Out of Playoffs
1943-44	50	15	6	4	...	7	17	1	...	22	23	5	...	178	187	49	4th,	Lost Final
1942-43	50	14	3	8	...	3	15	7	...	17	18	15	...	179	180	49	5th,	Out of Playoffs
1941-42	48	15	8	1	...	7	15	2	...	22	23	3	...	145	155	47	4th,	Lost Quarter-Final
1940-41	48	11	10	3	...	5	15	4	...	16	25	7	...	112	139	39	5th,	Lost Semi-Final
1939-40	48	15	7	2	...	8	12	4	...	23	19	6	...	112	120	52	4th,	Lost Quarter-Final
1938-39	48	5	13	6	...	7	15	2	...	12	28	8	...	91	132	32	7th,	Out of Playoffs
1937-38	**48**	**10**	**10**	**4**	**...**	**4**	**15**	**5**	**...**	**14**	**25**	**9**	**...**	**97**	**139**	**37**	**3rd, Amn. Div.**	**Won Stanley Cup**
1936-37	48	8	13	3	...	6	14	4	...	14	27	7	...	99	131	35	4th, Amn. Div.	Out of Playoffs
1935-36	48	15	7	2	...	6	12	6	...	21	19	8	...	93	92	50	3rd, Amn. Div.	Lost Quarter-Final
1934-35	48	12	9	3	...	14	8	2	...	26	17	5	...	118	88	57	2nd, Amn. Div.	Lost Quarter-Final
1933-34	**48**	**13**	**4**	**7**	**...**	**7**	**13**	**4**	**...**	**20**	**17**	**11**	**...**	**88**	**83**	**51**	**2nd, Amn. Div.**	**Won Stanley Cup**
1932-33	48	12	7	5	...	4	13	7	...	16	20	12	...	88	101	44	4th, Amn. Div.	Out of Playoffs
1931-32	48	13	5	6	...	5	14	5	...	18	19	11	...	86	101	47	2nd, Amn. Div.	Lost Quarter-Final
1930-31	44	13	8	1	...	11	9	2	...	24	17	3	...	108	78	51	2nd, Amn. Div.	Lost Final
1929-30	44	12	9	1	...	9	9	4	...	21	18	5	...	117	111	47	2nd, Amn. Div.	Lost Quarter-Final
1928-29	44	3	13	6	...	4	16	2	...	7	29	8	...	33	85	22	5th, Amn. Div.	Out of Playoffs
1927-28	44	2	18	2	...	5	16	1	...	7	34	3	...	68	134	17	5th, Amn. Div.	Out of Playoffs
1926-27	44	12	8	2	...	7	14	1	...	19	22	3	...	115	116	41	3rd, Amn. Div.	Lost Quarter-Final

2001-02 Player Personnel

FORWARDS	HT	WT	S	Place of Birth	Date	2000-01 Club
AMONTE, Tony	6-0	200	L	Hingham, MA	8/2/70	Chicago
BAINES, Ajay	5-10	178	L	Kamloops, B.C.	3/25/78	Norfolk
BELL, Mark	6-3	198	L	St. Paul's, Ont.	8/5/80	Chicago-Norfolk
CALDER, Kyle	5-11	180	L	Mannville, Alta.	1/5/79	Chicago-Norfolk
DAZE, Eric	6-6	234	L	Montreal, Que.	7/2/75	Chicago
DOWNEY, Aaron	6-1	216	R	Shelburne, Ont.	8/27/74	Chicago-Norfolk
DUBINSKY, Steve	6-0	190	L	Montreal, Que.	7/9/70	Chicago-Norfolk
HANKINSON, Casey	6-1	187	L	Edina, MN	5/8/76	Chicago-Norfolk
JONES, Ty	6-3	218	R	Richland, WA	2/22/79	Norfolk
KOROLEV, Igor	6-1	190	L	Moscow, USSR	9/6/70	Toronto
LEROUX, Jean-Yves	6-2	211	L	Montreal, Que.	6/24/76	Chicago
MARHA, Josef	6-0	176	L	Havlickuv, Czech.	6/2/76	Chicago-Norfolk
NYLANDER, Michael	6-1	195	L	Stockholm, Sweden	10/3/72	Chicago
PELUSO, Mike	6-1	208	R	Bismark, ND	9/2/74	Portland (AHL)-Worcester
PERROTT, Nathan	6-0	215	R	Owen Sound, Ont.	12/8/76	Norfolk
PROBERT, Bob	6-3	225	L	Windsor, Ont.	6/5/65	Chicago
RHEAUME, Pascal	6-1	209	L	Quebec, Que.	6/21/73	St. Louis-Worcester
RUUTU, Tuomo	6-0	201	L	Vantaa, Finland	2/16/83	HIFK Helsinki-Jokerit Helsinki
SOUZA, Mike	6-1	210	L	Melrose, MA	1/28/78	Norfolk
SULLIVAN, Steve	5-9	160	R	Timmins, Ont.	7/6/74	Chicago
THOMAS, Steve	5-10	185	L	Stockport, England	7/15/63	Toronto
VANDENBUSSCHE, Ryan	6-0	200	R	Simcoe, Ont.	2/28/73	Chicago
VON ARX, Reto	5-10	190	L	Egerkingen, Switz.	9/13/76	Chicago-Norfolk
VOROBIEV, Pavel	6-0	183	L	Karaganda, USSR	5/5/82	HC Yaroslavl
YAKOUBOV, Mikhail	6-3	208	L	Barnaul, USSR	2/16/82	Lada Togliatti
ZELEPUKIN, Valeri	6-1	200	L	Voskresensk, USSR	9/17/68	Chicago-Norfolk
ZHAMNOV, Alexei	6-1	200	L	Moscow, USSR	10/1/70	Chicago
DEFENSEMEN						
ALLISON, Jamie	6-1	200	L	Lindsay, Ont.	5/13/75	Chicago
BAUMGARTNER, Nolan	6-2	205	R	Calgary, Alta.	3/23/76	Chicago-Norfolk
DEAN, Kevin	6-3	210	L	Madison, WI	4/1/69	Chicago
KARPOVTSEV, Alexander	6-3	215	R	Moscow, USSR	4/7/70	Dynamo Moscow-Chicago
KLEMM, Jon	6-2	200	R	Cranbrook, B.C.	1/8/70	Colorado
McALPINE, Chris	6-0	210	R	Roseville, MN	12/1/71	Chicago-Norfolk
McCARTHY, Steve	6-0	197	L	Trail, B.C.	2/3/81	Chicago-Norfolk
MIRONOV, Boris	6-3	223	R	Moscow, USSR	3/21/72	Chicago
POAPST, Steve	6-0	200	L	Cornwall, Ont.	1/3/69	Chicago-Norfolk
SPACEK, Jaroslav	5-11	198	L	Rokycany, Czech.	2/11/74	Florida-Chicago
TOLKUNOV, Dmitri	6-2	200	R	Kiev, USSR	5/5/79	Norfolk
WILFORD, Marty	6-1	216	L	Cobourg, Ont.	4/17/77	Norfolk

GOALTENDERS	HT	WT	C	Place of Birth	Date	2000-01 Club
ANDERSSON, Craig	6-2	174	L	Park Ridge, IL	5/21/81	Guelph
LEIGHTON, Michael	6-2	175	L	Petrolia, Ont.	5/19/81	Windsor
MUNRO, Adam	6-1	194	L	St. George, Ont.	11/12/82	Erie
PASSMORE, Steve	5-9	165	L	Thunder Bay, Ont.	1/29/73	L.A.-Lowell (AHL)-Chi-Chicago (IHL)
THIBAULT, Jocelyn	5-11	170	L	Montreal, Que.	1/12/75	Chicago

Captains' History

Dick Irvin, 1926-27 to 1928-29; Duke Dukowski, 1929-30; Ty Arbour, 1930-31; Cy Wentworth, 1931-32; Helge Bostrom, 1932-33; Chuck Gardiner, 1933-34; no captain, 1934-35; Johnny Gottselig, 1935-36 to 1939-40; Earl Seibert, 1940-41, 1941-42; Doug Bentley, 1942-43, 1943-44; Clint Smith 1944-45; John Mariucci, 1945-46; Red Hamill, 1946-47; John Mariucci, 1947-48; Gaye Stewart, 1948-49; Doug Bentley, 1949-50; Jack Stewart, 1950-51, 1951-52; Bill Gadsby, 1952-53, 1953-54; Gus Mortson, 1954-55 to 1956-57; no captain, 1957-58; Ed Litzenberger, 1958-59 to 1960-61; Pierre Pilote, 1961-62 to 1967-68, no captain, 1968-69; Pat Stapleton, 1969-70; no captain, 1970-71 to 1974-75; Stan Mikita and Pit Martin, 1975-76; Stan Mikita, Pit Martin and Keith Magnuson, 1976-77; Keith Magnuson, 1977-78, 1978-79; Keith Magnuson and Terry Ruskowski, 1979-80; Terry Ruskowski, 1980-81, 1981-82; Darryl Sutter, 1982-83 to 1984-85; Darryl Sutter and Bob Murray, 1985-86; Darryl Sutter, 1986-87; no captain, 1987-88; Denis Savard and Dirk Graham, 1988-89; Dirk Graham, 1989-90 to 1994-95; Chris Chelios, 1995-96 to 1998-99; Doug Gilmour, 1999-2000; Tony Amonte, 2000-01 to date.

2000-01 Scoring

* - rookie

Regular Season

Pos	#	Player	Team	GP	G	A	Pts	+/–	PIM	PP	SH	GW	GT	S	%
C	26	Steve Sullivan	CHI	81	34	41	75	3	54	6	8	3	1	204	16.7
R	10	Tony Amonte	CHI	82	35	29	64	–22	54	9	1	3	1	256	13.7
C	92	Michael Nylander	CHI	82	25	39	64	7	32	4	0	5	0	176	14.2
L	55	Eric Daze	CHI	79	33	24	57	1	16	9	1	8	2	205	16.1
C	13	Alexei Zhamnov	CHI	63	13	36	49	–12	40	3	1	3	0	117	11.1
D	3	Jaroslav Spacek	FLA	12	2	1	3	–4	8	1	0	0	0	21	9.5
			CHI	50	5	18	23	7	20	2	0	1	0	85	5.9
			TOTAL	62	7	19	26	3	28	3	0	1	0	106	6.6
L	36	Chris Herperger	CHI	61	10	15	25	0	20	0	1	3	0	76	13.2
D	2	Boris Mironov	CHI	66	5	17	22	–14	42	3	0	0	0	143	3.5
L	24	Bob Probert	CHI	79	7	12	19	–13	103	1	0	0	1	45	15.6
D	4	Stephane Quintal	CHI	72	1	18	19	–9	60	0	0	0	0	109	0.9
C	22 *	Kyle Calder	CHI	43	5	10	15	–4	14	0	0	1	0	63	7.9
D	25	Alexander Karpovtsev	CHI	53	2	13	15	–4	39	1	0	0	0	52	3.8
D	6	Kevin Dean	CHI	69	0	11	11	–16	30	0	0	0	0	75	0.0
R	16	Steve Dubinsky	CHI	60	6	4	10	–4	33	0	1	0	0	70	8.6
L	23	Jean-Yves Leroux	CHI	59	4	4	8	–9	22	1	0	0	0	60	6.7
R	29	Valeri Zelepukin	CHI	36	3	4	7	–14	18	0	2	0	0	38	7.9
R	14	Ryan Vandenbussche	CHI	64	2	5	7	–8	146	0	0	0	0	24	8.3
D	39	Chris McAlpine	CHI	50	0	6	6	5	32	0	0	0	0	61	0.0
D	42	Steve Poapst	CHI	36	2	3	5	3	12	0	0	0	0	27	7.4
D	5 *	Steve McCarthy	CHI	44	0	5	5	–7	8	0	0	0	0	32	0.0
L	17 *	Reto Von Arx	CHI	19	3	1	4	–4	4	0	0	1	0	12	25.0
D	33	Jamie Allison	CHI	44	1	3	4	7	53	0	0	0	0	16	6.3
R	15	Blair Atcheynum	CHI	19	1	2	3	–7	2	0	0	0	0	18	5.6
C	11	Josef Marha	CHI	15	0	3	3	–4	6	0	0	0	0	17	0.0
G	41	Jocelyn Thibault	CHI	66	0	3	3	0	2	0	0	0	0	0	0.0
L	25	Kris King	CHI	13	1	0	1	–3	8	0	0	0	0	12	8.3
L	40 *	Casey Hankinson	CHI	11	0	1	1	–3	9	0	0	0	0	15	0.0
L	28 *	Mark Bell	CHI	13	0	1	1	0	4	0	0	0	0	14	0.0
G	30 *	Michel Larocque	CHI	3	0	0	0	0	0	0	0	0	0	0	0.0
R	49	Aaron Downey	CHI	3	0	0	0	–1	6	0	0	0	0	2	0.0
D	38 *	Nolan Baumgartner	CHI	8	0	0	0	–4	6	0	0	0	0	7	0.0
G	32	Robbie Tallas	CHI	12	0	0	0	0	0	0	0	0	0	0	0.0
G	37	Steve Passmore	L.A.	14	0	0	0	0	0	0	0	0	0	0	0.0
			CHI	6	0	0	0	0	4	0	0	0	0	0	0.0
			TOTAL	20	0	0	0	0	4	0	0	0	0	0	0.0
C	36	Mark Janssens	CHI	28	0	0	0	–8	33	0	0	0	0	15	0.0

Goaltending

No.	Goaltender	GPI	Mins	Avg	W	L	T	EN	SO	GA	SA	S%
37	Steve Passmore	6	340	2.47	0	4	1	0	0	14	147	.905
41	Jocelyn Thibault	66	3844	2.81	27	32	7	7	6	180	1711	.895
32	Robbie Tallas	12	627	3.35	2	7	0	1	0	35	265	.868
30	* Michel Larocque	3	152	3.55	0	2	0	0	0	9	59	.847
	Totals	**82**	**4981**	**2.96**	**29**	**45**	**8**	**8**	**6**	**246**	**2190**	**.888**

Coach

SUTTER, BRIAN

Coach, Chicago Blackhawks. Born in Viking, Alta., October 7, 1956.

Brian Sutter was hired as the head coach in Chicago on May 3, 2001. He is the second member of this storied family to have coached the Blackhawks (Darryl Sutter was the head coach of the Blackhawks from 1992 to 1995). The Sutter name has always been synonymous with intensity, honesty, tenacity, and hard work.

Following a 12-year playing career with the St. Louis Blues from 1976 to 1988, Sutter immediately joined the NHL coaching ranks by taking over the reigns of the team he had captained for nine of his 12 seasons. He spent four seasons as the coach of the Blues, posting a mark of 153-124-43 which then exceeded Scotty Bowman's club record for coaching victories. Sutter captured the Jack Adams Award as coach of the year in 1990-91.

Sutter became the head coach of the Boston Bruins in the 1992-93 season and immediately led the club to its first 50-win season in ten years. In his three seasons as the Bruins' chief mentor, Sutter had a coaching record of 120-73-23 for a .609 winning percentage. After leaving the coaching ranks for two seasons, Sutter returned behind the bench in his native province of Alberta as the head coach of the Calgary Flames for the 1997-98 season. He coached the Flames for three seasons.

As a player, Sutter was drafted by the St. Louis Blues with their second pick, 20th overall, in the 1976 Entry Draft. He wound up playing his entire 12-year NHL career with the Blues. A three time NHL All-Star Game selection, Sutter played 779 games and had 303 goals and 333 assists for 636 points. A great leader and an outstanding performer on the ice, Sutter's #11 was retired by the Blues on December 30, 1988.

Coaching Record

		Regular Season				Playoffs		
Season	Team	Games	W	L	T	Games	W	L
1988-89	St. Louis (NHL)	80	33	35	12	10	5	5
1989-90	St. Louis (NHL)	80	37	34	9	12	7	5
1990-91	St. Louis (NHL)	80	47	22	11	13	6	7
1991-92	St. Louis (NHL)	80	36	33	11	6	2	4
1992-93	Boston (NHL)	84	51	26	7	4	0	4
1993-94	Boston (NHL)	84	42	29	13	13	6	7
1994-95	Boston (NHL)	48	27	18	3	5	1	4
1997-98	Calgary (NHL)	82	26	41	15	....	....	....
1998-99	Calgary (NHL)	82	30	40	12	....	....	....
1999-2000	Calgary (NHL)	82	31	41	10	....	....	....
	NHL Totals	782	360	319	103	63	27	36

Club Records

Team

(Figures in brackets for season records are games played; records for fewest points, wins, ties, losses, goals, goals against are for 70 or more games)

Most Points	107	1970-71 (78), 1971-72 (78)
Most Wins	49	1970-71 (78), 1990-91 (80)
Most Ties	23	1973-74 (78)
Most Losses	51	1953-54 (70)
Most Goals	351	1985-86 (80)
Most Goals Against	363	1981-82 (80)
Fewest Points	31	1953-54 (70)
Fewest Wins	12	1953-54 (70)
Fewest Ties	6	1989-90 (80)
Fewest Losses	14	1973-74 (78)
Fewest Goals	*133	1953-54 (70)
Fewest Goals Against	164	1973-74 (78)
Longest Winning Streak		
Overall	8	Dec. 9-26/71, Jan. 4-21/81
Home	13	Nov. 11-Dec. 20/70
Away	7	Dec. 9-29/64
Longest Undefeated Streak		
Overall	15	Jan. 14-Feb. 16/67 (12 wins, 3 ties)
Home	18	Oct. 11-Dec. 20/70 (16 wins, 2 ties)
Away	12	Nov. 2-Dec. 16/67 (6 wins, 6 ties)
Longest Losing Streak		
Overall	13	Feb. 25-Oct. 11/51
Home	11	Feb. 8-Nov. 22/28
Away	17	Jan. 2-Oct. 7/54
Longest Winless Streak		
Overall	21	Dec. 17/50-Jan. 28/51 (18 losses, 3 ties)
Home	15	Dec. 16/28-Feb. 28/29 (11 losses, 4 ties)
Away	23	Dec. 19/50-Oct. 11/51 (21 losses, 2 ties)
Most Shutouts, Season	15	1969-70 (76)
Most PIM, Season	2,663	1991-92 (80)
Most Goals, Game	12	Jan. 30/69 (Chi. 12 at Phi. 0)

Individual

Most Seasons	22	Stan Mikita
Most Games	1,394	Stan Mikita
Most Goals, Career	604	Bobby Hull
Most Assists, Career	926	Stan Mikita
Most Points, Career	1,467	Stan Mikita (541G, 926A)
Most PIM, Career	1,495	Chris Chelios
Most Shutouts, Career	74	Tony Esposito
Longest Consecutive Games Streak	884	Steve Larmer (Oct. 6/82-Apr. 15/93)
Most Goals, Season	58	Bobby Hull (1968-69)
Most Assists, Season	87	Denis Savard (1981-82, 1987-88)
Most Points, Season	131	Denis Savard (1987-88; 44G, 87A)
Most PIM, Season	408	Mike Peluso (1991-92)
Most Points, Defenseman, Season	85	Doug Wilson (1981-82; 39G, 46A)
Most Points, Center, Season	131	Denis Savard (1987-88; 44G, 87A)
Most Points, Right Wing, Season	101	Steve Larmer (1990-91; 44G, 57A)
Most Points, Left Wing, Season	107	Bobby Hull (1968-69; 58G, 49A)
Most Points, Rookie, Season	90	Steve Larmer (1982-83; 43G, 47A)
Most Shutouts, Season	15	Tony Esposito (1969-70)
Most Goals, Game	5	Grant Mulvey (Feb. 3/82)
Most Assists, Game	6	Pat Stapleton (Mar. 30/69)
Most Points, Game	7	Max Bentley (Jan. 28/43; 4G, 3A), Grant Mulvey (Feb. 3/82; 5G, 2A)

* NHL Record.

Retired Numbers

1	Glenn Hall	1957-1967
9	Bobby Hull	1957-1972
18	Denis Savard	1980-1990, 1995-1997
21	Stan Mikita	1958-1980
35	Tony Esposito	1969-1984

All-time Record vs. Other Clubs

Regular Season

	At Home								On Road								Total							
	GP	W	L	T	OL	GF	GA	PTS	GP	W	L	T	OL	GF	GA	PTS	GP	W	L	T	OL	GF	GA	PTS
Anaheim	18	9	7	2	0	52	42	20	16	7	8	1	0	36	39	15	34	16	15	3	0	88	81	35
Atlanta	1	1	0	0	0	1	0	2	2	1	1	0	0	5	6	2	3	2	1	0	0	6	6	4
Boston	283	145	94	44	0	913	758	334	282	88	160	34	0	804	1020	210	565	233	254	78	0	1717	1778	544
Buffalo	49	26	16	6	1	159	136	59	51	13	32	6	0	131	193	32	100	39	48	12	1	290	329	91
Calgary	55	23	19	13	0	180	160	59	57	20	25	11	1	177	185	52	112	43	44	24	1	357	345	111
Carolina	27	16	8	3	0	114	78	35	29	12	14	3	0	90	94	27	56	28	22	6	0	204	172	62
Colorado	35	19	13	3	0	124	110	41	33	11	17	5	0	115	133	27	68	30	30	8	0	239	243	68
Columbus	2	2	0	0	0	7	1	4	3	2	0	0	1	11	8	5	5	4	0	0	1	18	9	9
Dallas	104	63	28	13	0	406	272	139	106	44	47	15	0	328	355	103	210	107	75	28	0	734	627	242
Detroit	330	150	129	51	0	989	927	351	327	97	199	31	0	814	1122	225	657	247	328	82	0	1803	2049	576
Edmonton	38	19	13	6	0	149	134	44	39	17	17	5	0	138	144	39	77	36	30	11	0	287	278	83
Florida	7	3	3	1	0	23	23	7	6	4	2	0	0	25	16	8	13	7	5	1	0	48	39	15
Los Angeles	69	32	28	9	0	246	207	73	68	30	30	8	0	235	232	68	137	62	58	17	0	481	439	141
Minnesota	2	0	2	0	0	4	9	0	2	1	1	0	0	3	4	2	4	1	3	0	0	7	13	2
Montreal	272	93	124	55	0	729	758	241	273	53	171	48	1	643	1055	155	545	146	295	103	1	1372	1813	396
Nashville	9	4	3	1	1	25	26	10	8	4	3	1	0	20	20	9	17	8	6	2	1	45	46	19
New Jersey	44	24	11	9	0	173	122	57	44	16	17	11	0	136	133	43	88	40	28	20	0	309	255	100
NY Islanders	46	25	16	5	0	156	150	55	45	13	17	15	0	136	156	41	91	38	33	20	0	292	306	96
NY Rangers	284	127	115	42	0	863	789	296	284	112	117	55	0	803	838	279	568	239	232	97	0	1666	1627	575
Ottawa	7	3	2	2	0	17	18	8	8	5	3	0	0	24	21	10	15	8	5	2	0	41	39	18
Philadelphia	58	25	14	19	0	203	167	69	59	16	32	11	0	155	191	43	117	41	46	30	0	358	358	112
Phoenix	42	25	10	7	0	175	118	57	44	15	25	4	0	137	153	34	86	40	35	11	0	312	271	91
Pittsburgh	57	38	10	9	0	233	155	85	57	23	27	7	0	187	204	53	114	61	37	16	0	420	359	138
St. Louis	110	61	34	15	0	413	332	137	107	37	53	17	0	330	360	91	217	98	87	32	0	743	692	228
San Jose	19	9	7	2	1	59	60	21	20	9	10	0	1	55	55	19	39	18	17	2	2	114	115	40
Tampa Bay	11	6	3	2	0	37	29	14	9	3	4	2	0	23	22	8	20	9	7	4	0	60	51	22
Toronto	316	156	118	42	0	966	826	354	313	96	163	54	0	816	1066	246	629	252	281	96	0	1782	1892	600
Vancouver	65	44	15	6	0	249	147	94	66	21	30	15	0	195	198	57	131	65	45	21	0	444	345	151
Washington	38	22	11	5	0	149	114	49	39	14	20	5	0	122	139	33	77	36	31	10	0	271	253	82
Defunct Clubs	139	79	40	20	0	408	268	178	140	52	67	21	0	316	346	125	279	131	107	41	0	724	614	303
Totals	**2537**	**1249**	**893**	**392**	**3**	**8222**	**6936**	**2893**	**2537**	**836**	**1312**	**385**	**4**	**7010**	**8508**	**2061**	**5074**	**2085**	**2205**	**777**	**7**	**15232**	**15444**	**4954**

Playoffs

	Series	W	L	GP	W	L	T	GF	GA	Last Mtg.	Round	Result
Boston	6	1	5	22	5	16	1	63	97	1978	QF	L 0-4
Buffalo	2	0	2	9	1	8	0	17	36	1980	QF	L 0-4
Calgary	3	1	2	12	5	7	0	33	37	1996	CQF	W 4-0
Colorado	2	0	2	12	4	8	0	28	49	1997	CQF	L 2-4
Dallas	6	4	2	33	19	14	0	120	118	1991	DSF	L 2-4
Detroit	14	8	6	69	38	31	0	210	190	1995	CF	L 1-4
Edmonton	4	1	3	20	8	12	0	77	102	1992	CF	W 4-0
Los Angeles	1	1	0	5	4	1	0	10	7	1974	QF	W 4-1
Montreal	17	5	12	81	29	50	2	185	261	1976	QF	L 0-4
NY Islanders	2	0	2	6	0	6	0	6	21	1979	QF	L 0-4
NY Rangers	5	4	1	24	14	10	0	66	54	1973	SF	W 4-1
Philadelphia	1	1	0	4	4	0	0	20	8	1971	QF	W 4-0
Pittsburgh	2	1	1	8	4	4	0	24	23	1992	F	L 0-4
St. Louis	9	7	2	45	27	18	0	166	129	1993	DSF	L 0-4
Toronto	9	3	6	38	15	22	1	89	111	1995	CQF	W 4-3
Vancouver	2	1	1	9	5	4	0	24	24	1995	CSF	W 4-0
Defunct Clubs	4	2	2	9	5	3	1	16	15			
Totals	**89**	**40**	**49**	**406**	**187**	**214**	**5**	**1154**	**1282**			

Calgary totals include Atlanta Flames, 1972-73 to 1979-80. Carolina totals include Hartford, 1979-80 to 1996-97.
Colorado totals include Quebec, 1979-80 to 1994-95. Dallas totals include Minnesota North Stars, 1967-68 to 1992-93.
New Jersey totals include Kansas City, 1974-75 to 1975-76, and Colorado Rockies, 1976-77 to 1981-82.
Phoenix totals include Winnipeg, 1979-80 to 1995-96.

Playoff Results 2001-1997

Year	Round	Opponent	Result	GF	GA
1997	CQF	Colorado	L 2-4	14	28

Abbreviations: Round: F – Final; **CF** – conference final; **CSF** – conference semi-final; **CQF** – conference quarter final; **DSF** division semi-final; **SF** – semi-final; **QF** – quarter-final.

2000-01 Results

Month	Date	Opponent	Score
Oct.	5	at Buffalo	2-4
	7	at Columbus	5-3
	12	Detroit	0-4
	14	at Montreal	4-5*
	15	Columbus	2-1
	18	NY Rangers	2-4
	20	Dallas	1-5
	21	at St. Louis	0-1
	26	Colorado	0-2
	28	Buffalo	1-3
	29	at Minnesota	3-2
Nov.	2	at Boston	4-5
	3	at Detroit	6-1
	5	Anaheim	4-2
	8	San Jose	2-3*
	10	Minnesota	2-5
	11	at Toronto	3-3
	14	at Vancouver	2-4
	16	at Calgary	5-2
	17	at Edmonton	3-3
	21	at Phoenix	4-1
	22	at San Jose	1-4
	24	at Minnesota	0-2
	27	at Detroit	6-5*
	30	Nashville	0-3
Dec.	1	at Nashville	2-1
	3	Columbus	5-0
	7	Minnesota	2-4
	9	at St. Louis	4-6
	10	St. Louis	1-6
	13	at Atlanta	1-3
	15	at Dallas	1-4
	16	at Nashville	3-0
	21	Vancouver	6-4
	23	at Ottawa	3-2
	27	Phoenix	1-1
	29	Detroit	3-2*
	31	at Carolina	1-2
Jan.	3	Vancouver	6-0
	5	Edmonton	1-2
	7	Tampa Bay	7-4
	9	at NY Islanders	6-3
	12	at Columbus	3-1
	14	Colorado	2-2
	17	Florida	5-0
	19	Washington	3-1
	21	Pittsburgh	0-4
	25	Philadelphia	1-5
	26	at Colorado	2-5
	28	at Vancouver	6-2
	31	at Edmonton	2-3
Feb.	1	at Calgary	3-5
	6	at Los Angeles	3-3
	7	at Anaheim	3-2
	10	at San Jose	2-3*
	11	at Phoenix	2-3
	14	San Jose	0-7
	16	St. Louis	6-2
	18	Los Angeles	3-0
	19	at NY Rangers	2-4
	21	Detroit	3-7
	23	Atlanta	1-0
	25	Toronto	6-4
	27	at Washington	3-2
Mar.	1	Los Angeles	2-2
	4	Carolina	3-6
	7	at Dallas	4-1
	9	at Anaheim	1-3
	10	at Los Angeles	2-2
	13	Dallas	0-3
	15	Nashville	3-2
	18	Anaheim	1-4
	22	Nashville	1-2*
	24	at St. Louis	1-5
	25	Calgary	1-3
	28	Ottawa	2-5
	29	at Pittsburgh	2-5
Apr.	1	Edmonton	3-3
	2	at New Jersey	3-4
	4	Calgary	2-5
	6	Toronto	0-1
	8	at Columbus	3-4*

* – Overtime

Entry Draft Selections 2001-1987

2001

Pick	
9	Tuomo Ruutu
29	Adam Munro
59	Matt Keith
73	Craig Andersson
104	Brent MacLellan
115	Vladimir Gusev
119	Alexei Zotkin
142	Tommi Jaminki
174	Alexander Golovin
186	Petr Puncochar
205	Teemu Jaaskelainen
216	Oleg Minakov
268	Jeff Miles

2000

Pick	
10	Mikhail Yakoubov
11	Pavel Vorobiev
49	Jonas Nordqvist
74	Igor Radulov
106	Scott Balan
117	Olli Malmivaara
151	Alexander Barkunov
177	Michael Ayers
193	Joey Martin
207	Cliff Loya
225	Vladislav Luchkin
240	Adam Berkhoel
262	Peter Flache
271	Reto Von Arx
291	Arne Ramholt

1999

Pick	
23	Steve McCarthy
46	Dimitri Levinski
63	Stepan Mokhov
134	Michael Jacobsen
165	Michael Leighton
194	Mattias Wennerberg
195	Yorick Treille
223	Andrew Carver

1998

Pick	
8	Mark Bell
94	Matthias Trattnig
156	Kent Huskins
158	Jari Viuhkola
166	Jonathan Pelletier
183	Tyler Arnason
210	Sean Griffin
238	Alexandre Couture
240	Andrei Yershov

1997

Pick	
13	Daniel Cleary
16	Ty Jones
39	Jeremy Reich
67	Mike Souza
110	Benjamin Simon
120	Peter Gardiner
130	Kyle Calder
147	Heath Gordon
174	Jerad Smith
204	Sergei Shikhanov
230	Chris Feil

1996

Pick	
31	Remi Royer
42	Jeff Paul
46	Geoff Peters
130	Andy Johnson
184	Mike Vellinga
210	Chris Twerdun
236	Andrei Kozyrev

1995

Pick	
19	Dmitri Nabokov
45	Christian Laflamme
71	Kevin McKay
82	Chris Van Dyk
97	Pavel Kriz
146	Marc Magliarditi
149	Marty Wilford
175	Steve Tardif
201	Casey Hankinson
227	Mike Pittman

1994

Pick	
14	Ethan Moreau
40	Jean-Yves Leroux
85	Steve McLaren
118	Marc Dupuis
144	Jim Enson
170	Tyler Prosofsky
196	Mike Josephson
222	Lubomir Jandera
248	Lars Weibel
263	Rob Mara

1993

Pick	
24	Eric Lecompte
50	Eric Manlow
54	Bogdan Savenko
76	Ryan Huska
90	Eric Daze
102	Patrik Pysz
128	Jonni Vauhkonen
180	Tom White
206	Sergei Petrov
232	Mike Rusk
258	Mike McGhan
284	Tom Noble

1992

Pick	
12	Sergei Krivokrasov
36	Jeff Shantz
41	Sergei Klimovich
89	Andy MacIntyre
113	Tim Hogan
137	Gerry Skrypec
161	Mike Prokopec
185	Layne Roland
209	David Hymovitz
233	Richard Raymond

1991

Pick	
22	Dean McAmmond
39	Michael Pomichter
44	Jamie Matthews
66	Bobby House
71	Igor Kravchuk
88	Zac Boyer
110	Maco Balkovec
112	Kevin St. Jacques
132	Jacques Auger
154	Scott Kirton
176	Roch Belley
198	Scott MacDonald
220	Alexander Andrievski
242	Mike Larkin
264	Scott Dean

1990

Pick	
16	Karl Dykhuis
37	Ivan Droppa
79	Chris Tucker
121	Brett Stickney
124	Derek Edgerly
163	Hugo Belanger
184	Owen Lessard
205	Erik Peterson
226	Steve Dubinsky
247	Dino Grossi

1989

Pick	
6	Adam Bennett
27	Michael Speer
48	Bob Kellogg
111	Tommi Pullola
132	Tracy Egeland
153	Milan Tichy
174	Jason Greyerbiehl
195	Matt Saunders
216	Mike Kozak
237	Michael Doneghey

1988

Pick	
8	Jeremy Roenick
50	Trevor Dam
71	Stefan Elvenas
92	Joe Cleary
113	Justin Lafayette
134	Craig Woodcroft
155	Jon Pojar
176	Mathew Hentges
197	Daniel Maurice
218	Dirk Tenzer
239	Andreas Lupzig

1987

Pick	
8	Jimmy Waite
29	Ryan McGill
50	Cam Russell
60	Mike Dagenais
92	Ulf Sandstrom
113	Mike McCormick
134	Stephen Tepper
155	John Reilly
176	Lance Werness
197	Dale Marquette
218	Bill Lacouture
239	Mike Lappin

Coaching History

Pete Muldoon, 1926-27; Barney Stanley and Hugh Lehman, 1927-28; Herb Gardiner and Dick Irvin, 1928-29; Tom Shaughnessy and Bill Tobin, 1929-30; Dick Irvin, 1930-31; Bill Tobin, 1931-32; Emil Iverson, Godfrey Matheson and Tommy Gorman, 1932-33; Tommy Gorman, 1933-34; Clem Loughlin, 1934-35 to 1936-37; Bill Stewart, 1937-38; Bill Stewart and Paul Thompson, 1938-39; Paul Thompson, 1939-40 to 1943-44; Paul Thompson and Johnny Gottselig, 1944-45; Johnny Gottselig, 1945-46, 1946-47; Johnny Gottselig and Charlie Conacher, 1947-48; Charlie Conacher, 1948-49, 1949-50; Ebbie Goodfellow, 1950-51, 1951-52; Sid Abel, 1952-53, 1953-54; Frank Eddolls, 1954-55; Dick Irvin, 1955-56; Tommy Ivan, 1956-57; Tommy Ivan and Rudy Pilous, 1957-58; Rudy Pilous, 1958-59 to 1962-63; Billy Reay, 1963-64 to 1975-76; Billy Reay and Bill White, 1976-77; Bob Pulford, 1977-78, 1978-79; Eddie Johnston, 1979-80; Keith Magnuson, 1980-81; Keith Magnuson and Bob Pulford, 1981-82; Orval Tessier, 1982-83, 1983-84; Orval Tessier and Bob Pulford, 1984-85; Bob Pulford, 1985-86, 1986-87; Bob Murdoch, 1987-88; Mike Keenan, 1988-89 to 1991-92; Darryl Sutter, 1992-93 to 1994-95; Craig Hartsburg, 1995-96 to 1997-98; Dirk Graham and Lorne Molleken, 1998-99; Lorne Molleken and Bob Pulford, 1999-2000; Alpo Suhonen, 2000-01; Brian Sutter, 2001-02.

General Manager

SMITH, MIKE
General Manager, Chicago Blackhawks.
Born in Potsdam, NY, August 31, 1945.

Mike Smith joined the Chicago Blackhawks as manager of hockey operations on December 12, 1999, and was officially named the club's general manager on September 22, 2000. Smith served as associate general manager of the Toronto Maple Leafs for two seasons (1997-98 and 1998-99) before joining the Blackhawks. Previously, he had served as a consultant under Bob Pulford with Chicago from 1995 to 1997. Smith held a variety of positions with the Winnipeg Jets from 1979 to 1994, including general manager. Under Smith, the Jets entered into a formal agreement with Sokol Kiev in 1989, the first of its kind for any NHL team.

Smith has a doctorate in Political Science and Russian Studies from Syracuse University. He has authored 10 books, mostly on coaching hockey.

Club Directory

United Center

Chicago Blackhawks
United Center
1901 W. Madison Street
Chicago, IL 60612
Phone **312/455-7000**
FAX 312/455-7041
www.chicagoblackhawks.com
Capacity: 20,500

President	William W. Wirtz
Senior Vice President	Robert J. Pulford
Vice President	Jack Davison
Vice President	Peter R. Wirtz
General Manager	Mike Smith
Assistant General Manager	Nick Beverley
Director of Professional Scouting	Joe Yannetti
Director of Amateur Scouting	Bill Lesuk
Director of Player Personnel	Dale Tallon
Head Coach	Brian Sutter
Assistant Coach	Denis Savard
Assistant Coach	Al Mac Adam
Asst. Coach, Strength & Cond.	Phil Walker
Goaltending Consultant	Vladislav Tretiak
Chief Amateur Scout	Michel Dumas
Amateur Scout	Bruce Franklin
Amateur Scout	Tim Higgins
Amateur Scout	Ron Anderson
European Scout	Sakari Pietela
Executive Assistant	Cindy Brueck
Manager of Team Services	Matt Colleran
Video Coordinator	Ike Rhodes
Medical Staff	
Club Doctors	Mark Bowen, Gordon Nuber, Greg Ewert
Team Dentist	Dr. Daniel Mackey, Dr. Dean Sana
Oral Surgeon	Dr. Eric Pulver
Eye Doctor	Dr. Robert Stein
Head Trainer	Michael Gapski
Equipment Manager	Troy Parchman
Asst. Equipment Mgr.	Bill Stehle
Asst. Equipment Mgr.	Lou Varga
Massage Therapist	Pawel Prylinski
Public Relations/Marketing	
Exec. Dir. of Communications	Jim De Maria
Dir. of Comm. Relations/PR Asst	Barbara Davidson
Manager of Public Relations	Tony Ommen
Exec. Dir. of Marketing and New Business Development	Jim Sofranko
Dir. of Corporate Sponsorships	Steve Waight
Acct. Exec., Corp. Sponsorship	David Stensby
Manager, Client Services	Kelly Bodnarchuk
Ex. Dir. of Fan Development, Operations and Charities	Carol Czaplicki
Mgr., Youth and Fan Development	Drew Stevenson
Manager, Game Operations	Mike Sullivan
Web Producer	Kellett McConville
Marketing Coordinator	Maxine Ohlava
Marketing Associate	Alison Tragesser
Administrative Assistant	Angela Armbruster
Finance	
Controller	Tracy Hernandez
Treasurer	Robert Rinkus
Accounting Manager	Deb Kulir
Accounting Clerk	Rita Loretto
Ticketing	
Director, Ticket Operations	James K. Bare
Director, Ticket Sales	Doug Ryan
Account Executives	Brad Bober, Dustin Corey, Jocelyn Gay, Katie Golem
Season Tickets Sales Manager	Steve Risnoy
Ticket Operations Manager	Kathie Raimondi
Administrative Assistant	Martha Webster
Miscellaneous Information	
Team Photographer	Bill Smith
Organist	Frank Pellico
Public Address Announcer	TBD
Executive Offices/Home Ice	United Center
Location of Press Box	South Side of United Center
Dimensions of Rink	200 feet by 85 feet
Ends of Rink	Plexi-glass extends above boards all around rink
Club Colors	Red, White & Black
Radio Station	WSCR (AM 670)
Television Station	Fox Sports Net Chicago
Broadcasters	Pat Foley, Bill Gardner

General Managers' History

Major Frederic McLaughlin, 1926-27 to 1941-42; Bill Tobin, 1942-43 to 1953-54; Tommy Ivan, 1954-55 to 1976-77; Bob Pulford, 1977-78 to 1989-90; Mike Keenan, 1990-91, 1991-92; Mike Keenan and Bob Pulford, 1992-93; Bob Pulford, 1993-94 to 1996-97; Bob Murray, 1997-98, 1998-99; Bob Murray and Bob Pulford, 1999-2000; Mike Smith, 2000-01 to date.

NHL Coaching Record

		Regular Season				Playoffs		
Season	Team	Games	W	L	T	Games	W	L
1980-81	Winnipeg	23	2	17	4	....	....	....
	NHL Totals	**23**	**2**	**17**	**4**	....	....	....

Colorado Avalanche

2000-01 Results: 52W-16L-10T-4OTL 118PTS. First, Northwest Division

The impressive depth of the Colorado Avalanche allowed them to overcome the loss of Peter Forsberg to a serious injury in the second round of the playoffs and still go on to win the Stanley Cup. Forsberg had 14 points in just 11 playoff games.

2001-02 Schedule

Month	Day	Date	Opponent
Oct.	Wed.	3	at Pittsburgh
	Tue.	9	Vancouver
	Thu.	11	at Edmonton
	Sat.	13	at Vancouver
	Tue.	16	Tampa Bay
	Thu.	18	Edmonton
	Sat.	20	at Columbus
	Sun.	21	at Chicago
	Tue.	23	Carolina
	Thu.	25	Vancouver
	Sat.	27	at Phoenix*
	Sun.	28	at Anaheim*
	Wed.	31	St. Louis
Nov.	Fri.	2	at Minnesota
	Sat.	3	at Toronto
	Tue.	6	at Montreal
	Thu.	8	at Ottawa
	Sat.	10	at Calgary
	Wed.	14	Minnesota
	Fri.	16	NY Islanders
	Sun.	18	at New Jersey*
	Tue.	20	at NY Rangers
	Wed.	21	at NY Islanders
	Sat.	24	Edmonton
	Tue.	27	Florida
	Fri.	30	at Vancouver
Dec.	Sat.	1	at Calgary
	Mon.	3	Ottawa
	Wed.	5	at Detroit
	Fri.	7	at Buffalo
	Sat.	8	at Columbus
	Mon.	10	Anaheim
	Wed.	12	Columbus
	Fri.	14	San Jose
	Sun.	16	at Minnesota*
	Wed.	19	Anaheim
	Fri.	21	Calgary
	Sun.	23	Minnesota
	Wed.	26	at Dallas
	Thu.	27	at Chicago
	Sat.	29	Philadelphia

Month	Day	Date	Opponent
Jan.	Tue.	1	at Nashville*
	Thu.	3	NY Rangers
	Sat.	5	at Detroit*
	Wed.	9	Chicago
	Sat.	12	at Edmonton
	Tue.	15	San Jose
	Thu.	17	Phoenix
	Sat.	19	at San Jose
	Mon.	21	Buffalo
	Wed.	23	at Edmonton
	Thu.	24	at Calgary
	Sat.	26	at Los Angeles*
	Mon.	28	Los Angeles
	Wed.	30	Nashville
Feb.	Mon.	4	Detroit
	Fri.	8	at Minnesota
	Sat.	9	Chicago
	Mon.	11	Boston
	Wed.	13	St. Louis
	Tue.	26	Calgary
	Thu.	28	Phoenix
Mar.	Sat.	2	Dallas*
	Mon.	4	New Jersey
	Wed.	6	Columbus
	Sat.	9	Los Angeles*
	Mon.	11	at St. Louis
	Thu.	14	at Atlanta
	Sat.	16	at Philadelphia*
	Sun.	17	at Nashville*
	Tue.	19	Washington
	Thu.	21	at Los Angeles
	Sat.	23	Detroit*
	Thu.	28	at San Jose
	Sat.	30	at Phoenix
Apr.	Mon.	1	Nashville
	Wed.	3	Atlanta
	Fri.	5	at Dallas
	Sun.	7	at St. Louis
	Tue.	9	Vancouver
	Fri.	12	at Anaheim
	Sun.	14	Dallas*

* Denotes afternoon game.

Franchise date: June 22, 1979
Transferred from Quebec to Denver, June 21, 1995

NORTHWEST DIVISION

23rd NHL Season

Year-by-Year Record

		Home				Road				Overall								
Season	GP	W	L	T	OL	W	L	T	OL	W	L	T	OL	GF	GA	Pts.	Finished	Playoff Result
2000-01	**82**	**28**	**6**	**5**	**2**	**24**	**10**	**5**	**2**	**52**	**16**	**10**	**4**	**270**	**192**	**118**	**1st, Northwest Div.**	**Won Stanley Cup**
1999-2000	82	25	12	4	0	17	16	7	1	42	28	11	1	233	201	96	1st, Northwest Div.	Lost Conf. Championship
1998-99	82	21	14	6	...	23	14	4	...	44	28	10	...	239	205	98	1st, Northwest Div.	Lost Conf. Championship
1997-98	82	21	10	10	...	18	16	7	...	39	26	17	...	231	205	95	1st, Pacific Div.	Lost Conf. Quarter-Final
1996-97	82	26	10	5	...	23	14	4	...	49	24	9	...	277	205	107	1st, Pacific Div.	Lost Conf. Championship
1995-96	**82**	**24**	**10**	**7**	**...**	**23**	**15**	**3**	**...**	**47**	**25**	**10**	**...**	**326**	**240**	**104**	**1st, Pacific Div.**	**Won Stanley Cup**
1994-95*	48	19	1	4	...	11	12	1	...	30	13	5	...	185	134	65	1st, Northeast Div.	Lost Conf. Quarter-Final
1993-94*	84	19	17	6	...	15	25	2	...	34	42	8	...	277	292	76	5th, Northeast Div.	Out of Playoffs
1992-93*	84	23	17	2	...	24	10	8	...	47	27	10	...	351	300	104	2nd, Adams Div.	Lost Div. Semi-Final
1991-92*	80	18	19	3	...	2	29	9	...	20	48	12	...	255	318	52	5th, Adams Div.	Out of Playoffs
1990-91*	80	9	23	8	...	7	27	6	...	16	50	14	...	236	354	46	5th, Adams Div.	Out of Playoffs
1989-90*	80	8	26	6	...	4	35	1	...	12	61	7	...	240	407	31	5th, Adams Div.	Out of Playoffs
1988-89*	80	16	20	4	...	11	26	3	...	27	46	7	...	269	342	61	5th, Adams Div.	Out of Playoffs
1987-88*	80	15	23	2	...	17	20	3	...	32	43	5	...	271	306	69	5th, Adams Div.	Out of Playoffs
1986-87*	80	20	13	7	...	11	26	3	...	31	39	10	...	267	276	72	4th, Adams Div.	Lost Div. Final
1985-86*	80	23	13	4	...	20	18	2	...	43	31	6	...	330	289	92	1st, Adams Div.	Lost Div. Semi-Final
1984-85*	80	24	12	4	...	17	18	5	...	41	30	9	...	323	275	91	2nd, Adams Div.	Lost Conf. Championship
1983-84*	80	24	11	5	...	18	17	5	...	42	28	10	...	360	278	94	3th, Adams Div.	Lost Div. Final
1982-83*	80	23	10	7	...	11	24	5	...	34	34	12	...	343	336	80	4th, Adams Div.	Lost Div. Semi-Final
1981-82*	80	24	13	3	...	9	18	13	...	33	31	16	...	356	345	82	4th, Adams Div.	Lost Conf. Championship
1980-81*	80	18	11	11	...	12	21	7	...	30	32	18	...	314	318	78	4th, Adams Div.	Lost Prelim. Round
1979-80*	80	17	16	7	...	8	28	4	...	25	44	11	...	248	313	61	5th, Adams Div.	Out of Playoffs

* Quebec Nordiques

2001-02 Player Personnel

FORWARDS	HT	WT	S	Place of Birth	Date	2000-01 Club
BABENKO, Yuri	6-1	200	L	Penza, USSR	1/2/78	Colorado-Hershey
DAW, Jeff	6-3	190	R	Carlisle, Ont.	2/28/72	Lowell-Cleveland
DRURY, Chris	5-10	180	R	Trumbull, CT	8/20/76	Colorado
FAIRCHILD, Kelly	5-11	180	L	Hibbing, MN	4/9/73	Hershey
FORSBERG, Peter	6-0	205	L	Ornskoldsvik, Sweden	7/20/73	Colorado
HEJDUK, Milan	5-11	185	R	Usti-nad-Labem, Czech.	2/14/76	Colorado
HINOTE, Dan	6-0	190	R	Leesburg, FL	1/30/77	Colorado
KRESTANOVICH, Jordan	6-1	170	L	Langley, B.C.	6/14/81	Calgary (WHL)-Hershey
KULESHOV, Mikhail	6-2	205	R	Perm, USSR	1/7/81	St. Petersburg-Hershey
LARSEN, Brad	6-0	200	L	Nakusp, B.C.	6/28/77	Colorado-Hershey
LAZAREV, Yevgeny	6-2	205	L	Kharkov, USSR	4/25/80	Hershey
MESSIER, Eric	6-2	200	L	Drummondville, Que.	10/29/73	Colorado
NEDOROST, Vaclav	6-1	190	L	Budejovice, Czech.	3/16/82	HC Budejovice
NIEMINEN, Ville	6-0	200	L	Tampere, Finland	4/6/77	Colorado-Hershey
PARKER, Scott	6-5	230	R	Hanford, CA	1/29/78	Colorado
PODEIN, Shjon	6-2	200	L	Rochester, MN	3/5/68	Colorado
REINPRECHT, Steve	6-0	190	L	Edmonton, AB	5/7/76	Los Angeles-Colorado
SAKIC, Joe	5-11	195	L	Burnaby, B.C.	7/7/69	Colorado
TANGUAY, Alex	6-0	190	L	Ste-Justine, Que.	11/21/79	Colorado
TIMMONS, K.C.	6-4	215	L	Victoria, B.C.	4/6/80	Hershey
VRBATA, Radim	6-1	185	R	Boleslav, Czech.	6/13/81	Shawinigan-Hershey
WILLSIE, Brian	6-1	195	R	London, Ont.	3/16/78	Hershey
YELLE, Stephane	6-1	190	L	Ottawa, Ont.	5/9/74	Colorado
DEFENSEMEN						
BERRY, Rick	6-2	210	L	Birtle, Man.	11/4/78	Colorado-Hershey
BLAKE, Rob	6-4	225	R	Simcoe, Ont.	12/10/69	Los Angeles-Colorado
de VRIES, Greg	6-3	215	L	Sundridge, Ont.	1/4/73	Colorado
FOOTE, Adam	6-2	215	R	Toronto, Ont.	7/10/71	Colorado
GILL, Todd	6-0	180	L	Cardinal, Ont.	11/9/65	Detroit-Cincinnati (AHL)
MUIR, Bryan	6-4	220	L	Winnipeg, Man.	6/8/73	T.B.-Detroit (IHL)-Col-Hershey
OBSUT, Jaroslav	6-1	200	L	Presov, Czech.	9/3/76	StL-Peoria-Wor
PAUL, Jeff	6-3	200	R	London, Ont.	3/1/78	Norfolk
RIAZANTSEV, Alexander	6-0	210	R	Moscow, USSR	3/15/80	Hershey
SKOULA, Martin	6-2	195	L	Litomerice, Czech.	10/28/79	Colorado

GOALTENDERS	HT	WT	C	Place of Birth	Date	2000-01 Club
AEBISCHER, David	6-1	190	L	Fribourg, Switz.	2/7/78	Colorado
ROY, Patrick	6-2	185	L	Quebec City, Que.	10/5/65	Colorado
SAUVE, Philippe	6-0	180	L	Buffalo, NY	2/27/80	Hershey

Captains' History

Marc Tardif, 1979-80, 1980-81; Robbie Ftorek and Andre Dupont, 1981-82; Mario Marois, 1982-83 to 1984-85; Mario Marois and Peter Stastny, 1985-86; Peter Stastny, 1986-87 to 1989-90; Joe Sakic and Steven Finn, 1990-91; Mike Hough, 1991-92; Joe Sakic, 1992-93 to date.

Coaching History

Jacques Demers, 1979-80; Maurice Filion and Michel Bergeron, 1980-81; Michel Bergeron, 1981-82 to 1986-87; Andre Savard and Ron Lapointe, 1987-88; Ron Lapointe and Jean Perron, 1988-89; Michel Bergeron, 1989-90; Dave Chambers, 1990-91; Dave Chambers and Pierre Page, 1991-92; Pierre Page, 1992-93, 1993-94; Marc Crawford, 1994-95 to 1997-98; Bob Hartley, 1998-99 to date.

Coach

HARTLEY, BOB
Coach, Colorado Avalanche. Born in Hawkesbury, Ont., September 7, 1960.

Bob Hartley became the second coach of the Colorado Avalanche and the 11th coach in franchise history when he was named to the position on June 30, 1998. In 2001, he led the team to its second Stanley Cup title. Before joining the Avalanche, Hartley spent four years as a head coach with the organization's American Hockey League affiliates in Cornwall and Hershey compiling a record of 151-136-33.

Hartley began his coaching career with the Hawksbury Hawks, where he won two Central Ontario Junior A championships in four seasons. In 1991 he became head coach of the Laval Titans of the Quebec Major Junior Hockey League, where he won another championship prior to becoming an assistant coach with the Cornwall Aces in 1993. He became head coach in Cornwall the following year and remained with the Avalanche affiliate after it relocated to Hershey for the 1996-97 season. Hartley coached Hershey to the Calder Cup championship that year. In addition to his on-ice success in Hershey, Hartley was known for his summer hockey camps and volunteer work within the community.

Coaching Record

		Regular Season				Playoffs		
Season	Team	Games	W	L	T	Games	W	L
1991-92	Laval (QMJHL)	70	38	27	5	10	4	6
1992-93	Laval (QMJHL)	70	43	25	2	13	12	1
1994-95	Cornwall (AHL)	80	38	33	9	15	8	7
1995-96	Cornwall (AHL)	80	34	39	7	8	3	5
1996-97	Hershey (AHL)	80	43	27	10	23	15	8
1997-98	Hershey (AHL)	80	36	37	7	7	3	4
1998-99	**Colorado (NHL)**	**82**	**44**	**28**	**10**	**19**	**11**	**8**
1999-2000	**Colorado (NHL)**	**82**	**42**	**29**	**11**	**17**	**11**	**6**
2000-01	**Colorado (NHL)**	**82**	**52**	**20**	**10**	**23**	**16**	**7***
	NHL Totals	**246**	**138**	**77**	**31**	**59**	**38**	**21**

* Stanley Cup win.

2000-01 Scoring

* - rookie

Regular Season

Pos	#	Player	Team	GP	G	A	Pts	+/–	PIM	PP	SH	GW	GT	S	%
C	19	Joe Sakic	COL	82	54	64	118	45	30	19	3	12	2	332	16.3
C	21	Peter Forsberg	COL	73	27	62	89	23	54	12	2	5	0	178	15.2
R	23	Milan Hejduk	COL	80	41	38	79	32	36	12	1	9	0	213	19.2
L	40	Alex Tanguay	COL	82	27	50	77	35	37	7	1	3	0	135	20.0
C	37	Chris Drury	COL	71	24	41	65	6	47	11	0	5	1	204	11.8
D	4	Rob Blake	L.A.	54	17	32	49	–8	69	9	0	1	1	223	7.6
			COL	13	2	8	10	11	8	1	0	1	0	44	4.5
			TOTAL	67	19	40	59	3	77	10	0	2	1	267	7.1
D	77	Raymond Bourque	COL	80	7	52	59	25	48	2	2	0	1	216	3.2
C	28	* Steve Reinprecht	L.A.	59	12	17	29	11	12	3	2	3	0	72	16.7
			COL	21	3	4	7	–1	2	0	0	0	0	28	10.7
			TOTAL	80	15	21	36	10	14	3	2	3	0	100	15.0
L	25	Shjon Podein	COL	82	15	17	32	7	68	0	0	3	0	137	10.9
D	41	Martin Skoula	COL	82	8	17	25	8	38	3	0	2	0	108	7.4
L	39	* Ville Nieminen	COL	50	14	8	22	8	38	2	0	3	0	68	20.6
D	7	Greg de Vries	COL	79	5	12	17	23	51	0	0	0	0	76	6.6
R	13	Dan Hinote	COL	76	5	10	15	1	51	1	0	1	0	69	7.2
D	24	Jon Klemm	COL	78	4	11	15	22	54	2	0	2	0	97	4.1
D	52	Adam Foote	COL	35	3	12	15	6	42	1	1	1	0	59	5.1
C	26	Stephane Yelle	COL	50	4	10	14	–3	20	0	1	0	0	54	7.4
L	29	Eric Messier	COL	64	5	7	12	–3	26	0	0	1	0	60	8.3
L	14	Dave Reid	COL	73	1	9	10	1	21	0	0	0	0	66	1.5
R	27	Scott Parker	COL	69	2	3	5	–2	155	0	0	1	0	35	5.7
G	33	Patrick Roy	COL	62	0	5	5	0	10	0	0	0	0	0	0.0
D	45	* Rick Berry	COL	19	0	4	4	5	38	0	0	0	0	10	0.0
D	44	Nolan Pratt	COL	46	1	2	3	2	40	0	0	1	0	26	3.8
D	2	Bryan Muir	T.B.	10	0	3	3	–7	15	0	0	0	0	14	0.0
			COL	8	0	0	0	0	4	0	0	0	0	3	0.0
			TOTAL	18	0	3	3	–7	19	0	0	0	0	17	0.0
L	11	Chris Dingman	COL	41	1	1	2	–3	108	0	0	0	0	33	3.0
G	1	* David Aebischer	COL	26	0	1	1	0	0	0	0	0	0	0	0.0
C	44	* Rob Shearer	COL	2	0	0	0	–2	0	0	0	0	0	0	0.0
C	63	Joel Prpic	COL	3	0	0	0	0	2	0	0	0	0	0	0.0
C	46	* Yuri Babenko	COL	3	0	0	0	0	0	0	0	0	0	2	0.0
L	9	* Brad Larsen	COL	9	0	0	0	1	0	0	0	0	0	3	0.0

Goaltending

No.	Goaltender	GPI	Mins	Avg	W	L	T	EN	SO	GA	SA	S%
33	Patrick Roy	62	3585	2.21	40	13	7	5	4	132	1513	.913
1	* David Aebischer	26	1393	2.24	12	7	3	3	3	52	538	.903
	Totals	**82**	**4993**	**2.31**	**52**	**20**	**10**	**8**	**7**	**192**	**2059**	**.907**

Playoffs

Pos	#	Player	Team	GP	G	A	Pts	+/–	PIM	PP	SH	GW	GT	S	%
C	19	Joe Sakic	COL	21	13	13	26	6	6	5	0	3	1	79	16.5
R	23	Milan Hejduk	COL	23	7	16	23	8	6	4	0	1	0	51	13.7
L	40	Alex Tanguay	COL	23	6	15	21	13	8	1	0	2	0	37	16.2
D	4	Rob Blake	COL	23	6	13	19	6	16	3	0	0	0	83	7.2
C	37	Chris Drury	COL	23	11	5	16	5	4	2	0	2	0	62	17.7
C	21	Peter Forsberg	COL	11	4	10	14	5	6	1	0	2	1	23	17.4
D	77	Raymond Bourque	COL	21	4	6	10	9	12	3	0	1	0	49	8.2
L	39	* Ville Nieminen	COL	23	4	6	10	–1	20	3	0	1	0	39	10.3
D	52	Adam Foote	COL	23	3	4	7	5	47	1	0	1	0	28	10.7
R	13	Dan Hinote	COL	23	2	4	6	4	21	0	0	0	0	16	12.5
C	28	* Steve Reinprecht	COL	22	2	3	5	0	2	0	0	0	0	14	14.3
L	25	Shjon Podein	COL	23	2	3	5	3	14	0	0	1	0	16	12.5
D	41	Martin Skoula	COL	23	1	4	5	1	8	0	0	0	0	14	7.1
L	29	Eric Messier	COL	23	2	2	4	0	14	0	0	0	0	20	10.0
L	11	Chris Dingman	COL	16	0	4	4	3	14	0	0	0	0	8	0.0
L	14	Dave Reid	COL	18	0	4	4	2	6	0	0	0	0	8	0.0
D	24	Jon Klemm	COL	22	1	2	3	7	16	0	0	1	0	14	7.1
C	26	Stephane Yelle	COL	23	1	2	3	2	8	0	0	1	1	23	4.3
G	33	Patrick Roy	COL	23	0	1	1	0	0	0	0	0	0	0	0.0
D	7	Greg de Vries	COL	23	0	1	1	5	20	0	0	0	0	20	0.0
G	1	* David Aebischer	COL	1	0	0	0	0	0	0	0	0	0	0	0.0
D	2	Bryan Muir	COL	3	0	0	0	0	0	0	0	0	0	0	0.0
R	27	Scott Parker	COL	4	0	0	0	0	2	0	0	0	0	0	0.0

Goaltending

No.	Goaltender	GPI	Mins	Avg	W	L	EN	SO	GA	SA	S%
1	* David Aebischer	1	1	0.00	0	0	0	0	0	0	.000
33	Patrick Roy	23	1451	1.70	16	7	0	4	41	622	.934
	Totals	**23**	**1455**	**1.69**	**16**	**7**	**0**	**4**	**41**	**622**	**.934**

Club Records

Team

(Figures in brackets for season records are games played; records for fewest points, wins, ties, losses, goals, goals against are for 70 or more games)

Most Points	**118**	2000-01 (82)
Most Wins	**52**	2000-01 (82)
Most Ties	**18**	1980-81 (80)
Most Losses	**61**	1989-90 (80)
Most Goals	**360**	1983-84 (80)
Most Goals Against	**407**	1989-90 (80)
Fewest Points	**31**	1989-90 (80)
Fewest Wins	**12**	1989-90 (80)
Fewest Ties	**5**	1987-88 (80)
Fewest Losses	**16**	2000-01 (82)
Fewest Goals	**231**	1997-98 (82)
Fewest Goals Against	**192**	2000-01 (82)
Longest Winning Streak		
Overall	**12**	Jan. 10-Feb. 7/99
Home	**10**	Nov. 26/83-Jan. 10/84, Mar. 6-Apr. 16/95
Away	**7**	Jan. 10-Feb. 7/99
Longest Undefeated Streak		
Overall	**12**	Dec. 23/96-Jan. 20/97 (9 wins, 3 ties), Jan. 10-Feb. 7/99 (12 wins)
Home	**14**	Nov. 19/83-Jan. 21/84 (11 wins, 3 ties)
Away	**10**	Jan. 10-Mar. 3/99 (8 wins, 2 ties)
Longest Losing Streak		
Overall	**14**	Oct. 21-Nov. 19/90
Home	**8**	Oct. 21-Nov. 24/90
Away	**18**	Jan. 18-Apr. 1/90
Longest Winless Streak		
Overall	**17**	Oct. 21-Nov. 25/90 (15 losses, 2 ties)
Home	**11**	Nov. 14-Dec. 26/89 (7 losses, 4 ties)
Away	**33**	Oct. 8/91-Feb. 27/92 (25 losses, 8 ties)
Most Shutouts, Season	**8**	1996-97 (82)
Most PIM, Season	**2,104**	1989-90 (80)
Most Goals, Game	**12**	Three times

Individual

Most Seasons	**13**	Joe Sakic
Most Games	**934**	Joe Sakic
Most Goals, Career	**457**	Joe Sakic
Most Assists, Career	**721**	Joe Sakic
Most Points, Career	**1,178**	Joe Sakic (457G, 721A)
Most PIM, Career	**1,562**	Dale Hunter
Most Shutouts, Career	**23**	Patrick Roy
Longest Consecutive Games Streak	**312**	Dale Hunter (Oct. 9/80-Mar. 13/84)
Most Goals, Season	**57**	Michel Goulet (1982-83)
Most Assists, Season	**93**	Peter Stastny (1981-82)
Most Points, Season	**139**	Peter Stastny (1981-82; 46G, 93A)
Most PIM, Season	**301**	Gord Donnelly (1987-88)
Most Points, Defenseman, Season	**82**	Steve Duchesne (1992-93; 20G, 62A)
Most Points, Center, Season	**139**	Peter Stastny (1981-82; 46G, 93A)
Most Points, Right Wing, Season	**103**	Jacques Richard (1980-81; 52G, 51A)
Most Points, Left Wing, Season	**121**	Michel Goulet (1983-84; 56G, 65A)
Most Points, Rookie, Season	**109**	Peter Stastny (1980-81; 39G, 70A)
Most Shutouts, Season	**7**	Patrick Roy (1996-97)
Most Goals, Game	**5**	Mats Sundin (Mar. 5/92), Mike Ricci (Feb. 17/94)
Most Assists, Game	**5**	Six times
Most Points, Game	**8**	Peter Stastny (Feb. 22/81; 4G, 4A), Anton Stastny (Feb. 22/81; 3G, 5A)

Records include Quebec Nordiques, 1979-80 through 1994-95.

Quebec Nordiques Retired Numbers

3	J.C. Tremblay	1972-1979
8	Marc Tardif	1979-1983
16	Michel Goulet	1979-1990

All-time Record vs. Other Clubs

Regular Season

	At Home								On Road								Total							
	GP	W	L	T	OL	GF	GA	PTS	GP	W	L	T	OL	GF	GA	PTS	GP	W	L	T	OL	GF	GA	PTS
Anaheim	15	8	4	3	0	52	41	19	15	8	4	3	0	38	34	19	30	16	8	6	0	90	75	38
Atlanta	2	1	1	0	0	8	6	2	2	2	0	0	0	7	4	4	4	3	1	0	0	15	10	6
Boston	63	23	34	6	0	227	263	52	61	21	31	9	0	189	238	51	124	44	65	15	0	416	501	103
Buffalo	62	30	20	11	1	223	192	72	61	17	35	9	0	197	242	43	123	47	55	20	1	420	434	115
Calgary	39	16	14	9	0	149	131	41	39	14	19	6	0	121	144	34	78	30	33	15	0	270	275	75
Carolina	63	37	17	9	0	266	189	83	61	25	24	12	0	211	201	62	124	62	41	21	0	477	390	145
Chicago	33	17	11	5	0	133	115	39	35	13	19	3	0	110	124	29	68	30	30	8	0	243	239	68
Columbus	2	2	0	0	0	8	3	4	2	2	0	0	0	9	3	4	4	4	0	0	0	17	6	8
Dallas	35	21	10	4	0	138	96	46	35	13	16	5	1	102	111	32	70	34	26	9	1	240	207	78
Detroit	36	19	13	4	0	137	124	42	34	12	20	1	1	106	129	26	70	31	33	5	1	243	253	68
Edmonton	39	19	17	3	0	157	152	41	38	14	21	3	0	115	163	31	77	33	38	6	0	272	315	72
Florida	9	3	3	3	0	25	22	9	9	8	1	0	0	39	24	16	18	11	4	3	0	64	46	25
Los Angeles	36	19	14	3	0	150	127	41	37	11	23	3	0	119	159	25	73	30	37	6	0	269	286	66
Minnesota	3	3	0	0	0	10	4	6	2	2	0	0	0	9	2	4	5	5	0	0	0	19	6	10
Montreal	62	31	26	5	0	209	216	67	62	16	37	9	0	195	256	41	124	47	63	14	0	404	472	108
Nashville	6	5	0	1	0	18	8	11	6	2	2	2	0	18	17	6	12	7	2	3	0	36	25	17
New Jersey	32	16	13	3	0	118	96	35	34	12	18	4	0	116	143	28	66	28	31	7	0	234	239	63
NY Islanders	32	19	11	2	0	121	96	40	30	13	16	1	0	104	120	27	62	32	27	3	0	225	216	67
NY Rangers	32	16	13	3	0	132	124	35	31	9	18	4	0	89	124	22	63	25	31	7	0	221	248	57
Ottawa	13	11	1	1	0	64	34	23	15	7	6	2	0	62	48	16	28	18	7	3	0	126	82	39
Philadelphia	32	11	9	12	0	118	113	34	32	8	21	2	1	87	120	19	64	19	30	14	1	205	233	53
Phoenix	35	16	15	4	0	123	125	36	34	15	13	6	0	127	127	36	69	31	28	10	0	250	252	72
Pittsburgh	31	16	13	2	0	138	121	34	34	14	15	5	0	139	139	33	65	30	28	7	0	277	260	67
St. Louis	35	18	11	5	1	123	99	42	34	10	21	3	0	105	137	23	69	28	32	8	1	228	236	65
San Jose	17	11	2	4	0	71	34	26	18	11	7	0	0	68	55	22	35	22	9	4	0	139	89	48
Tampa Bay	11	7	2	2	0	48	24	16	10	2	7	1	0	24	31	5	21	9	9	3	0	72	55	21
Toronto	29	17	7	5	0	111	87	39	32	14	14	4	0	127	109	32	61	31	21	9	0	238	196	71
Vancouver	39	19	13	7	0	133	110	45	39	19	14	6	0	155	136	44	78	38	27	13	0	288	246	89
Washington	31	14	13	4	0	99	110	32	32	11	17	4	0	104	129	26	63	25	30	8	0	203	239	58
Totals	**874**	**445**	**307**	**120**	**2**	**3309**	**2862**	**1012**	**874**	**325**	**439**	**107**	**3**	**2892**	**3269**	**760**	**1748**	**770**	**746**	**227**	**5**	**6201**	**6131**	**1772**

Playoffs

	Series	W	L	GP	W	L	T	GF	GA	Last Mtg.	Round	Result
Boston	2	1	1	11	5	6	0	36	37	1983	DSF	L 1-3
Buffalo	2	2	0	8	6	2	0	35	27	1985	DSF	W 3-2
Chicago	2	2	0	12	8	4	0	49	28	1997	CQF	W 4-2
Dallas	2	0	2	14	6	8	0	29	37	2000	CF	L 3-4
Detroit	4	3	1	23	14	9	0	66	54	2000	CSF	W 4-1
Edmonton	2	1	1	12	7	5	0	35	30	1990	CQF	L 3-4
Florida	1	1	0	4	4	0	0	15	4	1996	F	W 4-0
Hartford	2	1	1	9	4	5	0	34	35	1987	DSF	W 4-2
Los Angeles	1	1	0	7	4	3	0	17	10	2001	CSF	W 4-3
Montreal	5	2	3	31	14	17	0	85	105	1993	DSF	L 2-4
New Jersey	1	1	0	7	4	3	0	19	11	2001	F	W 4-3
NY Islanders	1	0	1	4	0	4	0	9	18	1982	CF	L 0-4
NY Rangers	1	0	1	6	2	4	0	19	25	1995	CQF	L 2-4
Philadelphia	2	0	2	11	4	7	0	29	39	1985	CF	L 2-4
Phoenix	1	1	0	5	4	1	0	17	10	2000	CQF	W 4-1
St. Louis	1	1	0	5	4	1	0	17	11	2001	CF	W 4-1
San Jose	1	1	0	6	4	2	0	19	17	1999	CQF	W 4-2
Vancouver	2	2	0	10	8	2	0	40	26	2001	CQF	W 4-0
Totals	**33**	**20**	**13**	**185**	**102**	**83**	**0**	**570**	**524**			

Playoff Results 2001-1997

Year	Round	Opponent	Result	GF	GA
2001	**F**	**New Jersey**	**W 4-3**	**19**	**11**
	CF	St. Louis	W 4-1	17	11
	CSF	Los Angeles	W 4-3	17	10
	CQF	Vancouver	W 4-0	16	9
2000	CF	Dallas	L 3-4	13	14
	CSF	Detroit	W 4-1	13	8
	CQF	Phoenix	W 4-1	17	10
1999	CF	Dallas	L 3-4	16	23
	CSF	Detroit	W 4-2	21	14
	CQF	San Jose	W 4-2	19	17
1998	CQF	Edmonton	L 3-4	16	19
1997	CF	Detroit	L 2-4	12	16
	CSF	Edmonton	W 4-1	19	11
	CQF	Chicago	W 4-2	28	14

Abbreviations: Round: F – Final; **CF** – conference final; **CSF** – conference semi-final; **CQF** – conference quarter-final; **DSF** – division semi-final.

Calgary totals include Atlanta Flames, 1979-80.
Dallas totals include Minnesota North Stars, 1979-80 to 1992-93.
Phoenix totals include Winnipeg, 1979-80 to 1995-96.

Carolina totals include Hartford, 1979-80 to 1996-97.
New Jersey totals include Colorado Rockies, 1979-80 to 1981-82.

2000-01 Results

Month	Day	Opponent	Score
Oct.	4	at Dallas	2-2
	7	at Edmonton	1-1
	10	at Calgary	3-1
	12	at Vancouver	5-2
	14	Columbus	3-1
	17	at Washington	4-3*
	18	at Columbus	5-1
	20	Florida	5-1
	25	Nashville	2-1*
	26	at Chicago	2-0
	28	Edmonton	4-2
	30	Phoenix	0-4
Nov.	1	at Vancouver	3-4
	3	Carolina	5-3
	7	Minnesota	2-0
	9	St. Louis	3-3
	11	Anaheim	3-1
	13	Pittsburgh	3-2*
	15	at Anaheim	3-0
	16	at Phoenix	3-6
	18	at Los Angeles	4-6
	22	Columbus	5-2
	25	Calgary	3-2*
	29	Phoenix	2-1
Dec.	1	Dallas	4-2
	3	at NY Rangers	6-3
	5	at New Jersey	1-6
	8	at Tampa Bay	2-0
	9	at Florida	4-2
	11	Tampa Bay	2-2
	13	Philadelphia	3-3
	15	Detroit	3-5
	19	Calgary	0-3
	21	Los Angeles	5-2
	23	Vancouver	3-2*
	26	at Nashville	2-5
	27	Edmonton	3-2
	29	Nashville	3-1
Jan.	2	Los Angeles	6-2
	4	San Jose	2-2
	6	at Carolina	2-2
	7	at Detroit	3-4*
	10	at Columbus	4-2
	12	at Minnesota	5-0
	14	at Chicago	2-2
	16	NY Islanders	4-1
	18	Vancouver	7-3
	20	at San Jose	2-1
	21	at Anaheim	4-2
	26	Chicago	5-2
	27	at Nashville	5-1
	30	at San Jose	3-1
Feb.	1	at Vancouver	3-5
	7	Washington	1-3
	9	Calgary	3-5
	10	St. Louis	3-4*
	13	at Montreal	3-2*
	15	at Ottawa	1-4
	17	at Toronto	5-5
	19	at Pittsburgh	5-1
	21	Boston	8-2
	23	Minnesota	4-1
	25	Atlanta	5-2
Mar.	3	Buffalo	2-3*
	4	at Phoenix	5-0
	6	at Atlanta	4-2
	8	at St. Louis	5-2
	10	at Dallas	2-3*
	11	Dallas	3-2
	13	New Jersey	3-6
	17	Detroit	5-3
	18	Minnesota	4-3
	20	San Jose	4-1
	22	at St. Louis	3-1
	24	at Boston	4-2
	28	at Edmonton	1-4
	29	at Calgary	1-0
	31	at Los Angeles	0-4
Apr.	2	Edmonton	5-3
	4	Anaheim	1-1
	7	at Detroit	3-4
	8	at Minnesota	4-2

* – Overtime

Entry Draft Selections 2001-1987

2001

Pick	
63	Peter Budaj
97	Danny Bois
130	Colt King
143	Frantisek Skladany
144	Cody McCormick
149	Mikko Viitanen
165	Pierre-Luc Emond
184	Scott Horvath
196	Charlie Stephens
227	Marek Svatos

2000

Pick	
14	Vaclav Nedorost
47	Jared Aulin
50	Sergei Soin
63	Agris Saviels
88	Kurt Sauer
92	Sergei Klyazmine
119	Brian Fahey
159	John-Michael Liles
189	Chris Bahen
221	Aaron Molnar
252	Darryl Bootland
266	Sean Kotary
285	Blake Ward

1999

Pick	
25	Mikhail Kuleshov
45	Martin Grenier
93	Branko Radivojevic
112	Sanny Lindstrom
122	Kristian Kovac
142	William Magnuson
152	Jordan Krestanovich
158	Anders Lovdahl
183	Riku Hahl
212	Radim Vrbata
240	Jeff Finger

1998

Pick	
12	Alex Tanguay
17	Martin Skoula
19	Robyn Regehr
20	Scott Parker
28	Ramzi Abid
38	Phillipe Sauve
53	Steve Moore
79	Yevgeny Lazarev
141	K.C. Timmons
167	Alexander Riazantsev

1997

Pick	
26	Kevin Grimes
53	Graham Belak
55	Rick Berry
78	Ville Nieminen
87	Brad Larsen
133	Aaron Miskovich
161	David Aebischer
217	Doug Schmidt
243	Kyle Kidney
245	Stephen Lafleur

1996

Pick	
25	Peter Ratchuk
51	Yuri Babenko
79	Mark Parrish
98	Ben Storey
107	Randy Petruk
134	Luke Curtin
146	Brian Willsie
160	Kai Fischer
167	Dan Hinote
176	Sami Pahlsson
188	Roman Pylner
214	Matthew Scorsune
240	Justin Clark

1995

Pick	
25	Marc Denis
51	Nic Beaudoin
77	John Tripp
81	Tomi Kallio
129	Brent Johnson
155	John Cirjak
181	Dan Smith
207	Tomi Hirvonen
228	Chris George

1994

Pick	
12	Wade Belak
22	Jeffrey Kealty
35	Josef Marha
61	Sebastien Bety
72	Chris Drury
87	Milan Hejduk
113	Tony Tuzzolino
139	Nicholas Windsor
165	Calvin Elfring
191	Jay Bertsch
217	Tim Thomas
243	Chris Pittman
285	Steven Low

1993

Pick	
10	Jocelyn Thibault
14	Adam Deadmarsh
49	Ashley Buckberger
75	Bill Pierce
101	Ryan Tocher
127	Anders Myrvold
137	Nicholas Checco
153	Christian Matte
179	David Ling
205	Petr Franek
231	Vincent Auger
257	Mark Pivetz
283	John Hillman

1992

Pick	
4	Todd Warriner
28	Paul Brousseau
29	Tuomas Gronman
52	Manny Fernandez
76	Ian McIntyre
100	Charlie Wasley
124	Paxton Schulte
148	Martin Lepage
172	Mike Jickling
196	Steve Passmore
220	Anson Carter
244	Aaron Ellis

1991

Pick	
1	Eric Lindros
24	Rene Corbet
46	Rich Brennan
68	Dave Karpa
90	Patrick Labrecque
103	Bill Lindsay
134	Mikael Johansson
156	Janne Laukkanen
157	Aaron Asp
178	Adam Bartell
188	Brent Brekke
200	Paul Koch
222	Doug Friedman
244	Eric Meloche

1990

Pick	
1	Owen Nolan
22	Ryan Hughes
43	Brad Zavisha
106	Jeff Parrott
127	Dwayne Norris
148	Andrei Kovalenko
158	Alexander Karpovtsev
169	Pat Mazzoli
190	Scott Davis
211	Mika Stromberg
232	Wade Klippenstein

1989

Pick	
1	Mats Sundin
22	Adam Foote
43	Stephane Morin
54	John Tanner
68	Niklas Andersson
76	Eric Dubois
85	Kevin Kaiser
106	Dan Lambert
127	Sergei Mylnikov
148	Paul Krake
169	Vyacheslav Bykov
190	Andrei Khomutov
211	Byron Witkowski
232	Noel Rahn

1988

Pick	
3	Curtis Leschyshyn
5	Daniel Dore
24	Stephane Fiset
45	Petri Aaltonen
66	Darin Kimble
87	Stephane Venne
108	Ed Ward
129	Valeri Kamensky
150	Sakari Lindfors
171	Dan Wiebe
213	Alexei Gusarov
234	Claude Lapointe

1987

Pick	
9	Bryan Fogarty
15	Joe Sakic
51	Jim Sprott
72	Kip Miller
93	Rob Mendel
114	Garth Snow
135	Tim Hanus
156	Jake Enebak
177	Jaroslav Sevcik
183	Ladislav Tresl
198	Darren Nauss
219	Mike Williams

General Managers' History

Maurice Filion, 1979-80 to 1987-88; Martin Madden, 1988-89; Martin Madden and Maurice Filion, 1989-90; Pierre Page, 1990-91 to 1993-94; Pierre Lacroix, 1994-95 to date.

President and General Manager

LACROIX, PIERRE
President and General Manager, Colorado Avalanche.
Born in Montreal, Que., August 3, 1948.

Pierre Lacroix was appointed to the general manager's post on May 24, 1994 after 21 years as a respected player agent. In his first season as general manager, his leadership was instrumental in moving the team from 11th to second place in the NHL. Lacroix's second season began with the club's move to Denver. He set out to improve the team and did so through acquisitions that brought Claude Lemieux, Sandis Ozolinsh, Patrick Roy and Mike Keane to Colorado. The revamped Avs finished atop the Pacific Division and went on to win the Stanley Cup. He was named NHL executive of the year by *The Hockey News* and became president of the club's hockey operations in August, 1995. The Avalanche have continued to rank among the NHL's top teams, and won the Stanley Cup again in 2001.

Club Directory

Pepsi Center

Colorado Avalanche
Pepsi Center
1000 Chopper Circle
Denver, CO 80204
Phone **303/405-1100**
FAX 303/893-0614
Press Box 303/575-1926
www.coloradoavalanche.com
Capacity: 18,007

Owner & Governor	E. Stanley Kroenke
Alternate Governor, President & General Manager	Pierre Lacroix
Assistant General Manager	Brian MacDonald
Head Coach	Bob Hartley
Assistant Coach	Jacques Cloutier
Assistant Coach	Bryan Trottier
Vice President of Player Personnel	Michel Goulet
Director of Hockey Administration	Charlotte Grahame
Team Services Assistant	Ronnie Jameson
Chief Scout	Jim Hammett
Pro Scout	Brad Smith
Scout	Yvon Gendron
Scout	Garth Joy
Scout	Steve Lyons
Scout	Don Paarup
Scout	Richard Pracey
Scout	Orval Tessier
European Scout	Joni Lehto
Computer Research Consultant	John Donohue
Strength & Conditioning Coach	Paul Goldberg
Head Athletic Trainer	Pat Karns
Kinesiologist	Matt Sokolowski
Massage Therapist	Gregorio Pradera
Equipment Manager	Wayne Flemming
Equipment Manager	Mark Miller
Assistant Equipment Manager	Dave Randolph
Communications Department	
Vice President of Communications & Team Services	Jean Martineau
Director of Special Projects & New Media	Hayne Ellis
Assistant Director of Communications	Damen Zier
Team Founded	1979 Quebec Nordiques – Relocated to Colorado 1995
Press Box Location	Northwest side – Press Box level
Practice Facility	South Suburban Family Sports Center
Minor League Affiliate	Hershey Bears (AHL)
Television Outlets	FOX Sports Net Rocky Mountain, KTVD UPN-20
Radio Flagship	KKFN AM-950

Hart Trophy winner Joe Sakic is the soul of the Colorado Avalanche. He trailed Jaromir Jagr by just three points (121-118) for the Art Ross Trophy, then led all playoff performers in scoring with 26 points in 21 games.

Columbus Blue Jackets

2000-01 Results: 28W-39L-9T-6OTL 71PTS. Fifth, Central Division

Year-by-Year Record

		Home				Road				Overall								
Season	GP	W	L	T	OL	W	L	T	OL	W	L	T	OL	GF	GA	Pts.	Finished	Playoff Result
2000-01	82	19	15	4	3	9	24	5	3	28	39	9	6	190	233	71	5th, Central Div.	Out of Playoffs

2001-02 Schedule

Oct.	Thu.	4	St. Louis
	Sat.	6	at Philadelphia
	Mon.	8	Philadelphia
	Fri.	12	Montreal
	Sun.	14	at Chicago
	Tue.	16	at Detroit
	Fri.	19	at Buffalo
	Sat.	20	Colorado
	Tue.	23	Los Angeles
	Thu.	25	Edmonton
	Sat.	27	at San Jose
	Tue.	30	at Vancouver
Nov.	Thu.	1	at Calgary
	Fri.	2	at Edmonton
	Tue.	6	Vancouver
	Fri.	9	Edmonton
	Sat.	10	at Boston
	Tue.	13	St. Louis
	Fri.	16	Anaheim
	Sat.	17	at Nashville
	Mon.	19	at Carolina
	Wed.	21	Detroit
	Fri.	23	Chicago
	Sun.	25	Calgary*
	Tue.	27	Phoenix
	Thu.	29	St. Louis
Dec.	Sat.	1	at St. Louis
	Wed.	5	at Florida
	Thu.	6	at Tampa Bay
	Sat.	8	Colorado
	Mon.	10	New Jersey
	Wed.	12	at Colorado
	Fri.	14	at Anaheim
	Sat.	15	at Los Angeles
	Mon.	17	at Phoenix
	Sat.	22	Dallas
	Thu.	27	at Detroit
	Sat.	29	Buffalo
	Mon.	31	Anaheim
Jan.	Thu.	3	at St. Louis
	Sun.	6	Nashville*
	Wed.	9	at Washington
	Thu.	10	at Chicago
	Sat.	12	Chicago
	Mon.	14	at NY Rangers
	Wed.	16	NY Rangers
	Fri.	18	Minnesota
	Sat.	19	at Nashville
	Mon.	21	Dallas
	Thu.	24	San Jose
	Sat.	26	Phoenix
	Mon.	28	at Dallas
	Wed.	30	at Anaheim
Feb.	Mon.	4	Boston
	Wed.	6	Ottawa
	Fri.	8	at Detroit
	Sat.	9	Nashville
	Tue.	12	Minnesota
	Tue.	26	Los Angeles
	Thu.	28	Pittsburgh
Mar.	Sat.	2	at Los Angeles*
	Sun.	3	at Phoenix*
	Wed.	6	at Colorado
	Fri.	8	NY Islanders
	Sun.	10	at Minnesota*
	Mon.	11	at Pittsburgh
	Thu.	14	Vancouver
	Sat.	16	Calgary
	Wed.	20	at Minnesota
	Thu.	21	Detroit
	Sat.	23	Washington
	Mon.	25	at Calgary
	Tue.	26	at Edmonton
	Thu.	28	at Vancouver
	Sat.	30	at San Jose
Apr.	Mon.	1	at Dallas
	Thu.	4	Nashville
	Sat.	6	at Montreal
	Mon.	8	at Toronto
	Wed.	10	San Jose
	Fri.	12	Atlanta
	Sun.	14	at Chicago*

* Denotes afternoon game.

Ron Tugnutt's 53 games in goal last season were the most he had played in the NHL since the 1990-91 season. His 2.44 goals-against average helped the Blue Jackets record a respectable 71 points in their inaugural season.

Franchise date: June 25, 1997

CENTRAL DIVISION

2nd NHL Season

2001-02 Player Personnel

FORWARDS	HT	WT	S	Place of Birth	Date	2000-01 Club
AUBIN, Serge	6-1	194	L	Val d'Or, Que.	2/15/75	Columbus
BELLEFEUILLE, Blake	5-10	208	R	Framingham, MA	12/27/77	Syracuse
DARCHE, Mathieu	6-1	225	L	St-Laurent, Que.	11/26/76	Columbus-Syracuse
DAVIDSON, Matt	6-2	190	R	Flin Flon, Man.	8/9/77	Columbus-Syracuse
DINEEN, Kevin	5-11	190	R	Quebec City, Que.	10/28/63	Columbus
HARKINS, Brett	6-1	185	L	North Ridgeville, OH	7/2/70	Houston
KNUTSEN, Espen	5-11	180	L	Oslo, Norway	1/12/72	Columbus
KRON, Robert	5-11	185	L	Brno, Czech.	2/27/67	Columbus
LING, David	5-9	185	R	Halifax, N.S.	1/9/75	Utah
McDONELL, Kent	6-0	200	R	Williamstown, Ont.	3/1/79	Dayton-Syracuse
MORAN, Brad	5-11	180	L	Abbotsford, B.C.	3/20/79	Syracuse
NEDOROST, Andrej	6-0	187	L	Trencin, Czech.	4/30/80	Keramicka Plzen
NIELSEN, Chris	6-1	190	R	Moshi, Tanzania	2/16/80	Columbus-Syracuse
PAROULEK, Martin	5-11	189	L	Uherske Hradiste, Czech.	11/4/79	HC Vsetin
PRONGER, Sean	6-2	205	L	Dryden, Ont.	11/30/72	Manitoba
REICH, Jeremy	6-1	190	L	Craik, Sask.	2/11/79	Syracuse
SANDERSON, Geoff	6-0	190	L	Hay River, N.W.T.	2/1/72	Columbus
SCHILL, Jonathan	6-1	201	L	Kitchener, Ont.	6/28/79	Syracuse-Dayton
SHELLEY, Jody	6-3	228	L	Yarmouth, N.S.	2/7/76	Columbus-Syracuse
SILLINGER, Mike	5-10	191	R	Regina, Sask.	6/29/71	Florida-Ottawa
SLOAN, Blake	5-10	196	R	Park Ridge, IL	7/27/75	Dal.-Houston-CBJ
SPANHEL, Martin	6-2	202	L	Zlin, Czech.	7/1/77	Columbus-Syracuse
VYBORNY, David	5-10	183	R	Jihlava, Czech.	6/2/75	Columbus
WHITNEY, Ray	5-10	175	R	Fort Saskatchewan, Alta.	5/8/72	Florida-Columbus
WRIGHT, Tyler	6-0	185	R	Canora, Sask.	4/6/73	Columbus
DEFENSEMEN						
BICANEK, Radim	6-1	195	L	Uherske Hradiste, Czech.	1/18/75	Columbus-Syracuse
GRAND-PIERRE, Jean-Luc	6-3	207	R	Montreal, Que.	2/2/77	Columbus
HEWARD, Jamie	6-2	207	R	Regina, Sask.	3/30/71	Columbus
KLESLA, Rostislav	6-2	198	L	Novy Jicin, Czech.	3/21/82	Columbus-Brampton
ODELEIN, Lyle	5-11	210	R	Quill Lake, Sask.	7/21/68	Columbus
PUSHOR, Jamie	6-3	218	R	Lethbridge, Alta.	2/11/73	Columbus
QUINT, Deron	6-2	219	L	Durham, NH	3/12/76	Columbus-Syracuse
SCOVILLE, Darryl	6-3	215	L	Swift Current, Sask.	10/13/75	Saint John
SRYUBKO, Andrei	6-3	205	L	Kiev, USSR	10/21/75	Syracuse
TIMANDER, Mattias	6-2	210	L	Solleftea, Sweden	4/16/74	Columbus
WARE, Jeff	6-4	220	L	Toronto, Ont.	5/19/77	Syracuse
WATSON, Dan	6-2	221	R	Glencoe, Ont.	10/5/79	Elmira-Syracuse
WESTCOTT, Duvie	5-11	180	R	Winnipeg, Man.	10/30/77	St. Cloud State

GOALTENDERS	HT	WT	C	Place of Birth	Date	2000-01 Club
DENIS, Marc	6-0	190	L	Montreal, Que.	8/1/77	Columbus
GARDNER, Greg	6-0	190	L	Mississauga, Ont.	11/21/75	Dayton-Syracuse
GOEHRING, Karl	5-7	155	L	Apple Valley, MN	8/23/78	North Dakota
LABBE, Jean-Francois	5-10	172	L	Sherbrooke, Que.	6/15/72	Hartford-Syracuse
TUGNUTT, Ron	5-11	160	L	Scarborough, Ont.	10/22/67	Columbus

2000-01 Scoring

* - rookie

Regular Season

Pos	#	Player	Team	GP	G	A	Pts	+/–	PIM	PP	SH	GW	GT	S	%
L	8	Geoff Sanderson	CBJ	68	30	26	56	4	46	9	0	7	0	199	15.1
C	21	Espen Knutsen	CBJ	66	11	42	53	–3	30	2	0	0	0	62	17.7
C	14	Ray Whitney	FLA	43	10	21	31	–16	28	5	0	0	0	117	8.5
			CBJ	3	0	3	3	–1	2	0	0	0	0	3	0.0
			TOTAL	46	10	24	34	–17	30	5	0	0	0	120	8.3
C	28	Tyler Wright	CBJ	76	16	16	32	–9	140	4	1	2	1	141	11.3
R	9 *	David Vyborny	CBJ	79	13	19	32	–9	22	5	0	1	0	125	10.4
C	10 *	Serge Aubin	CBJ	81	13	17	30	–20	107	0	0	2	1	110	11.8
D	6	Jamie Heward	CBJ	69	11	16	27	3	33	9	0	1	0	108	10.2
D	7	Deron Quint	CBJ	57	7	16	23	–19	16	3	0	0	0	148	4.7
R	25	Bruce Gardiner	CBJ	73	7	15	22	–1	78	0	0	1	0	60	11.7
C	18	Robert Kron	CBJ	59	8	11	19	4	10	0	1	1	0	134	6.0
R	29	Alex Selivanov	CBJ	59	8	11	19	–11	38	5	0	2	0	104	7.7
D	4	Lyle Odelein	CBJ	81	3	14	17	–16	118	1	0	0	0	104	2.9
D	33	Petteri Nummelin	CBJ	61	4	12	16	–11	10	2	0	0	0	99	4.0
R	11	Kevin Dineen	CBJ	66	8	7	15	2	126	0	0	3	0	74	10.8
D	5	Jamie Pushor	CBJ	75	3	10	13	7	94	0	1	0	0	64	4.7
D	37	Mattias Timander	CBJ	76	2	9	11	–8	24	0	0	1	0	68	2.9
C	22 *	Chris Nielsen	CBJ	29	4	5	9	4	4	0	0	1	1	36	11.1
R	15	Mike Maneluk	CBJ	39	5	1	6	–11	33	2	0	2	0	31	16.1
R	27	Blake Sloan	DAL	33	2	2	4	–2	4	0	0	1	0	29	6.9
			CBJ	14	1	0	1	–2	13	0	0	0	0	16	6.3
			TOTAL	47	3	2	5	–4	17	0	0	1	0	45	6.7
D	34	J-Luc Grand-Pierre	CBJ	64	1	4	5	–6	73	0	0	0	0	33	3.0
R	43	Jan Caloun	CBJ	11	0	3	3	–8	2	0	0	0	0	14	0.0
L	17	Steve Maltais	CBJ	26	0	3	3	–9	12	0	0	0	0	30	0.0
D	44 *	Rostislav Klesla	CBJ	8	2	0	2	–1	6	0	0	0	0	10	20.0
D	32	Radim Bicanek	CBJ	9	0	2	2	1	6	0	0	0	0	11	0.0
C	40 *	Bill Bowler	CBJ	9	0	2	2	–3	8	0	0	0	0	3	0.0
L	20 *	Martin Spanhel	CBJ	6	1	0	1	–1	2	0	0	0	0	8	12.5
G	31	Ron Tugnutt	CBJ	53	0	1	1	0	2	0	0	0	0	0	0.0
C	12	Ted Drury	CBJ	1	0	0	0	–3	0	0	0	0	0	3	0.0
L	36 *	Sean Selmser	CBJ	1	0	0	0	0	5	0	0	0	0	2	0.0
L	45 *	Jody Shelley	CBJ	1	0	0	0	0	10	0	0	0	0	0	0.0
D	24	Michael Gaul	CBJ	2	0	0	0	0	4	0	0	0	0	3	0.0
D	23	Kevin Dahl	CBJ	4	0	0	0	1	2	0	0	0	0	3	0.0
R	41 *	Matt Davidson	CBJ	5	0	0	0	2	0	0	0	0	0	2	0.0
L	19 *	Mathieu Darche	CBJ	9	0	0	0	–4	0	0	0	0	0	9	0.0
G	30 *	Marc Denis	CBJ	32	0	0	0	0	2	0	0	0	0	0	0.0

Goaltending

No.	Goaltender	GPI	Mins	Avg	W	L	T	EN	SO	GA	SA	S%
31	Ron Tugnutt	53	3129	2.44	22	25	5	5	4	127	1528	.917
30	* Marc Denis	32	1830	3.25	6	20	4	2	0	99	940	.895
	Totals	**82**	**4988**	**2.80**	**28**	**45**	**9**	**7**	**4**	**233**	**2475**	**.906**

Coaching History

Dave King, 2000-01 to date.

Coach

KING, DAVE

Coach, Columbus Blue Jackets. Born in Saskatoon, Sask., December 22, 1947.

Former Canadian national team coach Dave King was named the first head coach of the Columbus Blue Jackets on July 5, 2000. King joined the Blue Jackets after spending three seasons with the Montreal Canadiens organization.

King enjoyed a successful three-year stint as the head coach of the NHL's Calgary Flames from 1992 to 1995, guiding the club to consecutive Pacific Division titles in 1994 and 1995. He joined the Flames after spending nine seasons with the Canadian national hockey program. King coached Canada to the gold medal at the 1982 World Junior Championships and served as an assistant coach with the bronze medal-winning Team Canada at the 1982 World Championships. He later coached Canada at the Olympics in 1984, 1988 and 1992 and at the World Championships from 1989 to 1992.

King began his coaching career at the University of Saskatchewan in 1972-73. He then coached the Saskatoon Junior B Quakers to a pair of provincial and divisional championships from 1974 to 1976. After splitting the 1976-77 season between the Tier II Saskatoon Olympiques and Saskatoon Blades of the Western Hockey League, he joined the Billings Bighorns in 1977 and captured WHL Coach of the Year honors after leading the club to the 1978 WHL Finals. He then returned to the University of Saskatchewan, where he led the Huskies to three conference championships and the 1983 CIAU national title.

Coaching Record

		Regular Season or World Championships				Playoffs or Olympics			
Year	Team	Games	W	L	T	Games	W	L	T
1984	Canadian National	....	....	....	....	7	4	3	0
1987	Canadian National	10	3	5	2	....	....	....	....
1988	Canadian National	....	....	....	....	8	5	2	1
1989	Canadian National	10	7	3	0	....	....	....	....
1990	Canadian National	10	6	3	1	....	....	....	....
1991	Canadian National	10	5	2	3	....	....	....	....
1992	Canadian National	6	2	3	1	8	6	2	0
1992-93	**Calgary (NHL)**	**84**	**43**	**30**	**11**	**6**	**2**	**4**	....
1993-94	**Calgary (NHL)**	**84**	**42**	**29**	**13**	**7**	**3**	**4**	....
1994-95	**Calgary (NHL)**	**48**	**24**	**17**	**7**	**7**	**3**	**4**	....
2000-01	**Columbus (NHL)**	**82**	**28**	**45**	**9**	....	....	....	....
	NHL Totals	**298**	**137**	**121**	**40**	**20**	**8**	**12**	....

Club Records

Team

(Figures in brackets for season records are games played.)

Most Points **71** 2000-01 (82)
Most Wins **28** 2000-01 (82)
Most Ties **9** 2000-01 (82)
Most Losses **39** 2000-01 (82)
Most Goals **211** 2000-01 (82)
Most Goals Against **233** 2000-01 (82)
Fewest Points **71** 2000-01 (82)
Fewest Wins **28** 2000-01 (82)
Fewest Ties **9** 2000-01 (82)
Fewest Losses **39** 2000-01 (82)
Fewest Goals **211** 2000-01 (82)
Fewest Goals Against **233** 2000-01 (82)

Longest Winning Streak
Overall .... **4** Nov. 9-Nov. 16/00
Home .... **4** Mar. 24-Apr. 8/01
Away .... **2** Dec. 18-Dec. 23/00, Feb. 25-Mar. 1/01

Longest Undefeated Streak
Overall .... **4** Nov. 9-Nov. 16/00 (4 wins)
Home .... **5** Mar. 21-Apr. 8/01 (4 wins, 1 tie)
Away .... **2** Four times

Longest Losing Streak
Overall .... **8** Nov. 17-Dec. 3/00
Home .... **5** Oct. 7-Oct. 25/00, Nov. 17-Dec. 2/00
Away .... **5** Oct. 14-Nov. 1/00, Mar. 26-Apr. 6/01

Longest Winless Streak
Overall .... **8** Nov. 17-Dec. 3/00 (8 losses)
Home .... **5** Oct. 7-Oct. 25/00 (5 losses), Nov. 17-Dec. 2/00 (5 losses)
Away .... **7** Nov. 22-Dec. 16/00 (6 losses, 1 tie), Feb. 1-Feb. 24/01 (5 losses, 2 ties)

Most Shutouts, Season **4** 2000-01 (82)
Most PIM, Season **1,234** 2000-01 (82)
Most Goals, Game .... **7** Dec. 23/2000 (CBJ 7 at NYI 5), Mar. 9/01 (CBJ 7 at Fla. 6)

Individual

Most Seasons .... **1** Many players
Most Games .... **81** Serge Aubin, Lyle Odelein
Most Goals, Career .... **30** Geoff Sanderson
Most Assists, Career .... **42** Espen Knutsen
Most Points, Career .... **56** Geoff Sanderson (30G, 26A)
Most PIM, Career .... **140** Tyler Wright
Most Shutouts, Career .... **4** Ron Tugnutt
Most Goals, Season .... **30** Geoff Sanderson (2000-01)
Most Assists, Season .... **42** Espen Knutsen (2000-01)
Most Points, Season .... **56** Geoff Sanderson (2000-01; 30G, 26A)
Most PIM, Season .... **140** Tyler Wright (2000-01)
Most Points, Defenseman, Season .... **27** Jamie Heward (2000-01; 11G, 16A)
Most Points, Center, Season .... **53** Epsen Knutsen (2000-01; 11G, 42A)
Most Points, Right Wing, Season .... **42** Steve Heinze (2000-01; 22G, 20A)
Most Points, Left Wing, Season .... **56** Geoff Sanderson (2000-01; 30G, 26A)
Most Points, Rookie, Season .... **32** David Vyborny (2000-01; 13G, 19A)
Most Shutouts, Season .... **4** Ron Tugnutt (2000-01)
Most Goals, Game .... **3** Geoff Sanderson (Feb. 10/01), Deron Quint (Mar. 9/01), Tyler Wright (Mar. 16/01)
Most Assists, Game .... **5** Espen Knutsen (Mar. 24/01)
Most Points, Game .... **5** Espen Knutsen (Mar. 24/01; 5A)

Captains' History

Lyle Odelein, 2000-01 to date.

Geoff Sanderson's 30 goals last season nearly doubled Columbus's next-best scorer and were just 12 goals short of the expansion record set by Brian Bradley with Tampa Bay back in 1992-93.

2000-01 Results

Oct.	7	Chicago	3-5
	9	Los Angeles	1-7
	12	at Calgary	3-2
	14	at Colorado	1-3
	15	at Chicago	1-2
	18	Colorado	1-5
	21	at Pittsburgh	2-5
	22	Detroit	1-2*
	25	San Jose	1-3
	27	Washington	3-1
	28	at Detroit	1-4
	31	Los Angeles	4-1
Nov.	1	at Dallas	0-4
	4	at Ottawa	2-2
	5	Edmonton	2-4
	9	San Jose	5-2
	11	Phoenix	2-1
	14	Dallas	3-2
	16	at Nashville	5-1
	17	Florida	0-3
	19	Vancouver	1-6
	22	at Colorado	2-5
	24	at Dallas	0-3
	25	Dallas	2-4
	29	Philadelphia	3-4
Dec.	2	Atlanta	1-2
	3	at Chicago	0-5
	6	Anaheim	5-2
	8	Boston	3-2*
	10	at Phoenix	1-1
	13	at Anaheim	4-5*
	14	at San Jose	1-2
	16	at Vancouver	3-4
	18	at Montreal	2-0
	21	Ottawa	3-3
	23	at NY Islanders	7-5
	26	at St. Louis	0-5
	27	at New Jersey	2-2
	29	Carolina	3-1
	31	New Jersey	3-6
Jan.	3	Edmonton	5-2
	6	at Vancouver	3-4
	7	at Edmonton	2-4
	10	Colorado	2-4
	12	Chicago	1-3
	15	Minnesota	3-0
	17	at Minnesota	2-3*
	21	Tampa Bay	3-1
	23	at Buffalo	2-1
	27	Anaheim	2-1
	31	Detroit	2-3*
Feb.	1	at St. Louis	2-2
	6	St. Louis	2-2
	8	at Nashville	1-3
	10	Nashville	3-2
	12	NY Rangers	3-4
	14	at Toronto	2-2
	16	at Detroit	2-4
	17	Pittsburgh	2-3*
	20	at San Jose	2-3*
	21	at Phoenix	2-3
	24	at Los Angeles	1-3
	25	at Anaheim	5-2
	28	Phoenix	5-2
Mar.	1	at Nashville	5-2
	7	at Carolina	1-2
	9	at Florida	7-6*
	10	at Tampa Bay	1-4
	14	Calgary	3-0
	16	at Atlanta	3-0
	17	NY Islanders	3-3
	19	Nashville	1-2
	21	Vancouver	1-1
	24	Calgary	6-4
	26	at Edmonton	2-4
	27	at Calgary	0-3
	29	at Los Angeles	0-3
Apr.	1	St. Louis	2-1
	3	Detroit	2-1
	5	at St. Louis	1-4
	6	at Minnesota	2-3
	8	Chicago	4-3*

* – Overtime

All-time Record vs. Other Clubs

Regular Season

	At Home								On Road								Total							
	GP	W	L	T	OL	GF	GA	PTS	GP	W	L	T	OL	GF	GA	PTS	GP	W	L	T	OL	GF	GA	PTS
Anaheim	2	2	0	0	0	7	3	4	2	1	0	0	1	9	7	3	4	3	0	0	1	16	10	7
Atlanta	1	0	1	0	0	1	2	0	1	1	0	0	0	3	0	2	2	1	1	0	0	4	2	2
Boston	1	1	0	0	0	3	2	2	0	0	0	0	0	0	0	0	1	1	0	0	0	3	2	2
Buffalo	0	0	0	0	0	0	0	0	1	1	0	0	0	2	1	2	1	1	0	0	0	2	1	2
Calgary	2	2	0	0	0	9	4	4	2	1	1	0	0	3	5	2	4	3	1	0	0	12	9	6
Carolina	1	1	0	0	0	3	1	2	1	0	1	0	0	1	2	0	2	1	1	0	0	4	3	2
Chicago	3	1	2	0	0	8	11	2	2	0	2	0	0	1	7	0	5	1	4	0	0	9	18	2
Colorado	2	0	2	0	0	3	9	0	2	0	2	0	0	3	8	0	4	0	4	0	0	6	17	0
Dallas	2	1	1	0	0	5	6	2	2	0	2	0	0	0	7	0	4	1	3	0	0	5	13	2
Detroit	3	1	0	0	2	5	6	4	2	0	2	0	0	3	8	0	5	1	2	0	2	8	14	4
Edmonton	2	1	1	0	0	7	6	2	2	0	2	0	0	4	8	0	4	1	3	0	0	11	14	2
Florida	1	0	1	0	0	0	3	0	1	1	0	0	0	7	6	2	2	1	1	0	0	7	9	2
Los Angeles	2	1	1	0	0	5	8	2	2	0	2	0	0	1	6	0	4	1	3	0	0	6	14	2
Minnesota	1	1	0	0	0	3	0	2	2	0	1	0	1	4	6	1	3	1	1	0	1	7	6	3
Montreal	0	0	0	0	0	0	0	0	1	1	0	0	0	2	0	2	1	1	0	0	0	2	0	2
Nashville	2	1	1	0	0	4	4	2	3	2	1	0	0	11	6	4	5	3	2	0	0	15	10	6
New Jersey	1	0	1	0	0	3	6	0	1	0	0	1	0	2	2	1	2	0	1	1	0	5	8	1
NY Islanders	1	0	0	1	0	3	3	1	1	1	0	0	0	7	5	2	2	1	0	1	0	10	8	3
NY Rangers	1	0	1	0	0	3	4	0	0	0	0	0	0	0	0	0	1	0	1	0	0	3	4	0
Ottawa	1	0	0	1	0	3	3	1	1	0	0	1	0	2	2	1	2	0	0	2	0	5	5	2
Philadelphia	1	0	1	0	0	3	4	0	0	0	0	0	0	0	0	0	1	0	1	0	0	3	4	0
Phoenix	2	2	0	0	0	7	3	4	2	0	1	1	0	3	4	1	4	2	1	1	0	10	7	5
Pittsburgh	1	0	0	0	1	2	3	1	1	0	1	0	0	2	5	0	2	0	1	0	1	4	8	1
St. Louis	2	1	0	1	0	4	3	3	3	0	2	1	0	3	11	1	5	1	2	2	0	7	14	4
San Jose	2	1	1	0	0	6	5	2	2	0	1	0	1	3	5	1	4	1	2	0	1	9	10	3
Tampa Bay	1	1	0	0	0	3	1	2	1	0	1	0	0	1	4	0	2	1	1	0	0	4	5	2
Toronto	0	0	0	0	0	0	0	0	1	0	0	1	0	2	2	1	1	0	0	1	0	2	2	1
Vancouver	2	0	1	1	0	2	7	1	2	0	2	0	0	6	8	0	4	0	3	1	0	8	15	1
Washington	1	1	0	0	0	3	1	2	0	0	0	0	0	0	0	0	1	1	0	0	0	3	1	2
Totals	**41**	**19**	**15**	**4**	**3**	**105**	**108**	**45**	**41**	**9**	**24**	**5**	**3**	**85**	**125**	**26**	**82**	**28**	**39**	**9**	**6**	**190**	**233**	**71**

Entry Draft Selections 2001-2000

2001 Pick		2000 Pick	
8	Pascal Leclaire	4	Rostislav Klesla
38	Tim Jackman	69	Ben Knopp
53	Kiel McLeod	133	Petteri Nummelin
85	Aaron Johnson	138	Scott Heffernan
87	Per Mars	150	Tyler Kolarik
141	Cole Jarrett	169	Shane Bendera
173	Justin Aikins	200	Janne Jokila
187	Artem Vostrikov	231	Peter Zingoni
204	Raffaele Sannitz	278	Martin Paroulek
236	Ryan Bowness	286	Andrej Nedorost
242	Andrew Murray	292	Louis Mandeville

TM

General Managers' History

Doug MacLean, 2000-01 to date.

General Manager

MacLEAN, DOUG
General Manager, Columbus Blue Jackets.
Born in Summerside, P.E.I., April 12, 1954.

Doug MacLean joined the Columbus Blue Jackets in February, 1998, after a successful stint with the Florida Panthers that saw him lead the team to the Stanley Cup Finals in 1996 during his first season as head coach. He was selected as coach of the year by *The Hockey News* and was runner-up for the Jack Adams Award that same season.

MacLean began his NHL coaching career in 1986 as an assistant to Jacques Martin in St. Louis. He spent two seasons with the Blues before joining the Washington Capitals in 1988, assisting Bryan Murray behind the bench. He was named coach of the Capitals' American Hockey League affiliate in Baltimore for the final 35 games of the 1989-90 season.

The following season, MacLean joined Murray on the Detroit Red Wings, serving as an assistant coach for two years. In 1992, MacLean was named assistant general manager of the Red Wings and also served as general manager of the team's AHL affiliate in Adirondack for two years. MacLean followed Murray to the Panthers in 1994, becoming the expansion club's director of player development. He was named head coach on July 24, 1995.

A collegiate hockey player at the University of Prince Edward Island, MacLean graduated with a bachelor's degree in education. He also played for the Montreal Jr. Canadiens and was invited to training camp with the St. Louis Blues in 1974. Following his playing career, MacLean enrolled at the University of Western Ontario, where he received a master's degree in educational psychology. While attending Western, MacLean began his coaching career as an assistant with London of the Ontario Hockey League.

NHL Coaching Record

		Regular Season				Playoffs		
Season	Team	Games	W	L	T	Games	W	L
1995-96	Florida	82	41	31	10	22	12	10
1996-97	Florida	82	35	28	19	5	1	4
1997-98	Florida	23	7	12	4	....	....	....
	NHL Totals	**187**	**83**	**71**	**33**	**27**	**13**	**14**

Club Directory

Nationwide Arena

Columbus Blue Jackets
Nationwide Arena
200 W. Nationwide Blvd.
Columbus, Ohio 43215
Phone **614/246-4625**
FAX 614/246-4007
www.BlueJackets.com
Capacity: 18,136

Ownership

Majority Owner/Governor	John H. McConnell
Alternate Governor	John P. McConnell

Executive Staff

President/General Manager/Alternate Governor	Doug MacLean
Executive Vice-President/Assistant General Manager	Jim Clark
Sr. Vice-President of Business Development	Michael Humes
Vice-President of Marketing	David Paitson
Vice-President of Ticket Sales	Andy Silverman
Chief Financial Officer	T.J. LaMendola
General Counsel	Greg Kirstein

Hockey Operations

Head Coach	Dave King
Associate Coach	Newell Brown
Assistant Coach	Gerard Gallant
Goaltending Coach, Pro Scout	Rick Wamsley
Director of Amateur Scouting	Don Boyd
Assistant Director of Amateur Scouting	Paul Castron
Director of Pro Scouting	Bob Strumm
Manager of Hockey Operations	Chris MacFarland
Manager of Team Services	Jim Rankin
Video Coordinator	Dan Singleton
Administrative Assistant, Hockey Operations	Julie Uhler
Amateur Scouts	Sam McMaster, John Williams
Pro Scout	Peter Dineen
European Scout	Kjell Larsson
Regional Scouts	Brian Bates, Scott Fitzgerald, Erin Ginnell, Denis LeBlanc, John McNamara, Artem Telepin Nicholaevich, Bryan Raymond, Andrew Shaw, Wayne Smith, Milan Tichy
Head Athletic Trainer	Chris Mizer
Strength and Conditioning Coach	Mark Casterline
Equipment Manager	Tim LeRoy
Assistant Equipment Manager	Jamie Healy
Equipment Assistant	Andre Szucko

Business Operations

Executive Director of Sales	Paul D'Aiuto
Director of Communications	Todd Sharrock
Director of Client Services	Terri Murphy
Director of Advertising and Promotions	Marc Gregory
Director of Game Operations	Kimberly Kershaw
Director of Fan Development	J.D. Kershaw
Director of Community Development	Wendy Peterson
Business Development Manager	Scott Klein
Business Development Manager	Darlene Quebedeaux
Assistant Director of Communications	Jason Rothwell
Manager of Multimedia	Steve Ostaszewicz
Manager of Advertising and Promotions	Carson Woods
Graphic Designer/Manager of Print Production	Will Bennett
Client Services Managers	Brent Baker, John Sass
Legal/Immigration Associate	Kelley Kauffman
Manager of Video Services	Rich Davis
Game Operations Assistant	Matt Bettinger
Fan Development Coordinator	Joel Siegman
Mascot Coordinator	Jason Zumpano
Community Development Coordinator	Tracey Vogelpohl
Executive Assistant to Doug MacLean	Kari Pitzer
Executive Assistant to Michael Humes	Michelle LeVeque
Executive Assistant to David Paitson	Julie Sundquist
Administrative Assistant to Greg Kirstein	Nikki Ward

Finance

Controller	Rich Gross
Financial Analyst	Dana Fletcher
Staff Accountant	Nora Ludwig
Accounts Payable	Rose Phillips, Malika Dickerson
Accounts Receivable	Shelly Phillips
MIS Manager	Jim Connolly
Human Resources Manager	Harry Coder
Payroll Administrator	Vangie Bondy
General Manager, Facility Merchandising, Inc.	Jennifer Emerich
Team Store Manager, Facility Merchandising, Inc.	Karen Green
Warehouse Manager, Facility Merchandising, Inc.	Bill Bellville
Office Manager	Rachel Durham
Receptionist	Beth Carlisle

Ticket Operations

Director of Ticket Operations/Customer Service	Mark Morris
Director of Season Ticket Sales	Todd Taylor
Manager of Premium and Suite Services	Derrill Smith
Manager of Ticket Operations/Customer Service	Karen Bierley
Asst. Mgr. of Ticket Operations/Customer Service	Mark Metz
Account Executives – PSL	Celeste Leadingham, John Motto
Senior Account Executive – Group Sales	John Davis
Account Exec. – Group Sales	Heather Bardocz, Kristie Miller
Premium and Suite Services Coordinator	Brian Lane
Database Coordinator	Krista Vicars
Ticket Operations/Customer Service	Jack Decker, Tim O'Grady

Broadcasting

Director of Broadcasting	Russ Mollohan
Television Play-By-Play Announcer	Dan Kelly
Television Color Analyst	Steve Konroyd
Radio Play-By-Play Announcer	George Matthews
Radio Color Analyst	Bill Davidge

Dallas Stars

2000-01 Results: 48W-24L-8T-2OTL 106PTS. First, Pacific Division

A member of the Stars organization since 1991-92 when the team was still based in Minnesota, Derian Hatcher has been captain of the team since 1994-95 when he shared the "C" with Neal Broten.

2001-02 Schedule

Month	Day	Date	Opponent
Oct.	Fri.	5	Nashville
	Sun.	7	at Carolina*
	Tue.	9	Los Angeles
	Thu.	11	Vancouver
	Sat.	13	Calgary
	Wed.	17	at St. Louis
	Thu.	18	Phoenix
	Sat.	20	Chicago
	Wed.	24	at Pittsburgh
	Fri.	26	at Detroit
	Sun.	28	at NY Islanders*
	Mon.	29	at NY Rangers
	Wed.	31	Detroit
Nov.	Fri.	2	Nashville
	Sat.	3	at Nashville
	Wed.	7	San Jose
	Fri.	9	Phoenix
	Sun.	11	at Anaheim*
	Thu.	15	at Los Angeles
	Sat.	17	at San Jose
	Mon.	19	NY Islanders
	Wed.	21	Carolina
	Fri.	23	Philadelphia
	Sun.	25	at Minnesota*
	Thu.	29	at Calgary
Dec.	Sat.	1	at Edmonton
	Sun.	2	at Vancouver
	Wed.	5	Ottawa
	Fri.	7	Edmonton
	Wed.	12	Buffalo
	Fri.	14	Calgary
	Sat.	15	at Phoenix
	Mon.	17	San Jose
	Thu.	20	at Philadelphia
	Sat.	22	at Columbus
	Sun.	23	at Atlanta
	Wed.	26	Colorado
	Fri.	28	Washington
	Mon.	31	Boston
Jan.	Wed.	2	Atlanta
	Sat.	5	at St. Louis*
	Tue.	8	at Tampa Bay
	Wed.	9	at Florida
	Sat.	12	at Detroit*
	Sun.	13	at Minnesota
	Wed.	16	Detroit
	Fri.	18	Florida
	Sun.	20	at Chicago
	Mon.	21	at Columbus
	Wed.	23	Vancouver
	Fri.	25	Anaheim
	Mon.	28	Columbus
Feb.	Wed.	6	at Nashville
	Fri.	8	Edmonton
	Sun.	10	at Anaheim*
	Mon.	11	at Los Angeles
	Wed.	13	NY Rangers
	Tue.	26	at Phoenix
	Thu.	28	at Vancouver
Mar.	Sat.	2	at Colorado*
	Sun.	3	San Jose*
	Wed.	6	Los Angeles
	Fri.	8	Minnesota
	Sun.	10	New Jersey
	Tue.	12	at Washington
	Thu.	14	at Montreal
	Sat.	16	at Toronto
	Mon.	18	at Chicago
	Wed.	20	St. Louis
	Fri.	22	Phoenix
	Sun.	24	Anaheim*
	Tue.	26	at San Jose
	Thu.	28	at Calgary
	Sat.	30	at Edmonton
Apr.	Mon.	1	Columbus
	Wed.	3	St. Louis
	Fri.	5	Colorado
	Sun.	7	at Anaheim*
	Mon.	8	at Los Angeles
	Wed.	10	Minnesota
	Fri.	12	Chicago
	Sun.	14	at Colorado*

* Denotes afternoon game.

Franchise date: June 5, 1967

Transferred from Minnesota to Dallas, June 9, 1993.

WESTERN NHL CONFERENCE

PACIFIC DIVISION

35th NHL Season

Year-by-Year Record

		Home				Road				Overall								
Season	GP	W	L	T	OL	W	L	T	OL	W	L	T	OL	GF	GA	Pts.	Finished	Playoff Result
2000-01	82	26	10	5	0	22	14	3	2	48	24	8	2	241	187	106	1st, Pacific Div.	Lost Conf. Semi-Final
1999-2000	82	21	11	5	4	22	12	5	2	43	23	10	6	211	184	102	1st, Pacific Div.	Lost Final
1998-99	**82**	**29**	**8**	**4**	**...**	**22**	**11**	**8**	**...**	**51**	**19**	**12**	**...**	**236**	**168**	**114**	**1st, Pacific Div.**	**Won Stanley Cup**
1997-98	82	26	8	7	...	23	14	4	...	49	22	11	...	242	167	109	1st, Central Div.	Lost Conf. Final
1996-97	82	25	13	3	...	23	13	5	...	48	26	8	...	252	198	104	1st, Central Div.	Lost Conf. Quarter-Final
1995-96	82	14	18	9	...	12	24	5	...	26	42	14	...	227	280	66	6th, Central Div.	Out of Playoffs
1994-95	48	9	10	5	...	8	13	3	...	17	23	8	...	136	135	42	5th, Central Div.	Lost Conf. Quarter-Final
1993-94	84	23	12	7	...	19	17	6	...	42	29	13	...	286	265	97	3rd, Central Div.	Lost Conf. Semi-Final
1992-93*	84	18	17	7	...	18	21	3	...	36	38	10	...	272	293	82	5th, Norris Div.	Out of Playoffs
1991-92*	80	20	16	4	...	12	26	2	...	32	42	6	...	246	278	70	4th, Norris Div.	Lost Div. Semi-Final
1990-91*	80	19	15	6	...	8	24	8	...	27	39	14	...	256	266	68	4th, Norris Div.	Lost Final
1989-90*	80	26	12	2	...	10	28	2	...	36	40	4	...	284	291	76	4th, Norris Div.	Lost Div. Semi-Final
1988-89*	80	17	15	8	...	10	22	8	...	27	37	16	...	258	278	70	3rd, Norris Div.	Lost Div. Semi-Final
1987-88*	80	10	24	6	...	9	24	7	...	19	48	13	...	242	349	51	5th, Norris Div.	Out of Playoffs
1986-87*	80	17	20	3	...	13	20	7	...	30	40	10	...	296	314	70	5th, Norris Div.	Out of Playoffs
1985-86*	80	21	15	4	...	17	18	5	...	38	33	9	...	327	305	85	2nd, Norris Div.	Lost Div. Semi-Final
1984-85*	80	14	19	7	...	11	24	5	...	25	43	12	...	268	321	62	4th, Norris Div.	Lost Div. Final
1983-84*	80	22	14	4	...	17	17	6	...	39	31	10	...	345	344	88	1st, Norris Div.	Lost Conf. Championship
1982-83*	80	23	6	11	...	17	18	5	...	40	24	16	...	321	290	96	2nd, Norris Div.	Lost Div. Final
1981-82*	80	21	7	12	...	16	16	8	...	37	23	20	...	346	288	94	1st, Norris Div.	Lost Div. Semi-Final
1980-81*	80	23	10	7	...	12	18	10	...	35	28	17	...	291	263	87	3rd, Adams Div.	Lost Final
1979-80*	80	25	8	7	...	11	20	9	...	36	28	16	...	311	253	88	3rd, Adams Div.	Lost Semi-Final
1978-79*	80	19	15	6	...	9	25	6	...	28	40	12	...	257	289	68	4th, Adams Div.	Out Of Playoffs
1977-78*	80	12	24	4	...	6	29	5	...	18	53	9	...	218	325	45	5th, Smythe Div.	Out of Playoffs
1976-77*	80	17	14	9	...	6	25	9	...	23	39	18	...	240	310	64	2nd, Smythe Div.	Lost Prelim. Round
1975-76*	80	15	22	3	...	5	31	4	...	20	53	7	...	195	303	47	4th, Smythe Div.	Out of Playoffs
1974-75*	80	17	20	3	...	6	30	4	...	23	50	7	...	221	341	53	4th, Smythe Div.	Out of Playoffs
1973-74*	78	18	15	6	...	5	23	11	...	23	38	17	...	235	275	63	7th, West Div.	Out of Playoffs
1972-73*	78	26	8	5	...	11	22	6	...	37	30	11	...	254	230	85	3rd, West Div.	Lost Quarter-Final
1971-72*	78	22	11	6	...	15	18	6	...	37	29	12	...	212	191	86	2nd, West Div.	Lost Quarter-Final
1970-71*	78	16	15	8	...	12	19	8	...	28	34	16	...	191	223	72	4th, West Div.	Lost Semi-Final
1969-70*	76	11	16	11	...	8	19	11	...	19	35	22	...	224	257	60	3rd, West Div.	Lost Quarter-Final
1968-69*	76	11	21	6	...	7	22	9	...	18	43	15	...	189	270	51	6th, West Div.	Out of Playoffs
1967-68*	74	17	12	8	...	10	20	7	...	27	32	15	...	191	226	69	4th, West Div.	Lost Semi-Final

* Minnesota North Stars

2001-02 Player Personnel

FORWARDS	HT	WT	S	Place of Birth	Date	2000-01 Club
AUDETTE, Donald	5-8	190	R	Laval, Que.	9/23/69	Atlanta-Buffalo
DiMAIO, Rob	5-10	190	R	Calgary, Alta.	2/19/68	Carolina
GAINEY, Steve	6-0	185	L	Montreal, Que.	1/26/79	Dallas-Utah
HOGUE, Benoit	5-10	194	L	Repentigny, Que.	10/28/66	Dallas
KAMENSKY, Valeri	6-2	198	R	Voskresensk, USSR	4/18/66	NY Rangers
KAPANEN, Niko	5-9	180	L	Hattula, Finland	4/29/78	TPS Turku
KRISTOFFERSSON, Marcus	6-3	200	L	Ostersund, Sweden	1/22/79	Assat-Pori-Djurgardens IF
LANGENBRUNNER, Jamie	6-1	200	R	Duluth, MN	7/24/75	Dallas
LEHTINEN, Jere	6-0	200	R	Espoo, Finland	6/24/73	Dallas
LYASHENKO, Roman	6-0	189	R	Murmansk, Russia	5/2/79	Dallas-Utah
MANN, Cameron	6-0	195	R	Thompson, Man.	4/20/77	Boston-Prov (AHL)
MARSHALL, Grant	6-1	200	R	Mississauga, Ont.	6/9/73	Dallas
MODANO, Mike	6-3	205	L	Livonia, MI	6/7/70	Dallas
MONTGOMERY, Jim	5-10	180	R	Montreal, Que.	6/30/69	San Jose-Kentucky
MORGAN, Gavin	5-11	175	R	Scarborough, Ont.	7/9/76	Utah
MORROW, Brenden	5-11	200	L	Carlyle, Sask.	1/16/79	Dallas
MULLER, Kirk	6-0	205	L	Kingston, Ont.	2/8/66	Dallas
NIEUWENDYK, Joe	6-1	205	L	Oshawa, Ont.	9/10/66	Dallas
OTT, Steve	6-0	160	L	Summerside, P.E.I.	8/19/82	Windsor
SIM, Jonathan	5-10	184	L	New Glasgow, N.S.	9/29/77	Dallas-Utah
TURGEON, Pierre	6-1	199	L	Rouyn, Que.	8/28/69	St. Louis
VAN ALLEN, Shaun	6-1	204	L	Calgary, Alta.	8/29/67	Dallas
DEFENSEMEN						
ERSKINE, John	6-4	215	L	Kingston, Ont.	6/26/80	Utah
HATCHER, Derian	6-5	230	L	Sterling Heights, MI	6/4/72	Dallas
HAWGOOD, Greg	5-10	190	L	Edmonton, Alta.	8/10/68	Vancouver-Kansas City
HELENIUS, Sami	6-6	230	L	Helsinki, Finland	1/22/74	Dallas
LUKOWICH, Brad	6-1	200	L	Cranbrook, B.C.	8/12/76	Dallas
LUMME, Jyrki	6-1	209	L	Tampere, Finland	7/16/66	Phoenix
MATVICHUK, Richard	6-2	215	L	Edmonton, Alta.	2/5/73	Dallas
SYDOR, Darryl	6-1	205	L	Edmonton, Alta.	5/13/72	Dallas
WOTTON, Mark	6-1	195	L	Foxwarren, Man.	11/16/73	Dallas-Utah
ZUBOV, Sergei	6-1	200	R	Moscow, USSR	7/22/70	Dallas
GOALTENDERS	**HT**	**WT**	**C**	**Place of Birth**	**Date**	**2000-01 Club**
ALBAN, Chad	5-9	165	L	Kalamazoo, MI	4/27/76	Idaho-Grand Rapids-Utah
BACASHIHUA, Jason	5-11	167	L	Garden City, MI	9/20/82	Chicago (NAJHL)
BELFOUR, Ed	5-11	192	L	Carman, Man.	4/21/65	Dallas
TABARACCI, Rick	6-1	190	L	Toronto, Ont.	1/2/69	Utah
TURCO, Marty	5-11	183	L	Sault Ste. Marie, Ont.	8/13/75	Dallas

Coach

HITCHCOCK, KEN
Coach, Dallas Stars. Born in Edmonton, Alberta, December 17, 1951.

Ken Hitchcock coached the Dallas Stars to the first Stanley Cup championship in franchise history in 1999. That success culminated a season in which the Stars set franchise records with 51 victories (51-19-12) and 114 points, marking the third straight season in which Hitchcock's club established new highs in those categories. Since then, Dallas has remained among the NHL's best teams.

Named to his current position on January 8, 1996, Hitchcock had previously enjoyed winning seasons in every year at every level at which he had coached. He posted an incredible 575-69 mark in 10 seasons of Canadian Triple A midget hockey with Sherwood Park in suburban Edmonton, and then went on to record-breaking success with a .693 winning percentage in six seasons with Kamloops of the Western Hockey League. Hitchcock was the WHL coach of the year in 1986-87 and again in 1989-90, when he also added honors as Canadian Major Junior coach of the year.

After a three-year stint (1990-93) as an assistant coach for the Philadelphia Flyers, Hitchcock returned to head coaching duties in the International Hockey League before earning his promotion to Dallas.

Coaching Record

		Regular Season				Playoffs		
Season	Team	Games	W	L	T	Games	W	L
1984-85	Kamloops (WHL)	71	52	17	2	15	10	5
1985-86	Kamloops (WHL)	72	49	19	4	16	14	2
1986-87	Kamloops (WHL)	72	55	14	3	13	8	5
1987-88	Kamloops (WHL)	72	45	26	1	18	12	6
1988-89	Kamloops (WHL)	72	34	33	5	16	8	8
1989-90	Kamloops (WHL)	72	56	16	0	17	14	3
1993-94	Kalamazoo (IHL)	81	48	26	7	5	1	4
1994-95	Kalamazoo (IHL)	81	43	24	14	16	10	6
1995-96	Michigan (IHL)	40	19	10	11	....	....	....
	Dallas (NHL)	**43**	**15**	**23**	**5**	....	....	....
1996-97	**Dallas (NHL)**	**82**	**48**	**26**	**8**	**7**	**3**	**4**
1997-98	**Dallas (NHL)**	**82**	**49**	**22**	**11**	**17**	**10**	**7**
1998-99	**Dallas (NHL)**	**82**	**51**	**19**	**12**	**23**	**16**	**7***
1999-2000	**Dallas (NHL)**	**82**	**43**	**29**	**10**	**23**	**14**	**9**
2000-01	**Dallas (NHL)**	**82**	**48**	**26**	**8**	**10**	**4**	**6**
	NHL Totals	**453**	**254**	**145**	**54**	**80**	**46**	**34**

* Stanley Cup win.

2000-01 Scoring

* - rookie

Regular Season

Pos	#	Player	Team	GP	G	A	Pts	+/–	PIM	PP	SH	GW	GT	S	%
C	9	Mike Modano	DAL	81	33	51	84	26	52	8	3	7	1	208	15.9
R	16	Brett Hull	DAL	79	39	40	79	10	18	11	0	8	1	219	17.8
C	25	Joe Nieuwendyk	DAL	69	29	23	52	5	30	12	0	4	0	166	17.5
D	56	Sergei Zubov	DAL	79	10	41	51	22	24	6	0	1	1	173	5.8
D	5	Darryl Sydor	DAL	81	10	37	47	5	34	8	0	1	0	140	7.1
L	26	Jere Lehtinen	DAL	74	20	25	45	14	24	7	0	1	1	148	13.5
L	10	Brenden Morrow	DAL	82	20	24	44	18	128	7	0	6	0	121	16.5
R	29	Grant Marshall	DAL	75	13	24	37	1	64	4	0	1	0	93	14.0
R	15	Jamie Langenbrunner	DAL	53	12	18	30	4	57	3	2	4	0	104	11.5
L	17	Ted Donato	DAL	65	8	17	25	6	26	1	0	3	0	71	11.3
L	12	Mike Keane	DAL	67	10	14	24	4	35	1	0	1	0	64	15.6
C	27	Shaun Van Allen	DAL	59	7	16	23	5	16	0	2	3	0	51	13.7
D	2	Derian Hatcher	DAL	80	2	21	23	5	77	1	0	2	0	97	2.1
D	24	Richard Matvichuk	DAL	78	4	16	20	5	62	2	0	1	0	85	4.7
D	37	Brad Lukowich	DAL	80	4	10	14	28	76	0	0	2	0	43	9.3
C	33	Benoit Hogue	DAL	34	3	7	10	–1	26	0	0	0	0	35	8.6
L	22	Kirk Muller	DAL	55	1	9	10	–4	26	0	0	0	0	54	1.9
C	36	Roman Lyashenko	DAL	60	6	3	9	–1	45	0	0	1	0	48	12.5
R	55	* Tyler Bouck	DAL	48	2	5	7	–3	29	0	0	1	0	41	4.9
R	51	John MacLean	NYR	2	0	0	0	–2	0	0	0	0	0	0	0.0
			DAL	28	4	2	6	0	17	1	0	0	0	41	9.8
			TOTAL	30	4	2	6	–2	17	1	0	0	0	41	9.8
D	18	Grant Ledyard	T.B.	14	2	2	4	–5	12	0	0	0	0	12	16.7
			DAL	8	0	1	1	3	4	0	0	0	0	7	0.0
			TOTAL	22	2	3	5	–2	16	0	0	0	0	19	10.5
D	6	Sami Helenius	DAL	57	1	2	3	1	99	0	0	0	0	18	5.6
C	14	Jonathan Sim	DAL	15	0	3	3	–2	6	0	0	0	0	18	0.0
L	46	Jamie Wright	DAL	2	1	0	1	–3	0	0	0	0	0	4	25.0
G	20	Ed Belfour	DAL	63	0	1	1	0	4	0	0	0	0	0	0.0
D	34	Mark Wotton	DAL	1	0	0	0	0	0	0	0	0	0	0	0.0
L	42	* Steve Gainey	DAL	1	0	0	0	0	0	0	0	0	0	0	0.0
C	40	* Greg Leeb	DAL	2	0	0	0	–1	0	0	0	0	0	4	0.0
D	4	Gerald Diduck	DAL	14	0	0	0	4	18	0	0	0	0	8	0.0
D	28	* Richard Jackman	DAL	16	0	0	0	–6	18	0	0	0	0	10	0.0
G	35	* Marty Turco	DAL	26	0	0	0	0	12	0	0	0	0	0	0.0

Goaltending

No.	Goaltender	GPI	Mins	Avg	W	L	T	EN	SO	GA	SA	S%
35	* Marty Turco	26	1266	1.90	13	6	1	1	3	40	532	.925
20	Ed Belfour	63	3687	2.34	35	20	7	2	8	144	1508	.905
	Totals	**82**	**4970**	**2.26**	**48**	**26**	**8**	**3**	**11**	**187**	**2043**	**.908**

Playoffs

Pos	#	Player	Team	GP	G	A	Pts	+/–	PIM	PP	SH	GW	GT	S	%
C	9	Mike Modano	DAL	9	3	4	7	1	0	2	0	0	0	23	13.0
R	16	Brett Hull	DAL	10	2	5	7	–1	6	1	0	0	0	41	4.9
D	56	Sergei Zubov	DAL	10	1	5	6	2	4	0	0	0	0	22	4.5
L	12	Mike Keane	DAL	10	3	2	5	1	4	0	0	0	0	6	50.0
C	25	Joe Nieuwendyk	DAL	7	4	0	4	–2	4	1	0	1	0	18	22.2
R	15	Jamie Langenbrunner	DAL	10	2	2	4	2	6	0	0	1	1	22	9.1
L	22	Kirk Muller	DAL	10	1	3	4	0	12	0	0	1	1	18	5.6
D	5	Darryl Sydor	DAL	10	1	3	4	–2	0	1	0	0	0	20	5.0
R	51	John MacLean	DAL	10	2	1	3	–3	6	0	0	0	0	12	16.7
L	10	Brenden Morrow	DAL	10	0	3	3	1	12	0	0	0	0	14	0.0
C	27	Shaun Van Allen	DAL	8	0	2	2	1	8	0	0	0	0	10	0.0
C	33	Benoit Hogue	DAL	7	1	0	1	–4	6	0	0	1	1	3	33.3
L	26	Jere Lehtinen	DAL	10	1	0	1	–4	2	0	0	0	0	22	4.5
D	37	Brad Lukowich	DAL	10	1	0	1	2	4	0	0	0	0	14	7.1
L	17	Ted Donato	DAL	8	0	1	1	0	0	0	0	0	0	10	0.0
D	18	Grant Ledyard	DAL	9	0	1	1	2	4	0	0	0	0	11	0.0
D	2	Derian Hatcher	DAL	10	0	1	1	–7	16	0	0	0	0	13	0.0
D	6	Sami Helenius	DAL	1	0	0	0	0	0	0	0	0	0	0	0.0
C	36	Roman Lyashenko	DAL	1	0	0	0	0	0	0	0	0	0	1	0.0
R	55	* Tyler Bouck	DAL	1	0	0	0	0	0	0	0	0	0	1	0.0
R	29	Grant Marshall	DAL	9	0	0	0	–1	0	0	0	0	0	11	0.0
G	20	Ed Belfour	DAL	10	0	0	0	0	6	0	0	0	0	0	0.0
D	24	Richard Matvichuk	DAL	10	0	0	0	–2	14	0	0	0	0	8	0.0

Goaltending

No.	Goaltender	GPI	Mins	Avg	W	L	EN	SO	GA	SA	S%
20	Ed Belfour	10	671	2.24	4	6	1	0	25	277	.910
	Totals	**10**	**677**	**2.30**	**4**	**6**	**1**	**0**	**26**	**278**	**.906**

Coaching History

Wren Blair, 1967-68; Wren Blair and John Muckler, 1968-69; Wren Blair and Charlie Burns, 1969-70; Jackie Gordon, 1970-71 to 1972-73; Jackie Gordon and Parker MacDonald, 1973-74; Jackie Gordon and Charlie Burns, 1974-75; Ted Harris, 1975-76, 1976-77; Ted Harris, André Beaulieu and Lou Nanne, 1977-78; Harry Howell and Glen Sonmor, 1978-79; Glen Sonmor, 1979-80 to 1981-82; Glen Sonmor and Murray Oliver, 1982-83; Bill Mahoney, 1983-84, 1984-85; Lorne Henning, 1985-86; Lorne Henning and Glen Sonmor, 1986-87; Herb Brooks, 1987-88; Pierre Page, 1988-89, 1989-90; Bob Gainey, 1990-91 to 1994-95; Bob Gainey and Ken Hitchcock, 1995-96; Ken Hitchcock, 1996-97 to date.

Club Records

Team

(Figures in brackets for season records are games played; records for fewest points, wins, ties, losses, goals, goals against are for 70 or more games)

Most Points **114** 1998-99 (82)
Most Wins **51** 1998-99 (82)
Most Ties **22** 1969-70 (76)
Most Losses **53** 1975-76, 1977-78 (80)
Most Goals **346** 1981-82 (80)
Most Goals Against **349** 1987-88 (80)
Fewest Points **45** 1977-78 (80)
Fewest Wins **18** 1968-69 (76), 1977-78 (80)
Fewest Ties **4** 1989-90 (80)
Fewest Losses **19** 1998-99 (82)
Fewest Goals **189** 1968-69 (76)
Fewest Goals Against **167** 1997-98 (82)

Longest Winning Streak
Overall .... **7** Mar. 16-28/80, Mar. 16-Apr. 2/97, Nov. 22-Dec. 5/97
Home .... **11** Nov. 4-Dec. 27/72
Away .... **7** Three times

Longest Undefeated Streak
Overall .... **15** Dec. 6/98-Jan. 6/99 (12 wins, 3 ties)
Home .... **13** Oct. 28-Dec. 27/72 (12 wins, 1 tie), Nov. 21/79-Jan. 9/80 (10 wins, 3 ties), Jan. 17-Mar. 17/91 (11 wins, 2 ties)
Away .... **10** Jan. 12-Mar. 4/99 (8 wins, 2 ties)

Longest Losing Streak
Overall .... **10** Feb. 1-20/76
Home .... **6** Jan. 17-Feb. 4/70
Away .... **8** Oct. 19-Nov. 13/75, Jan. 28-Mar. 3/88

Longest Winless Streak
Overall .... **20** Jan. 15-Feb. 28/70 (15 losses, 5 ties)
Home .... **12** Jan. 17-Feb. 25/70 (8 losses, 4 ties)
Away .... **23** Oct. 25/74-Jan. 28/75 (19 losses, 4 ties)

Most Shutouts, Season **11** 2000-01 (82)
Most PIM, Season **2,313** 1987-88 (80)
Most Goals, Game .... **15** Nov. 11/81 (Wpg. 2 at Min. 15)

Individual

Most Seasons .... **16** Neal Broten
Most Games .... **992** Neal Broten
Most Goals, Career .... **382** Mike Modano
Most Assists, Career .... **593** Neal Broten
Most Points, Career .... **900** Mike Modano (382G, 518A)
Most PIM, Career .... **1,883** Shane Churla
Most Shutouts, Career .... **26** Cesare Maniago
Longest Consecutive Games Streak .... **442** Danny Grant (Dec. 4/68-Apr. 7/74)
Most Goals, Season .... **55** Dino Ciccarelli (1981-82), Brian Bellows (1989-90)
Most Assists, Season .... **76** Neal Broten (1985-86)
Most Points, Season .... **114** Bobby Smith (1981-82; 43G, 71A)
Most PIM, Season .... **382** Basil McRae (1987-88)
Most Points, Defenseman, Season .... **77** Craig Hartsburg (1981-82; 17G, 60A)
Most Points, Center, Season .... **114** Bobby Smith (1981-82; 43G, 71A)
Most Points, Right Wing, Season .... **106** Dino Ciccarelli (1981-82; 55G, 51A)
Most Points, Left Wing, Season .... **99** Brian Bellows (1989-90; 55G, 44A)
Most Points, Rookie, Season .... **98** Neal Broten (1981-82; 38G, 60A)
Most Shutouts, Season .... **9** Ed Belfour (1997-98)
Most Goals, Game .... **5** Tim Young (Jan. 15/79)
Most Assists, Game .... **5** Murray Oliver (Oct. 24/71), Larry Murphy (Oct. 17/89)
Most Points, Game .... **7** Bobby Smith (Nov. 11/81; 4G, 3A)

Records include Minnesota North Stars, 1967-68 through 1992-93.

Dallas Stars Retired Numbers

7	Neal Broten	1980-1995, 1996-1997

Minnesota North Stars Retired Numbers

8	Bill Goldsworthy	1967-1976
19	Bill Masterton	1967-1968

All-time Record vs. Other Clubs

Regular Season

	At Home								On Road								Total							
	GP	W	L	T	OL	GF	GA	PTS	GP	W	L	T	OL	GF	GA	PTS	GP	W	L	T	OL	GF	GA	PTS
Anaheim	19	16	2	1	0	80	33	33	19	11	8	0	0	50	44	22	38	27	10	1	0	130	77	55
Atlanta	1	1	0	0	0	2	1	2	2	2	0	0	0	7	4	4	3	3	0	0	0	9	5	6
Boston	59	17	29	13	0	173	217	47	58	9	40	9	0	140	249	27	117	26	69	22	0	313	466	74
Buffalo	52	25	21	6	0	166	153	56	50	13	26	11	0	133	179	37	102	38	47	17	0	299	332	93
Calgary	56	27	19	10	0	208	182	64	56	12	31	12	1	139	199	37	112	39	50	22	1	347	381	101
Carolina	27	16	10	1	0	109	81	33	29	14	11	4	0	107	96	32	56	30	21	5	0	216	177	65
Chicago	106	47	43	15	1	355	328	110	104	28	63	13	0	272	406	69	210	75	106	28	1	627	734	179
Colorado	35	17	11	5	2	111	102	41	35	10	20	4	1	96	138	25	70	27	31	9	3	207	240	66
Columbus	2	2	0	0	0	7	0	4	2	1	1	0	0	6	5	2	4	3	1	0	0	13	5	6
Detroit	100	50	35	15	0	355	300	115	100	36	50	14	0	325	387	86	200	86	85	29	0	680	687	201
Edmonton	39	20	13	6	0	144	117	46	38	12	17	8	1	127	156	33	77	32	30	14	1	271	273	79
Florida	6	3	1	2	0	21	16	8	7	3	3	1	0	21	19	7	13	6	4	3	0	42	35	15
Los Angeles	76	47	17	12	0	303	203	106	74	25	31	18	0	220	257	68	150	72	48	30	0	523	460	174
Minnesota	2	1	1	0	0	7	4	2	2	1	1	0	0	4	7	2	4	2	2	0	0	11	11	4
Montreal	57	16	30	11	0	147	201	43	56	11	37	8	0	137	245	30	113	27	67	19	0	284	446	73
Nashville	6	5	1	0	0	17	7	10	6	4	2	0	0	14	12	8	12	9	3	0	0	31	19	18
New Jersey	43	25	12	6	0	162	114	56	42	19	20	3	0	129	141	41	85	44	32	9	0	291	255	97
NY Islanders	45	18	19	7	1	133	163	44	45	14	23	8	0	129	166	36	90	32	42	15	1	262	329	80
NY Rangers	59	19	30	10	0	180	216	48	60	15	34	11	0	163	206	41	119	34	64	21	0	343	422	89
Ottawa	8	5	3	0	0	31	16	10	8	5	3	0	0	22	19	10	16	10	6	0	0	53	35	20
Philadelphia	64	27	23	14	0	211	207	68	64	9	41	14	0	145	249	32	128	36	64	28	0	356	456	100
Phoenix	47	23	17	7	0	176	143	53	46	23	20	3	0	157	149	49	93	46	37	10	0	333	292	102
Pittsburgh	63	36	21	6	0	243	212	78	61	19	36	6	0	176	229	44	124	55	57	12	0	419	441	122
St. Louis	109	49	39	21	0	369	326	119	111	30	60	20	1	315	406	81	220	79	99	41	1	684	732	200
San Jose	21	10	9	2	0	58	52	22	22	13	8	1	0	65	54	27	43	23	17	3	0	123	106	49
Tampa Bay	10	7	2	1	0	38	23	15	11	8	1	2	0	33	18	18	21	15	3	3	0	71	41	33
Toronto	95	49	35	11	0	362	302	109	100	35	49	16	0	314	351	86	195	84	84	27	0	676	653	195
Vancouver	65	34	19	12	0	244	198	80	65	25	30	10	0	197	238	60	130	59	49	22	0	441	436	140
Washington	38	19	11	8	0	141	103	46	38	15	15	8	0	118	117	38	76	34	26	16	0	259	220	84
Defunct Clubs	33	19	8	6	0	123	86	44	32	10	16	6	0	84	105	26	65	29	24	12	0	207	191	70
Totals	**1343**	**650**	**481**	**208**	**4**	**4676**	**4106**	**1512**	**1343**	**432**	**697**	**210**	**4**	**3845**	**4851**	**1078**	**2686**	**1082**	**1178**	**418**	**8**	**8521**	**8957**	**2590**

Playoffs

	Series	W	L	GP	W	L	T	GF	GA	Last Mtg.	Round	Result
Boston	1	1	0	3	3	0	0	20	13	1981	PR	W 3-0
Buffalo	3	2	1	13	8	5	0	39	37	1999	F	W 4-2
Calgary	1	1	0	6	4	2	0	25	18	1981	SF	W 4-2
Chicago	6	2	4	33	14	19	0	118	120	1991	DSF	W 4-2
Colorado	2	2	0	14	8	6	0	37	29	2000	CF	W 4-3
Detroit	3	0	3	18	6	12	0	40	55	1998	CF	L 2-4
Edmonton	7	5	2	36	23	13	0	98	93	2001	CQF	W 4-2
Los Angeles	1	1	0	7	4	3	0	26	21	1968	QF	W 4-3
Montreal	2	1	1	13	6	7	0	37	48	1980	QF	W 4-3
New Jersey	1	0	1	6	2	4	0	9	15	2000	F	L 2-4
NY Islanders	1	0	1	5	1	4	0	16	26	1981	F	L 1-4
Philadelphia	2	0	2	11	3	8	0	26	41	1980	SF	L 1-4
Pittsburgh	1	0	1	6	2	4	0	16	28	1991	F	L 2-4
St. Louis	12	6	6	66	34	32	0	197	187	2001	CSF	L 0-4
San Jose	2	2	0	11	8	3	0	31	19	2000	CSF	W 4-1
Toronto	2	2	0	7	6	1	0	35	26	1983	DSF	W 3-1
Vancouver	1	0	1	5	1	4	0	11	18	1994	CSF	L 1-4
Totals	**48**	**25**	**23**	**260**	**133**	**127**	**0**	**782**	**793**			

Playoff Results 2001-1997

Year	Round	Opponent	Result	GF	GA
2001	CSF	St. Louis	L 0-4	6	13
	CQF	Edmonton	W 4-2	16	13
2000	F	New Jersey	L 2-4	9	15
	CF	Colorado	W 4-3	14	13
	CSF	San Jose	W 4-1	15	7
	CQF	Edmonton	W 4-1	14	11
1999	**F**	**Buffalo**	**W 4-2**	**13**	**9**
	CF	Colorado	W 4-3	23	16
	CSF	St. Louis	W 4-2	17	12
	CQF	Edmonton	W 4-0	11	7
1998	CF	Detroit	L 2-4	11	15
	CSF	Edmonton	W 4-1	9	5
	CQF	San Jose	W 4-2	16	12
1997	CQF	Edmonton	L 3-4	18	21

Abbreviations: Round: F – Final; **CF** – conference final; **CSF** – conference semi-final; **CQF** – conference quarter-final; **DSF** – division semi-final; **SF** – semi-final; **QF** – quarter-final; **PR** – preliminary round.

Calgary totals include Atlanta Flames, 1972-73 to 1979-80. Carolina totals include Hartford, 1979-80 to 1996-97.
Colorado totals include Quebec, 1979-80 to 1994-95.
New Jersey totals include Kansas City, 1974-75 to 1975-76, and Colorado Rockies, 1976-77 to 1981-82.
Phoenix totals include Winnipeg, 1979-80 to 1995-96.

2000-01 Results

Oct.	4	Colorado	2-2		12	Detroit	2-3
	7	at Ottawa	1-3		14	at Tampa Bay	3-2
	9	at Toronto	3-1		15	at Florida	0-2
	10	at Carolina	2-5		17	Nashville	4-3*
	12	Philadelphia	4-1		19	Pittsburgh	6-5*
	14	Washington	3-0		21	at Phoenix	2-5
	18	San Jose	2-1		22	Vancouver	2-1
	20	at Chicago	5-1		24	New Jersey	1-4
	21	Los Angeles	4-3		26	San Jose	1-2
	25	Vancouver	2-6		30	at Los Angeles	0-8
	27	Phoenix	2-4	**Feb.**	1	at San Jose	4-2
	28	at St. Louis	3-4*		7	Edmonton	3-2
Nov.	1	Columbus	4-0		9	Minnesota	1-2
	3	at Phoenix	2-2		11	St. Louis	3-3
	11	Montreal	2-0		13	at Nashville	2-1
	14	at Columbus	2-3		14	Los Angeles	4-2
	15	at Buffalo	2-2		16	Anaheim	3-2*
	17	at Detroit	1-0		18	Detroit	1-2
	20	Tampa Bay	6-2		21	Minnesota	6-2
	22	at Nashville	1-0		23	Boston	5-4*
	24	Columbus	3-0		25	at Edmonton	2-3*
	25	at Columbus	4-2		26	at Calgary	2-3
	29	Calgary	3-4		28	at Vancouver	4-5
Dec.	1	at Colorado	2-4	**Mar.**	2	at Anaheim	5-2
	2	at Phoenix	5-2		4	Buffalo	4-1
	6	at San Jose	2-2		7	Chicago	1-4
	7	at Los Angeles	2-5		10	Colorado	3-2*
	10	at Anaheim	1-0		11	at Colorado	2-3
	13	Edmonton	5-2		13	at Chicago	3-0
	15	Chicago	4-1		16	Phoenix	1-1
	17	at Minnesota	0-6		18	Ottawa	5-1
	20	at New Jersey	1-4		19	at Minnesota	4-1
	21	at NY Islanders	3-1		21	Anaheim	8-0
	23	at Pittsburgh	8-2		23	NY Islanders	2-1
	27	Anaheim	3-1		25	St. Louis	1-1
	29	Los Angeles	1-4		28	at Vancouver	3-1
	31	NY Rangers	6-1		30	at Edmonton	5-4
Jan.	4	at Detroit	2-4		31	at Calgary	2-0
	6	at Boston	4-0	**Apr.**	2	Calgary	4-4
	8	at NY Rangers	2-1		4	Nashville	5-1
	10	at Atlanta	3-2		7	at San Jose	5-4*

* – Overtime

Entry Draft Selections 2001-1987

2001
Pick
26 Jason Bacashihua
70 Yared Hagos
92 Anthony Aquino
126 Daniel Volrab
161 Mike Smith
167 Michal Blazek
192 Jussi Jokinen
255 Marco Rosa
265 Dale Sullivan
285 Marek Tomica

2000
Pick
25 Steve Ott
60 Dan Ellis
68 Joel Lundqvist
91 Alexei Tereschenko
123 Vadim Khomitsky
139 Ruslan Bernikov
162 Artem Chernov
192 Ladislav Vlcek
219 Marco Tuokko
224 Antti Miettinen

1999
Pick
32 Mike Ryan
66 Dan Jancevski
96 Mathias Tjarnqvist
126 Jeff Bateman
156 Gregor Baumgartner
184 Justin Cox
186 Brett Draney
215 Jeff MacMillan
243 Brian Sullivan
265 Jamie Chamberlain
272 Mikhail Donika

1998
Pick
39 John Erskine
57 Tyler Bouck
86 Gabriel Karlsson
153 Pavel Patera
173 Niko Kapanen
200 Scott Perry

1997
Pick
25 Brenden Morrow
52 Roman Lyashenko
77 Steve Gainey
105 Marcus Kristoffersson
132 Teemu Elomo
160 Alexei Timkin
189 Jeff McKercher
216 Alexei Komarov
242 Brett McLean

1996
Pick
5 Richard Jackman
70 Jonathan Sim
90 Mike Hurley
112 Ryan Christie
113 Yevgeny Tsybuk
166 Eoin McInerney
194 Joel Kwiatkowski
220 Nick Bootland

1995
Pick
11 Jarome Iginla
37 Patrick Cote
63 Petr Buzek
69 Sergey Gusev
115 Wade Strand
141 Dominic Marleau
173 Jeff Dewar
193 Anatoli Koveshnikov
202 Sergei Luchinkin
219 Stephen Lowe

1994
Pick
20 Jason Botterill
46 Lee Jinman
98 Jamie Wright
124 Marty Turco
150 Evgeny Petrochinin
228 Marty Flichel
254 Jimmy Roy
280 Chris Szysky

1993
Pick
9 Todd Harvey
35 Jamie Langenbrunner
87 Chad Lang
136 Rick Mrozik
139 Per Svartvadet
165 Jeremy Stasiuk
191 Rob Lurtsema
243 Jordan Willis
249 Bill Lang
269 Cory Peterson

1992
Pick
34 Jarkko Varvio
58 Jeff Bes
88 Jere Lehtinen
130 Michael Johnson
154 Kyle Peterson
178 Juha Lind
202 Lars Edstrom
226 Jeff Romfo
250 Jeffrey Moen

1991
Pick
8 Richard Matvichuk
74 Mike Torchia
97 Mike Kennedy
118 Mark Lawrence
137 Geoff Finch
174 Michael Burkett
184 Derek Herlofsky
206 Tom Nemeth
228 Shayne Green
250 Jukka Suomalainen

1990
Pick
8 Derian Hatcher
50 Laurie Billeck
70 Cal McGowan
71 Frank Kovacs
92 Enrico Ciccone
113 Roman Turek
134 Jeff Levy
155 Doug Barrault
176 Joe Biondi
197 Troy Binnie
218 Ole-Eskild Dahlstrom
239 John McKersie

1989
Pick
7 Doug Zmolek
28 Mike Craig
60 Murray Garbutt
75 Jean-Francois Quintin
87 Pat MacLeod
91 Bryan Schoen
97 Rhys Hollyman
112 Scott Cashman
154 Jonathon Pratt
175 Kenneth Blum
196 Arturs Irbe
217 Tom Pederson
238 Helmut Balderis

1988
Pick
1 Mike Modano
40 Link Gaetz
43 Shaun Kane
64 Jeffrey Stolp
148 Ken MacArthur
169 Travis Richards
190 Ari Matilainen
211 Grant Bischoff
232 Trent Andison

1987
Pick
6 Dave Archibald
35 Scott McCrady
48 Kevin Kaminski
73 John Weisbrod
88 Teppo Kivela
109 D'arcy Norton
130 Timo Kulonen
151 Don Schmidt
172 Jarmo Myllys
193 Larry Olimb
214 Mark Felicio
235 Dave Shields

General Manager

GAINEY, BOB
Vice President of Hockey Operations/General Manager, Dallas Stars.
Born in Peterborough, Ont., December 13, 1953.

Named general manager of the team on June 8, 1992, Bob Gainey held the dual role of coach and g.m. for over three seasons before relinquishing his head coaching duties on January 8, 1996. He is the Stars' sixth general manager and was the team's 16th head coach. Gainey built Dallas into a Stanley Cup champion in 1999.

Under Gainey's tutelage, the Stars improved their regular-season record in each of his first four seasons as coach, going from 27 wins and 68 points in his first year to 42 wins and 97 points in 1993-94. In his first season, 1990-91, Gainey led the Stars through to the Stanley Cup finals, surprising Chicago and St. Louis and eliminating defending champion Edmonton before bowing in six games to Pittsburgh. He finished his reign behind the Stars bench with a 165-190-60 regular season record.

Elected to the Hockey Hall of Fame in 1992, Gainey was Montreal's first choice (eighth overall) in the 1973 Amateur Draft. During his 16-year career with the Canadiens, Gainey was a member of five Stanley Cup-winning teams and was named the Conn Smythe Trophy winner in 1979. He was a four-time recipient of the Frank Selke Trophy (1978-81), awarded to the League's top defensive forward, and participated in four NHL All-Star Games (1977, 1978, 1980 and 1981). He served as team captain for eight seasons (1981-89). During his career, he played in 1,160 regular-season games, registering 239 goals and 262 assists for 501 points. In addition, he tallied 73 points (25-48-73) in 182 post-season games.

NHL Coaching Record

		Regular Season				Playoffs		
Season	**Team**	**Games**	**W**	**L**	**T**	**Games**	**W**	**L**
1990-91	Minnesota	80	27	39	14	23	14	9
1991-92	Minnesota	80	32	42	6	7	3	4
1992-93	Minnesota	84	36	38	10	....	....	....
1993-94	Dallas	84	42	29	13	9	5	4
1994-95	Dallas	48	17	23	8	5	1	4
1995-96	Dallas	39	11	19	9	....	....	....
	NHL Totals	**415**	**165**	**190**	**60**	**44**	**23**	**21**

Club Directory

American Airlines Center

Dallas Stars
Office Address:
Dr Pepper StarCenter
211 Cowboys Parkway
Irving, TX 75063
Phone **972/831-2401**
FAX 972/868-2860
Ticket Information 214/GO STARS
www.dallasstars.com
Capacity: 18,532

Chairman of the Board & Owner	Thomas O. Hicks
President & Alternate Governor	James R. Lites
V.P. Hockey Operations & General Manager	Bob Gainey
Assistant General Manager	Doug Armstrong
Director, Hockey Operations	Les Jackson
Head Coach	Ken Hitchcock
Assistant Coach	Doug Jarvis
Assistant Coach	Rick Wilson
Assistant Coach	Craig Ludwig
Director, Media Relations	Larry Kelly
Manager, Media Relations	Mark Janko
Head Athletic Trainer	Dave Surprenant
Head Equipment Manager	Dave Smith
Assistant Equipment Manager	Steve Sumner
Strength and Conditioning Coach	J.J. McQueen
Assistant Athletic Trainer	Craig Lowry
Equipment Assistant	Mike Wrobolewski
Arena Address	2500 Victory Avenue, Dallas, TX 75201
Media Relations Phone	(972) 868-2818
Media Relations Fax	(972) 868-2860
Press Box Phone	(214) 665-4600
Press Box Fax	(214) 665-4601

Once again, it was Ed Belfour, shown at right, who was the main man in the Dallas nets, finishing with 35 wins in 63 games. Belfour's backup Marty Turco appeared in just 26 games but led the league with a 1.90 goals-against average and a save percentage of .925.

General Managers' History

Wren Blair, 1967-68 to 1973-74; Jack Gordon, 1974-75 to 1976-77; Lou Nanne, 1977-78 to 1987-88; Jack Ferreira, 1988-89, 1989-90; Bob Clarke 1990-91, 1991-92; Bob Gainey, 1992-93 to date.

Captains' History

Bob Woytowich, 1967-68; Elmer Vasko, 1968-69; Claude Larose, 1969-70; Ted Harris, 1970-71 to 1973-74; Bill Goldsworthy, 1974-75, 1975-76; Bill Hogaboam, 1976-77; Nick Beverley, 1977-78; J.P. Parise, 1978-79; Paul Shmyr, 1979-80, 1980-81; Tim Young, 1981-82; Craig Hartsburg, 1982-83; Craig Hartsburg and Brian Bellows, 1983-84; Craig Hartsburg, 1984-85 to 1987-88; Curt Fraser, Bob Rouse and Curt Giles, 1988-89; Curt Giles, 1989-90, 1990-91; Mark Tinordi, 1991-92 to 1993-94; Neal Broten and Derian Hatcher, 1994-95; Derian Hatcher, 1995-96 to date.

Detroit Red Wings

2000-01 Results: 49W-20L-9T-4OTL 111PTS. First, Central Division

Solid at both ends of the ice, Nicklas Lidstrom ranked second on the Red Wings with 71 points and became the first European-trained defenseman to win the Norris Trophy.

2001-02 Schedule

Oct.	Thu.	4	at San Jose	Jan.	Wed.	2	Anaheim
	Sat.	6	at Vancouver		Sat.	5	Colorado*
	Wed.	10	Calgary		Wed.	9	Vancouver
	Fri.	12	Buffalo		Sat.	12	Dallas*
	Sat.	13	at NY Islanders		Tue.	15	at Phoenix
	Tue.	16	Columbus		Wed.	16	at Dallas
	Thu.	18	Philadelphia		Fri.	18	Washington
	Sat.	20	Los Angeles		Sun.	20	Ottawa
	Wed.	24	Edmonton		Wed.	23	San Jose
	Fri.	26	Dallas		Fri.	25	Phoenix
	Sat.	27	at Nashville		Sat.	26	at St. Louis
	Tue.	30	at Carolina		Mon.	28	at Edmonton
	Wed.	31	at Dallas		Wed.	30	at Calgary
Nov.	Fri.	2	NY Islanders	Feb.	Mon.	4	at Colorado
	Sun.	4	at Chicago		Wed.	6	NY Rangers
	Wed.	7	at Phoenix		Fri.	8	Columbus
	Fri.	9	at Anaheim		Sat.	9	at Ottawa
	Sat.	10	at Los Angeles		Mon.	11	at Montreal
	Tue.	13	Carolina		Wed.	13	at Minnesota
	Fri.	16	Minnesota		Tue.	26	at Tampa Bay
	Sat.	17	Los Angeles		Wed.	27	at Florida
	Tue.	20	Nashville	Mar.	Sat.	2	at Pittsburgh*
	Wed.	21	at Columbus		Wed.	6	Toronto
	Fri.	23	St. Louis		Sat.	9	at St. Louis*
	Sun.	25	Chicago		Sun.	10	at Buffalo*
	Tue.	27	Calgary		Wed.	13	Edmonton
	Fri.	30	New Jersey		Sat.	16	at Boston*
Dec.	Sat.	1	at New Jersey		Sun.	17	at NY Rangers*
	Wed.	5	Colorado		Tue.	19	Anaheim
	Fri.	7	Phoenix		Thu.	21	at Columbus
	Mon.	10	at Calgary		Sat.	23	at Colorado*
	Thu.	13	at Edmonton		Mon.	25	at Nashville
	Sat.	15	at Vancouver		Thu.	28	Nashville
	Mon.	17	Chicago		Sat.	30	Atlanta
	Wed.	19	Vancouver	Apr.	Mon.	1	Toronto
	Fri.	21	San Jose		Wed.	3	at Anaheim
	Sun.	23	at Chicago		Thu.	4	at Los Angeles
	Wed.	26	at Minnesota		Sat.	6	at San Jose
	Thu.	27	Columbus		Wed.	10	Chicago
	Sat.	29	at Nashville		Sat.	13	at St. Louis*
	Mon.	31	Minnesota		Sun.	14	St. Louis*

* Denotes afternoon game.

Franchise date: September 25, 1926

CENTRAL DIVISION

76th NHL Season

Year-by-Year Record

		Home				Road				Overall								
Season	GP	W	L	T	OL	W	L	T	OL	W	L	T	OL	GF	GA	Pts.	Finished	Playoff Result
2000-01	82	27	9	3	2	22	11	6	2	49	20	9	4	253	202	111	1st, Central Div.	Lost Conf. Quarter-Final
1999-2000	82	28	9	3	1	20	13	7	1	48	22	10	2	278	210	108	2nd, Central Div.	Lost Conf. Semi-Final
1998-99	82	27	12	2	...	16	20	5	...	43	32	7	...	245	202	93	1st, Central Div.	Lost Conf. Semi-Final
1997-98	**82**	**25**	**8**	**8**	**...**	**19**	**15**	**7**	**...**	**44**	**23**	**15**	**...**	**250**	**196**	**103**	**2nd, Central Div.**	**Won Stanley Cup**
1996-97	**82**	**20**	**12**	**9**	**...**	**18**	**14**	**9**	**...**	**38**	**26**	**18**	**...**	**253**	**197**	**94**	**2nd, Central Div.**	**Won Stanley Cup**
1995-96	82	36	3	2	...	26	10	5	...	62	13	7	...	325	181	131	1st, Central Div.	Lost Conf. Championship
1994-95	48	17	4	3	...	16	7	1	...	33	11	4	...	180	117	70	1st, Central Div.	Lost Final
1993-94	84	23	13	6	...	23	17	2	...	46	30	8	...	356	275	100	1st, Central Div.	Lost Conf. Quarter-Final
1992-93	84	25	14	3	...	22	14	6	...	47	28	9	...	369	280	103	2nd, Norris Div.	Lost Div. Semi-Final
1991-92	80	24	12	4	...	19	13	8	...	43	25	12	...	320	256	98	1st, Norris Div.	Lost Div. Final
1990-91	80	26	14	0	...	8	24	8	...	34	38	8	...	273	298	76	3rd, Norris Div.	Lost Div. Semi-Final
1989-90	80	20	14	6	...	8	24	8	...	28	38	14	...	288	323	70	5th, Norris Div.	Out of Playoffs
1988-89	80	20	14	6	...	14	20	6	...	34	34	12	...	313	316	80	1st, Norris Div.	Lost Div. Semi-Final
1987-88	80	24	10	6	...	17	18	5	...	41	28	11	...	322	269	93	1st, Norris Div.	Lost Conf. Championship
1986-87	80	20	14	6	...	14	22	4	...	34	36	10	...	260	274	78	2nd, Norris Div.	Lost Conf. Championship
1985-86	80	10	26	4	...	7	31	2	...	17	57	6	...	266	415	40	5th, Norris Div.	Out of Playoffs
1984-85	80	19	14	7	...	8	27	5	...	27	41	12	...	313	357	66	3rd, Norris Div.	Lost Div. Semi-Final
1983-84	80	18	20	2	...	13	22	5	...	31	42	7	...	298	323	69	3rd, Norris Div.	Lost Div. Semi-Final
1982-83	80	14	19	7	...	7	25	8	...	21	44	15	...	263	344	57	5th, Norris Div.	Out of Playoffs
1981-82	80	15	19	6	...	6	28	6	...	21	47	12	...	270	351	54	6th, Norris Div.	Out of Playoffs
1980-81	80	16	15	9	...	3	28	9	...	19	43	18	...	252	339	56	5th, Norris Div.	Out of Playoffs
1979-80	80	14	21	5	...	12	22	6	...	26	43	11	...	268	306	63	5th, Norris Div.	Out of Playoffs
1978-79	80	15	17	8	...	8	24	8	...	23	41	16	...	252	295	62	5th, Norris Div.	Out of Playoffs
1977-78	80	22	11	7	...	10	23	7	...	32	34	14	...	252	266	78	2nd, Norris Div.	Lost Quarter-Final
1976-77	80	12	22	6	...	4	33	3	...	16	55	9	...	183	309	41	5th, Norris Div.	Out of Playoffs
1975-76	80	17	15	8	...	9	29	2	...	26	44	10	...	226	300	62	4th, Norris Div.	Out of Playoffs
1974-75	80	17	17	6	...	6	28	6	...	23	45	12	...	259	335	58	4th, Norris Div.	Out of Playoffs
1973-74	78	21	12	6	...	8	27	4	...	29	39	10	...	255	319	68	6th, East Div.	Out of Playoffs
1972-73	78	22	12	5	...	15	17	7	...	37	29	12	...	265	243	86	5th, East Div.	Out of Playoffs
1971-72	78	25	11	3	...	8	24	7	...	33	35	10	...	261	262	76	5th, East Div.	Out of Playoffs
1970-71	78	17	15	7	...	5	30	4	...	22	45	11	...	209	308	55	7th, East Div.	Out of Playoffs
1969-70	76	20	11	7	...	20	10	8	...	40	21	15	...	246	199	95	3rd, East Div.	Lost Quarter-Final
1968-69	76	23	8	7	...	10	23	5	...	33	31	12	...	239	221	78	5th, East Div.	Out of Playoffs
1967-68	74	18	15	4	...	9	20	8	...	27	35	12	...	245	257	66	6th, East Div.	Out of Playoffs
1966-67	70	21	11	3	...	6	28	1	...	27	39	4	...	212	241	58	5th,	Out of Playoffs
1965-66	70	20	8	7	...	11	19	5	...	31	27	12	...	221	194	74	4th,	Lost Final
1964-65	70	25	7	3	...	15	16	4	...	40	23	7	...	224	175	87	1st,	Lost Semi-Final
1963-64	70	23	9	3	...	7	20	8	...	30	29	11	...	191	204	71	4th,	Lost Final
1962-63	70	19	10	6	...	13	15	7	...	32	25	13	...	200	194	77	4th,	Lost Final
1961-62	70	17	11	7	...	6	22	7	...	23	33	14	...	184	219	60	5th,	Out of Playoffs
1960-61	70	15	13	7	...	10	16	9	...	25	29	16	...	195	215	66	4th,	Lost Final
1959-60	70	18	14	3	...	8	15	12	...	26	29	15	...	186	197	67	4th,	Lost Semi-Final
1958-59	70	13	17	5	...	12	20	3	...	25	37	8	...	167	218	58	6th,	Out of Playoffs
1957-58	70	16	11	8	...	13	18	4	...	29	29	12	...	176	207	70	3rd,	Lost Semi-Final
1956-57	70	23	7	5	...	15	13	7	...	38	20	12	...	198	157	88	1st,	Lost Semi-Final
1955-56	70	21	6	8	...	9	18	8	...	30	24	16	...	183	148	76	2nd,	Lost Final
1954-55	**70**	**25**	**5**	**5**	**...**	**17**	**12**	**6**	**...**	**42**	**17**	**11**	**...**	**204**	**134**	**95**	**1st,**	**Won Stanley Cup**
1953-54	**70**	**24**	**4**	**7**	**...**	**13**	**15**	**7**	**...**	**37**	**19**	**14**	**...**	**191**	**132**	**88**	**1st,**	**Won Stanley Cup**
1952-53	70	20	5	10	...	16	11	8	...	36	16	18	...	222	133	90	1st,	Lost Semi-Final
1951-52	**70**	**24**	**7**	**4**	**...**	**20**	**7**	**8**	**...**	**44**	**14**	**12**	**...**	**215**	**133**	**100**	**1st,**	**Won Stanley Cup**
1950-51	70	25	3	7	...	19	10	6	...	44	13	13	...	236	139	101	1st,	Lost Semi-Final
1949-50	**70**	**19**	**9**	**7**	**...**	**18**	**10**	**7**	**...**	**37**	**19**	**14**	**...**	**229**	**164**	**88**	**1st,**	**Won Stanley Cup**
1948-49	60	21	6	3	...	13	13	4	...	34	19	7	...	195	145	75	1st,	Lost Final
1947-48	60	16	9	5	...	14	9	7	...	30	18	12	...	187	148	72	2nd,	Lost Final
1946-47	60	14	10	6	...	8	17	5	...	22	27	11	...	190	193	55	4th,	Lost Semi-Final
1945-46	50	16	5	4	...	4	15	6	...	20	20	10	...	146	159	50	4th,	Lost Semi-Final
1944-45	50	19	5	1	...	12	9	4	...	31	14	5	...	218	161	67	2nd,	Lost Final
1943-44	50	18	5	2	...	8	13	4	...	26	18	6	...	214	177	58	2nd,	Lost Semi-Final
1942-43	**50**	**16**	**4**	**5**	**...**	**9**	**10**	**6**	**...**	**25**	**14**	**11**	**...**	**169**	**124**	**61**	**1st,**	**Won Stanley Cup**
1941-42	48	14	7	3	...	5	18	1	...	19	25	4	...	140	147	42	5th,	Lost Final
1940-41	48	14	5	5	...	7	11	6	...	21	16	11	...	112	102	53	3rd,	Lost Final
1939-40	48	11	10	3	...	5	16	3	...	16	26	6	...	90	126	38	5th,	Lost Semi-Final
1938-39	48	14	8	2	...	4	16	4	...	18	24	6	...	107	128	42	5th,	Lost Semi-Final
1937-38	48	8	10	6	...	4	15	5	...	12	25	11	...	99	133	35	4th, Amn. Div.	Out of Playoffs
1936-37	**48**	**14**	**5**	**5**	**...**	**11**	**9**	**4**	**...**	**25**	**14**	**9**	**...**	**128**	**102**	**59**	**1st, Amn. Div.**	**Won Stanley Cup**
1935-36	**48**	**14**	**5**	**5**	**...**	**10**	**11**	**3**	**...**	**24**	**16**	**8**	**...**	**124**	**103**	**56**	**1st, Amn. Div.**	**Won Stanley Cup**
1934-35	48	11	8	5	...	8	14	2	...	19	22	7	...	127	114	45	4th, Amn. Div.	Out of Playoffs
1933-34	48	15	5	4	...	9	9	6	...	24	14	10	...	113	98	58	1st, Amn. Div.	Lost Final
1932-33*	48	17	3	4	...	8	12	4	...	25	15	8	...	111	93	58	2nd, Amn. Div.	Lost Semi-Final
1931-32	48	15	3	6	...	3	17	4	...	18	20	10	...	95	108	46	3rd, Amn. Div.	Lost Quarter-Final
1930-31**	44	10	7	5	...	6	14	2	...	16	21	7	...	102	105	39	4th, Amn. Div.	Out of Playoffs
1929-30	44	9	10	3	...	5	14	3	...	14	24	6	...	117	133	34	4th, Amn. Div.	Out of Playoffs
1928-29	44	11	6	5	...	8	10	4	...	19	16	9	...	72	63	47	3rd, Amn. Div.	Lost Quarter-Final
1927-28	44	9	10	3	...	10	9	3	...	19	19	6	...	88	79	44	4th, Amn. Div.	Out of Playoffs
1926-27***	44	5	16	0	...	7	12	4	...	12	28	4	...	76	105	28	5th, Amn. Div.	Out of Playoffs

* Team name changed to Red Wings. ** Team name changed to Falcons. *** Team named Cougars.

2001-02 Player Personnel

FORWARDS	HT	WT	S	Place of Birth	Date	2000-01 Club
AVERY, Sean	5-10	185	L	North York, Ont.	4/10/80	Cincinnati (AHL)
BRULE, Steve	6-0	200	R	Montreal, Que.	1/15/75	Manitoba
BUTSAYEV, Yuri	6-1	183	L	Togliatti, USSR	10/11/78	Detroit-Cincinnati (AHL)
DANDENAULT, Mathieu	6-0	200	R	Sherbrooke, Que.	2/3/76	Detroit
DATSYUK, Pavel	5-11	180	L	Sverdlovsk, USSR	7/20/78	Ak Bars Kazan
DEVEREAUX, Boyd	6-2	195	L	Seaforth, Ont.	4/16/78	Detroit
DRAPER, Kris	5-11	190	L	Toronto, Ont.	5/24/71	Detroit
FEDOROV, Sergei	6-1	200	L	Pskov, USSR	12/13/69	Detroit
GILCHRIST, Brent	5-11	180	L	Moose Jaw, Sask.	4/3/67	Detroit
HOLMSTROM, Tomas	6-0	200	L	Pitea, Sweden	1/23/73	Detroit
LARIONOV, Igor	5-9	170	L	Voskresensk, USSR	12/3/60	Florida-Detroit
MALTBY, Kirk	6-0	180	R	Guelph, Ont.	12/22/72	Detroit
McCARTY, Darren	6-1	210	R	Burnaby, B.C.	4/1/72	Detroit
ROBITAILLE, Luc	6-1	215	L	Montreal, Que.	2/17/66	Los Angeles
SHANAHAN, Brendan	6-3	218	R	Mimico, Ont.	1/23/69	Detroit
VERBEEK, Pat	5-9	192	R	Sarnia, Ont.	5/24/64	Detroit
WILLIAMS, Jason	5-11	185	R	London, Ont.	8/11/80	Detroit-Cincinnati (AHL)
YZERMAN, Steve	5-11	185	R	Cranbrook, B.C.	5/9/65	Detroit
DEFENSEMEN						
CHELIOS, Chris	6-1	190	R	Chicago, IL	1/25/62	Detroit
DUCHESNE, Steve	5-11	195	L	Sept-Iles, Que.	6/30/65	Detroit
FISCHER, Jiri	6-5	225	L	Horovice, Czech.	7/31/80	Detroit-Cincinnati (AHL)
KUZNETSOV, Maxim	6-5	198	L	Pavlodar, USSR	3/24/77	Detroit
LIDSTROM, Nicklas	6-2	185	L	Vasteras, Sweden	4/28/70	Detroit
OLAUSSON, Fredrik	6-2	198	R	Dadesjo, Sweden	10/5/66	SC Bern
WALLIN, Jesse	6-2	190	L	Saskatoon, Sask.	3/10/78	Detroit-Cincinnati (AHL)
WIKSTROM, John	6-3	200	L	Lulea, Sweden	1/30/79	Cincinnati (AHL)
ZINGER, Dwayne	6-4	225	L	Coronation, Alta.	7/5/76	Cincinnati (AHL)

GOALTENDERS	HT	WT	C	Place of Birth	Date	2000-01 Club
ELLIOT, Jason	6-2	183	L	Inuvik, N.W.T.	11/10/75	Houston
HASEK, Dominik	5-11	180	L	Pardubice, Czech.	1/29/65	Buffalo
LEGACE, Manny	5-9	162	L	Toronto, Ont.	2/4/73	Detroit
OSGOOD, Chris	5-10	175	L	Peace River, Alta.	11/26/72	Detroit

Coach

BOWMAN, WILLIAM SCOTT (SCOTTY)
Coach, Detroit Red Wings. Born in Montreal, Que. September 18, 1933.

Scotty Bowman is entering his ninth season as coach of the Red Wings and his 30th as a coach in the NHL. Bowman equalled Toe Blake's record for coaches in 1998 when he guided the Detroit Red Wings to a second consecutive Stanley Cup championship. The victory gave Bowman his eighth title as a coach and the ninth of his career including his victory as director of player development with the Pittsburgh Penguins in 1991. Bowman, who is also the all-time coaching leader in both regular-season and playoff victories, is the first coach to win the Stanley Cup with three different teams.

Bowman began his NHL coaching career with the St. Louis Blues and led the team to the Stanley Cup finals three years in a row from 1968 to 1970. He was then appointed head coach of the Montreal Canadiens and led the team to five Stanley Cup titles in eight years.

Following an eight-season term as the general manager of the Buffalo Sabres, and a brief stint as a commentator for CBC Television, Bowman joined the Pittsburgh Penguins as director of player development, but returned to coaching when head coach Bob Johnson became ill in September, 1991. Bowman was elected to the Hockey Hall of Fame as a builder in 1991.

NHL Coaching Record

		Regular Season				Playoffs		
Season	Team	Games	W	L	T	Games	W	L
1967-68	St. Louis	58	23	21	14	18	8	10
1968-69	St. Louis	76	37	25	14	12	8	4
1969-70	St. Louis	76	37	27	12	16	8	8
1970-71	St. Louis	28	13	10	5	6	2	4
1971-72	Montreal	78	46	16	16	6	2	4
1972-73	Montreal	78	52	10	16	17	12	5*
1973-74	Montreal	78	45	24	9	6	2	4
1974-75	Montreal	80	47	14	19	11	6	5
1975-76	Montreal	80	58	11	11	13	12	1*
1976-77	Montreal	80	60	8	12	14	12	2*
1977-78	Montreal	80	59	10	11	15	12	3*
1978-79	Montreal	80	52	17	11	16	12	4*
1979-80	Buffalo	80	47	17	16	14	9	5
1981-82	Buffalo	35	18	10	7	4	1	3
1982-83	Buffalo	80	38	29	13	10	6	4
1983-84	Buffalo	80	48	25	7	3	0	3
1984-85	Buffalo	80	38	28	14	5	2	3
1985-86	Buffalo	37	18	18	1	....	....	....
1986-87	Buffalo	12	3	7	2	....	....	....
1991-92	Pittsburgh	80	39	32	9	21	16	5*
1992-93	Pittsburgh	84	56	21	7	12	7	5
1993-94	Detroit	84	46	30	8	7	3	4
1994-95	Detroit	48	33	11	4	18	12	6
1995-96	Detroit	82	62	13	7	19	10	9
1996-97	Detroit	82	38	26	18	20	16	4*
1997-98	Detroit	82	44	23	15	22	16	6*
1998-99	Detroit	77	39	32	6	10	6	4
1999-2000	Detroit	82	48	24	10	9	5	4
2000-01	Detroit	82	49	24	9	6	2	4
	NHL Totals	**2059**	**1193**	**563**	**303**	**330**	**207**	**123**

* Stanley Cup win.

2000-01 Scoring

* - rookie

Regular Season

Pos	#	Player	Team	GP	G	A	Pts	+/–	PIM	PP	SH	GW	GT	S	%
L	14	Brendan Shanahan	DET	81	31	45	76	9	81	15	1	7	1	278	11.2
D	5	Nicklas Lidstrom	DET	82	15	56	71	9	18	8	0	0	0	272	5.5
C	91	Sergei Fedorov	DET	75	32	37	69	12	40	14	2	7	1	268	11.9
R	20	Martin Lapointe	DET	82	27	30	57	3	127	13	0	8	0	181	14.9
C	19	Steve Yzerman	DET	54	18	34	52	4	18	5	0	7	0	155	11.6
L	96	Tomas Holmstrom	DET	73	16	24	40	–12	40	9	0	2	0	74	21.6
C	8	Igor Larionov	FLA	26	5	6	11	–11	10	2	0	0	0	15	33.3
			DET	39	4	25	29	6	28	2	0	1	0	31	12.9
			TOTAL	65	9	31	40	–5	38	4	0	1	0	46	19.6
L	13	Vyacheslav Kozlov	DET	72	20	18	38	9	30	4	0	5	1	187	10.7
R	15	Pat Verbeek	DET	67	15	15	30	0	73	7	0	0	0	113	13.3
D	11	Mathieu Dandenault	DET	73	10	15	25	11	38	2	0	2	0	95	10.5
C	33	Kris Draper	DET	75	8	17	25	17	38	0	1	1	0	123	6.5
D	28	Steve Duchesne	DET	54	6	19	25	9	48	2	0	0	0	76	7.9
R	25	Darren McCarty	DET	72	12	10	22	–5	123	1	1	3	1	118	10.2
R	17	Doug Brown	DET	60	9	13	22	0	14	2	1	1	0	91	9.9
D	55	Larry Murphy	DET	57	2	19	21	–6	12	0	0	1	0	81	2.5
L	18	Kirk Maltby	DET	79	12	7	19	16	22	1	3	3	0	119	10.1
C	21	Boyd Devereaux	DET	55	5	6	11	1	14	0	0	0	0	66	7.6
D	23	Todd Gill	DET	68	3	8	11	17	53	0	1	0	0	66	4.5
D	27	Aaron Ward	DET	73	4	5	9	–4	57	0	0	1	0	48	8.3
D	2	Jiri Fischer	DET	55	1	8	9	3	59	0	0	0	0	64	1.6
L	41	Brent Gilchrist	DET	60	1	8	9	–8	41	0	0	0	0	75	1.3
D	32	* Maxim Kuznetsov	DET	25	1	2	3	–1	23	0	0	0	0	17	5.9
C	29	* Jason Williams	DET	5	0	3	3	1	2	0	0	0	0	7	0.0
D	24	Chris Chelios	DET	24	0	3	3	4	45	0	0	0	0	26	0.0
C	22	Yuri Butsayev	DET	15	1	1	2	–2	4	0	0	0	0	18	5.6
G	34	Manny Legace	DET	39	0	2	2	0	4	0	0	0	0	0	0.0
D	3	* Jesse Wallin	DET	1	0	0	0	0	2	0	0	0	0	1	0.0
G	30	Chris Osgood	DET	52	0	0	0	0	8	0	0	0	0	0	0.0

Goaltending

No.	Goaltender	GPI	Mins	Avg	W	L	T	EN	SO	GA	SA	S%
34	Manny Legace	39	2136	2.05	24	5	5	1	2	73	909	.920
30	Chris Osgood	52	2834	2.69	25	19	4	1	1	127	1310	.903
	Totals	**82**	**4994**	**2.43**	**49**	**24**	**9**	**2**	**3**	**202**	**2221**	**.909**

Playoffs

Pos	#	Player	Team	GP	G	A	Pts	+/–	PIM	PP	SH	GW	GT	S	%
D	5	Nicklas Lidstrom	DET	6	1	7	8	1	0	0	0	0	0	15	6.7
C	91	Sergei Fedorov	DET	6	2	5	7	0	0	1	0	1	0	16	12.5
D	28	Steve Duchesne	DET	6	2	4	6	0	0	2	0	0	0	13	15.4
L	13	Vyacheslav Kozlov	DET	6	4	1	5	–2	2	2	0	0	0	14	28.6
L	14	Brendan Shanahan	DET	2	2	2	4	3	0	0	0	1	0	12	16.7
C	8	Igor Larionov	DET	6	1	3	4	–2	2	1	0	0	0	7	14.3
L	96	Tomas Holmstrom	DET	6	1	3	4	–1	8	1	0	0	0	6	16.7
R	15	Pat Verbeek	DET	5	2	0	2	–2	6	2	0	0	0	5	40.0
D	24	Chris Chelios	DET	5	1	0	1	–1	2	0	0	0	0	9	11.1
R	25	Darren McCarty	DET	6	1	0	1	1	2	0	0	0	0	10	10.0
L	41	Brent Gilchrist	DET	5	0	1	1	0	0	0	0	0	0	7	0.0
C	33	Kris Draper	DET	6	0	1	1	–3	2	0	0	0	0	7	0.0
D	55	Larry Murphy	DET	6	0	1	1	2	0	0	0	0	0	7	0.0
R	20	Martin Lapointe	DET	6	0	1	1	–4	8	0	0	0	0	9	0.0
D	11	Mathieu Dandenault	DET	6	0	1	1	–1	0	0	0	0	0	5	0.0
C	19	Steve Yzerman	DET	1	0	0	0	0	0	0	0	0	0	0	0.0
C	21	Boyd Devereaux	DET	2	0	0	0	–1	0	0	0	0	0	2	0.0
C	29	* Jason Williams	DET	2	0	0	0	2	0	0	0	0	0	2	0.0
R	17	Doug Brown	DET	4	0	0	0	–1	2	0	0	0	0	3	0.0
D	23	Todd Gill	DET	5	0	0	0	–5	8	0	0	0	0	4	0.0
D	2	Jiri Fischer	DET	5	0	0	0	–4	9	0	0	0	0	1	0.0
G	30	Chris Osgood	DET	6	0	0	0	0	0	0	0	0	0	0	0.0
L	18	Kirk Maltby	DET	6	0	0	0	–3	6	0	0	0	0	12	0.0

Goaltending

No.	Goaltender	GPI	Mins	Avg	W	L	EN	SO	GA	SA	S%
30	Chris Osgood	6	365	2.47	2	4	0	1	15	158	.905
	Totals	**6**	**367**	**2.45**	**2**	**4**	**0**	**1**	**15**	**158**	**.905**

Coaching History

Art Duncan, 1926-27; Jack Adams, 1927-28 to 1946-47; Tommy Ivan, 1947-48 to 1953-54; Jimmy Skinner, 1954-55 to 1956-57; Jimmy Skinner and Sid Abel, 1957-58; Sid Abel, 1958-59 to 1967-68; Bill Gadsby, 1968-69; Bill Gadsby and Sid Abel, 1969-70; Ned Harkness and Doug Barkley, 1970-71; Doug Barkley and John Wilson, 1971-72; John Wilson, 1972-73; Ted Garvin and Alex Delvecchio, 1973-74; Alex Delvecchio, 1974-75; Doug Barkley and Alex Delvecchio, 1975-76; Alex Delvecchio and Larry Wilson, 1976-77; Bobby Kromm, 1977-78, 1978-79; Bobby Kromm and Ted Lindsay, 1979-80; Ted Lindsay and Wayne Maxner, 1980-81; Wayne Maxner and Billy Dea, 1981-82; Nick Polano, 1982-83 to 1984-85; Harry Neale and Brad Park, 1985-86; Jacques Demers, 1986-87 to 1989-90; Bryan Murray, 1990-91 to 1992-93; Scotty Bowman, 1993-94 to 1997-98; Dave Lewis, Barry Smith (co-coaches) and Scotty Bowman, 1998-99; Scotty Bowman, 1999-2000 to date.

Club Records

Team

(Figures in brackets for season records are games played; records for fewest points, wins, ties, losses, goals, goals against are for 70 or more games)

Most Points	**131**	1995-96 (82)
Most Wins	***62**	1995-96 (82)
Most Ties	**18**	1952-53 (70), 1980-81 (80), 1996-97 (82)
Most Losses	**57**	1985-86 (80)
Most Goals	**369**	1992-93 (84)
Most Goals Against	**415**	1985-86 (80)
Fewest Points	**40**	1985-86 (80)
Fewest Wins	**16**	1976-77 (80)
Fewest Ties	**4**	1966-67 (70)
Fewest Losses	**13**	1950-51 (70), 1995-96 (82)
Fewest Goals	**167**	1958-59 (70)
Fewest Goals Against	**132**	1953-54 (70)
Longest Winning Streak		
Overall	**9**	Mar. 3-21/51, Feb. 27-Mar. 20/55, Dec. 12-31/95, Mar. 3-22/96
Home	**14**	Jan. 21-Mar. 25/65
Away	**7**	Mar. 25-Apr. 14/95, Feb. 18-Mar. 20/96
Longest Undefeated Streak		
Overall	**15**	Nov. 27-Dec. 28/52 (8 wins, 7 ties)
Home	**19**	Dec. 31/00-Apr.7/01 (17 wins, 2 ties)
Away	**15**	Oct. 18-Dec. 20/51 (10 wins, 5 ties)
Longest Losing Streak		
Overall	**14**	Feb. 24-Mar. 25/82
Home	**7**	Feb. 20-Mar. 25/82
Away	**14**	Oct. 19-Dec. 21/66
Longest Winless Streak		
Overall	**19**	Feb. 26-Apr. 3/77 (18 losses, 1 tie)
Home	**10**	Dec. 11/85-Jan. 18/86 (9 losses, 1 tie)
Away	**26**	Dec. 15/76-Apr. 3/77 (23 losses, 3 ties)
Most Shutouts, Season	**13**	1953-54 (70)
Most. PIM, Season	**2,393**	1985-86 (80)
Most Goals, Game	**15**	Jan. 23/44 (NYR 0 at Det. 15)

Individual

Most Seasons	**25**	Gordie Howe
Most Games	**1,687**	Gordie Howe
Most Goals, Career	**786**	Gordie Howe
Most Assists, Career	**1,023**	Gordie Howe
Most Points, Career	**1,809**	Gordie Howe (786G, 1,023A)
Most PIM, Career	**2,090**	Bob Probert
Most Shutouts, Career	**85**	Terry Sawchuk
Longest Consecutive Games Streak	**548**	Alex Delvecchio (Dec. 13/56-Nov. 11/64)
Most Goals, Season	**65**	Steve Yzerman (1988-89)
Most Assists, Season	**90**	Steve Yzerman (1988-89)
Most Points, Season	**155**	Steve Yzerman (1988-89; 65G, 90A)
Most PIM, Season	**398**	Bob Probert (1987-88)
Most Points, Defenseman, Season	**77**	Paul Coffey (1993-94; 14G, 63A)
Most Points, Center, Season	**155**	Steve Yzerman (1988-89; 65G, 90A)
Most Points, Right Wing, Season	**103**	Gordie Howe (1968-69; 44G, 59A)
Most Points, Left Wing, Season	**105**	John Ogrodnick (1984-85; 55G, 50A)
Most Points, Rookie, Season	**87**	Steve Yzerman (1983-84; 39G, 48A)
Most Shutouts, Season	**12**	Terry Sawchuk (1951-52, 1953-54, 1954-55), Glenn Hall (1955-56)
Most Goals, Game	**6**	Syd Howe (Feb. 3/44)
Most Assists, Game	***7**	Billy Taylor (Mar. 16/47)
Most Points, Game	**7**	Carl Liscombe (Nov. 5/42; 3G, 4A), Don Grosso (Feb. 3/44; 1G, 6A), Billy Taylor (Mar. 16/47; 7A)

* NHL Record.

Retired Numbers

1	Terry Sawchuk	1949-55, 57-64, 68-69
7	Ted Lindsay	1944-57, 64-65
9	Gordie Howe	1946-1971
10	Alex Delvecchio	1951-1973
12	Sid Abel	1938-43, 45-52

All-time Record vs. Other Clubs

Regular Season

	At Home								On Road								Total							
	GP	W	L	T	OL	GF	GA	PTS	GP	W	L	T	OL	GF	GA	PTS	GP	W	L	T	OL	GF	GA	PTS
Anaheim	16	12	1	3	0	63	39	27	16	9	5	2	0	50	35	20	32	21	6	5	0	113	74	47
Atlanta	2	2	0	0	0	7	2	4	2	2	0	0	0	13	5	4	4	4	0	0	0	20	7	8
Boston	283	153	78	52	0	950	716	358	285	90	152	43	0	759	1003	223	568	243	230	95	0	1709	1719	581
Buffalo	53	30	18	5	0	195	155	65	50	10	32	8	0	145	219	28	103	40	50	13	0	340	374	93
Calgary	53	27	16	10	0	198	161	64	54	17	31	6	0	165	217	40	107	44	47	16	0	363	378	104
Carolina	29	16	7	6	0	111	79	38	27	10	16	1	0	73	95	21	56	26	23	7	0	184	174	59
Chicago	327	199	96	31	1	1122	814	430	330	129	149	51	1	927	989	310	657	328	245	82	2	2049	1803	740
Colorado	34	21	12	1	0	129	106	43	36	13	19	4	0	124	137	30	70	34	31	5	0	253	243	73
Columbus	2	2	0	0	0	8	3	4	3	2	1	0	0	6	5	4	5	4	1	0	0	14	8	8
Dallas	100	50	36	14	0	387	325	114	100	35	50	15	0	300	355	85	200	85	86	29	0	687	680	199
Edmonton	38	20	15	3	0	145	133	43	38	13	19	6	0	143	156	32	76	33	34	9	0	288	289	75
Florida	6	3	1	2	0	24	18	8	7	4	1	2	0	22	14	10	13	7	2	4	0	46	32	18
Los Angeles	73	31	30	12	0	279	256	74	74	21	39	14	0	230	304	56	147	52	69	26	0	509	560	130
Minnesota	2	1	1	0	0	7	7	2	2	1	0	0	1	5	5	3	4	2	1	0	1	12	12	5
Montreal	279	130	96	53	0	803	714	313	280	66	171	43	0	632	990	175	559	196	267	96	0	1435	1704	488
Nashville	9	8	0	0	1	36	20	17	8	4	3	1	0	27	22	9	17	12	3	1	1	63	42	26
New Jersey	37	22	13	2	0	152	123	46	38	10	19	9	0	102	133	29	75	32	32	11	0	254	256	75
NY Islanders	42	23	17	2	0	152	132	48	44	18	23	3	0	130	158	39	86	41	40	5	0	282	290	87
NY Rangers	283	162	76	45	0	998	696	369	282	91	133	58	0	732	862	240	565	253	209	103	0	1730	1558	609
Ottawa	7	4	3	0	0	24	15	8	7	4	2	1	0	21	19	9	14	8	5	1	0	45	34	17
Philadelphia	57	29	18	10	0	203	178	68	57	13	33	11	0	166	227	37	114	42	51	21	0	369	405	105
Phoenix	45	22	17	6	0	181	157	50	43	15	16	12	0	137	135	42	88	37	33	18	0	318	292	92
Pittsburgh	64	39	13	12	0	246	175	90	62	15	43	4	0	183	274	34	126	54	56	16	0	429	449	124
St. Louis	102	46	39	17	0	370	316	109	102	28	54	19	1	277	357	76	204	74	93	36	1	647	673	185
San Jose	19	17	2	0	0	84	33	34	20	12	5	3	0	84	61	27	39	29	7	3	0	168	94	61
Tampa Bay	10	9	1	0	0	43	18	18	12	8	3	1	0	57	39	17	22	17	4	1	0	100	57	35
Toronto	319	166	106	46	1	951	783	379	314	104	163	47	0	842	1039	255	633	270	269	93	1	1793	1822	634
Vancouver	60	37	15	8	0	256	172	82	59	24	25	10	0	197	216	58	119	61	40	18	0	453	388	140
Washington	45	20	14	11	0	157	130	51	44	18	21	5	0	137	166	41	89	38	35	16	0	294	296	92
Defunct Clubs	141	76	40	25	0	430	307	177	141	49	63	29	0	364	375	127	282	125	103	54	0	794	682	304
Totals	**2537**	**1377**	**781**	**376**	**3**	**8711**	**6783**	**3133**	**2537**	**835**	**1291**	**408**	**3**	**7050**	**8612**	**2081**	**5074**	**2212**	**2072**	**784**	**6**	**15761**	**15395**	**5214**

Playoffs

	Series	W	L	GP	W	L	T	GF	GA	Last Mtg.	Round	Result
Anaheim	2	2	0	8	8	0	0	30	14	1999	CQF	W 4-0
Boston	7	3	4	33	14	19	0	98	96	1957	SF	L 1-4
Calgary	1	1	0	2	2	0	0	8	5	1978	PR	W 2-0
Chicago	14	6	8	69	31	38	0	190	210	1995	CF	W 4-1
Colorado	4	1	3	23	9	14	0	54	66	2000	CSF	L 1-4
Dallas	3	3	0	18	12	6	0	55	40	1998	CF	W 4-2
Edmonton	2	0	2	10	2	8	0	26	39	1988	CF	L 1-4
Los Angeles	2	1	1	10	6	4	0	32	21	2001	CQF	L 2-4
Montreal	12	7	5	62	29	33	0	149	161	1978	QF	L 1-4
New Jersey	1	0	1	4	0	4	0	7	16	1995	F	L 0-4
NY Rangers	5	4	1	23	13	10	0	57	49	1950	F	W 4-3
Philadelphia	1	1	0	4	4	0	0	16	6	1997	F	W 4-0
Phoenix	2	2	0	12	8	4	0	44	28	1998	CQF	W 4-2
St. Louis	6	4	2	35	20	15	0	111	92	1998	CSF	W 4-2
San Jose	2	1	1	11	7	4	0	51	27	1995	CSF	W 4-0
Toronto	23	11	12	117	59	58	0	321	311	1993	DSF	L 3-4
Washington	1	1	0	4	4	0	0	13	7	1998	F	W 4-0
Defunct Clubs	4	3	1	10	7	2	1	21	13			
Totals	**92**	**51**	**41**	**455**	**235**	**219**	**1**	**1283**	**1201**			

Playoff Results 2001-1997

Year	Round	Opponent	Result	GF	GA
2001	CQF	Los Angeles	L 2-4	17	15
2000	CSF	Colorado	L 1-4	8	13
	CQF	Los Angeles	W 4-0	15	6
1999	CSF	Colorado	L 2-4	14	21
	CQF	Anaheim	W 4-0	17	6
1998	**F**	**Washington**	**W 4-0**	**13**	**7**
	CF	Dallas	W 4-2	15	11
	CSF	St. Louis	W 4-2	23	13
	CQF	Phoenix	W 4-2	24	18
1997	**F**	**Philadelphia**	**W 4-0**	**16**	**6**
	CF	Colorado	W 4-2	16	12
	CSF	Anaheim	W 4-0	13	8
	CQF	St. Louis	W 4-2	13	12

Abbreviations: Round: F – Final; **CF** – conference final; **CSF** – conference semi-final; **CQF** – conference quarter-final; **DSF** – division semi-final; **SF** – semi-final; **QF** – quarter-final; **PR** – preliminary round.

Calgary totals include Atlanta Flames, 1972-73 to 1979-80.
Carolina totals include Hartford, 1979-80 to 1996-97.
Colorado totals include Quebec, 1979-80 to 1994-95.
Dallas totals include Minnesota North Stars, 1967-68 to 1992-93.
New Jersey totals include Kansas City, 1974-75 to 1975-76, and Colorado Rockies, 1976-77 to 1981-82.
Phoenix totals include Winnipeg, 1979-80 to 1995-96.

2000-01 Results

Month	Day	Opponent	Score	Month	Day	Opponent	Score
Oct.	5	at Calgary	4-3	**Jan.**	4	Dallas	4-2
	6	at Edmonton	1-2		5	at Minnesota	2-3*
	11	Edmonton	3-4		7	Colorado	4-3*
	12	at Chicago	4-0		9	Phoenix	2-2
	15	Calgary	2-4		12	at Dallas	3-2
	17	St. Louis	2-1		15	at San Jose	3-2
	19	Nashville	1-2*		16	at Vancouver	4-2
	21	Buffalo	5-4*		20	at Edmonton	1-2
	22	at Columbus	2-1*		21	at Calgary	2-4
	25	Tampa Bay	5-1		24	Nashville	4-3
	28	Columbus	4-1		26	Anaheim	3-2
	31	at Washington	2-6		30	at New Jersey	1-3
Nov.	1	at Montreal	4-2		31	at Columbus	3-2*
	3	Chicago	1-6	**Feb.**	6	Ottawa	4-2
	8	at Phoenix	4-2		8	Toronto	2-1
	11	at Los Angeles	2-2		10	at Toronto	3-3
	12	at Anaheim	3-2		14	Carolina	4-3*
	15	San Jose	4-1		16	Columbus	4-2
	17	Dallas	0-1		18	at Dallas	2-1
	18	at Nashville	2-3		20	at Nashville	3-3
	20	Nashville	6-3		21	at Chicago	7-3
	22	Boston	4-5		23	St. Louis	4-2
	24	Vancouver	3-2		25	Phoenix	6-3
	25	at NY Islanders	4-3		28	at Anaheim	3-1
	27	Chicago	5-6*	**Mar.**	2	at Phoenix	2-2
	29	at Atlanta	6-4		3	at Los Angeles	3-6
Dec.	1	at Florida	3-1		6	at Vancouver	4-3
	2	at Tampa Bay	0-3		10	at St. Louis	2-2
	6	Toronto	0-3		11	at Minnesota	3-2*
	8	Philadelphia	5-1		13	Vancouver	2-2
	10	Pittsburgh	3-4		15	Calgary	5-2
	13	Florida	3-3		17	at Colorado	3-5
	15	at Colorado	5-3		18	at San Jose	6-4
	16	at St. Louis	2-2		22	Minnesota	4-2
	18	Edmonton	4-3*		24	at NY Rangers	6-0
	20	San Jose	0-2		28	St. Louis	5-2
	22	Anaheim	2-1*		31	at Philadelphia	0-1
	23	at Boston	2-1*	**Apr.**	1	Washington	2-1*
	27	Minnesota	3-5		3	at Columbus	1-2
	29	at Chicago	2-3*		5	Atlanta	4-0
	31	Los Angeles	2-1		7	Colorado	4-3

* – Overtime

Entry Draft Selections 2001-1987

2001
Pick
62 Igor Grigorenko
121 Drew MacIntyre
129 Miroslav Blatak
157 Andreas Jamtin
195 Nick Pannoni
258 Dmitri Bykov
288 Francois Senez

2000
Pick
29 Niklas Kronwall
38 Tomas Kopecky
102 Stefan Liv
127 Dmitri Semenov
128 Alexander Seluyanov
130 Aaron Van Leusen
187 Per Backer
196 Paul Ballantyne
228 Jimmie Svensson
251 Todd Jackson
260 Yevgeny Bumagin

1999
Pick
120 Jari Tolsa
149 Andrei Maximenko
181 Kent McDonell
210 Henrik Zetterberg
238 Anton Borodkin
266 Ken Davis

1998
Pick
25 Jiri Fischer
55 Ryan Barnes
56 Tomek Valtonen
84 Jake McCracken
111 Brent Hobday
142 Calle Steen
151 Adam DeLeeuw
171 Pavel Datsyuk
198 Jeremy Goetzinger
226 David Petrasek
256 Petja Pietilainen

1997
Pick
49 Yuri Butsayev
76 Petr Sykora
102 Quintin Laing
129 John Wikstrom
157 B.J. Young
186 Mike Laceby
213 Steve Willejto
239 Greg Willers

1996
Pick
26 Jesse Wallin
52 Aren Miller
108 Johan Forsander
135 Michal Podolka
144 Magnus Nilsson
162 Alexandre Jacques
189 Colin Beardsmore
215 Craig Stahl
241 Eugeny Afanasiev

1995
Pick
26 Maxim Kuznetsov
52 Philippe Audet
58 Darryl Laplante
104 Anatoli Ustyugov
125 Chad Wilchynski
126 David Arsenault
156 Tyler Perry
182 Per Eklund
208 Andrei Samokhvalov
234 David Engblom

1994
Pick
23 Yan Golubovsky
49 Mathieu Dandenault
75 Sean Gillam
114 Frederic Deschenes
127 Doug Battaglia
153 Pavel Agarkov
205 Jason Elliot
231 Jeff Mikesch
257 Tomas Holmstrom
283 Toivo Suursoo

1993
Pick
5 Benoit Larose
22 Anders Eriksson
48 Jon Coleman
74 Kevin Hilton
97 John Jakopin
126 Norm Maracle
152 Tim Spitzig
178 Yuri Yeresko
204 Vitezslav Skuta
230 Ryan Shanahan
256 James Kosecki
282 Gordon Hunt

1992
Pick
22 Curtis Bowen
46 Darren McCarty
70 Sylvain Cloutier
118 Mike Sullivan
142 Jason MacDonald
166 Greg Scott
183 Justin Krall
189 C. J. Denomme
214 Jeff Walker
238 Dan McGillis
262 Ryan Bach

1991
Pick
10 Martin Lapointe
32 Jamie Pushor
54 Chris Osgood
76 Mike Knuble
98 Dimitri Motkov
142 Igor Malykhin
186 Jim Bermingham
208 Jason Firth
230 Bart Turner
252 Andrew Miller

1990
Pick
3 Keith Primeau
45 Vyacheslav Kozlov
66 Stewart Malgunas
87 Tony Burns
108 Claude Barthe
129 Jason York
150 Wes McCauley
171 Anthony Gruba
192 Travis Tucker
213 Brett Larson
234 John Hendry

1989
Pick
11 Mike Sillinger
32 Bob Boughner
53 Nicklas Lidstrom
74 Sergei Fedorov
95 Shawn McCosh
116 Dallas Drake
137 Scott Zygulski
158 Andy Suhy
179 Bob Jones
200 Greg Bignell
204 Rick Judson
221 Vladimir Konstantinov
242 Joseph Frederick
246 Jason Glickman

1988
Pick
17 Kory Kocur
38 Serge Anglehart
47 Guy Dupuis
59 Petr Hrbek
80 Sheldon Kennedy
143 Kelly Hurd
164 Brian McCormack
185 Jody Praznik
206 Glen Goodall
227 Darren Colbourne
248 Donald Stone

1987
Pick
11 Yves Racine
32 Gord Kruppke
41 Bob Wilkie
52 Dennis Holland
74 Mark Reimer
95 Radomir Brazda
116 Sean Clifford
137 Mike Gober
158 Kevin Scott
179 Mikko Haapakoski
200 Darin Bannister
221 Craig Quinlan
242 Tomas Jansson

Club Directory

Joe Louis Arena

Detroit Red Wings
Joe Louis Arena
600 Civic Center Drive
Detroit, MI 48226
Phone **313/396-7544**
FAX PR: 313/567-0296
Media Hotline: 313/396-7599
www.detroitredwings.com
Capacity: 20,053

Owner/Governor	Mike Ilitch
Owner/Secretary-Treasurer	Marian Ilitch
Senior Vice-President/Alternate Governor	Jim Devellano
Vice-President, Red Wings/President, Ilitch Holdings, Inc./Alternate Governor	Christopher Ilitch
President, Ilitch Holdings, Inc./Alternate Governor	Denise Ilitch
General Counsel	Rob Carr
General Manager/Alternate Governor	Ken Holland
Assistant General Manager	Jim Nill
Head Coach	Scotty Bowman
Associate Coach	Dave Lewis
Associate Coach	Barry Smith
Goaltending Consultant	Jim Bedard
Video Technician	Joe Kocur
NHL Scout	Dan Belisle
Pro Scout	Mark Howe
Pro Scout	Glenn Merkosky
Amateur Scout	Joe McDonnell
Amateur Scout	Bruce Haralson
Amateur Scout	Mark Leach
Director of European Scouting	Hakan Andersson
European Scout	Vladimir Havluj
Part-Time European Scout	Evgeni Erfilov
Part-Time Scout	Marty Stein
Executive Assistant	Nancy Beard
Administrative and Scouting Coordinator	David Kolb
Senior Director of Finance	Paul MacDonald
Accounting Assistant	Bridget Merritt
Athletic Therapist	John Wharton
Assistant Athletic Therapist	Piet Van Zant
Equipment Manager	Paul Boyer
Assistant Equipment Manager	Tim Abbott
Senior Director of Communications	John Hahn
Media Relations Manager	Michael Kuta
Community Relations Manager	Anne Marie Krappmann
Public Relations Assistant	Jennie Hagler
Team Photographer	Mark Hicks
Team Physicians	John Finley, D.O.; David Collon, M.D.
Team Dentist	C.J. Regula, D.M.D.
Radio Broadcasters, Team 1270 WXYT	Ken Kal, Paul Woods
Television Broadcasters, WKBD UPN-50 & FOX Sports Net Detroit	Ken Daniels, Mickey Redmond

General Manager

HOLLAND, KEN
General Manager, Detroit Red Wings. Born in Vernon, B.C., Nov. 10, 1955.

Ken Holland is entering his fifth season as a general manager and his 19th year with the Red Wings organization. In his four seasons as Detroit's general manager, Holland has established himself as one of the most innovative and aggressive GMs in the National Hockey League. Holland began his tenure as the club's general manager after serving as assistant general manager for the previous three seasons. Holland was elevated to his present position July 18, 1997.

In his new and expanded role, he oversees all aspects of hockey operations including all matters relating to player personnel, development, contract negotiations and player movements. Holland also continues to be Detroit's point person at the NHL Entry Draft, as he has for the past 11 years. In that capacity, he was instrumental in selecting such players as Vyacheslav Kozlov, Darren McCarty, Chris Osgood and Martin Lapointe, along with several other top prospects.

Holland has deftly handled several different front-office duties for the club over the past 19 years. At the conclusion of his playing days as a goaltender, spending most of his pro career at the American Hockey League level, Holland began his off-ice career in 1985 as a western Canada scout followed by five years as amateur scouting director before promotions leading to his current position as general manager.

A native of Vernon, BC, Holland played in the junior ranks for Medicine Hat (WHL) in 1974-75. He was Toronto's 13th pick (188th overall) in the 1975 draft but never saw action with the Maple Leafs. Holland twice signed with NHL teams as a free agent — in 1980 with Hartford and 1983 with Detroit. He spent most of his pro career with AHL clubs in Binghamton and Springfield, along with Adirondack, but did appear in four NHL games, making his debut with Hartford in 1980-81 and playing three contests for Detroit in 1983-84.

General Managers' History

Art Duncan and Duke Keats, 1926-27; Jack Adams, 1927-28 to 1961-62; Sid Abel, 1962-63 to 1969-70; Sid Abel and Ned Harkness, 1970-71; Ned Harkness, 1971-72 to 1973-74; Alex Delvecchio, 1974-75, 1975-76; Alex Delvecchio and Ted Lindsay, 1976-77; Ted Lindsay, 1977-78 to 1979-80; Jimmy Skinner, 1980-81, 1981-82; Jim Devellano, 1982-83 to 1989-90; Bryan Murray, 1990-91 to 1993-94; Jim Devellano (Senior Vice President), 1994-95 to 1996-97; Ken Holland, 1997-98 to date.

Captains' History

Art Duncan, 1926-27; Reg Noble, 1927-28 to 1929-30; George Hay, 1930-31; Carson Cooper, 1931-32; Larry Aurie, 1932-33; Herbie Lewis, 1933-34; Ebbie Goodfellow, 1934-35; Doug Young, 1935-36 to 1937-38; Ebbie Goodfellow, 1938-39 to 1940-41; Ebbie Goodfellow and Syd Howe, 1941-42; Sid Abel, 1942-43; Mud Bruneteau, Bill Hollett (co-captains), 1943-44; Bill Hollett, 1944-45; Bill Hollett and Sid Abel, 1945-46; Sid Abel, 1946-47 to 1951-52; Ted Lindsay, 1952-53 to 1955-56; Red Kelly, 1956-57, 1957-58; Gordie Howe, 1958-59 to 1961-62; Alex Delvecchio, 1962-63 to 1972-73; Alex Delvecchio, Nick Libett, Red Berenson, Gary Bergman, Ted Harris, Mickey Redmond and Larry Johnston, 1973-74; Marcel Dionne, 1974-75; Danny Grant and Terry Harper, 1975-76; Danny Grant and Dennis Polonich, 1976-77; Dan Maloney and Dennis Hextall, 1977-78; Dennis Hextall, Nick Libett and Paul Woods, 1978-79; Dale McCourt, 1979-80; Errol Thompson and Reed Larson, 1980-81; Reed Larson, 1981-82; Danny Gare, 1982-83 to 1985-86; Steve Yzerman, 1986-87 to date.

Edmonton Oilers

2000-01 Results: 39W-28L-12T-3OTL 93PTS. Second, Northwest Division

Year-by-Year Record

		Home				Road				Overall								
Season	GP	W	L	T	OL	W	L	T	OL	W	L	T	OL	GF	GA	Pts.	Finished	Playoff Result
2000-01	82	23	9	7	2	16	19	5	1	39	28	12	3	243	222	93	2nd, Northwest Div.	Lost Conf. Quarter-Final
1999-2000	82	18	11	9	3	14	15	7	5	32	26	16	8	226	212	88	2nd, Northwest Div.	Lost Conf. Quarter-Final
1998-99	82	17	19	5	...	16	18	7	...	33	37	12	...	230	226	78	2nd, Northwest Div.	Lost Conf. Quarter-Final
1997-98	82	20	16	5	...	15	21	5	...	35	37	10	...	215	224	80	3rd, Pacific Div.	Lost Conf. Semi-Final
1996-97	82	21	16	4	...	15	21	5	...	36	37	9	...	252	247	81	3rd, Pacific Div.	Lost Conf. Semi-Final
1995-96	82	15	21	5	...	15	23	3	...	30	44	8	...	240	304	68	5th, Pacific Div.	Out of Playoffs
1994-95	48	11	12	1	...	6	15	3	...	17	27	4	...	136	183	38	5th, Pacific Div.	Out of Playoffs
1993-94	84	17	22	3	...	8	23	11	...	25	45	14	...	261	305	64	6th, Pacific Div.	Out of Playoffs
1992-93	84	16	21	5	...	10	29	3	...	26	50	8	...	242	337	60	5th, Smythe Div.	Out of Playoffs
1991-92	80	22	13	5	...	14	21	5	...	36	34	10	...	295	297	82	3rd, Smythe Div.	Lost Conf. Championship
1990-91	80	22	15	3	...	15	22	3	...	37	37	6	...	272	272	80	3rd, Smythe Div.	Lost Conf. Championship
1989-90	**80**	**23**	**11**	**6**	**...**	**15**	**17**	**8**	**...**	**38**	**28**	**14**	**...**	**315**	**283**	**90**	**2nd, Smythe Div.**	**Won Stanley Cup**
1988-89	80	21	16	3	...	17	18	5	...	38	34	8	...	325	306	84	3rd, Smythe Div.	Lost Div. Semi-Final
1987-88	**80**	**28**	**8**	**4**	**...**	**16**	**17**	**7**	**...**	**44**	**25**	**11**	**...**	**363**	**288**	**99**	**2nd, Smythe Div.**	**Won Stanley Cup**
1986-87	**80**	**29**	**6**	**5**	**...**	**21**	**18**	**1**	**...**	**50**	**24**	**6**	**...**	**372**	**284**	**106**	**1st, Smythe Div.**	**Won Stanley Cup**
1985-86	80	32	6	2	...	24	11	5	...	56	17	7	...	426	310	119	1st, Smythe Div.	Lost Div. Final
1984-85	**80**	**26**	**7**	**7**	**...**	**23**	**13**	**4**	**...**	**49**	**20**	**11**	**...**	**401**	**298**	**109**	**1st, Smythe Div.**	**Won Stanley Cup**
1983-84	**80**	**31**	**5**	**4**	**...**	**26**	**13**	**1**	**...**	**57**	**18**	**5**	**...**	**446**	**314**	**119**	**1st, Smythe Div.**	**Won Stanley Cup**
1982-83	80	25	9	6	...	22	12	6	...	47	21	12	...	424	315	106	1st, Smythe Div.	Lost Final
1981-82	80	31	5	4	...	17	12	11	...	48	17	15	...	417	295	111	1st, Smythe Div.	Lost Div. Semi-Final
1980-81	80	17	13	10	...	12	22	6	...	29	35	16	...	328	327	74	4th, Smythe Div.	Lost Quarter-Final
1979-80	80	17	14	9	...	11	25	4	...	28	39	13	...	301	322	69	4th, Smythe Div.	Lost Prelim. Round

2001-02 Schedule

Oct.	Wed.	3	at Calgary
	Sat.	6	Phoenix
	Tue.	9	Chicago
	Thu.	11	Colorado
	Sat.	13	at Nashville
	Sun.	14	at Minnesota*
	Tue.	16	Toronto
	Thu.	18	at Colorado
	Sat.	20	Florida
	Mon.	22	Nashville
	Wed.	24	at Detroit
	Thu.	25	at Columbus
	Sat.	27	Vancouver
	Tue.	30	Montreal
Nov.	Fri.	2	Columbus
	Sun.	4	at Minnesota*
	Tue.	6	at Boston
	Fri.	9	at Columbus
	Sun.	11	at Carolina*
	Tue.	13	at Phoenix
	Fri.	16	Chicago
	Sat.	17	at Vancouver
	Tue.	20	St. Louis
	Thu.	22	Los Angeles
	Sat.	24	at Colorado
	Wed.	28	at Anaheim
	Thu.	29	at Los Angeles
Dec.	Sat.	1	Dallas
	Wed.	5	Anaheim
	Fri.	7	at Dallas
	Sat.	8	at Nashville
	Tue.	11	at San Jose
	Thu.	13	Detroit
	Fri.	14	Tampa Bay
	Sun.	16	at Philadelphia
	Tue.	18	at NY Islanders
	Thu.	20	at New Jersey
	Fri.	21	at Chicago
	Wed.	26	Calgary
	Fri.	28	Minnesota
	Sun.	30	New Jersey
	Mon.	31	at Calgary
Jan.	Wed.	2	NY Rangers
	Sat.	5	Vancouver
	Sun.	6	Montreal
	Thu.	10	Carolina
	Sat.	12	Colorado
	Mon.	14	at Chicago
	Tue.	15	at St. Louis
	Fri.	18	Anaheim
	Sat.	19	Pittsburgh
	Mon.	21	at San Jose*
	Wed.	23	Colorado
	Sat.	26	Toronto*
	Mon.	28	Detroit
	Wed.	30	at Vancouver
Feb.	Tue.	5	at Atlanta
	Thu.	7	at St. Louis
	Fri.	8	at Dallas
	Sun.	10	at Phoenix*
	Tue.	12	San Jose
	Thu.	28	Nashville
Mar.	Sat.	2	St. Louis
	Mon.	4	at Buffalo
	Wed.	6	at Tampa Bay
	Fri.	8	at Florida
	Sun.	10	at Washington*
	Wed.	13	at Detroit
	Thu.	14	at Ottawa
	Sat.	16	Washington
	Wed.	20	San Jose
	Sat.	23	Calgary
	Sun.	24	at Vancouver
	Tue.	26	Columbus
	Thu.	28	Los Angeles
	Sat.	30	Dallas
Apr.	Tue.	2	Minnesota
	Fri.	5	at Anaheim
	Sat.	6	at Los Angeles
	Wed.	10	Phoenix
	Fri.	12	Calgary
	Sun.	14	at Minnesota*

* Denotes afternoon game.

Franchise date: June 22, 1979

NORTHWEST DIVISION

23rd NHL Season

Acquired from the New York Islanders in a 2000 Draft day deal for Roman Hamrlik, Eric Brewer is developing into one of the top young defensemen in the NHL.

2001-02 Player Personnel

FORWARDS	HT	WT	S	Place of Birth	Date	2000-01 Club
BENDA, Jan	6-3	215	R	Reef, Belgium	3/28/72	Jokerit Helsinki
CARTER, Anson	6-1	200	R	Toronto, Ont.	6/6/74	Edmonton
CHIMERA, Jason	6-0	180	L	Edmonton, Alta.	5/2/79	Edmonton-Hamilton
CLEARY, Daniel	6-0	203	L	Carbonear, Nfld.	12/18/78	Edmonton
COMRIE, Mike	5-9	172	L	Edmonton, Alta.	9/11/80	Kootenay-Edmonton
COMRIE, Paul	5-11	192	L	Edmonton, Alta.	2/7/77	Edmonton
GREEN, Josh	6-4	212	L	Camrose, Alta.	11/16/77	Hamilton-Edmonton
GRIER, Mike	6-1	227	R	Detroit, MI	1/5/75	Edmonton
HECHT, Jochen	6-3	196	L	Mannheim, West Germany	6/21/77	St. Louis
HEMSKY, Ales	6-0	191	R	Pardubice, Czech.	8/13/83	Hull Olympiques
HENRICH, Michael	6-2	206	R	Thornhill, Ont.	3/3/80	Tallahasee-Hamilton
HINZ, Chad	5-10	190	R	Saskatoon, Sask.	3/21/79	Hamilton
HORCOFF, Shawn	6-1	202	L	Trail, B.C.	9/17/78	Edmonton-Hamilton
LARAQUE, Georges	6-3	240	R	Montreal, Que.	12/7/76	Edmonton
LEEB, Greg	5-9	165	L	Red Deer, Alta.	5/31/77	Dallas-Utah
MARCHANT, Todd	5-10	178	L	Buffalo, NY	8/12/73	Edmonton
McASLAN, Sean	6-1	190	R	Okotoks, Alta.	1/12/80	Calgary (WHL)
McDONALD, Kevin	5-11	198	R	Olds, Alta.	4/21/77	Florida (ECHL)-Roanoke
MIKHNOV, Alexei	6-5	198	L	Kiev, USSR	8/31/82	HC Moscow-THC Tver
MOREAU, Ethan	6-2	211	L	Huntsville, Ont.	9/22/75	Edmonton
MURRAY, Rem	6-2	195	L	Stratford, Ont.	10/9/72	Edmonton
PISANI, Fernando	6-1	185	L	Edmonton, Alta.	12/27/76	Hamilton
PITTIS, Domenic	5-11	190	L	Calgary, Alta.	10/1/74	Edmonton
REASONER, Marty	6-1	203	L	Rochester, NY	2/26/77	St. Louis-Worcester
REICHERT, Craig	6-1	200	R	Winnipeg, Man.	5/11/74	Dusseldorfer EG
RITA, Jani	6-1	206	L	Helsinki, Finland	7/25/81	Jokerit Helsinki
SARNO, Peter	5-11	185	L	Toronto, Ont.	7/26/79	Hamilton
SMYTH, Ryan	6-1	195	L	Banff, Alta.	2/21/76	Edmonton
SPIRIDONOV, Maxim	5-10	185	L	Moscow, USSR	4/7/78	Hamilton
SWANSON, Brian	5-10	185	L	Eagle River, AK	3/24/76	Edmonton-Hamilton
DEFENSEMEN						
BERGERON, Marc-Andre	5-9	185	L	St-Louis-de-France, Que.	10/13/80	Shawinigan
BREWER, Eric	6-3	220	L	Vernon, B.C.	4/17/79	Edmonton
BROWN, Sean	6-3	205	L	Oshawa, Ont.	11/5/76	Edmonton
BUTENSCHON, Sven	6-4	215	L	Itzehoe, West Germany	3/22/76	Pit-Wilkes-Barre-Edm
FERGUSON, Scott	6-1	202	L	Camrose, Alta.	1/6/73	Edmonton-Hamilton
HAJT, Chris	6-3	206	L	Saskatoon, Sask.	7/5/78	Edmonton-Hamilton
HENRY, Alex	6-5	220	L	Elliot Lake, Ont.	10/18/79	Hamilton
HORACEK, Jan	6-4	206	R	Benesov, Czech.	5/22/79	Worcester-Peoria
LIUBIMOV, Alexander	6-3	196	L	Ust-Kamenogorsk, USSR	2/15/80	Lada Togliatti
NASREDDINE, Alain	6-1	201	L	Montreal, Que.	7/10/75	Hamilton
NIINIMAA, Janne	6-1	220	L	Raahe, Finland	5/22/75	Edmonton
PISA, Ales	6-0	187	L	Pardibuce, Czech.	1/2/77	HC Pardubice
POTI, Tom	6-3	215	L	Worcester, MA	3/22/77	Edmonton
SEMENOV, Alexei	6-6	210	L	Murmansk, USSR	4/10/81	Sudbury Wolves
SMITH, Jason	6-3	210	R	Calgary, Alta.	11/2/73	Edmonton
STAIOS, Steve	6-1	200	R	Hamilton, Ont.	7/28/73	Atlanta
GOALTENDERS	**HT**	**WT**	**C**	**Place of Birth**	**Date**	**2000-01 Club**
CONKLIN, Ty	6-0	190	L	Anchorage, AK	3/30/76	New Hampshire
FOMITCHEV, Alexander	5-10	180	L	Moscow, USSR	2/19/79	Tall'see-Hamilton-Asheville
HEFFLER, Eric	6-3	190	L	Williamsville, NY	2/29/76	Hamilton-Greensboro
MARKKANEN, Jussi	5-11	183	L	Imatra, Finland	5/8/75	Tappara Tampere
SALO, Tommy	5-11	173	L	Surahammar, Sweden	2/1/71	Edmonton

Coaching History

Glen Sather, 1979-80; Bryan Watson and Glen Sather, 1980-81; Glen Sather, 1981-82 to 1988-89; John Muckler, 1989-90, 1990-91; Ted Green, 1991-92, 1992-93; Ted Green and Glen Sather, 1993-94; George Burnett and Ron Low, 1994-95; Ron Low, 1995-96 to 1998-99; Kevin Lowe, 1999-2000; Craig MacTavish, 2000-01 to date.

Coach

MacTAVISH, CRAIG
Coach, Edmonton Oilers. Born in London, Ont., August 15, 1958.

The Edmonton Oilers named Craig MacTavish as their head coach on June 22, 2000. He became the eighth person in the club's NHL history to hold the position. MacTavish joined Kevin Lowe and Glen Sather as head coaches who were former captains of the Oilers.

MacTavish played for 18 seasons in the NHL, including eight-and-three-quarter campaigns with the Oilers. He was instrumental in helping his teams win four Stanley Cup titles; three with Edmonton and one with the New York Rangers. Although he was the last player in the NHL to play without a helmet, MacTavish was known for his aggressive style, combined with above average skills.

MacTavish retired as a player in 1997 and was immediately named an assistant coach with the New York Rangers. He was with the Rangers for two seasons prior to joining the Oilers' coaching staff as an assistant under Kevin Lowe in 1999-2000.

Coaching Record

		Regular Season				Playoffs		
Season	**Team**	**Games**	**W**	**L**	**T**	**Games**	**W**	**L**
2000-01	**Edmonton (NHL)**	82	39	31	12	6	2	4
	NHL Totals	82	39	31	12	6	2	4

2000-01 Scoring

* - rookie

Regular Season

Pos	#	Player	Team	GP	G	A	Pts	+/–	PIM	PP	SH	GW	GT	S	%
C	39	Doug Weight	EDM	82	25	65	90	12	91	8	0	3	2	188	13.3
L	94	Ryan Smyth	EDM	82	31	39	70	10	58	11	0	6	1	245	12.7
D	44	Janne Niinimaa	EDM	82	12	34	46	6	90	8	0	1	0	122	9.8
R	22	Anson Carter	EDM	61	16	26	42	1	23	7	1	4	0	102	15.7
C	26	Todd Marchant	EDM	71	13	26	39	1	51	0	4	2	1	113	11.5
R	25	Mike Grier	EDM	74	20	16	36	11	20	2	3	2	1	124	16.1
L	17	Rem Murray	EDM	82	15	21	36	5	24	1	3	3	1	122	12.3
R	7	Daniel Cleary	EDM	81	14	21	35	5	37	2	0	2	1	107	13.1
D	5	Tom Poti	EDM	81	12	20	32	–4	60	6	0	3	0	161	7.5
C	34	Sergei Zholtok	MTL	32	1	10	11	–15	8	0	0	0	0	78	1.3
			EDM	37	4	16	20	8	22	1	0	0	0	61	6.6
			TOTAL	69	5	26	31	–7	30	1	0	0	0	139	3.6
R	27	Georges Laraque	EDM	82	13	16	29	5	148	1	0	1	1	73	17.8
D	55	Igor Ulanov	EDM	67	3	20	23	15	90	1	0	0	1	74	4.1
C	89 *	Mike Comrie	EDM	41	8	14	22	6	14	3	0	1	0	62	12.9
D	2	Eric Brewer	EDM	77	7	14	21	15	53	2	0	2	0	91	7.7
D	21	Jason Smith	EDM	82	5	15	20	14	120	1	1	0	0	140	3.6
L	18	Ethan Moreau	EDM	68	9	10	19	–6	90	0	1	3	0	97	9.3
C	36 *	Shawn Horcoff	EDM	49	9	7	16	8	10	0	0	2	0	42	21.4
C	14 *	Domenic Pittis	EDM	47	4	5	9	–5	49	0	0	2	0	42	9.5
D	23	Sean Brown	EDM	62	2	3	5	2	110	0	0	0	0	30	6.7
D	19	Sven Butenschon	PIT	5	0	1	1	1	2	0	0	0	0	6	0.0
			EDM	7	1	1	2	2	2	0	0	0	0	3	33.3
			TOTAL	12	1	2	3	3	4	0	0	0	0	9	11.1
C	37 *	Brian Swanson	EDM	16	1	1	2	–1	6	0	0	0	0	8	12.5
D	8	Frank Musil	EDM	13	0	2	2	–2	4	0	0	0	0	0	0.0
L	34 *	Michel Riesen	EDM	12	0	1	1	2	4	0	0	0	0	16	0.0
D	32	Scott Ferguson	EDM	20	0	1	1	2	13	0	0	0	0	8	0.0
G	35	Tommy Salo	EDM	73	0	1	1	0	4	0	0	0	0	0	0.0
D	19 *	Chris Hajt	EDM	1	0	0	0	–1	0	0	0	0	0	0	0.0
C	20 *	Jason Chimera	EDM	1	0	0	0	0	0	0	0	0	0	0	0.0
G	31	Joaquin Gage	EDM	5	0	0	0	0	0	0	0	0	0	0	0.0
L	29	Patrick Cote	EDM	6	0	0	0	–2	18	0	0	0	0	0	0.0
G	30	Dominic Roussel	ANA	13	0	0	0	0	0	0	0	0	0	0	0.0
			EDM	8	0	0	0	0	2	0	0	0	0	0	0.0
			TOTAL	21	0	0	0	0	2	0	0	0	0	0	0.0

Goaltending

No.	Goaltender	GPI	Mins	Avg	W	L	T	EN	SO	GA	SA	S%
35	Tommy Salo	73	4364	2.46	36	25	12	5	8	179	1856	.904
31	Joaquin Gage	5	260	3.46	2	2	0	1	0	15	125	.880
30	Dominic Roussel	8	348	3.62	1	4	0	1	0	21	151	.861
	Totals	**82**	**4997**	**2.67**	**39**	**31**	**12**	**7**	**8**	**222**	**2139**	**.896**

Playoffs

Pos	#	Player	Team	GP	G	A	Pts	+/–	PIM	PP	SH	GW	GT	S	%
L	94	Ryan Smyth	EDM	6	3	4	7	0	4	0	0	0	0	22	13.6
C	39	Doug Weight	EDM	6	1	5	6	0	17	0	0	0	0	18	5.6
D	2	Eric Brewer	EDM	6	1	5	6	–3	2	1	0	0	0	11	9.1
R	22	Anson Carter	EDM	6	3	1	4	1	4	1	0	1	0	13	23.1
C	89 *	Mike Comrie	EDM	6	1	2	3	0	0	1	0	1	1	7	14.3
L	17	Rem Murray	EDM	6	2	0	2	–2	6	1	0	0	0	15	13.3
R	27	Georges Laraque	EDM	6	1	1	2	2	8	0	0	0	0	5	20.0
R	7	Daniel Cleary	EDM	6	1	1	2	–2	8	1	0	0	0	6	16.7
D	21	Jason Smith	EDM	6	0	2	2	–3	6	0	0	0	0	6	0.0
D	44	Janne Niinimaa	EDM	6	0	2	2	–1	6	0	0	0	0	11	0.0
D	5	Tom Poti	EDM	6	0	2	2	2	2	0	0	0	0	7	0.0
C	34	Sergei Zholtok	EDM	3	0	0	0	–1	0	0	0	0	0	3	0.0
C	14 *	Domenic Pittis	EDM	3	0	0	0	–1	2	0	0	0	0	1	0.0
L	12	Josh Green	EDM	3	0	0	0	1	0	0	0	0	0	1	0.0
L	18	Ethan Moreau	EDM	4	0	0	0	–2	2	0	0	0	0	5	0.0
C	36 *	Shawn Horcoff	EDM	5	0	0	0	0	0	0	0	0	0	2	0.0
D	55	Igor Ulanov	EDM	6	0	0	0	–6	4	0	0	0	0	4	0.0
G	35	Tommy Salo	EDM	6	0	0	0	0	0	0	0	0	0	0	0.0
C	26	Todd Marchant	EDM	6	0	0	0	–3	4	0	0	0	0	7	0.0
R	25	Mike Grier	EDM	6	0	0	0	–2	8	0	0	0	0	6	0.0
D	32	Scott Ferguson	EDM	6	0	0	0	2	0	0	0	0	0	2	0.0

Goaltending

No.	Goaltender	GPI	Mins	Avg	W	L	EN	SO	GA	SA	S%
35	Tommy Salo	6	406	2.22	2	4	1	0	15	187	.920
	Totals	**6**	**407**	**2.36**	**2**	**4**	**1**	**0**	**16**	**188**	**.915**

Obtained from Boston for Bill Guerin on November 15, 2000, Anson Carter played just 61 games for the Oilers last season but still ranked fourth in team scoring.

Club Records

Team

(Figures in brackets for season records are games played; records for fewest points, wins, ties, losses, goals, goals against are for 70 or more games)

Most Points .... 119 — 1983-84 (80), 1985-86 (80)
Most Wins .... 57 — 1983-84 (80)
Most Ties .... 16 — 1980-81 (80), 1999-2000 (82)
Most Losses .... 50 — 1992-93 (84)
Most Goals .... *446 — 1983-84 (80)
Most Goals Against .... 337 — 1992-93 (84)
Fewest Points .... 60 — 1992-93 (84)
Fewest Wins .... 25 — 1993-94 (84)
Fewest Ties .... 5 — 1983-84 (80)
Fewest Losses .... 17 — 1981-82 (80), 1985-86 (80)
Fewest Goals .... 215 — 1997-98 (82)
Fewest Goals Against .... 212 — 1999-2000 (82)

Longest Winning Streak
- **Overall** .... 9 — Feb. 20-Mar. 13/01
- **Home** .... 8 — Jan. 19-Feb. 22/85, Feb. 24-Apr. 2/86
- **Away** .... 8 — Dec. 9/86-Jan. 17/87

Longest Undefeated Streak
- **Overall** .... 15 — Oct. 11-Nov. 9/84 (12 wins, 3 ties)
- **Home** .... 14 — Nov. 15/89-Jan. 6/90 (11 wins, 3 ties)
- **Away** .... 9 — Jan. 17-Mar. 2/82 (6 wins, 3 ties), Nov. 23/82-Jan. 18/83 (7 wins, 2 ties)

Longest Losing Streak
- **Overall** .... 11 — Oct. 16-Nov. 7/93
- **Home** .... 9 — Oct. 16-Nov. 24/93
- **Away** .... 9 — Nov. 25-Dec. 30/80

Longest Winless Streak
- **Overall** .... 14 — Oct. 11-Nov. 7/93 (13 losses, 1 tie)
- **Home** .... 9 — Oct. 16-Nov. 24/93 (9 losses)
- **Away** .... 9 — Three times

Most Shutouts, Season .... 8 — 1997-98 (82); 2000-01 (82)
Most PIM, Season .... 2,173 — 1987-88 (80)
Most Goals, Game .... 13 — Nov. 19/83 (N.J. 4 at Edm. 13), Nov. 8/85 (Van. 0 at Edm. 13)

Individual

Most Seasons .... 15 — Kevin Lowe
Most Games .... 1,037 — Kevin Lowe
Most Goals, Career .... 583 — Wayne Gretzky
Most Assists, Career .... 1,086 — Wayne Gretzky
Most Points, Career .... 1,669 — Wayne Gretzky (583G, 1,086A)
Most PIM, Career .... 1,747 — Kelly Buchberger
Most Shutouts, Career .... 14 — Curtis Joseph
Longest Consecutive Games Streak .... 521 — Craig MacTavish (Oct. 11/86-Jan. 2/93)
Most Goals, Season .... *92 — Wayne Gretzky (1981-82)
Most Assists, Season .... *163 — Wayne Gretzky (1985-86)
Most Points, Season .... *215 — Wayne Gretzky (1985-86; 52G, 163A)
Most PIM, Season .... 286 — Steve Smith (1987-88)
Most Points, Defenseman, Season .... 138 — Paul Coffey (1985-86; 48G, 90A)
Most Points, Center, Season .... *215 — Wayne Gretzky (1985-86; 52G, 163A)
Most Points, Right Wing, Season .... 135 — Jari Kurri (1984-85; 71G, 64A)
Most Points, Left Wing, Season .... 106 — Mark Messier (1982-83; 48G, 58A)
Most Points, Rookie, Season .... 75 — Jari Kurri (1980-81; 32G, 43A)
Most Shutouts, Season .... 8 — Curtis Joseph (1997-98), Tommy Salo (2000-01)
Most Goals, Game .... 5 — Wayne Gretzky (Feb. 18/81, Dec. 30/81, Dec. 15/84, Dec. 6/87), Jari Kurri (Nov. 19/83), Pat Hughes (Feb. 3/84)
Most Assists, Game .... *7 — Wayne Gretzky (Feb. 15/80, Dec. 11/85, Feb. 14/86)
Most Points, Game .... 8 — Wayne Gretzky (Nov. 19/83; 3G, 5A), (Jan. 4/84; 4G, 4A), Paul Coffey (Mar. 14/86; 2G, 6A)

* NHL Record.

Retired Numbers

3	Al Hamilton	1972-1980
99	Wayne Gretzky	1979-1988

Captains' History

Ron Chipperfield, 1979-80; Blair MacDonald and Lee Fogolin, 1980-81; Lee Fogolin, 1981-82, 1982-83; Wayne Gretzky, 1983-84 to 1987-88; Mark Messier, 1988-89 to 1990-91; Kevin Lowe, 1991-92; Craig MacTavish, 1992-93, 1993-94; Shayne Corson, 1994-95; Kelly Buchberger, 1995-96 to 1998-99; Doug Weight, 1999-2000, 2000-01.

All-time Record vs. Other Clubs

Regular Season

	At Home								On Road								Total							
	GP	W	L	T	OL	GF	GA	PTS	GP	W	L	T	OL	GF	GA	PTS	GP	W	L	T	OL	GF	GA	PTS
Anaheim	19	11	8	0	0	42	42	22	20	5	13	2	0	52	62	12	39	16	21	2	0	94	104	34
Atlanta	2	1	1	0	0	6	7	2	1	1	0	0	0	3	0	2	3	2	1	0	0	9	7	4
Boston	28	11	14	3	0	95	93	25	27	6	18	3	0	76	115	15	55	17	32	6	0	171	208	40
Buffalo	27	20	5	2	0	115	72	42	29	12	10	7	0	109	109	31	56	32	15	9	0	224	181	73
Calgary	73	39	23	10	1	291	245	89	73	27	39	7	0	260	310	61	146	66	62	17	1	551	555	150
Carolina	28	18	5	5	0	114	84	41	28	11	11	6	0	97	111	28	56	29	16	11	0	211	195	69
Chicago	39	17	17	5	0	144	138	39	38	13	19	6	0	134	149	32	77	30	36	11	0	278	287	71
Colorado	38	21	14	3	0	163	115	45	39	17	19	3	0	152	157	37	77	38	33	6	0	315	272	82
Columbus	2	2	0	0	0	8	4	4	2	1	1	0	0	6	7	2	4	3	1	0	0	14	11	6
Dallas	38	18	12	8	0	156	127	44	39	13	20	6	0	117	144	32	77	31	32	14	0	273	271	76
Detroit	38	19	13	6	0	156	143	44	38	15	19	3	1	133	145	34	76	34	32	9	1	289	288	78
Florida	5	2	2	1	0	14	12	5	7	1	4	2	0	16	19	4	12	3	6	3	0	30	31	9
Los Angeles	71	37	20	14	0	334	260	88	71	30	26	15	0	301	283	75	142	67	46	29	0	635	543	163
Minnesota	3	2	0	1	0	8	3	5	2	2	0	0	0	10	7	4	5	4	0	1	0	18	10	9
Montreal	31	15	16	0	0	99	98	30	28	9	15	4	0	89	100	22	59	24	31	4	0	188	198	52
Nashville	6	4	1	0	1	19	14	9	7	3	3	1	0	20	18	7	13	7	4	1	1	39	32	16
New Jersey	30	14	9	6	1	135	112	35	30	15	13	2	0	101	102	32	60	29	22	8	1	236	214	67
NY Islanders	28	16	7	5	0	105	82	37	28	7	12	9	0	105	117	23	56	23	19	14	0	210	199	60
NY Rangers	27	11	13	3	0	97	93	25	28	13	8	6	1	106	103	33	55	24	21	9	1	203	196	58
Ottawa	9	6	1	2	0	36	22	14	7	4	2	1	0	19	13	9	16	10	3	3	0	55	35	23
Philadelphia	27	14	8	5	0	96	81	33	29	7	20	2	0	79	126	16	56	21	28	7	0	175	207	49
Phoenix	66	41	19	6	0	290	218	88	65	34	26	4	1	290	265	73	131	75	45	10	1	580	483	161
Pittsburgh	28	21	6	1	0	144	94	43	29	12	14	3	0	124	113	27	57	33	20	4	0	268	207	70
St. Louis	38	20	15	3	0	143	132	43	38	16	16	5	1	143	140	38	76	36	31	8	1	286	272	81
San Jose	27	16	5	6	0	97	59	38	26	10	12	3	1	78	90	24	53	26	17	9	1	175	149	62
Tampa Bay	8	6	2	0	0	22	17	12	9	5	2	2	0	30	26	12	17	11	4	2	0	52	43	24
Toronto	38	20	11	6	1	165	126	47	35	14	19	2	0	148	146	30	73	34	30	8	1	313	272	77
Vancouver	73	47	18	7	1	336	227	102	74	36	28	9	1	300	274	82	147	83	46	16	2	636	501	184
Washington	27	13	10	4	0	111	87	30	27	9	16	2	0	91	113	20	54	22	26	6	0	202	200	50
Totals	**874**	**482**	**275**	**112**	**5**	**3541**	**2807**	**1081**	**874**	**348**	**405**	**115**	**6**	**3189**	**3364**	**817**	**1748**	**830**	**680**	**227**	**11**	**6730**	**6171**	**1898**

Playoffs

	Series	W	L	GP	W	L	T	GF	GA	Last Mtg.	Round	Result
Boston	2	2	0	9	8	1	0	41	20	1990	F	W 4-1
Calgary	5	4	1	30	19	11	0	132	96	1991	DSF	W 4-3
Chicago	4	3	1	20	12	8	0	102	77	1992	CF	L 0-4
Colorado	2	1	1	12	5	7	0	30	35	1998	CQF	W 4-3
Dallas	7	2	5	36	13	23	0	93	98	2001	CQF	L 2-4
Detroit	2	2	0	10	8	2	0	39	26	1988	CF	W 4-1
Los Angeles	7	5	2	36	24	12	0	154	127	1992	DSF	W 4-2
Montreal	1	1	0	3	3	0	0	15	6	1981	PR	W 3-0
NY Islanders	3	1	2	15	6	9	0	47	58	1984	F	W 4-1
Philadelphia	3	2	1	15	8	7	0	49	44	1987	F	W 4-3
Vancouver	2	2	0	9	7	2	0	35	20	1992	DF	W 4-2
Winnipeg	6	6	0	26	22	4	0	120	75	1990	DSF	W 4-3
Totals	**44**	**31**	**13**	**221**	**135**	**86**	**0**	**857**	**682**			

Calgary totals include Atlanta Flames, 1979-80.
Colorado totals include Quebec, 1979-80 to 1994-95.
New Jersey totals include Colorado Rockies, 1979-80 to 1981-82.

Playoff Results 2001-1997

Year	Round	Opponent	Result	GF	GA
2001	CQF	Dallas	L 2-4	13	16
2000	CQF	Dallas	L 1-4	11	14
1999	CQF	Dallas	L 0-4	7	11
1998	CSF	Dallas	L 1-4	5	9
	CQF	Colorado	W 4-3	19	16
1997	CSF	Colorado	L 1-4	11	19
	CQF	Dallas	W 4-3	21	18

Abbreviations: Round: F – Final; **CF** – conference final; **CSF** – conference semi-final; **CQF** – conference quarter-final; **DF** – division final; **DSF** – division semi-final; **PR** – preliminary round.

Carolina totals include Hartford, 1979-80 to 1996-97.
Dallas totals include Minnesota North Stars, 1979-80 to 1992-93.
Phoenix totals include Winnipeg, 1979-80 to 1995-96.

2000-01 Results

Oct.	6	Detroit	2-1
	7	Colorado	1-1
	10	at Montreal	2-5
	11	at Detroit	4-3
	13	Buffalo	3-2
	15	at Minnesota	5-3
	17	Boston	6-1
	19	Toronto	1-4
	22	Phoenix	3-3
	25	Atlanta	1-3
	27	at Anaheim	2-3
	28	at Colorado	2-4
	30	Anaheim	5-3
Nov.	1	Calgary	3-2
	3	Minnesota	3-0
	5	at Columbus	4-2
	7	at NY Rangers	3-4
	9	at Philadelphia	0-2
	11	at Pittsburgh	2-5
	12	at Minnesota	5-4*
	14	St. Louis	3-0
	17	Chicago	3-3
	19	Calgary	2-0
	22	at Toronto	3-4
	23	at Ottawa	5-3
	25	Anaheim	3-2
	29	Montreal	2-3
Dec.	2	at Vancouver	2-5
	3	San Jose	3-3
	6	Nashville	4-0
	9	Los Angeles	2-4
	13	at Dallas	2-5
	14	at Nashville	6-2
	16	at Washington	0-4
	18	at Detroit	3-4*
	20	Vancouver	3-2*
	22	at Calgary	1-1
	27	at Colorado	2-3
	28	at San Jose	2-2
	30	Montreal	3-2*
Jan.	1	at St. Louis	2-5
	3	at Columbus	2-5
	5	at Chicago	2-1
	7	Columbus	4-2
	10	Nashville	2-5
	12	Vancouver	2-3
	14	Ottawa	4-1
	16	at Nashville	2-1
	18	at St. Louis	1-4
	20	Detroit	2-1
	22	San Jose	2-2
	24	at San Jose	1-6
	26	Phoenix	1-1
	30	at Calgary	5-3
	31	Chicago	3-2
Feb.	7	at Dallas	2-3
	9	at Phoenix	0-2
	12	at Los Angeles	6-3
	14	at Anaheim	3-3
	16	NY Islanders	2-4
	17	Vancouver	5-6*
	20	Los Angeles	5-0
	24	at Calgary	3-1
	25	Dallas	3-2*
	28	St. Louis	5-3
Mar.	2	Minnesota	3-1
	7	Toronto	4-0
	9	at Buffalo	4-0
	11	at Carolina	3-2
	13	at Tampa Bay	5-4*
	14	at Florida	2-2
	17	New Jersey	5-6*
	19	Philadelphia	2-4
	21	at Los Angeles	7-0
	24	at Phoenix	4-7
	26	Columbus	4-2
	28	Colorado	4-1
	30	Dallas	4-5
Apr.	1	at Chicago	3-3
	2	at Colorado	3-5
	4	Minnesota	2-2
	7	at Vancouver	4-2

* – Overtime

Entry Draft Selections 2001-1987

2001

Pick	
13	Ales Hemsky
43	Doug Lynch
52	Ed Caron
84	Kenny Smith
133	Jussi Markkanen
154	Jake Brenk
185	Mikael Svensk
215	Dan Baum
248	Kari Haakana
272	Ales Pisa
278	Shay Stephenson

2000

Pick	
17	Alexei Mikhnov
35	Brad Winchester
83	Alexander Liubimov
113	Lou Dickenson
152	Paul Flache
184	Shaun Norrie
211	Joe Cullen
215	Matthew Lombardi
247	Jason Platt
274	Yevgeny Muratov

1999

Pick	
13	Jani Rita
36	Alexei Semenov
41	Tony Salmelainen
81	Adam Hauser
91	Mike Comrie
139	Jonathan Fauteux
171	Chris Legg
199	Christian Chartier
256	Tamas Groschl

1998

Pick	
13	Michael Henrich
67	Alex Henry
99	Shawn Horcoff
113	Kristian Antila
128	Paul Elliott
144	Oleg Smirnov
159	Trevor Ettinger
186	Michael Morrison
213	Christian Lefebvre
241	Maxim Spiridonov

1997

Pick	
14	Michel Riesen
41	Patrick Dovigi
68	Sergei Yerkovich
94	Jonas Elofsson
121	Jason Chimera
141	Peter Sarno
176	Kevin Bolibruck
187	Chad Hinz
205	Chris Kerr
231	Alexander Fomitchev

1996

Pick	
6	Boyd Devereaux
19	Matthieu Descoteaux
32	Chris Hajt
59	Tom Poti
114	Brian Urick
141	Bryan Randall
168	David Bernier
168	David Bernier
170	Brandon Lafrance
195	Fernando Pisani
221	John Hultberg

1995

Pick	
6	Steve Kelly
31	Georges Laraque
57	Lukas Zib
83	Mike Minard
109	Jan Snopek
161	Martin Cerven
187	Stephen Douglas
213	Jiri Antonin

1994

Pick	
4	Jason Bonsignore
6	Ryan Smyth
32	Mike Watt
53	Corey Neilson
60	Brad Symes
79	Adam Copeland
95	Jussi Tarvainen
110	Jon Gaskins
136	Terry Marchant
160	Curtis Sheptak
162	Dmitri Shulga
179	Chris Wickenheiser
185	Rob Guinn
188	Jason Reid
214	Jeremy Jablonski
266	Ladislav Benysek

1993

Pick	
7	Jason Arnott
16	Nick Stajduhar
33	David Vyborny
59	Kevin Paden
60	Alexander Kerch
111	Miroslav Satan
163	Alexander Zhurik
189	Martin Bakula
215	Brad Norton
241	Oleg Maltsev
267	Ilja Byakin

1992

Pick	
13	Joe Hulbig
37	Martin Reichel
61	Simon Roy
65	Kirk Maltby
96	Ralph Intranuovo
109	Joaquin Gage
157	Steve Gibson
181	Kyuin Shim
190	Colin Schmidt
205	Marko Tuomainen
253	Bryan Rasmussen

1991

Pick	
12	Tyler Wright
20	Martin Rucinsky
34	Andrew Verner
56	George Breen
78	Mario Nobili
93	Ryan Haggerty
144	David Oliver
166	Gary Kitching
210	Vegar Barlie
232	Yevgeny Belosheiken
254	Juha Riihijarvi

1990

Pick	
17	Scott Allison
38	Alexandre Legault
59	Joe Crowley
67	Joel Blain
101	Greg Louder
122	Keijo Sailynoja
143	Mike Power
164	Roman Mejzlik
185	Richard Zemlicka
206	Petr Korinek
227	invalid claim
248	Sami Nuutinen

1989

Pick	
15	Jason Soules
36	Richard Borgo
78	Josef Beranek
92	Peter White
120	Anatoli Semenov
140	Davis Payne
141	Sergei Yashin
162	Darcy Martini
225	Roman Bozek

1988

Pick	
19	Francois Leroux
39	Petro Koivunen
53	Trevor Sim
61	Collin Bauer
82	Cam Brauer
103	Don Martin
124	Len Barrie
145	Mike Glover
166	Shjon Podein
187	Tim Cole
208	Vladimir Zubkov
229	Darin MacDonald
250	Tim Tisdale

1987

Pick	
21	Peter Soberlak
42	Brad Werenka
63	Geoff Smith
64	Peter Eriksson
105	Shaun Van Allen
126	Radek Toupal
147	Tomas Srsen
168	Age Ellingsen
189	Gavin Armstrong
210	Mike Tinkham
231	Jeff Pauletti
241	Jesper Duus
252	Igor Vyazmikin

General Managers' History

Larry Gordon, 1979-80; Glen Sather, 1980-81 to 1999-2000; Kevin Lowe, 2000-01 to date.

General Manager

LOWE, KEVIN
General Manager, Edmonton Oilers. Born in Lachute, Que., April 15, 1959.

The Edmonton Oilers named Kevin Lowe as their general manager on June 9, 2000, filling the position left vacant when Glen Sather resigned on May 19th. Lowe moved into the front office after spending the 1999-2000 season as coach of the Oilers.

After a brilliant 19-year playing career with the Edmonton Oilers and New York Rangers, Kevin Lowe announced his retirement on July 30, 1998 and joined the Edmonton Oilers coaching staff. He replaced Ron Low as head coach on June 18, 1999.

Lowe was the Oilers' first-ever draft pick when he was selected 21st overall in the 1979 NHL Amateur Draft. He went on to play in 1,254 regular season games and 214 playoff games, winning six Stanley Cup championships; the first five with Edmonton (1984, 1985, 1987, 1988, 1990) followed by a sixth title with the Rangers in 1994.

Besides being the first draft choice in Oilers history, Lowe also scored the first goal in team history on October 10, 1979. He holds the Oilers' record for most games played in both the regular season (1,037) and playoffs (172), and became the sixth captain in team history in 1990-91. He was no less a leader off the ice, becoming the only player to win the King Clancy Memorial Trophy and the Budweiser/NHL Man of the Year Award in the same season (1989-90). Both awards are presented for leadership qualities and humanitarian contributions. His work with the Edmonton Christmas Bureau has set the standard for the Oilers' commitment to community involvement.

NHL Coaching Record

		Regular Season				Playoffs		
Season	Team	Games	W	L	T	Games	W	L
1999-2000	Edmonton	82	32	34	16	5	1	4
	NHL Totals	**82**	**32**	**34**	**16**	**5**	**1**	**4**

Club Directory

Skyreach Centre

Edmonton Oilers
11230 – 110 Street
Edmonton, Alberta T5G 3H7
Phone **780/414-4000**
Ticketing 780/414-4400
FAX 780/414-4659
www.edmontonoilers.com
Capacity: 16,839

Owner	Edmonton Investors Group Ltd.
Governor	Cal Nichols
Alternate Governors	Patrick R. LaForge, Kevin Lowe, Gordon Buchanan
President & Chief Executive Officer	Patrick R. LaForge
Executive Vice-President & General Manager	Kevin Lowe
Vice-President, Hockey Operations	Kevin Prendergast
Assistant General Manager	Scott Howson
Head Coach	Craig MacTavish
Assistant Coaches	Charlie Huddy, Bill Moores
Assistant Coach, Development	Mark Lamb
Goaltending Coach	Pete Peeters
Vice President, Public Relations, Hockey	Bill Tuele
Information Coordinator	Steve Knowles
Public Relations Coordinator, Hockey	Warren Suitor
Director of Research, Analysis and Software Development	Sean Draper
Video Coordinator	Brian Ross
Scouting Staff	Bill Dandy, Brad Davis, Lorne Davis, Morey Gare, Stu MacGregor, Bob Mancini, Chris McCarthy, Kent Nilsson, Gord Pell, Dave Semenko
Executive Assistant to the President	Donna Perman
Executive Assistant to the General Manager	Valerie Rendell
Administrative Assistant & Office Administrator	Cheryl Thomas
Receptionist/Administrative Assistant	Lisa Saskiw
Medical Training Staff	
Head Medical Trainer	Ken Lowe
Head Equipment Manager	Barrie Stafford
Equipment Manager	Lyle Kulchisky
Assistant Equipment Manager	Chris Delorey
Massage Therapist	Stewart Poirier
Team Medical Chief of Staff/Director of Glen Sather Sports Medicine Clinic	Dr. David C. Reid
Team Physician	Dr. Boris Boyko
Team Dermatologist	Dr. Don Groot
Team Dentists	Dr. Tony Sneazwell, Dr. Ben Eastwood
Fitness Consultants	Dr. Art Quinney, Dr. Gordon Bell
Physical Therapy Consultant	Dr. Dave Magee
Team Optometrist	Dr. Brent Saik
Strength & Conditioning Consultant	Daryl Duke
Finance	
Vice-President, Finance	Darryl Boessenkool
Controller	Jason Quilley
Facilities Manager	Craig Tkachuk
Manager Payroll & Benefits	Michelle Schwendeman
Financial Analyst	Colleen Rolston
Systems Administrators	Terry Rhoades, Rod Pruden
Finance Staff	Donna Chizen, Corinne McGregor, Lynn Schmidl, Sherry Smith
Marketing & Communications	
Vice-President, Marketing & Communications	Allan Watt
Director of Sales	Eric Upton
Director, Community Relations & Edmonton Oilers Help Foundation	Gillian Andries
Manager, Sponsorships and Sales	Brad MacGregor
National Accounts Manager	Matt Cummings
National Accounts Manager	Sean Price
Broadcast Sponsorship Coordinator	Nicole Baldwin
Director, Corporate Communications & Marketing	Natalie Minckler
Marketing & Promotions Manager	Melanie Harysh
Marketing & Communications Coordinator	Trena Jackson
Sponsorship & Sales Coordinator	Kristie Brown
Community Relations Coordinator	Heather Davidson
Director of Broadcast	Don Metz
Game Night Operations	Glenn Wiun
Game Night Supervisor	Marilyn Riddell
Publications Coordinator	Steve Sandor
New Media Production Manager	Andreas Schwabe
Properties	
Vice President, Properties	Darrell Holowaychuk
Properties Manager	Linda Malito
Product Manager	Brent Gibbs
Operations Manager	Doug Wadlow
Administrative Assistant	Nycole Kindree
Ticket Operations	
Director of Ticket Operations	John Yeomans
Box Office Manager	Bob Haromy
Ticket Client Services	Sheila McCaskill, Sandy Langley, Connie Lloyd, Chris Gosse
Suite Manager	Cathy Cookson
Ticket Sales	
Director of Ticket Sales	Michael Lake
Coordinator, Ticket Sales and Service	Jill Wolfe
Account Executives, Corporate Ticket Sales	Damon Bunting, Scott Jacques, Bruce Rakoczy, Jeff Tetz
Account Executives, Group Ticket Sales	Emiliano Diaz-Page, Marran Vogelesang
Miscellaneous	
Training Camp Site	Millennium Place; Sherwood Park, Alberta
Television	Sportsnet, CBXT TV
Radio Flagship Station	630 CHED (AM); Rod Phillips (Play-by-play) & Morley Scott (colour)

Florida Panthers

2000-01 Results: 22W-38L-13T-9OTL 66PTS. Third, Southeast Division

Year-by-Year Record

		Home				Road				Overall								
Season	GP	W	L	T	OL	W	L	T	OL	W	L	T	OL	GF	GA	Pts.	Finished	Playoff Result
2000-01	82	12	18	7	4	10	20	6	5	22	38	13	9	200	246	66	3rd, Southeast Div.	Out of Playoffs
1999-2000	82	26	9	4	2	17	18	2	4	43	27	6	6	244	209	98	2nd, Southeast Div.	Lost Conf. Quarter-Final
1998-99	82	17	17	7	...	13	17	11	...	30	34	18	...	210	228	78	2nd, Southeast Div.	Out of Playoffs
1997-98	82	11	24	6	...	13	19	9	...	24	43	15	...	203	256	63	6th, Atlantic Div.	Out of Playoffs
1996-97	82	21	12	8	...	14	16	11	...	35	28	19	...	221	201	89	3rd, Atlantic Div.	Lost Conf. Quarter-Final
1995-96	82	25	12	4	...	16	19	6	...	41	31	10	...	254	234	92	3rd, Atlantic Div.	Lost Final
1994-95	48	9	12	3	...	11	10	3	...	20	22	6	...	115	127	46	5th, Atlantic Div.	Out of Playoffs
1993-94	84	15	18	9	...	18	16	8	...	33	34	17	...	233	233	83	5th, Atlantic Div.	Out of Playoffs

2001-02 Schedule

Month	Day	Date	Opponent
Oct.	Thu.	4	at Philadelphia
	Sat.	6	NY Islanders
	Sun.	7	at Tampa Bay
	Wed.	10	Ottawa
	Sat.	13	Philadelphia
	Tue.	16	at Vancouver
	Thu.	18	at Calgary
	Sat.	20	at Edmonton
	Wed.	24	Washington
	Fri.	26	Los Angeles
	Sun.	28	at Pittsburgh
	Tue.	30	at NY Islanders
	Wed.	31	at NY Rangers
Nov.	Sat.	3	NY Rangers
	Wed.	7	Pittsburgh
	Sat.	10	Philadelphia
	Mon.	12	Buffalo
	Wed.	14	Toronto
	Fri.	16	at Buffalo
	Sat.	17	at Montreal
	Mon.	19	at Toronto
	Wed.	21	Anaheim
	Sat.	24	New Jersey
	Tue.	27	at Colorado
	Thu.	29	at Minnesota
Dec.	Sat.	1	Atlanta*
	Wed.	5	Columbus
	Sat.	8	Carolina
	Wed.	12	at Carolina
	Fri.	14	at New Jersey
	Sat.	15	at NY Islanders
	Mon.	17	at NY Rangers
	Wed.	19	Washington
	Sat.	22	St. Louis
	Wed.	26	at Atlanta
	Fri.	28	Boston
	Sat.	29	Toronto
	Mon.	31	Atlanta*
Jan.	Wed.	2	at Los Angeles
	Fri.	4	at Anaheim
	Sat.	5	at San Jose
	Mon.	7	at Washington
	Wed.	9	Dallas
	Fri.	11	Ottawa
	Sat.	12	Washington
	Wed.	16	Chicago
	Fri.	18	at Dallas
	Sat.	19	Atlanta
	Mon.	21	Montreal*
	Wed.	23	New Jersey
	Fri.	25	at Carolina
	Sat.	26	at Boston
	Wed.	30	Phoenix
Feb.	Mon.	4	NY Islanders
	Wed.	6	Tampa Bay
	Thu.	7	at Tampa Bay
	Sat.	9	at Boston*
	Tue.	12	at Nashville
	Wed.	13	at Chicago
	Tue.	26	at Washington
	Wed.	27	Detroit
Mar.	Sat.	2	at Tampa Bay
	Tue.	5	at Pittsburgh
	Fri.	8	Edmonton
	Sat.	9	Nashville
	Wed.	13	Calgary
	Fri.	15	Buffalo
	Sun.	17	at Ottawa*
	Wed.	20	Montreal
	Thu.	21	at Carolina
	Sat.	23	Boston
	Mon.	25	at New Jersey
	Tue.	26	at Montreal
	Thu.	28	at Ottawa
	Sat.	30	NY Rangers
Apr.	Wed.	3	Pittsburgh
	Fri.	5	at Buffalo
	Sat.	6	at Toronto
	Mon.	8	at Philadelphia
	Wed.	10	at Atlanta
	Fri.	12	Carolina
	Sun.	14	Tampa Bay*

* Denotes afternoon game.

Seen here celebrating one of his 59 goals with teammate Dan Boyle, Pavel Bure won the Rocket Richard Trophy for the second year in a row in 2000-01. This season, Bure will be joined in Florida by his brother Valeri.

Franchise date: June 14, 1993

SOUTHEAST DIVISION

9th NHL Season

2001-02 Player Personnel

FORWARDS	HT	WT	S	Place of Birth	Date	2000-01 Club
ADAMS, Kevyn	6-1	195	R	Washington, D.C.	10/8/74	Columbus-Florida
BURE, Pavel	5-10	189	L	Moscow, USSR	3/31/71	Florida
BURE, Valeri	5-10	185	R	Moscow, USSR	6/13/74	Calgary
HAGMAN, Niklas	6-0	190	L	Espoo, Finland	12/5/79	Karpat Oulu
HUSELIUS, Kristian	6-1	190	L	Haninge, Sweden	11/10/78	Vastra Frolunda
JOHNSON, Ryan	6-1	200	L	Thunder Bay, Ont.	6/14/76	Tampa Bay
JOKINEN, Olli	6-3	208	L	Kuopio, Finland	12/5/78	Florida
KOZLOV, Viktor	6-5	220	R	Togliatti, USSR	2/14/75	Florida
NILSON, Marcus	6-2	193	R	Balsta, Sweden	3/1/78	Florida
NOVOSELTSEV, Ivan	6-1	202	L	Golitsino, USSR	1/23/79	Florida-Louisville
PAYER, Serge	6-0	203	L	Rockland, Ont.	5/7/79	Florida-Louisville
SHVIDKI, Denis	6-2	213	L	Kharkov, USSR	11/21/80	Florida-Louisville
TETARENKO, Joey	6-2	212	R	Prince Albert, Sask.	3/3/78	Florida-Louisville
THOMPSON, Rocky	6-2	205	R	Calgary, Alta.	8/8/77	Florida-Louisville
WEISS, Stephen	6-0	183	L	Toronto, Ont.	4/3/83	Plymouth
WIEMER, Jason	6-1	220	L	Kimberley, B.C.	4/14/76	Calgary
WORRELL, Peter	6-6	245	L	Pierrefonds, Que.	8/18/77	Florida
DEFENSEMEN						
BOYLE, Dan	5-11	190	R	Ottawa, Ont.	7/12/76	Florida-Louisville
ELLIOTT, Paul	6-1	216	L	White Rock, B.C.	6/2/80	Kamloops-Regina
FERENCE, Brad	6-3	212	R	Calgary, Alta.	4/2/79	Florida-Louisville
HEDICAN, Bret	6-2	205	L	St. Paul, MN	8/10/70	Florida
JAKOPIN, John	6-5	239	R	Toronto, Ont.	5/16/75	Florida-Louisville
KRAJICEK, Lukas	6-2	182	L	Prostejov, Czech.	3/11/83	Peterborough
LAUS, Paul	6-1	212	R	Beamsville, Ont.	9/26/70	Florida
NORTON, Brad	6-4	225	L	Cambridge, MA	2/13/75	Hamilton
NORTON, Jeff	6-2	195	L	Acton, MA	11/25/65	Pittsburgh-San Jose
PITLICK, Lance	6-0	205	R	Minneapolis, MN	11/5/67	Florida
SVEHLA, Robert	6-1	210	R	Martin, Czech.	1/2/69	Florida
WARD, Lance	6-3	225	L	Lloydminster, Alta.	6/2/78	Florida-Louisville

GOALTENDERS	HT	WT	C	Place of Birth	Date	2000-01 Club
FLAHERTY, Wade	6-0	170	L	Terrace, B.C.	1/11/68	NY Islanders-Tampa Bay
KIDD, Trevor	6-2	190	L	Dugald, Man.	3/29/72	Florida
LUONGO, Roberto	6-3	198	L	Montreal, Que.	4/4/79	Florida-Louisville

Chosen fourth overall by the Islanders in 1997, Roberto Luongo began delivering on his promise in Florida last season with an impressive .920 save per-centage and a 2.44 goals-against average.

2000-01 Scoring

* - rookie

Regular Season

Pos	#	Player	Team	GP	G	A	Pts	+/–	PIM	PP	SH	GW	GT	S	%
R	10	Pavel Bure	FLA	82	59	33	92	–2	58	19	5	8	3	384	15.4
C	25	Viktor Kozlov	FLA	51	14	23	37	–4	10	6	0	2	0	139	10.1
L	18	Marcus Nilson	FLA	78	12	24	36	–3	74	0	0	2	0	141	8.5
C	44	Rob Niedermayer	FLA	67	12	20	32	–12	50	3	1	0	0	115	10.4
C	11	Kevyn Adams	CBJ	66	8	12	20	–4	52	0	0	1	0	84	9.5
			FLA	12	3	6	9	7	2	0	0	2	0	21	14.3
			TOTAL	78	11	18	29	3	54	0	0	3	0	105	10.5
C	13	Vaclav Prospal	OTT	40	1	12	13	1	12	0	0	0	0	68	1.5
			FLA	34	4	12	16	–2	10	1	0	0	0	68	5.9
			TOTAL	74	5	24	29	–1	22	1	0	0	0	136	3.7
D	24	Robert Svehla	FLA	82	6	22	28	–8	76	0	0	0	0	121	5.0
D	29	Anders Eriksson	CHI	13	2	3	5	–4	2	1	0	0	0	19	10.5
			FLA	60	0	21	21	2	28	0	0	0	0	80	0.0
			TOTAL	73	2	24	26	–2	30	1	0	0	0	99	2.0
L	17	Greg Adams	FLA	60	11	12	23	–3	10	2	0	1	0	66	16.7
C	9	Len Barrie	FLA	60	5	18	23	4	135	0	1	2	0	48	10.4
D	26	Dan Boyle	FLA	69	4	18	22	–14	28	1	0	0	0	83	4.8
D	4	Bret Hedican	FLA	70	5	15	20	–7	72	4	0	1	0	104	4.8
R	21	* Denis Shvidki	FLA	43	6	10	16	6	16	0	0	1	0	28	21.4
C	12	Olli Jokinen	FLA	78	6	10	16	–22	106	0	0	0	0	121	5.0
L	8	Peter Worrell	FLA	71	3	7	10	–10	248	0	0	0	0	86	3.5
R	39	* Ivan Novoseltsev	FLA	38	3	6	9	–5	16	0	0	0	0	34	8.8
C	19	* Serge Payer	FLA	43	5	1	6	0	21	0	1	0	0	34	14.7
D	36	* Joey Tetarenko	FLA	29	3	1	4	–1	44	0	0	0	0	21	14.3
D	3	Paul Laus	FLA	25	1	2	3	5	66	0	0	0	0	18	5.6
D	15	* John Jakopin	FLA	60	1	2	3	–4	62	0	0	0	0	23	4.3
D	2	Lance Pitlick	FLA	68	1	2	3	–5	42	0	0	0	0	24	4.2
D	5	Yan Golubovsky	FLA	6	0	2	2	3	2	0	0	0	0	4	0.0
D	49	* Lance Ward	FLA	30	0	2	2	–3	45	0	0	0	0	17	0.0
C	41	* Andrej Podkonicky	FLA	6	1	0	1	0	2	0	0	0	0	5	20.0
D	45	* Brad Ference	FLA	14	0	1	1	–10	14	0	0	0	0	5	0.0
D	7	Mike Wilson	FLA	19	0	1	1	–7	25	0	0	0	0	26	0.0
G	37	Trevor Kidd	FLA	42	0	1	1	0	6	0	0	0	0	0	0.0
R	43	Paul Brousseau	FLA	1	0	0	0	0	0	0	0	0	0	0	0.0
D	23	* Rocky Thompson	FLA	4	0	0	0	0	19	0	0	0	0	0	0.0
C	43	David Emma	FLA	6	0	0	0	–1	0	0	0	0	0	6	0.0
D	35	* Peter Ratchuk	FLA	8	0	0	0	–1	0	0	0	0	0	11	0.0
G	1	* Roberto Luongo	FLA	47	0	0	0	0	2	0	0	0	0	0	0.0

Goaltending

No.	Goaltender	GPI	Mins	Avg	W	L	T	EN	SO	GA	SA	S%
1	* Roberto Luongo	47	2628	2.44	12	24	7	6	5	107	1333	.920
37	Trevor Kidd	42	2354	3.31	10	23	6	3	1	130	1217	.893
	Totals	**82**	**5006**	**2.95**	**22**	**47**	**13**	**9**	**6**	**246**	**2559**	**.904**

General Managers' History

Bob Clarke, 1993-94; Bryan Murray, 1994-95 to 1999-2000; Bryan Murray and Bill Torrey, 2000-01; Bill Torrey, 2001-02.

General Manager

TORREY, BILL
President and General Manager, Florida Panthers.
Born in Montreal, PQ, June 23, 1934.

One of the most respected men in hockey, Bill Torrey is entering his ninth season as president of the Panthers. On December 28, 2000, he took on the job of general manager. Having built three different expansion teams from the ground up, he has spent 34 years in the NHL and was inducted into the Hockey Hall of Fame in 1995.

Under Torrey's guidance and direction, the Panthers have enjoyed tremendous success. In 1993-94, the team's inaugural season, he helped assemble a club that broke expansion records for wins (33), points (83) and winning percentage (.494). The Panthers also made it to the Stanley Cup Finals faster than any other post-1967 expansion team in NHL history, reaching the mark in 1995-96, their third year of existence. Torrey has worked diligently to grow the sport of hockey in the entire South Florida market. Youth hockey is booming in the area, with over 10,000 kids involved in the Panthers' Streetcats program.

Bill Torrey began his NHL career in 1967 as executive vice president of the expansion Oakland Seals. He then joined the expansion Islanders as general manager in 1972, becoming the first person hired by the organization. The Islanders evolved into one of hockey's great dynasties, as the team won four consecutive Stanley Cup titles at the start of the 1980s. It is this blueprint for success that Mr. Torrey has used in South Florida as he works toward building a strong, competitive and successful franchise. Torrey spent 21 years with the Islanders prior to joining the Panthers.

Club Records

Team

(Figures in brackets for season records are games played; records for fewest points, wins, ties, losses, goals, goals against are for 70 or more games)

Most Points	**98**	1999-2000 (82)
Most Wins	**43**	1999-2000 (82)
Most Ties	**19**	1996-97 (82)
Most Losses	**43**	1997-98 (82)
Most Goals	**254**	1995-96 (82)
Most Goals Against	**256**	1997-98 (82)
Fewest Points	**63**	1997-98 (82)
Fewest Wins	**22**	2000-01 (82)
Fewest Ties	**6**	1999-2000 (82)
Fewest Losses	**28**	1996-97 (82)
Fewest Goals	**200**	2000-01 (82)
Fewest Goals Against	**201**	1996-97 (82)
Longest Winning Streak		
Overall	**7**	Nov. 2-14/95
Home	**5**	Nov. 5-14/95
Away	**4**	Dec. 2-12/95, Nov. 13-Dec 1/96, Oct. 25-Nov. 22/97
Longest Undefeated Streak		
Overall	**12**	Oct. 5-30/96 (8 wins, 4 ties)
Home	**8**	Nov. 5-26/95 (7 wins, 1 tie)
Away	**7**	Twice
Longest Losing Streak		
Overall	**13**	Feb. 7-Mar. 23/98
Home	**6**	Feb. 25-Mar. 23/98
Away	**7**	Feb. 7-Mar. 21/98
Longest Winless Streak		
Overall	**15**	Feb. 1-Mar. 23/98 (14 losses, 1 tie)
Home	**8**	Feb. 1-Mar. 23/98 (7 losses, 1 tie)
Away	**16**	Jan. 2-Mar. 21/98 (12 losses, 4 ties)
Most Shutouts, Season	**6**	1994-95 (48), 2000-01 (82)
Most PIM, Season	**1,676**	1997-98 (82)
Most Goals, Game	**10**	Nov. 26/97 (Bos. 5 at Fla. 10)

Individual

Most Seasons	**8**	Scott Mellanby, Paul Laus, Rob Niedermayer
Most Games	**552**	Scott Mellanby
Most Goals, Career	**157**	Scott Mellanby
Most Assists, Career	**207**	Robert Svehla
Most Points, Career	**354**	Scott Mellanby (157G, 197A)
Most PIM, Career	**1,545**	Paul Laus
Most Shutouts, Career	**13**	John Vanbiesbrouck
Longest Consecutive Games Streak	**221**	Robert Svehla (Oct. 13/95-Mar. 4/98)
Most Goals, Season	**59**	Pavel Bure (2000-01)
Most Assists, Season	**53**	Viktor Kozlov (1999-2000)
Most Points, Season	**94**	Pavel Bure (1999-2000; 58G, 36A)
Most PIM, Season	**313**	Paul Laus (1996-97)
Most Points, Defenseman, Season	**57**	Robert Svehla (1995-96; 8G, 49A)
Most Points, Center, Season	**70**	Viktor Kozlov (1999-2000; 17G, 53A)
Most Points, Right Wing, Season	**94**	Pavel Bure (1999-2000; 58G, 36A)
Most Points, Left Wing, Season	**71**	Ray Whitney (1999-2000; 29G, 42A)
Most Points, Rookie, Season	**50**	Jesse Belanger (1993-94; 17G, 33A)
Most Shutouts, Season	**5**	Robert Luongo (2000-01)
Most Goals, Game	**4**	Mark Parrish (Oct. 30/98); Pavel Bure (Jan. 1/00, Feb. 10/01)
Most Assists, Game	**4**	Scott Mellanby (Nov. 26/97); Ray Whitney (Oct. 30/00)
Most Points, Game	**5**	Pavel Bure (Feb. 10/01; 4G, 1A)

Coaching History

Roger Neilson, 1993-94, 1994-95; Doug MacLean, 1995-96, 1996-97; Doug MacLean and Bryan Murray, 1997-98; Terry Murray, 1998-99, 1999-2000; Terry Murray and Duane Sutter, 2000-01; Duane Sutter, 2001-02.

Captains' History

Brian Skrudland, 1993-94 to 1996-97; Scott Mellanby, 1997-98 to 2000-01.

All-time Record vs. Other Clubs

Regular Season

	At Home								On Road								Total							
	GP	W	L	T	OL	GF	GA	PTS	GP	W	L	T	OL	GF	GA	PTS	GP	W	L	T	OL	GF	GA	PTS
Anaheim	5	2	1	2	0	13	13	6	7	4	2	0	1	24	22	9	12	6	3	2	1	37	35	15
Atlanta	5	2	2	1	0	14	12	5	5	1	1	2	1	16	14	5	10	3	3	3	1	30	26	10
Boston	15	8	7	0	0	45	40	16	16	8	5	3	0	46	40	19	31	16	12	3	0	91	80	35
Buffalo	15	8	7	0	0	46	47	16	17	3	11	2	1	26	54	9	32	11	18	2	1	72	101	25
Calgary	7	2	3	1	1	15	19	6	6	3	2	1	0	17	14	7	13	5	5	2	1	32	33	13
Carolina	18	6	3	7	2	48	36	21	17	8	7	1	1	51	54	18	35	14	10	8	3	99	90	39
Chicago	6	2	4	0	0	16	25	4	7	3	3	1	0	23	23	7	13	5	7	1	0	39	48	11
Colorado	9	1	8	0	0	24	39	2	9	3	3	3	0	22	25	9	18	4	11	3	0	46	64	11
Columbus	1	0	0	0	1	6	7	1	1	1	0	0	0	3	0	2	2	1	0	0	1	9	7	3
Dallas	7	3	3	1	0	19	21	7	6	1	3	2	0	16	21	4	13	4	6	3	0	35	42	11
Detroit	7	1	4	2	0	14	22	4	6	1	3	2	0	18	24	4	13	2	7	4	0	32	46	8
Edmonton	7	4	1	2	0	19	16	10	5	2	2	1	0	12	14	5	12	6	3	3	0	31	30	15
Los Angeles	6	3	0	3	0	18	9	9	7	3	4	0	0	23	22	6	13	6	4	3	0	41	31	15
Minnesota	1	1	0	0	0	2	1	2	1	0	0	1	0	0	0	1	2	1	0	1	0	2	1	3
Montreal	16	8	5	3	0	52	42	19	15	7	6	2	0	37	43	16	31	15	11	5	0	89	85	35
Nashville	2	2	0	0	0	7	3	4	3	2	0	1	0	8	5	5	5	4	0	1	0	15	8	9
New Jersey	19	7	8	4	0	44	43	18	18	4	9	3	2	38	56	13	37	11	17	7	2	82	99	31
NY Islanders	19	10	6	3	0	57	51	23	19	10	7	2	0	53	47	22	38	20	13	5	0	110	98	45
NY Rangers	19	9	9	1	0	51	50	19	18	6	8	4	0	47	55	16	37	15	17	5	0	98	105	35
Ottawa	16	9	5	1	1	56	47	20	16	7	7	2	0	45	45	16	32	16	12	3	1	101	92	36
Philadelphia	18	5	13	0	0	45	64	10	19	7	8	4	0	44	45	18	37	12	21	4	0	89	109	28
Phoenix	6	3	3	0	0	21	16	6	8	3	2	2	1	23	18	9	14	6	5	2	1	44	34	15
Pittsburgh	16	7	8	1	0	41	41	15	17	4	10	2	1	46	60	11	33	11	18	3	1	87	101	26
St. Louis	7	2	3	2	0	16	16	6	7	1	5	1	0	11	21	3	14	3	8	3	0	27	37	9
San Jose	7	2	0	5	0	20	14	9	7	2	3	2	0	17	17	6	14	4	3	7	0	37	31	15
Tampa Bay	20	14	3	3	0	60	36	31	20	10	6	4	0	58	43	24	40	24	9	7	0	118	79	55
Toronto	11	3	5	3	0	32	34	9	9	2	6	1	0	23	34	5	20	5	11	4	0	55	68	14
Vancouver	7	3	2	1	1	19	22	8	6	1	2	3	0	13	18	5	13	4	4	4	1	32	40	13
Washington	20	9	9	2	0	53	54	20	20	5	10	4	1	47	60	15	40	14	19	6	1	100	114	35
Totals	**312**	**136**	**122**	**48**	**6**	**873**	**840**	**326**	**312**	**112**	**135**	**56**	**9**	**807**	**894**	**289**	**624**	**248**	**257**	**104**	**15**	**1680**	**1734**	**615**

Playoffs

	Series	W	L	GP	W	L	T	GF	GA	Last Mtg.	Round	Result
Boston	1	1	0	5	4	1	0	22	16	1996	CQF	W 4-1
Colorado	1	0	1	4	0	4	0	4	15	1996	F	L 0-4
New Jersey	1	0	1	4	0	4	0	6	12	2000	CQF	L 0-4
NY Rangers	1	0	1	5	1	4	0	10	13	1997	CQF	L 1-4
Philadelphia	1	1	0	6	4	2	0	15	11	1996	CSF	W 4-2
Pittsburgh	1	1	0	7	4	3	0	20	15	1996	CF	W 4-3
Totals	**6**	**3**	**3**	**31**	**13**	**18**	**0**	**77**	**82**			

Playoff Results 2001-1997

Year	Round	Opponent	Result	GF	GA
2000	CQF	New Jersey	L 0-4	6	12
1997	CQF	NY Rangers	L 1-4	10	13

Abbreviations: Round: F – Final;
CF – conference final; **CSF** – conference semi-final;
CQF – conference quarter-final.

Colorado totals include Quebec, 1993-94 to 1994-95.
Phoenix totals include Winnipeg, 1993-94 to 1995-96.

Carolina totals include Hartford, 1993-94 to 1996-97.

2000-01 Results

Oct.	6	Vancouver	3-4*		9	at Carolina	3-7
	9	at Boston	2-4		12	Carolina	2-2
	13	Carolina	2-2		13	Philadelphia	1-4
	18	at Phoenix	1-2*		15	Dallas	2-0
	20	at Colorado	1-5		17	at Chicago	0-5
	22	at Minnesota	0-0		19	at Buffalo	0-1
	25	New Jersey	1-2		20	at Philadelphia	3-5
	27	at Nashville	3-3		22	at Boston	3-2
	28	Ottawa	3-1		24	at Washington	1-2
	30	at New Jersey	5-6*		26	Ottawa	4-5*
Nov.	1	NY Islanders	0-3		27	Tampa Bay	3-2*
	4	Washington	2-3		30	at Tampa Bay	3-4
	8	Montreal	2-4		31	Buffalo	5-2
	10	Calgary	3-3	**Feb.**	7	Minnesota	2-1
	13	Atlanta	1-4		9	NY Rangers	2-4
	15	at Carolina	4-1		10	at Atlanta	7-3
	17	at Columbus	3-0		14	Phoenix	4-3
	18	at Ottawa	2-5		16	Boston	2-1
	21	at Montreal	4-1		19	St. Louis	3-0
	24	at Tampa Bay	1-2		21	at Pittsburgh	2-3*
	25	Tampa Bay	2-1*		22	at Ottawa	2-4
	29	Carolina	1-2*		24	at NY Islanders	4-5
Dec.	1	Detroit	1-3		26	at New Jersey	3-5
	2	at St. Louis	2-5		28	at NY Rangers	2-4
	4	at Toronto	4-4	**Mar.**	2	Atlanta	3-4
	6	NY Islanders	1-4		3	at Atlanta	2-2
	8	at Atlanta	3-4*		7	San Jose	3-3
	9	Colorado	2-4		9	Columbus	6-7*
	13	at Detroit	3-3		11	at NY Islanders	4-1
	15	at Pittsburgh	4-1		14	Edmonton	2-2
	16	at Buffalo	2-3		16	Pittsburgh	3-6
	18	at NY Rangers	3-6		17	Toronto	3-5
	20	Pittsburgh	2-2		20	at Montreal	3-3
	22	New Jersey	0-2		21	at Toronto	3-1
	23	at Washington	3-5		23	Washington	4-1
	27	Philadelphia	2-5		28	Montreal	2-2
	29	Boston	3-0		30	Tampa Bay	2-4
	30	Toronto	1-4	**Apr.**	2	Buffalo	3-5
Jan.	3	at Anaheim	2-3*		3	at Philadelphia	2-1
	4	at Los Angeles	4-3		5	at Washington	0-3
	6	at San Jose	1-3		7	NY Rangers	3-0

* – Overtime

Entry Draft Selections 2001-1993

2001

Pick	
4	Stephen Weiss
24	Lukas Krajicek
34	Greg Watson
64	Tomas Malec
68	Grant McNeill
117	Mike Woodford
136	Billy Thompson
169	Dustin Johner
200	Toni Koivisto
231	Kyle Bruce
263	Jan Blanar
267	Ivan Majesky

2000

Pick	
58	Vladimir Sapozhnikov
77	Robert Fried
82	Sean O'Connor
115	Chris Eade
120	Davis Parley
190	Josh Olson
234	Janis Sprukts
253	Mathew Sommerfeld

1999

Pick	
12	Denis Shvidki
40	Alexander Auld
70	Niklas Hagman
80	Jean-Francois Laniel
103	Morgan McCormick
109	Rod Sarich
169	Brad Woods
198	Travis Eagles
227	Jonathon Charron

1998

Pick	
30	Kyle Rossiter
61	Joe DiPenta
63	Lance Ward
89	Ryan Jardine
117	Jaroslav Spacek
148	Chris Ovington
176	B.J. Ketcheson
203	Ian Jacobs
231	Adrian Wichser

1997

Pick	
20	Mike Brown
47	Kristian Huselius
56	Vratislav Cech
74	Nick Smith
95	Ivan Novoseltsev
127	Pat Parthenais
155	Keith Delaney
183	Tyler Palmer
211	Doug Schueller
237	Benoit Cote

1996

Pick	
20	Marcus Nilson
60	Chris Allen
65	Oleg Kvasha
82	Joey Tetarenko
129	Andrew Long
156	Gaetan Poirier
183	Alexandre Couture
209	Denis Khloptonov
235	Russell Smith

1995

Pick	
10	Radek Dvorak
36	Aaron MacDonald
62	Mike O'Grady
80	Dave Duerden
88	Daniel Tjarnqvist
114	Francois Cloutier
166	Peter Worrell
192	Filip Kuba
218	David Lemanowicz

1994

Pick	
1	Ed Jovanovski
27	Rhett Warrener
31	Jason Podollan
36	Ryan Johnson
84	David Nemirovsky
105	Dave Geris
157	Matt O'Dette
183	Jason Boudrias
235	Tero Lehtera
261	Per Gustafsson

1993

Pick	
5	Rob Niedermayer
41	Kevin Weekes
57	Chris Armstrong
67	Mikael Tjallden
78	Steve Washburn
83	Bill McCauley
109	Todd MacDonald
135	Alain Nasreddine
161	Trevor Doyle
187	Briane Thompson
213	Chad Cabana
239	John Demarco
265	Eric Montreuil

After a big year in 1999-2000, Viktor Kozlov played only 51 games last season but still ranked second among Panthers scorers.

Coach

SUTTER, DUANE
Coach, Florida Panthers. Born in Viking, Alta., March 16, 1960.

Duane Sutter became the interim head coach of the Florida Panthers on December 28, 2000 and was signed to a long-term deal on June 7, 2001. Prior to being named to the job, Sutter had spent more than two years as a pro scout for the club. He spent the previous three seasons as an assistant coach for the Panthers, including the 1995-96 Eastern Conference Championship team.

Duane is one of six Sutter brothers to have played in the NHL, and joins Brian and Darryl as the third family member to serve as a head coach.

A first-round draft pick of the New York Islanders (17th overall) in 1979, Duane Sutter played on four consecutive Stanley Cup winners with the Isles in the early 1980s. Nicknamed "Dog," he played 11 seasons in the NHL, eight with the Islanders and three with the Chicago Blackhawks, before retiring after the 1989-90 campaign. Duane appeared in 731 NHL games, recording 139 goals, 342 points and 1,333 penalty minutes. After completing his playing career, he spent two seasons as a scout for the Blackhawks, before taking over as head coach of the team's IHL affiliate, the Indianapolis Ice. In three years with the Ice, Duane compiled a record of 66-92-20 in 178 games.

Coaching Record

		Regular Season				Playoffs		
Season	Team	Games	W	L	T	Games	W	L
1992-93	Indianapolis (IHL)	16	6	5	5	5	1	4
1993-94	Indianapolis (IHL)	81	28	46	7	....	....	....
1994-95	Indianapolis (IHL)	81	32	41	8	....	....	....
2000-01	**Florida (NHL)**	**46**	**16**	**24**	**6**	....	....	....
	NHL Totals	**46**	**16**	**24**	**6**	....	....	....

Club Directory

National Car Rental Center

Florida Panthers
National Car Rental Center
One Panthers Parkway
Sunrise, FL 33323
Phone **954/835-7000**
FAX 954/835-7600
www.floridapanthers.com
Capacity: 19,250

Executive

Chairman of the Board/Chief Executive Officer	Alan Cohen
President, General Manager & Governor	William A. Torrey
Chief Operating Officer	Jeff Cogen
Chief Financial Officer	Bill Duffy
Senior Vice President	Steve Dangerfield
Vice President of Corporate Sales and Marketing Partnerships	Kimberly T. Sciarretta
Executive Assistant to Chairman of the Board and Chief Executive Officer	Athena Melfi
Executive Assistants to President	Deanna Cocozzelli, Cathy Stevenson
Executive Assistant to C.O.O. and Senior Vice President	Janine Shea
Executive Assistant to Chief Financial Officer and Director of Finance/Controller	Cathy Cuffe
Executive Assistant to Vice President of Corporate Sales and Marketing Partnerships	Susan Ferro

Hockey Operations

Assistant General Manager	Chuck Fletcher
Head Coach	Duane Sutter
Assistant Coaches	Paul Baxter, George Kingston
Executive Assistant, Hockey Operations	Vanessa Rey
Director of Amateur Scouting	Tim Murray
Director of Professional Player Evaluation	Michael Abbamont
Amateur Scouts	Darwin Bennett, Ron Harris, Todd Hearty, Wayne Meier, Marty Nanne, Sean O'Brien
Pro Scouts	Billy Dea, Joe Paterson
Chief European Scout	Pavel Routa
European Pro Scout	Slavomir Lener
Scouting & Video Coordinator	Brent Flahr
Head Medical Trainer	Stan Wong
Strength & Conditioning Coach	Ian Pyka
Head Equipment Manager	Mark Brennan
Associate Equipment Manager	Scott Tinkler
Equipment Staff	Jon Korman
Team Services Coordinator	Marni Share
Internist	Howard Bush, M.D.
Orthopedic Surgeon	Jeffrey Minkoff, M.D.
Assistant Orthopedist	Steve Stecker, M.D.
Massage Therapist	Mikhail Manchik
Plastic Surgeon	Harry K. Moon, M.D.
Team Dentist	Martin Robins, D.D.S.
Neuropsychologist	Kathleen Knee

Communications

Director of Broadcasting and Communications	Mike Hanson
Media Relations Manager	Randy Sieminski
Community Development Manager	Hillary Reynolds
Communications/Publications Coordinator	Michael Citro
Communications Coordinator	Mary Lou Veroline
Youth and Amateur Hockey Coordinator	Keith Martin
Administrative Assistant, Communications Department	Giselle Seoane

Corporate Sales and Client Services

Director of Client Services	Brette Sadler
Retail Sales Manager	Scott Baynes
Corporate Account Manager	Jason Camp
Corporate Account Coordinator	Marcie Maggio

Finance and Administration

Director of Information Technology	Kelly Moyer
Director of Finance/Controller	Evelyn Lopez
Office Manager	Laura Barrera
Accounting Manager	Michele Gilbert
Manager of Human Resources/Payroll	Carol Duncanson

Game Presentation/Promotions

Director of Game Presentation	Scott Cunningham
Game Presentation Producer	Marc Bick
Mascot Coordinator	Phil Crowhurst
Special Projects Coordinator	Eric Wasser
Game Presentation Coordinator	Angela Carrasco

Merchandise

Director of Merchandising	Ron Dennis
Retail Manager	Maria Cocozzelli
Buyer	Jessica Fong
Admin. Ass't to Director of Merchandising	Jean Marshall

Ticket Operations and Sales

Director of Group & Season Ticket Sales	Chris Gallagher
Director of Ticket & Game-Day Operations	Scott Wampold
Director of Suite & Club Level Services	Steve Woznick
Manager of Ticket Operations	Matt Coyne
Managers of Suite & Club Level Services	Kathy Stock, Peter Cameron
Group Sales Manager	Steve Golub
Senior Account Executive	Marcus Madlock
Account Executives	Dean Blixt, Chris Junghans, Marty Mulford, Topher Ollison
Sales Team Coordinator	Lauren Preziosi

Miscellaneous

Television	Fox Sports Net
Television Announcers	Jeff Rimer, Denis Potvin
Radio Flagship	WQAM (560 AM)
Radio Announcers	Jiggs McDonald, Randy Moller
Radio/"Inside the Panthers" Host	Steve Goldstein
Practice Facility	Incredible Ice

Los Angeles Kings

2000-01 Results: 38W-28L-13T-3OTL 92PTS. Third, Pacific Division

2001-02 Schedule

Month	Day	Date	Opponent	Month	Day	Date	Opponent
Oct.	Thu.	4	Phoenix		Mon.	7	at New Jersey
	Sun.	7	Minnesota*		Wed.	9	at NY Rangers
	Tue.	9	at Dallas		Thu.	10	at Boston
	Thu.	11	at St. Louis		Sat.	12	at San Jose*
	Sat.	13	Tampa Bay		Tue.	15	Nashville
	Tue.	16	Washington		Thu.	17	Buffalo
	Thu.	18	Anaheim		Sat.	19	NY Islanders*
	Sat.	20	at Detroit		Mon.	21	at Anaheim
	Tue.	23	at Columbus		Thu.	24	Minnesota
	Thu.	25	at Tampa Bay		Sat.	26	Colorado*
	Fri.	26	at Florida		Mon.	28	at Colorado
	Sun.	28	at Carolina*		Wed.	30	at Minnesota
	Tue.	30	at Chicago	**Feb.**	Mon.	4	Philadelphia
Nov.	Thu.	1	Chicago		Thu.	7	Carolina
	Sat.	3	Atlanta*		Fri.	8	at Phoenix
	Thu.	8	Calgary		Mon.	11	Dallas
	Sat.	10	Detroit		Wed.	13	Phoenix
	Thu.	15	Dallas		Tue.	26	at Columbus
	Sat.	17	at Detroit		Wed.	27	at Pittsburgh
	Sun.	18	at Minnesota*	**Mar.**	Sat.	2	Columbus*
	Tue.	20	at Calgary		Mon.	4	Ottawa
	Thu.	22	at Edmonton		Wed.	6	at Dallas
	Sat.	24	San Jose*		Thu.	7	at Nashville
	Thu.	29	Edmonton		Sat.	9	at Colorado*
Dec.	Sat.	1	Nashville*		Mon.	11	Chicago
	Mon.	3	Calgary		Thu.	14	St. Louis
	Thu.	6	St. Louis		Sat.	16	Pittsburgh*
	Sat.	8	at St. Louis		Mon.	18	at San Jose
	Sun.	9	at Chicago		Thu.	21	Colorado
	Tue.	11	at Nashville		Sat.	23	San Jose*
	Thu.	13	Vancouver		Sun.	24	at Phoenix*
	Sat.	15	Columbus		Tue.	26	at Vancouver
	Sun.	16	at Anaheim*		Thu.	28	at Edmonton
	Tue.	18	at Toronto		Sat.	30	at Calgary
	Thu.	20	at Ottawa	**Apr.**	Tue.	2	Vancouver
	Sat.	22	at Montreal		Thu.	4	Detroit
	Wed.	26	at Phoenix		Sat.	6	Edmonton
	Thu.	27	Anaheim		Mon.	8	Dallas
	Sat.	29	NY Rangers		Thu.	11	at Vancouver
Jan.	Wed.	2	Florida		Sat.	13	at San Jose*
	Sat.	5	at NY Islanders		Sun.	14	Anaheim*

* Denotes afternoon game.

Franchise date: June 5, 1967

PACIFIC DIVISION

35th NHL Season

Felix Potvin recaptured his star form in Los Angeles last season, posting a record of 13-5-5 with a 1.96 average and five shutouts in just 23 games. Potvin led the Kings on a late-season surge that led all the way to round two of the playoffs.

Year-by-Year Record

		Home				Road				Overall								
Season	GP	W	L	T	OL	W	L	T	OL	W	L	T	OL	GF	GA	Pts.	Finished	Playoff Result
2000-01	82	20	12	8	1	18	16	5	2	38	28	13	3	252	228	92	3rd, Pacific Div.	Lost Conf. Semi-Final
1999-2000	82	21	13	5	2	18	14	7	2	39	27	12	4	245	228	94	2nd, Pacific Div.	Lost Conf. Quater-Final
1998-99	82	18	20	3	...	14	25	2	...	32	45	5	...	189	222	69	5th, Pacific Div.	Out of Playoffs
1997-98	82	22	16	3	...	16	17	8	...	38	33	11	...	227	225	87	2nd, Pacific Div.	Lost Conf. Quater-Final
1996-97	82	18	16	7	...	10	27	4	...	28	43	11	...	214	268	67	6th, Pacific Div.	Out of Playoffs
1995-96	82	16	16	9	...	8	24	9	...	24	40	18	...	256	302	66	6th, Pacific Div.	Out of Playoffs
1994-95	48	7	11	6	...	9	12	3	...	16	23	9	...	142	174	41	4th, Pacific Div.	Out of Playoffs
1993-94	84	18	19	5	...	9	26	7	...	27	45	12	...	294	322	66	5th, Pacific Div.	Out of Playoffs
1992-93	84	22	15	5	...	17	20	5	...	39	35	10	...	338	340	88	3rd, Smythe Div.	Lost Final
1991-92	80	20	11	9	...	15	20	5	...	35	31	14	...	287	296	84	2nd, Smythe Div.	Lost Div. Semi-Final
1990-91	80	26	9	5	...	20	15	5	...	46	24	10	...	340	254	102	1st, Smythe Div.	Lost Div. Final
1989-90	80	21	16	3	...	13	23	4	...	34	39	7	...	338	337	75	4th, Smythe Div.	Lost Div. Final
1988-89	80	25	12	3	...	17	19	4	...	42	31	7	...	376	335	91	2nd, Smythe Div.	Lost Div. Final
1987-88	80	19	18	3	...	11	24	5	...	30	42	8	...	318	359	68	4th, Smythe Div.	Lost Div. Semi-Final
1986-87	80	20	17	3	...	11	24	5	...	31	41	8	...	318	341	70	4th, Smythe Div.	Lost Div. Semi-Final
1985-86	80	9	27	4	...	14	22	4	...	23	49	8	...	284	389	54	5th, Smythe Div.	Out of Playoffs
1984-85	80	20	14	6	...	14	18	8	...	34	32	14	...	339	326	82	4th, Smythe Div.	Lost Div. Semi-Final
1983-84	80	13	19	8	...	10	25	5	...	23	44	13	...	309	376	59	5th, Smythe Div.	Out of Playoffs
1982-83	80	20	13	7	...	7	28	5	...	27	41	12	...	308	365	66	5th, Smythe Div.	Out of Playoffs
1981-82	80	19	15	6	...	5	26	9	...	24	41	15	...	314	369	63	4th, Smythe Div.	Lost Div. Final
1980-81	80	22	11	7	...	21	13	6	...	43	24	13	...	337	290	99	2nd, Norris Div.	Lost Prelim. Round
1979-80	80	18	13	9	...	12	23	5	...	30	36	14	...	290	313	74	2nd, Norris Div.	Lost Prelim. Round
1978-79	80	20	13	7	...	14	21	5	...	34	34	12	...	292	286	80	3rd, Norris Div.	Lost Prelim. Round
1977-78	80	18	16	6	...	13	18	9	...	31	34	15	...	243	245	77	3rd, Norris Div.	Lost Prelim. Round
1976-77	80	20	13	7	...	14	18	8	...	34	31	15	...	271	241	83	2nd, Norris Div.	Lost Quarter-Final
1975-76	80	22	13	5	...	16	20	4	...	38	33	9	...	263	265	85	2nd, Norris Div.	Lost Quarter-Final
1974-75	80	22	7	11	...	20	10	10	...	42	17	21	...	269	185	105	2nd, Norris Div.	Lost Prelim. Round
1973-74	78	22	13	4	...	11	20	8	...	33	33	12	...	233	231	78	3rd, West Div.	Lost Quarter-Final
1972-73	78	21	11	7	...	10	25	4	...	31	36	11	...	232	245	73	6th, West Div.	Out of Playoffs
1971-72	78	14	23	2	...	6	26	7	...	20	49	9	...	206	305	49	7th, West Div.	Out of Playoffs
1970-71	78	17	14	8	...	8	26	5	...	25	40	13	...	239	303	63	5th, West Div.	Out of Playoffs
1969-70	76	12	22	4	...	2	30	6	...	14	52	10	...	168	290	38	6th, West Div.	Out of Playoffs
1968-69	76	19	14	5	...	5	28	5	...	24	42	10	...	185	260	58	4th, West Div.	Lost Semi-Final
1967-68	74	20	13	4	...	11	20	6	...	31	33	10	...	200	224	72	2nd, West Div.	Lost Quarter-Final

2001-02 Player Personnel

FORWARDS	HT	WT	S	Place of Birth	Date	2000-01 Club
AULIN, Jared	6-0	180	R	Calgary, Alta.	3/15/82	Kamloops
BEDNAR, Jaroslav	5-11	198	R	Prague, Czech.	11/8/76	HIFK Helsinki
BELANGER, Eric	6-0	185	L	Sherbrooke, Que.	12/16/77	Los Angeles-Lowell
BELANGER, Ken	6-4	225	L	Sault Ste. Marie, Ont.	5/14/74	Boston-Providence
BRENNAN, Kip	6-4	210	L	Kingston, Ont.	8/27/80	Lowell-Sudbury
BUCHBERGER, Kelly	6-2	210	L	Langenburg, Sask.	12/2/66	Los Angeles
CHARTRAND, Brad	5-11	191	L	Winnipeg, Man.	12/14/74	Los Angeles-Lowell
DEADMARSH, Adam	6-0	195	R	Trail, B.C.	5/10/75	Colorado-Los Angeles
EMERSON, Nelson	5-11	180	R	Hamilton, Ont.	8/17/67	Los Angeles
HEINZE, Steve	5-11	202	R	Lawrence, MA	1/30/70	Columbus-Buffalo
JOHNSON, Craig	6-2	200	L	St. Paul, MN	3/18/72	Los Angeles
KELLY, Steve	6-2	210	L	Vancouver, B.C.	10/26/76	New Jersey-Los Angeles
LAPERRIERE, Ian	6-1	201	R	Montreal, Que.	1/19/74	Los Angeles
MAIR, Adam	6-2	206	R	Hamilton, Ont.	2/15/79	Tor-St. John's-L.A.
MILLER, Nate	6-3	192	L	Anoka, MN	6/3/76	Lowell
MURRAY, Glen	6-3	225	R	Halifax, N.S.	11/1/72	Los Angeles
PALFFY, Ziggy	5-10	183	L	Skalica, Czech.	5/5/72	Los Angeles
PHILLIPS, Greg	6-2	205	R	Winnipeg, Man.	3/27/78	Lowell
ROBITAILLE, Randy	5-11	196	L	Ottawa, Ont.	10/12/75	Nashville-Milwaukee
SMITHSON, Jerred	6-2	190	R	Vernon, B.C.	2/4/79	Lowell
SMOLINSKI, Bryan	6-1	208	R	Toledo, OH	12/27/71	Los Angeles
STUMPEL, Jozef	6-3	225	R	Nitra, Czech.	7/20/72	Slovan Bratislava-Los Angeles
THOMAS, Scott	6-2	200	R	Buffalo, NY	1/18/70	Los Angeles-Manitoba
VALICEVIC, Rob	6-1	198	R	Detroit, MI	1/6/71	Nashville
DEFENSEMEN						
BOUCHER, Philippe	6-2	221	R	Ste-Apollinaire, Que.	3/24/73	Los Angeles-Manitoba
CORVO, Joe	6-0	205	R	Oak Park, IL	6/20/77	Lowell
HAUER, Brett	6-2	210	R	Richfield, MN	7/11/71	Manitoba
KARALAHTI, Jere	6-2	210	R	Helsinki, Finland	3/25/75	Los Angeles
LILJA, Andreas	6-3	222	L	Landskrona, Sweden	7/13/75	Los Angeles-Lowell
MILLER, Aaron	6-3	200	R	Buffalo, NY	8/11/71	Colorado-Los Angeles
MODRY, Jaroslav	6-2	215	L	Ceske-Budejovice, Czech.	2/27/71	Los Angeles
NORSTROM, Mattias	6-2	201	L	Stockholm, Sweden	1/2/72	Los Angeles
PUDLICK, Michael	6-3	190	L	Blaine, MN	2/24/78	Lowell
RULLIER, Joe	6-3	200	R	Montreal, Que.	1/28/80	Lowell
SCHNEIDER, Mathieu	5-10	192	L	New York, NY	6/12/69	Los Angeles
SEELEY, Richard	6-2	205	L	Powell River, B.C.	4/30/79	Lowell-Trenton
VISNOVSKY, Lubomir	5-10	183	L	Topolcany, Czech.	8/11/76	Los Angeles
ZIZKA, Tomas	6-1	198	L	Sternberk, Czech.	10/10/79	HCC Zlin

GOALTENDERS	HT	WT	C	Place of Birth	Date	2000-01 Club
COUSINEAU, Marcel	5-9	183	L	Delson, Que.	4/30/73	Lowell
FISET, Stephane	6-1	215	L	Montreal, Que.	6/17/70	Los Angeles-Lowell
POTVIN, Felix	6-1	190	L	Anjou, Que.	6/23/71	Vancouver-Los Angeles
SCOTT, Travis	6-2	185	L	Kanata, Ont.	9/14/75	Los Angeles-Lowell
STORR, Jamie	6-2	195	L	Brampton, Ont.	12/28/75	Los Angeles
VOLKOV, Alexei	6-1	195	L	Yekaterinburg, USSR	3/15/80	Lowell-New Orleans

General Managers' History

Larry Regan, 1967-68 to 1972-73; Larry Regan and Jake Milford, 1973-74; Jake Milford, 1974-75 to 1976-77; George Maguire, 1977-78 to 1982-83; George Maguire and Rogie Vachon, 1983-84; Rogie Vachon, 1984-85 to 1991-92; Nick Beverley, 1992-93, 1993-94; Sam McMaster, 1994-95 to 1996-97; Dave Taylor, 1997-98 to date.

General Manager

TAYLOR, DAVE
General Manager, Los Angeles Kings. Born in Levack, Ont., December 4, 1955.

No player in the history of the Kings ever wore the uniform with more distinction and class than Dave Taylor. For 17 seasons, Taylor gave his all, both on and off the ice, receiving All-Star status for his outstanding play.

Fittingly, after finishing his illustrious career during the 1993-94 season, Taylor remains a key part of the Kings organization, now serving as vice president and general manager for the NHL club. Taylor assumed his current responsibilities on April 22, 1997, becoming the seventh g.m. in team history. He joined the Kings front office four years earlier as an assistant to his predecessor, Sam McMaster.

An All-American hockey player while at Clarkson College, Taylor was relatively unknown when the Kings picked him in the 15th round of the 1975 draft. His grit and work ethic kept him around long enough to hook up with a center named Marcel Dionne, who virtually ignited Taylor's career. As a member of the renowned Triple Crown line with Dionne and left winger Charlie Simmer, Taylor became a prolific scorer and a fearsome checker. Taylor's NHL career stats include a Kings-record 1,111 games, 431 goals, 638 assists and 1,069 points.

A four-time NHL All-Star Game selection, Taylor served as the Kings captain for four seasons (1985-89). After posting career highs in goals (47) and points (112) during the 1980-81 season, Taylor earned a spot on the NHL Second All-Star Team. On April 3, 1995, Taylor's jersey No. 18 was retired, joining Rogie Vachon (No. 30) and Marcel Dionne (No. 16). For all his individual accomplishments in hockey, his crowning glory was reaching the Stanley Cup Finals with the 1992-93 Kings.

Away from the ice, Taylor has worked tirelessly for numerous charities throughout the years. Each year he hosts the Dave Taylor Golf Classic benefiting the Cystic Fibrosis Foundation, which annually raises more than $125,000. In 1991, the NHL honored Taylor's contributions to hockey and the community by awarding him both the Bill Masterton and King Clancy trophies.

2000-01 Scoring

* - rookie

Regular Season

Pos	#	Player	Team	GP	G	A	Pts	+/–	PIM	PP	SH	GW	GT	S	%
R	33	Ziggy Palffy	L.A.	73	38	51	89	22	20	12	4	8	0	217	17.5
L	20	Luc Robitaille	L.A.	82	37	51	88	10	66	16	1	4	1	235	15.7
C	21	Bryan Smolinski	L.A.	78	27	32	59	10	40	5	3	5	0	183	14.8
C	15	Jozef Stumpel	L.A.	63	16	39	55	20	14	9	0	6	0	95	16.8
D	10	Mathieu Schneider	L.A.	73	16	35	51	0	56	7	1	2	2	183	8.7
R	27	Glen Murray	L.A.	64	18	21	39	9	32	3	1	1	0	138	13.0
D	17 *	Lubomir Visnovsky	L.A.	81	7	32	39	16	36	3	0	3	0	105	6.7
R	28	Adam Deadmarsh	COL	39	13	13	26	–2	59	7	0	2	1	86	15.1
			L.A.	18	4	2	6	3	4	0	0	0	0	40	10.0
			TOTAL	57	17	15	32	1	63	7	0	2	1	126	13.5
R	7	Nelson Emerson	L.A.	78	11	11	22	–13	54	0	0	1	0	157	7.0
C	25 *	Eric Belanger	L.A.	62	9	12	21	14	16	1	2	1	0	80	11.3
R	9	Kelly Buchberger	L.A.	82	6	14	20	–10	75	0	0	1	0	66	9.1
D	44	Jaroslav Modry	L.A.	63	4	15	19	16	48	0	0	0	0	72	5.6
C	22	Ian Laperriere	L.A.	79	8	10	18	5	141	0	0	0	0	60	13.3
D	3	Aaron Miller	COL	56	4	9	13	19	29	0	0	0	0	49	8.2
			L.A.	13	0	5	5	3	14	0	0	0	0	10	0.0
			TOTAL	69	4	14	18	22	43	0	0	0	0	59	6.8
D	14	Mattias Norstrom	L.A.	82	0	18	18	10	60	0	0	0	0	59	0.0
L	23	Craig Johnson	L.A.	26	4	5	9	0	16	0	0	0	0	36	11.1
D	8	Jere Karalahti	L.A.	56	2	7	9	8	38	0	0	0	0	26	7.7
D	43	Philippe Boucher	L.A.	22	2	4	6	4	20	2	0	0	0	40	5.0
C	11	Steve Kelly	N.J.	24	2	2	4	0	21	0	0	0	0	18	11.1
			L.A.	11	1	0	1	0	4	0	0	0	0	4	25.0
			TOTAL	35	3	2	5	0	25	0	0	0	0	22	13.6
L	32	Stu Grimson	L.A.	72	3	2	5	–2	235	0	0	1	0	26	11.5
G	39	Felix Potvin	VAN	35	0	2	2	0	2	0	0	0	0	0	0.0
			L.A.	23	0	3	3	0	2	0	0	0	0	0	0.0
			TOTAL	58	0	5	5	0	4	0	0	0	0	0	0.0
R	51	Scott Thomas	L.A.	24	3	1	4	0	9	0	0	0	0	16	18.8
C	17 *	Tomas Vlasak	L.A.	10	1	3	4	4	2	0	0	0	0	15	6.7
C	24 *	Adam Mair	TOR	16	0	2	2	3	14	0	0	0	0	17	0.0
			L.A.	10	0	0	0	–3	6	0	0	0	0	5	0.0
			TOTAL	26	0	2	2	0	20	0	0	0	0	22	0.0
R	29	Brad Chartrand	L.A.	4	1	0	1	–2	2	0	0	1	0	6	16.7
R	12	Marko Tuomainen	L.A.	11	0	1	1	1	4	0	0	0	0	12	0.0
G	45 *	Travis Scott	L.A.	1	0	0	0	0	0	0	0	0	0	0	0.0
D	26	Richard Brennan	L.A.	2	0	0	0	–3	0	0	0	0	0	1	0.0
D	6 *	Andreas Lilja	L.A.	2	0	0	0	–2	4	0	0	0	0	1	0.0
G	35	Stephane Fiset	L.A.	7	0	0	0	0	2	0	0	0	0	0	0.0
G	1	Jamie Storr	L.A.	45	0	0	0	0	4	0	0	0	0	0	0.0

Goaltending

No.	Goaltender	GPI	Mins	Avg	W	L	T	EN	SO	GA	SA	S%
39	Felix Potvin	23	1410	1.96	13	5	5	0	5	46	571	.919
1	Jamie Storr	45	2498	2.74	19	18	6	7	4	114	1131	.899
37	Steve Passmore	14	718	3.09	3	8	1	2	1	37	310	.881
35	Stephane Fiset	7	318	3.58	3	0	1	0	0	19	129	.853
45	* Travis Scott	1	25	7.20	0	0	0	0	0	3	10	.700
	Totals	**82**	**4995**	**2.74**	**38**	**31**	**13**	**9**	**10**	**228**	**2160**	**.894**

Playoffs

Pos	#	Player	Team	GP	G	A	Pts	+/–	PIM	PP	SH	GW	GT	S	%
D	10	Mathieu Schneider	L.A.	13	0	9	9	4	10	0	0	0	0	34	0.0
R	33	Ziggy Palffy	L.A.	13	3	5	8	0	8	0	0	0	0	37	8.1
C	15	Jozef Stumpel	L.A.	13	3	5	8	1	10	2	0	1	0	24	12.5
L	20	Luc Robitaille	L.A.	13	4	3	7	1	10	1	0	1	0	24	16.7
R	27	Glen Murray	L.A.	13	4	3	7	–1	4	1	0	1	1	34	11.8
R	28	Adam Deadmarsh	L.A.	13	3	3	6	0	4	0	0	2	1	20	15.0
C	21	Bryan Smolinski	L.A.	13	1	5	6	–1	14	0	0	0	0	30	3.3
C	25 *	Eric Belanger	L.A.	13	1	4	5	3	2	0	0	1	1	18	5.6
R	7	Nelson Emerson	L.A.	13	2	2	4	1	4	0	0	0	0	22	9.1
C	22	Ian Laperriere	L.A.	13	1	2	3	1	12	0	0	0	0	13	7.7
D	14	Mattias Norstrom	L.A.	13	0	2	2	–4	18	0	0	0	0	5	0.0
R	9	Kelly Buchberger	L.A.	8	1	0	1	–1	2	0	0	0	0	5	20.0
D	44	Jaroslav Modry	L.A.	10	1	0	1	–1	4	1	0	1	1	12	8.3
R	51	Scott Thomas	L.A.	12	1	0	1	–1	4	1	0	0	0	6	16.7
D	3	Aaron Miller	L.A.	13	0	1	1	4	6	0	0	0	0	9	0.0
D	43	Philippe Boucher	L.A.	13	0	1	1	1	2	0	0	0	0	22	0.0
G	35	Stephane Fiset	L.A.	1	0	0	0	0	0	0	0	0	0	0	0.0
D	6 *	Andreas Lilja	L.A.	1	0	0	0	0	0	0	0	0	0	0	0.0
L	32	Stu Grimson	L.A.	5	0	0	0	0	4	0	0	0	0	1	0.0
C	11	Steve Kelly	L.A.	8	0	0	0	–1	2	0	0	0	0	1	0.0
D	17 *	Lubomir Visnovsky	L.A.	8	0	0	0	–1	0	0	0	0	0	6	0.0
G	39	Felix Potvin	L.A.	13	0	0	0	0	4	0	0	0	0	0	0.0
D	8	Jere Karalahti	L.A.	13	0	0	0	–7	18	0	0	0	0	10	0.0

Goaltending

No.	Goaltender	GPI	Mins	Avg	W	L	EN	SO	GA	SA	S%
35	Stephane Fiset	1	0	0.00	0	0	0	0	0	0	.000
39	Felix Potvin	13	812	2.44	7	6	1	2	33	361	.909
	Totals	**13**	**824**	**2.48**	**7**	**6**	**1**	**2**	**34**	**362**	**.906**

Captains' History

Bob Wall, 1967-68, 1968-69; Larry Cahan, 1969-70, 1970-71; Bob Pulford, 1971-72, 1972-73; Terry Harper, 1973-74, 1974-75; Mike Murphy, 1975-76 to 1980-81; Dave Lewis, 1981-82, 1982-83; Terry Ruskowski, 1983-84, 1984-85; Dave Taylor, 1985-86 to 1988-89; Wayne Gretzky, 1989-90 to 1991-92; Wayne Gretzky and Luc Robitaille, 1992-93; Wayne Gretzky, 1993-94, 1994-95; Wayne Gretzky and Rob Blake, 1995-96; Rob Blake, 1996-97 to 2000-01.

Club Records

Team

(Figures in brackets for season records are games played; records for fewest points, wins, ties, losses, goals, goals against are for 70 or more games)

Most Points	**105**	1974-75 (80)
Most Wins	**46**	1990-91 (80)
Most Ties	**21**	1974-75 (80)
Most Losses	**52**	1969-70 (76)
Most Goals	**376**	1988-89 (80)
Most Goals Against	**389**	1985-86 (80)
Fewest Points	**38**	1969-70 (76)
Fewest Wins	**14**	1969-70 (76)
Fewest Ties	**5**	1998-99 (82)
Fewest Losses	**17**	1974-75 (80)
Fewest Goals	**168**	1969-70 (76)
Fewest Goals Against	**185**	1974-75 (80)
Longest Winning Streak		
Overall	**8**	Oct. 21-Nov. 7/72
Home	**12**	Oct. 10-Dec. 5/92
Away	**8**	Dec. 18/74-Jan. 16/75
Longest Undefeated Streak		
Overall	**11**	Feb. 28-Mar. 24/74 (9 wins, 2 ties)
Home	**13**	Oct. 10-Dec. 8/92 (12 wins, 1 tie)
Away	**11**	Oct. 10-Dec. 11/74 (6 wins, 5 ties)
Longest Losing Streak		
Overall	**10**	Feb. 22-Mar. 9/84
Home	**9**	Feb. 8-Mar. 12/86
Away	**12**	Jan. 11-Feb. 15/70
Longest Winless Streak		
Overall	**17**	Jan. 29-Mar. 5/70 (13 losses, 4 ties)
Home	**9**	Jan. 29-Mar. 5/70 (8 losses, 1 tie), Feb. 8-Mar. 12/86 (9 losses)
Away	**21**	Jan. 11-Apr. 3/70 (17 losses, 4 ties)
Most Shutouts, Season	**10**	2000-01 (82)
Most PIM, Season	**2,228**	1990-91 (80)
Most Goals, Game	**12**	Nov. 28/84 (Van. 1 at L.A. 12)

Individual

Most Seasons	**17**	Dave Taylor
Most Games	**1,111**	Dave Taylor
Most Goals, Career	**550**	Marcel Dionne
Most Assists, Career	**757**	Marcel Dionne
Most Points Career	**1,307**	Marcel Dionne (550G, 757A)
Most PIM, Career	**1,846**	Marty McSorley
Most Shutouts, Career	**32**	Rogie Vachon
Longest Consecutive Games Streak	**324**	Marcel Dionne (Jan. 7/78-Jan. 9/82)
Most Goals, Season	**70**	Bernie Nicholls (1988-89)
Most Assists, Season	**122**	Wayne Gretzky (1990-91)
Most Points, Season	**168**	Wayne Gretzky (1988-89; 54G, 114A)
Most PIM, Season	**399**	Marty McSorley (1992-93)
Most Points, Defenseman, Season	**76**	Larry Murphy (1980-81; 16G, 60A)
Most Points, Center, Season	**168**	Wayne Gretzky (1988-89; 54G, 114A)
Most Points, Right Wing, Season	**112**	Dave Taylor (1980-81; 47G, 65A)
Most Points, Left Wing, Season	***125**	Luc Robitaille (1992-93; 63G, 62A)
Most Points, Rookie, Season	**84**	Luc Robitaille (1986-87; 45G, 39A)
Most Shutouts, Season	**8**	Rogie Vachon (1976-77)
Most Goals, Game	**4**	Sixteen times
Most Assists, Game	**6**	Bernie Nicholls (Dec. 1/88), Tomas Sandstrom (Oct. 9/93)
Most Points, Game	**8**	Bernie Nicholls (Dec. 1/88; 2G, 6A)

* NHL Record.

Coaching History

Red Kelly, 1967-68, 1968-69; Hal Laycoe and John Wilson, 1969-70; Larry Regan, 1970-71; Larry Regan and Fred Glover, 1971-72; Bob Pulford, 1972-73 to 1976-77; Ron Stewart, 1977-78; Bob Berry, 1978-79 to 1980-81; Parker MacDonald and Don Perry, 1981-82; Don Perry, 1982-83; Don Perry, Rogie Vachon and Roger Neilson, 1983-84; Pat Quinn, 1984-85, 1985-86; Pat Quinn and Mike Murphy 1986-87; Mike Murphy, Rogie Vachon and Robbie Ftorek, 1987-88; Robbie Ftorek, 1988-89; Tom Webster, 1989-90 to 1991-92; Barry Melrose, 1992-93, 1993-94; Barry Melrose and Rogie Vachon, 1994-95; Larry Robinson, 1995-96 to 1998-99; Andy Murray, 1999-2000 to date.

Retired Numbers

16	Marcel Dionne	1975-1987
18	Dave Taylor	1977-1994
30	Rogie Vachon	1971-1978

All-time Record vs. Other Clubs

Regular Season

	At Home								On Road								Total							
	GP	W	L	T	OL	GF	GA	PTS	GP	W	L	T	OL	GF	GA	PTS	GP	W	L	T	OL	GF	GA	PTS
Anaheim	22	11	8	3	0	65	59	25	22	6	11	5	0	51	73	17	44	17	19	8	0	116	132	42
Atlanta	2	1	0	0	1	10	7	3	2	2	0	0	0	9	3	4	4	3	0	0	1	19	10	7
Boston	59	21	31	7	0	204	216	49	60	11	43	6	0	169	282	28	119	32	74	13	0	373	498	77
Buffalo	52	21	22	9	0	180	180	51	51	15	27	9	0	150	208	39	103	36	49	18	0	330	388	90
Calgary	85	44	32	9	0	325	301	97	88	27	51	10	0	294	392	64	173	71	83	19	0	619	693	161
Carolina	28	15	10	3	0	119	110	33	28	11	13	4	0	111	108	26	56	26	23	7	0	230	218	59
Chicago	68	30	30	8	0	232	235	68	69	28	32	9	0	207	246	65	137	58	62	17	0	439	481	133
Colorado	37	23	11	3	0	159	119	49	36	14	19	3	0	127	150	31	73	37	30	6	0	286	269	80
Columbus	2	2	0	0	0	6	1	4	2	1	1	0	0	8	5	2	4	3	1	0	0	14	6	6
Dallas	74	31	25	18	0	257	220	80	76	17	46	12	1	203	303	47	150	48	71	30	1	460	523	127
Detroit	74	39	21	14	0	304	230	92	73	30	31	12	0	256	279	72	147	69	52	26	0	560	509	164
Edmonton	71	26	30	15	0	283	301	67	71	20	37	14	0	260	334	54	142	46	67	29	0	543	635	121
Florida	7	4	3	0	0	22	23	8	6	0	3	3	0	9	18	3	13	4	6	3	0	31	41	11
Minnesota	2	1	1	0	0	4	6	2	2	1	1	0	0	7	4	2	4	2	2	0	0	11	10	4
Montreal	63	18	36	9	0	195	251	45	62	8	43	11	0	158	284	27	125	26	79	20	0	353	535	72
Nashville	6	2	3	0	1	16	18	5	6	4	1	1	0	17	10	9	12	6	4	1	1	33	28	14
New Jersey	40	27	7	6	0	199	125	60	41	18	18	5	0	143	137	41	81	45	25	11	0	342	262	101
NY Islanders	43	21	15	7	0	159	137	49	42	14	24	4	0	119	155	32	85	35	39	11	0	278	292	81
NY Rangers	58	23	25	10	0	193	208	56	56	15	35	6	0	162	231	36	114	38	60	16	0	355	439	92
Ottawa	7	6	1	0	0	38	17	12	7	2	4	1	0	21	26	5	14	8	5	1	0	59	43	17
Philadelphia	63	20	35	8	0	187	216	48	62	16	39	7	0	156	239	39	125	36	74	15	0	343	455	87
Phoenix	66	23	31	11	1	264	268	58	68	25	33	10	0	231	273	60	134	48	64	21	1	495	541	118
Pittsburgh	67	42	17	8	0	258	178	92	70	22	38	10	0	220	258	54	137	64	55	18	0	478	436	146
St. Louis	72	33	28	11	0	248	214	77	72	17	45	10	0	185	272	44	144	50	73	21	0	433	486	121
San Jose	29	19	7	3	0	97	68	41	29	10	14	3	2	88	101	25	58	29	21	6	2	185	169	66
Tampa Bay	9	1	7	1	0	22	33	3	7	4	3	0	0	19	16	8	16	5	10	1	0	41	49	11
Toronto	64	34	21	9	0	230	187	77	66	21	34	11	0	217	261	53	130	55	55	20	0	447	448	130
Vancouver	93	50	29	14	0	378	290	114	91	30	45	15	1	290	348	76	184	80	74	29	1	668	638	190
Washington	45	26	13	6	0	178	138	58	44	19	18	7	0	165	182	45	89	45	31	13	0	343	320	103
Defunct Clubs	35	27	6	2	0	141	76	56	34	11	14	9	0	91	109	31	69	38	20	11	0	232	185	87
Totals	**1343**	**641**	**505**	**194**	**3**	**4973**	**4432**	**1479**	**1343**	**419**	**723**	**197**	**4**	**4143**	**5307**	**1039**	**2686**	**1060**	**1228**	**391**	**7**	**9116**	**9739**	**2518**

Playoffs

	Series	W	L	GP	W	L	T	GF	GA	Last Mtg.	Round	Result
Boston	2	0	2	13	5	8	0	38	56	1977	QF	L 2-4
Calgary	6	4	2	26	13	13	0	105	112	1993	DSF	W 4-2
Chicago	1	0	1	5	1	4	0	7	10	1974	QF	L 1-4
Colorado	1	0	1	7	3	4	0	10	17	2001	CSF	L 3-4
Dallas	1	0	1	7	3	4	0	21	26	1968	QF	L 3-4
Detroit	2	1	1	10	4	6	0	21	32	2001	CQF	W 4-2
Edmonton	7	2	5	36	12	24	0	127	154	1992	DSF	L 2-4
Montreal	1	0	1	5	1	4	0	12	15	1993	F	L 1-4
NY Islanders	1	0	1	4	1	3	0	10	21	1980	PR	L 1-3
NY Rangers	2	0	2	6	1	5	0	14	32	1981	PR	L 1-3
St. Louis	2	0	2	8	0	8	0	13	32	1998	CQF	L 0-4
Toronto	3	1	2	12	5	7	0	31	41	1993	CF	W 4-3
Vancouver	3	2	1	17	9	8	0	66	60	1993	DF	W 4-2
Defunct Clubs	1	1	0	7	4	3	0	23	25			
Totals	**33**	**11**	**22**	**163**	**62**	**101**	**0**	**498**	**633**			

Playoff Results 2001-1997

Year	Round	Opponent	Result	GF	GA
2001	CSF	Colorado	L 3-4	10	17
	CQF	Detroit	W 4-2	15	17
2000	CQF	Detroit	L 0-4	6	15
1998	CQF	St. Louis	L 0-4	8	16

Abbreviations: Round: F – Final; **CF** – conference final; **CSF** – conference semi-final; **CQF** – conference quarter-final; **DF** – division final; **DSF** – division semi-final; **QF** – quarter-final; **PR** – preliminary round.

Calgary totals include Atlanta Flames, 1972-73 to 1979-80. Carolina totals include Hartford, 1979-80 to 1996-97.
Colorado totals include Quebec, 1979-80 to 1994-95. Dallas totals include Minnesota North Stars, 1967-68 to 1992-93.
New Jersey totals include Kansas City, 1974-75 to 1975-76, and Colorado Rockies, 1976-77 to 1981-82.
Phoenix totals include Winnipeg, 1979-80 to 1995-96.

2000-01 Results

Oct.	6	at Washington	4-1		6	Calgary	5-0
	7	at Buffalo	3-5		11	Buffalo	3-2
	9	at Columbus	7-1		13	St. Louis	2-4
	11	St. Louis	4-4		16	at Ottawa	7-6*
	13	Boston	5-0		17	at Toronto	2-1
	15	Phoenix	5-6		20	at Carolina	6-3
	17	at Nashville	1-1		22	at Philadelphia	0-3
	19	at St. Louis	1-7		25	Calgary	0-3
	21	at Dallas	3-4		27	Minnesota	1-4
	23	at Anaheim	5-4*		30	Dallas	8-0
	25	Anaheim	6-2	**Feb.**	1	Nashville	4-6
	28	at Phoenix	1-3		6	Chicago	3-3
	31	at Columbus	1-4		8	Carolina	4-2
Nov.	2	at Atlanta	5-2		10	Washington	3-4
	4	at New Jersey	2-1		12	Edmonton	3-6
	5	at NY Islanders	4-1		14	at Dallas	2-4
	7	Phoenix	3-3		16	at Minnesota	4-0
	9	Vancouver	2-0		18	at Chicago	0-3
	11	Detroit	2-2		20	at Edmonton	0-5
	16	NY Islanders	5-1		22	at Calgary	2-0
	18	Colorado	6-4		24	Columbus	3-1
	23	New Jersey	1-6		27	at Nashville	2-1
	25	at Pittsburgh	2-2	**Mar.**	1	at Chicago	2-2
	26	at Boston	4-4		3	Detroit	6-3
	28	at NY Rangers	6-7		4	at Anaheim	0-4
Dec.	2	Minnesota	3-2		6	Montreal	4-3
	3	at Anaheim	0-4		8	Nashville	4-1
	7	Dallas	5-2		10	Chicago	2-2
	9	at Edmonton	4-2		14	at San Jose	4-1
	10	at Vancouver	2-1		17	San Jose	1-0*
	14	NY Rangers	5-5		19	Phoenix	6-2
	16	Tampa Bay	3-4		21	Edmonton	0-7
	19	Atlanta	6-7*		24	Anaheim	3-3
	21	at Colorado	2-5		26	San Jose	0-0
	22	at Minnesota	3-4		27	at San Jose	2-3*
	26	San Jose	1-2		29	Columbus	3-0
	28	at St. Louis	5-2		31	Colorado	4-0
	29	at Dallas	4-1	**Apr.**	2	Vancouver	3-1
	31	at Detroit	1-2		3	at Phoenix	2-2
Jan.	2	at Colorado	2-6		5	at Vancouver	2-3*
	4	Florida	3-4		7	at Calgary	3-2

* – Overtime

Entry Draft Selections 2001-1987

2001
Pick
18 Jens Karlsson
30 Dave Steckel
49 Mike Cammalleri
51 Jaroslav Bednar
83 Henrik Juntunen
116 Richard Petiot
152 Terry Denike
153 Tuukka Mantyla
214 Cristobal Huet
237 Mike Gabinet
277 Sebastien Laplante

2000
Pick
20 Alexander Frolov
54 Andreas Lilja
86 Yanick Lehoux
118 Lubomir Visnovsky
165 Nathan Marsters
201 Yevgeny Fedorov
206 Tim Eriksson
218 Craig Olynick
245 Dan Welch
250 Flavien Conne
282 Carl Grahn

1999
Pick
43 Andrei Shefer
74 Jason Crain
76 Frantisek Kaberle
92 Cory Campbell
104 Brian McGrattan
125 Daniel Johansson
133 Jean-Francois Nogues
193 Kevin Baker
222 George Parros
250 Noah Clarke

1998
Pick
21 Mathieu Biron
46 Justin Papineau
76 Alexei Volkov
103 Kip Brennan
133 Joe Rullier
163 Tomas Zizka
190 Tommi Hannus
217 Jim Henkel
248 Matthew Yeats

1997
Pick
3 Olli Jokinen
15 Matt Zultek
29 Scott Barney
83 Joe Corvo
99 Sean Blanchard
137 Richard Seeley
150 Jeff Katcher
193 Jay Kopischke
220 Konrad Brand

1996
Pick
30 Josh Green
37 Marian Cisar
57 Greg Phillips
84 Mikael Simons
96 Eric Belanger
120 Jesse Black
123 Peter Hogan
190 Stephen Valiquette
193 Kai Nurminen
219 Sebastien Simard

1995
Pick
3 Aki Berg
33 Don MacLean
50 Pavel Rosa
59 Vladimir Tsyplakov
118 Jason Morgan
137 Igor Melyakov
157 Benoit Larose
163 Juha Vuorivirta
215 Brian Stewart

1994
Pick
7 Jamie Storr
33 Matt Johnson
59 Vitali Yachmenev
111 Chris Schmidt
163 Luc Gagne
189 Andrew Dale
215 Jan Nemecek
241 Sergei Shalomai

1993
Pick
42 Shayne Toporowski
68 Jeff Mitchell
94 Bob Wren
105 Frederick Beaubien
117 Jason Saal
120 Tomas Vlasak
146 Jere Karalahti
172 Justin Martin
198 John-Tra Dillabough
224 Martin Strbak
250 Kimmo Timonen
276 Patrick Howald

1992
Pick
39 Justin Hocking
63 Sandy Allan
87 Kevin Brown
111 Jeff Shevalier
135 Rem Murray
207 Magnus Wernblom
231 Ryan Pisiak
255 Jukka Tiilikainen

1991
Pick
42 Guy Leveque
79 Keith Redmond
81 Alexei Zhitnik
108 Pauli Jaks
130 Brett Seguin
152 Kelly Fairchild
196 Craig Brown
218 Mattias Olsson
240 Andre Bouliane
262 Mike Gaul

1990
Pick
7 Darryl Sydor
28 Brandy Semchuk
49 Bill Berg
91 David Goverde
112 Erik Andersson
133 Robert Lang
154 Dean Hulett
175 Denis Leblanc
196 Patrik Ross
217 K.J.(Kevin) White
238 Troy Mohns

1989
Pick
39 Brent Thompson
81 Jim Maher
102 Eric Ricard
103 Thomas Newman
123 Daniel Rydmark
144 Ted Kramer
165 Sean Whyte
182 Jim Giacin
186 Martin Maskarinec
207 Jim Hiller
228 Steve Jaques
249 Kevin Sneddon

1988
Pick
7 Martin Gelinas
28 Paul Holden
49 John Van Kessel
70 Rob Blake
91 Jeff Robison
109 Micah Aivazoff
112 Robert Larsson
133 Jeff Kruesel
154 Timo Peltomaa
175 Jim Larkin
196 Brad Hyatt
217 Doug Laprade
238 Joe Flanagan

1987
Pick
4 Wayne McBean
27 Mark Fitzpatrick
43 Ross Wilson
90 Mike Vukonich
111 Greg Batters
132 Kyosti Karjalainen
174 Jeff Gawlicki
195 John Preston
216 Rostislav Vlach
237 Mikael Lindholm

Coach

MURRAY, ANDY
Coach, Los Angeles Kings. Born in Gladstone, Man., March 3, 1951.

Andy Murray became the 19th head coach in Kings history on June 14, 1999. His coaching experience dates back to 1974 and includes seven seasons as an NHL assistant or associate coach with the Winnipeg Jets (1993 to 1995), Minnesota North Stars (1990 to 1992) and Philadelphia Flyers (1988 to 1990). As an assistant coach in Minnesota, Murray reached the Stanley Cup Finals in 1991.

In addition to his NHL service, Murray brings to the Kings a tremendous amount of international coaching experience. As head coach of the Canadian national team, he guided his team to a 77-29-14 record and the gold medal in the 1997 World Hockey Championships.

From 1976 to 1978, Murray served his first head coaching position with the Brandon Travelers of the Manitoba Junior Hockey League. He moved on to become head coach for Brandon University from 1978 to 1981, leading the Bobcats to the #1 ranking in Canadian University hockey during his final year. In 1981-82, Murray moved to Switzerland, where for the next seven years he coached several Swiss-A Division teams.

Murray returned to North America as an assistant coach for the Hershey Bears of the American Hockey League in 1987 and helped guide the Bears to the 1988 Calder Cup Championship. In 1992, Murray returned to Europe to coach Lugano in Switzerland and then Eisbaren Berlin in Germany a year later. Most recently, Murray served as the head coach for Shattuck-St. Mary's in Faribault, Minnesota, where he led the prep school to a 70-9-2 record and the Midget Triple A USA Hockey national championship in 1998-99.

Coaching Record

		Regular Season				Playoffs		
Season	Team	Games	W	L	T	Games	W	L
1999-2000	Los Angeles (NHL)	82	39	31	12	4	0	4
2000-01	Los Angeles (NHL)	82	38	31	13	13	7	6
	NHL Totals	164	77	62	25	17	7	10

Club Directory

STAPLES Center

Los Angeles Kings
STAPLES Center
1111 South Figueroa Street
Los Angeles, CA 90015
Phone **213/742-7100**
GM FAX 310/535-4504
PR FAX 310/535-4507
www.lakings.com
Capacity: 18,118

Owners . . . . . Philip F. Anschutz, Edward P. Roski
President/Governor . . . . . Timothy J. Leiweke
Special Assistant to the President . . . . . Rogie Vachon
Manager of Special Services/Office of the President. . Lisa Tran
Assistant to the President . . . . . Jennifer Chapman

Hockey Operations
Senior Vice President/General Manager . . . . . Dave Taylor
Assistant General Manager . . . . . Kevin Gilmore
Director, Player Personnel . . . . . Bill O'Flaherty
Assistant to the General Manager . . . . . John Wolf
Executive Assistant to the General Manager . . . . . Marcia Galloway
Head Coach . . . . . Andy Murray
Assistant Coaches . . . . . Dave Tippett, Mark Hardy, Ray Bennett
Goaltending Consultant . . . . . Andy Nowicki
Director, Amateur Scouting . . . . . Al Murray
Director, Pro Scouting . . . . . Ace Bailey
Pro Scout - Director of European Evaluation . . . . . Rob Laird
Scouting Staff . . . . . Mark Bavis, Greg Drechsel, Vaclav Nedomansky, Parry Shockey, John Stanton, Ari Vuori, Michel Boucher, Gary Harker, Victor Tjumenev, Glen Williamson, Jim Cassidy, Mike Donnelly, Viacheslav Golovin, Jerry Sodomlak
Video Coordinator . . . . . Bill Gurney

Medical
Athletic Trainer . . . . . Peter Demers, ATC
Assistant Athletic Trainer . . . . . Rick Burrill, ATC
Rehabilitation Trainer . . . . . Robert Zolg, MPT, ATC
Head Speed-Strength and Conditioning Coach . . . . Joseph Horrigan, DC, CSCS
Assistant Speed-Strength and Conditioning Coach . Dave Good, CSCS, SSC
Nutrition Consultant . . . . . Doug Andersen, DC, CCN
Team Physician . . . . . Dr. Ronald Kvitne
Internist . . . . . Dr. Michael Mellman
Dentist . . . . . Dr. Jeffrey Hoy
Opthamologist . . . . . Dr. Howard Lazerson

Equipment Staff
Equipment Manager . . . . . Peter Millar
Assistant Equipment Manager . . . . . Rick Garcia, Dan Del Vecchio

Media Relations/Team Services
Director, Media Relations/Team Services . . . . . Mike Altieri
Manager, Media Relations/Team Services . . . . . Jeff Moeller
Media Relations Assistant . . . . . Lee Callans

Finance/Accounting/Ticket Operations
Executive Vice President, Chief Financial Officer. . . . Dan Beckerman
Director, Finance . . . . . Peter Mazur
Box Office Director . . . . . Larry Chu
Director of Payroll . . . . . Elcee Prendergast

Legal Department
Executive Vice President/General Counsel . . . . . Ted Fikre
Assistant General Counsel . . . . . Shawn Trell
Administrative Assistant to Executive Vice President, General Counsel . . . . . Frances Inomata

Human Resources
Vice President, Human Resources . . . . . Kevin McDowell
Director, Staffing & Development . . . . . Ed Perne
Director, Employee Services & Administration . . . . . Margaret Castaneda
Benefits Coordinator . . . . . Monica Franco

Sales & Marketing
Vice President, Sales & Marketing . . . . . Kurt J. Schwartzkopf
Director, Ticket Sales . . . . . Chris McGowan
Director, Entertainment and Special Events . . . . . Marianne Herman
Director, Group Sales . . . . . Carola Ross
Director, Corporate and Premium Seat Sales . . . . . Anthony Jones DeBerry
Manager, Marketing & Promotions . . . . . Shelby Russell
Manager, Corporate and Premium Seat Sales . . . . . Shawn Jeffers
Manager, Ticket Sales . . . . . Justin Apmadoc
Manager, Creative Services . . . . . Brooke Lingle
Graphic Designer . . . . . Lynette Fowler
Website Content Manager . . . . . Mark LaFerr
Account Manager, Corporate and Premium Seat Sales . . . . . Randy Bechtold
Community Development Manager . . . . . Kris Nakamura
Community Development Coordinator . . . . . Lara Frandzel
Fan Development Manager . . . . . Annie Camins
Fan Development Coordinator . . . . . Lee Barrett

Corporate Partnerships
Vice President, Client Services . . . . . Tracy Hartman
Director, Corporate Partnerships . . . . . Kevin Donovan
Account Executives . . . . . Jennifer Cordova, Damien Aveyan
Traffic Coordinator . . . . . Jennifer Tardiff

MIS/Merchandising
Chief Technical Officer . . . . . Vicki Kaplan
MIS Director . . . . . Ali Reza Shamma
Director of Merchandising . . . . . Alan Fey
Pro Shop Manager . . . . . Vince Spinosa

Broadcasting/Press Information
TV Play-by-Play Announcer-Fox Sports Net . . . . . Bob Miller
Radio Play-by-Play Announcer – ESPN Radio 1110-KSPN . . . . . Nick Nickson
TV Color Commentator – Fox Sports Net . . . . . Jim Fox
Radio Color Commentator – ESPN Radio 1110-KSPN . . . . . Daryl Evans
Training Center . . . . . HealthSouth Training Center

Minnesota Wild

2000-01 Results: 25W-39L-13T-5OTL 68PTS. Fifth, Northwest Division

Year-by-Year Record

		Home				Road				Overall								
Season	**GP**	**W**	**L**	**T**	**OL**	**W**	**L**	**T**	**OL**	**W**	**L**	**T**	**OL**	**GF**	**GA**	**Pts.**	**Finished**	**Playoff Result**
2000-01	82	14	13	10	4	11	26	3	1	25	39	13	5	168	210	68	5th, Northwest Div.	Out of Playoffs

2001-02 Schedule

Oct.	Sat.	6	at San Jose*		Sun.	6	Buffalo*
	Sun.	7	at Los Angeles*		Tue.	8	Montreal
	Wed.	10	Boston		Thu.	10	at Nashville
	Fri.	12	Chicago		Fri.	11	Anaheim
	Sun.	14	Edmonton*		Sun.	13	Dallas
	Tue.	16	San Jose		Tue.	15	at Carolina
	Fri.	19	St. Louis		Fri.	18	at Columbus
	Wed.	24	Carolina		Sat.	19	at Ottawa
	Sat.	27	at Calgary		Wed.	23	at Anaheim
	Tue.	30	at Nashville		Thu.	24	at Los Angeles
	Wed.	31	Nashville		Sat.	26	New Jersey*
Nov.	Fri.	2	Colorado		Mon.	28	Calgary
	Sun.	4	Edmonton*		Wed.	30	Los Angeles
	Tue.	6	at NY Rangers	**Feb.**	Tue.	5	at Toronto
	Thu.	8	at Boston		Wed.	6	at Washington
	Sun.	11	Vancouver*		Fri.	8	Colorado
	Tue.	13	Atlanta		Sun.	10	NY Islanders*
	Wed.	14	at Colorado		Tue.	12	at Columbus
	Fri.	16	at Detroit		Wed.	13	Detroit
	Sun.	18	Los Angeles*		Wed.	27	at Anaheim
	Tue.	20	at Phoenix	**Mar.**	Sat.	2	at Vancouver
	Wed.	21	at San Jose		Tue.	5	NY Rangers
	Fri.	23	Phoenix*		Thu.	7	at St. Louis
	Sun.	25	Dallas*		Fri.	8	at Dallas
	Tue.	27	Vancouver		Sun.	10	Columbus*
	Thu.	29	Florida		Tue.	12	Ottawa
Dec.	Sun.	2	St. Louis		Sun.	17	Phoenix*
	Wed.	5	at Chicago		Mon.	18	Calgary
	Sat.	8	at Philadelphia*		Wed.	20	Columbus
	Mon.	10	at Montreal		Sat.	23	at NY Islanders*
	Fri.	14	at Pittsburgh		Tue.	26	at St. Louis
	Sun.	16	Colorado*		Wed.	27	at Atlanta
	Tue.	18	Anaheim		Fri.	29	Chicago
	Sat.	22	at Vancouver		Sun.	31	at Chicago*
	Sun.	23	at Colorado	**Apr.**	Tue.	2	at Edmonton
	Wed.	26	Detroit		Thu.	4	at Calgary
	Fri.	28	at Edmonton		Fri.	5	at Vancouver
	Sat.	29	at Calgary		Mon.	8	San Jose
	Mon.	31	at Detroit		Wed.	10	at Dallas
Jan.	Wed.	2	Tampa Bay		Fri.	12	at Phoenix
	Fri.	4	Nashville		Sun.	14	Edmonton*

* Denotes afternoon game.

Wes Walz (above, left) returned from four years in Europe to join the Minnesota Wild for their inaugural season. He and Darby Hendrickson (above, right) each had 18 goals to tie rookie Marian Gaborik (right) for the team lead.

Franchise date: June 25, 1997

NORTHWEST DIVISION

2nd NHL Season

2001-02 Player Personnel

FORWARDS	HT	WT	S	Place of Birth	Date	2000-01 Club
ARONSON, Steve	6-1	205	R	Minnetonka, MN	7/15/78	Cleveland-Jackson
BARTOS, Peter	6-0	185	R	Martin, Czech.	9/5/73	Minnesota-Cleveland
BEAUFAIT, Mark	5-9	170	R	Livonia, MI	5/13/70	Orlando
BLOUIN, Sylvain	6-2	207	L	Montreal, Que.	5/21/74	Minnesota
BRUNETTE, Andrew	6-1	210	L	Sudbury, Ont.	8/24/73	Atlanta
CARTER, Shawn	6-3	210	L	Eagle River, WI	4/16/73	Houston
CAVANAUGH, Dan	6-1	190	R	Springfield, MA	3/3/80	Boston University
CAVOSIE, Marc	6-0	173	L	Albany, NY	8/6/81	RPI Engineers
DOWD, Jim	6-1	190	R	Brick, NJ	12/25/68	Minnesota
DUPUIS, Pascal	6-0	195	R	Laval, Quebec	4/7/79	Minnesota-Cleveland
FITZGERALD, Randy	5-11	174	L	Toronto, Ont.	9/5/79	Jackson Bandits
GABORIK, Marian	6-1	183	L	Trencin, Czech.	2/14/82	Minnesota
GARDINER, Peter	6-5	220	R	Toronto, Ont.	9/29/77	Jackson-Roanoke
GAVEY, Aaron	6-2	200	L	Sudbury, Ont.	2/22/74	Minnesota
GUSMANOV, Ravil	6-3	185	L	Naberezhnye Chelny, USSR	7/25/72	HC Magnitogorsk
HENDRICKSON, Darby	6-1	195	L	Richfield, MN	8/28/72	Minnesota
JOHNSON, Matt	6-5	232	L	Welland, Ont.	11/23/75	Minnesota
LAAKSONEN, Antti	6-0	180	L	Tammela, Finland	10/3/73	Minnesota
LAPLANTE, Darryl	6-0	198	L	Calgary, Alta.	3/28/77	Cleveland
LAROSE, Cory	6-0	188	L	Campbellton, N.B.	5/14/75	Jackson-Cleveland
McLEAN, Brett	5-11	194	L	Comox, B.C.	8/14/78	Cleveland
PARK, Richard	5-11	190	R	Seoul, S. Korea	5/27/76	Cleveland
PATERA, Pavel	6-1	172	L	Kladno, Czech.	9/6/71	Minnesota-Cleveland
ROEST, Stacy	5-9	185	R	Lethbridge, Alta.	3/15/74	Minnesota
SIMICEK, Roman	6-1	190	L	Ostrava, Czech.	11/4/71	Pittsburgh-Minnesota
STEWART, Cam	5-11	196	R	Kitchener, Ont.	9/18/71	Minnesota
SUSHINSKY, Maxim	5-8	165	L	St. Petersburg, USSR	7/1/74	Minnesota-Avangard Omsk
VIRTA, Tony	5-10	187	L	Hameenlinna, Finland	6/28/72	TPS Turku
WALLIN, Rickard	6-2	185	L	Stockholm, Sweden	4/19/80	Farjestads BK
WALZ, Wes	5-10	180	R	Calgary, Alta.	5/15/70	Minnesota
WANVIG, Kyle	6-2	219	R	Calgary, Alta.	1/29/81	Red Deer
ZHOLTOK, Sergei	6-2	191	R	Riga, Latvia	2/12/72	Montreal-Edmonton
DEFENSEMEN						
BENYSEK, Ladislav	6-2	190	L	Olomouc, Czech.	3/24/75	Minnesota
BOMBARDIR, Brad	6-1	205	L	Powell River, B.C.	5/5/72	Minnesota
BROWN, Brad	6-4	220	R	Baie Verte, Nfld.	12/27/75	NY Rangers
CROWLEY, Mike	5-11	190	L	Bloomington, MN	7/4/75	Anaheim-Grand Rapids
CULL, Trent	6-2	215	L	Brampton, Ont.	9/27/73	Wilkes-Barre
KUBA, Filip	6-3	205	L	Ostrava, Czech.	12/29/76	Minnesota
MARSHALL, Jason	6-2	200	R	Cranbrook, B.C.	2/22/71	Anaheim-Washington
MATTEUCCI, Mike	6-2	210	L	Trail, B.C.	12/27/71	Minnesota-Cleveland
MITCHELL, Willie	6-3	205	L	Port McNeill, B.C.	4/23/77	N.J.-Albany-Min
MURPHY, Curtis	5-8	185	R	Kerrobert, SK	12/3/75	Orlando
NYCHOLAT, Lawrence	6-0	192	L	Calgary, Alta.	5/7/79	Jackson-Cleveland
REITZ, Erik	6-0	192	R	Detroit, MI	7/29/82	Barrie
ROCHE, Travis	6-1	190	R	Grand Cache, Alta	6/17/78	North Dakota-Minnesota
SCHULTZ, Nick	6-0	187	L	Regina, Sask.	8/25/82	Prince Albert-Cleveland
SEKERAS, Lubomir	6-0	183	L	Trencin, Czech.	11/18/68	Minnesota
SUTTON, Andy	6-6	245	L	Edmonton, Alta.	3/10/75	Minnesota

GOALTENDERS	HT	WT	C	Place of Birth	Date	2000-01 Club
BROCHU, Martin	6-0	199	L	Anjou, Que.	3/10/73	Saint John
FERNANDEZ, Manny	6-0	180	L	Etobicoke, Ont.	8/27/74	Minnesota
GUSTAFSON, Derek	5-11	210	L	Gresham, OR	6/21/79	Min-Jackson-Clev
McLENNAN, Jamie	6-0	190	L	Edmonton, Alta.	6/30/71	Minnesota
ROLOSON, Dwayne	6-1	178	L	Simcoe, Ont.	10/12/69	Worcester

General Manager

RISEBROUGH, DOUG
Executive Vice President and General Manager, Minnesota Wild. Born in Guelph, Ont., January 29, 1954.

Doug Risebrough was hired as the first executive vice president and general manager of the Minnesota Wild on September 2, 1999. He is responsible for the club's overall hockey operations. After ending his 13-year NHL playing career with the Flames in 1987, Risebrough was named as assistant coach with Calgary and joined Terry Crisp behind the bench. Risebrough was appointed head coach of the Flames on May 18, 1990 and on May 16, 1991, he also assumed the role of general manager. Late in the 1991-92 campaign he directed his energies full-time to general manager, handing the coaching responsibilities over to Guy Charron for the balance of the season. Risebrough served as g.m. in Calgary through the start of the 1995-96 season.

Risebrough was Montreal's first selection, seventh overall, in the 1974 Amateur Draft. During his nine years with the Canadiens, he helped his club to four consecutive Stanley Cup championships between 1976 and 1979. He joined the Flames prior to the start of the club's 1982 training camp. During his NHL career, his clubs have won five Stanley Cup titles (1976-1979 as a player) and (1989 as an assistant coach with Calgary) and two Presidents' Trophies (1987-88 and 1988-89 as an assistant coach).

NHL Coaching Record

		Regular Season				Playoffs		
Season	Team	Games	W	L	T	Games	W	L
1990-91	Calgary	80	46	26	8	7	3	4
1991-92	Calgary	64	25	30	9	....	....	....
	NHL Totals	**144**	**71**	**56**	**17**	**7**	**3**	**4**

2000-01 Scoring

* - rookie

Regular Season

Pos	#	Player	Team	GP	G	A	Pts	+/–	PIM	PP	SH	GW	GT	S	%
L	10	* Marian Gaborik	MIN	71	18	18	36	–6	32	6	0	3	0	179	10.1
D	77	Lubomir Sekeras	MIN	80	11	23	34	–8	52	4	0	2	0	102	10.8
C	37	Wes Walz	MIN	82	18	12	30	–8	37	0	7	3	0	152	11.8
D	17	* Filip Kuba	MIN	75	9	21	30	–6	28	4	0	4	1	141	6.4
C	14	Darby Hendrickson	MIN	72	18	11	29	1	36	3	1	1	1	114	15.8
C	34	Jim Dowd	MIN	68	7	22	29	–6	80	0	0	0	1	92	7.6
L	24	Antti Laaksonen	MIN	82	12	16	28	–7	24	0	2	1	0	129	9.3
C	22	Stacy Roest	MIN	76	7	20	27	3	20	1	0	1	0	125	5.6
C	44	Aaron Gavey	MIN	75	10	14	24	–8	52	1	0	2	0	100	10.0
R	25	Sergei Krivokrasov	MIN	54	7	15	22	–1	20	2	0	1	0	107	6.5
C	16	Roman Simicek	PIT	29	3	6	9	–5	30	1	0	1	0	19	15.8
			MIN	28	2	4	6	–4	21	2	0	0	0	14	14.3
			TOTAL	57	5	10	15	–9	51	3	0	1	0	33	15.2
D	5	Brad Bombardir	MIN	70	0	15	15	–6	42	0	0	0	0	81	0.0
L	21	Cameron Stewart	MIN	54	4	9	13	–3	18	0	1	0	1	61	6.6
R	20	Maxim Sushinsky	MIN	30	7	4	11	–7	29	3	0	0	0	62	11.3
R	19	Jeff Nielsen	MIN	59	3	8	11	–16	4	1	0	1	0	82	3.7
D	2	* Willie Mitchell	N.J.	16	0	2	2	0	29	0	0	0	0	14	0.0
			MIN	17	1	7	8	4	11	0	0	0	0	16	6.3
			TOTAL	33	1	9	10	4	40	0	0	0	0	30	3.3
D	42	Andy Sutton	MIN	69	3	4	7	–11	131	2	0	0	0	64	4.7
D	3	* Ladislav Benysek	MIN	71	2	5	7	–11	38	1	0	0	0	48	4.2
L	45	Peter Bartos	MIN	13	4	2	6	2	6	1	0	1	0	18	22.2
L	36	Sylvain Blouin	MIN	41	3	2	5	–5	117	0	0	0	0	37	8.1
L	23	Pavel Patera	MIN	20	1	3	4	–8	4	0	0	0	0	14	7.1
L	12	Matt Johnson	MIN	50	1	1	2	–6	137	0	0	0	0	21	4.8
L	11	* Kai Nurminen	MIN	2	1	0	1	–1	2	0	0	0	0	1	100.0
L	11	* Pascal Dupuis	MIN	4	1	0	1	0	4	1	0	0	0	8	12.5
G	29	Jamie McLennan	MIN	38	0	1	1	0	4	0	0	0	0	0	0.0
D	15	J.J. Daigneault	MIN	1	0	0	0	–1	2	0	0	0	0	0	0.0
G	31	Zac Bierk	MIN	1	0	0	0	0	2	0	0	0	0	0	0.0
D	6	* Travis Roche	MIN	1	0	0	0	0	0	0	0	0	0	0	0.0
D	40	* Chris Armstrong	MIN	3	0	0	0	–3	0	0	0	0	0	4	0.0
R	26	* Christian Matte	MIN	3	0	0	0	0	2	0	0	0	0	8	0.0
D	28	Mike Matteucci	MIN	3	0	0	0	–2	2	0	0	0	0	3	0.0
G	30	* Derek Gustafson	MIN	4	0	0	0	0	0	0	0	0	0	0	0.0
C	32	Brian Bonin	MIN	7	0	0	0	–3	0	0	0	0	0	7	0.0
G	35	Manny Fernandez	MIN	42	0	0	0	0	6	0	0	0	0	0	0.0

Goaltending

No.	Goaltender	GPI	Mins	Avg	W	L	T	EN	SO	GA	SA	S%
35	Manny Fernandez	42	2461	2.24	19	17	4	1	4	92	1147	.920
30	* Derek Gustafson	4	239	2.51	1	3	0	1	0	10	97	.897
29	Jamie McLennan	38	2230	2.64	5	23	9	2	2	98	1032	.905
31	Zac Bierk	1	60	6.00	0	1	0	0	0	6	27	.778
	Totals	**82**	**5005**	**2.52**	**25**	**44**	**13**	**4**	**6**	**210**	**2307**	**.909**

Coach

LEMAIRE, JACQUES GERARD
Coach, Minnesota Wild. Born in LaSalle, Quebec, September 7, 1945.

The Minnesota Wild announced the signing of Jacques Lemaire as the club's first head coach on June 19, 2000. Lemaire had spent parts of the previous two seasons as a senior consultant to the general manager for the Montreal Canadiens, the franchise with which he captured eight Stanley Cup championships as a player.

Lemaire spent five seasons behind the New Jersey Devils bench and compiled a 199-122-57 mark. In 1994-95, he coached the Devils to their first Stanley Cup Championship. In his first season with the team (1993-94), he was awarded the Jack Adams Trophy as the NHL's outstanding coach.

Lemaire began his NHL coaching career with the Montreal Canadiens in 1983-84. The next year, he coached Montreal to the Adams Division Championship. He stepped aside as head coach following the 1984-85 campaign and moved to the front office where he held the position of assistant to the managing director for seven of his last eight years with the Canadiens. During that time, Lemaire played a role in Montreal's Stanley Cup Championships of 1986 and 1993.

Lemaire spent his entire NHL playing career with Montreal from 1967 to 1979. He then began his coaching career in Switzerland where he served as player/coach of the Sierre club. He returned to North America in 1981 and was named the first head coach of the Quebec Major Junior Hockey League's expansion Longueuil Chevaliers. In his only season at the helm (1982-83), Lemaire guided the team to the QMJHL finals.

Coaching Record

		Regular Season				Playoffs		
Season	Team	Games	W	L	T	Games	W	L
1979-80	Sierre (Switzerland)	UNAVAILABLE						
1980-81	Sierre (Switzerland)	UNAVAILABLE						
1982-83	Longueuil (QMJHL)	70	37	29	4	15	9	6
1983-84	**Montreal (NHL)**	**17**	**7**	**10**	**0**	**15**	**9**	**6**
1984-85	**Montreal (NHL)**	**80**	**41**	**27**	**12**	**12**	**6**	**6**
1993-94	**New Jersey (NHL)**	**84**	**47**	**25**	**12**	**20**	**11**	**9**
1994-95	**New Jersey (NHL)**	**48**	**22**	**18**	**8**	**20**	**16**	**4***
1995-96	**New Jersey (NHL)**	**82**	**37**	**33**	**12**	....	....	....
1996-97	**New Jersey (NHL)**	**82**	**45**	**23**	**14**	**10**	**5**	**5**
1997-98	**New Jersey (NHL)**	**82**	**48**	**23**	**11**	**6**	**2**	**4**
2000-01	**Minnesota (NHL)**	**82**	**25**	**44**	**13**	....	....	....
	NHL Totals	**557**	**272**	**203**	**82**	**83**	**49**	**34**

* Stanley Cup win.

Club Records

Team

(Figures in brackets for season records are games played.)

Most Points	**68**	2000-01 (82)
Most Wins	**25**	2000-01 (82)
Most Ties	**13**	2000-01 (82)
Most Losses	**39**	2000-01 (82)
Most Goals	**168**	2000-01 (82)
Most Goals Against	**210**	2000-01 (82)
Fewest Points	**68**	2000-01 (82)
Fewest Wins	**25**	2000-01 (82)
Fewest Ties	**13**	2000-01 (82)
Fewest Losses	**39**	2000-01 (82)
Fewest Goals	**168**	2000-01 (82)
Fewest Goals Against	**210**	2000-01 (82)
Longest Winning Streak		
Overall	**2**	Five times
Home	**2**	Three times
Away	**2**	Jan. 24-Jan. 27/01
Longest Undefeated Streak		
Overall	**8**	Dec. 17/00-Jan. 5/01 (5 wins, 3 ties)
Home	**9**	Dec. 13/00-Jan. 10/01 (5 wins, 4 ties)
Away	**2**	Jan. 24-Jan. 27/01 (2 wins)
Longest Losing Streak		
Overall	**5**	Mar. 11-Mar. 19/01
Home	**4**	Oct. 29-Nov. 15/00
Away	**5**	Mar. 15-Apr. 2/01
Longest Winless Streak		
Overall	**12**	Mar. 11-Apr. 4/01 (9 losses, 3 ties)
Home	**8**	Feb. 26-Mar. 28/01 (5 losses, 3 ties)
Away	**6**	Three times
Most Shutouts, Season	**6**	2000-01 (82)
Most PIM, Season		2000-01 (82)
Most Goals, Game	**6**	Oct. 18/2000 (T.B. 5 at Min. 6) Nov. 18/2000 (Min. 6 at Bos. 1) Dec. 17/2000 (Dal. 0 at Min. 6)

Individual

Most Seasons	**1**	Many players
Most Games	**82**	Wes Walz, Antti Laaksonen
Most Goals, Career	**18**	Marian Gaborik, Wes Walz, Darby Hendrickson
Most Assists, Career	**23**	Lubomir Sekeras
Most Points, Career	**36**	Marian Gaborik (18G, 18A)
Most PIM, Career	**137**	Matt Johnson
Most Shutouts, Career	**4**	Manny Fernandez
Most Goals, Season	**18**	Marian Gaborik (2000-01), Wes Walz (2000-01), Darby Hendrickson (2000-01)
Most Assists, Season	**23**	Lubomir Sekeras (2000-01)
Most Points, Season	**36**	Marian Gaborik (2000-01; 18G, 18A)
Most PIM, Season	**137**	Matt Johnson (2000-01)
Most Points, Defenseman, Season	**34**	Lubomir Sekeras (2000-01; 11G, 23A)
Most Points, Center, Season	**30**	Wes Walz (2000-01; 18G, 12A)
Most Points, Right Wing, Season	**22**	Sergei Krivokrasov (2000-01; 7G, 15A)
Most Points, Left Wing, Season	**36**	Marian Gaborik (2000-01; 18G, 18A)
Most Points, Rookie, Season	**36**	Marian Gaborik (2000-01; 18G, 18A)
Most Shutouts, Season	**4**	Manny Fernandez (2000-01)
Most Goals, Game	**3**	Antti Laaksonen (Nov. 26/00)
Most Assists, Game	**3**	Four times
Most Points, Game	**4**	Scott Pellerin (Oct. 18/00; 1G, 3A), Antti Laaksonen (Nov. 26/00; 3G, 1A)

General Managers' History

Doug Risebrough, 2000-01 to date.

Coaching History

Jacques Lemaire, 2000-01 to date.

Captains' History

No captain, 2000-01.

Goaltender Manny Fernandez complemented a tight defensive system that saw the Wild allow just 210 goals in their first season, 12th among the NHL's 30 teams.

All-time Record vs. Other Clubs

Regular Season

	At Home								On Road								Total							
	GP	W	L	T	OL	GF	GA	PTS	GP	W	L	T	OL	GF	GA	PTS	GP	W	L	T	OL	GF	GA	PTS
Anaheim	2	1	0	0	1	3	3	3	2	1	1	0	0	6	3	2	4	2	1	0	1	9	6	5
Atlanta	1	0	0	1	0	1	1	1	0	0	0	0	0	0	0	0	1	0	0	1	0	1	1	1
Boston	0	0	0	0	0	0	0	0	1	1	0	0	0	6	1	2	1	1	0	0	0	6	1	2
Buffalo	0	0	0	0	0	0	0	0	1	0	1	0	0	1	3	0	1	0	1	0	0	1	3	0
Calgary	3	1	1	1	0	4	3	3	2	1	0	1	0	4	3	3	5	2	1	2	0	8	6	6
Carolina	1	0	0	1	0	1	1	1	0	0	0	0	0	0	0	0	1	0	0	1	0	1	1	1
Chicago	2	1	1	0	0	4	3	2	2	2	0	0	0	9	4	4	4	3	1	0	0	13	7	6
Colorado	2	0	2	0	0	2	9	0	3	0	3	0	0	4	10	0	5	0	5	0	0	6	19	0
Columbus	2	2	0	0	0	6	4	4	1	0	1	0	0	0	3	0	3	2	1	0	0	6	7	4
Dallas	2	1	1	0	0	7	4	2	2	1	1	0	0	4	7	2	4	2	2	0	0	11	11	4
Detroit	2	1	0	0	1	5	5	3	2	1	1	0	0	7	7	2	4	2	1	0	1	12	12	5
Edmonton	2	0	1	0	1	7	10	1	3	0	2	1	0	3	8	1	5	0	3	1	1	10	18	2
Florida	1	0	0	1	0	0	0	1	1	0	1	0	0	1	2	0	2	0	1	1	0	1	2	1
Los Angeles	2	1	1	0	0	4	7	2	2	1	1	0	0	6	4	2	4	2	2	0	0	10	11	4
Montreal	0	0	0	0	0	0	0	0	1	0	0	1	0	2	2	1	1	0	0	1	0	2	2	1
Nashville	2	0	1	1	0	1	2	1	2	0	2	0	0	2	6	0	4	0	3	1	0	3	8	1
New Jersey	1	0	1	0	0	2	4	0	1	0	1	0	0	2	6	0	2	0	2	0	0	4	10	0
NY Islanders	1	1	0	0	0	3	2	2	1	1	0	0	0	4	1	2	2	2	0	0	0	7	3	4
NY Rangers	1	0	1	0	0	2	3	0	1	0	1	0	0	2	4	0	2	0	2	0	0	4	7	0
Ottawa	1	0	0	1	0	2	2	1	0	0	0	0	0	0	0	0	1	0	0	1	0	2	2	1
Philadelphia	1	0	0	1	0	3	3	1	1	0	1	0	0	0	3	0	2	0	1	1	0	3	6	1
Phoenix	2	0	1	1	0	2	4	1	2	0	2	0	0	1	6	0	4	0	3	1	0	3	10	1
Pittsburgh	1	1	0	0	0	4	2	2	1	0	1	0	0	1	2	0	2	1	1	0	0	5	4	2
St. Louis	2	0	0	1	1	3	4	2	2	0	2	0	0	1	7	0	4	0	2	1	1	4	11	2
San Jose	2	1	1	0	0	4	4	2	2	0	2	0	0	3	8	0	4	1	3	0	0	7	12	2
Tampa Bay	1	1	0	0	0	6	5	2	1	1	0	0	0	4	2	2	2	2	0	0	0	10	7	4
Toronto	0	0	0	0	0	0	0	0	1	0	1	0	0	1	6	0	1	0	1	0	0	1	6	0
Vancouver	3	1	1	1	0	8	9	3	2	1	0	0	1	6	6	3	5	2	1	1	1	14	15	6
Washington	1	1	0	0	0	3	0	2	1	0	1	0	0	1	2	0	2	1	1	0	0	4	2	2
Totals	**41**	**14**	**13**	**10**	**4**	**87**	**94**	**42**	**41**	**11**	**26**	**3**	**1**	**81**	**116**	**26**	**82**	**25**	**39**	**13**	**5**	**168**	**210**	**68**

2000-01 Results

Oct.	6	at Anaheim	1-3		10	Washington	3-0
	7	at Phoenix	1-4		12	Colorado	0-5
	11	Philadelphia	3-3		14	at NY Rangers	2-4
	13	at St. Louis	0-2		15	at Columbus	0-3
	15	Edmonton	3-5		17	Columbus	3-2*
	18	Tampa Bay	6-5		19	NY Islanders	3-2
	20	San Jose	1-3		21	New Jersey	2-4
	22	Florida	0-0		24	at Anaheim	5-0
	24	at Montreal	2-2		27	at Los Angeles	4-1
	25	at Toronto	1-6		30	at Vancouver	2-3*
	27	Calgary	3-1	**Feb.**	6	at Tampa Bay	4-2
	29	Chicago	2-3		7	at Florida	1-2
Nov.	3	at Edmonton	0-3		9	at Dallas	2-1
	5	at Calgary	3-2*		11	Pittsburgh	4-2
	7	at Colorado	0-2		14	at Pittsburgh	1-2
	8	Calgary	0-1		16	Los Angeles	0-4
	10	at Chicago	5-2		18	San Jose	3-1
	12	Edmonton	4-5*		21	at Dallas	2-6
	15	NY Rangers	2-3		23	at Colorado	1-4
	17	at Buffalo	1-3		24	at Nashville	1-2
	18	at Boston	6-1		26	Vancouver	2-5
	22	Calgary	1-1	**Mar.**	1	at Calgary	1-1
	24	Chicago	2-0		2	at Edmonton	1-3
	26	Vancouver	4-2		4	at Vancouver	4-3*
	28	at San Jose	1-4		6	St. Louis	3-3
	30	at Phoenix	0-2		8	at New Jersey	2-6
Dec.	2	at Los Angeles	2-3		9	at NY Islanders	4-1
	7	at Chicago	4-2		11	Detroit	2-3*
	8	Anaheim	0-1*		14	St. Louis	0-1*
	10	Nashville	1-2		15	at Philadelphia	0-3
	13	Carolina	1-1		18	at Colorado	3-4
	14	at Washington	1-2		19	Dallas	1-4
	17	Dallas	6-0		21	Nashville	0-0
	20	Ottawa	2-2		22	at Detroit	2-4
	22	Los Angeles	4-3		25	Vancouver	2-2
	27	at Detroit	5-3		28	Phoenix	0-2
	29	Phoenix	2-2		31	at Nashville	1-4
	31	Anaheim	3-2	**Apr.**	2	at San Jose	2-4
Jan.	3	Atlanta	1-1		4	at Edmonton	2-2
	5	Detroit	3-2*		6	Columbus	3-2
	6	at St. Louis	1-5		8	Colorado	2-4

* – Overtime

Entry Draft Selections 2001-2000

2001 Pick		2000 Pick	
6	Mikko Koivu	3	Marian Gaborik
36	Kyle Wanvig	33	Nick Schultz
74	Chris Heid	99	Marc Cavosie
93	Stephane Veilleux	132	Maxim Sushinsky
103	Tony Virta	199	Brian Passmore
202	Derek Boogaard	214	Peter Bartos
239	Jake Riddle	232	Lubomir Sekeras
		255	Eric Johansson

Originally selected by Tampa Bay in their inaugural season, Aaron Gavey was one of six Minnesota players to reach double digits in goals in year one.

Club Directory

Xcel Energy Center

Minnesota Wild
317 Washington Street
St. Paul, MN 55102
Phone **651/602-6000**
FAX 651/222-1055
Tickets 651/222-9453
www.wild.com/
Capacity: 18,064

Executive Management

Chairman	Bob Naegele, Jr.
Chief Executive Officer	Jac Sperling
President and Chief Operating Officer	Tod Leiweke
Exec. V.P./General Manager	Doug Risebrough
Chief Financial Officer	Martha Fuller
President of Saint Paul Arena Company	Chris Hansen
Vice President of Finance	Steve Calamia
Vice President of Corporate Partnerships	Laura Day
Vice President of Customer Sales and Service	Steve Griggs
Vice President of Information Technology	Brian Jore
Vice President of Marketing	Matt Majka
Vice President of Human Resources/ Customer Care	Mike Reeves
Vice President of Communications and Broadcasting	Bill Robertson
Vice President of Saint Paul Arena Company	Jim Ibister

Administration

Xcel Energy Center Project Director	Ray Chandler
Assistant Xcel Energy Center Project Director	Mark Anger
Manager of Special Projects	Kris Parod
Facilities Manager	Tim Wolfgram
Executive Assistant to the CEO	Heather Bernier
Executive Assistant to the President/COO	Stephanie Huseby
Executive Assistant to the CFO	Maggie Hobbs
Executive Assistant to the General Manager	Martha Trowbridge
Executive Assistant to the Arena President	CJ Neale

Coaching Staff

Head Coach	Jacques Lemaire
Assistant Coaches	Mike Ramsey, Mario Tremblay
Strength and Conditioning Coach	George Kinnear
Goaltending Consultant	Andre Lebrun

Hockey Operations

Director of Hockey Adminstration and Legal Affairs	Tom Lynn
Chief Amateur Scout	Tom Thompson
Coordinator of Amateur Scouting	Guy Lapointe
Scouts	Marc Chamard, Paul Charles, Chris Coveny, Frank Effinger, Branislav Gaborik, Glen Giovanucci, Ken Hoodikoff, Patrick Kipler, Jiri Koluch, David Mayville, Doug Mosher, Rick Pracey, Noel Rahn, Glen Sonmor, Bruce Southern, Thomas Steen, Rich Sutter, Matti Vaisanen
Head Athletic Therapist	Don Fuller
Head Equipment Manager	Tony DaCosta
Assistant Athletic Trainer	Mike Vogt
Assistant Equipment Manager	Brent Proulx
Video Coordinator	Todd Woodcroft
Hockey Operations Assistant	Tobin Wright
Hockey Operations Adminstrator	Cindy Sweiger
Hockey Operations Intern	Denny Scanlon
Medical Director	Dr. Sheldon Burns
Orthopedic Surgeon	Dr. Joel Boyd

Finance

Director of Finance	Brian Gramm
Accounting Manager	Anita Cunningham
Manager of Benefits and Payroll	Tim Case

Information Technology

Manager of Network Communications	Chris Monicatti

Corporate Partnerships

Director of Corporate Services	Carin Anderson
Director of Premium Service and Operations	Rachael Johnson
Manager of Service and Operations	Rob Asperheim

Customer Sales and Service

Director of Ticket Operations and Customer Service	Holly Cedarblade
Director of Group Sales	Kelly Harens
Director of Sales	Jamie Spencer

Marketing

Director of Events/Production	John Maher
Director of Retail Operations	Chris Poitras
Director of Advertising and Promotions	Wayne Peterson
Executive Director of the 10,000 Rinks Foundation	Heather McGinty
Director of Community Relations	Marlene Wall
Museum Curator	Roger Godin

Communications and Broadcasting

Director of Internet Services	Brian Hutchinson
Director of Publications/Creative Services	Brian Israel
Director of Broadcasting	Pat O'Connor
Manager of Media Relations/Team Services	Brad Smith
Manager of Arena Communications	Chris Kelleher
Manager, Corporate Communications and Internet Services	Aaron Sickman

Micellaneous

Training Site	Parade Ice Garden
Primary Affiliate	Houston Aeros (AHL)
Radio Network Flagship	WCCO (830 AM)
T.V. Networks	KMSP 9 (over-air), FOX Sports Net
Radio Play-by-Play Broadcaster	Bob Kurtz
Radio Color Analyst	Barry Buetel
Television Play-by-Play Broadcaster	Mike Goldberg
Television Color Analyst	Tom Reid
Team Photographer	Bruck Kluckhohn

Montreal Canadiens

2000-01 Results: 28W-40L-8T-6OTL 70PTS. Fifth, Northeast Division

Brian Savage (left) led the Canadiens with 21 goals last season while Oleg Petrov (right) tied Saku Koivu with 30 assists and 47 points.

2001-02 Schedule

Month	Day	Date	Opponent
Oct.	Thu.	4	at Ottawa
	Sat.	6	Toronto
	Tue.	9	Anaheim
	Fri.	12	at Columbus
	Sat.	13	New Jersey
	Mon.	15	NY Rangers
	Fri.	19	at Washington
	Sat.	20	Buffalo
	Fri.	26	at Buffalo
	Sat.	27	Philadelphia
	Tue.	30	at Edmonton
Nov.	Thu.	1	at Vancouver
	Sat.	3	at Calgary*
	Tue.	6	Colorado
	Thu.	8	Nashville
	Sat.	10	NY Islanders
	Sun.	11	at NY Rangers
	Tue.	13	at Boston
	Sat.	17	Florida
	Tue.	20	Boston
	Thu.	22	at Atlanta
	Sat.	24	Washington
	Tue.	27	Atlanta
	Thu.	29	at NY Islanders
Dec.	Sat.	1	NY Rangers
	Mon.	3	Chicago
	Wed.	5	New Jersey
	Sat.	8	Phoenix
	Mon.	10	Minnesota
	Wed.	12	at Atlanta
	Thu.	13	at Philadelphia
	Sat.	15	at Toronto
	Mon.	17	Tampa Bay
	Wed.	19	at Pittsburgh
	Thu.	20	at Boston
	Sat.	22	Los Angeles
	Wed.	26	at Buffalo
	Fri.	28	at St. Louis
	Sat.	29	at NY Islanders
Jan.	Thu.	3	at Vancouver
	Sat.	5	at Calgary*

Month	Day	Date	Opponent
	Sun.	6	at Edmonton
	Tue.	8	at Minnesota
	Thu.	10	NY Islanders
	Sat.	12	at Toronto
	Mon.	14	Philadelphia
	Wed.	16	Washington
	Thu.	17	at Carolina
	Sat.	19	at Tampa Bay
	Mon.	21	at Florida*
	Wed.	23	at Washington
	Sat.	26	Ottawa*
	Sun.	27	San Jose*
	Wed.	30	Boston
Feb.	Tue.	5	at New Jersey
	Thu.	7	Pittsburgh
	Sat.	9	at Toronto*
	Mon.	11	Detroit
	Tue.	26	Ottawa
	Wed.	27	at Chicago
Mar.	Sat.	2	Carolina
	Mon.	4	Atlanta
	Wed.	6	Boston
	Fri.	8	at Buffalo
	Sat.	9	Toronto
	Mon.	11	at NY Rangers
	Thu.	14	Dallas
	Sat.	16	Carolina
	Mon.	18	at Carolina
	Wed.	20	at Florida
	Fri.	22	at Tampa Bay
	Sat.	23	at Nashville
	Tue.	26	Florida
	Thu.	28	Tampa Bay
	Sat.	30	Pittsburgh
Apr.	Mon.	1	at Pittsburgh
	Thu.	4	at Philadelphia
	Sat.	6	Columbus
	Sun.	7	at Ottawa
	Tue.	9	Ottawa
	Fri.	12	at New Jersey
	Sat.	13	Buffalo

* Denotes afternoon game.

Franchise date: November 22, 1917

NORTHEAST DIVISION

85th NHL Season

Year-by-Year Record

Season	GP	Home W	Home L	Home T	Home OL	Road W	Road L	Road T	Road OL	Overall W	Overall L	Overall T	Overall OL	GF	GA	Pts.	Finished	Playoff Result
2000-01	82	15	20	4	2	13	20	4	4	28	40	8	6	206	232	70	5th, Northeast Div.	Out of Playoffs
1999-2000	82	18	17	5	1	17	17	4	3	35	34	9	4	196	194	83	4th, Northeast Div.	Out of Playoffs
1998-99	82	21	15	5	...	11	24	6	...	32	39	11	...	184	209	75	5th, Northeast Div.	Out of Playoffs
1997-98	82	15	17	9	...	22	15	4	...	37	32	13	...	235	208	87	4th, Northeast Div.	Lost Conf. Semi-Final
1996-97	82	17	17	7	...	14	19	8	...	31	36	15	...	249	276	77	4th, Northeast Div.	Lost Conf. Quarter-Final
1995-96	82	23	12	6	...	17	20	4	...	40	32	10	...	265	248	90	3rd, Northeast Div.	Lost Conf. Quarter-Final
1994-95	48	15	5	4	...	3	18	3	...	18	23	7	...	125	148	43	6th, Northeast Div.	Out of Playoffs
1993-94	84	26	12	4	...	15	17	10	...	41	29	14	...	283	248	96	3rd, Northeast Div.	Lost Conf. Quarter-Final
1992-93	**84**	**27**	**13**	**2**	**...**	**21**	**17**	**4**	**...**	**48**	**30**	**6**	**...**	**326**	**280**	**102**	**3rd, Adams Div.**	**Won Stanley Cup**
1991-92	80	27	8	5	...	14	20	6	...	41	28	11	...	267	207	93	1st, Adams Div.	Lost Div. Final
1990-91	80	23	12	5	...	16	18	6	...	39	30	11	...	273	249	89	2nd, Adams Div.	Lost Div. Final
1989-90	80	26	8	6	...	15	20	5	...	41	28	11	...	288	234	93	3rd, Adams Div.	Lost Div. Final
1988-89	80	30	6	4	...	23	12	5	...	53	18	9	...	315	218	115	1st, Adams Div.	Lost Final
1987-88	80	26	8	6	...	19	14	7	...	45	22	13	...	298	238	103	1st, Adams Div.	Lost Div. Final
1986-87	80	27	9	4	...	14	20	6	...	41	29	10	...	277	241	92	2nd, Adams Div.	Lost Conf. Championship
1985-86	**80**	**25**	**11**	**4**	**...**	**15**	**22**	**3**	**...**	**40**	**33**	**7**	**...**	**330**	**280**	**87**	**2nd, Adams Div.**	**Won Stanley Cup**
1984-85	80	24	10	6	...	17	17	6	...	41	27	12	...	309	262	94	1st, Adams Div.	Lost Div. Final
1983-84	80	19	19	2	...	16	21	3	...	35	40	5	...	286	295	75	4th, Adams Div.	Lost Conf. Championship
1982-83	80	25	6	9	...	17	18	5	...	42	24	14	...	350	286	98	2nd, Adams Div.	Lost Div. Semi-Final
1981-82	80	25	6	9	...	21	11	8	...	46	17	17	...	360	223	109	1st, Adams Div.	Lost Div. Semi-Final
1980-81	80	31	7	2	...	14	15	11	...	45	22	13	...	332	232	103	1st, Norris Div.	Lost Prelim. Round
1979-80	80	30	7	3	...	17	13	10	...	47	20	13	...	328	240	107	1st, Norris Div.	Lost Quarter-Final
1978-79	**80**	**29**	**6**	**5**	**...**	**23**	**11**	**6**	**...**	**52**	**17**	**11**	**...**	**337**	**204**	**115**	**1st, Norris Div.**	**Won Stanley Cup**
1977-78	**80**	**32**	**4**	**4**	**...**	**27**	**6**	**7**	**...**	**59**	**10**	**11**	**...**	**359**	**183**	**129**	**1st, Norris Div.**	**Won Stanley Cup**
1976-77	**80**	**33**	**1**	**6**	**...**	**27**	**7**	**6**	**...**	**60**	**8**	**12**	**...**	**387**	**171**	**132**	**1st, Norris Div.**	**Won Stanley Cup**
1975-76	**80**	**32**	**3**	**5**	**...**	**26**	**8**	**6**	**...**	**58**	**11**	**11**	**...**	**337**	**174**	**127**	**1st, Norris Div.**	**Won Stanley Cup**
1974-75	80	27	8	5	...	20	6	14	...	47	14	19	...	374	225	113	1st, Norris Div.	Lost Semi-Final
1973-74	78	24	12	3	...	21	12	6	...	45	24	9	...	293	240	99	2nd, East Div.	Lost Quarter-inal
1972-73	**78**	**29**	**4**	**6**	**...**	**23**	**6**	**10**	**...**	**52**	**10**	**16**	**...**	**329**	**184**	**120**	**1st, East Div.**	**Won Stanley Cup**
1971-72	78	29	3	7	...	17	13	9	...	46	16	16	...	307	205	108	3rd, East Div.	Lost Quarter-Final
1970-71	**78**	**29**	**7**	**3**	**...**	**13**	**16**	**10**	**...**	**42**	**23**	**13**	**...**	**291**	**216**	**97**	**3rd, East Div.**	**Won Stanley Cup**
1969-70	76	21	9	8	...	17	13	8	...	38	22	16	...	244	201	92	5th, East Div.	Out of Playoffs
1968-69	**76**	**26**	**7**	**5**	**...**	**20**	**12**	**6**	**...**	**46**	**19**	**11**	**...**	**271**	**202**	**103**	**1st, East Div.**	**Won Stanley Cup**
1967-68	**74**	**26**	**5**	**6**	**...**	**16**	**17**	**4**	**...**	**42**	**22**	**10**	**...**	**236**	**167**	**94**	**1st, East Div.**	**Won Stanley Cup**
1966-67	70	19	9	7	...	13	16	6	...	32	25	13	...	202	188	77	2nd,	Lost Final
1965-66	**70**	**23**	**11**	**1**	**...**	**18**	**10**	**7**	**...**	**41**	**21**	**8**	**...**	**239**	**173**	**90**	**1st,**	**Won Stanley Cup**
1964-65	**70**	**20**	**8**	**7**	**...**	**16**	**15**	**4**	**...**	**36**	**23**	**11**	**...**	**211**	**185**	**83**	**2nd,**	**Won Stanley Cup**
1963-64	70	22	7	6	...	14	14	7	...	36	21	13	...	209	167	85	1st,	Lost Semi-Final
1962-63	70	15	10	10	...	13	9	13	...	28	19	23	...	225	183	79	3rd,	Lost Semi-Final
1961-62	70	26	2	7	...	16	12	7	...	42	14	14	...	259	166	98	1st,	Lost Semi-Final
1960-61	70	24	6	5	...	17	13	5	...	41	19	10	...	254	188	92	1st,	Lost Semi-Final
1959-60	**70**	**23**	**4**	**8**	**...**	**17**	**14**	**4**	**...**	**40**	**18**	**12**	**...**	**255**	**178**	**92**	**1st,**	**Won Stanley Cup**
1958-59	**70**	**21**	**8**	**6**	**...**	**18**	**10**	**7**	**...**	**39**	**18**	**13**	**...**	**258**	**158**	**91**	**1st,**	**Won Stanley Cup**
1957-58	**70**	**23**	**8**	**4**	**...**	**20**	**9**	**6**	**...**	**43**	**17**	**10**	**...**	**250**	**158**	**96**	**1st,**	**Won Stanley Cup**
1956-57	**70**	**23**	**6**	**6**	**...**	**12**	**17**	**6**	**...**	**35**	**23**	**12**	**...**	**210**	**155**	**82**	**2nd,**	**Won Stanley Cup**
1955-56	**70**	**29**	**5**	**1**	**...**	**16**	**10**	**9**	**...**	**45**	**15**	**10**	**...**	**222**	**131**	**100**	**1st,**	**Won Stanley Cup**
1954-55	70	26	5	4	...	15	13	7	...	41	18	11	...	228	157	93	2nd,	Lost Final
1953-54	70	27	5	3	...	8	19	8	...	35	24	11	...	195	141	81	2nd,	Lost Final
1952-53	**70**	**18**	**12**	**5**	**...**	**10**	**11**	**14**	**...**	**28**	**23**	**19**	**...**	**155**	**148**	**75**	**2nd,**	**Won Stanley Cup**
1951-52	70	22	8	5	...	12	18	5	...	34	26	10	...	195	164	78	2nd,	Lost Final
1950-51	70	17	10	8	...	8	20	7	...	25	30	15	...	173	184	65	3rd,	Lost Final
1949-50	70	17	8	10	...	12	14	9	...	29	22	19	...	172	150	77	2nd,	Lost Semi-Final
1948-49	60	19	8	3	...	9	15	6	...	28	23	9	...	152	126	65	3rd,	Lost Semi-Final
1947-48	60	13	13	4	...	7	16	7	...	20	29	11	...	147	169	51	5th,	Out of Playoffs
1946-47	60	19	6	5	...	15	10	5	...	34	16	10	...	189	138	78	1st,	Lost Final
1945-46	**50**	**16**	**6**	**3**	**...**	**12**	**11**	**2**	**...**	**28**	**17**	**5**	**...**	**172**	**134**	**61**	**1st,**	**Won Stanley Cup**
1944-45	50	21	2	2	...	17	6	2	...	38	8	4	...	228	121	80	1st,	Lost Semi-Final
1943-44	**50**	**22**	**0**	**3**	**...**	**16**	**5**	**4**	**...**	**38**	**5**	**7**	**...**	**234**	**109**	**83**	**1st,**	**Won Stanley Cup**
1942-43	50	14	4	7	...	5	15	5	...	19	19	12	...	181	191	50	4th,	Lost Semi-Final
1941-42	48	12	10	2	...	6	17	1	...	18	27	3	...	134	173	39	6th,	Lost Quarter-Final
1940-41	48	11	9	4	...	5	17	2	...	16	26	6	...	121	147	38	6th,	Lost Quarter-Final
1939-40	48	5	14	5	...	5	19	0	...	10	33	5	...	90	167	25	7th,	Out of Playoffs
1938-39	48	8	11	5	...	7	13	4	...	15	24	9	...	115	146	39	6th,	Lost Quarter-Final
1937-38	48	13	4	7	...	5	13	6	...	18	17	13	...	123	128	49	3rd, Cdn. Div.	Lost Quarter-Final
1936-37	48	16	8	0	...	8	10	6	...	24	18	6	...	115	111	54	1st, Cdn. Div.	Lost Semi-Final
1935-36	48	5	11	8	...	6	15	3	...	11	26	11	...	82	123	33	4th, Cdn. Div.	Out of Playoffs
1934-35	48	11	11	2	...	8	12	4	...	19	23	6	...	110	145	44	3rd, Cdn. Div.	Lost Quarter-Final
1933-34	48	16	6	2	...	6	14	4	...	22	20	6	...	99	101	50	2nd, Cdn. Div.	Lost Quarter-Final
1932-33	48	15	5	4	...	3	20	1	...	18	25	5	...	92	115	41	3rd, Cdn. Div.	Lost Quarter-Final
1931-32	48	18	3	3	...	7	13	4	...	25	16	7	...	128	111	57	1st, Cdn. Div.	Lost Semi-Final
1930-31	**44**	**15**	**3**	**4**	**...**	**11**	**7**	**4**	**...**	**26**	**10**	**8**	**...**	**129**	**89**	**60**	**1st, Cdn. Div.**	**Won Stanley Cup**
1929-30	**44**	**13**	**5**	**4**	**...**	**8**	**9**	**5**	**...**	**21**	**14**	**9**	**...**	**142**	**114**	**51**	**2nd, Cdn. Div.**	**Won Stanley Cup**
1928-29	44	12	4	6	...	10	3	9	...	22	7	15	...	71	43	59	1st, Cdn. Div.	Lost Semi-Final
1927-28	44	12	7	3	...	14	4	4	...	26	11	7	...	116	48	59	1st, Cdn. Div.	Lost Semi-Final
1926-27	44	15	5	2	...	13	9	0	...	28	14	2	...	99	67	58	2nd, Cdn. Div.	Lost Semi-Final
1925-26	36	5	12	1	...	6	12	0	...	11	24	1	...	79	108	23	7th,	Out of Playoffs
1924-25	30	10	5	0	...	7	6	2	...	17	11	2	...	93	56	36	3rd,	Lost Final
1923-24	**24**	**10**	**2**	**0**	**...**	**3**	**9**	**0**	**...**	**13**	**11**	**0**	**...**	**59**	**48**	**26**	**2nd,**	**Won Stanley Cup**
1922-23	24	10	2	0	...	3	7	2	...	13	9	2	...	73	61	28	2nd,	Lost NHL Final
1921-22	24	8	3	1	...	4	8	0	...	12	11	1	...	88	94	25	3rd,	Out of Playoffs
1920-21	24	9	3	0	...	4	8	0	...	13	11	0	...	112	99	26	3rd and 2nd*	Out of Playoffs
1919-20	24	8	4	0	...	5	7	0	...	13	11	0	...	129	113	26	2nd and 3rd*	Out of Playoffs
1918-19	18	7	2	0	...	3	6	0	...	10	8	0	...	88	78	20	1st and 2nd*	Cup Final but no Decision
1917-18	22	8	3	0	...	5	6	0	...	13	9	0	...	115	84	26	1st and 3rd*	Lost NHL Final

* Season played in two halves with no combined standing at end.
From 1917-18 through 1925-26, NHL champions played against PCHA/WCHL champions for Stanley Cup.

2001-02 Player Personnel

FORWARDS	HT	WT	S	Place of Birth	Date	2000-01 Club
ASHAM, Arron	5-11	209	R	Portage La Prairie, Man.	4/13/78	Montreal-Quebec (AHL)
BELANGER, Francis	6-3	228	L	Bellefeuille, Que.	1/15/78	Phi (AHL)-Mtl-Que (AHL)
BRUNET, Benoit	6-0	203	L	Ste-Anne-de-Bellevue, Que.	8/24/68	Montreal
BULIS, Jan	6-1	208	L	Pardubice, Czech.	3/18/78	Wsh-Portland (AHL)-Mtl
CHOUINARD, Eric	6-3	205	L	Atlanta, GA	7/8/80	Montreal-Quebec (AHL)
DACKELL, Andreas	5-11	195	R	Gavle, Sweden	12/29/72	Ottawa
DARBY, Craig	6-3	197	R	Oneida, NY	9/26/72	Montreal
DELISLE, Xavier	5-11	193	R	Quebec City, Que.	5/24/77	Montreal-Quebec (AHL)
GRATTON, Benoit	5-11	194	L	Montreal, Que.	12/28/76	Calgary-Saint John
JUNEAU, Joe	6-0	198	L	Pont-Rouge, Que.	1/5/68	Phoenix
KILGER, Chad	6-3	215	L	Cornwall, Ont.	11/27/76	Edmonton-Montreal
KOIVU, Saku	5-10	180	L	Turku, Finland	11/23/74	Montreal
LANDRY, Eric	5-10	182	L	Gatineau, Que.	1/20/75	Montreal-Quebec (AHL)
ODJICK, Gino	6-3	217	L	Maniwaki, Que.	9/7/70	Philadelphia-Montreal
PERREAULT, Yanic	5-10	185	L	Sherbrooke, Que.	4/4/71	Toronto
PETROV, Oleg	5-9	171	L	Moscow, USSR	4/18/71	Montreal
POULIN, Patrick	6-1	216	L	Vanier, Que.	4/23/73	Montreal
RIBEIRO, Mike	6-0	177	L	Montreal, Que.	2/10/80	Montreal-Quebec (AHL)
RUCINSKY, Martin	6-1	205	L	Most, Czech.	3/11/71	Montreal
RYDER, Michael	6-1	191	R	St. John's, Nfld.	3/31/80	Tallahasee-Que (AHL)
SAVAGE, Brian	6-1	192	L	Sudbury, Ont.	2/24/71	Montreal
WARD, Jason	6-2	200	R	Chapleau, Ont.	1/16/79	Montreal-Quebec (AHL)
ZEDNIK, Richard	6-0	200	L	Bystrica, Czech.	1/6/76	Washington-Montreal
DEFENSEMEN						
BOUILLON, Francis	5-8	190	L	New York, NY	10/17/75	Montreal-Quebec (AHL)
BRISEBOIS, Patrice	6-1	203	R	Montreal, Que.	1/27/71	Montreal
DESCOTEAUX, Matthieu	6-4	208	L	Pierreville, Que.	9/23/77	Montreal-Quebec (AHL)
DYKHUIS, Karl	6-3	214	L	Sept-Iles, Que.	7/8/72	Montreal
GUREN, Miloslav	6-2	215	L	Uherske Hradiste, Czech.	9/24/76	Quebec (AHL)
MARKOV, Andrei	6-0	203	L	Voskresensk, USSR	12/20/78	Montreal-Quebec (AHL)
QUINTAL, Stephane	6-3	228	R	Boucherville, Que.	10/22/68	Chicago
RAZIN, Gennady	6-4	207	L	Kharkov, USSR	2/3/78	Quebec (AHL)
RIVET, Craig	6-2	207	R	North Bay, Ont.	9/13/74	Montreal
ROBIDAS, Stephane	5-11	189	R	Sherbrooke, Que.	3/3/77	Montreal
SOURAY, Sheldon	6-4	223	L	Elk Point, Alta.	7/13/76	Montreal
TRAVERSE, Patrick	6-4	204	L	Montreal, Que.	3/14/74	Ana-Bos-Mtl

GOALTENDERS	HT	WT	C	Place of Birth	Date	2000-01 Club
GARON, Mathieu	6-2	192	R	Chandler, Que.	1/9/78	Montreal-Quebec (AHL)
HACKETT, Jeff	6-1	198	L	London, Ont.	6/1/68	Montreal
THEODORE, Jose	5-11	182	R	Laval, Que.	9/13/76	Montreal-Quebec (AHL)

Coach

THERRIEN, MICHEL
Coach, Montreal Canadiens. Born in Montreal, Que., November 4, 1963.

Michel Therrien was named head coach of the Montreal Canadiens on November 20, 2000. He had joined the organization on June 10, 1997, as head coach of the AHL Fredericton Canadiens.

In his second season at the professional level in 1998-99, Therrien led the Fredericton Canadiens to the Eastern Conference finals, and was defeated in six games by the Calder Cup Champion Providence Bruins. Therrien became the first head coach of the AHL Québec Citadelles. He led the team to its first Division Championship with a 37-34-9 record in 1999-2000.

In 2000-2001, under Therrien, the Citadelles were leading the AHL Canadian Division, and second in the Eastern Conference with a 12-6-1-0 record when he was hired to replace Alain Vigneault as Canadiens' coach. Michel Therrien's career record in the AHL is 115-108-36 in 259 regular season games.

Before joining the Canadiens, Therrien coached the Laval Titan and the Granby Predateurs in the QMJHL, winning the Memorial Cup with Granby in 1996. He also reached the league finals twice with Laval in 1993-94 and 1994-95.

Coaching Record

		Regular Season				Playoffs		
Season	Team	Games	W	L	T	Games	W	L
1993-94	Laval (QMJHL)	72	49	22	1	21	14	7
1994-95	Laval (QMJHL)	72	48	22	2	20	14	6
1995-96	Granby (QMJHL)	70	56	12	2	21	17	4
1996-97	Granby (QMJHL)	70	44	20	6	5	1	4
1997-98	Fredericton (AHL)	80	33	32	15	4	1	3
1998-99	Fredericton (AHL)	80	33	36	11	15	9	6
1999-2000	Quebec (AHL)	80	37	34	9	3	0	3
2000-01	Quebec (AHL)	19	12	6	1	....	....	....
	Montreal (NHL)	**62**	**23**	**33**	**6**	....	....	....
	NHL Totals	**62**	**23**	**33**	**6**	....	....	....

2000-01 Scoring

* - rookie

Regular Season

Pos	#	Player	Team	GP	G	A	Pts	+/–	PIM	PP	SH	GW	GT	S	%
C	11	Saku Koivu	MTL	54	17	30	47	2	40	7	0	3	2	113	15.0
R	32	Oleg Petrov	MTL	81	17	30	47	–11	24	4	2	1	2	158	10.8
L	49	Brian Savage	MTL	62	21	24	45	–13	26	12	0	1	0	172	12.2
L	20	Richard Zednik	WSH	62	16	19	35	–2	61	4	0	3	1	155	10.3
			MTL	12	3	6	9	–2	10	1	0	0	0	23	13.0
			TOTAL	74	19	25	44	–4	71	5	0	3	1	178	10.7
L	26	Martin Rucinsky	MTL	57	16	22	38	–5	66	5	1	4	0	141	11.3
D	43	Patrice Brisebois	MTL	77	15	21	36	–31	28	11	0	4	0	178	8.4
C	25	Chad Kilger	EDM	34	5	2	7	–7	17	1	0	0	0	28	17.9
			MTL	43	9	16	25	–1	34	1	1	1	0	75	12.0
			TOTAL	77	14	18	32	–8	51	2	1	1	0	103	13.6
C	63	Craig Darby	MTL	78	12	16	28	–17	16	0	1	0	2	97	12.4
D	79 *	Andrei Markov	MTL	63	6	17	23	–6	18	2	0	0	0	82	7.3
C	38	Jan Bulis	WSH	39	5	13	18	0	26	1	0	0	0	41	12.2
			MTL	12	0	5	5	–1	0	0	0	0	0	20	0.0
			TOTAL	51	5	18	23	–1	26	1	0	0	0	61	8.2
C	37	Patrick Poulin	MTL	52	9	11	20	1	13	0	0	4	0	65	13.8
R	8	Jim Campbell	MTL	57	9	11	20	–3	53	6	0	1	0	81	11.1
D	28	Karl Dykhuis	MTL	67	8	9	17	9	44	2	0	1	0	66	12.1
D	54	Patrick Traverse	ANA	15	1	0	1	–6	6	0	0	0	0	7	14.3
			BOS	37	2	6	8	4	14	1	0	1	0	39	5.1
			MTL	19	2	3	5	–8	10	0	0	0	0	16	12.5
			TOTAL	71	5	9	14	–10	30	1	0	1	0	62	8.1
L	17	Benoit Brunet	MTL	35	3	11	14	–4	12	0	0	0	0	61	4.9
D	56 *	Stephane Robidas	MTL	65	6	6	12	0	14	1	0	0	0	77	7.8
C	78 *	Eric Landry	MTL	51	4	7	11	–9	43	2	0	0	0	54	7.4
D	44	Sheldon Souray	MTL	52	3	8	11	–11	95	0	0	2	0	103	2.9
L	47	Juha Lind	MTL	47	3	4	7	–4	4	0	0	2	0	36	8.3
D	51	Francis Bouillon	MTL	29	0	6	6	3	26	0	0	0	0	24	0.0
C	88 *	Xavier Delisle	MTL	14	3	2	5	–5	6	1	0	0	1	15	20.0
L	29	Gino Odjick	PHI	17	1	3	4	0	28	0	0	0	0	21	4.8
			MTL	13	1	0	1	0	44	0	0	0	0	11	9.1
			TOTAL	30	2	3	5	0	72	0	0	0	0	32	6.3
C	45	Arron Asham	MTL	46	2	3	5	–9	59	0	0	0	0	32	6.3
L	39	Johan Witehall	NYR	15	0	3	3	–5	8	0	0	0	0	16	0.0
			MTL	26	1	1	2	0	6	0	0	0	0	18	5.6
			TOTAL	41	1	4	5	–5	14	0	0	0	0	34	2.9
C	40 *	Eric Chouinard	MTL	13	1	3	4	0	0	1	0	0	0	11	9.1
D	52	Craig Rivet	MTL	26	1	2	3	–8	36	0	0	0	0	22	4.5
L	35	Andrei Bashkirov	MTL	18	0	3	3	–2	0	0	0	0	0	22	0.0
D	24	Christian Laflamme	MTL	39	0	3	3	–11	42	0	0	0	0	16	0.0
D	55 *	Matthieu Descoteaux	MTL	5	1	1	2	–2	4	1	0	0	0	6	16.7
G	60	Jose Theodore	MTL	59	1	0	1	0	6	0	0	0	0	1	100.0
D	29	Darryl Shannon	MTL	7	0	1	1	–4	6	0	0	0	0	6	0.0
G	31	Jeff Hackett	MTL	19	0	1	1	0	0	0	0	0	0	0	0.0
D	38	Barry Richter	MTL	2	0	0	0	–1	2	0	0	0	0	0	0.0
G	41	Eric Fichaud	MTL	2	0	0	0	0	0	0	0	0	0	0	0.0
C	71 *	Mike Ribeiro	MTL	2	0	0	0	0	2	0	0	0	0	3	0.0
D	39	Enrico Ciccone	MTL	3	0	0	0	–1	14	0	0	0	0	0	0.0
L	83 *	Eric Bertrand	MTL	3	0	0	0	0	0	0	0	0	0	0	0.0
C	46	Matt Higgins	MTL	6	0	0	0	–2	2	0	0	0	0	3	0.0
L	23 *	Francis Belanger	MTL	10	0	0	0	–3	29	0	0	0	0	2	0.0
G	30 *	Mathieu Garon	MTL	11	0	0	0	0	0	0	0	0	0	0	0.0
R	61	Jason Ward	MTL	12	0	0	0	3	12	0	0	0	0	4	0.0

Goaltending

No.	Goaltender	GPI	Mins	Avg	W	L	T	EN	SO	GA	SA	S%
30	* Mathieu Garon	11	589	2.44	4	5	1	1	2	24	233	.897
60	Jose Theodore	59	3298	2.57	20	29	5	6	2	141	1546	.909
31	Jeff Hackett	19	998	3.25	4	10	2	2	0	54	477	.887
41	Eric Fichaud	2	62	3.87	0	2	0	0	0	4	32	.875
	Totals	**82**	**4978**	**2.80**	**28**	**46**	**8**	**9**	**4**	**232**	**2297**	**.899**

Coaching History

Jack Laviolette, 1909-10; Adolphe Lecours, 1910-11; Napoleon Dorval, 1911-12, 1912-13; Jimmy Gardner, 1913-14, 1914-15; Newsy Lalonde, 1915-16 to 1920-21; Newsy Lalonde and Léo Dandurand, 1921-22; Léo Dandurand, 1922-23 to 1925-26; Cecil Hart, 1926-27 to 1931-32; Newsy Lalonde, 1932-33, 1933-34; Newsy Lalonde and Léo Dandurand, 1934-35; Sylvio Mantha, 1935-36; Cecil Hart, 1936-37, 1937-38; Cecil Hart and Jules Dugal, 1938-39; Babe Siebert, 1939*; Pit Lepine, 1939-40; Dick Irvin 1940-41 to 1954-55; Toe Blake, 1955-56 to 1967-68; Claude Ruel, 1968-69, 1969-70; Claude Ruel and Al MacNeil, 1970-71; Scotty Bowman, 1971-72 to 1978-79; Bernie Geoffrion and Claude Ruel, 1979-80; Claude Ruel, 1980-81; Bob Berry, 1981-82, 1982-83; Bob Berry and Jacques Lemaire, 1983-84; Jacques Lemaire, 1984-85; Jean Perron, 1985-86 to 1987-88; Pat Burns, 1988-89 to 1991-92; Jacques Demers, 1992-93 to 1994-95; Jacques Demers and Mario Tremblay, 1995-96; Mario Tremblay, 1996-97; Alain Vigneault, 1997-98 to 1999-2000; Alain Vigneault and Michel Therrien, 2000 -01; Michel Therrien, 2001-02.

* Named coach in summer but died before 1939-40 season began.

Captains' History

Jack Laviolette, 1909-10; Newsy Lalonde, 1910-11; Jack Laviolette, 1911-12; Newsy Lalonde, 1912-13; Jimmy Gardner, 1913-14, 1914-15; Howard McNamara, 1915-16; Newsy Lalonde, 1916-17 to 1921-22; Sprague Cleghorn, 1922-23 to 1924-25; Bill Coutu, 1925-26; Sylvio Mantha, 1926-27 to 1931-32; George Hainsworth, 1932-33; Sylvio Mantha, 1933-34 to 1935-36; Babe Siebert, 1936-37 to 1938-39; Walter Buswell, 1939-40; Toe Blake, 1940-41 to 1946-47; Toe Blake and Bill Durnan, 1947-48; Emile Bouchard, 1948-49 to 1955-56; Maurice Richard, 1956-57 to 1959-60; Doug Harvey, 1960-61; Jean Béliveau, 1961-62 to 1970-71; Henri Richard, 1971-72 to 1974-75; Yvan Cournoyer, 1975-76 to 1978-79; Serge Savard, 1979-80, 1980-81; Bob Gainey, 1981-82 to 1988-89; Guy Carbonneau and Chris Chelios (co-captains), 1989-90; Guy Carbonneau, 1990-91 to 1993-94; Kirk Muller and Mike Keane, 1994-95; Mike Keane and Pierre Turgeon, 1995-96; Pierre Turgeon and Vincent Damphousse, 1996-97; Vincent Damphousse, 1997-98, 1998-99; Saku Koivu, 1999-2000 to date.

Club Records

Team

(Figures in brackets for season records are games played; records for fewest points, wins, ties, losses, goals, goals against are for 70 or more games)

Most Points	*132	1976-77 (80)
Most Wins	60	1976-77 (80)
Most Ties	23	1962-63 (70)
Most Losses	40	1983-84 (80), 2000-01 (82)
Most Goals	387	1976-77 (80)
Most Goals Against	295	1983-84 (80)
Fewest Points	65	1950-51 (70)
Fewest Wins	25	1950-51 (70)
Fewest Ties	5	1983-84 (80)
Fewest Losses	*8	1976-77 (80)
Fewest Goals	155	1952-53 (70)
Fewest Goals Against	*131	1955-56 (70)
Longest Winning Streak		
Overall	12	Jan. 6-Feb. 3/68
Home	13	Nov. 2/43-Jan. 8/44, Jan. 30-Mar. 26/77
Away	8	Dec. 18/77-Jan. 18/78, Jan. 21-Feb. 21/82
Longest Undefeated Streak		
Overall	28	Dec. 18/77-Feb. 23/78 (23 wins, 5 ties)
Home	*34	Nov. 1/76-Apr. 2/77 (28 wins, 6 ties)
Away	*23	Nov. 27/74-Mar. 12/75 (14 wins, 9 ties)
Longest Losing Streak		
Overall	12	Feb. 13-Mar. 13/26
Home	7	Dec. 16/39-Jan. 18/40, Oct. 28-Nov. 25/00
Away	10	Jan. 16-Mar. 13/26
Longest Winless Streak		
Overall	12	Feb. 13-Mar. 13/26 (12 losses), Nov. 28-Dec. 29/35 (8 losses, 4 ties)
Home	15	Dec. 16/39-Mar. 7/40 (12 losses, 3 ties)
Away	12	Nov. 26/33-Jan. 28/34 (8 losses, 4 ties), Oct. 20/50-Dec. 13/51 (8 losses, 4 ties)
Most Shutouts, Season	*22	1928-29 (44)
Most PIM, Season	1,847	1995-96 (82)
Most Goals, Game	*16	Mar. 3/20 (Mtl. 16 at Que. 3)

Individual

Most Seasons	20	Henri Richard, Jean Béliveau
Most Games	1,256	Henri Richard
Most Goals, Career	544	Maurice Richard
Most Assists, Career	728	Guy Lafleur
Most Points, Career	1,246	Guy Lafleur (518G, 728A)
Most PIM, Career	2,248	Chris Nilan
Most Shutouts, Career	75	George Hainsworth
Longest Consecutive Games Streak	560	Doug Jarvis (Oct. 8/75-Apr. 4/82)
Most Goals, Season	60	Steve Shutt (1976-77), Guy Lafleur (1977-78)
Most Assists, Season	82	Peter Mahovlich (1974-75)
Most Points, Season	136	Guy Lafleur (1976-77; 56G, 80A)
Most PIM, Season	358	Chris Nilan (1984-85)
Most Points, Defenseman, Season	85	Larry Robinson (1976-77; 19G, 66A)
Most Points, Center, Season	117	Peter Mahovlich (1974-75; 35G, 82A)
Most Points, Right Wing, Season	136	Guy Lafleur (1976-77; 56G, 80A)
Most Points, Left Wing, Season	110	Mats Naslund (1985-86; 43G, 67A)
Most Points, Rookie, Season	71	Mats Naslund (1982-83; 26G, 45A), Kjell Dahlin (1985-86; 32G, 39A)
Most Shutouts, Season	*22	George Hainsworth (1928-29)
Most Goals, Game	6	Newsy Lalonde (Jan. 10/20)
Most Assists, Game	6	Elmer Lach (Feb. 6/43)
Most Points, Game	8	Maurice Richard (Dec. 28/44; 5G, 3A), Bert Olmstead (Jan. 9/54; 4G, 4A)

* NHL Record.

Retired Numbers

1	Jacques Plante	1952-1963
2	Doug Harvey	1947-1961
4	Jean Béliveau	1950-1971
7	Howie Morenz	1923-1937
9	Maurice Richard	1942-1960
10	Guy Lafleur	1971-1984
16	Henri Richard	1955-1975

All-time Record vs. Other Clubs

Regular Season

	At Home								On Road								Total							
	GP	W	L	T	OL	GF	GA	PTS	GP	W	L	T	OL	GF	GA	PTS	GP	W	L	T	OL	GF	GA	PTS
Anaheim	6	3	2	1	0	19	16	7	6	4	2	0	0	21	20	8	12	7	4	1	0	40	36	15
Atlanta	4	3	1	0	0	12	9	6	4	3	0	1	0	15	2	7	8	6	1	1	0	27	11	13
Boston	326	185	95	46	0	1101	774	416	327	121	148	56	2	886	963	300	653	306	243	102	2	1987	1737	716
Buffalo	95	53	30	12	0	370	285	118	94	28	47	19	0	257	295	75	189	81	77	31	0	627	580	193
Calgary	44	24	12	8	0	155	109	56	45	25	13	6	1	156	135	57	89	49	25	14	1	311	244	113
Carolina	69	46	15	7	1	291	196	100	72	35	27	9	1	258	217	80	141	81	42	16	2	549	413	180
Chicago	273	172	53	48	0	1055	643	392	272	124	93	55	0	758	729	303	545	296	146	103	0	1813	1372	695
Colorado	62	37	15	9	1	256	195	84	62	26	31	5	0	216	209	57	124	63	46	14	1	472	404	141
Columbus	1	0	1	0	0	0	2	0	0	0	0	0	0	0	0	0	1	0	1	0	0	0	2	0
Dallas	56	37	11	8	0	245	137	82	57	30	16	11	0	201	147	71	113	67	27	19	0	446	284	153
Detroit	280	171	66	43	0	990	632	385	279	96	129	53	1	714	803	246	559	267	195	96	1	1704	1435	631
Edmonton	28	15	8	4	1	100	89	35	31	16	14	0	1	98	99	33	59	31	22	4	2	198	188	68
Florida	15	6	7	2	0	43	37	14	16	5	8	3	0	42	52	13	31	11	15	5	0	85	89	27
Los Angeles	62	43	8	11	0	284	158	97	63	36	18	9	0	251	195	81	125	79	26	20	0	535	353	178
Minnesota	1	0	0	1	0	2	2	1	0	0	0	0	0	0	0	0	1	0	0	1	0	2	2	1
Nashville	2	2	0	0	0	7	4	4	2	0	1	1	0	3	8	1	4	2	1	1	0	10	12	5
New Jersey	48	29	13	6	0	170	126	64	48	24	21	3	0	183	144	51	96	53	34	9	0	353	270	115
NY Islanders	54	31	14	9	0	199	159	71	54	24	24	5	1	157	166	54	108	55	38	14	1	356	325	125
NY Rangers	284	188	57	39	0	1112	651	415	284	114	116	54	0	828	826	282	568	302	173	93	0	1940	1477	697
Ottawa	25	14	8	3	0	78	68	31	23	11	11	1	0	64	65	23	48	25	19	4	0	142	133	54
Philadelphia	68	34	20	14	0	245	206	82	67	25	26	16	0	202	204	66	135	59	46	30	0	447	410	148
Phoenix	28	24	3	1	0	139	63	49	27	11	9	7	0	104	89	29	55	35	12	8	0	243	152	78
Pittsburgh	76	57	10	9	0	364	193	123	76	36	27	13	0	267	229	85	152	93	37	22	0	631	422	208
St. Louis	57	40	10	7	0	248	154	87	56	28	13	15	0	195	144	71	113	68	23	22	0	443	298	158
San Jose	9	6	1	2	0	32	16	14	9	4	3	2	0	22	25	10	18	10	4	4	0	54	41	24
Tampa Bay	16	9	6	1	0	47	37	19	17	7	7	3	0	42	40	17	33	16	13	4	0	89	77	36
Toronto	325	197	88	40	0	1147	806	434	325	114	167	44	0	843	982	272	650	311	255	84	0	1990	1788	706
Vancouver	51	38	9	4	0	241	129	80	51	33	10	8	0	194	129	74	102	71	19	12	0	435	258	154
Washington	54	31	16	7	0	209	117	69	53	21	23	9	0	161	146	51	107	52	39	16	0	370	263	120
Defunct Clubs	231	148	58	25	0	779	469	321	230	98	97	35	0	586	606	231	461	246	155	60	0	1365	1075	552
Totals	**2650**	**1643**	**637**	**367**	**3**	**9940**	**6482**	**3656**	**2650**	**1099**	**1101**	**443**	**7**	**7724**	**7669**	**2648**	**5300**	**2742**	**1738**	**810**	**10**	**17664**	**14151**	**6304**

Playoffs

	Series	W	L	GP	W	L	T	GF	GA	Last Mtg.	Round	Result
Boston	28	21	7	139	87	52	0	430	339	1994	CQF	L 3-4
Buffalo	7	4	3	35	18	17	0	124	111	1998	CSF	L 0-4
Calgary	2	1	1	11	6	5	0	31	32	1989	F	L 2-4
Chicago	17	12	5	81	50	29	2	261	185	1976	QF	W 4-0
Colorado	5	3	2	31	17	14	0	105	85	1993	DSF	W 4-2
Dallas	2	1	1	13	7	6	0	48	37	1980	QF	L 3-4
Detroit	12	5	7	62	33	29	0	161	149	1978	QF	W 4-1
Edmonton	1	0	1	3	0	3	0	6	15	1981	PR	L 0-3
Hartford	5	5	0	27	19	8	0	96	70	1992	DSF	W 4-3
Los Angeles	1	1	0	5	4	1	0	15	12	1993	F	W 4-1
NY Islanders	4	3	1	22	14	8	0	64	55	1993	CF	W 4-1
NY Rangers	14	7	7	61	34	25	2	188	158	1996	CQF	L 2-4
New Jersey	1	0	1	5	1	4	0	11	22	1997	CQF	L 1-4
Philadelphia	4	3	1	21	14	7	0	72	52	1989	CF	W 4-2
Pittsburgh	1	1	0	6	4	2	0	18	15	1998	CQF	W 4-2
St. Louis	3	3	0	12	12	0	0	42	14	1977	QF	W 4-0
Toronto	15	8	7	71	42	29	0	215	160	1979	QF	W 4-0
Vancouver	1	1	0	5	4	1	0	20	9	1975	QF	W 4-1
Defunct Clubs	11*	6	4	28	15	9	4	70	71			
Totals	**134***	**85**	**48**	**638**	**381**	**249**	**8**	**1977**	**1591**			

* 1919 Final incomplete due to influenza epidemic.

Playoff Results 2001-1997

Year	Round	Opponent	Result	GF	GA
1998	CSF	Buffalo	L 0-4	10	17
	CQF	Pittsburgh	W 4-2	18	15
1997	CQF	New Jersey	L 1-4	11	22

Abbreviations: Round: F – Final; **CF** – conference final; **CSF** – conference semi-final; **CQF** – conference quarter-final; **DSF** – division semi-final; **QF** – quarter-final; **PR** – preliminary round.

Calgary totals include Atlanta Flames, 1972-73 to 1979-80.
Colorado totals include Quebec, 1979-80 to 1994-95.
Carolina totals include Hartford, 1979-80 to 1996-97.
Dallas totals include Minnesota North Stars, 1967-68 to 1992-93.
New Jersey totals include Kansas City, 1974-75 to 1975-76, and Colorado Rockies, 1976-77 to 1981-82.
Phoenix totals include Winnipeg, 1979-80 to 1995-96.

2000-01 Results

Oct.	6	at New Jersey	4-8
	7	at Toronto	0-2
	10	Edmonton	5-2
	11	at NY Rangers	1-3
	14	Chicago	5-4*
	17	Buffalo	4-3
	19	at Philadelphia	3-3
	21	Carolina	5-2
	24	Minnesota	2-2
	27	at NY Islanders	1-2
	28	NY Islanders	1-2
Nov.	1	Detroit	2-4
	3	at Buffalo	4-5
	4	NY Rangers	2-5
	8	at Florida	4-2
	10	at Tampa Bay	1-3
	11	at Dallas	0-2
	14	Tampa Bay	0-1
	17	at Washington	3-4
	18	Toronto	1-6
	21	Florida	1-4
	23	at Atlanta	6-0
	25	Buffalo	3-5
	27	Atlanta	3-2
	29	at Edmonton	3-2
	30	at Vancouver	4-3
Dec.	2	at Calgary	1-1
	5	Buffalo	2-3
	8	at Ottawa	0-1
	9	Ottawa	2-4
	13	Calgary	1-3
	15	at New Jersey	1-2
	16	Pittsburgh	4-4
	18	Columbus	0-2
	21	Nashville	4-2
	23	Toronto	2-5
	27	at Vancouver	2-3
	30	at Edmonton	2-3*
	31	at Calgary	4-5*
Jan.	2	at NY Islanders	3-0
	5	at Pittsburgh	4-3
	6	at Ottawa	3-4
	10	Boston	1-2
	12	at Atlanta	3-0
	13	Phoenix	5-2
	16	Carolina	2-3*
	18	Tampa Bay	3-1
	20	NY Rangers	2-2
	23	St. Louis	2-5
	24	at Pittsburgh	1-3
	27	Washington	4-2
	28	Ottawa	4-1
	31	at NY Rangers	2-4
Feb.	1	at Boston	3-0
	6	New Jersey	0-4
	10	NY Islanders	5-3
	11	at Buffalo	4-3
	13	Colorado	2-3*
	17	Washington	3-6
	18	at Ottawa	0-4
	21	Vancouver	1-2
	23	at Washington	1-3
	24	at Toronto	1-5
	27	at Philadelphia	3-2
	28	Pittsburgh	4-2
Mar.	3	Philadelphia	3-1
	6	at Los Angeles	3-4
	7	at Anaheim	2-4
	10	at Phoenix	3-3
	12	at San Jose	0-3
	14	at Carolina	6-3
	17	Boston	2-3
	20	Florida	3-3
	22	at Boston	2-3*
	24	Atlanta	2-3
	26	at Carolina	4-2
	28	at Florida	2-2
	29	at Tampa Bay	6-2
	31	Toronto	4-1
Apr.	2	at Boston	2-3*
	5	Philadelphia	3-2*
	7	New Jersey	0-2

* – Overtime

Entry Draft Selections 2001-1987

2001
Pick
7 Mike Komisarek
25 Alexander Perezhogin
37 Duncan Milroy
71 Tomas Plekanec
109 Martti Jarventie
171 Eric Himelfarb
266 Viktor Ujcik

2000
Pick
13 Ron Hainsey
16 Marcel Hossa
78 Josef Balej
79 Tyler Hanchuck
109 Johan Eneqvist
114 Christian Larrivee
145 Ryan Glenn
172 Scott Selig
182 Petr Chvojka
243 Joni Puurula
275 Jonathan Gauthier

1999
Pick
39 Alexander Buturlin
58 Matt Carkner
97 Chris Dyment
107 Evan Lindsay
136 Dusty Jamieson
145 Marc-Andre Thinel
150 Matt Shasby
167 Sean Dixon
196 Vadim Tarasov
225 Mikko Hyytia
253 Jerome Marois

1998
Pick
16 Eric Chouinard
45 Mike Ribeiro
75 Francois Beauchemin
132 Andrei Bashkirov
152 Gordie Dwyer
162 Andrei Markov
189 Andrei Kruchinin
201 Craig Murray
216 Michael Ryder
247 Darcy Harris

1997
Pick
11 Jason Ward
37 Gregor Baumgartner
65 Ilkka Mikkola
91 Daniel Tetrault
118 Konstantin Sidulov
122 Gennady Razin
145 Jonathan Desroches
172 Ben Guite
197 Petr Kubos
202 Andrei Sidyakin
228 Jarl Espen Ygranes

1996
Pick
18 Matt Higgins
44 Mathieu Garon
71 Arron Asham
92 Kim Staal
99 Etienne Drapeau
127 Daniel Archambault
154 Brett Clark
181 Timo Vertala
207 Mattia Baldi
233 Michel Tremblay

1995
Pick
8 Terry Ryan
60 Miloslav Guren
74 Martin Hohenberger
86 Jonathan Delisle
112 Niklas Anger
138 Boyd Olson
164 Stephane Robidas
190 Greg Hart
216 Eric Houde

1994
Pick
18 Brad Brown
44 Jose Theodore
54 Chris Murray
70 Marko Kiprusoff
74 Martin Belanger
96 Arto Kuki
122 Jimmy Drolet
148 Joel Irving
174 Jessie Rezansoff
200 Peter Strom
226 Tomas Vokoun
252 Chris Aldous
278 Ross Parsons

1993
Pick
21 Saku Koivu
47 Rory Fitzpatrick
73 Sebastien Bordeleau
85 Adam Wiesel
99 Jean-Francois Houle
113 Jeff Lank
125 Dion Darling
151 Darcy Tucker
177 David Ruhly
203 Alan Letang
229 Alexandre Duchesne
255 Brian Larochelle
281 Russell Guzior

1992
Pick
20 David Wilkie
33 Valeri Bure
44 Keli Corpse
68 Craig Rivet
82 Louis Bernard
92 Marc Lamothe
116 Don Chase
140 Martin Sychra
164 Christian Proulx
188 Michael Burman
212 Earl Cronan
236 Trent Cavicchi
260 Hiroyuki Miura

1991
Pick
17 Brent Bilodeau
28 Jim Campbell
43 Craig Darby
61 Yves Sarault
73 Vladimir Vujtek
83 Sylvain Lapointe
100 Brad Layzell
105 Tony Prpic
127 Oleg Petrov
149 Brady Kramer
171 Brian Savage
193 Scott Fraser
215 Greg MacEachern
237 Paul Lepler
259 Dale Hooper

1990
Pick
12 Turner Stevenson
39 Ryan Kuwabara
58 Charles Poulin
60 Robert Guillet
81 Gilbert Dionne
102 Paul Di Pietro
123 Craig Conroy
144 Stephen Rohr
165 Brent Fleetwood
186 Derek Maguire
207 Mark Kettelhut
228 John Uniac
249 Sergei Martynyuk

1989
Pick
13 Lindsay Vallis
30 Patrice Brisebois
41 Steve Larouche
51 Pierre Sevigny
83 Andre Racicot
104 Marc Deschamps
146 Craig Ferguson
167 Patrick Lebeau
188 Roy Mitchell
209 Ed Henrich
230 Justin Duberman
251 Steve Cadieux

1988
Pick
20 Eric Charron
34 Martin St. Amour
46 Neil Carnes
83 Patric Kjellberg
93 Peter Popovic
104 Jean-Claude Bergeron
125 Patrik Carnback
146 Tim Chase
167 Sean Hill
188 Harijs Vitolinsh
209 Yuri Krivokhizha
230 Kevin Dahl
251 Dave Kunda

1987
Pick
17 Andrew Cassels
33 John LeClair
38 Eric Desjardins
44 Mathieu Schneider
58 Francois Gravel
80 Kris Miller
101 Steve McCool
122 Les Kuntar
143 Rob Kelley
164 Will Geist
185 Eric Tremblay
206 Barry McKinlay
227 Ed Ronan
248 Bryan Herring

General Managers' History

Jack Laviolette and Joseph Cattarinich, 1909-1910; George Kennedy, 1910-11 to 1920-21; Leo Dandurand, 1921-22 to 1934-35; Ernest Savard, 1935-36; Cecil Hart, 1936-37 to 1938-39; Jules Dugal, 1939-40; Tom P. Gorman, 1940-41 to 1945-46; Frank J. Selke, 1946-47 to 1963-64; Sam Pollock, 1964-65 to 1977-78; Irving Grundman, 1978-79 to 1982-83; Serge Savard, 1983-84 to 1994-95; Serge Savard and Réjean Houle, 1995-96; Réjean Houle, 1996-97 to 1999-2000; Réjean Houle and Andre Savard, 2000-01; Andre Savard, 2001-02.

General Manager

SAVARD, ANDRE
General Manager, Montreal Canadiens.
Born in Témiscamingue, Que., February 9, 1953.

André Savard was named general manager of the Montreal Canadiens on November 20, 2000 after having joined the organization as Director of Hockey Personnel. He has tremendous experience in scouting and player development.

Savard has been associated with the NHL since 1973-74. Before joining the Canadiens, he spent five seasons with the Ottawa Senators organization, including the first four as head scout. In June of 1987, he became the first former Nordiques player to assume the Quebec head coaching position.

Savard played 12 seasons in the NHL. The Boston Bruins' first-round pick, sixth overall in 1973, he also played for the Buffalo Sabres and the Nordiques. In 790 NHL regular season games, he totalled 482 points (211 goals, 271 assists). He also added 31 points in 85 playoff games (13 goals, 18 assists). The former QMJHL star retired as a player after the 1984-85 season following a serious knee injury.

NHL Coaching Record

		Regular Season				Playoffs		
Season	Team	Games	W	L	T	Games	W	L
1987-88	Quebec	24	10	13	1	....	....	....

Club Directory

Molson Centre

Molson Centre
1260 de La Gauchetière Street W.
Montréal, QC H3B 5E8
Phone: **514/932-2582**
Fax Lines (all area code 514):
Hockey 932-8736
Team Services 989-2717
Media Relations 932-8285
Marketing 925-2145 or 932-9296
Children's Foundation 925-2144
www.canadiens.com
Capacity: 21,273

Executive Management
Chairman and Governor . . . George N. Gillett, Jr.
Vice-Chairman . . . Jeff Joyce
Consultant . . . Foster Gillett
President of Club de Hockey Canadien and L'Arena des Canadiens Inc. (Molson Centre) . . . Pierre Boivin
Executive Assistant to the President . . . Lise Beaudry
Executive Vice-President Hockey and General Manager . . . André Savard
Vice-President, Finance and Administration and Alternate Governor . . . Fred Steer
Executive Vice-President and General Manager, Entertainment . . . Aldo Giampaolo
Vice-President, Operations, L'Arena des Canadiens Inc. (Molson Centre) . . . Alain Gauthier

Hockey Operations
Assistant General Manager . . . Martin Madden
Head Coach . . . Michel Therrien
Assistant Coaches . . . Guy Carbonneau, Rick Green, Roland Melanson
Coordinator of Player Development - Special Projects . . Clément Jodoin
Pro-Scout Coordinator . . . Pierre Mondou
Amateur Scouting Coordinator . . . Pierre Dorion
Director of Team Services . . . Michèle Lapointe
Professional Scout . . . Doug Robinson
Amateur Scouts . . . Fred E. Bandel, Elmer Benning, William A. Berglund, Herb Hammond, Hannu Laine, Trent McCleary, Gerry O'Flaherty, Antonin Routa, Claude Ruel, Nikolai Vakourov
Exec. Asst. to Exec. V.P. & G.M., Hockey . . . Donna Stuart
Administrative Assistant, Team Services . . . Claudine Crépin

Medical and Training Staff
Club Physician and Chief Surgeon . . . Dr. David Mulder
Orthopaedist . . . Dr. Eric Lenczner
Ophthalmologist . . . Dr. John Little
Dentist . . . Dr. Pierre Desautels
General Physician . . . Dr. Vincent Lacroix
Head Athletic Therapist . . . Graham Rynbend
Assistant to the Head Athletic Therapist . . . Dominic Massi
Strength & Conditioning Coordinator . . . Scott Livingston
Equipment Manager . . . Pierre Gervais
Assistants to the Equipment Manager . . . Robert Boulanger, Pierre Ouellette
Video Supervisor . . . Mario Leblanc

Les Citadelles de Québec – AHL Affiliate
Address . . . Colisée de Québec, 250 Wilfrid Hamel Blvd, Québec, QC G1L 5A7 418/525-5333
President . . . Maurice Tanguay
General Manager . . . Raymond Bolduc
Head Coach . . . Éric Lavigne
Assistant Coach . . . Donald Dufresne
Goaltending Coach . . . Benoit Fortier
Director of Communications and Team Services . . . Nicole Bouchard

Communications
Director of Communications . . . Donald Beauchamp
Assistant to the Director of Communications . . . Dominick Saillant
Administrative Assistant . . . Sylvie Lambert

Marketing/Community Relations
Director of Marketing . . . Patrice St-Amour
Administrative Assistant . . . Louise Leman
Community Relations Manager . . . Frédérique Cardinal
Retail Operations and Promotion Manager . . . Luc Rocheleau
Game Presentation and Production Manager . . . Bob Levac

Ticket Sales
Executive Director, Sales . . . Richard Primeau
Season Ticket Sales Manager . . . Gilles Beauregard
Luxury Suites Manager . . . Gilbert Brault
Group Sales Manager . . . Pierre Constant

Advertising and Sponsorship Sales
EFFIX Inc. . . . François-Xavier Seigneur

Finance
Executive Director of Finance . . . Jacques Aubé
Controller, Budgeting & Analysis . . . Dennis McKinley
Controller, Financial Reporting . . . Françoise Brault
Accounting Supervisor/L'Arena des Canadiens Inc. . Paule Jolicoeur
Accounting Supervisor/Club de hockey Canadien Inc. . Marleine Bédard
Financial Analyst . . . Serge Rochon
Director of Information Technology . . . Pierre-Éric Belzile
Executive Assistant to the V.P. Finance . . . Susan Cryans

Ticketing Operations
Director, Ticket Office . . . Cathy D'Ascoli
Assistant Director, Ticket Office . . . Mike Tombs
Executive Assistant to the V.P. Operations . . . Maryse Cartwright

Entertainment
Executive Director, Events . . . Louise Laliberté
Exec. Asst. to Exec. V.P. & G.M., Entertainment . . . Vicki Mercuri

Broadcasting
Club trains at . . . Molson Centre
Play-by-play – Radio/TV . . . Claude Quenneville (SRC), Pierre Houde (RDS), André Côté (TQS), Pierre Rinfret (CKAC) French, Dino Sisto (CJAD-English), TBA (TSN-English)
TV Channels . . . CBFT (2), TQS (35) (French)
Cable TV . . . RDS (33) (French), TSN (28) (English)
Radio Stations . . . CKAC (730) (French), CJAD (800) (English)

Nashville Predators

2000-01 Results: 34W-36L-9T-3OTL 80PTS. Third, Central Division

Year-by-Year Record

		Home				Road				Overall								
Season	GP	W	L	T	OL	W	L	T	OL	W	L	T	OL	GF	GA	Pts.	Finished	Playoff Result
2000-01	82	16	18	7	0	18	18	2	3	34	36	9	3	186	200	80	3rd, Central Div.	Out of Playoffs
1999-2000	82	15	21	3	2	13	19	4	5	28	40	7	7	199	240	70	4th, Central Div.	Out of Playoffs
1998-99	82	15	22	4	...	13	25	3	...	28	47	7	...	190	261	63	4th, Central Div.	Out of Playoffs

2001-02 Schedule

Oct.	Fri.	5	at Dallas
	Sat.	6	St. Louis
	Thu.	11	Calgary
	Sat.	13	Edmonton
	Tue.	16	at Buffalo
	Thu.	18	Chicago
	Sat.	20	Boston
	Mon.	22	at Edmonton
	Tue.	23	at Vancouver
	Thu.	25	at Calgary
	Sat.	27	Detroit
	Tue.	30	Minnesota
	Wed.	31	at Minnesota
Nov.	Fri.	2	at Dallas
	Sat.	3	Dallas
	Thu.	8	at Montreal
	Sat.	10	at Ottawa
	Tue.	13	Buffalo
	Fri.	16	at Atlanta
	Sat.	17	Columbus
	Tue.	20	at Detroit
	Wed.	21	Chicago
	Fri.	23	Pittsburgh
	Tue.	27	at San Jose
	Thu.	29	at Phoenix
Dec.	Sat.	1	at Los Angeles*
	Sun.	2	at Anaheim*
	Thu.	6	Ottawa
	Sat.	8	Edmonton
	Tue.	11	Los Angeles
	Wed.	12	at NY Rangers
	Sat.	15	Chicago
	Thu.	20	Vancouver
	Sun.	23	San Jose*
	Wed.	26	Tampa Bay
	Sat.	29	Detroit
	Sun.	30	at St. Louis
Jan.	Tue.	1	Colorado*
	Thu.	3	at New Jersey
	Fri.	4	at Minnesota
	Sun.	6	at Columbus*
	Tue.	8	at Toronto
	Thu.	10	Minnesota
	Sat.	12	Anaheim
	Mon.	14	at Anaheim
	Tue.	15	at Los Angeles
	Thu.	17	Toronto
	Sat.	19	Columbus
	Mon.	21	Phoenix
	Wed.	23	at Carolina
	Thu.	24	at Philadelphia
	Sat.	26	Anaheim
	Mon.	28	at Vancouver
	Wed.	30	at Colorado
Feb.	Wed.	6	Dallas
	Fri.	8	Washington
	Sat.	9	at Columbus
	Tue.	12	Florida
	Tue.	26	San Jose
	Thu.	28	at Edmonton
Mar.	Sat.	2	at Calgary
	Tue.	5	at San Jose
	Thu.	7	Los Angeles
	Sat.	9	at Florida
	Sun.	10	at Tampa Bay
	Tue.	12	Vancouver
	Fri.	15	Phoenix
	Sun.	17	Colorado*
	Tue.	19	at St. Louis
	Thu.	21	New Jersey
	Sat.	23	Montreal
	Mon.	25	Detroit
	Wed.	27	at Chicago
	Thu.	28	at Detroit
	Sat.	30	St. Louis
Apr.	Mon.	1	at Colorado
	Wed.	3	at Chicago
	Thu.	4	at Columbus
	Sat.	6	Calgary
	Tue.	9	at St. Louis
	Thu.	11	NY Islanders
	Sun.	14	at Phoenix*

* Denotes afternoon game.

Once the backup to Martin Brodeur, Mike Dunham has begun to make a name for himself in Nashville. His .923 save percentage was second in the NHL last season as he helped the Predators post the league's seventh-best defensive record.

Franchise date: June 25, 1997

CENTRAL DIVISION

4th NHL Season

2001-02 Player Personnel

FORWARDS	HT	WT	S	Place of Birth	Date	2000-01 Club
ANDERSON, Erik	5-9	195	L	Plymouth, MI	3/6/78	St. Lawrence
ANDERSSON, Jonas	6-3	202	L	Stockholm, Sweden	2/24/81	Milwaukee
ARKHIPOV, Denis	6-3	210	L	Kazan, USSR	5/19/79	Nashville-Milwaukee
BARTEK, Martin	6-1	205	L	Kindgseed Jill, Czech.	7/17/80	Milwaukee-New Orleans
BOWLER, Bill	5-9	180	L	Toronto, Ont.	9/25/74	Columbus-Syracuse
CISAR, Marian	6-0	197	R	Bratislava, Czech.	2/25/78	Nashville-Milwaukee
CLASSEN, Greg	6-1	198	L	Aylsham, Sask.	8/24/77	Nashville-Milwaukee
ERAT, Martin	6-0	195	L	Trebic, Czech.	8/28/81	Saskatoon-Red Deer
FITZGERALD, Tom	6-0	195	R	Billerica, MA	8/28/68	Nashville
GOSSELIN, David	6-1	205	R	Levis, Que.	6/22/77	Milwaukee
GRIMSON, Stu	6-4	240	L	Kamloops, B.C.	5/20/65	Los Angeles
HARTNELL, Scott	6-2	208	L	Regina, Sask.	4/18/82	Nashville
JOHNSON, Greg	5-11	202	L	Thunder Bay, Ont.	3/16/71	Nashville
KJELLBERG, Patric	6-2	210	L	Trelleborg, Sweden	6/17/69	Nashville
KREVSUN, Alexandre	6-0	212	L	Togliatti, USSR	6/6/80	New Orleans
LEGWAND, David	6-2	190	L	Detroit, MI	8/17/80	Nashville
LUNDBOHM, Bryan	5-10	190	L	Roseau, MN	8/24/77	North Dakota
MOWERS, Mark	5-11	187	R	Whitesboro, NY	2/16/74	Milwaukee
ORSZAGH, Vladimir	5-11	173	L	Banska Bystrica, Czech.	5/24/77	Djurgardens IF
PANOV, Konstantin	6-0	193	L	Chelyabinsk, USSR	6/29/80	Kamloops
PAVLOV, Yevgeny	6-1	201	R	Togliatti, USSR	1/10/81	Lada Togliatti
RONNING, Cliff	5-8	165	L	Burnaby, B.C.	10/1/65	Nashville
SACHL, Petr	6-2	205	R	Jindrivichuk Hradec, Czech.	12/2/77	Milwaukee
SARAULT, Yves	6-1	190	L	Valleyfield, Que.	12/23/72	Atlanta-Orlando
STEVENSON, Jeremy	6-2	218	L	San Bernardino, CA	7/28/74	Nashville-Milwaukee
WALKER, Scott	5-10	196	R	Cambridge, Ont.	7/19/73	Nashville
YACHMENEV, Vitali	5-11	195	L	Chelyabinsk, USSR	1/8/75	Nashville
DEFENSEMEN						
BERENZWEIG, Bubba	6-1	217	L	Arlington Heights, IL	8/8/77	Nashville-Milwaukee
BOIKOV, Alexandre	6-0	200	L	Chelyabinsk, USSR	2/7/75	Nashville-Milwaukee
BRENNAN, Rich	6-2	200	R	Schenectady, NY	11/26/72	Los Angeles-Lowell
CHERNOV, Mikhail	6-2	205	R	Prokopjevsk, USSR	11/11/78	Philadelphia (AHL)
DELMORE, Andy	6-1	200	R	LaSalle, Ont.	12/26/76	Philadelphia
DURAK, Miroslav	6-4	212	R	Topolcany, Czech.	6/9/81	Sherbrooke-Acadie-Bathurst
EATON, Mark	6-2	205	L	Wilmington, DE	5/6/77	Nashville-Milwaukee
HELBLING, Timo	6-2	209	R	Basel, Switzerland	7/21/81	Windsor-Milwaukee
HOULDER, Bill	6-2	217	L	Thunder Bay, Ont.	3/11/67	Nashville
HULSE, Cale	6-3	220	R	Edmonton, Alta.	11/10/73	Nashville
LINTNER, Richard	6-3	212	R	Trencin, Czech.	11/15/77	Nashville
MORO, Marc	6-1	220	L	Toronto, Ont.	7/17/77	Nashville-Milwaukee
ROBERTSSON, Bert	6-3	205	L	Sodertalje, Sweden	6/30/74	NYR-Hartford-Houston-Milwaukee
SAUER, Kent	6-2	231	R	St. Cloud, MN	5/10/79	New Orleans-Milwaukee
SCHNABEL, Robert	6-5	233	L	Prague, Czech.	11/10/78	Springfield-Timra IK
SKRASTINS, Karlis	6-1	208	L	Riga, USSR	7/19/74	Nashville
SKRBEK, Pavel	6-3	217	L	Kladno, Czech.	8/9/78	Nashville-Milwaukee
TIMONEN, Kimmo	5-10	196	L	Kuopio, Finland	3/18/75	Nashville

GOALTENDERS	HT	WT	C	Place of Birth	Date	2000-01 Club
DUNHAM, Mike	6-3	200	L	Johnson City, NY	6/1/72	Nashville
FINLEY, Brian	6-3	205	R	Sault Ste. Marie, Ont.	7/13/81	Barrie-Brampton
LASAK, Jan	6-1	204	L	Zvolen, Czech.	4/10/79	Milwaukee
MASON, Chris	6-0	195	L	Red Deer, Alta.	4/20/76	Nashville-Milwaukee
VOKOUN, Tomas	6-0	195	R	Karlovy Vary, Czech.	7/2/76	Nashville

General Manager

POILE, DAVID
General Manager, Nashville Predators.
Born in Toronto, Ont., February 14, 1949.

Since joining the Predators as general manager on July 9, 1997, David Poile has made a commitment to building for the future, surrounding himself with one of the youngest and most talented staffs in the National Hockey League.

Prior to joining Nashville, Poile spent 15 seasons as vice president/general manager of the Washington Capitals. During his tenure in Washington, the Capitals made 14 post-season appearances, winning their only Patrick Division title in 1989 and advancing to the Conference Finals in 1990. During Poile's 15 years in Washington, the Capitals compiled a record of 594-454-132, finished second in the Patrick Division seven times and recorded 90-or-more points seven different seasons.

Poile started his professional hockey career as an administrative assistant for the Atlanta Flames in 1972, shortly after graduating from Northeastern University in Boston. At Northeastern, he was hockey team captain, leading scorer and most valuable player for two years.

In 1977, he was named assistant general manager of the Atlanta Flames (moved to Calgary in 1980), serving as the manager and coordinator of the Flames farm club.

Poile is a member of the NHL's general managers committee and was instrumental in the NHL's adoption of the instant replay rule in 1991. He was awarded *Inside Hockey*'s Man of the Year for his leadership on the issue. He was also twice honored as *The Sporting News* NHL Executive of the Year following the 1982-83 and 1983-84 seasons. Poile served as general manager of the 1998 and 1999 U.S. National Team for the International Ice Hockey Federation World Championships.

Poile was introduced to hockey by watching his father, Norman "Bud" Poile, play seven seasons in the NHL. Bud later became general manager for the Vancouver Canucks and the Philadelphia Flyers, both NHL expansion franchises at the time. In 1989, Bud was a co-winner of the Lester Patrick Award (an annual award for outstanding service to hockey in the United States), and was inducted into the Hockey Hall of Fame a year later.

2000-01 Scoring

* - rookie

Regular Season

Pos	#	Player	Team	GP	G	A	Pts	+/–	PIM	PP	SH	GW	GT	S	%
C	7	Cliff Ronning	NSH	80	19	43	62	4	28	6	0	4	0	237	8.0
R	24	Scott Walker	NSH	74	25	29	54	–2	66	9	3	1	1	159	15.7
L	10	Patric Kjellberg	NSH	81	14	31	45	–2	12	5	0	2	0	139	10.1
C	11	David Legwand	NSH	81	13	28	41	1	38	3	0	3	0	172	7.6
R	43	Vitali Yachmenev	NSH	78	15	19	34	–5	10	4	1	4	1	123	12.2
C	22	Greg Johnson	NSH	82	15	17	32	–6	46	1	0	4	0	97	15.5
R	39	* Marian Cisar	NSH	60	12	15	27	–7	45	5	0	1	0	97	12.4
C	27	Randy Robitaille	NSH	62	9	17	26	–11	12	5	0	0	0	121	7.4
D	44	Kimmo Timonen	NSH	82	12	13	25	–6	50	6	0	3	0	151	7.9
R	21	Tom Fitzgerald	NSH	82	9	9	18	–5	71	0	2	2	0	135	6.7
D	23	Bill Houlder	NSH	81	4	12	16	–7	40	0	1	1	1	78	5.1
R	17	* Scott Hartnell	NSH	75	2	14	16	–8	48	0	0	0	0	92	2.2
C	12	Robert Valicevic	NSH	60	8	6	14	–2	26	1	0	4	0	62	12.9
L	25	* Denis Arkhipov	NSH	40	6	7	13	0	4	0	0	0	0	42	14.3
D	3	Karlis Skrastins	NSH	82	1	11	12	–12	30	0	0	1	0	66	1.5
D	4	Mark Eaton	NSH	34	3	8	11	7	14	1	0	1	0	32	9.4
D	41	Richard Lintner	NSH	50	3	5	8	2	22	1	0	0	0	81	3.7
D	32	Cale Hulse	NSH	82	1	7	8	–5	128	0	0	1	0	93	1.1
C	9	* Greg Classen	NSH	27	2	4	6	–4	14	1	0	0	0	18	11.1
C	71	Sebastien Bordeleau	NSH	14	2	3	5	–4	14	0	0	0	0	20	10.0
L	16	Ville Peltonen	NSH	23	3	1	4	–7	2	0	0	0	0	38	7.9
L	19	Mike Watt	NSH	18	1	1	2	–2	8	0	0	1	0	18	5.6
L	28	Jeremy Stevenson	NSH	8	1	0	1	–1	39	0	0	0	0	6	16.7
L	36	* Sean Haggerty	NSH	3	0	1	1	1	0	0	0	0	0	2	0.0
G	30	* Chris Mason	NSH	1	0	0	0	0	0	0	0	0	0	0	0.0
D	49	Rory Fitzpatrick	NSH	2	0	0	0	–2	2	0	0	0	0	0	0.0
D	42	* Pavel Skrbek	NSH	5	0	0	0	1	4	0	0	0	0	2	0.0
D	26	* Bubba Berenzweig	NSH	5	0	0	0	0	0	0	0	0	0	0	0.0
D	33	* Marc Moro	NSH	6	0	0	0	1	12	0	0	0	0	1	0.0
D	38	* Alexandre Boikov	NSH	8	0	0	0	–1	13	0	0	0	0	3	0.0
G	29	Tomas Vokoun	NSH	37	0	0	0	0	2	0	0	0	0	0	0.0
G	1	Mike Dunham	NSH	48	0	0	0	0	2	0	0	0	0	0	0.0

Goaltending

No.	Goaltender	GPI	Mins	Avg	W	L	T	EN	SO	GA	SA	S%
30	* Chris Mason	1	59	2.03	0	1	0	0	0	2	20	.900
1	Mike Dunham	48	2810	2.28	21	21	4	2	4	107	1381	.923
29	Tomas Vokoun	37	2088	2.44	13	17	5	4	2	85	940	.910
	Totals	**82**	**4984**	**2.41**	**34**	**39**	**9**	**6**	**6**	**200**	**2347**	**.915**

Cliff Ronning has led the Predators in scoring in each of their first three seasons. His 43 assists last season established a franchise record.

Club Records

Team

(Figures in brackets for season records are games played; records for fewest points, wins, ties, losses, goals, goals against are for 70 or more games)

Most Points	**80**	2000-01 (82)
Most Wins	**34**	2000-01 (82)
Most Ties	**9**	2000-01 (82)
Most Losses	**47**	1998-99 (82)
Most Goals	**199**	1999-2000 (82)
Most Goals Against	**261**	1998-99 (82)
Fewest Points	**63**	1998-99 (82)
Fewest Wins	**28**	1998-99 (82), 1999-2000 (82)
Fewest Ties	**7**	1998-99 (82) 1999-2000 (82)
Fewest Losses	**36**	2000-01 (82)
Fewest Goals	**186**	2000-01 (82)
Fewest Goals Against	**200**	2000-01 (82)
Longest Winning Streak		
Overall	**4**	Dec. 26/99-Jan. 1/00, Jan. 29-Feb. 8/01
Home	**4**	Dec. 28/99-Jan. 8/00
Away	**3**	Feb. 12-24/99, Jan. 29-Feb. 1/01
Longest Undefeated Streak		
Overall	**8**	Dec. 18/99-Jan. 1/00
Home	**6**	Dec. 18/99-Jan. 8/00
Away	**3**	Seven times
Longest Losing Streak		
Overall	**7**	Nov. 20-Dec. 2/99
Home	**6**	Jan. 21-Feb. 15/99
Away	**5**	Twice
Longest Winless Streak		
Overall	**7**	Twice
Home	**9**	Jan. 21-Mar. 2/99
Away	**5**	Five times
Most Shutouts, Season	**6**	2000-01 (82)
Most PIM, Season	**1,420**	1998-99 (82)
Most Goals, Game	**7**	Nov. 26/00 (Nsh. 7 at Car. 4)

Individual

Most Seasons	**3**	Many players
Most Games	**244**	Tom Fitzgerald
Most Goals, Career	**63**	Cliff Ronning
Most Assists, Career	**114**	Cliff Ronning
Most Points, Career	**177**	Cliff Ronning (63G, 114A)
Most PIM, Career	**327**	Drake Berehowsky
Most Shutouts, Career	**5**	Mike Dunham
Longest Consecutive Games Streak	**213**	Tom Fitzgerald (Dec. 30/98-date)
Most Goals, Season	**26**	Cliff Ronning (1999-2000)
Most Assists, Season	**43**	Cliff Ronning (2000-01)
Most Points, Season	**62**	Cliff Ronning (1999-2000; 26G, 36A) (2000-01; 19G, 43A)
Most PIM, Season	**242**	Patrick Cote (1999-2000)
Most Points, Defenseman, Season	**33**	Kimmo Timonen (1999-2000; 8G, 25A)
Most Points, Center, Season	**62**	Cliff Ronning (1999-2000; 26G, 36A) (2000-01; 19G, 43A)
Most Points, Right Wing, Season	**54**	Scott Walker (2000-01; 25G, 29A)
Most Points, Left Wing, Season	**34**	Vitali Yachmenev (2000-01; 15G, 19A)
Most Points, Rookie, Season	**28**	David Legwand (1999-2000; 13G, 15A)
Most Shutouts, Season	**4**	Mike Dunham (2000-01)
Most Goals, Game	**3**	Rob Valicevic (Nov. 10/99), Scott Walker (Dec. 26/00)
Most Assists, Game	**3**	Six times
Most Points, Game	**4**	Four times

General Managers' History

David Poile, 1998-99 to date.

Coaching History

Barry Trotz, 1998-99 to date.

Captains' History

Tom Fitzgerald, 1998-99 to date.

Selected by Nashville in the 1998 Expansion Draft, Scott Walker led the club with a career-high 25 goals last season. His 29 assists were also a personal best.

2000-01 Results

Oct.	7	at Pittsburgh	3-1
	8	Pittsburgh	1-3
	13	Washington	3-1
	14	Carolina	2-1
	17	Los Angeles	1-1
	19	at Detroit	2-1*
	21	San Jose	3-5
	24	Vancouver	4-4
	25	at Colorado	1-2*
	27	Florida	3-3
	31	St. Louis	2-4
Nov.	2	at Philadelphia	3-1
	4	Anaheim	3-3
	7	at NY Islanders	1-2
	8	at New Jersey	4-3
	11	at Boston	2-2
	15	at Atlanta	0-1
	16	Columbus	1-5
	18	Detroit	3-2
	20	at Detroit	3-6
	22	Dallas	0-1
	24	St. Louis	0-4
	26	at Carolina	7-4
	28	Calgary	6-1
	30	at Chicago	3-0
Dec.	1	Chicago	1-2
	4	at Vancouver	3-6
	6	at Edmonton	0-4
	7	at Calgary	0-3
	10	at Minnesota	2-1
	12	Philadelphia	2-2
	14	Edmonton	2-6
	16	Chicago	0-3
	20	at Toronto	3-1
	21	at Montreal	2-4
	23	at NY Rangers	3-2*
	26	Colorado	5-2
	28	Anaheim	2-2
	29	at Colorado	1-3
Jan.	1	Vancouver	2-5
	4	at St. Louis	4-2
	6	Buffalo	0-2
	8	at Vancouver	1-2
	10	at Edmonton	5-2
	11	at Calgary	1-2
	13	at San Jose	5-3
	16	Edmonton	1-2
	17	at Dallas	3-4*
	19	Boston	1-0*
	21	St. Louis	3-1
	23	Atlanta	4-3
	24	at Detroit	3-4
	27	Colorado	1-5
	29	at Phoenix	5-2
	31	at Anaheim	3-0
Feb.	1	at Los Angeles	6-4
	8	Columbus	3-1
	10	at Columbus	2-3
	13	Dallas	1-2
	16	San Jose	0-2
	18	Tampa Bay	3-2
	20	Detroit	3-3
	21	at Washington	1-2
	24	Minnesota	2-1
	27	Los Angeles	1-2
Mar.	1	Columbus	2-5
	4	NY Rangers	5-2
	6	at Phoenix	1-5
	8	at Los Angeles	1-4
	10	at San Jose	3-0
	11	at Anaheim	0-1*
	15	at Chicago	2-3
	17	Phoenix	4-1
	19	at Columbus	2-1
	21	at Minnesota	0-0
	22	at Chicago	2-1*
	24	Ottawa	0-4
	29	Phoenix	4-3*
	31	Minnesota	4-1
Apr.	4	at Dallas	1-5
	5	Calgary	4-0
	7	at St. Louis	0-1

* – Overtime

All-time Record vs. Other Clubs

Regular Season

	At Home								On Road								Total							
	GP	W	L	T	OL	GF	GA	PTS	GP	W	L	T	OL	GF	GA	PTS	GP	W	L	T	OL	GF	GA	PTS
Anaheim	6	2	2	2	0	14	16	6	6	1	4	0	1	7	14	3	12	3	6	2	1	21	30	9
Atlanta	2	2	0	0	0	10	3	4	2	1	1	0	0	4	4	2	4	3	1	0	0	14	7	6
Boston	3	1	2	0	0	5	10	2	3	1	1	1	0	6	11	3	6	2	3	1	0	11	21	5
Buffalo	3	0	2	0	1	2	7	1	2	2	0	0	0	8	5	4	5	2	2	0	1	10	12	5
Calgary	7	4	3	0	0	23	15	8	6	1	2	1	2	13	18	5	13	5	5	1	2	36	33	13
Carolina	3	3	0	0	0	8	5	6	3	1	2	0	0	9	11	2	6	4	2	0	0	17	16	8
Chicago	8	3	4	1	0	20	20	7	9	4	4	1	0	26	25	9	17	7	8	2	0	46	45	16
Colorado	6	2	2	2	0	17	18	6	6	0	4	1	1	8	18	2	12	2	6	3	1	25	36	8
Columbus	3	1	2	0	0	6	11	2	2	1	1	0	0	4	4	2	5	2	3	0	0	10	15	4
Dallas	6	2	4	0	0	12	14	4	6	1	4	0	1	7	17	3	12	3	8	0	1	19	31	7
Detroit	8	3	4	1	0	22	27	7	9	1	7	0	1	20	36	3	17	4	11	1	1	42	63	10
Edmonton	7	3	3	1	0	18	20	7	6	2	4	0	0	14	19	4	13	5	7	1	0	32	39	11
Florida	3	0	2	1	0	5	8	1	2	0	2	0	0	3	7	0	5	0	4	1	0	8	15	1
Los Angeles	6	1	4	1	0	10	17	3	6	4	1	0	1	18	16	9	12	5	5	1	1	28	33	12
Minnesota	2	2	0	0	0	6	2	4	2	1	0	1	0	2	1	3	4	3	0	1	0	8	3	7
Montreal	2	1	0	1	0	8	3	3	2	0	2	0	0	4	7	0	4	1	2	1	0	12	10	3
New Jersey	2	0	2	0	0	2	6	0	3	2	1	0	0	8	9	4	5	2	3	0	0	10	15	4
NY Islanders	2	1	1	0	0	6	8	2	3	2	1	0	0	9	7	4	5	3	2	0	0	15	15	6
NY Rangers	2	1	1	0	0	9	9	2	3	1	2	0	0	5	12	2	5	2	3	0	0	14	21	4
Ottawa	2	0	2	0	0	1	7	0	2	1	1	0	0	3	4	2	4	1	3	0	0	4	11	2
Philadelphia	3	0	2	1	0	3	6	1	3	1	1	1	0	4	10	3	6	1	3	2	0	7	16	4
Phoenix	6	3	2	1	0	18	19	7	6	3	3	0	0	19	20	6	12	6	5	1	0	37	39	13
Pittsburgh	3	1	2	0	0	7	8	2	3	1	1	1	0	6	8	3	6	2	3	1	0	13	16	5
St. Louis	9	2	6	1	0	19	30	5	8	3	4	0	1	15	23	7	17	5	10	1	1	34	53	12
San Jose	6	2	4	0	0	12	19	4	6	3	3	0	0	18	15	6	12	5	7	0	0	30	34	10
Tampa Bay	3	1	2	0	0	7	8	2	2	1	0	1	0	7	4	3	5	2	2	1	0	14	12	5
Toronto	0	0	0	0	0	0	0	0	3	2	0	1	0	9	5	5	3	2	0	1	0	9	5	5
Vancouver	7	3	2	1	1	21	22	8	6	2	4	0	0	16	22	4	13	5	6	1	1	37	44	12
Washington	3	2	1	0	0	8	6	4	3	1	2	0	0	4	5	2	6	3	3	0	0	12	11	6
Totals	**123**	**46**	**61**	**14**	**2**	**299**	**344**	**108**	**123**	**44**	**62**	**9**	**8**	**276**	**357**	**105**	**246**	**90**	**123**	**23**	**10**	**575**	**701**	**213**

Entry Draft Selections 2001-1998

2001

Pick	
12	Dan Hamhuis
33	Timofei Shishkanov
42	Tomas Slovak
75	Denis Platonov
76	Oliver Setzinger
98	Jordin Tootoo
178	Anton Lavrentjev
240	Gustav Grasberg
271	Mikko Lehtonen

2000

Pick	
6	Scott Hartnell
36	Daniel Widing
72	Mattias Nilsson
89	Libor Pivko
131	Matt Hendricks
137	Mike Stuart
154	Matt Koalska
173	Tomas Harant
197	Zbynek Irgl
203	Jure Penko
236	Mats Christeen
284	Martin Hohener

1999

Pick	
6	Brian Finley
33	Jonas Andersson
52	Adam Hall
54	Andrew Hutchinson
61	Ed Hill
65	Jan Lasak
72	Brett Angel
121	Yevgeny Pavlov
124	Alexander Krevsun
131	Konstantin Panov
162	Timo Helbling
191	Martin Erat
205	Kyle Kettles
220	Miroslav Durak
248	Darren Haydar

1998

Pick	
2	David Legwand
60	Denis Arkhipov
85	Geoff Koch
88	Kent Sauer
138	Martin Beauchesne
147	Craig Brunel
202	Martin Bartek
230	Karlis Skrastins

Coach

TROTZ, BARRY
Coach, Nashville Predators. Born in Winnipeg, Man., July 15, 1962.

Barry Trotz realized his dream of becoming an NHL head coach on August 6, 1997, after serving four seasons as head coach and director of hockey operations for the American Hockey League's Portland Pirates. He and assistant Paul Gardner spent the 1997-98 season scouting in preparation for the inaugural season of the Nashville Predators.

Trotz began his coaching career in 1984 as assistant coach with the University of Manitoba for one season, before serving two seasons as the head coach and general manager of the Dauphin Kings Junior Hockey Club from 1985-87. He became head coach of the University of Manitoba during the 1987 season and also served as a scout for the Spokane Chiefs of the Western Hockey League that season. Trotz joined the Washington Capitals organization as their chief western scout during the 1988 season. The Winnipeg, Manitoba native was appointed an assistant coach of the Capitals' American Hockey League affiliate in Baltimore prior to the 1991 season before being named head coach prior to the 1992 season. When the franchise relocated to Portland, he guided the Pirates to two AHL Calder Cup Final appearances in the club's first four seasons. He led the Pirates to a league-best 43-27-10 record, captured the Calder Cup Championship and was named the American Hockey League Coach of the Year following the 1994-95 season.

In 1995, Trotz guided Portland to a new North American professional hockey league record 17-game unbeaten streak (14-0-3) to start the season. He was named head coach for the U.S. Team at the American Hockey League All-Star Game in 1996.

Prior to his coaching career, Trotz played junior hockey for the Western Hockey League's Regina Pats from 1979-83. During that time, he recorded 39 goals, 121 assists for 160 points, along with 490 penalty minutes in 204 games.

Coaching Record

		Regular Season				Playoffs		
Season	Team	Games	W	L	T	Games	W	L
1992-93	Baltimore (AHL)	80	28	40	12	7	3	4
1993-94	Portland (AHL)	80	43	27	10	8	6	2
1994-95	Portland (AHL)	80	46	22	12	7	3	4
1995-96	Portland (AHL)	80	32	38	10	24	14	10
1996-97	Portland (AHL)	80	37	33	10	5	2	3
1998-99	**Nashville (NHL)**	**82**	**28**	**47**	**7**	....	....	....
1999-2000	**Nashville (NHL)**	**82**	**28**	**47**	**7**	....	....	....
2000-01	**Nashville (NHL)**	**82**	**34**	**39**	**9**	....	....	....
	NHL Totals	**246**	**90**	**133**	**20**	....	....	....

Club Directory

Gaylord Entertainment Center

Nashville Predators
Gaylord Entertainment Center
501 Broadway
Nashville, TN 37203
Phone **615/770-2300**
FAX 615/770-2309
Ticket Information 615/770-PUCK
www.nashvillepredators.com
Capacity: 17,113

Owner, Chairman and Governor . . . . Craig Leipold
General Partner . . . . Nashville Predators, LLC
Limited Partner . . . . Gaylord Entertainment Company
President, COO and Alternate Governor . . . . Jack Diller
Exec. V.P./G.M. and Alternate Governor . . . . David Poile
Executive Vice President/Business Operations. . . . . . Tom Ward
Senior Vice President/Chief Financial Officer . . . . . . Ed Lang
Vice President/Communications & Development . . . Gerry Helper

Hockey Operations
Assistant General Manager . . . . Ray Shero
Head Coach . . . . Barry Trotz
Assistant Coaches . . . . Paul Gardner, Brent Peterson
Strength and Conditioning Coach . . . . Mark Nemish
Goaltending Coach . . . . Mitch Korn
Video Coach . . . . Robert Bouchard
Director of Player Personnel. . . . . Paul Fenton
Chief Amateur Scout. . . . . Craig Channell
Scouting Coordinator . . . . Dan MacKinnon
Professional Scout. . . . . Fred Devereaux
Amateur Scouts – Europe . . . Lucas Bergman, Alexei Dementiev, Martin Divis, Janne Kekalainen
Amateur Scouts - North America . . . . Luc Gauthier, Alan Hepple, Jeff Kealty, Rick Knickle, Mike Rooney, Greg Royce, Dennis Schueller
Head Athletic Trainer . . . . Dan Redmond
Equipment Manager . . . . Pete Rogers
Assistant Equipment Manager. . . . . Chris Scoppetto
Equipment Assistant . . . . Chris Moody
Locker Room Attendant . . . . Craig "Partner" Baugh
Massage Therapist . . . . Anthony Garrett
Nutritionist . . . . Donna Gurchiek
Manager of Team Services . . . . Gregory Harvey
Executive Assistant . . . . Kalli Quinn
Hockey Operations Assistant. . . . . Mike Corbett

Team Doctors
Dr. Michael J. Pagnani, MD, Dr. James W. McPherson Jr., DDS, Dr. Daniel Weikert, MD, Dr. Bryan D. Oslin, MD, Dr. Donald Griffin, MD, Dr. Gary S. Solomon, Ph. D., Dr. Carl Hampf, MD, Dr. Richard W. Garman, MD

Communications/Development
Communications Manager . . . . Ken Anderson
Communications Coordinator . . . . Tim Darling
Corporate Communications Coordinator. . . . . Cathy Lewandowski
Dir. Community Relations/Predators Foundation . . . Polly Pearce
Community Relations Manager . . . . Alexis Herbster
Community Relations Assistant . . . . Angel Winter
Manager, Amateur Hockey . . . . Marc Spigel
Graphic Artist, Communications & Development. . . Maggie Bizwell
Team Photographer . . . . John Russell

Business/Marketing/Corporate Sales
Vice President, Corporate Services. . . . . Susie Masotti
Director of Corporate Partnerships . . . . David Nivison
National Sales Director . . . . Jim Gibson
Corporate Sponsorship Sales, Account Executives . . Allison Gay, David Morse
Sponsor Services, Account Managers . . . . Evelyn Finch, Kristin Fricke, Tom Moulton
Premium Seating Manager . . . . Britt Kincheloe
Account Manager, Premium Seating . . . . Myron Murray
Director of Marketing . . . . Randy Campbell
Marketing and Special Events Manager. . . . . Christel Foley
Advertising Manager. . . . . Julia Robinson
Database Marketing Manager. . . . . Michael Vivelo
Marketing and Presentation Coordinator. . . . . Carrie Poss
Entertainment Coordinator . . . . Adam DeVault
Promotions Manager. . . . . Mark Iralson
Graphic Artist, Marketing . . . . Jennifer Sheets
Executive Assistant . . . . Linda Adams
Sponsor Sales Administrative Assistant . . . . Kelly Preuett

Finance/Human Resources
Director of Finance . . . . Beth Snider
Director of Human Resources . . . . Stephanie Ditenhafer
Administrator, Payroll & Accounting . . . . Susan Charnley
Accountant, Gaylord Entertainment Center. . . . . . . Tracy Hardes
Accountant, Team. . . . . Sjar Toney
Accounts Payable Clerk . . . . Carter Lynch
Accounting Coordinator . . . . Jonathan Norris
Manager, Internet Development . . . . Scott Pilkinton
Information Systems Manager. . . . . Jeff Beck
Computer Support Tech . . . . Wesley Green
Office Cordinator . . . . Laura Tucker
Executive Assistant . . . . Elaine Lewis

Broadcasting/Game Presentation
Vice President, Broadcasting . . . . John Guagliano
Director of Operations. . . . . Jimmy Corn
Producer . . . . Erik Barnhart
Game Presentation Manager. . . . . Bryan Shaffer
Broadcast and Entertainment Manager . . . . Susan Morgan
Video Presentation Manager . . . . Blake Grant
Production Assistant . . . . Robert Hill
Broadcasters . . . . Pete Weber, Terry Crisp

Ticket Operations
Vice President, Ticket Sales . . . . Scott Loft
Ticket Operations Manager . . . . Jamie Hall
Computer Operator . . . . Cordell Johnson
Business Development Manager . . . . Geoff Dunnuck
Club/Suite Sales Executive . . . . Tom Phillips
Corporate Account Execsutives . . . . Tony Hall, Nat Harden, Bob Milhizer, Jonathan Tuschl, Bill Walker
Fan Relations Manager . . . . Gene Connelly
Fan Relations Account Service Reps. . . . . Brad Gillispie, Elizabeth Mitchell, Tiffany Williams
Radio Flagship. . . . . WTN-FM (99.7 FM)
TV Flagship . . . . FOX Sports Net

New Jersey Devils

2000-01 Results: 48W-19L-12T-3OTL 111PTS. First, Atlantic Division

Year-by-Year Record

Season	GP	Home W	Home L	Home T	Home OL	Road W	Road L	Road T	Road OL	Overall W	Overall L	Overall T	Overall OL	GF	GA	Pts.	Finished	Playoff Result
2000-01	82	24	11	6	0	24	8	6	3	48	19	12	3	295	195	111	1st, Atlantic Div.	Lost Final
1999-2000	**82**	**28**	**9**	**3**	**1**	**17**	**15**	**5**	**4**	**45**	**24**	**8**	**5**	**251**	**203**	**103**	**2nd, Atlantic Div.**	**Won Stanley Cup**
1998-99	82	19	14	8	...	28	10	3	...	47	24	11	...	248	196	105	1st, Atlantic Div.	Lost Conf. Quarter-Final
1997-98	82	29	10	2	...	19	13	9	...	48	23	11	...	225	166	107	1st, Atlantic Div.	Lost Conf. Quarter-Final
1996-97	82	23	9	9	...	22	14	5	...	45	23	14	...	231	182	104	1st, Atlantic Div.	Lost Conf. Semi-Final
1995-96	82	22	17	2	...	15	16	10	...	37	33	12	...	215	202	86	6th, Atlantic Div.	Out of Playoffs
1994-95	**48**	**14**	**4**	**6**	**...**	**8**	**14**	**2**	**...**	**22**	**18**	**8**	**...**	**136**	**121**	**52**	**2nd, Atlantic Div.**	**Won Stanley Cup**
1993-94	84	29	11	2	...	18	14	10	...	47	25	12	...	306	220	106	2nd, Atlantic Div.	Lost Conf. Championship
1992-93	84	24	14	4	...	16	23	3	...	40	37	7	...	308	299	87	4th, Patrick Div.	Lost Div. Semi-Final
1991-92	80	24	12	4	...	14	19	3	...	38	31	11	...	289	259	87	4th, Patrick Div.	Lost Div. Semi-Final
1990-91	80	23	10	7	...	9	23	8	...	32	33	15	...	272	264	79	4th, Patrick Div.	Lost Div. Semi-Final
1989-90	80	22	15	3	...	15	19	6	...	37	34	9	...	295	288	83	2nd, Patrick Div.	Lost Div. Semi-Final
1988-89	80	17	18	5	...	10	23	7	...	27	41	12	...	281	325	66	5th, Patrick Div.	Out of Playoffs
1987-88	80	23	16	1	...	15	20	5	...	38	36	6	...	295	296	82	4th, Patrick Div.	Lost Conf. Championship
1986-87	80	20	17	3	...	9	28	3	...	29	45	6	...	293	368	64	6th, Patrick Div.	Out of Playoffs
1985-86	80	17	21	2	...	11	28	1	...	28	49	3	...	300	374	59	6th, Patrick Div.	Out of Playoffs
1984-85	80	13	21	6	...	9	27	4	...	22	48	10	...	264	346	54	5th, Patrick Div.	Out of Playoffs
1983-84	80	10	28	2	...	7	28	5	...	17	56	7	...	231	350	41	5th, Patrick Div.	Out of Playoffs
1982-83	80	11	20	9	...	6	29	5	...	17	49	14	...	230	338	48	5th, Patrick Div.	Out of Playoffs
1981-82**	80	14	21	5	...	4	28	8	...	18	49	13	...	241	362	49	5th, Smythe Div.	Out of Playoffs
1980-81**	80	15	16	9	...	7	29	4	...	22	45	13	...	258	344	57	5th, Smythe Div.	Out of Playoffs
1979-80**	80	12	20	8	...	7	28	5	...	19	48	13	...	234	308	51	6th, Smythe Div.	Out of Playoffs
1978-79**	80	8	24	8	...	7	29	4	...	15	53	12	...	210	331	42	4th, Smythe Div.	Out of Playoffs
1977-78**	80	17	14	9	...	2	26	12	...	19	40	21	...	257	305	59	2nd, Smythe Div.	Lost Prelim. Round
1976-77**	80	12	20	8	...	8	26	6	...	20	46	14	...	226	307	54	5th, Smythe Div.	Out of Playoffs
1975-76*	80	8	24	8	...	4	32	4	...	12	56	12	...	190	351	36	5th, Smythe Div.	Out of Playoffs
1974-75*	80	12	20	8	...	3	34	3	...	15	54	11	...	184	328	41	5th, Smythe Div.	Out of Playoffs

* Kansas City Scouts. ** Colorado Rockies.

2001-02 Schedule

Month	Day	Date	Opponent
Mar.	Sat.	17	Vancouver
Oct.	Sat.	6	at Washington
	Thu.	11	NY Islanders
	Sat.	13	at Montreal
	Wed.	17	at NY Rangers
	Thu.	18	San Jose
	Sat.	20	Ottawa
	Tue.	23	at Ottawa
	Sat.	27	Buffalo
	Tue.	30	at Boston
Nov.	Thu.	1	Phoenix
	Sat.	3	Boston*
	Wed.	7	Atlanta
	Fri.	9	Toronto
	Sat.	10	at Toronto
	Tue.	13	Pittsburgh
	Thu.	15	at Boston
	Sat.	17	Philadelphia*
	Sun.	18	Colorado*
	Tue.	20	at Philadelphia
	Fri.	23	at Tampa Bay
	Sat.	24	at Florida
	Tue.	27	at Pittsburgh
	Fri.	30	at Detroit
Dec.	Sat.	1	Detroit
	Tue.	4	Tampa Bay
	Wed.	5	at Montreal
	Sat.	8	Washington*
	Mon.	10	at Columbus
	Wed.	12	NY Islanders
	Fri.	14	Florida
	Sat.	15	at Ottawa
	Wed.	19	at NY Rangers
	Thu.	20	Edmonton
	Sat.	22	Ottawa*
	Wed.	26	Pittsburgh
	Sat.	29	at Vancouver
	Sun.	30	at Edmonton
Jan.	Tue.	1	St. Louis
	Thu.	3	Nashville
	Sat.	5	at Carolina
	Mon.	7	Los Angeles
	Wed.	9	Calgary
	Thu.	10	at Philadelphia
	Sat.	12	at Buffalo
	Tue.	15	Tampa Bay
	Thu.	17	NY Rangers
	Sat.	19	Carolina*
	Mon.	21	at Tampa Bay
	Wed.	23	at Florida
	Thu.	24	at Atlanta
	Sat.	26	at Minnesota*
	Tue.	29	at NY Islanders
	Wed.	30	Chicago
Feb.	Tue.	5	Montreal
	Thu.	7	Atlanta
	Sat.	9	at Pittsburgh*
	Sun.	10	Buffalo
	Tue.	12	at Buffalo
	Tue.	26	at NY Rangers
	Wed.	27	Philadelphia
Mar.	Fri.	1	Toronto
	Mon.	4	at Colorado
	Tue.	5	at Phoenix
	Fri.	8	at Anaheim
	Sun.	10	at Dallas
	Wed.	13	NY Islanders
	Sat.	16	NY Rangers*
	Wed.	20	at Chicago
	Thu.	21	at Nashville
	Sat.	23	Carolina*
	Mon.	25	Florida
	Wed.	27	at Pittsburgh
	Fri.	29	Washington
	Sat.	30	at Toronto
Apr.	Mon.	1	at NY Islanders
	Wed.	3	at Carolina
	Fri.	5	at Atlanta
	Sun.	7	Boston*
	Wed.	10	Philadelphia
	Fri.	12	Montreal
	Sat.	13	at Washington

* Denotes afternoon game.

Franchise date: June 11, 1974

Transferred from Denver to New Jersey, June 30, 1982.
Previously transferred from Kansas City to Denver.

ATLANTIC DIVISION

28th NHL Season

A hero of New Jersey's Stanley Cup victory in 2000, Jason Arnott averaged better than a point a game last season with 21 goals and 34 assists in 54 outings. Eight of his goals came on New Jersey's league-leading power-play.

2001-02 Player Personnel

FORWARDS	HT	WT	S	Place of Birth	Date	2000-01 Club
ARNOTT, Jason	6-4	225	R	Collingwood, Ont.	10/11/74	New Jersey
BERGLUND, Christian	5-11	185	L	Orebro, Sweden	3/12/80	Farjestads BK
BICEK, Jiri	5-10	190	L	Kosice, Czech.	12/3/78	New Jersey-Albany
BIRBRAER, Max	6-2	195	L	Ust-Kamenogorsk, USSR	12/15/80	Albany
BRYLIN, Sergei	5-10	190	L	Moscow, USSR	1/13/74	New Jersey
CAMERON, Scott	6-0	185	L	Sudbury, Ont.	4/11/81	North Bay
CLOUTHIER, Brett	6-5	225	L	Ottawa, Ont.	6/9/81	Kingston
CLOUTIER, Sylvain	6-0	200	L	Mont-Laurier, Que.	2/13/74	Albany
DAGENAIS, Pierre	6-5	215	L	Blainville, Que.	3/4/78	New Jersey-Albany
DRURY, Ted	6-2	210	L	Boston, MA	9/13/71	Columbus-Chi (IHL)
ELIAS, Patrik	6-1	195	L	Trebic, Czech.	4/13/76	New Jersey
FERRARO, Chris	5-9	175	R	Port Jefferson, NY	1/24/73	Albany
FOSTER, Adrian	6-1	200	L	Lethbridge, Alta.	1/15/82	Saskatoon
GIONTA, Brian	5-7	160	R	Rochester, NY	1/18/79	Boston College
GOMEZ, Scott	5-11	200	L	Anchorage, AK	12/23/79	New Jersey
GRON, Stanislav	6-2	205	L	Bratislava, Czech.	10/28/78	New Jersey-Albany
HOLIK, Bobby	6-4	230	R	Jihlava, Czech.	1/1/71	New Jersey
JEFFERSON, Mike	5-9	180	R	Brampton, Ont.	10/21/80	New Jersey-Albany
LeBLANC, Robin	6-1	177	R	Chur, Switz.	1/11/83	Baie Comeau
LEHOUX, Jason	6-2	220	L	Ste-Marie-Beauce, Que.	7/21/79	Albany
LEWIS, Carlyle	6-3	230	R	Middleton, N.S.	3/1/78	Albany
MADDEN, John	5-11	195	L	Barrie, Ont.	5/4/73	New Jersey
McCUTCHEON, Warren	6-4	190	L	Morden, Man.	8/6/82	Lethbridge
McKAY, Randy	6-2	210	R	Montreal, Que.	1/25/67	New Jersey
McKENZIE, Jim	6-4	230	L	Gull Lake, Sask.	11/3/69	New Jersey
NEMCHINOV, Sergei	6-1	205	L	Moscow, USSR	1/14/64	New Jersey
NOLAN, Brandon	6-0	175	L	Sault Ste. Marie, Ont.	7/18/83	Oshawa
PANDOLFO, Jay	6-1	190	L	Winchester, MA	12/27/74	New Jersey
POHANKA, Igor	6-3	185	L	Piestany, Czech.	7/5/83	Prince Albert
ROCHEFORT, Richard	5-10	195	R	North Bay, Ont.	1/7/77	Albany
RUPP, Mike	6-5	225	L	Cleveland, OH	1/13/80	Albany
SALOMONSSON, Andreas	6-0	185	L	Ornskoldsvik, Sweden	12/19/73	Djurgardens IF
SKRLAC, Rob	6-5	245	L	Port McNeill, B.C.	6/10/76	Albany
STEVENSON, Turner	6-3	225	R	Prince George, B.C.	5/18/72	New Jersey
SYKORA, Petr	6-0	190	L	Plzen, Czech.	11/19/76	New Jersey
DEFENSEMEN						
ALBELIN, Tommy	6-1	195	L	Stockholm, Sweden	5/21/64	Calgary
ANDREWS, Daryl	6-3	215	L	Campbell River, B.C.	4/27/77	Albany
BOUMEDIENNE, Josef	6-1	200	L	Stockholm, Sweden	1/12/78	Albany
COLE, Phil	6-4	195	L	Winnipeg, Man.	9/6/82	Lethbridge
COMMODORE, Mike	6-4	230	R	Fort Saskatchewan, Alta.	11/7/79	New Jersey-Albany
DANEYKO, Ken	6-1	215	L	Windsor, Ont.	4/17/64	New Jersey
DEZAINDE, Joel	6-0	200	L	Simcoe, Ont.	11/2/78	Mississippi
ENGELLAND, Deryk	6-2	205	R	Edmonton, Alta.	4/5/82	Moose Jaw
GOC, Sascha	6-2	225	R	Calw, West Germany	4/17/79	New Jersey-Albany
JOHNSTONE, Alex	6-1	205	L	Halifax, N.S.	12/28/79	Adirondack
JOKELA, Mikko	6-1	205	R	Lappeenranta, Finland	3/4/80	Sai-Lappeenranta-KooKoo Kouvola
LAKOS, Andre	6-6	230	R	Vienna, Austria	7/29/79	Albany
NEHRLING, Lucas	6-5	220	R	Peterborough, Ont.	8/14/79	Albany-Adirondack
NIEDERMAYER, Scott	6-1	200	L	Edmonton, Alta.	8/31/73	New Jersey
RAFALSKI, Brian	5-9	195	R	Dearborn, MI	9/28/73	New Jersey
STEVENS, Scott	6-2	215	L	Kitchener, Ont.	4/1/64	New Jersey
UCHEVATOV, Victor	6-4	205	L	Angarsk, USSR	2/10/83	HC Yaroslavl-2
WHITE, Colin	6-4	215	L	New Glasgow, N.S.	12/12/77	New Jersey

GOALTENDERS	HT	WT	C	Place of Birth	Date	2000-01 Club
AHONEN, Ari	6-1	185	L	Jyvaskyla, Finland	2/6/81	HIFK Helsinki
BRODEUR, Martin	6-2	205	L	Montreal, Que.	5/6/72	New Jersey
CLEMMENSEN, Scott	6-2	185	L	Des Moines, IA	7/23/77	Boston College
DAMPHOUSSE, Jean-Francois	6-0	180	L	St-Alexis-des-Monts, Que.	7/21/79	Albany
HENRY, Frederic	5-11	180	L	Cap-Rouge, Que.	8/9/77	Albany

General Managers' History

Sid Abel, 1974-75, 1975-76; Ray Miron, 1976-77 to 1980-81; Billy MacMillan, 1981-82, 1982-83; Billy MacMillan and Max McNab, 1983-84; Max McNab 1984-85 to 1986-87; Lou Lamoriello, 1987-88 to date.

General Manager

LAMORIELLO, LOU
CEO/President/General Manager, New Jersey Devils.
Born in Providence, RI, October 21, 1942.

Lou Lamoriello's life-long dedication to the game of hockey was rewarded in 1992 when he was named a recipient of the Lester Patrick Trophy for outstanding service to hockey in the United States. Lamoriello is entering his 15th season as president and general manager of the Devils following more than 20 years with Providence College as a player, coach and administrator. His trades, signings and draft choices helped lead the Devils to their first Stanley Cup championship in 1995 and another in 2000. A member of the varsity hockey Friars during his undergraduate days, he became an assistant coach with the college club after graduating in 1963. Lamoriello was later named head coach and in the ensuing 15 years, led his teams to a 248-179-13 record and appearances in 10 post-season tournaments, including the 1983 NCAA Final Four. Lamoriello also served a five-year term as athletic director at Providence and was a co-founder of Hockey East, one of the strongest collegiate hockey conferences in the U.S. He remained as athletic director until he was hired as president of the Devils on April 30, 1987. He assumed the dual responsibility of general manager on September 10, 1987. He was g.m. of Team USA for the first World Cup of Hockey in 1996 as the U.S. captured the championship. He was also the g.m. for the 1998 U.S. Olympic Team.

2000-01 Scoring

* - rookie

Regular Season

Pos	#	Player	Team	GP	G	A	Pts	+/–	PIM	PP	SH	GW	GT	S	%
L	26	Patrik Elias	N.J.	82	40	56	96	45	51	8	3	6	1	220	18.2
R	89	Alexander Mogilny	N.J.	75	43	40	83	10	43	12	0	7	0	240	17.9
R	17	Petr Sykora	N.J.	73	35	46	81	36	32	9	2	3	0	249	14.1
C	23	Scott Gomez	N.J.	76	14	49	63	–1	46	2	0	4	0	155	9.0
C	25	Jason Arnott	N.J.	54	21	34	55	23	75	8	0	3	2	138	15.2
C	18	Sergei Brylin	N.J.	75	23	29	52	25	24	3	1	0	2	130	17.7
D	28	Brian Rafalski	N.J.	78	9	43	52	36	26	6	0	1	1	142	6.3
C	16	Bobby Holik	N.J.	80	15	35	50	19	97	3	0	3	0	206	7.3
R	21	Randy McKay	N.J.	77	23	20	43	3	50	12	0	5	0	120	19.2
C	11	John Madden	N.J.	80	23	15	38	24	12	0	3	4	1	163	14.1
D	27	Scott Niedermayer	N.J.	57	6	29	35	14	22	1	0	5	0	87	6.9
D	4	Scott Stevens	N.J.	81	9	22	31	40	71	3	0	2	0	171	5.3
L	12	Sergei Nemchinov	N.J.	65	8	22	30	11	16	1	0	2	0	70	11.4
R	24	Turner Stevenson	N.J.	69	8	18	26	11	97	2	0	1	1	92	8.7
D	5 *	Colin White	N.J.	82	1	19	20	32	155	0	0	1	0	114	0.9
D	6	Sean O'Donnell	MIN	63	4	12	16	–2	128	1	0	2	0	58	6.9
			N.J.	17	0	1	1	2	33	0	0	0	0	9	0.0
			TOTAL	80	4	13	17	0	161	1	0	2	0	67	6.0
L	20	Jay Pandolfo	N.J.	63	4	12	16	3	16	0	0	0	0	57	7.0
C	22	Bob Corkum	L.A.	58	4	6	10	–12	18	1	0	0	0	47	8.5
			N.J.	17	3	1	4	4	4	0	0	0	0	19	15.8
			TOTAL	75	7	7	14	–8	22	1	0	0	0	66	10.6
D	2	Ken Sutton	N.J.	53	1	7	8	9	37	0	0	0	0	35	2.9
L	14 *	Pierre Dagenais	N.J.	9	3	2	5	1	6	1	0	1	0	20	15.0
D	6 *	Mike Commodore	N.J.	20	1	4	5	5	14	0	0	0	0	11	9.1
L	19	Jim McKenzie	N.J.	53	2	2	4	0	119	0	0	0	0	32	6.3
D	3	Ken Daneyko	N.J.	77	0	4	4	8	87	0	0	0	0	50	0.0
L	9 *	Jiri Bicek	N.J.	5	1	0	1	0	4	0	0	0	0	10	10.0
R	22	Ed Ward	N.J.	4	0	1	1	2	6	0	0	0	0	4	0.0
G	30	Martin Brodeur	N.J.	72	0	1	1	0	14	0	0	0	0	2	0.0
C	10 *	Stanislav Gron	N.J.	1	0	0	0	1	0	0	0	0	0	2	0.0
C	8 *	Mike Jefferson	N.J.	2	0	0	0	0	6	0	0	0	0	3	0.0
D	7 *	Sasha Goc	N.J.	11	0	0	0	7	4	0	0	0	0	7	0.0
G	34	John Vanbiesbrouck	NYI	44	0	0	0	0	8	0	0	0	0	0	0.0
			N.J.	4	0	0	0	0	0	0	0	0	0	0	0.0
			TOTAL	48	0	0	0	0	8	0	0	0	0	0	0.0

Goaltending

No.	Goaltender	GPI	Mins	Avg	W	L	T	EN	SO	GA	SA	S%
34	John Vanbiesbrouck	4	240	1.50	4	0	0	0	1	6	93	.935
30	Martin Brodeur	72	4297	2.32	42	17	11	2	9	166	1762	.906
31	Chris Terreri	10	453	2.78	2	5	1	0	0	21	167	.874
	Totals	**82**	**5001**	**2.34**	**48**	**22**	**12**	**2**	**10**	**195**	**2024**	**.904**

Playoffs

Pos	#	Player	Team	GP	G	A	Pts	+/–	PIM	PP	SH	GW	GT	S	%
L	26	Patrik Elias	N.J.	25	9	14	23	11	10	3	1	2	0	58	15.5
R	17	Petr Sykora	N.J.	25	10	12	22	15	12	2	2	2	0	71	14.1
D	28	Brian Rafalski	N.J.	25	7	11	18	10	7	1	0	3	1	47	14.9
C	16	Bobby Holik	N.J.	25	6	10	16	1	37	1	0	3	0	66	9.1
R	89	Alexander Mogilny	N.J.	25	5	11	16	3	8	1	0	2	0	76	6.6
C	25	Jason Arnott	N.J.	23	8	7	15	8	16	5	0	0	0	42	19.0
C	23	Scott Gomez	N.J.	25	5	9	14	7	24	0	0	0	0	70	7.1
R	21	Randy McKay	N.J.	19	6	3	9	3	8	2	0	1	1	31	19.4
D	4	Scott Stevens	N.J.	25	1	7	8	3	37	0	0	0	0	34	2.9
C	11	John Madden	N.J.	25	4	3	7	2	6	0	0	0	0	62	6.5
C	18	Sergei Brylin	N.J.	20	3	4	7	1	6	1	0	1	0	23	13.0
D	27	Scott Niedermayer	N.J.	21	0	6	6	7	14	0	0	0	0	29	0.0
L	20	Jay Pandolfo	N.J.	25	1	4	5	–1	4	0	0	0	0	19	5.3
R	24	Turner Stevenson	N.J.	23	1	3	4	2	20	0	0	1	0	14	7.1
L	12	Sergei Nemchinov	N.J.	25	1	3	4	0	4	0	0	0	0	16	6.3
C	22	Bob Corkum	N.J.	12	1	2	3	–2	0	0	0	0	0	11	9.1
D	6	Sean O'Donnell	N.J.	23	1	2	3	5	41	0	0	0	0	9	11.1
D	3	Ken Daneyko	N.J.	25	0	3	3	4	21	0	0	0	0	13	0.0
D	5 *	Colin White	N.J.	25	0	3	3	7	42	0	0	0	0	25	0.0
G	30	Martin Brodeur	N.J.	25	0	1	1	0	0	0	0	0	0	0	0.0
L	19	Jim McKenzie	N.J.	3	0	0	0	1	2	0	0	0	0	1	0.0
D	2	Ken Sutton	N.J.	6	0	0	0	1	13	0	0	0	0	7	0.0

Goaltending

No.	Goaltender	GPI	Mins	Avg	W	L	EN	SO	GA	SA	S%
30	Martin Brodeur	25	1505	2.07	15	10	0	4	52	507	.897
	Totals	**25**	**1513**	**2.06**	**15**	**10**	**0**	**4**	**52**	**507**	**.897**

Coaching History

Bep Guidolin, 1974-75; Bep Guidolin, Sid Abel and Eddie Bush, 1975-76; John Wilson, 1976-77; Pat Kelly, 1977-78; Pat Kelly and Aldo Guidolin, 1978-79; Don Cherry, 1979-80; Bill MacMillan, 1980-81; Bert Marshall and Marshall Johnston, 1981-82; Bill MacMillan, 1982-83; Bill MacMillan and Tom McVie, 1983-84; Doug Carpenter, 1984-85 to 1986-87; Doug Carpenter and Jim Schoenfeld, 1987-88; Jim Schoenfeld, 1988-89; Jim Schoenfeld and John Cunniff, 1989-90; John Cunniff and Tom McVie, 1990-91; Tom McVie, 1991-92; Herb Brooks, 1992-93; Jacques Lemaire, 1993-94 to 1997-98; Robbie Ftorek, 1998-99; Robbie Ftorek and Larry Robinson, 1999-2000; Larry Robinson, 2000-01 to date.

Captains' History

Simon Nolet, 1974-75 to 1976-77; Wilf Paiement, 1977-78; Gary Croteau, 1978-79; Mike Christie, Rene Robert and Lanny McDonald, 1979-80; Lanny McDonald, 1980-81; Lanny McDonald and Rob Ramage, 1981-82; Don Lever, 1982-83; Don Lever and Mel Bridgman, 1983-84; Mel Bridgman, 1984-85 to 1986-87; Kirk Muller, 1987-88 to 1990-91; Bruce Driver, 1991-92; Scott Stevens, 1992-93 to date.

Club Records

Team

(Figures in brackets for season records are games played; records for fewest points, wins, ties, losses, goals, goals against are for 70 or more games)

Most Points	111	2000-01 (82)
Most Wins	48	1997-98 (82), 2000-01 (82)
Most Ties	21	1977-78 (80)
Most Losses	56	1983-84 (80), 1975-76 (80)
Most Goals	308	1992-93 (84)
Most Goals Against	374	1985-86 (80)
Fewest Points	*36	1975-76 (80)
	41	1983-84 (80)
Fewest Wins	*12	1975-76 (80)
	17	1982-83 (80), 1983-84 (80)
Fewest Ties	3	1985-86 (80)
Fewest Losses	19	2000-01 (82)
Fewest Goals	*184	1974-75 (80)
	215	1995-96 (82)
Fewest Goals Against	166	1997-98 (82)
Longest Winning Streak		
Overall	13	Feb. 26-Mar. 23/01
Home	8	Oct. 9-Nov. 7/87
Away	**10	Feb. 27-Apr. 7/01
Longest Undefeated Streak		
Overall	13	Three times
Home	15	Jan. 8-Mar. 15/97 (9 wins, 6 tie)
Away	10	Feb. 27-Apr. 7/01 (10 wins)
Longest Losing Streak		
Overall	*14	Dec. 30/75-Jan. 29/76
	10	Oct. 14-Nov. 4/83
Home	9	Dec. 22/85-Feb. 6/86
Away	12	Oct. 19-Dec. 1/83
Longest Winless Streak		
Overall	*27	Feb. 12-Apr. 4/76 (21 losses, 6 ties)
	18	Oct. 20-Nov. 26/82 (14 losses 4 ties)
Home	*14	Feb. 12-Mar. 30/76 (10 losses, 4 ties), Feb. 4-Mar. 31/79 (12 losses, 2 ties)
	9	Dec. 22/85-Feb. 6/86 (9 losses)
Away	*32	Nov. 12/77-Mar. 15/78 (22 losses, 10 ties)
	14	Dec. 26/82-Mar. 5/83 (13 losses, 1 tie)
Most Shutouts, Season	13	1996-97 (82)
Most PIM, Season	2,494	1988-89 (80)
Most Goals, Game	9	Nine times

Individual

Most Seasons	18	Ken Daneyko
Most Games	1,147	Ken Daneyko
Most Goals, Career	347	John MacLean
Most Assists, Career	354	John MacLean
Most Points, Career	701	John MacLean (347G, 354A)
Most PIM, Career	2,426	Ken Daneyko
Most Shutouts, Career	51	Martin Brodeur
Longest Consecutive Games Streak	388	Ken Daneyko (Nov. 4/89-Mar. 29/94)
Most Goals, Season	46	Pat Verbeek (1987-88)
Most Assists, Season	60	Scott Stevens (1993-94)
Most Points, Season	96	Patrik Elias (2000-01; 40G, 56A)
Most PIM, Season	295	Krzysztof Oliwa (1997-98)
Most Points, Defenseman, Season	78	Scott Stevens (1993-94; 18G, 60A)
Most Points, Center, Season	94	Kirk Muller (1987-88; 37G, 57A)
Most Points, Right Wing, Season	*87	Wilf Paiement (1977-78; 31G, 56A)
	87	John MacLean (1988-89; 42G, 45A)
Most Points, Left Wing, Season	96	Patrik Elias (2000-01; 40G, 56A)
Most Points, Rookie, Season	70	Scott Gomez (1999-2000; 19G, 51A)
Most Shutouts, Season	10	Martin Brodeur (1996-97, 1997-98)
Most Goals, Game	4	Four times
Most Assists, Game	5	Greg Adams (Oct. 10/85), Kirk Muller (Mar. 25/87), Tom Kurvers (Feb. 13/89)
Most Points, Game	6	Kirk Muller (Nov. 29/86; 3G, 3A)

* Records include Kansas City Scouts and Colorado Rockies, 1974-75 through 1981-82.

** NHL Record.

All-time Record vs. Other Clubs

Regular Season

	At Home								On Road								Total							
	GP	W	L	T	OL	GF	GA	PTS	GP	W	L	T	OL	GF	GA	PTS	GP	W	L	T	OL	GF	GA	PTS
Anaheim	7	6	1	0	0	28	12	12	7	4	3	0	0	19	20	8	14	10	4	0	0	47	32	20
Atlanta	4	4	0	0	0	18	3	8	4	3	0	1	0	20	6	7	8	7	0	1	0	38	9	15
Boston	47	13	24	10	0	128	157	36	50	14	28	7	1	151	201	36	97	27	52	17	1	279	358	72
Buffalo	48	13	26	9	0	135	168	35	48	13	30	5	0	151	202	31	96	26	56	14	0	286	370	66
Calgary	42	13	26	3	0	118	157	29	41	6	27	8	0	107	179	20	83	19	53	11	0	225	336	49
Carolina	39	23	13	3	0	142	126	49	38	13	16	8	1	118	128	35	77	36	29	11	1	260	254	84
Chicago	44	17	16	11	0	133	136	45	44	11	24	9	0	122	173	31	88	28	40	20	0	255	309	76
Colorado	34	18	12	4	0	143	116	40	32	13	16	3	0	96	118	29	66	31	28	7	0	239	234	69
Columbus	1	0	0	1	0	2	2	1	1	1	0	0	0	6	3	2	2	1	0	1	0	8	5	3
Dallas	42	20	19	3	0	141	129	43	43	12	24	6	1	114	162	31	85	32	43	9	1	255	291	74
Detroit	38	19	10	9	0	133	102	47	37	13	22	2	0	123	152	28	75	32	32	11	0	256	254	75
Edmonton	30	13	15	2	0	102	101	28	30	10	14	6	0	112	135	26	60	23	29	8	0	214	236	54
Florida	18	11	4	3	0	56	38	25	19	8	7	4	0	43	44	20	37	19	11	7	0	99	82	45
Los Angeles	41	18	18	5	0	137	143	41	40	7	27	6	0	125	199	20	81	25	45	11	0	262	342	61
Minnesota	1	1	0	0	0	6	2	2	1	1	0	0	0	4	2	2	2	2	0	0	0	10	4	4
Montreal	48	21	24	3	0	144	183	45	48	13	28	6	1	126	170	33	96	34	52	9	1	270	353	78
Nashville	3	1	2	0	0	9	8	2	2	2	0	0	0	6	2	4	5	3	2	0	0	15	10	6
NY Islanders	76	30	35	11	0	253	273	71	77	15	52	10	0	222	335	40	153	45	87	21	0	475	608	111
NY Rangers	78	40	33	5	0	271	264	85	76	20	39	17	0	229	304	57	154	60	72	22	0	500	568	142
Ottawa	17	11	4	2	0	58	38	24	18	10	5	3	0	48	40	23	35	21	9	5	0	106	78	47
Philadelphia	75	39	29	7	0	267	268	85	77	21	48	8	0	201	308	50	152	60	77	15	0	468	576	135
Phoenix	27	11	10	6	0	89	82	28	29	6	20	3	0	77	110	15	56	17	30	9	0	166	192	43
Pittsburgh	73	34	26	13	0	273	252	81	71	28	38	4	1	249	274	61	144	62	64	17	1	522	526	142
St. Louis	44	20	17	7	0	142	127	47	44	10	26	7	1	134	187	28	88	30	43	14	1	276	314	75
San Jose	10	5	4	1	0	35	21	11	9	5	2	1	1	27	20	12	19	10	6	2	1	62	41	23
Tampa Bay	20	17	2	1	0	79	27	35	19	12	4	3	0	65	44	27	39	29	6	4	0	144	71	62
Toronto	40	14	13	13	0	141	126	41	42	10	28	4	0	132	174	24	82	24	41	17	0	273	300	65
Vancouver	46	20	20	6	0	147	149	46	46	9	26	11	0	128	171	29	92	29	46	17	0	275	320	75
Washington	73	34	31	7	1	227	219	76	73	22	46	5	0	209	290	49	146	56	77	12	1	436	509	125
Defunct Clubs	8	4	2	2	0	25	19	10	8	2	3	3	0	19	27	7	16	6	5	5	0	44	46	17
Totals	**1074**	**490**	**436**	**147**	**1**	**3582**	**3448**	**1128**	**1074**	**314**	**603**	**150**	**7**	**3183**	**4180**	**785**	**2148**	**804**	**1039**	**297**	**8**	**6765**	**7628**	**1913**

Playoffs

	Series	W	L	GP	W	L	T	GF	GA	Last Mtg.	Round	Result
Boston	3	2	1	18	11	7	0	55	52	1995	CQF	W 4-1
Buffalo	1	1	0	7	4	3	0	14	14	1994	CQF	W 4-3
Carolina	1	1	0	6	4	2	0	20	8	2001	CQF	W 4-2
Colorado	1	0	1	7	3	4	0	11	19	2001	F	L 3-4
Dallas	1	1	0	6	4	2	0	15	9	2000	F	W 4-2
Detroit	1	1	0	4	4	0	0	16	7	1995	F	W 4-0
Florida	1	1	0	4	4	0	0	12	6	2000	CQF	W 4-0
Montreal	1	1	0	5	4	1	0	22	11	1997	CQF	W 4-1
NY Islanders	1	1	0	6	4	2	0	23	18	1988	DSF	W 4-2
NY Rangers	3	0	3	19	7	12	0	46	56	1997	CSF	L 1-4
Ottawa	1	0	1	6	2	4	0	12	13	1998	CQF	L 2-4
Philadelphia	3	2	1	15	8	7	0	41	35	2000	CF	W 4-3
Pittsburgh	5	2	3	29	15	14	0	86	80	2001	CF	W 4-1
Toronto	2	2	0	13	8	5	0	37	27	2001	CSF	W 4-3
Washington	2	1	1	13	6	7	0	43	44	1990	DSF	L 2-4
Totals	**27**	**16**	**11**	**158**	**88**	**70**	**0**	**449**	**403**			

Playoff Results 2001-1997

Year	Round	Opponent	Result	GF	GA
2001	F	Colorado	L 3-4	11	19
	CF	Pittsburgh	W 4-1	17	7
	CSF	Toronto	W 4-3	21	18
	CQF	Carolina	W 4-2	20	8
2000	**F**	**Dallas**	**W 4-2**	**15**	**9**
	CF	Philadelphia	W 4-3	18	15
	CSF	Toronto	W 4-2	16	9
	CQF	Florida	W 4-0	12	6
1999	CQF	Pittsburgh	L 3-4	18	21
1998	CQF	Ottawa	L 2-4	12	13
1997	CSF	NY Rangers	L 1-4	5	10
	CQF	Montreal	W 4-1	22	11

Abbreviations: Round: F – Final; **CF** – conference final; **CSF** – conference semi-final; **CQF** – conference quarter-final; **DSF** – division semi-final.

Calgary totals include Atlanta Flames, 1974-75 to 1979-80.
Colorado totals include Quebec, 1979-80 to 1994-95.
Phoenix totals include Winnipeg, 1979-80 to 1995-96.
Carolina totals include Hartford, 1979-80 to 1996-97.
Dallas totals include Minnesota North Stars, 1974-75 to 1992-93.

2000-01 Results

Oct.	6	Montreal	8-4		13	Toronto	4-4
	13	at Ottawa	1-3		16	Boston	4-5
	14	Anaheim	4-2		18	at Philadelphia	7-1
	17	at Atlanta	3-3		20	Atlanta	3-2
	19	at Washington	2-5		21	at Minnesota	4-2
	21	Tampa Bay	7-2		24	at Dallas	4-1
	25	at Florida	2-1		25	at St. Louis	3-4*
	27	at Carolina	3-3		27	at Boston	3-4*
	28	at Pittsburgh	9-0		30	Detroit	3-1
	30	Florida	6-5*		31	at NY Islanders	2-3
Nov.	1	Philadelphia	1-1	**Feb.**	6	at Montreal	4-0
	2	at Toronto	3-5		8	at Ottawa	4-4
	4	Los Angeles	1-2		10	at Pittsburgh	4-5*
	8	Nashville	3-4		11	at NY Rangers	1-1
	10	Pittsburgh	2-4		14	Ottawa	2-3
	11	Buffalo	0-4		16	Pittsburgh	4-4
	14	San Jose	2-3		17	at Buffalo	1-5
	16	at Boston	3-2*		19	at Toronto	2-0
	18	Carolina	3-2*		22	Buffalo	0-1
	22	at Anaheim	5-2		23	at Carolina	2-3
	23	at Los Angeles	6-1		26	Florida	5-3
	25	at San Jose	3-2		27	at NY Islanders	4-1
	29	NY Rangers	5-2	**Mar.**	2	Carolina	7-3
Dec.	1	NY Islanders	0-0		4	Tampa Bay	6-0
	3	at NY Islanders	1-1		6	Ottawa	3-2*
	5	Colorado	6-1		8	Minnesota	6-2
	7	at Buffalo	2-5		10	at Philadelphia	3-2
	9	Washington	2-3		13	at Colorado	6-3
	11	Atlanta	4-0		14	at Phoenix	3-2
	15	Montreal	2-1		17	at Edmonton	6-5*
	16	at Philadelphia	3-6		19	at Calgary	4-2
	20	Dallas	4-1		21	NY Rangers	4-0
	22	at Florida	2-0		23	Vancouver	4-0
	23	at Tampa Bay	5-1		25	Pittsburgh	2-4
	27	Columbus	2-2		27	at Tampa Bay	7-1
	29	Washington	4-2		28	at Atlanta	4-2
	31	at Columbus	6-3		31	NY Rangers	3-4
Jan.	2	Philadelphia	1-1	**Apr.**	2	Chicago	4-3
	4	NY Islanders	4-2		3	at Washington	6-4
	6	at NY Rangers	5-5		6	Boston	5-2
	10	Phoenix	5-1		7	at Montreal	2-0

* – Overtime

Entry Draft Selections 2001-1987

2001
Pick
28 Adrian Foster
44 Igor Pohanka
48 Tuomas Pihlman
60 Victor Uchevatov
67 Robin LeBlanc
72 Brandon Nolan
128 Andrei Posnov
163 Andreas Salomonsson
194 James Massen
229 Aaron Voros
257 Yevgeny Gamalei

2000
Pick
22 David Hale
39 Teemu Laine
56 Alexander Suglobov
57 Matt DeMarchi
62 Paul Martin
67 Max Birbraer
76 Mike Rupp
125 Phil Cole
135 Mike Jefferson
164 Matus Kostur
194 Deryk Engelland
198 Ken Magowan
257 Warren McCutcheon

1999
Pick
27 Ari Ahonen
42 Mike Commodore
50 Brett Clouthier
95 Andre Lakos
100 Teemu Kesa
185 Scott Cameron
214 Chris Hartsburg
242 Justin Dziama

1998
Pick
26 Mike Van Ryn
27 Scott Gomez
37 Christian Berglund
82 Brian Gionta
96 Mikko Jokela
105 Pierre Dagenais
119 Anton But
143 Ryan Flinn
172 Jacques Lariviere
199 Erik Jensen
227 Marko Ahosilta
257 Ryan Held

1997
Pick
24 Jean-Francois Damphousse
38 Stanislav Gron
104 Lucas Nehrling
131 Jiri Bicek
159 Sascha Goc
188 Mathieu Benoit
215 Scott Clemmensen
241 Jan Srdinko

1996
Pick
10 Lance Ward
38 Wes Mason
41 Josh DeWolf
47 Pierre Dagenais
49 Colin White
63 Scott Parker
91 Josef Boumedienne
101 Josh MacNevin
118 Glenn Crawford
145 Sean Ritchlin
173 Daryl Andrews
199 Willie Mitchell
205 Jay Bertsch
225 Pasi Petrilainen

1995
Pick
18 Petr Sykora
44 Nathan Perrott
70 Sergei Vyshedkevich
78 David Gosselin
79 Alyn McCauley
96 Henrik Rehnberg
122 Chris Mason
148 Adam Young
174 Richard Rochefort
200 Frederic Henry
226 Colin O'Hara

1994
Pick
25 Vadim Sharifijanov
51 Patrik Elias
71 Sheldon Souray
103 Zdenek Skorepa
129 Christian Gosselin
134 Ryan Smart
155 Luciano Caravaggio
181 Jeff Williams
207 Eric Bertrand
233 Steve Sullivan
259 Scott Swanjord
269 Mike Hanson

1993
Pick
13 Denis Pederson
32 Jay Pandolfo
39 Brendan Morrison
65 Krzysztof Oliwa
110 John Guirestante
143 Steve Brule
169 Nikolai Zavarukhin
195 Thomas Cullen
221 Judd Lambert
247 Jimmy Provencher
273 Mike Legg

1992
Pick
18 Jason Smith
42 Sergei Brylin
66 Cale Hulse
90 Vitali Tomilin
94 Scott McCabe
114 Ryan Black
138 Dan Trebil
162 Geordie Kinnear
186 Stephane Yelle
210 Jeff Toms
234 Heath Weenk
258 Vladislav Yakovenko

1991
Pick
3 Scott Niedermayer
11 Brian Rolston
33 Donevan Hextall
55 Fredrik Lindquist
77 Bradley Willner
121 Curt Regnier
143 David Craievich
165 Paul Wolanski
187 Daniel Reimann
231 Kevin Riehl
253 Jason Hehr

1990
Pick
20 Martin Brodeur
24 David Harlock
29 Chris Gotziaman
53 Mike Dunham
56 Brad Bombardir
64 Mike Bodnarchuk
95 Dean Malkoc
104 Petr Kuchyna
116 Lubomir Kolnik
137 Chris McAlpine
179 Jaroslav Modry
200 Corey Schwab
221 Valeri Zelepukin
242 Todd Reirden

1989
Pick
5 Bill Guerin
18 Jason Miller
26 Jarrod Skalde
47 Scott Pellerin
89 Mike Heinke
110 David Emma
152 Sergei Starikov
173 Andre Faust
215 Jason Simon
236 Peter Larsson

1988
Pick
12 Corey Foster
23 Jeff Christian
54 Zdeno Ciger
65 Matt Ruchty
75 Scott Luik
96 Chris Nelson
117 Chad Johnson
138 Chad Erickson
159 Bryan Lafort
180 Sergei Svetlov
201 Bob Woods
207 Alexander Semak
222 Charles Hughes
244 Robert Wallwork

1987
Pick
2 Brendan Shanahan
23 Ricard Persson
65 Brian Sullivan
86 Kevin Dean
107 Ben Hankinson
128 Tom Neziol
149 Jim Dowd
170 John Blessman
191 Peter Fry
212 Alain Charland

Coach

ROBINSON, LARRY
Coach, New Jersey Devils. Born in Winchester, Ont., June 2, 1951.

On March 23, 2000, Larry Robinson was moved up from assistant coach to replace Robbie Ftorek as head coach in New Jersey. He went on to lead the Devils to the second Stanley Cup championship in franchise history that year, then guided the club back to the Finals in 2001. Previously, Robinson had been an assistant coach with the Devils when they won their first Stanley Cup title in 1995. He had first joined the Devils in 1993 following a one-year absence from hockey after concluding a 20-year NHL career that included six Stanley Cup championships and two Norris Trophy titles with the Montreal Canadiens.

Robinson returned to New Jersey for his second stint with the Devils when he was named to an assistant coaching position on May 26, 1999. He had spent the previous four seasons as the head coach of the Los Angeles Kings. Robinson spent the first 17 seasons of his Hall of Fame playing career with Montreal, before signing as a free agent with the Kings on July 25, 1989. He spent the final three years of his playing career with Los Angeles before retiring after the 1991-92 season.

Coaching Record

		Regular Season				Playoffs		
Season	Team	Games	W	L	T	Games	W	L
1995-96	Los Angeles (NHL)	82	24	40	18	....	....	....
1996-97	Los Angeles (NHL)	82	28	43	11	....	....	....
1997-98	Los Angeles (NHL)	82	38	33	11	4	0	4
1998-99	Los Angeles (NHL)	82	32	45	5	....	....	....
1999-2000	New Jersey (NHL)	8	4	4	0	23	16	7*
2000-01	New Jersey (NHL)	82	48	22	12	25	15	10
	NHL Totals	418	174	187	57	52	31	21

* Stanley Cup win.

Club Directory

Continental Airlines Arena

New Jersey Devils
Continental Airlines Arena
50 Route 120 North
P.O. Box 504
East Rutherford, NJ 07073
Phone **201/935-6050**
FAX 201/935-2127
www.newjerseydevils.com
Capacity: 19,040

CEO/President/General Manager	Louis A. Lamoriello
Executive Vice President	Peter S. McMullen
Executive Vice President	Chris Modrzynski
Vice President, Community Development/ Broadcasting	Glenn Adamo
Vice President, General Counsel	Joseph C. Benedetti
Vice President, Ticket Operations	Terry Farmer
Vice President, Corporate Partnerships	Kenneth F. Ferriter
Vice President, Sales/Marketing	Jason Siegel
Vice President, Finance	Scott Struble

Hockey Club Personnel

Head Coach	Larry Robinson
Assistant Coaches	Viacheslav Fetisov, Jay Leach
Goaltending Coach	Jacques Caron
Director, Scouting	David Conte
Assistant Director of Scouting	Claude Carrier
Scouting Staff	Glen Dirk, Milt Fisher, Ferny Flaman, Dennis Gendron, Dan Labraaten, Chris Lamoriello, Vladimir Lokotko, Joe Mahoney, Larry Perris, Marcel Pronovost, Lou Reycroft, Vaclav Slansky, Jr., Geoff Stevens, Ed Thomlinson, Les Widdifield
Pro Scouting Staff	Andre Boudrias, Bob Hoffmeyer, Kurt Kleinendorst, Jan Ludvig
Special Assignment Scout	John Cunniff
Hockey Operations Video Coordinator	Taran Singleton
Scouting Staff Assistant	Callie A. Smith
Medical Trainer	Bill Murray
Strength/Conditioning Coordinator	Michael Vasalani
Equipment Manager	Rich Matthews
Assistant Equipment Managers	Alex Abasto, Lou Centanni
Massage Therapist	Juergen Merz
Team Cardiologist	Dr. Joseph Niznik
Team Dentist	Dr. H. Hugh Gardy
Team Optometrist	Dr. Paul Berman
Team Orthopedists	Dr. Barry Fisher, Dr. Len Jaffe
Fitness Consultant	Vladimir Bure
Exercise Physiologist	Dr. Garret Caffrey
Physical Therapist	David Feniger
Video Consultant	Mitch Kaufman
Head Coach, Albany	Bob Carpenter
Assistant Coaches, Albany	Chris Terreri, Geordie Kinnear
Athletic Trainer, Albany	Curtis Bell
Equipment Manager, Albany	Jason McGrath

Administration

Hockey Operations Executive Assistant to the CEO/ President/General Manager	Marie Carnevale
Corporate Executive Assistant to the CEO/ President/General Manager	Mary K. Morrison
Staff Attorney	John Ruzich
Receptionists	Jelsa Belotta, Pat Maione
Corporate Staff Assistant	Christie Zdanowicz

Ticket Operations

Director, Ticket Operations	Tom Bates
Director, Customer Service/Season Ticket Accounts	Dave Beck
Customer Service Representative	Andrea Marchesani
Director, Group Sales	Neil Desormeaux
Group Account Manager	Rich Davis

Corporate Partnerships

Director, Corporate Accounts	Michael DeMartino
Account Manager, Corporate Partnerships	Michael Merolla
Staff Assistants, Corporate Partnerships	Matt Dugan, Mary Vesnesky

Marketing Department

Account Managers	Scott Bindemann, Erica Brask, Chris Brehm, Nicholas Durastanti, Fred Ewig, Todd Hyland, Justin Keshish, Geoffrey Lamm, Nick Mike-Mayer, Vincent Occhipinti, Charles Tabeek, James Winters
Assistant Director, Community Development	Paul Viola
Community Development Assistant	Andrew Schwartz
Coordinator, Game Entertainment	Bruce Cohn
Sales Receptionist	Elizabeth Grace
Merchandise Manager	David Perricone

Communications Department

Director, Information/Publications	Mike Levine
Director, Public Relations	Jeff Altstadter
Communications Assistant	Adam Manger

Finance Department

Assistant Controller	Craig Wolman
Staff Accountants	Jill Bach, Matt Courtney
Administrative Assistant	Eileen Musikant

Computer Operations

Director, Programming/Computer Operations	Jack Skelley
Systems Administrator	Mike Tukes
Director, Website Operations	Antonio Barrera
Assistant to Director, Website Operations	Chris Gerlach

Television/Radio

Television Outlet	FOX Sports Net New York
Broadcasters	Mike Emrick, Play-by-Play; Glenn Resch, Color
Radio Outlet	WABC 77AM
Broadcasters	Mike Miller, Play-by-Play; Randy Velischek, Color

New York Islanders

2000-01 Results: 21W-51L-7T-3OTL 52PTS. Fifth, Atlantic Division

In his first full season with the Islanders in 2000-01, Dave Scatchard scored 21 goals to rank second on the team behind Mariusz Czerkawski. Five of his goals were game-winners, a total that topped the team.

2001-02 Schedule

Oct.	Fri.	5	at Tampa Bay
	Sat.	6	at Florida
	Wed.	10	at Pittsburgh
	Thu.	11	at New Jersey
	Sat.	13	Detroit
	Wed.	17	at Carolina
	Thu.	18	Carolina
	Sat.	20	San Jose*
	Fri.	26	at Carolina
	Sun.	28	Dallas*
	Tue.	30	Florida
Nov.	Fri.	2	at Detroit
	Sat.	3	at Philadelphia
	Tue.	6	Tampa Bay
	Thu.	8	NY Rangers
	Sat.	10	at Montreal
	Wed.	14	at Pittsburgh
	Fri.	16	at Colorado
	Sat.	17	at Phoenix
	Mon.	19	at Dallas
	Wed.	21	Colorado
	Fri.	23	Toronto
	Sat.	24	Anaheim
	Tue.	27	Washington
	Thu.	29	Montreal
Dec.	Sat.	1	Buffalo
	Tue.	4	Philadelphia
	Thu.	6	at Philadelphia
	Fri.	7	at Chicago
	Tue.	11	Ottawa
	Wed.	12	at New Jersey
	Sat.	15	Florida
	Tue.	18	Edmonton
	Fri.	21	at NY Rangers
	Sat.	22	Boston
	Thu.	27	at Ottawa
	Sat.	29	Montreal
Jan.	Tue.	1	at Washington*
	Thu.	3	Pittsburgh
	Sat.	5	Los Angeles
	Sun.	6	at Atlanta
	Tue.	8	Calgary
	Thu.	10	at Montreal
	Sat.	12	at Boston
	Tue.	15	at Calgary
	Thu.	17	at San Jose
	Sat.	19	at Los Angeles*
	Tue.	22	NY Rangers
	Thu.	24	Pittsburgh
	Sat.	26	Tampa Bay
	Tue.	29	New Jersey
	Wed.	30	at NY Rangers
Feb.	Mon.	4	at Florida
	Tue.	5	St. Louis
	Thu.	7	Toronto
	Sun.	10	at Minnesota*
	Tue.	12	at Philadelphia
	Tue.	26	Boston
Mar.	Fri.	1	at Atlanta
	Sat.	2	Atlanta
	Mon.	4	Pittsburgh
	Thu.	7	Buffalo
	Fri.	8	at Columbus
	Sun.	10	Atlanta*
	Tue.	12	at Buffalo
	Wed.	13	at New Jersey
	Sat.	16	at Ottawa
	Tue.	19	at Toronto
	Thu.	21	Vancouver
	Sat.	23	Minnesota*
	Mon.	25	NY Rangers
	Wed.	27	Ottawa
	Thu.	28	at Toronto
	Sat.	30	at Washington
Apr.	Mon.	1	New Jersey
	Wed.	3	at Buffalo
	Thu.	4	at Boston
	Sat.	6	Washington
	Mon.	8	Carolina
	Thu.	11	at Nashville
	Fri.	12	at Tampa Bay
	Sun.	14	Philadelphia*

* Denotes afternoon game.

Franchise date: June 6, 1972

ATLANTIC DIVISION

30th NHL Season

Year-by-Year Record

		Home				Road				Overall								
Season	**GP**	**W**	**L**	**T**	**OL**	**W**	**L**	**T**	**OL**	**W**	**L**	**T**	**OL**	**GF**	**GA**	**Pts.**	**Finished**	**Playoff Result**
2000-01	82	12	27	1	1	9	24	6	2	21	51	7	3	185	268	52	5th, Atlantic Div.	Out of Playoffs
1999-2000	82	10	25	5	1	14	23	4	0	24	48	9	1	194	275	58	5th, Atlantic Div.	Out of Playoffs
1998-99	82	11	23	7	...	13	25	3	...	24	48	10	...	194	244	58	5th, Atlantic Div.	Out of Playoffs
1997-98	82	17	20	4	...	13	21	7	...	30	41	11	...	212	225	71	4th, Atlantic Div.	Out of Playoffs
1996-97	82	19	18	4	...	10	23	8	...	29	41	12	...	240	250	70	7th, Atlantic Div.	Out of Playoffs
1995-96	82	14	21	6	...	8	29	4	...	22	50	10	...	229	315	54	7th, Atlantic Div.	Out of Playoffs
1994-95	48	10	11	3	...	5	17	2	...	15	28	5	...	126	158	35	7th, Atlantic Div.	Out of Playoffs
1993-94	84	23	15	4	...	13	21	8	...	36	36	12	...	282	264	84	4th, Atlantic Div.	Lost Conf. Quarter-Final
1992-93	84	20	19	3	...	20	18	4	...	40	37	7	...	335	297	87	3rd, Patrick Div.	Lost Conf. Championship
1991-92	80	20	15	5	...	14	20	6	...	34	35	11	...	291	299	79	5th, Patrick Div.	Out of Playoffs
1990-91	80	15	19	6	...	10	26	4	...	25	45	10	...	223	290	60	6th, Patrick Div.	Out of Playoffs
1989-90	80	15	17	8	...	16	21	3	...	31	38	11	...	281	288	73	4th, Patrick Div.	Lost Div. Semi-Final
1988-89	80	19	18	3	...	9	29	2	...	28	47	5	...	265	325	61	6th, Patrick Div.	Out of Playoffs
1987-88	80	24	10	6	...	15	21	4	...	39	31	10	...	308	267	88	1st, Patrick Div.	Lost Div. Semi-Final
1986-87	80	20	15	5	...	15	18	7	...	35	33	12	...	279	281	82	3rd, Patrick Div.	Lost Div. Final
1985-86	80	22	11	7	...	17	18	5	...	39	29	12	...	327	284	90	3rd, Patrick Div.	Lost Div. Semi-Final
1984-85	80	26	11	3	...	14	23	3	...	40	34	6	...	345	312	86	3rd, Patrick Div.	Lost Div. Final
1983-84	80	28	11	1	...	22	15	3	...	50	26	4	...	357	269	104	1st, Patrick Div.	Lost Final
1982-83	**80**	**26**	**11**	**3**	**...**	**16**	**15**	**9**	**...**	**42**	**26**	**12**	**...**	**302**	**226**	**96**	**2nd, Patrick Div.**	**Won Stanley Cup**
1981-82	**80**	**33**	**3**	**4**	**...**	**21**	**13**	**6**	**...**	**54**	**16**	**10**	**...**	**385**	**250**	**118**	**1st, Patrick Div.**	**Won Stanley Cup**
1980-81	**80**	**23**	**6**	**11**	**...**	**25**	**12**	**3**	**...**	**48**	**18**	**14**	**...**	**355**	**260**	**110**	**1st, Patrick Div.**	**Won Stanley Cup**
1979-80	**80**	**26**	**9**	**5**	**...**	**13**	**19**	**8**	**...**	**39**	**28**	**13**	**...**	**281**	**247**	**91**	**2nd, Patrick Div.**	**Won Stanley Cup**
1978-79	80	31	3	6	...	20	12	8	...	51	15	14	...	358	214	116	1st, Patrick Div.	Lost Semi-Final
1977-78	80	29	3	8	...	19	14	7	...	48	17	15	...	334	210	111	1st, Patrick Div.	Lost Quarter-Final
1976-77	80	24	11	5	...	23	10	7	...	47	21	12	...	288	193	106	2nd, Patrick Div.	Lost Semi-Final
1975-76	80	24	8	8	...	18	13	9	...	42	21	17	...	297	190	101	2nd, Patrick Div.	Lost Semi-Final
1974-75	80	22	6	12	...	11	19	10	...	33	25	22	...	264	221	88	3rd, Patrick Div.	Lost Semi-Final
1973-74	78	13	17	9	...	6	24	9	...	19	41	18	...	182	247	56	8th, East Div.	Out of Playoffs
1972-73	78	10	25	4	...	2	35	2	...	12	60	6	...	170	347	30	8th, East Div.	Out of Playoffs

2001-02 Player Personnel

FORWARDS	HT	WT	S	Place of Birth	Date	2000-01 Club
BATES, Shawn	5-11	212	R	Melrose, MA	4/3/75	Boston-Prov (AHL)
BLAKE, Jason	5-10	185	L	Moorhead, MN	9/2/73	L.A.-Lowell (AHL)-NYI
CHARPENTIER, Marco	6-0	200	L	Montreal, Que.	1/23/80	Baie-Comeau
CZERKAWSKI, Mariusz	6-0	195	L	Radomsko, Poland	4/13/72	NY Islanders
GUITE, Ben	6-1	205	R	Montreal, Que.	7/17/78	Tallahasee
HUNTER, Trent	6-3	191	R	Red Deer, Alta.	7/5/80	Springfield
ISBISTER, Brad	6-4	227	R	Edmonton, Alta.	5/7/77	NY Islanders
KHARITONOV, Alexander	5-9	169	R	Moscow, USSR	3/30/76	Tampa Bay
KOLNIK, Juraj	5-10	182	R	Nitra, Czech.	11/13/80	Lowell (AHL)-NYI-Sprfld
KROG, Jason	5-11	191	R	Fernie, B.C.	10/9/75	NYI-Lowell (AHL)-Sprfld
KVASHA, Oleg	6-5	215	R	Moscow, USSR	7/26/78	NY Islanders
LAPOINTE, Claude	5-9	181	L	Lachine, Que.	10/11/68	NY Islanders
LINDGREN, Mats	6-2	202	L	Skelleftea, Sweden	10/1/74	NY Islanders
MAPLETOFT, Justin	6-1	180	L	Lloydminster, Sask.	1/11/81	Red Deer Rebels
MIKA, Petr	6-4	194	R	Prague, Czech.	2/12/79	Lowell-Springfield
PARRISH, Mark	5-11	191	R	Edina, MN	2/2/77	NY Islanders
PECA, Michael	5-11	190	R	Toronto, Ont.	3/26/74	Buffalo
PODOLLAN, Jason	6-1	198	R	Vernon, B.C.	2/18/76	Det (IHL)-Manitoba
ROCHE, Dave	6-4	230	L	Lindsay, Ont.	6/13/75	Saint John
SCATCHARD, Dave	6-2	220	R	Hinton, Alta.	2/20/76	NY Islanders
TORRES, Raffi	5-11	207	L	Toronto, Ont.	10/8/81	Brampton
TUOMAINEN, Marko	6-3	230	R	Kuopio, Finland	4/25/72	Lowell-Los Angeles
UPPER, Dmitri	6-1	185	R	Ust-Kamenogorsk, USSR	7/27/78	Torpedo Nizhny-Ak Bars Kazan
WEBB, Steve	6-0	195	R	Peterborough, Ont.	4/30/75	NY Islanders
YASHIN, Alexei	6-3	225	R	Sverdlovsk, USSR	11/5/73	Ottawa
DEFENSEMEN						
ARMSTRONG, Chris	6-0	205	L	Regina, Sask.	6/26/75	Minnesota-Cleveland
AUCOIN, Adrian	6-2	210	R	Ottawa, Ont.	7/3/73	Vancouver-Tampa Bay
CAIRNS, Eric	6-6	230	L	Oakville, Ont.	6/27/74	NY Islanders
GIROUX, Raymond	6-0	180	L	North Bay, Ont.	7/20/76	HIFK Helsinki-AIK Solna-Jokerit Helsinki
HALLER, Kevin	6-2	199	L	Trochu, Alta.	12/5/70	NY Islanders
HAMRLIK, Roman	6-2	215	L	Gottwaldov, Czech.	4/12/74	NY Islanders
JONSSON, Kenny	6-3	195	L	Angelholm, Sweden	10/6/74	NY Islanders
KIPRUSOFF, Marko	6-1	195	L	Turku, Finland	6/6/72	EHC Kloten
KOROLEV, Evgeny	6-1	186	L	Moscow, USSR	7/24/78	NYI-Chi (IHL)-Louisville
MARTINEK, Radek	6-1	200	R	Havlickuv Brod, Czech.	8/31/76	Budejovice
MEZEI, Branislav	6-4	221	L	Nitra, Czech.	10/8/80	NY Islanders-Lowell
SCHULTZ, Ray	6-2	200	L	Red Deer, Alta.	11/14/76	NY Islanders-Lowell-Cleveland
SUTTON, Ken	6-1	205	L	Edmonton, Alta.	11/5/69	New Jersey
TARNSTROM, Dick	6-2	200	L	Sundbyberg, Sweden	1/20/75	AIK Solna
GOALTENDERS	**HT**	**WT**	**C**	**Place of Birth**	**Date**	**2000-01 Club**
DiPIETRO, Rick	5-11	185	R	Winthrop, MA	9/19/81	NY Islanders-Chi (IHL)
SALFICKY, Dusan	6-1	185	L	Chrudim, Czech.	3/28/72	HCK Plzen
SNOW, Garth	6-3	200	L	Wrentham, MA	7/28/69	Pittsburgh-Wilkes-Barre
ST-GERMAIN, David	5-11	172	L	Charles-Lemoye, Que.	3/18/80	Baie-Comeau
VALIQUETTE, Stephen	6-5	190	L	Etobicoke, Ont.	8/20/77	Springfield

2000-01 Scoring

* - rookie

Regular Season

Pos	#	Player	Team	GP	G	A	Pts	+/–	PIM	PP	SH	GW	GT	S	%
R	21	Mariusz Czerkawski	NYI	82	30	32	62	–24	48	10	1	0	0	287	10.5
D	4	Roman Hamrlik	NYI	76	16	30	46	–20	92	5	1	4	0	232	6.9
C	38	Dave Scatchard	NYI	81	21	24	45	–9	114	4	0	5	1	176	11.9
C	18	Tim Connolly	NYI	82	10	31	41	–14	42	5	0	0	0	171	5.8
R	15	Brad Isbister	NYI	51	18	14	32	–19	59	7	1	4	0	129	14.0
C	13	Claude Lapointe	NYI	80	9	23	32	–2	56	1	1	1	1	94	9.6
R	27	Mark Parrish	NYI	70	17	13	30	–27	28	6	0	3	0	123	13.8
D	29	Kenny Jonsson	NYI	65	8	21	29	–22	30	5	0	0	0	91	8.8
R	11	Bill Muckalt	NYI	60	11	15	26	–4	33	1	0	2	1	90	12.2
L	12	Oleg Kvasha	NYI	62	11	9	20	–15	46	0	0	0	0	118	9.3
D	28	Garry Galley	NYI	56	6	14	20	–4	59	4	0	0	0	94	6.4
L	17 *	Taylor Pyatt	NYI	78	4	14	18	–17	39	1	0	2	0	86	4.7
C	14	Jason Blake	L.A.	17	1	3	4	–8	10	0	0	0	0	27	3.7
			NYI	30	4	8	12	–12	24	1	1	0	0	73	5.5
			TOTAL	47	5	11	16	–20	34	1	1	0	0	100	5.0
D	3	Zdeno Chara	NYI	82	2	7	9	–27	157	0	1	0	0	83	2.4
D	32	Aris Brimanis	NYI	56	0	8	8	–12	26	0	0	0	0	66	0.0
R	25 *	Juraj Kolnik	NYI	29	4	3	7	–8	12	0	0	0	0	38	10.5
C	10	Mats Lindgren	NYI	20	3	4	7	4	10	0	2	0	0	34	8.8
R	24	Mark Lawrence	NYI	36	3	4	7	–9	32	1	0	0	0	32	9.4
C	37	Steve Martins	T.B.	20	1	1	2	–9	13	0	0	0	0	18	5.6
			NYI	39	1	3	4	–7	20	0	1	0	0	28	3.6
			TOTAL	59	2	4	6	–16	33	0	1	0	0	46	4.3
D	7	Kevin Haller	NYI	30	1	5	6	5	56	0	0	0	0	19	5.3
D	2 *	Branislav Mezei	NYI	42	1	4	5	–5	53	0	0	0	0	29	3.4
D	33	Eric Cairns	NYI	45	2	2	4	–18	106	0	0	0	0	21	9.5
C	8 *	Jason Krog	NYI	9	0	3	3	4	0	0	0	0	0	7	0.0
L	16	Craig Berube	WSH	22	0	1	1	–3	18	0	0	0	0	8	0.0
			NYI	38	0	2	2	–5	54	0	0	0	0	27	0.0
			TOTAL	60	0	3	3	–8	72	0	0	0	0	35	0.0
D	39	Ray Schultz	NYI	13	0	2	2	–1	40	0	0	0	0	3	0.0
G	1 *	Rick DiPietro	NYI	20	0	2	2	0	6	0	0	0	0	0	0.0
R	20	Steve Webb	NYI	31	0	2	2	1	35	0	0	0	0	8	0.0
D	51 *	Anders Myrvold	NYI	12	0	1	1	–2	0	0	0	0	0	8	0.0
D	6	Mathieu Biron	NYI	14	0	1	1	2	12	0	0	0	0	10	0.0
D	36 *	Evgeny Korolev	NYI	8	0	0	0	0	6	0	0	0	0	11	0.0
C	49	Robert Petrovicky	NYI	11	0	0	0	–1	4	0	0	0	0	3	0.0
C	44	Jesse Belanger	NYI	12	0	0	0	–5	2	0	0	0	0	7	0.0
G	30	Chris Terreri	N.J.	10	0	0	0	0	0	0	0	0	0	0	0.0
			NYI	8	0	0	0	0	2	0	0	0	0	0	0.0
			TOTAL	18	0	0	0	0	2	0	0	0	0	0	0.0

Goaltending

No.	Goaltender	GPI	Mins	Avg	W	L	T	EN	SO	GA	SA	S%
30	Chris Terreri	8	443	2.44	2	4	1	2	0	18	205	.912
34	John Vanbiesbrouck	44	2390	3.01	10	25	5	4	1	120	1177	.898
31	Wade Flaherty	20	1017	3.30	6	10	0	3	1	56	470	.881
1	* Rick DiPietro	20	1083	3.49	3	15	1	2	0	63	515	.878
	Totals	**82**	**4968**	**3.24**	**21**	**54**	**7**	**11**	**2**	**268**	**2378**	**.887**

Coaching History

Phil Goyette and Earl Ingarfield, 1972-73; Al Arbour, 1973-74 to 1985-86; Terry Simpson, 1986-87, 1987-88; Terry Simpson and Al Arbour, 1988-89; Al Arbour, 1989-90 to 1993-94; Lorne Henning, 1994-95; Mike Milbury, 1995-96; Mike Milbury and Rick Bowness, 1996-97; Rick Bowness and Mike Milbury, 1997-98; Mike Milbury and Bill Stewart, 1998-99; Butch Goring, 1999-2000; Butch Goring and Lorne Henning, 2000-01; Peter Laviolette, 2001-02.

Coach

LAVIOLETTE, PETER
Coach, New York Islanders. Born in Norwood, MA, December 7, 1964.

Peter Laviolette was named the head coach of the New York Islanders on May 23, 2001, after having served as an assistant coach with the Boston Bruins under Pat Burns and Mike Keenan during the 2000-01 season. He had spent two years prior to that as the head coach of Boston's AHL affiliate in Providence. In 1998-99, he led that club to the winningest season in AHL history as they captured the Calder Cup championship. At the conclusion of that season, he was named the AHL's Outstanding Coach. In 1999-2000, he again led the AHL Bruins to a playoff berth, despite using over 80 players due to injuries and recalls to Boston.

Laviolette began his coaching career in 1997-98 with the ECHL's Wheeling Thunderbirds and led them to the playoff semifinals. Laviolette played four seasons of college hockey at Westfield (MA) State College. He turned professional in 1986-87 and spent most of his 11 pro seasons in the International and American Hockey Leagues, but played 12 NHL games with the New York Rangers in the 1988-89 season. Laviolette represented the United States on two Olympic Teams — playing in the 1988 Games in Calgary and captaining the 1994 squad in Lillehammer. He concluded his playing career with Providence, becoming the team's first captain in 1992-93.

Coaching Record

		Regular Season				Playoffs		
Season	Team	Games	W	L	T	Games	W	L
1997-98	Wheeling (ECHL)	70	37	24	9	15	8	7
1998-99	Providence (AHL)	80	56	16	8	19	15	4
1999-2000	Providence (AHL)	80	33	38	9	14	10	4

Acquired from Buffalo for Tim Connolly and Taylor Pyatt, the Islanders are hoping that Michael Peca's leadership skills will help them return to the playoffs.

Club Records

Team

(Figures in brackets for season records are games played; records for fewest points, wins, ties, losses, goals, goals against are for 70 or more games)

Most Points **118** 1981-82 (80)
Most Wins **54** 1981-82 (80)
Most Ties **22** 1974-75 (80)
Most Losses **60** 1972-73 (78)
Most Goals **385** 1981-82 (80)
Most Goals Against **347** 1972-73 (78)
Fewest Points **30** 1972-73 (78)
Fewest Wins **12** 1972-73 (78)
Fewest Ties **4** 1983-84 (80)
Fewest Losses **15** 1978-79 (80)
Fewest Goals **170** 1972-73 (78)
Fewest Goals Against **190** 1975-76 (80)
Longest Winning Streak
Overall .... **15** Jan. 21-Feb. 20/82
Home .... **14** Jan. 2-Feb. 27/82
Away .... **8** Feb. 27-Mar. 29/81
Longest Undefeated Streak
Overall .... **15** Jan. 21-Feb. 20/82 (15 wins), Nov. 4-Dec. 4/80 (13 wins, 2 ties)
Home .... **23** Oct. 17/78-Jan. 27/79 (19 wins, 4 ties), Jan. 2-Apr. 3/82 (21 wins, 2 ties)
Away .... **8** Four times
Longest Losing Streak
Overall .... **12** Dec. 27/72-Jan. 16/73, Nov. 22-Dec. 15/88
Home .... **7** Nov. 13-Dec. 14/99
Away .... **15** Jan. 20-Mar. 31/73
Longest Winless Streak
Overall .... **15** Nov. 22-Dec. 21/72 (12 losses, 3 ties)
Home .... **9** Mar. 2-Apr. 6/99 (7 losses, 2 ties)
Away .... **20** Nov. 3/72-Jan. 13/73 (19 losses, 1 tie)
Most Shutouts, Season **10** 1975-76 (80)
Most PIM, Season **1,857** 1986-87 (80)
Most Goals, Game .... **11** Dec. 20/83 (Pit. 3 at NYI 11), Mar. 3/84 (NYI 11 at Tor. 6)

Individual

Most Seasons .... **17** Billy Smith
Most Games .... **1,123** Bryan Trottier
Most Goals, Career .... **573** Mike Bossy
Most Assists, Career .... **853** Bryan Trottier
Most Points, Career .... **1,353** Bryan Trottier (500G, 853A)
Most PIM, Career .... **1,879** Mick Vukota
Most Shutouts, Career .... **25** Chico Resch
Longest Consecutive Games Streak .... **576** Bill Harris (Oct. 7/72-Nov. 30/79)
Most Goals, Season .... **69** Mike Bossy (1978-79)
Most Assists, Season .... **87** Bryan Trottier (1978-79)
Most Points, Season .... **147** Mike Bossy (1981-82; 64G, 83A)
Most PIM, Season .... **356** Brian Curran (1986-87)
Most Points, Defenseman, Season .... **101** Denis Potvin (1978-79; 31G, 70A)
Most Points, Center, Season .... **134** Bryan Trottier (1978-79; 47G, 87A)
Most Points, Right Wing, Season .... **147** Mike Bossy (1981-82; 64G, 83A)
Most Points, Left Wing, Season .... **100** John Tonelli (1984-85; 42G, 58A)
Most Points, Rookie, Season .... **95** Bryan Trottier (1975-76; 32G, 63A)
Most Shutouts, Season .... **7** Chico Resch (1975-76)
Most Goals, Game .... **5** Bryan Trottier (Dec. 23/78, Feb. 13/82), John Tonelli (Jan. 6/81)
Most Assists, Game .... **6** Mike Bossy (Jan. 6/81)
Most Points, Game .... **8** Bryan Trottier (Dec. 23/78; 5G, 3A)

Captains' History

Ed Westfall, 1972-73 to 1975-76; Ed Westfall and Clark Gillies, 1976-77; Clark Gillies, 1977-78, 1978-79; Denis Potvin, 1979-80 to 1986-87; Brent Sutter, 1987-88 to 1990-91; Brent Sutter and Pat Flatley, 1991-92; Pat Flatley, 1992-93 to 1995-96; no captain, 1996-97; Bryan McCabe and Trevor Linden, 1997-98; Trevor Linden, 1998-99; Kenny Jonsson, 1999-2000 to 2000-01.

Retired Numbers

5	Denis Potvin	1973-1988
9	Clark Gillies	1974-1986
22	Mike Bossy	1977-1987
23	Bob Nystrom	1972-1986
31	Billy Smith	1972-1989

All-time Record vs. Other Clubs

Regular Season

	At Home								On Road								Total							
	GP	W	L	T	OL	GF	GA	PTS	GP	W	L	T	OL	GF	GA	PTS	GP	W	L	T	OL	GF	GA	PTS
Anaheim	6	2	3	1	0	15	19	5	7	3	2	2	0	19	15	8	13	5	5	3	0	34	34	13
Atlanta	4	1	3	0	0	10	13	2	4	2	1	1	0	17	14	5	8	3	4	1	0	27	27	7
Boston	55	23	26	6	0	183	182	52	53	14	29	10	0	151	202	38	108	37	55	16	0	334	384	90
Buffalo	55	23	23	9	0	157	152	55	55	16	30	8	1	148	189	41	110	39	53	17	1	305	341	96
Calgary	48	25	14	9	0	185	131	59	48	13	24	11	0	142	171	37	96	38	38	20	0	327	302	96
Carolina	38	18	16	4	0	123	109	40	39	14	20	5	0	128	139	33	77	32	36	9	0	251	248	73
Chicago	45	17	13	15	0	156	136	49	46	16	25	5	0	150	156	37	91	33	38	20	0	306	292	86
Colorado	30	16	13	1	0	120	104	33	32	11	19	2	0	96	121	24	62	27	32	3	0	216	225	57
Columbus	1	0	1	0	0	5	7	0	1	0	0	1	0	3	3	1	2	0	1	1	0	8	10	1
Dallas	45	23	14	8	0	166	129	54	45	20	18	7	0	163	133	47	90	43	32	15	0	329	262	101
Detroit	44	23	18	3	0	158	130	49	42	17	23	2	0	132	152	36	86	40	41	5	0	290	282	85
Edmonton	28	12	7	9	0	117	105	33	28	7	16	5	0	82	105	19	56	19	23	14	0	199	210	52
Florida	19	7	10	2	0	47	53	16	19	6	10	3	0	51	57	15	38	13	20	5	0	98	110	31
Los Angeles	42	24	14	4	0	155	119	52	43	15	21	7	0	137	159	37	85	39	35	11	0	292	278	89
Minnesota	1	0	1	0	0	1	4	0	1	0	1	0	0	2	3	0	2	0	2	0	0	3	7	0
Montreal	54	25	24	5	0	166	157	55	54	14	31	9	0	159	199	37	108	39	55	14	0	325	356	92
Nashville	3	1	2	0	0	7	9	2	2	1	1	0	0	8	6	2	5	2	3	0	0	15	15	4
New Jersey	77	52	15	10	0	335	222	114	76	35	30	11	0	273	253	81	153	87	45	21	0	608	475	195
NY Rangers	88	53	27	7	1	352	273	114	88	27	51	10	0	266	337	64	176	80	78	17	1	618	610	178
Ottawa	18	3	10	4	1	59	71	11	17	4	9	4	0	46	58	12	35	7	19	8	1	105	129	23
Philadelphia	90	48	28	14	0	340	263	110	87	24	53	10	0	251	328	58	177	72	81	24	0	591	591	168
Phoenix	29	13	8	8	0	111	88	34	28	14	10	4	0	99	88	32	57	27	18	12	0	210	176	66
Pittsburgh	78	41	29	8	0	314	261	90	80	30	39	11	0	277	307	71	158	71	68	19	0	591	568	161
St. Louis	46	24	11	11	0	176	118	59	45	19	17	9	0	148	161	47	91	43	28	20	0	324	279	106
San Jose	10	5	4	1	0	38	33	11	9	5	3	1	0	31	22	11	19	10	7	2	0	69	55	22
Tampa Bay	19	8	10	1	0	54	60	17	20	8	9	2	1	59	54	19	39	16	19	3	1	113	114	36
Toronto	47	25	19	3	0	187	143	53	49	22	24	3	0	170	166	47	96	47	43	6	0	357	309	100
Vancouver	44	23	11	10	0	164	122	56	46	21	22	3	0	150	151	45	90	44	33	13	0	314	273	101
Washington	75	40	34	1	0	282	237	81	75	29	35	11	0	238	243	69	150	69	69	12	0	520	480	150
Defunct Clubs	13	11	0	2	0	75	33	24	13	4	5	4	0	35	41	12	26	15	5	6	0	110	74	36
Totals	**1152**	**586**	**408**	**156**	**2**	**4258**	**3483**	**1330**	**1152**	**411**	**578**	**161**	**2**	**3631**	**4033**	**985**	**2304**	**997**	**986**	**317**	**4**	**7889**	**7516**	**2315**

Playoffs

	Series	W	L	GP	W	L	T	GF	GA	Last Mtg.	Round	Result
Boston	2	?	0	11	8	3	0	49	35	1983	CF	W 4-2
Buffalo	3	3	0	16	12	4	0	59	45	1980	SF	W 4-2
Chicago	2	2	0	6	6	0	0	21	6	1979	QF	W 4-0
Colorado	1	1	0	4	4	0	0	18	9	1982	CF	W 4-0
Dallas	1	1	0	5	4	1	0	26	16	1981	F	W 4-1
Edmonton	3	2	1	15	9	6	0	58	47	1984	F	L 1-4
Los Angeles	1	1	0	4	3	1	0	21	10	1980	PR	W 3-1
Montreal	4	1	3	22	8	14	0	55	64	1993	CF	L 1-4
New Jersey	1	0	1	6	2	4	0	18	23	1988	DSF	L 2-4
NY Rangers	8	5	3	39	20	19	0	129	132	1994	CQF	L 0-4
Philadelphia	4	1	3	25	11	14	0	69	83	1987	DF	L 3-4
Pittsburgh	3	3	0	19	11	8	0	67	58	1993	DF	W 4-3
Toronto	2	1	1	10	6	4	0	33	20	1981	PR	W 3-0
Vancouver	2	2	0	6	6	0	0	26	14	1982	F	W 4-0
Washington	6	5	1	30	18	12	0	99	88	1993	DSF	W 4-2
Totals	**43**	**30**	**13**	**218**	**128**	**90**	**0**	**748**	**650**			

Calgary totals include Atlanta Flames, 1972-73 to 1979-80.
Carolina totals include Hartford, 1979-80 to 1996-97.
Colorado totals include Quebec, 1979-80 to 1994-95.
Dallas totals include Minnesota North Stars, 1972-73 to 1992-93.
New Jersey totals include Kansas City, 1974-75 to 1975-76, and Colorado Rockies, 1976-77 to 1981-82.
Phoenix totals include Winnipeg, 1979-80 to 1995-96.

Playoff Results 2001-1997

Year	Round	Opponent	Result	GF	GA

(Last playoff appearance: 1994)

Abbreviations: Round: F – Final; **CF** – conference final; **CQF** – conference quarter-final; **DF** – division final; **DSF** – division semi-final; **SF** – semi-final; **QF** – quarter-final; **PR** – preliminary round.

2000-01 Results

Oct.	6	at Tampa Bay	3-3		9	Chicago	3-6
	11	at Toronto	2-3		12	at Pittsburgh	3-4
	14	Calgary	0-2		13	Pittsburgh	6-5
	17	Anaheim	3-4		16	at Colorado	1-4
	20	at Atlanta	5-3		19	at Minnesota	2-3
	21	at Washington	4-4		21	at Atlanta	4-4
	27	Montreal	2-1		23	Ottawa	2-3
	28	at Montreal	2-1		26	at NY Rangers	3-2
	31	Boston	4-2		27	Buffalo	1-2
Nov.	1	at Florida	3-0		31	New Jersey	3-2
	3	at Tampa Bay	3-4*	**Feb.**	1	at Philadelphia	0-2
	5	Los Angeles	1-4		7	at Buffalo	1-2*
	7	Nashville	2-1		9	Philadelphia	2-5
	9	at Buffalo	0-3		10	at Montreal	3-5
	11	San Jose	0-4		12	at Ottawa	1-3
	16	at Los Angeles	1-5		14	Philadelphia	1-3
	18	at San Jose	3-5		16	at Edmonton	4-2
	19	at Anaheim	1-2		18	at Vancouver	2-3
	22	NY Rangers	3-4*		22	Philadelphia	4-3*
	24	at Washington	0-1		24	Florida	5-4
	25	Detroit	3-4		25	at Pittsburgh	1-6
	27	Tampa Bay	7-4		27	New Jersey	1-4
	30	Toronto	4-6	**Mar.**	1	Carolina	1-3
Dec.	1	at New Jersey	0-0		3	Tampa Bay	0-6
	3	New Jersey	1-1		5	at NY Rangers	5-2
	6	at Florida	4-1		6	Washington	1-5
	9	Atlanta	2-5		9	Minnesota	1-4
	10	at Philadelphia	2-5		11	Florida	1-4
	12	Washington	2-3		14	at Pittsburgh	3-1
	15	Toronto	3-2		17	at Columbus	3-3
	16	at Ottawa	0-6		18	at Carolina	1-2
	19	Carolina	2-1		20	at St. Louis	4-3*
	21	Dallas	1-3		23	at Dallas	1-2
	23	Columbus	5-7		25	at Phoenix	2-2
	27	Boston	2-5		28	at NY Rangers	2-4
	29	Atlanta	5-2		29	NY Rangers	4-6
	30	Buffalo	0-2		31	at Boston	2-4
Jan.	2	Montreal	0-3	**Apr.**	2	Pittsburgh	4-1
	4	at New Jersey	2-4		4	at Toronto	2-4
	6	Phoenix	1-2		6	Ottawa	3-4
	7	at Carolina	2-5		7	at Boston	2-4

* – Overtime

Entry Draft Selections 2001-1987

2001
Pick
101 Cory Stillman
132 Dusan Salficky
166 Andy Chiodo
197 Jan Holub
228 Mike Bray
260 Bryan Perez
280 Roman Kukhtinov
287 Juha-Pekka Ketola

2000
Pick
1 Rick DiPietro
5 Raffi Torres
101 Arto Tukio
105 Vladimir Gorbunov
136 Dmitri Upper
148 Kristofer Ottosson
202 Ryan Caldwell
264 Dmitri Altarev
267 Tomi Pettinen

1999
Pick
5 Tim Connolly
8 Taylor Pyatt
10 Branislav Mezei
28 Kristian Kudroc
78 Mattias Weinhandl
87 Brian Collins
101 Juraj Kolnik
102 Johan Halvardsson
130 Justin Mapletoft
140 Adam Johnson
163 Bjorn Melin
228 Radek Martinek
255 Brett Henning
268 Tyler Scott

1998
Pick
9 Mike Rupp
36 Chris Nielsen
95 Andy Burnham
123 Jiri Dopita
155 Kevin Clauson
182 Evgeny Korolev
209 Frederik Brindamour
237 Ben Blais
242 Jason Doyle
250 Radek Matejovsky

1997
Pick
4 Roberto Luongo
5 Eric Brewer
31 Jeff Zehr
59 Jarrett Smith
79 Robert Schnabel
85 Petr Mika
115 Adam Edinger
139 Bobby Leavins
166 Kris Knoblauch
196 Jeremy Symington
222 Ryan Clark

1996
Pick
3 Jean-Pierre Dumont
29 Dan Lacouture
56 Zdeno Chara
83 Tyrone Garner
109 Bubba Berenzweig
128 Petr Sachl
138 Todd Miller
165 J.R. Prestifilippo
192 Evgeny Korolev
218 Mike Muzechka

1995
Pick
2 Wade Redden
28 Jan Hlavac
41 D.J. Smith
106 Vladimir Orszagh
158 Andrew Taylor
210 David MacDonald
211 Mike Broda

1994
Pick
9 Brett Lindros
38 Jason Holland
63 Jason Strudwick
90 Brad Lukowich
112 Mark McArthur
116 Albert O'Connell
142 Jason Stewart
194 Mike Loach
203 Peter Hogardh
220 Gord Walsh
246 Kirk Dewaele
272 Dick Tarnstrom

1993
Pick
23 Todd Bertuzzi
40 Bryan McCabe
66 Vladimir Chebaturkin
92 Warren Luhning
118 Tommy Salo
144 Peter LeBoutillier
170 Darren Van Impe
196 Rod Hinks
222 Daniel Johansson
248 Stephane Larocque
274 Carl Charland

1992
Pick
5 Darius Kasparaitis
56 Jarrett Deuling
104 Thomas Klimt
105 Ryan Duthie
128 Derek Armstrong
152 Vladimir Grachev
159 Steve O'Rourke
176 Jason Widmer
200 Daniel Paradis
224 David Wainwright
248 Andrei Vasilyev

1991
Pick
4 Scott Lachance
26 Ziggy Palffy
48 Jamie McLennan
70 Milan Hnilicka
92 Steve Junker
114 Robert Valicevic
136 Andreas Johansson
158 Todd Sparks
180 John Johnson
202 Robert Canavan
224 Marcus Thuresson
246 Marty Schriner

1990
Pick
6 Scott Scissons
27 Chris Taylor
48 Dan Plante
90 Chris Marinucci
111 Joni Lehto
132 Michael Guilbert
153 Sylvain Fleury
174 John Joyce
195 Richard Enga
216 Martin Lacroix
237 Andy Shier

1989
Pick
2 Dave Chyzowski
23 Travis Green
44 Jason Zent
65 Brent Grieve
86 Jace Reed
90 Steve Young
99 Kevin O'Sullivan
128 Jon Larson
133 Brett Harkins
149 Phil Huber
170 Matthew Robbins
191 Vladimir Malakhov
212 Kelly Ens
233 Iain Fraser

1988
Pick
16 Kevin Cheveldayoff
29 Wayne Doucet
37 Sean Lebrun
58 Danny Lorenz
79 Andre Brassard
100 Paul Rutherford
111 Pavel Gross
121 Jason Rathbone
142 Yves Gaucher
163 Marty McInnis
173 Shorty Forrest
184 Jeff Blumer
205 Jeff Kampersal
226 Phillip Neururer
247 Joe Caprinni

1987
Pick
13 Dean Chynoweth
34 Jeff Hackett
55 Dean Ewen
76 George Maneluk
97 Petr Vlk
118 Rob DiMaio
139 Knut Walbye
160 Jeff Saterdalen
181 Shawn Howard
202 John Herlihy
223 Michael Erickson
244 Will Averill

General Managers' History

Bill Torrey, 1972-73 to 1991-92; Don Maloney, 1992-93 to 1994-95; Don Maloney and Mike Milbury, 1995-96; Mike Milbury, 1996-97 to date.

General Manager

MILBURY, MIKE
General Manager, New York Islanders. Born in Walpole, MA, June 17, 1952.

Milbury came to the Islanders with 20 years of professional hockey experience with the Boston Bruins — as a player, assistant coach, assistant general manager, general manager and coach on both the NHL and AHL levels. Milbury took over as general manager from Don Maloney on December 12, 1995.

His recent trades have brought the Islanders established stars like Alexei Yashin and Michael Peca as well as an abundance of young talent. In addition, his staff has used first round picks to take such players as Rick DiPietro (first overall, 2000).

Milbury joined the Boston organization after graduating from Colgate University with a degree in urban sociology and enjoyed a 10-year playing career with the team. He retired May 6, 1985 and took over as assistant coach. He returned to the ice late in the 1985-86 season when injuries decimated the Bruins defense.

Milbury's playing career concluded after the 1986-87 season and on July 16, 1987 he took over as coach of the Maine Mariners, Boston's top AHL affiliate. In his first year with the team he guided the Mariners to the AHL's Northern Division title and was named both AHL coach of the year and *The Hockey News* minor league coach of the year.

NHL Coaching Record

		Regular Season				Playoffs		
Season	Team	Games	W	L	T	Games	W	L
1989-90	Boston	80	46	25	9	21	13	8
1990-91	Boston	80	44	24	12	19	10	9
1995-96	NY Islanders	82	22	50	10	....	....	....
1996-97	NY Islanders	45	13	23	9	....	....	....
1997-98	NY Islanders	19	8	9	2	....	....	....
	NHL Totals	**306**	**133**	**131**	**42**	**40**	**23**	**17**

Club Directory

Nassau Veterans' Memorial Coliseum

New York Islanders
Nassau Veterans'
Memorial Coliseum
Uniondale, NY 11553
Phone **516/501-6700**
FAX 516/501-6746
www.newyorkislanders.com
Capacity: 16,297

Executive Directory

Owner and Governor	Charles B. Wang
Owner and Alternate Governor	Sanjay Kumar
Senior V.P. of Operations and Alternate Governor	Michael J. Picker
Senior Vice President of Sales and Marketing	Paul Lancey
Alternate Governor and General Counsel	Roy E. Reichbach
Alternate Governor	William M. Skehan
Executive Assistant	Theresa Dewar

Hockey Staff

General Manager	Mike Milbury
Asst. General Manager/Director of Player Personnel	Gordie Clark
Asst. General Manager/Director of Hockey Operations	Michael Santos, Esq.
Manager, Hockey Administration	Joanne Holewa
Assistant Manager of Player Contracts	Pam Genzardi
Head Coach	Peter Laviolette
Assistant Coaches	TBA
Head Amateur Scout	Tony Feltrin
Western Scout	Earl Ingarfield
Director of European Scouting	Anders Kallur
Director of Pro Scouting	Ken Morrow
Assistant Director of Pro Scouting	Kevin Maxwell
Scouting Staff	Jim Madigan, Mario Saraceno, Karel Pavlik, Doug Gibson, Brian Hunter, Harri Rindell, Harkie Singh, Nikolai Ladygin
Video Coordinator	Bob Smith

Medical Staff

Director of Medical Services	Dr. Elliot Pellman
Internist	Dr. Clifford Cooper
Team Orthopedists	Dr. Elliott Hershman, Dr. Kenneth Montgomery, Dr. David Gazzaniga
Team Dentists	Dr. Bruce Michnick, Dr. Jan Sherman

Training/Equipment Staff

Head Trainer	Rich Campbell
Strength and Conditioning Coach	Sean Donellan
Head Equipment Manager	Joe McMahon
Equipment Assistant	Bill Nichols
Lockerroom Attendants	Charles E. Nass, Matt Brager, Robert Dobrzeniecki, Arthur Verdi

Sales and Administration

Senior Vice President/CFO	Arthur McCarthy
Vice President of Administration	Janet L. Kask
Vice President of Communications	Chris Botta
Vice President of Corporate and Community Relations	Bill Kain
Director of Corporate Relations	Bob Nystrom
Director of Merchandise	Chris DiPierri
Director of Ticket Sales	Larry Fitzpatrick
Director of Game Operations	Tim Beach
Director of Corporate Sponsorships	Ted Van Zelst
Director of Executive Suites	Mary Dolan Grippo
Controller	Ralph Sellitti
Assistant Controller	Ginna Cotton
Customer Service Manager	Kerry Cornils
Payroll Manager	Christine Bowler
Staff Accountant	Heather Jabick, Laura Ferretti
Managers of Corporate Ticket Sales	Erik Scheibe, Brian Reynolds
Creative Services Manager	Mauricio Acosta
Manager of Multimedia and Team Services	Kerry Gwydir
Manager of Executive Suite Services	Linda Statkevicus
Manager of Game Operations and Events	Brad Preston
Manager of Broadcasting	Alice Vanderveldt
Team Store Managers	Danny DiPierri, Maryanne Steves, Krysta Mierzejewski
Group Sales Manager	Cliff Gault
Account Executive, Corporate Sales	Lee Jacobson
Corporate Account Executives	Anthony Mercogliano, Rob Olenchak
Customer Service Represenative	Jesse Mones
Group Sales Representative	Emily Derkasch
Account Executives	Mike Bellinzoni, Mike Clough, Steven Beisel, Andy Gilleece
Internet and Publications Coordinator	Nancy Koenig
Special Events Coordinator	Kevin Schwab
Creative Services Coordinator	Timothy Gilroy
Marketing Programs Coordinator	Jessica Rotoli
Media Relations Coordinator	Jamie Fabos
Ticket Coordinator	Maria Corvino
Assistant Ticket Coordinator	Adam Ortiz
Community Relations Coordinator	Heather Cozzens
Sponsor Services Coordinator	Lorraine Bittles
Administrative Services Coordinator	Sheriene Ahmed
Accounts Payable Bookkeeper	Janet Nelson
Receptionists	Chere O'Neill, Bonnie Dreher
Office Attendant	Todd Aronovitch

Team Information

Colors	Orange, Blue, White
Television Coverage	FOX SPORTS NEW YORK
TV Announcers	Howie Rose, Joe Micheletti
Radio	ONE-ON-ONE SPORTS 620 AM
Radio Announcers	Jim Cerny, Chris King

New York Rangers

2000-01 Results: 33W-43L-5T-1OTL 72PTS. Fourth, Atlantic Division

Theoren Fleury scored 30 goals and added 44 assists in 62 games.

2001-02 Schedule

Month	Day	Date	Game
Oct.	Fri.	5	at Carolina
	Sun.	7	Buffalo
	Wed.	10	Washington
	Sat.	13	at Ottawa
	Mon.	15	at Montreal
	Wed.	17	New Jersey
	Fri.	19	at Atlanta
	Sat.	20	at Tampa Bay
	Mon.	22	San Jose
	Thu.	25	at St. Louis
	Sat.	27	at Boston
	Mon.	29	Dallas
	Wed.	31	Florida
Nov.	Fri.	2	at Carolina
	Sat.	3	at Florida
	Tue.	6	Minnesota
	Thu.	8	at NY Islanders
	Sat.	10	at Buffalo
	Sun.	11	Montreal
	Wed.	14	Philadelphia
	Sat.	17	at Pittsburgh
	Sun.	18	Atlanta
	Tue.	20	Colorado
	Fri.	23	at Washington
	Sun.	25	Anaheim*
	Tue.	27	at Buffalo
	Thu.	29	Carolina
Dec.	Sat.	1	at Montreal
	Sun.	2	Tampa Bay
	Tue.	4	at Washington
	Thu.	6	Toronto
	Sat.	8	at Toronto
	Mon.	10	Carolina
	Wed.	12	Nashville
	Sat.	15	Buffalo
	Mon.	17	Florida
	Wed.	19	New Jersey
	Fri.	21	NY Islanders
	Sun.	23	Ottawa*
	Fri.	28	at San Jose
	Sat.	29	at Los Angeles
	Mon.	31	at Phoenix
Jan.	Wed.	2	at Edmonton
	Thu.	3	at Colorado
	Sat.	5	at Pittsburgh*
	Wed.	9	Los Angeles
	Sat.	12	at Philadelphia*
	Mon.	14	Columbus
	Wed.	16	at Columbus
	Thu.	17	at New Jersey
	Tue.	22	at NY Islanders
	Wed.	23	Boston
	Sat.	26	Washington*
	Mon.	28	Tampa Bay
	Wed.	30	NY Islanders
Feb.	Wed.	6	at Detroit
	Fri.	8	at Atlanta
	Sun.	10	Pittsburgh*
	Wed.	13	at Dallas
	Tue.	26	New Jersey
	Thu.	28	Ottawa
Mar.	Sat.	2	Philadelphia*
	Mon.	4	Calgary
	Tue.	5	at Minnesota
	Thu.	7	at Chicago
	Sat.	9	at Pittsburgh*
	Mon.	11	Montreal
	Wed.	13	Boston
	Sat.	16	at New Jersey*
	Sun.	17	Detroit*
	Tue.	19	Vancouver
	Thu.	21	at Ottawa
	Fri.	22	Atlanta
	Mon.	25	at NY Islanders
	Wed.	27	Philadelphia
	Sat.	30	at Florida
Apr.	Mon.	1	at Tampa Bay
	Thu.	4	at Toronto
	Sat.	6	at Boston*
	Mon.	8	Pittsburgh
	Wed.	10	Toronto
	Sat.	13	at Philadelphia*

* Denotes afternoon game.

Franchise date: May 15, 1926

ATLANTIC DIVISION

76th NHL Season

Year-by-Year Record

		Home				Road				Overall								
Season	GP	W	L	T	OL	W	L	T	OL	W	L	T	OL	GF	GA	Pts.	Finished	Playoff Result
2000-01	82	17	20	3	1	16	23	2	0	33	43	5	1	250	290	72	4th, Atlantic Div.	Out of Playoffs
1999-2000	82	15	20	5	1	14	18	7	2	29	38	12	3	218	246	73	4th, Atlantic Div.	Out of Playoffs
1998-99	82	17	19	5	...	16	19	6	...	33	38	11	...	217	227	77	4th, Atlantic Div.	Out of Playoffs
1997-98	82	14	18	9	...	11	21	9	...	25	39	18	...	197	231	68	5th, Atlantic Div.	Out of Playoffs
1996-97	82	21	14	6	...	17	20	4	...	38	34	10	...	258	231	86	4th, Atlantic Div.	Lost Conf. Final
1995-96	82	22	10	9	...	19	17	5	...	41	27	14	...	272	237	96	2nd, Atlantic Div.	Lost Conf. Semi-Final
1994-95	48	11	10	3	...	11	13	0	...	22	23	3	...	139	134	47	4th, Atlantic Div.	Lost Conf. Semi-Final
1993-94	**84**	**28**	**8**	**6**	**...**	**24**	**16**	**2**	**...**	**52**	**24**	**8**	**...**	**299**	**231**	**112**	**1st, Atlantic Div.**	**Won Stanley Cup**
1992-93	84	20	17	5	...	14	22	6	...	34	39	11	...	304	308	79	6th, Patrick Div.	Out of Playoffs
1991-92	80	28	8	4	...	22	17	1	...	50	25	5	...	321	246	105	1st, Patrick Div.	Lost Div. Final
1990-91	80	22	11	7	...	14	20	6	...	36	31	13	...	297	265	85	2nd, Patrick Div.	Lost Div. Semi-Final
1989-90	80	20	11	9	...	16	20	4	...	36	31	13	...	279	267	85	1st, Patrick Div.	Lost Div. Final
1988-89	80	21	17	2	...	16	18	6	...	37	35	8	...	310	307	82	3rd, Patrick Div.	Lost Div. Semi-Final
1987-88	80	22	13	5	...	14	21	5	...	36	34	10	...	300	283	82	5th, Patrick Div.	Out of Playoffs
1986-87	80	18	18	4	...	16	20	4	...	34	38	8	...	307	323	76	4th, Patrick Div.	Lost Div. Semi-Final
1985-86	80	20	18	2	...	16	20	4	...	36	38	6	...	280	276	78	4th, Patick Div.	Lost Conf. Championship
1984-85	80	16	18	6	...	10	26	4	...	26	44	10	...	295	345	62	4th, Patrick Div.	Lost Div. Semi-Final
1983-84	80	27	12	1	...	15	17	8	...	42	29	9	...	314	304	93	4th, Patrick Div.	Lost Div. Semi-Final
1982-83	80	24	13	3	...	11	22	7	...	35	35	10	...	306	287	80	4th, Patrick Div.	Lost Div. Final
1981-82	80	19	15	6	...	20	12	8	...	39	27	14	...	316	306	92	2nd, Patrick Div.	Lost Div. Final
1980-81	80	17	13	10	...	13	23	4	...	30	36	14	...	312	317	74	4th, Patrick Div.	Lost Semi-Final
1979-80	80	22	10	8	...	16	22	2	...	38	32	10	...	308	284	86	3rd, Patrick Div.	Lost Quarter-Final
1978-79	80	19	13	8	...	21	16	3	...	40	29	11	...	316	292	91	3rd, Patrick Div.	Lost Final
1977-78	80	18	15	7	...	12	22	6	...	30	37	13	...	279	280	73	4th, Patrick Div.	Lost Prelim. Round
1976-77	80	17	18	5	...	12	19	9	...	29	37	14	...	272	310	72	4th, Patrick Div.	Out of Playoffs
1975-76	80	16	16	8	...	13	26	1	...	29	42	9	...	262	333	67	4th, Patrick Div.	Out of Playoffs
1974-75	80	21	11	8	...	16	18	6	...	37	29	14	...	319	276	88	2nd, Patrick Div.	Lost Prelim. Round
1973-74	78	26	7	6	...	14	17	8	...	40	24	14	...	300	251	94	3rd, East Div.	Lost Semi-Final
1972-73	78	26	8	5	...	21	15	3	...	47	23	8	...	297	208	102	3rd, East Div.	Lost Semi-Final
1971-72	78	26	6	7	...	22	11	6	...	48	17	13	...	317	192	109	2nd, East Div.	Lost Final
1970-71	78	30	2	7	...	19	16	4	...	49	18	11	...	259	177	109	2nd, East Div.	Lost Semi-Final
1969-70	76	22	8	8	...	16	14	8	...	38	22	16	...	246	189	92	4th, East Div.	Lost Quarter-Final
1968-69	76	27	7	4	...	14	19	5	...	41	26	9	...	231	196	91	3rd, East Div.	Lost Quarter-Final
1967-68	74	22	8	7	...	17	15	5	...	39	23	12	...	226	183	90	2nd, East Div.	Lost Quarter-Final
1966-67	70	18	12	5	...	12	16	7	...	30	28	12	...	188	189	72	4th,	Lost Semi-Final
1965-66	70	12	16	7	...	6	25	4	...	18	41	11	...	195	261	47	6th,	Out of Playoffs
1964-65	70	8	19	8	...	12	19	4	...	20	38	12	...	179	246	52	5th,	Out of Playoffs
1963-64	70	14	13	8	...	8	25	2	...	22	38	10	...	186	242	54	5th,	Out of Playoffs
1962-63	70	12	17	6	...	10	19	6	...	22	36	12	...	211	233	56	5th,	Out of Playoffs
1961-62	70	16	11	8	...	10	21	4	...	26	32	12	...	195	207	64	4th,	Lost Semi-Final
1960-61	70	15	15	5	...	7	23	5	...	22	38	10	...	204	248	54	5th,	Out of Playoffs
1959-60	70	10	15	10	...	7	23	5	...	17	38	15	...	187	247	49	6th,	Out of Playoffs
1958-59	70	14	16	5	...	12	16	7	...	26	32	12	...	201	217	64	5th,	Out of Playoffs
1957-58	70	14	15	6	...	18	10	7	...	32	25	13	...	195	188	77	2nd,	Lost Semi-Final
1956-57	70	15	12	8	...	11	18	6	...	26	30	14	...	184	227	66	4th,	Lost Semi-Final
1955-56	70	20	7	8	...	12	21	2	...	32	28	10	...	204	203	74	3rd,	Lost Semi-Final
1954-55	70	10	12	13	...	7	23	5	...	17	35	18	...	150	210	52	5th,	Out of Playoffs
1953-54	70	18	12	5	...	11	19	5	...	29	31	10	...	161	182	68	5th,	Out of Playoffs
1952-53	70	11	14	10	...	6	23	6	...	17	37	16	...	152	211	50	6th,	Out of Playoffs
1951-52	70	16	13	6	...	7	21	7	...	23	34	13	...	192	219	59	5th,	Out of Playoffs
1950-51	70	14	11	10	...	6	18	11	...	20	29	21	...	169	201	61	5th,	Out of Playoffs
1949-50	70	19	12	4	...	9	19	7	...	28	31	11	...	170	189	67	4th,	Lost Final
1948-49	60	13	12	5	...	5	19	6	...	18	31	11	...	133	172	47	6th,	Out of Playoffs
1947-48	60	11	12	7	...	10	14	6	...	21	26	13	...	176	201	55	4th,	Lost Semi-Final
1946-47	60	11	14	5	...	11	18	1	...	22	32	6	...	167	186	50	5th,	Out of Playoffs
1945-46	50	8	12	5	...	5	16	4	...	13	28	9	...	144	191	35	6th,	Out of Playoffs
1944-45	50	7	11	7	...	4	18	3	...	11	29	10	...	154	247	32	6th,	Out of Playoffs
1943-44	50	4	17	4	...	2	22	1	...	6	39	5	...	162	310	17	6th,	Out of Playoffs
1942-43	50	7	13	5	...	4	18	3	...	11	31	8	...	161	253	30	6th,	Out of Playoffs
1941-42	48	15	8	1	...	14	9	1	...	29	17	2	...	177	143	60	1st,	Lost Semi-Final
1940-41	48	13	7	4	...	8	12	4	...	21	19	8	...	143	125	50	4th,	Lost Quarter-Final
1939-40	**48**	**17**	**4**	**3**	**...**	**10**	**7**	**7**	**...**	**27**	**11**	**10**	**...**	**136**	**77**	**64**	**2nd,**	**Won Stanley Cup**
1938-39	48	13	8	3	...	13	8	3	...	26	16	6	...	149	105	58	2nd,	Lost Semi-Final
1937-38	48	15	5	4	...	12	10	2	...	27	15	6	...	149	96	60	2nd, Amn. Div.	Lost Quarter-Final
1936-37	48	9	7	8	...	10	13	1	...	19	20	9	...	117	106	47	3rd, Amn. Div.	Lost Final
1935-36	48	11	6	7	...	8	11	5	...	19	17	12	...	91	96	50	4th, Amn. Div.	Out of Playoffs
1934-35	48	11	8	5	...	11	12	1	...	22	20	6	...	137	139	50	3rd, Amn. Div.	Lost Semi-Final
1933-34	48	11	7	6	...	10	12	2	...	21	19	8	...	120	113	50	3rd, Amn. Div.	Lost Quarter-Final
1932-33	**48**	**12**	**7**	**5**	**...**	**11**	**10**	**3**	**...**	**23**	**17**	**8**	**...**	**135**	**107**	**54**	**3rd, Amn. Div.**	**Won Stanley Cup**
1931-32	48	13	7	4	...	10	10	4	...	23	17	8	...	134	112	54	1st, Amn. Div.	Lost Final
1930-31	44	10	9	3	...	9	7	6	...	19	16	9	...	106	87	47	3rd, Amn. Div.	Lost Semi-Final
1929-30	44	11	5	6	...	6	12	4	...	17	17	10	...	136	143	44	3rd, Amn. Div.	Lost Semi-Final
1928-29	44	12	6	4	...	9	7	6	...	21	13	10	...	72	65	52	2nd, Amn. Div.	Lost Final
1927-28	**44**	**10**	**8**	**4**	**...**	**9**	**8**	**5**	**...**	**19**	**16**	**9**	**...**	**94**	**79**	**47**	**2nd, Amn. Div.**	**Won Stanley Cup**
1926-27	44	13	5	4	...	12	8	2	...	25	13	6	...	95	72	56	1st, Amn. Div.	Lost Quarter-Final

2001-02 Player Personnel

FORWARDS	HT	WT	S	Place of Birth	Date	2000-01 Club
CIGER, Zdeno	6-1	190	L	Martin, Czech.	10/19/69	HC Bratislava
DAWE, Jason	5-10	189	L	North York, Ont.	5/29/73	Hartford
DUERDEN, Dave	6-2	200	L	Oshawa, Ont.	4/11/77	Louisville-Hartford
DVORAK, Radek	6-1	194	R	Tabor, Czech.	3/9/77	NY Rangers
EKMAN, Nils	5-11	185	L	Stockholm, Sweden	3/11/76	Tampa Bay-Detroit (IHL)
FLEURY, Theoren	5-6	180	R	Oxbow, Sask.	6/29/68	NY Rangers
FREADRICH, Kyle	6-7	260	L	Edmonton, Alta.	12/28/78	Tampa Bay-Detroit (IHL)
GERNANDER, Ken	5-10	175	L	Coleraine, MN	6/30/69	Hartford
GROSEK, Michal	6-2	207	R	Vyskov, Czech.	6/1/75	NY Rangers-Hartford
HEISTEN, Barrett	6-1	189	L	Anchorage, AK	3/19/80	Seattle
JOHANSSON, Andreas	6-0	202	L	Hofors, Sweden	5/19/73	SC Bern
KANE, Boyd	6-2	218	L	Swift Current, Sask.	4/18/78	Charlotte-Hartford
LINDROS, Eric	6-4	236	R	London, Ont.	2/28/73	DID NOT PLAY
LUNDMARK, Jamie	6-0	174	R	Edmonton, Alta.	1/16/81	Seattle
MALHOTRA, Manny	6-2	210	L	Mississauga, Ont.	5/18/80	NY Rangers-Hartford
McCARTHY, Sandy	6-3	225	R	Toronto, Ont.	6/15/72	NY Rangers
MESSIER, Mark	6-1	210	L	Edmonton, Alta.	1/18/61	NY Rangers
NEDVED, Petr	6-3	195	L	Liberec, Czech.	12/9/71	NY Rangers
SAMUELSSON, Mikael	6-1	195	L	Mariefred, Sweden	12/23/76	San Jose-Kentucky
SCOTT, Richard	6-2	195	L	Orillia, Ont.	8/1/78	Hartford-Charlotte
SMYTH, Brad	6-0	195	R	Ottawa, Ont.	3/13/73	NY Rangers-Hartford
TOMS, Jeff	6-5	200	L	Swift Current, Sask.	6/4/74	NYI-Sprfld-NYR-Hart
ULMER, Layne	6-1	205	L	North Battleford, Sask.	9/14/80	Swift Current
YORK, Mike	5-10	185	R	Waterford, MI	1/3/78	NY Rangers

DEFENSEMEN	HT	WT	S	Place of Birth	Date	2000-01 Club
GAGNON, Sean	6-2	219	L	Sault Ste. Marie, Ont.	9/11/73	Ottawa-Grand Rapids
GOSSELIN, Christian	6-5	235	R	Laval, Que.	8/21/76	Kentucky
KARPA, Dave	6-1	210	R	Regina, Sask.	5/7/71	Carolina
KINCH, Matt	6-0	195	L	Red Deer, Alta.	2/17/80	Calgary (WHL)
KLOUCEK, Tomas	6-3	203	L	Prague, Czech.	3/7/80	NY Rangers-Hartford
LEETCH, Brian	6-1	190	L	Corpus Christi, TX	3/3/68	NY Rangers
LEFEBVRE, Sylvain	6-2	205	L	Richmond, Que.	10/14/67	NY Rangers
MALAKHOV, Vladimir	6-4	230	L	Ekaterinburg, USSR	8/30/68	NY Rangers
MOTTAU, Mike	6-0	192	L	Quincy, MA	3/19/78	NY Rangers-Hartford
NOVAK, Filip	6-0	174	L	Ceske Budejovice, Czech.	5/7/82	Regina
PURINTON, Dale	6-3	214	L	Fort Wayne, IN	10/11/76	NY Rangers-Hartford
RICHTER, Martin	6-1	196	R	Prostejov, Czech.	12/6/77	Sai-Lappeenranta-Hartford
ST. CROIX, Chris	6-1	199	R	Voorhees, NJ	5/2/79	Saint John
SMREK, Peter	6-1	215	L	Martin, Czech.	2/16/79	StL-Wor-NYR-Hart
ULANOV, Igor	6-3	211	L	Krasnokamsk, USSR	10/1/69	Edmonton
VAN IMPE, Darren	6-1	205	L	Saskatoon, Sask.	5/18/73	Boston
VIRTUE, Terry	6-0	207	R	Scarborough, Ont.	8/12/70	Hartford

GOALTENDERS	HT	WT	C	Place of Birth	Date	2000-01 Club
BLACKBURN, Dan	6-0	180	L	Montreal, Que.	5/20/83	Kootenay Ice
HOLMQVIST, Johan	6-3	190	L	Tolfta, Sweden	5/24/78	NY Rangers-Hartford
LABARBERA, Jason	6-2	205	L	Prince George, B.C.	1/18/80	NY Rangers-Hartford-Charlotte
RICHTER, Mike	5-11	185	L	Abington, PA	9/22/66	NY Rangers
YEREMEYEV, Vitali	5-10	167	L	Ust-Kamenogorsk, USSR	9/23/75	NY Rangers-Hartford-Charlotte

Captains' History

Bill Cook, 1926-27 to 1936-37; Art Coulter, 1937-38 to 1941-42; Ott Heller, 1942-43 to 1944-45; Neil Colville 1945-46 to 1948-49; Buddy O'Connor, 1949-50; Frank Eddolls, 1950-51; Frank Eddolls and Allan Stanley, 1951-52; Allan Stanley, 1952-53; Allan Stanley and Don Raleigh, 1953-54; Don Raleigh, 1954-55; Harry Howell, 1955-56, 1956-57; Red Sullivan, 1957-58 to 1960-61; Andy Bathgate, 1961-62, 1962-63; Andy Bathgate and Camille Henry, 1963-64; Camille Henry and Bob Nevin, 1964-65; Bob Nevin 1965-66 to 1970-71; Vic Hadfield, 1971-72 to 1973-74; Brad Park, 1974-75; Brad Park and Phil Esposito, 1975-76; Phil Esposito, 1976-77, 1977-78; Dave Maloney, 1978-79, 1979-80; Dave Maloney, Walt Tkaczuk and Barry Beck, 1980-81; Barry Beck, 1981-82 to 1985-86; Ron Greschner, 1986-87; Ron Greschner and Kelly Kisio, 1987-88; Kelly Kisio, 1988-89 to 1990-91; Mark Messier, 1991-92 to 1996-97; Brian Leetch, 1997-98 to 1999-2000; Mark Messier, 2000-01 to date.

Coaching History

Lester Patrick, 1926-27 to 1938-39; Frank Boucher, 1939-40 to 1947-48; Frank Boucher and Lynn Patrick, 1948-49; Lynn Patrick, 1949-50; Neil Colville, 1950-51; Neil Colville and Bill Cook, 1951-52; Bill Cook, 1952-53; Frank Boucher and Muzz Patrick, 1953-54; Muzz Patrick, 1954-55; Phil Watson, 1955-56 to 1958-59; Phil Watson and Alf Pike, 1959-60; Alf Pike, 1960-61; Doug Harvey, 1961-62; Muzz Patrick and Red Sullivan, 1962-63; Red Sullivan, 1963-64, 1964-65; Red Sullivan and Emile Francis, 1965-66; Emile Francis, 1966-67, 1967-68; Bernie Geoffrion and Emile Francis, 1968-69; Emile Francis, 1969-70 to 1972-73; Larry Popein and Emile Francis, 1973-74; Emile Francis, 1974-75; Ron Stewart and John Ferguson, 1975-76; John Ferguson, 1976-77; Jean-Guy Talbot, 1977-78; Fred Shero, 1978-79, 1979-80; Fred Shero and Craig Patrick, 1980-81; Herb Brooks, 1981-82 to 1983-84; Herb Brooks and Craig Patrick, 1984-85; Ted Sator, 1985-86; Ted Sator, Tom Webster and Phil Esposito, 1986-87; Michel Bergeron, 1987-88; Michel Bergeron and Phil Esposito, 1988-89; Roger Neilson, 1989-90 to 1991-92; Roger Neilson and Ron Smith, 1992-93; Mike Keenan, 1993-94; Colin Campbell, 1994-95 to 1996-97; Colin Campbell and John Muckler, 1997-98; John Muckler, 1998-99; John Muckler and John Tortorella, 1999-2000; Ron Low, 2000-01 to date.

General Managers' History

Lester Patrick, 1927-28 to 1945-46; Frank Boucher, 1946-47 to 1954-55; Muzz Patrick, 1955-56 to 1963-64; Emile Francis, 1964-65 to 1974-75; Emile Francis and John Ferguson, 1975-76; John Ferguson, 1976-77, 1977-78; John Ferguson and Fred Shero, 1978-79; Fred Shero, 1979-80; Fred Shero and Craig Patrick, 1980-81; Craig Patrick, 1981-82 to 1985-86; Phil Esposito, 1986-87 to 1988-89; Neil Smith, 1989-90 to 1999-2000; Glen Sather, 2000-01 to date.

2000-01 Scoring

* - rookie

Regular Season

Pos	#	Player	Team	GP	G	A	Pts	+/–	PIM	PP	SH	GW	GT	S	%
D	2	Brian Leetch	NYR	82	21	58	79	–18	34	10	1	3	1	241	8.7
C	93	Petr Nedved	NYR	79	32	46	78	10	54	9	1	5	0	230	13.9
R	14	Theoren Fleury	NYR	62	30	44	74	0	122	8	7	3	0	238	12.6
R	20	Radek Dvorak	NYR	82	31	36	67	9	20	5	2	3	0	230	13.5
C	11	Mark Messier	NYR	82	24	43	67	–25	89	12	3	2	0	131	18.3
L	27	Jan Hlavac	NYR	79	28	36	64	3	20	5	0	6	0	195	14.4
L	13	Valeri Kamensky	NYR	65	14	20	34	–18	36	6	0	1	0	129	10.9
C	18	Michael York	NYR	79	14	17	31	1	20	3	2	4	0	171	8.2
L	9	Adam Graves	NYR	82	10	16	26	–16	77	1	0	1	0	136	7.4
D	3	Kim Johnsson	NYR	75	5	21	26	–3	40	4	0	0	0	104	4.8
R	10	Sandy McCarthy	NYR	81	11	10	21	3	171	0	0	2	0	95	11.6
L	8	Michal Grosek	NYR	65	9	11	20	–10	61	2	0	0	0	84	10.7
D	24	Sylvain Lefebvre	NYR	71	2	13	15	3	55	0	0	0	0	39	5.1
C	6	Manny Malhotra	NYR	50	4	8	12	–10	31	0	0	2	0	46	8.7
D	47	Richard Pilon	NYR	69	2	9	11	–2	175	0	0	0	0	24	8.3
L	29	Jeff Toms	NYI	39	2	4	6	–7	10	0	0	0	0	37	5.4
			NYR	15	1	1	2	–3	0	0	0	0	0	12	8.3
			TOTAL	54	3	5	8	–10	10	0	0	0	0	49	6.1
C	26	Tim Taylor	NYR	38	2	5	7	–6	16	0	0	1	0	34	5.9
L	17	Colin Forbes	OTT	39	0	1	1	–3	31	0	0	0	0	26	0.0
			NYR	19	1	4	5	–3	15	0	0	0	0	20	5.0
			TOTAL	58	1	5	6	–6	46	0	0	0	0	46	2.2
D	25	* Peter Smrek	STL	6	2	0	2	1	2	0	0	1	0	5	40.0
			NYR	14	0	3	3	1	12	0	0	0	0	9	0.0
			TOTAL	20	2	3	5	2	14	0	0	1	0	14	14.3
D	22	* Tomas Kloucek	NYR	43	1	4	5	–3	74	0	0	0	0	22	4.5
D	4	Brad Brown	NYR	48	1	3	4	0	107	0	0	0	0	14	7.1
R	38	* Jeff Ulmer	NYR	21	3	0	3	–6	8	0	0	0	0	22	13.6
D	33	* Mike Mottau	NYR	18	0	3	3	–6	13	0	0	0	0	17	0.0
D	23	Vladimir Malakhov	NYR	3	0	2	2	0	4	0	0	0	0	6	0.0
D	5	* Dale Purinton	NYR	42	0	2	2	5	180	0	0	0	0	13	0.0
R	39	Brad Smyth	NYR	4	1	0	1	0	4	0	0	0	0	10	10.0
D	36	David Wilkie	NYR	1	0	0	0	–2	2	0	0	0	0	1	0.0
G	34	* Jason Labarbera	NYR	1	0	0	0	0	0	0	0	0	0	0	0.0
D	21	Bert Robertsson	NYR	2	0	0	0	–1	4	0	0	0	0	0	0.0
G	32	* Johan Holmqvist	NYR	2	0	0	0	0	2	0	0	0	0	0	0.0
D	39	Drew Bannister	NYR	3	0	0	0	–1	0	0	0	0	0	3	0.0
C	21	Derek Armstrong	NYR	3	0	0	0	0	0	0	0	0	0	6	0.0
D	21	Jason Doig	NYR	3	0	0	0	0	0	0	0	0	0	1	0.0
G	31	* Vitali Yeremeyev	NYR	4	0	0	0	0	0	0	0	0	0	0	0.0
R	37	* Tony Tuzzolino	NYR	6	0	0	0	–1	5	0	0	0	0	3	0.0
G	30	Kirk McLean	NYR	23	0	0	0	0	0	0	0	0	0	0	0.0
G	35	Mike Richter	NYR	45	0	0	0	0	0	0	0	0	0	0	0.0
G	31	Guy Hebert	ANA	41	0	0	0	0	0	0	0	0	0	0	0.0
			NYR	13	0	0	0	0	0	0	0	0	0	0	0.0
			TOTAL	54	0	0	0	0	0	0	0	0	0	0	0.0

Goaltending

No.	Goaltender	GPI	Mins	Avg	W	L	T	EN	SO	GA	SA	S%
34	* Jason Labarbera	1	10	0.00	0	0	0	0	0	0	2	1.000
35	Mike Richter	45	2635	3.28	20	21	3	5	0	144	1343	.893
31	Guy Hebert	13	735	3.43	5	7	1	2	0	42	409	.897
30	Kirk McLean	23	1220	3.49	8	10	1	0	0	71	639	.889
31	* Vitali Yeremeyev	4	212	4.53	0	4	0	0	0	16	104	.846
32	* Johan Holmqvist	2	119	5.04	0	2	0	0	0	10	71	.859
	Totals	**82**	**4966**	**3.50**	**33**	**44**	**5**	**7**	**0**	**290**	**2575**	**.887**

Coach

LOW, RON

Coach, New York Rangers. Born in Birtie, Man., June 21, 1950.

Ron Low was hired as head coach of the New York Rangers on July 12, 2000, after spending the 1999-2000 season with the Houston Aeros of the International Hockey League. He guided the club to the IHL Western Conference Finals.

Prior to his stint in Houston, Low served as head coach of the Edmonton Oilers, where he compiled a 139-162-40 mark in four-plus years behind the bench. As one of the NHL's youngest coaches, Low earned a reputation for successfully developing talented young prospects into solid NHL performers.

Low's history with Glen Sather and the Edmonton franchise dates back to the 1979-80 season, when the Oilers obtained him from the Quebec Nordiques. An NHL veteran of 11 years, Low's career in the crease saw him tend goal for Toronto, Washington, Detroit, Quebec, Edmonton and New Jersey from 1972 to 1985.

In 1985-86, Low was named player/assistant coach for the Nova Scotia Oilers, Edmonton's American Hockey League affiliate. Following two years as an assistant coach, he was named Nova Scotia's head coach in 1987-88 and kept that position when the team became the Cape Breton Oilers in 1988-89. He joined the NHL coaching ranks in August 1989 as an assistant coach for the Oilers, and was a member of the 1990 Stanley Cup championship team.

Coaching Record

		Regular Season				Playoffs		
Season	Team	Games	W	L	T	Games	W	L
1987-88	Nova Scotia (AHL)	80	35	36	9	5	1	4
1988-89	Cape Breton (AHL)	80	27	47	6	....	....	....
1994-95	**Edmonton (NHL)**	**13**	**5**	**7**	**1**	....	....	....
1995-96	**Edmonton (NHL)**	**82**	**30**	**44**	**8**	....	....	....
1996-97	**Edmonton (NHL)**	**82**	**36**	**37**	**9**	**12**	**5**	**7**
1997-98	**Edmonton (NHL)**	**82**	**35**	**37**	**10**	**12**	**5**	**7**
1998-99	**Edmonton (NHL)**	**82**	**33**	**37**	**12**	**4**	**0**	**4**
1999-2000	Houston (IHL)	82	44	29	9	11	6	5
2000-01	**NY Rangers (NHL)**	**82**	**33**	**44**	**5**	....	....	....
	NHL Totals	**423**	**172**	**206**	**45**	**28**	**10**	**18**

Club Records

Team

(Figures in brackets for season records are games played; records for fewest points, wins, ties, losses, goals, goals against are for 70 or more games)

Most Points	**112**	1993-94 (84)
Most Wins	**52**	1993-94 (84)
Most Ties	**21**	1950-51 (70)
Most Losses	**44**	1984-85 (80)
Most Goals	**321**	1991-92 (80)
Most Goals Against	**345**	1984-85 (80)
Fewest Points	**47**	1965-66 (70)
Fewest Wins	**17**	1952-53 (70), 1954-55 (70), 1959-60 (70)
Fewest Ties	**5**	1991-92 (80), 2000-01 (82)
Fewest Losses	**17**	1971-72 (78)
Fewest Goals	**150**	1954-55 (70)
Fewest Goals Against	**177**	1970-71 (78)
Longest Winning Streak		
Overall	**10**	Dec. 19/39-Jan. 13/40, Jan. 19-Feb. 10/73
Home	**14**	Dec. 19/39-Feb. 25/40
Away	**7**	Jan. 12-Feb. 12/35, Oct. 28-Nov. 29/78
Longest Undefeated Streak		
Overall	**19**	Nov. 23/39-Jan. 13/40 (14 wins, 5 ties)
Home	**26**	Mar. 29/70-Jan. 31/71 (19 wins, 7 ties)
Away	**11**	Nov. 5/39-Jan. 13/40 (6 wins, 5 ties)
Longest Losing Streak		
Overall	**11**	Oct. 30-Nov. 27/43
Home	**7**	Oct. 20-Nov. 14/76, Mar. 24-Apr. 14/93
Away	**10**	Oct. 30-Dec. 23/43
Longest Winless Streak		
Overall	**21**	Jan. 23-Mar. 19/44 (17 losses, 4 ties)
Home	**10**	Jan. 30-Mar. 19/44 (7 losses, 3 ties)
Away	**16**	Oct. 9-Dec. 20/52 (12 losses, 4 ties)
Most Shutouts, Season	**13**	1928-29 (44)
Most PIM, Season	**2,018**	1989-90 (80)
Most Goals, Game	**12**	Nov. 21/71 (Cal. 1 at NYR 12)

Individual

Most Seasons	**17**	Harry Howell
Most Games	**1,160**	Harry Howell
Most Goals, Career	**406**	Rod Gilbert
Most Assists, Career	**655**	Brian Leetch
Most Points, Career	**1,021**	Rod Gilbert (406G, 615A)
Most PIM, Career	**1,226**	Ron Greschner
Most Shutouts, Career	**49**	Ed Giacomin
Longest Consecutive Games Streak	**560**	Andy Hebenton (Oct. 7/55-Mar. 24/63)
Most Goals, Season	**52**	Adam Graves (1993-94)
Most Assists, Season	**80**	Brian Leetch (1991-92)
Most Points, Season	**109**	Jean Ratelle (1971-72; 46G, 63A)
Most PIM, Season	**305**	Troy Mallette (1989-90)
Most Points, Defenseman, Season	**102**	Brian Leetch (1991-92; 22G, 80A)
Most Points, Center, Season	**109**	Jean Ratelle (1971-72; 46G, 63A)
Most Points, Right Wing, Season	**97**	Rod Gilbert (1971-72; 43G, 54A), (1974-75; 36G, 61A)
Most Points, Left Wing, Season	**106**	Vic Hadfield (1971-72; 50G, 56A)
Most Points, Rookie, Season	**76**	Mark Pavelich (1981-82; 33G, 43A)
Most Shutouts, Season	**13**	John Ross Roach (1928-29)
Most Goals, Game	**5**	Don Murdoch (Oct. 12/76), Mark Pavelich (Feb. 23/83)
Most Assists, Game	**5**	Walt Tkaczuk (Feb. 12/72), Rod Gilbert (Mar. 2/75, Mar. 30/75, Oct. 8/76), Don Maloney (Jan. 3/87), Brian Leetch (Apr. 18/95), Wayne Gretzky (Feb. 15/99)
Most Points, Game	**7**	Steve Vickers (Feb. 18/76; 3G, 4A)

Retired Numbers

1	Ed Giacomin	1965-1976
7	Rod Gilbert	1960-1978

All-time Record vs. Other Clubs

Regular Season

	At Home								On Road								Total							
	GP	W	L	T	OL	GF	GA	PTS	GP	W	L	T	OL	GF	GA	PTS	GP	W	L	T	OL	GF	GA	PTS
Anaheim	6	2	3	1	0	17	18	5	7	1	6	0	0	19	30	2	13	3	9	1	0	36	48	7
Atlanta	4	2	2	0	0	13	15	4	4	4	0	0	0	18	9	8	8	6	2	0	0	31	24	12
Boston	296	128	113	55	0	902	835	311	292	93	157	42	0	818	1059	228	588	221	270	97	0	1720	1894	539
Buffalo	60	25	20	15	0	197	163	65	62	17	37	8	0	194	262	42	122	42	57	23	0	391	425	107
Calgary	49	23	21	5	0	174	174	51	48	11	27	10	0	146	215	32	97	34	48	15	0	320	389	83
Carolina	39	23	13	3	0	150	106	49	37	14	20	3	0	123	129	31	76	37	33	6	0	273	235	80
Chicago	284	117	112	55	0	838	803	289	284	115	127	42	0	789	863	272	568	232	239	97	0	1627	1666	561
Colorado	31	18	9	4	0	124	89	40	32	13	16	3	0	124	132	29	63	31	25	7	0	248	221	69
Columbus	0	0	0	0	0	0	0	0	1	1	0	0	0	4	3	2	1	1	0	0	0	4	3	2
Dallas	60	34	15	11	0	206	163	79	59	30	18	10	1	216	180	71	119	64	33	21	1	422	343	150
Detroit	282	133	91	58	0	862	732	324	283	76	162	45	0	696	998	197	565	209	253	103	0	1558	1730	521
Edmonton	28	9	13	6	0	103	106	24	27	13	11	3	0	93	97	29	55	22	24	9	0	196	203	53
Florida	18	8	6	4	0	55	47	20	19	9	9	1	0	50	51	19	37	17	15	5	0	105	98	39
Los Angeles	56	35	15	6	0	231	162	76	58	25	23	10	0	208	193	60	114	60	38	16	0	439	355	136
Minnesota	1	1	0	0	0	4	2	2	1	1	0	0	0	3	2	2	2	2	0	0	0	7	4	4
Montreal	284	116	114	54	0	826	828	286	284	57	188	39	0	651	1112	153	568	173	302	93	0	1477	1940	439
Nashville	3	2	0	0	1	12	5	5	2	1	1	0	0	9	9	2	5	3	1	0	1	21	14	7
New Jersey	76	39	20	17	0	304	229	95	78	33	40	5	0	264	271	71	154	72	60	22	0	568	500	166
NY Islanders	88	51	27	10	0	337	266	112	88	28	53	7	0	273	352	63	176	79	80	17	0	610	618	175
Ottawa	17	9	8	0	0	59	49	18	17	10	5	2	0	52	47	22	34	19	13	2	0	111	96	40
Philadelphia	102	44	35	23	0	330	297	111	101	37	50	14	0	284	333	88	203	81	85	37	0	614	630	199
Phoenix	28	17	9	2	0	125	100	36	29	13	12	4	0	98	100	30	57	30	21	6	0	223	200	66
Pittsburgh	93	47	37	9	0	371	318	103	92	40	38	14	0	348	338	94	185	87	75	23	0	719	656	197
St. Louis	59	44	9	6	0	243	140	94	60	28	23	9	0	193	174	65	119	72	32	15	0	436	314	159
San Jose	8	6	1	1	0	37	23	13	10	7	2	1	0	37	22	15	18	13	3	2	0	74	45	28
Tampa Bay	21	11	8	2	0	77	72	24	19	9	7	3	0	68	64	21	40	20	15	5	0	145	136	45
Toronto	277	118	103	56	0	851	808	292	276	82	154	39	1	724	953	204	553	200	257	95	1	1575	1761	496
Vancouver	52	37	10	5	0	232	133	79	50	33	14	3	0	203	160	69	102	70	24	8	0	435	293	148
Washington	76	36	31	8	1	289	265	81	78	31	38	9	0	259	290	71	154	67	69	17	1	548	555	152
Defunct Clubs	139	87	30	22	0	460	290	196	139	82	34	23	0	441	291	187	278	169	64	45	0	901	581	383
Totals	**2537**	**1222**	**875**	**438**	**2**	**8429**	**7238**	**2884**	**2537**	**914**	**1272**	**349**	**2**	**7405**	**8739**	**2179**	**5074**	**2136**	**2147**	**787**	**4**	**15834**	**15977**	**5063**

Playoffs

	Series	W	L	GP	W	L	T	GF	GA	Last Mtg.	Round	Result
Boston	9	3	6	42	18	22	2	104	114	1973	QF	W 4-1
Buffalo	1	0	1	3	1	2	0	6	11	1978	PR	L 1-2
Calgary	1	1	0	4	3	1	0	14	8	1980	PR	W 3-1
Chicago	5	1	4	24	10	14	0	54	66	1973	SF	L 1-4
Colorado	1	1	0	6	4	2	0	25	19	1995	CQF	W 4-2
Detroit	5	1	4	23	10	13	0	49	57	1950	F	L 3-4
Florida	1	1	0	5	4	1	0	13	10	1997	CQF	W 4-1
Los Angeles	2	2	0	6	5	1	0	32	14	1981	PR	W 3-1
Montreal	14	7	7	61	25	34	2	158	188	1996	CQF	W 4-2
New Jersey	3	3	0	19	12	7	0	56	46	1997	CSF	W 4-1
NY Islanders	8	3	5	39	19	20	0	132	129	1994	CQF	W 4-0
Philadelphia	10	4	6	47	20	27	0	153	158	1997	CF	L 1-4
Pittsburgh	3	0	3	15	3	12	0	45	64	1996	CSF	L 1-4
St. Louis	1	1	0	6	4	2	0	29	22	1981	QF	W 4-2
Toronto	8	5	3	35	19	16	0	86	86	1971	QF	W 4-2
Vancouver	1	1	0	7	4	3	0	21	19	1994	F	W 4-3
Washington	4	2	2	22	11	11	0	71	75	1994	CSF	W 4-1
Defunct	9	6	3	22	11	7	4	43	29			
Totals	**86**	**42**	**44**	**386**	**183**	**195**	**8**	**1091**	**1115**			

Calgary totals include Atlanta Flames, 1972-73 to 1979-80.
Colorado totals include Quebec, 1979-80 to 1994-95.
New Jersey totals include Kansas City, 1974-75 to 1975-76, and Colorado Rockies, 1976-77 to 1981-82.
Phoenix totals include Winnipeg, 1979-80 to 1995-96.
Carolina totals include Hartford, 1979-80 to 1996-97.
Dallas totals include Minnesota North Stars, 1967-68 to 1992-93.

Playoff Results 2001-1997

Year	Round	Opponent	Result	GF	GA
1997	CF	Philadelphia	L 1-4	13	20
	CSF	New Jersey	W 4-1	10	5
	CQF	Florida	W 4-1	13	10

Abbreviations: Round: F – Final;
CF – conference final; **CSF** – conference semi-final;
CQF – conference quarter-final; **SF** – semi-final;
QF – quarter-final; **PR** – preliminary round.

2000-01 Results

Oct.	7	at Atlanta	2-1		8	Dallas	1-2
	11	Montreal	3-1		13	at Boston	1-4
	14	at Pittsburgh	6-8		14	Minnesota	4-2
	16	Anaheim	3-4		16	Philadelphia	4-3*
	18	at Chicago	4-2		18	Toronto	2-1*
	22	Tampa Bay	2-4		20	at Montreal	2-2
	24	Philadelphia	4-5		22	at Carolina	5-2
	26	at Philadelphia	0-3		24	Carolina	2-3
	27	Pittsburgh	1-4		26	NY Islanders	2-3
	29	Boston	5-1		27	at Toronto	1-3
Nov.	1	Tampa Bay	6-1		29	Atlanta	2-7
	2	at Ottawa	5-6		31	Montreal	4-2
	4	at Montreal	5-2	**Feb.**	6	Buffalo	3-6
	7	Edmonton	4-3		9	at Florida	4-2
	9	at Washington	5-3		11	New Jersey	1-1
	12	Phoenix	0-2		12	at Columbus	4-3
	15	at Minnesota	3-2		17	at Tampa Bay	5-4
	17	at Vancouver	3-4		19	Chicago	4-2
	18	at Calgary	5-4*		23	at Pittsburgh	4-6
	21	Toronto	1-3		25	at Philadelphia	1-2
	22	at NY Islanders	4-3*		26	Ottawa	2-3
	24	at Buffalo	2-3		28	Florida	4-2
	26	Ottawa	3-2	**Mar.**	2	Pittsburgh	5-7
	28	Los Angeles	7-6		4	at Nashville	2-5
	29	at New Jersey	2-5		5	NY Islanders	2-5
Dec.	2	at Toronto	2-8		9	at Washington	3-5
	3	Colorado	3-6		10	at Ottawa	3-2
	6	Washington	3-2		12	Pittsburgh	3-3
	8	Buffalo	5-2		14	at Buffalo	3-6
	9	at Boston	4-6		17	at Philadelphia	1-2
	12	at San Jose	2-3		19	Washington	6-3
	14	at Los Angeles	5-5		21	at New Jersey	0-4
	15	at Anaheim	4-6		24	Detroit	0-6
	18	Florida	6-3		25	Boston	2-3
	20	St. Louis	3-6		28	NY Islanders	4-2
	23	Nashville	2-3*		29	at NY Islanders	6-4
	27	at Carolina	3-4		31	at New Jersey	4-3
	28	Atlanta	1-4	**Apr.**	1	at Atlanta	4-2
	31	at Dallas	1-6		4	Carolina	1-3
Jan.	4	at Phoenix	1-3		5	at Tampa Bay	4-3*
	6	New Jersey	5-5		7	at Florida	0-3

* – Overtime

Entry Draft Selections 2001-1987

2001

Pick	
10	Dan Blackburn
40	Fedor Tutin
79	Garth Murray
113	Bryce Lampman
139	Shawn Collymore
176	Marek Zidlicky
206	Petr Preucil
226	Pontus Petterstrom
230	Leonid Zhvachkin
238	Ryan Hollweg
269	Juris Stals

2000

Pick	
64	Filip Novak
95	Dominic Moore
112	Premysl Duben
140	Nathan Martz
143	Brandon Snee
175	Sven Helfenstein
205	Henrik Lundqvist
238	Dan Eberly
269	Martin Richter

1999

Pick	
4	Pavel Brendl
9	Jamie Lundmark
59	David Inman
79	Johan Asplund
90	Patrick Aufiero
137	Garrett Bembridge
177	Jay Dardis
197	Arto Laatikainen
226	Yevgeny Gusakov
251	Petter Henning
254	Alexei Bulatov

1998

Pick	
7	Manny Malhotra
40	Randy Copley
66	Jason Labarbera
114	Boyd Kane
122	Patrick Leahy
131	Tomas Kloucek
180	Stefan Lundqvist
207	Johan Witehall
235	Jan Mertzig

1997

Pick	
19	Stefan Cherneski
46	Wes Jarvis
73	Burke Henry
93	Tomi Kallarsson
126	Jason McLean
134	Johan Lindbom
136	Mike York
154	Shawn Degagne
175	Johan Holmqvist
182	Mike Mottau
210	Andrew Proskurnicki
236	Richard Miller

1996

Pick	
22	Jeff Brown
48	Daniel Goneau
76	Dmitri Subbotin
131	Colin Pepperall
158	Ola Sandberg
185	Jeff Dessner
211	Ryan McKie
237	Ronnie Sundin

1995

Pick	
39	Christian Dube
65	Mike Martin
91	Marc Savard
110	Alexei Vasiliev
117	Dale Purinton
143	Peter Slamiar
169	Jeff Heil
195	Ilja Gorokhov
221	Bob Maudie

1994

Pick	
26	Dan Cloutier
52	Rudolf Vercik
78	Adam Smith
100	Alexander Korobolin
104	Sylvain Blouin
130	Martin Ethier
135	Yuri Litvinov
156	David Brosseau
182	Alexei Lazarenko
208	Craig Anderson
209	Vitali Yeremeyev
234	Eric Boulton
260	Radoslav Kropac
267	Jamie Butt
286	Kim Johnsson

1993

Pick	
8	Niklas Sundstrom
34	Lee Sorochan
61	Maxim Galanov
86	Sergei Olimpiyev
112	Gary Roach
138	Dave Trofimenkoff
162	Sergei Kondrashkin
164	Todd Marchant
190	Eddy Campbell
216	Ken Shepard
242	Andrei Kudinov
261	Pavel Komarov
268	Maxim Smelnitsky

1992

Pick	
24	Peter Ferraro
48	Mattias Norstrom
72	Eric Cairns
85	Chris Ferraro
120	Dmitri Starostenko
144	David Dal Grande
168	Matt Oates
192	Mickey Elick
216	Daniel Brierley
240	Vladimir Vorobiev

1991

Pick	
15	Alexei Kovalev
37	Darcy Werenka
96	Corey Machanic
125	Fredrik Jax
128	Barry Young
147	John Rushin
169	Corey Hirsch
191	Vyacheslav Uvayev
213	Jamie Ram
235	Vitali Chinakhov
257	Brian Wiseman

1990

Pick	
13	Michael Stewart
34	Doug Weight
55	John Vary
69	Jeff Nielsen
76	Rick Willis
85	Sergei Zubov
99	Lubos Rob
118	Jason Weinrich
139	Brian Lonsinger
160	Todd Hedlund
181	Andrew Silverman
202	Jon Hillebrandt
223	Brett Lievers
244	Sergei Nemchinov

1989

Pick	
20	Steven Rice
40	Jason Prosofsky
45	Rob Zamuner
49	Louie DeBrusk
67	Jim Cummins
88	Aaron Miller
118	Joby Messier
139	Greg Leahy
160	Greg Spenrath
181	Mark Bavis
202	Roman Oksiuta
223	Steve Locke
244	Ken MacDermid

1988

Pick	
22	Troy Mallette
26	Murray Duval
68	Tony Amonte
99	Martin Bergeron
110	Dennis Vial
131	Mike Rosati
152	Eric Couvrette
194	Paul Cain
202	Eric Fenton
215	Peter Fiorentino
236	Keith Slifstein

1987

Pick	
10	Jay More
31	Daniel Lacroix
46	Simon Gagne
69	Mike Sullivan
94	Eric O'Borsky
115	Ludek Cajka
136	Clint Thomas
157	Charles Wiegand
178	Eric Burrill
199	David Porter
205	Brett Barnett
220	Lance Marciano

President and General Manager

SATHER, GLEN CAMERON
President and General Manager, New York Rangers
Born in High River, Alta., Sept. 2, 1943.

Glen Sather, who spent parts of four seasons with the New York Rangers as a player from 1970 to 1974, became the franchise's 12th president and 10th general manager on June 1, 2000. He joined the club following a 24-year career with the Edmonton Oilers, where he was the architect of five Stanley Cup Championships between 1984 and 1990. One of the most respected executives in the National Hockey League, Sather was honored for his tremendous achievements by becoming the first member of the Oilers organization to be selected to the Hockey Hall of Fame.

Named coach and vice president of hockey operations for the Oilers when the franchise joined the NHL in June of 1979, Sather became general manager and club president in May of 1980. He coached through the 1988-89 season and also returned for 60 games behind the bench in 1993-94. Sather-coached teams won the Stanley Cup four times in the 1980s. As general manager, Sather was instrumental in the Oilers' fifth Cup triumph in 1990.

He played for six different teams during a 10-year NHL career. He scored 80 goals in 658 games.

NHL Coaching Record

		Regular Season				Playoffs		
Season	Team	Games	W	L	T	Games	W	L
1979-80	Edmonton	80	28	39	13	3	0	3
1980-81	Edmonton	62	25	26	11	9	5	4
1981-82	Edmonton	80	48	17	15	5	2	3
1982-83	Edmonton	80	47	21	12	16	11	5
1983-84	Edmonton	80	57	18	5	19	15	4*
1984-85	Edmonton	80	49	20	11	18	15	3*
1985-86	Edmonton	80	56	17	7	10	6	4
1986-87	Edmonton	80	50	24	6	21	16	5*
1987-88	Edmonton	80	44	25	11	18	16	2*
1988-89	Edmonton	80	38	34	8	7	3	4
1993-94	Edmonton	60	22	27	11	....	....	....
	NHL Totals	**842**	**464**	**268**	**110**	**126**	**89**	**37**

* Stanley Cup win.

Club Directory

Madison Square Garden

New York Rangers
14th Floor
2 Pennsylvania Plaza
New York, New York 10121
Phone **212/465-6000**
PR FAX 212/465-6494
www.newyorkrangers.com
Capacity: 18,200

Office of the Chairman, Madison Square Garden
President and Chief Executive Officer, Cablevision Systems Corporation; Chairman, Madison Square Garden . . . . James L. Dolan
Vice Chairman, Cablevision Systems Corporation; Vice Chairman, Madison Square Garden . . . . Robert S. Lemle
President, Madison Square Garden/ Radio City Entertainment. . . . . Seth Abraham
President and General Manager, New York Knicks . . Scott Layden
President, Sports Team Operations . . . . Steve Mills
President and General Manager, New York Rangers . Glen Sather

Team Executive Management
Governor . . . . James L. Dolan
President and General Manager/ Alternate Governor . . . . Glen Sather
President, Sports Team Operation/ Alternate Governor . . . . Steve Mills
Executive Vice President and General Counsel, Madison Square Garden/Alternate Governor . . . . Kenneth W. Munoz
Senior Vice President, Legal Affairs, Madison Square Garden . . . . Marc Schoenfeld
Vice President, Operations. . . . . Mark Piazza
Vice President, Marketing . . . . Jeanie Baumgartner
Vice President, Controller . . . . John Cudmore
Vice President, Community Development . . . . Patricia Kerr
Vice President, Public Relations . . . . John Rosasco

Madison Square Garden Executive Management
President, MSG Facilities . . . . Robert Russo
Executive Vice President, Finance. . . . . Robert Pollichino
Executive Vice President, Advertising Sales . . . . Joe Gangone
Senior Vice President, Marketing . . . . Betsy Bruce
Senior Vice President, Business & Consumer Sales . . Joel Fisher
Senior Vice President, Communications. . . . . Barry Watkins

Hockey Club Personnel
Vice President, Player Development/ Assistant General Manager . . . . Don Maloney
Head Coach . . . . Ron Low
Assistant Coaches . . . . Ted Green, Walt Kyle
Goaltending Analyst . . . . Sam St. Laurent
Director, Player Personnel . . . . Tom Renney
Director, Hockey Administration and Scouting. . . . . Peter Stephan
Amateur Scouting Staff. . . . . Rich Brown, Ray Clearwater, Andre Beaulieu, Jan Gajdosik, Ernie Gare, Martin Madden Jr., Christer Rockstom, Bob Crocker, Jamie McDonald
Professional Scouting Staff . . . . Dave Brown, Harry Howell, Gilles Leger
Medical Trainer . . . . Jim Ramsay
Equipment Manager . . . . Acacio Marques
Assistant Equipment Manager. . . . . James Johnson
Massage Therapist . . . . Bruce Lifrieri
Strength and Conditioning Coordinator . . . . Mark Puttenvinck
Video Analyst . . . . Jerry Dineen
Practice Facility Manager. Pat Boller
Scouting Manager. . . . . Bill Short

Operations
Director, Business Operations . . . . Barbara Dand
Director, Team Operations . . . . Darren Blake
Executive Assistant to the President and G.M. . . . . . Sara Adamson
Operations Assistant . . . . Victor Saljanin
Operations Assistant . . . . Chris Smith

Public Relations
Director, Public Relations. Jason Vogel
Public Relations Coordinator . . . . Keith Soutar
Public Relations Coordinator . . . . Jennifer Schoenfeld

Marketing
Director, Marketing Partnerships . . . . Rob Scolaro
Game Presentation Coordinator . . . . Ryan Halkett
Manager, Marketing Partnerships . . . . Kelly Jutras
Manager, Website. . . . . Jeff Schwartzenberg
Marketing Coordinator . . . . Janet Duch
Marketing Assistant . . . . Adam Evert
Marketing Partnerships Assistant. . . . . Alessandra Savarese

Community Development
Director, Business Development . . . . Rob Capilli
Director, Special Projects/ Community Relations Representative. . . . . Rod Gilbert
Manager, Community Development . . . . Anthony Triano
Community Development Assistant. . . . . Jan Greenberg

Medical/Training Staff
Team Physician and Orthopedic Surgeon. . . . . Dr. Andrew Feldman
Assistant Team Physician. Dr. Anthony Maddalo
Medical Consultants . . . . Dr. Ronald Weissman
Team Dentists . . . . Drs. Irwin Mille, Don Soloman

Broadcasting and Miscellaneous
Television Network . . . . MSG Network
Radio Network . . . . MSG Radio
Practice Facility . . . . Rye Playland Ice Casino, Rye, NY 212/465-5850

Ottawa Senators

2000-01 Results: 48W-21L-9T-4OTL 109PTS. First, Northeast Division

Year-by-Year Record

		Home				Road				Overall								
Season	GP	W	L	T	OL	W	L	T	OL	W	L	T	OL	GF	GA	Pts.	Finished	Playoff Result
2000-01	82	26	7	5	3	22	14	4	1	48	21	9	4	274	205	109	1st, Northeast Div.	Lost Conf. Quarter-Final
1999-2000	82	24	10	5	2	17	18	6	0	41	28	11	2	244	210	95	2nd, Northeast Div.	Lost Conf. Quarter-Final
1998-99	82	22	11	8	...	22	12	7	...	44	23	15	...	239	179	103	1st, Northeast Div.	Lost Conf. Quarter-Final
1997-98	82	18	16	7	...	16	17	8	...	34	33	15	...	193	200	83	5th, Northeast Div.	Lost Conf. Semi-Final
1996-97	82	16	17	8	...	15	19	7	...	31	36	15	...	226	234	77	3rd, Northeast Div.	Lost Conf. Quarter-Final
1995-96	82	8	28	5	...	10	31	0	...	18	59	5	...	191	291	41	6th, Northeast Div.	Out of Playoffs
1994-95	48	5	16	3	...	4	18	2	...	9	34	5	...	117	174	23	7th, Northeast Div.	Out of Playoffs
1993-94	84	8	30	4	...	6	31	5	...	14	61	9	...	201	397	37	7th, Northeast Div.	Out of Playoffs
1992-93	84	9	29	4	...	1	41	0	...	10	70	4	...	202	395	24	6th, Adams Div.	Out of Playoffs

2001-02 Schedule

Oct.	Wed.	3	at Toronto
	Thu.	4	Montreal
	Sat.	6	at Buffalo
	Tue.	9	at Carolina
	Wed.	10	at Florida
	Sat.	13	NY Rangers
	Tue.	16	at Pittsburgh
	Thu.	18	Pittsburgh
	Sat.	20	at New Jersey
	Tue.	23	New Jersey
	Thu.	25	at Philadelphia
	Sat.	27	St. Louis
	Tue.	30	at Atlanta
Nov.	Sat.	3	Buffalo
	Thu.	8	Colorado
	Sat.	10	Nashville
	Tue.	13	at Washington
	Thu.	15	Carolina
	Sat.	17	Toronto
	Tue.	20	Vancouver
	Thu.	22	Calgary
	Sat.	24	Atlanta*
	Tue.	27	at St. Louis
Dec.	Sat.	1	Boston
	Mon.	3	at Colorado
	Wed.	5	at Dallas
	Thu.	6	at Nashville
	Sat.	8	Tampa Bay
	Tue.	11	at NY Islanders
	Thu.	13	Phoenix
	Sat.	15	New Jersey
	Tue.	18	at Carolina
	Thu.	20	Los Angeles
	Sat.	22	at New Jersey*
	Sun.	23	at NY Rangers*
	Wed.	26	at Boston
	Thu.	27	NY Islanders
	Sat.	29	at Pittsburgh
	Mon.	31	Chicago
Jan.	Thu.	3	Washington
	Sat.	5	at Toronto*
	Mon.	7	Toronto
	Wed.	9	at Atlanta
	Fri.	11	at Florida
	Sat.	12	at Tampa Bay
	Tue.	15	Philadelphia
	Thu.	17	at Boston
	Sat.	19	Minnesota
	Sun.	20	at Detroit
	Tue.	22	at Philadelphia
	Thu.	24	Boston
	Sat.	26	at Montreal*
	Wed.	30	Philadelphia
Feb.	Mon.	4	at Tampa Bay
	Wed.	6	at Columbus
	Fri.	8	at Buffalo
	Sat.	9	Detroit
	Tue.	12	Pittsburgh
	Tue.	26	at Montreal
	Thu.	28	at NY Rangers
Mar.	Sat.	2	Washington
	Mon.	4	at Los Angeles
	Thu.	7	at San Jose
	Sat.	9	at Phoenix*
	Sun.	10	at Anaheim*
	Tue.	12	at Minnesota
	Thu.	14	Edmonton
	Sat.	16	NY Islanders
	Sun.	17	Florida*
	Tue.	19	at Buffalo
	Thu.	21	NY Rangers
	Sat.	23	Atlanta
	Sun.	24	Buffalo*
	Wed.	27	at NY Islanders
	Thu.	28	Florida
	Sat.	30	Tampa Bay
Apr.	Tue.	2	Carolina
	Fri.	5	at Washington
	Sun.	7	Montreal
	Tue.	9	at Montreal
	Thu.	11	Boston
	Sat.	13	Toronto

* Denotes afternoon game.

Radek Bonk turned pro as a 17-year-old when he left the Czech Republic to play in the IHL in 1993. Ottawa selected him third overall in the NHL Entry Draft the following year. Bonk has scored 23 goals in each of the last two seasons.

Franchise date: December 16, 1991

EASTERN NHL CONFERENCE

NORTHEAST DIVISION

10th NHL Season

2001-02 Player Personnel

FORWARDS	HT	WT	S	Place of Birth	Date	2000-01 Club
ALFREDSSON, Daniel	5-11	195	R	Gothenburg, Sweden	12/11/72	Ottawa
ARVEDSON, Magnus	6-2	198	L	Karlstad, Sweden	11/25/71	Ottawa
BALA, Chris	6-1	180	L	Alexandria, VA	9/24/78	Harvard University
BONK, Radek	6-3	210	L	Krnov, Czech.	1/9/76	Ottawa
CIERNIK, Ivan	6-1	234	L	Levice, Czech.	10/30/77	Ottawa-Grand Rapids
DAHLMAN, Toni	5-11	194	R	Helsinki, Finland	9/3/79	Ilves Tampere
FISHER, Mike	6-1	193	R	Peterborough, Ont.	6/5/80	Ottawa
GIROUX, Alexandre	6-2	189	L	Quebec, Que.	6/16/81	Hull-Rouyn-Noranda
HAVLAT, Martin	6-1	190	L	Mlada Boleslav, Czech.	4/19/81	Ottawa
HERPERGER, Chris	6-0	190	L	Esterhazy, Sask.	2/24/74	Chicago-Norfolk
HOSSA, Marian	6-1	199	L	Stara Lubovna, Czech.	1/12/79	Ottawa
HYMOVITZ, David	5-11	170	L	Randolph, MA	5/30/74	Lowell
KELLY, Chris	6-0	179	L	Toronto, Ont.	11/11/80	London-Sudbury
LANGFELD, Josh	6-3	205	R	Fridley, MN	7/17/77	U. of Michigan
McEACHERN, Shawn	5-11	193	L	Waltham, MA	2/28/69	Ottawa
MUCKALT, Bill	6-1	200	R	Surrey, B.C.	7/15/74	NY Islanders
MURPHY, Joe	6-0	200	R	Didsbury, Alta.	1/21/75	Rochester
NEIL, Christopher	6-0	213	R	Markdale, Ont.	6/18/79	Grand Rapids
ROY, Andre	6-4	213	L	Port Chester, NY	2/8/75	Ottawa
SCHASTLIVY, Petr	6-1	204	L	Angarsk, USSR	4/18/79	Ottawa-Grand Rapids
SPEZZA, Jason	6-2	214	R	Mississauga, Ont.	6/13/83	Mississauga-Windsor
ULMER, Jeff	5-11	195	R	Wilcox, Sask.	4/27/77	NY Rangers-Hartford
VERMETTE, Antoine	6-1	184	L	St-Agapit, Quebec	7/20/82	Victoriaville
WHITE, Todd	5-10	194	L	Kanata, Ont.	5/21/75	Ottawa-Grand Rapids
DEFENSEMEN						
BROOKBANK, Wade	6-4	225	L	Lanigan, Sask.	9/29/77	Orlando-Oklahoma City
CHARA, Zdeno	6-9	255	L	Trencin, Czech.	3/18/77	NY Islanders
DEMIDOV, Ilja	6-3	185	L	Moscow, USSR	4/14/79	Grand Rapids
DOIG, Jason	6-3	228	R	Montreal, Que.	1/29/77	Hartford-NY Rangers
GRUDEN, John	6-0	203	L	Virginia, MN	6/4/70	Grand Rapids
HNIDY, Shane	6-2	210	R	Neepawa, Man.	11/8/75	Ottawa-Grand Rapids
KWIATKOWSKI, Joel	6-2	210	L	Kindersley, Sask.	3/22/77	Ottawa-Grand Rapids
LESCHYSHYN, Curtis	6-1	220	L	Thompson, Man.	9/21/69	Minnesota-Ottawa
PERSSON, Ricard	6-1	201	L	Ostersund, Sweden	8/24/69	Ottawa
PHILLIPS, Chris	6-3	215	L	Calgary, Alta.	3/9/78	Ottawa
RACHUNEK, Karel	6-2	202	R	Gottwaldov, Czech.	8/27/79	Ottawa
REDDEN, Wade	6-2	205	L	Lloydminster, Sask.	6/12/77	Ottawa
RICHARDS, Travis	6-1	195	L	Crystal, MN	3/22/70	Grand Rapids
RIVERS, Jamie	6-1	200	L	Ottawa, Ont.	3/16/75	Grand Rapids-Ottawa
SALO, Sami	6-3	215	R	Turku, Finland	9/2/74	Ottawa
VAUCLAIR, Julien	6-0	198	L	Delemont, Switzerland	10/2/79	HC Lugano

GOALTENDERS	HT	WT	C	Place of Birth	Date	2000-01 Club
CHOUINARD, Mathieu	6-1	211	L	Laval, Que.	4/11/80	Grand Rapids
HURME, Jani	6-0	187	L	Turku, Finland	1/7/75	Ottawa
LAJEUNESSE, Simon	6-0	175	L	Quebec City, Que.	1/22/81	Acadie-Bathurst-Val-d'Or
LALIME, Patrick	6-3	185	L	St-Bonaventure, Que.	7/7/74	Ottawa
PRUSEK, Martin	6-1	163	L	Ostrava, Czech.	12/11/75	HC Vitkovice

General Manager

JOHNSTON, MARSHALL
General Manager, Ottawa Senators. Born in Birch Hills, Sask., June 6, 1941.

Marshall Johnston was named general manager of the Ottawa Senators on June 8, 1999, replacing Rick Dudley. Johnston joined the Senators in July 1996 as director of player personnel. He worked through his first season in 1996-97 with the Senators' pro and amateur scouts and guided the staff during the 1997 NHL Entry Draft that saw the club pick Marian Hossa of Slovakia as its first selection, 12th overall.

After a successful seven-year NHL career on the ice (1967 to 1974), Johnston coached the California Golden Seals during parts of the 1973-74 and 1974-75 seasons. He then became head coach of Denver University, his alma mater, for four seasons, leading the Pioneers to the WCHA title and being named the Conference Coach of the Year in 1976-77.

Johnston joined the Colorado Rockies as assistant general manager and assistant coach on May 4, 1981 and served as head coach for the final 56 games of the 1981-82 season. Following the season, Johnston was named head coach of Canada's entry at the World Championships. After the Colorado franchise moved to New Jersey, he remained with the club as an assistant coach until being promoted to director of player personnel. He spent 10 years in New Jersey (1983 to 1993) as director of player personnel for the Devils, the 1995 Stanley Cup champions. While heading New Jersey's scouting department, the Devils drafted, among others, Scott Niedermayer, Brian Rolston, Martin Brodeur, Bill Guerin, Zdeno Ciger, Brendan Shanahan, Craig Wolanin, Sean Burke, Kirk Muller and Kirk McLean.

Johnston spent two years as executive director of CIPRO, a hockey scouting group jointly owned and operated by the Dallas Stars, Hartford Whalers, Philadelphia Flyers and Winnipeg Jets, prior to joining the New York Islanders' scouting staff in 1995-96.

NHL Coaching Record

		Regular Season				Playoffs		
Season	Team	Games	W	L	T	Games	W	L
1973-74	California	21	2	17	2	....	....	....
1974-75	California	48	11	28	9	....	....	....
1981-82	Colorado	56	15	32	9	....	....	....
	NHL Totals	**125**	**28**	**77**	**20**	....	....	....

2000-01 Scoring

* - rookie

Regular Season

Pos	#	Player	Team	GP	G	A	Pts	+/–	PIM	PP	SH	GW	GT	S	%
C	19	Alexei Yashin	OTT	82	40	48	88	10	30	13	2	10	1	263	15.2
R	18	Marian Hossa	OTT	81	32	43	75	19	44	11	2	7	0	249	12.9
L	15	Shawn McEachern	OTT	82	32	40	72	10	62	9	0	1	1	231	13.9
R	11	Daniel Alfredsson	OTT	68	24	46	70	11	30	10	0	3	1	206	11.7
C	14	Radek Bonk	OTT	74	23	36	59	27	52	5	2	3	0	139	16.5
D	6	Wade Redden	OTT	78	10	37	47	22	49	4	0	0	0	159	6.3
L	9 *	Martin Havlat	OTT	73	19	23	42	8	20	7	0	5	0	133	14.3
C	16	Mike Sillinger	FLA	55	13	21	34	–12	44	1	0	2	0	100	13.0
			OTT	13	3	4	7	1	4	0	0	0	0	19	15.8
			TOTAL	68	16	25	41	–11	48	1	0	2	0	119	13.4
L	7	Rob Zamuner	OTT	79	19	18	37	7	52	1	2	4	1	123	15.4
L	20	Magnus Arvedson	OTT	51	17	16	33	23	24	1	2	4	0	79	21.5
D	23 *	Karel Rachunek	OTT	71	3	30	33	17	60	3	0	0	0	77	3.9
R	10	Andreas Dackell	OTT	81	13	18	31	7	24	1	0	3	0	72	18.1
D	33	Jason York	OTT	74	6	16	22	7	72	3	0	2	0	133	4.5
C	12	Mike Fisher	OTT	60	7	12	19	–1	46	0	0	3	0	83	8.4
D	5	Sami Salo	OTT	31	2	16	18	9	10	1	0	0	0	61	3.3
D	4	Chris Phillips	OTT	73	2	12	14	8	31	2	0	0	0	77	2.6
D	2	Curtis Leschyshyn	MIN	54	2	3	5	–2	19	1	0	1	0	43	4.7
			OTT	11	0	4	4	7	0	0	0	0	0	8	0.0
			TOTAL	65	2	7	9	5	19	1	0	1	0	51	3.9
D	27	Ricard Persson	OTT	33	1	8	9	8	35	0	0	1	0	43	2.3
R	26	Andre Roy	OTT	64	3	5	8	1	169	0	0	0	0	33	9.1
D	22	Jamie Rivers	OTT	45	2	4	6	6	44	0	0	0	0	41	4.9
L	17	Eric Lacroix	NYR	46	2	3	5	–6	39	0	0	0	0	22	9.1
			OTT	9	0	1	1	0	4	0	0	0	0	10	0.0
			TOTAL	55	2	4	6	–6	43	0	0	0	0	32	6.3
C	28	Todd White	OTT	16	4	1	5	5	4	0	0	0	0	12	33.3
L	16 *	Petr Schastlivy	OTT	17	3	2	5	–1	6	0	0	0	0	32	9.4
D	34 *	Shane Hnidy	OTT	52	3	2	5	8	84	0	0	1	0	47	6.4
R	48 *	Ivan Ciernik	OTT	4	2	0	2	2	2	0	0	0	0	7	28.6
D	36 *	Joel Kwiatkowski	OTT	4	1	0	1	1	0	0	0	0	0	2	50.0
G	40	Patrick Lalime	OTT	60	0	1	1	0	2	0	0	0	0	0	0.0
G	30	Mike Fountain	OTT	1	0	0	0	0	0	0	0	0	0	0	0.0
D	3	Sean Gagnon	OTT	5	0	0	0	0	13	0	0	0	0	0	0.0
R	21	David Oliver	OTT	7	0	0	0	0	2	0	0	0	0	2	0.0
G	35 *	Jani Hurme	OTT	22	0	0	0	0	0	0	0	0	0	0	0.0

Goaltending

No.	Goaltender	GPI	Mins	Avg	W	L	T	EN	SO	GA	SA	S%
40	Patrick Lalime	60	3607	2.35	36	19	5	3	7	141	1640	.914
35	* Jani Hurme	22	1296	2.50	12	5	4	4	2	54	563	.904
30	Mike Fountain	1	59	3.05	0	1	0	0	0	3	25	.880
	Totals	**82**	**4977**	**2.47**	**48**	**25**	**9**	**7**	**9**	**205**	**2235**	**.908**

Playoffs

Pos	#	Player	Team	GP	G	A	Pts	+/–	PIM	PP	SH	GW	GT	S	%
R	18	Marian Hossa	OTT	4	1	1	2	1	4	0	0	0	0	12	8.3
L	15	Shawn McEachern	OTT	4	0	2	2	1	2	0	0	0	0	8	0.0
D	4	Chris Phillips	OTT	1	1	0	1	0	0	0	0	0	0	1	100.0
R	11	Daniel Alfredsson	OTT	4	1	0	1	0	2	0	0	0	0	13	7.7
L	17	Eric Lacroix	OTT	4	0	1	1	0	0	0	0	0	0	2	0.0
C	19	Alexei Yashin	OTT	4	0	1	1	1	0	0	0	0	0	12	0.0
C	12	Mike Fisher	OTT	4	0	1	1	–1	4	0	0	0	0	6	0.0
D	22	Jamie Rivers	OTT	1	0	0	0	0	4	0	0	0	0	2	0.0
D	34 *	Shane Hnidy	OTT	1	0	0	0	–1	0	0	0	0	0	0	0.0
D	27	Ricard Persson	OTT	2	0	0	0	0	0	0	0	0	0	2	0.0
C	14	Radek Bonk	OTT	2	0	0	0	–1	2	0	0	0	0	1	0.0
R	26	Andre Roy	OTT	2	0	0	0	0	16	0	0	0	0	0	0.0
L	20	Magnus Arvedson	OTT	2	0	0	0	0	0	0	0	0	0	1	0.0
C	28	Todd White	OTT	2	0	0	0	0	0	0	0	0	0	2	0.0
D	23 *	Karel Rachunek	OTT	3	0	0	0	–4	0	0	0	0	0	7	0.0
D	2	Curtis Leschyshyn	OTT	4	0	0	0	–1	0	0	0	0	0	5	0.0
C	16	Mike Sillinger	OTT	4	0	0	0	–3	2	0	0	0	0	3	0.0
D	33	Jason York	OTT	4	0	0	0	1	4	0	0	0	0	2	0.0
L	7	Rob Zamuner	OTT	4	0	0	0	–5	6	0	0	0	0	9	0.0
G	40	Patrick Lalime	OTT	4	0	0	0	0	0	0	0	0	0	0	0.0
D	6	Wade Redden	OTT	4	0	0	0	–3	0	0	0	0	0	11	0.0
R	10	Andreas Dackell	OTT	4	0	0	0	0	0	0	0	0	0	3	0.0
D	5	Sami Salo	OTT	4	0	0	0	0	0	0	0	0	0	14	0.0
L	9 *	Martin Havlat	OTT	4	0	0	0	–4	2	0	0	0	0	7	0.0

Goaltending

No.	Goaltender	GPI	Mins	Avg	W	L	EN	SO	GA	SA	S%
40	Patrick Lalime	4	251	2.39	0	4	0	0	10	99	.899
	Totals	**4**	**253**	**2.37**	**0**	**4**	**0**	**0**	**10**	**99**	**.899**

General Managers' History

Mel Bridgman, 1992-93; Randy Sexton, 1993-94, 1994-95; Randy Sexton and Pierre Gauthier, 1995-96; Pierre Gauthier, 1996-97, 1997-98; Rick Dudley, 1998-99; Marshall Johnston, 1999-2000 to date.

Club Records

Team

(Figures in brackets for season records are games played; records for fewest points, wins, ties, losses, goals, goals against are for 70 or more games)

Most Points .... 109 — 2000-01 (82)
Most Wins .... 48 — 2000-01 (82)
Most Ties .... 15 — 1996-97 (82), 1997-98 (82), 1998-99 (82)
Most Losses .... 70 — 1992-93 (84)
Most Goals .... 274 — 2000-01 (82)
Most Goals Against .... 397 — 1993-94 (84)
Fewest Points .... 24 — 1992-93 (84)
Fewest Wins .... 10 — 1992-93 (84)
Fewest Ties .... 4 — 1992-93 (84)
Fewest Losses .... 21 — 2000-01 (82)
Fewest Goals .... 191 — 1995-96 (82)
Fewest Goals Against .... 179 — 1998-99 (82)
Longest Winning Streak
Overall .... 5 — Jan. 6-14/99, Mar. 2-10/99
Home .... 7 — Feb. 13-Mar. 8/99
Away .... 5 — Apr. 3-19/98
Longest Undefeated Streak
Overall .... 11 — Dec. 28/98-Jan. 16/99 (8 wins, 3 ties)
Home .... 8 — Feb. 5-Mar. 20/98 (5 wins, 3 ties)
Away .... 7 — Twice

** NHL records do not include neutral site games

Longest Losing Streak
Overall .... 14 — Mar. 2-Apr. 7/93
Home .... *11 — Oct. 27-Dec. 8/93
Away .... *38 — Oct. 10/92-Apr. 3/93**
Longest Winless Streak
Overall .... 21 — Oct. 10-Nov. 23/92 (20 losses, 1 tie)
Home .... *17 — Oct. 28/95-Jan. 27/96 (15 losses, 2 ties)
Away .... *38 — Oct. 10/92-Apr. 3/93 (38 losses)
Most Shutouts, Season .... 9 — 2000-01 (82)
Most PIM, Season .... 1,716 — 1992-93 (84)
Most Goals, Game .... 9 — Jan. 31/99 (NYI 2 at Ott. 9), Mar. 8/99 (T.B. 3 at Ott. 9)

Individual

Most Seasons .... 7 — Alexei Yashin, Radek Bonk
Most Games, Career .... 504 — Alexei Yashin
Most Goals, Career .... 218 — Alexei Yashin
Most Assists, Career .... 273 — Alexei Yashin
Most Points, Career .... 491 — Alexei Yashin (218G, 273A)
Most PIM, Career .... 625 — Dennis Vial
Most Shutouts, Career .... 13 — Ron Tugnutt
Longest Consecutive Games Streak .... 210 — Alexei Yashin (Feb. 23/95-Apr. 17/99)
Most Goals, Season .... 44 — Alexei Yashin (1998-99)
Most Assists, Season .... 50 — Alexei Yashin (1998-99)
Most Points, Season .... 94 — Alexei Yashin (1998-99; 44G, 50A)
Most PIM, Season .... 318 — Mike Peluso (1992-93)
Most Points, Defenseman, Season .... 63 — Norm Maciver (1992-93; 17G, 46A)
Most Points, Center, Season .... 94 — Alexei Yashin (1998-99; 44G, 50A)
Most Points, Right Wing, Season .... 75 — Marian Hossa (2000-01; 32G, 43A)
Most Points, Left Wing, Season .... 72 — Shawn McEachern (2000-01; 32G, 40A)
Most Points, Rookie, Season .... 79 — Alexei Yashin (1993-94; 30G, 49A)
Most Shutouts, Season .... 7 — Patrick Lalime (2000-01)
Most Goals, Game .... 3 — Thirteen times
Most Assists, Game .... 4 — Alexei Yashin (Nov. 5/93), Vaclav Prospal (Mar. 21/00)
Most Points, Game .... 6 — Dan Quinn (Oct. 15/95; 3G, 3A)

* NHL Record.

Coaching History

Rick Bowness, 1992-93 to 1994-95; Rick Bowness, Dave Allison and Jacques Martin, 1995-96; Jacques Martin, 1996-97 to date.

Captains' History

Laurie Boschman, 1992-93; Brad Shaw, Mark Lamb and Gord Dineen, 1993-94; Randy Cunneyworth, 1994-95 to 1997-98; Alexei Yashin, 1998-99; Daniel Alfredsson, 1999-2000 to date.

Retired Numbers

8 Frank Finnigan 1924-1934

All-time Record vs. Other Clubs

Regular Season

	At Home								On Road								Total							
	GP	W	L	T	OL	GF	GA	PTS	GP	W	L	T	OL	GF	GA	PTS	GP	W	L	T	OL	GF	GA	PTS
Anaheim	7	3	3	1	0	21	18	7	6	1	3	2	0	9	16	4	13	4	6	3	0	30	34	11
Atlanta	4	3	0	1	0	24	10	7	4	3	1	0	0	17	14	6	8	6	1	1	0	41	24	13
Boston	23	6	14	3	0	52	79	15	25	7	15	3	0	73	98	17	48	13	29	6	0	125	177	32
Buffalo	25	6	12	6	1	53	73	19	23	5	16	2	0	29	75	12	48	11	28	8	1	82	148	31
Calgary	8	4	1	2	1	21	19	11	9	3	5	1	0	22	34	7	17	7	6	3	1	43	53	18
Carolina	23	8	11	3	1	59	67	20	21	3	16	2	0	39	66	8	44	11	27	5	1	98	133	28
Chicago	8	3	5	0	0	21	24	6	7	2	3	2	0	18	17	6	15	5	8	2	0	39	41	12
Colorado	15	6	7	2	0	48	62	14	13	1	11	1	0	34	64	3	28	7	18	3	0	82	126	17
Columbus	1	0	0	1	0	2	2	1	1	0	0	1	0	3	3	1	2	0	0	2	0	5	5	2
Dallas	8	3	5	0	0	19	22	6	8	3	5	0	0	16	31	6	16	6	10	0	0	35	53	12
Detroit	7	2	4	1	0	19	21	5	7	3	4	0	0	15	24	6	14	5	8	1	0	34	45	11
Edmonton	7	2	4	1	0	13	19	5	9	1	6	2	0	22	36	4	16	3	10	3	0	35	55	9
Florida	16	7	7	2	0	45	45	16	16	6	9	1	0	47	56	13	32	13	16	3	0	92	101	29
Los Angeles	7	4	1	1	1	26	21	10	7	1	6	0	0	17	38	2	14	5	7	1	1	43	59	12
Minnesota	0	0	0	0	0	0	0	0	1	0	0	1	0	2	2	1	1	0	0	1	0	2	2	1
Montreal	23	11	11	1	0	65	64	23	25	8	14	3	0	68	78	19	48	19	25	4	0	133	142	42
Nashville	2	1	1	0	0	4	3	2	2	2	0	0	0	7	1	4	4	3	1	0	0	11	4	6
New Jersey	18	5	9	3	1	40	48	14	17	4	10	2	1	38	58	11	35	9	19	5	2	78	106	25
NY Islanders	17	9	4	4	0	58	46	22	18	11	3	4	0	71	59	26	35	20	7	8	0	129	105	48
NY Rangers	17	5	10	2	0	47	52	12	17	8	9	0	0	49	59	16	34	13	19	2	0	96	111	28
Philadelphia	18	6	9	3	0	52	61	15	17	5	11	1	0	45	61	11	35	11	20	4	0	97	122	26
Phoenix	9	2	6	1	0	21	33	5	8	4	3	1	0	32	30	9	17	6	9	2	0	53	63	14
Pittsburgh	21	5	12	4	0	51	69	14	21	2	15	4	0	42	84	8	42	7	27	8	0	93	153	22
St. Louis	8	2	6	0	0	16	34	4	7	3	3	1	0	21	21	7	15	5	9	1	0	37	55	11
San Jose	8	3	1	4	0	27	23	10	7	3	4	0	0	10	12	6	15	6	5	4	0	37	35	16
Tampa Bay	17	10	7	0	0	64	41	20	17	9	7	1	0	57	51	19	34	19	14	1	0	121	92	39
Toronto	12	8	3	1	0	37	30	17	14	6	7	1	0	38	40	13	26	14	10	2	0	75	70	30
Vancouver	8	4	3	1	0	19	21	9	9	4	4	1	0	20	26	9	17	8	7	2	0	39	47	18
Washington	17	8	8	1	0	61	58	17	18	5	11	2	0	41	66	12	35	13	19	3	0	102	124	29
Totals	**354**	**136**	**164**	**49**	**5**	**985**	**1065**	**326**	**354**	**113**	**201**	**39**	**1**	**902**	**1220**	**266**	**708**	**249**	**365**	**88**	**6**	**1887**	**2285**	**592**

Playoffs

	Series	W	L	GP	W	L	T	GF	GA	Last Mtg.	Round	Result
Buffalo	2	0	2	11	3	8	0	19	26	1999	CQF	L 0-4
New Jersey	1	1	0	6	4	2	0	13	12	1998	CQF	W 4-2
Toronto	2	0	2	10	2	8	0	13	27	2001	CQF	L 0-4
Washington	1	0	1	5	1	4	0	7	18	1998	CSF	L 1-4
Totals	**6**	**1**	**5**	**32**	**10**	**22**	**0**	**52**	**83**			

Playoff Results 2001-1997

Year	Round	Opponent	Result	GF	GA
2001	CQF	Toronto	L 0-4	3	10
2000	CQF	Toronto	L 2-4	10	17
1999	CQF	Buffalo	L 0-4	6	12
1998	CSF	Washington	L 1-4	7	18
	CQF	New Jersey	W 4-2	13	12
1997	CQF	Buffalo	L 3-4	13	14

Abbreviations: Round: CSF – conference semi-final; **CQF** – conference quarter-final.

Colorado totals include Quebec, 1992-93 to 1994-95.
Dallas totals include Minnesota North Stars, 1992-93.
Carolina totals include Hartford, 1992-93 to 1996-97.
Phoenix totals include Winnipeg, 1992-93 to 1995-96.

2000-01 Results

Oct.	5	at Boston	4-4		13	at Calgary	5-2
	7	Dallas	3-1		14	at Edmonton	1-4
	13	New Jersey	3-1		16	Los Angeles	6-7*
	14	at Toronto	4-0		18	Washington	5-4
	17	at Philadelphia	6-1		20	Tampa Bay	3-0
	19	Pittsburgh	3-3		23	at NY Islanders	3-2
	21	Atlanta	6-6		25	at Tampa Bay	5-2
	25	at Pittsburgh	3-2		26	at Florida	5-4*
	27	at Tampa Bay	6-0		28	at Montreal	1-4
	28	at Florida	1-3		30	at Washington	1-1
	31	Toronto	4-3	**Feb.**	6	at Detroit	2-4
Nov.	2	NY Rangers	6-5		8	New Jersey	4-4
	4	Columbus	2-2		10	Buffalo	1-2*
	6	at Atlanta	3-2		12	NY Islanders	3-1
	9	at Boston	1-2		14	at New Jersey	3-2
	11	at Philadelphia	3-4		15	Colorado	4-1
	12	at Carolina	0-4		18	Montreal	4-0
	16	Carolina	0-1		19	at Buffalo	0-2
	18	Florida	5-2		22	Florida	4-2
	21	Boston	2-1		24	Vancouver	3-0
	23	Edmonton	3-5		26	at NY Rangers	3-2
	25	at Toronto	4-2		27	Buffalo	1-4
	26	at NY Rangers	2-3	**Mar.**	1	San Jose	8-4
	28	Buffalo	3-1		3	at Toronto	3-2*
Dec.	2	Philadelphia	5-3		6	at New Jersey	2-3*
	3	at Carolina	2-0		8	at Boston	5-3
	5	Pittsburgh	2-4		10	NY Rangers	2-3
	8	Montreal	1-0		11	at Washington	5-6
	9	at Montreal	4-2		14	Atlanta	8-1
	14	Calgary	4-2		16	Anaheim	4-1
	16	NY Islanders	6-0		18	at Dallas	1-5
	20	at Minnesota	2-2		21	at Phoenix	5-2
	21	at Columbus	3-3		22	at San Jose	2-1
	23	Chicago	2-3		24	at Nashville	4-0
	27	Washington	1-5		26	Philadelphia	3-3
	29	at Buffalo	0-2		28	at Chicago	5-2
	30	at Pittsburgh	3-5		30	Boston	5-4*
Jan.	2	St. Louis	3-1	**Apr.**	1	Carolina	2-3*
	4	Tampa Bay	8-3		3	at Atlanta	2-5
	6	Montreal	4-3		6	at NY Islanders	4-3
	10	at Vancouver	5-1		7	Toronto	5-3

* – Overtime

Entry Draft Selections 2001-1992

2001

Pick	
2	Jason Spezza
23	Tim Gleason
81	Neil Komadoski
99	Ray Emery
127	Christoph Schubert
162	Stefan Schauer
193	Brooks Laich
218	Jan Platil
223	Brandon Bochenski
235	Neil Petruic
256	Gregg Johnson
286	Toni Dahlman

2000

Pick	
21	Anton Volchenkov
45	Mathieu Chouinard
55	Antoine Vermette
87	Jan Bohac
122	Derrick Byfuglien
156	Greg Zanon
157	Grant Potulny
158	Sean Connolly
188	Jason Maleyko
283	James Demone

1999

Pick	
26	Martin Havlat
48	Simon Lajeunesse
62	Teemu Sainomaa
94	Chris Kelly
154	Andrew Ianiero
164	Martin Prusek
201	Mikko Ruutu
209	Layne Ulmer
213	Alexandre Giroux
269	Konstantin Gorovikov

1998

Pick	
15	Mathieu Chouinard
44	Mike Fisher
58	Chris Bala
74	Julien Vauclair
101	Petr Schastlivy
130	Gavin McLeod
161	Christopher Neil
188	Michel Periard
223	Sergei Verenikin
246	Rastislav Pavlikovsky

1997

Pick	
12	Marian Hossa
58	Jani Hurme
66	Josh Langfeld
119	Magnus Arvedson
146	Jeff Sullivan
173	Robin Bacul
203	Nick Gillis
229	Karel Rachunek

1996

Pick	
1	Chris Phillips
81	Antti-Jussi Niemi
136	Andreas Dackell
163	Francois Hardy
212	Erich Goldmann
216	Ivan Ciernik
239	Sami Salo

1995

Pick	
1	Bryan Berard
27	Marc Moro
53	Brad Larsen
89	Kevin Bolibruck
103	Kevin Boyd
131	David Hruska
183	Kaj Linna
184	Ray Schultz
231	Erik Kaminski

1994

Pick	
3	Radek Bonk
29	Stan Neckar
81	Bryan Masotta
131	Mike Gaffney
133	Daniel Alfredsson
159	Doug Sproule
210	Frederic Cassivi
211	Danny Dupont
237	Stephen MacKinnon
274	Antti Tormanen

1993

Pick	
1	Alexandre Daigle
27	Radim Bicanek
53	Patrick Charbonneau
91	Cosmo Dupaul
131	Rick Bodkin
157	Sergei Poleschuk
183	Jason Disher
209	Toby Kvalevog
227	Pavol Demitra
235	Rick Schuwerk

1992

Pick	
2	Alexei Yashin
25	Chad Penney
50	Patrick Traverse
73	Radek Hamr
98	Daniel Guerard
121	Al Sinclair
146	Jaroslav Miklenda
169	Jay Kenney
194	Claude Jr. Savoie
217	Jake Grimes
242	Tomas Jelinek
264	Petter Ronnqvist

Club Directory

Corel Centre

Ottawa Senators
Corel Centre
1000 Palladium Drive
Ottawa, Ontario
K2V 1A5
Phone **613/599-0250**
FAX 613/599-5562
www.ottawasenators.com
Capacity: 18,500

Chairman and Governor	Rod Bryden
President and CEO	Roy Mlakar
General Manager	Marshall Johnston
Assistant to the General Manager	Allison Vaughan
Director of Hockey Operations	Trevor Timmins
Director of Player Personnel	Jarmo Kekalainen
Director of Legal Relations	Peter Chiarelli
Chief Amateur Scout	Frank Jay
Head Coach	Jacques Martin
Assistant Coaches	Perry Pearn, Roger Neilson, Don Jackson
Strength & Conditioning & Video Coach	Randy Lee
Pro Scout/Goaltending Coach	Phil Myre
VP, Communications	Phil Legault
Manager, Communications	Ian Mendes
Coordinator, Communications	Tim Pattyson
Communications/Hockey Operations Assistant	Jennifer Vuong
Head Athletic Trainer	Kevin Wagner
Head Equipment Manager	John Gervais
Assistant Equipment Manager	Chris Cook
Massage Therapist	Brad Joyal
Professional scout	Bob Janecyk
Mental skills coach	John Phelan
Scouts	Dale Engel, George Fargher, Ken Williamson, Lewis Mongelluzzo, Patrick Savard, Boris Shagas, Ales Volek, Ilkka Ikonen
Radio	Sports Radio 1200 The Team (English), Radio 1150 (French)
Television	Sportsnet, New RO

Coach

MARTIN, JACQUES
Coach, Ottawa Senators. Born in St. Pascal, Ont., October 1, 1952.

Jacques Martin led the Ottawa Senators to their best regular season in team history in 2000-01, breaking team records for wins (48) and points (109) the club had established two years before.

When appointed the Senators' third head coach on January 24, 1996, Martin brought 10 years of NHL coaching experience, including five with the Quebec Nordiques, an organization often compared with the Senators, in that both teams were built around young, talented players requiring patience and teaching.

Martin's coaching career began at the collegiate level in 1976. He was appointed head coach of the Guelph Platers (now Storm) in 1985, winning the OHL title, the Memorial Cup and being named the OHL coach of the year. That summer, Martin became head coach of the St. Louis Blues. In his NHL rookie year, he lead the Blues to the Norris Division championship and, in two seasons with the Blues, posted a 66-71-23 record. He then spent two seasons as an assistant to Chicago's head coach Mike Keenan, before joining the Nordiques in 1990. With Quebec, he worked four years as assistant coach and one year (1993-94) as both head coach and general manager of the AHL Cornwall Aces.

Coaching Record

		Regular Season				Playoffs		
Season	**Team**	**Games**	**W**	**L**	**T**	**Games**	**W**	**L**
1983-84	Peterborough (OHL)	70	43	23	4	....	....	....
1984-85	Peterborough (OHL)	66	42	20	4	....	....	....
1985-86	Guelph (OHL)	66	41	23	2	....	....	....
1986-87	**St. Louis (NHL)**	**80**	**32**	**33**	**15**	**6**	**2**	**4**
1987-88	**St. Louis (NHL)**	**80**	**34**	**38**	**8**	**10**	**5**	**5**
1993-94	Cornwall (AHL)	80	33	36	11	13	8	5
1995-96	**Ottawa (NHL)**	**38**	**10**	**24**	**4**	....	....	....
1996-97	**Ottawa (NHL)**	**82**	**31**	**36**	**15**	**7**	**3**	**4**
1997-98	**Ottawa (NHL)**	**82**	**34**	**33**	**15**	**11**	**5**	**6**
1998-99	**Ottawa (NHL)**	**82**	**44**	**23**	**15**	**4**	**0**	**4**
1999-2000	**Ottawa (NHL)**	**82**	**41**	**30**	**11**	**6**	**2**	**4**
2000-01	**Ottawa (NHL)**	**82**	**48**	**25**	**9**	**4**	**0**	**4**
	NHL Totals	**608**	**274**	**242**	**92**	**48**	**17**	**31**

With a record of 36-19-5, Patrick Lalime shattered the previous club record of 22 wins by a netminder. The Senators won a club-record 48 games last season.

Philadelphia Flyers

2000-01 Results: 43W-25L-11T-3OTL 100PTS. Second, Atlantic Division

2001-02 Schedule

Month	Day	Date	Opponent	Month	Day	Date	Opponent
Oct.	Thu.	4	Florida		Thu.	10	New Jersey
	Sat.	6	Columbus		Sat.	12	NY Rangers*
	Mon.	8	at Columbus		Mon.	14	at Montreal
	Wed.	10	at Buffalo		Tue.	15	at Ottawa
	Sat.	13	at Florida		Thu.	17	Atlanta
	Tue.	16	at Atlanta		Sat.	19	at Toronto
	Thu.	18	at Detroit		Mon.	21	at Pittsburgh
	Sat.	20	Washington		Tue.	22	Ottawa
	Thu.	25	Ottawa		Thu.	24	Nashville
	Sat.	27	at Montreal		Sat.	26	Carolina
	Tue.	30	at Washington		Tue.	29	Pittsburgh
	Wed.	31	Pittsburgh		Wed.	30	at Ottawa
Nov.	Sat.	3	NY Islanders	**Feb.**	Mon.	4	at Los Angeles
	Tue.	6	at Chicago		Wed.	6	at Anaheim
	Thu.	8	at Tampa Bay		Sat.	9	at St. Louis
	Sat.	10	at Florida		Tue.	12	NY Islanders
	Wed.	14	at NY Rangers		Tue.	26	Chicago
	Thu.	15	Washington		Wed.	27	at New Jersey
	Sat.	17	at New Jersey*	**Mar.**	Sat.	2	at NY Rangers*
	Tue.	20	New Jersey		Mon.	4	at Boston
	Fri.	23	at Dallas		Thu.	7	Calgary
	Sun.	25	Vancouver		Fri.	8	at Tampa Bay
	Thu.	29	Boston		Sun.	10	Toronto
Dec.	Sat.	1	Tampa Bay		Tue.	12	at Toronto
	Tue.	4	at NY Islanders		Thu.	14	Buffalo
	Thu.	6	NY Islanders		Sat.	16	Colorado*
	Sat.	8	Minnesota*		Mon.	18	Tampa Bay
	Mon.	10	at Atlanta		Thu.	21	Anaheim
	Thu.	13	Montreal		Sat.	23	at Pittsburgh*
	Sat.	15	at Boston		Mon.	25	Toronto
	Sun.	16	Edmonton		Wed.	27	at NY Rangers
	Tue.	18	St. Louis		Thu.	28	at Carolina
	Thu.	20	Dallas		Sat.	30	Buffalo*
	Sat.	22	Carolina	**Apr.**	Mon.	1	at Buffalo
	Wed.	26	at Washington		Tue.	2	Boston
	Fri.	28	at Phoenix		Thu.	4	Montreal
	Sat.	29	at Colorado		Sat.	6	Pittsburgh
	Mon.	31	at Vancouver		Mon.	8	Florida
Jan.	Wed.	2	at San Jose		Wed.	10	at New Jersey
	Sun.	6	at Carolina*		Sat.	13	NY Rangers*
	Tue.	8	Atlanta		Sun.	14	at NY Islanders*

* Denotes afternoon game.

Franchise date: June 5, 1967

ATLANTIC DIVISION

35th NHL Season

Year-by-Year Record

		Home				Road				Overall								
Season	**GP**	**W**	**L**	**T**	**OL**	**W**	**L**	**T**	**OL**	**W**	**L**	**T**	**OL**	**GF**	**GA**	**Pts.**	**Finished**	**Playoff Result**
2000-01	82	26	11	4	0	17	14	7	3	43	25	11	3	240	207	100	2nd, Atlantic Div.	Lost Conf. Quarter-Final
1999-2000	82	25	6	7	3	20	16	5	0	45	22	12	3	237	179	105	1st, Atlantic Div.	Lost Conf. Championship
1998-99	82	21	9	11	...	16	17	8	...	37	26	19	...	231	196	93	2nd, Atlantic Div.	Lost Conf. Quarter-Final
1997-98	82	24	11	6	...	18	18	5	...	42	29	11	...	242	193	95	2nd, Atlantic Div.	Lost Conf. Quarter-Final
1996-97	82	23	12	6	...	22	12	7	...	45	24	13	...	274	217	103	2nd, Atlantic Div.	Lost Final
1995-96	82	27	9	5	...	18	15	8	...	45	24	13	...	282	208	103	1st, Atlantic Div.	Lost Conf. Semi-Final
1994-95	48	16	7	1	...	12	9	3	...	28	16	4	...	150	132	60	1st, Atlantic Div.	Lost Conf. Championship
1993-94	84	19	20	3	...	16	19	7	...	35	39	10	...	294	314	80	6th, Atlantic Div.	Out of Playoffs
1992-93	84	23	14	5	...	13	23	6	...	36	37	11	...	319	319	83	5th, Patrick Div.	Out of Playoffs
1991-92	80	22	11	7	...	10	26	4	...	32	37	11	...	252	273	75	6th, Patrick Div.	Out of Playoffs
1990-91	80	18	16	6	...	15	21	4	...	33	37	10	...	252	267	76	5th, Patrick Div.	Out of Playoffs
1989-90	80	17	19	4	...	13	20	7	...	30	39	11	...	290	297	71	6th, Patrick Div.	Out of Playoffs
1988-89	80	22	15	3	...	14	21	5	...	36	36	8	...	307	285	80	4th, Patrick Div.	Lost Conf. Championship
1987-88	80	20	14	6	...	18	19	3	...	38	33	9	...	292	292	85	3rd, Patrick Div.	Lost Div. Semi-Final
1986-87	80	29	9	2	...	17	17	6	...	46	26	8	...	310	245	100	1st, Patrick Div.	Lost Final
1985-86	80	33	6	1	...	20	17	3	...	53	23	4	...	335	241	110	1st, Patrick Div.	Lost Div. Semi-Final
1984-85	80	32	4	4	...	21	16	3	...	53	20	7	...	348	241	113	1st, Patrick Div.	Lost Final
1983-84	80	25	10	5	...	19	16	5	...	44	26	10	...	350	290	98	3rd, Patrick Div.	Lost Div. Semi-Final
1982-83	80	29	8	3	...	20	15	5	...	49	23	8	...	326	240	106	1st, Patrick Div.	Lost Div. Semi-Final
1981-82	80	25	10	5	...	13	21	6	...	38	31	11	...	325	313	87	3rd. Patrick Div.	Lost Div. Semi-Final
1980-81	80	23	9	8	...	18	15	7	...	41	24	15	...	313	249	97	2nd, Patrick Div.	Lost Quarter-Final
1979-80	80	27	5	8	...	21	7	12	...	48	12	20	...	327	254	116	1st, Patrick Div.	Lost Final
1978-79	80	26	10	4	...	14	15	11	...	40	25	15	...	281	248	95	2nd, Patrick Div.	Lost Quarter-Final
1977-78	80	29	6	5	...	16	14	10	...	45	20	15	...	296	200	105	2nd, Patrick Div.	Lost Semi-Final
1976-77	80	33	6	1	...	15	10	15	...	48	16	16	...	323	213	112	1st, Patrick Div.	Lost Semi-Final
1975-76	80	36	2	2	...	15	11	14	...	51	13	16	...	348	209	118	1st, Patrick Div.	Lost Final
1974-75	**80**	**32**	**6**	**2**	**...**	**19**	**12**	**9**	**...**	**51**	**18**	**11**	**...**	**293**	**181**	**113**	**1st, Patrick Div.**	**Won Stanley Cup**
1973-74	**78**	**28**	**6**	**5**	**...**	**22**	**10**	**7**	**...**	**50**	**16**	**12**	**...**	**273**	**164**	**112**	**1st, West Div.**	**Won Stanley Cup**
1972-73	78	27	8	4	...	10	22	7	...	37	30	11	...	296	256	85	2nd, West Div.	Lost Semi-Final
1971-72	78	19	13	7	...	7	25	7	...	26	38	14	...	200	236	66	5th, West Div.	Out of Playoffs
1970-71	78	20	10	9	...	8	23	8	...	28	33	17	...	207	225	73	3rd, West Div.	Lost Quarter-Final
1969-70	76	11	14	13	...	6	21	11	...	17	35	24	...	197	225	58	5th, West Div.	Out of Playoffs
1968-69	76	14	16	8	...	6	19	13	...	20	35	21	...	174	225	61	3rd, West Div.	Lost Quarter-Final
1967-68	74	17	13	7	...	14	19	4	...	31	32	11	...	173	179	73	1st, West Div.	Lost Quarter-Final

A member of the NHL's All-Rookie Team in 2000, speedster Simon Gagne topped his first-year totals with 27 goals and 32 assists in just 69 games last season.

2001-02 Player Personnel

FORWARDS	HT	WT	S	Place of Birth	Date	2000-01 Club
BOULERICE, Jesse	6-1	215	R	Plattsburgh, NY	8/10/78	Philadelphia (AHL)
BRENDL, Pavel	6-1	204	R	Opocno, Czech.	3/23/81	Calgary (WHL)
DIVISEK, Tomas	6-2	204	L	Most, Czech.	7/19/79	Phi-Phi (AHL)
DOPITA, Jiri	6-3	215	L	Sumperk, Czech.	12/2/68	Slovnaft Vsetin
FEDORUK, Todd	6-2	235	L	Redwater, Alta.	2/13/79	Phi (AHL)-Phi
FEDOTENKO, Ruslan	6-2	195	L	Kiev, Ukraine	1/18/79	Phi-Phi (AHL)
GAGNE, Simon	6-0	190	L	Ste. Foy, Que.	2/29/80	Philadelphia
GREIG, Mark	5-11	190	R	High River, Alta.	1/25/70	Phi-Phi (AHL)
HLAVAC, Jan	6-0	185	L	Prague, Czech.	9/20/76	NY Rangers
HUBACEK, Petr	6-2	183	R	Brno, Czech.	9/2/79	Phi-Phi (AHL)
LAW, Kirby	6-1	185	R	McCreary, Man.	3/11/77	Phi-Phi (AHL)
LeCLAIR, John	6-3	226	L	St. Albans, VT	7/5/69	Philadelphia
LEFEBVRE, Guillaume	6-1	200	L	Amos, Que.	5/7/81	Rouyn-Noranda
MANDERVILLE, Kent	6-3	200	L	Edmonton, Alta.	4/12/71	Philadelphia
MURRAY, Marty	5-9	180	L	Deloraine, Man.	2/16/75	Calgary-Saint John
PLETKA, Vaclav	5-11	182	L	Mlada Boleslav, Czech.	6/8/79	Philadelphia (AHL)
PRIMEAU, Keith	6-5	220	L	Toronto, Ont.	11/24/71	Philadelphia
RANHEIM, Paul	6-1	210	R	St. Louis, MO	1/25/66	Philadelphia
RECCHI, Mark	5-10	185	L	Kamloops, B.C.	2/1/68	Philadelphia
ROENICK, Jeremy	6-1	207	R	Boston, MA	1/17/70	Phoenix
TOCCHET, Rick	6-0	210	R	Scarborough, Ont.	4/9/64	Philadelphia
WATT, Mike	6-2	212	L	Seaforth, Ont.	3/31/76	Milwaukee-Nashville
WILLIAMS, Justin	6-1	190	R	Cobourg, Ont.	10/4/81	Philadelphia
ZULTEK, Matt	6-4	222	L	Windsor, Ont.	3/12/79	St. Thomas U.-Phi (AHL)
DEFENSEMEN						
BECKETT, Jason	6-3	205	R	Lethbridge, Alta.	7/23/80	Trenton-Phi (AHL)
DESJARDINS, Eric	6-1	205	R	Rouyn, Que.	6/14/69	Philadelphia
DiPENTA, Joe	6-3	225	L	Barrie, Ont.	2/25/79	Philadelphia (AHL)
FORBES, Ian	6-6	215	L	Brampton, Ont.	8/2/80	Trenton
JOHNSSON, Kim	6-1	178	L	Malmo, Sweden	3/16/76	NY Rangers
LESSARD, Francis	6-2	220	R	Montreal, Que.	5/30/79	Philadelphia (AHL)
McALLISTER, Chris	6-8	240	L	Saskatoon, Sask.	6/16/75	Philadelphia
McGILLIS, Dan	6-2	230	L	Hawkesbury, Ont.	7/1/72	Philadelphia
PETERS, Dan	5-10	183	L	Cottage Grove, MN	11/24/77	Philadelphia (AHL)
RICHARDSON, Luke	6-4	210	L	Ottawa, Ont.	3/26/69	Philadelphia
ST. JACQUES, Bruno	6-2	210	L	Montreal, Que.	8/22/80	Philadelphia (AHL)
SLANEY, John	6-0	189	L	St. John's, Nfld.	2/2/72	Wilkes-Barre-Phi (AHL)
THERIEN, Chris	6-5	235	L	Ottawa, Ont.	12/14/71	Philadelphia
TILEY, Brad	6-1	185	L	Markdale, Ont.	7/5/71	Phi-Phi (AHL)
VANDERMEER, Jim	6-1	208	L	Caroline, Alta.	2/21/80	Red Deer
WEINRICH, Eric	6-1	213	L	Roanoke, VA	12/19/66	Montreal-Boston

GOALTENDERS	HT	WT	C	Place of Birth	Date	2000-01 Club
BOUCHER, Brian	6-2	190	L	Woonsocket, RI	1/2/77	Philadelphia
CECHMANEK, Roman	6-3	187	L	Gottwaldov, Czech.	3/2/71	Phi-Phi (AHL)
LITTLE, Neil	6-1	193	L	Medicine Hat, Alta.	12/18/71	Philadelphia (AHL)
OUELLET, Maxime	6-2	195	L	Beauport, Que.	6/17/81	Phi-Phi (AHL)-Rouyn-Noranda

Captains' History

Lou Angotti, 1967-68; Ed Van Impe, 1968-69 to 1971-72; Ed Van Impe and Bobby Clarke, 1972-73; Bobby Clarke, 1973-74 to 1978-79; Mel Bridgman, 1979-80, 1980-81; Bill Barber, 1981-82; Bill Barber and Bobby Clarke, 1982-83; Bobby Clarke, 1983-84; Dave Poulin, 1984-85 to 1988-89; Dave Poulin and Ron Sutter, 1989-90; Ron Sutter, 1990-91; Rick Tocchet, 1991-92; no captain, 1992-93; Kevin Dineen, 1993-94; Eric Lindros, 1994-95 to 1998-99; Eric Lindros and Eric Desjardins, 1999-2000; Eric Desjardins, 2000-01 to date.

General Managers' History

Bud Poile, 1967-68, 1968-69; Bud Poile and Keith Allen, 1969-70; Keith Allen, 1970-71 to 1982-83; Bob McCammon, 1983-84; Bob Clarke, 1984-85 to 1989-90; Russ Farwell, 1990-91 to 1993-94; Bob Clarke, 1994-95 to date.

President and General Manager

CLARKE, ROBERT EARLE (BOB)
President/General Manager, Philadelphia Flyers.
Born in Flin Flon, Man., August 13, 1949.

Bob Clarke was named president and general manager of the Philadelphia Flyers on June 15, 1994. Clarke's appointment marked the second time he has served as the Flyers' general manager. The Flin Flon native was the Flyers' vice president and general manager from 1984-90. During his 13 years as the team's general manager, the Flyers have won six divisional titles, three conference championships, reached the Stanley Cup semifinals six times and the finals three times.

Prior to re-joining the Flyers' family in 1994, Clarke served as vice president and general manager of the Florida Panthers. In 1993-94, their first season in the NHL, the Panthers established NHL records for wins (33) and points (83) by an expansion franchise. Clarke also served as the vice president and general manager of the Minnesota North Stars from 1990-92, guiding the team to the Stanley Cup Finals in 1991.

As a player, the former Philadelphia captain led his club to Stanley Cup championships in 1974 and 1975 and captured numerous individual awards, including the Hart Trophy as the League's most valuable player in 1973, 1975 and 1976. The four-time All-Star also received the Bill Masterton Memorial Trophy (perseverance and dedication) in 1972 and the Frank J. Selke Trophy (top defensive forward) in 1983. He appeared in eight All-Star Games and was elected to the Hockey Hall of Fame in 1987. He was awarded the Lester Patrick Trophy in 1979-80 in recognition of his contribution to hockey in the United States. Clarke appeared in 1,144 regular season games, recording 358 goals and 852 assists for 1,210 points. He also added 119 points in 136 playoff games.

2000-01 Scoring

* - rookie

Regular Season

Pos	#	Player	Team	GP	G	A	Pts	+/–	PIM	PP	SH	GW	GT	S	%
R	8	Mark Recchi	PHI	69	27	50	77	15	33	7	1	8	0	191	14.1
C	25	Keith Primeau	PHI	71	34	39	73	17	76	11	0	4	1	165	20.6
C	12	Simon Gagne	PHI	69	27	32	59	24	18	6	0	7	1	191	14.1
C	18	Daymond Langkow	PHI	71	13	41	54	12	50	3	0	2	0	190	6.8
D	3	Daniel McGillis	PHI	82	14	35	49	13	86	4	0	4	0	207	6.8
D	37	Eric Desjardins	PHI	79	15	33	48	–3	50	6	1	4	1	187	8.0
L	26	* Ruslan Fedotenko	PHI	74	16	20	36	8	72	3	0	4	0	119	13.4
R	92	Rick Tocchet	PHI	60	14	22	36	10	83	5	0	2	0	76	18.4
L	9	Dean McAmmond	CHI	61	10	16	26	4	43	1	0	1	0	95	10.5
			PHI	10	1	1	2	–1	0	1	0	0	0	17	5.9
			TOTAL	71	11	17	28	3	43	2	0	1	0	112	9.8
R	14	* Justin Williams	PHI	63	12	13	25	6	22	0	0	0	0	99	12.1
C	15	Peter White	PHI	77	9	16	25	1	16	1	0	1	0	68	13.2
L	19	Paul Ranheim	PHI	80	10	7	17	2	14	0	2	0	1	123	8.1
D	23	Michal Sykora	PHI	49	5	11	16	9	26	1	1	1	0	71	7.0
R	11	Jody Hull	PHI	71	7	8	15	–1	10	0	2	2	0	78	9.0
C	28	Kent Manderville	PHI	82	5	10	15	–2	47	0	3	2	0	136	3.7
D	43	Andy Delmore	PHI	66	5	9	14	2	16	2	0	0	0	119	4.2
D	6	Chris Therien	PHI	73	2	12	14	22	48	1	0	0	0	103	1.9
L	10	John LeClair	PHI	16	7	5	12	2	0	3	0	2	0	48	14.6
L	29	* Todd Fedoruk	PHI	53	5	5	10	0	109	0	0	0	0	28	17.9
D	22	Luke Richardson	PHI	82	2	6	8	23	131	0	1	0	0	75	2.7
C	44	P.J. Stock	MTL	20	1	2	3	–1	32	0	0	0	0	9	11.1
			PHI	31	1	3	4	–2	78	0	0	0	0	18	5.6
			TOTAL	51	2	5	7	–3	110	0	0	0	0	27	7.4
L	42	Michel Picard	PHI	7	1	4	5	6	0	1	0	0	0	12	8.3
D	24	Chris McAllister	PHI	60	2	2	4	1	124	0	0	0	0	33	6.1
C	38	Derek Plante	PHI	12	1	2	3	0	4	0	0	0	0	20	5.0
R	9	Mark Greig	PHI	7	1	1	2	–2	4	0	0	0	0	7	14.3
C	21	* Petr Hubacek	PHI	6	1	0	1	–1	2	0	0	0	0	5	20.0
G	32	Roman Cechmanek	PHI	59	0	1	1	0	4	0	0	0	0	0	0.0
R	47	* Kirby Law	PHI	1	0	0	0	–1	0	0	0	0	0	0	0.0
D	2	Brad Tiley	PHI	2	0	0	0	–1	0	0	0	0	0	1	0.0
R	20	* Tomas Divisek	PHI	2	0	0	0	–1	0	0	0	0	0	2	0.0
G	49	* Maxime Ouellet	PHI	2	0	0	0	0	0	0	0	0	0	0	0.0
C	36	Steve Washburn	PHI	3	0	0	0	0	0	0	0	0	0	0	0.0
R	20	Keith Jones	PHI	8	0	0	0	–5	4	0	0	0	0	11	0.0
G	33	Brian Boucher	PHI	27	0	0	0	0	2	0	0	0	0	0	0.0

Goaltending

No.	Goaltender	GPI	Mins	Avg	W	L	T	EN	SO	GA	SA	S%
32	Roman Cechmanek	59	3431	2.01	35	15	6	2	10	115	1464	.921
49	* Maxime Ouellet	2	76	2.37	0	1	0	1	0	3	27	.889
33	Brian Boucher	27	1470	3.27	8	12	5	6	1	80	644	.876
	Totals	**82**	**5001**	**2.48**	**43**	**28**	**11**	**9**	**11**	**207**	**2144**	**.903**

Playoffs

Pos	#	Player	Team	GP	G	A	Pts	+/–	PIM	PP	SH	GW	GT	S	%
C	18	Daymond Langkow	PHI	6	2	4	6	–2	2	1	0	0	0	14	14.3
R	8	Mark Recchi	PHI	6	2	2	4	–3	2	1	0	1	0	18	11.1
C	12	Simon Gagne	PHI	6	3	0	3	–2	0	2	0	0	0	21	14.3
L	10	John LeClair	PHI	6	1	2	3	–2	2	0	0	0	0	13	7.7
C	28	Kent Manderville	PHI	6	1	2	3	2	2	0	0	0	0	8	12.5
C	25	Keith Primeau	PHI	4	0	3	3	–3	8	0	0	0	0	10	0.0
D	37	Eric Desjardins	PHI	6	1	1	2	–2	0	0	0	0	0	10	10.0
L	19	Paul Ranheim	PHI	6	0	2	2	2	2	0	0	0	0	4	0.0
D	43	Andy Delmore	PHI	2	1	0	1	–1	2	0	0	1	0	2	50.0
D	6	Chris Therien	PHI	6	1	0	1	–4	8	0	0	0	0	11	9.1
D	3	Daniel McGillis	PHI	6	1	0	1	–4	6	0	1	0	0	18	5.6
C	38	Derek Plante	PHI	5	0	1	1	–3	0	0	0	0	0	8	0.0
R	92	Rick Tocchet	PHI	6	0	1	1	–2	6	0	0	0	0	8	0.0
D	23	Michal Sykora	PHI	6	0	1	1	0	0	0	0	0	0	6	0.0
L	26	* Ruslan Fedotenko	PHI	6	0	1	1	–4	4	0	0	0	0	6	0.0
G	33	Brian Boucher	PHI	1	0	0	0	0	0	0	0	0	0	0	0.0
D	24	Chris McAllister	PHI	2	0	0	0	1	0	0	0	0	0	0	0.0
C	44	P.J. Stock	PHI	2	0	0	0	–2	0	0	0	0	0	0	0.0
L	29	* Todd Fedoruk	PHI	2	0	0	0	0	20	0	0	0	0	0	0.0
C	15	Peter White	PHI	3	0	0	0	–1	0	0	0	0	0	2	0.0
L	9	Dean McAmmond	PHI	4	0	0	0	0	2	0	0	0	0	4	0.0
R	11	Jody Hull	PHI	6	0	0	0	1	4	0	0	0	0	7	0.0
D	22	Luke Richardson	PHI	6	0	0	0	–3	4	0	0	0	0	6	0.0
G	32	Roman Cechmanek	PHI	6	0	0	0	0	0	0	0	0	0	0	0.0

Goaltending

No.	Goaltender	GPI	Mins	Avg	W	L	EN	SO	GA	SA	S%
32	Roman Cechmanek	6	347	3.11	2	4	0	0	18	165	.891
33	Brian Boucher	1	37	4.86	0	0	0	0	3	17	.824
	Totals	**6**	**384**	**3.28**	**2**	**4**	**0**	**0**	**21**	**182**	**.885**

Coaching History

Keith Allen, 1967-68, 1968-69; Vic Stasiuk, 1969-70, 1970-71; Fred Shero, 1971-72 to 1977-78; Bob McCammon and Pat Quinn, 1978-79; Pat Quinn, 1979-80, 1980-81; Pat Quinn and Bob McCammon, 1981-82; Bob McCammon, 1982-83, 1983-84; Mike Keenan, 1984-85 to 1987-88; Paul Holmgren, 1988-89 to 1990-91; Paul Holmgren and Bill Dineen, 1991-92; Bill Dineen, 1992-93; Terry Simpson, 1993-94; Terry Murray, 1994-95 to 1996-97; Wayne Cashman and Roger Neilson, 1997-98; Roger Neilson, 1998-99, 1999-2000; Craig Ramsay and Bill Barber, 2000-01; Bill Barber, 2001-02.

Club Records

Team

(Figures in brackets for season records are games played; records for fewest points, wins, ties, losses, goals, goals against are for 70 or more games)

Most Points	**118**	1975-76 (80)
Most Wins	**53**	1984-85 (80), 1985-86 (80)
Most Ties	***24**	1969-70 (76)
Most Losses	**39**	1993-94 (84)
Most Goals	**350**	1983-84 (80)
Most Goals Against	**319**	1992-93 (84)
Fewest Points	**58**	1969-70 (76)
Fewest Wins	**17**	1969-70 (76)
Fewest Ties	**4**	1985-86 (80)
Fewest Losses	**12**	1979-80 (80)
Fewest Goals	**173**	1967-68 (74)
Fewest Goals Against	**164**	1973-74 (78)
Longest Winning Streak		
Overall	**13**	Oct. 19-Nov. 17/85
Home	***20**	Jan. 4-Apr. 3/76
Away	**8**	Dec. 22/82-Jan. 16/83
Longest Undefeated Streak		
Overall	***35**	Oct. 14/79-Jan. 6/80 (25 wins, 10 ties)
Home	**26**	Oct. 11/79-Feb. 3/80 (19 wins, 7 ties)
Away	**16**	Oct. 20/79-Jan. 6/80 (11 wins, 5 ties)
Longest Losing Streak		
Overall	**6**	Mar. 25-Apr. 4/70, Dec. 5-Dec. 17/92, Jan. 25-Feb. 5/94
Home	**5**	Jan. 30-Feb. 15/69
Away	**8**	Oct. 25-Nov. 26/72
Longest Winless Streak		
Overall	**12**	Feb. 24-Mar. 16/99 (8 losses, 4 ties)
Home	**8**	Dec. 19/68-Jan. 18/69 (4 losses, 4 ties)
Away	**19**	Oct. 23/71-Jan. 27/72 (15 losses, 4 ties)
Most Shutouts, Season	**13**	1974-75 (80)
Most PIM, Season	**2,621**	1980-81 (80)
Most Goals, Game	**13**	Mar. 22/84 (Pit. 4 at Phi. 13), Oct. 18/84 (Van. 2 at Phi. 13)

Individual

Most Seasons	**15**	Bobby Clarke
Most Games	**1,144**	Bobby Clarke
Most Goals, Career	**420**	Bill Barber
Most Assists, Career	**852**	Bobby Clarke
Most Points, Career	**1,210**	Bobby Clarke (358G, 852A)
Most PIM, Career	**1,789**	Rick Tocchet
Most Shutouts, Career	**50**	Bernie Parent
Longest Consecutive Game Streak	**484**	Rod Brind'Amour (Feb. 24/93-Apr. 18/99)
Most Goals, Season	**61**	Reggie Leach (1975-76)
Most Assists, Season	**89**	Bobby Clarke (1974-75, 1975-76)
Most Points, Season	**123**	Mark Recchi (1992-93; 53G, 70A)
Most PIM, Season	***472**	Dave Schultz (1974-75)
Most Points, Defenseman, Season	**82**	Mark Howe (1985-86; 24G, 58A)
Most Points, Center, Season	**119**	Bobby Clarke (1975-76; 30G, 89A)
Most Points, Right Wing, Season	**123**	Mark Recchi (1992-93; 53G, 70A)
Most Points, Left Wing, Season	**112**	Bill Barber (1975-76; 50G, 62A)
Most Points, Rookie, Season	**82**	Mikael Renberg (1993-94; 38G, 44A)
Most Shutouts, Season	**12**	Bernie Parent (1973-74, 1974-75)
Most Goals, Game	**4**	Fourteen times
Most Assists, Game	**6**	Eric Lindros (Feb. 26/97)
Most Points, Game	**8**	Tom Bladon (Dec. 11/77; 4G, 4A)

* NHL Record.

Retired Numbers

1	Bernie Parent	1967-1971, 1973-1979
4	Barry Ashbee	1970-1974
7	Bill Barber	1972-1985
16	Bobby Clarke	1969-1984

All-time Record vs. Other Clubs

Regular Season

	At Home								On Road								Total							
	GP	W	L	T	OL	GF	GA	PTS	GP	W	L	T	OL	GF	GA	PTS	GP	W	L	T	OL	GF	GA	PTS
Anaheim	7	2	2	3	0	20	16	7	6	2	2	2	0	20	21	6	13	4	4	5	0	40	37	13
Atlanta	4	2	0	2	0	14	8	6	4	3	1	0	0	14	10	6	8	5	1	2	0	28	18	12
Boston	67	31	28	8	0	227	194	70	70	16	44	10	0	196	273	42	137	47	72	18	0	423	467	112
Buffalo	61	36	13	12	0	217	153	84	57	23	27	7	0	168	190	53	118	59	40	19	0	385	343	137
Calgary	49	33	13	3	0	195	130	69	51	17	25	9	0	167	204	43	100	50	38	12	0	362	334	112
Carolina	37	25	9	3	0	139	91	53	38	19	12	7	0	144	127	45	75	44	21	10	0	283	218	98
Chicago	59	32	16	11	0	191	155	75	58	14	25	19	0	167	203	47	117	46	41	30	0	358	358	122
Colorado	32	22	8	2	0	120	87	46	32	9	11	12	0	113	118	30	64	31	19	14	0	233	205	76
Columbus	0	0	0	0	0	0	0	0	1	1	0	0	0	4	3	2	1	1	0	0	0	4	3	2
Dallas	64	41	9	14	0	249	145	96	64	23	27	14	0	207	211	60	128	64	36	28	0	456	356	156
Detroit	57	33	13	11	0	227	166	77	57	18	29	10	0	178	203	46	114	51	42	21	0	405	369	123
Edmonton	29	20	7	2	0	126	79	42	27	8	14	5	0	81	96	21	56	28	21	7	0	207	175	63
Florida	19	8	7	4	0	45	44	20	18	13	5	0	0	64	45	26	37	21	12	4	0	109	89	46
Los Angeles	62	39	15	7	1	239	156	86	63	35	20	8	0	216	187	78	125	74	35	15	1	455	343	164
Minnesota	1	1	0	0	0	3	0	2	1	0	0	1	0	3	3	1	2	1	0	1	0	6	3	3
Montreal	67	26	24	16	1	204	202	69	68	20	33	14	1	206	245	55	135	46	57	30	2	410	447	124
Nashville	3	1	1	1	0	10	4	3	3	2	0	1	0	6	3	5	6	3	1	2	0	16	7	8
New Jersey	77	48	21	8	0	308	201	104	75	29	39	7	0	268	267	65	152	77	60	15	0	576	468	169
NY Islanders	87	53	23	10	1	328	251	117	90	28	47	14	1	263	340	71	177	81	70	24	2	591	591	188
NY Rangers	101	50	37	14	0	333	284	114	102	35	43	23	1	297	330	94	203	85	80	37	1	630	614	208
Ottawa	17	11	5	1	0	61	45	23	18	9	6	3	0	61	52	21	35	20	11	4	0	122	97	44
Phoenix	29	21	8	0	0	125	79	42	28	15	11	2	0	99	87	32	57	36	19	2	0	224	166	74
Pittsburgh	98	75	16	7	0	421	245	157	98	35	44	19	0	319	348	89	196	110	60	26	0	740	593	246
St. Louis	65	44	11	10	0	257	147	98	65	32	26	7	0	203	189	71	130	76	37	17	0	460	336	169
San Jose	9	6	2	1	0	32	20	13	9	7	1	1	0	28	15	15	18	13	3	2	0	60	35	28
Tampa Bay	19	12	1	6	0	66	31	30	20	12	7	1	0	62	54	25	39	24	8	7	0	128	85	55
Toronto	61	40	13	8	0	241	142	88	61	26	22	13	0	207	201	65	122	66	35	21	0	448	343	153
Vancouver	51	35	15	1	0	226	152	71	50	28	10	12	0	201	143	68	101	63	25	13	0	427	295	139
Washington	77	47	24	6	0	287	211	100	74	31	30	13	0	245	251	75	151	78	54	19	0	532	462	175
Defunct Clubs	34	24	4	6	0	137	67	54	35	13	14	8	0	102	89	34	69	37	18	14	0	239	156	88
Totals	**1343**	**818**	**345**	**177**	**3**	**5048**	**3505**	**1816**	**1343**	**523**	**575**	**242**	**3**	**4309**	**4508**	**1291**	**2686**	**1341**	**920**	**419**	**6**	**9357**	**8013**	**3107**

Playoffs

	Series	W	L	GP	W	L	T	GF	GA	Last Mtg.	Round	Result
Boston	4	2	2	20	9	11	0	57	60	1978	QF	L 1-4
Buffalo	7	5	2	37	23	14	0	110	96	2001	CQF	L 2-4
Calgary	2	1	1	11	7	4	0	43	28	1981	QF	L 3-4
Chicago	1	0	1	4	0	4	0	8	20	1971	QF	L 0-4
Colorado	2	2	0	11	7	4	0	39	29	1985	CF	W 4-2
Dallas	2	2	0	11	8	3	0	41	26	1980	SF	W 4-1
Detroit	1	0	1	4	0	4	0	6	16	1997	F	L 0-4
Edmonton	3	1	2	15	7	8	0	44	49	1987	F	L 3-4
Florida	1	0	1	6	2	4	0	11	15	1996	CSF	L 2-4
Montreal	4	1	3	21	6	15	0	52	72	1989	CF	L 2-4
New Jersey	3	1	2	15	7	8	0	35	41	2000	CF	L 3-4
NY Islanders	4	3	1	25	14	11	0	83	69	1987	DF	W 4-3
NY Rangers	10	6	4	47	27	20	0	158	153	1997	CF	W 4-1
Pittsburgh	3	3	0	18	12	6	0	66	51	2000	CSF	W 4-2
St. Louis	2	0	2	11	3	8	0	20	34	1969	QF	L 0-4
Tampa Bay	1	1	0	6	4	2	0	26	13	1996	CQF	W 4-2
Toronto	4	3	1	23	14	9	0	78	56	1999	CQF	L 2-4
Vancouver	1	1	0	3	2	1	0	15	9	1979	PR	W 2-1
Washington	3	1	2	16	7	9	0	55	65	1989	DSF	W 4-2
Totals	**58**	**33**	**25**	**304**	**160**	**144**	**0**	**946**	**902**			

Playoff Results 2001-1997

Year	Round	Opponent	Result	GF	GA
2001	CQF	Buffalo	L 2-4	13	21
2000	CF	New Jersey	L 3-4	15	18
	CSF	Pittsburgh	W 4-2	15	14
	CQF	Buffalo	W 4-1	14	8
1999	CQF	Toronto	L 2-4	11	9
1998	CQF	Buffalo	L 1-4	9	18
1997	F	Detroit	L 0-4	6	16
	CF	NY Rangers	W 4-1	20	13
	CSF	Buffalo	W 4-1	21	13
	CQF	Pittsburgh	W 4-1	20	13

Abbreviations: Round: F – Final; **CF** – conference final; **CSF** – conference semi-final; **CQF** – conference quarter-final; **DF** – division final; **DSF** – division semi-final; **SF** – semi-final; **QF** – quarter-final; **PR** – preliminary round.

Calgary totals include Atlanta Flames, 1972-73 to 1979-80. Carolina totals include Hartford, 1979-80 to 1996-97.
Colorado totals include Quebec, 1979-80 to 1994-95. Dallas totals include Minnesota North Stars, 1967-68 to 1992-93.
New Jersey totals include Kansas City, 1974-75 to 1975-76, and Colorado Rockies, 1976-77 to 1981-82.
Phoenix totals include Winnipeg, 1979-80 to 1995-96.

2000-01 Results

Month	Day	Opponent	Score	Month	Day	Opponent	Score
Oct.	5	Vancouver	6-3		8	at St. Louis	2-1*
	7	Boston	1-5		12	at Tampa Bay	3-0
	11	at Minnesota	3-3		13	at Florida	4-1
	12	at Dallas	1-4		16	at NY Rangers	3-4*
	14	at Phoenix	3-6		18	New Jersey	1-7
	17	Ottawa	1-6		20	Florida	5-3
	19	Montreal	3-3		22	Los Angeles	3-0
	21	Anaheim	3-4		25	at Chicago	5-1
	24	at NY Rangers	5-4		27	at Carolina	4-3
	26	NY Rangers	3-0		28	at Washington	2-4
	29	Washington	1-1		31	at Pittsburgh	5-1
Nov.	1	at New Jersey	1-1	**Feb.**	1	NY Islanders	2-0
	2	Nashville	1-3		6	at Boston	3-4
	4	Buffalo	3-0		7	at Pittsburgh	4-9
	8	at Pittsburgh	2-5		9	at NY Islanders	5-2
	9	Edmonton	2-0		14	at NY Islanders	3-1
	11	Ottawa	4-3		15	Toronto	5-2
	15	at Toronto	2-1*		17	Atlanta	5-1
	17	at Atlanta	3-2*		19	Carolina	4-0
	18	Washington	5-3		22	at NY Islanders	3-4*
	22	at Buffalo	3-1		24	Tampa Bay	0-0
	24	Pittsburgh	0-1		25	NY Rangers	2-1
	26	Phoenix	1-2		27	Montreal	2-3
	29	at Columbus	4-3	**Mar.**	1	Buffalo	2-0
	30	at Carolina	0-2		3	at Montreal	1-3
Dec.	2	at Ottawa	3-5		5	Boston	6-4
	6	Tampa Bay	6-3		8	Calgary	5-2
	8	at Detroit	1-5		10	New Jersey	2-3
	10	NY Islanders	5-2		13	St. Louis	5-2
	12	at Nashville	2-2		15	Minnesota	3-0
	13	at Colorado	3-3		17	NY Rangers	2-1
	16	New Jersey	6-3		19	at Edmonton	4-2
	19	at Boston	4-4		22	at Calgary	1-3
	21	San Jose	4-3		24	at Toronto	3-5
	23	Carolina	2-1*		26	at Ottawa	3-3
	27	at Florida	5-2		29	Toronto	1-2
	28	at Tampa Bay	3-4		31	Detroit	1-0
	30	at Washington	3-6	**Apr.**	3	Florida	1-2
Jan.	2	at New Jersey	1-1		5	at Montreal	2-3*
	5	at Atlanta	6-4		7	Pittsburgh	4-3*
	6	Atlanta	2-2		8	at Buffalo	2-1

* – Overtime

Entry Draft Selections 2001-1987

2001
Pick
27 Jeff Woywitka
95 Patrick Sharp
146 Jussi Timonen
150 Bernd Bruckler
158 Roman Malek
172 Denis Seidenberg
177 Andrei Razin
208 Thierry Douville
225 David Printz

2000
Pick
28 Justin Williams
94 Alexander Drozdetsky
171 Roman Cechmanek
195 Colin Shields
210 John Eichelberger
227 Guillaume Lefebvre
259 Regan Kelly
287 Milan Kopecky

1999
Pick
22 Maxime Ouellet
119 Jeff Feniak
160 Konstantin Rudenko
200 Pavel Kasparik
208 Vaclav Pletka
224 David Nystrom

1998
Pick
22 Simon Gagne
42 Jason Beckett
51 Ian Forbes
109 Jean-Philippe Morin
124 Francis Belanger
139 Garrett Prosofsky
168 Antero Niittymaki
175 Cam Ondrik
195 Tomas Divisek
222 Lubomir Pistek
243 Petr Hubacek
253 Bruno St. Jacques
258 Sergei Skrobot

1997
Pick
30 Jean-Marc Pelletier
50 Pat Kavanagh
62 Kris Mallette
103 Mikhail Chernov
158 Jordon Flodell
164 Todd Fedoruk
214 Marko Kauppinen
240 Par Styf

1996
Pick
15 Dainius Zubrus
64 Chester Gallant
124 Per-Ragna Bergqvist
133 Jesse Boulerice
187 Roman Malov
213 Jeff Milleker

1995
Pick
22 Brian Boucher
48 Shane Kenny
100 Radovan Somik
132 Dmitri Tertyshny
135 Jamie Sokolsky
152 Martin Spanhel
178 Martin Streit
204 Ruslan Shafikov
230 Jeff Lank

1994
Pick
62 Artem Anisimov
88 Adam Magarrell
101 Sebastien Vallee
140 Alex Selivanov
166 Colin Forbes
192 Derek Diener
202 Raymond Giroux
218 Johan Hedberg
244 Andre Payette
270 Jan Lipiansky

1993
Pick
36 Janne Niinimaa
71 Vaclav Prospal
77 Milos Holan
114 Vladimir Krechin
140 Mike Crowley
166 Aaron Israel
192 Paul Healey
218 Tripp Tracy
226 E.J. Bradley
244 Jeff Staples
270 Ken Hemenway

1992
Pick
7 Ryan Sittler
15 Jason Bowen
31 Denis Metlyuk
103 Vladislav Buljin
127 Roman Zolotov
151 Kirk Daubenspeck
175 Claude Jr. Jutras
199 Jonas Hakansson
223 Chris Herperger
247 Patrice Paquin

1991
Pick
6 Peter Forsberg
50 Yanick Dupre
86 Aris Brimanis
94 Yanick Degrace
116 Clayton Norris
122 Dmitry Yushkevich
138 Andrei Lomakin
182 James Bode
204 Josh Bartell
226 Neil Little
248 John Porco

1990
Pick
4 Mike Ricci
25 Chris Simon
40 Mikael Renberg
42 Terran Sandwith
44 Kimbi Daniels
46 Bill Armstrong
47 Chris Therien
52 Al Kinisky
88 Dan Kordic
109 Viacheslav Butsayev
151 Patrik Englund
172 Toni Porkka
193 Greg Hanson
214 Tommy Soderstrom
235 William Lund

1989
Pick
33 Greg Johnson
34 Patrik Juhlin
72 Reid Simpson
117 Niklas Eriksson
138 John Callahan Jr.
159 Sverre Sears
180 Glen Wisser
201 Al Kummu
222 Matt Brait
243 James Pollio

1988
Pick
14 Claude Boivin
35 Pat Murray
56 Craig Fisher
63 Dominic Roussel
77 Scott Lagrand
98 Edward O'Brien
119 Gordie Frantti
140 Jamie Cooke
161 Johan Salle
182 Brian Arthur
203 Jeff Dandretta
224 Scott Billey
245 Drahomir Kadlec

1987
Pick
20 Darren Rumble
30 Jeff Harding
62 Martin Hostak
83 Tomaz Eriksson
104 Bill Gall
125 Tony Link
146 Mark Strapon
167 Darryl Ingham
188 Bruce McDonald
209 Steve Morrow
230 Darius Rusnak
251 Dale Roehl

Coach

BARBER, BILL
Coach, Philadelphia Flyers. Born in Callander, Ont., July 11, 1952.

A member of the Flyers organization since being selected seventh overall in the 1972 Amateur Draft, Bill Barber began the 2000-01 season as an assistant coach with the team before being promoted to head coach on December 10, 2000. He went on to lead the Flyers to a 100-point season and win the Jack Adams Award as coach of the year.

Barber spent his entire 12-year playing career (1972-73 to 1983-84) with the Flyers and is the club's all-time leader with 420 goals. He also ranks high on the team's list in games played (903), assists (463) and points (883). Barber was a member of Philadelphia's Stanley Cup-winning teams in 1974 and 1975, and was elected to the Hockey Hall of Fame in 1990.

After retiring as a player, Barber worked for the Flyers as an assistant coach and as director of pro scouting. He became head coach of the Philadelphia Phantoms, the Flyers' AHL affiliate, in 1996-97, and held the job for four seasons. The Phantoms won the Calder Cup championship in 1997-98.

Coaching Record

		Regular Season				Playoffs		
Season	**Team**	**Games**	**W**	**L**	**T**	**Games**	**W**	**L**
1996-97	Philadelphia (AHL)	80	49	18	13	10	6	4
1997-98	Philadelphia (AHL)	80	47	21	12	20	15	5
1998-99	Philadelphia (AHL)	80	47	22	11	16	9	7
1999-2000	Philadelphia (AHL)	80	44	31	5	5	2	3
2000-01	**Philadelphia (NHL)**	**54**	**31**	**16**	**7**	**6**	**2**	**4**
	NHL Totals	**54**	**31**	**16**	**7**	**6**	**2**	**4**

Club Directory

First Union Center

Philadelphia Flyers
First Union Center
3601 South Broad Street
Philadelphia, PA 19148-5290
Phone **215/465-4500**
PR FAX 215/389-9403
www.philadelphiaflyers.com
Capacity: 19,523

Executive Management
Chairman . . . . Ed Snider
Limited Partners . . . . Pat Croce, Jay Snider, Sylvan and Fran Tobin
President and General Manager . . . . Bob Clarke
Chairman of the Board, Emeritus . . . . Joe Scott
Executive Vice President and
Chief Operating Officer . . . . Ron Ryan
Executive Vice President . . . . Keith Allen
Governor . . . . Ed Snider
Alternate Governors . . . . Bob Clarke, Ron Ryan, Phil Weinberg
Executive Assistants . . . . Lisa D'Aprile, Gina Pelle
Receptionist . . . . Maureen McGuckin

Hockey Club Personnel
Assistant General Manager . . . . Paul Holmgren
Head Coach . . . . Bill Barber
Assistant Coach . . . . E.J. McGuire
Assistant Coach . . . . Mike Stothers
Goaltending Coach . . . . Rejean Lemelin
Skating Coach . . . . David Roy
Chief Scout . . . . Dennis Patterson
Scouting Staff . . . . Serge Boudreault, John Chapman, Inge Hammarstrom, Simon Nolet, Chris Pryor, Vaclav Slansky, Evgeny Zimin
Pro Scouts . . . . Ron Hextall, Al Hill, Terry Murray
Assistant to the President . . . . Barry Hanrahan
Video Coordinator . . . . Steve Romanowski
Scouting Information Coordinator . . . . Bryan Hardenbergh
Massage Therapist . . . . Tom D'Ancona
Executive Assistant . . . . Dianna Taylor
Receptionist . . . . Sharon Allison

Medical/Training Staff
Team Physicians . . . . Arthur Bartolozzi, M.D., Jeff Hartzell, M.D., Gary Dorshimer, M.D., Guy Lanzi, D.M.D.
Athletic Trainer . . . . John Worley
Strength and Conditioning Instructor . . . . Jim McCrossin
Head Equipment Manager . . . . Jim Evers
Equipment Managers . . . . Anthony Oratorio, Harry Bricker, Luke Clarke

Public Relations
Director of Public Relations . . . . Zack Hill
Assistant Director of Public Relations . . . . Jill Lipson
Director of Media Services and Publications . . . . Joe Klueg
Director of Fan Services . . . . Joe Kadlec
Archivist . . . . Kerrianne Brady
Public Relations Assistant . . . . Kristin Lewandowski

Youth Hockey and Fan Development
Executive Director of Youth Hockey
and Fan Development . . . . Eric Turner
Director of Youth Hockey and Fan Development . . . Melissa Wilson

Sales/Marketing
Vice President, Sales . . . . Jack Betson
Vice President, Sales and Marketing . . . . Kathi Gillin
Director of Community Relations . . . . Linda Panasci
Director of Ticket Operations . . . . Cecilia Baker
Ticket Office Administration . . . . Joan Kadlec
Manager, Sales and Services . . . . Nicole Allison
Marketing Assistant . . . . Kevin Morley
Assistant Manager, Sales and Services . . . . Diane Smith
Manager of Game Presentation and Special Events . . Linda Held
Assistant to the VP, Sales and Marketing . . . . Debbie Brown

Finance
Director of Finance . . . . Dave Jablonski
Controller . . . . Lisa Cataldo
Payroll Accountant . . . . Susann Schaffer
Accounts Payable Manager . . . . Marilyn Trout

Advertising Sales
Vice President, Sales . . . . Joe Croce
Administrative Assistant . . . . Donna Schroeder
Director, Advertising Sales . . . . Jeffrey Kirk
General Sales Manager . . . . Brian Monihan
National Sales Manager . . . . Lee Stein
Senior Account Executive . . . . Joe Watson
Account Executives . . . . Sean Baedke, Nick Battista, Sarah Crafford, Mike Garrity, Robert Kasilowski, Traci Kloss, Bo Koelle, Ray Lyons, Steve Rex, Vince Santroni
Sponsorship Manager . . . . Maura Hood
Television Coordinator . . . . Shannan Reed
Manager of Contracts and Client Services . . . . Thea Vogel
Senior Account Coordinator . . . . Colleen Molloy
Account Coordinator . . . . Kim Windt
Director of Premium Seating . . . . Rick Campbell
Manager of Finance and Inventory . . . . Jimmy Dunk
Sales Executives . . . . Chris Genther, Pete Seelaus, Dennis Shea

Broadcasting
TV Play-by-Play, Analyst, Color Commentary . . . . . . Jim Jackson, Gary Dornhoefer, Steve Coates
Radio Play-by-Play, Color Analyst . . . . Tim Saunders, Brian Propp
Executive Producer/Director of Broadcasting . . . . . . Bryan Cooper
Associate Producer . . . . Jennifer Roman
Director, Flyers Game Operations . . . . Brian Mantai
Public Address Announcer . . . . Lou Nolan
TV Rightsholders . . . . Comcast SportsNet, UPN-57 WPSG-TV
Radio Rightsholder . . . . SportsRadio 610 WIP (610 AM)

Flyers Wives Charities
Executive Director . . . . Fran Tobin
Director . . . . Rita Johanson
Event Coordinator . . . . Susan Wechsler

Phoenix Coyotes

2000-01 Results: 35W-27L-17T-3OTL 90PTS. Fourth, Pacific Division

Sean Burke was touted as a Hart Trophy candidate through the first half of the 2000-01 season. In his busiest year since 1995-96, Burke recorded a career-best 2.27 goals-against average with a .922 save percentage that ranked third in the NHL.

2001-02 Schedule

Month	Day	Date	Opponent	Month	Day	Date	Opponent
Oct.	Thu.	4	at Los Angeles		Fri.	4	at San Jose
	Sat.	6	at Edmonton		Sun.	6	Tampa Bay
	Mon.	8	at Calgary		Wed.	9	San Jose
	Thu.	11	at Chicago		Tue.	15	Detroit
	Sat.	13	Washington		Thu.	17	at Colorado
	Tue.	16	Boston		Sat.	19	Buffalo
	Thu.	18	at Dallas		Mon.	21	at Nashville
	Sat.	20	Vancouver		Wed.	23	at Chicago
	Wed.	24	Anaheim		Fri.	25	at Detroit
	Sat.	27	Colorado*		Sat.	26	at Columbus
	Tue.	30	at Buffalo		Mon.	28	at Atlanta
Nov.	Thu.	1	at New Jersey		Wed.	30	at Florida
	Fri.	2	at Washington	**Feb.**	Mon.	4	at Vancouver
	Sun.	4	at Carolina*		Wed.	6	Chicago
	Wed.	7	Detroit		Fri.	8	Los Angeles
	Fri.	9	at Dallas		Sun.	10	Edmonton*
	Sat.	10	at St. Louis		Tue.	12	Calgary
	Tue.	13	Edmonton		Wed.	13	at Los Angeles
	Thu.	15	San Jose		Tue.	26	Dallas
	Sat.	17	NY Islanders		Thu.	28	at Colorado
	Tue.	20	Minnesota	**Mar.**	Sun.	3	Columbus*
	Fri.	23	at Minnesota*		Tue.	5	New Jersey
	Sat.	24	at St. Louis		Thu.	7	Vancouver
	Tue.	27	at Columbus		Sat.	9	Ottawa*
	Thu.	29	Nashville		Tue.	12	Chicago
Dec.	Sat.	1	Pittsburgh		Fri.	15	at Nashville
	Wed.	5	St. Louis		Sun.	17	at Minnesota*
	Fri.	7	at Detroit		Tue.	19	at Boston
	Sat.	8	at Montreal		Wed.	20	at Pittsburgh
	Tue.	11	at Toronto		Fri.	22	at Dallas
	Thu.	13	at Ottawa		Sun.	24	Los Angeles*
	Sat.	15	Dallas		Wed.	27	at Anaheim
	Mon.	17	Columbus		Thu.	28	Anaheim
	Wed.	19	Calgary		Sat.	30	Colorado
	Fri.	21	at Anaheim	**Apr.**	Mon.	1	St. Louis
	Sun.	23	Anaheim*		Thu.	4	at San Jose
	Wed.	26	Los Angeles		Sun.	7	at Vancouver
	Fri.	28	Philadelphia		Tue.	9	at Calgary
	Sun.	30	at San Jose*		Wed.	10	at Edmonton
	Mon.	31	NY Rangers		Fri.	12	Minnesota
Jan.	Thu.	3	Atlanta		Sun.	14	Nashville*

* Denotes afternoon game.

Franchise date: June 22, 1979

Transferred from Winnipeg to Phoenix, July 1, 1996

PACIFIC DIVISION

23rd NHL Season

Year-by-Year Record

		Home				Road				Overall								
Season	**GP**	**W**	**L**	**T**	**OL**	**W**	**L**	**T**	**OL**	**W**	**L**	**T**	**OL**	**GF**	**GA**	**Pts.**	**Finished**	**Playoff Result**
2000-01	82	21	11	7	2	14	16	10	1	35	27	17	3	214	212	90	4th, Pacific Div.	Out of Playoffs
1999-2000	82	22	16	2	1	17	15	6	3	39	31	8	4	232	228	90	3rd, Pacific Div.	Lost Conf. Quarter-Final
1998-99	82	23	13	5	...	16	18	7	...	39	31	12	...	205	197	90	2nd, Pacific Div.	Lost Conf. Quarter-Final
1997-98	82	19	16	6	...	16	19	6	...	35	35	12	...	224	227	82	4th, Central Div.	Lost Conf. Quarter-Final
1996-97	82	15	19	7	...	23	18	0	...	38	37	7	...	240	243	83	3rd, Central Div.	Lost Conf. Quarter-Final
1995-96*	82	22	16	3	...	14	24	3	...	36	40	6	...	275	291	78	5th, Central Div.	Lost Conf. Quarter-Final
1994-95*	48	10	10	4	...	6	15	3	...	16	25	7	...	157	177	39	6th, Central Div.	Out of Playoffs
1993-94*	84	15	23	4	...	9	28	5	...	24	51	9	...	245	344	57	6th, Central Div.	Out of Playoffs
1992-93*	84	23	16	3	...	17	21	4	...	40	37	7	...	322	320	87	4th, Smythe Div.	Lost Div. Semi-Final
1991-92*	80	20	14	6	...	13	18	9	...	33	32	15	...	251	244	81	4th, Smythe Div.	Lost Div. Semi-Final
1990-91*	80	17	18	5	...	9	25	6	...	26	43	11	...	260	288	63	5th, Smythe Div.	Out of Playoffs
1989-90*	80	22	13	5	...	15	19	6	...	37	32	11	...	298	290	85	3rd, Smythe Div.	Lost Div. Semi-Final
1988-89*	80	17	18	5	...	9	24	7	...	26	42	12	...	300	355	64	5th, Smythe Div.	Out of Playoffs
1987-88*	80	20	14	6	...	13	22	5	...	33	36	11	...	292	310	77	3rd, Smythe Div.	Lost Div. Semi-Final
1986-87*	80	25	12	3	...	15	20	5	...	40	32	8	...	279	271	88	3rd, Smythe Div.	Lost Div. Final
1985-86*	80	18	19	3	...	8	28	4	...	26	47	7	...	295	372	59	3rd, Smythe Div.	Lost Div. Semi-Final
1984-85*	80	21	13	6	...	22	14	4	...	43	27	10	...	358	332	96	2nd, Smythe Div.	Lost Div. Final
1983-84*	80	17	15	8	...	14	23	3	...	31	38	11	...	340	374	73	4th, Smythe Div.	Lost Div. Semi-Final
1982-83*	80	22	16	2	...	11	23	6	...	33	39	8	...	311	333	74	4th, Smythe Div.	Lost Div. Semi-Final
1981-82*	80	18	13	9	...	15	20	5	...	33	33	14	...	319	332	80	2nd, Norris Div.	Lost Div. Semi-Final
1980-81*	80	7	25	8	...	2	32	6	...	9	57	14	...	246	400	32	6th, Smythe Div.	Out of Playoffs
1979-80*	80	13	19	8	...	7	30	3	...	20	49	11	...	214	314	51	5th, Smythe Div.	Out of Playoffs

* Winnipeg Jets

2001-02 Player Personnel

FORWARDS	HT	WT	S	Place of Birth	Date	2000-01 Club
ABID, Ramzi	6-2	210	L	Montreal, Que.	3/24/80	Springfield
BEREZIN, Sergei	5-10	200	R	Voskresensk, USSR	11/5/71	Toronto
BOUCK, Tyler	6-0	196	L	Camrose, Alta.	1/13/80	Dallas-Utah
BRIERE, Daniel	5-10	181	R	Gatineau, Que.	10/6/77	Phoenix-Springfield
DOAN, Shane	6-2	223	R	Halkirk, Alta.	10/10/76	Phoenix
FABUS, Peter	6-1	191	L	Ilava, Czech.	7/15/79	Dukla Trencin
HANDZUS, Michal	6-5	210	L	Banska Bystrica, Czech.	3/11/77	St. Louis-Phoenix
JASPERS, Jason	5-11	185	L	Thunder Bay, Ont.	4/8/81	Sudbury
JOHNSON, Mike	6-2	200	R	Scarborough, Ont.	10/3/74	Tampa Bay-Phoenix
LANGKOW, Daymond	5-11	180	L	Edmonton, Alta	9/27/76	Philadelphia
LEMIEUX, Claude	6-1	226	R	Buckingham, Que.	7/16/65	Phoenix
LETOWSKI, Trevor	5-10	176	R	Thunder Bay, Ont.	4/5/77	Phoenix
MAY, Brad	6-1	209	L	Toronto, Ont.	11/29/71	Phoenix
NAGY, Ladislav	5-11	194	L	Saca, Czech.	6/1/79	St. Louis-Worcester-Phoenix
RADIVOJEVIC, Branko	6-1	200	R	Piestany, Czech.	11/24/80	Belleville
RALPH, Brad	6-2	206	L	Ottawa, Ont.	10/17/80	Phoenix-Springfield
SJOSTROM, Fredrik	6-0	194	L	Fargelanda, Sweden	5/6/83	Vastra Frolunda
SMITH, Wyatt	5-11	208	L	Thief River Falls, MN	2/13/77	Phoenix-Springfield
SULLIVAN, Mike	6-2	204	L	Marshfield, MA	2/27/68	Phoenix
TRUDEL, Jean-Guy	5-11	202	L	Sudbury, Ont.	10/18/75	Springfield
WARRINER, Todd	6-1	200	L	Blenheim, Ont.	1/3/74	Tampa Bay
WILSON, Landon	6-3	226	R	St. Louis, MO	3/13/75	Phoenix
ZAINULLIN, Ruslan	6-2	202	L	Kazan, USSR	2/14/82	Ak Bars Kazan
DEFENSEMEN						
BEZINA, Goran	6-4	220	L	Split, Yugoslavia	3/21/80	Fribourg-Gotteron
BOUCHARD, Joel	6-1	209	L	Montreal, Que.	1/23/74	Grand Rapids-Phoenix
CULLEN, David	6-2	209	R	St. Catharines, Ont.	12/30/76	Phoenix-Springfield
GRENIER, Martin	6-5	245	L	Laval, Que.	11/2/80	Quebec (QMJHL)-Victoriaville
LEACH, Jay	6-4	216	L	Syracuse, NY	9/2/79	Providence
MARA, Paul	6-4	210	L	Ridgewood, NJ	9/7/79	T.B.-Detroit (IHL)-Phx
MARKOV, Danny	6-1	190	L	Moscow, USSR	7/11/76	Toronto
NUMMINEN, Teppo	6-2	199	R	Tampere, Finland	7/3/68	Phoenix
SAFRONOV, Kirill	6-2	209	L	Leningrad, USSR	2/26/81	Springfield
SIMPSON, Todd	6-3	215	L	North Vancouver, B.C.	5/28/73	Florida-Phoenix
SUCHY, Radoslav	6-2	198	L	Kezmarok, Czech.	4/7/76	Phoenix
VAANANEN, Ossi	6-4	205	L	Vantaa, Finland	8/18/80	Phoenix
GOALTENDERS	**HT**	**WT**	**C**	**Place of Birth**	**Date**	**2000-01 Club**
BURKE, Sean	6-4	210	L	Windsor, Ont.	1/29/67	Phoenix
DesROCHERS, Patrick	6-4	207	L	Penetanguishene, Ont.	10/27/79	Springfield
ESCHE, Robert	6-1	200	L	Whitesboro, NY	1/22/78	Phoenix

2000-01 Scoring

* - rookie

Regular Season

Pos	#	Player	Team	GP	G	A	Pts	+/–	PIM	PP	SH	GW	GT	S	%
C	97	Jeremy Roenick	PHX	80	30	46	76	–1	114	13	0	7	1	192	15.6
R	19	Shane Doan	PHX	76	26	37	63	0	89	6	1	6	1	220	11.8
R	12	Mike Johnson	T.B.	64	11	27	38	–10	38	3	1	0	1	107	10.3
			PHX	12	2	3	5	0	4	1	0	0	0	17	11.8
			TOTAL	76	13	30	43	–10	42	4	1	0	1	124	10.5
L	90	Joe Juneau	PHX	69	10	23	33	–2	28	5	0	3	1	100	10.0
C	16	Michal Handzus	STL	36	10	14	24	11	12	3	2	2	0	58	17.2
			PHX	10	4	4	8	5	21	0	1	0	0	14	28.6
			TOTAL	46	14	18	32	16	33	3	3	2	0	72	19.4
R	28	Landon Wilson	PHX	70	18	13	31	3	92	2	0	3	1	123	14.6
D	27	Teppo Numminen	PHX	72	5	26	31	9	36	1	0	2	0	109	4.6
C	39	Travis Green	PHX	69	13	15	28	–11	63	3	0	0	0	113	11.5
R	22	Claude Lemieux	PHX	46	10	16	26	1	58	2	0	1	0	99	10.1
L	32	Brad May	PHX	62	11	14	25	10	107	0	0	0	0	83	13.3
D	21	Jyrki Lumme	PHX	58	4	21	25	3	44	0	0	0	1	77	5.2
C	36	Juha Ylonen	PHX	69	9	14	23	10	38	0	1	1	0	72	12.5
C	10	Trevor Letowski	PHX	77	7	15	22	–2	32	0	1	3	0	110	6.4
D	23	Paul Mara	T.B.	46	6	10	16	–17	40	2	0	1	0	58	10.3
			PHX	16	0	4	4	1	14	0	0	0	0	20	0.0
			TOTAL	62	6	14	20	–16	54	2	0	1	0	78	7.7
L	18	Mika Alatalo	PHX	70	7	12	19	1	22	0	0	1	0	64	10.9
C	17 *	Ladislav Nagy	STL	40	8	8	16	–2	20	2	0	2	0	59	13.6
			PHX	6	0	1	1	0	2	0	0	0	0	5	0.0
			TOTAL	46	8	9	17	–2	22	2	0	2	0	64	12.5
D	4 *	Ossi Vaananen	PHX	81	4	12	16	9	90	0	0	2	0	69	5.8
D	3	Keith Carney	PHX	82	2	14	16	15	86	0	0	0	0	65	3.1
C	8	Daniel Briere	PHX	30	11	4	15	–2	12	9	0	1	0	43	25.6
C	20 *	Wyatt Smith	PHX	42	3	7	10	7	13	0	1	0	0	40	7.5
D	15	Radoslav Suchy	PHX	72	0	10	10	1	22	0	0	0	0	33	0.0
C	26	Mike Sullivan	PHX	72	5	4	9	–6	16	0	3	0	0	59	8.5
D	2	Todd Simpson	FLA	25	1	3	4	0	74	0	0	1	0	26	3.8
			PHX	13	0	1	1	–4	12	0	0	0	0	9	0.0
			TOTAL	38	1	4	5	–4	86	0	0	1	0	35	2.9
D	6	Joel Bouchard	PHX	32	1	2	3	–8	22	0	0	0	0	26	3.8
G	42 *	Robert Esche	PHX	25	0	3	3	0	2	0	0	0	0	0	0.0
G	1	Sean Burke	PHX	62	0	1	1	0	16	0	0	0	0	0	0.0
L	31 *	Brad Ralph	PHX	1	0	0	0	0	0	0	0	0	0	0	0.0
D	2 *	David Cullen	PHX	2	0	0	0	1	0	0	0	0	0	0	0.0
R	14 *	Tavis Hansen	PHX	7	0	0	0	–1	4	0	0	0	0	2	0.0
L	29	Louie DeBrusk	PHX	39	0	0	0	–5	79	0	0	0	0	12	0.0

Goaltending

No.	Goaltender	GPI	Mins	Avg	W	L	T	EN	SO	GA	SA	S%
1	Sean Burke	62	3644	2.27	25	22	13	5	4	138	1766	.922
42	* Robert Esche	25	1350	3.02	10	8	4	1	2	68	657	.896
	Totals	**82**	**5010**	**2.54**	**35**	**30**	**17**	**6**	**6**	**212**	**2429**	**.913**

Coach

FRANCIS, BOB
Coach, Phoenix Coyotes. Born in North Battleford, Sask., December 5, 1958.

The Phoenix Coyotes named Bob Francis as the team's head coach on June 16, 1999. Francis became the 14th head coach in franchise history and the third since moving to Phoenix in 1996.

Francis joined the Coyotes after two successful seasons as an assistant coach with the Boston Bruins. The son of former NHL great Emile Francis joined the Bruins as an assistant on June 27, 1997. He had previously spent two seasons in the Boston organization as head coach of the Bruins' AHL affiliate in Providence.

Francis began his coaching career with the Calgary Flames organization in the 1986-87 season, first as a player/assistant coach with Calgary's IHL affiliate in Salt Lake City. Francis helped guide the Golden Eagles to the IHL championship, winning the Turner Cup that season and successfully defending its title the following year with Francis serving as a full-time assistant coach. In 1989-90, Francis became the Golden Eagles' head coach and held that position for four seasons. The highlight of his coaching career at Salt Lake City was a 50-win season during the 1990-91 campaign. When Calgary moved their development team to Saint John (AHL) in 1993-94, Francis moved as well and served as their head coach before joining Providence.

Before his move to the coaching ranks, Francis played four years of college hockey at the University of New Hampshire (ECAC). Francis spent most of his professional career at the minor-league level though he did play 14 NHL games with Detroit during the 1982-83 season.

Ossi Vaananen represented Finland at the 1999 World Junior Championships. He played his first professional season in his homeland in 1999-2000 and made a promising NHL debut last season.

Coaching Record

		Regular Season				Playoffs		
Season	Team	Games	W	L	T	Games	W	L
1989-90	Salt Lake (IHL)	82	37	36	9	10	5	5
1990-91	Salt Lake (IHL)	83	50	28	5	4	0	4
1991-92	Salt Lake (IHL)	82	33	40	9	5	1	4
1992-93	Salt Lake (IHL)	82	38	39	5	....	....	....
1993-94	Saint John (AHL)	80	37	33	10	7	3	4
1994-95	Saint John (AHL)	80	27	40	13	5	1	4
1995-96	Providence (AHL)	80	30	40	10	4	1	3
1996-97	Providence (AHL)	80	35	40	5	10	4	6
1999-2000	**Phoenix (NHL)**	**82**	**39**	**35**	**8**	**5**	**1**	**4**
2000-01	**Phoenix (NHL)**	**82**	**35**	**30**	**17**	....	....	....
	NHL Totals	**164**	**74**	**65**	**25**	**5**	**1**	**4**

Coaching History

Tom McVie and Bill Sutherland, 1979-80; Tom McVie, Bill Sutherland and Mike Smith, 1980-81; Tom Watt, 1981-82, 1982-83; Tom Watt and Barry Long, 1983-84; Barry Long, 1984-85; Barry Long and John Ferguson, 1985-86; Dan Maloney, 1986-87, 1987-88; Dan Maloney and Rick Bowness, 1988-89; Bob Murdoch, 1989-90, 1990-91; John Paddock, 1991-92 to 1993-94; John Paddock and Terry Simpson, 1994-95; Terry Simpson, 1995-96; Don Hay, 1996-97; Jim Schoenfeld, 1997-98, 1998-99; Bob Francis, 1999-2000 to date.

Club Records

Team

(Figures in brackets for season records are games played; records for fewest points, wins, ties, losses, goals, goals against are for 70 or more games)

Most Points .... 96 — 1984-85 (80)
Most Wins .... 43 — 1984-85 (80)
Most Ties .... 17 — 2000-01 (82)
Most Losses .... 57 — 1980-81 (80)
Most Goals .... 358 — 1984-85 (80)
Most Goals Against .... 400 — 1980-81 (80)
Fewest Points .... 32 — 1980-81 (80)
Fewest Wins .... 9 — 1980-81 (80)
Fewest Ties .... 6 — 1995-96 (82)
Fewest Losses .... 27 — 1984-85 (80), 2000-01 (82)
Fewest Goals .... 205 — 1998-99 (82)
Fewest Goals Against .... 197 — 1998-99 (82)

Longest Winning Streak
Overall .... 9 — Mar. 8-27/85
Home .... 9 — Dec. 27/92-Jan. 23/93
Away .... 8 — Feb. 25-Apr. 6/85

Longest Undefeated Streak
Overall .... 14 — Oct. 25-Nov. 28/98 (12 wins, 2 ties)
Home .... 11 — Dec. 23/83-Feb. 5/84 (6 wins, 5 ties), Oct. 15-Dec. 20/98 (10 wins, 1 tie)
Away .... 9 — Feb. 25-Apr. 7/85 (8 wins, 1 tie)

Longest Losing Streak
Overall .... 10 — Nov. 30-Dec. 20/80, Feb. 6-25/94
Home .... 5 — Oct. 29-Nov. 13/93, Mar. 13-23/00
Away .... 13 — Jan. 26-Apr. 14/94

Longest Winless Streak
Overall .... *30 — Oct. 19-Dec. 20/80 (23 losses, 7 ties)
Home .... 14 — Oct. 19-Dec. 14/80 (9 losses, 5 ties)
Away .... 18 — Oct. 10-Dec. 20/80 (16 losses, 2 ties)

Most Shutouts, Season .... 9 — 1998-99 (82)
Most PIM, Season .... 2,278 — 1987-88 (80)
Most Goals, Game .... 12 — Feb. 25/85 (Wpg. 12 at NYR 5)

Individual

Most Seasons .... 14 — Thomas Steen
Most Games .... 950 — Thomas Steen
Most Goals, Career .... 379 — Dale Hawerchuk
Most Assists, Career .... 553 — Thomas Steen
Most Points, Career .... 929 — Dale Hawerchuk (379G, 550A)
Most PIM, Career .... 1,508 — Keith Tkachuk
Most Shutouts, Career .... 21 — Nikolai Khabibulin
Longest Consecutive Games Streak .... 475 — Dale Hawerchuk (Dec. 19/82-Dec. 10/88)
Most Goals, Season .... 76 — Teemu Selanne (1992-93)
Most Assists, Season .... 79 — Phil Housley (1992-93)
Most Points, Season .... 132 — Teemu Selanne (1992-93; 76G, 56A)
Most PIM, Season .... 347 — Tie Domi (1993-94)
Most Points, Defenseman, Season .... 97 — Phil Housley (1992-93; 18G, 79A)
Most Points, Center, Season .... 130 — Dale Hawerchuk (1984-85; 53G, 77A)
Most Points, Right Wing, Season .... 132 — Teemu Selanne (1992-93; 76G, 56A)
Most Points, Left Wing, Season .... 98 — Keith Tkachuk (1995-96; 50G, 48A)
Most Points, Rookie, Season .... *132 — Teemu Selanne (1992-93; 76G, 56A)
Most Shutouts, Season .... 8 — Nikolai Khabibulin (1998-99)
Most Goals, Game .... 5 — Willy Lindstrom (Mar. 2/82), Alexei Zhamnov (Apr. 1/95)
Most Assists, Game .... 5 — Dale Hawerchuk (Mar. 6/84, Mar. 18/89, Mar. 4/90), Phil Housley (Jan. 18/93), Keith Tkachuk (Feb. 23/01)
Most Points, Game .... 6 — Willy Lindstrom (Mar. 2/82; 5G, 1A), Dale Hawerchuk (Dec. 14/83; 3G, 3A, Mar. 5/88; 2G, 4A, Mar. 18/89; 1G, 5A), Thomas Steen (Oct. 24/84; 2G, 4A), Ed Olczyk (Dec. 21/91; 2G, 4A)

* NHL Record.
Records include Winnipeg Jets, 1979-80 through 1995-96.

General Managers' History

John Ferguson, 1979-80 to 1987-88; John Ferguson and Mike Smith, 1988-89; Mike Smith, 1989-90 to 1992-93; Mike Smith and John Paddock, 1993-94; John Paddock, 1994-95, 1995-96; John Paddock and Bobby Smith, 1996-97; Bobby Smith, 1997-98 to 1999-2000; Bobby Smith and Cliff Fletcher, 2000-01; Cliff Fletcher, 2001-02.

Winnipeg Jets Retired Numbers

9	Bobby Hull	1972-1980
25	Thomas Steen	1981-1995

Captains' History

Lars-Erik Sjoberg, 1979-80; Morris Lukowich, 1980-81; Dave Christian, 1981-82; Dave Christian and Lucien DeBlois, 1982-83; Lucien DeBlois, 1983-84; Dale Hawerchuk, 1984-85 to 1988-89; Randy Carlyle, Dale Hawerchuk and Thomas Steen (tri-captains), 1989-90; Randy Carlyle and Thomas Steen (co-captains), 1990-91; Troy Murray, 1991-92; Troy Murray and Dean Kennedy, 1992-93; Dean Kennedy and Keith Tkachuk, 1993-94; Keith Tkachuk, 1994-95; Kris King, 1995-96; Keith Tkachuk, 1996-97 to 2000-01.

All-time Record vs. Other Clubs

Regular Season

	At Home								On Road								Total							
	GP	W	L	T	OL	GF	GA	PTS	GP	W	L	T	OL	GF	GA	PTS	GP	W	L	T	OL	GF	GA	PTS
Anaheim	18	8	9	1	0	58	58	17	19	7	9	2	1	52	54	17	37	15	18	3	1	110	112	34
Atlanta	2	2	0	0	0	9	3	4	1	1	0	0	0	3	2	2	3	3	0	0	0	12	5	6
Boston	28	12	14	2	0	98	100	26	28	4	21	3	0	87	129	11	56	16	35	5	0	185	229	37
Buffalo	27	13	12	2	0	86	88	28	28	3	20	5	0	71	121	11	55	16	32	7	0	157	209	39
Calgary	64	31	22	11	0	247	219	73	65	20	36	9	0	212	284	49	129	51	58	20	0	459	503	122
Carolina	30	13	14	2	1	106	110	29	27	9	12	6	0	84	99	24	57	22	26	8	1	190	209	53
Chicago	44	25	15	4	0	153	137	54	42	10	25	7	0	118	175	27	86	35	40	11	0	271	312	81
Colorado	34	13	15	6	0	127	127	32	35	15	16	4	0	125	123	34	69	28	31	10	0	252	250	66
Columbus	2	1	0	1	0	4	3	3	2	0	2	0	0	3	7	0	4	1	2	1	0	7	10	3
Dallas	46	20	23	3	0	149	157	43	47	17	23	7	0	143	176	41	93	37	46	10	0	292	333	84
Detroit	43	16	15	12	0	135	137	44	45	17	22	6	0	157	181	40	88	33	37	18	0	292	318	84
Edmonton	65	27	34	4	0	265	290	58	66	19	40	6	1	218	290	45	131	46	74	10	1	483	580	103
Florida	8	3	3	2	0	18	23	8	6	3	3	0	0	16	21	6	14	6	6	2	0	34	44	14
Los Angeles	68	33	25	10	0	273	231	76	66	32	23	11	0	268	264	75	134	65	48	21	0	541	495	151
Minnesota	2	2	0	0	0	6	1	4	2	1	0	1	0	4	2	3	4	3	0	1	0	10	3	7
Montreal	27	9	11	7	0	89	104	25	28	3	24	1	0	63	139	7	55	12	35	8	0	152	243	32
Nashville	6	3	2	0	1	20	19	7	6	2	2	1	1	19	18	6	12	5	4	1	2	39	37	13
New Jersey	29	20	6	3	0	110	77	43	27	10	11	6	0	82	89	26	56	30	17	9	0	192	166	69
NY Islanders	28	10	14	4	0	88	99	24	29	8	13	8	0	88	111	24	57	18	27	12	0	176	210	48
NY Rangers	29	12	13	4	0	100	98	28	28	9	17	2	0	100	125	20	57	21	30	6	0	200	223	48
Ottawa	8	3	4	1	0	30	32	7	9	6	2	1	0	33	21	13	17	9	6	2	0	63	53	20
Philadelphia	28	11	15	2	0	87	99	24	29	8	21	0	0	79	125	16	57	19	36	2	0	166	224	40
Pittsburgh	28	12	13	3	0	103	99	27	28	8	20	0	0	79	118	16	56	20	33	3	0	182	217	43
St. Louis	45	22	17	6	0	147	141	50	44	12	22	10	0	121	159	34	89	34	39	16	0	268	300	84
San Jose	27	15	8	3	1	85	70	34	24	10	12	2	0	78	83	22	51	25	20	5	1	163	153	56
Tampa Bay	9	6	3	0	0	28	19	12	8	5	3	0	0	30	24	10	17	11	6	0	0	58	43	22
Toronto	38	20	12	6	0	157	137	46	41	21	18	2	0	155	146	44	79	41	30	8	0	312	283	90
Vancouver	63	31	23	9	0	238	226	71	66	19	38	9	0	191	249	47	129	50	61	18	0	429	475	118
Washington	28	14	7	7	0	104	99	35	28	6	17	4	1	78	116	17	56	20	24	11	1	182	215	52
Totals	**874**	**407**	**349**	**115**	**3**	**3120**	**3003**	**932**	**874**	**285**	**472**	**113**	**4**	**2757**	**3451**	**687**	**1748**	**692**	**821**	**228**	**7**	**5877**	**6454**	**1619**

Playoffs

	Series	W	L	GP	W	L	T	GF	GA	Last Mtg.	Round	Result
Anaheim	1	0	1	7	3	4	0	17	17	1997	CQF	L 3-4
Calgary	3	2	1	13	7	6	0	45	43	1987	DSF	W 4-2
Colorado	1	0	1	5	1	4	0	10	17	2000	CQF	L 1-4
Detroit	2	0	2	12	4	8	0	28	44	1998	CQF	L 2-4
Edmonton	6	0	6	26	4	22	0	75	120	1990	DSF	L 3-4
St. Louis	2	0	2	11	4	7	0	29	39	1999	CQF	L 3-4
Vancouver	2	0	2	13	5	8	0	34	50	1993	DSF	L 2-4
Totals	**17**	**2**	**15**	**87**	**28**	**59**	**0**	**238**	**330**			

Playoff Results 2001-1997

Year	Round	Opponent	Result	GF	GA
2000	CQF	Colorado	L 1-4	10	17
1999	CQF	St. Louis	L 3-4	16	19
1998	CQF	Detroit	L 2-4	18	24
1997	CQF	Anaheim	L 3-4	17	17

Abbreviations: Round: CQF – conference quarter-final; **DSF** – division semi-final.

Calgary totals include Atlanta Flames, 1979-80.
Colorado totals include Quebec, 1979-80 to 1994-95.
New Jersey totals include Colorado Rockies, 1979-80 to 1981-82.
Carolina totals include Hartford, 1979-80 to 1996-97.
Dallas totals include Minnesota North Stars, 1979-80 to 1992-93.

2000-01 Results

Oct.	5	St. Louis	4-1		12	at Toronto	2-3
	7	Minnesota	4-1		13	at Montreal	2-5
	12	at San Jose	1-2		15	St. Louis	3-1
	14	Philadelphia	6-3		17	Pittsburgh	5-4
	15	at Los Angeles	6-5		19	at Anaheim	4-3
	18	Florida	2-1*		21	Dallas	5-2
	21	at Vancouver	3-2*		23	at Calgary	4-2
	22	at Edmonton	3-3		24	at Vancouver	2-6
	24	at Calgary	2-2		26	at Edmonton	1-1
	27	at Dallas	4-2		29	Nashville	2-5
	28	Los Angeles	3-1	**Feb.**	1	Anaheim	2-4
	30	at Colorado	4-0		7	Carolina	1-2*
Nov.	1	at Anaheim	1-1		9	Edmonton	2-0
	3	Dallas	2-2		11	Chicago	3-2
	7	at Los Angeles	3-3		13	at Tampa Bay	5-2
	8	Detroit	2-4		14	at Florida	3-4
	11	at Columbus	1-2		16	at Carolina	2-0
	12	at NY Rangers	2-0		18	Calgary	1-4
	14	at Washington	2-2		21	Columbus	3-2
	16	Colorado	6-3		23	at Buffalo	7-3
	18	Anaheim	2-6		25	at Detroit	3-6
	21	Chicago	1-4		27	at Boston	4-7
	25	at St. Louis	1-5		28	at Columbus	2-5
	26	at Philadelphia	2-1	**Mar.**	2	Detroit	2-2
	29	at Colorado	1-2		4	Colorado	0-5
	30	Minnesota	2-0		6	Nashville	5-1
Dec.	2	Dallas	2-5		8	Vancouver	3-2*
	6	Vancouver	1-1		10	Montreal	3-3
	10	Columbus	1-1		14	New Jersey	2-3
	14	Tampa Bay	3-2		16	at Dallas	1-1
	16	San Jose	1-2*		17	at Nashville	1-4
	20	Calgary	4-2		19	at Los Angeles	2-6
	22	Atlanta	5-1		21	Ottawa	2-5
	27	at Chicago	1-1		24	Edmonton	7-4
	29	at Minnesota	2-2		25	NY Islanders	2-2
	30	at St. Louis	1-2		28	at Minnesota	2-0
Jan.	1	San Jose	2-3		29	at Nashville	3-4*
	4	NY Rangers	3-1		31	San Jose	3-1
	6	at NY Islanders	2-1	**Apr.**	3	Los Angeles	2-2
	9	at Detroit	2-2		5	at San Jose	0-3
	10	at New Jersey	1-5		6	at Anaheim	5-2

* – Overtime

Entry Draft Selections 2001-1987

2001

Pick	
11	Fredrik Sjostrom
31	Matthew Spiller
45	Martin Podlesak
78	Beat Forster
148	David Klema
180	Scott Polaski
210	Steve Belanger
243	Frantisek Lukes
273	Severin Blindenbacher

2000

Pick	
19	Krys Kolanos
53	Alexander Tatarinov
85	Ramzi Abid
160	Nate Kiser
186	Brent Gauvreau
217	Igor Samoilov
249	Sami Venalainen
281	Peter Fabus

1999

Pick	
15	Scott Kelman
19	Kirill Safronov
53	Brad Ralph
71	Jason Jaspers
116	Ryan Lauzon
123	Preston Mizzi
168	Erik Lewerstrom
234	Goran Bezina
262	Alexei Litvinenko

1998

Pick	
14	Patrick Desrochers
43	Ossi Vaananen
73	Pat O'Leary
100	Ryan Vanbuskirk
115	Jay Leach
116	Josh Blackburn
129	Robert Schnabel
160	Rickard Wallin
187	Erik Westrum
214	Justin Hansen

1997

Pick	
43	Juha Gustafsson
96	Scott McCallum
123	Curtis Suter
151	Robert Francz
207	Alexander Andreyev
233	Wyatt Smith

1996

Pick	
11	Dan Focht
24	Daniel Briere
62	Per-Anton Lundstrom
119	Richard Lintner
139	Robert Esche
174	Trevor Letowski
200	Nicholas Lent
226	Marc-Etienne Hubert

1995

Pick	
7	Shane Doan
32	Marc Chouinard
34	Jason Doig
67	Brad Isbister
84	Justin Kurtz
121	Brian Elder
136	Sylvain Daigle
162	Paul Traynor
188	Jaroslav Obsut
189	Fredrik Loven
214	Rob Deciantis

1994

Pick	
30	Deron Quint
56	Dorian Anneck
58	Tavis Hansen
82	Steve Cheredaryk
108	Craig Mills
143	Steve Vezina
146	Chris Kibermanis
186	Ramil Saifullin
212	Henrik Smangs
238	Mike Mader
264	Jason Issel

1993

Pick	
15	Mats Lindgren
31	Scott Langkow
43	Alexei Budayev
79	Ruslan Batyrshin
93	Ravil Gusmanov
119	Larry Courville
145	Michal Grosek
171	Martin Woods
197	Adrian Murray
217	Vladimir Potapov
223	Ilja Stashenkov
228	Harijs Vitolinsh
285	Russ Hewson

1992

Pick	
17	Sergei Bautin
27	Boris Mironov
60	Jeremy Stevenson
84	Mark Visheau
132	Alexander Alexeyev
155	Artur Oktyabrev
156	Andrei Raisky
204	Nikolai Khabibulin
228	Yevgeny Garanin
229	Teemu Numminen
252	Andrei Karpovstev
254	Ivan Vologzhaninov

1991

Pick	
5	Aaron Ward
49	Dmitri Filimonov
91	Juha Ylonen
99	Yan Kaminsky
115	Jeff Sebastian
159	Jeff Ricciardi
181	Sean Gauthier
203	Igor Ulanov
225	Jason Jennings
247	Sergei Sorokin

1990

Pick	
19	Keith Tkachuk
35	Mike Muller
74	Roman Meluzin
75	Scott Levins
77	Alexei Zhamnov
98	Craig Martin
119	Daniel Jardemyr
140	John Lilley
161	Henrik Andersson
182	Rauli Raitanen
203	Mika Alatalo
224	Sergei Selyanin
245	Keith Morris

1989

Pick	
4	Stu Barnes
25	Dan Ratushny
46	Jason Cirone
62	Kris Draper
64	Mark Brownschidle
69	Allain Roy
109	Dan Bylsma
130	Pekka Peltola
131	Doug Evans
151	Jim Solly
172	Stephane Gauvin
193	Joe Larson
214	Bradley Podiak
235	Evgeny Davydov
240	Sergei Kharin

1988

Pick	
10	Teemu Selanne
31	Russell Romaniuk
52	Stephane Beauregard
73	Brian Hunt
94	Tony Joseph
101	Benoit Lebeau
115	Ronald Jones
127	Markus Akerblom
136	Jukka Marttila
157	Mark Smith
178	Mike Helber
199	Pavel Kostichkin
220	Kevin Heise
241	Kyle Galloway

1987

Pick	
16	Bryan Marchment
37	Patrik Ericksson
79	Don McLennan
96	Ken Gernander
100	Darrin Amundson
121	Joe Harwell
142	Todd Hartje
163	Markku Kyllonen
184	Jim Fernholz
226	Roger Rougelot
247	Hans Goran Elo

General Manager

FLETCHER, CLIFF
General Manager, Phoenix Coyotes.
Born in Montreal, Que., August 16, 1935.

Cliff Fletcher joined the Phoenix Coyotes during the 2000-01 season after working the previous two seasons as a senior advisor to the general manager of the Tampa Bay Lightning. A Stanley Cup winner with the Calgary Flames in 1989, Fletcher's NHL experience reaches back to 1967 when he became the Eastern Canada scout for the St. Louis Blues. He later became the club's assistant general manager.

Fletcher's hockey career began with the Montreal Junior Canadiens, and he scouted for 10 years in Sam Pollock's system. After his stay in St. Louis, Fletcher oversaw the beginning of the Atlanta Flames franchise in 1972. He was the club's general manager for 19 years, organizing the transfer of the team to Calgary in 1980. In the Flames' 11 seasons in Calgary with Fletcher at the helm, the club won two Presidents' Trophies, two Campbell Conference titles and two Smythe Division titles in addition to a Stanley Cup title. He also served as general manager of Team Canada in the 1981 Canada Cup.

From 1991 to 1997, Fletcher served as the chief operating officer, president and general manager of the Toronto Maple Leafs. In just his second season with the club, the Maple Leafs set team records with 44 wins and 99 points. Under Fletcher's direction, the Maple Leafs advanced to the Conference Championships in 1993 and 1994.

Fletcher was the first general manager to sign and bring a player from the Soviet Union to play in the NHL with official consent when Sergei Priakin joined the Flames in 1988.

Club Directory

America West Arena

Phoenix Coyotes
ALLTEL Ice Den
9375 E. Bell Road
Scottsdale, AZ 85260
Phone **480/473-5600**
FAX 480/473-5699
www.PhoenixCoyotes.com
Capacity: 16,210

Executive

Chairman and CEO	Steve Ellman
Managing Partner	Wayne Gretzky
President & Partner	Shawn Hunter
Executive VP & General Manager	Cliff Fletcher
Senior VP/Chief Financial Officer	Mark Peterson
Exec. Assistant to the President	Lisa Mardeusz
Exec. Assistant, Hockey Operations	Lesa Guth

Hockey Operations

Assistant General Manager	Laurence Gilman
Vice President of Scouting & Player Personnel	Dave Draper
Director of Amateur Scouting	Vaughn Karpan
Professional Scouts	Tom Kurvers, Warren Rychel
Director of Hockey Information	Igor Kuperman
Head Coach	Bob Francis
Assistant Coaches	Rick Bowness, Pat Conacher
Goaltending Coach	Benoit Allaire
Strength & Conditioning Coordinator	Stieg Theander
Amateur Scouts	Connie Broden, Shane Churla, Pelle Eklund, Keith Gretzky, Paul Henry, Blair Mackasey, Blair Reid, Evzen Slansky, Boris Yemeljanov
Athletic Therapist	Gord Hart
Massage Therapist	Jukka Nieminen
Equipment Manager	Stan Wilson
Assistant Equipment Managers	Tony Silva, Jason Rudee
Video Coordinator	Steve Peters
Team Physician	Matt Maddox, D.O.
Team Internist	Robert Luberto, D.O.
Team Dentists	Dr. Rick Lawson, Dr. Lawrence Emmott
Springfield Falcons (AHL) Head Coach	Marc Potvin
Springfield Falcons (AHL) Assistant Coach	Norm Maciver

Communications

Vice President of Media & Player Relations	Richard Nairn
Director of Media Relations	Rick Braunstein
Publications & Media Relations Coordinator	Ryan Lichtenfels

Broadcasting

TV Play-by-Play	Doug McLeod
TV Color Commentator	Charlie Simmer
Radio Play-by-Play	Curt Keilback
Radio Color Commentator	Jim Johnson
Broadcast Coordinator	Graham Taylor

Business Development

Vice President of Sales	Joe Levy
Director of Business Development	Vaibhav Gupta
Director of Suite Sales	Renee Tauer
Suite Sales Coordinator	TBA
Business Development Intern	Lauren Hill

Community Relations

Vice President of Communications/ Exec. Director of Coyotes Charities	Susan Kricun
Community/NHL Alumni Liaison	Jocelyn Lemieux
Community Relations Manager	Heather Bennett
Community Relations Assistant	Kelly Hilgart

Corporate Sales and Service

Director of Corporate Sales	Cullen Maxey
Manager of Corporate Sales	Kelly Staley
Corporate Account Executives	Justin Kemp, Jason Levy, Ashley Ritt, Amy Robertson

Finance and Administration

Controller	Joe Leibfried
Assistant Controller	Larry Silver
Payroll Administrator	Cheri Sedor
Accounting Assistant	Julie deWit
Administrative Assistant	Mary Jane DeBiasio
Receptionist	Tomi Stern

Marketing

Vice President of Marketing	Dave Groff
Director of Marketing	Brett Rogers
Marketing Coordinator	Jason Shughart
Marketing Assistant	TBA
Game Operations Coordinator	Jen Town
Manager of Fan Development	Brian Wilkinson

Ticket Sales and Service

Director of Ticket Operations	Dave Felsen
Box Office Manager	Kevin Prebil
Box Office Assistant	Karen Sabo
Director of Ticket Sales	Jim Willits
Ticket Sales Manager	Scott Newhouse
Account Executives	John Allen, Cortney Guinn, Randy Just, Neils Lund, E.A. McDonough, Tiffany Rojas, Tom Schimpf, Mike Wellington
Fan Relations Representatives	Adam Cresswell, Sarah Delp, Tudor Waddell
Sales Associate	Dan Schwimmer

Miscellaneous

Training Camp	Scottsdale, Arizona
Cable Television Station	FOX SPORTS NET Arizona
Broadcast Television Stations	KTVK (Ch. 3), KASW (WB-61)
Radio Stations	KDKB 93.3 FM, KDUS 1060 AM

Pittsburgh Penguins

2000-01 Results: 42W-28L-9T-3OTL 96PTS. Third, Atlantic Division

Year-by-Year Record

		Home				Road				Overall								
Season	GP	W	L	T	OL	W	L	T	OL	W	L	T	OL	GF	GA	Pts.	Finished	Playoff Result
2000-01	82	24	15	2	0	18	13	7	3	42	28	9	3	281	256	96	3rd, Atlantic Div.	Lost Conf. Championship
1999-2000	82	23	11	7	0	14	20	1	6	37	31	8	6	241	236	88	3rd, Atlantic Div.	Lost Conf. Semi-Final
1998-99	82	21	10	10	...	17	20	4	...	38	30	14	...	242	225	90	3rd, Atlantic Div.	Lost Conf. Semi-Final
1997-98	82	21	10	10	...	19	14	8	...	40	24	18	...	228	188	98	1st, Northeast Div.	Lost Conf. Quarter-Final
1996-97	82	25	11	5	...	13	25	3	...	38	36	8	...	285	280	84	2nd, Northeast Div.	Lost Conf. Quarter-Final
1995-96	82	32	9	0	...	17	20	4	...	49	29	4	...	362	284	102	1st, Northeast Div.	Lost Conf. Championship
1994-95	48	18	5	1	...	11	11	2	...	29	16	3	...	181	158	61	2nd, Northeast Div.	Lost Conf. Semi-Final
1993-94	84	25	9	8	...	19	18	5	...	44	27	13	...	299	285	101	1st, Northeast Div.	Lost Conf. Quarter-Final
1992-93	84	32	6	4	...	24	15	3	...	56	21	7	...	367	268	119	1st, Patrick Div.	Lost Div. Final
1991-92	**80**	**21**	**13**	**6**	**...**	**18**	**19**	**3**	**...**	**39**	**32**	**9**	**...**	**343**	**308**	**87**	**3rd, Patrick Div.**	**Won Stanley Cup**
1990-91	**80**	**25**	**12**	**3**	**...**	**16**	**21**	**3**	**...**	**41**	**33**	**6**	**...**	**342**	**305**	**88**	**1st, Patrick Div.**	**Won Stanley Cup**
1989-90	80	22	15	3	...	10	25	5	...	32	40	8	...	318	359	72	5th, Patrick Div.	Out of Playoffs
1988-89	80	24	13	3	...	16	20	4	...	40	33	7	...	347	349	87	2nd, Patrick Div.	Lost Div. Final
1987-88	80	22	12	6	...	14	23	3	...	36	35	9	...	319	316	81	6th, Patrick Div.	Out of Playoffs
1986-87	80	19	15	6	...	11	23	6	...	30	38	12	...	297	290	72	5th, Patrick Div.	Out of Playoffs
1985-86	80	20	15	5	...	14	23	3	...	34	38	8	...	313	305	76	5th, Patrick Div.	Out of Playoffs
1984-85	80	17	20	3	...	7	31	2	...	24	51	5	...	276	385	53	6th, Patrick Div.	Out of Playoffs
1983-84	80	7	29	4	...	9	29	2	...	16	58	6	...	254	390	38	6th, Patrick Div.	Out of Playoffs
1982-83	80	14	22	4	...	4	31	5	...	18	53	9	...	257	394	45	6th, Patrick Div.	Out of Playoffs
1981-82	80	21	11	8	...	10	25	5	...	31	36	13	...	310	337	75	4th, Patrick Div.	Lost Div. Semi-Final
1980-81	80	21	16	3	...	9	21	10	...	30	37	13	...	302	345	73	3rd, Norris Div.	Lost Prelim. Round
1979-80	80	20	13	7	...	10	24	6	...	30	37	13	...	251	303	73	3rd, Norris Div.	Lost Prelim. Round
1978-79	80	23	12	5	...	13	19	8	...	36	31	13	...	281	279	85	2nd, Norris Div.	Lost Quarter-Final
1977-78	80	16	15	9	...	9	22	9	...	25	37	18	...	254	321	68	4th, Norris Div.	Out of Playoffs
1976-77	80	22	12	6	...	12	21	7	...	34	33	13	...	240	252	81	3rd, Norris Div.	Lost Prelim. Round
1975-76	80	23	11	6	...	12	22	6	...	35	33	12	...	339	303	82	3rd, Norris Div.	Lost Prelim. Round
1974-75	80	25	5	10	...	12	23	5	...	37	28	15	...	326	289	89	3rd, Norris Div.	Lost Quarter-Final
1973-74	78	15	18	6	...	13	23	3	...	28	41	9	...	242	273	65	5th, West Div.	Out of Playoffs
1972-73	78	24	11	4	...	8	26	5	...	32	37	9	...	257	265	73	5th, West Div.	Out of Playoffs
1971-72	78	18	15	6	...	8	23	8	...	26	38	14	...	220	258	66	4th, West Div.	Lost Quarter-Final
1970-71	78	18	12	9	...	3	25	11	...	21	37	20	...	221	240	62	6th, West Div.	Out of Playoffs
1969-70	76	17	13	8	...	9	25	4	...	26	38	12	...	182	238	64	2nd, West Div.	Lost Semi-Final
1968-69	76	12	20	6	...	8	25	5	...	20	45	11	...	189	252	51	5th, West Div.	Out of Playoffs
1967-68	74	15	12	10	...	12	22	3	...	27	34	13	...	195	216	67	5th, West Div.	Out of Playoffs

2001-02 Schedule

Oct.	Wed.	3	Colorado		Tue.	8	Boston
	Sat.	6	Anaheim		Thu.	10	at Buffalo
	Wed.	10	NY Islanders		Sat.	12	St. Louis*
	Sun.	14	at Buffalo*		Tue.	15	at Vancouver
	Tue.	16	Ottawa		Thu.	17	at Calgary
	Thu.	18	at Ottawa		Sat.	19	at Edmonton
	Sat.	20	at St. Louis		Mon.	21	Philadelphia
	Tue.	23	at Atlanta		Wed.	23	Tampa Bay
	Wed.	24	Dallas		Thu.	24	at NY Islanders
	Sat.	27	at Toronto		Sat.	26	Atlanta*
	Sun.	28	Florida		Tue.	29	at Philadelphia
	Wed.	31	at Philadelphia		Wed.	30	San Jose*
Nov.	Thu.	1	Toronto	**Feb.**	Tue.	5	at Carolina
	Sat.	3	Tampa Bay		Thu.	7	at Montreal
	Tue.	6	at Carolina		Sat.	9	New Jersey*
	Wed.	7	at Florida		Sun.	10	at NY Rangers*
	Sat.	10	at Tampa Bay		Tue.	12	at Ottawa
	Tue.	13	at New Jersey		Wed.	27	Los Angeles
	Wed.	14	NY Islanders		Thu.	28	at Columbus
	Sat.	17	NY Rangers	**Mar.**	Sat.	2	Detroit*
	Wed.	21	Vancouver		Mon.	4	at NY Islanders
	Fri.	23	at Nashville		Tue.	5	Florida
	Sat.	24	Buffalo		Thu.	7	Carolina
	Tue.	27	New Jersey		Sat.	9	NY Rangers*
	Thu.	29	at San Jose		Mon.	11	Columbus
Dec.	Sat.	1	at Phoenix		Wed.	13	at Anaheim
	Tue.	4	at Toronto		Sat.	16	at Los Angeles*
	Thu.	6	at Boston		Mon.	18	at Atlanta
	Sat.	8	Atlanta		Wed.	20	Phoenix
	Tue.	11	at Washington		Sat.	23	Philadelphia*
	Wed.	12	Boston		Sun.	24	Washington
	Fri.	14	Minnesota		Wed.	27	New Jersey
	Sun.	16	Carolina*		Sat.	30	at Montreal
	Wed.	19	Montreal	**Apr.**	Mon.	1	Montreal
	Fri.	21	Washington		Wed.	3	at Florida
	Sat.	22	at Washington		Thu.	4	at Tampa Bay
	Wed.	26	at New Jersey		Sat.	6	at Philadelphia
	Sat.	29	Ottawa		Mon.	8	at NY Rangers
Jan.	Thu.	3	at NY Islanders		Wed.	10	Buffalo
	Sat.	5	NY Rangers*		Fri.	12	Toronto
	Sun.	6	at Chicago		Sat.	13	at Boston

* Denotes afternoon game.

Franchise date: June 5, 1967

ATLANTIC DIVISION

35th NHL Season

Pittsburgh acquired Johan Hedberg from San Jose on March 12, 2001 and summoned him from the Manitoba Moose to make his NHL debut. Hedberg went 7-1-1 in nine games down the stretch and starred for the Penguins in the playoffs.

2001-02 Player Personnel

FORWARDS	HT	WT	S	Place of Birth	Date	2000-01 Club
BEECH, Kris	6-2	178	L	Salmon Arm, B.C.	2/5/81	Washington-Cgy (WHL)
DOME, Robert	6-0	210	L	Skalica, Czech.	1/29/79	HCO Trinec-HC Kladno
FADRNY, Jan	6-0	182	R	Brno, Czech.	6/14/80	Brandon-Kelowna
GYORI, Dylan	5-11	190	L	Rimbey, Alta.	2/20/79	Wilkes-Barre
HRDINA, Jan	6-0	200	R	Hradec Kralove, Czech.	2/5/76	Pittsburgh
KOSTOPOULOS, Tom	6-0	205	R	Mississauga, Ont.	1/24/79	Wilkes-Barre
KOVALEV, Alexei	6-1	215	L	Togliatti, USSR	2/24/73	Pittsburgh
KRAFT, Milan	6-3	195	R	Plzen, Czech.	1/17/80	Pittsburgh-Wilkes-Barre
LaCOUTURE, Dan	6-3	210	L	Hyannis, MA	4/18/77	Edmonton-Pittsburgh
LANG, Robert	6-2	216	R	Teplice, Czech.	12/19/70	Pittsburgh
LEMIEUX, Mario	6-4	225	R	Montreal, Que.	10/5/65	Pittsburgh
MacDONALD, Jason	6-0	195	R	Charlottetown, P.E.I.	4/1/74	Wilkes-Barre
MATHIEU, Alexandre	6-2	177	L	Repentigny, Que.	2/12/79	Wilkes-Barre
MELOCHE, Eric	5-11	195	R	Montreal, Que.	5/1/76	Wilkes-Barre
MORAN, Ian	6-0	206	R	Cleveland, OH	8/24/72	Pittsburgh
MOROZOV, Aleksey	6-1	196	L	Moscow, USSR	2/16/77	Pittsburgh
OLIWA, Krzysztof	6-5	235	L	Tychy, Poland	4/12/73	Columbus-Pittsburgh
PARSONS, Steve	6-4	235	L	Vancouver, B.C.	3/12/75	Wheeling-Wilkes-Barre-Hershey
PETERSEN, Toby	5-10	196	L	Minneapolis, MN	10/27/78	Pittsburgh-Wilkes-Barre
PRIMEAU, Wayne	6-3	220	L	Scarborough, Ont.	6/4/76	Tampa Bay-Pittsburgh
SIVEK, Michal	6-3	209	L	Nachod, Czech.	1/21/81	Sparta Praha
SONNENBERG, Martin	6-0	184	L	Wetaskiwin, Alta.	1/23/78	Wilkes-Barre
STEVENS, Kevin	6-3	230	L	Brockton, MA	4/15/65	Philadelphia-Pittsburgh
STRAKA, Martin	5-9	176	L	Plzen, Czech.	9/3/72	Pittsburgh
SUROVY, Tomas	6-1	187	L	Banska Bystrica, Czech.	9/24/81	HC SKP Poprad
TIBBETTS, Billy	6-2	215	R	Boston, MA	10/14/74	Pittsburgh-Wilkes-Barre
VEROT, Darcy	6-0	190	L	Radville, Sask.	7/13/76	Wilkes-Barre
ZEVAKHIN, Alexander	6-0	187	L	Perm, USSR	12/30/78	Wilkes-Barre
DEFENSEMEN						
FERENCE, Andrew	5-10	190	L	Edmonton, Alta.	3/17/79	Wilkes-Barre-Pittsburgh
JONSSON, Hans	6-1	202	L	Jarved, Sweden	8/2/73	Pittsburgh
KASPARAITIS, Darius	5-11	212	L	Elektrenai, USSR	10/16/72	Pittsburgh
KOCI, David	6-6	216	L	Prague, Czech.	5/12/81	Prince George
LAUKKANEN, Janne	6-1	194	L	Lahti, Finland	3/19/70	Pittsburgh
LUPASCHUK, Ross	6-1	211	R	Edmonton, Alta.	1/19/81	Red Deer
MELICHAR, Josef	6-2	214	L	Ceske Budejovice, Czech.	1/20/79	Pittsburgh-Wilkes-Barre
MOORE, Mark	6-3	185	R	Windsor, Ont.	2/18/77	Wheeling-Charlotte-Wilkes-Barre
ORPIK, Brooks	6-3	217	L	Amherst, NY	9/26/80	Boston College
RATCHUK, Peter	6-1	185	L	Buffalo, NY	9/10/77	Florida-Louisville
ROBINSON, Darcy	6-3	229	R	Kamloops, B.C.	5/3/81	Saskatoon-Red Deer
ROZSIVAL, Michal	6-1	208	R	Vlasim, Czech.	9/3/78	Pittsburgh-Wilkes-Barre
SCUDERI, Rob	6-2	194	L	Syosset, NY	12/30/78	Boston College
WILSON, Mike	6-6	212	L	Brampton, Ont.	2/26/75	Florida-Louisville

GOALTENDERS	HT	WT	C	Place of Birth	Date	2000-01 Club
AUBIN, Jean-Sebastien	5-11	176	R	Montreal, Que.	7/17/77	Pittsburgh
CARON, Sebastian	6-1	160	L	Amqui, Que.	6/25/80	Wilkes-Barre
HEDBERG, Johan	5-11	185	L	Leksand, Sweden	5/5/73	Manitoba-Pittsburgh
TALLAS, Robbie	6-0	170	L	Edmonton, Alta.	3/20/73	Chi-Chi (IHL)-Norfolk

Coach

HLINKA, IVAN

Coach, Pittsburgh Penguins. Born in Most, Czechoslovakia, January 26, 1950.

The Pittsburgh Penguins named Ivan Hlinka as the 19th head coach in team history on June 21, 2000. He became the 16th different person to hold the head coaching title. Hlinka first joined the Penguins coaching staff as an associate coach on February 20, 2000.

Before joining the Penguins, Hlinka served as head coach of the Czech Republic national team, and is generally credited with building the country's ice hockey program into one of the finest in the world today. While serving as head coach, Hlinka led the team to two world championships and three Olympic medals in the 1990s. The high point of Hlinka's international coaching career came when he led the 1998 Czech Olympic Team to the country's first gold medal in hockey at the Winter Olympics in Nagano, Japan.

Hlinka began his professional playing career in 1966-67 with CHZ Litvinov in the Czech League, and quickly established himself as one of his country's top players. He also distinguished himself as a member of Czechoslovakia's national team during the 1970s and 1980s, playing in 11 World Championship tournaments and bringing home gold medals in 1972, 1976 and 1977. He also participated in the 1972 and 1976 Olympic Games, and was named the top forward at the 1976 Canada Cup tournament.

In 1981, Hlinka and fellow Czech Jiri Bubla made the transition to the NHL by joining the Vancouver Canucks. Hlinka returned to Europe in 1983 and finished out his playing career with EV Zug in the Swiss League from 1983 to 1985 before turning to coaching.

Coaching Record

		Regular Season				Playoffs		
Season	Team	Games	W	L	T	Games	W	L
1985-86	CHZ Litvinov (Czech)	34	20	10	4	....	....	....
1987-88	CHZ Litvinov (Czech)	34	18	13	3	....	....	....
1988-89	CHZ Litvinov (Czech)	34	13	15	6	....	....	....
1989-90	EHC Frieburg (Germany)	28	2	23	3	....	....	....
2000-01	**Pittsburgh (NHL)**	**82**	**42**	**31**	**9**	**18**	**9**	**9**
	NHL Totals	**82**	**42**	**31**	**9**	**18**	**9**	**9**

2000-01 Scoring

* - rookie

Regular Season

Pos	#	Player	Team	GP	G	A	Pts	+/–	PIM	PP	SH	GW	GT	S	%
R	68	Jaromir Jagr	PIT	81	52	69	121	19	42	14	1	10	1	317	16.4
R	27	Alexei Kovalev	PIT	79	44	51	95	12	96	12	2	9	1	307	14.3
C	82	Martin Straka	PIT	82	27	68	95	19	38	7	1	4	1	185	14.6
C	20	Robert Lang	PIT	82	32	48	80	20	28	10	0	2	0	177	18.1
C	66	Mario Lemieux	PIT	43	35	41	76	15	18	16	1	5	0	171	20.5
C	38	Jan Hrdina	PIT	78	15	28	43	19	48	3	0	1	1	89	16.9
L	25	Kevin Stevens	PHI	23	2	7	9	–2	18	0	0	0	0	31	6.5
			PIT	32	8	15	23	–4	55	2	0	0	0	76	10.5
			TOTAL	55	10	22	32	–6	73	2	0	0	0	107	9.3
L	18	Josef Beranek	PIT	70	9	14	23	–7	43	2	0	2	0	152	5.9
D	8	Hans Jonsson	PIT	58	4	18	22	11	22	2	0	0	0	44	9.1
C	15	Wayne Primeau	T.B.	47	2	13	15	–17	77	0	0	0	0	47	4.3
			PIT	28	1	6	7	0	54	0	0	0	0	30	3.3
			TOTAL	75	3	19	22	–17	131	0	0	0	0	77	3.9
D	5	Janne Laukkanen	PIT	50	3	17	20	9	34	0	0	0	0	58	5.2
R	95	Alexei Morozov	PIT	66	5	14	19	–8	6	0	0	1	0	72	6.9
D	11	Darius Kasparaitis	PIT	77	3	16	19	11	111	1	0	0	0	81	3.7
L	9	Rene Corbet	PIT	43	8	9	17	–3	57	2	0	1	1	85	9.4
D	7	Andrew Ference	PIT	36	4	11	15	6	28	1	0	1	0	47	8.5
C	14	* Milan Kraft	PIT	42	7	7	14	–6	8	1	1	1	1	63	11.1
C	37	Kip Miller	PIT	33	3	8	11	0	6	1	0	0	0	38	7.9
D	26	Frantisek Kucera	CBJ	48	2	5	7	–5	12	0	0	0	0	51	3.9
			PIT	7	0	2	2	–2	0	0	0	0	0	9	0.0
			TOTAL	55	2	7	9	–7	12	0	0	0	0	60	3.3
C	17	* Toby Petersen	PIT	12	2	6	8	3	4	0	0	1	0	25	8.0
R	24	Ian Moran	PIT	40	3	4	7	5	28	0	0	1	0	73	4.1
L	22	* Dan LaCouture	EDM	37	2	4	6	–2	29	0	0	1	0	22	9.1
			PIT	11	0	0	0	0	14	0	0	0	0	1	0.0
			TOTAL	48	2	4	6	–2	43	0	0	1	0	23	8.7
D	28	Michal Rozsival	PIT	30	1	4	5	3	26	0	0	0	0	17	5.9
L	29	Krzysztof Oliwa	CBJ	10	0	2	2	1	34	0	0	0	0	5	0.0
			PIT	26	1	2	3	–4	131	0	0	0	0	17	5.9
			TOTAL	36	1	4	5	–3	165	0	0	0	0	22	4.5
D	3	Marc Bergevin	STL	2	0	0	0	1	0	0	0	0	0	1	0.0
			PIT	36	1	4	5	5	26	0	0	0	0	11	9.1
			TOTAL	38	1	4	5	6	26	0	0	0	0	12	8.3
D	6	Bob Boughner	PIT	58	1	3	4	18	147	0	0	0	0	46	2.2
R	12	* William Tibbetts	PIT	29	1	2	3	–2	79	0	0	0	0	16	6.3
D	4	Bobby Dollas	S.J.	16	1	1	2	4	14	0	0	0	0	5	20.0
			PIT	5	0	0	0	0	4	0	0	0	0	6	0.0
			TOTAL	21	1	1	2	4	18	0	0	0	0	11	9.1
L	23	Steve McKenna	MIN	20	1	1	2	0	19	0	0	0	0	12	8.3
			PIT	34	0	0	0	–4	100	0	0	0	0	7	0.0
			TOTAL	54	1	1	2	–4	119	0	0	0	0	19	5.3
D	2	* Josef Melichar	PIT	18	0	2	2	–5	21	0	0	0	0	9	0.0
G	30	J-Sebastien Aubin	PIT	36	0	1	1	0	4	0	0	0	0	0	0.0
L	32	* Greg Crozier	PIT	1	0	0	0	0	0	0	0	0	0	0	0.0
R	16	Dennis Bonvie	PIT	3	0	0	0	–1	0	0	0	0	0	1	0.0
G	31	Rich Parent	PIT	7	0	0	0	0	0	0	0	0	0	0	0.0
G	1	Johan Hedberg	PIT	9	0	0	0	0	0	0	0	0	0	0	0.0
G	34	Garth Snow	PIT	35	0	0	0	0	8	0	0	0	0	0	0.0

Goaltending

No.	Goaltender	GPI	Mins	Avg	W	L	T	EN	SO	GA	SA	S%
1	Johan Hedberg	9	545	2.64	7	1	1	0	0	24	253	.905
34	Garth Snow	35	2032	2.98	14	15	4	1	3	101	1014	.900
31	Rich Parent	7	332	3.07	1	1	3	1	0	17	150	.887
30	J-Sebastien Aubin	36	2050	3.13	20	14	1	5	0	107	973	.890
	Totals	**82**	**4978**	**3.09**	**42**	**31**	**9**	**7**	**3**	**256**	**2397**	**.893**

Playoffs

Pos	#	Player	Team	GP	G	A	Pts	+/–	PIM	PP	SH	GW	GT	S	%
C	66	Mario Lemieux	PIT	18	6	11	17	4	4	1	0	3	0	39	15.4
C	82	Martin Straka	PIT	18	5	8	13	–1	8	3	0	2	2	47	10.6
R	68	Jaromir Jagr	PIT	16	2	10	12	4	18	2	0	0	0	38	5.3
R	27	Alexei Kovalev	PIT	18	5	5	10	–2	16	1	0	0	0	44	11.4
D	7	Andrew Ference	PIT	18	3	7	10	0	16	1	0	1	0	32	9.4
C	20	Robert Lang	PIT	16	4	4	8	2	4	0	0	0	0	25	16.0
C	38	Jan Hrdina	PIT	18	2	5	7	–4	8	0	0	0	0	13	15.4
L	25	Kevin Stevens	PIT	17	3	3	6	–4	20	2	0	1	0	19	15.8
R	95	Alexei Morozov	PIT	18	3	3	6	0	6	0	1	0	0	30	10.0
D	5	Janne Laukkanen	PIT	18	2	2	4	6	14	1	0	0	0	16	12.5
C	15	Wayne Primeau	PIT	18	1	3	4	–2	2	0	0	0	0	19	5.3
D	11	Darius Kasparaitis	PIT	17	1	1	2	–5	26	0	0	1	1	14	7.1
L	18	Josef Beranek	PIT	13	0	2	2	1	2	0	0	0	0	13	0.0
L	9	Rene Corbet	PIT	17	1	0	1	–5	12	0	0	1	0	14	7.1
D	3	Marc Bergevin	PIT	12	0	1	1	2	2	0	0	0	0	9	0.0
D	6	Bob Boughner	PIT	18	0	1	1	5	22	0	0	0	0	10	0.0
R	24	Ian Moran	PIT	18	0	1	1	–3	4	0	0	0	0	23	0.0
G	30	J-Sebastien Aubin	PIT	1	0	0	0	0	0	0	0	0	0	0	0.0
L	29	Krzysztof Oliwa	PIT	5	0	0	0	0	16	0	0	0	0	0	0.0
L	22	* Dan Lacouture	PIT	5	0	0	0	0	2	0	0	0	0	2	0.0
C	14	* Milan Kraft	PIT	8	0	0	0	–4	2	0	0	0	0	9	0.0
D	8	Hans Jonsson	PIT	16	0	0	0	–2	8	0	0	0	0	8	0.0
G	1	Johan Hedberg	PIT	18	0	0	0	0	0	0	0	0	0	0	0.0

Goaltending

No.	Goaltender	GPI	Mins	Avg	W	L	EN	SO	GA	SA	S%
30	J-Sebastien Aubin	1	1	0.00	0	0	0	0	0	0	.000
1	Johan Hedberg	18	1123	2.30	9	9	1	2	43	482	.911
	Totals	**18**	**1130**	**2.34**	**9**	**9**	**1**	**2**	**44**	**483**	**.909**

Club Records

Team

(Figures in brackets for season records are games played; records for fewest points, wins, ties, losses, goals, goals against are for 70 or more games)

Most Points	119	1992-93 (84)
Most Wins	56	1992-93 (84)
Most Ties	20	1970-71 (78)
Most Losses	58	1983-84 (80)
Most Goals	367	1992-93 (84)
Most Goals Against	394	1982-83 (80)
Fewest Points	38	1983-84 (80)
Fewest Wins	16	1983-84 (80)
Fewest Ties	4	1995-96 (82)
Fewest Losses	21	1992-93 (84)
Fewest Goals	182	1969-70 (76)
Fewest Goals Against	188	1997-98 (82)
Longest Winning Streak		
Overall	*17	Mar. 9-Apr. 10/93
Home	11	Jan. 5-Mar. 7/91
Away	7	Mar. 14-Apr. 9/93
Longest Undefeated Streak		
Overall	18	Mar. 9-Apr. 14/93 (17 wins, 1 tie)
Home	20	Nov. 30/74-Feb. 22/75 (12 wins, 8 ties)
Away	8	Mar. 14-Apr. 14/93 (7 wins, 1 tie)
Longest Losing Streak		
Overall	11	Jan. 22-Feb. 10/83
Home	7	Oct. 8-29/83
Away	18	Dec. 23/82-Mar. 4/83
Longest Winless Streak		
Overall	18	Jan. 2-Feb. 10/83 (17 losses, 1 tie)
Home	11	Oct. 8-Nov. 19/83 (9 losses, 2 ties)
Away	18	Oct. 25/70-Jan. 14/71 (11 losses, 7 ties), Dec. 23/82-Mar. 4/83 (18 losses)
Most Shutouts, Season	9	1998-99 (82)
Most PIM, Season	2,670	1988-89 (80)
Most Goals, Game	12	Mar. 15/75 (Wsh. 1 at Pit. 12), Dec. 26/91 (Tor. 1 at Pit. 12)

Individual

Most Seasons	13	Mario Lemieux
Most Games	806	Jaromir Jagr
Most Goals, Career	648	Mario Lemieux
Most Assists, Career	922	Mario Lemieux
Most Points, Career	1,570	Mario Lemieux (648G, 922A)
Most PIM, Career	1,023	Kevin Stevens
Most Shutouts, Career	22	Tom Barrasso
Longest Consecutive Games Streak	320	Ron Schock (Oct. 24/73-Apr. 3/77)
Most Goals, Season	85	Mario Lemieux (1988-89)
Most Assists, Season	114	Mario Lemieux (1988-89)
Most Points, Season	199	Mario Lemieux (1988-89; 85G, 114A)
Most PIM, Season	409	Paul Baxter (1981-82)
Most Points, Defenseman, Season	113	Paul Coffey (1988-89; 30G, 83A)
Most Points, Center, Season	199	Mario Lemieux (1988-89; 85G, 114A)
Most Points, Right Wing, Season	*149	Jaromir Jagr (1995-96; 62G, 87A)
Most Points, Left Wing, Season	123	Kevin Stevens (1991-92; 54G, 69A)
Most Points, Rookie, Season	100	Mario Lemieux (1984-85; 43G, 57A)
Most Shutouts, Season	7	Tom Barrasso (1997-98)
Most Goals, Game	5	Mario Lemieux (Three times)
Most Assists, Game	6	Ron Stackhouse (Mar. 8/75), Greg Malone (Nov. 28/79), Mario Lemieux (Three times)
Most Points, Game	8	Mario Lemieux (Oct. 15/88; 3G, 5A, Dec. 31/88; 5G, 3A)

* NHL Record.

Retired Numbers

21	Michel Brière	1969-1970

Captains' History

Ab McDonald, 1967-68; no captain, 1968-69 to 1972-73; Ron Schock, 1973-74 to 1976-77; Jean Pronovost, 1977-78; Orest Kindrachuk, 1978-79 to 1980-81; Randy Carlyle, 1981-82 to 1983-84; Mike Bullard, 1984-85, 1985-86; Mike Bullard and Terry Ruskowski, 1986-87; Dan Frawley and Mario Lemieux, 1987-88; Mario Lemieux, 1988-89 to 1993-94; Ron Francis, 1994-95; Mario Lemieux, 1995-96, 1996-97; Ron Francis, 1997-98; Jaromir Jagr, 1998-99 to 2000-01.

General Managers' History

Jack Riley, 1967-68 to 1969-70; Red Kelly, 1970-71; Red Kelly and Jack Riley, 1971-72; Jack Riley, 1972-73; Jack Riley and Jack Button, 1973-74; Jack Button, 1974-75; Wren Blair, 1975-76; Wren Blair and Baz Bastien, 1976-77; Baz Bastien, 1977-78 to 1982-83; Ed Johnston, 1983-84 to 1987-88; Tony Esposito, 1988-89; Tony Esposito and Craig Patrick, 1989-90; Craig Patrick, 1990-91 to date.

All-time Record vs. Other Clubs

Regular Season

	At Home								On Road								Total							
	GP	W	L	T	OL	GF	GA	PTS	GP	W	L	T	OL	GF	GA	PTS	GP	W	L	T	OL	GF	GA	PTS
Anaheim	7	4	1	2	0	25	22	10	6	3	2	0	1	22	20	7	13	7	3	2	1	47	42	17
Atlanta	4	4	0	0	0	17	5	8	4	4	0	0	0	18	10	8	8	8	0	0	0	35	15	16
Boston	74	31	28	15	0	260	264	77	72	13	53	6	0	204	325	32	146	44	81	21	0	464	589	109
Buffalo	65	32	17	16	0	245	205	80	65	17	32	16	0	180	263	50	130	49	49	32	0	425	468	130
Calgary	43	23	10	10	0	165	133	56	44	10	26	8	0	133	194	28	87	33	36	18	0	298	327	84
Carolina	40	21	14	5	0	176	150	47	42	20	19	3	0	164	164	43	82	41	33	8	0	340	314	90
Chicago	57	27	23	7	0	204	187	61	57	10	38	9	0	155	233	29	114	37	61	16	0	359	420	90
Colorado	34	15	14	5	0	139	139	35	31	13	15	2	1	121	138	29	65	28	29	7	1	260	277	64
Columbus	1	1	0	0	0	5	2	2	1	1	0	0	0	3	2	2	2	2	0	0	0	8	4	4
Dallas	61	36	19	6	0	229	176	78	63	21	35	6	1	212	243	49	124	57	54	12	1	441	419	127
Detroit	62	43	15	4	0	274	183	90	64	13	38	12	1	175	246	39	126	56	53	16	1	449	429	129
Edmonton	29	14	12	3	0	113	124	31	28	6	21	1	0	94	144	13	57	20	33	4	0	207	268	44
Florida	17	11	4	2	0	60	46	24	16	8	6	1	1	41	41	18	33	19	10	3	1	101	87	42
Los Angeles	70	38	22	10	0	258	220	86	67	17	42	8	0	178	258	42	137	55	64	18	0	436	478	128
Minnesota	1	1	0	0	0	2	1	2	1	0	1	0	0	2	4	0	2	1	1	0	0	4	5	2
Montreal	76	27	36	13	0	229	267	67	76	10	57	9	0	193	364	29	152	37	93	22	0	422	631	96
Nashville	3	1	1	1	0	8	6	3	3	2	1	0	0	8	7	4	6	3	2	1	0	16	13	7
New Jersey	71	39	28	4	0	274	249	82	73	26	34	13	0	252	273	65	144	65	62	17	0	526	522	147
NY Islanders	80	39	30	11	0	307	277	89	78	29	41	8	0	261	314	66	158	68	71	19	0	568	591	155
NY Rangers	92	38	40	14	0	338	348	90	93	37	47	9	0	318	371	83	185	75	87	23	0	656	719	173
Ottawa	21	15	2	4	0	84	42	34	21	12	5	4	0	69	51	28	42	27	7	8	0	153	93	62
Philadelphia	98	44	35	19	0	348	319	107	98	16	73	7	2	245	421	41	196	60	108	26	2	593	740	148
Phoenix	28	20	8	0	0	118	79	40	28	13	12	3	0	99	103	29	56	33	20	3	0	217	182	69
St. Louis	62	31	19	12	0	235	185	74	62	15	41	6	0	168	242	36	124	46	60	18	0	403	427	110
San Jose	7	3	3	1	0	34	25	7	10	6	2	2	0	50	20	14	17	9	5	3	0	84	45	21
Tampa Bay	17	12	3	2	0	72	42	26	17	8	7	2	0	51	48	18	34	20	10	4	0	123	90	44
Toronto	63	35	22	6	0	267	199	76	61	21	28	11	1	200	246	54	124	56	50	17	1	467	445	130
Vancouver	48	33	8	7	0	224	164	73	48	23	21	4	0	182	171	50	96	56	29	11	0	406	335	123
Washington	77	42	28	7	0	300	246	91	80	32	40	7	1	297	337	72	157	74	68	14	1	597	583	163
Defunct Clubs	35	22	6	7	0	148	93	51	34	13	10	11	0	108	101	37	69	35	16	18	0	256	194	88
Totals	**1343**	**702**	**448**	**193**	**0**	**5158**	**4398**	**1597**	**1343**	**419**	**747**	**168**	**9**	**4203**	**5354**	**1015**	**2686**	**1121**	**1195**	**361**	**9**	**9361**	**9752**	**2612**

Playoffs

	Series	W	L	GP	W	L	T	GF	GA	Last Mtg.	Round	Result
Boston	4	2	2	19	10	9	0	67	62	1992	CF	W 4-0
Buffalo	2	2	0	10	6	4	0	26	26	2001	CSF	W 4-3
Chicago	2	1	1	8	4	4	0	23	24	1992	F	W 4-0
Dallas	1	1	0	6	4	2	0	28	16	1991	F	W 4-2
Florida	1	0	1	7	3	4	0	15	20	1996	CF	L 3-4
Montreal	1	0	1	6	2	4	0	15	18	1998	CQF	L 2-4
New Jersey	5	3	2	29	14	15	0	80	86	2001	CF	L 1-4
NY Islanders	3	0	3	19	8	11	0	58	67	1993	DF	L 3-4
NY Rangers	3	3	0	15	12	3	0	64	45	1996	CSF	W 4-1
Philadelphia	3	0	3	18	6	12	0	51	66	2000	CSF	L 2-4
St. Louis	3	1	2	13	6	7	0	40	45	1981	PR	L 2-3
Toronto	3	0	3	12	4	8	0	27	39	1999	CSF	L 2-4
Washington	7	6	1	42	26	16	0	137	121	2001	CQF	W 4-2
Defunct Clubs	1	1	0	4	4	0	0	13	6			
Totals	**39**	**20**	**19**	**208**	**109**	**99**	**0**	**644**	**641**			

Playoff Results 2001-1997

Year	Round	Opponent	Result	GF	GA
2001	CF	New Jersey	L 1-4	7	17
	CSF	Buffalo	W 4-3	17	17
	CQF	Washington	W 4-2	14	10
2000	CSF	Philadelphia	L 2-4	14	15
	CQF	Washington	W 4-1	17	8
1999	CSF	Toronto	L 2-4	14	18
	CQF	New Jersey	W 4-3	21	18
1998	CQF	Montreal	L 2-4	15	18
1997	CQF	Philadelphia	L 1-4	13	20

Abbreviations: Round: F – Final; **CF** – conference final; **CSF** – conference semi-final; **CQF** – conference quarter-final; **DF** – division final; **PR** – preliminary round.

Calgary totals include Atlanta Flames, 1972-73 to 1979-80.
Colorado totals include Quebec, 1979-80 to 1994-95.
New Jersey totals include Kansas City, 1974-75 to 1975-76, and Colorado Rockies, 1976-77 to 1981-82.
Phoenix totals include Winnipeg, 1979-80 to 1995-96.
Carolina totals include Hartford, 1979-80 to 1996-97.
Dallas totals include Minnesota North Stars, 1967-68 to 1992-93.

2000-01 Results

Oct.	7	Nashville	1-3		9	at Boston	2-5
	8	at Nashville	3-1		12	NY Islanders	4-3
	13	Tampa Bay	3-2		13	at NY Islanders	5-6
	14	NY Rangers	8-6		15	Anaheim	3-2
	18	Carolina	2-3		17	at Phoenix	4-5
	19	at Ottawa	3-3		19	at Dallas	5-6*
	21	Columbus	5-2		21	at Chicago	4-0
	25	Ottawa	2-3		24	Montreal	3-1
	27	at NY Rangers	4-1		27	Atlanta	5-1
	28	New Jersey	0-9		30	at Atlanta	6-3
Nov.	1	at San Jose	2-3		31	Philadelphia	1-5
	3	at Vancouver	4-2	**Feb.**	7	Philadelphia	9-4
	4	at Calgary	1-1		10	New Jersey	5-4*
	8	Philadelphia	5-2		11	at Minnesota	2-4
	10	at New Jersey	4-2		14	Minnesota	2-1
	11	Edmonton	5-2		16	at New Jersey	4-4
	13	at Colorado	2-3*		17	at Columbus	3-2*
	16	at St. Louis	3-4		19	Colorado	1-5
	18	Atlanta	3-1		21	Florida	3-2*
	22	Carolina	1-3		23	NY Rangers	6-4
	24	at Philadelphia	1-0		25	NY Islanders	6-1
	25	Los Angeles	2-2		28	at Montreal	2-4
	28	at Boston	1-3	**Mar.**	2	at NY Rangers	7-5
Dec.	1	at Buffalo	6-4		3	at Washington	3-4
	2	Buffalo	2-3		7	Washington	3-4
	5	at Ottawa	4-2		8	at Atlanta	5-3
	6	Boston	2-3		10	Calgary	6-3
	9	at Toronto	1-5		12	at NY Rangers	3-3
	10	at Detroit	4-3		14	NY Islanders	1-3
	13	Toronto	4-7		16	at Florida	6-3
	15	Florida	1-4		17	at Tampa Bay	1-5
	16	at Montreal	4-4		20	Boston	2-2
	20	at Florida	2-2		23	at Carolina	3-5
	21	at Tampa Bay	1-1		25	at New Jersey	4-2
	23	Dallas	2-8		27	Buffalo	4-1
	26	at Buffalo	5-3		29	Chicago	5-2
	27	Toronto	5-0		31	St. Louis	5-3
	30	Ottawa	5-3	**Apr.**	2	at NY Islanders	1-4
Jan.	3	Washington	3-2		4	Tampa Bay	4-2
	5	Montreal	3-4		7	at Philadelphia	3-4*
	8	at Washington	5-3		8	at Carolina	6-4

* – Overtime

Entry Draft Selections 2001-1987

2001
Pick
21 Colby Armstrong
54 Noah Welch
86 Drew Fata
96 Alexandre Rouleau
120 Tomas Surovy
131 Ben Eaves
156 Andrew Schneider
217 Tomas Duba
250 Brandon Crawford-West

2000
Pick
18 Brooks Orpik
52 Shane Endicott
84 Peter Hamerlik
124 Michel Ouellet
146 David Koci
185 Patrick Foley
216 Jim Abbott
248 Steven Crampton
273 Roman Simicek
280 Nick Boucher

1999
Pick
18 Konstantin Koltsov
51 Matt Murley
57 Jeremy Van Hoof
86 Sebastian Caron
115 Ryan Malone
144 Tomas Skvaridlo
157 Vladimir Malenkikh
176 Doug Meyer
204 Tom Kostopoulos
233 Darcy Robinson
261 Andrew McPherson

1998
Pick
23 Milan Kraft
54 Alexander Zevakhin
80 David Cameron
110 Scott Myers
134 Rob Scuderi
169 Jan Fadrny
196 Joel Scherban
224 Mika Lehto
244 Toby Petersen
254 Matt Hussey

1997
Pick
17 Robert Dome
44 Brian Gaffaney
71 Josef Melichar
97 Alexandre Mathieu
124 Harlan Pratt
152 Petr Havelka
179 Mark Moore
208 Andrew Ference
234 Eric Lind

1996
Pick
23 Craig Hillier
28 Pavel Skrbek
72 Boyd Kane
77 Boris Protsenko
105 Michal Rozsival
150 Peter Bergman
186 Eric Meloche
238 Timo Seikkula

1995
Pick
24 Aleksey Morozov
76 Jean-Sebastien Aubin
102 Oleg Belov
128 Jan Hrdina
154 Alexei Kolkunov
180 Derrick Pyke
206 Sergei Voronov
232 Frank Ivankovic

1994
Pick
24 Chris Wells
50 Richard Park
57 Sven Butenschon
73 Greg Crozier
76 Alexei Krivchenkov
102 Tom O'Connor
128 Clint Johnson
154 Valentin Morozov
161 Serge Aubin
180 Drew Palmer
206 Boris Zelenko
232 Jason Godbout
258 Mikhail Kazakevich
284 Brian Leitza

1993
Pick
26 Stefan Bergkvist
52 Domenic Pittis
62 Dave Roche
104 Jonas Andersson-Junkka
130 Chris Kelleher
156 Patrick Lalime
182 Sean Selmser
208 Larry McMorran
234 Timothy Harberts
260 Leonid Toropchenko
286 Hans Jonsson

1992
Pick
19 Martin Straka
43 Marc Hussey
67 Travis Thiessen
91 Todd Klassen
115 Philippe DeRouville
139 Artem Kopot
163 Jan Alinc
187 Fran Bussey
211 Brian Bonin
235 Brian Callahan

1991
Pick
16 Markus Naslund
38 Rusty Fitzgerald
60 Shane Peacock
82 Joe Tamminen
104 Robert Melanson
126 Brian Clifford
148 Ed Patterson
170 Peter McLaughlin
192 Jeff Lembke
214 Chris Tok
236 Paul Dyck
258 Pasi Huura

1990
Pick
5 Jaromir Jagr
61 Joe Dziedzic
68 Chris Tamer
89 Brian Farrell
107 Ian Moran
110 Denis Casey
130 Mika Valila
131 Ken Plaquin
145 Pat Neaton
152 Petteri Koskimaki
173 Ladislav Karabin
194 Timothy Fingerhut
215 Michael Thompson
236 Brian Bruininks

1989
Pick
16 Jamie Heward
37 Paul Laus
58 John Brill
79 Todd Nelson
100 Tom Nevers
121 Mike Markovich
126 Mike Needham
142 Patrick Schafhauser
163 Dave Shute
184 Andrew Wolf
205 Greg Hagen
226 Scott Farrell
247 Jason Smart

1988
Pick
4 Darrin Shannon
25 Mark Major
62 Daniel Gauthier
67 Mark Recchi
88 Greg Andrusak
130 Troy Mick
151 Jeff Blaeser
172 Rob Gaudreau
193 David Pancoe
214 Cory Laylin
235 Darren Stolk

1987
Pick
5 Chris Joseph
26 Rick Tabaracci
47 Jamie Leach
68 Risto Kurkinen
89 Jeff Waver
110 Shawn McEachern
131 Jim Bodden
152 Jiri Kucera
173 Jack MacDougall
194 Daryn McBride
215 Mark Carlson
236 Ake Lilljebjorn

General Manager

PATRICK, CRAIG
General Manager, Pittsburgh Penguins. Born in Detroit, MI, May 20, 1946.

Known for his calm and patient management style, Craig Patrick has led the Penguins to two Stanley Cup championships, one Presidents' Trophy title and five division championships since taking over as general manager on December 5, 1989. In 2000, he and Mario Lemieux were recipients of the Lester Patrick Trophy for their contributions to hockey in the United States. He was elected to the Hockey Hall of Fame in 2001.

A member of one of hockey's most famous families — including grandfather Lester, father Lynn and uncle Muzz — Patrick played collegiate hockey at the University of Denver and captained the Pioneers to the NCAA championship in 1969. He played eight NHL seasons with four different teams, registering 72 goals and 163 points in 401 games before retiring in 1979. He made the transition to management and coaching when he landed the dual role of assistant coach and assistant g.m. of the 1980 U.S. Olympic Team that won the gold medal at Lake Placid.

Patrick joined the New York Rangers organization as director of operations in 1980 and became the youngest general manager in club history one year later. He served in that capacity through the 1985-86 season, leading his team to the playoffs every year.

Prior to joining the Penguins, Patrick spent two years as director of athletics and recreation at the University of Denver.

NHL Coaching Record

			Regular Season			Playoffs		
Season	**Team**	**Games**	**W**	**L**	**T**	**Games**	**W**	**L**
1980-81	NY Rangers	60	26	23	11	14	7	7
1984-85	NY Rangers	35	11	22	2	3	0	3
1989-90	Pittsburgh	54	22	26	6	....	....	....
1996-97	Pittsburgh	20	7	10	3	5	1	4
	NHL Totals	**169**	**66**	**81**	**22**	**22**	**8**	**14**

Club Directory

Mellon Arena

Pittsburgh Penguins
Mellon Arena
66 Mario Lemieux Place
Pittsburgh, PA 15219
Phone **412/642-1300**
FAX 412/642-1859
Media Relations FAX
412/642-1322
Capacity: 16,958

Ownership
Mario Lemieux and The Lemieux Group

Executive Committee
Chairman and CEO . . . . Mario Lemieux
President, Lemieux Group, LP/Governor. . . . . Ken Sawyer
President, Team Lemieux, LLC/Alternate Governor. . Tom Rooney
Executive Vice President/General Manager/
Alternate Governor . . . . Craig Patrick
Alternate Governors . . . . Ronald Burkle, Anthony Liberati

Administration
Vice President & General Counsel . . . . Ted Black
Executive Assistant . . . . Elaine Heufelder
Executive Assistant . . . . Fay McNamara
Receptionist . . . . Kelly Hart
Mailroom Supervisor . . . . Brett Hart

Hockey Operations
General Manager . . . . Craig Patrick
Assistant General Manager . . . . Ed Johnston
Head Coach . . . . Ivan Hlinka
Assistant Coaches . . . . Rick Kehoe, Joe Mullen, Randy Hillier
Goaltending Coach and Scout. . . . . Gilles Meloche
Head Scout . . . . Greg Malone
Scouts. . . . . Herb Brooks, Wayne Daniels, Chuck Grillo, Charlie Hodge, Mark Kelley, Neil Shea
Strength and Conditioning Coach . . . . John Welday
Equipment Manager . . . . Steve Latin
Trainers. . . . . Mark Mortland, Scott Johnson
Team Physician . . . . Dr. Charles Burke
Executive Assistant . . . . Tracey Botsford
Assistant Equipment Manager. . . . . Paul Flati
Equipment Staff . . . . Paul DeFazio
Head Coach, Wilkes-Barre/
Scranton Penguins (AHL) . . . . Glenn Patrick
Head Coach, Wheeling Nailers (ECHL). . . . . John Brophy

Communications and Marketing
Vice President, Communications/Marketing. . . . . . Tom McMillan
Director of Media Relations. . . . . Steve Bovino
Manager, Media Relations. . . . . Keith Wehner
Director of Marketing . . . . Brian Magness
Director of Public & Alumni Relations . . . . Cindy Himes
Director, Community Relations . . . . Renee Petrichevich
Director of Entertainment . . . . Paul Barto
Assistant Director, Entertainment . . . . Mike Wurman
Youth Hockey Coordinator . . . . Mark Shuttleworth

Finance
Vice President/Controller. . . . . Kevin Hart
Assistant Controller. . . . . Michael McCullough
Accounting Staff. . . . . Tawni Love, Troy Ussack, Andrea Winschel

Properties
Vice President of Properties. . . . . Mike Lee
Director of Publications. . . . . Brian Coe
Creative Director. . . . . Barb Pilarski
Multi Media Manager . . . . Chris DeVivo
Informational Services. . . . . Mia Scott

Ticketing
Vice President, Ticketing . . . . Mark Anderson
Director, Premium Seating. . . . . Terri Smith
Manager, Premium Services . . . . Michelle Follen
Assistant Manager, Premium Services . . . . Sherry Huggins
Senior Director, Ticketing . . . . James Santilli
Senior Director, Ticketing . . . . Chad Slencak
Manager, Ticket Sales . . . . Mike Guiffre
Director, Ticket Operations . . . . Laura Bryer
Box Office Manager . . . . Carol Coulson
Premium Seating Account Representative . . . . Bonnie Golinski

Corporate Sales
Vice President, Corporate Sales . . . . David Soltesz
Senior Director, Corporate Sponsorships . . . . Kimberly Bogesdorfer
Directors, Corporate Sponsorships. . . . . Carl D'Alicandro, Mark DeAndrea
Director, Corporate Sponsorships,
Lemieux Hockey Development. . . . . Terri Dobos Young
Manager, Sales Service . . . . Marie Mays
Assistant Manager, Sales Service . . . . Beth McQuiston

Broadcasting
TV Station. . . . . Fox Sports Net Pittsburgh
TV Announcers . . . . Mike Lange, Eddie Olczyk
Flagship Radio Station. . . . . 3WS (94.5 FM, 970 AM)
Radio Announcers. . . . . Paul Steigerwald, Bob Errey

Coaching History

Red Sullivan, 1967-68, 1968-69; Red Kelly, 1969-70 to 1971-72; Red Kelly and Ken Schinkel, 1972-73; Ken Schinkel and Marc Boileau, 1973-74; Marc Boileau, 1974-75; Marc Boileau and Ken Schinkel, 1975-76; Ken Schinkel, 1976-77; John Wilson, 1977-78 to 1979-80; Eddie Johnston, 1980-81 to 1982-83; Lou Angotti, 1983-84; Bob Berry, 1984-85 to 1986-87; Pierre Creamer, 1987-88; Gene Ubriaco, 1988-89; Gene Ubriaco and Craig Patrick, 1989-90; Bob Johnson, 1990-91, 1991-92; Scotty Bowman, 1991-92, 1992-93; Eddie Johnston, 1993-94 to 1995-96; Eddie Johnston and Craig Patrick, 1996-97; Kevin Constantine, 1997-98, 1998-99; Kevin Constantine and Herb Brooks, 1999-2000; Ivan Hlinka, 2000-01 to date.

St. Louis Blues

2000-01 Results: 43W-22L-12T-5OTL 103PTS. Second, Central Division

Year-by-Year Record

		Home				Road				Overall								
Season	GP	W	L	T	OL	W	L	T	OL	W	L	T	OL	GF	GA	Pts.	Finished	Playoff Result
2000-01	82	28	5	5	3	15	17	7	2	43	22	12	5	249	195	103	2nd, Central Div.	Lost Conf. Championship
1999-2000	82	24	9	7	1	27	10	4	0	51	19	11	1	248	165	114	1st, Central Div.	Lost Conf. Quarter-Final
1998-99	82	18	17	6	...	19	15	7	...	37	32	13	...	237	209	87	2nd, Central Div.	Lost Conf. Semi-Final
1997-98	82	26	10	5	...	19	19	3	...	45	29	8	...	256	204	98	3rd, Central Div.	Lost Conf. Semi-Final
1996-97	82	17	20	4	...	19	15	7	...	36	35	11	...	236	239	83	4th, Central Div.	Lost Conf. Quarter-Final
1995-96	82	15	17	9	...	17	17	7	...	32	34	16	...	219	248	80	4th, Central Div.	Lost Conf. Semi-Final
1994-95	48	16	6	2	...	12	9	3	...	28	15	5	...	178	135	61	2nd, Central Div.	Lost Conf. Quarter-Final
1993-94	84	23	11	8	...	17	22	3	...	40	33	11	...	270	283	91	4th, Central Div.	Lost Conf. Quarter-Final
1992-93	84	22	13	7	...	15	23	4	...	37	36	11	...	282	278	85	4th, Norris Div.	Lost Div. Final
1991-92	80	25	12	3	...	11	21	8	...	36	33	11	...	279	266	83	3rd, Norris Div.	Lost Div. Semi-Final
1990-91	80	24	9	7	...	23	13	4	...	47	22	11	...	310	250	105	2nd, Norris Div.	Lost Div. Final
1989-90	80	20	15	5	...	17	19	4	...	37	34	9	...	295	279	83	2nd, Norris Div.	Lost Div. Final
1988-89	80	22	11	7	...	11	24	5	...	33	35	12	...	275	285	78	2nd, Norris Div.	Lost Div. Final
1987-88	80	18	17	5	...	16	21	3	...	34	38	8	...	278	294	76	2nd, Norris Div.	Lost Div. Final
1986-87	80	21	12	7	...	11	21	8	...	32	33	15	...	281	293	79	1st, Norris Div.	Lost Div. Semi-Final
1985-86	80	23	11	6	...	14	23	3	...	37	34	9	...	302	291	83	3rd, Norris Div.	Lost Conf. Championship
1984-85	80	21	12	7	...	16	19	5	...	37	31	12	...	299	288	86	1st, Norris Div.	Lost Div. Semi-Final
1983-84	80	23	14	3	...	9	27	4	...	32	41	7	...	293	316	71	2nd, Norris Div.	Lost Div. Final
1982-83	80	16	16	8	...	9	24	7	...	25	40	15	...	285	316	65	4th, Norris Div.	Lost Div. Semi-Final
1981-82	80	22	14	4	...	10	26	4	...	32	40	8	...	315	349	72	3rd Norris Div.	Lost Div. Final
1980-81	80	29	7	4	...	16	11	13	...	45	18	17	...	352	281	107	1st, Smythe Div.	Lost Quarter-Final
1979-80	80	20	13	7	...	14	21	5	...	34	34	12	...	266	278	80	2nd, Smythe Div.	Lost Prelim. Round
1978-79	80	14	20	6	...	4	30	6	...	18	50	12	...	249	348	48	3rd, Smythe Div.	Out of Playoffs
1977-78	80	12	20	8	...	8	27	5	...	20	47	13	...	195	304	53	4th, Smythe Div.	Out of Playoffs
1976-77	80	22	13	5	...	10	26	4	...	32	39	9	...	239	276	73	1st, Smythe Div.	Lost Quarter-Final
1975-76	80	20	12	8	...	9	25	6	...	29	37	14	...	249	290	72	3rd, Smythe Div.	Lost Prelim. Round
1974-75	80	23	13	4	...	12	18	10	...	35	31	14	...	269	267	84	2nd, Smythe Div.	Lost Prelim. Round
1973-74	78	16	16	7	...	10	24	5	...	26	40	12	...	206	248	64	6th, West Div.	Out of Playoffs
1972-73	78	21	11	7	...	11	23	5	...	32	34	12	...	233	251	76	4th, West Div.	Lost Quarter-Final
1971-72	78	17	17	5	...	11	22	6	...	28	39	11	...	208	247	67	3rd, West Div.	Lost Semi-Final
1970-71	78	23	7	9	...	11	18	10	...	34	25	19	...	223	208	87	2nd, West Div.	Lost Quarter-Final
1969-70	76	24	9	5	...	13	18	7	...	37	27	12	...	224	179	86	1st, West Div.	Lost Final
1968-69	76	21	8	9	...	16	17	5	...	37	25	14	...	204	157	88	1st, West Div.	Lost Final
1967-68	74	18	12	7	...	9	19	9	...	27	31	16	...	177	191	70	3rd, West Div.	Lost Final

2001-02 Schedule

Oct.	Thu.	4	at Columbus
	Sat.	6	at Nashville
	Thu.	11	Los Angeles
	Sat.	13	at Toronto
	Wed.	17	Dallas
	Fri.	19	at Minnesota
	Sat.	20	Pittsburgh
	Mon.	22	Calgary
	Thu.	25	NY Rangers
	Sat.	27	at Ottawa
	Wed.	31	at Colorado
Nov.	Thu.	1	Carolina
	Sat.	3	Washington
	Tue.	6	San Jose
	Thu.	8	Vancouver
	Sat.	10	Phoenix
	Tue.	13	at Columbus
	Thu.	15	at Vancouver
	Sat.	17	at Calgary
	Tue.	20	at Edmonton
	Fri.	23	at Detroit
	Sat.	24	Phoenix
	Tue.	27	Ottawa
	Thu.	29	at Columbus
Dec.	Sat.	1	Columbus
	Sun.	2	at Minnesota
	Wed.	5	at Phoenix
	Thu.	6	at Los Angeles
	Sat.	8	Los Angeles
	Wed.	12	at Chicago
	Thu.	13	Toronto
	Sat.	15	Calgary
	Tue.	18	at Philadelphia
	Fri.	21	at Tampa Bay
	Sat.	22	at Florida
	Wed.	26	Chicago
	Fri.	28	Montreal
	Sun.	30	Nashville
Jan.	Tue.	1	at New Jersey
	Thu.	3	Columbus
	Sat.	5	Dallas*
	Tue.	8	at San Jose
	Wed.	9	at Anaheim
	Sat.	12	at Pittsburgh*
	Tue.	15	Edmonton
	Thu.	17	Vancouver
	Sat.	19	Boston
	Mon.	21	at Boston*
	Wed.	23	at Buffalo
	Fri.	25	at Chicago
	Sat.	26	Detroit
	Mon.	28	Anaheim
	Wed.	30	at Washington
Feb.	Tue.	5	at NY Islanders
	Thu.	7	Edmonton
	Sat.	9	Philadelphia
	Tue.	12	Atlanta
	Wed.	13	at Colorado
	Tue.	26	at Vancouver
	Thu.	28	at Calgary
Mar.	Sat.	2	at Edmonton
	Thu.	7	Minnesota
	Sat.	9	Detroit*
	Mon.	11	Colorado
	Wed.	13	at San Jose
	Thu.	14	at Los Angeles
	Sun.	17	at Anaheim*
	Tue.	19	Nashville
	Wed.	20	at Dallas
	Fri.	22	Anaheim
	Sun.	24	at Chicago*
	Tue.	26	Minnesota
	Thu.	28	Buffalo
	Sat.	30	at Nashville
Apr.	Mon.	1	at Phoenix
	Wed.	3	at Dallas
	Fri.	5	Chicago
	Sun.	7	Colorado
	Tue.	9	Nashville
	Thu.	11	San Jose
	Sat.	13	Detroit*
	Sun.	14	at Detroit*

* Denotes afternoon game.

Franchise date: June 5, 1967

CENTRAL DIVISION

35th NHL Season

It was lucky 13 for Scott Young in 2000-01 as his 13th NHL season proved to be his best. Young led the Blues with 40 goals (10 higher than his previous best) and also established a career high with 73 points.

2001-02 Player Personnel

FORWARDS	HT	WT	S	Place of Birth	Date	2000-01 Club
BORDELEAU, Sebastien	5-11	185	R	Vancouver, B.C.	2/15/75	Worcester-Nashville
CORSO, Daniel	5-10	187	L	Montreal, Que.	4/3/78	St. Louis-Worcester
DEMITRA, Pavol	5-11	203	L	Dubnica, Czech.	11/29/74	St. Louis
DRAKE, Dallas	6-1	187	L	Trail, B.C.	2/4/69	St. Louis
EASTWOOD, Mike	6-3	213	R	Ottawa, Ont.	7/1/67	St. Louis
KEANE, Mike	6-0	185	R	Winnipeg, Man.	5/29/67	Dallas
LOW, Reed	6-3	222	R	Moose Jaw, Sask.	6/21/76	St. Louis
MAYERS, Jamal	6-1	212	R	Toronto, Ont.	10/24/74	St. Louis
MELLANBY, Scott	6-1	205	R	Montreal, Que.	6/11/66	Florida-St. Louis
NASH, Tyson	6-0	185	L	Edmonton, Alta.	3/11/75	St. Louis
SIMPSON, Reid	6-2	216	L	Flin Flon, Man.	5/21/69	St. Louis
STILLMAN, Cory	6-0	194	L	Peterborough, Ont.	12/20/73	Calgary-St. Louis
TKACHUK, Keith	6-2	225	L	Melrose, MA	3/28/72	Phoenix-St. Louis
TKACZUK, Daniel	6-1	197	L	Toronto, Ont.	6/10/79	Calgary-Saint John
WEIGHT, Doug	5-11	200	L	Warren, MI	1/21/71	Edmonton
YOUNG, Scott	6-1	200	R	Clinton, MA	10/1/67	St. Louis
DEFENSEMEN						
FINLEY, Jeff	6-2	205	L	Edmonton, Alta.	4/14/67	St. Louis
HILL, Sean	6-0	203	R	Duluth, MN	2/14/70	St. Louis
KHAVANOV, Alexander	6-0	187	L	Ryazan, USSR	1/30/72	St. Louis
MacINNIS, Al	6-2	209	R	Inverness, N.S.	7/11/63	St. Louis
PILON, Rich	6-2	220	L	Saskatoon, Sask.	4/30/68	NY Rangers
PRONGER, Chris	6-6	220	L	Dryden, Ont.	10/10/74	St. Louis
SALVADOR, Bryce	6-2	215	L	Brandon, Man.	2/11/76	St. Louis
GOALTENDERS	**HT**	**WT**	**C**	**Place of Birth**	**Date**	**2000-01 Club**
BRATHWAITE, Fred	5-7	175	L	Ottawa, Ont.	11/24/72	Calgary
JOHNSON, Brent	6-2	200	L	Farmington, MI	3/12/77	St. Louis

Coaching History

Lynn Patrick and Scotty Bowman, 1967-68; Scotty Bowman, 1968-69, 1969-70; Al Arbour and Scotty Bowman, 1970-71; Sid Abel, Bill McCreary and Al Arbour, 1971-72; Al Arbour and Jean-Guy Talbot, 1972-73; Jean-Guy Talbot and Lou Angotti, 1973-74; Lou Angotti, Lynn Patrick and Garry Young, 1974-75; Garry Young, Lynn Patrick and Leo Boivin, 1975-76; Emile Francis, 1976-77; Leo Boivin and Barclay Plager, 1977-78; Barclay Plager, 1978-79; Barclay Plager and Red Berenson, 1979-80; Red Berenson, 1980-81; Red Berenson and Emile Francis, 1981-82; Emile Francis and Barclay Plager, 1982-83; Jacques Demers, 1983-84 to 1985-86; Jacques Martin, 1986-87, 1987-88; Brian Sutter, 1988-89 to 1991-92; Bob Plager and Bob Berry, 1992-93; Bob Berry, 1993-94; Mike Keenan, 1994-95, 1995-96; Mike Keenan, Jim Roberts and Joel Quenneville, 1996-97; Joel Quenneville, 1997-98 to date.

Coach

QUENNEVILLE, JOEL
Head Coach, St. Louis Blues. Born in Windsor, Ont., September 15, 1958.

Joel Quenneville was named head coach on January 6, 1997, becoming the 20th head coach in Blues history. His first game in St. Louis was on January 7, 1997. He won the Jack Adams Award as coach of the year in 1999-2000 after leading the Blues to the Presidents' Trophy with a club record 51 wins and 114 points. In 2000-01, he led the team to the Western Conference Finals.

Prior to joining the Blues the former NHL defenseman spent three seasons with the Colorado Avalanche organization as an assistant coach. He was instrumental in the Avalanche's drive for their first Stanley Cup championship during the 1995-96 season.

Prior to joining the Avalanche he was head coach for the Springfield Indians of the American Hockey League during the 1993-94 season. He retired from hockey after the 1991-92 season after serving the St. John's Maple Leafs (AHL) as a player/coach. Quenneville played 13 NHL seasons and finished with 803 career games played, 54 goals, 136 assists and 705 penalty minutes. His best years on the ice were spent with Hartford where he earned most valuable defenseman honors in 1984 and 1985. He played an integral part in helping Hartford win a divisional championship in 1986-87.

Coaching Record

		Regular Season				Playoffs		
Season	Team	Games	W	L	T	Games	W	L
1993-94	Springfield (AHL)	80	29	38	13	6	2	4
1996-97	**St. Louis (NHL)**	**40**	**18**	**15**	**7**	**6**	**2**	**4**
1997-98	**St. Louis (NHL)**	**82**	**45**	**29**	**8**	**10**	**6**	**4**
1998-99	**St. Louis (NHL)**	**82**	**37**	**32**	**13**	**13**	**6**	**7**
1999-2000	**St. Louis (NHL)**	**82**	**51**	**20**	**11**	**7**	**3**	**4**
2000-01	**St. Louis (NHL)**	**82**	**43**	**27**	**12**	**15**	**9**	**6**
	NHL Totals	**368**	**194**	**123**	**51**	**51**	**26**	**25**

2000-01 Scoring

* - rookie

Regular Season

Pos	#	Player	Team	GP	G	A	Pts	+/–	PIM	PP	SH	GW	GT	S	%
C	77	Pierre Turgeon	STL	79	30	52	82	14	37	11	0	6	1	171	17.5
L	7	Keith Tkachuk	PHX	64	29	42	71	6	108	15	0	4	1	230	12.6
			STL	12	6	2	8	–3	14	2	0	1	1	41	14.6
			TOTAL	76	35	44	79	3	122	17	0	5	2	271	12.9
R	48	Scott Young	STL	81	40	33	73	15	30	14	3	7	1	321	12.5
D	2	Al MacInnis	STL	59	12	42	54	23	52	6	1	3	0	218	5.5
L	12	Cory Stillman	CGY	66	21	24	45	–6	45	7	0	4	0	148	14.2
			STL	12	3	4	7	–2	6	3	0	0	0	26	11.5
			TOTAL	78	24	28	52	–8	51	10	0	4	0	174	13.8
D	44	Chris Pronger	STL	51	8	39	47	21	75	4	0	0	1	121	6.6
R	38	Pavol Demitra	STL	44	20	25	45	27	16	5	0	5	0	124	16.1
C	17	Jochen Hecht	STL	72	19	25	44	11	48	8	3	1	2	208	9.1
R	10	Dallas Drake	STL	82	12	29	41	18	71	2	0	3	0	142	8.5
D	29	Alexander Khavanov	STL	74	7	16	23	16	52	2	0	0	0	92	7.6
C	32	Mike Eastwood	STL	77	6	17	23	4	28	0	2	1	0	51	11.8
R	19	Scott Mellanby	FLA	40	4	9	13	–13	46	1	0	0	0	58	6.9
			STL	23	7	1	8	0	25	2	0	0	0	37	18.9
			TOTAL	63	11	10	21	–13	71	3	0	0	0	95	11.6
R	21	Jamal Mayers	STL	77	8	13	21	–3	117	0	0	0	0	132	6.1
L	9	Tyson Nash	STL	57	8	7	15	8	110	0	1	0	0	113	7.1
C	18	* Daniel Corso	STL	28	10	3	13	0	14	5	0	4	0	42	23.8
R	23	Lubos Bartecko	STL	50	5	8	13	–1	12	0	0	3	0	51	9.8
C	15	Marty Reasoner	STL	41	4	9	13	–5	14	0	0	0	0	65	6.2
D	6	Sean Hill	STL	48	1	10	11	5	51	0	0	0	0	47	2.1
D	37	Jeff Finley	STL	72	2	8	10	7	38	0	0	0	0	35	5.7
D	27	* Bryce Salvador	STL	75	2	8	10	–4	69	0	0	1	0	60	3.3
D	5	Alexei Gusarov	COL	9	0	1	1	2	6	0	0	0	0	4	0.0
			NYR	26	1	3	4	–2	6	0	0	0	0	21	4.8
			STL	16	0	4	4	–3	6	0	0	0	0	10	0.0
			TOTAL	51	1	8	9	–3	18	0	0	0	0	35	2.9
D	28	Todd Reirden	STL	38	2	4	6	–2	43	1	0	0	0	58	3.4
R	34	* Reed Low	STL	56	1	5	6	4	159	0	0	0	0	31	3.2
D	47	Darren Rumble	STL	12	0	4	4	7	27	0	0	0	0	11	0.0
L	33	Reid Simpson	STL	38	2	1	3	–3	96	0	0	1	0	23	8.7
D	55	Vlad Chebaturkin	STL	22	1	2	3	5	26	0	0	0	0	5	20.0
C	25	Pascal Rheaume	STL	8	2	0	2	–1	5	2	0	0	0	16	12.5
G	1	Roman Turek	STL	54	0	1	1	0	6	0	0	0	0	0	0.0
C	14	* Eric Boguniecki	STL	1	0	0	0	–1	0	0	0	0	0	1	0.0
D	7	* Mike Van Ryn	STL	1	0	0	0	–2	0	0	0	0	0	1	0.0
D	49	* Dale Clarke	STL	3	0	0	0	1	0	0	0	0	0	5	0.0
D	43	* Jaroslav Obsut	STL	4	0	0	0	1	2	0	0	0	0	3	0.0
D	36	Daniel Trebil	PIT	16	0	0	0	–1	7	0	0	0	0	17	0.0
			STL	10	0	0	0	1	0	0	0	0	0	9	0.0
			TOTAL	26	0	0	0	0	7	0	0	0	0	26	0.0
G	35	* Brent Johnson	STL	31	0	0	0	0	2	0	0	0	0	0	0.0

Goaltending

No.	Goaltender	GPI	Mins	Avg	W	L	T	EN	SO	GA	SA	S%
35	* Brent Johnson	31	1744	2.17	19	9	2	2	4	63	676	.907
1	Roman Turek	54	3232	2.28	24	18	10	7	6	123	1248	.901
	Totals	**82**	**5001**	**2.34**	**43**	**27**	**12**	**9**	**10**	**195**	**1933**	**.899**

Playoffs

Pos	#	Player	Team	GP	G	A	Pts	+/–	PIM	PP	SH	GW	GT	S	%
C	77	Pierre Turgeon	STL	15	5	10	15	8	2	1	0	0	0	30	16.7
R	48	Scott Young	STL	15	6	7	13	9	2	0	2	3	1	52	11.5
D	2	Al MacInnis	STL	15	2	8	10	2	18	2	0	0	0	67	3.0
L	7	Keith Tkachuk	STL	15	2	7	9	0	20	2	0	1	0	42	4.8
L	12	Cory Stillman	STL	15	3	5	8	0	8	1	0	1	1	35	8.6
D	44	Chris Pronger	STL	15	1	7	8	10	32	0	0	0	0	35	2.9
R	10	Dallas Drake	STL	15	4	2	6	1	16	0	1	1	0	21	19.0
R	19	Scott Mellanby	STL	15	3	3	6	–1	17	2	0	0	0	32	9.4
R	38	Pavol Demitra	STL	15	2	4	6	3	2	0	0	1	0	38	5.3
C	17	Jochen Hecht	STL	15	2	4	6	–3	4	0	0	0	0	19	10.5
D	29	Alexander Khavanov	STL	15	3	2	5	4	14	1	0	0	0	19	15.8
R	21	Jamal Mayers	STL	15	2	3	5	2	8	0	0	0	0	36	5.6
C	15	Marty Reasoner	STL	10	3	1	4	1	0	0	0	1	0	13	23.1
D	27	* Bryce Salvador	STL	14	2	0	2	–7	18	0	0	1	1	12	16.7
C	32	Mike Eastwood	STL	15	0	2	2	0	2	0	0	0	0	9	0.0
C	25	Pascal Rheaume	STL	3	0	1	1	1	0	0	0	0	0	4	0.0
C	18	* Daniel Corso	STL	12	0	1	1	–5	0	0	0	0	0	4	0.0
D	6	Sean Hill	STL	15	0	1	1	–1	12	0	0	0	0	16	0.0
D	28	Todd Reirden	STL	1	0	0	0	0	0	0	0	0	0	0	0.0
D	37	Jeff Finley	STL	2	0	0	0	–1	0	0	0	0	0	0	0.0
G	35	* Brent Johnson	STL	2	0	0	0	0	0	0	0	0	0	0	0.0
L	33	Reid Simpson	STL	5	0	0	0	0	2	0	0	0	0	1	0.0
D	5	Alexei Gusarov	STL	13	0	0	0	4	4	0	0	0	0	5	0.0
G	1	Roman Turek	STL	14	0	0	0	0	2	0	0	0	0	0	0.0

Goaltending

No.	Goaltender	GPI	Mins	Avg	W	L	EN	SO	GA	SA	S%
35	* Brent Johnson	2	62	1.94	0	1	0	0	2	36	.944
1	Roman Turek	14	908	2.05	9	5	1	0	31	382	.919
	Totals	**15**	**975**	**2.09**	**9**	**6**	**1**	**0**	**34**	**419**	**.919**

Captains' History

Al Arbour, 1967-68 to 1969-70; Red Berenson and Barclay Plager, 1970-71; Barclay Plager, 1971-72 to 1975-76; no captain, 1976-77; Red Berenson, 1977-78; Barry Gibbs, 1978-79; Brian Sutter, 1979-80 to 1987-88; Bernie Federko, 1988-89; Rick Meagher, 1989-90; Scott Stevens, 1990-91; Garth Butcher, 1991-92; Brett Hull, 1992-93 to 1994-95; Brett Hull, Shayne Corson and Wayne Gretzky, 1995-96; no captain, 1996-97; Chris Pronger, 1997-98 to date.

Club Records

Team

(Figures in brackets for season records are games played; records for fewest points, wins, ties, losses, goals, goals against are for 70 or more games)

Most Points	**114**	1999-2000 (82)
Most Wins	**51**	1999-2000 (82)
Most Ties	**19**	1970-71 (78)
Most Losses	**50**	1978-79 (80)
Most Goals	**352**	1980-81 (80)
Most Goals Against	**349**	1981-82 (80)
Fewest Points	**48**	1978-79 (80)
Fewest Wins	**18**	1978-79 (80)
Fewest Ties	**7**	1983-84 (80)
Fewest Losses	**18**	1980-81 (80)
Fewest Goals	**177**	1967-68 (74)
Fewest Goals Against	**157**	1968-69 (76)
Longest Winning Streak		
Overall	8	Nov. 24-Dec. 15/00
Home	9	Jan. 26-Feb. 26/91
Away	*10	Jan. 21-Mar. 2/00
Longest Undefeated Streak		
Overall	12	Nov. 10-Dec. 8/68 (5 wins, 7 ties), Nov. 24-Dec. 26/00 (11 wins, 1 tie)
Home	11	Four times
Away	11	Jan. 21-Mar. 4/00 (10 wins, 1 tie)
Longest Losing Streak		
Overall	7	Nov. 12-26/67, Feb. 12-25/89
Home	6	Nov. 23-Dec. 19/96
Away	10	Jan. 20-Mar. 8/82
Longest Winless Streak		
Overall	12	Jan. 17-Feb. 15/78 (10 losses, 2 ties)
Home	7	Dec. 28/82-Jan. 25/83 (5 losses, 2 ties)
Away	17	Jan. 23-Oct. 9/74 (13 losses, 4 ties)
Most Shutouts, Season	**13**	1968-69 (76)
Most PIM, Season	**2,041**	1990-91 (80)
Most Goals, Game	**11**	Feb. 26/94 (St.L. 11 at Ott. 1)

Individual

Most Seasons	**13**	Bernie Federko
Most Games	**927**	Bernie Federko
Most Goals, Career	**527**	Brett Hull
Most Assists, Career	**721**	Bernie Federko
Most Points, Career	**1,073**	Bernie Federko (352G, 721A)
Most PIM, Career	**1,786**	Brian Sutter
Most Shutouts, Career	**16**	Glenn Hall
Longest Consecutive Games Streak	**662**	Garry Unger (Feb. 7/71-Apr. 8/79)
Most Goals, Season	**86**	Brett Hull (1990-91)
Most Assists, Season	**90**	Adam Oates (1990-91)
Most Points, Season	**131**	Brett Hull (1990-91) (86G, 45A)
Most PIM, Season	**306**	Bob Gassoff (1975-76)
Most Points, Defenseman, Season	**78**	Jeff Brown (1992-93; 25G, 53A)
Most Points, Center, Season	**115**	Adam Oates (1990-91; 25G, 90A)
Most Points, Right Wing, Season	**131**	Brett Hull (1990-91; 86G, 45A)
Most Points, Left Wing, Season	**102**	Brendan Shanahan (1993-94; 52G, 50A)
Most Points, Rookie, Season	**73**	Jorgen Pettersson (1980-81; 37G, 36A)
Most Shutouts, Season	**8**	Glenn Hall (1968-69)
Most Goals, Game	**6**	Red Berenson (Nov. 7/68)
Most Assists, Game	**5**	Brian Sutter (Nov. 22/83), Bernie Federko (Feb. 27/88), Adam Oates (Jan. 26/91)
Most Points, Game	**7**	Red Berenson (Nov. 7/68; 6G, 1A), Garry Unger (Mar. 13/71; 3G, 4A)

* NHL Record.

Retired Numbers

3	Bob Gassoff	1973-1977
8	Barclay Plager	1967-1977
11	Brian Sutter	1976-1988
24	Bernie Federko	1976-1989

All-time Record vs. Other Clubs

Regular Season

	At Home								On Road								Total							
	GP	W	L	T	OL	GF	GA	PTS	GP	W	L	T	OL	GF	GA	PTS	GP	W	L	T	OL	GF	GA	PTS
Anaheim	16	8	5	3	0	53	44	19	16	11	4	1	0	52	38	23	32	19	9	4	0	105	82	42
Atlanta	1	1	0	0	0	4	1	2	2	2	0	0	0	11	5	4	3	3	0	0	0	15	6	6
Boston	57	25	23	9	0	182	194	59	57	13	35	9	0	153	244	35	114	38	58	18	0	335	438	94
Buffalo	48	27	14	7	0	174	123	61	49	14	29	6	0	151	195	34	97	41	43	13	0	325	318	95
Calgary	58	28	21	9	0	209	180	65	56	24	26	5	1	169	191	54	114	52	47	14	1	378	371	119
Carolina	29	17	9	3	0	113	90	37	29	16	11	2	0	92	87	34	58	33	20	5	0	205	177	71
Chicago	107	53	36	17	1	360	330	124	110	34	61	15	0	332	413	83	217	87	97	32	1	692	743	207
Colorado	34	21	10	3	0	137	105	45	35	12	18	5	0	99	123	29	69	33	28	8	0	236	228	74
Columbus	3	2	0	1	0	11	3	5	2	0	1	1	0	3	4	1	5	2	1	2	0	14	7	6
Dallas	111	61	30	20	0	406	315	142	109	39	49	21	0	326	369	99	220	100	79	41	0	732	684	241
Detroit	102	55	28	19	0	357	277	129	102	39	46	17	0	316	370	95	204	94	74	36	0	673	647	224
Edmonton	38	17	16	5	0	140	143	39	38	15	20	3	0	132	143	33	76	32	36	8	0	272	286	72
Florida	7	5	1	1	0	21	11	11	7	3	2	2	0	16	16	8	14	8	3	3	0	37	27	19
Los Angeles	72	45	17	10	0	272	185	100	72	28	33	11	0	214	248	67	144	73	50	21	0	486	433	167
Minnesota	2	2	0	0	0	7	1	4	2	1	0	1	0	4	3	3	4	3	0	1	0	11	4	7
Montreal	56	13	28	15	0	144	195	41	57	10	40	7	0	154	248	27	113	23	68	22	0	298	443	68
Nashville	8	5	3	0	0	23	15	10	9	6	2	1	0	30	19	13	17	11	5	1	0	53	34	23
New Jersey	44	27	10	7	0	187	134	61	44	17	20	7	0	127	142	41	88	44	30	14	0	314	276	102
NY Islanders	45	17	18	9	1	161	148	44	46	11	24	11	0	118	176	33	91	28	42	20	1	279	324	77
NY Rangers	60	23	28	9	0	174	193	55	59	9	44	6	0	140	243	24	119	32	72	15	0	314	436	79
Ottawa	7	3	3	1	0	21	21	7	8	6	2	0	0	34	16	12	15	9	5	1	0	55	37	19
Philadelphia	65	26	31	7	1	189	203	60	65	11	44	10	0	147	257	32	130	37	75	17	1	336	460	92
Phoenix	44	22	12	10	0	159	121	54	45	17	22	6	0	141	147	40	89	39	34	16	0	300	268	94
Pittsburgh	62	41	15	6	0	242	168	88	62	19	31	12	0	185	235	50	124	60	46	18	0	427	403	138
San Jose	22	15	5	1	1	78	50	32	18	14	3	1	0	65	42	29	40	29	8	2	1	143	92	61
Tampa Bay	9	8	1	0	0	35	20	16	11	5	4	2	0	37	32	12	20	13	5	2	0	72	52	28
Toronto	100	57	29	14	0	339	276	128	97	28	58	11	0	284	365	67	197	85	87	25	0	623	641	195
Vancouver	65	37	19	9	0	244	186	83	66	33	25	7	1	216	193	74	131	70	44	16	1	460	379	157
Washington	39	18	13	8	0	157	125	44	37	13	20	4	0	108	132	30	76	31	33	12	0	265	257	74
Defunct Clubs	32	25	4	3	0	131	55	53	33	11	10	12	0	95	100	34	65	36	14	15	0	226	155	87
Totals	**1343**	**704**	**429**	**206**	**4**	**4730**	**3912**	**1618**	**1343**	**461**	**684**	**196**	**2**	**3951**	**4796**	**1120**	**2686**	**1165**	**1113**	**402**	**6**	**8681**	**8708**	**2738**

Playoffs

	Series	W	L	GP	W	L	T	GF	GA	Last Mtg.	Round	Result
Boston	2	0	2	8	0	8	0	15	48	1972	SF	L 0-4
Buffalo	1	0	1	3	1	2	0	8	7	1976	PR	L 1-2
Calgary	1	0	1	7	3	4	0	22	28	1986	CF	L 3-4
Chicago	9	2	7	45	18	27	0	129	166	1993	DSF	W 4-0
Colorado	1	0	1	5	1	4	0	11	17	2001	CF	L 1-4
Dallas	12	6	6	66	32	34	0	187	197	2001	CSF	W 4-0
Detroit	6	2	4	35	15	20	0	92	111	1998	CSF	L 2-4
Los Angeles	2	2	0	8	8	0	0	32	13	1998	CQF	W 4-0
Montreal	3	0	3	12	0	12	0	14	42	1977	QF	L 0-4
NY Rangers	1	0	1	6	2	4	0	22	29	1981	QF	L 2-4
Philadelphia	2	2	0	11	8	3	0	34	20	1969	QF	W 4-0
Phoenix	2	2	0	11	7	4	0	39	29	1999	CQF	W 4-3
Pittsburgh	3	2	1	13	7	6	0	45	40	1981	PR	W 3-2
San Jose	2	1	1	13	7	6	0	38	31	2001	CQF	W 4-2
Toronto	5	3	2	31	17	14	0	88	90	1996	CQF	W 4-2
Vancouver	1	0	1	7	3	4	0	27	27	1995	CQF	L 3-4
Totals	**53**	**22**	**31**	**281**	**129**	**152**	**0**	**803**	**895**			

Playoff Results 2001-1997

Year	Round	Opponent	Result	GF	GA
2001	CF	Colorado	L 1-4	11	17
	CSF	Dallas	W 4-0	13	6
	CQF	San Jose	W 4-2	16	11
2000	CQF	San Jose	L 3-4	22	20
1999	CSF	Dallas	L 2-4	12	17
	CQF	Phoenix	W 4-3	19	16
1998	CSF	Detroit	L 2-4	13	23
	CQF	Los Angeles	W 4-0	16	8
1997	CQF	Detroit	L 2-4	12	13

Abbreviations: Round: CF – conference final; **CSF** – conference semi-final; **CQF** – conference quarter-final; **DSF** – division semi-final; **SF** – semi-final; **QF** – quarter-final; **PR** – preliminary round.

Calgary totals include Atlanta Flames, 1972-73 to 1979-80. Carolina totals include Hartford, 1979-80 to 1996-97.
Colorado totals include Quebec, 1979-80 to 1994-95. Dallas totals include Minnesota North Stars, 1967-68 to 1992-93.
New Jersey totals include Kansas City, 1974-75 to 1975-76, and Colorado Rockies, 1976-77 to 1981-82.
Phoenix totals include Winnipeg, 1979-80 to 1995-96.

2000-01 Results

Oct.	5	at Phoenix	1-4		13	at Los Angeles	4-2
	6	at San Jose	4-1		15	at Phoenix	1-3
	8	at Anaheim	5-1		18	Edmonton	4-1
	11	at Los Angeles	4-4		20	Vancouver	3-0
	13	Minnesota	2-0		21	at Nashville	1-3
	17	at Detroit	1-2		23	at Montreal	5-2
	19	Los Angeles	7-1		25	New Jersey	4-3*
	21	Chicago	1-0		27	San Jose	3-4*
	26	Calgary	4-3		29	Toronto	2-1
	28	Dallas	4-3*		30	at Boston	1-5
	29	at Carolina	4-1	**Feb.**	1	Columbus	2-2
	31	at Nashville	4-2		6	at Columbus	2-2
Nov.	2	Washington	2-0		8	Tampa Bay	4-1
	4	Toronto	0-0		10	at Colorado	4-3*
	9	at Colorado	3-3		11	at Dallas	3-3
	11	at Vancouver	5-2		15	Calgary	4-1
	14	at Edmonton	0-3		16	at Chicago	2-6
	16	Pittsburgh	4-3		19	at Florida	0-3
	18	Buffalo	4-1		20	at Tampa Bay	2-3
	21	Vancouver	3-4		23	at Detroit	2-4
	24	at Nashville	4-0		24	Boston	3-2*
	25	Phoenix	5-1		26	San Jose	7-2
	29	at Toronto	6-5*		28	at Edmonton	3-5
Dec.	2	Florida	5-2	**Mar.**	2	at Vancouver	2-3*
	5	Anaheim	1-0		3	at Calgary	2-3*
	9	Chicago	6-4		6	at Minnesota	3-3
	10	at Chicago	6-1		8	Colorado	2-5
	15	at Atlanta	6-3		10	Detroit	2-2
	16	Detroit	2-2		13	at Philadelphia	2-5
	20	at NY Rangers	6-3		14	at Minnesota	1-0*
	23	Anaheim	5-2		17	at Calgary	2-2
	26	Columbus	5-0		20	NY Islanders	3-4*
	28	Los Angeles	2-5		22	Colorado	1-3
	30	Phoenix	2-1		24	Chicago	5-1
Jan.	1	Edmonton	5-2		25	at Dallas	1-1
	2	at Ottawa	1-3		28	at Detroit	2-5
	4	Nashville	2-4		31	at Pittsburgh	3-5
	6	Minnesota	5-1	**Apr.**	1	at Columbus	1-2
	8	Philadelphia	1-2*		3	Carolina	2-2
	10	at Anaheim	4-2		5	Columbus	4-1
	11	at San Jose	3-6		7	Nashville	1-0

* – Overtime

Entry Draft Selections 2001-1987

2001
Pick
57 Jay McClement
89 Tuomas Nissinen
122 Igor Valeyev
159 Dmitri Semin
190 Brett Scheffelmaier
253 Petr Cajanek
270 Grant Jacobsen
283 Simon Skoog

2000
Pick
30 Jeff Taffe
65 David Morisset
75 Justin Papineau
96 Antoine Bergeron
129 Troy Riddle
167 Craig Weller
229 Brett Lutes
261 Reinhard Divis
293 Lauri Kinos

1999
Pick
17 Barret Jackman
85 Peter Smrek
114 Chad Starling
143 Trevor Byrne
180 Tore Vikingstad
203 Phil Osaer
221 Colin Hemingway
232 Alexander Khavanov
260 Brian McMeekin
270 James Desmarais

1998
Pick
24 Christian Backman
41 Maxim Linnik
83 Matt Walker
157 Brad Voth
170 Andrei Troschinsky
197 Brad Twordik
225 Yevgeny Pastukh
255 John Pohl

1997
Pick
40 Tyler Rennette
86 Didier Tremblay
98 Jan Horacek
106 Jame Pollock
149 Nicholas Bilotto
177 Ladislav Nagy
206 Bobby Haglund
232 Dmitri Plekhanov
244 Marek Ivan

1996
Pick
14 Marty Reasoner
67 Gordie Dwyer
95 Jonathan Zukiwsky
97 Andrei Petrakov
159 Stephen Wagner
169 Daniel Corso
177 Reed Low
196 Andrej Podkonicky
203 Tony Hutchins
229 Konstantin Shafranov

1995
Pick
49 Jochen Hecht
75 Scott Roche
101 Michal Handzus
127 Jeff Ambrosio
153 Denis Hamel
179 Jean-Luc Grand-Pierre
205 Derek Bekar
209 Libor Zabransky

1994
Pick
68 Stephane Roy
94 Tyler Harlton
120 Edvin Frylen
172 Roman Vopat
198 Steve Noble
224 Marc Stephan
250 Kevin Harper
276 Scott Fankhouser

1993
Pick
37 Maxim Bets
63 Jamie Rivers
89 Jamal Mayers
141 Todd Kelman
167 Mike Buzak
193 Eric Boguniecki
219 Mike Grier
245 Libor Prochazka
271 Alexander Vasilevski
275 Christer Olsson

1992
Pick
38 Igor Korolev
62 Vitali Karamnov
64 Vitali Prokhorov
86 Lee Leslie
134 Bob Lachance
158 Ian Laperriere
160 Lance Burns
180 Igor Boldin
182 Nick Naumenko
206 Todd Harris
230 Yuri Gunko
259 Wade Salzman

1991
Pick
27 Steve Staios
64 Kyle Reeves
65 Nathan LaFayette
87 Grayden Reid
109 Jeff Callinan
131 Bruce Gardiner
153 Terry Hollinger
175 Chris Kenady
197 Jed Fiebelkorn
219 Chris MacKenzie
241 Kevin Rappana
263 Mike Veisor

1990
Pick
33 Craig Johnson
54 Patrice Tardif
96 Jason Ruff
117 Kurtis Miller
138 Wayne Conlan
180 Parris Duffus
201 Steve Widmeyer
222 Joe Hawley
243 Joe Fleming

1989
Pick
9 Jason Marshall
31 Rick Corriveau
55 Denny Felsner
93 Daniel Laperriere
114 David Roberts
124 Derek Frenette
135 Jeff Batters
156 Kevin Plager
177 John Roderick
198 John Valo
219 Brian Lukowski

1988
Pick
9 Rod Brind'Amour
30 Adrien Plavsic
51 Rob Fournier
72 Jaan Luik
105 Dave Lacouture
114 Dan Fowler
135 Matt Hayes
156 John McCoy
177 Tony Twist
198 Bret Hedican
219 Heath DeBoer
240 Michael Francis

1987
Pick
12 Keith Osborne
54 Kevin Miehm
59 Robert Nordmark
75 Darren Smith
82 Andy Rymsha
117 Rob Robinson
138 Todd Crabtree
159 Guy Hebert
180 Robert Dumas
201 David Marvin
207 Andy Cesarski
222 Dan Rolfe
243 Ray Savard

Club Directory

Savvis Center

St. Louis Blues
Savvis Center
1401 Clark Avenue
St. Louis, MO 63103
Phone **314/622-2500**
FAX 314/622-2533
www.stlouisblues.com
Capacity: 19,022

Owner and Chairman	Bill Laurie
President and CEO	Mark Sauer
Sr. Vice President and General Manager	Larry Pleau
Vice President and Director of Hockey Operations	John Ferguson, Jr.
Head Coach	Joel Quenneville
Assistant Coaches	Mike Kitchen, Jim Roberts
Goaltending Coach	Keith Allain
Video Coach	Jamie Kompon
Athletic Trainer	Ray Barile
Equipment Manager	Bert Godin
Assistant Equipment Manager	Eric Bechtol
Massage Therapist	Jeff Wright
Exercise Physiologist	Dr. Howie Wenger
Sr. Vice President pf Marketing and Communications	Jim Woodcock
Director of Team Services	Mike Caruso
Director of Communications	Frank Buonomo
Assistant Director of Communications	Stan Richardson
Assistant Director of Communications	Greg Franklin
Team Photographer	Mark Buckner
Radio Station	KTRS 550 AM
Radio Broadcasters	Chris Kerber, Kelly Chase
Television Station	KPLR-TV WB 11
Television Broadcasters	Ken Wilson, Bernie Federko, Dan McLaughlin
Regional Sports Network	Fox Sports Net (Midwest)

Injuries limited Pavol Demitra to only 44 games in 2000-01, but the right winger still scored 20 goals (including five game winners) and finished with a plus/mius rating of +27.

General Manager

PLEAU, LARRY
General Manager, St. Louis Blues. Born in Lynn, MA, June 29, 1947.

Larry Pleau was named general manager on June 9, 1997, becoming the tenth person to hold that position in team history. He has built the Blues into one of the NHL's top teams, winning the President's Trophy in 1999-2000 and reaching the Western Conference Finals in 2000-01.

Pleau joined the Blues after spending eight seasons with the New York Rangers organization, most recently as vice president of player personnel. He joined the Rangers in 1989 as assistant general manager of player development. During Pleau's tenure in New York, the Rangers drafted NHL stars Sergei Zubov, Doug Weight, Alexei Kovalev, Niklas Sundstrom, Todd Marchant and Sergei Nemchinov, along with Corey Hirsch, Daniel Goneau and Mattias Norstrom. Prior to joining the Rangers, Pleau spent 17 seasons with the Hartford Whalers organization as a player, assistant coach, head coach, general manager and minor league general manager and head coach. He was also instrumental in drafting Ray Ferraro, Ron Francis, Kevin Dineen and Ulf Samuelsson while a member of the Whalers organization.

Pleau played three seasons with the Montreal Canadiens (1969-1972) in the National Hockey League before being the first player signed by the Hartford Whalers of the World Hockey Association. He was a center/left wing for the Whalers from 1972 until his retirement in 1979. He played in 468 regular season games for Hartford, accumulating 157 goals and 215 assists for 372 points. He also played for the 1968 United States Olympic Team, the 1969 U.S. National Team and for Team USA in the 1976 Canada Cup tournament.

NHL Coaching Record

		Regular Season				Playoffs		
Season	**Team**	**Games**	**W**	**L**	**T**	**Games**	**W**	**L**
1980-81	Hartford	20	6	12	2	....	....	....
1981-82	Hartford	80	21	41	18	....	....	....
1982-83	Hartford	18	4	13	1	....	....	....
1987-88	Hartford	26	13	13	0	6	2	4
1988-89	Hartford	80	37	38	5	4	0	4
	NHL Totals	**224**	**81**	**117**	**26**	**10**	**2**	**8**

General Managers' History

Lynn Patrick, 1967-68; Scotty Bowman, 1968-69 to 1970-71; Lynn Patrick, 1971-72; Sid Abel, 1972-73; Charles Catto, 1973-74; Gerry Ehman, 1974-75; Dennis Ball, 1975-76; Emile Francis, 1976-77 to 1982-83; Ron Caron, 1983-84 to 1993-94; Mike Keenan, 1994-95, 1995-96; Mike Keenan and Ron Caron, 1996-97; Larry Pleau, 1997-98 to date.

San Jose Sharks

2000-01 Results: 40W-27L-12T-3OTL 95PTS. Second, Pacific Division

Year-by-Year Record

Season	GP	Home W	Home L	Home T	Home OL	Road W	Road L	Road T	Road OL	Overall W	Overall L	Overall T	Overall OL	GF	GA	Pts.	Finished	Playoff Result
2000-01	82	22	14	4	1	18	13	8	2	40	27	12	3	217	192	95	2nd, Pacific Div.	Lost Conf. Quarter-Final
1999-2000	82	21	14	3	3	14	16	7	4	35	30	10	7	225	214	87	4th, Pacific Div.	Lost Conf. Semi-Final
1998-99	82	17	15	9	...	14	18	9	...	31	33	18	...	196	191	80	4th, Pacific Div.	Lost Conf. Quarter-Final
1997-98	82	17	19	5	...	17	19	5	...	34	38	10	...	210	216	78	4th, Pacific Div.	Lost Conf. Quarter-Final
1996-97	82	14	23	4	...	13	24	4	...	27	47	8	...	211	278	62	7th, Pacific Div.	Out of Playoffs
1995-96	82	12	26	3	...	8	29	4	...	20	55	7	...	252	357	47	7th, Pacific Div.	Out of Playoffs
1994-95	48	10	13	1	...	9	12	3	...	19	25	4	...	129	161	42	3rd, Pacific Div.	Lost Conf. Semi-Final
1993-94	84	19	13	10	...	14	22	6	...	33	35	16	...	252	265	82	3rd, Pacific Div.	Lost Conf. Semi-Final
1992-93	84	8	33	1	...	3	38	1	...	11	71	2	...	218	414	24	6th, Smythe Div.	Out of Playoffs
1991-92	80	14	23	3	...	3	35	2	...	17	58	5	...	219	359	39	6th, Smythe Div.	Out of Playoffs

2001-02 Schedule

Month	Day	Date	Opponent
Oct.	Thu.	4	Detroit
	Sat.	6	Minnesota*
	Thu.	11	Tampa Bay
	Sat.	13	Boston
	Tue.	16	at Minnesota
	Thu.	18	at New Jersey
	Sat.	20	at NY Islanders*
	Mon.	22	at NY Rangers
	Tue.	23	at Buffalo
	Thu.	25	at Chicago
	Sat.	27	Columbus
	Wed.	31	at Anaheim
Nov.	Thu.	1	Atlanta
	Sat.	3	Vancouver
	Tue.	6	at St. Louis
	Wed.	7	at Dallas
	Fri.	9	at Carolina
	Sun.	11	at Chicago
	Wed.	14	at Anaheim
	Thu.	15	at Phoenix
	Sat.	17	Dallas
	Wed.	21	Minnesota
	Sat.	24	at Los Angeles*
	Tue.	27	Nashville
	Thu.	29	Pittsburgh
	Fri.	30	at Anaheim
Dec.	Tue.	4	Calgary
	Thu.	6	at Calgary
	Sat.	8	at Vancouver
	Tue.	11	Edmonton
	Fri.	14	at Colorado
	Mon.	17	at Dallas
	Wed.	19	at Atlanta
	Fri.	21	at Detroit
	Sun.	23	at Nashville*
	Wed.	26	Anaheim
	Fri.	28	NY Rangers
	Sun.	30	Phoenix*
Jan.	Wed.	2	Philadelphia
	Fri.	4	Phoenix
	Sat.	5	Florida
	Tue.	8	St. Louis
	Wed.	9	at Phoenix
	Sat.	12	Los Angeles*
	Tue.	15	at Colorado
	Thu.	17	NY Islanders
	Sat.	19	Colorado
	Mon.	21	Edmonton*
	Wed.	23	at Detroit
	Thu.	24	at Columbus
	Sun.	27	at Montreal*
	Tue.	29	at Toronto
	Wed.	30	at Pittsburgh*
Feb.	Wed.	6	Calgary
	Fri.	8	Chicago
	Sun.	10	Carolina*
	Tue.	12	at Edmonton
	Tue.	26	at Nashville
	Thu.	28	at Washington
Mar.	Fri.	1	at Tampa Bay
	Sun.	3	at Dallas*
	Tue.	5	Nashville
	Thu.	7	Ottawa
	Sat.	9	Vancouver
	Sun.	10	at Vancouver
	Wed.	13	St. Louis
	Fri.	15	Washington
	Sat.	16	Chicago
	Mon.	18	Los Angeles
	Wed.	20	at Edmonton
	Thu.	21	at Calgary
	Sat.	23	at Los Angeles*
	Tue.	26	Dallas
	Thu.	28	Colorado
	Sat.	30	Columbus
Apr.	Tue.	2	Anaheim
	Thu.	4	Phoenix
	Sat.	6	Detroit
	Mon.	8	at Minnesota
	Wed.	10	at Columbus
	Thu.	11	at St. Louis
	Sat.	13	Los Angeles*

* Denotes afternoon game.

Brad Stuart was the runner-up to Scott Gomez for the Calder Trophy in 1999-2000 and continued his solid work on the Sharks blueline last year. Only Gary Suter had more points among San Jose defensemen.

Franchise date: May 9, 1990

WESTERN NHL CONFERENCE

PACIFIC DIVISION

11th NHL Season

2001-02 Player Personnel

FORWARDS	HT	WT	S	Place of Birth	Date	2000-01 Club
BRADLEY, Matt	6-2	195	R	Stittsville, Ont.	6/13/78	Kentucky-San Jose
CHEECHOO, Jonathan	6-0	205	R	Moose Factory, Ont.	7/15/80	Kentucky
COLAGIACOMO, Adam	6-2	200	R	Rexdale, Ont.	3/17/79	Kentucky
CRAIG, Mike	6-1	185	R	London, Ont.	6/6/71	Hershey
DAMPHOUSSE, Vincent	6-1	200	L	Montreal, Que.	12/17/67	San Jose
GOC, Marcel	6-0	189	L	Calw, West Germany	8/24/83	Schwenningen
GRAVES, Adam	6-0	205	L	Toronto, Ont.	4/12/68	NY Rangers
HARVEY, Todd	6-0	200	R	Hamilton, Ont.	2/17/75	San Jose
HYVONEN, Hannes	6-2	200	R	Oulu, Finland	8/29/75	HIFK Helsinki
KOROLYUK, Alexander	5-9	195	L	Moscow, USSR	1/15/76	Ak Bars Kazan-San Jose
KRAFT, Ryan	5-9	190	L	Bottineau, ND	11/7/75	Kentucky
LAPLANTE, Eric	6-0	185	L	St-Maurice, Que.	12/1/79	Kentucky
LUNDBOHM, Andy	6-3	225	L	Roseau, MN	3/24/77	Kentucky
MARLEAU, Patrick	6-2	210	L	Aneroid, Sask.	9/15/79	San Jose
MATTEAU, Stephane	6-4	215	L	Rouyn-Noranda, Que.	9/2/69	San Jose
MISCHLER, Greg	6-3	174	L	Holbrook, NY	9/15/78	Northeastern
NITTEL, Adam	6-2	225	R	Kitchener, Ont.	7/17/78	Dayton-Kentucky
NOLAN, Owen	6-1	210	R	Belfast, Ireland	2/12/72	San Jose
PRPIC, Joel	6-6	225	L	Sudbury, Ont.	9/25/74	Colorado-Hershey
RICCI, Mike	6-0	185	L	Scarborough, Ont.	10/27/71	San Jose
SELANNE, Teemu	6-0	204	R	Helsinki, Finland	7/3/70	Anaheim-San Jose
SMITH, Mark	5-10	205	L	Edmonton, Alta.	10/24/77	San Jose-Kentucky
STURM, Marco	6-0	195	L	Dingolfing, West Germany	9/8/78	San Jose
SUNDSTROM, Niklas	6-0	190	L	Ornskoldsvik, Sweden	6/6/75	San Jose
THORNTON, Scott	6-3	220	L	London, Ont.	1/9/71	San Jose
WISEMAN, Chad	6-0	190	L	Burlington, Ont.	3/25/81	Mississauga-Plymouth
ZALESAK, Miroslav	6-0	185	L	Skalica, Czech.	1/2/80	Kentucky
DEFENSEMEN						
BANCROFT, Steve	6-1	214	L	Toronto, Ont.	10/6/70	Kentucky
CARKNER, Matt	6-4	229	R	Winchester, Ont.	11/3/80	Peterborough
DAVISON, Rob	6-2	220	L	St. Catharines, Ont.	5/1/80	Kentucky
FIBIGER, Jesse	6-3	210	L	Victoria, B.C.	4/4/78	Minnesota-Duluth
HANNAN, Scott	6-2	220	L	Richmond, B.C.	1/23/79	San Jose
HEINS, Shawn	6-4	210	L	Eganville, Ont.	12/24/73	San Jose
JILLSON, Jeff	6-3	220	R	North Smithfield, RI	7/24/80	U. of Michigan
JINDRICH, Robert	5-11	195	L	Plzen, Czech.	10/14/76	Kentucky
MARCHMENT, Bryan	6-1	200	L	Scarborough, Ont.	5/1/69	San Jose
MULICK, Robert	6-2	210	R	Toronto, Ont.	10/23/79	Kentucky
RAGNARSSON, Marcus	6-1	215	L	Ostervala, Sweden	8/13/71	San Jose
RATHJE, Mike	6-5	245	L	Mannville, Alta.	5/11/74	San Jose
SMITH, Brandon	6-1	198	L	Hazelton, B.C.	2/25/73	Boston-Providence
STUART, Brad	6-2	215	L	Rocky Mountain House, Alta.	11/6/79	San Jose
SUTER, Gary	6-0	215	L	Madison, WI	6/24/64	San Jose

GOALTENDERS	HT	WT	C	Place of Birth	Date	2000-01 Club
KIELKUCKI, Marc	6-4	195	L	Brooklyn Park, MN	6/5/79	Air Force
KIPRUSOFF, Miikka	6-2	190	L	Turku, Finland	10/26/76	San Jose-Kentucky
NABOKOV, Evgeni	6-0	200	L	Ust-Kamenogorsk, USSR	7/25/75	San Jose
TOSKALA, Vesa	5-10	190	L	Tampere, Finland	5/20/77	Kentucky

Coach

SUTTER, DARRYL JOHN
Coach, San Jose Sharks. Born in Viking, Alta., August 19, 1958.

Darryl Sutter became the Sharks' fifth head coach on June 9, 1997. He led the club to a team-record 40 wins and 95 points in 2000-01. Sutter played eight NHL seasons, all with the Chicago Blackhawks (1979-87). He began his coaching career as an assistant in Chicago in 1987-88 before taking over as head coach of the Blackhawks' IHL affiliate that played in Saginaw (1988-89) and in Indianapolis (1989-90). His club won the IHL Turner Cup championship in 1990 and Sutter was named coach of the year.

He later served as an associate coach under Mike Keenan in Chicago in 1990-91 and 1991-92 and began a three-year tenure as head coach of the Blackhawks in 1992-93. As coach of Chicago, Sutter's teams reached the playoffs in all three seasons. He resigned as head coach following the 1994-95 season to spend more time with his family and worked as a consultant to the Blackhawks for special assignments in 1995-96 and 1996-97.

In 19 years of hockey as a player and coach, Sutter has never failed to qualify for post-season play. During his eight-year playing career, he scored 161 goals and added 118 assists in 406 regular-season games. He added 24 goals and 19 assists in 51 playoff games. Drafted 179th overall by Chicago in the 1978 NHL Entry Draft, he scored a remarkable 40 goals during his rookie season. The left winger served as team captain from 1982-83 until injuries forced his retirement after the 1986-87 season.

He is one of six brothers to play in the NHL. The others are Brian, Brent, Duane, Rich and Ron. All are involved in the Sutter Foundation which raises raises money for non-profit organizations in their home province of Alberta.

Coaching Record

		Regular Season				Playoffs		
Season	Team	Games	W	L	T	Games	W	L
1988-89	Saginaw (IHL)	82	46	26	10	6	2	4
1989-90	Indianapolis (IHL)	82	53	21	8	14	12	2
1992-93	**Chicago (NHL)**	**84**	**47**	**25**	**12**	**4**	**0**	**4**
1993-94	**Chicago (NHL)**	**84**	**39**	**36**	**9**	**6**	**2**	**4**
1994-95	**Chicago (NHL)**	**48**	**24**	**19**	**5**	**16**	**9**	**7**
1997-98	**San Jose (NHL)**	**82**	**34**	**38**	**10**	**6**	**2**	**4**
1998-99	**San Jose (NHL)**	**82**	**31**	**33**	**18**	**6**	**2**	**4**
1999-2000	**San Jose (NHL)**	**82**	**35**	**37**	**10**	**12**	**5**	**7**
2000-01	**San Jose (NHL)**	**82**	**40**	**30**	**12**	**6**	**2**	**4**
	NHL Totals	**544**	**250**	**218**	**76**	**56**	**22**	**34**

2000-01 Scoring

* - rookie

Regular Season

Pos	#	Player	Team	GP	G	A	Pts	+/–	PIM	PP	SH	GW	GT	S	%
R	8	Teemu Selanne	ANA	61	26	33	59	–8	36	10	0	5	1	202	12.9
			S.J.	12	7	6	13	1	0	2	0	2	0	31	22.6
			TOTAL	73	33	39	72	–7	36	12	0	7	1	233	14.2
C	14	Patrick Marleau	S.J.	81	25	27	52	7	22	5	0	6	0	146	17.1
R	11	Owen Nolan	S.J.	57	24	25	49	0	75	10	1	4	1	191	12.6
R	24	Niklas Sundstrom	S.J.	82	10	39	49	10	28	4	1	0	0	100	10.0
C	25	Vincent Damphousse	S.J.	45	9	37	46	17	62	4	0	3	0	101	8.9
C	18	Mike Ricci	S.J.	81	22	22	44	3	60	9	2	4	0	141	15.6
L	17	Scott Thornton	S.J.	73	19	17	36	4	114	4	0	1	1	159	11.9
D	20	Gary Suter	S.J.	68	10	24	34	8	84	4	0	1	0	157	6.4
L	19	Marco Sturm	S.J.	81	14	18	32	9	28	2	3	5	0	153	9.2
L	32	Stephane Matteau	S.J.	80	13	19	32	5	32	1	0	3	0	81	16.0
L	15	Alexander Korolyuk	S.J.	70	12	13	25	2	41	3	0	1	0	140	8.6
D	7	Brad Stuart	S.J.	77	5	18	23	10	56	1	0	2	1	119	4.2
R	9	Todd Harvey	S.J.	69	10	11	21	6	72	1	0	2	0	66	15.2
D	27	Bryan Marchment	S.J.	75	7	11	18	15	204	0	1	3	1	73	9.6
D	22	Scott Hannan	S.J.	75	3	14	17	10	51	0	0	1	0	96	3.1
D	10	Marcus Ragnarsson	S.J.	68	3	12	15	2	44	1	0	0	0	74	4.1
L	12	Bill Lindsay	CGY	52	1	9	10	–8	97	0	0	0	0	57	1.8
			S.J.	16	0	4	4	2	29	0	0	0	0	14	0.0
			TOTAL	68	1	13	14	–6	126	0	0	0	0	71	1.4
D	5	Jeff Norton	PIT	32	2	10	12	8	20	1	0	1	0	17	11.8
			S.J.	10	0	1	1	4	8	0	0	0	0	5	0.0
			TOTAL	42	2	11	13	12	28	1	0	1	0	22	9.1
D	40	Mike Rathje	S.J.	81	0	11	11	7	48	0	0	0	0	89	0.0
R	21	Tony Granato	S.J.	60	4	5	9	–1	65	1	0	1	0	85	4.7
D	23	Shawn Heins	S.J.	38	3	4	7	2	57	2	0	0	0	45	6.7
C	26	Jim Montgomery	S.J.	28	1	6	7	–1	19	1	0	0	0	17	5.9
C	16	* Mark Smith	S.J.	42	2	2	4	2	51	0	0	0	0	39	5.1
R	44	* Matt Bradley	S.J.	21	1	1	2	0	19	0	0	0	0	16	6.3
G	35	* Evgeni Nabokov	S.J.	66	0	2	2	0	8	0	0	0	0	1	0.0
L	29	Paul Kruse	S.J.	1	0	0	0	0	5	0	0	0	0	0	0.0
C	28	* Mikael Samuelsson	S.J.	4	0	0	0	0	0	0	0	0	0	3	0.0
G	34	* Miikka Kiprusoff	S.J.	5	0	0	0	0	0	0	0	0	0	0	0.0
G	31	Steve Shields	S.J.	21	0	0	0	0	2	0	0	0	0	0	0.0

Goaltending

No.	Goaltender	GPI	Mins	Avg	W	L	T	EN	SO	GA	SA	S%
34	* Miikka Kiprusoff	5	154	1.95	2	1	0	1	0	5	51	.902
35	* Evgeni Nabokov	66	3700	2.19	32	21	7	3	6	135	1582	.915
31	Steve Shields	21	1135	2.48	6	8	5	1	2	47	531	.911
	Totals	**82**	**5008**	**2.30**	**40**	**30**	**12**	**5**	**9**	**192**	**2169**	**.911**

Playoffs

Pos	#	Player	Team	GP	G	A	Pts	+/–	PIM	PP	SH	GW	GT	S	%
L	32	Stephane Matteau	S.J.	6	1	3	4	1	0	0	0	0	0	6	16.7
L	17	Scott Thornton	S.J.	6	3	0	3	1	8	0	0	1	0	15	20.0
C	25	Vincent Damphousse	S.J.	6	2	1	3	–1	14	0	1	0	0	15	13.3
C	18	Mike Ricci	S.J.	6	0	3	3	–1	0	0	0	0	0	10	0.0
R	24	Niklas Sundstrom	S.J.	6	0	3	3	1	2	0	0	0	0	5	0.0
C	14	Patrick Marleau	S.J.	6	2	0	2	1	4	0	0	0	0	12	16.7
R	11	Owen Nolan	S.J.	6	1	1	2	–5	8	0	0	1	0	26	3.8
R	8	Teemu Selanne	S.J.	6	0	2	2	2	2	0	0	0	0	5	0.0
L	19	Marco Sturm	S.J.	6	0	2	2	–2	0	0	0	0	0	7	0.0
R	21	Tony Granato	S.J.	4	1	0	1	0	4	0	0	0	0	5	20.0
D	7	Brad Stuart	S.J.	5	1	0	1	0	0	0	0	0	0	4	25.0
D	27	Bryan Marchment	S.J.	5	0	1	1	3	2	0	0	0	0	10	0.0
D	10	Marcus Ragnarsson	S.J.	5	0	1	1	0	8	0	0	0	0	5	0.0
D	5	Jeff Norton	S.J.	6	0	1	1	–2	2	0	0	0	0	3	0.0
D	40	Mike Rathje	S.J.	6	0	1	1	2	4	0	0	0	0	5	0.0
D	22	Scott Hannan	S.J.	6	0	1	1	–1	6	0	0	0	0	20	0.0
D	20	Gary Suter	S.J.	1	0	0	0	0	0	0	0	0	0	0	0.0
R	15	Alexander Korolyuk	S.J.	2	0	0	0	0	0	0	0	0	0	0	0.0
D	23	Shawn Heins	S.J.	2	0	0	0	–1	0	0	0	0	0	2	0.0
G	34	* Miikka Kiprusoff	S.J.	3	0	0	0	0	0	0	0	0	0	0	0.0
G	35	* Evgeni Nabokov	S.J.	4	0	0	0	0	0	0	0	0	0	0	0.0
L	12	Bill Lindsay	S.J.	6	0	0	0	0	16	0	0	0	0	4	0.0
R	9	Todd Harvey	S.J.	6	0	0	0	0	8	0	0	0	0	2	0.0

Goaltending

No.	Goaltender	GPI	Mins	Avg	W	L	EN	SO	GA	SA	S%
34	* Miikka Kiprusoff	3	149	2.01	1	1	1	0	5	79	.937
35	* Evgeni Nabokov	4	218	2.75	1	3	0	1	10	103	.903
	Totals	**6**	**370**	**2.59**	**2**	**4**	**1**	**1**	**16**	**183**	**.913**

Captains' History

Doug Wilson, 1991-92, 1992-93; Bob Errey, 1993-94; Bob Errey and Jeff Odgers, 1994-95; Jeff Odgers, 1995-96; Todd Gill, 1996-97, 1997-98; Owen Nolan, 1998-99 to date.

Coaching History

George Kingston, 1991-92, 1992-93; Kevin Constantine, 1993-94, 1994-95; Kevin Constantine and Jim Wiley, 1995-96; Al Sims, 1996-97; Darryl Sutter, 1997-98 to date.

Club Records

Team

(Figures in brackets for season records are games played; records for fewest points, wins, ties, losses, goals, goals against are for 70 or more games)

Most Points	**95**	2000-01 (82)
Most Wins	**40**	2000-01 (82)
Most Ties	**18**	1998-99 (82)
Most Losses	***71**	1992-93 (84)
Most Goals	**252**	1993-94 (84), 1995-96 (82)
Most Goals Against	**414**	1992-93 (84)
Fewest Points	**24**	1992-93 (84)
Fewest Wins	**11**	1992-93 (84)
Fewest Ties	***2**	1992-93 (84)
Fewest Losses	**33**	1998-99 (82)
Fewest Goals	**196**	1998-99 (82)
Fewest Goals Against	**191**	1998-99 (82)
Longest Winning Streak		
Overall	7	Mar. 24-Apr. 5/94
Home	5	Jan. 21-Feb. 15/95
Away	4	Four times
Longest Undefeated Streak		
Overall	9	Mar. 20-Apr. 5/94 (7 wins, 2 ties)
Home	7	Oct. 12-Nov. 22/00 (6 wins, 1 tie)
Away	10	Dec. 26/00-Feb. 16/01 (6 wins, 4 ties)
Longest Losing Streak		
Overall	***17**	Jan. 4-Feb. 12/93
Home	**9**	Nov. 19-Dec. 19/92
Away	**19**	Nov. 27/92-Feb. 12/93
Longest Winless Streak		
Overall	**20**	Dec. 29/92-Feb. 12/93 (19 losses, 1 tie)
Home	**9**	Nov. 19-Dec. 19/92 (9 losses)
Away	**19**	Nov. 27/92-Feb. 12/93 (19 losses)
Most Shutouts, Season	**9**	2000-01 (82)
Most PIM, Season	**2134**	1992-93 (84)
Most Goals, Game	**10**	Jan. 13/96 (S.J. 10 at Pit. 8)

Individual

Most Seasons	**8**	Mike Rathje
Most Games, Career	**512**	Jeff Friesen
Most Goals, Career	**161**	Owen Nolan
Most Assists, Career	**201**	Jeff Friesen
Most Points, Career	**350**	Jeff Friesen (149G, 201A)
Most PIM, Career	**1,001**	Jeff Odgers
Most Shutouts, Career	**10**	Steve Shields
Longest Consecutive Games Streak	**228**	Mike Ricci (Nov. 22/97-date)
Most Goals, Season	**44**	Owen Nolan (1999-2000)
Most Assists, Season	**52**	Kelly Kisio (1992-93)
Most Points, Season	**84**	Owen Nolan (1999-2000; 44G, 40A)
Most PIM, Season	**326**	Link Gaetz (1991-92)
Most Points, Defenseman, Season	**64**	Sandis Ozolnish (1993-94; 26G, 38A)
Most Points, Center, Season	**78**	Kelly Kisio (1992-93; 26G, 52A)
Most Points, Right Wing, Season	**84**	Owen Nolan (1999-2000; 44G, 40A)
Most Points, Left Wing, Season	**66**	Johan Garpenlov (1992-93; 22G, 44A)
Most Points, Rookie, Season	**59**	Pat Falloon (1991-92; 25G, 34A)
Most Shutouts, Season	**6**	Evgeni Nabokov (2000-01)
Most Goals, Game	**4**	Owen Nolan (Dec. 19/95)
Most Assists, Game	**4**	Three times
Most Points, Game	**6**	Owen Nolan (Oct. 4/99; 3G, 3A)

* NHL Record.

General Manager

LOMBARDI, DEAN
Executive Vice President and General Manager, San Jose Sharks.
Born in Holyoke, MA, March 5, 1958.

Dean Lombardi is the architect who built the San Jose hockey club. A charter member of the Sharks management team, Lombardi joined the club in 1990 as assistant general manager after having served in a similar capacity with the Minnesota North Stars. He was named San Jose's director of hockey operations on June 26, 1992 and became the club's general manager on March 6, 1996. As the team's top hockey executive, he oversees player personnel decisions, negotiates player contracts and coordinates the efforts of the Sharks' scouting and player evaluation departments.

Lombardi has spent considerable effort in building a professional scouting staff, reorganizing the amateur scouting department, and establishing a system to evaluate pro players at all levels. He has stood firm in building the Sharks through the draft, though trades have brought players like Owen Nolan, Vincent Damphousse and Adam Graves.

After the 1993-94 season that saw the Sharks post an NHL record single-season improvement of 58 points, Lombardi finished third in *The Hockey News* award voting for executive of the year.

General Managers' History

Jack Ferreira, 1991-92; Chuck Grillo (V.P. Director of Player Personnel), 1992-93 to 1995-96; Dean Lombardi, 1996-97 to date.

All-time Record vs. Other Clubs

Regular Season

	At Home								On Road								Total							
	GP	W	L	T	OL	GF	GA	PTS	GP	W	L	T	OL	GF	GA	PTS	GP	W	L	T	OL	GF	GA	PTS
Anaheim	22	10	10	2	0	67	66	22	22	11	9	2	0	72	60	24	44	21	19	4	0	139	126	46
Atlanta	2	1	0	1	0	6	3	3	1	1	0	0	0	3	0	2	3	2	0	1	0	9	3	5
Boston	9	2	5	2	0	24	34	6	8	0	6	2	0	19	29	2	17	2	11	4	0	43	63	8
Buffalo	9	5	1	3	0	34	31	13	9	0	9	0	0	25	46	0	18	5	10	3	0	59	77	13
Calgary	28	8	17	3	0	81	93	19	26	8	14	3	1	72	102	20	54	16	31	6	1	153	195	39
Carolina	9	5	4	0	0	40	29	10	9	5	4	0	0	21	28	10	18	10	8	0	0	61	57	20
Chicago	20	11	9	0	0	55	55	22	19	8	8	2	1	60	59	19	39	19	17	2	1	115	114	41
Colorado	18	7	11	0	0	55	68	14	17	2	11	4	0	34	71	8	35	9	22	4	0	89	139	22
Columbus	2	2	0	0	0	5	3	4	2	1	1	0	0	5	6	2	4	3	1	0	0	10	9	6
Dallas	22	8	12	1	1	54	65	18	21	9	10	2	0	52	58	20	43	17	22	3	1	106	123	38
Detroit	20	5	12	3	0	61	84	13	19	2	17	0	0	33	84	4	39	7	29	3	0	94	168	17
Edmonton	26	13	10	3	0	90	78	29	27	5	16	6	0	59	97	16	53	18	26	9	0	149	175	45
Florida	7	3	2	2	0	17	17	8	7	0	2	5	0	14	20	5	14	3	4	7	0	31	37	13
Los Angeles	29	16	10	3	0	101	88	35	29	7	18	3	1	68	97	18	58	23	28	6	1	169	185	53
Minnesota	2	2	0	0	0	8	3	4	2	1	1	0	0	4	4	2	4	3	1	0	0	12	7	6
Montreal	9	3	3	2	1	25	22	9	9	1	6	2	0	16	32	4	18	4	9	4	1	41	54	13
Nashville	6	3	3	0	0	15	18	6	6	4	2	0	0	19	12	8	12	7	5	0	0	34	30	14
New Jersey	9	3	5	1	0	20	27	7	10	4	5	1	0	21	35	9	19	7	10	2	0	41	62	16
NY Islanders	9	3	4	1	1	22	31	8	10	4	5	1	0	33	38	9	19	7	9	2	1	55	69	17
NY Rangers	10	2	7	1	0	22	37	5	8	1	6	1	0	23	37	3	18	3	13	2	0	45	74	8
Ottawa	7	4	3	0	0	12	10	8	8	1	3	4	0	23	27	6	15	5	6	4	0	35	37	14
Philadelphia	9	1	7	1	0	15	28	3	9	2	6	1	0	20	32	5	18	3	13	2	0	35	60	8
Phoenix	24	12	9	2	1	83	78	27	27	9	14	3	1	70	85	22	51	21	23	5	2	153	163	49
Pittsburgh	10	2	6	2	0	20	50	6	7	3	3	1	0	25	34	7	17	5	9	3	0	45	84	13
St. Louis	18	3	14	1	0	42	65	7	22	6	14	1	1	50	78	14	40	9	28	2	1	92	143	21
Tampa Bay	8	2	5	1	0	27	29	5	9	4	4	0	1	25	22	9	17	6	9	1	1	52	51	14
Toronto	14	5	7	2	0	30	38	12	16	4	11	1	0	41	62	9	30	9	18	3	0	71	100	21
Vancouver	28	9	14	5	0	82	95	23	26	6	16	4	0	62	97	16	54	15	30	9	0	144	192	39
Washington	8	4	3	1	0	22	22	9	9	4	5	0	0	25	28	8	17	8	8	1	0	47	50	17
Totals	**394**	**154**	**193**	**43**	**4**	**1135**	**1267**	**355**	**394**	**113**	**226**	**49**	**6**	**994**	**1380**	**281**	**788**	**267**	**419**	**92**	**10**	**2129**	**2647**	**636**

Playoffs

	Series	W	L	GP	W	L	T	GF	GA	Last Mtg.	Round	Result
Calgary	1	1	0	7	4	3	0	26	35	1995	CQF	W 4-3
Colorado	1	0	1	6	2	4	0	17	19	1999	CQF	L 2-4
Dallas	2	0	2	11	3	8	0	19	31	2000	CSF	L 1-4
Detroit	2	1	1	11	4	7	0	27	51	1995	CSF	L 0-4
St. Louis	2	1	1	13	6	7	0	31	38	2001	CQF	L 2-4
Toronto	1	0	1	7	3	4	0	21	26	1994	CSF	L 3-4
Totals	**9**	**3**	**6**	**55**	**22**	**33**	**0**	**141**	**200**			

Carolina totals include Hartford, 1991-92 to 1996-97.
Dallas totals include Minnesota North Stars, 1991-92 to 1992-93.

Playoff Results 2001-1997

Year	Round	Opponent	Result	GF	GA
2001	CQF	St. Louis	L 2-4	11	16
2000	CSF	Dallas	L 1-4	7	15
	CQF	St. Louis	W 4-3	20	22
1999	CQF	Colorado	L 2-4	17	19
1998	CQF	Dallas	L 2-4	12	16

Abbreviations: Round: CSF – conference semi-final; **CQF** – conference quarter-final.

Colorado totals include Quebec, 1991-92 to 1994-95.
Phoenix totals include Winnipeg, 1991-92 to 1995-96.

2000-01 Results

Oct.	6	St. Louis	1-4		11	St. Louis	6-3
	12	Phoenix	2-1		13	Nashville	3-5
	14	Boston	5-2		15	Detroit	2-3
	18	at Dallas	1-2		17	Calgary	4-4
	20	at Minnesota	3-1		20	Colorado	1-2
	21	at Nashville	5-3		22	at Edmonton	2-2
	24	at Carolina	3-2		24	Edmonton	6-1
	25	at Columbus	3-1		26	at Dallas	2-1
	28	Atlanta	2-2		27	at St. Louis	4-3*
Nov.	1	Pittsburgh	3-2		30	Colorado	1-3
	4	Carolina	4-1	**Feb.**	1	Dallas	2-4
	5	at Vancouver	2-2		6	at Calgary	1-1
	8	at Chicago	3-2*		8	at Vancouver	0-0
	9	at Columbus	2-5		10	Chicago	3-2*
	11	at NY Islanders	4-0		14	at Chicago	7-0
	14	at New Jersey	3-2		16	at Nashville	2-0
	15	at Detroit	1-4		18	at Minnesota	1-3
	18	NY Islanders	5-3		20	Columbus	3-2*
	22	Chicago	4-1		21	at Anaheim	0-1
	25	New Jersey	2-3		23	Anaheim	3-1
	28	Minnesota	4-1		26	at St. Louis	2-7
	30	Anaheim	3-2*		28	at Toronto	1-2
Dec.	3	at Edmonton	3-3	**Mar.**	1	at Ottawa	4-8
	4	at Calgary	8-0		3	at Boston	2-3
	6	Dallas	2-2		6	at Tampa Bay	1-2*
	8	Vancouver	1-6		7	at Florida	3-3
	12	NY Rangers	3-2		10	Nashville	0-3
	14	Columbus	2-1		12	Montreal	3-0
	16	at Phoenix	2-1*		14	Los Angeles	1-4
	18	at Washington	5-3		17	at Los Angeles	0-1*
	20	at Detroit	2-0		18	Detroit	4-6
	21	at Philadelphia	3-4		20	at Colorado	1-4
	23	at Buffalo	2-5		22	Ottawa	1-2
	26	at Los Angeles	2-1		26	at Los Angeles	0-0
	28	Edmonton	2-2		27	Los Angeles	3-2*
	30	Vancouver	3-6		29	Anaheim	7-4
Jan.	1	at Phoenix	3-2		31	at Phoenix	1-3
	3	Calgary	0-1	**Apr.**	2	Minnesota	4-2
	4	at Colorado	2-2		5	Phoenix	3-0
	6	Florida	3-1		7	Dallas	4-5*
	9	Buffalo	2-1		8	at Anaheim	4-1

* – Overtime

Entry Draft Selections 2001-1991

2001

Pick	
20	Marcel Goc
106	Christian Ehrhoff
107	Dimitri Patzold
140	Tomas Plihal
175	Ryan Clowe
182	Tom Cavanagh

2000

Pick	
41	Tero Maatta
104	Jon Disalvatore
142	Michal Pinc
166	Nolan Schaefer
183	Michal Macho
246	Chad Wiseman
256	Pasi Saarinen

1999

Pick	
14	Jeff Jillson
82	Mark Concannon
111	Willie Levesque
155	Nicholas Dimitrakos
229	Eric Betournay
241	Doug Murray
257	Hannes Hyvonen

1998

Pick	
3	Brad Stuart
29	Jonathan Cheechoo
65	Eric Laplante
98	Rob Davison
104	Miroslav Zalesak
127	Brandon Coalter
145	Mikael Samuelsson
185	Robert Mulick
212	Jim Fahey

1997

Pick	
2	Patrick Marleau
23	Scott Hannan
82	Adam Colagiacomo
107	Adam Nittel
163	Joe Dusbabek
192	Cam Severson
219	Mark Smith

1996

Pick	
2	Andrei Zyuzin
21	Marco Sturm
55	Terry Friesen
102	Matt Bradley
137	Michel Larocque
164	Jake Deadmarsh
191	Cory Cyrenne
217	David Thibeault

1995

Pick	
12	Teemu Riihijarvi
38	Peter Roed
64	Marko Makinen
90	Vesa Toskala
116	Miikka Kiprusoff
130	Michal Bros
140	Timo Hakanen
142	Jaroslav Kudrna
167	Brad Mehalko
168	Robert Jindrich
194	Ryan Kraft
220	Mikko Markkanen

1994

Pick	
11	Jeff Friesen
37	Angel Nikolov
66	Alexei Yegorov
89	Vaclav Varada
115	Brian Swanson
141	Alexander Korolyuk
167	Sergei Gorbachev
193	Eric Landry
219	Evgeni Nabokov
240	Tomas Pisa
245	Aniket Dhadphale
271	David Beauregard

1993

Pick	
6	Viktor Kozlov
28	Shean Donovan
45	Vlastimil Kroupa
58	Ville Peltonen
80	Alexander Osadchy
106	Andrei Buschan
132	Petri Varis
154	Fredrik Oduya
158	Anatoli Filatov
184	Todd Holt
210	Jonas Forsberg
236	Jeff Salajko
262	Jamie Matthews

1992

Pick	
3	Mike Rathje
10	Andrei Nazarov
51	Alexander Cherbayev
75	Jan Caloun
99	Marcus Ragnarsson
123	Michal Sykora
147	Eric Bellerose
171	Ryan Smith
195	Chris Burns
219	Alexander Kholomeyev
243	Victor Ignatjev

1991

Pick	
2	Pat Falloon
23	Ray Whitney
30	Sandis Ozolinsh
45	Dody Wood
67	Kerry Toporowski
89	Dan Ryder
111	Frank Nilsson
133	Jaroslav Otevrel
155	Dean Grillo
177	Corwin Saurdiff
199	Dale Craigwell
221	Aaron Kriss
243	Mikhail Kravets

Defenseman Marcus Ragnarsson is a six-year veteran on the Sharks blueline. He was a member of the 1998 Swedish Olympic hockey team in Nagano, Japan.

Club Directory

Compaq Center at San Jose

San Jose Sharks
Compaq Center at San Jose
525 West Santa Clara Street
San Jose, CA 95113
Phone **408/287-7070**
FAX 408/999-5797
www.sjsharks.com
Capacity: 17,496

Executive Staff

Owner & Chairman	George Gund III
Co-Owner	Gordon Gund
President & Chief Executive Officer	Greg Jamison
Executive Vice President of Business Operations	Malcolm Bordelon
Executive Vice President & GM (Compaq Center at San Jose)	Jim Goddard
Executive Vice President & General Counsel	Don Gralnek
Executive Vice President & General Manager (Sharks)	Dean Lombardi
Executive Vice President & Chief Financial Officer	Gregg Olson
Vice President of Corporate Partnerships	Greg Elliott
Vice President of Sales & Marketing	Kent Russell
Vice President of Building Operations	Rich Sotelo
Vice President and Assistant General Manager (Sharks)	Wayne Thomas
Executive Assistants	Tricia Nordquist, Michelle Simmons, Kristen Fuce

Hockey Operations

Head Coach	Darryl Sutter
Assistant Coach	Rich Preston
Assistant Coach	Lorne Molleken
Goaltender Coach	Warren Strelow
Director of Pro Development	Doug Wilson
Senior Professional Scout	John Ferguson
Professional Scout	Barry Long, Cap Raeder
Director of Amateur Scouting	Tim Burke
Chief Scout	Ray Payne
Special Assistant to the General Manager	Bob Berry
Assistant to the General Manager	Joe Will
Scouts	Pat Funk, Rob Grillo, Brian Gross, Karel Masopust, Ilkka Sinisalo
Executive Assistant	Brenda Will
Video Scouting Coordinator	Bob Friedlander
Team Services Coordinator	Aaron Abrams
Head Athletic Trainer	Ray Tufts, A.T.,C
Athletic Trainer	Tom Woodcock, A.T.,C,L
Strength & Conditioning Coordinator	Mac Read
Massage Therapist	Wes Howard
Equipment Manager	Mike Aldrich
Assistant Equipment Manager	Kurt Harvey
Equipment Assistant & Equipment Transportation	Roy Sneesby
Administrative Assistant	Cathy Hancock
Director of Hockey Operations, Cleveland	Jim Wiley
Head Coach, Cleveland	Roy Sommer
Assistant Coach, Cleveland	Nick Fotiu
Head Trainer, Cleveland	Dave Zenobi
Team Physician	Arthur J. Ting, M.D.
Team Dentist	Robert Bonahoom, D.D.S.
Team Vision Specialist	Vincent S. Zuccaro, O.D., F.A.A.O.
Medical Staff	Warren King, M.D., Mark Sontag, M.D., Will Straw, M.D.

Silicon Vally Sports & Entertainment/Business Operations

Director of Broadcasting	Frank Albin
Director of Media Relations	Ken Arnold
Media Relations Manager	Scott Emmert
Media Relations Coordinator	Ben Stephenson
Director of Marketing	Beth Brigino
Director of Ticket Operations	Mary Enriquez
Director of Ticket Sales	Andy Fiske
Director of Sponsorship Sales	TBD
Director of Community Development	Rob Jaynes
Director of Event Presentation	Jason Minsky
Director of Suite Hospitality	Jay O'Sullivan
Director of Internet Services	Roger Ross

The Sharks Foundation

Manager, The Sharks Foundation	Jackie Fuce

Finance

Director of Finance	Ken Caveney
Director of Information Technology	James Struckle
Human Resources Manager	Cathy Chandler

Building Operations

Director of Ticket Operations	Daniel DeBoer
Director of Booking & Events	Steve Kirsner, Chuck Ryder
Director of Guest Services	Ken Sweezey
Facilities Technical Director	Greg Carrolan
Director of Building Services	Monte Chavez
Chief Engineer	Mark Mullins

Miscellaneous

Television Station	FOX Sports Net
Radio Network Flagship	KFOX 98.5 (KUFX FM)
Television Play-By-Play Broadcaster	Randy Hahn
Television Color Analyst	Drew Remenda
Radio Play-By-Play Broadcaster	Dan Rusanowsky
Radio Color Analyst	Pete Stemkowski
Team Photographers	Don Smith, Rocky Widner
P.A. Announcer	Joe Ike
Mascot	S.J. Sharkie

Tampa Bay Lightning

2000-01 Results: 24W-47L-6T-5OTL 59PTS. Fifth, Southeast Division

Year-by-Year Record

Season	GP	Home W	Home L	Home T	Home OL	Road W	Road L	Road T	Road OL	Overall W	Overall L	Overall T	Overall OL	GF	GA	Pts.	Finished	Playoff Result
2000-01	82	17	19	3	2	7	28	3	3	24	47	6	5	201	280	59	5th, Southeast Div.	Out of Playoffs
1999-2000	82	13	20	4	4	6	27	5	3	19	47	9	7	204	310	54	4th, Southeast Div.	Out of Playoffs
1998-99	82	12	25	4	...	7	29	5	...	19	54	9	...	179	292	47	4th, Southeast Div.	Out of Playoffs
1997-98	82	11	23	7	...	6	32	3	...	17	55	10	...	151	269	44	7th, Atlantic Div.	Out of Playoffs
1996-97	82	15	18	8	...	17	22	2	...	32	40	10	...	217	247	74	6th, Atlantic Div.	Out of Playoffs
1995-96	82	22	14	5	...	16	18	7	...	38	32	12	...	238	248	88	5th, Atlantic Div.	Lost Conf. Quarter-Final
1994-95	48	10	14	0	...	7	14	3	...	17	28	3	...	120	144	37	6th, Atlantic Div.	Out of Playoffs
1993-94	84	14	22	6	...	16	21	5	...	30	43	11	...	224	251	71	7th, Atlantic Div.	Out of Playoffs
1992-93	84	12	27	3	...	11	27	4	...	23	54	7	...	245	332	53	6th, Norris Div.	Out of Playoffs

2001-02 Schedule

Oct.	Fri.	5	NY Islanders
	Sun.	7	Florida
	Thu.	11	at San Jose
	Sat.	13	at Los Angeles
	Sun.	14	at Anaheim*
	Tue.	16	at Colorado
	Sat.	20	NY Rangers
	Tue.	23	Washington
	Thu.	25	Los Angeles
	Sat.	27	at Atlanta
	Tue.	30	at Toronto
Nov.	Fri.	2	at Buffalo
	Sat.	3	at Pittsburgh
	Tue.	6	at NY Islanders
	Thu.	8	Philadelphia
	Sat.	10	Pittsburgh
	Thu.	15	Toronto
	Sat.	17	Carolina
	Tue.	20	Anaheim
	Wed.	21	at Washington
	Fri.	23	New Jersey
	Sun.	25	at Carolina*
	Tue.	27	at Boston
	Thu.	29	Atlanta
Dec.	Sat.	1	at Philadelphia
	Sun.	2	at NY Rangers
	Tue.	4	at New Jersey
	Thu.	6	Columbus
	Sat.	8	at Ottawa
	Mon.	10	at Vancouver
	Wed.	12	at Calgary
	Fri.	14	at Edmonton
	Mon.	17	at Montreal
	Fri.	21	St. Louis
	Wed.	26	at Nashville
	Thu.	27	Carolina
	Sat.	29	Boston
	Mon.	31	Toronto
Jan.	Wed.	2	at Minnesota
	Fri.	4	at Chicago
	Sun.	6	at Phoenix
	Tue.	8	Dallas
	Sat.	12	Ottawa
	Sun.	13	at Atlanta
	Tue.	15	at New Jersey
	Fri.	18	Chicago
	Sat.	19	Montreal
	Mon.	21	New Jersey
	Wed.	23	at Pittsburgh
	Fri.	25	at Buffalo
	Sat.	26	at NY Islanders
	Mon.	28	at NY Rangers
	Wed.	30	Carolina
Feb.	Mon.	4	Ottawa
	Wed.	6	at Florida
	Thu.	7	Florida
	Sat.	9	Washington
	Mon.	11	at Washington
	Tue.	26	Detroit
Mar.	Fri.	1	San Jose
	Sat.	2	Florida
	Wed.	6	Edmonton
	Fri.	8	Philadelphia
	Sun.	10	Nashville
	Tue.	12	at Atlanta
	Thu.	14	Calgary
	Sun.	17	Buffalo*
	Mon.	18	at Philadelphia
	Wed.	20	Atlanta
	Fri.	22	Montreal
	Sun.	24	Boston
	Tue.	26	at Toronto
	Thu.	28	at Montreal
	Sat.	30	at Ottawa
Apr.	Mon.	1	NY Rangers
	Wed.	3	at Washington
	Thu.	4	Pittsburgh
	Sun.	7	Buffalo*
	Tue.	9	at Boston
	Wed.	10	at Carolina
	Fri.	12	NY Islanders
	Sun.	14	at Florida*

* Denotes afternoon game.

Franchise date: December 16, 1991

SOUTHEAST DIVISION

10th NHL Season

Still six weeks shy of his 20th birthday at the time, Vincent Lecavalier became the youngest captain in NHL history when he was given the "C" in Tampa Bay on March 11, 2000. He had 23 goals in 68 games last season.

2001-02 Player Personnel

FORWARDS	HT	WT	S	Place of Birth	Date	2000-01 Club
AFANASENKOV, Dmitry	6-2	200	R	Arkhangelsk, USSR	5/12/80	Tampa Bay-Detroit (IHL)
ALEXEEV, Nikita	6-5	215	L	Murmansk, USSR	12/27/81	Erie
ANDREYCHUK, Dave	6-4	220	R	Hamilton, Ont.	9/29/63	Buffalo
BARNABY, Matthew	6-0	189	L	Ottawa, Ont.	5/4/73	Pittsburgh-Tampa Bay
CLYMER, Ben	6-1	195	R	Edina, MN	4/11/78	Tampa Bay-Detroit (IHL)
DWYER, Gordie	6-3	216	L	Dalhousie, NB	1/25/78	Tampa Bay-Detroit (IHL)
ELICH, Matt	6-3	196	R	Detroit, MI	9/22/79	Tampa Bay-Detroit (IHL)
HOLZINGER, Brian	5-11	190	R	Parma, OH	10/10/72	Tampa Bay
KEEFE, Sheldon	5-11	185	R	Brampton, Ont.	9/17/80	Tampa Bay-Detroit (IHL)
LECAVALIER, Vincent	6-4	205	L	Ile Bizard, Que.	4/21/80	Tampa Bay
MODIN, Fredrik	6-4	220	L	Sundsvall, Sweden	10/8/74	Tampa Bay
OLVESTAD, Jimmie	6-1	194	L	Stockholm, Sweden	2/16/80	Djurgardens IF
PROSPAL, Vaclav	6-2	195	L	Ceske-Budejovice, Czech.	2/17/75	Ottawa-Florida
RICHARDS, Brad	6-1	198	L	Montague, P.E.I.	5/2/80	Tampa Bay
ST-LOUIS, Martin	5-9	185	L	Laval, Que.	6/18/75	Tampa Bay
SVITOV, Alexander	6-3	198	L	Omsk, USSR	11/3/82	Avangard Omsk
TAYLOR, Tim	6-1	190	L	Stratford, Ont.	2/6/69	NY Rangers
YLONEN, Juha	6-1	189	L	Helsinki, Finland	2/13/72	Phoenix
ZIEGLER, Thomas	5-11	174	L	Zurich, Switz.	6/9/78	Tampa Bay-Detroit (IHL)
DEFENSEMEN						
BIRON, Mathieu	6-6	229	R	Lac St-Charles, Que.	4/29/80	NYI-Lowell (AHL)-Sprfld
CULLIMORE, Jassen	6-5	235	L	Simcoe, Ont.	12/4/72	Tampa Bay
JONES, Mike	6-3	190	L	Toledo, OH	5/18/76	Detroit (IHL)
KUBINA, Pavel	6-4	230	R	Celadna, Czech.	4/15/77	Tampa Bay
KUDROC, Kristian	6-6	240	R	Michalovce, Czech.	5/21/81	Tampa Bay-Detroit (IHL)
LEDYARD, Grant	6-2	195	L	Winnipeg, Man.	11/19/61	Tampa Bay-Dallas
NECKAR, Stan	6-1	214	L	Ceske Budejovice, Czech.	12/22/75	Phoenix-Tampa Bay
PRATT, Nolan	6-3	200	L	Fort McMurray, Alta.	8/14/75	Colorado
SARICH, Cory	6-3	193	R	Saskatoon, Sask.	8/16/78	Tampa Bay-Detroit (IHL)
SVOBODA, Petr	6-1	198	L	Most, Czech.	2/14/66	Tampa Bay
ZYUZIN, Andrei	6-1	210	R	Ufa, USSR	1/21/78	Tampa Bay-Detroit (IHL)
GOALTENDERS	**HT**	**WT**	**C**	**Place of Birth**	**Date**	**2000-01 Club**
KHABIBULIN, Nikolai	6-1	195	L	Sverdlovsk, USSR	1/13/73	Tampa Bay
KOCHAN, Dieter	6-1	180	L	Saskatoon, Sask.	5/11/74	Tampa Bay-Detroit (IHL)
WEEKES, Kevin	6-0	195	L	Toronto, Ont.	4/4/75	Tampa Bay

2000-01 Scoring

* - rookie

Regular Season

Pos	#	Player	Team	GP	G	A	Pts	+/–	PIM	PP	SH	GW	GT	S	%
C	19	* Brad Richards	T.B.	82	21	41	62	–10	14	7	0	3	0	179	11.7
L	33	Fredrik Modin	T.B.	76	32	24	56	–1	48	8	0	4	0	217	14.7
C	4	Vincent Lecavalier	T.B.	68	23	28	51	–26	66	7	0	3	0	165	13.9
C	26	Martin St. Louis	T.B.	78	18	22	40	–4	12	3	3	4	0	141	12.8
C	9	Brian Holzinger	T.B.	70	11	25	36	–9	64	3	0	2	0	87	12.6
D	13	Pavel Kubina	T.B.	70	11	19	30	–14	103	6	1	1	0	128	8.6
D	6	Adrian Aucoin	VAN	47	3	13	16	13	20	1	0	0	0	99	3.0
			T.B.	26	1	11	12	–8	25	1	0	0	0	60	1.7
			TOTAL	73	4	24	28	5	45	2	0	0	0	159	2.5
R	14	* Alexander Kharitonov	T.B.	66	7	15	22	–9	8	0	0	0	0	103	6.8
L	8	Todd Warriner	T.B.	64	10	11	21	–13	46	3	2	1	1	99	10.1
C	17	Ryan Johnson	T.B.	80	7	14	21	–20	44	1	0	0	0	71	9.9
L	28	Nils Ekman	T.B.	43	9	11	20	–15	40	2	1	1	0	72	12.5
D	30	Andrei Zyuzin	T.B.	64	4	16	20	–8	76	2	1	1	1	92	4.3
R	36	Matthew Barnaby	PIT	47	1	4	5	–7	168	0	0	0	0	38	2.6
			T.B.	29	4	4	8	–3	97	1	0	0	0	29	13.8
			TOTAL	76	5	8	13	–10	265	1	0	0	0	67	7.5
D	21	Cory Sarich	T.B.	73	1	8	9	–25	106	0	0	1	0	66	1.5
D	5	Jassen Cullimore	T.B.	74	1	6	7	–6	80	0	0	0	0	56	1.8
D	7	Ben Clymer	T.B.	23	5	1	6	–7	21	3	0	0	0	25	20.0
R	20	Stan Drulia	T.B.	34	2	4	6	–11	18	1	0	0	0	20	10.0
D	2	Stan Neckar	PHX	53	2	2	4	–2	63	0	0	1	0	16	12.5
			T.B.	16	0	2	2	–1	8	0	0	0	0	10	0.0
			TOTAL	69	2	4	6	–3	71	0	0	1	0	26	7.7
D	41	Maxim Galanov	T.B.	25	0	5	5	–5	8	0	0	0	0	10	0.0
R	27	* Sheldon Keefe	T.B.	49	4	0	4	–13	38	0	0	0	0	32	12.5
D	57	* Kristian Kudroc	T.B.	22	2	2	4	0	36	0	0	1	0	12	16.7
C	10	John Emmons	OTT	41	1	1	2	–5	20	0	0	0	0	28	3.6
			T.B.	12	1	1	2	0	22	0	0	0	0	9	11.1
			TOTAL	53	2	2	4	–5	42	0	0	0	0	37	5.4
D	23	Petr Svoboda	T.B.	19	1	3	4	–4	41	0	0	0	0	16	6.3
L	37	* Dimitry Afanasenkov	T.B.	9	1	1	2	1	4	0	0	0	0	8	12.5
D	62	* Kaspars Astashenko	T.B.	15	1	1	2	–4	4	0	0	0	0	4	25.0
D	32	Craig Millar	NSH	5	0	0	0	1	6	0	0	0	0	2	0.0
			T.B.	16	1	1	2	–8	10	0	0	1	0	10	10.0
			TOTAL	21	1	1	2	–7	16	0	0	1	0	12	8.3
D	11	Sergey Gusev	T.B.	16	1	0	1	–3	10	0	0	0	0	13	7.7
L	24	* Kyle Freadrich	T.B.	13	0	1	1	–1	36	0	0	0	0	3	0.0
L	34	* Gordie Dwyer	T.B.	28	0	1	1	–7	96	0	0	0	0	12	0.0
G	80	Kevin Weekes	T.B.	61	0	1	1	0	4	0	0	0	0	0	0.0
D	18	* Marek Posmyk	T.B.	1	0	0	0	–1	0	0	0	0	0	0	0.0
G	1	* Evgeny Konstantinov	T.B.	1	0	0	0	0	0	0	0	0	0	0	0.0
G	35	Nikolai Khabibulin	T.B.	2	0	0	0	0	0	0	0	0	0	0	0.0
C	43	* Thomas Ziegler	T.B.	5	0	0	0	–2	0	0	0	0	0	2	0.0
R	73	Matt Elich	T.B.	8	0	0	0	–5	0	0	0	0	0	7	0.0
G	35	* Dieter Kochan	T.B.	10	0	0	0	0	0	0	0	0	0	0	0.0
G	31	Wade Flaherty	NYI	20	0	0	0	0	2	0	0	0	0	0	0.0
			T.B.	2	0	0	0	0	0	0	0	0	0	0	0.0
			TOTAL	22	0	0	0	0	2	0	0	0	0	0	0.0

Goaltending

No.	Goaltender	GPI	Mins	Avg	W	L	T	EN	SO	GA	SA	S%
1	* Evgeny Konstantinov	1	0	0.00	0	0	0	0	0	0	0	.000
35	Nikolai Khabibulin	2	123	2.93	1	1	0	0	0	6	69	.913
80	Kevin Weekes	61	3378	3.14	20	33	3	8	4	177	1742	.898
35	* Dieter Kochan	10	314	3.44	0	3	0	1	0	18	138	.870
39	Dan Cloutier	24	1005	3.52	3	13	3	3	1	59	541	.891
31	Wade Flaherty	2	118	4.07	0	2	0	0	0	8	55	.855
	Totals	**82**	**4968**	**3.38**	**24**	**52**	**6**	**12**	**5**	**280**	**2557**	**.890**

Known in Toronto for the power of his shot, Fredrik Modin has become much more accurate with the Lightning, leading the team with 32 goals last year.

Coaching History

Terry Crisp, 1992-93 to 1996-97; Terry Crisp, Rick Paterson and Jacques Demers, 1997-98; Jacques Demers, 1998-99; Steve Ludzik, 1999-2000; Steve Ludzik and John Tortorella, 2000-01; John Tortorella, 2001-02.

Coach

TORTORELLA, JOHN
Coach, Tampa Bay Lightning. Born in Boston, MA, June 24, 1958.

After finishing out the 1999-2000 season as the interim coach of the New York Rangers, John Tortorella joined the Tampa Bay Lightning as an associate coach on July 7, 2000. He took over head coaching duties on January 6, 2001.

Prior to his season with the Rangers, Tortorella had spent two years as an assistant coach with the Phoenix Coyotes and eight years in the Buffalo Sabres organization. He was an assistant coach in Buffalo from 1989-90 to 1994-95, serving under current Tampa Bay general manager Rick Dudley until 1992. Tortorella served as the head coach of the Rochester Americans, Buffalo's AHL affiliate, in 1995-96 and 1996-97. He guided Rochester to the Calder Cup championship during his first season behind the bench.

Tortorella starred at the University of Maine for three seasons and was twice named a Conference All-Star. After playing hockey in Sweden, Tortorella played in the Atlantic Coast Hockey League with Virginia, Hampton Roads and Erie. He later spent two seasons (1986-87 and 1987-88) as the coach and general manager of the Virginia Lancers, compiling a record of 87-31 and winning the league championship and coach of the year honors during both campaigns. Following the 1987-88 season, Tortorella joined the Fort Wayne Komets of the IHL for their 1988 playoff run. He was an assistant coach with the New Haven Nighthawks of the AHL in 1988-89.

Coaching Record

		Regular Season				Playoffs		
Season	**Team**	**Games**	**W**	**L**	**T**	**Games**	**W**	**L**
1995-96	Rochester (AHL)	80	37	38	5	19	15	4
1996-97	Rochester (AHL)	80	40	30	9	10	6	4
1999-2000	**NY Rangers (NHL)**	**4**	**0**	**3**	**1**	....	....	....
2000-01	**Tampa Bay (NHL)**	**43**	**12**	**30**	**1**	....	....	....
	NHL Totals	**47**	**12**	**33**	**2**	....	....	....

Club Records

Team

(Figures in brackets for season records are games played; records for fewest points, wins, ties, losses, goals, goals against are for 70 or more games)

Most Points	**88**	1995-96 (82)
Most Wins	**38**	1995-96 (82)
Most Ties	**12**	1995-96 (82)
Most Losses	**55**	1997-98 (82)
Most Goals	**245**	1992-93 (84)
Most Goals Against	**332**	1992-93 (84)
Fewest Points	**44**	1997-98 (82)
Fewest Wins	**17**	1997-98 (82)
Fewest Ties	**6**	2000-01 (82)
Fewest Losses	**32**	1995-96 (82)
Fewest Goals	**151**	1997-98 (82)
Fewest Goals Against	**247**	1996-97 (82)
Longest Winning Streak		
Overall	**5**	Twice
Home	**6**	Feb. 15-Mar. 10/96
Away	**4**	Jan. 6-13/97
Longest Undefeated Streak		
Overall	**7**	Feb. 28-Mar. 13/96 (5 wins, 2 ties)
Home	**8**	Twice
Away	**6**	Dec. 28/93-Jan. 12/94 (5 wins, 1 tie)
Longest Losing Streak		
Overall	**13**	Jan. 3-Feb. 2/98
Home	**10**	Jan. 3-Feb. 26/98
Away	**11**	Oct. 24-Dec. 10/98
Longest Winless Streak		
Overall	**16**	Twice
Home	**11**	Jan. 2-Feb. 26/98 (10 losses, 1 tie)
Away	**17**	Dec. 2/99-Feb. 19/00 (14 losses, 3 ties)
Most Shutouts, Season	**6**	1996-97 (82)
Most PIM, Season	**1,823**	1997-98 (82)
Most Goals, Game	**8**	Nov. 22/00 (Atl. 2 at T.B. 8)

Individual

Most Seasons	**7**	Mikael Andersson, Rob Zamuner, Daren Puppa
Most Games, Career	**475**	Rob Zamuner
Most Goals, Career	**111**	Brian Bradley
Most Assists, Career	**189**	Brian Bradley
Most Points, Career	**300**	Brian Bradley (111G, 189A)
Most PIM, Career	**782**	Chris Gratton
Most Shutouts, Career	**12**	Daren Puppa
Longest Consecutive Games Streak	**226**	Rob Zamuner (Nov. 1/95-Mar. 30/98)
Most Goals, Season	**42**	Brian Bradley (1992-93)
Most Assists, Season	**56**	Brian Bradley (1995-96)
Most Points, Season	**86**	Brian Bradley (1992-93; 42G, 44A)
Most PIM, Season	**258**	Enrico Ciccone (1995-96)
Most Points, Defenseman, Season	**65**	Roman Hamrlik (1995-96; 16G, 49A)
Most Points, Center, Season	**86**	Brian Bradley (1992-93; 42G, 44A)
Most Points, Right Wing, Season	**60**	Dino Ciccarelli (1996-97; 35G, 25A)
Most Points, Left Wing, Season	**56**	Fredrik Modin (2000-01; 32G, 24A)
Most Points, Rookie, Season	**62**	Brad Richards (2000-01; 21G, 41A)
Most Shutouts, Season	**5**	Daren Puppa (1995-96)
Most Goals, Game	**4**	Chris Kontos (Oct. 7/92)
Most Assists, Game	**4**	Four times
Most Points, Game	**6**	Doug Crossman (Nov. 7/92; 3G, 3A)

Captains' History

No captain, 1992-93 to 1994-95; Paul Ysebaert, 1995-96, 1996-97; Paul Ysebaert and Mikael Renberg, 1997-98; Rob Zamuner, 1998-99; Bill Houlder, Chris Gratton and Vincent Lecavalier, 1999-2000; Vincent Lecavalier, 2000-01 to date.

All-time Record vs. Other Clubs

Regular Season

	At Home								On Road								Total							
	GP	W	L	T	OL	GF	GA	PTS	GP	W	L	T	OL	GF	GA	PTS	GP	W	L	T	OL	GF	GA	PTS
Anaheim	6	2	4	0	0	12	19	4	7	2	4	1	0	17	22	5	13	4	8	1	0	29	41	9
Atlanta	5	3	1	1	0	19	11	7	5	1	4	0	0	15	23	2	10	4	5	1	0	34	34	9
Boston	17	6	8	3	0	44	50	15	17	1	13	3	0	35	65	5	34	7	21	6	0	79	115	20
Buffalo	17	4	11	1	1	37	56	10	17	6	10	1	0	50	47	13	34	10	21	2	1	87	103	23
Calgary	9	4	4	1	0	28	30	9	7	2	4	0	1	14	25	5	16	6	8	1	1	42	55	14
Carolina	18	9	6	3	0	50	47	21	19	2	13	3	1	49	70	8	37	11	19	6	1	99	117	29
Chicago	9	4	3	2	0	22	23	10	11	3	6	2	0	29	37	8	20	7	9	4	0	51	60	18
Colorado	10	7	2	1	0	31	24	15	11	2	7	2	0	24	48	6	21	9	9	3	0	55	72	21
Columbus	1	1	0	0	0	4	1	2	1	0	1	0	0	1	3	0	2	1	1	0	0	5	4	2
Dallas	11	1	8	2	0	18	33	4	10	2	7	1	0	23	38	5	21	3	15	3	0	41	71	9
Detroit	12	3	8	1	0	39	57	7	10	1	9	0	0	18	43	2	22	4	17	1	0	57	100	9
Edmonton	9	2	4	2	1	26	30	7	8	2	6	0	0	17	22	4	17	4	10	2	1	43	52	11
Florida	20	6	10	4	0	43	58	16	20	3	12	3	2	36	60	11	40	9	22	7	2	79	118	27
Los Angeles	7	3	4	0	0	16	19	6	9	7	1	1	0	33	22	15	16	10	5	1	0	49	41	21
Minnesota	1	0	1	0	0	2	4	0	1	0	1	0	0	5	6	0	2	0	2	0	0	7	10	0
Montreal	17	7	6	3	1	40	42	18	16	6	9	1	0	37	47	13	33	13	15	4	1	77	89	31
Nashville	2	0	1	1	0	4	7	1	3	2	1	0	0	8	7	4	5	2	2	1	0	12	14	5
New Jersey	19	4	12	3	0	44	65	11	20	2	17	1	0	27	79	5	39	6	29	4	0	71	144	16
NY Islanders	20	10	8	2	0	54	59	22	19	10	7	1	1	60	54	22	39	20	15	3	1	114	113	44
NY Rangers	19	7	8	3	1	64	68	18	21	8	10	2	1	72	77	19	40	15	18	5	2	136	145	37
Ottawa	17	7	9	1	0	51	57	15	17	7	10	0	0	41	64	14	34	14	19	1	0	92	121	29
Philadelphia	20	7	11	1	1	54	62	16	19	1	12	6	0	31	66	8	39	8	23	7	1	85	128	24
Phoenix	8	3	5	0	0	24	30	6	9	3	6	0	0	19	28	6	17	6	11	0	0	43	58	12
Pittsburgh	17	7	8	2	0	48	51	16	17	3	12	2	0	42	72	8	34	10	20	4	0	90	123	24
St. Louis	11	4	5	2	0	32	37	10	9	1	8	0	0	20	35	2	20	5	13	2	0	52	72	12
San Jose	9	5	4	0	0	22	25	10	8	5	2	1	0	29	27	11	17	10	6	1	0	51	52	21
Toronto	14	2	12	0	0	28	52	4	15	6	8	1	0	38	53	13	29	8	20	1	0	66	105	17
Vancouver	8	3	4	0	1	28	32	7	7	0	6	1	0	12	34	1	15	3	10	1	1	40	66	8
Washington	21	5	15	1	0	46	72	11	21	5	12	4	0	47	78	14	42	10	27	5	0	93	150	25
Totals	**354**	**126**	**182**	**40**	**6**	**930**	**1121**	**298**	**354**	**93**	**218**	**37**	**6**	**849**	**1252**	**229**	**708**	**219**	**400**	**77**	**12**	**1779**	**2373**	**527**

Playoffs

	Series	W	L	GP	W	L	T	GF	GA	Last Mtg.	Round	Result
Philadelphia	1	0	1	6	2	4	0	13	26	1996	CQF	L 2-4
Totals	**1**	**0**	**1**	**6**	**2**	**4**	**0**	**13**	**26**			

Playoff Results 2001-1997

Year	Round	Opponent	Result	GF	GA

(Last playoff appearance: 1996)

Abbreviations: Round: CQF – conference quarter-final.

Carolina totals include Hartford, 1992-93 to 1996-97.
Dallas totals include Minnesota North Stars, 1992-93.

Colorado totals include Quebec, 1992-93 to 1994-95.
Phoenix totals include Winnipeg, 1992-93 to 1995-96.

2000-01 Results

Oct.	6	NY Islanders	3-3
	8	Vancouver	4-5
	13	at Pittsburgh	2-3
	15	Atlanta	5-2
	18	at Minnesota	5-6
	21	at New Jersey	2-7
	22	at NY Rangers	4-2
	25	at Detroit	1-5
	27	Ottawa	0-6
	31	at Carolina	5-6*
Nov.	1	at NY Rangers	1-6
	3	NY Islanders	4-3*
	5	Washington	5-2
	10	Montreal	3-1
	11	Calgary	3-4
	14	at Montreal	1-0
	17	at Toronto	2-2
	20	at Dallas	2-6
	22	Atlanta	8-2
	24	Florida	2-1
	25	at Florida	1-2*
	27	at NY Islanders	4-7
	29	at Washington	1-4
Dec.	1	at Atlanta	3-5
	2	Detroit	3-0
	6	at Philadelphia	3-6
	8	Colorado	0-2
	11	at Colorado	2-2
	14	at Phoenix	2-3
	16	at Los Angeles	4-3
	17	at Anaheim	1-3
	21	Pittsburgh	1-1
	23	New Jersey	1-5
	26	Carolina	3-2
	28	Philadelphia	4-3
	30	Boston	1-1
	31	Toronto	2-3
Jan.	3	at Carolina	2-3
	4	at Ottawa	3-8
	7	at Chicago	4-7
	10	at Toronto	3-1
	12	Philadelphia	0-3
	14	Dallas	2-3
	16	at Buffalo	1-3
	18	at Montreal	1-3
	20	at Ottawa	0-3
	21	at Columbus	1-3
	23	Washington	2-5
	25	Ottawa	2-5
	27	at Florida	2-3*
	29	at Carolina	2-5
	30	Florida	4-3
Feb.	1	Buffalo	4-2
	6	Minnesota	2-4
	8	at St. Louis	1-4
	10	at Boston	2-6
	13	Phoenix	2-5
	15	Boston	3-6
	17	NY Rangers	4-5
	18	at Nashville	2-3
	20	St. Louis	3-2
	24	at Philadelphia	0-0
	25	at Buffalo	4-5
Mar.	1	at Boston	1-3
	3	at NY Islanders	6-0
	4	at New Jersey	0-6
	6	San Jose	2-1*
	8	Carolina	1-0
	10	Columbus	4-1
	13	Edmonton	4-5*
	15	Toronto	3-2
	17	Pittsburgh	5-1
	21	at Atlanta	4-3
	22	Atlanta	0-2
	24	Washington	2-3
	27	New Jersey	1-7
	29	Montreal	2-6
	30	at Florida	4-2
Apr.	1	Buffalo	2-4
	4	at Pittsburgh	2-4
	5	NY Rangers	3-4*
	8	at Washington	1-2

* – Overtime

Entry Draft Selections 2001-1992

2001
Pick
3 Alexander Svitov
47 Alexander Polushin
61 Andreas Holmqvist
94 Evgeni Artukhin
123 Aaron Lobb
138 Paul Lynch
188 Arthur Femenella
219 Dennis Packard
222 Jeremy Van Hoof
252 J.F. Soucy
259 Dmitri Bezrukov
261 Vitali Smolyaninov
281 Ilja Solarev
289 Henrik Bergfors

2000
Pick
8 Nikita Alexeev
34 Ruslan Zainullin
81 Alexander Kharitonov
126 Johan Hagglund
161 Pavel Sedov
191 Aaron Gionet
222 Marek Priechodsky
226 Brian Eklund
233 Alexander Polukeyev
263 Thomas Ziegler

1999
Pick
47 Sheldon Keefe
67 Evgeny Konstantinov
75 Brett Scheffelmaier
88 Jimmie Olvestad
127 Kaspars Astashenko
148 Michal Lanicek
182 Fedor Fedorov
187 Ivan Rachunek
216 Erkki Rajamaki
244 Mikko Kuparinen

1998
Pick
1 Vincent Lecavalier
64 Brad Richards
72 Dmitry Afanasenkov
92 Eric Beaudoin
121 Curtis Rich
146 Sergei Kuznetsov
174 Brett Allan
194 Oak Hewer
221 Daniel Hulak
229 Chris Lyness
252 Martin Cibak

1997
Pick
7 Paul Mara
33 Kyle Kos
61 Matt Elich
108 Mark Thompson
109 Jan Sulc
112 Karel Betik
153 Andrei Skopintsev
168 Justin Jack
170 Eero Somervuori
185 Samuel St-Pierre
198 Shawn Skolney
224 Paul Comrie

1996
Pick
16 Mario Larocque
69 Curtis Tipler
125 Jason Robinson
152 Nikolai Ignatov
157 Xavier Delisle
179 Pavel Kubina

1995
Pick
5 Daymond Langkow
30 Mike McBain
56 Shane Willis
108 Konstantin Golokhvastov
134 Eduard Pershin
160 Cory Murphy
186 Joe Cardarelli
212 Zac Bierk

1994
Pick
8 Jason Wiemer
34 Colin Cloutier
55 Vadim Epanchintsev
86 Dmitri Klevakin
137 Daniel Juden
138 Bryce Salvador
164 Chris Maillet
190 Alexei Baranov
216 Yuri Smirnov
242 Shawn Gervais
268 Brian White

1993
Pick
3 Chris Gratton
29 Tyler Moss
55 Allan Egeland
81 Marian Kacir
107 Ryan Brown
133 Kiley Hill
159 Matthieu Raby
185 Ryan Nauss
211 Alexandre Laporte
237 Brett Duncan
263 Mark Szoke

1992
Pick
1 Roman Hamrlik
26 Drew Bannister
49 Brent Gretzky
74 Aaron Gavey
97 Brantt Myhres
122 Martin Tanguay
145 Derek Wilkinson
170 Dennis Maxwell
193 Andrew Kemper
218 Marc Tardif
241 Tom MacDonald

General Managers' History

Phil Esposito, 1992-93 to 1997-98; Jacques Demers, 1998-99; Rick Dudley, 1999-2000 to date.

General Manager

DUDLEY, RICK
General Manager, Tampa Bay Lightning.
Born in Toronto, Ont., January 31, 1949.

Rick Dudley was named vice president of hockey operations for Palace Sports and Entertainment (PS&E) on June 8, 1999 and took on the job of overseeing all aspects of Tampa Bay Lightning hockey operations when PS&E consummated its acquisition of the hockey club. On July 14, 1999, Dudley was officially named the club's general manager.

The hiring of Dudley in Tampa Bay was made possible after the Ottawa Senators reached a compensation agreement with Palace Sports and Entertainment. The move returned Dudley to his former employer (PS&E) after one season as the general manager in Ottawa. In his one season there, the Senators finished with 103 points, an increase of 20 points from the previous campaign. Ottawa finished with the third best overall record in the NHL during the 1998-99 season.

Before joining Ottawa, Dudley was the general manager of PS&E's Detroit Vipers in the International Hockey League. In Detroit, he served as general manager and head coach during the team's first two years of existence before concentrating solely on his front office work for the next two seasons.

Dudley is credited with finding the likes of Detroit's first two players in Petr Sykora and Miroslav Satan as well as bringing over 17-year-old phenom Sergei Samsonov. Samsonov helped lead the Vipers to the 1996 Turner Cup Championship and became the NHL's Rookie of the Year the following season.

A lifetime hockey man, Dudley was the head coach of the IHL's Phoenix Roadrunners in 1993-94. He took over the reigns of a last-place club and led them to the league's best record over the rest of the season. His other head coaching jobs came with the IHL's San Diego Gulls (1992-93), NHL's Buffalo Sabres (1989 to 1992), AHL's New Haven Nighthawks (1988-89), IHL's Flint Spirits (1986 to 1988), and ECHL's Carolina Thunderbirds (1981 to 1986). Dudley amassed a 476-196-51 lifetime record as a head coach.

His professional playing career spanned 13 seasons where he spent time in the AHL (Cleveland, Cincinnati, Fredericton), CHL (Iowa), IHL (Flint), WHA (Cincinnati) and NHL (Buffalo and Winnipeg).

NHL Coaching Record

		Regular Season				Playoffs		
Season	Team	Games	W	L	T	Games	W	L
1989-90	Buffalo	80	45	27	8	6	2	4
1990-91	Buffalo	80	31	30	9	6	2	4
1991-92	Buffalo	28	9	15	4	....	....	....
	NHL Totals	**188**	**85**	**72**	**31**	**12**	**4**	**8**

Club Directory

Ice Palace

Tampa Bay Lightning
Ice Palace
401 Channelside Drive
Tampa, FL 33602
Phone **813/301-6500**
FAX 813/301-1480
Ticket Info. 813/301-6600
www.icepalace.com
Capacity: 19,758

Executive Staff
Owner . . . . . Palace Sports & Entertainment, Bill Davidson
President of Palace Sports & Entertainment/Governor . . . . . Tom Wilson
President of Tampa Bay Lightning/ Alternate Governor . . . . . Ron Campbell
Senior Vice President of Sales and Marketing . . . . . Michael Yormark
Vice President of Administration . . . . . Sean Henry

Hockey Operations
Vice President of Hockey Operations/ General Manager . . . . . Rick Dudley
Assistant General Manager/Alternate Governor . . . . . Jay Feaster
Head Coach . . . . . John Tortorella
Associate Coach . . . . . Craig Ramsay
Goaltending Coach . . . . . Jeff Reese
Special Skills Coach . . . . . Paul Vincent
Head Scout . . . . . Jake Goertzen
Scouting Staff . . . . . Stephen Baker, Niklas Blomgren, Lou Clare, Serguei Grigorkin, Mike Guest, Randy Hansch, Dave Heitz, Karri Kettunen, Martin Loucher, Scott Luce, Dennis McIvor, John McLean, Craig Muni, Rick Paterson, Miroslav Prihoda, Grant Sonier, Buck Steele, John Torchetti, Luke Williams, Yuri Yanchenkov, Glen Zacharias
Director of Team Services . . . . . Phil Thibodeau
Head Medical Trainer . . . . . Dave Boyer
Strength & Conditioning Coach . . . . . Eric Lawson
Massage Therapist . . . . . Mike Griebel
Equipment Manager . . . . . Ray Thill
Assistant Equipment Managers . . . . . Dana Heinze, Jim Pickard
Video Coordinator . . . . . Nigel Kirwan
Hockey Operations Assistant . . . . . Kathy Paterson
Player Relations Coordinator . . . . . Ryan Belec
Team Physician . . . . . Dr. Richard Lehman
Assistant Coach, Springfield Falcons . . . . . Brad Shaw

Finance
Director of Finance . . . . . Brad Whalen
Finance Manager . . . . . Michelle Ekiss
Senior Accountants . . . . . Doug Riefler, Dave Weber
Accounts Payable . . . . . Tim Winans
Accounts Receivable . . . . . Alina Simonds
Staff Accountants . . . . . Kelly Dufresne, Jane Sheill

Sales
Vice President of Sales . . . . . Chad Estis
Director of Sales . . . . . Chris Gargani
Director of Group Events . . . . . Lynn Wittenburg
Director of Outside Sales . . . . . Doug Dawson
Marketing Database Manager . . . . . Damion Chatmon

Sales and Marketing
Vice President of Integrated Sales . . . . . Pedro Goncalves
Vice President of Marketing . . . . . Sean Flynn
Director of Promotions . . . . . Mark Gullett
Outside Entertainment Coordinator . . . . . Jason Franke
Marketing Manager . . . . . Eric Blankenship
Marketing Coordinators . . . . . Sandi Lundin, Justin Scott
Director of Client Services . . . . . Katherine Lesinski
Client Services Managers . . . . . Alaina Miller, Arleen Hernandez, Sean McHale
Executive Assistant . . . . . Lea Richmond
Corporate Marketing Sales Executive . . . . . Tom DeCaprio
Corporate Marketing Managers . . . . . Chris Hibbs, Ted Major, RJ Martino, Tim Zulawski
Director of Event Marketing . . . . . Holly Brown
Director of Sports Marketing . . . . . Bina Kumar
Vice President of Game Operations & Special Events . . . . . Killeen Mullen
Promotions Coordinator . . . . . Travis Flee
Game Operations Coordinator . . . . . Jim Mackes
Broadcasting Production Manager . . . . . Jim Ciotoli
Video Production Coordinator . . . . . Terry Levandoski
Director of Fan Development . . . . . David Cole
Director of Alumni . . . . . John Tucker
Director of Web Services . . . . . Martin Quessenberry
Web Marketing Coordinator . . . . . Jeff Pipech

Public Relations
Vice President of Public Relations . . . . . Bill Wickett
Director of Public Relations . . . . . Jay Preble
Public Relations Manager . . . . . Jay Levin
Community Relations Manager . . . . . Stephanie Hanchey

Broadcast Information
Director of Broadcasting & Programming . . . . . Jason Dixon
Television . . . . . Sunshine Network
Television Broadcasters . . . . . Rick Peckham, Bobby Taylor
Rinkside Reporter . . . . . Erin Andrews
Radio . . . . . WDAE AM 620
Radio Broadcasters . . . . . John Ahlers, Phil Esposito

Toronto Maple Leafs

2000-01 Results: 37W-29L-11T-5OTL 90PTS. Third, Northeast Division

Gary Roberts (left) and Bryan McCabe (right) were key acquisitions for Toronto last season. Roberts led the club with 29 goals, while McCabe was a valuable addition to the blueline corps.

2001-02 Schedule

Month	Day	Date	Opponent
Oct.	Wed.	3	Ottawa
	Sat.	6	at Montreal
	Mon.	8	Anaheim
	Thu.	11	at Carolina
	Sat.	13	St. Louis
	Tue.	16	at Edmonton
	Thu.	18	at Vancouver
	Sat.	20	at Calgary*
	Tue.	23	Boston
	Thu.	25	at Boston
	Sat.	27	Pittsburgh
	Tue.	30	Tampa Bay
Nov.	Thu.	1	at Pittsburgh
	Sat.	3	Colorado
	Tue.	6	Washington
	Fri.	9	at New Jersey
	Sat.	10	New Jersey
	Wed.	14	at Florida
	Thu.	15	at Tampa Bay
	Sat.	17	at Ottawa
	Mon.	19	Florida
	Wed.	21	at Buffalo
	Fri.	23	at NY Islanders
	Sat.	24	Boston
	Tue.	27	Carolina
	Fri.	30	at Chicago
Dec.	Sat.	1	Chicago
	Tue.	4	Pittsburgh
	Thu.	6	at NY Rangers
	Sat.	8	NY Rangers
	Tue.	11	Phoenix
	Thu.	13	at St. Louis
	Sat.	15	Montreal
	Tue.	18	Los Angeles
	Fri.	21	at Buffalo
	Sat.	22	Buffalo
	Wed.	26	at Carolina
	Fri.	28	at Atlanta
	Sat.	29	at Florida
	Mon.	31	at Tampa Bay
Jan.	Thu.	3	at Boston
	Sat.	5	Ottawa*
	Mon.	7	at Ottawa
	Tue.	8	Nashville
	Fri.	11	at Washington
	Sat.	12	Montreal
	Tue.	15	Atlanta
	Thu.	17	at Nashville
	Sat.	19	Philadelphia
	Tue.	22	at Calgary
	Fri.	25	at Vancouver
	Sat.	26	at Edmonton*
	Tue.	29	San Jose
	Wed.	30	at Atlanta
Feb.	Tue.	5	Minnesota
	Thu.	7	at NY Islanders
	Sat.	9	Montreal*
	Mon.	11	Atlanta
	Tue.	26	Carolina
Mar.	Fri.	1	at New Jersey
	Sat.	2	Buffalo
	Mon.	4	at Washington
	Wed.	6	at Detroit
	Sat.	9	at Montreal
	Sun.	10	at Philadelphia
	Tue.	12	Philadelphia
	Thu.	14	at Boston
	Sat.	16	Dallas
	Tue.	19	NY Islanders
	Thu.	21	Washington
	Sat.	23	Buffalo
	Mon.	25	at Philadelphia
	Tue.	26	Tampa Bay
	Thu.	28	NY Islanders
	Sat.	30	New Jersey
Apr.	Mon.	1	at Detroit
	Thu.	4	NY Rangers
	Sat.	6	Florida
	Mon.	8	Columbus
	Wed.	10	at NY Rangers
	Fri.	12	at Pittsburgh
	Sat.	13	at Ottawa

* Denotes afternoon game.

Franchise date: November 22, 1917

NORTHEAST DIVISION

85th NHL Season

Year-by-Year Record

		Home				Road				Overall								
Season	**GP**	**W**	**L**	**T**	**OL**	**W**	**L**	**T**	**OL**	**W**	**L**	**T**	**OL**	**GF**	**GA**	**Pts.**	**Finished**	**Playoff Result**
2000-01	82	19	11	7	4	18	18	4	1	37	29	11	5	232	207	90	3rd, Northeast Div.	Lost Conf. Semi-Final
1999-2000	82	24	12	5	0	21	15	2	3	45	27	7	3	246	222	100	1st, Northeast Div.	Lost Conf. Semi-Final
1998-99	82	23	13	5	...	22	17	2	...	45	30	7	...	268	231	97	2nd, Northeast Div.	Lost Conf. Championship
1997-98	82	16	20	5	...	14	23	4	...	30	43	9	...	194	237	69	6th, Central Div.	Out of Playoffs
1996-97	82	18	20	3	...	12	24	5	...	30	44	8	...	230	273	68	6th, Central Div.	Out of Playoffs
1995-96	82	19	15	7	...	15	21	5	...	34	36	12	...	247	252	80	3rd, Central Div.	Lost Conf. Quarter-Final
1994-95	48	15	7	2	...	6	12	6	...	21	19	8	...	135	146	50	4th, Central Div.	Lost Conf. Quarter-Final
1993-94	84	23	15	4	...	20	14	8	...	43	29	12	...	280	243	98	2nd, Central Div.	Lost Conf. Championship
1992-93	84	25	11	6	...	19	18	5	...	44	29	11	...	288	241	99	3rd, Norris Div.	Lost Conf. Championship
1991-92	80	21	16	3	...	9	27	4	...	30	43	7	...	234	294	67	5th, Norris Div.	Out of Playoffs
1990-91	80	15	21	4	...	8	25	7	...	23	46	11	...	241	318	57	5th, Norris Div.	Out of Playoffs
1989-90	80	24	14	2	...	14	24	2	...	38	38	4	...	337	358	80	3rd, Norris Div.	Lost Div. Semi-Final
1988-89	80	15	20	5	...	13	26	1	...	28	46	6	...	259	342	62	5th, Norris Div.	Out of Playoffs
1987-88	80	14	20	6	...	7	29	4	...	21	49	10	...	273	345	52	4th, Norris Div.	Lost Div. Semi-Final
1986-87	80	22	14	4	...	10	28	2	...	32	42	6	...	286	319	70	4th, Norris Div.	Lost Div. Final
1985-86	80	16	21	3	...	9	27	4	...	25	48	7	...	311	386	57	4th, Norris Div.	Lost Div. Final
1984-85	80	10	28	2	...	10	24	6	...	20	52	8	...	253	358	48	5th, Norris Div.	Out of Playoffs
1983-84	80	17	16	7	...	9	29	2	...	26	45	9	...	303	387	61	5th, Norris Div.	Out of Playoffs
1982-83	80	20	15	5	...	8	25	7	...	28	40	12	...	293	330	68	3rd, Norris Div.	Lost Div. Semi-Final
1981-82	80	12	20	8	...	8	24	8	...	20	44	16	...	298	380	56	5th, Norris Div.	Out of Playoffs
1980-81	80	14	21	5	...	14	16	10	...	28	37	15	...	322	367	71	5th, Adams Div.	Lost Prelim. Round
1979-80	80	17	19	4	...	18	21	1	...	35	40	5	...	304	327	75	4th, Adams Div.	Lost Prelim. Round
1978-79	80	20	12	8	...	14	21	5	...	34	33	13	...	267	252	81	3rd, Adams Div.	Lost Quarter-Final
1977-78	80	21	13	6	...	20	16	4	...	41	29	10	...	271	237	92	3rd, Adams Div.	Lost Semi-Final
1976-77	80	18	13	9	...	15	19	6	...	33	32	15	...	301	285	81	3rd, Adams Div.	Lost Quarter-Final
1975-76	80	23	12	5	...	11	19	10	...	34	31	15	...	294	276	83	3rd, Adams Div.	Lost Quarter-Final
1974-75	80	19	12	9	...	12	21	7	...	31	33	16	...	280	309	78	3rd, Adams Div.	Lost Quarter-Final
1973-74	78	21	11	7	...	14	16	9	...	35	27	16	...	274	230	86	4th, East Div.	Lost Quarter-Final
1972-73	78	20	12	7	...	7	29	3	...	27	41	10	...	247	279	64	6th, East Div.	Out of Playoffs
1971-72	78	21	11	7	...	12	20	7	...	33	31	14	...	209	208	80	4th, East Div.	Lost Quarter-Final
1970-71	78	24	9	6	...	13	24	2	...	37	33	8	...	248	211	82	4th, East Div.	Lost Quarter-Final
1969-70	76	18	13	7	...	11	21	6	...	29	34	13	...	222	242	71	6th, East Div.	Out of Playoffs
1968-69	76	20	8	10	...	15	18	5	...	35	26	15	...	234	217	85	4th, East Div.	Lost Quarter-Final
1967-68	74	24	9	4	...	9	22	6	...	33	31	10	...	209	176	76	5th, East Div.	Out of Playoffs
1966-67	**70**	**21**	**8**	**6**	**...**	**11**	**19**	**5**	**...**	**32**	**27**	**11**	**...**	**204**	**211**	**75**	**3rd,**	**Won Stanley Cup**
1965-66	70	22	9	4	...	12	16	7	...	34	25	11	...	208	187	79	3rd,	Lost Semi-Final
1964-65	70	17	15	3	...	13	11	11	...	30	26	14	...	204	173	74	4th,	Lost Semi-Final
1963-64	**70**	**22**	**7**	**6**	**...**	**11**	**18**	**6**	**...**	**33**	**25**	**12**	**...**	**192**	**172**	**78**	**3rd,**	**Won Stanley Cup**
1962-63	**70**	**21**	**8**	**6**	**...**	**14**	**15**	**6**	**...**	**35**	**23**	**12**	**...**	**221**	**180**	**82**	**1st,**	**Won Stanley Cup**
1961-62	**70**	**25**	**5**	**5**	**...**	**12**	**17**	**6**	**...**	**37**	**22**	**11**	**...**	**232**	**180**	**85**	**2nd,**	**Won Stanley Cup**
1960-61	70	21	6	8	...	18	13	4	...	39	19	12	...	234	176	90	2nd,	Lost Semi-Final
1959-60	70	20	9	6	...	15	17	3	...	35	26	9	...	199	195	79	2nd,	Lost Final
1958-59	70	17	13	5	...	10	19	6	...	27	32	11	...	189	201	65	4th,	Lost Final
1957-58	70	12	16	7	...	9	22	4	...	21	38	11	...	192	226	53	6th,	Out of Playoffs
1956-57	70	12	16	7	...	9	18	8	...	21	34	15	...	174	192	57	5th,	Out of Playoffs
1955-56	70	19	10	6	...	5	23	7	...	24	33	13	...	153	181	61	4th,	Lost Semi-Final
1954-55	70	14	10	11	...	10	14	11	...	24	24	22	...	147	135	70	3rd,	Lost Semi-Final
1953-54	70	22	6	7	...	10	18	7	...	32	24	14	...	152	131	78	3rd,	Lost Semi-Final
1952-53	70	17	12	6	...	10	18	7	...	27	30	13	...	156	167	67	5th,	Out of Playoffs
1951-52	70	17	10	8	...	12	15	8	...	29	25	16	...	168	157	74	3rd,	Lost Semi-Final
1950-51	**70**	**22**	**8**	**5**	**...**	**19**	**8**	**8**	**...**	**41**	**16**	**13**	**...**	**212**	**138**	**95**	**2nd,**	**Won Stanley Cup**
1949-50	70	18	9	8	...	13	18	4	...	31	27	12	...	176	173	74	3rd,	Lost Semi-Final
1948-49	**60**	**12**	**8**	**10**	**...**	**10**	**17**	**3**	**...**	**22**	**25**	**13**	**...**	**147**	**161**	**57**	**4th,**	**Won Stanley Cup**
1947-48	**60**	**22**	**3**	**5**	**...**	**10**	**12**	**8**	**...**	**32**	**15**	**13**	**...**	**182**	**143**	**77**	**1st,**	**Won Stanley Cup**
1946-47	**60**	**20**	**8**	**2**	**...**	**11**	**11**	**8**	**...**	**31**	**19**	**10**	**...**	**209**	**172**	**72**	**2nd,**	**Won Stanley Cup**
1945-46	50	10	13	2	...	9	11	5	...	19	24	7	...	174	185	45	5th,	Out of Playoffs
1944-45	**50**	**13**	**9**	**3**	**...**	**11**	**13**	**1**	**...**	**24**	**22**	**4**	**...**	**183**	**161**	**52**	**3rd,**	**Won Stanley Cup**
1943-44	50	13	11	1	...	10	12	3	...	23	23	4	...	214	174	50	3rd,	Lost Semi-Final
1942-43	50	17	6	2	...	5	13	7	...	22	19	9	...	198	159	53	3rd,	Lost Semi-Final
1941-42	**48**	**18**	**6**	**0**	**...**	**9**	**12**	**3**	**...**	**27**	**18**	**3**	**...**	**158**	**136**	**57**	**2nd,**	**Won Stanley Cup**
1940-41	48	16	5	3	...	12	9	3	...	28	14	6	...	145	99	62	2nd,	Lost Semi-Final
1939-40	48	15	3	6	...	10	14	0	...	25	17	6	...	134	110	56	3rd,	Lost Final
1938-39	48	13	8	3	...	6	12	6	...	19	20	9	...	114	107	47	3rd,	Lost Final
1937-38	48	13	6	5	...	11	9	4	...	24	15	9	...	151	127	57	1st, Cdn. Div.	Lost Final
1936-37	48	14	9	1	...	8	12	4	...	22	21	5	...	119	115	49	3rd, Cdn. Div.	Lost Quarter-Final
1935-36	48	15	4	5	...	8	15	1	...	23	19	6	...	126	106	52	2nd, Cdn. Div.	Lost Final
1934-35	48	16	6	2	...	14	8	2	...	30	14	4	...	157	111	64	1st, Cdn. Div.	Lost Final
1933-34	48	19	2	3	...	7	11	6	...	26	13	9	...	174	119	61	1st, Cdn. Div.	Lost Semi-Final
1932-33	48	16	4	4	...	8	14	2	...	24	18	6	...	119	111	54	1st, Cdn. Div.	Lost Final
1931-32	**48**	**17**	**4**	**3**	**...**	**6**	**14**	**4**	**...**	**23**	**18**	**7**	**...**	**155**	**127**	**53**	**2nd, Cdn. Div.**	**Won Stanley Cup**
1930-31	44	15	4	3	...	7	9	6	...	22	13	9	...	118	99	53	2nd, Cdn. Div.	Lost Quarter-Final
1929-30	44	10	8	4	...	7	13	2	...	17	21	6	...	116	124	40	4th, Cdn. Div.	Out of Playoffs
1928-29	44	15	5	2	...	6	13	3	...	21	18	5	...	85	69	47	3rd, Cdn. Div.	Lost Semi-Final
1927-28	44	9	8	5	...	9	10	3	...	18	18	8	...	89	88	44	4th, Cdn. Div.	Out of Playoffs
1926-27*	44	10	10	2	...	5	14	3	...	15	24	5	...	79	94	35	5th, Cdn. Div.	Out of Playoffs
1925-26	36	11	5	2	...	1	16	1	...	12	21	3	...	92	114	27	6th,	Out of Playoffs
1924-25	30	10	5	0	...	9	6	0	...	19	11	0	...	90	84	38	2nd,	Lost NHL S-Final
1923-24	24	7	5	0	...	3	9	0	...	10	14	0	...	59	85	20	3rd,	Out of Playoffs
1922-23	24	10	1	1	...	3	9	0	...	13	10	1	...	82	88	27	3rd,	Out of Playoffs
1921-22	**24**	**8**	**4**	**0**	**...**	**5**	**6**	**1**	**...**	**13**	**10**	**1**	**...**	**98**	**97**	**27**	**2nd,**	**Won Stanley Cup**
1920-21	24	9	3	0	...	6	6	0	...	15	9	0	...	105	100	30	2nd and 1st***	Lost NHL Final
1919-20**	24	8	4	0	...	4	8	0	...	12	12	0	...	119	106	24	3rd and 2nd***	Out of Playoffs
1918-19	18	5	4	0	...	0	9	0	...	5	13	0	...	64	92	10	3rd and 3rd***	Out of Playoffs
1917-18	**22**	**10**	**1**	**0**	**...**	**3**	**8**	**0**	**...**	**13**	**9**	**0**	**...**	**108**	**109**	**26**	**2nd and 1st*** **	**Won Stanley Cup**

* Name changed from St. Patricks to Maple Leafs. ** Name changed from Arenas to St. Patricks.
*** Season played in two halves with no combined standing at end.
From 1917-18 through 1925-26, NHL champions played against PCHA/WCHL champions for Stanley Cup.

2001-02 Player Personnel

FORWARDS	HT	WT	S	Place of Birth	Date	2000-01 Club
ANTROPOV, Nik	6-5	203	L	Vost, USSR	2/18/80	Toronto
BOYES, Brad	6-0	181	R	Mississauga, Ont.	4/17/82	Erie
CORSON, Shayne	6-1	202	L	Barrie, Ont.	8/13/66	Toronto
DOMI, Tie	5-10	200	R	Windsor, Ont.	11/1/69	Toronto
FARKAS, Jeff	6-0	185	L	Amherst, MA	1/24/78	Toronto-St. John's
GREEN, Travis	6-2	200	R	Castlegar, B.C.	12/20/70	Phoenix
HAKANSSON, Mikael	6-2	204	L	Stockholm, Sweden	5/31/74	St. John's
HOGLUND, Jonas	6-3	215	R	Hammaro, Swe.	8/29/72	Toronto
MacLEAN, Don	6-2	199	L	Sydney, N.S.	1/14/77	Toronto-St. John's
McCAULEY, Alyn	5-11	190	L	Brockville, Ont.	5/29/77	Toronto-St. John's
MILLS, Craig	6-0	190	R	Toronto, Ont.	8/27/76	Springfield
MOGILNY, Alexander	5-11	200	L	Khabarovsk, USSR	2/18/69	New Jersey
MURRAY, Chris	6-2	213	R	Port Hardy, B.C.	10/25/74	Worcester
REICHEL, Robert	5-10	185	L	Litvinov, Czech.	6/25/71	CHZ Litvinov
RENBERG, Mikael	6-2	218	L	Pitea, Sweden	5/5/72	Lulea HF
ROBERTS, Gary	6-1	190	L	North York, Ont.	5/23/66	Toronto
SUNDIN, Mats	6-4	220	R	Bromma, Sweden	2/13/71	Toronto
TUCKER, Darcy	5-11	185	L	Castor, Alta.	3/15/75	Toronto
VALK, Garry	6-1	200	L	Edmonton, Alta.	11/27/67	Toronto
WREN, Bob	5-10	185	L	Preston, Ont.	9/16/74	Anaheim-Cin (AHL)
DEFENSEMEN						
BELAK, Wade	6-5	222	R	Saskatoon, Sask.	7/3/76	Calgary-Toronto
BERG, Aki	6-3	215	L	Turku, Finland	7/28/77	Los Angeles-Toronto
BOUCHARD, Francois	6-0	189	R	Brossard, Que.	8/8/73	Djurgardens IF
CHARTIER, Christian	6-0	219	L	Russell, Man.	12/29/80	Prince George
COLAIACOVO, Carlo	6-1	184	L	Toronto, Ont.	1/27/83	Erie
CROSS, Cory	6-5	220	L	Lloydminster, Alta.	1/3/71	Toronto
DEMPSEY, Nathan	6-0	190	R	Spruce Grove, Alta.	7/14/74	Toronto-St. John's
ERIKSSON, Anders	6-2	220	L	Bollnas, Sweden	1/9/75	Chicago-Florida
GALANOV, Maxim	6-1	205	L	Krasnoyarsk, USSR	3/13/74	T.B.-Det (IHL)-Louisville
KABERLE, Tomas	6-2	190	L	Rakovnik, Czech.	3/2/78	Toronto
MANSON, Dave	6-2	200	L	Prince Albert, Sask.	1/27/67	Toronto
McCABE, Bryan	6-1	210	L	St. Catharines, Ont.	6/8/75	Toronto
PILAR, Karel	6-3	207	R	Prague, Czech.	12/23/77	CHZ Litvinov
SMITH, D.J.	6-2	205	L	Windsor, Ont.	5/13/77	St. John's
SVOBODA, Petr	6-3	200	R	Jihlava, Czech.	6/20/80	Toronto-St. John's
YAKUSHIN, Dmitri	6-0	200	L	Kharkov, USSR	1/21/78	St. John's
YUSHKEVICH, Dmitry	5-11	208	R	Yaroslavl, USSR	11/19/71	Toronto

GOALTENDERS	HT	WT	C	Place of Birth	Date	2000-01 Club
JOSEPH, Curtis	5-11	190	L	Keswick, Ont.	4/29/67	Toronto
MINARD, Mike	6-3	205	L	Owen Sound, Ont.	11/1/76	St. John's
TELLQVIST, Mikael	5-11	185	L	Sundbyberg, Sweden	9/19/79	Djurgardens IF
WAITE, Jimmy	6-1	180	L	Sherbrooke, Que.	4/15/69	St. John's

Coach and General Manager

QUINN, PAT
Coach and General Manager, Toronto Maple Leafs.
Born in Hamilton, Ont., January 29, 1943.

Pat Quinn became the 25th head coach of the Toronto Maple Leafs on June 26, 1998 and quickly turned the club's fortunes around. He earned a nomination for the Jack Adams Award as coach of the year in his first year behind the bench in Toronto after guiding the Leafs to a club record 45 victories. After the season, Quinn was named general manager on July 14, 1999. He is the first man since Punch Imlach in the 1960s to serve the dual role in Toronto. Quinn served as both coach and general manager during much of his time with the Vancouver Canucks. He led the Leafs to their first 100-point season in 1999-2000.

Quinn joined the Canucks as president and general manager in 1987 and took over the coaching reigns on January 31, 1991. He guided the Canucks to single-season records for wins (46) and points (101) in 1992-93, and led the team to the Stanley Cup Finals in 1994. Quinn had previously guided Philadelphia to the Stanley Cup Finals in 1980. He won the Jack Adams Award with the Flyers in 1979-80 and in Vancouver in 1992-93. He also coached in Los Angeles from 1984 to 1987.

Quinn spent the 1968-69 and 1969-70 seasons in a Maple Leafs uniform. He played 99 games for Toronto and later played for Vancouver and the Atlanta Flames. He holds a law degree from Widener University, Delaware School of Law.

NHL Coaching Record

		Regular Season				Playoffs		
Season	Team	Games	W	L	T	Games	W	L
1978-79	Philadelphia	30	18	8	4	8	3	5
1979-80	Philadelphia	80	48	12	20	19	13	6
1980-81	Philadelphia	80	41	24	15	12	6	6
1981-82	Philadelphia	72	34	29	9	....	....	....
1984-85	Los Angeles	80	34	32	14	3	0	3
1985-86	Los Angeles	80	23	49	8	....	....	....
1986-87	Los Angeles	42	18	20	4	....	....	....
1990-91	Vancouver	26	9	13	4	6	2	4
1991-92	Vancouver	80	42	26	12	13	6	7
1992-93	Vancouver	84	46	29	9	12	6	6
1993-94	Vancouver	84	41	40	3	24	15	9
1995-96	Vancouver	6	3	3	0	6	2	4
1998-99	Toronto	82	45	30	7	17	9	8
1999-2000	Toronto	82	45	30	7	12	6	6
2000-01	Toronto	82	37	34	11	11	7	4
	NHL Totals	**990**	**484**	**379**	**127**	**143**	**75**	**68**

2000-01 Scoring

* - rookie

Regular Season

Pos	#	Player	Team	GP	G	A	Pts	+/–	PIM	PP	SH	GW	GT	S	%
C	13	Mats Sundin	TOR	82	28	46	74	15	76	9	0	6	1	226	12.4
L	7	Gary Roberts	TOR	82	29	24	53	16	109	8	2	3	0	138	21.0
C	44	Yanic Perreault	TOR	76	24	28	52	0	52	5	0	2	0	134	17.9
L	94	Sergei Berezin	TOR	79	22	28	50	2	8	10	0	3	1	256	8.6
R	14	Jonas Hoglund	TOR	82	23	26	49	1	14	5	0	5	2	196	11.7
D	15	Tomas Kaberle	TOR	82	6	39	45	10	24	0	0	1	0	96	6.3
C	16	Darcy Tucker	TOR	82	16	21	37	6	141	2	0	4	0	122	13.1
L	32	Steve Thomas	TOR	57	8	26	34	0	46	1	0	1	0	140	5.7
C	22	Igor Korolev	TOR	73	10	19	29	3	28	2	0	0	0	78	12.8
D	24	Bryan McCabe	TOR	82	5	24	29	16	123	3	0	2	0	159	3.1
R	10	Garry Valk	TOR	74	8	18	26	4	46	1	0	2	0	87	9.2
L	27	Shayne Corson	TOR	77	8	18	26	1	189	0	0	2	0	102	7.8
D	36	Dmitry Yushkevich	TOR	81	5	19	24	–2	52	1	0	0	1	110	4.5
R	28	Tie Domi	TOR	82	13	7	20	2	214	1	0	1	0	60	21.7
C	9	Nik Antropov	TOR	52	6	11	17	5	30	0	0	1	0	71	8.5
D	55	Danny Markov	TOR	59	3	13	16	6	34	1	0	2	0	49	6.1
D	3	Dave Manson	TOR	74	4	7	11	13	93	0	0	0	0	70	5.7
L	43	Nathan Dempsey	TOR	25	1	9	10	13	4	1	0	0	0	31	3.2
D	4	Cory Cross	TOR	41	3	5	8	7	50	1	0	1	0	34	8.8
D	8	Aki Berg	L.A.	47	0	4	4	3	43	0	0	0	0	31	0.0
			TOR	12	3	0	3	–6	2	3	0	1	0	12	25.0
			TOTAL	59	3	4	7	–3	45	3	0	1	0	43	7.0
R	39	* Alexei Ponikarovsky	TOR	22	1	3	4	–1	14	0	0	0	0	21	4.8
D	23	* Petr Svoboda	TOR	18	1	2	3	–5	10	1	0	0	0	17	5.9
D	2	Wade Belak	CGY	23	0	0	0	–2	79	0	0	0	0	8	0.0
			TOR	16	1	1	2	–4	31	0	0	0	0	8	12.5
			TOTAL	39	1	1	2	–6	110	0	0	0	0	16	6.3
C	18	Alyn McCauley	TOR	14	1	0	1	0	0	0	0	0	0	13	7.7
C	37	* Donald MacLean	TOR	3	0	1	1	–2	2	0	0	0	0	2	0.0
G	31	Curtis Joseph	TOR	68	0	1	1	0	8	0	0	0	0	0	0.0
D	33	David Cooper	TOR	2	0	0	0	–1	0	0	0	0	0	3	0.0
C	19	* Jeff Farkas	TOR	2	0	0	0	–1	2	0	0	0	0	1	0.0
G	30	Glenn Healy	TOR	15	0	0	0	0	0	0	0	0	0	0	0.0

Goaltending

No.	Goaltender	GPI	Mins	Avg	W	L	T	EN	SO	GA	SA	S%
31	Curtis Joseph	68	4100	2.39	33	27	8	5	6	163	1907	.915
30	Glenn Healy	15	871	2.62	4	7	3	1	0	38	331	.885
	Totals	**82**	**4990**	**2.49**	**37**	**34**	**11**	**6**	**6**	**207**	**2244**	**.908**

Playoffs

Pos	#	Player	Team	GP	G	A	Pts	+/–	PIM	PP	SH	GW	GT	S	%
C	13	Mats Sundin	TOR	11	6	7	13	5	14	2	1	1	1	42	14.3
L	7	Gary Roberts	TOR	11	2	9	11	5	0	0	0	0	0	15	13.3
L	32	Steve Thomas	TOR	11	6	3	9	4	4	4	0	0	0	27	22.2
L	94	Sergei Berezin	TOR	11	2	5	7	1	2	0	0	2	0	24	8.3
C	44	Yanic Perreault	TOR	11	2	3	5	2	4	1	0	1	0	9	22.2
D	24	Bryan McCabe	TOR	11	2	3	5	5	16	1	0	0	0	17	11.8
D	15	Tomas Kaberle	TOR	11	1	3	4	4	0	0	0	1	0	17	5.9
D	36	Dmitry Yushkevich	TOR	11	0	4	4	–4	12	0	0	0	0	10	0.0
C	9	Nik Antropov	TOR	9	2	1	3	2	12	1	0	1	0	10	20.0
D	4	Cory Cross	TOR	11	2	1	3	–1	10	0	0	1	1	7	28.6
L	27	Shayne Corson	TOR	11	1	1	2	–1	14	0	0	0	0	12	8.3
D	55	Danny Markov	TOR	11	1	1	2	–3	12	0	0	0	0	7	14.3
C	16	Darcy Tucker	TOR	11	0	2	2	–2	6	0	0	0	0	17	0.0
D	8	Aki Berg	TOR	11	0	2	2	1	4	0	0	0	0	9	0.0
R	10	Garry Valk	TOR	5	1	0	1	–1	2	0	0	0	0	6	16.7
R	28	Tie Domi	TOR	8	0	1	1	0	20	0	0	0	0	3	0.0
D	3	Dave Manson	TOR	2	0	0	0	0	2	0	0	0	0	0	0.0
R	14	Jonas Hoglund	TOR	10	0	0	0	–4	4	0	0	0	0	8	0.0
C	18	Alyn McCauley	TOR	10	0	0	0	–4	2	0	0	0	0	3	0.0
G	31	Curtis Joseph	TOR	11	0	0	0	0	4	0	0	0	0	0	0.0
C	22	Igor Korolev	TOR	11	0	0	0	–3	0	0	0	0	0	4	0.0

Goaltending

No.	Goaltender	GPI	Mins	Avg	W	L	EN	SO	GA	SA	S%
31	Curtis Joseph	11	685	2.10	7	4	0	3	24	329	.927
	Totals	**11**	**686**	**2.10**	**7**	**4**	**0**	**3**	**24**	**329**	**.927**

Coaching History

Conn Smythe, 1927-28 to 1929-30; Conn Smythe and Art Duncan, 1930-31; Art Duncan and Dick Irvin, 1931-32; Dick Irvin, 1932-33 to 1939-40; Hap Day, 1940-41 to 1949-50; Joe Primeau, 1950-51 to 1952-53; King Clancy, 1953-54 to 1955-56; Howie Meeker, 1956-57; Billy Reay, 1957-58; Billy Reay and Punch Imlach, 1958-59; Punch Imlach, 1959-60 to 1968-69; John McLellan, 1969-70 to 1972-73; Red Kelly, 1973-74 to 1976-77; Roger Neilson, 1977-78, 1978-79; Floyd Smith, Dick Duff and Punch Imlach, 1979-80; Punch Imlach, Joe Crozier and Mike Nykoluk, 1980-81; Mike Nykoluk, 1981-82 to 1983-84; Dan Maloney, 1984-85, 1985-86; John Brophy, 1986-87, 1987-88; John Brophy and George Armstrong, 1988-89; Doug Carpenter, 1989-90; Doug Carpenter and Tom Watt, 1990-91; Tom Watt, 1991-92; Pat Burns, 1992-93 to 1994-95; Pat Burns and Nick Beverley, 1995-96; Mike Murphy, 1996-97, 1997-98; Pat Quinn, 1998-99 to date.

Club Records

Team

(Figures in brackets for season records are games played; records for fewest points, wins, ties, losses, goals, goals against are for 70 or more games)

Most Points	100	1999-2000 (82)
Most Wins	45	1998-99 (82), 1999-2000 (82)
Most Ties	22	1954-55 (70)
Most Losses	52	1984-85 (80)
Most Goals	337	1989-90 (80)
Most Goals Against	387	1983-84 (80)
Fewest Points	48	1984-85 (80)
Fewest Wins	20	1981-82 (80), 1984-85 (80)
Fewest Ties	4	1989-90 (80)
Fewest Losses	16	1950-51 (70)
Fewest Goals	147	1954-55 (70)
Fewest Goals Against	*131	1953-54 (70)
Longest Winning Streak		
Overall	10	Oct. 7-28/93
Home	9	Nov. 11-Dec. 26/53
Away	7	Nov. 14-Dec. 15/40, Dec. 4/60-Jan. 5/61
Longest Undefeated Streak		
Overall	11	Oct. 15-Nov. 8/50 (8 wins, 3 ties), Jan. 6-Feb. 1/94 (7 wins, 4 ties)
Home	18	Nov. 28/33-Mar. 10/34 (15 wins, 3 ties), Oct. 31/53-Jan. 23/54 (16 wins, 2 ties)
Away	9	Nov. 30/47-Jan. 11/48 (4 wins, 5 ties)
Longest Losing Streak		
Overall	10	Jan. 15-Feb. 8/67
Home	7	Nov. 11-Dec. 5/84
Away	11	Feb. 20-Apr. 1/88
Longest Winless Streak		
Overall	15	Dec. 26/87-Jan. 25/88 (11 losses, 4 ties)
Home	11	Dec. 19/87-Jan. 25/88 (7 losses, 4 ties)
Away	18	Oct. 6/82-Jan. 5/83 (13 losses, 5 ties)
Most Shutouts, Season	13	1953-54 (70)
Most PIM, Season	2,419	1989-90 (80)
Most Goals, Game	14	Mar. 16/57 (NYR 1 at Tor. 14)

Individual

Most Seasons	21	George Armstrong
Most Games	1,187	George Armstrong
Most Goals, Career	389	Darryl Sittler
Most Assists, Career	620	Borje Salming
Most Points, Career	916	Darryl Sittler (389G, 527A)
Most PIM, Career	1,670	Dave Williams
Most Shutouts, Career	62	Turk Broda
Longest Consecutive Games Streak	486	Tim Horton (Feb. 11/61-Feb. 4/68)
Most Goals, Season	54	Rick Vaive (1981-82)
Most Assists, Season	95	Doug Gilmour (1992-93)
Most Points, Season	127	Doug Gilmour (1992-93; 32G, 95A)
Most PIM, Season	365	Tie Domi (1997-98)
Most Points, Defenseman, Season	79	Ian Turnbull (1976-77; 22G, 57A)
Most Points, Center, Season	127	Doug Gilmour (1992-93; 32G, 95A)
Most Points, Right Wing, Season	97	Wilf Paiement (1980-81; 40G, 57A)
Most Points, Left Wing, Season	99	Dave Andreychuk (1993-94; 53G, 46A)
Most Points, Rookie, Season	66	Peter Ihnacak (1982-83; 28G, 38A)
Most Shutouts, Season	13	Harry Lumley (1953-54)
Most Goals, Game	6	Corb Denneny (Jan. 26/21), Darryl Sittler (Feb. 7/76)
Most Assists, Game	6	Babe Pratt (Jan. 8/44), Doug Gilmour (Feb. 13/93)
Most Points, Game	*10	Darryl Sittler (Feb. 7/76; 6G, 4A)

* NHL Record.

Retired Numbers

5	Bill Barilko	1946-1951
6	Ace Bailey	1926-1934

Honored Numbers

1	Turk Broda	1936-43, 45-52
	Johnny Bower	1958-1970
7	King Clancy	1930-1937
	Tim Horton	1949-50, 51-70
9	Charlie Conacher	1929-1938
	Ted Kennedy	1942-55, 56-57
10	Syl Apps	1936-43, 45-48
	George Armstrong	1949-50, 51-71

All-time Record vs. Other Clubs

Regular Season

	At Home								On Road								Total							
	GP	W	L	T	OL	GF	GA	PTS	GP	W	L	T	OL	GF	GA	PTS	GP	W	L	T	OL	GF	GA	PTS
Anaheim	13	7	2	4	0	39	27	18	10	5	4	1	0	27	29	11	23	12	6	5	0	66	56	29
Atlanta	3	2	1	0	0	12	5	4	3	2	1	0	0	9	6	4	6	4	2	0	0	21	11	8
Boston	291	151	89	51	0	987	754	353	290	86	156	47	1	766	951	220	581	237	245	98	1	1753	1705	573
Buffalo	59	24	25	10	0	181	206	58	61	17	39	5	0	163	252	39	120	41	64	15	0	344	458	97
Calgary	51	26	17	7	1	195	186	60	56	20	31	5	0	179	224	45	107	46	48	12	1	374	410	105
Carolina	30	10	15	5	0	105	112	25	31	9	17	5	0	103	131	23	61	19	32	10	0	208	243	48
Chicago	313	163	96	54	0	1066	816	380	316	118	156	42	0	826	966	278	629	281	252	96	0	1892	1782	658
Colorado	32	14	14	4	0	109	127	32	29	7	17	5	0	87	111	19	61	21	31	9	0	196	238	51
Columbus	1	0	0	1	0	2	2	1	0	0	0	0	0	0	0	0	1	0	0	1	0	2	2	1
Dallas	100	49	35	16	0	351	314	114	95	35	49	11	0	302	362	81	195	84	84	27	0	653	676	195
Detroit	314	163	104	47	0	1039	842	373	319	107	166	46	0	783	951	260	633	270	270	93	0	1822	1793	633
Edmonton	35	19	14	2	0	146	148	40	38	12	20	6	0	126	165	30	73	31	34	8	0	272	313	70
Florida	9	6	2	1	0	34	23	13	11	5	3	3	0	34	32	13	20	11	5	4	0	68	55	26
Los Angeles	66	34	21	11	0	261	217	79	64	21	34	9	0	187	230	51	130	55	55	20	0	448	447	130
Minnesota	1	1	0	0	0	6	1	2	0	0	0	0	0	0	0	0	1	1	0	0	0	6	1	2
Montreal	325	167	114	44	0	982	843	378	325	88	197	40	0	806	1147	216	650	255	311	84	0	1788	1990	594
Nashville	3	0	2	1	0	5	9	1	0	0	0	0	0	0	0	0	3	0	2	1	0	5	9	1
New Jersey	42	28	10	4	0	174	132	60	40	13	14	13	0	126	141	39	82	41	24	17	0	300	273	99
NY Islanders	49	24	22	3	0	166	170	51	47	19	25	3	0	143	187	41	96	43	47	6	0	309	357	92
NY Rangers	276	155	82	39	0	953	724	349	277	103	116	56	2	808	851	264	553	258	198	95	2	1761	1575	613
Ottawa	14	7	5	1	1	40	38	16	12	3	8	1	0	30	37	7	26	10	13	2	1	70	75	23
Philadelphia	61	22	25	13	1	201	207	58	61	13	39	8	1	142	241	35	122	35	64	21	2	343	448	93
Phoenix	41	18	21	2	0	146	155	38	38	12	20	6	0	137	157	30	79	30	41	8	0	283	312	68
Pittsburgh	61	29	21	11	0	246	200	69	63	22	35	6	0	199	267	50	124	51	56	17	0	445	467	119
St. Louis	97	58	27	11	1	365	284	128	100	29	57	14	0	276	339	72	197	87	84	25	1	641	623	200
San Jose	16	11	4	1	0	62	41	23	14	7	5	2	0	38	30	16	30	18	9	3	0	100	71	39
Tampa Bay	15	8	6	1	0	53	38	17	14	12	2	0	0	52	28	24	29	20	8	1	0	105	66	41
Vancouver	58	27	21	10	0	214	191	64	59	20	28	11	0	198	208	51	117	47	49	21	0	412	399	115
Washington	42	22	15	5	0	189	147	49	44	14	28	2	0	123	170	30	86	36	43	7	0	312	317	79
Defunct Clubs	232	158	53	21	0	860	515	337	233	84	120	29	0	607	745	197	465	242	173	50	0	1467	1260	534
Totals	**2650**	**1403**	**863**	**380**	**4**	**9189**	**7474**	**3190**	**2650**	**883**	**1387**	**376**	**4**	**7277**	**8958**	**2146**	**5300**	**2286**	**2250**	**756**	**8**	**16466**	**16432**	**5336**

Playoffs

	Series	W	L	GP	W	L	T	GF	GA	Last Mtg.	Round	Result
Boston	13	8	5	62	31	30	1	150	153	1974	QF	L 0-4
Buffalo	1	0	1	5	1	4	0	16	21	1999	CF	L 1-4
Calgary	1	1	0	2	2	0	0	9	5	1979	PR	W 2-0
Chicago	9	6	3	38	22	15	1	111	89	1995	CQF	L 3-4
Dallas	2	0	2	7	1	6	0	26	35	1983	DSF	L 1-3
Detroit	23	12	11	117	58	59	0	311	321	1993	DSF	W 4-3
Los Angeles	3	2	1	12	7	5	0	41	31	1993	CF	L 3-4
Montreal	15	7	8	71	29	42	0	160	215	1979	QF	L 0-4
New Jersey	2	0	2	13	5	8	0	27	37	2001	CSF	L 3-4
NY Islanders	2	1	1	10	4	6	0	20	33	1981	PR	L 0-3
NY Rangers	8	3	5	35	16	19	0	86	86	1971	QF	L 2-4
Ottawa	2	2	0	10	8	2	0	27	13	2001	CQF	W 4-0
Philadelphia	4	1	3	23	9	14	0	56	78	1999	CQF	W 4-2
Pittsburgh	3	3	0	12	8	4	0	39	27	1999	CSF	W 4-2
St. Louis	5	2	3	31	14	17	0	90	88	1996	CQF	L 2-4
San Jose	1	1	0	7	4	3	0	26	21	1994	CSF	W 4-3
Vancouver	1	0	1	5	1	4	0	9	16	1994	CF	L 1-4
Defunct	8	6	2	24	12	10	2	59	57			
Totals	**103**	**55**	**48**	**484**	**232**	**248**	**4**	**1263**	**1326**			

Playoff Results 2001-1997

Year	Round	Opponent	Result	GF	GA
2001	CSF	New Jersey	L 3-4	18	21
	CQF	Ottawa	W 4-0	10	3
2000	CSF	New Jersey	L 2-4	9	16
	CQF	Ottawa	W 4-2	17	10
1999	CF	Buffalo	L 1-4	16	21
	CSF	Pittsburgh	W 4-2	18	14
	CQF	Philadelphia	W 4-2	9	11

Abbreviations: Round: CF – conference final; **CSF** – conference semi-final; **CQF** – conference quarter-final; **DSF** – division semi-final; **QF** – quarter-final; **PR** – preliminary round.

Calgary totals include Atlanta Flames, 1972-73 to 1979-80.
Carolina totals include Hartford, 1979-80 to 1996-97.
Colorado totals include Quebec, 1979-80 to 1994-95.
Dallas totals include Minnesota North Stars, 1967-68 to 1992-93.
New Jersey totals include Kansas City, 1974-75 to 1975-76, and Colorado Rockies, 1976-77 to 1981-82.
Phoenix totals include Winnipeg, 1979-80 to 1995-96.

2000-01 Results

Month	Date		Opponent	Score
Oct.	7		Montreal	2-0
	9		Dallas	1-3
	11		NY Islanders	3-2
	14		Ottawa	0-4
	16	at	Vancouver	2-5
	19	at	Edmonton	4-1
	21	at	Calgary	2-1
	25		Minnesota	6-1
	27	at	Buffalo	1-2
	28	at	Boston	2-1*
	31	at	Ottawa	3-4
Nov.	2		New Jersey	5-3
	4	at	St. Louis	0-0
	5		Boston	7-1
	8		Carolina	5-0
	10	at	Carolina	1-3
	11		Chicago	3-3
	15		Philadelphia	1-2*
	17		Tampa Bay	2-2
	18	at	Montreal	6-1
	21	at	NY Rangers	3-1
	22		Edmonton	4-3
	25		Ottawa	2-4
	29		St. Louis	5-6*
	30	at	NY Islanders	6-4
Dec.	2		NY Rangers	8-2
	4		Florida	4-4
	6	at	Detroit	3-0
	9		Pittsburgh	5-1
	13	at	Pittsburgh	7-4
	15	at	NY Islanders	2-3
	16		Calgary	5-6*
	20		Nashville	1-3
	21	at	Boston	0-4
	23	at	Montreal	5-2
	26	at	Atlanta	3-5
	27	at	Pittsburgh	0-5
	30	at	Florida	4-1
	31	at	Tampa Bay	3-2
Jan.	3		Buffalo	1-1
	5	at	Buffalo	3-3
	6		Washington	2-3
	10		Tampa Bay	1-3
	12		Phoenix	3-2
	13	at	New Jersey	4-4
	17		Los Angeles	1-2
	18	at	NY Rangers	1-2*
	20		Buffalo	2-0
	24		Boston	1-2
	25	at	Atlanta	2-1*
	27		NY Rangers	3-1
	29	at	St. Louis	1-2
	31	at	Carolina	4-3
Feb.	1	at	Washington	4-5
	7		Atlanta	7-1
	8	at	Detroit	1-2
	10		Detroit	3-3
	14		Columbus	2-2
	15	at	Philadelphia	2-5
	17		Colorado	5-5
	19		New Jersey	0-2
	22		Vancouver	4-1
	24		Montreal	5-1
	25	at	Chicago	4-6
	28		San Jose	2-1
Mar.	1	at	Washington	3-2*
	3		Ottawa	2-3*
	6	at	Calgary	3-1
	7	at	Edmonton	0-4
	10	at	Vancouver	3-3
	14		Anaheim	3-2
	15	at	Tampa Bay	2-3
	17	at	Florida	5-3
	20	at	Buffalo	0-3
	21		Florida	1-3
	24		Philadelphia	5-3
	28		Boston	0-3
	29	at	Philadelphia	2-1
	31	at	Montreal	1-4
Apr.	4		NY Islanders	4-2
	6	at	Chicago	1-0
	7	at	Ottawa	3-5

* – Overtime

Entry Draft Selections 2001-1987

2001

Pick	
17	Carlo Colaiacovo
39	Karel Pilar
65	Brendan Bell
82	Jay Harrison
88	Nicolas Corbeil
134	Kyle Wellwood
168	Maxim Kondratjev
183	Jaroslav Sklenar
198	Ivan Kolozvary
213	Jan Chovan
246	Tomas Mojzis
276	Mike Knoepfli

2000

Pick	
24	Brad Boyes
51	Kris Vernarsky
70	Mikael Tellqvist
90	Jean-Francois Racine
100	Miguel Delisle
179	Vadim Sozinov
209	Markus Seikola
223	Lubos Velebny
254	Alexander Shinkar
265	Jean-Philippe Cote

1999

Pick	
24	Luca Cereda
60	Peter Reynolds
108	Mirko Murovic
110	Jon Zion
151	Vaclav Zavoral
161	Jan Sochor
211	Vladimir Kulikov
239	Pierre Hedin
267	Peter Metcalf

1998

Pick	
10	Nik Antropov
35	Petr Svoboda
69	Jamie Hodson
87	Alexei Ponikarovsky
126	Morgan Warren
154	Allan Rourke
181	Jonathan Gagnon
215	Dwight Wolfe
228	Michal Travnicek
236	Sergei Rostov

1997

Pick	
57	Jeff Farkas
84	Adam Mair
111	Frantisek Mrazek
138	Eric Gooldy
165	Hugo Marchand
190	Shawn Thornton
194	Russ Bartlett
221	Jonathan Hedstrom

1996

Pick	
36	Marek Posmyk
50	Francis Larivee
66	Mike Lankshear
68	Konstantin Kalmikov
86	Jason Sessa
103	Vladimir Antipov
110	Peter Cava
111	Brandon Sugden
140	Dmitri Yakushin
148	Chris Bogas
151	Lucio DeMartinis
178	Reggie Berg
204	Tomas Kaberle
230	Jared Hope

1995

Pick	
15	Jeff Ware
54	Ryan Pepperall
139	Doug Bonner
145	Yannick Tremblay
171	Marek Melenovsky
197	Mark Murphy
223	Danny Markov

1994

Pick	
16	Eric Fichaud
48	Sean Haggerty
64	Fredrik Modin
126	Mark Deyell
152	Karri White
178	Tommi Rajamaki
204	Rob Butler
256	Sergei Berezin
282	Doug Nolan

1993

Pick	
12	Kenny Jonsson
19	Landon Wilson
123	Zdenek Nedved
149	Paul Vincent
175	Jeff Andrews
201	David Brumby
253	Kyle Ferguson
279	Mikhail Lapin

1992

Pick	
8	Brandon Convery
23	Grant Marshall
77	Nikolai Borschevsky
95	Mark Raiter
101	Janne Gronvall
106	Chris Deruiter
125	Mikael Hakansson
149	Patrik Augusta
173	Ryan Vandenbussche
197	Wayne Clarke
221	Sergei Simonov
245	Nathan Dempsey

1991

Pick	
47	Yanic Perreault
69	Terry Chitaroni
102	Alexei Kudashov
113	Jeff Perry
120	Alexander Kuzminsky
135	Martin Prochazka
160	Dmitri Mironov
164	Robb McIntyre
167	Tomas Kucharcik
179	Guy Lehoux
201	Gary Miller
223	Johnathon Kelley
245	Chris O'Rourke

1990

Pick	
10	Drake Berehowsky
31	Felix Potvin
73	Darby Hendrickson
80	Greg Walters
115	Alexander Godynyuk
136	Eric Lacroix
157	Dan Stiver
178	Robert Horyna
199	Rob Chebator
220	Scott Malone
241	Nick Vachon

1989

Pick	
3	Scott Thornton
12	Rob Pearson
21	Steve Bancroft
66	Matt Martin
96	Keith Carney
108	David Burke
125	Michael Doers
129	Keith Merkler
150	Derek Langille
171	Jeffrey St. Laurent
192	Justin Tomberlin
213	Mike Jackson
234	Steve Chartrand

1988

Pick	
6	Scott Pearson
27	Tie Domi
48	Peter Ing
69	Ted Crowley
86	Len Esau
132	Matt Mallgrave
153	Peter Elvenas
174	Mike Delay
195	David Sacco
216	Mike Gregorio
237	Peter DeBoer

1987

Pick	
7	Luke Richardson
28	Daniel Marois
49	John McIntyre
71	Joe Sacco
91	Mike Eastwood
112	Damian Rhodes
133	Trevor Jobe
175	Brian Blad
196	Ron Bernacci
217	Ken Alexander
238	Alex Weinrich

Captains' History

Hap Day, 1927-28 to 1936-37; Charlie Conacher, 1937-38; Red Horner, 1938-39, 1939-40; Syl Apps, 1940-41 to 1942-43; Bob Davidson, 1943-44, 1944-45; Syl Apps, 1945-46 to 1947-48; Ted Kennedy, 1948-49 to 1954-55; Sid Smith, 1955-56; Jim Thomson, Ted Kennedy, 1956-57; George Armstrong, 1957-58 to 1968-69; Dave Keon, 1969-70 to 1974-75; Darryl Sittler, 1975-76 to 1980-81; Rick Vaive, 1981-82 to 1985-86; no captain, 1986-87 to 1988-89; Rob Ramage, 1989-90, 1990-91; Wendel Clark, 1991-92 to 1993-94; Doug Gilmour, 1994-95 to 1996-97; Mats Sundin, 1997-98 to date.

General Managers' History

Conn Smythe, 1927-28 to 1956-57; Hap Day, 1957-58; Punch Imlach, 1958-59 to 1968-69; Jim Gregory, 1969-70 to 1978-79; Punch Imlach, 1979-80, 1980-81; Punch Imlach and Gerry McNamara, 1981-82; Gerry McNamara, 1982-83 to 1987-88; Gord Stellick, 1988-89; Floyd Smith, 1989-90, 1990-91; Cliff Fletcher, 1991-92 to 1996-97; Ken Dryden, 1997-98, 1998-99; Pat Quinn, 1999-2000 to date.

Club Directory

Air Canada Centre

Toronto Maple Leafs
Air Canada Centre
40 Bay St., Suite 400
Toronto, Ontario M5J 2X2
Phone **416/815-5700**
FAX 416/359-9331
www.mapleleafs.com
Capacity: 18,819

Board of Directors

Steve A. Stavro (Chairman of the Board and NHL Governor), Brian P. Bellmore (Alternate NHL Governor), Dale Lastman, Robert G. Bertram, John MacIntyre, Dean Metcalf

Maple Leaf Sports & Entertainment Ltd.

Chairman of the Board and NHL Governor	Steve A. Stavro
Alternate NHL Governor	Brian P. Bellmore
President, Chief Executive Officer and Alternate NHL Governor	Richard Peddie
Executive Vice-President and Alternate NHL Governor	Ken Dryden
Sr. Vice-President and General Manager, Air Canada Centre	Bob Hunter
Sr. Vice-President, Business	Tom Anselmi
Sr. Vice-President, Chief Financial Officer	Ian Clarke
Vice-President, Sports Communications and Community Development	John Lashway
Vice-President, People	Mardi Walker
Vice-President, Regulatory Affairs and General Counsel	Robin Brudner
Vice-President, Sales and Service	Chris Overholt
Corporate Secretary	Paul Perantinos

Maple Leafs Management

President and Alternate NHL Governor	Ken Dryden
General Manager and Head Coach	Pat Quinn
Assistant to the President	Bill Watters
Director, Player Personnel	Mike Penny
Assistant Coaches	Keith Acton, Rick Ley
Development Coach	Paul Dennis
Community Representatives	Wendel Clark, Darryl Sittler
Chief European Scout	Thommie Bergman
Director, Amateur Scouting	Mark Hillier
Scouts	George Armstrong, Jim Bzdel, Bob Johnson, Garth Malarchuk, Murray Oliver, Mark Yannetti
European Scouts	Leonid Vaysfeld, Jan Kovac
Director, Hockey Operations	Casey Vanden Heuvel
Manager, Video Operations & Scouting	Reid Mitchell
Travel Co-ordinator	Mary Speck
Executive Assistant to President	Ann Clark
Executive Assistant to General Manager	Maria Tomasevic
Head Coach, St. John's AHL Affiliate	Lou Crawford
Assistant Coaches, St. John's AHL Affiliate	Kevin McClelland, Russ Adam
Alternate Practice Facility	Lake Shore Lions Arena

Maple Leafs Communications and Community Development

Vice-President, Sports Communications and Community Development	John Lashway
Director, Media Relations	Pat Park
Co-ordinators, Media Relations	Dave Griffiths, Reid Mitchell
Manager, Corporate Communications, MLSEL	Tara McCarthy
Director, Community Relations	Kristy Fletcher
Director, Leaf Community Fund	Angela McManus
Co-ordinators, Leaf Community Fund	Cora Mattholie, Veronica Love
Co-ordinators, Community Relations	Sefu Bernard, Paulette Minard
Manager, Game Presentation	Mike Ferriman
Manager, Game Operations	Nancy Gilks
Assistant, Game Operations	Shannon Nolan
Manager, Community Youth Outreach	Al Quance
Co-ordinator, Youth Hockey Development	Greg Schell
Alumni Relations	Jennifer Woods
Executive Assistant, Communications	Laura Leite

Maple Leafs Medical and Training Staff

Head Athletic Therapist	Chris Broadhurst
Athletic Therapist	Brent Smith
Equipment Manager	Brian Papineau
Assistant Equipment Managers	Bobby Hastings, Scott McKay
Team Doctors	Dr. Michael Clarfield, Dr. Darrell Ogilvie-Harris, Dr. Leith Douglas, Dr. Rob Devenyi, Dr. Simon McGrail
Team Dentist	Dr. Ernie Lewis
Team Psychologist	Robert Offenberger

Broadcast Information

Radio Play-By-Play	Joe Bowen, Dennis Beyak
Radio Analyst	Jim Ralph
Television Play-By-Play	Bob Cole, Joe Bowen
Television Analyst	Harry Neale
Radio Affiliation	Mojo Radio (AM 640)
TV Affiliation	CBC, TSN, Sportsnet

Air Canada Centre

Director, Building Operations	Diego Roccasalva
Director, Event Operations and Production	Jim Roe
Director, Event Personnel and Guest Services	Kim Bedier
Director, Programming and Event Marketing	Patti-Anne Tarlton
Director, Marketing	Beth Robertson
Director, Information Technology	Sasha Puric
Director, Ticket Operations	Donna Henderson
Manager, Video and Scoreboard Production	Curtis Emerson
Director, Executive Suites Services	Nancy Read
Director, Consumer Products	Jeff Newman
Executive Producer, New Media	John Shannon
Director of Business, New Media	Frank Bertolas
Director, Marketing Media	Alon Marcovici
Director, Corporate Sales	Dave Hopkinson

Vancouver Canucks

2000-01 Results: 36W-28L-11T-7OTL 90PTS. Third, Northwest Division

Year-by-Year Record

		Home				Road				Overall								
Season	GP	W	L	T	OL	W	L	T	OL	W	L	T	OL	GF	GA	Pts.	Finished	Playoff Result
2000-01	82	21	12	5	3	15	16	6	4	36	28	11	7	239	238	90	3rd, Northwest Div.	Lost Conf. Quarter-Final
1999-2000	82	16	14	5	6	14	15	10	2	30	29	15	8	227	237	83	3rd, Northwest Div.	Out of Playoffs
1998-99	82	14	21	6	...	9	26	6	...	23	47	12	...	192	258	58	4th, Northwest Div.	Out of Playoffs
1997-98	82	15	22	4	...	10	21	10	...	25	43	14	...	224	273	64	7th, Pacific Div.	Out of Playoffs
1996-97	82	20	17	4	...	15	23	3	...	35	40	7	...	257	273	77	4th, Pacific Div.	Out of Playoffs
1995-96	82	15	19	7	...	17	16	8	...	32	35	15	...	278	278	79	3rd, Pacific Div.	Lost Conf. Quarter-Final
1994-95	48	10	8	6	...	8	10	6	...	18	18	12	...	153	148	48	2nd, Pacific Div.	Lost Conf. Semi-Final
1993-94	84	20	19	3	...	21	21	0	...	41	40	3	...	279	276	85	2nd, Pacific Div.	Lost Final
1992-93	84	27	11	4	...	19	18	5	...	46	29	9	...	346	278	101	1st, Smythe Div.	Lost Div. Final
1991-92	80	23	10	7	...	19	16	5	...	42	26	12	...	285	250	96	1st, Smythe Div.	Lost Div. Final
1990-91	80	18	17	5	...	10	26	4	...	28	43	9	...	243	315	65	4th, Smythe Div.	Lost Div. Semi-Final
1989-90	80	13	16	11	...	12	25	3	...	25	41	14	...	245	306	64	5th, Smythe Div.	Out of Playoffs
1988-89	80	19	15	6	...	14	24	2	...	33	39	8	...	251	253	74	4th, Smythe Div.	Lost Div. Semi-Final
1987-88	80	15	20	5	...	10	26	4	...	25	46	9	...	272	320	59	5th, Smythe Div.	Out of Playoffs
1986-87	80	17	19	4	...	12	24	4	...	29	43	8	...	282	314	66	5th, Smythe Div.	Out of Playoffs
1985-86	80	17	18	5	...	6	26	8	...	23	44	13	...	282	333	59	4th, Smythe Div.	Lost Div. Semi-Final
1984-85	80	15	21	4	...	10	25	5	...	25	46	9	...	284	401	59	5th, Smythe Div.	Out of Playoffs
1983-84	80	20	16	4	...	12	23	5	...	32	39	9	...	306	328	73	3rd, Smythe Div.	Lost Div. Semi-Final
1982-83	80	20	12	8	...	10	23	7	...	30	35	15	...	303	309	75	3rd, Smythe Div.	Lost Div. Semi-Final
1981-82	80	20	8	12	...	10	25	5	...	30	33	17	...	290	286	77	2nd, Smythe Div.	Lost Final
1980-81	80	17	12	11	...	11	20	9	...	28	32	20	...	289	301	76	3rd, Smythe Div.	Lost Prelim. Round
1979-80	80	14	17	9	...	13	20	7	...	27	37	16	...	256	281	70	3rd, Smythe Div.	Lost Prelim. Round
1978-79	80	15	18	7	...	10	24	6	...	25	42	13	...	217	291	63	2nd, Smythe Div.	Lost Prelim. Round
1977-78	80	13	15	12	...	7	28	5	...	20	43	17	...	239	320	57	3rd, Smythe Div.	Out of Playoffs
1976-77	80	13	21	6	...	12	21	7	...	25	42	13	...	235	294	63	4th, Smythe Div.	Out of Playoffs
1975-76	80	22	11	7	...	11	21	8	...	33	32	15	...	271	272	81	2nd, Smythe Div.	Lost Prelim. Round
1974-75	80	23	12	5	...	15	20	5	...	38	32	10	...	271	254	86	1st, Smythe Div.	Lost Quarter-Final
1973-74	78	14	18	7	...	10	25	4	...	24	43	11	...	224	296	59	7th, East Div.	Out of Playoffs
1972-73	78	17	18	4	...	5	29	5	...	22	47	9	...	233	339	53	7th, East Div.	Out of Playoffs
1971-72	78	14	20	5	...	6	30	3	...	20	50	8	...	203	297	48	7th, East Div.	Out of Playoffs
1970-71	78	17	18	4	...	7	28	4	...	24	46	8	...	229	296	56	6th, East Div.	Out of Playoffs

2001-02 Schedule

Oct.	Thu.	4	Chicago		Mon.	31	Philadelphia
	Sat.	6	Detroit	**Jan.**	Thu.	3	Montreal
	Tue.	9	at Colorado		Sat.	5	at Edmonton
	Thu.	11	at Dallas		Tue.	8	at Buffalo
	Sat.	13	Colorado		Wed.	9	at Detroit
	Tue.	16	Florida		Sat.	12	Carolina
	Thu.	18	Toronto		Tue.	15	Pittsburgh
	Sat.	20	at Phoenix		Thu.	17	at St. Louis
	Sun.	21	at Anaheim*		Sat.	19	at Washington
	Tue.	23	Nashville		Mon.	21	at Carolina
	Thu.	25	at Colorado		Wed.	23	at Dallas
	Sat.	27	at Edmonton		Fri.	25	Toronto
	Tue.	30	Columbus		Sat.	26	at Calgary
Nov.	Thu.	1	Montreal		Mon.	28	Nashville
	Sat.	3	at San Jose		Wed.	30	Edmonton
	Tue.	6	at Columbus	**Feb.**	Mon.	4	Phoenix
	Thu.	8	at St. Louis		Fri.	8	at Calgary
	Fri.	9	at Chicago		Sat.	9	Calgary
	Sun.	11	at Minnesota*		Tue.	12	Boston
	Tue.	13	Chicago		Tue.	26	St. Louis
	Thu.	15	St. Louis		Thu.	28	Dallas
	Sat.	17	Edmonton	**Mar.**	Sat.	2	Minnesota
	Tue.	20	at Ottawa		Thu.	7	at Phoenix
	Wed.	21	at Pittsburgh		Sat.	9	at San Jose
	Fri.	23	at Boston*		Sun.	10	San Jose
	Sun.	25	at Philadelphia		Tue.	12	at Nashville
	Tue.	27	at Minnesota		Thu.	14	at Columbus
	Wed.	28	at Chicago		Sat.	16	at Atlanta
	Fri.	30	Colorado		Sun.	17	at New Jersey
Dec.	Sun.	2	Dallas		Tue.	19	at NY Rangers
	Thu.	6	Anaheim		Thu.	21	at NY Islanders
	Sat.	8	San Jose		Sun.	24	Edmonton
	Mon.	10	Tampa Bay		Tue.	26	Los Angeles
	Wed.	12	at Anaheim		Thu.	28	Columbus
	Thu.	13	at Los Angeles		Sat.	30	Anaheim
	Sat.	15	Detroit	**Apr.**	Tue.	2	at Los Angeles
	Wed.	19	at Detroit		Fri.	5	Minnesota
	Thu.	20	at Nashville		Sun.	7	Phoenix
	Sat.	22	Minnesota		Tue.	9	at Colorado
	Thu.	27	Calgary		Thu.	11	Los Angeles
	Sat.	29	New Jersey		Sat.	13	at Calgary

* Denotes afternoon game.

Franchise date: May 22, 1970

NORTHWEST DIVISION

32nd NHL Season

Ed Jovanovski launches his 6'2", 210-pound frame to trap Ottawa's Magnus Arvedson against the boards. A tough defenseman, Jovanovski also contributed a career-high 12 goals and 35 assists to the Vancouver offense last season.

2001-02 Player Personnel

FORWARDS	HT	WT	S	Place of Birth	Date	2000-01 Club
BERTUZZI, Todd	6-3	235	L	Sudbury, Ont.	2/2/75	Vancouver
BRASHEAR, Donald	6-2	225	L	Bedford, IN	1/7/72	Vancouver
BROWN, Mike	6-5	185	L	Surrey, B.C.	4/27/79	Vancouver-Kansas City
CASSELS, Andrew	6-1	185	L	Bramalea, Ont.	7/23/69	Vancouver
CHUBAROV, Artem	6-1	189	L	Gorky, USSR	12/12/79	Vancouver-Kansas City
COOKE, Matt	5-11	205	L	Belleville, Ont.	9/7/78	Vancouver
DAVIDSSON, Johan	6-1	190	R	Jonkoping, Sweden	1/6/76	Blues Espoo
DRUKEN, Harold	6-0	205	L	St. John's, Nfld.	1/26/79	Vancouver-Kansas City
HOLDEN, Josh	6-0	190	L	Calgary, Alta.	1/18/78	Kansas City-Vancouver
KARIYA, Steve	5-8	170	R	North Vancouver, B.C.	12/22/77	Vancouver-Kansas City
KLATT, Trent	6-1	210	R	Robbinsdale, MN	1/30/71	Vancouver
LEEB, Brad	5-11	180	R	Red Deer, Alta.	8/27/79	Kansas City
MORRISON, Brendan	5-11	190	L	Pitt Meadows, B.C.	8/15/75	Vancouver
NASLUND, Markus	5-11	195	L	Ornskoldsvik, Sweden	7/30/73	Vancouver
PEDERSON, Denis	6-2	205	R	Prince Albert, Sask.	9/10/75	Vancouver
REID, Brandon	5-8	165	R	Kirkland, Que.	3/9/81	Val d'or Foreurs
RUUTU, Jarkko	6-2	194	L	Vantaa, Finland	8/23/75	Vancouver-Kansas City
SAVAGE, Andre	6-0	195	R	Ottawa, Ont.	5/27/75	Boston-Prov (AHL)
SCHAEFER, Peter	5-11	195	L	Yellow Grass, Sask.	7/12/77	Vancouver
SEDIN, Daniel	6-1	200	L	Ornskoldsvik, Sweden	9/26/80	Vancouver
SEDIN, Henrik	6-2	200	L	Ornskoldsvik, Sweden	9/26/80	Vancouver
SHARIFIJANOV, Vadim	6-0	205	L	Ufa, USSR	12/23/75	Kansas City
VASILJEVS, Herbert	5-11	180	R	Riga, Latvia	5/27/76	Atlanta-Orlando
DEFENSEMEN						
ALLEN, Bryan	6-4	215	L	Kingston, Ont.	8/21/80	Vancouver-Kansas City
BARON, Murray	6-3	215	L	Prince George, B.C.	6/1/67	Vancouver
BEREHOWSKY, Drake	6-2	225	R	Toronto, Ont.	1/3/72	Nashville-Vancouver
BONNI, Ryan	6-4	190	L	Winnipeg, Man.	2/18/79	Kansas City
HELMER, Bryan	6-1	200	R	Sault Ste. Marie, Ont.	7/15/72	Vancouver-Kansas City
JOVANOVSKI, Ed	6-2	210	L	Windsor, Ont.	6/26/76	Vancouver
KOMARNISKI, Zenith	6-0	200	L	Edmonton, Alta.	8/13/78	Kansas City
LACHANCE, Scott	6-1	209	L	Charlottesville, VA	10/22/72	Vancouver
OHLUND, Mattias	6-2	220	L	Pitea, Sweden	9/9/76	Vancouver
SOPEL, Brent	6-1	205	R	Calgary, Alta.	1/7/77	Vancouver-Kansas City
GOALTENDERS	**HT**	**WT**	**C**	**Place of Birth**	**Date**	**2000-01 Club**
CLOUTIER, Dan	6-1	182	L	Mont-Laurier, Que.	4/22/76	T.B.-Detroit (IHL)-Van
MICHAUD, Alfie	5-10	177	L	Selkirk, Man.	11/6/76	Kansas City

2000-01 Scoring

* - rookie

Regular Season

Pos	#	Player	Team	GP	G	A	Pts	+/–	PIM	PP	SH	GW	GT	S	%
L	19	Markus Naslund	VAN	72	41	34	75	–2	58	18	1	5	0	277	14.8
C	25	Andrew Cassels	VAN	66	12	44	56	1	10	2	0	1	0	104	11.5
L	44	Todd Bertuzzi	VAN	79	25	30	55	–18	93	14	0	3	0	203	12.3
C	7	Brendan Morrison	VAN	82	16	38	54	2	42	3	2	3	3	179	8.9
D	55	Ed Jovanovski	VAN	79	12	35	47	–1	102	4	0	2	2	193	6.2
L	72	Peter Schaefer	VAN	82	16	20	36	4	22	3	4	2	0	163	9.8
L	22 *	Daniel Sedin	VAN	75	20	14	34	–3	24	10	0	3	0	127	15.7
R	26	Trent Klatt	VAN	77	13	20	33	8	31	3	0	1	0	140	9.3
C	15	Harold Druken	VAN	55	15	15	30	2	14	6	0	3	0	82	18.3
C	33 *	Henrik Sedin	VAN	82	9	20	29	–2	38	2	0	1	0	98	9.2
L	8	Donald Brashear	VAN	79	9	19	28	0	145	0	0	1	0	127	7.1
D	2	Mattias Ohlund	VAN	65	8	20	28	–16	46	1	1	4	0	136	5.9
C	24	Matt Cooke	VAN	81	14	13	27	5	94	0	2	0	0	121	11.6
D	17	Drake Berehowsky	NSH	66	6	18	24	–9	100	3	0	1	0	94	6.4
			VAN	14	1	1	2	0	21	1	0	0	0	13	7.7
			TOTAL	80	7	19	26	–9	121	4	0	1	0	107	6.5
D	3 *	Brent Sopel	VAN	52	4	10	14	4	10	0	0	1	0	57	7.0
D	14	Scott Lachance	VAN	76	3	11	14	5	46	0	0	0	0	55	5.5
C	20	Denis Pederson	VAN	61	4	8	12	0	65	0	1	3	0	70	5.7
D	23	Murray Baron	VAN	82	3	8	11	–13	63	0	0	1	0	56	5.4
C	9	Mike Stapleton	NYI	34	1	4	5	–5	2	0	0	0	0	22	4.5
			VAN	18	1	2	3	–6	8	1	0	0	0	9	11.1
			TOTAL	52	2	6	8	–11	10	1	0	0	0	31	6.5
D	4	Greg Hawgood	VAN	16	2	5	7	8	6	1	0	1	0	16	12.5
L	18	Steve Kariya	VAN	17	1	6	7	–1	8	1	0	0	0	22	4.5
L	37 *	Jarkko Ruutu	VAN	21	3	3	6	1	32	0	1	0	0	23	13.0
D	28	Bryan Helmer	VAN	20	2	4	6	0	18	0	0	0	0	28	7.1
D	34	Jason Strudwick	VAN	60	1	4	5	16	64	0	0	1	0	21	4.8
C	21	Josh Holden	VAN	10	1	0	1	0	0	0	0	0	0	12	8.3
L	27 *	Mike Brown	VAN	1	0	0	0	0	5	0	0	0	0	1	0.0
C	13	Artem Chubarov	VAN	1	0	0	0	–1	0	0	0	0	0	0	0.0
D	5 *	Bryan Allen	VAN	6	0	0	0	0	0	0	0	0	0	2	0.0
G	35	Bob Essensa	VAN	39	0	0	0	0	4	0	0	0	0	0	0.0
G	39	Dan Cloutier	T.B.	24	0	0	0	0	4	0	0	0	0	0	0.0
			VAN	16	0	0	0	0	0	0	0	0	0	0	0.0
			TOTAL	40	0	0	0	0	4	0	0	0	0	0	0.0

Goaltending

No.	Goaltender	GPI	Mins	Avg	W	L	T	EN	SO	GA	SA	S%
39	Dan Cloutier	16	914	2.43	4	6	5	0	0	37	348	.894
35	Bob Essensa	39	2059	2.68	18	12	3	4	1	92	854	.892
39	Felix Potvin	35	2006	3.08	14	17	3	2	1	103	914	.887
	Totals	**82**	**5006**	**2.85**	**36**	**35**	**11**	**6**	**2**	**238**	**2122**	**.888**

Playoffs

Pos	#	Player	Team	GP	G	A	Pts	+/–	PIM	PP	SH	GW	GT	S	%
L	44	Todd Bertuzzi	VAN	4	2	2	4	1	8	0	0	0	0	8	25.0
D	2	Mattias Ohlund	VAN	4	1	3	4	–5	6	1	0	0	0	10	10.0
C	33 *	Henrik Sedin	VAN	4	0	4	4	1	0	0	0	0	0	3	0.0
R	26	Trent Klatt	VAN	4	3	0	3	–3	0	2	0	0	0	13	23.1
C	7	Brendan Morrison	VAN	4	1	2	3	–2	0	1	0	0	0	11	9.1
L	22 *	Daniel Sedin	VAN	4	1	2	3	–1	0	0	0	0	0	4	25.0
D	55	Ed Jovanovski	VAN	4	1	1	2	–5	0	0	0	0	0	10	10.0
D	14	Scott Lachance	VAN	2	0	1	1	0	2	0	0	0	0	0	0.0
C	20	Denis Pederson	VAN	4	0	1	1	–1	4	0	0	0	0	4	0.0
C	15	Harold Druken	VAN	4	0	1	1	–5	0	0	0	0	0	6	0.0
L	37 *	Jarkko Ruutu	VAN	4	0	1	1	0	8	0	0	0	0	1	0.0
G	35	Bob Essensa	VAN	2	0	0	0	0	0	0	0	0	0	0	0.0
G	39	Dan Cloutier	VAN	2	0	0	0	0	0	0	0	0	0	0	0.0
D	34	Jason Strudwick	VAN	2	0	0	0	0	0	0	0	0	0	0	0.0
D	5 *	Bryan Allen	VAN	2	0	0	0	1	2	0	0	0	0	0	0.0
L	72	Peter Schaefer	VAN	3	0	0	0	–3	0	0	0	0	0	6	0.0
R	43 *	Pat Kavanagh	VAN	3	0	0	0	0	2	0	0	0	0	0	0.0
D	23	Murray Baron	VAN	4	0	0	0	–4	0	0	0	0	0	4	0.0
D	17	Drake Berehowsky	VAN	4	0	0	0	2	12	0	0	0	0	1	0.0
L	8	Donald Brashear	VAN	4	0	0	0	–2	0	0	0	0	0	4	0.0
D	3 *	Brent Sopel	VAN	4	0	0	0	–1	2	0	0	0	0	2	0.0
C	24	Matt Cooke	VAN	4	0	0	0	–3	4	0	0	0	0	1	0.0

Goaltending

No.	Goaltender	GPI	Mins	Avg	W	L	EN	SO	GA	SA	S%
35	Bob Essensa	2	122	2.95	0	2	0	0	6	58	.897
39	Dan Cloutier	2	117	4.62	0	2	1	0	9	57	.842
	Totals	**4**	**243**	**3.95**	**0**	**4**	**1**	**0**	**16**	**116**	**.862**

Coach

CRAWFORD, MARC

Coach, Vancouver Canucks. Born in Belleville, Ont., February 13, 1961.

Marc Crawford became the 15th head coach in Canucks history on January 24, 1999. Crawford began his NHL coaching career with the Quebec Nordiques in 1994 and won a Stanley Cup in 1996 when the team moved to Denver to become the Colorado Avalanche. With the win, Crawford became the third-youngest coach in NHL history to win a Stanley Cup. Crawford coached the Avalanche for two seasons after winning the Cup before leaving following the 1997-98 season. He began the 1998-99 season as a colour commentator for CBC's Hockey Night in Canada before joining the Canucks. He led the team to 83 points in his first full season behind the bench in 1999-2000, then guided the Canucks back into the playoffs in 2000-01.

Crawford was the head coach for Team Canada at the 1998 Olympic Winter Games in Nagano, Japan and he was an assistant coach with Canada's silver medal-winning team in the 1996 World Cup of Hockey. He began his coaching career when he was hired by Brian Burke as a playing assistant with Fredericton (AHL) for the 1987-88 season. At the end of the year he moved to Milwaukee where he served as an assistant coach for the Canucks' IHL minor league affiliate for the 1988-89 campaign. He then moved to Cornwall where he served as the Royals' general manager and head coach in 1989-90.

After two seasons with Cornwall, Crawford went on to coach the St. John's Maple Leafs of the AHL before joining the Nordiques in 1994. He received the 1995 Jack Adams Award as the NHL Coach of the Year, becoming the first rookie coach to win the award since it was inaugurated in 1974.

Crawford played every game of his six-year NHL career with the Vancouver Canucks, recording 19 goals and 31 assists in 176 games. He was a rookie on the Canucks team that made a run to the Stanley Cup finals to face the NY Islanders in 1982.

Coaching Record

		Regular Season				Playoffs		
Season	Team	Games	W	L	T	Games	W	L
1989-90	Cornwall (OHL)	66	24	38	4	6	2	4
1990-91	Cornwall (OHL)	66	23	42	1	....	....	....
1991-92	St. John's (AHL)	80	39	29	12	16	11	5
1992-93	St. John's (AHL)	80	41	26	13	9	4	5
1993-94	St. John's (AHL)	80	45	23	12	11	6	5
1994-95	**Quebec (NHL)**	**48**	**30**	**13**	**5**	**6**	**2**	**4**
1995-96	**Colorado (NHL)**	**82**	**47**	**25**	**10**	**22**	**16**	**6***
1996-97	**Colorado (NHL)**	**82**	**49**	**24**	**9**	**17**	**10**	**7**
1997-98	**Colorado (NHL)**	**82**	**39**	**26**	**17**	**7**	**3**	**4**
1998-99	**Vancouver (NHL)**	**37**	**8**	**23**	**6**	....	....	....
1999-2000	**Vancouver (NHL)**	**82**	**30**	**37**	**15**	....	....	....
2000-01	**Vancouver (NHL)**	**82**	**36**	**35**	**11**	**4**	**0**	**4**
	NHL Totals	**495**	**239**	**183**	**73**	**56**	**31**	**25**

* Stanley Cup win.

Coaching History

Hal Laycoe, 1970-71, 1971-72; Vic Stasiuk, 1972-73; Bill McCreary and Phil Maloney, 1973-74; Phil Maloney, 1974-75, 1975-76; Phil Maloney and Orland Kurtenbach, 1976-77; Orland Kurtenbach, 1977-78; Harry Neale, 1978-79 to 1980-81; Harry Neale and Roger Neilson, 1981-82; Roger Neilson, 1982-83; Roger Neilson and Harry Neale, 1983-84; Harry Neale and Bill Laforge, 1984-85; Tom Watt, 1985-86, 1986-87; Bob McCammon, 1987-88 to 1989-90; Bob McCammon and Pat Quinn, 1990-91; Pat Quinn, 1991-92 to 1993-94; Rick Ley, 1994-95; Rick Ley and Pat Quinn, 1995-96; Tom Renney, 1996-97; Tom Renney and Mike Keenan, 1997-98; Mike Keenan and Marc Crawford, 1998-99; Marc Crawford, 1999-2000 to date.

Club Records

Team

(Figures in brackets for season records are games played; records for fewest points, wins, ties, losses, goals, goals against are for 70 or more games)

Most Points	101	1992-93 (84)
Most Wins	46	1992-93 (84)
Most Ties	20	1980-81 (80)
Most Losses	50	1971-72 (78)
Most Goals	346	1992-93 (84)
Most Goals Against	401	1984-85 (80)
Fewest Points	48	1971-72 (78)
Fewest Wins	20	1971-72 (78), 1977-78 (80)
Fewest Ties	3	1993-94 (84)
Fewest Losses	26	1991-92 (80)
Fewest Goals	192	1998-99 (82)
Fewest Goals Against	237	1999-2000 (82)
Longest Winning Streak		
Overall	7	Feb. 10-23/89
Home	9	Nov. 6-Dec. 9/92
Away	5	Jan. 14-25/92, Oct. 6-Nov. 2/93
Longest Undefeated Streak		
Overall	10	Mar. 5-25/77 (5 wins, 5 ties)
Home	18	Nov. 4/92-Jan. 16/93 (16 wins, 2 ties)
Away	5	Five times
Longest Losing Streak		
Overall	10	Oct. 23-Nov. 11/97
Home	6	Dec. 18/70-Jan. 20/71
Away	12	Nov. 28/81-Feb. 6/82
Longest Winless Streak		
Overall	13	Nov. 9-Dec. 7/73 (10 losses, 3 ties)
Home	11	Dec. 18/70-Feb. 6/71 (10 losses, 1 tie)
Away	20	Jan. 2-Apr. 2/86 (14 losses, 6 ties)
Most Shutouts, Season	8	1974-75 (80)
Most PIM, Season	2,326	1992-93 (84)
Most Goals, Game	11	Mar. 28/71 (Cal. 5 at Van. 11), Nov. 25/86 (L.A. 5 at Van. 11), Mar. 1/92 (Cgy. 0 at Van. 11)

Individual

Most Seasons	13	Stan Smyl
Most Games	896	Stan Smyl
Most Goals, Career	262	Stan Smyl
Most Assists, Career	411	Stan Smyl
Most Points, Career	673	Stan Smyl (262G, 411A)
Most PIM, Career	2,127	Gino Odjick
Most Shutouts, Career	20	Kirk McLean
Longest Consecutive Games Streak	482	Trevor Linden (Oct. 4/90-Dec. 1/96)
Most Goals, Season	60	Pavel Bure (1992-93, 1993-94)
Most Assists, Season	62	André Boudrias (1974-75)
Most Points, Season	110	Pavel Bure (1992-93; 60G, 50A)
Most PIM, Season	372	Donald Brashear (1997-98)
Most Points, Defenseman, Season	63	Doug Lidster (1986-87; 12G, 51A)
Most Points, Center, Season	91	Patrik Sundstrom (1983-84; 38G, 53A)
Most Points, Right Wing, Season	110	Pavel Bure (1992-93; 60G, 50A)
Most Points, Left Wing, Season	81	Darcy Rota (1982-83; 42G, 39A)
Most Points, Rookie, Season	60	Ivan Hlinka (1981-82; 23G, 37A), Pavel Bure (1991-92; 34G, 26A)
Most Shutouts, Season	6	Gary Smith (1974-75), Garth Snow (1998-99)
Most Goals, Game	4	Nine times
Most Assists, Game	6	Patrik Sundstrom (Feb. 29/84)
Most Points, Game	7	Patrik Sundstrom (Feb. 29/84; 1G, 6A)

Retired Numbers

12	Stan Smyl	1978-1991

Captains' History

Orland Kurtenbach, 1970-71 to 1973-74; no captain, 1974-75; Andre Boudrias, 1975-76; Chris Oddleifson, 1976-77; Don Lever, 1977-78; Don Lever and Kevin McCarthy, 1978-79; Kevin McCarthy, 1979-80 to 1981-82; Stan Smyl, 1982-83 to 1989-90; Dan Quinn, Doug Lidster and Trevor Linden, 1990-91; Trevor Linden, 1991-92 to 1996-97; Mark Messier, 1997-98 to 1999-2000; Markus Naslund, 2000-01 to date.

General Managers' History

Bud Poile, 1970-71 to 1972-73; Hal Laycoe, 1973-74; Phil Maloney, 1974-75 to 1976-77; Jake Milford, 1977-78 to 1981-82; Harry Neale, 1982-83 to 1984-85; Jack Gordon, 1985-86, 1986-87; Pat Quinn, 1987-88 to 1997-98; Brian Burke, 1998-99 to date.

All-time Record vs. Other Clubs

Regular Season

	At Home								On Road								Total							
	GP	W	L	T	OL	GF	GA	PTS	GP	W	L	T	OL	GF	GA	PTS	GP	W	L	T	OL	GF	GA	PTS
Anaheim	20	13	6	1	0	73	47	27	19	8	5	6	0	62	48	22	39	21	11	7	0	135	95	49
Atlanta	1	0	0	1	0	1	1	1	2	1	1	0	0	8	9	2	3	1	1	1	0	9	10	3
Boston	49	16	25	8	0	162	201	40	49	6	36	7	0	115	208	19	98	22	61	15	0	277	409	59
Buffalo	50	24	16	10	0	186	160	58	50	17	25	8	0	146	181	42	100	41	41	18	0	332	341	100
Calgary	91	34	39	17	1	315	305	86	90	20	57	13	0	259	383	53	181	54	96	30	1	574	688	139
Carolina	28	12	10	6	0	96	79	30	27	10	12	5	0	90	87	25	55	22	22	11	0	186	166	55
Chicago	66	30	21	15	0	198	195	75	65	15	43	6	1	147	249	37	131	45	64	21	1	345	444	112
Colorado	39	14	18	6	1	136	155	35	39	13	18	7	1	110	133	34	78	27	36	13	2	246	288	69
Columbus	2	2	0	0	0	8	6	4	2	1	0	1	0	7	2	3	4	3	0	1	0	15	8	7
Dallas	65	30	25	10	0	238	197	70	65	19	34	12	0	198	244	50	130	49	59	22	0	436	441	120
Detroit	59	25	24	10	0	216	197	60	60	15	37	8	0	172	256	38	119	40	61	18	0	388	453	98
Edmonton	74	29	35	9	1	274	300	68	73	19	46	7	1	227	336	46	147	48	81	16	2	501	636	114
Florida	6	2	1	3	0	18	13	7	7	3	3	1	0	22	19	7	13	5	4	4	0	40	32	14
Los Angeles	91	46	30	15	0	348	290	107	93	29	49	14	1	290	378	73	184	75	79	29	1	638	668	180
Minnesota	2	1	0	0	1	6	6	3	3	1	1	1	0	9	8	3	5	2	1	1	1	15	14	6
Montreal	51	10	33	8	0	129	194	28	51	9	38	4	0	129	241	22	102	19	71	12	0	258	435	50
Nashville	6	4	2	0	0	22	16	8	7	3	3	1	0	22	21	7	13	7	5	1	0	44	37	15
New Jersey	46	26	9	11	0	171	128	63	46	20	20	6	0	149	147	46	92	46	29	17	0	320	275	109
NY Islanders	46	22	21	3	0	151	150	47	44	11	23	10	0	122	164	32	90	33	44	13	0	273	314	79
NY Rangers	50	14	33	3	0	160	203	31	52	10	37	5	0	133	232	25	102	24	70	8	0	293	435	56
Ottawa	9	4	4	1	0	26	20	9	8	3	4	1	0	21	19	7	17	7	8	2	0	47	39	16
Philadelphia	50	10	27	12	1	143	201	33	51	15	35	1	0	152	226	31	101	25	62	13	1	295	427	64
Phoenix	66	38	18	9	1	249	191	86	63	23	30	9	1	226	238	56	129	61	48	18	2	475	429	142
Pittsburgh	48	21	23	4	0	171	182	46	48	8	33	7	0	164	224	23	96	29	56	11	0	335	406	69
St. Louis	66	26	33	7	0	193	216	59	65	19	37	9	0	186	244	47	131	45	70	16	0	379	460	106
San Jose	26	16	6	4	0	97	62	36	28	14	9	5	0	95	82	33	54	30	15	9	0	192	144	69
Tampa Bay	7	6	0	1	0	34	12	13	8	5	3	0	0	32	28	10	15	11	3	1	0	66	40	23
Toronto	59	28	18	11	2	208	198	69	58	21	27	10	0	191	214	52	117	49	45	21	2	399	412	121
Washington	38	17	15	5	1	130	123	40	38	12	21	4	1	109	130	29	76	29	36	9	2	239	253	69
Defunct Clubs	19	14	3	2	0	82	48	30	19	10	8	1	0	71	68	21	38	24	11	3	0	153	116	51
Totals	**1230**	**534**	**495**	**192**	**9**	**4241**	**4096**	**1269**	**1230**	**360**	**695**	**169**	**6**	**3664**	**4819**	**895**	**2460**	**894**	**1190**	**361**	**15**	**7905**	**8915**	**2164**

Playoffs

	Series	W	L	GP	W	L	T	GF	GA	Last Mtg.	Round	Result
Buffalo	2	0	2	7	1	6	0	14	28	1981	PR	L 0-3
Calgary	5	2	3	25	12	13	0	80	82	1994	CQF	W 4-3
Chicago	2	1	1	9	4	5	0	24	24	1995	CSF	L 0-4
Colorado	2	0	2	10	2	8	0	26	40	2001	CQF	L 0-4
Dallas	1	1	0	5	4	1	0	18	11	1994	CSF	W 4-1
Edmonton	2	0	2	9	2	7	0	20	35	1992	DF	L 2-4
Los Angeles	3	1	2	17	8	9	0	60	66	1993	DF	L 2-4
Montreal	1	0	1	5	1	4	0	9	20	1975	QF	L 1-4
NY Islanders	2	0	2	6	0	6	0	14	26	1982	F	L 0-4
NY Rangers	1	0	1	7	3	4	0	19	21	1994	F	L 3-4
Philadelphia	1	0	1	3	1	2	0	9	15	1979	PR	L 1-2
St. Louis	1	1	0	7	4	3	0	27	27	1995	CQF	W 4-3
Toronto	1	1	0	5	4	1	0	16	9	1994	CF	W 4-1
Winnipeg	2	2	0	13	8	5	0	50	34	1993	DSF	W 4-2
Totals	**26**	**9**	**17**	**128**	**54**	**74**	**0**	**386**	**438**			

Playoff Results 2001-1997

Year	Round	Opponent	Result	GF	GA
2001	CQF	Colorado	L 0-4	9	16

Abbreviations: Round: F – Final; **CF** – conference final; **CSF** – conference semi-final; **CQF** – conference quarter-final; **DF** – division final; **DSF** – division semi-final; **QF** – quarter-final; **PR** – preliminary round.

Calgary totals include Atlanta Flames, 1972-73 to 1979-80. Carolina totals include Hartford, 1979-80 to 1996-97.
Colorado totals include Quebec, 1979-80 to 1994-95. Dallas totals include Minnesota North Stars, 1970-71 to 1992-93.
New Jersey totals include Kansas City, 1974-75 to 1975-76, and Colorado Rockies, 1976-77 to 1981-82.
Phoenix totals include Winnipeg, 1979-80 to 1995-96.

2000-01 Results

Oct.	5	at Philadelphia	3-6		8	Nashville	2-1
	6	at Florida	4-3*		10	Ottawa	1-5
	8	at Tampa Bay	5-4		12	at Edmonton	3-2
	12	Colorado	2-5		14	Calgary	5-1
	14	Buffalo	4-0		16	Detroit	2-4
	16	Toronto	5-2		18	at Colorado	3-7
	18	Calgary	4-1		20	at St. Louis	0-3
	21	Phoenix	2-3*		22	at Dallas	1-2
	24	at Nashville	4-4		24	Phoenix	6-2
	25	at Dallas	6-2		27	at Calgary	5-3
	27	Atlanta	1-1		28	Chicago	2-6
Nov.	1	Colorado	4-3		30	Minnesota	3-2*
	3	Pittsburgh	2-4	**Feb.**	1	Colorado	5-3
	5	San Jose	2-2		8	San Jose	0-0
	8	at Anaheim	7-2		10	Calgary	1-4
	9	at Los Angeles	0-2		14	Washington	3-4*
	11	St. Louis	2-5		17	at Edmonton	6-5*
	14	Chicago	4-2		18	NY Islanders	3-2
	17	NY Rangers	4-3		21	at Montreal	2-1
	19	at Columbus	6-1		22	at Toronto	1-4
	21	at St. Louis	4-3		24	at Ottawa	0-3
	22	at Washington	2-3*		26	at Minnesota	5-2
	24	at Detroit	2-3		28	Dallas	5-4
	26	at Minnesota	2-4	**Mar.**	2	St. Louis	3-2*
	28	Anaheim	4-1		4	Minnesota	3-4*
	30	Montreal	3-4		6	Detroit	3-4
Dec.	2	Edmonton	5-2		8	at Phoenix	2-3*
	4	Nashville	6-3		10	Toronto	3-3
	6	at Phoenix	1-1		13	at Detroit	2-2
	8	at San Jose	6-1		15	at Boston	2-2
	10	Los Angeles	1-2		16	at Buffalo	2-4
	16	Columbus	4-3		18	at Atlanta	5-3
	20	at Edmonton	2-3*		21	at Columbus	1-1
	21	at Chicago	4-6		23	at New Jersey	0-4
	23	at Colorado	2-3*		25	at Minnesota	2-2
	27	Montreal	3-2		28	Dallas	1-3
	29	at Calgary	0-5		30	Anaheim	2-2
	30	at San Jose	6-3	**Apr.**	1	at Anaheim	1-2
Jan.	1	at Nashville	5-2		2	at Los Angeles	1-3
	3	at Chicago	0-6		5	Los Angeles	3-2*
	6	Columbus	4-3		7	Edmonton	2-4

* – Overtime

Entry Draft Selections 2001-1987

2001

Pick	
16	R.J. Umberger
66	Fedor Fedorov
114	Yevgeny Gladskikh
151	Kevin Bieksa
212	Jason King
245	Konstantin Mikhailov

2000

Pick	
23	Nathan Smith
71	Thatcher Bell
93	Tim Branham
144	Pavel Duma
208	Brandon Reid
241	Nathan Barrett
272	Tim Smith

1999

Pick	
2	Daniel Sedin
3	Henrik Sedin
69	Rene Vydareny
129	Ryan Thorpe
172	Josh Reed
189	Kevin Swanson
218	Markus Kankaanpera
271	Darrell Hay

1998

Pick	
4	Bryan Allen
31	Artem Chubarov
68	Jarkko Ruutu
81	Justin Morrison
90	Regan Darby
136	David Ytfeldt
140	Rick Bertran
149	Paul Cabana
177	Vincent Malts
204	Greg Mischler
219	Curtis Valentine
232	Jason Metcalfe

1997

Pick	
10	Brad Ference
34	Ryan Bonni
36	Harold Druken
64	Kyle Freadrich
90	Chris Stanley
114	David Darguzas
117	Matt Cockell
144	Matt Cooke
148	Larry Shapley
171	Rod Leroux
201	Denis Martynyuk
227	Peter Brady

1996

Pick	
12	Josh Holden
75	Zenith Komarniski
93	Jonas Soling
121	Tyler Prosofsky
147	Nolan McDonald
175	Clint Cabana
201	Jeff Scissons
227	Lubomir Vaic

1995

Pick	
40	Chris McAllister
61	Larry Courville
66	Peter Schaefer
92	Lloyd Shaw
120	Todd Norman
144	Brent Sopel
170	Stewart Bodtker
196	Tyler Willis
222	Jason Cugnet

1994

Pick	
13	Mattias Ohlund
39	Robb Gordon
42	Dave Scatchard
65	Chad Allan
92	Mike Dubinsky
117	Yanick Dube
169	Yuri Kuznetsov
195	Rob Trumbley
221	Bill Muckalt
247	Tyson Nash
273	Robert Longpre

1993

Pick	
20	Mike Wilson
46	Rick Girard
98	Dieter Kochan
124	Scott Walker
150	Troy Creurer
176	Yevgeni Babariko
202	Sean Tallaire
254	Bert Robertsson
280	Sergei Tkachenko

1992

Pick	
21	Libor Polasek
40	Michael Peca
45	Mike Fountain
69	Jeff Connolly
93	Brent Tully
110	Brian Loney
117	Adrian Aucoin
141	Jason Clark
165	Scott Hollis
213	Sonny Mignacca
237	Mark Wotton
261	Aaron Boh

1991

Pick	
7	Alek Stojanov
29	Jassen Cullimore
51	Sean Pronger
95	Dan Kesa
117	John Namestnikov
139	Brent Thurston
161	Eric Johnson
183	David Neilson
205	Brad Barton
227	Jason Fitzsimmons
249	Xavier Majic

1990

Pick	
2	Petr Nedved
18	Shawn Antoski
23	Jiri Slegr
65	Darin Bader
86	Gino Odjick
128	Daryl Filipek
149	Paul O'Hagan
170	Mark Cipriano
191	Troy Neumier
212	Tyler Ertel
233	Karri Kivi

1989

Pick	
8	Jason Herter
29	Robert Woodward
71	Brett Hauer
113	Pavel Bure
134	James Revenberg
155	Rob Sangster
176	Sandy Moger
197	Gus Morschauser
218	Hayden O'Rear
239	Darcy Cahill
248	Jan Bergman

1988

Pick	
2	Trevor Linden
33	Leif Rohlin
44	Dane Jackson
107	Corrie D'Alessio
122	Phil Von Stefenelli
128	Dixon Ward
149	Greg Geldart
170	Roger Akerstrom
191	Paul Constantin
212	Chris Wolanin
233	Steffan Nilsson

1987

Pick	
24	Rob Murphy
45	Steve Veilleux
66	Doug Torrel
87	Sean Fabian
108	Garry Valk
129	Todd Fanning
150	Viktor Tyumenev
171	Greg Daly
192	John Fletcher
213	Roger Hansson
233	Neil Eisenhut
234	Matt Evo

President and General Manager

BURKE, BRIAN
President and General Manager, Vancouver Canucks.
Born in Providence, RI, June 30, 1955.

The Vancouver Canucks announced the appointment of Brian Burke to the position of president and general manager on June 22, 1998. Burke became the eighth general manager in Canucks history after serving as the National Hockey League's senior vice president and director of hockey operations for five years.

Burke's prior experience with the Canucks began when he was named vice president and director of hockey operations on June 2, 1987. Burke worked with former Canucks president and general manager Pat Quinn for five seasons and assisted in rebuilding Vancouver's team through his contract negotiation skills and his overseeing of the club's scouting systems and its minor league affiliates. Burke helped reshape the Canucks from a 59 point team in 1987-88, to a 96 point team in his final season of 1991-92. It was the first time since the 1974-75 regular season that the Canucks finished first in the Smythe Division.

Brian Burke was appointed general manager of the Hartford Whalers on May 26, 1992. In his only season in Hartford, Brian made a number of player moves, changed the team's uniform and completed a major draft-day trade in 1993. After acquiring the second overall selection from San Jose, Burke selected Chris Pronger who has developed into one of the NHL's premier defenceman.

Burke joined the NHL front office in September of 1993. In five years as NHL senior vice president, Burke was most visible in his role as the league's chief disciplinarian. He spent much of his time overseeing the league's on-ice officials and was responsible for many disciplinary decisions handed down by the NHL based on his interpretation of league rules. Brian worked closely with NHL commissioner Gary Bettman on the direction of the league and was a key member of the group that introduced NHL excitement to Japan when the Vancouver Canucks and Mighty Ducks of Anaheim opened the 1997-98 regular season in Tokyo.

Club Directory

General Motors Place

Vancouver Canucks
General Motors Place
800 Griffiths Way
Vancouver, B.C. V6B 6G1
Phone **604/899-4600**
FAX 604/899-4640
www.canucks.com
Capacity: 18,422

Executive

Chairman, OBSE; Governor, NHL	John E. McCaw Jr.
President, Chief Executive Officer, OBSE	Stanley B. McCammon
President & General Manager, Vancouver Canucks, Alternate Governor, NHL	Brian P. Burke
Chief Operating Officer, Alternate Governor, NHL	David Cobb
Senior Vice-President, Sales and Marketing	John Rizzardini
Vice President & General Manager, Arena Operations	Harvey Jones
Vice President, Finance	Victor de Bonis
Vice President, Broadcast and New Media	Chris Hebb
Vice President, Business Development	Ric Thomsen
Vice-President, Customer Sales & Service	John Rocha
Vice President, People Development	Susanne Haine

Hockey Operations

Senior Vice-President, Director Hockey Operations	David M. Nonis
Vice President, Player Personnel	Steve Tambellini
Head Coach	Marc Crawford
Assistant Coaches	Jack McIlhargey, Mike Johnston
General Manager, Manitoba Moose	Randy Carlyle
Head Coach, Manitoba Moose	Stan Smyl
Assistant Coach, Manitoba Moose	Barry Smith
Strength & Conditioning Coach	Peter Twist
Goaltending Consultant	Andy Moog
Assistant Coach, Video	Eric Crawford
Senior Editor, Alumni Liaison	Norm Jewison
Manager, Media Relations	Chris Brumwell
Coordinator, Media Relations	T.C. Carling
Assistant, Media Relations	Rob Viccars
Director, Community Relations	Veronica Varhaug
Coordinator, Community Relations	Allanah Mooney
Assistant, Community Relations	Regan McDonald
Executive Assistant to Brian Burke	Patti Timms
Executive Assistant to David Nonis	Chris Stephens

Scouting

Professional Scouts	Bob Murray, Shawn Dineen
European Scout	Thomas Gradin
Russian Scout	Sergei Chibisov
Amateur Scouts	Ron Delorme, Ken Slater, Jack McCartan, Barry Dean, Dave Morrison, Daryl Stanley, Jim Eagle, Mike McHugh, Tim Lenardon, Mario Marois
Scouting Information Coordinator	Jonathan Wall

Medical and Training Staff

Medical Trainer	Mike Burnstein
Assistant Medical Trainers	Jon Sanderson, Marty Dudgeon
Equipment Manager	Pat O'Neill
Assistant Equipment Manager	Darren Granger
Assistant Equipment Trainer	Jamie Hendricks
Game Dressing Room Attendants	Ron Shute, John Jukitch
Team Doctors	Dr. Rui Avelar, Dr. Bill Regan
Team Dentist	Dr. David Lawson
Team Chiropractor	Dr. Sid Sheard
Team Optometrist	Dr. Alan R. Boyco

Corporate Communications

Manager, Creative Services	Jackie Boucher
Photo Editor/Librarian	Kathy McAdam

Broadcasting

Director, Facilities and In-house Productions	Paul Brettell
Director, Production Services	Mike Hall

Business Development

Directors, Business Development	David Altman, Dave Cannon, Tom Mauthe
Director, Executive Suite Sales & Marketing	Chris Bradley
Sr. Manager, Suite and Sponsorship Services	Darren Moscovitch
Manager, Suite and Sponsorship Services	Shannon Soper
Manager, Hospitality Suite Sales & Service	Lara Grescoe

Legal

Corporate Counsel	James Conrad

Customer Sales & Service

Executive Assistant	Annabelle Kroes
Director, Customer Sales & Service	Caley Denton
Director, Customer Sales	Jordan Thorsteinson
Senior Managers, Customer Sales	Sharon Butler, Graham Wall
Managers, Customer Sales	Andrew Merai, Josh Bender, Marc Tourigny, Terry Craig, John Bellefeuille
Account Managers	Kevin Yeung , Paul Maaker, Andrew Marchand
Manager, Sales & Marketing	Rick Ramsbottom

Marketing and Game Operations

Director, Marketing	Paul Dal Monte
Manager, Game Presentation & Events	Karen Brydon

Finance, Administration and People Development

Director of Finance	Chris Samis
Executive Assistant to Victor de Bonis	Denise Ouang
Manager, People Development	Tracey Arnish
Assistant Controller	Patricia Bigonzi

Authentix, Fan Apparel and Collectibles

Senior Manager, Retail Operations	Dennis Kim
Merchandise Manager	Karen Saunders-Smith
Arena Store Manager	Alan Cook
Gate 5 Receptionist, OBSE	Lynn Bradley

Washington Capitals

2000-01 Results: 41W-27L-10T-4OTL 96PTS. First, Southeast Division

2001-02 Schedule

Oct.	Sat.	6	New Jersey
	Mon.	8	at Boston*
	Wed.	10	at NY Rangers
	Fri.	12	at Anaheim
	Sat.	13	at Phoenix
	Tue.	16	at Los Angeles
	Fri.	19	Montreal
	Sat.	20	at Philadelphia
	Tue.	23	at Tampa Bay
	Wed.	24	at Florida
	Fri.	26	at Atlanta
	Tue.	30	Philadelphia
Nov.	Fri.	2	Phoenix
	Sat.	3	at St. Louis
	Tue.	6	at Toronto
	Thu.	8	Carolina
	Sat.	10	Atlanta
	Tue.	13	Ottawa
	Thu.	15	at Philadelphia
	Sat.	17	Anaheim
	Wed.	21	Tampa Bay
	Fri.	23	NY Rangers
	Sat.	24	at Montreal
	Tue.	27	at NY Islanders
	Wed.	28	Buffalo
	Fri.	30	Carolina
Dec.	Sun.	2	at Carolina*
	Tue.	4	NY Rangers
	Thu.	6	at Atlanta
	Sat.	8	at New Jersey*
	Tue.	11	Pittsburgh
	Thu.	13	Boston
	Sat.	15	Atlanta
	Wed.	19	at Florida
	Fri.	21	at Pittsburgh
	Sat.	22	Pittsburgh
	Wed.	26	Philadelphia
	Fri.	28	at Dallas
	Sun.	30	Carolina*
Jan.	Tue.	1	NY Islanders*
	Thu.	3	at Ottawa
	Sat.	5	at Boston*
	Mon.	7	Florida
	Wed.	9	Columbus
	Fri.	11	Toronto
	Sat.	12	at Florida
	Mon.	14	Boston
	Wed.	16	at Montreal
	Fri.	18	at Detroit
	Sat.	19	Vancouver
	Tue.	22	at Atlanta
	Wed.	23	Montreal
	Sat.	26	at NY Rangers*
	Sun.	27	Buffalo*
	Wed.	30	St. Louis
Feb.	Wed.	6	Minnesota
	Fri.	8	at Nashville
	Sat.	9	at Tampa Bay
	Mon.	11	Tampa Bay
	Tue.	26	Florida
	Thu.	28	San Jose
Mar.	Sat.	2	at Ottawa
	Mon.	4	Toronto
	Wed.	6	Calgary
	Fri.	8	at Carolina
	Sun.	10	Edmonton*
	Tue.	12	Dallas
	Fri.	15	at San Jose
	Sat.	16	at Edmonton
	Tue.	19	at Colorado
	Thu.	21	at Toronto
	Sat.	23	at Columbus
	Sun.	24	at Pittsburgh
	Tue.	26	at Buffalo
	Fri.	29	at New Jersey
	Sat.	30	NY Islanders
Apr.	Wed.	3	Tampa Bay
	Fri.	5	Ottawa
	Sat.	6	at NY Islanders
	Tue.	9	Chicago
	Fri.	12	at Buffalo
	Sat.	13	New Jersey

* Denotes afternoon game.

Franchise date: June 11, 1974

SOUTHEAST DIVISION

28th NHL Season

Former Princeton star Jeff Halpern is a native of the DC area who has enjoyed great success in his first two seasons with Washington. Halpern had 21 goals and 21 assists in 2000-01 and his +13 rating was second on the team.

Year-by-Year Record

		Home				Road				Overall								
Season	**GP**	**W**	**L**	**T**	**OL**	**W**	**L**	**T**	**OL**	**W**	**L**	**T**	**OL**	**GF**	**GA**	**Pts.**	**Finished**	**Playoff Result**
2000-01	82	24	9	6	2	17	18	4	2	41	27	10	4	233	211	96	1st, Southeast Div.	Lost Conf. Quarter-Final
1999-2000	82	26	5	8	2	18	19	4	0	44	24	12	2	227	194	102	1st, Southeast Div.	Lost Conf. Quarter-Final
1998-99	82	16	23	2	...	15	22	4	...	31	45	6	...	200	218	68	3rd, Southeast Div.	Out of Playoffs
1997-98	82	23	12	6	...	17	18	6	...	40	30	12	...	219	202	92	3rd, Atlantic Div.	Lost Final
1996-97	82	19	17	5	...	14	23	4	...	33	40	9	...	214	231	75	5th, Atlantic Div.	Out of Playoffs
1995-96	82	21	15	5	...	18	17	6	...	39	32	11	...	234	204	89	4th, Atlantic Div.	Lost Conf. Quarter-Final
1994-95	48	15	6	3	...	7	12	5	...	22	18	8	...	136	120	52	3rd, Atlantic Div.	Lost Conf. Quarter-Final
1993-94	84	17	16	9	...	22	19	1	...	39	35	10	...	277	263	88	3rd, Atlantic Div.	Lost Conf. Semi-Final
1992-93	84	21	15	6	...	22	19	1	...	43	34	7		325	286	93	2nd, Patrick Div.	Lost Div. Semi-Final
1991-92	80	25	12	3	...	20	15	5	...	45	27	8	...	330	275	98	2nd, Patrick Div.	Lost Div. Semi-Final
1990-91	80	21	14	5	...	16	22	2	...	37	36	7	...	258	258	81	3rd, Patrick Div.	Lost Div. Final
1989-90	80	19	18	3	...	17	20	3	...	36	38	6	...	284	275	78	3rd, Patrick Div.	Lost Conf. Championship
1988-89	80	25	12	3	...	16	17	7	...	41	29	10	...	305	259	92	1st, Patrick Div.	Lost Div. Semi-Final
1987-88	80	22	14	4	...	16	19	5	...	38	33	9	...	281	249	85	2nd, Patrick Div.	Lost Div. Final
1986-87	80	22	15	3	...	16	17	7	...	38	32	10	...	285	278	86	2nd, Patrick Div.	Lost Div. Semi-Final
1985-86	80	30	8	2	...	20	15	5	...	50	23	7	...	315	272	107	2nd, Patrick Div.	Lost Div. Final
1984-85	80	27	11	2	...	19	14	7	...	46	25	9	...	322	240	101	2nd, Patrick Div.	Lost Div. Semi-Final
1983-84	80	26	11	3	...	22	16	2	...	48	27	5	...	308	226	101	2nd, Patrick Div.	Lost Div. Final
1982-83	80	22	12	6	...	17	13	10	...	39	25	16	...	306	283	94	3rd, Patrick Div.	Lost Div. Semi-Final
1981-82	80	16	16	8	...	10	25	5	...	26	41	13	...	319	338	65	5th, Patrick Div.	Out of Playoffs
1980-81	80	16	17	7	...	10	19	11	...	26	36	18	...	286	317	70	5th, Patrick Div.	Out of Playoffs
1979-80	80	20	14	6	...	7	26	7	...	27	40	13	...	261	293	67	5th, Patrick Div.	Out of Playoffs
1978-79	80	15	19	6	...	9	22	9	...	24	41	15	...	273	338	63	4th, Norris Div.	Out of Playoffs
1977-78	80	10	23	7	...	7	26	7	...	17	49	14	...	195	321	48	5th, Norris Div.	Out of Playoffs
1976-77	80	17	15	8	...	7	27	6	...	24	42	14	...	221	307	62	4th, Norris Div.	Out of Playoffs
1975-76	80	6	26	8	...	5	33	2	...	11	59	10	...	224	394	32	5th, Norris Div.	Out of Playoffs
1974-75	80	7	28	5	...	1	39	0	...	8	67	5	...	181	446	21	5th, Norris Div.	Out of Playoffs

2001-02 Player Personnel

FORWARDS	HT	WT	S	Place of Birth	Date	2000-01 Club
BONDRA, Peter	6-1	205	L	Luck, USSR	2/7/68	Washington
CORRINET, Chris	6-3	220	R	Derby, CT	10/29/78	Princeton Tigers-Port (AHL)
DAHLEN, Ulf	6-2	199	L	Ostersund, Sweden	1/12/67	Washington
FARRELL, Michael	6-1	205	R	Edina, MN	10/20/78	Portland (AHL)
FERRARO, Peter	5-10	180	R	Port Jefferson, NY	1/24/73	Providence (AHL)
HALPERN, Jeff	5-11	195	R	Potomac, MD	5/3/76	Washington
HLINKA, Martin	6-1	200	L	Bratislava, Czech.	9/25/76	Quad City-Port (AHL)
JAGR, Jaromir	6-2	234	L	Kladno, Czech.	2/15/72	Pittsburgh
KHRISTICH, Dmitri	6-2	195	R	Kiev, USSR	7/23/69	Toronto-Washington
KONOWALCHUK, Steve	6-1	207	L	Salt Lake City, UT	11/11/72	Washington
LINDEN, Trevor	6-4	215	R	Medicine Hat, Alta.	4/11/70	Montreal-Washington
METROPOLIT, Glen	5-10	200	R	Toronto, Ont.	6/25/74	Washington-Port (AHL)
MURPHY, Mark	5-11	200	L	Stoughton, MA	8/6/76	Portland (AHL)
NIKOLISHIN, Andrei	6-0	206	L	Vorkuta, USSR	3/25/73	Washington
OATES, Adam	5-11	188	R	Weston, Ont.	8/27/62	Washington
PETTINGER, Matt	6-1	205	L	Edmonton, Alta	10/22/80	Washington-Port (AHL)
SACCO, Joe	6-1	190	L	Medford, MA	2/4/69	Washington
SIMON, Chris	6-4	235	L	Wawa, Ont.	1/30/72	Washington
TVRDON, Roman	6-1	189	L	Trencin, Czech.	1/29/81	Spokane Chiefs
WHITFIELD, Trent	5-11	200	L	Estevan, Sask.	6/17/77	Washington-Port (AHL)
ZUBRUS, Dainius	6-4	227	L	Elektrenai, USSR	6/16/78	Montreal-Washington
DEFENSEMEN						
COTE, Sylvain	5-11	190	R	Quebec City, Que.	1/19/66	Washington
CUTTA, Jakub	6-3	207	L	Jablonec nad Nisou, Czech.	12/29/81	Washington-Swift Current
GONCHAR, Sergei	6-2	212	L	Chelyabinsk, USSR	4/13/74	Washington
JOHANSSON, Calle	5-11	208	L	Goteborg, Sweden	2/14/67	Washington
KLEE, Ken	6-1	212	R	Indianapolis, IN	4/24/71	Washington
KUCERA, Frantisek	6-2	205	R	Prague, Czech.	2/3/68	Columbus-Pittsburgh
MELANSON, Dean	5-11	190	R	Antigonish, N.S.	11/19/73	Phi (AHL)-Chi (IHL)-Port (AHL)
MIRONOV, Dmitri	6-4	224	R	Moscow, USSR	12/25/65	Washington-Houston
PEAT, Stephen	6-3	210	R	Princeton, B.C.	3/10/80	Portland (AHL)
REEKIE, Joe	6-3	220	L	Victoria, B.C.	2/22/65	Washington
ROHLOFF, Todd	6-3	213	L	Grand Rapids, IL	1/16/74	Portland (AHL)
WITT, Brendan	6-1	226	L	Humbolt, Sask.	2/20/75	Washington
YONKMAN, Nolan	6-5	218	R	Punnicht, Sask.	4/1/81	Kelowna Rockets-Brandon
ZETTLER, Rob	6-3	200	L	Sept Iles, Que.	3/8/68	Washington-Port (AHL)

GOALTENDERS	HT	WT	C	Place of Birth	Date	2000-01 Club
BILLINGTON, Craig	5-10	170	L	London, Ont.	9/11/66	Washington
CHARPENTIER, Sebastien	5-9	177	L	Drummondville, Que.	4/18/77	Portland (AHL)
HIRSCH, Corey	5-10	175	L	Medicine Hat, Alta.	8/10/72	Albany-Wsh-Cin (IHL)-Port (AHL)
KOLZIG, Olaf	6-3	225	L	Johannesburg, South Africa	4/9/70	Washington

General Manager

McPHEE, GEORGE
General Manager, Washington Capitals. Born in Guelph, Ont., July 2, 1958.

On June 9, 1997, George McPhee became the fifth general manager of the Washington Capitals. In his first year on the job, McPhee led the Caps to the Stanley Cup Finals for the first time in franchise history. He provides the Capitals with the leadership and knowledge to bring the Stanley Cup Finals back to Washington in the years to come.

A back injury forced McPhee to retire as an active player at the conclusion of the 1988-89 season, after a seven year playing career with the New York Rangers and New Jersey Devils. McPhee originally signed as a free agent with the Rangers in July, 1982, after graduating from Bowling Green State University with a business degree. McPhee did not waste any time in college, tallying 40 goals and 48 assists in his freshman season and easily winning CCHA rookie of the year honors. His outstanding collegiate hockey career was capped off when he was named the recipient of the Hobey Baker Award as the top U.S. collegiate player in his senior season. McPhee also earned All-America honors as a senior and finished his career at Bowling Green as the CCHA's all-time leading scorer with 114-153-267. He was the first player in CCHA history to make the Conference's all-academic team three straight seasons.

2000-01 Scoring

* - rookie

Regular Season

Pos	#	Player	Team	GP	G	A	Pts	+/–	PIM	PP	SH	GW	GT	S	%
C	77	Adam Oates	WSH	81	13	69	82	–9	28	5	0	4	0	72	18.1
R	12	Peter Bondra	WSH	82	45	36	81	8	60	22	4	8	0	305	14.8
D	55	Sergei Gonchar	WSH	76	19	38	57	12	70	8	0	2	0	241	7.9
R	10	Ulf Dahlen	WSH	73	15	33	48	11	6	6	0	2	1	145	10.3
L	22	Steve Konowalchuk	WSH	82	24	23	47	8	87	6	0	5	0	163	14.7
C	11	Jeff Halpern	WSH	80	21	21	42	13	60	2	1	5	2	110	19.1
R	8	Dmitri Khristich	TOR	27	3	6	9	8	8	2	0	0	0	23	13.0
			WSH	43	10	19	29	–8	8	4	0	4	0	54	18.5
			TOTAL	70	13	25	38	0	16	6	0	4	0	77	16.9
C	13	Andrei Nikolishin	WSH	81	13	25	38	9	34	4	0	2	1	145	9.0
C	16	Trevor Linden	MTL	57	12	21	33	–2	52	6	0	3	0	96	12.5
			WSH	12	3	1	4	2	8	0	0	0	0	30	10.0
			TOTAL	69	15	22	37	0	60	6	0	3	0	126	11.9
D	6	Calle Johansson	WSH	76	7	29	36	11	26	5	0	0	0	154	4.5
R	9	Dainius Zubrus	MTL	49	12	12	24	–7	30	3	0	0	0	70	17.1
			WSH	12	1	1	2	–4	7	1	0	0	0	13	7.7
			TOTAL	61	13	13	26	–11	37	4	0	0	0	83	15.7
L	17	Chris Simon	WSH	60	10	10	20	–12	109	4	0	2	0	123	8.1
D	3	Sylvain Cote	WSH	68	7	11	18	–3	18	1	1	1	0	86	8.1
L	14	Joe Sacco	WSH	69	7	7	14	4	48	0	0	0	0	81	8.6
D	29	Joe Reekie	WSH	74	2	9	11	14	77	0	0	1	0	59	3.4
D	15	Dmitri Mironov	WSH	36	3	5	8	–7	6	1	0	1	0	33	9.1
D	28	Jason Marshall	ANA	50	3	4	7	–12	105	2	1	1	0	38	7.9
			WSH	5	0	0	0	–1	17	0	0	0	0	5	0.0
			TOTAL	55	3	4	7	–13	122	2	1	1	0	43	7.0
D	19	Brendan Witt	WSH	72	3	3	6	2	101	0	0	0	0	87	3.4
D	2	Ken Klee	WSH	54	2	4	6	–5	60	0	0	0	1	58	3.4
C	23	* Trent Whitfield	WSH	61	2	4	6	3	35	0	0	0	0	47	4.3
R	9	Joe Murphy	WSH	14	1	5	6	–5	20	1	0	0	0	22	4.5
C	20	Glen Metropolit	WSH	15	1	5	6	–2	10	0	0	0	0	20	5.0
L	21	James Black	WSH	42	1	5	6	–3	4	0	0	0	0	34	2.9
C	26	Matthew Herr	WSH	22	2	3	5	3	17	0	0	1	0	20	10.0
D	24	Rob Zettler	WSH	29	0	4	4	0	55	0	0	0	0	17	0.0
R	25	Terry Yake	WSH	12	0	3	3	0	8	0	0	0	0	13	0.0
G	37	Olaf Kolzig	WSH	72	0	2	2	0	14	0	0	0	0	0	0.0
G	1	Craig Billington	WSH	12	0	1	1	0	0	0	0	0	0	0	0.0
G	30	Corey Hirsch	WSH	1	0	0	0	0	0	0	0	0	0	0	0.0
D	34	* Jakub Cutta	WSH	3	0	0	0	–1	0	0	0	0	0	1	0.0
C	16	* Kris Beech	WSH	4	0	0	0	–2	2	0	0	0	0	0	0.0
L	28	* Matt Pettinger	WSH	10	0	0	0	–1	2	0	0	0	0	6	0.0
R	74	Brantt Myhres	NSH	20	0	0	0	–5	28	0	0	0	0	1	0.0
			WSH	5	0	0	0	0	29	0	0	0	0	0	0.0
			TOTAL	25	0	0	0	–5	57	0	0	0	0	1	0.0

Goaltending

No.	Goaltender	GPI	Mins	Avg	W	L	T	EN	SO	GA	SA	S%
30	Corey Hirsch	1	20	0.00	1	0	0	0	0	0	8	1.000
1	Craig Billington	12	660	2.45	3	5	2	0	0	27	317	.915
37	Olaf Kolzig	72	4279	2.48	37	26	8	7	5	177	1941	.909
	Totals	**82**	**4986**	**2.54**	**41**	**31**	**10**	**7**	**5**	**211**	**2273**	**.907**

Playoffs

Pos	#	Player	Team	GP	G	A	Pts	+/–	PIM	PP	SH	GW	GT	S	%
L	22	Steve Konowalchuk	WSH	6	2	3	5	–1	14	2	0	0	0	9	22.2
C	11	Jeff Halpern	WSH	6	2	3	5	0	17	1	0	1	1	9	22.2
D	55	Sergei Gonchar	WSH	6	1	3	4	0	2	1	0	0	0	14	7.1
C	16	Trevor Linden	WSH	6	0	4	4	–3	14	0	0	0	0	17	0.0
D	6	Calle Johansson	WSH	6	1	2	3	–4	2	0	0	0	0	10	10.0
R	12	Peter Bondra	WSH	6	2	0	2	–2	2	2	0	1	0	25	8.0
D	19	Brendan Witt	WSH	6	2	0	2	–5	12	1	0	0	0	13	15.4
R	10	Ulf Dahlen	WSH	6	0	1	1	–2	2	0	0	0	0	10	0.0
D	2	Ken Klee	WSH	6	0	1	1	0	8	0	0	0	0	5	0.0
L	17	Chris Simon	WSH	6	0	1	1	–2	4	0	0	0	0	6	0.0
C	20	Glen Metropolit	WSH	1	0	0	0	–1	0	0	0	0	0	1	0.0
R	8	Dmitri Khristich	WSH	3	0	0	0	0	0	0	0	0	0	0	0.0
D	29	Joe Reekie	WSH	4	0	0	0	–1	4	0	0	0	0	0	0.0
D	3	Sylvain Cote	WSH	5	0	0	0	–1	2	0	0	0	0	4	0.0
C	23	* Trent Whitfield	WSH	5	0	0	0	0	2	0	0	0	0	3	0.0
G	37	Olaf Kolzig	WSH	6	0	0	0	0	0	0	0	0	0	0	0.0
C	77	Adam Oates	WSH	6	0	0	0	–4	0	0	0	0	0	6	0.0
L	14	Joe Sacco	WSH	6	0	0	0	–1	2	0	0	0	0	9	0.0
D	24	Rob Zettler	WSH	6	0	0	0	–1	0	0	0	0	0	4	0.0
C	13	Andrei Nikolishin	WSH	6	0	0	0	–3	2	0	0	0	0	9	0.0
R	9	Dainius Zubrus	WSH	6	0	0	0	1	2	0	0	0	0	7	0.0

Goaltending

No.	Goaltender	GPI	Mins	Avg	W	L	EN	SO	GA	SA	S%
37	Olaf Kolzig	6	375	2.24	2	4	0	1	14	153	.908
	Totals	**6**	**377**	**2.23**	**2**	**4**	**0**	**1**	**14**	**153**	**.908**

General Managers' History

Milt Schmidt, 1974-75; Milt Schmidt and Max McNab, 1975-76; Max McNab, 1976-77 to 1980-81; Max McNab and Roger Crozier, 1981-82; David Poile, 1982-83 to 1996-97; George McPhee, 1997-98 to date.

Club Records

Team

(Figures in brackets for season records are games played; records for fewest points, wins, ties, losses, goals, goals against are for 70 or more games)

Most Points **107** 1985-86 (80)
Most Wins **50** 1985-86 (80)
Most Ties **18** 1980-81 (80)
Most Losses **67** 1974-75 (80)
Most Goals **330** 1991-92 (80)
Most Goals Against ***446** 1974-75 (80)
Fewest Points ***21** 1974-75 (80)
Fewest Wins ***8** 1974-75 (80)
Fewest Ties **5** 1974-75 (80), 1983-84 (80)
Fewest Losses **23** 1985-86 (80)
Fewest Goals **181** 1974-75 (80)
Fewest Goals Against **202** 1997-98 (82)
Longest Winning Streak
Overall .... **10** Jan. 27-Feb. 18/84
Home .... **10** Jan. 4-Feb. 23/00
Away .... **6** Feb. 26-Apr. 1/84
Longest Undefeated Streak
Overall .... **14** Nov. 24-Dec. 23/82 (9 wins, 5 ties), Jan. 17-Feb. 18/84 (13 wins, 1 tie)
Home .... **13** Nov. 25/92-Jan. 31/93 (9 wins, 4 ties), Dec. 27/99-Feb. 23/00 (11 wins, 2 ties)
Away .... **10** Nov. 24/82-Jan. 8/83 (6 wins, 4 ties)
Longest Losing Streak
Overall .... ***17** Feb. 18-Mar. 26/75
Home .... ***11** Feb. 18-Mar. 30/75
Away .... **37** Oct. 9/74-Mar. 26/75
Longest Winless Streak
Overall .... **25** Nov. 29/75-Jan. 21/76 (22 losses, 3 ties)
Home .... **14** Dec. 3/75-Jan. 21/76 (11 losses, 3 ties)
Away .... **37** Oct. 9/74-Mar. 26/75 (37 losses)
Most Shutouts, Season **9** 1995-96 (82)
Most PIM, Season **2,204** 1989-90 (80)
Most Goals, Game .... **12** Feb. 6/90 (Que. 2 at Wsh. 12)

Individual

Most Seasons .... **13** Michal Pivonka, Kelly Miller, Calle Johansson
Most Games .... **940** Kelly Miller
Most Goals, Career .... **397** Mike Gartner
Most Assists, Career .... **418** Michal Pivonka
Most Points, Career .... **789** Mike Gartner (397G, 392A)
Most PIM, Career .... **2,003** Dale Hunter
Most Shutouts, Career .... **21** Olaf Kolzig
Longest Consecutive Games Streak .... **422** Bob Carpenter (Oct. 7/81-Nov. 22/86)
Most Goals, Season .... **60** Dennis Maruk (1981-82)
Most Assists, Season .... **76** Dennis Maruk (1981-82)
Most Points, Season .... **136** Dennis Maruk (1981-82; 60G, 76A)
Most PIM, Season .... **339** Alan May (1989-90)
Most Points, Defenseman, Season .... **81** Larry Murphy (1986-87; 23G, 58A)
Most Points, Center, Season .... **136** Dennis Maruk (1981-82; 60G, 76A)
Most Points, Right Wing, Season .... **102** Mike Gartner (1984-85; 50G, 52A)
Most Points, Left Wing, Season .... **87** Ryan Walter (1981-82; 38G, 49A)
Most Points, Rookie, Season .... **67** Bob Carpenter (1981-82; 32G, 35A), Chris Valentine (1981-82; 30G, 37A)
Most Shutouts, Season .... **9** Jim Carey (1995-96)
Most Goals, Game .... **5** Bengt Gustafsson (Jan. 8/84), Peter Bondra (Feb. 5/94)
Most Assists, Game .... **6** Mike Ridley (Jan. 7/89)
Most Points, Game .... **7** Dino Ciccarelli (Mar. 18/89; 4G, 3A)

* NHL Record.

Retired Numbers

5	Rod Langway	1982-1993
7	Yvon Labre	1974-1981
32	Dale Hunter	1987-1999

Coaching History

Jim Anderson, Red Sullivan and Milt Schmidt, 1974-75; Milt Schmidt and Tom McVie, 1975-76; Tom McVie, 1976-77, 1977-78; Danny Belisle, 1978-79; Danny Belisle and Gary Green, 1979-80; Gary Green, 1980-81; Gary Green, Roger Crozier and Bryan Murray, 1981-82; Bryan Murray, 1982-83 to 1988-89; Bryan Murray and Terry Murray, 1989-90; Terry Murray, 1990-91 to 1992-93; Terry Murray and Jim Schoenfeld, 1993-94; Jim Schoenfeld, 1994-95 to 1996-97; Ron Wilson, 1997-98 to date.

Captains' History

Doug Mohns, 1974-75; Bill Clement and Yvon Labre, 1975-76; Yvon Labre, 1976-77, 1977-78; Guy Charron, 1978-79; Ryan Walter, 1979-80 to 1981-82; Rod Langway, 1982-83 to 1991-92; Rod Langway and Kevin Hatcher, 1992-93; Kevin Hatcher, 1993-94; Dale Hunter, 1994-95 to 1998-99; Adam Oates, 1999-2000 to date.

All-time Record vs. Other Clubs

Regular Season

	At Home								On Road								Total							
	GP	W	L	T	OL	GF	GA	PTS	GP	W	L	T	OL	GF	GA	PTS	GP	W	L	T	OL	GF	GA	PTS
Anaheim	7	3	4	0	0	10	17	6	7	2	4	1	0	21	24	5	14	5	8	1	0	31	41	11
Atlanta	5	4	0	1	0	18	7	9	5	2	2	1	0	14	10	5	10	6	2	2	0	32	17	14
Boston	49	13	24	12	0	138	172	38	50	15	28	7	0	135	184	37	99	28	52	19	0	273	356	75
Buffalo	50	13	28	9	0	128	174	35	50	12	32	6	0	131	195	30	100	25	60	15	0	259	369	65
Calgary	38	19	14	5	0	143	132	43	37	6	24	7	0	89	156	19	75	25	38	12	0	232	288	62
Carolina	39	24	12	3	0	131	101	51	41	19	13	8	1	129	111	47	80	43	25	11	1	260	212	98
Chicago	39	20	14	5	0	139	122	45	38	11	22	5	0	114	149	27	77	31	36	10	0	253	271	72
Colorado	32	17	10	4	1	129	104	39	31	13	14	4	0	110	99	30	63	30	24	8	1	239	203	69
Columbus	0	0	0	0	0	0	0	0	1	0	1	0	0	1	3	0	1	0	1	0	0	1	3	0
Dallas	38	15	15	8	0	117	118	38	38	11	19	8	0	103	141	30	76	26	34	16	0	220	259	68
Detroit	44	21	18	5	0	166	137	47	45	14	19	11	1	130	157	40	89	35	37	16	1	296	294	87
Edmonton	27	16	9	2	0	113	91	34	27	10	13	4	0	87	111	24	54	26	22	6	0	200	202	58
Florida	20	11	5	4	0	60	47	26	20	9	9	2	0	54	53	20	40	20	14	6	0	114	100	46
Los Angeles	44	18	19	7	0	182	165	43	45	13	26	6	0	138	178	32	89	31	45	13	0	320	343	75
Minnesota	1	1	0	0	0	2	1	2	1	0	1	0	0	0	3	0	2	1	1	0	0	2	4	2
Montreal	53	23	21	9	0	146	161	55	54	16	31	7	0	117	209	39	107	39	52	16	0	263	370	94
Nashville	3	2	1	0	0	5	4	4	3	1	2	0	0	6	8	2	6	3	3	0	0	11	12	6
New Jersey	73	46	22	5	0	290	209	97	73	32	34	7	0	219	227	71	146	78	56	12	0	509	436	168
NY Islanders	75	35	29	11	0	243	238	81	75	34	40	1	0	237	282	69	150	69	69	12	0	480	520	150
NY Rangers	78	38	30	9	1	290	259	86	76	32	36	8	0	265	289	72	154	70	66	17	1	555	548	158
Ottawa	18	11	5	2	0	66	41	24	17	8	8	1	0	58	61	17	35	19	13	3	0	124	102	41
Philadelphia	74	30	31	13	0	251	245	73	77	24	47	6	0	211	287	54	151	54	78	19	0	462	532	127
Phoenix	28	18	6	4	0	116	78	40	28	7	14	7	0	99	104	21	56	25	20	11	0	215	182	61
Pittsburgh	80	41	31	7	1	337	297	90	77	28	42	7	0	246	300	63	157	69	73	14	1	583	597	153
St. Louis	37	20	13	4	0	132	108	44	39	13	18	8	0	125	157	34	76	33	31	12	0	257	265	78
San Jose	9	5	4	0	0	28	25	10	8	3	4	1	0	22	22	7	17	8	8	1	0	50	47	17
Tampa Bay	21	12	5	4	0	78	47	28	21	15	5	1	0	72	46	31	42	27	10	5	0	150	93	59
Toronto	44	28	13	2	1	170	123	59	42	15	22	5	0	147	189	35	86	43	35	7	1	317	312	94
Vancouver	38	22	12	4	0	130	109	48	38	16	17	5	0	123	130	37	76	38	29	9	0	253	239	85
Defunct Clubs	10	2	8	0	0	28	42	4	10	4	5	1	0	30	39	9	20	6	13	1	0	58	81	13
Totals	**1074**	**528**	**403**	**139**	**4**	**3786**	**3374**	**1199**	**1074**	**385**	**552**	**135**	**2**	**3233**	**3924**	**907**	**2148**	**913**	**955**	**274**	**6**	**7019**	**7298**	**2106**

Playoffs

	Series	W	L	GP	W	L	T	GF	GA	Last Mtg.	Round	Result
Boston	2	1	1	10	4	6	0	15	13	1998	CQF	W 4-2
Buffalo	1	1	0	6	4	2	0	13	11	1998	CF	W 4-2
Detroit	1	0	1	4	0	4	0	7	13	1998	F	L 0-4
New Jersey	2	1	1	13	7	6	0	44	43	1990	DSF	W 4-2
NY Islanders	6	1	5	30	12	18	0	88	89	1993	DSF	L 2-4
NY Rangers	4	2	2	22	11	11	0	75	71	1994	CSF	L 1-4
Ottawa	1	1	0	5	4	1	0	18	7	1998	CSF	W 4-1
Philadelphia	3	2	1	16	9	7	0	65	55	1989	DSF	L 2-4
Pittsburgh	7	1	6	42	16	26	0	121	137	2001	CQF	L 2-4
Totals	**27**	**10**	**17**	**148**	**67**	**81**	**0**	**452**	**464**			

Playoff Results 2001-1997

Year	Round	Opponent	Result	GF	GA
2001	CQF	Pittsburgh	L 2-4	10	14
2000	CQF	Pittsburgh	L 1-4	8	17
1998	F	Detroit	L 0-4	7	13
	CF	Buffalo	W 4-2	13	11
	CSF	Ottawa	W 4-1	18	7
	CQF	Boston	W 4-2	15	13

Abbreviations: Round: F – Final; **CF** – conference final; **CSF** – conference semi-final; **CQF** – conference quarter-final; **DSF** – division semi-final.

Calgary totals include Atlanta Flames, 1974-75 to 1979-80.
Carolina totals include Hartford, 1979-80 to 1996-97.
Colorado totals include Quebec, 1979-80 to 1994-95.
Dallas totals include Minnesota North Stars, 1974-75 to 1992-93.
New Jersey totals include Kansas City, 1974-75 to 1975-76, and Colorado Rockies, 1976-77 to 1981-82.
Phoenix totals include Winnipeg, 1979-80, 1995-96.

2000-01 Results

Oct.	6	Los Angeles	1-4		6	at Toronto	3-2
	7	at Carolina	3-3		8	Pittsburgh	3-5
	11	at Atlanta	3-3		10	at Minnesota	0-3
	13	at Nashville	1-3		13	Atlanta	4-1
	14	at Dallas	0-3		18	at Ottawa	4-5
	17	Colorado	3-4*		19	at Chicago	1-3
	19	New Jersey	5-2		23	at Tampa Bay	5-2
	21	NY Islanders	4-4		24	Florida	2-1
	26	at Boston	1-4		27	at Montreal	2-4
	27	at Columbus	1-3		28	Philadelphia	4-2
	29	at Philadelphia	1-1		30	Ottawa	1-1
	31	Detroit	6-2	Feb.	1	Toronto	5-4
Nov.	2	at St. Louis	0-2		7	at Colorado	3-1
	4	at Florida	3-2		9	at Anaheim	4-3
	5	at Tampa Bay	2-5		10	at Los Angeles	4-3
	9	NY Rangers	3-5		13	at Calgary	4-4
	12	Atlanta	2-2		14	at Vancouver	4-3*
	14	Phoenix	2-2		17	at Montreal	6-3
	17	Montreal	4-3		21	Nashville	2-1
	18	at Philadelphia	3-5		23	Montreal	3-1
	22	Vancouver	3-2*		24	at Carolina	2-1
	24	NY Islanders	1-0		27	Chicago	2-3
	25	at Atlanta	1-2	Mar.	1	Toronto	2-3*
	29	Tampa Bay	4-1		3	Pittsburgh	4-3
Dec.	1	Boston	3-2		6	at NY Islanders	5-1
	2	at Boston	2-0		7	at Pittsburgh	4-3
	6	at NY Rangers	2-3		9	NY Rangers	5-3
	9	at New Jersey	3-2		11	Ottawa	6-5
	12	at NY Islanders	3-2		13	Anaheim	0-2
	14	Minnesota	2-1		15	Carolina	0-3
	16	Edmonton	4-0		17	Buffalo	2-3
	18	San Jose	3-5		19	at NY Rangers	3-6
	20	Buffalo	2-2		23	at Florida	1-4
	21	at Buffalo	3-1		24	at Tampa Bay	3-2
	23	Florida	5-3		28	Carolina	7-0
	27	at Ottawa	5-1		30	at Carolina	3-4*
	29	at New Jersey	2-4	Apr.	1	at Detroit	1-2*
	30	Philadelphia	6-3		3	New Jersey	4-6
Jan.	1	Atlanta	4-2		5	Florida	3-0
	3	at Pittsburgh	2-3		6	at Buffalo	1-2
	5	Boston	1-1		8	Tampa Bay	2-1

* – Overtime

Entry Draft Selections 2001-1987

2001
Pick
58 Nathan Paetsch
90 Owen Fussey
125 Jeff Lucky
160 Artem Ternavsky
191 Zbynek Novak
221 John Oduya
249 Matt Maglione
254 Peter Polcik
275 Robert Muller
284 Viktor Hubl

2000
Pick
26 Brian Sutherby
43 Matt Pettinger
61 Jakub Cutta
121 Ryan Vanbuskirk
163 Ivan Nepryayev
289 Bjorn Nord

1999
Pick
7 Kris Beech
29 Michal Sivek
31 Charlie Stephens
34 Ross Lupaschuk
37 Nolan Yonkman
132 Roman Tvrdon
175 Kyle Clark
192 David Johansson
219 Maxim Orlov
249 Igor Schadilov

1998
Pick
49 Jomar Cruz
59 Todd Hornung
106 Krys Barch
107 Chris Corrinet
118 Mike Siklenka
125 Erik Wendell
179 Nathan Forster
193 Ratislav Stana
220 Michael Farrell
251 Blake Evans

1997
Pick
9 Nick Boynton
35 Jean-Francois Fortin
89 Curtis Cruickshank
116 Kevin Caulfield
143 Henrik Petre
200 Pierre-Luc Therrien
226 Matt Oikawa

1996
Pick
4 Alexandre Volchkov
17 Jaroslav Svejkovsky
43 Jan Bulis
58 Sergei Zimakov
74 Dave Weninger
78 Shawn McNeil
85 Justin Davis
126 Matthew Lahey
153 Andrew Van Bruggen
180 Michael Anderson
206 Oleg Orekhovsky
232 Chad Cavanagh

1995
Pick
17 Brad Church
23 Miika Elomo
43 Dwayne Hay
93 Sebastien Charpentier
95 Joel Theriault
105 Benoit Gratton
124 Joel Cort
147 Frederick Jobin
199 Vasili Turkovsky
225 Scott Swanson

1994
Pick
10 Nolan Baumgartner
15 Alexander Kharlamov
41 Scott Cherrey
93 Matt Herr
119 Yanick Jean
145 Dmitri Mekeshkin
171 Daniel Reja
197 Chris Patrick
223 John Tuohy
249 Richard Zednik
275 Sergei Tertyshny

1993
Pick
11 Brendan Witt
17 Jason Allison
69 Patrick Boileau
147 Frank Banham
173 Daniel Hendrickson
174 Andrew Brunette
199 Joel Poirier
225 Jason Gladney
251 Mark Seliger
277 Dany Bousquet

1992
Pick
14 Sergei Gonchar
32 Jim Carey
53 Stefan Ustorf
71 Martin Gendron
119 John Varga
167 Mark Matier
191 Mike Mathers
215 Brian Stagg
239 Gregory Callahan
263 Billy Jo MacPherson

1991
Pick
14 Pat Peake
21 Trevor Halverson
25 Eric Lavigne
36 Jeff Nelson
58 Steve Konowalchuk
80 Justin Morrison
146 Dave Morissette
168 Rick Corriveau
190 Trevor Duhaime
209 Rob Leask
212 Carl Leblanc
234 Rob Puchniak
256 Bill Kovacs

1990
Pick
9 John Slaney
30 Rod Pasma
51 Chris Longo
72 Randy Pearce
93 Brian Sakic
94 Mark Ouimet
114 Andrei Kovalev
135 Roman Kontsek
156 Peter Bondra
159 Steve Martell
177 Ken Klee
198 Michael Boback
219 Alan Brown
240 Todd Hlushko

1989
Pick
19 Olaf Kolzig
35 Byron Dafoe
59 Jim Mathieson
61 Jason Woolley
82 Trent Klatt
145 Dave Lorentz
166 Dean Holoien
187 Victor Gervais
208 Jiri Vykoukal
229 Sidorov Sidorov
250 Ken House

1988
Pick
15 Reggie Savage
36 Tim Taylor
41 Todd Bartley
57 Duane Derksen
78 Bob Krauss
120 Dmitri Khristich
141 Keith Jones
144 Brad Schlegel
162 Todd Hilditch
183 Petr Pavlas
192 Mark Sorensen
204 Claudio Scremin
225 Chris Venkus
246 Ron Pascucci

1987
Pick
36 Jeff Ballantyne
57 Steve Maltais
78 Tyler Larter
99 Pat Beauchesne
120 Rich Defreitas
141 Devon Oleniuk
162 Thomas Sjogren
204 Chris Clarke
225 Milos Vanik
240 Dan Brettschneider
246 Ryan Kummo

Coach

WILSON, RON
Coach, Washington Capitals. Born in Windsor, Ont., May 28, 1955.

In his first season as head coach of the Capitals, Wilson's team advanced to the Stanley Cup finals for the first time. He has also led the team to first place in the Southeast Division in 1999-2000 and 2000-01.

Prior to joining the Capitals, Wilson served as head coach in Anaheim for four years. He also spent three years in Vancouver as an assistant coach from 1990-93. Wilson also served as the head coach for Team USA, winners of the 1996 World Cup of Hockey.

Wilson has significant playing experience in professional, amateur and international hockey. He played four years at Providence College where he was a two-time All-American and became the NCAA's all-time leading scorer among defensemen with 250 points.

Wilson began his professional hockey career in 1976-77 with Dallas in the Central Hockey League. He joined the Toronto Maple Leafs in 1977-78, playing in 64 NHL contests over three seasons. Wilson then moved to Switzerland in 1980 and competed for the Swiss teams Kloten and Davos for six seasons. He signed with Minnesota as a free agent in 1985 where he played through 1988.

Although born in Canada, Wilson was raised in the United States and remains a U.S. citizen. He was a four-time player for U.S. National Teams (1975, 1981, 1983, 1987).

Coaching Record

		Regular Season				Playoffs		
Season	Team	Games	W	L	T	Games	W	L
1993-94	Anaheim (NHL)	84	33	46	5	....	....	....
1994-95	Anaheim (NHL)	48	16	27	5	....	....	....
1995-96	Anaheim (NHL)	82	35	39	8	....	....	....
1996-97	Anaheim (NHL)	82	36	33	13	11	4	7
1997-98	Washington (NHL)	82	40	30	12	21	12	9
1998-99	Washington (NHL)	82	31	45	6	....	....	....
1999-2000	Washington (NHL)	82	44	26	12	5	1	4
2000-01	Washington (NHL)	82	41	31	10	6	2	4
	NHL Totals	624	276	277	71	43	19	24

Club Directory

MCI Center

Washington Capitals
401 9th Street, NW
Washington, DC 20004
Phone **202/226-2200**
PR FAX 202/266-2360
www.washingtoncaps.com
Capacity: 18,672

Executive

Chairman & Majority Owner	Ted Leonsis
Owner, President & Governor	Dick Patrick
Owner	Raul Fernandez
Owner	Michael Jordan
Executive Assistant	Michelle Trostle

Hockey Operations

Vice President & General Manager	George McPhee
Director of Hockey Operations	Shawn Simpson
Director of Amateur Scouting	Ross Mahoney
Assistant to the General Manager	Frank Provenzano
Head Coach	Ron Wilson
Assistant Coaches	Tim Army, Tim Hunter
Goaltending Coach	Dave Prior
Strength & Conditioning Coach	Frank Costello
Director of Team Services	Todd Warren
Head Athletic Trainer	Greg Smith
Assistant Athletic Trainer	Tim Clark
Massage Therapist	Curt Millar
Team Physician	Ben Shaffer, MD
Head Equipment Manager	Doug Shearer
Assistant Equipment Manager	Craig Leydig
Equipment Assistant	Brian Metzger

Scouting Staff

Director, Amateur Scouting	Ross Mahoney
Pro Scouts	Archie Henderson, Brian MacLellan, Mike Backman
Ontario Scout	Steve Bowman
Western Scout	Dale Derkatch
Quebec Scout	Martin Pouliot
European Scouts	Ville Siren, Gleb Chistyakov, Vojtech Kucera
Western U.S.Scout	Ernie Vargas
Eastern U.S. Scout	Ed McColgan

Business Operations

Sr. Vice President, Business Operations	Declan J. Bolger
Special Adv., Strategy & Pres., washingtoncaps.com	Dean Silverman
Gen.Council and Corp.Secretary	George Stamas
Director, Operations	George Parr
Executive Assistant	Piper Sammons
Receptionist	Deborah Anderson
Mail Room Coordinator	Jennifer Whittington

Communications

Manager of Media Relations	Brian Potter
Manager of Information	Nate Ewell
Manager of Community Development	Stephanie Boyer
Executive Assistant	Stefanie Minor
Media Hotline	202/266-2365
MCI Center Phone	202/628-3200
MCI Center Press Box Phone	202/628-3200 ext. 7600
MCI Center Press Room Phone	202/628-3200 ext. 7500
MCI Center Press Room Fax	202/661-5011

Finance

Controller	Keith Burrows
Senior Accountant	Michael Mercer
Accounts Payable Manager	Jennifer Simpson
Staff Accountant	Jill Shannon

Marketing and Advertising

Senior Director, Marketing	John Vidalin
Director of Sponsorship Partnerships	Chris Hudgins
Director of Game Presentation	Mark Tamar
Promotions Manager	Missy Rentz
Fan Development Coordinator	Chris Lewis
Promotions Coordinator	Ryan Ahern
Marketing Coordinator	Shari Gulley
Mascot Coordinator	Desi Deceder
Game Operations Coordinator	Greg Hanover
Sr. Administrative Assistant	Kirsten Bergman

Sales

Vice President, Sales	Kevin Morgan
Senior Regional Sales Managers	Darren Bruening, Tim Munchmeyer, Tim Bronaugh
Regional Sales Managers	Mike Ragan, Letitia Petrillo, Greg Voss, Jyermal Jones, David Dzwonkowski, Doug Pristach, Scott Borden, Jay Wheeler, Jill Colby, Ryan Smith
Executive Assistant	Ingrid Harrell-Lee

Ticket Operations & Guest Services

Director, Ticket Operations & Guest Services	Laini Samuels
Assistant Director, Guest Services	Greg Monares
Manager, Ticket Operations	Chris Turns
Assistant Manager of Guest Services	Stacie Sandridge
Coordinators, Guest Services	Kim LaFollette, Crystal Jones
Ticket Operations Financial Coordinator	Mary Santos
Coordinators, Ticket Operations	Duane Harris, Eric Spat, Kelly Shultz
Arena	MCI Center, 601 F Street NW, Washington, DC 20004
Practice Facility	Piney Orchard Ice Arena, 8781 Piney Orchard Parkway, Odenton, MD 21113
Piney Orchard Phone	301/621-9111
Television	Comcast SportsNet and WB-50
Radio Flagship	TBD

2000-2001 Final Statistics

Standings

Abbreviations: GP – games played; **W** – wins; **L** – losses; **T** – ties; **OTL** – overtime losses; **GF** – goals for; **GA** – goals against; **PTS** – points.

EASTERN CONFERENCE

Northeast Division

	GP	W	L	T	OTL	GF	GA	PTS
Ottawa	82	48	21	9	4	274	205	109
Buffalo	82	46	30	5	1	218	184	98
Toronto	82	37	29	11	5	232	207	90
Boston	82	36	30	8	8	227	249	88
Montreal	82	28	40	8	6	206	232	70

Atlantic Division

	GP	W	L	T	OTL	GF	GA	PTS
New Jersey	82	48	19	12	3	295	195	111
Philadelphia	82	43	25	11	3	240	207	100
Pittsburgh	82	42	28	9	3	281	256	96
NY Rangers	82	33	43	5	1	250	290	72
NY Islanders	82	21	51	7	3	185	268	52

Southeast Division

	GP	W	L	T	OTL	GF	GA	PTS
Washington	82	41	27	10	4	233	211	96
Carolina	82	38	32	9	3	212	225	88
Florida	82	22	38	13	9	200	246	66
Atlanta	82	23	45	12	2	211	289	60
Tampa Bay	82	24	47	6	5	201	280	59

WESTERN CONFERENCE

Central Division

	GP	W	L	T	OTL	GF	GA	PTS
Detroit	82	49	20	9	4	253	202	111
St. Louis	82	43	22	12	5	249	195	103
Nashville	82	34	36	9	3	186	200	80
Chicago	82	29	40	8	5	210	246	71
Columbus	82	28	39	9	6	190	233	71

Pacific Division

	GP	W	L	T	OTL	GF	GA	PTS
Dallas	82	48	24	8	2	241	187	106
San Jose	82	40	27	12	3	217	192	95
Los Angeles	82	38	28	13	3	252	228	92
Phoenix	82	35	27	17	3	214	212	90
Anaheim	82	25	41	11	5	188	245	66

Northwest Division

	GP	W	L	T	OTL	GF	GA	PTS
Colorado	82	52	16	10	4	270	192	118
Edmonton	82	39	28	12	3	243	222	93
Vancouver	82	36	28	11	7	239	238	90
Calgary	82	27	36	15	4	197	236	73
Minnesota	82	25	39	13	5	168	210	68

After an off year in 1999-2000, Peter Bondra once again ranked among the NHL's elite scorers, collecting 45 goals including a league-leading 22 on the power play. Bondra had never before scored more than 12 power-play goals.

INDIVIDUAL LEADERS

Goal Scoring

Player	Team	GP	G
Pavel Bure	Florida	82	59
Joe Sakic	Colorado	82	54
Jaromir Jagr	Pittsburgh	81	52
Peter Bondra	Washington	82	45
Alexei Kovalev	Pittsburgh	79	44
Alexander Mogilny	New Jersey	75	43
Markus Naslund	Vancouver	72	41
Milan Hejduk	Colorado	80	41
Jeff O'Neill	Carolina	82	41

Assists

Player	Team	GP	A
Jaromir Jagr	Pittsburgh	81	69
Adam Oates	Washington	81	69
Martin Straka	Pittsburgh	82	68
Doug Weight	Edmonton	82	65
Joe Sakic	Colorado	82	64
Peter Forsberg	Colorado	73	62
Jason Allison	Boston	82	59
Brian Leetch	NY Rangers	82	58
Nicklas Lidstrom	Detroit	82	56
Patrik Elias	New Jersey	82	56

Power-play Goals

Player	Team	GP	PP
Peter Bondra	Washington	82	22
Joe Thornton	Boston	72	19
Joe Sakic	Colorado	82	19
Pavel Bure	Florida	82	19

Short-handed Goals

Player	Team	GP	SH
Steve Sullivan	Chicago	81	8
Theoren Fleury	NY Rangers	62	7
Wes Walz	Minnesota	82	7
Pavel Bure	Florida	82	5

Game-winning Goals

Player	Team	GP	GW
Joe Sakic	Colorado	82	12
Jaromir Jagr	Pittsburgh	81	10
Alexei Yashin	Ottawa	82	10
Alexei Kovalev	Pittsburgh	79	9
Milan Hejduk	Colorado	80	9

Game-tying Goals

Player	Team	GP	GT
Jarome Iginla	Calgary	77	3
Pavel Bure	Florida	82	3
Brendan Morrison	Vancouver	82	3

Shots

Player	Team	GP	S
Pavel Bure	Florida	82	384
Joe Sakic	Colorado	82	332
Scott Young	St. Louis	81	321
Jaromir Jagr	Pittsburgh	81	317
Alexei Kovalev	Pittsburgh	79	307
Peter Bondra	Washington	82	305
Bill Guerin	Edm., Bos.	85	289
Mariusz Czerkawski	NY Islanders	82	287
Brian Rolston	Boston	77	286
Brendan Shanahan	Detroit	81	278

Shooting Percentage

(minimum 82 shots)

Player	Team	GP	G	S	%
Gary Roberts	Toronto	82	29	138	21.0
Keith Primeau	Philadelphia	71	34	165	20.6
Mario Lemieux	Pittsburgh	43	35	171	20.5
Joe Thornton	Boston	72	37	181	20.4
Alex Tanguay	Colorado	82	27	135	20.0
Jason Allison	Boston	82	36	185	19.5
Milan Hejduk	Colorado	80	41	213	19.2
Randy McKay	New Jersey	77	23	120	19.2
Jeff Halpern	Washington	80	21	110	19.1

Penalty Minutes

Player	Team	GP	PIM
Matthew Barnaby	Pit., T.B.	76	265
Peter Worrell	Florida	71	248
Stu Grimson	Los Angeles	72	235
Andrei Nazarov	Ana., Bos.	79	229
Jeff Odgers	Atlanta	82	226

Plus/Minus

Player	Team	GP	+/–
Joe Sakic	Colorado	82	45
Patrik Elias	New Jersey	82	45
Scott Stevens	New Jersey	81	40
Petr Sykora	New Jersey	73	36
Brian Rafalski	New Jersey	78	36

Individual Leaders

Abbreviations: * – rookie eligible for Calder Trophy; **A** – assists; **G** – goals; **GP** – games played; **GT** – game-tying goals; **GW** – game-winning goals; **PIM** – penalties in minutes; **PP** – power play goals; **Pts** – points; **S** – shots on goal; **SH** – short-handed goals; **%** – percentage of shots on goal resulting in goals; **+/–** – difference between Goals For (**GF**) scored when a player is on the ice with his team at even strength or short-handed and Goals Against (**GA**) scored when the same player is on the ice with his team at even strength or on a power play.

Individual Scoring Leaders for Art Ross Trophy

Player	Team	GP	G	A	Pts	+/–	PIM	PP	SH	GW	GT	S	%
Jaromir Jagr	Pittsburgh	81	52	69	121	19	42	14	1	10	1	317	16.4
Joe Sakic	Colorado	82	54	64	118	45	30	19	3	12	2	332	16.3
Patrik Elias	New Jersey	82	40	56	96	45	51	8	3	6	1	220	18.2
Alexei Kovalev	Pittsburgh	79	44	51	95	12	96	12	2	9	1	307	14.3
Jason Allison	Boston	82	36	59	95	–8	85	11	3	6	0	185	19.5
Martin Straka	Pittsburgh	82	27	68	95	19	38	7	1	4	1	185	14.6
Pavel Bure	Florida	82	59	33	92	–2	58	19	5	8	3	384	15.4
Doug Weight	Edmonton	82	25	65	90	12	91	8	0	3	2	188	13.3
Ziggy Palffy	Los Angeles	73	38	51	89	22	20	12	4	8	0	217	17.5
Peter Forsberg	Colorado	73	27	62	89	23	54	12	2	5	0	178	15.2
Alexei Yashin	Ottawa	82	40	48	88	10	30	13	2	10	1	263	15.2
Luc Robitaille	Los Angeles	82	37	51	88	10	66	16	1	4	1	235	15.7
Bill Guerin	Edm., Bos.	85	40	45	85	7	140	11	1	5	0	289	13.8
Mike Modano	Dallas	81	33	51	84	26	52	8	3	7	1	208	15.9
Alexander Mogilny	New Jersey	75	43	40	83	10	43	12	0	7	0	240	17.9
Pierre Turgeon	St. Louis	79	30	52	82	14	37	11	0	6	1	171	17.5
Adam Oates	Washington	81	13	69	82	–9	28	5	0	4	0	72	18.1
Peter Bondra	Washington	82	45	36	81	8	60	22	4	8	0	305	14.8
Petr Sykora	New Jersey	73	35	46	81	36	32	9	2	3	0	249	14.1
Robert Lang	Pittsburgh	82	32	48	80	20	28	10	0	2	0	177	18.1
Milan Hejduk	Colorado	80	41	38	79	32	36	12	1	9	0	213	19.2
Brett Hull	Dallas	79	39	40	79	10	18	11	0	8	1	219	17.8
Keith Tkachuk	Phx., St.L.	76	35	44	79	3	122	17	0	5	2	271	12.9
Donald Audette	Atl., Buf.	76	34	45	79	–2	76	14	1	3	2	225	15.1
Brian Leetch	NY Rangers	82	21	58	79	–18	34	10	1	3	1	241	8.7
Petr Nedved	NY Rangers	79	32	46	78	10	54	9	1	5	0	230	13.9

Defencemen Scoring Leaders

Player	Team	GP	G	A	Pts	+/–	PIM	PP	SH	GW	GT	S	%
Brian Leetch	NY Rangers	82	21	58	79	–18	34	10	1	3	1	241	8.7
Nicklas Lidstrom	Detroit	82	15	56	71	9	18	8	0	0	0	272	5.5
Rob Blake	L.A., Col.	67	19	40	59	3	77	10	0	2	1	267	7.1
Raymond Bourque	Colorado	80	7	52	59	25	48	2	2	0	1	216	3.2
Sergei Gonchar	Washington	76	19	38	57	12	70	8	0	2	0	241	7.9
Al MacInnis	St. Louis	59	12	42	54	23	52	6	1	3	0	218	5.5
Oleg Tverdovsky	Anaheim	82	14	39	53	–11	32	8	0	3	2	188	7.4
Brian Rafalski	New Jersey	78	9	43	52	36	26	6	0	1	1	142	6.3
Mathieu Schneider	Los Angeles	73	16	35	51	0	56	7	1	2	2	183	8.7
Sergei Zubov	Dallas	79	10	41	51	22	24	6	0	1	1	173	5.8

Penguins teammates Robert Lang (left) and Alexei Kovalev were among four Pittsburgh players to crack the top 20 in scoring last season. Now an ex-Penguin, Jaromir Jagr won the Art Ross Trophy for the fourth straight season.

CONSECUTIVE SCORING STREAKS

Goals

Games	Player	Team	G
7	Pavel Bure	Florida	13
6	Jaromir Jagr	Pittsburgh	9
6	Daniel Briere	Phoenix	7
6	Joe Sakic	Colorado	6
5	Alexander Mogilny	New Jersey	8
5	Peter Forsberg	Colorado	7
5	Milan Hejduk	Colorado	7
5	Joe Thornton	Boston	7
5	Mario Lemieux	Pittsburgh	6
5	Scott Young	St. Louis	6
5	Ziggy Palffy	Los Angeles	6
5	Eric Daze	Chicago	6
5	Petr Sykora	New Jersey	5
5	Patrick Marleau	San Jose	5

Assists

Games	Player	Team	A
16	Jaromir Jagr	Pittsburgh	24
9	Petr Sykora	New Jersey	13
9	Jaromir Jagr	Pittsburgh	12
8	Rod Brind'Amour	Carolina	10
8	Patrik Elias	New Jersey	10
8	Alex Tanguay	Colorado	10
7	Milan Hejduk	Colorado	10
7	Sergei Berezin	Toronto	10
7	Ziggy Palffy	Los Angeles	9
7	Chris Pronger	St. Louis	9
7	Theoren Fleury	NY Rangers	8
7	Daniel Alfredsson	Ottawa	8
7	Mark Recchi	Philadelphia	7
7	Peter Forsberg	Colorado	7

Points

Games	Player	Team	G	A	PTS
16	Jaromir Jagr	Pittsburgh	7	24	31
14	Theoren Fleury	NY Rangers	6	15	21
13	Patrik Elias	New Jersey	12	13	25
13	Petr Sykora	New Jersey	6	17	23
11	Pavel Bure	Florida	15	7	22
11	Mark Recchi	Philadelphia	6	13	19
11	Joe Thornton	Boston	12	7	19
11	Alex Tanguay	Colorado	6	13	19
11	Adam Oates	Washington	3	13	16
10	Jaromir Jagr	Pittsburgh	11	12	23
10	V. Damphousse	San Jose	4	14	18
10	Joe Sakic	Colorado	9	9	18
10	Alexei Yashin	Ottawa	12	6	18
10	Keith Tkachuk	Phoenix	4	13	17
9	Marian Hossa	Ottawa	4	13	17
9	Mario Lemieux	Pittsburgh	8	8	16
9	Peter Forsberg	Colorado	9	7	16
9	Milan Hejduk	Colorado	6	10	16
9	Paul Kariya	Anaheim	5	10	15
9	Petr Sykora	New Jersey	8	5	13
9	Daniel Alfredsson	Ottawa	4	9	13
9	Kevin Stevens	Phi., Pit.	4	8	12
9	Martin Rucinsky	Montreal	5	6	11
9	D. Langkow	Philadelphia	2	7	9

Having been drafted back in 1994 and making his debut with 11 games played in 1999-2000, Evgeni Nabokov truly arrived in the NHL in 2000-01, posting 32 victories and a 2.19 goals-against average to win rookie of the year.

Leading all rookie scorers with 21 goals, 41 assists and 62 points, Tampa Bay's Brad Richards finished as the runner-up to Evgeni Nabokov in voting for the Calder Trophy.

Individual Rookie Scoring Leaders

Rookie	Team	GP	G	A	Pts	+/–	PIM	PP	SH	GW	GT	S	%
Brad Richards	Tampa Bay	82	21	41	62	–10	14	7	0	3	0	179	11.7
Shane Willis	Carolina	73	20	24	44	–6	45	9	0	6	0	172	11.6
Martin Havlat	Ottawa	73	19	23	42	8	20	7	0	5	0	133	14.3
Lubomir Visnovsky	Los Angeles	81	7	32	39	16	36	3	0	3	0	105	6.7
Marian Gaborik	Minnesota	71	18	18	36	–6	32	6	0	3	0	179	10.1
Ruslan Fedotenko	Philadelphia	74	16	20	36	8	72	3	0	4	0	119	13.4
Steve Reinprecht	L.A., Col.	80	15	21	36	10	14	3	2	3	0	100	15.0
Daniel Sedin	Vancouver	75	20	14	34	–3	24	10	0	3	0	127	15.7
Karel Rachunek	Ottawa	71	3	30	33	17	60	3	0	0	0	77	3.9
David Vyborny	Columbus	79	13	19	32	–9	22	5	0	1	0	125	10.4
Serge Aubin	Columbus	81	13	17	30	–20	107	0	0	2	1	110	11.8
Filip Kuba	Minnesota	75	9	21	30	–6	28	4	0	4	1	141	6.4
Henrik Sedin	Vancouver	82	9	20	29	–2	38	2	0	1	0	98	9.2
Tomi Kallio	Atlanta	56	14	13	27	–3	22	2	0	2	0	115	12.2
Marian Cisar	Nashville	60	12	15	27	–7	45	5	0	1	0	97	12.4

HockeyRules™

SALT LAKE 2002™

Goal Scoring

Name	Team	GP	G
Brad Richards	Tampa Bay	82	21
Shane Willis	Carolina	73	20
Daniel Sedin	Vancouver	75	20
Martin Havlat	Ottawa	73	19
Marian Gaborik	Minnesota	71	18
Ruslan Fedotenko	Philadelphia	74	16
Steve Reinprecht	L.A., Col.	80	15
Ville Nieminen	Colorado	50	14
Tomi Kallio	Atlanta	56	14
David Vyborny	Columbus	79	13
Serge Aubin	Columbus	81	13
Marian Cisar	Nashville	60	12
Justin Williams	Philadelphia	63	12
Daniel Corso	St. Louis	28	10

Assists

Name	Team	GP	A
Brad Richards	Tampa Bay	82	41
Lubomir Visnovsky	Los Angeles	81	32
Karel Rachunek	Ottawa	71	30
Shane Willis	Carolina	73	24
Martin Havlat	Ottawa	73	23
Filip Kuba	Minnesota	75	21
Steve Reinprecht	L.A., Col.	80	21
Ruslan Fedotenko	Philadelphia	74	20
Henrik Sedin	Vancouver	82	20
David Vyborny	Columbus	79	19
Colin White	New Jersey	82	19
Marian Gaborik	Minnesota	71	18
Dimitri Kalinin	Buffalo	79	18
Andrei Markov	Montreal	63	17
Serge Aubin	Columbus	81	17

Power-play Goals

Name	Team	GP	PP
Daniel Sedin	Vancouver	75	10
Shane Willis	Carolina	73	9
Martin Havlat	Ottawa	73	7
Brad Richards	Tampa Bay	82	7
Marian Gaborik	Minnesota	71	6
Daniel Corso	St. Louis	28	5
Marian Cisar	Nashville	60	5
David Vyborny	Columbus	79	5
Filip Kuba	Minnesota	75	4
Mike Comrie	Edmonton	41	3
Karel Rachunek	Ottawa	71	3
Ruslan Fedotenko	Philadelphia	74	3
Steve Reinprecht	L.A., Col.	80	3
Lubomir Visnovsky	Los Angeles	81	3

Short-handed Goals

Name	Team	GP	SH
Eric Belanger	Los Angeles	62	2
Steve Reinprecht	L.A., Col.	80	2
Jarkko Ruutu	Vancouver	21	1
Denis Hamel	Buffalo	41	1
Wyatt Smith	Phoenix	42	1
Milan Kraft	Pittsburgh	42	1
Serge Payer	Florida	43	1
Samuel Pahlsson	Bos., Ana.	76	1

Game-winning Goals

Name	Team	GP	GW
Shane Willis	Carolina	73	6
Martin Havlat	Ottawa	73	5
Daniel Corso	St. Louis	28	4
Ruslan Fedotenko	Philadelphia	74	4
Filip Kuba	Minnesota	75	4

Game-tying Goals

Name	Team	GP	GT
Xavier Delisle	Montreal	14	1
Chris Nielsen	Columbus	29	1
Milan Kraft	Pittsburgh	42	1
Petr Tenkrat	Anaheim	46	1
Filip Kuba	Minnesota	75	1
Serge Aubin	Columbus	81	1

Shots

Name	Team	GP	S
Marian Gaborik	Minnesota	71	179
Brad Richards	Tampa Bay	82	179
Shane Willis	Carolina	73	172
Filip Kuba	Minnesota	75	141
Martin Havlat	Ottawa	73	133
Daniel Sedin	Vancouver	75	127
David Vyborny	Columbus	79	125
Ruslan Fedotenko	Philadelphia	74	119
Tomi Kallio	Atlanta	56	115
Colin White	New Jersey	82	114

Shooting Percentage

(minimum 82 shots)

Name	Team	GP	G	S	%
Daniel Sedin	Vancouver	75	20	127	15.7
Steve Reinprecht	L.A., Col.	80	15	100	15.0
Martin Havlat	Ottawa	73	19	133	14.3
Ruslan Fedotenko	Philadelphia	74	16	119	13.4
Marian Cisar	Nashville	60	12	97	12.4
Tomi Kallio	Atlanta	56	14	115	12.2
Justin Williams	Philadelphia	63	12	99	12.1
Serge Aubin	Columbus	81	13	110	11.8
Brad Richards	Tampa Bay	82	21	179	11.7
Shane Willis	Carolina	73	20	172	11.6

Penalty Minutes

Name	Team	GP	PIM
Dale Purinton	NY Rangers	42	180
Reed Low	St. Louis	56	159
Colin White	New Jersey	82	155
Todd Fedoruk	Philadelphia	53	109
Serge Aubin	Columbus	81	107

Plus/Minus

Name	Team	GP	+/–
Colin White	New Jersey	82	32
Karel Rachunek	Ottawa	71	17
Lubomir Visnovsky	Los Angeles	81	16
Eric Belanger	Los Angeles	62	14
Steve Reinprecht	L.A., Col.	80	10
Ossi Vaananen	Phoenix	81	9

Three-or-More-Goal Games

Player	Team	Date	Final Score	G
Daniel Alfredsson	Ottawa	Mar. 1	S.J. 4 Ott. 8	3
Jason Allison	Boston	Mar. 31	NYI 2 Bos. 4	3
Donald Audette	Atlanta	Oct. 21	Atl. 6 Ott. 6	3
Donald Audette	Atlanta	Dec. 9	Atl. 5 NYI 2	3
Todd Bertuzzi	Vancouver	Dec. 30	Van. 6 S.J. 3	3
Rob Blake	Los Angeles	Dec. 14	NYR 5 L.A. 5	3
Peter Bondra	Washington	Dec. 27	Wsh. 5 Ott. 1	4
Peter Bondra	Washington	Feb. 1	Tor. 4 Wsh. 5	3
Peter Bondra	Washington	Mar. 9	NYR 3 Wsh. 5	3
Radek Bonk	Ottawa	Jan. 4	T.B. 3 Ott. 8	3
Rod Brind'Amour	Carolina	Jan. 7	NYI 2 Car. 5	3
Pavel Bure	Florida	Feb. 10	Fla. 7 Atl. 3	4
Pavel Bure	Florida	Feb. 14	Phx. 3 Fla. 4	3
Pavel Bure	Florida	Mar. 11	Fla. 4 NYI 1	3
Pavel Bure	Florida	Mar. 17	Tor. 5 Fla. 3	3
Andrew Cassels	Vancouver	Nov. 8	Van. 7 Ana. 2	3
Andreas Dackell	Ottawa	Oct. 21	Atl. 6 Ott. 6	3
Pavol Demitra	St. Louis	Dec. 20	St.L. 6 NYR 3	3
Shean Donovan	Atlanta	Nov. 29	Det. 6 Atl. 4	3
Harold Druken	Vancouver	Dec. 8	Van. 6 S.J. 1	3
Jean-Pierre Dumont	Buffalo	Dec. 12	Buf. 3 Bos. 0	3
Radek Dvorak	NY Rangers	Mar. 29	NYR 6 NYI 4	4
Patrik Elias	New Jersey	Dec. 5	Col. 1 N.J. 6	3
Patrik Elias	New Jersey	Mar. 17	N.J. 6 Edm. 5	3
Patrik Elias	New Jersey	Apr. 3	N.J. 6 Wsh. 4	3
Sergei Fedorov	Detroit	Nov. 22	Bos. 5 Det. 4	3
Ray Ferraro	Atlanta	Dec. 4	Bos. 4 Atl. 5	3
Ray Ferraro	Atlanta	Feb. 13	Buf. 4 Atl. 5	3
Theoren Fleury	NY Rangers	Nov. 1	T.B. 1 NYR 6	3
Michal Handzus	St. Louis	Dec. 23	Ana. 2 St.L. 5	3
Todd Harvey	San Jose	Dec. 18	S.J. 5 Wsh. 3	3
*Martin Havlat	Ottawa	Mar. 14	Atl. 1 Ott. 8	3
Steve Heinze	Buffalo	Mar. 16	Van. 2 Buf. 4	3
Jan Hlavac	NY Rangers	Jan. 6	N.J. 5 NYR 5	3
Jonas Hoglund	Toronto	Nov. 18	Tor. 6 Mtl. 1	3
Tomas Holmstrom	Detroit	Mar. 18	Det. 6 S.J. 4	3
Marian Hossa	Ottawa	Nov. 18	Fla. 2 Ott. 5	3
Brett Hull	Dallas	Mar. 18	Ott. 1 Dal. 5	3
Brett Hull	Dallas	Mar. 21	Ana. 0 Dal. 8	4
Jaromir Jagr	Pittsburgh	Oct. 14	NYR 6 Pit. 8	4
Jaromir Jagr	Pittsburgh	Dec. 16	Pit. 4 Mtl. 4	3
Jaromir Jagr	Pittsburgh	Mar. 10	Cgy. 3 Pit. 6	3
*Tomi Kallio	Atlanta	Nov. 4	Atl. 8 Bos. 3	3
Paul Kariya	Anaheim	Feb. 19	Cgy. 2 Ana. 6	3
Paul Kariya	Anaheim	Mar. 29	Ana. 4 S.J. 7	3
Steve Konowalchuk	Washington	Nov. 18	Wsh. 3 Phi. 5	3
Andrei Kovalenko	Boston	Jan. 9	Pit. 2 Bos. 5	3
Alexei Kovalev	Pittsburgh	Nov. 8	Phi. 2 Pit. 5	3
Alexei Kovalev	Pittsburgh	Feb. 7	Phi. 4 Pit. 9	3
Alexei Kovalev	Pittsburgh	Feb. 10	N.J. 4 Pit. 5	3
Alexei Kovalev	Pittsburgh	Feb. 23	NYR 4 Pit. 6	3
Antti Laaksonen	Minnesota	Nov. 26	Van. 2 Min. 4	3
Ian Laperriere	Los Angeles	Oct. 13	Bos. 0 L.A. 5	3
John Leclair	Philadelphia	Dec. 6	T.B. 3 Phi. 6	3
Jere Lehtinen	Dallas	Jan. 17	Nsh. 3 Dal. 4	3
Mario Lemieux	Pittsburgh	Jan. 24	Mtl. 1 Pit. 3	3
John Madden	New Jersey	Oct. 28	N.J. 9 Pit. 0	4
Marty McInnis	Anaheim	Oct. 23	L.A. 5 Ana. 4	3
Randy McKay	New Jersey	Oct. 28	N.J. 9 Pit. 0	4
Fredrik Modin	Tampa Bay	Oct. 22	T.B. 4 NYR 2	3
Alexander Mogilny	New Jersey	Jan. 4	NYI 2 N.J. 4	3
Markus Naslund	Vancouver	Jan. 14	Cgy. 1 Van. 5	3
Petr Nedved	NY Rangers	Feb. 17	NYR 5 T.B. 4	3
Joe Nieuwendyk	Dallas	Dec. 31	NYR 1 Dal. 6	3
Sandis Ozolinsh	Carolina	Mar. 4	Car. 6 Chi. 3	3
Ziggy Palffy	Los Angeles	Nov. 28	L.A. 6 NYR 7	3
Keith Primeau	Philadelphia	Mar. 8	Cgy. 2 Phi. 5	3
Deron Quint	Columbus	Mar. 9	CBJ 7 Fla. 6	3
Mike Ricci	San Jose	Apr. 7	Dal. 5 S.J. 4	3
Jeremy Roenick	Phoenix	Feb. 23	Phx. 7 Buf. 3	3
Joe Sakic	Colorado	Dec. 21	L.A. 2 Col. 5	3
Joe Sakic	Colorado	Apr. 2	Edm. 3 Col. 5	3
Geoff Sanderson	Columbus	Feb. 10	Nsh. 2 CBJ 3	3
Brian Savage	Montreal	Oct. 21	Car. 2 Mtl. 5	3
Teemu Selanne	Anaheim	Feb. 1	Ana. 4 Phx. 2	3
Teemu Selanne	San Jose	Mar. 29	Ana. 4 S.J. 7	3
Brendan Shanahan	Detroit	Mar. 15	Cgy. 2 Det. 5	4
Bryan Smolinski	Los Angeles	Jan. 16	L.A. 7 Ott. 6	3
Ryan Smyth	Edmonton	Nov. 14	St.L. 0 Edm. 3	3
Ryan Smyth	Edmonton	Jan. 14	Ott. 1 Edm. 4	3
Cory Stillman	Calgary	Nov. 29	Cgy. 4 Dal. 3	3
Martin Straka	Pittsburgh	Jan. 8	Pit. 5 Wsh. 3	3
Steve Sullivan	Chicago	Dec. 21	Van. 4 Chi. 6	3
Joe Thornton	Boston	Mar. 1	T.B. 1 Bos. 3	3
Scott Thornton	San Jose	Mar. 7	S.J. 3 Fla. 3	3
Keith Tkachuk	Phoenix	Dec. 20	Cgy. 2 Phx. 4	3
Pierre Turgeon	St. Louis	Dec. 15	St.L. 6 Atl. 3	3
Scott Walker	Nashville	Dec. 26	Col. 2 Nsh. 5	3
*Shane Willis	Carolina	Feb. 21	Atl. 3 Car. 6	3
Tyler Wright	Columbus	Mar. 16	CBJ 3 Atl. 0	3
Alexei Yashin	Ottawa	Jan. 6	Mtl. 3 Ott. 4	3
Richard Zednik	Washington	Oct. 31	Det. 2 Wsh. 6	3
Dainius Zubrus	Montreal	Oct. 14	Chi. 4 Mtl. 5	3

* indicates rookie

2000-2001 Penalty Shots

Scored

David Vyborny (Columbus) scored against Robbie Tallas (Chicago), October 15. Final score: Columbus 1 at Chicago 2.

David Legwand (Nashville) scored against Kirk McLean (NY Rangers), December 23. Final score: Nashville 3 at NY Rangers 2.

Martin Straka (Pittsburgh) scored against Damian Rhodes (Atlanta), January 30. Final score: Pittsburgh 6 at Atlanta 3.

Joe Nieuwendyk (Dallas) scored against Chris Osgood (Detroit), February 18. Final score: Detroit 2 at Dallas 1.

Ray Ferraro (Atlanta) scored against Arturs Irbe (Carolina), February 21. Final score: Atlanta 3 at Carolina 6.

Marty Reasoner (St. Louis) scored against Evgeni Nabokov (San Jose), February 26. Final score: San Jose 2 at St. Louis 7.

David Vyborny (Columbus) scored against Tomas Vokoun (Nashville), March 19. Final score: Nashville 2 at Columbus 1.

Martin Rucinsky (Montreal) scored against Kevin Weekes (Tampa Bay), March 29. Final score: Montreal 6 at Tampa Bay 2.

Joe Sacco (Washington) scored against Arturs Irbe (Carolina), March 30. Final score: Washington 3 at Carolina 4.

Stopped

Glenn Healy (Toronto) stopped Brad Isbister (NY Islanders), October 11. Final score: NY Islanders 2 at Toronto 3.

Joaquin Gage (Edmonton) stopped Scott Pellerin (Minnesota), October 15. Final score: Edmonton 5 at Minnesota 3.

Evgeni Nabokov (San Jose) stopped Martin Straka (Pittsburgh), November 1. Final score: Pittsburgh 2 at San Jose 3.

Dominik Hasek (Buffalo) stopped Dainius Zubrus (Montreal), November 3. Final score: Montreal 4 at Buffalo 5.

Steve Shields (San Jose) stopped Robert Kron (Columbus), November 9. Final score: San Jose 2 at Columbus 5.

Felix Potvin (Vancouver) stopped Maxim Sushinsky (Minnesota), November 26. Final score: Vancouver 2 at Minnesota 4.

John Vanbiesbrouck (NY Islanders) stopped Patrik Elias (New Jersey), December 1. Final score: NY Islanders 0 at New Jersey 0.

Ed Belfour (Dallas) stopped Alex Tanguay (Colorado), December 1. Final score: Dallas 2 at Colorado 4.

Mike Dunham (Nashville) stopped Gary Roberts (Toronto), December 20. Final score: Nashville 3 at Toronto 1.

Patrick Lalime (Ottawa) stopped Antti Laaksonen (Minnesota), December 20. Final score: Ottawa 2 at Minnesota 2.

Dan Cloutier (Tampa Bay) stopped Marian Hossa (Ottawa), January 4. Final score: Tampa Bay 3 at Ottawa 8.

Byron Dafoe (Boston) stopped Martin Straka (Pittsburgh), January 9. Final score: Pittsburgh 2 at Boston 5.

Dan Cloutier (Tampa Bay) stopped Daniel Alfredsson (Ottawa), January 20. Final score: Tampa Bay 0 at Ottawa 3.

Manny Fernandez (Minnesota) stopped Petr Sykora (New Jersey), January 21. Final score: New Jersey 4 at Minnesota 2.

Felix Potvin (Vancouver) stopped Brett Hull (Dallas), January 22. Final score: Vancouver 1 at Dallas 2.

Dominic Roussel (Edmonton) stopped Jeff Friesen (San Jose), January 24. Final score: Edmonton 1 at San Jose 6.

Martin Biron (Buffalo) stopped Mike Johnson (Tampa Bay), February 1. Final score: Buffalo 2 at Tampa Bay 4.

Martin Brodeur (New Jersey) stopped Dave Scatchard (NY Islanders), February 27. Final score: New Jersey 4 at NY Islanders 1.

Jean-Sebastien Aubin (Pittsburgh) stopped Martin Rucinsky (Montreal), February 28. Final score: Pittsburgh 2 at Montreal 4.

Marc Denis (Columbus) stopped Jeremy Roenick (Phoenix), February 28. Final score: Phoenix 2 at Columbus 5.

Norm Maracle (Atlanta) stopped Andrew Cassels (Vancouver), March 18. Final score: Vancouver 5 at Atlanta 3.

Tomas Vokoun (Nashville) stopped Alexei Zhamnov (Chicago), March 22. Final score: Nashville 2 at Chicago 1.

Fred Brathwaite (Calgary) stopped Ziggy Palffy (Los Angeles), April 7. Final score: Los Angeles 3 at Calgary 2.

Summary

32 penalty shots resulted in 9 goals

Goaltending Leaders

Minimum 26 games

Goals Against Average

Goaltender	Team	GPI	Mins	GA	Avg
*Marty Turco	Dallas	26	1266	40	1.90
Roman Cechmanek	Philadelphia	59	3431	115	2.01
Manny Legace	Detroit	39	2136	73	2.05
Dominik Hasek	Buffalo	67	3904	137	2.11
*Brent Johnson	St. Louis	31	1744	63	2.17

Save Percentage

Goaltender	Team	GPI	MINS	GA	SA	S%	W	L	T
*Marty Turco	Dallas	26	1266	40	532	.925	13	6	1
Mike Dunham	Nashville	48	2810	107	1381	.923	21	21	4
Sean Burke	Phoenix	62	3644	138	1766	.922	25	22	13
Dominik Hasek	Buffalo	67	3904	137	1726	.921	37	24	4
Roman Cechmanek	Philadelphia	59	3431	115	1464	.921	35	15	6

Wins

Goaltender	Team	GPI	MINS	W	L	T
Martin Brodeur	New Jersey	72	4297	42	17	11
Patrick Roy	Colorado	62	3585	40	13	7
Dominik Hasek	Buffalo	67	3904	37	24	4
Olaf Kolzig	Washington	72	4279	37	26	8
Arturs Irbe	Carolina	77	4406	37	29	9
Patrick Lalime	Ottawa	60	3607	36	19	5
Tommy Salo	Edmonton	73	4364	36	25	12
Roman Cechmanek	Philadelphia	59	3431	35	15	6
Ed Belfour	Dallas	63	3687	35	20	7

Shutouts

Goaltender	Team	GPI	MINS	SO	W	L	T
Dominik Hasek	Buffalo	67	3904	11	37	24	4
Roman Cechmanek	Philadelphia	59	3431	10	35	15	6
Martin Brodeur	New Jersey	72	4297	9	42	17	11
Ed Belfour	Dallas	63	3687	8	35	20	7
Tommy Salo	Edmonton	73	4364	8	36	25	12
Patrick Lalime	Ottawa	60	3607	7	36	19	5

Team-by-Team Point Totals

1996-97 to 2000-01

(Ranked by five-year point %)

	00-01	99-00	98-99	97-98	96-97	Pts%
Dallas	106	102	114	109	104	.652
New Jersey	111	103	105	107	104	.646
Colorado	118	96	98	95	107	.627
Detroit	111	108	93	103	94	.621
Philadelphia	100	105	93	95	103	.605
St. Louis	103	114	87	98	83	.591
Ottawa	109	95	103	83	77	.570
Pittsburgh	96	88	90	98	84	.556
Buffalo	98	85	91	89	92	.555
Phoenix	90	90	90	82	83	.530
Washington	96	102	68	92	75	.528
Toronto	90	100	97	69	68	.517
Edmonton	93	88	78	80	81	.512
Los Angeles	92	94	69	87	67	.499
Car./Hfd.	88	84	86	74	75	.496
Boston	88	73	91	91	61	.493
San Jose	95	87	80	78	62	.490
Florida	66	98	78	63	89	.480
Montreal	70	83	75	87	77	.478
Anaheim	66	83	83	65	85	.466
NY Rangers	72	73	77	68	86	.459
Chicago	71	78	70	73	81	.455
Vancouver	90	83	58	64	77	.454
Calgary	73	77	72	67	73	.441
Nashville	80	70	63	—	—	.433
Columbus	71	—	—	—	—	.433
Minnesota	68	—	—	—	—	.415
NY Islanders	52	58	58	71	70	.377
Tampa Bay	59	54	47	44	74	.339
Atlanta	60	39	—	—	—	.302

Team Record When Scoring First Goal of a Game

Team	GP	FG	W	L	T
Buffalo	82	50	38	8	4
Ottawa	82	50	36	7	7
Philadelphia	82	50	33	10	7
Los Angeles	82	48	30	9	9
Detroit	82	47	35	6	6
Dallas	82	45	36	4	5
Vancouver	82	45	27	10	8
Phoenix	82	45	24	9	12
Colorado	82	44	34	5	5
New Jersey	82	44	32	10	2
Tampa Bay	82	43	20	22	1
Columbus	82	43	19	19	5
St. Louis	82	41	32	5	4
NY Rangers	82	40	26	11	3
Carolina	82	40	25	10	5
Washington	82	39	30	5	4
Edmonton	82	39	27	9	3
Toronto	82	39	26	10	3
Nashville	82	38	26	8	4
San Jose	82	38	25	8	5
Calgary	82	38	21	11	6
Chicago	82	38	20	14	4
Boston	82	37	24	10	3
Anaheim	82	37	18	14	5
Florida	82	37	14	14	9
Pittsburgh	82	36	24	12	0
Minnesota	82	36	18	13	5
NY Islanders	82	35	17	15	3
Atlanta	82	34	18	11	5
Montreal	82	27	20	4	3

Team Plus/Minus Differential

Team	GF	PPGF	Net GF	GA	PPGA	Net GA	Goal Differential
New Jersey	295	71	**224**	195	49	**146**	+78
Colorado	270	80	**190**	192	59	**133**	+57
Ottawa	274	71	**203**	205	49	**156**	+47
St. Louis	249	72	**177**	195	57	**138**	+39
Philadelphia	240	55	**185**	207	55	**152**	+33
Dallas	241	72	**169**	187	49	**138**	+31
San Jose	217	57	**160**	192	61	**131**	+29
Pittsburgh	281	76	**205**	256	78	**178**	+27
Los Angeles	252	71	**181**	228	72	**156**	+25
Edmonton	243	59	**184**	222	62	**160**	+24
Toronto	232	57	**175**	207	55	**152**	+23
Detroit	253	85	**168**	202	55	**147**	+21
Buffalo	218	60	**158**	184	40	**144**	+14
Washington	233	75	**158**	211	62	**149**	+ 9
Phoenix	214	57	**157**	212	64	**148**	+ 9
Vancouver	239	71	**168**	238	74	**164**	+ 4
Nashville	186	51	**135**	200	49	**151**	-16
NY Rangers	250	65	**185**	290	86	**204**	-19
Boston	227	64	**163**	249	65	**184**	-21
Minnesota	168	36	**132**	210	57	**153**	-21
Chicago	210	41	**169**	246	52	**194**	-25
Florida	200	46	**154**	246	64	**182**	-28
Calgary	197	65	**132**	236	76	**160**	-28
Columbus	190	56	**134**	233	70	**163**	-29
Montreal	206	68	**138**	232	60	**172**	-34
Carolina	212	72	**140**	225	45	**180**	-40
Atlanta	211	54	**157**	289	90	**199**	-42
Anaheim	188	66	**122**	245	71	**174**	-52
NY Islanders	185	51	**134**	268	79	**189**	-55
Tampa Bay	201	53	**148**	280	72	**208**	-60

Team Record When Leading, Trailing, Tied

Team	Leading after 1 period			Leading after 2 periods			Trailing after 1 period			Trailing after 2 periods			Tied after 1 period			Tied after 2 periods		
	W	L	T	W	L	T	W	L	T	W	L	T	W	L	T	W	L	T
Anaheim	10	8	5	18	4	2	4	26	3	2	36	1	11	12	3	5	6	8
Atlanta	12	9	4	19	1	2	1	25	1	1	38	5	10	13	7	3	8	5
Boston	19	4	2	25	3	1	5	20	3	2	25	2	12	14	3	9	10	5
Buffalo	25	3	1	36	2	0	2	14	1	2	23	2	19	14	3	8	6	3
Calgary	14	6	1	22	3	5	1	22	5	2	30	3	12	12	9	3	7	7
Carolina	18	6	2	24	1	2	9	16	3	3	24	1	11	13	4	11	10	6
Chicago	14	7	2	19	3	1	4	22	4	1	35	2	11	16	2	9	7	5
Colorado	27	4	2	40	3	4	8	11	5	2	12	2	17	5	3	10	5	4
Columbus	17	8	2	22	3	3	4	22	3	1	32	2	7	15	4	5	10	4
Dallas	24	1	4	35	1	1	5	14	0	1	22	1	19	11	4	12	3	6
Detroit	20	3	2	32	0	2	7	13	1	6	18	2	22	8	6	11	6	5
Edmonton	16	4	3	29	3	2	5	15	3	2	21	6	18	12	6	8	7	4
Florida	8	6	5	13	6	7	3	24	0	2	34	2	11	17	8	7	7	4
Los Angeles	23	3	7	31	3	2	4	12	1	1	23	2	11	16	5	6	5	9
Minnesota	9	8	3	21	6	5	3	16	1	1	31	3	13	20	9	3	7	5
Montreal	16	3	1	23	2	1	4	26	5	2	36	6	8	17	2	3	8	1
Nashville	18	5	4	25	1	3	6	25	3	5	31	1	10	9	2	4	7	5
New Jersey	26	4	1	35	2	1	9	10	4	4	15	4	13	8	7	9	5	7
NY Islanders	7	6	1	13	4	2	5	26	3	1	44	1	9	22	3	7	6	4
NY Rangers	16	7	2	27	2	3	4	24	1	4	29	0	13	13	2	2	13	2
Ottawa	28	5	5	36	3	4	5	11	2	1	14	2	15	9	2	11	8	3
Philadelphia	20	6	4	31	5	2	5	15	3	4	19	4	18	7	4	8	4	5
Phoenix	16	6	6	29	1	8	8	16	2	3	19	2	11	8	9	3	10	7
Pittsburgh	22	8	0	26	3	0	10	16	7	4	26	4	10	7	2	12	2	5
San Jose	19	4	2	22	0	1	10	14	2	7	24	3	11	12	8	11	6	8
St. Louis	23	3	2	33	3	3	6	11	5	4	21	3	14	13	5	6	3	6
Tampa Bay	12	9	1	17	5	1	2	24	2	1	32	1	10	19	3	6	15	4
Toronto	22	7	3	27	5	1	7	18	4	5	23	3	8	9	4	5	6	7
Vancouver	22	5	4	26	3	5	5	19	3	4	24	4	9	11	4	6	8	2
Washington	23	2	3	27	1	4	9	19	4	4	22	4	9	10	3	10	8	2

Team Statistics

TEAMS' HOME-AND-ROAD RECORD

Eastern Conference

	Home								Road							
	GP	W	L	T	RT	GF	GA	PTS	GP	W	L	T	RT	GF	GA	PTS
N.J.	41	24	11	6	0	145	92	54	41	24	8	6	3	150	103	57
OTT	41	26	7	5	3	151	102	60	41	22	14	4	1	123	103	49
PHI	41	26	11	4	0	120	84	56	41	17	14	7	3	120	123	44
BUF	41	26	12	3	0	120	89	55	41	20	18	2	1	98	95	43
PIT	41	24	15	2	0	142	125	50	41	18	13	7	3	139	131	46
WSH	41	24	9	6	2	129	98	56	41	17	18	4	2	104	113	40
TOR	41	19	11	7	4	126	96	49	41	18	18	4	1	106	111	41
CAR	41	23	15	3	0	129	115	49	41	15	17	6	3	83	110	39
BOS	41	21	12	5	3	125	115	50	41	15	18	3	5	102	134	38
NYR	41	17	20	3	1	125	136	38	41	16	23	2	0	125	154	34
MTL	41	15	20	4	2	104	118	36	41	13	20	4	4	102	114	34
FLA	41	12	18	7	4	96	116	35	41	10	20	6	5	104	130	31
ATL	41	10	23	6	2	107	147	28	41	13	22	6	0	104	142	32
T.B.	41	17	19	3	2	109	125	39	41	7	28	3	3	92	155	20
NYI	41	12	27	1	1	96	142	26	41	9	24	6	2	89	126	26
Total	**615**	**296**	**230**	**65**	**24**	**1824**	**1700**	**681**	**615**	**234**	**275**	**70**	**36**	**1641**	**1844**	**574**

Western Conference

	GP	W	L	T	RT	GF	GA	PTS	GP	W	L	T	RT	GF	GA	PTS
COL	41	28	6	5	2	141	94	63	41	24	10	5	2	129	98	55
DET	41	27	9	3	2	134	101	59	41	22	11	6	2	119	101	52
DAL	41	26	10	5	0	132	85	57	41	22	14	3	2	109	102	49
ST.L.	41	28	5	5	3	133	76	64	41	15	17	7	2	116	119	39
S.J.	41	22	14	4	1	117	102	49	41	18	13	8	2	100	90	46
EDM	41	23	9	7	2	124	92	55	41	16	19	5	1	119	130	38
L.A.	41	20	12	8	1	140	111	49	41	18	16	5	2	112	117	43
VAN	41	21	12	5	3	124	113	50	41	15	16	6	4	115	125	40
PHX	41	21	11	7	2	114	100	51	41	14	16	10	1	100	112	39
NSH	41	16	18	7	0	92	102	39	41	18	18	2	3	94	98	41
CGY	41	12	18	9	2	95	110	35	41	15	18	6	2	102	126	38
CHI	41	14	21	4	2	94	123	34	41	15	19	4	3	116	123	37
CBJ	41	19	15	4	3	105	108	45	41	9	24	5	3	85	125	26
MIN	41	14	13	10	4	87	94	42	41	11	26	3	1	81	116	26
ANA	41	15	20	4	2	95	120	36	41	10	21	7	3	93	125	30
Total	**615**	**306**	**193**	**87**	**29**	**1727**	**1531**	**728**	**615**	**242**	**258**	**82**	**33**	**1590**	**1707**	**599**
	1230	**602**	**423**	**152**	**53**	**3551**	**3231**	**1409**	**1230**	**476**	**533**	**152**	**69**	**3231**	**3551**	**1173**

TEAMS' DIVISIONAL RECORD

Northeast Division

	Against Own Division								Against Other Divisions							
	GP	W	L	T	RT	GF	GA	PTS	GP	W	L	T	RT	GF	GA	PTS
OTT	20	13	5	1	1	56	44	28	62	35	16	8	3	218	161	81
BUF	20	11	7	2	0	51	39	24	62	35	23	3	1	167	145	74
TOR	20	7	10	2	1	46	48	17	62	30	19	9	4	186	159	73
BOS	20	11	6	1	2	46	49	25	62	25	24	7	6	181	200	63
MTL	20	5	13	0	2	44	63	12	62	23	27	8	4	162	169	58
Total	**100**	**47**	**41**	**6**	**6**	**243**	**243**	**106**	**310**	**148**	**109**	**35**	**18**	**914**	**834**	**349**

Atlantic Division

	GP	W	L	T	RT	GF	GA	PTS	GP	W	L	T	RT	GF	GA	PTS
N.J.	20	7	5	7	1	65	47	22	62	41	14	5	2	230	148	89
PHI	20	11	5	2	2	59	53	26	62	32	20	9	1	181	154	74
PIT	20	12	5	2	1	81	72	27	62	30	23	7	2	200	184	69
NYR	20	5	12	3	0	59	78	13	62	28	31	2	1	191	212	59
NYI	20	7	10	2	1	50	64	17	62	14	41	5	2	135	204	35
Total	**100**	**42**	**37**	**16**	**5**	**314**	**314**	**105**	**310**	**145**	**129**	**28**	**8**	**937**	**902**	**326**

Southeast Division

	GP	W	L	T	RT	GF	GA	PTS	GP	W	L	T	RT	GF	GA	PTS
WSH	20	12	4	3	1	59	42	28	62	29	23	7	3	174	169	68
CAR	20	11	5	4	0	59	50	26	62	27	27	5	3	153	175	62
FLA	20	5	10	3	2	49	58	15	62	17	28	10	7	151	188	51
ATL	20	6	10	4	0	51	68	16	62	17	35	8	2	160	221	44
T.B.	20	9	8	0	3	57	57	21	62	15	39	6	2	144	223	38
Total	**100**	**43**	**37**	**14**	**6**	**275**	**275**	**106**	**310**	**105**	**152**	**36**	**17**	**782**	**976**	**263**

Central Division

	GP	W	L	T	RT	GF	GA	PTS	GP	W	L	T	RT	GF	GA	PTS
DET	20	11	3	3	3	64	49	28	62	38	17	6	1	189	153	83
ST.L.	20	9	7	4	0	55	43	22	62	34	15	8	5	194	152	81
NSH	20	8	11	1	0	41	52	17	62	26	25	8	3	145	148	63
CHI	20	11	7	0	2	57	56	24	62	18	33	8	3	153	190	47
CBJ	20	6	10	2	2	39	56	16	62	22	29	7	4	151	177	55
Total	**100**	**45**	**38**	**10**	**7**	**256**	**256**	**107**	**310**	**138**	**119**	**37**	**16**	**832**	**820**	**329**

Pacific Division

	GP	W	L	T	RT	GF	GA	PTS	GP	W	L	T	RT	GF	GA	PTS
DAL	20	11	6	3	0	57	52	25	62	37	18	5	2	184	135	81
S.J.	20	11	5	2	2	45	38	26	62	29	22	10	1	172	154	69
L.A.	20	8	7	4	1	61	50	21	62	30	21	9	2	191	178	71
PHX	20	7	7	5	1	51	56	20	62	28	20	12	2	163	156	70
ANA	20	5	10	2	3	47	65	15	62	20	31	9	2	141	180	51
Total	**100**	**42**	**35**	**16**	**7**	**261**	**261**	**107**	**310**	**144**	**112**	**45**	**9**	**851**	**803**	**342**

Northwest Division

	GP	W	L	T	RT	GF	GA	PTS	GP	W	L	T	RT	GF	GA	PTS
COL	20	14	5	1	0	64	45	29	62	38	11	9	4	206	147	89
EDM	20	11	5	3	1	60	49	26	62	28	23	9	2	183	173	67
VAN	20	10	6	1	3	64	65	24	62	26	22	10	4	175	173	66
CGY	20	5	10	3	2	38	47	15	62	22	26	12	2	159	189	58
MIN	20	4	10	4	2	38	58	14	62	21	29	9	3	130	152	54
Total	**100**	**44**	**36**	**12**	**8**	**264**	**264**	**108**	**310**	**135**	**111**	**49**	**15**	**853**	**834**	**334**

TEAM STREAKS

Consecutive Wins

Games	Team	From	To
13	New Jersey	Feb. 26	Mar. 23
9	Colorado	Oct. 10	Oct. 28
9	Edmonton	Feb. 20	Mar. 13
8	St. Louis	Nov. 24	Dec. 15
7	St. Louis	Oct. 19	Nov. 2
7	Colorado	Jan. 16	Jan. 30
6	Philadelphia	Nov. 9	Nov. 22
6	New Jersey	Nov. 16	Nov. 29

Consecutive Home Wins

Games	Team	From	To
8	Detroit	Jan. 24	Feb. 25
7	Washington	Nov. 17	Dec. 16
7	New Jersey	Feb. 26	Mar. 23
6	St. Louis	Oct. 13	Nov. 2
6	Colorado	Nov. 11	Dec. 1
6	Philadelphia	Jan. 20	Feb. 19
6	Detroit	Mar. 15	Apr. 7
5	Phoenix	Oct. 5	Oct. 28
5	Buffalo	Oct. 25	Nov. 13
5	Philadelphia	Dec. 6	Dec. 23
5	Colorado	Dec. 21	Jan. 2
5	Boston	Feb. 6	Mar. 3
5	Ottawa	Feb. 12	Feb. 24
5	Edmonton	Feb. 20	Mar. 7
5	Anaheim	Mar. 4	Apr. 1
5	Buffalo	Mar. 14	Mar. 30

Consecutive Road Wins

Games	Team	From	To
10	New Jersey	Feb. 27	Apr. 7
6	Dallas	Mar. 13	Apr. 7
5	Colorado	Oct. 10	Oct. 26
5	Toronto	Nov. 18	Dec. 13
5	St. Louis	Nov. 24	Dec. 20
5	Washington	Feb. 14	Mar. 7

Consecutive Undefeated

Games	Team	W	T	From	To
13	Detroit	10	3	Jan. 31	Mar. 2
13	New Jersey	13	0	Feb. 26	Mar. 23
13	Dallas	10	3	Mar. 13	Apr. 7
12	Phoenix	7	5	Oct. 14	Nov. 7
12	St. Louis	11	1	Nov. 24	Dec. 26
12	Washington	10	2	Jan. 28	Feb. 24
11	Colorado	9	2	Oct. 4	Oct. 28
11	New Jersey	7	4	Dec. 20	Jan. 13
10	St. Louis	8	2	Oct. 19	Nov. 11
10	Colorado	9	1	Jan. 10	Jan. 30
10	Edmonton	9	1	Feb. 20	Mar. 14
9	Ottawa	6	3	Oct. 5	Oct. 27
9	San Jose	7	2	Oct. 20	Nov. 8
9	New Jersey	7	2	Nov. 16	Dec. 5
9	Carolina	7	2	Dec. 31	Jan. 18

Consecutive Home Undefeated

Games	Team	W	T	From	To
19	Detroit	17	2	Dec. 31	Apr. 7
11	Colorado	8	3	Nov. 3	Dec. 13
10	Buffalo	8	2	Oct. 5	Nov. 17
9	St. Louis	8	1	Oct. 13	Nov. 18
9	Washington	7	2	Nov. 12	Dec. 16
9	New Jersey	6	3	Dec. 11	Jan. 13
9	Minnesota	5	4	Dec. 13	Jan. 10
9	Carolina	8	1	Dec. 15	Jan. 18
9	Colorado	8	1	Dec. 21	Jan. 26
8	Philadelphia	7	1	Jan. 20	Feb. 25
8	Dallas	5	3	Mar. 10	Apr. 4

Consecutive Road Undefeated

Games	Team	W	T	From	To
10	San Jose	6	4	Dec. 26	Feb. 16
10	New Jersey	10	0	Feb. 27	Apr. 7
9	Washington	8	1	Feb. 7	Mar. 7
8	Phoenix	4	4	Oct. 15	Nov. 7
8	Edmonton	6	2	Feb. 12	Mar. 21
7	Colorado	5	2	Oct. 4	Oct. 26
7	Atlanta	3	4	Oct. 21	Nov. 13
7	New Jersey	6	1	Dec. 22	Jan. 24
7	Colorado	6	1	Jan. 10	Jan. 30
7	Detroit	4	3	Jan. 31	Mar. 2
6	San Jose	5	1	Oct. 20	Nov. 8
6	Pittsburgh	3	3	Dec. 10	Jan. 8
6	Dallas	6	0	Mar. 13	Apr. 7

TEAM PENALTIES

Abbreviations: GP – games played; **PEN** – total penalty minutes including bench minutes; **BMI** – total bench minor minutes; **AVG** – average penalty minutes/game calculated by dividing total penalty minutes by games played

Team	GP	PEN	BMI	AVG
NSH	82	944	8	11.5
CHI	82	1001	24	12.2
MTL	82	1020	18	12.4
DAL	82	1041	10	12.7
OTT	82	1062	10	13.0
CAR	82	1083	10	13.2
DET	82	1082	20	13.2
VAN	82	1113	22	13.6
ANA	82	1136	12	13.9
COL	82	1138	16	13.9
WSH	82	1141	10	13.9
PHI	82	1183	8	14.4
L.A.	82	1196	20	14.6
MIN	82	1200	26	14.6
CBJ	82	1234	20	15.0
N.J.	82	1235	18	15.1
BUF	82	1249	8	15.2
EDM	82	1287	10	15.7
BOS	82	1325	18	16.2
NYI	82	1339	14	16.3
PHX	82	1337	12	16.3
ST.L.	82	1345	14	16.4
S.J.	82	1364	10	16.6
CGY	82	1376	14	16.8
T.B.	82	1404	20	17.1
TOR	82	1430	6	17.4
ATL	82	1500	6	18.3
FLA	82	1509	10	18.4
NYR	82	1522	18	18.6
PIT	82	1585	12	19.3
Total	**1230**	**37381**	**424**	**30.4**

The New Jersey Devils were the NHL's most efficient team on the power-play in 2000-01. Petr Sykora helped lead the way, scoring nine of his career-high 35 goals when the Devils had a man advantage.

TEAMS' POWER-PLAY RECORD

Abbreviations: ADV – total advantages; **PPGF** – power-play goals for; **%** – calculated by dividing number of power-play goals by total advantages.

	Home					Road					Overall				
	Team	GP	ADV	PPGF	%	Team	GP	ADV	PPGF	%	Team	GP	ADV	PPGF	%
1	N.J.	41	155	40	25.8	COL	41	180	44	24.4	N.J.	82	310	71	22.9
2	WSH	41	188	46	24.5	DET	41	186	44	23.7	DET	82	384	85	22.1
3	PIT	41	187	41	21.9	N.J.	41	155	31	20.0	COL	82	363	80	22.0
4	ST.L.	41	196	42	21.4	DAL	41	171	32	18.7	WSH	82	353	75	21.2
5	DET	41	198	41	20.7	PIT	41	188	35	18.6	PIT	82	375	76	20.3
6	OTT	41	209	43	20.6	L.A.	41	169	31	18.3	DAL	82	367	72	19.6
7	DAL	41	196	40	20.4	NYR	41	176	32	18.2	L.A.	82	367	71	19.3
8	CAR	41	211	43	20.4	ANA	41	168	30	17.9	CAR	82	382	72	18.8
9	L.A.	41	198	40	20.2	WSH	41	165	29	17.6	ST.L.	82	385	72	18.7
10	COL	41	183	36	19.7	CGY	41	211	37	17.5	OTT	82	381	71	18.6
11	PHI	41	173	33	19.1	CAR	41	171	29	17.0	NYR	82	363	65	17.9
12	VAN	41	223	41	18.4	OTT	41	172	28	16.3	ANA	82	373	66	17.7
13	PHX	41	194	35	18.0	TOR	41	173	28	16.2	VAN	82	416	71	17.1
14	BUF	41	196	35	17.9	FLA	41	163	26	16.0	PHX	82	343	57	16.6
15	ATL	41	196	35	17.9	ST.L.	41	189	30	15.9	BOS	82	390	64	16.4
16	ANA	41	205	36	17.6	MTL	41	214	34	15.9	MTL	82	421	68	16.2
17	NYR	41	187	33	17.6	EDM	41	199	31	15.6	BUF	82	373	60	16.1
18	BOS	41	207	36	17.4	VAN	41	193	30	15.5	TOR	82	355	57	16.1
19	NSH	41	188	32	17.0	BOS	41	183	28	15.3	PHI	82	350	55	15.7
20	CBJ	41	219	37	16.9	PHX	41	149	22	14.8	CGY	82	435	65	14.9
21	MTL	41	207	34	16.4	BUF	41	177	25	14.1	EDM	82	398	59	14.8
22	TOR	41	182	29	15.9	CHI	41	161	22	13.7	CBJ	82	381	56	14.7
23	S.J	41	219	32	14.6	S.J	41	187	25	13.4	NSH	82	361	51	14.1
24	EDM	41	199	28	14.1	NYI	41	178	22	12.4	S.J	82	406	57	14.0
25	T.B.	41	214	30	14.0	PHI	41	177	22	12.4	ATL	82	395	54	13.7
26	NYI	41	208	29	13.9	CBJ	41	162	19	11.7	NYI	82	386	51	13.2
27	CGY	41	224	28	12.5	NSH	41	173	19	11.0	FLA	82	353	46	13.0
28	CHI	41	157	19	12.1	T.B.	41	210	23	11.0	CHI	82	318	41	12.9
29	FLA	41	190	20	10.5	MIN	41	176	17	9.7	T.B.	82	424	53	12.5
30	MIN	41	198	19	9.6	ATL	41	199	19	9.5	MIN	82	374	36	9.6
TOTAL		**1230**	**5907**	**1033**	**17.5**		**1230**	**5375**	**844**	**15.7**		**1230**	**11282**	**1877**	**16.6**

TEAMS' PENALTY KILLING RECORD

Abbreviations: TSH – total times short-handed; **PPGA** – power-play goals against; **%** – calculated by dividing times short minus power-play goals against by times short.

	Home					Road					Overall				
	Team	GP	TSH	PPGA	%	Team	GP	TSH	PPGA	%	Team	GP	TSH	PPGA	%
1	CAR	41	170	19	88.8	S.J	41	244	27	88.9	BUF	82	334	40	88.0
2	OTT	41	181	22	87.8	BUF	41	175	20	88.6	CAR	82	351	45	87.2
3	NSH	41	168	21	87.5	DET	41	205	26	87.3	OTT	82	361	49	86.4
4	BUF	41	159	20	87.4	DAL	41	165	23	86.1	DAL	82	355	49	86.2
5	MIN	41	193	25	87.0	CAR	41	181	26	85.6	S.J	82	441	61	86.2
6	TOR	41	174	23	86.8	OTT	41	180	27	85.0	DET	82	385	55	85.7
7	PHX	41	210	28	86.7	ST.L.	41	203	32	84.2	ST.L.	82	389	57	85.3
8	ST.L.	41	186	25	86.6	N.J.	41	176	28	84.1	PHX	82	432	64	85.2
9	EDM	41	169	23	86.4	PHX	41	222	36	83.8	NSH	82	331	49	85.2
10	DAL	41	190	26	86.3	WSH	41	213	35	83.6	TOR	82	366	55	85.0
11	FLA	41	189	27	85.7	TOR	41	192	32	83.3	N.J.	82	320	49	84.7
12	N.J.	41	144	21	85.4	COL	41	185	31	83.2	MIN	82	373	57	84.7
13	T.B.	41	205	30	85.4	NYI	41	239	41	82.8	WSH	82	391	62	84.1
14	CHI	41	150	22	85.3	NSH	41	163	28	82.8	CHI	82	323	52	83.9
15	PHI	41	158	24	84.8	CHI	41	173	30	82.7	FLA	82	398	64	83.9
16	WSH	41	178	27	84.8	VAN	41	200	35	82.5	EDM	82	382	62	83.8
17	MTL	41	155	24	84.5	FLA	41	209	37	82.3	T.B.	82	422	72	82.9
18	BOS	41	175	28	84.0	MIN	41	180	32	82.2	BOS	82	377	65	82.8
19	DET	41	180	29	83.9	ANA	41	202	36	82.2	COL	82	342	59	82.7
20	CGY	41	179	30	83.2	BOS	41	202	37	81.7	PHI	82	314	55	82.5
21	CBJ	41	179	30	83.2	EDM	41	213	39	81.7	MTL	82	337	60	82.2
22	S.J	41	197	34	82.7	PIT	41	224	43	80.8	NYI	82	445	79	82.2
23	L.A.	41	180	32	82.2	T.B.	41	217	42	80.6	ANA	82	390	71	81.8
24	COL	41	157	28	82.2	MTL	41	182	36	80.2	L.A.	82	382	72	81.2
25	NYI	41	206	38	81.6	L.A.	41	202	40	80.2	VAN	82	387	74	80.9
26	ANA	41	188	35	81.4	PHI	41	156	31	80.1	PIT	82	405	78	80.7
27	NYR	41	191	36	81.2	CBJ	41	184	40	78.3	CBJ	82	363	70	80.7
28	PIT	41	181	35	80.7	ATL	41	212	47	77.8	CGY	82	378	76	79.9
29	VAN	41	187	39	79.1	CGY	41	199	46	76.9	NYR	82	400	86	78.5
30	ATL	41	196	43	78.1	NYR	41	209	50	76.1	ATL	82	408	90	77.9
TOTAL		**1230**	**5375**	**844**	**84.3**		**1230**	**5907**	**1033**	**82.5**		**1230**	**11282**	**1877**	**83.4**

SHORT-HANDED GOALS FOR

	Home			Road			Overall		
	Team	GP	SHGF	Team	GP	SHGF	Team	GP	SHGF
1	MIN	41	10	CHI	41	8	NYR	82	16
2	L.A.	41	10	VAN	41	8	CHI	82	15
3	NYR	41	9	ST.L.	41	8	ST.L.	82	15
4	COL	41	8	NYI	41	8	L.A.	82	14
5	OTT	41	7	EDM	41	8	EDM	82	13
6	CHI	41	7	PHI	41	8	MIN	82	13
7	ST.L.	41	7	NYR	41	7	VAN	82	12
8	PHX	41	6	N.J.	41	7	COL	82	11
9	S.J.	41	6	DET	41	4	PHI	82	11
10	DET	41	6	MTL	41	4	OTT	82	10
11	T.B.	41	5	L.A.	41	4	DET	82	10
12	EDM	41	5	BOS	41	4	PHX	82	9
13	ATL	41	5	WSH	41	4	N.J.	82	9
14	NSH	41	5	PIT	41	4	T.B.	82	9
15	DAL	41	4	FLA	41	4	NYI	82	9
16	BOS	41	4	T.B.	41	4	ATL	82	9
17	FLA	41	4	ATL	41	4	BOS	82	8
18	ANA	41	4	COL	41	3	FLA	82	8
19	VAN	41	4	OTT	41	3	S.J.	82	8
20	BUF	41	3	MIN	41	3	DAL	82	7
21	PHI	41	3	DAL	41	3	PIT	82	7
22	PIT	41	3	PHX	41	3	NSH	82	7
23	CAR	41	3	CAR	41	3	BUF	82	6
24	CGY	41	2	BUF	41	3	WSH	82	6
25	N.J.	41	2	NSH	41	2	ANA	82	6
26	WSH	41	2	CBJ	41	2	CAR	82	6
27	TOR	41	2	ANA	41	2	MTL	82	5
28	CBJ	41	1	S.J.	41	2	CGY	82	3
29	MTL	41	1	CGY	41	1	CBJ	82	3
30	NYI	41	1	TOR	41	0	TOR	82	2
TOTAL		**1230**	**139**		**1230**	**128**		**1230**	**267**

SHORT-HANDED GOALS AGAINST

	Home			Road			Overall		
	Team	GP	SHGA	Team	GP	SHGA	Team	GP	SHGA
1	BOS	41	1	MTL	41	0	MTL	82	3
2	EDM	41	1	NSH	41	0	EDM	82	4
3	ST.L.	41	1	OTT	41	1	NSH	82	4
4	DAL	41	2	ATL	41	2	OTT	82	5
5	BUF	41	2	DET	41	3	BUF	82	5
6	N.J.	41	2	L.A.	41	3	PHX	82	6
7	T.B.	41	2	EDM	41	3	N.J.	82	6
8	PHX	41	3	CBJ	41	3	L.A.	82	6
9	WSH	41	3	PHX	41	3	DAL	82	7
10	TOR	41	3	BUF	41	3	BOS	82	7
11	MTL	41	3	NYI	41	4	DET	82	7
12	L.A.	41	3	WSH	41	4	ST.L.	82	7
13	VAN	41	3	NYR	41	4	WSH	82	7
14	COL	41	3	N.J.	41	4	ATL	82	8
15	PHI	41	4	DAL	41	5	CBJ	82	8
16	CGY	41	4	PIT	41	5	PHI	82	9
17	OTT	41	4	PHI	41	5	TOR	82	9
18	NSH	41	4	ANA	41	5	S.J.	82	10
19	DET	41	4	S.J.	41	5	COL	82	11
20	S.J.	41	5	CHI	41	6	VAN	82	11
21	CBJ	41	5	ST.L.	41	6	CGY	82	11
22	FLA	41	6	BOS	41	6	T.B.	82	11
23	PIT	41	6	TOR	41	6	PIT	82	11
24	ATL	41	6	MIN	41	7	CHI	82	12
25	CHI	41	6	FLA	41	7	NYR	82	12
26	MIN	41	7	CAR	41	7	FLA	82	13
27	ANA	41	8	CGY	41	7	ANA	82	13
28	NYR	41	8	COL	41	8	NYI	82	14
29	CAR	41	9	VAN	41	8	MIN	82	14
30	NYI	41	10	T.B.	41	9	CAR	82	16
TOTAL		**1230**	**128**		**1230**	**139**		**1230**	**267**

Overtime Results

1983-84 to 2000-01

Team	2000-01 GP	W	L	T	1999-2000 GP	W	L	T	1998-99 GP	W	L	T	1997-98 GP	W	L	T	1996-97 GP	W	L	T
ANA	20	4	5	11	18	3	3	12	17	1	3	13	20	3	4	13	16	3	0	13
ATL	16	2	2	12	11	0	4	7	...	...	...	...	...	...	...	...	...	...	...	...
BOS	20	4	8	8	26	1	6	19	17	2	2	13	17	3	1	13	15	3	3	9
BUF	10	4	1	5	20	5	4	11	23	3	3	17	21	3	1	17	21	5	4	12
CGY	22	3	4	15	26	11	5	10	16	3	1	12	22	4	3	15	16	3	4	9
CAR/HFD	18	6	3	9	14	4	0	10	24	1	5	18	12	2	2	8	18	3	4	11
CHI	15	2	5	8	17	5	2	10	15	1	2	12	18	1	4	13	19	1	5	13
COL/QUE	20	6	4	10	17	5	1	11	12	2	0	10	22	2	3	17	15	2	3	10
CBJ	18	3	6	9	...	...	...	...	...	...	...	...	...	...	...	...	...	...	...	...
DAL/MIN	16	6	2	8	19	3	6	10	16	3	1	12	17	5	1	11	15	4	3	8
DET	23	10	4	9	16	4	2	10	10	2	1	7	15	0	0	15	27	7	2	18
EDM	20	5	3	12	27	3	8	16	20	3	5	12	15	3	2	10	16	1	6	9
FLA	24	2	9	13	15	3	6	6	21	1	2	18	20	3	2	15	26	3	4	19
L.A.	19	3	3	13	21	5	4	12	12	5	2	5	16	3	2	11	14	0	3	11
MIN	22	4	5	13	...	...	...	...	...	...	...	...	...	...	...	...	...	...	...	...
MTL	16	2	6	8	17	4	4	9	15	0	4	11	20	3	4	13	21	2	4	15
NSH	17	5	3	9	18	4	7	7	10	1	2	7	...	...	...	...	...	...	...	...
N.J.	20	5	3	12	16	3	5	8	15	3	1	11	16	2	3	11	17	1	2	14
NYI	12	2	3	7	15	5	1	9	17	1	6	10	13	0	2	11	17	3	2	12
NYR	11	5	1	5	21	6	3	12	19	5	3	11	24	2	4	18	13	3	0	10
OTT	16	3	4	9	15	2	2	11	18	1	2	15	17	2	0	15	17	0	2	15
PHI	19	5	3	11	21	6	3	12	24	2	3	19	15	3	1	11	18	3	2	13
PHX/WPG	23	3	3	17	16	4	4	8	15	2	1	12	14	0	2	12	16	5	4	7
PIT	15	3	3	9	17	3	6	8	22	7	1	14	23	3	2	18	13	1	4	8
ST.L.	23	6	5	12	17	5	1	11	15	1	1	13	12	2	2	8	13	1	1	11
S.J.	22	7	3	12	21	4	7	10	21	1	2	18	12	0	2	10	12	3	1	8
T.B.	13	2	5	6	16	0	7	9	12	1	2	9	13	0	3	10	16	4	2	10
TOR	19	3	5	11	17	7	3	7	14	6	1	7	10	1	0	9	10	1	1	8
VAN	23	5	7	11	27	4	8	15	13	0	1	12	17	0	3	14	14	5	2	7
WSH	16	2	4	10	19	5	2	12	11	2	3	6	17	4	1	12	13	2	2	9
Totals	**274**	**122**		**152**	**260**	**114**		**146**	**222**	**60**		**162**	**219**	**54**		**165**	**214**	**70**		**144**

Team	1995-96 GP	W	L	T	1994-95 GP	W	L	T	1993-94 GP	W	L	T	1992-93 GP	W	L	T	1991-92 GP	W	L	T
ANA	16	6	2	8	7	2	0	5	12	2	5	5	...	...	...	...	...	...	...	...
ATL	...	...	...	...	...	...	...	...	...	...	...	...	...	...	...	...	...	...	...	...
BOS	19	2	6	11	8	2	3	3	17	2	2	13	15	5	3	7	20	6	2	12
BUF	15	2	6	7	9	1	1	7	13	0	4	9	18	4	4	10	16	2	2	12
CGY	16	2	3	11	9	1	1	7	18	3	2	13	19	4	4	11	19	2	5	12
CAR/HFD	14	2	3	9	9	1	1	7	14	4	1	9	18	3	9	6	18	2	3	13
CHI	19	1	4	14	7	2	0	5	16	2	5	9	16	1	3	12	19	2	2	15
COL/QUE	6	1	0	5	8	0	0	8	15	3	3	9	15	4	1	10	17	0	5	12
CBJ	...	...	...	...	...	...	...	...	...	...	...	...	...	...	...	...	...	...	...	...
DAL/MIN	15	1	0	14	9	0	1	8	22	6	3	13	10	0	0	10	8	0	2	6
DET	11	3	1	7	4	0	0	4	15	5	2	8	11	2	0	9	16	3	1	12
EDM	14	4	2	8	7	1	2	4	21	1	6	14	17	5	4	8	12	0	2	10
FLA	13	0	3	10	9	0	3	6	24	2	5	17	...	...	...	...	...	...	...	...
L.A.	23	3	2	18	9	0	0	9	18	3	3	12	13	2	1	10	16	1	1	14
MIN	...	...	...	...	...	...	...	...	...	...	...	...	...	...	...	...	...	...	...	...
MTL	15	2	3	10	10	1	2	7	19	3	2	14	14	5	3	6	20	6	3	11
NSH	...	...	...	...	...	...	...	...	...	...	...	...	...	...	...	...	...	...	...	...
N.J.	19	7	0	12	11	1	2	8	14	1	1	12	11	4	0	7	17	2	4	11
NYI	17	2	5	10	7	1	1	5	19	5	2	12	13	3	3	7	16	3	2	11
NYR	17	2	1	14	3	0	0	3	12	3	1	8	17	2	4	11	11	5	1	5
OTT	8	0	3	5	7	1	1	5	17	4	4	9	10	0	6	4	...	...	...	...
PHI	20	4	3	13	8	3	1	4	18	3	5	10	17	4	2	11	17	2	4	11
PHX/WPG	8	2	0	6	9	0	2	7	15	1	5	9	11	2	2	7	20	1	4	15
PIT	9	3	2	4	5	1	1	3	19	4	2	13	10	3	0	7	12	2	1	9
ST.L.	18	1	1	16	7	1	1	5	17	4	2	11	17	2	4	11	15	2	2	11
S.J.	9	1	1	7	5	1	0	4	19	2	1	16	10	3	5	2	9	1	3	5
T.B.	18	3	3	12	7	2	2	3	18	3	4	11	14	3	4	7	...	...	...	...
TOR	18	4	2	12	8	0	0	8	17	4	1	12	13	1	1	11	11	4	0	7
VAN	20	1	4	15	13	0	1	12	12	5	4	3	10	1	0	9	17	4	1	12
WSH	16	4	1	11	9	0	1	8	14	2	2	10	11	2	2	7	12	2	2	8
Totals	**201**	**64**		**137**	**101**	**26**		**75**	**214**	**74**		**140**	**165**	**65**		**100**	**169**	**52**		**117**

2000-2001

Home Team Wins:	69
Visiting Team Wins:	53

Team	1990-91 GP	W	L	T	1989-90 GP	W	L	T	1988-89 GP	W	L	T	1987-88 GP	W	L	T
ANA	...	...	...	...	...	...	...	...	...	...	...	...	...	...	...	...
ATL	...	...	...	...	...	...	...	...	...	...	...	...	...	...	...	...
BOS	17	5	0	12	14	3	2	9	19	3	2	14	14	4	4	6
BUF	24	3	2	19	15	4	3	8	13	2	4	7	12	0	1	11
CGY	15	3	4	8	21	3	3	15	17	5	3	9	15	2	4	9
CAR/HFD	9	1	1	7	9	0	0	9	10	1	4	5	12	3	2	7
CHI	12	3	1	8	10	2	2	6	17	2	3	12	15	4	2	9
COL/QUE	18	1	3	14	8	0	1	7	10	2	1	7	9	2	2	5
CBJ	...	...	...	...	...	...	...	...	...	...	...	...	...	...	...	...
DAL/MIN	17	0	3	14	11	3	4	4	17	0	1	16	16	1	2	13
DET	14	2	4	8	17	2	1	14	16	3	1	12	16	2	3	11
EDM	15	4	5	6	20	5	1	14	15	4	3	8	16	3	2	11
FLA	...	...	...	...	...	...	...	...	...	...	...	...	...	...	...	...
L.A.	16	4	2	10	12	3	2	7	14	6	1	7	12	1	3	8
MIN	...	...	...	...	...	...	...	...	...	...	...	...	...	...	...	...
MTL	17	3	3	11	17	4	2	11	11	2	0	9	16	1	2	13
NSH	...	...	...	...	...	...	...	...	...	...	...	...	...	...	...	...
N.J.	17	1	1	15	16	3	4	9	17	1	4	12	12	4	2	6
NYI	15	2	3	10	16	3	2	11	11	3	3	5	13	3	0	10
NYR	16	1	2	13	17	2	2	13	10	1	1	8	11	0	1	10
OTT	...	...	...	...	...	...	...	...	...	...	...	...	...	...	...	...
PHI	11	1	0	10	18	2	5	11	14	1	5	8	13	1	3	9
PHX/WPG	14	1	2	11	19	4	4	11	20	6	2	12	21	8	2	11
PIT	12	4	2	6	14	3	3	8	10	2	1	7	16	5	2	9
ST.L.	18	3	4	11	15	2	4	9	16	3	1	12	14	2	4	8
S.J.	...	...	...	...	...	...	...	...	...	...	...	...	...	...	...	...
T.B.	...	...	...	...	...	...	...	...	...	...	...	...	...	...	...	...
TOR	17	4	2	11	11	3	4	4	11	1	4	6	13	1	2	10
VAN	15	3	3	9	21	2	5	14	14	2	4	8	11	0	2	9
WSH	14	4	3	7	9	2	1	6	16	2	4	10	15	2	4	9
Totals	**166**	**54**		**112**	**155**	**55**		**100**	**149**	**52**		**97**	**146**	**49**		**97**

Team	1986-87 GP	W	L	T	1985-86 GP	W	L	T	1984-85 GP	W	L	T	1983-84 GP	W	L	T
ANA	...	...	...	...	...	...	...	...	...	...	...	...	...	...	...	...
ATL	...	...	...	...	...	...	...	...	...	...	...	...	...	...	...	...
BOS	12	2	3	7	17	2	3	12	18	4	4	10	7	1	0	6
BUF	13	1	4	8	9	1	2	6	17	0	3	14	13	5	1	7
CGY	4	1	0	3	12	1	2	9	14	1	1	12	18	4	0	14
CAR/HFD	9	2	0	7	7	1	2	4	17	4	4	9	15	2	3	10
CHI	15	1	0	14	12	3	1	8	12	2	3	7	9	0	1	8
COL/QUE	14	0	4	10	11	4	1	6	14	3	2	9	15	0	5	10
CBJ	...	...	...	...	...	...	...	...	...	...	...	...	...	...	...	...
DAL/MIN	14	2	2	10	15	4	2	9	15	1	2	12	18	5	3	10
DET	17	2	5	10	13	2	5	6	14	0	2	12	11	3	1	7
EDM	14	5	3	6	14	5	2	7	12	0	1	11	9	4	0	5
FLA	...	...	...	...	...	...	...	...	...	...	...	...	...	...	...	...
L.A.	12	2	2	8	14	3	3	8	19	3	2	14	17	1	3	13
MIN	...	...	...	...	...	...	...	...	...	...	...	...	...	...	...	...
MTL	16	2	4	10	14	1	6	7	18	3	3	12	7	1	1	5
NSH	...	...	...	...	...	...	...	...	...	...	...	...	...	...	...	...
N.J.	13	3	4	6	10	4	3	3	12	0	2	10	15	1	7	7
NYI	19	4	3	12	17	4	1	12	15	1	8	6	10	3	3	4
NYR	19	5	6	8	13	0	7	6	17	2	5	10	17	5	3	9
OTT	...	...	...	...	...	...	...	...	...	...	...	...	...	...	...	...
PHI	10	1	1	8	9	4	1	4	9	1	1	7	14	3	1	10
PHX/WPG	11	2	1	8	8	0	1	7	14	3	1	10	24	7	6	11
PIT	21	5	4	12	14	3	3	8	8	3	0	5	12	1	5	6
ST.L.	21	4	2	15	17	5	3	9	15	2	1	12	11	3	1	7
S.J.	...	...	...	...	...	...	...	...	...	...	...	...	...	...	...	...
T.B.	...	...	...	...	...	...	...	...	...	...	...	...	...	...	...	...
TOR	13	3	4	6	17	4	6	7	15	5	2	8	13	1	3	9
VAN	10	2	0	8	16	1	2	13	17	7	1	9	16	3	4	9
WSH	17	5	2	10	11	4	0	7	12	3	0	9	9	1	3	5
Totals	**147**	**54**		**93**	**135**	**56**		**79**	**152**	**48**		**104**	**140**	**54**		**86**

NHL Record Book

Year-By-Year Final Standings & Leading Scorers

*Stanley Cup winner

1917-18

First Half

Team	GP	W	L	T	GF	GA	PTS
Montreal	14	10	4	0	81	47	20
Toronto	14	8	6	0	71	75	16
Ottawa	14	5	9	0	67	79	10
**Mtl. Wanderers	6	1	5	0	17	35	2

**Montreal Arena burned down and Wanderers forced to withdraw from League. Montreal Canadiens and Toronto each counted a win for defaulted games with Wanderers.

Second Half

Team	GP	W	L	T	GF	GA	PTS
*Toronto	8	5	3	0	37	34	10
Ottawa	8	4	4	0	35	35	8
Montreal	8	3	5	0	34	37	6

Leading Scorers

Player	Club	GP	G	A	PTS	PIM
Malone, Joe	Montreal	20	44	4	48	30
Denneny, Cy	Ottawa	20	36	10	46	80
Noble, Reg	Toronto	20	30	10	40	35
Lalonde, Newsy	Montreal	14	23	7	30	51
Denneny, Corb	Toronto	21	20	9	29	14
Cameron, Harry	Toronto	21	17	10	27	28
Pitre, Didier	Montreal	20	17	6	23	29
Gerard, Eddie	Ottawa	20	13	7	20	26
Darragh, Jack	Ottawa	18	14	5	19	26
Nighbor, Frank	Ottawa	10	11	8	19	6
Meeking, Harry	Toronto	21	10	9	19	28

1918-19

First Half

Team	GP	W	L	T	GF	GA	PTS
• Montreal	10	7	3	0	57	50	14
Ottawa	10	5	5	0	39	39	10
Toronto	10	3	7	0	42	49	6

Second Half

Team	GP	W	L	T	GF	GA	PTS
Ottawa	8	7	1	0	32	14	14
Montreal	8	3	5	0	31	28	6
Toronto	8	2	6	0	22	43	4

• NHL Champion. Stanley Cup not awarded due to influenza epidemic.

Leading Scorers

Player	Club	GP	G	A	PTS	PIM
Lalonde, Newsy	Montreal	17	22	10	32	40
Cleghorn, Odie	Montreal	17	22	6	28	22
Nighbor, Frank	Ottawa	18	19	9	28	27
Denneny, Cy	Ottawa	18	18	4	22	58
Pitre, Didier	Montreal	17	14	5	19	12
Skinner, Alf	Toronto	17	12	4	16	26
Cameron, Harry	Tor., Ott.	14	11	3	14	35
Darragh, Jack	Ottawa	14	11	3	14	33
Randall, Ken	Toronto	15	8	6	14	27
Cleghorn, Sprague	Ottawa	18	7	6	13	27

All-Time Standings of NHL Teams

(ranked by percentage)

Active Clubs

Team	Games	Wins	Losses	Ties	OT Losses	Goals For	Goals Against	Points	Pts %	First Season
Montreal	5300	2742	1738	810	10	17664	14151	6304	.594	1917-18
Philadelphia	2686	1341	920	419	6	9357	8013	3107	.577	1967-68
Boston	5140	2444	1923	759	14	16763	15263	5661	.550	1924-25
Buffalo	2460	1158	916	381	5	8453	7612	2702	.549	1970-71
Edmonton	1748	830	680	227	11	6730	6171	1898	.540	1979-80
Calgary	2304	1039	909	347	9	8204	7687	2434	.526	1972-73
Detroit	5074	2212	2072	784	6	15761	15395	5214	.513	1926-27
St. Louis	2686	1165	1113	402	6	8681	8708	2738	.508	1967-68
Colorado	1748	770	746	227	5	6201	6131	1772	.504	1979-80
Toronto	5300	2286	2250	756	8	16466	16432	5336	.503	1917-18
NY Islanders	2304	997	986	317	4	7889	7516	2315	.501	1972-73
NY Rangers	5074	2136	2147	787	4	15834	15977	5063	.498	1926-27
Washington	2148	913	955	274	6	7019	7298	2106	.489	1974-75
Chicago	5074	2085	2205	777	7	15232	15444	4954	.487	1926-27
Florida	624	248	257	104	15	1680	1734	615	.486	1993-94
Pittsburgh	2686	1121	1195	361	9	9361	9752	2612	.485	1967-68
Dallas	2686	1082	1178	418	8	8521	8957	2590	.481	1967-68
Los Angeles	2686	1060	1228	391	7	9116	9739	2518	.467	1967-68
Phoenix	1748	692	821	228	7	5877	6454	1619	.461	1979-80
Anaheim	624	240	296	80	8	1658	1834	568	.449	1993-94
Carolina	1748	676	847	222	3	5543	6207	1577	.449	1979-80
New Jersey	2148	804	1039	297	8	6765	7628	1913	.443	1974-75
Vancouver	2460	894	1190	361	15	7905	8915	2164	.438	1970-71
Ottawa	708	249	365	88	6	1887	2285	592	.414	1992-93
Nashville	246	90	123	23	10	575	701	213	.414	1998-99
Columbus	82	28	39	9	6	190	233	71	.409	2000-01
San Jose	788	267	419	92	10	2129	2647	636	.397	1991-92
Minnesota	82	25	39	13	5	168	210	68	.388	2000-01
Tampa Bay	708	219	400	77	12	1779	2373	527	.368	1992-93
Atlanta	164	37	102	19	6	381	602	99	.292	99-2000

Defunct Clubs

Team	Games	Wins	Losses	Ties	Goals For	Goals Against	Points	Pts %	First Season	Last Season
Ottawa Senators	542	258	221	63	1458	1333	579	.534	1917-18	1933-34
Montreal Maroons	622	271	260	91	1474	1405	633	.509	1924-25	1937-38
NY/Brooklyn Americans	784	255	402	127	1643	2182	637	.406	1925-26	1941-42
Hamilton Tigers	126	47	78	1	414	475	95	.377	1920-21	1924-25
Cleveland Barons	160	47	87	26	470	617	120	.375	1976-77	1977-78
Pittsburgh Pirates	212	67	122	23	376	519	157	.370	1925-26	1929-30
Calif./Oakland Seals	698	182	401	115	1826	2580	479	.343	1967-68	1975-76
St. Louis Eagles	48	11	31	6	86	144	28	.292	1934-35	1934-35
Quebec Bulldogs	24	4	20	0	91	177	8	.167	1919-20	1919-20
Montreal Wanderers	6	1	5	0	17	35	2	.167	1917-18	1917-18
Philadelphia Quakers	44	4	36	4	76	184	12	.136	1930-31	1930-31

Calgary totals include Atlanta Flames, 1972-73 to 1979-80.
Carolina totals include Hartford, 1979-80 to 1996-97.
Colorado totals include Quebec, 1979-80 to 1994-95.
Dallas totals include Minnesota North Stars, 1967-68 to 1992-93.
Detroit totals include Cougars, 1926-27 to 1929-30, and Falcons, 1930-31 to 1931-32.
New Jersey totals include Kansas City, 1974-75 to 1975-76, and Colorado Rockies, 1976-77 to 1981-82.
Phoenix totals include Winnipeg, 1979-80 to 1995-96.
Toronto totals include Arenas, 1917-18 to 1918-19, and St. Patricks, 1919-20 to 1925-56.

1919-20

First Half

Team	GP	W	L	T	GF	GA	PTS
Ottawa	12	9	3	0	59	23	18
Montreal	12	8	4	0	62	51	16
Toronto	12	5	7	0	52	62	10
Quebec	12	2	10	0	44	81	4

Second Half

Team	GP	W	L	T	GF	GA	PTS
*Ottawa	12	10	2	0	62	41	20
Montreal	12	5	7	0	67	62	10
Toronto	12	7	5	0	67	44	14
Quebec	12	2	10	0	47	96	4

Leading Scorers

Player	Club	GP	G	A	PTS	PIM
Malone, Joe	Quebec	24	39	10	49	12
Lalonde, Newsy	Montreal	23	37	9	46	34
Nighbor, Frank	Ottawa	23	26	15	41	18
Denneny, Corb	Toronto	24	24	12	36	20
Darragh, Jack	Ottawa	23	22	14	36	22
Noble, Reg	Toronto	24	24	9	33	52
Arbour, Amos	Montreal	22	21	5	26	13
Wilson, Cully	Toronto	23	20	6	26	86
Pitre, Didier	Montreal	22	14	12	26	6
Broadbent, Punch	Ottawa	21	19	6	25	40

1920-21

First Half

Team	GP	W	L	T	GF	GA	PTS
*Ottawa	10	8	2	0	49	23	16
Toronto	10	5	5	0	39	47	10
Montreal	10	4	6	0	37	51	8
Hamilton	10	3	7	0	34	38	6

Second Half

Team	GP	W	L	T	GF	GA	PTS
Toronto	14	10	4	0	66	53	20
Montreal	14	9	5	0	75	48	18
Ottawa	14	6	8	0	48	52	12
Hamilton	14	3	11	0	58	94	6

Leading Scorers

Player	Club	GP	G	A	PTS	PIM
Lalonde, Newsy	Montreal	24	33	10	43	36
Dye, Babe	Ham., Tor.	24	35	5	40	32
Denneny, Cy	Ottawa	24	34	5	39	10
Malone, Joe	Hamilton	20	28	9	37	6
Nighbor, Frank	Ottawa	24	19	10	29	10
Noble, Reg	Toronto	24	19	8	27	54
Cameron, Harry	Toronto	24	18	9	27	35
Prodgers, Goldie	Hamilton	24	18	9	27	8
Denneny, Corb	Toronto	20	19	7	26	29
Darragh, Jack	Ottawa	24	11	15	26	20

1921-22

Team	GP	W	L	T	GF	GA	PTS
Ottawa	24	14	8	2	106	84	30
*Toronto	24	13	10	1	98	97	27
Montreal	24	12	11	1	88	94	25
Hamilton	24	7	17	0	88	105	14

Leading Scorers

Player	Club	GP	G	A	PTS	PIM
Broadbent, Punch	Ottawa	24	32	14	46	28
Denneny, Cy	Ottawa	22	27	12	39	20
Dye, Babe	Toronto	24	31	7	38	39
Cameron, Harry	Toronto	24	18	17	35	22
Malone, Joe	Hamilton	24	24	7	31	4
Denneny, Corb	Toronto	24	19	9	28	28
Noble, Reg	Toronto	24	17	11	28	19
Cleghorn, Sprague	Montreal	24	17	9	26	80
Boucher, Georges	Ottawa	23	13	12	25	12
Cleghorn, Odie	Montreal	23	21	3	24	26

1922-23

Team	GP	W	L	T	GF	GA	PTS
*Ottawa	24	14	9	1	77	54	29
Montreal	24	13	9	2	73	61	28
Toronto	24	13	10	1	82	88	27
Hamilton	24	6	18	0	81	110	12

Leading Scorers

Player	Club	GP	G	A	PTS	PIM
Dye, Babe	Toronto	22	26	11	37	19
Denneny, Cy	Ottawa	24	23	11	34	28
Boucher, Billy	Montreal	24	24	7	31	55
Adams, Jack	Toronto	23	19	9	28	42
Roach, Mickey	Hamilton	24	17	10	27	8
Cleghorn, Odie	Montreal	24	19	6	25	18
Boucher, Georges	Ottawa	24	14	9	23	58
Noble, Reg	Toronto	24	12	11	23	47
Wilson, Cully	Hamilton	23	16	5	21	46
Joliat, Aurel	Montreal	24	12	9	21	37

1923-24

Team	GP	W	L	T	GF	GA	PTS
Ottawa	24	16	8	0	74	54	32
*Montreal	24	13	11	0	59	48	26
Toronto	24	10	14	0	59	85	20
Hamilton	24	9	15	0	63	68	18

Leading Scorers

Player	Club	GP	G	A	PTS	PIM
Denneny, Cy	Ottawa	22	22	2	24	10
Boucher, Georges	Ottawa	21	13	10	23	38
Boucher, Billy	Montreal	23	16	6	22	48
Burch, Billy	Hamilton	24	16	6	22	6
Joliat, Aurel	Montreal	24	15	5	20	27
Dye, Babe	Toronto	19	16	3	19	23
Adams, Jack	Toronto	22	14	4	18	51
Noble, Reg	Toronto	23	12	5	17	79
Morenz, Howie	Montreal	24	13	3	16	20
Clancy, King	Ottawa	24	8	8	16	26

1924-25

Team	GP	W	L	T	GF	GA	PTS
Hamilton	30	19	10	1	90	60	39
Toronto	30	19	11	0	90	84	38
• Montreal	30	17	11	2	93	56	36
Ottawa	30	17	12	1	83	66	35
Mtl. Maroons	30	9	19	2	45	65	20
Boston	30	6	24	0	49	119	12

• NHL Champion (Stanley Cup won by Victoria Cougars, WCHL)

Leading Scorers

Player	Club	GP	G	A	PTS	PIM
Dye, Babe	Toronto	29	38	8	46	41
Denneny, Cy	Ottawa	29	27	15	42	16
Joliat, Aurel	Montreal	25	30	11	41	85
Morenz, Howie	Montreal	30	28	11	39	46
Green, Red	Hamilton	30	19	15	34	81
Adams, Jack	Toronto	27	21	10	31	67
Boucher, Billy	Montreal	30	17	13	30	92
Burch, Billy	Hamilton	27	20	7	27	10
Herbert, Jimmy	Boston	30	17	7	24	55
Smith, Hooley	Ottawa	30	10	13	23	81

1925-26

Team	GP	W	L	T	GF	GA	PTS
Ottawa	36	24	8	4	77	42	52
*Mtl. Maroons	36	20	11	5	91	73	45
Pittsburgh	36	19	16	1	82	70	39
Boston	36	17	15	4	92	85	38
NY Americans	36	12	20	4	68	89	28
Toronto	36	12	21	3	92	114	27
Montreal	36	11	24	1	79	108	23

Leading Scorers

Player	Club	GP	G	A	PTS	PIM
Stewart, Nels	Mtl. Maroons	36	34	8	42	119
Denneny, Cy	Ottawa	36	24	12	36	18
Cooper, Carson	Boston	36	28	3	31	10
Herbert, Jimmy	Boston	36	26	5	31	47
Morenz, Howie	Montreal	31	23	3	26	39
Adams, Jack	Toronto	36	21	5	26	52
Joliat, Aurel	Montreal	35	17	9	26	52
Burch, Billy	NY Americans	36	22	3	25	33
Smith, Hooley	Ottawa	28	16	9	25	53
Nighbor, Frank	Ottawa	35	12	13	25	40

1926-27

Canadian Division

Team	GP	W	L	T	GF	GA	PTS
*Ottawa	44	30	10	4	86	69	64
Montreal	44	28	14	2	99	67	58
Mtl. Maroons	44	20	20	4	71	68	44
NY Americans	44	17	25	2	82	91	36
Toronto	44	15	24	5	79	94	35

American Division

Team	GP	W	L	T	GF	GA	PTS
New York	44	25	13	6	95	72	56
Boston	44	21	20	3	97	89	45
Chicago	44	19	22	3	115	116	41
Pittsburgh	44	15	26	3	79	108	33
Detroit	44	12	28	4	76	105	28

Leading Scorers

Player	Club	GP	G	A	PTS	PIM
Cook, Bill	New York	44	33	4	37	58
Irvin, Dick	Chicago	43	18	18	36	34
Morenz, Howie	Montreal	44	25	7	32	49
Fredrickson, Frank	Det., Bos.	41	18	13	31	46
Dye, Babe	Chicago	41	25	5	30	14
Bailey, Ace	Toronto	42	15	13	28	82
Boucher, Frank	New York	44	13	15	28	17
Burch, Billy	NY Americans	43	19	8	27	40
Oliver, Harry	Boston	42	18	6	24	17
Keats, Duke	Bos., Det.	42	16	8	24	52

1927-28

Canadian Division

Team	GP	W	L	T	GF	GA	PTS
Montreal	44	26	11	7	116	48	59
Mtl. Maroons	44	24	14	6	96	77	54
Ottawa	44	20	14	10	78	57	50
Toronto	44	18	18	8	89	88	44
NY Americans	44	11	27	6	63	128	28

American Division

Team	GP	W	L	T	GF	GA	PTS
Boston	44	20	13	11	77	70	51
*New York	44	19	16	9	94	79	47
Pittsburgh	44	19	17	8	67	76	46
Detroit	44	19	19	6	88	79	44
Chicago	44	7	34	3	68	134	17

Leading Scorers

Player	Club	GP	G	A	PTS	PIM
Morenz, Howie	Montreal	43	33	18	51	66
Joliat, Aurel	Montreal	44	28	11	39	105
Boucher, Frank	New York	44	23	12	35	15
Hay, George	Detroit	42	22	13	35	20
Stewart, Nels	Mtl. Maroons	41	27	7	34	104
Gagne, Art	Montreal	44	20	10	30	75
Cook, Bun	New York	44	14	14	28	45
Carson, Bill	Toronto	32	20	6	26	36
Finnigan, Frank	Ottawa	38	20	5	25	34
Cook, Bill	New York	43	18	6	24	42
Keats, Duke	Det., Chi.	38	14	10	24	60

1928-29

Canadian Division

Team	GP	W	L	T	GF	GA	PTS
Montreal	44	22	7	15	71	43	59
NY Americans	44	19	13	12	53	53	50
Toronto	44	21	18	5	85	69	47
Ottawa	44	14	17	13	54	67	41
Mtl. Maroons	44	15	20	9	67	65	39

American Division

Team	GP	W	L	T	GF	GA	PTS
*Boston	44	26	13	5	89	52	57
New York	44	21	13	10	72	65	52
Detroit	44	19	16	9	72	63	47
Pittsburgh	44	9	27	8	46	80	26
Chicago	44	7	29	8	33	85	22

Leading Scorers

Player	Club	GP	G	A	PTS	PIM
Bailey, Ace	Toronto	44	22	10	32	78
Stewart, Nels	Mtl. Maroons	44	21	8	29	74
Cooper, Carson	Detroit	43	18	9	27	14
Morenz, Howie	Montreal	42	17	10	27	47
Blair, Andy	Toronto	44	12	15	27	41
Boucher, Frank	New York	44	10	16	26	8
Oliver, Harry	Boston	43	17	6	23	24
Cook, Bill	New York	43	15	8	23	41
Ward, Jimmy	Mtl. Maroons	43	14	8	22	46

Seven players tied with 19 points

1929-30

Canadian Division

Team	GP	W	L	T	GF	GA	PTS
Mtl. Maroons	44	23	16	5	141	114	51
*Montreal	44	21	14	9	142	114	51
Ottawa	44	21	15	8	138	118	50
Toronto	44	17	21	6	116	124	40
NY Americans	44	14	25	5	113	161	33

American Division

Team	GP	W	L	T	GF	GA	PTS
Boston	44	38	5	1	179	98	77
Chicago	44	21	18	5	117	111	47
New York	44	17	17	10	136	143	44
Detroit	44	14	24	6	117	133	34
Pittsburgh	44	5	36	3	102	185	13

Leading Scorers

Player	Club	GP	G	A	PTS	PIM
Weiland, Cooney	Boston	44	43	30	73	27
Boucher, Frank	New York	42	26	36	62	16
Clapper, Dit	Boston	44	41	20	61	48
Cook, Bill	New York	44	29	30	59	56
Kilrea, Hec	Ottawa	44	36	22	58	72
Stewart, Nels	Mtl. Maroons	44	39	16	55	81
Morenz, Howie	Montreal	44	40	10	50	72
Himes, Normie	NY Americans	44	28	22	50	15
Lamb, Joe	Ottawa	44	29	20	49	119
Gainor, Norm	Boston	42	18	31	49	39

1930-31

Canadian Division

Team	GP	W	L	T	GF	GA	PTS
*Montreal	44	26	10	8	129	89	60
Toronto	44	22	13	9	118	99	53
Mtl. Maroons	44	20	18	6	105	106	46
NY Americans	44	18	16	10	76	74	46
Ottawa	44	10	30	4	91	142	24

American Division

Team	GP	W	L	T	GF	GA	PTS
Boston	44	28	10	6	143	90	62
Chicago	44	24	17	3	108	78	51
New York	44	19	16	9	106	87	47
Detroit	44	16	21	7	102	105	39
Philadelphia	44	4	36	4	76	184	12

Leading Scorers

Player	Club	GP	G	A	PTS	PIM
Morenz, Howie	Montreal	39	28	23	51	49
Goodfellow, Ebbie	Detroit	44	25	23	48	32
Conacher, Charlie	Toronto	37	31	12	43	78
Cook, Bill	New York	43	30	12	42	39
Bailey, Ace	Toronto	40	23	19	42	46
Primeau, Joe	Toronto	38	9	32	41	18
Stewart, Nels	Mtl. Maroons	42	25	14	39	75
Boucher, Frank	New York	44	12	27	39	20
Weiland, Cooney	Boston	44	25	13	38	14
Cook, Bun	New York	44	18	17	35	72
Joliat, Aurel	Montreal	43	13	22	35	73

1931-32

Canadian Division

Team	GP	W	L	T	GF	GA	PTS
Montreal	48	25	16	7	128	111	57
*Toronto	48	23	18	7	155	127	53
Mtl. Maroons	48	19	22	7	142	139	45
NY Americans	48	16	24	8	95	142	40

American Division

Team	GP	W	L	T	GF	GA	PTS
New York	48	23	17	8	134	112	54
Chicago	48	18	19	11	86	101	47
Detroit	48	18	20	10	95	108	46
Boston	48	15	21	12	122	117	42

Leading Scorers

Player	Club	GP	G	A	PTS	PIM
Jackson, Busher	Toronto	48	28	25	53	63
Primeau, Joe	Toronto	46	13	37	50	25
Morenz, Howie	Montreal	48	24	25	49	46
Conacher, Charlie	Toronto	44	34	14	48	66
Cook, Bill	New York	48	34	14	48	33
Trottier, Dave	Mtl. Maroons	48	26	18	44	94
Smith, Reg	Mtl. Maroons	43	11	33	44	49
Siebert, Babe	Mtl. Maroons	48	21	18	39	64
Clapper, Dit	Boston	48	17	22	39	21
Joliat, Aurel	Montreal	48	15	24	39	46

1932-33

Canadian Division

Team	GP	W	L	T	GF	GA	PTS
Toronto	48	24	18	6	119	111	54
Mtl. Maroons	48	22	20	6	135	119	50
Montreal	48	18	25	5	92	115	41
NY Americans	48	15	22	11	91	118	41
Ottawa	48	11	27	10	88	131	32

American Division

Team	GP	W	L	T	GF	GA	PTS
Boston	48	25	15	8	124	88	58
Detroit	48	25	15	8	111	93	58
*New York	48	23	17	8	135	107	54
Chicago	48	16	20	12	88	101	44

Leading Scorers

Player	Club	GP	G	A	PTS	PIM
Cook, Bill	New York	48	28	22	50	51
Jackson, Busher	Toronto	48	27	17	44	43
Northcott, Baldy	Mtl. Maroons	48	22	21	43	30
Smith, Reg	Mtl. Maroons	48	20	21	41	66
Haynes, Paul	Mtl. Maroons	48	16	25	41	18
Joliat, Aurel	Montreal	48	18	21	39	53
Barry, Marty	Boston	48	24	13	37	40
Cook, Bun	New York	48	22	15	37	35
Stewart, Nels	Boston	47	18	18	36	62
Morenz, Howie	Montreal	46	14	21	35	32
Gagnon, Johnny	Montreal	48	12	23	35	64
Shore, Eddie	Boston	48	8	27	35	102
Boucher, Frank	New York	47	7	28	35	4

1933-34

Canadian Division

Team	GP	W	L	T	GF	GA	PTS
Toronto	48	26	13	9	174	119	61
Montreal	48	22	20	6	99	101	50
Mtl. Maroons	48	19	18	11	117	122	49
NY Americans	48	15	23	10	104	132	40
Ottawa	48	13	29	6	115	143	32

American Division

Team	GP	W	L	T	GF	GA	PTS
Detroit	48	24	14	10	113	98	58
*Chicago	48	20	17	11	88	83	51
New York	48	21	19	8	120	113	50
Boston	48	18	25	5	111	130	41

Leading Scorers

Player	Club	GP	G	A	PTS	PIM
Conacher, Charlie	Toronto	42	32	20	52	38
Primeau, Joe	Toronto	45	14	32	46	8
Boucher, Frank	New York	48	14	30	44	4
Barry, Marty	Boston	48	27	12	39	12
Dillon, Cecil	New York	48	13	26	39	10
Stewart, Nels	Boston	48	21	17	38	68
Jackson, Busher	Toronto	38	20	18	38	38
Joliat, Aurel	Montreal	48	22	15	37	27
Smith, Reg	Mtl. Maroons	47	18	19	37	58
Thompson, Paul	Chicago	48	20	16	36	17

1934-35

Canadian Division

Team	GP	W	L	T	GF	GA	PTS
Toronto	48	30	14	4	157	111	64
*Mtl. Maroons	48	24	19	5	123	92	53
Montreal	48	19	23	6	110	145	44
NY Americans	48	12	27	9	100	142	33
St. Louis	48	11	31	6	86	144	28

American Division

Team	GP	W	L	T	GF	GA	PTS
Boston	48	26	16	6	129	112	58
Chicago	48	26	17	5	118	88	57
New York	48	22	20	6	137	139	50
Detroit	48	19	22	7	127	114	45

Leading Scorers

Player	Club	GP	G	A	PTS	PIM
Conacher, Charlie	Toronto	47	36	21	57	24
Howe, Syd	St.L., Det.	50	22	25	47	34
Aurie, Larry	Detroit	48	17	29	46	24
Boucher, Frank	New York	48	13	32	45	2
Jackson, Busher	Toronto	42	22	22	44	27
Lewis, Herb	Detroit	47	16	27	43	26
Chapman, Art	NY Americans	47	9	34	43	4
Barry, Marty	Boston	48	20	20	40	33
Schriner, Sweeney	NY Americans	48	18	22	40	6
Stewart, Nels	Boston	47	21	18	39	45
Thompson, Paul	Chicago	48	16	23	39	20

1935-36

Canadian Division

Team	GP	W	L	T	GF	GA	PTS
Mtl. Maroons	48	22	16	10	114	106	54
Toronto	48	23	19	6	126	106	52
NY Americans	48	16	25	7	109	122	39
Montreal	48	11	26	11	82	123	33

American Division

Team	GP	W	L	T	GF	GA	PTS
*Detroit	48	24	16	8	124	103	56
Boston	48	22	20	6	92	83	50
Chicago	48	21	19	8	93	92	50
New York	48	19	17	12	91	96	50

Leading Scorers

Player	Club	GP	G	A	PTS	PIM
Schriner, Sweeney	NY Americans	48	19	26	45	8
Barry, Marty	Detroit	48	21	19	40	16
Thompson, Paul	Chicago	45	17	23	40	19
Thoms, Bill	Toronto	48	23	15	38	29
Conacher, Charlie	Toronto	44	23	15	38	74
Smith, Reg	Mtl. Maroons	47	19	19	38	75
Romnes, Doc	Chicago	48	13	25	38	6
Chapman, Art	NY Americans	47	10	28	38	14
Lewis, Herb	Detroit	45	14	23	37	25
Northcott, Baldy	Mtl. Maroons	48	15	21	36	41

1936-37

Canadian Division

Team	GP	W	L	T	GF	GA	PTS
Montreal	48	24	18	6	115	111	54
Mtl. Maroons	48	22	17	9	126	110	53
Toronto	48	22	21	5	119	115	49
NY Americans	48	15	29	4	122	161	34

American Division

Team	GP	W	L	T	GF	GA	PTS
*Detroit	48	25	14	9	128	102	59
Boston	48	23	18	7	120	110	53
New York	48	19	20	9	117	106	47
Chicago	48	14	27	7	99	131	35

Leading Scorers

Player	Club	GP	G	A	PTS	PIM
Schriner, Sweeney	NY Americans	48	21	25	46	17
Apps Sr., Syl	Toronto	48	16	29	45	10
Barry, Marty	Detroit	48	17	27	44	6
Aurie, Larry	Detroit	45	23	20	43	20
Jackson, Busher	Toronto	46	21	19	40	12
Gagnon, Johnny	Montreal	48	20	16	36	38
Gracie, Bob	Mtl. Maroons	47	11	25	36	18
Stewart, Nels	Bos., NYA	43	23	12	35	37
Thompson, Paul	Chicago	47	17	18	35	28
Cowley, Bill	Boston	46	13	22	35	4

1937-38

Canadian Division

Team	GP	W	L	T	GF	GA	PTS
Toronto	48	24	15	9	151	127	57
NY Americans	48	19	18	11	110	111	49
Montreal	48	18	17	13	123	128	49
Mtl. Maroons	48	12	30	6	101	149	30

American Division

Team	GP	W	L	T	GF	GA	PTS
Boston	48	30	11	7	142	89	67
New York	48	27	15	6	149	96	60
*Chicago	48	14	25	9	97	139	37
Detroit	48	12	25	11	99	133	35

Leading Scorers

Player	Club	GP	G	A	PTS	PIM
Drillon, Gordie	Toronto	48	26	26	52	4
Apps Sr., Syl	Toronto	47	21	29	50	9
Thompson, Paul	Chicago	48	22	22	44	14
Mantha, Georges	Montreal	47	23	19	42	12
Dillon, Cecil	New York	48	21	18	39	6
Cowley, Bill	Boston	48	17	22	39	8
Schriner, Sweeney	NY Americans	49	21	17	38	22
Thoms, Bill	Toronto	48	14	24	38	14
Smith, Clint	New York	48	14	23	37	0
Stewart, Nels	NY Americans	48	19	17	36	29
Colville, Neil	New York	45	17	19	36	11

1938-39

Team	GP	W	L	T	GF	GA	PTS
*Boston	48	36	10	2	156	76	74
New York	48	26	16	6	149	105	58
Toronto	48	19	20	9	114	107	47
NY Americans	48	17	21	10	119	157	44
Detroit	48	18	24	6	107	128	42
Montreal	48	15	24	9	115	146	39
Chicago	48	12	28	8	91	132	32

Leading Scorers

Player	Club	GP	G	A	PTS	PIM
Blake, Toe	Montreal	48	24	23	47	10
Schriner, Sweeney	NY Americans	48	13	31	44	20
Cowley, Bill	Boston	34	8	34	42	2
Smith, Clint	New York	48	21	20	41	2
Barry, Marty	Detroit	48	13	28	41	4
Apps Sr., Syl	Toronto	44	15	25	40	4
Anderson, Tom	NY Americans	48	13	27	40	14
Gottselig, Johnny	Chicago	48	16	23	39	15
Haynes, Paul	Montreal	47	5	33	38	27
Conacher, Roy	Boston	47	26	11	37	12
Carr, Lorne	NY Americans	46	19	18	37	16
Colville, Neil	New York	48	18	19	37	12
Watson, Phil	New York	48	15	22	37	42

1939-40

Team	GP	W	L	T	GF	GA	PTS
Boston	48	31	12	5	170	98	67
*New York	48	27	11	10	136	77	64
Toronto	48	25	17	6	134	110	56
Chicago	48	23	19	6	112	120	52
Detroit	48	16	26	6	90	126	38
NY Americans	48	15	29	4	106	140	34
Montreal	48	10	33	5	90	168	25

Leading Scorers

Player	Club	GP	G	A	PTS	PIM
Schmidt, Milt	Boston	48	22	30	52	37
Dumart, Woody	Boston	48	22	21	43	16
Bauer, Bobby	Boston	48	17	26	43	2
Drillon, Gordie	Toronto	43	21	19	40	13
Cowley, Bill	Boston	48	13	27	40	24
Hextall Sr., Bryan	New York	48	24	15	39	52
Colville, Neil	New York	48	19	19	38	22
Howe, Syd	Detroit	46	14	23	37	17
Blake, Toe	Montreal	48	17	19	36	48
Armstrong, Murray	NY Americans	48	16	20	36	12

Dit Clapper was a top-10 scorer with the Boston Bruins as a right winger in 1929-30 and 1931-32. He was later a three-time All-Star as a defenseman.

Best remembered for the three goals he scored in 21 seconds in 1951-52, Bill Mosienko was one of the NHL's top scorers during the mid 1940s.

1940-41

Team	GP	W	L	T	GF	GA	PTS
*Boston	48	27	8	13	168	102	67
Toronto	48	28	14	6	145	99	62
Detroit	48	21	16	11	112	102	53
New York	48	21	19	8	143	125	50
Chicago	48	16	25	7	112	139	39
Montreal	48	16	26	6	121	147	38
NY Americans	48	8	29	11	99	186	27

Leading Scorers

Player	Club	GP	G	A	PTS	PIM
Cowley, Bill	Boston	46	17	45	62	16
Hextall Sr., Bryan	New York	48	26	18	44	16
Drillon, Gordie	Toronto	42	23	21	44	2
Apps Sr., Syl	Toronto	41	20	24	44	6
Patrick, Lynn	New York	48	20	24	44	12
Howe, Syd	Detroit	48	20	24	44	8
Colville, Neil	New York	48	14	28	42	28
Wiseman, Eddie	Boston	48	16	24	40	10
Bauer, Bobby	Boston	48	17	22	39	2
Schriner, Sweeney	Toronto	48	24	14	38	6
Conacher, Roy	Boston	40	24	14	38	7
Schmidt, Milt	Boston	44	13	25	38	23

1941-42

Team	GP	W	L	T	GF	GA	PTS
New York	48	29	17	2	177	143	60
*Toronto	48	27	18	3	158	136	57
Boston	48	25	17	6	160	118	56
Chicago	48	22	23	3	145	155	47
Detroit	48	19	25	4	140	147	42
Montreal	48	18	27	3	134	173	39
Brooklyn	48	16	29	3	133	175	35

Leading Scorers

Player	Club	GP	G	A	PTS	PIM
Hextall Sr., Bryan	New York	48	24	32	56	30
Patrick, Lynn	New York	47	32	22	54	18
Grosso, Don	Detroit	48	23	30	53	13
Watson, Phil	New York	48	15	37	52	48
Abel, Sid	Detroit	48	18	31	49	45
Blake, Toe	Montreal	47	17	28	45	19
Thoms, Bill	Chicago	47	15	30	45	8
Drillon, Gordie	Toronto	48	23	18	41	6
Apps Sr., Syl	Toronto	38	18	23	41	0
Anderson, Tom	Brooklyn	48	12	29	41	54

1942-43

Team	GP	W	L	T	GF	GA	PTS
*Detroit	50	25	14	11	169	124	61
Boston	50	24	17	9	195	176	57
Toronto	50	22	19	9	198	159	53
Montreal	50	19	19	12	181	191	50
Chicago	50	17	18	15	179	180	49
New York	50	11	31	8	161	253	30

Leading Scorers

Player	Club	GP	G	A	PTS	PIM
Bentley, Doug	Chicago	50	33	40	73	18
Cowley, Bill	Boston	48	27	45	72	10
Bentley, Max	Chicago	47	26	44	70	2
Patrick, Lynn	New York	50	22	39	61	28
Carr, Lorne	Toronto	50	27	33	60	15
Taylor, Billy	Toronto	50	18	42	60	2
Hextall Sr., Bryan	New York	50	27	32	59	28
Blake, Toe	Montreal	48	23	36	59	28
Lach, Elmer	Montreal	45	18	40	58	14
O'Connor, Buddy	Montreal	50	15	43	58	2

1943-44

Team	GP	W	L	T	GF	GA	PTS
*Montreal	50	38	5	7	234	109	83
Detroit	50	26	18	6	214	177	58
Toronto	50	23	23	4	214	174	50
Chicago	50	22	23	5	178	187	49
Boston	50	19	26	5	223	268	43
New York	50	6	39	5	162	310	17

Leading Scorers

Player	Club	GP	G	A	PTS	PIM
Cain, Herb	Boston	48	36	46	82	4
Bentley, Doug	Chicago	50	38	39	77	22
Carr, Lorne	Toronto	50	36	38	74	9
Liscombe, Carl	Detroit	50	36	37	73	17
Lach, Elmer	Montreal	48	24	48	72	23
Smith, Clint	Chicago	50	23	49	72	4
Cowley, Bill	Boston	36	30	41	71	12
Mosienko, Bill	Chicago	50	32	38	70	10
Jackson, Art	Boston	49	28	41	69	8
Bodnar, Gus	Toronto	50	22	40	62	18

1944-45

Team	GP	W	L	T	GF	GA	PTS
Montreal	50	38	8	4	228	121	80
Detroit	50	31	14	5	218	161	67
*Toronto	50	24	22	4	183	161	52
Boston	50	16	30	4	179	219	36
Chicago	50	13	30	7	141	194	33
New York	50	11	29	10	154	247	32

Leading Scorers

Player	Club	GP	G	A	PTS	PIM
Lach, Elmer	Montreal	50	26	54	80	37
Richard, Maurice	Montreal	50	50	23	73	36
Blake, Toe	Montreal	49	29	38	67	15
Cowley, Bill	Boston	49	25	40	65	2
Kennedy, Ted	Toronto	49	29	25	54	14
Mosienko, Bill	Chicago	50	28	26	54	0
Carveth, Joe	Detroit	50	26	28	54	6
DeMarco Sr., Ab	New York	50	24	30	54	10
Smith, Clint	Chicago	50	23	31	54	0
Howe, Syd	Detroit	46	17	36	53	6

1945-46

Team	GP	W	L	T	GF	GA	PTS
*Montreal	50	28	17	5	172	134	61
Boston	50	24	18	8	167	156	56
Chicago	50	23	20	7	200	178	53
Detroit	50	20	20	10	146	159	50
Toronto	50	19	24	7	174	185	45
New York	50	13	28	9	144	191	35

Leading Scorers

Player	Club	GP	G	A	PTS	PIM
Bentley, Max	Chicago	47	31	30	61	6
Stewart, Gaye	Toronto	50	37	15	52	8
Blake, Toe	Montreal	50	29	21	50	2
Smith, Clint	Chicago	50	26	24	50	2
Richard, Maurice	Montreal	50	27	21	48	50
Mosienko, Bill	Chicago	40	18	30	48	12
DeMarco Sr., Ab	New York	50	20	27	47	20
Lach, Elmer	Montreal	50	13	34	47	34
Kaleta, Alex	Chicago	49	19	27	46	17
Taylor, Billy	Toronto	48	23	18	41	14
Horeck, Pete	Chicago	50	20	21	41	34

1946-47

Team	GP	W	L	T	GF	GA	PTS
Montreal	60	34	16	10	189	138	78
*Toronto	60	31	19	10	209	172	72
Boston	60	26	23	11	190	175	63
Detroit	60	22	27	11	190	193	55
New York	60	22	32	6	167	186	50
Chicago	60	19	37	4	193	274	42

Leading Scorers

Player	Club	GP	G	A	PTS	PIM
Bentley, Max	Chicago	60	29	43	72	12
Richard, Maurice	Montreal	60	45	26	71	69
Taylor, Billy	Detroit	60	17	46	63	35
Schmidt, Milt	Boston	59	27	35	62	40
Kennedy, Ted	Toronto	60	28	32	60	27
Bentley, Doug	Chicago	52	21	34	55	18
Bauer, Bobby	Boston	58	30	24	54	4
Conacher, Roy	Detroit	60	30	24	54	6
Mosienko, Bill	Chicago	59	25	27	52	2
Dumart, Woody	Boston	60	24	28	52	12

1947-48

Team	GP	W	L	T	GF	GA	PTS
*Toronto	60	32	15	13	182	143	77
Detroit	60	30	18	12	187	148	72
Boston	60	23	24	13	167	168	59
New York	60	21	26	13	176	201	55
Montreal	60	20	29	11	147	169	51
Chicago	60	20	34	6	195	225	46

Leading Scorers

Player	Club	GP	G	A	PTS	PIM
Lach, Elmer	Montreal	60	30	31	61	72
O'Connor, Buddy	New York	60	24	36	60	8
Bentley, Doug	Chicago	60	20	37	57	16
Stewart, Gaye	Tor., Chi.	61	27	29	56	83
Bentley, Max	Chi., Tor.	59	26	28	54	14
Poile, Bud	Tor., Chi.	58	25	29	54	17
Richard, Maurice	Montreal	53	28	25	53	89
Apps Sr., Syl	Toronto	55	26	27	53	12
Lindsay, Ted	Detroit	60	33	19	52	95
Conacher, Roy	Chicago	52	22	27	49	4

1948-49

Team	GP	W	L	T	GF	GA	PTS
Detroit	60	34	19	7	195	145	75
Boston	60	29	23	8	178	163	66
Montreal	60	28	23	9	152	126	65
*Toronto	60	22	25	13	147	161	57
Chicago	60	21	31	8	173	211	50
New York	60	18	31	11	133	172	47

Leading Scorers

Player	Club	GP	G	A	PTS	PIM
Conacher, Roy	Chicago	60	26	42	68	8
Bentley, Doug	Chicago	58	23	43	66	38
Abel, Sid	Detroit	60	28	26	54	49
Lindsay, Ted	Detroit	50	26	28	54	97
Conacher, Jim	Det., Chi.	59	26	23	49	43
Ronty, Paul	Boston	60	20	29	49	11
Watson, Harry	Toronto	60	26	19	45	0
Reay, Billy	Montreal	60	22	23	45	33
Bodnar, Gus	Chicago	59	19	26	45	14
Peirson, Johnny	Boston	59	22	21	43	45

1949-50

Team	GP	W	L	T	GF	GA	PTS
*Detroit	70	37	19	14	229	164	88
Montreal	70	29	22	19	172	150	77
Toronto	70	31	27	12	176	173	74
New York	70	28	31	11	170	189	67
Boston	70	22	32	16	198	228	60
Chicago	70	22	38	10	203	244	54

Leading Scorers

Player	Club	GP	G	A	PTS	PIM
Lindsay, Ted	Detroit	69	23	55	78	141
Abel, Sid	Detroit	69	34	35	69	46
Howe, Gordie	Detroit	70	35	33	68	69
Richard, Maurice	Montreal	70	43	22	65	114
Ronty, Paul	Boston	70	23	36	59	8
Conacher, Roy	Chicago	70	25	31	56	16
Bentley, Doug	Chicago	64	20	33	53	28
Peirson, Johnny	Boston	57	27	25	52	49
Prystai, Metro	Chicago	65	29	22	51	31
Guidolin, Bep	Chicago	70	17	34	51	42

The NHL's leading scorer in 1939-40, Milt Schmidt actually established a career high with 61 points in 1950-51. Red Wings goalie Terry Sawchuk spent his first full season in the NHL that same year.

1950-51

Team	GP	W	L	T	GF	GA	PTS
Detroit	70	44	13	13	236	139	101
*Toronto	70	41	16	13	212	138	95
Montreal	70	25	30	15	173	184	65
Boston	70	22	30	18	178	197	62
New York	70	20	29	21	169	201	61
Chicago	70	13	47	10	171	280	36

Leading Scorers

Player	Club	GP	G	A	PTS	PIM
Howe, Gordie	Detroit	70	43	43	86	74
Richard, Maurice	Montreal	65	42	24	66	97
Bentley, Max	Toronto	67	21	41	62	34
Abel, Sid	Detroit	69	23	38	61	30
Schmidt, Milt	Boston	62	22	39	61	33
Kennedy, Ted	Toronto	63	18	43	61	32
Lindsay, Ted	Detroit	67	24	35	59	110
Sloan, Tod	Toronto	70	31	25	56	105
Kelly, Red	Detroit	70	17	37	54	24
Smith, Sid	Toronto	70	30	21	51	10
Gardner, Cal	Toronto	66	23	28	51	42

1951-52

Team	GP	W	L	T	GF	GA	PTS
*Detroit	70	44	14	12	215	133	100
Montreal	70	34	26	10	195	164	78
Toronto	70	29	25	16	168	157	74
Boston	70	25	29	16	162	176	66
New York	70	23	34	13	192	219	59
Chicago	70	17	44	9	158	241	43

Leading Scorers

Player	Club	GP	G	A	PTS	PIM
Howe, Gordie	Detroit	70	47	39	86	78
Lindsay, Ted	Detroit	70	30	39	69	123
Lach, Elmer	Montreal	70	15	50	65	36
Raleigh, Don	New York	70	19	42	61	14
Smith, Sid	Toronto	70	27	30	57	6
Geoffrion, Bernie	Montreal	67	30	24	54	66
Mosienko, Bill	Chicago	70	31	22	53	10
Abel, Sid	Detroit	62	17	36	53	32
Kennedy, Ted	Toronto	70	19	33	52	33
Schmidt, Milt	Boston	69	21	29	50	57
Peirson, Johnny	Boston	68	20	30	50	30

1952-53

Team	GP	W	L	T	GF	GA	PTS
Detroit	70	36	16	18	222	133	90
*Montreal	70	28	23	19	155	148	75
Boston	70	28	29	13	152	172	69
Chicago	70	27	28	15	169	175	69
Toronto	70	27	30	13	156	167	67
New York	70	17	37	16	152	211	50

Leading Scorers

Player	Club	GP	G	A	PTS	PIM
Howe, Gordie	Detroit	70	49	46	95	57
Lindsay, Ted	Detroit	70	32	39	71	111
Richard, Maurice	Montreal	70	28	33	61	112
Hergesheimer, Wally	New York	70	30	29	59	10
Delvecchio, Alex	Detroit	70	16	43	59	28
Ronty, Paul	New York	70	16	38	54	20
Prystai, Metro	Detroit	70	16	34	50	12
Kelly, Red	Detroit	70	19	27	46	8
Olmstead, Bert	Montreal	69	17	28	45	83
Mackell, Fleming	Boston	65	27	17	44	63
McFadden, Jim	Chicago	70	23	21	44	29

1953-54

Team	GP	W	L	T	GF	GA	PTS
*Detroit	70	37	19	14	191	132	88
Montreal	70	35	24	11	195	141	81
Toronto	70	32	24	14	152	131	78
Boston	70	32	28	10	177	181	74
New York	70	29	31	10	161	182	68
Chicago	70	12	51	7	133	242	31

Leading Scorers

Player	Club	GP	G	A	PTS	PIM
Howe, Gordie	Detroit	70	33	48	81	109
Richard, Maurice	Montreal	70	37	30	67	112
Lindsay, Ted	Detroit	70	26	36	62	110
Geoffrion, Bernie	Montreal	54	29	25	54	87
Olmstead, Bert	Montreal	70	15	37	52	85
Kelly, Red	Detroit	62	16	33	49	18
Reibel, Earl	Detroit	69	15	33	48	18
Sandford, Ed	Boston	70	16	31	47	42
Mackell, Fleming	Boston	67	15	32	47	60
Mosdell, Kenny	Montreal	67	22	24	46	64
Ronty, Paul	New York	70	13	33	46	18

1954-55

Team	GP	W	L	T	GF	GA	PTS
*Detroit	70	42	17	11	204	134	95
Montreal	70	41	18	11	228	157	93
Toronto	70	24	24	22	147	135	70
Boston	70	23	26	21	169	188	67
New York	70	17	35	18	150	210	52
Chicago	70	13	40	17	161	235	43

Leading Scorers

Player	Club	GP	G	A	PTS	PIM
Geoffrion, Bernie	Montreal	70	38	37	75	57
Richard, Maurice	Montreal	67	38	36	74	125
Béliveau, Jean	Montreal	70	37	36	73	58
Reibel, Earl	Detroit	70	25	41	66	15
Howe, Gordie	Detroit	64	29	33	62	68
Sullivan, Red	Chicago	69	19	42	61	51
Olmstead, Bert	Montreal	70	10	48	58	103
Smith, Sid	Toronto	70	33	21	54	14
Mosdell, Kenny	Montreal	70	22	32	54	82
Lewicki, Danny	New York	70	29	24	53	8

1955-56

Team	GP	W	L	T	GF	GA	PTS
*Montreal	70	45	15	10	222	131	100
Detroit	70	30	24	16	183	148	76
New York	70	32	28	10	204	203	74
Toronto	70	24	33	13	153	181	61
Boston	70	23	34	13	147	185	59
Chicago	70	19	39	12	155	216	50

Leading Scorers

Player	Club	GP	G	A	PTS	PIM
Béliveau, Jean	Montreal	70	47	41	88	143
Howe, Gordie	Detroit	70	38	41	79	100
Richard, Maurice	Montreal	70	38	33	71	89
Olmstead, Bert	Montreal	70	14	56	70	94
Sloan, Tod	Toronto	70	37	29	66	100
Bathgate, Andy	New York	70	19	47	66	59
Geoffrion, Bernie	Montreal	59	29	33	62	66
Reibel, Earl	Detroit	68	17	39	56	10
Delvecchio, Alex	Detroit	70	25	26	51	24
Creighton, Dave	New York	70	20	31	51	43
Gadsby, Bill	New York	70	9	42	51	84

1956-57

Team	GP	W	L	T	GF	GA	PTS
Detroit	70	38	20	12	198	157	88
*Montreal	70	35	23	12	210	155	82
Boston	70	34	24	12	195	174	80
New York	70	26	30	14	184	227	66
Toronto	70	21	34	15	174	192	57
Chicago	70	16	39	15	169	225	47

Leading Scorers

Player	Club	GP	G	A	PTS	PIM
Howe, Gordie	Detroit	70	44	45	89	72
Lindsay, Ted	Detroit	70	30	55	85	103
Béliveau, Jean	Montreal	69	33	51	84	105
Bathgate, Andy	New York	70	27	50	77	60
Litzenberger, Ed	Chicago	70	32	32	64	48
Richard, Maurice	Montreal	63	33	29	62	74
McKenney, Don	Boston	69	21	39	60	31
Moore, Dickie	Montreal	70	29	29	58	56
Richard, Henri	Montreal	63	18	36	54	71
Ullman, Norm	Detroit	64	16	36	52	47

1957-58

Team	GP	W	L	T	GF	GA	PTS
*Montreal	70	43	17	10	250	158	96
New York	70	32	25	13	195	188	77
Detroit	70	29	29	12	176	207	70
Boston	70	27	28	15	199	194	69
Chicago	70	24	39	7	163	202	55
Toronto	70	21	38	11	192	226	53

Leading Scorers

Player	Club	GP	G	A	PTS	PIM
Moore, Dickie	Montreal	70	36	48	84	65
Richard, Henri	Montreal	67	28	52	80	56
Bathgate, Andy	New York	65	30	48	78	42
Howe, Gordie	Detroit	64	33	44	77	40
Horvath, Bronco	Boston	67	30	36	66	71
Litzenberger, Ed	Chicago	70	32	30	62	63
Mackell, Fleming	Boston	70	20	40	60	72
Béliveau, Jean	Montreal	55	27	32	59	93
Delvecchio, Alex	Detroit	70	21	38	59	22
McKenney, Don	Boston	70	28	30	58	22

1958-59

Team	GP	W	L	T	GF	GA	PTS
*Montreal	70	39	18	13	258	158	91
Boston	70	32	29	9	205	215	73
Chicago	70	28	29	13	197	208	69
Toronto	70	27	32	11	189	201	65
New York	70	26	32	12	201	217	64
Detroit	70	25	37	8	167	218	58

Leading Scorers

Player	Club	GP	G	A	PTS	PIM
Moore, Dickie	Montreal	70	41	55	96	61
Béliveau, Jean	Montreal	64	45	46	91	67
Bathgate, Andy	New York	70	40	48	88	48
Howe, Gordie	Detroit	70	32	46	78	57
Litzenberger, Ed	Chicago	70	33	44	77	37
Geoffrion, Bernie	Montreal	59	22	44	66	30
Sullivan, Red	New York	70	21	42	63	56
Hebenton, Andy	New York	70	33	29	62	8
McKenney, Don	Boston	70	32	30	62	20
Sloan, Tod	Chicago	59	27	35	62	79

1959-60

Team	GP	W	L	T	GF	GA	PTS
*Montreal	70	40	18	12	255	178	92
Toronto	70	35	26	9	199	195	79
Chicago	70	28	29	13	191	180	69
Detroit	70	26	29	15	186	197	67
Boston	70	28	34	8	220	241	64
New York	70	17	38	15	187	247	49

Leading Scorers

Player	Club	GP	G	A	PTS	PIM
Hull, Bobby	Chicago	70	39	42	81	68
Horvath, Bronco	Boston	68	39	41	80	60
Béliveau, Jean	Montreal	60	34	40	74	57
Bathgate, Andy	New York	70	26	48	74	28
Richard, Henri	Montreal	70	30	43	73	66
Howe, Gordie	Detroit	70	28	45	73	46
Geoffrion, Bernie	Montreal	59	30	41	71	36
McKenney, Don	Boston	70	20	49	69	28
Stasiuk, Vic	Boston	69	29	39	68	121
Prentice, Dean	New York	70	32	34	66	43

1960-61

Team	GP	W	L	T	GF	GA	PTS
Montreal	70	41	19	10	254	188	92
Toronto	70	39	19	12	234	176	90
*Chicago	70	29	24	17	198	180	75
Detroit	70	25	29	16	195	215	66
New York	70	22	38	10	204	248	54
Boston	70	15	42	13	176	254	43

Leading Scorers

Player	Club	GP	G	A	PTS	PIM
Geoffrion, Bernie	Montreal	64	50	45	95	29
Béliveau, Jean	Montreal	69	32	58	90	57
Mahovlich, Frank	Toronto	70	48	36	84	131
Bathgate, Andy	New York	70	29	48	77	22
Howe, Gordie	Detroit	64	23	49	72	30
Ullman, Norm	Detroit	70	28	42	70	34
Kelly, Red	Toronto	64	20	50	70	12
Moore, Dickie	Montreal	57	35	34	69	62
Richard, Henri	Montreal	70	24	44	68	91
Delvecchio, Alex	Detroit	70	27	35	62	26

1961-62

Team	GP	W	L	T	GF	GA	PTS
Montreal	70	42	14	14	259	166	98
*Toronto	70	37	22	11	232	180	85
Chicago	70	31	26	13	217	186	75
New York	70	26	32	12	195	207	64
Detroit	70	23	33	14	184	219	60
Boston	70	15	47	8	177	306	38

Leading Scorers

Player	Club	GP	G	A	PTS	PIM
Hull, Bobby	Chicago	70	50	34	84	35
Bathgate, Andy	New York	70	28	56	84	44
Howe, Gordie	Detroit	70	33	44	77	54
Mikita, Stan	Chicago	70	25	52	77	97
Mahovlich, Frank	Toronto	70	33	38	71	87
Delvecchio, Alex	Detroit	70	26	43	69	18
Backstrom, Ralph	Montreal	66	27	38	65	29
Ullman, Norm	Detroit	70	26	38	64	54
Hay, Bill	Chicago	60	11	52	63	34
Provost, Claude	Montreal	70	33	29	62	22

1962-63

Team	GP	W	L	T	GF	GA	PTS
*Toronto	70	35	23	12	221	180	82
Chicago	70	32	21	17	194	178	81
Montreal	70	28	19	23	225	183	79
Detroit	70	32	25	13	200	194	77
New York	70	22	36	12	211	233	56
Boston	70	14	39	17	198	281	45

Leading Scorers

Player	Club	GP	G	A	PTS	PIM
Howe, Gordie	Detroit	70	38	48	86	100
Bathgate, Andy	New York	70	35	46	81	54
Mikita, Stan	Chicago	65	31	45	76	69
Mahovlich, Frank	Toronto	67	36	37	73	56
Richard, Henri	Montreal	67	23	50	73	57
Béliveau, Jean	Montreal	69	18	49	67	68
Bucyk, John	Boston	69	27	39	66	36
Delvecchio, Alex	Detroit	70	20	44	64	8
Hull, Bobby	Chicago	65	31	31	62	27
Oliver, Murray	Boston	65	22	40	62	38

1963-64

Team	GP	W	L	T	GF	GA	PTS
Montreal	70	36	21	13	209	167	85
Chicago	70	36	22	12	218	169	84
*Toronto	70	33	25	12	192	172	78
Detroit	70	30	29	11	191	204	71
New York	70	22	38	10	186	242	54
Boston	70	18	40	12	170	212	48

Leading Scorers

Player	Club	GP	G	A	PTS	PIM
Mikita, Stan	Chicago	70	39	50	89	146
Hull, Bobby	Chicago	70	43	44	87	50
Béliveau, Jean	Montreal	68	28	50	78	42
Bathgate, Andy	NYR, Tor.	71	19	58	77	34
Howe, Gordie	Detroit	69	26	47	73	70
Wharram, Kenny	Chicago	70	39	32	71	18
Oliver, Murray	Boston	70	24	44	68	41
Goyette, Phil	New York	67	24	41	65	15
Gilbert, Rod	New York	70	24	40	64	62
Keon, Dave	Toronto	70	23	37	60	6

1964-65

Team	GP	W	L	T	GF	GA	PTS
Detroit	70	40	23	7	224	175	87
*Montreal	70	36	23	11	211	185	83
Chicago	70	34	28	8	224	176	76
Toronto	70	30	26	14	204	173	74
New York	70	20	38	12	179	246	52
Boston	70	21	43	6	166	253	48

Leading Scorers

Player	Club	GP	G	A	PTS	PIM
Mikita, Stan	Chicago	70	28	59	87	154
Ullman, Norm	Detroit	70	42	41	83	70
Howe, Gordie	Detroit	70	29	47	76	104
Hull, Bobby	Chicago	61	39	32	71	32
Delvecchio, Alex	Detroit	68	25	42	67	16
Provost, Claude	Montreal	70	27	37	64	28
Gilbert, Rod	New York	70	25	36	61	52
Pilote, Pierre	Chicago	68	14	45	59	162
Bucyk, John	Boston	68	26	29	55	24
Backstrom, Ralph	Montreal	70	25	30	55	41
Esposito, Phil	Chicago	70	23	32	55	44

1965-66

Team	GP	W	L	T	GF	GA	PTS
*Montreal	70	41	21	8	239	173	90
Chicago	70	37	25	8	240	187	82
Toronto	70	34	25	11	208	187	79
Detroit	70	31	27	12	221	194	74
Boston	70	21	43	6	174	275	48
New York	70	18	41	11	195	261	47

Leading Scorers

Player	Club	GP	G	A	PTS	PIM
Hull, Bobby	Chicago	65	54	43	97	70
Mikita, Stan	Chicago	68	30	48	78	58
Rousseau, Bobby	Montreal	70	30	48	78	20
Béliveau, Jean	Montreal	67	29	48	77	50
Howe, Gordie	Detroit	70	29	46	75	83
Ullman, Norm	Detroit	70	31	41	72	35
Delvecchio, Alex	Detroit	70	31	38	69	16
Nevin, Bob	New York	69	29	33	62	10
Richard, Henri	Montreal	62	22	39	61	47
Oliver, Murray	Boston	70	18	42	60	30

1966-67

Team	GP	W	L	T	GF	GA	PTS
Chicago	70	41	17	12	264	170	94
Montreal	70	32	25	13	202	188	77
*Toronto	70	32	27	11	204	211	75
New York	70	30	28	12	188	189	72
Detroit	70	27	39	4	212	241	58
Boston	70	17	43	10	182	253	44

Leading Scorers

Player	Club	GP	G	A	PTS	PIM
Mikita, Stan	Chicago	70	35	62	97	12
Hull, Bobby	Chicago	66	52	28	80	52
Ullman, Norm	Detroit	68	26	44	70	26
Wharram, Kenny	Chicago	70	31	34	65	21
Howe, Gordie	Detroit	69	25	40	65	53
Rousseau, Bobby	Montreal	68	19	44	63	58
Esposito, Phil	Chicago	69	21	40	61	40
Goyette, Phil	New York	70	12	49	61	6
Mohns, Doug	Chicago	61	25	35	60	58
Richard, Henri	Montreal	65	21	34	55	28
Delvecchio, Alex	Detroit	70	17	38	55	10

1967-68

East Division

Team	GP	W	L	T	GF	GA	PTS
*Montreal	74	42	22	10	236	167	94
New York	74	39	23	12	226	183	90
Boston	74	37	27	10	259	216	84
Chicago	74	32	26	16	212	222	80
Toronto	74	33	31	10	209	176	76
Detroit	74	27	35	12	245	257	66

West Division

Team	GP	W	L	T	GF	GA	PTS
Philadelphia	74	31	32	11	173	179	73
Los Angeles	74	31	33	10	200	224	72
St. Louis	74	27	31	16	177	191	70
Minnesota	74	27	32	15	191	226	69
Pittsburgh	74	27	34	13	195	216	67
Oakland	74	15	42	17	153	219	47

Leading Scorers

Player	Club	GP	G	A	PTS	PIM
Mikita, Stan	Chicago	72	40	47	87	14
Esposito, Phil	Boston	74	35	49	84	21
Howe, Gordie	Detroit	74	39	43	82	53
Ratelle, Jean	New York	74	32	46	78	18
Gilbert, Rod	New York	73	29	48	77	12
Hull, Bobby	Chicago	71	44	31	75	39
Ullman, Norm	Det., Tor.	71	35	37	72	28
Delvecchio, Alex	Detroit	74	22	48	70	14
Bucyk, John	Boston	72	30	39	69	8
Wharram, Kenny	Chicago	74	27	42	69	18

1968-69

East Division

Team	GP	W	L	T	GF	GA	PTS
*Montreal	76	46	19	11	271	202	103
Boston	76	42	18	16	303	221	100
New York	76	41	26	9	231	196	91
Toronto	76	35	26	15	234	217	85
Detroit	76	33	31	12	239	221	78
Chicago	76	34	33	9	280	246	77

West Division

Team	GP	W	L	T	GF	GA	PTS
St. Louis	76	37	25	14	204	157	88
Oakland	76	29	36	11	219	251	69
Philadelphia	76	20	35	21	174	225	61
Los Angeles	76	24	42	10	185	260	58
Pittsburgh	76	20	45	11	189	252	51
Minnesota	76	18	43	5	189	270	51

Leading Scorers

Player	Club	GP	G	A	PTS	PIM
Esposito, Phil	Boston	74	49	77	126	79
Hull, Bobby	Chicago	74	58	49	107	48
Howe, Gordie	Detroit	76	44	59	103	58
Mikita, Stan	Chicago	74	30	67	97	52
Hodge, Ken	Boston	75	45	45	90	75
Cournoyer, Yvan	Montreal	76	43	44	87	31
Delvecchio, Alex	Detroit	72	25	58	83	8
Berenson, Red	St. Louis	76	35	47	82	43
Béliveau, Jean	Montreal	69	33	49	82	55
Mahovlich, Frank	Detroit	76	49	29	78	38
Ratelle, Jean	New York	75	32	46	78	26

1969-70

East Division

Team	GP	W	L	T	GF	GA	PTS
Chicago	76	45	22	9	250	170	99
*Boston	76	40	17	19	277	216	99
Detroit	76	40	21	15	246	199	95
New York	76	38	22	16	246	189	92
Montreal	76	38	22	16	244	201	92
Toronto	76	29	34	13	222	242	71

West Division

Team	GP	W	L	T	GF	GA	PTS
St. Louis	76	37	27	12	224	179	86
Pittsburgh	76	26	38	12	182	238	64
Minnesota	76	19	35	22	224	257	60
Oakland	76	22	40	14	169	243	58
Philadelphia	76	17	35	24	197	225	58
Los Angeles	76	14	52	10	168	290	38

Leading Scorers

Player	Club	GP	G	A	PTS	PIM
Orr, Bobby	Boston	76	33	87	120	125
Esposito, Phil	Boston	76	43	56	99	50
Mikita, Stan	Chicago	76	39	47	86	50
Goyette, Phil	St. Louis	72	29	49	78	16
Tkaczuk, Walt	New York	76	27	50	77	38
Ratelle, Jean	New York	75	32	42	74	28
Berenson, Red	St. Louis	67	33	39	72	38
Parise, Jean-Paul	Minnesota	74	24	48	72	72
Howe, Gordie	Detroit	76	31	40	71	58
Mahovlich, Frank	Detroit	74	38	32	70	59
Balon, Dave	New York	76	33	37	70	100
McKenzie, John	Boston	72	29	41	70	114

1970-71

East Division

Team	GP	W	L	T	GF	GA	PTS
Boston	78	57	14	7	399	207	121
New York	78	49	18	11	259	177	109
*Montreal	78	42	23	13	291	216	97
Toronto	78	37	33	8	248	211	82
Buffalo	78	24	39	15	217	291	63
Vancouver	78	24	46	8	229	296	56
Detroit	78	22	45	11	209	308	55

West Division

Team	GP	W	L	T	GF	GA	PTS
Chicago	78	49	20	9	277	184	107
St. Louis	78	34	25	19	223	208	87
Philadelphia	78	28	33	17	207	225	73
Minnesota	78	28	34	16	191	223	72
Los Angeles	78	25	40	13	239	303	63
Pittsburgh	78	21	37	20	221	240	62
California	78	20	53	5	199	320	45

Leading Scorers

Player	Club	GP	G	A	PTS	PIM
Esposito, Phil	Boston	78	76	76	152	71
Orr, Bobby	Boston	78	37	102	139	91
Bucyk, John	Boston	78	51	65	116	8
Hodge, Ken	Boston	78	43	62	105	113
Hull, Bobby	Chicago	78	44	52	96	32
Ullman, Norm	Toronto	73	34	51	85	24
Cashman, Wayne	Boston	77	21	58	79	100
McKenzie, John	Boston	65	31	46	77	120
Keon, Dave	Toronto	76	38	38	76	4
Béliveau, Jean	Montreal	70	25	51	76	40
Stanfield, Fred	Boston	75	24	52	76	12

1971-72

East Division

Team	GP	W	L	T	GF	GA	PTS
*Boston	78	54	13	11	330	204	119
New York	78	48	17	13	317	192	109
Montreal	78	46	16	16	307	205	108
Toronto	78	33	31	14	209	208	80
Detroit	78	33	35	10	261	262	76
Buffalo	78	16	43	19	203	289	51
Vancouver	78	20	50	8	203	297	48

West Division

Team	GP	W	L	T	GF	GA	PTS
Chicago	78	46	17	15	256	166	107
Minnesota	78	37	29	12	212	191	86
St. Louis	78	28	39	11	208	247	67
Pittsburgh	78	26	38	14	220	258	66
Philadelphia	78	26	38	14	200	236	66
California	78	21	39	18	216	288	60
Los Angeles	78	20	49	9	206	305	49

Leading Scorers

Player	Club	GP	G	A	PTS	PIM
Esposito, Phil	Boston	76	66	67	133	76
Orr, Bobby	Boston	76	37	80	117	106
Ratelle, Jean	New York	63	46	63	109	4
Hadfield, Vic	New York	78	50	56	106	142
Gilbert, Rod	New York	73	43	54	97	64
Mahovlich, Frank	Montreal	76	43	53	96	36
Hull, Bobby	Chicago	78	50	43	93	24
Cournoyer, Yvan	Montreal	73	47	36	83	15
Bucyk, John	Boston	78	32	51	83	4
Clarke, Bobby	Philadelphia	78	35	46	81	87
Lemaire, Jacques	Montreal	77	32	49	81	26

1972-73

East Division

Team	GP	W	L	T	GF	GA	PTS
*Montreal	78	52	10	16	329	184	120
Boston	78	51	22	5	330	235	107
NY Rangers	78	47	23	8	297	208	102
Buffalo	78	37	27	14	257	219	88
Detroit	78	37	29	12	265	243	86
Toronto	78	27	41	10	247	279	64
Vancouver	78	22	47	9	233	339	53
NY Islanders	78	12	60	6	170	347	30

West Division

Team	GP	W	L	T	GF	GA	PTS
Chicago	78	42	27	9	284	225	93
Philadelphia	78	37	30	11	296	256	85
Minnesota	78	37	30	11	254	230	85
St. Louis	78	32	34	12	233	251	76
Pittsburgh	78	32	37	9	257	265	73
Los Angeles	78	31	36	11	232	245	73
Atlanta	78	25	38	15	191	239	65
California	78	16	46	16	213	323	48

Leading Scorers

Player	Club	GP	G	A	PTS	PIM
Esposito, Phil	Boston	78	55	75	130	87
Clarke, Bobby	Philadelphia	78	37	67	104	80
Orr, Bobby	Boston	63	29	72	101	99
MacLeish, Rick	Philadelphia	78	50	50	100	69
Lemaire, Jacques	Montreal	77	44	51	95	16
Ratelle, Jean	NY Rangers	78	41	53	94	12
Redmond, Mickey	Detroit	76	52	41	93	24
Bucyk, John	Boston	78	40	53	93	12
Mahovlich, Frank	Montreal	78	38	55	93	51
Pappin, Jim	Chicago	76	41	51	92	82

1973-74

East Division

Team	GP	W	L	T	GF	GA	PTS
Boston	78	52	17	9	349	221	113
Montreal	78	45	24	9	293	240	99
NY Rangers	78	40	24	14	300	251	94
Toronto	78	35	27	16	274	230	86
Buffalo	78	32	34	12	242	250	76
Detroit	78	29	39	10	255	319	68
Vancouver	78	24	43	11	224	296	59
NY Islanders	78	19	41	18	182	247	56

West Division

Team	GP	W	L	T	GF	GA	PTS
*Philadelphia	78	50	16	12	273	164	112
Chicago	78	41	14	23	272	164	105
Los Angeles	78	33	33	12	233	231	78
Atlanta	78	30	34	14	214	238	74
Pittsburgh	78	28	41	9	242	273	65
St. Louis	78	26	40	12	206	248	64
Minnesota	78	23	38	17	235	275	63
California	78	13	55	10	195	342	36

Leading Scorers

Player	Club	GP	G	A	PTS	PIM
Esposito, Phil	Boston	78	68	77	145	58
Orr, Bobby	Boston	74	32	90	122	82
Hodge, Ken	Boston	76	50	55	105	43
Cashman, Wayne	Boston	78	30	59	89	111
Clarke, Bobby	Philadelphia	77	35	52	87	113
Martin, Rick	Buffalo	78	52	34	86	38
Apps Jr., Syl	Pittsburgh	75	24	61	85	37
Sittler, Darryl	Toronto	78	38	46	84	55
MacDonald, Lowell	Pittsburgh	78	43	39	82	14
Park, Brad	NY Rangers	78	25	57	82	148
Hextall, Dennis	Minnesota	78	20	62	82	138

1974-75

PRINCE OF WALES CONFERENCE

Norris Division

Team	GP	W	L	T	GF	GA	PTS
Montreal	80	47	14	19	374	225	113
Los Angeles	80	42	17	21	269	185	105
Pittsburgh	80	37	28	15	326	289	89
Detroit	80	23	45	12	259	335	58
Washington	80	8	67	5	181	446	21

Adams Division

Team	GP	W	L	T	GF	GA	PTS
Buffalo	80	49	16	15	354	240	113
Boston	80	40	26	14	345	245	94
Toronto	80	31	33	16	280	309	78
California	80	19	48	13	212	316	51

CLARENCE CAMPBELL CONFERENCE

Patrick Division

Team	GP	W	L	T	GF	GA	PTS
*Philadelphia	80	51	18	11	293	181	113
NY Rangers	80	37	29	14	319	276	88
NY Islanders	80	33	25	22	264	221	88
Atlanta	80	34	31	15	243	233	83

Smythe Division

Team	GP	W	L	T	GF	GA	PTS
Vancouver	80	38	32	10	271	254	86
St. Louis	80	35	31	14	269	267	84
Chicago	80	37	35	8	268	241	82
Minnesota	80	23	50	7	221	341	53
Kansas City	80	15	54	11	184	328	41

Leading Scorers

Player	Club	GP	G	A	PTS	PIM
Orr, Bobby	Boston	80	46	89	135	101
Esposito, Phil	Boston	79	61	66	127	62
Dionne, Marcel	Detroit	80	47	74	121	14
Lafleur, Guy	Montreal	70	53	66	119	37
Mahovlich, Pete	Montreal	80	35	82	117	64
Clarke, Bobby	Philadelphia	80	27	89	116	125
Robert, Rene	Buffalo	74	40	60	100	75
Gilbert, Rod	NY Rangers	76	36	61	97	22
Perreault, Gilbert	Buffalo	68	39	57	96	36
Martin, Rick	Buffalo	68	52	43	95	72

Though overshadowed by Bobby Orr, Brad Park consistently ranked among the NHL's top-scoring defensemen, establishing career highs with 25 goals and 82 points in 1973-74.

1975-76

PRINCE OF WALES CONFERENCE

Norris Division

Team	GP	W	L	T	GF	GA	PTS
*Montreal	80	58	11	11	337	174	127
Los Angeles	80	38	33	9	263	265	85
Pittsburgh	80	35	33	12	339	303	82
Detroit	80	26	44	10	226	300	62
Washington	80	11	59	10	224	394	32

Adams Division

Team	GP	W	L	T	GF	GA	PTS
Boston	80	48	15	17	313	237	113
Buffalo	80	46	21	13	339	240	105
Toronto	80	34	31	15	294	276	83
California	80	27	42	11	250	278	65

CLARENCE CAMPBELL CONFERENCE

Patrick Division

Team	GP	W	L	T	GF	GA	PTS
Philadelphia	80	51	13	16	348	209	118
NY Islanders	80	42	21	17	297	190	101
Atlanta	80	35	33	12	262	237	82
NY Rangers	80	29	42	9	262	333	67

Smythe Division

Team	GP	W	L	T	GF	GA	PTS
Chicago	80	32	30	18	254	261	82
Vancouver	80	33	32	15	271	272	81
St. Louis	80	29	37	14	249	290	72
Minnesota	80	20	53	7	195	303	47
Kansas City	80	12	56	12	190	351	36

Leading Scorers

Player	Club	GP	G	A	PTS	PIM
Lafleur, Guy	Montreal	80	56	69	125	36
Clarke, Bobby	Philadelphia	76	30	89	119	13
Perreault, Gilbert	Buffalo	80	44	69	113	36
Barber, Bill	Philadelphia	80	50	62	112	104
Larouche, Pierre	Pittsburgh	76	53	58	111	33
Ratelle, Jean	Bos., NYR	80	36	69	105	18
Mahovlich, Pete	Montreal	80	34	71	105	76
Pronovost, Jean	Pittsburgh	80	52	52	104	24
Sittler, Darryl	Toronto	79	41	59	100	90
Apps Jr., Syl	Pittsburgh	80	32	67	99	24

1976-77

PRINCE OF WALES CONFERENCE

Norris Division

Team	GP	W	L	T	GF	GA	PTS
*Montreal	80	60	8	12	387	171	132
Los Angeles	80	34	31	15	271	241	83
Pittsburgh	80	34	33	13	240	252	81
Washington	80	24	42	14	221	307	62
Detroit	80	16	55	9	183	309	41

Adams Division

Team	GP	W	L	T	GF	GA	PTS
Boston	80	49	23	8	312	240	106
Buffalo	80	48	24	8	301	220	104
Toronto	80	33	32	15	301	285	81
Cleveland	80	25	42	13	240	292	63

CLARENCE CAMPBELL CONFERENCE

Patrick Division

Team	GP	W	L	T	GF	GA	PTS
Philadelphia	80	48	16	16	323	213	112
NY Islanders	80	47	21	12	288	193	106
Atlanta	80	34	34	12	264	265	80
NY Rangers	80	29	37	14	272	310	72

Smythe Division

Team	GP	W	L	T	GF	GA	PTS
St. Louis	80	32	39	9	239	276	73
Minnesota	80	23	39	18	240	310	64
Chicago	80	26	43	11	240	298	63
Vancouver	80	25	42	13	235	294	63
Colorado	80	20	46	14	226	307	54

Leading Scorers

Player	Club	GP	G	A	PTS	PIM
Lafleur, Guy	Montreal	80	56	80	136	20
Dionne, Marcel	Los Angeles	80	53	69	122	12
Shutt, Steve	Montreal	80	60	45	105	28
MacLeish, Rick	Philadelphia	79	49	48	97	42
Perreault, Gilbert	Buffalo	80	39	56	95	30
Young, Tim	Minnesota	80	29	66	95	58
Ratelle, Jean	Boston	78	33	61	94	22
McDonald, Lanny	Toronto	80	46	44	90	77
Sittler, Darryl	Toronto	73	38	52	90	89
Clarke, Bobby	Philadelphia	80	27	63	90	71

1977-78

PRINCE OF WALES CONFERENCE

Norris Division

Team	GP	W	L	T	GF	GA	PTS
*Montreal	80	59	10	11	359	183	129
Detroit	80	32	34	14	252	266	78
Los Angeles	80	31	34	15	243	245	77
Pittsburgh	80	25	37	18	254	321	68
Washington	80	17	49	14	195	321	48

Adams Division

Team	GP	W	L	T	GF	GA	PTS
Boston	80	51	18	11	333	218	113
Buffalo	80	44	19	17	288	215	105
Toronto	80	41	29	10	271	237	92
Cleveland	80	22	45	13	230	325	57

CLARENCE CAMPBELL CONFERENCE

Patrick Division

Team	GP	W	L	T	GF	GA	PTS
NY Islanders	80	48	17	15	334	210	111
Philadelphia	80	45	20	15	296	200	105
Atlanta	80	34	27	19	274	252	87
NY Rangers	80	30	37	13	279	280	73

Smythe Division

Team	GP	W	L	T	GF	GA	PTS
Chicago	80	32	29	19	230	220	83
Colorado	80	19	40	21	257	305	59
Vancouver	80	20	43	17	239	320	57
St. Louis	80	20	47	13	195	304	53
Minnesota	80	18	53	9	218	325	45

Leading Scorers

Player	Club	GP	G	A	PTS	PIM
Lafleur, Guy	Montreal	79	60	72	132	26
Trottier, Bryan	NY Islanders	77	46	77	123	46
Sittler, Darryl	Toronto	80	45	72	117	100
Lemaire, Jacques	Montreal	76	36	61	97	14
Potvin, Denis	NY Islanders	80	30	64	94	81
Bossy, Mike	NY Islanders	73	53	38	91	6
O'Reilly, Terry	Boston	77	29	61	90	211
Perreault, Gilbert	Buffalo	79	41	48	89	20
Clarke, Bobby	Philadelphia	71	21	68	89	83
McDonald, Lanny	Toronto	74	47	40	87	54
Paiement, Wilf	Colorado	80	31	56	87	114

1978-79

PRINCE OF WALES CONFERENCE

Norris Division

Team	GP	W	L	T	GF	GA	PTS
*Montreal	80	52	17	11	337	204	115
Pittsburgh	80	36	31	13	281	279	85
Los Angeles	80	34	34	12	292	286	80
Washington	80	24	41	15	273	338	63
Detroit	80	23	41	16	252	295	62

Adams Division

Team	GP	W	L	T	GF	GA	PTS
Boston	80	43	23	14	316	270	100
Buffalo	80	36	28	16	280	263	88
Toronto	80	34	33	13	267	252	81
Minnesota	80	28	40	12	257	289	68

CLARENCE CAMPBELL CONFERENCE

Patrick Division

Team	GP	W	L	T	GF	GA	PTS
NY Islanders	80	51	15	14	358	214	116
Philadelphia	80	40	25	15	281	248	95
NY Rangers	80	40	29	11	316	292	91
Atlanta	80	41	31	8	327	280	90

Smythe Division

Team	GP	W	L	T	GF	GA	PTS
Chicago	80	29	36	15	244	277	73
Vancouver	80	25	42	13	217	291	63
St. Louis	80	18	50	12	249	348	48
Colorado	80	15	53	12	210	331	42

Leading Scorers

Player	Club	GP	G	A	PTS	PIM
Trottier, Bryan	NY Islanders	76	47	87	134	50
Dionne, Marcel	Los Angeles	80	59	71	130	30
Lafleur, Guy	Montreal	80	52	77	129	28
Bossy, Mike	NY Islanders	80	69	57	126	25
MacMillan, Bob	Atlanta	79	37	71	108	14
Chouinard, Guy	Atlanta	80	50	57	107	14
Potvin, Denis	NY Islanders	73	31	70	101	58
Federko, Bernie	St. Louis	74	31	64	95	14
Taylor, Dave	Los Angeles	78	43	48	91	124
Gillies, Clark	NY Islanders	75	35	56	91	68

1979-80

PRINCE OF WALES CONFERENCE

Norris Division

Team	GP	W	L	T	GF	GA	PTS
Montreal	80	47	20	13	328	240	107
Los Angeles	80	30	36	14	290	313	74
Pittsburgh	80	30	37	13	251	303	73
Hartford	80	27	34	19	303	312	73
Detroit	80	26	43	11	268	306	63

Adams Division

Team	GP	W	L	T	GF	GA	PTS
Buffalo	80	47	17	16	318	201	110
Boston	80	46	21	13	310	234	105
Minnesota	80	36	28	16	311	253	88
Toronto	80	35	40	5	304	327	75
Quebec	80	25	44	11	248	313	61

CLARENCE CAMPBELL CONFERENCE

Patrick Division

Team	GP	W	L	T	GF	GA	PTS
Philadelphia	80	48	12	20	327	254	116
*NY Islanders	80	39	28	13	281	247	91
NY Rangers	80	38	32	10	308	284	86
Atlanta	80	35	32	13	282	269	83
Washington	80	27	40	13	261	293	67

Smythe Division

Team	GP	W	L	T	GF	GA	PTS
Chicago	80	34	27	19	241	250	87
St. Louis	80	34	34	12	266	278	80
Vancouver	80	27	37	16	256	281	70
Edmonton	80	28	39	13	301	322	69
Winnipeg	80	20	49	11	214	314	51
Colorado	80	19	48	13	234	308	51

Leading Scorers

Player	Club	GP	G	A	PTS	PIM
Dionne, Marcel	Los Angeles	80	53	84	137	32
Gretzky, Wayne	Edmonton	79	51	86	137	21
Lafleur, Guy	Montreal	74	50	75	125	12
Perreault, Gilbert	Buffalo	80	40	66	106	57
Rogers, Mike	Hartford	80	44	61	105	10
Trottier, Bryan	NY Islanders	78	42	62	104	68
Simmer, Charlie	Los Angeles	64	56	45	101	65
Stoughton, Blaine	Hartford	80	56	44	100	16
Sittler, Darryl	Toronto	73	40	57	97	62
MacDonald, Blair	Edmonton	80	46	48	94	6
Federko, Bernie	St. Louis	79	38	56	94	24

1980-81

PRINCE OF WALES CONFERENCE

Norris Division

Team	GP	W	L	T	GF	GA	PTS
Montreal	80	45	22	13	332	232	103
Los Angeles	80	43	24	13	337	290	99
Pittsburgh	80	30	37	13	302	345	73
Hartford	80	21	41	18	292	372	60
Detroit	80	19	43	18	252	339	56

Adams Division

Team	GP	W	L	T	GF	GA	PTS
Buffalo	80	39	20	21	327	250	99
Boston	80	37	30	13	316	272	87
Minnesota	80	35	28	17	291	263	87
Quebec	80	30	32	18	314	318	78
Toronto	80	28	37	15	322	367	71

CLARENCE CAMPBELL CONFERENCE

Patrick Division

Team	GP	W	L	T	GF	GA	PTS
*NY Islanders	80	48	18	14	355	260	110
Philadelphia	80	41	24	15	313	249	97
Calgary	80	39	27	14	329	298	92
NY Rangers	80	30	36	14	312	317	74
Washington	80	26	36	18	286	317	70

Smythe Division

Team	GP	W	L	T	GF	GA	PTS
St. Louis	80	45	18	17	352	281	107
Chicago	80	31	33	16	304	315	78
Vancouver	80	28	32	20	289	301	76
Edmonton	80	29	35	16	328	327	74
Colorado	80	22	45	13	258	344	57
Winnipeg	80	9	57	14	246	400	32

Leading Scorers

Player	Club	GP	G	A	PTS	PIM
Gretzky, Wayne	Edmonton	80	55	109	164	28
Dionne, Marcel	Los Angeles	80	58	77	135	70
Nilsson, Kent	Calgary	80	49	82	131	26
Bossy, Mike	NY Islanders	79	68	51	119	32
Taylor, Dave	Los Angeles	72	47	65	112	130
Stastny, Peter	Quebec	77	39	70	109	37
Simmer, Charlie	Los Angeles	65	56	49	105	62
Rogers, Mike	Hartford	80	40	65	105	32
Federko, Bernie	St. Louis	78	31	73	104	47
Richard, Jacques	Quebec	78	52	51	103	39
Middleton, Rick	Boston	80	44	59	103	16
Trottier, Bryan	NY Islanders	73	31	72	103	74

1981-82

CLARENCE CAMPBELL CONFERENCE

Norris Division

Team	GP	W	L	T	GF	GA	PTS
Minnesota	80	37	23	20	346	288	94
Winnipeg	80	33	33	14	319	332	80
St. Louis	80	32	40	8	315	349	72
Chicago	80	30	38	12	332	363	72
Toronto	80	20	44	16	298	380	56
Detroit	80	21	47	12	270	351	54

Smythe Division

Team	GP	W	L	T	GF	GA	PTS
Edmonton	80	48	17	15	417	295	111
Vancouver	80	30	33	17	290	286	77
Calgary	80	29	34	17	334	345	75
Los Angeles	80	24	41	15	314	369	63
Colorado	80	18	49	13	241	362	49

PRINCE OF WALES CONFERENCE

Adams Division

Team	GP	W	L	T	GF	GA	PTS
Montreal	80	46	17	17	360	223	109
Boston	80	43	27	10	323	285	96
Buffalo	80	39	26	15	307	273	93
Quebec	80	33	31	16	356	345	82
Hartford	80	21	41	18	264	351	60

Patrick Division

Team	GP	W	L	T	GF	GA	PTS
*NY Islanders	80	54	16	10	385	250	118
NY Rangers	80	39	27	14	316	306	92
Philadelphia	80	38	31	11	325	313	87
Pittsburgh	80	31	36	13	310	337	75
Washington	80	26	41	13	319	338	65

Leading Scorers

Player	Club	GP	G	A	PTS	PIM
Gretzky, Wayne	Edmonton	80	92	120	212	26
Bossy, Mike	NY Islanders	80	64	83	147	22
Stastny, Peter	Quebec	80	46	93	139	91
Maruk, Dennis	Washington	80	60	76	136	128
Trottier, Bryan	NY Islanders	80	50	79	129	88
Savard, Denis	Chicago	80	32	87	119	82
Dionne, Marcel	Los Angeles	78	50	67	117	50
Smith, Bobby	Minnesota	80	43	71	114	82
Ciccarelli, Dino	Minnesota	76	55	51	106	138
Taylor, Dave	Los Angeles	78	39	67	106	130

1982-83

CLARENCE CAMPBELL CONFERENCE

Norris Division

Team	GP	W	L	T	GF	GA	PTS
Chicago	80	47	23	10	338	268	104
Minnesota	80	40	24	16	321	290	96
Toronto	80	28	40	12	293	330	68
St. Louis	80	25	40	15	285	316	65
Detroit	80	21	44	15	263	344	57

Smythe Division

Team	GP	W	L	T	GF	GA	PTS
Edmonton	80	47	21	12	424	315	106
Calgary	80	32	34	14	321	317	78
Vancouver	80	30	35	15	303	309	75
Winnipeg	80	33	39	8	311	333	74
Los Angeles	80	27	41	12	308	365	66

PRINCE OF WALES CONFERENCE

Adams Division

Team	GP	W	L	T	GF	GA	PTS
Boston	80	50	20	10	327	228	110
Montreal	80	42	24	14	350	286	98
Buffalo	80	38	29	13	318	285	89
Quebec	80	34	34	12	343	336	80
Hartford	80	19	54	7	261	403	45

Patrick Division

Team	GP	W	L	T	GF	GA	PTS
Philadelphia	80	49	23	8	326	240	106
*NY Islanders	80	42	26	12	302	226	96
Washington	80	39	25	16	306	283	94
NY Rangers	80	35	35	10	306	287	80
New Jersey	80	17	49	14	230	338	48
Pittsburgh	80	18	53	9	257	394	45

Leading Scorers

Player	Club	GP	G	A	PTS	PIM
Gretzky, Wayne	Edmonton	80	71	125	196	59
Stastny, Peter	Quebec	75	47	77	124	78
Savard, Denis	Chicago	78	35	86	121	99
Bossy, Mike	NY Islanders	79	60	58	118	20
Dionne, Marcel	Los Angeles	80	56	51	107	22
Pederson, Barry	Boston	77	46	61	107	47
Messier, Mark	Edmonton	77	48	58	106	72
Goulet, Michel	Quebec	80	57	48	105	51
Anderson, Glenn	Edmonton	72	48	56	104	70
Nilsson, Kent	Calgary	80	46	58	104	10
Kurri, Jari	Edmonton	80	45	59	104	22

1983-84

CLARENCE CAMPBELL CONFERENCE

Norris Division

Team	GP	W	L	T	GF	GA	PTS
Minnesota	80	39	31	10	345	344	88
St. Louis	80	32	41	7	293	316	71
Detroit	80	31	42	7	298	323	69
Chicago	80	30	42	8	277	311	68
Toronto	80	26	45	9	303	387	61

Smythe Division

Team	GP	W	L	T	GF	GA	PTS
*Edmonton	80	57	18	5	446	314	119
Calgary	80	34	32	14	311	314	82
Vancouver	80	32	39	9	306	328	73
Winnipeg	80	31	38	11	340	374	73
Los Angeles	80	23	44	13	309	376	59

PRINCE OF WALES CONFERENCE

Adams Division

Team	GP	W	L	T	GF	GA	PTS
Boston	80	49	25	6	336	261	104
Buffalo	80	48	25	7	315	257	103
Quebec	80	42	28	10	360	278	94
Montreal	80	35	40	5	286	295	75
Hartford	80	28	42	10	288	320	66

Patrick Division

Team	GP	W	L	T	GF	GA	PTS
NY Islanders	80	50	26	4	357	269	104
Washington	80	48	27	5	308	226	101
Philadelphia	80	44	26	10	350	290	98
NY Rangers	80	42	29	9	314	304	93
New Jersey	80	17	56	7	231	350	41
Pittsburgh	80	16	58	6	254	390	38

Leading Scorers

Player	Club	GP	G	A	PTS	PIM
Gretzky, Wayne	Edmonton	74	87	118	205	39
Coffey, Paul	Edmonton	80	40	86	126	104
Goulet, Michel	Quebec	75	56	65	121	76
Stastny, Peter	Quebec	80	46	73	119	73
Bossy, Mike	NY Islanders	67	51	67	118	8
Pederson, Barry	Boston	80	39	77	116	64
Kurri, Jari	Edmonton	64	52	61	113	14
Trottier, Bryan	NY Islanders	68	40	71	111	59
Federko, Bernie	St. Louis	79	41	66	107	43
Middleton, Rick	Boston	80	47	58	105	14

1984-85

CLARENCE CAMPBELL CONFERENCE

Norris Division

Team	GP	W	L	T	GF	GA	PTS
St. Louis	80	37	31	12	299	288	86
Chicago	80	38	35	7	309	299	83
Detroit	80	27	41	12	313	357	66
Minnesota	80	25	43	12	268	321	62
Toronto	80	20	52	8	253	358	48

Smythe Division

Team	GP	W	L	T	GF	GA	PTS
*Edmonton	80	49	20	11	401	298	109
Winnipeg	80	43	27	10	358	332	96
Calgary	80	41	27	12	363	302	94
Los Angeles	80	34	32	14	339	326	82
Vancouver	80	25	46	9	284	401	59

PRINCE OF WALES CONFERENCE

Adams Division

Team	GP	W	L	T	GF	GA	PTS
Montreal	80	41	27	12	309	262	94
Quebec	80	41	30	9	323	275	91
Buffalo	80	38	28	14	290	237	90
Boston	80	36	34	10	303	287	82
Hartford	80	30	41	9	268	318	69

Patrick Division

Team	GP	W	L	T	GF	GA	PTS
Philadelphia	80	53	20	7	348	241	113
Washington	80	46	25	9	322	240	101
NY Islanders	80	40	34	6	345	312	86
NY Rangers	80	26	44	10	295	345	62
New Jersey	80	22	48	10	264	346	54
Pittsburgh	80	24	51	5	276	385	53

Leading Scorers

Player	Club	GP	G	A	PTS	PIM
Gretzky, Wayne	Edmonton	80	73	135	208	52
Kurri, Jari	Edmonton	73	71	64	135	30
Hawerchuk, Dale	Winnipeg	80	53	77	130	74
Dionne, Marcel	Los Angeles	80	46	80	126	46
Coffey, Paul	Edmonton	80	37	84	121	97
Bossy, Mike	NY Islanders	76	58	59	117	38
Ogrodnick, John	Detroit	79	55	50	105	30
Savard, Denis	Chicago	79	38	67	105	56
Federko, Bernie	St. Louis	76	30	73	103	27
Gartner, Mike	Washington	80	50	52	102	71

1985-86

CLARENCE CAMPBELL CONFERENCE

Norris Division

Team	GP	W	L	T	GF	GA	PTS
Chicago	80	39	33	8	351	349	86
Minnesota	80	38	33	9	327	305	85
St. Louis	80	37	34	9	302	291	83
Toronto	80	25	48	7	311	386	57
Detroit	80	17	57	6	266	415	40

Smythe Division

Team	GP	W	L	T	GF	GA	PTS
Edmonton	80	56	17	7	426	310	119
Calgary	80	40	31	9	354	315	89
Winnipeg	80	26	47	7	295	372	59
Vancouver	80	23	44	13	282	333	59
Los Angeles	80	23	49	8	284	389	54

PRINCE OF WALES CONFERENCE

Adams Division

Team	GP	W	L	T	GF	GA	PTS
Quebec	80	43	31	6	330	289	92
*Montreal	80	40	33	7	330	280	87
Boston	80	37	31	12	311	288	86
Hartford	80	40	36	4	332	302	84
Buffalo	80	37	37	6	296	291	80

Patrick Division

Team	GP	W	L	T	GF	GA	PTS
Philadelphia	80	53	23	4	335	241	110
Washington	80	50	23	7	315	272	107
NY Islanders	80	39	29	12	327	284	90
NY Rangers	80	36	38	6	280	276	78
Pittsburgh	80	34	38	8	313	305	76
New Jersey	80	28	49	3	300	374	59

Leading Scorers

Player	Club	GP	G	A	PTS	PIM
Gretzky, Wayne	Edmonton	80	52	163	215	52
Lemieux, Mario	Pittsburgh	79	48	93	141	43
Coffey, Paul	Edmonton	79	48	90	138	120
Kurri, Jari	Edmonton	78	68	63	131	22
Bossy, Mike	NY Islanders	80	61	62	123	14
Stastny, Peter	Quebec	76	41	81	122	60
Savard, Denis	Chicago	80	47	69	116	111
Naslund, Mats	Montreal	80	43	67	110	16
Hawerchuk, Dale	Winnipeg	80	46	59	105	44
Broten, Neal	Minnesota	80	29	76	105	47

1986-87

CLARENCE CAMPBELL CONFERENCE

Norris Division

Team	GP	W	L	T	GF	GA	PTS
St. Louis	80	32	33	15	281	293	79
Detroit	80	34	36	10	260	274	78
Chicago	80	29	37	14	290	310	72
Toronto	80	32	42	6	286	319	70
Minnesota	80	30	40	10	296	314	70

Smythe Division

Team	GP	W	L	T	GF	GA	PTS
*Edmonton	80	50	24	6	372	284	106
Calgary	80	46	31	3	318	289	95
Winnipeg	80	40	32	8	279	271	88
Los Angeles	80	31	41	8	318	341	70
Vancouver	80	29	43	8	282	314	66

PRINCE OF WALES CONFERENCE

Adams Division

Team	GP	W	L	T	GF	GA	PTS
Hartford	80	43	30	7	287	270	93
Montreal	80	41	29	10	277	241	92
Boston	80	39	34	7	301	276	85
Quebec	80	31	39	10	267	276	72
Buffalo	80	28	44	8	280	308	64

Patrick Division

Team	GP	W	L	T	GF	GA	PTS
Philadelphia	80	46	26	8	310	245	100
Washington	80	38	32	10	285	278	86
NY Islanders	80	35	33	12	279	281	82
NY Rangers	80	34	38	8	307	323	76
Pittsburgh	80	30	38	12	297	290	72
New Jersey	80	29	45	6	293	368	64

Leading Scorers

Player	Club	GP	G	A	PTS	PIM
Gretzky, Wayne	Edmonton	79	62	121	183	28
Kurri, Jari	Edmonton	79	54	54	108	41
Lemieux, Mario	Pittsburgh	63	54	53	107	57
Messier, Mark	Edmonton	77	37	70	107	73
Gilmour, Doug	St. Louis	80	42	63	105	58
Ciccarelli, Dino	Minnesota	80	52	51	103	92
Hawerchuk, Dale	Winnipeg	80	47	53	100	54
Goulet, Michel	Quebec	75	49	47	96	61
Kerr, Tim	Philadelphia	75	58	37	95	57
Bourque, Raymond	Boston	78	23	72	95	36

1987-88

CLARENCE CAMPBELL CONFERENCE

Norris Division

Team	GP	W	L	T	GF	GA	PTS
Detroit	80	41	28	11	322	269	93
St. Louis	80	34	38	8	278	294	76
Chicago	80	30	41	9	284	328	69
Toronto	80	21	49	10	273	345	52
Minnesota	80	19	48	13	242	349	51

Smythe Division

Team	GP	W	L	T	GF	GA	PTS
Calgary	80	48	23	9	397	305	105
*Edmonton	80	44	25	11	363	288	99
Winnipeg	80	33	36	11	292	310	77
Los Angeles	80	30	42	8	318	359	68
Vancouver	80	25	46	9	272	320	59

PRINCE OF WALES CONFERENCE

Adams Division

Team	GP	W	L	T	GF	GA	PTS
Montreal	80	45	22	13	298	238	103
Boston	80	44	30	6	300	251	94
Buffalo	80	37	32	11	283	305	85
Hartford	80	35	38	7	249	267	77
Quebec	80	32	43	5	271	306	69

Patrick Division

Team	GP	W	L	T	GF	GA	PTS
NY Islanders	80	39	31	10	308	267	88
Washington	80	38	33	9	281	249	85
Philadelphia	80	38	33	9	292	292	85
New Jersey	80	38	36	6	295	296	82
NY Rangers	80	36	34	10	300	283	82
Pittsburgh	80	36	35	9	319	316	81

Leading Scorers

Player	Club	GP	G	A	PTS	PIM
Lemieux, Mario	Pittsburgh	76	70	98	168	92
Gretzky, Wayne	Edmonton	64	40	109	149	24
Savard, Denis	Chicago	80	44	87	131	95
Hawerchuk, Dale	Winnipeg	80	44	77	121	59
Robitaille, Luc	Los Angeles	80	53	58	111	82
Stastny, Peter	Quebec	76	46	65	111	69
Messier, Mark	Edmonton	77	37	74	111	103
Carson, Jimmy	Los Angeles	80	55	52	107	45
Loob, Hakan	Calgary	80	50	56	106	47
Goulet, Michel	Quebec	80	48	58	106	56

1988-89

CLARENCE CAMPBELL CONFERENCE

Norris Division

Team	GP	W	L	T	GF	GA	PTS
Detroit	80	34	34	12	313	316	80
St. Louis	80	33	35	12	275	285	78
Minnesota	80	27	37	16	258	278	70
Chicago	80	27	41	12	297	335	66
Toronto	80	28	46	6	259	342	62

Smythe Division

Team	GP	W	L	T	GF	GA	PTS
*Calgary	80	54	17	9	354	226	117
Los Angeles	80	42	31	7	376	335	91
Edmonton	80	38	34	8	325	306	84
Vancouver	80	33	39	8	251	253	74
Winnipeg	80	26	42	12	300	355	64

PRINCE OF WALES CONFERENCE

Adams Division

Team	GP	W	L	T	GF	GA	PTS
Montreal	80	53	18	9	315	218	115
Boston	80	37	29	14	289	256	88
Buffalo	80	38	35	7	291	299	83
Hartford	80	37	38	5	299	290	79
Quebec	80	27	46	7	269	342	61

Patrick Division

Team	GP	W	L	T	GF	GA	PTS
Washington	80	41	29	10	305	259	92
Pittsburgh	80	40	33	7	347	349	87
NY Rangers	80	37	35	8	310	307	82
Philadelphia	80	36	36	8	307	285	80
New Jersey	80	27	41	12	281	325	66
NY Islanders	80	28	47	5	265	325	61

Leading Scorers

Player	Club	GP	G	A	PTS	PIM
Lemieux, Mario	Pittsburgh	76	85	114	199	100
Gretzky, Wayne	Los Angeles	78	54	114	168	26
Yzerman, Steve	Detroit	80	65	90	155	61
Nicholls, Bernie	Los Angeles	79	70	80	150	96
Brown, Rob	Pittsburgh	68	49	66	115	118
Coffey, Paul	Pittsburgh	75	30	83	113	193
Mullen, Joe	Calgary	79	51	59	110	16
Kurri, Jari	Edmonton	76	44	58	102	69
Carson, Jimmy	Edmonton	80	49	51	100	36
Robitaille, Luc	Los Angeles	78	46	52	98	65

1989-90

CLARENCE CAMPBELL CONFERENCE

Norris Division

Team	GP	W	L	T	GF	GA	PTS
Chicago	80	41	33	6	316	294	88
St. Louis	80	37	34	9	295	279	83
Toronto	80	38	38	4	337	358	80
Minnesota	80	36	40	4	284	291	76
Detroit	80	28	38	14	288	323	70

Smythe Division

Team	GP	W	L	T	GF	GA	PTS
Calgary	80	42	23	15	348	265	99
*Edmonton	80	38	28	14	315	283	90
Winnipeg	80	37	32	11	298	290	85
Los Angeles	80	34	39	7	338	337	75
Vancouver	80	25	41	14	245	306	64

PRINCE OF WALES CONFERENCE

Adams Division

Team	GP	W	L	T	GF	GA	PTS
Boston	80	46	25	9	289	232	101
Buffalo	80	45	27	8	286	248	98
Montreal	80	41	28	11	288	234	93
Hartford	80	38	33	9	275	268	85
Quebec	80	12	61	7	240	407	31

Patrick Division

Team	GP	W	L	T	GF	GA	PTS
NY Rangers	80	36	31	13	279	267	85
New Jersey	80	37	34	9	295	288	83
Washington	80	36	38	6	284	275	78
NY Islanders	80	31	38	11	281	288	73
Pittsburgh	80	32	40	8	318	359	72
Philadelphia	80	30	39	11	290	297	71

Leading Scorers

Player	Club	GP	G	A	PTS	PIM
Gretzky, Wayne	Los Angeles	73	40	102	142	42
Messier, Mark	Edmonton	79	45	84	129	79
Yzerman, Steve	Detroit	79	62	65	127	79
Lemieux, Mario	Pittsburgh	59	45	78	123	78
Hull, Brett	St. Louis	80	72	41	113	24
Nicholls, Bernie	L.A., NYR	79	39	73	112	86
Turgeon, Pierre	Buffalo	80	40	66	106	29
LaFontaine, Pat	NY Islanders	74	54	51	105	38
Coffey, Paul	Pittsburgh	80	29	74	103	95
Sakic, Joe	Quebec	80	39	63	102	27
Oates, Adam	St. Louis	80	23	79	102	30

1990-91

CLARENCE CAMPBELL CONFERENCE

Norris Division

Team	GP	W	L	T	GF	GA	PTS
Chicago	80	49	23	8	284	211	106
St. Louis	80	47	22	11	310	250	105
Detroit	80	34	38	8	273	298	76
Minnesota	80	27	39	14	256	266	68
Toronto	80	23	46	11	241	318	57

Smythe Division

Team	GP	W	L	T	GF	GA	PTS
Los Angeles	80	46	24	10	340	254	102
Calgary	80	46	26	8	344	263	100
Edmonton	80	37	37	6	272	272	80
Vancouver	80	28	43	9	243	315	65
Winnipeg	80	26	43	11	260	288	63

PRINCE OF WALES CONFERENCE

Adams Division

Team	GP	W	L	T	GF	GA	PTS
Boston	80	44	24	12	299	264	100
Montreal	80	39	30	11	273	249	89
Buffalo	80	31	30	19	292	278	81
Hartford	80	31	38	11	238	276	73
Quebec	80	16	50	14	236	354	46

Patrick Division

Team	GP	W	L	T	GF	GA	PTS
*Pittsburgh	80	41	33	6	342	305	88
NY Rangers	80	36	31	13	297	265	85
Washington	80	37	36	7	258	258	81
New Jersey	80	32	33	15	272	264	79
Philadelphia	80	33	37	10	252	267	76
NY Islanders	80	25	45	10	223	290	60

Leading Scorers

Player	Club	GP	G	A	PTS	PIM
Gretzky, Wayne	Los Angeles	78	41	122	163	16
Hull, Brett	St. Louis	78	86	45	131	22
Oates, Adam	St. Louis	61	25	90	115	29
Recchi, Mark	Pittsburgh	78	40	73	113	48
Cullen, John	Pit., Hfd.	78	39	71	110	101
Sakic, Joe	Quebec	80	48	61	109	24
Yzerman, Steve	Detroit	80	51	57	108	34
Fleury, Theoren	Calgary	79	51	53	104	136
MacInnis, Al	Calgary	78	28	75	103	90
Larmer, Steve	Chicago	80	44	57	101	79

1991-92

CLARENCE CAMPBELL CONFERENCE

Norris Division

Team	GP	W	L	T	GF	GA	PTS
Detroit	80	43	25	12	320	256	98
Chicago	80	36	29	15	257	236	87
St. Louis	80	36	33	11	279	266	83
Minnesota	80	32	42	6	246	278	70
Toronto	80	30	43	7	234	294	67

Smythe Division

Team	GP	W	L	T	GF	GA	PTS
Vancouver	80	42	26	12	285	250	96
Los Angeles	80	35	31	14	287	296	84
Edmonton	80	36	34	10	295	297	82
Winnipeg	80	33	32	15	251	244	81
Calgary	80	31	37	12	296	305	74
San Jose	80	17	58	5	219	359	39

PRINCE OF WALES CONFERENCE

Adams Division

Team	GP	W	L	T	GF	GA	PTS
Montreal	80	41	28	11	267	207	93
Boston	80	36	32	12	270	275	84
Buffalo	80	31	37	12	289	299	74
Hartford	80	26	41	13	247	283	65
Quebec	80	20	48	12	255	318	52

Patrick Division

Team	GP	W	L	T	GF	GA	PTS
NY Rangers	80	50	25	5	321	246	105
Washington	80	45	27	8	330	275	98
*Pittsburgh	80	39	32	9	343	308	87
New Jersey	80	38	31	11	289	259	87
NY Islanders	80	34	35	11	291	299	79
Philadelphia	80	32	37	11	252	273	75

Leading Scorers

Player	Club	GP	G	A	PTS	PIM
Lemieux, Mario	Pittsburgh	64	44	87	131	94
Stevens, Kevin	Pittsburgh	80	54	69	123	254
Gretzky, Wayne	Los Angeles	74	31	90	121	34
Hull, Brett	St. Louis	73	70	39	109	48
Robitaille, Luc	Los Angeles	80	44	63	107	95
Messier, Mark	NY Rangers	79	35	72	107	76
Roenick, Jeremy	Chicago	80	53	50	103	23
Yzerman, Steve	Detroit	79	45	58	103	64
Leetch, Brian	NY Rangers	80	22	80	102	26
Oates, Adam	St. L., Bos.	80	20	79	99	22

1992-93

CLARENCE CAMPBELL CONFERENCE

Norris Division

Team	GP	W	L	T	GF	GA	PTS
Chicago	84	47	25	12	279	230	106
Detroit	84	47	28	9	369	280	103
Toronto	84	44	29	11	288	241	99
St. Louis	84	37	36	11	282	278	85
Minnesota	84	36	38	10	272	293	82
Tampa Bay	84	23	54	7	245	332	53

Smythe Division

Team	GP	W	L	T	GF	GA	PTS
Vancouver	84	46	29	9	346	278	101
Calgary	84	43	30	11	322	282	97
Los Angeles	84	39	35	10	338	340	88
Winnipeg	84	40	37	7	322	320	87
Edmonton	84	26	50	8	242	337	60
San Jose	84	11	71	2	218	414	24

PRINCE OF WALES CONFERENCE

Adams Division

Team	GP	W	L	T	GF	GA	PTS
Boston	84	51	26	7	332	268	109
Quebec	84	47	27	10	351	300	104
*Montreal	84	48	30	6	326	280	102
Buffalo	84	38	36	10	335	297	86
Hartford	84	26	52	6	284	369	58
Ottawa	84	10	70	4	202	395	24

Patrick Division

Team	GP	W	L	T	GF	GA	PTS
Pittsburgh	84	56	21	7	367	268	119
Washington	84	43	34	7	325	286	93
NY Islanders	84	40	37	7	335	297	87
New Jersey	84	40	37	7	308	299	87
Philadelphia	84	36	37	11	319	319	83
NY Rangers	84	34	39	11	304	308	79

Leading Scorers

Player	Club	GP	G	A	PTS	PIM
Lemieux, Mario	Pittsburgh	60	69	91	160	38
LaFontaine, Pat	Buffalo	84	53	95	148	63
Oates, Adam	Boston	84	45	97	142	32
Yzerman, Steve	Detroit	84	58	79	137	44
Selanne, Teemu	Winnipeg	84	76	56	132	45
Turgeon, Pierre	NY Islanders	83	58	74	132	26
Mogilny, Alexander	Buffalo	77	76	51	127	40
Gilmour, Doug	Toronto	83	32	95	127	100
Robitaille, Luc	Los Angeles	84	63	62	125	100
Recchi, Mark	Philadelphia	84	53	70	123	95

1993-94

EASTERN CONFERENCE

Northeast Division

Team	GP	W	L	T	GF	GA	PTS
Pittsburgh	84	44	27	13	299	285	101
Boston	84	42	29	13	289	252	97
Montreal	84	41	29	14	283	248	96
Buffalo	84	43	32	9	282	218	95
Quebec	84	34	42	8	277	292	76
Hartford	84	27	48	9	227	288	63
Ottawa	84	14	61	9	201	397	37

Atlantic Division

Team	GP	W	L	T	GF	GA	PTS
*NY Rangers	84	52	24	8	299	231	112
New Jersey	84	47	25	12	306	220	106
Washington	84	39	35	10	277	263	88
NY Islanders	84	36	36	12	282	264	84
Florida	84	33	34	17	233	233	83
Philadelphia	84	35	39	10	294	314	80
Tampa Bay	84	30	43	11	224	251	71

WESTERN CONFERENCE

Central Division

Team	GP	W	L	T	GF	GA	PTS
Detroit	84	46	30	8	356	275	100
Toronto	84	43	29	12	280	243	98
Dallas	84	42	29	13	286	265	97
St. Louis	84	40	33	11	270	283	91
Chicago	84	39	36	9	254	240	87
Winnipeg	84	24	51	9	245	344	57

Pacific Division

Team	GP	W	L	T	GF	GA	PTS
Calgary	84	42	29	13	302	256	97
Vancouver	84	41	40	3	279	276	85
San Jose	84	33	35	16	252	265	82
Anaheim	84	33	46	5	229	251	71
Los Angeles	84	27	45	12	294	322	66
Edmonton	84	25	45	14	261	305	64

Leading Scorers

Player	Club	GP	G	A	PTS	PIM
Gretzky, Wayne	Los Angeles	81	38	92	130	20
Fedorov, Sergei	Detroit	82	56	64	120	34
Oates, Adam	Boston	77	32	80	112	45
Gilmour, Doug	Toronto	83	27	84	111	105
Bure, Pavel	Vancouver	76	60	47	107	86
Roenick, Jeremy	Chicago	84	46	61	107	125
Recchi, Mark	Philadelphia	84	40	67	107	46
Shanahan, Brendan	St. Louis	81	52	50	102	211
Andreychuk, Dave	Toronto	83	53	46	99	98
Jagr, Jaromir	Pittsburgh	80	32	67	99	61

1994-95

EASTERN CONFERENCE

Northeast Division

Team	GP	W	L	T	GF	GA	PTS
Quebec	48	30	13	5	185	134	65
Pittsburgh	48	29	16	3	181	158	61
Boston	48	27	18	3	150	127	57
Buffalo	48	22	19	7	130	119	51
Hartford	48	19	24	5	127	141	43
Montreal	48	18	23	7	125	148	43
Ottawa	48	9	34	5	117	174	23

Atlantic Division

Team	GP	W	L	T	GF	GA	PTS
Philadelphia	48	28	16	4	150	132	60
*New Jersey	48	22	18	8	136	121	52
Washington	48	22	18	8	136	120	52
NY Rangers	48	22	23	3	139	134	47
Florida	48	20	22	6	115	127	46
Tampa Bay	48	17	28	3	120	144	37
NY Islanders	48	15	28	5	126	158	35

WESTERN CONFERENCE

Central Division

Team	GP	W	L	T	GF	GA	PTS
Detroit	48	33	11	4	180	117	70
St. Louis	48	28	15	5	178	135	61
Chicago	48	24	19	5	156	115	53
Toronto	48	21	19	8	135	146	50
Dallas	48	17	23	8	136	135	42
Winnipeg	48	16	25	7	157	177	39

Pacific Division

Team	GP	W	L	T	GF	GA	PTS
Calgary	48	24	17	7	163	135	55
Vancouver	48	18	18	12	153	148	48
San Jose	48	19	25	4	129	161	42
Los Angeles	48	16	23	9	142	174	41
Edmonton	48	17	27	4	136	183	38
Anaheim	48	16	27	5	125	164	37

Leading Scorers

Player	Club	GP	G	A	PTS	PIM
Jagr, Jaromir	Pittsburgh	48	32	38	70	37
Lindros, Eric	Philadelphia	46	29	41	70	60
Zhamnov, Alexei	Winnipeg	48	30	35	65	20
Sakic, Joe	Quebec	47	19	43	62	30
Francis, Ron	Pittsburgh	44	11	48	59	18
Fleury, Theoren	Calgary	47	29	29	58	112
Coffey, Paul	Detroit	45	14	44	58	72
Renberg, Mikael	Philadelphia	47	26	31	57	20
LeClair, John	Mtl., Phi.	46	26	28	54	30
Messier, Mark	NY Rangers	46	14	39	53	40
Oates, Adam	Boston	48	12	41	53	8

1995-96

EASTERN CONFERENCE

Northeast Division

Team	GP	W	L	T	GF	GA	PTS
Pittsburgh	82	49	29	4	362	284	102
Boston	82	40	31	11	282	269	91
Montreal	82	40	32	10	265	248	90
Hartford	82	34	39	9	237	259	77
Buffalo	82	33	42	7	247	262	73
Ottawa	82	18	59	5	191	291	41

Atlantic Division

Team	GP	W	L	T	GF	GA	PTS
Philadelphia	82	45	24	13	282	208	103
NY Rangers	82	41	27	14	272	237	96
Florida	82	41	31	10	254	234	92
Washington	82	39	32	11	234	204	89
Tampa Bay	82	38	32	12	238	248	88
New Jersey	82	37	33	12	215	202	86
NY Islanders	82	22	50	10	229	315	54

WESTERN CONFERENCE

Central Division

Team	GP	W	L	T	GF	GA	PTS
Detroit	82	62	13	7	325	181	131
Chicago	82	40	28	14	273	220	94
Toronto	82	34	36	12	247	252	80
St. Louis	82	32	34	16	219	248	80
Winnipeg	82	36	40	6	275	291	78
Dallas	82	26	42	14	227	280	66

Pacific Division

Team	GP	W	L	T	GF	GA	PTS
*Colorado	82	47	25	10	326	240	104
Calgary	82	34	37	11	241	240	79
Vancouver	82	32	35	15	278	278	79
Anaheim	82	35	39	8	234	247	78
Edmonton	82	30	44	8	240	304	68
Los Angeles	82	24	40	18	256	302	66
San Jose	82	20	55	7	252	357	47

Leading Scorers

Player	Club	GP	G	A	PTS	PIM
Lemieux, Mario	Pittsburgh	70	69	92	161	54
Jagr, Jaromir	Pittsburgh	82	62	87	149	96
Sakic, Joe	Colorado	82	51	69	120	44
Francis, Ron	Pittsburgh	77	27	92	119	56
Forsberg, Peter	Colorado	82	30	86	116	47
Lindros, Eric	Philadelphia	73	47	68	115	163
Kariya, Paul	Anaheim	82	50	58	108	20
Selanne, Teemu	Wpg., Ana.	79	40	68	108	22
Mogilny, Alexander	Vancouver	79	55	52	107	16
Fedorov, Sergei	Detroit	78	39	68	107	48

One of the NHL's elite playmakers since first cracking the top 10 in scoring back in 1989-90, Adam Oates led the league with a career-high 97 assists in 1992-93.

1996-97

EASTERN CONFERENCE

Northeast Division

Team	GP	W	L	T	GF	GA	PTS
Buffalo	82	40	30	12	237	208	92
Pittsburgh	82	38	36	8	285	280	84
Ottawa	82	31	36	15	226	234	77
Montreal	82	31	36	15	249	276	77
Hartford	82	32	39	11	226	256	75
Boston	82	26	47	9	234	300	61

Atlantic Division

Team	GP	W	L	T	GF	GA	PTS
New Jersey	82	45	23	14	231	182	104
Philadelphia	82	45	24	13	274	217	103
Florida	82	35	28	19	221	201	89
NY Rangers	82	38	34	10	258	231	86
Washington	82	33	40	9	214	231	75
Tampa Bay	82	32	40	10	217	247	74
NY Islanders	82	29	41	12	240	250	70

WESTERN CONFERENCE

Central Division

Team	GP	W	L	T	GF	GA	PTS
Dallas	82	48	26	8	252	198	104
*Detroit	82	38	26	18	253	197	94
Phoenix	82	38	37	7	240	243	83
St. Louis	82	36	35	11	236	239	83
Chicago	82	34	35	13	223	210	81
Toronto	82	30	44	8	230	273	68

Pacific Division

Team	GP	W	L	T	GF	GA	PTS
Colorado	82	49	24	9	277	205	107
Anaheim	82	36	33	13	245	233	85
Edmonton	82	36	37	9	252	247	81
Vancouver	82	35	40	7	257	273	77
Calgary	82	32	41	9	214	239	73
Los Angeles	82	28	43	11	214	268	67
San Jose	82	27	47	8	211	278	62

Leading Scorers

Player	Club	GP	G	A	PTS	PIM
Lemieux, Mario	Pittsburgh	76	50	72	122	65
Selanne, Teemu	Anaheim	78	51	58	109	34
Kariya, Paul	Anaheim	69	44	55	99	6
LeClair, John	Philadelphia	82	50	47	97	58
Gretzky, Wayne	NY Rangers	82	25	72	97	28
Jagr, Jaromir	Pittsburgh	63	47	48	95	40
Sundin, Mats	Toronto	82	41	53	94	59
Palffy, Ziggy	NY Islanders	80	48	42	90	43
Francis, Ron	Pittsburgh	81	27	63	90	20
Shanahan, Brendan	Hfd., Det.	81	47	41	88	131

1997-98

EASTERN CONFERENCE

Northeast Division

Team	GP	W	L	T	GF	GA	PTS
Pittsburgh	82	40	24	18	228	188	98
Boston	82	39	30	13	221	194	91
Buffalo	82	36	29	17	211	187	89
Montreal	82	37	32	13	235	208	87
Ottawa	82	34	33	15	193	200	83
Carolina	82	33	41	8	200	219	74

Atlantic Division

Team	GP	W	L	T	GF	GA	PTS
New Jersey	82	48	23	11	225	166	107
Philadelphia	82	42	29	11	242	193	95
Washington	82	40	30	12	219	202	92
NY Islanders	82	30	41	11	212	225	71
NY Rangers	82	25	39	18	197	231	68
Florida	82	24	43	15	203	256	63
Tampa Bay	82	17	55	10	151	269	44

WESTERN CONFERENCE

Central Division

Team	GP	W	L	T	GF	GA	PTS
Dallas	82	49	22	11	242	167	109
*Detroit	82	44	23	15	250	196	103
St. Louis	82	45	29	8	256	204	98
Phoenix	82	35	35	12	224	227	82
Chicago	82	30	39	13	192	199	73
Toronto	82	30	43	9	194	237	69

Pacific Division

Team	GP	W	L	T	GF	GA	PTS
Colorado	82	39	26	17	231	205	95
Los Angeles	82	38	33	11	227	225	87
Edmonton	82	35	37	10	215	224	80
San Jose	82	34	38	10	210	216	78
Calgary	82	26	41	15	217	252	67
Anaheim	82	26	43	13	205	261	65
Vancouver	82	25	43	14	224	273	64

Leading Scorers

Player	Club	GP	G	A	PTS	PIM
Jagr, Jaromir	Pittsburgh	77	35	67	102	64
Forsberg, Peter	Colorado	72	25	66	91	94
Bure, Pavel	Vancouver	82	51	39	90	48
Gretzky, Wayne	NY Rangers	82	23	67	90	28
LeClair, John	Philadelphia	82	51	36	87	32
Palffy, Ziggy	NY Islanders	82	45	42	87	34
Francis, Ron	Pittsburgh	81	25	62	87	20
Selanne, Teemu	Anaheim	73	52	34	86	30
Allison, Jason	Boston	81	33	50	83	60
Stumpel, Jozef	Los Angeles	77	21	58	79	53

1998-99

EASTERN CONFERENCE

Northeast Division

Team	GP	W	L	T	GF	GA	PTS
Ottawa	82	44	23	15	239	179	103
Toronto	82	45	30	7	268	231	97
Boston	82	39	30	13	214	181	91
Buffalo	82	37	28	17	207	175	91
Montreal	82	32	39	11	184	209	75

Atlantic Division

Team	GP	W	L	T	GF	GA	PTS
New Jersey	82	47	24	11	248	196	105
Philadelphia	82	37	26	19	231	196	93
Pittsburgh	82	38	30	14	242	225	90
NY Rangers	82	33	38	11	217	227	77
NY Islanders	82	24	48	10	194	244	58

Southeast Division

Team	GP	W	L	T	GF	GA	PTS
Carolina	82	34	30	18	210	202	86
Florida	82	30	34	18	210	228	78
Washington	82	31	45	6	200	218	68
Tampa Bay	82	19	54	9	179	292	47

WESTERN CONFERENCE

Central Division

Team	GP	W	L	T	GF	GA	PTS
Detroit	82	43	32	7	245	202	93
St Louis	82	37	32	13	237	209	87
Chicago	82	29	41	12	202	248	70
Nashville	82	28	47	7	190	261	63

Pacific Division

Team	GP	W	L	T	GF	GA	PTS
*Dallas	82	51	19	12	236	168	114
Phoenix	82	39	31	12	205	197	90
Anaheim	82	35	34	13	215	206	83
San Jose	82	31	33	18	196	191	80
Los Angeles	82	32	45	5	189	222	69

Northwest Division

Team	GP	W	L	T	GF	GA	PTS
Colorado	82	44	28	10	239	205	98
Edmonton	82	33	37	12	230	226	78
Calgary	82	30	40	12	211	234	72
Vancouver	82	23	47	12	192	258	58

Leading Scorers

Player	Club	GP	G	A	PTS	PIM
Jagr, Jaromir	Pittsburgh	81	44	83	127	66
Selanne, Teemu	Anaheim	75	47	60	107	30
Kariya, Paul	Anaheim	82	39	62	101	40
Forsberg, Peter	Colorado	78	30	67	97	108
Sakic, Joe	Colorado	73	41	55	96	29
Yashin, Alexei	Ottawa	82	44	50	94	54
Lindros, Eric	Philadelphia	71	40	53	93	120
Fleury, Theoren	Cgy., Col.	75	40	53	93	86
Leclair, John	Philadelphia	76	43	47	90	30
Demitra, Pavol	St Louis	82	37	52	89	16

Paul Kariya first finished among the NHL's top-10 scorers in 1995-96. He has finished as high as third in scoring in 1996-97 and 1998-99.

Now a member of the New York Islanders, Alexei Yashin established career highs with 44 goals and 50 assists in 1998-99.

1999-2000

EASTERN CONFERENCE

Northeast Division

Team	GP	W	L	T	RT	GF	GA	PTS
Toronto	82	45	30	7	3	246	222	100
Ottawa	82	41	30	11	2	244	210	95
Buffalo	82	35	36	11	4	213	204	85
Montreal	82	35	38	9	4	196	194	83
Boston	82	24	39	19	6	210	248	73

Atlantic Division

Team	GP	W	L	T	RT	GF	GA	PTS
Philadelphia	82	45	25	12	3	237	179	105
*New Jersey	82	45	29	8	5	251	203	103
Pittsburgh	82	37	37	8	6	241	236	88
NY Rangers	82	29	41	12	3	218	246	73
NY Islanders	82	24	49	9	1	194	275	58

Southeast Division

Team	GP	W	L	T	RT	GF	GA	PTS
Washington	82	44	26	12	2	227	194	102
Florida	82	43	33	6	6	244	209	98
Carolina	82	37	35	10	0	217	216	84
Tampa Bay	82	19	54	9	7	204	310	54
Atlanta	82	14	61	7	4	170	313	39

WESTERN CONFERENCE

Central Division

Team	GP	W	L	T	RT	GF	GA	PTS
St. Louis	82	51	20	11	1	248	165	114
Detroit	82	48	24	10	2	278	210	108
Chicago	82	33	39	10	2	242	245	78
Nashville	82	28	47	7	7	199	240	70

Pacific Division

Team	GP	W	L	T	RT	GF	GA	PTS
Dallas	82	43	29	10	6	211	184	102
Los Angeles	82	39	31	12	4	245	228	94
Phoenix	82	39	35	8	4	232	228	90
San Jose	82	35	37	10	7	225	214	87
Anaheim	82	34	36	12	3	217	227	83

Northwest Division

Team	GP	W	L	T	RT	GF	GA	PTS
Colorado	82	42	29	11	1	233	201	96
Edmonton	82	32	34	16	8	226	212	88
Vancouver	82	30	37	15	8	227	237	83
Calgary	82	31	41	10	5	211	256	77

Leading Scorers

Player	Club	GP	G	A	PTS	PIM
Jagr, Jaromir	Pittsburgh	63	42	54	96	50
Bure, Pavel	Florida	74	58	36	94	16
Recchi, Mark	Philadelphia	82	28	63	91	50
Kariya, Paul	Anaheim	74	42	44	86	24
Selanne, Teemu	Anaheim	79	33	52	85	12
Nolan, Owen	San Jose	78	44	40	84	110
Amonte, Tony	Chicago	82	43	41	84	48
Modano, Mike	Dallas	77	38	43	81	48
Sakic, Joe	Colorado	60	28	53	81	28
Yzerman, Steve	Detroit	78	35	44	79	34

2000-2001

EASTERN CONFERENCE

Northeast Division

Team	GP	W	L	T	OTL	GF	GA	PTS
Ottawa	82	48	21	9	4	274	205	109
Buffalo	82	46	30	5	1	218	184	98
Toronto	82	37	29	11	5	232	207	90
Boston	82	36	30	8	8	227	249	88
Montreal	82	28	40	8	6	206	232	70

Atlantic Division

Team	GP	W	L	T	OTL	GF	GA	PTS
New Jersey	82	48	19	12	3	295	195	111
Philadelphia	82	43	25	11	3	240	207	100
Pittsburgh	82	42	28	9	3	281	256	96
NY Rangers	82	33	43	5	1	250	290	72
NY Islanders	82	21	51	7	3	185	268	52

Southeast Division

Team	GP	W	L	T	OTL	GF	GA	PTS
Washington	82	41	27	10	4	233	211	96
Carolina	82	38	32	9	3	212	225	88
Florida	82	22	38	13	9	200	246	66
Atlanta	82	23	45	12	2	211	289	60
Tampa Bay	82	24	47	6	5	201	280	59

WESTERN CONFERENCE

Central Division

Team	GP	W	L	T	OTL	GF	GA	PTS
Detroit	82	49	20	9	4	253	202	111
St. Louis	82	43	22	12	5	249	195	103
Nashville	82	34	36	9	3	186	200	80
Chicago	82	29	40	8	5	210	246	71
Columbus	82	28	39	9	6	190	233	71

Pacific Division

Team	GP	W	L	T	OTL	GF	GA	PTS
Dallas	82	48	24	8	2	241	187	106
San Jose	82	40	27	12	3	217	192	95
Los Angeles	82	38	28	13	3	252	228	92
Phoenix	82	35	27	17	3	214	212	90
Anaheim	82	25	41	11	5	188	245	66

Northwest Division

Team	GP	W	L	T	OTL	GF	GA	PTS
*Colorado	82	52	16	10	4	270	192	118
Edmonton	82	39	28	12	3	243	222	93
Vancouver	82	36	28	11	7	239	238	90
Calgary	82	27	36	15	4	197	236	73
Minnesota	82	25	39	13	5	168	210	68

Leading Scorers

Player	Club	GP	G	A	PTS	PIM
Jagr, Jaromir	Pittsburgh	81	52	69	121	42
Sakic, Joe	Colorado	82	54	64	118	30
Elias, Patrik	New Jersey	82	40	56	96	51
Kovalev, Alexei	Pittsburgh	79	44	51	95	96
Allison, Jason	Boston	82	36	59	95	85
Straka, Martin	Pittsburgh	82	27	68	95	38
Bure, Pavel	Florida	82	59	33	92	58
Weight, Doug	Edmonton	82	25	65	90	91
Palffy, Ziggy	Los Angeles	73	38	51	89	20
Forsberg, Peter	Colorado	73	27	62	89	54

Since making his NHL debut with one game played in 1995-96, Patrik Elias has improved his offensive totals in every season he has played. He was third in the league in scoring in 2000-01.

Note: Detailed statistics for 2000-2001 are listed in the Final Statistics, 2000-2001 section of the *NHL Guide & Record Book*. **See page 139.**

Owen Nolan established Sharks records with 40 goals and 84 points in 1999-2000. Entering the 2001-02 season, he is the only San Jose player to crack the top 10.

Team Records

Regular Season

FINAL STANDINGS

MOST POINTS, ONE SEASON:
132 — Montreal Canadiens, 1976-77. 60W-8L-12T. 80GP
131 — Detroit Red Wings, 1995-96. 62W-13L-7T. 82GP
129 — Montreal Canadiens, 1977-78. 59W-10L-11T. 80GP

BEST POINTS PERCENTAGE, ONE SEASON:
.875 — Boston Bruins, 1929-30. 38W-5L-1T. 77PTS in 44GP
.830 — Montreal Canadiens, 1943-44. 38W-5L-7T. 83PTS in 50GP
.825 — Montreal Canadiens, 1976-77. 60W-8L-12T. 132PTS in 80GP
.806 — Montreal Canadiens, 1977-78. 59W-10L-11T. 129PTS in 80GP
.800 — Montreal Canadiens, 1944-45. 38W-8L-4T. 80PTS in 50GP

FEWEST POINTS, ONE SEASON:
8 — Quebec Bulldogs, 1919-20. 4W-20L-0T. 24GP
10 — Toronto Arenas, 1918-19. 5W-13L-0T. 18GP
12 — Hamilton Tigers, 1920-21. 6W-18L-0T. 24GP
— Hamilton Tigers, 1922-23. 6W-18L-0T. 24GP
— Boston Bruins, 1924-25. 6W-24L-0T. 30GP
— Philadelphia Quakers, 1930-31. 4W-36L-4T. 44GP

FEWEST POINTS, ONE SEASON (MINIMUM 70-GAME SCHEDULE):
21 — Washington Capitals, 1974-75. 8W-67L-5T. 80GP
24 — Ottawa Senators, 1992-93. 10W-70L-4T. 84GP
— San Jose Sharks, 1992-93. 11W-71L-2T. 84GP
30 — NY Islanders, 1972-73. 12W-60L-6T. 78GP

WORST POINTS PERCENTAGE, ONE SEASON:
.131 — Washington Capitals, 1974-75. 8W-67L-5T. 21PTS in 80GP
.136 — Philadelphia Quakers, 1930-31. 4W-36L-4T. 12PTS in 44GP
.143 — Ottawa Senators, 1992-93. 10W-70L-4T. 24PTS in 84GP
.143 — San Jose Sharks, 1992-93. 11W-71L-2T. 24PTS in 84GP
.148 — Pittsburgh Pirates, 1929-30. 5W-36L-3T. 13PTS in 44GP

TEAM WINS

Most Wins

MOST WINS, ONE SEASON:
62 — Detroit Red Wings, 1995-96. 82GP
60 — Montreal Canadiens, 1976-77. 80GP
59 — Montreal Canadiens, 1977-78. 80GP

MOST HOME WINS, ONE SEASON:
36 — Philadelphia Flyers, 1975-76. 40GP
— Detroit Red Wings, 1995-96. 41GP
33 — Boston Bruins, 1970-71. 39GP
— Boston Bruins, 1973-74. 39GP
— Montreal Canadiens, 1976-77. 40GP
— Philadelphia Flyers, 1976-77. 40GP
— NY Islanders, 1981-82. 40GP
— Philadelphia Flyers, 1985-86. 40GP

MOST ROAD WINS, ONE SEASON:
28 — New Jersey Devils, 1998-99. 41GP
27 — Montreal Canadiens, 1976-77. 40GP
— Montreal Canadiens, 1977-78. 40GP
— St. Louis Blues, 1999-2000. 41GP
26 — Boston Bruins, 1971-72. 39GP
— Montreal Canadiens, 1975-76. 40GP
— Edmonton Oilers, 1983-84. 40GP
— Detroit Red Wings, 1995-96. 41GP

Fewest Wins

FEWEST WINS, ONE SEASON:
4 — Quebec Bulldogs, 1919-20. 24GP
— Philadelphia Quakers, 1930-31. 44GP
5 — Toronto Arenas, 1918-19. 18GP
— Pittsburgh Pirates, 1929-30. 44GP

FEWEST WINS, ONE SEASON (MINIMUM 70-GAME SCHEDULE):
8 — Washington Capitals, 1974-75. 80GP
9 — Winnipeg Jets, 1980-81. 80GP
10 — Ottawa Senators, 1992-93. 84GP

FEWEST HOME WINS, ONE SEASON:
2 — Chicago Blackhawks, 1927-28. 22GP
3 — Boston Bruins, 1924-25. 15GP
— Chicago Blackhawks, 1928-29. 22GP
— Philadelphia Quakers, 1930-31. 22GP

FEWEST HOME WINS, ONE SEASON (MINIMUM 70-GAME SCHEDULE):
6 — Chicago Blackhawks, 1954-55. 35GP
— Washington Capitals, 1975-76. 40GP
7 — Boston Bruins, 1962-63. 35GP
— Washington Capitals, 1974-75. 40GP
— Winnipeg Jets, 1980-81. 40GP
— Pittsburgh Penguins, 1983-84. 40GP

FEWEST ROAD WINS, ONE SEASON:
0 — Toronto Arenas, 1918-19. 9GP
— Quebec Bulldogs, 1919-20. 12GP
— Pittsburgh Pirates, 1929-30. 22GP
1 — Hamilton Tigers, 1921-22. 12GP
— Toronto St. Patricks, 1925-26. 18GP
— Philadelphia Quakers, 1930-31. 22GP
— NY Americans, 1940-41. 24GP
— Washington Capitals, 1974-75. 40GP
* — Ottawa Senators, 1992-93. 41GP

FEWEST ROAD WINS, ONE SEASON (MINIMUM 70-GAME SCHEDULE):
1 — Washington Capitals, 1974-75. 40GP
*** — Ottawa Senators,** 1992-93. 41GP
2 — Boston Bruins, 1960-61. 35GP
— Los Angeles Kings, 1969-70. 38GP
— NY Islanders, 1972-73. 39GP
— California Golden Seals, 1973-74. 39GP
— Colorado Rockies, 1977-78. 40GP
— Winnipeg Jets, 1980-81. 40GP
— Quebec Nordiques, 1991-92. 40GP

TEAM LOSSES

Fewest Losses

FEWEST LOSSES, ONE SEASON:
5 — Ottawa Senators, 1919-20. 24GP
— Boston Bruins, 1929-30. 44GP
— Montreal Canadiens, 1943-44. 50GP

FEWEST HOME LOSSES, ONE SEASON:
0 — Ottawa Senators, 1922-23. 12GP
— Montreal Canadiens, 1943-44. 25GP
1 — Toronto Arenas, 1917-18. 11GP
— Ottawa Senators, 1918-19. 9GP
— Ottawa Senators, 1919-20. 12GP
— Toronto St. Patricks, 1922-23. 12GP
— Boston Bruins, 1929-30. 22GP
— Boston Bruins, 1930-31. 22GP
— Montreal Canadiens, 1976-77. 40GP
— Quebec Nordiques, 1994-95. 24GP

FEWEST ROAD LOSSES, ONE SEASON:
3 — Montreal Canadiens, 1928-29. 22GP
4 — Ottawa Senators, 1919-20. 12GP
— Montreal Canadiens, 1927-28. 22GP
— Boston Bruins, 1929-30. 20GP
— Boston Bruins, 1940-41. 24GP

FEWEST LOSSES, ONE SEASON (MINIMUM 70-GAME SCHEDULE):
8 — Montreal Canadiens, 1976-77. 80GP
10 — Montreal Canadiens, 1972-73. 78GP
— Montreal Canadiens, 1977-78. 80GP
11 — Montreal Canadiens, 1975-76. 80GP

FEWEST HOME LOSSES, ONE SEASON (MINIMUM 70-GAME SCHEDULE):
1 — Montreal Canadiens, 1976-77. 40GP
2 — Montreal Canadiens, 1961-62. 35GP
— NY Rangers, 1970-71. 39GP
— Philadelphia Flyers, 1975-76. 40GP

FEWEST ROAD LOSSES, ONE SEASON (MINIMUM 70-GAME SCHEDULE):
6 — Montreal Canadiens, 1972-73. 39GP
— Montreal Canadiens, 1974-75. 40GP
— Montreal Canadiens, 1977-78. 40GP
7 — Detroit Red Wings, 1951-52. 35GP
— Montreal Canadiens, 1976-77. 40GP
— Philadelphia Flyers, 1979-80. 40GP

Most Losses

MOST LOSSES, ONE SEASON:
71 — San Jose Sharks, 1992-93. 84GP
70 — Ottawa Senators, 1992-93. 84GP
67 — Washington Capitals, 1974-75. 80GP
61 — Quebec Nordiques, 1989-90. 80GP
—Ottawa Senators, 1993-94. 84GP

MOST HOME LOSSES, ONE SEASON:
***32 — San Jose Sharks,** 1992-93. 41GP
29 — Pittsburgh Penguins, 1983-84. 40GP
* — Ottawa Senators, 1993-94. 41GP

MOST ROAD LOSSES, ONE SEASON:
***40 — Ottawa Senators,** 1992-93. 41GP
39 — Washington Capitals, 1974-75. 40GP
37 — California Seals, 1973-74. 39GP
* — San Jose Sharks, 1992-93. 41GP

* — Does not include neutral site games

TEAM TIES

Most Ties

MOST TIES, ONE SEASON:
24 — Philadelphia Flyers, 1969-70. 76GP
23 — Montreal Canadiens, 1962-63. 70GP
— Chicago Blackhawks, 1973-74. 78GP

MOST HOME TIES, ONE SEASON:
13 — NY Rangers, 1954-55. 35GP
— Philadelphia Flyers, 1969-70. 38GP
— California Golden Seals, 1971-72. 39GP
— California Golden Seals, 1972-73. 39GP
— Chicago Blackhawks, 1973-74. 39GP

MOST ROAD TIES, ONE SEASON:
15 — Philadelphia Flyers, 1976-77. 40GP
14 — Montreal Canadiens, 1952-53. 35GP
— Montreal Canadiens, 1974-75. 40GP
— Philadelphia Flyers, 1975-76. 40GP

Fewest Ties

FEWEST TIES, ONE SEASON (Since 1926-27):
1 — Boston Bruins, 1929-30. 44GP
2 — Montreal Canadians, 1926-27. 44GP
— NY Americans, 1926-27. 44GP
— Boston Bruins, 1938-39. 48GP
— NY Rangers, 1941-42. 48GP
— San Jose Sharks, 1992-93. 84GP

FEWEST TIES, ONE SEASON (MINIMUM 70-GAME SCHEDULE):
2 — San Jose Sharks, 1992-93. 84GP
3 — New Jersey Devils, 1985-86. 80GP
— Calgary Flames, 1986-87. 80GP
— Vancouver Canucks, 1993-94. 84GP

WINNING STREAKS

LONGEST WINNING STREAK, ONE SEASON:
17 Games — Pittsburgh Penguins, Mar. 9 - Apr. 10, 1993.
15 Games — NY Islanders, Jan. 21 - Feb. 20, 1982.
14 Games — Boston Bruins, Dec. 3, 1929 - Jan. 9, 1930.

LONGEST HOME WINNING STREAK, ONE SEASON:
20 Games — Boston Bruins, Dec. 3, 1929 - Mar. 18, 1930.
— Philadelphia Flyers, Jan. 4 - Apr. 3, 1976.

LONGEST ROAD WINNING STREAK, ONE SEASON:
10 Games — Buffalo Sabres, Dec. 10, 1983 - Jan. 23, 1984.
— St. Louis Blues, Jan. 21 - Mar. 2, 2000.
— New Jersey Devils, Feb. 27 - Apr. 7, 2001.
8 Games — Boston Bruins, Feb. 17 - Mar. 8, 1972.
— Los Angeles Kings, Dec. 18, 1974 - Jan. 16, 1975.
— Montreal Canadiens, Dec. 18, 1977 - Jan. 18, 1978.
— NY Islanders, Feb. 27 - Mar. 29, 1981.
— Montreal Canadiens, Jan. 21 - Feb. 21, 1982.
— Philadelphia Flyers, Dec. 22, 1982 - Jan. 16, 1983.
— Winnipeg Jets, Feb. 25 - Apr. 6, 1985.
— Edmonton Oilers, Dec. 9, 1986 - Jan. 17, 1987.
— Boston Bruins, Mar. 15 - Apr. 14, 1993.

LONGEST WINNING STREAK FROM START OF SEASON:
10 Games — Toronto Maple Leafs, 1993-94.
8 Games — Toronto Maple Leafs, 1934-35.
— Buffalo Sabres, 1975-76.
7 Games — Edmonton Oilers, 1983-84.
— Quebec Nordiques, 1985-86.
— Pittsburgh Penguins, 1986-87.
— Pittsburgh Penguins, 1994-95.

LONGEST HOME WINNING STREAK FROM START OF SEASON:
11 Games — Chicago Blackhawks, 1963-64.
10 Games — Ottawa Senators, 1925-26.
9 Games — Montreal Canadiens, 1953-54.
— Chicago Blackhawks, 1971-72.

LONGEST ROAD WINNING STREAK FROM START OF SEASON:
7 Games — Toronto Maple Leafs, Nov. 14 - Dec. 15, 1940.

LONGEST WINNING STREAK, INCLUDING PLAYOFFS:
15 Games — Detroit Red Wings, Feb. 27 - Apr. 5, 1955. Nine regular-season games, six playoff games.

LONGEST HOME WINNING STREAK, INCLUDING PLAYOFFS:
24 Games — Philadelphia Flyers, Jan. 4 - Apr. 25, 1976. Twenty regular-season games, four playoff games.

LONGEST ROAD WINNING STREAK, INCLUDING PLAYOFFS:
11 Games — New Jersey Devils, Feb. 27 - Apr. 17, 2001. Ten regular season games, one playoff game.

UNDEFEATED STREAKS

LONGEST UNDEFEATED STREAK, ONE SEASON:
35 Games — Philadelphia Flyers, Oct. 14, 1979 - Jan. 6, 1980. 25W-10T.
28 Games — Montreal Canadiens, Dec. 18, 1977 - Feb. 23, 1978. 23W-5T.
23 Games — Boston Bruins, Dec. 22, 1940 - Feb. 23, 1941. 15W-8T.
— Philadelphia Flyers, Jan. 29 - Mar. 18, 1976. 17W-6T.

LONGEST HOME UNDEFEATED STREAK, ONE SEASON:
34 Games — Montreal Canadiens, Nov. 1, 1976 - Apr. 2, 1977. 28W-6T.
27 Games — Boston Bruins, Nov. 22, 1970 - Mar. 20, 1971. 26W-1T.

LONGEST ROAD UNDEFEATED STREAK, ONE SEASON:
23 Games — Montreal Canadiens, Nov. 27, 1974 - Mar. 12, 1975. 14W-9T.
17 Games — Montreal Canadiens, Dec. 18, 1977 - Mar. 1, 1978. 14W-3T.
16 Games — Philadelphia Flyers, Oct. 20, 1979 - Jan. 6, 1980. 11W-5T.

LONGEST UNDEFEATED STREAK FROM START OF SEASON:
15 Games — Edmonton Oilers, 1984-85. 12W-3T.
14 Games — Montreal Canadiens, 1943-44. 11W-3T.
13 Games — Montreal Canadiens, 1972-73. 9W-4T.
— Pittsburgh Penguins, 1994-95. 12W-1T.

LONGEST HOME UNDEFEATED STREAK FROM START OF SEASON:
25 Games — Montreal Canadiens, Oct. 30, 1943 - Mar. 18, 1944. 22W-3T.

LONGEST ROAD UNDEFEATED STREAK FROM START OF SEASON:
15 Games — Detroit Red Wings, Oct. 18 - Dec. 20, 1951. 10W-5T.

LONGEST UNDEFEATED STREAK, INCLUDING PLAYOFFS:
21 Games — Pittsburgh Penguins, Mar. 9 - Apr. 22, 1993. 17W-1T in regular season and 3W in playoffs.

LONGEST HOME UNDEFEATED STREAK, INCLUDING PLAYOFFS:
38 Games — Montreal Canadiens, Nov. 1, 1976 - Apr. 26, 1977. 28W-6T in regular season and 4W in playoff.

LONGEST ROAD UNDEFEATED STREAK, INCLUDING PLAYOFFS:
13 Games — Montreal Canadiens, Feb. 26 - Apr. 20, 1980. 6W-4T in regular season and 3W in playoffs.
— NY Islanders, Mar. 16 - May 1, 1980. 3W-3T in regular season and 7W in playoffs.

LOSING STREAKS

LONGEST LOSING STREAK, ONE SEASON:
17 Games — Washington Capitals, Feb. 18 - Mar. 26, 1975.
— San Jose Sharks, Jan. 4 - Feb. 12, 1993.
15 Games — Philadelphia Quakers, Nov. 29, 1930 - Jan. 8, 1931.

LONGEST HOME LOSING STREAK, ONE SEASON:
11 Games — Boston Bruins, Dec. 8, 1924 - Feb. 17, 1925.
— Washington Capitals, Feb. 18 - Mar. 30, 1975.
— Ottawa Senators, Oct. 27 - Dec. 8, 1993.
— Atlanta Thrashers, Jan. 24-Mar. 16, 2000.

LONGEST ROAD LOSING STREAK, ONE SEASON:
***38 Games — Ottawa Senators,** Oct. 10, 1992 - Apr. 3, 1993.
37 Games — Washington Capitals, Oct. 9, 1974 - Mar. 26, 1975.

LONGEST LOSING STREAK FROM START OF SEASON:
11 Games — NY Rangers, 1943-44.
7 Games — Montreal Canadiens, 1938-39.
— Chicago Blackhawks, 1947-48.
— Washington Capitals, 1983-84.
— Chicago Blackhawks, 1997-98.

LONGEST HOME LOSING STREAK FROM START OF SEASON:
8 Games — Los Angeles Kings, Oct. 13 - Nov. 6, 1971.

LONGEST ROAD LOSING STREAK FROM START OF SEASON:
***38 Games — Ottawa Senators,** Oct. 10, 1992 - Apr. 3, 1993.

WINLESS STREAKS

LONGEST WINLESS STREAK, ONE SEASON:
30 Games — Winnipeg Jets, Oct. 19 - Dec. 20, 1980. 23L-7T.
27 Games — Kansas City Scouts, Feb. 12 - Apr. 4, 1976. 21L-6T.
25 Games — Washington Capitals, Nov. 29, 1975 - Jan. 21, 1976. 22L-3T.

LONGEST HOME WINLESS STREAK, ONE SEASON:
17 Games — Ottawa Senators, Oct. 28, 1995 - Jan. 27, 1996. 15L-2T.
— Atlanta Thrashers, Jan. 19 - Mar. 29, 2000. 15L-2T.
15 Games — Chicago Blackhawks, Dec. 16, 1928 - Feb. 28, 1929. 11L-4T.
— Montreal Canadiens, Dec. 16, 1939 - Mar. 7, 1940. 12L-3T.

LONGEST ROAD WINLESS STREAK, ONE SEASON:
***38 Games — Ottawa Senators,** Oct. 10, 1992 - Apr. 3, 1993. 38L-0T.
37 Games — Washington Capitals, Oct. 9, 1974 - Mar. 26, 1975. 37L-0T.

LONGEST WINLESS STREAK FROM START OF SEASON:
15 Games — NY Rangers, 1943-44. 14L-1T.
11 Games — Pittsburgh Pirates, 1927-28. 8L-3T.
— Minnesota North Stars, 1973-74. 5L-6T.
— San Jose Sharks, 1995-96. 7L-4T.

LONGEST HOME WINLESS STREAK FROM START OF SEASON:
11 Games — Pittsburgh Penguins, Oct. 8 - Nov. 19, 1983. 9L-2T.

LONGEST ROAD WINLESS STREAK FROM START OF SEASON:
***38 Games — Ottawa Senators,** Oct. 10, 1992 - Apr. 3, 1993. 38L-0T.

NON-SHUTOUT STREAKS

LONGEST NON-SHUTOUT STREAK:
264 Games — Calgary Flames, Nov. 12, 1981 - Jan. 9, 1985.
261 Games — Los Angeles Kings, Mar. 15, 1986 - Oct. 22, 1989.
244 Games — Washington Capitals, Oct. 31, 1989 - Nov. 11, 1993.
236 Games — NY Rangers, Dec. 20, 1989 - Dec. 13, 1992.
230 Games — Quebec Nordiques, Feb. 10, 1980 - Jan. 13, 1983.

LONGEST NON-SHUTOUT STREAK INCLUDING PLAYOFFS:
264 Games — Los Angeles Kings, Mar. 15, 1986 - Apr. 6, 1989. (5 playoff games in 1987; 5 in 1988; 2 in 1989).
262 Games — Chicago Blackhawks, Mar. 14, 1970 - Feb. 21, 1973. (8 playoff games in 1970; 18 in 1971; 8 in 1972).
251 Games — Quebec Nordiques, Feb. 10, 1980 - Jan. 13, 1983. (5 playoff games in 1981; 16 in 1982).
246 Games — Pittsburgh Penguins, Jan. 7, 1989 - Oct. 26, 1991. (11 playoff games in 1989; 24 in 1991).

TEAM GOALS

Most Goals

MOST GOALS, ONE SEASON:
446 — Edmonton Oilers, 1983-84. 80GP
426 — Edmonton Oilers, 1985-86. 80GP
424 — Edmonton Oilers, 1982-83. 80GP
417 — Edmonton Oilers, 1981-82. 80GP
401 — Edmonton Oilers, 1984-85. 80GP

MOST GOALS, ONE TEAM, ONE GAME:
16 — Montreal Canadiens, Mar. 3, 1920, at Quebec. Defeated Que. Bulldogs 16-3.

MOST GOALS, BOTH TEAMS, ONE GAME:
21 — Montreal Canadiens, Toronto St. Patricks, at Montreal, Jan. 10, 1920. Montreal won 14-7.
— Edmonton Oilers, Chicago Blackhawks, at Chicago, Dec. 11, 1985. Edmonton won 12-9.
20 — Edmonton Oilers, Minnesota North Stars, at Edmonton, Jan. 4, 1984. Edmonton won 12-8.
— Toronto Maple Leafs, Edmonton Oilers, at Toronto, Jan. 8, 1986. Toronto won 11-9.
19 — Montreal Wanderers, Toronto Arenas, at Montreal, Dec. 19, 1917. Montreal won 10-9.
— Montreal Canadiens, Quebec Bulldogs, at Quebec, Mar. 3, 1920. Montreal won 16-3.
— Montreal Canadiens, Hamilton Tigers, at Montreal, Feb. 26, 1921. Montreal won 13-6.
— Boston Bruins, NY Rangers, at Boston, Mar. 4, 1944. Boston won 10-9.
— Boston Bruins, Detroit Red Wings, at Detroit, Mar. 16, 1944. Detroit won 10-9.
— Vancouver Canucks, Minnesota North Stars, at Vancouver, Oct. 7, 1983. Vancouver won 10-9.

MOST GOALS, ONE TEAM, ONE PERIOD:
9 — Buffalo Sabres, Mar. 19, 1981, at Buffalo, second period during 14-4 win over Toronto.
8 — Detroit Red Wings, Jan. 23, 1944, at Detroit, third period during 15-0 win over NY Rangers.
— Boston Bruins, Mar. 16, 1969, at Boston, second period during 11-3 win over Toronto.
— NY Rangers, Nov. 21, 1971, at NY Rangers, third period during 12-1 win over California.
— Philadelphia Flyers, Mar. 31, 1973, at Philadelphia, second period during 10-2 win over NY Islanders.
— Buffalo Sabres, Dec. 21, 1975, at Buffalo, third period during 14-2 win over Washington.
— Minnesota North Stars, Nov. 11, 1981, at Minnesota, second period during 15-2 win over Winnipeg.
— Pittsburgh Penguins, Dec. 17, 1991, at Pittsburgh, second period during 10-2 win over San Jose.
— Washington Capitals, Feb. 3, 1999, at Washington, second period during 10-1 win over Tampa Bay.

MOST GOALS, BOTH TEAMS, ONE PERIOD:
12 — Buffalo Sabres, Toronto Maple Leafs, at Buffalo, March 19, 1981, second period. Buffalo scored 9 goals, Toronto 3. Buffalo won 14-4.
— Edmonton Oilers, Chicago Blackhawks, at Chicago, Dec. 11, 1985, second period. Edmonton scored 6 goals, Chicago 6. Edmonton won 12-9.
10 — NY Rangers, NY Americans, at NY Americans, March 16, 1939, third period. NY Rangers scored 7 goals, NY Americans 3. NY Rangers won 11-5.
— Toronto Maple Leafs, Detroit Red Wings, at Detroit, March 17, 1946, third period. Toronto scored 6 goals, Detroit 4. Toronto won 11-7.
— Vancouver Canucks, Buffalo Sabres, at Buffalo, Jan. 8, 1976, third period. Buffalo scored 6 goals, Vancouver 4. Buffalo won 8-5.
— Buffalo Sabres, Montreal Canadiens, at Montreal, Oct. 26, 1982, first period. Montreal scored 5 goals, Buffalo 5. 7-7 tie.
— Boston Bruins, Quebec Nordiques, at Quebec, Dec. 7, 1982, second period. Quebec scored 6 goals, Boston 4. Quebec won 10-5.
— Calgary Flames, Vancouver Canucks, at Vancouver, Jan. 16, 1987, first period. Vancouver scored 6 goals, Calgary 4. Vancouver won 9-5.
— Winnipeg Jets, Detroit Red Wings, at Detroit, Nov. 25, 1987, third period. Detroit scored 7 goals, Winnipeg 3. Detroit won 10-8.
— Chicago Blackhawks, St. Louis Blues, at St. Louis, March 15, 1988, third period. Chicago scored 5 goals, St. Louis 5. 7-7 tie.

MOST CONSECUTIVE GOALS, ONE TEAM, ONE GAME:
15 — Detroit Red Wings, Jan. 23, 1944, at Detroit. Defeated NY Rangers 15-0.

Fewest Goals

FEWEST GOALS, ONE SEASON:
33 — Chicago Blackhawks, 1928-29. 44GP
45 — Montreal Maroons, 1924-25. 30GP
46 — Pittsburgh Pirates, 1928-29. 44GP

FEWEST GOALS, ONE SEASON (MINIMUM 70-GAME SCHEDULE):
133 — Chicago Blackhawks, 1953-54. 70GP
147 — Toronto Maple Leafs, 1954-55. 70GP
— Boston Bruins, 1955-56. 70GP
150 — NY Rangers, 1954-55. 70GP

TEAM POWER-PLAY GOALS

MOST POWER-PLAY GOALS, ONE SEASON:
119 — Pittsburgh Penguins, 1988-89. 80GP
113 — Detroit Red Wings, 1992-93. 84GP
111 — NY Rangers, 1987-88. 80GP
110 — Pittsburgh Penguins, 1987-88. 80GP
— Winnipeg Jets, 1987-88, 80GP

TEAM SHORTHAND GOALS

MOST SHORTHAND GOALS, ONE SEASON:
36 — Edmonton Oilers, 1983-84. 80GP
28 — Edmonton Oilers, 1986-87. 80GP
27 — Edmonton Oilers, 1985-86. 80GP
— Edmonton Oilers, 1988-89. 80GP

TEAM GOALS-PER-GAME

HIGHEST GOALS-PER-GAME AVERAGE, ONE SEASON:
5.58 — Edmonton Oilers, 1983-84. 446G in 80GP
5.38 — Montreal Canadiens, 1919-20. 129G in 24GP
5.33 — Edmonton Oilers, 1985-86. 426G in 80GP
5.30 — Edmonton Oilers, 1982-83. 424G in 80GP
5.23 — Montreal Canadiens, 1917-18. 115G in 22GP

LOWEST GOALS-PER-GAME AVERAGE, ONE SEASON:
.75 — Chicago Blackhawks, 1928-29, 33G in 44GP
1.05 — Pittsburgh Pirates, 1928-29. 46G in 44GP
1.20 — NY Americans, 1928-29. 53G in 44GP

TEAM ASSISTS

MOST ASSISTS, ONE SEASON:
737 — Edmonton Oilers, 1985-86. 80GP
736 — Edmonton Oilers, 1983-84. 80GP
706 — Edmonton Oilers, 1981-82. 80GP

FEWEST ASSISTS, ONE SEASON (Since 1926-27):
45 — NY Rangers, 1926-27. 44GP

FEWEST ASSISTS, ONE SEASON (MINIMUM 70-GAME SCHEDULE):
206 — Chicago Blackhawks, 1953-54. 70GP

TEAM TOTAL POINTS

MOST SCORING POINTS, ONE SEASON:
1,182 — Edmonton Oilers, 1983-84. 80GP
1,163 — Edmonton Oilers, 1985-86. 80GP
1,123 — Edmonton Oilers, 1981-82. 80GP

MOST SCORING POINTS, ONE TEAM, ONE GAME:
40 — Buffalo Sabres, Dec. 21, 1975, at Buffalo. Buffalo defeated Washington 14-2, receiving 26A.
39 — Minnesota North Stars, Nov. 11, 1981, at Minnesota. Minnesota defeated Winnipeg 15-2, receiving 24A.
37 — Detroit Red Wings, Jan. 23, 1944, at Detroit. Detroit defeated NY Rangers 15-0, receiving 22A.
— Toronto Maple Leafs, Mar. 16, 1957, at Toronto. Toronto defeated NY Rangers 14-1, receiving 23A.
— Buffalo Sabres, Feb. 25, 1978, at Cleveland. Buffalo defeated Cleveland 13-3, receiving 24A.
— Calgary Flames, Feb. 10, 1993, at Calgary. Calgary defeated San Jose 13-1, receiving 24A.

MOST SCORING POINTS, BOTH TEAMS, ONE GAME:
62 — Edmonton Oilers, Chicago Blackhawks, at Chicago, Dec. 11, 1985. Edmonton won 12-9. Edmonton had 24A, Chicago, 17.
53 — Quebec Nordiques, Washington Capitals, at Washington, Feb. 22, 1981. Quebec won 11-7. Quebec had 22A, Washington, 13.
— Edmonton Oilers, Minnesota North Stars, at Edmonton, Jan. 4, 1984. Edmonton won 12-8. Edmonton had 20A, Minnesota 13.
— Minnesota North Stars, St. Louis Blues, at St. Louis, Jan. 27, 1984. Minnesota won 10-8. Minnesota had 19A, St. Louis 16.
— Toronto Maple Leafs, Edmonton Oilers, at Toronto, Jan. 8, 1986. Toronto won 11-9. Toronto had 17A, Edmonton 16.
52 — Mtl. Maroons, NY Americans, at NY Americans, Feb. 18, 1936. 8-8 tie. NY Americans had 20A, Montreal 16. (3A allowed for each goal.)
— Vancouver Canucks, Minnesota North Stars, at Vancouver, Oct. 7, 1983. Vancouver won 10-9. Vancouver had 16A, Minnesota 17.

MOST SCORING POINTS, ONE TEAM, ONE PERIOD:
23 — NY Rangers, Nov. 21, 1971, at NY Rangers, third period during 12-1 win over California. NY Rangers scored 8G and 15A.
— Buffalo Sabres, Dec. 21, 1975, at Buffalo, third period during 14-2 win over Washington. Buffalo scored 8G and 15A.
— Buffalo Sabres, March 19, 1981, at Buffalo, second period during 14-4 win over Toronto. Buffalo scored 9G and 14A.
22 — Detroit Red Wings, Jan. 23, 1944, at Detroit, third period during 15-0 win over NY Rangers. Detroit scored 8G and 14A.
— Boston Bruins, March 16, 1969, at Boston, second period during 11-3 win over Toronto Maple Leafs. Boston scored 8G and 14A.
— Minnesota North Stars, Nov. 11, 1981, at Minnesota, second period during 15-2 win over Winnipeg. Minnesota scored 8G and 14A.
— Pittsburgh Penguins, Dec. 17, 1991, at Pittsburgh, second period during 10-2 win over San Jose. Pittsburgh scored 8G and 14A.
— Washington Capitals, Feb. 3, 1999, at Washington, second period during 10-1 win over Tampa Bay. Washington scored 8G and 14A.

MOST SCORING POINTS, BOTH TEAMS, ONE PERIOD:
35 — Edmonton, Oilers, Chicago Blackhawks, at Chicago, Dec. 11, 1985, second period. Edmonton had 6G, 12A; Chicago, 6G, 11A. Edmonton won 12-9.
31 — Buffalo Sabres, Toronto Maple Leafs, at Buffalo, March 19, 1981, second period. Buffalo had 9G, 14A; Toronto, 3G, 5A. Buffalo won 14-4.
29 — Winnipeg Jets, Detroit Red Wings, at Detroit, Nov. 25, 1987, third period. Detroit had 7G, 13A; Winnipeg had 3G, 6A. Detroit won 10-8.
— Chicago Blackhawks, St. Louis Blues, at St. Louis, March 15, 1988, third period. St. Louis had 5G, 10A; Chicago had 5G, 9A. 7-7 tie.

FASTEST GOALS

FASTEST SIX GOALS, BOTH TEAMS
3 Minutes — Quebec Nordiques, Washington Capitals, at Washington, Feb. 22, 1981, second and third periods. Quebec scored 5G, Washington 1. Quebec won 11-7.
3 Minutes, 15 Seconds — Montreal Canadiens, Toronto Maple Leafs, at Montreal, Jan. 4, 1944, first period. Montreal scored 4G, Toronto 2. Montreal won 6-3.

FASTEST FIVE GOALS, BOTH TEAMS:
1 Minute, 24 Seconds — Chicago Blackhawks, Toronto Maple Leafs, at Toronto, Oct. 15, 1983, second period. Scorers: Gaston Gingras, Toronto, 16:49; Denis Savard, Chicago, 17:12; Steve Larmer, Chicago, 17:27; Savard, 17:42; John Anderson, Toronto, 18:13. Toronto won 10-8.
1 Minute, 39 Seconds — Detroit Red Wings, Toronto Maple Leafs, at Toronto, Nov. 15, 1944, third period. Scorers: Ted Kennedy, Toronto, 10:36 and 10:55; Hal Jackson, Detroit, 11:48; Steve Wochy, Detroit, 12:02; Don Grosso, Detroit, 12:15. Detroit won 8-4.

FASTEST FIVE GOALS, ONE TEAM:
2 Minutes, 7 Seconds — Pittsburgh Penguins, at Pittsburgh, Nov. 22, 1972, third period. Scorers: Bryan Hextall, 12:00; Jean Pronovost, 12:18; Al McDonough, 13:40; Ken Schinkel, 13:49; Ron Schock, 14:07. Pittsburgh defeated St. Louis 10-4.
2 Minutes, 37 Seconds — NY Islanders, at NY Islanders, Jan. 26, 1982, first period. Scorers: Duane Sutter, 1:31; John Tonelli, 2:30; Bryan Trottier, 2:46; Bryan Trottier, 3:31; Duane Sutter, 4:08. NY Islanders defeated Pittsburgh 9-2.
2 Minutes, 55 Seconds — Boston Bruins, at Boston, Dec. 19, 1974. Scorers: Bobby Schmautz, 19:13 (first period); Ken Hodge, 0:18; Phil Esposito, 0:43; Don Marcotte, 0:58; John Bucyk, 2:08 (second period). Boston defeated NY Rangers 11-3.

FASTEST FOUR GOALS, BOTH TEAMS:
53 Seconds — Chicago Blackhawks, Toronto Maple Leafs, at Toronto, Oct. 15, 1983, second period. Scorers: Gaston Gingras, Toronto, 16:49; Denis Savard, Chicago, 17:12; Steve Larmer, Chicago, 17:27; and Savard, 17:42. Toronto won 10-8.
57 Seconds — Quebec Nordiques, Detroit Red Wings, at Quebec, Jan. 27, 1990, first period. Scorers: Paul Gillis, Quebec, 18:01; Claude Loiselle, Quebec, 18:12; Joe Sakic, Quebec, 18:27; and Jimmy Carson, Detroit, 18:58. Detroit won 8-6.
1 Minute, 1 Second — Colorado Rockies, NY Rangers, at NY Rangers, Jan. 15, 1980, first period. Scorers: Doug Sulliman, NY Rangers, 7:52; Ed Johnstone, NY Rangers, 7:57; Warren Miller, NY Rangers, 8:20; Rob Ramage, Colorado, 8:53. 6-6 tie.
— Chicago Blackhawks, Toronto Maple Leafs, at Toronto, Oct. 15, 1983, second period. Scorers: Denis Savard, Chicago, 17:12; Steve Larmer, Chicago, 17:27; Savard, 17:42; John Anderson, Toronto, 18:13. Toronto won 10-8.

FASTEST FOUR GOALS, ONE TEAM:
1 Minute, 20 Seconds — Boston Bruins, at Boston, Jan. 21, 1945, second period. Scorers: Bill Thoms, 6:34; Frank Mario, 7:08 and 7:27; and Ken Smith, 7:54. Boston defeated NY Rangers 14-3.

FASTEST THREE GOALS, BOTH TEAMS:
15 Seconds — Minnesota North Stars, NY Rangers, at Minnesota, Feb. 10, 1983, second period. Scorers: Mark Pavelich, NY Rangers, 19:18; Ron Greschner, NY Rangers, 19:27; Willi Plett, Minnesota, 19:33. Minnesota won 7-5.
18 Seconds — Montreal Canadiens, NY Rangers, at Montreal, Dec. 12, 1963, first period. Scorers: Dave Balon, Montreal, 0:58; Gilles Tremblay, Montreal, 1:04; Camille Henry, NY Rangers, 1:16. Montreal won 6-4.
— California Golden Seals, Buffalo Sabres, at California, Feb. 1, 1976, third period. Scorers: Jim Moxey, California, 19:38; Wayne Merrick, California, 19:45; Danny Gare, Buffalo, 19:56. Buffalo won 9-5.

FASTEST THREE GOALS, ONE TEAM:
20 Seconds — Boston Bruins, at Boston, Feb. 25, 1971, third period. Scorers: John Bucyk, 4:50; Ed Westfall, 5:02; Ted Green, 5:10. Boston defeated Vancouver 8-3.
21 Seconds — Chicago Blackhawks, at New York, Mar. 23, 1952, third period. Bill Mosienko scored all three goals, at 6:09, 6:20 and 6:30. Chicago defeated NY Rangers 7-6.
— Washington Capitals, at Washington, Nov. 23, 1990, first period. Scorers: Michal Pivonka, 16:18; Stephen Leach, 16:29 and 16:39. Washington defeated Pittsburgh 7-3.

FASTEST THREE GOALS FROM START OF PERIOD, BOTH TEAMS:
1 Minute, 5 Seconds — Hartford Whalers, Montreal Canadiens, at Montreal, March 11, 1989, second period. Scorers: Kevin Dineen, Hartford, 0:11; Guy Carbonneau, Montreal, 0:36; Petr Svoboda, Montreal, 1:05. Montreal won 5-3.

FASTEST THREE GOALS FROM START OF PERIOD, ONE TEAM:
53 Seconds — Calgary Flames, at Calgary, Feb. 10, 1993, third period. Scorers: Gary Suter, 0:17; Chris Lindbergh, 0:40; Ron Stern, 0:53. Calgary defeated San Jose 13-1.

FASTEST TWO GOALS, BOTH TEAMS:
2 Seconds — St. Louis Blues, Boston Bruins, at Boston, Dec. 19, 1987, third period. Scorers: Ken Linseman, Boston, 19:50; Doug Gilmour, St. Louis, 19:52. St. Louis won 7-5.
3 Seconds — Chicago Blackhawks, Minnesota North Stars, at Minnesota, Nov. 5, 1988, third period. Scorers: Steve Thomas, Chicago, 6:03; Dave Gagner, Minnesota, 6:06. 5-5 tie.

FASTEST TWO GOALS, ONE TEAM:
4 Seconds — Montreal Maroons, at Montreal, Jan. 3, 1931, third period. Nels Stewart scored both goals, at 8:24 and 8:28. Mtl. Maroons defeated Boston 5-3.
— Buffalo Sabres, at Buffalo, Oct. 17, 1974, third period. Scorers: Lee Fogolin, 14:55; Don Luce, 14:59. Buffalo defeated California 6-1.
— Toronto Maple Leafs, at Quebec, Dec. 29, 1988, third period. Scorers: Ed Olczyk, 5:24; Gary Leeman, 5:28. Toronto defeated Quebec 6-5.
— Calgary Flames, at Quebec, Oct. 17, 1989, third period. Scorers: Doug Gilmour, 19:45; Paul Ranheim, 19:49. Calgary and Quebec tied 8-8.
— Winnipeg Jets, at Winnipeg, Dec. 15, 1995, second period. Deron Quint scored both goals, at 7:51 and 7:55. Winnipeg defeated Edmonton 9-4.

FASTEST TWO GOALS FROM START OF GAME, ONE TEAM:
24 Seconds — Edmonton Oilers, Mar. 28, 1982, at Los Angeles. Scorers: Mark Messier, 0:14; Dave Lumley, 0:24. Edmonton defeated Los Angeles 6-2.
29 Seconds — Pittsburgh Penguins, Dec. 6, 1980, at Pittsburgh. Scorers: George Ferguson, 0:17; Greg Malone, 0:29. Pittsburgh defeated Chicago 6-4.
32 Seconds — Calgary Flames, Mar. 11, 1987, at Hartford. Scorers: Doug Risebrough, 0:09; Colin Patterson, 0:32. Calgary defeated Hartford 6-1.

FASTEST TWO GOALS FROM START OF PERIOD, BOTH TEAMS:
14 Seconds — NY Rangers, Quebec Nordiques, at Quebec, Nov. 5, 1983, third period. Scorers: Andre Savard, Quebec, 0:08; Pierre Larouche, NY Rangers, 0:14. 4-4 tie.
26 Seconds — Buffalo Sabres, St. Louis Blues, at Buffalo, Jan. 3, 1993, third period. Scorers: Alexander Mogilny, Buffalo, 0:08; Phillippe Bozon, St. Louis, 0:26. Buffalo won 6-5.
28 Seconds — Boston Bruins, Montreal Canadiens, at Montreal, Oct. 11, 1989, third period. Scorers: Jim Wiemer, Boston 0:10; Tom Chorske, Montreal 0:28. Montreal won 4-2.

FASTEST TWO GOALS FROM START OF PERIOD, ONE TEAM:
21 Seconds — Chicago Blackhawks, Nov. 5, 1983, at Minnesota, second period. Scorers: Ken Yaremchuk, 0:12; Darryl Sutter, 0:21. Minnesota defeated Chicago 10-5.
30 Seconds — Washington Capitals, Jan. 27, 1980, at Washington, second period. Scorers: Mike Gartner, 0:08; Bengt Gustafsson, 0:30. Washington defeated NY Islanders 7-1.
31 Seconds —Buffalo Sabres, Jan. 10, 1974, at Buffalo, third period. Scorers: Rene Robert, 0:21; Rick Martin, 0:31. Buffalo defeated NY Rangers 7-2.
— NY Islanders, Feb. 22, 1986, at NY Islanders, third period. Scorers: Roger Kortko, 0:10; Bob Bourne, 0:31. NY Islanders defeated Detroit 5-2.

After Ken Linseman scored for the Boston Bruins at 19:50 of the third period on December 19, 1987, Doug Gilmour took just two seconds to respond for the St. Louis Blues.

50, 40, 30, 20-GOAL SCORERS

MOST 50-OR-MORE-GOAL SCORERS, ONE SEASON:

3 — Edmonton Oilers, 1983-84. Wayne Gretzky, 87; Glenn Anderson, 54; Jari Kurri, 52. 80GP
— Edmonton Oilers, 1985-86. Jari Kurri, 68; Glenn Anderson, 54; Wayne Gretzky, 52. 80GP
2 — Boston Bruins, 1970-71. Phil Esposito, 76; John Bucyk, 51. 78GP
— Boston Bruins, 1973-74. Phil Esposito, 68; Ken Hodge, 50. 78GP
— Philadelphia Flyers, 1975-76. Reggie Leach, 61; Bill Barber, 50. 80GP
— Pittsburgh Penguins, 1975-76. Pierre Larouche, 53; Jean Pronovost, 52. 80GP
— Montreal Canadiens, 1976-77. Steve Shutt, 60; Guy Lafleur, 56. 80GP
— Los Angeles Kings, 1979-80. Charlie Simmer, 56; Marcel Dionne, 53. 80GP
— Montreal Canadiens, 1979-80. Pierre Larouche, 50; Guy Lafleur, 50. 80GP
— Los Angeles Kings, 1980-81. Marcel Dionne, 58; Charlie Simmer, 56. 80GP
— Edmonton Oilers, 1981-82. Wayne Gretzky, 92; Mark Messier, 50. 80GP
— NY Islanders, 1981-82. Mike Bossy, 64; Bryan Trottier, 50. 80GP
— Edmonton Oilers, 1984-85. Wayne Gretzky, 73; Jari Kurri, 71. 80GP
— Washington Capitals, 1984-85. Bob Carpenter, 53; Mike Gartner, 50. 80GP
— Edmonton Oilers, 1986-87. Wayne Gretzky, 62; Jari Kurri, 54. 80GP
— Calgary Flames, 1987-88. Joe Nieuwendyk, 51; Hakan Loob, 50. 80GP
— Los Angeles Kings, 1987-88. Jimmy Carson, 55; Luc Robitaille, 53. 80GP
— Los Angeles Kings, 1988-89. Bernie Nicholls, 70; Wayne Gretzky, 54. 80GP
— Calgary Flames, 1988-89. Joe Nieuwendyk, 51; Joe Mullen, 51. 80GP
— Buffalo Sabres, 1992-93. Alexander Mogilny, 76; Pat LaFontaine, 53. 84GP
— Pittsburgh Penguins, 1992-93. Mario Lemieux, 69; Kevin Stevens, 55. 84GP
— St. Louis Blues, 1992-93. Brett Hull, 54; Brendan Shanahan, 51. 84GP
— St. Louis Blues, 1993-94. Brett Hull, 57; Brendan Shanahan, 52. 84GP
— Detroit Red Wings, 1993-94. Sergei Fedorov, 56; Ray Sheppard, 52. 84GP
— Pittsburgh Penguins, 1995-96. Mario Lemieux, 69; Jaromir Jagr, 62. 82GP

MOST 40-OR-MORE-GOAL SCORERS, ONE SEASON:

4 — Edmonton Oilers, 1982-83. Wayne Gretzky, 71; Glenn Anderson, 48; Mark Messier, 48; Jari Kurri, 45. 80GP
— Edmonton Oilers, 1983-84. Wayne Gretzky, 87; Glenn Anderson, 54; Jari Kurri, 52; Paul Coffey, 40. 80GP
— Edmonton Oilers, 1984-85. Wayne Gretzky, 73; Jari Kurri, 71; Mike Krushelnyski, 43; Glenn Anderson, 42. 80GP
— Edmonton Oilers, 1985-86. Jari Kurri, 68; Glenn Anderson, 54; Wayne Gretzky, 52; Paul Coffey, 48. 80GP
— Calgary Flames, 1987-88. Joe Nieuwendyk, 51; Hakan Loob, 50; Mike Bullard, 48; Joe Mullen, 40. 80GP
3 — Boston Bruins, 1970-71. Phil Esposito, 76; John Bucyk, 51; Ken Hodge, 43. 78GP
— NY Rangers, 1971-72. Vic Hadfield, 50; Jean Ratelle, 46; Rod Gilbert, 43. 78GP
— Buffalo Sabres, 1975-76. Danny Gare, 50; Rick Martin, 49; Gilbert Perreault, 44. 80GP
— Montreal Canadiens, 1979-80. Guy Lafleur, 50; Pierre Larouche, 50; Steve Shutt, 47. 80GP
— Buffalo Sabres, 1979-80. Danny Gare, 56; Rick Martin, 45; Gilbert Perreault, 40. 80GP
— Los Angeles Kings, 1980-81. Marcel Dionne, 58; Charlie Simmer, 56; Dave Taylor, 47. 80GP
— Los Angeles Kings, 1984-85. Marcel Dionne, 46; Bernie Nicholls, 46; Dave Taylor, 41. 80GP
— NY Islanders, 1984-85. Mike Bossy, 58; Brent Sutter, 42; John Tonelli; 42. 80GP
— Chicago Blackhawks, 1985-86. Denis Savard, 47; Troy Murray, 45; Al Secord, 40. 80GP
— Chicago Blackhawks, 1987-88. Denis Savard, 44; Rick Vaive, 43; Steve Larmer, 41. 80GP
— Edmonton Oilers, 1987-88. Craig Simpson, 43; Jari Kurri, 43; Wayne Gretzky, 40. 80GP
— Los Angeles Kings, 1988-89. Bernie Nicholls, 70; Wayne Gretzky, 54; Luc Robitaille, 46. 80GP
— Los Angeles Kings, 1990-91. Luc Robitaille, 45; Tomas Sandstrom, 45; Wayne Gretzky 41. 80GP
— Pittsburgh Penguins, 1991-92. Kevin Stevens, 54; Mario Lemieux, 44; Joe Mullen, 42. 80GP
— Pittsburgh Penguins, 1992-93. Mario Lemieux, 69; Kevin Stevens, 55; Rick Tocchet, 48. 84GP
— Calgary Flames, 1993-94. Gary Roberts, 41; Robert Reichel, 40; Theoren Fleury, 40. 84GP
— Pittsburgh Penguins, 1995-96. Mario Lemieux, 69; Jaromir Jagr, 62; Petr Nedved, 45. 82GP

MOST 30-OR-MORE GOAL SCORERS, ONE SEASON:

6 — Buffalo Sabres, 1974-75. Rick Martin, 52; Rene Robert, 40; Gilbert Perreault, 39; Don Luce, 33; Rick Dudley, Danny Gare, 31 each. 80GP
— NY Islanders, 1977-78. Mike Bossy, 53; Bryan Trottier, 46; Clark Gillies, 35; Denis Potvin, Bob Nystrom, Bob Bourne, 30 each. 80GP
— Winnipeg Jets, 1984-85. Dale Hawerchuk, 53; Paul MacLean, 41; Laurie Boschman, Brian Mullen, 32 each; Doug Smail, 31; Thomas Steen, 30. 80GP
5 — Chicago Blackhawks, 1968-69. 76GP
— Boston Bruins, 1970-71. 78GP
— Montreal Canadiens, 1971-72. 78GP
— Philadelphia Flyers, 1972-73. 78GP
— Boston Bruins, 1973-74. 78GP
— Montreal Canadiens, 1974-75. 80GP
— Montreal Canadiens, 1975-76. 80GP
— Pittsburgh Penguins, 1975-76. 80GP
— NY Islanders, 1978-79. 80GP
— Detroit Red Wings, 1979-80. 80GP
— Philadelphia Flyers, 1979-80. 80GP
— NY Islanders, 1980-81. 80GP
— St. Louis Blues, 1980-81. 80GP
— Chicago Blackhawks, 1981-82. 80GP
— Edmonton Oilers, 1981-82. 80GP
— Montreal Canadiens, 1981-82. 80GP
— Quebec Nordiques, 1981-82. 80GP
— Washington Capitals, 1981-82. 80GP
— Edmonton Oilers, 1982-83. 80GP
— Edmonton Oilers, 1983-84. 80GP
— Edmonton Oilers, 1984-85. 80GP
— Los Angeles Kings, 1984-85. 80GP
— Edmonton Oilers, 1985-86. 80GP
— Edmonton Oilers, 1986-87. 80GP
— Edmonton Oilers, 1987-88. 80GP
— Edmonton Oilers, 1988-89. 80GP
— Detroit Red Wings, 1991-92. 80GP
— NY Rangers, 1991-92. 80GP
— Pittsburgh Penguins, 1991-92. 80GP
— Detroit Red Wings, 1992-93. 84GP
— Pittsburgh Penguins, 1992-93. 84GP

MOST 20-OR-MORE GOAL SCORERS, ONE SEASON:

11 — Boston Bruins, 1977-78; Peter McNab, 41; Terry O'Reilly, 29; Bobby Schmautz, Stan Jonathan, 27 each; Jean Ratelle, Rick Middleton, 25 each; Wayne Cashman, 24; Gregg Sheppard, 23; Brad Park, 22; Don Marcotte, Bob Miller, 20 each. 80GP
10 — Boston Bruins, 1970-71. 78GP
— Montreal Canadiens, 1974-75. 80GP
— St. Louis Blues, 1980-81. 80GP

A member of Buffalo's "French Connection" line with Richard Martin and Gilbert Perreault, Rene Robert was one of six Sabres scorers to collect at least 30 goals in 1974-75.

100-POINT SCORERS

MOST 100 OR-MORE-POINT SCORERS, ONE SEASON:
4 — Boston Bruins, 1970-71, Phil Esposito, 76G-76A-152PTS; Bobby Orr, 37G-102A-139PTS; John Bucyk, 51G-65A-116PTS; Ken Hodge, 43G-62A-105PTS. 78GP
— Edmonton Oilers, 1982-83, Wayne Gretzky, 71G-125A-196PTS; Mark Messier, 48G-58A-106PTS; Glenn Anderson, 48G-56A-104PTS; Jari Kurri, 45G-59A-104PTS. 80GP
— Edmonton Oilers, 1983-84, Wayne Gretzky, 87G-118A-205PTS; Paul Coffey, 40G-86A-126PTS; Jari Kurri, 52G-61A-113PTS; Mark Messier, 37G-64A-101PTS. 80GP
— Edmonton Oilers,1985-86, Wayne Gretzky, 52G-163A-215PTS; Paul Coffey, 48G-90A-138PTS; Jari Kurri, 68G-63A-131PTS; Glenn Anderson, 54G-48A-102PTS. 80GP
— Pittsburgh Penguins,1992-93, Mario Lemieux, 69G-91A-160PTS; Kevin Stevens, 55G-56A-111PTS; Rick Tocchet, 48G-61A-109PTS; Ron Francis, 24G-76A-100PTS. 84GP
3 — Boston Bruins, 1973-74, Phil Esposito, 68G-77A-145PTS; Bobby Orr, 32G-90A-122PTS; Ken Hodge, 50G-55A-105PTS. 78GP
— NY Islanders, 1978-79, Bryan Trottier, 47G-87A-134PTS; Mike Bossy, 69G-57A-126PTS; Denis Potvin, 31G-70A-101PTS. 80GP
— Los Angeles Kings, 1980-81, Marcel Dionne, 58G-77A-135PTS; Dave Taylor, 47G-65A-112PTS; Charlie Simmer, 56G-49A-105PTS. 80GP
— Edmonton Oilers, 1984-85, Wayne Gretzky, 73G-135A-208PTS; Jari Kurri, 71G-64A-135PTS; Paul Coffey, 37G-84A-121PTS. 80GP
— NY Islanders, 1984-85. Mike Bossy, 58G-59A-117PTS; Brent Sutter, 42G-60A-102PTS; John Tonelli, 42G-58A-100PTS. 80GP
— Edmonton Oilers, 1986-87, Wayne Gretzky, 62G-121A-183PTS; Jari Kurri, 54G-54A-108PTS; Mark Messier, 37G-70A-107PTS. 80GP
— Pittsburgh Penguins, 1988-89, Mario Lemieux, 85G-114A-199PTS; Rob Brown, 49G-66A-115PTS; Paul Coffey, 30G-83A-113PTS. 80GP
— Pittsburgh Penguins, 1995-96, Mario Lemieux, 69G-92A-161PTS; Jaromir Jagr, 62G-87A-149PTS; Ron Francis, 27G-92A-119PTS. 82GP

SHOTS ON GOAL

MOST SHOTS, BOTH TEAMS, ONE GAME:
141 — NY Americans, Pittsburgh Pirates, Dec. 26, 1925, at NY Americans. NY Americans, who won game 3-1, had 73 shots; Pit. Pirates, 68 shots.

MOST SHOTS, ONE TEAM, ONE GAME:
83 — Boston Bruins, March 4, 1941, at Boston. Boston defeated Chicago 3-2.
73 — NY Americans, Dec. 26, 1925, at NY Americans. NY Americans defeated Pit. Pirates 3-1.
— Boston Bruins, March 21, 1991, at Boston. Boston tied Quebec 3-3.
72 — Boston Bruins, Dec. 10, 1970, at Boston. Boston defeated Buffalo 8-2.

MOST SHOTS, ONE TEAM, ONE PERIOD:
33 — Boston Bruins, March 4, 1941, at Boston, second period. Boston defeated Chicago 3-2.

TEAM GOALS AGAINST

Fewest Goals Against

FEWEST GOALS AGAINST, ONE SEASON:
42 — Ottawa Senators, 1925-26. 36GP
43 — Montreal Canadiens, 1928-29. 44GP
48 — Montreal Canadiens, 1923-24. 24GP
— Montreal Canadiens, 1927-28. 44GP

FEWEST GOALS AGAINST, ONE SEASON (MINIMUM 70-GAME SCHEDULE):
131 — Toronto Maple Leafs, 1953-54. 70GP
— Montreal Canadiens, 1955-56. 70GP
132 — Detroit Red Wings, 1953-54. 70GP
133 — Detroit Red Wings, 1951-52. 70GP
— Detroit Red Wings, 1952-53. 70GP

LOWEST GOALS-AGAINST-PER-GAME AVERAGE, ONE SEASON:
.98 — Montreal Canadiens, 1928-29. 43GA in 44GP.
1.09 — Montreal Canadiens, 1927-28. 48GA in 44GP.
1.17 — Ottawa Senators, 1925-26. 42GA in 36GP.

Most Goals Against

MOST GOALS AGAINST, ONE SEASON:
446 — Washington Capitals, 1974-75. 80GP
415 — Detroit Red Wings, 1985-86. 80GP
414 — San Jose Sharks, 1992-93. 84GP
407 — Quebec Nordiques, 1989-90. 80GP
403 — Hartford Whalers, 1982-83. 80GP

HIGHEST GOALS-AGAINST-PER-GAME AVERAGE, ONE SEASON:
7.38 — Quebec Bulldogs, 1919-20, 177GA in 24GP.
6.20 — NY Rangers, 1943-44, 310GA in 50GP.
5.58 — Washington Capitals, 1974-75, 446GA in 80GP.

MOST POWER-PLAY GOALS AGAINST, ONE SEASON:
122 — Chicago Blackhawks, 1988-89. 80GP
120 — Pittsburgh Penguins, 1987-88. 80GP
115 — New Jersey Devils, 1988-89. 80GP
— Ottawa Senators, 1992-93. 84GP
114 — Los Angeles Kings, 1992-93. 84GP

MOST SHORTHAND GOALS AGAINST, ONE SEASON:
22 — Pittsburgh Penguins, 1984-85. 80GP
— Minnesota North Stars, 1991-92. 80GP
— Colorado Avalanche, 1995-96. 82GP
21 — Calgary Flames, 1984-85. 80GP
— Pittsburgh Penguins, 1989-90. 80GP

SHUTOUTS

MOST SHUTOUTS, ONE SEASON:
22 — Montreal Canadiens, 1928-29. All by George Hainsworth. 44GP
16 — NY Americans, 1928-29. Roy Worters had 13; Flat Walsh 3. 44GP
15 — Ottawa Senators, 1925-26. All by Alex Connell. 36GP
— Ottawa Senators, 1927-28. All by Alex Connell. 44GP
— Boston Bruins, 1927-28. All by Hal Winkler. 44GP
— Chicago Blackhawks, 1969-70. All by Tony Esposito. 76GP

MOST CONSECUTIVE SHUTOUTS, ONE SEASON:
6 — Ottawa Senators, Jan. 31 - Feb. 18, 1928.

MOST CONSECUTIVE SHUTOUTS TO START SEASON:
5 — Toronto Maple Leafs, Nov. 13 - 22, 1930.

MOST GAMES SHUTOUT, ONE SEASON:
20 — Chicago Blackhawks, 1928-29. 44GP

MOST CONSECUTIVE GAMES SHUTOUT:
8 — Chicago Blackhawks, Feb. 7 - 28, 1929.

MOST CONSECUTIVE GAMES SHUTOUT TO START SEASON:
3 — Montreal Maroons, Nov. 11 - 18, 1930.

TEAM PENALTIES

MOST PENALTY MINUTES, ONE SEASON:
2,713 — Buffalo Sabres, 1991-92. 80GP
2,670 — Pittsburgh Penguins, 1988-89. 80GP
2,663 — Chicago Blackhawks, 1991-92. 80GP
2,643 — Calgary Flames, 1991-92. 80GP
2,621 — Philadelphia Flyers, 1980-81. 80GP

MOST PENALTIES, BOTH TEAMS, ONE GAME:
85 Penalties — Edmonton Oilers (44), Los Angeles Kings (41) at Los Angeles, Feb. 28, 1990. Edmonton received 26 minors, 7 majors, 6 10-minute misconducts, 4 game misconducts and 1 match penalty; Los Angeles received 26 minors, 9 majors, 3 10-minute misconducts and 3 game misconducts.

MOST PENALTY MINUTES, BOTH TEAMS, ONE GAME:
406 Minutes — Minnesota North Stars, Boston Bruins at Boston, Feb. 26, 1981. Minnesota received 18 minors, 13 majors, 4 10-minute misconducts and 7 game misconducts; a total of 211PIM. Boston received 20 minors, 13 majors, 3 10-minute misconducts and six game misconducts; a total of 195PIM.

MOST PENALTIES, ONE TEAM, ONE GAME:
44 — Edmonton Oilers, Feb. 28, 1990, at Los Angeles. Edmonton received 26 minors, 7 majors, 6 10-minute misconducts, 4 game misconducts and 1 match penalty.
42 — Minnesota North Stars, Feb. 26, 1981, at Boston. Minnesota received 18 minors, 13 majors, 4 10-minute misconducts and 7 game misconducts.
— Boston Bruins, Feb. 26, 1981, at Boston vs. Minnesota. Boston received 20 minors, 13 majors, 3 10-minute misconducts and 6 game misconducts.

MOST PENALTY MINUTES, ONE TEAM, ONE GAME:
211 — Minnesota North Stars, Feb. 26, 1981, at Boston. Minnesota received 18 minors, 13 majors, 4 10-minute misconducts and 7 game misconducts.

MOST PENALTIES, BOTH TEAMS, ONE PERIOD:
67 — Minnesota North Stars, Boston Bruins, at Boston, Feb. 26, 1981, first period. Minnesota received 15 minors, 8 majors, 4 10-minute misconducts and 7 game misconducts, a total of 34 penalties. Boston had 16 minors, 8 majors, 3 10-minute misconducts and 6 game misconducts, a total of 33 penalties.

MOST PENALTY MINUTES, BOTH TEAMS, ONE PERIOD:
372 — Los Angeles Kings, Philadelphia Flyers, at Philadelphia, March 11, 1979, first period. Philadelphia received 4 minors, 8 majors, 6 10-minute misconducts and 8 game misconducts for 188 minutes. Los Angeles received 2 minors, 8 majors, 6 10-minute misconducts and 8 game misconducts for 184 minutes.

MOST PENALTIES, ONE TEAM, ONE PERIOD:
34 — Minnesota North Stars, Feb. 26, 1981, at Boston, first period. 15 minors, 8 majors, 4 10-minute misconducts, 7 game misconducts.

MOST PENALTY MINUTES, ONE TEAM, ONE PERIOD:
188 — Philadelphia Flyers, March 11, 1979, at Philadelphia vs. Los Angeles, first period. Flyers received 4 minors, 8 majors, 6 10-minute misconducts and 8 game misconducts.

NHL Individual Scoring Records - History

Six individual scoring records stand as benchmarks in the history of the game: most goals, single-season and career; most assists, single-season and career; and most points, single-season and career. The evolution of these six records is traced here, beginning with 1917-18, the NHL's first season. New research has resulted in changes to scoring records in the NHL's first nine seasons.

MOST GOALS, ONE SEASON

44 —Joe Malone, Montreal, 1917-18.
Scored goal #44 against Toronto's Harry Holmes on March 2, 1918 and finished season with 44 goals.
50 —Maurice Richard, Montreal, 1944-45.
Scored goal #45 against Toronto's Frank McCool on February 25, 1945 and finished the season with 50 goals.
50 —Bernie Geoffrion, Montreal, 1960-61.
Scored goal #50 against Toronto's Cesare Maniago on March 16, 1961 and finished the season with 50 goals.
50 —Bobby Hull, Chicago, 1961-62.
Scored goal #50 against NY Rangers' Gump Worsley on March 25, 1962 and finished the season with 50 goals.
54 —Bobby Hull, Chicago, 1965-66.
Scored goal #51 against NY Rangers' Cesare Maniago on March 12, 1966 and finished the season with 54 goals.
58 —Bobby Hull, Chicago, 1968-69.
Scored goal #55 against Boston's Gerry Cheevers on March 20, 1969 and finished the season with 58 goals.
76 —Phil Esposito, Boston, 1970-71.
Scored goal #59 against Los Angeles' Denis DeJordy on March 11, 1971 and finished the season with 76 goals.
92 —Wayne Gretzky, Edmonton, 1981-82.
Scored goal #77 against Buffalo's Don Edwards on February 24, 1982 and finished the season with 92 goals.

MOST ASSISTS, ONE SEASON

10 —Cy Denneny, Ottawa, 1917-18.
—Reg Noble, Toronto, 1917-18.
—Harry Cameron, Toronto, 1917-18.
—Newsy Lalonde, Montreal, 1918-19.
15 —Frank Nighbor, Ottawa, 1919-20.
—Jack Darragh, Ottawa, 1920-21.
17 —Harry Cameron, Toronto, 1921-22.
18 —Dick Irvin, Chicago, 1926-27.
18 —Howie Morenz, Montreal, 1927-28.
36 —Frank Boucher, NY Rangers, 1929-30.
37 —Joe Primeau, Toronto, 1931-32.
45 —Bill Cowley, Boston, 1940-41.
45 —Bill Cowley, Boston, 1942-43.
49 —Clint Smith, Chicago, 1943-44.
54 —Elmer Lach, Montreal, 1944-45.
55 —Ted Lindsay, Detroit, 1949-50.
56 —Bert Olmstead, Montreal, 1955-56.
58 —Jean Beliveau, Montreal, 1960-61.
58 —Andy Bathgate, NY Rangers/Toronto, 1963-64.
59 —Stan Mikita, Chicago, 1964-65.
62 —Stan Mikita, Chicago, 1966-67.
77 —Phil Esposito, Boston, 1968-69.
87 —Bobby Orr, Boston, 1969-70.
102 —Bobby Orr, Boston, 1970-71.
109 —Wayne Gretzky, Edmonton, 1980-81.
120 —Wayne Gretzky, Edmonton, 1981-82.
125 —Wayne Gretzky, Edmonton, 1982-83.
135 —Wayne Gretzky, Edmonton, 1984-85.
163 —Wayne Gretzky, Edmonton, 1985-86.

MOST POINTS, ONE SEASON

48 —Joe Malone, Montreal, 1917-18.
49 —Joe Malone, Montreal, 1919-20.
51 —Howie Morenz, Montreal, 1927-28.
73 —Cooney Weiland, Boston, 1929-30.
73 —Doug Bentley, Chicago, 1942-43.
82 —Herb Cain, Boston, 1943-44.
86 —Gordie Howe, Detroit, 1950-51.
95 —Gordie Howe, Detroit, 1952-53.
96 —Dickie Moore, Montreal, 1958-59.
97 —Bobby Hull, Chicago, 1965-66.
97 —Stan Mikita, Chicago, 1966-67.
126 —Phil Esposito, Boston, 1968-69.
152 —Phil Esposito, Boston, 1970-71.
164 —Wayne Gretzky, Edmonton, 1980-81.
212 —Wayne Gretzky, Edmonton, 1981-82.
215 —Wayne Gretzky, Edmonton, 1985-86.

Gerry Cheevers was victimized by Bobby Hull when he broke his own record with goal #55 en route to 58 in 1968-69. Denis Dejordy (facing page) was the victim when Phil Esposito passed Hull with his 59th goal in 1970-71. Espo got 76 that year.

MOST REGULAR-SEASON GOALS, CAREER

44 —Joe Malone, 1917-18, Montreal.
Malone led the NHL in goals in the league's first season and finished with 44 goals in 22 games in 1917-18.
54 —Cy Denneny, 1918-19, Ottawa.
Denneny passed Malone during the 1918-19 season, finishing the year with a two-year total of 54 goals. He held the career goal- scoring mark until 1919-20.
143 —Joe Malone, Montreal, Quebec Bulldogs, Hamilton.
Malone passed Denneny in 1919-20 and remained the NHL's career goal-scoring leader until 1922-23.
248 —Cy Denneny, Ottawa, Boston.
Denneny passed Malone with goal #144 in 1922-23 and remained the NHL's career goal-scoring leader until his retirement. He finished with a career total of 248 goals.
271 —Howie Morenz, Montreal, Chicago, NY Rangers.
Morenz passed Denneny with goal #249 in 1933-34 and finished his career with 271 goals.
324 —Nels Stewart, Montreal Maroons, Boston, NY Americans.
Stewart passed Morenz with goal #272 in 1936-37 and remained the NHL's career goal-scoring leader until his retirement. He finished his career with 324 goals.
544 —Maurice Richard, Montreal.
Richard passed Nels Stewart with goal #325 on Nov. 8, 1952 and remained the NHL's career goal-scoring leader until his retirement. He finished his career with 544 goals.
801 —Gordie Howe, Detroit, Hartford.
Howe passed Richard with goal #545 on Nov. 10, 1963 and remained the NHL's career goal-scoring leader until his retirement. He finished his career with 801 goals.
894 —Wayne Gretzky, Edmonton, Los Angeles, St. Louis, NY Rangers.
Gretzky passed Gordie Howe with goal #802 on March 23, 1994. He retired as the NHL's current goal-scoring leader with 894.

MOST REGULAR-SEASON ASSISTS, CAREER

(minimum 100 assists)

100 —Frank Boucher, Ottawa, NY Rangers.
In 1930-31, Boucher became the first NHL player to reach the 100-assist milestone.

263 —Frank Boucher, Ottawa, NY Rangers.
Boucher retired as the NHL's career assist leader in 1938 with 253. He returned to the NHL in 1943-44 and remained the NHL's career assist leader until he was overtaken by Bill Cowley in 1943-44. He finished his career with 263 assists.

353 —Bill Cowley, St. Louis Eagles, Boston.
Cowley passed Boucher with assist #264 in 1943-44. He retired as the NHL's career assist leader in 1947 with 353.

408 —Elmer Lach, Montreal.
Lach passed Cowley with assist #354 in 1951-52. He retired as the NHL's career assist leader in 1954 with 408.

1,049 —Gordie Howe, Detroit, Hartford.
Howe passed Lach with assist #409 in 1957-58. He retired as the NHL's career assist leader in 1980 with 1,049.

1,963 —Wayne Gretzky, Edmonton, Los Angeles, St. Louis, NY Rangers.
Gretzky passed Howe with assist #1,050 in 1988-89. He retired as the NHL's current career assist leader with 1,963.

MOST REGULAR-SEASON POINTS, CAREER

(minimum 100 points)

100 —Joe Malone, Montreal, Quebec Bulldogs, Hamilton.
In 1919-20, Malone became the first player in NHL history to record 100 points.

200 —Cy Denneny, Ottawa.
In 1923-24, Denneny became the first player in NHL history to record 200 points.

300 —Cy Denneny, Ottawa.
In 1926-27, Denneny became the first player in NHL history to record 300 points.

333 —Cy Denneny, Ottawa, Boston.
Denneny retired as the NHL's career point-scoring leader in 1929 with 333 points.

472 —Howie Morenz, Montreal, Chicago, NY Rangers.
Morenz passed Cy Denneny with point #334 in 1931-32. At the time his career ended in 1937, he was the NHL's career point- scoring leader with 472 points.

515 —Nels Stewart, Montreal Maroons, Boston, NY Americans.
Stewart passed Morenz with point #473 in 1938-39. He retired as the NHL's career point-scoring leader in 1940 with 515 points.

528 —Syd Howe, Ottawa, Philadelphia Quakers, Toronto, St. Louis Eagles, Detroit.
Howe passed Nels Stewart with point #516 on March 8, 1945. He retired as the NHL's career point-scoring leader in 1946 with 528 points.

548 —Bill Cowley, St. Louis Eagles, Boston.
Cowley passed Syd Howe with point #529 on Feb. 12, 1947. He retired as the NHL's career point-scoring leader in 1947 with 548 points.

610 —Elmer Lach, Montreal.
Lach passed Bill Cowley with point #549 on Feb. 23, 1952. He remained the NHL's career point-scoring leader until he was overtaken by Maurice Richard in 1953-54. He finished his career with 623 points.

946 —Maurice Richard, Montreal.
Richard passed teammate Elmer Lach with point #611 on Dec. 12, 1953. He remained the NHL's career point-scoring leader until he was overtaken by Gordie Howe in 1959-60. He finished his career with 965 points.

1,850 —Gordie Howe, Detroit, Hartford.
Howe passed Richard with point #947 on Jan. 16, 1960. He retired as the NHL's career point-scoring leader in 1980 with 1,850 points.

2,857 —Wayne Gretzky, Edmonton, Los Angeles, St. Louis, NY Rangers.
Gretzky passed Howe with point #1,851 on Oct. 15, 1989. He retired as the NHL's current career points leader with 2,857.

Individual Records

Regular Season

SEASONS

MOST SEASONS:
26 — Gordie Howe, Detroit, 1946-47 – 1970-71; Hartford, 1979-80.
24 — Alex Delvecchio, Detroit, 1950-51 – 1973-74.
— Tim Horton, Toronto, NY Rangers, Pittsburgh, Buffalo, 1949-50, 1951-52 – 1973-74.
23 — John Bucyk, Detroit, Boston, 1955-56 – 1977-78.
22 — Dean Prentice, NY Rangers, Boston, Detroit, Pittsburgh, Minnesota, 1952-53 – 1973-74.
— Doug Mohns, Boston, Chicago, Minnesota, Atlanta, Washington, 1953-54 – 1974-75.
— Stan Mikita, Chicago, 1958-59 – 1979-80.
— Raymond Bourque, Boston, Colorado, 1979-80 – 2000-01.
— Mark Messier, Edmonton, NY Rangers, Vancouver, 1979-80 – 2000-01.

GAMES

MOST GAMES:
1,767 — Gordie Howe, Detroit, 1946-47 – 1970-71; Hartford, 1979-80.
1,616 — Larry Murphy, Los Angeles, Washington, Minnesota, Pittsburgh, Toronto, Detroit, 1980-81 – 2000-01.
1,612 — Raymond Bourque, Boston, Colorado, 1979-80 – 2000-01.

MOST GAMES, INCLUDING PLAYOFFS:
1,924 — Gordie Howe, Detroit, Hartford, 1,767 regular-season and 157 playoff games.
1,831 — Larry Murphy, Los Angeles, Washington, Minnesota, Pittsburgh, Toronto, Detroit, 1,616 regular-season and 215 playoff games.
1,826 — Raymond Bourque, Boston, Colorado, 1,612 regular-season and 214 playoff games.

MOST CONSECUTIVE GAMES:
964 — Doug Jarvis, Montreal, Washington, Hartford, from Oct. 8, 1975 – Oct. 10, 1987.
914 — Garry Unger, Toronto, Detroit, St. Louis, Atlanta, from Feb. 24, 1968 – Dec. 21, 1979.
884 — Steve Larmer, Chicago, from Oct. 6, 1982 – Apr. 15, 1993.
776 — Craig Ramsay, Buffalo, from Mar. 27, 1973 – Feb. 10, 1983.
630 — Andy Hebenton, NY Rangers, Boston, from Oct. 7, 1955 – Mar. 22, 1964.

GOALS

MOST GOALS:
894 — Wayne Gretzky, Edmonton, Los Angeles, St. Louis, NY Rangers, in 20 seasons, 1,487GP.
801 — Gordie Howe, Detroit, Hartford, in 26 seasons, 1,767GP.
731 — Marcel Dionne, Detroit, Los Angeles, NY Rangers, in 18 seasons, 1,348GP.
717 — Phil Esposito, Chicago, Boston, NY Rangers, in 18 seasons, 1,282GP.
708 — Mike Gartner, Washington, Minnesota, NY Rangers, Toronto, Phoenix, in 19 seasons, 1,432GP.

MOST GOALS, INCLUDING PLAYOFFS:
1,016 — Wayne Gretzky, Edmonton, Los Angeles, St. Louis, NY Rangers, 894 regular-season and 122 playoff goals.
869 — Gordie Howe, Detroit, Hartford, 801 regular-season and 68 playoff goals.
778 — Phil Esposito, Chicago, Boston, NY Rangers, 717 regular-season and 61 playoff goals.
752 — Marcel Dionne, Detroit, Los Angeles, NY Rangers, 731 regular-season and 21 playoff goals.

MOST GOALS, ONE SEASON:
92 — Wayne Gretzky, Edmonton, 1981-82. 80 game schedule.
87 — Wayne Gretzky, Edmonton, 1983-84. 80 game schedule.
86 — Brett Hull, St. Louis, 1990-91. 80 game schedule.
85 — Mario Lemieux, Pittsburgh, 1988-89. 80 game schedule.
76 — Phil Esposito, Boston, 1970-71. 78 game schedule.
— Alexander Mogilny, Buffalo, 1992-93. 84 game schedule.
— Teemu Selanne, Winnipeg, 1992-93. 84 game schedule.
73 — Wayne Gretzky, Edmonton, 1984-85. 80 game schedule.
72 — Brett Hull, St. Louis, 1989-90. 80 game schedule.
71 — Wayne Gretzky, Edmonton, 1982-83. 80 game schedule.
— Jari Kurri, Edmonton, 1984-85. 80 game schedule.
70 — Mario Lemieux, Pittsburgh, 1987-1988. 80 game schedule.
— Bernie Nicholls, Los Angeles, 1988-89. 80 game schedule.
— Brett Hull, St. Louis, 1991-92. 80 game schedule.

MOST GOALS, ONE SEASON, INCLUDING PLAYOFFS:
100 — Wayne Gretzky, Edmonton, 1983-84, 87G in 74 regular-season games and 13G in 19 playoff games.
97 — Wayne Gretzky, Edmonton, 1981-82, 92G in 80 regular-season games and 5G in 5 playoff games.
— Mario Lemieux, Pittsburgh, 1988-89, 85G in 76 regular-season games and 12G in 11 playoff games.
— Brett Hull, St. Louis, 1990-91, 86G in 78 regular-season games and 11G in 13 playoff games.
90 — Wayne Gretzky, Edmonton, 1984-85, 73G in 80 regular-season games and 17G in 18 playoff games.
— Jari Kurri, Edmonton, 1984-85, 71G in 80 regular-season games and 19G in 18 playoff games.
85 — Mike Bossy, NY Islanders, 1980-81, 68G in 79 regular-season games and 17G in 18 playoff games.
— Brett Hull, St. Louis, 1989-90, 72G in 80 regular-season games and 13G in 12 playoff games.
83 — Wayne Gretzky, Edmonton, 1982-83, 71G in 73 regular-season games and 12G in 16 playoff games.
— Alexander Mogilny, Buffalo, 1992-93, 76G in 77 regular-season games and 7G in 7 playoff games.

MOST GOALS, 50 GAMES FROM START OF SEASON:
61 — Wayne Gretzky, Edmonton, 1981-82. Oct. 7, 1981 - Jan. 22, 1982. (80-game schedule)
— Wayne Gretzky, Edmonton, 1983-84. Oct. 5, 1983 - Jan. 25, 1984. (80-game schedule)
54 — Mario Lemieux, Pittsburgh, 1988-89. Oct. 7, 1988 - Jan. 31, 1989. (80-game schedule)
53 — Wayne Gretzky, Edmonton, 1984-85. Oct. 11, 1984 - Jan. 28, 1985. (80-game schedule).
52 — Brett Hull, St. Louis, 1990-91. Oct. 4, 1990 - Jan. 26, 1991. (80-game schedule).
50 — Maurice Richard, Montreal, 1944-45. Oct. 28, 1944 - March 18, 1945. (50-game schedule)
— Mike Bossy, NY Islanders, 1980-81. Oct. 11, 1980 - Jan. 24, 1981. (80-game schedule)
— Brett Hull, St. Louis, 1991-92. Oct. 5, 1991 – Jan 28, 1992. (80 game schedule)

MOST GOALS, ONE GAME:
7 — Joe Malone, Que. Bulldogs, Jan. 31, 1920, at Quebec. Quebec 10, Toronto 6.
6 — Newsy Lalonde, Montreal, Jan. 10, 1920, at Montreal. Montreal 14, Toronto 7.
— Joe Malone, Que. Bulldogs, March 10, 1920, at Quebec. Quebec 10, Ottawa 4.
— Corb Denneny, Toronto, Jan. 26, 1921, at Toronto. Toronto 10, Hamilton 3.
— Cy Denneny, Ottawa, Mar. 7, 1921, at Ottawa. Ottawa 12, Hamilton 5.
— Syd Howe, Detroit, Feb. 3, 1944, at Detroit. Detroit 12, NY Rangers 2.
— Red Berenson, St. Louis, Nov. 7, 1968, at Philadelphia. St. Louis 8, Philadelphia 0.
— Darryl Sittler, Toronto, Feb. 7, 1976, at Toronto. Toronto 11, Boston 4.

Raymond Bourque's Stanley Cup victory with Colorado in 2001 capped a career that saw him play more games than anyone in NHL history except Gordie Howe and Larry Murphy. 1,518 of Bourque's 1,612 games were played with Boston.

Red Berenson, surrounded by teammates Jimmy Roberts (left) and Terry Crisp, set a record for goals in an NHL road game when he scored six for St. Louis against Philadelphia on November 7, 1968.

MOST GOALS, ONE ROAD GAME:

6 — Red Berenson, St. Louis, Nov. 7, 1968, at Philadelphia. St. Louis 8, Philadelphia 0.
5 — Joe Malone, Montreal, Dec. 19, 1917, at Ottawa. Montreal 9, Ottawa 4.
— Red Green, Hamilton, Dec. 5, 1924, at Toronto. Hamilton 10, Toronto 3.
— Babe Dye, Toronto, Dec. 22, 1924, at Boston. Toronto 10, Boston 2.
— Punch Broadbent, Mtl. Maroons, Jan. 7, 1925, at Hamilton. Mtl. Maroons 6, Hamilton 2.
— Don Murdoch, NY Rangers, Oct. 12, 1976, at Minnesota. NY Rangers 10, Minnesota 4.
— Tim Young, Minnesota, Jan. 15, 1979, at NY Rangers. Minnesota 8, NY Rangers 1.
— Willy Lindstrom, Winnipeg, Mar. 2, 1982, at Philadelphia. Winnipeg 7, Philadelphia 6.
— Bengt Gustafsson, Washington, Jan. 8, 1984, at Philadelphia. Washington 7, Philadelphia 1.
— Wayne Gretzky, Edmonton, Dec. 15, 1984, at St. Louis. Edmonton 8, St. Louis 2.
— Dave Andreychuk, Buffalo, Feb. 6, 1986, at Boston. Buffalo 8, Boston 6.
— Mats Sundin, Quebec, Mar. 5, 1992, at Hartford. Quebec 10, Hartford 4.
— Mario Lemieux, Pittsburgh, Apr. 9, 1993, at NY Rangers. Pittsburgh 10, NY Rangers 4.
— Mike Ricci, Quebec, Feb. 17, 1994, at San Jose. Quebec 8, San Jose 2.
— Alexei Zhamnov, Winnipeg, Apr. 1, 1995, at Los Angeles. Winnipeg 7, Los Angeles 7.

MOST GOALS, ONE PERIOD:

4 — Busher Jackson, Toronto, Nov. 20, 1934, at St. Louis, third period. Toronto 5, St. Louis Eagles 2.
— Max Bentley, Chicago, Jan. 28, 1943, at Chicago, third period. Chicago 10, NY Rangers 1.
— Clint Smith, Chicago, Mar. 4, 1945, at Chicago, third period. Chicago 6, Montreal 4.
— Red Berenson, St. Louis, Nov. 7, 1968, at Philadelphia, second period. St. Louis 8, Philadelphia 0.
— Wayne Gretzky, Edmonton, Feb. 18, 1981, at Edmonton, third period. Edmonton 9, St. Louis 2.
— Grant Mulvey, Chicago, Feb. 3, 1982, at Chicago, first period. Chicago 9, St. Louis 5.
— Bryan Trottier, NY Islanders, Feb. 13, 1982, at NY Islanders, second period. NY Islanders 8, Philadelphia 2.
— Al Secord, Chicago, Jan. 7, 1987, at Chicago, second period. Chicago 6, Toronto 4.
— Joe Nieuwendyk, Calgary, Jan. 11, 1989, at Calgary, second period. Calgary 8, Winnipeg 3.
— Peter Bondra, Washington, Feb. 5, 1994, at Washington, first period. Washington 6, Tampa Bay 3.
— Mario Lemieux, Pittsburgh, Jan. 26, 1997, at Montreal, third period. Pittsburgh 5, Montreal 2.

ASSISTS

MOST ASSISTS:

1,963 — Wayne Gretzky, Edmonton, Los Angeles, St. Louis, NY Rangers, in 20 seasons, 1,487GP.
1,169 — Raymond Bourque, Boston, Colorado, in 22 seasons, 1,612GP.
1,137 — Ron Francis, Hartford, Pittsburgh, Carolina, in 20 seasons, 1,489GP.
1,135 — Paul Coffey, Edmonton, Pittsburgh, Los Angeles, Detroit, Hartford, Philadelphia, Chicago, Carolina, Boston, in 21 seasons, in 1,409GP.
1,130 — Mark Messier, Edmonton, NY Rangers, Vancouver, in 22 seasons, 1,561GP.

MOST ASSISTS, INCLUDING PLAYOFFS:

2,223 — Wayne Gretzky, Edmonton, Los Angeles, St. Louis, NY Rangers, 1,963 regular-season and 260 playoff assists.
1,316 — Mark Messier, Edmonton, NY Rangers, Vancouver, 1,130 regular-season and 186 playoff assists.
1,308 — Raymond Bourque, Boston, Colorado, 1,169 regular season and 139 playoff assists.
1,272 — Paul Coffey, Edmonton, Pittsburgh, Los Angeles, Detroit, Hartford, Philadelphia, Chicago, Carolina, Boston, 1,135 regular-season and 137 playoff assists.
1,220 — Ron Francis, Hartford, Pittsburgh, Carolina, 1,137 regular-season and 83 playoff assists.

MOST ASSISTS, ONE SEASON:

163 — Wayne Gretzky, Edmonton, 1985-86. 80 game schedule.
135 — Wayne Gretzky, Edmonton, 1984-85. 80 game schedule.
125 — Wayne Gretzky, Edmonton, 1982-83. 80 game schedule.
122 — Wayne Gretzky, Los Angeles, 1990-91. 80 game schedule.
121 — Wayne Gretzky, Edmonton, 1986-87. 80 game schedule.
120 — Wayne Gretzky, Edmonton, 1981-82. 80 game schedule.
118 — Wayne Gretzky, Edmonton, 1983-84. 80 game schedule.
114 — Wayne Gretzky, Los Angeles, 1988-89. 80 game schedule.
— Mario Lemieux, Pittsburgh, 1988-89. 80 game schedule.
109 — Wayne Gretzky, Edmonton, 1980-81. 80 game schedule.
— Wayne Gretzky, Edmonton, 1987-88. 80 game schedule.
102 — Bobby Orr, Boston, 1970-71. 78 game schedule.
— Wayne Gretzky, Los Angeles, 1989-90. 80 game schedule.

MOST ASSISTS, ONE SEASON, INCLUDING PLAYOFFS:

174 — Wayne Gretzky, Edmonton, 1985-86, 163A in 80 regular-season games and 11A in 10 playoff games.
165 — Wayne Gretzky, Edmonton, 1984-85, 135A in 80 regular-season games and 30A in 18 playoff games.
151 — Wayne Gretzky, Edmonton, 1982-83, 125A in 80 regular-season games and 26A in 16 playoff games.
150 — Wayne Gretzky, Edmonton, 1986-87, 121A in 79 regular-season games and 29A in 21 playoff games.
140 — Wayne Gretzky, Edmonton, 1983-84, 118A in 74 regular-season games and 22A in 19 playoff games.
— Wayne Gretzky, Edmonton, 1987-88, 109A in 64 regular-season games and 31A in 19 playoff games.
133 — Wayne Gretzky, Los Angeles, 1990-91, 122A in 78 regular-season games and 11A in 12 playoff games.
131 — Wayne Gretzky, Los Angeles, 1988-89, 114A in 78 regular-season games and 17A in 11 playoff games.
127 — Wayne Gretzky, Edmonton, 1981-82, 120A in 80 regular-season games and 7A in 5 playoff games.
123 — Wayne Gretzky, Edmonton, 1980-81, 109A in 80 regular-season games and 14A in 9 playoff games.
121 — Mario Lemieux, Pittsburgh, 1988-89, 114A in 76 regular-season games and 7A in 11 playoff games.

MOST ASSISTS, ONE GAME:

7 — Billy Taylor, Detroit, Mar. 16, 1947, at Chicago. Detroit 10, Chicago 6.
— **Wayne Gretzky,** Edmonton, Feb. 15, 1980, at Edmonton. Edmonton 8, Washington 2.
— **Wayne Gretzky,** Edmonton, Dec. 11, 1985, at Chicago. Edmonton 12, Chicago 9.
— **Wayne Gretzky,** Edmonton, Feb. 14, 1986, at Edmonton. Edmonton 8, Quebec 2.
6 — Six assists have been recorded in one game on 24 occasions since Elmer Lach of Montreal first accomplished the feat vs. Boston on Feb. 6, 1943. The most recent player is Eric Lindros of Philadelphia (Feb. 26, 1997 at Ottawa)

MOST ASSISTS, ONE ROAD GAME:

7 — Billy Taylor, Detroit, Mar. 16, 1947, at Chicago. Detroit 10, Chicago 6.
— **Wayne Gretzky,** Edmonton, Dec. 11, 1985, at Chicago. Edmonton 12, Chicago 9.
6 — Bobby Orr, Boston, Jan. 1, 1973, at Vancouver. Boston 8, Vancouver 2.
— Patrik Sundstrom, Vancouver, Feb. 29, 1984, at Pittsburgh. Vancouver 9, Pittsburgh 5.
— Mario Lemieux, Pittsburgh, Dec. 5, 1992, at San Jose. Pittsburgh 9, San Jose 4.
— Eric Lindros, Philadelphia, Feb. 26, 1997, at Ottawa. Philadelphia 8, Ottawa 5.

MOST ASSISTS, ONE PERIOD:

5 — Dale Hawerchuk, Winnipeg, Mar. 6, 1984, at Los Angeles, second period. Winnipeg 7, Los Angeles 3.
4 — Four assists have been recorded in one period on 63 occasions since Mickey Roach of Hamilton first accomplished the feat vs. Toronto St. Pats on Feb. 23, 1921. Most recent player, Paul Kariya of Anaheim, (Dec. 16, 1998 vs Nashville).

POINTS

MOST POINTS:

2,857 — Wayne Gretzky, Edmonton, Los Angeles, St. Louis, NY Rangers, in 20 seasons, 1,487GP (894G-1963A).
1,850 — Gordie Howe, Detroit, Hartford, in 26 seasons, 1,767GP (801G-1049A).
1,781 — Mark Messier, Edmonton, NY Rangers, Vancouver, in 22 seasons, 1,561GP (651G-1,130A).
1,771 — Marcel Dionne, Detroit, Los Angeles, NY Rangers, in 18 seasons, 1,348GP (731G-1,040A).
1,624 — Ron Francis, Hartford, Pittsburgh, Carolina, in 20 seasons, 1,489GP (487G-1,137A).

MOST POINTS, INCLUDING PLAYOFFS:

3,239 — Wayne Gretzky, Edmonton, Los Angeles, St. Louis, NY Rangers, 2,857 regular-season and 382 playoff points.
2,076 — Mark Messier, Edmonton, NY Rangers, Vancouver, 1,781 regular-season and 295 playoff points.
2,010 — Gordie Howe, Detroit, Hartford, 1,850 regular-season and 160 playoff points.
1,816 — Marcel Dionne, Detroit, Los Angeles, NY Rangers, 1,771 regular-season and 45 playoff points.
1,766 — Steve Yzerman, Detroit, 1,614 regular-season and 152 playoff points.

MOST POINTS, ONE SEASON:

215 — Wayne Gretzky, Edmonton, 1985-86. 80 game schedule.
212 — Wayne Gretzky, Edmonton, 1981-82. 80 game schedule.
208 — Wayne Gretzky, Edmonton, 1984-85. 80 game schedule.
205 — Wayne Gretzky, Edmonton, 1983-84. 80 game schedule.
199 — Mario Lemieux, Pittsburgh, 1988-89. 80 game schedule.
196 — Wayne Gretzky, Edmonton, 1982-83. 80 game schedule.
183 — Wayne Gretzky, Edmonton, 1986-87. 80 game schedule.
168 — Mario Lemieux, Pittsburgh, 1987-88, 80 game schedule.
— Wayne Gretzky, Los Angeles, 1988-89. 80 game schedule.
164 — Wayne Gretzky, Edmonton, 1980-81. 80 game schedule.
163 — Wayne Gretzky, Los Angeles, 1990-91. 80 game schedule.
161 — Mario Lemieux, Pittsburgh, 1995-96. 82 game schedule.
160 — Mario Lemieux, Pittsburgh, 1992-93. 84 game schedule.

MOST POINTS, ONE SEASON, INCLUDING PLAYOFFS:

255 — Wayne Gretzky, Edmonton, 1984-85, 208PTS in 80 regular-season games and 47PTS in 18 playoff games.
240 — Wayne Gretzky, Edmonton, 1983-84, 205PTS in 74 regular-season games and 35PTS in 19 playoff games.
234 — Wayne Gretzky, Edmonton, 1982-83, 196PTS in 80 regular-season games and 38PTS in 16 playoff games.
— Wayne Gretzky, Edmonton, 1985-86, 215PTS in 80 regular-season games and 19PTS in 10 playoff games.
224 — Wayne Gretzky, Edmonton, 1981-82, 212PTS in 80 regular-season games and 12PTS in 5 playoff games.
218 — Mario Lemieux, Pittsburgh, 1988-89, 199PTS in 76 regular-season games and 19PTS in 11 playoff games.
217 — Wayne Gretzky, Edmonton, 1986-87, 183PTS in 79 regular-season games and 34PTS in 21 playoff games.
192 — Wayne Gretzky, Edmonton, 1987-88, 149PTS in 64 regular-season games and 43PTS in 19 playoff games.
190 — Wayne Gretzky, Los Angeles, 1988-89, 168PTS in 78 regular-season games and 22PTS in 11 playoff games.
188 — Mario Lemieux, Pittsburgh, 1995-96, 161PTS in 70 regular-season games and 27PTS in 18 playoff games.
185 — Wayne Gretzky, Edmonton, 1980-81, 164PTS in 80 regular-season games and 21PTS in 9 playoff games.

By setting up teammates for goals 1,963 times in his career, Wayne Gretzky collected more assists than any other NHL player has ever had points. Gretzky had seven assists in a single game three times in his career.

MOST POINTS, ONE GAME:
10 — Darryl Sittler, Toronto, Feb. 7, 1976, at Toronto, 6G-4A. Toronto 11, Boston 4.
8 — Maurice Richard, Montreal, Dec. 28, 1944, at Montreal, 5G-3A. Montreal 9, Detroit 1.
— Bert Olmstead, Montreal, Jan. 9, 1954, at Montreal, 4G-4A. Montreal 12, Chicago 1.
— Tom Bladon, Philadelphia, Dec. 11, 1977, at Philadelphia, 4G-4A. Philadelphia 11, Cleveland 1.
— Bryan Trottier, NY Islanders, Dec. 23, 1978, at NY Islanders, 5G-3A. NY Islanders 9, NY Rangers 4.
— Peter Stastny, Quebec, Feb. 22, 1981, at Washington, 4G-4A. Quebec 11, Washington 7.
— Anton Stastny, Quebec, Feb. 22, 1981, at Washington, 3G-5A. Quebec 11, Washington 7.
— Wayne Gretzky, Edmonton, Nov. 19, 1983, at Edmonton, 3G-5A. Edmonton 13, New Jersey 4.
— Wayne Gretzky, Edmonton, Jan. 4, 1984, at Edmonton, 4G-4A. Edmonton 12, Minnesota 8.
— Paul Coffey, Edmonton, Mar. 14, 1986, at Edmonton, 2G-6A. Edmonton 12, Detroit 3.
— Mario Lemieux, Pittsburgh, Oct. 15, 1988, at Pittsburgh, 2G-6A. Pittsburgh 9, St. Louis 2.
— Bernie Nicholls, Los Angeles, Dec. 1, 1988, at Los Angeles, 2G-6A. Los Angeles 9, Toronto 3.
— Mario Lemieux, Pittsburgh, Dec. 31, 1988, at Pittsburgh, 5G-3A. Pittsburgh 8, New Jersey 6.

MOST POINTS, ONE ROAD GAME:
8 — Peter Stastny, Quebec, Feb. 22, 1981, at Washington, 4G-4A. Quebec 11, Washington 7.
— **Anton Stastny,** Quebec, Feb. 22, 1981, at Washington, 3G-5A. Quebec 11, Washington 7.
7 — Red Green, Hamilton, Dec. 5, 1924, at Toronto, 5G-2A. Hamilton 10, Toronto 3.
— Billy Taylor, Detroit, Mar. 16, 1947, at Chicago, 7A. Detroit 10, Chicago 6.
— Red Berenson, St. Louis, Nov. 7, 1968, at Philadelphia, 6G-1A. St. Louis 8, Philadelphia 0.
— Gilbert Perreault, Buffalo, Feb. 1, 1976, at California, 2G-5A. Buffalo 9, California 5.
— Peter Stastny, Quebec, Apr. 1, 1982, at Boston, 3G-4A. Quebec 8, Boston 5.
— Wayne Gretzky, Edmonton, Nov. 6, 1983, at Winnipeg, 4G-3A. Edmonton 8, Winnipeg 5.
— Patrik Sundstrom, Vancouver, Feb. 29, 1984, at Pittsburgh, 1G-6A. Vancouver 9, Pittsburgh 5.
— Wayne Gretzky, Edmonton, Dec. 11, 1985, at Chicago, 7A, Edmonton 12, Chicago 9.
— Cam Neely, Boston, Oct. 16, 1988, at Chicago, 3G-4A. Boston 10, Chicago 3.
— Mario Lemieux, Pittsburgh, Jan. 21, 1989, at Edmonton, 2G-5A. Pittsburgh 7, Edmonton 4.
— Dino Ciccarelli, Washington, Mar. 18, 1989, at Hartford, 4G-3A. Washington 8, Hartford 2.
— Mats Sundin, Quebec, Mar. 5, 1992, at Hartford, 5G-2A. Quebec 10, Hartford 4.
— Mario Lemieux, Pittsburgh, Dec. 5, 1992, at San Jose, 1G-6A. Pittsburgh 9, San Jose 4.
— Eric Lindros, Philadelphia, Feb. 26, 1997, at Ottawa, 1G-6A. Philadelphia 8, Ottawa 5.

MOST POINTS, ONE PERIOD:
6 — Bryan Trottier, NY Islanders, Dec. 23, 1978, at NY Islanders, second period. 3G-3A. NY Islanders 9, NY Rangers 4.
5 — Les Cunningham, Chicago, Jan. 28, 1940, at Chicago, third period. 2G-3A. Chicago 8, Montreal 1.
— Max Bentley, Chicago, Jan. 28, 1943, at Chicago, third period. 4G-1A, Chicago 10, NY Rangers 1.
— Leo Labine, Boston, Nov. 28, 1954, at Boston, second period. 3G-2A. Boston 6, Detroit 2.
— Darryl Sittler, Toronto, Feb. 7, 1976, at Toronto, second period. 3G-2A. Toronto 11, Boston 4.
— Grant Mulvey, Chicago, Feb. 3, 1982, at Chicago, first period. 4G-1A. Chicago 9, St. Louis 5.
— Dale Hawerchuk, Winnipeg, Mar. 6, 1984, at Los Angeles, second period. 5A. Winnipeg 7, Los Angeles 3.
— Jari Kurri, Edmonton, Oct. 26, 1984, at Edmonton, second period. 2G-3A. Edmonton 8, Los Angeles 2.
— Pat Elynuik, Winnipeg, Jan. 20, 1989, at Winnipeg, second period. 2G-3A. Winnipeg 7, Pittsburgh 3.
— Ray Ferraro, Hartford, Dec. 9, 1989, at Hartford, first period. 3G-2A. Hartford 7, New Jersey 3.
— Stephane Richer, Montreal, Feb. 14, 1990, at Montreal, first period. 2G-3A. Montreal 10, Vancouver 1.
— Cliff Ronning, Vancouver, Apr. 15, 1993, at Los Angeles, third period. 3G-2A. Vancouver 8, Los Angeles 6.
— Peter Forsberg, Colorado, Mar. 3, 1999, at Florida, third period. 2G-3A. Colorado 7, Florida 5.

POWER-PLAY and SHORTHAND GOALS

MOST POWER-PLAY GOALS, ONE SEASON:
34 — Tim Kerr, Philadelphia, 1985-86. 80 game schedule.
32 — Dave Andreychuk, Buffalo, Toronto, 1992-93. 84 game schedule.
31 — Joe Nieuwendyk, Calgary, 1987-88. 80 game schedule.
— Mario Lemieux, Pittsburgh, 1988-89. 80 game schedule.
— Mario Lemieux, Pittsburgh, 1995-96. 82 game schedule.
29 — Michel Goulet, Quebec, 1987-88. 80 game schedule.
— Brett Hull, St. Louis, 1990-91. 80 game schedule.
— Brett Hull, St. Louis, 1992-93. 84 game schedule.

MOST SHORTHAND GOALS, ONE SEASON:
13 — Mario Lemieux, Pittsburgh, 1988-89. 80 game schedule.
12 — Wayne Gretzky, Edmonton, 1983-84. 80 game schedule.
11 — Wayne Gretzky, Edmonton, 1984-85. 80 game schedule.
10 — Marcel Dionne, Detroit, 1974-75. 80 game schedule.
— Mario Lemieux, Pittsburgh, 1987-88. 80 game schedule.
— Dirk Graham, Chicago, 1988-89. 80 game schedule.

MOST SHORTHAND GOALS, ONE GAME:
3 —Theoren Fleury, Calgary, Mar. 9, 1991, at St. Louis. Calgary 8, St. Louis 4.

OVERTIME SCORING

MOST OVERTIME GOALS, CAREER:
11 — Steve Thomas, Toronto, Chicago, NY Islanders, New Jersey.
10 — Mario Lemieux, Pittsburgh.
9 — Jaromir Jagr, Pittsburgh.
— Pierre Turgeon, Buffalo, NY Islanders, Montreal, St. Louis.
— Sergei Fedorov, Detroit.

MOST OVERTIME ASSISTS, CAREER:
15 — Wayne Gretzky, Edmonton, Los Angeles, St. Louis, NY Rangers.
— **Mark Messier,** Edmonton, NY Rangers, Vancouver.
13 — Raymond Bourque, Boston, Colorado.
— Doug Gilmour, St. Louis, Calgary, Toronto, New Jersey, Chicago, Buffalo.
— Adam Oates, Detroit, St. Louis, Boston, Washington.
12 — Scott Stevens, Washington, St. Louis, New Jersey.

MOST OVERTIME POINTS, CAREER:
23 — Mark Messier, Edmonton, NY Rangers, Vancouver. 8G-15A
21 — Steve Thomas, Toronto, Chicago, NY Islanders, New Jersey. 11G-10A
20 — Mario Lemieux, Pittsburgh. 10G-10A
18 — Raymond Bourque, Boston, Colorado. 5G-13A
— Adam Oates, Detroit, St. Louis, Boston, Washington. 5G-13A.
— Pierre Turgeon, Buffalo, NY Islanders, Montreal, St. Louis. 9G-9A
— Steve Yzerman, Detroit. 8G-10A
17 — Sergei Fedorov, Detroit. 9G-8A
— Wayne Gretzky, Edmonton, Los Angeles, St. Louis, NY Rangers. 2G-15A
16 — Doug Gilmour, St. Louis, Calgary, Toronto, New Jersey, Chicago, Buffalo. 3G-13A

SCORING BY A CENTER

MOST GOALS BY A CENTER, CAREER
894 — Wayne Gretzky, Edmonton, Los Angeles, St. Louis, NY Rangers, in 20 seasons.
731 — Marcel Dionne, Detroit, Los Angeles, NY Rangers, in 18 seasons.
717 — Phil Esposito, Chicago, Boston, NY Rangers, in 18 seasons.
651 — Mark Messier, Edmonton, NY Rangers, Vancouver, in 22 seasons.
648 — Mario Lemieux, Pittsburgh, in 13 seasons.

MOST GOALS BY A CENTER, ONE SEASON:
92 — Wayne Gretzky, Edmonton, 1981-82. 80 game schedule.
87 — Wayne Gretzky, Edmonton, 1983-84. 80 game schedule.
85 — Mario Lemieux, Pittsburgh, 1988-89. 80 game schedule.
76 — Phil Esposito, Boston, 1970-71. 78 game schedule.
73 — Wayne Gretzky, Edmonton, 1984-85. 80 game schedule.

Just 13 players in NHL history have had five or more points in a single period. The most recent was Peter Forsberg, who had two goals and three assists for Colorado in the third period of a 7-5 win over Florida on March 3, 1999.

MOST ASSISTS BY A CENTER, CAREER:
1,963 — Wayne Gretzky, Edmonton, Los Angeles, St. Louis, NY Rangers, in 20 seasons.
1,137 — Ron Francis, Hartford, Pittsburgh, Carolina, in 20 seasons.
1,130 — Mark Messier, Edmonton, NY Rangers, Vancouver, in 22 seasons.
1,040 — Marcel Dionne, Detroit, Los Angeles, NY Rangers, in 18 seasons.
969 — Steve Yzerman, Detroit, in 18 seasons.

MOST ASSISTS BY A CENTER, ONE SEASON:
163 — Wayne Gretzky, Edmonton, 1985-86. 80 game schedule.
135 — Wayne Gretzky, Edmonton, 1984-85. 80 game schedule.
125 — Wayne Gretzky, Edmonton, 1982-83. 80 game schedule.
122 — Wayne Gretzky, Los Angeles, 1990-91. 80 game schedule.
121 — Wayne Gretzky, Edmonton, 1986-87. 80 game schedule.

MOST POINTS BY A CENTER, CAREER:
2,857 — Wayne Gretzky, Edmonton, Los Angeles, St. Louis, NY Rangers, in 20 seasons.
1,781 — Mark Messier, Edmonton, NY Rangers, Vancouver, in 22 seasons.
1,771 — Marcel Dionne, Detroit, Los Angeles, NY Rangers, in 18 seasons.
1,624 — Ron Francis, Hartford, Pittsburgh, Carolina, in 20 seasons.
1,614 — Steve Yzerman, Detroit, in 18 seasons.

MOST POINTS BY A CENTER, ONE SEASON:
215 — Wayne Gretzky, Edmonton, 1985-86. 80 game schedule.
212 — Wayne Gretzky, Edmonton, 1981-82. 80 game schedule.
208 — Wayne Gretzky, Edmonton, 1984-85. 80 game schedule.
205 — Wayne Gretzky, Edmonton, 1983-84. 80 game schedule.
199 — Mario Lemieux, Pittsburgh, 1988-89. 80 game schedule.

SCORING BY A LEFT WING

MOST GOALS BY A LEFT WING, CAREER:
610 — Bobby Hull, Chicago, Winnipeg, Hartford, in 16 seasons.
590 — Luc Robitaille, Los Angeles, Pittsburgh, NY Rangers, in 15 seasons.
572 — Dave Andreychuk, Buffalo, Toronto, New Jersey, Boston, Colorado, in 19 seasons.
556 — John Bucyk, Detroit, Boston, in 23 seasons.
548 — Michel Goulet, Quebec, Chicago, in 15 seasons.

MOST GOALS BY A LEFT WING, ONE SEASON:
63 — Luc Robitaille, Los Angeles, 1992-93. 84 game schedule.
60 — Steve Shutt, Montreal, 1976-77. 80 game schedule.
58 — Bobby Hull, Chicago, 1968-69. 76 game schedule.
57 — Michel Goulet, Quebec, 1982-83. 80 game schedule.
56 — Charlie Simmer, Los Angeles, 1979-80. 80 game schedule.
— Charlie Simmer, Los Angeles, 1980-81. 80 game schedule.
— Michel Goulet, Quebec, 1983-84. 80 game schedule.

Elected to the Hockey Hall of Fame in 1998, Michel Goulet ranks fifth all-time in goals scored by a left winger. He also ranks among the top five in single-season scoring by a left winger.

MOST ASSISTS BY A LEFT WING, CAREER:
813 — John Bucyk, Detroit, Boston, in 23 seasons.
648 — Luc Robitaille, Los Angeles, Pittsburgh, NY Rangers, in 15 seasons.
637 — Dave Andreychuk, Buffalo, Toronto, New Jersey, Boston, Colorado, in 19 seasons.
604 — Michel Goulet, Quebec, Chicago, in 15 seasons.
579 — Brian Propp, Philadelphia, Boston, Minnesota, Hartford, in 15 seasons.

MOST ASSISTS BY A LEFT WING, ONE SEASON:
70 — Joe Juneau, Boston, 1992-93. 84 game schedule.
69 — Kevin Stevens, Pittsburgh, 1991-92. 80 game schedule.
67 — Mats Naslund, Montreal, 1985-86. 80 game schedule.
65 — John Bucyk, Boston, 1970-71. 78 game schedule.
— Michel Goulet, Quebec, 1983-84. 80 game schedule.
64 — Mark Messier, Edmonton, 1983-84. 80 game schedule.

MOST POINTS BY A LEFT WING, CAREER:
1,369 — John Bucyk, Detroit, Boston, in 23 seasons.
1,238 — Luc Robitaille, Los Angeles, Pittsburgh, NY Rangers, in 15 seasons.
1,209 — Dave Andreychuk, Buffalo, Toronto, New Jersey, Boston, Colorado, in 19 seasons.
1,170 — Bobby Hull, Chicago, Winnipeg, Hartford, in 16 seasons.
1,152 — Michel Goulet, Quebec, Chicago, in 15 seasons.

MOST POINTS BY A LEFT WING, ONE SEASON:
125 — Luc Robitaille, Los Angeles, 1992-93. 84 game schedule.
123 — Kevin Stevens, Pittsburgh, 1991-92. 80 game schedule.
121 — Michel Goulet, Quebec, 1983-84. 80 game schedule.
116 — John Bucyk, Boston, 1970-71. 78 game schedule.
112 — Bill Barber, Philadelphia, 1975-76. 80 game schedule.

SCORING BY A RIGHT WING

MOST GOALS BY A RIGHT WING, CAREER:
801 — Gordie Howe, Detroit, Hartford, in 26 seasons.
708 — Mike Gartner, Washington, Minnesota, NY Rangers, Toronto, Phoenix, in 19 seasons.
649 — Brett Hull, Calgary, St. Louis, Dallas, in 16 seasons.
608 — Dino Ciccarelli, Minnesota, Washington, Detroit, Tampa Bay, Florida, in 19 seasons.
601 — Jari Kurri, Edmonton, Los Angeles, NY Rangers, Anaheim, Colorado, in 17 seasons.

MOST GOALS BY A RIGHT WING, ONE SEASON:
86 — Brett Hull, St. Louis, 1990-91. 80 game schedule.
76 — Alexander Mogilny, Buffalo, 1992-93. 84 game schedule.
— Teemu Selanne, Winnipeg, 1992-93. 84 game schedule.
72 — Brett Hull, St. Louis, 1989-90. 80 game schedule.
71 — Jari Kurri, Edmonton, 1984-85. 80 game schedule.
70 — Brett Hull, St. Louis, 1991-92. 80 game schedule.

MOST ASSISTS BY A RIGHT WING, CAREER:
1,049 — Gordie Howe, Detroit, Hartford, in 26 seasons.
797 — Jari Kurri, Edmonton, Los Angeles, NY Rangers, Anaheim, Colorado, in 17 seasons.
793 — Guy Lafleur, Montreal, NY Rangers, Quebec, in 17 seasons.
640 — Jaromir Jagr, Pittsburgh, in 11 seasons.
638 — Dave Taylor, Los Angeles, in 17 seasons.

MOST ASSISTS BY A RIGHT WING, ONE SEASON:
87 — Jaromir Jagr, Pittsburgh, 1995-96. 82 game schedule.
83 — Mike Bossy, NY Islanders, 1981-82. 80 game schedule.
— Jaromir Jagr, Pittsburgh, 1998-99. 82 game schedule.
80 — Guy Lafleur, Montreal, 1976-77. 80 game schedule.
77 — Guy Lafleur, Montreal, 1978-79. 80 game schedule.

MOST POINTS BY A RIGHT WING, CAREER:
1,850 — Gordie Howe, Detroit, Hartford, in 26 seasons.
1,398 — Jari Kurri, Edmonton, Los Angeles, NY Rangers, Anaheim, Colorado, in 17 seasons.
1,353 — Guy Lafleur, Montreal, NY Rangers, Quebec, in 17 seasons.
1,335 — Mike Gartner, Washington, Minnesota, NY Rangers, Toronto, Phoenix, in 19 seasons.
1,200 — Dino Ciccarelli, Minnesota, Washington, Detroit, Tampa Bay, Florida, in 19 seasons.

MOST POINTS BY A RIGHT WING, ONE SEASON:
149 — Jaromir Jagr, Pittsburgh, 1995-96. 82 game schedule.
147 — Mike Bossy, NY Islanders, 1981-82. 80 game schedule.
136 — Guy Lafleur, Montreal, 1976-77. 80 game schedule.
135 — Jari Kurri, Edmonton, 1984-85. 80 game schedule.
132 — Guy Lafleur, Montreal, 1977-78. 80 game schedule.
— Teemu Selanne, Winnipeg, 1992-93. 84 game schedule.

SCORING BY A DEFENSEMAN

MOST GOALS BY A DEFENSEMAN, CAREER:
410 — Raymond Bourque, Boston, Colorado, in 22 seasons.
396 — Paul Coffey, Edmonton, Pittsburgh, Los Angeles, Detroit, Hartford, Philadelphia, Chicago, Carolina, Boston, in 21 seasons.
317 — Phil Housley, Buffalo, Winnipeg, St. Louis, Calgary, New Jersey, Washington, in 19 seasons.
313 — Al MacInnis, Calgary, St. Louis, in 20 seasons.
310 — Denis Potvin, NY Islanders, in 15 seasons.

MOST GOALS BY A DEFENSEMAN, ONE SEASON:
48 — Paul Coffey, Edmonton, 1985-86. 80 game schedule.
46 — Bobby Orr, Boston, 1974-75. 80 game schedule.
40 — Paul Coffey, Edmonton, 1983-84. 80 game schedule.
39 — Doug Wilson, Chicago, 1981-82. 80 game schedule.
37 — Bobby Orr, Boston, 1970-71. 78 game schedule.
— Bobby Orr, Boston, 1971-72. 78 game schedule.
— Paul Coffey, Edmonton, 1984-85. 80 game schedule.

MOST GOALS BY A DEFENSEMAN, ONE GAME:
5 — Ian Turnbull, Toronto, Feb. 2, 1977, at Toronto. Toronto 9, Detroit 1.
4 — Harry Cameron, Toronto, Dec. 26, 1917, at Toronto. Toronto 7, Montreal 5.
— Harry Cameron, Montreal, Mar. 3, 1920, at Quebec City. Montreal 16, Que. Bulldogs 3.
— Sprague Cleghorn, Montreal, Jan. 14, 1922, at Montreal. Montreal 10, Hamilton 6.
— Johnny McKinnon, Pit. Pirates, Nov. 19, 1929, at Pittsburgh. Pit. Pirates 10, Toronto 5.
— Hap Day, Toronto, Nov. 19, 1929, at Pittsburgh. Pit. Pirates 10, Toronto 5.
— Tom Bladon, Philadelphia, Dec. 11, 1977, at Philadelphia. Philadelphia 11, Cleveland 1.
— Ian Turnbull, Los Angeles, Dec. 12, 1981, at Los Angeles. Los Angeles 7, Vancouver 5.
— Paul Coffey, Edmonton, Oct. 26, 1984, at Calgary. Edmonton 6, Calgary 5.

MOST ASSISTS BY A DEFENSEMAN, CAREER:
1,169 — Raymond Bourque, Boston, Colorado, in 22 seasons.
1,135 — Paul Coffey, Edmonton, Pittsburgh, Los Angeles, Detroit, Hartford, Philadelphia, Chicago, Carolina, Boston, in 21 seasons.
929 — Larry Murphy, Los Angeles, Washington, Pittsburgh, Toronto, Detroit, in 21 seasons.
847 — Phil Housley, Buffalo, Winnipeg, St. Louis, Calgary, New Jersey, Washington, in 19 seasons.
845 — Al MacInnis, Calgary, St. Louis, in 20 seasons.

MOST ASSISTS BY A DEFENSEMAN, ONE SEASON:
102 — Bobby Orr, Boston, 1970-71. 78 game schedule.
90 — Bobby Orr, Boston, 1973-74. 78 game schedule.
— Paul Coffey, Edmonton, 1985-86. 80 game schedule.
89 — Bobby Orr, Boston, 1974-75. 80 game schedule.

MOST ASSISTS BY A DEFENSEMAN, ONE GAME:
6 — Babe Pratt, Toronto, Jan. 8, 1944, at Toronto. Toronto 12, Boston 3.
— Pat Stapleton, Chicago, Mar. 30, 1969, at Chicago. Chicago 9, Detroit 5.
— Bobby Orr, Boston, Jan. 1, 1973, at Vancouver. Boston 8, Vancouver 2.
— Ron Stackhouse, Pittsburgh, Mar. 8, 1975, at Pittsburgh. Pittsburgh 8, Philadelphia 2.
— Paul Coffey, Edmonton, Mar. 14, 1986, at Edmonton. Edmonton 12, Detroit 3.
— Gary Suter, Calgary, Apr. 4, 1986, at Calgary. Calgary 9, Edmonton 3.

MOST POINTS BY A DEFENSEMAN, CAREER:
1,579 — Raymond Bourque, Boston, Colorado, in 22 seasons.
1,531 — Paul Coffey, Edmonton, Pittsburgh, Los Angeles, Detroit, Hartford, Philadelphia, Chicago, Carolina, Boston, in 21 seasons.
1,216 — Larry Murphy, Los Angeles, Washington, Pittsburgh, Toronto, Detroit, in 21 seasons.
1,164 — Phil Housley, Buffalo, Winnipeg, St. Louis, Calgary, New Jersey, Washington, in 19 seasons.
1,158 — Al MacInnis, Calgary, St. Louis, in 20 seasons.

MOST POINTS BY A DEFENSEMAN, ONE SEASON:
139 — Bobby Orr, Boston, 1970-71. 78 game schedule.
138 — Paul Coffey, Edmonton, 1985-86. 80 game schedule.
135 — Bobby Orr, Boston, 1974-75. 80 game schedule.
126 — Paul Coffey, Edmonton, 1983-84. 80 game schedule.
122 — Bobby Orr, Boston, 1973-74. 78 game schedule.

MOST POINTS BY A DEFENSEMAN, ONE GAME:
8 — Tom Bladon, Philadelphia, Dec. 11, 1977, at Philadelphia. 4G-4A. Philadelphia 11, Cleveland 1.
— Paul Coffey, Edmonton, Mar. 14, 1986, at Edmonton. 2G-6A. Edmonton 12, Detroit 3.
7 — Bobby Orr, Boston, Nov. 15, 1973, at Boston. 3G-4A. Boston 10, NY Rangers 2.

SCORING BY A GOALTENDER

MOST POINTS BY A GOALTENDER, CAREER:
48 — Tom Barrasso, Buffalo, Pittsburgh, in 17 seasons. (48A)
46 — Grant Fuhr, Edmonton, Toronto, Buffalo, Los Angeles, St. Louis, in 19 seasons. (46A)

MOST POINTS BY A GOALTENDER, ONE SEASON:
14 — Grant Fuhr, Edmonton, 1983-84. (14A)
9 — Curtis Joseph, St. Louis, 1991-92. (9A)
8 — Mike Palmateer, Washington, 1980-81. (8A)
— Grant Fuhr, Edmonton, 1987-88. (8A)
— Ron Hextall, Philadelphia, 1988-89. (8A)
— Tom Barrasso, Pittsburgh, 1992-93. (8A)
7 — Ron Hextall, Philadelphia, 1987-88. (1G-6A)
— Mike Vernon, Calgary, 1987-88. (7A)

MOST POINTS BY A GOALTENDER, ONE GAME:
3 — Jeff Reese, Calgary, Feb. 10, 1993, at Calgary. Calgary 13, San Jose 1. (3A)

With 12 goals in 2000-01, Al MacInnis upped his career total to 313 and passed Denis Potvin for fourth place all-time among defensemen.

SCORING BY A ROOKIE

MOST GOALS BY A ROOKIE, ONE SEASON:
76 — Teemu Selanne, Winnipeg, 1992-93. 84 game schedule.
53 — Mike Bossy, NY Islanders, 1977-78. 80 game schedule.
51 — Joe Nieuwendyk, Calgary, 1987-88. 80 game schedule.
45 — Dale Hawerchuk, Winnipeg, 1981-82. 80 game schedule.
— Luc Robitaille, Los Angeles, 1986-87. 80 game schedule.

MOST GOALS BY A PLAYER IN HIS FIRST NHL SEASON, ONE GAME:
5 — Howie Meeker, Toronto, Jan. 8, 1947, at Toronto. Toronto 10, Chicago 4.
— Don Murdoch, NY Rangers, Oct. 12, 1976, at Minnesota. NY Rangers 10, Minnesota 4.

MOST GOALS BY A PLAYER IN HIS FIRST NHL GAME:
3 — Alex Smart, Montreal, Jan. 14, 1943, at Montreal. Montreal 5, Chicago 1.
— Real Cloutier, Quebec, Oct. 10, 1979, at Quebec. Atlanta 5, Quebec 3.

MOST ASSISTS BY A ROOKIE, ONE SEASON:
70 — Peter Stastny, Quebec, 1980-81. 80 game schedule.
— Joe Juneau, Boston, 1992-93. 84 game schedule.
63 — Bryan Trottier, NY Islanders, 1975-76. 80 game schedule.
62 — Sergei Makarov, Calgary, 1989-90. 80 game schedule.
60 — Larry Murphy, Los Angeles, 1980-81. 80 game schedule.

MOST ASSISTS BY A PLAYER IN HIS FIRST NHL SEASON, ONE GAME:
7 — Wayne Gretzky, Edmonton, Feb. 15, 1980, at Edmonton. Edmonton 8, Washington 2.
6 — Gary Suter, Calgary, Apr. 4, 1986, at Calgary. Calgary 9, Edmonton 3.

MOST ASSISTS BY A PLAYER IN HIS FIRST NHL GAME:
4 — Earl Reibel, Detroit, Oct. 8, 1953, at Detroit. Detroit 4, NY Rangers 1.
— Roland Eriksson, Minnesota, Oct. 6, 1976, at NY Rangers. NY Rangers 6, Minnesota 5.
3 — Al Hill, Philadelphia, Feb. 14, 1977, at Philadelphia. Philadelphia 6, St. Louis 4.

MOST POINTS BY A ROOKIE, ONE SEASON:
132 — Teemu Selanne, Winnipeg, 1992-93. 84 game schedule.
109 — Peter Stastny, Quebec, 1980-81. 80 game schedule.
103 — Dale Hawerchuk, Winnipeg, 1981-82. 80 game schedule.
102 — Joe Juneau, Boston, 1992-93. 84 game schedule.
100 — Mario Lemieux, Pittsburgh, 1984-85. 80 game schedule.

MOST POINTS BY A PLAYER IN HIS FIRST NHL SEASON, ONE GAME:
8 — Peter Stastny, Quebec, Feb. 22, 1981, at Washington. 4G-4A. Quebec 11, Washington 7.
— Anton Stastny, Quebec, Feb. 22, 1981, at Washington. 3G-5A. Quebec 11, Washington 7.
7 — Wayne Gretzky, Edmonton, Feb. 15, 1980, at Edmonton. 7A. Edmonton 8, Washington 2.
— Sergei Makarov, Calgary, Feb. 25, 1990, at Calgary. 2G-5A. Calgary 10, Edmonton 4.
6 — Wayne Gretzky, Edmonton, Mar. 29, 1980, at Toronto. 2G-4A. Edmonton 8, Toronto 5.
— Gary Suter, Calgary, Apr. 4, 1986, at Calgary. 6A. Calgary 9, Edmonton 3.

MOST POINTS BY A PLAYER IN HIS FIRST NHL GAME:
5 — Al Hill, Philadelphia, Feb. 14, 1977, at Philadelphia. 2G-3A. Philadelphia 6, St. Louis 4.
4 — Alex Smart, Montreal, Jan. 14, 1943, at Montreal. 3G-1A. Montreal 5, Chicago 1.
— Earl Reibel, Detroit, Oct. 8, 1953, at Detroit. 4A. Detroit 4, NY Rangers 1.
— Roland Eriksson, Minnesota, Oct. 6, 1976 at NY Rangers. 4A. NY Rangers 6, Minnesota 5.

SCORING BY A ROOKIE DEFENSEMAN

MOST GOALS BY A ROOKIE DEFENSEMAN, ONE SEASON:
23 — Brian Leetch, NY Rangers, 1988-89. 80 game schedule.
22 — Barry Beck, Col. Rockies, 1977-78. 80 game schedule.
19 — Reed Larson, Detroit, 1977-78. 80 game schedule.
— Phil Housley, Buffalo, 1982-83. 80 game schedule.

MOST ASSISTS BY A ROOKIE DEFENSEMAN, ONE SEASON:
60 — Larry Murphy, Los Angeles, 1980-81. 80 game schedule.
55 — Chris Chelios, Montreal, 1984-85. 80 game schedule.
50 — Stefan Persson, NY Islanders, 1977-78. 80 game schedule.
— Gary Suter, Calgary, 1985-86. 80 game schedule.
49 — Nicklas Lidstrom, Detroit, 1991-92. 80 game schedule.

MOST POINTS BY A ROOKIE DEFENSEMAN, ONE SEASON:
76 — Larry Murphy, Los Angeles, 1980-81. 80 game schedule.
71 — Brian Leetch, NY Rangers, 1988-89. 80 game schedule.
68 — Gary Suter, Calgary, 1985-86. 80 game schedule.
66 — Phil Housley, Buffalo, 1982-83. 80 game schedule.
65 — Raymond Bourque, Boston, 1979-80. 80 game schedule.

Consistency was the key to Mike Gartner's success, as 15 consecutive 30-goal seasons (and 17 overall in a 19-year career) resulted in his election to the Hockey Hall of Fame in 2001.

PER-GAME SCORING AVERAGES

HIGHEST GOALS-PER-GAME AVERAGE, CAREER (AMONG PLAYERS WITH 200 OR MORE GOALS):

.822 — Mario Lemieux, Pittsburgh, 648G, 788GP, from 1984-85 – 1996-97, 2000-01.
.762 — Mike Bossy, NY Islanders, 573G, 752GP, from 1977-78 – 1986-87.
.756 — Cy Denneny, Ottawa, Boston, 248G, 328GP, from 1917-18 – 1928-29.
.742 — Babe Dye, Toronto, Hamilton, Chicago, NY Americans, 201G, 271GP, from 1919-20 – 1930-31.
.645 — Pavel Bure, Vancouver, Florida, 384G, 595GP, from 1991-92 – 2000-01.
.637 — Brett Hull, Calgary, St. Louis, Dallas, 649G, 1,019GP, from 1985-86 – 2000-01.

HIGHEST GOALS-PER-GAME AVERAGE, ONE SEASON (AMONG PLAYERS WITH 20-OR-MORE GOALS):

2.20 — Joe Malone, Montreal, 1917-18, with 44G in 20GP.
1.80 — Cy Denneny, Ottawa, 1917-18, with 36G in 20GP.
1.64 — Newsy Lalonde, Montreal, 1917-18, with 23G in 14GP.
1.63 — Joe Malone, Quebec, 1919-20, with 39G in 24GP.
1.61 — Newsy Lalonde, Montreal, 1919-20, with 37G in 23GP.

HIGHEST GOALS-PER-GAME AVERAGE, ONE SEASON (AMONG PLAYERS WITH 50-OR-MORE GOALS):

1.18 — Wayne Gretzky, Edmonton, 1983-84, with 87G in 74GP.
1.15 — Wayne Gretzky, Edmonton, 1981-82, with 92G in 80GP.
— Mario Lemieux, Pittsburgh, 1992-93, with 69G in 60GP.
1.12 — Mario Lemieux, Pittsburgh, 1988-89, with 85G in 76GP.
1.10 — Brett Hull, St. Louis, 1990-91, with 86G in 78GP.
1.02 — Cam Neely, Boston, 1993-94, with 50G in 49GP.
1.00 — Maurice Richard, Montreal, 1944-45, with 50G in 50GP.

HIGHEST ASSISTS-PER-GAME AVERAGE, CAREER (AMONG PLAYERS WITH 300 OR MORE ASSISTS):

1.320 — Wayne Gretzky, Edmonton, Los Angeles, St. Louis, NY Rangers, 1,963A, 1,487GP from 1979-80 – 1998-99.
1.170 — Mario Lemieux, Pittsburgh, 922A, 788GP, from 1984-85 – 1996-97, 2000-01.
.982 — Bobby Orr, Boston, Chicago, 645A, 657GP from 1966-67 – 1978-79.
.882 — Peter Forsberg, Quebec, Colorado, 411A, 466GP, from 1994-95 – 2000-01.
.852 — Adam Oates, Detroit, St. Louis, Boston, Washington, 963A, 1,130GP, from 1984-85 – 2000-01.

HIGHEST ASSISTS-PER-GAME AVERAGE, ONE SEASON (AMONG PLAYERS WITH 35-OR-MORE ASSISTS):

2.04 — Wayne Gretzky, Edmonton, 1985-86, with 163A in 80GP.
1.70 — Wayne Gretzky, Edmonton, 1987-88, with 109A in 64GP.
1.69 — Wayne Gretzky, Edmonton, 1984-85, with 135A in 80GP.
1.59 — Wayne Gretzky, Edmonton, 1983-84, with 118A in 74GP.
1.56 — Wayne Gretzky, Edmonton, 1982-83, with 125A in 80GP.
1.56 — Wayne Gretzky, Los Angeles, 1990-91, with 122A in 78GP.
1.53 — Wayne Gretzky, Edmonton, 1986-87, with 121A in 79GP.
1.52 — Mario Lemieux, Pittsburgh, 1992-93, with 91A in 60GP.
1.50 — Wayne Gretzky, Edmonton, 1981-82, with 120A in 80GP.
1.50 — Mario Lemieux, Pittsburgh, 1988-89, with 114A in 76GP.

HIGHEST POINTS-PER-GAME AVERAGE, CAREER: (AMONG PLAYERS WITH 500 OR MORE POINTS):

1.992 — Mario Lemieux, Pittsburgh, 1,570PTS (648G-922A), 788GP, from 1984-85 – 1996-97, 2000-01.
1.921 — Wayne Gretzky, Edmonton, Los Angeles, St. Louis, NY Rangers, 2,857PTS (894G-1,963A), 1,487GP, from 1979-80 – 1998-99.
1.497 — Mike Bossy, NY Islanders, 1,126PTS (573G-553A), 752GP, from 1977-78 – 1986-87.
1.393 — Bobby Orr, Boston, Chicago, 915PTS (270G-645A), 657GP, from 1966-67 – 1978-79.
1.356 — Eric Lindros, Philadelphia, 659PTS (290G-369A), 486GP, from 1992-93 – 1999-2000.

HIGHEST POINTS-PER-GAME AVERAGE, ONE SEASON (AMONG PLAYERS WITH 50-OR-MORE POINTS):

2.77 — Wayne Gretzky, Edmonton, 1983-84, with 205PTS in 74GP.
2.69 — Wayne Gretzky, Edmonton, 1985-86, with 215PTS in 80GP.
2.67 — Mario Lemieux, Pittsburgh, 1992-93, with 160PTS in 60GP.
2.65 — Wayne Gretzky, Edmonton, 1981-82, with 212PTS in 80GP.
2.62 — Mario Lemieux, Pittsburgh, 1988-89, with 199PTS in 78GP.
2.60 — Wayne Gretzky, Edmonton, 1984-85, with 208PTS in 80GP.
2.45 — Wayne Gretzky, Edmonton, 1982-83, with 196PTS in 80GP.
2.33 — Wayne Gretzky, Edmonton, 1987-88, with 149PTS in 64GP.
2.32 — Wayne Gretzky, Edmonton, 1986-87, with 183PTS in 79GP.
2.30 — Mario Lemieux, Pittsburgh, 1995-96 with 161PTS in 70GP.
2.18 — Mario Lemieux, Pittsburgh, 1987-88 with 168PTS in 77GP.
2.15 — Wayne Gretzky, Los Angeles, 1988-89, with 168PTS in 78GP
2.09 — Wayne Gretzky, Los Angeles, 1990-91, with 163 PTS in 78GP.
2.08 — Mario Lemieux, Pittsburgh, 1989-90, with 123 PTS in 59GP.
2.05 — Wayne Gretzky, Edmonton, 1980-81, with 164PTS in 80GP.

SCORING PLATEAUS

MOST 20-OR-MORE GOAL SEASONS:

22 — Gordie Howe, Detroit, Hartford, in 26 seasons.
18 — Ron Francis, Hartford, Pittsburgh, Carolina, in 20 seasons.
17 — Marcel Dionne, Detroit, Los Angeles, NY Rangers, in 18 seasons.
— Mike Gartner, Washington, Minnesota, NY Rangers, Toronto, Phoenix, in 19 seasons.
— Wayne Gretzky, Edmonton, Los Angeles, St. Louis, NY Rangers, in 20 seasons.
— Mark Messier, Edmonton, NY Rangers, Vancouver, in 22 seasons.

MOST CONSECUTIVE 20-OR-MORE GOAL SEASONS:

22 — Gordie Howe, Detroit, 1949-50 – 1970-71.
17 — Marcel Dionne, Detroit, Los Angeles, NY Rangers, 1971-72 – 1987-88.
16 — Phil Esposito, Chicago, Boston, NY Rangers, 1964-65 – 1979-80.
15 — Mike Gartner, Washington, Minnesota, NY Rangers, Toronto, 1979-80 – 1993-94.
14 — Maurice Richard, Montreal, 1943-44 – 1956-57.
— Stan Mikita, Chicago, 1961-62 – 1974-75.
— Michel Goulet, Quebec, Chicago, 1979-80 – 1992-93.
— Dave Andreychuk, Buffalo, Toronto, New Jersey, 1983-84 – 1996-97.
— Brett Hull, St. Louis, Dallas, 1987-88 – 2000-01.

MOST 30-OR-MORE GOAL SEASONS:

17 — Mike Gartner, Washington, Minnesota, NY Rangers, Toronto, Phoenix, in 19 seasons.
14 — Gordie Howe, Detroit, Hartford, in 26 seasons.
— Marcel Dionne, Detroit, Los Angeles, NY Rangers, in 18 seasons.
— Wayne Gretzky, Edmonton, Los Angeles, St. Louis, NY Rangers, in 20 seasons.
13 — Bobby Hull, Chicago, Winnipeg, Hartford, in 16 seasons.
— Phil Esposito, Chicago, Boston, NY Rangers, in 18 seasons.

Joe Nieuwendyk was just the second rookie in NHL history to top 50 goals when he scored 51 times for Calgary in 1987-88. Nieuwendyk enters the 2001-02 season ninth among active scorers with 469 goals.

MOST CONSECUTIVE 30-OR-MORE GOAL SEASONS:
15 — Mike Gartner, Washington, Minnesota, NY Rangers, Toronto, 1979-80 – 1993-94.
13 — Bobby Hull, Chicago, 1959-60 – 1971-72.
— Phil Esposito, Boston, NY Rangers, 1967-68 – 1979-80.
— Wayne Gretzky, Edmonton, Los Angeles, 1979-80 – 1991-92.
12 — Marcel Dionne, Detroit, Los Angeles,1974-75 – 1985-86.

MOST 40-OR-MORE GOAL SEASONS:
12 — Wayne Gretzky, Edmonton, Los Angeles, St. Louis, NY Rangers, in 20 seasons.
10 — Marcel Dionne, Detroit, Los Angeles, NY Rangers, in 18 seasons.
— Mario Lemieux, Pittsburgh, in 13 seasons.
9 — Mike Bossy, NY Islanders, in 10 seasons.
— Mike Gartner, Washington, Minnesota, NY Rangers, Toronto, Phoenix, in 19 seasons.

MOST CONSECUTIVE 40-OR-MORE GOAL SEASONS:
12 — Wayne Gretzky, Edmonton, Los Angeles, 1979-80 – 1990-91.
9 — Mike Bossy, NY Islanders, 1977-78 – 1985-86.
8 — Luc Robitaille, Los Angeles, 1986-87 – 1993-94.
7 — Phil Esposito, Boston, 1968-69 – 1974-75.
— Michel Goulet, Quebec, 1981-82 – 1987-88.
— Jari Kurri, Edmonton, 1982-83 – 1988-89.

MOST 50-OR-MORE GOAL SEASONS:
9 — Mike Bossy, NY Islanders, in 10 seasons.
— Wayne Gretzky, Edmonton, Los Angeles, St. Louis, NY Rangers, in 20 seasons.
6 — Guy Lafleur, Montreal, NY Rangers, Quebec, in 17 seasons.
— Marcel Dionne, Detroit, Los Angeles, NY Rangers, in 18 seasons.
— Mario Lemieux, Pittsburgh, in 13 seasons.
5 — Bobby Hull, Chicago, Winnipeg, Hartford, in 16 seasons.
— Phil Esposito, Chicago, Boston, NY Rangers, in 18 seasons.
— Brett Hull, Calgary, St. Louis, Dallas, in 16 seasons.
— Steve Yzerman, Detroit, in 18 seasons.
— Pavel Bure, Vancouver, Florida, in 10 seasons.

MOST CONSECUTIVE 50-OR-MORE GOAL SEASONS:
9 — Mike Bossy, NY Islanders, 1977-78 – 1985-86.
8 — Wayne Gretzky, Edmonton, 1979-80 – 1986-87.
6 — Guy Lafleur, Montreal, 1974-75 – 1979-80.
5 — Phil Esposito, Boston, 1970-71 – 1974-75.
— Marcel Dionne, Los Angeles, 1978-79 – 1982-83.
— Brett Hull, St. Louis, 1989-90 – 1993-94.

MOST 60-OR-MORE GOAL SEASONS:
5 — Mike Bossy, NY Islanders, in 10 seasons.
— Wayne Gretzky, Edmonton, Los Angeles, St. Louis, NY Rangers, in 20 seasons.
4 — Phil Esposito, Chicago, Boston, NY Rangers, in 18 seasons.
— Mario Lemieux, Pittsburgh, in 13 seasons.

MOST CONSECUTIVE 60-OR-MORE GOAL SEASONS:
4 — Wayne Gretzky, Edmonton, 1981-82 – 1984-85.
3 — Mike Bossy, NY Islanders, 1980-81 – 1982-83.
— Brett Hull, St. Louis, 1989-90 – 1991-92.
2 — Phil Esposito, Boston, 1970-71 – 1971-72, 1973-74 – 1974-75.
— Jari Kurri, Edmonton, 1984-85 – 1985-86.
— Mario Lemieux, Pittsburgh, 1987-88 – 1988-89.
— Steve Yzerman, Detroit, 1988-89 – 1989-90.
— Pavel Bure, Vancouver, 1992-93 – 1993-94.

MOST 100-OR-MORE POINT SEASONS:
15 — Wayne Gretzky, Edmonton, Los Angeles, St. Louis, NY Rangers, in 20 seasons.
10 — Mario Lemieux, Pittsburgh, in 13 seasons.
8 — Marcel Dionne, Detroit, Los Angeles, NY Rangers, in 18 seasons.
7 — Mike Bossy, NY Islanders, in 10 seasons.
— Peter Stastny, Quebec, New Jersey, St. Louis, in 15 seasons.

MOST CONSECUTIVE 100-OR-MORE POINT SEASONS:
13 — Wayne Gretzky, Edmonton, Los Angeles, 1979-80 – 1991-92.
6 — Bobby Orr, Boston, 1969-70 – 1974-75.
— Guy Lafleur, Montreal, 1974-75 – 1979-80.
— Mike Bossy, NY Islanders,1980-81 – 1985-86.
— Peter Stastny, Quebec, 1980-81 – 1985-86.
— Mario Lemieux, Pittsburgh, 1984-85 – 1989-90.
— Steve Yzerman, Detroit, 1987-88 – 1992-93.

THREE-OR-MORE-GOAL GAMES

MOST THREE-OR-MORE GOAL GAMES, CAREER:
50 — Wayne Gretzky, Edmonton, Los Angeles, St. Louis, NY Rangers, in 20 seasons, 37 three-goal games, 9 four-goal games, 4 five-goal games.
40 — Mario Lemieux, Pittsburgh, in 13 seasons, 27 three-goal games, 10 four-goal games and 3 five-goal games.
39 — Mike Bossy, NY Islanders, in 10 seasons, 30 three-goal games, 9 four-goal games.
32 — Phil Esposito, Chicago, Boston, NY Rangers, in 18 seasons, 27 three-goal games, 5 four-goal games.
30 — Brett Hull, Calgary, St. Louis, Dallas, in 16 seasons, 27 three-goal games, 3 four-goal games.
28 — Bobby Hull, Chicago, Winnipeg, Hartford, in 16 seasons, 24 three-goal games, 4 four-goal games.
— Marcel Dionne, Detroit, Los Angeles, NY Rangers, in 18 seasons, 25 three-goal games, 3 four-goal games.

MOST THREE-OR-MORE GOAL GAMES, ONE SEASON:
10 — Wayne Gretzky, Edmonton, 1981-82. 6 three-goal games, 3 four-goal games, 1 five-goal game.
— Wayne Gretzky, Edmonton, 1983-84. 6 three-goal games, 4 four-goal games.
9 — Mike Bossy, NY Islanders, 1980-81. 6 three-goal games, 3 four-goal games.
— Mario Lemieux, Pittsburgh, 1988-89. 7 three-goal games, 1 four-goal game, 1 five-goal game.
8 — Brett Hull, St. Louis, 1991-92. 8 three-goal games.
7 — Joe Malone, Montreal, 1917-18. 2 three-goal games, 2 four-goal games, 3 five-goal games.
— Phil Esposito, Boston, 1970-71. 7 three-goal games.
— Rick Martin, Buffalo, 1975-76. 6 three-goal games, 1 four-goal game.
— Alexander Mogilny, Buffalo, 1992-93. 5 three-goal games, 2 four-goal games.

With a league-leading 59 goals in 2000-01, Pavel Bure became just the tenth player in NHL history to score 50 goals or more in at least five seasons. Bure was just one goal short of his career-high of 60 goals, which he has reached twice.

SCORING STREAKS

LONGEST CONSECUTIVE GOAL-SCORING STREAK:
16 Games — Punch Broadbent, Ottawa, 1921-22. 27 goals during streak.
14 Games — Joe Malone, Montreal, 1917-18. 35 goals during streak.
13 Games — Newsy Lalonde, Montreal, 1920-21. 24 goals during streak.
— Charlie Simmer, Los Angeles, 1979-80. 17 goals during streak.
12 Games — Cy Denneny, Ottawa, 1917-18. 23 goals during streak.
— Dave Lumley, Edmonton, 1981-82. 15 goals during streak.
— Mario Lemieux, Pittsburgh, 1992-93. 18 goals during streak.

LONGEST CONSECUTIVE ASSIST-SCORING STREAK:
23 Games — Wayne Gretzky, Los Angeles, 1990-91. 48A during streak.
18 Games — Adam Oates, Boston, 1992-93. 28A during streak.
17 Games — Wayne Gretzky, Edmonton, 1983-84. 38A during streak.
— Paul Coffey, Edmonton, 1985-86. 27A during streak.
— Wayne Gretzky, Los Angeles, 1989-90. 35A during streak.
16 Games — Jaromir Jagr, Pittsburgh, 2000-01. 24A during streak.

LONGEST CONSECUTIVE POINT SCORING STREAK:
51 Games — Wayne Gretzky, Edmonton, 1983-84. 61G-92A-153PTS during streak.
46 Games — Mario Lemieux, Pittsburgh, 1989-90. 39G-64A-103PTS during streak.
39 Games — Wayne Gretzky, Edmonton, 1985-86. 33G-75A-108PTS during streak.
30 Games — Wayne Gretzky, Edmonton, 1982-83. 24G-52A-76PTS during streak.
— Mats Sundin, Quebec, 1992-93. 21G-25A-46PTS during streak.
28 Games — Guy Lafleur, Montreal, 1976-77. 19G-42A-61PTS during streak.
— Wayne Gretzky, Edmonton, 1984-85. 20G-43A-63PTS during streak.
— Mario Lemieux, Pittsburgh, 1985-86. 21G-38A-59PTS during streak.
— Paul Coffey, Edmonton, 1985-86. 16G-39A-55PTS during streak.
— Steve Yzerman, Detroit, 1988-89. 29G-36A-65PTS during streak.

LONGEST CONSECUTIVE POINT-SCORING STREAK FROM START OF SEASON:
51 Games — Wayne Gretzky, Edmonton, 1983-84. 61G-92A-153PTS during streak which was stopped by goaltender Markus Mattsson and Los Angeles on Jan. 28, 1984.

LONGEST CONSECUTIVE POINT-SCORING STREAK BY A DEFENSEMAN:
28 Games — Paul Coffey, Edmonton, 1985-86. 16G-39A-55PTS during streak.
19 Games — Raymond Bourque, Boston, 1987-88. 6G-21A-27PTS during streak.
17 Games — Raymond Bourque, Boston, 1984-85. 4G-24A-28PTS during streak.
— Brian Leetch, NY Rangers, 1991-92. 5G-24A-29PTS during streak.
16 Games — Gary Suter, Calgary, 1987-88. 8G-17A-25PTS during streak.
15 Games — Bobby Orr, Boston, 1970-71. 10G-23A-33PTS during streak.
— Bobby Orr, Boston, 1973-74. 8G-15A-23PTS during streak.
— Steve Duchesne, Quebec, 1992-93. 4G-17A-21PTS during streak.
— Chris Chelios, Chicago, 1995-96. 4G-16A-20PTS during streak.

FASTEST GOALS AND ASSISTS

FASTEST GOAL FROM START OF A GAME:
5 Seconds — Doug Smail, Winnipeg, Dec. 20, 1981, at Winnipeg. Winnipeg 5, St. Louis 4.
— Bryan Trottier, NY Islanders, Mar. 22, 1984, at Boston. NY Islanders 3, Boston 3.
— Alexander Mogilny, Buffalo, Dec. 21, 1991, at Toronto. Buffalo 4, Toronto 1.
6 Seconds — Henry Boucha, Detroit, Jan. 28, 1973, at Montreal. Detroit 4, Montreal 2.
— Jean Pronovost, Pittsburgh, Mar. 25, 1976, at St. Louis. St. Louis 5, Pittsburgh 2.
7 Seconds — Charlie Conacher, Toronto, Feb. 6, 1932, at Toronto. Toronto 6, Boston 0.
— Danny Gare, Buffalo, Dec. 17, 1978, at Buffalo. Buffalo 6, Vancouver 3.
— Dave Williams, Los Angeles, Feb. 14, 1987 at Los Angeles. Los Angeles 5, Harford 2.
8 Seconds — Ron Martin, NY Americans, Dec. 4, 1932, at NY Americans. NY Americans 4, Montreal 2.
— Chuck Arnason, Col. Rockies, Jan. 28, 1977, at Atlanta. Col. Rockies 3, Atlanta 3.
— Wayne Gretzky, Edmonton, Dec. 14, 1983, at NY Rangers. Edmonton 9, NY Rangers 4.
— Gaetan Duchesne, Washington, Mar. 14, 1987, at St. Louis. Washington 3, St. Louis 3.
— Tim Kerr, Philadelphia, Mar. 7, 1989, at Philadelphia. Philadelphia 4, Edmonton 4.
— Grant Ledyard, Buffalo, Dec. 4, 1991, at Winnipeg. Buffalo 4, Winnipeg 4.
— Brent Sutter, Chicago, Feb. 5, 1995, at Vancouver. Chicago 9, Vancouver 4.
— Paul Kariya, Anaheim, Mar. 9, 1997, at Colorado. Anaheim 2, Colorado 2.
— Tony Hrkac, Dallas, Nov. 7, 1998, at Los Angeles. Dallas 4, Los Angeles 3.
— Sergei Fedorov, Detroit, Nov. 21, 1998, at Vancouver. Detroit 4, Vancouver 2.

FASTEST GOAL FROM START OF A PERIOD:
4 Seconds — Claude Provost, Montreal, Nov. 9, 1957, at Montreal, second period. Montreal 4, Boston 2.
— Denis Savard, Chicago, Jan. 12, 1986, at Chicago, third period. Chicago 4, Hartford 2.

FASTEST GOAL BY A PLAYER IN HIS FIRST NHL GAME:
15 Seconds — Gus Bodnar, Toronto, Oct. 30, 1943. Toronto 5, NY Rangers 2.
18 Seconds — Danny Gare, Buffalo, Oct. 10, 1974. Buffalo 9, Boston 5.
20 Seconds — Alexander Mogilny, Buffalo, Oct. 5, 1989. Buffalo 4, Quebec 3.

FASTEST TWO GOALS:
4 Seconds — Nels Stewart, Mtl. Maroons, Jan. 3, 1931, at Montreal at 8:24 and 8:28, third period. Mtl. Maroons 5, Boston 3.
— Deron Quint, Winnipeg, Dec. 15, 1995, at Winnipeg at 7:51 and 7:55, second period. Winnipeg 9, Edmonton 4.
5 Seconds — Pete Mahovlich, Montreal, Feb. 20, 1971, at Montreal at 12:16 and 12:21, third period. Montreal 7, Chicago 1.
6 Seconds — Jim Pappin, Chicago, Feb. 16, 1972, at Chicago at 2:57 and 3:03, third period. Chicago 3, Philadelphia 3.
— Ralph Backstrom, Los Angeles, Nov. 2, 1972, at Los Angeles at 8:30 and 8:36, third period. Los Angeles 5, Boston 2.
— Lanny McDonald, Calgary, Mar. 22, 1984, at Calgary at 16:23 and 16:29, first period. Detroit 6, Calgary 4.
— Sylvain Turgeon, Hartford, Mar. 28, 1987, at Hartford at 13:59 and 14:05, second period. Hartford 5, Pittsburgh 4.

FASTEST THREE GOALS:
21 Seconds — Bill Mosienko, Chicago, Mar. 23, 1952, at NY Rangers, against goaltender Lorne Anderson. Mosienko scored at 6:09, 6:20 and 6:30 of third period, all with both teams at full strength. Chicago 7, NY Rangers 6.
44 Seconds — Jean Béliveau, Montreal, Nov. 5, 1955, at Montreal, against goaltender Terry Sawchuk. Béliveau scored at :42, 1:08 and 1:26 of second period, all with Montreal holding a 6-4 man advantage. Montreal 4, Boston 2.

FASTEST THREE ASSISTS:
21 Seconds — Gus Bodnar, Chicago, Mar. 23, 1952, at NY Rangers, Bodnar assisted on Bill Mosienko's three goals at 6:09, 6:20 and 6:30 of third period. Chicago 7, NY Rangers 6.
44 Seconds — Bert Olmstead, Montreal, Nov. 5, 1955, at Montreal, Olmstead assisted on Jean Béliveau's three goals at :42, 1:08 and 1:26 of second period. Montreal 4, Boston 2.

SHOTS ON GOAL

MOST SHOTS ON GOAL, ONE SEASON:
550 — Phil Esposito, Boston, 1970-71. 78 game schedule.
429 — Paul Kariya, Anaheim, 1998-99. 82 game schedule.
426 — Phil Esposito, Boston, 1971-72. 78 game schedule.
414 — Bobby Hull, Chicago, 1968-69. 76 game schedule.

PENALTIES

MOST PENALTY MINUTES, CAREER:
3,966 — Dave Williams, Toronto, Vancouver, Detroit, Los Angeles, Hartford, in 14 seasons, 962GP.
3,565 — Dale Hunter, Quebec, Washington, Colorado, in 19 seasons, 1,407GP.
3,381 — Marty McSorley, Pittsburgh, Edmonton, Los Angeles, NY Rangers, San Jose, Boston, in 17 seasons, 961GP.
3,146 — Tim Hunter, Calgary, Quebec, Vancouver, San Jose, in 16 seasons, 815GP.
3,124 — Bob Probert, Detroit, Chicago, in 16 seasons, 874GP.

MOST PENALTY MINUTES, CAREER, INCLUDING PLAYOFFS:
4,421 — Dave Williams, Toronto, Vancouver, Detroit, Los Angeles, Hartford, 3,966 in regular-season; 455 in playoffs.
4,294 — Dale Hunter, Quebec, Washington, Colorado, 3,565 in regular-season; 729 in playoffs.
3,755 — Marty McSorley, Pittsburgh, Edmonton, Los Angeles, NY Rangers, San Jose, Boston, 3,381 in regular-season; 374 in playoffs.
3,584 — Chris Nilan, Montreal, NY Rangers, Boston, 3,043 in regular-season; 541 in playoffs.
3,572 — Tim Hunter, Calgary, Quebec, Vancouver, San Jose, 3,146 in regular-season; 426 in playoffs.

MOST PENALTY MINUTES, ONE SEASON:
472 — Dave Schultz, Philadelphia, 1974-75.
409 — Paul Baxter, Pittsburgh, 1981-82.
408 — Mike Peluso, Chicago, 1991-92.
405 — Dave Schultz, Los Angeles, Pittsburgh, 1977-78.

MOST PENALTIES, ONE GAME:
10 — Chris Nilan, Boston, Mar. 31, 1991, at Boston against Hartford. 6 minors, 2 majors, 1 10-minute misconduct, 1 game misconduct.
9 — Jim Dorey, Toronto, Oct. 16, 1968, at Toronto against Pittsburgh. 4 minors, 2 majors, 2 10-minute misconducts, 1 game misconduct.
— Dave Schultz, Pittsburgh, Apr. 6, 1978, at Detroit. 5 minors, 2 majors, 2 10-minute misconducts.
— Randy Holt, Los Angeles, Mar. 11, 1979, at Philadelphia. 1 minor, 3 majors, 2 10-minute misconducts, 3 game misconducts.
— Russ Anderson, Pittsburgh, Jan. 19, 1980, at Pittsburgh. 3 minors, 3 majors, 3 game misconducts.
— Kim Clackson, Quebec, Mar. 8, 1981, at Quebec. 4 minors, 3 majors, 2 game misconducts.
— Terry O'Reilly, Boston, Dec. 19, 1984, at Hartford. 5 minors, 3 majors, 1 game misconduct.
— Larry Playfair, Los Angeles, Dec. 9, 1986, at NY Islanders. 6 minors, 2 majors, 1 10-minute misconduct.
— Marty McSorley, Los Angeles, Apr. 14, 1992, at Vancouver. 5 minors, 2 majors, 1 10-minute misconduct, 1 game misconduct.

MOST PENALTY MINUTES, ONE GAME:
67 — Randy Holt, Los Angeles, Mar. 11, 1979, at Philadelphia. 1 minor, 3 majors, 2 10-minute misconducts, 3 game misconducts.
55 — Frank Bathe, Philadelphia, Mar. 11, 1979, at Philadelphia. 3 majors, 2 10-minute misconducts, 2 game misconducts.
51 — Russ Anderson, Pittsburgh, Jan. 19, 1980, at Pittsburgh. 3 minors, 3 majors, 3 game misconducts.

MOST PENALTIES, ONE PERIOD:
9 — Randy Holt, Los Angeles, Mar. 11, 1979, at Philadelphia, first period. 1 minor, 3 majors, 2 10-minute misconducts, 3 game misconducts.

MOST PENALTY MINUTES, ONE PERIOD:
67 — Randy Holt, Los Angeles, Mar. 11, 1979, at Philadelphia, first period. 1 minor, 3 majors, 2 10-minute misconducts, 3 game misconducts.

GOALTENDING

MOST GAMES APPEARED IN BY A GOALTENDER, CAREER:
971 — Terry Sawchuk, Detroit, Boston, Toronto, Los Angeles, NY Rangers from 1949-50 – 1969-70.
906 — Glenn Hall, Detroit, Chicago, St. Louis from 1952-53 – 1970-71.
903 — Patrick Roy, Montreal, Colorado from 1984-85 – 2000-01.
886 — Tony Esposito, Montreal, Chicago from 1968-69 – 1983-84.
868 — Grant Fuhr, Edmonton, Toronto, Buffalo, Los Angeles, St. Louis, Calgary from 1981-82 – 1999-2000.

MOST CONSECUTIVE COMPLETE GAMES BY A GOALTENDER:
502 — Glenn Hall, Detroit, Chicago. Played 502 games from beginning of 1955-56 season - first 12 games of 1962-63. In his 503rd straight game, Nov. 7, 1962, at Chicago, Hall was removed from the game against Boston with a back injury in the first period.

MOST GAMES APPEARED IN BY A GOALTENDER, ONE SEASON:
79 — Grant Fuhr, St. Louis, 1995-96.
77 — Martin Brodeur, New Jersey, 1995-96.
— Bill Ranford, Edmonton, Boston, 1995-96.
— Arturs Irbe, Carolina, 2000-01.
75 — Grant Fuhr, Edmonton, 1987-88.
— Arturs Irbe, Carolina, 1999-2000.

MOST MINUTES PLAYED BY A GOALTENDER, CAREER:
57,194 — Terry Sawchuk, Detroit, Boston, Toronto, Los Angeles, NY Rangers, from 1949-50 – 1969-70.

MOST MINUTES PLAYED BY A GOALTENDER, ONE SEASON:
4,433 — Martin Brodeur, New Jersey, 1995-96.

MOST SHUTOUTS, CAREER:
103 — Terry Sawchuk, Detroit, Boston, Toronto, Los Angeles, NY Rangers in 21 seasons.
94 — George Hainsworth, Montreal, Toronto in 10 seasons.
84 — Glenn Hall, Detroit, Chicago, St. Louis in 16 seasons.

MOST SHUTOUTS, ONE SEASON:
22 — George Hainsworth, Montreal, 1928-29. 44GP
15 — Alex Connell, Ottawa, 1925-26. 36GP
— Alex Connell, Ottawa, 1927-28. 44GP
— Hal Winkler, Boston, 1927-28. 44GP
— Tony Esposito, Chicago, 1969-70. 63GP
14 — George Hainsworth, Montreal, 1926-27. 44GP

LONGEST SHUTOUT SEQUENCE BY A GOALTENDER:
461 Minutes, 29 Seconds — Alex Connell, Ottawa, 1927-28, six consecutive shutouts. (Forward passing not permitted in attacking zones in 1927-28.)
343 Minutes, 5 Seconds — George Hainsworth, Montreal, 1928-29, four consecutive shutouts. (Forward passing not permitted in attacking zones in 1928-29.)
324 Minutes, 40 Seconds — Roy Worters, NY Americans, 1930-31, four consecutive shutouts.
309 Minutes, 21 Seconds — Bill Durnan, Montreal, 1948-49, four consecutive shutouts.

MOST WINS BY A GOALTENDER, CAREER:
484 — Patrick Roy, Montreal, Colorado, in 17 seasons. 903GP
447 — Terry Sawchuk, Detroit, Boston, Toronto, Los Angeles, NY Rangers, in 21 seasons. 972GP
435 — Jacques Plante, Montreal, NY Rangers, St. Louis, Toronto, Boston, in 18 seasons. 837GP
423 — Tony Esposito, Montreal, Chicago, in 16 seasons. 886GP

MOST WINS BY A GOALTENDER, ONE SEASON:
47 — Bernie Parent, Philadelphia, 1973-74. 73GP
44 — Bernie Parent, Philadelphia, 1974-75. 68GP
— Terry Sawchuk, Detroit, 1950-51. 70GP
— Terry Sawchuk, Detroit, 1951-52. 70GP

LONGEST WINNING STREAK BY A GOALTENDER, ONE SEASON:
17 — Gilles Gilbert, Boston, 1975-76.
14 — Tiny Thompson, Boston, 1929-30.
— Ross Brooks, Boston, 1973-74.
— Don Beaupre, Minnesota, 1985-86.
— Tom Barrasso, Pittsburgh, 1992-93.

LONGEST UNDEFEATED STREAK BY A GOALTENDER, ONE SEASON:
32 Games — Gerry Cheevers, Boston, 1971-72. 24W-8T
31 Games — Pete Peeters, Boston, 1982-83. 26W-5T
27 Games — Pete Peeters, Philadelphia, 1979-80. 22W-5T
23 Games — Frank Brimsek, Boston, 1940-41. 15W-8T
— Chico Resch, NY Islanders, 1978-79. 15W-8T
— Grant Fuhr, Edmonton, 1981-82. 15W-8T

LONGEST UNDEFEATED STREAK BY A GOALTENDER IN HIS FIRST NHL SEASON:
23 Games — Grant Fuhr, 1981-82. 15W-8T.

LONGEST UNDEFEATED STREAK BY A GOALTENDER FROM START OF CAREER:
16 Games — Patrick Lalime, Pittsburgh, 1996-97. 14W-2T.

MOST 40-OR-MORE WIN SEASONS BY A GOALTENDER:
3 — Terry Sawchuk, Detroit, Boston, Toronto, Los Angeles, NY Rangers, in 21 seasons.
— Jacques Plante, Montreal, NY Rangers, St. Louis, Toronto, Boston, in 18 seasons.
— Martin Brodeur, New Jersey, in 9 seasons.
2 — Bernie Parent, Boston, Philadelphia, Toronto, in 13 seasons.
— Ken Dryden, Montreal, in 8 seasons.
— Ed Belfour, Chicago, San Jose, Dallas, in 13 seasons.

MOST CONSECUTIVE 40-OR-MORE WIN SEASONS BY A GOALTENDER:
2 — Terry Sawchuk, Detroit, 1950-51 – 1951-52.
— Bernie Parent, Philadelphia, 1973-74 – 1974-75.
— Ken Dryden, Montreal, 1975-76 – 1976-77.
— Martin Brodeur, New Jersey, 1999-2000 – 2000-01.

MOST 30-OR-MORE WIN SEASONS BY A GOALTENDER:
11 — Patrick Roy, Montreal, Colorado, in 17 seasons.
8 — Tony Esposito, Montreal, Chicago, in 16 seasons.
7 — Jacques Plante, Montreal, NY Rangers, St. Louis, Toronto, Boston, in 18 seasons.
— Ken Dryden, Montreal, in 8 seasons.
— Ed Belfour, Chicago, San Jose, Dallas, in 13 seasons.

MOST CONSECUTIVE 30-OR-MORE WIN SEASONS BY A GOALTENDER:
7 — Tony Esposito, Chicago, 1969-70 – 1975-76.
6 — Jacques Plante, Montreal, 1954-55 – 1959-60.
— Patrick Roy, Montreal, Colorado, 1995-96 – 2000-01.
— Martin Brodeur, New Jersey, 1995-96 – 2000-01.
5 — Terry Sawchuk, Detroit, 1950-51 – 1954-55.
— Ken Dryden, Montreal, 1974-75 – 1978-79.

MOST LOSSES BY A GOALTENDER, CAREER:
352 — Gump Worsley, NY Rangers, Montreal, Minnesota, in 21 seasons. 861GP
351 — Gilles Meloche, Chicago, California, Cleveland, Minnesota, Pittsburgh, in 18 seasons. 788GP
343 — John Vanbiesbrouck, NY Rangers, Florida, Philadelphia, NY Islanders, New Jersey, in 19 seasons. 877GP
332 — Terry Sawchuk, Detroit, Boston, Toronto, Los Angeles, NY Rangers, in 21 seasons. 972GP

MOST LOSSES BY A GOALTENDER, ONE SEASON:
48 — Gary Smith, California, 1970-71.
47 — Al Rollins, Chicago, 1953-54.

By leading the league with 42 victories in 2000-01, Martin Brodeur joined Jacques Plante and Terry Sawchuk as the only goaltenders to win 40 games or more three times. Brodeur is one of only four goalies with back-to-back 40-win seasons.

Active NHL Players' Three-or-More-Goal Games

Teemu Selanne had a pair of three-goal games last season, one for the Mighty Ducks in February and one against them in March after his trade to San Jose.

Regular Season

Teams named are the ones the players were with at the time of their multiple-scoring games. Players listed alphabetically.

Player	Team	3-Goals	4-Goals	5-Goals
Adams, Greg	Vancouver	1	1	—
Alfredsson, Daniel	Ottawa	2	—	—
Allison, Jason	Boston	4	—	—
Amonte, Tony	NYR, Chi.	7	—	—
Andersson, Mikael	Tampa Bay	1	—	—
Andersson, Niklas	NY Islanders	1	—	—
Andreychuk, Dave	Buf., Tor., Bos.	7	3	1
Antropov, Nik	Toronto	1	—	—
Arnott, Jason	Edmonton	2	—	—
Arvedson, Magnus	Ottawa	1	—	—
Audette, Donald	Buf., Atl.	4	—	—
Barnes, Stu	Wpg., Pit.	3	—	—
Battaglia, Bates	Carolina	1	—	—
Beranek, Josef	Philadelphia	1	—	—
Berezin, Sergei	Toronto	2	—	—
Bertuzzi, Todd	Vancouver	1	—	—
Blake, Rob	Los Angeles	1	—	—
Bondra, Peter	Washington	11	5	1
Bonk, Radek	Ottawa	1	—	—
Brind'Amour, Rod	Phi., Car.	2	—	—
Brown, Doug	Detroit	1	—	—
Brown, Rob	Pittsburgh	7	—	—
Buchberger, Kelly	Edmonton	1	—	—
Bure, Pavel	Van., Fla.	16	3	—
Bure, Valeri	Calgary	1	—	—
Butsayev, Viacheslav	Philadelphia	1	—	—
Carter, Anson	Boston	1	—	—
Cassels, Andrew	Vancouver	1	—	—
Conroy, Craig	St. Louis	1	—	—
Corson, Shayne	Mtl., Edm.	3	—	—
Craven, Murray	Philadelphia	3	—	—
Czerkawski, Mariusz	Edm., NYI	3	—	—
Dackell, Andreas	Ottawa	1	—	—
Dahlen, Ulf	NYR, Min., S.J.	4	—	—
Damphousse, Vincent	Tor., Edm., Mtl., S.J.	11	1	—
Dawe, Jason	Buffalo	2	—	—
Daze, Eric	Chicago	1	1	—
Deadmarsh, Adam	Colorado	1	—	—
Demitra, Pavol	St. Louis	2	—	—
Devereaux, Boyd	Edmonton	1	—	—
Dineen, Kevin	Hfd., Phi.	9	1	—
Dionne, Gilbert	Montreal	1	—	—
Donovan, Shean	Atlanta	1	—	—
Druken, Harold	Vancouver	1	—	—
Duchesne, Steve	L.A., Phi., St.L.	3	—	—
Dumont, Jean-Pierre	Chi., Buf.	2	—	—
Dvorak, Radek	NY Rangers	1	1	—
Eastwood, Mike	St. Louis	1	—	—
Elias, Patrik	New Jersey	3	—	—
Emerson, Nelson	Winnipeg	1	—	—
Fedorov, Sergei	Detroit	2	1	1
Ferraro, Ray	Hfd., NYI, NYR, Atl.	9	1	—
Fleury, Theoren	Cgy., Col., NYR	15	—	—
Forsberg, Peter	Colorado	4	—	—
Francis, Ron	Hfd., Pit.	10	1	—
Friesen, Jeff	San Jose	2	—	—
Garpenlov, Johan	Det., S.J., Fla.	2	1	—
Gelinas, Martin	Edm., Van.	2	1	—
Gilchrist, Brent	Montreal	1	—	—
Gilmour, Doug	St.L., Tor.	3	—	—
Gomez, Scott	New Jersey	1	—	—
Gonchar, Sergei	Washington	1	—	—
Granato, Tony	NYR, L.A., S.J.	6	1	—
Gratton, Chris	Tampa Bay	1	—	—
Graves, Adam	Edm., NYR	6	—	—
Green, Travis	NY Islanders	1	—	—
Grier, Mike	Edmonton	1	—	—
Grosek, Michal	Buffalo	1	—	—
Guerin, Bill	New Jersey	1	—	—
Handzus, Michal	St. Louis	1	—	—
Harvey, Todd	Dal., S.J.	2	—	—
Hatcher, Kevin	Wsh., Dal.	2	—	—
Havlat, Martin	Ottawa	1	—	—
Heinze, Steve	Bos., Buf.	5	—	—
Hlavac, Jan	NY Rangers	2	—	—
Hoglund, Jonas	Toronto	1	—	—
Hogue, Benoit	NY Islanders	1	—	—
Holik, Bobby	New Jersey	3	—	—
Holmstrom, Tomas	Detroit	1	—	—
Hossa, Marian	Ottawa	1	—	—
Housley, Phil	Buffalo	2	—	—
Hull, Brett	Cgy., St.L., Dal.	27	3	—
Hull, Jody	Hartford	1	—	—
Jagr, Jaromir	Pittsburgh	8	1	—
Juneau, Joe	Bos., Wsh.	2	—	—
Kallio, Tomi	Atlanta	1	—	—
Kamensky, Valeri	Colorado	5	—	—
Kapanen, Sami	Carolina	2	—	—
Kariya, Paul	Anaheim	5	—	—
Khristich, Dimitri	Wsh., Bos.	3	—	—
King, Derek	NYI, Tor.	6	1	—
Klatt, Trent	Philadelphia	1	—	—
Konowalchuk, Steve	Washington	3	—	—
Korolev, Igor	Winnipeg	1	—	—
Kovalenko, Andrei	Que., Bos.	2	—	—
Kovalev, Alexei	NYR, Pit.	6	—	—
Kozlov, Viktor	Florida	1	—	—
Kozlov, Vyacheslav	Detroit	2	1	—
Laaksonen, Antti	Minnesota	1	—	—
Lacroix, Eric	Colorado	1	—	—
Laperriere, Ian	Los Angeles	1	—	—
Lapointe, Martin	Detroit	1	—	—
Laraque, Georges	Edmonton	1	—	—
Larionov, Igor	Van., S.J.	4	—	—
Larouche, Steve	Ottawa	1	—	—
LeClair, John	Philadelphia	8	2	—
Lehtinen, Jere	Dallas	1	—	—
Lemieux, Claude	Mtl., N.J., Col.	7	—	—
Lemieux, Mario	Pittsburgh	27	10	3
Linden, Trevor	Van., Mtl.	5	—	—
Lindros, Eric	Philadelphia	10	1	—
MacInnis, Al	Cgy., St. L.	3	—	—
MacLean, John	New Jersey	6	—	—
Madden, John	New Jersey	—	1	—
Malakhov, Vladimir	Montreal	1	—	—
Maltby, Kirk	Detroit	1	—	—
Manderville, Kent	Hartford	1	—	—
McEachern, Shawn	Ottawa	1	—	—
McInnis, Marty	Cgy., Ana.	2	—	—
McKay, Randy	New Jersey	1	1	—
McKenzie, Jim	Phoenix	1	—	—
Messier, Mark	Edm., NYR	15	4	—
Miller, Kevin	Det., St.L., S.J.	4	—	—
Modano, Mike	Min., Dal.	6	1	—
Modin, Fredrik	Tampa Bay	1	—	—
Mogilny, Alexander	Buf., Van., N.J.	13	2	—
Morozov, Alexei	Pittsburgh	1	—	—
Muller, Kirk	N.J., Mtl., Tor.	7	—	—
Murray, Glen	Los Angeles	2	—	—
Murray, Rem	Edmonton	1	—	—
Naslund, Markus	Pit., Van.	4	—	—
Nedved, Petr	Pit., NYR	5	1	—
Nemchinov, Sergei	NY Rangers	1	—	—
Nieuwendyk, Joe	Cgy., Dal.	9	3	1
Nolan, Owen	Que., S.J.	9	1	—
Noonan, Brian	Chi., NYR	3	1	—
Nylander, Michael	Hfd., Chi.	1	1	—
Oates, Adam	Bos., Wsh.	6	1	—
Odelein, Lyle	Montreal	1	—	—
Oliver, David	Edmonton	1	—	—
O'Neill, Jeff	Hartford	1	—	—
Ozolinsh, Sandis	Col., Car.	2	—	—
Palffy, Ziggy	NYI, L.A.	7	—	—
Parrish, Mark	Florida	—	1	—
Peca, Michael	Buffalo	1	—	—
Perreault, Yanic	L.A., Tor.	2	1	—
Plante, Derek	Buffalo	1	—	—
Podein, Shjon	Colorado	1	—	—
Primeau, Keith	Philadelphia	1	—	—
Probert, Bob	Detroit	1	—	—
Quint, Deron	Columbus	1	—	—
Ranheim, Paul	Calgary	1	—	—
Recchi, Mark	Pit., Mtl.	3	—	—
Reichel, Robert	Cgy., NYI	5	—	—
Reid, Dave	Bos., Dal.	2	—	—
Renberg, Mikael	Phi., T.B.	2	—	—
Ricci, Mike	Que., S.J.	1	—	1
Roberts, Gary	Cgy., Car.	10	1	—
Robitaille, Luc	L.A., Pit.	11	3	—
Roenick, Jeremy	Chi., Phx.	7	2	—
Rolston, Brian	New Jersey	1	—	—
Ronning, Cliff	St.L., Van.	3	—	—
Rucinsky, Martin	Montreal	2	—	—
Sakic, Joe	Que., Col.	10	1	—
Salo, Sami	Ottawa	1	—	—
Samsonov, Sergei	Boston	1	—	—
Sanderson, Geoff	Har., Buf., CBJ	7	—	—
Satan, Miroslav	Buffalo	3	—	—
Savage, Brian	Montreal	5	1	—
Savard, Marc	Calgary	—	1	—
Selanne, Teemu	Wpg., Ana., S.J.	16	2	—
Selivanov, Alexander	Edmonton	2	1	—
Shanahan, Brendan	N.J., St.L., Hfd., Det.	12	1	—
Sheppard, Ray	Buf., Det., S.J., Fla.	12	—	—
Smolinski, Bryan	Bos., L.A.	2	—	—
Smyth, Ryan	Edmonton	4	—	—
Stevens, Kevin	Pit., NYR	9	2	—
Stillman, Cory	Calgary	2	—	—
Straka, Martin	Pittsburgh	4	—	—
Stumpel, Jozef	Bos., L.A.	2	—	—
Sturm, Marco	San Jose	1	—	—
Sullivan, Steve	Tor., Chi.	1	1	—
Sundin, Mats	Que., Tor.	5	—	1
Svejkovsky, Jaroslav	Washington	—	1	—
Sydor, Darryl	Dallas	1	—	—
Sylvester, Dean	Atlanta	1	—	—
Thomas, Steve	Chi., NYI	4	2	—
Thornton, Joe	Boston	1	—	—
Thornton, Scott	San Jose	1	—	—
Titov, German	Calgary	2	—	—
Tkachuk, Keith	Phoenix	7	2	—
Tocchet, Rick	Phi., Pit., L.A., Bos.	12	2	—
Turcotte, Darren	NY Rangers	4	—	—
Turgeon, Pierre	Buf., NYI, Mtl., St.L.	15	—	—
Valicevic, Robert	Nashville	1	—	—
Valk, Garry	Anaheim	1	—	—
Verbeek, Pat	N.J., Hfd., NYR, Dal.	11	1	—
Walker, Scott	Nashville	1	—	—
Ward, Dixon	Buffalo	1	—	—
Weight, Doug	Edmonton	1	—	—
Wesley, Glen	Boston	1	—	—
Wiemer, Jason	Tampa Bay	1	—	—
Willis, Shane	Carolina	1	—	—
Wright, Tyler	Columbus	1	—	—
Yachmenev, Vitali	Los Angeles	1	—	—
Yake, Terry	Anaheim	1	—	—
Yashin, Alexei	Ottawa	6	—	—
Yegorov, Alexei	San Jose	1	—	—
Young, Scott	Que., Col.	4	—	—
Yzerman, Steve	Detroit	17	1	—
Zamuner, Rob	Tampa Bay	1	—	—
Zednik, Richard	Washington	1	—	—
Zhamnov, Alexei	Wpg., Chi.	5	—	1
Zubrus, Dainus	Montreal	1	—	—

Top 100 All-Time Goal-Scoring Leaders

* active player

	Player	Seasons	Games	Goals	Goals per game
1.	**Wayne Gretzky**, Edm., L.A., St.L., NYR	20	1487	**894**	.601
2.	**Gordie Howe**, Det., Hfd.	26	1767	**801**	.453
3.	**Marcel Dionne**, Det., L.A., NYR	18	1348	**731**	.542
4.	**Phil Esposito**, Chi., Bos., NYR	18	1282	**717**	.559
5.	**Mike Gartner**, Wsh., Min., NYR, Tor., Phx.	19	1432	**708**	.494
* 6.	**Mark Messier**, Edm., NYR, Van.	22	1561	**651**	.417
* 7.	**Brett Hull**, Cgy., St.L., Dal.	16	1019	**649**	.637
* 8.	**Mario Lemieux**, Pit.	13	788	**648**	.822
* 9.	**Steve Yzerman**, Det.	18	1310	**645**	.492
10.	**Bobby Hull**, Chi., Wpg., Hfd.	16	1063	**610**	.574
11.	**Dino Ciccarelli**, Min., Wsh., Det., T.B., Fla.	19	1232	**608**	.494
12.	**Jari Kurri**, Edm., L.A., NYR, Ana., Col.	17	1251	**601**	.480
* 13.	**Luc Robitaille**, L.A., Pit., NYR	15	1124	**590**	.525
14.	**Mike Bossy**, NYI	10	752	**573**	.762
* 15.	**Dave Andreychuk**, Buf., Tor., N.J., Bos., Col.	19	1361	**572**	.420
16.	**Guy Lafleur**, Mtl., NYR, Que.	17	1126	**560**	.497
17.	**John Bucyk**, Det., Bos.	23	1540	**556**	.361
18.	**Michel Goulet**, Que., Chi.	15	1089	**548**	.503
19.	**Maurice Richard**, Mtl.	18	978	**544**	.556
20.	**Stan Mikita**, Chi.	22	1394	**541**	.388
21.	**Frank Mahovlich**, Tor., Det., Mtl.	18	1181	**533**	.451
22.	**Bryan Trottier**, NYI, Pit.	21	1279	**524**	.410
23.	**Dale Hawerchuk**, Wpg., Buf., St.L., Phi.	16	1188	**518**	.436
* 24.	**Pat Verbeek**, N.J., Hfd., NYR, Dal., Det.	19	1360	**515**	.379
25.	**Gilbert Perreault**, Buf.	17	1191	**512**	.430
26.	**Jean Beliveau**, Mtl.	20	1125	**507**	.451
27.	**Joe Mullen**, St.L., Cgy., Pit., Bos.	17	1062	**502**	.473
28.	**Lanny McDonald**, Tor., Col., Cgy.	16	1111	**500**	.450
29.	**Glenn Anderson**, Edm., Tor., NYR, St.L.	16	1129	**498**	.441
30.	**Jean Ratelle**, NYR, Bos.	21	1281	**491**	.383
31.	**Norm Ullman**, Det., Tor.	20	1410	**490**	.348
* 32.	**Ron Francis**, Hfd., Pit., Car.	20	1489	**487**	.327
33.	**Brian Bellows**, Min., Mtl., T.B., Ana., Wsh.	17	1188	**485**	.408
34.	**Darryl Sittler**, Tor., Phi., Det.	15	1096	**484**	.442
35.	**Bernie Nicholls**, L.A., NYR, Edm., N.J., Chi., S.J.	18	1127	**475**	.421
36.	**Denis Savard**, Chi., Mtl., T.B.	18	1196	**473**	.395
* 37.	**Joe Nieuwendyk**, Cgy., Dal.	15	952	**469**	.493
38.	**Pat LaFontaine**, NYI, Buf., NYR	15	865	**468**	.541
* 39.	**Brendan Shanahan**, N.J., St.L., Hfd., Det.	14	1028	**466**	.453
* 40.	**Joe Sakic**, Que., Col.	13	934	**457**	.489
41.	**Alex Delvecchio**, Det.	25	1549	**456**	.294
* 42.	**Pierre Turgeon**, Buf., NYI, Mtl., St.L.	14	1008	**453**	.449
43.	**Peter Stastny**, Que., N.J., St.L.	15	977	**450**	.461
44.	**Rick Middleton**, NYR, Bos.	14	1005	**448**	.446
45.	**Steve Larmer**, Chi., NYR	15	1006	**441**	.438
46.	**Rick Vaive**, Van., Tor., Chi., Buf.	13	876	**441**	.503
* 47.	**Rick Tocchet**, Phi., Pit., L.A., Bos., Wsh., Phx.	17	1130	**440**	.389
* 48.	**Jaromir Jagr**, Pit.	11	806	**439**	.545
49.	**Dave Taylor**, L.A.	17	1111	**431**	.388
* 50.	**Doug Gilmour**, St.L., Cgy., Tor., N.J., Chi., Buf.	18	1342	**429**	.320
51.	**Yvan Cournoyer**, Mtl.	16	968	**428**	.442
52.	**Brian Propp**, Phi., Bos., Min., Hfd.	15	1016	**425**	.418
53.	**Steve Shutt**, Mtl., L.A.	13	930	**424**	.456
54.	**Bill Barber**, Phi.	14	903	**420**	.465
* 55.	**Theoren Fleury**, Cgy., Col., NYR	13	948	**419**	.442
56.	**Garry Unger**, Tor., Det., St.L., Atl., L.A., Edm.	16	1105	**413**	.374
57.	**Raymond Bourque**, Bos., Col.	22	1612	**410**	.254
* 58.	**John MacLean**, N.J., S.J., NYR, Dal.	18	1174	**410**	.349
* 59.	**Jeremy Roenick**, Chi., Phx.	13	908	**408**	.449
60.	**Stephane Richer**, Mtl., N.J., T.B., St.L.	16	986	**407**	.413
61.	**Rod Gilbert**, NYR	18	1065	**406**	.381
62.	**John Ogrodnick**, Det., Que., NYR	14	928	**402**	.433
63.	**Paul Coffey**, Edm., Pit., L.A., Det., Hfd., Phi., Chi., Car., Bos.	21	1409	**396**	.281
64.	**Dave Keon**, Tor., Hfd.	18	1296	**396**	.306
* 65.	**Alexander Mogilny**, Buf., Van., N.J.	12	780	**396**	.508
66.	**Pierre Larouche**, Pit., Mtl., Hfd., NYR	14	812	**395**	.486
67.	**Cam Neely**, Van., Bos.	13	726	**395**	.544
* 68.	**Ray Ferraro**, Hfd., NYI, NYR, L.A., Atl.	17	1182	**394**	.333
69.	**Tomas Sandstrom**, NYR, L.A., Pit., Det., Ana.	15	983	**394**	.401
70.	**Bernie Geoffrion**, Mtl., NYR	16	883	**393**	.445
71.	**Jean Pronovost**, Pit., Atl., Wsh.	14	998	**391**	.392
72.	**Dean Prentice**, NYR, Bos., Det., Pit., Min.	22	1378	**391**	.284
* 73.	**Mark Recchi**, Pit., Phi., Mtl.	13	932	**388**	.416
* 74.	**Steve Thomas**, Tor., Chi., NYI, N.J.	17	1076	**386**	.359
* 75.	**Pavel Bure**, Van., Fla.	10	595	**384**	.645
76.	**Rick Martin**, Buf., L.A.	11	685	**384**	.561
* 77.	**Peter Bondra**, Wsh.	11	754	**382**	.507
* 78.	**Mike Modano**, Min., Dal.	13	868	**382**	.440
79.	**Reggie Leach**, Bos., Cal., Phi., Det.	13	934	**381**	.408
* 80.	**Teemu Selanne**, Wpg., Ana., S.J.	9	637	**379**	.595
81.	**Ted Lindsay**, Det., Chi.	17	1068	**379**	.355
* 82.	**Vincent Damphousse**, Tor., Edm., Mtl., S.J.	15	1132	**377**	.333
83.	**Butch Goring**, L.A., NYI, Bos.	19	1107	**375**	.339
84.	**Rick Kehoe**, Tor., Pit.	18	906	**371**	.409
85.	**Tim Kerr**, Phi., NYR, Hfd.	13	655	**370**	.565
86.	**Bernie Federko**, St.L., Det.	14	1000	**369**	.369
87.	**Geoff Courtnall**, Bos., Edm., Wsh., St.L., Van.	17	1048	**367**	.350
88.	**Jacques Lemaire**, Mtl.	16	853	**366**	.429
89.	**Peter McNab**, Buf., Bos., Van., N.J.	14	954	**363**	.381
90.	**Brent Sutter**, NYI, Chi.	18	1111	**363**	.327
91.	**Ivan Boldirev**, Bos., Cal., Chi., Atl., Van., Det.	15	1052	**361**	.343
92.	**Bobby Clarke**, Phi.	20	1144	**358**	.313
93.	**Henri Richard**, Mtl.	20	1256	**358**	.285
94.	**Bobby Smith**, Min., Mtl.	15	1077	**357**	.331
95.	**Ray Sheppard**, Buf., NYR, Det., S.J., Fla., Car.	13	817	**357**	.437
96.	**Dennis Maruk**, Cal., Cle., Min., Wsh.	14	888	**356**	.401
97.	**Wilf Paiement**, K.C., Col., Tor., Que., NYR, Buf., Pit.	14	946	**356**	.376
* 98.	**Mats Sundin**, Que., Tor.	11	848	**356**	.420
99.	**Mike Foligno**, Det., Buf., Tor., Fla.	16	1018	**355**	.349
*100.	**Claude Lemieux**, Mtl., N.J., Col., Phx.	18	1047	**355**	.339

After three-and-a-half years of retirement, Mario Lemieux left the boardroom for the dressing room and returned to the ice on December 27, 2000. He scored against Toronto that night and went on to notch 35 goals in just 43 games.

Top 100 Active Goal-Scoring Leaders

	Player	Seasons	Games	Goals	Goals per game
1.	**Mark Messier**, Edm., NYR, Van.	22	1561	**651**	.417
2.	**Brett Hull**, Cgy., St.L., Dal.	16	1019	**649**	.637
3.	**Mario Lemieux**, Pit.	13	788	**648**	.822
4.	**Steve Yzerman**, Det.	18	1310	**645**	.492
5.	**Luc Robitaille**, L.A., Pit., NYR	15	1124	**590**	.525
6.	**Dave Andreychuk**, Buf., Tor., N.J., Bos., Col.	19	1361	**572**	.420
7.	**Pat Verbeek**, N.J., Hfd., NYR, Dal., Det.	19	1360	**515**	.379
8.	**Ron Francis**, Hfd., Pit., Car.	20	1489	**487**	.327
9.	**Joe Nieuwendyk**, Cgy., Dal.	15	952	**469**	.493
10.	**Brendan Shanahan**, N.J., St.L., Hfd., Det.	14	1028	**466**	.453
11.	**Joe Sakic**, Que., Col.	13	934	**457**	.489
12.	**Pierre Turgeon**, Buf., NYI, Mtl., St.L.	14	1008	**453**	.449
13.	**Rick Tocchet**, Phi., Pit., L.A., Bos., Wsh., Phx.	17	1130	**440**	.389
14.	**Jaromir Jagr**, Pit.	11	806	**439**	.545
15.	**Doug Gilmour**, St.L., Cgy., Tor., N.J., Chi., Buf.	18	1342	**429**	.320
16.	**Theoren Fleury**, Cgy., Col., NYR	13	948	**419**	.442
17.	**John MacLean**, N.J., S.J., NYR, Dal.	18	1174	**410**	.349
18.	**Jeremy Roenick**, Chi., Phx.	13	908	**408**	.449
19.	**Alexander Mogilny**, Buf., Van., N.J.	12	780	**396**	.508
20.	**Ray Ferraro**, Hfd., NYI, NYR, L.A., Atl.	17	1182	**394**	.333
21.	**Mark Recchi**, Pit., Phi., Mtl.	13	932	**388**	.416
22.	**Steve Thomas**, Tor., Chi., NYI, N.J.	17	1076	**386**	.359
23.	**Pavel Bure**, Van., Fla.	10	595	**384**	.645
24.	**Mike Modano**, Min., Dal.	13	868	**382**	.440
25.	**Peter Bondra**, Wsh.	11	754	**382**	.507
26.	**Teemu Selanne**, Wpg., Ana., S.J.	9	637	**379**	.595
27.	**Vincent Damphousse**, Tor., Edm., Mtl., S.J.	15	1132	**377**	.333
28.	**Mats Sundin**, Que., Tor.	11	848	**356**	.420
29.	**Claude Lemieux**, Mtl., N.J., Col., Phx.	18	1047	**355**	.339
30.	**Greg Adams**, N.J., Van., Dal., Phx., Fla.	17	1056	**355**	.336
31.	**Kevin Dineen**, Hfd., Phi., Car., Ott., CBJ	17	1125	**350**	.311
32.	**Kirk Muller**, N.J., Mtl., NYI, Tor., Fla., Dal.	17	1216	**346**	.285
33.	**Gary Roberts**, Cgy., Car., Tor.	15	874	**343**	.392
34.	**Sergei Fedorov**, Det.	11	747	**333**	.446
35.	**Keith Tkachuk**, Wpg., Phx., St.L.	10	652	**329**	.505
36.	**Kevin Stevens**, Pit., Bos., L.A., NYR, Phi.	14	842	**328**	.390
37.	**Tony Amonte**, NYR, Chi.	11	779	**325**	.417
38.	**Phil Housley**, Buf., Wpg., St.L., Cgy., N.J., Wsh.	19	1357	**317**	.234
39.	**Adam Oates**, Det., St.L., Bos., Wsh.	16	1130	**316**	.280
40.	**John LeClair**, Mtl., Phi.	11	681	**316**	.464
41.	**Al MacInnis**, Cgy., St.L.	20	1262	**313**	.248
42.	**Trevor Linden**, Van., NYI, Mtl., Wsh.	13	928	**303**	.327
43.	**Adam Graves**, Det., Edm., NYR	14	989	**303**	.306
44.	**Rod Brind'Amour**, St.L., Phi., Car.	13	902	**302**	.335
45.	**Eric Lindros**, Phi.	8	486	**290**	.597
46.	**Larry Murphy**, L.A., Wsh., Min., Pit., Tor., Det.	21	1615	**287**	.178
47.	**Scott Mellanby**, Phi., Edm., Fla., St.L.	16	1079	**285**	.264
48.	**Owen Nolan**, Que., Col., S.J.	11	700	**278**	.397
49.	**Scott Young**, Hfd., Pit., Que., Col., Ana., St.L.	13	903	**274**	.303
50.	**Cliff Ronning**, St.L., Van., Phx., Nsh.	15	936	**261**	.279
51.	**Ulf Dahlen**, NYR, Min., Dal., S.J., Chi., Wsh.	12	834	**261**	.313
52.	**Derek King**, NYI, Hfd., Tor., St.L., Ott.	15	830	**261**	.314
53.	**Geoff Sanderson**, Hfd., Car., Van., Buf., CBJ	11	724	**255**	.352
54.	**Dmitri Khristich**, Wsh., L.A., Bos., Tor.	11	750	**250**	.333
55.	**Shayne Corson**, Mtl., Edm., St.L., Tor.	16	1019	**249**	.244
56.	**Tony Granato**, NYR, L.A., S.J.	13	773	**248**	.321
57.	**Paul Kariya**, Ana.	7	442	**243**	.550
58.	**Donald Audette**, Buf., L.A., Atl.	12	597	**235**	.394
59.	**Petr Nedved**, Van., St.L., NYR, Pit.	10	652	**234**	.359
60.	**Joe Murphy**, Det., Edm., Chi., St.L., S.J., Bos., Wsh.	15	779	**233**	.299
61.	**Ziggy Palffy**, NYI, L.A.	8	468	**233**	.498
62.	**Kevin Hatcher**, Wsh., Dal., Pit., NYR, Car.	17	1157	**227**	.196
63.	**Steve Duchesne**, L.A., Phi., Que., St.L., Ott., Det.	15	1049	**224**	.214
64.	**Keith Primeau**, Det., Hfd., Car., Phi.	11	691	**220**	.318
65.	**Alexei Yashin**, Ott.	8	504	**218**	.433
66.	**Martin Gelinas**, Edm., Que., Van., Car.	13	823	**218**	.265
67.	**Bill Guerin**, N.J., Edm., Bos.	10	655	**215**	.328
68.	**Benoit Hogue**, Buf., NYI, Tor., Dal., T.B., Phx.	14	805	**215**	.267
69.	**Bobby Holik**, Hfd., N.J.	11	797	**215**	.270
70.	**Shawn McEachern**, Pit., L.A., Bos., Ott.	10	675	**212**	.314
71.	**Alexei Kovalev**, NYR, Pit.	9	626	**209**	.334
72.	**Robert Reichel**, Cgy., NYI, Phx.	8	602	**209**	.347

With 487 goals entering the 2001-02 season, Ron Francis needs to score 13 more times to join just four other player in NHL history with at least 500 goals and 1,000 assists. Steve Yzerman needs 31 assists to accomplish the same feat.

	Player	Seasons	Games	Goals	Goals per game
73.	**Brian Leetch**, NYR	14	939	**205**	.218
74.	**Ron Sutter**, Phi., St.L., Que., NYI, Bos., S.J., Cgy.	19	1093	**205**	.188
75.	**Vyacheslav Kozlov**, Det.	10	607	**202**	.333
76.	**Alexei Zhamnov**, Wpg., Chi.	9	589	**200**	.340
77.	**Gary Suter**, Cgy., Chi., S.J.	16	1063	**197**	.185
78.	**Mike Ricci**, Phi., Que., Col., S.J.	11	789	**196**	.248
79.	**Valeri Kamensky**, Que., Col., NYR	10	583	**193**	.331
80.	**Rob Brown**, Pit., Hfd., Chi., Dal., L.A.	11	543	**190**	.350
81.	**Nelson Emerson**, St.L., Wpg., Hfd., Car., Chi., Ott., Atl., L.A.	11	730	**190**	.260
82.	**Scott Stevens**, Wsh., St.L., N.J.	19	1434	**188**	.131
83.	**Doug Weight**, NYR, Edm.	11	706	**180**	.255
84.	**Stu Barnes**, Wpg., Fla., Pit., Buf.	10	671	**180**	.268
85.	**Bryan Smolinski**, Bos., Pit., NYI, L.A.	9	601	**178**	.296
86.	**Jason Arnott**, Edm., N.J.	8	525	**175**	.333
87.	**Andrei Kovalenko**, Que., Col., Mtl., Edm., Phi., Car., Bos.	9	620	**173**	.279
88.	**Peter Forsberg**, Que., Col.	7	466	**169**	.363
89.	**Chris Chelios**, Mtl., Chi., Det.	18	1181	**168**	.142
90.	**Martin Rucinsky**, Edm., Que., Col., Mtl.	10	599	**167**	.279
91.	**Miroslav Satan**, Edm., Buf.	6	461	**167**	.362
92.	**Markus Naslund**, Pit., Van.	8	549	**167**	.304
93.	**Dave Reid**, Bos., Tor., Dal., Col.	18	961	**165**	.172
94.	**Andrew Cassels**, Mtl., Hfd., Cgy., Van.	12	794	**163**	.205
95.	**Bob Probert**, Det., Chi.	16	874	**162**	.185
96.	**Eric Daze**, Chi.	7	445	**162**	.364
97.	**Doug Brown**, N.J., Pit., Det.	15	854	**160**	.187
98.	**Martin Straka**, Pit., Ott., NYI, Fla.	9	603	**159**	.264
99.	**Steve Heinze**, Bos., CBJ, Buf.	10	594	**158**	.266
100.	**Mariusz Czerkawski**, Bos., Edm., NYI	8	504	**155**	.308

Top 100 All-Time Assist Leaders

* active player

	Player	Seasons	Games	Assists	Assists per game
1.	**Wayne Gretzky**, Edm., L.A., St.L., NYR	20	1487	**1963**	1.320
2.	**Raymond Bourque**, Bos., Col.	22	1612	**1169**	.725
* 3.	**Ron Francis**, Hfd., Pit., Car.	20	1489	**1137**	.764
4.	**Paul Coffey**, Edm., Pit., L.A., Det., Hfd., Phi., Chi., Car., Bos.	21	1409	**1135**	.806
* 5.	**Mark Messier**, Edm., NYR, Van.	22	1561	**1130**	.724
6.	**Gordie Howe**, Det., Hfd.	26	1767	**1049**	.594
7.	**Marcel Dionne**, Det., L.A., NYR	18	1348	**1040**	.772
* 8.	**Steve Yzerman**, Det.	18	1310	**969**	.740
* 9.	**Adam Oates**, Det., St.L., Bos., Wsh.	16	1130	**963**	.852
* 10.	**Larry Murphy**, L.A., Wsh., Min., Pit., Tor., Det.	21	1615	**929**	.575
11.	**Stan Mikita**, Chi.	22	1394	**926**	.664
* 12.	**Mario Lemieux**, Pit.	13	788	**922**	1.170
* 13.	**Doug Gilmour**, St.L., Cgy., Tor., N.J., Chi., Buf.	18	1342	**914**	.681
14.	**Bryan Trottier**, NYI, Pit.	21	1279	**901**	.704
15.	**Dale Hawerchuk**, Wpg., Buf., St.L., Phi.	16	1188	**891**	.750
16.	**Phil Esposito**, Chi., Bos., NYR	18	1282	**873**	.681
17.	**Denis Savard**, Chi., Mtl., T.B.	18	1196	**865**	.723
18.	**Bobby Clarke**, Phi.	20	1144	**852**	.745
* 19.	**Phil Housley**, Buf., Wpg., St.L., Cgy., N.J., Wsh.	19	1357	**847**	.624
* 20.	**Al MacInnis**, Cgy., St.L.	20	1262	**845**	.670
21.	**Alex Delvecchio**, Det.	25	1549	**825**	.533
22.	**Gilbert Perreault**, Buf.	17	1191	**814**	.683
23.	**John Bucyk**, Det., Bos.	23	1540	**813**	.528
24.	**Jari Kurri**, Edm., L.A., NYR, Ana., Col.	17	1251	**797**	.637
25.	**Guy Lafleur**, Mtl., NYR, Que.	17	1126	**793**	.704
26.	**Peter Stastny**, Que., N.J., St.L.	15	977	**789**	.808
27.	**Jean Ratelle**, NYR, Bos.	21	1281	**776**	.606
28.	**Bernie Federko**, St.L., Det.	14	1000	**761**	.761
29.	**Larry Robinson**, Mtl., L.A.	23	1384	**750**	.542
30.	**Denis Potvin**, NYI	15	1060	**742**	.700
31.	**Norm Ullman**, Det., Tor.	20	1410	**739**	.524
32.	**Bernie Nicholls**, L.A., NYR, Edm., N.J., Chi., S.J.	18	1127	**734**	.651
* 33.	**Joe Sakic**, Que., Col.	13	934	**721**	.772
34.	**Jean Beliveau**, Mtl.	20	1125	**712**	.633
35.	**Dale Hunter**, Que., Wsh., Col.	20	1407	**697**	.495
* 36.	**Pierre Turgeon**, Buf., NYI, Mtl., St.L.	14	1008	**692**	.687
37.	**Henri Richard**, Mtl.	20	1256	**688**	.548
38.	**Brad Park**, NYR, Bos., Det.	17	1113	**683**	.614
39.	**Bobby Smith**, Min., Mtl.	15	1077	**679**	.630
* 40.	**Scott Stevens**, Wsh., St.L., N.J.	19	1434	**671**	.468
* 41.	**Vincent Damphousse**, Tor., Edm., Mtl., S.J.	15	1132	**668**	.590
* 42.	**Chris Chelios**, Mtl., Chi., Det.	18	1181	**667**	.565
* 43.	**Brian Leetch**, NYR	14	939	**655**	.698
* 44.	**Luc Robitaille**, L.A., Pit., NYR	15	1124	**648**	.577
45.	**Bobby Orr**, Bos., Chi.	12	657	**645**	.982
* 46.	**Jaromir Jagr**, Pit.	11	806	**640**	.794
47.	**Dave Taylor**, L.A.	17	1111	**638**	.574
48.	**Darryl Sittler**, Tor., Phi., Det.	15	1096	**637**	.581
49.	**Borje Salming**, Tor., Det.	17	1148	**637**	.555
* 50.	**Dave Andreychuk**, Buf., Tor., N.J., Bos., Col.	19	1361	**637**	.468
51.	**Neal Broten**, Min., Dal., N.J., L.A.	17	1099	**634**	.577
52.	**Mike Gartner**, Wsh., Min., NYR, Tor., Phx.	19	1432	**627**	.438
53.	**Andy Bathgate**, NYR, Tor., Det., Pit.	17	1069	**624**	.584
* 54.	**Mark Recchi**, Pit., Phi., Mtl.	13	932	**622**	.667
55.	**Rod Gilbert**, NYR	18	1065	**615**	.577
* 56.	**Gary Suter**, Cgy., Chi., S.J.	16	1063	**615**	.579
57.	**Michel Goulet**, Que., Chi.	15	1089	**604**	.555
58.	**Glenn Anderson**, Edm., Tor., NYR, St.L.	16	1129	**601**	.532
59.	**Dino Ciccarelli**, Min., Wsh., Det., T.B., Fla.	19	1232	**592**	.481
60.	**Doug Wilson**, Chi., S.J.	16	1024	**590**	.576
61.	**Dave Keon**, Tor., Hfd.	18	1296	**590**	.455
62.	**Dave Babych**, Wpg., Hfd., Van., Phi., L.A.	19	1195	**581**	.486
63.	**Brian Propp**, Phi., Bos., Min., Hfd.	15	1016	**579**	.570
* 64.	**Kirk Muller**, N.J., Mtl., NYI, Tor., Fla., Dal.	17	1216	**577**	.475
* 65.	**Theoren Fleury**, Cgy., Col., NYR	13	948	**573**	.604
66.	**Steve Larmer**, Chi., NYR	15	1006	**571**	.568
67.	**Frank Mahovlich**, Tor., Det., Mtl.	18	1181	**570**	.483
68.	**Craig Janney**, Bos., St.L., S.J., Wpg., Phx., T.B., NYI	12	760	**563**	.741
69.	**Joe Mullen**, St.L., Cgy., Pit., Bos.	17	1062	**561**	.528
70.	**Bobby Hull**, Chi., Wpg., Hfd.	16	1063	**560**	.527
71.	**Thomas Steen**, Wpg.	14	950	**553**	.582
72.	**Mike Bossy**, NYI	10	752	**553**	.735

Only Mario Lemieux (1.170) comes close to approaching Wayne Gretzky's assists-per-game rate of 1.320. Among the NHL's top 100 assist leaders, Bobby Orr (#45) has the next-best ratio with .982 assists per game.

	Player	Seasons	Games	Assists	Assist per game
73.	**Ken Linseman**, Phi., Edm., Bos., Tor.	14	860	**551**	.641
74.	**Tom Lysiak**, Atl., Chi.	13	919	**551**	.600
75.	**Mark Howe**, Hfd., Phi., Det.	16	929	**545**	.587
76.	**Pat LaFontaine**, NYI, Buf., NYR	15	865	**545**	.630
77.	**Red Kelly**, Det., Tor.	21	1316	**542**	.412
78.	**Rick Middleton**, NYR, Bos.	14	1005	**540**	.537
* 79.	**Jeremy Roenick**, Chi., Phx.	13	908	**539**	.594
80.	**Brian Bellows**, Min., Mtl., T.B., Ana., Wsh.	17	1188	**537**	.452
* 81.	**Brett Hull**, Cgy., St.L., Dal.	16	1019	**534**	.524
* 82.	**Pat Verbeek**, N.J., Hfd., NYR, Dal., Det.	19	1360	**528**	.388
83.	**Dennis Maruk**, Cal., Cle., Min., Wsh.	14	888	**522**	.588
* 84.	**Mike Modano**, Min., Dal.	13	868	**518**	.597
85.	**Wayne Cashman**, Bos.	23	1027	**516**	.502
86.	**Butch Goring**, L.A., NYI, Bos.	19	1107	**513**	.463
87.	**John Tonelli**, NYI, Cgy., L.A., Chi., Que.	14	1028	**511**	.497
* 88.	**Rick Tocchet**, Phi., Pit., L.A., Bos., Wsh., Phx.	17	1130	**510**	.451
* 89.	**Steve Duchesne**, L.A., Phi., Que., St.L., Ott., Det.	15	1049	**510**	.486
90.	**Lanny McDonald**, Tor., Col., Cgy.	16	1111	**506**	.455
* 91.	**Mats Sundin**, Que., Tor.	11	848	**506**	.597
92.	**Ivan Boldirev**, Bos., Cal., Chi., Atl., Van., Det.	15	1052	**505**	.480
93.	**Randy Carlyle**, Tor., Pit., Wpg.	19	1055	**499**	.473
* 94.	**Murray Craven**, Det., Phi., Hfd., Van., Chi., S.J.	18	1071	**493**	.460
* 95.	**Brendan Shanahan**, N.J., St.L., Hfd., Det.	14	1028	**489**	.476
96.	**Pit Martin**, Det., Bos., Chi., Van.	17	1101	**485**	.441
97.	**Pete Mahovlich**, Det., Mtl., Pit.	16	884	**485**	.549
* 98.	**Cliff Ronning**, St.L., Van., Phx., Nsh.	15	936	**482**	.515
* 99.	**Steve Thomas**, Tor., Chi., NYI, N.J.	17	1076	**480**	.446
* 100.	**Rod Brind'Amour**, St.L., Phi., Car.	13	902	**479**	.531

Top 100 Active Assist Leaders

	Player	Seasons	Games	Assists	Assists per game
1.	**Ron Francis**, Hfd., Pit., Car.	20	1489	**1137**	.764
2.	**Mark Messier**, Edm., NYR, Van.	22	1561	**1130**	.724
3.	**Steve Yzerman**, Det.	18	1310	**969**	.740
4.	**Adam Oates**, Det., St.L., Bos., Wsh.	16	1130	**963**	.852
5.	**Larry Murphy**, L.A., Wsh., Min., Pit., Tor., Det.	21	1615	**929**	.575
6.	**Mario Lemieux**, Pit.	13	788	**922**	1.170
7.	**Doug Gilmour**, St.L., Cgy., Tor., N.J., Chi., Buf.	18	1342	**914**	.681
8.	**Phil Housley**, Buf., Wpg., St.L., Cgy., N.J., Wsh.	19	1357	**847**	.624
9.	**Al MacInnis**, Cgy., St.L.	20	1262	**845**	.670
10.	**Joe Sakic**, Que., Col.	13	934	**721**	.772
11.	**Pierre Turgeon**, Buf., NYI, Mtl., St.L.	14	1008	**692**	.687
12.	**Scott Stevens**, Wsh., St.L., N.J.	19	1434	**671**	.468
13.	**Vincent Damphousse**, Tor., Edm., Mtl., S.J.	15	1132	**668**	.590
14.	**Chris Chelios**, Mtl., Chi., Det.	18	1181	**667**	.565
15.	**Brian Leetch**, NYR	14	939	**655**	.698
16.	**Luc Robitaille**, L.A., Pit., NYR	15	1124	**648**	.577
17.	**Jaromir Jagr**, Pit.	11	806	**640**	.794
18.	**Dave Andreychuk**, Buf., Tor., N.J., Bos., Col.	19	1361	**637**	.468
19.	**Mark Recchi**, Pit., Phi., Mtl.	13	932	**622**	.667
20.	**Gary Suter**, Cgy., Chi., S.J.	16	1063	**615**	.579
21.	**Kirk Muller**, N.J., Mtl., NYI, Tor., Fla., Dal.	17	1216	**577**	.475
22.	**Theoren Fleury**, Cgy., Col., NYR	13	948	**573**	.604
23.	**Jeremy Roenick**, Chi., Phx.	13	908	**539**	.594
24.	**Brett Hull**, Cgy., St.L., Dal.	16	1019	**534**	.524
25.	**Pat Verbeek**, N.J., Hfd., NYR, Dal., Det.	19	1360	**528**	.388
26.	**Mike Modano**, Min., Dal.	13	868	**518**	.597
27.	**Rick Tocchet**, Phi., Pit., L.A., Bos., Wsh., Phx.	17	1130	**510**	.451
28.	**Steve Duchesne**, L.A., Phi., Que., St.L., Ott., Det.	15	1049	**510**	.486
29.	**Mats Sundin**, Que., Tor.	11	848	**506**	.597
30.	**Brendan Shanahan**, N.J., St.L., Hfd., Det.	14	1028	**489**	.476
31.	**Cliff Ronning**, St.L., Van., Phx., Nsh.	15	936	**482**	.515
32.	**Steve Thomas**, Tor., Chi., NYI, N.J.	17	1076	**480**	.446
33.	**Rod Brind'Amour**, St.L., Phi., Car.	13	902	**479**	.531
34.	**Garry Galley**, L.A., Wsh., Bos., Phi., Buf., NYI	17	1149	**475**	.413
35.	**Sergei Fedorov**, Det.	11	747	**470**	.629
36.	**Ray Ferraro**, Hfd., NYI, NYR, L.A., Atl.	17	1182	**467**	.395
37.	**Doug Weight**, NYR, Edm.	11	706	**467**	.661
38.	**James Patrick**, NYR, Hfd., Cgy., Buf.	18	1100	**463**	.421
39.	**Kevin Hatcher**, Wsh., Dal., Pit., NYR, Car.	17	1157	**450**	.389
40.	**Alexander Mogilny**, Buf., Van., N.J.	12	780	**445**	.571
41.	**Joe Nieuwendyk**, Cgy., Dal.	15	952	**440**	.462
42.	**Nicklas Lidstrom**, Det.	10	775	**431**	.556
43.	**John MacLean**, N.J., S.J., NYR, Dal.	18	1174	**426**	.363
44.	**Teemu Selanne**, Wpg., Ana., S.J.	9	637	**422**	.662
45.	**Fredrik Olausson**, Wpg., Edm., Ana., Pit.	14	931	**415**	.446
46.	**Andrew Cassels**, Mtl., Hfd., Cgy., Van.	12	794	**413**	.520
47.	**Peter Forsberg**, Que., Col.	7	466	**411**	.882
48.	**Igor Larionov**, Van., S.J., Det., Fla.	11	728	**400**	.549
49.	**Calle Johansson**, Buf., Wsh.	14	1008	**398**	.395
50.	**Kevin Dineen**, Hfd., Phi., Car., Ott., CBJ	17	1125	**397**	.353
51.	**Trevor Linden**, Van., NYI, Mtl., Wsh.	13	928	**397**	.428
52.	**Kevin Stevens**, Pit., Bos., L.A., NYR, Phi.	14	842	**393**	.467
53.	**Greg Adams**, N.J., Van., Dal., Phx., Fla.	17	1056	**388**	.367
54.	**Shayne Corson**, Mtl., Edm., St.L., Tor.	16	1019	**386**	.379
55.	**Sergei Zubov**, NYR, Pit., Dal.	9	617	**373**	.605
56.	**Eric Lindros**, Phi.	8	486	**369**	.759
57.	**Claude Lemieux**, Mtl., N.J., Col., Phx.	18	1047	**369**	.352
58.	**Teppo Numminen**, Wpg., Phx.	13	944	**367**	.389
59.	**Eric Desjardins**, Mtl., Phi.	13	906	**365**	.403
60.	**Joe Juneau**, Bos., Wsh., Buf., Ott., Phx.	10	616	**362**	.588
61.	**Gary Roberts**, Cgy., Car., Tor.	15	874	**359**	.411
62.	**Scott Mellanby**, Phi., Edm., Fla., St.L.	16	1079	**356**	.330
63.	**Glen Wesley**, Bos., Hfd., Car.	14	1026	**353**	.344
64.	**Derek King**, NYI, Hfd., Tor., St.L., Ott.	15	830	**351**	.423
65.	**Alexei Zhamnov**, Wpg., Chi.	9	589	**348**	.591
66.	**Petr Svoboda**, Mtl., Buf., Phi., T.B., Tor.	17	1046	**343**	.328
67.	**Scott Young**, Hfd., Pit., Que., Col., Ana., St.L.	13	903	**335**	.371
68.	**Jyrki Lumme**, Mtl., Van., Phx.	13	846	**334**	.395
69.	**Tony Amonte**, NYR, Chi.	11	779	**333**	.427
70.	**Ron Sutter**, Phi., St.L., Que., NYI, Bos., S.J., Cgy.	19	1093	**329**	.301

Tiny but talented, 5'6" Theoren Fleury has collected 573 assists in his career, ranking him 22nd among active players. Fleury's best season as a playmaker came in 1992-93 when he set up 66 goals for the Calgary Flames.

	Player		Games	Assists	Assists per game
71.	**Jeff Norton**, NYI, S.J., St.L., Edm., T.B., Fla., Pit.	14	767	**327**	.426
72.	**Dmitri Khristich**, Wsh., L.A., Bos., Tor.	11	750	**325**	.433
73.	**Benoit Hogue**, Buf., NYI, Tor., Dal., T.B., Phx.	14	805	**313**	.389
74.	**John LeClair**, Mtl., Phi.	11	681	**311**	.457
75.	**Ulf Dahlen**, NYR, Min., Dal., S.J., Chi., Wsh.	12	834	**305**	.366
76.	**Keith Tkachuk**, Wpg., Phx., St.L.	10	652	**302**	.463
77.	**Sylvain Cote**, Hfd., Wsh., Tor., Chi., Dal.	17	1100	**302**	.275
78.	**Rob Blake**, L.A., Col.	12	675	**299**	.443
79.	**Robert Reichel**, Cgy., NYI, Phx.	8	602	**298**	.495
80.	**Pavel Bure**, Van., Fla.	10	595	**296**	.497
81.	**Petr Nedved**, Van., St.L., NYR, Pit.	10	652	**296**	.454
82.	**Joe Murphy**, Det., Edm., Chi., St.L., S.J., Bos., Wsh.	15	779	**295**	.379
83.	**Mathieu Schneider**, Mtl., NYI, Tor., NYR, L.A.	13	781	**295**	.378
84.	**Nelson Emerson**, St.L., Wpg., Hfd., Car., Chi., Ott., Atl., L.A.	11	730	**291**	.399
85.	**Martin Straka**, Pit., Ott., NYI, Fla.	9	603	**290**	.481
86.	**Owen Nolan**, Que., Col., S.J.	11	700	**289**	.413
87.	**Paul Kariya**, Ana.	7	442	**288**	.652
88.	**Valeri Kamensky**, Que., Col., NYR	10	583	**287**	.492
89.	**Sandis Ozolinsh**, S.J., Col., Car.	9	578	**286**	.495
90.	**Dave Manson**, Chi., Edm., Wpg., Phx., Mtl., Dal., Tor.	15	1056	**286**	.271
91.	**Zarley Zalapski**, Pit., Hfd., Cgy., Mtl., Phi.	12	637	**285**	.447
92.	**Peter Bondra**, Wsh.	11	754	**282**	.374
93.	**Bobby Holik**, Hfd., N.J.	11	797	**282**	.354
94.	**Jozef Stumpel**, Bos., L.A.	10	535	**281**	.525
95.	**Mike Ricci**, Phi., Que., Col., S.J.	11	789	**279**	.354
96.	**Mike Keane**, Mtl., Col., NYR, Dal.	13	954	**277**	.290
97.	**Keith Primeau**, Det., Hfd., Car., Phi.	11	691	**276**	.399
98.	**Scott Niedermayer**, N.J.	10	654	**274**	.419
99.	**Alexei Kovalev**, NYR, Pit.	9	626	**273**	.436
100.	**Alexei Yashin**, Ott.	8	504	**273**	.542

Top 100 All-Time Point Leaders

* active player

	Player	Seasons	Games	Goals	Assists	Points	Points per game
1.	**Wayne Gretzky**, Edm., L.A., St.L., NYR	20	1487	894	1963	2857	1.921
2.	**Gordie Howe**, Det., Hfd.	26	1767	801	1049	1850	1.047
* 3.	**Mark Messier**, Edm., NYR, Van.	22	1561	651	1130	1781	1.141
4.	**Marcel Dionne**, Det., L.A., NYR	18	1348	731	1040	1771	1.314
* 5.	**Ron Francis**, Hfd., Pit., Car.	20	1489	487	1137	1624	1.091
* 6.	**Steve Yzerman**, Det.	18	1310	645	969	1614	1.232
7.	**Phil Esposito**, Chi., Bos., NYR	18	1282	717	873	1590	1.240
8.	**Raymond Bourque**, Bos., Col.	22	1612	410	1169	1579	.980
* 9.	**Mario Lemieux**, Pit.	13	788	648	922	1570	1.992
10.	**Paul Coffey**, Edm., Pit., L.A., Det., Hfd., Phi., Chi., Car., Bos.	21	1409	396	1135	1531	1.087
11.	**Stan Mikita**, Chi.	22	1394	541	926	1467	1.052
12.	**Bryan Trottier**, NYI, Pit.	21	1279	524	901	1425	1.114
13.	**Dale Hawerchuk**, Wpg., Buf., St.L., Phi.	16	1188	518	891	1409	1.186
14.	**Jari Kurri**, Edm., L.A., NYR, Ana., Col.	17	1251	601	797	1398	1.118
15.	**John Bucyk**, Det., Bos.	23	1540	556	813	1369	.889
16.	**Guy Lafleur**, Mtl., NYR, Que.	17	1126	560	793	1353	1.202
* 17.	**Doug Gilmour**, St.L., Cgy., Tor., N.J., Chi., Buf.	18	1342	429	914	1343	1.001
18.	**Denis Savard**, Chi., Mtl., T.B.	18	1196	473	865	1338	1.119
19.	**Mike Gartner**, Wsh., Min., NYR, Tor., Phx.	19	1432	708	627	1335	.932
20.	**Gilbert Perreault**, Buf.	17	1191	512	814	1326	1.113
21.	**Alex Delvecchio**, Det.	25	1549	456	825	1281	.827
* 22.	**Adam Oates**, Det., St.L., Bos., Wsh.	16	1130	316	963	1279	1.132
23.	**Jean Ratelle**, NYR, Bos.	21	1281	491	776	1267	.989
24.	**Peter Stastny**, Que., N.J., St.L.	15	977	450	789	1239	1.268
* 25.	**Luc Robitaille**, L.A., Pit., NYR	15	1124	590	648	1238	1.101
26.	**Norm Ullman**, Det., Tor.	20	1410	490	739	1229	.872
27.	**Jean Beliveau**, Mtl.	20	1125	507	712	1219	1.084
* 28.	**Larry Murphy**, L.A., Wsh., Min., Pit., Tor., Det.	21	1615	287	929	1216	.753
29.	**Bobby Clarke**, Phi.	20	1144	358	852	1210	1.058
30.	**Bernie Nicholls**, L.A., NYR, Edm., N.J., Chi., S.J.	18	1127	475	734	1209	1.073
* 31.	**Dave Andreychuk**, Buf., Tor., N.J., Bos., Col.	19	1361	572	637	1209	.888
32.	**Dino Ciccarelli**, Min., Wsh., Det., T.B., Fla.	19	1232	608	592	1200	.974
* 33.	**Brett Hull**, Cgy., St.L., Dal.	16	1019	649	534	1183	1.161
* 34.	**Joe Sakic**, Que., Col.	13	934	457	721	1178	1.261
35.	**Bobby Hull**, Chi., Wpg., Hfd.	16	1063	610	560	1170	1.101
* 36.	**Phil Housley**, Buf., Wpg., St.L., Cgy., N.J., Wsh.	19	1357	317	847	1164	.858
* 37.	**Al MacInnis**, Cgy., St.L.	20	1262	313	845	1158	.918
38.	Michel Goulet, Que., Chi.	15	1089	548	604	1152	1.058
* 39.	**Pierre Turgeon**, Buf., NYI, Mtl., St.L.	14	1008	453	692	1145	1.136
40.	**Bernie Federko**, St.L., Det.	14	1000	369	761	1130	1.130
41.	**Mike Bossy**, NYI	10	752	573	553	1126	1.497
42.	**Darryl Sittler**, Tor., Phi., Det.	15	1096	484	637	1121	1.023
43.	**Frank Mahovlich**, Tor., Det., Mtl.	18	1181	533	570	1103	.934
44.	**Glenn Anderson**, Edm., Tor., NYR, St.L.	16	1129	498	601	1099	.973
* 45.	**Jaromir Jagr**, Pit.	11	806	439	640	1079	1.339
46.	**Dave Taylor**, L.A.	17	1111	431	638	1069	.962
47.	**Joe Mullen**, St.L., Cgy., Pit., Bos.	17	1062	502	561	1063	1.001
48.	**Denis Potvin**, NYI	15	1060	310	742	1052	.992
49.	**Henri Richard**, Mtl.	20	1256	358	688	1046	.833
* 50.	**Vincent Damphousse**, Tor., Edm., Mtl., S.J.	15	1132	377	668	1045	.923
* 51.	**Pat Verbeek**, N.J., Hfd., NYR, Dal., Det.	19	1360	515	528	1043	.767
52.	**Bobby Smith**, Min., Mtl.	15	1077	357	679	1036	.962
53.	**Brian Bellows**, Min., Mtl., T.B., Ana., Wsh.	17	1188	485	537	1022	.860
54.	**Rod Gilbert**, NYR	18	1065	406	615	1021	.959
55.	**Dale Hunter**, Que., Wsh., Col	20	1407	323	697	1020	.725
56.	**Pat LaFontaine**, NYI, Buf., NYR	15	865	468	545	1013	1.171
57.	**Steve Larmer**, Chi., NYR	15	1006	441	571	1012	1.006
* 58.	**Mark Recchi**, Pit., Phi., Mtl.	13	932	388	622	1010	1.084
59.	**Lanny McDonald**, Tor., Col., Cgy.	16	1111	500	506	1006	.905
60.	**Brian Propp**, Phi., Bos., Min., Hfd.	15	1016	425	579	1004	.988
* 61.	**Theoren Fleury**, Cgy., Col., NYR	13	948	419	573	992	1.046
62.	**Rick Middleton**, NYR, Bos.	14	1005	448	540	988	.983
63.	**Dave Keon**, Tor., Hfd.	18	1296	396	590	986	.761
64.	**Andy Bathgate**, NYR, Tor., Det., Pit.	17	1069	349	624	973	.910
65.	**Maurice Richard**, Mtl.	18	978	544	421	965	.987
66.	**Larry Robinson**, Mtl., L.A.	23	1384	208	750	958	.692
* 67.	**Brendan Shanahan**, N.J., St.L., Hfd., Det.	14	1028	466	489	955	.929
* 68.	**Rick Tocchet**, Phi., Pit., L.A., Bos., Wsh., Phx.	17	1130	440	510	950	.841
* 69.	**Jeremy Roenick**, Chi., Phx.	13	908	408	539	947	1.043
* 70.	**Kirk Muller**, N.J., Mtl., NYI, Tor., Fla., Dal.	17	1216	346	577	923	.759
71.	**Neal Broten**, Min., Dal., N.J., L.A.	17	1099	289	634	923	.840
72.	**Bobby Orr**, Bos., Chi.	12	657	270	645	915	1.393
* 73.	**Joe Nieuwendyk**, Cgy., Dal.	15	952	469	440	909	.955
* 74.	**Mike Modano**, Min., Dal.	13	868	382	518	900	1.037
75.	**Brad Park**, NYR, Bos., Det.	17	1113	213	683	896	.805
76.	**Butch Goring**, L.A., NYI, Bos.	19	1107	375	513	888	.802
77.	**Bill Barber**, Phi.	14	903	420	463	883	.978
78.	**Dennis Maruk**, Cal., Cle., Min., Wsh.	14	888	356	522	878	.989
79.	**Ivan Boldirev**, Bos., Cal., Chi., Atl., Van., Det.	15	1052	361	505	866	.823
* 80.	**Steve Thomas**, Tor., Chi., NYI, N.J.	17	1076	386	480	866	.805
81.	**Yvan Cournoyer**, Mtl.	16	968	428	435	863	.892
* 82.	**Mats Sundin**, Que., Tor.	11	848	356	506	862	1.017
* 83.	**Ray Ferraro**, Hfd., NYI, NYR, L.A., Atl.	17	1182	394	467	861	.728
* 84.	**Brian Leetch**, NYR	14	939	205	655	860	.916
85.	**Dean Prentice**, NYR, Bos., Det., Pit., Min.	22	1378	391	469	860	.624
* 86.	**Scott Stevens**, Wsh., St.L., N.J.	19	1434	188	671	859	.599
87.	**Tomas Sandstrom**, NYR, L.A., Pit., Det., Ana.	15	983	394	462	856	.871
88.	**Ted Lindsay**, Det., Chi.	17	1068	379	472	851	.797
89.	**Tom Lysiak**, Atl., Chi.	13	919	292	551	843	.917
* 90.	**Alexander Mogilny**, Buf., Van., N.J.	12	780	396	445	841	1.078
91.	**John Tonelli**, NYI, Cgy., L.A., Chi., Que.	14	1028	325	511	836	.813
* 92.	**John MacLean**, N.J., S.J., NYR, Dal.	18	1174	410	426	836	.712
93.	**Jacques Lemaire**, Mtl.	16	853	366	469	835	.979
* 94.	**Chris Chelios**, Mtl., Chi., Det.	18	1181	168	667	835	.707
95.	**Brent Sutter**, NYI, Chi.	18	1111	363	466	829	.746
96.	**Doug Wilson**, Chi., S.J.	16	1024	237	590	827	.808
97.	**John Ogrodnick**, Det., Que., NYR	14	928	402	425	827	.891
98.	**Red Kelly**, Det., Tor.	21	1316	281	542	823	.625
99.	**Bernie Geoffrion**, Mtl., NYR	16	883	393	429	822	.931
100.	**Pierre Larouche**, Pit., Mtl., Hfd., NYR	14	812	395	427	822	1.012

At the time of his retirement in 1968, Bernie Geoffrion ranked eighth all-time in NHL scoring with 822 points. Entering the 2001-02 season, "Boom Boom" now ranks 99th.

Top 100 Active Points Leaders

By leading the expansion Columbus Blue Jackets in scoring with 30 goals and 26 assists in just 68 games last season, Geoff Sanderson climbed into 80th spot among the NHL's top 100 active points leaders.

	Player	Seasons	Games	Goals	Assists	Points	Points per game
1.	**Mark Messier**, Edm., NYR, Van.	22	1561	651	1130	**1781**	1.141
2.	**Ron Francis**, Hfd., Pit., Car.	20	1489	487	1137	**1624**	1.091
3.	**Steve Yzerman**, Det.	18	1310	645	969	**1614**	1.232
4.	**Mario Lemieux**, Pit.	13	788	648	922	**1570**	1.992
5.	**Doug Gilmour**, St.L., Cgy., Tor., N.J., Chi., Buf.	18	1342	429	914	**1343**	1.001
6.	**Adam Oates**, Det., St.L., Bos., Wsh.	16	1130	316	963	**1279**	1.132
7.	**Luc Robitaille**, L.A., Pit., NYR	15	1124	590	648	**1238**	1.101
8.	**Larry Murphy**, L.A., Wsh., Min., Pit., Tor., Det.	21	1615	287	929	**1216**	.753
9.	**Dave Andreychuk**, Buf., Tor., N.J., Bos., Col.	19	1361	572	637	**1209**	.888
10.	**Brett Hull**, Cgy., St.L., Dal.	16	1019	649	534	**1183**	1.161
11.	**Joe Sakic**, Que., Col.	13	934	457	721	**1178**	1.261
12.	**Phil Housley**, Buf., Wpg., St.L., Cgy., N.J., Wsh.	19	1357	317	847	**1164**	.858
13.	**Al MacInnis**, Cgy., St.L.	20	1262	313	845	**1158**	.918
14.	**Pierre Turgeon**, Buf., NYI, Mtl., St.L.	14	1008	453	692	**1145**	1.136
15.	**Jaromir Jagr**, Pit.	11	806	439	640	**1079**	1.339
16.	**Vincent Damphousse**, Tor., Edm., Mtl., S.J.	15	1132	377	668	**1045**	.923
17.	**Pat Verbeek**, N.J., Hfd., NYR, Dal., Det.	19	1360	515	528	**1043**	.767
18.	**Mark Recchi**, Pit., Phi., Mtl.	13	932	388	622	**1010**	1.084
19.	**Theoren Fleury**, Cgy., Col., NYR	13	948	419	573	**992**	1.046
20.	**Brendan Shanahan**, N.J., St.L., Hfd., Det.	14	1028	466	489	**955**	.929
21.	**Rick Tocchet**, Phi., Pit., L.A., Bos., Wsh., Phx.	17	1130	440	510	**950**	.841
22.	**Jeremy Roenick**, Chi., Phx.	13	908	408	539	**947**	1.043
23.	**Kirk Muller**, N.J., Mtl., NYI, Tor., Fla., Dal.	17	1216	346	577	**923**	.759
24.	**Joe Nieuwendyk**, Cgy., Dal.	15	952	469	440	**909**	.955
25.	**Mike Modano**, Min., Dal.	13	868	382	518	**900**	1.037
26.	**Steve Thomas**, Tor., Chi., NYI, N.J.	17	1076	386	480	**866**	.805
27.	**Mats Sundin**, Que., Tor.	11	848	356	506	**862**	1.017
28.	**Ray Ferraro**, Hfd., NYI, NYR, L.A., Atl.	17	1182	394	467	**861**	.728
29.	**Brian Leetch**, NYR	14	939	205	655	**860**	.916
30.	**Scott Stevens**, Wsh., St.L., N.J.	19	1434	188	671	**859**	.599
31.	**Alexander Mogilny**, Buf., Van., N.J.	12	780	396	445	**841**	1.078
32.	**John MacLean**, N.J., S.J., NYR, Dal.	18	1174	410	426	**836**	.712
33.	**Chris Chelios**, Mtl., Chi., Det.	18	1181	168	667	**835**	.707
34.	**Gary Suter**, Cgy., Chi., S.J.	16	1063	197	615	**812**	.764
35.	**Sergei Fedorov**, Det.	11	747	333	470	**803**	1.075
36.	**Teemu Selanne**, Wpg., Ana., S.J.	9	637	379	422	**801**	1.257
37.	**Rod Brind'Amour**, St.L., Phi., Car.	13	902	302	479	**781**	.866
38.	**Kevin Dineen**, Hfd., Phi., Car., Ott., CBJ	17	1125	350	397	**747**	.664
39.	**Cliff Ronning**, St.L., Van., Phx., Nsh.	15	936	261	482	**743**	.794
40.	**Greg Adams**, N.J., Van., Dal., Phx., Fla.	17	1056	355	388	**743**	.704
41.	**Steve Duchesne**, L.A., Phi., Que., St.L., Ott., Det.	15	1049	224	510	**734**	.700
42.	**Claude Lemieux**, Mtl., N.J., Col., Phx.	18	1047	355	369	**724**	.691
43.	**Kevin Stevens**, Pit., Bos., L.A., NYR, Phi.	14	842	328	393	**721**	.856
44.	**Gary Roberts**, Cgy., Car., Tor.	15	874	343	359	**702**	.803
45.	**Trevor Linden**, Van., NYI, Mtl., Wsh.	13	928	303	397	**700**	.754
46.	**Pavel Bure**, Van., Fla.	10	595	384	296	**680**	1.143
47.	**Kevin Hatcher**, Wsh., Dal., Pit., NYR, Car.	17	1157	227	450	**677**	.585
48.	**Peter Bondra**, Wsh.	11	754	382	282	**664**	.881
49.	**Eric Lindros**, Phi.	8	486	290	369	**659**	1.356
50.	**Tony Amonte**, NYR, Chi.	11	779	325	333	**658**	.845
51.	**Doug Weight**, NYR, Edm.	11	706	180	467	**647**	.916
52.	**Scott Mellanby**, Phi., Edm., Fla., St.L.	16	1079	285	356	**641**	.594
53.	**Shayne Corson**, Mtl., Edm., St.L., Tor.	16	1019	249	386	**635**	.623
54.	**Keith Tkachuk**, Wpg., Phx., St.L.	10	652	329	302	**631**	.968
55.	**John LeClair**, Mtl., Phi.	11	681	316	311	**627**	.921
56.	**Derek King**, NYI, Hfd., Tor., St.L., Ott.	15	830	261	351	**612**	.737
57.	**Scott Young**, Hfd., Pit., Que., Col., Ana., St.L.	13	903	274	335	**609**	.674
58.	**Garry Galley**, L.A., Wsh., Bos., Phi., Buf., NYI	17	1149	125	475	**600**	.522
59.	**James Patrick**, NYR, Hfd., Cgy., Buf.	18	1100	136	463	**599**	.545
60.	**Peter Forsberg**, Que., Col.	7	466	169	411	**580**	1.245
61.	**Andrew Cassels**, Mtl., Hfd., Cgy., Van.	12	794	163	413	**576**	.725
62.	**Dmitri Khristich**, Wsh., L.A., Bos., Tor.	11	750	250	325	**575**	.767
63.	**Adam Graves**, Det., Edm., NYR	14	989	303	264	**567**	.573
64.	**Nicklas Lidstrom**, Det.	10	775	136	431	**567**	.732
65.	**Owen Nolan**, Que., Col., S.J.	11	700	278	289	**567**	.810
66.	**Ulf Dahlen**, NYR, Min., Dal., S.J., Chi., Wsh.	12	834	261	305	**566**	.679
67.	**Fredrik Olausson**, Wpg., Edm., Ana., Pit.	14	931	143	415	**558**	.599
68.	**Alexei Zhamnov**, Wpg., Chi.	9	589	200	348	**548**	.930
69.	**Igor Larionov**, Van., S.J., Det., Fla.	11	728	147	400	**547**	.751
70.	**Ron Sutter**, Phi., St.L., Que., NYI, Bos., S.J., Cgy.	19	1093	205	329	**534**	.489
71.	**Paul Kariya**, Ana.	7	442	243	288	**531**	1.201
72.	**Petr Nedved**, Van., St.L., NYR, Pit.	10	652	234	296	**530**	.813
73.	**Joe Murphy**, Det., Edm., Chi., St.L., S.J., Bos., Wsh.	15	779	233	295	**528**	.678
74.	**Benoit Hogue**, Buf., NYI, Tor., Dal., T.B., Phx.	14	805	215	313	**528**	.656
75.	**Calle Johansson**, Buf., Wsh.	14	1008	114	398	**512**	.508
76.	**Robert Reichel**, Cgy., NYI, Phx.	8	602	209	298	**507**	.842
77.	**Joe Juneau**, Bos., Wsh., Buf., Ott., Phx.	10	616	137	362	**499**	.810
78.	**Bobby Holik**, Hfd., N.J.	11	797	215	282	**497**	.624
79.	**Keith Primeau**, Det., Hfd., Car., Phi.	11	691	220	276	**496**	.718
80.	**Geoff Sanderson**, Hfd., Car., Van., Buf., CBJ	11	724	255	238	**493**	.681
81.	**Tony Granato**, NYR, L.A., S.J.	13	773	248	244	**492**	.636
82.	**Alexei Yashin**, Ott.	8	504	218	273	**491**	.974
83.	**Ziggy Palffy**, NYI, L.A.	8	468	233	253	**486**	1.038
84.	**Eric Desjardins**, Mtl., Phi.	13	906	117	365	**482**	.532
85.	**Alexei Kovalev**, NYR, Pit.	9	626	209	273	**482**	.770
86.	**Nelson Emerson**, St.L., Wpg., Hfd., Car., Chi., Ott., Atl., L.A.	11	730	190	291	**481**	.659
87.	**Valeri Kamensky**, Que., Col., NYR	10	583	193	287	**480**	.823
88.	**Mike Ricci**, Phi., Que., Col., S.J.	11	789	196	279	**475**	.602
89.	**Glen Wesley**, Bos., Hfd., Car.	14	1026	118	353	**471**	.459
90.	**Sergei Zubov**, NYR, Pit., Dal.	9	617	93	373	**466**	.755
91.	**Teppo Numminen**, Wpg., Phx.	13	944	89	367	**456**	.483
92.	**Martin Straka**, Pit., Ott., NYI, Fla.	9	603	159	290	**449**	.745
93.	**Donald Audette**, Buf., L.A., Atl.	12	597	235	212	**447**	.749
94.	**Shawn McEachern**, Pit., L.A., Bos., Ott.	10	675	212	232	**444**	.658
95.	**Martin Gelinas**, Edm., Que., Van., Car.	13	823	218	221	**439**	.533
96.	**Rob Blake**, L.A., Col.	12	675	140	299	**439**	.650
97.	**Rob Brown**, Pit., Hfd., Chi., Dal., L.A.	11	543	190	248	**438**	.807
98.	**Bill Guerin**, N.J., Edm., Bos.	10	655	215	223	**438**	.669
99.	**Jyrki Lumme**, Mtl., Van., Phx.	13	846	104	334	**438**	.518
100.	**Mike Keane**, Mtl., Col., NYR, Dal.	13	954	149	277	**426**	.447

All-Time Games Played Leaders

Regular Season

* active player

		Player	Team	Seasons	GP
	1.	Gordie Howe	Detroit	25	1687
			Hartford	1	80
			Total	**26**	**1,767**
*	2.	Larry Murphy	Los Angeles	3¼	242
			Washington	5½	453
			Minnesota	1¾	121
			Pittsburgh	4½	336
			Toronto	1¾	151
			Detroit	4¼	312
			Total	**21**	**1,615**
	3.	Raymond Bourque	Boston	20¾	1,518
			Colorado	1¼	94
			Total	**22**	**1,612**
*	4.	Mark Messier	Edmonton	12	851
			NY Rangers	7	503
			Vancouver	3	207
			Total	**22**	**1,561**
	5.	**Alex Delvecchio**	**Detroit**	**24**	**1,549**
	6.	John Bucyk	Detroit	2	104
			Boston	21	1,436
			Total	**23**	**1,540**
*	7.	Ron Francis	Hartford	9¾	714
			Pittsburgh	7¼	533
			Carolina	3	242
			Total	**20**	**1,489**
	8.	Wayne Gretzky	Edmonton	9	696
			Los Angeles	7¾	539
			St. Louis	¼	18
			NY Rangers	3	234
			Total	**20**	**1,487**
	9.	Tim Horton	Toronto	19¾	1,185
			NY Rangers	1¼	93
			Pittsburgh	1	44
			Buffalo	2	124
			Total	**24**	**1,446**
*	10.	Scott Stevens	Washington	8	601
			St. Louis	1	78
			New Jersey	10	755
			Total	**19**	**1,434**
	11.	Mike Gartner	Washington	9¾	758
			Minnesota	1	80
			NY Rangers	4	322
			Toronto	2¼	130
			Phoenix	2	142
			Total	**19**	**1,432**
	12.	Harry Howell	NY Rangers	17	1,160
			Oakland	1	55
			California	½	28
			Los Angeles	2½	168
			Total	**21**	**1,411**
	13.	Norm Ullman	Detroit	12½	875
			Toronto	7½	535
			Total	**20**	**1,410**
	14.	Paul Coffey	Edmonton	7	532
			Pittsburgh	4¾	331
			Los Angeles	¾	60
			Detroit	3½	231
			Hartford	¼	20
			Philadelphia	1¾	94
			Chicago	¼	10
			Carolina	1¾	113
			Boston	1	18
			Total	**21**	**1,409**
	15.	Dale Hunter	Quebec	7	523
			Washington	11¾	872
			Colorado	¼	12
			Total	**19**	**1,407**
	16.	**Stan Mikita**	**Chicago**	**22**	**1,394**
	17.	Doug Mohns	Boston	11	710
			Chicago	6½	415
			Minnesota	2½	162
			Atlanta	1	28
			Washington	1	75
			Total	**22**	**1,390**
	18.	Larry Robinson	Montreal	17	1,202
			Los Angeles	3	182
			Total	**20**	**1,384**
	19.	Dean Prentice	NY Rangers	10½	666
			Boston	3	170
			Detroit	3½	230
			Pittsburgh	2	144
			Minnesota	3	168
			Total	**22**	**1,378**
*	20.	Dave Andreychuk	Buffalo	11½	837
			Toronto	3¼	223
			New Jersey	3¼	224
			Boston	¾	63
			Colorado	¼	14
			Total	**19**	**1,361**
*	21.	Pat Verbeek	New Jersey	7	463
			Hartford	5¾	433
			NY Rangers	1¼	88
			Dallas	3	241
			Detroit	2	135
			Total	**19**	**1,360**
*	22.	Phil Housley	Buffalo	8	608
			Winnipeg	3	232
			St. Louis	1	26
			Calgary	4¾	328
			New Jersey	¼	22
			Washington	2	141
			Total	**19**	**1,357**
	23.	Ron Stewart	Toronto	13	838
			Boston	2	126
			St. Louis	½	19
			NY Rangers	4	306
			Vancouver	1	42
			NY Islanders	½	22
			Total	**21**	**1,353**
	24.	Marcel Dionne	Detroit	4	309
			Los Angeles	11¾	921
			NY Rangers	2¼	118
			Total	**18**	**1,348**
*	25.	Doug Gilmour	St. Louis	5	384
			Calgary	3½	266
			Toronto	5¼	392
			New Jersey	1¼	83
			Chicago	1¾	135
			Buffalo	1¼	82
			Total	**18**	**1,342**
	26.	Guy Carbonneau	Montreal	13	912
			St. Louis	1	42
			Dallas	5	364
			Total	**19**	**1,318**
	27.	Red Kelly	Detroit	12½	846
			Toronto	7½	470
			Total	**20**	**1,316**
*	28.	**Steve Yzerman**	**Detroit**	**18**	**1,310**
	29.	Dave Keon	Toronto	15	1,062
			Hartford	3	234
			Total	**18**	**1,296**
	30.	Phil Esposito	Chicago	4	235
			Boston	8¼	625
			NY Rangers	5¾	422
			Total	**18**	**1,282**
	31.	Jean Ratelle	NY Rangers	15¼	862
			Boston	5¾	419
			Total	**21**	**1,281**
	32.	Bryan Trottier	NY Islanders	15	1,123
			Pittsburgh	3	156
			Total	**18**	**1,279**
*	33.	Al MacInnis	Calgary	13	803
			St. Louis	7	459
			Total	**20**	**1,262**
	34.	**Henri Richard**	**Montreal**	**20**	**1,256**
	35.	Craig Ludwig	Montreal	8	597
			NY Islanders	1	75
			Minnesota	2	151
			Dallas	6	433
			Total	**17**	**1,256**
	36.	Kevin Lowe	Edmonton	15	1,037
			NY Rangers	4	217
			Total	**19**	**1,254**
	37.	Jari Kurri	Edmonton	10	754
			Los Angeles	4¾	331
			NY Rangers	¼	14
			Anaheim	1	82
			Colorado	1	70
			Total	**17**	**1,251**
	38.	Bill Gadsby	Chicago	8½	468
			NY Rangers	6½	457
			Detroit	5	323
			Total	**20**	**1,248**
	39.	Allan Stanley	NY Rangers	6¼	307
			Chicago	1¾	111
			Boston	2	129
			Toronto	10	633
			Philadelphia	1	64
			Total	**21**	**1,244**
	40.	Dino Ciccarelli	Minnesota	8¾	602
			Washington	3¼	223
			Detroit	4	254
			Tampa Bay	1½	111
			Florida	1½	42
			Total	**19**	**1,232**
	41.	Eddie Westfall	Boston	11	734
			NY Islanders	7	493
			Total	**18**	**1,227**
	42.	Brad McCrimmon	Boston	3	228
			Philadelphia	5	367
			Calgary	3	231
			Detroit	3	203
			Hartford	3	156
			Phoenix	1	37
			Total	**18**	**1,222**
	43.	Eric Nesterenko	Toronto	5	206
			Chicago	16	1,013
			Total	**21**	**1,219**
*	44.	Kirk Muller	New Jersey	7	556
			Montreal	3¾	267
			NY Islanders	¾	27
			Toronto	1¼	102
			Florida	2¼	162
			Dallas	2	102
			Total	**17**	**1,216**
	45.	Marcel Pronovost	Detroit	16	983
			Toronto	5	223
			Total	**21**	**1,206**
	46.	Denis Savard	Chicago	12¾	881
			Montreal	3	210
			Tampa Bay	1¾	105
			Total	**17**	**1,196**
	47.	Dave Babych	Winnipeg	5¼	390
			Hartford	5¾	349
			Vancouver	6¾	409
			Philadelphia	1	39
			Los Angeles	¼	8
			Total	**19**	**1,195**
	48.	**Gilbert Perrault**	**Buffalo**	**17**	**1,191**
	49.	Dale Hawerchuk	Winnipeg	9	713
			Buffalo	5	342
			St. Louis	¾	66
			Philadelphia	1¼	67
			Total	**16**	**1,188**
	50.	Brian Bellows	Minnesota	10	753
			Montreal	3	200
			Tampa Bay	1¼	86
			Anaheim	¾	62
			Washington	2	87
			Total	**17**	**1,188**
	51.	**George Armstrong**	**Toronto**	**21**	**1,187**
*	52.	Ray Ferraro	Hartford	6¼	442
			NY Islanders	4¾	316
			NY Rangers	¾	65
			Los Angeles	3¼	197
			Atlanta	2	162
			Total	**17**	**1,182**
	53.	Frank Mahovlich	Toronto	11¾	720
			Detroit	2¾	198
			Montreal	3½	263
			Total	**18**	**1,181**
*	54.	Chris Chelios	Montreal	7	402
			Chicago	8¾	664
			Detroit	2¼	115
			Total	**18**	**1,181**
	55.	Bob Carpenter	Washington	6¼	490
			NY Rangers	½	28
			Los Angeles	1¾	120
			Boston	3½	187
			New Jersey	6	353
			Total	**18**	**1,178**
	56.	Don Marshall	Montreal	10	585
			NY Rangers	7	479
			Buffalo	1	62
			Toronto	1	50
			Total	**19**	**1,176**
*	57.	John MacLean	New Jersey	13¼	934
			San Jose	¾	51
			NY Rangers	2¼	161
			Dallas	¾	28
			Total	**17**	**1,174**
	58.	**Bob Gainey**	**Montreal**	**16**	**1,160**
*	59.	Kevin Hatcher	Washington	10	685
			Dallas	2	121
			Pittsburgh	3	220
			NY Rangers	1	74
			Carolina	1	57
			Total	**17**	**1,157**
	60.	Leo Boivin	Toronto	3¼	137
			Boston	11½	717
			Detroit	1½	85
			Pittsburgh	1½	114
			Minnesota	1½	97
			Total	**19**	**1,150**
*	61.	Garry Galley	Los Angeles	5½	361
			Washington	1½	76
			Boston	3½	257
			Philadelphia	3¼	236
			Buffalo	2¼	163
			NY Islanders	1	56
			Total	**17**	**1,149**
	62.	Borje Salming	Toronto	16	1,099
			Detroit	1	49
			Total	**17**	**1,148**
*	63.	**Ken Daneyko**	**New Jersey**	**17**	**1,147**
	64.	**Bobby Clarke**	**Philadelphia**	**15**	**1,144**
*	65.	Vincent Damphousse	Toronto	5	394
			Edmonton	1	80
			Montreal	6¾	519
			San Jose	2¼	139
			Total	**15**	**1,132**

	Player	Team	Seasons	GP
* 66.	**Rick Tocchet**	Philadelphia	9	607
		Pittsburgh	2¼	150
		Los Angeles	1½	80
		Boston	1¼	67
		Washington	¼	13
		Phoenix	2¾	213
		Total	**17**	**1,130**
* 67.	**Adam Oates**	Detroit	4	246
		St. Louis	2¾	195
		Boston	5	368
		Washington	4¼	321
		Total	**16**	**1,130**
68.	**Glenn Anderson**	Edmonton	11½	845
		Toronto	2¾	221
		NY Rangers	¼	12
		St. Louis	1½	51
		Total	**16**	**1,129**
69.	**Dave Ellett**	Winnipeg	6¼	475
		Toronto	6½	446
		New Jersey	¼	20
		Boston	2	136
		St. Louis	1	52
		Total	**16**	**1,129**
70.	**Bob Nevin**	Toronto	5¾	250
		NY Rangers	7¼	505
		Minnesota	2	138
		Los Angeles	3	235
		Total	**18**	**1,128**
71.	**Jamie Macoun**	Calgary	8½	586
		Toronto	6¼	466
		Detroit	1¼	76
		Total	**16**	**1,128**
72.	**Murray Oliver**	Detroit	2½	101
		Boston	6½	429
		Toronto	3	226
		Minnesota	5	371
		Total	**17**	**1,127**
73.	**Bernie Nicholls**	Los Angeles	8½	602
		NY Rangers	1¾	104
		Edmonton	1¼	95
		New Jersey	1½	84
		Chicago	2	107
		San Jose	3	135
		Total	**18**	**1,127**
74.	**Guy Lafleur**	Montreal	14	961
		NY Rangers	1	67
		Quebec	2	98
		Total	**17**	**1,126**
75.	**Jean Beliveau**	**Montreal**	**20**	**1,125**
* 76.	**Kevin Dineen**	Hartford	8¾	587
		Philadelphia	4¼	284
		Carolina	2	121
		Ottawa	1	67
		Columbus	1	66
		Total	**17**	**1,125**
* 77.	**Luc Robitaille**	Los Angeles	12	932
		Pittsburgh	1	46
		NY Rangers	2	146
		Total	**15**	**1,124**
78.	**Doug Harvey**	Montreal	14	890
		NY Rangers	3	151
		Detroit	1	2
		St. Louis	1	70
		Total	**19**	**1,113**
79.	**Brad Park**	NY Rangers	7½	465
		Boston	7½	501
		Detroit	2	147
		Total	**17**	**1,113**
80.	**Lanny McDonald**	Toronto	6½	477
		Colorado	1¾	142
		Calgary	7¾	441
		Total	**16**	**1,111**
81.	**Dave Taylor**	**Los Angeles**	**17**	**1,111**
82.	**Brent Sutter**	NY Islanders	11¼	694
		Chicago	6¾	417
		Total	**18**	**1,111**
83.	**Butch Goring**	Los Angeles	10¾	736
		NY Islanders	4¾	332
		Boston	½	39
		Total	**16**	**1,107**
84.	**Garry Unger**	Toronto	½	15
		Detroit	3	216
		St. Louis	8½	662
		Atlanta	1	79
		Los Angeles	¾	58
		Edmonton	2¼	75
		Total	**16**	**1,105**
85.	**Pit Martin**	Detroit	3¼	119
		Boston	1¾	111
		Chicago	10¼	740
		Vancouver	1¾	131
		Total	**17**	**1,101**
* 86.	**Sylvain Cote**	Hartford	7	382
		Washington	7¾	551
		Toronto	1½	94
		Chicago	½	45
		Dallas	¼	28
		Total	**17**	**1,100**
* 87.	**James Patrick**	NY Rangers	10¼	671
		Hartford	½	47
		Calgary	4¼	217
		Buffalo	3	165
		Total	**18**	**1,100**
88.	**Neal Broten**	Minnesota	13	876
		Dallas	2	116
		New Jersey	1¾	88
		Los Angeles	¼	19
		Total	**17**	**1,099**
89.	**Jay Wells**	Los Angeles	9	604
		Philadelphia	1¾	126
		Buffalo	2	85
		NY Rangers	3¼	186
		St. Louis	1	76
		Tampa Bay	1	21
		Total	**18**	**1,098**
90.	**Gordie Roberts**	Hartford	1½	107
		Minnesota	7	555
		Philadelphia	¼	11
		St. Louis	2½	166
		Pittsburgh	1¾	134
		Boston	2	124
		Total	**15**	**1,097**
91.	**Darryl Sittler**	Toronto	11½	844
		Philadelphia	2½	191
		Detroit	1	61
		Total	**15**	**1,096**
92.	**Craig MacTavish**	Boston	5	217
		Edmonton	8¾	701
		NY Rangers	¼	12
		Philadelphia	1¾	100
		St. Louis	1¼	63
		Total	**17**	**1,093**
* 93.	**Ron Sutter**	Philadelphia	9	555
		St. Louis	2½	163
		Quebec	½	37
		NY Islanders	1	27
		Boston	1	18
		San Jose	4	272
		Calgary	1	21
		Total	**19**	**1,093**
94.	**Michel Goulet**	Quebec	10¾	813
		Chicago	4¼	276
		Total	**15**	**1,089**
95.	**Carol Vadnais**	Montreal	2	42
		Oakland	2	152
		California	1¾	94
		Boston	3½	263
		NY Rangers	6¾	485
		New Jersey	1	51
		Total	**17**	**1,087**
96.	**Brad Marsh**	Atlanta	2	160
		Calgary	1¼	97
		Philadelphia	6¾	514
		Toronto	2¾	181
		Detroit	1¼	75
		Ottawa	1	59
		Total	**15**	**1,086**
97.	**Ulf Samuelsson**	Hartford	6¾	463
		Pittsburgh	4¼	277
		NY Rangers	3¾	287
		Detroit	¼	4
		Philadelphia	1	49
		Total	**16**	**1,080**
98.	**Bob Pulford**	Toronto	14	947
		Los Angeles	2	132
		Total	**16**	**1,079**
* 99.	**Scott Mellanby**	Philadelphia	6	355
		Edmonton	2	149
		Florida	7¾	552
		St. Louis	¼	23
		Total	**16**	**1,079**
100.	**Bobby Smith**	Minnesota	8¼	572
		Montreal	6¾	505
		Total	**15**	**1,077**
* 101.	**Steve Thomas**	Toronto	6	377
		Chicago	4¼	231
		NY Islanders	3¾	275
		New Jersey	3	193
		Total	**17**	**1,076**
102.	**Doug Bodger**	Pittsburgh	4¼	299
		Buffalo	7	479
		San Jose	2¼	166
		New Jersey	½	49
		Los Angeles	1	65
		Vancouver	1	13
		Total	**16**	**1,071**
103.	**Murray Craven**	Detroit	2	46
		Philadelphia	7¼	523
		Hartford	1½	128
		Vancouver	1¼	88
		Chicago	3	157
		San Jose	3	129
		Total	**18**	**1,071**
104.	**Craig Ramsay**	**Buffalo**	**14**	**1,070**
105.	**Mike Ramsey**	Buffalo	13¾	911
		Pittsburgh	1¼	77
		Detroit	3	82
		Total	**18**	**1,070**
106.	**Andy Bathgate**	NY Rangers	11¾	719
		Toronto	1¼	70
		Detroit	2	130
		Pittsburgh	2	150
		Total	**17**	**1,069**
107.	**Ted Lindsay**	Detroit	14	862
		Chicago	3	206
		Total	**17**	**1,068**
108.	**Terry Harper**	Montreal	10	554
		Los Angeles	3	234
		Detroit	4	252
		St. Louis	1	11
		Colorado	1	15
		Total	**19**	**1,066**
109.	**Rod Gilbert**	**NY Rangers**	**18**	**1,065**
110.	**Bobby Hull**	Chicago	15	1,036
		Winnipeg	2/3	18
		Hartford	1/3	9
		Total	**16**	**1,063**
* 111.	**Gary Suter**	Calgary	8½	617
		Chicago	4½	301
		San Jose	3	145
		Total	**16**	**1,063**
112.	**Joe Mullen**	St. Louis	4½	301
		Calgary	4½	345
		Pittsburgh	6	379
		Boston	1	37
		Total	**16**	**1,062**
113.	**Bob Rouse**	Minnesota	5¾	351
		Washington	2	130
		Toronto	3¼	237
		Detroit	4	247
		San Jose	2	96
		Total	**17**	**1,061**
114.	**Denis Potvin**	**NY Islanders**	**15**	**1,060**
115.	**Kelly Miller**	NY Rangers	2½	117
		Washington	12½	940
		Total	**15**	**1,057**
116.	**Jean Guy Talbot**	Montreal	13	791
		Minnesota	¼	4
		Detroit	½	32
		St. Louis	2½	172
		Buffalo	¾	57
		Total	**17**	**1,056**
* 117.	**Greg Adams**	New Jersey	3	186
		Vancouver	7¾	489
		Dallas	3¼	177
		Phoenix	2	144
		Florida	1	60
		Total	**17**	**1,056**
* 118.	**Dave Manson**	Chicago	6¼	431
		Edmonton	2¾	219
		Winnipeg	2¼	139
		Phoenix	¾	66
		Montreal	1½	101
		Dallas	½	26
		Toronto	1	74
		Total	**15**	**1,056**
119.	**Randy Carlyle**	Toronto	2	94
		Pittsburgh	5¾	397
		Winnipeg	9¼	564
		Total	**17**	**1,055**
120.	**Ivan Boldirev**	Boston	1¼	13
		California	2¾	191
		Chicago	4¾	384
		Atlanta	1	65
		Vancouver	2¾	216
		Detroit	2½	183
		Total	**15**	**1,052**
* 121.	**Steve Duchesne**	Los Angeles	5¾	442
		Philadelphia	1¼	89
		Quebec	1	82
		St. Louis	3	163
		Ottawa	2	140
		Detroit	2	133
		Total	**15**	**1,049**
122.	**Geoff Courtnall**	Boston	4¾	259
		Edmonton	¼	12
		Washington	2	159
		St. Louis	5¾	326
		Washington	4¼	292
		Total	**17**	**1,048**
123.	**Eddie Shack**	NY Rangers	2¼	141
		Toronto	8¾	504
		Boston	2	120
		Los Angeles	1¼	84
		Buffalo	1½	111
		Pittsburgh	1¼	87
		Total	**17**	**1,047**
* 124.	**Claude Lemieux**	Montreal	7	281
		New Jersey	5¾	423
		Colorado	4¼	297
		Phoenix	1	46
		Total	**18**	**1,047**
125.	**Rob Ramage**	Colorado	3	234
		St. Louis	5¾	441
		Calgary	1¼	80
		Toronto	2	160
		Minnesota	1	34
		Tampa Bay	¾	66
		Montreal	½	14
		Philadelphia	¾	15
		Total	**15**	**1,044**
126.	**Serge Savard**	Montreal	15	917
		Winnipeg	2	123
		Total	**17**	**1,040**
127.	**Ron Ellis**	**Toronto**	**16**	**1,034**
128.	**Harold Snepsts**	Vancouver	11¾	781
		Minnesota	1	71
		Detroit	3	120
		St. Louis	1¼	61
		Total	**17**	**1,033**

	Player	Team	Seasons	GP
129.	**Ralph Backstrom**	Montreal	14½	844
		Los Angeles	2¼	172
		Chicago	¼	16
		Total	**17**	**1,032**
130.	**Ed Olczyk**	Chicago	5	322
		Toronto	3¼	257
		Winnipeg	3½	214
		NY Rangers	2¼	103
		Los Angeles	¾	67
		Pittsburgh	1¼	68
		Total	**16**	**1,031**
131.	**Dick Duff**	Toronto	9¾	582
		NY Rangers	¾	43
		Montreal	5	305
		Los Angeles	¾	39
		Buffalo	1¾	61
		Total	**18**	**1,030**
* 132.	**Marc Bergevin**	Chicago	4¼	266
		NY Islanders	1¾	76
		Hartford	2	79
		Tampa Bay	3	205
		Detroit	1	70
		St. Louis	4	296
		Pittsburgh	1	38
		Total	**17**	**1,030**
133.	**Russ Courtnall**	Toronto	5¼	309
		Montreal	3¾	250
		Minnesota	1	84
		Dallas	1½	116
		Vancouver	2¼	141
		NY Rangers	¼	14
		Los Angeles	2	115
		Total	**16**	**1,029**
* 134.	**Luke Richardson**	Toronto	4	278
		Edmonton	6	436
		Philadelphia	4	315
		Total	**14**	**1,029**
135.	**John Tonelli**	NY Islanders	7¾	584
		Calgary	2¼	161
		Los Angeles	3	231
		Chicago	¾	33
		Quebec	¼	19
		Total	**14**	**1,028**
136.	**Gaetan Duchesne**	Washington	6	451
		Quebec	2	150
		Minnesota	4	297
		San Jose	1¾	117
		Florida	¼	13
		Total	**14**	**1,028**
* 137.	**Brendan Shanahan**	New Jersey	4	281
		St. Louis	4	277
		Hartford	1¼	76
		Detroit	4¾	394
		Total	**14**	**1,028**
* 138.	**Petr Svoboda**	Montreal	7¾	534
		Buffalo	3	139
		Philadelphia	3¾	232
		Tampa Bay	2½	123
		Total	**17**	**1,028**
139.	**Wayne Cashman**	**Boston**	**17**	**1,027**
* 140.	**Glen Wesley**	Boston	7	537
		Hartford	3	184
		Carolina	4	305
		Total	**14**	**1,026**
141.	**Doug Wilson**	Chicago	14	938
		San Jose	2	86
		Total	**16**	**1,024**
142.	**Jim Neilson**	NY Rangers	12	810
		California	2	98
		Cleveland	2	115
		Total	**16**	**1,023**
143.	**Keith Acton**	Montreal	4¼	228
		Minnesota	4¼	343
		Edmonton	1	72
		Philadelphia	4½	303
		Washington	¼	6
		NY Islanders	¾	71
		Total	**15**	**1,023**
144.	**Don Lever**	Vancouver	7 2/3	593
		Atlanta	1/3	28
		Calgary	1¼	85
		Colorado	¾	59
		New Jersey	3	216
		Buffalo	2	39
		Total	**15**	**1,020**
* 145.	**Shayne Corson**	Montreal	10¾	662
		Edmonton	3	192
		St. Louis	1¼	88
		Toronto	1	77
		Total	**16**	**1,019**
* 146.	**Brett Hull**	Calgary	1¾	57
		St. Louis	10¼	744
		Dallas	3	218
		Total	**15**	**1,019**
147.	**Mike Foligno**	Detroit	2½	186
		Buffalo	9	664
		Toronto	2¾	129
		Florida	¾	39
		Total	**15**	**1,018**
148.	**Charlie Huddy**	Edmonton	11	694
		Los Angeles	3¼	226
		Buffalo	2½	85
		St. Louis	¼	12
		Total	**17**	**1,017**
149.	**Phil Russell**	Chicago	6¾	504
		Atlanta	1¼	93
		Calgary	3	229
		New Jersey	2¾	172
		Buffalo	1¼	18
		Total	**15**	**1,016**
150.	**Brian Propp**	Philadelphia	10¾	790
		Boston	¼	14
		Minnesota	3	147
		Hartford	1	65
		Total	**15**	**1,016**
151.	**Laurie Boschman**	Toronto	2¾	187
		Edmonton	1	73
		Winnipeg	7¼	526
		New Jersey	2	153
		Ottawa	1	70
		Total	**14**	**1,009**
152.	**Dave Christian**	Winnipeg	4	230
		Washington	6½	504
		Boston	1½	128
		St. Louis	1	78
		Chicago	2	69
		Total	**15**	**1,009**
153.	**Dave Lewis**	NY Islanders	6¾	514
		Los Angeles	3¼	221
		New Jersey	3	209
		Detroit	2	64
		Total	**15**	**1,008**
154.	**Bob Murray**	**Chicago**	**15**	**1,008**
* 155.	**Calle Johansson**	Buffalo	1¾	118
		Washington	12¼	890
		Total	**14**	**1,008**
* 156.	**Pierre Turgeon**	Buffalo	4¼	322
		NY Islanders	3½	255
		Montreal	1½	104
		St. Louis	4¾	327
		Total	**14**	**1,008**
157.	**Jim Roberts**	Montreal	9 2/3	611
		St. Louis	5 1/3	395
		Total	**15**	**1,006**
158.	**Steve Larmer**	Chicago	13	891
		NY Rangers	2	115
		Total	**15**	**1,006**
159.	**Rick Middleton**	NY Rangers	2	124
		Boston	12	881
		Total	**14**	**1,005**
160.	**Claude Provost**	**Montreal**	**15**	**1,005**
161.	**Ryan Walter**	Washington	4	307
		Montreal	9	604
		Vancouver	2	92
		Total	**15**	**1,003**
162.	**Vic Hadfield**	NY Rangers	13	839
		Pittsburgh	3	163
		Total	**16**	**1,002**
163.	**Bernie Federko**	St. Louis	14	927
		Detroit	1	73
		Total	**15**	**1,000**

All-Time Penalty-Minute Leaders

* active player

(Regular season. Minimum 2,000 minutes)

	Player	Seasons	Games	Penalty Minutes	Mins. per game
1.	**Tiger Williams**, Tor., Van., Det., L.A., Hfd.	14	962	**3966**	4.12
2.	**Dale Hunter**, Que., Wsh., Col.	20	1407	**3565**	2.53
* 3.	**Marty McSorley**, Pit., Edm., L.A., NYR, S.J., Bos.	17	961	**3381**	3.52
4.	**Tim Hunter**, Cgy., Que., Van., S.J.	17	815	**3146**	3.86
* 5.	**Bob Probert**, Det., Chi.	16	874	**3124**	3.57
6.	**Chris Nilan**, Mtl., NYR, Bos.	13	688	**3043**	4.42
* 7.	**Rick Tocchet**, Phi., Pit., L.A., Bos., Wsh., Phx.	17	1130	**2944**	2.61
* 8.	**Rob Ray**, Buf.	12	777	**2897**	3.73
* 9.	**Craig Berube**, Phi., Tor., Cgy., Wsh., NYI	15	933	**2885**	3.09
* 10.	**Tie Domi**, Tor., NYR, Wpg.	12	710	**2870**	4.04
* 11.	**Pat Verbeek**, N.J., Hfd., NYR, Dal., Det.	19	1360	**2833**	2.08
* 12.	**Dave Manson**, Chi., Edm., Wpg., Phx., Mtl., Dal., Tor.	15	1056	**2759**	2.61
* 13.	**Scott Stevens**, Wsh., St.L., N.J.	19	1434	**2678**	1.87
14.	**Willi Plett**, Atl., Cgy., Min., Bos.	13	834	**2572**	3.08
15.	**Joe Kocur**, Det., NYR, Van.	16	820	**2519**	3.07
* 16.	**Gino Odjick**, Van., NYI, Phi., Mtl.	11	569	**2463**	4.33
17.	**Basil McRae**, Que., Tor., Det., Min., T.B., St.L., Chi.	16	576	**2457**	4.27
18.	**Ulf Samuelsson**, Hfd., Pit., NYR, Det., Phi.	16	1080	**2453**	2.27
* 19.	**Chris Chelios**, Mtl., Chi., Det.	18	1181	**2430**	2.06
* 20.	**Ken Daneyko**, N.J.	18	1147	**2426**	2.12
21.	**Jay Wells**, L.A., Phi., Buf., NYR, St.L., T.B.	18	1098	**2359**	2.15
22.	**Garth Butcher**, Van., St.L., Que., Tor.	14	897	**2302**	2.57
23.	**Shane Churla**, Hfd., Cgy., Min., Dal., L.A., NYR	12	488	**2301**	4.72
24.	**Dave Schultz**, Phi., L.A., Pit., Buf.	9	535	**2294**	4.29
25.	**Laurie Boschman**, Tor., Edm., Wpg., N.J., Ott.	14	1009	**2265**	2.24
26.	**Ken Baumgartner**, L.A., NYI, Tor., Ana., Bos.	13	696	**2244**	3.22
27.	**Rob Ramage**, Col., St.L., Cgy., Tor., Min., T.B., Mtl., Phi.	15	1044	**2226**	2.13
28.	**Bryan Watson**, Mtl., Det., Oak., Pit., St.L., Wsh.	16	878	**2212**	2.52
* 29.	**Gary Roberts**, Cgy., Car., Tor.	15	874	**2188**	2.50
* 30.	**Shayne Corson**, Mtl., Edm., St.L., Tor.	16	1019	**2159**	2.12
* 31.	**Kevin Dineen**, Hfd., Phi., Car., Ott., CBJ	17	1125	**2155**	1.92
32.	**Steve Smith**, Edm., Chi., Cgy.	17	804	**2139**	2.66
33.	**Terry O'Reilly**, Bos.	14	891	**2095**	2.35
34.	**Al Secord**, Bos., Chi., Tor., Phi.	12	766	**2093**	2.73
35.	**Ron Stern**, Van., Cgy., S.J.	13	638	**2077**	3.26
36.	**Mick Vukota**, NYI, T.B., Mtl.	11	574	**2071**	3.61
37.	**Gord Donnelly**, Que., Wpg., Buf., Dal.	12	554	**2069**	3.73
* 38.	**Jeff Odgers**, S.J., Bos., Col., Atl.	10	701	**2058**	2.94
39.	**Mike Foligno**, Det., Buf., Tor., Fla.	16	1018	**2049**	2.01
40.	**Phil Russell**, Chi., Atl., Cgy., N.J., Buf.	17	1016	**2038**	2.01
* 41.	**Stu Grimson**, Cgy., Chi., Ana., Det., Hfd., Car., L.A.	13	699	**2037**	2.91
42.	**Kris King**, Det., NYR, Wpg., Phx., Tor., Chi.	14	849	**2030**	2.39
43.	**Kelly Chase**, St.L., Hfd., Tor.	11	458	**2017**	4.40
* 44.	**Scott Mellanby**, Phi., Edm., Fla., St.L.	16	1079	**2016**	1.87
45.	**Harold Snepsts**, Van., Min., Det., St.L.	18	1033	**2009**	1.94
* 46.	**Lyle Odelein**, Mtl., N.J., Phx., CBJ	12	802	**2003**	2.50

Goaltending Records

All-Time Shutout Leaders

Goaltender	Team	Seasons	Games	Shutouts
Terry Sawchuk	Detroit	14	734	85
(1949-1970)	Boston	2	102	11
	Toronto	3	91	4
	Los Angeles	1	36	2
	NY Rangers	1	8	1
	Total	21	971	**103**
George Hainsworth	Montreal	7½	318	75
(1926-1937)	Toronto	3½	147	19
	Total	11	465	**94**
Glenn Hall	Detroit	4	148	17
(1952-1971)	Chicago	10	618	51
	St. Louis	4	140	16
	Total	18	906	**84**
Jacques Plante	Montreal	11	556	58
(1952-1973)	NY Rangers	2	98	5
	St. Louis	2	69	10
	Toronto	2¾	106	7
	Boston	¼	8	2
	Total	18	837	**82**
Tiny Thompson	Boston	10¼	468	74
(1928-1940)	Detroit	1¾	85	7
	Total	12	553	**81**
Alex Connell	Ottawa	8	293	64
(1924-1937)	Detroit	1	48	6
	NY Americans	1	1	0
	Mtl. Maroons	2	75	11
	Total	12	417	**81**
Tony Esposito	Montreal	1	13	2
(1968-1984)	Chicago	15	873	74
	Total	16	886	**76**
Lorne Chabot	NY Rangers	2	80	21
(1926-1937)	Toronto	5	214	33
	Montreal	1	47	8
	Chicago	1	48	8
	Mtl. Maroons	1	16	2
	NY Americans	1	6	1
	Total	11	411	**73**
Harry Lumley	Detroit	6½	324	26
(1943-1960)	NY Rangers	½	1	0
	Chicago	2	134	5
	Toronto	4	267	34
	Boston	3	78	6
	Total	16	804	**71**
Roy Worters	Pittsburgh Pirates	3	123	22
(1925-1937)	NY Americans	9	360	45
	* Montreal		1	0
	Total	12	484	**67**
Turk Broda (1936-1952)	Toronto	14	629	**62**
John Ross Roach	Toronto	7	222	13
(1921-1935)	NY Rangers	4	89	30
	Detroit	3	180	15
	Total	14	491	**58**
Clint Benedict	Ottawa	7	158	19
(1917-1930)	Mtl. Maroons	6	204	38
	Total	13	362	**57**
Ed Belfour	Chicago	7⅔	415	30
(1988-2001)	San Jose	⅓	13	1
	Dallas	4	247	26
	Total	12	675	**57**
Dominik Hasek	Chicago	2	25	1
(1990-2001)	Buffalo	9	491	55
	Total	11	516	**56**
Bernie Parent	Boston	2	57	1
(1965-1979)	Philadelphia	9½	486	50
	Toronto	1½	65	3
	Total	13	608	**54**
Ed Giacomin	NY Rangers	10¼	539	49
(1965-1978)	Detroit	2¾	71	5
	Total	13	610	**54**
Patrick Roy	Montreal	11½	551	29
(1984-2001)	Colorado	5½	352	23
	Total	17	903	**52**
David Kerr	Mtl. Maroons	3	101	11
(1930-1941)	NY Americans	1	1	0
	NY Rangers	7	324	40
	Total	11	426	**51**
Rogie Vachon	Montreal	5¼	206	13
(1966-1982)	Los Angeles	6¾	389	32
	Detroit	2	109	4
	Boston	2	91	2
	Total	16	795	**51**
Martin Brodeur (1991-2001)	New Jersey	9	519	**51**
Ken Dryden (1970-1979)	Montreal	8	397	**46**
Gump Worsley	NY Rangers	10	582	24
(1952-1974)	Montreal	6½	172	16
	Minnesota	4½	107	3
	Total	21	861	**43**
Charlie Gardiner (1927-1934)	Chicago	7	316	**42**
Frank Brimsek	Boston	9	444	35
(1938-1950)	Chicago	1	70	5
	Total	10	514	**40**
John Vanbiesbrouck	NY Rangers	11	449	16
(1981-2001)	Florida	5	268	13
	Philadelphia	2	112	9
	NY Islanders	¾	44	1
	New Jersey	¼	4	1
	Total	19	877	**40**
Johnny Bower	NY Rangers	3	77	5
(1953-1970)	Toronto	12	475	32
	Total	15	552	**37**
Tom Barrasso	Buffalo	5¼	226	13
(1983-2000)	Pittsburgh	11½	460	22
	Ottawa	¼	7	0
	Total	17	733	**35**

*Played 1 game for Canadiens in 1929-30.

Ten or More Shutouts, One Season

Number of Shutouts	Goaltender	Team	Season	Length of Schedule
22	George Hainsworth	Montreal	1928-29	44
15	Alex Connell	Ottawa	1925-26	36
	Alex Connell	Ottawa	1927-28	44
	Hal Winkler	Boston	1927-28	44
	Tony Esposito	Chicago	1969-70	76
14	George Hainsworth	Montreal	1926-27	44
13	Clint Benedict	Mtl. Maroons	1926-27	44
	Alex Connell	Ottawa	1926-27	44
	George Hainsworth	Montreal	1927-28	44
	John Ross Roach	NY Rangers	1928-29	44
	Roy Worters	NY Americans	1928-29	44
	Harry Lumley	Toronto	1953-54	70
	Dominik Hasek	Buffalo	1997-98	82
12	Tiny Thompson	Boston	1928-29	44
	Lorne Chabot	Toronto	1928-29	44
	Charlie Gardiner	Chicago	1930-31	44
	Terry Sawchuk	Detroit	1951-52	70
	Terry Sawchuk	Detroit	1953-54	70
	Terry Sawchuk	Detroit	1954-55	70
	Glenn Hall	Detroit	1955-56	70
	Bernie Parent	Philadelphia	1973-74	78
	Bernie Parent	Philadelphia	1974-75	80
11	Lorne Chabot	NY Rangers	1927-28	44
	Harry Holmes	Detroit	1927-28	44
	Clint Benedict	Mtl. Maroons	1928-29	44
	Joe Miller	Pittsburgh Pirates	1928-29	44
	Tiny Thompson	Boston	1932-33	48
	Terry Sawchuk	Detroit	1950-51	70
	Dominik Hasek	**Buffalo**	**2000-01**	**82**
10	Lorne Chabot	NY Rangers	1926-27	44
	Roy Worters	Pittsburgh Pirates	1927-28	44
	Dolly Dolson	Detroit	1928-29	44
	John Ross Roach	Detroit	1932-33	48
	Charlie Gardiner	Chicago	1933-34	48
	Tiny Thompson	Boston	1935-36	48
	Frank Brimsek	Boston	1938-39	48
	Bill Durnan	Montreal	1948-49	60
	Gerry McNeil	Montreal	1952-53	70
	Harry Lumley	Toronto	1952-53	70
	Tony Esposito	Chicago	1973-74	78
	Ken Dryden	Montreal	1976-77	80
	Martin Brodeur	New Jersey	1996-97	82
	Martin Brodeur	New Jersey	1997-98	82
	Byron Dafoe	Boston	1998-99	82
	Roman Cechmanek	**Philadelphia**	**2000-01**	**82**

All-Time Win Leaders

(Minimum 215 Wins)

Wins	Goaltender	GP	Dec.	Losses	Ties
484	* Patrick Roy	903	871	277	110
447	Terry Sawchuk	971	949	330	172
435	Jacques Plante	837	827	247	145
423	Tony Esposito	886	880	306	151
407	Glenn Hall	906	896	326	163
403	Grant Fuhr	868	812	295	114
383	* Mike Vernon	763	738	264	91
372	Andy Moog	713	669	209	88
372	John Vanbiesbrouck	877	834	343	119
355	Rogie Vachon	795	773	291	127
353	* Tom Barrasso	733	693	259	81
343	* Ed Belfour	675	647	215	89
335	Gump Worsley	861	837	352	150
330	Harry Lumley	803	801	329	142
317	* Curtis Joseph	655	636	243	76
305	Billy Smith	680	643	233	105
302	Turk Broda	629	627	224	101
296	Ron Hextall	608	579	214	69
294	Mike Liut	663	639	271	74
289	Ed Giacomin	610	594	208	97
286	* Martin Brodeur	519	504	142	76
286	Dan Bouchard	655	631	232	113
284	Tiny Thompson	553	553	194	75
272	* Mike Richter	598	566	226	68
271	Bernie Parent	608	590	198	121
271	Kelly Hrudey	677	624	265	88
270	Gilles Meloche	788	752	351	131
268	Don Beaupre	667	620	277	75
258	Ken Dryden	397	389	57	74
252	Frank Brimsek	514	514	182	80
250	Johnny Bower	552	535	195	90
247	* Dominik Hasek	516	493	174	72
246	George Hainsworth	465	465	145	74
246	Pete Peeters	489	452	155	51
245	* Kirk McLean	612	579	262	72
243	* Sean Burke	633	603	274	86
240	Bill Ranford	647	595	279	76
236	Reggie Lemelin	507	461	162	63
234	Eddie Johnston	592	571	257	80
231	Glenn Resch	571	537	224	82
230	Gerry Cheevers	418	406	102	74
225	* Ken Wregget	575	526	248	53
221	* Chris Osgood	389	377	110	46
219	John Ross Roach	492	491	204	68
215	Greg Millen	604	588	284	89

* active player

Active Shutout Leaders

(Minimum 21 Shutouts)

Goaltender	Teams	Seasons	Games	Shutouts
Ed Belfour	Chi., S.J., Dal.	12	675	**57**
Dominik Hasek	Chicago, Buffalo	11	516	**56**
Patrick Roy	Montreal, Colorado	17	903	**52**
Martin Brodeur	New Jersey	9	519	**51**
Tom Barrasso	Buf., Pit., Ott.	17	733	**35**
Curtis Joseph	St.L., Edm., Tor.	12	655	**32**
Chris Osgood	Detroit	8	389	**30**
Arturs Irbe	S.J., Dal., Van., Car.	10	473	**30**
Guy Hebert	St.L., Ana., NYR	10	491	**28**
Sean Burke	N.J., Hfd., Car., Van., Phi., Fla., Phx.	13	633	**26**
Mike Vernon	Cgy., Det., S.J., Fla.	18	763	**26**
Tommy Salo	NY Islanders, Edmonton	7	343	**24**
Byron Dafoe	Wsh., L.A., Bos.	9	316	**22**
Jeff Hackett	NYI, S.J., Chi., Mtl.	12	422	**22**
Mike Richter	NY Rangers	12	598	**22**
Kirk McLean	N.J., Van., Car., Fla., NYR	16	612	**22**
Nikolai Khabibulin	Wpg., Phx., T.B.	6	286	**21**
Olaf Kolzig	Washington	10	344	**21**
Jocelyn Thibault	Que., Col., Mtl., Chi.	8	393	**21**

Goals Against Average Leaders

(Minimum 13 games played, 1994-95; minimum 26 games played, 1992-93 to 1993-94; 25 games played, 1926-27 to 1991-92, 1995-96 to date; 15 games played, 1917-18 to 1925-26.)

Season	Goaltender and Club	GP	Mins.	GA	SO	AVG.
2000-01	Marty Turco, Dallas	26	1,266	40	3	1.90
1999-2000	Brian Boucher, Philadelphia	35	2,038	65	4	1.91
1998-99	Ron Tugnutt, Ottawa	43	2,508	75	3	1.79
1997-98	Ed Belfour, Dallas	61	3,581	112	9	1.88
1996-97	Martin Brodeur, New Jersey	67	3,838	120	10	1.88
1995-96	Ron Hextall, Philadelphia	53	3,102	112	4	2.17
1994-95	Dominik Hasek, Buffalo	41	2,416	85	5	2.11
1993-94	Dominik Hasek, Buffalo	58	3,358	109	7	1.95
1992-93	Felix Potvin, Toronto	48	2,781	116	2	2.50
1991-92	Patrick Roy, Montreal	67	3,935	155	5	2.36
1990-91	Ed Belfour, Chicago	74	4,127	170	4	2.47
1989-90	Mike Liut, Hartford, Washington	37	2,161	91	4	2.53
1988-89	Patrick Roy, Montreal	48	2,744	113	4	2.47
1987-88	Pete Peeters, Washington	35	1,896	88	2	2.78
1986-87	Brian Hayward, Montreal	37	2,178	102	1	2.81
1985-86	Bob Froese, Philadelphia	51	2,728	116	5	2.55
1984-85	Tom Barrasso, Buffalo	54	3,248	144	5	2.66
1983-84	Pat Riggin, Washington	41	2,299	102	4	2.66
1982-83	Pete Peeters, Boston	62	3,611	142	8	2.36
1981-82	Denis Herron, Montreal	27	1,547	68	3	2.64
1980-81	Richard Sevigny, Montreal	33	1,777	71	2	2.40
1979-80	Bob Sauve, Buffalo	32	1,880	74	4	2.36
1978-79	Ken Dryden, Montreal	47	2,814	108	5	2.30
1977-78	Ken Dryden, Montreal	52	3,071	105	5	2.05
1976-77	Michel Larocque, Montreal	26	1,525	53	4	2.09
1975-76	Ken Dryden, Montreal	62	3,580	121	8	2.03
1974-75	Bernie Parent, Philadelphia	68	4,041	137	12	2.03
1973-74	Bernie Parent, Philadelphia	73	4,314	136	12	1.89
1972-73	Ken Dryden, Montreal	54	3,165	119	6	2.26
1971-72	Tony Esposito, Chicago	48	2,780	82	9	1.77
1970-71	Jacques Plante, Toronto	40	2,329	73	4	1.88
1969-70	Ernie Wakely, St. Louis	30	1,651	58	4	2.11
1968-69	Jacques Plante, St. Louis	37	2,139	70	5	1.96
1967-68	Gump Worsley, Montreal	40	2,213	73	6	1.98
1966-67	Glenn Hall, Chicago	32	1,664	66	2	2.38
1965-66	Johnny Bower, Toronto	35	1,998	75	3	2.25
1964-65	Johnny Bower, Toronto	34	2,040	81	3	2.38
1963-64	Johnny Bower, Toronto	51	3,009	106	5	2.11
1962-63	Don Simmons, Toronto	28	1,680	69	1	2.46
1961-62	Jacques Plante, Montreal	70	4,200	166	4	2.37
1960-61	Charlie Hodge, Montreal	30	1,800	74	4	2.47
1959-60	Jacques Plante, Montreal	69	4,140	175	3	2.54
1958-59	Jacques Plante, Montreal	67	4,000	144	9	2.16
1957-58	Jacques Plante, Montreal	57	3,386	119	9	2.11
1956-57	Jacques Plante, Montreal	61	3,660	122	9	2.00
1955-56	Jacques Plante, Montreal	64	3,840	119	7	1.86
1954-55	Harry Lumley, Toronto	69	4,140	134	8	1.94
1953-54	Harry Lumley, Toronto	69	4,140	128	13	1.86
1952-53	Terry Sawchuk, Detroit	63	3,780	120	9	1.90
1951-52	Terry Sawchuk, Detroit	70	4,200	133	12	1.90
1950-51	Al Rollins, Toronto	40	2,367	70	5	1.77
1949-50	Bill Durnan, Montreal	64	3,840	141	8	2.20
1948-49	Bill Durnan, Montreal	60	3,600	126	10	2.10
1947-48	Turk Broda, Toronto	60	3,600	143	5	2.38
1946-47	Bill Durnan, Montreal	60	3,600	138	4	2.30
1945-46	Bill Durnan, Montreal	40	2,400	104	4	2.60
1944-45	Bill Durnan, Montreal	50	3,000	121	1	2.42
1943-44	Bill Durnan, Montreal	50	3,000	109	2	2.18
1942-43	Johnny Mowers, Detroit	50	3,010	124	6	2.47
1941-42	Frank Brimsek, Boston	47	2,930	115	3	2.35
1940-41	Turk Broda, Toronto	48	2,970	99	5	2.00
1939-40	Dave Kerr, NY Rangers	48	3,000	77	8	1.54
1938-39	Frank Brimsek, Boston	43	2,610	68	10	1.56
1937-38	Tiny Thompson, Boston	48	2,970	89	7	1.80
1936-37	Norman Smith, Detroit	48	2,980	102	6	2.05
1935-36	Tiny Thompson, Boston	48	2,930	82	10	1.68
1934-35	Lorne Chabot, Chicago	48	2,940	88	8	1.80
1933-34	Wilf Cude, Detroit, Montreal	30	1,920	47	5	1.47
1932-33	Tiny Thompson, Boston	48	3,000	88	11	1.76
1931-32	Chuck Gardiner, Chicago	48	2,989	92	4	1.85
1930-31	Roy Worters, NY Americans	44	2,760	74	8	1.61
1929-30	Tiny Thompson, Boston	44	2,680	98	3	2.19
1928-29	George Hainsworth, Montreal	44	2,800	43	22	0.92
1927-28	George Hainsworth, Montreal	44	2,730	48	13	1.05
1926-27	Clint Benedict, Mtl. Maroons	43	2,748	65	13	1.42
1925-26	Alex Connell, Ottawa	36	2,251	42	15	1.12
1924-25	Georges Vezina, Montreal	30	1,860	56	5	1.81
1923-24	Georges Vezina, Montreal	24	1,459	48	3	1.97
1922-23	Clint Benedict, Ottawa	24	1,478	54	4	2.18
1921-22	Clint Benedict, Ottawa	24	1,508	84	2	3.34
1920-21	Clint Benedict, Ottawa	24	1,457	75	2	3.09
1919-20	Clint Benedict, Ottawa	24	1,444	64	5	2.66
1918-19	Clint Benedict, Ottawa	18	1,113	53	2	2.86
1917-18	Georges Vezina, Montreal	21	1,282	84	1	3.93

All-Time Regular Season NHL Coaching Register

Regular Season, 1917-2001

Coach	Team	Games Coached	Wins	Losses	Ties	Year	Cup Wins	Career
Abel, Sid	Chicago	140	39	79	22	2		
	Detroit	811	340	339	132	12		
	St. Louis	10	3	6	1	1		
	Kansas City	3	0	3	0	1		
	Total	964	382	427	155	16		1952-76
Adams, Jack	Detroit	964	413	390	161	20	3	1927-47
Allen, Keith	Philadelphia	150	51	67	32	2		1967-69
Allison, Dave	Ottawa	25	2	22	1	1		1995-96
Anderson, Jim	Washington	54	4	45	5	1		1974-75
Angotti, Lou	St. Louis	32	6	20	6	2		
	Pittsburgh	80	16	58	6	1		
	Total	112	22	78	12	3		1973-84
Arbour, Al	St. Louis	107	42	40	25	3		
	NY Islanders	1499	739	537	223	19	4	
	Total	1606	781	577	248	22	4	1970-94
Armstrong, George	Toronto	47	17	26	4	1		1988-89
Barber, Bill	Philadelphia	54	31	16	7	1		2000-01
Barkley, Doug	Detroit	77	20	46	11	3		1970-76
Beaulieu, Andre	Minnesota	32	6	23	3	1		1977-78
Belisle, Danny	Washington	96	28	51	17	2		1978-80
Berenson, Red	St. Louis	204	100	72	32	3		1979-82
Bergeron, Michel	Quebec	634	265	283	86	8		
	NY Rangers	158	73	67	18	2		
	Total	792	338	350	104	10		1980-90
Berry, Bob	Los Angeles	240	107	94	39	3		
	Montreal	223	116	71	36	3		
	Pittsburgh	240	88	127	25	3		
	St. Louis	157	73	63	21	2		
	Total	860	384	355	121	11		1978-94
Beverley, Nick	Toronto	17	9	6	2	1		1995-96
Blackburn, Don	Hartford	140	42	63	35	2		1979-81
Blair, Wren	Minnesota	147	48	65	34	3		1967-70
Blake, Toe	Montreal	914	500	255	159	13	8	1955-68
Boileau, Marc	Pittsburgh	151	66	61	24	3		1973-76
Boivin, Leo	St. Louis	97	28	53	16	2		1975-78
Boucher, Frank	NY Rangers	527	181	263	83	11	1	1939-54
Boucher, Georges	Mtl. Maroons	12	6	5	1	1		
	Ottawa	48	13	29	6	1		
	St. Louis	35	9	20	6	1		
	Boston	70	22	32	16	1		
	Total	165	50	86	29	4		1930-50
Bowman, Scotty	St. Louis	238	110	83	45	4		
	Montreal	634	419	110	105	8	5	
	Buffalo	404	210	134	60	7		
	Pittsburgh	164	95	53	16	2	1	
	Detroit	619	359	183	77	8	2	
	Total	2059	1193	563	303	29	8	1967-01
Bowness, Rick	Winnipeg	28	8	17	3	1		
	Boston	80	36	32	12	1		
	Ottawa	235	39	178	18	4		
	NY Islanders	100	38	50	12	2		
	Total	443	121	277	45	8		1988-98
Brooks, Herb	NY Rangers	285	131	113	41	4		
	Minnesota	80	19	48	13	1		
	New Jersey	84	40	37	7	1		
	Pittsburgh	58	29	24	5	1		
	Total	507	219	222	66	7		1981-00
Brophy, John	Toronto	193	64	111	18	3		1986-89
Burnett, George	Edmonton	35	12	20	3	1		1994-95
Burns, Charlie	Minnesota	86	22	50	14	2		1969-75
Burns, Pat	Montreal	320	174	104	42	4		
	Toronto	281	133	107	41	4		
	Boston	254	105	103	46	4		
	Total	855	412	314	129	12		1988-01
Bush, Eddie	Kansas City	32	1	23	8	1		1975-76
Campbell, Colin	NY Rangers	269	118	108	43	4		1994-98
Carpenter, Doug	New Jersey	290	100	166	24	4		
	Toronto	91	39	47	5	2		
	Total	381	139	213	29	6		1984-91
Carroll, Dick	Toronto	40	18	22	0	2	1	1917-19
Carroll, Frank	Toronto	24	15	9	0	1		1920-21
Cashman, Wayne	Philadelphia	61	32	20	9	1		1997-98
Chambers, Dave	Quebec	98	19	64	15	2		1990-92
Charron, Guy	Calgary	16	6	7	3	1		
	Anaheim	49	14	28	7	1		
	Total	65	20	35	10	2		1991-01
Cheevers, Gerry	Boston	376	204	126	46	5		1980-85
Cherry, Don	Boston	400	231	105	64	5		
	Colorado	80	19	48	13	1		
	Total	480	250	153	77	6		1974-80
Clancy, King	Mtl. Maroons	18	6	11	1	1		
	Toronto	210	80	81	49	3		
	Total	228	86	92	50	4		1937-56
Clapper, Dit	Boston	230	102	88	40	4		1945-49
Cleghorn, Odie	Pittsburgh	168	62	86	20	4		1925-29
Cleghorn, Sprague	Mtl. Maroons	48	19	22	7	1		1931-32

Coach	Team	Games Coached	Wins	Losses	Ties	Years	Cup Wins	Career
Conacher, Charlie	Chicago	162	56	84	22	3		1947-50
Conacher, Lionel	NY Americans	44	14	25	5	1		1929-30
Constantine, Kevin	San Jose	157	55	78	24	3		
	Pittsburgh	188	86	67	35	3		
	Total	345	141	145	59	6		1993-00
Cook, Bill	NY Rangers	117	34	59	24	2		1951-53
Crawford, Marc	Quebec	48	30	13	5	1		
	Colorado	246	135	75	36	3	1	
	Vancouver	201	74	95	32	3		
	Total	495	239	183	73	7	1	1994-01
Creamer, Pierre	Pittsburgh	80	36	35	9	1		1987-88
Creighton, Fred	Atlanta	348	156	136	56	5		
	Boston	73	40	20	13	1		
	Total	421	196	156	69	6		1974-80
Crisp, Terry	Calgary	240	144	63	33	3	1	
	Tampa Bay	391	142	204	45	6		
	Total	631	286	267	78	9	1	1987-98
Crozier, Joe	Buffalo	192	77	80	35	3		
	Toronto	40	13	22	5	1		
	Total	232	90	102	40	4		1971-81
Crozier, Roger	Washington	1	0	1	0	1		1981-82
Cunniff, John	Hartford	13	3	9	1	1		
	New Jersey	133	59	56	18	2		
	Total	146	62	65	19	3		1982-91
Curry, Alex	Ottawa	36	24	8	4	1		1925-26
Dandurand, Leo	Montreal	163	78	76	9	6	1	1921-35
Day, Hap	Toronto	546	259	206	81	10	5	1940-50
Dea, Billy	Detroit	11	3	8	0	1		1981-82
Delvecchio, Alex	Detroit	245	82	131	32	4		1973-77
Demers, Jacques	Quebec	80	25	44	11	1		
	St. Louis	240	106	106	28	3		
	Detroit	320	137	136	47	4		
	Montreal	221	107	87	27	4	1	
	Tampa Bay	145	34	94	17	2		
	Total	1006	409	467	130	14	1	1979-99
Denneny, Cy	Boston	44	26	13	5	1	1	
	Ottawa	48	11	27	10	1		
	Total	92	37	40	15	2	1	1928-33
Dineen, Bill	Philadelphia	140	60	60	20	2		1991-93
Dudley, Rick	Buffalo	188	85	72	31	3		1989-92
Duff, Dick	Toronto	2	0	2	0	1		1979-80
Dugal, Jules	Montreal	18	9	6	3	1		1938-39
Duncan, Art	Detroit	33	10	21	2	1		
	Toronto	47	21	16	10	2	1	
	Total	80	31	37	12	3	1	1926-32
Dutton, Red	NY Americans	288	90	151	47	6		
	Brooklyn	48	16	29	3	1		
	Total	336	106	180	50	7		1935-42
Eddolls, Frank	Chicago	70	13	40	17	1		1954-55
Esposito, Phil	NY Rangers	45	24	21	0	2		1986-89
Evans, Jack	California	80	27	42	11	1		
	Cleveland	160	47	87	26	2		
	Hartford	374	163	174	37	5		
	Total	614	237	303	74	8		1975-88
Fashoway, Gordie	Oakland	10	4	5	1	1		1967-68
Ferguson, John	NY Rangers	121	43	59	19	2		
	Winnipeg	14	7	6	1	1		
	Total	135	50	65	20	3		1975-86
Filion, Maurice	Quebec	6	1	3	2	1		1980-81
Francis, Bob	Phoenix	164	74	65	25	2		1999-01
Francis, Emile	NY Rangers	654	342	209	103	10		
	St. Louis	124	46	64	14	3		
	Total	778	388	273	117	13		1965-83
Fraser, Curt	Atlanta	164	37	108	19	2		1999-01
Fredrickson, Frank	Pittsburgh	44	5	36	3	1		1929-30
Ftorek, Robbie	Los Angeles	132	65	56	11	2		
	New Jersey	156	88	49	19	2		
	Total	288	153	105	30	4		1987-00
Gadsby, Bill	Detroit	78	35	31	12	2		1968-70
Gainey, Bob	Minnesota	244	95	119	30	3		
	Dallas	171	70	71	30	3		
	Total	415	165	190	60	6		1990-96
Gardiner, Herb	Chicago	32	5	23	4	1		1929-30
Gardner, Jimmy	Hamilton	30	19	10	1	1		1924-25
Garvin, Ted	Detroit	11	2	8	1	1		1973-74
Geoffrion, Bernie	NY Rangers	43	22	18	3	1		
	Atlanta	208	77	92	39	3		
	Montreal	30	15	9	6	1		
	Total	281	114	119	48	5		1968-80
Gerard, Eddie	Ottawa	22	9	13	0	1		
	Mtl. Maroons	294	129	122	43	7	1	
	NY Americans	92	34	40	18	2		
	St. Louis	13	2	11	0	1		
	Total	421	174	186	61	11	1	1917-35
Gilbert, Greg	Calgary	14	4	8	2	1		2000-01
Gill, David	Ottawa	132	64	41	27	3	1	1926-29
Glover, Fred	Oakland	152	51	76	25	2		
	California	204	45	131	28	4		
	Los Angeles	68	18	42	8	1		
	Total	424	114	249	61	7		1968-74
Goodfellow, Ebbie	Chicago	140	30	91	19	2		1950-52
Gordon, Jackie	Minnesota	289	116	123	50	5		1970-75
Goring, Butch	Boston	93	42	38	13	2		
	NY Islanders	147	41	92	14	2		
	Total	240	83	130	27	4		1985-01

Coach	Team	Games Coached	Wins	Losses	Ties	Years	Cup Wins	Career
Gorman, Tommy	NY Americans	80	31	33	16	2		
	Chicago	73	28	28	17	2	1	
	Mtl. Maroons	174	74	71	29	4	1	
	Total	327	133	132	62	8	2	1925-38
Gottselig, Johnny	Chicago	187	62	105	20	4		1944-48
Goyette, Phil	NY Islanders	48	6	38	4	1		1972-73
Graham, Dirk	Chicago	59	16	35	8	1		1998-99
Green, Gary	Washington	157	50	78	29	3		1979-82
Green, Pete	Ottawa	150	94	52	4	6	3	1919-25
Green, Shorty	NY Americans	44	11	27	6	1		1927-28
Green, Ted	Edmonton	188	65	102	21	3		1991-94
Guidolin, Aldo	Colorado	59	12	39	8	1		1978-79
Guidolin, Bep	Boston	104	72	23	9	2		
	Kansas City	125	26	84	15	2		
	Total	229	98	107	24	4		1972-76
Harkness, Ned	Detroit	38	12	22	4	1		1970-71
Harris, Ted	Minnesota	179	48	104	27	3		1975-78
Hart, Cecil	Montreal	394	196	125	73	9	2	1926-39
Hartley, Bob	Colorado	246	138	77	31	3	1	1998-01
Hartsburg, Craig	Chicago	246	104	102	40	3		
	Anaheim	197	80	88	29	3		
	Total	443	184	190	69	6		1995-01
Harvey, Doug	NY Rangers	70	26	32	12	1		1961-62
Hay, Don	Phoenix	82	38	37	7	1		
	Calgary	68	23	32	13	1		
	Total	150	61	69	20	2		1996-01
Heffernan, Frank	Toronto	12	5	7	0	1		1919-20
Henning, Lorne	Minnesota	158	68	72	18	2		
	NY Islanders	65	19	39	7	2		
	Total	223	87	111	25	4		1985-01
Hitchcock, Ken	Dallas	453	254	145	54	6	1	1995-01
Hlinka, Ivan	Pittsburgh	82	42	31	9	1		2000-01
Holmgren, Paul	Philadelphia	264	107	126	31	4		
	Hartford	161	54	93	14	4		
	Total	425	161	219	45	8		1988-96
Howell, Harry	Minnesota	11	3	6	2	1		1978-79
Imlach, Punch	Toronto	770	370	275	125	12	4	
	Buffalo	119	32	62	25	2		
	Total	889	402	337	150	14	4	1958-80
Ingarfield, Earl	NY Islanders	30	6	22	2	1		1972-73
Inglis, Bill	Buffalo	56	28	18	10	1		1978-79
Irvin, Dick	Chicago	126	45	62	19	3		
	Toronto	427	216	152	59	9	1	
	Montreal	896	431	313	152	15	3	
	Total	1449	692	527	230	27	4	1928-56
Ivan, Tommy	Detroit	470	262	118	90	7	3	
	Chicago	103	26	56	21	2		
	Total	573	288	174	111	9	3	1947-58
Iverson, Emil	Chicago	21	8	7	6	1		1932-33
Johnson, Bob	Calgary	400	193	155	52	5		
	Pittsburgh	80	41	33	6	1	1	
	Total	480	234	188	58	6	1	1982-91
Johnson, Tom	Boston	208	142	43	23	3	1	1970-73
Johnston, Eddie	Chicago	80	34	27	19	1		
	Pittsburgh	516	232	224	60	7		
	Total	596	266	251	79	8		1979-97
Johnston, Marshall	California	69	13	45	11	2		
	Colorado	56	15	32	9	1		
	Total	125	28	77	20	3		1973-82
Kasper, Steve	Boston	164	66	78	20	2		1995-97
Keats, Duke	Detroit	11	2	7	2	1		1926-27
Keenan, Mike	Philadelphia	320	190	102	28	4		
	Chicago	320	153	126	41	4		
	NY Rangers	84	52	24	8	1	1	
	St. Louis	163	75	66	22	3		
	Vancouver	108	36	54	18	2		
	Boston	74	33	34	7	1		
	Total	1069	539	406	124	15	1	1984-01
Kelly, Pat	Colorado	101	22	54	25	2		1977-79
Kelly, Red	Los Angeles	150	55	75	20	2		
	Pittsburgh	274	90	132	52	4		
	Toronto	318	133	123	62	4		
	Total	742	278	330	134	10		1967-77
King, Dave	Calgary	216	109	76	31	3		
	Columbus	82	28	45	9	1		
	Total	298	137	121	40	4		1992-01
Kingston, George	San Jose	164	28	129	7	2		1991-93
Kish, Larry	Hartford	49	12	32	5	1		1982-83
Kromm, Bobby	Detroit	231	79	111	41	3		1977-80
Kurtenbach, Orland	Vancouver	125	36	62	27	2		1976-78
LaForge, Bill	Vancouver	20	4	14	2	1		1984-85
Lalonde, Newsy	Montreal	207	96	97	14	8		
	NY Americans	44	17	25	2	1		
	Ottawa	88	31	45	12	2		
	Total	339	144	167	28	11		1917-35
Lapointe, Ron	Quebec	89	33	50	6	2		1987-89
Laycoe, Hal	Los Angeles	24	5	18	1	1		
	Vancouver	156	44	96	16	2		
	Total	180	49	114	17	3		1969-72
Lehman, Hugh	Chicago	21	3	17	1	1		1927-28
Lemaire, Jacques	Montreal	97	48	37	12	2		
	New Jersey	378	199	122	57	5	1	
	Minnesota	82	25	44	13	1		
	Total	557	272	203	82	8	1	1983-01
Lepine, Pit	Montreal	48	10	33	5	1		1939-40
LeSueur, Percy	Hamilton	10	3	7	0	1		1923-24
Lewis, Dave*	Detroit	5	4	1	0	1		1998-99

*Results shared with co-coach Barry Smith

Coach	Team	Games Coached	Wins	Losses	Ties	Years	Cup Wins	Career
Ley, Rick	Hartford	160	69	71	20	2		
	Vancouver	124	47	50	27	2		
	Total	284	116	121	47	4		1989-96
Lindsay, Ted	Detroit	29	5	21	3	2		1979-81
Long, Barry	Winnipeg	205	87	93	25	3		1983-86
Loughlin, Clem	Chicago	144	61	63	20	3		1934-37
Low, Ron	Edmonton	341	139	162	40	5		
	NY Rangers	82	33	44	5	1		
	Total	423	172	206	45	6		1994-01
Lowe, Kevin	Edmonton	82	32	34	16	1		1999-00
Ludzik, Steve	Tampa Bay	121	31	76	14	2		1999-01
MacDonald, Parker	Minnesota	61	20	30	11	1		
	Los Angeles	42	13	24	5	1		
	Total	103	33	54	16	2		1973-82
MacLean, Doug	Florida	187	83	71	33	3		1995-98
MacMillan, Bill	Colorado	80	22	45	13	1		
	New Jersey	100	19	67	14	2		
	Total	180	41	112	27	3		1980-84
MacNeil, Al	Montreal	55	31	15	9	1	1	
	Atlanta	80	35	32	13	1		
	Calgary	160	68	61	31	2		
	Total	295	134	108	53	4	1	1970-82
MacTavish, Craig	Edmonton	82	39	31	12	1		2000-01
Magnuson, Keith	Chicago	132	49	57	26	2		1980-82
Mahoney, Bill	Minnesota	93	42	39	12	2		1983-85
Maloney, Dan	Toronto	160	45	100	15	2		
	Winnipeg	212	91	93	28	3		
	Total	372	136	193	43	5		1984-89
Maloney, Phil	Vancouver	232	95	105	32	4		1973-77
Mantha, Sylvio	Montreal	48	11	26	11	1		1935-36
Marshall, Bert	Colorado	24	3	17	4	1		1981-82
Martin, Jacques	St. Louis	160	66	71	23	2		
	Ottawa	448	208	171	69	6		
	Total	608	274	242	92	8		1986-01
Matheson, Godfrey	Chicago	2	0	2	0	1		1932-33
Maurice, Paul	Hartford	152	61	72	19	2		
	Carolina	328	142	141	45	4		
	Total	480	203	213	64	6		1995-01
Maxner, Wayne	Detroit	129	34	68	27	2		1980-82
McCammon, Bob	Philadelphia	218	119	68	31	4		
	Vancouver	294	102	156	36	4		
	Total	512	221	224	67	8		1978-91
McCreary, Bill	St. Louis	24	6	14	4	1		
	Vancouver	41	9	25	7	1		
	California	32	8	20	4	1		
	Total	97	23	59	15	3		1971-75
McGuire, Pierre	Hartford	67	23	37	7	1		1993-94
McLellan, John	Toronto	310	126	139	45	4		1969-73
McVie, Tom	Washington	204	49	122	33	3		
	Winnipeg	105	20	67	18	2		
	New Jersey	153	57	74	22	3		
	Total	462	126	263	73	8		1975-92
Meeker, Howie	Toronto	70	21	34	15	1		1956-57
Melrose, Barry	Los Angeles	209	79	101	29	3		1992-95
Milbury, Mike	Boston	160	90	49	21	2		
	NY Islanders	191	56	111	24	4		
	Total	351	146	160	45	6		1989-99
Molleken, Lorne	Chicago	47	18	21	8	2		1998-00
Muckler, John	Minnesota	35	6	23	6	1		
	Edmonton	160	75	65	20	2	1	
	Buffalo	268	125	109	34	4		
	NY Rangers	185	70	91	24	3		
	Total	648	276	288	84	10	1	1968-00
Muldoon, Pete	Chicago	44	19	22	3	1		1926-27
Munro, Dunc	Mtl. Maroons	76	37	29	10	2		1929-31
Murdoch, Bob	Chicago	80	30	41	9	1		
	Winnipeg	160	63	75	22	2		
	Total	240	93	116	31	3		1987-91
Murphy, Mike	Los Angeles	65	20	37	8	2		
	Toronto	164	60	87	17	2		
	Total	229	80	124	25	4		1986-98
Murray, Andy	Los Angeles	164	77	62	25	2		1999-01
Murray, Bryan	Washington	672	343	246	83	9		
	Detroit	244	124	91	29	3		
	Florida	59	17	31	11	1		
	Total	975	484	368	123	13		1981-98
Murray, Terry	Washington	325	163	134	28	5		
	Philadelphia	212	118	64	30	3		
	Florida	200	79	90	31	3		
	Total	737	360	288	89	11		1989-01
Nanne, Lou	Minnesota	29	7	18	4	1		1977-78
Neale, Harry	Vancouver	407	142	189	76	6		
	Detroit	35	8	23	4	1		
	Total	442	150	212	80	7		1978-86
Neilson, Roger	Toronto	160	75	62	23	2		
	Buffalo	80	39	20	21	1		
	Vancouver	133	51	61	21	3		
	Los Angeles	28	8	17	3	1		
	NY Rangers	280	141	104	35	4		
	Florida	132	53	56	23	2		
	Philadelphia	185	92	60	33	3		
	Total	998	459	380	159	16		1977-00
Nolan, Ted	Buffalo	164	73	72	19	2		1995-97
Nykoluk, Mike	Toronto	280	89	144	47	4		1980-84
O'Donohue, George	Toronto	29	15	13	1	2	1	1921-23
O'Reilly, Terry	Boston	227	115	86	26	3		1986-89
Oliver, Murray	Minnesota	41	21	12	8	2		1981-83
Olmstead, Bert	Oakland	64	11	37	16	1		1967-68

Coach	Team	Games Coached	Wins	Losses	Ties	Years	Cup Wins	Career
Paddock, John	**Winnipeg**	**281**	**106**	**138**	**37**	**4**		**1991-95**
Page, Pierre	Minnesota	160	63	77	20	2		
	Quebec	230	98	103	29	3		
	Calgary	164	66	78	20	2		
	Anaheim	82	26	43	13	1		
	Total	**636**	**253**	**301**	**82**	**8**		**1988-98**
Park, Brad	**Detroit**	**45**	**9**	**34**	**2**	**1**		**1985-86**
Paterson, Rick	**Tampa Bay**	**8**	**0**	**8**	**0**	**1**		**1997-98**
Patrick, Craig	NY Rangers	95	37	45	13	2		
	Pittsburgh	74	29	36	9	2		
	Total	**169**	**66**	**81**	**22**	**4**		**1980-97**
Patrick, Frank	**Boston**	**96**	**48**	**36**	**12**	**2**		**1934-36**
Patrick, Lester	**NY Rangers**	**604**	**281**	**216**	**107**	**13**	**2**	**1926-39**
Patrick, Lynn	NY Rangers	107	40	51	16	2		
	Boston	310	117	130	63	5		
	St. Louis	26	8	15	3	3		
	Total	**443**	**165**	**196**	**82**	**10**		**1948-76**
Patrick, Muzz	**NY Rangers**	**136**	**43**	**66**	**27**	**4**		**1953-63**
Perron, Jean	Montreal	240	126	84	30	3	1	
	Quebec	47	16	26	5	1		
	Total	**287**	**142**	**110**	**35**	**4**	**1**	**1985-89**
Perry, Don	**Los Angeles**	**168**	**52**	**85**	**31**	**3**		**1981-84**
Pike, Alf	**NY Rangers**	**123**	**36**	**66**	**21**	**2**		**1959-61**
Pilous, Rudy	**Chicago**	**387**	**162**	**151**	**74**	**6**	**1**	**1957-63**
Plager, Barclay	**St. Louis**	**178**	**49**	**96**	**33**	**4**		**1977-83**
Plager, Bob	**St. Louis**	**11**	**4**	**6**	**1**	**1**		**1992-93**
Pleau, Larry	**Hartford**	**224**	**81**	**117**	**26**	**5**		**1980-89**
Polano, Nick	**Detroit**	**240**	**79**	**127**	**34**	**3**		**1982-85**
Popein, Larry	**NY Rangers**	**41**	**18**	**14**	**9**	**1**		**1973-74**
Powers, Eddie	**Toronto**	**66**	**31**	**32**	**3**	**2**		**1924-26**
Primeau, Joe	**Toronto**	**210**	**97**	**71**	**42**	**3**	**1**	**1950-53**
Pronovost, Marcel	**Buffalo**	**104**	**52**	**29**	**23**	**2**		**1977-79**
Pulford, Bob	Los Angeles	396	178	150	68	5		
	Chicago	433	185	180	68	7		
	Total	**829**	**363**	**330**	**136**	**12**		**1972-00**
Quenneville, Joel	**St. Louis**	**368**	**194**	**123**	**51**	**5**		**1996-01**
Querrie, Charles	**Toronto**	**72**	**29**	**38**	**5**	**3**		**1922-27**
Quinn, Mike	**Quebec**	**24**	**4**	**20**	**0**	**1**		**1919-20**
Quinn, Pat	Philadelphia	262	141	73	48	4		
	Los Angeles	202	75	101	26	3		
	Vancouver	280	141	111	28	5		
	Toronto	246	127	94	25	3		
	Total	**990**	**484**	**379**	**127**	**15**		**1978-01**
Ramsay, Craig	Buffalo	21	4	15	2	1		
	Philadelphia	28	12	12	4	1		
	Total	**49**	**16**	**27**	**6**	**2**		**1986-01**
Randall, Ken	**Hamilton**	**14**	**6**	**8**	**0**	**1**		**1923-24**
Reay, Billy	Toronto	90	26	50	14	2		
	Chicago	1012	516	335	161	14		
	Total	**1102**	**542**	**385**	**175**	**16**		**1957-77**
Regan, Larry	**Los Angeles**	**88**	**27**	**47**	**14**	**2**		**1970-72**
Renney, Tom	**Vancouver**	**101**	**39**	**53**	**9**	**2**		**1996-98**
Risebrough, Doug	**Calgary**	**144**	**71**	**56**	**17**	**2**		**1990-92**
Roberts, Jim	Buffalo	45	21	16	8	1		
	Hartford	80	26	41	13	1		
	St. Louis	9	3	3	3	1		
	Total	**134**	**50**	**60**	**24**	**3**		**1981-97**
Robinson, Larry	Los Angeles	328	122	161	45	4		
	New Jersey	90	52	26	12	2	1	
	Total	**418**	**174**	**187**	**57**	**6**	**1**	**1995-01**
Rodden, Mike	**Toronto**	**2**	**0**	**2**	**0**	**1**		**1926-27**
Romeril, Alex	**Toronto**	**13**	**7**	**5**	**1**	**1**		**1926-27**
Ross, Art	Mtl. Wanderers	6	1	5	0	1		
	Hamilton	24	6	18	0	1		
	Boston	728	361	277	90	16	1	
	Total	**758**	**368**	**300**	**90**	**18**	**1**	**1917-45**
Ruel, Claude	**Montreal**	**305**	**172**	**82**	**51**	**5**	**2**	**1968-81**
Ruff, Lindy	**Buffalo**	**328**	**154**	**124**	**50**	**4**		**1997-01**
Sather, Glen	**Edmonton**	**842**	**464**	**268**	**110**	**11**	**4**	**1979-94**
Sator, Ted	NY Rangers	99	41	48	10	2		
	Buffalo	207	96	89	22	3		
	Total	**306**	**137**	**137**	**32**	**5**		**1985-89**
Savard, Andre	**Quebec**	**24**	**10**	**13**	**1**	**1**		**1987-88**
Schinkel, Ken	**Pittsburgh**	**203**	**83**	**92**	**28**	**4**		**1972-77**
Schmidt, Milt	Boston	726	245	360	121	11		
	Washington	44	5	34	5	2		
	Total	**770**	**250**	**394**	**126**	**13**		**1954-76**
Schoenfeld, Jim	Buffalo	43	19	19	5	1		
	New Jersey	124	50	59	15	3		
	Washington	249	113	102	34	4		
	Phoenix	164	74	66	24	2		
	Total	**580**	**256**	**248**	**78**	**10**		**1985-99**
Shaughnessy, Tom	**Chicago**	**21**	**10**	**8**	**3**	**1**		**1929-30**
Shero, Fred	Philadelphia	554	308	151	95	7	2	
	NY Rangers	180	82	74	24	3		
	Total	**734**	**390**	**225**	**119**	**10**	**2**	**1971-81**
Simpson, Joe	**NY Americans**	**144**	**42**	**72**	**30**	**3**		**1932-35**
Simpson, Terry	NY Islanders	187	81	82	24	3		
	Philadelphia	84	35	39	10	1		
	Winnipeg	97	43	47	7	2		
	Total	**368**	**159**	**168**	**41**	**6**		**1986-96**
Sims, Al	**San Jose**	**82**	**27**	**47**	**8**	**1**		**1996-97**
Sinden, Harry	**Boston**	**327**	**153**	**116**	**58**	**6**	**1**	**1966-85**
Skinner, Jimmy	**Detroit**	**247**	**123**	**78**	**46**	**4**	**1**	**1954-58**
Smeaton, Cooper	**Philadelphia**	**44**	**4**	**36**	**4**	**1**		**1930-31**
Smith, Alf	**Ottawa**	**18**	**12**	**6**	**0**	**1**		**1918-19**
Smith, Barry*	**Detroit**	**5**	**4**	**1**	**0**	**1**		**1998-99**

*Results shared with co-coach Dave Lewis

Coach	Team	Games Coached	Wins	Losses	Ties	Years	Cup Wins	Career
Smith, Floyd	Buffalo	241	143	62	36	4		
	Toronto	68	30	33	5	1		
	Total	**309**	**173**	**95**	**41**	**5**		**1971-80**
Smith, Mike	**Winnipeg**	**23**	**2**	**17**	**4**	**1**		**1980-81**
Smith, Ron	**NY Rangers**	**44**	**15**	**22**	**7**	**1**		**1992-93**
Smythe, Conn	**Toronto**	**134**	**57**	**57**	**20**	**4**		**1927-31**
Sonmor, Glen	**Minnesota**	**417**	**174**	**161**	**82**	**7**		**1978-87**
Sproule, Harry	**Toronto**	**12**	**7**	**5**	**0**	**1**		**1919-20**
Stanley, Barney	**Chicago**	**23**	**4**	**17**	**2**	**1**		**1927-28**
Stasiuk, Vic	Philadelphia	154	45	68	41	2		
	California	75	21	38	16	1		
	Vancouver	78	22	47	9	1		
	Total	**307**	**88**	**153**	**66**	**4**		**1969-73**
Stewart, Bill	**Chicago**	**69**	**22**	**35**	**12**	**2**	**1**	**1937-39**
Stewart, Bill	**NY Islanders**	**37**	**11**	**19**	**7**	**1**		**1998-99**
Stewart, Ron	NY Rangers	39	15	20	4	1		
	Los Angeles	80	31	34	15	1		
	Total	**119**	**46**	**54**	**19**	**2**		**1975-78**
Suhonen, Alpo	**Chicago**	**82**	**29**	**45**	**8**	**1**		**2000-01**
Sullivan, Red	NY Rangers	196	58	103	35	4		
	Pittsburgh	150	47	79	24	2		
	Washington	18	2	16	0	1		
	Total	**364**	**107**	**198**	**59**	**7**		**1962-75**
Sutherland, Bill	**Winnipeg**	**32**	**7**	**22**	**3**	**2**		**1979-81**
Sutter, Brian	St. Louis	320	153	124	43	4		
	Boston	216	120	73	23	3		
	Calgary	246	87	122	37	3		
	Total	**782**	**360**	**319**	**103**	**10**		**1988-00**
Sutter, Darryl	Chicago	216	110	80	26	3		
	San Jose	328	140	138	50	4		
	Total	**544**	**250**	**218**	**76**	**7**		**1992-01**
Sutter, Duane	**Florida**	**46**	**16**	**24**	**6**	**1**		**2000-01**
Talbot, Jean-Guy	St. Louis	120	52	53	15	2		
	NY Rangers	80	30	37	13	1		
	Total	**200**	**82**	**90**	**28**	**3**		**1972-78**
Tessier, Orval	**Chicago**	**213**	**99**	**93**	**21**	**3**		**1982-85**
Therrien, Michel	**Montreal**	**62**	**23**	**33**	**6**	**1**		**2000-01**
Thompson, Paul	**Chicago**	**272**	**104**	**127**	**41**	**7**		**1938-45**
Thompson, Percy	**Hamilton**	**48**	**13**	**35**	**0**	**2**		**1920-22**
Tobin, Bill	**Chicago**	**71**	**29**	**29**	**13**	**2**		**1929-32**
Tortorella, John	NY Rangers	4	0	3	1	1		
	Tampa Bay	43	12	30	1	1		
	Total	**47**	**12**	**33**	**2**	**2**		**1999-01**
Tremblay, Mario	**Montreal**	**159**	**71**	**63**	**25**	**2**		**1995-97**
Trotz, Barry	**Nashville**	**246**	**90**	**133**	**20**	**3**		**1998-01**
Ubriaco, Gene	**Pittsburgh**	**106**	**50**	**47**	**9**	**2**		**1988-90**
Vachon, Rogie	**Los Angeles**	**10**	**4**	**3**	**3**	**3**		**1983-95**
Vigneault, Alain	**Montreal**	**266**	**109**	**122**	**35**	**4**		**1997-01**
Watson, Bryan	**Edmonton**	**18**	**4**	**9**	**5**	**1**		**1980-81**
Watson, Phil	NY Rangers	295	119	124	52	5		
	Boston	84	16	55	13	2		
	Total	**379**	**135**	**179**	**65**	**7**		**1955-63**
Watt, Tom	Winnipeg	181	72	85	24	3		
	Vancouver	160	52	87	21	2		
	Toronto	149	52	80	17	2		
	Total	**490**	**176**	**252**	**62**	**7**		**1981-92**
Webster, Tom	NY Rangers	18	5	9	4	1		
	Los Angeles	240	115	94	31	3		
	Total	**258**	**120**	**103**	**35**	**4**		**1986-92**
Weiland, Cooney	**Boston**	**96**	**58**	**20**	**18**	**2**	**1**	**1939-41**
White, Bill	**Chicago**	**46**	**16**	**24**	**6**	**1**		**1976-77**
Wiley, Jim	**San Jose**	**57**	**17**	**37**	**3**	**1**		**1995-96**
Wilson, Johnny	Los Angeles	52	9	34	9	1		
	Detroit	145	67	56	22	2		
	Colorado	80	20	46	14	1		
	Pittsburgh	240	91	105	44	3		
	Total	**517**	**187**	**241**	**89**	**7**		**1969-80**
Wilson, Larry	**Detroit**	**36**	**3**	**29**	**4**	**1**		**1976-77**
Wilson, Ron	Anaheim	296	120	145	31	4		
	Washington	328	156	132	40	4		
	Total	**624**	**276**	**277**	**71**	**7**		**1993-00**
Young, Garry	California	12	2	7	3	1		
	St. Louis	98	41	41	16	2		
	Total	**110**	**43**	**48**	**19**	**3**		**1972-76**

Ivan Hlinka (left) and Alpo Suhonen (right) were the first two Europeans to become NHL head coaches in 2000-01. Hlinka will be back in Pittsburgh in 2001-02, but Suhonen stepped down in Chicago due to health reasons.

Year-by-Year Individual Regular-Season Leaders

Season	Goals	G	Assists	A	Points	Pts.	Penalty Minutes	PIM
1917-18	Joe Malone	44	Cy Denneny	10	Joe Malone	48	Joe Hall	100
			Reg Noble	10				
			Harry Cameron	10				
1918-19	Newsy Lalonde	23	Newsy Lalonde	10	Newsy Lalonde	33	Joe Hall	135
			Eddie Gerard	10				
1919-20	Joe Malone	39	Frank Nighbor	15	Joe Malone	49	Cully Wilson	86
1920-21	Babe Dye	35	Jack Darragh	15	Newsy Lalonde	43	Bert Corbeau	86
1921-22	Punch Broadbent	32	Punch Broadbent	14	Punch Broadbent	46	Sprague Cleghorn	63
			Leo Reise	14				
1922-23	Babe Dye	26	Edmond Bouchard	12	Babe Dye	37	Georges Boucher	58
1923-24	Cy Denneny	22	King Clancy	8	Cy Denneny	23	Bert Corbeau	55
1924-25	Babe Dye	38	Cy Denneny	15	Babe Dye	44	Billy Boucher	92
1925-26	Nels Stewart	34	Frank Nighbor	13	Nels Stewart	42	Bert Corbeau	121
1926-27	Bill Cook	33	Dick Irvin	18	Bill Cook	37	Nels Stewart	133
1927-28	Howie Morenz	33	Howie Morenz	18	Howie Morenz	51	Eddie Shore	165
1928-29	Ace Bailey	22	Frank Boucher	16	Ace Bailey	32	Red Dutton	139
1929-30	Cooney Weiland	43	Frank Boucher	36	Cooney Weiland	73	Joe Lamb	119
1930-31	Charlie Conacher	31	Joe Primeau	32	Howie Morenz	51	Harvey Rockburn	118
1931-32	Charlie Conacher	34	Joe Primeau	37	Busher Jackson	53	Red Dutton	107
	Bill Cook	34						
1932-33	Bill Cook	28	Frank Boucher	28	Bill Cook	50	Red Horner	144
1933-34	Charlie Conacher	32	Joe Primeau	32	Charlie Conacher	52	Red Horner	126 *
1934-35	Charlie Conacher	36	Art Chapman	34	Charlie Conacher	57	Red Horner	125
1935-36	Charlie Conacher	23	Art Chapman	28	Sweeney Schriner	45	Red Horner	167
	Bill Thoms	23						
1936-37	Larry Aurie	23	Syl Apps Sr.	29	Sweeney Schriner	46	Red Horner	124
	Nels Stewart	23						
1937-38	Gordie Drillon	26	Syl Apps Sr.	29	Gordie Drillon	52	Red Horner	82 *
1938-39	Roy Conacher	26	Bill Cowley	34	Toe Blake	47	Red Horner	85
1939-40	Bryan Hextall Sr.	24	Milt Schmidt	30	Milt Schmidt	52	Red Horner	87
1940-41	Bryan Hextall Sr.	26	Bill Cowley	45	Bill Cowley	62	Jimmy Orlando	99
1941-42	Lynn Patrick	32	Phil Watson	37	Bryan Hextall Sr.	56	Jimmy Orlando	81 **
1942-43	Doug Bentley	33	Bill Cowley	45	Doug Bentley	73	Jimmy Orlando	89 *
1943-44	Doug Bentley	38	Clint Smith	49	Herb Cain	82	Mike McMahon Sr.	98
1944-45	Maurice Richard	50	Elmer Lach	54	Elmer Lach	80	Pat Egan	86
1945-46	Gaye Stewart	37	Elmer Lach	34	Max Bentley	61	Jack Stewart	73
1946-47	Maurice Richard	45	Billy Taylor	46	Max Bentley	72	Gus Mortson	133
1947-48	Ted Lindsay	33	Doug Bentley	37	Elmer Lach	61	Bill Barilko	147
1948-49	Sid Abel	28	Doug Bentley	43	Roy Conacher	68	Bill Ezinicki	145
1949-50	Maurice Richard	43	Ted Lindsay	55	Ted Lindsay	78	Bill Ezinicki	144
1950-51	Gordie Howe	43	Gordie Howe	43	Gordie Howe	86	Gus Mortson	142
1951-52	Gordie Howe	47	Elmer Lach	50	Gordie Howe	86	Gus Kyle	127
1952-53	Gordie Howe	49	Gordie Howe	46	Gordie Howe	95	Maurice Richard	112
1953-54	Maurice Richard	37	Gordie Howe	48	Gordie Howe	81	Gus Mortson	132
1954-55	Maurice Richard	38	Bert Olmstead	48	Bernie Geoffrion	75	Fernie Flaman	150
	Bernie Geoffrion	38						
1955-56	Jean Beliveau	47	Bert Olmstead	56	Jean Beliveau	88	Lou Fontinato	202
1956-57	Gordie Howe	44	Ted Lindsay	55	Gordie Howe	89	Gus Mortson	147
1957-58	Dickie Moore	36	Henri Richard	52	Dickie Moore	84	Lou Fontinato	152
1958-59	Jean Beliveau	45	Dickie Moore	55	Dickie Moore	96	Ted Lindsay	184
1959-60	Bobby Hull	39	Don McKenney	49	Bobby Hull	81	Carl Brewer	150
1960-61	Bernie Geoffrion	50	Jean Beliveau	58	Bernie Geoffrion	95	Pierre Pilote	165
1961-62	Bobby Hull	50	Andy Bathgate	56	Bobby Hull	84	Lou Fontinato	167
					Andy Bathgate	84		
1962-63	Gordie Howe	38	Henri Richard	50	Gordie Howe	86	Howie Young	273
1963-64	Bobby Hull	43	Andy Bathgate	58	Stan Mikita	89	Vic Hadfield	151
1964-65	Norm Ullman	42	Stan Mikita	59	Stan Mikita	87	Carl Brewer	177
1965-66	Bobby Hull	54	Stan Mikita	48	Bobby Hull	97	Reggie Fleming	166
			Bobby Rousseau	48				
			Jean Beliveau	48				
1966-67	Bobby Hull	52	Stan Mikita	62	Stan Mikita	97	John Ferguson	177
1967-68	Bobby Hull	44	Phil Esposito	49	Stan Mikita	87	Barclay Plager	153
1968-69	Bobby Hull	58	Phil Esposito	77	Phil Esposito	126	Forbes Kennedy	219
1969-70	Phil Esposito	43	Bobby Orr	87	Bobby Orr	120	Keith Magnuson	213
1970-71	Phil Esposito	76	Bobby Orr	102	Phil Esposito	152	Keith Magnuson	291
1971-72	Phil Esposito	66	Bobby Orr	80	Phil Esposito	133	Bryan Watson	212
1972-73	Phil Esposito	55	Phil Esposito	75	Phil Esposito	130	Dave Schultz	259
1973-74	Phil Esposito	68	Bobby Orr	90	Phil Esposito	145	Dave Schultz	348
1974-75	Phil Esposito	61	Bobby Orr	89	Bobby Orr	135	Dave Schultz	472
			Bobby Clarke	89				
1975-76	Reggie Leach	61	Bobby Clarke	89	Guy Lafleur	125	Steve Durbano	370
1976-77	Steve Shutt	60	Guy Lafleur	80	Guy Lafleur	136	Dave Williams	338
1977-78	Guy Lafleur	60	Bryan Trottier	77	Guy Lafleur	132	Dave Schultz	405
1978-79	Mike Bossy	69	Bryan Trottier	87	Bryan Trottier	134	Dave Williams	298
1979-80	Charlie Simmer	56	Wayne Gretzky	86	Marcel Dionne	137	Jimmy Mann	287
	Danny Gare	56			Wayne Gretzky	137		
	Blaine Stoughton	56						
1980-81	Mike Bossy	68	Wayne Gretzky	109	Wayne Gretzky	164	Dave Williams	343
1981-82	Wayne Gretzky	92	Wayne Gretzky	120	Wayne Gretzky	212	Paul Baxter	409
1982-83	Wayne Gretzky	71	Wayne Gretzky	125	Wayne Gretzky	196	Randy Holt	275
1983-84	Wayne Gretzky	87	Wayne Gretzky	118	Wayne Gretzky	205	Chris Nilan	338
1984-85	Wayne Gretzky	73	Wayne Gretzky	135	Wayne Gretzky	208	Chris Nilan	358
1985-86	Jari Kurri	68	Wayne Gretzky	163	Wayne Gretzky	215	Joey Kocur	377
1986-87	Wayne Gretzky	62	Wayne Gretzky	121	Wayne Gretzky	183	Tim Hunter	361
1987-88	Mario Lemieux	70	Wayne Gretzky	109	Mario Lemieux	168	Bob Probert	398
1988-89	Mario Lemieux	85	Mario Lemieux	114	Mario Lemieux	199	Tim Hunter	375
			Wayne Gretzky	114				
1989-90	Brett Hull	72	Wayne Gretzky	102	Wayne Gretzky	142	Basil McRae	351
1990-91	Brett Hull	86	Wayne Gretzky	122	Wayne Gretzky	163	Rob Ray	350
1991-92	Brett Hull	70	Wayne Gretzky	90	Mario Lemieux	131	Mike Peluso	408
1992-93	Teemu Selanne	76	Adam Oates	97	Mario Lemieux	160	Marty McSorley	399
	Alexander Mogilny	76						
1993-94	Pavel Bure	60	Wayne Gretzky	92	Wayne Gretzky	130	Tie Domi	347
1994-95	Peter Bondra	34	Ron Francis	48	Jaromir Jagr	70	Enrico Ciccone	225
					Eric Lindros	70		
1995-96	Mario Lemieux	69	Mario Lemieux	92	Mario Lemieux	161	Matthew Barnaby	335
			Ron Francis	92				
1996-97	Keith Tkachuk	52	Mario Lemieux	72	Mario Lemieux	122	Gino Odjick	371
			Wayne Gretzky	72				
1997-98	Teemu Selanne	52	Jaromir Jagr	67	Jaromir Jagr	102	Donald Brashear	372
	Peter Bondra	52	Wayne Gretzky	67				
1998-99	Teemu Selanne	47	Jaromir Jagr	83	Jaromir Jagr	127	Rob Ray	261
99-2000	Pavel Bure	58	Mark Recchi	63	Jaromir Jagr	96	Denny Lambert	219
2000-01	Pavel Bure	59	Jaromir Jagr	69	Jaromir Jagr	121	Matthew Barnaby	265
			Adam Oates	69				

* Match Misconduct penalty not included in total penalty minutes. ** Three Match Misconduct penalties not included in total penalty minutes.
1946-47 was the first season that a Match penalty was automaticaly written into the player's total penalty minutes as 20 minutes.
Beginning in 1947-48 all penalties, Match, Game Misconduct, and Misconduct, are written as 10 minutes.

One Season Scoring Records

Goals-Per-Game Leaders, One Season

(Among players with 20 goals or more in one season)

Player	Team	Season	Games	Goals	Average
Joe Malone	Montreal	1917-18	20	44	2.20
Cy Denneny	Ottawa	1917-18	20	36	1.80
Newsy Lalonde	Montreal	1917-18	14	23	1.64
Joe Malone	Quebec	1919-20	24	39	1.63
Newsy Lalonde	Montreal	1919-20	23	37	1.61
Reg Noble	Toronto	1917-18	20	30	1.50
Babe Dye	Ham., Tor.	1920-21	24	35	1.46
Cy Denneny	Ottawa	1920-21	24	34	1.42
Joe Malone	Hamilton	1920-21	20	28	1.40
Newsy Lalonde	Montreal	1920-21	24	33	1.38
Punch Broadbent	Ottawa	1921-22	24	32	1.33
Babe Dye	Toronto	1924-25	29	38	1.31
Newsy Lalonde	Montreal	1918-19	17	22	1.29
Odie Cleghorn	Montreal	1918-19	17	22	1.29
Babe Dye	Toronto	1921-22	24	31	1.29
Cy Denneny	Ottawa	1921-22	22	27	1.23
Aurel Joliat	Montreal	1924-25	25	30	1.20
Babe Dye	Toronto	1922-23	22	26	1.18
Wayne Gretzky	Edmonton	1983-84	74	87	1.18
Wayne Gretzky	Edmonton	1981-82	80	92	1.15
Mario Lemieux	Pittsburgh	1992-93	60	69	1.15
Frank Nighbor	Ottawa	1919-20	23	26	1.13
Mario Lemieux	Pittsburgh	1988-89	76	85	1.12
Brett Hull	St. Louis	1990-91	78	86	1.10
Cam Neely	Boston	1993-94	49	50	1.02
Reg Noble	Toronto	1919-20	24	24	1.00
Corb Denneny	Toronto	1919-20	24	24	1.00
Joe Malone	Hamilton	1921-22	24	24	1.00
Billy Boucher	Montreal	1922-23	24	24	1.00
Cy Denneny	Ottawa	1923-24	22	22	1.00
Maurice Richard	Montreal	1944-45	50	50	1.00
Alexander Mogilny	Buffalo	1992-93	77	76	0.99
Mario Lemieux	Pittsburgh	1995-96	70	69	0.99
Cooney Weiland	Boston	1929-30	44	43	0.98
Phil Esposito	Boston	1970-71	78	76	0.97
Jari Kurri	Edmonton	1984-85	73	71	0.97

Of the 16 players in NHL history to have averaged more than a goal per game for an entire season, 11 did so prior to 1925. Frank Nighbor turned the trick with 26 goals in 23 games for Ottawa in 1919-20.

Assists-Per-Game Leaders, One Season

(Among players with 35 assists or more in one season)

Player	Team	Season	Games	Assists	Average
Wayne Gretzky	Edmonton	1985-86	80	163	2.04
Wayne Gretzky	Edmonton	1987-88	64	109	1.70
Wayne Gretzky	Edmonton	1984-85	80	135	1.69
Wayne Gretzky	Edmonton	1983-84	74	118	1.59
Wayne Gretzky	Edmonton	1982-83	80	125	1.56
Wayne Gretzky	Los Angeles	1990-91	78	122	1.56
Wayne Gretzky	Edmonton	1986-87	79	121	1.53
Mario Lemieux	Pittsburgh	1992-93	60	91	1.52
Wayne Gretzky	Edmonton	1981-82	80	120	1.50
Mario Lemieux	Pittsburgh	1988-89	76	114	1.50
Adam Oates	St. Louis	1990-91	61	90	1.48
Wayne Gretzky	Los Angeles	1988-89	78	114	1.46
Wayne Gretzky	Los Angeles	1989-90	73	102	1.40
Wayne Gretzky	Edmonton	1980-81	80	109	1.36
Mario Lemieux	Pittsburgh	1991-92	64	87	1.36
Mario Lemieux	Pittsburgh	1989-90	59	78	1.32
Bobby Orr	Boston	1970-71	78	102	1.31
Mario Lemieux	Pittsburgh	1995-96	70	92	1.31
Mario Lemieux	Pittsburgh	1987-88	77	98	1.27
Bobby Orr	Boston	1973-74	74	90	1.22
Wayne Gretzky	Los Angeles	1991-92	74	90	1.22
Ron Francis	Pittsburgh	1995-96	77	92	1.19
Mario Lemieux	Pittsburgh	1985-86	79	93	1.18
Bobby Clarke	Philadelphia	1975-76	76	89	1.17
Peter Stastny	Quebec	1981-82	80	93	1.16
Adam Oates	Boston	1992-93	84	97	1.15
Doug Gilmour	Toronto	1992-93	83	95	1.14
Wayne Gretzky	Los Angeles	1993-94	81	92	1.14
Paul Coffey	Edmonton	1985-86	79	90	1.14
Bobby Orr	Boston	1969-70	76	87	1.14
Bryan Trottier	NY Islanders	1978-79	76	87	1.14
Bobby Orr	Boston	1972-73	63	72	1.14
Bill Cowley	Boston	1943-44	36	41	1.14
Pat LaFontaine	Buffalo	1992-93	84	95	1.13
Steve Yzerman	Detroit	1988-89	80	90	1.13
Paul Coffey	Pittsburgh	1987-88	46	52	1.13
Bobby Orr	Boston	1974-75	80	89	1.11
Bobby Clarke	Philadelphia	1974-75	80	89	1.11
Paul Coffey	Pittsburgh	1988-89	75	83	1.11
Wayne Gretzky	Los Angeles	1992-93	45	49	1.11
Denis Savard	Chicago	1982-83	78	86	1.10
Denis Savard	Chicago	1981-82	80	87	1.09
Denis Savard	Chicago	1987-88	80	87	1.09
Wayne Gretzky	Edmonton	1979-80	79	86	1.09
Ron Francis	Pittsburgh	1994-95	44	48	1.09
Paul Coffey	Edmonton	1983-84	80	86	1.08
Elmer Lach	Montreal	1944-45	50	54	1.08
Peter Stastny	Quebec	1985-86	76	81	1.07
Jaromir Jagr	Pittsburgh	1995-96	82	87	1.06
Mark Messier	Edmonton	1989-90	79	84	1.06
Peter Forsberg	Colorado	1995-96	82	86	1.05
Paul Coffey	Edmonton	1984-85	80	84	1.05
Marcel Dionne	Los Angeles	1979-80	80	84	1.05
Bobby Orr	Boston	1971-72	76	80	1.05
Mike Bossy	NY Islanders	1981-82	80	83	1.04
Adam Oates	Boston	1993-94	77	80	1.04
Phil Esposito	Boston	1968-69	74	77	1.04
Bryan Trottier	NY Islanders	1983-84	68	71	1.04
Pete Mahovlich	Montreal	1974-75	80	82	1.03
Kent Nilsson	Calgary	1980-81	80	82	1.03
Peter Stastny	Quebec	1982-83	75	77	1.03
Jaromir Jagr	Pittsburgh	1998-99	81	83	1.02
Doug Gilmour	Toronto	1993-94	83	84	1.01
Bernie Nicholls	Los Angeles	1988-89	79	80	1.01
Guy Lafleur	Montreal	1979-80	74	75	1.01
Guy Lafleur	Montreal	1976-77	80	80	1.00
Marcel Dionne	Los Angeles	1984-85	80	80	1.00
Brian Leetch	NY Rangers	1991-92	80	80	1.00
Bryan Trottier	NY Islanders	1977-78	77	77	1.00
Mike Bossy	NY Islanders	1983-84	67	67	1.00
Jean Ratelle	NY Rangers	1971-72	63	63	1.00
Steve Yzerman	Detroit	1993-94	58	58	1.00
Ron Francis	Hartford	1985-86	53	53	1.00
Guy Chouinard	Calgary	1980-81	52	52	1.00
Elmer Lach	Montreal	1943-44	48	48	1.00

Points-Per-Game Leaders, One Season

(Among players with 50 points or more in one season)

Player	Team	Season	Games	Points	Average
Wayne Gretzky	Edmonton	1983-84	74	205	2.77
Wayne Gretzky	Edmonton	1985-86	80	215	2.69
Mario Lemieux	Pittsburgh	1992-93	60	160	2.67
Wayne Gretzky	Edmonton	1981-82	80	212	2.65
Mario Lemieux	Pittsburgh	1988-89	76	199	2.62
Wayne Gretzky	Edmonton	1984-85	80	208	2.60
Wayne Gretzky	Edmonton	1982-83	80	196	2.45
Wayne Gretzky	Edmonton	1987-88	64	149	2.33
Wayne Gretzky	Edmonton	1986-87	79	183	2.32
Mario Lemieux	Pittsburgh	1995-96	70	161	2.30
Mario Lemieux	Pittsburgh	1987-88	77	168	2.18
Wayne Gretzky	Los Angeles	1988-89	78	168	2.15
Wayne Gretzky	Los Angeles	1990-91	78	163	2.09
Mario Lemieux	Pittsburgh	1989-90	59	123	2.08
Wayne Gretzky	Edmonton	1980-81	80	164	2.05
Mario Lemieux	Pittsburgh	1991-92	64	131	2.05
Bill Cowley	Boston	1943-44	36	71	1.97
Phil Esposito	Boston	1970-71	78	152	1.95
Wayne Gretzky	Los Angeles	1989-90	73	142	1.95
Steve Yzerman	Detroit	1988-89	80	155	1.94
Bernie Nicholls	Los Angeles	1988-89	79	150	1.90
Adam Oates	St. Louis	1990-91	61	115	1.89
Phil Esposito	Boston	1973-74	78	145	1.86
Jari Kurri	Edmonton	1984-85	73	135	1.85
Mike Bossy	NY Islanders	1981-82	80	147	1.84
Jaromir Jagr	Pittsburgh	1995-96	82	149	1.82
Mario Lemieux	Pittsburgh	1985-86	79	141	1.78
Bobby Orr	Boston	1970-71	78	139	1.78
Jari Kurri	Edmonton	1983-84	64	113	1.77
Mario Lemieux	**Pittsburgh**	**2000-01**	**43**	**76**	**1.77**
Pat LaFontaine	Buffalo	1992-93	84	148	1.76
Bryan Trottier	NY Islanders	1978-79	76	134	1.76
Mike Bossy	NY Islanders	1983-84	67	118	1.76
Paul Coffey	Edmonton	1985-86	79	138	1.75
Phil Esposito	Boston	1971-72	76	133	1.75
Peter Stastny	Quebec	1981-82	80	139	1.74
Wayne Gretzky	Edmonton	1979-80	79	137	1.73
Jean Ratelle	NY Rangers	1971-72	63	109	1.73
Marcel Dionne	Los Angeles	1979-80	80	137	1.71
Herb Cain	Boston	1943-44	48	82	1.71
Guy Lafleur	Montreal	1976-77	80	136	1.70
Dennis Maruk	Washington	1981-82	80	136	1.70
Phil Esposito	Boston	1968-69	74	126	1.70
Guy Lafleur	Montreal	1974-75	70	119	1.70
Mario Lemieux	Pittsburgh	1986-87	63	107	1.70
Adam Oates	Boston	1992-93	84	142	1.69
Bobby Orr	Boston	1974-75	80	135	1.69
Marcel Dionne	Los Angeles	1980-81	80	135	1.69
Guy Lafleur	Montreal	1977-78	78	132	1.69
Guy Lafleur	Montreal	1979-80	74	125	1.69
Rob Brown	Pittsburgh	1988-89	68	115	1.69
Jari Kurri	Edmonton	1985-86	78	131	1.68
Brett Hull	St. Louis	1990-91	78	131	1.68
Phil Esposito	Boston	1972-73	78	130	1.67
Cooney Weiland	Boston	1929-30	44	73	1.66
Alexander Mogilny	Buffalo	1992-93	77	127	1.65
Peter Stastny	Quebec	1982-83	75	124	1.65
Bobby Orr	Boston	1973-74	74	122	1.65
Kent Nilsson	Calgary	1980-81	80	131	1.64
Denis Savard	Chicago	1987-88	80	131	1.64
Wayne Gretzky	Los Angeles	1991-92	74	121	1.64
Steve Yzerman	Detroit	1992-93	84	137	1.63
Marcel Dionne	Los Angeles	1978-79	80	130	1.63
Dale Hawerchuk	Winnipeg	1984-85	80	130	1.63
Mark Messier	Edmonton	1989-90	79	129	1.63
Bryan Trottier	NY Islanders	1983-84	68	111	1.63
Pat LaFontaine	Buffalo	1991-92	57	93	1.63
Charlie Simmer	Los Angeles	1980-81	65	105	1.62
Guy Lafleur	Montreal	1978-79	80	129	1.61
Bryan Trottier	NY Islanders	1981-82	80	129	1.61
Phil Esposito	Boston	1974-75	79	127	1.61
Steve Yzerman	Detroit	1989-90	79	127	1.61
Peter Stastny	Quebec	1985-86	76	122	1.61
Mario Lemieux	Pittsburgh	1996-97	76	122	1.61
Michel Goulet	Quebec	1983-84	75	121	1.61
Wayne Gretzky	Los Angeles	1993-94	81	130	1.60
Bryan Trottier	NY Islanders	1977-78	77	123	1.60
Bobby Orr	Boston	1972-73	63	101	1.60
Guy Chouinard	Calgary	1980-81	52	83	1.60
Elmer Lach	Montreal	1944-45	50	80	1.60
Pierre Turgeon	NY Islanders	1992-93	83	132	1.59
Steve Yzerman	Detroit	1987-88	64	102	1.59
Mike Bossy	NY Islanders	1978-79	80	126	1.58
Paul Coffey	Edmonton	1983-84	80	126	1.58
Marcel Dionne	Los Angeles	1984-85	80	126	1.58
Bobby Orr	Boston	1969-70	76	120	1.58
Eric Lindros	Philadelphia	1995-96	73	115	1.58
Charlie Simmer	Los Angeles	1979-80	64	101	1.58
Teemu Selanne	Winnipeg	1992-93	84	132	1.57
Jaromir Jagr	Pittsburgh	1998-99	81	127	1.57
Bobby Clarke	Philadelphia	1975-76	76	119	1.57
Guy Lafleur	Montreal	1975-76	80	125	1.56
Dave Taylor	Los Angeles	1980-81	72	112	1.56
Denis Savard	Chicago	1982-83	78	121	1.55
Ron Francis	Pittsburgh	1995-96	77	119	1.55
Mike Bossy	NY Islanders	1985-86	80	123	1.54
Kevin Stevens	Pittsburgh	1991-92	80	123	1.54
Bobby Orr	Boston	1971-72	76	117	1.54
Mike Bossy	NY Islanders	1984-85	76	117	1.54
Kevin Stevens	Pittsburgh	1992-93	72	111	1.54
Doug Bentley	Chicago	1943-44	50	77	1.54
Doug Gilmour	Toronto	1992-93	83	127	1.53
Marcel Dionne	Los Angeles	1976-77	80	122	1.53
Jaromir Jagr	Pittsburgh	99-2000	63	96	1.52
Eric Lindros	Philadelphia	1996-97	52	79	1.52
Eric Lindros	Philadelphia	1994-95	46	70	1.52
Marcel Dionne	Detroit	1974-75	80	121	1.51
Dale Hawerchuk	Winnipeg	1987-88	80	121	1.51
Paul Coffey	Pittsburgh	1988-89	75	113	1.51
Jaromir Jagr	Pittsburgh	1996-97	63	95	1.51

With 76 points in just 43 games in 2000-01, Mario Lemieux averaged 1.77 points per game in his comeback season. Lemieux's greatest points-per-game rate (2.67) came in 1992-93 when he had 160 points in just 60 games.

A Hall-of-Fame career was launched when John Ferguson and the Winnipeg Jets selected Dale Hawerchuk first overall in the 1981 Entry Draft. Hawerchuk had 45 goals and 58 assists for 103 points as a rookie in 1981-82.

Rookie Scoring Records

All-Time Top 50 Goal-Scoring Rookies

	Rookie	Team	Position	Season	GP	G	A	PTS
1.	* Teemu Selanne	Winnipeg	Right wing	1992-93	84	**76**	56	132
2.	* Mike Bossy	NY Islanders	Right wing	1977-78	73	**53**	38	91
3.	* Joe Nieuwendyk	Calgary	Center	1987-88	75	**51**	41	92
4.	* Dale Hawerchuk	Winnipeg	Center	1981-82	80	**45**	58	103
	* Luc Robitaille	Los Angeles	Left wing	1986-87	79	**45**	39	84
6.	Rick Martin	Buffalo	Left wing	1971-72	73	**44**	30	74
	Barry Pederson	Boston	Center	1981-82	80	**44**	48	92
8.	* Steve Larmer	Chicago	Right wing	1982-83	80	**43**	47	90
	* Mario Lemieux	Pittsburgh	Center	1984-85	73	**43**	57	100
10.	Eric Lindros	Philadelphia	Center	1992-93	61	**41**	34	75
11.	Darryl Sutter	Chicago	Left wing	1980-81	76	**40**	22	62
	Sylvain Turgeon	Hartford	Left wing	1983-84	76	**40**	32	72
	Warren Young	Pittsburgh	Left wing	1984-85	80	**40**	32	72
14.	* Eric Vail	Atlanta	Left wing	1974-75	72	**39**	21	60
	Anton Stastny	Quebec	Left wing	1980-81	80	**39**	46	85
	* Peter Stastny	Quebec	Center	1980-81	77	**39**	70	109
	Steve Yzerman	Detroit	Center	1983-84	80	**39**	48	87
18.	* Gilbert Perreault	Buffalo	Center	1970-71	78	**38**	34	72
	Neal Broten	Minnesota	Center	1981-82	73	**38**	60	98
	Ray Sheppard	Buffalo	Right wing	1987-88	74	**38**	27	65
	Mikael Renberg	Philadelphia	Left wing	1993-94	83	**38**	44	82
22.	Jorgen Pettersson	St. Louis	Left wing	1980-81	62	**37**	36	73
	Jimmy Carson	Los Angeles	Center	1986-87	80	**37**	42	79
24.	Mike Foligno	Detroit	Right wing	1979-80	80	**36**	35	71
	Mike Bullard	Pittsburgh	Center	1981-82	75	**36**	27	63
	Paul MacLean	Winnipeg	Right wing	1981-82	74	**36**	25	61
	Tony Granato	NY Rangers	Right wing	1988-89	78	**36**	27	63
28.	Marian Stastny	Quebec	Right wing	1981-82	74	**35**	54	89
	Brian Bellows	Minnesota	Right wing	1982-83	78	**35**	30	65
	Tony Amonte	NY Rangers	Right wing	1991-92	79	**35**	34	69
31.	Nels Stewart	Mtl. Maroons	Center	1925-26	36	**34**	8	42
	* Danny Grant	Minnesota	Left wing	1968-69	75	**34**	31	65
	Norm Ferguson	Oakland	Right wing	1968-69	76	**34**	20	54
	Brian Propp	Philadelphia	Left wing	1979-80	80	**34**	41	75
	Wendel Clark	Toronto	Left wing	1985-86	66	**34**	11	45
	* Pavel Bure	Vancouver	Right wing	1991-92	65	**34**	26	60
37.	* Willi Plett	Atlanta	Right wing	1976-77	64	**33**	23	56
	Dale McCourt	Detroit	Center	1977-78	76	**33**	39	72
	Mark Pavelich	NY Rangers	Center	1981-82	79	**33**	43	76
	Ron Flockhart	Philadelphia	Center	1981-82	72	**33**	39	72
	Steve Bozek	Los Angeles	Center	1981-82	71	**33**	23	56
	Jason Arnott	Edmonton	Center	1993-94	78	**33**	35	68
43.	Bill Mosienko	Chicago	Right wing	1943-44	50	**32**	38	70
	Michel Bergeron	Detroit	Right wing	1975-76	72	**32**	27	59
	* Bryan Trottier	NY Islanders	Center	1975-76	80	**32**	63	95
	Don Murdoch	NY Rangers	Right wing	1976-77	59	**32**	24	56
	Jari Kurri	Edmonton	Left wing	1980-81	75	**32**	43	75
	Bobby Carpenter	Washington	Center	1981-82	80	**32**	35	67
	Kjell Dahlin	Montreal	Right wing	1985-86	77	**32**	39	71
	Petr Klima	Detroit	Left wing	1985-86	74	**32**	24	56
	Darren Turcotte	NY Rangers	Right wing	1989-90	76	**32**	34	66
	Joe Juneau	Boston	Center	1992-93	84	**32**	70	102

* Calder Trophy Winner

All-Time Top 50 Point-Scoring Rookies

	Rookie	Team	Position	Season	GP	G	A	PTS
1.	* Teemu Selanne	Winnipeg	Right wing	1992-93	84	76	56	**132**
2.	* Peter Stastny	Quebec	Center	1980-81	77	39	70	**109**
3.	* Dale Hawerchuk	Winnipeg	Center	1981-82	80	45	58	**103**
4.	Joe Juneau	Boston	Center	1992-93	84	32	70	**102**
5.	* Mario Lemieux	Pittsburgh	Center	1984-85	73	43	57	**100**
6.	Neal Broten	Minnesota	Center	1981-82	73	38	60	**98**
7.	* Bryan Trottier	NY Islanders	Center	1975-76	80	32	63	**95**
8.	Barry Pederson	Boston	Center	1981-82	80	44	48	**92**
	* Joe Nieuwendyk	Calgary	Center	1987-88	75	51	41	**92**
10.	* Mike Bossy	NY Islanders	Right wing	1977-78	73	53	38	**91**
11.	* Steve Larmer	Chicago	Right wing	1982-83	80	43	47	**90**
12.	Marian Stastny	Quebec	Right wing	1981-82	74	35	54	**89**
13.	Steve Yzerman	Detroit	Center	1983-84	80	39	48	**87**
14.	* Sergei Makarov	Calgary	Right wing	1989-90	80	24	62	**86**
15.	Anton Stastny	Quebec	Left wing	1980-81	80	39	46	**85**
16.	* Luc Robitaille	Los Angeles	Left wing	1986-87	79	45	39	**84**
17.	Mikael Renberg	Philadelphia	Left wing	1993-94	83	38	44	**82**
18.	Jimmy Carson	Los Angeles	Center	1986-87	80	37	42	**79**
	Sergei Fedorov	Detroit	Center	1990-91	77	31	48	**79**
	Alexei Yashin	Ottawa	Center	1993-94	83	30	49	**79**
21.	Marcel Dionne	Detroit	Center	1971-72	78	28	49	**77**
22.	Larry Murphy	Los Angeles	Defense	1980-81	80	16	60	**76**
	Mark Pavelich	NY Rangers	Center	1981-82	79	33	43	**76**
	Dave Poulin	Philadelphia	Center	1983-84	73	31	45	**76**
25.	Brian Propp	Philadelphia	Left wing	1979-80	80	34	41	**75**
	Jari Kurri	Edmonton	Left wing	1980-81	75	32	43	**75**
	Denis Savard	Chicago	Center	1980-81	76	28	47	**75**
	Mike Modano	Minnesota	Center	1989-90	80	29	46	**75**
	Eric Lindros	Philadelphia	Center	1992-93	61	41	34	**75**
30.	Rick Martin	Buffalo	Left wing	1971-72	73	44	30	**74**
	* Bobby Smith	Minnesota	Center	1978-79	80	30	44	**74**
32.	Jorgen Pettersson	St. Louis	Left wing	1980-81	62	37	36	**73**
33.	* Gilbert Perreault	Buffalo	Center	1970-71	78	38	34	**72**
	Dale McCourt	Detroit	Center	1977-78	76	33	39	**72**
	Ron Flockhart	Philadelphia	Center	1981-82	72	33	39	**72**
	Sylvain Turgeon	Hartford	Left wing	1983-84	76	40	32	**72**
	Warren Young	Pittsburgh	Left wing	1984-85	80	40	32	**72**
	Carey Wilson	Calgary	Center	1984-85	74	24	48	**72**
	Alexei Zhamnov	Winnipeg	Center	1992-93	68	25	47	**72**
40.	Mike Foligno	Detroit	Right wing	1979-80	80	36	35	**71**
	Dave Christian	Winnipeg	Center	1980-81	80	28	43	**71**
	Mats Naslund	Montreal	Left wing	1982-83	74	26	45	**71**
	Kjell Dahlin	Montreal	Right wing	1985-86	77	32	39	**71**
	* Brian Leetch	NY Rangers	Defense	1988-89	68	23	48	**71**
45.	Bill Mosienko	Chicago	Right wing	1943-44	50	32	38	**70**
	* Scott Gomez	New Jersey	Center	99-2000	82	19	51	**70**
47.	Roland Eriksson	Minnesota	Center	1976-77	80	25	44	**69**
	Tony Amonte	NY Rangers	Right wing	1991-92	79	35	34	**69**
49.	Jude Drouin	Minnesota	Center	1970-71	75	16	52	**68**
	Pierre Larouche	Pittsburgh	Center	1974-75	79	31	37	**68**
	Ron Francis	Hartford	Center	1981-82	59	25	43	**68**
	* Gary Suter	Calgary	Defense	1985-86	80	18	50	**68**
	Jason Arnott	Edmonton	Center	1993-94	84	33	35	**68**

Bobby Hull

Marcel Dionne

Jari Kurri

50-Goal Seasons

Player	Team	Date of 50th Goal	Score	Goaltender	Player's Game No.	Team Game No.	Total Goals	Total Games	Age When First 50th Scored (Yrs. & Mos.)
Maurice Richard	Mtl.	18-3-45	Mtl. 4 at Bos. 2	Harvey Bennett	50	50	50	50	23.7
Bernie Geoffrion	Mtl.	16-3-61	Tor. 2 at Mtl. 5	Cesare Maniago	62	68	50	64	30.1
Bobby Hull	Chi.	25-3-62	Chi. 1 at NYR 4	Gump Worsley	70	70	50	70	23.2
Bobby Hull	Chi.	2-3-66	Det. 4 at Chi. 5	Hank Bassen	52	57	54	65	
Bobby Hull	Chi.	18-3-67	Chi. 5 at Tor. 9	Bruce Gamble	63	66	52	66	
Bobby Hull	Chi.	5-3-69	NYR 4 at Chi. 4	Ed Giacomin	64	66	58	74	
Phil Esposito	Bos.	20-2-71	Bos. 4 at L.A. 5	Denis DeJordy	58	58	76	78	29.0
John Bucyk	Bos.	16-3-71	Bos. 11 at Det. 4	Roy Edwards	69	69	51	78	35.10
Phil Esposito	Bos.	20-2-72	Bos. 3 at Chi. 1	Tony Esposito	60	60	66	76	
Bobby Hull	Chi.	2-4-72	Det. 1 at Chi. 6	Andy Brown	78	78	50	78	
Vic Hadfield	NYR	2-4-72	Mtl. 6 at NYR 5	Denis DeJordy	78	78	50	78	31.6
Phil Esposito	Bos.	25-3-73	Buf. 1 at Bos. 6	Roger Crozier	75	75	55	78	
Mickey Redmond	Det.	27-3-73	Det. 8 at Tor. 1	Ron Low	73	75	52	76	25.3
Rick MacLeish	Phi.	1-4-73	Phi. 4 at Pit. 5	Cam Newton	78	78	50	78	23.2
Phil Esposito	Bos.	20-2-74	Bos. 5 at Min. 5	Cesare Maniago	56	56	68	78	
Mickey Redmond	Det.	23-3-74	NYR 3 at Det 5	Ed Giacomin	69	71	51	76	
Ken Hodge	Bos.	6-4-74	Bos. 2 at Mtl. 6	Michel Larocque	75	77	50	76	29.10
Rick Martin	Buf.	7-4-74	St. L. 2 at Buf. 5	Wayne Stephenson	78	78	52	78	22.9
Phil Esposito	Bos.	8-2-75	Bos. 8 at Det. 5	Jim Rutherford	54	54	61	79	
Guy Lafleur	Mtl.	29-3-75	K.C. 1 at Mtl. 4	Denis Herron	66	76	53	70	23.6
Danny Grant	Det.	2-4-75	Wsh. 3 at Det. 8	John Adams	78	78	50	80	29.2
Rick Martin	Buf.	3-4-75	Bos. 2 at Buf. 4	Ken Broderick	67	79	52	68	
Reggie Leach	Phi.	14-3-76	Atl. 1 at Phi. 6	Dan Bouchard	69	69	61	80	25.11
Jean Pronovost	Pit.	24-3-76	Bos. 5 at Pit. 5	Gilles Gilbert	74	74	52	80	30.3
Guy Lafleur	Mtl.	27-3-76	K.C. 2 at Mtl. 8	Denis Herron	76	76	56	80	
Bill Barber	Phi.	3-4-76	Buf. 2 at Phi. 5	Al Smith	79	79	50	80	23.9
Pierre Larouche	Pit.	3-4-76	Wsh. 5 at Pit. 4	Ron Low	75	79	53	76	20.5
Danny Gare	Buf.	4-4-76	Tor. 2 at Buf. 5	Gord McRae	79	80	50	79	21.11
Steve Shutt	Mtl.	1-3-77	Mtl. 5 at NYI 4	Chico Resch	65	65	60	80	24.8
Guy Lafleur	Mtl.	6-3-77	Mtl. 1 at Buf. 4	Don Edwards	68	68	56	80	
Marcel Dionne	L.A.	2-4-77	Min. 2 at L.A. 7	Pete LoPresti	79	79	53	80	25.8
Guy Lafleur	Mtl.	8-3-78	Wsh. 3 at Mtl. 4	Jim Bedard	63	65	60	78	
Mike Bossy	NYI	1-4-78	Wsh. 2 at NYI 3	Bernie Wolfe	69	76	53	73	21.2
Mike Bossy	NYI	24-2-79	Det. 1 at NYI 3	Rogie Vachon	58	58	69	80	
Marcel Dionne	L.A.	11-3-79	L.A. 3 at Phi. 6	Wayne Stephenson	68	68	59	80	
Guy Lafleur	Mtl.	31-3-79	Pit. 3 at Mtl. 5	Denis Herron	76	76	52	80	
Guy Chouinard	Atl.	6-4-79	NYR 2 at Atl. 9	John Davidson	79	79	50	80	22.5
Marcel Dionne	L.A.	12-3-80	L.A. 2 at Pit. 4	Nick Ricci	70	70	53	80	
Mike Bossy	NYI	16-3-80	NYI 6 at Chi. 1	Tony Esposito	68	71	51	75	
Charlie Simmer	L.A.	19-3-80	Det. 3 at L.A. 4	Jim Rutherford	57	73	56	64	26.0
Pierre Larouche	Mtl.	25-3-80	Chi. 4 at Mtl. 8	Tony Esposito	72	75	50	73	
Danny Gare	Buf.	27-3-80	Det. 1 at Buf. 10	Jim Rutherford	71	75	56	76	
Blaine Stoughton	Hfd.	28-3-80	Hfd. 4 at Van. 4	Glen Hanlon	75	75	56	80	27.0
Guy Lafleur	Mtl.	2-4-80	Mtl. 7 at Det. 2	Rogie Vachon	72	78	50	74	
Wayne Gretzky	Edm.	2-4-80	Min. 1 at Edm. 1	Gary Edwards	78	79	51	79	19.2
Reggie Leach	Phi.	3-4-80	Wsh. 2 at Phi. 4	empty net	75	79	50	76	
Mike Bossy	NYI	24-1-81	Que. 3 at NYI 7	Ron Grahame	50	50	68	79	
Charlie Simmer	L.A.	26-1-81	L.A. 7 at Que. 5	Michel Dion	51	51	56	65	
Marcel Dionne	L.A.	8-3-81	L.A. 4 at Wpg. 1	Markus Mattsson	68	68	58	80	
Wayne Babych	St. L.	12-3-81	St. L. 3 at Mtl. 4	Richard Sevigny	70	68	54	78	22.9
Wayne Gretzky	Edm.	15-3-81	Edm. 3 at Cgy. 3	Pat Riggin	69	69	55	80	
Rick Kehoe	Pit.	16-3-81	Pit. 7 at Edm. 6	Eddie Mio	70	70	55	80	29.7
Jacques Richard	Que.	29-3-81	Mtl. 0 at Que. 4	Richard Sevigny	76	75	52	78	28.6
Dennis Maruk	Wsh.	5-4-81	Det. 2 at Wsh. 7	Larry Lozinski	80	80	50	80	25.3
Wayne Gretzky	Edm.	30-12-81	Phi. 5 at Edm. 7	empty net	39	39	92	80	
Dennis Maruk	Wsh.	21-2-82	Wpg. 3 at Wsh. 6	Doug Soetaert	61	61	60	80	
Mike Bossy	NYI	4-3-82	Tor. 1 at NYI 10	Michel Larocque	66	66	64	80	
Dino Ciccarelli	Min.	8-3-82	St. L. 1 at Min. 8	Mike Liut	67	68	55	76	22.1
Rick Vaive	Tor.	24-3-82	St. L. 3 at Tor. 4	Mike Liut	72	75	54	77	22.10
Blaine Stoughton	Hfd.	28-3-82	Min. 5 at Hfd. 2	Gilles Meloche	76	76	52	80	
Rick Middleton	Bos.	28-3-82	Bos. 5 at Buf. 9	Paul Harrison	72	77	51	75	28.11
Marcel Dionne	L.A.	30-3-82	Cgy. 7 at L.A. 5	Pat Riggin	75	77	50	78	
Mark Messier	Edm.	31-3-82	L.A. 3 at Edm. 7	Mario Lessard	78	79	50	78	21.3
Bryan Trottier	NYI	3-4-82	Phi. 3 at NYI 6	Pete Peeters	79	79	50	80	25.9
Lanny McDonald	Cgy.	18-2-83	Cgy. 1 at Buf. 5	Bob Sauve	60	60	66	80	30.0
Wayne Gretzky	Edm.	19-2-83	Edm. 10 at Pit. 7	Nick Ricci	60	60	71	80	
Michel Goulet	Que.	5-3-83	Hfd. 3 at Que. 10	Mike Veisor	67	67	57	80	22.11
Mike Bossy	NYI	12-3-83	Wsh. 2 at NYI 6	Al Jensen	70	71	60	79	
Marcel Dionne	L.A.	17-3-83	Que. 3 at L.A. 4	Dan Bouchard	71	71	56	80	
Al Secord	Chi.	20-3-83	Tor. 3 at Chi. 7	Mike Palmateer	73	73	54	80	25.0
Rick Vaive	Tor.	30-3-83	Tor. 4 at Det. 2	Gilles Gilbert	76	78	51	78	
Wayne Gretzky	Edm.	7-1-84	Hfd. 3 at Edm. 5	Greg Millen	42	42	87	74	
Michel Goulet	Que.	8-3-84	Que. 8 at Pit. 6	Denis Herron	63	69	56	75	
Rick Vaive	Tor.	14-3-84	Min. 3 at Tor. 3	Gilles Meloche	69	72	52	76	
Mike Bullard	Pit.	14-3-84	Pit. 6 at L.A. 7	Markus Mattsson	71	72	51	76	23.0
Jari Kurri	Edm.	15-3-84	Edm. 2 at Mtl. 3	Rick Wamsley	57	73	52	64	23.10
Glenn Anderson	Edm.	21-3-84	Hfd. 3 at Edm. 5	Greg Millen	76	76	54	80	23.6
Tim Kerr	Phi.	22-3-84	Pit. 4 at Phi. 13	Denis Herron	74	75	54	79	24.3
Mike Bossy	NYI	31-3-84	NYI 3 at Wsh. 1	Pat Riggin	67	79	51	67	
Wayne Gretzky	Edm.	26-1-85	Pit. 3 at Edm. 6	Denis Herron	49	49	73	80	
Jari Kurri	Edm.	3-2-85	Hfd. 3 at Edm. 6	Greg Millen	50	53	71	73	
Mike Bossy	NYI	5-3-85	Phi. 5 at NYI 4	Bob Froese	61	65	58	76	
Michel Goulet	Que.	6-3-85	Buf. 3 at Que. 4	Tom Barrasso	62	73	55	69	
Tim Kerr	Phi.	7-3-85	Wsh. 6 at Phi. 9	Pat Riggin	63	65	54	74	
John Ogrodnick	Det.	13-3-85	Det. 6 at Edm. 7	Grant Fuhr	69	69	55	79	25.9
Bob Carpenter	Wsh.	21-3-85	Wsh. 2 at Mtl. 3	Steve Penney	72	72	53	80	21.9

Player	Team	Date of 50th Goal	Score		Goaltender	Player's Game No.	Team Game No.	Total Goals	Total Games	Age When First 50th Scored (Yrs. & Mos.)
Dale Hawerchuk	Wpg.	29-3-85	Chi. 5	at Wpg. 5	W. Skorodenski	77	77	53	80	21.11
Mike Gartner	Wsh.	7-4-85	Pit. 3	at Wsh. 7	Brian Ford	80	80	50	80	25.5
Jari Kurri	Edm.	4-3-86	Edm. 6	at Van. 2	Richard Brodeur	63	65	68	78	
Mike Bossy	NYI	11-3-86	Cgy. 4	at NYI 8	Rejean Lemelin	67	67	61	80	
Glenn Anderson	Edm.	14-3-86	Det. 3	at Edm. 12	Greg Stefan	63	71	54	72	
Michel Goulet	Que.	17-3-86	Que. 8	at Mtl. 6	Patrick Roy	67	72	53	75	
Wayne Gretzky	Edm.	18-3-86	Wpg. 2	at Edm. 6	Brian Hayward	72	72	52	80	
Tim Kerr	Phi.	20-3-86	Pit. 1	at Phi. 5	Roberto Romano	68	72	58	76	
Wayne Gretzky	Edm.	4-2-87	Edm. 6	at Min. 5	Don Beaupre	55	55	62	79	
Dino Ciccarelli	Min.	7-3-87	Pit. 7	at Min. 3	Gilles Meloche	66	66	52	80	
Mario Lemieux	Pit.	12-3-87	Que. 3	at Pit. 6	Mario Gosselin	53	70	54	63	21.5
Tim Kerr	Phi.	17-3-87	NYR 1	at Phi. 4	J. Vanbiesbrouck	67	71	58	75	
Jari Kurri	Edm.	17-3-87	N.J. 4	at Edm. 7	Craig Billington	69	70	54	79	
Mario Lemieux	Pit.	2-2-88	Wsh. 2	at Pit. 3	Pete Peeters	51	54	70	77	
Steve Yzerman	Det.	1-3-88	Buf. 0	at Det. 4	Tom Barrasso	64	64	50	64	22.10
Joe Nieuwendyk	Cgy.	12-3-88	Buf. 4	at Cgy. 10	Tom Barrasso	66	70	51	75	21.5
Craig Simpson	Edm.	15-3-88	Buf. 4	at Edm. 6	Jacques Cloutier	71	71	56	80	21.1
Jimmy Carson	L.A.	26-3-88	Chi. 5	at L.A. 9	Darren Pang	77	77	55	88	19.8
Luc Robitaille	L.A.	1-4-88	L.A. 6	at Cgy. 3	Mike Vernon	79	79	53	80	21.10
Hakan Loob	Cgy.	3-4-88	Min. 1	at Cgy. 4	Don Beaupre	80	80	50	80	27.9
Stephane Richer	Mtl.	3-4-88	Mtl. 4	at Buf. 4	Tom Barrasso	72	80	50	72	21.10
Mario Lemieux	Pit.	20-1-89	Pit. 3	at Wpg. 7	Pokey Reddick	44	46	85	76	
Bernie Nicholls	L.A.	28-1-89	Edm. 7	at L.A. 6	Grant Fuhr	51	51	70	79	27.7
Steve Yzerman	Det.	5-2-89	Det. 6	at Wpg. 2	Pokey Reddick	55	55	65	80	
Wayne Gretzky	L.A.	4-3-89	Phi. 2	at L.A. 6	Ron Hextall	66	67	54	78	
Joe Nieuwendyk	Cgy.	21-3-89	NYI 1	at Cgy. 4	Mark Fitzpatrick	72	74	51	77	
Joe Mullen	Cgy.	31-3-89	Wpg. 1	at Cgy. 4	Bob Essensa	78	79	51	79	32.1
Brett Hull	St. L.	6-2-90	Tor. 4	at St. L. 6	Jeff Reese	54	54	72	80	25.6
Steve Yzerman	Det.	24-2-90	Det. 3	at NYI 3	Glenn Healy	63	63	62	79	
Cam Neely	Bos.	10-3-90	Bos. 3	at NYI 3	Mark Fitzpatrick	69	71	55	76	24.9
Luc Robitaille	L.A.	31-3-90	L.A. 3	at Van. 6	Kirk McLean	79	79	52	80	
Brian Bellows	Min.	22-3-90	Min. 5	at Det. 1	Tim Cheveldae	75	75	55	80	25.6
Pat LaFontaine	NYI	24-3-90	NYI 5	at Edm. 5	Bill Ranford	71	77	54	74	25.1
Stephane Richer	Mtl.	24-3-90	Mtl. 4	at Hfd. 7	Peter Sidorkiewicz	75	77	51	75	
Gary Leeman	Tor.	28-3-90	NYI 6	at Tor. 3	Mark Fitzpatrick	78	78	51	80	26.1
Brett Hull	St. L.	25-1-91	St. L. 9	at Det. 4	David Gagnon	49	49	86	78	
Cam Neely	Bos.	26-3-91	Bos. 7	at Que. 4	empty net	67	78	51	69	
Theoren Fleury	Cgy.	26-3-91	Van. 2	at Cgy. 7	Bob Mason	77	77	51	79	22.9
Steve Yzerman	Det.	30-3-91	NYR 5	at Det. 6	Mike Richter	79	79	51	80	
Brett Hull	St. L.	28-1-92	St. L. 3	at L.A. 3	Kelly Hrudey	50	50	70	73	
Jeremy Roenick	Chi.	7-3-92	Chi. 2	at Bos. 1	Daniel Berthiaume	67	67	53	80	22.2
Kevin Stevens	Pit.	24-3-92	Pit. 3	at Det. 4	Tim Cheveldae	74	74	54	80	26.11
Gary Roberts	Cgy.	31-3-92	Edm. 2	at Cgy. 5	Bill Ranford	73	77	53	76	25.10
Alexander Mogilny	Buf.	3-2-93	Hfd. 2	at Buf. 3	Sean Burke	46	53	76	77	23.11
Teemu Selanne	Wpg.	28-2-93	Min. 6	at Wpg. 7	Darcy Wakaluk	63	63	76	84	22.6
Pavel Bure	Van.	1-3-93	Van. 5	at Buf. 2*	Grant Fuhr	63	63	60	83	21.11
Steve Yzerman	Det.	10-3-93	Det. 6	at Edm. 3	Bill Ranford	70	70	58	84	
Luc Robitaille	L.A.	15-3-93	L.A. 4	at Buf. 2	Grant Fuhr	69	69	63	84	
Brett Hull	St. L.	20-3-93	St. L. 2	at L.A. 3	Robb Stauber	73	73	54	80	
Mario Lemieux	Pit.	21-3-93	Pit. 6	at Edm. 4**	Ron Tugnutt	48	72	69	60	
Kevin Stevens	Pit.	21-3-93	Pit. 6	at Edm. 4**	Ron Tugnutt	62	72	55	72	
Dave Andreychuk	Tor.	23-3-93	Tor. 5	at Wpg. 4	Bob Essensa	72	73	54	83	29.6
Pat LaFontaine	Buf.	28-3-93	Ott. 1	at Buf. 3	Peter Sidorkiewicz	75	75	53	84	
Pierre Turgeon	NYI	2-4-93	NYI 3	at NYR 2	Mike Richter	75	76	58	83	23.8
Mark Recchi	Phi.	3-4-93	T.B. 2	at Phi. 6	J-C Bergeron	77	77	53	84	25.2
Jeremy Roenick	Chi.	15-4-93	Tor. 2	at Chi. 3	Felix Potvin	84	84	50	84	
Brendan Shanahan	St. L.	15-4-93	T.B. 5	at St. L. 6	Pat Jablonski	71	84	51	71	24.3
Cam Neely	Bos.	7-3-94	Wsh. 3	at Bos. 6	Don Beaupre	44	66	50	49	
Sergei Fedorov	Det.	15-3-94	Van. 2	at Det. 5	Kirk McLean	67	69	56	82	24.3
Pavel Bure	Van.	23-3-94	Van. 6	at L.A. 3	empty net	65	73	60	76	
Adam Graves	NYR	23-3-94	NYR 5	at Edm. 3	Bill Ranford	74	74	51	84	25.11
Dave Andreychuk	Tor	24-3-94	S.J. 2	at Tor. 1	Arturs Irbe	73	74	53	83	
Brett Hull	St. L.	25-3-94	Dal. 3	at St. L. 5	Andy Moog	71	74	52	81	
Ray Sheppard	Det.	29-3-94	Hfd. 2	at Det. 6	Sean Burke	74	76	52	82	27.10
Brendan Shanahan	St. L.	12-4-94	St. L. 5	at Dal. 9	Andy Moog	80	83	52	81	
Mike Modano	Dal.	12-4-94	St. L. 5	at Dal. 9	Curtis Joseph	75	83	50	76	23.11
Mario Lemieux	Pit.	23-2-96	Hfd. 4	at Pit. 5	Sean Burke	50	59	69	70	
Jaromir Jagr	Pit.	23-2-96	Hfd. 4	at Pit. 5	Sean Burke	59	59	62	82	24.0
Alexander Mogilny	Van.	29-2-96	St. L. 2	at Van. 2	Grant Fuhr	60	63	55	79	
Peter Bondra	Wsh.	3-4-96	Wsh. 5	at Buf. 1	Andrei Trefilov	62	77	52	67	28.1
Joe Sakic	Col.	7-4-96	Col. 4	at Dal. 1	empty net	79	79	51	82	26.7
John LeClair	Phi.	10-4-96	Phi. 5	at N.J. 1	Corey Schwab	80	80	51	82	26.7
Keith Tkachuk	Wpg.	12-4-96	L.A. 3	at Wpg. 5	empty net	75	81	50	76	24.0
Paul Kariya	Ana.	14-4-96	Wpg. 2	at Ana. 5	N. Khabibulin	82	82	50	82	21.5
Keith Tkachuk	Phx.	6-4-97	Phx. 1	at Col. 2	Patrick Roy	78	79	52	81	
Teemu Selanne	Ana.	9-4-97	L.A. 1	at Ana. 4	empty net	77	81	51	78	
Mario Lemieux	Pit.	11-4-97	Pit. 2	at Fla. 4	J. Vanbiesbrouck	75	81	50	76	
John LeClair	Phi.	13-4-97	N.J. 4	at Phi. 5	Mike Dunham	82	82	50	82	
Teemu Selanne	Ana.	25-3-98	Ana. 3	at Chi. 2	Jeff Hackett	66	71	52	73	
John LeClair	Phi.	13-4-98	Phi. 1	at Buf. 2	Dominik Hasek	79	79	51	82	
Pavel Bure	Van.	17-4-98	Cgy. 4	at Van. 2	Dwayne Roloson	81	81	51	82	
Peter Bondra	Wsh.	18-4-98	Wsh. 4	at Car. 3	Mike Fountain	75	80	52	76	
Pavel Bure	Fla.	18-3-00	Fla. 4	at NYI 2	empty net	63	71	58	74	
Pavel Bure	Fla.	16-3-01	Pit. 6	at Fla. 3	Johan Hedberg	72	72	59	82	
Joe Sakic	Col.	4-4-01	Ana. 1	at Col. 1	J-S Giguere	80	80	54	82	
Jaromir Jagr	Pit.	4-4-01	T.B. 2	at Pit. 4	Kevin Weekes	80	80	52	81	

* neutral site game played at Hamilton; ** neutral site game played at Cleveland

John Ogrodnick

Steve Yzerman

Pavel Bure

Gordie Howe

Jean Ratelle

Mike Rogers

100-Point Seasons

Player	Team	Date of 100th Point	G or A	Score		Player's Game No.	Team Game No.	Points G - A PTS	Total Games	Age when first 100th point scored (Yrs. & Mos.)
Phil Esposito	Bos.	2-3-69	(G)	Pit. 0	at Bos. 4	60	62	49-77 — 126	74	27.1
Bobby Hull	Chi.	20-3-69	(G)	Chi. 5	at Bos. 5	71	71	58-49 — 107	76	30.2
Gordie Howe	Det.	30-3-69	(G)	Det. 5	at Chi. 9	76	76	44-59 — 103	76	41.0
Bobby Orr	Bos.	15-3-70	(G)	Det. 5	at Bos. 5	67	67	33-87 — 120	76	22.11
Phil Esposito	Bos.	6-2-71	(A)	Buf. 3	at Bos. 4	51	51	76-76 — 152	78	
Bobby Orr	Bos.	20-2-71	(A)	Bos. 4	at L.A. 5	58	58	37-102 — 139	78	
John Bucyk	Bos.	13-3-71	(G)	Bos. 6	at Van. 3	68	68	51-65 — 116	78	35.10
Ken Hodge	Bos.	21-3-71	(A)	Buf. 7	at Bos. 5	72	72	43-62 — 105	78	26.9
Jean Ratelle	NYR	18-2-72	(A)	NYR 2	at Cal. 2	58	58	46-63 — 109	63	31.4
Phil Esposito	Bos.	19-2-72	(A)	Bos. 6	at Min. 4	59	59	66-67 — 133	76	
Bobby Orr	Bos.	2-3-72	(A)	Van. 3	at Bos. 7	64	64	37-80 — 117	76	
Vic Hadfield	NYR	25-3-72	(A)	NYR 3	at Mtl. 3	74	74	50-56 — 106	78	31.5
Phil Esposito	Bos.	3-3-73	(A)	Bos. 1	at Mtl. 5	64	64	55-75 — 130	78	
Bobby Clarke	Phi.	29-3-73	(G)	Atl. 2	at Phi. 4	76	76	37-67 — 104	78	23.7
Bobby Orr	Bos.	31-3-73	(G)	Bos. 3	at Tor. 7	62	77	29-72 — 101	63	
Rick MacLeish	Phi.	1-4-73	(G)	Phi. 4	at Pit. 5	78	78	50-50 — 100	78	23.3
Phil Esposito	Bos.	13-2-74	(A)	Bos. 9	at Cal. 6	53	53	68-77 — 145	78	
Bobby Orr	Bos.	12-3-74	(A)	Buf. 0	at Bos. 4	62	66	32-90 — 122	74	
Ken Hodge	Bos.	24-3-74	(A)	Mtl. 3	at Bos. 6	72	72	50-55 — 105	76	
Phil Esposito	Bos.	8-2-75	(A)	Bos. 8	at Det. 5	54	54	61-66 — 127	79	
Bobby Orr	Bos.	13-2-75	(A)	Bos. 1	at Buf. 3	57	57	46-89 — 135	80	
Guy Lafleur	Mtl.	7-3-75	(G)	Wsh. 4	at Mtl. 8	56	66	53-66 — 119	70	24.6
Pete Mahovlich	Mtl.	9-3-75	(G)	Mtl. 5	at NYR 3	67	67	35-82 — 117	80	29.5
Marcel Dionne	Det.	9-3-75	(A)	Det. 5	at Phi. 8	67	67	47-74 — 121	80	23.7
Bobby Clarke	Phi.	22-3-75	(A)	Min. 0	at Phi. 4	72	72	27-89 — 116	80	
Rene Robert	Buf.	5-4-75	(A)	Buf. 4	at Tor. 2	74	80	40-60 — 100	74	26.4
Guy Lafleur	Mtl.	10-3-76	(G)	Mtl. 5	at Chi. 1	69	69	56-69 — 125	80	
Bobby Clarke	Phi.	11-3-76	(A)	Buf. 1	at Phi. 6	64	68	30-89 — 119	76	
Bill Barber	Phi.	18-3-76	(A)	Van. 2	at Phi. 3	71	71	50-62 — 112	80	23.8
Gilbert Perreault	Buf.	21-3-76	(A)	K.C. 1	at Buf. 3	73	73	44-69 — 113	80	25.4
Pierre Larouche	Pit.	24-3-76	(G)	Bos. 5	at Pit. 5	70	74	53-58 — 111	76	20.4
Pete Mahovlich	Mtl.	28-3-76	(A)	Mtl. 2	at Bos. 2	77	77	34-71 — 105	80	
Jean Ratelle	Bos.	30-3-76	(G)	Buf. 4	at Bos. 4	77	77	36-69 — 105	80	
Jean Pronovost	Pit.	3-4-76	(A)	Wsh. 5	at Pit. 4	79	79	52-52 — 104	80	30.4
Darryl Sittler	Tor.	3-4-76	(A)	Bos. 4	at Tor. 2	78	79	41-59 — 100	79	25.7
Guy Lafleur	Mtl.	26-2-77	(A)	Cle. 3	at Mtl. 5	63	63	56-80 — 136	80	
Marcel Dionne	L.A.	5-3-77	(G)	Pit. 3	at L.A. 3	67	67	53-69 — 122	80	
Steve Shutt	Mtl.	27-3-77	(A)	Mtl. 6	at Det. 0	77	77	60-45 — 105	80	24.9
Bryan Trottier	NYI	25-2-78	(A)	Chi. 1	at NYI 7	59	60	46-77 — 123	77	21.7
Guy Lafleur	Mtl.	28-2-78	(G)	Det. 3	at Mtl. 9	69	61	60-72 — 132	78	
Darryl Sittler	Tor.	12-3-78	(A)	Tor. 7	at Pit. 1	67	67	45-72 — 117	80	
Guy Lafleur	Mtl.	27-2-79	(A)	Mtl. 3	at NYI 7	61	61	52-77 — 129	80	
Bryan Trottier	NYI	6-3-79	(A)	Buf. 3	at NYI 2	59	63	47-87 — 134	76	
Marcel Dionne	L.A.	8-3-79	(G)	L.A. 4	at Buf. 6	66	66	59-71 — 130	80	
Mike Bossy	NYI	11-3-79	(G)	NYI 4	at Bos. 4	66	66	69-57 — 126	80	22.2
Bob MacMillan	Atl.	15-3-79	(A)	Atl. 4	at Phi. 5	68	69	37-71 — 108	79	26.6
Guy Chouinard	Atl.	30-3-79	(G)	L.A. 3	at Atl. 5	75	75	50-57 — 107	80	22.5
Denis Potvin	NYI	8-4-79	(A)	NYI 5	at NYR 2	73	80	31-70 — 101	73	25.5
Marcel Dionne	L.A.	6-2-80	(A)	L.A. 3	at Hfd. 7	53	53	53-84 — 137	80	
Guy Lafleur	Mtl.	10-2-80	(A)	Mtl. 3	at Bos. 2	55	55	50-75 — 125	74	
Wayne Gretzky	Edm.	24-2-80	(A)	Bos. 4	at Edm. 2	61	62	51-86 — 137	79	19.2
Bryan Trottier	NYI	30-3-80	(A)	NYI 9	at Que. 6	75	77	42-62 — 104	78	
Gilbert Perreault	Buf.	1-4-80	(A)	Buf. 5	at Atl. 2	77	77	40-66 — 106	80	
Mike Rogers	Hfd.	4-4-80	(A)	Que. 2	at Hfd. 9	79	79	44-61 — 105	80	25.5
Charlie Simmer	L.A.	5-4-80	(G)	Van. 5	at L.A. 3	64	80	56-45 — 101	64	26.0
Blaine Stoughton	Hfd.	6-4-80	(A)	Det. 3	at Hfd. 5	80	80	56-44 — 100	80	27.0
Wayne Gretzky	Edm.	6-2-81	(G)	Wpg. 4	at Edm. 10	53	53	55-109 — 164	80	
Marcel Dionne	L.A.	12-2-81	(A)	L.A. 5	at Chi. 5	58	58	58-77 — 135	80	
Charlie Simmer	L.A.	14-2-81	(A)	Bos. 5	at L.A. 4	59	59	56-49 — 105	65	
Kent Nilsson	Cgy.	27-2-81	(G)	Hfd. 1	at Cgy. 5	64	64	49-82 — 131	80	24.6
Mike Bossy	NYI	3-3-81	(G)	Edm. 8	at NYI 8	65	66	68-51 — 119	79	
Dave Taylor	L.A.	14-3-81	(G)	Min. 4	at L.A. 10	63	70	47-65 — 112	72	25.3
Mike Rogers	Hfd.	22-3-81	(G)	Tor. 3	at Hfd. 3	74	74	40-65 — 105	80	
Bernie Federko	St. L.	28-3-81	(A)	Buf. 4	at St. L. 7	74	76	31-73 — 104	78	24.10
Rick Middleton	Bos.	28-3-81	(A)	Chi. 2	at Bos. 5	76	76	44-59 — 103	80	27.4
Jacques Richard	Que.	29-3-81	(G)	Mtl. 0	at Que. 4	75	76	52-51 — 103	78	28.6
Bryan Trottier	NYI	29-3-81	(G)	NYI 5	at Wsh. 4	69	76	31-72 — 103	73	
Peter Stastny	Que.	29-3-81	(A)	Mtl. 0	at Que. 4	73	76	39-70 — 109	77	24.6
Wayne Gretzky	Edm.	27-12-81	(G)	L.A. 3	at Edm. 10	38	38	92-120 — 212	80	
Mike Bossy	NYI	13-2-82	(A)	Phi. 2	at NYI 8	55	55	64-83 — 147	80	
Peter Stastny	Que.	16-2-82	(A)	Wpg. 3	at Que. 7	60	60	46-93 — 139	80	
Dennis Maruk	Wsh.	20-2-82	(G)	Wsh. 3	at Min. 7	60	60	60-76 — 136	80	26.3
Bryan Trottier	NYI	23-2-82	(G)	Chi. 1	at NYI 5	61	61	50-79 — 129	80	
Denis Savard	Chi.	27-2-82	(A)	Chi. 5	at L.A. 3	64	64	32-87 — 119	80	21.1
Bobby Smith	Min.	3-3-82	(A)	Det. 4	at Min. 6	66	66	43-71 — 114	80	24.1
Marcel Dionne	L.A.	6-3-82	(G)	L.A. 6	at Hfd. 7	64	66	50-67 — 117	78	
Dave Taylor	L.A.	20-3-82	(A)	Pit. 5	at L.A. 7	71	72	39-67 — 106	78	
Dale Hawerchuk	Wpg.	24-3-82	(G)	L.A. 3	at Wpg.	74	74	45-58 — 103	80	18.11
Dino Ciccarelli	Min.	27-3-82	(A)	Min. 6	at Bos. 5	72	76	55-52 — 107	76	21.8
Glenn Anderson	Edm.	28-3-82	(G)	Edm. 6	at L.A. 2	78	78	38-67 — 105	80	21.7
Mike Rogers	NYR	2-4-82	(G)	Pit. 7	at NYR 5	79	79	38-65 — 103	80	

Player	Team	Date of 100th Point	G or A	Score		Player's Game No.	Team Game No.	Points G - A PTS	Total Games	Age when first 100th point scored (Yrs. & Mos.)
Wayne Gretzky	Edm.	5-1-83	(A)	Edm. 8	at Wpg. 3	42	42	71-125 — 196	80	
Mike Bossy	NYI	3-3-83	(A)	Tor. 1	at NYI. 5	66	67	60-58 — 118	79	
Peter Stastny	Que.	5-3-83	(A)	Hfd. 3	at Que. 10	62	67	47-77 — 124	75	
Denis Savard	Chi.	6-3-83	(G)	Mtl. 4	at Chi. 5	65	67	35-86 — 121	78	
Mark Messier	Edm.	23-3-83	(G)	Edm. 4	at Wpg. 7	73	76	48-58 — 106	77	22.2
Barry Pederson	Bos.	26-3-83	(A)	Hfd. 4	at Bos. 7	73	76	46-61 — 107	77	22.0
Marcel Dionne	L.A.	26-3-83	(A)	Edm. 9	at L.A. 3	75	75	56-51 — 107	80	
Michel Goulet	Que.	27-3-83	(A)	Que. 6	at Buf. 6	77	77	57-48 — 105	80	22.11
Glenn Anderson	Edm.	29-3-83	(A)	Edm. 7	at Van. 4	70	78	48-56 — 104	72	
Jari Kurri	Edm.	29-3-83	(A)	Edm. 7	at Van. 4	78	78	45-59 — 104	80	22.10
Kent Nilsson	Cgy.	29-3-83	(G)	L.A. 3	at Cgy. 5	78	78	46-58 — 104	80	
Wayne Gretzky	Edm.	18-12-83	(G)	Edm. 7	at Wpg. 5	34	34	87-118 — 205	74	
Paul Coffey	Edm.	4-3-84	(A)	Mtl. 1	at Edm. 6	68	68	40-86 — 126	80	22.9
Michel Goulet	Que.	4-3-84	(A)	Que. 1	at Buf. 1	62	67	56-65 — 121	75	
Jari Kurri	Edm.	7-3-84	(G)	Chi. 4	at Edm. 7	53	69	52-61 — 113	64	
Peter Stastny	Que.	8-3-84	(A)	Que. 8	at Pit. 6	69	69	46-73 — 119	80	
Mike Bossy	NYI	8-3-84	(G)	Tor. 5	at NYI 9	56	68	51-67 — 118	67	
Barry Pederson	Bos.	14-3-84	(A)	Bos. 4	at Det. 2	71	71	39-77 — 116	80	
Bryan Trottier	NYI	18-3-84	(G)	NYI 4	at Hfd. 5	62	73	40-71 — 111	68	
Bernie Federko	St. L.	20-3-84	(A)	Wpg. 3	at St. L. 9	75	76	41-66 — 107	79	
Rick Middleton	Bos.	27-3-84	(G)	Bos. 6	at Que. 4	77	77	47-58 — 105	80	
Dale Hawerchuk	Wpg.	27-3-84	(G)	Wpg. 3	at L.A. 3	77	77	37-65 — 102	80	
Mark Messier	Edm.	27-3-84	(G)	Edm. 9	at Cgy. 2	72	79	37-64 — 101	73	
Wayne Gretzky	Edm.	29-12-84	(A)	Det. 3	at Edm. 6	35	35	73-135 — 208	80	
Jari Kurri	Edm.	29-1-85	(G)	Edm. 4	at Cgy. 2	48	51	71-64 — 135	73	
Mike Bossy	NYI	23-2-85	(G)	Bos. 1	at NYI 7	56	60	58-59 — 117	76	
Dale Hawerchuk	Wpg.	25-2-85	(A)	Wpg. 12	at NYR 5	64	64	53-77 — 130	80	
Marcel Dionne	L.A.	5-3-85	(A)	Pit. 0	at L.A. 6	66	66	46-80 — 126	80	
Brent Sutter	NYI	12-3-85	(A)	NYI 6	at St. L. 5	68	68	42-60 — 102	72	22.10
John Ogrodnick	Det.	22-3-85	(A)	NYR 3	at Det. 5	73	73	55-50 — 105	79	25.9
Paul Coffey	Edm.	26-3-85	(G)	Edm. 7	at NYI 5	74	74	37-84 — 121	80	
Denis Savard	Chi.	29-3-85	(A)	Chi. 5	at Wpg. 5	75	76	38-67 — 105	79	
Peter Stastny	Que.	2-4-85	(A)	Bos. 4	at Que. 6	74	77	32-68 — 100	75	
Bernie Federko	St. L.	4-4-85	(A)	NYR 5	at St. L. 4	74	78	30-73 — 103	76	
John Tonelli	NYI	6-4-85	(G)	N.J. 5	at NYI 5	80	80	42-58 — 100	80	28.1
Paul MacLean	Wpg.	6-4-85	(A)	Wpg. 6	at Edm. 5	78	79	41-60 — 101	79	27.1
Bernie Nicholls	L.A.	6-4-85	(A)	Van. 4	at L.A. 4	80	80	46-54 — 100	80	22.9
Mike Gartner	Wsh.	7-4-85	(G)	Pit. 3	at Wsh. 7	80	80	50-52 — 102	80	25.6
Mario Lemieux	Pit.	7-4-85	(G)	Pit. 3	at Wsh. 7	73	80	43-57 — 100	73	19.6
Wayne Gretzky	Edm.	4-1-86	(A)	Hfd. 3	at Edm. 4	39	39	52-163 — 215	80	
Mario Lemieux	Pit.	15-2-86	(G)	Van. 4	at Pit. 9	55	56	48-93 — 141	79	
Paul Coffey	Edm.	19-2-86	(A)	Tor. 5	at Edm. 9	59	60	48-90 — 138	79	
Peter Stastny	Que.	1-3-86	(A)	Buf. 8	at Que. 4	66	68	41-81 — 122	76	
Jari Kurri	Edm.	2-3-86	(G)	Phi. 1	at Edm. 2	62	64	68-63 — 131	78	
Mike Bossy	NYI	8-3-86	(G)	Wsh. 6	at NYI 2	65	65	61-62 — 123	80	
Denis Savard	Chi.	12-3-86	(A)	Buf. 7	at Chi. 6	69	69	47-69 — 116	80	
Mats Naslund	Mtl.	13-3-86	(A)	Mtl. 2	at Bos. 3	70	70	43-67 — 110	80	26.4
Michel Goulet	Que.	24-3-86	(A)	Que. 1	at Min. 0	70	75	53-50 — 103	75	
Glenn Anderson	Edm.	25-3-86	(G)	Edm. 7	at Det. 2	66	74	54-48 — 102	72	
Neal Broten	Min.	26-3-86	(A)	Min. 6	at Tor. 1	76	76	29-76 — 105	80	26.4
Dale Hawerchuk	Wpg.	31-3-86	(A)	Wpg. 5	at L.A. 2	78	78	46-59 — 105	80	
Bernie Federko	St. L.	5-4-86	(G)	Chi. 5	at St. L. 7	79	79	34-68 — 102	80	
Wayne Gretzky	Edm.	11-1-87	(A)	Cgy. 3	at Edm. 5	42	42	62-121 — 183	79	
Jari Kurri	Edm.	14-3-87	(A)	Buf. 3	at Edm. 5	67	68	54-54 — 108	79	
Mario Lemieux	Pit.	18-3-87	(A)	St. L. 4	at Pit. 5	55	72	54-53 — 107	63	
Mark Messier	Edm.	19-3-87	(A)	Edm. 4	at Cgy. 5	71	71	37-70 — 107	77	
Dino Ciccarelli	Min.	30-3-87	(A)	NYR 6	at Min. 5	78	78	52-51 — 103	80	
Doug Gilmour	St. L.	2-4-87	(A)	Buf. 3	at St. L. 5	78	78	42-63 — 105	80	23.10
Dale Hawerchuk	Wpg.	5-4-87	(A)	Wpg. 3	at Cgy. 1	80	80	47-53 — 100	80	
Mario Lemieux	Pit.	20-1-88	(G)	Plt. 8	at Chi. 3	45	48	70-98 — 168	77	
Wayne Gretzky	Edm.	11-2-88	(G)	Edm. 7	at Van. 2	43	56	40-109 — 149	64	
Denis Savard	Chi.	12-2-88	(A)	St. L. 3	at Chi. 4	57	57	44-87 — 131	80	
Dale Hawerchuk	Wpg.	23-2-88	(G)	Wpg. 4	at Pit. 3	61	61	44-77 — 121	80	
Steve Yzerman	Det.	27-2-88	(A)	Det. 4	at Que. 5	63	63	50-52 — 102	64	22.10
Peter Stastny	Que.	8-3-88	(A)	Hfd. 4	at Que. 6	63	67	46-65 — 111	76	
Mark Messier	Edm.	15-3-88	(A)	Buf. 4	at Edm. 6	68	71	37-74 — 111	77	
Jimmy Carson	L.A.	26-3-88	(A)	Chi. 5	at L.A. 9	77	77	55-52 — 107	80	19.8
Hakan Loob	Cgy.	26-3-88	(A)	Van. 1	at Cgy. 6	76	76	50-56 — 106	80	27.9
Mike Bullard	Cgy.	26-3-88	(A)	Van. 1	at Cgy. 6	76	76	48-55 — 103	79	27.1
Michel Goulet	Que.	27-3-88	(A)	Pit. 6	at Que. 3	76	76	48-58 — 106	80	
Luc Robitaille	L.A.	30-3-88	(G)	Cgy. 7	at L.A. 9	78	78	53-58 — 111	80	22.1
Mario Lemieux	Pit.	31-12-88	(A)	N.J. 6	at Pit. 8	36	38	85-114 — 199	76	
Wayne Gretzky	L.A.	21-1-89	(A)	L.A. 4	at Hfd. 5	47	48	54-114 — 168	78	
Bernie Nicholls	L.A.	21-1-89	(A)	L.A. 4	at Hfd. 5	48	48	70-80 — 150	79	
Steve Yzerman	Det.	27-1-89	(G)	Tor. 1	at Det. 8	50	50	65-90 — 155	80	
Rob Brown	Pit.	16-3-89	(A)	Pit. 2	at N.J. 1	60	72	49-66 — 115	68	20.11
Paul Coffey	Pit.	20-3-89	(A)	Pit. 2	at Min. 7	69	74	30-83 — 113	75	
Joe Mullen	Cgy.	23-3-89	(A)	L.A. 2	at Cgy. 4	74	75	51-59 — 110	79	32.1
Jari Kurri	Edm.	29-3-89	(A)	Edm. 5	at Van. 2	75	79	44-58 — 102	76	
Jimmy Carson	Edm.	2-4-89	(A)	Edm. 2	at Cgy. 4	80	80	49-51 — 100	80	
Mario Lemieux	Pit.	28-1-90	(G)	Pit. 2	at Buf. 7	50	50	45-78 — 123	59	
Wayne Gretzky	L.A.	30-1-90	(A)	N.J. 2	at L.A. 5	51	51	40-102 — 142	73	
Steve Yzerman	Det.	19-2-90	(A)	Mtl. 5	at Det. 5	61	61	62-65 — 127	79	
Mark Messier	Edm.	20-2-90	(A)	Edm. 4	at Van. 2	62	62	45-84 — 129	79	
Brett Hull	St. L.	3-3-90	(A)	NYI 4	at St. L. 5	67	67	72-41 — 113	80	25.7
Bernie Nicholls	NYR	12-3-90	(A)	L.A. 6	at NYR 2	70	71	39-73 — 112	79	
Pierre Turgeon	Buf.	25-3-90	(G)	N.J. 4	at Buf. 3	76	76	40-66 — 106	80	20.7
Paul Coffey	Pit.	25-3-90	(A)	Pit. 2	at Hfd. 4	77	77	29-74 — 103	80	
Pat LaFontaine	NYI	27-3-90	(G)	Cgy. 4	at NYI 2	72	78	54-51 — 105	74	25.1
Adam Oates	St. L.	29-3-90	(G)	Pit 4	at St. L. 5	79	79	23-79 — 102	80	27.7

Kent Nilsson

Mats Naslund

Pat LaFontaine

Alexander Mogilny

Joe Sakic

Doug Weight

Player	Team	Date of 100th Point	G or A	Score		Player's Game No.	Team Game No.	Points G - A PTS	Total Games	Age when first 100th point scored (Yrs. & Mos.)
Joe Sakic	Que.	31-3-90	(G)	Hfd. 3	at Que. 2	79	79	39-63 — 102	80	20.8
Ron Francis	Hfd.	31-3-90	(G)	Hfd. 3	at Que. 2	79	79	32-69 — 101	80	27.0
Luc Robitaille	L.A.	1-4-90	(A)	L.A. 4	at Cgy. 8	80	80	52-49 — 101	80	
Wayne Gretzky	L.A.	30-1-91	(A)	N.J. 4	at L.A. 2	50	51	41-122 — 163	78	
Brett Hull	St. L.	23-2-91	(G)	Bos. 2	at St. L. 9	60	62	86-45 — 131	78	
Mark Recchi	Pit.	5-3-91	(G)	Van. 1	at Pit. 4	66	67	40-73 — 113	78	23.1
Steve Yzerman	Det.	10-3-91	(G)	Det. 4	at St. L. 1	72	72	51-57 — 108	80	
John Cullen	Hfd.	16-3-91	(G)	N.J. 2	at Hfd. 6	71	71	39-71 — 110	78	26.7
Adam Oates	St. L.	17-3-91	(A)	St. L. 4	at Chi. 6	54	73	25-90 — 115	61	
Joe Sakic	Que.	19-3-91	(G)	Edm. 7	at Que. 6	74	74	48-61 — 109	80	
Steve Larmer	Chi.	24-3-91	(A)	Min. 4	at Chi. 5	76	76	44-57 — 101	80	29.9
Theoren Fleury	Cgy.	26-3-91	(G)	Van. 2	at Cgy. 7	77	77	51-53 — 104	79	22.9
Al MacInnis	Cgy.	28-3-91	(A)	Edm. 4	at Cgy. 4	78	78	28-75 — 103	78	27.8
Brett Hull	St. L.	2-3-92	(G)	St. L. 5	at Van. 3	66	66	70-39 — 109	73	
Wayne Gretzky	L.A.	3-3-92	(A)	Phi. 1	at L.A. 4	60	66	31-90 — 121	74	
Kevin Stevens	Pit.	7-3-92	(A)	Pit. 3	at L.A. 5	66	66	54-69 — 123	80	26.11
Mario Lemieux	Pit.	10-3-92	(A)	Cgy. 2	at Pit. 5	53	67	44-87 — 131	64	
Luc Robitaille	L.A.	17-3-92	(A)	Wpg. 4	at L.A. 5	73	73	44-63 — 107	80	
Mark Messier	NYR	22-3-92	(G)	N.J. 3	at NYR 6	74	75	35-72 — 107	79	
Jeremy Roenick	Chi.	29-3-92	(A)	Tor. 1	at Chi. 5	77	77	53-50 — 103	80	22.2
Steve Yzerman	Det.	14-4-92	(G)	Det. 7	at Min. 4	79	80	45-58 — 103	79	
Brian Leetch	NYR	16-4-92	(G)	Pit. 1	at NYR 7	80	80	22-80 — 102	80	24.1
Mario Lemieux	Pit.	31-12-92	(G)	Tor. 3	at Pit. 3	38	39	69-91 — 160	60	
Pat LaFontaine	Buf.	10-2-93	(A)	Buf. 6	at Wpg. 2	55	55	53-95 — 148	84	
Adam Oates	Bos.	14-2-93	(A)	Bos. 3	at T.B. 3	58	58	45-97 — 142	84	
Steve Yzerman	Det.	24-2-93	(A)	Det. 7	at Buf. 10	64	64	58-79 — 137	84	
Pierre Turgeon	NYI	28-2-93	(G)	NYI 7	at Hfd. 6	62	63	58-74 — 132	83	
Doug Gilmour	Tor.	3-3-93	(A)	Min. 1	at Tor. 3	64	64	32-95 — 127	83	
Alexander Mogilny	Buf.	5-3-93	(A)	Hfd. 4	at Buf. 2	58	65	76-51 — 127	77	24.1
Mark Recchi	Phi.	7-3-93	(G)	Phi. 3	at N.J. 7	66	66	53-70 — 123	84	
Teemu Selanne	Wpg.	9-3-93	(G)	Wpg. 4	at T.B. 2	68	68	76-56 — 132	84	22.7
Luc Robitaille	L.A.	15-3-93	(A)	L.A. 4	at Buf. 2	69	69	63-62 — 125	84	
Kevin Stevens	Pit.	23-3-93	(A)	S.J. 2	at Pit. 7	63	73	55-56 — 111	72	
Mats Sundin	Que.	27-3-93	(G)	Phi. 3	at Que. 8	71	75	47-67 — 114	80	22.1
Pavel Bure	Van.	1-4-93	(G)	Van. 5	at T.B. 3	77	77	60-50 — 110	83	22.0
Jeremy Roenick	Chi.	4-4-93	(G)	St. L. 4	at Chi. 5	79	79	50-57 — 107	84	
Craig Janney	St. L.	4-4-93	(G)	St. L. 4	at Chi. 5	79	79	24-82 — 106	84	25.7
Rick Tocchet	Pit.	7-4-93	(G)	Mtl. 3	at Pit. 4	77	81	48-61 — 109	80	28.11
Joe Sakic	Que.	8-4-93	(A)	Que. 2	at Bos. 6	75	81	48-57 — 105	78	
Ron Francis	Pit.	9-4-93	(A)	Pit. 10	at NYR 4	82	82	24-76 — 100	84	
Brett Hull	St. L.	11-4-93	(G)	Min. 1	at St. L. 5	78	82	54-47 — 101	80	
Theoren Fleury	Cgy.	11-4-93	(G)	Cgy. 3	at Van. 6	82	82	34-66 — 100	83	
Joe Juneau	Bos.	14-4-93	(A)	Bos. 4	at Ott. 2	84	84	32-70 — 102	84	25.3
Wayne Gretzky	L.A.	14-2-94	(A)	Bos. 3	at L.A. 2	56	56	38-92 — 130	81	
Sergei Fedorov	Det.	1-3-94	(A)	Cgy. 2	at Det. 5	63	63	56-64 — 120	82	24.2
Doug Gilmour	Tor.	23-3-94	(G)	Tor. 1	at Fla. 1	74	74	27-84 — 111	83	
Adam Oates	Bos.	26-3-94	(A)	Mtl. 3	at Bos. 6	68	75	32-80 — 112	77	
Mark Recchi	Phi.	27-3-94	(A)	Ana. 3	at Phi. 2	76	76	40-67 — 107	84	
Pavel Bure	Van.	28-3-94	(A)	Tor. 2	at Van. 3	68	76	60-47 — 107	76	
Jeremy Roenick	Chi.	31-3-94	(G)	Chi. 3	at Wsh. 6	78	78	46-61 — 107	84	
Brendan Shanahan	St. L.	12-4-94	(G)	St. L. 5	at Dal. 9	80	83	52-50 — 102	81	25.2
Mario Lemieux	Pit.	16-1-96	(G)	Col. 5	at Pit. 2	38	44	69-92 — 161	70	
Jaromir Jagr	Pit.	6-2-96	(G)	Bos. 5	at Pit. 6	52	52	62-87 — 149	82	23.12
Ron Francis	Pit.	9-3-96	(A)	N.J. 4	at Pit. 3	61	66	27-92 — 119	77	
Peter Forsberg	Col.	9-3-96	(A)	Col. 7	at Van. 5	68	68	30-86 — 116	82	22.7
Joe Sakic	Col.	17-3-96	(A)	Edm. 1	at Col. 8	70	70	51-69 — 120	82	
Teemu Selanne	Ana.	25-3-96	(A)	Ana. 1	at Det. 5	70	73	40-68 — 108	79	
Alexander Mogilny	Van.	25-3-96	(A)	L.A. 1	at Van. 4	72	75	55-52 — 107	79	
Eric Lindros	Phi.	25-3-96	(A)	Hfd. 0	at Phi. 3	65	73	47-68 — 115	73	23.0
Wayne Gretzky	St. L.	28-3-96	(A)	N.J. 4	at St. L. 4	76	75	23-79 — 102	80	
Doug Weight	Edm.	30-3-96	(G)	Tor. 4	at Edm. 3	76	76	25-79 — 104	82	25.3
Sergei Fedorov	Det.	2-4-96	(A)	Det. 3	at S.J. 6	72	76	39-68 — 107	78	
Paul Kariya	Ana.	7-4-96	(G)	Ana. 5	at S.J. 3	78	78	50-58 — 108	82	21.5
Mario Lemieux	Pit.	8-3-97	(A)	Phi. 2	at Pit. 3	61	65	50-72 — 122	76	
Teemu Selanne	Ana.	1-4-97	(A)	Chi. 3	at Ana. 3	74	78	51-58 — 109	78	
Jaromir Jagr	Pit.	15-4-98	(G)	T.B. 1	at Pit. 5	76	80	35-67 — 102	77	
Jaromir Jagr	Pit.	13-3-99	(G)	Phi. 0	at Pit. 4	65	65	44-83 — 127	81	
Teemu Selanne	Ana.	5-4-99	(A)	Ana. 2	at Det. 3	69	76	47-60 — 107	75	
Paul Kariya	Ana.	17-4-99	(G)	Ana. 3	at S.J. 3	82	82	39-62 — 101	82	
Jaromir Jagr	Pit.	10-3-01	(G)	Cgy. 3	at Pit. 6	68	68	52-69-121	81	
Joe Sakic	Col.	18-3-01	(G)	Min. 3	at Col. 4	72	72	54-64-118	82	

Five-or-more-Goal Games

Player	Team	Date	Score		Opposing Goaltender
SEVEN GOALS					
Joe Malone	Quebec Bulldogs	Jan. 31/20	Tor. 6	at Que. 10	Ivan Mitchell
SIX GOALS					
Newsy Lalonde	Montreal	Jan. 10/20	Tor. 7	at Mtl. 14	Ivan Mitchell
Joe Malone	Quebec Bulldogs	Mar. 10/20	Ott. 4	at Que. 10	Clint Benedict
Corb Denneny	Toronto St. Pats	Jan. 26/21	Ham. 3	at Tor. 10	Howard Lockhart
Cy Denneny	Ottawa Senators	Mar. 7/21	Ham. 5	at Ott. 12	Howard Lockhart
Syd Howe	Detroit	Feb. 3/44	NYR 2	at Det. 12	Ken McAuley
Red Berenson	St. Louis	Nov. 7/68	St. L. 8	at Phil 0	Doug Favell
Darryl Sittler	Toronto	Feb. 7/76	Bos. 4	at Tor. 11	Dave Reece
FIVE GOALS					
Joe Malone	Montreal	Dec. 19/17	Mtl. 7	at Ott. 4	Clint Benedict
Harry Hyland	Mtl. Wanderers	Dec. 19/17	Tor. 9	at Mtl. W. 10	Art Brooks
Joe Malone	Montreal	Jan. 12/18	Ott. 4	at Mtl. 9	Clint Benedict
Joe Malone	Montreal	Feb. 2/18	Tor. 2	at Mtl. 11	Harry Holmes
Mickey Roach	Toronto St. Pats	Mar. 6/20	Que. 2	at Tor. 11	Frank Brophy
Newsy Lalonde	Montreal	Feb. 16/21	Ham. 5	at Mtl. 10	Howard Lockhart
Babe Dye	Toronto St. Pats	Dec. 16/22	Mtl. 2	at Tor. 7	Georges Vezina
Red Green	Hamilton Tigers	Dec. 5/24	Ham. 10	at Tor. 3	John Ross Roach
Babe Dye	Toronto St. Pats	Dec. 22/24	Tor. 10	at Bos. 1	Charles Stewart
Punch Broadbent	Mtl. Maroons	Jan. 7/25	Mtl. 6	at Ham. 2	Jake Forbes
Pit Lepine	Montreal	Dec. 14/29	Ott. 4	at Mtl. 6	Alex Connell
Howie Morenz	Montreal	Mar. 18/30	NYA 3	at Mtl. 8	Roy Worters
Charlie Conacher	Toronto	Jan. 19/32	NYA 3	at Tor. 11	Roy Worters
Ray Getliffe	Montreal	Feb. 6/43	Bos. 3	at Mtl. 8	Frank Brimsek
Maurice Richard	Montreal	Dec. 28/44	Det. 1	at Mtl. 9	Harry Lumley
Howie Meeker	Toronto	Jan. 8/47	Chi. 4	at Tor. 10	Paul Bibeault
Bernie Geoffrion	Montreal	Feb. 19/55	NYR 2	at Mtl. 10	Gump Worsley
Bobby Rousseau	Montreal	Feb. 1/64	Det. 3	at Mtl. 9	Roger Crozier
Yvan Cournoyer	Montreal	Feb. 15/75	Chi. 3	at Mtl. 12	Mike Veisor
Don Murdoch	NY Rangers	Oct. 12/76	NYR 10	at Min. 4	Gary Smith
Ian Turnbull	Toronto	Feb. 2/77	Det. 1	at Tor. 9	Ed Giacomin (2) Jim Rutherford (3)
Bryan Trottier	NY Islanders	Dec. 23/78	NYR 4	at NYI 9	Wayne Thomas (4) John Davidson (1)
Tim Young	Minnesota	Jan. 15/79	Min. 8	at NYR 1	Doug Soetaert (3) Wayne Thomas (2)

Player	Team	Date	Score		Opposing Goaltender
John Tonelli	NY Islanders	Jan. 6/81	Tor. 3	at NYI 6	Jiri Crha (4) empty net (1)
Wayne Gretzky	Edmonton	Feb. 18/81	St. L. 2	at Edm. 9	Mike Liut (3) Ed Staniowski (2)
Wayne Gretzky	Edmonton	Dec. 30/81	Phi. 5	at Edm. 7	Pete Peeters (4) empty net (1)
Grant Mulvey	Chicago	Feb. 3/82	St. L. 5	at Chi. 9	Mike Liut (4) Gary Edwards (1)
Bryan Trottier	NY Islanders	Feb. 13/82	Phi. 2	at NYI 8	Pete Peeters
Willy Lindstrom	Winnipeg	Mar. 2/82	Wpg. 7	at Phi. 6	Pete Peeters
Mark Pavelich	NY Rangers	Feb. 23/83	Hfd. 3	at NYR 11	Greg Millen
Jari Kurri	Edmonton	Nov. 19/83	N.J. 4	at Edm. 13	Chico Resch (3) Ron Low (2)
Bengt Gustafsson	Washington	Jan. 8/84	Wsh. 7	at Phi. 1	Pelle Lindbergh
Pat Hughes	Edmonton	Feb. 3/84	Cgy. 5	at Edm. 10	Don Edwards (3) Reggie Lemelin (2)
Wayne Gretzky	Edmonton	Dec. 15/84	Edm. 8	at St. L. 2	Rick Wamsley (4) Mike Liut(1)
Dave Andreychuk	Buffalo	Feb. 6/86	Buf. 8	at Bos. 6	Pat Riggin (1) Doug Keans (4)
Wayne Gretzky	Edmonton	Dec. 6/87	Min. 4	at Edm. 10	Don Beaupre (4) Kari Takko (1)
Mario Lemieux	Pittsburgh	Dec. 31/88	N.J. 6	at Pit. 8	Bob Sauve (3) Chris Terreri (2)
Joe Nieuwendyk	Calgary	Jan. 11/89	Wpg. 3	at Cgy. 8	Daniel Berthiaume
Mats Sundin	Quebec	Mar. 5/92	Que. 10	at Hfd. 4	Peter Sidorkiewicz (3) Kay Whitmore (2)
Mario Lemieux	Pittsburgh	Apr. 9/93	Pit. 10	at NYR 4	Corey Hirsch (3) Mike Richter (2)
Peter Bondra	Washington	Feb. 5/94	T.B. 3	at Wsh. 6	Daren Puppa (4) Pat Jablonski (1)
Mike Ricci	Quebec	Feb. 17/94	Que. 8	at S.J. 2	Arturs Irbe (3) Jimmy Waite (2)
Alexei Zhamnov	Winnipeg	Apr. 1/95	Wpg. 7	at L.A. 7	Kelly Hrudey (3) Grant Fuhr (2)
Mario Lemieux	Pittsburgh	Mar. 26/96	St. L. 4	at Pit. 8	Grant Fuhr (1) Jon Casey (4)
Sergei Fedorov	Detroit	Dec. 26/96	Wsh. 4	at Det. 5	Jim Carey

Players' 500th Goals

Regular Season

Player	Team	Date	Game No.	Score		Opposing Goaltender	Total Goals	Total Games
Maurice Richard	Montreal	Oct. 19/57	863	Chi. 1	at Mtl. 3	Glenn Hall	544	978
Gordie Howe	Detroit	Mar. 14/62	1,045	Det. 2	at NYR 3	Gump Worsley	801	1,767
Bobby Hull	Chicago	Feb. 21/70	861	NYR. 2	at Chi. 4	Ed Giacomin	610	1,063
Jean Béliveau	Montreal	Feb. 11/71	1,101	Min. 2	at Mtl. 6	Gilles Gilbert	507	1,125
Frank Mahovlich	Montreal	Mar. 21/73	1,105	Van. 2	at Mtl. 3	Dunc Wilson	533	1,181
Phil Esposito	Boston	Dec. 22/74	803	Det. 4	at Bos. 5	Jim Rutherford	717	1,282
John Bucyk	Boston	Oct. 30/75	1,370	St. L. 2	at Bos. 3	Yves Bélanger	556	1,540
Stan Mikita	Chicago	Feb. 27/77	1,221	Van. 4	at Chi. 3	Cesare Maniago	541	1,394
Marcel Dionne	Los Angeles	Dec. 14/82	887	L.A. 2	at Wsh. 7	Al Jensen	731	1,348
Guy Lafleur	Montreal	Dec. 20/83	918	Mtl. 6	at N.J. 0	Chico Resch	560	1,126
Mike Bossy	NY Islanders	Jan. 2/86	647	Bos. 5	at NYI 7	empty net	573	752
Gilbert Perreault	Buffalo	Mar. 9/86	1,159	N.J. 3	at Buf. 4	Alain Chevrier	512	1,191
Wayne Gretzky	Edmonton	Nov. 22/86	575	Van. 2	at Edm. 5	empty net	894	1,487
Lanny McDonald	Calgary	Mar. 21/89	1,107	NYI 1	at Cgy. 4	Mark Fitzpatrick	500	1,111
Bryan Trottier	NY Islanders	Feb. 13/90	1,104	Cgy. 4	at NYI 2	Rick Wamsley	524	1,279
Mike Gartner	NY Rangers	Oct. 14/91	936	Wsh. 5	at NYR 3	Mike Liut	708	1,432
Michel Goulet	Chicago	Feb. 16/92	951	Cgy. 5	at Chi. 5	Jeff Reese	548	1,089
Jari Kurri	Los Angeles	Oct. 17/92	833	Bos. 6	at L.A. 8	empty net	601	1,251
Dino Ciccarelli	Detroit	Jan. 8/94	946	Det. 6	at L.A. 3	Kelly Hrudey	608	1,232
*Mario Lemieux	Pittsburgh	Oct. 26/95	605	Pit. 7	at NYI 5	Tommy Soderstrom	648	788
*Mark Messier	NY Rangers	Nov. 6/95	1,141	Cgy. 2	at NYR 4	Rick Tabaracci	651	1,561
*Steve Yzerman	Detroit	Jan. 17/96	906	Col. 2	at Det. 3	Patrick Roy	645	1,310
Dale Hawerchuk	St. Louis	Jan. 31/96	1,103	St. L. 4	at Tor. 0	Felix Potvin	518	1,188
*Brett Hull	St. Louis	Dec. 22/96	693	L.A. 4	at St. L. 7	Stephane Fiset	649	1,019
Joe Mullen	Pittsburgh	Mar. 14/97	1,052	Pit. 3	at Col. 6	Patrick Roy	502	1,062
*Dave Andreychuk	New Jersey	Mar. 15/97	1,070	Wsh. 2	at N.J. 3	Bill Ranford	572	1,361
*Luc Robitaille	Los Angeles	Jan. 7/99	928	Buf. 2	at L.A. 4	Dwayne Roloson	590	1,124
*Pat Verbeek	Detroit	Mar. 22/00	1,285	Cgy. 2	at Det. 2	Fred Brathwaite	515	1,360

No NHL player has scored five goals in a single game since Sergei Fedorov did the deed for Detroit. Fedorov scored all five goals in the Red Wings' 5-4 win over Washington on December 26, 1996.

Players' 1,000th Points

Regular Season

Player	Team	Date	Game No.	G or A	Score		Total Points G A PTS	Total Games
Gordie Howe	Detroit	Nov. 27/60	938	(A)	Tor. 0	at Det. 2	801-1,049–1,850	1,767
Jean Béliveau	Montreal	Mar. 3/68	911	(G)	Mtl. 2	at Det. 5	507-712–1,219	1,125
Alex Delvecchio	Detroit	Feb. 16/69	1,143	(A)	LA 3	at Det. 6	456-825–1,281	1,549
Bobby Hull	Chicago	Dec. 13/70	909	(A)	Min. 2	at Chi. 5	610-560–1,170	1,063
Norm Ullman	Toronto	Oct. 16/71	1,113	(A)	NYR 5	at Tor. 3	490-739–1,229	1,410
Stan Mikita	Chicago	Oct. 15/72	924	(A)	St. L. 3	at Chi. 1	541-926–1,467	1,394
John Bucyk	Boston	Nov. 9/72	1,144	(G)	Det. 3	at Bos. 8	556-813–1,369	1,540
Frank Mahovlich	Montreal	Feb. 17/73	1,090	(A)	Phi. 7	at Mtl. 6	533-570–1,103	1,181
Henri Richard	Montreal	Dec. 20/73	1,194	(A)	Mtl. 2	at Buf. 2	358-688–1,046	1,256
Phil Esposito	Boston	Feb. 15/74	745	(A)	Bos. 4	at Van. 2	717-873–1,590	1,282
Rod Gilbert	NY Rangers	Feb. 19/77	1,027	(G)	NYR 2	at NYI 5	406-615–1,021	1,065
Jean Ratelle	Boston	Apr. 3/77	1,007	(A)	Tor. 4	at Bos. 7	491-776–1,267	1,281
Marcel Dionne	Los Angeles	Jan. 7/81	740	(G)	L.A. 5	at Hfd. 3	731-1,040–1,771	1,348
Guy Lafleur	Montreal	Mar. 4/81	720	(G)	Mtl. 9	at Wpg. 3	560-793–1,353	1,126
Bobby Clarke	Philadelphia	Mar. 19/81	922	(G)	Bos. 3	at Phi. 5	358-852–1,210	1,144
Gilbert Perreault	Buffalo	Apr. 3/82	871	(A)	Buf. 5	at Mtl.4	512-814–1,326	1,191
Darryl Sittler	Philadelphia	Jan. 20/83	927	(G)	Cgy 2	at Phi. 5	484-637–1,121	1,096
Wayne Gretzky	Edmonton	Dec. 19/84	424	(A)	L.A. 3	at Edm. 7	894-1,963–2,875	1,487
Bryan Trottier	NY Islanders	Jan. 29/85	726	(G)	Min. 4	at NYI 4	524-901–1,425	1,279
Mike Bossy	NY Islanders	Jan. 24/86	656	(A)	NYI 7	at Wsh. 5	573-553–1,126	752
Denis Potvin	NY Islanders	Apr. 4/87	987	(G)	Buf. 6	at NYI 6	310-742–1,052	1,060
Bernie Federko	St. Louis	Mar. 19/88	855	(A)	Hfd. 5	at St. L. 3	369-761–1,130	1,000
Lanny McDonald	Calgary	Mar. 7/89	1,101	(G)	Wpg. 5	at Cgy. 9	500-506–1,006	1,111
Peter Stastny	Quebec	Oct. 19/89	682	(G)	Que. 5	at Chi. 3	450-789–1,239	977
Jari Kurri	Edmonton	Jan. 2/90	716	(A)	Edm. 6	at St. L. 4	601-797–1,398	1,251
Denis Savard	Chicago	Mar. 11/90	727	(A)	St. L. 6	at Chi. 4	473-865–1,338	1,196
Paul Coffey	Pittsburgh	Dec. 22/90	770	(A)	Pit. 4	at NYI 3	396-1,135–1,531	1,409
*Mark Messier	Edmonton	Jan. 13/91	822	(A)	Edm. 5	at Phi. 3	651-1,130–1,781	1,561
Dave Taylor	Los Angeles	Feb. 5/91	930	(A)	L.A. 3	at Phi. 2	431-638–1,069	1,111
Michel Goulet	Chicago	Feb. 23/91	878	(G)	Chi. 3	at Min. 3	548-604–1,152	1,089
Dale Hawerchuk	Buffalo	Mar. 8/91	781	(G)	Chi. 5	at Buf. 3	518-891–1,409	1,188
Bobby Smith	Minnesota	Nov. 30/91	986	(A)	Min. 4	at Tor. 3	357-679–1,036	1,077
Mike Gartner	NY Rangers	Jan. 4/92	971	(G)	NYR 4	at N.J. 6	708-627–1,335	1,432
Raymond Bourque	Boston	Feb. 29/92	933	(A)	Wsh. 5	at Bos. 5	410-1,169–1,579	1,612
*Mario Lemieux	Pittsburgh	Mar. 24/92	513	(A)	Pit. 3	at Det. 4	648-922–1,570	788
Glenn Anderson	Toronto	Feb. 22/93	954	(G)	Tor. 8	at Van. 1	498-601–1,099	1,129
*Steve Yzerman	Detroit	Feb. 24/93	737	(A)	Det. 7	at Buf. 10	645-969–1,614	1,310
*Ron Francis	Pittsburgh	Oct. 28/93	893	(G)	Que. 7	at Pit. 3	487-1,137–1,624	1,489
Bernie Nicholls	New Jersey	Feb. 13/94	858	(G)	N.J. 3	at T.B. 3	475-734–1,209	1,127
Dino Ciccarelli	Detroit	Mar. 9/94	957	(G)	Det. 5	at Cgy. 1	608-592–1,200	1,232
Brian Propp	Hartford	Mar. 19/94	1,008	(G)	Hfd. 5	at Phi. 3	425-579–1,004	1,016
Joe Mullen	Pittsburgh	Feb. 7/95	935	(A)	Fla. 3	at Pit. 7	502-561–1,063	1,062
Steve Larmer	NY Rangers	Mar. 8/95	983	(A)	N.J. 4	at NYR 6	441-571–1,012	1,006
*Doug Gilmour	Toronto	Dec. 23/95	935	(A)	Edm. 1	at Tor. 6	429-914–1,343	1,342
*Larry Murphy	Toronto	Mar. 27/96	1,228	(G)	Tor. 6	at Van. 2	287-929–1,216	1,615
*Dave Andreychuk	New Jersey	Apr. 7/96	998	(G)	NYR 2	at N.J. 4	572-637–1,209	1,361
*Adam Oates	Washington	Oct. 8/97	830	(G)	Wsh. 6	at NYI 3	316-963–1,279	1,130
*Phil Housley	Washington	Nov. 8/97	1,081	(A)	Edm. 1	at Wsh. 2	317-847–1,164	1,357
Dale Hunter	Washington	Jan. 9/98	1,308	(A)	Phi. 1	at Wsh. 4	323-697–1,020	1,407
Pat Lafontaine	NY Rangers	Jan. 22/98	847	(G)	Phi. 4	at NYR 3	468-545–1,013	865
*Luc Robitaille	Los Angeles	Jan. 29/98	882	(A)	Cgy. 3	at L.A. 5	590-648–1,238	1,124
*Al MacInnis	St. Louis	Apr. 7/98	1,056	(A)	St. L. 3	at Det. 5	313-845–1,158	1,262
*Brett Hull	Dallas	Nov. 14/98	815	(A)	Dal. 3	at Bos. 1	649-534–1,183	1,019
Brian Bellows	Washington	Jan. 2/99	1,147	(A)	Tor. 2	at Wsh. 5	485-537–1,022	1,188
*Pierre Turgeon	St. Louis	Oct. 9/99	881	(G)	St. L. 4	at Edm. 3	453-692–1,145	1,008
*Joe Sakic	Colorado	Dec. 27/99	810	(A)	St. L. 1	at Col. 5	457-721–1,178	934
*Pat Verbeek	Detroit	Feb. 27/00	1,275	(A)	T.B. 1	at Det. 3	515-528–1,043	1,360
*V. Damphousse	San Jose	Oct. 14/00	1,090	(A)	Bos. 2	at S.J. 5	377-668-1,045	1,132
*Jaromir Jagr	Pittsburgh	Dec. 30/00	763	(G)	Ott. 3	at Pit. 5	439-640-1,079	806
*Mark Recchi	Philadelphia	Mar. 13/01	920	(A)	St. L. 2	at Phi. 5	388-622-1,010	932

*Active

Vincent Damphousse (top), Jaromir Jagr (center) and Mark Recchi (above) each reached the 1,000-point plateau during the 2000-01 season.

Individual Awards

Hart Memorial Trophy

Art Ross Trophy

Calder Memorial Trophy

James Norris Memorial Trophy

HART MEMORIAL TROPHY

An annual award "to the player adjudged to be the most valuable to his team." Winner selected in a poll by the Professional Hockey Writers' Association in the 30 NHL cities at the end of the regular schedule. The winner receives $10,000 and the runners-up $6,000 and $4,000.

History: The Hart Memorial Trophy was presented by the National Hockey League in 1960 after the original Hart Trophy was retired to the Hockey Hall of Fame. The original Hart Trophy was donated to the NHL in 1923 by Dr. David A. Hart, father of Cecil Hart, former manager-coach of the Montreal Canadiens.

2000-01 Winner: **Joe Sakic, Colorado Avalanche**
Runners-up: **Mario Lemieux, Pittsburgh Penguins**
Jaromir Jagr, Pittsburgh Penguins

Center Joe Sakic of the Colorado Avalanche added a chapter to the rich history of the Hart Memorial Trophy by capturing his first such award in his 13th season. No other player in the 78-year history of the Hart Trophy has played as many NHL seasons as Sakic before winning hockey's highest individual honor for the first time. As well, Sakic joins Mark Messier, Wayne Gretzky and Bobby Clarke as only the fourth player in NHL history to captain his club to a Stanley Cup championship and capture the Hart Trophy in the same season. Sakic received a total of 53 first-place votes and 585 points to finish well ahead of Mario Lemieux (eight first place votes, 272 points) and Jaromir Jagr (210 points).

Sakic led his club to the Presidents' Trophy with a franchise-record 118 points, and finished second in the NHL scoring race with 118 points (54 goals, 64 assists) in 82 games. He led all players in power-play points (46) and game-winning goals (12), and tied for the League lead in plus-minus (+45). Sakic's best previous results in Hart Trophy voting were seventh-place finishes in 1990-91 and 1995-96.

CALDER MEMORIAL TROPHY

An annual award "to the player selected as the most proficient in his first year of competition in the National Hockey League." Winner selected in a poll by the Professional Hockey Writers' Association at the end of the regular schedule. The winner receives $10,000 and the runners-up $6,000 and $4,000.

History: From 1936-37 until his death in 1943, Frank Calder, NHL President, bought a trophy each year to be given permanently to the outstanding rookie. After Calder's death, the NHL presented the Calder Memorial Trophy in his memory and the trophy is to be kept in perpetuity. To be eligible for the award, a player cannot have played more than 25 games in any single preceding season nor in six or more games in each of any two preceding seasons in any major professional league. Beginning in 1990-91, to be eligible for this award a player must not have attained his twenty-sixth birthday by September 15th of the season in which he is eligible.

2000-01 Winner: **Evgeni Nabokov, San Jose Sharks**
Runners-up: **Brad Richards, Tampa Bay Lightning**
Martin Havlat, Ottawa Senators

Goaltender Evgeni Nabokov of the San Jose Sharks was elected the winner of the Calder Memorial Trophy. Nabokov received 50 of 62 first-place votes and was the second choice on seven other ballots for a total of 565 points. Tampa Bay's Brad Richards finished second in the balloting with nine first-place votes and 416 points. Martin Havlat of Ottawa received two first-place votes and 240 points.

Nabokov posted a 32-21-7 record with a 2.19 goals-against average and a .915 save percentage in 66 games for San Jose. The Sharks' ninth choice, 219th overall, in the 1994 Entry Draft, Nabokov is the first Calder Trophy winner in franchise history. He was just the second San Jose player to be named a Calder finalist, following defenseman Brad Stuart who was runner-up behind Scott Gomez last year.

ART ROSS TROPHY

An annual award "to the player who leads the league in scoring points at the end of the regular season." The winner receives $10,000 and the runners-up $6,000 and $4,000.

History: Arthur Howie Ross, former manager-coach of the Boston Bruins, presented the trophy to the National Hockey League in 1947. If two players finish the schedule with the same number of points, the trophy is awarded in the following manner: 1. Player with most goals. 2. Player with fewer games played. 3. Player scoring first goal of the season.

2000-01 Winner: **Jaromir Jagr, Pittsburgh Penguins**
Runners-up: **Joe Sakic, Colorado Avalanche**
Patrik Elias, New Jersey Devils

Right winger Jaromir Jagr of the Pittsburgh Penguins won the Art Ross Trophy for the fourth consecutive time. Jagr tallied 121 points (52 goals, 69 assists) in 81 games, helping the Penguins reach the Stanley Cup Playoffs for the 11th consecutive season. Jagr had 36 multiple-point games, tied for the League lead in assists (69) and posted a 16-game assist streak from January 9 to February 16 — the longest since Adam Oates had an 18-game streak with Boston in 1992-93. Jagr edged out Joe Sakic, who finished second in the League with 118 points (54 goals, 64 assists). Patrik Elias of the Devils placed third in the scoring race with 96 points (40 goals, 56 assists).

Jagr, who also won in 1995, joins a group of four scoring greats to have won the Art Ross Trophy five or more times: Wayne Gretzky (10), Gordie Howe (six), Mario Lemieux (six) and Phil Esposito (five).

JAMES NORRIS MEMORIAL TROPHY

An annual award "to the defense player who demonstrates throughout the season the greatest all-round ability in the position." Winner selected in a poll by the Professional Hockey Writers' Association at the end of the regular schedule. The winner receives $10,000 and the runners-up $6,000 and $4,000.

History: The James Norris Memorial Trophy was presented in 1953 by the four children of the late James Norris in memory of the former owner-president of the Detroit Red Wings.

2000-01 Winner: **Nicklas Lidstrom, Detroit Red Wings**
Runners-up: **Raymond Bourque, Colorado Avalanche**
Scott Stevens, New Jersey Devils

After finishing as the runner-up for three consecutive seasons, Nicklas Lidstrom of the Detroit Red Wings won the Norris Trophy for the first time in his career. Lidstrom was a near-unanimous choice. He was named the top selection on 56 of 62 ballots and second on five of the other six for 600 points. Colorado's Raymond Bourque (four first-place votes, 251 points) was runner-up for the sixth time in his 22-year career. Scott Stevens had one first-place vote and 203 points to finish third in the balloting.

Lidstrom finished second in scoring among defencemen with 71 points (15 goals, 56 assists) in 82 games and averaged 28:26 of ice time per game, second in the NHL. A native of Vasteras, Sweden, Lidstrom in the first European-trained Norris Trophy winner. Two European defensemen — Borje Salming (1977, 1980) and Vladimir Konstantinov (1997) — had finished as high as second in Norris Trophy voting.

Vezina Trophy

Lady Byng Memorial Trophy

Frank J. Selke Trophy

Conn Smythe Trophy

VEZINA TROPHY

An annual award "to the goalkeeper adjudged to be the best at his position" as voted by the general managers of each of the 30 clubs. Over-all winner receives $10,000, runners-up $6,000 and $4,000.

History: Leo Dandurand, Louis Letourneau and Joe Cattarinich, former owners of the Montreal Canadiens, presented the trophy to the National Hockey League in 1926-27 in memory of Georges Vezina, outstanding goalkeeper of the Canadiens who collapsed during an NHL game on November 28, 1925, and died of tuberculosis a few months later. Until the 1981-82 season, the goalkeeper(s) of the team allowing the fewest number of goals during the regular season were awarded the Vezina Trophy.

2000-01 Winner: Dominik Hasek, Buffalo Sabres
Runners-up: Roman Cechmanek, Philadelphia Flyers
Martin Brodeur, New Jersey Devils

Dominik Hasek of the Buffalo Sabres captured the Vezina Trophy for the sixth time in his career. Only Jacques Plante, who won or shared the Vezina Trophy seven times under the pre-1981-82 format, has earned the award more often. Hasek was named on 25 of 30 ballots and received nine first-place votes for 85 points, edging second-place Roman Cechmanek of the Philadelphia Flyers (seven first place votes, 65 points). Martin Brodeur also had seven first-place votes, but just 42 points in all.

Hasek's 37 victories were tied for third in the League as he posted a record of 37-24-4 in 67 games. He led the League with 11 shutouts, while his 2.11 goals-against average and .921 save percentage both ranked fourth. By helping the Sabres allow a League-low 184 goals, Hasek also earned the William Jennings Trophy.

CONN SMYTHE TROPHY

An annual award "to the most valuable player for his team in the playoffs." Winner selected by the Professional Hockey Writers' Association at the conclusion of the final game in the Stanley Cup Finals. The winner receives $10,000.

History: Presented by Maple Leaf Gardens Limited in 1964 to honor Conn Smythe, the former coach, manager, president and owner-governor of the Toronto Maple Leafs.

2000-01 Winner: Patrick Roy, Colorado Avalanche

Colorado Avalanche goaltender Patrick Roy became the NHL's first three-time winner of the Conn Smythe Trophy. Roy appeared in each of Colorado's 23 playoff games, posting a 16-7 record, 1.70 goals-against average, .934 save percentage and four shutouts. He held the opposition to one goal or less in 13 of his 23 games. In the Stanley Cup Finals, Roy was 4-3 with a 1.58 goals-against average, two shutouts and a .938 save percentage.

LADY BYNG MEMORIAL TROPHY

An annual award "to the player adjudged to have exhibited the best type of sportsmanship and gentlemanly conduct combined with a high standard of playing ability." Winner selected in a poll by the Professional Hockey Writers' Association at the end of the regular schedule. The winner receives $10,000 and the runners-up $6,000 and $4,000.

History: Lady Byng, wife of Canada's Governor-General at the time, presented the Lady Byng Trophy in 1925. After Frank Boucher of the New York Rangers won the award seven times in eight seasons, he was given the trophy to keep and Lady Byng donated another trophy in 1936. After Lady Byng's death in 1949, the National Hockey League presented a new trophy, changing the name to Lady Byng Memorial Trophy.

2000-01 Winner: Joe Sakic, Colorado Avalanche
Runners-up: Nicklas Lidstrom, Detroit Red Wings
Adam Oates, Washington Capitals

Joe Sakic of the Colorado Avalanche won the Lady Byng Memorial Trophy for the first time in his career. Sakic received 15 first-place votes and 312 points to edge Detroit's Nicklas Lidstrom, who had 21 first-place votes but only 308 points overall, in the closest Lady Byng voting in League history. Although this marks his first career victory, Sakic has earned Lady Byng Trophy votes in 11 of his 13 NHL seasons, and finished second to Wayne Gretzky in 1991-92.

FRANK J. SELKE TROPHY

An annual award "to the forward who best excels in the defensive aspects of the game." Winner selected in a poll by the Professional Hockey Writers' Association at the end of the regular schedule. The winner receives $10,000 and the runners-up $6,000 and $4,000.

History: Presented to the National Hockey League in 1977 by the Board of Governors of the NHL in honor of Frank J. Selke, one of the great architects of NHL championship teams.

2000-01 Winner: John Madden, New Jersey Devils
Runners-up: Joe Sakic, Colorado Avalanche
Mike Modano, Dallas Stars

New Jersey Devils center John Madden captured the Frank J. Selke Trophy in just his second full NHL season. Madden received 14 first-place votes and 269 points to edge Colorado Avalanche center Joe Sakic, who polled more first-place votes (15) but 20 fewer voting points (249).

After leading the Devils with six shorthanded goals in 1999-2000, Madden tallied three in 2000-01 to share the club lead with Patrik Elias. Overall, Madden tallied 23 goals and posted a +24 rating, fourth among Devils forwards. He is the first Frank Selke Trophy winner in franchise history.

WILLIAM M. JENNINGS TROPHY

An annual award "to the goalkeeper(s) having played a minimum of 25 games for the team with the fewest goals scored against it." Winners selected on regular-season play. Overall winner receives $10,000, runners-up $6,000 and $4,000.

History: The Jennings Trophy was presented in 1981-82 by the National Hockey League's Board of Governors to honor the late William M. Jennings, longtime governor and president of the New York Rangers and one of the great builders of hockey in the United States.

2000-01 Winner: Dominik Hasek, Buffalo Sabres
Runners-up: Ed Belfour and Marty Turco, Dallas Stars
Evgeni Nabokov, San Jose Sharks (tied with)
Patrick Roy and David Aebischer, Colorado Avalanche

Goaltender Dominik Hasek of the Buffalo Sabres collected the William M. Jennings Trophy for the second time in his career, having shared the award with Grant Fuhr in 1994. Hasek led all goaltenders in shutouts (11), tied for third in wins (37) and placed fourth in both goals-against average (2.11) and save percentage (.921). The Sabres allowed just 184 goals in 82 games en route to a 46-30-5-1 record for 98 points, their highest total since 1989-90. The Dallas Stars goaltending tandem of Ed Belfour and Marty Turco finished runner-up to Hasek with 187 goals against. Both San Jose and Colorado surrendered 192 goals.

LESTER B. PEARSON AWARD

An annual award presented to the NHL's outstanding player as selected by the members of the National Hockey League Players' Association. The winner receives $20,000, and the two finalists receive $10,000 each to donate to the grassroots hockey program of their choice, through the NHLPA's Goals & Dreams Fund

History: The award was first presented in 1970-71 by the NHLPA in honor of the late Lester B. Pearson, former Prime Minister of Canada.

2000-2001 Winner: Joe Sakic, Colorado Avalanche
Finalists: Jaromir Jagr, Pittsburgh Penguins
Mario Lemieux, Pittsburgh Penguins

Joe Sakic of the Colorado Avalanche won the Lester B. Pearson for the first time. Sakic designated his $20,000 to the Burnaby Minor Hockey Association. Jaromir Jagr designate his $10,000 to the Kladno Hockey Club in the Czech Republic. Mario Lemieux donated $5,000 to Pittsburgh Street Pals and $5,000 to Hockey in the Hood, two Pittsburgh area hockey programs.

William M. Jennings Trophy

Jack Adams Award

Bill Masterton Trophy

Lester Patrick Trophy

Lester B. Pearson Award

JACK ADAMS AWARD

An annual award presented by the National Hockey League Broadcasters' Association to "the NHL coach adjudged to have contributed the most to his team's success." Winner selected by a poll among members of the NHL Broadcasters' Association at the end of the regular season. The winner receives $1,000 from the NHLBA.

History: The award was presented by the NHL Broadcasters' Association in 1974 to commemorate the late Jack Adams, coach and general manager of the Detroit Red Wings, whose lifetime dedication to hockey serves as an inspiration to all who aspire to further the game.

2000-01 Winner: **Bill Barber, Philadelphia Flyers**
Runners-up: **Scotty Bowman, Detroit Red Wings**
Jacques Martin, Ottawa Senators

Philadelphia Flyers head coach Bill Barber captured the Jack Adams Award as coach of the year. Barber polled 125 points, including 17 first-place votes, to finish ahead of Detroit's Scotty Bowman (95 points, 14 first-place votes) and Ottawa's Jacques Martin (92, 10). He becomes the first Jack Adams winner to have taken over behind the bench in mid-season and the eighth winner to capture the award in his first NHL season as head coach.

Barber took over in Philadelphia on December 10 and led the Flyers to a 31-13-7-3 record in 54 games, including a 5-0-3 mark in his first eight games. The Flyers finished the season with 100 points and a second-place finish in the Atlantic Division.

BILL MASTERTON MEMORIAL TROPHY

An annual award under the trusteeship of the Professional Hockey Writers' Association to "the National Hockey League player who best exemplifies the qualities of perseverance, sportsmanship and dedication to hockey." Winner selected by a poll among the 30 chapters of the PHWA at the end of the regular season. A $2,500 grant from the PHWA is awarded annually to the Bill Masterton Scholarship Fund, based in Bloomington, MN, in the name of the Masterton Trophy winner.

History: The trophy was presented by the NHL Writers' Association in 1968 to commemorate the late Bill Masterton, a player with the Minnesota North Stars, who exhibited to a high degree the qualities of perseverance, sportsmanship and dedication to hockey, and who died January 15, 1968.

2000-01 Winner: **Adam Graves, New York Rangers**

New York Rangers forward Adam Graves was the recipient of the Masteron Trophy. Over the previous calendar year, Graves' infant son and his father passed away, but the veteran left winger remained the ever-present heart and soul of his team. Graves' dedication to his teammates, the fans, his sport and his charitable endeavors has been unwavering.

LESTER PATRICK TROPHY

An annual award "for outstanding service to hockey in the United States." Eligible recipients are players, officials, coaches, executives and referees. Winners are selected by an award committee consisting of the commissioner of the NHL, an NHL governor, a representative of the New York Rangers, a member of the Hockey Hall of Fame builder's section, a member of the Hockey Hall of Fame player's section, a member of the U.S. Hockey Hall of Fame, a member of the NHL Broadcasters' Association and a member of the Professional Hockey Writers' Association. Each except the League Commissioner is rotated annually. The winner receives a miniature of the trophy.

History: Presented by the New York Rangers in 1966 to honor the late Lester Patrick, longtime general manager and coach of the New York Rangers, whose teams finished out of the playoffs only once in his first 16 years with the club.

2000-01 Winners: **Scotty Bowman**
David Poile
Gary Bettman

The winningest coach in NHL history, Scotty Bowman concluded his 29th NHL season, and his eighth as head coach of the Detroit Red Wings, in 2000-01. Bowman has had his name engraved on the Stanley Cup nine times, eight as head coach, including five with the Montreal Canadiens (1973, 1976, 1977, 1978, 1979), one with the Pittsburgh Penguins (1992) and two in Detroit (1996, 1997). In 1990-91, he helped the Penguins win the Cup as Pittsburgh's director of player development and recruitment. Bowman also is one of only three head coaches in professional sports to win championships with three different teams. The others were professional football coach Guy Chamberlain (Canton, 1922, 1923; Cleveland, 1924; and Frankford, 1926) and CFL coach Don Matthews (British Columbia, 1985; Baltimore, 1995; and Toronto, 1996, 1997).

With nearly 30 years of experience as a hockey executive, David Poile has had a hand in bringing the NHL to three U.S. markets — Atlanta, Washington and, most recently, Nashville. Poile spent 15 seasons as vice president and general manager of the Washington Capitals; under his direction, the Capitals made 14 postseason appearances, won the Patrick Division title in 1989 and advanced to the Conference Finals in 1990. Poile also served USA Hockey as general manager of the 1998 and 1999 U.S. National Teams that competed in the International Ice Hockey Federation World Championships. He and his father, Norman "Bud" Poile, are the sixth father-son combination to receive the Lester Patrick Award, joining Craig and Lynn Patrick; Bill and Arthur Wirtz; James D. and James Norris Sr.; Bruce and James Norris Sr.; and Weston W. and Charles F. Adams.

In his first eight seasons as the NHL's first Commissioner, Gary Bettman has enlarged significantly the League's "franchise footprint" in the United States. Under his direction, the NHL has grown from 24 teams to 30 overall and has reached 21 U.S. markets, up from the 14 in place in February, 1993, when Bettman took office. His tenure has seen the NHL return to Atlanta and Minnesota's Twin Cities area, while franchises also have been placed in Nashville, Dallas, Phoenix, Raleigh, and Columbus.

Bettman secured the League's first U.S. national television agreement in 20 years, signing broadcast contracts with FOX and ESPN/ESPN 2. In 1998, the League signed a multi-tiered, multi-year partnership with ABC and ESPN. Additionally, the League has grown dramatically in the areas of sponsorships, business partnerships, Internet and technological advancements, grassroots initiatives, youth programs and international participation.

King Clancy Memorial Trophy

Bud Light Plus-Minus Award

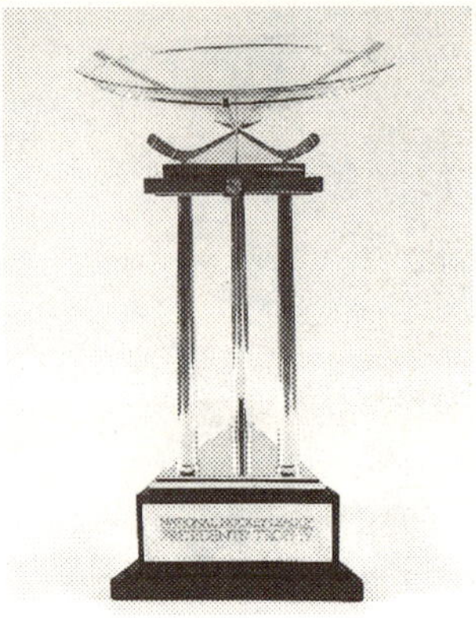

Presidents' Trophy

Maurice "Rocket" Richard Trophy

KING CLANCY MEMORIAL TROPHY

An annual award "to the player who best exemplifies leadership qualities on and off the ice and has made a noteworthy humanitarian contribution in his community."

History: The King Clancy Memorial Trophy was presented to the National Hockey League by the Board of Governors in 1988 to honor the late Frank "King" Clancy.

2000-01 Winner: **Shjon Podein**, Colorado Avalanche

Colorado Avalanche left winger Shjon Podein was the 2000-01 recipient of the King Clancy Memorial Trophy. Through his enthusiastic involvement in all aspects of his own charitable foundation, his efforts to promote education and the countless hours he spends enriching the lives of children, Podein has stood out as the consummate model of a caring community representative.

In 1997, Podein founded the Shjon Podein Children's Foundation in his hometown of Rochester, MN, raising funds for children's charities ranging from medical research to equipping underprivileged youth hockey players. Last season the Foundation supported the introduction of hockey to 40 low-income Denver children.

Podein also serves as spokesperson for the Denver Post Newspaper in Education program "Learning is the Goal," making numerous appearances at local schools to discuss and reinforce with students the ideas of teamwork, respect and pride in their work. He also supports the Read Team program, visiting elementary schools and reading to students, and served as spokesperson for the NHL Cool School program as part of the 2001 NHL All-Star Weekend festivities in Denver.

PRESIDENTS' TROPHY

An annual award to the club finishing the regular-season with the best overall record. The winner receives $350,000, to be split between the team and its players.

History: Presented to the National Hockey League in 1985-86 by the NHL Board of Governors to recognize the team compiling the top regular-season record.

2000-01 Winner: **Colorado Avalanche**
Runners-up: **Detroit Red Wings**
New Jersey Devils

The Colorado Avalanche finished first in the Northwest Division (for their sixth straight divisional title) and in the Western Conference with a record of 52-16-10-4, amassing 118 points and breaking club records for wins (previously 49) and points (107) set when the club last won the Presidents' Trophy in 1997. The Avalanche went on to win the Stanley Cup, becoming just the fifth team to win both honors since the Presidents' Trophy was introduced in 1986. The Detroit Red Wings had the NHL's next-best record at 49-20-9-4 for 111 points. New Jersey finished 48-19-12-3 and also had 111 points.

MAURICE "ROCKET" RICHARD TROPHY

An annual award "presented to the player finishing the regular season as the League's goal-scoring leader."

History: A gift to the NHL from the Montreal Canadiens in 1999, the Maurice "Rocket" Richard Trophy honors one of the game's greatest stars. During his 18-year career with the Canadiens from 1942-43 through 1959-60, Richard was the first player in NHL history to score 50 goals in a season and 500 in his career. He played on eight Stanley Cup champions and led the League in goal scoring five times.

2000-01 Winner: **Pavel Bure, Florida Panthers**
Runners-up: **Joe Sakic, Colorado Avalanche**
Jaromir Jagr, Pittsburgh Penguins

Right winger Pavel Bure of the Florida Panthers won the Maurice "Rocket" Richard Trophy for the second consecutive season. Bure tallied 59 goals, just one shy of his single-season high, and became just the 12th player in NHL history to capture goal-scoring championships in consecutive seasons. Bure accounted for 29.5% of Florida's goals (59 of 200), easily the highest percentage in the League's modern era. Bure surpassed the mark of St. Louis sniper Brett Hull, who tallied 27.7% of the Blues' goals (86 of 310) in 1990-91. Bure also led the League in shots on goal with 384 in 82 games.

Finishing second behind Bure in goals was Joe Sakic, who scored 54 times to surpass his career high of 51 from 1995-96. Jaromir Jagr had 52 goals to surpass 50 for the first time since scoring 62 in 1995-96.

BUD LIGHT PLUS-MINUS AWARD

An annual award "to the player, having played a minimum of 60 games, who leads the League in plus/minus statistics" at the end of the regular season.
Bud Light will contribute $5,000 on behalf of the winner to the charity of his choice.

History: This award was first presented to the NHL in 1997-98 by Anheuser-Busch Inc. to recognize the League leader in plus-minus statistics. Plus-minus statistics are calculated by giving a player a "plus" when on-ice for an even-strength or short-handed goal scored by his team. He receives a "minus" when on-ice for an even-strength or short-handed goal scored by the opposing team. A plus-minus award has been presented since the 1982-83 season.

2000-01 Winners: **Joe Sakic, Colorado Avalanche (tie)**
Patrik Elias, New Jersey Devils (tie)
Runner-up: **Scott Stevens, New Jersey Devils**

Forwards Patrik Elias of the New Jersey Devils and Joe Sakic of the Colorado Avalanche, whose +45 ratings led all National Hockey League players, are the co-winners of the 2000-01 Bud Light Plus-Minus Award. Elias and Sakic were followed by three members of the Devils: defenseman and team captain Scott Stevens (+40), forward Petr Sykora (+36) and defenseman Brian Rafalski (+33). In all, the New Jersey Devils had five players in the top 10. Two Colorado teammates joined Sakic in the top 10 while the Dallas Stars and Ottawa Senators each placed one in the top group.

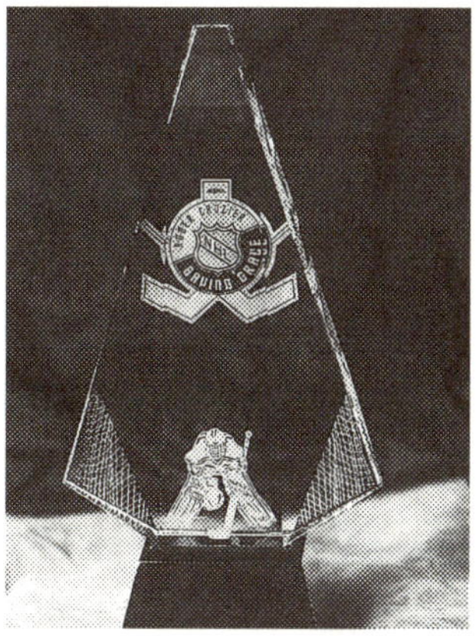

MBNA Roger Crozier Saving Grace Award

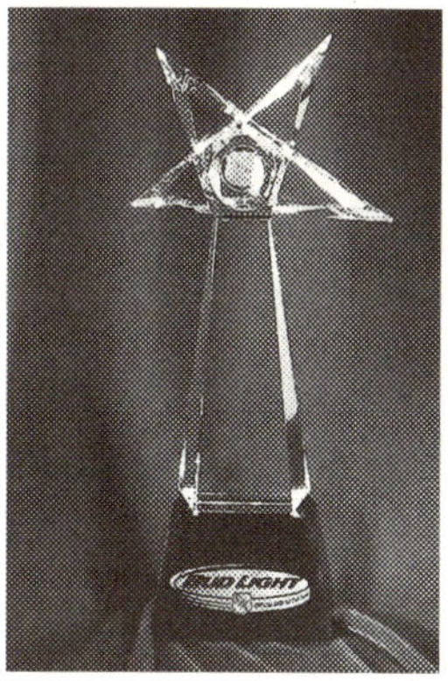

Bud Light NHL All-Star Game MVP Award

MBNA ROGER CROZIER SAVING GRACE AWARD

An award "presented to the goaltender having played a minimum of 25 games with the NHL's best save percentage during the regular season." The winner receives $25,000 to be donated to the youth hockey or educational program of his choice.

History: This award was first presented to the league in 1999-2000 by MBNA Corporation. It is named for Roger Crozier, one of the NHL's top goaltenders during his career. Crozier joined MBNA America Bank in 1983. He passed away on Jan. 11, 1996. Save percentage is calculated by dividing total saves by total shots faced.

2000-01 Winner: **Marty Turco, Dallas Stars**
Runners-up: **Mike Dunham, Nashville Predators**
Sean Burke, Phoenix Coyotes

Dallas Stars goaltender Marty Turco earned the MBNA Roger Crozier Saving Grace Award with a .925 save percentage. He edged Mike Dunham of the Nashville Predators (.923) and Sean Burke of the Phoenix Coyotes (.922), as well as Dominik Hasek of the Buffalo Sabres and first-year goaltender Roman Cechmanek of the Philadelphia Flyers, each of whom finished with a .921 save percentage. Turco's check for $25,000 will be donated to the charities of his choice: the Soo Pee Wee Hockey League (Sault Ste. Marie, Ontario) and to Big Brothers and Big Sisters of Dallas.

BUD LIGHT NHL ALL-STAR GAME MVP AWARD

1962 Eddie Shack, Tor.
1963 Frank Mahovlich, Tor.
1964 Jean Beliveau, Mtl.
1965 Gordie Howe, Det..
1967 Henri Richard, Mtl.
1968 Bruce Gamble, Tor.
1969 Frank Mahovlich, Det.
1970 Bobby Hull, Chi.
1971 Bobby Hull, Chi.
1972 Bobby Orr, Bos.
1973 Greg Polis, Pit.
1974 Garry Unger, St.L.
1975 Syl Apps Jr., Pit.
1976 Peter Mahovlich, Mtl.
1977 Rick Martin, Buf.
1978 Billy Smith, NYI
1980 Reggie Leach, Phi.
1981 Mike Liut, St.L.
1982 Mike Bossy, NYI
1983 Wayne Gretzky, Edm.
1984 Don Maloney, NYR
1985 Mario Lemieux, Pit.
1986 Grant Fuhr, Edm.
1988 Mario Lemieux, Pit.
1989 Wayne Gretzky, L.A.
1990 Mario Lemieux, Pit.
1991 Vincent Damphousse, Tor.
1992 Brett Hull, St.L.
1993 Mike Gartner, NYR
1994 Mike Richter, NYR
1996 Raymond Bourque, Bos.
1997 Mark Recchi, Mtl.
1998 Teemu Selanne, Ana.
1999 Wayne Gretzky, NYR
2000 Pavel Bure, Fla.
2001 Bill Guerin, Bos.

NHL AWARD MONEY BREAKDOWN — 2000-01

(Players on each club determine how team award money is divided.)

TEAM AWARDS

Stanley Cup Playoffs	Number of Clubs	Share Per Club	Total
Conference Quarter-Final Losers	8	$ 237,500	$1,900,000
Conference Semi-Final Losers	4	412,500	1,650,000
Conference Championship Losers	2	902,500	1,805,000
Stanley Cup Loser	1	1,467,500	1,467,500
Stanley Cup Winners	1	2,142,500	2,142,500
TOTAL PLAYOFF AWARD MONEY			$8,965,000

Final Standings, Regular Season	Number of Clubs	Share Per Club	Total
Presidents' Trophy			
Club's Share	1	$ 100,000	$ 100,000
Players' Share	1	250,000	250,000
Conference First Place*	2	500,000	1,000,000
Conference Second Place*	2	375,000	750,000
Conference Third Place*	2	250,000	500,000
Conference Fourth Place*	2	125,000	250,000
*based on points.			
TOTAL REGULAR-SEASON AWARD MONEY			$2,850,000

INDIVIDUAL AWARDS	Winner	First Runner-up	Second Runner-up
Hart, Calder, Norris, Ross, Vezina, Byng, Selke, Jennings, Masterton Trophies	$10,000	$6,000	$4,000
King Clancy Trophy	$ 3,000	$1,000	
Conn Smythe Trophy	$10,000		
TOTAL INDIVIDUAL AWARD MONEY			$194,000

ALL-STARS	Number of winners	Per Player	Total
First Team All-Stars	6	$10,000	$ 60,000
Second Team All-Stars	6	5,000	$ 30,000
TOTAL ALL-STAR AWARD MONEY			$ 90,000
TOTAL AWARD MONEY			**$12,099,000**

2000-01 NHL Player of the Week/Month Award Winners

Player of the Week

Week Ending	Player
Oct. 15	**Patrick Roy**, Colorado
Oct. 22	**Trevor Linden**, Montreal
Oct. 29	**Scott Young**, St. Louis
Nov. 5	**Theoren Fleury**, NY Rangers
Nov. 12	**Alexei Kovalev**, Pittsburgh
Nov. 19	**Tommy Salo**, Edmonton
Nov. 26	**Sergei Fedorov**, Detroit
Dec. 3	**Patrick Lalime**, Ottawa
Dec. 10	**Marc Denis**, Columbus
Dec. 17	**Olaf Kolzig**, Washington
Dec. 23	**Adam Oates**, Washington
Dec. 31	**Mario Lemieux**, Pittsburgh and **Jaromir Jagr**, Pittsburgh
Jan. 7	**Michael Nylander**, Chicago
Jan. 14	**Roman Cechmanek**, Philadelphia
Jan. 21	**Alex Tanguay**, Colorado
Jan. 28	**Evgeni Nabokov**, San Jose
Feb. 11	**Alexei Kovalev**, Pittsburgh
Feb. 18	**Patrick Lalime**, Ottawa
Feb. 25	**Peter Forsberg**, Colorado
Mar. 4	**Patrik Elias**, New Jersey
Mar. 11	**Tommy Salo**, Edmonton
Mar. 18	**Ron Tugnutt**, Columbus
Mar. 25	**Joe Sakic**, Colorado
Apr. 1	**Felix Potvin**, Los Angeles
Apr. 8	**Joe Sakic**, Colorado

Player of the Month

Month	Player
October	**Sean Burke**, Phoenix
November	**Jaromir Jagr**, Pittsburgh
December	**Donald Audette**, Atlanta
January	**Mario Lemieux**, Pittsburgh
February	**Alexei Kovalev**, Pittsburgh
March	**Jaromir Jagr**, Pittsburgh

Rookie of the Month

Month	Player
October	**Brad Richards**, Tampa Bay
November	**Evgeni Nabokov**, San Jose
December	**Evgeni Nabokov**, San Jose
January	**Karel Rachunek**, Ottawa
February	**Shane Willis**, Carolina
March	**Martin Havlat**, Ottawa

NATIONAL HOCKEY LEAGUE INDIVIDUAL AWARD WINNERS

ART ROSS TROPHY

	Winner	Runner-up
2001	Jaromir Jagr, Pit.	Joe Sakic, Col.
2000	Jaromir Jagr, Pit.	Pavel Bure, Fla.
1999	Jaromir Jagr, Pit.	Teemu Selanne, Ana.
1998	Jaromir Jagr, Pit.	Peter Forsberg, Col.
1997	Mario Lemieux, Pit.	Teemu Selanne, Ana.
1996	Mario Lemieux, Pit.	Jaromir Jagr, Pit.
1995	Jaromir Jagr, Pit.	Eric Lindros, Phi.
1994	Wayne Gretzky, L.A.	Sergei Fedorov, Det.
1993	Mario Lemieux, Pit.	Pat LaFontaine, Buf.
1992	Mario Lemieux, Pit.	Kevin Stevens, Pit.
1991	Wayne Gretzky, L.A.	Brett Hull, St.L.
1990	Wayne Gretzky, L.A.	Mark Messier, Edm.
1989	Mario Lemieux, Pit.	Wayne Gretzky, L.A.
1988	Mario Lemieux, Pit.	Wayne Gretzky, Edm.
1987	Wayne Gretzky, Edm.	Jari Kurri, Edm.
1986	Wayne Gretzky, Edm.	Mario Lemieux, Pit.
1985	Wayne Gretzky, Edm.	Jari Kurri, Edm.
1984	Wayne Gretzky, Edm.	Paul Coffey, Edm.
1983	Wayne Gretzky, Edm.	Peter Stastny, Que.
1982	Wayne Gretzky, Edm.	Mike Bossy, NYI
1981	Wayne Gretzky, Edm.	Marcel Dionne, L.A.
1980	Marcel Dionne, L.A.	Wayne Gretzky, Edm.
1979	Bryan Trottier, NYI	Marcel Dionne, L.A.
1978	Guy Lafleur, Mtl.	Bryan Trottier, NYI
1977	Guy Lafleur, Mtl.	Marcel Dionne, L.A.
1976	Guy Lafleur, Mtl.	Bobby Clarke, Phi.
1975	Bobby Orr, Bos.	Phil Esposito, Bos.
1974	Phil Esposito, Bos.	Bobby Orr, Bos.
1973	Phil Esposito, Bos.	Bobby Clarke, Phi.
1972	Phil Esposito, Bos.	Bobby Orr, Bos.
1971	Phil Esposito, Bos.	Bobby Orr, Bos.
1970	Bobby Orr, Bos.	Phil Esposito, Bos.
1969	Phil Esposito, Bos.	Bobby Hull, Chi.
1968	Stan Mikita, Chi.	Phil Esposito, Bos.
1967	Stan Mikita, Chi.	Bobby Hull, Chi.
1966	Bobby Hull, Chi.	Stan Mikita, Chi.
1965	Stan Mikita, Chi.	Norm Ullman, Det.
1964	Stan Mikita, Chi.	Bobby Hull, Chi.
1963	Gordie Howe, Det.	Andy Bathgate, NYR
1962	Bobby Hull, Chi.	Andy Bathgate, NYR
1961	Bernie Geoffrion, Mtl.	Jean Beliveau, Mtl.
1960	Bobby Hull, Chi.	Bronco Horvath, Bos.
1959	Dickie Moore, Mtl.	Jean Beliveau, Mtl.
1958	Dickie Moore, Mtl.	Henri Richard, Mtl.
1957	Gordie Howe, Det.	Ted Lindsay, Det.
1956	Jean Beliveau, Mtl.	Gordie Howe, Det.
1955	Bernie Geoffrion, Mtl.	Maurice Richard, Mtl.
1954	Gordie Howe, Det.	Maurice Richard, Mtl.
1953	Gordie Howe, Det.	Ted Lindsay, Det.
1952	Gordie Howe, Det.	Ted Lindsay, Det.
1951	Gordie Howe, Det.	Maurice Richard, Mtl.
1950	Ted Lindsay, Det.	Sid Abel, Det.
1949	Roy Conacher, Chi.	Doug Bentley, Chi.
1948*	Elmer Lach, Mtl.	Buddy O'Connor, NYR
1947	Max Bentley, Chi.	Maurice Richard, Mtl.
1946	Max Bentley, Chi.	Gaye Stewart, Tor.
1945	Elmer Lach, Mtl.	Maurice Richard, Mtl.
1944	Herb Cain, Bos.	Doug Bentley, Chi.
1943	Doug Bentley, Chi.	Bill Cowley, Bos.
1942	Bryan Hextall Sr., NYR	Lynn Patrick, NYR
1941	Bill Cowley, Bos.	Bryan Hextall Sr., NYR
1940	Milt Schmidt, Bos.	Woody Dumart, Bos.
1939	Toe Blake, Mtl.	Sweeney Schriner, NYA
1938	Gordie Drillon, Tor.	Syl Apps Sr., Tor.
1937	Sweeney Schriner, NYA	Syl Apps Sr., Tor.
1936	Sweeney Schriner, NYA	Marty Barry, Det.
1935	Charlie Conacher, Tor.	Syd Howe, St.L-Det.
1934	Charlie Conacher, Tor.	Joe Primeau, Tor
1933	Bill Cook, NYR	Harvey Jackson, Tor.
1932	Busher Jackson, Tor.	Joe Primeau, Tor.
1931	Howie Morenz, Mtl.	Ebbie Goodfellow, Det.
1930	Cooney Weiland, Bos.	Frank Boucher, NYR
1929	Ace Bailey, Tor.	Nels Stewart, Mtl.M
1928	Howie Morenz, Mtl.	Aurel Joliat, Mtl.
1927	Bill Cook, NYR	Dick Irvin, Chi.
1926	Nels Stewart, Mtl.M.	Cy Denneny, Ott.
1925	Babe Dye, Tor.	Cy Denneny, Ott.
1924	Cy Denneny, Ott.	Billy Boucher, Mtl.
1923	Babe Dye, Tor.	Cy Denneny, Ott.
1922	Punch Broadbent, Ott.	Cy Denneny, Ott.
1921	Newsy Lalonde, Mtl.	Babe Dye, Ham., Tor.
1920	Joe Malone, Que.	Newsy Lalonde, Mtl.
1919	Newsy Lalonde, Mtl.	Odie Cleghorn, Mtl.
1918	Joe Malone, Mtl.	Cy Denneny, Ott.

* Trophy first awarded in 1948.
Scoring leaders listed from 1918 to 1947.

HART TROPHY

	Winner	Runner-up
2001	Joe Sakic, Col.	Mario Lemieux, Pit.
2000	Chris Pronger, St.L.	Jaromir Jagr, Pit.
1999	Jaromir Jagr, Pit.	Alexei Yashin, Ott.
1998	Dominik Hasek, Buf.	Jaromir Jagr, Pit.
1997	Dominik Hasek, Buf.	Paul Kariya, Ana.
1996	Mario Lemieux, Pit.	Mark Messier, NYR
1995	Eric Lindros, Phi.	Jaromir Jagr, Pit.
1994	Sergei Fedorov, Det.	Dominik Hasek, Buf.
1993	Mario Lemieux, Pit.	Doug Gilmour, Tor.
1992	Mark Messier, NYR	Patrick Roy, Mtl.
1991	Brett Hull, St.L.	Wayne Gretzky, L.A.
1990	Mark Messier, Edm.	Raymond Bourque, Bos.
1989	Wayne Gretzky, L.A.	Mario Lemieux, Pit.
1988	Mario Lemieux, Pit.	Grant Fuhr, Edm.
1987	Wayne Gretzky, Edm.	Raymond Bourque, Bos.
1986	Wayne Gretzky, Edm.	Mario Lemieux, Pit.
1985	Wayne Gretzky, Edm.	Dale Hawerchuk, Wpg.
1984	Wayne Gretzky, Edm.	Rod Langway, Wsh.
1983	Wayne Gretzky, Edm.	Pete Peeters, Bos.
1982	Wayne Gretzky, Edm.	Bryan Trottier, NYI
1981	Wayne Gretzky, Edm.	Mike Liut, St.L.
1980	Wayne Gretzky, Edm.	Marcel Dionne, L.A.
1979	Bryan Trottier, NYI	Guy Lafleur, Mtl
1978	Guy Lafleur, Mtl.	Bryan Trottier, NYI
1977	Guy Lafleur, Mtl.	Bobby Clarke, Phi.
1976	Bobby Clarke, Phi.	Denis Potvin, NYI
1975	Bobby Clarke, Phi.	Rogie Vachon, L.A.
1974	Phil Esposito, Bos.	Bernie Parent, Phi.
1973	Bobby Clarke, Phi.	Phil Esposito, Bos.
1972	Bobby Orr, Bos.	Ken Dryden, Mtl.
1971	Bobby Orr, Bos.	Phil Esposito, Bos.
1970	Bobby Orr, Bos.	Tony Esposito, Chi.
1969	Phil Esposito, Bos.	Jean Beliveau, Mtl.
1968	Stan Mikita, Chi.	Jean Beliveau, Mtl.
1967	Stan Mikita, Chi.	Ed Giacomin, NYR
1966	Bobby Hull, Chi.	Jean Beliveau, Mtl.
1965	Bobby Hull, Chi.	Norm Ullman, Det.
1964	Jean Beliveau, Mtl.	Bobby Hull, Chi.
1963	Gordie Howe, Det.	Stan Mikita, Chi.
1962	Jacques Plante, Mtl.	Doug Harvey, NYR
1961	Bernie Geoffrion, Mtl.	Johnny Bower, Tor.
1960	Gordie Howe, Det.	Bobby Hull, Chi.
1959	Andy Bathgate, NYR	Gordie Howe, Det.
1958	Gordie Howe, Det.	Andy Bathgate, NYR
1957	Gordie Howe, Det.	Jean Beliveau, Mtl.
1956	Jean Beliveau, Mtl.	Tod Sloan, Tor.
1955	Ted Kennedy, Tor.	Harry Lumley, Tor.
1954	Al Rollins, Chi.	Red Kelly, Det.
1953	Gordie Howe, Det.	Al Rollins, Chi.
1952	Gordie Howe, Det.	Elmer Lach, Mtl.
1951	Milt Schmidt, Bos.	Maurice Richard, Mtl.
1950	Chuck Rayner, NYR	Ted Kennedy, Tor.
1949	Sid Abel, Det.	Bill Durnan, Mtl.
1948	Buddy O'Connor, NYR	Frank Brimsek, Bos.
1947	Maurice Richard, Mtl.	Milt Schmidt, Bos.
1946	Max Bentley, Chi.	Gaye Stewart, Tor.
1945	Elmer Lach, Mtl.	Maurice Richard, Mtl.
1944	Babe Pratt, Tor.	Bill Cowley, Bos.
1943	Bill Cowley, Bos.	Doug Bentley, Chi.
1942	Tom Anderson, Bro.	Syl Apps Sr., Tor.
1941	Bill Cowley, Bos.	Dit Clapper, Bos.
1940	Ebbie Goodfellow, Det.	Syl Apps Sr., Tor.
1939	Toe Blake, Mtl.	Syl Apps Sr., Tor.
1938	Eddie Shore, Bos.	Paul Thompson, Chi.
1937	Babe Siebert, Mtl.	Lionel Conacher, Mtl.M
1936	Eddie Shore, Bos.	Hooley Smith, Mtl.M
1935	Eddie Shore, Bos.	Charlie Conacher, Tor.
1934	Aurel Joliat, Mtl.	Lionel Conacher, Chi.
1933	Eddie Shore, Bos.	Bill Cook, NYR
1932	Howie Morenz, Mtl.	Ching Johnson, NYR
1931	Howie Morenz, Mtl.	Eddie Shore, Bos.
1930	Nels Stewart, Mtl.M.	Lionel Hitchman, Bos.
1929	Roy Worters, NYA	Ace Bailey, Tor.
1928	Howie Morenz, Mtl.	Roy Worters, Pit.
1927	Herb Gardiner, Mtl.	Bill Cook, NYR
1926	Nels Stewart, Mtl.M.	Sprague Cleghorn, Bos.
1925	Billy Burch, Ham.	Howie Morenz, Mtl.
1924	Frank Nighbor, Ott.	Sprague Cleghorn, Mtl.

BILL MASTERTON TROPHY WINNERS

2001	Adam Graves	NY Rangers
2000	Ken Daneyko	New Jersey
1999	John Cullen	Tampa Bay
1998	Jamie McLennan	St. Louis
1997	Tony Granato	San Jose
1996	Gary Roberts	Calgary
1995	Pat LaFontaine	Buffalo
1994	Cam Neely	Boston
1993	Mario Lemieux	Pittsburgh
1992	Mark Fitzpatrick	NY Islanders
1991	Dave Taylor	Los Angeles
1990	Gord Kluzak	Boston
1989	Tim Kerr	Philadelphia
1988	Bob Bourne	Los Angeles
1987	Doug Jarvis	Hartford
1986	Charlie Simmer	Boston
1985	Anders Hedberg	NY Rangers
1984	Brad Park	Detroit
1983	Lanny McDonald	Calgary
1982	Glenn Resch	Colorado
1981	Blake Dunlop	St. Louis
1980	Al MacAdam	Minnesota
1979	Serge Savard	Montreal
1978	Butch Goring	Los Angeles
1977	Ed Westfall	NY Islanders
1976	Rod Gilbert	NY Rangers
1975	Don Luce	Buffalo
1974	Henri Richard	Montreal
1973	Lowell MacDonald	Pittsburgh
1972	Bobby Clarke	Phiiladelphia
1971	Jean Ratelle	NY Rangers
1970	Pit Martin	Chicago
1969	Ted Hampson	Oakland
1968	Claude Provost	Montreal

PRESIDENTS' TROPHY

	Winner	Runner-up
2001	Colorado Avalanche	Detroit Red Wings
2000	St. Louis Blues	Detroit Red Wings
1999	Dallas Stars	New Jersey Devils
1998	Dallas Stars	New Jersey Devils
1997	Colorado Avalanche	Dallas Stars
1996	Detroit Red Wings	Colorado Avalanche
1995	Detroit Red Wings	Quebec Nordiques
1994	New York Rangers	New Jersey Devils
1993	Pittsburgh Penguins	Boston Bruins
1992	New York Rangers	Washington Capitals
1991	Chicago Blackhawks	St. Louis Blues
1990	Boston Bruins	Calgary Flames
1989	Calgary Flames	Montreal Canadiens
1988	Calgary Flames	Montreal Canadiens
1987	Edmonton Oilers	Philadelphia Flyers
1986	Edmonton Oilers	Philadelphia Flyers

LADY BYNG TROPHY

	Winner	Runner-up
2001	Joe Sakic, Col.	Nicklas Lidstrom, Det.
2000	Pavol Demitra, St.L.	Nicklas Lidstrom, Det.
1999	Wayne Gretzky, NYR.	Nicklas Lidstrom, Det.
1998	Ron Francis, Pit.	Teemu Selanne, Ana.
1997	Paul Kariya, Ana.	Teemu Selanne, Ana.
1996	Paul Kariya, Ana.	Adam Oates, Bos.
1995	Ron Francis, Pit.	Adam Oates, Bos.
1994	Wayne Gretzky, L.A.	Adam Oates, Bos.
1993	Pierre Turgeon, NYI	Adam Oates, Bos.
1992	Wayne Gretzky, L.A.	Joe Sakic, Que.
1991	Wayne Gretzky, L.A.	Brett Hull, St.L.
1990	Brett Hull, St.L.	Wayne Gretzky, L.A.
1989	Joe Mullen, Cgy.	Wayne Gretzky, L.A.
1988	Mats Naslund, Mtl.	Wayne Gretzky, Edm.
1987	Joe Mullen, Cgy.	Wayne Gretzky, Edm.
1986	Mike Bossy, NYI	Jari Kurri, Edm.
1985	Jari Kurri, Edm.	Joe Mullen, St.L.
1984	Mike Bossy, NYI	Rick Middleton, Bos.
1983	Mike Bossy, NYI	Rick Middleton, Bos.
1982	Rick Middleton, Bos.	Mike Bossy, NYI
1981	Rick Kehoe, Pit.	Wayne Gretzky, Edm.
1980	Wayne Gretzky, Edm.	Marcel Dionne, L.A.
1979	Bob MacMillan, Atl.	Marcel Dionne, L.A.
1978	Butch Goring, L.A.	Peter McNab, Bos.
1977	Marcel Dionne, L.A.	Jean Ratelle, Bos.
1976	Jean Ratelle, NYR-Bos.	Jean Pronovost, Pit.
1975	Marcel Dionne, Det.	John Bucyk, Bos.
1974	John Bucyk, Bos.	Lowell MacDonald, Pit.
1973	Gilbert Perreault, Buf.	Jean Ratelle, NYR
1972	Jean Ratelle, NYR	John Bucyk, Bos.
1971	John Bucyk, Bos.	Dave Keon, Tor.
1970	Phil Goyette, St.L.	John Bucyk, Bos.
1969	Alex Delvecchio, Det.	Ted Hampson, Oak.
1968	Stan Mikita, Chi.	John Bucyk, Bos.
1967	Stan Mikita, Chi.	Dave Keon, Tor.
1966	Alex Delvecchio, Det.	Bobby Rousseau, Mtl.
1965	Bobby Hull, Chi.	Alex Delvecchio, Det.
1964	Ken Wharram, Chi.	Dave Keon, Tor.
1963	Dave Keon, Tor.	Camille Henry, NYR
1962	Dave Keon, Tor.	Claude Provost, Mtl.
1961	Red Kelly, Tor.	Norm Ullman, Det.
1960	Don McKenney, Bos.	Andy Hebenton, NYR
1959	Alex Delvecchio, Det.	Andy Hebenton, NYR
1958	Camille Henry, NYR	Don Marshall, Mtl.
1957	Andy Hebenton, NYR	Earl Reibel, Det.
1956	Earl Reibel, Det.	Floyd Curry, Mtl.
1955	Sid Smith, Tor.	Danny Lewicki, NYR
1954	Red Kelly, Det.	Don Raleigh, NYR
1953	Red Kelly, Det.	Wally Hergesheimer, NYR
1952	Sid Smith, Tor.	Red Kelly, Det.
1951	Red Kelly, Det.	Woody Dumart, Bos.
1950	Edgar Laprade, NYR	Red Kelly, Det.
1949	Bill Quackenbush, Det.	Harry Watson, Tor.
1948	Buddy O'Connor, NYR	Syl Apps Sr., Tor.
1947	Bobby Bauer, Bos.	Syl Apps Sr., Tor.
1946	Toe Blake, Mtl.	Clint Smith, Chi.
1945	Bill Mosienko, Chi.	Syd Howe, Det.
1944	Clint Smith, Chi.	Herb Cain, Bos.
1943	Max Bentley, Chi.	Buddy O'Connor, Mtl.
1942	Syl Apps Sr., Tor.	Gordie Drillon, Tor.
1941	Bobby Bauer, Bos.	Gordie Drillon, Tor.
1940	Bobby Bauer, Bos.	Clint Smith, NYR
1939	Clint Smith, NYR	Marty Barry, Det.
1938	Gordie Drillon, Tor.	Clint Smith, NYR
1937	Marty Barry, Det.	Gordie Drillon, Tor.
1936	Doc Romnes, Chi.	Sweeney Schriner, NYA
1935	Frank Boucher, NYR	Russ Blinco, Mtl.M
1934	Frank Boucher, NYR	Joe Primeau, Tor.
1933	Frank Boucher, NYR	Joe Primeau, Tor.
1932	Joe Primeau, Tor.	Frank Boucher, NYR
1931	Frank Boucher, NYR	Normie Himes, NYA
1930	Frank Boucher, NYR	Normie Himes, NYA
1929	Frank Boucher, NYR	Harold Darragh, Pit.
1928	Frank Boucher, NYR	George Hay, Det.
1927	Billy Burch, NYA	Dick Irvin, Chi.
1926	Frank Nighbor, Ott.	Billy Burch, NYA
1925	Frank Nighbor, Ott.	none

KING CLANCY MEMORIAL TROPHY WINNERS

2001	Shjon Podein	Colorado
2000	Curtis Joseph	Toronto
1999	Rob Ray	Buffalo
1998	Kelly Chase	St. Louis
1997	Trevor Linden	Vancouver
1996	Kris King	Winnipeg
1995	Joe Nieuwendyk	Calgary
1994	Adam Graves	NY Rangers
1993	Dave Poulin	Boston
1992	Raymond Bourque	Boston
1991	Dave Taylor	Los Angeles
1990	Kevin Lowe	Edmonton
1989	Bryan Trottier	NY Islanders
1988	Lanny McDonald	Calgary

VEZINA TROPHY

	Winner	Runner-up
2001	Dominik Hasek, Buf.	Roman Cechmanek, Phi.
2000	Olaf Kolzig, Wsh.	Roman Turek, St.L.
1999	Dominik Hasek, Buf.	Curtis Joseph, Tor.
1998	Dominik Hasek, Buf.	Martin Brodeur, N.J.
1997	Dominik Hasek, Buf.	Martin Brodeur, N.J.
1996	Jim Carey, Wsh.	Chris Osgood, Det.
1995	Dominik Hasek, Buf.	Ed Belfour, Chi.
1994	Dominik Hasek, Buf.	John Vanbiesbrouck, Fla.
1993	Ed Belfour, Chi.	Tom Barrasso, Pit.
1992	Patrick Roy, Mtl.	Kirk McLean, Van.
1991	Ed Belfour, Chi.	Patrick Roy, Mtl.
1990	Patrick Roy, Mtl.	Daren Puppa, Buf.
1989	Patrick Roy, Mtl.	Mike Vernon, Cgy.
1988	Grant Fuhr, Edm.	Tom Barrasso, Buf.
1987	Ron Hextall, Phi.	Mike Liut, Hfd.
1986	John Vanbiesbrouck, NYR	Bob Froese, Phi.
1985	Pelle Lindbergh, Phi.	Tom Barrasso, Buf.
1984	Tom Barrasso, Buf.	Reggie Lemelin, Cgy.
1983	Pete Peeters, Bos.	Rollie Melanson, NYI
1982	Billy Smith, NYI	Grant Fuhr, Edm.
1981	Richard Sevigny, Mtl.	Pete Peeters, Phi.
	Denis Herron, Mtl.	Rick St. Croix, Phi.
	Michel Larocque, Mtl.	
1980	Bob Sauve, Buf.	Gerry Cheevers, Bos.
	Don Edwards, Buf.	Gilles Gilbert, Bos.
1979	Ken Dryden, Mtl.	Chico Resch, NYI
	Michel Larocque, Mtl.	Billy Smith, NYI
1978	Ken Dryden, Mtl.	Bernie Parent, Phi.
	Michel Larocque, Mtl.	Wayne Stephenson, Phi.
1977	Ken Dryden, Mtl.	Chico Resch, NYI
	Michel Larocque, Mtl.	Billy Smith, NYI
1976	Ken Dryden, Mtl.	Chico Resch, NYI
		Billy Smith, NYI
1975	Bernie Parent, Phi.	Rogie Vachon, L.A.
		Gary Edwards, L.A.
1974	Bernie Parent, Phi. (tie)	Gilles Gilbert, Bos.
	Tony Esposito, Chi. (tie)	
1973	Ken Dryden, Mtl.	Ed Giacomin, NYR
		Gilles Villemure, NYR
1972	Tony Esposito, Chi.	Cesare Maniago, Min.
	Gary Smith, Chi.	Gump Worsley, Min.
1971	Ed Giacomin, NYR	Tony Esposito, Chi.
	Gilles Villemure, NYR	
1970	Tony Esposito, Chi.	Jacques Plante, St.L.
		Ernie Wakely, St.L.
1969	Jacques Plante, St.L.	Ed Giacomin, NYR
	Glenn Hall, St.L.	
1968	Gump Worsley, Mtl.	Johnny Bower, Tor.
	Rogie Vachon, Mtl.	Bruce Gamble, Tor.
1967	Glenn Hall, Chi.	Charlie Hodge, Mtl.
	Denis Dejordy, Chi.	
1966	Gump Worsley, Mtl.	Glenn Hall, Chi.
	Charlie Hodge, Mtl.	
1965	Terry Sawchuk, Tor.	Roger Crozier, Det.
	Johnny Bower, Tor.	
1964	Charlie Hodge, Mtl.	Glenn Hall, Chi.
1963	Glenn Hall, Chi.	Johnny Bower, Tor.
		Don Simmons, Tor.
1962	Jacques Plante, Mtl.	Johnny Bower, Tor.
1961	Johnny Bower, Tor.	Glenn Hall, Chi.
1960	Jacques Plante, Mtl.	Glenn Hall, Chi.
1959	Jacques Plante, Mtl.	Johnny Bower, Tor.
		Ed Chadwick, Tor.
1958	Jacques Plante, Mtl.	Gump Worsley, NYR
		Marcel Paille, NYR
1957	Jacques Plante, Mtl.	Glenn Hall, Det.
1956	Jacques Plante, Mtl.	Glenn Hall, Det.
1955	Terry Sawchuk, Det.	Harry Lumley, Tor.
1954	Harry Lumley, Tor.	Terry Sawchuk, Det.
1953	Terry Sawchuk, Det.	Gerry McNeil, Mtl.
1952	Terry Sawchuk, Det.	Al Rollins, Tor.
1951	Al Rollins, Tor.	Terry Sawchuk, Det.
1950	Bill Durnan, Mtl.	Harry Lumley, Det.
1949	Bill Durnan, Mtl.	Harry Lumley, Det.
1948	Turk Broda, Tor.	Harry Lumley, Det.
1947	Bill Durnan, Mtl.	Turk Broda, Tor.
1946	Bill Durnan, Mtl.	Frank Brimsek, Bos.
1945	Bill Durnan, Mtl.	Frank McCool, Tor. (tie)
		Harry Lumley, Det. (tie)
1944	Bill Durnan, Mtl.	Paul Bibeault, Tor.
1943	Johnny Mowers, Det.	Turk Broda, Tor.
1942	Frank Brimsek, Bos.	Turk Broda, Tor.
1941	Turk Broda, Tor.	Frank Brimsek, Bos. (tie)
		Johnny Mowers, Det. (tie)
1940	Dave Kerr, NYR	Frank Brimsek, Bos.
1939	Frank Brimsek, Bos.	Dave Kerr, NYR
1938	Tiny Thompson, Bos.	Dave Kerr, NYR
1937	Normie Smith, Det.	Dave Kerr, NYR
1936	Tiny Thompson, Bos.	Mike Karakas, Chi.
1935	Lorne Chabot, Chi.	Alex Connell, Mtl.M
1934	Charlie Gardiner, Chi.	Wilf Cude, Det.
1933	Tiny Thompson, Bos.	John Ross Roach, Det.
1932	Charlie Gardiner, Chi.	Alex Connell, Det.
1931	Roy Worters, NYA	Charlie Gardiner, Chi.
1930	Tiny Thompson, Bos.	Charlie Gardiner, Chi.
1929	George Hainsworth, Mtl.	Tiny Thompson, Bos.
1928	George Hainsworth, Mtl.	Alex Connell, Ott.
1927	George Hainsworth, Mtl.	Clint Benedict, Mtl.M

CALDER MEMORIAL TROPHY WINNERS

	Winner	Runner-up
2001	Evgeni Nabokov, S.J.	Brad Richards, T.B.
2000	Scott Gomez, N.J.	Brad Stuart, S.J.
1999	Chris Drury, Col.	Marian Hossa, Ott.
1998	Sergei Samsonov, Bos.	Mattias Ohlund, Van.
1997	Bryan Berard, NYI	Jarome Iginla, Cgy.
1996	Daniel Alfredsson, Ott.	Eric Daze, Chi.
1995	Peter Forsberg, Que.	Jim Carey, Wsh.
1994	Martin Brodeur, N.J.	Jason Arnott, Edm.
1993	Teemu Selanne, Wpg.	Joe Juneau, Bos.
1992	Pavel Bure, Van.	Nicklas Lidstrom, Det
1991	Ed Belfour, Chi.	Sergei Fedorov, Det.
1990	Sergei Makarov, Cgy.	Mike Modano, Min.
1989	Brian Leetch, NYR	Trevor Linden, Van.
1988	Joe Nieuwendyk, Cgy.	Ray Sheppard, Buf.
1987	Luc Robitaille, L.A.	Ron Hextall, Phi.
1986	Gary Suter, Cgy.	Wendel Clark, Tor.
1985	Mario Lemieux, Pit.	Chris Chelios, Mtl.
1984	Tom Barrasso, Buf.	Steve Yzerman, Det.
1983	Steve Larmer, Chi.	Phil Housley, Buf.
1982	Dale Hawerchuk, Wpg.	Barry Pederson, Bos.
1981	Peter Stastny, Que.	Larry Murphy, L.A.
1980	Raymond Bourque, Bos.	Mike Foligno, Det.
1979	Bobby Smith, Min	Ryan Walter, Wsh.
1978	Mike Bossy, NYI	Barry Beck, Col.
1977	Willi Plett, Atl.	Don Murdoch, NYR
1976	Bryan Trottier, NYI	Chico Resch, NYI
1975	Eric Vail, Atl.	Pierre Larouche, Pit.
1974	Denis Potvin, NYI	Tom Lysiak, Atl.
1973	Steve Vickers, NYR	Bill Barber, Phi.
1972	Ken Dryden, Mtl.	Rick Martin, Buf.
1971	Gilbert Perreault, Buf.	Jude Drouin, Min.
1970	Tony Esposito, Chi.	Bill Fairbairn, NYR
1969	Danny Grant, Min.	Norm Ferguson, Oak.
1968	Derek Sanderson, Bos.	Jacques Lemaire, Mtl.
1967	Bobby Orr, Bos.	Ed Van Impe, Chi.
1966	Brit Selby, Tor.	Bert Marshall, Det.
1965	Roger Crozier, Det.	Ron Ellis, Tor.
1964	Jacques Laperriere, Mtl.	John Ferguson, Mtl.
1963	Kent Douglas, Tor.	Doug Barkley, Det.
1962	Bobby Rousseau, Mtl.	Cliff Pennington, Bos.
1961	Dave Keon, Tor.	Bob Nevin, Tor.
1960	Bill Hay, Chi.	Murray Oliver, Det.
1959	Ralph Backstrom, Mtl.	Carl Brewer, Tor.
1958	Frank Mahovlich, Tor.	Bobby Hull, Chi.
1957	Larry Regan, Bos.	Ed Chadwick, Tor.
1956	Glenn Hall, Det.	Andy Hebenton, NYR
1955	Ed Litzenberger, Chi.	Don McKenney, Bos.
1954	Camille Henry, NYR	Earl Reibel, Det.
1953	Gump Worsley, NYR	Gord Hannigan, Tor.
1952	Bernie Geoffrion, Mtl.	Hy Buller, NYR
1951	Terry Sawchuk, Det.	Al Rollins, Tor.
1950	Jack Gelineau, Bos.	Phil Maloney, Bos.
1949	Pentti Lund, NYR	Allan Stanley, NYR
1948	Jim McFadden, Det.	Pete Babando, Bos.
1947	Howie Meeker, Tor.	Jim Conacher, Det.
1946	Edgar Laprade, NYR	George Gee, Chi.
1945	Frank McCool, Tor.	Ken Smith, Bos.
1944	Gus Bodnar, Tor.	Bill Durnan, Mtl.
1943	Gaye Stewart, Tor.	Glen Harmon, Mtl.
1942	Grant Warwick, NYR	Buddy O'Connor, Mtl.
1941	Johnny Quilty, Mtl.	Johnny Mowers, Det.
1940	Kilby MacDonald, NYR	Wally Stanowski, Tor.
1939	Frank Brimsek, Bos.	Roy Conacher, Bos.
1938	Cully Dahlstrom, Chi.	Murph Chamberlain, Tor.
1937	Syl Apps Sr., Tor.	Gordie Drillon, Tor.
1936	Mike Karakas, Chi.	Bucko McDonald, Det.
1935	Sweeney Schriner, NYA	Bert Connolly, NYR
1934	Russ Blinko, Mtl.M.	none
1933	Carl Voss, Det.	none

FRANK J. SELKE TROPHY WINNERS

	Winner	Runner-up
2001	John Madden, N.J.	Joe Sakic, Col.
2000	Steve Yzerman, Det.	Michal Handzus, St.L.
1999	Jere Lehtinen, Dal.	Magnus Arvedson, Ott.
1998	Jere Lehtinen, Dal.	Michael Peca, Buf.
1997	Michael Peca, Buf.	Peter Forsberg, Col.
1996	Sergei Fedorov, Det.	Ron Francis, Pit.
1995	Ron Francis, Pit.	Esa Tikkanen, St.L.
1994	Sergei Fedorov, Det.	Doug Gilmour, Tor.
1993	Doug Gilmour, Tor.	Dave Poulin, Bos.
1992	Guy Carbonneau, Mtl.	Sergei Fedorov, Det.
1991	Dirk Graham, Chi.	Esa Tikkanen, Edm.
1990	Rick Meagher, St.L.	Guy Carbonneau, Mtl.
1989	Guy Carbonneau, Mtl.	Esa Tikkanen, Edm.
1988	Guy Carbonneau, Mtl.	Steve Kasper, Bos.
1987	Dave Poulin, Phi.	Guy Carbonneau, Mtl.
1986	Troy Murray, Chi.	Ron Sutter, Phi.
1985	Craig Ramsay, Buf.	Doug Jarvis, Wsh.
1984	Doug Jarvis, Wsh.	Bryan Trottier, NYI
1983	Bobby Clarke, Phi.	Jari Kurri, Edm.
1982	Steve Kasper, Bos.	Bob Gainey, Mtl.
1981	Bob Gainey, Mtl.	Craig Ramsay, Buf.
1980	Bob Gainey, Mtl.	Craig Ramsay, Buf.
1979	Bob Gainey, Mtl.	Don Marcotte, Bos.
1978	Bob Gainey, Mtl.	Craig Ramsay, Buf.

CONN SMYTHE TROPHY WINNERS

2001	Patrick Roy	Colorado
2000	Scott Stevens	New Jersey
1999	Joe Nieuwendyk	Dallas
1998	Steve Yzerman	Detroit
1997	Mike Vernon	Detroit
1996	Joe Sakic	Colorado
1995	Claude Lemieux	New Jersey
1994	Brian Leetch	NY Rangers
1993	Patrick Roy	Montreal
1992	Mario Lemieux	Pittsburgh
1991	Mario Lemieux	Pittsburgh
1990	Bill Ranford	Edmonton
1989	Al MacInnis	Calgary
1988	Wayne Gretzky	Edmonton
1987	Ron Hextall	Philadelphia
1986	Patrick Roy	Montreal
1985	Wayne Gretzky	Edmonton
1984	Mark Messier	Edmonton
1983	Billy Smith	NY Islanders
1982	Mike Bossy	NY Islanders
1981	Butch Goring	NY Islanders
1980	Bryan Trottier	NY Islanders
1979	Bob Gainey	Montreal
1978	Larry Robinson	Montreal
1977	Guy Lafleur	Montreal
1976	Reggie Leach	Philadelphia
1975	Bernie Parent	Philadelphia
1974	Bernie Parent	Philadelphia
1973	Yvan Cournoyer	Montreal
1972	Bobby Orr	Boston
1971	Ken Dryden	Montreal
1970	Bobby Orr	Boston
1969	Serge Savard	Montreal
1968	Glenn Hall	St. Louis
1967	Dave Keon	Toronto
1966	Roger Crozier	Detroit

JAMES NORRIS TROPHY WINNERS

	Winner	Runner-up
2001	Nicklas Lidstrom, Det.	Raymond Bourque, Col.
2000	Chris Pronger, St.L.	Nicklas Lidstrom, Det.
1999	Al MacInnis, St.L.	Nicklas Lidstrom, Det.
1998	Rob Blake, L.A.	Nicklas Lidstrom, Det.
1997	Brian Leetch, NYR	V. Konstantinov, Det.
1996	Chris Chelios, Chi.	Raymond Bourque, Bos.
1995	Paul Coffey, Det.	Chris Chelios, Chi.
1994	Raymond Bourque, Bos.	Scott Stevens, N.J.
1993	Chris Chelios, Chi.	Raymond Bourque, Bos.
1992	Brian Leetch, NYR	Raymond Bourque, Bos.
1991	Raymond Bourque, Bos.	Al MacInnis, Cgy.
1990	Raymond Bourque, Bos.	Al MacInnis, Cgy.
1989	Chris Chelios, Mtl	Paul Coffey, Pit.
1988	Raymond Bourque, Bos.	Scott Stevens, Wsh.
1987	Raymond Bourque, Bos.	Mark Howe, Phi.
1986	Paul Coffey, Edm.	Mark Howe, Phi.
1985	Paul Coffey, Edm.	Raymond Bourque, Bos.
1984	Rod Langway, Wsh.	Paul Coffey, Edm.
1983	Rod Langway, Wsh.	Mark Howe, Phi.
1982	Doug Wilson, Chi.	Raymond Bourque, Bos.
1981	Randy Carlyle, Pit.	Denis Potvin, NYI
1980	Larry Robinson, Mtl.	Borje Salming, Tor.
1979	Denis Potvin, NYI	Larry Robinson, Mtl.
1978	Denis Potvin, NYI	Brad Park, Bos.
1977	Larry Robinson, Mtl.	Borje Salming, Tor.
1976	Denis Potvin, NYI	Brad Park, NYR-Bos.
1975	Bobby Orr, Bos.	Denis Potvin, NYI
1974	Bobby Orr, Bos.	Brad Park, NYR
1973	Bobby Orr, Bos.	Guy Lapointe, Mtl.
1972	Bobby Orr, Bos.	Brad Park, NYR
1971	Bobby Orr, Bos.	Brad Park, NYR
1970	Bobby Orr, Bos.	Brad Park, NYR
1969	Bobby Orr, Bos.	Tim Horton, Tor.
1968	Bobby Orr, Bos.	J.C. Tremblay, Mtl
1967	Harry Howell, NYR	Pierre Pilote, Chi.
1966	Jacques Laperriere, Mtl.	Pierre Pilote, Chi.
1965	Pierre Pilote, Chi.	Jacques Laperriere, Mtl.
1964	Pierre Pilote, Chi.	Tim Horton, Tor.
1963	Pierre Pilote, Chi.	Carl Brewer, Tor.
1962	Doug Harvey, NYR	Pierre Pilote, Chi.
1961	Doug Harvey, Mtl.	Marcel Pronovost, Det.
1960	Doug Harvey, Mtl.	Allan Stanley, Tor.
1959	Tom Johnson, Mtl.	Bill Gadsby, NYR
1958	Doug Harvey, Mtl.	Bill Gadsby, NYR
1957	Doug Harvey, Mtl.	Red Kelly, Det.
1956	Doug Harvey, Mtl.	Bill Gadsby, NYR
1955	Doug Harvey, Mtl.	Red Kelly, Det.
1954	Red Kelly, Det.	Doug Harvey, Mtl.

MAURICE "ROCKET" RICHARD TROPHY WINNER

2001	Pavel Bure	Florida
2000	Pavel Bure	Florida
1999	Teemu Selanne	Anaheim

LESTER PATRICK TROPHY WINNERS

2001	Scotty Bowman
	David Poile
	Gary Bettman
2000	Mario Lemieux
	Craig Patrick
	Lou Vairo
1999	Harry Sinden
	1998 U.S. Olympic Women's Hockey Team
1998	Peter Karmanos
	Neal Broten
	John Mayasich
	Max McNab
1997	Seymour H. Knox III
	Bill Cleary
	Pat LaFontaine
1996	George Gund
	Ken Morrow
	Milt Schmidt
1995	Joe Mullen
	Brian Mullen
	Bob Fleming
1994	Wayne Gretzky
	Robert Ridder
1993	*Frank Boucher
	*Mervyn "Red" Dutton
	Bruce McNall
	Gil Stein
1992	Al Arbour
	Art Berglund
	Lou Lamoriello
1991	Rod Gilbert
	Mike Ilitch
1990	Len Ceglarski
1989	Dan Kelly
	Lou Nanne
	*Lynn Patrick
	Bud Poile
1988	Keith Allen
	Fred Cusick
	Bob Johnson
1987	*Hobey Baker
	Frank Mathers
1986	John MacInnes
	Jack Riley
1985	Jack Butterfield
	Arthur M. Wirtz
1984	John A. Ziegler, Jr.
	*Arthur Howie Ross
1983	Bill Torrey
1982	Emile P. Francis
1981	Charles M. Schulz
1980	Bobby Clarke
	Edward M. Snider
	Frederick A. Shero
	1980 U.S. Olympic Hockey Team
1979	Bobby Orr
1978	Phil Esposito
	Tom Fitzgerald
	William T. Tutt
	William W. Wirtz
1977	John P. Bucyk
	Murray A. Armstrong
	John Mariucci
1976	Stanley Mikita
	George A. Leader
	Bruce A. Norris
1975	Donald M. Clark
	William L. Chadwick
	Thomas N. Ivan
1974	Alex Delvecchio
	Murray Murdoch
	*Weston W. Adams, Sr.
	*Charles L. Crovat
1973	Walter L. Bush, Jr.
1972	Clarence S. Campbell
	John A. "Snooks" Kelly
	Ralph "Cooney" Weiland
	*James D. Norris
1971	William M. Jennings
	*John B. Sollenberger
	*Terrance G. Sawchuk
1970	Edward W. Shore
	*James C. V. Hendy
1969	Robert M. Hull
	*Edward J. Jeremiah
1968	Thomas F. Lockhart
	*Walter A. Brown
	*Gen. John R. Kilpatrick
1967	Gordon Howe
	*Charles F. Adams
	*James Norris, Sr.
1966	J.J. "Jack" Adams

* awarded posthumously

BUD LIGHT PLUS-MINUS AWARD WINNERS

2001	Patrik Elias	New Jersey
	Joe Sakic	Colorado
2000	Chris Pronger	St. Louis
1999	John LeClair	Philadelphia
1998	Chris Pronger	St. Louis

WILLIAM M. JENNINGS TROPHY WINNERS

	Winner	Runner-up
2001	Dominik Hasek, Buf.	Ed Belfour, Dal.
		Marty Turco
2000	Roman Turek, St.L.	John Vanbiesbrouck, Phi.
		Brian Boucher
1999	Ed Belfour, Dal.	Dominik Hasek, Buf.
	Roman Turek	
1998	Martin Brodeur, N.J.	Ed Belfour, Dal.
1997	Martin Brodeur, N.J.	Chris Osgood, Det.
	Mike Dunham	Mike Vernon
1996	Chris Osgood, Det.	Martin Brodeur, N.J.
	Mike Vernon	
1995	Ed Belfour, Chi.	Mike Vernon, Det.
		Chris Osgood
1994	Dominik Hasek, Buf.	Martin Brodeur, N.J.
	Grant Fuhr	Chris Terreri
1993	Ed Belfour, Chi.	Felix Potvin, Tor.
		Grant Fuhr
1992	Patrick Roy, Mtl.	Ed Belfour, Chi.
1991	Ed Belfour, Chi.	Patrick Roy, Mtl.
1990	Andy Moog, Bos.	Patrick Roy, Mtl.
	Reggie Lemelin	Brian Hayward
1989	Patrick Roy, Mtl.	Mike Vernon, Cgy.
	Brian Hayward	Rick Wamsley
1988	Patrick Roy, Mtl.	Clint Malarchuk, Wsh.
	Brian Hayward	Pete Peeters
1987	Patrick Roy, Mtl.	Ron Hextall, Phi.
	Brian Hayward	
1986	Bob Froese, Phi.	Al Jensen, Wsh.
	Darren Jensen	Pete Peeters
1985	Tom Barrasso, Buf.	Pat Riggin, Wsh.
	Bob Sauve	
1984	Al Jensen, Wsh.	Tom Barrasso, Buf.
	Pat Riggin	Bob Sauve
1983	Rollie Melanson, NYI	Pete Peeters, Bos.
	Billy Smith	
1982	Rick Wamsley, Mtl.	Billy Smith, NYI
	Denis Herron	Rollie Melanson

LESTER B. PEARSON AWARD WINNERS

2001	Joe Sakic	Colorado
2000	Jaromir Jagr	Pittsburgh
1999	Jaromir Jagr	Pittsburgh
1998	Dominik Hasek	Buffalo
1997	Dominik Hasek	Buffalo
1996	Mario Lemieux	Pittsburgh
1995	Eric Lindros	Philadelphia
1994	Sergei Fedorov	Detroit
1993	Mario Lemieux	Pittsburgh
1992	Mark Messier	NY Rangers
1991	Brett Hull	St. Louis
1990	Mark Messier	Edmonton
1989	Steve Yzerman	Detroit
1988	Mario Lemieux	Pittsburgh
1987	Wayne Gretzky	Edmonton
1986	Mario Lemieux	Pittsburgh
1985	Wayne Gretzky	Edmonton
1984	Wayne Gretzky	Edmonton
1983	Wayne Gretzky	Edmonton
1982	Wayne Gretzky	Edmonton
1981	Mike Liut	St. Louis
1980	Marcel Dionne	Los Angeles
1979	Marcel Dionne	Los Angeles
1978	Guy Lafleur	Montreal
1977	Guy Lafleur	Montreal
1976	Guy Lafleur	Montreal
1975	Bobby Orr	Boston
1974	Phil Esposito	Boston
1973	Bobby Clarke	Philadelphia
1972	Jean Ratelle	NY Rangers
1971	Phil Esposito	Boston

JACK ADAMS AWARD WINNERS

	Winner	Runner-up
2001	Bill Barber, Phi.	Scotty Bowman, Det.
2000	Joel Quenneville, St.L.	Alain Vigneault, Mtl.
1999	Jacques Martin, Ott.	Pat Quinn, Tor.
1998	Pat Burns, Bos.	Larry Robinson, L.A.
1997	Ted Nolan, Buf.	Ken Hitchcock, Dal.
1996	Scotty Bowman, Det.	Doug MacLean, Fla.
1995	Marc Crawford, Que.	Scotty Bowman, Det.
1994	Jacques Lemaire, N.J.	Kevin Constantine, S.J.
1993	Pat Burns, Tor.	Brian Sutter, Bos.
1992	Pat Quinn, Van.	Roger Neilson, NYR
1991	Brian Sutter, St.L.	Tom Webster, L.A.
1990	Bob Murdoch, Wpg.	Mike Milbury, Bos.
1989	Pat Burns, Mtl.	Bob McCammon, Van.
1988	Jacques Demers, Det.	Terry Crisp, Cgy.
1987	Jacques Demers, Det.	Jack Evans, Hfd.
1986	Glen Sather, Edm.	Jacques Demers, St.L.
1985	Mike Keenan, Phi.	Barry Long, Wpg.
1984	Bryan Murray, Wsh.	Scotty Bowman, Buf.
1983	Orval Tessier, Chi.	
1982	Tom Watt, Wpg.	
1981	Red Berenson, St.L.	Bob Berry, L.A.
1980	Pat Quinn, Phi.	
1979	Al Arbour, NYI	Fred Shero, NYR
1978	Bobby Kromm, Det.	Don Cherry, Bos.
1977	Scotty Bowman, Mtl.	Tom McVie, Wsh.
1976	Don Cherry, Bos.	
1975	Bob Pulford, L.A.	
1974	Fred Shero, Phi.	

NHL Amateur and Entry Draft

History

Year	Site	Date	Total Players Drafted
1963	Queen Elizabeth Hotel	June 5	21
1964	Queen Elizabeth Hotel	June 11	24
1965	Queen Elizabeth Hotel	April 27	11
1966	Mount Royal Hotel	April 25	24
1967	Queen Elizabeth Hotel	June 7	18
1968	Queen Elizabeth Hotel	June 13	24
1969	Queen Elizabeth Hotel	June 12	84
1970	Queen Elizabeth Hotel	June 11	115
1971	Queen Elizabeth Hotel	June 10	117
1972	Queen Elizabeth Hotel	June 8	152
1973	Mount Royal Hotel	May 15	168
1974	NHL Montreal Office	May 28	247
1975	NHL Montreal Office	June 3	217
1976	NHL Montreal Office	June 1	135
1977	NHL Montreal Office	June 14	185
1978	Queen Elizabeth Hotel	June 15	234
1979	Queen Elizabeth Hotel	August 9	126
1980	Montreal Forum	June 11	210
1981	Montreal Forum	June 10	211
1982	Montreal Forum	June 9	252
1983	Montreal Forum	June 8	242
1984	Montreal Forum	June 9	250
1985	Toronto Convention Centre	June 15	252
1986	Montreal Forum	June 21	252
1987	Joe Louis Sports Arena	June 13	252
1988	Montreal Forum	June 11	252
1989	Metropolitan Sports Center	June 17	252
1990	B. C. Place	June 16	250
1991	Memorial Auditorium	June 9	264
1992	Montreal Forum	June 20	264
1993	Colisée de Québec	June 26	286
1994	Hartford Civic Center	June 28-29	286
1995	Edmonton Coliseum	July 8	234
1996	Kiel Center	June 22	241
1997	Civic Arena	June 21	246
1998	Marine Midland Arena	June 27	258
1999	FleetCenter	June 26	272
2000	Saddledome	June 24-25	293
2001	National Car Rental Center	June 23-24	289

* The NHL Amateur Draft became the NHL Entry Draft in 1979

First Selections

Year	Player	Pos	Drafted By	Drafted From	Age
1969	Rejean Houle	LW	Montreal	Montreal Jr. Canadiens	19.8
1970	Gilbert Perreault	C	Buffalo	Montreal Jr. Canadiens	19.7
1971	Guy Lafleur	RW	Montreal	Quebec Remparts	19.9
1972	Billy Harris	RW	NY Islanders	Toronto Marlboros	20.4
1973	Denis Potvin	D	NY Islanders	Ottawa 67's	19.7
1974	Greg Joly	D	Washington	Regina Pats	20.0
1975	Mel Bridgman	C	Philadelphia	Victoria Cougars	20.1
1976	Rick Green	D	Washington	London Knights	20.3
1977	Dale McCourt	C	Detroit	St. Catharines Fincups	20.4
1978	Bobby Smith	C	Minnesota	Ottawa 67's	20.4
1979	Rob Ramage	D	Colorado	London Knights	20.5
1980	Doug Wickenheiser	C	Montreal	Regina Pats	19.2
1981	Dale Hawerchuk	C	Winnipeg	Cornwall Royals	18.2
1982	Gord Kluzak	D	Boston	Nanaimo Islanders	18.3
1983	Brian Lawton	C	Minnesota	Mount St. Charles HS	18.11
1984	Mario Lemieux	C	Pittsburgh	Laval Voisins	18.8
1985	Wendel Clark	LW/D	Toronto	Saskatoon Blades	18.7
1986	Joe Murphy	C	Detroit	Michigan State	18.8
1987	Pierre Turgeon	C	Buffalo	Granby Bisons	17.10
1988	Mike Modano	C	Minnesota	Prince Albert Raiders	18.0
1989	Mats Sundin	RW	Quebec	Nacka IK (Sweden)	18.4
1990	Owen Nolan	RW	Quebec	Cornwall Royals	18.4
1991	Eric Lindros	C	Quebec	Oshawa Generals	18.3
1992	Roman Hamrlik	D	Tampa Bay	ZPS Zlin (Czech.)	18.2
1993	Alexandre Daigle	C	Ottawa	Victoriaville Tigres	18.5
1994	Ed Jovanovski	D	Florida	Windsor Spitfires	18.0
1995	Bryan Berard	D	Ottawa	Detroit Jr. Red Wings	18.4
1996	Chris Phillips	D	Ottawa	Prince Albert Raiders	18.3
1997	Joe Thornton	C	Boston	Sault Ste. Marie	17.11
1998	Vincent Lecavalier	C	Tampa Bay	Rimouski Oceanic	18.2
1999	Patrik Stefan	C	Atlanta	Long Beach Ice Dogs	18.9
2000	Rick DiPietro	G	NY Islanders	Boston University	18.9
2001	Ilya Kovalchuk	LW	Atlanta	Krylja Sovetov (Russia)	18.2

Top prospects heading into the 2001 NHL Entry Draft, wearing the jerseys of their 2000-01 teams: Left to right, front row, Pascal Leclaire (Halifax Mooseheads, G, selected 8th overall by Columbus), Jason Spezza (Windsor Spitfires, C, 2nd by Ottawa), Dan Blackburn (Kootenay Ice, G, 10th by NY Rangers); back row, Stephen Weiss (Plymouth Whalers, C, 4th by Florida), Mike Komisarek (U. of Michigan, D, 7th by Montreal), R.J. Umberger (Ohio State, C, 16th by Vancouver), Dan Hamhuis (Prince George Cougars, D, 12th by Nashville).

Draft Summary

Following is a summary of the number of players drafted from the Ontario Hockey League (OHL), Western Hockey League (WHL), Quebec Major Junior Hockey League (QMJHL), United States Colleges, United States High Schools, European Leagues and other Leagues throughout North America since 1969:

	OHL	WHL	QMJHL	US Colleges	US HS	International	Other
1969	36	20	11	7	0	1	9
1970	51	22	13	16	0	0	13
1971	41	28	13	22	0	0	13
1972	46	44	30	21	0	0	11
1973	56	49	24	25	0	0	14
1974	69	66	40	41	0	6	25
1975	55	57	28	59	0	6	12
1976	47	33	18	26	0	8	3
1977	42	44	40	49	0	5	5
1978	59	48	22	73	0	16	16
1979	48	37	19	15	0	6	1
1980	73	41	24	42	7	13	10
1981	59	37	28	21	17	32	17
1982	60	55	17	20	47	35	18
1983	57	41	24	14	35	34	37
1984	55	38	16	22	44	40	36
1985	59	47	15	20	48	31	31
1986	66	32	22	22	40	28	42
1987	32	36	17	40	69	38	20
1988	32	30	22	48	56	39	25
1989	39	44	16	48	47	38	20
1990	39	33	14	38	57	53	16
1991	43	40	25	43	37	55	21
1992	57	45	22	9	25	84	22
1993	60	44	23	17	33	78	31
1994	45	66	28	6	28	80	33
1995	54	55	35	5	2	69	14
1996	51	54	31	25	6	58	16
1997	52	63	19	26	4	63	19
1998	50	44	41	27	7	75	14
1999	52	40	20	36	9	94	21
2000	39	41	21	35	7	123	27
2001	41	45	26	24	8	119	26
Total	**1665**	**1419**	**764**	**942**	**633**	**1327**	**638**

Total Drafted, 1969-2001: 7,099

Ontario Hockey League

Club	'69	'70	'71	'72	'73	'74	'75	'76	'77	'78	'79	'80	'81	'82	'83	'84	'85	'86	'87	'88	'89	'90	'91	'92	'93	'94	'95	'96	'97	'98	'99	'00	'01	Total
Peterborough	5	5	4	5	9	4	8	1	4	6	9	10	3	5	7	3	9	2	5	2	2	4	3	4	4	2	5	4	5	1	4	1	2	147
Oshawa	5	4	3	5	5	7	6	6	1	3	3	2	9	5	5	6	6	6	3	2	4	2	4	4	4	1	10	1	3	4	3	2	1	135
Kitchener	1	6	2	8	4	13	3	1	3	4	4	4	5	5	8	4	6	3	2	1	7	5	3	1	4	2	4	2	3	5	–	1	1	125
Ottawa	2	4	3	4	6	5	6	5	5	5	3	8	4	9	2	2	3	3	2	1	–	5	5	6	4	1	1	2	5	2	6	2	3	124
London	4	9	1	5	6	6	3	5	4	3	6	2	5	5	3	7	1	3	2	6	3	3	1	3	4	1	1	4	1	8	4	1	2	122
Sudbury	–	–	–	–	6	6	4	5	4	4	3	7	2	4	–	2	5	3	1	–	1	2	8	2	10	2	2	1	3	5	5	–	2	99
S.S. Marie	–	–	–	–	4	5	2	5	1	5	3	3	8	1	6	4	5	7	1	2	3	1	2	7	3	4	3	4	1	4	1	1	1	97
Kingston	–	–	–	–	–	4	4	6	4	9	2	8	5	2	1	3	3	4	1	1	–	2	2	3	5	2	3	4	4	1	4	–	2	89
Niagara Falls	4	2	1	4	–	–	–	–	2	3	5	8	6	6	–	–	–	–	–	–	4	4	4	4	4	3	2	6	–	–	–	–	–	72
Windsor	–	–	–	–	–	–	–	2	1	4	2	3	5	3	2	2	3	7	–	5	2	1	–	3	–	3	4	1	5	1	2	2	2	65
Guelph	–	–	–	–	–	–	–	–	–	–	–	–	–	–	1	5	3	8	2	–	4	–	–	2	2	7	5	6	1	5	3	1	4	59
North Bay	–	–	–	–	–	–	–	–	–	–	–	–	–	–	4	4	3	3	3	3	1	4	2	5	2	7	2	1	1	2	2	2	3	54
Belleville	–	–	–	–	–	–	–	–	–	–	–	–	–	–	3	4	4	5	2	–	4	2	1	4	–	3	3	–	5	2	5	1	3	51
Det./Plymouth	–	–	–	–	–	–	–	–	–	–	–	–	–	–	–	–	–	–	–	–	–	–	2	2	7	2	6	3	4	2	2	6	3	39
Owen Sound	–	–	–	–	–	–	–	–	–	–	–	–	–	–	–	–	–	–	–	–	–	1	1	2	4	3	2	3	2	1	–	1	–	20
Barrie	–	–	–	–	–	–	–	–	–	–	–	–	–	–	–	–	–	–	–	–	–	–	–	–	–	–	–	2	4	3	6	3	1	19
Sarnia	–	–	–	–	–	–	–	–	–	–	–	–	–	–	–	–	–	–	–	–	–	–	–	–	–	–	1	7	2	3	1	3	1	18
Erie	–	–	–	–	–	–	–	–	–	–	–	–	–	–	–	–	–	–	–	–	–	–	–	–	–	–	–	–	3	1	2	3	2	11
Brampton	–	–	–	–	–	–	–	–	–	–	–	–	–	–	–	–	–	–	–	–	–	–	–	–	–	–	–	–	–	–	2	6	3	11
St. Michael's	–	–	–	–	–	–	–	–	–	–	–	–	–	–	–	–	–	–	–	–	–	–	–	–	–	–	–	–	–	–	–	1	5	6
Mississauga	–	–	–	–	–	–	–	–	–	–	–	–	–	–	–	–	–	–	–	–	–	–	–	–	–	–	–	–	–	–	–	2	–	2

Teams no longer operating

Club	'69	'70	'71	'72	'73	'74	'75	'76	'77	'78	'79	'80	'81	'82	'83	'84	'85	'86	'87	'88	'89	'90	'91	'92	'93	'94	'95	'96	'97	'98	'99	'00	'01	Total
Toronto	3	7	6	5	6	8	4	4	7	5	4	10	2	6	4	4	3	4	1	2	2	–	–	–	–	–	–	–	–	–	–	–	–	97
Hamilton	2	3	5	4	6	4	7	3	–	8	1	–	–	–	–	–	3	6	4	4	–	–	2	–	–	–	–	–	–	–	–	–	–	62
St. Catharines	5	5	8	5	4	7	8	4	6	–	–	–	–	–	–	–	–	–	–	–	–	–	–	–	–	–	–	–	–	–	–	–	–	52
Cornwall	–	–	–	–	–	–	–	–	–	–	–	–	–	7	4	3	2	2	3	3	2	3	3	5	–	–	–	–	–	–	–	–	–	37
Brantford	–	–	–	–	–	–	–	–	–	–	3	8	5	2	7	2	–	–	–	–	–	–	–	–	–	–	–	–	–	–	–	–	–	27
Montreal	5	6	8	1	–	–	–	–	–	–	–	–	–	–	–	–	–	–	–	–	–	–	–	–	–	–	–	–	–	–	–	–	–	20
Newmarket	–	–	–	–	–	–	–	–	–	–	–	–	–	–	–	–	–	–	–	–	–	–	–	–	3	2	–	–	–	–	–	–	–	5

Year	Total Ontario Drafted	Total Players Drafted	Ontario %
1969	36	84	42.9
1970	51	115	44.3
1971	41	117	35.0
1972	46	152	30.3
1973	56	168	33.3
1974	69	247	27.9
1975	55	217	25.3
1976	47	135	34.8
1977	42	185	22.7
1978	59	234	25.2
1979	48	126	38.1
1980	73	210	34.8
1981	59	211	28.0
1982	60	252	23.8
1983	57	242	23.6
1984	55	250	22.0
1985	59	252	23.4
1986	66	252	26.2
1987	32	252	12.7
1988	32	252	12.7
1989	39	252	15.5
1990	39	250	15.6
1991	43	264	16.3
1992	57	264	21.6
1993	60	286	21.0
1994	45	286	15.7
1995	54	234	23.1
1996	51	241	21.1
1997	52	246	21.1
1998	50	258	19.4
1999	52	272	19.1
2000	39	293	13.3
2001	41	289	14.2
Total	**1665**	**7388**	**22.5**

Western Hockey League

Club	'69	'70	'71	'72	'73	'74	'75	'76	'77	'78	'79	'80	'81	'82	'83	'84	'85	'86	'87	'88	'89	'90	'91	'92	'93	'94	'95	'96	'97	'98	'99	'00	'01	Total
Regina	–	–	5	5	1	8	5	3	1	4	1	3	5	6	8	4	4	3	2	–	5	1	–	4	–	3	2	4	3	2	4	2	2	100
Saskatoon	1	–	1	3	8	4	5	3	4	1	2	2	3	5	5	3	1	5	4	4	3	2	2	3	2	4	2	2	2	2	4	1	4	97
Portland	–	–	–	–	–	–	–	–	4	8	7	8	6	7	7	5	2	4	3	1	4	1	1	4	4	3	2	1	3	3	1	6	–	95
Medicine Hat	–	–	–	4	6	4	5	3	5	4	–	4	2	1	2	1	6	2	5	1	4	1	3	3	1	6	2	7	2	3	1	–	2	90
Kamloops	–	–	–	–	–	4	4	4	4	–	–	–	–	2	4	4	4	4	3	1	5	4	6	3	2	9	5	4	3	1	4	4	2	90
Brandon	–	3	1	5	2	7	4	–	3	1	10	5	2	2	1	3	2	1	3	3	–	1	1	1	2	5	6	2	5	4	–	–	2	87
Lethbridge	–	–	–	–	–	–	3	2	3	5	4	1	4	7	2	1	5	1	–	3	3	4	7	3	4	3	3	1	5	1	–	3	1	79
Seattle	–	–	–	–	–	–	–	–	–	4	2	3	–	6	–	1	3	1	2	4	2	6	3	2	4	5	5	1	8	2	6	4	5	79
Prince Albert	–	–	–	–	–	–	–	–	–	–	–	–	–	4	2	2	6	6	1	3	3	4	6	2	5	3	4	3	5	3	3	2	4	71
Spokane	–	–	–	–	–	–	–	–	–	–	–	–	1	–	–	–	–	–	1	3	2	1	5	7	4	4	4	5	4	1	1	2	3	48
Swift Current	1	–	1	–	3	6	–	–	–	–	–	–	–	–	–	–	–	–	5	2	2	2	1	1	5	4	4	1	2	2	1	3	1	47
Moose Jaw	–	–	–	–	–	–	–	–	–	–	–	–	–	–	–	–	4	1	3	–	3	1	2	3	2	3	4	4	4	2	1	5	3	45
Tri-City	–	–	–	–	–	–	–	–	–	–	–	–	–	–	–	–	–	–	–	–	4	3	3	5	2	2	6	6	1	4	1	2	2	41
Red Deer	–	–	–	–	–	–	–	–	–	–	–	–	–	–	–	–	–	–	–	–	–	–	–	–	3	5	2	4	3	5	1	1	6	30
Kelowna	–	–	–	–	–	–	–	–	–	–	–	–	–	–	–	–	–	–	–	–	–	–	–	–	–	–	–	4	7	2	2	1	1	17
Calgary	–	–	–	–	–	–	–	–	–	–	–	–	–	–	–	–	–	–	–	–	–	–	–	–	–	–	–	3	–	3	6	4	1	17
Prince George	–	–	–	–	–	–	–	–	–	–	–	–	–	–	–	–	–	–	–	–	–	–	–	–	–	–	2	2	2	4	2	–	4	16
Kootenay	–	–	–	–	–	–	–	–	–	–	–	–	–	–	–	–	–	–	–	–	–	–	–	–	–	–	–	–	–	–	2	1	2	5
Edmonton	–	–	–	–	–	–	–	–	–	–	–	–	–	–	–	–	–	–	–	–	–	–	–	–	–	–	–	–	4	–	–	–	–	4

Teams no longer operating

Club	'69	'70	'71	'72	'73	'74	'75	'76	'77	'78	'79	'80	'81	'82	'83	'84	'85	'86	'87	'88	'89	'90	'91	'92	'93	'94	'95	'96	'97	'98	'99	'00	'01	Total
Victoria	–	–	–	2	2	5	7	4	3	3	1	8	6	2	3	4	2	1	2	4	4	2	–	1	2	2	–	–	–	–	–	–	–	70
Calgary	3	5	2	7	4	8	4	4	4	3	–	2	5	4	3	3	3	2	–	–	–	–	–	–	–	–	–	–	–	–	–	–	–	66
New Westm'r	–	–	–	6	8	7	9	5	8	6	5	1	–	–	–	2	1	1	2	1	–	–	–	–	–	–	–	–	–	–	–	–	–	62
Flin Flon	4	4	5	2	4	7	4	3	1	5	–	–	–	–	–	–	–	–	–	–	–	–	–	–	–	–	–	–	–	–	–	–	–	39
Winnipeg	3	2	4	2	5	4	4	–	4	–	–	–	1	4	1	–	–	–	–	–	–	–	–	–	–	–	–	–	–	–	–	–	–	34
Edmonton	4	4	5	6	6	2	3	2	–	–	2	–	–	–	–	–	–	–	–	–	–	–	–	–	–	–	–	–	–	–	–	–	–	34
Billings	–	–	–	–	–	–	–	–	–	4	3	4	2	–	–	–	–	–	–	–	–	–	–	–	–	–	–	–	–	–	–	–	–	13
Estevan	4	4	4	–	–	–	–	–	–	–	–	–	–	–	–	–	–	–	–	–	–	–	–	–	–	–	–	–	–	–	–	–	–	12
Tacoma	–	–	–	–	–	–	–	–	–	–	–	–	–	–	–	–	–	–	–	–	–	–	–	3	2	5	2	–	–	–	–	–	–	12
Kelowna	–	–	–	–	–	–	–	–	–	–	–	–	–	–	2	4	5	–	–	–	–	–	–	–	–	–	–	–	–	–	–	–	–	11
Nanaimo	–	–	–	–	–	–	–	–	–	–	–	–	–	5	1	–	–	–	–	–	–	–	–	–	–	–	–	–	–	–	–	–	–	6
Vancouver	–	–	–	2	–	–	–	–	–	–	–	–	–	–	–	–	–	–	–	–	–	–	–	–	–	–	–	–	–	–	–	–	–	2

Year	Total Western Drafted	Total Players Drafted	Western %
1969	20	84	23.8
1970	22	115	19.1
1971	28	117	23.9
1972	44	152	28.9
1973	49	168	29.2
1974	66	247	26.7
1975	57	217	26.3
1976	33	135	24.4
1977	44	185	23.8
1978	48	234	20.5
1979	37	126	29.4
1980	41	210	19.5
1981	37	211	17.5
1982	55	252	21.8
1983	41	242	16.9
1984	37	250	14.8
1985	48	252	19.0
1986	32	252	12.7
1987	36	252	14.3
1988	30	252	11.9
1989	44	252	17.5
1990	33	250	13.2
1991	40	264	15.2
1992	45	264	17.0
1993	44	286	15.4
1994	66	286	23.0
1995	55	234	23.5
1996	54	241	22.4
1997	63	246	25.6
1998	44	258	17.0
1999	40	272	14.7
2000	41	293	14.0
2001	45	289	15.5
Total	**1419**	**7388**	**19.2**

Both Ryan Smyth (far left) and Derek Morris (left) are products of the Western Hockey League. Edmonton selected Smyth sixth overall from Moose Jaw in 1994. Calgary grabbed Morris from Regina with the 13th pick in 1996.

Quebec Major Junior Hockey League

Club	'69	'70	'71	'72	'73	'74	'75	'76	'77	'78	'79	'80	'81	'82	'83	'84	'85	'86	'87	'88	'89	'90	'91	'92	'93	'94	'95	'96	'97	'98	'99	'00	'01	Total
Shawinigan	3	2	1	6	1	5	3	–	3	–	–	2	2	5	5	2	–	2	1	–	2	–	2	3	1	1	2	4	1	3	1	1	1	65
Sherbrooke	–	–	2	2	4	3	7	5	6	3	4	1	5	2	–	–	–	–	–	–	–	–	–	–	3	2	4	–	1	5	–	–	3	62
Hull	–	–	–	–	–	–	3	2	2	3	–	3	1	–	3	1	–	4	3	2	2	3	3	3	3	1	3	3	–	3	4	–	2	57
Drummondville	2	4	1	4	2	1	–	–	–	–	–	–	–	–	–	1	2	2	2	4	1	–	4	2	2	1	4	3	2	2	–	1	1	48
Chicoutimi	–	–	–	–	–	1	–	–	5	1	1	3	6	1	3	–	3	1	2	2	1	1	–	1	1	3	2	–	2	1	–	1	1	43
Granby	–	–	–	–	–	–	–	–	–	–	–	–	–	2	1	3	2	2	4	–	2	–	2	–	1	5	2	3	1	–	–	–	–	30
Victoriaville	–	–	–	–	–	–	–	–	–	–	–	–	–	–	–	–	–	–	–	4	–	1	–	2	6	1	1	3	2	1	2	3	1	27
Beauport	–	–	–	–	–	–	–	–	–	–	–	–	–	–	–	–	–	–	–	–	–	–	1	3	1	3	7	3	3	–	–	–	–	21
Val D'Or	–	–	–	–	–	–	–	–	–	–	–	–	–	–	–	–	–	–	–	–	–	–	–	–	–	1	2	4	2	–	3	2	2	16
St. Hyacinthe	–	–	–	–	–	–	–	–	–	–	–	–	–	–	–	–	–	–	–	–	–	3	1	2	1	4	–	4	–	–	–	–	–	15
Halifax	–	–	–	–	–	–	–	–	–	–	–	–	–	–	–	–	–	–	–	–	–	–	–	–	–	–	3	1	3	3	–	2	3	15
Rimouski	–	–	–	–	–	–	–	–	–	–	–	–	–	–	–	–	–	–	–	–	–	–	–	–	–	–	–	–	–	5	2	2	4	13
Quebec	–	–	–	–	–	–	–	–	–	–	–	–	–	–	–	–	–	–	–	–	–	–	–	–	–	–	–	–	–	4	3	–	3	10
Rouyn-Noranda	–	–	–	–	–	–	–	–	–	–	–	–	–	–	–	–	–	–	–	–	–	–	–	–	–	–	–	–	–	3	1	4	–	8
Baie-Comeau	–	–	–	–	–	–	–	–	–	–	–	–	–	–	–	–	–	–	–	–	–	–	–	–	–	–	–	–	–	3	–	2	3	8
Moncton	–	–	–	–	–	–	–	–	–	–	–	–	–	–	–	–	–	–	–	–	–	–	–	–	–	–	–	1	1	2	2	–	–	6
Cape Breton	–	–	–	–	–	–	–	–	–	–	–	–	–	–	–	–	–	–	–	–	–	–	–	–	–	–	–	–	–	3	–	1	1	5
Montreal	–	–	–	–	–	–	–	–	–	–	–	–	–	–	–	–	–	–	–	–	–	–	–	–	–	–	–	–	–	–	–	2	1	3
Acadie-Bathurst	–	–	–	–	–	–	–	–	–	–	–	–	–	–	–	–	–	–	–	–	–	–	–	–	–	–	–	–	–	–	2	–	–	2

Teams no longer operating

Club	'69	'70	'71	'72	'73	'74	'75	'76	'77	'78	'79	'80	'81	'82	'83	'84	'85	'86	'87	'88	'89	'90	'91	'92	'93	'94	'95	'96	'97	'98	'99	'00	'01	Total
Laval	–	–	–	1	–	2	1	1	4	2	1	–	–	2	1	2	–	5	3	1	3	3	4	1	2	5	4	2	1	3	–	–	–	54
Quebec	1	1	2	4	6	6	1	3	7	1	3	2	2	1	2	2	3	–	–	–	–	–	–	–	–	–	–	–	–	–	–	–	–	47
Trois Rivieres	–	1	2	2	2	2	3	2	6	3	2	2	2	1	3	–	3	–	1	3	3	1	2	1	–	–	–	–	–	–	–	–	–	47
Cornwall	2	1	2	6	4	8	1	3	1	6	1	5	5	–	–	–	–	–	–	–	–	–	–	–	–	–	–	–	–	–	–	–	–	45
Montreal	–	–	–	–	4	4	8	1	3	2	4	3	–	3	–	–	–	–	–	–	–	–	–	–	–	–	–	–	–	–	–	–	–	32
Sorel	2	3	1	3	1	8	1	1	3	–	–	–	5	–	–	–	–	–	–	–	–	–	–	–	–	–	–	–	–	–	–	–	–	28
Verdun	–	1	1	2	–	–	–	–	–	1	3	3	–	–	3	3	–	3	0	3	1	–	–	3	–	–	–	–	–	–	–	–	–	27
St. Jean	–	–	–	–	–	–	–	–	–	–	–	–	–	–	2	–	1	1	0	3	1	–	3	1	2	1	1	–	–	–	–	–	–	16
Longueuil	–	–	–	–	–	–	–	–	–	–	–	–	–	–	1	2	1	2	1	–	–	2	3	–	–	–	–	–	–	–	–	–	–	12
St. Jerome	1	–	1	–	–	–	–	–	–	–	–	–	–	–	–	–	–	–	–	–	–	–	–	–	–	–	–	–	–	–	–	–	–	2

Year	Total Quebec Drafted	Total Players Drafted	Quebec %
1969	11	84	13.1
1970	13	115	11.3
1971	13	117	11.1
1972	30	152	19.7
1973	24	168	14.3
1974	40	247	16.2
1975	28	217	12.9
1976	18	135	13.3
1977	40	185	21.6
1978	22	234	9.4
1979	19	126	15.1
1980	24	210	11.4
1981	28	211	13.3
1982	17	252	6.7
1983	24	242	9.9
1984	16	250	6.4
1985	15	252	5.9
1986	22	252	8.7
1987	17	252	6.7
1988	22	252	8.7
1989	16	252	6.3
1990	14	250	5.6
1991	25	264	9.5
1992	22	264	8.3
1993	23	286	8.0
1994	28	286	9.7
1995	35	234	14.9
1996	31	241	12.8
1997	19	246	7.7
1998	41	258	15.9
1999	20	272	7.3
2000	21	293	7.1
2001	26	289	9.0
Total	**764**	**7388**	**10.3**

United States Colleges

Club	'69	'70	'71	'72	'73	'74	'75	'76	'77	'78	'79	'80	'81	'82	'83	'84	'85	'86	'87	'88	'89	'90	'91	'92	'93	'94	'95	'96	'97	'98	99	'00	'01	Total
Minnesota	1	3	2	–	–	9	4	4	5	5	2	3	1	1	1	–	–	2	1	1	1	–	–	–	–	–	2	3	2	1	3	3	–	60
Michigan	1	–	–	–	2	2	3	3	1	6	–	4	–	–	–	1	1	–	1	2	3	5	4	2	1	1	–	3	1	3	2	1	2	55
Michigan Tech	–	–	3	1	2	5	4	4	1	2	1	4	–	1	–	2	2	2	1	1	2	1	2	–	1	2	–	1	–	–	–	–	1	46
Boston U.	–	4	–	–	1	1	1	1	4	5	1	–	1	–	–	1	1	2	2	3	1	2	2	1	1	–	1	1	1	2	3	1	2	46
Denver	1	3	2	4	2	3	1	2	2	2	2	1	–	1	–	–	1	2	4	1	1	–	–	–	–	–	–	–	3	–	1	–	–	39
Wisconsin	–	1	2	4	5	4	4	2	3	–	1	–	3	2	–	1	1	–	1	–	1	–	1	–	–	–	–	–	–	–	2	3	–	41
Michigan State	–	–	1	–	1	1	1	1	–	–	–	2	–	2	–	2	–	1	1	4	4	5	4	1	1	1	–	1	1	1	2	2	–	40
North Dakota	2	3	3	1	4	2	1	–	1	2	3	3	1	–	–	1	–	–	–	–	2	1	1	–	–	–	–	–	2	–	1	1	–	35
Clarkson	–	–	2	2	1	–	2	–	2	2	1	1	1	1	1	1	–	–	1	1	1	3	2	1	1	–	–	–	–	3	1	1	–	32
Providence	–	–	–	–	–	–	3	2	3	4	–	5	4	1	2	–	1	1	–	–	–	1	–	–	–	–	–	–	1	2	–	2	–	32
Harvard	–	–	2	–	–	–	2	–	2	2	–	–	–	1	1	–	2	–	1	1	2	–	–	–	2	1	–	3	1	2	1	2	2	30
Boston College	–	1	–	–	–	–	1	1	–	5	–	2	1	1	–	–	–	1	2	–	2	–	–	–	–	–	–	2	3	3	–	3	2	30
New Hampshire	–	–	–	1	1	3	6	–	4	1	1	2	1	1	1	2	–	–	–	1	–	–	–	–	–	–	–	–	1	–	1	2	–	29
Cornell	–	–	–	2	1	1	–	1	1	1	–	1	1	1	–	1	2	–	1	2	5	2	–	–	–	–	–	–	1	–	2	2	–	28
Colorado	2	1	–	–	–	1	3	1	2	2	–	1	–	–	–	3	–	1	–	1	–	2	–	–	–	–	1	–	–	3	1	2	1	28
Notre Dame	–	–	2	3	–	–	7	2	–	3	1	1	–	–	–	–	–	–	–	–	–	–	–	–	–	–	–	1	2	–	2	1	1	26
Bowling Green	–	–	–	–	–	1	3	2	1	1	1	1	–	–	1	–	–	–	–	3	2	1	3	1	–	–	–	–	1	1	1	–	1	25
RPI	–	–	–	–	1	–	–	–	1	3	–	1	2	1	1	–	1	–	2	2	–	–	3	1	–	–	–	–	1	–	2	2	1	25
Lake Superior	–	–	–	–	1	1	1	–	–	3	–	–	–	–	–	1	–	3	–	3	2	3	1	–	1	–	–	1	1	–	1	–	–	23
W. Michigan	–	–	–	–	–	–	–	–	2	–	–	2	–	–	2	2	–	2	1	1	1	1	4	–	2	–	–	–	1	1	–	–	–	22
St. Lawrence	–	–	–	–	–	–	1	–	1	4	–	–	–	3	–	1	1	1	1	1	1	1	2	–	1	–	–	1	1	–	1	–	–	22
Vermont	–	–	–	–	1	–	4	–	1	1	–	1	1	–	1	1	2	–	–	1	–	–	1	–	–	1	–	1	–	–	–	–	2	19
Northern Mich.	–	–	–	–	–	–	–	–	–	4	–	1	2	1	–	–	–	–	4	1	2	–	1	–	–	–	–	1	–	–	–	1	–	18
Maine	–	–	–	–	–	–	–	–	–	–	–	–	–	1	1	–	–	1	–	3	2	1	–	–	1	–	–	1	1	1	4	1	–	18
Ohio State	–	–	–	–	–	–	–	–	2	1	–	–	–	–	–	1	–	–	2	2	–	1	1	1	1	–	–	1	1	–	1	–	2	17
Miami of Ohio	–	–	–	–	–	–	–	–	–	–	–	–	–	–	–	–	1	–	2	4	2	–	2	1	1	–	–	–	–	1	–	–	1	15
Minn.-Duluth	–	–	2	1	–	–	–	–	1	1	–	–	1	–	–	–	–	–	–	2	1	2	1	–	–	–	–	–	–	1	–	–	–	13
Brown	–	–	–	–	1	2	1	–	3	2	–	–	–	1	–	–	–	–	–	–	–	–	1	–	–	–	–	–	–	–	–	1	–	12
Colgate	–	–	–	–	–	1	–	–	–	2	1	–	–	–	–	–	–	–	–	1	1	2	2	–	–	–	–	–	–	–	–	–	–	10
Yale	–	–	–	1	–	–	1	–	–	2	–	1	–	–	–	–	–	1	2	–	1	–	–	–	1	–	–	–	–	–	–	–	–	10
Northeastern	–	–	–	–	–	1	–	–	–	1	–	1	–	–	1	–	1	1	–	–	1	1	–	–	–	–	–	–	–	1	1	–	–	10
Princeton	–	–	–	–	–	–	–	1	–	–	1	–	1	1	–	1	–	–	–	1	–	1	–	–	–	1	–	–	–	–	1	–	–	1	10

Colleges with fewer than 10 players drafted:

8 - Ferris State; **7** - Merrimack; **6** - Illinois-Chicago, St. Louis, Dartmouth, Lowell; **5** - Pennsylvania, Union College; **4** - Alaska-Anchorage, Union College; **3** - Babson College, St. Cloud State; **2** - Alaska-Fairbanks, Nebraska-Omaha; **1** - Air Force, American International College, Army, Bemidji State, Greenway, Hamilton, Mankato State, Mass.-Amherst, St. Anselen College, St. Thomas, Salem State, San Diego U., Wisconsin-River Falls.

Year	Total College Drafted	Total Players Drafted	College %
1969	7	84	8.3
1970	16	115	13.9
1971	22	117	18.8
1972	21	152	13.8
1973	25	168	14.9
1974	41	247	16.6
1975	59	217	26.7
1976	26	135	19.3
1977	49	185	26.5
1978	73	234	31.2
1979	15	126	11.9
1980	42	210	20.0
1981	21	211	10.0
1982	20	252	7.9
1983	14	242	5.8
1984	22	250	8.8
1985	20	252	7.9
1986	22	252	8.7
1987	40	252	15.9
1988	48	252	19.0
1989	48	252	19.0
1990	38	250	15.2
1991	43	264	16.3
1992	9	264	3.4
1993	17	286	5.9
1994	6	286	2.1
1995	5	234	2.1
1996	25	241	10.4
1997	26	246	10.5
1998	27	258	10.4
1999	36	272	13.2
2000	35	293	11.9
2001	24	289	8.3
Total	**942**	**7388**	**12.7**

United States High Schools (10 or more players drafted)

Club	'80	'81	'82	'83	'84	'85	'86	'87	'88	'89	'90	'91	'92	'93	'94	'95	'96	'97	'98	'99	'00	'01	Total
Northwood Prep (NY)	–	–	2	1	–	2	2	4	1	1	3	1	–	1	1	–	–	–	–	–	1	–	20
Belmont Hill (MA)	–	–	–	1	–	2	1	2	1	3	2	1	2	–	1	–	–	–	–	–	–	–	16
Cushing Acad. (MA)	–	–	–	–	1	–	–	–	3	2	3	1	–	2	2	–	1	1	–	–	–	1	17
Edina (MN)	–	1	4	2	2	–	–	1	2	2	1	–	1	–	–	–	–	–	–	–	–	–	16
Hill-Murray (MN)	–	–	–	–	3	–	3	3	–	2	3	–	–	–	1	–	–	–	–	–	–	–	15
Mount St. Charles (RI)	–	1	–	3	1	–	2	1	2	1	1	–	–	–	–	–	–	–	–	–	–	–	12
Culver Mil. Acad. (IN)	–	–	–	–	–	–	–	2	1	2	2	1	2	2	–	–	–	–	–	–	–	–	12
Catholic Memorial (MA)	–	–	–	–	–	2	–	1	1	2	–	–	2	1	2	–	–	–	1	–	–	–	12
Canterbury (CT)	–	–	–	–	–	–	2	–	3	–	2	–	2	1	–	–	–	–	–	–	–	–	10
Matignon (MA)	1	1	1	–	3	–	–	3	–	–	–	1	–	–	–	–	–	–	–	–	–	–	10
Roseau (MN)	1	–	1	1	1	–	1	–	–	1	3	1	–	–	–	–	–	–	–	–	–	–	10
Deerfield (IL)	–	–	–	–	1	1	–	1	1	2	–	1	–	–	–	–	–	–	–	1	2	–	10
Choate (CT)	–	–	–	–	–	1	–	2	3	–	1	1	1	–	–	–	–	–	–	–	1	–	10
Hotchkiss (CT)	–	–	–	–	–	1	–	–	1	–	1	–	–	–	3	1	2	–	–	–	–	1	10

Year	Total USHS Drafted	Total Players Drafted	USHS %
1980	7	210	3.3
1981	17	211	8.1
1982	47	252	18.6
1983	35	242	14.5
1984	44	250	17.6
1985	48	252	19.1
1986	40	252	15.9
1987	69	252	27.4
1988	56	252	22.2
1989	47	252	18.7
1990	57	250	22.8
1991	37	264	14.0
1992	25	264	9.5
1993	33	286	11.5
1994	28	286	9.7
1995	2	234	0.9
1996	6	241	2.4
1997	4	246	1.6
1998	7	258	2.7
1999	9	272	3.3
2000	7	293	2.4
2001	8	289	2.7
Total	**633**	**7388**	**8.5**

International

Country	'69	'70	'71	'72	'73	'74	'75	'76	'77	'78	'79	'80	'81	'82	'83	'84	'85	'86	'87	'88	'89	'90	'91	'92	'93	'94	'95	'96	'97	'98	'99	'00	'01	Total
USSR/CIS/Russia	–	–	–	–	–	–	1	–	–	2	–	–	–	3	5	1	2	1	2	11	18	14	25	45	31	35	27	17	16	22	29	44	36	387
Sweden	–	–	–	–	–	5	2	5	2	8	5	9	14	14	10	14	16	9	15	14	9	7	11	11	18	17	8	16	14	19	24	24	14	334
Czech Republic and Slovakia	–	–	–	–	–	–	–	–	–	–	2	1	–	4	13	13	8	6	11	5	8	21	9	17	15	18	21	14	17	20	20	28	28	308
Finland	1	–	–	–	–	1	3	2	3	2	–	4	12	5	9	10	4	10	6	7	3	9	6	8	9	8	12	7	11	12	17	19	29	229
Germany	–	–	–	–	–	–	–	–	–	2	–	–	2	–	1	2	1	–	1	2	–	–	1	1	3	1	1	3	1	–	–	1	7	31
Switzerland	–	–	–	–	–	–	–	1	–	–	–	–	–	–	–	–	–	–	–	–	–	–	1	–	2	1	–	1	3	2	3	7	5	26
Norway	–	–	–	–	–	–	–	–	–	–	–	–	–	–	–	–	–	–	2	–	–	2	1	–	–	–	–	–	1	–	–	–	–	6
Denmark	–	–	–	–	–	–	–	–	–	–	–	–	–	–	–	–	–	1	1	–	–	–	–	–	–	–	–	–	–	–	–	–	–	2
Scotland	–	–	–	–	–	–	–	–	–	–	–	–	–	–	–	–	–	1	–	–	–	–	–	–	–	–	–	–	–	–	–	–	–	1
Poland	–	–	–	–	–	–	–	–	–	–	–	–	–	–	–	–	–	–	–	–	–	–	1	–	–	–	–	–	–	–	–	–	–	1
Japan	–	–	–	–	–	–	–	–	–	–	–	–	–	–	–	–	–	–	–	–	–	–	–	1	–	–	–	–	–	–	–	–	–	1
Hungary	–	–	–	–	–	–	–	–	–	–	–	–	–	–	–	–	–	–	–	–	–	–	–	–	–	–	–	–	–	–	1	–	–	1

Year	Total Int'l Drafted	Total Players Drafted	Int'l %
1969	1	84	1.2
1970	0	115	0
1971	0	117	0
1972	0	152	0
1973	0	168	0
1974	6	247	2.4
1975	6	217	2.8
1976	8	135	5.9
1977	5	185	2.7
1978	16	234	6.8
1979	6	126	4.8
1980	13	210	6.2
1981	32	211	15.2
1982	35	252	13.9
1983	34	242	14.0
1984	40	250	17.6
1985	31	252	12.3
1986	28	252	11.1
1987	38	252	15.1
1988	39	252	15.5
1989	38	252	15.1
1990	53	250	21.2
1991	55	264	20.8
1992	84	264	31.4
1993	78	286	27.3
1994	80	286	27.9
1995	69	234	29.5
1996	58	241	24.0
1997	63	246	25.6
1998	75	258	29.0
1999	94	272	34.5
2000	123	293	42.0
2001	119	289	41.1
Total	**1208**	**7099**	**17.9**

Russia/C.I.S.

Club	'74	'75	'76	'77	'78	'79	'80	'81	'82	'83	'84	'85	'86	'87	'88	'89	'90	'91	'92	'93	'94	'95	'96	'97	'98	99	'00	'01	Total
CSKA Moscow	–	–	–	–	1	–	–	–	1	4	–	1	1	1	5	8	3	4	7	3	5	2	3	–	1	3	–	–	53
Dynamo Moscow	–	–	–	–	–	–	–	–	–	–	–	–	–	–	2	3	4	7	10	2	1	7	1	1	1	2	2	–	43
Krylja Sovetov Moscow	–	–	–	–	–	–	–	–	–	–	–	–	–	–	1	1	2	4	3	1	5	3	2	1	1	2	1	1	28
Spartak Moscow	–	–	–	–	–	–	–	–	1	–	–	1	–	1	–	–	–	1	4	–	6	1	–	–	–	1	–	6	22
Lokomotiv-2 Yaroslavl[6]	–	–	–	–	–	–	–	–	–	–	–	–	–	–	–	–	–	–	–	–	–	1	2	2	4	–	9	1	19
Lokomotiv Yaroslavl[6]	–	–	–	–	–	–	–	–	–	–	–	–	–	–	–	–	1	2	–	–	1	5	1	1	3	1	1	–	16
Traktor Chelyabinsk	–	–	–	–	–	–	–	–	–	–	–	–	–	–	–	2	–	–	2	7	1	1	–	1	1	–	–	–	15
Dynamo-2 Moscow	–	–	–	–	–	–	–	–	–	–	–	–	–	–	–	–	–	–	2	1	2	–	–	3	3	–	4	–	15
Khimik Voskresensk	–	–	–	–	–	–	–	–	–	1	–	–	–	–	–	1	3	1	2	–	1	–	–	–	2	–	1	1	13
Lada Togliatti	–	–	–	–	–	–	–	–	–	–	–	–	–	–	–	–	–	–	1	2	–	–	1	3	1	2	2	–	12
Sokol Kiev	–	–	–	–	–	–	–	–	–	–	1	–	–	–	1	–	1	2	3	1	–	2	–	–	–	–	–	–	11
SKA St. Peterburg[2]	–	–	–	–	1	–	–	–	1	–	–	–	–	–	–	–	–	2	1	–	1	–	–	–	–	2	1	2	11
Pardaugava Riga[1]	–	1	–	–	–	–	–	–	–	–	–	–	–	–	1	2	–	1	4	1	–	–	–	–	–	–	–	–	10
Severstal Cherepovets[5]	–	–	–	–	–	–	–	–	–	–	–	–	–	–	–	–	–	–	1	1	–	1	1	–	–	5	1	–	10
Torpedo Ust Kamenogorsk	–	–	–	–	–	–	–	–	–	–	–	–	–	–	–	–	–	–	1	1	2	1	–	–	2	1	–	–	8
Salavat Yulayev Ufa	–	–	–	–	–	–	–	–	–	–	–	–	–	–	–	–	–	–	–	2	2	1	1	1	–	–	1	–	8
Avangard Omsk	–	–	–	–	–	–	–	–	–	–	–	–	–	–	–	–	–	–	–	–	3	–	1	–	–	–	1	3	8
HC CSKA Moscow	–	–	–	–	–	–	–	–	–	–	–	–	–	–	–	–	–	–	–	–	–	–	–	–	–	2	5	–	7
CSKA-2 Moscow	–	–	–	–	–	–	–	–	–	–	–	–	–	–	–	–	–	–	–	–	1	–	2	2	–	–	–	–	5
Kristall Elektrostal	–	–	–	–	–	–	–	–	–	–	–	–	–	–	–	–	–	–	3	–	–	–	–	1	–	–	–	1	5
Metallurg Novokuznetsk	–	–	–	–	–	–	–	–	–	–	–	–	–	–	–	–	–	–	–	–	–	–	–	–	–	2	2	1	5
Neftekhimik Nizhnekamsk	–	–	–	–	–	–	–	–	–	–	–	–	–	–	–	–	–	–	–	–	–	–	–	1	–	–	2	2	5
Lada-2 Togliatti	–	–	–	–	–	–	–	–	–	–	–	–	–	–	–	–	–	–	–	–	–	–	–	–	–	1	2	2	5
Tivali Minsk[3]	–	–	–	–	–	–	–	–	–	–	–	–	–	–	1	–	–	–	–	2	1	–	–	–	–	–	–	–	4
Torpedo Nizhny Novgorod[4]	–	–	–	–	–	–	–	–	–	–	–	–	–	–	–	–	1	–	2	–	–	–	–	–	–	–	1	–	4
Molot Perm	–	–	–	–	–	–	–	–	–	–	–	–	–	–	–	–	–	–	–	–	1	1	–	–	–	–	1	1	4
AK Bars Kazan	–	–	–	–	–	–	–	–	–	–	–	–	–	–	–	–	–	–	–	–	1	–	–	–	1	–	1	1	4
Avtomobilist Yekaterinburg	–	–	–	–	–	–	–	–	–	–	–	–	–	–	–	–	–	–	–	–	–	–	1	–	1	1	–	–	3
CSK VVS Samara	–	–	–	–	–	–	–	–	–	–	–	–	–	–	–	–	–	–	–	–	–	1	–	–	–	1	–	1	3
Avangard-2 Omsk	–	–	–	–	–	–	–	–	–	–	–	–	–	–	–	–	–	–	–	–	–	–	–	–	–	–	–	3	3
Metallurg Magnitogorsk	–	–	–	–	–	–	–	–	–	–	–	–	–	–	–	–	–	–	–	–	–	–	–	–	–	–	–	3	3
Dizelist Penza	–	–	–	–	–	–	–	–	–	–	–	–	–	–	–	–	–	–	1	–	–	–	–	–	–	–	1	–	2
Severstal-2 Cherepovets	–	–	–	–	–	–	–	–	–	–	–	–	–	–	–	–	–	–	–	–	–	–	–	–	–	1	1	–	2
Metallurg-2 Novokuznetsk	–	–	–	–	–	–	–	–	–	–	–	–	–	–	–	–	–	–	–	–	–	–	–	–	–	–	2	–	2
Kristall Saratov	–	–	–	–	–	–	–	–	–	–	–	–	–	–	–	–	–	–	–	1	–	–	–	–	–	–	–	1	2
Ak-Bars-2 Kazan	–	–	–	–	–	–	–	–	–	–	–	–	–	–	–	–	–	–	–	–	–	–	–	–	–	1	–	1	2

Former club names: [1]–Dynamo Riga, HC Riga, [2]–SKA Leningrad, [3]–Dynamo Minsk, [4]–Torpedo Gorky, [5]–Metallurg Cherepovets, [6]–Torpedo Yaroslavl

Teams with one player selected:

Amur Khabarovsk, Argus Moscow, Dynamo Khazov, Dynamo-81 Riga, Izohets St. Petersburg, Khimik Novopolotsk, Krylja Sovetov-2 Moscow, Mechel Chelyabinsk, Neftekhimik Nizhnekamsk, Salavat Novoil Ufa, SKA-2 St. Petersburg, Sibir-2 Novosibirsk-1, THC Tver, Vityaz Podolsk, Vityaz-2 Podolsk.

Sweden

Club	'74	'75	'76	'77	'78	'79	'80	'81	'82	'83	'84	'85	'86	'87	'88	'89	'90	'91	'92	'93	'94	'95	'96	'97	'98	'99	'00	'01	Total
Djurgarden Stockholm	1	1	1	–	–	1	2	–	1	2	1	–	1	2	–	1	1	2	1	1	–	3	2	2	–	1	4	1	32
MoDo Hockey Ornskoldsvik	–	–	1	–	–	1	–	–	1	–	2	–	–	1	–	–	–	2	2	5	–	–	3	3	–	7	3	–	31
Farjestad Karlstad	–	–	–	2	2	–	1	2	1	1	1	2	–	–	–	1	–	1	2	1	–	2	–	3	6	1	–	1	30
Leksand	1	–	–	–	–	1	–	–	1	–	2	2	1	1	2	1	–	2	–	2	2	–	1	–	2	–	5	–	26
AIK Solna	–	–	1	–	1	1	–	2	3	1	–	4	–	–	–	–	1	1	1	–	1	–	–	1	1	3	–	1	23
Vastra Frolunda Goteborg	–	–	–	–	–	–	–	–	–	–	2	1	–	1	1	1	–	–	1	–	3	1	1	–	1	2	4	3	22
Brynas Gavle	1	–	–	–	1	1	1	1	–	1	2	–	–	4	–	–	–	–	–	1	–	–	1	1	2	1	1	2	21
HV 71 Jonkoping	–	–	–	–	–	–	–	1	–	–	–	–	–	1	1	–	1	–	–	–	2	–	2	1	4	3	1	–	17
Sodertalje	–	–	–	–	1	–	–	1	1	1	2	2	2	–	–	2	–	–	–	1	–	–	–	–	1	–	1	1	16
Skelleftea	–	1	1	–	–	–	–	1	1	2	1	–	–	–	1	–	–	–	–	1	–	–	–	1	–	–	–	–	10
Lulea	–	–	–	–	–	–	1	1	–	–	–	–	1	1	1	–	–	–	1	–	–	–	–	1	1	–	2	–	10
Rogle Angelholm	–	–	–	–	–	–	–	–	–	–	–	–	–	1	2	–	–	–	–	2	2	1	–	–	–	1	–	–	9
Vasteras	–	–	–	–	–	–	–	–	–	–	–	–	–	–	2	2	1	1	–	1	1	–	–	–	–	–	1	–	9
Malmo	–	–	–	–	–	–	–	–	–	–	–	–	–	–	1	–	–	–	1	1	1	–	2	–	–	1	1	–	8
Sundsvall Timra[1]	–	–	–	–	–	–	1	2	–	–	–	1	1	–	–	–	–	–	–	–	1	–	–	–	–	1	–	–	7
Bjorkloven Umea	–	–	–	–	–	–	2	1	–	–	–	1	–	–	1	–	–	–	–	–	–	–	–	–	–	–	–	–	5
Orebro	–	–	1	–	1	–	–	–	–	1	–	1	–	1	–	–	–	–	–	–	–	–	–	–	–	–	–	–	5
Hammarby Stockholm	–	–	–	–	–	–	1	1	–	–	–	–	–	–	–	–	–	–	–	1	1	–	–	–	1	–	–	1	6
Nacka	–	–	–	–	–	–	–	–	–	–	–	–	1	–	–	1	–	–	2	–	–	–	–	–	–	–	–	–	4
Mora	–	–	–	–	–	–	–	–	–	1	–	–	1	–	–	–	–	–	–	–	–	–	1	1	–	–	–	1	5
Huddinge	–	–	–	–	–	–	–	–	–	–	–	–	–	–	–	–	–	1	–	–	–	–	2	–	–	1	–	1	5
Falun	–	–	–	–	–	–	–	1	–	–	–	–	–	–	1	–	–	1	–	–	–	–	–	–	–	–	–	–	3
Team Kiruna	–	–	–	–	1	–	–	–	1	–	–	–	–	–	–	–	–	–	–	1	–	–	–	–	–	–	–	–	3
Boden	1	–	–	–	–	–	–	–	–	–	–	–	1	–	–	–	–	–	–	–	1	–	–	–	–	–	–	–	3
Pitea	–	–	–	–	–	–	–	–	1	–	–	–	–	–	–	–	1	–	–	–	1	–	–	–	–	–	–	–	3
Troja	–	–	–	–	–	–	–	–	–	–	–	1	–	–	1	–	–	–	–	–	–	–	–	–	–	1	–	–	3
Grums	–	–	–	–	–	–	–	–	–	–	–	–	–	–	–	–	–	–	–	–	1	–	–	–	–	1	1	–	3
Ostersund	–	–	–	–	–	–	–	–	–	–	–	1	–	1	–	–	–	–	–	–	–	–	–	–	–	–	–	–	2

Former club names: [1]–Timra

Teams with one player selected:

Almtuna, Danderyd Hockey, Fagersta, Karskoga, Morrum, Stocksund, S/G Hockey 83 Gavle, Talje, Tingsryd, Tunabro, Uppsala, Vallentuna, Vita Hasten.

Czech Republic and Slovakia

Club	'69	'70	'71	'72	'73	'74	'75	'76	'77	'78	'79	'80	'81	'82	'83	'84	'85	'86	'87	'88	'89	'90	'91	'92	'93	'94	'95	'96	'97	'98	'99	'00	'01	Total
Chemopetrol Litvinov[1]	–	–	–	–	–	–	–	–	–	–	–	–	–	3	1	2	–	–	–	–	2	2	1	3	2	4	2	2	2	1	1	–	1	29
Dukla Jihlava	–	–	–	–	–	–	–	–	–	–	–	–	–	2	4	3	1	–	3	1	1	3	2	1	1	1	2	2	–	–	–	1	–	28
HC Ceske Budejovice[6]	–	–	–	–	–	–	–	–	–	–	–	–	–	2	1	1	–	–	1	–	1	2	–	–	1	2	3	1	2	1	1	3	2	24
Slavia Praha	–	–	–	–	–	–	–	–	–	–	–	–	–	–	–	1	–	–	–	–	–	–	–	–	1	–	–	–	4	5	2	3	5	21
Dukla Trencin	–	–	–	–	–	–	–	–	–	–	–	–	–	–	–	1	–	–	–	1	1	2	–	2	2	–	1	2	1	–	2	3	2	20
Sparta Praha	–	–	–	–	–	–	–	–	–	–	–	–	–	1	–	2	1	1	1	2	1	2	–	1	1	–	1	–	1	1	–	1	2	19
Slovan Bratislava	–	–	–	–	–	–	–	–	–	1	1	–	–	2	–	–	1	1	1	–	–	1	–	–	–	3	–	1	1	1	2	2	–	18
ZPS Zlin[2]	–	–	–	–	–	–	–	–	–	–	–	–	–	–	1	–	1	1	1	–	–	–	2	2	1	–	2	–	1	2	2	–	2	18
HC Kladno[7]	–	–	–	–	–	–	–	–	–	–	–	–	2	1	–	1	–	1	–	–	–	1	2	–	1	2	–	2	–	–	2	1	1	17
HC Vitkovice[8]	–	–	–	–	–	–	–	–	–	1	–	–	1	–	–	–	–	–	–	–	–	1	–	1	3	1	1	1	–	1	1	1	–	13
HC Kosice[3]	–	–	–	–	–	–	–	–	–	–	–	–	1	2	–	2	–	1	–	–	–	2	–	–	–	–	–	1	1	1	1	–	1	13
Interconex Plzen[9]	–	–	–	–	–	–	–	–	–	–	–	–	–	–	–	–	–	1	–	–	1	1	–	3	–	1	1	–	–	1	–	1	1	11
HC Pardubice[4]	–	–	–	–	–	–	–	–	–	–	–	–	–	–	2	–	2	–	1	–	–	–	–	–	–	2	1	–	1	–	–	–	1	10
Zetor Brno	–	–	–	–	–	–	–	–	–	–	–	–	–	–	–	–	1	–	3	–	–	2	–	1	–	–	–	–	–	1	–	–	–	8
HC Olomouc[5]	–	–	–	–	–	–	–	–	–	–	–	–	–	–	–	–	–	–	–	–	1	–	–	2	–	1	2	–	–	1	–	–	–	7
ZTK Zvolen	–	–	–	–	–	–	–	–	–	–	–	–	–	–	–	–	–	–	–	–	–	–	–	1	–	–	1	1	–	–	2	2	–	7
HC Vsetin	–	–	–	–	–	–	–	–	–	–	–	–	–	–	–	–	–	–	–	–	–	–	–	–	–	–	–	–	2	1	–	2	2	7
AC Nitra	–	–	–	–	–	–	–	–	–	–	–	–	–	–	–	–	–	–	–	–	–	–	2	–	1	–	–	1	–	1	–	–	1	6
ZTS Martin	–	–	–	–	–	–	–	–	–	–	–	–	–	–	–	–	–	–	–	1	–	–	–	–	–	–	2	–	–	–	–	1	1	5
Zelezarny Trinec	–	–	–	–	–	–	–	–	–	–	–	–	–	–	–	–	–	–	–	–	–	–	–	–	–	–	–	–	–	–	1	1	1	4
IS Banska Bystrica	–	–	–	–	–	–	–	–	–	–	–	–	–	–	–	–	–	–	–	–	–	–	–	–	–	1	1	–	–	–	–	–	–	2
ZPA Presov	–	–	–	–	–	–	–	–	–	–	–	–	–	–	–	–	–	–	–	–	–	–	–	–	1	–	–	–	1	–	–	–	–	2
Partizan Liptovsky Mikulas	–	–	–	–	–	–	–	–	–	–	–	–	–	–	–	–	–	–	–	–	–	1	–	–	–	–	–	–	–	1	–	–	–	2
VTJ Pisek	–	–	–	–	–	–	–	–	–	–	–	–	–	–	–	–	–	–	–	–	–	1	–	–	–	–	–	–	–	–	1	–	–	2
Michalovce	–	–	–	–	–	–	–	–	–	–	–	–	–	–	–	–	–	–	–	–	–	–	–	–	–	–	–	–	–	–	2	–	–	2
Ingstav Brno	–	–	–	–	–	–	–	–	–	–	–	–	–	–	–	–	1	–	–	–	–	–	–	–	–	–	–	–	–	–	–	–	1	2
HC Karlovy Vary	–	–	–	–	–	–	–	–	–	–	–	–	–	–	–	–	–	–	–	–	–	–	–	–	–	–	–	–	–	–	–	1	1	2
HC Liberec	–	–	–	–	–	–	–	–	–	–	–	–	–	–	–	–	–	–	–	–	–	–	–	–	–	–	–	–	–	–	–	–	2	2

Former club names: [1]–CHZ Litvinov, [2]–TJ Gottwaldov, TJ Zlin, [3]–VSZ Kosice, [4]–Tesla Pardubice, [5]–DS Olomouc, [6]–Motor Ceske Budejovice, [7]–Poldi Kladno, [8]–TJ Vitkovice, [9]–Skoda Plzen

Teams with one player selected:
Banik Sokolov, Havlickuv Brod, KLH Chomutov, HC Havirov, KC SKP Poprad, KC Skalica, HK Trnava, KHM Zvolen.

Finland

Club	'69	'70	'71	'72	'73	'74	'75	'76	'77	'78	'79	'80	'81	'82	'83	'84	'85	'86	'87	'88	'89	'90	'91	'92	'93	'94	'95	'96	'97	'98	'99	'00	'01	Total
TPS Turku	–	–	–	–	–	–	–	–	–	–	–	1	6	–	–	–	1	1	–	–	–	–	–	–	3	2	3	1	3	3	1	3	3	31
HIFK Helsinki	1	–	–	–	–	–	1	–	1	–	–	–	1	1	2	2	1	–	–	2	1	–	–	–	2	–	1	–	1	2	4	2	2	27
Ilves Tampere	–	–	–	–	–	–	–	–	1	2	–	–	2	–	2	2	–	1	–	1	–	1	1	–	–	–	2	–	–	2	1	3	4	25
Jokerit Helsinki	–	–	–	–	–	–	–	–	–	–	–	2	1	–	–	1	–	–	1	1	–	2	–	3	–	1	–	1	1	1	3	3	4	25
Tappara Tampere	–	–	–	–	–	1	–	–	–	–	–	–	–	2	–	–	–	4	–	1	–	1	–	–	–	–	1	1	2	–	–	1	2	16
Lukko Rauma	–	–	–	–	–	–	–	2	1	–	–	–	–	–	2	–	1	–	1	–	–	1	–	1	–	–	–	–	–	–	2	1	3	15
Karpat Oulu	–	–	–	–	–	–	–	–	–	–	–	1	–	1	–	1	–	2	2	–	–	–	1	–	1	–	–	–	1	1	–	–	3	14
Assat Pori	–	–	–	–	–	–	2	–	–	–	–	–	1	–	2	2	–	–	–	1	–	1	–	–	1	1	1	–	–	1	–	–	–	13
Kiekko-Espoo	–	–	–	–	–	–	–	–	–	–	–	–	–	–	–	–	–	–	–	1	–	1	1	2	–	2	1	–	1	–	2	–	2	12
HPK Hameenlinna	–	–	–	–	–	–	–	–	–	–	–	–	–	–	–	–	–	–	–	–	1	–	–	2	–	–	–	–	1	1	1	3	1	10
JyP HT Jyvaskyla	–	–	–	–	–	–	–	–	–	–	–	–	–	–	–	–	–	–	1	–	–	–	–	–	–	–	–	2	1	–	3	–	1	8
KalPa Kuopio	–	–	–	–	–	–	–	–	–	–	–	–	–	–	–	–	–	–	1	–	–	–	–	–	1	2	–	–	–	1	–	1	2	8
Reipas Lahti	–	–	–	–	–	–	–	–	–	–	–	–	–	1	1	1	–	–	–	–	–	–	2	–	1	–	–	1	–	–	–	–	–	7
SaiPa Lappeenranta	–	–	–	–	–	–	–	–	–	–	–	–	1	–	–	–	–	–	–	–	–	1	–	–	–	–	–	–	–	–	–	1	1	4
Kiekoo-67 Turku	–	–	–	–	–	–	–	–	–	–	–	–	–	–	–	–	–	–	–	–	–	–	–	–	–	–	3	–	–	–	–	–	–	3
Sapko Savonlinna	–	–	–	–	–	–	–	–	–	–	–	–	–	–	–	–	1	1	–	–	–	–	–	–	–	–	–	–	–	–	–	–	–	2
Sport Vaasa	–	–	–	–	–	–	–	–	–	–	–	–	–	–	–	–	–	1	–	–	1	–	–	–	–	–	–	–	–	–	–	–	–	2

Teams with one player selected:
Ahmat Hyvinkaa, GrIFK Kauniainen, Koo Koo Kouvola, S-Kiekko Seinajoki, Junkkarit Kalajoki, Hermes Kokkola.

2001 Entry Draft Analysis

Country of Origin

Country	Players Drafted
Canada	106
USA	41
Russia	36
Czech Republic	31
Finland	23
Sweden	17
Slovakia	15
Germany	6
Switzerland	5
Kazakhstan	3
Austria	2
Latvia	1
Ukraine	1
Slovenia	1
France	1

Birth Year

Year	Players Drafted
1983	123
1982	94
1981	42
1980	4
1979	2
1978	2
1977	7
1976	3
1975	5
1974	1
1973	3
1972	3

Position

Position	Players Drafted
Defense	95
Center	67
Right Wing	52
Left Wing	41
Goaltender	34

Note: Players drafted in the international category played outside North America in their draft year. European-born players drafted from the OHL, QMJHL, WHL or U.S. Colleges are not counted as International players. See Country of Origin, at left.

Notes on 2001 First Round Selections

1. ATLANTA • **ILYA KOVALCHUK** • RW • A big, strong player with impressive speed, quickness and acceleration, Ilya Kovalchuk is the first Russian player to be selected number one in the NHL Entry Draft. Kovalchuk has excellent hockey sense, and with his outstanding puckhandling skills he is a very good playmaker and a dangerous scorer. Kovalchuk led the Russian team to a gold medal at the Under-18 World Championships with 11 goals in six games. He is projected to be a potential franchise player.

2. OTTAWA • **JASON SPEZZA** • C • The top-rated North American prospect in the draft, Jason Spezza possesses outstanding hockey sense and is an excellent playmaker who is very confident with the puck. Spezza is a mature and disciplined player who has the ability to dominate a game and control the play. He is one of only four players to represent Canada at the World Junior Championships as a 16-year-old (2000).

3. TAMPA BAY • **ALEXANDER SVITOV** • C • The youngest player in the Russian elite league when he broke in as a 16-year-old in 1999-2000, Alexander Svitov is a creative playmaker who can excel in a physical game. A very good skater with a powerful stride, Svitov plays at a very high skill level and is used in all game situations. Excellent on face-offs, he uses his impressive size (6'3", 198 pounds) to advantage.

4. FLORIDA • **STEPHEN WEISS** • C • Often compared to Steve Yzerman and Joe Sakic, Stephen Weiss is an effortless skater with excellent speed. A superb passer with a quick, accurate wrist shot, he is dangerous around the opponent's net but is also aware of his defensive responsibilities. Weiss is an effective forechecker who is willing to sacrifice himself to make a play. He is strong in the faceoff circle.

5. ANAHEIM • **STANISLAV CHISTOV** • RW • Though he is only 5'9" and weighs just 169 pounds, Stanislav Chistov is a good competitor and hard worker who plays with intensity. One of the best pure talents to be available in the draft, Chistov is an excellent skater with impressive speed and agility. He has good vision and strong hockey instincts, making him a very strong puckhandler and creative playmaker.

6. MINNESOTA • **MIKKO KOIVU** • C • The brother of Saku Koivu, Mikko Koivu stands four inches taller at 6'2" and weighs 183 pounds. Though not an overly physical player, Koivu will sacrifice himself to make the play and moves well through traffic. He has a high overall skill level and is an excellent passer with very good hockey sense. Koivu captained the Finnish team at the 2001 Under-18 World Championships.

7. MONTREAL • **MIKE KOMISAREK** • D • The top-rated defenseman in the draft, Mike Komisarek is a graduate of USA Hockey's National Team Develop-ment Program. At 6'4" and 225 pounds, he enjoys the physical aspects of the game and is a punishing checker who has an intimidating presence on the ice. Komisarek also has a hard and accurate slapshot and is a good skater who can join in on the rush.

8. COLUMBUS • **PASCAL LECLAIRE** • G • Rated as the top North American goaltending prospect despite injuries during the 2000-01 season, Pascal Leclaire is a competitive netminder who likes to challenge the shooter. He plays the angles extremely well and uses an effective butterfly style. Leclaire sees the puck well in traffic and has a fast glove hand. He has a great work ethic and very strong athletic ability.

9. CHICAGO • **TUOMO RUUTU** • C • The third member of his family to be drafted in the last four years (Jarkko, 68th overall in 1998; Mikko 201st in 2000), Tuomo Ruutu was the youngest player in the top Finnish league last season. A strong skater with impressive quickness, Ruutu is an excellent two-way player with a great work ethic. He handles the puck well in traffic and like to play a physical game.

10. NY RANGERS • **DAN BLACKBURN** • G • The youngest winner of the Western Hockey League's player-of-the-year award at 16 in 1999-2000, Dan Blackburn is a very consistent goaltender who is a good skater and has excellent flexibility, agility and lateral movement. He has a very good glove hand and is extremely quick to regain his feet. Blackburn has good rebound control and also handles the puck well.

11. PHOENIX • **FREDRIK SJOSTROM** • RW • A good team player with a lot of character, Fredrik Sjostrom is an excellent skater with impressive speed and good balance. He is an offensive-minded player with good hockey sense and a high overall skill level. Sjostrom has very strong puckhandling and passing skills and he is effective in the corners and along the boards. He represented Sweden at both the Under-18 World Championships and the World Juniors in 2000-01.

12. NASHVILLE • **DAN HAMHUIS** • D • A very skilled and intelligent defenseman, Dan Hamhuis anticipates the play very well and makes good decisions. He is a very good, well-balanced skater with good agility and excellent speed. Hamhuis has a hard and accurate shot and is a confident puck carrier who is capable of leading a rush. He is also a physical player who is a good open-ice hitter and is tough along the boards.

13. EDMONTON • **ALES HEMSKY** • RW • A native of the Czech Republic, Ales Hemsky led all rookies in the Quebec Major Junior Hockey League with 64 assists and 100 points in 2000-01. Hemsky is an excellent skater with a very smooth stride and impressive speed and agility. He is a confident and patient puck carrier, and has a quick, accurate wrist shot as well as a powerful slapshot. Hemsky's father coaches Pardubice in the Czech elite league.

14. CALGARY • **CHUCK KOBASEW** • RW • Named the top rookie in Hockey East last season, Chuck Kobasew was also the NCAA leader in game-winning goals and helped Boston College win the NCAA title. A former British Columbia junior star, Kobasew is a creative offensive player who is very dangerous around the net. He is also a good competitor who works well in the corners and plays the body.

15. CAROLINA • **IGOR KNYAZEV** • D • The captain of Russia's gold medal-winning Under-18 World Championship team, Igor Knyazev is an offensive-minded defenseman who does not back down from a physical game. He is a strong skater with good mob-ility who has the ability to lead the offensive attack. Knyazev plays a strong positional game in his own zone and anticipates the play very well.

16. VANCOUVER • **R.J. UMBERGER** • C • A graduate of the U.S. National Team Development Program who went on to become the CCHA rookie of the year with Ohio State, R.J. Umberger is a 6'2", 200-pounder who uses good speed and acceleration to dominate one-on-one situations. Umberger is a smooth and powerful skater with a heavy wrist shot and a quick release. He is a confident and talented puckhandler.

17. TORONTO • **CARLO COLAIACOVO** • D • A very determined player who can lift teammates with his effort, Carlo Colaiacovo has an excellent feel for the game. An intelligent defenseman who plays with poise and patience, Colaiacovo is an excellent skater who has the ability to join in the rush and can be a threat when pinching from the point. He has a hard and accurate shot and is effective on the power-play.

18. LOS ANGELES • **JENS KARLSSON** • RW • At 6'3" and 205 pounds, Jens Karlsson is a big, strong winger who has the ability to dominate games. He starred as a Swedish junior but had a difficult time making the transition to the elite league in 2000-01, though he did come on strong in the playoffs. Karlsson played for Sweden at the Under-18 World Championships.

19. BOSTON • **SHAONE MORRISONN** • D • Rated 58th among North American prospects at midseason, Shaone Morrisonn moved up 17 spots by year's end and wound up being selected 19th in the draft. An excellent skater with good acceleration, Morrisonn plays at a very high skill level and has the ability to lead the offensive attack. At 6'3" and 182 pounds, he is not an overly physical player but effectively takes his man. Morrisonn has a good shot from the point.

20. SAN JOSE • **MARCEL GOC** • C • A rookie in the German elite league as a 16-year-old in 1999-2000, Marcel Goc is a hard worker who is very effective along the boards and in the corners. A good skater who seldom gets knocked down, Goc has good puck-handling skills and works well in heavy traffic. He has excellent hockey sense and strong playmaking ability. He is good on the face-off and cool under pressure.

21. PITTSBURGH • **COLBY ARMSTRONG** • RW • A very good skater with a long, smooth stride, Colby Armstrong was a member of the Red Deer Rebels, winners of the Memorial Cup in 2001. Armstrong is a good playmaker with strong passing skills who works well in heavy traffic. He is a natural goal-scorer with a quick, accurate shot and is very strong in one-on-one situations. Armstrong anticipates the play very well and is a very good two-way player.

22. BUFFALO • **JIRI NOVOTNY** • C • The captain of the Czech Republic team at the Under-18 World Championships, Jiri Novotny is a smooth skater with good speed and acceleration. He is creative with strong puckhandling skills and a very good understanding of the game. Novotny is very good in one-on-one situations and is excellent on face-offs. He is a reliable and hard-working player.

23. OTTAWA • **TIM GLEASON** • D • An excellent skater with impressive power, balance, speed and mobility, Tim Gleason is an offensive defenseman with solid puckhandling skills. He is an aggressive player who enjoys the physical aspects of the game and is a punishing checker. Gleason also passes the puck with authority and has a very hard shot. He is very effective four-on-four and when killing penalties.

24. FLORIDA • **LUKAS KRAJICEK** • D • A native of the Czech Republic who was named rookie of the year with the Peterborough Petes of the OHL in 2000-01, Lukas Krajicek is a very good skater with exceptional lateral movement. He has excellent hockey sense and can lead a rush with his strong puckhandling skills. Krajicek is a dedicated and hard-working player who reacts very quickly in defensive situations.

25. MONTREAL • **ALEXANDER PEREZHOGIN** • C • A natural goal-scorer with a wide variety of shots, Alexander Perezhogin is an offensive threat every time he steps on the ice. A member of the Russian team that won gold at the Under-18 World Championships, Perezhogin is a typically fast Russian forward, but he needs to improve his overall physical strength. He is a very good puckhandler with good hockey sense.

26. DALLAS • **JASON BACASHIHUA** • G • With a good combination of balance and speed, Jason Bacashihua is a goaltender with good lateral move-ment. He remains cool under pressure, but at 5'11" and just 167 pounds, he needs to bulk up. Considered a top NCAA prospect, Bacashihua has instead spent the last two seasons playing U.S. junior hockey and is expected to move up to major junior with the Plymouth Whalers in 2001-02.

27. PHILADELPHIA • **JEFF WOYWITKA** • D • A member of the Memorial Cup champion Red Deer Rebels, Jeff Woywitka is a 6'2", 209-pound defenseman who is very solid on his skates. Woywitka is a strong skater with good lateral movement who is aware of all his options when in possession of the puck. He uses his partner effectively when in the defensive zone and has a hard shot from the point.

28. NEW JERSEY • **ADRIAN FOSTER** • LW • Before suffering an abdominal injury that has sidelined him for most of the past two seasons, Adrian Foster was being compared favorably with former teammate Dany Heatly, who was selected second overall in the 2000 Entry Draft. At 6'1" and 200 pounds, Foster is a natural talent with a lot of desire and grit. Despite his injury, he is seen to have tremendous potential.

29. CHICAGO • **ADAM MUNRO** • G • Finishing among the OHL's leaders in most categories, including a league-leading .920 save percentage, Adam Munro is strong on his skates and excellent at playing the angles. He likes to play at the top of his crease and has a good glove hand. Munro uses the paddle-down technique very well and is good at controlling rebounds. He has good instincts and reads the play well.

30. LOS ANGELES • **DAVE STECKEL** • C • At 6'5" and 210 pounds, David Steckel is an intimidating presence on the ice and takes advantage of his reach when controlling the puck. A graduate of the U.S. National Team Development Program, Steckel is an aggressive and tenacious forechecker who is a deceptively fast skater. He is a good goal-scorer who drives hard to the net and stands his ground in the slot.

NHL IMAGES PHOTO

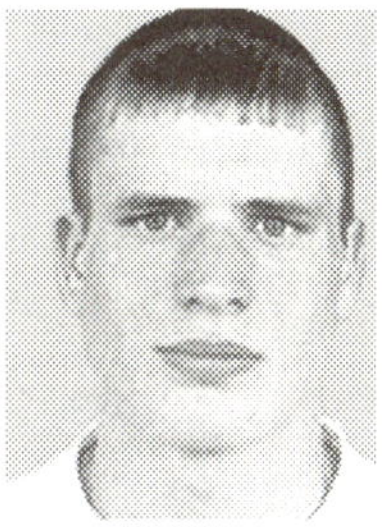

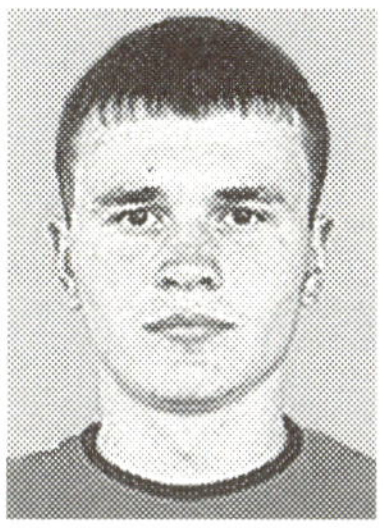

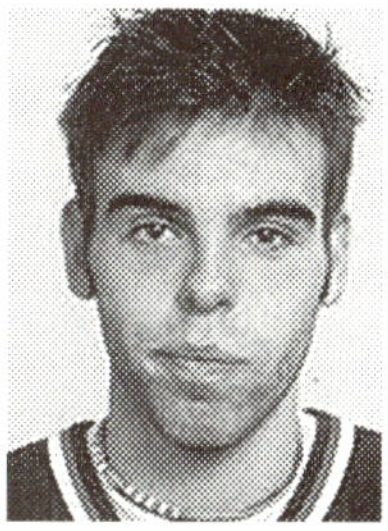

NHL IMAGES PHOTO

Players selected first through tenth in the 2001 NHL Entry Draft: (All rows left to right):
Top row: 1. Ilya Kovalchuk, LW, Atlanta; 2. Jason Spezza, C, Ottawa.
Second row: 3. Alexander Svitov, C, Tampa Bay; 4. Stephen Weiss, C, Florida.
Third row: 5. Stanislav Chistov, LW, Anaheim; 6. Mikko Koivu, C, Minnesota.
Fourth row: 7. Mike Komisarek, D, Montreal; 8. Pascal Leclaire, G, Columbus.
Fifth row: 9. Tuomo Ruutu, C, Chicago; 10. Dan Blackburn, G, NY Rangers.

2001 Entry Draft

Transferred draft choice notation:

Example: Col.-Ana. represents a draft choice transferred **from** Colorado **to** Anaheim.

Pick	Player	Claimed By	Amateur Club	Position
ROUND #1				
1.	KOVALCHUK, Ilya	Atl.	Krylja Sovetov	LW
2.	SPEZZA, Jason	NYI-Ott.	Windsor	C
3.	SVITOV, Alexander	T.B.	Omsk	C
4.	WEISS, Stephen	Fla.	Plymouth	C
5.	CHISTOV, Stanislav	Ana.	Omsk	LW
6.	KOIVU, Mikko	Min.	TPS Turku	C
7.	KOMISAREK, Mike	Mtl.	U. of Michigan	D
8.	LECLAIRE, Pascal	CBJ	Halifax	G
9.	RUUTU, Tuomo	Chi.	Jokerit	C
10.	BLACKBURN, Dan	NYR	Kootenay	G
11.	SJOSTROM, Fredrik	Cgy.-Phx.	V. Frolunda	RW
12.	HAMHUIS, Dan	Nsh.	Prince George	D
13.	HEMSKY, Ales	Bos.-Edm.	Hull	RW
14.	KOBASEW, Chuck	Phx.-Cgy.	Boston College	RW
15.	KNYAZEV, Igor	Car.	Spartak	D
16.	UMBERGER, R.J.	Van.	Ohio State	C
17.	COLAIACOVO, Carlo	Tor.	Erie	D
18.	KARLSSON, Jens	L.A.	V. Frolunda	LW
19.	MORRISONN, Shaone	Edm.-Bos.	Kamloops	D
20.	GOC, Marcel	S.J.	Schwenningen	C
21.	ARMSTRONG, Colby	Pit.	Red Deer	RW
22.	NOVOTNY, Jiri	Buf.	Budejovice	C
23.	GLEASON, Tim	Phi.-Ott.	Windsor	D
24.	KRAJICEK, Lukas	St.L.-N.J.-Fla.	Peterborough	D
25.	PEREZHOGIN, Alexander	Wsh.-Mtl.	Omsk 2	RW
26.	BACASHIHUA, Jason	Dal.	Chicago Jr.	G
27.	WOYWITKA, Jeff	Ott.-Phi.	Red Deer	D
28.	FOSTER, Adrian	N.J.	Saskatoon	LW
29.	MUNRO, Adam	Det.-Chi.	Erie	G
30.	STECKEL, David	Col.-L.A.	Ohio State	LW/C
ROUND #2				
31.	SPILLER, Matthew	NYI-T.B.-Phx.	Seattle	D
32.	ROY, Derek	T.B.-Buf.	Kitchener	C
33.	SHISHKANOV, Timofei	Atl.-Van.-Nsh.	Spartak	LW
34.	WATSON, Greg	Fla.	Prince Albert	C/LW
35.	POPOVIC, Mark	Ana.	Toronto St. Michael's	D
36.	WANVIG, Kyle	Min.	Red Deer	RW
37.	MILROY, Duncan	Mtl.	Swift Current	RW
38.	JACKMAN, Tim	CBJ	Mankato State	RW
39.	PILAR, Karel	Chi.-Tor.	Litvinov	D
40.	TUTIN, Fedor	NYR	SKA St.Petersburg	D
41.	TARATUKHIN, Andrei	Cgy.-Ana.-Phx.-Cgy.	Omsk 2	C
42.	SLOVAK, Tomas	Nsh.	Kosice	D
43.	LYNCH, Doug	Bos.-Edm.	Red Deer	D
44.	POHANKA, Igor	Phx.-Fla.-N.J.	Prince Albert	C
45.	PODLESAK, Martin	Phx.	Lethbridge	LW
46.	ZIGOMANIS, Mike	Car.	Kingston	C
47.	POLUSHIN, Alexander	Van.-T.B.	Tver	RW
48.	PIHLMAN, Tuomas	Van.-Fla.-N.J.	JYP	RW
49.	CAMMALLERI, Mike	Tor.-L.A.	U. of Michigan	C
50.	THORBURN, Chris	Buf.	North Bay	C
51.	BEDNAR, Jaroslav	L.A.	HIFK	RW
52.	CARON, Edward	Edm.	Phillips-Exeter	LW
53.	McLEOD, Kiel	S.J.-Mtl.-CBJ	Kelowna	C
54.	WELCH, Noah	Pit.	St. Sebastian's	D
55.	POMINVILLE, Jason	Buf.	Shawinigan	RW
56.	MEDVEDEV, Andrei	Phi.-Fla.-Cgy.	Spartak	G
57.	McCLEMENT, Jay	St.L.	Brampton	C
58.	PAETSCH, Nathan	Wsh.	Moose Jaw	D
59.	KEITH, Matt	Dal.-Chi.	Spokane	RW
60.	UCHEVATOV, Victor	Ott.-N.J.	Yaroslavl 2	D
61.	HOLMQVIST, Andreas	N.J.-Mtl.-Wsh.-T.B.	Hammarby	D
62.	GRIGORENKO, Igor	Det.	Samara	RW
63.	BUDAJ, Peter	Col.	Toronto St. Michael's	G
ROUND #3				
64.	MALEC, Tomas	NYI-Fla.	Rimouski	D
65.	BELL, Brendan	T.B.-Wsh.-Tor.	Ottawa	D
66.	FEDOROV, Fedor	Atl.-Van.	Sudbury	LW
67.	LEBLANC, Robin	N.J.	Baie Comeau	RW
68.	MCNEILL, Grant	Fla.	Prince Albert	D
69.	STEPP, Joel	Ana.	Red Deer	C/LW
70.	HAGOS, Yared	Min.-Dal.	AIK Jr.	C
71.	PLEKANEC, Tomas	Mtl.	Kladno	LW
72.	NOLAN, Brandon	CBJ-N.J.	Oshawa	C/LW
73.	ANDERSSON, Craig	Chi.	Guelph	G
74.	HEID, Chris	NYR-Min.	Spokane	D
75.	PLATONOV, Denis	Cgy.-Nsh.	Saratov	F
76.	SETZINGER, Oliver	Nsh.	Ilves	C
77.	McLACHLAN, Darren	Bos.	Seattle	LW
78.	FORSTER, Beat	Phx. N.J. Phx.	Davos	D
79.	MURRAY, Garth	Car.-Min.-NYR	Regina	C/LW
80.	GARNETT, Michael	Van.-Atl.	Saskatoon	G
81.	KOMADOSKI, Neil	N.J.-Ott.	U. of Notre Dame	D
82.	HARRISON, Jay	Tor.	Brampton	D
83.	JUNTUNEN, Henrik	L.A.	Karpat Jr.	RW
84.	SMITH, Kenny	Edm.	Harvard	D
85.	JOHNSON, Aaron	S.J.-Min.-Atl.-Pit.-CBJ	Rimouski	D
86.	FATA, Drew	Pit.	Toronto St. Michael's	D
87.	MARS, Per	Buf.-CBJ	Brynas	C
88.	CORBEIL, Nicolas	Phi.-Chi.-Tor.	Sherbrooke	C
89.	NISSINEN, Tuomas	St.L.	KalPa Jr.	G
90.	FUSSEY, Owen	Wsh.	Calgary	RW
91.	ESTRADA, Kevin	Car.	Chilliwack	LW
92.	AQUINO, Anthony	Dal.	Merrimack	RW
93.	VEILLEUX, Stephane	Ott.-Min.	Val D'Or	C
94.	ARTUKHIN, Evgeni	N.J.-Ott.-T.B.	Podolsk	RW
95.	SHARP, Patrick	Det.-Nsh.-Phi.	U. of Vermont	C
96.	ROULEAU, Alexandre	Pit.	Val D'Or	D
97.	BOIS, Danny	Col.	London	RW

ROUND #4

Pick	Player	Claimed By	Amateur Club	Position
98.	TOOTOO, Jordin	NYI-Phi.-Nsh.	Brandon	RW
99.	EMERY, Ray	T.B.-Ott.	Sault Ste Marie	G
100.	SIPOTZ, Brian	Atl.	Miami University	D
101.	STILLMAN, Cory	Fla.-NYI	Kingston	C
102.	PARSSINEN, Timo	Ana.	HPK	LW
103.	VIRTA, Tony	Min.	TPS	RW
104.	MacLELLAN, Brent	Mtl.-Chi.	Rimouski	D
105.	KORSUNOV, Vladimir	CBJ-Ana.	Spartak	D
106.	EHRHOFF, Christian	Chi.-S.J.	Krefeld	D
107.	PATZOLD, Dimitri	NYR-S.J.	Erding	G
108.	MAKI, Tomi	Cgy.	Jokerit Jr.	RW
109.	JARVENTIE, Martti	Mtl.	TPS	D
110.	ZEPP, Rob	Nsh.-Phi.-Car.	Plymouth	G
111.	KALTIAINEN, Matti	Bos.	Blues Jr.	G
112.	GAJIC, Milan	Phx.-N.J.-Atl.	Burnaby	C
113.	LAMPMAN, Bryce	Car.-NYR	Omaha	D
114.	GLADSKIKH, Yevgeny	Van.	Magnitogorsk	RW
115.	GUSEV, Vladimir	Tor.-Chi.	Sibir 2	D
116.	PETIOT, Richard	L.A.	Camrose	D
117.	WOODFORD, Michael	CBJ-Fla.	Cushing Academy	RW
118.	ROGERS, Brandon	Edm.-Wsh.-Ana.	Hotchkiss	D
119.	ZOTKIN, Alexei	S.J.-Chi.	Magnitogorsk	LW
120.	SUROVY, Tomas	Pit.	Poprad	C
121.	MacINTYRE, Drew	Det.	Sherbrooke	G
122.	VALEYEV, Igor	Buf.-Atl.-St.L.	North Bay	LW
123.	LOBB, Aaron	Phi.-T.B.	London	RW
124.	SHASTIN, Yegor	St.L.-Cgy.	Omsk	LW
125.	LUCKY, Jeff	Wsh.	Spokane	RW
126.	VOLRAB, Daniel	Dal.	Sparta Praha Jr.	C
127.	SCHUBERT, Christoph	Ott.	Munchen	D
128.	POSNOV, Andrei	N.J.	Krylja Sovetov	LW
129.	BLATAK, Miroslav	Det.	Zlin	D
130.	KING, Colt	Col.	Guelph	LW
131.	EAVES, Ben	Pit.	Boston College	C

ROUND #5

Pick	Player	Claimed By	Amateur Club	Position
132.	SALFICKY, Dusan	NYI	Plzen	G
133.	MARKKANEN, Jussi	Edm.	Tappara	G
134.	WELLWOOD, Kyle	T.B.-Tor.	Belleville	C
135.	STUART, Colin	Atl.	Colorado College	C
136.	THOMPSON, Billy	Fla.	Prince George	G
137.	PERREAULT, Joel	Ana.	Baie Comeau	C
138.	LYNCH , Paul	Phi.-T.B.	Valley Jr. Warriors	D
139.	COLLYMORE, Shawn	Min.-NYR	Quebec	RW
140.	PLIHAL, Tomas	Mtl.-Buf.-S.J.	Liberec Jr.	C
141.	JARRETT, Cole	CBJ	Plymouth	D
142.	JAMINKI, Tommi	Chi.	Blues Jr.	LW
143.	SKLADANY, Frantisek	NYR-Col.	Boston University	LW
144.	McCORMICK, Cody	Col.	Belleville	C/RW
145.	HAKEWILL, James	Cgy.	Westminster High	D
146.	TIMONEN, Jussi	Nsh.-Phi.	KalPa Jr.	D
147.	JAKES, Jiri	Bos.	Brandon	RW
148.	KLEMA, David	Phx.	Des Moines	C
149.	VIITANEN, Mikko	Car.-Col.	Ahmat	L
150.	BRUCKLER, Bernd	Phi.	Tri-City	G
151.	BIEKSA, Kevin	Van.	Bowling Green	D
152.	DENIKE, Terry	Tor.-T.B.-L.A.	Weyburn	G
153.	MANTYLA, Tuukka	L.A.	Tappara	D
154.	BRENK, Jake	Edm.	Breck	C
155.	VONDRKA, Michal	S.J.-Buf.	Budejovice	LW
156.	SCHNEIDER, Andy	Pit.	Lincoln	D
157.	JAMTIN, Andreas	Buf.-CBJ-Cgy.-Det.	Farjestad Jr.	RW
158.	MALEK, Roman	Phi.	Slavia Praha	G
159.	SEMIN, Dmitri	St.L.	Spartak	F
160.	TERNAVSKY, Artem	Wsh.	Sherbrooke	D
161.	SMITH, Mike	Dal.	Sudbury	G
162.	SCHAUER, Stefan	Ott.	Riessersee	D
163.	SALOMONSSON, Andreas	N.J.	Djurgarden	C
164.	TRUBACHEV, Yuri	Det.-Cgy.	SKA St. Petersburg	C
165.	EMOND, Pierre-Luc	Col.	Drummondville	C

ROUND #6

Pick	Player	Claimed By	Amateur Club	Position
166.	CHIODO, Andy	NYI	Toronto St. Michael's	G
167.	BLAZEK, Michal	T.B.-Dal.	Vsetin Jr.	D
168.	KONDRATJEV, Maxim	Atl.-Tor.	Togliatti 2	D
169.	JOHNER, Dustin	Fla.	Seattle	C
170.	TABACEK, Jan	Ana.	Martin	D
171.	HIMELFARB, Eric	Min.-Mtl.	Sarnia	C
172.	SEIDENBERG, Denis	Mtl.-Phi.	Mannheim	D
173.	AIKINS, Justin	CBJ	Langley	C
174.	GOLOVIN, Alexander	Chi.	Omsk 2	LW
175.	CLOWE, Ryan	S.J.	Rimouski	RW
176.	ZIDLICKY, Marek	NYR	HIFK	D
177.	RAZIN, Andrei	Cgy.-Phi.	Magnitogorsk	C
178.	LAVRENTJEV, Anton	Nsh.	Kazan 2	D
179.	ALBERTS, Andrew	Bos.	Waterloo	D
180.	POLASKI, Scott	Phx.	Sioux City	RW
181.	BOISCLAIR, Daniel	Car.	Cape Breton	G
182.	CAVANAGH, Tom	Van.-S.J.	Phillips-Exeter	RW
183.	SKLENAR, Jaroslav	Tor.	Brno	RW
184.	HORVATH, Scott	L.A.-T.B.-Col.	U. Mass-Amherst	RW
185.	SVENSK, Mikael	Edm.	V. Frolunda Jr.	D
186.	PUNCOCHAR, Petr	S.J.-Chi.	Karlovy Vary Jr.	D
187.	VOSTRIKOV, Artem	Pit.-CBJ	Togliatti 2	C
188.	FEMENELLA, Art	Buf.-L.A.-T.B.	Sioux City	D
189.	NURMINEN, Pasi	Phi.-Atl.	Jokerit	G
190.	SCHEFFELMAIER, Brett	St.L.	Medicine Hat	D
191.	NOVAK, Zbynek	Wsh.	Slavia Jr.	LW
192.	JOKINEN, Jussi	Dal.	Karpat Jr.	F
193.	LAICH, Brooks	Ott.	Moose Jaw	C
194.	MASSEN, James	N.J.	Sioux Falls	RW
195.	PANNONI, Nick	Det.	Seattle	G
196.	STEPHENS, Charlie	Col.	Guelph	C/RW

ROUND #7

Pick	Player	Claimed By	Amateur Club	Position
197.	HOLUB, Jan	NYI	Liberec Jr.	D
198.	KOLOZVARY, Ivan	T.B.-Tor.	Trencin	F
199.	SUDERMAN, Matt	Atl.	Saskatoon	D
200.	KOIVISTO, Toni	Fla.	Lukko	W
201.	FITZRANDOLPH, Colin	Ana.-Atl.	Phillips-Exeter	C
202.	BOOGAARD, Derek	Min.	Prince George	F
203.	ARCHER, Andrew	Mtl.	Guelph	D
204.	SANNITZ, Raffaele	CBJ	Lugano	F
205.	JAASKELAINEN, Teemu	Chi.	Ilves Jr.	D
206.	PREUCIL, Petr	NYR	Quebec	C
207.	BEMBRIDGE, Garett	Cgy.	Saskatoon	RW
208.	DOUVILLE, Thierry	Nsh.-Phi.	Baie Comeau	D
209.	SIGALET, Jordan	Bos.	Victoria	G
210.	BELANGER, Steve	Phx.	Kamloops	G
211.	CURRY, Sean	Car.	Tri-City	D
212.	KING, Jason	Van.	Halifax	RW
213.	CHOVAN, Jan	Tor.	Belleville	G
214.	HUET, Cristobal	L.A.	Lugano	G
215.	BAUM, Dan	Edm.	Prince George	C/LW
216.	MINAKOV, Oleg	S.J.-Chi.	Elektrostal	RW
217.	DUBA, Tomas	Pit.	Sparta Praha Jr.	G
218.	PLATIL, Jan	Buf.-T.B.-Ott.	Barrie	D
219.	PACKARD, Dennis	Phi.-T.B.	Harvard	LW
220.	MOSS, David	St.L.-Cgy.	Cedar Rapids	LW
221.	ODUYA, John	Wsh.	Victoriaville	D
222.	VAN HOOF, Jeremy	Dal.-T.B.	Ottawa	D
223.	BOCHENSKI, Brandon	Ott.	Lincoln	RW
224.	MARTENSSON, Tony	N.J.-Ana.	Brynas	RW
225.	PRINTZ, David	Ott.-Phi.	Great Falls	D
226.	PETTERSTRM, Pontus	Det.-Cgy.-NYR	Tingsryd	LW
227.	SVATOS, Marek	Col.	Kootenay	RW

ROUND #8

Pick	Player	Claimed By	Amateur Club	Position
228.	BRAY, Mike	NYI	Quebec	RW
229.	VOROS, Aaron	T.B.-N.J.	Victoria	C
230.	ZHVACHKIN, Leonid	Atl.-NYR	Podolsk 2	D
231.	BRUCE, Kyle	Fla.	Prince Albert	RW
232.	GERBER, Martin	Ana.	Langnau	G
233.	CAMPBELL, Joe	Min.-S.-J.-Cgy.	Des Moines	D
234.	ASLUND, Calle	S.J.-Buf.	Huddinge Jr.	D
235.	PETRUIC, Neil	Mtl.-Ott.	Kindersley	D
236.	BOWNESS, Ryan	CBJ	Brampton	RW
237.	GABINET, Mike	Chi.-L.A.	U. of Nebraska-Omaha	D
238.	HOLLWEG, Ryan	NYR	Medicine Hat	C
239.	RIDDLE, Jake	Cgy.-Min.	Seattle	LW
240.	GRASBERG, Gustav	Nsh.	Mora	C
241.	JURCINA, Milan	Bos.	Halifax	D
242.	MURRAY, Andrew	CBJ	Selkirk	C
243.	LUKES, Frantisek	Phx.	Toronto St. Michael's	LW
244.	TREVISANI, Carter	Car.	Ottawa	D
245.	MIKHAILOV, Konstantin	Van.	Neftekhimik	C
246.	MOJZIS, Tomas	Tor.	Moose Jaw	D
247.	DUBEC, Marek	L.A.-Buf.	Vsetin	F
248.	HAAKANA, Kari	Edm.	Jokerit	D
249.	MAGLIONE, Matt	S.J.-Wsh.	Princeton	D
250.	CRAWFORD-WEST, Brandon	Pit.	Texas Tornado	G
251.	HAMALAINEN, Ville	Buf.-Cgy.	SaiPa	W
252.	SOUCY, Jean Francois	Phi.-T.B.	Montreal	C
253.	CAJANEK, Petr	St.L.	Zlin	LW
254.	POLCIK, Peter	Wsh.	Nitra	LW
255.	ROSA, Marco	Dal.	Merrimack	C
256.	JOHNSON, Gregg	Ott.	Boston University	C
257.	GAMALEI, Yevgeny	N.J.	Khimik	D
258.	BYKOV, Dmitri	Det.	Kazan	D
259.	BEZRUKOV, Dmitri	Col.-T.B.	Neftekhimik	LW

ROUND #9

Pick	Player	Claimed By	Amateur Club	Position
260.	PEREZ, Bryan	NYI	Michigan Tech	LW
261.	SMOLYANINOV, Vitali	T.B.	Neftekhimik 2	LW
262.	CARTELLI, Mario	Atl.	Trinec	D
263.	BLANAR, Jan	Fla.	Trencin Jr.	D
264.	PARENTEAU, Pierre	Ana.	Chicoutimi	C
265.	SULLIVAN, Dale	Min.-Dal.	Hull	RW
266.	UJCIK, Viktor	Mtl.	Slavia Praha	W
267.	MAJESKY, Ivan	CBJ-Fla.	Ilves	R
268.	MILES, Jeff	Chi.	U. of Vermont	C
269.	STALS, Juris	NYR	Lukko Jr.	LW
270.	JACOBSEN, Grant	Cgy.-St.L.	Regina	C
271.	LEHTONEN, Mikko	Nsh.	Karpat	D
272.	PISA, Ales	Bos.-Edm.	Pardubice	D
273.	BLINDENBACHER, Severin	Phx.	Kloten	D
274.	REYNOLDS, Peter	Car.	North Bay	D
275.	MULLER, Robert	Van.-NYI-Wsh.	Mannheim	G
276.	KNOEPFLI, Mike	Tor.	Georgetown	LW
277.	LAPLANTE, Sebastien	L.A.	Rayside-Balfour	G
278.	STEPHENSON, Shay	Edm.	Red Deer	LW
279.	JORDE, Ryan	S.J.-Buf.	Tri-City	D
280.	KUKHTINOV, Roman	Pit.-NYI	Novokuznetsk	D
281.	SOLAREV, Ilja	Buf.-T.B.	Perm	LW
282.	RODMAN, Marcel	Phi.-Bos.	Peterborough	RW
283.	SKOOG, Simon	St.L.	Morrum	D
284.	HUBL, Viktor	Wsh.	Slavia Praha	W
285.	TOMICA, Marek	Dal.	Slavia Praha	W
286.	DAHLMAN, Tony	Ott.	Ilves	RW
287.	KETOLA, Juha-Pekka	N.J.-NYI	Lukko Jr.	C
288.	SENEZ, Francois	Det.	R.P.I.	D
289.	BERGFORS, Henrik	Col.-T.B.	Sodertalje Jr.	D

First Two Rounds, 2000-1969 Entry/Amateur Drafts

2000

FIRST ROUND

Selection	Claimed By	Amateur Club	
1. DiPIETRO, Rick	NYI	Boston University	G
2. HEATLEY, Dany	Atl.	U. of Wisconsin	LW
3. GABORIK, Marian	Min.	Dukla Trencin	LW
4. KLESLA, Rostislav	CBJ	Brampton	D
5. TORRES, Raffi	T.B.-NYI	Brampton	LW
6. HARTNELL, Scott	Nsh.	Prince Albert	RW
7. JONSSON, Lars	Bos.	Leksand Jr.	D
8. ALEXEEV, Nikita	NYR-T.B.	Erie	RW
9. KRAHN, Brent	Cgy.	Calgary	G
10. YAKOUBOV, Mikhail	Chi.	Lada Togliatti 2	C
11. VOROBJEV, Pavel	Van.-Chi.	Yaroslavl	RW
12. SMIRNOV, Alexei	Ana.	Tver	LW
13. HAINSEY, Ron	Mtl.	Mass.-Lowell	D
14. NEDOROST, Vaclav	Car.-Col.	Budejovice	C
15. KRYUKOV, Artem	Buf.	Yaroslavl 2	C
16. HOSSA, Marcel	S.J.-Mtl.	Portland	C
17. MIKHNOV, Alexei	Edm.	Yaroslavl 2	W
18. ORPIK, Brooks	Pit.	Boston College	D
19. KOLANOS, Krystofer	Phx.	Boston College	C
20. FROLOV, Alexander	L.A.	Yaroslavl 2	LW
21. VOLCHENKOV, Anton	Ott.	HC Moscow	D
22. HALE, David	Col.-N.J.	Sioux City	D
23. SMITH, Nathan	Fla.-Van.	Swift Current	C
24. BOYES, Brad	Tor.	Erie	C
25. OTT, Steve	Dal.	Windsor	C
26. SUTHERBY, Brian	Wsh.	Moose Jaw	C
27. SAMUELSSON, Martin	N.J.-Col.-Bos.	MoDo Jr.	W
28. WILLIAMS, Justin	Phi.	Plymouth	RW
29. KRONWALL, Niklas	Det.	Djurgarden	D
30. TAFFE, Jeff	St.L.	U. of Minnesota	C

SECOND ROUND

Selection	Claimed By	Amateur Club	
31. NIKULIN, Ilja	Atl.	Tver	D
32. KURKA, Tomas	CBJ-Col.-Car.	Plymouth	LW
33. SCHULTZ, Nick	Min.	Prince Albert	D
34. ZAINULLAN, Ruslan	T.B.	Kazan	RW
35. WINCHESTER, Brad	NYI-Edm.	U. of Wisconsin	LW
36. WIDING, Daniel	Nsh.	Leksand Jr.	RW
37. HILBERT, Andy	Bos.	U. of Michigan	C
38. KOPECKY, Tomas	NYR-Det.	Dukla Trencin	C
39. LAINE, Teemu	Van.-NYI-N.J.	Jokerit	RW
40. FOSTER, Kurtis	Cgy.	Peterborough	D
41. MAATTA, Tero	Chi-S.J.	Jokerit Jr.	D
42. USTRNUL, Libor	Van.-Atl.	Plymouth	D
43. PETTINGER, Matt	Ana.-Cgy.-Wsh.	Calgary	LW
44. BRYZGALOV, Ilja	Mtl.-Ana.	Lada Togliatti	G
45. CHOUINARD, Mathieu	Ott.	Shawinigan	G
46. STOLL, Jarret	Col.-Cgy.	Kootenay	C
47. AULIN, Jared	Car.-Col.	Kamloops	C
48. DICAIRE, Gerard	Buf.	Seattle	D
49. NORDQVIST, Jonas	S.J.-Chi.	Leksand Jr.	C
50. SOIN, Sergei	Col.	Krylja Sovetov	C
51. VERNARSKY, Kris	Edm.-Tor.	Plymouth	C
52. ENDICOTT, Shane	Pit.	Seattle	C
53. TATARINOV, Alexander	Phx.	Yaroslavl 2	RW
54. LILJA, Andreas	L.A.	Malmo	D
55. VERMETTE, Antoine	Ott.	Victoriaville	C
56. SUGLOBOV, Alexander	N.J.	Yaroslavl 2	C
57. DeMARCHI, Matt	Col.-N.J.	U. of Minnesota	D
58. SAPOZHNIKOV, Vladimir	Fla.	Novokuznetsk 2	D
59. HUML, Ivan	Tor.-Bos.	Langley	LW
60. ELLIS, Dan	Dal.	Omaha	G
61. CUTTA, Jakub	Wsh.	Swift Current	D
62. MARTIN, Paul	N.J.	Elk River HS	D
63. SAVIELS, Argis	Phi.-Car.-Col.	Owen Sound	D
64. NOVAK, Filip	Det.-NYR	Regina	D
65. MORISSET, David	St.L.	Seattle	RW

1999

FIRST ROUND

Selection	Claimed By	Amateur Club	
1. STEFAN, Patrik	T.B.-Van.-Atl.	Long Beach	C
2. SEDIN, Daniel	Atl.-Van.	MoDo	LW
3. SEDIN, Henrik	Van.	MoDo	C
4. BRENDL, Pavel	Chi.-Van.-T.B.-NYR	Calgary	RW
5. CONNOLLY, Tim	NYI	Erie	C
6. FINLEY, Brian	Nsh.	Barrie	G
7. BEECH, Kris	Wsh.	Calgary	C
8. PYATT, Taylor	L.A.-NYI	Sudbury	LW
9. LUNDMARK, Jamie	Cgy.-NYR	Moose Jaw	C
10. MEZEI, Branislav	Mtl.-NYI	Belleville	D
11. SAPRYKIN, Oleg	NYR-Cgy.	Seattle	C
12. SHVIDKY, Denis	Fla.	Barrie	RW
13. RITA, Jani	Edm.	Jokerit Helsinki	RW
14. JILLSON, Jeff	S.J.	U. of Michigan	D
15. KELMAN, Scott	Ana.-Phx.	Seattle	C
16. TANABE, David	Car.	U. of Wisconsin	D
17. JACKMAN, Barret	St.L.	Regina	D
18. KOLTSOV, Konstantin	Pit.	Cherepovets	LW
19. SAFRONOV, Kirill	Phx.	St. Petersburg	D
20. HEISTEN, Barrett	Buf.	U. of Maine	LW
21. BOYNTON, Nicholas	Bos.	Ottawa	D
22. OUELLET, Maxime	Phi.	Quebec	G
23. MCCARTHY, Steve	Det.-Chi.	Kootenay	D
24. CEREDA, Luca	Tor.	Ambri	C
25. KULESHOV, Mikhail	Col.	Cherepovets	LW
26. HAVLAT, Martin	Ott.	Trinec	C
27. AHONEN, Ari	N.J.	JyP HT Jr.	G
28. KUDROC, Kristian	Dal.-NYI	Michalovce	D

SECOND ROUND

Selection	Claimed By	Amateur Club	
29. SIVEK, Michal	T.B.-Wsh.	HC Kladno Jr.	C
30. SELLARS, Luke	Atl.	Ottawa	D
31. STEPHENS, Charlie	Van.-Col.-Wsh.	Guelph	F
32. RYAN, Michael	NYI-Dal.	Boston College HS	C
33. ANDERSSON, Jonas	Nsh.	AIK Solna Jr.	RW
34. LUPASCHUK, Ross	Wsh.	Prince Albert	D
35. BARTOVIC, Milan	L.A.-Buf.	Dukla Trencin Jrs.	RW
36. SEMENOV, Alexei	Edm.	Sudbury	D
37. YONKMAN, Nolan	Wsh.	Kelowna	D
38. CAVANAUGH, Dan	Cgy.	Boston University	F
39. BUTURLIN, Alexander	Mtl.	CSKA Moscow Jr.	LW
40. AULD, Alexander	St.L.-Fla.	North Bay	G
41. SALMELAINEN, Tony	Edm.	HIFK Helsinki	LW
42. COMMODORE, Mike	N.J.	U. of North Dakota	D
43. SHEFER, Andrei	L.A.	Cherepovets	LW
44. LEOPOLD, Jordan	NYR-Ott.-Ana.	U. of Minnesota	D
45. GRENIER, Martin	Fla.-Nsh.-Col.	Quebec	D
46. LEVINSKY, Dmitri	Chi.	Cherepovets	RW
47. KEEFE, Sheldon	S.J.-Det.-T.B.	Barrie	RW
48. LAJEUNESSE, Simon	Ana.-Ott.	Moncton	G
49. LYSAK, Brett	Car.	Regina	C
50. CLOUTHIER, Brett	St.L.-N.J.	Kingston	LW
51. MURLEY, Matt	Pit.	R.P.I.	LW
52. HALL, Adam	Nsh.	Michigan State	RW
53. RALPH, Brad	Phx.	Oshawa	LW
54. HUTCHINSON, Andrew	Col.-Nsh.	Michigan State	D
55. JANIK, Doug	Buf.	U. of Maine	D
56. ZULTEK, Matt	Bos.	Ottawa	LW
57. VAN HOOF, Jeremy	Pit.	Ottawa	D
58. CARKNER, Matt	Phi.-Mtl.	Peterborough	D
59. INMAN, David	Det.-NYR	U. of Notre Dame	C
60. REYNOLDS, Peter	Tor.	London	D
61. HILL, Ed	Col.-Nsh.	Barrie	D
62. SAINOMAA, Teemu	Ott.	Jokerit Helsinki Jr.	LW
63. MOKHOV, Stepan	N.J.-Chi.	Cherepovets	D
64. ZIGOMANIS, Michael	Dal.-Buf.	Kingston	C
65. LASAK, Jan	Nsh.	ZTK Zvolen Jr.	G
66. JANCEVSKI, Dan	St.L.-Dal.	London	D

1998

FIRST ROUND

Selection	Claimed By	Amateur Club	
1. LECAVALIER, Vincent	Fla.-S.J.-T.B.	Rimouski	C
2. LEGWAND, David	T.B.-S.J.-Nsh.	Plymouth	C
3. STUART, Brad	Nsh.-S.J.	Regina	D
4. ALLEN, Bryan	Van.	Oshawa	D
5. VISHNEVSKY, Vitaly	Ana.	Torpedo-2 Yaroslavl	D
6. FATA, Rico	Cgy.	London	C
7. MALHOTRA, Manny	NYR	Guelph	C
8. BELL, Mark	Tor.-Chi.	Ottawa	LW
9. RUPP, Michael	NYI	Erie	LW
10. ANTROPOV, Nikolai	Chi.-Tor.	Torpedo Ust-Kamenogorsk	C
11. HEEREMA, Jeff	Car.	Sarnia	RW
12. TANGUAY, Alex	S.J.-Col.	Halifax	C
13. HENRICH, Michael	Edm.	Barrie	RW
14. DESROCHERS, Patrick	Phx.	Sarnia	G
15. CHOUINARD, Mathieu	Ott.	Shawinigan	G
16. CHOUINARD, Eric	Mtl.	Quebec	C
17. SKOULA, Martin	L.A.-Col.	Barrie	D
18. KALININ, Dimitri	Buf.	Traktor Chelyabinsk	D
19. REGEHER, Robyn	Bos.-Col.	Kamloops	D
20. PARKER, Scott	Wsh.-Col.	Kelowna	D
21. BIRON, Mathieu	Col.-L.A.	Shawinigan	D
22. GAGNE, Simon	Phi.-T.B.-Phi.	Quebec	C
23. KRAFT, Milan	T.B.	Keramika Plzen Jr.	C
24. BACKMAN, Christian	St.L.	Vastra Frolunda Jr.	D
25. FISCHER, Jiri	Det.	Hull	D
26. VAN RYN, Mike	N.J.	U. of Michigan	D
27. GOMEZ, Scott	Dal.-N.J.	Tri-City	C

SECOND ROUND

Selection	Claimed By	Amateur Club	
28. ABID, Ramzi	T.B.-Col.	Chicoutimi	LW
29. CHEECHOO, Jonathon	Nsh.-S.J.	Belleville	RW
30. ROSSITER, Kyle	Fla.	Spokane	D
31. CHUBAROV, Artem	Van.	Dynamo Moscow	C
32. PEAT, Stephen	Ana.	Red Deer	D
33. BETTS, Blair	Cgy.	Prince George	C
34. PETERS, Andrew	NYR-Buf.	Oshawa	LW
35. SVOBODA, Petr	Tor.	Havlickuv Brod	D
36. NEILSON, Chris	NYI	Calgary	C
37. BERGLUND, Christian	N.J.	Farjestad Karlstad Jr.	C
38. SAUVE, Philippe	Chi-Col.	Rimouski	G
39. ERSKINE, John	Car.-N.J.-Dal.	London	D
40. COPLEY, Randy	NYR	Cape Breton	RW
41. LINNIK, Maxim	S.J.-Det.-St.L.	St. Thomas Jr. B	D
42. BECKETT, Jason	Edm.-Phi.	Seattle	D
43. VAANANEN, Ossi	Phx.	Jokerit Helsinki Jr.	D
44. FISHER, Mike	Ott.	Sudbury	C
45. RIBEIRO, Mike	Mtl.	Rouyn-Noranda	C
46. PAPINEAU, Justin	L.A.	Belleville	C
47. MILLEY, Norman	Buf.	Sudbury	RW
48. GIRARD, Jonathon	Bos.	Laval	D
49. CRUZ, Jomar	Wsh.	Brandon	G
50. KRISTEK, Jaroslav	Col.-S.J.-Buf.	ZPS Zlin	RW
51. FORBES, Ian	Phi.	Guelph	D
52. ALLEN, Bobby	Bos.	Boston College	D
53. MOORE, Steve	Col.	Harvard	C
54. ZEVAKHIN, Alexander	Pit.	CSKA Moscow	RW
55. BARNES, Ryan	St.L-Det.	Sudbury	LW
56. VALTONEN, Tomek	Det.	Ilves Tampere Jr.	LW
57. BOUCK, Tyler	N.J.-Dal.	Prince George	RW
58. BALA, Chris	Dal.-Phi.-Ott.	Harvard	LW

When the Islanders took him in 2000, Rick DiPietro (right) became the first goalie to be selected #1 overall since the NHL Draft became universal in 1969. Jarome Iginla (far right) was drafted 11th by Dallas in 1995, but has become a star in Calgary.

1997

FIRST ROUND

Selection	Claimed By	Amateur Club	
1. THORNTON, Joe	Bos.	Sault Ste. Marie	C
2. MARLEAU, Patrick	S.J.	Seattle	C
3. JOKINEN, Olli	L.A.	HIFK Helsinki	C
4. LUONGO, Roberto	Tor.-NYI	Val D'Or	G
5. BREWER, Eric	NYI	Prince George	D
6. TKACZUK, Daniel	Cgy.	Barrie	C
7. MARA, Paul	T.B.	Sudbury	D
8. SAMSONOV, Sergei	Car.-Bos.	Detroit	LW
9. BOYNTON, Nicholas	Wsh.	Ottawa	D
10. FERENCE, Brad	Van.	Spokane	D
11. WARD, Jason	Mtl.	Erie	C
12. HOSSA, Marian	Ott.	Dukla Trencin	RW
13. CLEARY, Daniel	Chi.	Belleville	LW
14. RIESEN, Michel	Edm.	Biel-Bienne	LW
15. ZULTEK, Matt	St.L-Edm.-St.L.-L.A.	Ottawa	LW
16. JONES, Ty	Pho.-Chi.	Spokane	RW
17. DOME, Robert	Pit.	Long Beach/ Las Vegas	RW
18. HOLMQVIST, Mikael	Ana.	Djurgarden	C
19. CHERNESKI, Stefan	NYR	Brandon	RW
20. BROWN, Mike	Fla.	Red Deer	C
21. NORONEN, Mika	Buf.	Tappara Tampere	G
22. TSELIOS, Nikos	Det.-Car.	Belleville	D
23. HANNAN, Scott	Phi.-Car.-S.J.	Kelowna	D
24. DAMPHOUSSE, J-F	N.J.	Moncton	G
25. MORROW, Brenden	Dal.	Portland	LW
26. GRIMES, Kevin	Col.	Kingston	D

SECOND ROUND

Selection	Claimed By	Amateur Club	
27. CLYMER, Ben	Bos.	U. of Minnesota	D
28. DEFAUW, Brad	S.J.-Car.	U. of North Dakota	LW
29. BARNEY, Scott	L.A.	Peterborough	C
30. PELLETIER, Jean-Marc	Tor.-Phi.	Cornell U.	G
31. ZEHR, Jeff	NYI	Windsor	LW
32. LINDSAY, Evan	Cgy.	Prince Albert	G
33. KOS, Kyle	T.B.	Red Deer	D
34. BONNI, Ryan	Car.-Van.	Saskatoon	D
35. FORTIN, J-F	Wsh.	Sherbrooke	D
36. DRUKEN, Harold	Van.	Detroit	LW
37. BAUMGARTNER, Gregor	Mtl.	Laval	C
38. GRON, Stanislav	Ott.-N.J.	Slovan Bratislava Jr.	C
39. REICH, Jeremy	Chi.	Seattle	C
40. RENNETTE, Tyler	St.L.	North Bay	C
41. DOVIGI, Patrick	Edm.	Erie	G
42. TRIPP, John	St.L.-Cgy.	Oshawa	RW
43. GUSTAFSSON, Juha	Pho.	Kiekko-Espoo Jr.	D
44. GAFFANEY, Brian	Pit.	North Iowa Jr. A	D
45. BALMOCHNYKH, Maxim	Ana.	Lada Togliatti	LW
46. JARVIS, Wes	NYR	Kitchener	D
47. HUSELIUS, Kristian	Fla.	Farjestad Karlstad	LW
48. TALLINDER, Henrik	Buf.	AIK Solna	D
49. BUTSAYEV, Yuri	Det.	Lada Togliatti	C
50. KAVANAGH, Pat	Phi.	Peterborough	RW
51. KOKOREV, Dmitri	N.J.-Car.-Cgy.	Dynamo-2 Moscow	D
52. LYASHENKO, Roman	Dal.	Torpedo Yaroslavl	C
53. BELAK, Graham	Col.	Edmonton	D

1996

FIRST ROUND

Selection	Claimed By	Amateur Club	
1. PHILLIPS, Chris	Ott.	Prince Albert	D
2. ZYUZIN, Andrei	S.J.	Salavat Yulayev Ufa	D
3. DUMONT, Jean-Pierre	NYI	Val d'Or	RW
4. VOLCHKOV, Alexander	L.A.-Wsh.	Barrie	C
5. JACKMAN, Richard	Dal.	Sault Ste. Marie	D
6. DEVEREAUX, Boyd	Edm.	Kitchener	C
7. RASMUSSEN, Erik	Buf.	U. of Minnesota	C
8. AITKEN, Johnathan	Hfd.-Bos.	Medicine Hat	D
9. SALEI, Ruslan	Ana.	Las Vegas	D
10. WARD, Lance	N.J.	Red Deer	D
11. FOCHT, Dan	Pho.	Tri-City	D
12. HOLDEN, Josh	Van.	Regina	C
13. MORRIS, Derek	Cgy.	Regina	D
14. REASONER, Marty	St.L.-Edm.-St.L.	Boston College	C
15. ZUBRUS, Dainius	Tor.-Phi.	Pembroke	RW
16. LAROCQUE, Mario	T.B.	Hull	D
17. SVEJKOVSKY, Jaroslav	Wsh.	Tri-City	RW
18. HIGGINS, Matt	Mtl.	Moose Jaw	C
19. DESCOTEAUX, Matthieu	Bos.-Edm.	Shawinigan	D
20. NILSON, Marcus	Fla.	Djurgarden	C
21. STURM, Marco	Chi.-S.J.	Landshut	C
22. BROWN, Jeff	NYR	Sarnia	D
23. HILLIER, Craig	Pit.	Ottawa	G
24. BRIERE, Daniel	Phi.-Pho.	Drummondville	C
25. RATCHUK, Peter	Col.	Shattuck St. Mary's	D
26. WALLIN, Jesse	Det.	Red Deer	D

SECOND ROUND

Selection	Claimed By	Amateur Club	
27. SARICH, Cory	Ott.-St.L.-Buf.	Saskatoon	D
28. SKRBEK, Pavel	S.J.-N.J.-Pit.	HC Kladno	D
29. LACOUTURE, Dan	NYI	Jr. Whalers	LW
30. GREEN, Josh	L.A.	Medicine Hat	LW
31. ROYER, Remi	Dal.-Pho.-S.J.-Chi.	St-Hyacinthe	D
32. HAJT, Chris	Edm.	Guelph	D
33. VAN OENE, Darren	Buf.	Brandon	LW
34. WASYLUK, Trevor	Hfd.	Medicine Hat	LW
35. CULLEN, Matt	Ana.	St. Cloud State	C
36. POSMYK, Marek	N.J.-Tor.	Dukla Jihlava	D
37. CISAR, Marian	Pho.-L.A.	Slovan Bratislava	W
38. MASON, Wesley	Van.-N.J.	Sarnia	LW
39. BRIGLEY, Travis	Cgy.	Lethbridge	LW
40. BEGIN, Steve	St.L.-Cgy.	Val d'Or	C
41. DEWOLF, Joshua	Tor.-Pit.-N.J.	Twin Cities	D
42. PAUL, Jeff	T.B.-Chi.	Niagara Falls	D
43. BULIS, Jan	Wsh.	Barrie	C
44. GARON, Mathieu	Mtl.	Victoriaville	G
45. KUSTER, Henry	Bos.	Medicine Hat	RW
46. PETERS, Geoff	Fla.-S.J.-Chi.	Niagara Falls	C
47. DAGENAIS, Pierre	Chi.-T.B.-N.J.	Moncton	LW
48. GONEAU, Daniel	NYR	Granby	LW
49. WHITE, Colin	Pit.-N.J.	Hull	D
50. LARIVEE, Francis	Phi.-Tor.	Laval	G
51. BABENKO, Yuri	Col.	Krylja Sovetov	C
52. MILLER, Aren	Det.	Spokane	G

1995

FIRST ROUND

Selection	Claimed By	Amateur Club	
1. BERARD, Bryan	Ott.	Detroit	D
2. REDDEN, Wade	NYI	Brandon	D
3. BERG, Aki-Petteri	L.A.	Kiekko-67 Turku	D
4. KILGER, Chad	Ana.	Kingston	C
5. LANGKOW, Daymond	T.B.	Tri-City	C
6. KELLY, Steve	Edm.	Prince Albert	C
7. DOAN, Shane	Wpg.	Kamloops	RW
8. RYAN, Terry	Mtl.	Tri-City	LW
9. McLAREN, Kyle	Hfd.-Bos.	Tacoma	D
10. DVORAK, Radek	Fla.	HC Ceske Budejovice	W
11. IGINLA, Jarome	Dal.	Kamloops	C
12. RIIHIJARVI, Teemu	S.J.	Kiekko-Espoo Jr.	LW
13. GIGUERE, J-Sebastien	NYR-Hfd.	Halifax	G
14. McKEE, Jay	Van.-Buf.	Niagara Falls	D
15. WARE, Jeff	Tor.	Oshawa	D
16. BIRON, Martin	Buf.	Beauport	G
17. CHURCH, Brad	Wsh.	Prince Albert	LW
18. SYKORA, Petr	N.J.	Detroit	C
19. NABOKOV, Dmitri	Chi.	Krylja Sovetov	C
20. GAUTHIER, Denis Jr.	Cgy.	Drummondville	D
21. BROWN, Sean	Bos.	Belleville	D
22. BOUCHER, Brian	Phi.	Tri-City	G
23. ELOMO, Miika	St.L.-Wsh.	Kiekko-67 Turku	LW
24. MOROZOV, Alexei	Pit.	Krylja Sovetov	RW
25. DENIS, Marc	Col.	Chicoutimi	G
26. KUZNETSOV, Maxim	Det.	Dynamo Moscow	D

SECOND ROUND

Selection	Claimed By	Amateur Club	
27. MORO, Marc	Ott.	Kingston	D
28. HLAVAC, Jan	NYI	Sparta Praha	LW
29. WESENBERG, Brian	Ana.	Guelph	RW
30. McBAIN, Mike	T.B.	Red Deer	D
31. LARAQUE, Georges	Edm.	St-Jean	RW
32. CHOUINARD, Marc	Wpg.	Beauport	C
33. MacLEAN, Donald	L.A.	Beauport	C
34. DOIG, Jason	Mtl.-Wpg.	Laval	D
35. FEDOTOV, Sergei	Hfd.	Dynamo Moscow	D
36. MacDONALD, Aaron	Fla.	Swift Current	G
37. COTE, Patrick	Dal.	Beauport	LW
38. ROED, Peter	S.J.	White Bear Lake	C
39. DUBE, Christian	NYR	Sherbrooke	C
40. McALLISTER, Chris	Van.	Saskatoon	D
41. SMITH, Denis (D.J.)	Tor.-NYI	Windsor	D
42. DUTIAUME, Mark	Buf.	Brandon	LW
43. HAY, Dwayne	Wsh.	Guelph	LW
44. PERROTT, Nathan	N.J.	Oshawa	RW
45. LAFLAMME, Christian	Chi.	Beauport	D
46. SMIRNOV, Pavel	Cgy.	Molot Perm	RW/C
47. SCHAFER, Paxton	Bos.	Medicine Hat	G
48. KENNY, Shane	Phi.	Owen Sound	D
49. HECHT, Jochen	St.L.	Mannheim	C
50. ROSA, Pavel	Pit.-L.A.	Litvinov Jr.	RW
51. BEAUDOIN, Nic	Col.	Detroit	LW
52. AUDET, Philippe	Det.	Granby	LW

1994

FIRST ROUND

Selection	Claimed By	Amateur Club	
1. JOVANOVSKI, Ed	Fla.	Windsor	D
2. TVERDOVSKY, Oleg	Ana.	Soviet Wings	D
3. BONK, Radek	Ott.	Las Vegas	C
4. BONSIGNORE, Jason	Wpg.-Edm.	Niagara Falls	C
5. O'NEILL, Jeff	Hfd.	Guelph	C
6. SMYTH, Ryan	Edm.	Moose Jaw	LW
7. STORR, Jamie	L.A.	Owen Sound	G
8. WIEMER, Jason	T.B.	Portland	LW
9. LINDROS, Brett	Que.-NYI	Kingston	RW
10. BAUMGARTNER, Nolan	Phi.-Que.-Tor.-Wsh.	Kamloops	D
11. FRIESEN, Jeff	S.J.	Regina	LW
12. BELAK, Wade	NYI-Que.	Saskatoon	D
13. OHLUND, Mattias	Van.	Pitea	D
14. MOREAU, Ethan	Chi.	Niagara Falls	LW
15. KHARLAMOV, Alexander	Wsh.	CSKA Moscow	C
16. FICHAUD, Eric	St.L.-Wsh.-Tor.	Chicoutimi	G
17. PRIMEAU, Wayne	Buf.	Owen Sound	C
18. BROWN, Brad	Mtl.	North Bay	C
19. DINGMAN, Chris	Cgy.	Brandon	LW
20. BOTTERILL, Jason	Dal.	U. of Michigan	LW
21. RYABCHIKOV, Evgeni	Bos.	Molot Perm	G
22. KEALTY, Jeffrey	Tor.-Que.	Catholic Memorial	D
23. GOLUBOVSKY, Yan	Det.	CSKA Jr. Moscow	D
24. WELLS, Chris	Pit.	Seattle	G
25. SHARIFIJANOV, Vadim	N.J.	Salavat Yulayev Ufa	RW
26. CLOUTIER, Dan	NYR	Sault Ste. Marie	G

SECOND ROUND

Selection	Claimed By	Amateur Club	
27. WARRENER, Rhett	Fla.	Saskatoon	D
28. DAVIDSSON, Johan	Ana.	HV 71	C
29. NECKAR, Stanislav	Ott.	Ceske Budejovice	D
30. QUINT, Deron	Wpg.	Seattle	D
31. PODOLLAN, Jason	Hfd.-Fla.	Spokane	C
32. WATT, Mike	Edm.	Stratford Jr. B	LW
33. JOHNSON, Matt	L.A.	Peterborough	LW
34. CLOUTIER, Colin	T.B.	Brandon	C
35. MARHA, Josef	Que.	Dukla Jihlava	C
36. JOHNSON, Ryan	Phi.-Fla.	Thunder Bay Jr. A	C
37. NIKOLOV, Angel	S.J.	Litvinov	D
38. HOLLAND, Jason	NYI	Kamloops	D
39. GORDON, Robb	Van.	Powell River Jr. A	C
40. LEROUX, Jean-Yves	Chi.	Beauport	LW
41. CHERREY, Scott	Wsh.	North Bay	LW
42. SCATCHARD, Dave	St.L.-Van.	Portland	C
43. BROWN, Curtis	Buf.	Moose Jaw	C
44. THEODORE, Jose	Mtl.	St-Jean	G
45. RYABYKIN, Dmitri	Cgy.	Dynamo-2	D
46. JINMAN, Lee	Dal.	North Bay	C
47. GONEAU, Daniel	Bos.	Laval	LW
48. HAGGERTY, Sean	Tor.	Detroit	LW
49. DANDENAULT, Mathieu	Det.	Sherbrooke	RW
50. PARK, Richard	Pit.	Belleville	C
51. ELIAS, Patrik	N.J.	Kladno	LW
52. VERCIK, Rudolf	NYR	Slovan Bratislava	LW

1993

FIRST ROUND

Selection	Claimed By	Amateur Club	
1. DAIGLE, Alexandre	Ott.	Victoriaville	C
2. PRONGER, Chris	S.J.-Hfd.	Peterborough	D
3. GRATTON, Chris	T.B.	Kingston	C
4. KARIYA, Paul	Ana.	University of Maine	LW
5. NIEDERMAYER, Rob	Fla.	Medicine Hat	C
6. KOZLOV, Viktor	Hfd.-S.J.	Dynamo Moscow	LW
7. ARNOTT, Jason	Edm.	Oshawa	C
8. SUNDSTROM, Niklas	NYR	MoDo	LW
9. HARVEY, Todd	Dal.	Detroit	C
10. THIBAULT, Jocelyn	Phi.-Que.	Sherbrooke	G
11. WITT, Brendan	St. L.-Wsh.	Seattle	D
12. JONSSON, Kenny	Buf.-Tor.	Rogle Angelholm	D
13. PEDERSON, Denis	N.J.	Prince Albert	C
14. DEADMARSH, Adam	NYI-Que.	Portland	C
15. LINDGREN, Mats	Wpg.	Skelleftea	C
16. STAJDUHAR, Nick	L.A.-Edm.	London	D
17. ALLISON, Jason	Wsh.	London	C
18. MATTSSON, Jesper	Cgy.	Malmo	C
19. WILSON, Landon	Tor.	Dubuque Jr. A	RW
20. WILSON, Mike	Van.	Sudbury	D
21. KOIVU, Saku	Mtl.	TPS Turku	C
22. ERIKSSON, Anders	Det.	MoDo	D
23. BERTUZZI, Todd	Que.-NYI	Guelph	C
24. LECOMPTE, Eric	Chi.	Hull	LW
25. ADAMS, Kevyn	Bos.	Miami-Ohio	C
26. BERGQVIST, Stefan	Pit.	Leksand	D

SECOND ROUND

Selection	Claimed By	Amateur Club	
27. BICANEK, Radim	Ott.	Dukla Jihlava	D
28. DONOVAN, Shean	S.J.	Ottawa	RW
29. MOSS, Tyler	T.B.	Kingston	G
30. TSULYGIN, Nikolai	Ana.	Salavat Yulayev Ufa	D
31. LANGKOW, Scott	Fla.-Wpg.	Portland	G
32. PANDOLFO, Jay	Hfd.-N.J.	Boston University	LW
33. VYBORNY, David	Edm.	Sparta Praha	C
34. SOROCHAN, Lee	NYR	Lethbridge	D
35. LANGENBRUNNER, Jamie	Dal.	Cloquet	C
36. NIINIMAA, Janne	Phi.	Karpat Oulu	D
37. BETS, Maxim	St. L.	Spokane	LW
38. TSYGUROV, Denis	Buf.	Lada Togliatti	D
39. MORRISON, Brendan	N.J.	Penticton T-II Jr. A	C
40. McCABE, Bryan	NYI	Spokane	D
41. WEEKES, Kevin	Wpg.-Fla.	Owen Sound	G
42. TOPOROWSKI, Shayne	L.A.	Prince Albert	RW
43. BUDAYEV, Alexei	Wsh.-Wpg.	Kristall Elektrostal	C
44. ALLISON, Jamie	Cgy.	Detroit	D
45. KROUPA, Vlastimil	Tor.-Hfd.-S.J.	Chemopetrol Litvinov	D
46. GIRARD, Rick	Van.	Swift Current	C
47. FITZPATRICK, Rory	Mtl.	Sudbury	D
48. COLEMAN, Jonathan	Det.	Andover Academy	D
49. BUCKBERGER, Ashley	Que.	Swift Current	RW
50. MANLOW, Eric	Chi.	Kitchener	C
51. ALVEY, Matt	Bos.	Springfield Jr. B	RW
52. PITTIS, Domenic	Pit.	Lethbridge	C

1992

FIRST ROUND

Selection	Claimed By	Amateur Club	
1. HAMRLIK, Roman	T.B.	ZPS Zlin	D
2. YASHIN, Alexei	Ott.	Dynamo Moscow	C
3. RATHJE, Mike	S.J.	Medicine Hat	D
4. WARRINER, Todd	Que.	Windsor	LW
5. KASPARAITIS, Darius	Tor.-NYI	Dynamo Moscow	D
6. STILLMAN, Cory	Cgy.	Windsor	C
7. SITTLER, Ryan	Phi.	Nichols	LW
8. CONVERY, Brandon	NYI-Tor.	Sudbury	C
9. PETROVICKY, Robert	Hfd.	Dukla Trencin	C
10. NAZAROV, Andrei	Min.-S.J.	Dynamo Moscow	LW
11. COOPER, David	Buf.	Medicine Hat	D
12. KRIVOKRASOV, Sergei	Wpg.-Chi.	CSKA Moscow	RW
13. HULBIG, Joe	Edm.	St. Sebastian's	LW
14. GONCHAR, Sergei	St.L.-Wsh.	Chelyabinsk	D
15. BOWEN, Jason	L.A.-Pit.-Phi.	Tri-City	LW
16. KVARTALNOV, Dmitri	Bos.	San Diego	LW
17. BAUTIN, Sergei	Chi.-Wpg.	Dynamo Moscow	D
18. SMITH, Jason	N.J.	Regina	D
19. STRAKA, Martin	Pit.	Skoda Plzen	C
20. WILKIE, David	Mtl.	Kamloops	D
21. POLASEK, Libor	Van.	TJ Vitkovice	C
22. BOWEN, Curtis	Det.	Ottawa	LW
23. MARSHALL, Grant	Wsh.-Tor.	Ottawa	RW
24. FERRARO, Peter	NYR	Waterloo Jr. A	C

SECOND ROUND

Selection	Claimed By	Amateur Club	
25. PENNEY, Chad	Ott.	North Bay	LW
26. BANNISTER, Drew	T.B.	Sault Ste. Marie	D
27. MIRONOV, Boris	S.J.-Chi.-Wpg.	CSKA Moscow	D
28. BROUSSEAU, Paul	Que.	Hull	RW
29. GRONMAN, Toumas	Tor.-Que.	Tacoma	D
30. O'SULLIVAN, Chris	Cgy.	Catholic Memorial	D
31. METLYUK, Denis	Phi.	Lada Togliatti	C
32. CAREY, Jim	NYI-Tor.-Wsh.	Catholic Memorial	G
33. BURE, Valeri	Hfd.-Mtl.	Spokane	LW
34. VARVIO, Jarkko	Min.	HPK	RW
35. CIERNY, Jozef	Buf.	ZTK Zvolen	LW
36. SHANTZ, Jeff	Wpg.-Chi.	Regina	C
37. REICHEL, Martin	Edm.	Freiburg	RW
38. KOROLEV, Igor	St.L.	Dynamo Moscow	RW
39. HOCKING, Justin	L.A.	Spokane	D
40. PECA, Mike	Bos.-Van.	Ottawa	C
41. KLIMOVICH, Sergei	Chi.	Dynamo Moscow	C
42. BRYLIN, Sergei	N.J.	CSKA Moscow	C
43. HUSSEY, Marc	Pit.	Moose Jaw	D
44. CORPSE, Keli	Mtl.	Kingston	C
45. FOUNTAIN, Michael	Van.	Oshawa	G
46. McCARTY, Darren	Det.	Belleville	RW
47. NIKOLISHIN, Andrei	Wsh.-Hfd.	Dynamo Moscow	LW
48. NORSTROM, Mattias	NYR	AIK	D

1991

FIRST ROUND

Selection	Claimed By	Amateur Club	
1. LINDROS, Eric	Que.	Oshawa	C
2. FALLOON, Pat	S.J.	Spokane	RW
3. NIEDERMAYER, Scott	Tor.-N.J.	Kamloops	D
4. LACHANCE, Scott	NYI	Boston University	D
5. WARD, Aaron	Wpg.	U. of Michigan	D
6. FORSBERG, Peter	Phi.	MoDo	C
7. STOJANOV, Alex	Van.	Hamilton	RW
8. MATVICHUK, Richard	Min.	Saskatoon	D
9. POULIN, Patrick	Hfd.	St. Hyacinthe	LW
10. LAPOINTE, Martin	Det.	Laval	RW
11. ROLSTON, Brian	N.J.	Detroit Comp. Jr. A	C
12. WRIGHT, Tyler	Edm.	Swift Current	C
13. BOUCHER, Phillipe	Buf.	Granby	D
14. PEAKE, Pat	Wsh.	Detroit	C
15. KOVALEV, Alexei	NYR	D'amo Moscow	RW
16. NASLUND, Markus	Pit.	MoDo	RW
17. BILODEAU, Brent	Mtl.	Seattle	D
18. MURRAY, Glen	Bos.	Sudbury	RW
19. SUNDBLAD, Niklas	Cgy.	AIK	RW
20. RUCINSKY, Martin	L.A.-Edm.	CHZ Litvinov	LW
21. HALVERSON, Trevor	St.L.-Wsh.	North Bay	LW
22. McAMMOND, Dean	Chi.	Prince Albert	C

SECOND ROUND

Selection	Claimed By	Amateur Club	
23. WHITNEY, Ray	S.J.	Spokane	C
24. CORBET, Rene	Que.	Drummondville	LW
25. LAVIGNE, Eric	Tor.-Que.-Wsh.	Hull	D
26. PALFFY, Zigmund	NYI	AC Nitra	LW
27. STAIOS, Steve	Wpg.-St.L.	Niagara Falls	D
28. CAMPBELL, Jim	Phi.-Mtl.	Northwood Prep	C
29. CULLIMORE, Jassen	Van.	Peterborough	D
30. OZOLINSH, Sandis	Min.-S.J.	Dynamo Riga	D
31. HAMRLIK, Martin	Hfd.	TJ Zin	D
32. PUSHOR, Jamie	Det.	Lethbridge	D
33. HEXTALL, Donevan	N.J.	Prince Albert	LW
34. VERNER, Andrew	Edm.	Peterborough	G
35. DAWE, Jason	Buf.	Peterborough	LW
36. NELSON, Jeff	Wsh.	Prince Albert	C
37. WERENKA, Darcy	NYR	Lethbridge	D
38. FITZGERALD, Rusty	Pit.	Duluth East HS	C
39. POMICHTER, Michael	Mtl.-Chi.	Springfield Jr. B	C
40. STUMPEL, Jozef	Bos.	AC Nitra	RW
41. GROLEAU, Francois	Cgy.	Shawinigan	D
42. LEVEQUE, Guy	L.A.	Cornwall	C
43. DARBY, Craig	St.L.-Mtl.	Albany Academy	C
44. MATTHEWS, Jamie	Chi.	Sudbury	C

1990

FIRST ROUND

Selection	Claimed By	Amateur Club	
1. NOLAN, Owen	Que.	Cornwall	RW
2. NEDVED, Petr	Van.	Seattle	C
3. PRIMEAU, Keith	Det.	Niagara Falls	C
4. RICCI, Mike	Phi.	Peterborough	C
5. JAGR, Jaromir	Pit.	Poldi Kladno	LW
6. SCISSONS, Scott	NYI	Saskatoon	C
7. SYDOR, Darryl	L.A.	Kamloops	D
8. HATCHER, Derian	Min.	North Bay	D
9. SLANEY, John	Wsh.	Cornwall	D
10. BEREHOWSKY, Drake	Tor.	Kingston	D
11. KIDD, Trevor	N.J.-Cgy.	Brandon	G
12. STEVENSON, Turner	St.L.-Mtl.	Seattle	RW
13. STEWART, Michael	NYR	Michigan State	D
14. MAY, Brad	Wpg.-Buf.	Niagara Falls	LW
15. GREIG, Mark	Hfd.	Lethbridge	RW
16. DYKHUIS, Karl	Chi.	Hull	D
17. ALLISON, Scott	Edm.	Prince Albert	C
18. ANTOSKI, Shawn	Mtl.-St.L.-Van.	North Bay	LW
19. TKACHUK, Keith	Buf.-Wpg.	Malden Catholic	LW
20. BRODEUR, Martin	Cgy.-N.J.	St. Hyacinthe	G
21. SMOLINSKI, Bryan	Bos.	Michigan State	C

SECOND ROUND

Selection	Claimed By	Amateur Club	
22. HUGHES, Ryan	Que.	Cornell	C
23. SLEGR, Jiri	Van.	CHZ Litvinov	D
24. HARLOCK, David	Det.-Cgy.-N.J.	U. of Michigan	D
25. SIMON, Chris	Phi.	Ottawa	LW
26. PERREAULT, Nicolas P.	Pit.-Cgy.	Hawkesbury Jr. A	D
27. TAYLOR, Chris	NYI	London	C
28. SEMCHUK, Brandy	L.A.	Canadian National	RW
29. GOTZIAMAN, Chris	Min.-Cgy.-N.J.	Roseau	RW
30. PASMA, Rod	Wsh.	Cornwall	D
31. POTVIN, Felix	Tor.	Chicoutimi	G
32. VIITAKOSKI, Vesa	N.J.-Cgy.	SaiPa	LW
33. JOHNSON, Craig	St.L.	Hill-Murray HS	C
34. WEIGHT, Doug	NYR	Lake Superior	C
35. MULLER, Mike	Wpg.	Wayzata	D
36. SANDERSON, Geoff	Hfd.	Swift Current	C
37. DROPPA, Ivan	Chi.	Partizan	D
38. LEGAULT, Alexandre	Edm.	Boston University	RW
39. KUWABARA, Ryan	Mtl.	Ottawa	RW
40. RENBERG, Mikael	Buf.-Phi.	Pitea	LW
41. BELZILE, Etienne	Cgy.	Cornell	D
42. SANDWITH, Terran	Bos.-Phi.	Tri-City	D

1989

FIRST ROUND

Selection	Claimed By	Amateur Club	
1. SUNDIN, Mats	Que.	Nacka	RW
2. CHYZOWSKI, Dave	NYI	Kamloops	LW
3. THORNTON, Scott	Tor.	Belleville	C
4. BARNES, Stu	Wpg.	Tri-City	C
5. GUERIN, Bill	N.J.	Springfield Jr. B	RW
6. BENNETT, Adam	Chi.	Sudbury	D
7. ZMOLEK, Doug	Min.	John Marshall	D
8. HERTER, Jason	Van.	U. of North Dakota	D
9. MARSHALL, Jason	St.L.	Vernon Jr. A	D
10. HOLIK, Robert	Hfd.	Dukla Jihlava	C
11. SILLINGER, Mike	Det.	Regina	C
12. PEARSON, Rob	Phi.-Tor.	Belleville	RW
13. VALLIS, Lindsay	NYR-Mtl.	Seattle	RW
14. HALLER, Kevin	Buf.	Regina	D
15. SOULES, Jason	Edm.	Niagara Falls	D
16. HEWARD, Jamie	Pit.	Regina	RW
17. STEVENSON, Shayne	Bos.	Kitchener	RW
18. MILLER, Jason	L.A.-Edm.-N.J.	Medicine Hat	C
19. KOLZIG, Olaf	Wsh.	Tri-City	G
20. RICE, Steven	Mtl.-NYR	Kitchener	RW
21. BANCROFT, Steve	Cgy.-Tor.	Belleville	D

SECOND ROUND

Selection	Claimed By	Amateur Club	
22. FOOTE, Adam	Que.	Sault Ste. Marie	D
23. GREEN, Travis	NYI	Spokane	C
24. MANDERVILLE, Kent	Tor.-Cgy.	Notre Dame Jr. A	LW
25. RATUSHNY, Dan	Wpg.	Cornell	D
26. SKALDE, Jarrod	N.J.	Oshawa	C
27. SPEER, Michael	Chi.	Guelph	D
28. CRAIG, Mike	Min.	Oshawa	RW
29. WOODWARD, Robert	Van.	Deerfield	LW
30. BRISEBOIS, Patrice	St.L.-Mtl.	Laval	D
31. CORRIVEAU, Rick	Hfd.-St.L.	London	D
32. BOUGHNER, Bob	Det.	Sault Ste. Marie	D
33. JOHNSON, Greg	Phi.	Thunder Bay Jr. A	C
34. JUHLIN, Patrik	NYR-Phi.	Vasteras	LW
35. DAFOE, Byron	Buf.-Wsh.	Portland	D
36. BORGO, Richard	Edm.	Kitchener	G
37. LAUS, Paul	Pit.	Niagara Falls	D
38. PARSON, Mike	Bos.	Guelph	G
39. THOMPSON, Brent	L.A.	Medicine Hat	D
40. PROSOFSKY, Jason	Wsh.-NYR	Medicine Hat	RW
41. LAROUCHE, Steve	Mtl.	Trois-Rivieres	C
42. DRURY, Ted	Cgy.	Fairfield Prep	C

1988

FIRST ROUND

Selection	Claimed By	Amateur Club	
1. MODANO, Mike	Min.	Prince Albert	C
2. LINDEN, Trevor	Van.	Medicine Hat	RW
3. LESCHYSHYN, Curtis	Que.	Saskatoon	D
4. SHANNON, Darrin	Pit.	Windsor	LW
5. DORE, Daniel	NYR-Que.	Drummondville	RW
6. PEARSON, Scott	Tor.	Kingston	LW
7. GELINAS, Martin	L.A.	Hull	LW
8. ROENICK, Jeremy	Chi.	Thayer Academy	C
9. BRIND'AMOUR, Rod	St.L.	Notre Dame Jr. A	C
10. SELANNE, Teemu	Wpg.	Jokerit	RW
11. GOVEDARIS, Chris	Hfd.	Toronto	LW
12. FOSTER, Corey	N.J.	Peterborough	D
13. SAVAGE, Joel	Buf.	Victoria	RW
14. BOIVIN, Claude	Phi.	Drummondville	LW
15. SAVAGE, Reginald	Wsh.	Victoriaville	C
16. CHEVELDAYOFF, Kevin	NYI	Brandon	D
17. KOCUR, Kory	Det.	Saskatoon	RW
18. CIMETTA, Robert	Bos.	Toronto	LW
19. LEROUX, Francois	Edm.	St. Jean	D
20. CHARRON, Eric	Mtl.	Trois-Rivieres	D
21. MUZZATTI, Jason	Cgy.	Michigan State	G

SECOND ROUND

Selection	Claimed By	Amateur Club	
22. MALLETTE, Troy	Min.-NYR	Sault Ste. Marie	C
23. CHRISTIAN, Jeff	Van.-N.J.	London	LW
24. FISET, Stephane	Que.	Victoriaville	G
25. MAJOR, Mark	Pit.	North Bay	D
26. DUVAL, Murray	NYR	Spokane	RW
27. DOMI, Tie	Tor.	Peterborough	RW
28. HOLDEN, Paul	L.A.	London	D
29. DOUCET, Wayne	Chi. NYI	Hamilton	LW
30. PLAVSIC, Adrien	St.L.	U. of New Hampshire	D
31. ROMANIUK, Russell	Wpg.	St. Boniface Jr. A	LW
32. RICHTER, Barry	Hfd.	Culver Academy	D
33. ROHLIN, Leif	N.J.-Van.	Vasteras	D
34. ST. AMOUR, Martin	Buf.-Mtl.	Verdun	LW
35. MURRAY, Pat	Phi.	Michigan State	LW
36. TAYLOR, Tim	Wsh.	London	C
37. LEBRUN, Sean	NYI	New Westminster	LW
38. ANGLEHART, Serge	Det.	Drummondville	D
39. KOIVUNEN, Petro	Bos.-Edm.	Espoo	C
40. GAETZ, Link	Edm.-Min.	Spokane	D
41. BARTLEY, Wade	Mtl.-St.L.-Wsh.	Dauphin Jr. A	D
42. HARKINS, Todd	Cgy.	Miami-Ohio	RW

1987

FIRST ROUND

Selection	Claimed By	Amateur Club	
1. TURGEON, Pierre	Buf.	Granby	C
2. SHANAHAN, Brendan	N.J.	London	C
3. WESLEY, Glen	Van.-Bos.	Portland	D
4. McBEAN, Wayne	Min.-L.A.	Medicine Hat	D
5. JOSEPH, Chris	Pit.	Seattle	D
6. ARCHIBALD, David	L.A.-Min.	Portland	C/LW
7. RICHARDSON, Luke	Tor.	Peterborough	D
8. WAITE, Jimmy	Chi.	Chicoutimi	G
9. FOGARTY, Bryan	Que.	Kingston	D
10. MORE, Jayson	NYR	New Westminster	D
11. RACINE, Yves	Det.	Longueuil	D
12. OSBORNE, Keith	St.L.	North Bay	RW
13. CHYNOWETH, Dean	NYI	Medicine Hat	D
14. QUINTAL, Stephane	Bos.	Granby	D
15. SAKIC, Joe	Wsh.-Que.	Swift Current	C
16. MARCHMENT, Bryan	Wpg.	Belleville	D
17. CASSELS, Andrew	Mtl.	Ottawa	C
18. HULL, Jody	Hfd.	Peterborough	RW
19. DEASLEY, Bryan	Cgy.	U. of Michigan	LW
20. RUMBLE, Darren	Phi.	Kitchener	D
21. SOBERLAK, Peter	Edm.	Swift Current	LW

SECOND ROUND

Selection	Claimed By	Amateur Club	
22. MILLER, Brad	Buf.	Regina	D
23. PERSSON, Rickard	N.J.	Ostersund	D
24. MURPHY, Rob	Van.	Laval	C
25. MATTEAU, Stephane	Min.-Cgy.	Hull	LW
26. TABARACCI, Richard	Pit.	Cornwall	G
27. FITZPATRICK, Mark	L.A.	Medicine Hat	G
28. MAROIS, Daniel	Tor.	Chicoutimi	RW
29. McGILL, Ryan	Chi.	Swift Current	D
30. HARDING, Jeff	Que.-Phi.	St. Michael's Jr. B	LW
31. LACROIX, Daniel	NYR	Granby	LW
32. KRUPPKE, Gordon	Det.	Prince Albert	D
33. LECLAIR, John	St.L.-Mtl.	Bellows Academy	D
34. HACKETT, Jeff	NYI	Oshawa	G
35. McCRADY, Scott	Bos.-Min.	Medicine Hat	D
36. BALLANTYNE, Jeff	Wsh.	Ottawa	D
37. ERICKSSON, Patrik	Wpg.	Brynas	C
38. DESJARDINS, Eric	Mtl.	Granby	D
39. BURT, Adam	Hfd.	North Bay	D
40. GRANT, Kevin	Cgy.	Kitchener	D
41. WILKIE, Bob	Phi.-Det.	Swift Current	D
42. WERENKA, Brad	Edm.	N. Michigan	D

1986

FIRST ROUND

Selection	Claimed By	Amateur Club	
1. MURPHY, Joe	Det.	Michigan State	C
2. CARSON, Jimmy	L.A.	Verdun	C
3. BRADY, Neil	N.J.	Medicine Hat	C
4. ZALAPSKI, Zarley	Pit.	Canadian National	D
5. ANDERSON, Shawn	Buf.	Canadian National	D
6. DAMPHOUSSE, Vincent	Tor.	Laval	LW
7. WOODLEY, Dan	Van.	Portland	C
8. ELYNUIK, Pat	Wpg.	Prince Albert	RW
9. LEETCH, Brian	NYR	Avon Old Farms HS	D
10. LEMIEUX, Jocelyn	St.L.	Laval	RW
11. YOUNG, Scott	Hfd.	Boston University	RW
12. BABE, Warren	Min.	Lethbridge	LW
13. JANNEY, Craig	Bos.	Boston College	C
14. SANIPASS, Everett	Chi.	Verdun	LW
15. PEDERSON, Mark	Mtl.	Medicine Hat	LW
16. PELAWA, George	Cgy.	Bemidji HS	RW
17. FITZGERALD, Tom	NYI	Austin Prep	C
18. McRAE, Ken	Que.	Sudbury	C
19. GREENLAW, Jeff	Wsh.	Canadian National	LW
20. HUFFMAN, Kerry	Phi.	Guelph	D
21. ISSEL, Kim	Edm.	Prince Albert	RW

SECOND ROUND

Selection	Claimed By	Amateur Club	
22. GRAVES, Adam	Det.	Windsor	C
23. SEPPO, Jukka	L.A.-Phi.	Sport	LW
24. COPELAND, Todd	N.J.	Belmont Hill HS	D
25. CAPUANO, Dave	Pit.	Mt. St. Charles HS	C
26. BROWN, Greg	Buf.	St. Mark's	D
27. BRUNET, Benoit	Tor.-Mtl.	Hull	LW
28. HAWLEY, Kent	Van.-Phi.	Ottawa	C
29. NUMMINEN, Teppo	Wpg.	Tappara	D
30. WILKINSON, Neil	NYR-Min.	Selkirk	D
31. POSMA, Mike	St.L.	Buffalo Jr. A	D
32. LaFORGE, Marc	Hfd.	Kingston	D
33. KOLSTAD, Dean	Min.	Prince Albert	D
34. TIRKKONEN, Pekka	Bos.	SaPKo	C
35. KURZAWSKI, Mark	Chi.	Windsor	D
36. SHANNON, Darryl	Mtl.-Tor.	Windsor	D
37. GLYNN, Brian	Cgy.	Saskatoon	D
38. VASKE, Dennis	NYI	Armstrong HS	D
39. ROUTHIER, Jean-Marc	Que.	Hull	RW
40. SEFTEL, Steve	Wsh.	Kingston	LW
41. GUERARD, Stephane	Phi.-Que.	Shawinigan	D
42. NICHOLS, Jamie	Edm.	Portland	LW

1985

FIRST ROUND

Selection	Claimed By	Amateur Club	
1. CLARK, Wendel	Tor.	Saskatoon	D
2. SIMPSON, Craig	Pit.	Michigan State	C
3. WOLANIN, Craig	N.J.	Kitchener	D
4. SANDLAK, Jim	Van.	London	RW
5. MURZYN, Dana	Hfd.	Calgary	D
6. DALGARNO, Brad	Min.-NYI	Hamilton	RW
7. DAHLEN, Ulf	NYR	Ostersund	C
8. FEDYK, Brent	Det.	Regina	RW
9. DUNCANSON, Craig	L.A.	Sudbury	LW
10. GRATTON, Dan	Bos.-L.A.	Oshawa	C
11. MANSON, David	Chi.	Prince Albert	D
12. CHARBONNEAU, Jose	St.L.-Mtl.	Drummondville	RW
13. KING, Derek	NYI	Sault Ste. Marie	LW
14. JOHANSSON, Calle	Buf.	V. Frolunda	D
15. LATTA, Dave	Que.	Kitchener	LW
16. CHORSKE, Tom	Mtl.	Minneapolis SW HS	LW
17. BIOTTI, Chris	Cgy.	Belmont Hill HS	D
18. STEWART, Ryan	Wpg.	Kamloops	C
19. CORRIVEAU, Yvon	Wsh.	Toronto	LW
20. METCALFE, Scott	Edm.	Kingston	LW
21. SEABROOKE, Glen	Phi.	Peterborough	C

SECOND ROUND

Selection	Claimed By	Amateur Club	
22. SPANGLER, Ken	Tor.	Calgary	D
23. GIFFIN, Lee	Pit.	Oshawa	RW
24. BURKE, Sean	N.J.	Toronto	G
25. GAMBLE, Troy	Van.	Medicine Hat	G
26. WHITMORE, Kay	Hfd.	Peterborough	G
27. NIEUWENDYK, Joe	Min.-Cgy.	Cornell	C
28. RICHTER, Mike	NYR	Northwood Prep.	G
29. SHARPLES, Jeff	Det.	Kelowna	D
30. EDLUND, Par	L.A.	Bjorkloven	RW
31. COTE, Alain	Bos.	Quebec	D
32. WEINRICH, Eric	Chi.-N.J.	North Yarmouth	D
33. RICHARD, Todd	Mtl.	Armstrong HS	D
34. LAUER, Brad	NYI	Regina	RW
35. HOGUE, Benoit	Buf.	St-Jean	C
36. LAFRENIERE, Jason	Que.	Hamilton	C
37. RAGLAN, Herb	Mtl.-St.L.	Kingston	RW
38. WENAAS, Jeff	Cgy.	Medicine Hat	C
39. OHMAN, Roger	Wpg.	Leksand	D
40. DRUCE, John	Wsh.	Peterborough	RW
41. CARNELLEY, Todd	Edm.	Kamloops	D
42. RENDALL, Bruce	Phi.	Chatham	LW

1984

FIRST ROUND

Selection	Claimed By	Amateur Club	
1. LEMIEUX, Mario	Pit.	Laval	C
2. MULLER, Kirk	N.J.	Cdn. Nat./Guelph	C
3. OLCZYK, Ed	L.A.-Chi.	U.S. National	RW
4. IAFRATE, Al	Tor.	U.S. National/Belleville	D
5. SVOBODA, Petr	Hfd.-Mtl.	CHZ	D
6. REDMOND, Craig	Chi.-L.A.	Canadian National	D
7. BURR, Shawn	Det.	Kitchener	C
8. CORSON, Shayne	St.L.-Mtl.	Brantford	C
9. BODGER, Doug	Wpg.-Pit.	Kamloops Jr. A	D
10. DAIGNEAULT, J.J.	Van.	Cdn. Nat./Longueuil	D
11. COTE, Sylvain	Mtl.-Hfd.	Quebec	D
12. ROBERTS, Gary	Cgy.	Ottawa	LW
13. QUINN, David	Min.	Kent HS	D
14. CARKNER, Terry	NYR	Peterborough	D
15. STIENBURG, Trevor	Que.	Guelph	C
16. BELANGER, Roger	Phi.-Pit.	Kingston	D
17. HATCHER, Kevin	Wsh.	North Bay	D
18. ANDERSSON, Mikael	Buf.	V. Frolunda	C
19. PASIN, Dave	Bos.	Prince Albert	RW
20. MacPHERSON, Duncan	NYI	Saskatoon	D
21. ODELEIN, Selmar	Edm.	Regina	D

SECOND ROUND

Selection	Claimed By	Amateur Club	
22. SMYTH, Greg	Phi.	London	D
23. BILLINGTON, Craig	N.J.	Belleville	G
24. WILKS, Brian	L.A.	Kitchener	C
25. GILL, Todd	Tor.	Windsor	D
26. BENNING, Brian	Hfd.-St.L.	Portland	D
27. MELLANBY, Scott	Chi.-Phi.	Henry Carr Jr. B	RW
28. HOUDA, Doug	Det.	Calgary	D
29. RICHER, Stephane	St.L.-Mtl.	Granby	C
30. DOURIS, Peter	Wpg.	U. of New Hampshire	C
31. ROHLICEK, Jeff	Van.	Portland	LW
32. HRKAC, Anthony	Mtl.-St.L.	Orillia Jr. A	C
33. SABOURIN, Ken	Cgy.	Sault Ste. Marie	D
34. LEACH, Stephen	Min.-Wsh.	Matignon HS	RW
35. HELMINEN, Raimo	NYR	Ilves	C
36. BROWN, Jeff	Que.	Sudbury	D
37. CHYCHRUN, Jeff	Phi.	Kingston	D
38. RANHEIM, Paul	Wsh.-Cgy.	Edina HS	C
39. TRAPP, Doug	Buf.	Regina	LW
40. PODLOSKI, Ray	Bos.	Portland	C
41. MELANSON, Bruce	NYI	Oshawa	RW
42. REAUGH, Daryl	Edm.	Kamloops Jr. A	G

1983

FIRST ROUND

Selection	Claimed By	Amateur Club	
1. LAWTON, Brian	Pit.-Min.	Mount St. Charles HS	C
2. TURGEON, Sylvain	Hfd.	Hull	C
3. LaFONTAINE, Pat	N.J.-NYI	Verdun	C
4. YZERMAN, Steve	Det.	Peterborough	C
5. BARRASSO, Tom	St.L.-L.A.-Buf.	Acton-Boxboro HS	G
6. MacLEAN, John	L.A.-N.J.	Oshawa	RW
7. COURTNALL, Russ	Tor.	Victoria	C
8. McBAIN, Andrew	Wpg.	North Bay	RW
9. NEELY, Cam	Van.	Portland	RW
10. LACOMBE, Normand	Cgy.-Buf.	New Hampshire	RW
11. CREIGHTON, Adam	Que.-Buf.	Ottawa	C
12. GAGNER, Dave	NYR	Brantford	C
13. QUINN, Dan	Buf.-Cgy.	Belleville	C
14. DOLLAS, Bobby	Wsh.-Wpg.	Laval	D
15. ERREY, Bob	Min.-Pit.	Peterborough	LW
16. DIDUCK, Gerald	NYI	Lethbridge	D
17. TURCOTTE, Alfie	Mtl.	Portland	C
18. CASSIDY, Bruce	Chi.	Ottawa	D
19. BEUKEBOOM, Jeff	Edm.	Sault Ste. Marie	D
20. JENSEN, David	Phi.-Hfd.	Lawrence	C
21. MARKWART, Nevin	Bos.	Regina	LW

SECOND ROUND

Selection	Claimed By	Amateur Club	
22. CHARLESWORTH, Todd	Pit.	Oshawa	D
23. SIREN, Ville	Hfd.	Ilves	D
24. EVANS, Shawn	N.J.	Peterborough	D
25. LAMBERT, Lane	Det.	Saskatoon	RW
26. LEMIEUX, Claude	St.L.-Mtl.	Trois-Rivières	RW
27. MOMESSO, Sergio	L.A.-Mtl.	Shawinigan	C
28. JACKSON, Jeff	Tor.	Brantford	LW
29. BERRY, Brad	Wpg.	St. Albert	D
30. BRUCE, Dave	Van.	Kitchener	RW
31. TUCKER, John	Cgy.-Buf.	Kitchener	C
32. HEROUX, Yves	Que.	Chicoutimi	RW
33. HEATH, Randy	NYR	Portland	LW
34. HAJDU, Richard	Wsh.-Buf.	Kamloops Jr. A	LW
35. FRANCIS, Todd	Mtl.	Brantford	RW
36. PARKS, Malcolm	Min.	St. Albert	C
37. McKECHNEY, Garnet	NYI	Kitchener	RW
38. MUSIL, Frantisek	Mtl.-Min.	Tesla	D
39. PRESLEY, Wayne	Chi.	Kitchener	RW
40. GOLDEN, Mike	Edm.	Reading HS	C
41. ZEZEL, Peter	Phi.	Toronto	C
42. JOHNSTON, Greg	Bos.	Toronto	RW

1982

FIRST ROUND

Selection	Claimed By	Amateur Club	
1. KLUZAK, Gord	Col.-Bos.	Nanaimo	D
2. BELLOWS, Brian	Det.-Min.	Kitchener	RW
3. NYLUND, Gary	Tor.	Portland	D
4. SUTTER, Ron	Hfd.-Phi.	Lethbridge	C
5. STEVENS, Scott	L.A.-Wsh.	Kitchener	D
6. HOUSLEY, Phil	Wsh.-Buf.	S. St. Paul HS	D
7. YAREMCHUK, Ken	Chi.	Portland	C
8. TROTTIER, Rocky	St.L.-N.J.	Nanaimo	RW
9. CYR, Paul	Cgy.-Buf.	Victoria	LW
10. SUTTER, Rich	Pit.	Lethbridge	RW
11. PETIT, Michel	Van.	Sherbrooke	D
12. KYTE, Jim	Wpg.	Cornwall	D
13. SHAW, David	Que.	Kitchener	D
14. LAWLESS, Paul	Phi.-Hfd.	Windsor	LW
15. KONTOS, Chris	NYR	Toronto	C
16. ANDREYCHUK, Dave	Buf.	Oshawa	LW
17. CRAVEN, Murray	Min.-Det.	Medicine Hat	C
18. DANEYKO, Ken	Bos.-N.J.	Seattle	D
19. HEROUX, Alain	Mtl.	Chicoutimi	LW
20. PLAYFAIR, Jim	Edm.	Portland	D
21. FLATLEY, Pat	NYI	U. of Wisconsin	RW

SECOND ROUND

Selection	Claimed By	Amateur Club	
22. CURRAN, Brian	Col.-Bos.	Portland	D
23. COURTEAU, Yves	Det.	Laval	RW
24. LEEMAN, Gary	Tor.	Regina	D
25. IHNACAK, Peter	Hfd.-Tor.	Sparta	C
26. ANDERSON, Mike	L.A.-Buf.	N. St. Paul HS	C
27. HEIDT, Mike	Wsh.-L.A.	Calgary	D
28. BADEAU, Rene	St.L.-Chi.	Quebec	D
29. REIERSON, Dave	Cgy.	Prince Albert	D
30. JOHANSSON, Jens	Buf.	Pitea	D
31. GAUVREAU, Jocelyn	Pit.-Mtl.	Granby	D
32. CARLSON, Kent	Van.-Mtl.	St. Lawrence University	D
33. MALEY, David	Wpg.-Mtl.	Edina HS	C
34. GILLIS, Paul	Que.	Niagara Falls	C
35. PATERSON, Mark	Phi.-Hfd.	Ottawa	D
36. SANDSTROM, Tomas	NYR	Farjestads	RW
37. KROMM, Richard	Buf.-Cgy.	Portland	LW
38. HRYNEWICH, Tim	Min.-Pit.	Sudbury	LW
39. BYERS, Lyndon	Bos.	Regina	RW
40. SANDELIN, Scott	Mtl.	Hibbing HS	D
41. GRAVES, Steve	Edm.	Sault Ste. Marie	C
42. SMITH, Vern	NYI	Lethbridge	D

1981

FIRST ROUND

Selection	Claimed By	Amateur Club	
1. HAWERCHUK, Dale	Wpg.	Cornwall	C
2. SMITH, Doug	Det.-L.A.	Ottawa	C
3. CARPENTER, Bobby	Col.-Wsh.	St. John's HS	C
4. FRANCIS, Ron	Hfd.	Sault Ste. Marie	C
5. CIRELLA, Joe	Wsh.-Col.	Oshawa	D
6. BENNING, Jim	Tor.	Portland	D
7. HUNTER, Mark	Pit.-Mtl.	Brantford	RW
8. FUHR, Grant	Edm.	Victoria	G
9. PATRICK, James	NYR	Prince Albert	D
10. BUTCHER, Garth	Van.	Regina	D
11. MOLLER, Randy	Que.	Lethbridge	D
12. TANTI, Tony	Chi.	Oshawa	RW
13. MEIGHAN, Ron	Min.	Niagara Falls	D
14. LEVEILLE, Normand	Bos.	Chicoutimi	LW
15. MacINNIS, Allan	Cgy.	Kitchener	D
16. SMITH, Steve	Phi.	Sault Ste. Marie	D
17. DUDACEK, Jiri	Buf.	Poldi Kladno	RW
18. DELORME, Gilbert	L.A.-Mtl.	Chicoutimi	D
19. INGMAN, Jan	Mtl.	Farjestad	LW
20. RUFF, Marty	St.L.	Lethbridge	D
21. BOUTILIER, Paul	NYI	Sherbrooke	D

SECOND ROUND

Selection	Claimed By	Amateur Club	
22. ARNIEL, Scott	Wpg.	Cornwall	LW
23. LOISELLE, Claude	Det.	Windsor	C
24. YAREMCHUK, Gary	Col.-Tor.	Portland	C
25. GRIFFIN, Kevin	Hfd.-Chi.	Portland	LW
26. CHERNOMAZ, Rich	Wsh.-Col.	Victoria	C
27. DONNELLY, Dave	Tor.-Min.	St. Albert	C
28. GATZOS, Steve	Pit.	Sault Ste. Marie	RW
29. STRUEBY, Todd	Edm.	Regina	LW
30. ERIXON, Jan	NYR	Skelleftea	RW
31. SANDS, Mike	Van.-Min.	Sudbury	G
32. ERIKSSON, Lars	Que.-Mtl.	Brynas	G
33. HIRSCH, Tom	Chi.-Min.	Patrick Henry HS	D
34. PREUSS, Dave	Min.	St. Thomas Academy	RW
35. DUFOUR, Luc	Bos.	Chicoutimi	RW
36. NORDIN, Hakan	Cgy.-St.L.	Farjestad	D
37. COSTELLO, Rich	Phi.	Natick HS	C
38. VIRTA, Hannu	Buf.	TPS	D
39. KENNEDY, Dean	L.A.	Brandon	D
40. CHELIOS, Chris	Mtl.	Moose Jaw	D
41. WAHLSTEN, Jali	St.L.-Min.	TPS	C
42. DINEEN, Gord	NYI	Sault Ste. Marie	D

1980

FIRST ROUND

Selection	Claimed By	Amateur Club	
1. WICKENHEISER, Doug	Col.-Mtl.	Regina	C
2. BABYCH, Dave	Wpg.	Portland	D
3. SAVARD, Denis	Que.-Chi.	Montreal	C
4. MURPHY, Larry	Det.-L.A.	Peterborough	D
5. VEITCH, Darren	Wsh.	Regina	D
6. COFFEY, Paul	Edm.	Kitchener	D
7. LANZ, Rick	Van.	Oshawa	D
8. ARTHUR, Fred	Hfd.	Cornwall	D
9. BULLARD, Mike	Pit.	Brantford	C
10. FOX, Jimmy	L.A.	Ottawa	RW
11. BLAISDELL, Mike	Tor.-Det.	Regina	RW
12. WILSON, Rik	St.L.	Kingston	D
13. CYR, Denis	Cgy.	Montreal	RW
14. MALONE, Jim	NYR	Toronto	C
15. DUPONT, Jerome	Chi.	Toronto	D
16. PALMER, Brad	Min.	Victoria	LW
17. SUTTER, Brent	NYI	Red Deer	C
18. PEDERSON, Barry	Bos.	Victoria	C
19. GAGNE, Paul	Mtl.-Col.	Windsor	LW
20. PATRICK, Steve	Buf.	Brandon	RW
21. STOTHERS, Mike	Phi.	Kingston	D

SECOND ROUND

Selection	Claimed By	Amateur Club	
22. WARD, Joe	Col.	Seattle	C
23. MANTHA, Moe	Wpg.	Toronto	D
24. ROCHEFORT, Normand	Que.	Quebec	D
25. MUNI, Craig	Det.-Tor.	Kingston	D
26. McGILL, Bob	Wsh.-Tor.	Victoria	D
27. NATTRESS, Ric	Edm.-Mtl.	Brantford	D
28. LUDZIK, Steve	Van.-Chi.	Niagara Falls	C
29. GALARNEAU, Michel	Hfd.	Hull	C
30. SOLHEIM, Ken	Pit.-Chi.	Medicine Hat	LW
31. CURTALE, Tony	L.A.-Cgy.	Brantford	D
32. LaVALLEE, Kevin	Tor.-Cgy.	Brantford	LW
33. TERRION, Greg	St.L.-L.A.	Brantford	LW
34. MORRISON, Dave	Cgy.-L.A.	Peterborough	RW
35. ALLISON, Mike	NYR	Sudbury	LW
36. DAWES, Len	Chi.	Victoria	D
37. BEAUPRE, Don	Min.	Sudbury	G
38. HRUDEY, Kelly	NYI	Medicine Hat	G
39. KONROYD, Steve	Cgy.	Oshawa	D
40. CHABOT, John	Mtl.	Hull	C
41. MOLLER, Mike	Buf.	Lethbridge	RW
42. FRASER, Jay	Phi.	Ottawa	LW

1979

FIRST ROUND

Selection	Claimed By	Amateur Club	
1. RAMAGE, Rob	Col.	London	D
2. TURNBULL, Perry	St.L.	Portland	C
3. FOLIGNO, Mike	Det.	Sudbury	RW
4. GARTNER, Mike	Wsh.	Niagara Falls	RW
5. VAIVE, Rick	Van.	Sherbrooke	RW
6. HARTSBURG, Craig	Min.	Sault St. Marie	D
7. BROWN, Keith	Chi.	Portland	D
8. BOURQUE, Raymond	L.A.-Bos.	Verdun	D
9. BOSCHMAN, Laurie	Tor.	Brandon	C
10. McCARTHY, Tom	Wsh.-Min.	Oshawa	LW
11. RAMSEY, Mike	Buf.	U. of Minnesota	D
12. REINHART, Paul	Atl.	Kitchener	D
13. SULLIMAN, Doug	NYR	Kitchener	RW
14. PROPP, Brian	Phi.	Brandon	LW
15. McCRIMMON, Brad	Bos.	Brandon	D
16. WELLS, Jay	Mtl.-L.A.	Kingston	D
17. SUTTER, Duane	NYI	Lethbridge	RW
18. ALLISON, Ray	Hfd.	Brandon	RW
19. MANN, Jimmy	Wpg.	Sherbrooke	RW
20. GOULET, Michel	Que.	Quebec	LW
21. LOWE, Kevin	Edm.	Quebec	D

SECOND ROUND

Selection	Claimed By	Amateur Club	
22. WESLEY, Blake	Col.-Phi.	Portland	D
23. PEROVICH, Mike	St.L.-Atl.	Brandon	D
24. RAUSSE, Errol	Det.-Wsh.	Seattle	LW
25. JONSSON, Tomas	Wsh.-NYI	MoDo	D
26. ASHTON, Brent	Van.	Saskatoon	LW
27. GINGRAS, Gaston	Min.-Mtl.	Hamilton	D
28. TRIMPER, Tim	Chi.	Peterborough	LW
29. HOPKINS, Dean	L.A.	London	RW
30. HARDY, Mark	Tor.-L.A.	Montreal	D
31. MARSHALL, Paul	Wsh.-Pit.	Brantford	LW
32. RUFF, Lindy	Buf.	Lethbridge	D
33. RIGGIN, Pat	Atl.	London	G
34. HOSPODAR, Ed	NYR	Ottawa	D
35. LINDBERGH, Pelle	Phi.	AIK Solna	G
36. MORRISON, Doug	Bos.	Lethbridge	RW
37. NASLUND, Mats	Mtl.	Brynas IFK	LW
38. CARROLL, Billy	NYI	London	C
39. SMITH, Stuart	Hfd.	Peterborough	D
40. CHRISTIAN, Dave	Wpg.	U. of North Dakota	C
41. HUNTER, Dale	Que.	Sudbury	C
42. BROTEN, Neal	Min.	U. of Minnesota	C

1978

FIRST ROUND

Selection	Claimed By	Amateur Club	
1. SMITH, Bobby	Min.	Ottawa	C
2. WALTER, Ryan	Wsh.	Seattle	LW
3. BABYCH, Wayne	St.L.	Portland	RW
4. DERLAGO, Bill	Van.	Brandon	C
5. GILLIS, Mike	Col.	Kingston	LW
6. WILSON, Behn	Pit.-Phi.	Kingston	D
7. LINSEMAN, Ken	NYR-Phi.	Kingston	C
8. GEOFFRION, Danny	L.A.-Mtl.	Cornwall	RW
9. HUBER, Willie	Det.	Hamilton	D
10. HIGGINS, Tim	Chi.	Ottawa	RW
11. MARSH, Brad	Atl.	London	D
12. PETERSON, Brent	Tor.-Det.	Portland	C
13. PLAYFAIR, Larry	Buf.	Portland	D
14. LUCAS, Danny	Phi.	Sault Ste. Marie	RW
15. TAMBELLINI, Steve	NYI	Lethbridge	C
16. SECORD, Al	Bos.	Hamilton	LW
17. HUNTER, Dave	Mtl.	Sudbury	LW
18. COULIS, Tim	Wsh.	Hamilton	LW

SECOND ROUND

Selection	Claimed By	Amateur Club	
19. PAYNE, Steve	Min.	Ottawa	LW
20. MULVEY, Paul	Wsh.	Portland	RW
21. QUENNEVILLE, Joel	Tor.	Windsor	D
22. FRASER, Curt	Van.	Victoria	LW
23. MacKINNON, Paul	Wsh.	Peterborough	D
24. CHRISTOFF, Steve	Min.	U. of Minnesota	C
25. MEEKER, Mike	Pit.	Peterborough	RW
26. MALONEY, Don	NYR	Kitchener	LW
27. MALINOWSKI, Merlin	Col.	Medicine Hat	C
28. HICKS, Glenn	Det.	Flin Flon	LW
29. LECUYER, Doug	Chi.	Portland	LW
30. YAKIWCHUK, Dale	Mtl.	Portland	C
31. JENSEN, Al	Det.	Hamilton	G
32. McKEGNEY, Tony	Buf.	Kingston	LW
33. SIMURDA, Mike	Phi.	Kingston	RW
34. JOHNSTON, Randy	NYI	Peterborough	D
35. NICOLSON, Graeme	Bos.	Cornwall	D
36. CARTER, Ron	Mtl.	Sherbrooke	RW

1977

FIRST ROUND

Selection	Claimed By	Amateur Club	
1. McCOURT, Dale	Det.	St. Catharines	C
2. BECK, Barry	Col.	New Westminster	D
3. PICARD, Robert	Wsh.	Montreal	D
4. GILLIS, Jere	Van.	Sherbrooke	LW
5. CROMBEEN, Mike	Cle.	Kingston	RW
6. WILSON, Doug	Chi.	Ottawa	D
7. MAXWELL, Brad	Min.	New Westminster	D
8. DEBLOIS, Lucien	NYR	Sorel	C
9. CAMPBELL, Scott	St.L.	London	D
10. NAPIER, Mark	Atl.-Mtl.	Toronto	RW
11. ANDERSON, John	Tor.	Toronto	RW
12. JOHANSEN, Trevor	Pit.-Tor.	Toronto	D
13. DUGUAY, Ron	L.A.-NYR	Sudbury	C
14. SEILING, Ric	Buf.	St. Catharines	RW
15. BOSSY, Mike	NYI	Laval	RW
16. FOSTER, Dwight	Bos.	Kitchener	C/RW
17. McCARTHY, Kevin	Phi.	Winnipeg	D
18. DUPONT, Norm	Mtl.	Montreal	C

SECOND ROUND

Selection	Claimed By	Amateur Club	
19. SAVARD, Jean	Det.-Chi.	Quebec	C
20. ZAHARKO, Miles	Col.-Atl.	New Westminister	D
21. LOFTHOUSE, Mark	Wsh.	New Westminster	RW
22. BANDURA, Jeff	Van.	Portland	D
23. CHICOINE, Daniel	Cle.	Sherbrooke	RW
24. GLADNEY, Bob	Chi.-Tor.	Oshawa	D
25. SEMENKO, Dave	Min.	Brandon	LW
26. KEATING, Mike	NYR	St. Catherines	LW
27. LABATTE, Neil	St.L.	Toronto	D
28. LAURENCE, Don	Atl.	Kitchener	C
29. SAGANIUK, Rocky	Tor.	Lethbridge	RW
30. HAMILTON, Jim	Pit.	London	RW
31. HILL, Brian	L.A.-Atl.	Medicine Hat	RW
32. ARESHENKOFF, Ron	Buf.	Medicine Hat	C
33. TONELLI, John	NYI	Toronto	LW
34. PARRO, Dave	Bos.	Saskatoon	G
35. GORENCE, Tom	Phi.	U. of Minnesota	RW
36. LANGWAY, Rod	Mtl.	U. of New Hampshire	D

1976

FIRST ROUND

Selection	Claimed By	Amateur Club	
1. GREEN, Rick	K.C.-Wsh.	London	D
2. CHAPMAN, Blair	Pit.	Saskatoon	RW
3. SHARPLEY, Glen	Min.	Hull	C
4. WILLIAMS, Fred	Det.	Saskatoon	C
5. JOHANSSON, Bjorn	Cal.	Sweden	D
6. MURDOCH, Don	NYR	Medicine Hat	RW
7. FEDERKO, Bernie	St.L.	Saskatoon	C
8. SHAND, Dave	Van.-Atl.	Peterborough	D
9. CLOUTIER, Real	Chi.	Quebec	RW
10. PHILLIPOFF, Harold	Atl.	New Westminster	LW
11. GARDNER, Paul	Pit.-K.C.	Oshawa	C
12. LEE, Peter	Tor.-Mtl.	Ottawa	RW
13. SCHUTT, Rod	L.A.-Mtl.	Sudbury	LW
14. McKENDRY, Alex	NYI	Sudbury	LW
15. CARROLL, Greg	Buf.-Wsh.	Medicine Hat	C
16. PACHAL, Clayton	Bos.	New Westminster	C
17. SUZOR, Mark	Phi.	Kingston	D
18. BAKER, Bruce	Mtl.	Ottawa	RW

SECOND ROUND

Selection	Claimed By	Amateur Club	
19. MALONE, Greg	Wsh.-Pit.	Oshawa	C
20. SUTTER, Brian	K.C.-St.L.	Lethbridge	LW
21. CLIPPINGDALE, Steve	Min.-L.A.	New Westminster	LW
22. LARSON, Reed	Det.	U. of Minnesota	D
23. STENLUND, Vern	Cal.	London	C
24. FARRISH, Dave	NYR	Sudbury	D
25. SMRKE, John	St.L.	Toronto	LW
26. MANNO, Bob	Van.	St. Catharines	D
27. McDILL, Jeff	Chi.	Victoria	RW
28. SIMPSON, Bobby	Atl.	Sherbrooke	LW
29. MARSH, Peter	Pit.	Sherbrooke	RW
30. CARLYLE, Randy	Tor.	Sudbury	D
31. ROBERTS, Jim	L.A.-Min.	Ottawa	LW
32. KASZYCKI, Mike	NYI	Sault Ste. Marie	C
33. KOWAL, Joe	Buf.	Hamilton	LW
34. GLOECKNER, Larry	Bos.	Victoria	D
35. CALLANDER, Drew	Phi.	Regina	C
36. MELROSE, Barry	Mtl.	Kamloops	D

1975

FIRST ROUND

Selection	Claimed By	Amateur Club	
1. BRIDGMAN, Mel	Wsh.-Phi.	Victoria	C
2. DEAN, Barry	K.C.	Medicine Hat	LW
3. KLASSEN, Ralph	Cal.	Saskatoon	C
4. MAXWELL, Brian	Min.	Medicine Hat	D
5. LAPOINTE, Rick	Det.	Victoria	D
6. ASHBY, Don	Tor.	Calgary	C
7. VAYDIK, Greg	Chi.	Medicine Hat	C
8. MULHERN, Richard	Atl.	Sherbrooke	D
9. SADLER, Robin	St.L.-Mtl.	Edmonton	D
10. BLIGHT, Rick	Van.	Brandon	RW
11. PRICE, Pat	NYI	Saskatoon	D
12. DILLON, Wayne	NYR	Toronto	C
13. LAXTON, Gord	Pit.	New Westminster	G
14. HALWARD, Doug	Bos.	Peterborough	D
15. MONDOU, Pierre	L.A.-Mtl.	Montreal	C
16. YOUNG, Tim	Mtl.-L.A.	Ottawa	C
17. SAUVE, Bob	Buf.	Laval	G
18. FORSYTH, Alex	Phi.-Wsh.	Kingston	C

SECOND ROUND

Selection	Claimed By	Amateur Club	
19. SCAMURRA, Peter	Wsh.	Peterborough	D
20. CAIRNS, Don	K.C.	Victoria	LW
21. MARUK, Dennis	Cal.	London	C
22. ENGBLOM, Brian	Min.-Mtl.	U. of Wisconsin	D
23. ROLLINS, Jerry	Det.	Winnipeg	D
24. JARVIS, Doug	Tor.	Peterborough	C
25. ARNDT, Daniel	Chi.	Saskatoon	LW
26. BOWNESS, Rick	Atl.	Montreal	RW
27. STANIOWSKI, Ed	St.L.	Regina	G
28. GASSOFF, Brad	Van.	Kamloops	D
29. SALVIAN, David	NYI	St. Catharines	RW
30. SOETAERT, Doug	NYR	Edmonton	G
31. ANDERSON, Russ	Pit.	U. of Minnesota	D
32. SMITH, Barry	Bos.	New Westminster	C
33. BUCYK, Terry	L.A.	Lethbridge	RW
34. GREENBANK, Kelvin	Mtl.	Winnipeg	RW
35. BREITENBACH, Ken	Buf.	St. Catharines	D
36. MASTERS, Jamie	Phi.-St.L.	Ottawa	D

1974

FIRST ROUND

Selection	Claimed By	Amateur Club	
1. JOLY, Greg	Wsh.	Regina	D
2. PAIEMENT, Wilfred	K.C.	St. Catharines	RW
3. HAMPTON, Rick	Cal.	St. Catharines	D
4. GILLIES, Clark	NYI	Regina	LW
5. CONNOR, Cam	Van.-Mtl.	Flin Flon	RW
6. HICKS, Doug	Min.	Flin Flon	D
7. RISEBROUGH, Doug	St.L.-Mtl.	Kitchener	C
8. LAROUCHE, Pierre	Pit.	Sorel	C
9. LOCHEAD, Bill	Det.	Oshawa	LW
10. CHARTRAW, Rick	Atl.-Mtl.	Kitchener	D
11. FOGOLIN, Lee	Buf.	Oshawa	D
12. TREMBLAY, Mario	L.A.-Mtl.	Montreal	RW
13. VALIQUETTE, Jack	Tor.	Sault Ste. Marie	C
14. MALONEY, Dave	NYR	Kitchener	D
15. McTAVISH, Gord	Mtl.	Sudbury	C
16. MULVEY, Grant	Chi.	Calgary	RW
17. CHIPPERFIELD, Ron	Phi.-Cal.	Brandon	C
18. LARWAY, Don	Bos.	Swift Current	RW

SECOND ROUND

Selection	Claimed By	Amateur Club	
19. MARSON, Mike	Wsh.	Sudbury	LW
20. BURDON, Glen	K.C.	Regina	C
21. AFFLECK, Bruce	Cal.	U. of Denver	D
22. TROTTIER, Bryan	NYI	Swift Current	C
23. SEDLBAUER, Ron	Van.	Kitchener	LW
24. NANTAIS, Rick	Min.	Quebec	LW
25. HOWE, Mark	St.L.-Bos.	Toronto	D
26. HESS, Bob	Pit.-St.L.	New Westminster	D
27. COSSETTE, Jacques	Det.-Pit.	Sorel	RW
28. CHOUINARD, Guy	Atl.	Quebec	C
29. GARE, Danny	Buf.	Calgary	RW
30. MacGREGOR, Gary	L.A.-Mtl.	Cornwall	C
31. WILLIAMS, Dave	Tor.	Swift Current	LW
32. GRESCHNER, Ron	NYR	New Westminster	D
33. LUPIEN, Gilles	Mtl.	Montreal	D
34. DAIGLE, Alain	Chi.	Trois-Rivières	RW
35. McLEAN, Don	Phi.	Sudbury	D
36. STURGEON, Peter	Bos.	Kitchener	LW

1973

FIRST ROUND

Selection	Claimed By	Amateur Club	
1. POTVIN, Denis	NYI	Ottawa	D
2. LYSIAK, Tom	Cal.-Mtl.-Atl.	Medicine Hat	C
3. VERVERGAERT, Dennis	Van.	London	RW
4. McDONALD, Lanny	Tor.	Medicine Hat	RW
5. DAVIDSON, John	Atl.-Mtl.-St.L.	Calgary	G
6. SAVARD, Andre	L.A.-Bos.	Quebec	C
7. STOUGHTON, Blaine	Pit.	Flin Flon	RW
8. GAINEY, Bob	St.L.-Mtl.	Peterborough	LW
9. DAILEY, Bob	Min.-Mtl.-Van.	Toronto	D
10. NEELY, Bob	Phi.-Tor.	Peterborough	LW
11. RICHARDSON, Terry	Det.	New Westminster	G
12. TITANIC, Morris	Buf.	Sudbury	LW
13. ROTA, Darcy	Chi.	Edmonton	LW
14. MIDDLETON, Rick	NYR	Oshawa	RW
15. TURNBULL, Ian	Bos.-Tor.	Ottawa	D
16. MERCREDI, Vic	Mtl.-Atl.	New Westminster	C

SECOND ROUND

Selection	Claimed By	Amateur Club	
17. GOLDUP, Glen	NYI-Mtl.	Toronto	RW
18. DUNLOP, Blake	Cal.-Min.	Ottawa	C
19. BORDELEAU, Paulin	Van.	Toronto	RW
20. GOODENOUGH, Larry	Tor.-Phi.	London	D
21. VAIL, Eric	Atl.	Sudbury	LW
22. MARRIN, Peter	L.A.-Mtl.	Toronto	C
23. BIANCHIN, Wayne	Pit.	Flin Flon	LW
24. PESUT, George	St.L.	Saskatoon	D
25. ROGERS, John	Min.	Edmonton	RW
26. LEVINS, Brent	Phi.	Swift Current	
27. CAMPBELL, Colin	Det.-Pit.	Peterborough	D
28. LANDRY, Jean	Buf.	Quebec	D
29. THOMAS, Reg	Chi.	London	LW
30. HICKEY, Pat	NYR	Hamilton	LW
31. JONES, Jim	Bos.	Peterborough	RW
32. ANDRUFF, Ron	Mtl.	Flin Flon	C

1972

FIRST ROUND

Selection	Claimed By	Amateur Club	
1. HARRIS, Billy	NYI	Toronto	RW
2. RICHARD, Jacques	Atl.	Quebec	LW
3. LEVER, Don	Van.	Niagara Falls	C
4. SHUTT, Steve	L.A.-Mtl.	Toronto	LW
5. SCHOENFELD, Jim	Buf.	Niagara Falls	D
6. LAROCQUE, Michel	Cal.-Mtl.	Ottawa	G
7. BARBER, Bill	Phi.	Kitchener	LW
8. GARDNER, Dave	Pit.-Min.-Mtl.	Toronto	C
9. MERRICK, Wayne	St.L.	Ottawa	C
10. BLANCHARD, Albert	Det.-NYR	Kitchener	LW
11. FERGUSON, George	Tor.	Toronto	C
12. BYERS, Jerry	Min.	Kitchener	LW
13. RUSSELL, Phil	Chi.	Edmonton	D
14. VAN BOXMEER, John	Mtl.	Guelph	D
15. MacMILLAN, Bobby	NYR	St. Catharines	RW
16. BLOOM, Mike	Bos.	St. Catharines	LW

SECOND ROUND

Selection	Claimed By	Amateur Club	
17. HENNING Lorne	NYI	New Westminster	C
18. BIALOWAS, Dwight	Atl.	Regina	D
19. McSHEFFREY, Brian	Van.	Ottawa	RW
20. KOZAK, Don	L.A.	Edmonton	RW
21. SACHARUK, Larry	Buf.-NYR	Saskatoon	D
22. CASSIDY, Tom	Cal.	Kitchener	C
23. BLADON, Tom	Phi.	Edmonton	D
24. LYNCH, Jack	Pit.	Oshawa	D
25. CARRIERE, Larry	St.L.-Buf.	Loyola College	D
26. GUITE, Pierre	Det.	St. Catharines	LW
27. OSBURN, Randy	Tor.	London	LW
28. WEIR, Stan	Min.-Cal.	Medicine Hat	C
29. OGILVIE, Brian	Chi.	Edmonton	C
30. LUKOWICH, Bernie	Mtl.-Pit.	New Westminster	RW
31. VILLEMURE, Rene	NYR	Shawinigan	LW
32. ELDER, Wayne	Bos.	London	D

1971

FIRST ROUND

Selection	Claimed By	Amateur Club	
1. LAFLEUR, Guy	Cal.-Mtl.	Quebec	RW
2. DIONNE, Marcel	Det.	St. Catharines	C
3. GUEVREMONT, Jocelyn	Van.	Montreal	D
4. CARR, Gene	Pit.-St.L.	Flin Flon	C
5. MARTIN, Rick	Buf.	Montreal	LW
6. JONES, Ron	L.A.-Bos.	Edmonton	D
7. ARNASON, Chuck	Min.-Mtl.	Flin Flon	RW
8. WRIGHT, Larry	Phi.	Regina	C
9. PLANTE, Pierre	Tor.-Phi.	Drummondville	RW
10. VICKERS, Steve	St.L.-NYR	Toronto	LW
11. WILSON, Murray	Mtl.	Ottawa	LW
12. SPRING, Dan	Chi.	Edmonton	C
13. DURBANO, Steve	NYR	Toronto	D
14. O'REILLY, Terry	Bos.	Oshawa	RW

SECOND ROUND

Selection	Claimed By	Amateur Club	
15. BAIRD, Ken	Cal.	Flin Flon	D
16. BOUCHA, Henry	Det.	U.S. Nationals	C
17. LALONDE, Bobby	Van.	Montreal	C
18. McKENZIE, Brian	Pit.	St. Catharines	LW
19. RAMSAY, Craig	Buf.	Peterborough	LW
20. ROBINSON, Larry	L.A.-Mtl.	Kitchener	D
21. NORRISH, Rod	Min.	Regina	LW
22. KEHOE, Rick	Phi.-Tor.	Hamilton	RW
23. FORTIER, Dave	Tor.	St. Catharines	D
24. DEGUISE, Michel	St.L.-Mtl.	Sorel	G
25. FRENCH, Terry	Mtl.	Ottawa	C
26. KRYSKOW, Dave	Chi.	Edmonton	LW
27. WILLIAMS, Tom	NYR	Hamilton	LW
28. RIDLEY, Curt	Bos.	Portage	G

1970

FIRST ROUND

Selection	Claimed By	Amateur Club	
1. PERREAULT, Gilbert	Buf.	Montreal	C
2. TALLON, Dale	Van.	Toronto	D
3. LEACH, Reg	L.A.-Bos.	Flin Flon	LW
4. MacLEISH, Rick	Phi.-Bos.	Peterborough	C
5. MARTINIUK, Ray	Oak.-Mtl.	Flin Flon	G
6. LEFLEY, Chuck	Min.-Mtl.	Canadian National	C
7. POLIS, Greg	Pit.	Estevan	LW
8. SITTLER, Darryl	Tor.	London	C
9. PLUMB, Ron	Bos.	Peterborough	D
10. ODDLEIFSON, Chris	St.L.-Oak.	Winnipeg	C
11. GRATTON, Norm	Mtl.-NYR	Montreal	LW
12. LAJEUNESSE, Serge	Det.	Montreal	RW
13. STEWART, Bob	Bos.	Oshawa	D
14. MALONEY, Dan	Chi.	London	LW

SECOND ROUND

Selection	Claimed By	Amateur Club	
15. DEADMARSH, Butch	Buf.	Brandon	LW
16. HARGREAVES, Jim	Van.	Winnipeg	D
17. HARVEY, Fred	L.A.-Min.	Hamilton	RW
18. CLEMENT, Bill	Phi.	Ottawa	C
19. LAFRAMBOISE, Pete	Oak.	Ottawa	C
20. BARRETT, Fred	Min.	Toronto	D
21. STEWART, John	Pit.	Flin Flon	LW
22. THOMPSON, Errol	Tor.	Charlottetown	LW
23. KEOGAN, Murray	St.L.	U. of Minnesota	C
24. McDONOUGH, Al	Mtl.-L.A.	St. Catharines	RW
25. MURPHY, Mike	NYR	Toronto	RW
26. GUINDON, Bobby	Det.	Montreal	LW
27. BOUCHARD, Dan	Bos.	London	G
28. ARCHAMBAULT, Mike	Chi.	Drummondville	LW

1969

FIRST ROUND

Selection	Claimed By	Amateur Club	
1. HOULE, Rejean	Mtl.	Montreal	LW
2. TARDIF, Marc	Mtl.	Montreal	LW
3. TANNAHILL, Don	Min.-Bos.	Niagara Falls	LW
4. SPRING, Frank	Pit.-Bos.	Edmonton	RW
5. REDMOND, Dick	L.A.-Mtl.-Min.	St. Catharines	D
6. CURRIER, Bob	Phi.	Cornwall	C
7. FEATHERSTONE, Tony	Oak.	Peterborough	RW
8. DUPONT, André	St.L.-NYR	Montreal	D
9. MOSER, Ernie	Det.-Tor.	Estevan	RW
10. RUTHERFORD, Jim	Det.	Hamilton	G
11. BOLDIREV, Ivan	Bos.	Oshawa	C
12. JARRY, Pierre	NYR	Ottawa	LW
13. BORDELEAU, J.-P.	Chi.	Montreal	RW
14. O'BRIEN, Dennis	Min.	St. Catharines	D

SECOND ROUND

Selection	Claimed By	Amateur Club	
15. KESSELL, Rick	Pit.	Oshawa	C
16. HOGANSON, Dale	L.A.	Estevan	D
17. CLARKE, Bobby	Phi.	Flin Flon	C
18. STACKHOUSE, Ron	Oak.	Peterborough	D
19. LOWE, Mike	St.L.	Loyola College	
20. BRINDLEY, Doug	Tor.	Niagara Falls	C
21. GARWASIUK, Ron	Det.	Regina	LW
22. QUOQUOCHI, Art	Bos.	Montreal	
23. WILSON, Bert	NYR	London	LW
24. ROMANCHYCH, Larry	Chi.	Flin Flon	RW
25. GILBERT, Gilles	Min.	London	G
26. BRIERE, Michel	Pit.	Shawinigan Falls	C
27. BODDY, Greg	L.A.	Edmonton	D
28. BROSSART, Bill	Phi.	Estevan	D

Craig Ramsay (right) was selected 19th overall by Buffalo in 1971. Bill Barber (far right) went to the Flyers with the seventh pick in 1972. Barber replaced Ramsay as the Philadelphia coach in 2000-01 and went on to win the Jack Adams Award.

NHL All-Stars

Active Players' All-Star Selection Records

	First Team Selections		Second Team Selections		Total
GOALTENDERS					
Dominik Hasek	(6)	1993-94; 1994-95; 1996-97; 1997-98; 1998-99; 2000-01.	(0)		6
Patrick Roy	(3)	1988-89; 1989-90; 1991-92.	(2)	1987-88; 1990-91.	5
Ed Belfour	(2)	1990-91; 1992-93.	(1)	1994-95.	3
Tom Barrasso	(1)	1983-84	(2)	1984-85, 1992-93	3
Martin Brodeur	(0)		(2)	1996-97; 1997-98.	2
Olaf Kolzig	(1)	99-2000.	(0)		1
Mike Vernon	(0)		(1)	1988-89.	1
Kirk McLean	(0)		(1)	1991-92.	1
Chris Osgood	(0)		(1)	1995-96.	1
Byron Dafoe	(0)		(1)	1998-99.	1
Roman Turek	(0)		(1)	99-2000.	1
Roman Cechmanek	(0)		(1)	2000-01.	1
DEFENSEMEN					
Chris Chelios	(4)	1988-89; 1992-93; 1994-95; 1995-96.	(2)	1990-91; 1996-97.	6
Al MacInnis	(3)	1989-90; 1990-91; 1998-99.	(3)	1986-87; 1988-89; 1993-94.	6
Scott Stevens	(2)	1987-88; 1993-94.	(3)	1991-92; 1996-97; 2000-01.	5
Brian Leetch	(2)	1991-92; 1996-97.	(3)	1990-91; 1993-94; 1995-96.	5
Nicklas Lidstrom	(4)	1997-98; 1998-99; 99-2000; 2000-01.	(0)		4
Rob Blake	(1)	1997-98.	(2)	99-2000; 2000-01.	3
Larry Murphy	(0)		(3)	1986-87; 1992-93; 1994-95.	3
Chris Pronger	(1)	99-2000.	(1)	1997-98.	2
Eric Desjardins	(0)		(2)	1998-99; 99-2000.	2
Sandis Ozolinsh	(1)	1996-97.	(0)		1
Gary Suter	(0)		(1)	1987-88.	1
Phil Housley	(0)		(1)	1991-92.	1
Scott Niedermayer	(0)		(1)	1997-98.	1
CENTERS					
Mario Lemieux	(5)	1987-88; 1988-89; 1992-93; 1995-96; 1996-97.	(4)	1985-86; 1986-87; 1991-92; 2000-01.	9
Mark Messier	(2)	1989-90; 1991-92.	(0)		2
Peter Forsberg	(2)	1997-98; 1998-99.	(0)		2
Eric Lindros	(1)	1994-95.	(1)	1995-96.	2
Sergei Fedorov	(1)	1993-94.	(0)		1
Steve Yzerman	(1)	99-2000.	(0)		1
Joe Sakic	(1)	2000-01.	(0)		1
Adam Oates	(0)		(1)	1990-91.	1
Alexei Zhamnov	(0)		(1)	1994-95.	1
Alexei Yashin	(0)		(1)	1998-99.	1
Mike Modano	(0)		(1)	99-2000.	1
RIGHT WINGERS					
Jaromir Jagr	(6)	1994-95; 1995-96; 1997-98; 1998-99; 99-2000; 2000-01.	(1)	1996-97.	7
Teemu Selanne	(2)	1992-93; 1996-97.	(2)	1997-98; 1998-99.	4
Brett Hull	(3)	1989-90; 1990-91; 1991-92.	(0)		3
Pavel Bure	(1)	1993-94.	(2)	99-2000; 2000-01.	3
Alexander Mogilny	(0)		(2)	1992-93; 1995-96.	2
Mark Recchi	(0)		(1)	1991-92.	1
Theoren Fleury	(0)		(1)	1994-95.	1
LEFT WINGERS					
Luc Robitaille	(5)	1987-88; 1988-89; 1989-90; 1990-91; 1992-93.	(3)	1986-87; 1991-92; 2000-01.	8
John LeClair	(2)	1994-95, 1997-98.	(3)	1995-96; 1996-97; 1998-99.	5
Paul Kariya	(3)	1995-96; 1996-97; 1998-99.	(1)	99-2000.	4
Mark Messier	(2)	1981-82; 1982-83.	(1)	1983-84.	3
Kevin Stevens	(1)	1991-92.	(2)	1990-91; 1992-93.	3
Brendan Shanahan	(2)	1993-94; 99-2000.	(0)		2
Keith Tkachuk	(0)		(2)	1994-95; 1997-98.	2
Patrik Elias	(1)	2000-01.	(0)		1
Adam Graves	(0)		(1)	1993-94.	1

Leading NHL All-Stars 1930-31 to 2000-01

Player	Pos	Team	NHL Seasons	First Team Selections	Second Team Selections	Total Selections
Howe, Gordie	RW	Detroit	26	12	9	21
Bourque, Raymond	D	Bos., Col.	22	13	6	19
Gretzky, Wayne	C	Edm., L.A., NYR	20	8	7	15
Richard, Maurice	RW	Montreal	18	8	6	14
Hull, Bobby	LW	Chicago	16	10	2	12
Harvey, Doug	D	Mtl., NYR	19	10	1	11
Hall, Glenn	G	Det., Chi., St.L.	18	7	4	11
Beliveau, Jean	C	Montreal	20	6	4	10
Seibert, Earl	D	NYR, Chi.	15	4	6	10
Orr, Bobby	D	Boston	12	8	1	9
Lindsay, Ted	LW	Detroit	17	8	1	9
* Lemieux, Mario	C	Pittsburgh	13	5	4	9
Mahovlich, Frank	LW	Tor., Det., Mtl.	18	3	6	9
Shore, Eddie	D	Boston	14	7	1	8
Esposito, Phil	C	Boston	18	6	2	8
Kelly, Red	D	Detroit	20	6	2	8
Mikita, Stan	C	Chicago	22	6	2	8
Bossy, Mike	RW	NY Islanders	10	5	3	8
Pilote, Pierre	D	Chicago	14	5	3	8
* Robitaille, Luc	LW	Los Angeles	15	5	3	8
Coffey, Paul	D	Edm., Pit., Det.	20	4	4	8
Brimsek, Frank	G	Boston	10	2	6	8
* Jagr, Jaromir	RW	Pittsburgh	11	6	1	7
Potvin, Denis	D	NY Islanders	15	5	2	7
Park, Brad	D	NYR, Bos.	17	5	2	7
Plante, Jacques	G	Mtl., Tor.	18	3	4	7
Gadsby, Bill	D	Chi., NYR, Det.	20	3	4	7
Sawchuk, Terry	G	Detroit	21	3	4	7
Durnan, Bill	G	Montreal	7	6	0	6
* Hasek, Dominik	G	Buffalo	11	6	0	6
Lafleur, Guy	RW	Montreal	16	6	0	6
Dryden, Ken	G	Montreal	8	5	1	6
* Chelios, Chris	D	Mtl., Chi.	17	4	2	6
* MacInnis, Al	D	Cgy., St.L.	19	3	3	6
Clapper, Dit	RW/D	Boston	20	3	3	6
Robinson, Larry	D	Montreal	20	3	3	6
Horton, Tim	D	Toronto	24	3	3	6
Salming, Borje	D	Toronto	17	1	5	6
Cowley, Bill	C	Boston	13	4	1	5
Jackson, Busher	LW	Toronto	15	4	1	5
* Messier, Mark	LW/C	Edm., NYR	21	4	1	5
Conacher, Charlie	RW	Toronto	12	3	2	5
Stewart, Jack	D	Detroit	12	3	2	5
Blake, Toe	LW	Montreal	14	3	2	5
Lach, Elmer	C	Montreal	14	3	2	5
Quackenbush, Bill	D	Det., Bos.	14	3	2	5
Goulet, Michel	LW	Quebec	15	3	2	5
Esposito, Tony	G	Chicago	16	3	2	5
Reardon, Ken	D	Montreal	7	2	3	5
Apps Sr., Syl	C	Toronto	10	2	3	5
* LeClair, John	LW	Mtl., Phi.	10	2	3	5
* Leetch, Brian	D	NY Rangers	11	2	3	5
Giacomin, Ed	G	NY Rangers	13	2	3	5
Kurri, Jari	RW	Edmonton	16	2	3	5
* Roy, Patrick	G	Montreal	16	2	3	5
* Stevens, Scott	D	Wsh., N.J.	19	2	3	5

* Active

Position Leaders in All-Star Selections

Position	Player	First Team	Second Team	Total
GOAL	Glenn Hall	7	4	11
	Frank Brimsek	2	6	8
	Jacques Plante	3	4	7
	Terry Sawchuk	3	4	7
	Bill Durnan	6	0	6
	* Dominik Hasek	6	0	6
	Ken Dryden	5	1	6
DEFENSE	Raymond Bourque	13	6	19
	Doug Harvey	10	1	11
	Earl Seibert	4	6	10
	Bobby Orr	8	1	9
	Eddie Shore	7	1	8
	Red Kelly	6	2	8
	Pierre Pilote	5	3	8
	Paul Coffey	4	4	8

Position	Player	First Team	Second Team	Total
LEFT WING	Bobby Hull	10	2	12
	Ted Lindsay	8	1	9
	Frank Mahovlich	3	6	9
	* Luc Robitaille	5	3	8
	Busher Jackson	4	1	5
	Toe Blake	3	2	5
	Michel Goulet	3	2	5
RIGHT WING	Gordie Howe	12	9	21
	Maurice Richard	8	6	14
	Mike Bossy	5	3	8
	* Jaromir Jagr	6	1	7
	Guy Lafleur	6	0	6
CENTER	Wayne Gretzky	8	7	15
	Jean Beliveau	6	4	10
	* Mario Lemieux	5	4	9
	Phil Esposito	6	2	8
	Stan Mikita	6	2	8

* active player

All-Star Teams

1930-2001

Voting for the NHL All-Star Team is conducted among the representatives of the Professional Hockey Writers' Association at the end of the season.

Following is a list of the First and Second All-Star Teams since their inception in 1930-31.

2000-2001

First Team		Second Team
Hasek, Dominik, Buf.	G	Cechmanek, Roman, Phi.
Lidstrom, Nicklas, Det.	D	Blake, Rob, L.A., Col.
Bourque, Raymond, Col.	D	Stevens, Scott, N.J.
Sakic, Joe, Col.	C	Lemieux, Mario, Pit.
Jagr, Jaromir, Pit.	RW	Bure, Pavel, Fla.
Elias, Patrik, N.J.	LW	Robitaille, Luc, L.A.

1999-2000

First Team		Second Team
Kolzig, Olaf, Wsh.	G	Turek, Roman, St. L.
Pronger, Chris, St. L.	D	Blake, Rob, L.A.
Lindstrom, Nicklas, Det.	D	Desjardins, Eric, Phi.
Yzerman, Steve, Det.	C	Modano, Mike, Dal.
Jagr, Jaromir, Pit.	RW	Bure, Pavel, Fla.
Shanahan, Brendan, Det.	LW	Kariya, Paul, Ana.

1998-99

First Team		Second Team
Hasek, Dominik, Buf.	G	Dafoe, Byron, Bos.
MacInnis, Al, St. L.	D	Bourque, Raymond, Bos.
Lindstrom, Nicklas, Det.	D	Desjardins, Eric, Phi.
Forsberg, Peter, Col.	C	Yashin, Alexei, Ott.
Jagr, Jaromir, Pit.	RW	Selanne, Teemu, Ana.
Kariya, Paul, Ana.	LW	LeClair, John, Phi.

1997-98

First Team		Second Team
Hasek, Dominik, Buf.	G	Brodeur, Martin, N.J.
Lidstrom, Nicklas, Det.	D	Pronger, Chris, St.L.
Blake, Rob, L.A.	D	Niedermayer, Scott, N.J.
Forsberg, Peter, Col.	C	Gretzky, Wayne, NYR
Jagr, Jaromir, Pit.	RW	Selanne, Teemu, Ana.
LeClair, John, Phi.	LW	Tkachuk, Keith, Phx.

1996-97

First Team		Second Team
Hasek, Dominik, Buf.	G	Brodeur, Martin, N.J.
Leetch, Brian, NYR	D	Chelios, Chris, Chi.
Ozolinsh, Sandis, Col.	D	Stevens, Scott, N.J.
Lemieux, Mario, Pit.	C	Gretzky, Wayne, NYR
Selanne, Teemu, Ana.	RW	Jagr, Jaromir, Pit.
Kariya, Paul, Ana.	LW	LeClair, John, Phi.

1995-96

First Team		Second Team
Carey, Jim, Wsh.	G	Osgood, Chris, Det.
Chelios, Chris, Chi.	D	Konstantinov, V., Det.
Bourque, Raymond, Bos.	D	Leetch, Brian, NYR.
Lemieux, Mario, Pit.	C	Lindros, Eric, Phi.
Jagr, Jaromir, Pit.	RW	Mogilny, Alexander, Van.
Kariya, Paul, Ana.	LW	LeClair, John, Phi.

1994-95

First Team		Second Team
Hasek, Dominik, Buf.	G	Belfour, Ed, Chi.
Coffey, Paul, Det.	D	Bourque, Raymond, Bos.
Chelios, Chris, Chi.	D	Murphy, Larry, Pit.
Lindros, Eric, Phi.	C	Zhamnov, Alexei, Wpg.
Jagr, Jaromir, Pit.	RW	Fleury, Theoren, Cgy.
LeClair, John, Mtl., Phi.	LW	Tkachuk, Keith, Wpg.

1993-94

First Team		Second Team
Hasek, Dominik, Buf.	G	Vanbiesbrouck, John, Fla.
Bourque, Raymond, Bos.	D	MacInnis, Al, Cgy.
Stevens, Scott, N.J.	D	Leetch, Brian, NYR
Fedorov, Sergei, Det.	C	Gretzky, Wayne, L.A.
Bure, Pavel, Van.	RW	Neely, Cam, Bos.
Shanahan, Brendan, St. L.	LW	Graves, Adam, NYR

1992-93

First Team		Second Team
Belfour, Ed, Chi.	G	Barrasso, Tom, Pit.
Chelios, Chris, Chi.	D	Murphy, Larry, Pit.
Bourque, Raymond, Bos.	D	Iafrate, Al, Wsh.
Lemieux, Mario, Pit.	C	LaFontaine, Pat, Buf.
Selanne, Teemu, Wpg.	RW	Mogilny, Alexander, Buf.
Robitaille, Luc, L.A.	LW	Stevens, Kevin, Pit.

1991-92

First Team		Second Team
Roy, Patrick, Mtl.	G	McLean, Kirk, Van.
Leetch, Brian, NYR	D	Housley, Phil, Wpg.
Bourque, Raymond, Bos.	D	Stevens, Scott, N.J.
Messier, Mark, NYR	C	Lemieux, Mario, Pit.
Hull, Brett, St. L.	RW	Recchi, Mark, Pit., Phi.
Stevens, Kevin, Pit.	LW	Robitaille, Luc, L.A.

1990-91

First Team		Second Team
Belfour, Ed, Chi.	G	Roy, Patrick, Mtl.
Bourque, Raymond, Bos.	D	Chelios, Chris, Chi.
MacInnis, Al, Cgy.	D	Leetch, Brian, NYR
Gretzky, Wayne, L.A.	C	Oates, Adam, St. L.
Hull, Brett, St. L.	RW	Neely, Cam, Bos.
Robitaille, Luc, L.A.	LW	Stevens, Kevin, Pit.

1989-90

First Team		Second Team
Roy, Patrick, Mtl.	G	Puppa, Daren, Buf.
Bourque, Raymond, Bos.	D	Coffey, Paul, Pit.
MacInnis, Al, Cgy.	D	Wilson, Doug, Chi.
Messier, Mark, Edm.	C	Gretzky, Wayne, L.A.
Hull, Brett, St. L.	RW	Neely, Cam, Bos.
Robitaille, Luc, L.A.	LW	Bellows, Brian, Min.

1988-89

First Team		Second Team
Roy, Patrick, Mtl.	G	Vernon, Mike, Cgy.
Chelios, Chris, Mtl.	D	MacInnis, Al, Cgy.
Coffey, Paul, Pit.	D	Bourque, Raymond, Bos.
Lemieux, Mario, Pit.	C	Gretzky, Wayne, L.A.
Mullen, Joe, Cgy.	RW	Kurri, Jari, Edm.
Robitaille, Luc, L.A.	LW	Gallant, Gerard, Det.

1987-88

First Team		Second Team
Fuhr, Grant, Edm.	G	Roy, Patrick, Mtl.
Bourque, Raymond, Bos.	D	Suter, Gary, Cgy.
Stevens, Scott, Wsh.	D	McCrimmon, Brad, Cgy.
Lemieux, Mario, Pit.	C	Gretzky, Wayne, Edm.
Loob, Hakan, Cgy.	RW	Neely, Cam, Bos.
Robitaille, Luc, L.A.	LW	Goulet, Michel, Que.

1986-87

First Team		Second Team
Hextall, Ron, Phi.	G	Liut, Mike, Hfd.
Bourque, Raymond, Bos.	D	Murphy, Larry, Wsh.
Howe, Mark, Phi.	D	MacInnis, Al, Cgy.
Gretzky, Wayne, Edm.	C	Lemieux, Mario, Pit.
Kurri, Jari, Edm.	RW	Kerr, Tim, Phi.
Goulet, Michel, Que.	LW	Robitaille, Luc, L.A.

1985-86

First Team		Second Team
Vanbiesbrouck, John, NYR	G	Froese, Bob, Phi.
Coffey, Paul, Edm.	D	Robinson, Larry, Mtl.
Howe, Mark, Phi.	D	Bourque, Raymond, Bos.
Gretzky, Wayne, Edm.	C	Lemieux, Mario, Pit.
Bossy, Mike, NYI	RW	Kurri, Jari, Edm.
Goulet, Michel, Que.	LW	Naslund, Mats, Mtl.

1984-85

First Team		Second Team
Lindbergh, Pelle, Phi.	G	Barrasso, Tom, Buf.
Coffey, Paul, Edm.	D	Langway, Rod, Wsh.
Bourque, Raymond, Bos.	D	Wilson, Doug, Chi.
Gretzky, Wayne, Edm.	C	Hawerchuk, Dale, Wpg.
Kurri, Jari, Edm.	RW	Bossy, Mike, NYI
Ogrodnick, John, Det.	LW	Tonelli, John, NYI

1983-84

First Team		Second Team
Barrasso, Tom, Buf.	G	Riggin, Pat, Wsh.
Langway, Rod, Wsh.	D	Coffey, Paul, Edm.
Bourque, Raymond, Bos.	D	Potvin, Denis, NYI
Gretzky, Wayne, Edm.	C	Trottier, Bryan, NYI
Bossy, Mike, NYI	RW	Kurri, Jari, Edm.
Goulet, Michel, Que.	LW	Messier, Mark, Edm.

1982-83

First Team		Second Team
Peeters, Pete, Bos.	G	Melanson, Rollie, NYI
Howe, Mark, Phi.	D	Bourque, Raymond, Bos.
Langway, Rod, Wsh.	D	Coffey, Paul, Edm.
Gretzky, Wayne, Edm.	C	Savard, Denis, Chi.
Bossy, Mike, NYI	RW	McDonald, Lanny, Cgy.
Messier, Mark, Edm.	LW	Goulet, Michel, Que.

1981-82

First Team		Second Team
Smith, Billy, NYI	G	Fuhr, Grant, Edm.
Wilson, Doug, Chi.	D	Coffey, Paul, Edm.
Bourque, Raymond, Bos.	D	Engblom, Brian, Mtl.
Gretzky, Wayne, Edm.	C	Trottier, Bryan, NYI
Bossy, Mike, NYI	RW	Middleton, Rick, Bos.
Messier, Mark, Edm.	LW	Tonelli, John, NYI

Roman Cechmanek was a first-year sensation for the Flyers in 2000-01. Though too old to qualify for the Calder Trophy (which went to fellow netminder Evgeni Nabokov of San Jose), Cechmanek earned honors as a Second-Team All-Star.

Raymond Bourque, NHL All-Star, 1979-80 to 2000-01

ca. 1980

2001

1982

1995

SUPERSTAR DEFENSEMAN RAYMOND BOURQUE retired on the highest of notes at the end of the 2001 playoffs, hoisting the Stanley Cup in the traditional winner's pose.

Bourque's spectacular accomplishments leap out when his career totals are examined. He leads all defensemen with 410 goals and 1,169 assists for 1,579 points in 22 NHL seasons and was a 19-time All-Star Team selection, earning a First Team berth on 13 occasions.

A member of the Boston Bruins from 1979 to 2000, he was the NHL's rookie of the year in 1979-80 and went on to win the Norris Trophy as the League's top defenseman on five occasions.

Traded to Colorado on March 6, 2000, he appeared in the 2001 NHL All-Star Game in Denver and was a major contributor to the Avalanche's 2001 playoff run with ten points, three power-play goals and a plus/minus rating of +9.

1980-81

First Team		Second Team
Liut, Mike, St.L.	G	Lessard, Mario, L.A.
Potvin, Denis, NYI	D	Robinson, Larry, Mtl.
Carlyle, Randy, Pit.	D	Bourque, Raymond, Bos.
Gretzky, Wayne, Edm.	C	Dionne, Marcel, L.A.
Bossy, Mike, NYI	RW	Taylor, Dave, L.A.
Simmer, Charlie, L.A.	LW	Barber, Bill, Phi.

1979-80

First Team		Second Team
Esposito, Tony, Chi.	G	Edwards, Don, Buf.
Robinson, Larry, Mtl.	D	Salming, Borje, Tor.
Bourque, Raymond, Bos.	D	Schoenfeld, Jim, Buf.
Dionne, Marcel, L.A.	C	Gretzky, Wayne, Edm.
Lafleur, Guy, Mtl.	RW	Gare, Danny, Buf.
Simmer, Charlie, L.A.	LW	Shutt, Steve, Mtl.

1978-79

First Team		Second Team
Dryden, Ken, Mtl.	G	Resch, Glenn, NYI
Potvin, Denis, NYI	D	Salming, Borje, Tor.
Robinson, Larry, Mtl.	D	Savard, Serge, Mtl.
Trottier, Bryan, NYI	C	Dionne, Marcel, L.A.
Lafleur, Guy, Mtl.	RW	Bossy, Mike, NYI
Gillies, Clark, NYI	LW	Barber, Bill, Phi.

1977-78

First Team		Second Team
Dryden, Ken, Mtl.	G	Edwards, Don, Buf.
Potvin, Denis, NYI	D	Robinson, Larry, Mtl.
Park, Brad, Bos.	D	Salming, Borje, Tor.
Trottier, Bryan, NYI	C	Sittler, Darryl, Tor.
Lafleur, Guy, Mtl.	RW	Bossy, Mike, NYI
Gillies, Clark, NYI	LW	Shutt, Steve, Mtl.

1976-77

First Team		Second Team
Dryden, Ken, Mtl.	G	Vachon, Rogie, L.A.
Robinson, Larry, Mtl.	D	Potvin, Denis, NYI
Salming, Borje, Tor.	D	Lapointe, Guy, Mtl.
Dionne, Marcel, L.A.	C	Perreault, Gilbert, Buf.
Lafleur, Guy, Mtl.	RW	McDonald, Lanny, Tor.
Shutt, Steve, Mtl.	LW	Martin, Rick, Buf.

1975-76

First Team		Second Team
Dryden, Ken, Mtl.	G	Resch, Glenn, NYI
Potvin, Denis, NYI	D	Salming, Borje, Tor.
Park, Brad, Bos.	D	Lapointe, Guy, Mtl.
Clarke, Bobby, Phi.	C	Perreault, Gilbert, Buf.
Lafleur, Guy, Mtl.	RW	Leach, Reggie, Phi.
Barber, Bill, Phi.	LW	Martin, Rick, Buf.

1974-75

First Team		Second Team
Parent, Bernie, Phi.	G	Vachon, Rogie, L.A.
Orr, Bobby, Bos.	D	Lapointe, Guy, Mtl.
Potvin, Denis, NYI	D	Salming, Borje, Tor.
Clarke, Bobby, Phi.	C	Esposito, Phil, Bos.
Lafleur, Guy, Mtl.	RW	Robert, René, Buf.
Martin, Rick, Buf.	LW	Vickers, Steve, NYR

1973-74

First Team		Second Team
Parent, Bernie, Phi.	G	Esposito, Tony, Chi.
Orr, Bobby, Bos.	D	White, Bill, Chi.
Park, Brad, NYR	D	Ashbee, Barry, Phi.
Esposito, Phil, Bos.	C	Clarke, Bobby, Phi.
Hodge, Ken, Bos.	RW	Redmond, Mickey, Det.
Martin, Rick, Buf.	LW	Cashman, Wayne, Bos.

1972-73

First Team		Second Team
Dryden, Ken, Mtl.	G	Esposito, Tony, Chi.
Orr, Bobby, Bos.	D	Park, Brad, NYR
Lapointe, Guy, Mtl.	D	White, Bill, Chi.
Esposito, Phil, Bos.	C	Clarke, Bobby, Phi.
Redmond, Mickey, Det.	RW	Cournoyer, Yvan, Mtl.
Mahovlich, Frank, Mtl.	LW	Hull, Dennis, Chi.

1971-72

First Team		Second Team
Esposito, Tony, Chi.	G	Dryden, Ken, Mtl.
Orr, Bobby, Bos.	D	White, Bill, Chi.
Park, Brad, NYR	D	Stapleton, Pat, Chi.
Esposito, Phil, Bos.	C	Ratelle, Jean, NYR
Gilbert, Rod, NYR	RW	Cournoyer, Yvan, Mtl.
Hull, Bobby, Chi.	LW	Hadfield, Vic, NYR

1970-71

First Team		Second Team
Giacomin, Ed, NYR	G	Plante, Jacques, Tor.
Orr, Bobby, Bos.	D	Park, Brad, NYR
Tremblay, J.C., Mtl.	D	Stapleton, Pat, Chi.
Esposito, Phil, Bos.	C	Keon, Dave, Tor.
Hodge, Ken, Bos.	RW	Cournoyer, Yvan, Mtl.
Bucyk, John, Bos.	LW	Hull, Bobby, Chi.

1969-70

First Team		Second Team
Esposito, Tony, Chi.	G	Giacomin, Ed, NYR
Orr, Bobby, Bos.	D	Brewer, Carl, Det.
Park, Brad, NYR	D	Laperriere, Jacques, Mtl.
Esposito, Phil, Bos.	C	Mikita, Stan, Chi.
Howe, Gordie, Det.	RW	McKenzie, John, Bos.
Hull, Bobby, Chi.	LW	Mahovlich, Frank, Det.

1968-69

First Team		Second Team
Hall, Glenn, St.L.	G	Giacomin, Ed, NYR
Orr, Bobby, Bos.	D	Green, Ted, Bos.
Horton, Tim, Tor.	D	Harris, Ted, Mtl.
Esposito, Phil, Bos.	C	Béliveau, Jean, Mtl.
Howe, Gordie, Det.	RW	Cournoyer, Yvan, Mtl.
Hull, Bobby, Chi.	LW	Mahovlich, Frank, Det.

1967-68

First Team		Second Team
Worsley, Gump, Mtl.	G	Giacomin, Ed, NYR
Orr, Bobby, Bos.	D	Tremblay, J.C., Mtl.
Horton, Tim, Tor.	D	Neilson, Jim, NYR
Mikita, Stan, Chi.	C	Esposito, Phil, Bos.
Howe, Gordie, Det.	RW	Gilbert, Rod, NYR
Hull, Bobby, Chi.	LW	Bucyk, John, Bos.

1966-67

First Team		Second Team
Giacomin, Ed, NYR	G	Hall, Glenn, Chi.
Pilote, Pierre, Chi.	D	Horton, Tim, Tor.
Howell, Harry, NYR	D	Orr, Bobby, Bos.
Mikita, Stan, Chi.	C	Ullman, Norm, Det.
Wharram, Kenny, Chi.	RW	Howe, Gordie, Det.
Hull, Bobby, Chi.	LW	Marshall, Don, NYR

1965-66

First Team		Second Team
Hall, Glenn, Chi.	G	Worsley, Gump, Mtl.
Laperriere, Jacques, Mtl.	D	Stanley, Allan, Tor.
Pilote, Pierre, Chi.	D	Stapleton, Pat, Chi.
Mikita, Stan, Chi.	C	Béliveau, Jean, Mtl.
Howe, Gordie, Det.	RW	Rousseau, Bobby, Mtl.
Hull, Bobby, Chi.	LW	Mahovlich, Frank, Tor.

1964-65

First Team		Second Team
Crozier, Roger, Det.	G	Hodge, Charlie, Mtl.
Pilote, Pierre, Chi.	D	Gadsby, Bill, Det.
Laperriere, Jacques, Mtl.	D	Brewer, Carl, Tor.
Ullman, Norm, Det.	C	Mikita, Stan, Chi.
Provost, Claude, Mtl.	RW	Howe, Gordie, Det.
Hull, Bobby, Chi.	LW	Mahovlich, Frank, Tor.

1963-64

First Team		Second Team
Hall, Glenn, Chi.	G	Hodge, Charlie, Mtl.
Pilote, Pierre, Chi.	D	Vasko, Elmer, Chi.
Horton, Tim, Tor.	D	Laperriere, Jacques, Mtl.
Mikita, Stan, Chi.	C	Béliveau, Jean, Mtl.
Wharram, Kenny, Chi.	RW	Howe, Gordie, Det.
Hull, Bobby, Chi.	LW	Mahovlich, Frank, Tor.

1962-63

First Team		Second Team
Hall, Glenn, Chi.	G	Sawchuk, Terry, Det.
Pilote, Pierre, Chi.	D	Horton, Tim, Tor.
Brewer, Carl, Tor.	D	Vasko, Elmer, Chi.
Mikita, Stan, Chi.	C	Richard, Henri, Mtl.
Howe, Gordie, Det.	RW	Bathgate, Andy, NYR
Mahovlich, Frank, Tor.	LW	Hull, Bobby, Chi.

1961-62

First Team		Second Team
Plante, Jacques, Mtl.	G	Hall, Glenn, Chi.
Harvey, Doug, NYR	D	Brewer, Carl, Tor.
Talbot, Jean-Guy, Mtl.	D	Pilote, Pierre, Chi.
Mikita, Stan, Chi.	C	Keon, Dave, Tor.
Bathgate, Andy, NYR	RW	Howe, Gordie, Det.
Hull, Bobby, Chi.	LW	Mahovlich, Frank, Tor.

1960-61

First Team		Second Team
Bower, Johnny, Tor.	G	Hall, Glenn, Chi.
Harvey, Doug, Mtl.	D	Stanley, Allan, Tor.
Pronovost, Marcel, Det.	D	Pilote, Pierre, Chi.
Béliveau, Jean, Mtl.	C	Richard, Henri, Mtl.
Geoffrion, Bernie, Mtl.	RW	Howe, Gordie, Det.
Mahovlich, Frank, Tor.	LW	Moore, Dickie, Mtl.

1959-60

First Team		Second Team
Hall, Glenn, Chi.	G	Plante, Jacques, Mtl.
Harvey, Doug, Mtl.	D	Stanley, Allan, Tor.
Pronovost, Marcel, Det.	D	Pilote, Pierre, Chi.
Béliveau, Jean, Mtl.	C	Horvath, Bronco, Bos.
Howe, Gordie, Det.	RW	Geoffrion, Bernie, Mtl.
Hull, Bobby, Chi.	LW	Prentice, Dean, NYR

1958-59

First Team		Second Team
Plante, Jacques, Mtl.	G	Sawchuk, Terry, Det.
Johnson, Tom, Mtl.	D	Pronovost, Marcel, Det.
Gadsby, Bill, NYR	D	Harvey, Doug, Mtl.
Béliveau, Jean, Mtl.	C	Richard, Henri, Mtl.
Bathgate, Andy, NYR	RW	Howe, Gordie, Det.
Moore, Dickie, Mtl.	LW	Delvecchio, Alex, Det.

1957-58

First Team		Second Team
Hall, Glenn, Chi.	G	Plante, Jacques, Mtl.
Harvey, Doug, Mtl.	D	Flaman, Fern, Bos.
Gadsby, Bill, NYR	D	Pronovost, Marcel, Det.
Richard, Henri, Mtl.	C	Béliveau, Jean, Mtl.
Howe, Gordie, Det.	RW	Bathgate, Andy, NYR
Moore, Dickie, Mtl.	LW	Henry, Camille, NYR

1956-57

First Team		Second Team
Hall, Glenn, Det.	G	Plante, Jacques, Mtl.
Harvey, Doug, Mtl.	D	Flaman, Fern, Bos.
Kelly, Red, Det.	D	Gadsby, Bill, NYR
Béliveau, Jean, Mtl.	C	Litzenberger, Ed, Chi.
Howe, Gordie, Det.	RW	Richard, Maurice, Mtl.
Lindsay, Ted, Det.	LW	Chevrefils, Real, Bos.

1955-56

First Team		Second Team
Plante, Jacques, Mtl.	G	Hall, Glenn, Det.
Harvey, Doug, Mtl.	D	Kelly, Red, Det.
Gadsby, Bill, NYR	D	Johnson, Tom, Mtl.
Béliveau, Jean, Mtl.	C	Sloan, Tod, Tor.
Richard, Maurice, Mtl.	RW	Howe, Gordie, Det.
Lindsay, Ted, Det.	LW	Olmstead, Bert, Mtl.

1954-55

First Team		Second Team
Lumley, Harry, Tor.	G	Sawchuk, Terry, Det.
Harvey, Doug, Mtl.	D	Goldham, Bob, Det.
Kelly, Red, Det.	D	Flaman, Fern, Bos.
Béliveau, Jean, Mtl.	C	Mosdell, Kenny, Mtl.
Richard, Maurice, Mtl.	RW	Geoffrion, Bernie, Mtl.
Smith, Sid, Tor.	LW	Lewicki, Danny, NYR

Stan Mikita (#21), Pierre Pilote (#3) and Glenn Hall (#1)

Carl Brewer

Gordie Howe

Frank Mahovolich

1962-63 NHL First All-Star Team

BLACKHAWKS TEAMMATES Stan Mikita, Pierre Pilote and Glenn Hall in the photo above all rank highly in career All-Star selections at their position. Mikita and Pilote were eight-time All-Stars – Mikita at center and Pilote on defense – while Hall tops all goaltenders with 11 selections. All three were chosen to the First Team together three times in the 1960s. Frank Mahovlich (at left, bottom), Gordie Howe (at left, center) and Carl Brewer (far left) joined them in 1962-63. Mahovlich earned nine career All-Star berths, while Howe holds the all-time record with 21 selections. His mark of 12 appearances on the First Team was surpassed by Raymond Bourque in 2000-01.

1953-54

First Team		Second Team
Lumley, Harry, Tor.	G	Sawchuk, Terry, Det.
Kelly, Red, Det.	D	Gadsby, Bill, Chi.
Harvey, Doug, Mtl.	D	Horton, Tim, Tor.
Mosdell, Kenny, Mtl.	C	Kennedy, Ted, Tor.
Howe, Gordie, Det.	RW	Richard, Maurice, Mtl.
Lindsay, Ted, Det.	LW	Sandford, Ed, Bos.

1952-53

First Team		Second Team
Sawchuk, Terry, Det.	G	McNeil, Gerry, Mtl.
Kelly, Red, Det.	D	Quackenbush, Bill, Bos.
Harvey, Doug, Mtl.	D	Gadsby, Bill, Chi.
Mackell, Fleming, Bos.	C	Delvecchio, Alex, Det.
Howe, Gordie, Det.	RW	Richard, Maurice, Mtl.
Lindsay, Ted, Det.	LW	Olmstead, Bert, Mtl.

1951-52

First Team		Second Team
Sawchuk, Terry, Det.	G	Henry, Jim, Bos.
Kelly, Red, Det.	D	Buller, Hy, NYR
Harvey, Doug, Mtl.	D	Thomson, Jimmy, Tor.
Lach, Elmer, Mtl.	C	Schmidt, Milt, Bos.
Howe, Gordie, Det.	RW	Richard, Maurice, Mtl.
Lindsay, Ted, Det.	LW	Smith, Sid, Tor.

1950-51

First Team		Second Team
Sawchuk, Terry, Det.	G	Rayner, Chuck, NYR
Kelly, Red, Det.	D	Thomson, Jimmy, Tor.
Quackenbush, Bill, Bos.	D	Reise Jr., Leo, Det.
Schmidt, Milt, Bos.	C	Abel, Sid, Det.
	(tied)	Kennedy, Ted, Tor.
Howe, Gordie, Det.	RW	Richard, Maurice, Mtl.
Lindsay, Ted, Det.	LW	Smith, Sid, Tor.

1949-50

First Team		Second Team
Durnan, Bill, Mtl.	G	Rayner, Chuck, NYR
Mortson, Gus, Tor.	D	Reise Jr., Leo, Det.
Reardon, Ken, Mtl.	D	Kelly, Red, Det.
Abel, Sid, Det.	C	Kennedy, Ted, Tor.
Richard, Maurice, Mtl.	RW	Howe, Gordie, Det.
Lindsay, Ted, Det.	LW	Leswick, Tony, NYR

1948-49

First Team		Second Team
Durnan, Bill, Mtl.	G	Rayner, Chuck, NYR
Quackenbush, Bill, Det.	D	Harmon, Glen, Mtl.
Stewart, Jack, Det.	D	Reardon, Ken, Mtl.
Abel, Sid, Det.	C	Bentley, Doug, Chi.
Richard, Maurice, Mtl.	RW	Howe, Gordie, Det.
Conacher, Roy, Chi.	LW	Lindsay, Ted, Det.

1947-48

First Team		Second Team
Broda, Turk, Tor.	G	Brimsek, Frank, Bos.
Quackenbush, Bill, Det.	D	Reardon, Ken, Mtl.
Stewart, Jack, Det.	D	Colville, Neil, NYR
Lach, Elmer, Mtl.	C	O'Connor, Buddy, NYR
Richard, Maurice, Mtl.	RW	Poile, Bud, Chi.
Lindsay, Ted, Det.	LW	Stewart, Gaye, Chi.

1946-47

First Team		Second Team
Durnan, Bill, Mtl.	G	Brimsek, Frank, Bos.
Reardon, Ken, Mtl.	D	Stewart, Jack, Det.
Bouchard, Butch, Mtl.	D	Quackenbush, Bill, Det.
Schmidt, Milt, Bos.	C	Bentley, Max, Chi.
Richard, Maurice, Mtl.	RW	Bauer, Bobby, Bos.
Bentley, Doug, Chi.	LW	Dumart, Woody, Bos.

1945-46

First Team		Second Team
Durnan, Bill, Mtl.	G	Brimsek, Frank, Bos.
Crawford, Jack, Bos.	D	Reardon, Ken, Mtl.
Bouchard, Butch, Mtl.	D	Stewart, Jack, Det.
Bentley, Max, Chi.	C	Lach, Elmer, Mtl.
Richard, Maurice, Mtl.	RW	Mosienko, Bill, Chi.
Stewart, Gaye, Tor.	LW	Blake, Toe, Mtl.
Irvin, Dick, Mtl.	Coach	Gottselig, Johnny, Chi.

1944-45

First Team		Second Team
Durnan, Bill, Mtl.	G	Karakas, Mike, Chi.
Bouchard, Butch, Mtl.	D	Harmon, Glen, Mtl.
Hollett, Flash, Det.	D	Pratt, Babe, Tor.
Lach, Elmer, Mtl.	C	Cowley, Bill, Bos.
Richard, Maurice, Mtl.	RW	Mosienko, Bill, Chi.
Blake, Toe, Mtl.	LW	Howe, Syd, Det.
Irvin, Dick, Mtl.	Coach	Adams, Jack, Det.

1943-44

First Team		Second Team
Durnan, Bill, Mtl.	G	Bibeault, Paul, Tor.
Seibert, Earl, Chi.	D	Bouchard, Butch, Mtl.
Pratt, Babe, Tor.	D	Clapper, Dit, Bos.
Cowley, Bill, Bos.	C	Lach, Elmer, Mtl.
Carr, Lorne, Tor.	RW	Richard, Maurice, Mtl.
Bentley, Doug, Chi.	LW	Cain, Herb, Bos.
Irvin, Dick, Mtl.	Coach	Day, Hap, Tor.

1942-43

First Team		Second Team
Mowers, Johnny, Det.	G	Brimsek, Frank, Bos.
Seibert, Earl, Chi.	D	Crawford, Jack, Bos.
Stewart, Jack, Det.	D	Hollett, Flash, Bos.
Cowley, Bill, Bos.	C	Apps Sr., Syl, Tor.
Carr, Lorne, Tor.	RW	Hextall Sr., Bryan, NYR
Bentley, Doug, Chi.	LW	Patrick, Lynn, NYR
Adams, Jack, Det.	Coach	Ross, Art, Bos.

1941-42

First Team		Second Team
Brimsek, Frank, Bos.	G	Broda, Turk, Tor.
Seibert, Earl, Chi.	D	Egan, Pat, Bro.
Anderson, Tom, Bro.	D	McDonald, Bucko, Tor.
Apps Sr., Syl, Tor.	C	Watson, Phil, NYR
Hextall Sr., Bryan, NYR	RW	Drillon, Gordie, Tor.
Patrick, Lynn, NYR	LW	Abel, Sid, Det.
Boucher, Frank, NYR	Coach	Thompson, Paul, Chi.

1940-41

First Team		Second Team
Broda, Turk, Tor.	G	Brimsek, Frank, Bos.
Clapper, Dit, Bos.	D	Seibert, Earl, Chi.
Stanowski, Wally, Tor.	D	Heller, Ott, NYR
Cowley, Bill, Bos.	C	Apps Sr., Syl, Tor.
Hextall Sr., Bryan, NYR	RW	Bauer, Bobby, Bos.
Schriner, Sweeney, Tor.	LW	Dumart, Woody, Bos.
Weiland, Cooney, Bos.	Coach	Irvin, Dick, Mtl.

1939-40

First Team		Second Team
Kerr, Dave, NYR	G	Brimsek, Frank, Bos.
Clapper, Dit, Bos.	D	Coulter, Art, NYR
Goodfellow, Ebbie, Det.	D	Seibert, Earl, Chi.
Schmidt, Milt, Bos.	C	Colville, Neil, NYR
Hextall Sr., Bryan, NYR	RW	Bauer, Bobby, Bos.
Blake, Toe, Mtl.	LW	Dumart, Woody, Bos.
Thompson, Paul, Chi.	Coach	Boucher, Frank, NYR

1938-39

First Team		Second Team
Brimsek, Frank, Bos.	G	Robertson, Earl, NYA
Shore, Eddie, Bos.	D	Seibert, Earl, Chi.
Clapper, Dit, Bos.	D	Coulter, Art, NYR
Apps Sr., Syl, Tor.	C	Colville, Neil, NYR
Drillon, Gordie, Tor.	RW	Bauer, Bobby, Bos.
Blake, Toe, Mtl.	LW	Gottselig, Johnny, Chi.
Ross, Art, Bos.	Coach	Dutton, Red, NYA

1937-38

First Team		Second Team
Thompson, Tiny, Bos.	G	Kerr, Dave, NYR
Shore, Eddie, Bos.	D	Coulter, Art, NYR
Siebert, Babe, Mtl.	D	Seibert, Earl, Chi.
Cowley, Bill, Bos.	C	Apps Sr., Syl, Tor.
Dillon, Cecil, NYR	RW	
Drillon, Gordie, Tor.	(tied)	
Thompson, Paul, Chi.	LW	Blake, Toe, Mtl.
Patrick, Lester, NYR	Coach	Ross, Art, Bos.

1936-37

First Team		Second Team
Smith, Normie, Det.	G	Cude, Wilf, Mtl.
Siebert, Babe, Mtl.	D	Seibert, Earl, Chi.
Goodfellow, Ebbie, Det.	D	Conacher, Lionel, Mtl. M.
Barry, Marty, Det.	C	Chapman, Art, NYA
Aurie, Larry, Det.	RW	Dillon, Cecil, NYR
Jackson, Busher, Tor.	LW	Schriner, Sweeney, NYA
Adams, Jack, Det.	Coach	Hart, Cecil, Mtl.

1935-36

First Team		Second Team
Thompson, Tiny, Bos.	G	Cude, Wilf, Mtl.
Shore, Eddie, Bos.	D	Seibert, Earl, Chi.
Siebert, Babe, Bos.	D	Goodfellow, Ebbie, Det.
Smith, Hooley, Mtl. M.	C	Thoms, Bill, Tor.
Conacher, Charlie, Tor.	RW	Dillon, Cecil, NYR
Schriner, Sweeney, NYA	LW	Thompson, Paul, Chi.
Patrick, Lester, NYR	Coach	Gorman, Tommy, Mtl. M.

1934-35

First Team		Second Team
Chabot, Lorne, Chi.	G	Thompson, Tiny, Bos.
Shore, Eddie, Bos.	D	Wentworth, Cy, Mtl. M.
Seibert, Earl, NYR	D	Coulter, Art, Chi.
Boucher, Frank, NYR	C	Weiland, Cooney, Det.
Conacher, Charlie, Tor.	RW	Clapper, Dit, Bos.
Jackson, Busher, Tor.	LW	Joliat, Aurel, Mtl.
Patrick, Lester, NYR	Coach	Irvin, Dick, Tor.

1933-34

First Team		Second Team
Gardiner, Chuck, Chi.	G	Worters, Roy, NYA
Clancy, King, Tor.	D	Shore, Eddie, Bos.
Conacher, Lionel, Chi.	D	Johnson, Ching, NYR
Boucher, Frank, NYR	C	Primeau, Joe, Tor.
Conacher, Charlie, Tor.	RW	Cook, Bill, NYR
Jackson, Busher, Tor.	LW	Joliat, Aurel, Mtl.
Patrick, Lester, NYR	Coach	Irvin, Dick, Tor.

1932-33

First Team		Second Team
Roach, John Ross, Det.	G	Gardiner, Chuck, Chi.
Shore, Eddie, Bos.	D	Clancy, King, Tor.
Johnson, Ching, NYR	D	Conacher, Lionel, Mtl. M.
Boucher, Frank, NYR	C	Morenz, Howie, Mtl.
Cook, Bill, NYR	RW	Conacher, Charlie, Tor.
Northcott, Baldy, Mtl M.	LW	Jackson, Busher, Tor.
Patrick, Lester, NYR	Coach	Irvin, Dick, Tor.

1931-32

First Team		Second Team
Gardiner, Chuck, Chi.	G	Worters, Roy, NYA
Shore, Eddie, Bos.	D	Mantha, Sylvio, Mtl.
Johnson, Ching, NYR	D	Clancy, King, Tor.
Morenz, Howie, Mtl.	C	Smith, Hooley, Mtl. M.
Cook, Bill, NYR	RW	Conacher, Charlie, Tor.
Jackson, Busher, Tor.	LW	Joliat, Aurel, Mtl.
Patrick, Lester, NYR	Coach	Irvin, Dick, Tor.

1930-31

First Team		Second Team
Gardiner, Chuck, Chi.	G	Thompson, Tiny, Bos.
Shore, Eddie, Bos.	D	Mantha, Sylvio, Mtl.
Clancy, King, Tor.	D	Johnson, Ching, NYR
Morenz, Howie, Mtl.	C	Boucher, Frank, NYR
Cook, Bill, NYR	RW	Clapper, Dit, Bos.
Joliat, Aurel, Mtl.	LW	Cook, Bun, NYR
Patrick, Lester, NYR	Coach	Irvin, Dick, Chi.

In 1929, Roy Worters became the first goalie to win the Hart Trophy as MVP. He won the Vezina Trophy in 1931 and was a Second-Team All-Star in 1932 and 1934.

All-Star Game Results

Year	Venue	Score	Coaches	Attendance
2001	Colorado	North America 14, World 12	Joel Quenneville, Jacques Martin	18,646
2000	Toronto	World 9, North America 4	Scotty Bowman, Pat Quinn	19,300
1999	Tampa Bay	North America 8, World 6	Lindy Ruff, Ken Hitchcock	19,758
1998	Vancouver	North America 8, World 7	Jacques Lemaire, Ken Hitchcock	18,422
1997	San Jose	East 11, West 7	Doug MacLean, Ken Hitchcock	17,422
1996	Boston	East 5, West 4	Doug MacLean, Scotty Bowman	17,565
1994	NY Rangers	East 9, West 8	Jacques Demers, Barry Melrose	18,200
1993	Montreal	Wales 16, Campbell 6	Scotty Bowman, Mike Keenan	17,137
1992	Philadelphia	Campbell 10, Wales 6	Bob Gainey, Scotty Bowman	17,380
1991	Chicago	Campbell 11, Wales 5	John Muckler, Mike Milbury	18,472
1990	Pittsburgh	Wales 12, Campbell 7	Pat Burns, Terry Crisp	16,236
1989	Edmonton	Campbell 9, Wales 5	Glen Sather, Terry O'Reilly	17,503
1988	St. Louis	Wales 6, Campbell 5 OT	Mike Keenan, Glen Sather	17,878
1986	Hartford	Wales 4, Campbell 3 OT	Mike Keenan, Glen Sather	15,100
1985	Calgary	Wales 6, Campbell 4	Al Arbour, Glen Sather	16,825
1984	New Jersey	Wales 7, Campbell 6	Al Arbour, Glen Sather	18,939
1983	NY Islanders	Campbell 9, Wales 3	Roger Neilson, Al Arbour	15,230
1982	Washington	Wales 4, Campbell 2	Al Arbour, Glen Sonmor	18,130
1981	Los Angeles	Campbell 4, Wales 1	Pat Quinn, Scotty Bowman	15,761
1980	Detroit	Wales 6, Campbell 3	Scotty Bowman, Al Arbour	21,002
1978	Buffalo	Wales 3, Campbell 2 OT	Scotty Bowman, Fred Shero	16,433
1977	Vancouver	Wales 4, Campbell 3	Scotty Bowman, Fred Shero	15,607
1976	Philadelphia	Wales 7, Campbell 5	Floyd Smith, Fred Shero	16,436
1975	Montreal	Wales 7, Campbell 1	Bep Guidolin, Fred Shero	16,080
1974	Chicago	West 6, East 4	Billy Reay, Scotty Bowman	16,426
1973	NY Rangers	East 5, West 4	Tom Johnson, Billy Reay	16,986
1972	Minnesota	East 3, West 2	Al MacNeil, Billy Reay	15,423
1971	Boston	West 2, East 1	Scotty Bowman, Harry Sinden	14,790
1970	St. Louis	East 4, West 1	Claude Ruel, Scotty Bowman	16,587
1969	Montreal	East 3, West 3	Toe Blake, Scotty Bowman	16,260
1968	Toronto	Toronto 4, All-Stars 3	Punch Imlach, Toe Blake	15,753
1967	Montreal	Montreal 3, All-Stars 0	Toe Blake, Sid Abel	14,284
1965	Montreal	All-Stars 5, Montreal 2	Billy Reay, Toe Blake	13,529
1964	Toronto	All-Stars 3, Toronto 2	Sid Abel, Punch Imlach	14,232
1963	Toronto	All-Stars 3, Toronto 3	Sid Abel, Punch Imlach	14,034
1962	Toronto	Toronto 4, All-Stars 1	Punch Imlach, Rudy Pilous	14,236
1961	Chicago	All-Stars 3, Chicago 1	Sid Abel, Rudy Pilous	14,534
1960	Montreal	All-Stars 2, Montreal 1	Punch Imlach, Toe Blake	13,949
1959	Montreal	Montreal 6, All-Stars 1	Toe Blake, Punch Imlach	13,818
1958	Montreal	Montreal 6, All-Stars 3	Toe Blake, Milt Schmidt	13,989
1957	Montreal	All-Stars 5, Montreal 3	Milt Schmidt, Toe Blake	13,003
1956	Montreal	All-Stars 1, Montreal 1	Jim Skinner, Toe Blake	13,095
1955	Detroit	Detroit 3, All-Stars 1	Jim Skinner, Dick Irvin	10,111
1954	Detroit	All-Stars 2, Detroit 2	King Clancy, Jim Skinner	10,689
1953	Montreal	All-Stars 3, Montreal 1	Lynn Patrick, Dick Irvin	14,153
1952	Detroit	1st Team 1, 2nd Team 1	Tommy Ivan, Dick Irvin	10,680
1951	Toronto	1st Team 2, 2nd Team 2	Joe Primeau, Dick Irvin	11,469
1950	Detroit	Detroit 7, All-Stars 1	Tommy Ivan, Lynn Patrick	9,166
1949	Toronto	All-Stars 3, Toronto 1	Tommy Ivan, Hap Day	13,541
1948	Chicago	All-Stars 3, Toronto 1	Tommy Ivan, Hap Day	12,794
1947	Toronto	All-Stars 4, Toronto 3	Dick Irvin, Hap Day	14,169

There was no All-Star contest during the calendar year of 1966 because the game was moved from the start of season to mid-season. In 1979, the Challenge Cup series between the Soviet Union and Team NHL replaced the All-Star Game. In 1987, Rendez-Vous '87, two games between the Soviet Union and Team NHL replaced the All-Star Game. Rendez-Vous '87 scores: game one, NHL All-Stars 4, Soviet Union 3; game two, Soviet Union 5, NHL All-Stars 3. There was no All-Star Game in 1995 due to a labor disruption.

2000-01 All-Star Game Summary

February 4, 2001 at Denver North America 14, World 12

PLAYERS ON ICE: **North America** — Brodeur, Burke, Roy, Bourque, R. Blake, Jovanovski, Leetch, S. Niedermayer, S. Stevens, Jas. Allison, Amonte, Audette, Fleury, Gagne, Guerin, B. Hull, P. Kariya, M. Lemieux, L. Robitaille, Sakic, Weight

The World — Cechmanek, Hasek, Nabokov, Lidstrom, Ozolinsh, Gonchar, Niinimaa, Numminen, Ragnarsson, P. Bure, Forsberg, Bonk, Fedorov, Hejduk, Hossa, Kovalev, Modin, Naslund, Palffy, Samsonov, Sundin

SUMMARY

First Period

1. North America	Fleury (1)	(Kariya, S. Stevens)	0:49
2. World	Sundin (1)	(Modin, Lidstrom)	8:01
3. North America	Guerin (1)	(Weight)	11:22
4. North America	Robitaille (1)	(Allison, Blake)	12:00
5. World	Sundin (2)	(Modin, Numminen)	17:05
6. World	Forsberg (1)	(Samsonov)	17:26

PENALTIES: None

Second Period

7. World	Naslund (1)	(Gonchar, Hossa)	2:40
8. North America	Amonte (1)	(Weight)	3:25
9. North America	M. Lemieux (1)	(S. Stevens)	4:53
10. North America	Sakic (1)	(Kariya, Fleury)	6:59
11. World	Samsonov (1)	(Forsberg, Lidstrom)	8:08
12. North America	Amonte (2)	(Guerin, Leetch)	8:36
13. North America	Guerin (2)	(Amonte)	14:36
14. World	Palffy (1)	(Modin, Sundin)	17:01
15. North America	Robitaille (1)	(Audette)	18:13
16. World	Fedorov (1)	(P. Bure, Kovalev)	19:35

PENALTIES: None

Third Period

17. World	Hejduk (1)	(Ozolinsh, Forsberg)	1:05
18. North America	Weight (1)	(Amonte, Guerin)	2:56
19. North America	Gagne (1)	(Hull, M. Lemieux)	5:16
20. World	Bonk (1)	(Naslund, Hossa)	5:50
21. World	Fedorov (2)	(P. Bure, Numminen)	8:55
22. North America	Fleury (2)	(Kariya)	12:03
23. World	Kovalev (1)	(Sundin, Gonchar)	15:57
24. North America	Gagne (2)	(unassisted)	17:07
25. North America	Guerin (3)	(Jovanoski, Weight)	17:58
26. World	Lidstrom (1)	(Palffy, Modin)	19:35

PENALTIES: None

SHOTS ON GOAL BY:

North America	17	20	16	**53**
World	11	11	23	**45**

	Goaltenders:	Time	SA	GA	ENG	Dec
N. America	Roy	20:00	11	3	0	
N. America	Burke	20:00	11	4	0	
N. America	Brodeur	20:00	23	5	0	W
World	Hasek	20:00	17	3	0	
World	Cechmanek	20:00	20	6	0	
World	Nabokov	20:00	16	5	0	L

PP Conversions: North America 0/0; World 0/0.

Referees: Mick McGeough, Richard Trottier Linesmen: Randy Mitton, Mark Wheler

Attendance: 18,646.

NHL ALL-ROOKIE TEAM

Voting for the NHL All-Rookie Team is conducted among the representatives of the Professional Hockey Writers' Association at the end of the season. The rookie all-star team was first selected for the 1982-83 season.

2000-01

Evgeni Nabokov, San Jose — *Goal*
Lubomir Visnovsky, Los Angeles — *Defense*
Colin White, New Jersey — *Defense*
Martin Havlat, Ottawa — *Forward*
Brad Richards, Tampa Bay — *Forward*
Shane Willis, Carolina — *Forward*

1999-2000

Brian Boucher, Philadelphia — *Goal*
Brian Rafalski, New Jersey — *Defense*
Brad Stuart, San Jose — *Defense*
Simon Gagne, Philadelphia — *Forward*
Scott Gomez, New Jersey — *Forward*
Michael York, NY Rangers — *Forward*

1997-98

Jamie Storr, Los Angeles — *Goal*
Mattias Ohlund, Vancouver — *Defense*
Derek Morris, Calgary — *Defense*
Sergei Samsonov, Boston — *Forward*
Patrick Elias, New Jersey — *Forward*
Mike Johnson, Toronto — *Forward*

1995-96

Corey Hirsch, Vancouver — *Goal*
Ed Jovanovski, Florida — *Defense*
Kyle McLaren, Boston — *Defense*
Daniel Alfredsson, Ottawa — *Forward*
Eric Daze, Chicago — *Forward*
Petr Sykora, New Jersey — *Forward*

1993-94

Martin Brodeur, New Jersey — *Goal*
Chris Pronger, Hartford — *Defense*
Boris Mironov, Wpg./Edm. — *Defense*
Jason Arnott, Edmonton — *Center*
Mikael Renberg, Philadelphia — *Wing*
Oleg Petrov, Montreal — *Wing*

1998-99

Jamie Storr, Los Angeles
Tom Poti, Edmonton
Sami Salo, Ottawa
Chris Drury, Colorado
Milan Hejduk, Colorado
Marian Hossa, Ottawa

1996-97

Patrick Lalime, Pittsburgh
Bryan Berard, NY Islanders
Janne Niinimaa, Philadelphia
Jarome Iginla, Calgary
Jim Campbell, St. Louis
Sergei Berezin, Toronto

1994-95

Jim Carey, Washington
Chris Therien, Philadelphia
Kenny Jonsson, Toronto
Peter Forsberg, Quebec
Jeff Friesen, San Jose
Paul Kariya, Anaheim

1992-93

Felix Potvin, Toronto
Vladimir Malakhov, NY Islanders
Scott Niedermayer, New Jersey
Eric Lindros, Philadelphia
Teemu Selanne, Winnipeg
Joe Juneau, Boston

1991-92

Dominik Hasek, Chicago — *Goal*
Nicklas Lidstrom, Detroit — *Defense*
Vladimir Konstantinov, Detroit — *Defense*
Kevin Todd, New Jersey — *Center*
Tony Amonte, NY Rangers — *Right Wing*
Gilbert Dionne, Montreal — *Left Wing*

1989-90

Bob Essensa, Winnipeg — *Goal*
Brad Shaw, Hartford — *Defense*
Geoff Smith, Edmonton — *Defense*
Mike Modano, Minnesota — *Center*
Sergei Makarov, Calgary — *Right Wing*
Rod Brind'Amour, St. Louis — *Left Wing*

1987-88

Darren Pang, Chicago — *Goal*
Glen Wesley, Boston — *Defense*
Calle Johansson, Buffalo — *Defense*
Joe Nieuwendyk, Calgary — *Center*
Ray Sheppard, Buffalo — *Right Wing*
Iain Duncan, Winnipeg — *Left Wing*

1985-86

Patrick Roy, Montreal — *Goal*
Gary Suter, Calgary — *Defense*
Dana Murzyn, Hartford — *Defense*
Mike Ridley, NY Rangers — *Center*
Kjell Dahlin, Montreal — *Right Wing*
Wendel Clark, Toronto — *Left Wing*

1983-84

Tom Barrasso, Buffalo — *Goal*
Thomas Eriksson, Philadelphia — *Defense*
Jamie Macoun, Calgary — *Defense*
Steve Yzerman, Detroit — *Center*
Hakan Loob, Calgary — *Right Wing*
Sylvain Turgeon, Hartford — *Left Wing*

1990-91

Ed Belfour, Chicago
Eric Weinrich, New Jersey
Rob Blake, Los Angeles
Sergei Fedorov, Detroit
Ken Hodge, Boston
Jaromir Jagr, Pittsburgh

1988-89

Peter Sidorkiewicz, Hartford
Brian Leetch, NY Rangers
Zarley Zalapski, Pittsburgh
Trevor Linden, Vancouver
Tony Granato, NY Rangers
David Volek, NY Islanders

1986-87

Ron Hextall, Philadelphia
Steve Duchesne, Los Angeles
Brian Benning, St. Louis
Jimmy Carson, Los Angeles
Jim Sandlak, Vancouver
Luc Robitaille, Los Angeles

1984-85

Steve Penney, Montreal
Chris Chelios, Montreal
Bruce Bell, Quebec
Mario Lemieux, Pittsburgh
Tomas Sandstrom, NY Rangers
Warren Young, Pittsburgh

1982-83

Pelle Lindbergh, Philadelphia
Scott Stevens, Washington
Phil Housley, Buffalo
Dan Daoust, Mtl./Tor.
Steve Larmer, Chicago
Mats Naslund, Montreal

All-Star Game Records 1947 through 2001

TEAM RECORDS

MOST GOALS, BOTH TEAMS, ONE GAME:
26 — North America 14, World 12, 2001 at Colorado
22 — Wales 16, Campbell 6, 1993 at Montreal
19 — Wales 12, Campbell 7, 1990 at Pittsburgh
18 — East 11, West 7, 1997 at San Jose
17 — East 9, West 8, 1994 at NY Rangers
16 — Campbell 11, Wales 5, 1991 at Chicago
— Campbell 10, Wales 6, 1992 at Philadelphia
15 — North America 8, World 7, 1998 at Vancouver

FEWEST GOALS, BOTH TEAMS, ONE GAME:
2 — NHL All-Stars 1, Montreal Canadiens 1, 1956 at Montreal
— First Team All-Stars 1, Second Team All-Stars 1, 1952 at Detroit
3 — West 2, East 1, 1971 at Boston
— Montreal Canadiens 3, NHL All-Stars 0, 1967 at Montreal
— NHL All-Stars 2, Montreal Canadiens 1, 1960 at Montreal

MOST GOALS, ONE TEAM, ONE GAME:
16 — Wales 16, Campbell 6, 1993 at Montreal
14 — North America 14, World 12, 2001 at Colorado
12 — Wales 12, Campbell 7, 1990 at Pittsburgh
— World 12, North America 14, 2001 at Colorado
11 — Campbell 11, Wales 5, 1991 at Chicago
— East 11, West 7, 1997 at San Jose

FEWEST GOALS, ONE TEAM, ONE GAME:
0 — NHL All-Stars 0, Montreal Canadiens 3, 1967 at Montreal
1 — 17 times (1981, 1975, 1971, 1970, 1962, 1961, 1960, 1959, both teams 1956, 1955, 1953, both teams 1952, 1950, 1949, 1948)

MOST SHOTS, BOTH TEAMS, ONE GAME (SINCE 1955):

102 — 1994 at NY Rangers	—	East 9 (56 shots), West 8 (46 shots)
98 — 2001 at Colorado	—	North America 14 (53 shots), World 12 (45 shots)
90 — 1993 at Montreal	—	Wales 16 (49 shots), Campbell 6 (41 shots)
87 — 1990 at Pittsburgh	—	Wales 12 (45 shots), Campbell 7 (42 shots)
— 1997 at San Jose	—	East 11 (41 shots), West 7 (46 shots)

FEWEST SHOTS, BOTH TEAMS, ONE GAME (SINCE 1955):

52 — 1978 at Buffalo	—	Campbell 2 (12 shots) Wales 3 (40 shots)
53 — 1960 at Montreal	—	NHL All-Stars 2 (27 shots) Montreal Canadiens 1 (26 shots)
55 — 1956 at Montreal	—	NHL All-Stars 1 (28 shots) Montreal Canadiens 1 (27 shots)
— 1971 at Boston	—	West 2 (28 shots) East 1 (27 shots)

MOST SHOTS, ONE TEAM, ONE GAME (SINCE 1955):

56 — 1994 at NY Rangers	—	East (9-8 vs. West)
53 — 2001 at Colorado	—	North America (14-12 vs. World)
49 — 1993 at Montreal	—	Wales (16-6 vs. Campbell)
— 1999 at Tampa Bay	—	North America (8-6 vs. World)
48 — 2000 at Toronto	—	World (9-4 vs. North America)

FEWEST SHOTS, ONE TEAM, ONE GAME (SINCE 1955):

12 — 1978 at Buffalo	—	Campbell (2-3 vs. Wales)
17 — 1970 at St. Louis	—	West (1-4 vs. East)
23 — 1961 at Chicago	—	Chicago Black Hawks (1-3 vs. NHL All-Stars)
24 — 1976 at Philadelphia	—	Campbell (5-7 vs. Wales)

MOST POWER-PLAY GOALS, BOTH TEAMS, ONE GAME (SINCE 1950):

3 — 1953 at Montreal	—	NHL All-Stars 3 (2 power-play goals), Montreal Canadiens 1 (1 power-play goal)
— 1954 at Detroit	—	NHL All-Stars 2 (1 power-play goal) Detroit Red Wings 2 (2 power-play goals)
— 1958 at Montreal	—	NHL All-Stars 3 (1 power-play goal) Montreal Canadiens 6 (2 power-play goals)

FEWEST POWER-PLAY GOALS, BOTH TEAMS, ONE GAME (SINCE 1950):
0 — 19 times (1952, 1959, 1960, 1967, 1968, 1969, 1972, 1973, 1976, 1980, 1981, 1984, 1985, 1992, 1994, 1996, 1999, 2000, 2001)

FASTEST TWO GOALS, BOTH TEAMS, FROM START OF GAME:
37 seconds — 1970 at St. Louis — Jacques Laperriere of East scored at 0:20 and Dean Prentice of West scored at 0:37. Final score: East 4, West 1.

2:15 — 1998 at Vancouver — Teemu Selanee scored at 0:53 and Jaromir Jagr scored at 2:15 for World. Final score: North America 8, World 7.

3:37 — 1993 at Montreal — Mike Gartner scored at 3:15 and at 3:37 for Wales. Final score: Wales 16, Campbell 6.

FASTEST TWO GOALS, BOTH TEAMS:
8 seconds — 1997 at San Jose — Owen Nolan scored at 18:54 and 19:02 of second period for West. Final Score: East 11, West 7.

10 seconds — 1976 at Philadelphia — Dennis Ververgaert scored at 4:33 and at 4:43 of third period for Campbell. Final score: Wales 7, Campbell 5.

13 seconds — 1998 at Vancouver — Teemu Selanne scored at 4:00 of first period for World and John LeClair scored at 4:13 for North America. Final score: North America 8, World 7.

FASTEST THREE GOALS, BOTH TEAMS:
1:08 — 1993 at Montreal — all by Wales — Mike Gartner scored at 3:15 and at 3:37 of first period; Peter Bondra scored at 4:23. Final score: Wales 16, Campbell 6.

1:14 — 1994 at NY Rangers — Bob Kudelski scored at 9:46 of first period for East; Sergei Fedorov scored at 10:20 for West; Eric Lindros scored at 11:00 for East. Final score: East 9, West 8.

1:23 — 1999 at Tampa Bay — Mats Sundin scored at 2:57 of third period for World; Darryl Sydor scored at 4:02 for North America; Sergei Zubov scored at 4:20 for World. Final score: North America 8, World 6.

FASTEST FOUR GOALS, BOTH TEAMS:
2:24 — 1997 at San Jose — Brendan Shanahan scored at 16:38 of second period for West; Dale Hawerchuk scored at 17:28 for East; Owen Nolan scored at 18:54 and 19:02 for West. Final score: East 11, West 7.

3:04 — 1997 at San Jose — Mark Recchi scored at 15:32 of first period for East; Dale Hawerchuk scored at 16:19 for East; Pavel Bure scored at 17:36 for West; Paul Kariya scored at 18:36 for West. Final score: East 11, West 7.

3:20 — 1998 at Vancouver — Teemu Selanne scored at 0:53 of first period for World; Jaromir Jagr scored at 2:15 for World; Selanne scored at 4:00 for World; John LeClair scored at 4:13 for North America. Final score: North America 8, World 7.

FASTEST TWO GOALS, ONE TEAM, FROM START OF GAME:
2:15 — 1998 at Vancouver — World — Teemu Selanee scored at 0:53 and Jaromir Jagr scored at 2:15. Final score: North America 8, World 7.

3:37 — 1993 at Montreal — Wales — Mike Gartner scored at 3:15 and at 3:37. Final score: Wales 16, Campbell 6.

4:19 — 1980 at Detroit — Wales — Larry Robinson scored at 3:58 and Steve Payne scored at 4:19. Final score: Wales 6, Campbell 3.

FASTEST TWO GOALS, ONE TEAM:
8 seconds — 1997 at San Jose — West — Owen Nolan scored at 18:54 and at 19:02 of second period. Final score: East 11, West 7.

10 seconds — 1976 at Philadelphia — Campbell — Dennis Ververgaert scored at 4:33 and at 4:43 of third period. Final score: Wales 7, Campbell 5.

14 seconds — 1989 at Edmonton — Campbell — Steve Yzerman and Gary Leeman scored at 17:21 and 17:35 of second period. Final score: Campbell 9, Wales 5.

FASTEST THREE GOALS, ONE TEAM:
1:08 — 1993 at Montreal — Wales — Mike Gartner scored at 3:15 and 3:37 of first period; Peter Bondra scored at 4:23. Final score: Wales 16, Campbell 6.

1:32 — 1980 at Detroit — Wales — Ron Stackhouse scored at 11:40 of third period; Craig Hartsburg scored at 12:40; Reed Larson scored at 13:12. Final score: Wales 6, Campbell 3.

1:42 — 1993 at Montreal — Wales — Alexander Mogilny scored at 11:40 of first period; Pierre Turgeon scored at 13:05; Mike Gartner scored at 13:22. Final score: Wales 16, Campbell 6.

FASTEST FOUR GOALS, ONE TEAM:
4:19 — 1992 at Philadelphia — Campbell — Brian Bellows scored at 7:40 of second period; Jeremy Roenick scored at 8:13; Theoren Fleury scored at 11:06, Brett Hull scored at 11:59. Final score: Campbell 10, Wales 6.

4:26 — 1980 at Detroit — Wales — Ron Stackhouse scored at 11:40 of third period; Craig Hartsburg scored at 12:40; Reed Larson scored at 13:12; Real Cloutier scored at 16:06. Final score: Wales 6, Campbell 3.

4:29 — 1999 at Tampa Bay — North America — Paul Kariya scored at 16:45 of first period; Mark Recchi scored at 17:18; Raymond Bourque scored at 0:17 of second period; Wayne Gretzky scored at 1:14. Final score: North America 8, World 6.

MOST GOALS, BOTH TEAMS, ONE PERIOD:
10 — 1997 at San Jose — Second period — East (6), West (4). Final score: East 11, West 7.

— 2001 at Colorado — Second period — North America (6), World (4). Final score: North America 14, World 12.

— 2001 at Colorado — Third period — North America (5), World (5). Final score: North America 14, World 12.

9 — 1990 at Pittsburgh — First period — Wales (7), Campbell (2). Final score: Wales 12, Campbell 7.

MOST GOALS, ONE TEAM, ONE PERIOD:
7 — 1990 at Pittsburgh — First period — Wales. Final score: Wales 12, Campbell 7.
6 — 1983 at NY Islanders — Third period — Campbell. Final score: Campbell 9, Wales 3.
— 1992 at Philadelphia — Second Period — Campbell. Final score: Campbell 10, Wales 6.
— 1993 at Montreal — First period — Wales. Final score: Wales 16, Campbell 6.
— 1993 at Montreal — Second period — Wales. Final score: Wales 16, Campbell 6.
— 1997 at San Jose — Second period — East. Final score: East 11, West 7.
— 2001 at Colorado — Second period — North America. Final score: North America 14, World 12.

MOST SHOTS, BOTH TEAMS, ONE PERIOD:
39 — 1994 at NY Rangers — Second period — West (21), East (18). Final score: East 9, West 8.
— 2001 at Colorado — Third period — World (23), North America (16). Final score: North America 14, World 12.
36 — 1990 at Pittsburgh — Third period — Campbell (22), Wales (14). Final score: Wales 12, Campbell 7.
— 1994 at NY Rangers — First period — East (19), West (17). Final score: East 9, West 8.

MOST SHOTS, ONE TEAM, ONE PERIOD:
23 — 2001 at Colorado — Third period — World. Final score: North America 14, World 12.
22 — 1990 at Pittsburgh — Third period — Campbell. Final score: Wales 12, Campbell 7.
— 1991 at Chicago — Third Period — Wales. Final score: Campbell 11, Wales 5.
— 1993 at Montreal — First period — Wales. Final score: Wales 16, Campbell 6.

FEWEST SHOTS, BOTH TEAMS, ONE PERIOD:
9 — 1971 at Boston — Third period — East (2), West (7). Final score: West 2, East 1.
— 1980 at Detroit — Second period — Campbell (4), Wales (5). Final score: Wales 6, Campbell 3.
13 — 1982 at Washington — Third period — Campbell (6), Wales (7). Final score: Wales 4, Campbell 2.
14 — 1978 at Buffalo — First period — Campbell (7), Wales (7). Final score: Wales 3, Campbell 2.
— 1986 at Hartford — First period — Campbell (6), Wales (8). Final score: Wales 4, Campbell 3.

FEWEST SHOTS, ONE TEAM, ONE PERIOD:
2 — 1971 at Boston — Third period — East. Final score: West 2, East 1.
— 1978 at Buffalo — Second period — Campbell. Final score: Wales 3, Campbell 2.
3 — 1978 at Buffalo — Third period — Campbell. Final score: Wales 3, Campbell 2.
4 — 1955 at Detroit — First period — NHL All-Stars. Final score: Detroit Red Wings 3, NHL All-Stars 1.
— 1980 at Detroit — Second period — Campbell. Final score: Wales 6, Campbell 3.

INDIVIDUAL RECORDS

Games

MOST GAMES PLAYED:
23 — Gordie Howe from 1948 through 1980
19 — Raymond Bourque from 1981 through 2001
18 — Wayne Gretzky from 1980 through 1999
15 — Frank Mahovlich from 1959 through 1974
14 — Paul Coffey from 1982 through 1997
— Mark Messier from 1982 through 2000

Goals

MOST GOALS (CAREER):
13 — Wayne Gretzky in 18GP
12 — Mario Lemieux in 9GP
10 — Gordie Howe in 23GP
8 — Luc Robitaille in 8GP
— Frank Mahovlich in 15GP

MOST GOALS, ONE GAME:
4 — Wayne Gretzky, Campbell, 1983
— Mario Lemieux, Wales, 1990
— Vince Damphousse, Campbell, 1991
— Mike Gartner, Wales, 1993
3 — Ted Lindsay, Detroit, 1950
— Mario Lemieux, Wales, 1988
— Pierre Turgeon, Wales, 1993
— Mark Recchi, East, 1997
— Owen Nolan, West, 1997
— Teemu Selanne, World, 1998
— Pavel Bure, World, 2000
— Bill Guerin, North America, 2001

MOST GOALS, ONE PERIOD:
4 — Wayne Gretzky, Campbell, Third period, 1983
3 — Mario Lemieux, Wales, First period, 1990
— Vince Damphousse, Campbell, Third period, 1991
— Mike Gartner, Wales, First period, 1993

Assists

MOST ASSISTS (CAREER):
13 — Mark Messier in 14GP
— Raymond Bourque in 19GP
12 — Adam Oates in 5GP
— Joe Sakic in 8GP
— Wayne Gretzky in 18GP

MOST ASSISTS, ONE GAME:
5 — Mats Naslund, Wales, 1988
4 — Raymond Bourque, Wales, 1985
— Adam Oates, Campbell, 1991
— Adam Oates, Wales, 1993
— Mark Recchi, Wales, 1993
— Pierre Turgeon, East, 1994
— Fredrik Modin, World, 2001

MOST ASSISTS, ONE PERIOD:
4 — Adam Oates, Wales, First period, 1993
3 — Mark Messier, Campbell, Third period, 1983

Mike Bullard, Denis Savard, Rick Vaive, Mike O'Connell and Gilbert Perreault battle for the puck in front of Glenn "Chico" Resch as the Wales team battles the Campbells in the 1984 All-Star Game.

Points

MOST POINTS, CAREER:
25 — Wayne Gretzky (13G-12A in 18GP)
22 — Mario Lemieux (12G-10A in 9GP)
19 — Gordie Howe (10G-9A in 23GP)
18 — Mark Messier (5G-13A in 14GP)
17 — Raymond Bourque (4G-13A in 19GP)

MOST POINTS, ONE GAME:
6 — Mario Lemieux, Wales, 1988 (3G-3A)
5 — Mats Naslund, Wales, 1988 (5A)
— Adam Oates, Campbell, 1991 (1G-4A)
— Mike Gartner, Wales, 1993 (4G-1A)
— Mark Recchi, Wales, 1993 (1G-4A)
— Pierre Turgeon, Wales, 1993 (3G-2A)
— Bill Guerin, North America, 2001 (3G-2A)

MOST POINTS, ONE PERIOD:
4 — Wayne Gretzky, Campbell, Third period, 1983 (4G)
— Mike Gartner, Wales, First period, 1993 (3G-1A)
— Adam Oates, Wales, First period, 1993 (4A)
3 — Gordie Howe, NHL All-Stars, Second period, 1965 (1G-2A)
— Pete Mahovlich, Wales, First period, 1976 (1G-2A)
— Mark Messier, Campbell, Third period, 1983 (3A)
— Mario Lemieux, Wales, Second period, 1988 (1G-2A)
— Mario Lemieux, Wales, First period, 1990 (3G)
— Vince Damphousse, Campbell, Third period, 1991 (3G)
— Mark Recchi, Wales, Second period, 1993 (1G-2A)
— Tony Amonte, North America, Second period, 2001 (2G-1A)

Power-Play Goals

MOST POWER-PLAY GOALS, CAREER:
6 — Gordie Howe in 23GP
3 — Bobby Hull in 12GP
— Maurice Richard in 13GP

Fastest Goals

FASTEST GOAL FROM START OF GAME:
19 seconds — Ted Lindsay, Detroit, 1950
20 seconds — Jacques Laperriere, East, 1970
21 seconds — Mario Lemieux, Wales, 1990
36 seconds — Chico Maki, West, 1971
37 seconds — Dean Prentice, West, 1970

FASTEST GOAL FROM START OF A PERIOD:
17 seconds — Raymond Bourque, North America, 1999 (second period)
19 seconds — Ted Lindsay, Detroit, 1950 (first period)
— Rick Tocchet, Wales, 1993 (second period)
20 seconds — Jacques Laperriere, East, 1970 (first period)
21 seconds — Mario Lemieux, Wales, 1990 (first period)
26 seconds — Wayne Gretzky, Campbell, 1982 (second period)

FASTEST TWO GOALS (ONE PLAYER) FROM START OF GAME:
3:37 — Mike Gartner, Wales, 1993, at 3:15 and 3:37.
4:00 — Teemu Selanne, World, 1998, at 0:53 and 4:00
5:25 — Wally Hergesheimer, NHL All-Stars, 1953, at 4:06 and 5:25.

FASTEST TWO GOALS (ONE PLAYER) FROM START OF A PERIOD:
3:37 — Mike Gartner, Wales, 1993, at 3:15 and 3:37 of first period.
4:00 — Teemu Selanne, World, 1998, at 0:53 and 4:00 of first period.
4:43 — Dennis Ververgaert, Campbell, 1976, at 4:33 and 4:43 of third period.

FASTEST TWO GOALS (ONE PLAYER):
8 seconds — Owen Nolan, West, 1997. Scored at 18:54 and 19:02 of second period.
10 seconds — Dennis Ververgaert, Campbell, 1976. Scored at 4:33 and 4:43 of third period.
22 seconds — Mike Gartner, Wales, 1993. Scored at 3:15 and 3:37 of first period.

Penalties

MOST PENALTY MINUTES:
25 — Gordie Howe in 23GP
21 — Gus Mortson in 9GP
16 — Harry Howell in 7GP

Goaltenders

MOST GAMES PLAYED:
13 — Glenn Hall from 1955-1969
11 — Terry Sawchuk from 1950-1968
9 — Patrick Roy from 1988-2001
8 — Jacques Plante from 1956-1970
6 — Ed Giacomin from 1967-1973
— Tony Esposito from 1970-1980
— Grant Fuhr from 1982-1989
— Martin Brodeur from 1996-2001

MOST MINUTES PLAYED:
540 — Glenn Hall in 13GP
467 — Terry Sawchuk in 11GP
370 — Jacques Plante in 8GP
210 — Patrick Roy in 9GP
209 — Turk Broda in 4GP

MOST GOALS AGAINST:
27 — Patrick Roy in 9GP
22 — Glenn Hall in 13GP
21 — Mike Vernon in 5GP
19 — Terry Sawchuk in 11GP
18 — Jacques Plante in 8GP
— Andy Moog in 4GP

BEST GOALS-AGAINST-AVERAGE AMONG THOSE WITH AT LEAST TWO GAMES PLAYED:
0.68 — Gilles Villemure in 3GP
1.49 — Gerry McNeil in 3GP
1.50 — Johnny Bower in 4GP
1.51 — Frank Brimsek in 2GP
1.64 — Gump Worsley in 4GP
2.03 — Don Edwards in 2GP

As Stanley Cup champions four times in the early 1950s, the Red Wings got three opportunities to battle the NHL All-Stars. Detroit was a 7-1 winner in 1950, then had a tie in 1954 and another victory in 1955.

Hockey Hall of Fame

(Year of induction is listed after each Honoured Members name)

Mike Gartner scored 708 goals in his career, fifth in NHL history. He enters the Hockey Hall of Fame in 2001 with fellow players Dale Hawerchuk, Jari Kurri and Viachelsav Fetisov. Craig Patrick will be inducted as a builder.

Location: BCE Place, at the corner of Front and Yonge Streets in the heart of downtown Toronto. Easy access from all major highways running into Toronto. Close to TTC and Union Station.

Telephone: administration (416) 360-7735; information (416) 360-7765.

Summer and Christmas/March break hours: Monday to Saturday 9:30 a.m. to 6 p.m.; Sunday 10:00 a.m. to 6 p.m.

Fall/Winter/Spring hours (except Christmas/March break): Monday to Friday 10 a.m. to 5 p.m.; Saturday 9:30 a.m. to 6 p.m.; Sunday 10:30 a.m. to 5 p.m.

The Hockey Hall of Fame can be booked for private functions after hours.

Website address: www.hhof.com

History: The Hockey Hall of Fame was established in 1943. Members were first honoured in 1945. On August 26, 1961, the Hockey Hall of Fame opened its doors to the public in a building located on the grounds of the Canadian National Exhibition in Toronto. The Hockey Hall of Fame relocated to its new site at BCE Place and welcomed the hockey world on June 18, 1993.

Honour Roll: There are 324 Honoured Members in the Hockey Hall of Fame. 222 have been inducted as players, 88 as builders and 14 as Referees/Linesmen. In addition, there are 66 media honourees.

Founding Sponsors: Special thanks to Blockbuster Video, Coca-Cola Ltd., Ford of Canada, Household Financial Services, IBM Corporation, Imperial Oil, Kodak Canada Inc., London Life Insurance Company, Molson Breweries, The Sports Network Inc. (TSN/RDS), The Toronto Sun Publishing Corporation, WorldCom.

PLAYERS

* Abel, Sidney Gerald 1969
* Adams, John James "Jack" 1959
* Apps, Charles Joseph Sylvanus "Syl" 1961
Armstrong, George Edward 1975
* Bailey, Irvine Wallace "Ace" 1975
* Bain, Donald H. "Dan" 1945
* Baker, Hobart "Hobey" 1945
Barber, William Charles "Bill" 1990
* Barry, Martin J. "Marty" 1965
Bathgate, Andrew James "Andy" 1978
* Bauer, Robert Theodore "Bobby" 1996
Béliveau, Jean Arthur 1972
* Benedict, Clinton S. 1965
* Bentley, Douglas Wagner 1964
* Bentley, Maxwell H. L. 1966
* Blake, Hector Toe 1966
Boivin, Leo Joseph 1986
* Boon, Richard R. "Dickie" 1952
Bossy, Michael 1991
Bouchard, Butch Joseph "Butch" 1966
* Boucher, Frank 1958
* Boucher, George "Buck" 1960
Bower, John William 1976
* Bowie, Russell 1945
* Brimsek, Francis Charles 1966
* Broadbent, Harry L. "Punch" 1962
* Broda, Walter Edward "Turk" 1967
Bucyk, John Paul 1981
* Burch, Billy 1974
* Cameron, Harold Hugh "Harry" 1962
Cheevers, Gerald Michael "Gerry" 1985
* Clancy, Francis Michael "King" 1958
* Clapper, Aubrey "Dit" 1947
Clarke, Robert "Bobby" 1987
* Cleghorn, Sprague 1958
* Colville, Neil MacNeil 1967
* Conacher, Charles W. 1961
* Conacher, Lionel Pretoria 1994
* Conacher, Roy Gordon 1998
* Connell, Alex 1958
* Cook, Fred "Bun" 1995
* Cook, William Osser 1952
Coulter, Arthur Edmund 1974
Cournoyer, Yvan Serge 1982
* Cowley, William Mailes 1968
* Crawford, Samuel Russell "Rusty" 1962
* Darragh, John Proctor "Jack" 1962
* Davidson, Allan M. "Scotty" 1950
* Day, Clarence Henry Hap 1961
Delvecchio, Alex 1977
* Denneny, Cyril "Cy" 1959
Dionne, Marcel 1992
* Drillon, Gordon Arthur 1975
* Drinkwater, Charles Graham 1950
Dryden, Kenneth Wayne 1983
Dumart, Woodrow "Woody" 1992
* Dunderdale, Thomas 1974
* Durnan, William Ronald 1964
* Dutton, Mervyn A. "Red" 1958
* Dye, Cecil Henry "Babe" 1970
Esposito, Anthony James "Tony" 1988
Esposito, Philip Anthony 1984
* Farrell, Arthur F. 1965
Fetisov, Viacheslav 2001
Flaman, Ferdinand Charles "Fern" 1990
* Foyston, Frank 1958
* Fredrickson, Frank 1958
Gadsby, William Alexander 1970
Gainey, Bob 1992
* Gardiner, Charles Robert "Chuck" 1945
* Gardiner, Herbert Martin "Herb" 1958
* Gardner, James Henry "Jimmy" 1962
Gartner, Michael Alfred 2001
Geoffrion, Jos. A. Bernard "Boom Boom" 1972
* Gerard, Eddie 1945
Giacomin, Edward "Eddie" 1987
Gilbert, Rodrigue Gabriel "Rod" 1982
* Gilmour, Hamilton Livingstone "Billy" 1962
* Goheen, Frank Xavier "Moose" 1952
* Goodfellow, Ebenezer R. "Ebbie" 1963
Goulet, Michel 1998
* Grant, Michael "Mike" 1950
* Green, Wilfred "Shorty" 1962
Gretzky, Wayne Douglas 1999
* Griffis, Silas Seth "Si" 1950
* Hainsworth, George 1961
Hall, Glenn Henry 1975
* Hall, Joseph Henry 1961
* Harvey, Douglas Norman 1973
Hawerchuk, Dale Martin 2001
* Hay, George 1958
* Hern, William Milton "Riley" 1962
* Hextall, Bryan Aldwyn 1969
* Holmes, Harry Hap 1972
* Hooper, Charles Thomas "Tom" 1962
Horner, George Reginald "Red" 1965
* Horton, Miles Gilbert "Tim" 1977
Howe, Gordon 1972
* Howe, Sydney Harris 1965
Howell, Henry Vernon "Harry" 1979
Hull, Robert Marvin 1983
* Hutton, John Bower "Bouse" 1962
* Hyland, Harry M. 1962
* Irvin, James Dickenson "Dick" 1958
* Jackson, Harvey "Busher" 1971
* Johnson, Ernest "Moose" 1952
* Johnson, Ivan "Ching" 1958
Johnson, Thomas Christian 1970
* Joliat, Aurel 1947
* Keats, Gordon "Duke" 1958
Kelly, Leonard Patrick "Red" 1969
Kennedy, Theodore Samuel "Teeder" 1966
Keon, David Michael 1986
Kurri, Jari 2001
Lach, Elmer James 1966
Lafleur, Guy Damien 1988
* Lalonde, Edouard Charles "Newsy" 1950
Laperriere, Jacques 1987
Lapointe, Guy 1993
Laprade, Edgar 1993
* Laviolette, Jean Baptiste "Jack" 1962
* Lehman, Hugh 1958
Lemaire, Jacques Gerard 1984
Lemieux, Mario 1997
* LeSueur, Percy 1961
* Lewis, Herbert A. 1989
Lindsay, Robert Blake Theodore "Ted" 1966
* Lumley, Harry 1980
* MacKay, Duncan "Mickey" 1952
Mahovlich, Frank William 1981
* Malone, Joseph "Joe" 1950
* Mantha, Sylvio 1960
* Marshall, John "Jack" 1965
* Maxwell, Fred G. "Steamer" 1962
McDonald, Lanny 1992
* McGee, Frank 1945
* McGimsie, William George "Billy" 1962
* McNamara, George 1958
Mikita, Stanley 1983
Moore, Richard Winston "Dickie" 1974
* Moran, Patrick Joseph "Paddy" 1958
* Morenz, Howie 1945
* Mosienko, William "Billy" 1965
Mullen, Joseph P. 2000
* Nighbor, Frank 1947
* Noble, Edward Reginald "Reg" 1962
* O'Connor, Herbert William "Buddy" 1988
* Oliver, Harry 1967
Olmstead, Murray Bert "Bert" 1985
Orr, Robert Gordon 1979
Parent, Bernard Marcel 1984
Park, Douglas Bradford "Brad" 1988
* Patrick, Joseph Lynn 1980
* Patrick, Lester 1947
Perreault, Gilbert 1990
* Phillips, Tommy 1945
Pilote, Joseph Albert Pierre Paul 1975
* Pitre, Didier "Pit" 1962
* Plante, Joseph Jacques Omer 1978

Potvin, Denis 1991
* Pratt, Walter "Babe" 1966
* Primeau, A. Joseph 1963
Pronovost, Joseph René Marcel 1978
Pulford, Bob 1991
* Pulford, Harvey 1945
* Quackenbush, Hubert George "Bill" 1976
* Rankin, Frank 1961
Ratelle, Joseph Gilbert Yvan Jean "Jean" 1985
Rayner, Claude Earl "Chuck" 1973
Reardon, Kenneth Joseph 1966
Richard, Joseph Henri 1979
* Richard, Joseph Henri Maurice "Rocket" 1961
* Richardson, George Taylor 1950
* Roberts, Gordon 1971
Robinson, Larry 1995
* Ross, Arthur Howie 1945
* Russel, Blair 1965
* Russell, Ernest 1965
* Ruttan, J.D. "Jack" 1962
Salming, Borje Anders 1996
Savard, Denis Joseph 2000
Savard, Serge A. 1986
* Sawchuk, Terrance Gordon "Terry" 1971
* Scanlan, Fred 1965
Schmidt, Milton Conrad "Milt" 1961
* Schriner, David "Sweeney" 1962
* Seibert, Earl Walter 1963
* Seibert, Oliver Levi 1961
* Shore, Edward W. "Eddie" 1947
Shutt, Stephen 1993
* Siebert, Albert C. "Babe" 1964
* Simpson, Harold Edward "Bullet Joe" 1962
Sittler, Darryl Glen 1989
* Smith, Alfred E. 1962
Smith, Clint 1991
* Smith, Reginald "Hooley" 1972
* Smith, Thomas James 1973
Smith, William John "Billy" 1993
Stanley, Allan Herbert 1981
* Stanley, Russell "Barney" 1962
Stastny, Peter 1998
* Stewart, John Sherratt "Black Jack" 1964
* Stewart, Nelson "Nels" 1962
* Stuart, Bruce 1961
* Stuart, Hod 1945
* Taylor, Frederic "Cyclone" (O.B.E.) 1947
* Thompson, Cecil R. "Tiny" 1959
Tretiak, Vladislav 1989
* Trihey, Col. Harry J. 1950
Trottier, Bryan 1997
Ullman, Norman V. Alexander "Norm" 1982
* Vezina, Georges 1945
* Walker, John Phillip "Jack" 1960
* Walsh, Martin "Marty" 1962
* Watson, Harry E. 1962
Watson, Harry 1994
* Weiland, Ralph "Cooney" 1971
* Westwick, Harry 1962
* Whitcroft, Fred 1962
* Wilson, Gordon Allan "Phat" 1962
Worsley, Lorne John "Gump" 1980
* Worters, Roy 1969

BUILDERS

* Adams, Charles 1960
* Adams, Weston W. 1972
* Aheam, Thomas Franklin "Frank" 1962
* Ahearne, John Francis "Bunny" 1977
* Allan, Sir Montagu (C.V.O.) 1945
Allen, Keith 1992
Arbour, Alger Joseph "Al" 1996
* Ballard, Harold Edwin 1977
* Bauer, Father David 1989
* Bickell, John Paris 1978
Bowman, Scotty 1991
* Brown, George V. 1961
* Brown, Walter A. 1962
* Buckland, Frank 1975
Bush, Walter Sr. 2000
Butterfield, Jack Arlington 1980
* Calder, Frank 1947
* Campbell, Angus D. 1964
* Campbell, Clarence Sutherland 1966
* Cattarinich, Joseph 1977
* Dandurand, Joseph Viateur "Leo" 1963
* Dilio, Francis Paul 1964
* Dudley, George S. 1958
* Dunn, James A. 1968
Francis, Emile 1982
* Gibson, Dr. John L. "Jack" 1976
* Gorman, Thomas Patrick "Tommy" 1963
* Griffiths, Frank A. 1993
* Hanley, William 1986
* Hay, Charles 1974
* Hendy, James C. 1968
* Hewitt, Foster 1965
* Hewitt, William Abraham 1947
* Hume, Fred J. 1962
* Imlach, George "Punch" 1984
* Ivan, Thomas N. 1974
* Jennings, William M. 1975
* Johnson, Bob 1992
* Juckes, Gordon W. 1979
* Kilpatrick, Gen. John Reed 1960
* Knox, Seymour H. III 1993
* Leader, George Alfred 1969
* LeBel, Robert 1970
* Lockhart, Thomas F. 1965
* Loicq, Paul 1961
* Mariucci, John 1985
Mathers, Frank 1992
* McLaughlin, Major Frederic 1963
* Milford, John "Jake" 1984
Molson, Hon. Hartland de Montarville 1973
Morrison, Ian "Scotty" 1999
* Murray, Monsignor Athol 1998
* Nelson, Francis 1947
* Norris, Bruce A. 1969
* Norris, Sr., James 1958
* Norris, James Dougan 1962
* Northey, William M. 1947
* O'Brien, John Ambrose 1962
O'Neill, Brian 1994
* Page, Fred 1993
Patrick, Craig 2001
* Patrick, Frank 1958
* Pickard, Allan W. 1958
* Pilous, Rudy 1985
Poile, Norman "Bud" 1990
Pollock, Samuel Patterson Smyth 1978
* Raymond, Sen. Donat 1958
* Robertson, John Ross 1947
* Robinson, Claude C. 1947
* Ross, Philip D. 1976
Sabetzki, Dr. Gunther 1995
Sather, Glen 1997
* Selke, Frank J. 1960
Sinden, Harry James 1983
* Smith, Frank D. 1962
* Smythe, Conn 1958
Snider, Edward M. 1988
* Stanley of Preston, Lord (G.C.B.) 1945
* Sutherland, Cap. James T. 1947
* Tarasov, Anatoli V. 1974
Torrey, Bill 1995
* Turner, Lloyd 1958
* Tutt, William Thayer 1978
* Voss, Carl Potter 1974
* Waghorn, Fred C. 1961
* Wirtz, Arthur Michael 1971
Wirtz, William W. "Bill" 1976
Ziegler, John A. Jr. 1987

REFEREES/LINESMEN

Armstrong, Neil 1991
Ashley, John George 1981
Chadwick, William L. 1964
D'Amico, John 1993
* Elliott, Chaucer 1961
* Hayes, George William 1988
* Hewitson, Robert W. 1963
* Ion, Fred J. "Mickey" 1961
Pavelich, Matt 1987
* Rodden, Michael J. "Mike" 1962
* Smeaton, J. Cooper 1961
Storey, Roy Alvin "Red" 1967
Udvari, Frank Joseph 1973
Van Hellemond, Andy 1999

Hockey Hall of Fame Game
Saturday, November 10, 2001
New Jersey Devils vs.
Toronto Maple Leafs at
Air Canada Centre in Toronto.

Elmer Ferguson Memorial Award Winners

In recognition of distinguished members of the newspaper profession whose words have brought honor to journalism and to hockey. Selected by the Professional Hockey Writers' Association.

* Barton, Charlie, Buffalo-Courier Express 1985
* Beauchamp, Jacques, Montreal Matin/Journal de Montréal 1984
* Brennan, Bill, Detroit News 1987
* Burchard, Jim, New York World Telegram 1984
* Burnett, Red, Toronto Star 1984
* Carroll, Dink, Montreal Gazette 1984
* Coleman, Jim, Southam Newspapers 1984
Conway, Russ, Eagle-Tribune 1999
* Damata, Ted, Chicago Tribune 1984
Delano, Hugh, New York Post 1991
Desjardins, Marcel, Montréal La Presse 1984
Duhatschek, Eric, Calgary Herald/Globe and Mail 2001
* Dulmage, Jack, Windsor Star 1984
Dunnell, Milt, Toronto Star 1984
* Ferguson, Elmer, Montreal Herald/Star 1984
Fisher, Red, Montreal Star/Gazette 1985
* Fitzgerald, Tom, Boston Globe 1984
Frayne, Trent, Toronto Telegram/Globe and Mail/Sun 1984
Gatecliff, Jack, St. Catherines Standard 1995
Gross, George, Toronto Telegram/Sun 1985
Johnston, Dick, Buffalo News 1986
* Laney, Al, New York Herald-Tribune 1984
Larochelle, Claude, Le Soleil 1989
L'Esperance, Zotique, Journal de Montréal/le Petit Journal 1985
* MacLeod, Rex, Toronto Globe and Mail/Star 1987
Matheson, Jim, Edmonton Journal 2000
* Mayer, Charles, Journal de Montréal/la Patrie 1985
McKenzie, Ken, The Hockey News 1997
Monahan, Leo, Boston Daily Record/Record-American/Herald American 1986
Moriarty, Tim, UPI/Newsday 1986
* Nichols, Joe, New York Times 1984
* O'Brien, Andy, Weekend Magazine 1985
Orr, Frank, Toronto Star 1989
Olan, Ben, New York Associated Press 1987
* O'Meara, Basil, Montreal Star 1984
Pedneault, Yvon, La Presse/Journal de Montréal 1998
Proudfoot, Jim, Toronto Star 1988
Raymond, Bertrand, Journal de Montréal 1990
Rosa, Fran, Boston Globe 1987
Strachan, Al, Globe and Mail/Toronto Sun 1993
* Vipond, Jim, Toronto Globe and Mail 1984
Walter, Lewis, Detroit Times 1984
Young, Scott, Toronto Globe and Mail/Telegram 1988

Foster Hewitt Memorial Award Winners

In recognition of members of the radio and television industry who made outstanding contributions to their profession and the game during their career in hockey broadcasting. Selected by the NHL Broadcasters' Association.

Cole, Bob, Hockey Night in Canada 1996
Cusick, Fred, Boston 1984
* Darling, Ted, Buffalo 1994
* Gallivan, Danny, Montreal 1984
Garneau, Richard, Montreal 1999
* Hart, Gene, Philadelphia 1997
* Hewitt, Foster, Toronto 1984
Irvin, Dick, Montreal 1988
* Kelly, Dan, St. Louis 1989
Lange, Mike, Pittsburgh 2001
* Lecavelier, René, Montreal 1984
Lynch, Budd, Detroit 1985
Martyn, Bruce, Detroit 1991
McDonald, Jiggs, Los Angeles, Atlanta, NY Islanders 1990
McFarlane, Brian, Hockey Night in Canada 1995
* McKnight, Wes, Toronto 1986
Meeker, Howie, Hockey Night in Canada 1998
Miller, Bob, Los Angeles 2000
Pettit, Lloyd, Chicago 1986
Robson, Jim, Vancouver 1992
Shaver, Al, Minnesota 1993
* Smith, Doug, Montreal 1985
Wilson, Bob, Boston 1987

* Deceased

United States Hockey Hall of Fame

The United States Hockey Hall of Fame was opened on June 21, 1973 as the national shrine of American Hockey. It is dedicated to honoring the sport of ice hockey in the United States by preserving those precious memories and legends of the game. It is located in Eveleth, Minnesota, 60 miles north of Duluth on Highway 53. The facility is open Monday to Saturday, 9 a.m. to 5 p.m. and Sundays from 10 a.m. to 3 p.m. Admission is $6.00 for adults, $5.00 for seniors and youths (13-17) and $4.00 for children (6-12). Call for any further information: 1-800-443-7825 or 218-744-5167. Web site address: www.ushockeyhall.com

There are now 107 enshrined members consisting of 63 players, 22 coaches, 19 administrators, one player/administrator, one referee and one team. New members are inducted annually in the fall and must have made a significant contribution towards hockey in the United States during the course of their career. A special Wayne Gretzky Award pays tribute to international individuals who have made major contributions to hockey in the USA. Support for the Hall of Fame comes from sponsorships, admissions, gift store sales, special events and grants from the hockey community and government agencies.

PLAYERS

* Abel, Clarence "Taffy" 1973
* Baker, Hobart "Hobey" 1973

Bartholome, Earl 1977
* Bessone, Peter 1978

Blake, Robert 1985
Boucha, Henry 1995
* Brimsek, Frank 1973

Broten, Neal 2000
Cavanagh, Joe 1994
* Chaisson, Ray 1974
* Chase, John P. 1973

Christian, Roger 1989
Christian, William "Bill" 1984
Cleary, Robert 1981
Cleary, William 1976
* Conroy, Anthony 1975

Curran, Mike 1998
* Dahlstrom, Carl "Cully" 1973
* Desjardins, Victor 1974
* Desmond, Richard 1988
* Dill, Robert 1979
* Everett, Doug 1974

Ftorek, Robbie 1991
* Garrison, John B. 1973

Garrity, Jack 1986
* Goheen, Frank "Moose" 1973

Grant, Wally 1994
* Harding, Austin "Austie" 1975
* Iglehart, Stewart 1975
* Johnson, Virgil 1974
* Karakas, Mike 1973

Kirrane, Jack 1987
* Lane, Myles J. 1973

Langevin, David R. 1993
Langway, Rod 1999
Larson, Reed 1996
* Linder, Joseph 1975
* LoPresti, Sam L. 1973
* Mariucci, John 1973

Matchefts, John 1991
* Mather, Bruce 1998

Mayasich, John 1976
McCartan, Jack 1983
* Moe, William 1974

Morrow, Ken 1995
* Moseley, Fred 1975

Mullen, Joe 1998
* Murray, Sr., Hugh "Muzz" 1987
* Nelson, Hubert "Hub" 1978
* Nyrop, William D. 1997
* Olson , Eddie 1977
* Owen, Jr., George 1973
* Palmer, Winthrop 1973

Paradise, Robert 1989
* Purpur, Clifford "Fido" 1974

Riley, William 1977
Roberts, Gordie 1999
* Romnes, Elwin "Doc" 1973
* Rondeau, Richard 1985

Sheehy, Timothy K. 1997
* Williams, Thomas 1981
* Winters, Frank "Coddy" 1973
* Yackel, Ken 1986

COACHES

* Almquist, Oscar 1983

Bessone, Amo 1992
Brooks, Herbert 1990
Ceglarski, Len 1992
* Fullerton, James 1992

Gambucci, Sergio 1996
* Gordon, Malcolm K. 1973

Harkness, Nevin D. "Ned" 1994
Heyliger, Victor 1974
* Holt, Jr. Charles E. 1997

Ikola, Willard 1990
* Jeremiah, Edward J. 1973
* Johnson, Bob 1991
* Kelley, John "Snooks" 1974

Kelley, John H. "Jack" 1993
Patrick, Craig 1996
Pleban, Jon "Connie" 1990
Riley, Jack 1979
* Ross, Larry 1988
* Thompson, Clifford, R. 1973
* Stewart, William 1982
* Winsor, Alfred "Ralph" 1973

ADMINISTRATORS

* Brown, George V. 1973
* Brown, Walter A. 1973

Bush, Walter 1980
* Clark, Donald 1978

Claypool, James 1995
* Gibson, J.C. "Doc" 1973
* Jennings, William M. 1981
* Kahler, Nick 1980
* Lockhart, Thomas F. 1973
* Marvin, Cal 1982

Palazzari, Doug 2000
Pleau, Larry 2000
* Ridder, Robert 1976
* Schulz, Charles M. 1993

Trumble, Harold 1985
* Tutt, William Thayer 1973

Watson, Sid 1999
Wirtz, William W. "Bill" 1984
* Wright, Lyle Z.1973

PLAYER/ADMINISTRATOR

Nanne, Lou 1998

REFEREE

Chadwick, William 1974

TEAM

1960 U.S. Olympic Team, 2000

*Deceased

Neal Broten was the first American-born NHL player to top 100 points in a single season (1985-86). He won an Olympic gold medal with the 1980 "Miracle on Ice" team and later earned a Stanley Cup ring with the New Jersey Devils in 1995.

NHL League and Team Websites

National Hockey League	www.nhl.com
NHL Games on Radio	www.nhl.com/intheslot/listen/radio/index.html
NHL Site for Kids	www.nhl.com/kids
NHL Merchandise Shop	www.shop.nhl.com
NHL Trivia	nhltrivia.buzztime.com
NHL Job Postings	hockeyjobs.nhl.com
Hockey Fights Cancer	www.nhl.com/nhlhq/hockeyfightscancer/index.html

Official NHL Team Websites:

Anaheim	www.mightyducks.com
Atlanta	www.atlantathrashers.com
Boston	www.bostonbruins.com
Buffalo	www.sabres.com
Calgary	www.calgaryflames.com
Carolina	www.caneshockey.com
Chicago	www.chicagoblackhawks.com
Colorado	www.coloradoavalanche.com
Columbus	www.columbusbluejackets.com
Dallas	www.dallasstars.com
Detroit	www.detroitredwings.com
Edmonton	www.edmontonoilers.com
Florida	www.floridapanthers.com
Los Angeles	www.lakings.com
Minnesota	www.wild.com
Montreal	www.canadiens.com
Nashville	www.nashvillepredators.com
New Jersey	www.newjerseydevils.com
NY Islanders	www.newyorkislanders.com
NY Rangers	www.newyorkrangers.com
Ottawa	www.ottawasenators.com
Philadelphia	www.philadelphiaflyers.com
Phoenix	www.phoenixcoyotes.com
Pittsburgh	www.pittsburghpenguins.com
St. Louis	www.stlouisblues.com
San Jose	www.sj-sharks.com
Tampa Bay	www.tampabaylightning.com
Toronto	www.torontomapleleafs.com
Vancouver	www.canucks.com
Washington	www.washingtoncaps.com

2001 Stanley Cup Playoffs

Results

CONFERENCE QUARTER-FINALS
(Best-of-seven series)

Eastern Conference

Series 'A'

Thu Apr 12	Carolina 1	at	New Jersey 5
Sun Apr 15	Carolina 0	at	New Jersey 2
Tue Apr 17	New Jersey 4	at	Carolina 0
Wed Apr 18	New Jersey 2	at	Carolina 3*
Fri Apr 20	Carolina 3	at	New Jersey 2
Sun Apr 22	New Jersey 5	at	Carolina 1

*Rod Brind'Amour Scored at 0:46 of Overtime

(New Jersey Won Series 4-2)

Series 'B'

Fri Apr 13	Toronto 1	at	Ottawa 0*
Sat Apr 14	Toronto 3	at	Ottawa 0
Mon Apr 16	Ottawa 2	at	Toronto 3**
Wed Apr 18	Ottawa 1	at	Toronto 3

*Mats Sundin Scored at 10:49 of Overtime
**Cory Cross Scored at 2:16 of Overtime

(Toronto Won Series 4-0)

Series 'C'

Thu Apr 12	Pittsburgh 0	at	Washington 1
Sat Apr 14	Pittsburgh 2	at	Washington 1
Mon Apr 16	Washington 0	at	Pittsburgh 3
Wed Apr 18	Washington 4	at	Pittsburgh 3*
Sat Apr 21	Pittsburgh 2	at	Washington 1
Mon Apr 23	Washington 3	at	Pittsburgh 4**

*Jeff Halpern Scored at 4:01 of Overtime
**Martin Straka Scored at 13:04 of Overtime

(Pittsburgh Won Series 4-2)

Series 'D'

Wed Apr 11	Buffalo 2	at	Philadelphia 1
Sat Apr 14	Buffalo 4	at	Philadelphia 3*
Mon Apr 16	Philadelphia 3	at	Buffalo 2
Tue Apr 17	Philadelphia 3	at	Buffalo 4**
Thu Apr 19	Buffalo 1	at	Philadelphia 3
Sat Apr 21	Philadelphia 0	at	Buffalo 8

*Jay McKee Scored at 18:02 of Overtime
**Curtis Brown Scored at 6:13 of Overtime

(Buffalo Won Series 4-2)

Western Conference

Series 'E'

Thu Apr 12	Vancouver 4	at	Colorado 5
Sat Apr 14	Vancouver 1	at	Colorado 2
Mon Apr 16	Colorado 4	at	Vancouver 3*
Wed Apr 18	Colorado 5	at	Vancouver 1

*Peter Forsberg Scored at 2:50 of Overtime

(Colorado Won Series 4-0)

Series 'F'

Wed Apr 11	Los Angeles 3	at	Detroit 5
Sat Apr 14	Los Angeles 0	at	Detroit 4
Sun Apr 15	Detroit 1	at	Los Angeles 2
Wed Apr 18	Detroit 3	at	Los Angeles 4*
Sat Apr 21	Los Angeles 3	at	Detroit 2
Mon Apr 23	Detroit 2	at	Los Angeles 3**

*Eric Belanger Scored at 2:36 of Overtime
**Adam Deadmarsh Scored at 4:48 of Overtime

(Los Angeles Won Series 4-2)

Series 'G'

Wed Apr 11	Edmonton 1	at	Dallas 2*
Sat Apr 14	Edmonton 4	at	Dallas 3
Sun Apr 15	Dallas 3	at	Edmonton 2**
Tue Apr 17	Dallas 1	at	Edmonton 2***
Thu Apr 19	Edmonton 3	at	Dallas 4****
Sat Apr 21	Dallas 3	at	Edmonton 1

*Jamie Langenbrunner Scored at 2:08 of Overtime
**Benoit Hogue Scored at 19:48 of Overtime
***Mike Comrie Scored at 17:19 of Overtime
****Kirk Muller Scored at 8:01 of Overtime

(Dallas Won Series 4-2)

Series 'H'

Thu Apr 12	San Jose 1	at	St. Louis 3
Sat Apr 14	San Jose 1	at	St. Louis 0
Mon Apr 16	St. Louis 6	at	San Jose 3
Tue Apr 17	St. Louis 2	at	San Jose 3
Thu Apr 19	San Jose 2	at	St. Louis 3*
Sat Apr 21	St. Louis 2	at	San Jose 1

*Bryce Salvador Scored at 9:54 of Overtime

(St. Louis Won Series 4-2)

CONFERENCE SEMI-FINALS
(Best-of-seven series)

Eastern Conference

Series 'I'

Thu Apr 26	Toronto 2	at	New Jersey 0
Sat Apr 28	Toronto 5	at	New Jersey 6*
Tue May 1	New Jersey 3	at	Toronto 2**
Thu May 3	New Jersey 1	at	Toronto 3
Sat May 5	Toronto 3	at	New Jersey 2
Mon May 7	New Jersey 4	at	Toronto 2
Wed May 9	Toronto 1	at	New Jersey 5

*Randy McKay Scored at 5:31 of Overtime
**Brian Rafalski Scored at 7:00 of Overtime

(New Jersey Won Series 4-3)

Series 'J'

Thu Apr 26	Pittsburgh 3	at	Buffalo 0
Sat Apr 28	Pittsburgh 3	at	Buffalo 1
Mon Apr 30	Buffalo 4	at	Pittsburgh 1
Wed May 2	Buffalo 5	at	Pittsburgh 2
Sat May 5	Pittsburgh 2	at	Buffalo 3*
Tue May 8	Buffalo 2	at	Pittsburgh 3**
Thu May 10	Pittsburgh 3	at	Buffalo 2***

*Stu Barnes Scored at 8:34 of Overtime
**Martin Straka Scored at 11:29 of Overtime
***Darius Kasparaitis Scored at 13:01 of Overtime

(Pittsburgh Won Series 4-3)

Western Conference

Series 'K'

Thu Apr 26	Los Angeles 4	at	Colorado 3*
Sat Apr 28	Los Angeles 0	at	Colorado 2
Mon Apr 30	Colorado 4	at	Los Angeles 3
Wed May 2	Colorado 3	at	Los Angeles 0
Fri May 4	Los Angeles 1	at	Colorado 0
Sun May 6	Colorado 0	at	Los Angeles 1**
Wed May 9	Los Angeles 1	at	Colorado 5

*Jaroslav Modry Scored at 14:23 of Overtime
**Glen Murray Scored at 22:41 of Overtime

(Colorado Won Series 4-3)

Series 'L'

Fri Apr 27	St. Louis 4	at	Dallas 2
Sun Apr 29	St. Louis 2	at	Dallas 1
Tue May 1	Dallas 2	at	St. Louis 3*
Thu May 3	Dallas 1	at	St. Louis 4

*Cory Stillman Scored at 29:26 of Overtime

(St. Louis Won Series 4-0)

CONFERENCE FINALS
(Best-of-seven series)

Eastern Conference

Series 'M'

Sat May 12	Pittsburgh 1	at	New Jersey 3
Tue May 15	Pittsburgh 4	at	New Jersey 2
Thu May 17	New Jersey 3	at	Pittsburgh 0
Sat May 19	New Jersey 5	at	Pittsburgh 0
Tue May 22	Pittsburgh 2	at	New Jersey 4

(New Jersey Won Series 4-1)

Western Conference

Series 'N'

Sat May 12	St. Louis 1	at	Colorado 4
Mon May 14	St. Louis 2	at	Colorado 4
Wed May 16	Colorado 3	at	St. Louis 4*
Fri May 18	Colorado 4	at	St. Louis 3**
Mon May 21	St. Louis 1	at	Colorado 2***

*Scott Young Scored at 30:27 of Overtime
**Stephane Yelle Scored at 4:23 of Overtime
***Joe Sakic Scored at 0:24 of Overtime

(Colorado Won Series 4-1)

STANLEY CUP CHAMPIONSHIP
(Best-of-seven series)

Series 'O'

Sat May 26	New Jersey 0	at	Colorado 5
Tue May 29	New Jersey 2	at	Colorado 1
Thu May 31	Colorado 3	at	New Jersey 1
Sat June 2	Colorado 2	at	New Jersey 3
Mon June 4	New Jersey 4	at	Colorado 1
Thu June 7	Colorado 4	at	New Jersey 0
Sat June 9	New Jersey 1	at	Colorado 3

(Colorado Won Series 4-3)

Team Playoff Records

	GP	W	L	GF	GA	%
Colorado	23	16	7	69	41	.696
New Jersey	25	15	10	69	52	.600
St. Louis	15	9	6	40	34	.600
Pittsburgh	18	9	9	38	44	.500
Toronto	11	7	4	28	24	.636
Buffalo	13	7	6	38	30	.538
Los Angeles	13	7	6	25	34	.538
Dallas	10	4	6	22	26	.400
Detroit	6	2	4	17	15	.333
Edmonton	6	2	4	13	16	.333
Washington	6	2	4	10	14	.333
San Jose	6	2	4	11	16	.333
Philadelphia	6	2	4	13	21	.333
Carolina	6	2	4	8	20	.333
Vancouver	4	0	4	9	16	.000
Ottawa	4	0	4	3	10	.000

Individual Leaders

Abbreviations: ***–** rookie eligible for Calder Trophy; **A** – assists; **G** – goals; **GP** – Games Played; **OT** – overtime goals; **GW** – game-winning goals; **PIM** – penalties in minutes; **PP** – power play goals; **Pts** – points; **S** – shots on goal; **SH** – short-handed goals; **%** – percentage of shots resulting in goals; +/– – difference between Goals For (**GF**) scored when a player is on the ice with his team at even strength or short-handed and Goals Against (**GA**) scored when the same player is on the ice with his team at even strength or on a power play.

Playoff Scoring Leaders

Player	Team	GP	G	A	PTS	+/–	PIM	PP	SH	GW	OT	S	%
Joe Sakic	Colorado	21	13	13	26	6	6	5	0	3	1	79	16.5
Patrik Elias	New Jersey	25	9	14	23	11	10	3	1	2	0	58	15.5
Milan Hejduk	Colorado	23	7	16	23	8	6	4	0	1	0	51	13.7
Petr Sykora	New Jersey	25	10	12	22	15	12	2	2	2	0	71	14.1
Alex Tanguay	Colorado	23	6	15	21	13	8	1	0	2	0	37	16.2
Rob Blake	Colorado	23	6	13	19	6	16	3	0	0	0	83	7.2
Brian Rafalski	New Jersey	25	7	11	18	10	7	1	0	3	1	47	14.9
Mario Lemieux	Pittsburgh	18	6	11	17	4	4	1	0	3	0	39	15.4
Chris Drury	Colorado	23	11	5	16	5	4	2	0	2	0	62	17.7
Bobby Holik	New Jersey	25	6	10	16	1	37	1	0	3	0	66	9.1
Alexander Mogilny	New Jersey	25	5	11	16	3	8	1	0	2	0	76	6.6
Jason Arnott	New Jersey	23	8	7	15	8	16	5	0	0	0	42	19.0
Pierre Turgeon	St. Louis	15	5	10	15	8	2	1	0	0	0	30	16.7
Scott Gomez	New Jersey	25	5	9	14	7	24	0	0	0	0	70	7.1
Peter Forsberg	Colorado	11	4	10	14	5	6	1	0	2	1	23	17.4
Mats Sundin	Toronto	11	6	7	13	5	14	2	1	1	1	42	14.3
Scott Young	St. Louis	15	6	7	13	9	2	0	2	3	1	52	11.5
Martin Straka	Pittsburgh	18	5	8	13	–1	8	3	0	2	2	47	10.6
Miroslav Satan	Buffalo	13	3	10	13	4	8	1	0	0	0	40	7.5
Jaromir Jagr	Pittsburgh	16	2	10	12	4	18	2	0	0	0	38	5.3
Gary Roberts	Toronto	11	2	9	11	5	0	0	0	0	0	15	13.3

Playoff Defencemen Scoring Leaders

Player	Team	GP	G	A	PTS	+/–	PIM	PP	SH	GW	OT	S	%
Rob Blake	Colorado	23	6	13	19	6	16	3	0	0	0	83	7.2
Brian Rafalski	New Jersey	25	7	11	18	10	7	1	0	3	1	47	14.9
Raymond Bourque	Colorado	21	4	6	10	9	12	3	0	1	0	49	8.2
Andrew Ference	Pittsburgh	18	3	7	10	0	16	1	0	1	0	32	9.4
Al MacInnis	St. Louis	15	2	8	10	2	18	2	0	0	0	67	3.0
Mathieu Schneider	Los Angeles	13	0	9	9	4	10	0	0	0	0	34	.0
Nicklas Lidstrom	Detroit	6	1	7	8	1	0	0	0	0	0	15	6.7
Chris Pronger	St. Louis	15	1	7	8	10	32	0	0	0	0	35	2.9
Scott Stevens	New Jersey	25	1	7	8	3	37	0	0	0	0	34	2.9
Adam Foote	Colorado	23	3	4	7	5	47	1	0	1	0	28	10.7
Alexei Zhitnik	Buffalo	13	1	6	7	–3	12	0	0	0	0	18	5.6

GOALTENDING LEADERS

Goals Against Average

Goaltender	Team	GPI	Mins	GA	Avg.
Patrick Roy	Colorado	23	1451	41	1.70
Roman Turek	St. Louis	14	908	31	2.05
Martin Brodeur	New Jersey	25	1505	52	2.07
Dominik Hasek	Buffalo	13	833	29	2.09
Curtis Joseph	Toronto	11	685	24	2.10

Wins

Goaltender	Team	GPI	Mins	W	L
Patrick Roy	Colorado	23	1451	16	7
Martin Brodeur	New Jersey	25	1505	15	10
Roman Turek	St. Louis	14	908	9	5
Johan Hedberg	Pittsburgh	18	1123	9	9
Curtis Joseph	Toronto	11	685	7	4
Felix Potvin	Los Angeles	13	812	7	6
Dominik Hasek	Buffalo	13	833	7	6

Save Percentage

Goaltender	Team	GPI	Mins	GA	SA	S%	W	L
Patrick Roy	Colorado	23	1451	41	622	.934	16	7
Curtis Joseph	Toronto	11	685	24	329	.927	7	4
Roman Turek	St. Louis	14	908	31	382	.919	9	5
Dominik Hasek	Buffalo	13	833	29	347	.916	7	6
Johan Hedberg	Pittsburgh	18	1123	43	482	.911	9	9

Shutouts

Goaltender	Team	GPI	Mins	SO
Patrick Roy	Colorado	23	1451	4
Martin Brodeur	New Jersey	25	1505	4
Curtis Joseph	Toronto	11	685	3
Felix Potvin	Los Angeles	13	812	2
Johan Hedberg	Pittsburgh	18	1123	2

Goal Scoring

Name	Team	GP	G
Joe Sakic	Colorado	21	13
Chris Drury	Colorado	23	11
Petr Sykora	New Jersey	25	10
Patrik Elias	New Jersey	25	9
Jason Arnott	New Jersey	23	8
Milan Hejduk	Colorado	23	7
Brian Rafalski	New Jersey	25	7
Mats Sundin	Toronto	11	6
Steve Thomas	Toronto	11	6
Chris Gratton	Buffalo	13	6
Scott Young	St. Louis	15	6
Mario Lemieux	Pittsburgh	18	6
Randy McKay	New Jersey	19	6
Rob Blake	Colorado	23	6
Alex Tanguay	Colorado	23	6
Bobby Holik	New Jersey	25	6

Assists

Name	Team	GP	A
Milan Hejduk	Colorado	23	16
Alex Tanguay	Colorado	23	15
Patrik Elias	New Jersey	25	14
Joe Sakic	Colorado	21	13
Rob Blake	Colorado	23	13
Petr Sykora	New Jersey	25	12
Mario Lemieux	Pittsburgh	18	11
Alexander Mogilny	New Jersey	25	11
Brian Rafalski	New Jersey	25	11
Peter Forsberg	Colorado	11	10
Miroslav Satan	Buffalo	13	10
Pierre Turgeon	St. Louis	15	10
Jaromir Jagr	Pittsburgh	16	10
Bobby Holik	New Jersey	25	10

Power-play Goals

Name	Team	GP	PP
Joe Sakic	Colorado	21	5
Jason Arnott	New Jersey	23	5
Steve Thomas	Toronto	11	4
Milan Hejduk	Colorado	23	4
Steve Heinze	Buffalo	13	3
Martin Straka	Pittsburgh	18	3
Raymond Bourque	Colorado	21	3
Rob Blake	Colorado	23	3
*Ville Nieminen	Colorado	23	3
Patrik Elias	New Jersey	25	3

Game-winning Goals

Name	Team	GP	GW
Scott Young	St. Louis	15	3
Mario Lemieux	Pittsburgh	18	3
Joe Sakic	Colorado	21	3
Bobby Holik	New Jersey	25	3
Brian Rafalski	New Jersey	25	3

Short-handed Goals

Name	Team	GP	SH
Curtis Brown	Buffalo	13	2
Scott Young	St. Louis	15	2
Petr Sykora	New Jersey	25	2
Vincent Damphousse	San Jose	6	1
Daniel McGillis	Philadelphia	6	1
Mats Sundin	Toronto	11	1
Dallas Drake	St. Louis	15	1
Alexei Morozov	Pittsburgh	18	1
Patrik Elias	New Jersey	25	1

Overtime Goals

Name	Team	GP	OT
Martin Straka	Pittsburgh	18	2

Shots

Name	Team	GP	S
Rob Blake	Colorado	23	83
Joe Sakic	Colorado	21	79
Alexander Mogilny	New Jersey	25	76
Petr Sykora	New Jersey	25	71
Scott Gomez	New Jersey	25	70

Plus/Minus

Name	Team	GP	+/–
Petr Sykora	New Jersey	25	15
Alex Tanguay	Colorado	23	13
Patrik Elias	New Jersey	25	11
Chris Pronger	St. Louis	15	10
Brian Rafalski	New Jersey	25	10

TEAMS' PLAYOFF HOME/ROAD RECORD

	HOME						ROAD					
	GP	W	L	GF	GA	%	GP	W	L	GF	GA	%
COL	13	9	4	37	22	.692	10	7	3	32	19	.700
N.J.	13	7	6	35	31	.538	12	8	4	34	21	.667
ST.L.	7	5	2	20	14	.714	8	4	4	20	20	.500
PIT	8	3	5	16	26	.375	10	6	4	22	18	.600
TOR	5	3	2	13	11	.600	6	4	2	15	13	.667
BUF	7	3	4	20	17	.429	6	4	2	18	13	.667
L.A.	6	4	2	13	13	.667	7	3	4	12	21	.429
DAL	5	2	3	12	14	.400	5	2	3	10	12	.400
DET	3	2	1	11	6	.667	3	0	3	6	9	.000
EDM	3	1	2	5	7	.333	3	1	2	8	9	.333
WSH	3	1	2	3	4	.333	3	1	2	7	10	.333
S.J.	3	1	2	7	10	.333	3	1	2	4	6	.333
PHI	3	1	2	7	7	.333	3	1	2	6	14	.333
CAR	3	1	2	4	11	.333	3	1	2	4	9	.333
VAN	2	0	2	4	9	.000	2	0	2	5	7	.000
OTT	2	0	2	0	4	.000	2	0	2	3	6	.000
Total	**86**	**43**	**43**	**207**	**206**	**.500**	**8**	**43**	**43**	**206**	**207**	**.500**

TEAM PENALTIES

Abbreviations: GP – games played; **PIM** – total penalty minutes, including bench penalties; **TBPM** – total bench penalty minutes; **AVG** – average penalty minutes per game.

Team	GP	PIM	TBPM	AVG
DET	6	57	0	9.5
BUF	13	138	2	10.6
COL	23	256	6	11.1
L.A.	13	146	4	11.2
DAL	10	116	2	11.6
PIT	18	214	2	11.9
OTT	4	48	0	12.0
ST.L.	15	183	0	12.2
PHI	6	74	0	12.3
VAN	4	50	0	12.5
TOR	11	146	2	13.3
N.J.	25	334	2	13.4
EDM	6	83	0	13.8
S.J.	6	88	0	14.7
WSH	6	91	0	15.2
CAR	6	115	0	19.2
Total (2 teams)	**86**	**2139**	**20**	**24.9**

TEAMS' POWER-PLAY RECORD

Abbreviations: ADV-total advantages; **PPGF**-power play goals for; **%** arrived by dividing number of power-play goals by total advantages.

HOME

TEAM	GP	ADV	PPGF	%
1 DET	3	12	5	41.7
2 PHI	3	9	3	33.3
3 WSH	3	11	3	27.3
4 TOR	5	22	6	27.3
5 COL	13	66	17	25.8
6 BUF	7	35	8	22.9
7 VAN	2	10	2	20.0
8 L.A.	6	29	5	17.2
9 PIT	8	35	6	17.1
10 CAR	3	19	3	15.8
11 N.J.	13	57	7	12.3
12 DAL	5	25	3	12.0
13 ST.L.	7	32	3	9.4
14 EDM	3	16	1	6.3
15 OTT	2	11	0	.0
16 S.J.	3	12	0	.0
Total	**86**	**401**	**72**	**18.0**

ROAD

TEAM	GP	ADV	PPGF	%
WSH	3	11	4	36.4
VAN	2	6	2	33.3
DET	3	15	4	26.7
EDM	3	15	4	26.7
N.J.	12	44	9	20.5
ST.L.	8	30	6	20.0
PIT	10	26	5	19.2
TOR	6	17	3	17.6
PHI	3	8	1	12.5
BUF	6	16	2	12.5
COL	10	50	6	12.0
DAL	5	18	2	11.1
L.A.	7	21	1	4.8
OTT	2	5	0	.0
CAR	3	10	0	.0
S.J.	3	10	0	.0
Total	**86**	**302**	**49**	**16.2**

OVERALL

TEAM	GP	ADV	PPGF	%
DET	6	27	9	33.3
WSH	6	22	7	31.8
VAN	4	16	4	25.0
PHI	6	17	4	23.5
TOR	11	39	9	23.1
COL	23	116	23	19.8
BUF	13	51	10	19.6
PIT	18	61	11	18.0
EDM	6	31	5	16.1
N.J.	25	101	16	15.8
ST.L.	15	62	9	14.5
L.A.	13	50	6	12.0
DAL	10	43	5	11.6
CAR	6	29	3	10.3
OTT	4	16	0	.0
S.J.	6	22	0	.0
Total	**86**	**703**	**121**	**17.2**

TEAMS' PENALTY KILLING RECORD

Abbreviations: TSH – Total times short-handed; **PPGA** – power-play goals against; **%** arrived by dividing times short minus power-play goals against by times short.

HOME

Team	GP	TSH	PPGA	%
1 OTT	2	5	0	100.0
2 DET	3	6	0	100.0
3 STL	7	25	2	92.0
4 EDM	3	12	1	91.7
5 BUF	7	23	3	87.0
6 CAR	3	13	2	84.6
7 L.A	6	31	5	83.9
8 N.J	13	43	7	83.7
9 COL	13	43	7	83.7
10 WSH	3	6	1	83.3
11 PHI	3	6	1	83.3
12 DAL	5	24	4	83.3
13 TOR	5	17	3	82.4
14 VAN	2	9	2	77.8
15 PIT	8	27	7	74.1
16 S.J	3	12	4	66.7
Total	**86**	**302**	**49**	**83.8**

ROAD

Team	GP	TSH	PPGA	%
CAR	3	11	0	100.0
S.J	3	15	1	93.3
DAL	5	23	2	91.3
TOR	6	31	3	90.3
COL	10	49	6	87.8
STL	8	39	6	84.6
N.J	12	61	10	83.6
PIT	10	46	9	80.4
DET	3	14	3	78.6
EDM	3	14	3	78.6
BUF	6	21	5	76.2
WSH	3	15	4	73.3
L.A	7	32	9	71.9
VAN	2	10	3	70.0
OTT	2	8	3	62.5
PHI	3	12	5	58.3
Total	**86**	**401**	**72**	**82.0**

OVERALL

Team	GP	TSH	PPGA	%
CAR	6	24	2	91.7
TOR	11	48	6	87.5
STL	15	64	8	87.5
DAL	10	47	6	87.2
COL	23	92	13	85.9
DET	6	20	3	85.0
EDM	6	26	4	84.6
N.J	25	104	17	83.7
BUF	13	44	8	81.8
S.J	6	27	5	81.5
PIT	18	73	16	78.1
L.A	13	63	14	77.8
OTT	4	13	3	76.9
WSH	6	21	5	76.2
VAN	4	19	5	73.7
PHI	6	18	6	66.7
Total	**86**	**703**	**121**	**82.8**

SHORT HAND GOALS

Team	Games	Goals For
ST.L.	15	3
N.J.	25	3
BUF	13	2
PHI	6	1
S.J.	6	1
TOR	11	1
PIT	18	1
OTT	4	0
VAN	4	0
CAR	6	0
WSH	6	0
DET	6	0
EDM	6	0
DAL	10	0
L.A.	13	0
COL	23	0
Total	**86**	**12**

Team	Games	Goals Against
L.A.	13	0
TOR	11	0
WSH	6	0
PHI	6	0
DET	6	0
EDM	6	0
OTT	4	0
VAN	4	0
ST.L.	15	1
BUF	13	1
DAL	10	1
CAR	6	1
S.J.	6	1
N.J.	25	2
COL	23	2
PIT	18	3
Total	**86**	**12**

Colorado's Patrick Roy led all playoff netminders in every major statistical category en route to becoming the first player to win the Conn Smythe Trophy as playoff MVP three times.

Stanley Cup Record Book

History: The Stanley Cup, the oldest trophy competed for by professional athletes in North America, was donated by Frederick Arthur, Lord Stanley of Preston and son of the Earl of Derby, in 1893. Lord Stanley purchased the trophy for 10 guineas ($50 at that time) for presentation to the amateur hockey champions of Canada. Since 1910, when the National Hockey Association took possession of the Stanley Cup, the trophy has been the symbol of professional hockey supremacy. It has been competed for only by NHL teams since 1926-27 and has been under the exclusive control of the NHL since 1947.

Stanley Cup Standings

1918-2001

(ranked by Cup wins)

Teams	Cup Wins	Yrs.	Series	Wins	Losses	Games	Wins	Losses	Ties	Goals For	Goals Against	Winning %
Montreal	23[1]	72	134[2]	85	48	638	381	249	8	1977	1591	.603
Toronto	13	61	103	55	48	484	232	248	4	1263	1362	.484
Detroit	9	50	92	51	41	455	235	219	1	1283	1201	.518
Boston	5	59	101	47	54	494	236	252	6	1448	1464	.484
Edmonton	5	18	44	31	13	221	135	86	0	857	682	.611
NY Rangers	4	48	86	42	44	386	183	195	8	1091	1114	.484
NY Islanders	4	17	43	30	13	218	128	90	0	748	650	.587
Chicago	3	52	89	40	49	406	187	214	5	1171	1298	.467
Philadelphia	2	27	58	33	25	304	160	144	0	946	902	.526
Pittsburgh	2	21	39	20	19	208	109	99	0	644	641	.524
Colorado[3]	2	15	33	20	13	185	102	83	0	570	524	.551
New Jersey[4]	2	13	27	16	11	158	88	70	0	449	403	.557
Dallas[5]	1	24	48	25	23	260	133	127	0	782	793	.512
Calgary[6]	1	21	32	12	20	156	69	87	0	529	573	.442
St. Louis	0	31	53	22	31	281	129	152	0	803	895	.459
Buffalo	0	25	42	17	25	209	99	110	0	626	639	.474
Los Angeles	0	22	33	11	22	163	62	101	0	498	633	.380
Vancouver	0	17	26	9	17	128	54	74	0	386	438	.422
Washington	0	17	27	10	17	148	67	81	0	452	464	.453
Phoenix[7]	0	15	17	2	15	87	28	59	0	238	330	.322
Carolina[8]	0	10	11	1	10	61	22	39	0	161	213	.361
San Jose	0	6	9	3	6	55	22	33	0	141	200	.400
Ottawa	0	5	6	1	5	32	10	22	0	52	83	.313
Florida	0	3	6	3	3	31	13	18	0	77	82	.419
Anaheim	0	2	3	1	2	15	4	11	0	31	47	.267
Tampa Bay	0	1	1	0	1	6	2	4	0	13	26	.333

1 Montreal also won the Stanley Cup in 1916.
2 1919 final incomplete due to influenza epidemic.
3 Includes totals of Quebec 1979-95.
4 Includes totals of Colorado Rockies 1976-82.
5 Includes totals of Minnesota North Stars 1967-93.
6 Includes totals of Atlanta Flames 1972-80.
7 Includes totals of Winnipeg 1979-96.
8 Includes totals of Hartford 1979-97.

Stanley Cup Winners Prior to Formation of NHL in 1917

Season	Champions	Manager	Coach
1916-17	Seattle Metropolitans	Pete Muldoon	Pete Muldoon
1915-16	Montreal Canadiens	George Kennedy	George Kennedy
1914-15	Vancouver Millionaires	Frank Patrick	Frank Patrick
1913-14	Toronto Blueshirts	Jack Marshall	Scotty Davidson*
1912-13**	Quebec Bulldogs	M.J. Quinn	Joe Malone*
1911-12	Quebec Bulldogs	M.J. Quinn	C. Nolan
1910-11	Ottawa Senators		Bruce Stuart*
1909-10	Montreal Wanderers	R. R. Boon	Pud Glass*
1908-09	Ottawa Senators		Bruce Stuart*
1907-08	Montreal Wanderers	R. R. Boon	Cecil Blachford
1906-07	Montreal Wanderers (Mar. 1907)	R. R. Boon	Cecil Blachford
1906-07	Kenora Thistles (Jan./Mar. 1907)	F.A. Hudson	Tommy Phillips*
1905-06	Montreal Wanderers (Mar. 1906)	Cecil Blachford*	
1905-06	Ottawa Silver Seven (Feb. 1906)		A. T. Smith
1904-05	Ottawa Silver Seven		A. T. Smith
1903-04	Ottawa Silver Seven		A. T. Smith
1902-03	Ottawa Silver Seven (Mar. 1903)		A. T. Smith
1902-03	Montreal A.A.A. (Feb. 1903)		C. McKerrow
1901-02	Montreal A.A.A. (Mar. 1902)		C. McKerrow
1901-02	Winnipeg Victorias (Jan. 1902)		
1900-01	Winnipeg Victorias		D. H. Bain*
1899-1900	Montreal Shamrocks		H.J. Trihey*
1898-99	Montreal Shamrocks (Mar. 1899)		H.J. Trihey*
1898-99	Montreal Victorias (Feb. 1899)		Mike Grant*
1897-98	Montreal Victorias		F. Richardson
1896-97	Montreal Victorias		Mike Grant*
1895-96	Montreal Victorias (Dec. 1896)		Mike Grant*
1895-96	Winnipeg Victorias (Feb. 1896)		J.C. G. Armytage
1894-95	Montreal Victorias		Mike Grant*
1893-94	Montreal A.A.A.		
1892-93	Montreal A.A.A.		

* In the early years the teams were frequently run by the Captain. *Indicates Captain
** Victoria defeated Quebec in challenge series. No official recognition.

Stanley Cup Winners

Year	W-L-T in Finals	Winner	Coach	Finalist	Coach
2001	4-3	Colorado	Bob Hartley	New Jersey	Larry Robinson
2000	4-2	New Jersey	Larry Robinson	Dallas	Ken Hitchcock
1999	4-2	Dallas	Ken Hitchcock	Buffalo	Lindy Ruff
1998	4-0	Detroit	Scotty Bowman	Washington	Ron Wilson
1997	4-0	Detroit	Scotty Bowman	Philadelphia	Terry Murray
1996	4-0	Colorado	Marc Crawford	Florida	Doug MacLean
1995	4-0	New Jersey	Jacques Lemaire	Detroit	Scotty Bowman
1994	4-3	NY Rangers	Mike Keenan	Vancouver	Pat Quinn
1993	4-1	Montreal	Jacques Demers	Los Angeles	Barry Melrose
1992	4-0	Pittsburgh	Scotty Bowman	Chicago	Mike Keenan
1991	4-2	Pittsburgh	Bob Johnson	Minnesota	Bob Gainey
1990	4-1	Edmonton	John Muckler	Boston	Mike Milbury
1989	4-2	Calgary	Terry Crisp	Montreal	Pat Burns
1988	4-0	Edmonton	Glen Sather	Boston	Terry O'Reilly
1987	4-3	Edmonton	Glen Sather	Philadelphia	Mike Keenan
1986	4-1	Montreal	Jean Perron	Calgary	Bob Johnson
1985	4-1	Edmonton	Glen Sather	Philadelphia	Mike Keenan
1984	4-1	Edmonton	Glen Sather	NY Islanders	Al Arbour
1983	4-0	NY Islanders	Al Arbour	Edmonton	Glen Sather
1982	4-0	NY Islanders	Al Arbour	Vancouver	Roger Neilson
1981	4-1	NY Islanders	Al Arbour	Minnesota	Glen Sonmor
1980	4-2	NY Islanders	Al Arbour	Philadelphia	Pat Quinn
1979	4-1	Montreal	Scotty Bowman	NY Rangers	Fred Shero
1978	4-2	Montreal	Scotty Bowman	Boston	Don Cherry
1977	4-0	Montreal	Scotty Bowman	Boston	Don Cherry
1976	4-0	Montreal	Scotty Bowman	Philadelphia	Fred Shero
1975	4-2	Philadelphia	Fred Shero	Buffalo	Floyd Smith
1974	4-2	Philadelphia	Fred Shero	Boston	Bep Guidolin
1973	4-2	Montreal	Scotty Bowman	Chicago	Billy Reay
1972	4-2	Boston	Tom Johnson	NY Rangers	Emile Francis
1971	4-3	Montreal	Al MacNeil	Chicago	Billy Reay
1970	4-0	Boston	Harry Sinden	St. Louis	Scotty Bowman
1969	4-0	Montreal	Claude Ruel	St. Louis	Scotty Bowman
1968	4-0	Montreal	Toe Blake	St. Louis	Scotty Bowman
1967	4-2	Toronto	Punch Imlach	Montreal	Toe Blake
1966	4-2	Montreal	Toe Blake	Detroit	Sid Abel
1965	4-3	Montreal	Toe Blake	Chicago	Billy Reay
1964	4-3	Toronto	Punch Imlach	Detroit	Sid Abel
1963	4-1	Toronto	Punch Imlach	Detroit	Sid Abel
1962	4-2	Toronto	Punch Imlach	Chicago	Rudy Pilous
1961	4-2	Chicago	Rudy Pilous	Detroit	Sid Abel
1960	4-0	Montreal	Toe Blake	Toronto	Punch Imlach
1959	4-1	Montreal	Toe Blake	Toronto	Punch Imlach
1958	4-2	Montreal	Toe Blake	Boston	Milt Schmidt
1957	4-1	Montreal	Toe Blake	Boston	Milt Schmidt
1956	4-1	Montreal	Toe Blake	Detroit	Jimmy Skinner
1955	4-3	Detroit	Jimmy Skinner	Montreal	Dick Irvin
1954	4-3	Detroit	Tommy Ivan	Montreal	Dick Irvin
1953	4-1	Montreal	Dick Irvin	Boston	Lynn Patrick
1952	4-0	Detroit	Tommy Ivan	Montreal	Dick Irvin
1951	4-1	Toronto	Joe Primeau	Montreal	Dick Irvin
1950	4-3	Detroit	Tommy Ivan	NY Rangers	Lynn Patrick
1949	4-0	Toronto	Hap Day	Detroit	Tommy Ivan
1948	4-0	Toronto	Hap Day	Detroit	Tommy Ivan
1947	4-2	Toronto	Hap Day	Montreal	Dick Irvin
1946	4-1	Montreal	Dick Irvin	Boston	Dit Clapper
1945	4-3	Toronto	Hap Day	Detroit	Jack Adams
1944	4-0	Montreal	Dick Irvin	Chicago	Paul Thompson
1943	4-0	Detroit	Jack Adams	Boston	Art Ross
1942	4-3	Toronto	Hap Day	Detroit	Jack Adams
1941	4-0	Boston	Cooney Weiland	Detroit	Ebbie Goodfellow
1940	4-2	NY Rangers	Frank Boucher	Toronto	Dick Irvin
1939	4-1	Boston	Art Ross	Toronto	Dick Irvin
1938	3-1	Chicago	Bill Stewart	Toronto	Dick Irvin
1937	3-2	Detroit	Jack Adams	NY Rangers	Lester Patrick
1936	3-1	Detroit	Jack Adams	Toronto	Dick Irvin
1935	3-0	Mtl. Maroons	Tommy Gorman	Toronto	Dick Irvin
1934	3-1	Chicago	Tommy Gorman	Detroit	Herbie Lewis
1933	3-1	NY Rangers	Lester Patrick	Toronto	Dick Irvin
1932	3-0	Toronto	Dick Irvin	NY Rangers	Lester Patrick
1931	3-2	Montreal	Cecil Hart	Chicago	Dick Irvin
1930	2-0	Montreal	Cecil Hart	Boston	Art Ross
1929	2-0	Boston	Cy Denneny	NY Rangers	Lester Patrick
1928	3-2	NY Rangers	Lester Patrick	Mtl. Maroons	Eddie Gerard
1927	2-0-2	Ottawa	Dave Gill	Boston	Art Ross

The National Hockey League assumed control of Stanley Cup competition after 1926

Year	W-L-T in Finals	Winner	Coach	Finalist	Coach
1926	3-1	Mtl. Maroons	Eddie Gerard	Victoria	Lester Patrick
1925	3-1	Victoria	Lester Patrick	Montreal	Leo Dandurand
1924	2-0	Montreal	Leo Dandurand	Cgy. Tigers	Eddie Oatman
	2-0			Van. Maroons	Art Duncan/Frank Patrick
1923	2-0	Ottawa	Pete Green	Edm. Eskimos	Ken McKenzie
	3-1			Van. Maroons	Lloyd Cook/Frank Patrick
1922	3-2	Tor. St. Pats	George O'Donoghue	Van. Millionaires	Lloyd Cook/Frank Patrick
1921	3-2	Ottawa	Pete Green	Van. Millionaires	Lloyd Cook/Frank Patrick
1920	3-2	Ottawa	Pete Green	Seattle	Pete Muldoon
1919	2-2-1	No decision - series between Montreal and Seattle cancelled due to influenza epidemic			
1918	3-2	Tor. Arenas	Dick Carroll	Van. Millionaires	Frank Patrick

Championship Trophies

PRINCE OF WALES TROPHY

Beginning with the 1993-94 season, the club which advances to the Stanley Cup Finals as the winner of the Eastern Conference Championship is presented with the Prince of Wales Trophy.

History: His Royal Highness, the Prince of Wales, donated the trophy to the National Hockey League in 1924. From 1927-28 through 1937-38, the award was presented to the team finishing first in the American Division of the NHL. From 1938-39, when the NHL reverted to one section, to 1966-67, it was presented to the team winning the NHL regular-season championship. With expansion in 1967-68, it again became a divisional trophy, awarded to the regular-season champions of the East Division through to the end of the 1973-74 season. Beginning in 1974-75, it was awarded to the regular-season winner of the conference bearing the name of the trophy. From 1981-82 to 1992-93 the trophy was presented to the playoff champion in the Wales Conference. Since 1993-94, the trophy has been presented to the playoff champion in the Eastern Conference.

2000-2001 Winner: New Jersey Devils

The New Jersey Devils won their second consecutive Prince of Wales Trophy on May 22, 2001 after defeating the Pittsburgh Penguins 4-2 at home in game five of the Eastern Conference Championship series. Before defeating the Penguins, the Devils had series wins over the Carolina Panthers and Toronto Maple Leafs.

PRINCE OF WALES TROPHY WINNERS

2000-01	New Jersey Devils	1961-62	Montreal Canadiens
99-2000	New Jersey Devils	1960-61	Montreal Canadiens
1998-99	Buffalo Sabres	1959-60	Montreal Canadiens
1997-98	Washington Capitals	1958-59	Montreal Canadiens
1996-97	Philadelphia Flyers	1957-58	Montreal Canadiens
1995-96	Florida Panthers	1956-57	Detroit Red Wings
1994-95	New Jersey Devils	1955-56	Montreal Canadiens
1993-94	New York Rangers	1954-55	Detroit Red Wings
1992-93	Montreal Canadiens	1953-54	Detroit Red Wings
1991-92	Pittsburgh Penguins	1952-53	Detroit Red Wings
1990-91	Pittsburgh Penguins	1951-52	Detroit Red Wings
1989-90	Boston Bruins	1950-51	Detroit Red Wings
1988-89	Montreal Canadiens	1949-50	Detroit Red Wings
1987-88	Boston Bruins	1948-49	Detroit Red Wings
1986-87	Philadelphia Flyers	1947-48	Toronto Maple Leafs
1985-86	Montreal Canadiens	1946-47	Montreal Canadiens
1984-85	Philadelphia Flyers	1945-46	Montreal Canadiens
1983-84	New York Islanders	1944-45	Montreal Canadiens
1982-83	New York Islanders	1943-44	Montreal Canadiens
1981-82	New York Islanders	1942-43	Detroit Red Wings
1980-81	Montreal Canadiens	1941-42	New York Rangers
1979-80	Buffalo Sabres	1940-41	Boston Bruins
1978-79	Montreal Canadiens	1939-40	Boston Bruins
1977-78	Montreal Canadiens	1938-39	Boston Bruins
1976-77	Montreal Canadiens	1937-38	Boston Bruins
1975-76	Montreal Canadiens	1936-37	Detroit Red Wings
1974-75	Buffalo Sabres	1935-36	Detroit Red Wings
1973-74	Boston Bruins	1934-35	Boston Bruins
1972-73	Montreal Canadiens	1933-34	Detroit Red Wings
1971-72	Boston Bruins	1932-33	Boston Bruins
1970-71	Boston Bruins	1931-32	New York Rangers
1969-70	Chicago Blackhawks	1930-31	Boston Bruins
1968-69	Montreal Canadiens	1929-30	Boston Bruins
1967-68	Montreal Canadiens	1928-29	Boston Bruins
1966-67	Chicago Blackhawks	1927-28	Boston Bruins
1965-66	Montreal Canadiens	1926-27	Ottawa Senators
1964-65	Detroit Red Wings	1925-26	Montreal Maroons
1963-64	Montreal Canadiens	1924-25	Montreal Canadiens
1962-63	Toronto Maple Leafs	1923-24	Montreal Canadiens

Prince of Wales Trophy

Clarence S. Campbell Bowl

Stanley Cup

CLARENCE S. CAMPBELL BOWL

Beginning with the 1993-94 season, the club which advances to the Stanley Cup Finals as the winner of the Western Conference Championship is presented with the Clarence S. Campbell Bowl.

History: Presented by the member clubs in 1968 for perpetual competition by the National Hockey League in recognition of the services of Clarence S. Campbell, President of the NHL from 1946 to 1977. From 1967-68 through 1973-74, the trophy was awarded to the regular-season champions of the West Division. Beginning in 1974-75, it was awarded to the regular-season winner of the conference bearing the name of the trophy. From 1981-82 to 1992-93 the trophy was presented to the playoff champion in the Campbell Conference. Since 1993-94, the trophy has been presented to the playoff champion in the Western Conference. The trophy itself is a hallmark piece made of sterling silver and was crafted by a British silversmith in 1878.

2000-2001 Winner: Colorado Avalanche

The Colorado Avalanche won their first Clarence Campbell Bowl since 1996 on May 21, 2001 after defeating the St. Louis Blues 2-1 in overtime in game five of the Western Conference Championship series. Before defeating the Blues, the Avalanche had series wins over the Vancouver Canucks and Los Angeles Kings.

CLARENCE S. CAMPBELL BOWL WINNERS

2000-01	Colorado Avalanche	1983-84	Edmonton Oilers
99-2000	Dallas Stars	1982-83	Edmonton Oilers
1998-99	Dallas Stars	1981-82	Vancouver Canucks
1997-98	Detroit Red Wings	1980-81	New York Islanders
1996-97	Detroit Red Wings	1979-80	Philadelphia Flyers
1995-96	Colorado Avalanche	1978-79	New York Islanders
1994-95	Detroit Red Wings	1977-78	New York Islanders
1993-94	Vancouver Canucks	1976-77	Philadelphia Flyers
1992-93	Los Angeles Kings	1975-76	Philadelphia Flyers
1991-92	Chicago Blackhawks	1974-75	Philadelphia Flyers
1990-91	Minnesota North Stars	1973-74	Philadelphia Flyers
1989-90	Edmonton Oilers	1972-73	Chicago Blackhawks
1988-89	Calgary Flames	1971-72	Chicago Blackhawks
1987-88	Edmonton Oilers	1970-71	Chicago Blackhawks
1986-87	Edmonton Oilers	1969-70	St. Louis Blues
1985-86	Calgary Flames	1968-69	St. Louis Blues
1984-85	Edmonton Oilers	1967-68	Philadelphia Flyers

Stanley Cup Winners

Rosters and Final Series Scores

2000-01 — Colorado Avalanche — Joe Sakic (Captain), David Aebischer, Rob Blake, Raymond Bourque, Greg de Vries, Chris Dingman, Chris Drury, Adam Foote, Peter Forsberg, Milan Hejduk, Dan Hinote, Jon Klemm, Eric Messier, Bryan Muir, Ville Nieminen, Scott Parker, Shjon Podein, Nolan Pratt, David Reid, Steven Reinprecht, Patrick Roy, Martin Skoula, Alex Tanguay, Stephane Yelle, E. Stanley Kroenke (Owner/Governor), Pierre Lacroix (President and General Manager), Bob Hartley (Head Coach), Jacques Cloutier (Assistant Coach), Bryan Trottier (Assistant Coach), Paul Fixter (Video Coach), Francois Giguere (Vice President of Hockey Operations), Brian MacDonald (Assistant General Manager), Michel Goulet (Vice President of Player Personnel), Jean Martineau (Vice President of Communications/Team Services), Pat Karns (Head Athletic Trainer), Matthew Sokolowski (Assistant Athletic Trainer), Wayne Flemming (Equipment Manager), Mark Miller (Equipment Manager), Dave Randolph (Assistant Equipment Manager), Paul Goldberg (Strength and Conditioning Coach), Gregorio Pradera (Massage Therapist), Brad Smith (Pro Scout), Jim Hammett (Chief Scout), Garth Joy, Steve Lyons, Joni Lehto, Orval Tessier (Scouts), Charlotte Grahame (Director of Hockey Operations).

Scores: May 26, at Colorado - Colorado 5, New Jersey 0; May 29, at Colorado - New Jersey 2, Colorado 1; May 31, at New Jersey - Colorado 3, New Jersey 1; June 2, at New Jersey - New Jersey 3, Colorado 2; June 4, at Colorado - New Jersey 4, Colorado 1; June 7, at New Jersey - Colorado 4, New Jersey 0; June 9, at Colorado - Colorado 3, New Jersey 1.

1999-2000 — New Jersey Devils — Scott Stevens (Captain), Jason Arnott, Brad Bombardir, Martin Brodeur, Steve Brule, Sergei Brylin, Ken Daneyko, Patrik Elias, Scott Gomez, Bobby Holik, Steve Kelly, Claude Lemieux, John Madden, Vladimir Malakhov, Randy McKay, Alexander Mogilny, Sergei Nemchinov, Scott Niedermayer, Krzysztof Oliwa, Jay Pandolfo, Brian Rafalski, Ken Sutton, Petr Sykora, Chris Terreri, Colin White, Dr. John J. McMullen (Owner/Chairman), Peter S. McMullen (Owner), Lou Lamoriello (President/General Manager), Larry Robinson (Head Coach), Viacheslav Fetisov (Assistant Coach), Bob Carpenter (Assistant Coach), Jacques Caron (Goaltending Coach), John Cunniff (AHL Coach), David Conte (Director of Scouting), Milt Fisher (Scout), Claude Carrier (Assistant Director of Scouting), Dan Labraaten (Scout), Marcel Pronovost (Scout), Bob Hoffmeyer (Pro Scout), Dr. Barry Fisher (Orthopedist), Dennis Gendron (AHL Assistant Coach), Robbie Ftorek (Coach), Vladimir Bure (Consultant), Taran Singleton (Hockey Operations), Marie Carnevale (Hockey Operations), Callie Smith (Hockey Operations), Bill Murray (Medical Trainer), Michael Vasalani (Strength/Conditioning Coordinator), Dana McGuane (Equipment Manager), Juergen Merz (Massage Therapist), Harry Bricker (Assistant Equipment Manager), Lou Centanni (Assistant Equipment Manager).

Scores: May 30, at New Jersey - New Jersey 7, Dallas 3; June 1, at New Jersey - Dallas 2, New Jersey 1; June 3, at Dallas - New Jersey 2, Dallas 1; June 5, at Dallas - New Jersey 3, Dallas 1; June 8, at New Jersey - Dallas 1 - New Jersey 0; at Dallas, New Jersey 2 - Dallas 1.

1998-99 — Dallas Stars — Derian Hatcher (Captain), Ed Belfour, Guy Carbonneau, Shawn Chambers, Benoit Hogue, Tony Hrkac, Brett Hull, Mike Keane, Jamie Langenbrunner, Jere Lehtinen, Craig Ludwig, Grant Marshall, Richard Matvichuk, Mike Modano, Joe Nieuwendyk, Derek Plante, Dave Reid, Jon Sim, Brian Skrudland, Blake Sloan, Darryl Sydor, Roman Turek, Pat Verbeek, Sergei Zubov, Thomas Hicks (Chairman of the Board and Owner), Jim Lites (President), Bob Gainey (Vice President, Hockey Operations and General Manager), Doug Armstrong (Assistant General Manager), Craig Button (Director of Player Personnel), Ken Hitchcock (Head Coach), Doug Jarvis (Assistant Coach), Rick Wilson (Assistant Coach), Rick McLaughlin (Vice President and Chief Financial Officer), Jeff Cogen (Vice President, Marketing and Promotion), Bill Strong (Vice President, Marketing and Broadcasting), Tim Bernhardt (Director of Amateur Scouting), Doug Overton (Director of Pro Scouting), Bob Gernander (Chief Scout), Stu MacGregor (Western Scout), Dave Suprenant (Medical Trainer), Dave Smith (Equipment Manager), Rich Matthews (Equipment Manager), J.J. McQueen (Strength and Conditioning Coach), Rick St. Croix (Goaltending Consultant), Dan Stuchal (Director of Team Services), Larry Kelly (Director of Public Relations).

Scores: June 8, at Dallas - Buffalo 3, Dallas 2; June 10, at Dallas - Dallas 4, Buffalo 2; June 12, at Buffalo - Dallas 2, Buffalo 1; June 15, at Buffalo - Buffalo 2, Dallas 1; June 17, at Dallas - Dallas 2, Buffalo 0; June 19, at Buffalo - Dallas 2, Buffalo 1.

1997-98 — Detroit Red Wings — Steve Yzerman (Captain), Doug Brown, Mathieu Dandenault, Kris Draper, Anders Eriksson, Sergei Fedorov, Viacheslav Fetisov, Brent Gilchrist, Kevin Hodson, Tomas Holmstrom, Michael Knuble, Joey Kocur, Vladimir Konstantinov, Vyacheslav Kozlov, Martin Lapointe, Igor Larionov, Nicklas Lidstrom, Jamie Macoun, Kirk Maltby, Darren McCarty, Dmitri Mironov, Larry Murphy, Chris Osgood, Bob Rouse, Brendan Shanahan, Aaron Ward, Mike Ilitch, (Owner/Chairman), Marian Ilitch (Owner), Atanas Ilitch (Vice President), Christopher Ilitch (Vice President), Denise Ilitch, Ronald Ilitch, Michael Ilitch Jr., Lisa Ilitch Murray, Carole Ilitch Trepeck, Jim Devellano (Senior Vice President), Scotty Bowman (Head Coach), Ken Holland (General Manager), Don Waddell (Assistant General Manager), Barry Smith (Associate Coach), Dave Lewis (Associate Coach), Jim Bedard (Goaltending Consultant), Jim Nill (Director of Player Development), Dan Belisle (Pro Scout), Mark Howe (Pro Scout), Hakan Andersson (Director of European Scouting), Mark Leach (USA Scout), Moe McDonnell (Eastern Scout), Bruce Haralson (Western Scout), John Wharton (Athletic Trainer), Paul Boyer (Equipment Manager) Tim Abbott (Assistant Equipment Manager), Bob Huddleston (Masseur), Sergei Mnatsakanov (Masseur), Wally Crossman (Dressing Room Assistant).

Scores: June 9, at Detroit — Detroit 2, Washington 1; June 11, at Detroit — Detroit 5, Washington 4; June 13, at Washington — Detroit 2, Washington 1; June 16, at Washington — Detroit 4, Washington 1.

1996-97 — Detroit Red Wings — Steve Yzerman (Captain), Doug Brown, Mathieu Dandenault, Kris Draper, Sergei Fedorov, Viacheslav Fetisov, Kevin Hodson, Tomas Holmstrom, Joe Kocur, Vladimir Konstantinov, Vyacheslav Kozlov, Martin Lapointe, Igor Larionov, Nicklas Lidstrom, Kirk Maltby, Darren McCarty, Larry Murphy, Chris Osgood, Jamie Pushor, Bob Rouse, Tomas Sandstrom, Brendan Shanahan, Tim Taylor, Mike Vernon, Aaron Ward, Mike Ilitch (Owner/Chairman), Marian Ilitch (Owner), Atanas Ilitch (Vice President), Christopher Ilitch (Vice President), Denise Ilitch Lites, Ronald Ilitch, Michael Ilitch, Jr., Lisa Ilitch Murray, Carole Ilitch Trepeck, Jim Devellano (Senior Vice President), Scotty Bowman (Head Coach/Director of Player Personnel), Ken Holland (Assistant General Manager), Barry Smith (Associate Coach), Dave Lewis (Associate Coach), Mike Krushelnyski (Assistant Coach). Jim Nill (Director of Player Development), Dan Belisle (Pro Scout), Mark Howe (Pro Scout), Hakan Andersson (Director of European Scouting), John Wharton (Athletic Trainer), Paul Boyer (Equipment Manager) Tim Abbott (Assistant Equipment Manager), Sergei Mnatsakanov (Masseur).

Scores: May 31, at Philadelphia — Detroit 4, Philadelphia 2; June 3, at Philadelphia — Detroit 4, Philadelphia 2; June 5, at Detroit — Detroit 6, Philadelphia 1; June 7, at Detroit — Detroit 2, Philadelphia 1.

1995-96 — Colorado Avalanche — Joe Sakic (Captain), Rene Corbet, Adam Deadmarsh, Stephane Fiset, Adam Foote, Peter Forsberg, Alexei Gusarov, Dave Hannan, Valeri Kamensky, Mike Keane, Jon Klemm, Uwe Krupp, Sylvain Lefebvre, Claude Lemieux, Curtis Leschyshyn, Troy Murray, Sandis Ozolinsh, Mike Ricci, Patrick Roy, Warren Rychel, Chris Simon, Craig Wolanin, Stephane Yelle, Scott Young, Charlie Lyons (Chairman, CEO), Pierre Lacroix (Exec. V.P., G.M.), Marc Crawford (Head Coach), Joel Quenneville (Assistant Coach), Jacques Cloutier (Assistant Coach), Francois Giguere (Assistant General Manager), Michel Goulet (Director of Player Personnel), Dave Draper (Chief Scout), Jean Martineau (Director of Public Relations), Pat Karns (Trainer), Matthew Sokolowski (Assistant Trainer), Rob McLean (Equipment Manager), Mike Kramer (Assistant Equipment Manager), Brock Gibbins (Assistant Equipment Manager), Skip Allen (Strength and Conditioning Coach), Paul Fixter (Video Coordinator), Leo Vyssokov (Massage Therapist).

Scores: June 4, at Colorado — Colorado 3, Florida 1; June 6, at Colorado — Colorado 8, Florida 1; June 8, at Florida — Colorado 3, Florida 2; June 10, at Florida — Colorado 1, Florida 0.

1994-95 — New Jersey Devils — Scott Stevens (Captain), Tommy Albelin, Martin Brodeur, Neil Broten, Sergei Brylin, Bob Carpenter, Shawn Chambers, Tom Chorske, Danton Cole, Ken Daneyko, Kevin Dean, Jim Dowd, Bruce Driver (Alternate Captain), Bill Guerin, Bobby Holik, Claude Lemieux, John MacLean (Alternate Captain), Chris McAlpine, Randy McKay, Scott Niedermayer, Mike Peluso, Stephane J.J. Richer, Brian Rolston, Chris Terreri, Valeri Zelepukin, Dr. John J. McMullen (Owner/Chairman), Peter S. McMullen (Owner), Lou Lamoriello (President/General Manager), Jacques Lemaire (Head Coach), Jacques Caron (Goaltender Coach), Dennis Gendron (Assistant Coach), Larry Robinson (Assistant Coach), Robbie Ftorek (AHL Coach), Alex Abasto (Assistant Equipment Manager), Bob Huddleston (Massage Therapist), David Nichols (Equipment Manager), Ted Schuch (Medical Trainer), Mike Vasalani (Strength Coach), David Conte (Director of Scouting) Claude Carrier (Scout), Milt Fisher (Scout), Dan Labraaten (Scout), Marcel Pronovost (Scout).

Scores: June 17, at Detroit — New Jersey 2, Detroit 1; June 20, at Detroit — New Jersey 4, Detroit 2; June 22, at New Jersey — New Jersey 5, Detroit 2; June 24, at New Jersey — New Jersey 5, Detroit 2.

1993-94 — New York Rangers — Mark Messier (Captain), Brian Leetch, Kevin Lowe, Adam Graves, Steve Larmer, Glenn Anderson, Jeff Beukeboom, Greg Gilbert, Mike Hartman, Glenn Healy, Mike Hudson, Alexander Karpovtsev, Joe Kocur, Alexei Kovalev, Nick Kypreos, Doug Lidster, Stephane Matteau, Craig MacTavish, Sergei Nemchinov, Brian Noonan, Ed Olczyk, Mike Richter, Esa Tikkanen, Jay Wells, Sergei Zubov, Neil Smith (President, General Manager and Governor), Robert Gutkowski, Stanley Jaffe, Kenneth Munoz (Governors), Larry Pleau (Assistant General Manager), Mike Keenan (Head Coach), Colin Campbell (Associate Coach), Dick Todd (Assistant Coach), Matthew Loughren (Manager, Team Operations), Barry Watkins (Director, Communications), Christer Rockstrom, Tony Feltrin, Martin Madden, Herb Hammond, Darwin Bennett (Scouts), Dave Smith, Joe Murphy, Mike Folga, Bruce Lifrieri (Trainers).

Scores: May 31, at New York — Vancouver 3, NY Rangers 2; June 2, at New York — NY Rangers 3, Vancouver 1; June 4, at Vancouver — NY Rangers 5, Vancouver 1; June 7, at Vancouver — NY Rangers 4, Vancouver 2; June 9, at New York — Vancouver 6, at NY Rangers 3; June 11, at Vancouver — Vancouver 4, NY Rangers 1; June 14, at New York — NY Rangers 3, Vancouver 2.

1992-93 — Montreal Canadiens — Guy Carbonneau (Captain), Patrick Roy, Mike Keane, Eric Desjardins, Stephan Lebeau, Mathieu Schneider, Jean-Jacques Daigneault, Denis Savard, Lyle Odelein, Todd Ewen, Kirk Muller, John LeClair, Gilbert Dionne, Benoit Brunet, Patrice Brisebois, Paul Di Pietro, Andre Racicot, Donald Dufresne, Mario Roberge, Sean Hill, Ed Ronan, Kevin Haller, Vincent Damphousse, Brian Bellows, Gary Leeman, Rob Ramage, Ronald Corey (President), Serge Savard (Managing Director & Vice-President Hockey), Jacques Demers (Head Coach), Jacques Laperriere (Assistant Coach), Charles Thiffault (Assistant Coach), Francois Allaire (Goaltending Instructor), Jean Béliveau (Senior Vice-President, Corporate Affairs), Fred Steer (Vice-President, Finance & Adminstration), Aldo Giampaolo (Vice-President, Operations), Bernard Brisset (Vice-President, Marketing & Communications), André Boudrias (Assistant to the Managing Director & Director of Scouting), Jacques Lemaire (Assistant to the Managing Director), Gaeten Lefebvre (Athletic Trainer), John Shipman (Assistant to the Athletic Trainer), Eddy Palchak (Equipment Manager), Pierre Gervais (Assistant to the Equipment Manager), Robert Boulanger (Assistant to the Equipment Manager), Pierre Ouellete (Assistant to the Equipment Manager).

Scores: June 1, at Montreal — Los Angeles 4, Montreal 1; June 2, at Montreal — Montreal 3, Los Angeles 2; June 5, at Los Angeles — Montreal 4, Los Angeles 3; June 7, at Los Angeles — Montreal 3, Los Angeles 2; June 9, at Montreal — Montreal 4, Los Angeles 1.

1991-92 — Pittsburgh Penguins — Mario Lemieux (Captain), Ron Francis, Bryan Trottier, Kevin Stevens, Bob Errey, Phil Bourque, Troy Loney, Rick Tocchet, Joe Mullen, Jaromir Jagr, Jiri Hrdina, Shawn McEachern, Ulf Samuelsson, Kjell Samuelsson, Larry Murphy, Gord Roberts, Jim Paek, Paul Stanton, Tom Barrasso, Ken Wregget, Jay Caufield, Jamie Leach, Wendell Young, Grant Jennings, Peter Taglianetti, Jock Callander, Dave Michayluk, Mike Needham, Jeff Chychrun, Ken Priestlay, Jeff Daniels, Howard Baldwin (Owner and President), Morris Belzberg (Owner), Thomas Ruta (Owner), Donn Patton (Executive Vice President and Chief Financial Officer), Paul Martha (Executive Vice President and General Counsel), Craig Patrick (Executive Vice President and General Manager), Bob Johnson (Coach), Scotty Bowman (Director of Player Development and Coach), Barry Smith, Rick Kehoe, Pierre McGuire, Gilles Meloche, Rick Paterson (Assistant Coaches), Steve Latin (Equipment Manager), Skip Thayer (Trainer), John Welday (Strength and Conditioning Coach), Greg Malone, Les Binkley, Charlie Hodge, John Gill, Ralph Cox (Scouts).

Scores: May 26, at Pittsburgh — Pittsburgh 5, Chicago 4; May 28, at Pittsburgh — Pittsburgh 3, Chicago 1; May 30, at Chicago — Pittsburgh 1, Chicago 0; June 1, at Chicago — Pittsburgh 6, Chicago 5.

1990-91 — Pittsburgh Penguins — Mario Lemieux (Captain), Paul Coffey, Randy Hillier, Bob Errey, Tom Barrasso, Phil Bourque, Jay Caufield, Ron Francis, Randy Gilhen, Jiri Hrdina, Jaromir Jagr, Grant Jennings, Troy Loney, Joe Mullen, Larry Murphy, Jim Paek, Frank Pietrangelo, Barry Pederson, Mark Recchi, Gordie Roberts, Ulf Samuelsson, Paul Stanton, Kevin Stevens, Peter Taglianetti, Bryan Trottier, Scott Young, Wendell Young, Edward J. DeBartolo, Sr. (Owner), Marie D. DeBartolo York (President), Paul Martha (Vice-President & General Counsel), Craig Patrick (General Manager), Scotty Bowman (Director of Player Development & Recruitment), Bob Johnson (Coach), Rick Kehoe (Assistant Coach), Gilles Meloche (Goaltending Coach & Scout), Rick Paterson (Assistant Coach), Barry Smith (Assistant Coach), Steve Latin (Equipment Manager), Skip Thayer (Trainer), John Welday (Strength & Conditioning Coach), Greg Malone (Scout).

Scores: May 15, at Pittsburgh — Minnesota 5, Pittsburgh 4; May 17, at Pittsburgh — Pittsburgh 4, Minnesota 1; May 19, at Minnesota — Minnesota 3, Pittsburgh 1; May 21, at Minnesota — Pittsburgh 5, Minnesota 3; May 23, at Pittsburgh — Pittsburgh 6, Minnesota 4; May 25, at Minnesota — Pittsburgh 8, Minnesota 0.

1989-90 — Edmonton Oilers — Kevin Lowe, Steve Smith, Jeff Beukeboom, Mark Lamb, Joe Murphy, Glenn Anderson, Mark Messier, Adam Graves, Craig MacTavish, Kelly Buchberger, Jari Kurri, Craig Simpson, Martin Gelinas, Randy Gregg, Charlie Huddy, Geoff Smith, Reijo Ruotsalainen, Craig Muni, Bill Ranford, Dave Brown, Pokey Reddick, Petr Klima, Esa Tikkanen, Grant Fuhr, Peter Pocklington (Owner), Glen Sather (President/General Manager), John Muckler (Coach), Ted Green (Co-Coach), Ron Low (Ass't Coach), Bruce MacGregor (Ass't General Manager), Barry Fraser (Director of Player Personnel), John Blackwell (Director of Operations, AHL), Ace Bailey, Ed Chadwick, Lorne Davis, Harry Howell, Matti Vaisanen and Albert Reeves (Scouts), Bill Tuele (Director of Public Relations), Werner Baum (Controller), Dr. Gordon Cameron (Medical Chief of Staff), Dr. David Reid (Team Physician), Barrie Stafford (Athletic Trainer), Ken Lowe (Athletic Therapist), Stuart Poirier (Massage Therapist), Lyle Kulchisky (Ass't Trainer).

Scores: May 15, at Boston — Edmonton 3, Boston 2; May 18, at Boston — Edmonton 7, Boston 2; May 20, at Edmonton — Boston 2, Edmonton 1; May 22, at Edmonton — Edmonton 5, Boston 1; May 24, at Boston — Edmonton 4, Boston 1.

1988-89 — Calgary Flames — Mike Vernon, Rick Wamsley, Al MacInnis, Brad McCrimmon, Dana Murzyn, Ric Nattress, Joe Mullen, Lanny McDonald (Co-captain), Gary Roberts, Colin Patterson, Hakan Loob, Theoren Fleury, Jiri Hrdina, Tim Hunter (Ass't. captain), Gary Suter, Mark Hunter, Jim Peplinski (Co-captain), Joe Nieuwendyk, Brian MacLellan, Joel Otto, Jamie Macoun, Doug Gilmour, Rob Ramage. Norman Green, Harley Hotchkiss, Norman Kwong, Sonia Scurfield, B.J. Seaman, D.K. Seaman (Owners), Cliff Fletcher (President and General Manager), Al MacNeil (Ass't General Manager), Al Coates (Ass't to the President), Terry Crisp (Head Coach), Doug Risebrough, Tom Watt (Ass't Coaches), Glenn Hall (Goaltending Consultant), Jim Murray (Trainer), Bob Stewart (Equipment Manager), Al Murray (Ass't Trainer).
Scores: May 14, at Calgary — Calgary 3, Montreal 2; May 17, at Calgary— Montreal 4, Calgary 2; May 19, at Montreal — Montreal 4, Calgary 3; May 21, at Montreal — Calgary 4, Montreal 2; May 23, at Calgary — Calgary 3, Montreal 2; May 25, at Montreal — Calgary 4, Montreal 2.

1987-88 — Edmonton Oilers — Keith Acton, Glenn Anderson, Jeff Beukeboom, Geoff Courtnall, Grant Fuhr, Randy Gregg, Wayne Gretzky, Dave Hannan, Charlie Huddy, Mike Krushelnyski, Jari Kurri, Normand Lacombe, Kevin Lowe, Craig MacTavish, Kevin McClelland, Marty McSorley, Mark Messier, Craig Muni, Bill Ranford, Craig Simpson, Steve Smith, Esa Tikkanen, Peter Pocklington (Owner), Glen Sather (General Manager/Coach), John Muckler (Co-Coach), Ted Green (Ass't Coach), Bruce MacGregor (Ass't General Manager), Barry Fraser (Director of Player Personnel), Bill Tuele (Director of Public Relations), Dr. Gordon Cameron (Team Physician), Peter Millar (Athletic Therapist), Barrie Stafford (Trainer), Juergen Mers (Massage Therapist), Lyle Kulchisky (Ass't Trainer).
Scores: May 18, at Edmonton — Edmonton 2, Boston 1; May 20, at Edmonton — Edmonton 4, Boston 2; May 22, at Boston — Edmonton 6, Boston 3; May 24, at Boston — Boston 3, Edmonton 3 (suspended due to power failure); May 26, at Edmonton — Edmonton 6, Boston 3.

1986-87 — Edmonton Oilers — Glenn Anderson, Jeff Beukeboom, Kelly Buchberger, Paul Coffey, Grant Fuhr, Randy Gregg, Wayne Gretzky, Charlie Huddy, Dave Hunter, Mike Krushelnyski, Jari Kurri, Moe Lemay, Kevin Lowe, Craig MacTavish, Kevin McClelland, Marty McSorley, Mark Messier, Andy Moog, Craig Muni, Kent Nilsson, Jaroslav Pouzar, Reijo Ruotsalainen, Steve Smith, Esa Tikkanen, Peter Pocklington (Owner), Glen Sather (General Manager/Coach), John Muckler (Co-Coach), Ted Green (Ass't. Coach), Ron Low (Ass't. Coach), Bruce MacGregor (Ass't. General Manager), Barry Fraser (Director of Player Personnel), Peter Millar (Athletic Therapist), Barrie Stafford (Trainer), Lyle Kulchisky (Ass't Trainer).
Scores: May 17, at Edmonton — Edmonton 4, Philadelphia 2; May 20, at Edmonton — Edmonton 3, Philadelphia 2; May 22, at Philadelphia — Philadelphia 5, Edmonton 3; May 24, at Philadelphia — Edmonton 4, Philadelphia 1; May 26, at Edmonton — Philadelphia 4, Edmonton 3; May 28, at Philadelphia — Philadelphia 3, Edmonton 2; May 31, at Edmonton — Edmonton 3, Philadelphia 1.

1985-86 — Montreal Canadiens — Bob Gainey, Doug Soetaert, Patrick Roy, Rick Green, David Maley, Ryan Walter, Serge Boisvert, Mario Tremblay, Bobby Smith, Craig Ludwig, Tom Kurvers, Kjell Dahlin, Larry Robinson, Guy Carbonneau, Chris Chelios, Petr Svoboda, Mats Naslund, Lucien DeBlois, Steve Rooney, Gaston Gingras, Mike Lalor, Chris Nilan, John Kordic, Claude Lemieux, Mike McPhee, Brian Skrudland, Stephane Richer, Ronald Corey (President), Serge Savard (General Manager), Jean Perron (Coach), Jacques Laperrière (Ass't. Coach), Jean Béliveau (Vice President), Francois-Xavier Seigneur (Vice President), Fred Steer (Vice President), Jacques Lemaire (Ass't. General Manager), André Boudrias (Ass't. General Manager), Claude Ruel (Scouting), Yves Belanger (Athletic Therapist), Gaetan Lefebvre (Ass't. Athletic Therapist), Eddy Palchak (Trainer), Sylvain Toupin (Ass't. Trainer).
Scores: May 16, at Calgary — Calgary 5, Montreal 2; May 18, at Calgary — Montreal 3, Calgary 2; May 20, at Montreal — Montreal 5, Calgary 3; May 22, at Montreal — Montreal 1, Calgary 0; May 24, at Calgary — Montreal 4, Calgary 3.

1984-85 — Edmonton Oilers — Glenn Anderson, Bill Carroll, Paul Coffey, Lee Fogolin, Grant Fuhr, Randy Gregg, Wayne Gretzky, Charlie Huddy, Pat Hughes, Dave Hunter, Don Jackson, Mike Krushelnyski, Jari Kurri, Willy Lindstrom, Kevin Lowe, Dave Lumley, Kevin McClelland, Larry Melnyk, Mark Messier, Andy Moog, Mark Napier, Jaroslav Pouzar, Dave Semenko, Esa Tikkanen, Peter Pocklington (Owner), Glen Sather (General Manager/Coach), John Muckler (Ass't. Coach), Ted Green (Ass't. Coach), Bruce MacGregor (Ass't. General Manager), Barry Fraser (Director of Player Personnel/Chief Scout), Peter Millar (Athletic Therapist), Barrie Stafford, Lyle Kulchisky (Trainers)
Scores: May 21, at Philadelphia — Philadelphia 4, Edmonton 1; May 23, at Philadelphia — Edmonton 3, Philadelphia 1; May 25, at Edmonton — Edmonton 4, Philadelphia 3; May 28, at Edmonton — Edmonton 5, Philadelphia 3; May 30, at Edmonton — Edmonton 8, Philadelphia 3.

1983-84 — Edmonton Oilers — Glenn Anderson, Paul Coffey, Pat Conacher, Lee Fogolin, Grant Fuhr, Randy Gregg, Wayne Gretzky, Charlie Huddy, Pat Hughes, Dave Hunter, Don Jackson, Jari Kurri, Willy Lindstrom, Ken Linseman, Kevin Lowe, Dave Lumley, Kevin McClelland, Mark Messier, Andy Moog, Jaroslav Pouzar, Dave Semenko, Peter Pocklington (Owner), Glen Sather (General Manager/Coach), John Muckler (Ass't. Coach), Ted Green (Ass't. Coach), Bruce MacGregor (Ass't. General Manager), Barry Fraser (Director of Player Personnel/Chief Scout), Peter Millar (Athletic Therapist), Barrie Stafford (Trainer)
Scores: May 10, at New York — Edmonton 1, NY Islanders 0; May 12, at New York — NY Islanders 6, Edmonton 1; May 15, at Edmonton — Edmonton 7, NY Islanders 2; May 17, at Edmonton — Edmonton 7, NY Islanders 2; May 19, at Edmonton — Edmonton 5, NY Islanders 2.

1982-83 — New York Islanders — Mike Bossy, Bob Bourne, Paul Boutilier, Billy Carroll, Greg Gilbert, Clark Gillies, Butch Goring, Mats Hallin, Tomas Jonsson, Anders Kallur, Gord Lane, Dave Langevin, Mike McEwen, Rollie Melanson, Wayne Merrick, Ken Morrow, Bob Nystrom, Stefan Persson, Denis Potvin, Billy Smith, Brent Sutter, Duane Sutter, John Tonelli, Bryan Trottier, Al Arbour (coach), Lorne Henning (ass't coach), Bill Torrey (general manager), Ron Waske, Jim Pickard (trainers)
Scores: May 10, at Edmonton — NY Islanders 2, Edmonton 0; May 12, at Edmonton — NY Islanders 6, Edmonton 3; May 14, at New York — NY Islanders 5, Edmonton 1; May 17, at New York — NY Islanders 4, Edmonton 2

1981-82 — New York Islanders — Mike Bossy, Bob Bourne, Billy Carroll, Butch Goring, Greg Gilbert, Clark Gillies, Tomas Jonsson, Anders Kallur, Gord Lane, Dave Langevin, Hector Marini, Mike McEwen, Rollie Melanson, Wayne Merrick, Ken Morrow, Bob Nystrom, Stefan Persson, Denis Potvin, Billy Smith, Brent Sutter, Duane Sutter, John Tonelli, Bryan Trottier, Al Arbour (coach), Lorne Henning (ass't coach), Bill Torrey (general manager), Jim Devellano (ass't. general manager/dir. of scouting), Ron Waske, Jim Pickard (trainers)
Scores: May 8, at New York — NY Islanders 6, Vancouver 5; May 11, at New York — NY Islanders 6, Vancouver 4; May 13, at Vancouver — NY Islanders 3, Vancouver 0; May 16, at Vancouver — NY Islanders 3, Vancouver 1

1980-81 — New York Islanders — Denis Potvin, Mike McEwen, Ken Morrow, Gord Lane, Bob Lorimer, Stefan Persson, Dave Langevin, Mike Bossy, Bryan Trottier, Butch Goring, Wayne Merrick, Clark Gillies, John Tonelli, Bob Nystrom, Bill Carroll, Bob Bourne, Hector Marini, Anders Kallur, Duane Sutter, Garry Howatt, Lorne Henning, Billy Smith, Rollie Melanson, Al Arbour (coach), Bill Torrey (general manager), Jim Devellano (chief scout), Ron Waske, Jim Pickard (trainers).
Scores: May 12, at New York — NY Islanders 6, Minnesota 3; May 14, at New York — NY Islanders 6, Minnesota 3; May 17, at Minnesota — NY Islanders 7, Minnesota 5; May 19, at Minnesota— Minnesota 4, NY Islanders 2; May 21, at New York — NY Islanders 5, Minnesota 1.

1979-80 — New York Islanders — Gord Lane, Jean Potvin, Bob Lorimer, Denis Potvin, Stefan Persson, Ken Morrow, Dave Langevin, Duane Sutter, Garry Howatt, Clark Gillies, Lorne Henning, Wayne Merrick, Bob Bourne, Steve Tambellini, Bryan Trottier, Mike Bossy, Bob Nystrom, John Tonelli, Anders Kallur, Butch Goring, Alex McKendry, Glenn Resch, Billy Smith, Al Arbour (coach), Bill Torrey (general manager), Jim Devellano (chief scout), Ron Waske, Jim Pickard (trainers).
Scores: May 13, at Philadelphia — NY Islanders 4, Philadelphia 3; May 15, at Philadelphia — Philadelphia 8, NY Islanders 3; May 17, at New York — NY Islanders 6, Philadelphia 2; May 19, at New York — NY Islanders 5, Philadelphia 2; May 22 at Philadelphia — Philadelphia 6, NY Islanders 3; May 24, at New York — NY Islanders 5, Philadelphia 4.

1978-79 — Montreal Canadiens — Ken Dryden, Larry Robinson, Serge Savard, Guy Lapointe, Brian Engblom, Gilles Lupien, Rick Chartraw, Guy Lafleur, Steve Shutt, Jacques Lemaire, Yvan Cournoyer, Réjean Houle, Pierre Mondou, Bob Gainey, Doug Jarvis, Yvon Lambert, Doug Risebrough, Pierre Larouche, Mario Tremblay, Cam Connor, Pat Hughes, Rod Langway, Mark Napier, Michel Larocque, Richard Sévigny, Scotty Bowman (coach), Irving Grundman (managing director), Eddy Palchak, Pierre Meilleur (trainers).
Scores: May 13, at Montreal — NY Rangers 4, Montreal 1; May 15, at Montreal — Montreal 6, NY Rangers 2; May 17, at New York — Montreal 4, NY Rangers 1; May 19, at New York — Montreal 4, NY Rangers 3; May 21, at Montreal — Montreal 4, NY Rangers 1.

1977-78 — Montreal Canadiens — Ken Dryden, Larry Robinson, Serge Savard, Guy Lapointe, Bill Nyrop, Pierre Bouchard, Brian Engblom, Gilles Lupien, Rick Chartraw, Guy Lafleur, Steve Shutt, Jacques Lemaire, Yvan Cournoyer, Réjean Houle, Pierre Mondou, Bob Gainey, Doug Jarvis, Yvon Lambert, Doug Risebrough, Pierre Larouche, Mario Tremblay, Michel Larocque, Murray Wilson, Scotty Bowman (coach), Sam Pollock (general manager), Eddy Palchak, Pierre Meilleur (trainers).
Scores: May 13, at Montreal — Montreal 4, Boston 1; May 16, at Montreal — Montreal 3, Boston 2; May 18, at Boston — Boston 4, Montreal 0; May 21, at Boston — Boston 4, Montreal 3; May 23, at Montreal — Montreal 4, Boston 1; May 25, at Boston — Montreal 4, Boston 1.

1976-77 — Montreal Canadiens — Ken Dryden, Guy Lapointe, Larry Robinson, Serge Savard, Jimmy Roberts, Rick Chartraw, Bill Nyrop, Pierre Bouchard, Brian Engblom, Yvan Cournoyer, Guy Lafleur, Jacques Lemaire, Steve Shutt, Pete Mahovlich, Murray Wilson, Doug Jarvis, Yvon Lambert, Bob Gainey, Doug Risebrough, Mario Tremblay, Rejean Houle, Pierre Mondou, Mike Polich, Michel Larocque, Scotty Bowman (coach), Sam Pollock (general manager), Eddy Palchak, Pierre Meilleur (trainers).
Scores: May 7, at Montreal — Montreal 7, Boston 3; May 10, at Montreal — Montreal 3, Boston 0; May 12, at Boston — Montreal 4, Boston 2; May 14, at Boston — Montreal 2, Boston 1.

1975-76 — Montreal Canadiens — Ken Dryden, Serge Savard, Guy Lapointe, Larry Robinson, Bill Nyrop, Pierre Bouchard, Jimmy Roberts, Guy Lafleur, Steve Shutt, Pete Mahovlich, Yvan Cournoyer, Jacques Lemaire, Yvon Lambert, Bob Gainey, Doug Jarvis, Doug Risebrough, Murray Wilson, Mario Tremblay, Rick Chartraw, Michel Larocque, Scotty Bowman (coach), Sam Pollock (general manager), Eddy Palchak, Pierre Meilleur (trainers).
Scores: May 9, at Montreal — Montreal 4, Philadelphia 3; May 11, at Montreal — Montreal 2, Philadelphia 1; May 13, at Philadelphia — Montreal 3, Philadelphia 2; May 16, at Philadelphia — Montreal 5, Philadelphia 3.

1974-75 — Philadelphia Flyers — Bernie Parent, Wayne Stephenson, Ed Van Impe, Tom Bladon, André Dupont, Joe Watson, Jimmy Watson, Ted Harris, Larry Goodenough, Rick MacLeish, Bobby Clarke, Bill Barber, Reggie Leach, Gary Dornhoefer, Ross Lonsberry, Bob Kelly, Terry Crisp, Don Saleski, Dave Schultz, Orest Kindrachuk, Bill Clement, Fred Shero (coach), Keith Allen (general manager), Frank Lewis, Jim McKenzie (trainers).
Scores: May 15, at Philadelphia — Philadelphia 4, Buffalo 1; May 18, at Philadelphia — Philadelphia 2, Buffalo 1; May 20, at Buffalo — Buffalo 5, Philadelphia 4; May 22, at Buffalo — Buffalo 4, Philadelphia 2; May 25, at Philadelphia — Philadelphia 5, Buffalo 1; May 27, at Buffalo — Philadelphia 2, Buffalo 0.

1973-74 — Philadelphia Flyers — Bernie Parent, Ed Van Impe, Tom Bladon, André Dupont, Joe Watson, Jimmy Watson, Barry Ashbee, Bill Barber, Dave Schultz, Don Saleski, Gary Dornhoefer, Terry Crisp, Bobby Clarke, Simon Nolet, Ross Lonsberry, Rick MacLeish, Bill Flett, Orest Kindrachuk, Bill Clement, Bob Kelly, Bruce Cowick, Al MacAdam, Bobby Taylor, Fred Shero (coach), Keith Allen (general manager), Frank Lewis, Jim McKenzie (trainers).
Scores: May 7, at Boston — Boston 3, Philadelphia 2; May 9, at Boston — Philadelphia 3, Boston 2; May 12, at Philadelphia — Philadelphia 4, Boston 1; May 14, at Philadelphia — Philadelphia 4, Boston 2; May 16, at Boston — Boston 5, Philadelphia 1; May 19, at Philadelphia — Philadelphia 1, Boston 0.

1972-73 — Montreal Canadiens — Ken Dryden, Guy Lapointe, Serge Savard, Larry Robinson, Jacques Laperrière, Bob Murdoch, Pierre Bouchard, Jimmy Roberts, Yvan Cournoyer, Frank Mahovlich, Jacques Lemaire, Pete Mahovlich, Marc Tardif, Henri Richard, Réjean Houle, Guy Lafleur, Chuck Lefley, Claude Larose, Murray Wilson, Steve Shutt, Michel Plasse, Scotty Bowman (coach), Sam Pollock (general manager), Ed Palchak, Bob Williams (trainers).
Scores: April 29, at Montreal — Montreal 8, Chicago 3; May 1, at Montreal — Montreal 4, Chicago 1; May 3, at Chicago — Chicago 7, Montreal 4; May 6, at Chicago — Montreal 4, Chicago 0; May 8, at Montreal — Chicago 8, Montreal 7; May 10, at Chicago — Montreal 6, Chicago 4.

1971-72 — Boston Bruins — Gerry Cheevers, Eddie Johnston, Bobby Orr, Ted Green, Carol Vadnais, Dallas Smith, Don Awrey, Phil Esposito, Ken Hodge, John Bucyk, Mike Walton, Wayne Cashman, Garnet Bailey, Derek Sanderson, Fred Stanfield, Ed Westfall, John McKenzie, Don Marcotte, Garry Peters, Chris Hayes, Tom Johnson (coach), Milt Schmidt (general manager), Dan Canney, John Forristall (trainers).
Scores: April 30, at Boston — Boston 6, NY Rangers 5; May 2, at Boston — Boston 2, NY Rangers 1; May 4, at New York — NY Rangers 5, Boston 2; May 7, at New York — Boston 3, NY Rangers 2; May 9, at Boston — NY Rangers 3, Boston 2; May 11, at New York — Boston 3, NY Rangers 0.

1970-71 — Montreal Canadiens — Ken Dryden, Rogie Vachon, Jacques Laperrière, J.C. Tremblay, Guy Lapointe, Terry Harper, Pierre Bouchard, Jean Béliveau, Marc Tardif, Yvan Cournoyer, Réjean Houle, Claude Larose, Henri Richard, Phil Roberto, Pete Mahovlich, Leon Rochefort, John Ferguson, Bobby Sheehan, Jacques Lemaire, Frank Mahovlich, Bob Murdoch, Chuck Lefley, Al MacNeil (coach), Sam Pollock (general manager), Yvon Belanger, Ed Palchak (trainers).
Scores: May 4, at Chicago — Chicago 2, Montreal 1; May 6, at Chicago — Chicago 5, Montreal 3; May 9, at Montreal — Montreal 4, Chicago 2; May 11, at Montreal — Montreal 5, Chicago 2; May 13, at Chicago — Chicago 2, Montreal 0; May 16, at Montreal — Montreal 4, Chicago 3; May 18, at Chicago — Montreal 3, Chicago 2.

1969-70 — Boston Bruins — Gerry Cheevers, Eddie Johnston, Bobby Orr, Rick Smith, Dallas Smith, Bill Speer, Gary Doak, Don Awrey, Phil Esposito, Ken Hodge, John Bucyk, Wayne Carleton, Wayne Cashman, Derek Sanderson, Fred Stanfield, Ed Westfall, John McKenzie, Jim Lorentz, Don Marcotte, Bill Lesuk, Dan Schock, Harry Sinden (coach), Milt Schmidt (general manager), Dan Canney, John Forristall (trainers).
Scores: May 3, at St. Louis — Boston 6, St. Louis 1; May 5, at St. Louis — Boston 6, St. Louis 2; May 7, at Boston — Boston 4, St. Louis 1; May 10, at Boston — Boston 4, St. Louis 3.

1968-69 — Montreal Canadiens — Gump Worsley, Rogie Vachon, Jacques Laperrière, J.C. Tremblay, Ted Harris, Serge Savard, Terry Harper, Larry Hillman, Jean Béliveau, Ralph Backstrom, Dick Duff, Yvan Cournoyer, Claude Provost, Bobby Rousseau, Henri Richard, John Ferguson, Christian Bordeleau, Mickey Redmond, Jacques Lemaire, Lucien Grenier, Tony Esposito, Claude Ruel (coach), Sam Pollock (general manager), Larry Aubut, Eddy Palchak (trainers).
Scores: April 27, at Montreal — Montreal 3, St. Louis 1; April 29, at Montreal — Montreal 3, St. Louis 1; May 1 at St. Louis — Montreal 4, St. Louis 0; May 4, at St. Louis — Montreal 2, St. Louis 1.

1967-68 — Montreal Canadiens — Gump Worsley, Rogie Vachon, Jacques Laperrière, J.C. Tremblay, Ted Harris, Serge Savard, Terry Harper, Carol Vadnais, Jean Béliveau, Gilles Tremblay, Ralph Backstrom, Dick Duff, Claude Larose, Yvan Cournoyer, Claude Provost, Bobby Rousseau, Henri Richard, John Ferguson, Danny Grant, Jacques Lemaire, Mickey Redmond, Toe Blake (coach), Sam Pollock (general manager), Larry Aubut, Eddy Palchak (trainers).
Scores: May 5, at St. Louis — Montreal 3, St. Louis 2; May 7, at St. Louis — Montreal 1, St. Louis 0; May 9, at Montreal — Montreal 4, St. Louis 3; May 11, at Montreal — Montreal 3, St. Louis 2.

1966-67 — Toronto Maple Leafs — Johnny Bower, Terry Sawchuk, Larry Hillman, Marcel Pronovost, Tim Horton, Bob Baun, Aut Erickson, Allan Stanley, Red Kelly, Ron Ellis, George Armstrong, Pete Stemkowski, Dave Keon, Mike Walton, Jim Pappin, Bob Pulford, Brian Conacher, Eddie Shack, Frank Mahovlich, Milan Marcetta, Larry Jeffrey, Bruce Gamble, Punch Imlach (manager-coach), Bob Haggart (trainer).
Scores: April 20, at Montreal — Toronto 2, Montreal 6; April 22, at Montreal — Toronto 3, Montreal 0; April 25, at Toronto — Toronto 3, Montreal 2; April 27, at Toronto — Toronto 2, Montreal 6; April 29, at Montreal — Toronto 4, Montreal 1; May 2, at Toronto — Toronto 3, Montreal 1.

1965-66 — Montreal Canadiens — Gump Worsley, Charlie Hodge, Jean-Claude Tremblay, Ted Harris, Jean-Guy Talbot, Terry Harper, Jacques Laperrière, Noel Price, Jean Béliveau, Ralph Backstrom, Dick Duff, Gilles Tremblay, Claude Larose, Yvan Cournoyer, Claude Provost, Bobby Rousseau, Henri Richard, Dave Balon, John Ferguson, Leon Rochefort, Jim Roberts, Toe Blake (coach), Sam Pollock (general manager), Larry Aubut, Andy Galley (trainers).
Scores: April 24, at Montreal — Detroit 3, Montreal 2; April 26, at Montreal — Detroit 5, Montreal 2; April 28, at Detroit — Montreal 4, Detroit 2; May 1, at Detroit — Montreal 2, Detroit 1; May 3, at Montreal — Montreal 5, Detroit 1; May 5, at Detroit — Montreal 3, Detroit 2.

1964-65 — Montreal Canadiens — Gump Worsley, Charlie Hodge, Jean-Claude Tremblay, Ted Harris, Jean-Guy Talbot, Terry Harper, Jacques Laperrière, Jean Gauthier, Noel Picard, Jean Béliveau, Ralph Backstrom, Dick Duff, Claude Larose, Yvan Cournoyer, Claude Provost, Bobby Rousseau, Henri Richard, Dave Balon, John Ferguson, Red Berenson, Jim Roberts, Toe Blake (coach), Sam Pollock (general manager), Larry Aubut, Andy Galley (trainers).
Scores: April 17, at Montreal — Montreal 3, Chicago 2; April 20, at Montreal — Montreal 2, Chicago 0; April 22, at Chicago — Montreal 1, Chicago 3; April 25, at Chicago — Montreal 1, Chicago 5; April 7, at Montreal — Montreal 6, Chicago 0; April 29, at Chicago — Montreal 1, Chicago 2; May 1, at Montreal — Montreal 4, Chicago 0.

1963-64 — Toronto Maple Leafs — Johnny Bower, Don Simmons, Carl Brewer, Tim Horton, Bob Baun, Allan Stanley, Larry Hillman, Al Arbour, Red Kelly, Gerry Ehman, Andy Bathgate, George Armstrong, Ron Stewart, Dave Keon, Billy Harris, Don McKenney, Jim Pappin, Bob Pulford, Eddie Shack, Frank Mahovlich, Ed Litzenberger, Punch Imlach (manager-coach), Bob Haggert (trainer).
Scores April 11, at Toronto — Toronto 3, Detroit 2; April 14, at Toronto — Toronto 3, Detroit 4; April 16, at Detroit — Toronto 3, Detroit 4; April 18, at Detroit — Toronto 4, Detroit 2; April 21, at Toronto — Toronto 1, Detroit 2; April 23, at Detroit — Toronto 4, Detroit 3; April 25, at Toronto — Toronto 4, Detroit 0.

1962-63 — Toronto Maple Leafs — Johnny Bower, Don Simmons, Carl Brewer, Tim Horton, Kent Douglas, Allan Stanley, Bob Baun, Larry Hillman, Red Kelly, Dick Duff, George Armstrong, Bob Nevin, Ron Stewart, Dave Keon, Billy Harris, Bob Pulford, Eddie Shack, Ed Litzenberger, Frank Mahovlich, John MacMillan, Punch Imlach (manager-coach), Bob Haggert (trainer).
Scores: April 9, at Toronto — Toronto 4, Detroit 2; April 11, at Toronto — Toronto 4, Detroit 2; April 14, at Detroit — Toronto 2, Detroit 3; April 16, at Detroit — Toronto 4, Detroit 2; April 18, at Toronto — Toronto 3, Detroit 1.

1961-62 — Toronto Maple Leafs — Johnny Bower, Don Simmons, Carl Brewer, Tim Horton, Bob Baun, Allan Stanley, Al Arbour, Larry Hillman, Red Kelly, Dick Duff, George Armstrong, Frank Mahovlich, Bob Nevin, Ron Stewart, Billy Harris, Bert Olmstead, Bob Pulford, Eddie Shack, Dave Keon, Ed Litzenberger, John MacMillan, Punch Imlach (manager-coach), Bob Haggert (trainer).
Scores: April 10, at Toronto — Toronto 4, Chicago 1; April 12, at Toronto — Toronto 3, Chicago 2; April 15, at Chicago — Toronto 0, Chicago 3; April 17, at Chicago — Toronto 1, Chicago 4; April 19, at Toronto —Toronto 8, Chicago 4; April 22, at Chicago — Toronto 2, Chicago 1.

1960-61 — Chicago Black Hawks — Glenn Hall, Al Arbour, Pierre Pilote, Elmer Vasko, Jack Evans, Dollard St. Laurent, Reggie Fleming, Tod Sloan, Ron Murphy, Ed Litzenberger, Bill Hay, Wayne Hillman, Bobby Hull, Ab McDonald, Eric Nesterenko, Kenny Wharram, Earl Balfour, Stan Mikita, Murray Balfour, Chico Maki, Wayne Hicks, Tommy Ivan (manager), Rudy Pilous (coach), Nick Garen (trainer).
Scores: April 6, at Chicago — Chicago 3, Detroit 2; April 8, at Detroit — Detroit 3, Chicago 1; April 10, at Chicago — Chicago 3, Detroit 1; April 12, at Detroit — Detroit 2, Chicago 1; April 14, at Chicago — Chicago 6, Detroit 3; April 16, at Detroit — Chicago 5, Detroit 1.

1959-60 — Montreal Canadiens — Jacques Plante, Charlie Hodge, Doug Harvey, Tom Johnson, Bob Turner, Jean-Guy Talbot, Albert Langlois, Ralph Backstrom, Jean Béliveau, Marcel Bonin, Bernie Geoffrion, Phil Goyette, Bill Hicke, Don Marshall, Ab McDonald, Dickie Moore, André Pronovost, Claude Provost, Henri Richard, Maurice Richard, Frank Selke (manager), Toe Blake (coach), Hector Dubois, Larry Aubut (trainers).
Scores: April 7, at Montreal — Montreal 4, Toronto 2; April 9, at Montreal — Montreal 2, Toronto 1; April 12, at Toronto — Montreal 5, Toronto 2; April 14, at Toronto — Montreal 4, Toronto 0.

1958-59 — Montreal Canadiens — Jacques Plante, Charlie Hodge, Doug Harvey, Tom Johnson, Bob Turner, Jean-Guy Talbot, Albert Langlois, Bernie Geoffrion, Ralph Backstrom, Bill Hicke, Maurice Richard, Dickie Moore, Claude Provost, Ab McDonald, Henri Richard, Marcel Bonin, Phil Goyette, Don Marshall, André Pronovost, Jean Béliveau, Frank Selke (manager), Toe Blake (coach), Hector Dubois, Larry Aubut (trainers).
Scores: April 9, at Montreal — Montreal 5, Toronto 3; April 11, at Montreal — Montreal 3, Toronto 1; April 14, at Toronto — Toronto 3, Montreal 2; April 16, at Toronto — Montreal 3, Toronto 2; April 18, at Montreal — Montreal 5, Toronto 3.

The "Old Pappies." Veteran members of the 1967 Stanley Cup champion Toronto Maple Leafs photographed in Maple Leaf Gardens. Left to right (kneeling) goaltenders Johnny Bower and Terry Sawchuk; (standing) coach Punch Imlach, Marcel Pronovost, captain George Armstrong, Red Kelly and Allan Stanley.

1957-58 — Montreal Canadiens — Jacques Plante, Gerry McNeil, Doug Harvey, Tom Johnson, Bob Turner, Dollard St-Laurent, Jean-Guy Talbot, Albert Langlois, Jean Béliveau, Bernie Geoffrion, Maurice Richard, Dickie Moore, Claude Provost, Floyd Curry, Bert Olmstead, Henri Richard, Marcel Bonin, Phil Goyette, Don Marshall, André Pronovost, Connie Broden, Frank Selke (manager), Toe Blake (coach), Hector Dubois, Larry Aubut (trainers).
Scores: April 8, at Montreal —Montreal 2, Boston 1; April 10, at Montreal — Boston 5, Montreal 2; April 13, at Boston — Montreal 3, Boston 0; April 15, at Boston — Boston 3, Montreal 1; April 17, at Montreal — Montreal 3, Boston 2; April 20, at Boston — Montreal 5, Boston 3.

1956-57 — Montreal Canadiens — Jacques Plante, Gerry McNeil, Doug Harvey, Tom Johnson, Bob Turner, Dollard St. Laurent, Jean-Guy Talbot, Jean Béliveau, Bernie Geoffrion, Floyd Curry, Dickie Moore, Maurice Richard, Claude Provost, Bert Olmstead, Henri Richard, Phil Goyette, Don Marshall, André Pronovost, Connie Broden, Frank Selke (manager), Toe Blake (coach), Hector Dubois, Larry Aubut (trainers).
Scores: April 6, at Montreal — Montreal 5, Boston 1; April 9, at Montreal — Montreal 1, Boston 0; April 11, at Boston — Montreal 4, Boston 2; April 14, at Boston — Boston 2, Montreal 0; April 16, at Montreal — Montreal 5, Boston 1.

1955-56 — Montreal Canadiens — Jacques Plante, Doug Harvey, Butch Bouchard, Bob Turner, Tom Johnson, Jean-Guy Talbot, Dollard St. Laurent, Jean Béliveau, Bernie Geoffrion, Bert Olmstead, Floyd Curry, Jackie Leclair, Maurice Richard, Dickie Moore, Henri Richard, Kenny Mosdell, Don Marshall, Claude Provost, Frank Selke (manager), Toe Blake (coach), Hector Dubois (trainer).
Scores: March 31, at Montreal — Montreal 6, Detroit 4; April 3, at Montreal — Montreal 5, Detroit 1; April 5, at Detroit — Detroit 3, Montreal 1; April 8, at Detroit — Montreal 3, Detroit 0; April 10, at Montreal — Montreal 3, Detroit 1.

1954-55 — Detroit Red Wings — Terry Sawchuk, Red Kelly, Bob Goldham, Marcel Pronovost, Benny Woit, Jim Hay, Larry Hillman, Ted Lindsay, Tony Leswick, Gordie Howe, Alex Delvecchio, Marty Pavelich, Glen Skov, Earl Reibel, John Wilson, Bill Dineen, Vic Stasiuk, Marcel Bonin, Jack Adams (manager), Jimmy Skinner (coach), Carl Mattson (trainer).
Scores: April 3, at Detroit — Detroit 4, Montreal 2; April 5, at Detroit — Detroit 7, Montreal 1, April 7, at Montreal — Montreal 4, Detroit 2; April 9, at Montreal — Montreal 5, Detroit 3; April 10, at Detroit — Detroit 5, Montreal 1; April 12, at Montreal — Montreal 6, Detroit 3; April 14, at Detroit — Detroit 3, Montreal 1.

1953-54 — Detroit Red Wings — Terry Sawchuk, Red Kelly, Bob Goldham, Benny Woit, Marcel Pronovost, Al Arbour, Keith Allen, Ted Lindsay, Tony Leswick, Gordie Howe, Marty Pavelich, Alex Delvecchio, Gilles Dube, Metro Prystai, Glen Skov, Johnny Wilson, Bill Dineen, Jimmy Peters Sr., Earl Reibel, Vic Stasiuk, Jack Adams (manager), Tommy Ivan (coach), Carl Mattson (trainer).
Scores: April 4, at Detroit — Detroit 3, Montreal 1; April 6, at Detroit — Montreal 3, Detroit 1; April 8, at Montreal — Detroit 5, Montreal 2; April 10, at Montreal — Detroit 2, Montreal 0; April 11, at Detroit — Montreal 1, Detroit 0; April 13, at Montreal — Montreal 4, Detroit 1; April 16, at Detroit — Detroit 2, Montreal 1.

1952-53 — Montreal Canadiens — Gerry McNeil, Jacques Plante, Doug Harvey, Butch Bouchard, Tom Johnson, Dollard St. Laurent, Bud MacPherson, Maurice Richard, Elmer Lach, Paul Meger, Bert Olmstead, Bernie Geoffrion, Floyd Curry, Paul Masnick, Billy Reay, Dickie Moore, Kenny Mosdell, Dick Gamble, Johnny McCormack, Lorne Davis, Calum MacKay, Eddie Mazur, Frank Selke (manager), Dick Irvin (coach), Hector Dubois (trainer).
Scores: April 9, at Montreal — Montreal 4, Boston 2; April 11, at Montreal — Boston 4, Montreal 1; April 12, at Boston — Montreal 3, Boston 0; April 14, at Boston — Montreal 7, Boston 3; April 16, at Montreal — Montreal 1, Boston 0.

1951-52 — Detroit Red Wings — Terry Sawchuk, Bob Goldham, Benny Woit, Red Kelly, Leo Reise Jr., Marcel Pronovost, Ted Lindsay, Tony Leswick, Gordie Howe, Metro Prystai, Marty Pavelich, Sid Abel, Glen Skov, Alex Delvecchio, John Wilson, Vic Stasiuk, Larry Zeidel, Jack Adams (manager) Tommy Ivan (coach), Carl Mattson (trainer).
Scores: April 10, at Montreal — Detroit 3, Montreal 1; April 12, at Montreal — Detroit 2, Montreal 1; April 13, at Detroit — Detroit 3, Montreal 0; April 15, at Detroit — Detroit 3, Montreal 0.

1950-51 — Toronto Maple Leafs — Turk Broda, Al Rollins, Jim Thomson, Gus Mortson, Bill Barilko, Bill Juzda, Fern Flaman, Hugh Bolton, Ted Kennedy, Sid Smith, Tod Sloan, Cal Gardner, Howie Meeker, Harry Watson, Max Bentley, Joe Klukay, Danny Lewicki, Ray Timgren, Fleming Mackell, Johnny McCormack, Bob Hassard, Conn Smythe (manager), Joe Primeau (coach), Tim Daly (trainer).
Scores: April 11, at Toronto — Toronto 3, Montreal 2; April 14, at Toronto — Montreal 3, Toronto 2; April 17, at Montreal — Toronto 2, Montreal 1; April 19, at Montreal — Toronto 3, Montreal 2; April 21, at Toronto — Toronto 3, Montreal 2.

1949-50 — Detroit Red Wings — Harry Lumley, Jack Stewart, Leo Reise Jr., Clare Martin, Doug McKay, Al Dewsbury, Lee Fogolin, Marcel Pronovost, Red Kelly, Ted Lindsay, Sid Abel, Gordie Howe, George Gee, Jimmy Peters Sr., Marty Pavelich, Jim McFadden, Pete Babando, Max McNab, Gerry Couture, Joe Carveth, Steve Black, John Wilson, Larry Wilson, Jack Adams (manager), Tommy Ivan (coach), Carl Mattson (trainer).
Scores: April 11, at Detroit — Detroit 4, NY Rangers 1; April 13, at Toronto* — NY Rangers 3, Detroit 1; April 15, at Toronto — Detroit 4, NY Rangers 0; April 18, at Detroit — NY Rangers 4, Detroit 3; April 20, at Detroit — NY Rangers 2, Detroit 1; April 22, at Detroit — Detroit 5, NY Rangers 4; April 23, at Detroit — Detroit 4, NY Rangers 3.

* Ice was unavailable in Madison Square Garden and Rangers elected to play second and third games on Toronto ice.

1948-49 — Toronto Maple Leafs — Turk Broda, Jim Thomson, Gus Mortson, Bill Barilko, Garth Boesch, Bill Juzda, Ted Kennedy, Howie Meeker, Vic Lynn, Harry Watson, Bill Ezinicki, Cal Gardner, Max Bentley, Joe Klukay, Sid Smith, Don Metz, Ray Timgren, Fleming Mackell, Harry Taylor, Bob Dawes, Tod Sloan, Conn Smythe (manager), Hap Day (coach), Tim Daly (trainer).
Scores: April 8, at Detroit — Toronto 3, Detroit 2; April 10, at Detroit — Toronto 3, Detroit 1; April 13, at Toronto — Toronto 3, Detroit 1; April 16, at Toronto — Toronto 3, Detroit 1.

A powerful defenseman over the course of his 15-year career, Butch Bouchard celebrated Stanley Cup victories with the Canadiens in 1944, 1946, 1953 and 1956.

1947-48 — Toronto Maple Leafs — Turk Broda, Jim Thomson, Wally Stanowski, Garth Boesch, Bill Barilko, Gus Mortson, Phil Samis, Syl Apps Sr., Bill Ezinicki, Harry Watson, Ted Kennedy, Howie Meeker, Vic Lynn, Nick Metz, Max Bentley, Joe Klukay, Les Costello, Don Metz, Sid Smith, Conn Smythe (manager), Hap Day (coach), Tim Daly (trainer).
Scores: April 7, at Toronto — Toronto 5, Detroit 3; April 10, at Toronto — Toronto 4, Detroit 2; April 11, at Detroit — Toronto 2, Detroit 0; April 14, at Detroit — Toronto 7, Detroit 2.

1946-47 — Toronto Maple Leafs — Turk Broda, Garth Boesch, Gus Mortson, Jim Thomson, Wally Stanowski, Bill Barilko, Harry Watson, Bud Poile, Ted Kennedy, Syl Apps Sr., Don Metz, Nick Metz, Bill Ezinicki, Vic Lynn, Howie Meeker, Gaye Stewart, Joe Klukay, Gus Bodnar, Bob Goldham, Conn Smythe (manager), Hap Day (coach), Tim Daly (trainer).
Scores: April 8, at Montreal — Montreal 6, Toronto 0; April 10, at Montreal — Toronto 4, Montreal 0; April 12, at Toronto — Toronto 4, Montreal 2; April 15, at Toronto — Toronto 2, Montreal 1; April 17, at Montreal — Montreal 3, Toronto 1; April 19, at Toronto — Toronto 2, Montreal 1.

1945-46 — Montreal Canadiens — Elmer Lach, Toe Blake, Maurice Richard, Bob Fillion, Dutch Hiller, Murph Chamberlain, Ken Mosdell, Buddy O'Connor, Glen Harmon, Jimmy Peters Sr., Butch Bouchard, Billy Reay, Ken Reardon, Leo Lamoureux, Frank Eddolls, Gerry Plamondon, Bill Durnan, Tommy Gorman (manager), Dick Irvin (coach), Ernie Cook (trainer).
Scores: March 30, at Montreal — Montreal 4, Boston 3; April 2, at Montreal — Montreal 3, Boston 2; April 4, at Boston — Montreal 4, Boston 2; April 7, at Boston — Boston 3, Montreal 2; April 9, at Montreal — Montreal 6, Boston 3.

1944-45 — Toronto Maple Leafs — Don Metz, Frank McCool, Wally Stanowski, Reg Hamilton, Elwyn Morris, Johnny McCreedy, Tommy O'Neill, Ted Kennedy, Babe Pratt, Gus Bodnar, Art Jackson, Jack McLean, Mel Hill, Nick Metz, Bob Davidson, Sweeney Schriner, Lorne Carr, Conn Smythe (manager), Frank Selke (business manager), Hap Day (coach), Tim Daly (trainer).
Scores: April 6, at Detroit — Toronto 1, Detroit 0; April 8, at Detroit — Toronto 2, Detroit 0; April 12, at Toronto — Toronto 1, Detroit 0; April 14, at Toronto — Detroit 5, Toronto 3; April 19, at Detroit — Detroit 2, Toronto 0; April 21, at Toronto — Detroit 1, Toronto 0; April 22, at Detroit — Toronto 2, Detroit 1.

1943-44 — Montreal Canadiens — Toe Blake, Maurice Richard, Elmer Lach, Ray Getliffe, Murph Chamberlain, Phil Watson, Butch Bouchard, Glen Harmon, Buddy O'Connor, Jerry Heffernan, Mike McMahon Sr., Leo Lamoureux, Fernand Majeau, Bob Fillion, Bill Durnan, Tommy Gorman (manager), Dick Irvin (coach), Ernie Cook (trainer).
Scores: April 4, at Montreal — Montreal 5, Chicago 1; April 6, at Chicago — Montreal 3, Chicago 1; April 9, at Chicago — Montreal 3, Chicago 2; April 13, at Montreal — Montreal 5, Chicago 4.

1942-43 — Detroit Red Wings — Jack Stewart, Jimmy Orlando, Sid Abel, Alex Motter, Harry Watson, Joe Carveth, Mud Bruneteau, Eddie Wares, Johnny Mowers, Cully Simon, Don Grosso, Carl Liscombe, Connie Brown, Syd Howe, Les Douglas, Hal Jackson, Joe Fisher, Jack Adams (manager), Ebbie Goodfellow (playing-coach), Honey Walker (trainer).
Scores: April 1, at Detroit — Detroit 6, Boston 2; April 4, at Detroit — Detroit 4, Boston 3; April 7, at Boston — Detroit 4, Boston 0; April 8, at Boston — Detroit 2, Boston 0.

1941-42 — Toronto Maple Leafs — Wally Stanowski, Syl Apps Sr., Bob Goldham, Gordie Drillon, Hank Goldup, Ernie Dickens, Sweeney Schriner, Bucko McDonald, Bob Davidson, Nick Metz, Bingo Kampman, Don Metz, Gaye Stewart, Turk Broda, Johnny McCreedy, Lorne Carr, Pete Langelle, Billy Taylor, Conn Smythe (manager), Hap Day (coach), Frank Selke (business manager), Tim Daly (trainer).
Scores: April 4, at Toronto — Detroit 3, Toronto 2; April 7, at Toronto — Detroit 4, Toronto 2; April 9, at Detroit — Detroit 5, Toronto 2; April 12, at Detroit — Toronto 4, Detroit 3; April 14, at Toronto — Toronto 9, Detroit 3; April 16, at Detroit — Toronto 3, Detroit 0; April 18, at Toronto — Toronto 3, Detroit 1.

1940-41 — Boston Bruins — Bill Cowley, Des Smith, Dit Clapper, Frank Brimsek, Flash Hollett, John Crawford, Bobby Bauer, Pat McReavy, Herb Cain, Mel Hill, Milt Schmidt, Woody Dumart, Roy Conacher, Terry Reardon, Art Jackson, Eddie Wiseman, Art Ross (manager), Cooney Weiland (coach), Win Green (trainer).
Scores: April 6, at Boston — Detroit 2, Boston 3; April 8, at Boston — Detroit 1, Boston 2; April 10, at Detroit — Boston 4, Detroit 2; April 12, at Detroit — Boston 3, Detroit 1.

1939-40 — New York Rangers — Dave Kerr, Art Coulter, Ott Heller, Alex Shibicky, Mac Colville, Neil Colville, Phil Watson, Lynn Patrick, Clint Smith, Muzz Patrick, Babe Pratt, Bryan Hextall Sr., Kilby Macdonald, Dutch Hiller, Alf Pike, Sanford Smith, Lester Patrick (manager), Frank Boucher (coach), Harry Westerby (trainer).
Scores: April 2, at New York — NY Rangers 2, Toronto 1; April 3, at New York — NY Rangers 6, Toronto 2; April 6, at Toronto — NY Rangers 1, Toronto 2; April 9, at Toronto — NY Rangers 0, Toronto 3; April 11, at Toronto — NY Rangers 2, Toronto 1; April 13, at Toronto — NY Rangers 3, Toronto 2.

1938-39 — Boston Bruins — Bobby Bauer, Mel Hill, Flash Hollett, Roy Conacher, Gord Pettinger, Charlie Sands, Milt Schmidt, Woody Dumart, Jack Crawford, Ray Getliffe, Frank Brimsek, Eddie Shore, Dit Clapper, Bill Cowley, Jack Portland, Red Hamill, Cooney Weiland, Art Ross (manager-coach), Win Green (trainer).
Scores: April 6, at Boston — Toronto 1, Boston 2; April 9, at Boston — Toronto 3, Boston 2; April 11, at Toronto — Toronto 1, Boston 3; April 13, at Toronto — Toronto 0, Boston 2; April 16, at Boston — Toronto 1, Boston 3.

1937-38 — Chicago Black Hawks — Art Wiebe, Carl Voss, Hal Jackson, Mike Karakas, Mush March, Jack Shill, Earl Seibert, Cully Dahlstrom, Alex Levinsky, Johnny Gottselig, Lou Trudel, Pete Palangio, Bill MacKenzie, Doc Romnes, Paul Thompson, Roger Jenkins, Alf Moore, Bert Connolly, Virgil Johnson, Paul Goodman, Bill Stewart (manager-coach), Eddie Froelich (trainer).
Scores: April 5, at Toronto — Chicago 3, Toronto 1; April 7, at Toronto — Chicago 1, Toronto 5; April 10, at Chicago — Chicago 2, Toronto 1; April 12, at Chicago — Chicago 4, Toronto 1.

1936-37 — Detroit Red Wings — Norman Smith, Pete Kelly, Larry Aurie, Herbie Lewis, Hec Kilrea, Mud Bruneteau, Syd Howe, Wally Kilrea, Jimmy Franks, Bucko McDonald, Gord Pettinger, Ebbie Goodfellow, John Gallagher, Ralph Bowman, John Sorrell, Marty Barry, Earl Robertson, John Sherf, Howard Mackie, Jack Adams (manager-coach), Honey Walker (trainer).
Scores: April 6, at New York — Detroit 1, NY Rangers 5; April 8, at Detroit — Detroit 4, NY Rangers 2; April 11, at Detroit — Detroit 0, NY Rangers 1; April 13, at Detroit — Detroit 1, NY Rangers 0; April 15, at Detroit — Detroit 3, NY Rangers 0.

1935-36 — Detroit Red Wings — John Sorrell, Syd Howe, Marty Barry, Herbie Lewis, Mud Bruneteau, Wally Kilrea, Hec Kilrea, Gord Pettinger, Bucko McDonald, Ralph Bowman, Pete Kelly, Doug Young, Ebbie Goodfellow, Norman Smith, Jack Adams (manager-coach), Honey Walker (trainer).
Scores: April 5, at Detroit — Detroit 3, Toronto 1; April 7, at Detroit — Detroit 9, Toronto 4; April 9, at Toronto — Detroit 3, Toronto 4; April 11, at Toronto — Detroit 3, Toronto 2.

1934-35 — Montreal Maroons — Lionel Conacher, Cy Wentworth, Alex Connell, Toe Blake, Stewart Evans, Earl Robinson, Bill Miller, Dave Trottier, Jimmy Ward, Larry Northcott, Hooley Smith, Russ Blinco, Allan Shields, Sammy McManus, Gus Marker, Bob Gracie, Herb Cain, Tommy Gorman (manager-coach), Bill O'Brien (trainer).
Scores: April 4, at Toronto — Mtl. Maroons 3, Toronto 2; April 6, at Toronto — Mtl. Maroons 3, Toronto 1; April 9, at Montreal — Mtl. Maroons 4, Toronto 1.

1933-34 — Chicago Black Hawks — Clarence Abel, Rosie Couture, Lou Trudel, Lionel Conacher, Paul Thompson, Leroy Goldsworthy, Art Coulter, Roger Jenkins, Don McFayden, Tom Cook, Doc Romnes, Johnny Gottselig, Mush March, Johnny Sheppard, Chuck Gardiner (captain), Bill Kendall, Tommy Gorman (manager-coach), Eddie Froelich (trainer).
Scores: April 3, at Detroit — Chicago 2, Detroit 1; April 5, at Detroit — Chicago 4, Detroit 1; April 8, at Chicago — Detroit 5, Chicago 2; April 10, at Chicago — Chicago 1, Detroit 0.

1932-33 — New York Rangers — Ching Johnson, Butch Keeling, Frank Boucher, Art Somers, Babe Siebert, Bun Cook, Andy Aitkenhead, Ott Heller, Oscar Asmundson, Gord Pettinger, Doug Brennan, Cecil Dillon, Bill Cook (captain), Murray Murdoch, Earl Seibert, Lester Patrick (manager-coach), Harry Westerby (trainer).
Scores: April 4, at New York — NY Rangers 5, Toronto 1; April 8, at Toronto — NY Rangers 3, Toronto 1; April 11, at Toronto — Toronto 3, NY Rangers 2; April 13, at Toronto — NY Rangers 1, Toronto 0.

1931-32 — Toronto Maple Leafs — Charlie Conacher, Harvey Jackson, King Clancy, Andy Blair, Red Horner, Lorne Chabot, Alex Levinsky, Joe Primeau, Hal Darragh, Hal Cotton, Frank Finnigan, Hap Day, Ace Bailey, Bob Gracie, Fred Robertson, Earl Miller, Conn Smythe (manager), Dick Irvin (coach), Tim Daly (trainer).
Scores: April 5, at New York — Toronto 6, NY Rangers 4; April 7, at Boston* — Toronto 6, NY Rangers 2; April 9, at Toronto — Toronto 6, NY Rangers 4.

* Ice was unavailable in Madison Square Garden and Rangers elected to play the second game on neutral ice.

1930-31 — Montreal Canadiens — George Hainsworth, Wildor Larochelle, Marty Burke, Sylvio Mantha, Howie Morenz, Johnny Gagnon, Aurel Joliat, Armand Mondou, Pit Lepine, Albert Leduc, Georges Mantha, Art Lesieur, Nick Wasnie, Bert McCaffrey, Gus Rivers, Jean Pusie, Léo Dandurand (manager), Cecil Hart (coach), Ed Dufour (trainer).
Scores: April 3, at Chicago — Montreal 2, Chicago 1; April 5, at Chicago — Chicago 2, Montreal 1; April 9, at Montreal — Chicago 3, Montreal 2; April 11, at Montreal — Montreal 4, Chicago 2; April 14, at Montreal — Montreal 2, Chicago 0.

1929-30 — Montreal Canadiens — George Hainsworth, Marty Burke, Sylvio Mantha, Howie Morenz, Bert McCaffrey, Aurel Joliat, Albert Leduc, Pit Lepine, Wildor Larochelle, Nick Wasnie, Gerald Carson, Armand Mondou, Georges Mantha, Gus Rivers, Léo Dandurand (manager), Cecil Hart (coach), Ed Dufour (trainer).
Scores: April 1, at Boston — Montreal 3, Boston 0; April 3, at Montreal — Montreal 4, Boston 3.

1928-29 — Boston Bruins — Tiny Thompson, Eddie Shore, Lionel Hitchman, Perk Galbraith, Eric Pettinger, Frank Fredrickson, Mickey Mackay, Red Green, Dutch Gainor, Harry Oliver, Eddie Rodden, Dit Clapper, Cooney Weiland, Lloyd Klein, Cy Denneny, Bill Carson, George Owen, Myles Lane, Art Ross (manager-coach), Win Green (trainer).
Scores: March 28, at Boston — Boston 2, NY Rangers 0; March 29, at New York — Boston 2, NY Rangers 1.

1927-28 — New York Rangers — Lorne Chabot, Clarence Abel, Leon Bourgault, Ching Johnson, Bill Cook, Bun Cook, Frank Boucher, Bill Boyd, Murray Murdoch, Paul Thompson, Alex Gray, Joe Miller, Patsy Callighen, Lester Patrick (manager-coach), Harry Westerby (trainer).
Scores: April 5, at Montreal — Mtl. Maroons 2, NY Rangers 0; April 7, at Montreal — NY Rangers 2, Mtl. Maroons 1; April 10, at Montreal — Mtl. Maroons 2, NY Rangers 0; April 12, at Montreal — NY Rangers 1, Mtl. Maroons 0; April 14, at Montreal — NY Rangers 2, Mtl. Maroons 1.

1926-27 — Ottawa Senators — Alex Connell, King Clancy, Georges Boucher, Ed Gorman, Frank Finnigan, Alex Smith, Hec Kilrea, Hooley Smith, Cy Denneny, Frank Nighbor, Jack Adams, Milt Halliday, Dave Gill (manager-coach).
Scores: April 7, at Boston — Ottawa 0, Boston 0; April 9, at Boston — Ottawa 3, Boston 1; April 11, at Ottawa — Boston 1, Ottawa 1; April 13, at Ottawa — Ottawa 3, Boston 1.

1925-26 — Montreal Maroons — Clint Benedict, Reg Noble, Frank Carson, Dunc Munro, Nels Stewart, Harry Broadbent, Babe Siebert, Chuck Dinsmore, Bill Phillips, Hobie Kitchen, Sam Rothschield, Albert Holway, George Horne, Bernie Brophy, Eddie Gerard (manager-coach), Bill O'Brien (trainer).
Scores: March 30, at Montreal — Mtl. Maroons 3, Victoria 0; April 1, at Montreal — Mtl. Maroons 3, Victoria 0; April 3, at Montreal — Victoria 3, Mtl. Maroons 2; April 6, at Montreal — Mtl. Maroons 2, Victoria 0.

The series in the spring of 1926 ended the annual playoffs between the champions of the East and the champions of the West. Since 1926-27 the annual playoffs in the National Hockey League have decided the Stanley Cup champions.

1924-25 — Victoria Cougars — Harry Holmes, Clem Loughlin, Gord Fraser, Frank Fredrickson, Jack Walker, Wilf Hart, Harold Halderson, Frank Foyston, Wally Elmer, Harry Meeking, Jocko Anderson, Lester Patrick (manager-coach).
Scores: March 21, at Victoria — Victoria 5, Montreal 2; March 23, at Vancouver — Victoria 3, Montreal 1; March 27, at Victoria — Montreal 4, Victoria 2; March 30, at Victoria — Victoria 6, Montreal 1.

1923-24 — Montreal Canadiens — Georges Vezina, Sprague Cleghorn, Billy Couture, Howie Morenz, Aurel Joliat, Billy Boucher, Odie Cleghorn, Sylvio Mantha, Bobby Boucher, Billy Bell, Billy Cameron, Joe Malone, Charles Fortier, Leo Dandurand (manager-coach).
Scores: March 18, at Montreal — Montreal 3, Van. Maroons 2; March 20, at Montreal — Montreal 2, Van. Maroons 1. March 22, at Montreal — Montreal 6, Cgy. Tigers 1; March 25, at Ottawa* — Montreal 3, Cgy. Tigers 0.

* Game transferred to Ottawa to benefit from artificial ice surface.

Even before there was an NHL, there was the Montreal Canadiens. Hockey's most storied franchise was formed for the 1909-10 season of the National Hockey Association and won the Stanley Cup for the first time in 1916.

1922-23 — Ottawa Senators — Georges Boucher, Lionel Hitchman, Frank Nighbor, King Clancy, Harry Helman, Clint Benedict, Jack Darragh, Eddie Gerard, Cy Denneny, Harry Broadbent, Tommy Gorman (manager), Pete Green (coach), F. Dolan (trainer).
Scores: March 16, at Vancouver — Ottawa 1, Van. Maroons 0; March 19, at Vancouver — Van. Maroons 4, Ottawa 1; March 23, at Vancouver — Ottawa 3, Van. Maroons 2; March 26, at Vancouver — Ottawa 5, Van. Maroons 1; March 29, at Vancouver — Ottawa 2, Edm. Eskimos 1; March 31, at Vancouver — Ottawa 1, Edm. Eskimos 0.

1921-22 — Toronto St. Pats — Ted Stackhouse, Corb Denneny, Rod Smylie, Lloyd Andrews, John Ross Roach, Harry Cameron, Billy Stuart, Babe Dye, Ken Randall, Reg Noble, Eddie Gerard (borrowed for one game from Ottawa), Stan Jackson, Nolan Mitchell, Charlie Querrie (manager), George O'Donoghue (coach).
Scores: March 17, at Toronto — Van. Millionaires 4, Toronto 3; March 20, at Toronto — Toronto 2, Van. Millionaires 1; March 23, at Toronto — Van. Millionaires 3, Toronto 0; March 25, at Toronto — Toronto 6, Van. Millionaires 0; March 28, at Toronto — Toronto 5, Van. Millionaires 1.

1920-21 — Ottawa Senators — Jack McKell, Jack Darragh, Morley Bruce, Georges Boucher, Eddie Gerard, Clint Benedict, Sprague Cleghorn, Frank Nighbor, Harry Broadbent, Cy Denneny, Leth Graham, Tommy Gorman (manager),Pete Green (coach), F. Dolan (trainer).
Scores: March 21, at Vancouver — Van. Millionaires 2, Ottawa 1; March 24, at Vancouver — Ottawa 4, Van. Millionaires 3; March 28, at Vancouver — Ottawa 3, Van. Millionaires 2; March 31, at Vancouver — Van. Millionaires 3, Ottawa 2; April 4, at Vancouver — Ottawa 2, Van. Millionaires 1

1919-20 — Ottawa Senators — Jack McKell, Jack Darragh, Morley Bruce, Horrace Merrill, Georges Boucher, Eddie Gerard, Clint Benedict, Sprague Cleghorn, Frank Nighbor, Harry Broadbent, Cy Denneny, Tommy Gorman (manager), Pete Green (coach).
Scores: March 22, at Ottawa — Ottawa 3, Seattle 2; March 24, at Ottawa — Ottawa 3, Seattle 0; March 27, at Ottawa — Seattle 3, Ottawa 1; March 30, at Toronto* — Seattle 5, Ottawa 2; April 1, at Toronto* — Ottawa 6, Seattle 1.

* Games transferred to Toronto to benefit from artificial ice surface.

1918-19 — No decision, Series halted by Spanish influenza epidemic, illness of several players and death of Joe Hall of Montreal Canadiens from flu. Five games had been played when the series was halted, each team having won two and tied one. The results are shown:
Scores: March 19, at Seattle — Seattle 7, Montreal 0; March 22, at Seattle — Montreal 4, Seattle 2; March 24, at Seattle — Seattle 7, Montreal 2; March 26, at Seattle — Montreal 0, Seattle 0; March 30, at Seattle — Montreal 4, Seattle 3.

1917-18 — Toronto Arenas — Rusty Crawford, Harry Meeking, Ken Randall, Corb Denneny, Harry Cameron, Jack Adams, Alf Skinner, Harry Mummery, Harry Holmes, Reg Noble, Sammy Hebert, Jack Marks, Jack Coughlin, Charlie Querrie (manager), Dick Carroll (coach), Frank Carroll (trainer).
Scores: March 20, at Toronto — Toronto 5, Van. Millionaires 3; March 23, at Toronto — Van. Millionaires 6, Toronto 4; March 26, at Toronto — Toronto 6, Van. Millionaires 3; March 28, at Toronto — Van. Millionaires 8, Toronto 1; March 30, at Toronto — Toronto 2, Van. Millionaires 1.

1916-17 — Seattle Metropolitans — Harry Holmes, Ed Carpenter, Cully Wilson, Jack Walker, Bernie Morris, Frank Foyston, Roy Rickey, Jim Riley, Bobby Rowe (captain), Peter Muldoon (manager).
Scores: March 17, at Seattle — Montreal 8, Seattle 4; March 20, at Seattle — Seattle 6, Montreal 1; March 23, at Seattle — Seattle 4, Montreal 1; March 25, at Seattle — Seattle 9, Montreal 1.

1915-16 — Montreal Canadiens — Georges Vezina, Bert Corbeau, Jack Laviolette, Newsy Lalonde, Louis Berlinguette, Goldie Prodgers, Howard McNamara, Didier Pitre, Skene Ronan, Amos Arbour, Georges Poulin, Jacques Fournier, George Kennedy (manager).
Scores: March 20, at Montreal — Portland 2, Montreal 0; March 22, at Montreal — Montreal 2, Portland 1; March 25, at Montreal — Montreal 6, Portland 3; March 28, at Montreal — Portland 6, Montreal 5; March 30, at Montreal — Montreal 2, Portland 1.

1914-15 — Vancouver Millionaires — Kenny Mallen, Frank Nighbor, Fred (Cyclone) Taylor, Hughie Lehman, Lloyd Cook, Mickey MacKay, Barney Stanley, Jim Seaborn, Si Griffis (captain), Jean Matz, Frank Patrick (playing manager).
Scores: March 22, at Vancouver — Van. Millionaires 6, Ottawa 2; March 24, at Vancouver — Van. Millionaires 8, Ottawa 3; March 26, at Vancouver — Van. Millionaires 12, Ottawa 3.

1913-14 — Toronto Blueshirts — Con Corbeau, F. Roy McGiffen, Jack Walker, George McNamara, Cully Wilson, Frank Foyston, Harry Cameron, Harry Holmes, Alan M. Davidson (captain), Harriston, Jack Marshall (playing-manager), Frank and Dick Carroll (trainers).
Scores: March 14, at Toronto — Toronto 5, Victoria 2; March 17, at Toronto — Toronto 6, Victoria 5; March 19, at Toronto — Toronto 2, Victoria 1.

1912-13 — Quebec Bulldogs — Joe Malone, Joe Hall, Paddy Moran, Harry Mummery, Tommy Smith, Jack Marks, Russell Crawford, Billy Creighton, Jeff Malone, Rocket Power, M.J. Quinn (manager), D. Beland (trainer).
Scores: March 8, at Quebec — Que. Bulldogs 14, Sydney 3; March 10, at Quebec — Que. Bulldogs 6, Sydney 2.

Victoria challenged Quebec but the Bulldogs refused to put the Stanley Cup in competition so the two teams played an exhibition series with Victoria winning two games to one by scores of 7-5, 3-6, 6-1. It was the first meeting between the Eastern champions and the Western champions. The following year, and until the Western Hockey League disbanded after the 1926 playoffs, the Cup went to the winner of the series between East and West.

1911-12 — Quebec Bulldogs — Goldie Prodgers, Joe Hall, Walter Rooney, Paddy Moran, Jack Marks, Jack McDonald, Eddie Oatman, George Leonard, Joe Malone (captain), C. Nolan (coach), M.J. Quinn (manager), D. Beland (trainer).
Scores: March 11, at Quebec — Que. Bulldogs 9, Moncton 3; March 13, at Quebec — Que. Bulldogs 8, Moncton 0.

Prior to 1912, teams could challenge the Stanley Cup champions for the title, thus there was more than one Championship Series played in most of the seasons between 1894 and 1911.

1910-11 — Ottawa Senators — Hamby Shore, Percy LeSueur, Jack Darragh, Bruce Stuart, Marty Walsh, Bruce Ridpath, Fred Lake, Albert (Dubby) Kerr, Alex Currie, Horace Gaul.
Scores: March 13, at Ottawa — Ottawa 7, Galt 4; March 16, at Ottawa — Ottawa 13, Port Arthur 4.

1909-10 — Montreal Wanderers — Cecil W. Blachford, Ernie (Moose) Johnson, Ernie Russell, Riley Hern, Harry Hyland, Jack Marshall, Frank (Pud) Glass (captain), Jimmy Gardner, R. R. (Dickie) Boon (manager).
Scores: March 12, at Montreal — Mtl. Wanderers 7, Berlin (Kitchener) 3.

1908-09 — Ottawa Senators — Fred Lake, Percy LeSueur, Fred (Cyclone) Taylor, H.L. (Billy) Gilmour, Albert Kerr, Edgar Dey, Marty Walsh, Bruce Stuart (captain).
Scores: Ottawa, as champions of the Eastern Canada Hockey Association took over the Stanley Cup in 1909 and, although a challenge was accepted by the Cup trustees from Winnipeg Shamrocks, games could not be arranged because of the lateness of the season. No other challenges were made in 1909. The following season — 1909-10 — however, the Senators accepted two challenges as defending Cup Champions. The first was against Galt in a two-game, total-goals series, and the second against Edmonton, also a two-game, total-goals series. Results: January 5, at Ottawa —Ottawa 12, Galt 3; January 7, at Ottawa — Ottawa 3, Galt 1. January 18, at Ottawa — Ottawa 8, Edm. Eskimos 4; January 20, at Ottawa — Ottawa 13, Edm. Eskimos 7.

1907-08 — Montreal Wanderers — Riley Hern, Art Ross, Walter Smaill, Frank (Pud) Glass, Bruce Stuart, Ernie Russell, Ernie (Moose) Johnson, Cecil Blachford (captain), Tom Hooper, Larry Gilmour, Ernie Liffiton, R.R. (Dickie) Boon (manager).
Scores: Wanderers accepted four challenges for the Cup: January 9, at Montreal — Mtl. Wanderers 9, Ott. Victorias 3; January 13, at Montreal — Mtl. Wanderers 13, Ott. Victorias 1; March 10, at Montreal — Mtl. Wanderers 11, Wpg. Maple Leafs 5; March 12, at Montreal — Mtl. Wanderers 9, Wpg. Maple Leafs 3; March 14, at Montreal — Mtl. Wanderers 6, Toronto (OPHL) 4. At start of following season, 1908-09, Wanderers were challenged by Edmonton. Results: December 28, at Montreal — Mtl. Wanderers 7, Edm. Eskimos 3; December 30, at Montreal — Edm. Eskimos 7, Mtl. Wanderers 6. Total goals: Mtl. Wanderers 13, Edm. Eskimos 10.

1906-07 — (March 25) — **Montreal Wanderers** — W.S. (Billy) Strachan, Riley Hern, Lester Patrick, Hod Stuart, Frank (Pud) Glass, Ernie Russell, Cecil Blachford (captain), Ernie (Moose) Johnson, Rod Kennedy, Jack Marshall, R.R. (Dickie) Boon (manager).

1906-07 — (March 18) — **Kenora Thistles** — Eddie Geroux, Si Griffis, Tom Hooper, Fred Whitcroft, Alf Smith, Harry Westwick, Roxy Beaudro, Tom Phillips (captain), Russell Phillips.
Scores: March 16, at Winnipeg — Kenora 8, Brandon 6; March 18, at Winnipeg — Kenora 4, Brandon 1; March 23, at Winnipeg — Mtl. Wanderers 7, Kenora 2; March 25, at Winnipeg — Kenora 6, Mtl. Wanderers 5. Total goals: Mtl. Wanderers 12, Kenora 8.

1906-07 — (January) — **Kenora Thistles** — Eddie Geroux, Art Ross, Si Griffis, Tom Hooper, Billy McGimsie, Roxy Beaudro, Tom Phillips (captain), Joe Hall, Russell Phillips.
Scores: January 17, at Montreal — Kenora 4, Mtl. Wanderers 2; Jan. 21, at Montreal — Kenora 8, Mtl. Wanderers 6.

1905-06 — (March) — **Montreal Wanderers** — Henri Menard, Billy Strachan, Rod Kennedy, Lester Patrick, Frank (Pud) Glass, Ernie Russell, Ernie (Moose) Johnson, Cecil Blachford (captain), Josh Arnold, R.R. (Dickie) Boon (manager).
Scores: March 14, at Montreal — Mtl. Wanderers 9, Ottawa 1; March 17, at Ottawa — Ottawa 9, Mtl. Wanderers 3. Total goals: Mtl. Wanderers 12, Ottawa 10. Wanderers accepted a challenge from New Glasgow, N.S., prior to the start of the 1906-07 season. Results: December 27, at Montreal — Mtl. Wanderers 10, New Glasgow 3; December 29, at Montreal — Mtl. Wanderers 7, New Glasgow 2.

1905-06 — (February) — **Ottawa Silver Seven** — Harvey Pulford (captain), Arthur Moore, Harry Westwick, Frank McGee, Alf Smith (playing coach), Billy Gilmour, Billy Hague, Percy LeSueur, Harry Smith, Tommy Smith, Dion, Ebbs.
Scores: February 27, at Ottawa — Ottawa 16, Queen's University 7; February 28, at Ottawa — Ottawa 12, Queen's University 7; March 6, at Ottawa — Ottawa 6, Smiths Falls 5; March 8, at Ottawa — Ottawa 8, Smiths Falls 2.

1904-05 — Ottawa Silver Seven — Dave Finnie, Harvey Pulford (captain), Arthur Moore, Harry Westwick, Frank McGee, Alf Smith (playing coach), Billy Gilmour, Frank White, Horace Gaul, Hamby Shore, Bones Allen.
Scores: January 13, at Ottawa — Ottawa 9, Dawson City 2; January 16, at Ottawa — Ottawa 23, Dawson City 2; March 7, at Ottawa — Rat Portage 9, Ottawa 3; March 9, at Ottawa — Ottawa 4, Rat Portage 2; March 11, at Ottawa — Ottawa 5, Rat Portage 4.

1903-04 — Ottawa Silver Seven — S.C. (Suddy) Gilmour, Arthur Moore, Frank McGee, J.B. (Bouse) Hutton, H.L. (Billy) Gilmour, Jim McGee, Harry Westwick, E. H. (Harvey) Pulford (captain), Scott, Alf Smith (playing coach).
Scores: December 30, at Ottawa — Ottawa 9, Wpg. Rowing Club 1; January 1, at Ottawa — Wpg. Rowing Club 6, Ottawa 2; January 4, at Ottawa — Ottawa 2, Wpg. Rowing Club 0. February 23, at Ottawa — Ottawa 6, Tor. Marlboros 3; February 25, at Ottawa — Ottawa 11, Tor. Marlboros 2; March 2, at Montreal — Ottawa 5, Mtl. Wanderers 5. Following the tie game, a new two-game series was ordered to be played in Ottawa but the Wanderers refused unless the tie game was replayed in Montreal. When no settlement could be reached, the series was abandoned and Ottawa retained the Cup and accepted a two-game challenge from Brandon. Results: (both games at Ottawa), March 9, Ottawa 6, Brandon 3; March 11, Ottawa 9, Brandon 3.

1902-03 — (March) — **Ottawa Silver Seven** — S.C. (Suddy) Gilmour, P.T. (Percy) Sims, J.B. (Bouse) Hutton, D.J. (Dave) Gilmour, H.L. (Billy) Gilmour, Harry Westwick, Frank McGee, F.H. Wood, A.A. Fraser, Charles D. Spittal, E.H. (Harvey) Pulford (captain), Arthur Moore, Alf Smith (coach.)
Scores: March 7, at Montreal — Ottawa 1, Mtl. Victorias 1; March 10, at Ottawa — Ottawa 8, Mtl. Victorias 0. Total goals: Ottawa 9, Mtl. Victorias 1; March 12, at Ottawa — Ottawa 6, Rat Portage 2; March 14, at Ottawa — Ottawa 4, Rat Portage 2.

1902-03 — (February) — **Montreal AAA** — Tom Hodge, R.R. (Dickie) Boon, W.C. (Billy) Nicholson, Tom Phillips, Art Hooper, W.J. (Billy) Bellingham, Charles A. Liffiton, Jack Marshall, Jim Gardner, Cecil Blachford, George Smith.
Scores: January 29, at Montreal — Mtl. AAA 8, Wpg. Victorias 1; January 31, at Montreal — Wpg. Victorias 2, Mtl. AAA 2; February 2, at Montreal — Wpg. Victorias 4, Mtl. AAA 2; February 4, at Montreal — Mtl. AAA 5, Wpg. Victorias 1.

1901-02 — (March) — **Montreal AAA** — Tom Hodge, R.R. (Dickie) Boon, William C. (Billy) Nicholson, Archie Hooper, W.J. (Billy) Bellingham, Charles A. Liffiton, Jack Marshall, Roland Elliott, Jim Gardner.
Scores: March 13, at Winnipeg — Wpg. Victorias 1, Mtl. AAA 0; March 15, at Winnipeg — Mtl. AAA 5, Wpg. Victorias 0; March 17, at Winnipeg — Mtl. AAA 2, Wpg. Victorias 1.

1901-02 — (January) — **Winnipeg Victorias** — Burke Wood, A.B. (Tony) Gingras, Charles W. Johnstone, R.M. (Rod) Flett, Magnus L. Flett, Dan Bain (captain), Fred Scanlon, F. Cadham, G. Brown.
Scores: January 21, at Winnipeg — Wpg. Victorias 5, Tor Wellingtons 3; January 23, at Winnipeg — Wpg. Victorias 5, Tor. Wellingtons 3.

1900-01 — Winnipeg Victorias — Burke Wood, Jack Marshall, A.B. (Tony) Gingras, Charles W. Johnstone, R.M. (Rod) Flett, Magnus L. Flett, Dan Bain (captain), Art Brown.
Scores: January 29, at Montreal — Wpg. Victorias 4, Mtl. Shamrocks 3; January 31, at Montreal — Wpg. Victorias 2, Mtl. Shamrocks 1.

1899-1900 — Montreal Shamrocks — Joe McKenna, Frank Tansey, Frank Wall, Art Farrell, Fred Scanlon, Harry Trihey (captain), Jack Brannen.
Scores: February 12, at Montreal — Mtl. Shamrocks 4, Wpg. Victorias 3; February 14, at Montreal — Wpg. Victorias 3, Mtl. Shamrocks 2; February 16, at Montreal — Mtl. Shamrocks 5, Wpg. Victorias 4; March 5, at Montreal — Mtl. Shamrocks 10, Halifax 2; March 7, at Montreal — Mtl. Shamrocks 11, Halifax 0.

1898-99 — (March) — **Montreal Shamrocks** — Jim McKenna, Frank Tansey, Frank Wall, Harry Trihey (captain), Art Farrell, Fred Scanlon, Jack Brannen, John Dobby, Charles Hoerner.
Scores: March 14, at Montreal — Mtl. Shamrocks 6, Queen's University 2.

1898-99 — (February) — **Montreal Victorias** — Gordon Lewis, Mike Grant, Graham Drinkwater, Cam Davidson, Bob McDougall, Ernie McLea, Frank Richardson, Jack Ewing, Russell Bowie, Douglas Acer, Fred McRobie.
Scores: February 15, at Montreal — Mtl. Victorias 2, Wpg. Victorias 1; February 18, at Montreal — Mtl. Victorias 3, Wpg. Victorias 2.

1897-98 — Montreal Victorias — Gordon Lewis, Hartland McDougall, Mike Grant, Graham Drinkwater, Cam Davidson, Bob McDougall, Ernie McLea, Frank Richardson (captain), Jack Ewing. The Victorias as champions of the Amateur Hockey Association, retained the Cup and were not called upon to defend it.

1896-97 — Montreal Victorias — Gordon Lewis, Harold Henderson, Mike Grant (captain), Cam Davidson, Graham Drinkwater, Robert McDougall, Ernie McLea, Shirley Davidson, Hartland McDougall, Jack Ewing, Percy Molson, David Gillilan, McLellan.
Scores: December 27, at Montreal — Mtl. Victorias 15, Ott. Capitals 2.

1895-96 — (December) — **Montreal Victorias** — Harold Henderson, Mike Grant (captain), Robert McDougall, Graham Drinkwater, Shirley Davidson, Ernie McLea, W. Wallace, Robert Jones, Cam Davidson, David Gillilan, Stanley Willett.
Scores: December 30, at Winnipeg — Mtl. Victorias 6, Wpg. Victorias 5.

1895-96 — (February) — **Winnipeg Victorias** — George "Whitey" Merritt, Rod Flett, Fred Higginbotham, Jack Armitage (captain), Colin "Tote" Campbell, Dan Bain, Bobby Benson, Attie Howard.
Scores: February 14, at Montreal — Wpg. Victorias 2, Mtl. Victorias 0.

1894-95 — Montreal Victorias — Robert Jones, Harold Henderson, Mike Grant (captain), Shirley Davidson, Bob McDougall, Norman Rankin, Graham Drinkwater, Roland Elliot, William Pullan, Hartland McDougall, Jim Fenwick, A. McDougall. Montreal Victorias, as champions of the Amateur Hockey Association, were prepared to defend the Stanley Cup. However, the Stanley Cup trustees had already accepted a challenge match between the 1894 champion Montreal AAA and Queen's University. It was declared that if Montreal AAA defeated Queen's University, Montreal Victorias would be declared Stanley Cup champions. If Queen's University won, the Cup would go to the university club. In a game played March 9, 1895, Montreal AAA defeated Queen's University 5-1. As a result, Montreal Victorias were awarded the Stanley Cup.

1893-94 — Montreal AAA — Herbert Collins, Allan Cameron, George James, Billy Barlow, Clare Mussen, Archie Hodgson, Haviland Routh, Alex Irving, James Stewart, E. O'Brien, A.C. (Toad) Wand, A.B. Kingan.
Scores: March 17, at Mtl. Victorias — Mtl. AAA 3, Mtl. Victorias 2; March 22, at Montreal — Mtl. AAA 3, Ott. Capitals 1.

1892-93 — Montreal AAA — Tom Paton, James Stewart, Allan Cameron, Haviland Routh, Archie Hodgson, Billy Barlow, A.B. Kingan, G.S. Lowe.
In accordance with the terms governing the presentation of the Stanley Cup, it was awarded for the first time to the Montreal AAA as champions of the Amateur Hockey Association in 1893. Once Montreal AAA had been declared holders of the Stanley Cup, any Canadian hockey team could challenge for the trophy.

All-Time NHL Playoff Formats

1917-18 — The regular-season was split into two halves. The winners of both halves faced each other in a two-game, total-goals series for the NHL championship and the right to meet the PCHA champion in the best-of-five Stanley Cup Finals.

1918-19 — Same as 1917-18, except that the Stanley Cup Finals was extended to a best-of-seven series.

1919-20 — Same as 1917-1918, except that Ottawa won both halves of the split regular-season schedule to earn an automatic berth into the best-of-five Stanley Cup Finals against the PCHA champions.

1921-22 — The top two teams at the conclusion of the regular-season faced each other in a two-game, total-goals series for the NHL championship. The NHL champion then moved on to play the winner of the PCHA-WCHL playoff series in the best-of-five Stanley Cup Finals.

1922-23 — The top two teams at the conclusion of the regular-season faced each other in a two-game, total-goals series for the NHL championship. The NHL champion then moved on to play the PCHA champion in the best-of-three Stanley Cup Semi-Finals, and the winner of the Semi-Finals played the WCHL champion, which had been given a bye, in the best-of-three Stanley Cup Finals.

1923-24 — The top two teams at the conclusion of the regular-season faced each other in a two-game, total-goals series for the NHL championship. The NHL champion then moved on to play the loser of the PCHA-WCHL playoff (the winner of the PCHA-WCHL playoff earned a bye into the Stanley Cup Finals) in the best-of-three Stanley Cup Semi-Finals. The winner of this series met the PCHA-WCHL playoff winner in the best-of-three Stanley Cup Finals.

1924-25 — The first place team (Hamilton) at the conclusion of the regular-season was supposed to play the winner of a two-game, total goals series between the second (Toronto) and third (Montreal) place clubs. However, Hamilton refused to abide by this new format, demanding greater compensation than offered by the League. Thus, Toronto and Montreal played their two-game, total-goals series, and the winner (Montreal) earned the NHL title and then played the WCHL champion (Victoria) in the best-of-five Stanley Cup Finals.

1925-26 — The format which was intended for 1924-25 went into effect. The winner of the two-game, total-goals series between the second and third place teams squared off against the first place team in the two-game, total-goals NHL championship series. The NHL champion then moved on to play the WHL champion in the best-of-five Stanley Cup Finals.

After the 1925-26 season, the NHL was the only major professional hockey league still in existence and consequently took over sole control of the Stanley Cup competition.

1926-27 — The 10-team league was divided into two divisions — Canadian and American — of five teams apiece. In each division, the winner of the two-game, total-goals series between the second and third place teams faced the first place team in a two-game, total-goals series for the division title. The two division title winners then met in the best-of-five Stanley Cup Finals.

1928-29 — Both first place teams in the two divisions played each other in a best-of-five series. Both second place teams in the two divisions played each other in a two-game, total-goals series as did the two third place teams. The winners of these latter two series then played each other in a best-of-three series for the right to meet the winner of the series between the two first place clubs. This Stanley Cup Final was a best-of-three.

Series A: First in Canadian Division versus first in American (best-of-five)
Series B: Second in Canadian Division versus second in American (two-game, total-goals)
Series C: Third in Canadian Division versus third in American (two-game, total-goals)
Series D: Winner of Series B versus winner of Series C (best-of-three)
Series E: Winner of Series A versus winner of Series D (best of three) for Stanley Cup

1931-32 — Same as 1928-29, except that Series D was changed to a two-game, total-goals format and Series E was changed to best of five.

1936-37 — Same as 1931-32, except that Series B, C, and D were each best-of-three.

1938-39 — With the NHL reduced to seven teams, the two-division system was replaced by one seven-team league. Based on final regular-season standings, the following playoff format was adopted:

Series A: First versus Second (best-of-seven)
Series B: Third versus Fourth (best-of-three)
Series C: Fifth versus Sixth (best-of-three)
Series D: Winner of Series B versus winner of Series C (best-of-three)
Series E: Winner of Series A versus winner of Series D (best-of-seven)

1942-43 — With the NHL reduced to six teams (the "original six"), only the top four finishers qualified for playoff action. The best-of-seven Semi-Finals pitted Team #1 vs Team #3 and Team #2 vs Team #4. The winners of each Semi-Final series met in the best-of-seven Stanley Cup Finals.

1967-68 — When it doubled in size from 6 to 12 teams, the NHL once again was divided into two divisions — East and West — of six teams apiece. The top four clubs in each division qualified for the playoffs (all series were best-of-seven):

Series A: Team #1 (East) vs Team #3 (East)
Series B: Team #2 (East) vs Team #4 (East)
Series C: Team #1 (West) vs Team #3 (West)
Series D: Team #2 (West) vs Team #4 (West)
Series E: Winner of Series A vs winner of Series B
Series F: Winner of Series C vs winner of Series D
Series G: Winner of Series E vs Winner of Series F

1970-71 — Same as 1967-68 except that Series E matched the winners of Series A and D, and Series F matched the winners of Series B and C.

1971-72 — Same as 1970-71, except that Series A and C matched Team #1 vs Team #4, and Series B and D matched Team #2 vs Team #3.

1974-75 — With the League now expanded to 18 teams in four divisions, a completely new playoff format was introduced. First, the #2 and #3 teams in each of the four divisions were pooled together in the Preliminary round. These eight (#2 and #3) clubs were ranked #1 to #8 based on regular-season record:

Series A: Team #1 vs Team #8 (best-of-three)
Series B: Team #2 vs Team #7 (best-of-three)
Series C: Team #3 vs Team #6 (best-of-three)
Series D: Team #4 vs Team #5 (best-of-three)
The winners of this Preliminary round then pooled together with the four division winners, which had received byes into this Quarter-Final round. These eight teams were again ranked #1 to #8 based on regular-season record:
Series E: Team #1 vs Team #8 (best-of-seven)
Series F: Team #2 vs Team #7 (best-of-seven)
Series G: Team #3 vs Team #6 (best-of-seven)
Series H: Team #4 vs Team #5 (best-of-seven)
The four Quarter-Finals winners, which moved on to the Semi-Finals, were then ranked #1 to #4 based on regular season record:
Series I: Team #1 vs Team #4 (best-of-seven)
Series J: Team #2 vs Team #3 (best-of-seven)
Series K: Winner of Series I vs winner of Series J (best-of-seven)

1977-78 — Same as 1974-75, except that the Preliminary round consisted of the #2 teams in the four divisions and the next four teams based on regular-season record (not their standings within their divisions).

1979-80 — With the addition of four WHA franchises, the League expanded its playoff structure to include 16 of its 21 teams. The four first place teams in the four divisions automatically earned playoff berths. Among the 17 other clubs, the top 12, according to regular-season record, also earned berths. All 16 teams were then pooled together and ranked #1 to #16 based on regular-season record:

Series A: Team #1 vs Team #16 (best-of-five)
Series B: Team #2 vs Team #15 (best-of-five)
Series C: Team #3 vs Team #14 (best-of-five)
Series D: Team #4 vs Team #13 (best-of-five)
Series E: Team #5 vs Team #12 (best-of-five)
Series F: Team #6 vs Team #11 (best-of-five)
Series G: Team #7 vs Team #10 (best-of-five)
Series H: Team #8 vs Team # 9 (best-of-five)
The eight Preliminary round winners, ranked #1 to #8 based on regular-season record, moved on to the Quarter-Finals:
Series I: Team #1 vs Team #8 (best-of-seven)
Series J: Team #2 vs Team #7 (best-of-seven)
Series K: Team #3 vs Team #6 (best-of-seven)
Series L: Team #4 vs Team #5 (best-of-seven)
The four Quarter-Finals winners, ranked #1 to #4 based on regular-season record, moved on to the semi-finals:
Series M: Team #1 vs Team #4 (best-of-seven)
Series N: Team #2 vs Team #3 (best-of-seven)
Series O: Winner of Series M vs winner of Series N (best-of-seven)

1981-82 — The first four teams in each division earned playoff berths. In each division, the first-place team opposed the fourth-place team and the second-place team opposed the third-place team in a best-of-five Division Semi-Final series (DSF). In each division, the two winners of the DSF met in a best-of-seven Division Final series (DF). The two DF winners in each conference met in a best-of-seven Conference Final series (CF). In the Prince of Wales Conference, the Adams Division winner opposed the Patrick Division winner; in the Clarence Campbell Conference, the Smythe Division winner opposed the Norris Division winner. The two CF winners met in a best-of-seven Stanley Cup Final (F) series.

1986-87 — Division Semi-Final series changed from best-of-five to best-of-seven.

1993-94 — The NHL's playoff draw is conference-based rather than division-based. At the conclusion of the regular season, the top eight teams in each of the Eastern and Western Conferences qualify for the playoffs. The teams that finish in first place in each of the League's divisions are seeded first and second in each conference's playoff draw and are assured of home ice advantage in the first two playoff rounds. The remaining teams are seeded based on their regular-season point totals. In each conference, the team seeded #1 plays #8; #2 vs. #7; #3 vs. #6; and #4 vs. #5. All series are best-of-seven with home ice rotating on a 2-2-1-1-1 basis, with the exception of matchups between Central and Pacific Division teams. These matchups will be played on a 2-3-2 basis to reduce travel. In a 2-3-2 series, the team with the most points will have its choice to start the series at home or on the road. The Eastern Conference champion will face the Western Conference champion in the Stanley Cup Final.

1994-95 — Same as 1993-94, except that in first, second or third-round playoff series involving Central and Pacific Division teams, the team with the better record has the choice of using either a 2-3-2 or a 2-2-1-1-1 format. When a 2-3-2 format is selected, the higher-ranked team also has the choice of playing games 1, 2, 6 and 7 at home or playing games 3, 4 and 5 at home. The format for the Stanley Cup Final remains 2-2-1-1-1.

1998-99 — The NHL's clubs are re-aligned into two conferences each consisting of three divisions. The number of teams qualifying for the Stanley Cup Playoffs remains unchanged at 16.

First-round playoff berths will be awarded to the first-place team in each division as well as to the next five best teams based on regular-season point totals in each conference. The three division winners in each conference will be seeded first through third, in order of points, for the playoffs and the next five best teams, in order of points, will be seeded fourth through eighth. In each conference, the team seeded #1 will play #8; #2 vs. #7; #3 vs. #6; and #4 vs. #5 in the quarterfinal round. Home-ice in the Conference Quarterfinals is granted to those teams seeded first through fourth in each conference.

In the Conference Semifinals and Conference Finals, teams will be re-seeded according to the same criteria as the Conference Quarterfinals. Higher seeded teams will have home-ice advantage.

Home-ice advantage for the Stanley Cup Finals will be determined by points.

All series remain best-of-seven.

The 1955-56 Montreal Canadiens look stylish in the fashions of the day. The Canadiens were in the midst of a stretch that would seem them reach the Finals for 10 straight years and win the Stanley Cup six times, including five in a row.

Team Records

1918-2001

GAMES PLAYED

MOST GAMES PLAYED BY ALL TEAMS, ONE PLAYOFF YEAR:
92 — 1991. There were 51 DSF, 24 DF, 11 CF and 6 F games.
90 — 1994. There were 48 CQF, 23 CSF, 12 CF and 7 F games.
87 — 1987. There were 44 DSF, 25 DF, 11 CF and 7 F games.

MOST GAMES PLAYED, ONE TEAM, ONE PLAYOFF YEAR:
26 — Philadelphia Flyers, 1987. Won DSF 4-2 against NY Rangers, DF 4-3 against NY Islanders, CF 4-2 against Montreal, and lost F 4-3 against Edmonton.
25 — New Jersey Devils, 2001. Won CQF 4-2 against Carolina, CSF 4-3 against Toronto, CF 4-1 against Pittsburgh, and lost F 4-3 against Colorado.
24 — Pittsburgh Penguins,1991. Won DSF 4-3 against New Jersey, DF 4-1 against Washington, CF 4-2 against Boston, and F 4-2 against Minnesota.
— Los Angeles Kings, 1993. Won DSF 4-2 against Calgary, DF 4-2 against Vancouver, CF 4-3 against Toronto, and lost F 4-1 against Montreal.
— Vancouver Canucks, 1994. Won CQF 4-3 against Calgary, CSF 4-1 against Dallas, CF 4-1 against Toronto, and lost F 4-3 against NY Rangers.

PLAYOFF APPEARANCES

MOST STANLEY CUP CHAMPIONSHIPS:
23 — Montreal Canadiens 1924-30-31-44-46-53-56-57-58-59-60-65-66-68-69-71-73-76-77-78-79-86-93
13 — Toronto Maple Leafs 1918-22-32-42-45-47-48-49-51-62-63-64-67
9 — Detroit Red Wings 1936-37-43-50-52-54-55-97-98

MOST CONSECUTIVE STANLEY CUP CHAMPIONSHIPS:
5 — Montreal Canadiens (1956-57-58-59-60)
4 — Montreal Canadiens (1976-77-78-79)
— NY Islanders (1980-81-82-83)

MOST FINAL SERIES APPEARANCES:
32 — Montreal Canadiens in 84-year history.
21 — Toronto Maple Leafs in 84-year history.
— Detroit Red Wings in 74-year history.

MOST CONSECUTIVE FINAL SERIES APPEARANCES:
10 — Montreal Canadiens, (1951-60, inclusive)
5 — Montreal Canadiens, (1965-69, inclusive)
— NY Islanders, (1980-84, inclusive)

MOST YEARS IN PLAYOFFS:
72 — Montreal Canadiens in 84-year history.
61 — Toronto Maple Leafs in 84-year history.
59 — Boston Bruins in 77-year history.

MOST CONSECUTIVE PLAYOFF APPEARANCES:
29 — Boston Bruins (1968-96, inclusive)
28 — Chicago Blackhawks (1970-97, inclusive)
24 — Montreal Canadiens (1971-94, inclusive)
22 — St. Louis Blues (1980-2001, inclusive)
21 — Montreal Canadiens (1949-69, inclusive)

TEAM WINS

MOST HOME WINS, ONE TEAM, ONE PLAYOFF YEAR:
11 — Edmonton Oilers, 1988 in 11 home games.
10 — Edmonton Oilers, 1985 in 10 home games.
— Montreal Canadiens, 1986 in 11 home games.
— Montreal Canadiens, 1993 in 11 home games.

MOST ROAD WINS, ONE TEAM, ONE PLAYOFF YEAR:
10 — New Jersey Devils, 1995. Won three at Boston in CQF; two at Pittsburgh in CSF; three at Philadelphia in CF; and two at Detroit in F series.
— **New Jersey Devils,** 2000. Won two at Florida in CQF; two at Toronto in CSF; three at Philadelphia in CF; and three at Dallas in F series.
8 — NY Islanders, 1980. Won two at Los Angeles in PR; three at Boston in QF; two at Buffalo in SF; and one at Philadelphia in F series.
— Philadelphia Flyers, 1987. Won two at NY Rangers in DSF; two at NY Islanders in DF; three at Montreal in CF; and one at Edmonton in F series.
— Edmonton Oilers, 1990. Won one at Winnipeg in DSF; two at Los Angeles in DF; two at Chicago in CF and three at Boston in F series.
— Pittsburgh Penguins, 1992. Won two at Washington in DSF; two at NY Rangers in DF; two at Boston in CF; and two at Chicago in F series.
— Vancouver Canucks, 1994. Won three at Calgary in CQF; two at Dallas in CSF; one at Toronto in CF; and two at NY Rangers in F series.
— Colorado Avalanche, 1996. Won two at Vancouver in CQF; two at Chicago in CSF; two at Detroit in CF; and two at Florida in F series.
— Detroit Red Wings, 1998. Won two at Phoenix in CQF; three at St. Louis in CSF; one at Dallas in CF; and two at Washington in F series.
— Colorado Avalanche, 1999. Won three at San Jose in CQF; three at Detroit in CSF; and two at Dallas in CF.
— New Jersey Devils, 2001. Won two at Carolina in CQF; two at Toronto in CSF; two at Pittsburgh in CF; and two at Colorado in F series.

MOST ROAD WINS, ALL TEAMS, ONE PLAYOFF YEAR:
46 — 1987. Of 87 games played, road teams won 46 (22 DSF, 14 DF, 8 CF and 2 in Stanley Cup final).

MOST OVERTIME WINS, ONE TEAM, ONE PLAYOFF YEAR:
10 — Montreal Canadiens, 1993. Two against Quebec in DSF; three against Buffalo in DF; two against NY Islanders in CF; and three against Los Angeles in F. Montreal played 20 games.
6 — NY Islanders, 1980. One against Los Angeles in PR; two against Boston in QF; one against Buffalo in SF; and two against Philadelphia in F. Islanders played 21 games.
— Vancouver Canucks, 1994. Three against Calgary in CQF; one against Dallas in CSF; one against Toronto in CF; and one against NY Rangers in F. Vancouver played 24 games.

MOST OVERTIME WINS AT HOME, ONE TEAM, ONE PLAYOFF YEAR:
4 — St. Louis Blues, 1968. Won one vs. Philadelphia in QF and three vs. Minnesota in SF.
— **Montreal Canadiens, 1993.** Won one vs. Quebec in DSF, one vs. Buffalo in DF, one vs. NY Islanders in CF and one vs. Los Angeles in F series.

MOST OVERTIME WINS ON THE ROAD, ONE TEAM, ONE PLAYOFF YEAR:
6 — Montreal Canadiens, 1993. Won one vs. Quebec in DSF, two vs. Buffalo in DF, one vs. NY Islanders in CF and two vs. Los Angeles in F series.

TEAM LOSSES

MOST LOSSES, ONE TEAM, ONE PLAYOFF YEAR:
11 — Philadelphia Flyers, 1987. Lost two vs. NY Rangers in DSF; three vs. NY Islanders in DF; two vs. Montreal in CF; and four vs. Edmonton in F series.

MOST HOME LOSSES, ONE TEAM, ONE PLAYOFF YEAR:
6 — Philadelphia Flyers, 1987. Lost one vs. NY Rangers in DSF; two vs. NY Islanders in DF; two vs. Montreal in CF; and one vs. Edmonton in F series.
— Washington Capitals, 1998. Lost two vs. Boston in CQF; two vs. Buffalo in CF; and two vs. Detroit in F series.
— Colorado Avalanche, 1999. Lost two vs. San Jose in CQF; two vs. Detroit in CSF; and two vs. Dallas in CF series.
— New Jersey Devils, 2001. Lost one vs. Carolina in CQF; two vs. Toronto in CSF; one vs. Pittsburgh in CF series; and two vs Colorado in F series.

MOST ROAD LOSSES, ONE TEAM, ONE PLAYOFF YEAR:
6 — St. Louis Blues, 1968. Lost two at Philadelphia in QF; two at Minnesota in SF; and two at Montreal in F series.
— **St. Louis Blues, 1970.** Lost two at Minnesota in QF; two at Pittsburgh in SF; and two at Boston in F series.
— **NY Islanders, 1984.** Lost one at NY Rangers in DSF; two at Montreal in CF; and three at Edmonton in F series.
— **Los Angeles Kings, 1993.** Lost one at Calgary in DSF; one at Vancouver in DF; two at Toronto in CF; and two at Montreal in F series.

MOST OVERTIME LOSSES, ONE TEAM, ONE PLAYOFF YEAR:
4 — Montreal Canadiens, 1951. Lost four vs. Toronto in F series.
— St. Louis Blues, 1968. Lost one vs. Philadelphia in QF; one vs. Minnesota in SF; and two vs. Montreal in F series.
— Los Angeles Kings, 1991. Lost one vs. Vancouver in DSF; and three vs. Edmonton in DF series.
— Los Angeles Kings, 1993. Lost one vs. Toronto in CF; and three vs. Montreal in F series.
— Philadelphia Flyers, 1996. Lost two vs. Tampa Bay in CQF; and two vs. Florida in CSF series.

MOST OVERTIME LOSSES AT HOME, ONE TEAM, ONE PLAYOFF YEAR:
2 — Two overtime losses at home by one team in one playoff year has occurred 40 times. The Pittsburgh Penguins are the most recent team to equal this mark when they lost twice in overtime at home to the Philadelphia Flyers in the 2000 Stanley Cup CSF series.

MOST OVERTIME LOSSES ON THE ROAD, ONE TEAM, ONE PLAYOFF YEAR:
3 — Los Angeles Kings, 1991. Lost one at Vancouver in DSF; and two at Edmonton in DF series.
— **St. Louis Blues, 1996.** Lost two at Toronto in CQF; and one at Detroit in CSF series.
— **Dallas Stars, 1999.** Lost two at St. Louis in CSF; and one at Colorado in CF series.

A record-tying four overtime losses, including three in the finals, helped to dash the Stanley Cup dreams of coach Barry Melrose and the 1993 Los Angeles Kings.

PLAYOFF WINNING STREAKS

LONGEST PLAYOFF WINNING STREAK:
14 — Pittsburgh Penguins. Streak started May 9, 1992, at Pittsburgh with a 5-4 win in fourth game of DF series against NY Rangers, won by Pittsburgh 4-2. Continued with a four-game win over Boston in 1992 CF and a four-game sweep of Chicago in 1992 F. Pittsburgh then won the first three games of 1993 DSF versus New Jersey. New Jersey ended the streak April 25, 1993, at New Jersey with a 4-1 win.
12 — Edmonton Oilers. Streak started May 15, 1984, at Edmonton with a 7-2 win in third game of F series against NY Islanders, won by Edmonton 4-1. Continued with a three-game sweep of Los Angeles in 1985 DSF and a four game sweep of Winnipeg in 1985 DF. Edmonton then won the first two games of 1985 CF versus Chicago. Chicago ended the streak May 9, 1985, at Chicago with a 5-2 win.

MOST CONSECUTIVE WINS, ONE TEAM, ONE PLAYOFF YEAR:
11 — Chicago Blackhawks in 1992. Chicago won last three games of DSF against St. Louis to win series 4-2 and then defeated Detroit 4-0 in DF and Edmonton 4-0 in CF.
— Pittsburgh Penguins in 1992. Pittsburgh won last three games of DF against NY Rangers to win series 4-2 and then defeated Boston 4-0 in CF and Chicago 4-0 in F.
— Montreal Canadiens in 1993. Montreal won last four games of DSF against Quebec to win series 4-2, defeated Buffalo 4-0 in DF and won first three games of CF against NY Islanders.

PLAYOFF LOSING STREAKS

LONGEST PLAYOFF LOSING STREAK:
16 Games — Chicago Blackhawks. Streak started in 1975 QF against Buffalo when Chicago lost last two games. Then Chicago lost four games to Montreal in 1976 QF; two games to NY Islanders in 1977 PR; four games to Boston in 1978 QF and four games to NY Islanders in 1979 QF. Streak ended on April 8, 1980 when Chicago defeated St. Louis 3-2 in the opening game of their 1980 PR series.
14 Games — Los Angeles Kings. Streak started when the Kings lost four consecutive games in the 1993 Stanley Cup Finals against Montreal. The Kings failed to qualify for the playoffs for the next four years. Los Angeles lost four straight games to St. Louis in the 1998 CQF and failed to qualify for the 1999 playoffs. They were defeated in four straight games by Detroit in the 2000 CQF series. Los Angeles lost the first two games of their 2001 CQF series against Detroit before defeating Detroit 2-1 on April 15, 2001 to end the streak.

CUP CRAZY

MOST GOALS IN A SERIES, ONE TEAM

MOST GOALS, ONE TEAM, ONE PLAYOFF SERIES:
44 — Edmonton Oilers in 1985 CF. Edmonton won best-of-seven series 4-2, outscoring Chicago 44-25.
35 — Edmonton Oilers in 1983 DF. Edmonton won best-of-seven series 4-1, outscoring Calgary 35-13.
— Calgary Flames in 1995 CQF. Calgary lost best-of-seven series 4-3, outscoring San Jose 35-26.

MOST GOALS, ONE TEAM, TWO-GAME SERIES:
11 — Buffalo Sabres in 1977 PR. Buffalo won best-of-three series 2-0, outscoring Minnesota 11-3.
— Toronto Maple Leafs in 1978 PR. Toronto won best-of-three series 2-0, outscoring Los Angeles 11-3.
10 — Boston Bruins in 1927 QF. Boston won two-game total goal series 10-5.

MOST GOALS, ONE TEAM, THREE-GAME SERIES:
23 — Chicago Blackhawks in 1985 DSF. Chicago won best-of-five series 3-0, outscoring Detroit 23-8.
20 — Minnesota North Stars in 1981 PR. Minnesota won best-of-five series 3-0, outscoring Boston 20-13.
— NY Islanders in 1981 PR. New York won best-of-five series 3-0, outscoring Toronto 20-4.

MOST GOALS, ONE TEAM, FOUR-GAME SERIES:
28 — Boston Bruins in 1972 SF. Boston won best-of-seven series 4-0, outscoring St. Louis 28-8.

MOST GOALS, ONE TEAM, FIVE-GAME SERIES:
35 — Edmonton Oilers in 1983 DF. Edmonton won best-of-seven series 4-1, outscoring Calgary 35-13.
32 — Edmonton Oilers in 1987 DSF. Edmonton won best-of-seven series 4-1, outscoring Los Angeles 32-20.
28 — NY Rangers in 1979 QF. NY Rangers won best-of-seven series 4-1, outscoring Philadelphia 28-8.

MOST GOALS, ONE TEAM, SIX-GAME SERIES:
44 — Edmonton Oilers in 1985 CF. Edmonton won best-of-seven series 4-2, outscoring Chicago 44-25.
33 — Chicago Blackhawks in 1985 DF. Chicago won best-of-seven series 4-2, outscoring Minnesota 33-29.
— Montreal Canadiens in 1973 F. Montreal won best-of-seven series 4-2, outscoring Chicago 33-23.
— Los Angeles Kings in 1993 DSF. Los Angeles won best-of-seven series 4-2, outscoring Calgary 33-28.

MOST GOALS, ONE TEAM, SEVEN-GAME SERIES:
35 — Calgary Flames in 1995 CQF. Calgary lost best-of-seven series 4-3, outscoring San Jose 35-26.
33 — Philadelphia Flyers in 1976 QF. Philadelphia won best-of-seven series 4-3, outscoring Toronto 33-23.
— Boston Bruins in 1983 DF. Boston won best-of-seven series 4-3, outscoring Buffalo 33-23.
— Edmonton Oilers in 1984 DF. Edmonton won best-of-seven series 4-3, outscoring Calgary 33-27.

Phil Housley set up nine goals in a seven-game series when Calgary scored a record 35 times against San Jose. Unfortunately for the Flames, the Sharks still managed to take the series four games to three.

FEWEST GOALS IN A SERIES, ONE TEAM

FEWEST GOALS, ONE TEAM, TWO-GAME SERIES:
0 — NY Americans in 1929 SF. Lost two-game total-goal series 1-0 against NY Rangers.
— Chicago Blackhawks in 1935 SF. Lost two-game total-goal series 1-0 against Mtl. Maroons.
— Mtl. Maroons in 1937 SF. Lost best-of-three series 2-0 to NY Rangers while being outscored 5-0.
— NY Americans in 1939 QF. Lost best-of-three series 2-0 to Toronto while being outscored 6-0.

FEWEST GOALS, ONE TEAM, THREE-GAME SERIES:
1 — Mtl. Maroons in 1936 SF. Lost best-of-five series 3-0 to Detroit and were outscored 6-1.

FEWEST GOALS, ONE TEAM, FOUR-GAME SERIES:
2 — Boston Bruins in 1935 SF. Lost best-of-five series 3-1 to Toronto and were outscored 7-2.
— Montreal Canadiens in 1952 F. Lost best-of-seven series 4-0 to Detroit and were outscored 11-2.

FEWEST GOALS, ONE TEAM, FIVE-GAME SERIES:
5 — NY Rangers in 1928 F. NY Rangers won best-of-five series 3-2, while being outscored by Mtl. Maroons 6-5.
— Boston Bruins in 1995 CQF. New Jersey won best-of-seven series 4-1, while outscoring Boston 14-5.
— New Jersey Devils in 1997 CSF. NY Rangers won best-of-seven series 4-1, while outscoring New Jersey 10-5.

FEWEST GOALS, ONE TEAM, SIX-GAME SERIES:
5 — Boston Bruins in 1951 SF. Toronto won best-of-seven series 4-1 with 1 tie, outscoring Boston 17-5.

FEWEST GOALS, ONE TEAM, SEVEN-GAME SERIES:
9 — Toronto Maple Leafs, in 1945 F. Toronto won best-of- seven series 4-3; teams tied in scoring 9-9.
— Detroit Red Wings, in 1945 F. Toronto won best-of-seven series 4-3; teams tied in scoring 9-9.

MOST GOALS IN A SERIES, BOTH TEAMS

MOST GOALS, BOTH TEAMS, ONE PLAYOFF SERIES:
69 — Edmonton Oilers, Chicago Blackhawks in 1985 CF. Edmonton won best-of-seven series 4-2, outscoring Chicago 44-25.
62 — Chicago Blackhawks, Minnesota North Stars in 1985 DF. Chicago won best-of-seven series 4-2, outscoring Minnesota 33-29.
61 — Los Angeles Kings, Calgary Flames in 1993 DSF. Los Angeles won best-of-seven series 4-2, outscoring Calgary 33-28.
— San Jose Sharks, Calgary Flames in 1995 CQF. San Jose won best-of-seven series 4-3, while being outscored 35-26.

MOST GOALS, BOTH TEAMS, TWO-GAME SERIES:
17 — Toronto St. Patricks, Montreal Canadiens in 1918 NHL F. Toronto won two-game total goal series 10-7.
15 — Boston Bruins, Chicago Blackhawks in 1927 QF. Boston won two-game total goal series 10-5.
— Pittsburgh Penguins, St. Louis Blues in 1975 PR. Pittsburgh won best-of-three series 2-0, outscoring St. Louis 9-6.

MOST GOALS, BOTH TEAMS, THREE-GAME SERIES:
33 — Minnesota North Stars, Boston Bruins in 1981 PR. Minnesota won best-of-five series 3-0, outscoring Boston 20-13.
31 — Chicago Blackhawks, Detroit Red Wings in 1985 DSF. Chicago won best-of-five series 3-0, outscoring Detroit 23-8.
28 — Toronto Maple Leafs, NY Rangers in 1932 F. Toronto won best-of-five series 3-0, outscoring NY Rangers 18-10.

MOST GOALS, BOTH TEAMS, FOUR-GAME SERIES:
36 — Boston Bruins, St. Louis Blues in 1972 SF. Boston won best-of-seven series 4-0, outscoring St. Louis 28-8.
— Minnesota North Stars, Toronto Maple Leafs in 1983 DSF. Minnesota won best-of-five series 3-1; teams tied in scoring 18-18.
— Edmonton Oilers, Chicago Blackhawks in 1983 CF. Edmonton won best-of-seven series 4-0, outscoring Chicago 25-11.
35 — NY Rangers, Los Angeles Kings in 1981 PR. NY Rangers won best-of-five series 3-1, outscoring Los Angeles 23-12.

MOST GOALS, BOTH TEAMS, FIVE-GAME SERIES:
52 — Edmonton Oilers, Los Angeles Kings in 1987 DSF. Edmonton won best-of-seven series 4-1, outscoring Los Angeles 32-20.
50 — Los Angeles Kings, Edmonton Oilers in 1982 DSF. Los Angeles won best-of-five series 3-2, outscoring Edmonton 27-23.
48 — Edmonton Oilers, Calgary Flames in 1983 DF. Edmonton won best-of-seven series 4-1, outscoring Calgary 35-13.
— Calgary Flames, Los Angeles Kings in 1988 DSF. Calgary won best-of-seven series 4-1, outscoring Los Angeles 30-18.

MOST GOALS, BOTH TEAMS, SIX-GAME SERIES:
69 — Edmonton Oilers, Chicago Blackhawks in 1985 CF. Edmonton won best-of-seven series 4-2, outscoring Chicago 44-25.
62 — Chicago Blackhawks, Minnesota North Stars in 1985 DF. Chicago won best-of-seven series 4-2, outscoring Minnesota 33-29.
61 — Los Angeles Kings, Calgary Flames in 1993 DSF. Los Angeles won best-of-seven series 4-2, outscoring Calgary 33-28.

MOST GOALS, BOTH TEAMS, SEVEN-GAME SERIES:
61 — San Jose Sharks, Calgary Flames in 1995 CQF. San Jose won best-of-seven series 4-3, while being outscored 35-26.
60 — Edmonton Oilers, Calgary Flames in 1984 DF. Edmonton won best-of-seven series 4-3, outscoring Calgary 33-27.

FEWEST GOALS IN A SERIES, BOTH TEAMS

FEWEST GOALS, BOTH TEAMS, TWO-GAME SERIES:
1 — NY Rangers, NY Americans in 1929 SF. NY Rangers defeated NY Americans 1-0 in two-game, total-goal series.
— Mtl. Maroons, Chicago Blackhawks in 1935 SF. Mtl. Maroons defeated Chicago 1-0 in two-game, total-goal series.

FEWEST GOALS, BOTH TEAMS, THREE-GAME SERIES:
7 — Boston Bruins, Montreal Canadiens in 1929 SF. Boston won best-of-five series 3-0, outscoring Montreal 5-2.
— Detroit Red Wings, Montreal Maroons in 1936 SF. Detroit won best-of-five series 3-0, outscoring Mtl. Maroons 6-1.

FEWEST GOALS, BOTH TEAMS, FOUR-GAME SERIES:
9 — Toronto Maple Leafs, Boston Bruins in 1935 SF. Toronto won best-of-five series 3-1, outscoring Boston 7-2.

FEWEST GOALS, BOTH TEAMS, FIVE-GAME SERIES:
11 — NY Rangers, Montreal Maroons in 1928 F. NY Rangers won best-of-five series 3-2, while being outscored by Mtl. Maroons 6-5.

FEWEST GOALS, BOTH TEAMS, SIX-GAME SERIES:
20 — Toronto Maple Leafs, Philadelphia Flyers in 1999 CQF. Toronto won best-of-seven series 4-2, while being outscored by Philadelphia 11-9.

FEWEST GOALS, BOTH TEAMS, SEVEN-GAME SERIES:
18 — Toronto Maple Leafs, Detroit Red Wings in 1945 F. Toronto won best-of-seven series 4-3; teams tied in scoring 9-9.

MOST GOALS IN A GAME OR PERIOD

MOST GOALS, ONE TEAM, ONE GAME:
13 — Edmonton Oilers at Edmonton, April 9, 1987. Edmonton 13, Los Angeles 3. Edmonton won best-of-seven DSF 4-1.
12 — Los Angeles Kings at Los Angeles, April 10, 1990. Los Angeles 12, Calgary 4. Los Angeles won best-of-seven DSF 4-2.
11 — Montreal Canadiens at Montreal, March 30, 1944. Montreal 11, Toronto 0. Montreal won best-of-seven SF 4-1.
— Edmonton Oilers at Edmonton, May 4, 1985. Edmonton 11, Chicago 2. Edmonton won best-of-seven CF 4-2.

MOST GOALS, ONE TEAM, ONE PERIOD:
7 — Montreal Canadiens, March 30, 1944, at Montreal in third period, during 11-0 win against Toronto.

MOST GOALS, BOTH TEAMS, ONE GAME:
18 — Los Angeles Kings, Edmonton Oilers at Edmonton, April 7, 1982. Los Angeles 10, Edmonton 8. Los Angeles won best-of-five DSF 3-2.
17 — Pittsburgh Penguins, Philadelphia Flyers at Pittsburgh, April 25, 1989. Pittsburgh 10, Philadelphia 7. Philadelphia won best-of-seven DF 4-3.
16 — Edmonton Oilers, Los Angeles Kings at Edmonton, April 9, 1987. Edmonton 13, Los Angeles 3. Edmonton won best-of-seven DSF 4-1.
— Los Angeles Kings, Calgary Flames at Los Angeles, April 10, 1990. Los Angeles 12, Calgary 4. Los Angeles won best-of-seven DF 4-2.

MOST GOALS, BOTH TEAMS, ONE PERIOD:
9 — NY Rangers, Philadelphia Flyers, at Philadelphia, April 24, 1979, third period. NY Rangers won 8-3, scoring six of nine third-period goals.
— Los Angeles Kings, Calgary Flames, at Los Angeles, April 10, 1990, second period. Los Angeles won 12-4, scoring five of nine second-period goals.
8 — Chicago Blackhawks, Montreal Canadiens, at Montreal, May 8, 1973, second period. Chicago won 8-7, scoring five of eight second-period goals.
— Chicago Blackhawks, Edmonton Oilers, at Chicago, May 12, 1985, first period. Chicago won 8-6, scoring five of eight first-period goals.
— Edmonton Oilers, Winnipeg Jets, at Edmonton, April 6, 1988, third period. Edmonton won 7-4, scoring six of eight third-period goals.
— Hartford Whalers, Montreal Canadiens, at Hartford, April 10, 1988, third period. Hartford won 7-5, scoring five of eight third-period goals.
— Vancouver Canucks, NY Rangers, at NY Rangers, June 9, 1994, third period. Vancouver won 6-3, scoring five of eight third-period goals.

TEAM POWER-PLAY GOALS

MOST POWER-PLAY GOALS BY ALL TEAMS, ONE PLAYOFF YEAR:
199 — 1988 in 83 games.

MOST POWER-PLAY GOALS, ONE TEAM, ONE PLAYOFF YEAR:
35 — Minnesota North Stars, 1991 in 23 games.
32 — Edmonton Oilers, 1988 in 18 games.
31 — NY Islanders, 1981 in 18 games.

MOST POWER-PLAY GOALS, ONE TEAM, ONE SERIES:
15 — NY Islanders in 1980 F against Philadelphia. NY Islanders won series 4-2.
— Minnesota North Stars in 1991 DSF against Chicago. Minnesota won series 4-2.
13 — NY Islanders in 1981 QF against Edmonton. NY Islanders won series 4-2.
— Calgary Flames in 1986 CF against St. Louis. Calgary won series 4-3.
12 — Toronto Maple Leafs in 1976 QF against Philadelphia. Philadelphia won series 4-3.

MOST POWER-PLAY GOALS, BOTH TEAMS, ONE SERIES:
21 — NY Islanders, Philadelphia Flyers in 1980 F, won by NY Islanders 4-2. NY Islanders had 15 and Philadelphia 6.
— NY Islanders, Edmonton Oilers in 1981 QF, won by NY Islanders 4-2. NY Islanders had 13 and Edmonton 8.
— Philadelphia Flyers, Pittsburgh Penguins in 1989 DF, won by Philadelphia 4-3. Philadelphia had 11 and Pittsburgh 10.
— Minnesota North Stars, Chicago Blackhawks in 1991 DSF, won by Minnesota 4-2. Minnesota had 15 and Chicago 6.
20 — Toronto Maple Leafs, Philadelphia Flyers in 1976 QF, won by Philadelphia 4-3. Toronto had 12 and Philadelphia 8.

MOST POWER-PLAY GOALS, ONE TEAM, ONE GAME:
6 — Boston Bruins, April 2, 1969, at Boston against Toronto. Boston won 10-0.

MOST POWER-PLAY GOALS, BOTH TEAMS, ONE GAME:
8 — Minnesota North Stars, St. Louis Blues, April 24, 1991 at Minnesota. Minnesota had 4, St. Louis 4. Minnesota won 8-4.
7 — Minnesota North Stars, Edmonton Oilers, April 28, 1984 at Minnesota. Minnesota had 4, Edmonton 3. Edmonton won 8-5.
— Philadelphia Flyers, NY Rangers, April 13, 1985 at NY Rangers. Philadelphia had 4, NY Rangers 3. Philadelphia won 6-5.
— Edmonton Oilers, Chicago Blackhawks, May 14, 1985 at Edmonton. Chicago had 5, Edmonton 2. Edmonton won 10-5.
— Edmonton Oilers, Los Angeles Kings, April 9, 1987 at Edmonton. Edmonton had 5, Los Angeles 2. Edmonton won 13-3.
— Vancouver Canucks, Calgary Flames, April 9, 1989 at Vancouver. Vancouver had 4, Calgary 3. Vancouver won 5-3.

MOST POWER-PLAY GOALS, ONE TEAM, ONE PERIOD:
4 — Toronto Maple Leafs, March 26, 1936, second period against Boston at Toronto. Toronto won 8-3.
— Minnesota North Stars, April 28, 1984, second period against Edmonton at Minnesota. Edmonton won 8-5.
— Boston Bruins, April 11, 1991, third period against Hartford at Boston. Boston won 6-1.
— Minnesota North Stars, April 24, 1991, second period against St. Louis at Minnesota. Minnesota won 8-4.
— St. Louis Blues, April 27, 1998, third period at Los Angeles. St. Louis won 4-3.

MOST POWER-PLAY GOALS, BOTH TEAMS, ONE PERIOD:
5 — Minnesota North Stars, Edmonton Oilers, April 28, 1984, second period, at Minnesota. Minnesota had 4 and Edmonton 1. Edmonton won 8-5.
— Vancouver Canucks, Calgary Flames, April 9, 1989, third period, at Vancouver. Vancouver had 3 and Calgary 2. Vancouver won 5-3.
— Minnesota North Stars, St. Louis Blues, April 24, 1991, second period, at Minnesota. Minnesota had 4 and St. Louis 1. Minnesota won 8-4.

TEAM SHORTHAND GOALS

MOST SHORTHAND GOALS BY ALL TEAMS, ONE PLAYOFF YEAR:
33 — 1988, in 83 games.

MOST SHORTHAND GOALS, ONE TEAM, ONE PLAYOFF YEAR:
10 — Edmonton Oilers, 1983, in 16 games.
9 — NY Islanders, 1981, in 19 games.
8 — Philadelphia Flyers, 1989, in 19 games.

MOST SHORTHAND GOALS, ONE TEAM, ONE SERIES:
6 — Calgary Flames in 1995 against San Jose in best-of-seven CQF won by San Jose 4-3.
— Vancouver Canucks in 1995 against St. Louis in best-of-seven CQF won by Vancouver 4-3.
5 — NY Rangers in 1979 against Philadelphia in best-of-seven QF won by NY Rangers 4-1.
— Edmonton Oilers in 1983 against Calgary in best-of-seven DF won by Edmonton 4-1.

MOST SHORTHAND GOALS, BOTH TEAMS, ONE SERIES:
7 — Boston Bruins (4), NY Rangers (3), in 1958 SF won by Boston 4-2.
— Edmonton Oilers (5), Calgary Flames (2), in 1983 DF won by Edmonton 4-1.
— Vancouver Canucks (6), St. Louis Blues (1), in 1995 CQF won by Vancouver 4-3.

MOST SHORTHAND GOALS, ONE TEAM, ONE GAME:
3 — Boston Bruins, April 11, 1981, at Minnesota. Minnesota won 6-3.
— NY Islanders, April 17, 1983, at NY Rangers. NY Rangers won 7-6.
— Toronto Maple Leafs, May 8, 1994, at San Jose. Toronto won 8-3.

MOST SHORTHAND GOALS, BOTH TEAMS, ONE GAME:
4 — Boston Bruins, Minnesota North Stars, April 11, 1981, at Minnesota. Boston had 3 shorthand goals, Minnesota 1. Minnesota won 6-3.
— NY Islanders, NY Rangers, April 17, 1983, at NY Rangers. NY Islanders had 3 shorthand goals, NY Rangers 1. NY Rangers won 7-6.
— San Jose Sharks, Toronto Maple Leafs, May 8, 1994, at San Jose. Toronto had 3 shorthand goals, San Jose 1. Toronto won 8-3.
3 — Toronto Maple Leafs, Detroit Red Wings, April 5, 1947, at Toronto. Toronto had 2 shorthand goals, Detroit 1. Toronto won 6-1.
— NY Rangers, Boston Bruins, April 1, 1958, at Boston. NY Rangers had 2 shorthand goals, Boston 1. NY Rangers won 5-2.
— Minnesota North Stars, Philadelphia Flyers, May 4, 1980, at Minnesota. Minnesota had 2 shorthand goals, Philadelphia 1. Philadelphia won 5-3.
— Edmonton Oilers, Winnipeg Jets, April 9, 1988, at Winnipeg. Winnipeg had 2 shorthand goals, Edmonton 1. Winnipeg won 6-4.
— New Jersey Devils, NY Islanders, April 14, 1988, at New Jersey. NY Islanders had 2 shorthand goals, New Jersey 1. New Jersey won 6-5.
— Montreal Canadiens, New Jersey Devils, April 17, 1997, at New Jersey. Montreal had 2 shorthand goals, New Jersey 1. New Jersey won 5-2.
— Dallas Stars, San Jose Sharks, May 5, 2000, at San Jose. Dallas had 2 shorthand goals, San Jose 1. Dallas won 5-4.

MOST SHORTHAND GOALS, ONE TEAM, ONE PERIOD:
2 — Toronto Maple Leafs, April 5, 1947, at Toronto against Detroit, first period. Toronto won 6-1.
— Toronto Maple Leafs, April 13, 1965, at Toronto against Montreal, first period. Montreal won 4-3.
— Boston Bruins, April 20, 1969, at Boston against Montreal, first period. Boston won 3-2.
— Boston Bruins, April 8, 1970, at Boston against NY Rangers, second period. Boston won 8-2.
— Boston Bruins, April 30, 1972, at Boston against NY Rangers, first period. Boston won 6-5.
— Chicago Blackhawks, May 3, 1973, at Chicago against Montreal, first period. Chicago won 7-4.
— Montreal Canadiens, April 23, 1978, at Detroit, first period. Montreal won 8-0.
— NY Islanders, April 8, 1980, at NY Islanders against Los Angeles, second period. NY Islanders won 8-1.
— Los Angeles Kings, April 9, 1980, at NY Islanders, first period. Los Angeles won 6-3.
— Boston Bruins, April 13, 1980, at Pittsburgh, second period. Boston won 8-3.
— Minnesota North Stars, May 4, 1980, at Minnesota against Philadelphia, second period. Philadelphia won 5-3.
— Boston Bruins, April 11, 1981, at Minnesota, third period. Minnesota won 6-3.
— NY Islanders, May 12, 1981, at NY Islanders against Minnesota, first period. NY Islanders won 6-3.
— Montreal Canadiens, April 7, 1982, at Montreal against Quebec, third period. Montreal won 5-1.
— Edmonton Oilers, April 24, 1983, at Edmonton against Chicago, third period. Edmonton won 8-4.
— Winnipeg Jets, April 14, 1985, at Calgary, second period. Winnipeg won 5-3.
— Boston Bruins, April 6, 1988, at Boston against Buffalo, first period. Boston won 7-3.
— NY Islanders, April 14, 1988, at New Jersey, third period. New Jersey won 6-5.
— Detroit Red Wings, April 29, 1993, at Toronto, second period. Detroit won 7-3.
— Toronto Maple Leafs, May 8, 1994, at San Jose, third period. Toronto won 8-3.
— Calgary Flames, May 11, 1995, at San Jose, first period. Calgary won 9-2.
— Vancouver Canucks, May 15, 1995, at St. Louis, second period. Vancouver won 6-5.
— Montreal Canadiens, April 17, 1997, at New Jersey, second period. New Jersey won 5-2.
— Philadelphia Flyers, April 26, 1997, at Philadelphia against Pittsburgh, first period. Philadelphia won 6-3.
— Phoenix Coyotes, April 24, 1998, at Detroit, second period. Phoenix won 7-4.
— Buffalo Sabres, April 27, 1998, at Buffalo against Philadelphia, second period. Buffalo won 6-1.
— San Jose Sharks, April 30, 1999, at Colorado, third period. San Jose won 7-3.

MOST SHORTHAND GOALS, BOTH TEAMS, ONE PERIOD:
3 — Toronto Maple Leafs, Detroit Red Wings, April 5, 1947, at Toronto, first period. Toronto had 2 shorthand goals, Detroit 1. Toronto won 6-1.
— Toronto Maple Leafs, San Jose Sharks, May 8, 1994, at San Jose, third period. Toronto had 2 shorthand goals, San Jose 1. Toronto won 8-3.

FASTEST GOALS

FASTEST FIVE GOALS, BOTH TEAMS:
3 Minutes, 6 Seconds — Chicago Blackhawks, Minnesota North Stars at Chicago, April 21, 1985. Keith Brown scored for Chicago at 1:12 of second period; Ken Yaremchuk, Chicago, 1:27; Dino Ciccarelli, Minnesota, 2:48; Tony McKegney, Minnesota, 4:07; and Curt Fraser, Chicago, 4:18. Chicago won 6-2 and best-of-seven DF 4-2.
3 Minutes, 20 Seconds — Minnesota North Stars, Philadelphia Flyers at Philadelphia, April 29, 1980. Paul Shmyr scored for Minnesota at 13:20 of first period; Steve Christoff, Minnesota, 13:59; Ken Linseman, Philadelphia, 14:54; Tom Gorence, Philadelphia, 15:36; and Linseman, 16:40. Minnesota won 6-5. Philadelphia won best-of-seven SF 4-1.
4 Minutes — Detroit Red Wings, Los Angeles Kings at Detroit, April 15, 2000. Brendan Shanahan scored for Detroit at 0:55 of first period; Martin Lapointe, Detroit, 1:33; Luc Robitaille, Los Angeles, 2:04; Kris Draper, Detroit, 3:32; and Ziggy Palffy, Los Angeles, 4:55. Detroit won 8-5 and best-of-seven CQF 4-0.

FASTEST FIVE GOALS, ONE TEAM:
3 Minutes, 36 Seconds — Montreal Canadiens at Montreal, March 30, 1944, against Toronto. Toe Blake scored at 7:58 and 8:37 of third period; Maurice Richard, 9:17; Ray Getliffe, 10:33; and Buddy O'Connor, 11:34. Montreal won 11-0 and best-of-seven SF 4-1.

FASTEST FOUR GOALS, BOTH TEAMS:
1 Minute, 33 Seconds — Philadelphia Flyers, Toronto Maple Leafs at Philadelphia, April 20, 1976. Don Saleski scored for Philadelphia at 10:04 of second period; Bob Neely, Toronto, 10:42; Gary Dornhoefer, Philadelphia, 11:24; and Don Saleski, 11:37. Philadelphia won 7-1 and best-of-seven QF 4-3.
1 Minute, 34 seconds — Montreal Canadiens, Calgary Flames at Montreal, May 20, 1986. Joel Otto scored for Calgary at 17:59 of first period; Bobby Smith, Montreal, 18:25; Mats Naslund, Montreal, 19:17; and Bob Gainey, Montreal, 19:33. Montreal won 5-3 and best-of-seven F 4-1.
1 Minute, 38 Seconds — Boston Bruins, Philadelphia Flyers at Philadelphia, April 26, 1977. Gregg Sheppard scored for Boston at 14:01 of second period; Mike Milbury, Boston, 15:01; Gary Dornhoefer, Philadelphia, 15:16; and Jean Ratelle, Boston, 15:39. Boston won 5-4 and best-of-seven SF 4-0.

FASTEST FOUR GOALS, ONE TEAM:
2 Minutes, 35 Seconds — Montreal Canadiens at Montreal, March 30, 1944, against Toronto. Toe Blake scored at 7:58 and 8:37 of third period; Maurice Richard, 9:17; and Ray Getliffe, 10:33. Montreal won 11-0 and best-of-seven SF 4-1.

FASTEST THREE GOALS, BOTH TEAMS:
21 Seconds — Edmonton Oilers, Chicago Blackhawks at Edmonton, May 7, 1985. Behn Wilson scored for Chicago at 19:22 of third period, Jari Kurri at 19:36 and Glenn Anderson at 19:43 for Edmonton. Edmonton won 7-3 and best-of-seven CF 4-2.
27 Seconds — Phoenix Coyotes, Detroit Red Wings at Detroit, April 24, 1998. Jeremy Roenick scored for Phoenix at 13:24 of the second period. Mathieu Dandenault scored for Detroit at 13:32, and Keith Tkachuk scored for Phoenix at 13:51. Phoenix won 7-4, Detroit won the best-of-seven CQF 4-2.
30 Seconds — Chicago Blackhawks, Pittsburgh Penguins at Chicago, June 1, 1992. Dirk Graham scored for Chicago at 6:21 of first period, Kevin Stevens for Pittsburgh at 6:33 and Dirk Graham at 6:51. Pittsburgh won 6-5 and best-of-seven F 4-0.

FASTEST THREE GOALS, ONE TEAM:
23 Seconds — Toronto Maple Leafs at Toronto, April 12, 1979, against Atlanta. Darryl Sittler scored at 4:04 and 4:16 of first period and Ron Ellis at 4:27. Leafs won 7-4 and best-of-three PR 2-0.
38 Seconds — NY Rangers at NY Rangers, April 12, 1986 against Philadelphia. Jim Wiemer scored at 12:29 of third period, Bob Brooke at 12:43 and Ron Greschner at 13:07. NY Rangers won 5-2 and best-of-five DSF 3-2.
— Colorado Avalanche at Vancouver, April 18, 2001. Peter Forsberg scored at 9:11 of third period, Joe Sakic at 9:28 and Eric Messier at 9:49. Colorado won 5-1 and best-of-seven CQF 4-0.

FASTEST TWO GOALS, BOTH TEAMS:
5 Seconds — Pittsburgh Penguins, Buffalo Sabres at Buffalo, April 14, 1979. Gilbert Perreault scored for Buffalo at 12:59 and Jim Hamilton for Pittsburgh at 13:04 of first period. Pittsburgh won 4-3 and best-of-three PR 2-1.
8 Seconds — Minnesota North Stars, St. Louis Blues at Minnesota, April 9, 1989. Bernie Federko scored for St. Louis at 2:28 and Perry Berezan for Minnesota at 2:36 of third period. Minnesota won 5-4. St. Louis won best-of-seven DSF 4-1.
— Phoenix Coyotes, Detroit Red Wings at Detroit, April 24, 1998. Jeremy Roenick scored for Phoenix at 13:24 and Mathieu Dandenault for Detroit at 13:32 of second period. Phoenix won 7-4. Detroit won best-of-seven CQF 4-2.
9 Seconds — NY Islanders, Washington Capitals at Washington, April 10, 1986. Bryan Trottier scored for NY Islanders at 18:26 and Scott Stevens for Washington at 18:35 of second period. Washington won 5-2, and best-of-five DSF 3-0.
— Buffalo Sabres, Toronto Maple Leafs at Toronto, May 23, 1999. Vaclav Varada scored for Buffalo at 4:23 and Mats Sundin for Toronto at 4:32 of first period. Buffalo won 5-4, and best-of-seven CF 4-1.

FASTEST TWO GOALS, ONE TEAM:
5 Seconds — Detroit Red Wings at Detroit, April 11, 1965, against Chicago. Norm Ullman scored at 17:35 and 17:40, second period. Detroit won 4-2. Chicago won best-of-seven SF 4-3.

Curtis Joseph (top) and Olaf Kolzig (above) were two of the goalies that helped set a playoff record in 2001 for the most shutouts in one year. Joseph had three of the record 19 whitewashes while Kolzig had one.

OVERTIME

SHORTEST OVERTIME:
9 Seconds — Montreal Canadiens, Calgary Flames at Calgary, May 18, 1986. Montreal won 3-2 on Brian Skrudland's goal and captured the best-of-seven F 4-1.
11 Seconds — NY Islanders, NY Rangers at NY Rangers, April 11, 1975. NY Islanders won 4-3 on Jean-Paul Parise's goal and captured the best-of-three PR 2-1.

LONGEST OVERTIME:
116 Minutes, 30 Seconds — Detroit Red Wings, Mtl. Maroons at Montreal, March 24, 25, 1936. Detroit 1, Mtl. Maroons 0. Mud Bruneteau scored, assisted by Hec Kilrea, at 16:30 of sixth overtime period, or after 176 minutes, 30 seconds from start of game, which ended at 2:25 a.m. Detroit won best-of-five SF 3-0.

MOST OVERTIME GAMES, ONE PLAYOFF YEAR:
28 — 1993. Of 85 games played, 28 went into overtime.
26 — 2001. Of 86 games played, 26 went into overtime.
21 — 1999. Of 86 games played, 21 went into overtime.
19 — 1996. Of 86 games played, 19 went into overtime.
— 1998. Of 82 games played, 19 went into overtime.

FEWEST OVERTIME GAMES, ONE PLAYOFF YEAR:
0 — 1963. None of the 16 games went into overtime, the only year since 1926 that no overtime was required in any playoff series.

MOST OVERTIME GAMES, ONE SERIES:
5 — Toronto Maple Leafs, Montreal Canadiens in 1951. Toronto won best-of-seven F 4-1.
4 — Toronto Maple Leafs, Boston Bruins in 1933. Toronto won best-of-five SF 3-2.
— Boston Bruins, NY Rangers in 1939. Boston won best-of-seven SF 4-3.
— St. Louis Blues, Minnesota North Stars in 1968. St. Louis won best-of-seven SF 4-3.
— Dallas Stars, St. Louis Blues in 1999. Dallas won best-of-seven CSF 4-2.
— Dallas Stars, Edmonton Oilers in 2001. Dallas won best-of-seven CQF 4-2.

THREE-OR-MORE GOAL GAMES

MOST THREE-OR-MORE GOAL GAMES BY ALL TEAMS, ONE PLAYOFF YEAR:
12 — 1983 in 66 games.
— **1988** in 83 games.
11 — 1985 in 70 games.
— 1992 in 86 games.

MOST THREE-OR-MORE GOAL GAMES, ONE TEAM, ONE PLAYOFF YEAR:
6 — Edmonton Oilers in 16 games, 1983.
— **Edmonton Oilers** in 18 games, 1985.

SHUTOUTS

MOST SHUTOUTS, ONE PLAYOFF YEAR, ALL TEAMS:
19 — 2001. Of 86 games played, Colorado and New Jersey had 4 each, Toronto had 3, Pittsburgh and Los Angeles had 2 each, while Buffalo, Washington, Detroit and San Jose had 1 each.
18 — 1997. Of 82 games played, Colorado and NY Rangers had 3 each, Edmonton, St. Louis and New Jersey had 2 each, while Anaheim, Buffalo, Detroit, Florida, Ottawa and Phoenix had 1 each.
16 — 1994. Of 90 games played, NY Rangers and Vancouver had 4 each, Toronto had 3, Buffalo had 2, while Washington, Detroit and New Jersey had 1 each.

FEWEST SHUTOUTS, ONE PLAYOFF YEAR, ALL TEAMS:
0 — 1959. 18 games played.

MOST SHUTOUTS, BOTH TEAMS, ONE SERIES:
5 — 1945 F, Toronto Maple Leafs, Detroit Red Wings. Toronto had 3 shutouts, Detroit 2. Toronto won best-of-seven series 4-3.
— **1950 SF, Toronto Maple Leafs, Detroit Red Wings.** Toronto had 3 shutouts, Detroit 2. Detroit won best-of-seven series 4-3.

TEAM PENALTIES

FEWEST PENALTIES, BOTH TEAMS, BEST-OF-SEVEN SERIES:
19 — Detroit Red Wings, Toronto Maple Leafs in 1945 F, won by Toronto 4-3. Detroit received 10 minors, Toronto had 9 minors.

FEWEST PENALTIES, ONE TEAM, BEST-OF-SEVEN SERIES:
9 — Toronto Maple Leafs in 1945 F, won by Toronto 4-3 against Detroit.

MOST PENALTIES, BOTH TEAMS, ONE SERIES:
219 — New Jersey Devils, Washington Capitals in 1988 DF won by New Jersey 4-3. New Jersey received 98 minors, 11 majors, 9 misconducts and 1 match penalty. Washington received 80 minors, 11 majors, 8 misconducts and 1 match penalty.

MOST PENALTY MINUTES, BOTH TEAMS, ONE SERIES:
656 — New Jersey Devils, Washington Capitals in 1988 DF won by New Jersey 4-3. New Jersey had 351 minutes; Washington 305.

MOST PENALTIES, ONE TEAM, ONE SERIES:
119 — New Jersey Devils in 1988 DF won by New Jersey against Washington. New Jersey received 98 minors, 11 majors, 9 misconducts and 1 match penalty.

MOST PENALTY MINUTES, ONE TEAM, ONE SERIES:
351 — New Jersey Devils in 1988 DF won by New Jersey 4-3 against Washington.

MOST PENALTIES, BOTH TEAMS, ONE GAME:
66 — Detroit Red Wings, St. Louis Blues at St. Louis, April 12, 1991. Detroit received 33 penalties; St. Louis 33. St. Louis won 6-1.
62 — New Jersey Devils, Washington Capitals at New Jersey, April 22, 1988. New Jersey received 32 penalties; Washington 30. New Jersey won 10-4.

MOST PENALTY MINUTES, BOTH TEAMS, ONE GAME:
298 Minutes — Detroit Red Wings, St. Louis Blues at St. Louis, April 12, 1991. Detroit received 33 penalties for 152 minutes; St. Louis 33 penalties for 146 minutes. St. Louis won 6-1.
267 Minutes — NY Rangers, Los Angeles Kings at Los Angeles, April 9, 1981. NY Rangers received 31 penalties for 142 minutes; Los Angeles 28 penalties for 125 minutes. Los Angeles won 5-4.

MOST PENALTIES, ONE TEAM, ONE GAME:
33 — Detroit Red Wings, at St. Louis, April 12,1991. St. Louis won 6-1.
— **St. Louis Blues,** at St. Louis, April 12, 1991. St. Louis won 6-1.
32 — New Jersey Devils, at Washington, April 22,1988. New Jersey won 10-4.
31 — NY Rangers, at Los Angeles, April 9, 1981. Los Angeles won 5-4.
30 — Philadelphia Flyers, at Toronto, April 15, 1976. Toronto won 5-4.

MOST PENALTY MINUTES, ONE TEAM, ONE GAME:
152 — Detroit Red Wings, at St. Louis, April 12, 1991. St. Louis won 6-1.
146 — St. Louis Blues, at St. Louis, April 12, 1991. St. Louis won 6-1.
142 — NY Rangers, at Los Angeles, April 9, 1981. Los Angeles won 5-4.

MOST PENALTIES, BOTH TEAMS, ONE PERIOD:
43 — NY Rangers, Los Angeles Kings at Los Angeles, April 9, 1981, first period. NY Rangers had 24 penalties; Los Angeles 19. Los Angeles won 5-4.

MOST PENALTY MINUTES, BOTH TEAMS, ONE PERIOD:
248 — NY Islanders, Boston Bruins at Boston, April 17, 1980, first period. Each team received 124 minutes. NY Islanders won 5-4.

MOST PENALTIES, ONE TEAM, ONE PERIOD:
24 — NY Rangers, at Los Angeles, April 9, 1981, first period. Los Angeles won 5-4.

MOST PENALTY MINUTES, ONE TEAM, ONE PERIOD:
125 — NY Rangers, at Los Angeles, April 9, 1981, first period. Los Angeles won 5-4.

Individual Records

GAMES PLAYED

MOST YEARS IN PLAYOFFS:
21 — Raymond Bourque, Boston, Colorado (1980-96 incl.; 98-01 incl.)
20 — Gordie Howe, Detroit, Hartford
— Larry Robinson, Montreal, Los Angeles
19 — Red Kelly, Detroit, Toronto
— Larry Murphy, Los Angeles, Washington, Minnesota, Pittsburgh, Toronto, Detroit

MOST CONSECUTIVE YEARS IN PLAYOFFS:
20 — Larry Robinson, Montreal, Los Angeles (1973-92, inclusive).
18 — Larry Murphy, Los Angeles, Washington, Minnesota, Pittsburgh, Toronto, Detroit (1984-2001, inclusive).
17 — Brad Park, NY Rangers, Boston, Detroit (1969-85, inclusive).
— Raymond Bourque, Boston (1980-96, inclusive).
16 — Jean Beliveau, Montreal (1954-69, inclusive).
— Bob Gainey, Montreal (1974-89, inclusive).
— Dale Hunter, Quebec, Washington (1981-96, inclusive)

MOST PLAYOFF GAMES:
236 — Mark Messier, Edmonton, NY Rangers
231 — Guy Carbonneau, Montreal, St. Louis, Dallas
227 — Larry Robinson, Montreal, Los Angeles
225 — Glenn Anderson, Edmonton, Toronto, NY Rangers, St. Louis
221 — Bryan Trottier, NY Islanders, Pittsburgh
— Claude Lemieux, Montreal, New Jersey, Colorado

GOALS

MOST GOALS IN PLAYOFFS (CAREER):
122 — Wayne Gretzky, Edmonton, Los Angeles, St. Louis, NY Rangers
109 — Mark Messier, Edmonton, NY Rangers
106 — Jari Kurri, Edmonton, Los Angeles, NY Rangers, Anaheim
93 — Glenn Anderson, Edmonton, Toronto, NY Rangers, St. Louis
90 — Brett Hull, Calgary, St. Louis, Dallas

MOST GOALS, ONE PLAYOFF YEAR:
19 — Reggie Leach, Philadelphia, 1976. 16 games.
— Jari Kurri, Edmonton, 1985. 18 games.
18 — Joe Sakic, Colorado, 1996. 22 games.
17 — Newsy Lalonde, Montreal, 1919. 10 games.
— Mike Bossy, NY Islanders, 1981. 18 games.
— Steve Payne, Minnesota, 1981. 19 games.
— Mike Bossy, NY Islanders, 1982. 19 games.
— Mike Bossy, NY Islanders, 1983. 19 games
— Wayne Gretzky, Edmonton, 1985. 18 games.
— Kevin Stevens, Pittsburgh, 1991. 24 games.

MOST GOALS IN ONE SERIES (OTHER THAN FINAL):
12 — Jari Kurri, Edmonton, in 1985 CF, 6 games vs. Chicago.
11 — Newsy Lalonde, Montreal, in 1919 NHL F, 5 games vs. Ottawa.
10 — Tim Kerr, Philadelphia, in 1989 DF, 7 games vs. Pittsburgh.
9 — Reggie Leach, Philadelphia, in 1976 SF, 5 games vs. Boston.
— Bill Barber, Philadelphia, in 1980 SF, 5 games vs. Minnesota.
— Mike Bossy, NY Islanders, in 1983 CF, 6 games vs. Boston.
— Mario Lemieux, Pittsburgh, in 1989 DF, 7 games vs. Philadelphia.

MOST GOALS IN FINAL SERIES (NHL PLAYERS ONLY):
9 — Babe Dye, Toronto, in 1922, 5 games vs. Van. Millionaires.
8 — Alf Skinner, Toronto, in 1918, 5 games vs. Van. Millionaires.
7 — Jean Beliveau, Montreal, in 1956, 5 games vs. Detroit.
— Mike Bossy, NY Islanders, in 1982, 4 games vs. Vancouver.
— Wayne Gretzky, Edmonton, in 1985, 5 games vs. Philadelphia.

MOST GOALS, ONE GAME:
5 — Newsy Lalonde, Montreal, March 1, 1919, at Montreal. Final score: Montreal 6, Ottawa 3.
— Maurice Richard, Montreal, March 23, 1944, at Montreal. Final score: Montreal 5, Toronto 1.
— Darryl Sittler, Toronto, April 22, 1976, at Toronto. Final score: Toronto 8, Philadelphia 5.
— Reggie Leach, Philadelphia, May 6, 1976, at Philadelphia. Final score: Philadelphia 6, Boston 3.
— Mario Lemieux, Pittsburgh, April 25, 1989, at Pittsburgh. Final score: Pittsburgh 10, Philadelphia 7.

MOST GOALS, ONE PERIOD:
4 — Tim Kerr, Philadelphia, April 13, 1985, at NY Rangers, second period. Final score: Philadelphia 6, NY Rangers 5.
— Mario Lemieux, Pittsburgh, April 25, 1989, at Pittsburgh vs. Philadelphia, first period. Final score: Pittsburgh 10, Philadelphia 7.

ASSISTS

MOST ASSISTS IN PLAYOFFS (CAREER):
260 — Wayne Gretzky, Edmonton, Los Angeles, St. Louis, NY Rangers
186 — Mark Messier, Edmonton, NY Rangers
139 — Raymond Bourque, Boston, Colorado
137 — Paul Coffey, Edmonton, Pittsburgh, Los Angeles, Detroit, Philadelphia, Carolina
127 — Jari Kurri, Edmonton, Los Angeles, NY Rangers, Anaheim

MOST ASSISTS, ONE PLAYOFF YEAR:
31 — Wayne Gretzky, Edmonton, 1988. 19 games.
30 — Wayne Gretzky, Edmonton, 1985. 18 games.
29 — Wayne Gretzky, Edmonton, 1987. 21 games.
28 — Mario Lemieux, Pittsburgh, 1991. 23 games.
26 — Wayne Gretzky, Edmonton, 1983. 16 games.

MOST ASSISTS IN ONE SERIES (OTHER THAN FINAL):
14 — Rick Middleton, Boston, in 1983 DF, 7 games vs. Buffalo.
— Wayne Gretzky, Edmonton, in 1985 CF, 6 games vs. Chicago.
13 — Wayne Gretzky, Edmonton, in 1987 DSF, 5 games vs. Los Angeles.
— Doug Gilmour, Toronto, in 1994 CSF, 7 games vs. San Jose.
11 — Al MacInnis, Calgary, in 1984 DF, 7 games vs. Edmonton.
— Mark Messier, Edmonton, in 1989 DSF, 7 games vs. Los Angeles.
— Mike Ridley, Washington, in 1992 DSF, 7 games vs. Pittsburgh.
— Ron Francis, Pittsburgh, in 1995 CQF, 7 games vs. Washington.
10 — Fleming Mackell, Boston, in 1958 SF, 6 games vs. NY Rangers.
— Stan Mikita, Chicago, in 1962 SF, 6 games vs. Montreal.
— Bob Bourne, NY Islanders, in 1983 DF, 6 games vs. NY Rangers.
— Wayne Gretzky, Edmonton, in 1988 DSF, 5 games vs. Winnipeg.
— Mario Lemieux, Pittsburgh, in 1992 DSF, 6 games vs. Washington.

MOST ASSISTS IN FINAL SERIES:
10 — Wayne Gretzky, Edmonton, in 1988, 4 games plus suspended game vs. Boston.
9 — Jacques Lemaire, Montreal, in 1973, 6 games vs. Chicago.
— Wayne Gretzky, Edmonton, in 1987, 7 games vs. Philadelphia.
— Larry Murphy, Pittsburgh, in 1991, 6 games vs. Minnesota.

MOST ASSISTS, ONE GAME:
6 — Mikko Leinonen, NY Rangers, April 8, 1982, at NY Rangers. Final score: NY Rangers 7, Philadelphia 3.
— Wayne Gretzky, Edmonton, April 9, 1987, at Edmonton. Final score: Edmonton 13, Los Angeles 3.
5 — Toe Blake, Montreal, March 23, 1944, at Montreal. Final score: Montreal 5, Toronto 1.
— Maurice Richard, Montreal, March 27, 1956, at Montreal. Final score: Montreal 7, NY Rangers 0.
— Bert Olmstead, Montreal, March 30, 1957, at Montreal. Final score: Montreal 8, NY Rangers 3.
— Don McKenney, Boston, April 5, 1958, at Boston. Final score: Boston 8, NY Rangers 2.
— Stan Mikita, Chicago, April 4, 1973, at Chicago. Final score: Chicago 7, St. Louis 1.
— Wayne Gretzky, Edmonton, April 8, 1981, at Montreal. Final score: Edmonton 6, Montreal 3.
— Paul Coffey, Edmonton, May 14, 1985, at Edmonton. Final score: Edmonton 10, Chicago 5.
— Doug Gilmour, St. Louis, April 15, 1986, at Minnesota. Final score: St. Louis 6, Minnesota 3.
— Risto Siltanen, Quebec, April 14, 1987, at Hartford. Final score: Quebec 7, Hartford 5.
— Patrik Sundstrom, New Jersey, April 22, 1988, at New Jersey. Final score: New Jersey 10, Washington 4.
— Geoff Courtnall, St. Louis, April 23, 1998, at St. Louis. Final score: St. Louis 8, Los Angeles 3.

MOST ASSISTS, ONE PERIOD:
3 — Three assists by one player in one period of a playoff game has been recorded on 73 occasions. Alexander Mogilny of the New Jersey Devils is the most recent to equal this mark with 3 assists in the second period against Toronto, April 28, 2001. Final score: New Jersey 6, Toronto 5.
— Wayne Gretzky has had 3 assists in one period 5 times; Raymond Bourque, 3 times; Toe Blake, Jean Beliveau, Doug Harvey and Bobby Orr, twice. Nick Metz of Toronto was the first player to be credited with 3 assists in one period of a playoff game Mar. 21, 1941 at Toronto vs. Boston.

POINTS

MOST POINTS IN PLAYOFFS (CAREER):
382 — Wayne Gretzky, Edmonton, Los Angeles, St. Louis, NY Rangers, 122G, 260A
295 — Mark Messier, Edmonton, NY Rangers, 109G, 186A
233 — Jari Kurri, Edmonton, Los Angeles, NY Rangers, Anaheim, 106G, 127A
214 — Glenn Anderson, Edmonton, Toronto, NY Rangers, St. Louis, 93G, 121A
196 — Paul Coffey, Edmonton, Pittsburgh, Los Angeles, Detroit, Philadelphia, Carolina, 59G, 137A

MOST POINTS, ONE PLAYOFF YEAR:
47 — Wayne Gretzky, Edmonton, in 1985. 17 goals, 30 assists in 18 games.
44 — Mario Lemieux, Pittsburgh, in 1991. 16 goals, 28 assists in 23 games.
43 — Wayne Gretzky, Edmonton, in 1988. 12 goals, 31 assists in 19 games.
40 — Wayne Gretzky, Los Angeles, in 1993. 15 goals, 25 assists in 24 games.
38 — Wayne Gretzky, Edmonton, in 1983. 12 goals, 26 assists in 16 games.

MOST POINTS IN ONE SERIES (OTHER THAN FINAL):

19 — Rick Middleton, Boston, in 1983 DF, 7 games vs. Buffalo. 5 goals, 14 assists.
18 — Wayne Gretzky, Edmonton, in 1985 CF, 6 games vs. Chicago. 4 goals, 14 assists.
17 — Mario Lemieux, Pittsburgh, in 1992 DSF, 6 games vs. Washington. 7 goals, 10 assists.
16 — Barry Pederson, Boston, in 1983 DF, 7 games vs. Buffalo. 7 goals, 9 assists.
— Doug Gilmour, Toronto, in 1994 CSF, 7 games vs. San Jose. 3 goals, 13 assists.
15 — Jari Kurri, Edmonton, in 1985 CF, 6 games vs. Chicago. 12 goals, 3 assists.
— Wayne Gretzky, Edmonton, in 1987 DSF, 5 games vs. Los Angeles. 2 goals, 13 assists.
— Tim Kerr, Philadelphia, in 1989 DF, 7 games vs. Pittsburgh. 10 goals, 5 assists.
— Mario Lemieux, Pittsburgh, in 1991 CF, 6 games vs. Boston. 6 goals, 9 assists.

MOST POINTS IN FINAL SERIES:

13 — Wayne Gretzky, Edmonton, in 1988, 4 games plus suspended game vs. Boston. 3 goals, 10 assists.
12 — Gordie Howe, Detroit, in 1955, 7 games vs. Montreal. 5 goals, 7 assists.
— Yvan Cournoyer, Montreal, in 1973, 6 games vs. Chicago. 6 goals, 6 assists.
— Jacques Lemaire, Montreal, in 1973, 6 games vs. Chicago. 3 goals, 9 assists.
— Mario Lemieux, Pittsburgh, in 1991, 5 games vs. Minnesota. 5 goals, 7 assists.

MOST POINTS, ONE GAME:

8 — Patrik Sundstrom, New Jersey, April 22, 1988, at New Jersey during 10-4 win over Washington. Sundstrom had 3 goals, 5 assists.
— Mario Lemieux, Pittsburgh, April 25, 1989, at Pittsburgh during 10-7 win over Philadelphia. Lemieux had 5 goals, 3 assists.
7 — Wayne Gretzky, Edmonton, April 17, 1983, at Calgary during 10-2 win. Gretzky had 4 goals, 3 assists.
— Wayne Gretzky, Edmonton, April 25,1985, at Winnipeg during 8-3 win. Gretzky had 3 goals, 4 assists.
— Wayne Gretzky, Edmonton, April 9, 1987, at Edmonton during 13-3 win over Los Angeles. Gretzky had 1 goal, 6 assists.
6 — Dickie Moore, Montreal, March 25, 1954, at Montreal during 8-1 win over Boston. Moore had 2 goals, 4 assists.
— Phil Esposito, Boston, April 2, 1969, at Boston during 10-0 win over Toronto. Esposito had 4 goals, 2 assists.
— Darryl Sittler, Toronto, April 22, 1976, at Toronto during 8-5 win over Philadelphia. Sittler had 5 goals, 1 assist.
— Guy Lafleur, Montreal, April 11, 1977, at Montreal during 7-2 win over St. Louis. Lafleur had 3 goals, 3 assists.
— Mikko Leinonen, NY Rangers, April 8, 1982, at NY Rangers during 7-3 win over Philadelphia. Leinonen had 6 assists.
— Paul Coffey, Edmonton, May 14, 1985, at Edmonton during 10-5 win over Chicago. Coffey had 1 goal, 5 assists.
— John Anderson, Hartford, April 12, 1986, at Hartford during 9-4 win over Quebec. Anderson had 2 goals, 4 assists.
— Mario Lemieux, Pittsburgh, April 23, 1992, at Pittsburgh during 6-4 win over Washington. Lemieux had 3 goals, 3 assists.
— Geoff Courtnall, St. Louis Blues, April 23, 1998, at St. Louis during 8-3 win over Los Angeles. Courtnall had 1 goal, 5 assists.

MOST POINTS, ONE PERIOD:

4 — Maurice Richard, Montreal, March 29, 1945, at Montreal vs. Toronto. Third period, 3 goals, 1 assist. Final score: Montreal 10, Toronto 3.
— Dickie Moore, Montreal, March 25, 1954, at Montreal vs. Boston. First period, 2 goals, 2 assists. Final score: Montreal 8, Boston 1.
— Barry Pederson, Boston, April 8, 1982, at Boston vs. Buffalo. Second period, 3 goals, 1 assist. Final score: Boston 7, Buffalo 3.
— Peter McNab, Boston, April 11, 1982, at Buffalo. Second period, 1 goal, 3 assists. Final score: Boston 5, Buffalo 2.
— Tim Kerr, Philadelphia, April 13, 1985, at NY Rangers. Second period, 4 goals. Final score: Philadelphia 6, NY Rangers 5.
— Ken Linseman, Boston, April 14, 1985, at Boston vs. Montreal. Second period, 2 goals, 2 assists. Final score: Boston 7, Montreal 6.
— Wayne Gretzky, Edmonton, April 12, 1987, at Los Angeles. Third period, 1 goal, 3 assists. Final score: Edmonton 6, Los Angeles 3.
— Glenn Anderson, Edmonton, April 6, 1988, at Edmonton vs. Winnipeg. Third period, 3 goals, 1 assist. Final score: Edmonton 7, Winnipeg 4.
— Mario Lemieux, Pittsburgh, April 25, 1989, at Pittsburgh vs. Philadelphia. First period, 4 goals. Final score: Pittsburgh 10, Philadelphia 7.
— Dave Gagner, Minnesota, April 8, 1991, at Minnesota vs. Chicago. First period, 2 goals, 2 assists. Final score: Chicago 6, Minnesota 5.
— Mario Lemieux, Pittsburgh, April 23, 1992, at Pittsburgh vs. Washington. Second period, 2 goals, 2 assists. Final score: Pittsburgh 6, Washington 4.
— Alexander Mogilny, New Jersey, April 28, 2001, at New Jersey vs. Toronto. Second period, 1 goal, 3 assists. Final score: New Jersey 6, Toronto 5.

POWER-PLAY GOALS

MOST POWER-PLAY GOALS IN PLAYOFFS (CAREER):

35 — Mike Bossy, NY Islanders
34 — Dino Ciccarelli, Minnesota, Washington, Detroit
— Wayne Gretzky, Edmonton, Los Angeles, St. Louis, NY Rangers
— Brett Hull, St. Louis, Dallas
29 — Mario Lemieux, Pittsburgh

MOST POWER-PLAY GOALS, ONE PLAYOFF YEAR:

9 — Mike Bossy, NY Islanders, 1981. 18 games against Toronto, Edmonton, NY Rangers and Minnesota.
— Cam Neely, Boston, 1991. 19 games against Hartford, Montreal and Pittsburgh.
8 — Tim Kerr, Philadelphia, 1989. 19 games.
— John Druce, Washington, 1990. 15 games.
— Brian Propp, Minnesota, 1991. 23 games.
— Mario Lemieux, Pittsburgh, 1992. 15 games.

MOST POWER-PLAY GOALS, ONE PLAYOFF SERIES:

6 — Chris Kontos, Los Angeles, 1989, DSF vs. Edmonton, won by Los Angeles 4-3.
5 — Andy Bathgate, Detroit, 1966, SF vs. Chicago, won by Detroit 4-2.
— Denis Potvin, NY Islanders, 1981, QF vs. Edmonton, won by NY Islanders 4-2.
— Ken Houston, Calgary, 1981, QF vs. Philadelphia, won by Calgary 4-3.
— Rick Vaive, Chicago, 1988, DSF vs. St. Louis, won by St. Louis 4-1.
— Tim Kerr, Philadelphia, 1989, DF vs. Pittsburgh, won by Philadelphia 4-3.
— Mario Lemieux, Pittsburgh, 1989, DF vs. Philadelphia, won by Philadelphia 4-3.
— John Druce, Washington, 1990, DF vs. NY Rangers, won by Washington 4-1.
— Pat LaFontaine, Buffalo, 1992, DSF vs. Boston, won by Boston 4-3.
— Adam Graves, NY Rangers, 1996, CQF vs Montreal, won by NY Rangers 4-2.

MOST POWER-PLAY GOALS, ONE GAME:

3 — Syd Howe, Detroit, March 23, 1939, at Detroit vs. Montreal. Detroit won 7-3.
— Sid Smith, Toronto, April 10, 1949, at Detroit. Toronto won 3-1.
— Phil Esposito, Boston, April 2, 1969, at Boston vs. Toronto. Boston won 10-0.
— John Bucyk, Boston, April 21, 1974, at Boston vs. Chicago. Boston won 8-6.
— Denis Potvin, NY Islanders, April 17, 1981, at NY Islanders vs. Edmonton. NY Islanders won 6-3.
— Tim Kerr, Philadelphia, April 13, 1985, at NY Rangers. Philadelphia won 6-5.
— Jari Kurri, Edmonton, April 9, 1987, at Edmonton vs. Los Angeles. Edmonton won 13-3.
— Mark Johnson, New Jersey, April 22, 1988, at New Jersey vs. Washington. New Jersey won 10-4.
— Dino Ciccarelli, Detroit, April 29, 1993, at Toronto. Detroit won 7-3.
— Dino Ciccarelli, Detroit, May 11, 1995, at Dallas. Detroit won 5-1.
— Valeri Kamensky, Colorado, April 24, 1997, at Colorado vs. Chicago. Colorado won 7-0.

MOST POWER-PLAY GOALS, ONE PERIOD:

3 — Tim Kerr, Philadelphia, April 13, 1985, at NY Rangers, second period in 6-5 win.
2 — Two power-play goals have been scored by one player in one period on 53 occasions. Charlie Conacher of Toronto was the first to score two power-play goals in one period, setting the mark on March 26, 1936. Brendan Shanahan of the Detroit Red Wings is the most recent to equal this mark with two power-play goals May 3, 1998, at Phoenix, first period in 5-2 win.

SHORTHAND GOALS

MOST SHORTHAND GOALS IN PLAYOFFS (CAREER):

14 — Mark Messier, Edmonton, NY Rangers
11 — Wayne Gretzky, Edmonton, Los Angeles, St. Louis
10 — Jari Kurri, Edmonton, Los Angeles, NY Rangers
8 — Ed Westfall, Boston, NY Islanders
— Hakan Loob, Calgary

MOST SHORTHAND GOALS, ONE PLAYOFF YEAR:

3 — Derek Sanderson, Boston, 1969. 1 against Toronto in QF, won by Boston 4-0; 2 against Montreal in SF, won by Montreal, 4-2.
— Bill Barber, Philadelphia, 1980. All against Minnesota in SF, won by Philadelphia 4-1.
— Lorne Henning, NY Islanders, 1980. 1 against Boston in QF, won by NY Islanders 4-1; 1 against Buffalo in SF, won by NY Islanders 4-2, 1 against Philadelphia in F, won by NY Islanders 4-2.
— Wayne Gretzky, Edmonton, 1983. 2 against Winnipeg in DSF, won by Edmonton 3-0; 1 against Calgary in DF, won by Edmonton 4-1.
— Wayne Presley, Chicago, 1989. All against Detroit in DSF, won by Chicago 4-2.
— Todd Marchant, Edmonton, 1997. 1 against Dallas in CQF, won by Edmonton 4-3; 2 against Colorado in CSF, won by Colorado 4-1.

Though they came close, not even Wayne Gretzky or Mario Lemieux were able to break Rick Middleton's record of 19 points in a single playoff series. Middleton ran up the score during Boston's seven-game victory over Buffalo in 1983.

MOST SHORTHAND GOALS, ONE PLAYOFF SERIES:

3 — Bill Barber, Philadelphia, 1980, SF vs. Minnesota, won by Philadelphia 4-1.
— Wayne Presley, Chicago, 1989, DSF vs. Detroit, won by Chicago 4-2.
2 — Mac Colville, NY Rangers, 1940, SF vs. Boston, won by NY Rangers 4-2.
— Jerry Toppazzini, Boston, 1958, SF vs. NY Rangers, won by Boston 4-2.
— Dave Keon, Toronto, 1963, F vs. Detroit, won by Toronto 4-1.
— Bob Pulford, Toronto, 1964, F vs. Detroit, won by Toronto 4-3.
— Serge Savard, Montreal, 1968, F vs. St. Louis, won by Montreal 4-0.
— Derek Sanderson, Boston, 1969, SF vs. Montreal, won by Montreal 4-2.
— Bryan Trottier, NY Islanders, 1980, PR vs. Los Angeles, won by NY Islanders 3-1.
— Bobby Lalonde, Boston, 1981, PR vs. Minnesota, won by Minnesota 3-0.
— Butch Goring, NY Islanders, 1981, SF vs. NY Rangers, won by NY Islanders 4-0.
— Wayne Gretzky, Edmonton, 1983, DSF vs. Winnipeg, won by Edmonton 3-0.
— Mark Messier, Edmonton, 1983, DF vs. Calgary, won by Edmonton 4-1.
— Jari Kurri, Edmonton, 1983, CF vs. Chicago, won by Edmonton 4-0.
— Wayne Gretzky, Edmonton, 1985, DF vs. Winnipeg, won by Edmonton 4-0.
— Kevin Lowe, Edmonton, 1987, F vs. Philadelphia, won by Edmonton 4-3.
— Bob Gould, Washington, 1988, DSF vs. Philadelphia, won by Washington 4-3.
— Dave Poulin, Philadelphia, 1989, DF vs. Pittsburgh, won by Philadelphia 4-3.
— Russ Courtnall, Montreal, 1991, DF vs. Boston, won by Boston 4-3.
— Sergei Fedorov, Detroit, 1992, DSF vs. Minnesota, won by Detroit 4-3.
— Mark Messier, NY Rangers, 1992, DSF vs. New Jersey, won by NY Rangers 4-3.
— Tom Fitzgerald, NY Islanders, 1993, DF vs. Pittsburgh, won by NY Islanders 4-3.
— Mark Osborne, Toronto, 1994, CSF vs. San Jose, won by Toronto 4-3.
— Tony Amonte, Chicago, 1997, CQF vs. Colorado, won by Colorado 4-2.
— Brian Rolston, New Jersey, 1997, CQF vs. Montreal, won by New Jersey 4-1.
— Rod Brind'Amour, Philadelphia, 1997, CQF vs. Pittsburgh, won by Philadelphia 4-1.
— Todd Marchant, Edmonton, 1997, CSF vs. Colorado, won by Colorado 4-1.
— Jeremy Roenick, Phoenix, 1998, CQF vs. Detroit, won by Detroit 4-2.
— Vincent Damphousse, San Jose, 1999, CQF vs. Colorado, won by Colorado 4-2.
— Dixon Ward, Buffalo, 1999, CF vs. Toronto, won by Buffalo 4-1.
— Curtis Brown, Buffalo, 2001, CSF vs. Pittsburgh, won by Pittsburgh 4-3.

MOST SHORTHAND GOALS, ONE GAME:

2 — Dave Keon, Toronto, April 18, 1963, at Toronto, in 3-1 win vs. Detroit.
— Bryan Trottier, NY Islanders, April 8, 1980, at NY Islanders, in 8-1 win vs. Los Angeles.
— Bobby Lalonde, Boston, April 11, 1981, at Minnesota, in 6-3 loss vs. Minnesota.
— Wayne Gretzky, Edmonton, April 6, 1983, at Edmonton, in 6-3 win vs. Winnipeg.
— Jari Kurri, Edmonton, April 24, 1983, at Edmonton, in 8-3 win vs. Chicago.
— Mark Messier, NY Rangers, April 21, 1992, at NY Rangers, in 7-3 loss vs. New Jersey.
— Tom Fitzgerald, NY Islanders, May 8, 1993, at NY Islanders, in 6-5 win vs. Pittsburgh.
— Rod Brind'Amour, Philadelphia, April 26, 1997, at Philadelphia, in 6-3 win vs. Pittsburgh.
— Jeremy Roenick, Phoenix, April 24, 1998, at Detroit, in 7-4 win by Phoenix.
— Vincent Damphousse, San Jose, April 30, 1999, at Colorado, in 7-3 win by San Jose.

MOST SHORTHAND GOALS, ONE PERIOD:

2 — Bryan Trottier, NY Islanders, April 8, 1980, second period at NY Islanders in 8-1 win vs. Los Angeles.
— Bobby Lalonde, Boston, April 11, 1981, third period at Minnesota in 6-3 loss vs. Minnesota.
— Jari Kurri, Edmonton, April 24, 1983, third period at Edmonton in 8-4 win vs. Chicago.
— Rod Brind'Amour, Philadelphia, April 26, 1997, first period at Philadelphia in 6-3 win vs. Pittsburgh.
— Jeremy Roenick, Phoenix, April 24, 1998, second period at Detroit in 7-4 win by Phoenix.
— Vincent Damphousse, San Jose, April 30, 1999, third period at Colorado in 7-3 win by San Jose.

GAME-WINNING GOALS

MOST GAME-WINNING GOALS IN PLAYOFFS (CAREER):

24 — Wayne Gretzky, Edmonton, Los Angeles, St. Louis, NY Rangers
21 — Brett Hull, St. Louis, Dallas
19 — Claude Lemieux, Montreal, New Jersey, Colorado
18 — Maurice Richard, Montreal
17 — Mike Bossy, NY Islanders
— Glenn Anderson, Edmonton, Toronto, NY Rangers, St. Louis

MOST GAME-WINNING GOALS, ONE PLAYOFF YEAR:

6 — Joe Sakic, Colorado, 1996. 22 games.
— Joe Nieuwendyk, Dallas, 1999. 23 games.
5 — Mike Bossy, NY Islanders, 1983. 19 games.
— Jari Kurri, Edmonton, 1987. 21 games.
— Bobby Smith, Minnesota, 1991. 23 games.
— Mario Lemieux, Pittsburgh, 1992. 15 games.

MOST GAME-WINNING GOALS, ONE PLAYOFF SERIES:

4 — Mike Bossy, NY Islanders, 1983, CF vs. Boston, won by NY Islanders 4-2.

OVERTIME GOALS

MOST OVERTIME GOALS IN PLAYOFFS (CAREER):

6 — Maurice Richard, Montreal (1 in 1946; 3 in 1951; 1 in 1957; 1 in 1958.)
5 — Glenn Anderson, Edmonton, Toronto, St. Louis
4 — Bob Nystrom, NY Islanders
— Dale Hunter, Quebec, Washington
— Wayne Gretzky, Edmonton, Los Angeles
— Stephane Richer, Montreal, New Jersey
— Joe Murphy, Edmonton, Chicago
— Esa Tikkanen, Edmonton, NY Rangers
— Jaromir Jagr, Pittsburgh
— Kirk Muller, Montreal, Dallas
— Joe Sakic, Colorado

MOST OVERTIME GOALS, ONE PLAYOFF YEAR:

3 — Mel Hill, Boston, 1939. All against NY Rangers in best-of-seven SF, won by Boston 4-3.
— Maurice Richard, Montreal, 1951. 2 against Detroit in best-of-seven SF, won by Montreal 4-2; 1 against Toronto best-of-seven F, won by Toronto 4-1.

MOST OVERTIME GOALS, ONE PLAYOFF SERIES:

3 — Mel Hill, Boston, 1939, SF vs. NY Rangers, won by Boston 4-3. Hill scored at 59:25 of overtime March 21 for a 2-1 win; at 8:24, March 23 for a 3-2 win; and at 48:00, April 2 for a 2-1 win.

Bob Nystrom, who celebrates a goal against Vancouver in the 1982 Stanley Cup finals, was a key part of the New York Islanders' Stanley Cup dynasty. Nystrom scored four overtime goals in his playoff career.

SCORING BY A DEFENSEMAN

MOST GOALS BY A DEFENSEMAN, ONE PLAYOFF YEAR:
12 — Paul Coffey, Edmonton, 1985. 18 games.
11 — Brian Leetch, NY Rangers, 1994. 23 games.
9 — Bobby Orr, Boston, 1970. 14 games.
— Brad Park, Boston, 1978. 15 games.
8 — Denis Potvin, NY Islanders, 1981. 18 games.
— Raymond Bourque, Boston, 1983. 17 games.
— Denis Potvin, NY Islanders, 1983. 20 games.
— Paul Coffey, Edmonton, 1984. 19 games.

MOST GOALS BY A DEFENSEMAN, ONE GAME:
3 — Bobby Orr, Boston, April 11, 1971, at Montreal. Final score: Boston 5, Montreal 2.
— Dick Redmond, Chicago, April 4, 1973, at Chicago. Final score: Chicago 7, St. Louis 1.
— Denis Potvin, NY Islanders, April 17, 1981, at NY Islanders. Final score: NY Islanders 6, Edmonton 3.
— Paul Reinhart, Calgary, April 14, 1983, at Edmonton. Final score: Edmonton 6, Calgary 3.
— Doug Halward, Vancouver, April 7, 1984, at Vancouver. Final score: Vancouver 7, Calgary 0.
— Paul Reinhart, Calgary, April 8, 1984, at Vancouver. Final score: Calgary 5, Vancouver 1.
— Al Iafrate, Washington, April 26, 1993, at Washington. Final score: Washington 6, NY Islanders 4.
— Eric Desjardins, Montreal, June 3, 1993, at Montreal. Final score: Montreal 3, Los Angeles 2.
— Gary Suter, Chicago, April 24, 1994, at Chicago. Final score: Chicago 4, Toronto 3.
— Brian Leetch, NY Rangers, May 22, 1995, at Philadelphia. Final score: Philadelphia 4, NY Rangers 3.
— Andy Delmore, Philadelphia, May 7, 2000, at Philadelphia. Final score: Philadelphia 6, Pittsburgh 3.

MOST ASSISTS BY A DEFENSEMAN, ONE PLAYOFF YEAR:
25 — Paul Coffey, Edmonton, 1985. 18 games.
24 — Al MacInnis, Calgary, 1989. 22 games.
23 — Brian Leetch, NY Rangers, 1994. 23 games.
19 — Bobby Orr, Boston, 1972. 15 games.
18 — Raymond Bourque, Boston, 1988. 23 games.
— Raymond Bourque, Boston, 1991. 19 games.
— Larry Murphy, Pittsburgh, 1991. 23 games.

MOST ASSISTS BY A DEFENSEMAN, ONE GAME:
5 — Paul Coffey, Edmonton, May 14, 1985 at Edmonton vs. Chicago. Edmonton won 10-5.
— Risto Siltanen, Quebec, April 14, 1987 at Hartford. Quebec won 7-5.

MOST POINTS BY A DEFENSEMAN, ONE PLAYOFF YEAR:
37 — Paul Coffey, Edmonton, in 1985. 12 goals, 25 assists in 18 games.
34 — Brian Leetch, NY Rangers, in 1994. 11 goals, 23 assists in 23 games.
31 — Al MacInnis, Calgary, in 1989. 7 goals, 24 assists in 22 games.
25 — Denis Potvin, NY Islanders, in 1981. 8 goals, 17 assists in 18 games.
— Raymond Bourque, Boston, in 1991. 7 goals, 18 assists in 19 games.

MOST POINTS BY A DEFENSEMAN, ONE GAME:
6 — Paul Coffey, Edmonton, May 14, 1985 at Edmonton vs. Chicago. 1 goal, 5 assists. Edmonton won 10-5.
5 — Eddie Bush, Detroit, April 9, 1942, at Detroit vs. Toronto. 1 goal, 4 assists. Detroit won 5-2.
— Bob Dailey, Philadelphia, May 1, 1980, at Philadelphia vs. Minnesota. 1 goal, 4 assists. Philadelphia won 7-0.
— Denis Potvin, NY Islanders, April 17, 1981, at NY Islanders vs. Edmonton. 3 goals, 2 assists. NY Islanders won 6-3.
— Risto Siltanen, Quebec, April 14, 1987, at Hartford. 5 assists. Quebec won 7-5.

SCORING BY A ROOKIE

MOST GOALS BY A ROOKIE, ONE PLAYOFF YEAR:
14 — Dino Ciccarelli, Minnesota, 1981. 19 games.
11 — Jeremy Roenick, Chicago, 1990. 20 games.
10 — Claude Lemieux, Montreal, 1986. 20 games.
9 — Pat Flatley, NY Islanders, 1984. 21 games
8 — Steve Christoff, Minnesota, 1980. 14 games.
— Brad Palmer, Minnesota, 1981. 19 games.
— Mike Krushelnyski, Boston, 1983. 17 games.
— Bob Joyce, Boston, 1988. 23 games.

MOST POINTS BY A ROOKIE, ONE PLAYOFF YEAR:
21 — Dino Ciccarelli, Minnesota, in 1981. 14 goals, 7 assists in 19 games.
20 — Don Maloney, NY Rangers, in 1979. 7 goals, 13 assists in 18 games.

THREE-OR-MORE-GOAL GAMES

MOST THREE-OR-MORE-GOAL GAMES IN PLAYOFFS (CAREER):
10 — Wayne Gretzky, Edmonton, Los Angeles, NY Rangers. Eight three-goal games; two four-goal games.
7 — Maurice Richard, Montreal. Four three-goal games; two four-goal games; one five-goal game.
— Jari Kurri, Edmonton. Six three-goal games; one four-goal game.
6 — Dino Ciccarelli, Minnesota, Washington, Detroit. Five three-goal games; one four-goal game.
5 — Mike Bossy, NY Islanders. Four three-goal games; one four-goal game.

MOST THREE-OR-MORE-GOAL GAMES, ONE PLAYOFF YEAR:
4 — Jari Kurri, Edmonton, 1985. 1 four-goal game, 3 three-goal games.
3 — Mark Messier, Edmonton, 1983. 3 three-goal games.
— Mike Bossy, NY Islanders, 1983. 1 four-goal game, 2 three-goal games
2 — Newsy Lalonde, Montreal, 1919. 1 five-goal game, 1 four-goal game.
— Maurice Richard, Montreal, 1944. 1 five-goal game; 1 three-goal game.
— Doug Bentley, Chicago, 1944. 2 three-goal games.
— Norm Ullman, Detroit, 1964. 2 three-goal games.
— Phil Esposito, Boston, 1970. 2 three-goal games.
— Pit Martin, Chicago, 1973. 2 three-goal games.
— Rick MacLeish, Philadelphia, 1975. 2 three-goal games.
— Lanny McDonald, Toronto, 1977. 1 four-goal game; 1 three-goal game.
— Wayne Gretzky, Edmonton, 1981. 2 three-goal games.
— Wayne Gretzky, Edmonton, 1983. 2 four-goal games.
— Wayne Gretzky, Edmonton, 1985. 2 three-goal games.
— Petr Klima, Detroit, 1988. 2 three-goal games.
— Cam Neely, Boston, 1991. 2 three-goal games.
— Wayne Gretzky, NY Rangers, 1997. 2 three-goal games.
— Daniel Alfredsson, Ottawa, 1998. 2 three-goal games.

MOST THREE-OR-MORE-GOAL GAMES, ONE PLAYOFF SERIES:
3 — Jari Kurri, Edmonton, 1985, CF vs. Chicago, won by Edmonton 4-2. Kurri scored 3 G May 7 at Edmonton in 7-3 win, 3 G May 14 at Edmonton in 10-5 win and 4 G May 16 at Chicago in 8-2 win.
2 — Doug Bentley, Chicago, 1944, SF vs. Detroit, won by Chicago 4-1. Bentley scored 3 G Mar. 28 at Chicago in 7-1 win and 3 G Mar. 30 at Detroit in 5-2 win.
— Norm Ullman, Detroit, 1964, SF vs. Chicago, won by Detroit 4-3. Ullman scored 3 G Mar. 29 at Chicago in 7-1 win and 3 G April 7 at Detroit in 7-2 win.
— Mark Messier, Edmonton, 1983, DF vs. Calgary, won by Edmonton 4-1. Messier scored 4 G April 14 at Edmonton in 6-3 win and 3 G April 17 at Calgary in 10-2 win.
— Mike Bossy, NY Islanders, 1983, CF vs. Boston, won by NY Islanders 4-2. Bossy scored 3 G May 3 at NY Islanders in 8-3 win and 4 G May 7 at New York in 8-4 win.

SCORING STREAKS

LONGEST CONSECUTIVE GOAL-SCORING STREAK, ONE PLAYOFF YEAR:
10 Games — Reggie Leach, Philadelphia, 1976. Streak started April 17 at Toronto and ended May 9 at Montreal. He scored one goal in each of eight games; two in one game; and five in another; a total of 15 goals.

LONGEST CONSECUTIVE POINT-SCORING STREAK, ONE PLAYOFF YEAR:
18 games — Bryan Trottier, NY Islanders, 1981. 11 goals, 18 assists, 29 points.
17 games — Wayne Gretzky, Edmonton, 1988. 12 goals, 29 assists, 41 points.
— Al MacInnis, Calgary, 1989. 7 goals, 19 assists, 26 points.

LONGEST CONSECUTIVE POINT-SCORING STREAK, MORE THAN ONE PLAYOFF YEAR:
27 games — Bryan Trottier, NY Islanders, 1980, 1981 and 1982. 7 games in 1980 (3 G, 5 A, 8 PTS), 18 games in 1981 (11 G, 18 A, 29 PTS), and two games in 1982 (2 G, 3 A, 5 PTS). Total points, 42.
19 games — Wayne Gretzky, Edmonton, Los Angeles, 1988 and 1989. 17 games in 1988 (12 G, 29 A, 41 PTS with Edmonton), 2 games in 1989 (1 G, 2 A, 3 PTS with Los Angeles). Total points, 44.

FASTEST GOALS

FASTEST GOAL FROM START OF GAME:
6 Seconds — Don Kozak, Los Angeles, April 17, 1977, at Los Angeles vs. Boston and goaltender Gerry Cheevers. Los Angeles won 7-4.
7 Seconds — Bob Gainey, Montreal, May 5, 1977, at NY Islanders vs. goaltender Chico Resch. Montreal won 2-1.
— Terry Murray, Philadelphia, April 12, 1981, at Quebec vs. goaltender Dan Bouchard. Quebec won 4-3 in overtime.
8 Seconds — Stan Smyl, Vancouver, April 7, 1982, at Vancouver vs. Calgary and goaltender Pat Riggin. Vancouver won 5-3.

FASTEST GOAL FROM START OF PERIOD (OTHER THAN FIRST):
6 Seconds — Pelle Eklund, Philadelphia, April 25, 1989, at Pittsburgh vs. goaltender Tom Barrasso, second period. Pittsburgh won 10-7.
9 Seconds — Bill Collins, Minnesota, April 9, 1968, at Minnesota vs. Los Angeles and goaltender Wayne Rutledge, third period. Minnesota won 7-5.
— Dave Balon, Minnesota, April 25, 1968, at St. Louis vs. goaltender Glenn Hall, third period. Minnesota won 5-1.
— Murray Oliver, Minnesota, April 8, 1971, at St. Louis vs. goaltender Ernie Wakely, third period. St. Louis won 4-2.
— Clark Gillies, NY Islanders, April 15, 1977, at Buffalo vs. goaltender Don Edwards, third period. NY Islanders won 4-3.
— Eric Vail, Atlanta, April 11, 1978, at Atlanta vs. Detroit and goaltender Ron Low, third period. Detroit won 5-3.
— Stan Smyl, Vancouver, April 10, 1979, at Philadelphia vs. goaltender Wayne Stephenson, third period. Vancouver won 3-2.
— Wayne Gretzky, Edmonton, April 6, 1983, at Edmonton vs. Winnipeg and goaltender Brian Hayward, second period. Edmonton won 6-3.
— Mark Messier, Edmonton, April 16, 1984, at Calgary vs. goaltender Don Edwards, third period. Edmonton won 5-3.
— Brian Skrudland, Montreal, May 18, 1986, at Calgary vs. goaltender Mike Vernon, first overtime period. Montreal won 3-2.

FASTEST TWO GOALS:
5 Seconds — Norm Ullman, Detroit, April 11, 1965, at Detroit vs. Chicago and goaltender Glenn Hall. Ullman scored at 17:35 and 17:40 of second period. Detroit won 4-2.

FASTEST TWO GOALS FROM START OF A GAME:
1 Minute, 8 Seconds — Dick Duff, Toronto, April 9, 1963, at Toronto vs. Detroit and goaltender Terry Sawchuk. Duff scored at 0:49 and 1:08. Final score: Toronto 4, Detroit 2.

FASTEST TWO GOALS FROM START OF A PERIOD:
35 Seconds — Pat LaFontaine, NY Islanders, May 19, 1984, at Edmonton vs. goaltender Andy Moog. LaFontaine scored at 0:13 and 0:35 of third period. Final score: Edmonton 5, NY Islanders 2.

PENALTIES

MOST PENALTY MINUTES IN PLAYOFFS (CAREER):
729 — Dale Hunter, Quebec, Washington, Colorado
541 — Chris Nilan, Montreal, NY Rangers, Boston
517 — Claude Lemieux, Montreal, New Jersey, Colorado
471 — Rick Tocchet, Philadelphia, Pittsburgh, Boston, Phoenix
466 — Willi Plett, Atlanta, Calgary, Minnesota, Boston

MOST PENALTIES, ONE GAME:
8 — Forbes Kennedy, Toronto, April 2, 1969, at Boston. Four minors, 2 majors, 1 10-minute misconduct, 1 game misconduct. Final score: Boston 10, Toronto 0.
— Kim Clackson, Pittsburgh, April 14, 1980, at Boston. Five minors, 2 majors, 1 10-minute misconduct. Final score: Boston 6, Pittsburgh 2

MOST PENALTY MINUTES, ONE GAME:
42 — Dave Schultz, Philadelphia, April 22, 1976, at Toronto. One minor, 2 majors, 1 10-minute misconduct and 2 game-misconducts. Final score: Toronto 8, Philadelphia 5.

MOST PENALTIES, ONE PERIOD AND MOST PENALTY MINUTES, ONE PERIOD:
6 Penalties; 39 Minutes — Ed Hospodar, NY Rangers, April 9, 1981, at Los Angeles, first period. Two minors, 1 major, 1 10-minute misconduct, 2 game misconducts. Final score: Los Angeles 5, NY Rangers 4.

GOALTENDING

MOST PLAYOFF GAMES APPEARED IN BY A GOALTENDER (CAREER):
219 — Patrick Roy, Montreal, Colorado
150 — Grant Fuhr, Edmonton, Buffalo, St. Louis
141 — Ed Belfour, Chicago, Dallas
138 — Mike Vernon, Calgary, Detroit, San Jose, Florida
132 — Billy Smith, NY Islanders
— Andy Moog, Edmonton, Boston, Dallas, Montreal

MOST MINUTES PLAYED BY A GOALTENDER (CAREER):
13,545 — Patrick Roy, Montreal, Colorado
8,834 — Grant Fuhr, Edmonton, Buffalo, St. Louis
8,639 — Ed Belfour, Chicago, Dallas
8,214 — Mike Vernon, Calgary, Detroit, San Jose, Florida
7,645 — Billy Smith, NY Islanders

MOST MINUTES PLAYED BY A GOALTENDER, ONE PLAYOFF YEAR:
1,544 — Kirk McLean, Vancouver, 1994. 24 games.
— Ed Belfour, Dallas, 1999. 23 games.
1,540 — Ron Hextall, Philadelphia, 1987. 26 games.
1,505 — Mike Richter, NY Rangers, 1994. 23 games.
1,477 — Martin Brodeur, New Jersey, 2001. 25 games.

MOST SHUTOUTS IN PLAYOFFS (CAREER):
19 — Patrick Roy, Montreal, Colorado
15 — Clint Benedict, Ottawa, Mtl. Maroons
14 — Jacques Plante, Montreal, St. Louis
13 — Turk Broda, Toronto
12 — Terry Sawchuk, Detroit, Los Angeles
— Martin Brodeur, New Jersey
— Curtis Joseph, St. Louis, Edmonton, Toronto

MOST SHUTOUTS, ONE PLAYOFF YEAR:
4 — Clint Benedict, Mtl. Maroons, 1926. 8 games.
— Clint Benedict, Mtl. Maroons, 1928. 9 games.
— Dave Kerr, NY Rangers, 1937. 9 games.
— Frank McCool, Toronto, 1945. 13 games.
— Terry Sawchuk, Detroit, 1952. 8 games.
— Bernie Parent, Philadelphia, 1975. 17 games.
— Ken Dryden, Montreal, 1977. 14 games.
— Mike Richter, NY Rangers, 1994. 23 games.
— Kirk McLean, Vancouver, 1994. 24 games.
— Olaf Kolzig, Washington, 1998. 21 games.
— Ed Belfour, Dallas, 2000. 23 games.
— Patrick Roy, Colorado, 2001. 23 games.
— Martin Brodeur, New Jersey, 2001. 25 games.

MOST SHUTOUTS, ONE PLAYOFF SERIES:
3 — Clint Benedict, Mtl. Maroons, in 1926 F, 4 games vs. Victoria.
— Dave Kerr, NY Rangers, in 1940 SF, 6 games vs. Boston.
— Frank McCool, Toronto, in 1945 F, 7 games vs. Detroit.
— Turk Broda, Toronto, in 1950 SF, 7 games vs. Detroit.
— Felix Potvin, Toronto, in 1994 CQF, 6 games vs. Chicago.
— Martin Brodeur, New Jersey, in 1995 CQF, 5 games vs. Boston.

MOST WINS BY A GOALTENDER, (CAREER):
137 — Patrick Roy, Montreal, Colorado
92 — Grant Fuhr, Edmonton, Buffalo, St. Louis
88 — Billy Smith, NY Islanders
80 — Ken Dryden, Montreal
79 — Ed Belfour, Chicago, Dallas

MOST WINS BY A GOALTENDER, ONE PLAYOFF YEAR:
16 — Sixteen wins by a goaltender in one playoff year has been recorded on 13 occasions. Patrick Roy of the Colorado Avalance is the most recent to equal this mark, posting a record of 16 wins, 7 losses in 23 games in 2001. It was first accomplished by Grant Fuhr in 1988.

MOST CONSECUTIVE WINS BY A GOALTENDER, MORE THAN ONE PLAYOFF YEAR:
14 — Tom Barrasso, Pittsburgh, 1992, 1993; 3 wins against NY Rangers in 1992 DF, won by Pittsburgh 4-2; 4 wins against Boston in 1992 CF, won by Pittsburgh 4-0; 4 wins against Chicago in 1992 F, won by Pittsburgh 4-0; 3 wins against New Jersey in 1993 DSF, won by Pittsburgh 4-1.

MOST CONSECUTIVE WINS BY A GOALTENDER, ONE PLAYOFF YEAR:
11 — Ed Belfour, Chicago, 1992. 3 wins against St. Louis in DSF, won by Chicago 4-2; 4 wins against Detroit in DF, won by Chicago 4-0; and 4 wins against Edmonton in CF, won by Chicago 4-0.
— Tom Barrasso, Pittsburgh, 1992. 3 wins against NY Rangers in DF, won by Pittsburgh 4-2; 4 wins against Boston in CF, won by Pittsburgh 4-0; and 4 wins against Chicago in F, won by Pittsburgh 4-0.
— Patrick Roy, Montreal, 1993. 4 wins against Quebec in DSF, won by Montreal 4-2; 4 wins against Buffalo in DF, won by Montreal 4-0; and 3 wins against NY Islanders in CF, won by Montreal 4-1.

LONGEST SHUTOUT SEQUENCE:
248 Minutes, 32 Seconds — Normie Smith, Detroit, 1936. In best-of-five SF, Smith shut out Mtl. Maroons twice, 1-0, March 24, in 116:30 overtime; shut out Maroons 3-0 in second game, March 26; and was scored against at 12:02 of first period, March 29, by Gus Marker. Detroit won SF 3-0.

MOST CONSECUTIVE SHUTOUTS:
3 — Clint Benedict, Mtl. Maroons, 1926. Benedict shut out Ottawa 1-0, Mar. 27; he then shut out Victoria twice, 3-0, Mar. 30; 3-0, Apr. 1. Mtl. Maroons won NHL F vs. Ottawa 2 goals to 1 and won the best-of-five F vs. Victoria 3-1.
— John Ross Roach, NY Rangers, 1929. Roach shut out NY Americans twice, 0-0, Mar. 19; 1-0, Mar. 21; he then shut out Toronto 1-0, Mar. 24. NY Rangers won QF vs. NY Americans 1 goal to 0 and won the best-of-three SF vs. Toronto 2-0.
— Frank McCool, Toronto, 1945. McCool shut out Detroit 1-0, April 6; 2-0, April 8; 1-0, April 12. Toronto won the best-of-seven F 4-3.

Early Playoff Records

1893-1918

Team Records

MOST GOALS, BOTH TEAMS, ONE GAME:
25 — Ottawa Silver Seven, Dawson City at Ottawa, Jan. 16, 1905. Ottawa 23, Dawson City 2. Ottawa won best-of-three series 2-0.

MOST GOALS, ONE TEAM, ONE GAME:
23 — Ottawa Silver Seven at Ottawa, Jan. 16, 1905. Ottawa defeated Dawson City 23-2.

MOST GOALS, BOTH TEAMS, BEST-OF-THREE SERIES:
42 — Ottawa Silver Seven, Queen's University at Ottawa, 1906. Ottawa defeated Queen's 16-7, Feb. 27, and 12-7, Feb. 28.

MOST GOALS, ONE TEAM, BEST-OF-THREE SERIES:
32 — Ottawa Silver Seven in 1905 at Ottawa. Defeated Dawson City 9-2, Jan. 13, and 23-2, Jan. 16.

MOST GOALS, BOTH TEAMS, BEST-OF-FIVE SERIES:
39 — Toronto Arenas, Vancouver Millionaires at Toronto, 1918. Toronto won 5-3, Mar. 20; 6-3, Mar. 26; 2-1, Mar. 30. Vancouver won 6-4, Mar. 23, and 8-1, Mar. 28. Toronto scored 18 goals; Vancouver 21.

MOST GOALS, ONE TEAM, BEST-OF-FIVE SERIES:
26 — Vancouver Millionaires in 1915 at Vancouver. Defeated Ottawa Senators 6-2, Mar. 22; 8-3, Mar. 24; and 12-3, Mar. 26.

Individual Records

MOST GOALS IN PLAYOFFS:
63 — Frank McGee, Ottawa Silver Seven, in 22 playoff games. Seven goals in four games, 1903; 21 goals in eight games, 1904; 18 goals in four games, 1905; 17 goals in six games, 1906.

MOST GOALS, ONE PLAYOFF SERIES:
15 — Frank McGee, Ottawa Silver Seven, in two games in 1905 at Ottawa. Scored one goal, Jan. 13, in 9-2 victory over Dawson City and 14 goals, Jan. 16, in 23-2 victory.

MOST GOALS, ONE PLAYOFF GAME:
14 — Frank McGee, Ottawa Silver Seven, Jan. 16, 1905 at Ottawa in 23-2 victory over Dawson City.

FASTEST THREE GOALS:
40 Seconds — Marty Walsh, Ottawa Senators, at Ottawa, March 16, 1911, at 3:00, 3:10, and 3:40 of third period. Ottawa defeated Port Arthur 13-4.

All-Time Playoff Goal Leaders since 1918

(40 or more goals)

Player	Teams	Yrs.	GP	G
Wayne Gretzky	Edm., L.A., St.L., NYR	16	208	122
*Mark Messier	Edm., NYR, Van.	17	236	109
Jari Kurri	Edm., L.A., NYR, Ana., Col.	15	200	106
Glenn Anderson	Edm., Tor., NYR, St.L.	15	225	93
*Brett Hull	Cgy., St.L., Dal.	16	163	90
Mike Bossy	NYI	10	129	85
Maurice Richard	Mtl.	15	133	82
*Claude Lemieux	Mtl., N.J., Col., Phx.	15	221	80
Jean Beliveau	Mtl.	17	162	79
*Mario Lemieux	Pit.	8	107	76
Dino Ciccarelli	Min., Wsh., Det., T.B., Fla.	14	141	73
Esa Tikkanen	Edm., NYR, St.L., N.J., Van., Fla., Wsh.	13	186	72
Bryan Trottier	NYI, Pit.	17	221	71
Gordie Howe	Det., Hfd.	20	157	68
Denis Savard	Chi., Mtl., T.B.	16	169	66
*Jaromir Jagr	Pit.	11	140	65
Yvan Cournoyer	Mtl.	12	147	64
Brian Propp	Phi., Bos., Min., Hfd.	13	160	64
Bobby Smith	Min., Mtl.	13	184	64
Bobby Hull	Chi., Wpg., Hfd.	14	119	62
Phil Esposito	Chi., Bos., NYR	15	130	61
Jacques Lemaire	Mtl.	11	145	61
*Steve Yzerman	Det.	16	154	61
Joe Mullen	St.L., Cgy., Pit., Bos.	15	143	60
Stan Mikita	Chi.	18	155	59
Paul Coffey	Edm., Pit., L.A., Det., Hfd., Phi., Chi., Car., Bos.	16	194	59
Guy Lafleur	Mtl., NYR, Que.	14	128	58
Bernie Geoffrion	Mtl., NYR	16	132	58
Cam Neely	Van., Bos.	9	93	57
*Joe Nieuwendyk	Cgy., Dal.	13	127	57
*Joe Sakic	Que., Col.	8	114	56
Steve Larmer	Chi., NYR	13	140	56
*Doug Gilmour	St.L., Cgy., Tor., N.J., Chi., Buf.	16	170	56
Denis Potvin	NYI	14	185	56
Rick MacLeish	Phi., Hfd., Pit., Det.	11	114	54
Bill Barber	Phi.	11	129	53
Stephane Richer	Mtl., N.J., T.B., St.L.	12	131	53
*Luc Robitaille	L.A., Pit., NYR	13	132	53
*Rick Tocchet	Phi., Pit., L.A., Bos., Wsh., Phx.	13	145	52
Frank Mahovlich	Tor., Det., Mtl.	14	137	51
Brian Bellows	Min., Mtl., T.B., Ana., Wsh.	13	143	51
Steve Shutt	Mtl., L.A.	12	99	50
*Steve Thomas	Tor., Chi., NYI, N.J.	13	142	49
Henri Richard	Mtl.	18	180	49
Reggie Leach	Bos., Cal., Phi., Det.	8	94	47
Ted Lindsay	Det., Chi.	16	133	47
Clark Gillies	NYI, Buf.	13	164	47
*Kevin Stevens	Pit., Bos., L.A., NYR, Phi.	7	103	46
Dickie Moore	Mtl., Tor., St.L.	14	135	46
Rick Middleton	NYR, Bos.	12	114	45
*Mike Modano	Min., Dal.	10	127	45
*Jeremy Roenick	Chi., Phx.	12	100	44
Lanny McDonald	Tor., Col., Cgy.	13	117	44
*Sergei Fedorov	Det.	11	135	44
Ken Linseman	Phi., Edm., Bos., Tor.	11	113	43
Mike Gartner	Wsh., Min., NYR, Tor., Phx.	15	122	43
*Peter Forsberg	Que., Col.	7	95	42
*Brendan Shanahan	N.J., St.L., Hfd., Det.	12	112	42
*Vyacheslav Kozlov	Det.	9	114	42
Bernie Nicholls	L.A., NYR, Edm., N.J., Chi., S.J.	13	118	42
Bobby Clarke	Phi.	13	136	42
Dale Hunter	Que., Wsh., Col.	18	186	42
John Bucyk	Det., Bos.	14	124	41
Raymond Bourque	Bos., Col.	21	214	41
Tim Kerr	Phi., NYR, Hfd.	10	81	40
Peter McNab	Buf., Bos., Van., N.J.	10	107	40
*Ron Francis	Hfd., Pit., Car.	15	136	40
Bob Bourne	NYI, L.A.	13	139	40
John Tonelli	NYI, Cgy., L.A., Chi., Que.	13	172	40

* Active

All-Time Playoff Assist Leaders since 1918

(60 or more assists)

Player	Teams	Yrs.	GP	A
Wayne Gretzky	Edm., L.A., St.L., NYR	16	208	260
*Mark Messier	Edm., NYR, Van.	17	236	186
Raymond Bourque	Bos., Col.	21	214	139
Paul Coffey	Edm., Pit., L.A., Det., Hfd., Phi., Chi., Car., Bos.	16	194	137
Jari Kurri	Edm., L.A., NYR, Ana., Col.	15	200	127
*Doug Gilmour	St.L., Cgy., Tor., N.J., Chi., Buf.	16	170	122
Glenn Anderson	Edm., Tor., NYR, St.L.	15	225	121
Larry Robinson	Mtl., L.A.	20	227	116
*Larry Murphy	L.A., Wsh., Min., Pit., Tor., Det.	20	215	115
*Al MacInnis	Cgy., St.L.	17	164	113
Bryan Trottier	NYI, Pit.	17	221	113
Denis Savard	Chi., Mtl., T.B.	16	169	109
Denis Potvin	NYI	14	185	108
*Adam Oates	Det., St.L., Bos., Wsh.	13	137	103
*Sergei Fedorov	Det.	11	135	97
Jean Beliveau	Mtl.	17	162	97
*Mario Lemieux	Pit.	8	107	96
Bobby Smith	Min., Mtl.	13	184	96
*Chris Chelios	Mtl., Chi., Det.	17	187	93
Gordie Howe	Det., Hfd.	20	157	92
*Steve Yzerman	Det.	16	154	91
Stan Mikita	Chi.	18	155	91
Brad Park	NYR, Bos., Det.	17	161	90
Craig Janney	Bos., St.L., S.J., Wpg., Phx., T.B., NYI	11	120	86
*Scott Stevens	Wsh., St.L., N.J.	18	203	86
Brian Propp	Phi., Bos., Min., Hfd.	13	160	84
*Ron Francis	Hfd., Pit., Car.	15	136	83
*Jaromir Jagr	Pit.	11	140	82
Henri Richard	Mtl.	18	180	80
Jacques Lemaire	Mtl.	11	145	78
Ken Linseman	Phi., Edm., Bos., Tor.	11	113	77
Bobby Clarke	Phi.	13	136	77
*Claude Lemieux	Mtl., N.J., Col., Phx.	15	221	77
Guy Lafleur	Mtl., NYR, Que.	14	128	76
Phil Esposito	Chi., Bos., NYR	15	130	76
*Brett Hull	Cgy., St.L., Dal.	16	163	76
Dale Hunter	Que., Wsh., Col.	18	186	76
Mike Bossy	NYI	10	129	75
Steve Larmer	Chi., NYR	13	140	75
John Tonelli	NYI, Cgy., L.A., Chi., Que.	13	172	75
*Joe Sakic	Que., Col.	8	114	73
Peter Stastny	Que., N.J., St.L.	12	93	72
Bernie Nicholls	L.A., NYR, Edm., N.J., Chi., S.J.	13	118	72
Brian Bellows	Min., Mtl., T.B., Ana., Wsh.	13	143	71
Gilbert Perreault	Buf.	11	90	70
Geoff Courtnall	Bos., Edm., Wsh., St.L., Van.	15	156	70
Dale Hawerchuk	Wpg., Buf., St.L., Phi.	15	97	69
Alex Delvecchio	Det.	14	121	69
*Sergei Zubov	NYR, Pit., Dal.	8	125	68
Bobby Hull	Chi., Wpg., Hfd.	14	119	67
Frank Mahovlich	Tor., Det., Mtl.	14	137	67
Bobby Orr	Bos., Chi.	8	74	66
Bernie Federko	St.L., Det.	11	91	66
*Peter Forsberg	Que., Col.	7	95	66
Jean Ratelle	NYR, Bos.	15	123	66
Charlie Huddy	Edm., L.A., Buf., St.L.	14	183	66
*Mike Modano	Min., Dal.	10	127	64
*Nicklas Lidstrom	Det.	10	129	64
*Luc Robitaille	L.A., Pit., NYR	13	132	64
Dickie Moore	Mtl., Tor., St.L.	14	135	64
Doug Harvey	Mtl., NYR, Det., St.L.	15	137	64
Neal Broten	Min., Dal., N.J., L.A.	13	135	63
Yvan Cournoyer	Mtl.	12	147	63
John Bucyk	Det., Bos.	14	124	62
*Brian Leetch	NYR	7	82	61
Doug Wilson	Chi., S.J.	12	95	61
*Sandis Ozolinsh	S.J., Col., Car.	8	113	61
*Kevin Stevens	Pit., Bos., L.A., NYR, Phi.	7	103	60
*Igor Larionov	Van., S.J., Det., Fla.	10	127	60
Bernie Geoffrion	Mtl., NYR	16	132	60
*Rick Tocchet	Phi., Pit., L.A., Bos., Wsh., Phx.	13	145	60
Esa Tikkanen	Edm., NYR, St.L., N.J., Van., Fla., Wsh.	13	186	60

All-Time Playoff Point Leaders since 1918

(100 or more points)

Player	Teams	Yrs.	GP	G	A	Pts.
Wayne Gretzky	Edm., L.A., St.L., NYR	16	208	122	260	382
*Mark Messier	Edm., NYR, Van.	17	236	109	186	295
Jari Kurri	Edm., L.A., NYR, Ana., Col.	15	200	106	127	233
Glenn Anderson	Edm., Tor., NYR, St.L.	15	225	93	121	214
Paul Coffey	Edm., Pit., L.A., Det., Hfd., Phi., Chi., Car., Bos.	16	194	59	137	196
Bryan Trottier	NYI, Pit.	17	221	71	113	184
Raymond Bourque	Bos., Col.	21	214	41	139	180
*Doug Gilmour	St.L., Cgy., Tor., N.J., Chi., Buf.	16	170	56	122	178
Jean Beliveau	Mtl.	17	162	79	97	176
Denis Savard	Chi., Mtl., T.B.	16	169	66	109	175
*Mario Lemieux	Pit.	8	107	76	96	172
*Brett Hull	Cgy., St.L., Dal.	16	163	90	76	166
Denis Potvin	NYI	14	185	56	108	164
Mike Bossy	NYI	10	129	85	75	160
Gordie Howe	Det., Hfd.	20	157	68	92	160
Bobby Smith	Min., Mtl.	13	184	64	96	160
*Claude Lemieux	Mtl., N.J., Col., Phx.	15	221	80	77	157
*Steve Yzerman	Det.	16	154	61	91	152
*Al MacInnis	Cgy., St.L.	17	164	39	113	152
*Larry Murphy	L.A., Wsh., Min., Pit., Tor., Det.	20	215	37	115	152
Stan Mikita	Chi.	18	155	59	91	150
Brian Propp	Phi., Bos., Min., Hfd.	13	160	64	84	148
*Jaromir Jagr	Pit.	11	140	65	82	147
Larry Robinson	Mtl., L.A.	20	227	28	116	144
*Sergei Fedorov	Det.	11	135	44	97	141
*Adam Oates	Det., St.L., Bos., Wsh.	13	137	38	103	141
Jacques Lemaire	Mtl.	11	145	61	78	139
Phil Esposito	Chi., Bos., NYR	15	130	61	76	137
Guy Lafleur	Mtl., NYR, Que.	14	128	58	76	134
Esa Tikkanen	Edm., NYR, St.L., N.J., Van., Fla., Wsh.	13	186	72	60	132
Steve Larmer	Chi., NYR	13	140	56	75	131
*Joe Sakic	Que., Col.	8	114	56	73	129
Bobby Hull	Chi., Wpg., Hfd.	14	119	62	67	129
Henri Richard	Mtl.	18	180	49	80	129
Yvan Cournoyer	Mtl.	12	147	64	63	127
Maurice Richard	Mtl.	15	133	82	44	126
Brad Park	NYR, Bos., Det.	17	161	35	90	125
*Ron Francis	Hfd., Pit., Car.	15	136	40	83	123
Brian Bellows	Min., Mtl., T.B., Ana., Wsh.	13	143	51	71	122
*Chris Chelios	Mtl., Chi., Det.	17	187	29	93	122
Ken Linseman	Phi., Edm., Bos., Tor.	11	113	43	77	120
Bobby Clarke	Phi.	13	136	42	77	119
Bernie Geoffrion	Mtl., NYR	16	132	58	60	118
Frank Mahovlich	Tor., Det., Mtl.	14	137	51	67	118
Dino Ciccarelli	Min., Wsh., Det., T.B., Fla.	14	141	73	45	118
Dale Hunter	Que., Wsh., Col.	18	186	42	76	118
*Luc Robitaille	L.A., Pit., NYR	13	132	53	64	117
John Tonelli	NYI, Cgy., L.A., Chi., Que.	13	172	40	75	115
Bernie Nicholls	L.A., NYR, Edm., N.J., Chi., S.J.	13	118	42	72	114
*Rick Tocchet	Phi., Pit., L.A., Bos., Wsh., Phx.	13	145	52	60	112
Craig Janney	Bos., St.L., S.J., Wpg., Phx., T.B., NYI	11	120	24	86	110
Dickie Moore	Mtl., Tor., St.L.	14	135	46	64	110
*Mike Modano	Min., Dal.	10	127	45	64	109
Geoff Courtnall	Bos., Edm., Wsh., St.L., Van.	15	156	39	70	109
*Scott Stevens	Wsh., St.L., N.J.	18	203	23	86	109
*Peter Forsberg	Que., Col.	7	95	42	66	108
Bill Barber	Phi	11	129	53	55	108
Rick MacLeish	Phi., Hfd., Pit., Det.	11	114	54	53	107
*Kevin Stevens	Pit., Bos., L.A., NYR, Phi.	7	103	46	60	106
Joe Mullen	St.L., Cgy., Pit., Bos.	15	143	60	46	106
Peter Stastny	Que., N.J., St.L.	12	93	33	72	105
Alex Delvecchio	Det.	14	121	35	69	104
Gilbert Perreault	Buf.	11	90	33	70	103
John Bucyk	Det., Bos.	14	124	41	62	103
Bernie Federko	St.L., Det.	11	91	35	66	101
Rick Middleton	NYR, Bos.	12	114	45	55	100
*Joe Nieuwendyk	Cgy., Dal.	13	127	57	43	100

Three-or-more-Goal Games, Playoffs 1918–2001

Player	Team	Date	City	Total Goals	Opposing Goaltender	Score	
Wayne Gretzky (10)	Edm.	Apr. 11/81	Edm.	3	Richard Sevigny	Edm. 6	Mtl. 2
		Apr. 19/81	Edm.	3	Billy Smith	Edm. 5	NYI 2
		Apr. 6/83	Edm.	4	Brian Hayward	Edm. 6	Wpg. 3
		Apr. 17/83	Cgy.	4	Rejean Lemelin	Edm. 10	Cgy. 2
		Apr. 25/85	Wpg.	3	Bryan Hayward (2) Marc Behrend (1)	Edm. 8	Wpg. 3
		May 25/85	Edm.	3	Pelle Lindbergh	Edm. 4	Phi. 3
		Apr. 24/86	Cgy.	3	Mike Vernon	Edm. 7	Cgy. 4
	L.A.	May 29/93	Tor.	3	Felix Potvin	L.A. 5	Tor. 4
	NYR	Apr. 23/97	NYR	3	John Vanbiesbrouck	NYR 3	Fla. 2
		May 18/97	Phi.	3	Garth Snow	NYR 5	Phi. 4
Maurice Richard (7)	Mtl.	Mar. 23/44	Mtl.	5	Paul Bibeault	Mtl. 5	Tor. 1
		Apr. 7/44	Chi.	3	Mike Karakas	Mtl. 3	Chi. 1
		Mar. 29/45	Mtl.	4	Frank McCool	Mtl. 10	Tor. 3
		Apr. 14/53	Bos.	3	Gord Henry	Mtl. 7	Bos. 3
		Mar. 20/56	Mtl.	3	Gump Worsley	Mtl. 7	NYR 1
		Apr. 6/57	Mtl.	4	Don Simmons	Mtl. 5	Bos. 1
		Apr. 1/58	Det.	3	Terry Sawchuk	Mtl. 4	Det. 3
Jari Kurri (7)	Edm.	Apr. 4/84	Edm.	3	Doug Soetaert (1) Mike Veisor (2)	Edm. 9	Wpg. 2
		Apr. 25/85	Wpg.	3	Brian Hayward (2) Marc Behrend (1)	Edm. 8	Wpg. 3
		May 7/85	Edm.	3	Murray Bannerman	Edm. 7	Chi. 3
		May 14/85	Edm.	3	Murray Bannerman	Edm. 10	Chi. 5
		May 16/85	Chi.	4	Murray Bannerman	Edm. 8	Chi. 2
		Apr. 9/87	Edm.	4	Rollie Melanson (2) Darren Eliot (2)	Edm. 13	L.A. 3
		May 18/90	Bos.	3	Andy Moog (2) Reggie Lemelin (1)	Edm. 7	Bos. 2
Dino Ciccarelli (6)	Min.	May 5/81	Min.	3	Pat Riggin	Min. 7	Cgy. 4
		Apr. 10/82	Min.	3	Murray Bannerman	Min. 7	Chi. 1
	Wsh.	Apr. 5/90	N.J.	3	Sean Burke	Wsh. 5	N.J. 4
		Apr. 25/92	Pit.	4	Tom Barrasso (1) Ken Wreggett (3)	Wsh. 7	Pit. 2
	Det.	Apr. 29/93	Tor.	3	Felix Potvin (2) Daren Puppa (1)	Det. 7	Tor. 3
		May 11/95	Dal.	3	Andy Moog (2) Darcy Wakaluk (1)	Det. 5	Dal. 1
Mike Bossy (5)	NYI	Apr. 16/79	NYI	3	Tony Esposito	NYI 6	Chi. 2
		May 8/82	NYI	3	Richard Brodeur	NYI 6	Van. 5
		Apr. 10/83	Wsh.	3	Al Jensen	NYI 6	Wsh. 3
		May 3/83	NYI	3	Pete Peeters	NYI 8	Bos. 3
		May 7/83	NYI	4	Pete Peeters	NYI 8	Bos. 4
Phil Esposito (4)	Bos.	Apr. 2/69	Bos.	4	Bruce Gamble	Bos. 10	Tor. 0
		Apr. 8/70	Bos.	3	Ed Giacomin	Bos. 8	NYR 2
		Apr. 19/70	Chi.	3	Tony Esposito	Bos. 6	Chi. 3
		Apr. 8/75	Bos.	3	Tony Esposito (2) Michel Dumas (1)	Bos. 8	Chi. 2
Mark Messier (4)	Edm.	Apr. 14/83	Edm.	4	Reggie Lemelin	Edm. 6	Cgy. 3
		Apr. 17/83	Cgy.	3	Reggie Lemelin (1) Don Edwards (2)	Edm. 10	Cgy. 2
		Apr. 26/83	Edm.	3	Murray Bannerman	Edm. 8	Chi. 2
	NYR	May 25/94	N.J.	3	Martin Brodeur (2) ENG (1)	NYR 4	N.J. 2
Steve Yzerman (4)	Det.	Apr. 6/89	Det.	3	Alain Chevrier	Chi. 5	Det. 4
		Apr. 4/91	St. L.	3	Vincent Riendeau (2)	Det. 6	St. L. 3
		May 8/96	St. L.	3	Jon Casey	St.L. 5	Det. 4
		Apr. 21/99	Det.	3	Guy Hebert (2) Pat Jablonski (1)	Det.. 5	Ana. 3
Bernie Geoffrion (3)	Mtl.	Mar. 27/52	Mtl.	3	Jim Henry	Mtl. 4	Bos. 0
		Apr. 7/55	Mtl.	3	Terry Sawchuk	Mtl. 4	Det. 2
		Mar. 30/57	Mtl.	3	Gump Worsley	Mtl. 8	NYR 3
Norm Ullman (3)	Det.	Mar. 29/64	Chi.	3	Glenn Hall	Det. 5	Chi. 4
		Apr. 7/64	Det.	3	Glenn Hall (2) Denis DeJordy (1)	Det. 7	Chi. 2
		Apr. 11/65	Det.	3	Glenn Hall	Det. 4	Chi. 2
John Bucyk (3)	Bos.	May 3/70	St. L.	3	Jacques Plante (1) Ernie Wakely (2)	Bos. 6	St. L. 1
		Apr. 20/72	Bos.	3	Jacques Caron (1) Ernie Wakely (2)	Bos. 10	St. L. 2
		Apr. 21/74	Bos.	3	Tony Esposito	Bos. 8	Chi. 6
Rick MacLeish (3)	Phi.	Apr. 11/74	Phi.	3	Phil Myre	Phi. 5	Atl. 1
		Apr. 13/75	Phi.	3	Gord McRae	Phi. 6	Tor. 3
		May 13/75	Phi.	3	Chico Resch	Phi. 4	NYI 1
Denis Savard (3)	Chi.	Apr. 19/82	Chi.	3	Mike Liut	Chi. 7	StL. 4
		Apr. 10/86	Chi.	4	Ken Wregget	Tor. 6	Chi. 4
		Apr. 9/88	St. L.	3	Greg Millen	Chi. 6	St. L. 3
Tim Kerr (3)	Phi.	Apr. 13/85	NYR	4	Glen Hanlon	Phi. 6	NYR 5
		Apr. 20/87	Phi.	3	Kelly Hrudey	Phi. 4	NYI 2
		Apr. 19/89	Pit.	3	Tom Barrasso	Phi. 4	Pit. 2
Cam Neely (3)	Bos.	Apr. 9/87	Mtl.	3	Patrick Roy	Mtl. 4	Bos. 3
		Apr. 5/91	Bos.	3	Peter Sidorkiewicz	Bos. 4	Hfd. 3
		Apr. 25/91	Bos.	3	Patrick Roy	Bos. 4	Mtl. 1
Petr Klima (3)	Det.	Apr. 7/88	Tor.	3	Alan Bester (2) Ken Wregett (1)	Det. 6	Tor. 2
		Apr. 21/88	St. L.	3	Greg Millen	Det. 6	St. L. 0
	Edm.	May 4/91	Edm.	3	Jon Casey	Edm. 7	Min. 2
Esa Tikkanen (3)	Edm.	May 22/88	Edm.	3	Reggie Lemelin	Edm. 6	Bos. 3
		Apr. 16/91	Cgy.	3	Mike Vernon	Edm. 5	Cgy. 4
		Apr. 26/92	L.A.	3	Kelly Hrudey	Edm. 5	L.A. 2
					Tom Askey (1)		
Mario Lemieux (3)	Pit.	Apr. 25/89	Pit.	5	Ron Hextall	Pit. 10	Phi. 7
		Apr. 23/92	Pit.	3	Don Beaupre	Pit. 6	Wsh. 4
		May 11/96	Pit.	3	Mike Richter	Pit. 7	NYR 3
Mike Gartner (3)	NYR	Apr. 13/90	NYR	3	Mark Fitzpatrick (2) Glenn Healy (1)	NYR 6	NYI 5
		Apr. 27/92	NYR	3	Chris Terreri	NYR 8	N.J. 5
	Tor.	Apr. 25/96	Tor.	3	Jon Casey	Tor. 5	St.L. 4

Player	Team	Date	City	Total Goals	Opposing Goaltender	Score	
Newsy Lalonde (2)	Mtl.	Mar. 1/19	Mtl.	5	Clint Benedict	Mtl. 6	Ott. 3
		Mar. 22/19	Sea.	4	Harry Holmes	Mtl. 4	Sea. 2
Howie Morenz (2)	Mtl.	Mar. 22/24	Mtl.	3	Charles Reid	Mtl. 6	Cgy.T. 1
		Mar. 27/25	Mtl.	3	Harry Holmes	Mtl. 4	Vic. 2
Toe Blake (2)	Mtl.	Mar. 22/38	Mtl.	3	Mike Karakas	Mtl. 6	Chi. 4
		Mar. 26/46	Chi.	3	Mike Karakas	Mtl. 7	Chi. 2
Doug Bentley (2)	Chi.	Mar. 28/44	Chi.	3	Connie Dion	Chi. 7	Det. 1
		Mar. 30/44	Det.	3	Connie Dion	Chi. 5	Det. 2
Ted Kennedy (2)	Tor.	Apr. 14/45	Tor.	3	Harry Lumley	Det. 5	Tor. 3
		Mar. 27/48	Tor.	4	Frank Brimsek	Tor. 5	Bos. 3
Bobby Hull (2)	Chi.	Apr. 7/63	Det.	3	Terry Sawchuk	Det. 7	Chi. 4
		Apr. 9/72	Pit.	3	Jim Rutherford	Chi. 6	Pit. 5
F. St. Marseille (2)	St. L.	Apr. 28/70	St. L.	3	Al Smith	St. L. 5	Pit. 0
		Apr. 6/72	Min.	3	Cesare Maniago	Min. 6	St. L. 5
Pit Martin (2)	Chi.	Apr. 4/73	Chi.	3	Wayne Stephenson	Chi. 7	St. L. 1
		May 10/73	Chi.	3	Ken Dryden	Mtl. 6	Chi. 4
Yvan Cournoyer (2)	Mtl.	Apr. 5/73	Mtl.	3	Dave Dryden	Mtl. 7	Buf. 3
		Apr. 11/74	Mtl.	3	Ed Giacomin	Mtl. 4	NYR 1
Guy Lafleur (2)	Mtl.	May 1/75	Mtl.	3	Roger Crozier (1) Gerry Desjardins (2)	Mtl. 7	Buf. 0
		Apr. 11/77	Mtl.	3	Ed Staniowski	Mtl. 7	St. L. 2
Lanny McDonald (2)	Tor.	Apr. 9/77	Pit.	3	Denis Herron	Tor. 5	Pit. 2
		Apr. 17/77	Tor.	4	Wayne Stephenson	Phi. 6	Tor. 5
Butch Goring (2)	L.A.	Apr. 9/77	L.A.	3	Phil Myre	L.A. 4	Atl. 2
	NYI	May 17/81	Min.	3	Gilles Meloche	NYI 7	Min. 5
Bryan Trottier (2)	NYI	Apr. 8/80	NYI	3	Doug Keans	NYI 8	L.A. 1
		Apr. 9/81	NYI	3	Michel Larocque	NYI 5	Tor. 1
Bill Barber (2)	Phi.	May 4/80	Min.	4	Gilles Meloche	Phi. 5	Min. 3
		Apr. 9/81	Phi.	3	Dan Bouchard	Phi. 8	Que. 5
Brian Propp (2)	Phi.	Apr. 22/81	Phi.	3	Pat Riggin	Phi. 9	Cgy. 4
		Apr. 21/85	Phi.	3	Billy Smith	Phi. 5	NYI 2
Paul Reinhart (2)	Cgy	Apr. 14/83	Edm.	3	Andy Moog	Edm. 6	Cgy. 3
		Apr. 8/84	Van	3	Richard Brodeur	Cgy. 5	Van. 1
Peter Stastny (2)	Que.	Apr. 5/83	Bos.	3	Pete Peeters	Bos. 4	Que. 3
		Apr. 11/87	Que.	3	Mike Liut (2) Steve Weeks (1)	Que. 5	Hfd. 1
Glenn Anderson (2)	Edm.	Apr. 26/83	Edm.	4	Murray Bannerman	Edm. 8	Chi. 2
		Apr. 6/88	Wpg.	3	Daniel Berthiaume	Edm. 7	Wpg. 4
Michel Goulet (2)	Que.	Apr. 23/85	Que.	3	Steve Penney	Que. 7	Mtl. 6
		Apr. 12/87	Que.	3	Mike Liut	Que. 4	Hfd. 1
Peter Zezel (2)	Phi.	Apr. 13/86	NYR	3	John Vanbiesbrouck	Phi. 7	NYR 1
	St. L.	Apr. 11/89	St. L.	3	Jon Casey (2) Kari Takko (1)	St. L. 6	Min. 1
Geoff Courtnall (2)	Van.	Apr. 4/91	L.A.	3	Kelly Hrudey	Van. 6	L.A. 5
		Apr. 30/92	Van.	3	Rick Tabaracci	Van. 5	Win. 0
Joe Sakic (2)	Que.	May 6/95	Que.	3	Mike Richter	Que. 5	NYR 4
	Col.	Apr. 25/96	Col.	3	Corey Hirsch	Col. 5	Van. 4
Daniel Alfredsson (2)	Ott.	Apr. 28/98	Ott.	3	Martin Brodeur	Ott. 4	N.J. 3
		May 11/98	Ott.	3	Olaf Kolzig	Ott. 4	Wsh. 3
Harry Meeking	Tor.	Mar. 11/18	Tor.	3	Georges Vezina	Tor. 7	Mtl. 3
Alf Skinner	Tor.	Mar. 23/18	Tor.	3	Hugh Lehman	Van.M. 6	Tor. 4
Joe Malone	Mtl.	Feb. 23/19	Mtl.	3	Clint Benedict	Mtl. 8	Ott. 4
Odie Cleghorn	Mtl.	Feb. 27/19	Ott.	3	Clint Benedict	Mtl. 5	Ott. 3
Jack Darragh	Ott.	Apr. 1/20	Tor.	3	Harry Holmes	Ott. 6	Sea. 1
George Boucher	Ott.	Mar. 10/21	Ott.	3	Jake Forbes	Ott. 5	Tor. 0
Babe Dye	Tor.	Mar. 28/22	Tor.	4	Hugh Lehman	Tor. 5	Van.M. 1
Percy Galbraith	Bos.	Mar. 31/27	Bos.	3	Hugh Lehman	Bos. 4	Chi. 4
Busher Jackson	Tor.	Apr. 5/32	NYR	3	John Ross Roach	Tor. 6	NYR 4
Frank Boucher	NYR	Apr. 9/32	Tor.	3	Lorne Chabot	Tor. 6	NYR 4
Charlie Conacher	Tor.	Mar. 26/36	Tor.	3	Tiny Thompson	Tor. 8	Bos. 3
Syd Howe	Det.	Mar. 23/39	Det.	3	Claude Bourque	Det. 7	Mtl. 3
Bryan Hextall Sr.	NYR	Apr. 3/40	NYR	3	Turk Broda	NYR 6	Tor. 2
Joe Benoit	Mtl.	Mar. 22/41	Mtl.	3	Sam LoPresti	Mtl. 4	Chi. 3
Syl Apps Sr.	Tor.	Mar. 25/41	Tor.	3	Frank Brimsek	Tor. 7	Bos. 2
Jack McGill	Bos.	Mar. 29/42	Bos.	3	Johnny Mowers	Det. 6	Bos. 4
Don Metz	Tor.	Apr. 14/42	Tor.	3	Johnny Mowers	Tor. 9	Det. 3
Mud Bruneteau	Det.	Apr. 1/43	Det.	3	Frank Brimsek	Det. 6	Bos. 2
Don Grosso	Det.	Apr. 7/43	Bos.	3	Frank Brimsek	Det. 4	Bos. 0
Carl Liscombe	Det.	Apr. 3/45	Bos.	4	Paul Bibeault	Det. 5	Bos. 3
Billy Reay	Mtl.	Apr. 1/47	Bos.	4	Frank Brimsek	Mtl. 5	Bos. 1
Gerry Plamondon	Mtl.	Mar. 24/49	Det.	3	Harry Lumley	Mtl. 4	Det. 3
Sid Smith	Tor.	Apr. 10/49	Det.	3	Harry Lumley	Tor. 3	Det. 1
Pentti Lund	NYR	Apr. 2/50	NYR	3	Bill Durnan	NYR 4	Mtl. 1
Ted Lindsay	Det.	Apr. 5/55	Det.	4	Charlie Hodge (1) Jacques Plante (3)	Det. 7	Mtl. 1
Gordie Howe	Det.	Apr. 10/55	Det.	3	Jacques Plante	Det. 5	Mtl. 1
Phil Goyette	Mtl.	Mar. 25/58	Mtl.	3	Terry Sawchuk	Mtl. 8	Det. 1
Jerry Toppazzini	Bos.	Apr. 5/58	Bos.	3	Gump Worsley	Bos. 8	NYR 2
Bob Pulford	Tor.	Apr. 19/62	Tor.	3	Glenn Hall	Tor. 8	Chi. 4
Dave Keon	Tor.	Apr. 9/64	Mtl.	3	Charlie Hodge	Tor. 3	Mtl. 1
Henri Richard	Mtl.	Apr. 20/67	Mtl.	3	Terry Sawchuk (2) Johnny Bower (1)	Mtl. 6	Tor. 2
Rosaire Paiement	Phi.	Apr. 13/68	Phi.	3	Glenn Hall (1) Seth Martin (2)	Phi. 6	St. L. 1
Jean Beliveau	Mtl.	Apr. 20/68	Mtl.	3	Denis DeJordy	Mtl. 4	Chi. 1
Red Berenson	St. L.	Apr. 15/69	St. L.	3	Gerry Desjardins	St. L. 4	L.A. 0
Ken Schinkel	Pit.	Apr. 11/70	Oak.	3	Gary Smith	Pit. 5	Oak. 2
Jim Pappin	Chi.	Apr. 11/71	Phi.	3	Bruce Gamble	Chi. 6	Phi. 2
Bobby Orr	Bos.	Apr. 11/71	Mtl.	3	Ken Dryden	Bos. 5	Mtl. 2
Jacques Lemaire	Mtl.	Apr. 20/71	Mtl.	3	Gump Worsley	Mtl. 7	Min. 2
Vic Hadfield	NYR	Apr. 22/71	NYR	3	Tony Esposito	NYR 4	Chi. 1
Fred Stanfield	Bos.	Apr. 18/72	Bos.	3	Jacques Caron	Bos. 6	St. L. 1
Ken Hodge	Bos.	Apr. 30/72	Bos.	3	Ed Giacomin	Bos. 6	NYR 5
Steve Vickers	NYR	Apr. 10/73	Bos.	3	Ross Brooks (2) Eddie Johnston (1)	NYR 6	Bos. 3
Dick Redmond	Chi.	Apr. 4/73	Chi.	3	Wayne Stephenson	Chi. 7	St. L. 1
Tom Williams	L.A.	Apr. 14/74	L.A.	3	Mike Veisor	L.A. 5	Chi. 1
Marcel Dionne	L.A.	Apr. 15/76	L.A.	3	Gilles Gilbert	L.A. 6	Bos. 4

Player	Team	Date	City	Total Goals	Opposing Goaltender	Score	
Don Saleski	Phi.	Apr. 20/76	Phi.	3	Wayne Thomas	Phi. 7	Tor. 1
Darryl Sittler	Tor.	Apr. 22/76	Tor.	5	Bernie Parent	Tor. 8	Phi. 5
Reggie Leach	Phi.	May 6/76	Phi.	5	Gilles Gilbert	Phi. 6	Bos. 3
Jim Lorentz	Buf.	Apr. 7/77	Min.	3	Pete LoPresti (2)		
					Gary Smith (1)	Buf. 7	Min. 1
Bobby Schmautz	Bos.	Apr. 11/77	Bos.	3	Rogie Vachon	Bos. 8	L.A. 3
Billy Harris	NYI	Apr. 23/77	Mtl.	3	Ken Dryden	Mtl. 4	NYI 3
George Ferguson	Tor.	Apr. 11/78	Tor.	3	Rogie Vachon	Tor. 7	L.A. 3
Jean Ratelle	Bos.	May 3/79	Bos.	3	Ken Dryden	Bos. 4	Mtl. 3
Stan Jonathan	Bos.	May 8/79	Bos.	3	Ken Dryden	Bos. 5	Mtl. 2
Ron Duguay	NYR	Apr. 20/80	NYR	3	Pete Peeters	NYR 4	Phi. 2
Steve Shutt	Mtl.	Apr. 22/80	Mtl.	3	Gilles Meloche	Mtl. 6	Min. 2
Gilbert Perreault	Buf.	May 6/80	NYI	3	Billy Smith (2)		
					ENG (1)	Buf. 7	NYI 4
Paul Holmgren	Phi.	May 15/80	Phil	3	Billy Smith	Phi. 8	NYI 3
Steve Payne	Min.	Apr. 8/81	Bos.	3	Rogie Vachon	Min. 5	Bos. 4
Denis Potvin	NYI	Apr. 17/81	NYI	3	Andy Moog	NYI 6	Edm. 3
Barry Pederson	Bos.	Apr. 8/82	Bos.	3	Don Edwards	Bos. 7	Buf. 3
Duane Sutter	NYI	Apr. 15/83	NYI	3	Glen Hanlon	NYI 5	NYR 0
Doug Halward	Van.	Apr. 7/84	Van.	3	Reggie Lemelin (2)		
					Don Edwards (1)	Van. 7	Cgy. 0
Jorgen Pettersson	St. L.	Apr. 8/84	Det.	3	Eddie Mio	St. L. 3	Det. 2
Clark Gillies	NYI	May 12/84	NYI	3	Grant Fuhr	NYI 6	Edm. 1
Ken Linseman	Bos.	Apr. 14/85	Bos.	3	Steve Penney	Bos. 7	Mtl. 6
Dave Andreychuk	Buf.	Apr. 14/85	Buf.	3	Dan Bouchard	Buf. 7	Que. 4
Greg Paslawski	St. L.	Apr. 15/86	Min.	3	Don Beaupre	St. L. 6	Min. 3
Doug Risebrough	Cgy.	May 4/86	Cgy.	3	Rick Wamsley	Cgy. 8	St. L. 2
Mike McPhee	Mtl.	Apr. 11/87	Bos.	3	Doug Keans	Mtl. 5	Bos. 4
John Ogrodnick	Que.	Apr. 14/87	Hfd.	3	Mike Liut	Que. 7	Hfd. 5
Pelle Eklund	Phi.	May 10/87	Mtl.	3	Patrick Roy (1)		
					Brian Hayward (2)	Phi. 6	Mtl. 3
John Tucker	Buf.	Apr. 9/88	Bos.	4	Andy Moog	Buf. 6	Bos. 2
Tony Hrkac	St. L.	Apr. 10/88	St. L.	4	Darren Pang	St. L. 6	Chi. 5
Hakan Loob	Cgy.	Apr. 10/88	Cgy.	3	Glenn Healy	Cgy. 7	L.A. 3
Ed Olczyk	Tor.	Apr. 12/88	Tor.	3	Greg Stefan (2)		
					Glen Hanlon (1)	Tor. 6	Det. 5
Aaron Broten	N.J.	Apr. 20/88	N.J.	3	Pete Peeters	N.J. 5	Wsh. 2
Mark Johnson	N.J.	Apr. 22/88	Wsh.	4	Pete Peeters	N.J. 10	Wsh. 4
Patrik Sundstrom	N.J.	Apr. 22/88	Wsh.	3	Pete Peeters (2)		
					Clint Malarchuk (1)	N.J. 10	Wsh. 4
Bob Brooke	Min.	Apr. 5/89	St. L.	3	Greg Millen	St. L. 4	Min. 3
Chris Kontos	L.A.	Apr. 6/89	L.A.	3	Grant Fuhr	L.A. 5	Edm. 2
Wayne Presley	Chi.	Apr. 13/89	Chi.	3	Greg Stefan (1)		
					Glen Hanlon (2)	Chi. 7	Det. 1
Tony Granato	L.A.	Apr. 10/90	L.A.	3	Mike Vernon (1)		
					Rick Wamsley (2)	L.A. 12	Cgy. 4
Tomas Sandstrom	L.A.	Apr. 10/90	L.A.	3	Mike Vernon (1)		
					Rick Wamsley (2)	L.A. 12	Cgy. 4
Dave Taylor	L.A.	Apr. 10/90	L.A.	3	Mike Vernon (1)		
					Rick Wamsley (2)	L.A. 12	Cgy. 4
Bernie Nicholls	NYR	Apr. 19/90	NYR	3	Mike Liut	NYR 7	Wsh. 3
John Druce	Wsh.	Apr. 21/90	NYR	3	John Vanbiesbrouck	Wsh. 6	NYR 3
Adam Oates	St. L.	Apr. 12/91	St. L.	3	Tim Chevaldae	St. L. 6	Det. 1
Luc Robitaille	L.A.	Apr. 26/91	L.A.	3	Grant Fuhr	L.A. 5	Edm. 2
Ron Francis	Pit.	May 9/92	Pit.	3	Mike Richter (2)		
					John V'brouck (1)	Pit. 5	NYR. 4
Dirk Graham	Chi.	June 1/92	Chi.	3	Tom Barrasso	Pit. 5	Chi. 2
Joe Murphy	Edm.	May 6/92	Edm.	3	Kirk McLean	Edm. 5	Van. 2
Ray Sheppard	Det.	Apr. 24/92	Min.	3	Jon Casey	Min. 5	Det. 2
Kevin Stevens	Pit.	May 21/92	Bos.	4	Andy Moog	Pit. 5	Bos. 2
Pavel Bure	Van.	Apr. 28/92	Wpg.	3	Rick Tabaracci	Van. 8	Wpg. 3
Brian Noonan	Chi.	Apr. 18/93	Chi.	3	Curtis Joseph	St. L. 4	Chi. 3
Dale Hunter	Wsh.	Apr. 20/93	Wsh.	3	Glenn Healy	NYI 5	Wsh. 4
Teemu Selanne	Wpg.	Apr. 23/93	Wpg.	3	Kirk McLean	Wpg. 5	Van. 4
Ray Ferraro	NYI	Apr. 26/93	Wsh.	4	Don Beaupre	Wsh. 6	NYI 4
Al Iafrate	Wsh.	Apr. 26/93	Wsh.	3	Glenn Healy (2)		
					Mark Fitzpatrick (1)	Wsh. 6	NYI 4
Paul Di Pietro	Mtl.	Apr. 28/93	Mtl.	3	Ron Hextall	Mtl. 6	Que. 2
Wendel Clark	Tor.	May 27/93	L.A.	3	Kelly Hrudey	L.A. 5	Tor. 4
Eric Desjardins	Mtl.	Jun. 3/93	Mtl.	3	Kelly Hrudey	Mtl. 3	L.A. 2
Tony Amonte	Chi.	Apr. 23/94	Chi.	4	Felix Potvin	Chi. 5	Tor. 4
Gary Suter	Chi.	Apr. 24/94	Chi.	3	Felix Potvin	Chi. 4	Tor. 3
Ulf Dahlen	S.J.	May 6/94	S.J.	3	Felix Potvin	S.J. 5	Tor. 2
Mike Sullivan	Cgy.	May 11/95	S.J.	3	Arturs Irbe (2)		
					Wade Flaherty (1)	Cgy. 9	S.J. 2
Theoren Fleury	Cgy.	May 13/95	S.J.	4	Arturs Irbe (3)		
					ENG (1)	Cgy. 6	S.J. 4
Brendan Shanahan	St. L.	May 13/95	Van.	3	Kirk McLean	St. L. 5	Van. 2
John LeClair	Phi.	May 21/95	Phi.	3	Mike Richter	Phi. 5	NYR 4
Brian Leetch	NYR	May 22/95	Phi.	3	Ron Hextall	Phi. 4	NYR 3
Trevor Linden	Van.	Apr. 25/96	Col.	3	Patrick Roy	Col. 5	Van. 4
Jaromir Jagr	Pit.	May 11/96	Pit.	3	Mike Richter	Pit. 7	NYR 3
Peter Forsberg	Col.	Jun. 6/96	Col.	3	John Vanbiesbrouck	Col. 8	Fla. 1
Valeri Zelepukin	N.J.	Apr. 22/97	Mtl.	3	Jocelyn Thibault	N.J. 6	Mtl. 4
Valeri Kamensky	Col.	Apr. 24/97	Col.	3	Jeff Hackett (2)		
					Chris Terreri (1)	Col. 7	Chi. 0
Eric Lindros	Phi.	May 20/97	NYR	3	Mike Richter	Phi. 6	NYR 3
Matthew Barnaby	Buf.	May 10/98	Buf.	3	Andy Moog (2)	Buf. 6	Mtl. 3
					ENG (1)		
Martin Straka	Pit.	Apr. 25/99	Pit.	3	Martin Brodeur	Pit. 4	N.J. 2
Martin Lapointe	Det.	Apr. 15/00	Det.	3	Stephane Fiset (2)	Det. 8	L.A. 5
					Jamie Storr (1)		
Doug Weight	Edm.	Apr. 16/00	Edm.	3	Ed Belfour	Edm. 5	Dal. 2
Bill Guerin	Edm.	Apr. 18/00	Edm.	3	Ed Belfour	Dal. 4	Edm. 3
Scott Young	St. L.	Apr. 23/00	S.J.	3	Steve Shields	St. L. 6	S.J. 2
Andy Delmore	Phi.	May 7/00	Phi.	3	Ron Tugnutt (2)	Phi. 6	Pit. 3
					Peter Skudra (1)		

Leading Playoff Scorers, 1918–2001

Season	Player and Club	Games Played	Goals	Assists	Points
2000-01	Joe Sakic, Colorado	21	13	13	26
99-2000	Brett Hull, Dallas	23	11	13	24
1998-99	Peter Forsberg, Colorado	19	8	16	24
1997-98	Steve Yzerman, Detroit	22	6	18	24
1996-97	Eric Lindros, Philadelphia	19	12	14	26
1995-96	Joe Sakic, Colorado	22	18	16	34
1994-95	Sergei Fedorov, Detroit	17	7	17	24
1993-94	Brian Leetch, NY Rangers	23	11	23	34
1992-93	Wayne Gretzky, Los Angeles	24	15	25	40
1991-92	Mario Lemieux, Pittsburgh	15	16	18	34
1990-91	Mario Lemieux, Pittsburgh	23	16	28	44
1989-90	Craig Simpson, Edmonton	22	16	15	31
	Mark Messier, Edmonton	22	9	22	31
1988-89	Al MacInnis, Calgary	22	7	24	31
1987-88	Wayne Gretzky, Edmonton	19	12	31	43
1986-87	Wayne Gretzky, Edmonton	21	5	29	34
1985-86	Doug Gilmour, St. Louis	19	9	12	21
	Bernie Federko, St. Louis	19	7	14	21
1984-85	Wayne Gretzky, Edmonton	18	17	30	47
1983-84	Wayne Gretzky, Edmonton	19	13	22	35
1982-83	Wayne Gretzky, Edmonton	16	12	26	38
1981-82	Bryan Trottier, NY Islanders	19	6	23	29
1980-81	Mike Bossy, NY Islanders	18	17	18	35
1979-80	Bryan Trottier, NY Islanders	21	12	17	29
1978-79	Jacques Lemaire, Montreal	16	11	12	23
	Guy Lafleur, Montreal	16	10	13	23
1977-78	Guy Lafleur, Montreal	15	10	11	21
	Larry Robinson, Montreal	15	4	17	21
1976-77	Guy Lafleur, Montreal	14	9	17	26
1975-76	Reggie Leach, Philadelphia	16	19	5	24
1974-75	Rick MacLeish, Philadelphia	17	11	9	20
1973-74	Rick MacLeish, Philadelphia	17	13	9	22
1972-73	Yvan Cournoyer, Montreal	17	15	10	25
1971-72	Phil Esposito, Boston	15	9	15	24
	Bobby Orr, Boston	15	5	19	24
1970-71	Frank Mahovlich, Montreal	20	14	13	27
1969-70	Phil Esposito, Boston	14	13	14	27
1968-69	Phil Esposito, Boston	10	8	10	18
1967-68	Bill Goldsworthy, Minnesota	14	8	7	15
1966-67	Jim Pappin, Toronto	12	7	8	15
1965-66	Norm Ullman, Detroit	12	6	9	15
1964-65	Bobby Hull, Chicago	14	10	7	17
1963-64	Gordie Howe, Detroit	14	9	10	19
1962-63	Gordie Howe, Detroit	11	7	9	16
	Norm Ullman, Detroit	11	4	12	16
1961-62	Stan Mikita, Chicago	12	6	15	21
1960-61	Gordie Howe, Detroit	11	4	11	15
	Pierre Pilote, Chicago	12	3	12	15
1959-60	Henri Richard, Montreal	8	3	9	12
	Bernie Geoffrion, Montreal	8	2	10	12
1958-59	Dickie Moore, Montreal	11	5	12	17
1957-58	Fleming Mackell, Boston	12	5	14	19
1956-57	Bernie Geoffrion, Montreal	11	11	7	18
1955-56	Jean Béliveau, Montreal	10	12	7	19
1954-55	Gordie Howe, Detroit	11	9	11	20
1953-54	Dickie Moore, Montreal	11	5	8	13
1952-53	Ed Sanford, Boston	11	8	3	11
1951-52	Ted Lindsay, Detroit	8	5	2	7
	Floyd Curry, Montreal	11	4	3	7
	Metro Prystai, Detroit	8	2	5	7
	Gordie Howe, Detroit	8	2	5	7
1950-51	Maurice Richard, Montreal	11	9	4	13
	Max Bentley, Toronto	11	2	11	13
1949-50	Pentti Lund, NY Rangers	12	6	5	11
1948-49	Gordie Howe, Detroit	11	8	3	11
1947-48	Ted Kennedy, Toronto	9	8	6	14
1946-47	Maurice Richard, Montreal	10	6	5	11
1945-46	Elmer Lach, Montreal	9	5	12	17
1944-45	Joe Carveth, Detroit	14	5	6	11
1943-44	Toe Blake, Montreal	9	7	11	18
1942-43	Carl Liscombe, Detroit	10	6	8	14
1941-42	Don Grosso, Detroit	12	8	6	14
1940-41	Milt Schmidt, Boston	11	5	6	11
1939-40	Phil Watson, NY Rangers	12	3	6	9
	Neil Colville, NY Rangers	12	2	7	9
1938-39	Bill Cowley, Boston	12	3	11	14
1937-38	Johnny Gottselig, Chicago	10	5	3	8
1936-37	Marty Barry, Detroit	10	4	7	11
1935-36	Frank Boll, Toronto	9	7	3	10
1934-35	Baldy Northcott, Mtl. Maroons	7	4	1	5
	Busher Jackson, Toronto	7	3	2	5
	Cy Wentworth, Mtl. Maroons	7	3	2	5
1933-34	Larry Aurie, Detroit	9	3	7	10
1932-33	Cecil Dillon, NY Rangers	8	8	2	10
1931-32	Frank Boucher, NY Rangers	7	3	6	9
1930-31	Cooney Weiland, Boston	5	6	3	9
1929-30	Marty Barry, Boston	6	3	3	6
	Cooney Weiland, Boston	6	1	5	6
1928-29	Andy Blair, Toronto	4	3	0	3
	Butch Keeling, NY Rangers	6	3	0	3
	Ace Bailey, Toronto	4	1	2	3
1927-28	Frank Boucher, NY Rangers	9	7	3	10
1926-27	Harry Oliver, Boston	8	4	2	6
	Percy Galbraith, Boston	8	3	3	6
	Frank Fredrickson, Boston	8	2	4	6
1925-26	Nels Stewart, Mtl. Maroons	8	6	3	9
1924-25	Howie Morenz, Montreal	6	7	1	8
1923-24	Howie Morenz, Montreal	6	7	2	9
1922-23	Punch Broadbent, Ottawa	8	6	1	7
1921-22	Babe Dye, Toronto	7	11	2	13
1920-21	Cy Denneny, Ottawa	7	4	2	6
1919-20	Frank Nighbor, Ottawa	5	6	1	7
	Jack Darragh, Ottawa	5	5	2	7
1918-19	Newsy Lalonde, Montreal	10	17	1	18
1917-18	Alf Skinner, Toronto	7	8	1	9

Overtime Games since 1918

Abbreviations: Teams/Cities: — **Ana.** - Anaheim; **Atl.** - Atlanta; **Bos.** - Boston; **Buf.** - Buffalo; **Cgy.** - Calgary; **Cgy. T.** - Calgary Tigers (Western Canada Hockey League); **Chi.** - Chicago; **Col.** - Colorado; **Dal.** - Dallas; **Det.** - Detroit; **Edm.** - Edmonton; **Edm. E.** - Edmonton Eskimos (WCHL); **Fla.** - Florida; **Hfd.** - Hartford; **K.C.** - Kansas City; **L.A.** - Los Angeles; **Min.** - Minnesota; **Mtl.** - Montreal; **Mtl.M.** - Montreal Maroons; **N.J.** - New Jersey; **NYA** - NY Americans; **NYI** - New York Islanders; **NYR** - New York Rangers; **Oak.** - Oakland; **Ott.** - Ottawa; **Phi.** - Philadelphia; **Phx.** - Phoenix; **Pit.** - Pittsburgh; **Que.** - Quebec; **St. L.** - St. Louis; **Sea.** - Seattle Metropolitans (Pacific Coast Hockey Association); **S.J.** - San Jose; **T.B.** - Tampa Bay; **Tor.** - Toronto; **Van.** - Vancouver; **Van. M** - Vancouver Millionaires (PCHA); **Vic.** - Victoria Cougars (WCHL); **Wpg.** - Winnipeg; **Wsh.** - Washington.

SERIES — **CF** - conference final; **CSF** - conference semi-final; **CQF** - conference quarter-final; **DF** - division final; **DSF** - division semi-final; **F** - final; **PR** - preliminary round; **QF** - quarter final; **SF** - semi-final.

Date	City	Series	Score		Scorer	Overtime	Series Winner
Mar. 26/19	Sea.	F	Mtl. 0	Sea. 0	no scorer	20:00	
Mar. 30/19	Sea.	F	Mtl. 4	Sea. 3	Odie Cleghorn	15:57	
Mar. 20/22	Tor.	F	Tor 2	Van.M. 1	Babe Dye	4:50	Tor.
Mar. 29/23	Van.	F	Ott. 2	Edm.E. 1	Cy Denneny	2:08	Ott.
Mar. 31/27	Mtl.	QF	Mtl. 1	Mtl. M. 0	Howie Morenz	12:05	Mtl.
Apr. 7/27	Bos.	F	Ott. 0	Bos. 0	no scorer	20:00	Ott.
Apr. 11/27	Ott.	F	Bos. 1	Ott. 1	no scorer	20:00	Ott.
Apr. 3/28	Mtl.	QF	Mtl. M. 1	Mtl. 0	Russ Oatman	8:20	Mtl. M.
Apr. 7/28	Mtl.	F	NYR 2	Mtl. M. 1	Frank Boucher	7:05	NYR
Mar. 21/29	NYR	QF	NYR 1	NYA 0	Butch Keeling	29:50	NYR
Mar. 26/29	Tor.	SF	NYR 2	Tor. 1	Frank Boucher	2:03	NYR
Mar. 20/30	Mtl.	SF	Bos. 2	Mtl. M. 1	Harry Oliver	45:35	Bos.
Mar. 25/30	Bos.	SF	Mtl. M. 1	Bos. 0	Archie Wilcox	26:27	Bos.
Mar. 26/30	Mtl.	QF	Chi. 2	Mtl. 2	Howie Morenz (Mtl.)	51:43	Mtl.
Mar. 28/30	Mtl.	SF	Mtl. 2	NYR 1	Gus Rivers	68:52	Mtl.
Mar. 24/31	Bos.	SF	Bos. 5	Mtl. 4	Cooney Weiland	18:56	Mtl.
Mar. 26/31	Chi.	QF	Chi. 2	Tor. 1	Stew Adams	19:20	Chi.
Mar. 28/31	Mtl.	SF	Mtl. 4	Bos. 3	Georges Mantha	5:10	Mtl.
Apr. 1/31	Mtl.	SF	Mtl. 3	Bos. 2	Wildor Larochelle	19:00	Mtl.
Apr. 5/31	Chi.	F	Chi. 2	Mtl. 1	Johnny Gottselig	24:50	Mtl.
Apr. 9/31	Mtl.	F	Chi. 3	Mtl. 2	Cy Wentworth	53:50	Mtl.
Mar. 26/32	Mtl.	SF	NYR 4	Mtl. 3	Fred Cook	59:32	NYR
Apr. 2/32	Tor.	SF	Tor. 3	Mtl. M. 2	Bob Gracie	17:59	Tor.
Mar. 25/33	Bos.	SF	Bos. 2	Tor. 1	Marty Barry	14:14	Tor.
Mar. 28/33	Bos.	SF	Tor. 1	Bos. 0	Busher Jackson	15:03	Tor.
Mar. 30/33	Tor.	SF	Bos. 2	Tor. 1	Eddie Shore	4:23	Tor.
Apr. 3/33	Tor.	SF	Tor. 1	Bos. 0	Ken Doraty	104:46	Tor.
Apr. 13/33	Tor.	F	NYR 1	Tor. 0	Bill Cook	7:33	NYR
Mar. 22/34	Tor.	SF	Det. 2	Tor. 1	Herbie Lewis	1:33	Det.
Mar. 25/34	Chi.	QF	Chi. 1	Mtl. 1	Mush March (Chi)	11:05	Chi.
Apr. 3/34	Det.	F	Chi. 2	Det. 1	Paul Thompson	21:10	Chi.
Apr. 10/34	Chi.	F	Chi. 1	Det. 0	Mush March	30:05	Chi.
Mar. 23/35	Bos.	SF	Bos. 1	Tor. 0	Dit Clapper	33:26	Tor.
Mar. 26/35	Chi.	QF	Mtl. M. 1	Chi. 0	Baldy Northcott	4:02	Mtl. M.
Mar. 30/35	Tor.	SF	Tor. 2	Bos. 1	Pep Kelly	1:36	Tor.
Apr. 4/35	Tor.	F	Mtl. M. 3	Tor. 2	Dave Trottier	5:28	Mtl. M.
Mar. 24/36	Mtl.	SF	Det. 1	Mtl. M. 0	Mud Bruneteau	116:30	Det.
Apr. 9/36	Tor.	F	Tor. 4	Det. 3	Buzz Boll	0:31	Det.
Mar. 25/37	NYR	QF	NYR 2	Tor. 1	Babe Pratt	13:05	NYR
Apr. 1/37	Mtl.	SF	Det. 2	Mtl. 1	Hec Kilrea	51:49	Det.
Mar. 22/38	NYR	QF	NYA 2	NYR 1	Johnny Sorrell	21:25	NYA
Mar. 24/38	Tor.	SF	Tor. 1	Bos. 0	George Parsons	21:31	Tor.
Mar. 26/38	Mtl.	QF	Chi. 3	Mtl. 2	Paul Thompson	11:49	Chi.
Mar. 27/38	NYR	QF	NYA 3	NYR 2	Lorne Carr	60:40	NYA
Mar. 29/38	Bos.	SF	Tor. 3	Bos. 2	Gordie Drillon	10:04	Tor.
Mar. 31/38	Chi.	SF	Chi. 1	NYA 0	Cully Dahlstrom	33:01	Chi.
Mar. 21/39	NYR	SF	Bos. 2	NYR 1	Mel Hill	59:25	Bos.
Mar. 23/39	Bos.	SF	Bos. 3	NYR 2	Mel Hill	8:24	Bos.
Mar. 26/39	Det.	QF	Det. 1	Mtl. 0	Marty Barry	7:47	Det.
Mar. 30/39	Bos.	SF	NYR 2	Bos. 1	Clint Smith	17:19	Bos.
Apr. 1/39	Tor.	SF	Tor. 5	Det. 4	Gordie Drillon	5:42	Tor.
Apr. 2/39	Bos.	SF	Bos. 2	NYR 1	Mel Hill	48:00	Bos.
Apr. 9/39	Bos.	F	Tor. 3	Bos. 2	Doc Romnes	10:38	Bos.
Mar. 19/40	Det.	QF	Det. 2	NYA 1	Syd Howe	0:25	Det.
Mar. 19/40	Tor.	QF	Tor. 3	Chi. 2	Syl Apps Sr.	6:35	Tor.
Apr. 2/40	NYR	F	NYR 2	Tor. 1	Alf Pike	15:30	NYR
Apr. 11/40	Tor.	F	NYR 2	Tor. 1	Muzz Patrick	31:43	NYR
Apr. 13/40	Tor.	F	NYR 3	Tor. 2	Bryan Hextall Sr.	2:07	NYR
Mar. 20/41	Det.	QF	Det. 2	NYR 1	Gus Giesebrecht	12:01	Det.
Mar. 22/41	Mtl.	QF	Mtl. 4	Chi. 3	Charlie Sands	34:04	Chi.
Mar. 29/41	Bos.	SF	Tor. 2	Bos. 1	Pete Langelle	17:31	Bos.
Mar. 30/41	Chi.	SF	Det. 2	Chi. 1	Gus Giesebrecht	9:15	Det.
Mar. 22/42	Chi.	QF	Bos. 2	Chi. 1	Des Smith	6:51	Bos.
Mar. 21/43	Bos.	SF	Bos. 5	Mtl. 4	Don Gallinger	12:30	Bos.
Mar. 23/43	Det.	SF	Tor. 3	Det. 2	Jack McLean	70:18	Det.
Mar. 25/43	Mtl.	SF	Bos. 3	Mtl. 2	Harvey Jackson	3:20	Bos.
Mar. 30/43	Tor.	SF	Det. 3	Tor. 2	Adam Brown	9:21	Det.
Mar. 30/43	Bos.	SF	Bos. 5	Mtl. 4	Ab DeMarco	3:41	Bos.
Apr. 13/44	Mtl.	F	Mtl. 5	Chi. 4	Toe Blake	9:12	Mtl.
Mar. 27/45	Tor.	SF	Tor. 4	Mtl. 3	Gus Bodnar	12:36	Tor.
Mar. 29/45	Det.	SF	Det. 3	Bos. 2	Mud Bruneteau	17:12	Det.
Apr. 21/45	Tor.	F	Det. 1	Tor. 0	Ed Bruneteau	14:16	Tor.
Mar. 28/46	Bos.	SF	Bos. 4	Det. 3	Don Gallinger	9:51	Bos.
Mar. 30/46	Mtl.	F	Mtl. 4	Bos. 3	Maurice Richard	9:08	Mtl.
Apr. 2/46	Mtl.	F	Mtl. 3	Bos. 2	Jim Peters	16:55	Mtl.
Apr. 7/46	Bos.	F	Bos. 3	Mtl. 2	Terry Reardon	15:13	Mtl.
Mar. 26/47	Tor.	SF	Tor. 3	Det. 2	Howie Meeker	3:05	Tor.
Mar. 27/47	Mtl.	SF	Mtl. 2	Bos. 1	Kenny Mosdell	5:38	Mtl.
Apr. 3/47	Mtl.	SF	Mtl. 4	Bos. 3	John Quilty	36:40	Mtl.
Apr. 15/47	Tor.	F	Tor. 2	Mtl. 1	Syl Apps Sr.	16:36	Tor.
Mar. 24/48	Tor.	SF	Tor. 5	Bos. 4	Nick Metz	17:03	Tor.
Mar. 22/49	Det.	SF	Det. 2	Mtl. 1	Max McNab	44:52	Det.
Mar. 24/49	Det.	SF	Mtl. 4	Det. 3	Gerry Plamondon	2:59	Det.
Mar. 26/49	Tor.	SF	Bos. 5	Tor. 4	Woody Dumart	16:14	Tor.
Apr. 8/49	Det.	F	Tor. 3	Det. 2	Joe Klukay	17:31	Tor.
Apr. 4/50	Tor.	SF	Det. 2	Tor. 1	Leo Reise Sr.	20:38	Det.
Apr. 4/50	Mtl.	SF	Mtl. 3	NYR 2	Elmer Lach	15:19	NYR
Apr. 9/50	Det.	SF	Det. 1	Tor. 0	Leo Reise	8:39	Det.
Apr. 18/50	Det.	F	NYR 4	Det. 3	Don Raleigh	8:34	Det.
Apr. 20/50	Det.	F	NYR 2	Det. 1	Don Raleigh	1:38	Det.
Apr. 23/50	Det.	F	Det. 4	NYR 3	Pete Babando	28:31	Det.
Mar. 27/51	Det.	SF	Mtl. 3	Det. 2	Maurice Richard	61:09	Mtl.
Mar. 29/51	Det.	SF	Mtl. 1	Det. 0	Maurice Richard	42:20	Mtl.
Mar. 31/51	Tor.	SF	Bos. 1	Tor. 1	no scorer	20:00	Tor.
Apr. 11/51	Tor.	F	Tor. 3	Mtl. 2	Sid Smith	5:51	Tor.
Apr. 14/51	Tor.	F	Mtl. 3	Tor. 2	Maurice Richard	2:55	Tor.
Apr. 17/51	Mtl.	F	Tor. 2	Mtl. 1	Ted Kennedy	4:47	Tor.
Apr. 19/51	Mtl.	F	Tor. 3	Mtl. 2	Harry Watson	5:15	Tor.
Apr. 21/51	Tor.	F	Tor. 3	Mtl. 2	Bill Barilko	2:53	Tor.
Apr. 6/52	Bos.	SF	Mtl. 3	Bos. 2	Paul Masnick	27:49	Mtl.
Mar. 29/53	Bos.	SF	Bos. 2	Det. 1	Jack McIntyre	12:29	Bos.
Mar. 29/53	Chi.	SF	Chi. 2	Mtl. 1	Al Dewsbury	5:18	Mtl.
Apr. 16/53	Mtl.	F	Mtl. 1	Bos. 0	Elmer Lach	1:22	Mtl.
Apr. 1/54	Det.	SF	Det. 4	Tor. 3	Ted Lindsay	21:01	Det.
Apr. 11/54	Det.	F	Mtl. 1	Det. 0	Kenny Mosdell	5:45	Det.
Apr. 16/54	Det.	F	Det. 2	Mtl. 1	Tony Leswick	4:29	Det.
Mar. 29/55	Bos.	SF	Mtl. 4	Bos. 3	Don Marshall	3:05	Mtl.
Mar. 24/56	Tor.	SF	Det. 5	Tor. 4	Ted Lindsay	4:22	Det.
Mar. 28/57	NYR	SF	NYR 4	Mtl. 3	Andy Hebenton	13:38	Mtl.
Apr. 4/57	Mtl.	SF	Mtl. 4	NYR 3	Maurice Richard	1:11	Mtl.
Mar. 27/58	NYR	SF	Bos. 4	NYR 3	Jerry Toppazzini	4:46	Bos.
Mar. 30/58	Det.	SF	Mtl. 2	Det. 1	André Pronovost	11:52	Mtl.
Apr. 17/58	Mtl.	F	Mtl. 3	Bos. 2	Maurice Richard	5:45	Mtl.
Mar. 28/59	Tor.	SF	Tor. 3	Bos. 2	Gerry Ehman	5:02	Tor.
Mar. 31/59	Tor.	SF	Tor. 3	Bos. 2	Frank Mahovlich	11:21	Tor.
Apr. 14/59	Tor.	F	Tor. 3	Mtl. 2	Dick Duff	10:06	Mtl.
Mar. 26/60	Mtl.	SF	Mtl. 4	Chi. 3	Doug Harvey	8:38	Mtl.
Mar. 27/60	Det.	SF	Tor. 5	Det. 4	Frank Mahovlich	43:00	Tor.
Mar. 29/60	Det.	SF	Det. 2	Tor. 1	Gerry Melnyk	1:54	Tor.
Mar. 22/61	Tor.	SF	Tor. 3	Det. 2	George Armstrong	24:51	Det.
Mar. 26/61	Chi.	SF	Chi. 2	Mtl. 1	Murray Balfour	52:12	Chi.
Apr. 5/62	Tor.	SF	Tor. 3	NYR 2	Red Kelly	24:23	Tor.
Apr. 2/64	Det.	SF	Chi. 3	Det. 2	Murray Balfour	8:21	Det.
Apr. 14/64	Tor.	F	Det. 4	Tor. 3	Larry Jeffrey	7:52	Tor.
Apr. 23/64	Det.	F	Tor. 4	Det. 3	Bob Baun	1:43	Tor.
Apr. 6/65	Tor.	SF	Tor. 3	Mtl. 2	Dave Keon	4:17	Mtl.
Apr. 13/65	Tor.	SF	Mtl. 4	Tor. 3	Claude Provost	16:33	Mtl.
May 5/66	Det.	F	Mtl. 3	Det. 2	Henri Richard	2:20	Mtl.
Apr. 13/67	NYR	SF	Mtl. 2	NYR 1	John Ferguson	6:28	Mtl.
Apr. 25/67	Tor.	F	Tor. 3	Mtl. 2	Bob Pulford	28:26	Tor.
Apr. 10/68	St. L.	QF	St. L. 3	Phi. 2	Larry Keenan	24:10	St. L.
Apr. 16/68	St. L.	QF	Phi. 2	St. L. 1	Don Blackburn	31:18	St. L.
Apr. 16/68	Min.	QF	Min. 4	L.A. 3	Milan Marcetta	9:11	Min.
Apr. 22/68	Min.	SF	Min. 3	St. L. 2	Parker MacDonald	3:41	St. L.
Apr. 27/68	St. L.	SF	St. L. 4	Min. 3	Gary Sabourin	1:32	St. L.
Apr. 28/68	Mtl.	SF	Mtl. 4	Chi. 3	Jacques Lemaire	2:14	Mtl.
Apr. 29/68	St. L.	SF	St. L. 3	Min. 2	Bill McCreary	17:27	St. L.
May 3/68	St. L.	SF	St. L. 2	Min. 1	Ron Schock	22:50	St. L.
May 5/68	St. L.	F	Mtl. 3	St. L. 2	Jacques Lemaire	1:41	Mtl.
May 9/68	Mtl.	F	Mtl. 4	St. L. 3	Bobby Rousseau	1:13	Mtl.
Apr. 2/69	Oak.	QF	L.A. 5	Oak. 4	Ted Irvine	0:19	L.A.
Apr. 10/69	Mtl.	SF	Mtl. 3	Bos. 2	Ralph Backstrom	0:42	Mtl.
Apr. 13/69	Mtl.	SF	Mtl. 4	Bos. 3	Mickey Redmond	4:55	Mtl.
Apr. 24/69	Bos.	SF	Mtl. 2	Bos. 1	Jean Béliveau	31:28	Mtl.
Apr. 12/70	Oak.	QF	Pit. 3	Oak. 2	Michel Briere	8:28	Pit.
May 10/70	Bos.	F	Bos. 4	St. L. 3	Bobby Orr	0:40	Bos.
Apr. 15/71	Tor.	QF	NYR 2	Tor. 1	Bob Nevin	9:07	NYR
Apr. 18/71	Chi.	SF	NYR 2	Chi. 1	Pete Stemkowski	1:37	Chi.
Apr. 27/71	Chi.	SF	Chi. 3	NYR 2	Bobby Hull	6:35	Chi.
Apr. 29/71	NYR	SF	NYR 3	Chi. 2	Pete Stemkowski	41:29	Chi.
May 4/71	Chi.	F	Chi. 2	Mtl. 1	Jim Pappin	21:11	Mtl.
Apr. 6/72	Bos.	QF	Tor. 4	Bos. 3	Jim Harrison	2:58	Bos.
Apr. 6/72	Min.	QF	Min. 6	St. L. 5	Bill Goldsworthy	1:36	St. L.
Apr. 9/72	Pit.	QF	Chi. 6	Pit. 5	Pit Martin	0:12	Chi.
Apr. 16/72	Min.	QF	St. L. 2	Min. 1	Kevin O'Shea	10:07	St. L.
Apr. 1/73	Mtl.	QF	Buf. 3	Mtl. 2	René Robert	9:18	Mtl.
Apr. 10/73	Phi.	QF	Phi. 3	Min. 2	Gary Dornhoefer	8:35	Phi.
Apr. 14/73	Mtl.	SF	Phi. 5	Mtl. 4	Rick MacLeish	2:56	Mtl.
Apr. 17/73	Mtl.	SF	Mtl. 4	Phi. 3	Larry Robinson	6:45	Mtl.
Apr. 14/74	Tor.	QF	Bos. 4	Tor. 3	Ken Hodge	1:27	Bos.
Apr. 14/74	Atl.	QF	Phi. 4	Atl. 3	Dave Schultz	5:40	Phi.
Apr. 16/74	Mtl.	QF	NYR 3	Mtl. 2	Ron Harris	4:07	NYR
Apr. 23/74	Chi.	SF	Chi. 4	Bos. 3	Jim Pappin	3:48	Bos.
Apr. 28/74	NYR	SF	NYR 2	Phi. 1	Rod Gilbert	4:20	Phi.
May 9/74	Bos.	F	Phi. 3	Bos. 2	Bobby Clarke	12:01	Phi.
Apr. 8/75	L.A.	PR	L.A. 3	Tor. 2	Mike Murphy	8:53	Tor.
Apr. 10/75	Tor.	PR	Tor. 3	L.A. 2	Blaine Stoughton	10:19	Tor.
Apr. 10/75	Chi.	PR	Chi. 4	Bos. 3	Ivan Boldirev	7:33	Chi.
Apr. 11/75	NYR	PR	NYI 4	NYR 3	Jean-Paul Parise	0:11	NYI
Apr. 19/75	Tor.	QF	Phi. 4	Tor. 3	André Dupont	1:45	Phi.
Apr. 17/75	Chi.	QF	Chi. 5	Buf. 4	Stan Mikita	2:31	Buf.
Apr. 22/75	Mtl.	QF	Mtl. 5	Van. 4	Guy Lafleur	17:06	Mtl.
May 1/75	Phi.	SF	Phi. 5	NYI 4	Bobby Clarke	2:56	Phi.
May 7/75	NYI	SF	NYI 4	Phi. 3	Jude Drouin	1:53	Phi.
Apr. 27/75	Buf.	SF	Buf. 6	Mtl. 5	Danny Gare	4:42	Buf.
May 6/75	Buf.	SF	Buf. 5	Mtl. 4	René Robert	5:56	Buf.
May 20/75	Buf.	F	Buf. 5	Phi. 4	René Robert	18:29	Phi.
Apr. 8/76	Buf.	PR	Buf. 3	St. L. 2	Danny Gare	11:43	Buf.
Apr. 9/76	Buf.	PR	Buf. 2	St. L. 1	Don Luce	14:27	Buf.
Apr. 13/76	Bos.	QF	L.A. 3	Bos. 2	Butch Goring	0:27	Bos.
Apr. 13/76	Buf.	QF	Buf. 3	NYI 2	Danny Gare	14:04	NYI
Apr. 22/76	L.A.	QF	L.A. 4	Bos. 3	Butch Goring	18:28	Bos.
Apr. 29/76	Phi.	SF	Phi. 2	Bos. 1	Reggie Leach	13:38	Phi.
Apr. 15/77	Tor.	QF	Phi. 4	Tor. 3	Rick MacLeish	2:55	Phi.
Apr. 17/77	Tor.	QF	Phi. 6	Tor. 5	Reggie Leach	19:10	Phi.
Apr. 24/77	Phi.	SF	Bos. 4	Phi. 3	Rick Middleton	2:57	Bos.
Apr. 26/77	Phi.	SF	Bos. 5	Phi. 4	Terry O'Reilly	30:07	Bos.
May 3/77	Mtl.	SF	NYI 4	Mtl. 3	Billy Harris	3:58	Mtl.

Date	City	Series	Score		Scorer	Overtime	Series Winner
May 14/77	Bos.	F	Mtl. 2	Bos. 1	Jacques Lemaire	4:32	Mtl.
Apr. 11/78	Phi.	PR	Phi. 3	Col. 2	Mel Bridgman	0:23	Phi.
Apr. 13/78	NYR	PR	NYR 4	Buf. 3	Don Murdoch	1:37	Buf.
Apr. 19/78	Bos.	QF	Bos. 4	Chi. 3	Terry O'Reilly	1:50	Bos.
Apr. 19/78	NYI	QF	NYI 3	Tor. 2	Mike Bossy	2:50	Tor.
Apr. 21/78	Chi.	QF	Bos. 4	Chi. 3	Peter McNab	10:17	Bos.
Apr. 25/78	NYI	QF	NYI 2	Tor. 1	Bob Nystrom	8:02	Tor.
Apr. 29/78	NYI	QF	Tor. 2	NYI 1	Lanny McDonald	4:13	Tor.
May 2/78	Bos.	SF	Bos. 3	Phi. 2	Rick Middleton	1:43	Bos.
May 16/78	Mtl.	F	Mtl. 3	Bos. 2	Guy Lafleur	13:09	Mtl.
May 21/78	Bos.	F	Bos. 4	Mtl. 3	Bobby Schmautz	6:22	Mtl.
Apr. 12/79	L.A.	PR	NYR 2	L.A. 1	Phil Esposito	6:11	NYR
Apr. 14/79	Buf.	PR	Pit. 4	Buf. 3	George Ferguson	0:47	Pit.
Apr. 16/79	Phi.	QF	Phi. 3	NYR 2	Ken Linseman	0:44	NYR
Apr. 18/79	NYI	QF	NYI 1	Chi. 0	Mike Bossy	2:31	NYI
Apr. 21/79	Tor.	QF	Mtl. 4	Tor. 3	Cam Connor	25:25	Mtl.
Apr. 22/79	Tor.	QF	Mtl. 5	Tor. 4	Larry Robinson	4:14	Mtl.
Apr. 28/79	NYI	SF	NYI 4	NYR 3	Denis Potvin	8:02	NYR
May 3/79	NYR	SF	NYI 3	NYR 2	Bob Nystrom	3:40	NYR
May 3/79	Bos.	SF	Bos. 4	Mtl. 3	Jean Ratelle	3:46	Mtl.
May 10/79	Mtl.	SF	Mtl. 5	Bos. 4	Yvon Lambert	9:33	Mtl.
May 19/79	NYR	F	Mtl. 4	NYR 3	Serge Savard	7:25	Mtl.
Apr. 8/80	NYR	PR	NYR 2	Atl. 1	Steve Vickers	0:33	NYR
Apr. 8/80	Phi.	PR	Phi. 4	Edm. 3	Bobby Clarke	8:06	Phi.
Apr. 8/80	Chi.	PR	Chi. 3	St. L. 2	Doug Lecuyer	12:34	Chi.
Apr. 11/80	Hfd.	PR	Mtl. 4	Hfd. 3	Yvon Lambert	0:29	Mtl.
Apr. 11/80	Tor.	PR	Min. 4	Tor. 3	Al MacAdam	0:32	Min.
Apr. 11/80	L.A.	PR	NYI 4	L.A. 3	Ken Morrow	6:55	NYI
Apr. 11/80	Edm.	PR	Phi. 3	Edm. 2	Ken Linseman	23:56	Phi.
Apr. 16/80	Bos.	QF	NYI 2	Bos. 1	Clark Gillies	1:02	NYI
Apr. 17/80	Bos.	QF	NYI 5	Bos. 4	Bob Bourne	1:24	NYI
Apr. 21/80	NYI	QF	Bos. 4	NYI 3	Terry O'Reilly	17:13	NYI
May 1/80	Buf.	SF	NYI 2	Buf. 1	Bob Nystrom	21:20	NYI
May 13/80	Phi.	F	NYI 4	Phi. 3	Denis Potvin	4:07	NYI
May 24/80	NYI	F	NYI 5	Phi. 4	Bob Nystrom	7:11	NYI
Apr. 8/81	Buf.	PR	Buf. 3	Van. 2	Alan Haworth	5:00	Buf.
Apr. 8/81	Bos.	PR	Min. 5	Bos. 4	Steve Payne	3:34	Min.
Apr. 11/81	Chi.	PR	Cgy. 5	Chi. 4	Willi Plett	35:17	Cgy.
Apr. 12/81	Que.	PR	Que. 4	Phi. 3	Dale Hunter	0:37	Phi.
Apr. 14/81	St. L.	PR	St. L. 4	Pit. 3	Mike Crombeen	25:16	St. L.
Apr. 16/81	Buf.	QF	Min. 4	Buf. 3	Steve Payne	0:22	Min.
Apr. 20/81	Min.	QF	Buf. 5	Min. 4	Craig Ramsay	16:32	Min.
Apr. 20/81	Edm.	QF	NYI 5	Edm. 4	Ken Morrow	5:41	NYI
Apr. 7/82	Min.	DSF	Chi. 3	Min. 2	Greg Fox	3:34	Chi.
Apr. 8/82	Edm.	DSF	Edm. 3	L.A. 2	Wayne Gretzky	6:20	L.A.
Apr. 8/82	Van.	DSF	Van. 2	Cgy. 1	Dave Williams	14:20	Van.
Apr. 10/82	Pit.	DSF	Pit. 2	NYI 1	Rick Kehoe	4:14	NYI
Apr. 10/82	L.A.	DSF	L.A. 6	Edm. 5	Daryl Evans	2:35	L.A.
Apr. 13/82	Mtl.	DSF	Que. 3	Mtl. 2	Dale Hunter	0:22	Que.
Apr. 13/82	NYI	DSF	NYI 4	Pit. 3	John Tonelli	6:19	NYI
Apr. 16/82	Van.	DF	L.A. 3	Van. 2	Steve Bozek	4:33	Van.
Apr. 18/82	Que.	DF	Que. 3	Bos. 2	Wilf Paiement	11:44	Que.
Apr. 18/82	NYR	DF	NYI 4	NYR 3	Bryan Trottier	3:00	NYI
Apr. 18/82	L.A.	DF	Van. 4	L.A. 3	Colin Campbell	1:23	Van.
Apr. 21/82	St. L.	DF	St. L. 3	Chi. 2	Bernie Federko	3:28	Chi.
Apr. 23/82	Que.	DF	Bos. 6	Que. 5	Peter McNab	10:54	Que.
Apr. 27/82	Chi.	CF	Van. 2	Chi. 1	Jim Nill	28:58	Van.
May 1/82	Que.	CF	NYI 5	Que. 4	Wayne Merrick	16:52	NYI
May 8/82	NYI	F	NYI 6	Van. 5	Mike Bossy	19:58	NYI
Apr. 5/83	Bos.	DSF	Bos. 4	Que. 3	Barry Pederson	1:46	Bos.
Apr. 6/83	Cgy.	DSF	Cgy. 4	Van. 3	Eddy Beers	12:27	Cgy.
Apr. 7/83	Min.	DSF	Min. 5	Tor. 4	Bobby Smith	5:03	Min.
Apr. 10/83	Tor.	DSF	Min. 5	Tor. 4	Dino Ciccarelli	8:05	Min.
Apr. 10/83	Van.	DSF	Cgy. 4	Van. 3	Greg Meredith	1:06	Cgy.
Apr. 18/83	Min.	DF	Chi. 4	Min. 3	Rich Preston	10:34	Chi.
Apr. 24/83	Bos.	DF	Bos. 3	Buf. 2	Brad Park	1:52	Bos.
Apr. 5/84	Edm.	DSF	Edm. 5	Wpg. 4	Randy Gregg	0:21	Edm.
Apr. 7/84	Det.	DSF	St. L. 4	Det. 3	Mark Reeds	37:07	St. L.
Apr. 8/84	Det.	DSF	St. L. 3	Det. 2	Jorgen Pettersson	2:42	St. L.
Apr. 10/84	NYI	DSF	NYI 3	NYR 2	Ken Morrow	8:56	NYI
Apr. 13/84	Min.	DF	St. L. 4	Min. 3	Doug Gilmour	16:16	Min.
Apr. 13/84	Edm.	DF	Cgy. 6	Edm. 5	Carey Wilson	3:42	Edm.
Apr. 13/84	NYI	DF	NYI 5	Wsh. 4	Anders Kallur	7:35	NYI
Apr. 16/84	Mtl.	DF	Que. 4	Mtl. 3	Bo Berglund	3:00	Mtl.
Apr. 20/84	Cgy.	DF	Cgy. 5	Edm. 4	Lanny McDonald	1:04	Edm.
Apr. 22/84	Min.	DF	Min. 4	St. L. 3	Steve Payne	6:00	Min.
Apr. 10/85	Phi.	DSF	Phi. 5	NYR 4	Mark Howe	8:01	Phi.
Apr. 10/85	Wsh.	DSF	Wsh. 4	NYI 3	Alan Haworth	2:28	NYI
Apr. 10/85	Edm.	DSF	Edm. 3	L.A. 2	Lee Fogolin	3:01	Edm.
Apr. 10/85	Wpg.	DSF	Wpg. 5	Cgy. 4	Brian Mullen	7:56	Wpg.
Apr. 11/85	Wsh.	DSF	Wsh. 2	NYI 1	Mike Gartner	21:23	NYI
Apr. 13/85	L.A.	DSF	Edm. 4	L.A. 3	Glenn Anderson	0:46	Edm.
Apr. 18/85	Mtl.	DF	Que. 2	Mtl. 1	Mark Kumpel	12:23	Que.
Apr. 23/85	Que.	DF	Que. 7	Mtl. 6	Dale Hunter	18:36	Que.
May 2/85	Mtl.	DF	Que. 3	Mtl. 2	Peter Stastny	2:22	Que.
Apr. 25/85	Min.	DF	Chi. 7	Min. 6	Darryl Sutter	21:57	Chi.
Apr. 28/85	Chi.	DF	Min. 5	Chi. 4	Dennis Maruk	1:14	Chi.
Apr. 30/85	Min.	DF	Chi. 6	Min. 5	Darryl Sutter	15:41	Chi.
May 5/85	Que.	CF	Que. 2	Phi. 1	Peter Stastny	6:20	Phi.
Apr. 9/86	Que.	DSF	Hfd. 3	Que. 2	Sylvain Turgeon	2:36	Hfd.
Apr. 12/86	Wpg.	DSF	Cgy. 4	Wpg. 3	Lanny McDonald	8:25	Cgy.
Apr. 17/86	Wsh.	DF	NYR 4	Wsh. 3	Brian MacLellan	1:16	NYR
Apr. 20/86	Edm.	DF	Edm. 6	Cgy. 5	Glenn Anderson	1:04	Cgy.
Apr. 23/86	Hfd.	DF	Hfd. 2	Mtl. 1	Kevin Dineen	1:07	Mtl.
Apr. 23/86	NYR	DF	NYR 6	Wsh. 5	Bob Brooke	2:40	NYR
Apr. 26/86	St L.	DF	St L. 4	Tor. 3	Mark Reeds	7:11	St L.
Apr. 29/86	Mtl.	DF	Mtl. 2	Hfd. 1	Claude Lemieux	5:55	Mtl.
May 5/86	NYR	CF	Mtl. 4	NYR 3	Claude Lemieux	9:41	Mtl.
May 12/86	St L.	CF	St L. 6	Cgy. 5	Doug Wickenheiser	7:30	Cgy.
May 18/86	Cgy.	F	Mtl. 3	Cgy. 2	Brian Skrudland	0:09	Mtl.
Apr. 8/87	Hfd.	DSF	Hfd. 3	Que. 2	Paul MacDermid	2:20	Que.
Apr. 9/87	Mtl.	DSF	Mtl. 4	Bos. 3	Mats Naslund	2:38	Mtl.
Apr. 9/87	St. L.	DSF	Tor. 3	St. L. 2	Rick Lanz	10:17	Tor.
Apr. 11/87	Wpg.	DSF	Cgy. 3	Wpg. 2	Mike Bullard	3:53	Wpg.
Apr. 11/87	Chi.	DSF	Det. 4	Chi. 3	Shawn Burr	4:51	Det.
Apr. 16/87	Que.	DSF	Que. 5	Hfd. 4	Peter Stastny	6:05	Que.
Apr. 18/87	Wsh.	DSF	NYI 3	Wsh. 2	Pat LaFontaine	68:47	NYI
Apr. 21/87	Edm.	DF	Edm. 3	Wpg. 2	Glenn Anderson	0:36	Edm.
Apr. 26/87	Que.	DF	Mtl. 3	Que. 2	Mats Naslund	5:30	Mtl.
Apr. 27/87	Tor.	DF	Tor. 3	Det. 2	Mike Allison	9:31	Det.
May 4/87	Phi.	CF	Phi. 4	Mtl. 3	Ilkka Sinislao	9:11	Phi.
May 20/87	Edm.	F	Edm. 3	Phi. 2	Jari Kurri	6:50	Edm.
Apr. 6/88	NYI	DSF	NYI 4	N.J. 3	Pat LaFontaine	6:11	N.J.
Apr. 10/88	Phi.	DSF	Phi. 5	Wsh. 4	Murray Craven	1:18	Wsh.
Apr. 10/88	N.J.	DSF	NYI 5	N.J. 4	Brent Sutter	15:07	N.J.
Apr. 10/88	Buf.	DSF	Buf. 6	Bos. 5	John Tucker	5:32	Bos.
Apr. 12/88	Det.	DSF	Tor. 6	Det. 5	Ed Olczyk	0:34	Det.
Apr. 16/88	Wsh.	DSF	Wsh. 5	Phi. 4	Dale Hunter	5:57	Wsh.
Apr. 21/88	Cgy.	DF	Edm. 5	Cgy. 4	Wayne Gretzky	7:54	Edm.
May 4/88	Bos.	CF	N.J. 3	Bos. 2	Doug Brown	17:46	Bos.
May 9/88	Det.	CF	Edm. 4	Det. 3	Jari Kurri	11:02	Edm.
Apr. 5/89	St. L.	DSF	St. L. 4	Min. 3	Brett Hull	11:55	St. L.
Apr. 5/89	Cgy.	DSF	Van. 4	Cgy. 3	Paul Reinhart	2:47	Cgy.
Apr. 6/89	St. L.	DSF	St. L. 4	Min. 3	Rick Meagher	5:30	St. L.
Apr. 6/89	Det.	DSF	Chi. 5	Det. 4	Duane Sutter	14:36	Chi.
Apr. 8/89	Hfd.	DSF	Mtl. 5	Hfd. 4	Stephane Richer	5:01	Mtl.
Apr. 8/89	Phi.	DSF	Wsh. 4	Phi. 3	Kelly Miller	0:51	Phi.
Apr. 9/89	Hfd.	DSF	Mtl. 4	Hfd. 3	Russ Courtnall	15:12	Mtl.
Apr. 15/89	Cgy.	DSF	Cgy. 4	Van. 3	Joel Otto	19:21	Cgy.
Apr. 18/89	Cgy.	DF	Cgy. 4	L.A. 3	Doug Gilmour	7:47	Cgy.
Apr. 19/89	Mtl.	DF	Mtl. 3	Bos. 2	Bobby Smith	12:24	Mtl.
Apr. 20/89	St. L.	DF	St. L. 5	Chi. 4	Tony Hrkac	33:49	Chi.
Apr. 21/89	Phi.	DF	Pit. 4	Phi. 3	Phil Bourque	12:08	Phi.
May 8/89	Chi.	CF	Cgy. 2	Chi. 1	Al MacInnis	15:05	Cgy.
May 9/89	Mtl.	CF	Phi. 2	Mtl. 1	Dave Poulin	5:02	Mtl.
May 19/89	Mtl.	F	Mtl. 4	Cgy. 3	Ryan Walter	38:08	Cgy.
Apr. 5/90	N.J.	DSF	Wsh. 5	N.J. 4	Dino Ciccarelli	5:34	Wsh.
Apr. 6/90	Edm.	DSF	Edm. 3	Wpg. 2	Mark Lamb	4:21	Edm.
Apr. 8/90	Tor.	DSF	St. L. 6	Tor. 5	Sergio Momesso	6:04	St. L.
Apr. 8/90	L.A.	DSF	L.A. 2	Cgy. 1	Tony Granato	8:37	L.A.
Apr. 9/90	Mtl.	DSF	Mtl. 2	Buf. 1	Brian Skrudland	12:35	Mtl.
Apr. 9/90	NYI	DSF	NYI 4	NYR 3	Brent Sutter	20:59	NYR
Apr. 10/90	Wpg.	DSF	Wpg. 4	Edm. 3	Dave Ellett	21:08	Edm.
Apr. 14/90	L.A.	DSF	L.A. 4	Cgy. 3	Mike Krushelnyski	23:14	L.A.
Apr. 15/90	Hfd.	DSF	Hfd. 3	Bos. 2	Kevin Dineen	12:30	Bos.
Apr. 21/90	Bos.	DF	Bos. 5	Mtl. 4	Garry Galley	3:42	Bos.
Apr. 24/90	L.A.	DF	Edm. 6	L.A. 5	Joe Murphy	4:42	Edm.
Apr. 25/90	Wsh.	DF	Wsh. 4	NYR 3	Rod Langway	0:34	Wsh.
Apr. 27/90	NYR	DF	Wsh. 2	NYR 1	John Druce	6:48	Wsh.
May 15/90	Bos.	F	Edm. 3	Bos. 2	Petr Klima	55:13	Edm.
Apr. 4/91	Chi.	DSF	Min. 4	Chi. 3	Brian Propp	4:14	Min.
Apr. 5/91	Pit.	DSF	Pit. 5	N.J. 4	Jaromir Jagr	8:52	Pit.
Apr. 6/91	L.A.	DSF	L.A. 3	Van. 2	Wayne Gretzky	11:08	L.A.
Apr. 8/91	Van.	DSF	Van. 2	L.A. 1	Cliff Ronning	3:12	L.A.
Apr. 11/91	NYR	DSF	Wsh. 5	NYR 4	Dino Ciccarelli	6:44	Wsh.
Apr. 11/91	Mtl.	DSF	Mtl. 4	Buf. 3	Russ Courtnall	5:56	Mtl.
Apr. 14/91	Edm.	DSF	Cgy. 2	Edm. 1	Theoren Fleury	4:40	Edm.
Apr. 16/91	Cgy.	DSF	Edm. 5	Cgy. 4	Esa Tikkanen	6:58	Edm.
Apr. 18/91	L.A.	DF	L.A. 4	Edm. 3	Luc Robitaille	2:13	Edm.
Apr. 19/91	Bos.	DF	Mtl. 4	Bos. 3	Stephane Richer	0:27	Bos.
Apr. 19/91	Pit.	DF	Pit. 7	Wsh. 6	Kevin Stevens	8:10	Pit.
Apr. 20/91	L.A.	DF	Edm. 4	L.A. 3	Petr Klima	24:48	Edm.
Apr. 22/91	Edm.	DF	Edm. 4	L.A. 3	Esa Tikkanen	20:48	Edm.
Apr. 27/91	Mtl.	DF	Mtl. 3	Bos. 2	Shayne Corson	17:47	Bos.
Apr. 28/91	Edm.	DF	Edm. 4	L.A. 3	Craig MacTavish	16:57	Edm.
May 3/91	Bos.	CF	Bos. 5	Pit. 4	Vladimir Ruzicka	8:14	Pit.
Apr. 21/92	Bos.	DSF	Bos. 3	Buf. 2	Adam Oates	11:14	Bos.
Apr. 22/92	Min.	DSF	Det. 5	Min. 4	Yves Racine	1:15	Det.
Apr. 22/92	St. L.	DSF	St. L. 5	Chi. 4	Brett Hull	23:33	Chi.
Apr. 25/92	Buf.	DSF	Bos. 5	Buf. 4	Ted Donato	2:08	Bos.
Apr. 28/92	Min.	DSF	Det. 1	Min. 0	Sergei Fedorov	16:13	Det.
Apr. 29/92	Hfd.	DSF	Hfd. 2	Mtl. 1	Yvon Corriveau	0:24	Mtl.
May 1/92	Mtl.	DSF	Mtl. 3	Hfd. 2	Russ Courtnall	25:26	Mtl.
May 3/92	Van.	DF	Edm. 4	Van. 3	Joe Murphy	8:36	Edm.
May 5/92	Mtl.	DF	Bos. 3	Mtl. 2	Peter Douris	3:12	Bos.
May 7/92	Pit.	DF	NYR 6	Pit. 5	Kris King	1:29	Pit.
May 9/92	Pit.	DF	Pit. 5	NYR 4	Ron Francis	2:47	Pit.
May 17/92	Pit.	CF	Pit. 4	Bos. 3	Jaromir Jagr	9:44	Pit.
May 20/92	Edm.	CF	Chi. 4	Edm. 3	Jeremy Roenick	2:45	Chi.
Apr. 18/93	Bos.	DSF	Buf. 5	Bos. 4	Bob Sweeney	11:03	Buf.
Apr. 18/93	Que.	DSF	Que. 3	Mtl. 2	Scott Young	16:49	Mtl.
Apr. 20/93	Wsh.	DSF	NYI 5	Wsh. 4	Brian Mullen	34:50	NYI
Apr. 22/93	Mtl.	DSF	Mtl. 2	Que. 1	Vincent Damphousse	10:30	Mtl.
Apr. 22/93	Buf.	DSF	Buf. 4	Bos. 3	Yuri Khmylev	1:05	Buf.
Apr. 22/93	NYI	DSF	NYI 4	Wsh. 3	Ray Ferraro	4:46	NYI
Apr. 24/93	Buf.	DSF	Buf. 6	Bos. 5	Brad May	4:48	Buf.
Apr. 24/93	NYI	DSF	NYI 4	Wsh. 3	Ray Ferraro	25:40	NYI
Apr. 25/93	St. L.	DSF	St. L. 4	Chi. 3	Craig Janney	10:43	St. L.
Apr. 26/93	Que.	DSF	Mtl. 5	Que. 4	Kirk Muller	8:17	Mtl.
Apr. 27/93	Det.	DSF	Tor. 5	Det. 4	Mike Foligno	2:05	Tor.
Apr. 27/93	Van.	DSF	Wpg. 4	Van. 3	Teemu Selanne	6:18	Van.
Apr. 29/93	Wpg.	DSF	Van. 4	Wpg. 3	Greg Adams	4:30	Van.
May 1/93	Det.	DSF	Tor. 4	Det. 3	Nikolai Borschevsky	2:35	Tor.
May 3/93	Tor.	DF	Tor. 2	St. L. 1	Doug Gilmour	23:16	Tor.
May 4/93	Mtl.	DF	Mtl. 4	Buf. 3	Guy Carbonneau	2:50	Mtl.
May 5/93	Tor.	DF	St. L. 2	Tor. 1	Jeff Brown	23:03	Tor.
May 6/93	Buf.	DF	Mtl. 4	Buf. 3	Gilbert Dionne	8:28	Mtl.
May 8/93	Buf.	DF	Mtl. 4	Buf. 3	Kirk Muller	11:37	Mtl.
May 11/93	Van.	DF	L.A. 4	Van. 3	Gary Shuchuk	26:31	L.A.
May 14/93	Pit.	DF	NYI 4	Pit. 3	Dave Volek	5:16	NYI
May 18/93	Mtl.	CF	Mtl. 4	NYI 3	Stephan Lebeau	26:21	Mtl.
May 20/93	NYI	CF	Mtl. 2	NYI 1	Guy Carbonneau	12:34	Mtl.
May 25/93	Tor.	CF	Tor. 3	L.A. 2	Glenn Anderson	19:20	L.A.
May 27/93	L.A.	CF	L.A. 5	Tor. 4	Wayne Gretzky	1:41	L.A.

Date	City	Series	Score		Scorer	Overtime	Series Winner
Jun. 3/93	Mtl.	F	Mtl. 3	L.A. 2	Eric Desjardins	0:51	Mtl.
Jun. 5/93	L.A.	F	Mtl. 4	L.A. 3	John LeClair	0:34	Mtl.
Jun. 7/93	L.A.	F	Mtl. 3	L.A. 2	John LeClair	14:37	Mtl.
Apr. 20/94	Tor.	CQF	Tor. 1	Chi. 0	Todd Gill	2:15	Tor.
Apr. 22/94	St. L.	CQF	Dal. 5	St. L. 4	Paul Cavallini	8:34	Dal.
Apr. 24/94	Chi.	CQF	Chi. 4	Tor. 3	Jeremy Roenick	1:23	Tor.
Apr. 25/94	Bos.	CQF	Mtl. 2	Bos. 1	Kirk Muller	17:18	Bos.
Apr. 26/94	Cgy.	CQF	Van. 2	Cgy. 1	Geoff Courtnall	7:15	Van.
Apr. 27/94	Buf.	CQF	Buf. 1	N.J. 0	Dave Hannan	65:43	N.J.
Apr. 28/94	Van.	CQF	Van. 3	Cgy. 2	Trevor Linden	16:43	Van.
Apr. 30/94	Cgy.	CQF	Van. 4	Cgy. 3	Pavel Bure	22:20	Van.
May 3/94	N.J.	CSF	Bos. 6	N.J. 5	Don Sweeney	9:08	N.J.
May 7/94	Bos.	CSF	N.J. 5	Bos. 4	Stephane Richer	14:19	N.J.
May 8/94	Van.	CSF	Van. 2	Dal. 1	Sergio Momesso	11:01	Van.
May 12/94	Tor.	CSF	Tor. 3	S.J. 2	Mike Gartner	8:53	Tor.
May 15/94	NYR	CF	N.J. 4	NYR 3	Stephane Richer	35:23	NYR
May 16/94	Tor.	CF	Tor. 3	Van. 2	Peter Zezel	16:55	Van.
May 19/94	N.J.	CF	NYR 3	N.J. 2	Stephane Matteau	26:13	NYR
May 24/94	Van.	CF	Van. 4	Tor. 3	Greg Adams	20:14	Van.
May 27/94	NYR	CF	NYR 2	N.J. 1	Stephane Matteau	24:24	NYR
May 31/94	NYR	F	Van. 3	NYR 2	Greg Adams	19:26	NYR
May 7/95	Phi.	CQF	Phi. 4	Buf. 3	Karl Dykhuis	10:06	Phi.
May 9/95	Cgy.	CQF	S.J. 5	Cgy. 4	Ulf Dahlen	12:21	S.J.
May 12/95	NYR	CQF	NYR 3	Que. 2	Steve Larmer	8:09	NYR
May 12/95	N.J.	CQF	N.J. 1	Bos. 0	Randy McKay	8:51	N.J.
May 14/95	Pit.	CQF	Pit. 6	Wsh. 5	Luc Robitaille	4:30	Pit.
May 15/95	St. L.	CQF	Van. 6	St. L. 5	Cliff Ronning	1:48	Van.
May 17/95	Tor.	CQF	Tor. 5	Chi. 4	Randy Wood	10:00	Chi.
May 19/95	Cgy.	CQF	S.J. 5	Cgy. 4	Ray Whitney	21:54	S.J.
May 21/95	Phi.	CSF	Phi. 5	NYR 4	Eric Desjardins	7:03	Phi.
May 21/95	Chi.	CSF	Chi. 2	Van. 1	Joe Murphy	9:04	Chi.
May 22/95	Phi.	CSF	Phi. 4	NYR 3	Kevin Haller	0:25	Phi.
May 25/95	Van.	CSF	Chi. 3	Van. 2	Chris Chelios	6:22	Chi.
May 26/95	N.J.	CSF	N.J. 2	Pit. 1	Neal Broten	18:36	N.J.
May 27/95	Van.	CSF	Chi. 4	Van. 3	Chris Chelios	5:35	Chi.
Jun. 1/95	Det.	CF	Det. 2	Chi. 1	Nicklas Lidstrom	1:01	Det.
Jun. 6/95	Chi.	CF	Det. 4	Chi. 3	Vladimir Konstantinov	29:25	Det.
Jun. 7/95	N.J.	CF	Phi. 3	N.J. 2	Eric Lindros	4:19	N.J.
Jun. 11/95	Det.	CF	Det. 2	Chi. 1	Vyacheslav Kozlov	22:25	Det.
Apr. 16/96	NYR	CQF	Mtl. 3	NYR 2	Vincent Damphousse	5:04	NYR
Apr. 18/96	Tor.	CQF	Tor. 5	St. L. 4	Mats Sundin	4:02	St. L.
Apr. 18/96	Phi.	CQF	T.B. 2	Phi. 1	Brian Bellows	9:05	Phi.
Apr. 21/96	St. L.	CQF	St. L. 3	Tor. 2	Glenn Anderson	1:24	St. L.
Apr. 21/96	T.B.	CQF	T.B. 5	Phi. 4	Alexander Selivanov	2:04	Phi.
Apr. 23/96	Cgy.	CQF	Chi. 2	Cgy. 1	Joe Murphy	50:02	Chi.
Apr. 24/96	Wsh.	CQF	Pit. 3	Wsh. 2	Petr Nedved	79:15	Pit.
Apr. 25/96	Col.	CQF	Col. 5	Van. 4	Joe Sakic	0:51	Col.
Apr. 25/96	Tor.	CQF	Tor. 5	St. L. 4	Mike Gartner	7:31	St. L.
May 2/96	Col.	CSF	Chi. 3	Col. 2	Jeremy Roenick	6:29	Col.
May 6/96	Chi.	CSF	Chi. 4	Col. 3	Sergei Krivokrasov	0:46	Col.
May 8/96	St. L.	CSF	St. L. 5	Det. 4	Igor Kravchuk	3:23	Det.
May 8/96	Chi.	CSF	Col. 3	Chi. 2	Joe Sakic	44:33	Col.
May 9/96	Fla.	CSF	Fla. 4	Phi. 3	Dave Lowry	4:06	Fla.
May 12/96	Phi.	CSF	Fla. 2	Phi. 1	Mike Hough	28:05	Fla.
May 13/96	Chi.	CSF	Col. 4	Chi. 3	Sandis Ozolinsh	25:18	Col.
May 16/96	Det.	CSF	Det. 1	St. L. 0	Steve Yzerman	21:15	Det.
May 19/96	Det.	CF	Col. 3	Det. 2	Mike Keane	17:31	Col.
Jun. 10/96	Fla.	F	Col. 1	Fla. 0	Uwe Krupp	44:31	Col.
Apr. 20/97	Chi.	CQF	Chi. 4	Col. 3	Sergei Krivokrasov	31:03	Col.
Apr. 20/97	Edm.	CQF	Edm. 4	Dal. 3	Kelly Buchberger	9:15	Edm.
Apr. 22/97	NYR	CQF	NYR 4	Fla. 3	Esa Tikkanen	16:29	NYR
Apr. 23/97	Ott.	CQF	Ott. 1	Buf. 0	Daniel Alfredsson	2:34	Buf.
Apr. 24/97	Mtl.	CQF	Mtl. 4	N.J. 3	Patrice Brisebois	47:37	N.J.
Apr. 25/97	Fla.	CQF	NYR 3	Fla. 2	Esa Tikkanen	12:02	NYR
Apr. 25/97	Dal.	CQF	Edm. 1	Dal. 0	Ryan Smyth	20:22	Edm.
Apr. 27/97	Phx.	CQF	Ana. 3	Phx. 2	Paul Kariya	7:29	Ana.
Apr. 29/97	Buf.	CQF	Buf. 3	Ott. 2	Derek Plante	5:24	Buf.
Apr. 29/97	Dal.	CQF	Edm. 4	Dal. 3	Todd Marchant	12:26	Edm.
May 2/97	Det.	CSF	Det. 2	Ana. 1	Martin Lapointe	0:59	Det.
May 4/97	Det.	CSF	Det. 3	Ana. 2	Vyacheslav Kozlov	41:31	Det.
May 8/97	Ana.	CSF	Det. 3	Ana. 2	Brendan Shanahan	37:03	Det.
May 9/97	Phi.	CSF	Buf. 5	Phi. 4	Ed Ronan	6:24	Phi.
May 9/97	Edm.	CSF	Col. 3	Edm. 2	Claude Lemieux	8:35	Col.
May 11/97	N.J.	CSF	NYR 2	N.J. 1	Adam Graves	14:08	NYR
Apr. 22/98	N.J.	CQF	OTT. 2	N.J. 1	Bruce Gardiner	5:58	Ott.
Apr. 23/98	Pit.	CQF	Mtl. 3	Pit. 2	Benoit Brunet	18:43	Mtl.
Apr. 24/98	Wsh.	CQF	Bos. 4	Wsh. 3	Darren Van Impe	20:54	Wsh.
Apr. 26/98	Ott.	CQF	Ott. 2	N.J. 1	Alexei Yashin	2:47	Ott.
Apr. 26/98	Bos.	CQF	Wsh. 3	Bos. 2	Joe Juneau	26:31	Wsh.
Apr. 26/98	Edm.	CQF	Col. 5	Edm. 4	Joe Sakic	15:25	Edm.
Apr. 28/98	S.J.	CQF	S.J. 1	Dal. 0	Andrei Zyuzin	6:31	Dal.
May 1/98	Phi.	CQF	Buf. 3	Phi. 2	Michal Grosek	5:40	Buf.
May 2/98	S.J.	CQF	Dal. 3	S.J. 2	Mike Keane	3:43	Dal.
May 3/98	Bos.	CQF	Wsh. 3	Bos. 2	Brian Bellows	15:24	Wsh.
May 3/98	Buf.	CSF	Buf. 3	Mtl. 2	Geoff Sanderson	2:37	Buf.
May 11/98	Edm.	CSF	Dal. 1	Edm. 0	Benoit Hogue	13:07	Dal.
May 12/98	Mtl.	CSF	Buf. 5	Mtl. 4	Michael Peca	21:24	Buf.
May 12/98	St.L.	CSF	Det. 3	St.L. 2	Brendan Shanahan	31:12	Det.
May 25/98	Wsh.	CF	Wsh. 3	Buf. 2	Todd Krygier	3:01	Wsh.
May 28/98	Buf.	CF	Wsh. 4	Buf. 3	Peter Bondra	9:37	Wsh.
Jun. 3/98	Dal.	CF	Dal. 3	Det. 2	Jamie Langenbrunner	0:46	Det.
Jun. 4/98	Buf.	CF	Wsh. 3	Buf. 2	Joe Juneau	6:24	Wsh.
Jun. 11/98	Det.	F	Det. 5	Wsh. 4	Kris Draper	15:24	Det.
Apr. 23/99	Ott.	CQF	Buf. 3	Ott. 2	Miroslav Satan	30:35	Buf.
Apr. 24/99	Car.	CQF	Car. 3	Bos. 2	Ray Sheppard	17:05	Bos.
Apr. 24/99	Phx.	CQF	Phx. 4	St. L. 3	Shane Doan	8:58	St. L.
Apr. 26/99	S.J.	CQF	Col. 2	S.J. 1	Milan Hejduk	7:53	Col.
Apr. 27/99	Edm.	CQF	Dal. 3	Edm. 2	Joe Nieuwendyk	57:34	Dal.
Apr. 30/99	Tor.	CQF	Tor. 2	Phi. 1	Yanic Perreault	11:51	Tor.
Apr. 30/99	Car.	CQF	Bos. 4	Car. 3	Anson Carter	34:45	Bos.
Apr. 30/99	Phx..	CQF	St.L. 2	Phx. 1	Scott Young	5:43	St.L.
May 2/99	Pit.	CQF	Pit. 3	N.J. 2	Jaromir Jagr	8:59	Pit.
May 3/99	S.J.	CQF	Col. 3	S.J. 2	Milan Hejduk	13:12	Col.
May 4/99	Phx.	CQF	St. L. 1	Phx. 0	Pierre Turgeon	17:59	St. L.
May 7/99	Col.	CSF	Det. 3	Col. 2	Kirk Maltby	4:18	Col.
May 8/99	Dal.	CSF	Dal. 5	St. L. 4	Joe Nieuwendyk	8:22	Dal.
May 10/99	St.L.	CSF	St. L. 3	Dal. 2	Pavol Demitra	2:43	Dal.
May 12/99	St.L.	CSF	St. L. 3	Dal. 2	Pierre Turgeon	5:52	Dal.
May 13/99	Pit.	CSF	Tor. 3	Pit. 2	Sergei Berezin	2:18	Tor.
May 17/99	Pit.	CSF	Tor. 4	Pit. 3	Garry Valk	1:57	Tor.
May 17/99	St.L.	CSF	Dal. 2	St. L. 1	Mike Mondano	2:21	Dal.
May 28/99	Col.	CF	Col. 3	Dal. 2	Chris Drury	19:29	Dal.
Jun. 8/99	Dal.	F	Buf. 3	Dal. 2	Jason Woolley	15:30	Dal.
Jun. 19/99	Buf.	F	Dal. 2	Buf. 1	Brett Hull	54:51	Dal.
Apr. 15/00	Pit.	CQF	Pit. 2	Wsh. 1	Jaromir Jagr	5:49	Pit.
Apr. 18/00	Buf.	CQF	Buf. 3	Phi. 2	Stu Barnes	4:42	Phi.
Apr. 22/00	Tor.	CQF	Tor. 2	Ott. 1	Steve Thomas	14:47	Tor.
May 2/00	Pit.	CSF	Phi. 4	Pit. 3	Andy Delmore	11:01	Phi.
May 3/00	Det.	CSF	Col. 3	Det. 2	Chris Drury	10:21	Col.
May 4/00	Pit.	CSF	Phi. 2	Pit. 1	Keith Primeau	92:01	Phi.
May 23/00	Dal.	CF	Dal. 3	Col. 2	Joe Nieuwendyk	12:10	Dal.
Jun. 8/00	N.J.	F	Dal. 1	N.J. 0	Mike Modano	46:21	N.J.
Jun. 10/00	Dal.	F	N.J. 2	Dal. 1	Jason Arnott	28:20	N.J.
Apr. 11/01	Dal.	CQF	Dal. 2	Edm. 1	Jamie Langenbrunner	2:08	Dal
Apr. 13/01	Ott.	CQF	Tor. 1	Ott. 0	Mats Sundin	10:49	Tor
Apr. 14/01	Phi.	CQF	Buf. 4	Phi. 3	Jay McKee	18:02	Buf.
Apr. 15/01	Edm.	CQF	Dal. 3	Edm. 2	Benoit Hogue	19:48	Dal.
Apr. 16/01	Tor.	CQF	Tor. 3	Ott. 2	Cory Cross	2:16	Tor.
Apr. 16/01	Van.	CQF	Col. 4	Van. 3	Peter Forsberg	2:50	Col.
Apr. 17/01	Buf.	CQF	Buf. 4	Phi. 3	Curtis Brown	6:13	Buf.
Apr. 17/01	Edm.	CQF	Edm. 2	Dal. 1	Mike Comrie	17:19	Dal.
Apr. 18/01	Car.	CQF	Car. 3	N.J. 2	Rod Brind'Amour	:46	N.J.
Apr. 18/01	Pit.	CQF	Wsh. 4	Pit. 3	Jeff Halpern	4:01	Pit.
Apr. 18/01	L.A.	CQF	L.A. 4	Det. 3	Eric Belanger	2:36	L.A
Apr. 19/01	Dal.	CQF	Dal. 4	Edm. 3	Kirk Muller	8:01	Dal.
Apr. 19/01	St.L.	CQF	St.L. 3	S.J. 2	Bryce Salvador	9:54	St.L.
Apr. 23/01	Pit.	CQF	Pit. 4	Wsh. 3	Martin Straka	13:04	Pit.
Apr. 23/01	L.A.	CQF	L.A. 3	Det. 2	Adam Deadmarsh	4:48	L.A.
Apr. 26/01	Col.	CSF	L.A. 4	Col. 3	Jaroslav Modry	14:23	Col.
Apr. 28/01	N.J.	CSF	N.J. 6	Tor. 5	Randy McKay	5:31	N.J.
May 1/01	Tor.	CSF	N.J. 3	Tor. 2	Brian Rafalski	7:00	N.J.
May 1/01	St.L.	CSF	St.L. 3	Dal. 2	Cory Stillman	29:26	St.L.
May 5/01	Buf.	CSF	Buf. 3	Pit. 2	Stu Barnes	8:34	Pit.
May 6/01	L.A.	CSF	L.A. 1	Col. 0	Glen Murray	22:41	Col.
May 8/01	Pit.	CSF	Pit. 3	Buf. 2	Martin Straka	11:29	Pit.
May 10/01	Buf.	CSF	Pit. 3	Buf. 2	Darius Kasparaitis	13:01	Pit.
May 16/01	St.L.	CF	St.L. 4	Col. 3	Scott Young	30:27	Col.
May 18/01	St.L.	CF	Col. 4	St.L. 3	Stephane Yelle	4:23	Col.
May 21/01	Col.	CF	Col. 2	St.L. 1	Joe Sakic	:24	Col.

The Los Angeles Kings shocked the Detroit Red Wings in the opening round of the 2001 playoffs. Adam Deadmarsh scored the series-winning goal in overtime of game six.

NHL Playoff Coaching Records

Coach	Team	Games Coached	Wins	Losses	Ties	Playoff Years	Cup Wins	Career
Abel, Sid	Chicago	7	3	4	0	1		
	Detroit	69	29	40	0	8		
	Total	76	32	44	0	9		1952-76
Adams, Jack	Detroit	105	52	52	1	15	3	1927-47
Allen, Keith	Philadelphia	11	3	8	0	2		1967-69
Arbour, Al	St. Louis	11	4	7	0	1		
	NY Islanders	198	119	79	0	15	4	
	Total	209	123	86	0	16	4	1970-94
Barber, Bill	Philadelphia	6	2	4	0	1		2000-01
Berenson, Red	St. Louis	14	5	9	0	2		1979-82
Bergeron, Michel	Quebec	68	31	37	0	7		1980-90
Berry, Bob	Los Angeles	10	2	8	0	3		
	Montreal	8	2	6	0	2		
	St. Louis	15	7	8	0	2		
	Total	33	11	22	0	7		1978-94
Beverley, Nick	Toronto	6	2	4	0	1		1995-96
Blackburn, Don	Hartford	3	0	3	0	1		1979-81
Blair, Wren	Minnesota	14	7	7	0	1		1967-70
Blake, Toe	Montreal	119	82	37	0	13	8	1955-68
Boileau, Marc	Pittsburgh	9	5	4	0	1		1973-76
Boivin, Leo	St. Louis	3	1	2	0	1		1975-78
Boucher, Frank	NY Rangers	27	13	14	0	4	1	1939-54
Boucher, Georges	Mtl. Maroons	2	0	2	0	1		1930-50
Bowman, Scotty	St. Louis	52	26	26	0	4		
	Montreal	98	70	28	0	8	5	
	Buffalo	36	18	18	0	5		
	Pittsburgh	33	23	10	0	2	1	
	Detroit	111	70	41	0	8	2	
	Total	330	207	123	0	27	8	1967-01
Bowness, Rick	Boston	15	8	7	0	1		1988-98
Brooks, Herb	NY Rangers	24	12	12	0	3		
	New Jersey	5	1	4	0	1		
	Pittsburgh	11	6	5	0	1		
	Total	40	19	21	0	5		1981-00
Brophy, John	Toronto	19	9	10	0	2		1986-89
Burns, Charlie	Minnesota	6	2	4	0	1		1969-75
Burns, Pat	Montreal	56	30	26	0	4		
	Toronto	46	23	23	0	3		
	Boston	18	8	10	0	3		
	Total	120	61	59	0	9		1988-01
Campbell, Colin	NY Rangers	36	18	18	0	3		1994-98
Carpenter, Doug	Toronto	5	1	4	0	1		1984-91
Carroll, Dick	Toronto	9	4	5	0	2	1	1917-19
Cheevers, Gerry	Boston	34	15	19	0	4		1980-85
Cherry, Don	Boston	55	31	24	0	5		1974-80
Clancy, King	Toronto	14	2	12	0	3		1937-56
Clapper, Dit	Boston	25	8	17	0	4		1945-49
Cleghorn, Odie	Pittsburgh	4	1	2	1	2		1925-29
Cleghorn, Sprague	Mtl. Maroons	4	1	1	2	1		1931-32
Constantine, Kevin	San Jose	25	11	14	0	2		
	Pittsburgh	19	8	11	0	2		
	Total	44	19	25	0	4		1993-00
Crawford, Marc	Quebec	6	2	4	0	1		
	Colorado	46	29	17	0	3	1	
	Vancouver	4	0	4	0	1		
	Total	56	31	25	0	5	1	1994-01
Creighton, Fred	Atlanta	9	2	7	0	4		1974-80
Crisp, Terry	Calgary	37	22	15	0	3	1	
	Tampa Bay	6	2	4	0	1		
	Total	43	24	19	0	4	1	1987-98
Crozier, Joe	Buffalo	6	2	4	0	1		1971-81
Cunniff, John	New Jersey	6	2	4	0	1		1982-91
Curry, Alex	Ottawa	2	0	1	1	1		1925-26
Dandurand, Leo	Montreal	16	10	6	0	4	1	1921-35
Day, Hap	Toronto	80	49	31	0	9	5	1940-50
Demers, Jacques	St. Louis	33	16	17	0	3		
	Detroit	38	20	18	0	3		
	Montreal	27	19	8	0	2	1	
	Total	98	55	43	0	8	1	1979-99
Denneny, Cy	Boston	5	5	0	0	1	1	1928-33
Dudley, Rick	Buffalo	12	4	8	0	2		1989-92
Dugal, Jules	Montreal	3	1	2	0	1		1938-39
Duncan, Art	Toronto	2	0	1	1	1	1	1926-32
Dutton, Red	NY Americans	16	6	10	0	4		1935-42
Esposito, Phil	NY Rangers	10	2	8	0	2		1986-89
Evans, Jack	Hartford	16	8	8	0	2		1975-88
Ferguson, John	Winnipeg	3	0	3	0	1		1975-86
Francis, Bob	Phoenix	5	1	4	0	1		1999-01
Francis, Emile	NY Rangers	75	34	41	0	9		
	St. Louis	14	5	9	0	2		
	Total	89	39	50	0	11		1965-83
Ftorek, Robbie	Los Angeles	16	5	11	0	2		
	New Jersey	7	3	4	0	1		
	Total	23	8	15	0	3		1987-00
Gainey, Bob	Minnesota	30	17	13	0	2		
	Dallas	14	6	8	0	2		
	Total	44	23	21	0	4		1990-96
Geoffrion, Bernie	Atlanta	4	0	4	0	1		1968-80
Gerard, Eddie	Mtl. Maroons	25	11	9	5	5	1	1917-35
Gill, David	Ottawa	8	3	2	3	2	1	1926-29
Glover, Fred	Oakland	11	3	8	0	2		1968-74
Gordon, Jackie	Minnesota	25	11	14	0	3		1970-75
Goring, Butch	Boston	3	0	3	0	1		1985-01
Gorman, Tommy	NY Americans	2	0	1	1	1		
	Chicago	8	6	1	1	1	1	
	Mtl. Maroons	15	7	6	2	3	1	
	Total	25	13	8	4	5	2	1925-38
Gottselig, Johnny	Chicago	4	0	4	0	1		1944-48
Green, Pete	Ottawa	26	14	9	3	6	3	1919-25
Green, Ted	Edmonton	16	8	8	0	1		1991-94
Guidolin, Bep	Boston	21	11	10	0	2		1972-76
Harris, Ted	Minnesota	2	0	2	0	1		1975-78
Hart, Cecil	Montreal	37	16	17	4	8	2	1926-39
Hartley, Bob	Colorado	59	38	21	0	3	1	1998-01
Hartsburg, Craig	Chicago	16	8	8	0	2		
	Anaheim	4	0	4	0	1		
	Total	20	8	12	0	3		1995-01
Harvey, Doug	NY Rangers	6	2	4	0	1		1961-62
Hay, Don	Phoenix	7	3	4	0	1		1996-01
Henning, Lorne	Minnesota	5	2	3	0	1		1985-01
Hitchcock, Ken	Dallas	80	47	33	0	5	1	1995-01
Hlinka, Ivan	Pittsburgh	18	9	9	0	1		2000-01
Holmgren, Paul	Philadelphia	19	10	9	0	1		1988-96
Imlach, Punch	Toronto	92	44	48	0	11	4	1958-80
Inglis, Bill	Buffalo	3	1	2	0	1		1978-79
Irvin, Dick	Chicago	9	5	3	1	1		
	Toronto	66	33	32	1	9	1	
	Montreal	115	62	53	0	14	3	
	Total	190	100	88	2	24	4	1928-56
Ivan, Tommy	Detroit	67	36	31	0	7	3	1947-58
Johnson, Bob	Calgary	52	25	27	0	5		
	Pittsburgh	24	16	8	0	1	1	
	Total	76	41	35	0	6	1	1982-91
Johnson, Tom	Boston	22	15	7	0	2	1	1970-73
Johnston, Eddie	Chicago	7	3	4	0	1		
	Pittsburgh	46	22	24	0	5		
	Total	53	25	28	0	6		1979-97
Kasper, Steve	Boston	5	1	4	0	1		1995-97
Keenan, Mike	Philadelphia	57	32	25	0	4		
	Chicago	60	33	27	0	4		
	NY Rangers	23	16	7	0	1	1	
	St. Louis	20	10	10	0	2		
	Total	160	91	69	0	11	1	1984-01
Kelly, Pat	Colorado	2	0	2	0	1		1977-79
Kelly, Red	Los Angeles	18	7	11	0	2		
	Pittsburgh	14	6	8	0	2		
	Toronto	30	11	19	0	4		
	Total	62	24	38	0	8		1967-77
King, Dave	Calgary	20	8	12	0	3		1992-01
Kromm, Bobby	Detroit	7	3	4	0	1		1977-80
Lalonde, Newsy	Montreal	16	7	6	3	4		
	Ottawa	2	0	1	1	1		
	Total	18	7	7	4	5		1917-35
Lemaire, Jacques	Montreal	27	15	12	0	2		
	New Jersey	56	34	22	0	4	1	
	Total	83	49	34	0	6	1	1983-01
Ley, Rick	Hartford	13	5	8	0	2		
	Vancouver	11	4	7	0	1		
	Total	24	9	15	0	3		1989-96
Long, Barry	Winnipeg	11	3	8	0	2		1983-86
Loughlin, Clem	Chicago	4	1	2	1	2		1934-37
Low, Ron	Edmonton	28	10	18	0	3		1994-01
Lowe, Kevin	Edmonton	5	1	4	0	1		1999-00
MacLean, Doug	Florida	27	13	14	0	2		1995-98
MacNeil, Al	Montreal	20	12	8	0	1	1	
	Atlanta	4	1	3	0	1		
	Calgary	19	9	10	0	2		
	Total	43	22	21	0	4	1	1970-82
MacTavish, Craig	Edmonton	6	2	4	0	1		2000-01
Magnuson, Keith	Chicago	3	0	3	0	1		1980-82
Mahoney, Bill	Minnesota	16	7	9	0	1		1983-85
Maloney, Dan	Toronto	10	6	4	0	1		
	Winnipeg	15	5	10	0	2		
	Total	25	11	14	0	3		1984-89
Maloney, Phil	Vancouver	7	1	6	0	2		1973-77
Martin, Jacques	St. Louis	16	7	9	0	2		
	Ottawa	32	10	22	0	4		
	Total	48	17	31	0	7		1986-01
Maurice, Paul	Carolina	12	4	8	0	2		1995-01
McCammon, Bob	Philadelphia	10	1	9	0	3		
	Vancouver	7	3	4	0	1		
	Total	17	4	13	0	4		1978-91
McLellan, John	Toronto	11	3	8	0	2		1969-73
McVie, Tom	New Jersey	14	6	8	0	2		1975-92
Melrose, Barry	Los Angeles	24	13	11	0	1		1992-95
Milbury, Mike	Boston	40	23	17	0	2		1989-98
Muckler, John	Edmonton	40	25	15	0	2	1	
	Buffalo	27	11	16	0	4		
	Total	67	36	31	0	6	1	1968-00
Muldoon, Pete	Chicago	2	0	1	1	1		1926-27
Munro, Dunc	Mtl. Maroons	4	1	3	0	1		1929-31
Murdoch, Bob	Chicago	5	1	4	0	1		
	Winnipeg	7	3	4	0	1		
	Total	12	4	8	0	2		1987-91
Murphy, Mike	Los Angeles	5	1	4	0	1		1986-98
Murray, Andy	Los Angeles	17	7	10	0	2		1999-01

Coach	Team	Games Coached	Wins	Losses	Ties	Playoff Year	Cup Wins	Career
Murray, Bryan	Washington	53	24	29	0	7		
	Detroit	25	10	15	0	3		
	Total	**78**	**34**	**44**	**0**	**10**		**1981-98**
Murray, Terry	Washington	39	18	21	0	4		
	Philadelphia	46	28	18	0	3		
	Florida	4	0	4	0	1		
	Total	**89**	**46**	**43**	**0**	**8**		**1989-01**
Neale, Harry	**Vancouver**	**14**	**3**	**11**	**0**	**4**		**1978-86**
Neilson, Roger	Toronto	19	8	11	0	2		
	Buffalo	8	4	4	0	1		
	Vancouver	21	12	9	0	2		
	NY Rangers	29	13	16	0	3		
	Philadelphia	29	14	15	0	3		
	Total	**106**	**51**	**55**	**0**	**11**		**1977-00**
Nolan, Ted	**Buffalo**	**12**	**5**	**7**	**0**	**1**		**1995-97**
Nykoluk, Mike	**Toronto**	**7**	**1**	**6**	**0**	**2**		**1980-84**
O'Donoghue, George	**Toronto**	**7**	**4**	**2**	**1**	**1**		**1921-23**
O'Reilly, Terry	**Boston**	**37**	**17**	**19**	**1**	**3**		**1986-89**
Oliver, Murray	**Minnesota**	**13**	**5**	**8**	**0**	**2**		**1981-83**
Paddock, John	**Winnipeg**	**13**	**5**	**8**	**0**	**2**		**1991-95**
Page, Pierre	Minnesota	12	4	8	0	2		
	Quebec	6	2	4	0	1		
	Calgary	4	0	4	0	1		
	Total	**22**	**6**	**16**	**0**	**4**		**1988-98**
Patrick, Craig	NY Rangers	17	7	10	0	2		
	Pittsburgh	5	1	4	0	1		
	Total	**22**	**8**	**14**	**0**	**3**		**1980-97**
Patrick, Frank	**Boston**	**6**	**2**	**4**	**0**	**2**		**1934-36**
Patrick, Lester	**NY Rangers**	**65**	**32**	**26**	**7**	**12**	**2**	**1926-39**
Patrick, Lynn	NY Rangers	12	7	5	0	1		
	Boston	28	9	18	1	4		
	Total	**40**	**16**	**23**	**1**	**5**		**1948-76**
Perron, Jean	**Montreal**	**48**	**30**	**18**	**0**	**3**	**1**	**1985-89**
Perry, Don	**Los Angeles**	**10**	**4**	**6**	**0**	**1**		**1981-84**
Pilous, Rudy	**Chicago**	**41**	**19**	**22**	**0**	**5**	**1**	**1957-63**
Plager, Barclay	**St. Louis**	**4**	**1**	**3**	**0**	**1**		**1977-83**
Pleau, Larry	**Hartford**	**10**	**2**	**8**	**0**	**2**		**1980-89**
Polano, Nick	**Detroit**	**7**	**1**	**6**	**0**	**2**		**1982-85**
Powers, Eddie	**Toronto**	**2**	**0**	**2**	**0**	**1**		**1924-26**
Primeau, Joe	**Toronto**	**15**	**8**	**6**	**1**	**2**	**1**	**1950-53**
Pronovost, Marcel	**Buffalo**	**8**	**3**	**5**	**0**	**1**		**1977-79**
Pulford, Bob	Los Angeles	26	10	16	0	4		
	Chicago	45	17	28	0	6		
	Total	**71**	**27**	**44**	**0**	**10**		**1972-00**
Quenneville, Joel	**St. Louis**	**51**	**26**	**25**	**0**	**5**		**1996-01**
Quinn, Pat	Philadelphia	39	22	17	0	3		
	Los Angeles	3	0	3	0	1		
	Vancouver	61	31	30	0	5		
	Toronto	40	22	18	0	3		
	Total	**143**	**75**	**68**	**0**	**12**		**1978-01**
Reay, Billy	**Chicago**	**116**	**56**	**60**	**0**	**12**		**1957-77**
Risebrough, Doug	**Calgary**	**7**	**3**	**4**	**0**	**1**		**1990-92**
Roberts, Jim	**Hartford**	**7**	**3**	**4**	**0**	**1**		**1981-97**
Robinson, Larry	Los Angeles	4	0	4	0	1		
	New Jersey	48	31	17	0	2	1	
	Total	**52**	**31**	**21**	**0**	**3**	**1**	**1995-01**

Coach	Team	Games Coached	Wins	Losses	Ties	Playoff Years	Cup Wins	Career
Ross, Art	**Boston**	**65**	**27**	**33**	**5**	**11**	**1**	**1917-45**
Ruel, Claude	**Montreal**	**27**	**18**	**9**	**0**	**3**	**2**	**1968-81**
Ruff, Lindy	**Buffalo**	**54**	**32**	**22**	**0**	**4**		**1997-01**
Sather, Glen	**Edmonton**	**127**	**89**	**37**	**1**	**10**	**4**	**1979-94**
Sator, Ted	NY Rangers	16	8	8	0	1		
	Buffalo	11	3	8	0	2		
	Total	**27**	**11**	**16**	**0**	**3**		**1985-89**
Schinkel, Ken	**Pittsburgh**	**6**	**2**	**4**	**0**	**2**		**1972-77**
Schmidt, Milt	**Boston**	**34**	**15**	**19**	**0**	**4**		**1954-76**
Schoenfeld, Jim	New Jersey	20	11	9	0	1		
	Washington	24	10	14	0	3		
	Phoenix	13	5	8	0	2		
	Total	**57**	**26**	**31**	**0**	**6**		**1985-99**
Shero, Fred	Philadelphia	83	48	35	0	6	2	
	NY Rangers	27	15	12	0	2		
	Total	**110**	**63**	**47**	**0**	**8**	**2**	**1971-81**
Simpson, Terry	NY Islanders	20	9	11	0	2		
	Winnipeg	6	2	4	0	1		
	Total	**26**	**11**	**15**	**0**	**3**		**1986-96**
Sinden, Harry	**Boston**	**43**	**24**	**19**	**0**	**5**	**1**	**1966-85**
Skinner, Jimmy	**Detroit**	**26**	**14**	**12**	**0**	**3**	**1**	**1954-58**
Smith, Alf	**Ottawa**	**5**	**1**	**4**	**0**	**1**		**1918-19**
Smith, Floyd	**Buffalo**	**32**	**16**	**16**	**0**	**3**		**1971-80**
Smythe, Conn	**Toronto**	**4**	**2**	**2**	**0**	**1**		**1927-31**
Sonmor, Glen	**Minnesota**	**43**	**25**	**18**	**0**	**3**		**1978-87**
Stasiuk, Vic	**Philadelphia**	**4**	**0**	**4**	**0**	**1**		**1969-73**
Stewart, Bill	**Chicago**	**10**	**7**	**3**	**0**	**1**	**1**	**1937-39**
Stewart, Ron	**Los Angeles**	**2**	**0**	**2**	**0**	**1**		**1975-78**
Sutter, Brian	St. Louis	41	20	21	0	4		
	Boston	22	7	15	0	3		
	Total	**63**	**27**	**36**	**0**	**7**		**1988-00**
Sutter, Darryl	Chicago	26	11	15	0	3		
	San Jose	30	11	19	0	4		
	Total	**56**	**22**	**34**	**0**	**7**		**1992-01**
Talbot, Jean-Guy	St. Louis	5	1	4	0	1		
	NY Rangers	3	1	2	0	1		
	Total	**8**	**2**	**6**	**0**	**2**		**1972-78**
Tessier, Orval	**Chicago**	**18**	**9**	**9**	**0**	**2**		**1982-85**
Thompson, Paul	**Chicago**	**19**	**7**	**12**	**0**	**4**		**1938-45**
Tobin, Bill	**Chicago**	**4**	**1**	**2**	**1**	**2**		**1929-32**
Tremblay, Mario	**Montreal**	**11**	**3**	**8**	**0**	**2**		**1995-97**
Ubriaco, Gene	**Pittsburgh**	**11**	**7**	**4**	**0**	**1**		**1988-90**
Vigneault, Alain	**Montreal**	**10**	**4**	**6**	**0**	**1**		**1997-01**
Watson, Phil	**NY Rangers**	**16**	**4**	**12**	**0**	**3**		**1955-63**
Watt, Tom	Winnipeg	7	1	6	0	2		
	Vancouver	3	0	3	0	1		
	Total	**10**	**1**	**9**	**0**	**3**		**1981-92**
Webster, Tom	**Los Angeles**	**28**	**12**	**16**	**0**	**3**		**1986-92**
Weiland, Cooney	**Boston**	**17**	**10**	**7**	**0**	**2**	**1**	**1939-41**
White, Bill	**Chicago**	**2**	**0**	**2**	**0**	**1**		**1976-77**
Wilson, Johnny	**Pittsburgh**	**12**	**4**	**8**	**0**	**2**		**1969-80**
Wilson, Ron	Anaheim	11	4	7	0	1		
	Washington	32	15	17	0	3		
	Total	**43**	**19**	**24**	**0**	**4**		**1993-01**
Young, Garry	**St. Louis**	**2**	**0**	**2**	**0**	**1**		**1972-76**

Bob Hartley (left) led the Colorado Avalanche to their second Stanley Cup victory in 2001. Marc Crawford (right), who led Colorado to its first title in 1996, guided Vancouver back into the playoffs for the first time since that season.

Penalty Shots in Stanley Cup Playoff Games

Date	Player	Goaltender	Scored	Final Score	Series
Mar. 25/37	Lionel Conacher, Mtl. Maroons	Tiny Thompson, Boston	No	Mtl. M. 0 at Bos. 4	QF
Apr. 15/37	Alex Shibicky, NY Rangers	Earl Robertson, Detroit	No	NYR 0 at Det. 3	F
Apr. 13/44	Virgil Johnson, Chicago	Bill Durnan, Montreal	No	Chi. 4 at Mtl. 5*	F
Apr. 9/68	Wayne Connelly, Minnesota	Terry Sawchuk, Los Angeles	Yes	L.A. 5 at Min. 7	QF
Apr. 27/68	Jim Roberts, St. Louis	Cesare Maniago, Minnesota	No	St. L. 4 at Min. 3	SF
May 16/71	Frank Mahovlich, Montreal	Tony Esposito, Chicago	No	Chi. 3 at Mtl. 4	F
May 7/75	Bill Barber, Philadelphia	Chico Resch, NY Islanders	No	Phi. 3 at NYI 4*	SF
Apr. 20/79	Mike Walton, Chicago	Chico Resch, NY Islanders	No	NYI 4 at Chi. 0	QF
Apr. 9/81	Peter McNab, Boston	Don Beaupre, Minnesota	No	Min. 5 at Bos. 4*	PR
Apr. 17/81	Anders Hedberg, NY Rangers	Mike Liut, St. Louis	Yes	NYR 6 at St. L. 4	QF
Apr. 9/83	Denis Potvin, NY Islanders	Pat Riggin, Washington	No	NYI 6 at Wsh. 2	DSF
Apr. 28/84	Wayne Gretzky, Edmonton	Don Beaupre, Minnesota	Yes	Edm. 8 at Min. 5	CF
May 1/84	Mats Naslund, Montreal	Billy Smith, NY Islanders	No	Mtl. 1 at NYI 3	CF
Apr. 14/85	Bob Carpenter, Washington	Billy Smith, NY Islanders	No	Wsh. 4 at NYI. 6	DF
May 28/85	Ron Sutter, Philadelphia	Grant Fuhr, Edmonton	No	Phi. 3 at Edm. 5	F
May 30/85	Dave Poulin, Philadelphia	Grant Fuhr, Edmonton	No	Phi. 3 at Edm. 8	F
Apr. 9/88	John Tucker, Buffalo	Andy Moog, Boston	Yes	Bos. 2 at Buf. 6	DSF
Apr. 9/88	Petr Klima, Detroit	Allan Bester, Toronto	Yes	Det. 6 at Tor. 3	DSF
Apr. 8/89	Neal Broten, Minnesota	Greg Millen, St. Louis	Yes	St. L. 5 at Min. 3	DSF
Apr. 4/90	Al MacInnis, Calgary	Kelly Hrudey, Los Angeles	Yes	L.A. 5 at Cgy. 3	DSF
Apr. 5/90	Randy Wood, NY Islanders	Mike Richter, NY Rangers	No	NYI 1 at NYR 2	DSF
May 3/90	Kelly Miller, Washington	Andy Moog, Boston	No	Wsh. 3 at Bos. 5	CF
May 18/90	Petr Klima, Edmonton	Reggie Lemelin, Boston	No	Edm. 7 at Bos. 2	F
Apr. 6/91	Basil McRae, Minnesota	Ed Belfour, Chicago	Yes	Min. 2 at Chi. 5	DSF
Apr. 10/91	Steve Duchesne, Los Angeles	Kirk McLean, Vancouver	Yes	L.A. 6 at Van. 1	DSF
May 11/92	Jaromir Jagr, Pittsburgh	John Vanbiesbrouck, NYR	Yes	Pit. 3 at NYR 2	DF
May 13/92	Shawn McEachern, Pittsburgh	John Vanbiesbrouck, NYR	No	NYR 1 at Pit. 5	DF
June 7/94	Pavel Bure, Vancouver	Mike Richter, NYR	No	NYR 4 at Van. 2	F
May 9/95	Patrick Poulin, Chicago	Felix Potvin, Toronto	No	Tor. 3 at Chi. 0	CQF
May 10/95	Michal Pivonka, Washington	Tom Barrasso, Pittsburgh	No	Pit. 2 at Wsh. 6	CQF
Apr. 24/96	Joe Juneau, Washington	Ken Wregget, Pittsburgh	No	Pit. 3 at Wsh. 2**	CQF
May 11/97	Eric Lindros, Philadelphia	Steve Shields, Buffalo	Yes	Phi. 6 at Buf. 3	CSF
Apr. 23/98	Alexei Morozov, Pittsburgh	Andy Moog, Montreal	No	Mtl. 3 at Pit. 2**	CQF
Apr. 22/99	Mats Sundin, Toronto	John Vanbiesbrouck, Phi.	No	Phi. 3 at Tor. 0	CQF
May 29/99	Mats Sundin, Toronto	Dominik Hasek, Buffalo	Yes	Tor. 2 at Buf. 5	CF
Apr. 16/00	Eric Desjardins, Philadelphia	Dominik Hasek, Buffalo	No	Phi. 2 at Buf. 0	CQF
Apr. 11/01	Mark Recchi, Philadelphia	Dominik Hasek, Buffalo	No	Buf. 2 at Phi. 1	CQF
May 2/01	Martin Straka, Pittsburgh	Dominik Hasek, Buffalo	No	Buf. 5 at Pit. 2	CSF
May 12/01	Joe Sakic, Colorado	Roman Turek, St. Louis	Yes	St. L. 1 at Col. 4	CF

* Game was decided in overtime, but shot taken during regulation time.
** Shot taken in overtime.

Pittsburgh's Martin Straka was one of two shooters that Dominik Hasek stopped on penalty shots in last year's playoffs. Four of the last five playoff penalty shots have come against the former Sabres netminder.

Ten Longest Overtime Games

Date	City	Series	Score		Scorer	Overtime	Series Winner
Mar. 24/36	Mtl.	SF	Det. 1	Mtl. M. 0	Mud Bruneteau	116:30	Det.
Apr. 3/33	Tor.	SF	Tor. 1	Bos. 0	Ken Doraty	104:46	Tor.
May 4/00	Pit.	CSF	Phi. 2	Pit. 1	Keith Primeau	92:01	Phi.
Apr. 24/96	Wsh.	CQF	Pit. 3	Wsh. 2	Petr Nedved	79:15	Pit.
Mar. 23/43	Det.	SF	Tor. 3	Det. 2	Jack McLean	70:18	Det.
Mar. 28/30	Mtl.	SF	Mtl. 2	NYR 1	Gus Rivers	68:52	Mtl.
Apr. 18/87	Wsh.	DSF	NYI 3	Wsh. 2	Pat LaFontaine	68:47	NYI
Apr. 27/94	Buf.	CQF	Buf. 1	N.J. 0	Dave Hannan	65:43	N.J.
Mar. 27/51	Det.	SF	Mtl. 3	Det. 2	Maurice Richard	61:09	Mtl.
Mar. 27/38	NYR	QF	NYA 3	NYR 2	Lorne Carr	60:40	NYA

Overtime Record of Current Teams

(Listed by number of OT games played)

	Overall				Home					Road				
Team	GP	W	L	T	GP	W	L	T	Last OT Game	GP	W	L	T	Last OT Game
Montreal	120	69	49	2	55	36	18	1	May 12/98	65	33	31	1	May 8/98
Boston	98	38	57	3	45	20	24	1	May 3/98	53	18	33	2	Apr. 30/99
Toronto	97	51	45	1	61	33	27	1	May 1/01	36	18	18	0	Apr. 28/01
Detroit	66	31	35	0	39	16	23	0	May 3/00	27	15	12	0	Apr. 23/01
NY Rangers	63	30	33	0	27	12	15	0	Apr. 22/97	36	18	18	0	May 11/97
Chicago	62	30	30	2	30	16	13	1	Apr. 20/97	32	14	17	1	May 2/96
Philadelphia	50	24	26	0	22	11	11	0	Apr. 17/01	28	13	15	0	May 4/00
Dallas[1]	50	23	27	0	23	10	13	0	Apr. 19/01	27	13	14	0	May 1/01
St. Louis	49	27	22	0	26	20	6	0	May 18/01	23	7	16	0	May 21/01
Buffalo	46	25	21	0	26	16	10	0	May 10/01	20	9	11	0	May 8/01
Colorado[2]	40	24	16	0	16	9	7	0	May 21/01	24	15	9	0	May 18/01
NY Islanders	38	29	9	0	17	14	3	0	May 20/93	21	15	6	0	May 18/93
Edmonton	38	21	17	0	21	11	10	0	Apr. 17/01	17	10	7	0	Apr. 19/01
Los Angeles	34	16	18	0	19	11	8	0	May 6/01	15	5	10	0	Apr. 26/01
Vancouver	30	13	17	0	13	5	8	0	Apr. 16/01	17	8	9	0	Apr. 25/96
Calgary[3]	30	11	19	0	14	4	10	0	Apr. 23/96	16	7	9	0	Apr. 28/94
Washington	29	14	15	0	10	5	5	0	May 25/98	19	9	10	0	Apr. 23/01
Pittsburgh	28	15	13	0	18	10	8	0	May 8/01	10	5	5	0	May 10/01
New Jersey[4]	25	8	17	0	11	3	8	0	Apr. 28/01	14	5	9	0	May 1/01
Carolina[5]	14	7	7	0	10	6	4	0	Apr. 18/01	4	1	3	0	May 1/92
Phoenix[6]	12	5	7	0	8	3	5	0	May 4/99	4	2	2	0	Apr. 27/93
San Jose	8	3	5	0	4	1	3	0	May 3/99	4	2	2	0	Apr. 19/01
Ottawa	6	2	4	0	3	1	2	0	Apr. 13/01	3	1	2	0	Apr. 16/01
Florida	5	2	3	0	3	1	2	0	Apr. 25/97	2	1	1	0	Apr. 22/97
Anaheim	4	1	3	0	1	0	1	0	May 8/97	3	1	2	0	May 4/97
Tampa Bay	2	2	0	0	1	1	0	0	Apr. 21/96	1	1	0	0	Apr. 18/96

[1] Totals include those of Minnesota North Stars 1967-93.
[2] Totals include those of Quebec 1979-95.
[3] Totals include those of Atlanta Flames 1972-80.
[4] Totals include those of Kansas City and Colorado Rockies 1974-82.
[5] Totals include those of Hartford 1979-97.
[6] Totals include those of Winnipeg 1979-96.

Joe Sakic scored the series-winning goal just 24 seconds into overtime when Colorado knocked off St. Louis in a five-game Western Conference Final. The Stanley Cup champs posted a 3-3 record in overtime games in the 2001 playoffs.

Late Additions to Player Register

GUITE, Ben (GWIGHT, BEHN) **NYI**

Right wing. Shoots right. 6'1'', 205 lbs. Born, Montreal, Que., July 17, 1978.
(Montreal's 8th choice, 172nd overall, in 1997 Entry Draft).

			Regular Season					Playoffs				
Season	Club	League	GP	G	A	TP	PIM	GP	G	A	TP	PIM
1996-97	U. of Maine	H-East	34	7	7	14	21	....	....	....	....	....
1997-98	U. of Maine	H-East	32	6	12	18	20	....	....	....	....	....
1998-99	U. of Maine	H-East	40	12	16	28	30	....	....	....	....	....
99-2000	U. of Maine	H-East	40	22	14	36	36	....	....	....	....	....
2000-01	Tallahassee	ECHL	68	11	18	29	34	....	....	....	....	....

Signed as a free agent by **NY Islanders**, August, 2001.

TARNSTROM, Dick (TAHRN-struhm, DIHK) **NYI**

Defense. Shoots left. 6'2'', 200 lbs. Born, Sundbyberg, Sweden. January 20, 1975.
(NY Islanders' 12th choice, 272nd overall, in 1994 Entry Draft).

			Regular Season					Playoffs				
Season	Club	League	GP	G	A	TP	PIM	GP	G	A	TP	PIM
1992-93	AIK Solna	Sweden	3	0	0	0	0	....	....	....	....	....
1993-94	AIK Solna	Sweden	33	1	4	5	....	....	....	....	....	....
1994-95	AIK Solna	Sweden	37	8	4	12	26	....	....	....	....	....
1995-96	AIK Solna	Sweden	40	0	5	5	32	....	....	....	....	....
1996-97	AIK Solna	Sweden	49	5	3	8	38	7	0	1	1	6
1997-98	AIK Solna	Sweden	45	2	12	14	30	....	....	....	....	....
1998-99	AIK Solna	Sweden	47	9	14	23	36	....	....	....	....	....
99-2000	AIK Solna	Sweden	42	7	15	22	20	....	....	....	....	....
2000-01	AIK Solna	Sweden	50	10	18	28	28	5	0	0	0	8

KIPRUSOFF, Marko (KIHP-roo-sawf, MAR-koh) **NYI**

Defense. Shoots left. 6'1'', 195 lbs. Born, Turku, Finland. June 6, 1972.
(Montreal's 4th choice, 70th overall, in 1994 Entry Draft).

			Regular Season					Playoffs				
Season	Club	League	GP	G	A	TP	PIM	GP	G	A	TP	PIM
1990-91	TPS Turku	Finn-Jr.	17	2	9	11	2	....	....	....	....	....
	TuTo Turku	Finland-2	22	4	8	12	0	....	....	....	....	....
	TPS Turku	Finland	3	0	0	0	0	....	....	....	....	....
1991-92	TPS Turku	Finland	23	0	2	2	0	....	....	....	....	....
	Kiekko Turku	Finland-2	4	0	0	0	4	....	....	....	....	....
	Hameenlinna	Finland	3	0	0	0	0	....	....	....	....	....
1992-93	TPS Turku	Finland	43	3	7	10	14	12	2	3	5	6
	Kiekko Turku	Finland-2	1	0	1	1	2	....	....	....	....	....
1993-94	TPS Turku	Finland	48	5	19	24	8	11	0	6	6	4
1994-95	TPS Turku	Finland	50	10	21	31	16	13	0	9	9	2
1995-96	**Montreal**	**NHL**	**24**	**0**	**4**	**4**	**8**	**....**	**....**	**....**	**....**	**....**
	Fredericton	AHL	28	4	10	14	2	10	2	5	7	2
1996-97	Malmo	Sweden	50	10	18	28	24	4	0	0	0	0
1997-98	Malmo	Sweden	46	7	16	23	23	....	....	....	....	....
1998-99	TPS Turku	Finland	49	15	22	37	12	10	3	6	9	0
99-2000	TPS Turku	Finland	53	6	27	33	10	11	0	3	3	0
2000-01	EHC Kloten	Switz.	43	6	20	26	10	9	2	7	9	2

Signed as a free agent by **NY Islanders**, June 15, 2001.

ARMSTRONG, Chris Signed as a free agent by **NY Islanders**, August 8, 2001.

HERR, Matt Signed as a free agent by **Florida**, August 21, 2001.

HULL, Brett Signed as a free agent by **Detroit**, August 22, 2001.

LAFLAMME, Christian Signed as a free agent by **St. Louis**, August 21, 2001.

PODOLLAN, Jason Signed as a free agent by **NY Islanders**, August, 2001.

ROCHE, Dave Signed as a free agent by **NY Islanders**, August 17, 2001.

TOBLER, Ryan Signed as a free agent by **Tampa Bay**, August 21, 2001.

TUOMAINEN, Marko Signed as a free agent by **NY Islanders**, July 18, 2001.

League Abbreviations

AAHA	Alberta Amateur Hockey Association
AAHL	Alaska Amateur Hockey League
ACHL	Atlantic Coast Hockey League
AFHL	American Frontier Hockey League
AHL	American Hockey League
AJHL	Alberta Junior Hockey Leagues
Alpenliga	Alpenliga (Austria, Italy, Slovenia 1994-1999)
AMHL	Alberta Midget AAA Hockey League
AUAA	Atlantic University Athletic Association
BCAHA	British Columbia Amateur Hockey Association
BCJHL	British Columbia Junior Hockey League
CCHA	Central Collegiate Hockey Association
CEGEP	Quebec College Prep
CHA	College Hockey America
CHL	Central Hockey League
CIS	Commonwealth of Independent States
ColHL	Colonial Hockey League
CWUAA	Canadian Western University Athletic Association
DEB	Deutsche Eishockey Bundesliga
DEL	Deutsche Eishockey Liga
ECAC	Eastern College Athletic Conference
ECHL	East Coast Hockey League
EJHL	Eastern Junior Hockey League
EuroHL	European Hockey League
G.N.	Great Northern
GPAC	Great Plains Athletic Conference
H-East	Hockey East
HJHL	Heritage Junior Hockey League
Hi-School	High School (also H.S.)
IEL	Internationale Eishockey Liga
IHL	International Hockey League
IJHL	Interstate Junior Hockey League
KIDHL	Kootenay International Junior B Hockey League
MAAC	Metro Atlantic Athletic Conference
MAHA	Manitoba Amateur Hockey Association
MBHL	Metropolitan Boston Hockey League
MEHL	Midwest Elite Hockey League
MIAC	Minnesota Intercollegiate Athletic Conference
MJHL	Manitoba Junior Hockey League
MJrHL	Maritime Junior Major Hockey League
MMHL	Manitoba Midget AAA Hockey League
MNHL	Michigan National Hockey League
MTJHL	Metropolitan Toronto Junior Hockey League
MTHL	Metro Toronto Hockey League
NAJHL	North American Junior Hockey League
Nat-Team	National Team (also Nt.-Team)
NBAHA	New Brunswick Amateur Hockey Association
NCAA	National Collegiate Athletic Association
NEJHL	New England Junior Hockey League
NFAHA	Newfoundland Amateur Hockey Association
NHL	National Hockey League
NOHA	Northern Ontario Hockey Association
NOJHL	Northern Ontario Junior Hockey League
NSMHL	Nova Scotia Midget AAA Hockey League
OCJHL	Ontario Central Junior A Hockey League
OHL	Ontario Hockey League
OJHL-B	Ontario Junior B Hockey Leagues
OMHA	Ontario Minor Hockey Association
OMJHL	Ontario Major Junior Hockey League
OPJHL	Ontario Provincial Junior A Hockey League
OUAA	Ontario Universities Athletic Association
QAAA	Quebec Amateur Athletic Association
QAHA	Quebec Amateur Hockey Association
QJHL	Quebec Junior Hockey League
QMJHL	Quebec Major Junior Hockey League
PCJHL	Pacific Coast Junior Hockey League
PIJHL	Pacific International Junior Hockey League
RMJHL	Rocky Mountain Junior Hockey League
SAHA	Saskatchewan Amateur Hockey Association
SJHL	Saskatchewan Junior Hockey League
SMHL	Saskatchewan Midget AAA Hockey League
SSJHL	Southern Saskatchewan Junior B Hockey League
SunHL	Sunshine Hockey League
TBAHA	Thunder Bay Amateur Hockey Association
TBJHL	Thunder Bay Junior Hockey League
TBMHL	Thunder Bay Midget Hockey League
UHL	United Hockey League
USAHA	United States Amateur Hockey Association
USDP	United States National Development Under-18 Program
USDP-17	United States National Development Under-17 Program
USHL	United States (Junior A) Hockey League
VIJHL	Vancouver Island Junior Hockey League
WCHA	Western Collegiate Hockey Association
WCHL	West Coast Hockey League
WHA	World Hockey Association
WHL	Western Hockey League
WNYHA	Western New York Hockey Association
WPHL	Western Professional Hockey League
WSJHL	Western States Junior Hockey League
X-Games	Exhibition Games, Series or Season

2001-02 Prospect Register

Note: The 2001-02 Prospect Register lists forwards and defensemen only. Goaltenders are listed separately. The Prospect Register lists every player drafted in the first five rounds of the 2001 Entry Draft, players on NHL Reserve Lists and other players who have not yet played in the NHL. Trades and roster changes are current as of August 20, 2001.

Abbreviations: A – assists; **G** – goals; **GP** – games played; **Lea** – league; **PIM** – penalties in minutes; **TP** – total points; ***** – league-leading total.

NHL Player Register begins on page 338.

Goaltender Register begins on page 575.

League Abbreviations are listed on page 274.

ABBOTT, Jim — PIT.

Left wing. Shoots left. 6'1", 185 lbs. Born, New York, NY, May 3, 1980.
(Pittsburgh's 7th choice, 216th overall, in 2000 Entry Draft).

			Regular Season					Playoffs				
Season	Club	Lea	GP	G	A	TP	PIM	GP	G	A	TP	PIM
1997-98	Pittsburgh	MTJHL	50	30	23	53	138	....	....	....	....	....
1998-99	St. Louis Sting	NAJHL	56	*45	33	78	35	9	7	2	9	12
99-2000	New Hampshire	H-East	28	7	6	13	22	....	....	....	....	....
2000-01	New Hampshire	H-East	33	10	12	22	52	....	....	....	....	....

NAJHL First All-Star Team (1999)

ABID, Ramzi (a-BIHD, RAM-zee) — PHX.

Left wing. Shoots left. 6'2", 210 lbs. Born, Montreal, Que., March 24, 1980.
(Phoenix's 3rd choice, 85th overall, in 2000 Entry Draft).

			Regular Season					Playoffs				
Season	Club	Lea	GP	G	A	TP	PIM	GP	G	A	TP	PIM
1995-96	Richelieu Selectes	QAAA	42	10	14	24	18	4	1	2	3	2
1996-97	Chicoutimi	QMJHL	65	13	24	37	141	21	2	12	14	28
1997-98	Chicoutimi	QMJHL	68	50	*85	*135	266	6	3	4	7	10
1998-99	Chicoutimi	QMJHL	21	11	15	26	97	....	....	....	....	....
	Acadie-Bathurst	QMJHL	24	14	22	36	102	23	14	20	34	*84
99-2000	Acadie-Bathurst	QMJHL	13	10	11	21	61	....	....	....	....	....
	Halifax	QMJHL	59	57	80	137	148	10	10	13	23	18
2000-01	Springfield	AHL	17	6	4	10	38	....	....	....	....	....

• Re-entered NHL Entry Draft. Originally Colorado's 5th choice, 28th overall, in 1998 Entry Draft.

QMJHL First All-Star Team (1998, 2000) • Canadian Major Junior First All-Star Team (2000) • Won Ed Chynoweth Trophy (Memorial Cup Tournament Leading Scorer) (2000)

• Missed majority of 2000-01 season recovering from hand injury originally suffered in game vs. Louisville (AHL), October 27, 2000.

ABRAHAMSSON, Elias (AH-brah-ham-suhn, eh-LEE-ahs)

Defense. Shoots left. 6'3", 240 lbs. Born, Uppsala, Sweden, June 15, 1977.
(Boston's 6th choice, 132nd overall, in 1996 Entry Draft).

			Regular Season					Playoffs				
Season	Club	Lea	GP	G	A	TP	PIM	GP	G	A	TP	PIM
1993-94	Uppsala AIS	Swede-2	1	0	0	0	0	....	....	....	....	....
1994-95	Halifax	QMJHL	25	0	3	3	41	....	....	....	....	....
1995-96	Halifax	QMJHL	64	3	11	14	268	6	2	2	4	8
1996-97	Halifax	QMJHL	30	4	10	14	231	18	4	9	13	74
1997-98	Providence Bruins	AHL	29	0	1	1	47	....	....	....	....	....
1998-99	Providence Bruins	AHL	75	2	9	11	184	4	0	0	0	7
99-2000	Providence Bruins	AHL	19	1	1	2	45	....	....	....	....	....
	Hamilton Bulldogs	AHL	56	1	3	4	90	10	0	1	1	4
2000-01	Providence Bruins	AHL	39	2	2	4	54	14	0	0	0	20

• Missed majority of 1996-97 and 1997-98 seasons recovering from shoulder injury suffered at Boston Bruins training camp, September 28, 1996.

ADDUONO, Jeremy (uh-DOO-noh, JAIR-eh-mee) — BUF.

Right wing. Shoots right. 6', 183 lbs. Born, Thunder Bay, Ont., August 4, 1978.
(Buffalo's 8th choice, 184th overall, in 1997 Entry Draft).

			Regular Season					Playoffs				
Season	Club	Lea	GP	G	A	TP	PIM	GP	G	A	TP	PIM
1994-95	Thunder Bay	USHL	40	11	10	21	8	....	....	....	....	....
1995-96	Sudbury Wolves	OHL	66	15	22	37	14	....	....	....	....	....
1996-97	Sudbury Wolves	OHL	66	29	40	69	24	....	....	....	....	....
1997-98	Sudbury Wolves	OHL	66	37	69	106	40	10	5	5	10	10
1998-99	Canada	Nat-Team	44	10	18	28	10	....	....	....	....	....
99-2000	Rochester	AHL	51	23	22	45	20	21	6	11	17	2
2000-01	Rochester	AHL	76	24	30	54	53	4	1	0	1	4

AHMAOJA, Timo (ahkh-mah-OH-yah, TIH-moo) — ANA.

Defense. Shoots right. 6'1", 180 lbs. Born, Jyvaskyla, Finland, August 8, 1978.
(Anaheim's 5th choice, 172nd overall, in 1996 Entry Draft).

			Regular Season					Playoffs				
Season	Club	Lea	GP	G	A	TP	PIM	GP	G	A	TP	PIM
1993-94	JyP Jyvaskyla-C	Finn-Jr.	32	6	9	15	34	6	2	0	2	4
1994-95	JyP Jyvaskyla-B	Finn-Jr.	6	1	3	4	8	....	....	....	....	....
	JyP Jyvaskyla	Finn-Jr.	30	1	1	2	2	7	0	0	0	0
1995-96	JyP Jyvaskyla	Finn-Jr.	28	0	7	7	16	6	1	0	1	2
	JyP Jyvaskyla	Finland	4	0	0	0	4	....	....	....	....	....
1996-97	JyP Jyvaskyla	Finn-Jr.	19	4	5	9	24	....	....	....	....	....
	JyP Jyvaskyla	Finland	35	0	4	4	8	....	....	....	....	....
1997-98	JyP Jyvaskyla	Finland	10	0	0	0	4	....	....	....	....	....
	Diskos Jyvaskyla	Finland-2	23	1	2	3	14	....	....	....	....	....
	Lukko Rauma	Finland	10	0	0	0	0	....	....	....	....	....
1998-99	KalPa Kuopio	Finn-Jr.	3	0	1	1	10	....	....	....	....	....
	KalPa Kuopio	Finland	52	0	1	1	16	....	....	....	....	....
99-2000	Pelicans Lahti	Finland	29	0	0	0	4	....	....	....	....	....
2000-01	Assat-Pori	Finland	32	1	3	4	10	....	....	....	....	....
	HPK Hameenlinna	Finland	21	1	0	1	12	....	....	....	....	....

AHOSILTA, Marko (ah-hoh-SIHL-tuh, mahr-KOH) — N.J.

Center. Shoots left. 5'8", 165 lbs. Born, Kuopio, Finland, January 24, 1980.
(New Jersey's 11th choice, 227th overall, in 1998 Entry Draft).

			Regular Season					Playoffs				
Season	Club	Lea	GP	G	A	TP	PIM	GP	G	A	TP	PIM
1994-95	KalPa Kuopio-C	Finn-Jr.	13	4	6	10	10	....	....	....	....	....
1995-96	KalPa Kuopio	Finn-Jr.	12	4	8	12	10	....	....	....	....	....
1996-97	KalPa Kuopio	Finn-Jr.	35	15	21	36	36	5	2	0	2	2
1997-98	KalPa Kuopio	Finn-Jr.	14	14	13	27	10	....	....	....	....	....
	KalPa Kuopio	Finland	2	0	0	0	0	....	....	....	....	....
1998-99	KalPa Kuopio	Finland	1	0	0	0	0	....	....	....	....	....
	KalPa Kuopio	Finn-Jr.	24	7	7	14	10	....	....	....	....	....
99-2000	KalPa Kuopio	Finn-Jr.	10	6	4	10	8	....	....	....	....	....
	KJT-Jarvenpaa	Finland-2	30	19	5	24	14	....	....	....	....	....
2000-01			DID NOT PLAY									

ALEXEEV, Nikita (uh-LEHX-ee-ehv, nih-KEE-tuh) — T.B.

Right wing. Shoots left. 6'5", 215 lbs. Born, Murmansk, USSR, December 27, 1981.
(Tampa Bay's 1st choice, 8th overall, in 2000 Entry Draft).

			Regular Season					Playoffs				
Season	Club	Lea	GP	G	A	TP	PIM	GP	G	A	TP	PIM
1996-97	Krylja Sovetov	Russia-Jr.	45	4	6	10	8	....	....	....	....	....
1997-98	Krylja Sovetov-2	Russia-3	61	11	4	15	36	....	....	....	....	....
1998-99	Erie Otters	OHL	61	17	18	35	14	5	1	1	2	4
99-2000	Erie Otters	OHL	64	24	29	53	42	13	4	3	7	6
2000-01	Erie Otters	OHL	64	31	41	72	45	12	7	7	14	12

ALINC, Jan (AHL-lihnch, YAHN) — PIT.

Center. Shoots left. 6'2", 190 lbs. Born, Louny, Czech., May 27, 1972.
(Pittsburgh's 7th choice, 163rd overall, in 1992 Entry Draft).

			Regular Season					Playoffs				
Season	Club	Lea	GP	G	A	TP	PIM	GP	G	A	TP	PIM
1990-91	CHZ Litvinov	Czech.	7	1	1	2	....	....	....	....	....	....
1991-92	CHZ Litvinov	Czech.	45	21	16	37	24	....	....	....	....	....
1992-93	CHZ Litvinov	Czech.	36	16	13	29	....	....	....	....	....	....
1993-94	CHZ Litvinov	Cze-Rep	36	16	25	41	....	4	1	4	5	....
	Czech-Republic	Olympics	6	2	0	2	4	....	....	....	....	....
1994-95	CHZ Litvinov	Cze-Rep	42	16	32	48	50	4	3	2	5	2
1995-96	CHZ Litvinov	Cze-Rep	38	15	29	44	....	16	2	5	7	....
1996-97	Assat-Pori	Finland	47	9	16	25	16	4	0	4	4	2
1997-98	Assat-Pori	Finland	15	2	8	10	10	....	....	....	....	....
	CHZ Litvinov	Cze-Rep	33	12	32	44	14	4	1	2	3	12
1998-99	MoDo Hockey	Sweden	48	7	11	18	22	9	1	0	1	0
99-2000	CHZ Litvinov	Cze-Rep	48	19	15	34	72	6	0	1	1	25
2000-01	Slavia Praha	Cze-Rep	44	12	35	47	18	11	1	6	7	0

ALLAN, Chad (AHL-lan, CHAD)

Defense. Shoots left. 6'1", 200 lbs. Born, Saskatoon, Sask., July 12, 1976.
(Vancouver's 4th choice, 65th overall, in 1994 Entry Draft).

			Regular Season					Playoffs				
Season	Club	Lea	GP	G	A	TP	PIM	GP	G	A	TP	PIM
1991-92	Saskatoon Blaze	SMHL	36	5	16	21	64	....	....	....	....	....
	Saskatoon Blades	WHL	1	0	0	0	2	....	....	....	....	....
1992-93	Saskatoon Blades	WHL	69	2	10	12	67	9	0	0	0	25
1993-94	Saskatoon Blades	WHL	70	6	16	22	123	16	1	1	2	21
1994-95	Saskatoon Blades	WHL	63	14	29	43	95	9	0	3	3	2
1995-96	Saskatoon Blades	WHL	57	8	30	38	106	4	0	0	0	5
1996-97	Syracuse Crunch	AHL	73	3	10	13	83	3	0	1	1	0
1997-98	Syracuse Crunch	AHL	73	2	10	12	121	5	0	0	0	4
1998-99	Syracuse Crunch	AHL	60	2	8	10	98	....	....	....	....	....
99-2000	Syracuse Crunch	AHL	76	3	18	21	100	4	0	0	0	0
2000-01	St. John's Leafs	AHL	73	4	5	9	50	4	1	1	2	9

WHL East First All-Star Team (1995) • WHL East Second All-Star Team (1996)

ALLEN, Bobby (AHL-lehn, BAW-bee) BOS.

Defense. Shoots left. 6'1", 205 lbs. Born, Braintree, MA, November 14, 1978.
(Boston's 2nd choice, 52nd overall, in 1998 Entry Draft).

			Regular Season					Playoffs				
Season	Club	Lea	GP	G	A	TP	PIM	GP	G	A	TP	PIM
1996-97	Cushing Academy	Hi-School	36	11	33	44	28	....	....	....	....	....
1997-98	Boston College	H-East	40	7	21	28	49	....	....	....	....	....
1998-99	Boston College	H-East	43	9	23	32	34	....	....	....	....	....
99-2000	Boston College	H-East	42	4	23	27	40	....	....	....	....	....
2000-01	Boston College	H-East	42	5	18	23	28	....	....	....	....	....

Hockey East Second All-Star Team (2000) • Hockey East First All-Star Team (2001) • NCAA East First All-American Team (2001)

ALTAREV, Dmitri (al-ta-REHV, dih-MEE-tree) NYI

Left wing. Shoots left. 6'3", 191 lbs. Born, Penza, USSR, August 12, 1980.
(NY Islanders' 8th choice, 264th overall, in 2000 Entry Draft).

			Regular Season					Playoffs				
Season	Club	Lea	GP	G	A	TP	PIM	GP	G	A	TP	PIM
1997-98	Dizelist Penza-2	Russia-3	57	15	8	23	83	....	....	....	....	....
1998-99	Dizelist Penza-3	Russia-4	6	2	0	2	8	....	....	....	....	....
	Dizelist Penza-2	Russia-3	35	4	3	7	30	....	....	....	....	....
99-2000	Dizelist Penza-2	Russia-3	44	10	8	18	25	....	....	....	....	....
2000-01	Torpedo Nizhny	Russia	36	1	2	3	26	....	....	....	....	....

ANDERSON, Erik (AN-duhr-suhn) NSH.

Center. Shoots left. 5'9", 195 lbs. Born, Plymouth, MI, March 6, 1978.

			Regular Season					Playoffs				
Season	Club	Lea	GP	G	A	TP	PIM	GP	G	A	TP	PIM
1995-96	Stratford Cullitons	OJHL-B	38	29	43	72	10	....	....	....	....	....
1996-97	Stratford Cullitons	OJHL-B	48	54	*91	*145	40	....	....	....	....	....
1997-98	St. Lawrence	ECAC	33	5	13	18	12	....	....	....	....	....
1998-99	St. Lawrence	ECAC	39	10	30	40	18	....	....	....	....	....
99-2000	St. Lawrence	ECAC	36	14	25	39	20	....	....	....	....	....
2000-01	St. Lawrence	ECAC	32	17	34	51	4	....	....	....	....	....

ECAC Player of the Year (2001) • All-ECAC First All-Star Team (2001)

Signed as a free agent by **Nashville**, July 5, 2001.

ANDERSSON, Jonas (AN-duhr-suhn, JOH-nas) NSH.

Right wing. Shoots left. 6'3", 202 lbs. Born, Stockholm, Sweden, February 24, 1981.
(Nashville's 2nd choice, 33rd overall, in 1999 Entry Draft).

			Regular Season					Playoffs				
Season	Club	Lea	GP	G	A	TP	PIM	GP	G	A	TP	PIM
1997-98	AIK Solna	Swede-Jr.	33	14	16	30	32	....	....	....	....	....
1998-99	AIK Solna	Swede-Jr.	16	3	7	10	18	....	....	....	....	....
	London Knights	Britain	12	2	3	5	0	....	....	....	....	....
99-2000	North Bay	OHL	67	31	36	67	27	6	2	2	4	2
	Milwaukee	IHL	2	1	0	1	0	2	0	0	0	2
2000-01	Milwaukee	IHL	52	6	7	13	44	5	0	0	0	2

ANDERSSON-JUNKKA, Jonas (AN-duhr-suhn-JUHNK-ka, JOH-nuh)

Defense. Shoots right. 6'2", 170 lbs. Born, Kiruna, Sweden, May 4, 1975.
(Pittsburgh's 4th choice, 104th overall, in 1993 Entry Draft).

			Regular Season					Playoffs				
Season	Club	Lea	GP	G	A	TP	PIM	GP	G	A	TP	PIM
1991-92	Kiruna IK	Swede-2	1	0	0	0	0	....	....	....	....	....
1992-93	Kiruna IK	Swede-2	30	3	7	10	32	....	....	....	....	....
1993-94	Kiruna IK	Swede-2	32	6	10	16	84	....	....	....	....	....
1994-95	Vastra Frolunda	Sweden	19	0	2	2	2	....	....	....	....	....
1995-96	Vastra Frolunda	Sweden	31	3	1	4	20	13	1	0	1	6
1996-97	MoDo Hockey	Sweden	12	1	3	4	10	....	....	....	....	....
1997-98	MoDo Hockey	Sweden	35	5	5	10	12	1	0	0	0	0
1998-99	Kiekko-Espoo	Finland	34	4	4	8	20	....	....	....	....	....
	HPK Hameenlinna	Finland	16	1	5	6	16	8	3	1	4	8
99-2000	HPK Hameenlinna	Finland	54	13	18	31	72	8	1	4	5	20
2000-01	Syracuse Crunch	AHL	58	5	14	19	49	2	0	0	0	0

Selected by **Columbus** from **Pittsburgh** in Expansion Draft, June 23, 2000.

ANDREWS, Daryl (AN-drews, DAI-rihl) N.J.

Defense. Shoots left. 6'3", 215 lbs. Born, Campbell River, B.C., April 27, 1977.
(New Jersey's 11th choice, 173rd overall, in 1996 Entry Draft).

			Regular Season					Playoffs				
Season	Club	Lea	GP	G	A	TP	PIM	GP	G	A	TP	PIM
1995-96	Melfort Mustangs	SJHL	55	2	12	14	51	....	....	....	....	....
1996-97	Western Michigan	CCHA	37	6	20	26	86	....	....	....	....	....
1997-98	Western Michigan	CCHA	36	3	0	3	81	....	....	....	....	....
1998-99	Western Michigan	CCHA	33	3	11	14	42	....	....	....	....	....
99-2000	Western Michigan	CCHA	36	3	16	19	52	....	....	....	....	....
	Albany River Rats	AHL	9	0	2	2	9	5	0	0	0	0
2000-01	Albany River Rats	AHL	80	2	8	10	49	....	....	....	....	....

ANDREYEV, Alexander (an-DRAY-ehv, AHL-ihx-ander) PHX.

Defense. Shoots left. 6'4", 219 lbs. Born, Riga, Latvia, September 14, 1979.
(Phoenix's 5th choice, 207th overall, in 1997 Entry Draft).

			Regular Season					Playoffs				
Season	Club	Lea	GP	G	A	TP	PIM	GP	G	A	TP	PIM
1996-97	Essamika Riga	Latvia	5	0	0	0	6	....	....	....	....	....
	Weyburn Wings	SJHL	13	0	1	1	81	....	....	....	....	....
1997-98	Prince George	WHL	23	0	1	1	30	....	....	....	....	....
1998-99	Moose Jaw	WHL	60	11	11	22	80	5	0	0	0	4
99-2000	Mississippi	ECHL	21	1	2	3	43	....	....	....	....	....
	B.C. Icemen	UHL	21	1	3	4	80	6	0	0	0	4
2000-01	B.C. Icemen	UHL	66	0	9	9	146	....	....	....	....	....

ANGELSTAD, Mel (AN-gehl-stahd, MEHL)

Left wing. Shoots left. 6'2", 214 lbs. Born, Saskatoon, Sask., October 31, 1972.

			Regular Season					Playoffs				
Season	Club	Lea	GP	G	A	TP	PIM	GP	G	A	TP	PIM
1988-89	Allan Legionaires	MAHA	35	15	23	38	256	....	....	....	....	....
1989-90	Warman Valley	MJHL	38	1	5	6	411	....	....	....	....	....
1990-91	Flin Flon Bombers	MJHL	62	6	11	17	463	....	....	....	....	....
1991-92	Dauphin Kings	MJHL	44	8	29	37	*296	....	....	....	....	....
1992-93	Thunder Bay	ColHL	45	2	5	7	256	5	0	0	0	10
	Nashville Knights	ECHL	1	0	0	0	14	....	....	....	....	....
1993-94	Thunder Bay	ColHL	58	1	20	21	374	9	1	2	3	65
	P.E.I. Senators	AHL	1	0	0	0	5	....	....	....	....	....
1994-95	Thunder Bay	ColHL	46	0	8	8	317	7	0	3	3	62
	P.E.I. Senators	AHL	3	0	0	0	16	....	....	....	....	....
1995-96	Thunder Bay	ColHL	51	3	3	6	335	16	0	6	6	94
	Phoenix	IHL	5	0	0	0	43	....	....	....	....	....
1996-97	Thunder Bay	ColHL	66	10	21	31	422	7	0	1	1	21
1997-98	Fort Worth	WPHL	19	1	6	7	102	....	....	....	....	....
	Las Vegas	IHL	3	0	0	0	5	....	....	....	....	....
	Orlando	IHL	63	1	3	4	321	8	0	0	0	29
1998-99	Michigan K-Wings	IHL	78	3	5	8	421	5	1	0	1	16
99-2000	Michigan K-Wings	IHL	33	3	4	7	144	....	....	....	....	....
2000-01	Manitoba Moose	IHL	67	1	5	6	232	8	0	0	0	26

Signed as a free agent by **Dallas**, July 29, 1998.

ANGER, Niklas (AN-guhr, NIHK-lahs) MTL.

Right wing. Shoots left. 6'1", 185 lbs. Born, Gavle, Sweden, July 31, 1977.
(Montreal's 5th choice, 112th overall, in 1995 Entry Draft).

			Regular Season					Playoffs				
Season	Club	Lea	GP	G	A	TP	PIM	GP	G	A	TP	PIM
1994-95	Djurgardens IF	Swede-Jr.	30	14	12	26	26	....	....	....	....	....
	Djurgardens IF	Sweden	1	0	0	0	0	....	....	....	....	....
1995-96	Djurgardens IF	Sweden	10	0	0	0	2	....	....	....	....	....
1996-97	Arlanda HK	Swede-2	16	5	9	14	6	....	....	....	....	....
	Linkopings HC	Swede-2	7	2	1	3	10	....	....	....	....	....
	Djurgardens IF	Sweden	4	0	0	0	0	....	....	....	....	....
1997-98	Djurgardens IF	Sweden	45	2	5	7	37	12	0	1	1	2
1998-99	AIK Solna	Sweden	47	6	6	12	16	....	....	....	....	....
99-2000	AIK Solna	Sweden	50	11	13	24	14	....	....	....	....	....
2000-01	AIK Solna	Sweden	50	5	10	15	22	5	0	1	1	2

ANISIMOV, Artem (ah-NIH-sih-mohv, AHR-tehm) MIN.

Defense. Shoots left. 6'1", 187 lbs. Born, Kazan, USSR, July 27, 1976.
(Philadelphia's 1st choice, 62nd overall, in 1994 Entry Draft).

			Regular Season					Playoffs				
Season	Club	Lea	GP	G	A	TP	PIM	GP	G	A	TP	PIM
1993-94	Ak Bars Kazan	CIS	38	0	1	1	12	5	0	0	0	0
1994-95	Ak Bars Kazan	CIS	46	3	2	5	55	1	0	0	0	0
1995-96	Ak Bars Kazan	CIS	30	0	2	2	8	....	....	....	....	....
1996-97	Ak Bars Kazan	Russia	5	0	1	1	2	....	....	....	....	....
1997-98	Ak Bars Kazan	Russia	44	0	0	0	26	....	....	....	....	....
1998-99	Ak Bars Kazan	Russia	39	0	4	4	10	9	0	0	0	2
99-2000	Ak Bars Kazan	Russia	11	0	1	1	2	5	1	1	2	4
2000-01	Ak Bars Kazan	Russia	4	1	0	1	6	....	....	....	....	....
	Amur Khabarovsk	Russia	16	1	0	1	12	....	....	....	....	....

Selected by **Minnesota** from **Philadelphia** in Expansion Draft, June 23, 2000.

ANTIPOV, Vladimir (an-TIH-pahv, vla-DIH-meer) TOR.

Right wing. Shoots left. 5'11", 180 lbs. Born, Appatity, USSR, January 17, 1978.
(Toronto's 6th choice, 103rd overall, in 1996 Entry Draft).

			Regular Season					Playoffs				
Season	Club	Lea	GP	G	A	TP	PIM	GP	G	A	TP	PIM
1995-96	Torpedo Yaroslavl	CIS-2	39	14	11	25	....	....	....	....	....	....
1996-97	HC Yaroslavl-2	Russia-3	14	3	4	7	26	....	....	....	....	....
	Torpedo Yaroslavl	Russia	27	6	4	10	22	2	0	0	0	0
1997-98	Torpedo Yaroslavl	Russia	41	9	3	12	57	....	....	....	....	....
	Torpedo Yaroslavl	EuroHL	7	0	2	2	2	....	....	....	....	....
1998-99	Torpedo Yaroslavl	Russia	42	7	13	20	30	10	2	2	4	10
99-2000	St. John's Leafs	AHL	45	6	7	13	14	....	....	....	....	....
	South Carolina	ECHL	4	0	4	4	2	....	....	....	....	....
	Long Beach	IHL	16	3	3	6	18	1	0	0	0	0
2000-01	St. John's Leafs	AHL	9	1	1	2	2	....	....	....	....	....
	HC Yaroslavl	Russia	22	5	5	10	56	11	2	1	3	8

Released by **Toronto** and signed as a free agent by **Locomotiv Yaroslavl** (Russia) with **Toronto** retaining NHL rights, November 14, 2000.

APPS, Syl (APPS, sihl) TOR.

Center. Shoots right. 6', 195 lbs. Born, Pittsburgh, PA, June 2, 1976.

			Regular Season					Playoffs				
Season	Club	Lea	GP	G	A	TP	PIM	GP	G	A	TP	PIM
1994-95	St. Michael's	MTJHL	6	3	1	4	2	....	....	....	....	....
1995-96	Princeton Tigers	ECAC	26	4	6	10	30	....	....	....	....	....
1996-97	Princeton Tigers	ECAC	27	3	6	9	40	....	....	....	....	....
1997-98	Princeton Tigers	ECAC	35	10	8	18	65	....	....	....	....	....
1998-99	Princeton Tigers	ECAC	34	13	21	34	45	....	....	....	....	....
99-2000	St. John's Leafs	AHL	58	5	7	12	87	....	....	....	....	....
2000-01	St. John's Leafs	AHL	69	6	8	14	73	4	0	0	0	0

Signed as a free agent by **Toronto**, July 22, 1999.

AQUINO, Anthony (a-KEE-noh, AN-thuh-nee) DAL.

Right wing. Shoots right. 5'10", 180 lbs. Born, Toronto, Ont., August 1, 1982.
(Dallas' 3rd choice, 92nd overall, in 2001 Entry Draft).

			Regular Season					Playoffs				
Season	Club	Lea	GP	G	A	TP	PIM	GP	G	A	TP	PIM
1997-98	Mississauga	OPJHL	50	10	13	23	14	....	....	....	....	....
1998-99	Bramalea Blues	OPJHL	47	31	44	75	31	....	....	....	....	....
99-2000	Merrimack	H-East	36	15	14	29	12	....	....	....	....	....
2000-01	Merrimack	H-East	38	17	25	42	22	....	....	....	....	....

Hockey East All-Rookie Team (2000) • Hockey East Second All-Star Team (2001)

ARMSTRONG, Colby (AHRM-stawng, KOHL-bee) PIT.

Right wing. Shoots right. 6'1", 180 lbs. Born, Lloydminster, Sask., November 23, 1982.
(Pittsburgh's 1st choice, 21st overall, in 2001 Entry Draft).

			Regular Season					Playoffs				
Season	Club	Lea	GP	G	A	TP	PIM	GP	G	A	TP	PIM
1998-99	Saskatoon AAA	SMHL	33	21	19	40	103	....	....	....	....	....
	Red Deer Rebels	WHL	1	0	1	1	0	....	....	....	....	....
99-2000	Red Deer Rebels	WHL	68	13	25	38	122	2	0	1	1	11
2000-01	Red Deer Rebels	WHL	72	36	42	78	156	21	6	6	12	29

ARNASON, Tyler (AHR-na-suhn, TIGH-luhr) CHI.

Center. Shoots left. 5'11", 207 lbs. Born, Oklahoma City, OK, March 16, 1979.
(Chicago's 6th choice, 183rd overall, in 1998 Entry Draft).

			Regular Season					Playoffs				
Season	Club	Lea	GP	G	A	TP	PIM	GP	G	A	TP	PIM
1996-97	Winnipeg Blues	MJHL	50	35	50	85	15	6	3	3	6	18
1997-98	Fargo-Moorhead	USHL	52	37	45	82	16	4	1	1	2	2
1998-99	St. Cloud State	WCHA	38	14	17	31	16	....	....	....	....	....
99-2000	St. Cloud State	WCHA	39	19	30	49	18	....	....	....	....	....
2000-01	St. Cloud State	WCHA	41	28	28	56	14	....	....	....	....	....

Won MJHL Rookie of the Year Award (1997) • USHL First All-Star Team (1998) • WCHA All-Rookie Team (1999) • WCHA Second All-Star Team (2000)

ARONSON, Steve (AIR-uhn-suhn, STEEV) MIN.

Right wing. Shoots right. 6'1", 205 lbs. Born, Minnetonka, MN, July 15, 1978.

			Regular Season					Playoffs				
Season	Club	Lea	GP	G	A	TP	PIM	GP	G	A	TP	PIM
1996-97	U. of St. Thomas	MIAC	27	11	25	36	44	....	....	....	....	....
1997-98	U. of St. Thomas	MIAC	28	32	25	57	41	....	....	....	....	....
1998-99	U. of St. Thomas	MIAC	31	23	37	60	73	....	....	....	....	....
99-2000	U. of St. Thomas	MIAC	33	38	53	91	72	....	....	....	....	....
2000-01	Cleveland	IHL	64	9	17	26	23	4	1	0	1	0
	Jackson Bandits	ECHL	3	0	1	1	2	....	....	....	....	....

MIAC All-Conference Team (1997, 1998, 1999, 2000) • NCAA-3 First Team All-American (1998, 1999, 2000) • Won MIAC Most Valuable Player Award (1999, 2000) • Won NCAA-3 Player of the Year Award (2000)

Signed as a free agent by **Minnesota**, May 4, 2000.

ARTUKHIN, Evgeni (ahr-TYEW-khin, yehv-GEH-nee) T.B.

Right wing. Shoots left. 6'4", 213 lbs. Born, Moscow, USSR, April 4, 1983.
(Tampa Bay's 4th choice, 94th overall, in 2001 Entry Draft).

			Regular Season					Playoffs				
Season	Club	Lea	GP	G	A	TP	PIM	GP	G	A	TP	PIM
99-2000	Vityaz Podolsk-2	Russia-3	26	9	8	17	46	....	....	....	....	....
	Vityaz Podolsk	Russia-2	3	0	0	0	2	....	....	....	....	....
2000-01	Vityaz Podolsk	Russia	24	0	1	1	14	....	....	....	....	....

AUFIERO, Patrick (ow-fee-AIR-oh, PAT-rihk) NYR

Defense. Shoots right. 6'2", 186 lbs. Born, Winchester, MA, July 1, 1980.
(NY Rangers' 5th choice, 90th overall, in 1999 Entry Draft).

			Regular Season					Playoffs				
Season	Club	Lea	GP	G	A	TP	PIM	GP	G	A	TP	PIM
1995-96	Winchester High	Hi-School	25	13	18	31	....	....	....	....	....	....
1996-97	Winchester High	Hi-School	27	27	21	48	....	....	....	....	....	....
1997-98	Team USA	USDP	56	10	11	21	111	....	....	....	....	....
1998-99	Boston University	H-East	22	3	4	7	14	....	....	....	....	....
99-2000	Boston University	H-East	38	3	20	23	37	....	....	....	....	....
2000-01	Boston University	H-East	34	5	8	13	30	....	....	....	....	....

Hockey East Second All-Star Team (2000)

AULIN, Jared (AW-lihn, JAIR-ehd) L.A.

Center. Shoots right. 6', 180 lbs. Born, Calgary, Alta., March 15, 1982.
(Colorado's 2nd choice, 47th overall, in 2000 Entry Draft).

			Regular Season					Playoffs				
Season	Club	Lea	GP	G	A	TP	PIM	GP	G	A	TP	PIM
1997-98	Airdrie Xtreme	AAHA	55	42	61	103	60	....	....	....	....	....
	Kamloops Blazers	WHL	2	0	0	0	0	....	....	....	....	....
1998-99	Kamloops Blazers	WHL	55	7	19	26	23	13	1	3	4	2
99-2000	Kamloops Blazers	WHL	57	17	38	55	70	4	0	1	1	6
2000-01	Kamloops Blazers	WHL	70	31	*77	108	62	4	0	2	2	0

WHL West First All-Star Team (2001)

Traded to **LA Kings** by **Colorado** to complete transaction that sent Rob Blake and Steve Reinprecht to Colorado (February 21, 2001), March 22, 2001.

AVERY, Sean DET.

Center. Shoots left. 5'10", 185 lbs. Born, North York, Ont., April 10, 1980.

			Regular Season					Playoffs				
Season	Club	Lea	GP	G	A	TP	PIM	GP	G	A	TP	PIM
1995-96	Markham	OMHA	70	34	81	115	180	....	....	....	....	....
	Markham Waxers	OJHL	1	0	0	0	4	....	....	....	....	....
1996-97	Owen Sound	OHL	58	10	21	31	86	4	1	0	1	4
1997-98	Owen Sound	OHL	47	13	41	54	105	....	....	....	....	....
1998-99	Owen Sound	OHL	28	22	23	45	70	....	....	....	....	....
	Kingston	OHL	33	14	25	39	88	5	1	3	4	13
99-2000	Kingston	OHL	55	28	56	84	215	5	2	2	4	26
2000-01	Cincinnati Ducks	AHL	58	8	15	23	304	4	1	0	1	19

Signed as a free agent by **Detroit**, September 21, 1999.

BABY, Stephan (BAY-bee, STEE-vehn) ATL.

Right wing. Shoots right. 6'5", 225 lbs. Born, Chicago, IL, January 31, 1980.
(Atlanta's 8th choice, 188th overall, in 1999 Entry Draft).

			Regular Season					Playoffs				
Season	Club	Lea	GP	G	A	TP	PIM	GP	G	A	TP	PIM
1997-98	Green Bay	USHL	56	17	17	34	85	4	1	3	4	8
1998-99	Green Bay	USHL	55	23	24	47	83	6	1	1	2	4
99-2000	Cornell Big Red	ECAC	31	4	10	14	52	....	....	....	....	....
2000-01	Cornell Big Red	ECAC	32	8	20	28	47	....	....	....	....	....

BACKER, Per (BAK-uhr, PAIR) DET.

Right wing. Shoots left. 6'1", 161 lbs. Born, Grums, Sweden, January 4, 1982.
(Detroit's 7th choice, 187th overall, in 2000 Entry Draft).

			Regular Season					Playoffs				
Season	Club	Lea	GP	G	A	TP	PIM	GP	G	A	TP	PIM
1998-99	Grums BK	Swede-2	17	1	1	2	4	....	....	....	....	....
99-2000	Grums BK	Swede-2	46	12	10	22	24	....	....	....	....	....
2000-01	Bofors IK	Swede-2	41	20	15	35	47	....	....	....	....	....

BACKMAN, Christian (BAK-man, KRIH-stan) ST.L.

Defense. Shoots left. 6'4", 198 lbs. Born, Alingsas, Sweden, April 28, 1980.
(St. Louis' 1st choice, 24th overall, in 1998 Entry Draft).

			Regular Season					Playoffs				
Season	Club	Lea	GP	G	A	TP	PIM	GP	G	A	TP	PIM
1996-97	Vastra Frolunda	Swede-Jr.	26	2	5	7	16	....	....	....	....	....
1997-98	Vastra Frolunda	Swede-Jr.	28	5	14	19	12	2	0	1	1	4
1998-99	Vastra Frolunda	Swede-Jr.	4	0	2	2	4	....	....	....	....	....
	Vastra Frolunda	Sweden	49	0	4	4	4	4	0	0	0	0
99-2000	Gislaved SK	Swede-2	21	5	2	7	8	....	....	....	....	....
	Vastra Frolunda	Sweden	27	1	0	1	14	5	0	0	0	0
2000-01	Vastra Frolunda	Sweden	50	1	10	11	32	3	0	2	2	2

BAHEN, Chris (BAY-hehn, KRIHS) COL.

Defense. Shoots left. 6', 180 lbs. Born, Monttreal, Que., November 16, 1980.
(Colorado's 10th choice, 189th overall, in 2000 Entry Draft).

			Regular Season					Playoffs				
Season	Club	Lea	GP	G	A	TP	PIM	GP	G	A	TP	PIM
1994-95	Thornhill AA	OMHA	40	12	38	50	82	....	....	....	....	....
1995-96	Thornhill AA	OMHA	40	18	51	69	96	....	....	....	....	....
1996-97	Thornhill AAA	OMHA	40	23	42	65	108	....	....	....	....	....
1997-98	Thornhill Rattlers	MTJHL	45	5	9	14	131	....	....	....	....	....
1998-99	Milton Merchants	OPJHL	32	3	14	17	20	....	....	....	....	....
99-2000	Clarkson Knights	ECAC	34	8	10	18	54	....	....	....	....	....
2000-01	Clarkson Knights	ECAC	34	3	7	10	45	....	....	....	....	....

BAINES, Ajay CHI.

Center. Shoots left. 5'10", 178 lbs. Born, Kamloops, B.C., March 25, 1978.

			Regular Season					Playoffs				
Season	Club	Lea	GP	G	A	TP	PIM	GP	G	A	TP	PIM
1994-95	Kamloops Blaze	BCAHA	52	45	79	124	139	....	....	....	....	....
1995-96	Kamloops Blazers	WHL	68	14	29	43	43	....	....	....	....	....
1996-97	Kamloops Blazers	WHL	70	32	43	75	106	5	4	1	5	6
1997-98	Kamloops Blazers	WHL	72	34	25	59	88	....	....	....	....	....
1998-99	Kamloops Blazers	WHL	72	33	32	65	145	15	7	6	13	20
99-2000	Greenville Growl	ECHL	67	24	31	55	102	15	2	5	7	13
2000-01	Norfolk Admirals	AHL	73	18	18	36	92	9	0	1	1	2

Signed as a free agent by **Chicago**, August 1, 2001.

BALA, Chris (BA-la, KRIHS) OTT.

Left wing. Shoots left. 6'1", 180 lbs. Born, Alexandria, VA, September 24, 1978.
(Ottawa's 3rd choice, 58th overall, in 1998 Entry Draft).

			Regular Season					Playoffs				
Season	Club	Lea	GP	G	A	TP	PIM	GP	G	A	TP	PIM
1996-97	Hill-Murray	Hi-School	23	28	33	61	36	....	....	....	....	....
1997-98	Harvard University	ECAC	33	16	14	30	23	....	....	....	....	....
1998-99	Harvard University	ECAC	28	5	10	15	16	....	....	....	....	....
99-2000	Harvard University	ECAC	30	10	14	24	18	....	....	....	....	....
2000-01	Harvard University	ECAC	32	14	16	30	24	....	....	....	....	....

BALAN, Scott (BAY-luhn, SKAWT) CHI.

Defense. Shoots right. 6'3", 191 lbs. Born, Medicine Hat, Alta., May 29, 1982.
(Chicago's 5th choice, 106th overall, in 2000 Entry Draft).

			Regular Season					Playoffs				
Season	Club	Lea	GP	G	A	TP	PIM	GP	G	A	TP	PIM
1997-98	Regina Chiefs	AMHL	56	6	25	31	139	....	....	....	....	....
	Regina Pats	WHL	1	0	1	1	0	....	....	....	....	....
1998-99	Regina Pats	WHL	63	1	8	9	42	....	....	....	....	....
99-2000	Regina Pats	WHL	67	3	11	14	157	7	0	1	1	17
2000-01	Regina Pats	WHL	42	2	5	7	69	....	....	....	....	....
	Saskatoon	WHL	28	0	5	5	49	....	....	....	....	....

Traded to **Saskatoon** by **Regina** with future considerations for Garnet Exelby, January 15, 2001.

BALEJ, Josef (BAH-lay, YOH-zehf) MTL.

Right wing. Shoots right. 6', 187 lbs. Born, Myjava, Czech., February 22, 1982.
(Montreal's 3rd choice, 78th overall, in 2000 Entry Draft).

			Regular Season					Playoffs				
Season	Club	Lea	GP	G	A	TP	PIM	GP	G	A	TP	PIM
1997-98	Dukla Trencin	Slovak-Jr.	52	57	40	97	60	....	....	....	....	....
1998-99	Thunder Bay	USHL	38	8	7	15	9	....	....	....	....	....
	Rochester	USHL	17	0	1	1	2	....	....	....	....	....
99-2000	Portland	WHL	65	22	23	45	33	....	....	....	....	....
2000-01	Portland	WHL	46	32	21	53	18	16	9	6	15	6

BALLANTYNE, Paul (BAL-uhn-tughn, PAWL) DET.

Defense. Shoots right. 6'3", 200 lbs. Born, Waterloo, Ont., July 16, 1982.
(Detroit's 8th choice, 196th overall, in 2000 Entry Draft).

			Regular Season					Playoffs				
Season	Club	Lea	GP	G	A	TP	PIM	GP	G	A	TP	PIM
1997-98	Waterloo Lions	OMHA	30	4	16	20	55	....	....	....	....	....
	Waterloo Siskins	OPJHL	1	0	0	0	0	....	....	....	....	....
1998-99	Sault Ste. Marie	OHL	53	0	6	6	33	5	1	0	1	4
99-2000	Sault Ste. Marie	OHL	58	4	15	19	60	17	2	3	5	17
2000-01	Sault Ste. Marie	OHL	63	12	28	40	60	....	....	....	....	....

BARBER, Greg (BAHR-buhr, GREHG) BOS.

Right wing. Shoots right. 6', 185 lbs. Born, Dawson Creek, B.C., May 26, 1980.
(Boston's 7th choice, 207th overall, in 1999 Entry Draft).

			Regular Season					Playoffs				
Season	Club	Lea	GP	G	A	TP	PIM	GP	G	A	TP	PIM
1996-97	Kelowna	BCAHA	54	36	48	84	90	....	....	....	....	....
1997-98	Victoria Salsa	BCJHL	60	15	22	37	24	7	2	2	4	4
1998-99	Victoria Salsa	BCJHL	60	41	41	82	95	....	....	....	....	....
99-2000	U. of Denver	WCHA	40	7	8	15	24	....	....	....	....	....
2000-01	U. of Denver	WCHA	35	7	8	15	22	....	....	....	....	....

BARCH, Krys (BAHR-ch, KRIHS) WSH.

Left wing. Shoots left. 6'2", 200 lbs. Born, Guelph, Ont., March 26, 1980.
(Washington's 3rd choice, 106th overall, in 1998 Entry Draft).

			Regular Season					Playoffs				
Season	Club	Lea	GP	G	A	TP	PIM	GP	G	A	TP	PIM
1995-96	Georgetown	OPJHL	41	6	8	14	10	....	....	....	....	....
1996-97	Georgetown	OPJHL	51	18	26	44	58	....	....	....	....	....
1997-98	London Knights	OHL	65	9	27	36	62	16	4	3	7	16
1998-99	London Knights	OHL	66	18	20	38	66	25	9	17	26	15
99-2000	London Knights	OHL	56	23	26	49	78	....	....	....	....	....
	Portland Pirates	AHL	....	....	....	....	....	4	0	2	2	2
2000-01	Portland Pirates	AHL	76	10	15	25	91	2	0	0	0	0

BARKUNOV, Alexander (bahr-koo-NAHF, al-ehx-AN-duhr) **CHI.**

Defense. Shoots right. 6'1", 199 lbs. Born, Novosibirsk, USSR, May 13, 1981.
(Chicago's 7th choice, 151st overall, in 2000 Entry Draft).

			Regular Season					Playoffs				
Season	Club	Lea	GP	G	A	TP	PIM	GP	G	A	TP	PIM
1996-97	HC Yaroslavl-2	Russia-3	1	0	0	0	0	....	....	....	....	....
1997-98	Torpedo Yaroslavl	Russia-2	20	1	1	2	6	....	....	....	....	....
1998-99	HC Yaroslavl-2	Russia-3	19	0	3	3	8	....	....	....	....	....
99-2000	Torpedo Yaroslavl	Russia-2	38	5	9	14	16	....	....	....	....	....
2000-01	HC Yaroslavl	Russia	34	5	1	6	10	2	0	0	0	2

BARNES, Ryan (BAHR-nz, RIGH-uhn) **DET.**

Left wing. Shoots left. 6'1", 201 lbs. Born, Dunnville, Ont., January 30, 1980.
(Detroit's 2nd choice, 55th overall, in 1998 Entry Draft).

			Regular Season					Playoffs				
Season	Club	Lea	GP	G	A	TP	PIM	GP	G	A	TP	PIM
1996-97	Quinte Hawks	MTJHL	46	15	19	34	245	....	....	....	....	....
1997-98	Sudbury Wolves	OHL	46	13	18	31	111	10	0	2	2	24
1998-99	Sudbury Wolves	OHL	8	2	0	2	*23	....	....	....	....	....
	St. Michael's	OHL	31	11	14	25	*215	....	....	....	....	....
	Barrie Colts	OHL	24	16	14	30	*161	12	2	4	6	40
99-2000	Barrie Colts	OHL	31	17	12	29	98	25	7	7	14	49
2000-01	Cincinnati Ducks	AHL	1	0	0	0	7	....	....	....	....	....
	Toledo Storm	ECHL	16	2	4	6	31	....	....	....	....	....

• Missed majority of 2000-01 season recovering from head injury suffered in training camp, September, 2000.

BARRETT, Nathan (BAIR-uht, NAY-thun) **VAN.**

Center. Shoots left. 5'11", 192 lbs. Born, Vancouver, B.C., August 3, 1981.
(Vancouver's 6th choice, 241st overall, in 2000 Entry Draft).

			Regular Season					Playoffs				
Season	Club	Lea	GP	G	A	TP	PIM	GP	G	A	TP	PIM
1996-97	Langley Bantams	BCAHA	90	107	109	216	96	....	....	....	....	....
1997-98	Tri-City Americans	WHL	47	1	1	2	23	....	....	....	....	....
1998-99	Tri-City Americans	WHL	33	9	9	18	19	....	....	....	....	....
	Lethbridge	WHL	22	12	9	21	19	4	1	0	1	0
99-2000	Lethbridge	WHL	72	44	38	82	38	....	....	....	....	....
2000-01	Lethbridge	WHL	70	46	53	99	66	5	1	1	2	6

WHL East Second All-Star Team (2001)

BARTEK, Martin (BAHR-tehk, MAHR-tehn) **NSH.**

Center. Shoots left. 6'1", 205 lbs. Born, Kindgseed Jill, Czech., July 17, 1980.
(Nashville's 7th choice, 202nd overall, in 1998 Entry Draft).

			Regular Season					Playoffs				
Season	Club	Lea	GP	G	A	TP	PIM	GP	G	A	TP	PIM
1995-96	HKm Zvolen	Slovak-Jr.	46	75	43	118	....	....	....	....	....	....
1996-97	Kings Edgehill	Hi-School	35	45	40	85	32	....	....	....	....	....
1997-98	Rouyn-Noranda	QMJHL	28	9	19	28	12	....	....	....	....	....
	Rimouski Oceanic	QMJHL	13	3	4	7	6	....	....	....	....	....
	Sherbrooke	QMJHL	25	11	12	23	38	....	....	....	....	....
1998-99	HKm Zvolen	Slovak-Jr.	17	14	17	31	89	....	....	....	....	....
	HKm Zvolen	Slovakia	28	10	8	18	18	2	1	0	1	0
99-2000	Moncton Wildcats	QMJHL	69	32	44	76	36	16	10	13	23	24
2000-01	Milwaukee	IHL	14	1	0	1	2	....	....	....	....	....
	New Orleans	ECHL	51	30	33	63	16	8	5	4	9	4

BARTLETT, Russ (BAHRT-leht, RUHS) **TOR.**

Center. Shoots left. 6'2", 185 lbs. Born, Windham, NH, February 10, 1978.
(Toronto's 7th choice, 194th overall, in 1997 Entry Draft).

			Regular Season					Playoffs				
Season	Club	Lea	GP	G	A	TP	PIM	GP	G	A	TP	PIM
1996-97	Phillips-Exeter	Hi-School	31	27	63	90	24	....	....	....	....	....
1997-98	Boston University	H-East	38	8	11	19	44	....	....	....	....	....
1998-99	Boston University	H-East	35	12	20	32	18	....	....	....	....	....
99-2000	St. Lawrence	ECAC	DID NOT PLAY – TRANSFERRED COLLEGES									
2000-01	St. Lawrence	ECAC	37	18	25	43	20	....	....	....	....	....

BARTOVIC, Milan (BAHR-tuh-vihch, MIH-lan) **BUF.**

Right wing. Shoots left. 6', 194 lbs. Born, Trencin, Czech., April 9, 1981.
(Buffalo's 2nd choice, 35th overall, in 1999 Entry Draft).

			Regular Season					Playoffs				
Season	Club	Lea	GP	G	A	TP	PIM	GP	G	A	TP	PIM
1997-98	Dukla Trencin	Slovak-Jr.	26	2	6	8	27	....	....	....	....	....
1998-99	Dukla Trencin	Slovak-Jr.	46	36	35	71	62	6	9	3	12	10
99-2000	Tri-City Americans	WHL	18	8	9	17	12	....	....	....	....	....
	Brandon	WHL	38	18	22	40	28	....	....	....	....	....
2000-01	Brandon	WHL	34	15	25	40	40	6	1	2	3	8
	Rochester	AHL	2	1	1	2	0	4	0	1	1	2

• Missed majority of 2000-01 season recovering from shoulder injury originally suffered in game vs. Red Deer (WHL), October 10, 2000.

BATEMAN, Jeff (BAYT-mahn, JEHF) **DAL.**

Center. Shoots left. 5'11", 179 lbs. Born, Belleville, Ont., August 29, 1981.
(Dallas' 4th choice, 126th overall, in 1999 Entry Draft).

			Regular Season					Playoffs				
Season	Club	Lea	GP	G	A	TP	PIM	GP	G	A	TP	PIM
1996-97	Belleville Petes	OMHA	51	102	64	166	....	....	....	....	....	....
1997-98	Wellington Dukes	MTJHL	50	26	35	61	68	....	....	....	....	....
1998-99	Brampton	OHL	68	23	35	58	27	....	....	....	....	....
99-2000	Brampton	OHL	64	23	41	64	62	6	2	1	3	4
2000-01	Brampton	OHL	53	15	44	59	81	9	5	7	12	18

BATOVSKY, Zoltan (ba-TAWV-skee, ZOHL-tan)

Right wing. Shoots left. 5'11", 186 lbs. Born, Slovad, Czech., March 27, 1979.

			Regular Season					Playoffs				
Season	Club	Lea	GP	G	A	TP	PIM	GP	G	A	TP	PIM
1996-97	HC Bystricka	Slovak-Jr.	50	29	38	67	....	....	....	....	....	....
1997-98	Drummondville	QMJHL	69	22	43	65	112	....	....	....	....	....
1998-99	Drummondville	QMJHL	62	29	42	71	126	....	....	....	....	....
99-2000	Drummondville	QMJHL	63	27	60	87	151	16	10	19	29	12
2000-01	Kentucky	AHL	79	9	19	28	36	3	0	2	2	0

Signed as a free agent by **San Jose**, June 24, 2000. • Died of injuries suffered in automobile accident, August 8, 2001.

BAUMGARTNER, Gregor (BAWM-gahrt-nuhr, GREHG-ohr) **DAL.**

Left wing. Shoots left. 6'2", 192 lbs. Born, Leoben, Austria, July 13, 1979.
(Dallas' 5th choice, 156th overall, in 1999 Entry Draft).

			Regular Season					Playoffs				
Season	Club	Lea	GP	G	A	TP	PIM	GP	G	A	TP	PIM
1993-94	Ste-Foy AA	QAHA	55	37	33	70	....	....	....	....	....	....
1994-95	Ste-Foy Governors	QAAA	43	28	29	57	2	12	9	4	13	2
1995-96	Clarkson Knights	ECAC	7	0	1	1	0	....	....	....	....	....
	Gatineau Elites	QAAA	15	8	11	19	6	4	3	2	5	....
1996-97	Laval Titan	QMJHL	68	19	45	64	15	3	0	0	0	0
1997-98	Laval Titan	QMJHL	68	31	51	82	10	16	5	12	17	6
1998-99	Acadie-Bathurst	QMJHL	68	33	58	91	14	23	8	8	16	8
99-2000	Michigan K-Wings	IHL	59	6	9	15	11	....	....	....	....	....
2000-01	Utah Grizzlies	IHL	31	3	2	5	4	....	....	....	....	....
	Idaho Steelheads	WCHL	4	2	2	4	2	....	....	....	....	....
	Oklahoma City	CHL	6	2	3	5	8	....	....	....	....	....

• Re-entered NHL Entry Draft. Originally Montreal' 2nd choice, 37th overall, in 1997 Entry Draft.
• Left **Clarkson University** and signed as a free agent by **Gatineau Intrepide** (QAAA), December 7, 1995.

BAYDA, Ryan (BAY-duh, RIGH-uhn) **CAR.**

Left wing. Shoots left. 5'11", 185 lbs. Born, Saskatoon, Sask., December 9, 1980.
(Carolina's 2nd choice, 80th overall, in 2000 Entry Draft).

			Regular Season					Playoffs				
Season	Club	Lea	GP	G	A	TP	PIM	GP	G	A	TP	PIM
1995-96	Saskatoon Flyers	SAHA	60	85	74	159	85	....	....	....	....	....
1996-97	Saskatoon	SMHL	44	22	23	45	18	....	....	....	....	....
1997-98	Saskatoon	SMHL	41	29	49	78	103	....	....	....	....	....
1998-99	Vernon Vipers	BCJHL	45	24	58	82	15	....	....	....	....	....
99-2000	North Dakota	WCHA	44	17	23	40	30	....	....	....	....	....
2000-01	North Dakota	WCHA	46	25	34	59	48	....	....	....	....	....

Won BCJHL Rookie of the Year Award (1999) • WCHA All-Rookie Team (2000) • WCHA Second All-Star Team (2001)

BEAUCHEMIN, Francois (boh-sheh-MEH, frahn-SWUH) **MTL.**

Defense. Shoots left. 6', 206 lbs. Born, Sorel, Que., June 4, 1980.
(Montreal's 3rd choice, 75th overall, in 1998 Entry Draft).

			Regular Season					Playoffs				
Season	Club	Lea	GP	G	A	TP	PIM	GP	G	A	TP	PIM
1995-96	Richelieu Regents	QAAA	40	9	23	32	59	....	....	....	....	....
1996-97	Laval Titan	QMJHL	66	7	21	28	132	3	0	0	0	2
1997-98	Laval Titan	QMJHL	70	12	35	47	132	16	1	3	4	23
1998-99	Acadie-Bathurst	QMJHL	31	4	17	21	53	23	2	16	18	55
99-2000	Acadie-Bathurst	QMJHL	38	11	36	47	64	....	....	....	....	....
	Moncton Wildcats	QMJHL	33	8	31	39	35	16	2	11	13	14
2000-01	Quebec Citadelles	AHL	56	3	6	9	44	....	....	....	....	....

QMJHL Second All-Star Team (2000)

BEAUDOIN, Eric (boh-DWEH, AIR-ihk) **FLA.**

Left wing. Shoots left. 6'5", 204 lbs. Born, Ottawa, Ont., May 3, 1980.
(Tampa Bay's 4th choice, 92nd overall, in 1998 Entry Draft).

			Regular Season					Playoffs				
Season	Club	Lea	GP	G	A	TP	PIM	GP	G	A	TP	PIM
1996-97	Ottawa Jr. Sens	OCJHL	54	12	19	31	55	....	....	....	....	....
1997-98	Guelph Storm	OHL	62	9	13	22	43	12	3	2	5	4
1998-99	Guelph Storm	OHL	66	28	43	71	79	11	5	3	8	12
99-2000	Guelph Storm	OHL	68	38	34	72	126	6	3	0	3	2
2000-01	Louisville Panthers	AHL	71	15	10	25	78	....	....	....	....	....

Traded to **Florida** by **Tampa Bay** for Florida's 7th round choice (Marek Priechodsky) in 2000 Entry Draft, June 1, 2000.

BECKETT, Jason (Beh-keht, JAY-suhn) **PHI.**

Defense. Shoots right. 6'3", 205 lbs. Born, Lethbridge, Alta., July 23, 1980.
(Philadelphia's 2nd choice, 42nd overall, in 1998 Entry Draft).

			Regular Season					Playoffs				
Season	Club	Lea	GP	G	A	TP	PIM	GP	G	A	TP	PIM
1996-97	Lethbridge Y-Men	AMHL	34	7	10	17	118	....	....	....	....	....
1997-98	Seattle T-Birds	WHL	71	1	11	12	241	5	0	0	0	16
1998-99	Seattle T-Birds	WHL	70	4	26	30	195	11	0	1	1	40
99-2000	Seattle T-Birds	WHL	70	3	15	18	183	7	1	1	2	12
2000-01	Trenton Titans	ECHL	17	2	2	4	24	15	0	1	1	26
	Philadelphia	AHL	56	2	10	12	107	....	....	....	....	....

BEDNAR, Jaroslav (BEHD-nahr, YA-roh-slahv) **L.A.**

Right wing. Shoots right. 5'11", 198 lbs. Born, Prague, Czech., November 8, 1976.
(Los Angeles' 4th choice, 51st overall, in 2001 Entry Draft).

			Regular Season					Playoffs				
Season	Club	Lea	GP	G	A	TP	PIM	GP	G	A	TP	PIM
1994-95	Slavia Praha	Cze-Rep	20	6	7	13	4	3	0	0	0	0
1995-96	Slavia Praha	Cze-Rep	20	3	1	4	6	3	0	0	0	0
1996-97	Slavia Praha	Cze-Rep	45	18	12	30	18	....	....	....	....	....
1997-98	Slavia Praha	Cze-Rep	14	2	5	7	6	....	....	....	....	....
	HC Plzen	Cze-Rep	34	26	15	41	16	5	2	4	6	4
	HC Plzen	EuroHL	....	....	....	....	....	5	4	2	6	4
1998-99	Sparta Praha	Cze-Rep	52	23	14	37	30	8	5	2	7	0
99-2000	JyP Jyvaskyla	Finland	53	34	28	62	56	....	....	....	....	....
2000-01	HIFK Helsinki	Finland	56	*32	28	60	51	5	3	1	4	0

BELL, Brendan (BEHL, BREHN-duhn) **TOR.**

Defense. Shoots left. 6', 198 lbs. Born, Ottawa, Ont., March 31, 1983.
(Toronto's 3rd choice, 65th overall, in 2001 Entry Draft).

			Regular Season					Playoffs				
Season	Club	Lea	GP	G	A	TP	PIM	GP	G	A	TP	PIM
1998-99	Ottawa Jr. Sens	OCJHL	54	7	20	27	46	....	....	....	....	....
99-2000	Ottawa 67's	OHL	48	1	32	33	34	5	0	1	1	4
2000-01	Ottawa 67's	OHL	68	7	32	39	59	20	1	11	12	22

OCJHL All-Rookie Team (1999) • Won OCJHL Rookie of the Year Award (1999)

BELL, Thatcher (BEHL, THA-tchuhr) **VAN.**

Center. Shoots left. 6', 172 lbs. Born, Charlottetown, P.E.I., February 1, 1982.
(Vancouver's 2nd choice, 71st overall, in 2000 Entry Draft).

			Regular Season					Playoffs				
Season	Club	Lea	GP	G	A	TP	PIM	GP	G	A	TP	PIM
1997-98	U.C.C. Blues	Hi-School	44	35	50	85	....	....	....	....	....	....
1998-99	Rimouski Oceanic	QMJHL	64	16	38	54	67	11	3	1	4	0
99-2000	Rimouski Oceanic	QMJHL	53	26	43	69	61	5	0	0	0	15
2000-01	Rimouski Oceanic	QMJHL	46	27	32	59	77	11	6	7	13	14

BELLEFEUILLE, Blake (BEHL-fay, BLAYK) **CBJ**

Right wing. Shoots right. 5'10", 208 lbs. Born, Framingham, MA, December 27, 1977.

			Regular Season					Playoffs				
Season	Club	Lea	GP	G	A	TP	PIM	GP	G	A	TP	PIM
1994-95	Framingham High	Hi-School	20	42	50	92	....	....	....	....	....	....
1995-96	Framingham High	Hi-School	20	31	60	91	....	....	....	....	....	....
1996-97	Boston College	H-East	34	16	19	35	20	....	....	....	....	....
1997-98	Boston College	H-East	41	19	20	39	35	....	....	....	....	....
1998-99	Boston College	H-East	43	24	25	49	80	....	....	....	....	....
99-2000	Boston College	H-East	39	18	31	49	28	....	....	....	....	....
2000-01	Syracuse Crunch	AHL	50	5	5	10	18	5	0	0	0	0

• All-time leading scorer in Massachusetts High-School history with career totals of 120-182-302. • Hockey East Second All-Star Team (2000)

Signed as a free agent by **Columbus**, May 26, 2000.

BEMBRIDGE, Garrett (bem-BRIHDJ, GAHR-reht) **CGY.**

Right wing. Shoots right. 6', 180 lbs. Born, Melfort, Sask., July 6, 1981.
(Calgary's 8th choice, 207th overall, in 2001 Entry Draft).

			Regular Season					Playoffs				
Season	Club	Lea	GP	G	A	TP	PIM	GP	G	A	TP	PIM
1997-98	Saskatoon Blaze	SMHL	44	29	45	74	74	....	....	....	....	....
	Saskatoon Blades	WHL	6	1	1	2	0	1	0	0	0	0
1998-99	Saskatoon Blades	WHL	68	23	27	50	30	....	....	....	....	....
99-2000	Saskatoon Blades	WHL	72	27	31	58	41	11	5	5	10	2
2000-01	Saskatoon Blades	WHL	72	38	40	78	40	....	....	....	....	....

• Re-entered NHL Entry Draft. Originally NY Rangers's 6th choice, 137th overall, in 1999 Entry Draft.

BENOIT, Mathieu (behn-WAH, MAT-hew)

Right wing. Shoots right. 5'11", 200 lbs. Born, St-Clec, Que., July 12, 1979.
(New Jersey's 6th choice, 188th overall, in 1997 Entry Draft).

			Regular Season					Playoffs				
Season	Club	Lea	GP	G	A	TP	PIM	GP	G	A	TP	PIM
1993-94	Salaberry Lions	QAHA	32	72	42	114	22	....	....	....	....	....
1994-95	Lac St-Louis	QAAA	44	21	33	54	34	8	0	2	2	2
1995-96	Chicoutimi	QMJHL	61	6	14	20	17	17	0	0	0	0
1996-97	Chicoutimi	QMJHL	64	35	36	71	22	9	2	2	4	0
1997-98	Chicoutimi	QMJHL	59	56	61	117	32	6	2	3	5	2
1998-99	Chicoutimi	QMJHL	36	39	14	53	28	....	....	....	....	....
	Acadie-Bathurst	QMJHL	32	23	33	56	6	23	*20	*21	*41	16
99-2000	Acadie-Bathurst	QMJHL	20	29	10	39	38	....	....	....	....	....
	Moncton Wildcats	QMJHL	33	28	34	62	21	16	15	15	30	6
	Albany River Rats	AHL	1	0	0	0	0	....	....	....	....	....
2000-01	Hartford	AHL	9	1	0	1	0	....	....	....	....	....
	Charlotte	ECHL	62	43	30	73	16	5	3	3	6	10

QMJHL First All-Star Team (1998) • QMJHL Second All-Star Team (1999, 2000)

BERG, Reggie (BUHRG, REH-jee) **CAR.**

Center. Shoots left. 5'10", 180 lbs. Born, Coon Rapids, MN, September 18, 1976.
(Toronto's 12th choice, 178th overall, in 1996 Entry Draft).

			Regular Season					Playoffs				
Season	Club	Lea	GP	G	A	TP	PIM	GP	G	A	TP	PIM
1993-94	Des Moines	USHL	27	13	24	37	48	....	....	....	....	....
1994-95	Des Moines	USHL	35	30	35	65	75	12	11	8	19	12
1995-96	U. of Minnesota	WCHA	40	23	11	34	69	....	....	....	....	....
1996-97	U. of Minnesota	WCHA	38	11	26	37	48	....	....	....	....	....
1997-98	U. of Minnesota	WCHA	39	20	19	39	53	....	....	....	....	....
1998-99	U. of Minnesota	WCHA	43	20	28	48	64	....	....	....	....	....
99-2000	Florida Everblades	ECHL	52	27	25	52	64	5	2	1	3	6
	Orlando	IHL	2	0	0	0	0	....	....	....	....	....
2000-01	Cincinnati	IHL	3	0	0	0	2	....	....	....	....	....
	Lowell	AHL	30	6	7	13	22	....	....	....	....	....
	Florida Everblades	ECHL	33	19	29	48	39	5	1	3	4	6

WCHA Second All-Star Team (1998)

Signed as a free agent by **Carolina**, August 21, 2000.

BERGERON, Antoine (BAIR-zhuhr-uhn, ahn-TWAHN) **ST.L.**

Defense. Shoots left. 6'2", 212 lbs. Born, Valcourt, Que., December 14, 1981.
(St. Louis' 4th choice, 96th overall, in 2000 Entry Draft).

			Regular Season					Playoffs				
Season	Club	Lea	GP	G	A	TP	PIM	GP	G	A	TP	PIM
1996-97	Magog Selectes	QAAA	34	4	11	15	20	....	....	....	....	....
1997-98	Magog Selectes	QAAA	17	7	10	17	39	10	3	4	7	12
1998-99	Rimouski Oceanic	QMJHL	20	0	4	4	28	....	....	....	....	....
	Victoriaville Tigres	QMJHL	30	3	6	9	73	2	0	0	0	0
99-2000	Victoriaville Tigres	QMJHL	24	2	8	10	30	....	....	....	....	....
	Val-d'Or Foreurs	QMJHL	8	3	1	4	10	....	....	....	....	....
2000-01	Val-d'Or Foreurs	QMJHL	36	16	26	42	95	....	....	....	....	....
	Acadie-Bathurst	QMJHL	26	8	19	27	72	19	6	10	16	46

Traded to **Acadie-Bathurst** by **Val-d'Or** with J-F Laniel, Eric Labelle and future considerations for Simon Lajeunesse and the return of Val-d'Or's 4th choice (previously acquired, Val d'Or selected Mathieu Curadeau) in 2001 QMJHL Midget Draft, January 7, 2001.

BERGERON, Marc-Andre (BAIR-zhur-uhn, MAHRK-AWN-dray) **EDM.**

Defense. Shoots left. 5'9", 185 lbs. Born, St-Louis-de-France, Que., October 13, 1980.

			Regular Season					Playoffs				
Season	Club	Lea	GP	G	A	TP	PIM	GP	G	A	TP	PIM
1997-98	Baie-Comeau	QMJHL	40	6	14	20	48	....	....	....	....	....
1998-99	Baie-Comeau	QMJHL	46	8	14	22	57	....	....	....	....	....
	Shawinigan	QMJHL	24	6	7	13	66	5	2	2	4	24
99-2000	Shawinigan	QMJHL	70	24	50	74	173	13	4	7	11	45
2000-01	Shawinigan	QMJHL	69	42	59	101	185	10	4	11	15	24

QMJHL First All-Star Team (2001) • Canadian Major Junior First All-Star Team (2001) • Canadian Major Junior Defenseman of the Year (2001)

Signed as a free agent by **Edmonton**, July 20, 2001.

BERGLUND, Christian (BUHRG-luhnd, KRIH-stan) **N.J.**

Right wing. Shoots left. 5'11", 185 lbs. Born, Orebro, Sweden, March 12, 1980.
(New Jersey's 3rd choice, 37th overall, in 1998 Entry Draft).

			Regular Season					Playoffs				
Season	Club	Lea	GP	G	A	TP	PIM	GP	G	A	TP	PIM
1994-95	Kariskoga IK	Swede-4	20	14	13	27	....	....	....	....	....	....
1995-96	Kristinehamn SK	Swede-3	23	8	8	16	12	....	....	....	....	....
1996-97	Farjestads BK	Swede-Jr.	21	2	3	5	24	....	....	....	....	....
1997-98	Farjestads BK	Swede-Jr.	29	23	19	42	88	2	0	0	0	0
	Farjestads BK	Sweden	1	0	0	0	0	....	....	....	....	....
1998-99	Farjestads BK	Swede-Jr.	5	3	4	7	22	....	....	....	....	....
	Farjestads BK	Sweden	37	2	4	6	37	4	1	0	1	4
99-2000	Farjestads BK	Swede-Jr.	5	3	5	8	8	....	....	....	....	....
	Bofors IK	Swede-2	6	2	0	2	12	....	....	....	....	....
	Farjestads BK	Sweden	43	8	6	14	44	7	2	1	3	10
2000-01	Farjestads BK	Sweden	49	17	20	37	*142	16	7	7	14	22

BERNIKOV, Ruslan (BAIR-nih-kahf, roos-LAHN) **DAL.**

Right wing. Shoots left. 6'3", 198 lbs. Born, Vidnoye, USSR, December 4, 1977.
(Dallas' 6th choice, 139th overall, in 2000 Entry Draft).

			Regular Season					Playoffs				
Season	Club	Lea	GP	G	A	TP	PIM	GP	G	A	TP	PIM
1996-97	D'amo Moscow-2	Russia-3	32	11	4	15	20	....	....	....	....	....
	Dynamo Moscow	Russia	2	0	0	0	0	....	....	....	....	....
1997-98	Yekaterinburg-2	Russia-3	2	1	1	2	0	....	....	....	....	....
	HC Yekaterinburg	Russia	43	7	7	14	55	....	....	....	....	....
1998-99	Dynamo Moscow	Russia	6	0	1	1	2	....	....	....	....	....
	Krylja Sovetov	Russia	20	3	1	4	24	....	....	....	....	....
	CSKA Moscow	Russia	1	0	0	0	0	....	....	....	....	....
	HC Cherepovets	Russia	5	0	0	0	0	1	0	0	0	0
99-2000	Dynamo Moscow	Russia	6	2	1	3	2	....	....	....	....	....
	Amur Khabarovsk	Russia	14	3	6	9	10	5	3	1	4	2
2000-01	Amur Khabarovsk	Russia	33	1	4	5	40	....	....	....	....	....

BERTI, Chris (BUHR-tee, KRIHS) **BOS.**

Center. Shoots left. 6'5", 206 lbs. Born, Scarborough, Ont., October 6, 1981.
(Boston's 9th choice, 204th overall, in 2000 Entry Draft).

			Regular Season					Playoffs				
Season	Club	Lea	GP	G	A	TP	PIM	GP	G	A	TP	PIM
1996-97	Oshawa Legion	OMHA	40	16	31	47	43	....	....	....	....	....
1997-98	Sarnia Jacks	OJHL-B	8	4	3	7	2	....	....	....	....	....
	Sarnia Sting	OHL	59	2	7	9	9	5	0	0	0	0
1998-99	Sarnia Sting	OHL	68	10	12	22	114	6	0	1	1	0
99-2000	Sarnia Sting	OHL	62	8	11	19	131	7	1	0	1	13
2000-01	Sarnia Sting	OHL	25	5	10	15	38	....	....	....	....	....
	Erie Otters	OHL	19	0	6	6	42	15	3	5	8	33

Traded to **Erie** by **Sarnia** for Riley Moher, January 6, 2001.

BETTS, Blair (BEHTS, BLAIR) **CGY.**

Center. Shoots left. 6'1", 200 lbs. Born, Edmonton, Alta., February 16, 1980.
(Calgary's 2nd choice, 33rd overall, in 1998 Entry Draft).

			Regular Season					Playoffs				
Season	Club	Lea	GP	G	A	TP	PIM	GP	G	A	TP	PIM
1995-96	Sherwood Park	AMHL	34	22	19	41	69	....	....	....	....	....
1996-97	Prince George	WHL	58	12	18	30	19	15	2	2	4	6
1997-98	Prince George	WHL	71	35	41	76	38	11	4	6	10	8
1998-99	Prince George	WHL	42	20	22	42	39	7	3	2	5	8
99-2000	Prince George	WHL	44	24	35	59	38	13	11	11	22	6
2000-01	Saint John Flames	AHL	75	13	15	28	28	19	2	3	5	4

BEZINA, Goran (BEH-zee-nuh, GOH-ran) **PHX.**

Defense. Shoots left. 6'4", 220 lbs. Born, Split, Yugoslavia, March 21, 1980.
(Phoenix's 8th choice, 234th overall, in 1999 Entry Draft).

			Regular Season					Playoffs				
Season	Club	Lea	GP	G	A	TP	PIM	GP	G	A	TP	PIM
1998-99	Fribourg-Gotteron	Switz-Jr.	22	11	6	17	64	....	....	....	....	....
	Fribourg-Gotteron	Switz.	38	0	0	0	14	4	0	0	0	2
	Fribourg-Gotteron	EuroHL	6	0	0	0	0	....	....	....	....	....
99-2000	Fribourg-Gotteron	Switz-Jr.	2	0	1	1	16	2	1	1	2	8
	Fribourg-Gotteron	Switz.	44	3	6	9	10	4	0	0	0	6
2000-01	Fribourg-Gotteron	Switz.	44	10	10	20	44	5	1	1	2	12

BIEKSA, Kevin (BEEKS-ah, KEH-vihn) **VAN.**

Defense. Shoots right. 6'1", 180 lbs. Born, Grimsby, Ont., June 16, 1981.
(Vancouver's 4th choice, 151st overall, in 2001 Entry Draft).

			Regular Season					Playoffs				
Season	Club	Lea	GP	G	A	TP	PIM	GP	G	A	TP	PIM
1997-98	Burlington	OPJHL	27	0	3	3	10	....	....	....	....	....
1998-99	Burlington	OPJHL	49	8	29	37	83	....	....	....	....	....
99-2000	Burlington	OPJHL	49	6	27	33	139	....	....	....	....	....
2000-01	Bowling Green	CCHA	35	4	9	13	90	....	....	....	....	....

BIRBRAER, Max (beer-BRIEGH-uhr, max) **N.J.**

Left wing. Shoots left. 6'2", 195 lbs. Born, Ust-Kamenogorsk, USSR, December 15, 1980.
(New Jersey's 6th choice, 67th overall, in 2000 Entry Draft).

			Regular Season					Playoffs				
Season	Club	Lea	GP	G	A	TP	PIM	GP	G	A	TP	PIM
1997-98	Shelburne Wolves	MTJHL	12	7	11	18	8	....	....	....	....	....
1998-99	Shelburne Wolves	OPJHL	35	20	22	42	25	....	....	....	....	....
99-2000	Newmarket 87's	OPJHL	47	50	32	82	52	....	....	....	....	....
2000-01	Albany River Rats	AHL	50	7	6	13	24	....	....	....	....	....

BIZYAYEV, Vasili (bihz-AY-yehv, va-SEE-lee) **BUF.**

Right wing. Shoots left. 6'1", 185 lbs. Born, Moscow, USSR, June 6, 1982.
(Buffalo's 5th choice, 213th overall, in 2000 Entry Draft).

			Regular Season					Playoffs				
Season	Club	Lea	GP	G	A	TP	PIM	GP	G	A	TP	PIM
99-2000	HC Moscow	Russia-2	STATISTICS NOT AVAILABLE									
2000-01	Kitchener	OHL	53	10	14	24	10	....	....	....	....	....

BLAIS, Ben (BLAYS, BEHN) NYI

Defense. Shoots left. 6'4", 195 lbs. Born, Berlin, NH, February 16, 1978.
(NY Islanders' 8th choice, 237th overall, in 1998 Entry Draft).

			Regular Season					Playoffs				
Season	Club	Lea	GP	G	A	TP	PIM	GP	G	A	TP	PIM
1997-98	Salisbury School	Hi-School	20	5	21	26	....	....	....	....	....	....
	Walpole Stars	EJHL	34	7	18	25	75	....	....	....	....	....
1998-99	St. Lawrence	ECAC	3	0	1	1	6	....	....	....	....	....
99-2000	Quinnipiac College	MAAC	DID NOT PLAY – TRANSFERRED COLLEGES									
2000-01	Quinnipiac College	MAAC	33	3	11	14	54	....	....	....	....	....

Won EJHL Defenseman of the Year Award (1998) • MAAC All-Tournament Team (2001)

BLATAK, Miroslav (BLAT-ak, MEER-oh-slahv) DET.

Defense. Shoots left. 5'11", 172 lbs. Born, Gottwaldov, Czech., May 25, 1982.
(Detroit's 3rd choice, 129th overall, in 2001 Entry Draft).

			Regular Season					Playoffs				
Season	Club	Lea	GP	G	A	TP	PIM	GP	G	A	TP	PIM
99-2000	HC Vsetin-B	Cze-Rep	30	0	0	0	12	....	....	....	....	....
	HC Vsetin-Jr.	Cze-Rep	12	0	2	2	10	....	....	....	....	....
2000-01	HC Vsetin-B	Cze-Rep	33	7	8	15	56	....	....	....	....	....
	HC Vsetin-Jr.	Cze-Rep	12	2	4	6	54	7	0	6	6	6
	HC Zlin	Cze-Rep	8	0	2	2	0	6	0	0	0	0

BLATNY, Zdenek (BLAT-nee, z-DEHN-ehk) ATL.

Center. Shoots left. 6'1", 195 lbs. Born, Brno, Czech., January 14, 1981.
(Atlanta's 3rd choice, 68th overall, in 1999 Entry Draft).

			Regular Season					Playoffs				
Season	Club	Lea	GP	G	A	TP	PIM	GP	G	A	TP	PIM
1997-98	Kometa Brno-Jr.	Cze-Rep	42	22	21	43	40	....	....	....	....	....
1998-99	Seattle T-Birds	WHL	44	18	15	33	25	11	4	0	4	24
99-2000	Seattle T-Birds	WHL	7	4	5	9	12	....	....	....	....	....
	Kootenay Ice	WHL	61	43	39	82	119	21	10	*17	27	46
2000-01	Kootenay Ice	WHL	58	37	48	85	120	11	8	10	18	24

WHL East Second All-star Team (2000)

BOHAC, Jan (BOH-hach, YAHN) OTT.

Center. Shoots left. 6'4", 201 lbs. Born, Tabor, Czech., February 3, 1982.
(Ottawa's 4th choice, 87th overall, in 2000 Entry Draft).

			Regular Season					Playoffs				
Season	Club	Lea	GP	G	A	TP	PIM	GP	G	A	TP	PIM
1997-98	Slavia Praha-Jr.	Cze-Rep	39	8	12	20	12	....	....	....	....	....
1998-99	Slavia Praha-Jr.	Cze-Rep	35	6	6	12	10	....	....	....	....	....
	Slavia Praha	Cze-Rep	2	0	0	0	0	....	....	....	....	....
99-2000	Slavia Praha-Jr.	Cze-Rep	22	7	8	15	6	7	0	1	1	4
	Slavia Praha	Cze-Rep	25	1	2	3	4	....	....	....	....	....
2000-01	Slavia Praha	Cze-Rep	19	2	0	2	0	2	0	0	0	0

BOIS, Danny (BOIZ, DA-nee) COL.

Right wing. Shoots right. 6', 190 lbs. Born, Thunder Bay, Ont., June 1, 1983.
(Colorado's 2nd choice, 97th overall, in 2001 Entry Draft).

			Regular Season					Playoffs				
Season	Club	Lea	GP	G	A	TP	PIM	GP	G	A	TP	PIM
1998-99	Thunder Bay	TBMHL	15	7	12	19	28	....	....	....	....	....
99-2000	Wellington Dukes	OPJHL	37	15	20	35	115	....	....	....	....	....
2000-01	London Knights	OHL	66	21	16	37	218	5	2	1	3	19

OHL Second All-Rookie Team (2001)

BOISVERT, Hugo (bwuh-VAIR, HEW-goh)

Center. Shoots left. 6', 200 lbs. Born, St-Eustache, Que., February 11, 1976.

			Regular Season					Playoffs				
Season	Club	Lea	GP	G	A	TP	PIM	GP	G	A	TP	PIM
1994-95	Cornwall Colts	OCJHL	27	13	19	32	26	....	....	....	....	....
1995-96	Cornwall Colts	OCJHL	54	40	90	130	102	15	15	20	35	44
1996-97	Ohio State	CCHA	38	11	27	38	44	....	....	....	....	....
1997-98	Ohio State	CCHA	42	23	*35	58	70	....	....	....	....	....
1998-99	Ohio State	CCHA	41	24	27	51	54	....	....	....	....	....
99-2000	Canada	Nat-Team	39	10	14	24	12	....	....	....	....	....
2000-01	Orlando	IHL	68	6	12	18	41	16	4	5	9	23

CCHA First All-Star Team (1998, 1999) • NCAA West First All-American Team (1998) • NCAA West Second All-American Team (1999)

Signed as a free agent by **Atlanta**, June 25, 1999.

BOLIBRUCK, Kevin (BOH-lee-bruhk, KEH-vihn)

Defense. Shoots left. 6'1", 200 lbs. Born, Peterborough, Ont., February 8, 1977.
(Edmonton's 7th choice, 176th overall, in 1997 Entry Draft).

			Regular Season					Playoffs				
Season	Club	Lea	GP	G	A	TP	PIM	GP	G	A	TP	PIM
1993-94	Thorold Hawks	OJHL-B	38	6	18	24	78	....	....	....	....	....
1994-95	Peterborough	OHL	66	2	16	18	88	11	1	1	2	14
1995-96	Peterborough	OHL	57	6	21	27	105	24	3	6	9	46
1996-97	Peterborough	OHL	46	4	26	30	63	11	3	3	6	14
1997-98	Canada	Nat-Team	49	2	5	7	65	....	....	....	....	....
1998-99	Hamilton Bulldogs	AHL	64	1	6	7	42	11	0	1	1	4
99-2000	Hamilton Bulldogs	AHL	54	1	4	5	67	10	0	1	1	4
2000-01	Rochester	AHL	76	2	5	7	52	3	0	0	0	0

• Re-entered NHL Entry Draft. Originally Ottawa's 4th choice, 89th overall, in 1995 Entry Draft.

OHL First All-Star Team (1996)

Rights traded to **Chicago** by **Ottawa** with Denis Chasse and Ottawa's 6th round choice (later traded back to Ottawa - Ottawa selected Christopher Neil) in 1998 Entry Draft for Mike Prokopec, March 18, 1997. Signed as a free agent by **Rochester** (AHL), September 20, 2000.

BOOGAARD, Derek MIN.

Left wing. Shoots left. 6' 6", 249 lbs. Born, Saskatoon, Sask., June 23, 1982.
(Minnesota's 6th choice, 202nd overall, in 2001 Entry Draft).

			Regular Season					Playoffs				
Season	Club	Lea	GP	G	A	TP	PIM	GP	G	A	TP	PIM
1998-99	Regina Caps	SSJHL	35	2	3	5	166	....	....	....	....	....
99-2000	Regina Pats	WHL	5	0	0	0	17	....	....	....	....	....
	Prince George	WHL	33	0	0	0	149	....	....	....	....	....
2000-01	Prince George	WHL	61	1	8	9	245	6	1	0	1	31

Traded to **Prince George** by **Regina** for Jonanthan Parker, October 26, 1999.

BOOTLAND, Darryl (BOOT-land, DAIR-ihl) COL.

Right wing. Shoots right. 6'1", 200 lbs. Born, Toronto, Ont., November 2, 1981.
(Colorado's 12th choice, 252nd overall, in 2000 Entry Draft).

			Regular Season					Playoffs				
Season	Club	Lea	GP	G	A	TP	PIM	GP	G	A	TP	PIM
1997-98	Orangeville	OJHL-B	44	22	26	48	177	....	....	....	....	....
1998-99	Barrie Colts	OHL	38	18	11	29	89	....	....	....	....	....
	St. Michael's	OHL	28	12	6	18	80	....	....	....	....	....
99-2000	St. Michael's	OHL	65	24	30	54	166	....	....	....	....	....
2000-01	St. Michael's	OHL	56	32	33	65	136	11	3	1	4	20

BOOTLAND, Nick (BOOT-land, NIHK)

Left wing. Shoots left. 6'3", 215 lbs. Born, Shelbourne, Ont., July 31, 1978.
(Dallas' 8th choice, 220th overall, in 1996 Entry Draft).

			Regular Season					Playoffs				
Season	Club	Lea	GP	G	A	TP	PIM	GP	G	A	TP	PIM
1994-95	Orangeville	OJHL-B	47	11	10	21	57	....	....	....	....	....
1995-96	Guelph Storm	OHL	64	8	7	15	90	16	1	0	1	21
1996-97	Guelph Storm	OHL	64	35	23	58	117	18	11	7	18	36
1997-98	Guelph Storm	OHL	64	23	37	60	128	12	7	6	13	22
1998-99	Hershey Bears	AHL	62	3	6	9	122	....	....	....	....	....
99-2000	Hershey Bears	AHL	59	5	13	18	108	14	2	2	4	26
2000-01	Hershey Bears	AHL	71	6	8	14	110	12	1	3	4	2

Signed as a free agent by **Colorado**, August 6, 1998.

BOUCHARD, Francois (BOO-shahrd, fran-SWUH) TOR.

Defense. Shoots right. 6', 189 lbs. Born, Brossard, Que., August 8, 1973.
(Tampa Bay's 1st choice, 8th overall, in 1994 Supplemental Draft).

			Regular Season					Playoffs				
Season	Club	Lea	GP	G	A	TP	PIM	GP	G	A	TP	PIM
1989-90	Richelieu Riverains	QAAA	39	4	22	26	....	4	1	1	2	....
1990-91			STATISTICS NOT AVAILABLE									
1991-92	Northeastern	H-East	34	4	9	13	28	....	....	....	....	....
1992-93	Northeastern	H-East	26	4	6	10	20	....	....	....	....	....
1993-94	Northeastern	H-East	39	15	15	30	34	....	....	....	....	....
1994-95	Northeastern	H-East	31	7	16	23	39	....	....	....	....	....
1995-96	Charlotte	ECHL	66	9	18	27	64	16	4	4	8	18
1996-97	Karpat Oulu	Finland-2	50	22	20	42	6	....	....	....	....	....
1997-98	HPK Hameenlinna	Finland	10	1	0	1	20	....	....	....	....	....
	Augsburger EV	DEL	36	7	9	16	36	....	....	....	....	....
1998-99	Karpat Oulu	Finland-2	42	6	19	25	60	5	1	0	1	2
99-2000	MoDo Hockey	Sweden	41	2	6	8	38	13	0	0	0	16
2000-01	Djurgardens IF	Sweden	48	10	11	21	58	16	2	3	5	14

Hockey East First All-Star Team (1992) • NCAA All-Eat Team (1992)

Signed as a free agent by **Toronto**, July 16, 2001.

BOULERICE, Jesse (BOO-luhr-ighs, JEHS-see) PHI.

Right wing. Shoots right. 6'1", 215 lbs. Born, Plattsburgh, NY, August 10, 1978.
(Philadelphia's 4th choice, 133rd overall, in 1996 Entry Draft).

			Regular Season					Playoffs				
Season	Club	Lea	GP	G	A	TP	PIM	GP	G	A	TP	PIM
1994-95	Hawkesbury	OCJHL	46	1	8	9	160	....	....	....	....	....
1995-96	Detroit Whalers	OHL	64	2	5	7	150	16	0	0	0	12
1996-97	Detroit Whalers	OHL	33	10	14	24	209	....	....	....	....	....
1997-98	Plymouth Whalers	OHL	53	20	23	43	170	13	2	4	6	35
1998-99	Philadelphia	AHL	24	1	2	3	82	....	....	....	....	....
	New Orleans	ECHL	12	0	1	1	38	....	....	....	....	....
99-2000	Philadelphia	AHL	40	3	4	7	85	4	0	2	2	4
	Trenton Titans	ECHL	25	8	8	16	90	....	....	....	....	....
2000-01	Philadelphia	AHL	60	3	4	7	256	10	1	1	2	28

BOUMEDIENNE, Josef (BOO-mih-dyehn, JOH-sehf) N.J.

Defense. Shoots left. 6'1", 200 lbs. Born, Stockholm, Sweden, January 12, 1978.
(New Jersey's 7th choice, 91st overall, in 1996 Entry Draft).

			Regular Season					Playoffs				
Season	Club	Lea	GP	G	A	TP	PIM	GP	G	A	TP	PIM
1994-95	Huddinge IF	Swede-Jr.	10	0	2	2	57	....	....	....	....	....
1995-96	Huddinge IK	Swede-Jr.	25	2	4	6	66	....	....	....	....	....
	Huddinge IK	Swede-Jr.	7	0	0	0	14	....	....	....	....	....
1996-97	Sodertalje SK	Sweden	32	1	1	2	32	....	....	....	....	....
1997-98	Sodertalje SK	Sweden	26	3	3	6	28	....	....	....	....	....
1998-99	Tappara Tampere	Finland	51	6	8	14	119	....	....	....	....	....
99-2000	Tappara Tampere	Finland	50	8	24	32	160	4	1	2	3	10
2000-01	Albany River Rats	AHL	79	8	28	36	117	....	....	....	....	....

BOWEN, Eric (BOW-ehn, AIR-ihk) ATL.

Right wing. Shoots right. 6'2", 225 lbs. Born, Canoga Park, CA, October 30, 1981.
(Atlanta's 12th choice, 244th overall, in 2000 Entry Draft).

			Regular Season					Playoffs				
Season	Club	Lea	GP	G	A	TP	PIM	GP	G	A	TP	PIM
1998-99	Team USA	USDP-17	49	2	7	9	99	....	....	....	....	....
	Team USA	USDP	3	0	0	0	2	....	....	....	....	....
99-2000	Portland	WHL	69	2	5	7	184	....	....	....	....	....
2000-01	Portland	WHL	34	5	5	10	107	....	....	....	....	....
	Kootenay Ice	WHL	22	1	3	4	71	....	....	....	....	....

Traded to **Kootenay** by **Portland** for future considerations, January 6, 2001.

BOYES, Brad (BOIZ, BRAD) TOR.

Center. Shoots right. 6', 181 lbs. Born, Mississauga, Ont., April 17, 1982.
(Toronto's 1st choice, 24th overall, in 2000 Entry Draft).

			Regular Season					Playoffs				
Season	Club	Lea	GP	G	A	TP	PIM	GP	G	A	TP	PIM
1997-98	Mississauga Reps	MTHL	44	27	50	77	....	....	....	....	....	....
1998-99	Erie Otters	OHL	59	24	36	60	30	5	1	2	3	10
99-2000	Erie Otters	OHL	68	36	46	82	38	13	6	8	14	10
2000-01	Erie Otters	OHL	59	45	45	90	42	15	10	13	23	8

OHL Second All-Rookie Team (1999) • CHL Scholastic Player of the Year (2000) • OHL Second All-Star Team (2001)

BRANHAM, Tim (BRA-nuhm, TIHM) VAN.

Defense. Shoots left. 6'2", 185 lbs. Born, Minoqua, WI, May 10, 1981.
(Vancouver's 3rd choice, 93rd overall, in 2000 Entry Draft).

			Regular Season					Playoffs				
Season	Club	Lea	GP	G	A	TP	PIM	GP	G	A	TP	PIM
1997-98	Danville Wings	NAJHL	54	2	7	9	72	5	0	0	0	4
1998-99	Soo Indians	NAJHL	19	2	2	4	30	4	0	0	0	2
99-2000	Soo Indians	NAJHL	22	5	11	16	32	....	....	....	....	....
	Barrie Colts	OHL	38	3	16	19	46	25	4	7	11	17
2000-01	Barrie Colts	OHL	68	7	25	32	77	3	0	1	1	6

BRENDL, Pavel (BREHN-duhl, PAH-vehl) PHI.

Right wing. Shoots right. 6'1", 204 lbs. Born, Opocno, Czech., March 23, 1981.
(NY Rangers' 1st choice, 4th overall, in 1999 Entry Draft).

			Regular Season					Playoffs				
Season	Club	Lea	GP	G	A	TP	PIM	GP	G	A	TP	PIM
1996-97	HC Olomouc-Jr.	Cze-Rep	40	35	17	52	....	....	....	....	....	....
1997-98	HC Olomouc-Jr.	Cze-Rep	38	29	23	52	....	....	....	....	....	....
	HC Olomouc-2	Cze-Rep	12	1	1	2	....	....	....	....	....	....
1998-99	Calgary Hitmen	WHL	68	*73	61	*134	40	20	*21	*25	*46	18
99-2000	Calgary Hitmen	WHL	61	*59	52	111	94	10	7	12	19	8
	Hartford	AHL	....	....	....	....	....	2	0	0	0	0
2000-01	Calgary Hitmen	WHL	49	40	35	75	66	10	7	6	13	6

WHL East First All-Star Team (1999) • Canadian Major Junior First All-Star Team (1999) • Canadian Major Junior Rookie of the Year (1999) • Memorial Cup All-Star Team (1999) • WHL East Second All-Star Team (2000)

Traded to **Philadelphia** by **NY Rangers** with Jan Hlavac, Kim Johnsson and NY Rangers' 3rd round choice in 2003 Entry Draft for the rights to Eric Lindros and a conditional 1st round choice in 2003 Entry Draft, August 20, 2001.

BRENK, Jake (BREHNK, JAYK) EDM.

Center. Shoots right. 6'2", 187 lbs. Born, Detroit Lakes, MN, April 16, 1982.
(Edmonton's 6th choice, 154th overall, in 2001 Entry Draft).

			Regular Season					Playoffs				
Season	Club	Lea	GP	G	A	TP	PIM	GP	G	A	TP	PIM
99-2000	Breck High	Hi-School	28	18	23	41	....	....	....	....	....	....
2000-01	Breck High	Hi-School	22	28	30	58	22	....	....	....	....	....

BRENNAN, Kip (BREHN-nan, KIHP) L.A.

Left wing. Shoots left. 6'4", 210 lbs. Born, Kingston, Ont., August 27, 1980.
(Los Angeles' 4th choice, 103rd overall, in 1998 Entry Draft).

			Regular Season					Playoffs				
Season	Club	Lea	GP	G	A	TP	PIM	GP	G	A	TP	PIM
1995-96	St. Michael's	OPJHL	40	0	11	11	155	....	....	....	....	....
1996-97	Windsor Spitfires	OHL	42	0	10	10	156	5	0	1	1	16
1997-98	Windsor Spitfires	OHL	24	0	7	7	103	....	....	....	....	....
	Sudbury Wolves	OHL	24	0	3	3	85	....	....	....	....	....
1998-99	Sudbury Wolves	OHL	38	9	12	21	160	....	....	....	....	....
99-2000	Sudbury Wolves	OHL	55	16	16	32	228	12	3	3	6	67
2000-01	Lowell	AHL	23	2	3	5	117	....	....	....	....	....
	Sudbury Wolves	OHL	27	7	14	21	94	12	5	6	11	*92

• Returned to **Sudbury** (OHL) by **Lowell** (AHL), January 10, 2001.

BROOKBANK, Wade OTT.

Defense. Shoots left. 6'4", 225 lbs. Born, Lanigan, Sask., September 29, 1977.

			Regular Season					Playoffs				
Season	Club	Lea	GP	G	A	TP	PIM	GP	G	A	TP	PIM
1997-98	Melville	SJHL	58	8	21	29	330	....	....	....	....	....
	Anchorage Aces	WCHL	7	0	0	0	46	4	0	0	0	20
1998-99	Anchorage Aces	WCHL	56	0	4	4	337	....	....	....	....	....
99-2000	Oklahoma City	CHL	68	3	9	12	354	7	1	1	2	29
2000-01	Orlando	IHL	29	0	1	1	122	4	0	0	0	6
	Oklahoma City	CHL	46	1	13	14	267	5	0	0	0	24

Signed as a free agent by **Orlando** (IHL), September 1, 2000. • Signed as a free agent by **Ottawa**, July 27, 2001.

BROS, Michal (BROHSH, MEE-khahl) MIN.

Center. Shoots right. 6'1", 195 lbs. Born, Olomouc, Czech., January 25, 1976.
(San Jose's 6th choice, 130th overall, in 1995 Entry Draft).

			Regular Season					Playoffs				
Season	Club	Lea	GP	G	A	TP	PIM	GP	G	A	TP	PIM
1994-95	HC Olomouc-Jr.	Cze-Rep	34	29	32	61	....	....	....	....	....	....
1995-96	HC Olomouc	Cze-Rep	35	8	11	19	....	4	2	0	2	....
1996-97	HC Olomouc	Cze-Rep	50	13	14	27	28	....	....	....	....	....
1997-98	Petra Vsetin	Cze-Rep	47	14	18	32	28	10	3	1	4	2
	Petra Vsetin	EuroHL	9	3	0	3	2	....	....	....	....	....
1998-99	Slovnaft Vsetin	Cze-Rep	42	10	18	28	18	12	1	3	4	....
99-2000	Sparta Praha	Cze-Rep	49	6	30	36	49	9	1	3	4	4
2000-01	Sparta Praha	Cze-Rep	27	3	13	16	22	13	4	6	10	8

Selected by **Minnesota** from **San Jose** in Expansion Draft, June 23, 2000.

BROWN, Jeff (BROWN, JEHF) NYR

Defense. Shoots right. 6'2", 218 lbs. Born, Mississauga, Ont., April 24, 1978.
(NY Rangers' 1st choice, 22nd overall, in 1996 Entry Draft).

			Regular Season					Playoffs				
Season	Club	Lea	GP	G	A	TP	PIM	GP	G	A	TP	PIM
1993-94	Thornhill Islanders	MTJHL	47	6	18	24	96	....	....	....	....	....
1994-95	Sarnia Sting	OHL	58	2	14	16	52	4	0	2	2	2
1995-96	Sarnia Sting	OHL	65	8	20	28	111	10	1	2	3	12
1996-97	Sarnia Sting	OHL	35	5	14	19	60	....	....	....	....	....
	London Knights	OHL	28	1	17	18	32	....	....	....	....	....
1997-98	London Knights	OHL	63	12	42	54	96	15	1	4	5	26
1998-99	Canada	Nat-Team	13	0	2	2	8	....	....	....	....	....
	Hartford	AHL	9	0	2	2	21	....	....	....	....	....
	Charlotte	ECHL	12	1	2	3	20	....	....	....	....	....
99-2000	Hartford	AHL	6	0	0	0	2	....	....	....	....	....
	Charlotte	ECHL	51	7	18	25	107	....	....	....	....	....
2000-01	Hartford	AHL	3	0	0	0	2	....	....	....	....	....
	New Haven	UHL	67	7	16	23	116	8	1	2	3	8

MTJHL Bauer Division Future Star (1994) • OHL Third All-Star Team (1998)

BROWN, Marc (BROWN, MAHRK) ST.L.

Left wing. Shoots left. 6'1", 196 lbs. Born, Surrey, B.C., March 10, 1979.

			Regular Season					Playoffs				
Season	Club	Lea	GP	G	A	TP	PIM	GP	G	A	TP	PIM
1995-96	Abbotsford Pilots	PIJHL	35	20	15	35	15	....	....	....	....	....
1996-97	Spokane Chiefs	WHL	52	4	8	12	37	2	0	0	0	0
1997-98	Spokane Chiefs	WHL	41	10	15	25	34	....	....	....	....	....
	Prince Albert	WHL	23	6	8	14	21	....	....	....	....	....
1998-99	Prince Albert	WHL	72	35	45	80	47	14	12	6	18	6
99-2000	Worcester	AHL	72	13	11	24	24	17	3	1	4	0
2000-01	Worcester	AHL	34	9	10	19	27	10	0	1	1	6

Signed as a free agent by **St. Louis**, September 24, 1999. • Missed majority of 2000-01 season recovering from abdominal injury suffered in training camp, September 27, 2000.

BRUNEL, Craig (broo-NEHL, KRAYG) BUF.

Right wing. Shoots right. 6', 200 lbs. Born, Winnipeg, Man., November 12, 1979.
(Buffalo's 12th choice, 263rd overall, in 1999 Entry Draft).

			Regular Season					Playoffs				
Season	Club	Lea	GP	G	A	TP	PIM	GP	G	A	TP	PIM
1995-96	Notre Dame	SMHL	36	4	9	13	79	....	....	....	....	....
1996-97	Prince Albert	WHL	57	5	2	7	208	4	0	0	0	13
1997-98	Prince Albert	WHL	58	6	12	18	247	....	....	....	....	....
1998-99	Prince Albert	WHL	50	10	8	18	173	14	4	2	6	48
99-2000	Prince Albert	WHL	17	0	2	2	59	....	....	....	....	....
	Red Deer Rebels	WHL	35	3	2	5	140	4	0	1	1	22
2000-01	Rochester	AHL	37	3	2	5	96	....	....	....	....	....
	South Carolina	ECHL	8	0	3	3	34	....	....	....	....	....
	Long Beach	WCHL	6	2	0	2	57	....	....	....	....	....

• Re-entered NHL Entry Draft. Originally Nashville's 6th choice, 147th overall, in 1998 Entry Draft.

BULATOV, Alexei (boo-LA-tahf, al-EHX-ay) NYR

Right wing. Shoots left. 6'1", 185 lbs. Born, Sverdlovsk, USSR, January 24, 1978.
(NY Rangers' 11th choice, 254th overall, in 1999 Entry Draft).

			Regular Season					Playoffs				
Season	Club	Lea	GP	G	A	TP	PIM	GP	G	A	TP	PIM
1996-97	HC Yekaterinburg	Russia-2	22	6	6	12	10	....	....	....	....	....
	HC Yekaterinburg	Russia	20	2	4	6	2	....	....	....	....	....
1997-98	HC Yekaterinburg	Russia-2	22	7	6	13	14	....	....	....	....	....
	HC Yekaterinburg	Russia	15	5	3	8	10	....	....	....	....	....
1998-99	HC Yekaterinburg	Russia-2	47	21	16	37	24	....	....	....	....	....
99-2000	HC Cherepovets	Russia	9	1	0	1	0	....	....	....	....	....
	Salavat Ufa	Russia	6	0	3	3	2	....	....	....	....	....
	CSK Samara	Russia	6	0	0	0	2	....	....	....	....	....
2000-01	Ust-Novokuznetsk	Russia	32	2	3	5	4	....	....	....	....	....

BUMAGIN, Yevgeny (boo-MA-gihn, yehv-GEH-nee) DET.

Center. Shoots left. 6', 170 lbs. Born, Belgorod, USSR, April 7, 1982.
(Detroit's 11th choice, 260th overall, in 2000 Entry Draft).

			Regular Season					Playoffs				
Season	Club	Lea	GP	G	A	TP	PIM	GP	G	A	TP	PIM
1997-98	Lada Togliatti-2	Russia-3	7	0	0	0	2	....	....	....	....	....
1998-99	Lada Togliatti-2	Russia-3	40	7	8	15	22	....	....	....	....	....
99-2000	Lada Togliatti-2	Russia-3	36	23	8	31	....	....	....	....	....	....
2000-01	CSK Samara	Russia-2	13	1	0	1	10	....	....	....	....	....

BURNETT, Garrett (buhr-NEHT, GAIR-eht)

Left wing. Shoots left. 6'3", 230 lbs. Born, Coquitlam, B.C., September 23, 1975.

			Regular Season					Playoffs				
Season	Club	Lea	GP	G	A	TP	PIM	GP	G	A	TP	PIM
1993-94	Trail Smokies	RIJHL	26	2	1	3	248	....	....	....	....	....
1994-95	Sault Ste. Marie	OHL	14	0	1	1	78	....	....	....	....	....
	Kitchener	OHL	22	0	1	1	74	3	0	1	1	23
1995-96	Utica Blizzard	ColHL	15	0	1	1	78	....	....	....	....	....
	Oklahoma City	CHL	3	0	0	0	20	....	....	....	....	....
	Tulsa Oilers	CHL	6	1	0	1	94	....	....	....	....	....
	Nashville Knights	ECHL	3	0	0	0	22	....	....	....	....	....
	Jacksonville	ECHL	8	0	1	1	38	1	0	0	0	0
1996-97	Knoxville	ECHL	50	5	11	16	321	....	....	....	....	....
1997-98	Johnstown Chiefs	ECHL	34	1	1	2	331	....	....	....	....	....
	Philadelphia	AHL	14	1	2	3	129	....	....	....	....	....
1998-99	Kentucky	AHL	31	1	0	1	186	....	....	....	....	....
99-2000	Kentucky	AHL	58	3	3	6	*506	4	0	0	0	31
2000-01	Cleveland	IHL	54	2	4	6	250	....	....	....	....	....

Signed as a free agent by **San Jose**, July 2, 1998.

BUT, Anton (BOOT, AN-tawn) N.J.

Left wing. Shoots left. 6'1", 190 lbs. Born, Kharkov, USSR, July 3, 1980.
(New Jersey's 7th choice, 119th overall, in 1998 Entry Draft).

			Regular Season					Playoffs				
Season	Club	Lea	GP	G	A	TP	PIM	GP	G	A	TP	PIM
1995-96	Torpedo Yaroslavl	Russia-2	60	30	12	42	10	....	....	....	....	....
1996-97	HC Yaroslavl-2	Russia-3	70	30	20	50	20	....	....	....	....	....
1997-98	Torpedo Yaroslavl	Russia-2	48	12	5	17	28	....	....	....	....	....
1998-99	Torpedo Yaroslavl	Russia	5	0	0	0	0	....	....	....	....	....
	Torpedo Yaroslavl	Russia-2	22	12	8	20	59	....	....	....	....	....
99-2000	Torpedo Yaroslavl	Russia	26	2	5	7	16	8	2	1	3	0
	Torpedo Yaroslavl	Russia-2	1	0	0	0	2	....	....	....	....	....
2000-01	HC Yaroslavl	Russia	42	14	6	20	14	11	1	3	4	8

BUTURLIN, Alexander (boo-tuhr-LIHN, AL-ehx-an-DEHR) MTL.

Right wing. Shoots left. 5'11", 182 lbs. Born, Moscow, USSR, September 3, 1981.
(Montreal's 1st choice, 39th overall, in 1999 Entry Draft).

			Regular Season					Playoffs				
Season	Club	Lea	GP	G	A	TP	PIM	GP	G	A	TP	PIM
1997-98	HC Moscow-2	Russia-3	50	12	15	27	46	....	....	....	....	....
	CSKA Moscow	Russia	2	0	0	0	0	....	....	....	....	....
1998-99	CSKA Moscow	Russia	16	1	0	1	6	3	1	0	1	2
99-2000	Sarnia Sting	OHL	57	20	27	47	46	7	4	2	6	12
2000-01	Sarnia Sting	OHL	57	28	37	65	27	4	3	1	4	0

BYFUGLIEN, Derrick (bigh-FEWG-lehn, DEHR-ihk) OTT.

Defense. Shoots left. 6'1", 212 lbs. Born, Roseau, MN, December 23, 1980.
(Ottawa's 5th choice, 122nd overall, in 2000 Entry Draft).

			Regular Season					Playoffs				
Season	Club	Lea	GP	G	A	TP	PIM	GP	G	A	TP	PIM
1998-99	Roseau Rams	Hi-School	20	15	19	34		....	....	....	....	....
	Fargo-Moorhead	USHL	12	2	3	5	71	....	....	....	....	....
99-2000	Fargo-Moorhead	USHL	50	5	11	16	106	....	....	....	....	....
2000-01	North Dakota	WCHA	6	0	1	1	2	....	....	....	....	....
	Erie Otters	OHL	31	1	4	5	37	15	3	1	4	29

• Left **University of North Dakota** and signed as a free agent by **Erie** (OHL), December 27, 2000.

BYRNE, Trevor (BUHR-ne, TREH-vohr) ST.L.

Defense. Shoots left. 6'3", 205 lbs. Born, Hingham, MA, May 7, 1980.
(St. Louis' 4th choice, 143rd overall, in 1999 Entry Draft).

			Regular Season					Playoffs				
Season	Club	Lea	GP	G	A	TP	PIM	GP	G	A	TP	PIM
1997-98	Deerfield Academy	Hi-School	25	5	14	19	16	....	....	....	....	....
1998-99	Deerfield Academy	Hi-School	25	9	19	28	22	....	....	....	....	....
99-2000	Dartmouth College	ECAC	30	3	9	12	40	....	....	....	....	....
2000-01	Dartmouth College	ECAC	34	5	21	26	52	....	....	....	....	....

ECAC Second All-Star Team (2001)

CABANA, Paul (CA-ba-NA, PAWL) VAN.

Right wing. Shoots right. 6'1", 185 lbs. Born, Calgary, Alta., September 28, 1978.
(Vancouver's 8th choice, 149th overall, in 1998 Entry Draft).

			Regular Season					Playoffs				
Season	Club	Lea	GP	G	A	TP	PIM	GP	G	A	TP	PIM
1996-97	Fort McMurray	AJHL	58	24	22	46	....	3	1	3	4	2
1997-98	Fort McMurray	AJHL	52	48	32	80	111	....	....	....	....	....
1998-99	Michigan Tech	WCHA	38	12	9	21	50	....	....	....	....	....
99-2000	Michigan Tech	WCHA	36	10	5	15	94	....	....	....	....	....
2000-01	Michigan Tech	WCHA	35	15	6	21	41	....	....	....	....	....

AJHL All-Rookie Team (1997) • AJHL First All-Star Team (1998)

CALDWELL, Ryan (KAWLD-wehl, RIGH-uhn) NYI

Defense. Shoots left. 6'2", 174 lbs. Born, Deloraine, Man., June 15, 1981.
(NY Islanders' 7th choice, 202nd overall, in 2000 Entry Draft).

			Regular Season					Playoffs				
Season	Club	Lea	GP	G	A	TP	PIM	GP	G	A	TP	PIM
1998-99	Shattack-St. Mary	Hi-School	29	24	55	79	22	....	....	....	....	....
99-2000	Thunder Bay	USHL	46	3	20	23	152	....	....	....	....	....
2000-01	U. of Denver	WCHA	36	3	20	23	76	....	....	....	....	....

WCHA All-Rookie Team (2001)

CAMERON, Scott (KAM-erh-RAWN, SCAWT) N.J.

Center. Shoots left. 6', 185 lbs. Born, Sudbury, Ont., April 11, 1981.
(New Jersey's 6th choice, 185th overall, in 1999 Entry Draft).

			Regular Season					Playoffs				
Season	Club	Lea	GP	G	A	TP	PIM	GP	G	A	TP	PIM
1997-98	Port Colborne	OJHL-B	40	16	35	51	73	....	....	....	....	....
1998-99	Barrie Colts	OHL	66	10	32	42	14	12	2	2	4	2
99-2000	Barrie Colts	OHL	21	2	4	6	19	....	....	....	....	....
	North Bay	OHL	49	26	28	54	13	6	3	0	3	4
	Albany River Rats	AHL	3	1	0	1	0	1	0	0	0	0
2000-01	North Bay	OHL	68	37	43	80	45	4	0	1	1	2

CAMMALLERI, Mike (kam-UH-LAIR-ee, MIGHK) L.A.

Center. Shoots left. 5'9", 180 lbs. Born, Richmond Hill, Ont., June 8, 1982.
(Los Angeles' 3rd choice, 49th overall, in 2001 Entry Draft).

			Regular Season					Playoffs				
Season	Club	Lea	GP	G	A	TP	PIM	GP	G	A	TP	PIM
1997-98	Bramalea Blues	OPJHL	46	36	52	88	30	....	....	....	....	....
1998-99	Bramalea Blues	OPJHL	41	31	72	103	51	....	....	....	....	....
99-2000	U. of Michigan	CCHA	39	13	13	26	32	....	....	....	....	....
2000-01	U. of Michigan	CCHA	42	*29	32	61	24	....	....	....	....	....

Won OPJHL Rookie of the Year Award (1998) • CCHA First All-Star Team (2001) • NCAA West Second All-American Team (2001)

CAMPBELL, Eddy ST.L.

Defense. Shoots left. 6'2", 212 lbs. Born, Worcester, MA, November 26, 1974.
(NY Rangers' 9th choice, 190th overall, in 1993 Entry Draft).

			Regular Season					Playoffs				
Season	Club	Lea	GP	G	A	TP	PIM	GP	G	A	TP	PIM
1992-93	Omaha Lancers	USHL	42	9	19	28	160	....	....	....	....	....
1993-94	U. of Mass-Lowell	H-East	40	8	16	24	114	....	....	....	....	....
1994-95	U. of Mass-Lowell	H-East	34	6	24	30	105	....	....	....	....	....
1995-96	U. of Mass-Lowell	H-East	39	6	33	39	*107	....	....	....	....	....
1996-97	Binghamton	AHL	74	5	17	22	108	4	0	0	0	2
1997-98	Hartford	AHL	9	0	1	1	9	14	0	2	2	33
	Fort Wayne	IHL	50	10	5	15	147	....	....	....	....	....
1998-99	Hartford	AHL	18	0	3	3	24	7	0	3	3	14
	Fort Wayne	IHL	46	1	16	17	137	....	....	....	....	....
99-2000	Orlando	IHL	81	2	7	9	217	3	0	0	0	6
2000-01	Worcester	AHL	78	5	27	32	207	10	1	0	1	10

Signed as a free agent by **St. Louis**, July 1, 2001.

CARKNER, Matt (KARK-nehr, MAT) S.J.

Defense. Shoots right. 6'4", 229 lbs. Born, Winchester, Ont., November 3, 1980.
(Montreal's 2nd choice, 58th overall, in 1999 Entry Draft).

			Regular Season					Playoffs				
Season	Club	Lea	GP	G	A	TP	PIM	GP	G	A	TP	PIM
1996-97	Winchester Hawks	OJHL-B	29	1	18	19	....	....	....	....	....	....
1997-98	Peterborough	OHL	57	0	6	6	121	4	0	0	0	2
1998-99	Peterborough	OHL	60	2	16	18	173	5	0	0	0	20
99-2000	Peterborough	OHL	62	3	13	16	177	5	0	1	1	6
2000-01	Peterborough	OHL	53	8	8	16	128	7	0	3	3	25

Signed as a free agent by **San Jose**, June 6, 2001.

CARON, Ed (kahr-OHN, EHD) EDM.

Left wing. Shoots left. 6'2", 214 lbs. Born, Nashua, NH, April 30, 1982.
(Edmonton's 3rd choice, 52nd overall, in 2001 Entry Draft).

			Regular Season					Playoffs				
Season	Club	Lea	GP	G	A	TP	PIM	GP	G	A	TP	PIM
1998-99	Phillips Exeter	Hi-School	31	39	30	69	28	....	....	....	....	....
99-2000	Phillips Exeter	Hi-School	26	22	26	48	24	....	....	....	....	....
2000-01	Phillips Exeter	Hi-School	17	30	20	50	42	....	....	....	....	....

CARTER, Shawn (KAR-tuhr, SHAWN) MIN.

Center. Shoots left. 6'3", 210 lbs. Born, Eagle River, WI, April 16, 1973.

			Regular Season					Playoffs				
Season	Club	Lea	GP	G	A	TP	PIM	GP	G	A	TP	PIM
1991-92	Omaha Lancers	USHL	43	6	5	11	16	10	4	3	7	10
1992-93	U. of Wisconsin	WCHA	5	1	0	1	4	....	....	....	....	....
1993-94	U. of Wisconsin	WCHA	16	2	2	4	24	....	....	....	....	....
1994-95	U. of Wisconsin	WCHA	43	15	13	28	98	....	....	....	....	....
1995-96	U. of Wisconsin	WCHA	40	17	28	45	50	....	....	....	....	....
1996-97	Orlando	IHL	53	22	25	47	40	....	....	....	....	....
	St. John's Leafs	AHL	18	5	6	11	15	7	1	2	3	6
1997-98	St. John's Leafs	AHL	80	14	16	30	117	4	1	0	1	4
1998-99	Orlando	IHL	79	13	26	39	103	17	1	4	5	10
99-2000	Orlando	IHL	81	20	30	50	120	6	0	2	2	4
2000-01	Houston Aeros	IHL	82	23	36	59	54	7	2	5	7	2

Signed as a free agent by **Toronto**, February 14, 1997. Signed as a free agent by **Orlando** (IHL), September 10, 1998. Signed as a free agent by **Houston** (IHL), August 17, 2000. Signed as a free agent by **Minnesota**, June 13, 2001.

CASS, Bill (KAS, BIHL) ANA.

Defense. Shoots left. 6', 208 lbs. Born, Hingham, MA, September 30, 1980.
(Anaheim's 5th choice, 153rd overall, in 2000 Entry Draft).

			Regular Season					Playoffs				
Season	Club	Lea	GP	G	A	TP	PIM	GP	G	A	TP	PIM
1997-98	Team USA	USDP	38	4	9	13	75	2	0	0	0	0
1998-99	Team USA	USDP	41	0	6	6	22	....	....	....	....	....
99-2000	Boston College	H-East	41	1	8	9	26	....	....	....	....	....
2000-01	Boston College	H-East	40	0	6	6	52	....	....	....	....	....

CAVANAUGH, Dan (KAV-a-NAW, DAN) MIN.

Center. Shoots right. 6'1", 190 lbs. Born, Springfield, MA, March 3, 1980.
(Calgary's 2nd choice, 38th overall, in 1999 Entry Draft).

			Regular Season					Playoffs				
Season	Club	Lea	GP	G	A	TP	PIM	GP	G	A	TP	PIM
1995-96	New England	EJHL	43	8	7	15	....	....	....	....	....	....
1996-97	New England	EJHL	56	23	46	69	....	....	....	....	....	....
1997-98	New England	EJHL	38	31	*47	*78	58	13	8	12	30	....
1998-99	Boston University	H-East	36	6	8	14	60	....	....	....	....	....
99-2000	Boston University	H-East	40	9	25	34	62	....	....	....	....	....
2000-01	Boston University	H-East	35	7	21	28	43	....	....	....	....	....

Won EJHL Most Valuable Player Award (1998)

Rights traded to **Minnesota** by **Calgary** with Calgary's 8th round choice (Jake Riddle) in 2001 Entry Draft for Mike Vernon, June 23, 2000.

CAVOSIE, Marc (kuh-VOI-see, MAHRK) MIN.

Left wing. Shoots left. 6', 173 lbs. Born, Albany, NY, August 6, 1981.
(Minnesota's 3rd choice, 99th overall, in 2000 Entry Draft).

			Regular Season					Playoffs				
Season	Club	Lea	GP	G	A	TP	PIM	GP	G	A	TP	PIM
1995-96	Albany Academy	Hi-School	22	8	27	31	....	....	....	....	....	....
1996-97	Albany Academy	Hi-School	28	26	45	71	....	....	....	....	....	....
1997-98	Albany Academy	Hi-School	28	38	33	71	....	....	....	....	....	....
1998-99	Albany Academy	Hi-School	28	23	20	43	32	....	....	....	....	....
99-2000	RPI Engineers	ECAC	29	11	17	28	10	....	....	....	....	....
2000-01	RPI Engineers	ECAC	28	13	16	29	47	....	....	....	....	....

CECH, Vratislav (CHEHKH, VUHR-atih-SLAV) BOS.

Defense. Shoots left. 6'3", 196 lbs. Born, Tabor, Czech., January 28, 1979.
(Florida's 3rd choice, 56th overall, in 1997 Entry Draft).

			Regular Season					Playoffs				
Season	Club	Lea	GP	G	A	TP	PIM	GP	G	A	TP	PIM
1995-96	HC Brno-Jr.	Cze-Rep	37	10	13	23	....	....	....	....	....	....
1996-97	Kitchener	OHL	57	5	19	24	72	13	1	2	3	12
1997-98	Kitchener	OHL	63	9	33	42	66	6	2	2	4	13
1998-99	Kitchener	OHL	66	6	21	27	73	1	0	1	1	4
99-2000	Providence Bruins	AHL	3	0	1	1	0	....	....	....	....	....
	Greenville Growl	ECHL	55	7	15	22	51	15	0	5	5	16
2000-01	Greenville Growl	ECHL	64	10	19	29	96	....	....	....	....	....
	Providence Bruins	AHL	4	0	0	0	2	....	....	....	....	....

Signed as a free agent by **Boston**, July 22, 1999.

CEREDA, Luca (suh-REH-duh, LOO-ka) TOR.

Center. Shoots left. 6'2", 202 lbs. Born, Lugano, Switzerland, September 7, 1981.
(Toronto's 1st choice, 24th overall, in 1999 Entry Draft).

			Regular Season					Playoffs				
Season	Club	Lea	GP	G	A	TP	PIM	GP	G	A	TP	PIM
1996-97	Ambri-Piotta	Switz-Jr.	35	13	8	21	....	....	....	....	....	....
1997-98	Ambri-Piotta	Switz-Jr.	28	17	27	44	24	....	....	....	....	....
1998-99	Ambri-Piotta	Switz-Jr.	3	4	3	7	20	....	....	....	....	....
	Ambri-Piotta	Switz.	38	6	10	16	8	15	0	6	6	4
99-2000	Ambri-Piotta	Switz.	44	1	5	6	14	9	0	1	1	2
2000-01	Ottawa 67's	OHL	DID NOT PLAY									

• Missed entire 2000-01 season recovering from heart surgery, September, 2000.

CHAGODAYEV, Alexandr (cheh-goh-digh-ehv, al-ehx-AN-duhr) ANA.

Center. Shoots left. 6'1", 185 lbs. Born, Perm, USSR, January 15, 1981.
(Anaheim's 3rd choice, 105th overall, in 1999 Entry Draft).

			Regular Season					Playoffs				
Season	Club	Lea	GP	G	A	TP	PIM	GP	G	A	TP	PIM
1997-98	HC Moscow	Russia-2	5	1	0	1	0	....	....	....	....	....
	CSKA Moscow	Russia	1	0	0	0	0	....	....	....	....	....
1998-99	HC Moscow	Russia-2	35	9	9	18	16	....	....	....	....	....
99-2000	HC Moscow	Russia-2	40	5	7	12	....	....	....	....	....	....
2000-01	Krylja Sovetov	Russia-2	7	0	1	1	0	....	....	....	....	....
	St. Petersburg	Russia	8	0	1	1	0	....	....	....	....	....
	HC Yaroslavl	Russia	6	2	0	2	2	....	....	....	....	....
	Salavat Yulayev	Russia	1	0	0	0	0	....	....	....	....	....

CHALMERS, James PHI.

Center. Shoots left. 6'2", 200 lbs. Born, Mississauga, Ont., August 19, 1977.

			Regular Season					Playoffs				
Season	Club	Lea	GP	G	A	TP	PIM	GP	G	A	TP	PIM
1995-96	Shelburne HTI	MTJHL	14	5	5	10	17	....	....	....	....	....
1996-97	Shelburne HTI	MTJHL	40	35	24	59	58	....	....	....	....	....
	Summerside Caps	MJrHL	32	24	21	45	56	....	....	....	....	....
1997-98	Nebraska-Omaha	NCAA-2	30	8	12	20	20	....	....	....	....	....
1998-99	Nebraska-Omaha	NCAA-2	28	6	11	17	53	....	....	....	....	....
99-2000	Nebraska-Omaha	CCHA	37	5	8	13	72	....	....	....	....	....
2000-01	Nebraska-Omaha	CCHA	37	6	15	21	96	....	....	....	....	....

Signed as a free agent by **Philadelphia**, June 14, 2001.

CHARPENTIER, Marco (shar-PUHNT-yay, MAHR-koh) NYI

Center. Shoots left. 6', 200 lbs. Born, Montreal, Que., January 23, 1980.

			Regular Season					Playoffs				
Season	Club	Lea	GP	G	A	TP	PIM	GP	G	A	TP	PIM
1996-97	Mtl-Bourassa	QAAA	42	15	23	38	28	....	....	....	....	....
1997-98	Quebec Remparts	QMJHL	55	4	7	11	12	3	0	1	1	0
1998-99	Quebec Remparts	QMJHL	12	4	7	11	4	....	....	....	....	....
	Baie-Comeau	QMJHL	52	16	23	39	34	....	....	....	....	....
99-2000	Baie-Comeau	QMJHL	72	51	62	113	39	6	3	2	5	16
2000-01	Baie-Comeau	QMJHL	71	57	55	112	88	11	9	10	19	10

Signed as a free agent by **NY Islanders**, December 12, 2000.

CHARRON, Craig (shah-ROHN, KRAYG)

Center. Shoots right. 5'10", 175 lbs. Born, North Easton, MA, November 15, 1967.
(Montreal's 1st choice, 25th overall, in 1989 Supplemental Draft).

			Regular Season					Playoffs				
Season	Club	Lea	GP	G	A	TP	PIM	GP	G	A	TP	PIM
1986-87	U. Mass-Lowell	H-East	36	11	16	27	48	....	....	....	....	....
1987-88	U. Mass-Lowell	H-East	39	22	18	40	32	....	....	....	....	....
1988-89	U. Mass-Lowell	H-East	32	14	21	35	32	....	....	....	....	....
1989-90	U. Mass-Lowell	H-East	35	17	29	46	10	....	....	....	....	....
1990-91	Winston-Salem	ECHL	30	11	16	27	10	....	....	....	....	....
	Albany Choppers	IHL	5	0	2	2	0	....	....	....	....	....
	Fredericton	AHL	24	2	5	7	4	5	0	3	3	0
1991-92	Cincinnati	ECHL	64	41	55	96	97	9	5	5	10	10
1992-93	Birmingham Bulls	ECHL	23	9	17	26	18	....	....	....	....	....
	Cincinnati	IHL	27	6	8	14	8	....	....	....	....	....
1993-94	Olofstroms IK	Swede-2	32	38	34	72	66	....	....	....	....	....
1994-95	Dayton Bombers	ECHL	48	35	47	82	82	9	9	13	22	10
	Kalamazoo Wings	IHL	2	0	0	0	0	....	....	....	....	....
	Fort Wayne	IHL	2	1	0	1	4	....	....	....	....	....
	Cornwall Aces	AHL	6	5	0	5	0	2	0	0	0	0
1995-96	Rochester	AHL	72	43	52	95	79	19	7	10	17	12
1996-97	Rochester	AHL	72	24	41	65	42	10	8	8	16	2
1997-98	Rochester	AHL	75	25	53	78	51	4	1	1	2	0
1998-99	Lowell	AHL	71	22	39	61	41	3	1	2	3	8
99-2000	St. John's Leafs	AHL	32	11	18	29	14	....	....	....	....	....
	Lowell	AHL	22	8	13	21	14	7	2	3	5	4
2000-01	Rochester	AHL	73	18	32	50	53	4	0	1	1	2

Won Fred T. Hunt Award (Sportsmanship - AHL) (1998)

Signed as a free agent by **NY Islanders**, September 3, 1998. Traded to **Toronto** by **NY Islanders** for Niklas Andersson, August 17, 1999. Traded to **Los Angeles** by **Toronto** for Donald MacLean, February 23, 2000. Signed as a free agent by **Rochester** (AHL), July 20, 2000.

CHARTIER, Christian (SHAR-tee-yay, KRIHS-t'yehn) **TOR.**

Defense. Shoots left. 6', 219 lbs. Born, Russell, Man., December 29, 1980.
(Edmonton's 8th choice, 199th overall, in 1999 Entry Draft).

			Regular Season					Playoffs				
Season	Club	Lea	GP	G	A	TP	PIM	GP	G	A	TP	PIM
1995-96	Yellowhead Pass	MMHL	36	8	23	31	68	....	....	....	....	....
1996-97	Saskatoon Blades	WHL	64	2	23	25	32	....	....	....	....	....
1997-98	Saskatoon Blades	WHL	68	8	33	41	43	6	0	3	3	12
1998-99	Saskatoon Blades	WHL	62	2	14	16	71	....	....	....	....	....
99-2000	Saskatoon Blades	WHL	11	2	2	4	4	....	....	....	....	....
	Prince George	WHL	57	16	36	52	60	13	4	9	13	12
2000-01	Prince George	WHL	63	12	56	68	99	6	1	4	5	6

WHL West Second All-Star Team (2000) • WHL West First All-Star Team (2001)

Signed as a free agent by **Toronto**, June 25, 2001.

CHEECHOO, Jonathan (CHEE-choo, JAWN-ah-thuhn) **S.J.**

Right wing. Shoots right. 6', 205 lbs. Born, Moose Factory, Ont., July 15, 1980.
(San Jose's 2nd choice, 29th overall, in 1998 Entry Draft).

			Regular Season					Playoffs				
Season	Club	Lea	GP	G	A	TP	PIM	GP	G	A	TP	PIM
1996-97	Kitchener	OJHL-B	43	35	41	76	33	....	....	....	....	....
1997-98	Belleville Bulls	OHL	64	31	45	76	62	10	4	2	6	10
1998-99	Belleville Bulls	OHL	63	35	47	82	74	21	15	15	30	27
99-2000	Belleville Bulls	OHL	66	45	46	91	102	16	5	12	17	16
2000-01	Kentucky	AHL	75	32	34	66	63	3	0	0	0	0

CHERNOV, Artem (chair-NAHF, AR-tehm) **DAL.**

Center. Shoots left. 5'10", 176 lbs. Born, Novokuznetsk, USSR, April 28, 1982.
(Dallas' 7th choice, 162nd overall, in 2000 Entry Draft).

			Regular Season					Playoffs				
Season	Club	Lea	GP	G	A	TP	PIM	GP	G	A	TP	PIM
1997-98	Novokuznetsk-2	Russia-3	4	0	0	0	0	....	....	....	....	....
1998-99	Novokuznetsk-2	Russia-4	32	9	7	16	14	....	....	....	....	....
99-2000	Ust-Novokuznetsk	Russia	10	2	3	5	0	5	0	0	0	0
2000-01	Ust-Novokuznetsk	Russia	44	15	17	32	30	....	....	....	....	....

CHERNOV, Mikhail (chair-NAHF, mihk-AIL) **NSH.**

Defense. Shoots right. 6'2", 205 lbs. Born, Prokopjevsk, USSR, November 11, 1978.
(Philadelphia's 4th choice, 103rd overall, in 1997 Entry Draft).

			Regular Season					Playoffs				
Season	Club	Lea	GP	G	A	TP	PIM	GP	G	A	TP	PIM
1995-96	HC Novisibirsk	CIS-2	40	2	7	9	10	....	....	....	....	....
1996-97	HC Yaroslavl-2	Russia-3	33	4	2	6	40	....	....	....	....	....
	Torpedo Yaroslavl	Russia	5	0	0	0	0	....	....	....	....	....
1997-98	Torpedo Yaroslavl	Russia	7	0	0	0	4	....	....	....	....	....
1998-99	Philadelphia	AHL	56	4	3	7	98	14	1	0	1	8
99-2000	Philadelphia	AHL	67	10	6	16	54	5	1	2	3	22
2000-01	Philadelphia	AHL	50	8	12	20	32	6	1	2	3	4

Traded to **Nashville** by **Philadelphia** for Mike Watt, May 24, 2001.

CHISTOV, Stanislav (chihs-TAHV, STAHN-his-LAHV) **ANA.**

Left wing. Shoots right. 5'9", 169 lbs. Born, Chelyabinsk, USSR, April 17, 1983.
(Anaheim's 1st choice, 5th overall, in 2001 Entry Draft).

			Regular Season					Playoffs				
Season	Club	Lea	GP	G	A	TP	PIM	GP	G	A	TP	PIM
1998-99	HK Chelyabinsk-2	Russia-4	1	0	0	0	0	....	....	....	....	....
	Georgetown	OPJHL	14	10	7	17	21	....	....	....	....	....
99-2000	Avangard Omsk	Russia-Jr.	5	4	3	7	8	....	....	....	....	....
	VDV Omsk-2	Russia-3	18	12	4	16	24	....	....	....	....	....
	HC Novokznetsk	Russia-2	9	7	4	11	18	....	....	....	....	....
	Avangard Omsk	Russia	3	1	0	1	2	....	....	....	....	....
2000-01	VDV Omsk-2	Russia-3	8	5	4	9	2	....	....	....	....	....
	Avangard Omsk	Russia	24	4	8	12	12	5	0	0	0	2

CHRISTEEN, Mats (KRIHS-teen, MATS) **NSH.**

Defense. Shoots left. 6'1", 181 lbs. Born, Sodertalje, Sweden, February 13, 1982.
(Nashville's 11th choice, 236th overall, in 2000 Entry Draft).

			Regular Season					Playoffs				
Season	Club	Lea	GP	G	A	TP	PIM	GP	G	A	TP	PIM
99-2000	Sodertalje SK-B	Swede-Jr.	5	0	1	1	8	....	....	....	....	....
	Sodertalje SK	Swede-Jr.	30	1	0	1	30	4	1	0	1	6
2000-01	Sodertalje SK	Swede-Jr.	19	2	8	10	16	....	....	....	....	....
	Sodertalje SK	Swede-2	15	0	3	3	4	....	....	....	....	....

CIBAK, Martin (TSEE-bak, MAHR-tihn) **T.B.**

Center. Shoots left. 6'1", 195 lbs. Born, Liptovmikulas, Czech., May 17, 1980.
(Tampa Bay's 11th choice, 252nd overall, in 1998 Entry Draft).

			Regular Season					Playoffs				
Season	Club	Lea	GP	G	A	TP	PIM	GP	G	A	TP	PIM
1995-96	HK Liptovsky	Slovak-Jr.	48	38	35	73	....	....	....	....	....	....
1996-97	HK Liptovsky	Slovak-Jr.	45	22	18	40	....	....	....	....	....	....
1997-98	HK Liptovsky	Slovak-Jr.	42	31	21	52	....	....	....	....	....	....
	HK Liptovsky	Slovakia	28	1	3	4	10	....	....	....	....	....
1998-99	Medicine Hat	WHL	66	21	26	47	72	....	....	....	....	....
99-2000	Medicine Hat	WHL	58	16	29	45	77	....	....	....	....	....
2000-01	Detroit Vipers	IHL	79	10	28	38	88	....	....	....	....	....

CLARK, Kyle (KLAHRK, KIGHLE) **WSH.**

Right wing. Shoots right. 6'7", 210 lbs. Born, Burlington, VT, February 14, 1980.
(Washington's 7th choice, 175th overall, in 1999 Entry Draft).

			Regular Season					Playoffs				
Season	Club	Lea	GP	G	A	TP	PIM	GP	G	A	TP	PIM
1997-98	Team USA	USDP	65	14	11	25	287	....	....	....	....	....
1998-99	Harvard University	ECAC	20	0	2	2	30	....	....	....	....	....
99-2000	Harvard University	ECAC	22	0	3	3	30	....	....	....	....	....
2000-01	Harvard University	ECAC	18	0	2	2	20	....	....	....	....	....
	Portland Pirates	AHL	2	0	0	0	2	....	....	....	....	....
	Richmond	ECHL	18	1	2	3	110	3	0	0	0	5

CLARK, Ryan (KLAHRK, RIGH-yan) **NYI**

Defense. Shoots left. 6'3", 205 lbs. Born, Edmonton, Alta., October 30, 1977.
(NY Islanders' 11th choice, 222nd overall, in 1997 Entry Draft).

			Regular Season					Playoffs				
Season	Club	Lea	GP	G	A	TP	PIM	GP	G	A	TP	PIM
1996-97	Sioux City	USHL	1	0	0	0	15	....	....	....	....	....
	Lincoln Stars	USHL	34	6	7	13	79	14	0	5	5	16
1997-98	Notre Dame	CCHA	38	0	6	6	22	....	....	....	....	....
1998-99	Notre Dame	CCHA	14	1	2	3	26	....	....	....	....	....
99-2000	Notre Dame	CCHA	36	1	3	4	60	....	....	....	....	....
2000-01	Notre Dame	CCHA	33	0	2	2	79	....	....	....	....	....

CLARKE, Noah (KLAHRK, NOH-uh) **L.A.**

Left wing. Shoots left. 5'9", 175 lbs. Born, LaVerne, CA, June 11, 1979.
(Los Angeles' 10th choice, 250th overall, in 1999 Entry Draft).

			Regular Season					Playoffs				
Season	Club	Lea	GP	G	A	TP	PIM	GP	G	A	TP	PIM
1996-97	Shattuck-St. Mary	Hi-School	30	33	44	77	....	....	....	....	....	....
1997-98	Des Moines	USHL	54	19	30	49	29	12	2	9	11	23
1998-99	Des Moines	USHL	52	31	32	63	47	13	8	2	10	16
99-2000	Colorado College	WCHA	39	17	20	37	30	....	....	....	....	....
2000-01	Colorado College	WCHA	41	12	20	32	22	....	....	....	....	....

USHL All-Rookie Team (1998) • USHL First All-Star Team (1999) • Won Curt Hammer Award (Most Gentlemanly Player - USHL) (1999) • WCHA All-Rookie Team (2000)

CLAUSON, Kevin (KLAW-sohn, KEH-vihn) **NYI**

Defense. Shoots left. 6'5", 210 lbs. Born, Lebanon, NH, November 13, 1978.
(NY Islanders' 5th choice, 155th overall, in 1998 Entry Draft).

			Regular Season					Playoffs				
Season	Club	Lea	GP	G	A	TP	PIM	GP	G	A	TP	PIM
1996-97	Boston Bulldogs	MBHL	60	17	41	58	....	....	....	....	....	....
1997-98	Western Michigan	CCHA	36	1	1	2	56	....	....	....	....	....
1998-99	Western Michigan	CCHA	12	0	1	1	14	....	....	....	....	....
99-2000	U. of Maine	H-East	7	0	0	0	2	....	....	....	....	....
2000-01	U. of Maine	H-East	39	2	8	10	24	....	....	....	....	....

• Ruled ineligible to play first semester of 1999-2000 season under NCAA transfer rules.

CLOUTHIER, Brett (KLOO-tyay, BREHT) **N.J.**

Left wing. Shoots left. 6'5", 225 lbs. Born, Ottawa, Ont., June 9, 1981.
(New Jersey's 3rd choice, 50th overall, in 1999 Entry Draft).

			Regular Season					Playoffs				
Season	Club	Lea	GP	G	A	TP	PIM	GP	G	A	TP	PIM
1997-98	Kanata Lasers	OCJHL	50	12	10	22	135	....	....	....	....	....
1998-99	Kingston	OHL	64	8	14	22	227	5	1	1	2	4
99-2000	Kingston	OHL	65	13	26	39	266	5	2	0	2	17
2000-01	Kingston	OHL	68	28	29	57	165	4	1	0	1	10

COLAGIACOMO, Adam (coh-lah-JAH-coh-moh, A-dam) **S.J.**

Right wing. Shoots right. 6'2", 200 lbs. Born, Rexdale, Ont., March 17, 1979.
(San Jose's 3rd choice, 82nd overall, in 1997 Entry Draft).

			Regular Season					Playoffs				
Season	Club	Lea	GP	G	A	TP	PIM	GP	G	A	TP	PIM
1994-95	North York	MTJHL	33	39	20	59	48	....	....	....	....	....
1995-96	London Knights	OHL	66	28	38	66	88	....	....	....	....	....
1996-97	London Knights	OHL	26	11	11	22	37	....	....	....	....	....
	Oshawa 67's	OHL	23	14	10	24	32	13	1	5	6	4
1997-98	Oshawa 67's	OHL	58	25	31	56	80	7	1	0	1	2
1998-99	Plymouth Whalers	OHL	67	40	68	108	89	10	6	9	15	14
99-2000	Kentucky	AHL	42	5	8	13	27	1	1	0	1	0
	New Orleans	ECHL	18	7	7	14	12	3	0	2	2	2
2000-01	Kentucky	AHL	67	10	11	21	48	2	0	0	0	0

COLAIACOVO, Carlo (koh-lee-A-KOH-voh, KAR-loh) **TOR.**

Defense. Shoots left. 6'1", 184 lbs. Born, Toronto, Ont., January 27, 1983.
(Toronto's 1st choice, 17th overall, in 2001 Entry Draft).

			Regular Season					Playoffs				
Season	Club	Lea	GP	G	A	TP	PIM	GP	G	A	TP	PIM
1998-99	Mississauga Reps	MTHL	44	10	12	23	28	....	....	....	....	....
99-2000	Erie Otters	OHL	52	4	18	22	12	13	2	4	6	9
2000-01	Erie Otters	OHL	62	12	27	39	59	14	4	7	11	16

COLE, Erik (KOHL, AIR-ihk) **CAR.**

Left wing. Shoots left. 6'1", 200 lbs. Born, Oswego, NY, November 6, 1978.
(Carolina's 3rd choice, 71st overall, in 1998 Entry Draft).

			Regular Season					Playoffs				
Season	Club	Lea	GP	G	A	TP	PIM	GP	G	A	TP	PIM
1995-96	Oswego Bucs	Hi-School	40	49	41	90	....	....	....	....	....	....
1996-97	Des Moines	USHL	48	30	34	64	140	5	2	0	2	6
1997-98	Clarkson Knights	ECAC	34	11	20	31	55	....	....	....	....	....
1998-99	Clarkson Knights	ECAC	36	*22	20	42	50	....	....	....	....	....
99-2000	Clarkson Knights	ECAC	33	19	11	30	46	....	....	....	....	....
	Cincinnati	IHL	9	4	3	7	2	7	1	1	2	2
2000-01	Cincinnati	IHL	69	23	20	43	28	5	1	0	1	2

ECAC First All-Star Team (1999) • NCAA East Second All-American Team (1999) • ECAC Second All-Star Team (2000)

COLE, Phil (KOHL, FIHL) N.J.

Defense. Shoots left. 6'4", 195 lbs. Born, Winnipeg, Man., September 6, 1982.
(New Jersey's 8th choice, 125th overall, in 2000 Entry Draft).

			Regular Season					Playoffs				
Season	Club	Lea	GP	G	A	TP	PIM	GP	G	A	TP	PIM
1997-98	Winnipeg Sharks	MMHL	45	0	18	18	68	5	0	4	4	2
1998-99	Lethbridge	WHL	45	2	1	3	64	4	0	0	0	0
99-2000	Lethbridge	WHL	51	1	6	7	112	....	....	....	....	....
2000-01	Lethbridge	WHL	63	6	15	21	129	1	0	0	0	2

COLEMAN, Jon (KOHL-man, JAWN)

Defense. Shoots right. 6'1", 205 lbs. Born, Boston, MA, March 9, 1975.
(Detroit's 2nd choice, 48th overall, in 1993 Entry Draft).

			Regular Season					Playoffs				
Season	Club	Lea	GP	G	A	TP	PIM	GP	G	A	TP	PIM
1992-93	Phillips Academy	Hi-School	24	14	33	47	40	....	....	....	....	....
1993-94	Boston University	H-East	29	1	14	15	26	....	....	....	....	....
1994-95	Boston University	H-East	40	5	23	28	42	....	....	....	....	....
1995-96	Boston University	H-East	40	7	31	38	58	....	....	....	....	....
1996-97	Boston University	H-East	39	5	27	32	20	....	....	....	....	....
1997-98	Detroit Vipers	IHL	1	0	0	0	0	....	....	....	....	....
	Adirondack	AHL	54	2	29	31	23	2	0	0	0	0
1998-99	Adirondack	AHL	72	12	26	38	32	3	0	0	0	0
99-2000	Kentucky	AHL	66	1	14	15	43	9	2	4	6	2
2000-01	Providence	AHL	49	4	15	19	14	....	....	....	....	....
	Orlando	IHL	19	1	7	8	6	12	0	1	1	2

Hockey East Second All-Star Team (1996, 1997) • NCAA East Second All-American Team (1996) • NCAA East First All-American Team (1997)

Signed as a free agent by **San Jose**, August 26, 1999. Signed as a free agent by **Providence** (AHL), December 12, 2000. Loaned to **Orlando** (IHL) by **Providence** (AHL) for future considerations, March 9. 2001.

COLLINS, Brian (kAW-lihns, BRIGH-uhn) NYI

Center. Shoots left. 6'1", 190 lbs. Born, Worcester, MA, September 13, 1980.
(NY Islanders' 6th choice, 87th overall, in 1999 Entry Draft).

			Regular Season					Playoffs				
Season	Club	Lea	GP	G	A	TP	PIM	GP	G	A	TP	PIM
1998-99	St. John's Prep	Hi-School	28	38	35	73	20	....	....	....	....	....
99-2000	Boston University	H-East	42	13	11	24	61	....	....	....	....	....
2000-01	Boston University	H-East	37	14	16	30	16	....	....	....	....	....

COLLYMORE, Shawn (KAW-lee-mohr, SHAWN) NYR

Right wing. Shoots right. 5'11", 180 lbs. Born, Ville de Lasalle, Que., May 2, 1983.
(NY Rangers' 5th choice, 139th overall, in 2001 Entry Draft).

			Regular Season					Playoffs				
Season	Club	Lea	GP	G	A	TP	PIM	GP	G	A	TP	PIM
99-2000	Quebec Remparts	QMJHL	64	8	16	24	22	11	0	2	2	0
2000-01	Quebec Remparts	QMJHL	71	24	43	67	32	4	0	3	3	0

CONCANNON, Mark (KAHN-kan-nuhn, MAHRK) S.J.

Left wing. Shoots left. 6', 200 lbs. Born, Boston, MA, June 12, 1980.
(San Jose's 2nd choice, 82nd overall, in 1999 Entry Draft).

			Regular Season					Playoffs				
Season	Club	Lea	GP	G	A	TP	PIM	GP	G	A	TP	PIM
1997-98	Hull High	Hi-School	20	38	35	73	....	....	....	....	....	....
1998-99	Winchendon	Hi-School	26	23	38	61	11	....	....	....	....	....
99-2000	U. Mass-Lowell	H-East	23	4	3	7	8	....	....	....	....	....
2000-01	U. Mass-Lowell	H-East	19	2	7	9	6	....	....	....	....	....

CONNE, Flavien (KAW-neh, FLA-vee-ehn) L.A.

Center. Shoots left. 5'9", 176 lbs. Born, Geneva, Switz., April 1, 1980.
(Los Angeles' 10th choice, 250th overall, in 2000 Entry Draft).

			Regular Season					Playoffs				
Season	Club	Lea	GP	G	A	TP	PIM	GP	G	A	TP	PIM
1995-96	Geneve-Servette	Switz-Jr.	22	39	27	56	32	....	....	....	....	....
1996-97	Geneve-Servette	Switz-2	30	9	8	17	8	5	1	1	2	4
1997-98	Geneve-Servette	Switz-Jr.	37	15	12	27	57	3	0	2	2	2
	Geneve-Servette	Switz-2	9	11	6	17	12	....	....	....	....	....
	Ambri-Piotta	Switz.	1	0	0	0	0	....	....	....	....	....
1998-99	Fribourg-Gotteron	Switz-Jr.	1	1	1	2	2	....	....	....	....	....
	Fribourg-Gotteron	Switz.	37	14	14	28	59	4	4	1	5	6
	Fribourg-Gotteron	EuroHL	3	0	0	0	0	....	....	....	....	....
99-2000	Fribourg-Gotteron	Switz.	44	19	22	41	38	4	0	1	1	0
2000-01	HC Lugano	Switz.	42	9	14	23	8	15	2	6	8	37

CONNOLLY, Sean (KAW-nuhl-lee, SHAWN) OTT.

Defense. Shoots right. 6'1", 187 lbs. Born, Dearborne, MI, October 8, 1980.
(Ottawa's 8th choice, 158th overall, in 2000 Entry Draft).

			Regular Season					Playoffs				
Season	Club	Lea	GP	G	A	TP	PIM	GP	G	A	TP	PIM
1997-98	Markham Waxers	MTJHL	45	10	28	38	181	....	....	....	....	....
1998-99	North-Michigan	CCHA	33	4	18	22	62	....	....	....	....	....
99-2000	North-Michigan	CCHA	35	2	14	16	64	....	....	....	....	....
2000-01	North-Michigan	CCHA	38	5	14	19	80	....	....	....	....	....

COOK, Jesse (KUK, JEH-see) CGY.

Defense. Shoots right. 6'6", 210 lbs. Born, Denver, CO, October 11, 1979.
(Calgary's 6th choice, 153rd overall, in 1999 Entry Draft).

			Regular Season					Playoffs				
Season	Club	Lea	GP	G	A	TP	PIM	GP	G	A	TP	PIM
1997-98	Calgary Royals	AJHL	34	5	24	29	35	3	1	2	3	4
1998-99	U. of Denver	WCHA	33	0	10	10	22	....	....	....	....	....
99-2000	U. of Denver	WCHA	41	2	12	14	40	....	....	....	....	....
2000-01	U. of Denver	WCHA	37	2	15	17	22	....	....	....	....	....

CORAZZINI, Carl BOS.

Left wing. Shoots right. 5'9", 170 lbs. Born, Framingham, MA, April 21, 1979.

			Regular Season					Playoffs				
Season	Club	Lea	GP	G	A	TP	PIM	GP	G	A	TP	PIM
1996-97	St. Sebastian's	Hi-School	25	29	31	60	....	....	....	....	....	....
1997-98	Boston University	H-East	36	9	6	15	4	....	....	....	....	....
1998-99	Boston University	H-East	37	15	9	24	12	....	....	....	....	....
99-2000	Boston University	H-East	42	22	20	42	44	....	....	....	....	....
2000-01	Boston University	H-East	35	16	20	36	48	....	....	....	....	....

All Hockey East Rookie Team (1998) • Hockey East First All-Star Team (2001)

Signed as a free agent by **Boston**, August 8, 2001.

CORBEIL, Nicolas (kohr-BAY, NIH-coh-las), TOR.

Center. Shoots right. 5'10", 177 lbs. Born, Laval, Que., March 30, 1983.
(Toronto's 5th choice, 88th overall, in 2001 Entry Draft).

			Regular Season					Playoffs				
Season	Club	Lea	GP	G	A	TP	PIM	GP	G	A	TP	PIM
99-2000	Sherbrooke	QMJHL	64	9	12	21	28	5	1	0	1	0
2000-01	Sherbrooke	QMJHL	68	33	51	84	159	3	1	3	4	4

CORRINET, Chris (KOHR-rih-neht, KRIHS) WSH.

Right wing. Shoots right. 6'3", 220 lbs. Born, Derby, CT, October 29, 1978.
(Washington's 4th choice, 107th overall, in 1998 Entry Draft).

			Regular Season					Playoffs				
Season	Club	Lea	GP	G	A	TP	PIM	GP	G	A	TP	PIM
1996-97	Deerfield Prep	Hi-School	16	6	15	21	10	....	....	....	....	....
1997-98	Princeton Tigers	ECAC	31	3	6	9	22	....	....	....	....	....
1998-99	Princeton Tigers	ECAC	32	10	6	16	38	....	....	....	....	....
99-2000	Princeton Tigers	ECAC	30	10	14	24	41	....	....	....	....	....
2000-01	Princeton Tigers	ECAC	31	13	12	25	30	....	....	....	....	....
	Portland Pirates	AHL	6	0	1	1	4	2	1	0	1	0

CORVO, Joe (KOHR-voh, JOH-sehf) L.A.

Defense. Shoots right. 6', 205 lbs. Born, Oak Park, IL, June 20, 1977.
(Los Angeles' 4th choice, 83rd overall, in 1997 Entry Draft).

			Regular Season					Playoffs				
Season	Club	Lea	GP	G	A	TP	PIM	GP	G	A	TP	PIM
1995-96	Western Michigan	CCHA	41	5	25	30	38	....	....	....	....	....
1996-97	Western Michigan	CCHA	37	12	21	33	85	....	....	....	....	....
1997-98	Western Michigan	CCHA	32	5	12	17	93	....	....	....	....	....
1998-99	Springfield	AHL	50	5	15	20	32	....	....	....	....	....
	Hampton Roads	ECHL	5	0	0	0	15	4	0	1	1	0
99-2000					DID NOT PLAY							
2000-01	Lowell	AHL	77	10	23	33	31	4	3	1	4	0

CCHA All-Rookie Team (1996) • CCHA Second All-Star Team (1997)
• Missed entire 1999-2000 season after failing to come to contract terms with **LA Kings**

COTE, Jean-Philippe (KOH-tay, zhawn-fihl-EEP) TOR.

Defense. Shoots left. 6'1", 195 lbs. Born, Charlesbourg, Que., April 22, 1982.
(Toronto's 10th choice, 265th overall, in 2000 Entry Draft).

			Regular Season					Playoffs				
Season	Club	Lea	GP	G	A	TP	PIM	GP	G	A	TP	PIM
1998-99	Ste-Foy Governors	QAAA	38	10	24	34	34	17	1	8	9	17
	Quebec Remparts	QMJHL	8	0	0	0	2	....	....	....	....	....
99-2000	Quebec Remparts	QMJHL	34	0	10	10	15	....	....	....	....	....
	Cape Breton	QMJHL	28	0	4	4	21	4	0	1	1	4
2000-01	Cape Breton	QMJHL	71	6	29	35	90	12	0	0	0	18

COURTNEY, Ryan (KOHRT-nee, RIGH-uhn) BUF.

Left wing. Shoots left. 6'2", 195 lbs. Born, Peterborough, Ont., March 8, 1982.
(Buffalo's 8th choice, 277th overall, in 2000 Entry Draft).

			Regular Season					Playoffs				
Season	Club	Lea	GP	G	A	TP	PIM	GP	G	A	TP	PIM
1997-98	Peterborough	OMHA	48	25	30	55	48	....	....	....	....	....
1998-99	Windsor Spitfires	OHL	60	7	10	17	13	5	0	0	0	7
99-2000	Windsor Spitfires	OHL	65	10	22	32	44	12	0	1	1	9
2000-01	Windsor Spitfires	OHL	14	3	7	10	7	....	....	....	....	....
	Mississauga	OHL	49	6	16	22	23	....	....	....	....	....

Traded to **Mississauga** by **Windsor** with Tyler Eady for Jason Spezza, Mark Rideout and Mike Jannes, November 15, 2000.

COX, Justin (KAWKS, JUH-stihn) DAL.

Right wing. Shoots right. 6', 165 lbs. Born, Merritt, B.C., March 13, 1981.
(Dallas' 6th choice, 184th overall, in 1999 Entry Draft).

			Regular Season					Playoffs				
Season	Club	Lea	GP	G	A	TP	PIM	GP	G	A	TP	PIM
1996-97	Spruce Grove	AMHL	78	57	92	149	86	....	....	....	....	....
1997-98	Prince George	WHL	40	1	4	5	15	2	0	0	0	0
1998-99	Prince George	WHL	72	9	13	22	51	7	1	0	1	13
99-2000	Prince George	WHL	71	33	38	71	74	13	2	4	6	16
2000-01	Prince George	WHL	71	30	38	68	91	6	3	4	7	20

CRAIN, Jason (KRAYN, JAY-suhn) L.A.

Defense. Shoots left. 6'3", 190 lbs. Born, Pittsburgh, PA, January 3, 1980.
(Los Angeles' 2nd choice, 74th overall, in 1999 Entry Draft).

			Regular Season					Playoffs				
Season	Club	Lea	GP	G	A	TP	PIM	GP	G	A	TP	PIM
1996-97	St. Thomas Stars	OJHL-B	50	9	18	27	67	....	....	....	....	....
1997-98	St. Thomas Stars	OJHL-B	43	6	33	39	49	....	....	....	....	....
1998-99	Ohio State	CCHA	41	3	14	17	18	....	....	....	....	....
99-2000	Ohio State	CCHA	35	2	9	11	32	....	....	....	....	....
2000-01	Ohio State	CCHA	36	2	4	6	36	....	....	....	....	....

CRAMPTON, Steven (KRAMP-tuhn, STEE-vehn) PIT.

Right wing. Shoots right. 6'2", 197 lbs. Born, Winnipeg, Man., April 12, 1982.
(Pittsburgh's 8th choice, 248th overall, in 2000 Entry Draft).

			Regular Season					Playoffs				
Season	Club	Lea	GP	G	A	TP	PIM	GP	G	A	TP	PIM
1997-98	Winnipeg Sharks	MAHA	29	33	38	71	76	....	....	....	....	....
1998-99	Moose Jaw	WHL	52	7	5	12	31	9	1	1	2	4
99-2000	Moose Jaw	WHL	69	22	20	42	91	4	0	3	3	9
2000-01	Moose Jaw	WHL	72	26	33	59	153	4	1	2	3	6

CRONIN, John (KROH-nihhn, JAWN) BOS.

Defense. Shoots right. 6'2", 200 lbs. Born, Duxbury, MA, May 1, 1980.
(Boston's 8th choice, 236th overall, in 1999 Entry Draft).

			Regular Season					Playoffs				
Season	Club	Lea	GP	G	A	TP	PIM	GP	G	A	TP	PIM
1997-98	Nobles-Greenough	Hi-School	30	8	22	30	14	....	....	....	....	....
1998-99	Nobles-Greenough	Hi-School	30	8	26	34	24	....	....	....	....	....
99-2000	Boston University	H-East	28	3	5	8	26	....	....	....	....	....
2000-01	Boston University	H-East	37	2	11	13	36	....	....	....	....	....

CULL, Trent (KUHL, TREHNT) MIN.

Defense. Shoots left. 6'2", 215 lbs. Born, Brampton, Ont., September 27, 1973.

			Regular Season					Playoffs				
Season	Club	Lea	GP	G	A	TP	PIM	GP	G	A	TP	PIM
1988-89	Georgetown	OJHL-B	36	1	5	6	51					
1989-90	Owen Sound	OHL	57	0	5	5	53	12	0	2	2	11
1990-91	Owen Sound	OHL	24	1	2	3	19					
	Windsor Spitfires	OHL	33	1	6	7	34	11	0	0	0	8
1991-92	Windsor Spitfires	OHL	32	0	6	6	66					
	Kingston	OHL	18	0	0	0	31					
1992-93	Kingston	OHL	60	11	28	39	144	16	2	8	10	37
1993-94	Kingston	OHL	50	2	30	32	147	6	0	1	1	6
1994-95	St. John's Leafs	AHL	43	0	1	1	53					
	Brantford Smoke	ColHL	4	0	0	0	14					
1995-96	St. John's Leafs	AHL	46	2	1	3	118	4	0	0	0	6
1996-97	St. John's Leafs	AHL	75	4	5	9	219	8	0	1	1	18
1997-98	Houston Aeros	IHL	72	4	8	12	201	4	0	0	0	4
1998-99	Houston Aeros	IHL	72	2	14	16	232	19	0	2	2	34
99-2000	Springfield	AHL	28	0	2	2	74					
	Houston Aeros	IHL	35	2	7	9	133	5	0	0	0	24
2000-01	Wilkes-Barre	AHL	71	11	15	26	166	21	3	2	5	28

Signed as a free agent by **Toronto**, June 4, 1994. Signed as a free agent by **Phoenix**, August 26, 1999. Signed as a free agent by **Pittsburgh**, August 28, 2000. Signed as a free agent by **Minnesota**, July 13, 2001.

CULLEN, Joe (KUH-lehn, JOH) EDM.

Center. Shoots left. 6'1", 190 lbs. Born, Virginia, MN, February 14, 1981.
(Edmonton's 7th choice, 211th overall, in 2000 Entry Draft).

			Regular Season					Playoffs				
Season	Club	Lea	GP	G	A	TP	PIM	GP	G	A	TP	PIM
1997-98	Moorehead High	Hi-School	23	18	18	36	....					
1998-99	Team USA	USDP	52	11	15	26	33					
99-2000	Colorado College	WCHA	29	4	6	10	30					
2000-01	Colorado College	WCHA	34	8	12	20	38					

DAHLMAN, Toni OTT.

Right wing. Shoots right. 5'11", 194 lbs. Born, Helsinki, Finland, September 3, 1979.
(Ottawa's 12th choice, 286th overall, in 2001 Entry Draft).

			Regular Season					Playoffs				
Season	Club	Lea	GP	G	A	TP	PIM	GP	G	A	TP	PIM
1996-97	Karhu-Kissat	Finn-Jr.	24	22	18	30	6					
1997-98	Jokerit Helsinki	Finn-Jr.	21	13	11	24	14	7	2	2	4	0
1998-99	Jokerit Helsinki	Finn-Jr.	33	10	22	32	6	9	4	3	7	2
	Jokerit Helsinki	Finland	5	0	0	0	0	3	0	1	1	0
99-2000	Jokerit Helsinki	Finn-Jr.	12	6	8	14	4	12	7	7	14	4
	Hermes Kokkula	Finland-2	23	6	3	9	4					
	Jokerit Helsinki	Finland	1	0	0	0	0					
2000-01	Ilves Tampere	Finland	56	10	18	28	16	9	3	2	5	2

DARBY, Regan (DAHR-bee, REE-gan) VAN.

Defense. Shoots left. 6'2", 200 lbs. Born, Estevan, Sask., July 17, 1980.
(Vancouver's 5th choice, 90th overall, in 1998 Entry Draft).

			Regular Season					Playoffs				
Season	Club	Lea	GP	G	A	TP	PIM	GP	G	A	TP	PIM
1996-97	Swift Current	SMHL	36	10	20	30	210					
1997-98	Spokane Chiefs	WHL	7	0	1	1	28					
	Tri-City Americans	WHL	32	1	2	3	125					
1998-99	Tri-City Americans	WHL	38	2	4	6	152					
	Red Deer Rebels	WHL	19	1	6	7	90	9	0	1	1	18
99-2000	Red Deer Rebels	WHL	18	3	6	9	79					
	Prince Albert	WHL	44	1	9	10	143	6	0	1	1	23
2000-01	Kansas City	IHL	55	1	5	6	164					

DARDIS, Jay (DAHR-dihs, JAY) NYR

Center. Shoots right. 6'3", 190 lbs. Born, Proctor, MN, July 4, 1981.
(NY Rangers' 7th choice, 177th overall, in 1999 Entry Draft).

			Regular Season					Playoffs				
Season	Club	Lea	GP	G	A	TP	PIM	GP	G	A	TP	PIM
1998-99	Proctor High	Hi-School	26	23	36	59	32					
99-2000	Waterloo Hawks	USHL	17	3	4	7	18					
	Rochester	USHL	22	4	4	8	10					
2000-01	Rochester	USHL	49	11	10	21	78					

DATSYUK, Pavel (daht-SOOK, PAH-vehl) DET.

Center. Shoots left. 5'11", 180 lbs. Born, Sverdlovsk, USSR, July 20, 1978.
(Detroit's 8th choice, 171st overall, in 1998 Entry Draft).

			Regular Season					Playoffs				
Season	Club	Lea	GP	G	A	TP	PIM	GP	G	A	TP	PIM
1996-97	HC Yekaterinburg	Russia	18	2	2	4	4					
	HC Yekaterinburg	Russia-2	36	12	10	22	12					
1997-98	HC Yekaterinburg	Russia	24	3	5	8	4					
	HC Yekaterinburg	Russia-2	22	7	8	15	4					
1998-99	HC Yekaterinburg	Russia-3	22	12	15	27	12					
	HC Yekaterinburg	Russia-2	13	9	8	17	2	9	3	7	10	10
99-2000	HC Yekaterinburg	Russia	15	1	3	4	4					
2000-01	Ak Bars Kazan	Russia	42	9	18	27	10	4	0	1	1	2

• Spent majority of 1999-2000 season on **Ak Bars Kazan** (Russia) taxi squad.

DAVIS, Greg ST.L.

Left wing. Shoots right. 6'4", 195 lbs. Born, Calgary, Alta., July 26, 1979.

			Regular Season					Playoffs				
Season	Club	Lea	GP	G	A	TP	PIM	GP	G	A	TP	PIM
1997-98	Olds Grizzlies	AJHL	56	12	21	33	37	8	0	2	2	10
1998-99	Olds Grizzlies	AJHL	61	19	28	47	97					
99-2000	McGill University	CIAU	38	23	16	39	22					
2000-01	McGill University	CIAU	33	30	35	65	38					

Signed as a free agent by **St. Louis**, May 5, 2001.

DAVIS, Ken (DAY-vihs, KEHN) DET.

Right wing. Shoots right. 6'4", 210 lbs. Born, Calgary, Alta., March 20, 1981.
(Detroit's 6th choice, 266th overall, in 1999 Entry Draft).

			Regular Season					Playoffs				
Season	Club	Lea	GP	G	A	TP	PIM	GP	G	A	TP	PIM
1996-97	Calgary Royals	AMHL	54	24	27	51	84					
1997-98	Portland	WHL	66	8	11	19	27	14	1	0	1	7
1998-99	Portland	WHL	72	13	14	27	76	4	0	1	1	11
99-2000	Portland	WHL	6	1	2	3	18					
	Medicine Hat	WHL	61	23	10	33	86					
2000-01	Medicine Hat	WHL	69	19	15	34	75					

DAVIS, Wade (DAY-vihs, WAYD) CGY.

Defense. Shoots right. 6'4", 185 lbs. Born, Kamloops, B.C., April 13, 1982.
(Calgary's 5th choice, 141st overall, in 2000 Entry Draft).

			Regular Season					Playoffs				
Season	Club	Lea	GP	G	A	TP	PIM	GP	G	A	TP	PIM
1997-98	Fernie Ghostriders	RMJHL	42	8	17	25	19					
	Calgary Hitmen	WHL	2	0	0	0	0	1	0	0	0	0
1998-99	Calgary Hitmen	WHL	38	0	2	2	21	2	0	0	0	0
99-2000	Calgary Hitmen	WHL	61	3	15	18	59	13	0	2	2	15
2000-01	Calgary Hitmen	WHL	67	11	21	32	77	12	0	2	2	16

DAVISON, Rob (DAY-vihs-ohn, RAWB) S.J.

Defense. Shoots left. 6'2", 220 lbs. Born, St. Catharines, Ont., May 1, 1980.
(San Jose's 4th choice, 98th overall, in 1998 Entry Draft).

			Regular Season					Playoffs				
Season	Club	Lea	GP	G	A	TP	PIM	GP	G	A	TP	PIM
1995-96	St. Michael's	OPJHL	21	0	0	0	21					
1996-97	St. Michael's	OPJHL	45	2	6	8	93					
1997-98	North Bay	OHL	59	0	11	11	200					
1998-99	North Bay	OHL	59	2	17	19	150	4	0	1	1	12
99-2000	North Bay	OHL	67	4	6	10	194	6	0	1	1	8
2000-01	Kentucky	AHL	72	0	4	4	230	3	0	0	0	0

DAW, Jeff (DAW, JEHF) COL.

Center. Shoots right. 6'3", 190 lbs. Born, Carlisle, Ont., February 28, 1972.

			Regular Season					Playoffs				
Season	Club	Lea	GP	G	A	TP	PIM	GP	G	A	TP	PIM
1989-90	Milton Merchants	OPJHL	42	19	29	48	2					
1990-91	Milton Merchants	OPJHL	34	21	41	62	22					
1991-92	Milton Merchants	OPJHL	41	33	33	66	20					
1992-93	U. Mass-Lowell	H-East	37	12	18	30	14					
1993-94	U. Mass-Lowell	H-East	40	6	12	18	12					
1994-95	U. Mass-Lowell	H-East	40	27	15	42	24					
1995-96	U. Mass-Lowell	H-East	40	23	28	51	10					
1996-97	Wheeling Nailers	ECHL	13	3	8	11	26					
	Hamilton Bulldogs	AHL	56	11	8	19	39	19	4	5	9	0
1997-98	Hamilton Bulldogs	AHL	79	28	35	63	20	9	6	3	9	0
1998-99	Hamilton Bulldogs	AHL	66	18	29	47	10	11	0	3	3	4
99-2000	Cleveland	IHL	9	4	1	5	2					
	Houston Aeros	IHL	44	9	8	17	12					
	Lowell	AHL	10	0	5	5	4	7	1	2	3	6
2000-01	Lowell	AHL	65	28	28	56	33	3	0	1	1	2
	Cleveland	IHL	8	2	3	5	2					

Signed as a free agent by **Edmonton**, August 1, 1996. Signed as a free agent by **Chicago**, July 22, 1999. Traded to **Lowell** (AHL) by **Houston** (IHL) with Chicago retaining NHL rights for Dave Hymotitz, March 17, 2000. Selected by **Minnesota** from **Chicago** in Expansion Draft, June 23, 2000. Signed as a free agent by **Colorado**, July 23, 2001.

DeCECCO, Bret (duh-CHEHK-oh, BREHT)

Right wing. Shoots right. 5'10", 189 lbs. Born, Edmonton, Alta., May 20, 1980.
(Buffalo's 10th choice, 206th overall, in 1999 Entry Draft).

			Regular Season					Playoffs				
Season	Club	Lea	GP	G	A	TP	PIM	GP	G	A	TP	PIM
1994-95	Edmonton Ice	AAHA	52	185	120	205	....					
1995-96	Sherwood Park	AMHL	35	32	32	64	75					
	Seattle T-Birds	WHL	6	3	1	4	8	4	1	0	1	4
1996-97	Seattle T-Birds	WHL	54	17	19	36	40	15	7	1	8	9
1997-98	Seattle T-Birds	WHL	71	36	56	92	84	3	0	0	0	0
1998-99	Seattle T-Birds	WHL	72	57	43	100	81	11	1	4	5	21
99-2000	Seattle T-Birds	WHL	51	29	26	55	56	4	4	2	6	4
2000-01	Seattle T-Birds	WHL	6	2	3	5	8					
	Kootenay Ice	WHL	51	32	28	60	61	11	6	11	17	12

WHL West Second All-Star Team (1999)

Traded to **Kootenay** by **Seattle** with Brennan Evans for Dion Lassu, Brad Tutschek and future considerations, October 31, 2000.

DEFAUW, Brad (duh-FOU, BRAD) CAR.

Left wing. Shoots left. 6'2", 210 lbs. Born, Edina, MN, November 10, 1977.
(Carolina's 2nd choice, 28th overall, in 1997 Entry Draft).

			Regular Season					Playoffs				
Season	Club	Lea	GP	G	A	TP	PIM	GP	G	A	TP	PIM
1995-96	Apple Collegiate	Hi-School	28	21	34	55	14					
1996-97	North Dakota	WCHA	37	7	6	13	39					
1997-98	North Dakota	WCHA	36	9	11	20	34					
1998-99	North Dakota	WCHA	34	11	12	23	64					
99-2000	North Dakota	WCHA	43	13	9	22	52					
2000-01	Cincinnati	IHL	82	20	31	51	39	4	2	0	2	8

DEGERMAN, Tommi (DEH-guhr-mahn,TAW-mee) ANA.

Left wing. Shoots left. 6'2", 200 lbs. Born, Vihti, Finland, February 23, 1976.
(Anaheim's 8th choice, 235th overall, in 1997 Entry Draft).

			Regular Season					Playoffs				
Season	Club	Lea	GP	G	A	TP	PIM	GP	G	A	TP	PIM
1992-93	Kiekko-Espoo-B	Finn-Jr.	35	14	17	31	4	5	3	4	*7	0
1993-94	Kiekko-Espoo-B	Finn-Jr.	13	8	5	13	14					
	Kiekko-Espoo	Finn-Jr.	34	2	6	8	14					
1994-95	Kiekko-Espoo	Finn-Jr.	26	4	7	11	14	5	1	0	1	4
1995-96	Kiekko-Espoo	Finn-Jr.	36	11	15	26	14					
1996-97	Kiekko-Espoo	Finn-Jr.	3	3	0	3	0					
	Pelicans Lahti	Finland-2	4	0	4	4	0					
	Kiekko-Espoo	Finland	23	2	0	2	2					
	Boston University	H-East	17	6	10	16	19					
1997-98	Boston University	H-East	35	12	20	32	37					
1998-99	Boston University	H-East	27	12	9	21	24					
99-2000	Boston University	H-East	42	19	24	43	18					
2000-01	KJT-Jarvenpaa	Finland-2	15	1	5	6	10					
	Blues Espoo	Finland	1	0	0	0	0					

DELEEUW, Adam (DEH-lee-EW, A-dam) DET.

Left wing. Shoots left. 6', 206 lbs. Born, Brampton, Ont., February 29, 1980.
(Detroit's 7th choice, 151st overall, in 1998 Entry Draft).

			Regular Season					Playoffs				
Season	Club	Lea	GP	G	A	TP	PIM	GP	G	A	TP	PIM
1996-97	Brampton Caps	OPJHL	45	11	17	28	97					
1997-98	Barrie Colts	OHL	56	10	6	16	224					
1998-99	Barrie Colts	OHL	39	15	16	31	146					
	St. Michael's	OHL	29	10	5	15	55					
99-2000	St. Michael's	OHL	45	11	19	30	107					
	Dayton Bombers	ECHL	2	0	0	0	2	3	0	0	0	2
2000-01	St. Michael's	OHL	54	11	14	25	122	18	1	1	2	21

DELISLE, Miguel (duh-LIGHL, mih-GEHL) TOR.

Right wing. Shoots right. 6'2", 202 lbs. Born, Cornwall, Ont., April 6, 1982.
(Toronto's 5th choice, 100th overall, in 2000 Entry Draft).

			Regular Season					Playoffs				
Season	Club	Lea	GP	G	A	TP	PIM	GP	G	A	TP	PIM
1997-98	Caledon Canucks	MTJHL	46	20	24	44	142	....	....	....	....	....
1998-99	Ottawa 67's	OHL	57	16	17	33	34	9	1	0	1	4
99-2000	Ottawa 67's	OHL	54	20	29	49	73	11	4	1	5	28
2000-01	Ottawa 67's	OHL	61	34	38	72	89	20	8	17	25	30

DeMARCHI, Matt (dih-MAHR-shee, MAT) N.J.

Defense. Shoots left. 6'3", 180 lbs. Born, Bemidji, MN, May 4, 1981.
(New Jersey's 4th choice, 57th overall, in 2000 Entry Draft).

			Regular Season					Playoffs				
Season	Club	Lea	GP	G	A	TP	PIM	GP	G	A	TP	PIM
1997-98	North Iowa	USHL	34	1	2	3	66	10	0	1	1	19
1998-99	North Iowa	USHL	53	4	14	18	131	....	....	....	....	....
99-2000	U. of Minnesota	WCHA	39	1	6	7	82	....	....	....	....	....
2000-01	U. of Minnesota	WCHA	39	4	9	13	*149	....	....	....	....	....

DEMIDOV, Ilja (deh-MEE-dahf, ihl-YA) OTT.

Defense. Shoots left. 6'3", 185 lbs. Born, Moscow, USSR, April 14, 1979.
(Calgary's 10th choice, 140th overall, in 1997 Entry Draft).

			Regular Season					Playoffs				
Season	Club	Lea	GP	G	A	TP	PIM	GP	G	A	TP	PIM
1995-96	Dynamo Moscow	CIS-2	10	0	14	14	....	....	....	....	....	....
1996-97	D'amo Moscow-2	Russia-3	32	1	0	1	60	....	....	....	....	....
1997-98	Oshawa Generals	OHL	61	4	16	20	67	7	0	1	1	2
1998-99	Oshawa Generals	OHL	62	4	23	27	72	15	2	5	7	24
99-2000	Oshawa Generals	OHL	62	11	37	48	105	5	0	2	2	24
2000-01	Grand Rapids	IHL	54	1	4	5	65	2	0	1	1	21

Signed as a free agent by **Ottawa**, February 25, 2000.

DENISOV, Denis (den-NEES-ahf, deh-NEES) BUF.

Left wing. Shoots left. 6', 183 lbs. Born, Kalinin, USSR, December 31, 1981.
(Buffalo's 4th choice, 149th overall, in 2000 Entry Draft).

			Regular Season					Playoffs				
Season	Club	Lea	GP	G	A	TP	PIM	GP	G	A	TP	PIM
1997-98	CSKA Moscow	Russia	7	0	0	0	4	....	....	....	....	....
1998-99	HC Moscow	Russia-2	42	1	6	7	16	....	....	....	....	....
99-2000	HC Moscow	Russia-2	39	1	8	9	16	....	....	....	....	....
2000-01	HC Moscow	Russia-2	41	0	3	3	6	....	....	....	....	....

DESMARAIS, James (deh-mahr-AY, JAYMZ) ST.L.

Center. Shoots right. 5'10", 170 lbs. Born, Montreal, Que., May 4, 1979.
(St. Louis' 10th choice, 270th overall, in 1999 Entry Draft).

			Regular Season					Playoffs				
Season	Club	Lea	GP	G	A	TP	PIM	GP	G	A	TP	PIM
1994-95	Lac St-Louis	QAAA	1	0	0	0	0	....	....	....	....	....
1995-96	Lac St-Louis	QAAA	44	19	23	42	42	....	....	....	....	....
1996-97	Laval Titan	QMJHL	67	12	21	33	32	3	0	0	0	4
1997-98	Laval Titan	QMJHL	68	33	40	73	56	15	6	5	11	12
1998-99	Rouyn-Noranda	QMJHL	66	62	73	135	127	11	6	7	13	14
99-2000	Peoria	ECHL	59	26	33	59	51	....	....	....	....	....
	Worcester	AHL	8	0	2	2	0	....	....	....	....	....
2000-01	Springfield	AHL	37	8	16	24	6	....	....	....	....	....
	BC Icemen	UHL	33	17	23	40	18	....	....	....	....	....

QMJHL First All-Star Team (1999)

DESSNER, Jeff (DEHS-nehr, JEHF) ATL.

Defense. Shoots left. 6'2", 195 lbs. Born, Skokie, IL, April 16, 1977.
(NY Rangers' 6th choice, 185th overall, in 1996 Entry Draft).

			Regular Season					Playoffs				
Season	Club	Lea	GP	G	A	TP	PIM	GP	G	A	TP	PIM
1995-96	Taft Eagles	Hi-School	25	12	18	30	....	....	....	....	....	....
1996-97	U. of Wisconsin	WCHA	DID NOT PLAY – INJURED									
1997-98	U. of Wisconsin	WCHA	19	1	3	4	43	....	....	....	....	....
1998-99	U. of Wisconsin	WCHA	37	7	14	21	46	....	....	....	....	....
99-2000	U. of Wisconsin	WCHA	40	11	15	26	59	....	....	....	....	....
2000-01	U. of Wisconsin	WCHA	39	7	12	19	58	....	....	....	....	....

WCHA First All-Star Team (2000) • NCAA West First All-American Team (2000)

• Missed entire 1996-97 season recovering from back surgery, June, 1996. Traded to **Atlanta** by **NY Rangers** for Atlanta's 8th round choice (Leonid Zhvachkin) in 2001 Entry Draft, June 23, 2001.

DEZAINDE, Joel N.J.

Defense. Shoots left. 6', 200 lbs. Born, Simcoe, Ont., November 2, 1978.

			Regular Season					Playoffs				
Season	Club	Lea	GP	G	A	TP	PIM	GP	G	A	TP	PIM
1993-94	Oshwekin Eagles	OJHL-B	47	4	2	6	111	....	....	....	....	....
1994-95	London Knights	OHL	53	0	4	4	60	4	0	3	3	0
1995-96	London Knights	OHL	64	9	33	42	99	....	....	....	....	....
1996-97	Owen Sound	OHL	34	6	8	14	39	....	....	....	....	....
	Belleville Bulls	OHL	29	5	12	17	35	6	1	5	6	8
1997-98	Belleville Bulls	OHL	65	13	45	58	81	10	3	5	8	16
1998-99	Mississauga	OHL	24	4	20	24	35	....	....	....	....	....
	Barrie Colts	OHL	36	15	33	48	52	12	2	9	11	....
99-2000	Arkansas	WPHL	51	15	25	40	57	....	....	....	....	....
	Detroit Vipers	IHL	14	1	2	3	20	....	....	....	....	....
2000-01	Mississippi	ECHL	58	10	38	48	77	....	....	....	....	....

Signed try-out contract and invited to training camp by **New Jersey**, May 2, 2001.

DICAIRE, Gerard (dih-KAIR, zhehr-AHR) BUF.

Defense. Shoots left. 6'2", 198 lbs. Born, Faro, Yukon, September 14, 1982.
(Buffalo's 2nd choice, 48th overall, in 2000 Entry Draft).

			Regular Season					Playoffs				
Season	Club	Lea	GP	G	A	TP	PIM	GP	G	A	TP	PIM
1997-98	Tumber Ridge	NWJHL	35	15	28	43	63	....	....	....	....	....
1998-99	Prince George	BCJHL	51	6	22	28	28	....	....	....	....	....
99-2000	Seattle T-Birds	WHL	68	11	25	36	38	7	0	1	1	6
2000-01	Seattle T-Birds	WHL	69	15	36	51	33	9	0	2	2	2

WHL West Second All-Star Team (2001)

DICKENSON, Lou (DIH-kehn-suhn, LOO) EDM.

Center. Shoots left. 6'1", 192 lbs. Born, Ottawa, Ont., August 15, 1982.
(Edmonton's 4th choice, 113th overall, in 2000 Entry Draft).

			Regular Season					Playoffs				
Season	Club	Lea	GP	G	A	TP	PIM	GP	G	A	TP	PIM
1997-98	South Ottawa	OMHA	36	37	37	74	40	....	....	....	....	....
1998-99	Mississauga	OHL	62	19	27	46	12	....	....	....	....	....
99-2000	Mississauga	OHL	66	21	25	46	46	....	....	....	....	....
2000-01	London Knights	OHL	35	12	13	25	23	....	....	....	....	....
	Kingston	OHL	25	4	6	10	10	4	1	0	1	4

Traded to **London** by **Mississauga** with Mississauga's 5th round choice in 2002 OHL Priority Draft for Brett Angel, Dan Sullivan and Chris Osborne, August 21, 2000. Traded to **Kingston** by **London** with London's 10th round choice (Dayne Davis) in 2001 OHL Midget Draft for Sean McMorrow and Kingston's 2nd round choice (Gerald Coleman) in 2001 OHL Midget Draft, January 8, 2001.

DIETRICH, Brandon (DEE-trihk, BRAN-duhn) NYR

Right wing. Shoots right. 6', 190 lbs. Born, Waterloo, Ont., March 22, 1978.

			Regular Season					Playoffs				
Season	Club	Lea	GP	G	A	TP	PIM	GP	G	A	TP	PIM
1995-96	Waterloo Siskins	OJHL-B	19	2	11	13	2	....	....	....	....	....
1996-97	Elmira Kings	OJHL-B	48	24	34	58	92	....	....	....	....	....
1997-98	Elmira Kings	OJHL-B	48	51	48	99	72	....	....	....	....	....
1998-99	St. Lawrence	ECAC	39	20	19	39	22	....	....	....	....	....
99-2000	St. Lawrence	ECAC	36	15	26	41	20	....	....	....	....	....
2000-01	Hartford	AHL	44	3	8	11	11	....	....	....	....	....
	Charlotte	ECHL	20	2	9	11	19	5	5	1	6	6

ECAC First All-Star Team (2000) • NCAA East Second All-American Team (2000)

Signed as a free agent by **NY Rangers**, June 29, 2000.

DiLAURO, Raymond (dih-LAW-roh, RAY-muhnd) ATL.

Defense. Shoots right. 6'2", 220 lbs. Born, Bensalem, PA, July 13, 1979.
(Atlanta's 11th choice, 246th overall, in 1999 Entry Draft).

			Regular Season					Playoffs				
Season	Club	Lea	GP	G	A	TP	PIM	GP	G	A	TP	PIM
1997-98	Sports Academy	X-Games	32	17	50	67	....	....	....	....	....	....
1998-99	St. Lawrence	ECAC	35	4	8	12	12	....	....	....	....	....
99-2000	St. Lawrence	ECAC	37	3	9	12	22	....	....	....	....	....
2000-01	St. Lawrence	ECAC	34	3	11	14	28	....	....	....	....	....

DIMITRAKOS, Nicholas (DIH-mih-tra-kohs, NIK-oh-lahs) S.J.

Right wing. Shoots right. 5'11", 190 lbs. Born, Boston, MA, May 21, 1979.
(San Jose's 4th choice, 155th overall, in 1999 Entry Draft).

			Regular Season					Playoffs				
Season	Club	Lea	GP	G	A	TP	PIM	GP	G	A	TP	PIM
1994-95	Matignon High	Hi-School	23	10	12	22	....	....	....	....	....	....
1995-96	Matignon High	Hi-School	25	12	28	40	....	....	....	....	....	....
1996-97	Matignon High	Hi-School	25	23	32	55	....	....	....	....	....	....
1997-98	Avon Old Farms	Hi-School	26	27	28	55	....	....	....	....	....	....
1998-99	U. of Maine	H-East	35	8	19	27	33	....	....	....	....	....
99-2000	U. of Maine	H-East	32	11	16	27	16	....	....	....	....	....
2000-01	U. of Maine	H-East	29	11	14	25	43	....	....	....	....	....

NCAA Championship All-Tournament Team (1999)

DiPENTA, Joe (DIH-pehn-tah, JOH) PHI.

Defense. Shoots left. 6'3", 225 lbs. Born, Barrie, Ont., February 25, 1979.
(Florida's 2nd choice, 61st overall, in 1998 Entry Draft).

			Regular Season					Playoffs				
Season	Club	Lea	GP	G	A	TP	PIM	GP	G	A	TP	PIM
1996-97	Smiths Falls	OCJHL	54	13	22	35	92	....	....	....	....	....
1997-98	Boston University	H-East	38	2	16	18	50	....	....	....	....	....
1998-99	Boston University	H-East	36	2	15	17	72	....	....	....	....	....
99-2000	Halifax	QMJHL	63	13	43	56	83	10	3	4	7	26
2000-01	Philadelphia	AHL	71	3	5	8	65	10	1	2	3	15

Signed as a free agent by **Philadelphia**, July 12, 2000.

DiROBERTO, Torrey (DIH-raw-buhr-toh, TOHR-ree) ANA.

Center. Shoots left. 5'11", 186 lbs. Born, Utica, NY, April 17, 1978.
(Buffalo's 6th choice, 128th overall, in 1997 Entry Draft).

			Regular Season					Playoffs				
Season	Club	Lea	GP	G	A	TP	PIM	GP	G	A	TP	PIM
1994-95	Indianapolis Colts	MEHL	56	38	52	90	36	....	....	....	....	....
1995-96	Seattle T-Birds	WHL	70	16	19	35	118	5	0	2	2	8
1996-97	Seattle T-Birds	WHL	72	37	44	81	91	15	9	5	14	8
1997-98	Seattle T-Birds	WHL	43	14	21	35	48	5	0	2	2	14
1998-99	Seattle T-Birds	WHL	66	25	42	67	100	11	4	4	8	14
99-2000	Cincinnati Ducks	AHL	73	18	16	34	41	....	....	....	....	....
	Huntington	ECHL	3	1	1	2	6	....	....	....	....	....
	Dayton Bombers	ECHL	1	0	1	1	0	....	....	....	....	....
2000-01	Baton Rouge	ECHL	3	0	3	3	2	....	....	....	....	....
	Cincinnati Ducks	AHL	67	11	13	24	86	3	0	1	1	2

Signed as a free agent by **Anaheim**, July 1, 1999.

DISALVATORE, Jon (dih-sal-vuh-TOH-ray, JAWN) S.J.

Right wing. Shoots right. 6'1", 180 lbs. Born, Bangor, ME, March 30, 1981.
(San Jose's 2nd choice, 104th overall, in 2000 Entry Draft).

			Regular Season					Playoffs				
Season	Club	Lea	GP	G	A	TP	PIM	GP	G	A	TP	PIM
1997-98	New England	EJHL	38	24	41	65	....	....	....	....	....	....
1998-99	New England	EJHL	48	44	76	*120	38	....	....	....	....	....
99-2000	Providence	H-East	38	15	12	27	12	....	....	....	....	....
2000-01	Providence	H-East	36	9	16	25	29	....	....	....	....	....

EJHL First All-Star Team (1999) • Won EJHL MVP Award (1999)

DOBRYSHKIN, Yuri (doh-BRIHSH-kihn, yew-REE) ATL.

Left wing. Shoots right. 6', 189 lbs. Born, Penza, USSR, July 19, 1979.
(Atlanta's 7th choice, 159th overall, in 1999 Entry Draft).

			Regular Season					Playoffs				
Season	Club	Lea	GP	G	A	TP	PIM	GP	G	A	TP	PIM
1996-97	Krylja Sovetov-2	Russia-3	35	13	5	18	42	....	....	....	....	....
	Krylja Sovetov	Russia	2	0	0	0	0	2	0	0	0	0
1997-98	Krylja Sovetov-2	Russia-3	26	12	5	17	68	....	....	....	....	....
	Krylja Sovetov	Russia	22	4	0	4	12	....	....	....	....	....
1998-99	Krylja Sovetov	Russia	50	11	5	16	86	....	....	....	....	....
99-2000	Ak Bars Kazan	Russia	27	6	9	15	24	17	2	0	2	10
2000-01	Ak Bars Kazan	Russia	40	10	5	15	32	4	2	0	2	2

DOMAN, Matt (DOH-man, MAT) **CGY.**

Right wing. Shoots right. 6'1", 218 lbs. Born, St. Cloud, MN, February 10, 1980.
(Calgary's 5th choice, 135th overall, in 1999 Entry Draft).

			Regular Season					Playoffs				
Season	Club	Lea	GP	G	A	TP	PIM	GP	G	A	TP	PIM
1997-98	Team USA	USDP	55	24	22	46	208	....	....	....	....	....
1998-99	U. of Wisconsin	WCHA	34	5	5	10	52	....	....	....	....	....
99-2000	U. of Wisconsin	WCHA	22	1	12	13	53	....	....	....	....	....
2000-01	U. of Wisconsin	WCHA	41	9	10	19	68	....	....	....	....	....

DONIKA, Mikhail (DAW-nih-ka, mihk-high-EHL) **DAL.**

Defense. Shoots left. 6', 185 lbs. Born, Yaroslavl, USSR, May 15, 1979.
(Dallas' 11th choice, 272nd overall, in 1999 Entry Draft).

			Regular Season					Playoffs				
Season	Club	Lea	GP	G	A	TP	PIM	GP	G	A	TP	PIM
1996-97	HC Yaroslavl-2	Russia-3	15	3	5	8	6	....	....	....	....	....
	Torpedo Yaroslavl	Russia	22	1	0	1	6	2	0	0	0	0
1997-98	Torpedo Yaroslavl	Russia-2	19	1	2	3	32	....	....	....	....	....
	Torpedo Yaroslavl	Russia	30	0	2	2	14	....	....	....	....	....
1998-99	HC Yaroslavl-2	Russia-3	6	2	1	3	4	....	....	....	....	....
	Torpedo Yaroslavl	Russia	37	0	1	1	10	....	....	....	....	....
99-2000	Torpedo Yaroslavl	Russia	35	0	1	1	22	10	0	0	0	4
2000-01	Dynamo Moscow	Russia	43	1	3	4	12	....	....	....	....	....

DOPITA, Jiri (doh-PEE-tuh, YIH-ree) **PHI.**

Center. Shoots left. 6'3", 215 lbs. Born, Sumperk, Czech., December 2, 1968.
(NY Islanders' 4th choice, 123rd overall, in 1998 Entry Draft).

			Regular Season					Playoffs				
Season	Club	Lea	GP	G	A	TP	PIM	GP	G	A	TP	PIM
1989-90	Dukla Jihlava	Czech.	5	1	2	3	0	....	....	....	....	....
1990-91	HC Olomouc	Czech.	42	11	13	24	26	....	....	....	....	....
1991-92	HC Olomouc	Czech.	38	24	20	44	28	3	1	4	5	0
1992-93	HC Olomouc	Czech.	28	12	17	29	16	....	....	....	....	....
	EHC Berlin	DEL	11	7	8	15	49	4	3	5	8	5
1993-94	EHC Berlin	DEL	42	23	21	44	52	....	....	....	....	....
	HC Olomouc	Cze-Rep	....	....	....	....	....	12	4	7	11	....
1994-95	EHC Berlin	DEL	42	28	40	68	55	....	....	....	....	....
1995-96	HC Petra Vsetin	Cze-Rep	38	19	20	39	20	13	9	11	20	10
1996-97	HC Petra Vsetin	Cze-Rep	52	*30	31	61	55	10	7	4	11	22
1997-98	HC Petra Vsetin	Cze-Rep	52	21	34	55	64	10	*12	6	18	4
	HC Petra Vsetin	EuroHL	6	2	4	6	4	....	....	....	....	....
1998-99	Slovnaft Vsetin	Cze-Rep	50	19	32	51	43	12	1	6	7	....
99-2000	Slovnaft Vsetin	Cze-Rep	49	*30	29	59	83	9	0	4	4	6
	Slovnaft Vsetin	EuroHL	3	0	2	2	2	....	....	....	....	....
2000-01	Slovnaft Vsetin	Cze-Rep	46	19	31	50	53	14	8	*13	*21	18

• Re-entered NHL Entry Draft. Originally Boston' 4th choice, 133rd overall, in 1992 Entry Draft.

Rights traded to **Florida** by **NY Islanders** for San Jose's 5th round choice (previously acquired, NY Islanders selected Adam Johnson) in 1999 Entry Draft, June 26, 1999. Rights traded to **Philadelphia** by **Florida** for Philadelphia's 2nd round choice (later traded to Calgary - Calgary selected Andrei Medvedev) in 2001 Entry Draft, June 23, 2001.

DOULL, Doug (DOOL, DUHG) **TOR.**

Left wing. Shoots left. 6'2", 216 lbs. Born, Glace Bay, N.S., May 31, 1974.

			Regular Season					Playoffs				
Season	Club	Lea	GP	G	A	TP	PIM	GP	G	A	TP	PIM
1990-91	Wexford Waxers	OMHL	39	22	36	58	141	....	....	....	....	....
1991-92	Belleville Bulls	OHL	62	6	11	17	123	....	....	....	....	....
1992-93	Belleville Bulls	OHL	65	19	37	56	143	....	....	....	....	....
1993-94	Belleville Bulls	OHL	62	13	24	37	143	....	....	....	....	....
1994-95	Belleville Bulls	OHL	29	7	12	19	71	16	2	13	15	39
1995-96	St. Mary's Huskies	AUAA	11	4	4	8	54	....	....	....	....	....
1996-97	St. Mary's Huskies	AUAA	18	3	10	13	138	....	....	....	....	....
1997-98	St. Mary's Huskies	AUAA	25	4	11	15	227	....	....	....	....	....
1998-99	Michigan K-Wings	IHL	55	4	11	15	227	3	1	1	2	4
99-2000	Detroit Vipers	IHL	17	0	2	2	69	....	....	....	....	....
	Manitoba Moose	IHL	45	4	4	8	184	2	0	0	0	2
2000-01	Manchester Storm	Britain	15	1	6	7	51	....	....	....	....	....
	Saint John	AHL	49	3	10	13	167	16	0	1	1	32

Signed as a free agent by **Manchester** (Britain), August 15, 2000. Signed to a 25-game tryout contract by **Saint John** (AHL) after securing release from **Manchester** (Britain), December 19, 2000. Signed as a free agent by **Saint John** (AHL), February 18, 2001. Signed as a free agent by **Toronto**, July 25, 2001.

DRANEY, Brett (DRAY-nee, BREHT) **DAL.**

Left wing. Shoots left. 6'1", 185 lbs. Born, Merritt, B.C., March 12, 1981.
(Dallas' 7th choice, 186th overall, in 1999 Entry Draft).

			Regular Season					Playoffs				
Season	Club	Lea	GP	G	A	TP	PIM	GP	G	A	TP	PIM
1996-97	Kamloops JV's	BCAHA	43	69	73	132	54	....	....	....	....	....
1997-98	Kamloops Blazers	WHL	42	2	2	4	16	7	0	0	0	0
1998-99	Kamloops Blazers	WHL	58	7	10	17	48	15	1	1	2	8
99-2000	Kamloops Blazers	WHL	62	18	27	45	63	4	1	1	2	11
2000-01	Medicine Hat	WHL	57	20	28	48	84	....	....	....	....	....

Traded to **Medicine Hat** by **Kamloops** for Paul Elliot and Kevin Labbe, September 7, 2000.

DROZDETSKY, Alexander (drawz-DEHT-skee, al-ehx-AN-duhr) **PHI.**

Right wing. Shoots left. 6', 180 lbs. Born, Moscow, USSR, October 11, 1981.
(Philadelphia's 2nd choice, 94th overall, in 2000 Entry Draft).

			Regular Season					Playoffs				
Season	Club	Lea	GP	G	A	TP	PIM	GP	G	A	TP	PIM
1997-98	St. Petersburg-2	Russia-3	19	0	1	1	0	....	....	....	....	....
1998-99	St. Petersburg-2	Russia-3	24	5	3	8	12	....	....	....	....	....
99-2000	St. Petersburg-2	Russia-3	4	4	1	5	2	....	....	....	....	....
	St. Petersburg	Russia	32	2	0	2	10	4	0	0	0	0
2000-01	St. Petersburg	Russia	42	6	7	13	74	....	....	....	....	....

DUBEN, Premysl (DUH-behn, PREHM-uh-suhl) **NYR**

Defense. Shoots left. 6'3", 220 lbs. Born, Jihlava, Czech., October 5, 1981.
(NY Rangers' 3rd choice, 112th overall, in 2000 Entry Draft).

			Regular Season					Playoffs				
Season	Club	Lea	GP	G	A	TP	PIM	GP	G	A	TP	PIM
1997-98	Dukla Jihlava-Jr.	Cze-Rep	25	1	6	7	34	....	....	....	....	....
1998-99	Dukla Jihlava-Jr.	Cze-Rep	41	1	5	6	18	....	....	....	....	....
99-2000	Dukla Jihlava-Jr.	Cze-Rep	27	4	2	6	36	....	....	....	....	....
	Dukla Jihlava-2	Cze-Rep	19	0	1	1	10	14	0	1	1	4
2000-01	Baie-Comeau	QMJHL	32	0	8	8	36	9	1	0	1	12

DUDA, Radek (DOO-duh, RA-dehk) **CGY.**

Right wing. Shoots left. 6'1", 193 lbs. Born, Skolov, Czech., January 28, 1979.
(Calgary's 7th choice, 192nd overall, in 1998 Entry Draft).

			Regular Season					Playoffs				
Season	Club	Lea	GP	G	A	TP	PIM	GP	G	A	TP	PIM
1994-95	Sokolov Praha-Jr.	Cze-Rep	36	67	37	104	....	....	....	....	....	....
1995-96	Sparta Praha-Jr.	Cze-Rep	39	15	10	25	....	....	....	....	....	....
1996-97	Sparta Praha-Jr.	Cze-Rep	21	9	14	23	....	....	....	....	....	....
	Sparta Praha-2	Cze-Rep	1	0	0	0	....	....	....	....	....	....
	Sparta Praha	Cze-Rep	....	....	....	....	....	1	0	0	0	0
1997-98	Sparta Praha	Cze-Rep	39	3	3	6	41	10	0	2	2	6
1998-99	Regina Pats	WHL	65	24	31	55	139	....	....	....	....	....
99-2000	Lethbridge	WHL	69	42	64	106	193	....	....	....	....	....
2000-01	HCK Plzen	Cze-Rep	24	5	6	11	49	....	....	....	....	....
	Sparta Praha	Cze-Rep	18	2	1	3	66	....	....	....	....	....

DUMA, Pavel (DOO-muh, PAH-vehl) **VAN.**

Center. Shoots left. 6'1", 183 lbs. Born, Karaganda, USSR, June 20, 1981.
(Vancouver's 4th choice, 144th overall, in 2000 Entry Draft).

			Regular Season					Playoffs				
Season	Club	Lea	GP	G	A	TP	PIM	GP	G	A	TP	PIM
1997-98	Nizhnekamsk-2	Russia-3	36	6	2	8	18	....	....	....	....	....
1998-99	Nizhnekamsk-2	Russia-4	34	13	12	25	20	....	....	....	....	....
	HC Nizhnekamsk	Russia	4	0	0	0	2	3	0	2	2	2
99-2000	HC Nizhnekamsk	Russia	29	2	5	7	14	....	....	....	....	....
	Ak Bars Kazan	Russia	8	0	1	1	2	7	0	0	0	2
2000-01	HC Nizhnekamsk	Russia	31	3	1	4	22	....	....	....	....	....

DuPONT, Micki (DOO-pawnt, MIH-kee) **CGY.**

Defense. Shoots right. 5'9", 180 lbs. Born, Calgary, Alta., April 15, 1980.
(Calgary's 9th choice, 270th overall, in 2000 Entry Draft).

			Regular Season					Playoffs				
Season	Club	Lea	GP	G	A	TP	PIM	GP	G	A	TP	PIM
1995-96	Calgary Blazers	AMHL	35	10	35	45	68	....	....	....	....	....
1996-97	Kamloops Blazers	WHL	59	8	27	35	39	5	0	4	4	8
1997-98	Kamloops Blazers	WHL	71	13	41	54	91	7	0	1	1	10
1998-99	Kamloops Blazers	WHL	59	8	27	35	110	15	2	8	10	22
99-2000	Kamloops Blazers	WHL	70	26	62	88	156	4	0	2	2	17
	Long Beach	IHL	1	0	0	0	0	....	....	....	....	....
	San Diego Gulls	WCHL	....	....	....	....	....	7	2	2	4	0
2000-01	Saint John Flames	AHL	67	8	21	29	28	19	1	9	10	14

DURAK, Miroslav (DOO-rak, MEE-roh-slav) **NSH.**

Defense. Shoots right. 6'4", 212 lbs. Born, Topolcany, Czech., June 9, 1981.
(Nashville's 14th choice, 220th overall, in 1999 Entry Draft).

			Regular Season					Playoffs				
Season	Club	Lea	GP	G	A	TP	PIM	GP	G	A	TP	PIM
1997-98	Slovan Bratislava	Slovak-Jr.	36	4	10	14	34	....	....	....	....	....
1998-99	Slovan Bratislava	Slovak-Jr.	38	1	7	8	48	....	....	....	....	....
99-2000	Des Moines	USHL	55	5	6	11	93	9	2	1	3	12
2000-01	Sherbrooke	QMJHL	34	0	17	17	24	....	....	....	....	....
	Acadie-Bathurst	QMJHL	27	5	13	18	95	18	4	3	7	45

Traded to **Acadie-Bathurst** by **Sherbrooke** for future considerations, January 5, 2001.

DWYER, Jeff (DWIGH-uhr, JEHF) **ATL.**

Defense. Shoots left. 6'2", 205 lbs. Born, Greenwich, CT, November 22, 1980.
(Atlanta's 8th choice, 178th overall, in 2000 Entry Draft).

			Regular Season					Playoffs				
Season	Club	Lea	GP	G	A	TP	PIM	GP	G	A	TP	PIM
1996-97	Choate-Rosemary	Hi-School	28	5	11	16	....	....	....	....	....	....
1997-98	Choate-Rosemary	Hi-School	28	9	14	23	....	....	....	....	....	....
1998-99	Choate-Rosemary	Hi-School	27	8	22	30	....	....	....	....	....	....
99-2000	Choate-Rosemary	Hi-School	25	11	30	41	25	....	....	....	....	....
2000-01	Yale University	ECAC	31	3	18	21	16	....	....	....	....	....

DYMENT, Chris (DIGH-mehnt, KRIHS) **MTL.**

Defense. Shoots right. 6'3", 210 lbs. Born, Stoneham, MA, October 24, 1979.
(Montreal's 3rd choice, 97th overall, in 1999 Entry Draft).

			Regular Season					Playoffs				
Season	Club	Lea	GP	G	A	TP	PIM	GP	G	A	TP	PIM
1997-98	Reading High	Hi-School	22	22	22	44	15	....	....	....	....	....
1998-99	Boston University	H-East	25	1	5	6	16	....	....	....	....	....
99-2000	Boston University	H-East	42	11	20	31	42	....	....	....	....	....
2000-01	Boston University	H-East	37	1	10	11	38	....	....	....	....	....

Hockey East First All-Star Team (2000) • NCAA East Second All-American Team (2000)

EADE, Chris (EED, KRIHS) **FLA.**

Defense. Shoots right. 6'1", 204 lbs. Born, Etobicoke, Ont., April 20, 1982.
(Florida's 4th choice, 115th overall, in 2000 Entry Draft).

			Regular Season					Playoffs				
Season	Club	Lea	GP	G	A	TP	PIM	GP	G	A	TP	PIM
1997-98	Oshawa Legion	MTJHL	45	10	13	23	186	....	....	....	....	....
1998-99	North Bay	OHL	46	1	6	7	32	4	0	0	0	0
99-2000	North Bay	OHL	58	5	25	30	64	3	0	0	0	4
2000-01	North Bay	OHL	64	3	26	29	117	4	1	2	3	4
	Louisville Panthers	AHL	4	0	0	0	0	....	....	....	....	....

EAVES, Ben (EEVZ, BEHN) **PIT.**

Center. Shoots right. 5'8", 174 lbs. Born, Minneapolis, MN, March 27, 1982.
(Pittsburgh's 6th choice, 131st overall, in 2001 Entry Draft).

			Regular Season					Playoffs				
Season	Club	Lea	GP	G	A	TP	PIM	GP	G	A	TP	PIM
1998-99	Minnesota Selects	USAHA	71	68	88	156	12	....	....	....	....	....
99-2000	Shattuck-St. Mary	Hi-School	57	47	71	118	16	....	....	....	....	....
2000-01	Boston College	H-East	40	13	26	39	12	....	....	....	....	....

EBERLY, Dan (EH-bur-lee, DAN) **NYR**

Defense. Shoots left. 6', 180 lbs. Born, Newton, MA, October 28, 1980.
(NY Rangers' 8th choice, 238th overall, in 2000 Entry Draft).

			Regular Season					Playoffs				
Season	Club	Lea	GP	G	A	TP	PIM	GP	G	A	TP	PIM
99-2000	RPI Engineers	ECAC	21	2	5	7	8	....	....	....	....	....
2000-01	RPI Engineers	ECAC	28	3	8	11	20	....	....	....	....	....

EDINGER, Adam (EH-dihn-juhr, A-dam) NYI

Center. Shoots left. 6'2", 210 lbs. Born, Toledo, OH, September 21, 1977.
(NY Islanders' 7th choice, 115th overall, in 1997 Entry Draft).

			Regular Season					Playoffs				
Season	Club	Lea	GP	G	A	TP	PIM	GP	G	A	TP	PIM
1994-95	Leamington Flyers	OJHL-B	38	19	62	81	100	....	....	....	....	....
1995-96	Leamington Flyers	OJHL-B	45	45	50	95	120	....	....	....	....	....
1996-97	Bowling Green	CCHA	34	11	18	29	42	....	....	....	....	....
1997-98	Bowling Green	CCHA	27	9	13	22	62	....	....	....	....	....
1998-99	Bowling Green	CCHA	38	23	25	48	36	....	....	....	....	....
99-2000	Bowling Green	CCHA	36	14	18	32	34	....	....	....	....	....
	Trenton Titans	ECHL	3	3	1	4	0	....	....	....	....	....
2000-01	New Orleans	ECHL	58	31	45	76	63	8	8	5	13	8

CCHA First All-Star Team (1999)

EHRHOFF, Christian (AIR-hawf, KRIHS-tyan) S.J.

Defense. Shoots left. 6'2", 187 lbs. Born, Moers, West Germany, July 6, 1982.
(San Jose's 2nd choice, 106th overall, in 2001 Entry Draft).

			Regular Season					Playoffs				
Season	Club	Lea	GP	G	A	TP	PIM	GP	G	A	TP	PIM
1998-99	Krefeld Pinguine	DEL-Jr.	22	10	14	24	46	....	....	....	....	....
99-2000	EV Duisburg	DEB-2	41	3	12	15	50	....	....	....	....	....
	Krefeld Pinguine	DEL	9	1	0	1	6	3	0	0	0	0
2000-01	EV Duisburg	DEB-2	6	1	2	3	12	....	....	....	....	....
	Krefeld Pinguine	DEL	58	3	11	14	73	....	....	....	....	....

EICHELBERGER, John (IGH-kehl-buhr-guhr, JAWN) PHI.

Center. Shoots left. 6'2", 185 lbs. Born, Atlanta, GA, February 23, 1981.
(Philadelphia's 5th choice, 210th overall, in 2000 Entry Draft).

			Regular Season					Playoffs				
Season	Club	Lea	GP	G	A	TP	PIM	GP	G	A	TP	PIM
1997-98	Team USA	USDP	65	11	28	34	54	....	....	....	....	....
1998-99	Team USA	USDP	31	5	11	16	24	....	....	....	....	....
99-2000	Green Bay	USHL	49	19	50	69	58	....	....	....	....	....
2000-01	U. of Wisconsin	WCHA	25	0	5	5	2	....	....	....	....	....

ELLIOTT, Paul (EHL-lee-awt, PAWL) FLA.

Defense. Shoots left. 6'1", 216 lbs. Born, White Rock, B.C., June 2, 1980.
(Edmonton's 5th choice, 128th overall, in 1998 Entry Draft).

			Regular Season					Playoffs				
Season	Club	Lea	GP	G	A	TP	PIM	GP	G	A	TP	PIM
1995-96	Surrey Eagles	BCAHA	45	23	60	83	77	....	....	....	....	....
	Lethbridge	WHL	2	0	0	0	0	....	....	....	....	....
1996-97	Lethbridge	WHL	46	0	8	8	17	1	0	0	0	0
1997-98	Lethbridge	WHL	48	4	18	22	35	....	....	....	....	....
	Medicine Hat	WHL	24	7	9	16	12	....	....	....	....	....
1998-99	Medicine Hat	WHL	71	11	36	47	80	....	....	....	....	....
99-2000	Medicine Hat	WHL	66	15	28	43	91	....	....	....	....	....
2000-01	Kamloops Blazers	WHL	40	10	33	43	37	....	....	....	....	....
	Regina Pats	WHL	27	8	17	25	51	6	0	4	4	2

Memorial Cup All-Star Team (2001)

Traded to **Kamloops** by **Medicine Hat** with Kevin Labbe for Brett Draney, September 7, 2000. Traded to **Regina** by **Kamloops** for Shawn Belle, January 11, 2001. Signed as a free agent by **Florida**, July 3, 2001.

ELOFSSON, Jonas (EHL-uhf-suhn, YOHuhs) CHI.

Defense. Shoots left. 6'1", 180 lbs. Born, Ulricehamn, Sweden, January 31, 1979.
(Edmonton's 4th choice, 94th overall, in 1997 Entry Draft).

			Regular Season					Playoffs				
Season	Club	Lea	GP	G	A	TP	PIM	GP	G	A	TP	PIM
1995-96	Farjestads BK	Swede-Jr.	26	6	11	17	18	....	....	....	....	....
1996-97	Farjestads BK	Sweden	3	0	0	0	0	5	0	1	1	0
	Farjestads BK	EuroHL	2	1	1	2	0	....	....	....	....	....
1997-98	Farjestads BK	Sweden	29	3	2	5	14	12	0	1	1	6
	Farjestads BK	EuroHL	7	1	1	2	4	....	....	....	....	....
1998-99	Farjestads BK	Sweden	40	2	7	9	18	4	0	0	0	0
	Farjestads BK	EuroHL	5	1	0	1	4	....	....	....	....	....
99-2000	Farjestads BK	Sweden	47	3	6	9	44	4	0	0	0	6
2000-01	HV Jonkoping	Sweden	30	1	3	4	12	....	....	....	....	....
	TPS Turku	Finland	10	0	0	0	0	....	....	....	....	....

Traded to **Chicago** by **Edmonton** with Boris Mironov and Dean McAmmond for Chad Kilger, Daniel Cleary, Ethan Moreau and Christian Laflamme, March 20, 1999.

ELOMO, Teemu (eh-LOH-moh, TEE-moo) DAL.

Left wing. Shoots left. 5'11", 176 lbs. Born, Turku, Finland, January 13, 1979.
(Dallas' 5th choice, 132nd overall, in 1997 Entry Draft).

			Regular Season					Playoffs				
Season	Club	Lea	GP	G	A	TP	PIM	GP	G	A	TP	PIM
1993-94	TPS Turku-C	Finn-Jr.	34	7	25	32	56	....	....	....	....	....
1994-95	TPS Turku-C	Finn-Jr.	24	19	22	41	82	....	....	....	....	....
	TPS Turku-B	Finn-Jr.	8	5	2	7	12	2	1	0	1	0
1995-96	TPS Turku-B	Finn-Jr.	17	9	8	17	28	....	....	....	....	....
	TPS Turku	Finn-Jr.	2	0	0	0	0	....	....	....	....	....
	Kiekko-67	Finland-2	11	1	0	1	14	6	2	0	2	8
1996-97	TPS Turku	Finn-Jr.	9	6	2	8	16	....	....	....	....	....
	Kiekko-67	Finland-2	15	4	3	7	24	....	....	....	....	....
	TPS Turku	Finland	6	0	1	1	0	3	0	0	0	2
1997-98	TPS Turku	Finland	26	3	3	6	14	3	1	0	1	2
	TPS Turku	EuroHL	3	0	0	0	2	....	....	....	....	....
1998-99	TPS Turku	Finland	34	4	8	12	16	5	0	0	0	2
99-2000	TPS Turku	Finland	52	9	7	16	28	11	3	2	5	0
2000-01	TPS Turku	Finland	56	2	10	12	44	10	1	3	4	0

EMOND, Pierre-Luc (ee-MOHN, pee-AIR-LOOK) COL.

Center. Shoots left. 6', 195 lbs. Born, Valleyfield, Que., October 10, 1982.
(Colorado's 7th choice, 165th overall, in 2001 Entry Draft).

			Regular Season					Playoffs				
Season	Club	Lea	GP	G	A	TP	PIM	GP	G	A	TP	PIM
1998-99	Gatineau Intrepide	QAAA	42	7	17	24	24	....	....	....	....	....
99-2000	Drummondville	QMJHL	58	8	11	19	74	16	6	3	9	10
2000-01	Drummondville	QMJHL	62	10	36	46	110	6	2	0	2	10

ENDICOTT, Shane (ehn-DIH-kawt, SHAYN) PIT.

Center. Shoots left. 6'4", 200 lbs. Born, Saskatoon, Sask., December 21, 1981.
(Pittsburgh's 2nd choice, 52nd overall, in 2000 Entry Draft).

			Regular Season					Playoffs				
Season	Club	Lea	GP	G	A	TP	PIM	GP	G	A	TP	PIM
1997-98	Saskatoon AAA	SMHL	43	31	32	63	42	....	....	....	....	....
	Seattle T-Birds	WHL	....	....	....	....	....	5	0	0	0	0
1998-99	Seattle T-Birds	WHL	72	13	26	39	27	11	0	1	1	0
99-2000	Seattle T-Birds	WHL	70	23	32	55	62	7	1	6	7	6
2000-01	Seattle T-Birds	WHL	72	36	43	79	86	9	4	5	9	12

ENEQVIST, Johan (EHN-uh-kvist, YOH-han) MTL.

Center. Shoots left. 6', 183 lbs. Born, Nacka, Sweden, January 21, 1982.
(Montreal's 5th choice, 109th overall, in 2000 Entry Draft).

			Regular Season					Playoffs				
Season	Club	Lea	GP	G	A	TP	PIM	GP	G	A	TP	PIM
99-2000	Leksands IF-B	Swede-Jr.	5	1	1	2	28	....	....	....	....	....
	Leksands IF	Swede-Jr.	36	10	13	23	36	2	0	0	0	0
2000-01	Leksands IF	Swede-2	21	19	15	34	2	2	1	1	2	4
	Leksands IF	Sweden	2	0	0	0	0	....	....	....	....	....
	Leksands IF	Swede-Jr.	....	....	....	....	....	2	0	0	0	2

ENGELLAND, Deryk (ehn-GUHL-uhnd, DEH-rihk) N.J.

Defense. Shoots right. 6'2", 205 lbs. Born, Edmonton, Alta., April 5, 1982.
(New Jersey's 11th choice, 194th overall, in 2000 Entry Draft).

			Regular Season					Playoffs				
Season	Club	Lea	GP	G	A	TP	PIM	GP	G	A	TP	PIM
1998-99	Moose Jaw	WHL	2	0	0	0	0	....	....	....	....	....
99-2000	Moose Jaw	WHL	55	0	5	5	62	4	0	0	0	0
2000-01	Moose Jaw	WHL	65	4	11	15	157	4	0	0	0	10

ERAT, Martin (EE-rat, mahr-TIHN) NSH.

Left wing. Shoots left. 6', 195 lbs. Born, Trebic, Czech., August 28, 1981.
(Nashville's 12th choice, 191st overall, in 1999 Entry Draft).

			Regular Season					Playoffs				
Season	Club	Lea	GP	G	A	TP	PIM	GP	G	A	TP	PIM
1997-98	ZPS Zlin-Jr.	Cze-Rep	46	35	30	65	....	....	....	....	....	....
1998-99	ZPS Zlin-Jr.	Cze-Rep	35	21	23	44	....	....	....	....	....	....
	ZPS Zlin	Cze-Rep	5	0	0	0	2	....	....	....	....	....
99-2000	Saskatoon Blades	WHL	66	27	26	53	82	11	4	8	12	16
2000-01	Saskatoon Blades	WHL	31	19	35	54	48	....	....	....	....	....
	Red Deer Rebels	WHL	17	4	24	28	24	22	*15	*21	*36	32

Traded to **Red Deer** by **Saskatoon** with Darcy Robinson and Cam Ondik for Michael Garnett, Justin Wallin, Martin Vymazzi and future considerations, January 11, 2001.

ERIKSSON, Tim (AIR-ihk-suhn, TIHM) L.A.

Center. Shoots left. 5'9", 161 lbs. Born, Sodertalje, Sweden, February 5, 1982.
(Los Angeles' 7th choice, 206th overall, in 2000 Entry Draft).

			Regular Season					Playoffs				
Season	Club	Lea	GP	G	A	TP	PIM	GP	G	A	TP	PIM
1997-98	Sodertalje SK	Swede-Jr.	11	7	12	19	10	....	....	....	....	....
1998-99	Vastra Frolunda	Swede-Jr.	29	7	8	15	6	....	....	....	....	....
99-2000	Vastra Frolunda	Swede-Jr.	36	16	25	41	82	....	....	....	....	....
2000-01	Hammarby IF	Switz-Jr.	1	2	1	3	0	....	....	....	....	....
	Hammarby IF	Switz-2	38	9	22	31	10	14	2	4	6	8

ERSKINE, John (AIR-skign, JAWN) DAL.

Defense. Shoots left. 6'4", 215 lbs. Born, Kingston, Ont., June 26, 1980.
(Dallas' 1st choice, 39th overall, in 1998 Entry Draft).

			Regular Season					Playoffs				
Season	Club	Lea	GP	G	A	TP	PIM	GP	G	A	TP	PIM
1996-97	Quinte Hawks	MTJHL	48	4	16	20	241	....	....	....	....	....
1997-98	London Knights	OHL	55	0	9	9	205	16	0	5	5	25
1998-99	London Knights	OHL	57	8	12	20	208	25	5	10	15	38
99-2000	London Knights	OHL	58	12	31	43	177	....	....	....	....	....
2000-01	Utah Grizzlies	IHL	77	1	8	9	284	....	....	....	....	....

OHL First All-Star Team (2000)

ESTRADA, Kevin (eh-STRA-duh, KEH-vihn) CAR.

Right wing. Shoots left. 5'11", 185 lbs. Born, Surrey, B.C., May 28, 1982.
(Carolina's 3rd choice, 91st overall, in 2001 Entry Draft).

			Regular Season					Playoffs				
Season	Club	Lea	GP	G	A	TP	PIM	GP	G	A	TP	PIM
1997-98	Chilliwack Chiefs	BCJHL	35	1	5	6	17	....	....	....	....	....
1998-99	Chilliwack Chiefs	BCJHL	DID NOT PLAY – INJURED									
99-2000	Chilliwack Chiefs	BCJHL	45	9	20	29	29	30	6	27	33	14
2000-01	Chilliwack Chiefs	BCJHL	59	34	*84	*118	65	....	....	....	....	....

BCJHL Coastal Conference First All-Star Team (2001)

EVANS, Blake (EH-vans, BLAYK) ST.L.

Center. Shoots right. 6'1", 221 lbs. Born, Kindersley, Sask., July 2, 1980.
(Washington's 10th choice, 251st overall, in 1998 Entry Draft).

			Regular Season					Playoffs				
Season	Club	Lea	GP	G	A	TP	PIM	GP	G	A	TP	PIM
1995-96	Saskatoon	SMHL	41	15	23	38	84	....	....	....	....	....
1996-97	Spokane Chiefs	WHL	53	4	7	11	19	7	0	0	0	0
1997-98	Spokane Chiefs	WHL	16	6	5	11	29	....	....	....	....	....
	Tri-City Americans	WHL	57	13	29	42	102	....	....	....	....	....
1998-99	Tri-City Americans	WHL	72	18	29	47	131	12	0	4	4	16
99-2000	Tri-City Americans	WHL	72	27	43	70	110	4	1	0	1	6
2000-01	Tri-City Americans	WHL	40	28	31	59	70	....	....	....	....	....
	Regina Pats	WHL	27	24	19	43	50	6	6	2	8	8

WHL East Second All-Star Team (2001)

Traded to **Regina** by **Tri-City** with Jeff Feniak for Shawn Bell, Joey Bastien, Justin Lucyshyn and future considerations, January 8, 2001. Signed as a free agent by **St. Louis**, April 11, 2001.

EVANS, David (EHV-vuhns, DAY-vihd) CAR.

Center. Shoots right. 6'3", 185 lbs. Born, Albany, NY, February 17, 1980.
(Carolina's 7th choice, 231st overall, in 1999 Entry Draft).

			Regular Season					Playoffs				
Season	Club	Lea	GP	G	A	TP	PIM	GP	G	A	TP	PIM
1997-98	Capital District	X-Games	51	53	60	113	....	....	....	....	....	....
1998-99	Clarkson Knights	ECAC	33	6	10	16	6	....	....	....	....	....
99-2000	Clarkson Knights	ECAC	34	11	17	28	18	....	....	....	....	....
2000-01	Clarkson Knights	ECAC	33	12	19	31	8	....	....	....	....	....

EXELBY, Garnet (EHX-uhl-bee, GAHR-neht) **ATL.**

Defense. Shoots left. 6'1", 200 lbs. Born, Craik, Sask., August 16, 1981.
(Atlanta's 9th choice, 217th overall, in 1999 Entry Draft).

			Regular Season					Playoffs				
Season	Club	Lea	GP	G	A	TP	PIM	GP	G	A	TP	PIM
1997-98	Winnipeg Blues	MJHL	46	5	11	16	110	....	....	....	....	....
1998-99	Saskatoon Blades	WHL	61	5	3	8	91	....	....	....	....	....
99-2000	Saskatoon Blades	WHL	63	1	8	9	79	11	0	2	2	21
2000-01	Saskatoon Blades	WHL	43	5	10	15	110	....	....	....	....	....
	Regina Pats	WHL	22	2	8	10	51	6	0	2	2	2

Traded to **Regina** by **Saskatoon** for Scott Balan and future considerations, January 15, 2001.

FABUS, Peter (fah-BUSH, PEE-tuhr) **PHX.**

Center. Shoots left. 6'1", 191 lbs. Born, Ilava, Czech., July 15, 1979.
(Phoenix's 8th choice, 281st overall, in 2000 Entry Draft).

			Regular Season					Playoffs				
Season	Club	Lea	GP	G	A	TP	PIM	GP	G	A	TP	PIM
1997-98	HK Dubnica	Slovak-Jr.	28	9	14	23	96	....	....	....	....	....
	HK Dubnica	Slovak-2	34	4	4	8	24	....	....	....	....	....
1998-99	HK Zilina	Slovak-2	26	7	8	15	24	....	....	....	....	....
99-2000	Dukla Trencin	Slovakia	54	20	11	31	34	5	1	1	2	0
2000-01	Dukla Trencin	Slovakia	52	31	22	53	94	14	4	6	10	60

FADRNY, Jan (FAHD-uhr-nee, YAN) **PIT.**

Center. Shoots right. 6', 182 lbs. Born, Brno, Czech., June 14, 1980.
(Pittsburgh's 6th choice, 169th overall, in 1998 Entry Draft).

			Regular Season					Playoffs				
Season	Club	Lea	GP	G	A	TP	PIM	GP	G	A	TP	PIM
1995-96	Kometa Brno-Jr.	Cze-Rep	36	22	15	37	26	....	....	....	....	....
1996-97	HC Olomouc-Jr.	Cze-Rep	38	16	24	40	32	....	....	....	....	....
1997-98	Slavia Praha-Jr.	Cze-Rep	14	7	4	11	12	....	....	....	....	....
	Slavia Praha	Cze-Rep	18	1	1	2	2	3	0	0	0	4
1998-99	Brandon	WHL	45	4	17	21	36	5	1	2	3	4
99-2000	Brandon	WHL	55	26	25	51	56	....	....	....	....	....
2000-01	Brandon	WHL	2	1	1	2	6	....	....	....	....	....
	Kelowna Rockets	WHL	56	32	45	77	58	6	3	4	7	8

Traded to **Kelowna** by **Brandon** with Bart Rushmer for Nolan Yonkman and Kelowna's 6th round choice (Jeff Wollin) in 2001 WHL Bantam Draft, October 12, 2000.

FAHEY, Brian (FAY-hee, BRIGH-uhn) **COL.**

Defense. Shoots right. 6', 200 lbs. Born, Des Plaines, IL, March 2, 1981.
(Colorado's 7th choice, 119th overall, in 2000 Entry Draft).

			Regular Season					Playoffs				
Season	Club	Lea	GP	G	A	TP	PIM	GP	G	A	TP	PIM
1997-98	Team USA	USDP	68	7	21	28	57	....	....	....	....	....
1998-99	Team USA	USDP	52	9	9	18	34	....	....	....	....	....
99-2000	U. of Wisconsin	WCHA	41	6	11	17	42	....	....	....	....	....
2000-01	U. of Wisconsin	WCHA	38	1	5	6	16	....	....	....	....	....

WCHA All-Rookie Team (2000)

FAHEY, Jim (FA-hee, JIHM) **S.J.**

Defense. Shoots right. 6', 215 lbs. Born, Boston, MA, May 11, 1979.
(San Jose's 9th choice, 212th overall, in 1998 Entry Draft).

			Regular Season					Playoffs				
Season	Club	Lea	GP	G	A	TP	PIM	GP	G	A	TP	PIM
1997-98	Catholic Knights	Hi-School	24	12	32	44	28	....	....	....	....	....
1998-99	Northeastern	H-East	32	5	13	18	34	....	....	....	....	....
99-2000	Northeastern	H-East	36	3	17	20	62	....	....	....	....	....
2000-01	Northeastern	H-East	36	4	23	27	48	....	....	....	....	....

Hockey East Second All-Star Team (2001)

FARRELL, Michael (FAHR-ehl, MIHK-ehl) **WSH.**

Right wing. Shoots right. 6'1", 205 lbs. Born, Edina, MN, October 20, 1978.
(Washington's 9th choice, 220th overall, in 1998 Entry Draft).

			Regular Season					Playoffs				
Season	Club	Lea	GP	G	A	TP	PIM	GP	G	A	TP	PIM
1997-98	Providence	H-East	33	5	8	13	32	....	....	....	....	....
1998-99	Providence	H-East	29	3	12	15	51	....	....	....	....	....
99-2000	Providence	H-East	36	3	6	9	71	....	....	....	....	....
	Portland Pirates	AHL	7	2	0	2	0	4	0	1	1	0
2000-01	Portland Pirates	AHL	79	6	18	24	61	3	0	2	2	2

FAST, Brad (FAST, BRAD) **CAR.**

Defense. Shoots left. 6', 185 lbs. Born, Fort St. John, B.C., February 21, 1980.
(Carolina's 2nd choice, 84th overall, in 1999 Entry Draft).

			Regular Season					Playoffs				
Season	Club	Lea	GP	G	A	TP	PIM	GP	G	A	TP	PIM
1994-95	Fort St. John	BCAHA	40	9	26	35	40	....	....	....	....	....
1995-96	Fort St. John	BCAHA	60	53	52	105	70	....	....	....	....	....
1996-97	Prince George	BCJHL	49	3	7	10	19	....	....	....	....	....
1997-98	Prince George	BCJHL	59	10	33	43	22	....	....	....	....	....
1998-99	Prince George	BCJHL	59	27	46	73	....	....	....	....	....	....
99-2000	Michigan State	CCHA	42	5	9	14	20	....	....	....	....	....
2000-01	Michigan State	CCHA	42	4	24	28	16	....	....	....	....	....

FATA, Drew (FA-tuh, DROO) **PIT.**

Defense. Shoots left. 6'1", 211 lbs. Born, Sault Ste. Marie, Ont., July 28, 1983.
(Pittsburgh's 3rd choice, 86th overall, in 2001 Entry Draft).

			Regular Season					Playoffs				
Season	Club	Lea	GP	G	A	TP	PIM	GP	G	A	TP	PIM
99-2000	St. Michael's B's	OPJHL	49	9	18	27	144	....	....	....	....	....
2000-01	St. Michael's	OHL	58	5	15	20	134	18	1	3	4	26

OHL Second All-Rookie Team (2001)

FEDOROV, Fedor (FEH-duh-rahf, feh-DUHR) **VAN.**

Left wing. Shoots left. 6'3", 202 lbs. Born, Appatity, USSR, June 11, 1981.
(Vancouver's 2nd choice, 66th overall, in 2001 Entry Draft).

			Regular Season					Playoffs				
Season	Club	Lea	GP	G	A	TP	PIM	GP	G	A	TP	PIM
1997-98	Detroit Caesars	MNHL	13	3	7	10	18	....	....	....	....	....
1998-99	Port Huron	UHL	42	2	5	7	20	....	....	....	....	....
99-2000	Windsor Spitfires	OHL	60	7	10	17	115	12	1	0	1	4
2000-01	Sudbury Wolves	OHL	67	33	45	78	88	12	4	6	10	36

• Re-entered NHL Entry Draft. Originally Tampa Bay's 7th choice, 182nd overall, in 1999 Entry Draft.

Traded to **Sudbury** by **Windsor** for future considerations, September 16, 2001.

FEDOROV, Yevgeny (FEH-duh-rahf, yehv-GEH-nee) **L.A.**

Center. Shoots left. 5'10", 187 lbs. Born, Sverdlovsk, USSR, November 11, 1980.
(Los Angeles' 6th choice, 201st overall, in 2000 Entry Draft).

			Regular Season					Playoffs				
Season	Club	Lea	GP	G	A	TP	PIM	GP	G	A	TP	PIM
1997-98	Krylja Sovetov-2	Russia-3	20	1	6	7	48	....	....	....	....	....
	Krylja Sovetov	Russia	32	1	0	1	12	....	....	....	....	....
1998-99	Krylja Sovetov	Russia	52	5	3	8	61	....	....	....	....	....
99-2000	Molot-Perm	Russia	37	5	5	10	20	3	0	1	1	4
2000-01	Molot-Perm	Russia	43	9	9	18	18	....	....	....	....	....

FERGUSON, Troy (fuhr-GUH-suhn, TROI) **CAR.**

Right wing. Shoots right. 5'9", 165 lbs. Born, Calgary, Alta., September 30, 1980.
(Carolina's 7th choice, 276th overall, in 2000 Entry Draft).

			Regular Season					Playoffs				
Season	Club	Lea	GP	G	A	TP	PIM	GP	G	A	TP	PIM
1996-97	Kitchener	OJHL-B	47	14	15	29	16	....	....	....	....	....
1997-98	Team USA	USDP	54	11	9	20	14	....	....	....	....	....
1998-99	Team USA	USDP-17	24	3	10	13	14	....	....	....	....	....
	Team USA	USDP	29	4	4	8	20	....	....	....	....	....
99-2000	Michigan State	CCHA	42	5	7	12	10	....	....	....	....	....
2000-01	Michigan State	CCHA	41	4	10	14	12	....	....	....	....	....

FIBIGER, Jesse (feh-BEH-gehr, JEH-see) **S.J.**

Defense. Shoots left. 6'3", 210 lbs. Born, Victoria, B.C., April 4, 1978.
(Anaheim's 5th choice, 178th overall, in 1998 Entry Draft).

			Regular Season					Playoffs				
Season	Club	Lea	GP	G	A	TP	PIM	GP	G	A	TP	PIM
1996-97	Victoria Salsa	BCJHL	53	6	18	24	88	....	....	....	....	....
1997-98	Minnesota-Duluth	WCHA	40	3	6	9	82	....	....	....	....	....
1998-99	Minnesota-Duluth	WCHA	36	4	16	20	61	....	....	....	....	....
99-2000	Minnesota-Duluth	WCHA	37	4	6	10	83	....	....	....	....	....
2000-01	Minnesota-Duluth	WCHA	37	0	8	8	56	....	....	....	....	....

Signed as a free agent by **San Jose**, August 15, 2001.

FILIPOWICZ, Jayme (fihl-ih-POW-its, JAY-mee)

Defense. Shoots left. 6'2", 215 lbs. Born, Arlington Heights, IL, June 15, 1976.

			Regular Season					Playoffs				
Season	Club	Lea	GP	G	A	TP	PIM	GP	G	A	TP	PIM
1994/96	Dubuque Saints	USHL	127	18	55	73	....	....	....	....	....	....
1996-97	New Hampshire	H-East	35	3	16	19	43	....	....	....	....	....
1997-98	New Hampshire	H-East	38	3	28	31	47	....	....	....	....	....
1998-99	New Hampshire	H-East	41	8	30	38	56	....	....	....	....	....
99-2000	Milwaukee	IHL	76	9	23	32	118	3	0	1	1	0
2000-01	Milwaukee	IHL	68	0	13	13	101	2	0	0	0	2

• Statistics for USHL's Dubuque Fighting Saints are career totals for 1994-1996 seasons. • Hockey East First All-Star Team (1999) • NCAA East Second All-American Team (1999) • NCAA Championship All-Tournament Team (1999)

Signed as a free agent by **Nashville**, June 17, 1999.

FINGER, Jeff (FIHN-guhr, JEHF) **COL.**

Defense. Shoots left. 6'1", 195 lbs. Born, Hancock, MI, December 18, 1979.
(Colorado's 11th choice, 240th overall, in 1999 Entry Draft).

			Regular Season					Playoffs				
Season	Club	Lea	GP	G	A	TP	PIM	GP	G	A	TP	PIM
1997-98	Green Bay	USHL	51	5	9	14	208	4	0	0	0	18
1998-99	Green Bay	USHL	54	11	28	39	199	6	0	3	3	14
99-2000	Green Bay	USHL	55	13	35	48	15	5	1	6	7	22
2000-01	St. Cloud State	WCHA	41	4	5	9	84	....	....	....	....	....

FINNSTROM, Johan (FIHN-struhm, YOH-hahn) **CGY.**

Defense. Shoots left. 6'3", 205 lbs. Born, Broby, Sweden, March 27, 1976.
(Calgary's 5th choice, 97th overall, in 1994 Entry Draft).

			Regular Season					Playoffs				
Season	Club	Lea	GP	G	A	TP	PIM	GP	G	A	TP	PIM
1993-94	Rogle Angelholm	Sweden	7	1	1	2	2	....	....	....	....	....
1994-95	Rogle Angelholm	Sweden	19	0	0	0	10	....	....	....	....	....
1995-96	Rogle Angelholm	Sweden	18	0	0	0	10	....	....	....	....	....
1996-97	Rogle Angelholm	Swede-2	31	1	5	6	59	....	....	....	....	....
1997-98	Lulea HF	Sweden	45	0	1	1	17	3	0	0	0	0
	Lulea HF	EuroHL	6	0	0	0	4	....	....	....	....	....
1998-99	Lulea HF	Sweden	49	1	8	9	63	9	0	4	4	12
99-2000	Lulea HF	Sweden	46	1	4	5	71	9	0	0	0	4
2000-01	Lulea HF	Sweden	46	1	6	7	40	12	0	2	2	12

FITZGERALD, Randy (FIHTZ-jer-awld, RAN-dee) **MIN.**

Left wing. Shoots left. 5'11", 174 lbs. Born, Toronto, Ont., September 5, 1979.
(Carolina's 8th choice, 199th overall, in 1997 Entry Draft).

			Regular Season					Playoffs				
Season	Club	Lea	GP	G	A	TP	PIM	GP	G	A	TP	PIM
1995-96	Markham Waxers	OPJHL	46	17	17	34	79	....	....	....	....	....
1996-97	Detroit Whalers	OHL	65	12	18	30	123	5	0	1	1	13
1997-98	Plymouth Whalers	OHL	54	11	24	35	104	15	6	3	9	46
1998-99	Plymouth Whalers	OHL	64	15	34	49	144	11	3	7	10	16
99-2000	Plymouth Whalers	OHL	50	18	24	42	89	23	13	10	23	47
2000-01	Jackson Bandits	ECHL	21	1	0	1	23	....	....	....	....	....

Signed as a free agent by **Minnesota**, June 14, 2000. • Missed majority of 2000-01 recovering from wrist injury suffered in training camp, September 29, 2000.

FLACHE, Paul (FLAK, PAWL) **EDM.**

Defense. Shoots right. 6'5", 195 lbs. Born, Toronto, Ont., March 4, 1982.
(Edmonton's 5th choice, 152nd overall, in 2000 Entry Draft).

			Regular Season					Playoffs				
Season	Club	Lea	GP	G	A	TP	PIM	GP	G	A	TP	PIM
1998-99	Cobourg Cougars	OPJHL	41	1	6	7	50	....	....	....	....	....
99-2000	Brampton	OHL	54	1	0	1	59	6	0	0	0	8
2000-01	Brampton	OHL	68	8	16	24	100	9	1	1	2	18

FLACHE, Peter (FLACH, PEE-tuhr) **CHI.**

Center. Shoots left. 6'5", 190 lbs. Born, Toronto, Ont., March 4, 1982.
(Chicago's 13th choice, 262nd overall, in 2000 Entry Draft).

			Regular Season					Playoffs				
Season	Club	Lea	GP	G	A	TP	PIM	GP	G	A	TP	PIM
1998-99	Cobourg Cougars	OPJHL	45	4	5	9	30	....	....	....	....	....
99-2000	Guelph Storm	OHL	56	3	6	9	40	....	....	....	....	....
2000-01	Guelph Storm	OHL	53	3	3	6	32	4	1	0	1	0

FOCHT, Dan (FOHKT, DAN) **PHX.**

Defense. Shoots left. 6'6", 234 lbs. Born, Regina, Sask., December 31, 1977.
(Phoenix's 1st choice, 11th overall, in 1996 Entry Draft).

			Regular Season					Playoffs				
Season	Club	Lea	GP	G	A	TP	PIM	GP	G	A	TP	PIM
1994-95	Saskatoon Blaze	SMHL	33	6	12	18	98					
1995-96	Tri-City Americans	WHL	63	6	12	18	161	11	1	1	2	23
1996-97	Tri-City Americans	WHL	28	0	5	5	92					
	Regina Pats	WHL	22	2	2	4	59	5	0	2	2	8
	Springfield	AHL	1	0	0	0	2					
1997-98	Springfield	AHL	61	2	5	7	125	3	0	0	0	4
1998-99	Mississippi	ECHL	2	0	0	0	6					
	Springfield	AHL	30	0	2	2	58	3	1	0	1	10
99-2000	Jokerit Helsinki	Finland	2	0	0	0	0					
	Mississippi	ECHL	4	0	1	1	0					
	Springfield	AHL	44	2	9	11	86	5	0	1	1	2
2000-01	Springfield	AHL	69	0	6	6	156					

FOLEY, Patrick (FOH-lee, PAT-rihk) **PIT.**

Left wing. Shoots left. 6', 216 lbs. Born, Boston, MA, January 24, 1981.
(Pittsburgh's 6th choice, 185th overall, in 2000 Entry Draft).

			Regular Season					Playoffs				
Season	Club	Lea	GP	G	A	TP	PIM	GP	G	A	TP	PIM
1996-97	St. Sebastian's	Hi-School	23	11	12	23						
1997-98	St. Sebastian's	Hi-School	25	17	24	41						
	Team USA	USDP	8	3	3	6	8					
1998-99	Team USA	USDP-17	52	7	9	16	146					
99-2000	New Hampshire	H-East	30	3	7	10	61					
2000-01	New Hampshire	H-East	DID NOT PLAY – INJURED									

• Missed entire 2000-01 season recovering from head injury originally suffered in game vs. U. Mass-Lowell (H-East), February 4, 2000.

FORBES, Ian (FOHRBZ, EE-an) **PHI.**

Defense. Shoots left. 6'6", 215 lbs. Born, Brampton, Ont., August 2, 1980.
(Philadelphia's 3rd choice, 51st overall, in 1998 Entry Draft).

			Regular Season					Playoffs				
Season	Club	Lea	GP	G	A	TP	PIM	GP	G	A	TP	PIM
1996-97	Mississauga Reps	MTHL	39	10	32	42	178					
1997-98	Guelph Fire	OJHL-B	3	0	1	1	19					
	Guelph Storm	OHL	61	2	3	5	164	12	0	0	0	16
1998-99	Guelph Storm	OHL	60	1	8	9	182	5	0	1	1	8
99-2000	Guelph Storm	OHL	62	2	7	9	143	6	0	0	0	11
2000-01	Trenton Titans	ECHL	33	0	2	2	133					

FORREST, J.D. (FOH-rehst, JAY-DEE) **CAR.**

Defense. Shoots left. 5'8", 167 lbs. Born, Westchester, NY, April 15, 1981.
(Carolina's 5th choice, 181st overall, in 2000 Entry Draft).

			Regular Season					Playoffs				
Season	Club	Lea	GP	G	A	TP	PIM	GP	G	A	TP	PIM
1997-98	Team USA	USDP	74	7	26	33	41					
1998-99	Team USA	USDP-17	2	1	0	1	4					
	Team USA	USDP	48	5	21	26	34					
99-2000	Team USA	USDP-17	49	6	28	34	36					
	Team USA	USDP	8	0	0	0	2					
2000-01	Boston College	H-East	38	6	17	23	40					

NAJHL All-League First All-Star Team (2000)

FORSANDER, Johan (fohr-SAHN-duhr, YOH-hahn) **DET.**

Left wing. Shoots left. 6'1", 174 lbs. Born, Jonkoping, Sweden, April 28, 1978.
(Detroit's 3rd choice, 108th overall, in 1996 Entry Draft).

			Regular Season					Playoffs				
Season	Club	Lea	GP	G	A	TP	PIM	GP	G	A	TP	PIM
1994-95	HV Jonkoping	Swede-Jr.	25	2	2	4	6					
1995-96	HV Jonkoping	Swede-Jr.	27	15	8	23	12					
	HV Jonkoping	Sweden	6	0	0	0	0	3	0	0	0	2
1996-97	HV Jonkoping	Sweden	44	3	2	5	6	5	0	0	0	0
1997-98	HV Jonkoping	Sweden	46	3	2	5	12	5	0	0	0	0
1998-99	HV Jonkoping	Sweden	48	5	4	9	6					
99-2000	HV Jonkoping	Sweden	48	9	9	18	6	6	0	0	0	4
2000-01	HV Jonkoping	Sweden	DID NOT PLAY – INJURED									

• Missed entire 2000-01 season recovering from foot injury suffered in training camp, September 2, 2000.

FORSTER, Beat (FOHRS-tuhr, BEE-at) **PHX.**

Defense. Shoots left. 6'1", 209 lbs. Born, Herisau, Switz., February 2, 1983.
(Phoenix's 4th choice, 78th overall, in 2001 Entry Draft).

			Regular Season					Playoffs				
Season	Club	Lea	GP	G	A	TP	PIM	GP	G	A	TP	PIM
99-2000	HC Davos	Switz-Jr.	34	4	15	19	40	6	1	0	1	6
2000-01	HC Davos	Switz-Jr.	27	6	7	13	44					
	HC Davos	Switz.	7	0	0	0	6	3	0	0	0	2

FORSTER, Nathan (FOHRS-tuhr, NAY-than) **WSH.**

Defense. Shoots right. 6'1", 195 lbs. Born, Vancouver, B.C., July 3, 1980.
(Washington's 7th choice, 179th overall, in 1998 Entry Draft).

			Regular Season					Playoffs				
Season	Club	Lea	GP	G	A	TP	PIM	GP	G	A	TP	PIM
1995-96	Victoria Lions	BCAHA	49	25	48	73	122					
1996-97	Seattle T-Birds	WHL	22	1	2	3	39	4	0	0	0	0
1997-98	Seattle T-Birds	WHL	68	1	12	13	153	5	0	1	1	8
1998-99	Seattle T-Birds	WHL	65	5	17	22	153	10	0	2	2	26
99-2000	Seattle T-Birds	WHL	51	9	28	37	104	7	1	4	5	30
2000-01	Richmond	ECHL	30	2	7	9	55					
	Portland Pirates	AHL	27	0	2	2	25	3	0	0	0	0

FORTIER, Francois (FOHR-tyay, fran-SWUH) **NYR**

Left wing. Shoots left. 5'11", 194 lbs. Born, Beauport, Que., June 13, 1979.

			Regular Season					Playoffs				
Season	Club	Lea	GP	G	A	TP	PIM	GP	G	A	TP	PIM
1995-96	Ste-Foy Governors	QAAA	41	16	17	33	36					
1996-97	Sherbrooke	QMJHL	62	21	16	37	74	3	0	2	2	2
1997-98	Sherbrooke	QMJHL	70	36	52	88	42					
1998-99	Sherbrooke	QMJHL	48	36	40	76	8	13	6	9	15	4
	Hartford	AHL	1	0	0	0	0					
99-2000	Hartford	AHL	63	6	9	15	14					
2000-01	Hartford	AHL	28	2	6	8	8					
	Charlotte	ECHL	7	1	5	6	15					
	Quebec Citadelles	AHL	28	5	5	10	17					

Signed as a free agent by **NY Rangers**, October 5, 1998.

FORTIN, Jean-Francois (fohr-TEHN, ZHAWN-fran-SWUH) **WSH.**

Defense. Shoots right. 6'2", 200 lbs. Born, Laval, Que., March 15, 1979.
(Washington's 2nd choice, 35th overall, in 1997 Entry Draft).

			Regular Season					Playoffs				
Season	Club	Lea	GP	G	A	TP	PIM	GP	G	A	TP	PIM
1993-94	Laval-Laurentide	QAHA	31	8	20	28	32					
1994-95	Abitibi Foresters	QAAA	44	2	14	16	34	10	2	2	4	
1995-96	Sherbrooke	QMJHL	69	7	15	22	40	7	2	6	8	2
1996-97	Sherbrooke	QMJHL	59	7	30	37	89	2	0	1	1	14
1997-98	Sherbrooke	QMJHL	55	12	25	37	37					
1998-99	Sherbrooke	QMJHL	64	17	33	50	78	12	5	13	18	20
99-2000	Portland Pirates	AHL	43	3	5	8	44	2	0	0	0	0
	Hampton Roads	ECHL	7	0	2	2	0					
2000-01	Portland Pirates	AHL	32	1	7	8	22	1	0	0	0	0
	Richmond	ECHL	15	0	4	4	2					

FOSTER, Adrian (FAW-stuhr, AY-dree-uhn) **N.J.**

Left wing. Shoots left. 6'1", 200 lbs. Born, Lethbridge, Alta., January 15, 1982.
(New Jersey's 1st choice, 28th overall, in 2001 Entry Draft).

			Regular Season					Playoffs				
Season	Club	Lea	GP	G	A	TP	PIM	GP	G	A	TP	PIM
1997-98	Calgary Buffaloes	AMHL	36	26	54	80	50	9	3	14	17	18
1998-99	Calgary Canucks	AJHL	18	15	17	32	18					
99-2000	Saskatoon Blades	WHL	7	1	2	3	6					
2000-01	Saskatoon Blades	WHL	5	0	5	5	4					

• Missed majority of 1998-99 season recovering from ankle injury. • Missed majority of 1999-2000 and 2000-01 seasons recovering from abdominal injury, October, 1999.

FOSTER, Kurtis (FAW-stuhr, KUHR-this) **CGY.**

Defense. Shoots right. 6'5", 205 lbs. Born, Carp, Ont., November 24, 1981.
(Calgary's 2nd choice, 40th overall, in 2000 Entry Draft).

			Regular Season					Playoffs				
Season	Club	Lea	GP	G	A	TP	PIM	GP	G	A	TP	PIM
1997-98	Ottawa Valley	OMHA	36	7	18	25	88					
	Peterborough	OHL	39	1	1	2	45	4	0	0	0	2
1998-99	Peterborough	OHL	54	2	13	15	59	5	0	0	0	6
99-2000	Peterborough	OHL	68	6	18	24	116	5	1	2	3	4
2000-01	Peterborough	OHL	62	17	24	41	78	7	1	1	2	10

FRANCZ, Robert (FRANZ, RAW-behrt) **PHX.**

Left wing. Shoots left. 6'2", 214 lbs. Born, Bad Muskau, East Germany, March 30, 1978.
(Phoenix's 4th choice, 151st overall, in 1997 Entry Draft).

			Regular Season					Playoffs				
Season	Club	Lea	GP	G	A	TP	PIM	GP	G	A	TP	PIM
1995-96	Augsburger EV	DEL-Jr.	7	1	1	2	62					
	Augsburger EV	DEL	36	0	1	1	43	6	0	0	0	0
1996-97	Peterborough	OHL	60	9	21	30	149	8	1	1	2	17
1997-98	Peterborough	OHL	60	24	27	51	135	4	1	0	1	10
1998-99	Peterborough	OHL	65	25	32	57	171	5	0	2	2	12
	Springfield	AHL	2	1	0	1	4	1	0	0	0	0
99-2000	Springfield	AHL	36	0	3	3	89	2	0	0	0	0
	Mississippi Wolves	ECHL	16	7	4	11	56					
2000-01	Springfield	AHL	24	2	1	3	26					
	Mississippi Wolves	ECHL	32	9	15	24	56					

FRIED, Robert (FREED, RAW-buhrt) **FLA.**

Right wing. Shoots right. 6'2", 210 lbs. Born, Philadelphia, PA, March 8, 1981.
(Florida's 2nd choice, 77th overall, in 2000 Entry Draft).

			Regular Season					Playoffs				
Season	Club	Lea	GP	G	A	TP	PIM	GP	G	A	TP	PIM
1998-99	Deerfield Prep	Hi-School	24	13	20	33	28					
99-2000	Deerfield Prep	Hi-School	26	25	20	45	35					
2000-01	Harvard University	ECAC	30	4	1	5	22					

FROGREN, Jonas (FREW-grehn, YOH-nuhs) **CGY.**

Defense. Shoots left. 6'1", 190 lbs. Born, Falun, Sweden, August 28, 1980.
(Calgary's 8th choice, 206th overall, in 1998 Entry Draft).

			Regular Season					Playoffs				
Season	Club	Lea	GP	G	A	TP	PIM	GP	G	A	TP	PIM
1996-97	Farjestads BK	Swede-Jr.	20	2	7	9	4					
1997-98	Farjestads BK	Swede-Jr.	28	5	6	11	12	2	1	0	1	0
1998-99	Farjestads BK	Swede-Jr.	14	1	5	6	12					
	Farjestads BK	Sweden	22	0	0	0	2					
99-2000	Bofors IF	Swede-2	43	2	7	9	40					
2000-01	Farjestads BK	Sweden	49	3	0	3	10	16	0	0	0	4

FROLOV, Alexander (froh-LAHF, al-ehx-AN-duhr) **L.A.**

Left wing. Shoots right. 6'4", 191 lbs. Born, Moscow, USSR, June 19, 1982.
(Los Angeles' 1st choice, 20th overall, in 2000 Entry Draft).

			Regular Season					Playoffs				
Season	Club	Lea	GP	G	A	TP	PIM	GP	G	A	TP	PIM
1998-99	Krylja Sovetov	Russia	1	0	0	0	0					
99-2000	HC Yaroslavl-2	Russia-3	36	27	13	40	30					
2000-01	Krylja Sovetov	Russia-2	44	20	19	39	8					

FRYLEN, Edvin (FREE-ew-lihn, EHD-vihn) **ST.L.**

Defense. Shoots left. 6'3", 217 lbs. Born, Jarfalla, Sweden, December 23, 1975.
(St. Louis' 3rd choice, 120th overall, in 1994 Entry Draft).

			Regular Season					Playoffs				
Season	Club	Lea	GP	G	A	TP	PIM	GP	G	A	TP	PIM
1990-91	Vasteras IK	Sweden	16	5	3	8	16					
1991-92	Vasteras IK	Sweden	2	0	0	0	0					
1992-93	Vasteras IK	Sweden	29	0	2	2	14	3	0	0	0	0
1993-94	Vasteras IK	Sweden	32	1	0	1	26					
1994-95	Ahvesta IK	Swede-2	9	4	2	6	20					
	Vasteras IK	Sweden	25	2	1	3	14	4	0	0	0	4
1995-96	Vasteras IK	Sweden	39	8	5	13	16					
1996-97	Vasteras IK	Sweden	47	8	3	11	32					
1997-98	Vasteras IK	Sweden	46	4	7	11	36					
1998-99	Vasteras IK	Sweden	50	6	20	26	36					
99-2000	Linkopings HC	Sweden	45	10	6	16	30					
2000-01	Djurgardens IF	Sweden	47	7	6	13	34	16	1	2	3	16

FUSSEY, Owen (FOO-see, OH-when) WSH.

Right wing. Shoots left. 6', 185 lbs. Born, Winnipeg, Man., April 2, 1983.
(Washington's 2nd choice, 90th overall, in 2001 Entry Draft).

			Regular Season					Playoffs				
Season	Club	Lea	GP	G	A	TP	PIM	GP	G	A	TP	PIM
1998-99	Winnipeg Warriors	MMHL	40	38	33	71	24	....	....	....	....	....
99-2000	Calgary Hitmen	WHL	51	7	6	13	35	12	3	4	7	2
2000-01	Calgary Hitmen	WHL	48	15	10	25	33	12	2	1	3	6

GAFFANEY, Brian (GAF-an-nee, BRIGH-uhn) PIT.

Defense. Shoots left. 6'5", 205 lbs. Born, Alexandria, MN, October 4, 1977.
(Pittsburgh's 2nd choice, 44th overall, in 1997 Entry Draft).

			Regular Season					Playoffs				
Season	Club	Lea	GP	G	A	TP	PIM	GP	G	A	TP	PIM
1995-96	Alexandria High	Hi-School	27	10	29	39	28	....	....	....	....	....
1996-97	North Iowa	USHL	48	8	13	21	49	11	0	0	0	61
1997-98	St. Cloud State	WCHA	26	0	2	2	37	....	....	....	....	....
1998-99	St. Cloud State	WCHA	37	3	5	8	45	....	....	....	....	....
99-2000	St. Cloud State	WCHA	38	1	4	5	51	....	....	....	....	....
2000-01	St. Cloud State	WCHA	32	2	1	3	44	....	....	....	....	....
	Wilkes-Barre	AHL	2	0	1	1	0	1	0	0	0	0

GAGNON, Jonathan (GAN-YAW, JAWN-ah-thuhn) TOR.

Center. Shoots left. 6'1", 190 lbs. Born, Montreal, Que., May 20, 1980.
(Toronto's 7th choice, 181st overall, in 1998 Entry Draft).

			Regular Season					Playoffs				
Season	Club	Lea	GP	G	A	TP	PIM	GP	G	A	TP	PIM
1996-97	Val-d'Or Foreurs	QMJHL	65	5	15	20	35	13	1	0	1	2
1997-98	Val-d'Or Foreurs	QMJHL	40	9	19	28	54	....	....	....	....	....
	Cape Breton	QMJHL	29	6	7	13	25	4	2	3	5	12
1998-99	Cape Breton	QMJHL	68	27	37	64	39	5	2	4	6	2
99-2000	Rouyn-Noranda	QMJHL	10	0	1	1	14	....	....	....	....	....
	Cape Breton	QMJHL	26	8	12	20	25	....	....	....	....	....
	Halifax	QMJHL	19	11	4	15	37	....	....	....	....	....
	Drummondville	QMJHL	27	16	21	37	38	14	4	12	16	8
2000-01	Pensacola	ECHL	70	24	15	39	52	....	....	....	....	....

GAJIC, Milan (GAY-jihk, MEE-lan) ATL.

Center. Shoots right. 5'11", 182 lbs. Born, Vancouver, B.C., June 1, 1981.
(Atlanta's 4th choice, 112th overall, in 2001 Entry Draft).

			Regular Season					Playoffs				
Season	Club	Lea	GP	G	A	TP	PIM	GP	G	A	TP	PIM
1997-98	Merritt	BCJHL	51	6	14	20	....	....	....	....	....	....
1998-99	Burnaby Bulldogs	BCJHL	56	29	30	59	41	....	....	....	....	....
99-2000	Burnaby Bulldogs	BCJHL	56	34	47	81	42	....	....	....	....	....
2000-01	Burnaby Bulldogs	BCJHL	50	46	52	98	84	....	....	....	....	....

GAMACHE, Simon (ga-MOHSH, see-MOHN) ATL.

Center. Shoots left. 5'10", 185 lbs. Born, Montreal, Que., January 3, 1981.
(Atlanta's 14th choice, 290th overall, in 2000 Entry Draft).

			Regular Season					Playoffs				
Season	Club	Lea	GP	G	A	TP	PIM	GP	G	A	TP	PIM
1997-98	Levis Elites	QAAA	42	28	26	54	....	4	1	1	2	....
1998-99	Val d'Or Foreurs	QMJHL	70	19	43	62	54	6	1	2	3	4
99-2000	Val d'Or Foreurs	QMJHL	72	64	79	143	74	....	....	....	....	....
2000-01	Val-d'Or Foreurs	QMJHL	72	*74	*110	*184	70	21	*22	*35	*57	18

Canadian Major Junior Second All-Star Team (2000) • QMJHL First All-Star Team (2001) • Won Michel Briere Trophy (MVP - QMJHL) (2001) • Canadian Major Junior First All-Star Team (2001) • Canadian Major Junior Player of the Year (2001) • Sheetrock CHL Top Scorer Award (2001) • Memorial Cup All-Star Team (2001) • Won Ed Chynoweth Trophy (Memorial Cup Tournament Leading Scorer) (2001)

GARDINER, Peter (GAHR-din-uhr, PEE-tuhr) MIN.

Right wing. Shoots right. 6'5", 220 lbs. Born, Toronto, Ont., September 29, 1977.
(Chicago's 6th choice, 120th overall, in 1997 Entry Draft).

			Regular Season					Playoffs				
Season	Club	Lea	GP	G	A	TP	PIM	GP	G	A	TP	PIM
1993-94	Wexford Raiders	OPJHL	2	1	1	2	0	....	....	....	....	....
1994-95	Wexford Raiders	OPJHL	44	7	15	22	34	....	....	....	....	....
1995-96	Wexford Raiders	OPJHL	44	18	28	46	113	....	....	....	....	....
1996-97	RPI Engineers	ECAC	36	10	21	31	47	....	....	....	....	....
1997-98	RPI Engineers	ECAC	35	10	9	19	52	....	....	....	....	....
1998-99	RPI Engineers	ECAC	37	17	21	38	76	....	....	....	....	....
99-2000	RPI Engineers	ECAC	36	11	13	24	62	....	....	....	....	....
2000-01	Jackson Bandits	ECHL	5	0	0	0	2	....	....	....	....	....
	Roanoke Express	ECHL	58	15	19	34	130	....	....	....	....	....

Signed as a free agent by **Minnesota**, June 7, 2000.

GAUSTAD, Paul (GAW-stad, PAWL) BUF.

Center/Left wing. Shoots left. 6'3", 180 lbs. Born, Fargo, ND, February 3, 1982.
(Buffalo's 6th choice, 220th overall, in 2000 Entry Draft).

			Regular Season					Playoffs				
Season	Club	Lea	GP	G	A	TP	PIM	GP	G	A	TP	PIM
1998-99	Portland Hawks	USAHA	45	47	53	100	81	....	....	....	....	....
99-2000	Portland	WHL	56	6	8	14	110	....	....	....	....	....
2000-01	Portland	WHL	70	11	30	41	168	16	10	6	16	59

GAUTHIER, Jonathan (GOH-tyay, JAWN-ah-thuhn)

Defense. Shoots left. 6'1", 187 lbs. Born, Hauterive, Que., February 16, 1980.
(Montreal's 11th choice, 275th overall, in 2000 Entry Draft).

			Regular Season					Playoffs				
Season	Club	Lea	GP	G	A	TP	PIM	GP	G	A	TP	PIM
1996-97	Jonquiere Elites	QAAA	43	14	23	37	....	5	3	3	6	....
1997-98	Moncton Alpines	QMJHL	51	1	7	8	37	....	....	....	....	....
1998-99	Moncton	QMJHL	39	5	8	13	41	....	....	....	....	....
	Rouyn-Noranda	QMJHL	22	2	13	15	25	11	2	4	6	14
99-2000	Rouyn-Noranda	QMJHL	70	32	49	81	104	11	3	7	10	18
2000-01	Rouyn-Noranda	QMJHL	69	30	45	75	176	9	1	5	6	22

GAUVREAU, Brent (GAWV-roh, BREHNT) PHX.

Right wing. Shoots right. 6'3", 196 lbs. Born, Sudbury, Ont., June 29, 1980.
(Phoenix's 5th choice, 186th overall, in 2000 Entry Draft).

			Regular Season					Playoffs				
Season	Club	Lea	GP	G	A	TP	PIM	GP	G	A	TP	PIM
1995-96	Sudbury Cubs	NOHA	61	43	49	92	68	....	....	....	....	....
1996-97	Oshawa Generals	OHL	59	8	13	21	13	18	1	5	6	2
1997-98	Oshawa Generals	OHL	66	25	42	67	39	7	3	1	4	2
1998-99	Oshawa Generals	OHL	68	33	62	95	57	15	9	11	20	15
99-2000	Oshawa Generals	OHL	59	34	53	87	74	5	1	2	3	4
	Saint John Flames	AHL	2	0	0	0	0	....	....	....	....	....
2000-01	Springfield	AHL	1	0	0	0	0	....	....	....	....	....
	Mississippi	ECHL	67	11	21	32	63	....	....	....	....	....

• Re-entered NHL Entry Draft. Originally Calgary's 6th choice, 120th overall, in 1998 Entry Draft.

GELLARD, Mike BOS.

Left wing. Shoots left. 6'1", 193 lbs. Born, Markham, Ont., October 10, 1978.

			Regular Season					Playoffs				
Season	Club	Lea	GP	G	A	TP	PIM	GP	G	A	TP	PIM
1995-96	Thornhill Islanders	MTJHL	49	15	24	39	2	16	6	9	15	0
1996-97	Thornhill Islanders	MTJHL	43	29	37	66	4	9	3	10	13	0
1997-98	St. Lawrence	ECAC	31	4	6	10	18	....	....	....	....	....
1998-99	St. Lawrence	ECAC	39	10	11	21	22	....	....	....	....	....
99-2000	St. Lawrence	ECAC	36	14	22	36	36	....	....	....	....	....
2000-01	St. Lawrence	ECAC	37	19	38	57	14	....	....	....	....	....

Won MTJHL Central Sportsmanlike Player of the Year Award (1997) • MTJHL Metro All-Star Team (1997) • ECAC First All-Star Team (2001) • Won ECAC Defensive Player of the Year Award (2001)

Signed as a free agent by **Boston**, August 2, 2001.

GILLIS, Nick (GIHL-LIHS, NIHK) OTT.

Right wing. Shoots right. 6', 188 lbs. Born, Cambridge, MA, February 20, 1978.
(Ottawa's 7th choice, 203rd overall, in 1997 Entry Draft).

			Regular Season					Playoffs				
Season	Club	Lea	GP	G	A	TP	PIM	GP	G	A	TP	PIM
1993-94	Boston Terriers	X-Games	60	58	70	128	112	....	....	....	....	....
1994-95	Cushing Academy	Hi-School	28	15	38	53	62	....	....	....	....	....
	Central-Mass	MBHL	8	14	10	24	....	....	....	....	....	....
1995-96	Cushing Academy	Hi-School	34	34	58	92	47	....	....	....	....	....
1996-97	Cushing Academy	Hi-School	32	30	54	84	27	....	....	....	....	....
1997-98	Boston University	H-East	34	8	12	20	43	....	....	....	....	....
1998-99	Boston University	H-East	33	3	16	19	37	....	....	....	....	....
99-2000	Boston University	H-East	42	8	18	26	26	....	....	....	....	....
2000-01	Boston University	H-East	35	7	7	14	16	....	....	....	....	....

GIONET, Aaron (jee-AWN-eht, AIR-ruhn) T.B.

Defense. Shoots right. 6'2", 191 lbs. Born, Port McNeil, B.C., June 28, 1982.
(Tampa Bay's 6th choice, 191st overall, in 2000 Entry Draft).

			Regular Season					Playoffs				
Season	Club	Lea	GP	G	A	TP	PIM	GP	G	A	TP	PIM
1997-98	Campbell River	VIJHL	8	1	0	1	35	....	....	....	....	....
1998-99	Kamloops Blazers	WHL	53	1	1	2	70	....	....	....	....	....
99-2000	Kamloops Blazers	WHL	68	5	6	11	243	4	0	0	0	8
2000-01	Kamloops Blazers	WHL	68	5	2	7	231	4	0	0	0	6

GIONTA, Brian (jee-OHN-tuh, BRIGH-uhn) N.J.

Right wing. Shoots right. 5'7", 160 lbs. Born, Rochester, NY, January 18, 1979.
(New Jersey's 4th choice, 82nd overall, in 1998 Entry Draft).

			Regular Season					Playoffs				
Season	Club	Lea	GP	G	A	TP	PIM	GP	G	A	TP	PIM
1994-95	Rochester	NEJHL	28	*52	37	*89	....	....	....	....	....	....
1995-96	Niagara Scenics	MTJHL	51	47	44	91	59	....	....	....	....	....
1996-97	Niagara Scenics	MTJHL	50	57	70	127	101	6	6	11	17	21
1997-98	Boston College	H-East	40	30	32	62	44	....	....	....	....	....
1998-99	Boston College	H-East	39	27	33	60	46	....	....	....	....	....
99-2000	Boston College	H-East	42	*33	23	56	66	....	....	....	....	....
2000-01	Boston College	H-East	43	*33	21	*54	47	....	....	....	....	....

Won MTJHL Player of the Year Award (1997) • Won Hockey East Rookie of the Year Award (1998) • Hockey East Second All-Star Team (1998) • NCAA East Second All-American Team (1998) • Hockey East First All-Star Team (1999, 2000, 2001) • NCAA East First All-American Team (1999, 2000, 2001)

GIROUX, Alexandre (ZHIH-roo, al-ehx-AN-dreh) OTT.

Center. Shoots left. 6'2", 189 lbs. Born, Quebec, Que., June 16, 1981.
(Ottawa's 9th choice, 213th overall, in 1999 Entry Draft).

			Regular Season					Playoffs				
Season	Club	Lea	GP	G	A	TP	PIM	GP	G	A	TP	PIM
1997-98	Ste-Foy Governors	QAAA	42	28	30	58	96	....	....	....	....	....
1998-99	Hull Olympiques	QMJHL	67	15	22	37	124	22	2	2	4	8
99-2000	Hull Olympiques	QMJHL	72	52	47	99	117	15	12	6	18	30
2000-01	Hull Olympiques	QMJHL	38	31	32	63	62	....	....	....	....	....
	Rouyn-Noranda	QMJHL	25	13	14	27	56	9	2	6	8	22

Traded to **Rouyn-Noranda** by **Hull** for Maxime Talbot, Dominic D'amour and Rouyn-Noranda's first choice (Charles Fontaine) in 2001 QMJHL Midget Draft, January 8, 2001.

GLADSKIKH, Evgeny (glad-SKEEKH, ehv-GEH-nee) VAN.

Right wing. Shoots left. 6', 176 lbs. Born, Magnitogorsk, USSR, April 24, 1982.
(Vancouver's 3rd choice, 114th overall, in 2001 Entry Draft).

			Regular Season					Playoffs				
Season	Club	Lea	GP	G	A	TP	PIM	GP	G	A	TP	PIM
1998-99	Magnitogorsk-2	Russia-4	16	3	3	6	6	....	....	....	....	....
99-2000	Magnitogorsk-2	Russia-3	39	17	2	19	74	....	....	....	....	....
	HC Magnitogorsk	Russia	1	0	0	0	0	....	....	....	....	....
2000-01	Magnitogorsk-2	Russia-4	11	10	7	17	6	....	....	....	....	....
	HC Magnitogorsk	Russia	31	3	5	8	10	12	0	2	2	2

GLEASON, Tim (GLEE-suhn, TIHM) OTT.

Defense. Shoots left. 6'1", 205 lbs. Born, Southfield, MI, January 29, 1983.
(Ottawa's 2nd choice, 23rd overall, in 2001 Entry Draft).

			Regular Season					Playoffs				
Season	Club	Lea	GP	G	A	TP	PIM	GP	G	A	TP	PIM
1998-99	Leamington	OJHL-B	52	5	26	31	76	....	....	....	....	....
99-2000	Windsor Spitfires	OHL	55	5	13	18	101	12	2	4	6	14
2000-01	Windsor Spitfires	OHL	47	8	28	36	124	9	1	2	3	23

GLENN, Ryan (GLEHN, RIGH-unh) **MTL.**

Defense. Shoots left. 6'3", 210 lbs. Born, New Westminster, B.C., June 7, 1980.
(Montreal's 7th choice, 145th overall, in 2000 Entry Draft).

			Regular Season					Playoffs				
Season	**Club**	**Lea**	**GP**	**G**	**A**	**TP**	**PIM**	**GP**	**G**	**A**	**TP**	**PIM**
99-2000	Walpole Jr. Stars	EJHL	42	19	40	59	54	8	4	13	17	....
2000-01	St. Lawrence	ECAC	37	3	1	4	34	....	....	....	....	....

EJHL First All-Star Team (2000) • Won EJHL Defencemen of the Year Award (2000)

GOC, Marcel (GAWCH, mahr-SEHL) **S.J.**

Center. Shoots left. 6', 189 lbs. Born, Calw, West Germany, August 24, 1983.
(San Jose's 1st choice, 20th overall, in 2001 Entry Draft).

			Regular Season					Playoffs				
Season	**Club**	**Lea**	**GP**	**G**	**A**	**TP**	**PIM**	**GP**	**G**	**A**	**TP**	**PIM**
1998-99	Schwenningen	DEL-Jr.	12	23	10	33	12	....	....	....	....	....
99-2000	Schwenningen	DEL	51	0	3	3	4	11	1	1	2	2
2000-01	Schwenningen	DEL	58	13	28	41	12	....	....	....	....	....

GODARD, Eric (GAW-duhrd, AIR-ihk) **FLA.**

Right wing. Shoots right. 6'4", 227 lbs. Born, Vernon, B.C., March 7, 1980.

			Regular Season					Playoffs				
Season	**Club**	**Lea**	**GP**	**G**	**A**	**TP**	**PIM**	**GP**	**G**	**A**	**TP**	**PIM**
1997-98	Lethbridge	WHL	7	0	0	0	26	2	0	0	0	0
1998-99	Lethbridge	WHL	66	2	5	7	213	4	0	0	0	14
99-2000	Lethbridge	WHL	60	3	5	8	*310	....	....	....	....	....
	Louisville Panthers	AHL	4	0	1	1	16	....	....	....	....	....
2000-01	Louisville Panthers	AHL	45	0	0	0	132	....	....	....	....	....

Signed as a free agent by **Florida**, September 24, 1999.

GOLDADE, Aaron (GOHLD-ayd, AIR-ruhn) **BUF.**

Center. Shoots left. 6', 180 lbs. Born, Prince Albert, Sask., July 30, 1980.
(Buffalo's 6th choice, 137th overall, in 1998 Entry Draft).

			Regular Season					Playoffs				
Season	**Club**	**Lea**	**GP**	**G**	**A**	**TP**	**PIM**	**GP**	**G**	**A**	**TP**	**PIM**
1995-96	Prince Albert	AMHL	44	31	38	69	26	....	....	....	....	....
1996-97	Brandon	WHL	59	4	10	14	51	6	0	1	1	0
1997-98	Brandon	WHL	66	19	16	35	58	16	0	2	2	22
1998-99	Brandon	WHL	64	27	33	60	56	5	0	1	1	8
99-2000	Brandon	WHL	56	14	28	42	33	....	....	....	....	....
2000-01	Brandon	WHL	65	22	34	56	84	6	2	2	4	16

GORBUNOV, Vladimir (gohr-buh-NAHF, vla-DIH-meer) **NYI**

Center. Shoots left. 6', 174 lbs. Born, Moscow, USSR, April 22, 1982.
(NY Islanders' 4th choice, 105th overall, in 2000 Entry Draft).

			Regular Season					Playoffs				
Season	**Club**	**Lea**	**GP**	**G**	**A**	**TP**	**PIM**	**GP**	**G**	**A**	**TP**	**PIM**
99-2000	HC Moscow	Russia-2	22	11	7	18	32	....	....	....	....	....
2000-01	HC Moscow	Russia-2	43	10	14	24	63	....	....	....	....	....

GORNICK, Brian (GOHR-nihk, BRIGH-uhn) **ANA.**

Center. Shoots left. 6'4", 200 lbs. Born, St. Paul, MN, March 17, 1980.
(Anaheim's 7th choice, 258th overall, in 1999 Entry Draft).

			Regular Season					Playoffs				
Season	**Club**	**Lea**	**GP**	**G**	**A**	**TP**	**PIM**	**GP**	**G**	**A**	**TP**	**PIM**
1998-99	Air Force Falcons	CHA	34	10	11	21	20	....	....	....	....	....
99-2000	Air Force Falcons	CHA	39	13	25	38	26	....	....	....	....	....
2000-01	Air Force Falcons	CHA	36	16	17	33	18	....	....	....	....	....

CHA First All-Star Team (2001)

GOROVIKOV, Konstantin (goh-roh-vih-KAHF, kawn-stehn-TEEN) **OTT.**

Center. Shoots left. 5'11", 172 lbs. Born, Novosibirsk, USSR, August 31, 1977.
(Ottawa's 10th choice, 269th overall, in 1999 Entry Draft).

			Regular Season					Playoffs				
Season	**Club**	**Lea**	**GP**	**G**	**A**	**TP**	**PIM**	**GP**	**G**	**A**	**TP**	**PIM**
1994-95	St. Petersburg-2	CIS-3	38	6	5	11	22	....	....	....	....	....
	St. Petersburg	CIS	13	1	0	1	4	2	0	0	0	0
1995-96	St. Petersburg-2	CIS-3	3	2	0	2	0	....	....	....	....	....
	St. Petersburg	CIS	45	2	4	6	18	2	0	0	0	0
1996-97	St. Petersburg	Russia	37	4	2	6	20	....	....	....	....	....
1997-98	St. Petersburg	Russia	44	6	12	18	22	....	....	....	....	....
1998-99	St. Petersburg	Russia	42	12	7	19	14	....	....	....	....	....
99-2000	Grand Rapids	IHL	57	9	14	23	30	8	1	0	1	4
2000-01	Grand Rapids	IHL	68	7	19	26	48	....	....	....	....	....

GOSSELIN, Christian (gawz-LEH, KRIHST-an) **NYR**

Defense. Shoots right. 6'5", 235 lbs. Born, Laval, Que., August 21, 1976.
(New Jersey's 5th choice, 129th overall, in 1994 Entry Draft).

			Regular Season					Playoffs				
Season	**Club**	**Lea**	**GP**	**G**	**A**	**TP**	**PIM**	**GP**	**G**	**A**	**TP**	**PIM**
1992-93	Hull Olympiques	QMJHL	49	1	3	4	24	....	....	....	....	....
1993-94	St-Hyacinthe	QMJHL	12	3	2	5	16	....	....	....	....	....
1994-95	St-Hyacinthe	QMJHL	60	5	10	15	202	5	0	0	0	11
1995-96	Laval Titan	QMJHL	21	1	8	9	69	....	....	....	....	....
1996-97	Macon Whoopies	CHL	63	8	10	18	229	5	0	0	0	29
1997-98	Pensacola	ECHL	42	6	5	11	181	18	0	1	1	52
	Fredericton	AHL	6	0	0	0	17	....	....	....	....	....
1998-99	Kentucky	AHL	31	1	1	2	107	....	....	....	....	....
99-2000	Kentucky	AHL	68	0	4	4	266	9	0	0	0	34
2000-01	Kentucky	AHL	42	2	3	5	145	3	0	1	1	6

Signed as a free agent by **San Jose**, July 15, 1998. Traded to **NY Rangers** by **San Jose** with Mikael Samuelsson for Adam Graves and future considerations, June 24, 2001.

GREEN, Mike (GREEN, MIGHK) **FLA.**

Center/Right wing. Shoots right. 5'11", 192 lbs. Born, Calgary, AB, August 23, 1979.

			Regular Season					Playoffs				
Season	**Club**	**Lea**	**GP**	**G**	**A**	**TP**	**PIM**	**GP**	**G**	**A**	**TP**	**PIM**
1996-97	Calgary Stars	AMHL	35	34	27	61	78	....	....	....	....	....
	Edmonton Ice	WHL	7	0	2	2	0	....	....	....	....	....
1997-98	Edmonton Ice	WHL	71	15	26	41	16	....	....	....	....	....
1998-99	Kootenay Ice	WHL	71	35	45	80	37	7	2	2	4	4
99-2000	Kootenay Ice	WHL	69	43	49	92	63	21	9	16	25	20
2000-01	Port Huron	UHL	11	1	5	6	6	....	....	....	....	....
	Louisville Panthers	AHL	24	2	1	3	4	....	....	....	....	....
	Knoxville Speed	UHL	48	18	24	42	35	1	0	0	0	0

WHL East Second All-Star Team (2000)

Signed as a free agent by **Florida**, April 7, 2000.

GRENIER, Martin (GREH-nyay, MAHR-tihn) **PHX.**

Defense. Shoots left. 6'5", 245 lbs. Born, Laval, Que., November 2, 1980.
(Colorado's 2nd choice, 45th overall, in 1999 Entry Draft).

			Regular Season					Playoffs				
Season	**Club**	**Lea**	**GP**	**G**	**A**	**TP**	**PIM**	**GP**	**G**	**A**	**TP**	**PIM**
1996-97	Laval-Laurentide	QAAA	34	3	16	19	117	13	0	4	4	....
1997-98	Quebec Remparts	QMJHL	61	4	11	15	202	14	0	2	2	36
1998-99	Quebec Remparts	QMJHL	60	7	18	25	*479	13	0	4	4	29
99-2000	Quebec Remparts	QMJHL	67	11	35	46	302	7	1	4	5	27
2000-01	Quebec Remparts	QMJHL	26	5	16	21	82	....	....	....	....	....
	Victoriaville Tigres	QMJHL	28	9	19	28	108	13	2	8	10	51

Traded to **Victoriaville** by **Quebec** for Daniel Masse, Daniel Houle and Victoriaville's 1st round choice (Jeff MacAuley) in 2001 QMJHL Midget Draft, January 12, 2001. Traded to **Boston** by **Colorado** with Brian Rolston, Sami Pahlsson and New Jersey's 1st round choice (previously acquired, Boston selected Martin Samuelsson) in 2000 Entry Draft for Ray Bourque and Dave Andreychuk, March 6, 2000. Signed as a free agent by **Phoenix**, June 27, 2001.

GRIGORENKO, Igor (grih-goh-REHN-koh, EE-gohr) **DET.**

Right wing. Shoots right. 5'10", 178 lbs. Born, Togliatti, USSR, April 9, 1983.
(Detroit's 1st choice, 62nd overall, in 2001 Entry Draft).

			Regular Season					Playoffs				
Season	**Club**	**Lea**	**GP**	**G**	**A**	**TP**	**PIM**	**GP**	**G**	**A**	**TP**	**PIM**
1998-99	Lada Togliatti-2	Russia-4	19	3	3	6	2	....	....	....	....	....
99-2000	Lada Togliatti-2	Russia-3	38	17	18	35	36	....	....	....	....	....
2000-01	Lada Togliatti-2	Russia-3	6	5	4	9	....	....	....	....	....	....
	CSK Samara	Russia-2	39	10	10	20	....	....	....	....	....	....
	Lada Togliatti	Russia	....	....	....	....	....	5	1	0	1	4

GROSCHL, Tamas (GROH-shuhl, TAW-mahsh) **EDM.**

Right wing. Shoots left. 6'2", 183 lbs. Born, Budapest, Hungary, August 21, 1980.
(Edmonton's 9th choice, 256th overall, in 1999 Entry Draft).

			Regular Season					Playoffs				
Season	**Club**	**Lea**	**GP**	**G**	**A**	**TP**	**PIM**	**GP**	**G**	**A**	**TP**	**PIM**
199-00	Leksands IF	Swede-Jr.	33	15	14	29	46	....	....	....	....	....
1998-99	UTE Budapest	Hungary	STATISTICS NOT AVAILABLE									
99-2000	Team Hungary	Nat-Team	11	4	5	9	35	....	....	....	....	....
	Leksands IF	Sweden	2	0	0	0	0	....	....	....	....	....
2000-01	Augusta Lynx	ECHL	59	5	11	16	52	3	0	0	0	0

GUSAKOV, Yevgeny (goo-sawk-KAHF, yehv-GEH-nee) **NYR**

Right wing. Shoots left. 6'6", 225 lbs. Born, Togliatti, USSR, March 6, 1981.
(NY Rangers' 9th choice, 226th overall, in 1999 Entry Draft).

			Regular Season					Playoffs				
Season	**Club**	**Lea**	**GP**	**G**	**A**	**TP**	**PIM**	**GP**	**G**	**A**	**TP**	**PIM**
1997-98	Lada Togliatti-2	Russia-3	24	4	2	6	10	....	....	....	....	....
1998-99	Lada Togliatti-2	Russia-4	42	12	3	15	28	....	....	....	....	....
99-2000	Baie-Comeau	QMJHL	61	25	22	47	135	6	5	1	6	10
2000-01	Lada Togliatti	Russia	1	0	0	0	0	....	....	....	....	....

GUSEV, Vladimir (GOO-sehv, vla-DIH-meer) **CHI.**

Defense. Shoots left. 6'1", 205 lbs. Born, Novosibirsk, USSR, November 24, 1982.
(Chicago's 6th choice, 115th overall, in 2001 Entry Draft).

			Regular Season					Playoffs				
Season	**Club**	**Lea**	**GP**	**G**	**A**	**TP**	**PIM**	**GP**	**G**	**A**	**TP**	**PIM**
99-2000	Novokuznetsk-2	Russia-3	21	1	0	1	0	....	....	....	....	....
	HC Novokuznetsk	Russia	....	....	....	....	....	3	0	0	0	0
2000-01	Amur Khabarovsk	Russia	1	0	0	0	0	....	....	....	....	....
	Sibir Novosibirsk-2	Russia-3	STATISTICS NOT AVAILABLE									
	Sibir Novosibirsk	Russia-2	1	0	0	0	0	....	....	....	....	....

GUSTAFSSON, Juha (GOOS-tahf-suhn, YOO-huh) **PHX.**

Defense. Shoots left. 6'3", 200 lbs. Born, Helsinki, Finland, April 26, 1979.
(Phoenix's 1st choice, 43rd overall, in 1997 Entry Draft).

			Regular Season					Playoffs				
Season	**Club**	**Lea**	**GP**	**G**	**A**	**TP**	**PIM**	**GP**	**G**	**A**	**TP**	**PIM**
1994-95	Kiekko-Espoo-B	Finn-Jr.	24	1	4	5	26	....	....	....	....	....
	Kiekko-Espoo	Finn-Jr.	2	0	0	0	0	4	0	0	0	4
1995-96	Kiekko-Espoo	Finn-Jr.	33	1	5	6	28	4	0	0	0	2
	Kiekko-Espoo	Finland	1	0	0	0	0	....	....	....	....	....
1996-97	Kiekko-Espoo	Finn-Jr.	32	1	3	4	30	....	....	....	....	....
	Kiekko-Espoo	Finland	3	0	0	0	0	3	0	0	0	0
1997-98	Kiekko-Espoo	Finn-Jr.	33	3	3	6	18	....	....	....	....	....
	Kiekko-Espoo	Finland	2	0	0	0	0	....	....	....	....	....
1998-99	Ahmat Hyvinkaa	Finland-2	37	3	7	10	36	....	....	....	....	....
99-2000	Blues Espoo	Finland	33	1	4	5	26	....	....	....	....	....
2000-01	KJT Jarvenpaa	Finland-2	6	2	1	3	4	....	....	....	....	....
	Blues Espoo	Finland	46	1	2	3	34	....	....	....	....	....

GYORI, Dylan (GIH-ree, DIH-luhn) **PIT.**

Center. Shoots left. 5'11", 190 lbs. Born, Rimbey, Alta., February 20, 1979.

			Regular Season					Playoffs				
Season	**Club**	**Lea**	**GP**	**G**	**A**	**TP**	**PIM**	**GP**	**G**	**A**	**TP**	**PIM**
1994-95	Red Deer Chiefs	AMHL	36	36	27	63	61	....	....	....	....	....
	Tri-City Americans	WHL	3	0	0	0	0	....	....	....	....	....
1995-96	Tri-City Americans	WHL	50	12	13	25	26	10	0	0	0	2
1996-97	Tri-City Americans	WHL	72	29	27	56	95	....	....	....	....	....
1997-98	Tri-City Americans	WHL	72	33	54	87	81	....	....	....	....	....
1998-99	Tri-City Americans	WHL	69	53	65	118	112	12	7	11	18	25
99-2000	Wilkes-Barre	AHL	36	2	2	4	23	....	....	....	....	....
	Richmond	ECHL	29	11	20	31	50	3	1	0	1	6
2000-01	Wilkes-Barre	AHL	70	5	15	20	86	18	1	3	4	24

WHL West First All-Star Team (1999)

Signed as a free agent by **Pittsburgh**, August 19, 1999.

HAGGLUND, Johan (HAG-luhnd, YOH-hahn) **T.B.**

Center. Shoots left. 6'2", 196 lbs. Born, Ornskoldsvik, Sweden, June 9, 1982.
(Tampa Bay's 4th choice, 126th overall, in 2000 Entry Draft).

			Regular Season					Playoffs				
Season	**Club**	**Lea**	**GP**	**G**	**A**	**TP**	**PIM**	**GP**	**G**	**A**	**TP**	**PIM**
1998-99	Modo Hockey	Swede-Jr.	28	16	22	38	52	....	....	....	....	....
99-2000	Modo Hockey-B	Swede-Jr.	7	1	2	3	8	....	....	....	....	....
	Modo Hockey	Swede-Jr.	35	7	10	17	75	2	1	0	1	0
2000-01	Modo Hockey	Swede-Jr.	21	9	9	18	66	....	....	....	....	....

HAGMAN, Niklas (HAG-muhn, NIHK-las) FLA.

Left wing. Shoots left. 6', 190 lbs. Born, Espoo, Finland, December 5, 1979.
(Florida's 3rd choice, 70th overall, in 1999 Entry Draft).

			Regular Season					Playoffs				
Season	Club	Lea	GP	G	A	TP	PIM	GP	G	A	TP	PIM
1994-95	HIFK Helsinki-C	Finn-Jr.	28	30	15	45	40	4	2	0	2	6
1995-96	HIFK Helsinki-B	Finn-Jr.	26	12	21	33	32	4	3	0	3	2
	HIFK Helsinki	Finn-Jr.	12	3	1	4	0	....	....	....	....	....
1996-97	HIFK Helsinki	Finn-Jr.	30	13	12	25	30	4	1	1	2	0
1997-98	HIFK Helsinki	Finn-Jr.	26	9	5	14	16	....	....	....	....	....
	HIFK Helsinki	Finland	8	1	0	1	0	....	....	....	....	....
1998-99	HIFK Helsinki	Finn-Jr.	14	4	9	13	43	....	....	....	....	....
	HIFK Helsinki	EuroHL	1	0	1	1	0	....	....	....	....	....
	HIFK Helsinki	Finland	17	1	1	2	14	....	....	....	....	....
	Kiekko-Espoo	Finland	14	1	1	2	2	4	1	0	1	0
99-2000	Karpat Oulu	Finland-2	41	17	18	35	12	7	4	2	6	....
2000-01	Karpat Oulu	Finland	56	28	18	46	32	8	3	1	4	0

HAGOS, Yared (HA-gohs, YAIR-ehd) DAL.

Center. Shoots left. 6'1", 202 lbs. Born, Stockholm, Sweden, March 27, 1983.
(Dallas' 2nd choice, 70th overall, in 2001 Entry Draft).

			Regular Season					Playoffs				
Season	Club	Lea	GP	G	A	TP	PIM	GP	G	A	TP	PIM
1998-99	AIK Solna	Swede-Jr.	32	8	12	20	22	....	....	....	....	....
99-2000	AIK Solna-B	Swede-Jr.	13	4	6	10	6	....	....	....	....	....
	AIK Solna	Swede-Jr.	17	6	4	10	10	....	....	....	....	....
2000-01	AIK Solna	Swede-Jr.	24	8	13	21	46	2	2	1	3	2
	AIK Solna	Sweden	....	....	....	....	....	5	0	0	0	0

HAHL, Riku (HAHL, REE-koo) COL.

Center. Shoots left. 6', 190 lbs. Born, Hameenlinna, Finland, November 1, 1980.
(Colorado's 9th choice, 183rd overall, in 1999 Entry Draft).

			Regular Season					Playoffs				
Season	Club	Lea	GP	G	A	TP	PIM	GP	G	A	TP	PIM
1995-96	Hameenlinna-C	Finn-Jr.	32	18	30	48	28	....	....	....	....	....
1996-97	Hameenlinna-B	Finn-Jr.	32	19	24	43	22	....	....	....	....	....
	HPK Hameenlinna	Finn-Jr.	2	0	1	1	2	6	2	0	2	2
1997-98	Hameenlinna-B	Finn-Jr.	10	5	14	19	6	....	....	....	....	....
	HPK Hameenlinna	Finn-Jr.	35	13	6	19	12	....	....	....	....	....
1998-99	HPK Hameenlinna	Finn-Jr.	6	0	2	2	6	....	....	....	....	....
	HPK Hameenlinna	Finland	28	0	1	1	0	8	0	0	0	2
99-2000	HPK Hameenlinna	Finn-Jr.	12	1	6	7	8	9	5	4	9	16
	HPK Hameenlinna	Finland	50	4	3	7	18	8	0	0	0	2
2000-01	HPK Hameenlinna	Finn-Jr.	2	1	3	4	0	....	....	....	....	....
	HPK Hameenlinna	Finland	55	3	9	12	32	....	....	....	....	....

HAINSEY, Ron (HAYN-zee, RAWN) MTL.

Defense. Shoots left. 6'3", 200 lbs. Born, Bolton, CT, March 24, 1981.
(Montreal's 1st choice, 13th overall, in 2000 Entry Draft).

			Regular Season					Playoffs				
Season	Club	Lea	GP	G	A	TP	PIM	GP	G	A	TP	PIM
1997-98	Team USA	USDP	66	6	15	21	44	....	....	....	....	....
1998-99	Team USA	USDP	48	5	12	17	45	....	....	....	....	....
99-2000	U. Mass-Lowell	H-East	30	3	8	11	20	....	....	....	....	....
2000-01	U. Mass-Lowell	H-East	33	10	26	36	51	....	....	....	....	....
	Quebec Citadelles	AHL	4	1	0	1	0	1	0	0	0	0

Hockey East First All-Star Team (2001) • NCAA East Second All-American Team (2001)

HAJEK, David (HIGH-ehk, DAV-vihd) CGY.

Defense. Shoots left. 5'11", 165 lbs. Born, Chomutov, Czech., June 13, 1980.
(Calgary's 8th choice, 239th overall, in 2000 Entry Draft).

			Regular Season					Playoffs				
Season	Club	Lea	GP	G	A	TP	PIM	GP	G	A	TP	PIM
1996-97	KLH Chomotov-Jr.	Cze-Rep	36	8	14	22	30	4	0	0	0	2
1997-98	KLH Chomotov-Jr.	Cze-Rep	36	3	9	12	18	....	....	....	....	....
1998-99	Melville	SJHL	25	10	19	29	....	....	....	....	....	....
	Spokane Chiefs	WHL	27	0	3	3	10	....	....	....	....	....
99-2000	KLH Chomotov-Jr.	Cze-Rep	7	1	5	6	14	....	....	....	....	....
	KLH Chomotov-2	Cze-Rep	28	1	5	6	14	12	1	3	4	10
2000-01	HC Kladno	Cze-Rep	40	1	1	2	66	....	....	....	....	....

HAKANSSON, Mikael (HAK-ahn-suhn, mihk-AIL) TOR.

Center. Shoots left. 6'2", 204 lbs. Born, Stockholm, Sweden, May 31, 1974.
(Toronto's 7th choice, 125th overall, in 1992 Entry Draft).

			Regular Season					Playoffs				
Season	Club	Lea	GP	G	A	TP	PIM	GP	G	A	TP	PIM
1990-91	Nacka IK	Swede-2	27	2	5	7	6	....	....	....	....	....
1991-92	Nacka IK	Swede-2	29	3	15	18	24	....	....	....	....	....
1992-93	Djurgardens IF	Sweden	40	0	1	1	6	3	0	0	0	0
1993-94	Djurgardens IF	Sweden	37	3	3	6	12	4	0	0	0	0
1994-95	MoDo Hockey	Sweden	37	3	7	10	16	....	....	....	....	....
1995-96	MoDo Hockey	Sweden	40	8	4	12	18	8	2	0	2	0
1996-97	Djurgardens IF	Sweden	48	8	12	20	12	4	0	0	0	0
1997-98	Djurgardens IF	Sweden	43	9	2	11	8	15	3	0	3	14
1998-99	Djurgardens IF	Sweden	48	13	12	25	14	4	1	0	1	0
	Djurgardens IF	EuroHL	6	0	1	1	20	....	....	....	....	....
99-2000	Djurgardens IF	Sweden	48	17	17	34	26	13	3	8	11	12
2000-01	St. John's Leafs	AHL	64	10	40	50	46	4	0	0	0	0

Signed as a free agent by **Djurgardens IF** (Sweden) with **Toronto** retaining NHL rights, August 2, 2001.

HAKEWILL, James (HAYK-wihl, JAYMZ) CGY.

Defense. Shoots left. 6'3", 205 lbs. Born, Wilmette, IL, June 7, 1982.
(Calgary's 6th choice, 145th overall, in 2001 Entry Draft).

			Regular Season					Playoffs				
Season	Club	Lea	GP	G	A	TP	PIM	GP	G	A	TP	PIM
99-2000	Westminster High	Hi-School	23	3	13	16	22	....	....	....	....	....
2000-01	Westminster High	Hi-School	23	4	15	19	30	....	....	....	....	....

HALE, David (HAYL, DAY-vihd) N.J.

Defense. Shoots left. 6'2", 204 lbs. Born, Colorado Springs, CO, June 18, 1981.
(New Jersey's 1st choice, 22nd overall, in 2000 Entry Draft).

			Regular Season					Playoffs				
Season	Club	Lea	GP	G	A	TP	PIM	GP	G	A	TP	PIM
1997-98	Colorado North	Hi-School	25	11	33	44	154	....	....	....	....	....
1998-99	Sioux City	USHL	56	3	15	18	127	5	0	0	0	18
99-2000	Sioux City	USHL	54	6	18	24	187	5	0	2	2	6
2000-01	North Dakota	WCHA	44	4	5	9	79	....	....	....	....	....

USHL First All-Star Team (2000)

HALL, Adam (HAWL, A-dam) NSH.

Right wing. Shoots right. 6'3", 205 lbs. Born, Kalamazoo, MI, August 14, 1980.
(Nashville's 3rd choice, 52nd overall, in 1999 Entry Draft).

			Regular Season					Playoffs				
Season	Club	Lea	GP	G	A	TP	PIM	GP	G	A	TP	PIM
1996-97	Bramalea Blues	OPJHL	43	9	14	23	92	....	....	....	....	....
1997-98	Team USA	USDP	71	42	23	65	63	....	....	....	....	....
1998-99	Michigan State	CCHA	36	16	7	23	74	....	....	....	....	....
99-2000	Michigan State	CCHA	40	*26	13	39	38	....	....	....	....	....
2000-01	Michigan State	CCHA	42	18	12	30	42	....	....	....	....	....

CCHA Second All-Star Team (2000)

HALL, Todd (HAWL, TAWD) NYR

Left wing. Shoots left. 6'1", 200 lbs. Born, Hamden, CT, January 22, 1973.
(Hartford's 3rd choice, 53rd overall, in 1991 Entry Draft).

			Regular Season					Playoffs				
Season	Club	Lea	GP	G	A	TP	PIM	GP	G	A	TP	PIM
1990-91	Hamden High	Hi-School	23	10	15	25	12	....	....	....	....	....
1991-92	Boston College	H-East	33	2	10	12	14	....	....	....	....	....
1992-93	Boston College	H-East	34	2	10	12	22	....	....	....	....	....
1993-94	New Hampshire	H-East	DID NOT PLAY – TRANSFERRED COLLEGES									
1994-95	New Hampshire	H-East	36	8	18	26	16	....	....	....	....	....
1995-96	New Hampshire	H-East	31	4	26	30	10	....	....	....	....	....
1996-97	Binghamton	AHL	40	3	7	10	12	4	0	1	1	0
	Charlotte	ECHL	13	0	2	2	8	....	....	....	....	....
1997-98	Hartford	AHL	73	7	18	25	26	8	0	1	1	8
1998-99	Hartford	AHL	72	14	15	29	12	1	0	0	0	0
99-2000	Hartford	AHL	74	11	34	45	14	23	2	6	8	8
2000-01	Hartford	AHL	79	5	12	17	13	5	0	0	0	2

Hockey East Second All-Star Team (1996)

Signed as a free agent by **NY Rangers**, July 28, 1997.

HALVARDSSON, Johan (HAL-vahrds-sohn, YOH-hahn) NYI

Defense. Shoots left. 6'3", 198 lbs. Born, Jonkoping, Sweden, December 26, 1979.
(NY Islanders' 8th choice, 102nd overall, in 1999 Entry Draft).

			Regular Season					Playoffs				
Season	Club	Lea	GP	G	A	TP	PIM	GP	G	A	TP	PIM
1997-98	HV Jonkoping	Swede-Jr.	28	5	5	10	65	....	....	....	....	....
1998-99	HV Jonkoping	Sweden	17	1	2	3	33	....	....	....	....	....
99-2000	HV Jonkoping	Sweden	46	0	3	3	75	5	0	0	0	8
2000-01	HV Jonkoping	Sweden	33	0	0	0	24	....	....	....	....	....

HAMHUIS, Dan (HAM-yoos, DAN) NSH.

Defense. Shoots left. 6', 196 lbs. Born, Smithers, B.C., December 13, 1982.
(Nashville's 1st choice, 12th overall, in 2001 Entry Draft).

			Regular Season					Playoffs				
Season	Club	Lea	GP	G	A	TP	PIM	GP	G	A	TP	PIM
1997-98	Smithers A's	BCAHA	59	59	72	131	59	....	....	....	....	....
1998-99	Prince George	WHL	56	1	3	4	45	7	1	2	3	8
99-2000	Prince George	WHL	70	10	23	33	140	13	2	3	5	35
2000-01	Prince George	WHL	62	13	47	60	125	6	2	3	5	15

WHL West First All-Star Team (2001)

HANNUS, Tommi (HA-nuhs, TAW-mee) L.A.

Center. Shoots right. 6', 180 lbs. Born, Vantaa, Finland, June 27, 1980.
(Los Angeles' 7th choice, 190th overall, in 1998 Entry Draft).

			Regular Season					Playoffs				
Season	Club	Lea	GP	G	A	TP	PIM	GP	G	A	TP	PIM
1994-95	TPS Turku-C	Finn-Jr.	27	24	13	37	43	....	....	....	....	....
1995-96	TPS Turku-C	Finn-Jr.	29	34	22	56	67	....	....	....	....	....
	TPS Turku-B	Finn-Jr.	1	1	0	1	2	....	....	....	....	....
1996-97	TPS Turku	Finn-Jr.	27	7	7	14	6	....	....	....	....	....
	TPS Turku-B	Finn-Jr.	18	7	7	14	6	6	4	2	6	10
1997-98	TPS Turku	Finn-Jr.	19	6	3	9	4	....	....	....	....	....
	TPS Turku-B	Finn-Jr.	9	5	4	9	8	....	....	....	....	....
1998-99	TPS Turku	Finn-Jr.	8	5	4	9	22	....	....	....	....	....
	TuTo Turku	Finland-2	18	6	4	10	16	8	0	2	2	8
99-2000	TPS Turku	Finn-Jr.	3	4	3	7	6	....	....	....	....	....
	TuTo Turku	Finland-2	27	11	6	17	20	....	....	....	....	....
	Assat-Pori	Finland	13	1	0	1	4	....	....	....	....	....
2000-01	TuTo Turku	Finland-2	29	9	8	17	16	11	*7	7	14	*24

HARANT, Tomas (HAH-rant, TAW-mahsh) NSH.

Defense. Shoots left. 6'3", 200 lbs. Born, Zilina, Czech., April 28, 1980.
(Nashville's 8th choice, 173rd overall, in 2000 Entry Draft).

			Regular Season					Playoffs				
Season	Club	Lea	GP	G	A	TP	PIM	GP	G	A	TP	PIM
1997-98	SKP Zilina	Slovak-Jr.	41	5	7	12	72	....	....	....	....	....
	SKP Zilina	Slovak-2	5	0	0	0	0	....	....	....	....	....
1998-99	SKP Zilina	Slovak-Jr.	33	1	6	7	108	....	....	....	....	....
99-2000	SKP Zilina	Slovak-2	26	0	3	3	34	....	....	....	....	....
2000-01	HCO Trinec-Jr.	Cze-Rep	5	1	2	3	8	1	0	0	0	4
	HCO Trinec	Cze-Rep	15	1	2	3	14	....	....	....	....	....

HARDER, Mike (HAHR-duhr, MIGHK)

Center. Shoots right. 6', 185 lbs. Born, Winnipeg, Man., February 8, 1973.

			Regular Season					Playoffs				
Season	Club	Lea	GP	G	A	TP	PIM	GP	G	A	TP	PIM
1993-94	Colgate University	ECAC	33	21	25	46	14	....	....	....	....	....
1994-95	Colgate University	ECAC	36	22	36	58	13	....	....	....	....	....
1995-96	Colgate University	ECAC	32	23	32	55	26	....	....	....	....	....
1996-97	Colgate University	ECAC	33	22	33	55	20	....	....	....	....	....
	Hamilton Bulldogs	AHL	2	0	1	1	0	....	....	....	....	....
	Milwaukee	IHL	7	1	3	4	6	2	0	1	1	0
1997-98	Milwaukee	IHL	62	20	17	37	32	....	....	....	....	....
	Springfield	AHL	3	2	0	2	2	....	....	....	....	....
	Rochester	AHL	8	4	2	6	0	4	3	2	5	8
1998-99	Rochester	AHL	79	31	48	79	39	20	2	9	11	23
99-2000	Hartford	AHL	56	18	21	39	33	12	0	4	4	4
2000-01	Hartford	AHL	36	10	19	29	27	....	....	....	....	....
	Louisville Panthers	AHL	38	13	24	37	8	....	....	....	....	....

ECAC Second All-Star Team (1995, 1996) • ECAC First All-Star Team (1997) • NCAA East Second All-American Team (1997)

Signed as a free agent by **NY Rangers**, August 2, 1999.

HARIKKALA, Jaakko (HAHR-ee-kuh-lah, YAH-koh) **BOS.**

Defense. Shoots left. 6'2", 215 lbs. Born, Kalanti, Finland, March 30, 1981.
(Boston's 4th choice, 118th overall, in 1999 Entry Draft).

			Regular Season					Playoffs				
Season	Club	Lea	GP	G	A	TP	PIM	GP	G	A	TP	PIM
1997-98	Jaa-Kotkat-2	Finland-3	5	0	2	2	8	....	....	....	....	....
	Jaa-Kotkat	Finland-2	45	2	6	8	65	....	....	....	....	....
1998-99	Lukko Rauma	Finn-Jr.	11	1	3	4	22	....	....	....	....	....
	Lukko Rauma	Finland	35	0	0	0	10	....	....	....	....	....
99-2000	Lukko Rauma	Finland	24	0	0	0	2	....	....	....	....	....
2000-01	Lukko Rauma	Finn-Jr.	2	2	0	2	2	....	....	....	....	....
	Jaa-Kotkat	Finland-2	10	0	2	2	16	....	....	....	....	....
	Lukko Rauma	Finland	10	0	0	0	0	....	....	....	....	....

HARLTON, Tyler (HAHRL-tawn, TIGH-luhr) **TOR.**

Defense. Shoots left. 6'2", 212 lbs. Born, Pense, Sask., January 11, 1976.
(St. Louis' 2nd choice, 94th overall, in 1994 Entry Draft).

			Regular Season					Playoffs				
Season	Club	Lea	GP	G	A	TP	PIM	GP	G	A	TP	PIM
1993-94	Vernon Vipers	BCJHL	60	3	18	21	102	....	....	....	....	....
1994-95	Michigan State	CCHA	39	1	3	4	55	....	....	....	....	....
1995-96	Michigan State	CCHA	39	1	6	7	51	....	....	....	....	....
1996-97	Michigan State	CCHA	39	2	9	11	75	....	....	....	....	....
1997-98	Michigan State	CCHA	44	1	12	13	68	....	....	....	....	....
1998-99	Worcester	AHL	58	2	5	7	94	....	....	....	....	....
	Peoria Riverman	ECHL	6	0	2	2	40	....	....	....	....	....
99-2000	Worcester	AHL	3	0	0	0	4	....	....	....	....	....
	St. John's Leafs	AHL	56	2	6	8	62	....	....	....	....	....
2000-01	St. John's Leafs	AHL	80	5	18	23	68	4	0	0	0	0

CCHA First All-Star Team (1998) • NCAA West Second All-American Team (1998)

Traded to **Toronto** by **St. Louis** with future considerations for Derek King, October 20, 1999.

HARRISON, Jay (HAIR-ih-suhn, JAY) **TOR.**

Defense. Shoots left. 6'3", 200 lbs. Born, Oshawa, Ont., November 3, 1982.
(Toronto's 4th choice, 82nd overall, in 2001 Entry Draft).

			Regular Season					Playoffs				
Season	Club	Lea	GP	G	A	TP	PIM	GP	G	A	TP	PIM
1997-98	Oshawa Legion	MTJHL	42	1	11	12	143	....	....	....	....	....
1998-99	Brampton	OHL	63	1	14	15	108	....	....	....	....	....
99-2000	Brampton	OHL	68	2	18	20	139	6	0	2	2	15
2000-01	Brampton	OHL	53	4	15	19	112	9	1	1	2	17

HARTSBURG, Chris (HAHRTZ-buhrg, KRIHS) **N.J.**

Center. Shoots right. 6', 190 lbs. Born, Edina, MN, May 30, 1980.
(New Jersey's 7th choice, 214th overall, in 1999 Entry Draft).

			Regular Season					Playoffs				
Season	Club	Lea	GP	G	A	TP	PIM	GP	G	A	TP	PIM
1995-96	Cambridge Hawks	OPJHL	46	12	15	27	10	....	....	....	....	....
1996-97	Cambridge Hawks	OPJHL	47	14	19	33	29	....	....	....	....	....
1997-98	Omaha Lancers	USHL	54	16	19	35	58	12	2	2	4	20
1998-99	Colorado College	WCHA	34	6	4	10	60	....	....	....	....	....
99-2000	Colorado College	WCHA	33	3	2	5	50	....	....	....	....	....
2000-01	Colorado College	WCHA	41	8	7	15	38	....	....	....	....	....

HARVEY, Paul (HAHR-vee, PAWL) **FLA.**

Right wing. Shoots right. 6'4", 205 lbs. Born, South Boston, MA, August 8, 1978.

			Regular Season					Playoffs				
Season	Club	Lea	GP	G	A	TP	PIM	GP	G	A	TP	PIM
1996-97	Syracuse Crunch	MTJHL	23	18	31	49	196	....	....	....	....	....
1997-98	Erie Otters	OHL	31	3	6	9	64	6	0	1	1	0
1998-99	Erie Otters	OHL	61	16	17	33	132	5	1	0	1	15
99-2000	Louisville Panthers	AHL	34	2	7	9	50	2	0	0	0	0
	Port Huron Cats	UHL	16	1	5	6	22	3	1	0	1	2
2000-01	Louisville Panthers	AHL	34	2	5	7	37	....	....	....	....	....
	Port Huron Cats	UHL	11	9	3	12	2	....	....	....	....	....

Signed as a free agent by **Florida**, June 16, 1999

HAVELKA, Petr (huh-VEHL-kah, PEE-tuhr) **PIT.**

Left wing. Shoots left. 6'2", 187 lbs. Born, Most, Czech., March 4, 1979.
(Pittsburgh's 6th choice, 152nd overall, in 1997 Entry Draft).

			Regular Season					Playoffs				
Season	Club	Lea	GP	G	A	TP	PIM	GP	G	A	TP	PIM
1995-96	Sparta Praha-Jr.	Cze-Rep	40	15	10	25	....	....	....	....	....	....
1996-97	Sparta Praha-Jr.	Cze-Rep	22	14	13	27	....	....	....	....	....	....
	Sparta Praha	Cze-Rep	....	....	....	....	....	1	0	0	0	0
1997-98	Sparta Praha-Jr.	Cze-Rep	DID NOT PLAY – INJURED									
1998-99	Sparta Praha-Jr.	Cze-Rep	5	7	3	10	....	4	1	1	2	....
	Velvana Kladno	Cze-Rep	5	0	0	0	0	....	....	....	....	....
99-2000	Sparta Praha-Jr.	Cze-Rep	2	1	0	1	0	....	....	....	....	....
	HC Medvedi-2	Cze-Rep	5	2	4	6	29	....	....	....	....	....
	Velvana Kladno	Cze-Rep	6	1	2	3	2	....	....	....	....	....
	Sparta Praha	Cze-Rep	10	0	1	1	0	3	0	0	0	0
2000-01	HC Medvedi-2	Cze-Rep	3	0	0	0	0	....	....	....	....	....
	Sparta Praha	Cze-Rep	....	....	....	....	....	7	1	0	1	2

HAY, Darrell (HAY, DAIR-ehl) **VAN.**

Defense. Shoots right. 6', 190 lbs. Born, Kamloops, B.C, April 2, 1980.
(Vancouver's 8th choice, 271st overall, in 1999 Entry Draft).

			Regular Season					Playoffs				
Season	Club	Lea	GP	G	A	TP	PIM	GP	G	A	TP	PIM
1995-96	Kamloops Lions	BCAHA	65	34	57	91	155	....	....	....	....	....
1996-97	Tri-City Americans	WHL	61	0	10	10	41	....	....	....	....	....
1997-98	Tri-City Americans	WHL	71	5	33	38	90	....	....	....	....	....
1998-99	Tri-City Americans	WHL	72	13	49	62	87	12	2	10	12	22
99-2000	Tri-City Americans	WHL	64	15	36	51	85	4	0	1	1	8
2000-01	Florida Everblades	ECHL	40	5	4	9	26	5	2	1	3	0
	Kansas City	IHL	9	0	0	0	19	....	....	....	....	....

WHL West Second All-Star Team (2000)

HAYDAR, Darren (HAY-duhr, DAIR-ehn) **NSH.**

Right wing. Shoots left. 5'8", 166 lbs. Born, Toronto, Ont., October 22, 1979.
(Nashville's 14th choice, 248th overall, in 1999 Entry Draft).

			Regular Season					Playoffs				
Season	Club	Lea	GP	G	A	TP	PIM	GP	G	A	TP	PIM
1995-96	Milton Merchants	OPJHL	6	1	2	3	4	....	....	....	....	....
1996-97	Milton Merchants	OPJHL	51	32	68	100	68	....	....	....	....	....
1997-98	Milton Merchants	OPJHL	51	*71	*69	*140	65	....	....	....	....	....
1998-99	New Hampshire	H-East	41	31	30	61	34	....	....	....	....	....
99-2000	New Hampshire	H-East	38	22	19	41	42	....	....	....	....	....
2000-01	New Hampshire	H-East	39	18	23	41	38	....	....	....	....	....

Won OPJHL Player of the Year Award (1998) • OPJHL First All-Star Team (1998) • Hockey East Second All-Star Team (1999, 2000)

HEALEY, Eric (HEE-lee, AIR-ihk)

Left wing. Shoots left. 5'11", 196 lbs. Born, Hull, MA, January 20, 1975.

			Regular Season					Playoffs				
Season	Club	Lea	GP	G	A	TP	PIM	GP	G	A	TP	PIM
1993-94	New England	NEJHL	37	61	76	137	....	....	....	....	....	....
1994-95	RPI Engineers	ECAC	37	13	11	24	35	....	....	....	....	....
1995-96	RPI Engineers	ECAC	35	18	22	40	57	....	....	....	....	....
1996-97	RPI Engineers	ECAC	36	30	26	56	63	....	....	....	....	....
1997-98	RPI Engineers	ECAC	35	21	27	48	42	....	....	....	....	....
1998-99	Saint John Flames	AHL	64	14	24	38	77	....	....	....	....	....
	Orlando	IHL	13	5	4	9	13	8	1	0	1	12
99-2000	Springfield	AHL	32	14	15	29	51	1	0	0	0	2
2000-01	Springfield	AHL	66	16	17	33	53	....	....	....	....	....

ECAC Second All-Star Team (1997) • NCAA East Second All-American Team (1997, 1998) • ECAC First All-Star Team (1998)

Signed as a free agent by **Calgary**, September 22, 1998. Signed as a free agent by **Phoenix**, July 26, 1999.

HEATLEY, Dany (HEET-lee, DA-nee) **ATL.**

Left wing. Shoots left. 6'2", 210 lbs. Born, Freiburg, West Germany, January 21, 1981.
(Atlanta's 1st choice, 2nd overall, in 2000 Entry Draft).

			Regular Season					Playoffs				
Season	Club	Lea	GP	G	A	TP	PIM	GP	G	A	TP	PIM
1996-97	Calgary Blazers	AAHA	25	30	42	72	26	....	....	....	....	....
1997-98	Calgary Buffaloes	AMHL	36	39	42	*91	34	10	10	12	*22	30
1998-99	Calgary Canucks	AJHL	60	*70	56	*126	91	13	*22	13	*35	6
99-2000	U. of Wisconsin	WCHA	38	28	28	56	32	....	....	....	....	....
2000-01	U. of Wisconsin	WCHA	39	24	33	57	74	....	....	....	....	....

Air Canada Cup MVP (1997) • AJHL Player of the Year (1999) • Canadian Junior "A" Player of the Year (1999) • WCHA First All-Star Team (2000) • WCHA Rookie of the Year (2000) • NCAA West Second All-American Team (2000) • WCHA Second All-Star Team (2001) • NCAA West First All-American Team (2001)

HEDIN, Pierre (heh-DEEN, PEE-air) **TOR.**

Defense. Shoots left. 6'1", 198 lbs. Born, Ornskoldsvik, Sweden, February 19, 1978.
(Toronto's 8th choice, 239th overall, in 1999 Entry Draft).

			Regular Season					Playoffs				
Season	Club	Lea	GP	G	A	TP	PIM	GP	G	A	TP	PIM
1994-95	MoDo Hockey	Swede-Jr.	21	0	3	3	20	....	....	....	....	....
1996-97	MoDo Hockey	Sweden	19	1	2	3	6	....	....	....	....	....
1997-98	MoDo Hockey	Swede-Jr.	7	1	6	7	10	....	....	....	....	....
	MoDo Hockey	Sweden	29	2	1	3	26	9	1	1	2	4
1998-99	MoDo Hockey	Sweden	41	6	5	11	28	13	1	1	2	12
99-2000	MoDo Hockey	Sweden	48	9	5	14	36	13	0	2	2	8
2000-01	MoDo Hockey	Sweden	46	5	8	13	59	7	3	0	3	4

HEDSTROM, Jonathan (HEHD-struhm, JAWN-ah-thuhn) **ANA.**

Right wing. Shoots left. 6', 200 lbs. Born, Skelleftea, Sweden, December 27, 1977.
(Toronto's 8th choice, 221st overall, in 1997 Entry Draft).

			Regular Season					Playoffs				
Season	Club	Lea	GP	G	A	TP	PIM	GP	G	A	TP	PIM
1995-96	HV Skelleftea	Swede-2	7	0	0	0	0	....	....	....	....	....
1996-97	HV Skelleftea	Swede-Jr.	9	4	4	8	....	....	....	....	....	....
	HV Skelleftea	Swede-2	12	1	1	2	10	6	0	0	0	2
1997-98	HV Skelleftea	Swede-Jr.	1	0	0	0	2	....	....	....	....	....
	HV Skelleftea	Swede-2	16	2	3	5	....	....	....	....	....	....
1998-99	Skelleftea AIK	Swede-2	36	15	28	43	74	....	....	....	....	....
99-2000	Lulea HF	Sweden	48	9	17	26	46	9	2	1	3	12
2000-01	Lulea HF	Sweden	46	9	19	28	68	12	1	6	7	16

Rights traded to **Anaheim** by **Toronto** for Anaheim's 6th (Vadim Sozinov) and 7th (Markus Seikola) round choices in 2000 Entry Draft, June 25, 2000.

HEEREMA, Jeff (HEER-eh-muh, JEHF) **CAR.**

Right wing. Shoots right. 6'1", 190 lbs. Born, Thunder Bay, Ont., January 17, 1980.
(Carolina's 1st choice, 11th overall, in 1998 Entry Draft).

			Regular Season					Playoffs				
Season	Club	Lea	GP	G	A	TP	PIM	GP	G	A	TP	PIM
1996-97	Thunder Bay	TBMHL	54	42	29	71	112	....	....	....	....	....
1997-98	Sarnia Sting	OHL	63	32	40	72	88	5	4	1	5	10
1998-99	Sarnia Sting	OHL	62	31	39	70	113	6	5	1	6	0
99-2000	Sarnia Sting	OHL	67	36	41	77	62	7	4	2	6	10
2000-01	Cincinnati	IHL	73	17	16	33	42	4	0	0	0	0

HEFFERNAN, Scott (HEH-fuhr-nuhn, SKAWT) **CBJ**

Defense. Shoots left. 6'5", 187 lbs. Born, Montreal, Que., March 9, 1982.
(Columbus' 4th choice, 138th overall, in 2000 Entry Draft).

			Regular Season					Playoffs				
Season	Club	Lea	GP	G	A	TP	PIM	GP	G	A	TP	PIM
1998-99	Pembroke Kings	OCJHL	44	3	5	8	51	....	....	....	....	....
99-2000	Sarnia Sting	OHL	55	5	10	15	24	7	0	1	1	4
2000-01	Sarnia Sting	OHL	51	2	20	22	30	4	0	1	1	0

HEID, Chris (HIGHD, KRIHS) **MIN.**

Defense. Shoots left. 6'2", 205 lbs. Born, Langley, B.C., March 14, 1983.
(Minnesota's 3rd choice, 74th overall, in 2001 Entry Draft).

			Regular Season					Playoffs				
Season	Club	Lea	GP	G	A	TP	PIM	GP	G	A	TP	PIM
1998-99	Kamloops	BCAHA	58	26	34	60	65	....	....	....	....	....
	Spokane Chiefs	WHL	1	0	0	0	0	....	....	....	....	....
99-2000	Spokane Chiefs	WHL	44	1	7	8	25	6	0	0	0	4
2000-01	Spokane Chiefs	WHL	51	2	15	17	76	12	0	4	4	12

HEISTEN, Barrett (HIGH-stehn, BAIR-reht) **NYR**

Left wing. Shoots left. 6'1", 189 lbs. Born, Anchorage, AK, March 19, 1980.
(Buffalo's 1st choice, 20th overall, in 1999 Entry Draft).

			Regular Season					Playoffs				
Season	Club	Lea	GP	G	A	TP	PIM	GP	G	A	TP	PIM
1996-97	Anchorage Stars	AAHL	39	35	29	64	....	....	....	....	....	....
1997-98	Team USA	USDP	50	11	26	37	245	....	....	....	....	....
1998-99	U. of Maine	H-East	34	12	16	28	72	....	....	....	....	....
99-2000	U. of Maine	H-East	37	13	24	37	86	....	....	....	....	....
2000-01	Seattle T-Birds	WHL	58	20	57	77	61	9	2	6	8	20

• Left **University of Maine** (H-East) and signed with **Seattle** (WHL) who had selected him 80th overall in 1998 WHL Bantam Draft, August 7, 2000. Signed as a free agent by **NY Rangers**, June 16, 2001.

HELBLING, Timo (HEHL-blihng, TEE-moh) **NSH.**

Defense. Shoots right. 6'2", 209 lbs. Born, Basel, Switzerland, July 21, 1981.
(Nashville's 11th choice, 162nd overall, in 1999 Entry Draft).

			Regular Season					Playoffs				
Season	Club	Lea	GP	G	A	TP	PIM	GP	G	A	TP	PIM
1997-98	HC Davos	Switz-Jr.	34	6	6	12	38	....	....	....	....	....
1998-99	HC Davos	Switz-Jr.	28	5	10	15	116	2	1	3	4	35
	HC Davos	Switz.	44	0	0	0	8	4	0	0	0	0
99-2000	HC Davos	Switz.	44	0	0	0	49	5	0	0	0	0
2000-01	Windsor Spitfires	OHL	54	7	14	21	90	7	0	2	2	11
	Milwaukee	IHL	....	....	....	....	....	1	0	0	0	0

HELFENSTEIN, Sven (hehl-fehn-SHTIGHN, SVEHN) **NYR**

Left wing. Shoots right. 5'10", 176 lbs. Born, Winterthur, Switzerland, July 30, 1982.
(NY Rangers' 6th choice, 175th overall, in 2000 Entry Draft).

			Regular Season					Playoffs				
Season	Club	Lea	GP	G	A	TP	PIM	GP	G	A	TP	PIM
1997-98	EHC Kloten	Switz-Jr.	31	6	8	14	14	....	....	....	....	....
1998-99	EHC Kloten	Switz-Jr.	33	25	18	43	14	7	5	3	8	2
	EHC Kloten	Switz.	2	0	0	0	0	....	....	....	....	....
99-2000	EHC Kloten	Switz.	40	6	3	9	28	6	0	1	1	0
2000-01	EHC Kloten	Switz.	8	1	1	2	0	....	....	....	....	....
	Chaux-de-Fonds	Switz.	23	2	8	10	6	12	1	3	4	6

HEMINGWAY, Colin (HEH-mihng-way, CAW-lihn) **ST.L.**

Right wing. Shoots right. 6', 170 lbs. Born, Regina, Sask., August 12, 1980.
(St. Louis' 7th choice, 221st overall, in 1999 Entry Draft).

			Regular Season					Playoffs				
Season	Club	Lea	GP	G	A	TP	PIM	GP	G	A	TP	PIM
1996-97	Port Coquitlam	PIJHL	34	23	24	47	52	....	....	....	....	....
1997-98	South Surrey	BCJHL	58	12	16	28	46	....	....	....	....	....
1998-99	South Surrey	BCJHL	59	40	64	104	52	....	....	....	....	....
99-2000	New Hampshire	H-East	22	3	5	8	6	....	....	....	....	....
2000-01	New Hampshire	H-East	37	9	18	27	16	....	....	....	....	....

HEMSKY, Ales (HEHM-skee, ahl-EHSH) **EDM.**

Right wing. Shoots right. 6', 191 lbs. Born, Pardubice, Czech., August 13, 1983.
(Edmonton's 1st choice, 13th overall, in 2001 Entry Draft).

			Regular Season					Playoffs				
Season	Club	Lea	GP	G	A	TP	PIM	GP	G	A	TP	PIM
99-2000	HC Pardubice-Jr.	Cze-Rep	45	20	36	56	54	7	4	14	18	36
	HC Pardubice	Cze-Rep	4	0	1	1	0	....	....	....	....	....
2000-01	Hull Olympiques	QMJHL	68	36	64	100	67	5	2	3	5	2

HENDRICKS, Matt (HEHN-drihks, MAT) **NSH.**

Center. Shoots left. 6', 195 lbs. Born, Blaine, MN, June 17, 1981.
(Nashville's 5th choice, 131st overall, in 2000 Entry Draft).

			Regular Season					Playoffs				
Season	Club	Lea	GP	G	A	TP	PIM	GP	G	A	TP	PIM
1998-99	Blaine High	Hi-School	22	23	34	57	42	....	....	....	....	....
99-2000	Blaine High	Hi-School	21	23	30	53	28	....	....	....	....	....
2000-01	St. Cloud State	WCHA	37	3	9	12	23	....	....	....	....	....

HENKEL, Jim (HEHN-kehl, JIHM) **L.A.**

Center. Shoots left. 6'2", 180 lbs. Born, Red Bank, NJ, May 25, 1979.
(Los Angeles' 8th choice, 217th overall, in 1998 Entry Draft).

			Regular Season					Playoffs				
Season	Club	Lea	GP	G	A	TP	PIM	GP	G	A	TP	PIM
1997-98	New England	EJHL	37	34	37	71	....	11	7	17	24	....
1998-99	RPI Engineers	ECAC	20	0	4	4	14	....	....	....	....	....
99-2000	RPI Engineers	ECAC	34	2	5	7	28	....	....	....	....	....
2000-01	RPI Engineers	ECAC	34	11	19	30	44	....	....	....	....	....

HENNING, Brett (HEH-nihng, BREHT) **NYI**

Center. Shoots left. 6'1", 203 lbs. Born, Huntington, NY, May 7, 1980.
(NY Islanders' 13th choice, 255th overall, in 1999 Entry Draft).

			Regular Season					Playoffs				
Season	Club	Lea	GP	G	A	TP	PIM	GP	G	A	TP	PIM
1995-96	Cambridge Hawks	OJHL-B	46	8	26	34	49	....	....	....	....	....
1996-97	Cambridge Hawks	OJHL-B	43	11	21	32	70	....	....	....	....	....
1997-98	Team USA	USDP	71	13	31	44	96	....	....	....	....	....
1998-99	Notre Dame	CCHA	38	4	6	10	30	....	....	....	....	....
99-2000	Notre Dame	CCHA	36	3	7	10	16	....	....	....	....	....
2000-01	Notre Dame	CCHA	15	1	2	3	14	....	....	....	....	....

HENNING, Petter (HEH-nihng, PEH-tehr) **NYR**

Right wing. Shoots left. 6', 209 lbs. Born, Ornskoldsvik, Sweden, September 15, 1980.
(NY Rangers' 10th choice, 251st overall, in 1999 Entry Draft).

			Regular Season					Playoffs				
Season	Club	Lea	GP	G	A	TP	PIM	GP	G	A	TP	PIM
1997-98	MoDo Hockey	Swede-Jr.	27	7	6	13	12	....	....	....	....	....
1998-99	MoDo Hockey	Swede-Jr.	38	10	10	20	74	....	....	....	....	....
	MoDo Hockey	Sweden	1	0	0	0	0	....	....	....	....	....
99-2000	Skelleftea AIK	Swede-Jr.	3	1	0	1	0	....	....	....	....	....
	Skelleftea AIK	Sweden	8	0	0	0	2	....	....	....	....	....
2000-01	Tingsryd IK	Swede-2	40	3	5	8	18	3	0	0	0	6

HENRICH, Michael (HEHN-rihch, MIGH-kuhl) **EDM.**

Right wing. Shoots right. 6'2", 206 lbs. Born, Thornhill, Ont., March 3, 1980.
(Edmonton's 1st choice, 13th overall, in 1998 Entry Draft).

			Regular Season					Playoffs				
Season	Club	Lea	GP	G	A	TP	PIM	GP	G	A	TP	PIM
1995-96	Wexford Raiders	MTJHL	4	1	0	1	0	....	....	....	....	....
1996-97	Barrie Colts	OHL	52	9	15	24	19	9	0	5	5	0
1997-98	Barrie Colts	OHL	66	41	22	63	75	5	1	3	4	0
1998-99	Barrie Colts	OHL	62	38	33	71	42	12	0	2	2	4
99-2000	Barrie Colts	OHL	66	38	48	86	69	25	10	18	28	30
2000-01	Tallahassee	ECHL	6	1	1	2	0	....	....	....	....	....
	Hamilton Bulldogs	AHL	73	5	10	15	36	....	....	....	....	....

HENRY, Alex (HEHN-ree, AL-ehx) **EDM.**

Defense. Shoots left. 6'5", 220 lbs. Born, Elliot Lake, Ont., October 18, 1979.
(Edmonton's 2nd choice, 67th overall, in 1998 Entry Draft).

			Regular Season					Playoffs				
Season	Club	Lea	GP	G	A	TP	PIM	GP	G	A	TP	PIM
1995-96	Timmins Titans	NOHA	30	2	4	11	15	....	....	....	....	....
	Timmins Bears	NOJHA	2	0	0	0	0	....	....	....	....	....
1996-97	London Knights	OHL	61	1	10	11	65	....	....	....	....	....
1997-98	London Knights	OHL	62	5	9	14	97	16	0	3	3	14
1998-99	London Knights	OHL	68	5	23	28	105	25	3	10	13	22
99-2000	Hamilton Bulldogs	AHL	60	1	0	1	69	....	....	....	....	....
2000-01	Hamilton Bulldogs	AHL	56	2	3	5	87	....	....	....	....	....

HENRY, Burke (HEHN-ree, BUHRK) **CGY.**

Defense. Shoots left. 6'3", 190 lbs. Born, Ste. Rose, Man., January 21, 1979.
(NY Rangers' 3rd choice, 73rd overall, in 1997 Entry Draft).

			Regular Season					Playoffs				
Season	Club	Lea	GP	G	A	TP	PIM	GP	G	A	TP	PIM
1995-96	Brandon	WHL	50	6	11	17	58	19	0	4	4	19
1996-97	Brandon	WHL	55	6	25	31	81	6	1	3	4	4
1997-98	Brandon	WHL	72	18	65	83	153	18	3	16	19	37
1998-99	Brandon	WHL	68	18	58	76	151	5	1	6	7	9
99-2000	Hartford	AHL	64	3	12	15	47	5	0	0	0	2
2000-01	Hartford	AHL	80	8	30	38	133	5	0	0	0	2

WHL East First All-Star Team (1998) • WHL East Second All-Star Team (1999)

Traded to **Calgary** by **NY Rangers** for Chris St. Croix, June 23, 2001.

HENTUNEN, Jukka (HEHN-too-nehn, YOO-kuh) **CGY.**

Right wing. Shoots right. 5'10", 194 lbs. Born, Joroinen, Finland, May 3, 1974.
(Calgary's 7th choice, 176th overall, in 2000 Entry Draft).

			Regular Season					Playoffs				
Season	Club	Lea	GP	G	A	TP	PIM	GP	G	A	TP	PIM
1993-94	Kiekko Warkaus	Finland-3	24	11	7	18	12	....	....	....	....	....
1994-95	Kiekko Warkaus	Finland-3	29	23	23	46	28	....	....	....	....	....
1995-96	Diskos Jyvaskyla	Finland-2	53	28	24	52	18	....	....	....	....	....
1996-97	Hermes Kokkola	Finland-2	35	10	13	23	43	3	1	0	1	0
1997-98	Hermes Kokkola	Finland-2	49	19	16	35	36	3	3	3	6	0
1998-99	Hermes Kokkola	Finland-2	1	0	0	0	0	....	....	....	....	....
	HPK Hameenlinna	Finland	41	13	21	34	32	8	1	4	5	12
99-2000	HPK Hameenlinna	Finland	53	17	28	45	76	8	4	2	6	12
2000-01	Jokerit Helsinki	Finland	56	27	28	55	24	5	1	0	1	4

HILBERT, Andy (HIHL-buhrt, AN-dee) **BOS.**

Center. Shoots left. 5'11", 190 lbs. Born, Howell, MI, February 6, 1981.
(Boston's 3rd choice, 37th overall, in 2000 Entry Draft).

			Regular Season					Playoffs				
Season	Club	Lea	GP	G	A	TP	PIM	GP	G	A	TP	PIM
1997-98	Team USA	USDP	75	34	30	64	148	....	....	....	....	....
1998-99	Team USA	USDP	46	23	35	58	140	....	....	....	....	....
99-2000	U. of Michigan	CCHA	35	17	15	32	39	....	....	....	....	....
2000-01	U. of Michigan	CCHA	42	26	38	64	72	....	....	....	....	....

CCHA First All-Star Team (2001) • NCAA West First All-American Team (2001)

HINZ, Chad (HIHNZ, CHAD) **EDM.**

Right wing. Shoots right. 5'10", 190 lbs. Born, Saskatoon, Sask., March 21, 1979.
(Edmonton's 8th choice, 187th overall, in 1997 Entry Draft).

			Regular Season					Playoffs				
Season	Club	Lea	GP	G	A	TP	PIM	GP	G	A	TP	PIM
1994-95	Saskatoon AAA	SMHL	29	25	21	46	41	....	....	....	....	....
1995-96	Moose Jaw	WHL	70	22	32	54	65	....	....	....	....	....
1996-97	Moose Jaw	WHL	72	37	47	84	47	12	4	1	5	11
1997-98	Moose Jaw	WHL	72	20	57	77	45	4	1	2	3	2
1998-99	Moose Jaw	WHL	71	42	*75	117	40	11	4	12	16	12
	Hamilton Bulldogs	AHL	3	0	0	0	2	....	....	....	....	....
99-2000	Hamilton Bulldogs	AHL	18	1	4	5	2	5	1	0	1	0
	Tallahassee	ECHL	49	15	25	40	35	....	....	....	....	....
2000-01	Hamilton Bulldogs	AHL	78	13	22	35	30	....	....	....	....	....

WHL East First All-Star Team (1999)

HIRVONEN, Tomi (HIHR-voh-nehn, TAW-mee) **COL.**

Center. Shoots left. 5'11", 185 lbs. Born, Tampere, Finland, January 11, 1977.
(Colorado's 8th choice, 207th overall, in 1995 Entry Draft).

			Regular Season					Playoffs				
Season	Club	Lea	GP	G	A	TP	PIM	GP	G	A	TP	PIM
1992-93	Ilves Tampere-C	Finn-Jr	34	32	20	52	71	....	....	....	....	....
1993-94	Ilves Tampere-B	Finn-Jr	28	13	14	27	96	....	....	....	....	....
	Ilves Tampere	Finn-Jr.	1	0	0	0	0	....	....	....	....	....
1994-95	Ilves Tampere-B	Finn-Jr.	6	1	5	6	14	....	....	....	....	....
	Ilves Tampere	Finn-Jr.	28	9	13	22	30	8	4	2	6	14
1995-96	Ilves Tampere	Finn-Jr.	5	2	2	4	37	7	5	10	15	8
	KooVee Tampere	Finland-2	7	4	1	5	26	....	....	....	....	....
	Ilves Tampere	Finland	28	1	0	1	24	....	....	....	....	....
1996-97	Ilves Tampere	Finn-Jr.	5	2	2	4	37	4	1	3	4	8
	Ilves Tampere	Finland	40	0	7	7	22	6	0	0	0	4
1997-98	Ilves Tampere	Finland	48	10	12	22	54	9	0	0	0	2
	Ilves Tampere	Finn-Jr.	....	....	....	....	....	2	5	0	5	4
1998-99	Ilves Tampere	Finland	50	5	15	20	94	4	0	0	0	8
	Ilves Tampere	EuroHL	6	1	3	4	2	....	....	....	....	....
99-2000	Ilves Tampere	Finland	45	4	7	11	62	3	0	1	1	6
2000-01	JyP Jyvaskyla	Finland	52	5	8	13	76	....	....	....	....	....

HLINKA, Martin (huh-LIHN-kuh, MAHR-tihn) WSH.

Left wing. Shoots left. 6'1", 200 lbs. Born, Bratislava, Czech., September 25, 1976.

Season	Club	Lea	Regular Season GP	G	A	TP	PIM	Playoffs GP	G	A	TP	PIM
1995-96	Augsburg College	NCAA	15	6	5	11	....	....	....	....	....	....
1996-97	Augsburg College	NCAA	24	14	23	37	....	....	....	....	....	....
1997-98	Augsburg College	NCAA	24	14	30	44	....	....	....	....	....	....
1998-99	Augsburg College	NCAA	22	6	27	33	24	....	....	....	....	....
	Quad City	UHL	2	1	1	2	0	1	0	0	0	0
99-2000	Quad City	UHL	71	21	46	67	74	14	0	7	7	24
	Chicago Wolves	IHL	1	0	0	0	0	....	....	....	....	....
2000-01	Quad City	UHL	11	4	10	14	0	5	1	1	2	....
	Portland Pirates	AHL	60	13	19	32	50	3	1	2	3	2

MIAC First All-Star Team (1997, 1998, 1999) • MIAC All-Conference All-Star Team (1999) • Also played football at Augsburg College and holds every school single season and career record for field goals attempted, field goals made and total points scored. • UHL All-Rookie Team (2000)

Selected by **Quad City** (UHL) in UHL Over-age Priority Draft, March 12, 1999. Signed as a free agent by **Portland** (AHL), November 10, 2000. Signed as a free agent by **Washington**, May 3, 2001.

HOHENER, Martin (HOH-ehn-uhr, MAHR-tihn) NSH.

Defense. Shoots left. 6'1", 192 lbs. Born, Zurich, Switz., June 23, 1980.
(Nashville's 12th choice, 284th overall, in 2000 Entry Draft).

Season	Club	Lea	Regular Season GP	G	A	TP	PIM	Playoffs GP	G	A	TP	PIM
1996-97	EHC Kloten	Switz-Jr.	37	4	7	11	....	....	....	....	....	....
1997-98	EHC Kloten	Switz-Jr.	25	2	9	11	31	....	....	....	....	....
	EHC Bulach	Switz-2	4	0	0	0	0	....	....	....	....	....
1998-99	EHC Kloten	Switz-Jr.	21	5	8	13	22	2	1	0	1	2
	EHC Kloten	Switz.	20	0	1	1	2	9	0	1	1	0
99-2000	EHC Kloten	Switz.	44	4	2	6	20	5	0	1	1	2
2000-01	EHC Kloten	Switz.	35	4	5	9	32	9	0	1	1	6

HOLLIS, Scott (HAWL-lihs, SKAWT)

Right wing. Shoots right. 6', 185 lbs. Born, Kingston, Ont., September 18, 1972.
(Vancouver's 9th choice, 165th overall, in 1992 Entry Draft).

Season	Club	Lea	Regular Season GP	G	A	TP	PIM	Playoffs GP	G	A	TP	PIM
1988-89	Kingston Lions	OMHA	14	14	14	28	15	....	....	....	....	....
1989-90	Oshawa Generals	OHL	50	4	6	10	33	9	0	1	1	2
1990-91	Oshawa Generals	OHL	66	24	33	57	91	16	5	3	8	20
1991-92	Oshawa Generals	OHL	66	47	54	101	183	7	7	3	10	8
1992-93	Oshawa Generals	OHL	62	49	53	102	148	13	8	15	23	22
1993-94	Las Vegas	IHL	23	3	1	4	65	....	....	....	....	....
	Knoxville	ECHL	29	20	16	36	99	3	3	1	4	8
1994-95	Adirondack	AHL	48	12	15	27	118	....	....	....	....	....
1995-96	Toledo Storm	ECHL	7	7	11	18	5	....	....	....	....	....
	Adirondack	AHL	55	18	17	37	111	3	0	1	1	4
1996-97	San Antonio	IHL	73	17	17	34	187	9	1	1	2	6
1997-98	San Antonio	IHL	19	15	6	21	21	....	....	....	....	....
	Orlando	IHL	48	16	23	39	68	17	5	4	9	30
1998-99	Orlando	IHL	3	1	1	2	6	....	....	....	....	....
	Long Beach	IHL	13	2	5	7	21	....	....	....	....	....
	Las Vegas	IHL	53	20	25	45	67	....	....	....	....	....
99-2000	SB Rosenheim	DEL	63	21	16	37	80	....	....	....	....	....
2000-01	Syracuse Crunch	AHL	38	10	10	20	92	....	....	....	....	....
	Houston Aeros	IHL	22	7	6	13	22	7	1	0	1	10

Signed as a free agent by **Columbus**, August 7, 2000.

HOLMQVIST, Andreas (HOHLM-kvihst, ahn-DRAY-uhs) T.B.

Defense. Shoots right. 6'4", 190 lbs. Born, Stockholm, Sweden, July 23, 1981.
(Tampa Bay's 3rd choice, 61st overall, in 2001 Entry Draft).

Season	Club	Lea	Regular Season GP	G	A	TP	PIM	Playoffs GP	G	A	TP	PIM
99-2000	Hammarby IF	Swede-Jr.	33	8	12	20	16	6	1	2	3	4
2000-01	Hammarby IF	Swede-Jr.	47	6	15	21	40	....	....	....	....	....

HOLMQVIST, Mikael (HOHLM-kvihst, MIHK-al) ANA.

Center. Shoots left. 6'3", 189 lbs. Born, Stockholm, Sweden, June 8, 1979.
(Anaheim's 1st choice, 18th overall, in 1997 Entry Draft).

Season	Club	Lea	Regular Season GP	G	A	TP	PIM	Playoffs GP	G	A	TP	PIM
1995-96	Djurgardens IF	Swede-Jr.	24	7	2	9	4	....	....	....	....	....
1996-97	Djurgardens IF	Swede-Jr.	39	29	35	64	110	....	....	....	....	....
	Djurgardens IF	Sweden	9	0	0	0	0	....	....	....	....	....
1997-98	Farjestads BK	Sweden	41	2	3	5	6	7	0	0	0	0
	Farjestads BK	EuroHL	5	2	2	4	2	....	....	....	....	....
1998-99	Farjestads BK	Swede-Jr.	2	2	2	4	2	....	....	....	....	....
	Farjestads BK	EuroHL	3	0	0	0	0	1	0	0	0	0
	Farjestads BK	Sweden	15	0	0	0	6	....	....	....	....	....
	Hammarby IF	Swede-2	3	2	0	2	0	....	....	....	....	....
99-2000	TPS Turku	Finland	54	12	3	15	14	11	2	3	5	4
2000-01	TPS Turku	Finland	46	4	5	9	8	10	1	3	4	2

HORACEK, Jan (HOHR-uh-chehk, YAN) EDM.

Defense. Shoots right. 6'4", 206 lbs. Born, Benesov, Czech., May 22, 1979.
(St. Louis' 3rd choice, 98th overall, in 1997 Entry Draft).

Season	Club	Lea	Regular Season GP	G	A	TP	PIM	Playoffs GP	G	A	TP	PIM
1995-96	Slavia Praha-Jr.	Cze-Rep	18	1	5	6	0	....	....	....	....	....
	HC Karlovy-2	Cze-Rep	11	0	0	0	0	....	....	....	....	....
	Slavia Praha	Cze-Rep	8	0	1	1	4	....	....	....	....	....
1996-97	Slavia Praha-Jr.	Cze-Rep	25	4	14	18	....	....	....	....	....	....
	HC Beroun-2	Cze-Rep	2	0	0	0	....	....	....	....	....	....
	Slavia Praha	Cze-Rep	9	0	0	0	6	3	0	0	0	0
1997-98	Moncton Wildcats	QMJHL	54	3	18	21	146	10	1	5	6	20
1998-99	Slavia Praha	Cze-Rep	1	0	0	0	2	....	....	....	....	....
	Worcester	AHL	53	1	13	14	119	4	0	0	0	6
99-2000	Worcester	AHL	68	1	8	9	145	9	0	0	0	2
2000-01	Worcester	AHL	11	0	1	1	20	2	0	0	0	2
	Peoria	ECHL	6	0	3	3	8	....	....	....	....	....

• Missed majority of 2000-01 season recovering from wrist surgery, October 23, 2000. Traded to **Edmonton** by **St. Louis** with Marty Reasoner and Jochen Hecht for Doug Weight and Michel Riesen, July 1, 2001.

HOSSA, Marcel (HOH-sah, MAHR-sehl) MTL.

Center. Shoots left. 6'2", 211 lbs. Born, Ilava, Czech., October 12, 1981.
(Montreal's 2nd choice, 16th overall, in 2000 Entry Draft).

Season	Club	Lea	Regular Season GP	G	A	TP	PIM	Playoffs GP	G	A	TP	PIM
1996-97	Dukla Trencin	Slovak-Jr.	45	30	21	51	30	....	....	....	....	....
1997-98	Dukla Trencin	Slovak-Jr.	39	11	38	49	44	....	....	....	....	....
1998-99	Portland	WHL	70	7	14	21	66	2	0	0	0	2
99-2000	Portland	WHL	60	24	29	53	58	....	....	....	....	....
2000-01	Portland	WHL	58	34	56	90	58	16	5	7	12	14

WHL West Second All-Star Team (2001)

HOUSE, Bobby (HOWSE, BAW-bee) TOR.

Right wing. Shoots right. 6'1", 205 lbs. Born, Whitehorse, Yukon, January 7, 1973.
(Chicago's 4th choice, 66th overall, in 1991 Entry Draft).

Season	Club	Lea	Regular Season GP	G	A	TP	PIM	Playoffs GP	G	A	TP	PIM
1988-89	Whitehorse Elks	AAHL	28	36	27	63	28	....	....	....	....	....
1989-90	Spokane Chiefs	WHL	64	18	16	34	74	5	0	0	0	6
1990-91	Spokane Chiefs	WHL	38	11	19	30	63	....	....	....	....	....
	Brandon	WHL	23	18	7	25	14	....	....	....	....	....
1991-92	Brandon	WHL	71	35	42	77	133	....	....	....	....	....
1992-93	Brandon	WHL	61	57	39	96	87	4	2	2	4	0
1993-94	Indianapolis Ice	IHL	42	10	8	18	51	....	....	....	....	....
	Flint Generals	ColHL	4	3	3	6	0	....	....	....	....	....
1994-95	Columbus Chill	ECHL	9	11	6	17	2	....	....	....	....	....
	Indianapolis Ice	IHL	26	2	3	5	26	....	....	....	....	....
	Albany River Rats	AHL	26	4	7	11	12	8	1	1	2	0
1995-96	Albany River Rats	AHL	77	37	49	86	57	4	0	0	0	4
1996-97	Albany River Rats	AHL	68	18	16	34	65	16	3	2	5	23
1997-98	Albany River Rats	AHL	19	10	10	20	10	....	....	....	....	....
	Hershey Bears	AHL	20	2	6	8	8	....	....	....	....	....
	Quebec Rafales	IHL	24	5	7	12	12	....	....	....	....	....
	Syracuse Crunch	AHL	9	5	6	11	6	5	2	0	2	4
1998-99	Augusta Lynx	ECHL	5	1	0	1	15	....	....	....	....	....
	Albany River Rats	AHL	1	0	0	0	0	....	....	....	....	....
	Springfield	AHL	56	11	18	29	27	3	1	0	1	2
99-2000	St. John's Leafs	AHL	68	24	29	53	46	....	....	....	....	....
2000-01	St. John's Leafs	AHL	65	36	33	69	49	....	....	....	....	....

WHL East Second All-Star Team (1993) • AHL Second All-Star Team (2001)

Traded to **New Jersey** by **Chicago** for cash, May 21, 1996. Signed as a free agent by **Toronto**, August 20, 1999.

HUML, Ivan (HUH-muhl, ee-VAHN) BOS.

Left wing. Shoots left. 6'2", 195 lbs. Born, Kladno, Czech., September 6, 1981.
(Boston's 4th choice, 59th overall, in 2000 Entry Draft).

Season	Club	Lea	Regular Season GP	G	A	TP	PIM	Playoffs GP	G	A	TP	PIM
1996-97	HC Kladno-Jr.	Cze-Rep	37	16	3	19	....	....	....	....	....	....
1997-98	HC Kladno-Jr.	Cze-Rep	46	37	24	61	....	....	....	....	....	....
	HC Kladno	Cze-Rep	1	0	0	0	0	....	....	....	....	....
1998-99	HC Kladno-Jr.	Cze-Rep	18	6	6	12	....	....	....	....	....	....
	Langley Hornets	BCJHL	33	23	17	40	41	....	....	....	....	....
99-2000	Langley Hornets	BCJHL	49	53	51	104	72	....	....	....	....	....
2000-01	Providence Bruins	AHL	79	13	6	19	28	17	0	0	0	2

HUNTER, Trent (HUHN-tuhr, TREHNT) NYI

Right wing. Shoots right. 6'3", 191 lbs. Born, Red Deer, Alta., July 5, 1980.
(Anaheim's 4th choice, 150th overall, in 1998 Entry Draft).

Season	Club	Lea	Regular Season GP	G	A	TP	PIM	Playoffs GP	G	A	TP	PIM
1996-97	Red Deer Chiefs	AMHL	42	30	25	55	50	....	....	....	....	....
1997-98	Prince George	WHL	60	13	14	27	34	8	1	0	1	4
1998-99	Prince George	WHL	50	18	20	38	34	7	2	5	7	2
99-2000	Prince George	WHL	67	46	49	95	47	13	7	15	22	6
2000-01	Springfield	AHL	57	18	17	35	14	....	....	....	....	....

WHL West First All-Star Team (2000)

Traded to **NY Islanders** by **Anaheim** for Columbus' 4th round choice (previously acquired, Anaheim selected Jonas Ronnqvist) in 2000 Entry Draft, May 23, 2000.

HUSELIUS, Kristian (hoo-SAY-lee-oos, KRIHST-yan) FLA.

Right wing. Shoots left. 6'1", 190 lbs. Born, Haninge, Sweden, November 10, 1978.
(Florida's 2nd choice, 47th overall, in 1997 Entry Draft).

Season	Club	Lea	Regular Season GP	G	A	TP	PIM	Playoffs GP	G	A	TP	PIM
1994-95	Hammarby IF	Swede-Jr.	17	6	2	8	2	....	....	....	....	....
1995-96	Hammarby IF	Swede-Jr.	25	13	8	21	14	....	....	....	....	....
	Hammarby IF	Sweden	6	1	0	1	0	....	....	....	....	....
1996-97	Farjestads BK	Sweden	13	2	0	2	4	5	1	0	1	0
1997-98	Farjestads BK	Sweden	34	2	1	3	2	11	0	0	0	0
	Farjestads BK	EuroHL	5	2	3	5	0	....	....	....	....	....
1998-99	Farjestads BK	Sweden	28	4	4	8	4	....	....	....	....	....
	Farjestads BK	EuroHL	6	2	2	4	8	1	0	0	0	0
	Vastra Frolunda	Sweden	20	2	2	4	2	4	1	0	1	0
99-2000	Vastra Frolunda	Sweden	50	21	23	44	20	5	2	2	4	8
2000-01	Vastra Frolunda	Sweden	49	*32	*35	*67	26	5	4	5	9	14

HUSKINS, Kent (HUHS-kihns, KEHNT) CHI.

Defense. Shoots left. 6'2", 190 lbs. Born, Ottawa, Ont., May 4, 1979.
(Chicago's 3rd choice, 156th overall, in 1998 Entry Draft).

Season	Club	Lea	Regular Season GP	G	A	TP	PIM	Playoffs GP	G	A	TP	PIM
1995-96	Kanata Lasers	OCJHL	49	6	21	27	18	....	....	....	....	....
1996-97	Kanata Lasers	OCJHL	53	11	36	47	89	....	....	....	....	....
1997-98	Clarkson Knights	ECAC	35	2	8	10	46	....	....	....	....	....
1998-99	Clarkson Knights	ECAC	37	5	11	16	28	....	....	....	....	....
99-2000	Clarkson Knights	ECAC	28	2	16	18	30	....	....	....	....	....
2000-01	Clarkson Knights	ECAC	35	6	28	34	22	....	....	....	....	....

ECAC First All-Star Team (2000, 2001) • NCAA East First All-American Team (2001)

HUSSEY, Matt (HUH-see, MAT) PIT.

Center. Shoots left. 6'2", 195 lbs. Born, New Haven, CT, May 28, 1979.
(Pittsburgh's 10th choice, 254th overall, in 1998 Entry Draft).

Season	Club	Lea	Regular Season GP	G	A	TP	PIM	Playoffs GP	G	A	TP	PIM
1996-97	Wayzata High	Hi-School	48	34	31	65	....	....	....	....	....	....
1997-98	Avon Old Farms	Hi-School	26	26	23	49	20	....	....	....	....	....
1998-99	U. of Wisconsin	WCHA	37	10	5	15	18	....	....	....	....	....
99-2000	U. of Wisconsin	WCHA	35	5	11	16	8	....	....	....	....	....
2000-01	U. of Wisconsin	WCHA	40	9	11	20	24	....	....	....	....	....

HUTCHINSON, Andrew (HUHT-chihn-suhn, AN-droo) NSH.

Defense. Shoots right. 6'2", 190 lbs. Born, Evanston, IL, March 24, 1980.
(Nashville's 4th choice, 54th overall, in 1999 Entry Draft).

			Regular Season					Playoffs				
Season	Club	Lea	GP	G	A	TP	PIM	GP	G	A	TP	PIM
1996-97	Detroit Caesars	NAJHL	82	15	41	56	....	....	....	....	....	....
1997-98	Team USA	USDP	59	7	21	28	53	....	....	....	....	....
1998-99	Michigan State	CCHA	37	3	12	15	26	....	....	....	....	....
99-2000	Michigan State	CCHA	42	5	12	17	64	....	....	....	....	....
2000-01	Michigan State	CCHA	42	5	19	24	46	....	....	....	....	....

CCHA Second All-Star Team (2001)

HYACINTHE, Seneque (high-a-SIHNT, SHE-nehk)

Left wing. Shoots left. 5'11", 180 lbs. Born, Montreal, Que., February 22, 1981.
(Buffalo's 9th choice, 178th overall, in 1999 Entry Draft).

			Regular Season					Playoffs				
Season	Club	Lea	GP	G	A	TP	PIM	GP	G	A	TP	PIM
1996-97	Mtl-Bourassa	QAAA	31	20	19	39	....	16	9	13	22	....
1997-98	Laval Titan	QMJHL	65	10	8	18	37	8	3	2	5	2
1998-99	Acadie-Bathurst	QMJHL	31	13	17	30	70	....	....	....	....	....
	Val-d'Or Foreurs	QMJHL	32	11	16	27	36	4	0	2	2	2
99-2000	Val-d'Or Foreurs	QMJHL	49	15	30	45	43	....	....	....	....	....
2000-01	Val-d'Or Foreurs	QMJHL	66	32	54	86	68	21	10	17	27	22

HYMOVITZ, David (HIH-moh-vihtz, DAY-vihd) OTT.

Left wing. Shoots left. 5'11", 170 lbs. Born, Boston, MA, May 30, 1974.
(Chicago's 9th choice, 209th overall, in 1992 Entry Draft).

			Regular Season					Playoffs				
Season	Club	Lea	GP	G	A	TP	PIM	GP	G	A	TP	PIM
1991-92	Thayer Academy	Hi-School	26	28	21	49	22	....	....	....	....	....
1992-93	Boston College	H-East	37	7	6	13	6	....	....	....	....	....
1993-94	Boston College	H-East	36	18	14	32	18	....	....	....	....	....
1994-95	Boston College	H-East	35	21	19	40	22	....	....	....	....	....
1995-96	Boston College	H-East	36	26	18	44	32	....	....	....	....	....
1996-97	Columbus Chill	ECHL	58	39	32	71	29	5	4	1	5	2
	Indianapolis Ice	IHL	6	0	1	1	0	1	0	0	0	0
1997-98	Indianapolis Ice	IHL	63	11	15	26	20	5	1	1	2	6
1998-99	Indianapolis Ice	IHL	78	46	30	76	42	5	2	3	5	2
99-2000	Lowell	AHL	67	19	17	36	30	....	....	....	....	....
	Houston Aeros	IHL	18	10	3	13	16	11	3	4	7	8
2000-01	Lowell	AHL	60	14	15	29	52	4	2	1	3	17

IHL Second All-Star Team (1999)

Signed as a free agent by **LA Kings**, June 10, 1999. Traded to **Houston** (IHL) by **Lowell** (AHL) with LA Kings retaining NHL rights for Jeff Daw , March 17, 2000. Signed as a free agent by **Ottawa**, July 13, 2001.

HYVONEN, Hannes (HOO-voh-nuhn, HAH-nuhs) S.J.

Right wing. Shoots right. 6'2", 200 lbs. Born, Oulu, Finland, August 29, 1975.
(San Jose's 7th choice, 257th overall, in 1999 Entry Draft).

			Regular Season					Playoffs				
Season	Club	Lea	GP	G	A	TP	PIM	GP	G	A	TP	PIM
1993-94	Karpat Oulu	Finn-Jr.	35	15	13	28	26	3	0	0	0	0
	Karpat Oulu	Finland-2	3	3	1	4	2	....	....	....	....	....
1994-95	TPS Turku	Finn-Jr.	10	8	2	10	64	....	....	....	....	....
	Kiekko-67	Finn-Jr.	1	1	0	1	0	....	....	....	....	....
	Kiekko-67	Finland-2	16	4	2	6	10	....	....	....	....	....
	TPS Turku	Finland	9	4	3	7	16	5	0	0	0	7
1995-96	Kiekko-67	Finland-2	2	1	0	1	8	....	....	....	....	....
	TPS Turku	Finland	30	11	5	16	49	7	0	1	1	28
1996-97	TPS Turku	Finland	41	10	5	15	48	10	4	2	6	14
1997-98	TPS Turku	Finland	29	2	6	8	71	2	0	0	0	0
1998-99	Blues Espoo	Finland	52	23	18	41	74	4	2	1	3	2
99-2000	Blues Espoo	Finland	18	5	2	7	*89	....	....	....	....	....
	HIFK Helsinki	Finland	22	2	2	4	*100	9	4	0	4	8
2000-01	HIFK Helsinki	Finland	56	14	12	26	34	5	0	0	0	8

HYYTIA, Mikko (HOO-tee-a, MEE-koh) MTL.

Center. Shoots left. 6', 180 lbs. Born, Jyvaskyla, Finland, July 12, 1981.
(Montreal's 10th choice, 225th overall, in 1999 Entry Draft).

			Regular Season					Playoffs				
Season	Club	Lea	GP	G	A	TP	PIM	GP	G	A	TP	PIM
1997-98	JyP Jyvaskyla	Finn-Jr.	36	11	15	26	14	5	2	1	3	2
1998-99	JyP Jyvaskyla-B	Finn-Jr.	27	32	15	47	53	....	....	....	....	....
	JyP Jyvaskyla	Finn-Jr.	12	2	7	9	4	....	....	....	....	....
99-2000	JyP Jyvaskyla-B	Finn-Jr.	7	3	3	6	4	....	....	....	....	....
	JyP Jyvaskyla	Finn-Jr.	1	0	0	0	0	....	....	....	....	....
2000-01	JyP Jyvaskyla	Finn-Jr.	27	8	18	26	26	6	2	1	3	2
	JyP Jyvaskyla	Finland	20	1	0	1	2	....	....	....	....	....

INMAN, David (IHN-man, DAY-vihd) NYR

Center. Shoots left. 6'1", 180 lbs. Born, New York, NY, June 13, 1980.
(NY Rangers' 3rd choice, 59th overall, in 1999 Entry Draft).

			Regular Season					Playoffs				
Season	Club	Lea	GP	G	A	TP	PIM	GP	G	A	TP	PIM
1995-96	Wexford Raiders	MTJHL	4	2	1	3	0	....	....	....	....	....
1996-97	Wexford Raiders	MTJHL	43	32	56	88	59	....	....	....	....	....
1997-98	Wexford Raiders	MTJHL	37	36	44	80	82	....	....	....	....	....
1998-99	Notre Dame	CCHA	38	10	10	20	74	....	....	....	....	....
99-2000	Notre Dame	CCHA	32	13	7	20	12	....	....	....	....	....
2000-01	Notre Dame	CCHA	37	11	6	17	10	....	....	....	....	....

IRGL, Zbynek (UHR-guhl, ZBIH-nehk) NSH.

Center. Shoots right. 5'11", 174 lbs. Born, Vitkovice, Czech., November 29, 1980.
(Nashville's 9th choice, 197th overall, in 2000 Entry Draft).

			Regular Season					Playoffs				
Season	Club	Lea	GP	G	A	TP	PIM	GP	G	A	TP	PIM
1996-97	HC Vitkovice-Jr.	Cze-Rep	43	44	22	66	....	....	....	....	....	....
1997-98	HC Vitkovice-Jr.	Cze-Rep	37	17	10	27	....	....	....	....	....	....
1998-99	HC Vitkovice-Jr.	Cze-Rep	18	9	8	17	....	....	....	....	....	....
	HC Vitkovice	Cze-Rep	33	2	2	4	6	4	0	0	0	....
99-2000	Dukla Jihlava-2	Cze-Rep	1	0	0	0	0	....	....	....	....	....
	HC Vitkovice	Cze-Rep	47	7	5	12	10	....	....	....	....	....
2000-01	HC Vitkovice	Cze-Rep	37	0	1	1	8	4	0	0	0	0

ISOSALO, Samu (ee-soh-SA-low, SA-moo) ATL.

Right wing. Shoots left. 6'3", 205 lbs. Born, Rauma, Finland, October 10, 1981.
(Atlanta's 10th choice, 230th overall, in 2000 Entry Draft).

			Regular Season					Playoffs				
Season	Club	Lea	GP	G	A	TP	PIM	GP	G	A	TP	PIM
1996-97	Lukko Rauma-B	Finn-Jr.	21	5	6	11	45	....	....	....	....	....
1997-98	Lukko Rauma	Finn-Jr.	34	21	19	40	48	....	....	....	....	....
1998-99	North Bay	OHL	59	13	12	25	19	4	0	0	0	4
99-2000	North Bay	OHL	48	17	25	42	26	3	0	0	0	0
2000-01	Lukko Rauma	Finn-Jr.	14	11	9	20	42	3	1	2	3	0
	Jaa-Kotkat	Finland-2	3	2	1	3	2	....	....	....	....	....
	Lukko Rauma	Finland	31	1	1	2	33	1	0	0	0	0

JACKMAN, Barret (JAK-man, BAIR-reht) ST.L.

Defense. Shoots left. 6'1", 200 lbs. Born, Trail, B.C., March 5, 1981.
(St. Louis' 1st choice, 17th overall, in 1999 Entry Draft).

			Regular Season					Playoffs				
Season	Club	Lea	GP	G	A	TP	PIM	GP	G	A	TP	PIM
1996-97	Beaver Valley	VIJHL	32	22	25	47	180	....	....	....	....	....
1997-98	Regina Pats	WHL	68	2	11	13	224	9	0	3	3	32
1998-99	Regina Pats	WHL	70	8	36	44	259	....	....	....	....	....
99-2000	Regina Pats	WHL	53	9	37	46	175	6	1	1	2	19
	Worcester	AHL	....	....	....	....	....	2	0	0	0	13
2000-01	Regina Pats	WHL	43	9	27	36	138	6	0	3	3	8

WHL East Second All-Star Team (2000)

JACKMAN, Tim (JAK-man, TIHM) CBJ

Right wing. Shoots right. 6'2", 190 lbs. Born, Minot, ND, November 14, 1981.
(Columbus' 2nd choice, 38th overall, in 2001 Entry Draft).

			Regular Season					Playoffs				
Season	Club	Lea	GP	G	A	TP	PIM	GP	G	A	TP	PIM
1998-99	Park Center High	Hi-School	22	22	22	44	....	....	....	....	....	....
99-2000	Park Center High	Hi-School	19	34	22	56	....	....	....	....	....	....
	Twin Cities	USHL	25	11	9	20	58	13	8	5	13	12
2000-01	MSU-Mankato	WCHA	37	11	14	25	92	....	....	....	....	....

Minnesota High School All-Conference Team (1999, 2000) • Minnesota All-State Team (2000)

JACKSON, Todd (JAK-suhn, TAWD) DET.

Right wing. Shoots right. 5'11", 170 lbs. Born, Syracuse, NY, April 10, 1981.
(Detroit's 10th choice, 251st overall, in 2000 Entry Draft).

			Regular Season					Playoffs				
Season	Club	Lea	GP	G	A	TP	PIM	GP	G	A	TP	PIM
1998-99	Team USA	USDP	53	11	9	20	56	....	....	....	....	....
99-2000	Team USA	USDP-17	29	8	10	18	25	....	....	....	....	....
	Team USA	USDP	23	8	6	14	12	....	....	....	....	....
2000-01	U. of Maine	H-East	39	4	8	12	8	....	....	....	....	....

JACOBS, Ian (JAY-cawbs, EE-an) FLA.

Right wing. Shoots right. 6'4", 207 lbs. Born, Walpole Island, Ont., May 16, 1980.
(Florida's 8th choice, 203rd overall, in 1998 Entry Draft).

			Regular Season					Playoffs				
Season	Club	Lea	GP	G	A	TP	PIM	GP	G	A	TP	PIM
1996-97	Chatham	OJHL-B	48	15	16	31	85	....	....	....	....	....
1997-98	Ottawa 67's	OHL	61	7	8	15	23	9	0	0	0	4
1998-99	Ottawa 67's	OHL	63	7	17	24	46	9	1	2	3	7
99-2000	Ottawa 67's	OHL	59	13	26	39	56	11	1	3	4	11
2000-01	Port Huron	UHL	68	9	18	27	34	....	....	....	....	....

JACOBSEN, Michael (JAY-cawbs, MIGH-kuhl)

Defense. Shoots left. 6'1", 207 lbs. Born, Thunder Bay, Ont., July 24, 1981.
(Chicago's 4th choice, 134th overall, in 1999 Entry Draft).

			Regular Season					Playoffs				
Season	Club	Lea	GP	G	A	TP	PIM	GP	G	A	TP	PIM
1996-97	Thunder Bay	TBAHA	71	28	42	70	40	....	....	....	....	....
1997-98	Belleville Bulls	OHL	56	7	14	21	14	10	0	3	3	0
1998-99	Belleville Bulls	OHL	68	5	27	32	33	21	0	4	4	10
99-2000	Belleville Bulls	OHL	68	9	40	49	18	16	2	5	7	7
2000-01	Belleville Bulls	OHL	63	16	34	50	24	10	2	4	6	4

JAKES, Jiri (YA-kesh, YOO-ree) BOS.

Right wing. Shoots left. 6'4", 210 lbs. Born, Prague, Czech., October 4, 1982.
(Boston's 4th choice, 147th overall, in 2001 Entry Draft).

			Regular Season					Playoffs				
Season	Club	Lea	GP	G	A	TP	PIM	GP	G	A	TP	PIM
99-2000	HC Sparta-Jr	Cze-Rep	27	5	7	12	....	....	....	....	....	....
2000-01	Brandon	WHL	64	22	16	38	73	6	1	1	2	4

JAMINKI, Tommi (yah-MIHN-kee,TAW-mee) CHI.

Left wing. Shoots right. 6', 180 lbs. Born, Turku, Finland, February 11, 1983.
(Chicago's 8th choice, 142nd overall, in 2001 Entry Draft).

			Regular Season					Playoffs				
Season	Club	Lea	GP	G	A	TP	PIM	GP	G	A	TP	PIM
99-2000	KJT Kerawa	Finn-Jr.	35	9	10	19	106	....	....	....	....	....
2000-01	Blues Espoo	Finn-Jr.	36	6	6	12	16	....	....	....	....	....

JAMTIN, Andreas (yahm-TEEN, ahn-DRAY-uhs) DET.

Right wing. Shoots left. 5'11", 185 lbs. Born, Stockholm, Sweden, May 4, 1983.
(Detroit's 4th choice, 157th overall, in 2001 Entry Draft).

			Regular Season					Playoffs				
Season	Club	Lea	GP	G	A	TP	PIM	GP	G	A	TP	PIM
1998-99	AIK Solna	Swede-Jr.	44	33	29	62	105	....	....	....	....	....
99-2000	Farjestad Karlstad	Swede-Jr.	28	6	6	12	36	....	....	....	....	....
2000-01	Farjestad Karlstad	Swede-Jr.	14	8	6	14	85	....	....	....	....	....
	Farjestad Karlstad	Sweden	1	0	0	0	0	....	....	....	....	....

JANCEVSKI, Dan (jan-SEHV-skee, DAN) DAL.

Defense. Shoots left. 6'3", 222 lbs. Born, Windsor, Ont., June 15, 1981.
(Dallas' 2nd choice, 66th overall, in 1999 Entry Draft).

			Regular Season					Playoffs				
Season	Club	Lea	GP	G	A	TP	PIM	GP	G	A	TP	PIM
1995-96	Riverside Regents	OMHA	59	9	22	31	67	....	....	....	....	....
1996-97	Windsor Lions	OMHA	47	6	20	26	99	....	....	....	....	....
1997-98	Tecumseh	OJHL-B	49	3	11	14	145	....	....	....	....	....
1998-99	London Knights	OHL	68	2	12	14	115	25	1	7	8	24
99-2000	London Knights	OHL	59	8	15	23	138	....	....	....	....	....
2000-01	London Knights	OHL	39	4	23	27	95	....	....	....	....	....
	Sudbury Wolves	OHL	31	3	14	17	45	12	0	9	9	17

Traded to **Sudbury** by **London** with Chris Kelly for Dennis Wideman and future considerations, January 10, 2001.

JANIK, Doug (JAN-nihk, DUHG) **BUF.**

Defense. Shoots left. 6'1", 198 lbs. Born, Agawam, MA, March 26, 1980.
(Buffalo's 3rd choice, 55th overall, in 1999 Entry Draft).

			Regular Season					Playoffs				
Season	Club	Lea	GP	G	A	TP	PIM	GP	G	A	TP	PIM
1995-96	Springfield	EJHL	48	16	38	54	....	....	....	....	....	....
1996-97	Springfield	EJHL	39	12	24	36	22	11	5	9	14	10
1997-98	Team USA	USDP	65	8	26	34	105	....	....	....	....	....
1998-99	U. of Maine	H-East	35	3	13	16	44	....	....	....	....	....
99-2000	U. of Maine	H-East	36	6	14	20	54	....	....	....	....	....
2000-01	U. of Maine	H-East	39	3	15	18	52	....	....	....	....	....

JARDINE, Ryan (JAHR-dighn, RIGH-yan) **FLA.**

Left wing. Shoots left. 6', 210 lbs. Born, Ottawa, Ont., March 15, 1980.
(Florida's 4th choice, 89th overall, in 1998 Entry Draft).

			Regular Season					Playoffs				
Season	Club	Lea	GP	G	A	TP	PIM	GP	G	A	TP	PIM
1996-97	Kanata Lasers	OCJHL	52	30	27	57	76	....	....	....	....	....
1997-98	Sault Ste. Marie	OHL	65	28	32	60	16	....	....	....	....	....
1998-99	Sault Ste. Marie	OHL	68	27	34	61	56	5	0	1	1	6
99-2000	Sault Ste. Marie	OHL	65	43	34	77	58	17	11	8	19	16
2000-01	Louisville Panthers	AHL	77	12	14	26	38	....	....	....	....	....

JARRETT, Cole (JAIR-reht, KOHL) **CBJ**

Defense. Shoots left. 5'10", 200 lbs. Born, Sault Ste. Marie, Ont., January 4, 1983.
(Columbus' 6th choice, 141st overall, in 2001 Entry Draft).

			Regular Season					Playoffs				
Season	Club	Lea	GP	G	A	TP	PIM	GP	G	A	TP	PIM
1998-99	Waterloo Siskins	OJHL-B	44	6	10	16	43	....	....	....	....	....
99-2000	Plymouth	OHL	57	3	7	10	47	23	3	7	10	19
2000-01	Plymouth	OHL	60	12	36	48	98	19	6	12	18	29

JARVENTIE, Martti (yar-VEHN-tee-eh, MAHR-tee) **MTL.**

Defense. Shoots left. 5'11", 185 lbs. Born, Tampere, Finland, April 4, 1976.
(Montreal's 5th choice, 109th overall, in 2001 Entry Draft).

			Regular Season					Playoffs				
Season	Club	Lea	GP	G	A	TP	PIM	GP	G	A	TP	PIM
1992-93	Ilves Tampere-B	Finn-Jr.	27	1	4	5	92	....	....	....	....	....
	Ilves Tampere	Finn-Jr.	12	0	1	1	6	....	....	....	....	....
1993-94	Ilves Tampere-B	Finn-Jr.	5	2	2	4	14	....	....	....	....	....
	Ilves Tampere	Finn-Jr.	36	7	6	13	34	6	1	2	3	....
1994-95	Ilves Tampere	Finn-Jr.	9	2	2	4	26	....	....	....	....	....
	Ilves Tampere	Finland	37	1	6	7	18	....	....	....	....	....
	Ilves Tampere	Finland-2	7	0	1	1	0	....	....	....	....	....
1995-96	Ilves Tampere	Finland	21	2	1	3	30	....	....	....	....	....
	Ilves Tampere	Finn-Jr.	3	2	2	4	4	....	....	....	....	....
	KooVee Tampere	Finland-2	3	0	0	0	2	....	....	....	....	....
	Lukko Rauma	Finland	15	0	1	1	10	....	....	....	....	....
1996-97	Ilves Tampere	Finn-Jr.	2	0	0	0	2	....	....	....	....	....
	Ilves Tampere	Finland	44	2	11	13	34	6	0	1	1	0
1997-98	Ilves Tampere	Finland	37	2	5	7	22	9	2	2	4	14
1998-99	Ilves Tampere	Finland	43	2	4	6	56	4	0	0	0	0
99-2000	Ilves Tampere	Finland	50	14	14	28	77	3	1	1	2	2
2000-01	TPS Turku	Finland	56	5	14	19	71	10	1	2	3	4

JARVIS, Wes (JAHR-vihs, WEHS) **NYR**

Defense. Shoots left. 6'5", 215 lbs. Born, Toronto, Ont., April 16, 1979.
(NY Rangers' 2nd choice, 46th overall, in 1997 Entry Draft).

			Regular Season					Playoffs				
Season	Club	Lea	GP	G	A	TP	PIM	GP	G	A	TP	PIM
1993-94	Ottawa Jr. Sens	OCJHL	42	22	43	65	52	....	....	....	....	....
1994-95	Ottawa Jr. Sens	OCJHL	45	23	48	71	48	....	....	....	....	....
1995-96	Gloucester	OCJHL	43	3	6	9	73	....	....	....	....	....
1996-97	Kitchener	OHL	56	4	8	12	108	13	0	4	4	25
1997-98	Kitchener	OHL	47	10	18	28	112	1	0	0	0	2
1998-99	Kitchener	OHL	52	5	18	23	80	1	0	0	0	2
99-2000	Canada	Nat-Team	43	2	5	7	50	....	....	....	....	....
2000-01	Hartford	AHL	20	1	2	3	24	....	....	....	....	....
	Charlotte	ECHL	39	4	8	12	185	3	0	1	1	10

JASPERS, Jason (JAS-puhrs, JAY-suhn) **PHX.**

Center/Left wing. Shoots left. 5'11", 185 lbs. Born, Thunder Bay, Ont., April 8, 1981.
(Phoenix's 4th choice, 71st overall, in 1999 Entry Draft).

			Regular Season					Playoffs				
Season	Club	Lea	GP	G	A	TP	PIM	GP	G	A	TP	PIM
1996-97	Thunder Bay	TBAHA	70	51	69	120	67	....	....	....	....	....
1997-98	Thunder Bay	TBAHA	72	45	75	120	90	....	....	....	....	....
1998-99	Sudbury Wolves	OHL	68	28	33	61	81	4	2	1	3	13
99-2000	Sudbury Wolves	OHL	68	46	61	107	107	12	4	6	10	27
2000-01	Sudbury Wolves	OHL	63	42	42	84	77	12	3	16	19	18

OHL Second All-Star Team (2000)

JENSEN, Erik (JEHN-sehn, AIR-ihk) **N.J.**

Right wing. Shoots right. 6'1", 195 lbs. Born, Madison, WI, September 4, 1979.
(New Jersey's 10th choice, 199th overall, in 1998 Entry Draft).

			Regular Season					Playoffs				
Season	Club	Lea	GP	G	A	TP	PIM	GP	G	A	TP	PIM
1997-98	Des Moines	USHL	41	12	14	26	90	....	....	....	....	....
1998-99	Des Moines	USHL	26	5	11	16	62	14	4	3	7	35
99-2000	U. of Wisconsin	WCHA	22	3	3	6	30	....	....	....	....	....
2000-01	U. of Wisconsin	WCHA	39	6	7	13	57	....	....	....	....	....

JILLSON, Jeff (JIHL-sohn, JEHF) **S.J.**

Defense. Shoots right. 6'3", 220 lbs. Born, North Smithfield, RI, July 24, 1980.
(San Jose's 1st choice, 14th overall, in 1999 Entry Draft).

			Regular Season					Playoffs				
Season	Club	Lea	GP	G	A	TP	PIM	GP	G	A	TP	PIM
1995-96	Mount St. Charles	Hi-School	15	8	7	15	15	5	1	1	2	4
1996-97	Mount St. Charles	Hi-School	15	16	14	30	20	4	0	4	4	6
1997-98	Mount St. Charles	Hi-School	15	10	13	23	32	5	4	5	9	6
1998-99	U. of Michigan	CCHA	38	5	19	24	71	....	....	....	....	....
99-2000	U. of Michigan	CCHA	38	8	26	34	115	....	....	....	....	....
2000-01	U. of Michigan	CCHA	43	10	20	30	74	....	....	....	....	....

Rhode Island All-State First All-Star Team (1996, 1997, 1998) • CCHA All-Rookie Team (1999) • CCHA First All-Star Team (2000, 2001) • NCAA West First All-American Team (2000) • NCAA West Second All-American Team (2001)

JINDRICH, Robert (IHN-drihkh, RAW-buhrt) **S.J.**

Defense. Shoots left. 5'11", 195 lbs. Born, Plzen, Czech., October 14, 1976.
(San Jose's 10th choice, 168th overall, in 1995 Entry Draft).

			Regular Season					Playoffs				
Season	Club	Lea	GP	G	A	TP	PIM	GP	G	A	TP	PIM
1993-94	ZKZ Plzen	Cze-Rep	18	0	2	2	....	....	....	....	....	....
1994-95	ZKZ Plzen	Cze-Rep	11	1	0	1	4	....	....	....	....	....
1995-96	ZKZ Plzen	Cze-Rep	37	1	3	4	....	3	0	0	0	....
1996-97	ZKZ Plzen	Cze-Rep	49	7	9	16	44	....	....	....	....	....
1997-98	HC Beroun-2	Cze-Rep	13	4	2	6	0	....	....	....	....	....
	ZKZ Plzen	Cze-Rep	39	1	6	7	18	4	0	0	0	0
1998-99	ZKZ Plzen	Cze-Rep	52	6	12	18	24	5	1	0	1	....
99-2000	Kentucky	AHL	78	2	21	23	51	9	0	4	4	6
2000-01	Kentucky	AHL	62	4	16	20	36	2	0	0	0	0

JOHANSSON, Daniel (yoh-HAN-suhn, DAN-yehl) **L.A.**

Center. Shoots left. 5'11", 176 lbs. Born, Ornskoldsvik, Sweden, July 5, 1981.
(Los Angeles' 6th choice, 125th overall, in 1999 Entry Draft).

			Regular Season					Playoffs				
Season	Club	Lea	GP	G	A	TP	PIM	GP	G	A	TP	PIM
1997-98	MoDo Hockey	Swede-Jr.	6	0	0	0	0	....	....	....	....	....
1998-99	MoDo Hockey	Swede-Jr.	43	10	19	29	....	....	....	....	....	....
99-2000	MoDo Hockey	Swede-Jr.	35	11	21	32	34	....	....	....	....	....
	MoDo Hockey	EuroHL	2	0	0	0	0	....	....	....	....	....
2000-01	Bodens IK	Swede-2	36	4	3	7	10	4	0	0	0	0

JOHANSSON, David (yoh-HAHN-suhn) **WSH.**

Defense. Shoots left. 6', 176 lbs. Born, Lidingo, Sweden, June 15, 1981.
(Washington's 8th choice, 192nd overall, in 1999 Entry Draft).

			Regular Season					Playoffs				
Season	Club	Lea	GP	G	A	TP	PIM	GP	G	A	TP	PIM
1997-98	AIK Solna	Swede-Jr.	13	0	1	1	10	....	....	....	....	....
1998-99	AIK Solna	Swede-Jr.	33	5	5	10	30	....	....	....	....	....
99-2000	Kelowna Rockets	WHL	62	3	24	27	36	2	0	0	0	0
2000-01	AIK Solna	Swede-Jr.	10	0	3	3	37	....	....	....	....	....
	AIK Solna	Sweden	37	4	2	6	57	4	0	1	1	0

JOHANSSON, Eric (joh-HAHN-suhn, AIR-ihk) **MIN.**

Center. Shoots left. 6', 190 lbs. Born, Edmonton, Alta., January 7, 1982.
(Minnesota's 9th choice, 255th overall, in 2000 Entry Draft).

			Regular Season					Playoffs				
Season	Club	Lea	GP	G	A	TP	PIM	GP	G	A	TP	PIM
1997-98	Edmonton CAC	AMHA	22	13	10	23	19	....	....	....	....	....
1998-99	Tri-City Americans	WHL	48	8	14	22	20	6	1	1	2	2
99-2000	Tri-City Americans	WHL	72	24	36	60	38	4	0	0	0	2
2000-01	Tri-City Americans	WHL	72	36	44	80	72	....	....	....	....	....

JOHANSSON, Tobias (yoh-HAHN-suhn, TOH-bigh-as) **ANA.**

Left wing. Shoots left. 5'11", 180 lbs. Born, Malmo, Sweden, October 22, 1977.
(Anaheim's 7th choice, 224th overall, in 1996 Entry Draft).

			Regular Season					Playoffs				
Season	Club	Lea	GP	G	A	TP	PIM	GP	G	A	TP	PIM
1995-96	Malmo IF	Swede-Jr.	30	7	13	20	38	....	....	....	....	....
1996-97	Malmo IF	Swede-Jr.	15	6	8	14	63	....	....	....	....	....
1997-98	Tranas AIF	Swede-2	31	7	2	9	18	....	....	....	....	....
1998-99	Tranas AIF	Swede-2	32	11	5	16	28	....	....	....	....	....
99-2000	Tranas AIF	Swede-2	30	8	5	13	73	....	....	....	....	....
	Tranas AIF	Sweden	14	2	3	5	10	....	....	....	....	....
2000-01	Tranas AIF	Swede-2	42	23	11	34	50	3	0	0	0	0

JOHNSON, Aaron (JAWN-suhn, AIR-ruhn) **CBJ**

Defense. Shoots left. 6', 186 lbs. Born, Port Hawkesbury, N.S., April 30, 1983.
(Columbus' 4th choice, 85th overall, in 2001 Entry Draft).

			Regular Season					Playoffs				
Season	Club	Lea	GP	G	A	TP	PIM	GP	G	A	TP	PIM
99-2000	Rimouski Oceanic	QMJHL	63	1	14	15	57	8	0	0	0	0
2000-01	Rimouski Oceanic	QMJHL	64	12	41	53	128	11	2	4	6	35

JOHNSON, Adam (JAWN-suhn, A-duhm) **NYI**

Defense. Shoots left. 6'6", 220 lbs. Born, Minneapolis, MN, August 2, 1980.
(NY Islanders' 10th choice, 140th overall, in 1999 Entry Draft).

			Regular Season					Playoffs				
Season	Club	Lea	GP	G	A	TP	PIM	GP	G	A	TP	PIM
1998-99	Greenway High	Hi-School	17	5	13	18	32	....	....	....	....	....
99-2000	Tri-City Americans	WHL	52	0	3	3	90	4	0	1	1	4
2000-01	Tri-City Americans	WHL	13	1	3	4	32	....	....	....	....	....
	Lethbridge	WHL	44	5	6	11	88	5	0	2	2	17

Traded to **Lethbridge** by **Tri-City** with Ryley Layden for Ryan Jorde and Colin Johnson, October 25, 2000.

JOHNSTONE, Alex (JAWN-stohn, AL-ehx) **N.J.**

Defense. Shoots left. 6'1", 205 lbs. Born, Halifax, N.S., December 28, 1979.

			Regular Season					Playoffs				
Season	Club	Lea	GP	G	A	TP	PIM	GP	G	A	TP	PIM
1996-97	Halifax	QMJHL	39	1	5	6	213	18	1	0	1	48
1997-98	Halifax	QMJHL	66	3	10	13	390	5	0	2	2	8
1998-99	Halifax	QMJHL	60	1	8	9	248	5	0	1	1	4
99-2000	Albany River Rats	AHL	13	0	0	0	22	....	....	....	....	....
	Augusta Lynx	ECHL	21	0	2	2	88	....	....	....	....	....
2000-01	Adirondack	UHL	72	2	8	10	240	1	0	0	0	0

Signed as a free agent by **New Jersey**, August 8, 1998.

JOKELA, Mikko (YOH-kih-lah, MIH-koh) **N.J.**

Defense. Shoots right. 6'1", 205 lbs. Born, Lappeenranta, Finland, March 4, 1980.
(New Jersey's 5th choice, 96th overall, in 1998 Entry Draft).

			Regular Season					Playoffs				
Season	Club	Lea	GP	G	A	TP	PIM	GP	G	A	TP	PIM
1994-95	KalPa Kuopio-C	Finn-Jr.	29	7	12	19	36	....	....	....	....	....
1995-96	KalPa Kuopio-C	Finn-Jr.	23	10	19	29	103	6	3	5	8	4
	KalPa Kuopio-B	Finn-Jr.	9	2	1	3	20	....	....	....	....	....
	KalPa Kuopio	Finn-Jr.	11	2	1	3	20	....	....	....	....	....
1996-97	KalPa Kuopio-B	Finn-Jr.	11	3	2	5	8	5	1	1	2	4
	KalPa Kuopio	Finn-Jr.	22	2	4	6	4	....	....	....	....	....
	KalPa Kuopio-2	Finn-Jr.	....	....	....	....	....	12	0	1	1	14
1997-98	HIFK Helsinki	Finn-Jr.	22	2	5	7	14	....	....	....	....	....
	Hermes HT	Finland-2	6	0	1	1	2	....	....	....	....	....
	HIFK Helsinki	Finland	16	0	0	0	0	....	....	....	....	....
1998-99	KalPa Kuopio	Finn-Jr.	1	0	1	1	2	....	....	....	....	....
	KalPa Kuopio	Finland	42	1	2	3	18	....	....	....	....	....
	HIFK Helsinki	Finland	3	0	0	0	2	....	....	....	....	....
	KalPa Kuopio	Finland-2	....	....	....	....	....	6	0	0	0	2
99-2000	Sai-Lappeenranta	Finland	48	0	5	5	50	....	....	....	....	....
	Sai-Lappeenranta	Finn-Jr.	....	....	....	....	....	1	0	0	0	0
2000-01	Sai-Lappeenranta	Finn-Jr.	4	2	2	4	2	3	0	0	0	2
	KooKoo Kouvola	Finland-2	5	3	0	3	0	....	....	....	....	....
	Sai-Lappeenranta	Finland	50	1	0	1	24	....	....	....	....	....

JOKILA, Janne (YOHK-ih-luh, YAHN-ee) **CBJ**

Left wing. Shoots left. 5'9", 174 lbs. Born, Turku, Finland, April 22, 1982.
(Columbus' 7th choice, 200th overall, in 2000 Entry Draft).

			Regular Season					Playoffs				
Season	Club	Lea	GP	G	A	TP	PIM	GP	G	A	TP	PIM
1997-98	TPS Turku	Finn-Jr.	30	11	10	21	28	6	3	1	4	2
1998-99	TPS Turku	Finn-Jr.	36	17	15	32	77	....	....	....	....	....
99-2000	TPS Turku	Finn-Jr.	35	10	7	17	32	....	....	....	....	....
2000-01	TPS Turku	Finn-Jr.	22	15	15	30	30	2	0	1	1	4
	TPS Turku	Finland	2	0	0	0	0	....	....	....	....	....
	Sai-Lappeenranta	Finland	8	1	1	2	0	....	....	....	....	....

JONES, Mike (JOHNZ, MIGHK) **T.B.**

Defense. Shoots left. 6'3", 190 lbs. Born, Toledo, OH, May 18, 1976.

			Regular Season					Playoffs				
Season	Club	Lea	GP	G	A	TP	PIM	GP	G	A	TP	PIM
1994-95	Cleveland Barons	NAJHL	45	15	33	48	....	....	....	....	....	....
1995-96	Cleveland Barons	NAJHL	46	25	*45	70	....	....	....	....	....	....
1996-97	Bowling Green	CCHA	27	1	6	7	47	....	....	....	....	....
1997-98	Bowling Green	CCHA	28	3	12	15	69	....	....	....	....	....
1998-99	Bowling Green	CCHA	38	8	21	29	80	....	....	....	....	....
99-2000	Bowling Green	CCHA	34	6	13	19	71	....	....	....	....	....
2000-01	Detroit Vipers	IHL	71	9	17	26	41	....	....	....	....	....

Won NAJHL Defenseman of the Year Award (1996) • CCHA Second All-Star Team (1999)

Signed as a free agent by **Tampa Bay**, April 13, 2000.

JONSSON, Lars (YAWN-suhn, LARZ) **BOS.**

Defense. Shoots left. 6'1", 198 lbs. Born, Borlange, Sweden, January 2, 1982.
(Boston's 1st choice, 7th overall, in 2000 Entry Draft).

			Regular Season					Playoffs				
Season	Club	Lea	GP	G	A	TP	PIM	GP	G	A	TP	PIM
1998-99	Leksands IF	Swede-Jr.	40	4	8	12	42	....	....	....	....	....
99-2000	Leksands IF	Swede-Jr.	34	16	22	38	50	2	0	0	0	0
	Leksands IF	Sweden	5	0	0	0	4	....	....	....	....	....
2000-01	Leksands IF	Swede-Jr.	7	1	3	4	6	....	....	....	....	....
	Leksands IF	Sweden	31	2	1	3	12	....	....	....	....	....

JUNTUNEN, Henrik (YUN-tuh-nehn, HEHN-rihk) **L.A.**

Right wing. Shoots right. 6'2", 185 lbs. Born, Goteborg, Sweden, April 24, 1983.
(Los Angeles' 5th choice, 83rd overall, in 2001 Entry Draft).

			Regular Season					Playoffs				
Season	Club	Lea	GP	G	A	TP	PIM	GP	G	A	TP	PIM
99-2000	Karpat Oulu	Finn-Jr.	34	16	7	23	18	5	0	0	0	2
2000-01	Karpat Oulu	Finn-Jr.	17	4	4	8	12	....	....	....	....	....
	Karpat Oulu	Finland	....	....	....	....	....	2	0	0	0	0

KACZOWKA, David (kuh-ZOW-kuh, DAY-vihd) **ATL.**

Left wing. Shoots left. 6'2", 205 lbs. Born, Regina, Sask., July 5, 1981.
(Atlanta's 4th choice, 98th overall, in 1999 Entry Draft).

			Regular Season					Playoffs				
Season	Club	Lea	GP	G	A	TP	PIM	GP	G	A	TP	PIM
1997-98	Prince Albert	SAHA	56	5	13	18	334	....	....	....	....	....
1998-99	Seattle T-Birds	WHL	60	3	2	5	247	9	0	0	0	24
99-2000	Seattle T-Birds	WHL	63	3	3	6	211	1	0	0	0	0
2000-01	Regina Pats	WHL	63	4	6	10	*414	6	0	0	0	6

Traded to **Regina** by **Seattle** for Regina's 3rd round choice in 2002 WHL Bantam Draft, September 3, 2000.

KAHNBERG, Magnus (KAHN-buhrg, MAHG-nus) **CAR.**

Left wing. Shoots right. 6'1", 185 lbs. Born, Goteborg, Sweden, February 25, 1980.
(Carolina's 6th choice, 212th overall, in 2000 Entry Draft).

			Regular Season					Playoffs				
Season	Club	Lea	GP	G	A	TP	PIM	GP	G	A	TP	PIM
1997-98	Vastra Frolunda	Swede-Jr.	39	21	13	34	14	10	5	8	13	6
1998-99	Vastra Frolunda	Swede-Jr.	34	23	18	41	4	4	1	1	2	0
99-2000	Vastra Frolunda	Swede-Jr.	35	45	21	66	30	6	7	4	11	4
	Vastra Frolunda	Sweden	4	0	0	0	0	....	....	....	....	....
2000-01	Vastra Frolunda	Swede-Jr.	2	2	1	3	2	....	....	....	....	....
	Vastra Frolunda	Sweden	50	8	6	14	6	5	0	0	0	2

KALLARSSON, Tomi (KAL-ahr-suhn, TAW-mee) **NYR**

Defense. Shoots left. 6'3", 194 lbs. Born, Lempaala, Finland, March 15, 1979.
(NY Rangers' 4th choice, 93rd overall, in 1997 Entry Draft).

			Regular Season					Playoffs				
Season	Club	Lea	GP	G	A	TP	PIM	GP	G	A	TP	PIM
1994-95	Tappara Tampere	Finn-Jr.	22	9	4	13	26	....	....	....	....	....
1995-96	Tappara Tampere	Finn-Jr.	31	3	5	8	24	6	0	0	0	0
1996-97	HPK Hameenlinna	Finn-Jr.	31	1	3	4	26	6	0	0	0	2
1997-98	HPK Hameenlinna	Finn-Jr.	32	5	9	14	71	....	....	....	....	....
	Pelicans Lahti	Finland-2	3	0	0	0	0	....	....	....	....	....
	HPK Hameenlinna	Finland	12	0	0	0	2	....	....	....	....	....
1998-99	HPK Hameenlinna	Finn-Jr.	2	0	1	1	6	....	....	....	....	....
	Ahmat Hyvinkaa	Finland-2	21	2	7	9	52	....	....	....	....	....
	HPK Hameenlinna	Finland	25	0	0	0	22	8	0	0	0	8
99-2000	HPK Hameenlinna	Finn-Jr.	3	2	2	4	4	....	....	....	....	....
	HPK Hameenlinna	Finland	50	0	5	5	58	8	0	0	0	4
2000-01	Timra IK	Sweden	37	0	0	0	54	....	....	....	....	....

KALMIKOV, Konstantin (kahl-mih-KAHV, KAWN-stan-tihn)

Left wing. Shoots right. 6'4", 205 lbs. Born, Kharkov, USSR, June 14, 1978.
(Toronto's 4th choice, 68th overall, in 1996 Entry Draft).

			Regular Season					Playoffs				
Season	Club	Lea	GP	G	A	TP	PIM	GP	G	A	TP	PIM
1994-95	Druzhba-78	Russia	65	51	55	106	45	....	....	....	....	....
1995-96	Flint Generals	ColHL	38	4	12	16	16	....	....	....	....	....
	Detroit Falcons	ColHL	5	0	1	1	0	....	....	....	....	....
1996-97	Sudbury Wolves	OHL	66	22	34	56	25	....	....	....	....	....
	St. John's Leafs	AHL	2	0	0	0	0	....	....	....	....	....
1997-98	Sudbury Wolves	OHL	66	32	32	64	21	10	7	2	9	2
1998-99	St. John's Leafs	AHL	52	3	4	7	4	....	....	....	....	....
99-2000	St. John's Leafs	AHL	76	8	20	28	21	....	....	....	....	....
2000-01	St. John's Leafs	AHL	47	7	10	17	8	....	....	....	....	....
	Detroit Vipers	IHL	18	2	1	3	2	....	....	....	....	....

Traded to **Tampa Bay** by **Toronto** for Maxim Galanov, February 20, 2001.

KANE, Boyd (KAYN, BOIYD) **NYR**

Left wing. Shoots left. 6'2", 218 lbs. Born, Swift Current, Sask., April 18, 1978.
(NY Rangers' 4th choice, 114th overall, in 1998 Entry Draft).

			Regular Season					Playoffs				
Season	Club	Lea	GP	G	A	TP	PIM	GP	G	A	TP	PIM
1994-95	Regina Pats	WHL	25	6	5	11	6	4	0	0	0	0
1995-96	Regina Pats	WHL	72	21	42	63	155	11	5	7	12	12
1996-97	Regina Pats	WHL	66	25	50	75	154	5	1	1	2	15
1997-98	Regina Pats	WHL	68	48	45	93	133	9	5	7	12	29
1998-99	Hartford	AHL	56	3	5	8	23	....	....	....	....	....
	Charlotte	ECHL	12	5	6	11	14	....	....	....	....	....
99-2000	Charlotte	ECHL	47	10	19	29	110	....	....	....	....	....
	Hartford	AHL	8	0	0	0	9	....	....	....	....	....
	B.C. Icemen	UHL	3	0	2	2	4	1	0	0	0	0
2000-01	Charlotte	ECHL	12	9	8	17	6	....	....	....	....	....
	Hartford	AHL	56	11	17	28	81	5	2	0	2	2

• Re-entered NHL Entry Draft. Originally Pittsburgh' 3rd choice, 72nd overall, in 1996 Entry Draft.

KANKAANPERA, Markus (kan-kahn-PEHR-a, MAHR-kus) **VAN.**

Defense. Shoots left. 6'1", 191 lbs. Born, Skelleftea, Sweden, April 27, 1980.
(Vancouver's 7th choice, 218th overall, in 1999 Entry Draft).

			Regular Season					Playoffs				
Season	Club	Lea	GP	G	A	TP	PIM	GP	G	A	TP	PIM
1996-97	JyP Jyvaskyla	Finn-Jr.	33	3	5	8	83	....	....	....	....	....
1997-98	JyP Jyvaskyla-B	Finn-Jr.	13	4	10	14	18	5	3	2	5	6
	JyP Jyvaskyla	Finn-Jr.	32	0	0	0	2	....	....	....	....	....
1998-99	JyP Jyvaskyla	Finn-Jr.	1	0	0	0	4	....	....	....	....	....
	JyP Jyvaskyla	Finland	50	0	2	2	85	3	0	0	0	0
99-2000	JyP Jyvaskyla	Finn-Jr.	3	1	1	2	2	3	0	1	1	6
	JyP Jyvaskyla	Finland	47	0	5	5	87	....	....	....	....	....
2000-01	JyP Jyvaskyla	Finland	53	5	4	9	60	....	....	....	....	....

KAPANEN, Niko (KA-pah-nehn, NEE-KOH) **DAL.**

Center. Shoots left. 5'9", 180 lbs. Born, Hattula, Finland, April 29, 1978.
(Dallas' 5th choice, 173rd overall, in 1998 Entry Draft).

			Regular Season					Playoffs				
Season	Club	Lea	GP	G	A	TP	PIM	GP	G	A	TP	PIM
1992-93	Hameenlinna-C	Finn-Jr.	14	14	6	20	2	....	....	....	....	....
1993-94	Hameenlinna-C	Finn-Jr.	2	0	1	1	0	....	....	....	....	....
	HPK Hameenlinna	Finn-Jr.	31	17	33	50	34	....	....	....	....	....
1994-95	Hameenlinna-B	Finn-Jr.	37	19	44	63	40	....	....	....	....	....
1995-96	Hameenlinna-B	Finn-Jr.	10	6	6	12	8	....	....	....	....	....
	HPK Hameenlinna	Finn-Jr.	26	15	22	37	34	....	....	....	....	....
	HPK Hameenlinna	Finland	7	1	0	1	0	....	....	....	....	....
1996-97	HPK Hameenlinna	Finn-Jr.	5	1	7	8	2	2	0	1	1	2
	HPK Hameenlinna	Finland	41	6	9	15	12	10	4	5	9	2
	HPK Hameenlinna	EuroHL	6	3	0	3	4	1	0	0	0	0
1997-98	HPK Hameenlinna	Finn-Jr.	2	1	1	2	0	....	....	....	....	....
	HPK Hameenlinna	Finland	48	8	18	26	44	....	....	....	....	....
1998-99	HPK Hameenlinna	Finland	53	14	29	43	49	8	3	4	7	4
99-2000	HPK Hameenlinna	Finland	53	20	28	48	40	8	1	9	10	4
2000-01	TPS Turku	Finland	56	11	21	32	20	10	2	1	3	4

KARLIN, Mattias (KAR-lihn, MAT-teeuhs) **BOS.**

Center/Right wing. Shoots left. 5'11", 183 lbs. Born, Domsjo, Sweden, July 4, 1979.
(Boston's 4th choice, 54th overall, in 1997 Entry Draft).

			Regular Season					Playoffs				
Season	Club	Lea	GP	G	A	TP	PIM	GP	G	A	TP	PIM
1995-96	MoDo Hockey	Swede-Jr.	30	12	23	35	16	....	....	....	....	....
1996-97	MoDo Hockey	Sweden	6	0	0	0	0	....	....	....	....	....
1997-98	MoDo Hockey	Sweden	32	0	2	2	8	1	0	0	0	0
1998-99	MoDo Hockey	Sweden	50	2	5	7	14	13	1	1	2	4
99-2000	MoDo Hockey	Sweden	42	0	5	5	10	12	0	0	0	2
2000-01	Providence Bruins	AHL	68	3	12	15	28	16	1	2	3	2

KARLSSON, Gabriel (KARLS-suhn, ga-BREE-ehl) **DAL.**

Center. Shoots left. 6'1", 189 lbs. Born, Borlange, Sweden, January 22, 1980.
(Dallas' 3rd choice, 86th overall, in 1998 Entry Draft).

			Regular Season					Playoffs				
Season	Club	Lea	GP	G	A	TP	PIM	GP	G	A	TP	PIM
1996-97	HV Jonkoping	Swede-Jr.	25	7	9	16	....	....	....	....	....	....
1997-98	HV Jonkoping	Swede-Jr.	27	11	15	26	32	....	....	....	....	....
	HV Jonkoping	Sweden	1	0	0	0	0	....	....	....	....	....
1998-99	HV Jonkoping	Swede-Jr.	12	4	9	13	4	....	....	....	....	....
	HV Jonkoping	Sweden	33	2	1	3	2	....	....	....	....	....
99-2000	HV Jonkoping	Sweden	50	5	3	8	12	6	0	0	0	2
2000-01	Assat-Pori	Finland	17	2	2	4	6	....	....	....	....	....
	Leksands IF	Sweden	35	9	8	17	10	....	....	....	....	....

KARLSSON, Jens (KARLS-suhn, YEHNZ) **L.A.**

Left wing. Shoots right. 6'3", 205 lbs. Born, Goteborg, Sweden, November 7, 1982.
(Los Angeles' 1st choice, 18th overall, in 2001 Entry Draft).

			Regular Season					Playoffs				
Season	Club	Lea	GP	G	A	TP	PIM	GP	G	A	TP	PIM
1997-98	Vastra Frolunda	Swede-Jr.	17	2	3	5	4	....	....	....	....	....
1998-99	Vastra Frolunda	Swede-Jr.	32	27	17	44	110	4	2	2	4	0
99-2000	Vastra Frolunda	Swede-Jr.	33	25	14	39	100	4	2	2	4	0
2000-01	Vastra Frolunda	Swede-Jr.	15	8	7	15	97	1	0	1	1	2
	Molndal IF	Swede-2	5	1	1	2	35	....	....	....	....	....
	Vastra Frolunda	Sweden	19	2	0	2	4	....	....	....	....	....

KASPARIK, Pavel (kas-PAHR-ihk, PAH-vehl) **PHI.**

Center. Shoots left. 6'2", 198 lbs. Born, Pisek, Czech., November 11, 1979.
(Philadelphia's 4th choice, 200th overall, in 1999 Entry Draft).

			Regular Season					Playoffs				
Season	Club	Lea	GP	G	A	TP	PIM	GP	G	A	TP	PIM
1996-97	IHC Pisek-Jr.	Cze-Rep	36	12	5	17	....	....	....	....	....	....
1997-98	IHC Pisek-Jr.	Cze-Rep	39	21	19	40	....	....	....	....	....	....
	IHC Pisek-2	Cze-Rep	15	3	3	6	....	....	....	....	....	....
1998-99	IHC Pisek-Jr.	Cze-Rep	7	2	3	5	....	....	....	....	....	....
	IHC Pisek-2	Cze-Rep	51	20	23	43	....	....	....	....	....	....
99-2000	IHC Pisek-2	Cze-Rep	24	6	9	15	....	....	....	....	....	....
	HC Havirov	Cze-Rep	1	0	0	0	0	....	....	....	....	....
	Sparta Praha	Cze-Rep	22	1	1	2	0	....	....	....	....	....
2000-01	Karlovy Vary	Cze-Rep	29	1	2	3	20	....	....	....	....	....
	Sparta Praha	Cze-Rep	19	5	1	6	18	13	2	0	2	12

KAUPPINEN, Marko (KOW-pih-nehn, MAHR-koh) **PHI.**

Defense. Shoots left. 6', 178 lbs. Born, Mikkeli, Finland, March 23, 1979.
(Philadelphia's 7th choice, 214th overall, in 1997 Entry Draft).

			Regular Season					Playoffs				
Season	Club	Lea	GP	G	A	TP	PIM	GP	G	A	TP	PIM
1994-95	Jukurit Mikkeli-C	Finn-Jr.	31	12	11	23	48	....	....	....	....	....
1995-96	Jukurit Mikkeli	Finland-3	19	1	5	6	10	3	0	0	0	0
1996-97	JyP Jyvaskyla	Finn-Jr.	29	2	3	5	14	7	0	0	0	29
1997-98	JyP Jyvaskyla	Finn-Jr.	16	2	4	6	16	....	....	....	....	....
	Diskos Jyvaskyla	Finland-2	2	2	1	3	0	....	....	....	....	....
	JyP Jyvaskyla	Finland	33	2	6	8	26	....	....	....	....	....
1998-99	JyP Jyvaskyla	Finn-Jr.	3	2	1	3	6	....	....	....	....	....
	JyP Jyvaskyla	Finland	49	5	7	12	56	3	0	0	0	6
99-2000	Jokerit Helsinki	Finn-Jr.	5	0	3	3	8	1	1	0	1	4
	Jokerit Helsinki	Finland	47	4	9	13	16	10	1	3	4	2
2000-01	AIK Solna	Sweden	4	0	0	0	4	....	....	....	....	....
	Jokerit Helsinki	Finland	48	5	7	12	41	5	0	0	0	8

KEITH, Matt ((KEETH, MAT) **CHI.**

Right wing. Shoots right. 6'2", 194 lbs. Born, Edmonton, Alta., April 11, 1983.
(Chicago's 3rd choice, 59th overall, in 2001 Entry Draft).

			Regular Season					Playoffs				
Season	Club	Lea	GP	G	A	TP	PIM	GP	G	A	TP	PIM
1998-99	Banff Icemen	HJHL		STATISTICS NOT AVAILABLE								
	Spokane Chiefs	WHL	7	1	0	1	4	....	....	....	....	....
99-2000	Spokane Chiefs	WHL	39	1	3	4	37	15	1	2	3	11
2000-01	Spokane Chiefs	WHL	33	13	14	27	63	12	1	3	4	14

• Missed majority of 2000-01 season recovering from shoulder injury originally suffered in game vs. Kamloops, September 22, 2000.

KELLEHER, Chris (KEH-leh-huhr, KRIHS) **BOS.**

Defense. Shoots left. 6'1", 210 lbs. Born, Cambridge, MA, March 23, 1975.
(Pittsburgh's 5th choice, 130th overall, in 1993 Entry Draft).

			Regular Season					Playoffs				
Season	Club	Lea	GP	G	A	TP	PIM	GP	G	A	TP	PIM
1990-91	Belmont Hill	Hi-School	20	4	23	27	14	....	....	....	....	....
1991-92	St. Sebastien's	Hi-School	28	7	27	34	12	....	....	....	....	....
1992-93	St. Sebastien's	Hi-School	25	8	30	38	16	....	....	....	....	....
1993-94	St. Sebastien's	Hi-School	24	10	21	31	....	....	....	....	....	....
1994-95	Boston University	H-East	35	3	17	20	62	....	....	....	....	....
1995-96	Boston University	H-East	37	7	18	25	43	....	....	....	....	....
1996-97	Boston University	H-East	39	10	24	34	54	....	....	....	....	....
1997-98	Boston University	H-East	37	4	26	30	40	....	....	....	....	....
1998-99	Syracuse Crunch	AHL	45	1	4	5	43	....	....	....	....	....
99-2000	Wilkes-Barre	AHL	67	0	12	12	40	....	....	....	....	....
2000-01	Wilkes-Barre	AHL	66	6	13	19	37	21	7	18	*25	4

NCAA East Second All-American Team (1997, 1998) • Hockey East Second All-Star Team (1998)

Signed as a free agent by **Boston**, July 24, 2001.

KELLY, Chris (KEHL-lee, KRIHS) **OTT.**

Center/Left wing. Shoots left. 6', 179 lbs. Born, Toronto, Ont., November 11, 1980.
(Ottawa's 4th choice, 94th overall, in 1999 Entry Draft).

			Regular Season					Playoffs				
Season	Club	Lea	GP	G	A	TP	PIM	GP	G	A	TP	PIM
1995-96	Toronto Marlies	MTHL	42	25	45	70	25	....	....	....	....	....
1996-97	Aurora Tigers	MTJHL	49	14	20	34	11	....	....	....	....	....
1997-98	London Knights	OHL	54	15	14	29	4	16	4	5	9	12
1998-99	London Knights	OHL	68	36	41	77	60	25	9	17	26	22
99-2000	London Knights	OHL	63	29	43	72	57	....	....	....	....	....
2000-01	London Knights	OHL	31	21	34	55	46	....	....	....	....	....
	Sudbury Wolves	OHL	19	5	16	21	17	12	11	5	16	14

Traded to **Sudbury** by **London** with Dan Jancevski for Dennis Wideman and future considerations, January 10, 2001.

KELLY, Regan (KEHL-lee, REE-guhn) **TOR.**

Defense. Shoots left. 6'2", 185 lbs. Born, Watrous, Sask., March 9, 1981.
(Philadelphia's 7th choice, 259th overall, in 2000 Entry Draft).

			Regular Season					Playoffs				
Season	Club	Lea	GP	G	A	TP	PIM	GP	G	A	TP	PIM
1997-98	Tisdale Trojans	SMHL	41	2	13	15	24	....	....	....	....	....
1998-99	Nipawin Hawks	SJHL	52	4	14	18	30	....	....	....	....	....
99-2000	Nipawin Hawks	SJHL	46	8	21	29	20	....	....	....	....	....
2000-01	Providence	H-East	36	4	21	25	58	....	....	....	....	....

SJHL All-Rookie Team (1999) • Hockey East All-Rookie Team (2001) • Hockey East All-Tournament Team (2001)

Rights traded to **Toronto** by **Philadelphia** for Chris McAllister, September 26, 2000.

KESA, Teemu (KEH-sah, TEE-moo) **N.J.**

Defense. Shoots right. 6', 185 lbs. Born, Helsinki, Finland, June 7, 1981.
(New Jersey's 5th choice, 100th overall, in 1999 Entry Draft).

			Regular Season					Playoffs				
Season	Club	Lea	GP	G	A	TP	PIM	GP	G	A	TP	PIM
1996-97	Tappara Tampere	Finn-Jr.	32	1	5	6	58	4	1	0	4	29
1997-98	Ilves Tampere-B	Finn-Jr.	33	8	1	9	78	....	....	....	....	....
1998-99	Ilves Tampere-B	Finn-Jr.	24	4	5	9	146	....	....	....	....	....
	Ilves Tampere	Finn-Jr.	6	0	1	1	10	....	....	....	....	....
99-2000	Ilves Tampere	Finn-Jr.	31	1	7	8	92	....	....	....	....	....
	Ilves Tampere	Finland	5	0	0	0	8	....	....	....	....	....
2000-01	Ilves Tampere	Finn-Jr.	4	1	0	1	4	....	....	....	....	....
	Sport Vassa	Finland-2	1	0	1	1	0	....	....	....	....	....

KHOMITSKY, Vadim (khoh-MIHT-skee, va-DEEM) **DAL.**

Defense. Shoots left. 6'1", 185 lbs. Born, Voskresensk, USSR, July 21, 1982.
(Dallas' 5th choice, 123rd overall, in 2000 Entry Draft).

			Regular Season					Playoffs				
Season	Club	Lea	GP	G	A	TP	PIM	GP	G	A	TP	PIM
1998-99	HK Voskresensk	Russia	9	0	0	0	10	....	....	....	....	....
99-2000	HK Voskresensk	Russia-2	17	0	0	0	31	....	....	....	....	....
	HC Moscow	Russia-2	11	0	1	1	10	....	....	....	....	....
2000-01	HC Moscow	Russia-2	44	2	7	9	89	....	....	....	....	....

KIDNEY, Kyle (KIHD-nee, KIGHL) **COL.**

Left wing. Shoots left. 6'2", 240 lbs. Born, Ithaca, NY, January 11, 1978.
(Colorado's 9th choice, 243rd overall, in 1997 Entry Draft).

			Regular Season					Playoffs				
Season	Club	Lea	GP	G	A	TP	PIM	GP	G	A	TP	PIM
1996-97	Salisbury High	Hi-School	28	27	35	62	....	....	....	....	....	....
1997-98	U. Mass-Lowell	H-East	33	3	8	11	38	....	....	....	....	....
1998-99	U. Mass-Lowell	H-East	30	3	7	10	58	....	....	....	....	....
99-2000	U. Mass-Lowell	H-East	28	4	7	11	26	....	....	....	....	....
2000-01	U. Mass-Lowell	H-East	37	10	18	28	88	....	....	....	....	....

KINCH, Matt (KIHNCH, MAT-thew) **NYR**

Defense. Shoots left. 6', 195 lbs. Born, Red Deer, Alta., February 17, 1980.
(Buffalo's 8th choice, 146th overall, in 1999 Entry Draft).

			Regular Season					Playoffs				
Season	Club	Lea	GP	G	A	TP	PIM	GP	G	A	TP	PIM
1995-96	Red Deer Chiefs	AMHL	35	6	17	23	31	....	....	....	....	....
	Calgary Hitmen	WHL	1	0	1	1	2	....	....	....	....	....
1996-97	Calgary Hitmen	WHL	64	10	22	32	31	....	....	....	....	....
1997-98	Calgary Hitmen	WHL	55	7	24	31	13	18	3	2	5	4
1998-99	Calgary Hitmen	WHL	68	14	69	83	16	21	8	15	23	59
99-2000	Calgary Hitmen	WHL	62	14	61	75	24	13	2	12	14	8
2000-01	Calgary Hitmen	WHL	70	18	66	84	52	12	3	6	9	6

WHL East First All-Star Team (1999) • Memorial Cup All-Star Team (1999) • WHL East Second All-Star Team (2000) • WHL East First All-Star Team (2001) • Canadian Major Junior First All-Star Team (2001)

Signed as a free agent by **NY Rangers**, June 26, 2001.

KING, Colt (KIHNG, KOHLT) **COL.**

Left wing. Shoots left. 6'2", 220 lbs. Born, Thunder Bay, Ont., March 4, 1983.
(Colorado's 3rd choice, 130th overall, in 2001 Entry Draft).

			Regular Season					Playoffs				
Season	Club	Lea	GP	G	A	TP	PIM	GP	G	A	TP	PIM
1998-99	St. Thomas Stars	OJHL-B	41	11	13	24	89	....	....	....	....	....
99-2000	Guelph Storm	OHL	53	2	2	4	41	6	0	0	0	5
2000-01	Guelph Storm	OHL	65	25	27	52	129	4	0	1	1	8

KINOS, Lauri (KEE-nohs, LOH-ree) **ST.L.**

Defense. Shoots left. 6'2", 195 lbs. Born, Jyvaskyla, Finland, June 29, 1980.
(St. Louis' 9th choice, 293rd overall, in 2000 Entry Draft).

			Regular Season					Playoffs				
Season	Club	Lea	GP	G	A	TP	PIM	GP	G	A	TP	PIM
1996-97	Diskos Jyvaskyla	Finn-Jr.	24	2	0	2	32	....	....	....	....	....
1997-98	JyP Jyvaskyla	Finn-Jr.	29	8	6	14	30	2	0	0	0	0
1998-99	JyP Jyvaskyla	Finn-Jr.	27	3	1	4	30	....	....	....	....	....
99-2000	Montreal Rocket	QMJHL	69	12	17	29	80	5	1	1	2	6
2000-01	Worcester IceCats	AHL	11	0	0	0	8	....	....	....	....	....
	Peoria Rivermen	ECHL	55	4	12	16	56	9	0	1	1	6

KISER, Nate (KIGH-zuhr, NAT) **PHX.**

Defense. Shoots right. 6'1", 202 lbs. Born, Southgate, MI, May 4, 1982.
(Phoenix's 4th choice, 160th overall, in 2000 Entry Draft).

			Regular Season					Playoffs				
Season	Club	Lea	GP	G	A	TP	PIM	GP	G	A	TP	PIM
1998-99	Det-Compuware	NAJHL	32	2	3	5	46	....	....	....	....	....
99-2000	Plymouth Whalers	OHL	63	3	5	8	102	23	1	1	2	18
2000-01	Plymouth Whalers	OHL	62	1	8	9	105	13	0	1	1	26

KLEMA, David (KLEE-mah, DAY-vihd) **PHX.**

Center. Shoots left. 6', 178 lbs. Born, Roseau, MN, April 3, 1982.
(Phoenix's 5th choice, 148th overall, in 2001 Entry Draft).

			Regular Season					Playoffs				
Season	Club	Lea	GP	G	A	TP	PIM	GP	G	A	TP	PIM
1998-99	Roseau Rams	Hi-School	28	25	35	63	....	....	....	....	....	....
99-2000	Roseau Rams	Hi-School	28	16	31	47	8	....	....	....	....	....
	Fargo-Moorhead	USHL	6	0	2	2	4	....	....	....	....	....
	Des Moines	USHL	4	1	1	2	0	6	1	1	2	0
2000-01	Des Moines	USHL	56	13	40	53	58	3	1	0	1	0

KLYAZMIN, Sergei (klee-YAZ-mihn, SAIR-gay) COL.

Left wing. Shoots left. 6'3", 190 lbs. Born, Moscow, USSR, March 1, 1982.
(Colorado's 6th choice, 92nd overall, in 2000 Entry Draft).

			Regular Season					Playoffs				
Season	Club	Lea	GP	G	A	TP	PIM	GP	G	A	TP	PIM
1998-99	Krylja Sovetov-2	Russia-3	21	1	4	5	14					
99-2000	D'amo Moscow-2	Russia-3	16	3	2	5	18					
2000-01	Halifax	QMJHL	65	33	28	61	76	6	1	2	3	16

KNOPP, Ben (KUH-nawp, BEHN) CBJ

Right wing. Shoots right. 6', 185 lbs. Born, Calgary, Alta., April 8, 1982.
(Columbus' 2nd choice, 69th overall, in 2000 Entry Draft).

			Regular Season					Playoffs				
Season	Club	Lea	GP	G	A	TP	PIM	GP	G	A	TP	PIM
1997-98	Calgary Buffaloes	AMHL	35	28	48	76	34	10	10	6	16	30
1998-99	Calgary Canucks	AJHL	55	37	45	82	161	6	6	6	12	6
99-2000	Moose Jaw	WHL	72	30	30	60	101	4	2	2	4	4
2000-01	Moose Jaw	WHL	58	22	34	56	105	4	0	0	0	11

KNYAZEV, Igor (kuh-NYA-zhev, EE-gohr) CAR.

Defense. Shoots left. 6', 191 lbs. Born, Elektrostal, USSR, January 27, 1983.
(Carolina's 1st choice, 15th overall, in 2001 Entry Draft).

			Regular Season					Playoffs				
Season	Club	Lea	GP	G	A	TP	PIM	GP	G	A	TP	PIM
99-2000	Krylja Sovetov-2	Russia-3	13	2	4	6	74					
	Krylja Sovetov	Russia-2	26	1	1	2	6					
2000-01	Krylja Sovetov	Russia-2	42	6	3	9	64	11	0	2	2	37

KOALSKA, Matt (KOHL-skuh, MAT) NSH.

Center. Shoots left. 6'1", 190 lbs. Born, St. Paul, MN, May 16, 1980.
(Nashville's 7th choice, 154th overall, in 2000 Entry Draft).

			Regular Season					Playoffs				
Season	Club	Lea	GP	G	A	TP	PIM	GP	G	A	TP	PIM
1998-99	Hill-Murray	Hi-School	26	20	50	70	18					
99-2000	Twin Cities	USHL	57	24	34	58	19	13	5	5	10	4
2000-01	U. of Minnesota	WCHA	42	10	24	34	36					

First All-Conference Schoolboy Team (1999) • First All-State Schoolboy Team (1999)

KOBASEW, Chuck (KOH-buh-soo, CHUK) CGY.

Right wing. Shoots right. 5'11", 195 lbs. Born, Osoyoos, B.C., April 17, 1982.
(Calgary's 1st choice, 14th overall, in 2001 Entry Draft).

			Regular Season					Playoffs				
Season	Club	Lea	GP	G	A	TP	PIM	GP	G	A	TP	PIM
1997-98	Osoyoos Heat	KIJHL	6	2	2	4	2					
1998-99	Osoyoos Heat	KIJHL	23	25	24	49	....					
	Penticton	BCJHL	30	11	17	28	18					
99-2000	Penticton	BCJHL	58	*54	52	106	83					
2000-01	Boston College	H-East	43	27	22	49	38					

BCJHL First All-Star Team (2000) • Won BCJHL Interior Division MVP Award (2000) • Hockey East Second All-Star Team (2001) • NCAA Championship All-Tournament Team (2001) • NCAA Championship Tournament MVP (2001)

Rights traded to **Kelowna** by **Prince George** for Chuck Di Ubaldo and future considerations, August 1, 2001. • Left **Boston College** and signed with **Kelowna** (WHL), August 13, 2001.

KOCH, Geoff (KAWCH, JEHF)

Left wing. Shoots left. 6'1", 190 lbs. Born, Exeter, NH, June 27, 1979.
(Nashville's 3rd choice, 85th overall, in 1998 Entry Draft).

			Regular Season					Playoffs				
Season	Club	Lea	GP	G	A	TP	PIM	GP	G	A	TP	PIM
1994-95	Phillips Exeter	Hi-School	24	32	20	52	51					
1995-96	Phillips Exeter	Hi-School	28	37	40	77	48					
1996-97	Phillips Exeter	Hi-School	22	30	30	60	62					
1997-98	U. of Michigan	CCHA	43	5	6	11	51					
1998-99	U. of Michigan	CCHA	40	4	12	16	101					
99-2000	U. of Michigan	CCHA	36	12	16	28	56					
2000-01	U. of Michigan	CCHA	40	10	16	26	36					

KOCI, David (KOH-chee, DAY-vihd) PIT.

Defense. Shoots left. 6'6", 216 lbs. Born, Prague, Czech., May 12, 1981.
(Pittsburgh's 5th choice, 146th overall, in 2000 Entry Draft).

			Regular Season					Playoffs				
Season	Club	Lea	GP	G	A	TP	PIM	GP	G	A	TP	PIM
1997-98	Sparta Praha-Jr.	Cze-Rep	41	2	9	11	105					
1998-99	HC Hvezda-Jr.	Cze-Rep	22	1	3	4	36					
	Sparta Praha-Jr.	Cze-Rep	7	0	0	0	4					
99-2000	Sparta Praha-Jr.	Cze-Rep	47	0	6	6	124					
2000-01	Prince George	WHL	70	2	7	9	155	6	0	0	0	20

KOIVU, Mikko (KOI-voo, MEE-koh) MIN.

Center. Shoots left. 6'2", 183 lbs. Born, Turku, Finland, March 12, 1983.
(Minnesota's 1st choice, 6th overall, in 2001 Entry Draft).

			Regular Season					Playoffs				
Season	Club	Lea	GP	G	A	TP	PIM	GP	G	A	TP	PIM
99-2000	TPS Turku	Finn-Jr.	41	8	17	25	40	13	1	4	5	8
2000-01	TPS Turku	Finn-Jr.	26	9	36	45	26	4	2	2	4	8
	TPS Turku	Finland	21	0	1	1	2					

KOKOREV, Dimitri (KOH-koh-rehf, DEH-mee-tree) CGY.

Defense. Shoots left. 6'3", 198 lbs. Born, Moscow, USSR, January 9, 1979.
(Calgary's 4th choice, 51st overall, in 1997 Entry Draft).

			Regular Season					Playoffs				
Season	Club	Lea	GP	G	A	TP	PIM	GP	G	A	TP	PIM
1996-97	D'amo Moscow-2	Russia-3	27	2	4	6	24					
	Dynamo Moscow	Russia	1	0	0	0	0					
1997-98	Dynamo Moscow	Russia-2	24	1	2	3	20					
1998-99	Dynamo Moscow	Russia	26	0	1	1	20	8	1	0	1	0
	Dynamo Moscow	Russia-2	14	0	2	2	20					
99-2000	THK Tver	Russia-2	20	6	3	9	32					
	Dynamo Moscow	Russia	22	0	1	1	14	1	0	0	0	0
2000-01	Dynamo Moscow	Russia	5	0	1	1	4					

KOLANOS, Krys (koh-LA-nohs, KRIHS) PHX.

Center. Shoots right. 6'2", 196 lbs. Born, Calgary, Alta., July 27, 1981.
(Phoenix's 1st choice, 19th overall, in 2000 Entry Draft).

			Regular Season					Playoffs				
Season	Club	Lea	GP	G	A	TP	PIM	GP	G	A	TP	PIM
1996-97	Calgary Flames	AAHA	24	24	35	59	....					
1997-98	Calgary Buffaloes	AMHL	34	34	43	77	29					
1998-99	Calgary Royals	AJHL	58	43	67	110	98					
99-2000	Boston College	H-East	42	16	16	32	48					
2000-01	Boston College	H-East	41	25	25	50	54					

AJHL First All-Star Team (1999) • Won AJHL Rookie of the Year Award (1999) • Hockey East All-Rookie Team (2000) • Hockey East Second All-Star Team (2001) • NCAA East Second All-American Team (2001) • NCAA Championship All-Tournament Team (2001)

KOLARIK, Tyler (koh-LAHR-ihk, TIGH-luhr) CBJ

Center. Shoots right. 5'10", 190 lbs. Born, Philadelphia, PA, January 26, 1981.
(Columbus' 5th choice, 150th overall, in 2000 Entry Draft).

			Regular Season					Playoffs				
Season	Club	Lea	GP	G	A	TP	PIM	GP	G	A	TP	PIM
99-2000	Deerfield Academy	Hi-School	26	31	22	53	8					
	NY/Mid-Atlantic	MBHL	3	4	3	7	0					
2000-01	Harvard University	ECAC	32	13	15	28	36					

KOLTSOV, Konstantin (KOHLT-sahv, KOHN-stan-tihn) PIT.

Right wing. Shoots left. 6', 187 lbs. Born, Minsk, USSR, April 17, 1981.
(Pittsburgh's 1st choice, 18th overall, in 1999 Entry Draft).

			Regular Season					Playoffs				
Season	Club	Lea	GP	G	A	TP	PIM	GP	G	A	TP	PIM
1997-98	HC Cherepovets-2	Russia-3	44	11	12	23	16					
	HC Cherepovets	Russia	2	0	0	0	2					
1998-99	HC Cherepovets-3	Russia-4	2	0	1	1	2					
	HC Cherepovets-2	Russia-3	11	1	4	5	18					
	HC Cherepovets	Russia	33	3	0	3	8	1	0	0	0	2
99-2000	HC Novokuznetsk	Russia	30	3	4	7	12	11	1	1	2	6
2000-01	Ak Bars Kazan	Russia	24	7	8	15	10	2	0	0	0	4

KOMADOSKI, Neil (koh-mah-DAW-skee, NEEL) OTT.

Defense. Shoots left. 6'1", 212 lbs. Born, Chesterfield, MO, February 10, 1982.
(Ottawa's 3rd choice, 81st overall, in 2001 Entry Draft).

			Regular Season					Playoffs				
Season	Club	Lea	GP	G	A	TP	PIM	GP	G	A	TP	PIM
1997-98	Aurora Tigers	OPJHL	1	0	0	0	0					
1998-99	Team USA	USDP	50	8	7	15	202					
99-2000	Team USA	USDP	49	3	11	14	222					
2000-01	Notre Dame	CCHA	30	2	5	7	106					

KOMAROV, Alexei (KOH-muh-rahf, al-EHX-ay) DAL.

Defense. Shoots left. 6'4", 194 lbs. Born, Moscow, USSR, June 11, 1978.
(Dallas' 8th choice, 216th overall, in 1997 Entry Draft).

			Regular Season					Playoffs				
Season	Club	Lea	GP	G	A	TP	PIM	GP	G	A	TP	PIM
1996-97	D'amo Moscow-2	Russia-3	32	2	3	5	12					
1997-98	HC Yekaterinburg	Russia-2	22	0	1	1	14					
	HC Yekaterinburg	Russia	19	0	0	0	6					
1998-99	Krylja Sovetov	Russia	21	1	0	1	6					
99-2000	Krylja Sovetov	Russia-2	32	0	5	5	22					
2000-01	Krylja Sovetov	Russia-2	33	2	5	7	28	12	0	3	3	8

KOMISAREK, Mike (koh-mih-SAIR-ehk, MIGHK) MTL.

Defense. Shoots right. 6'4", 225 lbs. Born, Islip Terrace, NY, January 19, 1982.
(Montreal's 1st choice, 7th overall, in 2001 Entry Draft).

			Regular Season					Playoffs				
Season	Club	Lea	GP	G	A	TP	PIM	GP	G	A	TP	PIM
1998-99	New England	EJHL	53	17	24	51	....					
99-2000	Team USA	USDP	51	5	8	13	124					
2000-01	U. of Michigan	CCHA	41	4	12	16	77					

KOPECKY, Milan (koh-PEHTS-kee, MEE-lan) PHI.

Left wing. Shoots left. 6', 180 lbs. Born, Kolin, Czech., May 11, 1981.
(Philadelphia's 8th choice, 287th overall, in 2000 Entry Draft).

			Regular Season					Playoffs				
Season	Club	Lea	GP	G	A	TP	PIM	GP	G	A	TP	PIM
1998-99	Slavia Praha-Jr.	Cze-Rep.	49	14	21	35	....					
99-2000	Slavia Praha-Jr.	Cze-Rep.	36	17	7	24	24	7	5	3	8	0
	Slavia Praha	Cze-Rep.	2	0	0	0	0					

KOPECKY, Tomas (koh-PEHTS-kee, TAW-mahsh) DET.

Center. Shoots left. 6'3", 187 lbs. Born, Ilava, Czech., February 5, 1982.
(Detroit's 2nd choice, 38th overall, in 2000 Entry Draft).

			Regular Season					Playoffs				
Season	Club	Lea	GP	G	A	TP	PIM	GP	G	A	TP	PIM
1997-98	Dukla Trencin	Slovak-Jr.	41	19	22	41	....					
1998-99	Dukla Trencin	Slovak-Jr.	44	13	16	29	18					
99-2000	Dukla Trencin	Slovak-Jr.	14	8	9	17	36					
	Dukla Trencin	Slovakia	52	3	4	7	24	5	0	0	0	0
2000-01	Lethbridge	WHL	49	22	28	50	52	5	1	1	2	6
	Cincinnati Ducks	AHL	1	0	0	0	0					

KORSUNOV, Vladimir (KOHR-suhn-ahv, vla-DIH-meer) ANA.

Defense. Shoots left. 6'2", 202 lbs. Born, Moscow, USSR, March 16, 1983.
(Anaheim's 5th choice, 105th overall, in 2001 Entry Draft).

			Regular Season					Playoffs				
Season	Club	Lea	GP	G	A	TP	PIM	GP	G	A	TP	PIM
1998-99	Krylja Sovetov-2	Russia-3	22	1	11	12	60					
2000-01	Krylja Sovetov	Russia-2	10	0	0	0	2					

KOS, Kyle (KOHS, KIGHL) T.B.

Defense. Shoots left. 6'3", 207 lbs. Born, Hope, B.C., May 25, 1979.
(Tampa Bay's 2nd choice, 33rd overall, in 1997 Entry Draft).

			Regular Season					Playoffs				
Season	Club	Lea	GP	G	A	TP	PIM	GP	G	A	TP	PIM
1994-95	Notre Dame	SMHL	35	15	25	40	25	....	....	....	....	....
1995-96	Notre Dame	SJHL	40	2	10	12	22	....	....	....	....	....
1996-97	Red Deer Rebels	WHL	64	2	18	20	40	10	0	0	0	8
1997-98	Red Deer Rebels	WHL	71	7	33	40	102	5	0	3	3	4
1998-99	Red Deer Rebels	WHL	37	3	17	20	56	....	....	....	....	....
	Kamloops Blazers	WHL	28	6	14	20	42	9	0	0	0	8
99-2000	Detroit Vipers	IHL	44	1	2	3	77	....	....	....	....	....
	Utah Grizzlies	IHL	12	0	1	1	24	2	0	1	1	0
2000-01	Detroit Vipers	IHL	46	0	9	9	165	....	....	....	....	....

KOSICK, Mark (KOHS-ihk, MAHRK) CAR.

Center. Shoots left. 5'11", 190 lbs. Born, Victoria, B.C., March 25, 1979.
(Carolina's 9th choice, 211th overall, in 1998 Entry Draft).

			Regular Season					Playoffs				
Season	Club	Lea	GP	G	A	TP	PIM	GP	G	A	TP	PIM
1996-97	Victoria Salsa	BCJHL	54	21	37	58	12	....	....	....	....	....
1997-98	U. of Michigan	CCHA	45	14	32	46	18	....	....	....	....	....
1998-99	U. of Michigan	CCHA	42	12	23	35	14	....	....	....	....	....
99-2000	U. of Michigan	CCHA	37	18	16	34	16	....	....	....	....	....
2000-01	U. of Michigan	CCHA	41	14	17	31	14	....	....	....	....	....

NCAA Championship All-Tournament Team (2000)

KOSTOPOULOS, Tom (kaw-STAWP-oh-lihs, TAWM) PIT.

Right wing. Shoots right. 6', 205 lbs. Born, Mississauga, Ont., January 24, 1979.
(Pittsburgh's 9th choice, 204th overall, in 1999 Entry Draft).

			Regular Season					Playoffs				
Season	Club	Lea	GP	G	A	TP	PIM	GP	G	A	TP	PIM
1995-96	Brampton Blues	OPJHL	24	9	9	18	28	....	....	....	....	....
1996-97	London Knights	OHL	64	13	12	25	67	....	....	....	....	....
1997-98	London Knights	OHL	66	24	26	50	108	16	6	4	10	26
1998-99	London Knights	OHL	66	27	60	87	114	25	19	16	35	32
99-2000	Wilkes-Barre	AHL	76	26	32	58	121	....	....	....	....	....
2000-01	Wilkes-Barre	AHL	80	16	36	52	120	21	3	9	12	6

KOTALIK, Ales (KOH-tuh-lihk, AH-lehsh) BUF.

Right wing. Shoots right. 6'1", 198 lbs. Born, Jindrichuv Hradec, Czech., December 23, 1978.
(Buffalo's 7th choice, 164th overall, in 1998 Entry Draft).

			Regular Season					Playoffs				
Season	Club	Lea	GP	G	A	TP	PIM	GP	G	A	TP	PIM
1993-94	HC Budejovice-Jr.	Cze-Rep	28	12	12	24	....	....	....	....	....	....
1994-95	HC Budejovice-Jr.	Cze-Rep	36	26	17	43	....	....	....	....	....	....
1995-96	HC Budejovice-Jr.	Cze-Rep	28	6	7	13	....	....	....	....	....	....
1996-97	HC Budejovice-Jr.	Cze-Rep	36	15	16	31	24	....	....	....	....	....
1997-98	HC Budejovice	Cze-Rep	47	9	7	16	14	....	....	....	....	....
1998-99	HC Budejovice	Cze-Rep	41	8	13	21	16	3	0	0	0	....
99-2000	HC Budejovice	Cze-Rep	43	7	12	19	34	3	0	1	1	6
2000-01	HC Budejovice	Cze-Rep	52	19	29	48	54	....	....	....	....	....

KOTARY, Sean (koh-TAH-ree, SHAWN) COL.

Center. Shoots right. 6', 190 lbs. Born, New Hartford, NY, April 28, 1981.
(Colorado's 13th choice, 266th overall, in 2000 Entry Draft).

			Regular Season					Playoffs				
Season	Club	Lea	GP	G	A	TP	PIM	GP	G	A	TP	PIM
1995/98	New Hartford	Hi-School	74	54	55	109	....	....	....	....	....	....
1998-99	Loomis-Chaffe	Hi-School	25	32	26	58	....	....	....	....	....	....
99-2000	Northwood Prep	Hi-School	41	49	57	106	21	....	....	....	....	....
2000-01	Bowling Green	CCHA	5	0	0	0	4	....	....	....	....	....

• Statistics for **New Hartford High School** are career totals from the 1995-1998 seasons

KOVAC, Kristian (KOH-vach, KRIHST-yan) COL.

Right wing. Shoots right. 6'2", 205 lbs. Born, Kosice, Czech., January 1, 1981.
(Colorado's 5th choice, 122nd overall, in 1999 Entry Draft).

			Regular Season					Playoffs				
Season	Club	Lea	GP	G	A	TP	PIM	GP	G	A	TP	PIM
1997-98	HC Kosice	Slovak-Jr.	47	22	11	33	103	....	....	....	....	....
1998-99	HC Kosice	Slovak-Jr.	39	30	20	50	73	2	1	0	1	2
	HC Kosice	Slovakia	6	0	0	0	2	....	....	....	....	....
99-2000	Victoriaville Tigres	QMJHL	65	11	18	29	50	5	0	0	0	4
2000-01	Victoriaville Tigres	QMJHL	51	10	20	30	38	13	2	3	5	4

KOVALCHUK, Ilya (koh-vuhl-CHOOK, IHL-yuh) ATL.

Left wing. Shoots right. 6'2", 202 lbs. Born, Tver, USSR, April 15, 1983.
(Atlanta's 1st choice, 1st overall, in 2001 Entry Draft).

			Regular Season					Playoffs				
Season	Club	Lea	GP	G	A	TP	PIM	GP	G	A	TP	PIM
99-2000	Krylja Sovetov-2	Russia-3	2	2	1	3	14	....	....	....	....	....
	Krylja Sovetov	Russia-2	49	12	5	17	75	....	....	....	....	....
2000-01	Krylja Sovetov	Russia-2	39	25	18	43	78	12	14	4	18	38

KRAFT, Ryan (KRAFT, RIGH-uhn) S.J.

Center. Shoots left. 5'9", 190 lbs. Born, Bottineau, ND, November 7, 1975.
(San Jose's 11th choice, 194th overall, in 1995 Entry Draft).

			Regular Season					Playoffs				
Season	Club	Lea	GP	G	A	TP	PIM	GP	G	A	TP	PIM
1993-94	Moorhead High	Hi-School	25	40	45	85	....	....	....	....	....	....
1994-95	U. of Minnesota	WCHA	44	13	33	46	44	....	....	....	....	....
1995-96	U. of Minnesota	WCHA	41	13	24	37	24	....	....	....	....	....
1996-97	U. of Minnesota	WCHA	42	25	21	46	37	....	....	....	....	....
1997-98	U. of Minnesota	WCHA	32	11	26	37	16	....	....	....	....	....
1998-99	Richmond	ECHL	63	28	36	64	35	18	10	10	20	4
99-2000	Richmond	ECHL	44	32	35	67	32	....	....	....	....	....
	Cleveland	IHL	1	0	1	1	0	....	....	....	....	....
	Kentucky	AHL	15	7	6	13	2	5	3	1	4	0
2000-01	Kentucky	AHL	77	38	50	88	36	3	2	0	2	0

WCHA All-Rookie Team (1995) • WCHA All-Academic Team (1996) • AHL Second All-Star Team (2001) • Won Dudley "Red" Garrett Memorial Trophy (Top Rookie - AHL) (2001)

KRAJICEK, Lukas (KRIGH-ee-chehk, LOO-kahsh) FLA.

Defense. Shoots left. 6'2", 182 lbs. Born, Prostejov, Czech., March 11, 1983.
(Florida's 2nd choice, 24th overall, in 2001 Entry Draft).

			Regular Season					Playoffs				
Season	Club	Lea	GP	G	A	TP	PIM	GP	G	A	TP	PIM
1998-99	ZPS Zlin-Jr.	Cze-Rep	48	8	18	26	40	....	....	....	....	....
99-2000	Det-Compuware	NAJHL	53	5	22	27	61	5	0	1	1	18
2000-01	Peterborough	OHL	61	8	27	35	53	7	0	5	5	0

OHL All-Rookie Team (2001)

KRESTANOVICH, Jordan (KREH-sta-noh-vihtch, JOHR-dan) COL.

Left wing. Shoots left. 6'1", 170 lbs. Born, Langley, B.C., June 14, 1981.
(Colorado's 7th choice, 152nd overall, in 1999 Entry Draft).

			Regular Season					Playoffs				
Season	Club	Lea	GP	G	A	TP	PIM	GP	G	A	TP	PIM
1996-97	Surrey Chiefs	BCAHA	55	79	81	160	....	....	....	....	....	....
1997-98	Calgary Hitmen	WHL	22	1	0	1	0	13	0	0	0	0
1998-99	Calgary Hitmen	WHL	62	6	13	19	10	20	3	8	11	4
99-2000	Calgary Hitmen	WHL	72	19	24	43	22	13	7	7	14	4
	Hershey Bears	AHL	....	....	....	....	....	1	0	0	0	0
2000-01	Calgary Hitmen	WHL	70	40	60	100	32	12	8	4	12	8
	Hershey Bears	AHL	....	....	....	....	....	2	0	0	0	0

KREVSUN, Alexandre (KREHV-sihn, al-ehx-AN-duhr) NSH.

Right wing. Shoots left. 6', 212 lbs. Born, Togliatti, USSR, June 6, 1980.
(Nashville's 9th choice, 124th overall, in 1999 Entry Draft).

			Regular Season					Playoffs				
Season	Club	Lea	GP	G	A	TP	PIM	GP	G	A	TP	PIM
1996-97	Lada Togliatti	Russia	2	0	0	0	0	....	....	....	....	....
1997-98	Lada Togliatti-2	Russia-3	37	10	5	15	24	....	....	....	....	....
1998-99	Lada Togliatti-2	Russia-4	24	10	4	14	30	....	....	....	....	....
	CSK Samara-2	Russia-4	8	4	0	4	4	....	....	....	....	....
	CSK Samara	Russia	5	0	2	2	4	2	0	0	0	0
99-2000	CSK Samara-2	Russia-4	1	0	0	0	0	....	....	....	....	....
	Krylja Sovetov	Russia-2	14	1	1	2	16	....	....	....	....	....
2000-01	New Orleans	ECHL	48	8	13	21	24	4	0	0	0	0

KRISTEK, Jaroslav (KRIHSH-tehk, YAH-roh-slahv) BUF.

Right wing. Shoots left. 6'2", 190 lbs. Born, Zlin, Czech., March 16, 1980.
(Buffalo's 4th choice, 50th overall, in 1998 Entry Draft).

			Regular Season					Playoffs				
Season	Club	Lea	GP	G	A	TP	PIM	GP	G	A	TP	PIM
1995-96	ZPS Zlin-Jr.	Cze-Rep	34	33	20	53	....	....	....	....	....	....
1996-97	ZPS Zlin-Jr.	Cze-Rep	44	28	27	55	....	....	....	....	....	....
1997-98	ZPS Zlin-Jr.	Cze-Rep	7	8	5	13	....	....	....	....	....	....
	HC Prostejov-2	Cze-Rep	4	0	0	0	....	....	....	....	....	....
	ZPS Zlin	Cze-Rep	37	2	8	10	20	....	....	....	....	....
1998-99	Tri-City Americans	WHL	70	38	48	86	55	12	4	3	7	2
99-2000	Tri-City Americans	WHL	45	26	25	51	16	2	0	0	0	0
2000-01	Rochester	AHL	35	5	3	8	20	....	....	....	....	....

KRISTOFFERSSON, Marcus (KRIHST-aw-fuhr-SOHN, MAHRK) DAL.

Right wing. Shoots left. 6'3", 200 lbs. Born, Ostersund, Sweden, January 22, 1979.
(Dallas' 4th choice, 105th overall, in 1997 Entry Draft).

			Regular Season					Playoffs				
Season	Club	Lea	GP	G	A	TP	PIM	GP	G	A	TP	PIM
1995-96	Mora IK	Swede-Jr.	16	2	2	4	28	....	....	....	....	....
	Mora IK	Swede-2	26	1	0	1	20	5	0	0	0	2
1996-97	Mora IK	Swede-2	33	1	5	6	26	....	....	....	....	....
1997-98	Mora IK	Swede-2	27	7	6	13	40	....	....	....	....	....
1998-99	HV Jonkoping	Swede-Jr.	3	0	1	1	27	....	....	....	....	....
	HV Jonkoping	Sweden	34	0	1	1	65	....	....	....	....	....
99-2000	HV Jonkoping	Swede-Jr.	7	5	9	14	41	....	....	....	....	....
	HV Jonkoping	Sweden	10	0	0	0	0	....	....	....	....	....
	Blues Espoo	Finland	29	7	4	11	42	1	1	0	1	0
2000-01	Assat-Pori	Finland	9	1	0	1	16	....	....	....	....	....
	Djurgardens IF	Sweden	29	4	2	6	72	12	2	2	4	45

KRONWALL, Niklas (KRAHN-wuhl, NIHK-las) DET.

Defense. Shoots left. 5'11", 165 lbs. Born, Stockholm, Sweden, January 12, 1981.
(Detroit's 1st choice, 29th overall, in 2000 Entry Draft).

			Regular Season					Playoffs				
Season	Club	Lea	GP	G	A	TP	PIM	GP	G	A	TP	PIM
1996-97	Djurgardens IF	Swede-Jr.	1	0	0	0	0	....	....	....	....	....
1997-98	Djurgardens IF	Swede-Jr.	27	4	3	7	71	2	0	0	0	2
1998-99	Huddinge IK	Swede-2	24	1	1	2	24	....	....	....	....	....
99-2000	Djurgardens IF	Sweden	37	1	4	5	16	8	0	0	0	8
2000-01	Djurgardens IF	Sweden	31	1	9	10	32	15	0	1	1	8

KRUCHININ, Andrei (kroo-CHIHN-ihn, AWN-dray) MTL.

Defense. Shoots left. 5'11", 187 lbs. Born, Karaganda, USSR, May 18, 1978.
(Montreal's 7th choice, 189th overall, in 1998 Entry Draft).

			Regular Season					Playoffs				
Season	Club	Lea	GP	G	A	TP	PIM	GP	G	A	TP	PIM
1996-97	Lada Togliatti	Russia	19	0	1	1	8	11	0	0	0	0
1997-98	Lada Togliatti	Russia	43	0	4	4	73	....	....	....	....	....
1998-99	Lada Togliatti	Russia	41	1	4	5	56	6	0	1	1	2
99-2000	CSK Samara	Russia	6	1	0	1	0	....	....	....	....	....
	Lada Togliatti	Russia	25	1	2	3	24	6	1	0	1	4
2000-01	Molot-Perm	Russia	14	1	3	4	10	....	....	....	....	....
	Lada Togliatti	Russia	14	0	2	2	12	3	0	0	0	0

KRYUKOV, Artem (KREE-oo-kahf, AHR-tehm) BUF.

Center. Shoots left. 6'3", 187 lbs. Born, Novosibirsk, USSR, March 5, 1982.
(Buffalo's 1st choice, 15th overall, in 2000 Entry Draft).

			Regular Season					Playoffs				
Season	Club	Lea	GP	G	A	TP	PIM	GP	G	A	TP	PIM
1997-98	Torpedo Yaroslavl	Russia-2	7	0	0	0	2	....	....	....	....	....
1998-99	HC Yaroslavl-2	Russia-3	20	2	2	4	6	....	....	....	....	....
99-2000	HC Yaroslavl-2	Russia-3	14	1	1	2	12	....	....	....	....	....
	Torpedo Yaroslavl	Russia	3	0	0	0	4	....	....	....	....	....
2000-01	HC Yaroslavl-2	Russia-3	6	0	0	0	2	11	0	0	0	8
	St. Petersburg	Russia	14	0	2	2	14	....	....	....	....	....

KUCERA, Jiri (kuh-CHEH-rah, YUHREE) PIT.

Center. Shoots left. 5'11", 180 lbs. Born, Bratislava, Czech., March 28, 1966.
(Pittsburgh's 8th choice, 152nd overall, in 1987 Entry Draft).

			Regular Season					Playoffs				
Season	Club	Lea	GP	G	A	TP	PIM	GP	G	A	TP	PIM
1984-85	Skoda Pizen	Czech.	40	6	6	12	4	....	....	....	....	....
1985-86	Dukla Jihlava	Czech.	30	6	4	10	....	....	....	....	....	....
1986-87	Dukla Jihlava	Czech.	43	13	12	25	18	....	....	....	....	....
1987-88	Skoda Plzen	Czech.	41	21	24	45	22	....	....	....	....	....
1988-89	Skoda Plzen	Czech.	40	20	15	35	22	....	....	....	....	....
1989-90	Skoda Plzen	Czech.	47	13	24	37	....	....	....	....	....	....
1990-91	Tappara Tampere	Finland	44	23	34	57	26	3	0	2	2	4
1991-92	Tappara Tampere	Finland	44	22	20	42	8	....	....	....	....	....
1992-93	Tappara Tampere	Finland	48	22	32	54	20	....	....	....	....	....
1993-94	Tappara Tampere	Finland	47	16	26	42	37	10	7	5	12	4
	Olympics	Cze-Rep	8	6	2	8	4	....	....	....	....	....
1994-95	Lulea HF	Sweden	40	15	12	27	24	9	2	7	9	8
1995-96	Lulea HF	Sweden	39	15	19	34	38	12	4	6	10	6
1996-97	ZKZ Plzen	Cze-Rep	43	10	23	33	28	....	....	....	....	....
1997-98	EHC Kloten	Switz.	38	8	22	30	18	7	1	2	3	2
1998-99	Lulea HF	Sweden	44	7	21	28	52	5	2	1	3	4
99-2000	Lulea HF	Sweden	47	13	21	34	34	9	1	1	2	6
2000-01	Lulea HF	Sweden	34	10	8	18	8	....	....	....	....	....

KULESHOV, Mikhail (koo-leh-SHAWV, mihk-AIL) COL.

Left wing. Shoots right. 6'2", 205 lbs. Born, Perm, USSR, January 7, 1981.
(Colorado's 1st choice, 25th overall, in 1999 Entry Draft).

			Regular Season					Playoffs				
Season	Club	Lea	GP	G	A	TP	PIM	GP	G	A	TP	PIM
1997-98	Avangard Omsk-2	Russia-3	12	12	3	15	12	....	....	....	....	....
	Avangard Omsk	Russia	4	1	0	1	4	....	....	....	....	....
1998-99	HC Cherepovets-3	Russia-4	3	2	1	3	32	....	....	....	....	....
	HC Cherepovets-2	Russia-3	25	7	5	12	12	....	....	....	....	....
	HC Cherepovets	Russia	15	2	0	2	8	3	0	0	0	4
99-2000	HC Cherepovets	Russia	8	0	0	0	4	3	0	0	0	2
2000-01	St. Petersburg	Russia	7	0	0	0	8	....	....	....	....	....
	Hershey Bears	AHL	3	0	0	0	4	11	1	0	1	0

KUPARINEN, Mikko (koo-PAHR-ai-nehn, MEE-koh) T.B.

Defense. Shoots left. 6'4", 213 lbs. Born, Kerava, Finland, March 29, 1977.
(Tampa Bay's 10th choice, 244th overall, in 1999 Entry Draft).

			Regular Season					Playoffs				
Season	Club	Lea	GP	G	A	TP	PIM	GP	G	A	TP	PIM
1994-95	Hameenlinna-B	Finn-Jr.	31	4	7	11	16	....	....	....	....	....
1995-96	Hameenlinna-B	Finn-Jr.	19	5	6	11	8	....	....	....	....	....
1996-97	HPK Hameenlinna	Finn-Jr.	35	0	6	6	38	4	0	0	0	2
	HPK Hameenlinna	Finland	1	0	1	1	2	....	....	....	....	....
1997-98	HPK Hameenlinna	Finn-Jr.	28	2	4	6	18	....	....	....	....	....
1998-99	Ahmat Hyvinkas	Finland-2	3	0	0	0	2	....	....	....	....	....
	HPK Hameenlinna	Finland	33	0	3	3	52	....	....	....	....	....
	Grand Rapids	IHL	19	0	2	2	35	....	....	....	....	....
99-2000	HIFK Helsinki	Finland	28	0	2	2	49	9	0	0	0	0
	Detroit Vipers	IHL	5	0	0	0	2	....	....	....	....	....
	Long Beach	IHL	4	0	0	0	4	....	....	....	....	....
2000-01	Detroit Vipers	IHL	43	1	5	6	73	....	....	....	....	....
	Johnstown Chiefs	ECHL	13	1	4	5	10	....	....	....	....	....

Traded to **Atlanta** by **Tampa Bay** for future considerations, October 29, 1999. Traded to **Tampa Bay** by **Atlanta** for Chris McAlpine, March 11, 2000.

KURKA, Tomas (KUHR-kuh, TAW-mahsh) CAR.

Left wing. Shoots left. 5'11", 190 lbs. Born, Most, Czech., December 14, 1981.
(Carolina's 1st choice, 32nd overall, in 2000 Entry Draft).

			Regular Season					Playoffs				
Season	Club	Lea	GP	G	A	TP	PIM	GP	G	A	TP	PIM
1996-97	CHZ Litvinov-Jr.	Cze-Rep	38	25	20	45	20	....	....	....	....	....
1997-98	CHZ Litvinov-Jr.	Cze-Rep	44	38	23	61	90	....	....	....	....	....
1998-99	CHZ Litvinov-Jr.	Cze-Rep	42	23	16	39	47	....	....	....	....	....
	CHZ Litvinov	Cze-Rep	6	0	0	0	0	....	....	....	....	....
99-2000	Plymouth Whalers	OHL	64	36	28	64	37	17	7	6	13	6
2000-01	Plymouth Whalers	OHL	47	15	29	44	20	16	8	13	21	13

KUZNETSOV, Sergei (kooz-NEHT-zahv, SAIR-gay) PHX.

Center. Shoots left. 6'1", 180 lbs. Born, Yaroslavl, USSR, January 29, 1980.
(Tampa Bay's 6th choice, 146th overall, in 1998 Entry Draft).

			Regular Season					Playoffs				
Season	Club	Lea	GP	G	A	TP	PIM	GP	G	A	TP	PIM
1995-96	Torpedo Yaroslavl	Russia-Jr.	28	14	14	28	20	....	....	....	....	....
1996-97	Torpedo Yaroslavl	Russia-3	62	16	15	31	35	....	....	....	....	....
1997-98	Torpedo Yaroslavl	Russia-2	42	10	13	23	30	....	....	....	....	....
1998-99	Peterborough	OHL	65	8	17	25	39	5	2	1	3	2
99-2000	Peterborough	OHL	68	33	32	65	54	5	0	4	4	2
2000-01	Mississippi	ECHL	55	11	17	28	34	....	....	....	....	....
	Springfield	AHL	22	0	4	4	10	....	....	....	....	....

Signed as a free agent by **Phoenix**, August 15, 2000.

LAATIKAINEN, Arto (lah-tee-KIGH-nuhn, AHR-toh) NYR

Defense. Shoots left. 6', 187 lbs. Born, Espoo, Finland, May 24, 1980.
(NY Rangers' 8th choice, 197th overall, in 1999 Entry Draft).

			Regular Season					Playoffs				
Season	Club	Lea	GP	G	A	TP	PIM	GP	G	A	TP	PIM
1996-97	Blues Espoo	Finn-Jr.	34	2	9	11	34	....	....	....	....	....
1997-98	Blues Espoo-B	Finn-Jr.	7	2	1	3	6	....	....	....	....	....
	Blues Espoo	Finn-Jr.	35	7	9	16	24	5	2	0	2	2
1998-99	Blues Espoo	Finn-Jr.	3	0	1	1	4	1	1	1	2	0
	Blues Espoo	Finland	48	0	6	6	14	4	0	2	2	2
99-2000	Blues Espoo	Finn-Jr.	1	0	0	0	2	....	....	....	....	....
	Blues Espoo	Finland	51	6	5	11	12	4	1	0	1	4
2000-01	Blues Espoo	Finland	54	5	9	14	38	....	....	....	....	....

LAINE, Teemu (LIGH-neh, TEE-moo) N.J.

Right wing. Shoots left. 6', 200 lbs. Born, Helsinki, Finland, August 9, 1982.
(New Jersey's 2nd choice, 39th overall, in 2000 Entry Draft).

			Regular Season					Playoffs				
Season	Club	Lea	GP	G	A	TP	PIM	GP	G	A	TP	PIM
1998-99	Jokerit Helsinki	Finn-Jr.	29	20	17	37	83	6	0	2	2	6
99-2000	Jokerit Helsinki	Finn-Jr.	23	5	9	14	42	....	....	....	....	....
	Jokerit Helsinki	Finland	14	1	1	2	8	....	....	....	....	....
2000-01	Jokerit Helsinki	Finn-Jr.	4	1	2	3	18	1	0	0	0	0
	Kiekko-Vantta	Finland-2	18	2	4	6	30	....	....	....	....	....
	Jokerit Helsinki	Finland	25	3	2	5	10	5	1	0	1	2

LAKOS, Andre (LA-kaws, AWN-dray) N.J.

Defense. Shoots right. 6'6", 230 lbs. Born, Vienna, Austria, July 29, 1979.
(New Jersey's 4th choice, 95th overall, in 1999 Entry Draft).

			Regular Season					Playoffs				
Season	Club	Lea	GP	G	A	TP	PIM	GP	G	A	TP	PIM
1995-96	Mtl-Bourassa	QAAA	40	2	13	15	68	....	....	....	....	....
1996-97	Shelburne Wolves	MTJHL	36	5	12	17	47	....	....	....	....	....
1997-98	St. Michael's	OHL	49	2	10	12	54	....	....	....	....	....
1998-99	Barrie Colts	OHL	62	4	23	27	40	12	3	3	6	8
99-2000	Albany River Rats	AHL	65	1	7	8	41	5	0	2	2	4
2000-01	Albany River Rats	AHL	51	1	20	21	29	....	....	....	....	....

LAMPMAN, Bryce (LAMP-man, BRIGHS) NYR

Defense. Shoots left. 6'1", 193 lbs. Born, Rochester, MN, August 31, 1982.
(NY Rangers' 4th choice, 113th overall, in 2001 Entry Draft).

			Regular Season					Playoffs				
Season	Club	Lea	GP	G	A	TP	PIM	GP	G	A	TP	PIM
1998-99	Rochester	USHL	53	3	8	11	33	....	....	....	....	....
99-2000	Rochester	USHL	10	0	0	0	14	....	....	....	....	....
	Omaha Lancers	USHL	11	1	2	3	38	4	0	0	0	0
2000-01	Omaha Lancers	USHL	55	10	11	21	77	12	1	4	5	12

LANGFELD, Josh (LANG-fehld, JAWSH) OTT.

Right wing. Shoots right. 6'3", 205 lbs. Born, Fridley, MN, July 17, 1977.
(Ottawa's 3rd choice, 66th overall, in 1997 Entry Draft).

			Regular Season					Playoffs				
Season	Club	Lea	GP	G	A	TP	PIM	GP	G	A	TP	PIM
1995-96	Great Falls	AFJHL	45	45	40	85	105	....	....	....	....	....
1996-97	Lincoln Stars	USHL	38	35	23	58	100	14	8	*13	*21	42
1997-98	U. of Michigan	CCHA	46	19	17	36	66	....	....	....	....	....
1998-99	U. of Michigan	CCHA	41	21	14	35	84	....	....	....	....	....
99-2000	U. of Michigan	CCHA	39	9	21	30	56	....	....	....	....	....
2000-01	U. of Michigan	CCHA	42	16	12	28	44	....	....	....	....	....

NCAA Championship All-Tournament Team (1998)

LAPLANTE, Eric (LA-plawnt, AIR-ihk) S.J.

Left wing. Shoots left. 6', 185 lbs. Born, St-Maurice, Que., December 1, 1979.
(San Jose's 3rd choice, 65th overall, in 1998 Entry Draft).

			Regular Season					Playoffs				
Season	Club	Lea	GP	G	A	TP	PIM	GP	G	A	TP	PIM
1995-96	Cap-d-Madelaine	QAAA	41	13	18	31	138	....	....	....	....	....
1996-97	Halifax	QMJHL	68	20	30	50	245	18	3	11	14	28
1997-98	Halifax	QMJHL	40	19	22	41	193	....	....	....	....	....
1998-99	Drummondville	QMJHL	42	14	25	39	258	....	....	....	....	....
	Quebec Remparts	QMJHL	23	4	17	21	58	13	8	7	15	45
99-2000	Quebec Remparts	QMJHL	47	24	35	59	234	10	3	5	8	*83
2000-01	Kentucky	AHL	62	5	8	13	181	3	0	0	0	6

LAROSE, Cory (la-ROHZ, KOH-ree) MIN.

Left wing. Shoots left. 6', 188 lbs. Born, Campbellton, N.B., May 14, 1975.

			Regular Season					Playoffs				
Season	Club	Lea	GP	G	A	TP	PIM	GP	G	A	TP	PIM
1995-96	Langley Thunder	BCJHL	54	28	46	74	61	....	....	....	....	....
1996-97	U. of Maine	H-East	35	10	27	37	32	....	....	....	....	....
1997-98	U. of Maine	H-East	34	15	25	40	22	....	....	....	....	....
1998-99	U. of Maine	H-East	38	21	31	52	34	....	....	....	....	....
99-2000	U. of Maine	H-East	39	15	*36	51	45	....	....	....	....	....
2000-01	Jackson Bandits	ECHL	63	21	32	53	73	5	2	2	4	12
	Cleveland	IHL	4	1	1	2	6	....	....	....	....	....

BCJHL Playoff MVP (1996) • Hockey East First All-Star Team (2000) • NCAA East Second All-American Team (2000)

Signed as a free agent by **Minnesota**, May 10, 2000.

LARRIVEE, Christian (la-ree-VAY, krihs-TYEH) MTL.

Center. Shoots left. 6'3", 192 lbs. Born, Gaspe, Que., August 25, 1982.
(Montreal's 6th choice, 114th overall, in 2000 Entry Draft).

			Regular Season					Playoffs				
Season	Club	Lea	GP	G	A	TP	PIM	GP	G	A	TP	PIM
1998-99	Jonquiere Aces	QAAA	42	26	36	62	10	....	....	....	....	....
99-2000	Chicoutimi	QMJHL	69	8	15	23	18	....	....	....	....	....
2000-01	Chicoutimi	QMJHL	72	32	48	80	46	7	3	1	4	4

LAUZON, Ryan (LOH-zohn, RIGH-yan) PHX.

Center. Shoots left. 5'9", 182 lbs. Born, Halifax, N.S., October 8, 1980.
(Phoenix's 5th choice, 116th overall, in 1999 Entry Draft).

			Regular Season					Playoffs				
Season	Club	Lea	GP	G	A	TP	PIM	GP	G	A	TP	PIM
1995-96	Halifax Hawks	NSMHL	89	96	128	224	....	....	....	....	....	....
1996-97	Hull Olympiques	QMJHL	65	8	10	18	16	14	1	0	1	0
1997-98	Hull Olympiques	QMJHL	64	33	56	89	37	11	8	13	21	2
1998-99	Hull Olympiques	QMJHL	57	21	47	68	36	23	3	20	23	10
99-2000	Hull Olympiques	QMJHL	49	24	35	59	37	15	6	8	14	8
2000-01	Springfield	AHL	37	5	10	15	6	....	....	....	....	....

LAZAREV, Yevgeny (LA-zahr-ehv, YEHV-geh-nee) COL.

Right wing. Shoots left. 6'2", 205 lbs. Born, Kharkov, USSR, April 25, 1980.
(Colorado's 8th choice, 79th overall, in 1998 Entry Draft).

			Regular Season					Playoffs				
Season	Club	Lea	GP	G	A	TP	PIM	GP	G	A	TP	PIM
1995-96	Torpedo Yaroslavl	Russia 2	60	32	30	62	45	....	....	....	....	....
1996-97	HC Yaroslavl-2	Russia-3	44	18	15	33	38	16	23	21	44	22
	Torpedo Yaroslavl	Russia	1	0	0	0	0	....	....	....	....	....
1997-98	Kitchener	OJHL-B	11	9	13	22	19	5	5	2	7	17
1998-99	Hershey Bears	AHL	53	6	15	21	18	....	....	....	....	....
99-2000	Hershey Bears	AHL	46	2	11	13	44	8	0	1	1	2
	Pensacola	ECHL	11	3	5	8	23	....	....	....	....	....
2000-01	Hershey Bears	AHL	80	17	21	38	50	12	3	8	11	10

LEACH, Jay (LEECH, JAY) PHX.

Defense. Shoots left. 6'4", 216 lbs. Born, Syracuse, NY, September 2, 1979.
(Phoenix's 5th choice, 115th overall, in 1998 Entry Draft).

			Regular Season					Playoffs				
Season	Club	Lea	GP	G	A	TP	PIM	GP	G	A	TP	PIM
1994-95	John Marshall	Hi-School	10	0	0	0	14	....	....	....	....	....
1995-96	John Marshall	Hi-School	11	1	2	3	8	4	0	0	0	0
	Capital District	NAJHL	53	3	8	11	33	....	....	....	....	....
1996-97	Capital District	NAJHL	57	8	50	58	140	....	....	....	....	....
1997-98	Providence	H-East	32	0	8	8	29	....	....	....	....	....
1998-99	Providence	H-East	33	1	8	9	42	....	....	....	....	....
99-2000	Providence	H-East	37	1	9	10	101	....	....	....	....	....
2000-01	Providence	H-East	40	4	21	25	104	....	....	....	....	....

Hockey East All-Academic Team (2000)

LEAHY, Patrick (LEH-hey, PAT-rihk) NYR

Right wing. Shoots right. 6'3", 190 lbs. Born, Brighton, MA, June 9, 1979.
(NY Rangers' 5th choice, 122nd overall, in 1998 Entry Draft).

			Regular Season					Playoffs				
Season	Club	Lea	GP	G	A	TP	PIM	GP	G	A	TP	PIM
1996-97	Boston College	Hi-School	25	24	24	48	....	....	....	....	....	....
1997-98	U. of Miami-Ohio	CCHA	28	0	1	1	24	....	....	....	....	....
1998-99	U. of Miami-Ohio	CCHA	34	10	20	30	40	....	....	....	....	....
99-2000	U. of Miami-Ohio	CCHA	36	16	22	38	89	....	....	....	....	....
2000-01	U. of Miami-Ohio	CCHA	37	13	19	32	14	....	....	....	....	....

LeBLANC, Robin (luh-BLAWNK, RAW-bihn) N.J.

Right wing. Shoots right. 6'1", 177 lbs. Born, Chur, Switz., January 11, 1983.
(New Jersey's 5th choice, 67th overall, in 2001 Entry Draft).

			Regular Season					Playoffs				
Season	Club	Lea	GP	G	A	TP	PIM	GP	G	A	TP	PIM
99-2000	Baie Comeau	QMJHL	51	6	11	17	40	5	2	1	3	8
2000-01	Baie Comeau	QMJHL	61	24	38	62	33	11	7	8	15	8

LEFEBVRE, Guillaume (luh-FAYV, GEE-ohm) PHI.

Left wing. Shoots left. 6'1", 200 lbs. Born, Amos, Que., May 7, 1981.
(Philadelphia's 6th choice, 227th overall, in 2000 Entry Draft).

			Regular Season					Playoffs				
Season	Club	Lea	GP	G	A	TP	PIM	GP	G	A	TP	PIM
1996-97	Amos Forestiers	QAAA	40	7	12	19	....	....	....	....	....	....
1997-98	Amos Forestiers	QAAA	42	12	16	28	100	6	4	5	9	....
1998-99	Shawinigan	QMJHL	40	3	1	4	49	....	....	....	....	....
	Cape Breton	QMJHL	24	2	7	9	13	5	0	1	1	0
99-2000	Cape Breton	QMJHL	44	26	28	54	82	....	....	....	....	....
	Quebec Remparts	QMJHL	2	3	1	4	0	....	....	....	....	....
	Rouyn-Noranda	QMJHL	25	4	11	15	39	11	4	0	4	25
2000-01	Rouyn-Noranda	QMJHL	61	24	43	67	160	9	3	1	4	22

LEGAULT, Jay (LEH-goh, JAY) ANA.

Left wing. Shoots left. 6'4", 214 lbs. Born, Peterborough, Ont., May 15, 1979.
(Anaheim's 3rd choice, 72nd overall, in 1997 Entry Draft).

			Regular Season					Playoffs				
Season	Club	Lea	GP	G	A	TP	PIM	GP	G	A	TP	PIM
1994-95	Peterborough AA	OMHA	34	41	70	111	68	....	....	....	....	....
1995-96	Oshawa Generals	OHL	61	2	11	13	37	5	0	1	1	8
1996-97	Oshawa Generals	OHL	39	13	26	39	50	....	....	....	....	....
	London Knights	OHL	28	6	13	19	37	....	....	....	....	....
1997-98	London Knights	OHL	61	39	56	95	87	16	1	8	9	34
1998-99	London Knights	OHL	65	43	51	94	99	25	8	18	26	40
99-2000	Cincinnati Ducks	AHL	70	15	19	34	75	....	....	....	....	....
	Dayton Bombers	ECHL	2	0	0	0	2	....	....	....	....	....
2000-01	Baton Rouge	ECHL	8	3	5	8	6	....	....	....	....	....
	Cincinnati Ducks	AHL	57	18	19	37	44	4	0	3	3	0

LEGG, Chris (LEHG, KRIHS) EDM.

Center. Shoots left. 5'11", 177 lbs. Born, London, Ont., February 19, 1980.
(Edmonton's 7th choice, 171st overall, in 1999 Entry Draft).

			Regular Season					Playoffs				
Season	Club	Lea	GP	G	A	TP	PIM	GP	G	A	TP	PIM
1996-97	London Nationals	OJHL-B	43	6	16	22	31	....	....	....	....	....
1997-98	London Nationals	OJHL-B	50	36	32	68	45	....	....	....	....	....
1998-99	London Nationals	OJHL-B	52	38	40	78	28	....	....	....	....	....
99-2000	Brown University	ECAC	23	2	3	5	4	....	....	....	....	....
2000-01	Brown University	ECAC	26	3	5	8	6	....	....	....	....	....

LEHOUX, Jason (luh-HOO, JAY-suhn) N.J.

Right wing. Shoots left. 6'2", 220 lbs. Born, Ste-Marie-Beauce, Que., July 21, 1979.

			Regular Season					Playoffs				
Season	Club	Lea	GP	G	A	TP	PIM	GP	G	A	TP	PIM
1995-96	Cap-d-Madeleine	QAAA	42	22	23	45	....	5	2	1	3	16
1996-97	Rimouski Oceanic	QMJHL	16	1	2	3	111	....	....	....	....	....
1997-98	Rouyn-Noranda	QMJHL	28	6	1	7	95	6	3	1	4	6
1998-99	Rouyn-Noranda	QMJHL	64	13	20	33	288	6	1	2	3	49
99-2000	Rouyn-Noranda	QMJHL	14	4	7	11	54	....	....	....	....	....
	Hull Olympiques	QMJHL	29	11	7	18	109	15	6	4	10	14
2000-01	Albany River Rats	AHL	52	8	7	15	101	....	....	....	....	....

Signed as a free agent by **New Jersey**, June 27, 2000.

LEHOUX, Yanick (luh-HOO, YAH-nihk) L.A.

Center. Shoots right. 6', 170 lbs. Born, Montreal, Que., April 8, 1982.
(Los Angeles' 3rd choice, 86th overall, in 2000 Entry Draft).

			Regular Season					Playoffs				
Season	Club	Lea	GP	G	A	TP	PIM	GP	G	A	TP	PIM
1997-98	Cap-d-Madelaine	QAAA	42	29	50	79	26	....	....	....	....	....
1998-99	Baie-Comeau	QMJHL	63	10	20	30	31	....	....	....	....	....
99-2000	Baie-Comeau	QMJHL	67	31	61	92	14	6	1	2	3	2
2000-01	Baie-Comeau	QMJHL	70	67	68	135	62	11	8	16	24	0

LEOPOLD, Jordan (LEE-oh-pohld, JOHR-dan) CGY.

Defense. Shoots left. 6', 193 lbs. Born, Golden Valley, MN, August 3, 1980.
(Anaheim's 1st choice, 44th overall, in 1999 Entry Draft).

			Regular Season					Playoffs				
Season	Club	Lea	GP	G	A	TP	PIM	GP	G	A	TP	PIM
1995-96	Armstrong High	Hi-School	19	11	14	25	30	....	....	....	....	....
1996-97	Armstrong High	Hi-School	30	24	36	60	....	....	....	....	....	....
1997-98	Team USA	USDP	60	11	12	23	16	....	....	....	....	....
1998-99	U. of Minnesota	WCHA	39	7	16	23	20	....	....	....	....	....
99-2000	U. of Minnesota	WCHA	39	6	18	24	20	....	....	....	....	....
2000-01	U. of Minnesota	WCHA	42	12	37	49	38	....	....	....	....	....

WCHA All-Rookie Team (1999) • WCHA Second All-Star Team (2000) • WCHA First All-Star Team (2001) • NCAA West First All-American Team (2001)

Traded to **Calgary** by **Anaheim** for Andrei Nazarov and Calgary's 2nd round choice (later traded to Phoenix - later traded back to Calgary - Calgary selected Andrei Taratukhin) in 2001 Entry Draft, September 26, 2000.

LEPHART, Mike PHI.

Left wing. Shoots right. 5'11", 194 lbs. Born, Niskayuna, NY, April 3, 1977.

			Regular Season					Playoffs				
Season	Club	Lea	GP	G	A	TP	PIM	GP	G	A	TP	PIM
1994-95	Springfield Pics	EJHL	45	20	30	50	....	....	....	....	....	....
1995-96	Omaha Lancers	USHL	45	12	12	24	40	....	....	....	....	....
1996-97	Omaha Lancers	USHL	54	40	50	*90	76	10	4	5	9	16
1997-98	Boston College	H-East	40	15	12	27	24	....	....	....	....	....
1998-99	Boston College	H-East	36	11	16	27	28	....	....	....	....	....
99-2000	Boston College	H-East	42	14	19	33	66	....	....	....	....	....
2000-01	Boston College	H-East	43	15	19	34	46	....	....	....	....	....

USHL First All-Star Team (1997) • Hockey East All-Academic Team (2000, 2001) • Hockey East Defensive Player-of-the-Year (2001)

Signed as a free agent by **Philadelphia**, June 11, 2001.

LESSARD, Francis (leh-SAHR, FRAN-sihs) PHI.

Defense. Shoots right. 6'2", 220 lbs. Born, Montreal, Que., May 30, 1979.
(Carolina's 3rd choice, 80th overall, in 1997 Entry Draft).

			Regular Season					Playoffs				
Season	Club	Lea	GP	G	A	TP	PIM	GP	G	A	TP	PIM
1995-96	Laval Regents	QAAA	41	5	7	12	73	....	....	....	....	....
1996-97	Val-d'Or Foreurs	QMJHL	66	1	9	10	287	....	....	....	....	....
1997-98	Val-d'Or Foreurs	QMJHL	63	3	20	23	338	19	1	6	7	*101
1998-99	Drummondville	QMJHL	53	12	36	48	295	....	....	....	....	....
99-2000	Philadelphia	AHL	78	4	8	12	416	5	0	1	1	7
2000-01	Philadelphia	AHL	64	3	7	10	330	10	0	0	0	33

Memorial Cup All-Star Team (1998)

Traded to **Philadelphia** by **Carolina** for Philadelphia's 8th round choice (Antti Jokella) in 1999 Entry Draft, May 25, 1999.

LEVESQUE, Willie (luh-VEHK, WIHL-lee) S.J.

Right wing. Shoots right. 6', 195 lbs. Born, Oak Bluffs, MA, January 22, 1980.
(San Jose's 3rd choice, 111th overall, in 1999 Entry Draft).

			Regular Season					Playoffs				
Season	Club	Lea	GP	G	A	TP	PIM	GP	G	A	TP	PIM
1997-98	Team USA	USDP	60	12	24	36	118	....	....	....	....	....
1998-99	Northeastern	H-East	34	12	10	22	38	....	....	....	....	....
99-2000	Northeastern	H-East	33	9	13	22	45	....	....	....	....	....
2000-01	Northeastern	H-East	35	13	16	29	62	....	....	....	....	....

Hockey East All-Rookie Team (1999) • Hockey East All-Academic Team (2000)

LEVINSKI, Dimitri (leh-VOHN-skee, DEH-mih-TREE) CHI.

Right wing. Shoots left. 6'1", 183 lbs. Born, Ust-Kamenogorsk, USSR, June 23, 1981.
(Chicago's 2nd choice, 46th overall, in 1999 Entry Draft).

			Regular Season					Playoffs				
Season	Club	Lea	GP	G	A	TP	PIM	GP	G	A	TP	PIM
1996-97	VDV Omsk-2	Russia-3	15	6	2	8	8	....	....	....	....	....
1997-98	VDV Omsk-2	Russia-3	18	5	2	7	8	....	....	....	....	....
1998-99	HC Cherepovets-3	Russia-4	3	2	0	2	2	....	....	....	....	....
	HC Cherepovets-2	Russia-3	26	4	2	6	39	....	....	....	....	....
	HC Cherepovets	Russia	1	0	0	0	0	....	....	....	....	....
99-2000	St. Petersburg	Russia	25	0	2	2	4	4	0	0	0	0
2000-01	Amur Khabarovsk	Russia-2	8	5	3	8	16	....	....	....	....	....
	Amur Khabarovsk	Russia	22	0	2	2	2	....	....	....	....	....

LEWERSTROM, Erik (LEH-vuhr-struhm, AIR-ihk) PHX.

Defense. Shoots left. 6'2", 198 lbs. Born, Grums, Sweden, May 28, 1980.
(Phoenix's 7th choice, 168th overall, in 1999 Entry Draft).

			Regular Season					Playoffs				
Season	Club	Lea	GP	G	A	TP	PIM	GP	G	A	TP	PIM
1996-97	Grums IK	Swede-2	1	0	0	0	0	....	....	....	....	....
1997-98	Grums IK	Swede-2	4	0	0	0	2	....	....	....	....	....
1998-99	Grums IK	Swede-2	29	3	9	12	42	....	....	....	....	....
99-2000	Grums IK	Swede-2	37	5	7	12	88	....	....	....	....	....
2000-01	Farjestads BK	Swede-Jr.	1	0	0	0	0	....	....	....	....	....
	Farjestads BK	Sweden	45	4	0	4	45	14	0	0	0	27

LEWIS, Carlyle (LOO-ihs, KAHR-lighl) N.J.

Right wing. Shoots right. 6'3", 230 lbs. Born, Middleton, N.S., March 1, 1978.

			Regular Season					Playoffs				
Season	Club	Lea	GP	G	A	TP	PIM	GP	G	A	TP	PIM
1994-95	Summerside Caps	MJrHL	20	3	5	8	63	....	....	....	....	....
1995-96	Beaufort Harfangs	QMJHL	30	0	2	2	90	1	0	0	0	0
1996-97	Beaufort Harfangs	QMJHl	66	7	8	15	353	4	1	1	2	7
1997-98	Laval Titans	QMJHL	59	9	13	22	310	16	1	3	4	53
1998-99	Halifax	QMJHL	65	20	27	47	425	5	1	1	2	18
99-2000	Albany River Rats	AHL	69	1	2	3	181	4	0	0	0	0
2000-01	Albany River Rats	AHL	68	1	7	8	175	....	....	....	....	....

Signed as a free agent by **New Jersey**, January 26, 1999.

LILES, John-Michael (LIGH-uhls, JAWN-MIGHK-uhl) COL.

Defense. Shoots left. 5'10", 185 lbs. Born, Zionsville, IN, November 25, 1980.
(Colorado's 8th choice, 159th overall, in 2000 Entry Draft).

			Regular Season					Playoffs				
Season	Club	Lea	GP	G	A	TP	PIM	GP	G	A	TP	PIM
1997-98	Team USA	USDP	67	6	14	20	44	....	....	....	....	....
1998-99	Team USA	USDP-17	13	2	5	7	6	....	....	....	....	....
	Team USA	USDP	46	4	14	18	47	....	....	....	....	....
99-2000	Michigan State	CCHA	40	8	20	28	26	....	....	....	....	....
2000-01	Michigan State	CCHA	42	7	18	25	28	....	....	....	....	....

CCHA Second All-Star Team (2001)

LIND, Eric (LIHND, AIR-ihk) PIT.

Defense. Shoots right. 6'1", 198 lbs. Born, New Canaan, CT, March 12, 1978.
(Pittsburgh's 9th choice, 234th overall, in 1997 Entry Draft).

			Regular Season					Playoffs				
Season	**Club**	**Lea**	**GP**	**G**	**A**	**TP**	**PIM**	**GP**	**G**	**A**	**TP**	**PIM**
1994-95	Avon Old Farms	Hi-School	22	5	15	20	....	....	....	....	....	....
1995-96	Avon Old Farms	Hi-School	40	9	19	28	20	....	....	....	....	....
1996-97	Avon Old Farms	Hi-School	23	9	28	37	50	....	....	....	....	....
	Des Moines	USHL	14	2	3	5	10	....	....	....	....	....
1997-98	New Hampshire	H-East	33	1	11	12	63	....	....	....	....	....
1998-99	New Hampshire	H-East	41	3	9	12	20	....	....	....	....	....
99-2000	New Hampshire	H-East	38	1	3	4	18	....	....	....	....	....
2000-01	New Hampshire	H-East	39	4	9	13	30	....	....	....	....	....

LINDSTROM, Andreas (LIHND-struhm, an-DRAY-uhs) BOS.

Right wing. Shoots left. 5'9", 165 lbs. Born, Lulea, Sweden, September 1, 1982.
(Boston's 12th choice, 279th overall, in 2000 Entry Draft).

			Regular Season					Playoffs				
Season	**Club**	**Lea**	**GP**	**G**	**A**	**TP**	**PIM**	**GP**	**G**	**A**	**TP**	**PIM**
99-2000	Lulea HF	Swede-Jr.	9	2	2	4	14	....	....	....	....	....
2000-01	Lulea HF	Swede-Jr.	21	8	6	14	18	....	....	....	....	....
	Lulea HF	Sweden	3	0	0	0	0	8	1	0	1	0

LINDSTROM, Sanny (LIHND-struhm, SAN-nee) COL.

Defense. Shoots left. 6'2", 205 lbs. Born, Stockholm, Sweden, December 24, 1979.
(Colorado's 4th choice, 112th overall, in 1999 Entry Draft).

			Regular Season					Playoffs				
Season	**Club**	**Lea**	**GP**	**G**	**A**	**TP**	**PIM**	**GP**	**G**	**A**	**TP**	**PIM**
1997-98	Huddinge IK	Swede-2	32	6	6	12	46	....	....	....	....	....
1998-99	Huddinge IK	Swede-2	37	4	4	8	65	....	....	....	....	....
99-2000	Hershey Bears	AHL	42	1	2	3	57	....	....	....	....	....
	Baton Rouge	ECHL	11	1	2	3	16	....	....	....	....	....
2000-01	Hershey Bears	AHL	24	0	0	0	61	....	....	....	....	....
	Quad City	UHL	5	1	1	2	10	....	....	....	....	....

• Missed majority of 2000-01 season recovering from knee injury originally suffered in practice, March 5, 2000.

LINGREN, Steve (LIHN-grehn, STEEV)

Defense. Shoots left. 6', 193 lbs. Born, Lake Cowichin, B.C., July 23, 1973.

			Regular Season					Playoffs				
Season	**Club**	**Lea**	**GP**	**G**	**A**	**TP**	**PIM**	**GP**	**G**	**A**	**TP**	**PIM**
1991-92	Victoria Cougars	WHL	70	4	14	18	103	....	....	....	....	....
1992-93	Victoria Cougars	WHL	72	10	43	53	148	....	....	....	....	....
1993-94	Victoria Cougars	WHL	56	14	21	35	118	....	....	....	....	....
	Kalamazoo Wings	IHL	2	0	0	0	0	....	....	....	....	....
1994-95	Dayton Bombers	ECHL	64	11	23	34	128	9	2	8	10	16
	Kalamazoo	IHL	4	0	0	0	0	....	....	....	....	....
1995-96	Dayton Bombers	ECHL	51	15	28	43	83	....	....	....	....	....
	Cornwall Aces	AHL	1	0	1	1	0	....	....	....	....	....
	Michigan K-Wings	IHL	2	0	0	0	0	....	....	....	....	....
1996-97	Dayton Bombers	ECHL	9	2	5	7	15	....	....	....	....	....
	Hershey Bears	AHL	40	3	10	13	67	12	1	2	3	8
1997-98	Hershey Bears	AHL	63	12	18	30	89	....	....	....	....	....
1998-99	Kentucky	AHL	74	11	19	30	60	12	0	4	4	0
99-2000	Kansas City	IHL	75	10	15	25	54	....	....	....	....	....
2000-01	Kansas City	IHL	66	5	14	19	50	....	....	....	....	....

ECHL First All-Star Team (1996)

Signed as a free agent by **San Jose**, August 3, 1998.

LITVINENKO, Alexei (liht-vihn-EHN-koh, al-EHX-ay) PHX.

Defense. Shoots left. 6'4", 180 lbs. Born, Ust-Kamenogorsk, USSR, March 7, 1980.
(Phoenix's 9th choice, 262nd overall, in 1999 Entry Draft).

			Regular Season					Playoffs				
Season	**Club**	**Lea**	**GP**	**G**	**A**	**TP**	**PIM**	**GP**	**G**	**A**	**TP**	**PIM**
1997-98	Kamenogorsk-2	Russia-3	12	0	0	0	8	....	....	....	....	....
	Ust-Kamenogorsk	Russia-2	2	0	0	0	0	....	....	....	....	....
1998-99	Kamenogorsk-2	Russia-4	31	3	4	7	52	....	....	....	....	....
	Kamenogorsk-2	Russia-3	16	0	4	4	14	....	....	....	....	....
99-2000	Dynamo Moscow	Russia	7	0	0	0	4	....	....	....	....	....
2000-01	Dynamo Moscow	Russia	6	0	0	0	0	....	....	....	....	....
	HC Yekaterinburg	Russia	26	0	0	0	42	....	....	....	....	....

LIUBIMOV, Alexander (loo-BEE-mahf, al-ehx-AN-duhr) EDM.

Defense. Shoots left. 6'3", 196 lbs. Born, Ust-Kamenogorsk, USSR, February 15, 1980.
(Edmonton's 3rd choice, 83rd overall, in 2000 Entry Draft).

			Regular Season					Playoffs				
Season	**Club**	**Lea**	**GP**	**G**	**A**	**TP**	**PIM**	**GP**	**G**	**A**	**TP**	**PIM**
1995-96	Ust-Kamenogorsk	CIS-Jr.	30	9	5	14	20	....	....	....	....	....
	Kamenogorsk-2	CIS-3	2	0	0	0	0	....	....	....	....	....
1996-97	Lada Togliatti	Russia-Jr.		STATISTICS NOT AVAILABLE								
	Lada Togliatti-2	Russia-3		STATISTICS NOT AVAILABLE								
	Lada Togliatti	Russia	2	0	0	0	0	....	....	....	....	....
1997-98	Lada Togliatti-2	Russia-3	38	7	6	13	63	....	....	....	....	....
1998-99	Lada Togliatti-2	Russia-4	44	5	4	9	36	....	....	....	....	....
99-2000	CSK Samara	Russia	17	0	1	1	14	....	....	....	....	....
	Lada Togliatti	Russia	8	0	0	0	6	7	0	1	1	2
2000-01	Lada Togliatti	Russia	23	1	2	3	8	....	....	....	....	....

LOBB, Aaron (LAWB, AIR-ruhn) T.B.

Right wing. Shoots right. 6'4", 193 lbs. Born, Brucefield, Ont., June 10, 1983.
(Tampa Bay's 5th choice, 123rd overall, in 2001 Entry Draft).

			Regular Season					Playoffs				
Season	**Club**	**Lea**	**GP**	**G**	**A**	**TP**	**PIM**	**GP**	**G**	**A**	**TP**	**PIM**
1998-99	Strathroy Rockets	OJHL-B	39	6	14	20	30	....	....	....	....	....
99-2000	London Knights	OHL	58	2	9	11	23	....	....	....	....	....
2000-01	London Knights	OHL	67	23	25	48	93	5	0	2	2	12

LOMBARDI, Matthew EDM.

Center. Shoots left. 5'11", 191 lbs. Born, Montreal, Que., March 18, 1982.
(Edmonton's 7th choice, 215th overall, in 2000 Entry Draft).

			Regular Season					Playoffs				
Season	**Club**	**Lea**	**GP**	**G**	**A**	**TP**	**PIM**	**GP**	**G**	**A**	**TP**	**PIM**
1997-98	Gatineau Elites	QAAA	42	10	13	23	....	13	4	7	11	....
1998-99	Victoriaville Tigres	QMJHL	47	6	10	16	8	5	0	0	0	0
99-2000	Victoriaville Tigres	QMJHL	65	18	26	44	28	6	0	0	0	6
2000-01	Victoriaville Tigres	QMJHL	72	28	39	67	66	13	12	6	18	10

LOVDAHL, Anders (LUHV-duhl, AN-duhrs) COL.

Center. Shoots left. 6'4", 190 lbs. Born, Borlange, Sweden, February 4, 1981.
(Colorado's 8th choice, 158th overall, in 1999 Entry Draft).

			Regular Season					Playoffs				
Season	**Club**	**Lea**	**GP**	**G**	**A**	**TP**	**PIM**	**GP**	**G**	**A**	**TP**	**PIM**
1997-98	HV Jonkoping	Swede-Jr.	26	5	5	10	18	....	....	....	....	....
1998-99	HV Jonkoping	Swede-Jr.		DID NOT PLAY – INJURED								
99-2000	Calgary Hitmen	WHL	36	5	9	14	28	....	....	....	....	....
	Moose Jaw	WHL	31	3	0	3	8	4	0	0	0	2
2000-01	Tranas AIF	Swede-2	16	3	4	7	4	....	....	....	....	....

LOVEN, Fredrik (LUH-vehn, FREHD-rihk) PHX.

Center. Shoots left. 6'2", 183 lbs. Born, Stockholm, Sweden, March 14, 1977.
(Winnipeg's 10th choice, 189th overall, in 1995 Entry Draft).

			Regular Season					Playoffs				
Season	**Club**	**Lea**	**GP**	**G**	**A**	**TP**	**PIM**	**GP**	**G**	**A**	**TP**	**PIM**
1994-95	Djurgardens IF	Swede-Jr.	29	6	10	16	14	....	....	....	....	....
1995-96	Djurgardens IF	Sweden	4	0	0	0	0	4	0	0	0	0
1996-97	Djurgardens IF	Swede-Jr.	4	2	2	4	8	....	....	....	....	....
	Arlanda IK	Swede-2	5	0	3	3	4	....	....	....	....	....
	Djurgardens IF	Sweden	7	0	0	0	0	....	....	....	....	....
1997-98	Bjorkloven IF	Swede-2	32	5	6	11	8	14	0	2	2	10
1998-99	Hammarby IF	Swede-2	37	8	17	25	47	5	2	0	2	4
99-2000	Hammarby IF	Swede-2	45	2	8	10	34	2	0	0	0	0
2000-01	Hammarby IF	Swede-2	39	3	4	7	12	5	0	3	3	4

Signed as a free agent by **Tingsryds AIF** (Sweden-2), August 8, 2001.

LOYA, Cliff (LOI-uh, KLIHF) CHI.

Defense. Shoots left. 6'2", 200 lbs. Born, Pittsburgh, PA, May 8, 1981.
(Chicago's 10th choice, 207th overall, in 2000 Entry Draft).

			Regular Season					Playoffs				
Season	**Club**	**Lea**	**GP**	**G**	**A**	**TP**	**PIM**	**GP**	**G**	**A**	**TP**	**PIM**
1998-99	Shattuck-St. Mary	Hi-School	52	7	29	36	34	....	....	....	....	....
99-2000	U. of Maine	H-East	31	0	5	5	22	....	....	....	....	....
2000-01	U. of Maine	H-East	36	1	2	3	28	....	....	....	....	....

LUCHINKIN, Sergei (loo-CHIHN-kihn, SAIR-gay) CBJ

Left wing. Shoots left. 5'11", 172 lbs. Born, Dmitrov, USSR, October 16, 1976.
(Dallas' 9th choice, 202nd overall, in 1995 Entry Draft).

			Regular Season					Playoffs				
Season	**Club**	**Lea**	**GP**	**G**	**A**	**TP**	**PIM**	**GP**	**G**	**A**	**TP**	**PIM**
1994-95	Dynamo Moscow	CIS	6	1	0	1	4	....	....	....	....	....
1995-96	Dynamo Moscow	CIS	21	6	2	8	14	10	0	1	1	6
1996-97	Dynamo Moscow	Russia	18	1	5	6	4	....	....	....	....	....
1997-98	Dynamo Moscow	EuroHL	1	0	0	0	0	....	....	....	....	....
	Dynamo Moscow	Russia	6	0	1	1	0	....	....	....	....	....
	Krylja Sovetov	Russia	10	0	1	1	4	....	....	....	....	....
1998-99	Krylja Sovetov	Russia	33	4	5	9	18	....	....	....	....	....
99-2000	Krylja Sovetov-2	Russia-3	1	2	0	2	2	....	....	....	....	....
	Krylja Sovetov	Russia-2	58	19	17	36	54	....	....	....	....	....
2000-01	Krylja Sovetov	Russia-2	57	23	18	41	46	....	....	....	....	....

Selected by **Columbus** from **Dallas** in Expansion Draft, June 23, 2000.

LUCHKIN, Vladislav (LOOCH-kihn, VLA-dihs-lav) CHI.

Center. Shoots left. 6'1", 185 lbs. Born, Cherepovets, USSR, February 3, 1982.
(Chicago's 11th choice, 225th overall, in 2000 Entry Draft).

			Regular Season					Playoffs				
Season	**Club**	**Lea**	**GP**	**G**	**A**	**TP**	**PIM**	**GP**	**G**	**A**	**TP**	**PIM**
1997-98	HC Cherepovets-2	Russia-3	23	2	5	7	12	....	....	....	....	....
1998-99	HC Cherepovets-2	Russia-3	25	6	4	10	8	....	....	....	....	....
	HC Cherepovets-3	Russia-4	8	1	3	4	10	....	....	....	....	....
99-2000	HC Cherepovets-2	Russia-3	30	23	10	33	36	....	....	....	....	....
2000-01	HC Cherepovets	Russia	28	2	3	5	10	6	2	0	2	4

LUCKY, Jeff (LUH-kee, JEHF) WSH.

Right wing. Shoots right. 6'1", 193 lbs. Born, Regina, Sask., March 17, 1983.
(Washington's 3rd choice, 125th overall, in 2001 Entry Draft).

			Regular Season					Playoffs				
Season	**Club**	**Lea**	**GP**	**G**	**A**	**TP**	**PIM**	**GP**	**G**	**A**	**TP**	**PIM**
1998-99	Yorkton Mallers	SMHL	42	28	40	68	4	8	6	7	13	0
	Spokane Chiefs	WHL	1	0	0	0	0	....	....	....	....	....
99-2000	Spokane Chiefs	WHL	57	8	10	18	12	13	1	0	1	2
2000-01	Spokane Chiefs	WHL	53	20	21	41	26	....	....	....	....	....

LUNDBOHM, Andy (LUHND-bawm, AN-dee) S.J.

Center. Shoots left. 6'3", 225 lbs. Born, Roseau, MN, March 24, 1977.

			Regular Season					Playoffs				
Season	**Club**	**Lea**	**GP**	**G**	**A**	**TP**	**PIM**	**GP**	**G**	**A**	**TP**	**PIM**
1995-96	Army Knights	NCAA	37	21	25	46	42	....	....	....	....	....
1996-97	Army Knights	NCAA	29	19	27	46	16	....	....	....	....	....
1997-98	Army Knights	NCAA	31	19	25	44	42	....	....	....	....	....
1998-99	Army Knights	NCAA	26	17	15	32	30	....	....	....	....	....
99-2000	New Orleans	ECHL	12	2	2	4	4	....	....	....	....	....
	Kentucky	AHL	22	2	1	3	8	2	0	0	0	5
2000-01	Kentucky	AHL	63	7	15	22	41	....	....	....	....	....

Signed as a free agent by **San Jose**, June 11, 1999.

LUNDBOHM, Bryan (LUHND-bawm, BRIGH-uhn) NSH.

Center. Shoots left. 5'10", 190 lbs. Born, Roseau, MN, August 24, 1977.

			Regular Season					Playoffs				
Season	**Club**	**Lea**	**GP**	**G**	**A**	**TP**	**PIM**	**GP**	**G**	**A**	**TP**	**PIM**
1996-97	Lincoln Stars	USHL	52	13	33	45	33	14	8	4	12	33
1997-98	Lincoln Stars	USHL	55	26	38	64	10	9	2	7	9	0
1998-99	North Dakota	WCHA	32	2	9	11	4	....	....	....	....	....
99-2000	North Dakota	WCHA	44	22	22	44	14	....	....	....	....	....
2000-01	North Dakota	WCHA	46	*32	27	69	38	....	....	....	....	....

USHL First All-Star Team (1998) • WCHA First All-Star Team (2001) • NCAA West Second All-American Team (2001) • NCAA Championship All-Tournament Team (2001)

Signed as a free agent by **Nashville**, May 1, 2001.

LUNDMARK, Jamie (LUHND-mahrk, JAY-mee) NYR

Center. Shoots right. 6', 174 lbs. Born, Edmonton, Alta., January 16, 1981.
(NY Rangers' 2nd choice, 9th overall, in 1999 Entry Draft).

			Regular Season					Playoffs				
Season	Club	Lea	GP	G	A	TP	PIM	GP	G	A	TP	PIM
1996-97	St. Albert Saints	AJHL	35	10	9	19	8	....	....	....	....	....
1997-98	St. Albert Saints	AJHL	57	33	58	91	171	19	13	18	31	5
1998-99	Moose Jaw	WHL	70	40	51	91	121	11	5	4	9	24
99-2000	Moose Jaw	WHL	37	21	27	48	33	....	....	....	....	....
2000-01	Seattle T-Birds	WHL	52	35	42	77	49	9	4	4	8	16

WHL All-Rookie Team (1999) • WHL East Second All-Star Team (1999) • WHL West First All-Star Team (2001)

Traded to **Seattle** by **Moose Jaw** for Scott Kellman, October 27, 2000.

LUNDQVIST, Joel (LOOND-kvihst, JOHL) DAL.

Center. Shoots left. 6', 185 lbs. Born, Are, Sweden, March 2, 1982.
(Dallas' 3rd choice, 68th overall, in 2000 Entry Draft).

			Regular Season					Playoffs				
Season	Club	Lea	GP	G	A	TP	PIM	GP	G	A	TP	PIM
1997-98	Rogle BK	Swede-Jr.	59	36	40	76	....	....	....	....	....	....
1998-99	Vasta Frolunda	Swede-Jr.	32	26	38	64	37	4	3	1	4	2
99-2000	Vasta Frolunda-B	Swede-Jr.	4	2	4	6	4	....	....	....	....	....
	Vasta Frolunda	Swede-Jr.	25	7	12	19	2	6	2	3	5	2
2000-01	Vastra Frolunda	Swede-Jr.	9	4	10	14	12	....	....	....	....	....
	Molndals HS	Swede-2	6	5	1	6	0	....	....	....	....	....
	Vastra Frolunda	Sweden	9	0	0	0	0	....	....	....	....	....

LUNDQVIST, Stefan (LUHND-kvihst, STEH-fan) NYR

Right wing. Shoots left. 6'3", 209 lbs. Born, Gavle, Sweden, February 18, 1978.
(NY Rangers' 7th choice, 180th overall, in 1998 Entry Draft).

			Regular Season					Playoffs				
Season	Club	Lea	GP	G	A	TP	PIM	GP	G	A	TP	PIM
1994-95	Avesta BK	Swede-2	3	0	1	1	0	....	....	....	....	....
1995-96	Avesta BK	Swede-3	27	24	13	37	10	....	....	....	....	....
1996-97	Avesta BK	Swede-3	31	37	29	66	....	....	....	....	....	....
1997-98	Brynas IF	Swede-Jr.	21	23	15	38	2	....	....	....	....	....
	Brynas IF	Sweden	27	2	2	4	0	1	0	0	0	0
1998-99	Brynas IF	Sweden	13	0	0	0	0	....	....	....	....	....
	Uppsala ALF	Swede-2	15	7	8	15	0	....	....	....	....	....
	Mora IK	Swede-2	23	10	7	17	22	4	2	2	4	2
99-2000	Brynas IF	Sweden	48	6	4	10	12	11	1	0	1	0
	Brynas IF	EuroHL	6	1	1	2	2	....	....	....	....	....
2000-01	Skelleftea AIK	Sweden	35	21	11	32	14	1	0	0	0	0

LUNDSTROM, Per-Anton (LUHND-struhm, PAIR-AN-tawn) PHX.

Defense. Shoots left. 6'2", 185 lbs. Born, Umea, Sweden, September 29, 1977.
(Phoenix's 3rd choice, 62nd overall, in 1996 Entry Draft).

			Regular Season					Playoffs				
Season	Club	Lea	GP	G	A	TP	PIM	GP	G	A	TP	PIM
1993-94	AIK Tegs	Swede-3	13	4	4	8	8	....	....	....	....	....
1994-95	MoDo Hockey	Swede-Jr.	20	3	4	7	18	....	....	....	....	....
1995-96	MoDo Hockey	Swede-Jr.	25	3	3	6	28	2	1	0	1	4
	MoDo Hockey	Sweden	19	1	1	2	29	4	0	0	0	2
1996-97	MoDo Hockey	Sweden	35	0	0	0	42	....	....	....	....	....
1997-98	Bjorkloven IF	Swede-2	31	6	13	19	71	....	....	....	....	....
1998-99	Bjorkloven IF	Sweden	39	1	2	3	36	....	....	....	....	....
99-2000	AIK Solna	Sweden	50	4	5	9	48	....	....	....	....	....
2000-01	AIK Solna	Sweden	50	2	4	6	63	3	1	0	1	0

LUPASCHUK, Ross (LOO-puhs-chuhk, RAWS) PIT.

Defense. Shoots right. 6'1", 211 lbs. Born, Edmonton, Alta., January 19, 1981.
(Washington's 4th choice, 34th overall, in 1999 Entry Draft).

			Regular Season					Playoffs				
Season	Club	Lea	GP	G	A	TP	PIM	GP	G	A	TP	PIM
1996-97	Edmonton Mets	AAHA	65	5	22	27	87	....	....	....	....	....
1997-98	Prince Albert	WHL	67	6	12	18	170	....	....	....	....	....
1998-99	Prince Albert	WHL	67	8	20	28	127	14	4	9	13	16
99-2000	Prince Albert	WHL	22	8	8	16	42	....	....	....	....	....
	Red Deer Rebels	WHL	46	13	27	40	116	4	0	1	1	10
2000-01	Red Deer Rebels	WHL	65	28	37	65	135	22	5	10	15	54

WHL East Second All-Star Team (2001) • Memorial Cup All-Star Team (2001)

Traded to **Pittsburgh** by **Washington** with Kris Beech, Michal Sivek and future considerations for Jaromir Jagr and Frantisek Kucera, July 11, 2001.

LUTES, Brett (LOOTZ, BREHT) ST.L.

Left wing. Shoots left. 6', 182 lbs. Born, Moncton, NB, February 2, 1982.
(St. Louis' 7th choice, 229th overall, in 2000 Entry Draft).

			Regular Season					Playoffs				
Season	Club	Lea	GP	G	A	TP	PIM	GP	G	A	TP	PIM
99-2000	Montreal Rocket	QMJHL	4	2	1	3	0	....	....	....	....	....
2000-01	Montreal Rocket	QMJHL	72	29	38	67	34	....	....	....	....	....

LYNCH, Doug (LIHNCH, DUHG) EDM.

Defense. Shoots left. 6'3", 205 lbs. Born, North Vancouver, B.C., April 4, 1983.
(Edmonton's 2nd choice, 43rd overall, in 2001 Entry Draft).

			Regular Season					Playoffs				
Season	Club	Lea	GP	G	A	TP	PIM	GP	G	A	TP	PIM
1998-99	Port Coquitlam	BCAHA	45	47	48	95	120	....	....	....	....	....
	Red Deer Rebels	WHL	2	0	1	1	2	....	....	....	....	....
99-2000	Red Deer Rebels	WHL	65	9	5	14	57	4	0	0	0	5
2000-01	Red Deer Rebels	WHL	72	12	37	49	181	21	1	9	10	30

LYNCH, Paul (LIHNCH, PAWL) T.B.

Defense. Shoots left. 6'4", 195 lbs. Born, Salem, MA, April 23, 1982.
(Tampa Bay's 6th choice, 138th overall, in 2001 Entry Draft).

			Regular Season					Playoffs				
Season	Club	Lea	GP	G	A	TP	PIM	GP	G	A	TP	PIM
99-2000	Brooks High	Hi-School	23	21	25	46	34	....	....	....	....	....
2000-01	Valley Warriors	EJHL	21	3	4	7	143	....	....	....	....	....

LYSAK, Brett (LIGH-sak, BREHT) CAR.

Center. Shoots left. 6', 190 lbs. Born, Edmonton, Alta., December 30, 1980.
(Carolina's 2nd choice, 49th overall, in 1999 Entry Draft).

			Regular Season					Playoffs				
Season	Club	Lea	GP	G	A	TP	PIM	GP	G	A	TP	PIM
1995-96	St. Albert Saints	AMHL	35	20	23	43	68	....	....	....	....	....
1996-97	Regina Pats	WHL	66	11	14	25	41	5	0	1	1	5
1997-98	Regina Pats	WHL	70	22	38	60	82	9	6	2	8	8
1998-99	Regina Pats	WHL	61	39	49	88	84	....	....	....	....	....
99-2000	Regina Pats	WHL	70	38	40	78	24	7	5	4	9	2
2000-01	Regina Pats	WHL	64	35	48	83	44	6	5	1	6	4

WHL East Second All-Star Team (1999) • Memorial Cup All-Star Team (2001)

MAATTA, Tero (MAH-tuh, TEH-roh) S.J.

Defense. Shoots left. 6'1", 205 lbs. Born, Vantaa, Finland, January 2, 1982.
(San Jose's 1st choice, 41st overall, in 2000 Entry Draft).

			Regular Season					Playoffs				
Season	Club	Lea	GP	G	A	TP	PIM	GP	G	A	TP	PIM
1997-98	Jokerit Helsinki	Finn-Jr.	28	4	7	11	10	2	0	0	0	2
1998-99	Jokerit Helsinki	Finn-Jr.	38	4	8	12	75	8	1	3	4	6
99-2000	Jokerit Helsinki	Finn-Jr.	31	4	4	8	53	....	....	....	....	....
2000-01	Blues Espoo	Finland	44	4	4	8	24	....	....	....	....	....

MacDONALD, Jason PIT.

Right wing. Shoots right. 6', 195 lbs. Born, Charlottetown, P.E.I., April 1, 1974.
(Detroit's 5th choice, 142nd overall, in 1992 Entry Draft).

			Regular Season					Playoffs				
Season	Club	Lea	GP	G	A	TP	PIM	GP	G	A	TP	PIM
1989-90	Charlottetown	MJrHL	29	11	29	40	206	....	....	....	....	....
1990-91	North Bay	OHL	57	12	15	27	126	10	3	3	6	15
1991-92	North Bay	OHL	17	5	8	13	50	....	....	....	....	....
	Owen Sound	OHL	42	17	19	36	129	5	0	3	3	16
1992-93	Owen Sound	OHL	56	46	43	89	197	8	6	5	11	28
1993-94	Owen Sound	OHL	66	55	61	116	177	9	7	11	18	36
	Adirondack	AHL	....	....	....	....	....	1	0	0	0	0
1994-95	Adirondack	AHL	68	14	21	35	238	4	0	0	0	2
1995-96	Adirondack	AHL	43	9	13	22	99	....	....	....	....	....
	Toledo Storm	ECHL	9	5	5	10	26	9	3	1	4	39
1996-97	Adirondack	AHL	1	0	0	0	2	....	....	....	....	....
	Fredericton	AHL	63	22	25	47	189	....	....	....	....	....
1997-98	Canada	Nat-Team	51	15	20	35	133	....	....	....	....	....
	Saint John Flames	AHL	6	2	0	2	27	11	1	3	4	17
1998-99	Manitoba Moose	IHL	82	25	27	52	283	5	2	2	4	13
99-2000	Manitoba Moose	IHL	30	5	10	15	77	....	....	....	....	....
	Orlando	IHL	29	7	7	14	113	4	0	0	0	19
2000-01	Wilkes-Barre	AHL	74	17	16	33	290	17	1	3	4	*66

OHL Second All-Star Team (1994)

Traded to **Montreal** by **Detroit** for cash, November 8, 1996. Signed as a free agent by **Pittsburgh**, July 18, 2001.

MACHO, Michal (MA-khoh, MEE-khuhl) S.J.

Center. Shoots right. 6'1", 169 lbs. Born, Martin, Czech., January 17, 1982.
(San Jose's 5th choice, 183rd overall, in 2000 Entry Draft).

			Regular Season					Playoffs				
Season	Club	Lea	GP	G	A	TP	PIM	GP	G	A	TP	PIM
1997-98	Martimex Martin	Slovak-Jr.	55	44	58	102	....	....	....	....	....	....
1998-99	King's Edge Hill	Hi-School	50	45	55	100	....	....	....	....	....	....
99-2000	MHC Martin	Slovak-Jr.	30	38	44	82	....	....	....	....	....	....
	MHC Martin	Slovak-2	8	1	5	6	4	....	....	....	....	....
2000-01	MHC Martin	Slovakia	37	5	10	15	12	3	1	1	2	2

MacINTYRE, Dave (MAK-ihn-TIGHR, DAYV)

Defense. Shoots left. 5'11", 190 lbs. Born, New Glasgow, N.S., October 20, 1968.

			Regular Season					Playoffs				
Season	Club	Lea	GP	G	A	TP	PIM	GP	G	A	TP	PIM
1987-88	New Hampshire	H-East	30	5	5	10	30	....	....	....	....	....
1988-89	New Hampshire	H-East	33	0	4	4	24	....	....	....	....	....
1989-90	New Hampshire	H-East	37	5	15	20	20	....	....	....	....	....
1990-91	New Hampshire	H-East	34	4	14	18	10	....	....	....	....	....
	Johnstown Chiefs	ECHL	....	....	....	....	....	7	0	4	4	0
1991-92	Johnstown Chiefs	ECHL	63	21	37	58	84	6	1	2	3	4
	Moncton Hawks	AHL	6	0	1	1	0	11	2	2	4	16
1992-93	Dayton Bombers	ECHL	6	2	4	6	10	....	....	....	....	....
	Moncton Hawks	AHL	50	5	17	22	37	2	0	0	0	0
1993-94	Salt Lake City	IHL	71	9	27	36	69	....	....	....	....	....
1994-95	Peoria Rivermen	IHL	71	10	31	41	52	8	2	3	5	0
1995-96	Peoria Rivermen	IHL	74	11	35	46	60	6	0	0	0	8
1996-97	San Antonio	IHL	76	17	36	53	104	8	1	4	5	2
1997-98	San Antonio	IHL	19	4	10	14	12	....	....	....	....	....
	Milwaukee	IHL	12	6	2	8	8	....	....	....	....	....
	Orlando	IHL	19	0	10	10	25	....	....	....	....	....
1998-99	Long Beach	IHL	3	0	0	0	0	....	....	....	....	....
	Berlin Capitals	DEL	12	1	3	4	8	....	....	....	....	....
99-2000	JyP Jyvaskyla	Finland	31	2	6	8	70	....	....	....	....	....
2000-01	Sprinfield Falcons	AHL	20	2	12	14	14	....	....	....	....	....

Signed as a free agent by **Phoenix**, August 3, 2000.

MacISAAC, Dave (muh-KIGH-zuhk, DAYV)

Defense. Shoots left. 6'2", 225 lbs. Born, Cambridge, MA, April 23, 1972.

			Regular Season					Playoffs				
Season	Club	Lea	GP	G	A	TP	PIM	GP	G	A	TP	PIM
1992-93	U. of Maine	H-East	35	5	32	37	14	....	....	....	....	....
1993-94	U. of Maine	H-East	31	4	20	24	22	....	....	....	....	....
1994-95	U. of Maine	H-East	44	5	13	18	44	....	....	....	....	....
	Milwaukee	IHL	2	0	0	0	5	9	0	2	2	2
1995-96	Milwaukee	IHL	71	7	16	23	165	....	....	....	....	....
1996-97	Philadelphia	AHL	61	3	15	18	187	10	0	1	1	31
1997-98	Philadelphia	AHL	80	7	21	28	241	18	5	13	18	20
1998-99	Philadelphia	AHL	47	6	15	21	98	16	2	5	7	50
99-2000	Lowell	AHL	77	1	25	26	179	7	0	1	1	4
2000-01	Kentucky	AHL	73	9	24	33	178	3	0	0	0	6

Signed as a free agent by **Philadelphia**, July 30, 1996. Signed as a free agent by **LA Kings**, August 25, 1999. Signed as a free agent by **San Jose**, August 10, 2000.

MacKENZIE, Derek (muh-KEHN-zee, DAIR-ehk) **ATL.**

Center. Shoots left. 5'11", 180 lbs. Born, Sudbury, Ont., June 11, 1981.
(Atlanta's 6th choice, 128th overall, in 1999 Entry Draft).

				Regular Season					Playoffs			
Season	Club	Lea	GP	G	A	TP	PIM	GP	G	A	TP	PIM
1996-97	Rayside-Balfour	NOJHA	40	23	32	55	40	....	....	....	....	....
1997-98	Sudbury Wolves	OHL	59	9	11	20	26	....	....	....	....	....
1998-99	Sudbury Wolves	OHL	68	22	65	87	74	4	2	4	6	2
99-2000	Sudbury Wolves	OHL	68	24	33	57	110	12	5	9	14	16
2000-01	Sudbury Wolves	OHL	62	40	49	89	89	12	6	8	14	16

MacLELLAN, Brent (mak-LEHL-uhn, BREHNT) **CHI.**

Defense. Shoots right. 6'4", 218 lbs. Born, Halifax, N.S., March 23, 1983.
(Chicago's 5th choice, 104th overall, in 2001 Entry Draft).

				Regular Season					Playoffs			
Season	Club	Lea	GP	G	A	TP	PIM	GP	G	A	TP	PIM
99-2000	Rimouski	QMJHL	69	2	13	15	98	14	2	1	3	4
2000-01	Rimouski	QMJHL	62	7	19	26	155	11	0	0	0	41

MacMILLAN, Jeff (muhk-MIHL-uhn, JEHF) **DAL.**

Defense. Shoots left. 6'3", 202 lbs. Born, Durham, Ont., March 30, 1979.
(Dallas' 8th choice, 215th overall, in 1999 Entry Draft).

				Regular Season					Playoffs			
Season	Club	Lea	GP	G	A	TP	PIM	GP	G	A	TP	PIM
1995-96	Hanover Barons	OJHL-C	29	7	13	20	26	....	....	....	....	....
1996-97	Oshawa Generals	OHL	39	0	4	4	15	15	0	0	0	4
1997-98	Oshawa Generals	OHL	64	3	12	15	72	7	0	3	3	11
1998-99	Oshawa Generals	OHL	65	3	18	21	109	15	3	6	9	28
99-2000	Michigan K-Wings	IHL	53	0	3	3	54	....	....	....	....	....
	Fort Wayne	UHL	7	1	1	2	25	9	0	2	2	10
2000-01	Utah Grizzlies	IHL	81	5	15	20	105	....	....	....	....	....

MacNEIL, Ian (muhk-NEEL, EE-an) **CAR.**

Center. Shoots left. 6'2", 190 lbs. Born, Halifax, N.S., April 27, 1977.
(Hartford's 3rd choice, 85th overall, in 1995 Entry Draft).

				Regular Season					Playoffs			
Season	Club	Lea	GP	G	A	TP	PIM	GP	G	A	TP	PIM
1993-94	Whitby Lions	OMHA	50	30	22	52	102	....	....	....	....	....
1994-95	Oshawa 67's	OHL	60	7	21	28	62	7	0	2	2	0
1995-96	Oshawa 67's	OHL	49	15	17	32	54	5	1	2	3	8
1996-97	Oshawa 67's	OHL	64	23	20	43	96	18	2	3	5	37
1997-98	New Haven	AHL	68	12	21	33	67	3	1	0	1	10
1998-99	New Haven	AHL	47	6	4	10	62	....	....	....	....	....
99-2000	Cincinnati	IHL	81	19	18	37	100	11	3	2	5	25
2000-01	Cincinnati	IHL	82	17	22	39	139	5	0	1	1	4

Rights transferred to **Carolina** after **Hartford** franchise relocated, June 25, 1997.

MAGLIONE, Matt **WSH.**

Defense. Shoots left. 6' 1", 185 lbs. Born, Syracuse, NY, April 20, 1982.
(Washington's 7th choice, 249th overall, in 2001 Entry Draft).

				Regular Season					Playoffs			
Season	Club	Lea	GP	G	A	TP	PIM	GP	G	A	TP	PIM
1996-97	Syracuse Crunch	MTJHL	40	0	4	4	20	....	....	....	....	....
1997-98	Syracuse Crunch	MTJHL	40	3	13	16	86	....	....	....	....	....
1998-99	Auburn Jr. Crunch	OPJHL	44	12	24	36	44	....	....	....	....	....
99-2000	Team USA	USDP	48	4	6	10	23	....	....	....	....	....
2000-01	Princeton Tigers	ECAC	30	4	5	9	12	....	....	....	....	....

MAGNUSON, Will (MAG-nuh-sohn, Wihl-ee-am) **COL.**

Defense. Shoots right. 6'5", 235 lbs. Born, Anchorage, AK, February 19, 1980.
(Colorado's 6th choice, 142nd overall, in 1999 Entry Draft).

				Regular Season					Playoffs			
Season	Club	Lea	GP	G	A	TP	PIM	GP	G	A	TP	PIM
1997-98	Team USA	USDP	69	2	15	17	62	....	....	....	....	....
1998-99	Lake Superior	CCHA	32	0	1	1	44	....	....	....	....	....
99-2000	Lake Superior	CCHA	27	0	2	2	38	....	....	....	....	....
2000-01	Lake Superior	CCHA	33	0	3	3	54	....	....	....	....	....

MAGOWAN, Ken (muh-GOW-uhn, KEHN) **N.J.**

Left wing. Shoots left. 6'2", 207 lbs. Born, Kelowna, B.C., July 22, 1981.
(New Jersey's 11th choice, 198th overall, in 2000 Entry Draft).

				Regular Season					Playoffs			
Season	Club	Lea	GP	G	A	TP	PIM	GP	G	A	TP	PIM
1996-97	Kelowna Rockets	BCAHA	57	68	66	134	78	....	....	....	....	....
1997-98	Kelowna Vikings	BCAHA	47	45	45	90	80	....	....	....	....	....
1998-99	Vernon Vipers	BCJHL	60	15	25	40	40	....	....	....	....	....
99-2000	Vernon Vipers	BCJHL	58	31	36	68	....	....	....	....	....	....
2000-01	Boston University	H-East	34	5	1	6	22	....	....	....	....	....

BCJHL Interior First All-Star Team (1999)

MAKELA, Tuukka (MA-kuh-luh TUH-kuh) **BOS.**

Defense. Shoots left. 6'2", 202 lbs. Born, Helsinki, Finland, May 24, 1982.
(Boston's 5th choice, 66th overall, in 2000 Entry Draft).

				Regular Season					Playoffs			
Season	Club	Lea	GP	G	A	TP	PIM	GP	G	A	TP	PIM
1997-98	HIFK Helsinki	Finn-Jr.	5	0	0	0	4	....	....	....	....	....
1998-99	HIFK Helsinki	Finn-Jr.	32	1	1	2	20	3	0	1	1	0
99-2000	HIFK Helsinki	Finn-Jr.	36	2	5	7	22	....	....	....	....	....
2000-01	Montreal Rocket	QMJHL	9	2	1	3	14	....	....	....	....	....

• Missed majority of 2000-01 season recovering from head injury suffered in game vs. Rouyn-Noranda (QMJHL), September 20, 2000.

MAKI, Tomi (MA-kee, TAW-mee) **CGY.**

Right wing. Shoots left. 5'11", 172 lbs. Born, Helsinki, Finland, August 19, 1983.
(Calgary's 4th choice, 108th overall, in 2001 Entry Draft).

				Regular Season					Playoffs			
Season	Club	Lea	GP	G	A	TP	PIM	GP	G	A	TP	PIM
99-2000	Jokerit Helsinki	Finn-Jr.	33	6	1	7	12	3	0	0	0	0
2000-01	Jokerit Helsinki	Finn-Jr.	39	7	8	15	10	2	0	0	0	2

MALEC, Tomas (MA-lehts, TAW-mahsh) **FLA.**

Defense. Shoots left. 6'2", 193 lbs. Born, Skalica, Czech., May 13, 1982.
(Florida's 4th choice, 64th overall, in 2001 Entry Draft).

				Regular Season					Playoffs			
Season	Club	Lea	GP	G	A	TP	PIM	GP	G	A	TP	PIM
99-2000	HK 36 Skalica	Slovak-Jr.	46	6	5	11	150	....	....	....	....	....
2000-01	Rimouski Oceanic	QMJHL	64	13	50	63	198	11	0	11	11	26

MALENKIKH, Vladimir (MAH-lihn-keh, vla-DIH-meer_ **PIT.**

Defense. Shoots left. 6'1", 187 lbs. Born, Togliatti, USSR, October 1, 1980.
(Pittsburgh's 7th choice, 157th overall, in 1999 Entry Draft).

				Regular Season					Playoffs			
Season	Club	Lea	GP	G	A	TP	PIM	GP	G	A	TP	PIM
1997-98	Lada Togliatti-2	Russia-3	39	6	4	10	112	....	....	....	....	....
1998-99	Lada Togliatti-2	Russia-3	38	6	3	9	68	....	....	....	....	....
	Lada Togliatti	Russia	9	0	0	0	2	....	....	....	....	....
99-2000	CSK Samara	Russia	7	0	1	1	14	....	....	....	....	....
2000-01	Lada Togliatti	Russia	25	1	1	2	14	5	0	0	0	26

MALEYKO, Jason (muh-LAY-koh, JAY-suhn) **OTT.**

Defense. Shoots left. 6'3", 211 lbs. Born, Windsor, Ont., May 24, 1980.
(Ottawa's 9th choice, 188th overall, in 2000 Entry Draft).

				Regular Season					Playoffs			
Season	Club	Lea	GP	G	A	TP	PIM	GP	G	A	TP	PIM
1996-97	Leamington Flyers	OJHL-B	36	3	10	13	113	....	....	....	....	....
	Windsor Spitfires	OHL	9	0	3	3	2	4	1	0	0	0
1997-98	Oshawa Generals	OHL	64	4	4	8	152	7	0	1	1	4
1998-99	Brampton	OHL	68	7	25	32	155	....	....	....	....	....
99-2000	Brampton	OHL	63	5	27	32	108	6	0	4	4	8
2000-01	Brampton	OHL	63	11	30	41	78	9	2	3	5	10

MALLETTE, Carl (muh-LEHT, KAHRL) **ATL.**

Center. Shoots right. 6'1", 188 lbs. Born, Pointe Claire, Que., November 17, 1981.
(Atlanta's 4th choice, 107th overall, in 2000 Entry Draft).

				Regular Season					Playoffs			
Season	Club	Lea	GP	G	A	TP	PIM	GP	G	A	TP	PIM
1996-97	Lac St-Louis	QAAA	32	14	22	36	35	7	2	6	8	16
1997-98	Victoriaville Tigres	QMJHL	55	8	7	15	30	6	1	1	2	4
1998-99	Victoriaville Tigres	QMJHL	62	27	46	73	51	6	1	2	3	2
99-2000	Victoriaville Tigres	QMJHL	69	49	76	125	97	6	6	3	9	28
2000-01	Victoriaville Tigres	QMJHL	61	28	55	83	99	13	10	8	18	42

MALMIVAARA, Olli (mal-MIH-vah-ruh, OH-lee) **CHI.**

Defense. Shoots left. 6'5", 213 lbs. Born, Kajaani, Finland, March 13, 1982.
(Chicago's 6th choice, 117th overall, in 2000 Entry Draft).

				Regular Season					Playoffs			
Season	Club	Lea	GP	G	A	TP	PIM	GP	G	A	TP	PIM
1998-99	Jokerit Helsinki	Finn-Jr.	35	1	8	9	10	7	0	0	0	2
99-2000	Jokerit Helsinki	Finn-Jr.	27	3	3	6	12	....	....	....	....	....
2000-01	Jokerit Helsinki	Finn-Jr.	33	10	13	23	24	2	0	0	0	0
	Kiekko-Vantaa	Finland-2	4	1	0	1	2	....	....	....	....	....
	Jokerit Helsinki	Finland	5	0	0	0	2	....	....	....	....	....

MALONE, Ryan (MA-lohne, RIGH-yan) **PIT.**

Left wing. Shoots left. 6'3", 190 lbs. Born, Pittsburgh, PA, December 1, 1979.
(Pittsburgh's 5th choice, 115th overall, in 1999 Entry Draft).

				Regular Season					Playoffs			
Season	Club	Lea	GP	G	A	TP	PIM	GP	G	A	TP	PIM
1997-98	Shattuck-St. Mary	Hi-School	50	41	44	85	69	....	....	....	....	....
1998-99	Omaha Lancers	USHL	51	14	22	36	81	....	....	....	....	....
99-2000	St. Cloud State	WCHA	38	9	21	30	68	....	....	....	....	....
2000-01	St. Cloud State	WCHA	36	7	18	25	52	....	....	....	....	....

MAMANE, Shawn (muh-MA-nee, SHAWN) **ST.L.**

Left wing. Shoots left. 6', 195 lbs. Born, Montreal, Que., February 26, 1979.

				Regular Season					Playoffs			
Season	Club	Lea	GP	G	A	TP	PIM	GP	G	A	TP	PIM
1997-98	Laval Titan	QMJHL	15	2	1	3	8	....	....	....	....	....
	Nipawin Hawks	SJHL	36	3	6	9	111	....	....	....	....	....
1998-99	Nipawin Hawks	SJHL	STATISTICS NOT AVAILABLE									
99-2000	Nipawin Hawks	SJHL	35	35	25	58	79	....	....	....	....	....
	Wayne State	CHA	DID NOT PLAY – FRESHMAN									
	Worcester	AHL	1	0	0	0	0	....	....	....	....	....
2000-01	Peoria Rivermen	ECHL	19	9	8	17	47	....	....	....	....	....
	Worcester	AHL	51	4	6	10	68	4	0	0	0	2

Signed as a free agent by **St. Louis**, April 18, 2000.

MANDEVILLE, Louis (MAN-deh-vihl, LOO-ee) **CBJ**

Defense. Shoots left. 6'2", 193 lbs. Born, Sorel, Que., May 3, 1982.
(Columbus' 11th choice, 292nd overall, in 2000 Entry Draft).

				Regular Season					Playoffs			
Season	Club	Lea	GP	G	A	TP	PIM	GP	G	A	TP	PIM
1998-99	Charles-Lemoyne	QAAA	41	10	28	38	48	....	....	....	....	....
99-2000	Rouyn-Noranda	QMJHL	50	5	11	16	31	11	2	1	3	4
2000-01	Rouyn-Noranda	QMJHL	42	2	15	17	59	....	....	....	....	....
	Halifax	QMJHL	28	2	20	22	36	6	0	4	4	6

Traded to **Halifax** by **Rouyn-Noranda** with Sebastien Laprise for Halifax's 2nd (Guillaume Desbiens) and 3rd (Daniel Leblanc) round choices in 2001 QMJHL Midget Draft, January 9, 2001.

MANNING, Paul (MAN-nihng, PAWL) **CBJ**

Defense. Shoots left. 6'4", 193 lbs. Born, Red Deer, Alta., April 15, 1979.
(Calgary's 3rd choice, 62nd overall, in 1998 Entry Draft).

				Regular Season					Playoffs			
Season	Club	Lea	GP	G	A	TP	PIM	GP	G	A	TP	PIM
1995-96	Red Deer Chiefs	AMHL	32	8	32	40	....	....	....	....	....	....
1996-97	Red Deer Vipers	HJHL	36	9	33	42	....	....	....	....	....	....
1997-98	Colorado College	WCHA	30	1	5	6	16	....	....	....	....	....
1998-99	Colorado College	WCHA	41	3	10	13	75	....	....	....	....	....
99-2000	Colorado College	WCHA	39	6	17	23	26	....	....	....	....	....
2000-01	Colorado College	WCHA	34	2	28	30	48	....	....	....	....	....

WCHA Second All-Star Team (2001)

Rights traded to **Columbus** by **Calgary** for Buffalo's 5th round choice (previously acquired, later traded to Detroit - Detroit selected Andreas Jamtin) in 2001 Entry Draft, June 24, 2001.

MANTYLA, Tuukka (man-TYEW-la, TOO-OO-kuh) L.A.

Defense. Shoots left. 5'9", 172 lbs. Born, Tampere, Finland, May 25, 1981.
(Los Angeles' 8th choice, 153rd overall, in 2001 Entry Draft).

			Regular Season					Playoffs				
Season	Club	Lea	GP	G	A	TP	PIM	GP	G	A	TP	PIM
1995-96	HC Tampere-C	Finn-Jr.	32	2	2	4	28	....	....	....	....	....
1996-97	HC Tampere-C	Finn-Jr.	32	12	25	37	52	4	1	2	3	4
	HC Tampere-B	Finn-Jr.	2	0	0	0	2	....	....	....	....	....
1997-98	HC Tampere-B	Finn-Jr.	31	2	23	25	49	....	....	....	....	....
	Tappara Tampere	Finn-Jr.	2	0	0	0	0	6	0	0	0	4
1998-99	HC Tampere-B	Finn-Jr.	10	4	4	8	42	....	....	....	....	....
	Tappara Tampere	Finn-Jr.	34	5	13	18	42	....	....	....	....	....
99-2000	Tappara Tampere	Finn-Jr.	7	2	5	7	22	5	2	5	7	4
	Tappara Tampere	Finland	43	2	8	10	16	4	0	0	0	0
2000-01	Tappara Tampere	Finland	53	6	14	20	32	10	2	2	4	10

MAPLETOFT, Justin (MAPLE-tawft, JUH-stihn) NYI

Center. Shoots left. 6'1", 180 lbs. Born, Lloydminster, Sask., January 11, 1981.
(NY Islanders' 9th choice, 130th overall, in 1999 Entry Draft).

			Regular Season					Playoffs				
Season	Club	Lea	GP	G	A	TP	PIM	GP	G	A	TP	PIM
1996-97	Calgary Royals	AMHL	36	25	36	51	....	....	....	....	....	....
	Red Deer Rebels	WHL	2	0	0	0	0	....	....	....	....	....
1997-98	Red Deer Rebels	WHL	65	9	4	13	41	....	....	....	....	....
1998-99	Red Deer Rebels	WHL	72	24	22	46	81	....	....	....	....	....
99-2000	Red Deer Rebels	WHL	72	39	57	96	135	4	2	1	3	28
2000-01	Red Deer Rebels	WHL	70	43	*77	*120	111	22	13	*21	34	59

WHL East First All-Star Team (2000, 2001) • Canadian Major Junior First All-Star Team (2001)

MAROIS, Jerome (MAIR-wuh, jair-OHM) MTL.

Left wing. Shoots left. 6', 199 lbs. Born, Quebec, Que., January 27, 1981.
(Montreal's 11th choice, 253rd overall, in 1999 Entry Draft).

			Regular Season					Playoffs				
Season	Club	Lea	GP	G	A	TP	PIM	GP	G	A	TP	PIM
1996-97	Ste-Foy Governors	QAAA	44	29	24	53	....	10	8	8	16	....
1997-98	Quebec Remparts	QMJHL	55	5	12	17	12	12	2	0	2	2
1998-99	Quebec Remparts	QMJHL	52	8	15	23	48	12	0	4	4	13
99-2000	Cape Breton	QMJHL	66	28	34	62	95	4	2	1	3	14
2000-01	Rouyn-Noranda	QMJHL	68	36	47	83	119	6	1	0	1	17

Traded to **Rouyn-Noranda** by **Cape Breton** with Cape Breton's 8th round choice (Etienne Gagner) in 2001 QMJHL Midget Draft for Kevin Cloutier and Hull's 4th round choice (acquired earlier, Cape Breton selected Marc-Olivier Vary) in 2000 QMJHL Midget Draft.

MARS, Per (MAHRZ, PAIR) CBJ

Center. Shoots left. 6'3", 202 lbs. Born, Froson, Sweden, October 23, 1982.
(Columbus' 5th choice, 87th overall, in 2001 Entry Draft).

			Regular Season					Playoffs				
Season	Club	Lea	GP	G	A	TP	PIM	GP	G	A	TP	PIM
2000-01	Brynas IF	Swede-Jr.	23	7	7	14	62	....	....	....	....	....
	Brynas IF	Sweden	6	0	0	0	0	2	0	0	0	0

MARTIN, Joey (MAHR-tihn, JOH-ee) CHI.

Defense. Shoots left. 6'3", 198 lbs. Born, Fridley, MN, July 17, 1981.
(Chicago's 9th choice, 193rd overall, in 2000 Entry Draft).

			Regular Season					Playoffs				
Season	Club	Lea	GP	G	A	TP	PIM	GP	G	A	TP	PIM
1998-99	Buffalo-Minnesota	Hi-School	23	10	9	19	19	....	....	....	....	....
99-2000	Omaha Lancers	USHL	56	1	4	5	41	4	0	0	0	0
2000-01	U. of Minnesota	WCHA	18	0	2	2	2					

MARTIN, Mike (MAHR-tihn, MIGHK) CGY.

Defense. Shoots right. 6'2", 205 lbs. Born, Stratford, Ont., October 27, 1976.
(NY Rangers' 2nd choice, 65th overall, in 1995 Entry Draft).

			Regular Season					Playoffs				
Season	Club	Lea	GP	G	A	TP	PIM	GP	G	A	TP	PIM
1991-92	Stratford	OJHL-B	16	2	3	5	14	....	....	....	....	....
1992-93	Windsor Spitfires	OHL	61	2	7	9	80	....	....	....	....	....
1993-94	Windsor Spitfires	OHL	64	2	29	31	94	4	1	2	3	4
1994-95	Windsor Spitfires	OHL	53	9	28	37	79	10	1	3	4	21
1995-96	Windsor Spitfires	OHL	65	19	48	67	128	7	0	6	6	14
1996-97	Binghamton	AHL	62	2	7	9	45	3	0	1	1	2
1997-98	Hartford	AHL	60	4	11	15	70	4	0	0	0	2
1998-99	Fort Wayne	IHL	75	6	20	26	89	2	0	0	0	4
99-2000	Michigan K-Wings	IHL	74	8	15	23	99	....	....	....	....	....
2000-01	Saint John Flames	AHL	60	7	16	23	69	16	1	2	3	14

Signed as a free agent by **Calgary**, August 18, 2000.

MARTIN, Paul (MAHR-tihn, PAWL) N.J.

Defense. Shoots left. 6'1", 170 lbs. Born, Minneapolis, MN, March 5, 1981.
(New Jersey's 5th choice, 62nd overall, in 2000 Entry Draft).

			Regular Season					Playoffs				
Season	Club	Lea	GP	G	A	TP	PIM	GP	G	A	TP	PIM
1998-99	Elk River High	Hi-School	24	9	11	20	....	....	....	....	....	....
99-2000	Elk River High	Hi-School	24	15	35	50	26	....	....	....	....	....
2000-01	U. of Minnesota	WCHA	38	3	17	20	8	....	....	....	....	....

Minnesota High School Player of the Year (1999)

MARTINEK, Radek (MAHR-tih-nehk, RA-dehk) NYI

Defense. Shoots right. 6', 196 lbs. Born, Havlickuv Brod, Czech., August 31, 1976.
(NY Islanders' 12th choice, 228th overall, in 1999 Entry Draft).

			Regular Season					Playoffs				
Season	Club	Lea	GP	G	A	TP	PIM	GP	G	A	TP	PIM
1996-97	HC Budejovice	Cze-Rep	52	3	5	8	40	5	0	1	1	2
1997-98	HC Budejovice	Cze-Rep	42	2	7	9	36	....	....	....	....	....
1998-99	HC Budejovice	Cze-Rep	52	12	13	25	50	3	0	2	2	....
99-2000	HC Budejovice	Cze-Rep	45	5	18	23	24	3	0	0	0	6
2000-01	HC Budejovice	Cze-Rep	44	8	10	18	45	....	....	....	....	....

MARTYNYUK, Denis (mahr-tih-nyook, DEH-nihs) VAN.

Left wing. Shoots left. 6'3", 190 lbs. Born, Kapfenberg, Austria, July 26, 1979.
(Vancouver's 11th choice, 201st overall, in 1997 Entry Draft).

			Regular Season					Playoffs				
Season	Club	Lea	GP	G	A	TP	PIM	GP	G	A	TP	PIM
1994-95	CSKA Moscow	Russia-Jr.	34	25	25	50	20	....	....	....	....	....
1995-96	CSKA Moscow	Russia-Jr.	36	10	15	25	20	....	....	....	....	....
	HC Moscow	Russia-2	25	2	5	7	20	....	....	....	....	....
1996-97	HC Moscow-2	Russia-3	41	7	4	11	12	....	....	....	....	....
	CSKA Moscow	Russia	3	1	0	1	0	....	....	....	....	....
1997-98	Krylja Sovetov-2	Russia-3	45	9	5	14	34	....	....	....	....	....
1998-99	Krylja Sovetov	Russia	17	0	0	0	8	....	....	....	....	....
99-2000	Krylja Sovetov	Russia-2	STATISTICS NOT AVAILABLE									
2000-01	Krylja Sovetov-2	Russia-3	6	1	3	4	0	....	....	....	....	....
	Amur Khabarovsk	Russia	1	0	0	0	0	....	....	....	....	....

MARTZ, Nathan (MAHRTZ, NAY-thun) NYR

Center. Shoots left. 6'3", 169 lbs. Born, Chilliwack, B.C., March 4, 1981.
(NY Rangers' 4th choice, 140th overall, in 2000 Entry Draft).

			Regular Season					Playoffs				
Season	Club	Lea	GP	G	A	TP	PIM	GP	G	A	TP	PIM
1997-98	Chilliwack Chiefs	BCJHL	59	8	13	21	86	....	....	....	....	....
1998-99	Chilliwack Chiefs	BCJHL	59	20	38	58	....	....	....	....	....	....
99-2000	Chilliwack Chiefs	BCJHL	59	35	75	110	97	....	....	....	....	....
2000-01	New Hampshire	H-East	37	5	14	19	20	....	....	....	....	....

MASON, Wes (MAY-suhn, WEHS)

Left wing. Shoots left. 6'2", 180 lbs. Born, Windsor, Ont., December 12, 1977.
(New Jersey's 2nd choice, 38th overall, in 1996 Entry Draft).

			Regular Season					Playoffs				
Season	Club	Lea	GP	G	A	TP	PIM	GP	G	A	TP	PIM
1992-93	Port Stanley	OJHL-D	38	19	39	58	88	....	....	....	....	....
1993-94	Chatham	OJHL-B	52	26	47	73	123	....	....	....	....	....
1994-95	Sarnia Sting	OHL	38	1	8	9	50	2	0	0	0	9
1995-96	Sarnia Sting	OHL	63	23	45	68	97	10	3	2	5	16
1996-97	Sarnia Sting	OHL	66	45	46	91	72	12	7	11	18	10
1997-98	Sarnia Sting	OHL	2	1	0	1	4	....	....	....	....	....
	Sudbury Wolves	OHL	9	3	8	11	12	....	....	....	....	....
	Kingston	OHL	38	10	19	29	38	10	0	2	2	4
1998-99	Albany River Rats	AHL	27	4	4	8	36	....	....	....	....	....
	Augusta Lynx	ECHL	30	13	14	27	75	2	1	0	1	6
99-2000	Augusta Lynx	ECHL	28	18	20	38	41	....	....	....	....	....
	Orlando	IHL	33	11	15	26	30	....	....	....	....	....
	Louisville Panthers	AHL	8	1	2	3	2	3	0	0	0	0
2000-01	Orlando	IHL	45	13	14	27	52	16	6	7	13	24

Traded to **Atlanta** by **New Jersey** with Eric Bertrand for Sylvain Cloutier, Jeff Williams and Atlanta's 7th round choice (Ken Magovan) in 2000 Entry Draft, November 1, 1999.

MATEJOVSKY, Radek (ma-teh-YAHV-skee, ra-DEHK) NYI

Right wing. Shoots right. 6'1", 187 lbs. Born, Praha, Czech., November 17, 1977.
(NY Islanders' 9th choice, 250th overall, in 1998 Entry Draft).

			Regular Season					Playoffs				
Season	Club	Lea	GP	G	A	TP	PIM	GP	G	A	TP	PIM
1992-93	HC Budejovice-Jr.	Cze-Rep	25	38	24	62	....	....	....	....	....	....
1993-94	Slavia Praha-Jr.	Cze-Rep	45	30	26	56	....	....	....	....	....	....
1994-95	Slavia Praha-Jr.	Cze-Rep	28	7	8	15	12	....	....	....	....	....
1995-96	Slavia Praha-Jr.	Cze-Rep	47	37	21	58	24	....	....	....	....	....
1996-97	Slavia Praha-Jr.	Cze-Rep	4	1	1	2	....	....	....	....	....	....
	HC Beroun-2	Cze-Rep	12	3	1	4	18	....	....	....	....	....
	Slavia Praha	Cze-Rep	41	3	4	7	10	3	0	0	0	0
1997-98	Slavia Praha	Cze-Rep	52	9	4	13	24	3	0	0	0	0
1998-99	Dukla Jihlava	Cze-Rep	52	12	10	22	57	....	....	....	....	....
99-2000	Slavia Praha	Cze-Rep	25	4	3	7	22	....	....	....	....	....
	HC Pardubice	Cze-Rep	25	2	4	6	18	3	0	0	0	0
2000-01	Slavia Praha	Cze-Rep	39	6	8	14	63	11	1	2	3	18

MATHIEU, Alexandre (mah-TYOO, al-ehx-AN-duhr) PIT.

Left wing. Shoots left. 6'2", 177 lbs. Born, Repentigny, Que., February 12, 1979.
(Pittsburgh's 4th choice, 97th overall, in 1997 Entry Draft).

			Regular Season					Playoffs				
Season	Club	Lea	GP	G	A	TP	PIM	GP	G	A	TP	PIM
1995-96	Laval-Laurentide	QAAA	44	6	24	30	....	15	2	9	11	....
1996-97	Halifax	QMJHL	70	12	22	34	16	18	2	5	7	2
1997-98	Halifax	QMJHL	68	35	41	76	52	5	1	1	2	4
1998-99	Halifax	QMJHL	69	21	27	48	90	5	0	1	1	4
99-2000	Wilkes-Barre	AHL	52	4	4	8	18	....	....	....	....	....
2000-01	Wilkes-Barre	AHL	77	11	17	28	32	16	4	2	6	14

MAXIMENKO, Andrei (max-EE-mehn-koh, AWN-dray) DET.

Left wing. Shoots right. 5'11", 172 lbs. Born, Moscow, USSR, January 10, 1981.
(Detroit's 2nd choice, 149th overall, in 1999 Entry Draft).

			Regular Season					Playoffs				
Season	Club	Lea	GP	G	A	TP	PIM	GP	G	A	TP	PIM
1997-98	Krylja Sovetov-2	Russia-3	42	2	4	6	12	....	....	....	....	....
1998-99	Krylja Sovetov	Russia	28	1	2	3	24	....	....	....	....	....
99-2000	Krylja Sovetov-2	Russia-3	6	4	2	6	26	....	....	....	....	....
	Krylja Sovetov	Russia-2	39	6	7	13	41	....	....	....	....	....
2000-01	Krylja Sovetov	Russia-2	28	2	5	7	8	....	....	....	....	....

McASLAN, Sean (mikk-AZ-luhnd, SHAWN) EDM.

Right wing. Shoots right. 6'1", 190 lbs. Born, Okootoks, Alta., January 12, 1980.

			Regular Season					Playoffs				
Season	Club	Lea	GP	G	A	TP	PIM	GP	G	A	TP	PIM
1996-97	Calgary Hitmen	WHL	26	2	3	5	22	....	....	....	....	....
1997-98	Calgary Hitmen	WHL	69	8	16	24	83	....	....	....	....	....
1998-99	Calgary Hitmen	WHL	71	7	16	23	110	21	2	1	3	18
99-2000	Calgary Hitmen	WHL	72	18	16	34	117	13	4	2	6	49
2000-01	Calgary Hitmen	WHL	51	21	32	53	137	12	3	5	8	29

Signed as a free agent by **Edmonton**, March 14, 2001.

McCAMBRIDGE, Keith (muh-KAYM-brihdj, KEETH)

Defense. Shoots left. 6'2", 205 lbs. Born, Thompson, Man., February 1, 1974.
(Calgary's 10th choice, 201st overall, in 1994 Entry Draft).

			Regular Season					Playoffs				
Season	Club	Lea	GP	G	A	TP	PIM	GP	G	A	TP	PIM
1991-92	Swift Current	WHL	72	1	4	5	84	8	0	0	0	2
1992-93	Swift Current	WHL	70	0	6	6	87	17	0	1	1	27
1993-94	Swift Current	WHL	71	0	10	10	179	7	0	0	0	4
1994-95	Swift Current	WHL	48	5	7	12	120	....	....	....	....	....
	Kamloops Blazers	WHL	21	0	6	6	90	21	0	5	5	49
1995-96	Saint John Flames	AHL	48	1	3	4	89	16	0	0	0	6
1996-97	Saint John Flames	AHL	56	2	1	3	109	....	....	....	....	....
1997-98	Saint John Flames	AHL	56	4	4	8	118	....	....	....	....	....
	Las Vegas	IHL	10	0	1	1	16	4	0	0	0	9
1998-99	Las Vegas	IHL	18	1	2	3	56	....	....	....	....	....
	Long Beach	IHL	52	2	5	7	200	8	0	0	0	20
99-2000	Providence Bruins	AHL	47	0	2	2	135	....	....	....	....	....
	Manitoba Moose	IHL	3	0	1	1	4	....	....	....	....	....
2000-01	Providence Bruins	AHL	63	1	5	6	215	10	0	0	0	18

Signed as free agent by **Boston**, August 20, 1999.

McCANN, Sean (muh-KAN, SHAWN)

Defense. Shoots right. 6', 195 lbs. Born, North York, Ont., September 18, 1971.
(Florida's 1st choice, 1st overall, in 1994 Supplemental Draft).

			Regular Season					Playoffs				
Season	Club	Lea	GP	G	A	TP	PIM	GP	G	A	TP	PIM
1988-89	Thornhill T-Birds	MTJHL	37	2	12	14	153	....	....	....	....	....
1989-90	Thornhill T-Birds	MTJHL	42	12	19	31	111	....	....	....	....	....
1990-91	Harvard University	ECAC	28	2	9	11	88	....	....	....	....	....
1991-92	Harvard University	ECAC	27	4	10	14	51	....	....	....	....	....
1992-93	Harvard University	ECAC	31	4	5	9	38	....	....	....	....	....
1993-94	Harvard University	ECAC	33	22	17	39	82	....	....	....	....	....
1994-95	Cincinnati	IHL	76	10	12	22	58	10	0	2	2	8
1995-96	Carolina	AHL	80	14	33	47	61	....	....	....	....	....
1996-97	Grand Rapids	IHL	76	8	26	34	46	5	0	0	0	2
1997-98	Milwaukee	IHL	33	6	11	17	37	....	....	....	....	....
	Orlando	IHL	26	5	3	8	30	....	....	....	....	....
1998-99	Orlando	IHL	42	4	9	13	28	....	....	....	....	....
	Springfield	AHL	31	8	15	23	31	3	0	1	1	4
99-2000	Springfield	AHL	62	5	38	43	77	....	....	....	....	....
	Syracuse Crunch	AHL	11	0	9	9	12	4	0	2	2	0
2000-01	Houston Aeros	IHL	82	12	18	30	50	7	1	2	3	0

ECAC First All-Star Team (1994) • NCAA East First All-American Team (1994) • NCAA Final Four All-Tournament Team (1994) • NCAA Final Four Tournament Most Valuable Player (1994)

Signed as a free agent by **Phoenix**, August, 1999. Loaned to **Syracuse** (AHL) by **Springfield** (AHL) for loan of Martin Gendron, March 15, 2000. Signed as a free agent by **Atlanta**, July 19, 2000.

McCARTHY, Jeremiah CAR.

Defense. Shoots left. 6', 210 lbs. Born, Boston, MA, March 1, 1976.

			Regular Season					Playoffs				
Season	Club	Lea	GP	G	A	TP	PIM	GP	G	A	TP	PIM
1994-95	Harvard University	ECAC	25	3	5	8	4	....	....	....	....	....
1995-96	Harvard University	ECAC	32	4	12	16	20	....	....	....	....	....
1996-97	Harvard University	ECAC	32	4	9	13	22	....	....	....	....	....
1997-98	Harvard University	ECAC	28	11	10	21	38	....	....	....	....	....
1998-99	Peoria Rivermen	ECHL	6	1	2	3	6	....	....	....	....	....
	Worcester	AHL	59	5	10	15	37	4	0	2	2	0
99-2000	Missouri	UHL	33	10	25	35	45	....	....	....	....	....
	Springfield	AHL	43	5	9	14	16	5	1	1	2	0
2000-01	Cincinnati	IHL	69	6	12	18	34	3	0	0	0	0

Signed as a free agent by **Carolina**, August 21, 2000.

McCLEMENT, Jay (muh-KLEHM-ehnt, JAY) ST.L.

Center. Shoots left. 6'1", 193 lbs. Born, Kingston, Ont., March 2, 1983.
(St. Louis' 1st choice, 57th overall, in 2001 Entry Draft).

			Regular Season					Playoffs				
Season	Club	Lea	GP	G	A	TP	PIM	GP	G	A	TP	PIM
1997-98	Kingston	OPJHL	48	3	8	11	15	....	....	....	....	....
1998-99	Kingston	OPJHL	51	25	28	53	34	....	....	....	....	....
99-2000	Brampton	OHL	63	13	16	29	34	6	0	4	4	8
2000-01	Brampton	OHL	66	30	19	49	61	9	4	2	6	10

McCORMICK, Cody (muh-KOHR-mihk, KOH-dee) COL.

Center. Shoots right. 6'2", 200 lbs. Born, London, Ont., April 18, 1983.
(Colorado's 5th choice, 144th overall, in 2001 Entry Draft).

			Regular Season					Playoffs				
Season	Club	Lea	GP	G	A	TP	PIM	GP	G	A	TP	PIM
1998-99	Elgin Middlesex	OMHA	58	22	40	62	81	....	....	....	....	....
99-2000	Belleville Bulls	OHL	45	3	4	7	42	9	1	0	1	10
2000-01	Belleville Bulls	OHL	66	7	16	23	135	10	1	1	2	23

McCUTCHEON, Warren (muh-KUHCH-uhn, WAW-rehn) N.J.

Center. Shoots left. 6'4", 190 lbs. Born, Morden, Man., August 6, 1982.
(New Jersey's 13th choice, 257th overall, in 2000 Entry Draft).

			Regular Season					Playoffs				
Season	Club	Lea	GP	G	A	TP	PIM	GP	G	A	TP	PIM
1998-99	Pembina Valley	MMHL	32	22	23	45	....	....	....	....	....	....
99-2000	Lethbridge	WHL	62	2	4	6	39	....	....	....	....	....
2000-01	Lethbridge	WHL	69	17	29	46	69	4	1	0	1	11

McDONALD, Brent (muhk-DAW-nuhld, BREHNT) CAR.

Center. Shoots right. 5'11", 180 lbs. Born, Olds, Alta., October 7, 1979.
(Carolina's 10th choice, 239th overall, in 1998 Entry Draft).

			Regular Season					Playoffs				
Season	Club	Lea	GP	G	A	TP	PIM	GP	G	A	TP	PIM
1994-95	Red Deer Royals	AAHA	26	16	24	40	55	....	....	....	....	....
1995-96	Red Deer Rebels	WHL	68	1	7	8	55	6	0	1	1	2
1996-97	Red Deer Rebels	WHL	69	11	17	28	94	16	4	3	7	38
1997-98	Red Deer Rebels	WHL	69	18	27	45	93	5	0	2	2	4
1998-99	Red Deer Rebels	WHL	38	17	18	35	64	....	....	....	....	....
	Prince George	WHL	34	13	13	26	40	7	1	1	2	18
99-2000	Prince George	WHL	7	1	3	4	6	....	....	....	....	....
	Spokane Chiefs	WHL	61	28	30	58	77	15	5	8	13	42
2000-01	Florida Everblades	ECHL	67	11	11	22	55	5	1	0	1	4

McDONALD, Kevin (muhk-DAW-nuhld, KEH-vihn) EDM.

Right wing. Shoots right. 5'11", 198 lbs. Born, Olds, Alta., April 21, 1977.

			Regular Season					Playoffs				
Season	Club	Lea	GP	G	A	TP	PIM	GP	G	A	TP	PIM
1994-95	Olds Grizzlies	AJHL	35	7	6	13	193	....	....	....	....	....
	Kamloops Blazers	WHL	6	1	1	2	27	....	....	....	....	....
1995-96	Regina Pats	WHL	70	11	19	30	200	11	0	1	1	17
1996-97	Edmonton Ice	WHL	4	0	0	0	12	....	....	....	....	....
	Medicine Hat	WHL	67	25	24	49	188	4	1	0	1	14
1997-98	Medicine Hat	WHL	47	15	7	22	167	....	....	....	....	....
	Seattle T-birds	WHL	23	11	9	20	138	5	1	0	1	21
1998-99	Florida Everblades	ECHL	41	17	24	41	153	6	3	2	5	10
	New Haven	AHL	8	0	0	0	14	....	....	....	....	....
99-2000	Florida Everblades	ECHL	DID NOT PLAY – INJURED									
2000-01	Florida Everblades	ECHL	13	1	2	3	67	....	....	....	....	....
	Roanoke Express	ECHL	57	8	12	20	296	5	0	0	0	4

• Missed entire 1999-2000 season recovering from knee surgery, June, 1999. Traded to **Roanoke** (ECHL) by **Florida** (ECHL) for Colin Anderson, November 15, 2000. Signed as a free agent by **Edmonton**, May 29, 2001.

McDONELL, Kent (MUHK-dawn-EHL, KEHNT) CBJ

Right wing. Shoots right. 6', 200 lbs. Born, Williamstown, Ont., March 1, 1979.
(Detroit's 3rd choice, 181st overall, in 1999 Entry Draft).

			Regular Season					Playoffs				
Season	Club	Lea	GP	G	A	TP	PIM	GP	G	A	TP	PIM
1995-96	Cornwall Colts	OCJHL	33	21	14	35	64	....	....	....	....	....
1996-97	Guelph Storm	OHL	56	7	5	12	57	16	0	2	2	4
1997-98	Guelph Storm	OHL	64	28	23	51	76	12	7	4	11	18
1998-99	Guelph Storm	OHL	60	31	38	69	110	11	4	3	7	36
99-2000	Guelph Storm	OHL	56	35	35	70	100	6	1	4	5	6
2000-01	Dayton Bombers	ECHL	28	16	9	25	94	3	0	0	0	4
	Syracuse Crunch	AHL	32	3	3	6	36	3	1	0	1	0

• Re-entered NHL Entry Draft. Originally Carolina's 9th choice, 225th overall, in 1997 Entry Draft.
Traded to **Columbus** by **Detroit** for future considerations, August 14, 2000.

McGRATTAN, Brian (muhk-GRA-tuhn, BRIGH-uhn)

Right wing. Shoots right. 6'3", 210 lbs. Born, Hamilton, Ont., September 2, 1981.
(Los Angeles' 5th choice, 104th overall, in 1999 Entry Draft).

			Regular Season					Playoffs				
Season	Club	Lea	GP	G	A	TP	PIM	GP	G	A	TP	PIM
1997-98	Guelph Royals	OJHL-B	15	4	3	7	94	....	....	....	....	....
	Guelph Storm	OHL	25	3	2	5	11	....	....	....	....	....
1998-99	Guelph Storm	OHL	6	1	3	4	15	....	....	....	....	....
	Sudbury Wolves	OHL	53	7	10	17	153	4	0	0	0	8
99-2000	Sudbury Wolves	OHL	25	2	8	10	79	....	....	....	....	....
	Mississauga	OHL	42	9	13	22	166	....	....	....	....	....
2000-01	Mississauga	OHL	31	20	9	29	83	....	....	....	....	....

• Missed majority of 2000-01 season recovering from knee injury suffered in game vs. Kingston (OHL), January 1, 2001.

McKERCHER, Jeff (muh-KUHR-chur, JEHF) DAL.

Defense. Shoots right. 6'2", 218 lbs. Born, Cornwall, Ont., January 14, 1979.
(Dallas' 7th choice, 189th overall, in 1997 Entry Draft).

			Regular Season					Playoffs				
Season	Club	Lea	GP	G	A	TP	PIM	GP	G	A	TP	PIM
1995-96	Cornwall Colts	OCJHL	53	1	16	17	33	....	....	....	....	....
1996-97	Barrie Colts	OHL	60	1	4	5	32	9	0	1	1	13
1997-98	Barrie Colts	OHL	51	0	2	2	21	6	0	0	0	2
1998-99	Sault Ste. Marie	OHL	8	0	0	0	0	....	....	....	....	....
	Peterborough	OHL	57	1	7	8	22	5	0	0	0	4
99-2000	Fort Wayne	UHL	72	2	7	9	55	11	0	4	4	4
2000-01	Mississippi	ECHL	16	2	3	5	14	....	....	....	....	....
	Augusta Lynx	ECHL	2	0	1	1	0	....	....	....	....	....

McLACHLAN, Darren (muhk-LAWK-luhn, DAIR-rehn) BOS.

Left wing. Shoots left. 6'1", 230 lbs. Born, Penticton, B.C., February 16, 1983.
(Boston's 2nd choice, 77th overall, in 2001 Entry Draft).

			Regular Season					Playoffs				
Season	Club	Lea	GP	G	A	TP	PIM	GP	G	A	TP	PIM
1998-99	Campbell River	VIJHL	31	15	25	40	212	....	....	....	....	....
	Seattle T-Birds	WHL	2	0	1	1	7	....	....	....	....	....
99-2000	Seattle T-Birds	WHL	54	5	1	6	175	7	0	0	0	9
2000-01	Seattle T-Birds	WHL	42	10	9	19	161	9	1	3	4	18

McLAREN, Steve (muh-KLAIR-uhn, STEEV) ST.L.

Left wing. Shoots left. 6', 200 lbs. Born, Owen Sound, Ont., February 3, 1975.
(Chicago's 3rd choice, 85th overall, in 1994 Entry Draft).

			Regular Season					Playoffs				
Season	Club	Lea	GP	G	A	TP	PIM	GP	G	A	TP	PIM
1992-93	North Bay	NOJHA	30	15	18	33	110	....	....	....	....	....
1993-94	North Bay	OHL	55	2	15	17	130	18	0	3	3	50
1994-95	North Bay	OHL	27	3	10	13	119	6	2	1	3	23
1995-96	Indianapolis Ice	IHL	54	1	2	3	170	3	0	0	0	2
1996-97	Indianapolis Ice	IHL	63	2	5	7	309	4	0	0	0	10
1997-98	Indianapolis Ice	IHL	61	3	5	8	208	5	0	0	0	24
1998-99	Philadelphia	AHL	52	4	3	7	216	7	0	0	0	2
99-2000	Philadelphia	AHL	64	1	2	3	247	....	....	....	....	....
2000-01	Philadelphia	AHL	48	3	1	4	177	8	0	0	0	38

Signed as a free agent by **Philadelphia**, August 24, 1998. Signed as a free agent by **St. Louis**, July 16, 2001.

McLEAN, Brett (muh-CLAYN, BREHT) MIN.

Center. Shoots left. 5'11", 194 lbs. Born, Comox, B.C., August 14, 1978.
(Dallas' 9th choice, 242nd overall, in 1997 Entry Draft).

			Regular Season					Playoffs				
Season	Club	Lea	GP	G	A	TP	PIM	GP	G	A	TP	PIM
1993-94	Notre Dame	SAHA	71	109	124	233	70	....	....	....	....	....
1994-95	Tacoma Rockets	WHL	67	11	23	34	33	4	0	1	1	0
1995-96	Kelowna Rockets	WHL	71	37	42	79	60	6	2	2	4	6
1996-97	Kelowna Rockets	WHL	72	44	60	104	98	6	4	2	6	12
1997-98	Kelowna Rockets	WHL	54	42	45	87	91	7	4	5	9	17
1998-99	Kelowna Rockets	WHL	44	32	38	70	46	....	....	....	....	....
	Brandon	WHL	21	15	16	31	20	5	1	6	7	8
	Cincinnati Ducks	AHL	7	0	3	3	6	....	....	....	....	....
99-2000	Johnstown Chiefs	ECHL	8	4	7	11	6	....	....	....	....	....
	Saint John Flames	AHL	72	15	23	38	115	3	0	1	1	2
2000-01	Cleveland	IHL	74	20	24	44	54	4	0	0	0	18

Signed as a free agent by **Calgary**, September, 1999. Signed as a free agent by **Minnesota**, July 13, 2000.

McLEOD, Kiel (muk-KLOWD, KIGHL) CBJ

Center. Shoots right. 6'5", 211 lbs. Born, Ft. Saskatchewan, Alta., December 30, 1982.
(Columbus' 3rd choice, 53rd overall, in 2001 Entry Draft).

			Regular Season					Playoffs				
Season	Club	Lea	GP	G	A	TP	PIM	GP	G	A	TP	PIM
1997-98	North Delta	BCAHA	55	57	55	112	202	....	....	....	....	....
1998-99	Kelowna Rockets	WHL	55	12	15	27	48	6	0	1	1	2
99-2000	Kelowna Rockets	WHL	59	17	13	30	100	5	2	1	3	2
2000-01	Kelowna Rockets	WHL	65	38	28	66	94	4	4	1	5	8

McMEEKIN, Brian (muhk-MEE-khin, BRIGH-uhn) ST.L.

Defense. Shoots right. 6'4", 195 lbs. Born, Trail, B.C., June 20, 1979.
(St. Louis' 9th choice, 260th overall, in 1999 Entry Draft).

			Regular Season					Playoffs				
Season	Club	Lea	GP	G	A	TP	PIM	GP	G	A	TP	PIM
1997-98	Trail Smokies	BCJHL	49	4	7	11	66	10	0	1	1	10
1998-99	Cornell Big Red	ECAC	26	0	1	1	12	....	....	....	....	....
99-2000	Cornell Big Red	ECAC	11	0	1	1	8	....	....	....	....	....
2000-01	Cornell Big Red	ECAC	31	2	1	3	24	....	....	....	....	....

McMORROW, Sean (muhk-MOHR-roh, SHAWN) BUF.

Defense. Shoots right. 6'4", 194 lbs. Born, Vancouver, B.C., January 19, 1982.
(Buffalo's 7th choice, 258th overall, in 2000 Entry Draft).

			Regular Season					Playoffs				
Season	Club	Lea	GP	G	A	TP	PIM	GP	G	A	TP	PIM
1998-99	Pickering Panthers	OPJHL	35	2	10	12	175	....	....	....	....	....
99-2000	Sarnia Sting	OHL	31	0	1	1	75	....	....	....	....	....
	Kitchener	OHL	31	0	1	1	67	4	0	0	0	12
2000-01	Mississauga	OHL	13	0	0	0	34	....	....	....	....	....
	Kingston	OHL	7	0	1	1	22	....	....	....	....	....
	London Knights	OHL	29	0	3	3	75	5	0	0	0	0

Traded to **Mississauga** by **Kitchener** with Michael Wehrstedt and Brent Labre for Marcus Smith and Kitchener's 1st round choice (later traded back to Kitchener - Kitchener selected Vasily Bizyayev) in 2000 CHL Import Draft, July 2, 2000. Traded to **Kingston** by **Mississauga** for Matt Timmons, December 13, 2000. Traded to **London** by **Kingston** with Kingston's 2nd round choice (Gerald Coleman) in 2001 OHL Midget Draft for Lou Dickenson and London's 10th round choice (Dayne Davis) in 2001 OHL Midget Draft, January 8, 2001.

McNEILL, Grant (muhk-NEEL, GRANT) FLA.

Defense. Shoots left. 6'2", 210 lbs. Born, Vermillion, Alta., June 8, 1983.
(Florida's 5th choice, 68th overall, in 2001 Entry Draft).

			Regular Season					Playoffs				
Season	Club	Lea	GP	G	A	TP	PIM	GP	G	A	TP	PIM
99-2000	Prince Albert	WHL	58	1	1	2	43	6	0	1	1	0
2000-01	Prince Albert	WHL	61	2	6	8	280	....	....	....	....	....

McPHERSON, Andrew (muhk-FUHR-suhn, AN-droo) PIT.

Left wing. Shoots left. 6'2", 175 lbs. Born, Ottawa, Ont., April 28, 1979.
(Pittsburgh's 11th choice, 261st overall, in 1999 Entry Draft).

			Regular Season					Playoffs				
Season	Club	Lea	GP	G	A	TP	PIM	GP	G	A	TP	PIM
1997-98	Dauphin Kings	MJHL	61	24	37	61	132	....	....	....	....	....
1998-99	RPI Engineers	ECAC	29	5	4	9	12	....	....	....	....	....
99-2000	RPI Engineers	ECAC	37	10	6	16	22	....	....	....	....	....
2000-01	RPI Engineers	ECAC	31	5	6	11	34	....	....	....	....	....

McRAE, Mark (muh-KRAY, MAHRK) ATL.

Defense. Shoots right. 6', 175 lbs. Born, Toronto, Ont., April 29, 1981.
(Atlanta's 13th choice, 288th overall, in 2000 Entry Draft).

			Regular Season					Playoffs				
Season	Club	Lea	GP	G	A	TP	PIM	GP	G	A	TP	PIM
1997-98	Brampton Caps	OPJHL	46	23	41	64	25	....	....	....	....	....
1998-99	Brampton Caps	OPJHL	50	34	40	74	29	....	....	....	....	....
99-2000	Cornell Big Red	ECAC	27	5	16	21	10	....	....	....	....	....
2000-01	Cornell Big Red	ECAC	33	8	11	19	14	....	....	....	....	....

McRAE, Matt (muh-KRAY, MAT) ATL.

Center. Shoots right. 6', 180 lbs. Born, Toronto, Ont., April 29, 1981.
(Atlanta's 6th choice, 147th overall, in 2000 Entry Draft).

			Regular Season					Playoffs				
Season	Club	Lea	GP	G	A	TP	PIM	GP	G	A	TP	PIM
1997-98	Brampton Caps	OPJHL	50	26	26	52	22	....	....	....	....	....
1998-99	Brampton Caps	OPJHL	50	34	40	74	29	....	....	....	....	....
99-2000	Cornell Big Red	ECAC	31	8	16	24	22	....	....	....	....	....
2000-01	Cornell Big Red	ECAC	27	3	6	9	10	....	....	....	....	....

MEHALKO, Brad NYR

Right wing. Shoots right. 6'1", 190 lbs. Born, Enchant, Alta., November 4, 1977.
(San Jose's 9th choice, 167th overall, in 1995 Entry Draft).

			Regular Season					Playoffs				
Season	Club	Lea	GP	G	A	TP	PIM	GP	G	A	TP	PIM
1992-93	Lethbridge Elite	AAHA	54	41	54	95	146	....	....	....	....	....
1993-94	Lethbridge	WHL	62	9	9	18	48	....	....	....	....	....
1994-95	Lethbridge	WHL	52	11	15	26	83	....	....	....	....	....
1995-96	Lethbridge	WHL	48	15	37	52	97	....	....	....	....	....
	Prince George	WHL	23	6	15	21	30	....	....	....	....	....
1996-97	Prince George	WHL	58	16	29	45	104	15	1	8	9	29
1997-98	Calgary Hitmen	WHL	55	26	49	75	107	....	....	....	....	....
1998-99	Tacoma	WCHL	49	14	22	36	75	....	....	....	....	....
	Las Vegas	IHL	8	1	0	1	7	....	....	....	....	....
99-2000	Canada	Nat-Team	56	10	21	31	86	....	....	....	....	....
	Kansas City	IHL	11	1	3	4	2	....	....	....	....	....
2000-01	Charlotte	ECHL	26	8	11	19	47	....	....	....	....	....
	Hartford	AHL	27	4	7	11	60	3	0	0	0	10

MELENOVSKY, Marek (meh-leh-NAHF-skee, MAIR-ehk) TOR.

Center. Shoots left. 5'10", 180 lbs. Born, Humpolec, Czech., March 30, 1977.
(Toronto's 5th choice, 171st overall, in 1995 Entry Draft).

			Regular Season					Playoffs				
Season	Club	Lea	GP	G	A	TP	PIM	GP	G	A	TP	PIM
1994-95	Dukla Jihlava-Jr.	Cze-Rep	28	23	11	34	....	....	....	....	....	....
	Dukla Jihlava	Cze-Rep	3	0	0	0	0	5	1	3	4	0
1995-96	Dukla Jihlava	Cze-Rep	33	3	3	6	....	5	1	2	3	....
1996-97	Dukla Jihlava	Cze-Rep	46	5	13	18	22	....	....	....	....	....
	St. John's Leafs	AHL	2	1	2	3	0	2	0	0	0	0
1997-98	Dukla Jihlava	Cze-Rep	18	10	14	24	30	....	....	....	....	....
1998-99	Dukla Jihlava	Cze-Rep	52	7	10	17	26	....	....	....	....	....
	Dukla Jihlava	EuroHL	6	0	2	2	2	....	....	....	....	....
99-2000	HCF Havirov	Cze-Rep	49	12	12	24	32	....	....	....	....	....
2000-01	HCF Havirov	Cze-Rep	48	22	20	42	43	....	....	....	....	....

MELIN, Bjorn (MEH-lihn, b-YUHRN) NYI

Right wing. Shoots right. 6'1", 178 lbs. Born, Jonkoping, Sweden, July 4, 1981.
(NY Islanders' 11th choice, 163rd overall, in 1999 Entry Draft).

			Regular Season					Playoffs				
Season	Club	Lea	GP	G	A	TP	PIM	GP	G	A	TP	PIM
1997-98	HV Jonkoping	Swede-Jr.	8	0	3	3	2	....	....	....	....	....
1998-99	HV Jonkoping	Swede-Jr.	30	12	7	19	50	....	....	....	....	....
99-2000	HV Jonkoping	Swede-Jr.	24	19	16	35	70	....	....	....	....	....
	HV Jonkoping	Sweden	23	3	0	3	2	5	0	0	0	0
2000-01	HV Jonkoping	Swede-Jr.	10	6	5	11	66	....	....	....	....	....
	HV Jonkoping	Sweden	43	2	1	3	26	....	....	....	....	....

MELOCHE, Eric (muh-LAWSH, AIR-ihk) PIT.

Right wing. Shoots right. 5'11", 195 lbs. Born, Montreal, Que., May 1, 1976.
(Pittsburgh's 7th choice, 186th overall, in 1996 Entry Draft).

			Regular Season					Playoffs				
Season	Club	Lea	GP	G	A	TP	PIM	GP	G	A	TP	PIM
1994-95	Cornwall Colts	OCJHL	40	7	15	22	51	....	....	....	....	....
1995-96	Cornwall Colts	OCJHL	64	68	53	121	162	....	....	....	....	....
1996-97	Ohio State	CCHA	39	12	11	23	78	....	....	....	....	....
1997-98	Ohio State	CCHA	42	26	22	48	86	....	....	....	....	....
1998-99	Ohio State	CCHA	35	11	16	27	87	....	....	....	....	....
99-2000	Ohio State	CCHA	36	20	11	31	*138	....	....	....	....	....
2000-01	Wilkes-Barre	AHL	79	20	20	40	72	21	6	10	16	17

MERRICK, Andrew (MEHR-rihk, AN-droo) CAR.

Center. Shoots left. 5'11", 202 lbs. Born, Syosset, NY, March 23, 1978.
(Carolina's 6th choice, 169th overall, in 1997 Entry Draft).

			Regular Season					Playoffs				
Season	Club	Lea	GP	G	A	TP	PIM	GP	G	A	TP	PIM
1994-95	Sarnia Jacks	OJHL-B	47	25	37	62	161	....	....	....	....	....
1995-96	Sarnia Jacks	OJHL-B	49	29	27	56	116	....	....	....	....	....
1996-97	U. of Michigan	CCHA	36	3	10	13	42	....	....	....	....	....
1997-98	U. of Michigan	CCHA	33	4	3	7	74	....	....	....	....	....
1998-99	U. of Michigan	CCHA	32	1	3	4	61	....	....	....	....	....
99-2000	U. of Michigan	CCHA	16	2	3	5	36	....	....	....	....	....
2000-01	Muskegon Fury	UHL	49	7	7	14	69	....	....	....	....	....
	Missouri	UHL	20	1	4	5	33	1	0	0	0	0

METCALF, Peter (MEHT-kaf, PEE-tuhr) TOR.

Defense. Shoots left. 6', 190 lbs. Born, Colorado Springs, CO, February 25, 1979.
(Toronto's 9th choice, 267th overall, in 1999 Entry Draft).

			Regular Season					Playoffs				
Season	Club	Lea	GP	G	A	TP	PIM	GP	G	A	TP	PIM
1997-98	Cushing Academy	Hi-School	25	18	48	66	....	....	....	....	....	....
1998-99	U. of Maine	H-East	33	6	17	23	34	....	....	....	....	....
99-2000	U. of Maine	H-East	40	4	17	21	56	....	....	....	....	....
2000-01	U. of Maine	H-East	31	5	9	14	44	....	....	....	....	....

METHOT, Francois (meh-THOH, FRAN-swaw) BUF.

Center. Shoots right. 6', 184 lbs. Born, Montreal, Que., April 26, 1978.
(Buffalo's 4th choice, 54th overall, in 1996 Entry Draft).

			Regular Season					Playoffs				
Season	Club	Lea	GP	G	A	TP	PIM	GP	G	A	TP	PIM
1993-94	Mtl-Bourassa	QAAA	44	17	38	55	....	4	3	1	4	4
1994-95	St-Hyacinthe	QMJHL	60	14	38	52	22	5	0	1	1	0
1995-96	St-Hyacinthe	QMJHL	68	32	62	94	22	12	6	6	12	4
1996-97	Rouyn-Noranda	QMJHL	47	21	30	51	22	....	....	....	....	....
	Shawinigan	QMJHL	18	8	17	25	2	7	2	6	8	2
1997-98	Shawinigan	QMJHL	36	23	42	65	10	6	1	3	4	5
1998-99	Rochester	AHL	58	5	8	13	8	9	0	1	1	0
99-2000	Rochester	AHL	80	14	18	32	20	21	2	4	6	16
2000-01	Rochester	AHL	79	22	33	55	35	4	1	3	4	0

MEYER, Doug (MIGH-yuhr, DUHG) PIT.

Left wing. Shoots left. 6'1", 197 lbs. Born, Bloomington, MN, February 21, 1980.
(Pittsburgh's 8th choice, 176th overall, in 1999 Entry Draft).

			Regular Season					Playoffs				
Season	Club	Lea	GP	G	A	TP	PIM	GP	G	A	TP	PIM
1997-98	Team USA	USDP	68	21	16	37	30	....	....	....	....	....
1998-99	U. of Minnesota	WCHA	36	4	4	8	18	....	....	....	....	....
99-2000	U. of Minnesota	WCHA	26	1	3	4	18	....	....	....	....	....
2000-01	Des Moines	USHL	50	29	27	56	36	3	0	0	0	15

• Ruled academically ineligible to play 2000-01 season by University of Minnesota, May 1, 2000.

MIETTINEN, Antti (mih-EHT-tih-nehn, AN-tee) DAL.

Center. Shoots right. 5'11", 180 lbs. Born, Hameenlinna, Finland, July 3, 1980.
(Dallas' 10th choice, 224th overall, in 2000 Entry Draft).

			Regular Season					Playoffs				
Season	Club	Lea	GP	G	A	TP	PIM	GP	G	A	TP	PIM
1996-97	Hameenlinna-B	Finn-Jr.	36	24	29	53	34	....	....	....	....	....
1997-98	Hameenlinna-B	Finn-Jr.	34	13	28	41	63	8	1	0	1	2
	HPK Hameenlinna	Finn-Jr.	8	1	0	1	2	....	....	....	....	....
1998-99	HPK Hameenlinna	Finn-Jr.	35	17	22	39	28	....	....	....	....	....
	FPS Forssa	Finland-2	4	3	1	4	6	....	....	....	....	....
	HPK Hameenlinna	Finland	13	0	0	0	2	4	0	0	0	0
99-2000	HPK Hameenlinna	Finn-Jr.	16	11	13	24	16	....	....	....	....	....
	HPK Hameenlinna	Finland	39	2	1	3	8	7	1	0	1	0
2000-01	HPK Hameenlinna	Finn-Jr.	4	3	10	13	2	....	....	....	....	....
	HPK Hameenlinna	Finland	55	13	11	24	20	....	....	....	....	....

MIETTINEN, Tommi (mih-EHT-tih-nehn,TAW-mee) ANA.

Center. Shoots left. 5'10", 165 lbs. Born, Kuopio, Finland, December 3, 1975.
(Anaheim's 9th choice, 236th overall, in 1994 Entry Draft).

			Regular Season					Playoffs				
Season	Club	Lea	GP	G	A	TP	PIM	GP	G	A	TP	PIM
1991-92	KalPa Kuopio	Finn-Jr.	37	9	16	25	12	....	....	....	....	....
1992-93	KalPa Kuopio-B	Finn-Jr.	7	3	8	11	2	....	....	....	....	....
	KalPa Kuopio	Finn-Jr.	26	16	27	43	14	....	....	....	....	....
	KalPa Kuopio	Finland	14	0	0	0	0	....	....	....	....	....
1993-94	KalPa Kuopio	Finn-Jr.	9	5	9	14	10	....	....	....	....	....
	KalPa Kuopio	Finland	47	5	7	12	14	....	....	....	....	....
1994-95	KalPa Kuopio	Finn-Jr.	2	1	3	4	2	....	....	....	....	....
	KalPa Kuopio	Finland	48	13	16	29	26	3	1	1	2	2
1995-96	TPS Turku	Finland	36	3	10	13	10	10	2	1	3	29
1996-97	TPS Turku	Finland	41	6	15	21	6	12	3	4	7	8
1997-98	TPS Turku	Finland	42	8	6	14	26	4	0	0	0	0
	TPS Turku	EuroHL	3	0	0	0	2	....	....	....	....	....
1998-99	TPS Turku	Finland	54	10	17	27	26	10	4	4	8	0
99-2000	Ilves-Tampere	Finland	54	13	20	33	24	....	....	....	....	....
2000-01	Ilves-Tampere	Finland	55	10	20	30	38	9	0	1	1	4

MIKHNOV, Alexei (MIHKH-nahf, al-EHX-ay) **EDM.**

Left wing. Shoots left. 6'5", 198 lbs. Born, Kiev, USSR, August 31, 1982.
(Edmonton's 1st choice, 17th overall, in 2000 Entry Draft).

			Regular Season					Playoffs				
Season	Club	Lea	GP	G	A	TP	PIM	GP	G	A	TP	PIM
1997-98	Torpedo Yaroslavl	Russia-2	6	0	0	0	0	....	....	....	....	....
1998-99	Hk Yaroslavl-2	Russia-3	14	2	2	4	4	....	....	....	....	....
99-2000	Hk Yaroslavl-2	Russia-3	53	24	17	41	10	....	....	....	....	....
2000-01	HC Moscow	Russia-2	4	0	0	0	2	....	....	....	....	....
	THC Tver	Russia-2	22	5	11	16	6	....	....	....	....	....

MIKKOLA, Ilkka (mih-KOHLA, IHL-ka) **MTL.**

Defense. Shoots left. 6', 189 lbs. Born, Oulu, Finland, January 18, 1979.
(Montreal's 3rd choice, 65th overall, in 1997 Entry Draft).

			Regular Season					Playoffs				
Season	Club	Lea	GP	G	A	TP	PIM	GP	G	A	TP	PIM
1993-94	Karpat Oulu-C	Finn-Jr.	22	3	6	9	4	4	0	1	1	4
1994-95	Karpat Oulu-C	Finn-Jr.	31	17	27	44	24	3	0	0	0	8
1995-96	Karpat Oulu-B	Finn-Jr.	4	2	0	2	0	....	....	....	....	....
	Karpat Oulu	Finn-Jr.	21	2	3	5	20	....	....	....	....	....
	Karpat Oulu	Finland-2	10	0	4	4	29	2	0	0	0	2
1996-97	Karpat Oulu	Finn-Jr.	40	7	12	19	32	6	0	0	0	4
1997-98	Karpat Oulu	Finn-Jr.	8	4	2	6	10	....	....	....	....	....
	Karpat Oulu	Finland-2	27	7	2	9	34	....	....	....	....	....
1998-99	TPS Turku	Finland	42	1	3	4	41	10	1	0	1	6
99-2000	TPS Turku	Finland	54	2	6	8	48	11	0	0	0	6
2000-01	TPS Turku	Finland	37	3	6	9	22	10	0	1	1	4

MILLER, Nate (MIHL-luhr, NAYT) **L.A.**

Right wing. Shoots left. 6'3", 192 lbs. Born, Anoka, MN, June 3, 1976.

			Regular Season					Playoffs				
Season	Club	Lea	GP	G	A	TP	PIM	GP	G	A	TP	PIM
1995-96	Twin Cities	USHL	53	25	34	59	91	....	....	....	....	....
1996-97	U. of Minnesota	WCHA	40	5	9	14	36	....	....	....	....	....
1997-98	U. of Minnesota	WCHA	39	8	6	14	42	....	....	....	....	....
1998-99	U. of Minnesota	WCHA	43	6	8	14	70	....	....	....	....	....
99-2000	U. of Minnesota	WCHA	41	16	19	35	38	....	....	....	....	....
2000-01	Lowell	AHL	80	15	10	25	61	4	0	0	0	2

Signed as a free agent by **LA Kings**, August 11, 2000.

MILLEY, Norman (MIHL-lee, NOHR-man) **BUF.**

Right wing. Shoots right. 6', 200 lbs. Born, Toronto, Ont., February 14, 1980.
(Buffalo's 3rd choice, 47th overall, in 1998 Entry Draft).

			Regular Season					Playoffs				
Season	Club	Lea	GP	G	A	TP	PIM	GP	G	A	TP	PIM
1995-96	Toronto Wings	MTHL	42	42	36	78	....	....	....	....	....	....
	St. Michael's B's	OPJHL	5	2	1	3	0	....	....	....	....	....
1996-97	Sudbury Wolves	OHL	61	30	32	62	15	....	....	....	....	....
1997-98	Sudbury Wolves	OHL	62	33	41	74	48	10	0	1	1	4
1998-99	Sudbury Wolves	OHL	68	52	68	120	47	4	2	3	5	4
99-2000	Sudbury Wolves	OHL	68	*52	60	112	47	12	8	11	19	6
2000-01	Rochester	AHL	77	20	27	47	56	4	0	0	0	2

OHL Second All-Star Team (1999) • OHL First All-Star Team (2000) • Canadian Major Junior First All-Star Team (2000)

MILROY, Duncan (MIHL-roi, DUHN-can) **MTL.**

Right wing. Shoots right. 6', 197 lbs. Born, Edmonton, Alta., February 8, 1983.
(Montreal's 3rd choice, 37th overall, in 2001 Entry Draft).

			Regular Season					Playoffs				
Season	Club	Lea	GP	G	A	TP	PIM	GP	G	A	TP	PIM
1998-99	Edmonton Leafs	AMHL	34	34	36	70	73	....	....	....	....	....
	Swift Current	WHL	3	0	0	0	0	....	....	....	....	....
99-2000	Swift Current	WHL	68	15	15	30	20	12	3	5	8	12
2000-01	Swift Current	WHL	68	38	54	92	51	19	9	12	21	6

MISCHLER, Greg (MIH-schluhr, GREHG) **S.J.**

Center. Shoots left. 6'3", 174 lbs. Born, Holbrook, NY, September 15, 1978.
(Vancouver's 10th choice, 204th overall, in 1998 Entry Draft).

			Regular Season					Playoffs				
Season	Club	Lea	GP	G	A	TP	PIM	GP	G	A	TP	PIM
1997-98	Northeastern	H-East	39	7	13	20	22	....	....	....	....	....
1998-99	Northeastern	H-East	33	8	15	23	36	....	....	....	....	....
99-2000	Northeastern	H-East	34	9	14	23	22	....	....	....	....	....
2000-01	Northeastern	H-East	36	10	*32	42	34	....	....	....	....	....

Signed as a free agent by **San Jose**, June 13, 2001.

MISKOVICH, Aaron (MIHS-kuh-vihch, AIR-ruhn) **COL.**

Center. Shoots left. 5'10", 185 lbs. Born, Grand Rapids, MN, April 28, 1978.
(Colorado's 6th choice, 133rd overall, in 1997 Entry Draft).

			Regular Season					Playoffs				
Season	Club	Lea	GP	G	A	TP	PIM	GP	G	A	TP	PIM
1996-97	Grand Rapids High	Hi-School	30	34	50	84	....	....	....	....	....	....
	Green Bay	USHL	14	4	9	13	14	3	0	1	1	6
1997-98	U. of Minnesota	WCHA	28	4	8	12	14	....	....	....	....	....
1998-99	U. of Minnesota	WCHA	42	11	11	22	36	....	....	....	....	....
99-2000	U. of Minnesota	WCHA	41	16	16	32	24	....	....	....	....	....
2000-01	U. of Minnesota	WCHA	41	12	12	24	41	....	....	....	....	....

Compiled career totals of 100-83-117-200 at Grand Rapids High School. • Minnesota High School Player of the Year (1997)

MITCHELL, Kevin (MIHT-chehl, KEH vihn)

Defense. Shoots left. 5'11", 190 lbs. Born, Bronx, NY, June 5, 1980.
(Calgary's 9th choice, 234th overall, in 1998 Entry Draft).

			Regular Season					Playoffs				
Season	Club	Lea	GP	G	A	TP	PIM	GP	G	A	TP	PIM
1996-97	Cambridge Hawks	OJHL-B	47	30	28	58	140	....	....	....	....	....
1997-98	Guelph Storm	OHL	65	10	46	56	73	12	1	7	8	14
1998-99	Guelph Storm	OHL	68	26	52	78	107	11	3	10	13	29
99-2000	Guelph Storm	OHL	68	19	58	77	94	6	1	2	3	10
2000-01	Oshawa Generals	OHL	54	10	29	39	139	....	....	....	....	....
	Hamilton Bulldogs	AHL	8	0	3	3	2	....	....	....	....	....

OHL Second All-Star Team (1999, 2000)

Traded to **Oshawa** by **Guelph** with Jon Hedberg, Chris Whitley and Guelph's 3rd round choice (Chris Hulit) in 2001 OHL Midget Draft for Andrew Archer, Nick Lees and Oshawa's 5th round choice in 2002 OHL Priority Draft, September 29, 2000.

MOEN, Travis (MOH-ehn, TRA-vihs) **CGY.**

Left wing. Shoots left. 6'2", 198 lbs. Born, Swift Current, Sask., April 6, 1982.
(Calgary's 6th choice, 155th overall, in 2000 Entry Draft).

			Regular Season					Playoffs				
Season	Club	Lea	GP	G	A	TP	PIM	GP	G	A	TP	PIM
1998-99	Swift Current	SMHL		STATISTICS NOT AVAILABLE								
	Kelowna Rockets	WHL	4	0	0	0	0	....	....	....	....	....
99-2000	Kelowna Rockets	WHL	66	9	6	15	96	5	1	1	2	2
2000-01	Kelowna Rockets	WHL	40	8	8	16	106	....	....	....	....	....

MOKHOV, Stepan (MOH-khohv, STEH-pan) **CHI.**

Defense. Shoots left. 6'2", 190 lbs. Born, Ust-Kamenogorsk, USSR, January 22, 1981.
(Chicago's 3rd choice, 63rd overall, in 1999 Entry Draft).

			Regular Season					Playoffs				
Season	Club	Lea	GP	G	A	TP	PIM	GP	G	A	TP	PIM
1997-98	Avangard Omsk-2	Russia-3	18	0	1	1	8	....	....	....	....	....
1998-99	HC Cherepovets-2	Russia-3	25	2	0	2	34	....	....	....	....	....
	HC Cherepovets-3	Russia-4	3	0	0	0	6	....	....	....	....	....
	HC Cherepovets	Russia	1	0	0	0	0	....	....	....	....	....
99-2000	HC Novokuznetsk	Russia	18	0	1	1	6	14	1	0	1	4
2000-01	Krylja Sovetov	Russia-2	30	0	5	5	4	....	....	....	....	....

MOORE, Dominic (MOOR, DOHM-ih-nihk) **NYR**

Center. Shoots left. 6', 180 lbs. Born, Thornhill, Ont., August 3, 1980.
(NY Rangers' 2nd choice, 95th overall, in 2000 Entry Draft).

			Regular Season					Playoffs				
Season	Club	Lea	GP	G	A	TP	PIM	GP	G	A	TP	PIM
1996-97	Thornhill Islanders	MTJHL	29	4	6	10	48	1	0	1	1	0
1997-98	Aurora Tigers	OPJHL	51	10	15	25	16	....	....	....	....	....
1998-99	Aurora Tigers	OPJHL	51	34	53	87	70	....	....	....	....	....
99-2000	Harvard University	ECAC	30	12	24	28	16	....	....	....	....	....
2000-01	Harvard University	ECAC	32	15	28	43	40	....	....	....	....	....

ECAC All-Rookie Team (2000) • ECAC Second All-Star Team (2001)

MOORE, Mark (MOOR, MAHRK) **PIT.**

Defense. Shoots right. 6'3", 185 lbs. Born, Windsor, Ont., February 18, 1977.
(Pittsburgh's 7th choice, 179th overall, in 1997 Entry Draft).

			Regular Season					Playoffs				
Season	Club	Lea	GP	G	A	TP	PIM	GP	G	A	TP	PIM
1995-96	Thornhill Islanders	MTJHL	50	12	19	31	51	18	4	5	9	0
1996-97	Harvard University	ECAC	22	5	2	7	16	....	....	....	....	....
1997-98	Harvard University	ECAC	32	1	3	4	90	....	....	....	....	....
1998-99	Harvard University	ECAC	32	1	2	3	82	....	....	....	....	....
99-2000	Harvard University	ECAC	28	0	2	2	48	....	....	....	....	....
2000-01	Wheeling Nailers	ECHL	20	0	2	2	19	....	....	....	....	....
	Charlotte	ECHL	7	0	0	0	4	....	....	....	....	....
	Wilkes-Barre	AHL	11	0	0	0	2	3	0	0	0	0

MOORE, Steve (MOOR, STEEV) **COL.**

Center. Shoots right. 6'2", 205 lbs. Born, Windsor, Ont., September 22, 1978.
(Colorado's 7th choice, 53rd overall, in 1998 Entry Draft).

			Regular Season					Playoffs				
Season	Club	Lea	GP	G	A	TP	PIM	GP	G	A	TP	PIM
1995-96	Thornhill Islanders	MTJHL	50	25	27	52	57	18	4	5	9	....
1996-97	Thornhill Islanders	MTJHL	50	34	52	86	52	13	10	11	21	2
1997-98	Harvard University	ECAC	33	10	23	33	46	....	....	....	....	....
1998-99	Harvard University	ECAC	30	18	13	31	34	....	....	....	....	....
99-2000	Harvard University	ECAC	27	10	16	26	53	....	....	....	....	....
2000-01	Harvard University	ECAC	32	7	26	33	43	....	....	....	....	....

MORAN, Brad (moh-RAN, BRAD) **CBJ**

Center. Shoots left. 5'11", 180 lbs. Born, Abbotsford, B.C., March 20, 1979.
(Buffalo's 8th choice, 191st overall, in 1998 Entry Draft).

			Regular Season					Playoffs				
Season	Club	Lea	GP	G	A	TP	PIM	GP	G	A	TP	PIM
1994-95	Abbotsford	BCAHA	56	66	93	159	40	....	....	....	....	....
1995-96	Calgary Hitmen	WHL	70	13	31	44	28	....	....	....	....	....
1996-97	Calgary Hitmen	WHL	72	30	36	66	61	....	....	....	....	....
1997-98	Calgary Hitmen	WHL	72	53	49	102	64	18	10	8	18	20
1998-99	Calgary Hitmen	WHL	71	60	58	118	96	21	17	*25	42	26
99-2000	Calgary Hitmen	WHL	72	48	*72	*120	84	13	7	15	22	18
2000-01	Syracuse Crunch	AHL	71	11	19	30	30	5	3	4	7	2

WHL East First All-Star Team (1999, 2000)

Signed as a free agent by **Columbus**, June 5, 2000.

MORGAN, Gavin **DAL.**

Center. Shoots right. 5'11", 175 lbs. Born, Scarborough, Ont., July 9, 1976.

			Regular Season					Playoffs				
Season	Club	Lea	GP	G	A	TP	PIM	GP	G	A	TP	PIM
1992-93	Wexford Raiders	MTJHL	3	0	1	1	0	....	....	....	....	....
1993-94	Wexford Raiders	MTJHL	49	18	32	50	91	....	....	....	....	....
1994-95	Wexford Raiders	MTJHL	49	26	39	65	170	....	....	....	....	....
1995-96	U. of Denver	WCHA	28	2	9	11	47	....	....	....	....	....
1996-97	U. of Denver	WCHA	41	8	15	23	46	....	....	....	....	....
1997-98	U. of Denver	WCHA	37	9	8	17	42	....	....	....	....	....
1998-99	U. of Denver	WCHA	40	13	16	29	85	....	....	....	....	....
99-2000	Idalo Steelheads	WCHL	54	17	33	50	150	3	0	3	3	4
	Long Beach	IHL	7	0	1	1	10	....	....	....	....	....
	Utah Grizzlies	IHL	10	0	2	2	4	2	1	0	1	2
2000-01	Utah Grizzlies	IHL	79	7	14	21	187	....	....	....	....	....

Signed as a free agent by **Idaho** (WCHL), August 25, 1999. Signed as a free agent by **Utah** (IHL), June 26, 2000. Signed as a free agent by **Dallas**, July 6, 2001.

MORISSET, David (moh-rih-SEHT, DAY-vihd) **FLA.**

Right wing. Shoots right. 6'2", 195 lbs. Born, Langley, B.C., April 6, 1981.
(St. Louis' 2nd choice, 65th overall, in 2000 Entry Draft).

			Regular Season					Playoffs				
Season	Club	Lea	GP	G	A	TP	PIM	GP	G	A	TP	PIM
1997-98	Seattle T-Birds	WHL	58	6	2	8	104	5	1	0	1	6
1998-99	Seattle T-Birds	WHL	17	4	0	4	31	11	1	1	2	22
99-2000	Seattle T-Birds	WHL	60	23	34	57	69	7	3	4	7	12
2000-01	Seattle T-Birds	WHL	61	32	36	68	95	9	4	2	6	12

• Missed majority of 1998-99 season recovering from shoulder injury suffered in practice, November, 1998. • Rights traded to **Florida** by **St. Louis** with St. Louis' 5th round pick in 2002 Entry Draft for Scott Mellanby, February 9, 2001.

MORRISON, Justin (MOHR-rihs-OHN, JUHS-tihn) **VAN.**

Right wing. Shoots right. 6'3", 205 lbs. Born, Los Angeles, CA, September 10, 1979.
(Vancouver's 4th choice, 81st overall, in 1998 Entry Draft).

			Regular Season					Playoffs				
Season	**Club**	**Lea**	**GP**	**G**	**A**	**TP**	**PIM**	**GP**	**G**	**A**	**TP**	**PIM**
1996-97	Omaha Lancers	USHL	62	12	24	36	44	10	2	4	6	8
1997-98	Colorado College	WCHA	42	4	9	13	8	....	....	....	....	....
1998-99	Colorado College	WCHA	38	23	15	38	33	....	....	....	....	....
99-2000	Colorado College	WCHA	38	7	19	26	28	....	....	....	....	....
2000-01	Colorado College	WCHA	41	21	14	35	42	....	....	....	....	....

MORRISONN, Shaone (MOHR-rih-sohn, SHAY-ohn) **BOS.**

Defense. Shoots left. 6'3", 182 lbs. Born, Vancouver, B.C., December 23, 1982.
(Boston's 1st choice, 19th overall, in 2001 Entry Draft).

			Regular Season					Playoffs				
Season	**Club**	**Lea**	**GP**	**G**	**A**	**TP**	**PIM**	**GP**	**G**	**A**	**TP**	**PIM**
99-2000	Kamloops	WHL	57	1	6	7	80	4	0	0	0	6
2000-01	Kamloops	WHL	61	13	25	38	132	4	0	0	0	6

MOSOVSKY, Karel (moh-SAWV-skee, KA-rehl) **BUF.**

Left wing. Shoots right. 6'3", 201 lbs. Born, Piesk, Czech., August 22, 1981.
(Buffalo's 6th choice, 117th overall, in 1999 Entry Draft).

			Regular Season					Playoffs				
Season	**Club**	**Lea**	**GP**	**G**	**A**	**TP**	**PIM**	**GP**	**G**	**A**	**TP**	**PIM**
1997-98	HC Budejovice-Jr.	Cze-Rep	36	15	17	32	52	....	....	....	....	....
1998-99	Regina Pats	WHL	68	26	25	51	58	....	....	....	....	....
99-2000	Regina Pats	WHL	56	24	34	58	80	7	3	1	4	12
2000-01	Regina Pats	WHL	61	25	26	51	59	6	1	3	4	8

MRAZEK, Frantisek (muh-RA-zehk, FRAN-tih-SEHK) **TOR.**

Left wing. Shoots left. 6'4", 211 lbs. Born, Ceske-Budejovice, Czech., May 16, 1979.
(Toronto's 3rd choice, 111th overall, in 1997 Entry Draft).

			Regular Season					Playoffs				
Season	**Club**	**Lea**	**GP**	**G**	**A**	**TP**	**PIM**	**GP**	**G**	**A**	**TP**	**PIM**
1995-96	HC Budejovice-Jr.	Cze-Rep	19	8	3	11	....	....	....	....	....	....
1996-97	HC Budejovice-Jr.	Cze-Rep	40	18	15	33	....	....	....	....	....	....
1997-98	Red Deer Rebels	WHL	65	30	24	54	71	5	1	0	1	2
1998-99	Red Deer Rebels	WHL	60	34	42	76	79	9	6	4	10	16
99-2000	St. John's Leafs	AHL	1	0	0	0	0	....	....	....	....	....
2000-01	St. John's Leafs	AHL	51	4	9	13	24	....	....	....	....	....

• Missed majority of 1999-2000 season recovering from knee injury suffered in training camp, October 1, 1999.

MULICK, Robert (muhl-LIHK, RAW-buhrt) **S.J.**

Defense. Shoots right. 6'2", 210 lbs. Born, Toronto, Ont., October 23, 1979.
(San Jose's 8th choice, 185th overall, in 1998 Entry Draft).

			Regular Season					Playoffs				
Season	**Club**	**Lea**	**GP**	**G**	**A**	**TP**	**PIM**	**GP**	**G**	**A**	**TP**	**PIM**
1994-95	Mississauga Reps	MTHL	52	8	23	31	80	....	....	....	....	....
1995-96	Sault Ste. Marie	OHL	54	0	3	3	58	3	0	0	0	0
1996-97	Sault Ste. Marie	OHL	60	2	8	10	49	11	0	1	1	12
1997-98	Sault Ste. Marie	OHL	61	0	10	10	109	....	....	....	....	....
1998-99	Sault Ste. Marie	OHL	66	1	12	13	83	5	0	1	1	10
99-2000	Kentucky	AHL	52	0	0	0	52	9	0	0	0	10
2000-01	Kentucky	AHL	71	0	6	6	55	2	0	0	0	0

MURATOV, Yevgeny (muhr-A-tahf, ehv-GEH-nee) **EDM.**

Left wing. Shoots right. 5'10", 178 lbs. Born, Nizhny Tagil, USSR, January 28, 1981.
(Edmonton's 10th choice, 274th overall, in 2000 Entry Draft).

			Regular Season					Playoffs				
Season	**Club**	**Lea**	**GP**	**G**	**A**	**TP**	**PIM**	**GP**	**G**	**A**	**TP**	**PIM**
1997-98	HC Nizhnekamsk-2	Russia-3	39	7	7	14	2	....	....	....	....	....
1998-99	HC Nizhnekamsk-2	Russia-3	37	26	9	35	32	....	....	....	....	....
	HC Nizhnekamsk	Russia	4	0	0	0	0	3	1	0	1	2
99-2000	HC Nizhnekamsk	Russia	29	9	7	16	2	....	....	....	....	....
	Ak Bars Kazan	Russia	8	2	2	4	2	9	0	0	0	2
2000-01	HC Nizhnekamsk	Russia	42	9	8	17	14	4	0	0	0	0

MURLEY, Matt (MUHR-lee, MAT) **PIT.**

Left wing. Shoots left. 6'1", 192 lbs. Born, Troy, NY, December 17, 1979.
(Pittsburgh's 2nd choice, 51st overall, in 1999 Entry Draft).

			Regular Season					Playoffs				
Season	**Club**	**Lea**	**GP**	**G**	**A**	**TP**	**PIM**	**GP**	**G**	**A**	**TP**	**PIM**
1996-97	Syracuse Crunch	MTJHL	48	52	58	110	111	....	....	....	....	....
1997-98	Syracuse Crunch	MTJHL	49	56	70	126	103	....	....	....	....	....
1998-99	RPI Engineers	ECAC	36	17	32	49	32	....	....	....	....	....
99-2000	RPI Engineers	ECAC	35	9	29	38	42	....	....	....	....	....
2000-01	RPI Engineers	ECAC	34	*24	18	42	34	....	....	....	....	....

MURPHY, Curtis **MIN.**

Defense. Shoots right. 5'8", 185 lbs. Born, Kerrobert, SK, December 3, 1975.

			Regular Season					Playoffs				
Season	**Club**	**Lea**	**GP**	**G**	**A**	**TP**	**PIM**	**GP**	**G**	**A**	**TP**	**PIM**
1993-94	Nipawin Hawks	SJHL	60	21	33	54	....	....	....	....	....	....
1994-95	North Dakota	WCHA	33	6	10	16	28	....	....	....	....	....
1995-96	North Dakota	WCHA	38	6	12	18	58	....	....	....	....	....
1996-97	North Dakota	WCHA	43	12	30	42	36	....	....	....	....	....
1997-98	North Dakota	WCHA	39	8	34	42	78	....	....	....	....	....
99-2000	Orlando	IHL	80	22	35	57	60	17	4	5	9	16
2000-01	Orlando	IHL	51	19	30	49	55	10	2	9	11	12

WCHA First All-Star Team (1997, 1998) • NCAA West Second All-American Team (1997) • WCHA Player of the Year (1998) • WCHA All-Tournament Team (1998) • NCAA West First All-American Team (1998) • IHL First All-Star Team (2001)

Signed as a free agent by **Minnesota**, June 18, 2001.

MURPHY, Joe **OTT.**

Right wing. Shoots right. 6', 200 lbs. Born, Didsbury, Alta., January 21, 1975.

			Regular Season					Playoffs				
Season	**Club**	**Lea**	**GP**	**G**	**A**	**TP**	**PIM**	**GP**	**G**	**A**	**TP**	**PIM**
1993-94	Olds Grizzlies	AJHL	52	34	38	72	121	....	....	....	....	....
1994-95	Olds Grizzlies	AJHL	52	30	29	59	65	....	....	....	....	....
1995-96	U. of Denver	WCHA	29	1	6	7	16	....	....	....	....	....
1996-97	U. of Denver	WCHA	36	8	14	22	40	....	....	....	....	....
1997-98	U. of Denver	WCHA	38	7	14	21	60	....	....	....	....	....
1998-99	U. of Denver	WCHA	33	3	13	16	25	....	....	....	....	....
	Huntsville	CHL	....	....	....	....	....	13	1	5	6	20
99-2000	Roanoke Express	ECHL	34	12	19	31	34	....	....	....	....	....
	Rochester	AHL	32	0	6	6	8	21	4	2	6	27
2000-01	Rochester	AHL	74	20	15	35	43	4	0	1	1	4

Signed as a free agent by **Buffalo**, July 28, 1998. Signed as a free agent by **Ottawa**, August 1, 2001.

MURPHY, Mark (MUHR-fee, MAHRK) **WSH.**

Left wing. Shoots left. 5'11", 200 lbs. Born, Stoughton, MA, August 6, 1976.
(Toronto's 6th choice, 197th overall, in 1995 Entry Draft).

			Regular Season					Playoffs				
Season	**Club**	**Lea**	**GP**	**G**	**A**	**TP**	**PIM**	**GP**	**G**	**A**	**TP**	**PIM**
1994-95	Stratford Cullitons	OJHL-B	47	52	56	108	64	....	....	....	....	....
1995-96	Stratford Cullitons	OJHL-B	1	0	0	0	0	....	....	....	....	....
	RPI Engineers	ECAC	32	1	1	2	50	....	....	....	....	....
1996-97	RPI Engineers	ECAC	34	9	18	27	56	....	....	....	....	....
1997-98	RPI Engineers	ECAC	35	8	27	35	63	....	....	....	....	....
1998-99	RPI Engineers	ECAC	37	11	30	41	76	....	....	....	....	....
99-2000	Wilkes-Barre	AHL	38	11	22	33	35	....	....	....	....	....
	Trenton Titans	ECHL	37	21	18	39	60	12	2	8	10	17
	Philadelphia	AHL	....	....	....	....	....	2	0	0	0	0
2000-01	Portland Pirates	AHL	76	29	41	70	92	3	2	0	2	2

Signed as a free agent by **Washington**, July 13, 2000.

MURPHY, Ryan (MUHR-fee, RIGH-yan) **CAR.**

Left wing. Shoots left. 6'1", 192 lbs. Born, Van Nuys, CA, March 21, 1979.
(Carolina's 4th choice, 113th overall, in 1999 Entry Draft).

			Regular Season					Playoffs				
Season	**Club**	**Lea**	**GP**	**G**	**A**	**TP**	**PIM**	**GP**	**G**	**A**	**TP**	**PIM**
1995-96	Thornhill Islanders	MTJHL	32	13	16	29	49	1	0	0	0	0
1996-97	Thornhill Islanders	MTJHL	41	22	32	54	36	12	7	8	15	....
1997-98	Bowling Green	CCHA	36	3	9	12	27	....	....	....	....	....
1998-99	Bowling Green	CCHA	34	10	23	33	38	....	....	....	....	....
99-2000	Bowling Green	CCHA	36	9	10	19	63	....	....	....	....	....
2000-01	Bowling Green	CCHA	38	23	15	38	22	....	....	....	....	....

MURRAY, Craig (MUHR-ray, KRAYG) **MTL.**

Center. Shoots left. 6', 175 lbs. Born, Souris, Man., February 22, 1979.
(Montreal's 8th choice, 201st overall, in 1998 Entry Draft).

			Regular Season					Playoffs				
Season	**Club**	**Lea**	**GP**	**G**	**A**	**TP**	**PIM**	**GP**	**G**	**A**	**TP**	**PIM**
1994-95	Penticton Pats	BCAHA	60	74	76	150	42	....	....	....	....	....
1995-96	Penticton	BCJHL	55	14	6	20	54	....	....	....	....	....
1996-97	Penticton	BCJHL	45	25	31	56	39	....	....	....	....	....
1997-98	Penticton	BCJHL	57	45	52	97	50	7	6	8	14	14
1998-99	U. of Michigan	CCHA	16	0	1	1	6	....	....	....	....	....
99-2000	U. of Michigan	CCHA	23	2	1	3	12	....	....	....	....	....
2000-01	U. of Michigan	CCHA	42	10	7	17	32	....	....	....	....	....

MURRAY, Doug (MUH-ree, DUHG) **S.J.**

Defense. Shoots left. 6'3", 220 lbs. Born, Bromma, Sweden, March 12, 1980.
(San Jose's 6th choice, 241st overall, in 1999 Entry Draft).

			Regular Season					Playoffs				
Season	**Club**	**Lea**	**GP**	**G**	**A**	**TP**	**PIM**	**GP**	**G**	**A**	**TP**	**PIM**
1998-99	NY Apple Core	EJHL	60	17	47	64	62	....	....	....	....	....
99-2000	Cornell Big Red	ECAC	32	3	6	9	38	....	....	....	....	....
2000-01	Cornell Big Red	ECAC	25	5	13	18	39	....	....	....	....	....

MURRAY, Garth (MUH-ree, GARTH) **NYR**

Center. Shoots left. 6'1", 205 lbs. Born, Regina, Sask., September 17, 1982.
(NY Rangers' 3rd choice, 79th overall, in 2001 Entry Draft).

			Regular Season					Playoffs				
Season	**Club**	**Lea**	**GP**	**G**	**A**	**TP**	**PIM**	**GP**	**G**	**A**	**TP**	**PIM**
1997-98	Calgary Buffaloes	AMHL	56	26	34	60	110	....	....	....	....	....
	Regina Pats	WHL	4	0	0	0	2	2	0	0	0	0
1998-99	Regina Pats	WHL	60	3	5	8	101	....	....	....	....	....
99-2000	Regina Pats	WHL	68	14	26	40	155	7	1	1	2	7
2000-01	Regina Pats	WHL	72	28	16	44	183	6	1	1	2	10

NAUMENKO, Nick (NAH-mehn-koh, NIHK)

Defense. Shoots right. 5'11", 185 lbs. Born, Chicago, IL, July 7, 1974.
(St. Louis' 9th choice, 182nd overall, in 1992 Entry Draft).

			Regular Season					Playoffs				
Season	**Club**	**Lea**	**GP**	**G**	**A**	**TP**	**PIM**	**GP**	**G**	**A**	**TP**	**PIM**
1991-92	Dubuque Saints	USHL	24	6	19	25	4	....	....	....	....	....
1992-93	North Dakota	WCHA	38	10	24	34	26	....	....	....	....	....
1993-94	North Dakota	WCHA	32	4	22	26	22	....	....	....	....	....
1994-95	North Dakota	WCHA	39	13	26	39	78	....	....	....	....	....
1995-96	North Dakota	WCHA	37	11	30	41	32	....	....	....	....	....
1996-97	Worcester	AHL	54	6	22	28	72	1	0	0	0	0
1997-98	Worcester	AHL	71	12	34	46	63	11	1	7	8	8
1998-99	Utah Grizzlies	IHL	20	4	3	7	20	....	....	....	....	....
	Las Vegas	IHL	34	5	16	21	37	....	....	....	....	....
	Kansas City	IHL	21	3	8	11	4	3	1	2	3	4
99-2000	Kansas City	IHL	54	9	27	36	79	....	....	....	....	....
2000-01	Cleveland	IHL	77	5	45	50	60	4	0	0	0	4

WCHA First All-Star Team (1995, 1996)

Signed as a free agent by **Minnesota**, September 6, 2000.

NEDOROST, Andrej (NEHD-ohr-ohst, awn-DRAY) CBJ

Center. Shoots left. 6', 187 lbs. Born, Trencin, Czech., April 30, 1980.
(Columbus' 10th choice, 286th overall, in 2000 Entry Draft).

			Regular Season					Playoffs				
Season	Club	Lea	GP	G	A	TP	PIM	GP	G	A	TP	PIM
1996-96	Dukla Trencin	Slovak-Jr.	40	50	35	85	....	....	....	....	....	....
1996-97	Dukla Trencin	Slovak-Jr.	45	15	16	31	....	....	....	....	....	....
1997-98	Dukla Trencin	Slovak-Jr.	45	27	22	49	61	....	....	....	....	....
	Dukla Trencin	Slovakia	1	0	0	0	0	....	....	....	....	....
1998-99	ESC Essen	DEB-Jr.	17	37	18	55	43	....	....	....	....	....
	ESC Essen	DEB	30	3	5	8	22	....	....	....	....	....
99-2000	ESC Essen	DEL	66	7	5	12	44	....	....	....	....	....
2000-01	Keramicka Plzen	Cze-Rep	33	10	8	18	22	....	....	....	....	....

NEDOROST, Vaclav (neh-DOHR-uhst, VA-tslav) COL.

Center. Shoots left. 6'1", 190 lbs. Born, Budejovice, Czech., March 16, 1982.
(Colorado's 1st choice, 14th overall, in 2000 Entry Draft).

			Regular Season					Playoffs				
Season	Club	Lea	GP	G	A	TP	PIM	GP	G	A	TP	PIM
1997-98	HC Budejovice-Jr.	Cze-Rep	43	30	23	53	20	....	....	....	....	....
1998-99	HC Budejovice-Jr.	Cze-Rep	39	6	15	21	20	....	....	....	....	....
	HC Budejovice	Cze-Rep	7	0	2	2	0	....	....	....	....	....
99-2000	HC Budejovice-Jr.	Cze-Rep	14	4	7	11	4	....	....	....	....	....
	HC Budejovice	Cze-Rep	38	8	6	14	6	3	0	0	0	0
2000-01	HC Budejovice	Cze-Rep	36	3	12	15	14	....	....	....	....	....

NEHRLING, Lucas (NEHR-lihng, LEW-cas) N.J.

Defense. Shoots right. 6'5", 220 lbs. Born, Peterborough, Ont., August 14, 1979.
(New Jersey's 3rd choice, 104th overall, in 1997 Entry Draft).

			Regular Season					Playoffs				
Season	Club	Lea	GP	G	A	TP	PIM	GP	G	A	TP	PIM
1995-96	Quinte Hawks	OMHA	25	0	9	9	59	....	....	....	....	....
1996-97	Sarnia Sting	OHL	63	3	12	15	74	12	0	2	2	23
1997-98	Sarnia Sting	OHL	22	0	2	2	46	....	....	....	....	....
	Kingston	OHL	39	1	8	9	83	12	0	1	1	19
1998-99	Kingston	OHL	2	0	1	1	13	....	....	....	....	....
	Guelph Storm	OHL	60	5	14	19	131	11	0	1	1	35
99-2000	Augusta Lynx	ECHL	9	1	0	1	12	....	....	....	....	....
	Arkansas	ECHL	16	0	1	1	51	....	....	....	....	....
	Muskegon Fury	UHL	22	1	2	3	86	2	0	0	0	2
	Albany River Rats	AHL	18	0	0	0	27	4	0	0	0	0
2000-01	Albany River Rats	AHL	33	1	1	2	92	....	....	....	....	....
	Adirondack	UHL	23	1	4	5	99	5	0	1	1	19

NEIL, Christopher (NEEL, KRIHS-toh-fuhr) OTT.

Right wing. Shoots right. 6', 213 lbs. Born, Markdale, Ont., June 18, 1979.
(Ottawa's 7th choice, 161st overall, in 1998 Entry Draft).

			Regular Season					Playoffs				
Season	Club	Lea	GP	G	A	TP	PIM	GP	G	A	TP	PIM
1995-96	Orangeville	OJHL-B	43	15	15	30	50	....	....	....	....	....
1996-97	North Bay	OHL	65	13	16	29	150	....	....	....	....	....
1997-98	North Bay	OHL	59	26	29	55	231	....	....	....	....	....
1998-99	North Bay	OHL	66	26	46	72	215	4	1	0	1	15
99-2000	Mobile Mysticks	ECHL	4	0	2	2	39	....	....	....	....	....
	Grand Rapids	IHL	51	9	10	19	301	8	0	2	2	24
2000-01	Grand Rapids	IHL	78	15	21	36	354	10	2	2	4	22

NEPRYAYEV, Ivan (neh-pree-YIGH-ehv, IGH-van) WSH.

Center. Shoots left. 6'1", 178 lbs. Born, Yaroslavl, USSR, February 4, 1982.
(Washington's 5th choice, 163rd overall, in 2000 Entry Draft).

			Regular Season					Playoffs				
Season	Club	Lea	GP	G	A	TP	PIM	GP	G	A	TP	PIM
1997-98	HC Yaroslavl-2	Russia-2	6	0	0	0	0	....	....	....	....	....
1998-99	HC Yaroslavl-2	Russia-3	15	1	0	1	0	....	....	....	....	....
99-2000	HC Yaroslavl-2	Russia-3	40	8	14	22	....	....	....	....	....	....
2000-01	Torpedo Yaroslavl	Russia	10	0	0	0	2	....	....	....	....	....

NEWMAN, Jared (NOO-muhn, JAH-rehd) CAR.

Defense. Shoots right. 6'2", 201 lbs. Born, Detroit, MI, March 7, 1982.
(Carolina's 4th choice, 110th overall, in 2000 Entry Draft).

			Regular Season					Playoffs				
Season	Club	Lea	GP	G	A	TP	PIM	GP	G	A	TP	PIM
1997-98	Plymouth	NAJHL	49	1	4	5	69	....	....	....	....	....
1998-99	Plymouth Whalers	OHL	66	2	15	17	57	11	1	2	3	9
99-2000	Plymouth Whalers	OHL	50	1	15	16	123	23	0	5	5	34
2000-01	Plymouth Whalers	OHL	34	0	4	4	114	6	0	3	3	26

NIELSEN, Evan (NEEL-suhn, EH-vuhn) ATL.

Defense. Shoots right. 6'2", 195 lbs. Born, Evanston, IL, May 28, 1981.
(Atlanta's 11th choice, 242nd overall, in 2000 Entry Draft).

			Regular Season					Playoffs				
Season	Club	Lea	GP	G	A	TP	PIM	GP	G	A	TP	PIM
1996-97	Evanston High	Hi-School	23	14	17	31	....	....	....	....	....	....
1997-98	Taft High	Hi-School	20	5	12	17	....	....	....	....	....	....
1998-99	Taft High	Hi-School	20	7	5	12	12	....	....	....	....	....
99-2000	Notre Dame	CCHA	48	4	10	14	63	....	....	....	....	....
2000-01	Notre Dame	CCHA	37	2	10	12	54	....	....	....	....	....

NIKOLOV, Angel (NIH-koh-lohv, AYN-jehl) S.J.

Defense. Shoots left. 6'2", 205 lbs. Born, Most, Czech., November 18, 1975.
(San Jose's 2nd choice, 37th overall, in 1994 Entry Draft).

			Regular Season					Playoffs				
Season	Club	Lea	GP	G	A	TP	PIM	GP	G	A	TP	PIM
1993-94	CHZ Litvinov	Cze-Rep	10	2	2	4	....	3	0	0	0	....
1994-95	CHZ Litvinov	Cze-Rep	41	1	4	5	18	4	0	0	0	27
1995-96	CHZ Litvinov	Cze-Rep	40	1	7	8	....	10	0	1	1	....
1996-97	CHZ Litvinov	Cze-Rep	47	0	9	9	44	....	....	....	....	....
1997-98	CHZ Litvinov	Cze-Rep	51	1	4	5	53	4	0	3	3	27
1998-99	CHZ Litvinov	Cze-Rep	51	5	12	17	54	....	....	....	....	....
99-2000	CHZ Litvinov	Cze-Rep	51	6	15	21	32	7	1	2	3	2
2000-01	CHZ Litvinov	Cze-Rep	48	5	11	16	85	6	0	1	1	6

NIKULIN, Ilja (nij-KOO-lihn, ihl-YUH) ATL.

Defense. Shoots left. 6'3", 210 lbs. Born, Moscow, USSR, March 12, 1982.
(Atlanta's 2nd choice, 31st overall, in 2000 Entry Draft).

			Regular Season					Playoffs				
Season	Club	Lea	GP	G	A	TP	PIM	GP	G	A	TP	PIM
1998-99	D'amo Moscow-2	Russia-3	23	0	2	2	18	....	....	....	....	....
99-2000	D'amo Moscow-2	Russia-3	4	2	1	3	10	....	....	....	....	....
	THC Tver	Russia-2	39	3	6	9	84	....	....	....	....	....
2000-01	Dynamo Moscow	Russia	44	0	4	4	61	....	....	....	....	....

NILSSON, Magnus (NIHL-suhn, MAG-nuhs) DET.

Right wing. Shoots left. 6'1", 187 lbs. Born, Finspang, Sweden, February 1, 1978.
(Detroit's 5th choice, 144th overall, in 1996 Entry Draft).

			Regular Season					Playoffs				
Season	Club	Lea	GP	G	A	TP	PIM	GP	G	A	TP	PIM
1995-96	Vita Hasten	Swede-2	28	3	3	6	16	....	....	....	....	....
1996-97	Malmo IF	Swede-Jr.	14	10	9	19	45	....	....	....	....	....
	Malmo IF	Sweden	12	0	0	0	0	....	....	....	....	....
1997-98	Malmo IF	Sweden	45	6	1	7	6	....	....	....	....	....
1998-99	Malmo IF	Sweden	42	0	0	0	10	4	0	0	0	0
99-2000	Malmo IF	Sweden	44	5	5	10	63	6	0	0	0	25
2000-01	Louisiana	ECHL	68	13	11	24	66	11	3	2	5	8

NILSSON, Mattias (NIHL-suhn, MA-tee-uhs) NSH.

Defense. Shoots left. 6'3", 195 lbs. Born, Ornskoldsvik, Sweden, February 16, 1982.
(Nashville's 3rd choice, 72nd overall, in 2000 Entry Draft).

			Regular Season					Playoffs				
Season	Club	Lea	GP	G	A	TP	PIM	GP	G	A	TP	PIM
1997-98	Modo Hockey	Swede-Jr.	40	20	14	34	34	....	....	....	....	....
1998-99	Modo Hockey	Swede-Jr.	30	7	7	14	26	....	....	....	....	....
99-2000	Modo Hockey	Swede-Jr.	33	5	5	10	56	2	0	0	0	0
2000-01	Modo Hockey	Swede-Jr.	18	2	3	5	62	....	....	....	....	....

NITTEL, Adam (nih-TEHL, A-dam) S.J.

Right wing. Shoots right. 6'2", 225 lbs. Born, Kitchener, Ont., July 17, 1978.
(San Jose's 4th choice, 107th overall, in 1997 Entry Draft).

			Regular Season					Playoffs				
Season	Club	Lea	GP	G	A	TP	PIM	GP	G	A	TP	PIM
1994-95	Guelph Platers	OJHL-B	36	1	8	9	92	....	....	....	....	....
1995-96	Royal York	OPJHL	32	8	8	16	93	....	....	....	....	....
	Niagara Falls	OHL	39	3	3	6	74	10	0	3	3	39
1996-97	Erie Otters	OHL	46	8	11	19	194	....	....	....	....	....
1997-98	Erie Otters	OHL	48	11	17	28	*309	7	0	0	0	19
1998-99	Mississauga	OHL	34	15	16	31	235	....	....	....	....	....
	Sault Ste. Marie	OHL	21	3	8	11	101	5	1	2	3	30
99-2000	Kentucky	AHL	29	2	4	6	116	....	....	....	....	....
	New Orleans	ECHL	26	2	3	5	96	3	0	1	1	28
2000-01	Dayton Bombers	ECHL	9	0	0	0	30	....	....	....	....	....
	Kentucky	AHL	40	2	0	2	203	....	....	....	....	....

NOLAN, Brandon (NOH-lan, BRAN-duhn) N.J.

Center. Shoots left. 6', 175 lbs. Born, Sault Ste. Marie, Ont., July 18, 1983.
(New Jersey's 6th choice, 72nd overall, in 2001 Entry Draft).

			Regular Season					Playoffs				
Season	Club	Lea	GP	G	A	TP	PIM	GP	G	A	TP	PIM
99-2000	St. Catharines	OJHL-B	47	18	13	31	10	....	....	....	....	....
2000-01	Oshawa Generals	OHL	52	15	23	38	21	....	....	....	....	....

NORDGREN, Niklas (NORHD-grehn, NIHK-lahs) CAR.

Left wing. Shoots right. 5'11", 190 lbs. Born, Ornskoldsvik, Sweden, June 28, 1979.
(Carolina's 7th choice, 195th overall, in 1997 Entry Draft).

			Regular Season					Playoffs				
Season	Club	Lea	GP	G	A	TP	PIM	GP	G	A	TP	PIM
1995-96	MoDo Hockey-B	Swede-Jr.	30	37	27	64	....	....	....	....	....	....
1996-97	MoDo Hockey	Swede-Jr.	22	14	6	20	....	....	....	....	....	....
	MoDo Hockey	Sweden	5	0	0	0	0	....	....	....	....	....
1997-98	MoDo Hockey	Swede-Jr.	28	15	15	30	52	....	....	....	....	....
1998-99	MoDo Hockey	Swede-2	22	7	4	11	22	3	2	1	3	0
	MoDo Hockey	Sweden	7	0	0	0	2	....	....	....	....	....
99-2000	Sundsvall IK	Swede-2	27	21	11	32	58	....	....	....	....	....
	MoDo Hockey	EuroHL	1	0	0	0	0	1	0	0	0	0
2000-01	Sundsvall IK	Swede-2	35	22	19	41	45	....	....	....	....	....

NORDQVIST, Jonas (NAWRD-kvihst, YOH-nuhs) CHI.

Center. Shoots left. 6'2", 198 lbs. Born, Leksand, Sweden, April 26, 1982.
(Chicago's 3rd choice, 49th overall, in 2000 Entry Draft).

			Regular Season					Playoffs				
Season	Club	Lea	GP	G	A	TP	PIM	GP	G	A	TP	PIM
1997-98	Leksands IF	Swede-Jr.	42	26	35	61	....	....	....	....	....	....
1998-99	Leksands IF	Swede-Jr.	32	14	25	39	....	....	....	....	....	....
99-2000	Leksands IF	Swede-Jr.	34	15	24	39	32	2	0	0	0	2
	Leksands IF	Sweden	3	0	0	0	0	....	....	....	....	....
2000-01	Leksands IF	Swede-Jr.	10	6	13	19	6	5	1	6	7	2
	Leksands IF	Sweden	42	3	4	7	4	....	....	....	....	....

NORRIE, Shaun (NAW-ree, SHAWN) EDM.

Right wing. Shoots right. 6'2", 190 lbs. Born, Calgary, Alta., September 15, 1982.
(Edmonton's 6th choice, 184th overall, in 2000 Entry Draft).

			Regular Season					Playoffs				
Season	Club	Lea	GP	G	A	TP	PIM	GP	G	A	TP	PIM
1998-99	Calgary Royals	AMHL	36	29	37	66	60	....	....	....	....	....
	Calgary Hitmen	WHL	4	0	0	0	0	5	0	0	0	0
99-2000	Calgary Hitmen	WHL	67	12	13	25	94	13	3	2	5	8
2000-01	Calgary Hitmen	WHL	72	24	24	48	106	12	1	2	3	18

NORTON, Brad (NOHR-tohn, BRAD) FLA.

Defense. Shoots left. 6'4", 225 lbs. Born, Cambridge, MA, February 13, 1975.
(Edmonton's 9th choice, 215th overall, in 1993 Entry Draft).

			Regular Season					Playoffs				
Season	Club	Lea	GP	G	A	TP	PIM	GP	G	A	TP	PIM
1992-93	Cushing Academy	Hi-School	31	10	26	36	....	....	....	....	....	....
1994-95	U. Mass-Amherst	H-East	30	0	6	6	89	....	....	....	....	....
1995-96	U. Mass-Amherst	H-East	34	4	12	16	99	....	....	....	....	....
1996-97	U. Mass-Amherst	H-East	35	2	16	18	88	....	....	....	....	....
1997-98	U. Mass-Amherst	H-East	20	2	13	15	28	....	....	....	....	....
	Detroit Vipers	IHL	33	1	4	5	56	22	0	2	2	87
1998-99	Hamilton Bulldogs	AHL	58	1	8	9	134	11	0	1	1	6
99-2000	Hamilton Bulldogs	AHL	40	5	12	17	104	10	1	4	5	26
2000-01	Hamilton Bulldogs	AHL	46	3	15	18	114	....	....	....	....	....

Signed as a free agent by **Florida**, July 27, 2001.

NOVAK, Filip (NOH-vak, FIH-lihp) NYR

Defense. Shoots left. 6', 174 lbs. Born, Ceske Budejovice, Czech., May 7, 1982.
(NY Rangers' 1st choice, 64th overall, in 2000 Entry Draft).

			Regular Season					Playoffs				
Season	Club	Lea	GP	G	A	TP	PIM	GP	G	A	TP	PIM
1998-99	HC Budejovice-Jr.	Cze-Rep	68	8	10	18	34	....	....	....	....	....
99-2000	Regina Pats	WHL	47	7	32	39	70	7	1	4	5	5
2000-01	Regina Pats	WHL	64	17	50	67	75	6	1	4	5	6

WHL East Second All-Star Team (2001)

NOVOTNY, Jiri (NOH-vaht-nee, YOO-ree) **BUF.**

Center. Shoots right. 6'2", 185 lbs. Born, Pelhrimov, Czech., August 12, 1983.
(Buffalo's 1st choice, 22nd overall, in 2001 Entry Draft).

			Regular Season					Playoffs				
Season	Club	Lea	GP	G	A	TP	PIM	GP	G	A	TP	PIM
99-2000	HC Budejovice-Jr.	Cze-Rep	39	11	12	23	14	....	....	....	....	....
2000-01	HC Budejovice-Jr.	Cze-Rep	33	10	10	20	....	....	....	....	....	....

NOWAK, Brett (NOH-wak, BREHT) **BOS.**

Center. Shoots left. 6'2", 192 lbs. Born, New Haven, CT, May 20, 1981.
(Boston's 7th choice, 102nd overall, in 2000 Entry Draft).

			Regular Season					Playoffs				
Season	Club	Lea	GP	G	A	TP	PIM	GP	G	A	TP	PIM
1997-98	Hotchkiss Prep	Hi-School	21	24	42	66	42	....	....	....	....	....
1998-99	Hotchkiss Prep	Hi-School	20	21	36	57	6	....	....	....	....	....
99-2000	Harvard University	ECAC	26	6	11	17	20	....	....	....	....	....
2000-01	Harvard University	ECAC	24	7	9	16	26	....	....	....	....	....

NUUTINEN, Sami (NOO-tih-nehn, SA-mee) **EDM.**

Defense. Shoots left. 6'1", 189 lbs. Born, Espoo, Finland, June 11, 1971.
(Edmonton's 12th choice, 248th overall, in 1990 Entry Draft).

			Regular Season					Playoffs				
Season	Club	Lea	GP	G	A	TP	PIM	GP	G	A	TP	PIM
1988-89	Kiekko Espoo	Finn-Jr.	6	1	7	8	10	4	2	4	6	2
	Kiekko Espoo	Finland-2	39	18	10	28	46	....	....	....	....	....
1989-90	Kiekko Espoo	Finn-Jr.	8	3	5	8	6	5	3	1	4	8
	Kiekko Espoo	Finland-2	40	8	15	23	....	....	....	....	....	....
1990-91	K-Kissat	Finland-2	3	1	0	1	0	....	....	....	....	....
	HIFK Helsinki	Finland	27	1	3	4	6	3	0	0	0	0
1991-92	HIFK Helsinki	Finland	44	5	6	11	10	9	0	1	1	4
1992-93	Kiekko Espoo	Finland	48	7	11	18	59	....	....	....	....	....
1993-94	Kiekko Espoo	Finland	46	9	15	24	36	....	....	....	....	....
1994-95	Kiekko Espoo	Finland	50	8	24	32	38	4	0	1	1	0
1995-96	Kiekko Espoo	Finland	49	7	7	14	54	....	....	....	....	....
1996-97	Vasteras IK	Sweden	50	7	7	14	22	....	....	....	....	....
1997-98	Kiekko Espoo	Finland	48	4	17	21	51	8	0	2	2	6
1998-99	Jokerit Helsinki	Finland	54	10	18	28	22	3	0	2	2	0
99-2000	SB Rosenheim	DEL	52	2	11	13	16	....	....	....	....	....
2000-01	HPK Hameenlinna	Finland	48	3	6	9	52	....	....	....	....	....

NYCHOLAT, Lawrence (NIH-coh-lat, LAW-rehnts) **MIN.**

Defense. Shoots left. 6', 192 lbs. Born, Calgary, Alta., May 7, 1979.

			Regular Season					Playoffs				
Season	Club	Lea	GP	G	A	TP	PIM	GP	G	A	TP	PIM
1995-96	Notre Dame	SMHL	42	10	36	46	66	....	....	....	....	....
1996-97	Swift Current	WHL	67	8	13	21	82	10	0	0	0	24
1997-98	Swift Current	WHL	71	13	35	48	108	1	0	0	0	0
1998-99	Swift Current	WHL	72	16	44	60	125	6	2	2	4	12
99-2000	Swift Current	WHL	70	22	58	80	92	2	0	0	0	0
2000-01	Jackson Bandits	ECHL	5	1	2	3	5	....	....	....	....	....
	Cleveland	IHL	42	3	7	10	69	4	0	0	0	2

Signed as a free agent by **Minnesota**, August 31, 2000.

NYSTROM, David (NEW-strawm, DAY-vihd) **PHI.**

Left wing. Shoots right. 6', 174 lbs. Born, Hagersten, Sweden, February 21, 1980.
(Philadelphia's 6th choice, 224th overall, in 1999 Entry Draft).

			Regular Season					Playoffs				
Season	Club	Lea	GP	G	A	TP	PIM	GP	G	A	TP	PIM
1996-97	Vastra Frolunda	Swede-Jr.	23	6	2	8	....	....	....	....	....	....
1997-98	Vastra Frolunda	Swede-Jr.	29	17	18	35	26	2	0	0	0	0
1998-99	Vastra Frolunda	Swede-Jr.	28	15	16	31	20	....	....	....	....	....
99-2000	Troja IF Ljungby	Swede-2	45	20	15	35	34	2	0	0	0	0
2000-01	Troja IF Ljungby	Swede-2	38	20	11	31	30	4	0	0	0	0

O'CONNOR, Sean (oh-KAW-nuhr, SHAWN) **FLA.**

Right wing. Shoots right. 6'3", 220 lbs. Born, Victoria, B.C., October 19, 1981.
(Florida's 3rd choice, 82nd overall, in 2000 Entry Draft).

			Regular Season					Playoffs				
Season	Club	Lea	GP	G	A	TP	PIM	GP	G	A	TP	PIM
1995-96	Victoria RRC	BCAHA	60	23	45	68	70	....	....	....	....	....
1996-97	Victoria RRC	BCAHA	50	59	73	132	190	....	....	....	....	....
1997-98	Victoria Salsa	BCJHL	50	9	17	26	145	....	....	....	....	....
1998-99	Victoria Salsa	BCJHL	53	17	18	35	197	....	....	....	....	....
99-2000	Moose Jaw	WHL	51	5	8	13	166	2	0	0	0	2
2000-01	Moose Jaw	WHL	71	34	15	49	192	4	0	1	1	15

O'LEARY, Pat (OH-leer-ree, PAT) **PHX.**

Center. Shoots left. 6'2", 190 lbs. Born, Minneapolis, MN, September 2, 1979.
(Phoenix's 3rd choice, 73rd overall, in 1998 Entry Draft).

			Regular Season					Playoffs				
Season	Club	Lea	GP	G	A	TP	PIM	GP	G	A	TP	PIM
1996-97	Robbinsdale	Hi-School	22	28	27	55	42	....	....	....	....	....
1997-98	Robbinsdale	Hi-School	24	22	27	49	28	....	....	....	....	....
1998-99	U. of Minnesota	WCHA	17	0	2	2	8	....	....	....	....	....
99-2000	U. of Minnesota	WCHA	25	6	1	7	8	....	....	....	....	....
2000-01	U. of Minnesota	WCHA	38	5	4	9	44	....	....	....	....	....

OLSON, Josh (OHL-suhn, JAWSH) **FLA.**

Left wing. Shoots left. 6'5", 233 lbs. Born, Grand Forks, ND, July 13, 1981.
(Florida's 6th choice, 190th overall, in 2000 Entry Draft).

			Regular Season					Playoffs				
Season	Club	Lea	GP	G	A	TP	PIM	GP	G	A	TP	PIM
99-2000	Fargo-Moorhead	USHL	18	2	5	7	37	....	....	....	....	....
	Omaha Lancers	USHL	43	6	7	13	44	4	0	0	0	4
2000-01	Portland	WHL	72	22	38	60	86	16	5	4	9	17

OLVESTAD, Jimmie (OHL-vuh-stahd, JIHM-mee) **T.B.**

Left wing. Shoots left. 6'1", 194 lbs. Born, Stockholm, Sweden, February 16, 1980.
(Tampa Bay's 4th choice, 88th overall, in 1999 Entry Draft).

			Regular Season					Playoffs				
Season	Club	Lea	GP	G	A	TP	PIM	GP	G	A	TP	PIM
1996-97	Huddinge IF	Swede-Jr.	40	15	16	31	....	....	....	....	....	....
1997-98	Djurgardens IF	Swede-Jr.	10	3	3	6	10	....	....	....	....	....
	Huddinge IF	Swede-2	11	0	0	0	6	....	....	....	....	....
1998-99	Djurgardens IF	Sweden	44	2	4	6	18	4	0	0	0	8
99-2000	Djurgardens IF	Sweden	50	6	3	9	34	13	1	2	3	12
2000-01	Djurgardens IF	Sweden	50	7	8	15	79	16	7	2	9	14

OLYNICK, Craig (oh-LIHN-ihk, KRAYG) **L.A.**

Defense. Shoots right. 6'1", 185 lbs. Born, Saskatoon, Sask., August 21, 1982.
(Los Angeles' 8th choice, 218th overall, in 2000 Entry Draft).

			Regular Season					Playoffs				
Season	Club	Lea	GP	G	A	TP	PIM	GP	G	A	TP	PIM
1997-98	Humboldt	SAHA	57	37	72	109	230	....	....	....	....	....
1998-99	Seattle T-Birds	WHL	51	1	9	10	89	11	0	0	0	14
99-2000	Seattle T-Birds	WHL	65	1	9	10	120	7	1	0	1	17
2000-01	Seattle T-Birds	WHL	62	5	20	25	105	9	0	2	2	14

OREKHOVSKY, Oleg (oh-reh-KHOHV-skee, OH-lehg) **MIN.**

Defense. Shoots right. 6', 183 lbs. Born, Krasnoyarsk, USSR, November 3, 1977.
(Washington's 11th choice, 206th overall, in 1996 Entry Draft).

			Regular Season					Playoffs				
Season	Club	Lea	GP	G	A	TP	PIM	GP	G	A	TP	PIM
1994-95	Dynamo Moscow	CIS	30	0	1	1	18	....	....	....	....	....
1995-96	Dynamo Moscow	CIS	22	1	2	3	14	8	0	0	0	6
1996-97	Dynamo Moscow	Russia	32	4	2	6	16	4	2	1	3	2
1997-98	Dynamo Moscow	EuroHL	7	2	1	3	12	....	....	....	....	....
	Dynamo Moscow	Russia	40	4	5	9	34	....	....	....	....	....
1998-99	Dynamo Moscow	EuroHL	3	1	1	2	2	6	0	0	0	6
	Dynamo Moscow	Russia	42	1	1	2	22	16	1	2	3	6
99-2000	Dynamo Moscow	EuroHL	6	1	0	1	2	....	....	....	....	....
	Dynamo Moscow	Russia	37	3	6	9	38	15	1	0	1	4
2000-01	Dynamo Moscow	Russia	40	2	4	6	44	....	....	....	....	....

Selected by **Minnesota** from **Washington** in Expansion Draft, June 23, 2000.

ORLOV, Maxim (ohr-LAHF, max-EEM) **WSH.**

Center. Shoots left. 6', 176 lbs. Born, Moscow, USSR, March 31, 1981.
(Washington's 9th choice, 219th overall, in 1999 Entry Draft).

			Regular Season					Playoffs				
Season	Club	Lea	GP	G	A	TP	PIM	GP	G	A	TP	PIM
1998-99	CSKA Moscow	Russia	2	0	0	0	2	1	0	0	0	0
99-2000	CSKA Moscow	Russia	25	0	0	0	2	2	0	0	0	2
2000-01	CSKA Moscow	Russia	41	5	4	9	14	....	....	....	....	....

ORPIK, Brooks (OHR-pihk, BRUKS) **PIT.**

Defense. Shoots left. 6'3", 217 lbs. Born, Amherst, NY, September 26, 1980.
(Pittsburgh's 1st choice, 18th overall, in 2000 Entry Draft).

			Regular Season					Playoffs				
Season	Club	Lea	GP	G	A	TP	PIM	GP	G	A	TP	PIM
1996-97	Thayer Academy	Hi-School	20	4	1	5	....	....	....	....	....	....
1997-98	Thayer Academy	Hi-School	22	0	7	7	....	....	....	....	....	....
1998-99	Boston College	H-East	41	1	10	11	*96	....	....	....	....	....
99-2000	Boston College	H-East	38	1	9	10	102	....	....	....	....	....
2000-01	Boston College	H-East	40	0	20	20	*124	....	....	....	....	....

OTT, Steve (AWT, STEEV) **DAL.**

Center. Shoots left. 6', 160 lbs. Born, Summerside, P.E.I., August 19, 1982.
(Dallas' 1st choice, 25th overall, in 2000 Entry Draft).

			Regular Season					Playoffs				
Season	Club	Lea	GP	G	A	TP	PIM	GP	G	A	TP	PIM
1998-99	Leamington Flyers	OJHL-B	48	14	30	44	110	....	....	....	....	....
99-2000	Windsor Spitfires	OHL	66	23	39	62	131	12	3	5	8	21
2000-01	Windsor Spitfires	OHL	55	50	37	87	164	9	3	8	11	27

OTTOSSON, Kristofer (AW-toh-suhn, KRIHS-tuh-fuhr) **NYI**

Right wing. Shoots left. 5'10", 187 lbs. Born, Stockholm, Sweden, January 9, 1976.
(NY Islanders' 6th choice, 148th overall, in 2000 Entry Draft).

			Regular Season					Playoffs				
Season	Club	Lea	GP	G	A	TP	PIM	GP	G	A	TP	PIM
1993-94	Djurgardens IF	Swede-Jr.	13	3	6	9	4	....	....	....	....	....
1994-95	Djurgardens IF	Swede-Jr.	15	8	23	31	2	....	....	....	....	....
	Djurgardens IF	Sweden	30	0	0	0	2	3	0	0	0	0
1995-96	Djurgardens IF	Swede-Jr.	15	5	12	17	4	....	....	....	....	....
	Djurgardens IF	Sweden	32	1	0	1	2	2	0	0	0	0
1996-97	Arlanda HC	Swede-2	6	6	0	6	0	....	....	....	....	....
	Djurgardens IF	Sweden	20	0	0	0	2	....	....	....	....	....
	Huddinge IF	Swede-2	13	1	3	4	2	2	0	1	1	0
1997-98	Huddinge IF	Swede-2	30	17	20	37	14	....	....	....	....	....
1998-99	Huddinge IF	Swede-2	41	15	19	34	16	....	....	....	....	....
99-2000	Djurgardens IF	Sweden	47	25	15	40	12	13	7	2	9	2
2000-01	Djurgardens IF	Sweden	46	17	24	41	14	14	*7	4	11	4

OUELLET, Michel (oo-LEHT, mih-SHEHL) **PIT.**

Right wing. Shoots right. 6'1", 182 lbs. Born, Rimouski, Que., March 5, 1982.
(Pittsburgh's 4th choice, 124th overall, in 2000 Entry Draft).

			Regular Season					Playoffs				
Season	Club	Lea	GP	G	A	TP	PIM	GP	G	A	TP	PIM
1997-98	Jonquiere Elites	QAAA	33	20	32	52	52	....	....	....	....	....
1998-99	Rimouski Oceanic	QMJHL	28	7	13	20	10	11	0	1	1	6
99-2000	Rimouski Oceanic	QMJHL	72	36	53	89	38	14	4	5	9	14
2000-01	Rimouski Oceanic	QMJHL	63	42	50	92	50	11	6	7	13	8

PAETSCH, Nathan (PASH, NAY-thuhn) **WSH.**

Defense. Shoots left. 6', 195 lbs. Born, Humboldt, Sask., March 30, 1983.
(Washington's 1st choice, 58th overall, in 2001 Entry Draft).

			Regular Season					Playoffs				
Season	Club	Lea	GP	G	A	TP	PIM	GP	G	A	TP	PIM
1998-99	Tisdale Trojans	SMHL	74	20	55	75	120	....	....	....	....	....
	Moose Jaw	WHL	2	0	0	0	0	....	....	....	....	....
99-2000	Moose Jaw	WHL	68	9	35	44	49	4	0	1	1	0
2000-01	Moose Jaw	WHL	70	8	54	62	118	4	1	2	3	6

PANDOLFO, Mike (pan-DAHL-foh, MIGHK) **BUF.**

Left wing. Shoots left. 6'3", 226 lbs. Born, Winchester, MA, September 15, 1979.
(Buffalo's 5th choice, 77th overall, in 1998 Entry Draft).

			Regular Season					Playoffs				
Season	Club	Lea	GP	G	A	TP	PIM	GP	G	A	TP	PIM
1996-97	St. Sebastian's	Hi-School	32	27	28	55	30	....	....	....	....	....
1997-98	St. Sebastien's	Hi-School	28	29	23	52	18	....	....	....	....	....
1998-99	Boston University	H-East	34	13	4	17	26	....	....	....	....	....
99-2000	Boston University	H-East	41	13	10	23	37	....	....	....	....	....
2000-01	Boston University	H-East	37	16	13	29	30	....	....	....	....	....

PANOV, Konstantin (PAN-ahv, KAWN-stan-tihn) **NSH.**

Right wing. Shoots left. 6', 193 lbs. Born, Chelyabinsk, USSR, June 29, 1980.
(Nashville's 10th choice, 131st overall, in 1999 Entry Draft).

			Regular Season					Playoffs				
Season	Club	Lea	GP	G	A	TP	PIM	GP	G	A	TP	PIM
1996-97	HC Nadezhda	Russia-3	25	18	30	48	22	....	....	....	....	....
1997-98	Yunior-T Kurgan	Russia-3	20	7	3	10	6	....	....	....	....	....
	HC Chelyabinsk	Russia	6	2	0	2	4	2	0	0	0	0
1998-99	Kamloops Blazers	WHL	62	33	30	63	62	13	5	3	8	10
99-2000	Kamloops Blazers	WHL	64	43	30	73	47	....	....	....	....	....
2000-01	Kamloops Blazers	WHL	69	44	56	100	54	4	1	0	1	2

WHL West Second All-Star Team (2000) • WHL West First All-Star Team (2001)

PANZER, Jeff (PAN-zuhr, JEHF) **ST.L.**

Center. Shoots left. 5'10", 160 lbs. Born, Grand Forks, ND, April 7, 1978.

			Regular Season					Playoffs				
Season	Club	Lea	GP	G	A	TP	PIM	GP	G	A	TP	PIM
1996-97	Fargo-Moorhead	USHL	49	30	40	70	52	6	3	7	10	0
1997-98	North Dakota	WCHA	37	14	23	37	18	....	....	....	....	....
1998-99	North Dakota	WCHA	37	21	26	47	14	....	....	....	....	....
99-2000	North Dakota	WCHA	44	19	*44	63	16	....	....	....	....	....
2000-01	North Dakota	WCHA	46	26	*55	*81	28	....	....	....	....	....

WCHA Second All-Star Team (1999) • WCHA First All-Star Team (2000, 2001) • NCAA West First All-American Team (2000, 2001)

Signed as a free agent by **St. Louis**, April 30, 2001.

PAPINEAU, Justin (PA-pee-noh, JUHS-tihn) **ST.L.**

Center. Shoots left. 5'10", 178 lbs. Born, Ottawa, Ont., January 15, 1980.
(St. Louis' 3rd choice, 75th overall, in 2000 Entry Draft).

			Regular Season					Playoffs				
Season	Club	Lea	GP	G	A	TP	PIM	GP	G	A	TP	PIM
1995-96	Ottawa Jr. Sens	OCJHL	52	31	19	50	51	....	....	....	....	....
1996-97	Belleville Bulls	OHL	50	10	32	42	32	....	....	....	....	....
1997-98	Belleville Bulls	OHL	66	41	53	94	34	10	5	9	14	6
1998-99	Belleville Bulls	OHL	68	52	47	99	28	21	*21	*30	*51	20
99-2000	Belleville Bulls	OHL	60	40	36	76	52	16	4	12	16	16
2000-01	Worcester	AHL	43	7	22	29	33	11	7	3	10	8

• Re-entered NHL Entry Draft. Originally Los Angeles' 2nd choice, 46th overall, in 1998 Entry Draft.

PAROULEK, Martin (pa-ROH-oo-lek, MAHR-tihn) **CBJ**

Right wing. Shoots left. 5'11", 189 lbs. Born, Uherske Hradiste, Czech., November 4, 1979.
(Columbus' 9th choice, 278th overall, in 2000 Entry Draft).

			Regular Season					Playoffs				
Season	Club	Lea	GP	G	A	TP	PIM	GP	G	A	TP	PIM
1998-99	HC Vsetin-Jr.	Cze-Rep	45	25	19	44	....	....	....	....	....	....
	HC Vsetin	Cze-Rep.	11	1	1	2	....	7	0	1	1	0
99-2000	HC Vsetin	Cze-Rep.	48	11	14	25	24	8	1	1	2	4
2000-01	HC Vsetin	Cze-Rep.	28	10	4	14	16	14	3	3	6	10

PARROS, George (PAIR-ohs, JOHRJ) **L.A.**

Right wing. Shoots right. 6'4", 210 lbs. Born, Washington, PA, December 29, 1979.
(Los Angeles' 9th choice, 222nd overall, in 1999 Entry Draft).

			Regular Season					Playoffs				
Season	Club	Lea	GP	G	A	TP	PIM	GP	G	A	TP	PIM
1998-99	Chicago Freeze	NAJHL	54	30	20	50	126	....	....	....	....	....
99-2000	Princeton Tigers	ECAC	27	4	2	6	14	....	....	....	....	....
2000-01	Princeton Tigers	ECAC	31	7	10	17	38	....	....	....	....	....

NAJHL All-Rookie Team (1999) • Won NAJHL Rookie of the Year Award (1999)

PARSONS, Steve **PIT.**

Left wing. Shoots left. 6'4", 235 lbs. Born, Vancouver, B.C., March 12, 1975.

			Regular Season					Playoffs				
Season	Club	Lea	GP	G	A	TP	PIM	GP	G	A	TP	PIM
1994-95	Laval Titans	QMJHL	27	0	1	1	176	14	0	0	0	52
1995-96	Nanaimo	BCJHL	48	18	36	54	275	....	....	....	....	....
1996-97	Reno Renegades	WCHL	7	0	1	1	27	....	....	....	....	....
	Bakersfield Fog	WCHL	5	0	1	1	38	....	....	....	....	....
1997-98	Concordia College	ACAC	STATISTICS NOT AVAILABLE									
1998-99	Concordia College	ACAC	25	6	20	26	178	....	....	....	....	....
99-2000	Madison Monsters	UHL	39	3	6	9	241	....	....	....	....	....
	Milwaukee	IHL	2	0	1	1	2	....	....	....	....	....
	Fort Wayne	UHL	17	0	3	3	108	11	0	0	0	29
2000-01	Wheeling	ECHL	19	5	4	9	178	....	....	....	....	....
	Wilkes-Barre	AHL	4	0	0	0	12	....	....	....	....	....
	Hershey Bears	AHL	30	1	0	1	98	1	0	0	0	0

Signed to 25-game contract by **Wilkes-Barre** (AHL), October 4, 2000. Released by **Wilkes-Barre** (AHL) and assigned to **Wheeling** (ECHL), November 6, 2000. Signed to 25-game try-out contract by **Hershey** (AHL), January 9, 2001. Signed as a free agent by **Pittsburgh**, July 30, 2001.

PARSSINEN, Timo (pahr-SIH-nehn, TEE-moh) **ANA.**

Left wing. Shoots left. 5'10", 176 lbs. Born, Lohjan mlk., Finland, January 19, 1977.
(Anaheim's 4th choice, 102nd overall, in 2001 Entry Draft).

			Regular Season					Playoffs				
Season	Club	Lea	GP	G	A	TP	PIM	GP	G	A	TP	PIM
1994-95	TuTu Turku	Finn-Jr.	14	9	6	15	33	....	....	....	....	....
	TuTu Turku	Finland	1	1	0	1	0	....	....	....	....	....
1995-96	TuTu Turku	Finn-Jr.	14	18	15	33	12	11	12	6	18	36
	TuTu Turku	Finland	7	0	0	0	4	....	....	....	....	....
1996-97	TuTu Turku	Finland-2	39	21	29	50	30	....	....	....	....	....
	TuTu Turku	Finn-Jr.	....	....	....	....	....	9	2	14	16	36
1997-98	Hermes Kokkola	Finland-2	46	29	39	68	66	3	1	0	1	4
1998-99	HPK Hameenlinna	Finland	46	15	24	39	46	8	2	3	5	8
99-2000	HPK Hameenlinna	Finland	53	25	27	52	60	8	5	5	10	8
2000-01	HPK Hameenlinna	Finland	54	18	31	49	48	....	....	....	....	....

PAUL, Jeff (PAWL, JEHF) **COL.**

Defense. Shoots right. 6'3", 200 lbs. Born, London, Ont., March 1, 1978.
(Chicago's 2nd choice, 42nd overall, in 1996 Entry Draft).

			Regular Season					Playoffs				
Season	Club	Lea	GP	G	A	TP	PIM	GP	G	A	TP	PIM
1993-94	Woodstock	OJHL-C	36	1	6	7	73	....	....	....	....	....
1994-95	Niagara Falls	OHL	57	3	10	13	64	6	0	2	2	0
1995-96	Niagara Falls	OHL	48	1	7	8	81	10	0	4	4	37
1996-97	Erie Otters	OHL	60	4	23	27	152	5	2	0	2	12
1997-98	Erie Otters	OHL	48	3	17	20	108	7	0	2	2	13
1998-99	Portland Pirates	AHL	6	0	0	0	4	....	....	....	....	....
	Indianapolis Ice	IHL	55	0	7	7	120	7	0	2	2	12
99-2000	Cleveland	IHL	69	6	6	12	210	9	1	0	1	12
2000-01	Norfolk Admirals	AHL	59	5	6	11	171	9	0	2	2	12

Signed as a free agent by **Colorado**, August 8, 2001.

PAVLOV, Yevgeny (pahv-lohv, YEHV-jeh-nee) **NSH.**

Center. Shoots right. 6'1", 201 lbs. Born, Togliatti, USSR, January 10, 1981.
(Nashville's 8th choice, 121st overall, in 1999 Entry Draft).

			Regular Season					Playoffs				
Season	Club	Lea	GP	G	A	TP	PIM	GP	G	A	TP	PIM
1997-98	Lada Togliatti-2	Russia-3	27	8	1	9	4	....	....	....	....	....
1998-99	Lada Togliatti-2	Russia-4	33	17	3	20	8	....	....	....	....	....
	Lada Togliatti	Russia	9	0	1	1	2	....	....	....	....	....
99-2000	Lada Togliatti-2	Russia-3	55	30	17	47	18	....	....	....	....	....
	Salavat Ufa	Russia	5	1	0	1	10	....	....	....	....	....
	Lada Togliatti	Russia	2	0	0	0	0	1	0	0	0	0
2000-01	Lada Togliatti	Russia	28	2	1	3	4	....	....	....	....	....

PEAT, Stephen (PEET, STEEV-vuhn) **WSH.**

Defense. Shoots right. 6'3", 210 lbs. Born, Princeton, B.C., March 10, 1980.
(Anaheim's 2nd choice, 32nd overall, in 1998 Entry Draft).

			Regular Season					Playoffs				
Season	Club	Lea	GP	G	A	TP	PIM	GP	G	A	TP	PIM
1995-96	Langley Thunder	BCJHL	59	5	15	20	112	....	....	....	....	....
	Red Deer Rebels	WHL	1	0	0	0	0	....	....	....	....	....
1996-97	Red Deer Rebels	WHL	68	3	14	17	161	16	0	2	2	22
1997-98	Red Deer Rebels	WHL	63	6	12	18	189	5	0	0	0	8
1998-99	Red Deer Rebels	WHL	31	2	6	8	98	....	....	....	....	....
	Tri-City Americans	WHL	5	0	0	0	19	....	....	....	....	....
99-2000	Tri-City Americans	WHL	12	0	2	2	48	....	....	....	....	....
	Calgary Hitmen	WHL	23	0	8	8	100	13	0	1	1	33
2000-01	Portland Pirates	AHL	6	0	0	0	16	....	....	....	....	....

Rights traded to **Washington** by **Anaheim** for Washington's 4th round choice (later traded to Montreal - later traded to Pittsburgh - Pittsburgh selected Michel Ouellet) in 2000 Entry Draft, June 1, 2000.

PECKER, Cory (PEH-kuhr, KOH-ree)

Center. Shoots right. 6', 190 lbs. Born, Montreal, Que., March 20, 1981.
(Calgary's 7th choice, 166th overall, in 1999 Entry Draft).

			Regular Season					Playoffs				
Season	Club	Lea	GP	G	A	TP	PIM	GP	G	A	TP	PIM
1995-96	Lac St-Louis	QAAA	5	0	0	0	0	....	....	....	....	....
1996-97	Lac St-Louis	QAAA	40	30	40	70	....	7	4	2	6	....
1997-98	Sault Ste. Marie	OHL	29	3	4	7	15	....	....	....	....	....
1998-99	Sault Ste. Marie	OHL	68	25	34	59	24	5	1	2	3	2
99-2000	Sault Ste. Marie	OHL	65	33	36	69	38	12	6	8	14	8
2000-01	Sault Ste. Marie	OHL	31	24	16	40	37	....	....	....	....	....
	Erie Otters	OHL	30	17	22	39	32	15	14	9	23	16

OHL Second All-Star Team (2001)

• Missed majority of 1997-98 season after being diagnosed with Chron's Disease. • Traded to **Erie** by **Sault Ste. Marie** for Troy Ilijow, Patrick Lamesse and Erie's 4th round choice in 2002 OHL Priority Draft, January 3, 2001.

PELUSO, Mike (puh-LOO-soh, MIGHK) **CHI.**

Right wing. Shoots right. 6'1", 208 lbs. Born, Bismark, ND, September 2, 1974.
(Calgary's 12th choice, 253rd overall, in 1994 Entry Draft).

			Regular Season					Playoffs				
Season	Club	Lea	GP	G	A	TP	PIM	GP	G	A	TP	PIM
1993-94	Omaha Lancers	USHL	48	36	29	65	77	....	....	....	....	....
1994-95	Minnesota-Duluth	WCHA	38	11	23	34	38	....	....	....	....	....
1995-96	Minnesota-Duluth	WCHA	38	25	19	44	64	....	....	....	....	....
1996-97	Minnesota-Duluth	WCHA	37	20	20	40	53	....	....	....	....	....
1997-98	Minnesota-Duluth	WCHA	40	24	21	45	100	....	....	....	....	....
1998-99	Portland Pirates	AHL	26	7	6	13	6	....	....	....	....	....
99-2000	Portland Pirates	AHL	71	25	29	54	86	4	2	0	2	0
2000-01	Portland Pirates	AHL	19	12	10	22	17	....	....	....	....	....
	Worcester	AHL	44	17	23	40	22	11	3	3	6	4

WCHA Second All-Star Team (1997)

Signed as a free agent by **Washington**, October 9, 1998. Traded to **St. Louis** by **Washington** with future considerations for Derek Bekar and future considerations, November 29, 2000. Signed as a free agent by **Chicago**, August 1, 2001.

PEREZHOGIN, Alexander (pehr-eh-ZHO-ghin, al-ehx-AN-duhr) **MTL.**

Right wing. Shoots left. 6', 185 lbs. Born, Ust-Kamenogorsk, USSR, August 10, 1983.
(Montreal's 2nd choice, 25th overall, in 2001 Entry Draft).

			Regular Season					Playoffs				
Season	Club	Lea	GP	G	A	TP	PIM	GP	G	A	TP	PIM
1998-99	VDV Omsk-2	Russia-3	4	0	1	1	0	....	....	....	....	....
	Avangard Omsk	Russia-2	22	12	11	23	12	....	....	....	....	....
99-2000	Avangard Omsk	Russia-2	22	12	11	23	12	....	....	....	....	....
	Avangard Omsk	Russia	1	0	0	0	0	....	....	....	....	....
2000-01	Avangard Omsk	Russia-Jr.	6	1	5	6	4	....	....	....	....	....
	VDV Omsk-2	Russia-3	41	47	24	71	40	....	....	....	....	....
	Avangard Omsk	Russia	....	....	....	....	....	1	0	0	0	0

PERIARD, Michel (pair-EE-ahr, mee-SHEHL) FLA.

Defense. Shoots left. 6', 178 lbs. Born, Montreal, Que., November 10, 1979.
(Ottawa's 8th choice, 188th overall, in 1998 Entry Draft).

			Regular Season					Playoffs				
Season	Club	Lea	GP	G	A	TP	PIM	GP	G	A	TP	PIM
1996-97	Charles-Lemoyne	QAAA	40	8	15	23	64	15	7	20	27	....
1997-98	Shawinigan	QMJHL	68	14	30	44	64	5	0	0	0	18
1998-99	Shawinigan	QMJHL	64	14	40	54	90	6	1	2	3	4
99-2000	Rimouski Oceanic	QMJHL	70	25	75	100	58	14	5	17	22	16
2000-01	Louisville Panthers	AHL	7	0	1	1	0	....	....	....	....	....
	Port Huron	UHL	23	1	8	9	30	....	....	....	....	....
	Rockford IceHogs	UHL	31	3	14	17	20	....	....	....	....	....

QMJHL First All-Star Team (2000) • Canadian Major Junior First All-Star Team (2000) • Memorial Cup All-Star Team (2000)

Signed as a free agent by **Florida**, August 1, 2000.

PERREAULT, Joel ANA.

Right wing. Shoots right. 6'1", 163 lbs. Born, Montreal, Que., April 6, 1983.
(Anaheim's 7th choice, 137th overall, in 2001 Entry Draft).

			Regular Season					Playoffs				
Season	Club	Lea	GP	G	A	TP	PIM	GP	G	A	TP	PIM
2000-01	Baie Comeau	QMJHL	68	10	14	24	46	11	1	1	2	10

PERROTT, Nathan (PEHR-roht, NAY-than) CHI.

Right wing. Shoots right. 6', 215 lbs. Born, Owen Sound, Ont., December 8, 1976.
(New Jersey's 2nd choice, 44th overall, in 1995 Entry Draft).

			Regular Season					Playoffs				
Season	Club	Lea	GP	G	A	TP	PIM	GP	G	A	TP	PIM
1992-93	Walkerton	OJHL-C	25	6	13	19	45	....	....	....	....	....
1993-94	St. Mary's	OJHL-B	41	11	26	37	249	....	....	....	....	....
1994-95	Oshawa Generals	OHL	63	18	28	46	233	2	1	1	2	9
1995-96	Oshawa Generals	OHL	59	30	32	62	158	5	2	3	5	8
	Albany River Rats	AHL	4	0	0	0	12	....	....	....	....	....
1996-97	Oshawa Generals	OHL	5	1	0	1	17	....	....	....	....	....
	Sault Ste. Marie	OHL	37	18	23	41	120	11	5	5	10	60
1997-98	Indianapolis Ice	IHL	31	4	3	7	76	....	....	....	....	....
	Jacksonville	ECHL	30	6	8	14	135	....	....	....	....	....
1998-99	Indianapolis Ice	IHL	72	14	11	25	307	7	3	1	4	45
99-2000	Cleveland	IHL	65	12	9	21	248	9	2	1	3	19
2000-01	Norfolk Admirals	AHL	73	11	17	28	268	9	2	0	2	18

Signed as a free agent by **Chicago**, August 27, 1997.

PERRY, Scott (PEHR-ree, SCAWT) DAL.

Center. Shoots left. 6', 180 lbs. Born, Boston, MA, October 12, 1978.
(Dallas' 6th choice, 200th overall, in 1998 Entry Draft).

			Regular Season					Playoffs				
Season	Club	Lea	GP	G	A	TP	PIM	GP	G	A	TP	PIM
1996-97	Thayer Academy	Hi-School	STATISTICS NOT AVAILABLE									
1997-98	Boston University	H-East	38	5	12	17	18	....	....	....	....	....
1998-99	Boston University	H-East	33	4	8	12	26	....	....	....	....	....
99-2000	Boston University	H-East	40	0	3	3	18	....	....	....	....	....
2000-01	Boston University	H-East	23	0	3	3	8	....	....	....	....	....

PETERS, Andrew (PEE-tuhrs, AN-droo) BUF.

Left wing. Shoots left. 6'4", 213 lbs. Born, St. Catharines, Ont., May 5, 1980.
(Buffalo's 2nd choice, 34th overall, in 1998 Entry Draft).

			Regular Season					Playoffs				
Season	Club	Lea	GP	G	A	TP	PIM	GP	G	A	TP	PIM
1996-97	Georgetown	OPJHL	46	11	16	27	65	....	....	....	....	....
1997-98	Oshawa Generals	OHL	60	11	7	18	220	7	2	0	2	19
1998-99	Oshawa Generals	OHL	54	14	10	24	137	15	2	7	9	36
99-2000	Kitchener	OHL	42	6	13	19	95	4	0	1	1	14
2000-01	Rochester	AHL	49	0	4	4	118	....	....	....	....	....

PETERS, Dan (PEE-tuhrs, DAN) PHI.

Defense. Shoots left. 5'10", 183 lbs. Born, Cottage Grove, MN, November 24, 1977.

			Regular Season					Playoffs				
Season	Club	Lea	GP	G	A	TP	PIM	GP	G	A	TP	PIM
1995-96	Omaha Lancers	USHL	54	11	36	47	....	....	....	....	....	....
1996-97	Colorado College	WCHA	36	4	12	16	62	....	....	....	....	....
1997-98	Colorado College	WCHA	37	5	16	21	108	....	....	....	....	....
1998-99	Colorado College	WCHA	36	8	21	29	82	....	....	....	....	....
99-2000	Colorado College	WCHA	27	2	8	10	58	....	....	....	....	....
2000-01	Philadelphia	AHL	73	2	14	16	71	6	1	4	5	8

WCHA Second All-Star Team (1999)

Signed as a free agent by **Philadelphia**, May 5, 2000.

PETERS, Geoff (PEE-tuhrs, JEHF)

Center. Shoots left. 6'1", 185 lbs. Born, Hamilton, Ont., April 30, 1978.
(Chicago's 3rd choice, 46th overall, in 1996 Entry Draft).

			Regular Season					Playoffs				
Season	Club	Lea	GP	G	A	TP	PIM	GP	G	A	TP	PIM
1993-94	Wexford Hawks	MTHL	34	39	26	65	26	....	....	....	....	....
1994-95	Niagara Falls	OHL	57	11	9	20	37	6	2	0	2	4
1995-96	Niagara Falls	OHL	64	25	34	59	51	10	4	4	8	8
1996-97	Erie Otters	OHL	28	12	10	22	39	5	1	3	4	7
1997-98	Erie Otters	OHL	31	15	11	26	36	....	....	....	....	....
	North Bay	OHL	20	11	14	25	22	....	....	....	....	....
	Indianapolis Ice	IHL	2	0	0	0	10	....	....	....	....	....
1998-99	Canada	Nat-Team	38	9	4	13	50	....	....	....	....	....
	Portland Pirates	AHL	4	1	1	2	9	....	....	....	....	....
99-2000	Cleveland	IHL	68	10	4	14	87	7	0	3	3	4
2000-01	Norfolk Admirals	AHL	73	11	10	21	48	6	0	1	1	6

PETIOT, Richard (PEH-tee-awt, RIH-chuhrd) L.A.

Defense. Shoots left. 6'2", 190 lbs. Born, Daysland, Alta., August 20, 1982.
(Los Angeles' 6th choice, 116th overall, in 2001 Entry Draft).

			Regular Season					Playoffs				
Season	Club	Lea	GP	G	A	TP	PIM	GP	G	A	TP	PIM
99-2000	Camrose Nordics	AAHA	STATISTICS NOT AVAILABLE									
2000-01	Camrose Kodiacs	AJHL	55	8	16	24	81	8	2	1	3	8

AJHL All-Rookie Team (2001) • AJHL South Second All-Star Team (2001)

PETRAKOV, Andrei (peh-trah-KAHF, AN-dray) ST.L.

Right wing. Shoots left. 6', 204 lbs. Born, Sverdlovsk, USSR, April 26, 1976.
(St. Louis' 4th choice, 97th overall, in 1996 Entry Draft).

			Regular Season					Playoffs				
Season	Club	Lea	GP	G	A	TP	PIM	GP	G	A	TP	PIM
1992-93	HC Yekaterinburg	CIS	5	0	0	0	0	1	0	0	0	0
1993-94	HC Yekaterinburg	CIS	35	4	2	6	10	....	....	....	....	....
1994-95	HC Yekaterinburg	CIS	11	1	1	2	6	1	0	0	0	0
1995-96	HC Yekaterinburg	CIS-2	52	17	6	23	14	....	....	....	....	....
1996-97	HC Yekaterinburg	Russia	14	6	1	7	6	....	....	....	....	....
	HC Magnitogorsk	Russia	18	4	0	4	8	6	0	0	0	0
1997-98	CSK Samara	Russia	9	0	0	0	4	....	....	....	....	....
	HC Magnitogorsk	Russia	29	9	11	20	0	....	....	....	....	....
1998-99	Worcester	AHL	4	0	1	1	2	....	....	....	....	....
	HC Magnitogorsk	Russia	10	4	4	8	8	15	4	8	12	4
	Muskegon Fury	UHL	5	4	3	7	0	....	....	....	....	....
	Fort Wayne	IHL	11	2	4	6	0	....	....	....	....	....
99-2000	HC Magnitogorsk	Russia	27	9	12	21	20	2	0	1	1	2
2000-01	HC Magnitogorsk	Russia	10	2	4	6	4	....	....	....	....	....
	Peoria Rivermen	ECHL	12	2	2	4	0	....	....	....	....	....

PETRASEK, David (PEH-truh-sehk, DAY-vihd) DET.

Defense. Shoots right. 6', 187 lbs. Born, Jonkoping, Sweden, February 1, 1976.
(Detroit's 10th choice, 226th overall, in 1998 Entry Draft).

			Regular Season					Playoffs				
Season	Club	Lea	GP	G	A	TP	PIM	GP	G	A	TP	PIM
1993-94	HV Jonkoping	Swede-Jr.	14	3	3	6	26	....	....	....	....	....
1994-95	HV Jonkoping	Swede-Jr.	19	8	9	17	55	....	....	....	....	....
	HV Jonkoping	Sweden	30	0	1	1	6	11	0	0	0	0
1995-96	HV Jonkoping	Swede-Jr.	12	1	5	6	16	....	....	....	....	....
	HV Jonkoping	Sweden	36	0	1	1	14	1	0	0	0	0
1996-97	HV Jonkoping	Swede-Jr.	3	0	0	0	....	....	....	....	....	....
	HV Jonkoping	Sweden	49	2	4	6	14	5	0	0	0	4
1997-98	HV Jonkoping	Sweden	43	6	7	13	80	5	2	2	4	14
1998-99	HV Jonkoping	Sweden	45	3	4	7	48	....	....	....	....	....
99-2000	HV Jonkoping	Sweden	46	4	6	10	54	5	1	1	2	41
2000-01	Malmo IF	Sweden	47	7	7	14	74	9	1	1	2	8

PETRE, Henrik (PEH-truh, HEHN-rihk) WSH.

Defense. Shoots left. 6'1", 187 lbs. Born, Stockholm, Sweden, April 9, 1979.
(Washington's 5th choice, 143rd overall, in 1997 Entry Draft).

			Regular Season					Playoffs				
Season	Club	Lea	GP	G	A	TP	PIM	GP	G	A	TP	PIM
1995-96	Djurgardens IF	Swede-Jr.	21	6	4	10	8	....	....	....	....	....
1996-97	Djurgardens IF	Swede-Jr.	20	7	6	13	....	....	....	....	....	....
1997-98	Huddinge IF	Swede-2	30	4	4	8	30	....	....	....	....	....
	Djurgardens IF	Sweden	3	0	0	0	0	....	....	....	....	....
1998-99	Huddinge IF	Swede-2	14	0	1	1	20	....	....	....	....	....
	Djurgardens IF	Sweden	9	0	0	0	10	....	....	....	....	....
99-2000	Brynas IF	Sweden	47	3	3	6	73	11	1	0	1	12
	Brynas IF	EuroHL	5	0	2	2	4	....	....	....	....	....
2000-01	Brynas IF	Sweden	27	2	3	5	20	4	0	1	1	27

PETRILAINEN, Pasi (peh-trih-LAI-nehn, PAH-see) N.J.

Defense. Shoots left. 5'10", 185 lbs. Born, Tampere, Finland, May 5, 1978.
(New Jersey's 14th choice, 225th overall, in 1996 Entry Draft).

			Regular Season					Playoffs				
Season	Club	Lea	GP	G	A	TP	PIM	GP	G	A	TP	PIM
1992-93	Tappara Tampere	Finn-Jr.	1	0	0	0	2	....	....	....	....	....
1993-94	HC Tampere-C	Finn-Jr.	30	6	20	26	36	7	2	4	6	4
	Tappara Tampere	Finn-Jr.	2	0	0	0	0	....	....	....	....	....
1994-95	HC Tampere-B	Finn-Jr.	8	1	5	6	4	7	1	3	4	2
	Tappara Tampere	Finn-Jr.	14	3	4	7	6	....	....	....	....	....
	Tappara Tampere	Finland	25	3	0	3	14	....	....	....	....	....
1995-96	Tappara Tampere	Finn-Jr.	5	0	2	2	4	....	....	....	....	....
	Tappara Tampere	Finland	40	0	4	4	18	4	0	0	0	2
	HC Tampere-B	Finn-Jr.	....	....	....	....	....	1	1	1	2	2
1996-97	Tappara Tampere	Finland	43	2	9	11	46	3	0	0	0	2
1997-98	Tappara Tampere	Finland	48	4	7	11	34	4	0	0	0	4
1998-99	Tappara Tampere	Finland	35	3	3	6	26	....	....	....	....	....
99-2000	Tappara Tampere	Finland	39	1	9	10	22	4	0	1	1	0
2000-01	Timra IK	Sweden	49	3	10	13	22	....	....	....	....	....

PETROCHININ, Evgeny (peht-roh-CHIH-nihn, ehv-GEH-nee) DAL.

Defense. Shoots left. 6'2", 190 lbs. Born, Murmansk, USSR, February 7, 1976.
(Dallas' 5th choice, 150th overall, in 1994 Entry Draft).

			Regular Season					Playoffs				
Season	Club	Lea	GP	G	A	TP	PIM	GP	G	A	TP	PIM
1993-94	Krylja Sovetov	CIS	2	0	0	0	0	....	....	....	....	....
1994-95	Krylja Sovetov	CIS	45	0	2	2	14	....	....	....	....	....
1995-96	Krylja Sovetov	CIS	50	5	17	22	18	5	3	0	3	0
1996-97	Krylja Sovetov	Russia	32	5	6	11	52	....	....	....	....	....
1997-98	Krylja Sovetov	Russia	46	12	6	18	100	....	....	....	....	....
1998-99	Krylja Sovetov	Russia	21	4	6	10	14	....	....	....	....	....
	Ak Bars Kazan	Russia	6	0	2	2	2	9	1	1	2	24
99-2000	HC Novokuznetsk	Russia	33	7	10	17	38	14	2	1	3	26
2000-01	HC Cherepovets	Russia	40	8	7	15	38	9	2	0	2	40

PETTINEN, Tomi (peh-TIHN-ehn, TAW-mee) NYI

Defense. Shoots left. 6'3", 211 lbs. Born, Ylojarvi, Finland, June 17, 1977.
(NY Islanders' 9th choice, 267th overall, in 2000 Entry Draft).

			Regular Season					Playoffs				
Season	Club	Lea	GP	G	A	TP	PIM	GP	G	A	TP	PIM
1993-94	Ilves Tampere-C	Finn-Jr.	31	2	2	4	4	....	....	....	....	....
1994-95	Ilves Tampere-B	Finn-Jr.	31	1	6	7	46	4	0	0	0	2
	Ilves Tampere	Finn-Jr.	1	0	0	0	0	....	....	....	....	....
1995-96	Ilves Tampere	Finn-Jr.	21	0	0	0	64	....	....	....	....	....
	Ilves Tampere-2	Finn-Jr.	....	....	....	....	....	12	1	1	2	18
1996-97	Ilves Tampere	Finn-Jr.	26	3	8	11	44	....	....	....	....	....
	Ilves Tampere	Finland	16	1	0	1	12	....	....	....	....	....
1997-98	Ilves Tampere	Finn-Jr.	14	1	4	5	24	....	....	....	....	....
	Ilves Tampere	Finland	3	0	0	0	0	....	....	....	....	....
	Lukko Rauma	Finn-Jr.	11	2	6	8	14	....	....	....	....	....
	Lukko Rauma	Finland-2	4	0	0	0	2	....	....	....	....	....
	Lukko Rauma	Finland	27	0	2	2	16	....	....	....	....	....
1998-99	Hermes Kokkala	Finland-2	42	8	6	14	76	3	0	0	0	6
	HIFK Helsinki	Finland	4	0	0	0	2	....	....	....	....	....
99-2000	Ilves Tampere	Finland	51	1	6	7	78	3	1	2	3	2
2000-01	Ilves Tampere	Finland	56	2	2	4	86	9	0	0	0	4

PHILLIPS, Greg (FIHL-ihps, GREHG) **L.A.**

Right wing. Shoots right. 6'2", 205 lbs. Born, Winnipeg, Man., March 27, 1978.
(Los Angeles' 3rd choice, 57th overall, in 1996 Entry Draft).

			Regular Season					Playoffs				
Season	Club	Lea	GP	G	A	TP	PIM	GP	G	A	TP	PIM
1993-94	Winnipeg Lions	MAHA	21	12	4	16	51	....	....	....	....	....
1994-95	Saskatoon Blades	WHL	64	3	5	8	94	10	0	0	0	4
1995-96	Saskatoon Blades	WHL	67	21	24	45	132	4	1	2	3	2
1996-97	Saskatoon Blades	WHL	34	17	19	36	64	....	....	....	....	....
1997-98	Saskatoon Blades	WHL	47	24	28	52	116	....	....	....	....	....
	Brandon	WHL	22	10	21	31	49	18	11	11	22	58
1998-99	Springfield	AHL	63	16	13	29	74	3	0	0	0	4
99-2000	Lowell	AHL	62	20	10	30	140	7	3	0	3	10
2000-01	Lowell	AHL	33	5	5	10	33	....	....	....	....	....

PIHLMAN, Tuomas (PIHL-mahn, too-AH-muhs) **N.J.**

Right wing. Shoots left. 6'2", 205 lbs. Born, Espoo, Finland, November 13, 1982.
(New Jersey's 3rd choice, 48th overall, in 2001 Entry Draft).

			Regular Season					Playoffs				
Season	Club	Lea	GP	G	A	TP	PIM	GP	G	A	TP	PIM
1997-98	JyP Jyvaskyla-B	Finn-Jr.	30	2	5	7	18	4	1	3	4	6
1998-99	JyP Jyvaskyla-B	Finn-Jr.	35	21	20	41	64	6	1	1	2	12
99-2000	JyP Jyvaskyla	Finn-Jr.	20	4	4	8	54	4	0	0	0	8
	JyP Jyvaskyla	Finland	17	0	0	0	18	....	....	....	....	....
2000-01	JyP Jyvaskyla	Finn-Jr.	1	1	0	1	0	....	....	....	....	....
	JyP Jyvaskyla	Finland	47	3	6	9	59	....	....	....	....	....

PILAR, Karel (PEE-lahr, KAH-rehl) **TOR.**

Defense. Shoots right. 6'3", 207 lbs. Born, Prague, Czech., December 23, 1977.
(Toronto's 2nd choice, 39th overall, in 2001 Entry Draft).

			Regular Season					Playoffs				
Season	Club	Lea	GP	G	A	TP	PIM	GP	G	A	TP	PIM
99-2000	CHZ Litvinov	Cze-Rep	49	2	12	14	53	7	0	0	0	4
2000-01	CHZ Litvinov	Cze-Rep	52	12	26	38	52	4	1	1	2	25

PINC, Michal (PIHNTS, MIH-khuhl) **S.J.**

Center. Shoots left. 5'11", 180 lbs. Born, Litvinov, Czech., December 2, 1981.
(San Jose's 3rd choice, 142nd overall, in 2000 Entry Draft).

			Regular Season					Playoffs				
Season	Club	Lea	GP	G	A	TP	PIM	GP	G	A	TP	PIM
1997-98	CHZ Litvinov-Jr	Cze-Rep	47	18	36	54	....	....	....	....	....	....
1998-99	CHZ Litvinov-Jr	Cze-Rep	41	24	17	41	....	....	....	....	....	....
	CHZ Litvinov	Cze-Rep	7	0	0	0	4	....	....	....	....	....
99-2000	Hull Olympiques	QMJHL	31	11	27	38	67	....	....	....	....	....
	Rouyn-Noranda	QMJHL	27	8	16	24	64	11	0	5	5	18
2000-01	Rouyn-Noranda	QMJHL	64	16	46	62	220	9	0	3	3	12

PIROS, Kamil (PIH-ruhsh, KA-mihl) **ATL.**

Center. Shoots left. 6'1", 195 lbs. Born, Most, Czech., November 20, 1978.
(Buffalo's 9th choice, 212th overall, in 1997 Entry Draft).

			Regular Season					Playoffs				
Season	Club	Lea	GP	G	A	TP	PIM	GP	G	A	TP	PIM
1993-94	HC Most-Jr.	Cze-Rep	16	12	10	22	....	....	....	....	....	....
	CHZ Litvinov-Jr.	Cze-Rep	22	6	13	19	....	....	....	....	....	....
1994-95	CHZ Litvinov-Jr.	Cze-Rep	40	27	16	43	....	....	....	....	....	....
1995-96	CHZ Litvinov-Jr.	Cze-Rep	42	16	13	29	....	....	....	....	....	....
1996-97	CHZ Litvinov-Jr.	Cze-Rep	3	2	1	3	....	....	....	....	....	....
	CHZ Litvinov	Cze-Rep	38	4	9	13	10	....	....	....	....	....
1997-98	CHZ Litvinov	Cze-Rep	14	0	1	1	2	....	....	....	....	....
	HC Vitkovice	Cze-Rep	26	2	9	11	14	....	....	....	....	....
1998-99	CHZ Litvinov	Cze-Rep	41	7	9	16	10	....	....	....	....	....
99-2000	CHZ Litvinov	Cze-Rep	40	8	8	16	18	7	0	3	3	2
2000-01	CHZ Litvinov	Cze-Rep	48	11	13	24	28	6	1	1	2	2

Rights traded to **Atlanta** by **Buffalo** with Buffalo's 4th round choice (later traded to St. Louis - St. Louis selected Igor Valeyev) in 2001 Entry Draft for Donald Audette, March 13, 2001.

PISA, Ales (PEE-sha, al-EHSH **EDM.**

Defense. Shoots left. 6', 187 lbs. Born, Pardibuce, Czech., January 2, 1977.
(Edmonton's 10th choice, 272nd overall, in 2001 Entry Draft).

			Regular Season					Playoffs				
Season	Club	Lea	GP	G	A	TP	PIM	GP	G	A	TP	PIM
1993-94	HC Pardubice	Cze-Rep	2	0	0	0	0	....	....	....	....	....
1994-95	HC Pardubice	Cze-Rep	22	0	0	0	18	2	0	0	0	0
1995-96	HC Pardubice	Cze-Rep	33	0	4	4	82	....	....	....	....	....
1996-97	HC Pardubice	Cze-Rep	41	4	2	6	70	6	0	2	2	6
1997-98	HC Pardubice	Cze-Rep	50	4	9	13	107	3	0	0	0	4
1998-99	HC Pardubice	Cze-Rep	48	7	12	19	74	3	0	1	1	....
99-2000	HC Pardubice	Cze-Rep	51	5	11	16	58	1	0	0	0	4
2000-01	HC Pardubice	Cze-Rep	47	10	13	23	75	7	2	2	4	4

PISANI, Fernando (pih-ZAN-ee, FUHR-nan-DOH) **EDM.**

Center/Left wing. Shoots left. 6'1", 185 lbs. Born, Edmonton, Alta., December 27, 1976.
(Edmonton's 9th choice, 195th overall, in 1996 Entry Draft).

			Regular Season					Playoffs				
Season	Club	Lea	GP	G	A	TP	PIM	GP	G	A	TP	PIM
1994-95	Bonnyville	AJHL	56	30	55	85	105	....	....	....	....	....
1995-96	St. Albert Saints	AJHL	58	40	63	103	134	18	7	22	29	28
1996-97	Providence	H-East	35	12	18	30	36	....	....	....	....	....
1997-98	Providence	H-East	36	16	18	34	20	....	....	....	....	....
1998-99	Providence	H-East	38	14	37	51	42	....	....	....	....	....
99-2000	Providence	H-East	38	14	24	38	56	....	....	....	....	....
2000-01	Hamilton Bulldogs	AHL	52	12	13	25	28	....	....	....	....	....

PIVKO, Libor (PIHV-koh, LEE-bohr) **NSH.**

Left wing. Shoots left. 6'2", 205 lbs. Born, Novy Vicin, Czech., March 29, 1980.
(Nashville's 4th choice, 89th overall, in 2000 Entry Draft).

			Regular Season					Playoffs				
Season	Club	Lea	GP	G	A	TP	PIM	GP	G	A	TP	PIM
1995-96	HC Opava-Jr.	Cze-Rep	37	19	14	33	30	....	....	....	....	....
1996-97	HC Opava-Jr.	Cze-Rep	16	12	9	21	22	....	....	....	....	....
1997-98	HC Opava-Jr.	Cze-Rep	37	15	11	26	36	....	....	....	....	....
1998-99	HC Opava-Jr.	Cze-Rep	38	21	14	35	....	....	....	....	....	....
	HC Opava	Cze-Rep	5	0	1	1	0	....	....	....	....	....
99-2000	HC Havirov-Jr.	Cze-Rep	5	1	3	4	4	....	....	....	....	....
	HC Havirov	Cze-Rep	40	11	11	22	41	....	....	....	....	....
	HC Brno-3	Cze-Rep	....	....	....	....	....	4	3	4	7	0
2000-01	HCF Havirov	Cze-Rep	45	7	12	19	58	....	....	....	....	....

PLATONOV, Denis (PLAH-tah-nahv, DIHN-ihs) **NSH.**

Center. Shoots left. 6'1", 194 lbs. Born, Saratov, USSR, November 6, 1981.
(Nashville's 4th choice, 75th overall, in 2001 Entry Draft).

			Regular Season					Playoffs				
Season	Club	Lea	GP	G	A	TP	PIM	GP	G	A	TP	PIM
1997-98	Kristall Saratov-2	Russia-3	20	4	2	6	34	....	....	....	....	....
1998-99	Kristall Saratov	Russia-2	14	1	0	1	61	....	....	....	....	....
99-2000	Kristall Saratov-2	Russia-3	5	0	0	0	37	....	....	....	....	....
	Kristall Saratov	Russia-2	32	9	4	13	60	....	....	....	....	....
2000-01	Kristall Saratov	Russia-2	51	14	6	20	75	....	....	....	....	....

PLATT, Jason (PLAT, JAY-suhn) **EDM.**

Defense. Shoots left. 6'1", 210 lbs. Born, San Francisco, CA, April 29, 1981.
(Edmonton's 9th choice, 247th overall, in 2000 Entry Draft).

			Regular Season					Playoffs				
Season	Club	Lea	GP	G	A	TP	PIM	GP	G	A	TP	PIM
1998-99	Omaha Lancers	USHL	56	2	9	11	65	11	0	0	0	8
99-2000	Omaha Lancers	USHL	49	1	6	7	65	4	0	0	0	9
2000-01	Providence	H-East	26	0	2	2	12	....	....	....	....	....

PLEKANEC, Tomas (pleh-KA-nyehts, TAW-mahsh) **MTL.**

Left wing. Shoots left. 5'9", 189 lbs. Born, Kladno, Czech., October 31, 1982.
(Montreal's 4th choice, 71st overall, in 2001 Entry Draft).

			Regular Season					Playoffs				
Season	Club	Lea	GP	G	A	TP	PIM	GP	G	A	TP	PIM
1998-99	HC Kladno	Cze-Rep	3	0	0	0	0	....	....	....	....	....
99-2000	HC Kladno-Jr.	Cze-Rep	43	14	16	30	....	....	....	....	....	....
2000-01	HC Kladno	Cze-Rep	47	9	9	18	24	....	....	....	....	....

PLETKA, Vaclav (PLEHT-kuh, VA-tslav) **PHI.**

Right wing. Shoots left. 5'11", 182 lbs. Born, Mlada Boleslav, Czech., June 8, 1979.
(Philadelphia's 5th choice, 208th overall, in 1999 Entry Draft).

			Regular Season					Playoffs				
Season	Club	Lea	GP	G	A	TP	PIM	GP	G	A	TP	PIM
1995-96	Mlada Boleslav-Jr.	Cze-Rep	35	22	17	39	....	....	....	....	....	....
1996-97	Mlada Boleslav-Jr.	Cze-Rep	37	28	13	41	....	....	....	....	....	....
1997-98	Mlada Boleslav-Jr.	Cze-Rep	36	23	25	48	....	....	....	....	....	....
1998-99	HC Trinec-Jr.	Cze-Rep	20	11	5	16	....	....	....	....	....	....
	HC Trinec	Cze-Rep	50	15	11	26	20	10	2	1	3	....
99-2000	HC Trinec	Cze-Rep	51	28	21	49	62	4	2	2	4	2
2000-01	Philadelphia	AHL	71	20	21	41	51	10	1	3	4	4

PLIHAL, Tomas (PLEE-hahl, TAW-mahsh) **S.J.**

Center. Shoots left. 6'1", 176 lbs. Born, Frydlant v Cechach, Czech., March 28, 1983.
(San Jose's 4th choice, 140th overall, in 2001 Entry Draft).

			Regular Season					Playoffs				
Season	Club	Lea	GP	G	A	TP	PIM	GP	G	A	TP	PIM
2000-01	HC Liberec-Jr.	Cze-Rep	33	16	12	28	....	....	....	....	....	....

PODHRADSKY, Peter (pohd-RAD-skee, PEE-tuhr) **ANA.**

Defense. Shoots right. 6'2", 182 lbs. Born, Bratislava, Czech., December 10, 1979.
(Anaheim's 4th choice, 134th overall, in 2000 Entry Draft).

			Regular Season					Playoffs				
Season	Club	Lea	GP	G	A	TP	PIM	GP	G	A	TP	PIM
1995-96	HC Bratislava-Jr.	Slovakia	50	14	17	31	....	....	....	....	....	....
1996-97	HC Bratislava-Jr.	Slovakia	41	2	6	8	28	....	....	....	....	....
1997-98	HC Bratislava-Jr.	Slovakia	48	11	13	24	58	....	....	....	....	....
1998-99	HC Bratislava-Jr.	Slovakia	25	9	14	23	57	2	0	1	1	0
	HC Bratislava	Slovakia	23	1	4	5	37	4	0	0	0	0
99-2000	HK Trnava-2	Slovakia	1	0	0	0	0	....	....	....	....	....
	HC Bratislava	Slovakia	40	4	11	15	63	8	1	0	1	2
2000-01	Cincinnati Ducks	AHL	59	4	5	9	27	2	0	0	0	0

PODLESAK, Martin (PAWD-leh-shahk, MAHR-tihn) **PHX.**

Left wing. Shoots left. 6'5", 202 lbs. Born, Melnik, Czech., September 26, 1982.
(Phoenix's 3rd choice, 45th overall, in 2001 Entry Draft).

			Regular Season					Playoffs				
Season	Club	Lea	GP	G	A	TP	PIM	GP	G	A	TP	PIM
99-2000	Sparta Praha-Jr.	Cze-Rep	24	6	5	11	....	11	6	2	8	....
2000-01	Tri-City Americans	WHL	39	13	13	26	36	....	....	....	....	....
	Lethbridge	WHL	21	8	6	14	23	3	1	1	2	2

Traded to **Lethbridge** by **Tri-City** for Derrick Atkinson, Tri-Cities' 1st choice (Brett Festerling) in 2001 WHL Draft and Tri-Cities' 1st choice (Sergei Lavrentiev) in 2001 CHL Import Draft, January 15, 2001.

POHANKA, Igor (poh-HAHN-kah, EE-gohr) **N.J.**

Center. Shoots left. 6'3", 185 lbs. Born, Piestany, Czech., July 5, 1983.
(New Jersey's 2nd choice, 44th overall, in 2001 Entry Draft).

			Regular Season					Playoffs				
Season	Club	Lea	GP	G	A	TP	PIM	GP	G	A	TP	PIM
99-2000	HC Bratislava	Slovak-Jr.	57	36	41	77	62	....	....	....	....	....
2000-01	Prince Albert	WHL	70	16	33	49	24	....	....	....	....	....

POHL, John (PAWL, JAWN) **ST.L.**

Center. Shoots right. 6', 186 lbs. Born, Rochester, MN, June 29, 1979.
(St. Louis' 8th choice, 255th overall, in 1998 Entry Draft).

			Regular Season					Playoffs				
Season	Club	Lea	GP	G	A	TP	PIM	GP	G	A	TP	PIM
1997-98	Red Wing High	Hi-School	28	30	77	107	18	....	....	....	....	....
	Twin Cities	USHL	10	5	3	8	10	....	....	....	....	....
1998-99	U. of Minnesota	WCHA	42	7	10	17	18	....	....	....	....	....
99-2000	U. of Minnesota	WCHA	41	18	41	59	26	....	....	....	....	....
2000-01	U. of Minnesota	WCHA	38	19	26	45	24	....	....	....	....	....

Minnesota High School Player of the Year (1998) • WCHA Second All-Star Team (2000)

POLLOCK, Jame (PAWL-lawk, JAYM) **ST.L.**

Defense. Shoots right. 6'1", 210 lbs. Born, Quebec, Que., June 16, 1979.
(St. Louis' 4th choice, 106th overall, in 1997 Entry Draft).

			Regular Season					Playoffs				
Season	Club	Lea	GP	G	A	TP	PIM	GP	G	A	TP	PIM
1994-95	Victoria Legion	BCAHA	43	22	56	78	96	....	....	....	....	....
1995-96	Seattle T-Birds	WHL	32	0	1	1	15	....	....	....	....	....
1996-97	Seattle T-Birds	WHL	66	15	19	34	94	15	3	5	8	16
1997-98	Seattle T-Birds	WHL	66	11	36	47	78	5	0	1	1	17
1998-99	Seattle T-Birds	WHL	59	10	32	42	78	11	3	4	7	8
99-2000	Worcester	AHL	56	12	12	24	50	9	5	3	8	6
2000-01	Worcester	AHL	55	15	8	23	36	11	1	7	8	10

POLUSHIN, Alexander (puh-LOOSH-ihn, al-ehx-AN-duhr) **T.B.**

Right wing. Shoots left. 6'3", 198 lbs. Born, Kirovo-Chepetsk, USSR, May 8, 1983.
(Tampa Bay's 2nd choice, 47th overall, in 2001 Entry Draft).

			Regular Season					Playoffs				
Season	Club	Lea	GP	G	A	TP	PIM	GP	G	A	TP	PIM
99-2000	D'amo Moscow-2	Russia-3	18	4	3	7	14	....	....	....	....	....
	Krylja Sovetov	Russia-2	14	1	0	1	2	....	....	....	....	....
2000-01	THC Tver	Russia-2	38	10	5	15	10	....	....	....	....	....

POMINVILLE, Jason (paw-MIHN-vihl, JAY-suhn) **BUF.**

Right wing. Shoots right. 5'11", 174 lbs. Born, Repentigny, Que., November 30, 1982.
(Buffalo's 4th choice, 55th overall, in 2001 Entry Draft).

			Regular Season					Playoffs				
Season	Club	Lea	GP	G	A	TP	PIM	GP	G	A	TP	PIM
1998-99	Rive Nord Elites	QAHA	STATISTICS NOT AVAILABLE									
	Shawinigan	QMJHL	2	0	0	0	0	....	....	....	....	....
99-2000	Shawinigan	QMJHL	60	4	17	21	12	13	2	3	5	0
2000-01	Shawinigan	QMJHL	71	46	67	113	24	10	6	6	12	0

POPOVIC, Mark (poh-PUH-vihk, MAHRK) **ANA.**

Defense. Shoots left. 6'1", 194 lbs. Born, Stoney Creek, Ont., October 11, 1982.
(Anaheim's 2nd choice, 35th overall, in 2001 Entry Draft).

			Regular Season					Playoffs				
Season	Club	Lea	GP	G	A	TP	PIM	GP	G	A	TP	PIM
1997-98	Mississauga	OPJHL	51	10	16	26	32	....	....	....	....	....
1998-99	St. Michael's	OHL	60	6	26	32	46	....	....	....	....	....
99-2000	St. Michael's	OHL	68	11	29	40	68	....	....	....	....	....
2000-01	St. Michael's	OHL	61	7	35	42	54	18	3	5	8	22

OHL Second All-Rookie Team (1998)

POSNOV, Andrei (pawz-NAWF, AN-dray) **N.J.**

Left wing. Shoots right. 6', 185 lbs. Born, Moscow, USSR, November 19, 1981.
(New Jersey's 7th choice, 128th overall, in 2001 Entry Draft).

			Regular Season					Playoffs				
Season	Club	Lea	GP	G	A	TP	PIM	GP	G	A	TP	PIM
1998-99	Krylja Sovetov-3	Russia-4	9	3	1	4	8	....	....	....	....	....
99-2000	Krylja Sovetov-2	Russia-3	26	7	8	15	52	....	....	....	....	....
2000-01	Krylja Sovetov	Russia-2	15	0	5	5	4	....	....	....	....	....

POTULNY, Grant (puh-TUHL-nee, GRANT) **OTT.**

Center. Shoots left. 6'2", 194 lbs. Born, Grand Forks, ND, March 4, 1980.
(Ottawa's 7th choice, 157th overall, in 2000 Entry Draft).

			Regular Season					Playoffs				
Season	Club	Lea	GP	G	A	TP	PIM	GP	G	A	TP	PIM
1998-99	Lincoln Stars	USHL	46	7	11	18	76	10	2	1	3	7
99-2000	Lincoln Stars	USHL	56	25	30	55	85	10	3	4	7	4
2000-01	U. of Minnesota	WCHA	42	22	11	33	38	....	....	....	....	....

PRATT, Harlan (PRAT, HAR-lahn) **CAR.**

Defense. Shoots left. 6'1", 195 lbs. Born, Fort McMurray, Alta., December 10, 1978.
(Pittsburgh's 5th choice, 124th overall, in 1997 Entry Draft).

			Regular Season					Playoffs				
Season	Club	Lea	GP	G	A	TP	PIM	GP	G	A	TP	PIM
1994-95	Seattle T-Birds	WHL	33	1	0	1	17	1	0	0	0	0
1995-96	Red Deer Rebels	WHL	60	2	3	5	22	10	0	0	0	4
1996-97	Red Deer Rebels	WHL	2	0	0	0	2	....	....	....	....	....
	Prince Albert	WHL	65	7	26	33	49	4	1	1	2	4
1997-98	Prince Albert	WHL	37	6	14	20	12	....	....	....	....	....
	Regina Pats	WHL	24	2	6	8	23	9	2	2	4	2
1998-99	Portland	WHL	10	1	3	4	10	....	....	....	....	....
	Toledo Storm	ECHL	61	4	35	39	32	3	0	0	0	0
99-2000	Florida Everblades	ECHL	68	4	29	33	38	5	0	1	1	2
2000-01	Cincinnati	IHL	73	6	23	29	45	2	0	1	1	2

Signed as a free agent by **Carolina**, August 21, 2000.

PRESTBERG, Pelle (PEHST-buhrg, PEHL-lee) **ANA.**

Left wing. Shoots left. 5'10", 170 lbs. Born, Jonkoping, Sweden, February 5, 1975.
(Anaheim's 7th choice, 233rd overall, in 1998 Entry Draft).

			Regular Season					Playoffs				
Season	Club	Lea	GP	G	A	TP	PIM	GP	G	A	TP	PIM
1990-91	IFK Munkfors	Swede-3	3	0	3	3	....	....	....	....	....	....
1991-92	IFK Munkfors	Swede-3	26	6	10	16	18	....	....	....	....	....
1992-93	IFK Munkfors	Swede-3	36	8	8	16	20	....	....	....	....	....
1993-94	Sunne IK	Swede-3	32	8	6	14	16	....	....	....	....	....
1994-95	IFK Munkfors	Swede-3	27	13	9	22	44	....	....	....	....	....
1995-96	IFK Munkfors	Swede-3	30	20	11	31	32	....	....	....	....	....
1996-97	IFK Munkfors	Swede-3	32	28	10	38	50	....	....	....	....	....
1997-98	Farjestads BK	Sweden	45	29	15	44	22	12	*9	2	11	8
1998-99	Farjestads BK	Sweden	48	18	15	33	28	4	0	1	1	4
99-2000	Farjestads BK	Sweden	48	13	9	22	26	7	1	1	2	18
2000-01	Vastra Frolunda	Sweden	50	14	9	23	18	5	0	0	0	8

PRIECHODSKY, Marek (pree-HOHD-skee, MA-rehk) **T.B.**

Defense. Shoots left. 6'2", 194 lbs. Born, Bratislava, Czech., October 24, 1979.
(Tampa Bay's 7th choice, 222nd overall, in 2000 Entry Draft).

			Regular Season					Playoffs				
Season	Club	Lea	GP	G	A	TP	PIM	GP	G	A	TP	PIM
1997-98	HC Bratislava	Slovak-Jr.	33	1	3	4	24	....	....	....	....	....
1998-99	HC Bratislava	Slovak-Jr.	STATISTICS NOT AVAILABLE									
99-2000	HK Trnava	Slovak-2	28	2	8	10	54	....	....	....	....	....
	HC Bratislava	Slovakia	6	0	0	0	2	....	....	....	....	....
2000-01	HC Bratislava	Slovakia	44	0	5	5	6	....	....	....	....	....

PUDLICK, Michael (PUHD-lihk, MIGHK-uhl) **L.A.**

Defense. Shoots left. 6'3", 190 lbs. Born, Blaine, MN, February 24, 1978.

			Regular Season					Playoffs				
Season	Club	Lea	GP	G	A	TP	PIM	GP	G	A	TP	PIM
1995-96	Blaine High	Hi-School	25	9	30	39	....	....	....	....	....	....
1996-97	Twin Cities	USHL	49	10	19	29	93	5	0	2	2	4
1997-98	Twin Cities	USHL	50	3	14	17	138	....	....	....	....	....
1998-99	St. Cloud State	WCHA	37	13	12	25	74	....	....	....	....	....
99-2000	St. Cloud State	WCHA	40	8	22	30	65	....	....	....	....	....
2000-01	Lowell	AHL	57	7	13	20	39	4	0	1	1	2

WCHA First All-Star Team (2000) • NCAA West Second All-American Team (2000)

Signed as a free agent by **LA Kings** April 5, 2000.

RACHUNEK, Ivan (ra-KHOO-nuhk, EE-vahn) **T.B.**

Right wing. Shoots left. 5'10", 172 lbs. Born, Gottwaldov, Czech., July 6, 1981.
(Tampa Bay's 8th choice, 187th overall, in 1999 Entry Draft).

			Regular Season					Playoffs				
Season	Club	Lea	GP	G	A	TP	PIM	GP	G	A	TP	PIM
1997-98	Barum Zlin-Jr.	Cze-Rep	48	15	25	40	172	....	....	....	....	....
1998-99	Barum Zlin-Jr.	Cze-Rep	40	37	22	59	70	....	....	....	....	....
	Barum Zlin	Cze-Rep	5	0	0	0	0	....	....	....	....	....
99-2000	Barum Zlin	Cze-Rep	5	0	1	1	2	....	....	....	....	....
	Windsor Spitfires	OHL	15	2	2	4	21	....	....	....	....	....
2000-01	HCC Zlin	Cze-Rep	50	8	9	17	95	6	1	0	1	8

RADIVOJEVIC, Branko (ra-dih-VOI-uh-vihch, BRAN-koh) **PHX.**

Right wing. Shoots right. 6'1", 200 lbs. Born, Piestany, Czech., November 24, 1980.
(Colorado's 3rd choice, 93rd overall, in 1999 Entry Draft).

			Regular Season					Playoffs				
Season	Club	Lea	GP	G	A	TP	PIM	GP	G	A	TP	PIM
1997-98	Dukla Trencin	Slovak-Jr.	52	30	31	61	50	....	....	....	....	....
	Dukla Trencin	Slovakia	1	0	0	0	2	....	....	....	....	....
1998-99	Belleville Bulls	OHL	68	20	38	58	61	21	7	17	24	18
99-2000	Belleville Bulls	OHL	59	23	49	72	86	16	5	8	13	32
2000-01	Belleville Bulls	OHL	61	34	70	104	77	10	6	10	16	18

OHL First All-Star Team (2001)

Signed as a free agent by **Phoenix**, June 19, 2001.

RADULOV, Igor (rah-DOO-lahf, EE-gohr) **CHI.**

Left wing. Shoots left. 6', 194 lbs. Born, Nizhny Tagil, USSR, August 23, 1982.
(Chicago's 4th choice, 74th overall, in 2000 Entry Draft).

			Regular Season					Playoffs				
Season	Club	Lea	GP	G	A	TP	PIM	GP	G	A	TP	PIM
1997-98	Torpedo Yaroslavl	Russia-2	5	0	2	2	4	....	....	....	....	....
1998-99	HC Yaroslavl-2	Russia-3	21	2	3	5	4	....	....	....	....	....
99-2000	HC Yaroslavl-2	Russia-3	31	17	16	33	....	....	....	....	....	....
2000-01	Kristov Saratov	Russia-2	STATISTICS NOT AVAILABLE									
	St. Petersburg	Russia	8	1	0	1	6	....	....	....	....	....

RAJAMAKI, Erkki (righ-ya-MA-kee, UHR-kee) **T.B.**

Left wing. Shoots left. 6'2", 205 lbs. Born, Vantaa, Finland, October 30, 1978.
(Tampa Bay's 9th choice, 216th overall, in 1999 Entry Draft).

			Regular Season					Playoffs				
Season	Club	Lea	GP	G	A	TP	PIM	GP	G	A	TP	PIM
1996-97	Kiekko-Vantaa-B	Finn-Jr.	33	14	19	33	32	....	....	....	....	....
1997-98	HIFK Helsinki	Finn-Jr.	14	1	2	3	2	....	....	....	....	....
	Kiekko-Vantaa-B	Finn-Jr.	....	....	....	....	....	10	3	0	3	2
1998-99	HIFK Helsinki-B	Finn-Jr.	14	2	2	4	8	....	....	....	....	....
	HIFK Helsinki	Finland	14	0	0	0	2	....	....	....	....	....
	HIFK Helsinki	Finn-Jr.	....	....	....	....	....	13	7	3	10	45
99-2000	Colgate University	ECAC	31	1	6	7	20	....	....	....	....	....
2000-01	HIFK Helsinki	Finland	50	1	2	3	10	5	0	0	0	2

RAJAMAKI, Tommi (righ-YAH-ma-kee, TAW-mee) **CBJ**

Defense. Shoots left. 6'2", 205 lbs. Born, Pori, Finland, February 29, 1976.
(Toronto's 6th choice, 178th overall, in 1994 Entry Draft).

			Regular Season					Playoffs				
Season	Club	Lea	GP	G	A	TP	PIM	GP	G	A	TP	PIM
1994-95	Assat-Pori	Finn-Jr.	29	11	17	28	30	....	....	....	....	....
	Assat-Pori	Finland	12	4	1	5	8	7	0	1	1	2
1995-96	Assat-Pori	Finland	45	5	2	7	26	3	0	0	0	6
1996-97	Assat-Pori	Finland	46	0	1	1	16	4	0	0	0	2
1997-98	TPS Turku	Finland	46	1	1	2	24	4	0	0	0	0
1998-99	TPS Turku	Finland	53	3	3	6	24	10	0	0	0	6
99-2000	TPS Turku	Finland	53	2	6	8	51	11	0	1	1	2
	TPS Turku	EuroHL	6	0	3	3	0	5	0	0	0	0
2000-01	TPS Turku	Finland	56	6	3	9	20	10	1	1	2	2

Selected by **Columbus** from **Toronto** in Expansion Draft, June 23, 2000.

RAKHMATULLIN, Ashkat (rahkh-ma-TOO-lihn, ahs-KHAHT) **MIN.**

Left wing. Shoots left. 5'11", 165 lbs. Born, Ufa, USSR, May 31, 1978.
(Hartford's 10th choice, 231st overall, in 1996 Entry Draft).

			Regular Season					Playoffs				
Season	Club	Lea	GP	G	A	TP	PIM	GP	G	A	TP	PIM
1996-97	Ufa-Salavat	Russia	28	1	3	4	8	3	0	0	0	0
1997-98	Ufa-Salavat	Russia	14	0	1	1	6	....	....	....	....	....
1998-99	Asheville Smoke	UHL	31	6	10	16	23	4	1	0	1	0
	Fayetteville	CHL	4	0	0	0	4	....	....	....	....	....
	Florida Everblades	ECHL	6	0	1	1	2	....	....	....	....	....
99-2000	Ufa-Salavat	Russia	34	5	8	13	14	....	....	....	....	....
2000-01	Ufa-Salavat	Russia	44	7	15	22	22	....	....	....	....	....

Rights transferred to **Carolina** after **Hartford** franchise relocated, June 25, 1997. Traded to **Minnesota** by **Carolina** with Carolina's 3rd round choice (later traded to NY Rangers - NY Rangers selected Garth Murray) in 2001 Entry Draft and future considerations for Scott Pellerin, March 1, 2001.

RAMHOLT, Arne (RAM-hohlt, AHR-neh)

Defense. Shoots right. 6'3", 215 lbs. Born, Zurich, Switz., May 20, 1976.
(Chicago's 15th choice, 291st overall, in 2000 Entry Draft).

			Regular Season					Playoffs				
Season	Club	Lea	GP	G	A	TP	PIM	GP	G	A	TP	PIM
1993-94	ZSC Zurich	Switz-Jr.	15	0	0	0	2	....	....	....	....	....
1994-95	ZSC Zurich	Switz-Jr.	25	0	2	2	4	11	0	0	0	0
1995-96	ZSC Zurich	Switz-Jr.	5	0	0	0	0	....	....	....	....	....
1996-97	ZSC Zurich	Switz-2	5	0	0	0	0	....	....	....	....	....
1997-98	St. Lawrence	ECAC	14	0	0	0	2	....	....	....	....	....
1998-99	GC Zurich	Switz-2	29	5	10	15	24	....	....	....	....	....
	ZSC Zurich	Switz.	5	0	0	0	2	....	....	....	....	....
	EHC Kloten	Switz.	8	0	0	0	2	12	0	1	1	8
99-2000	EHC Kloten	Switz.	34	0	4	4	12	7	0	2	2	16
2000-01	Norfolk Admirals	AHL	62	3	8	11	25					

RAZIN, Andrei (RAH-zihn, AN-dray) PHI.

Center. Shoots left. 5'11", 180 lbs. Born, Togliatti, Russia, October 23, 1973.
(Philadelphia's 7th choice, 177th overall, in 2001 Entry Draft).

			Regular Season					Playoffs				
Season	Club	Lea	GP	G	A	TP	PIM	GP	G	A	TP	PIM
1990-91	Mayak Samara	USSR-3	2	0	0	0	2	....	....	....	....	....
1991-92	Mayak Samara-2	CIS-3	41	15	16	31	26	....	....	....	....	....
	Lada Togliatti	CIS	7	0	0	0	2	....	....	....	....	....
1992-93	Mayak Samara-2	CIS-3	29	8	7	15	12	....	....	....	....	....
	Lada Togliatti	CIS	12	1	2	3	0	1	0	0	0	0
1993-94	Lada Togliatti-2	CIS-3	4	4	0	4	0	....	....	....	....	....
	Lada Togliatti	CIS	15	1	1	2	0	....	....	....	....	....
1994-95	HC Magnitogorsk	CIS	49	11	14	25	12	7	3	2	5	16
1995-96	HC Magnitogorsk	CIS-2	5	3	0	3	0	....	....	....	....	....
	HC Magnitogorsk	CIS	40	6	11	17	28	4	0	0	0	2
1996-97	Magnitogorsk-2	Russia-3	4	5	3	8	4	....	....	....	....	....
	CSK Samara	Russia	32	7	8	15	12	2	0	1	1	2
1997-98	Magnitogorsk-2	Russia-3	1	1	2	3	0	....	....	....	....	....
	HC Magnitogorsk	Russia	46	6	32	38	12	....	....	....	....	....
1998-99	Magnitogorsk-2	Russia-3	1	2	2	4	0	....	....	....	....	....
	HC Magnitogorsk	Russia	39	7	25	32	14	16	4	3	7	6
99-2000	Magnitogorsk-2	Russia-3	4	3	5	8	0	....	....	....	....	....
	HC Magnitogorsk	Russia	29	11	10	21	8	12	3	2	5	4
2000-01	HC Magnitogorsk	Russia	44	16	31	47	78	12	7	6	13	20

RAZIN, Gennady (RAH-zihn, gen-AH-dee) MTL.

Defense. Shoots left. 6'4", 207 lbs. Born, Kharkov, USSR, February 3, 1978.
(Montreal's 6th choice, 122nd overall, in 1997 Entry Draft).

			Regular Season					Playoffs				
Season	Club	Lea	GP	G	A	TP	PIM	GP	G	A	TP	PIM
1995-96	St. Albert Saints	AJHL	52	3	16	19	113	18	1	10	11	8
1996-97	Kamloops Blazers	WHL	63	7	19	26	56	3	0	0	0	4
1997-98	Kamloops Blazers	WHL	70	2	11	13	64	7	0	0	0	4
1998-99	Fredericton	AHL	48	0	3	3	16	4	0	0	0	2
99-2000	Quebec Citadelles	AHL	66	2	9	11	29	3	0	0	0	0
2000-01	Quebec Citadelles	AHL	69	3	19	22	25	9	0	0	0	4

READY, Ryan (REH-dee, RIGH-yan) VAN.

Left wing. Shoots left. 6'2", 195 lbs. Born, Peterborough, Ont., November 7, 1978.
(Calgary's 8th choice, 100th overall, in 1997 Entry Draft).

			Regular Season					Playoffs				
Season	Club	Lea	GP	G	A	TP	PIM	GP	G	A	TP	PIM
1994-95	Peterborough	OPJHL	48	20	33	53	65	....	....	....	....	....
1995-96	Belleville Bulls	OHL	63	5	13	18	54	10	0	2	2	2
1996-97	Belleville Bulls	OHL	66	23	24	47	102	6	1	3	4	4
1997-98	Belleville Bulls	OHL	66	33	39	72	80	10	5	2	7	12
1998-99	Belleville Bulls	OHL	63	33	59	92	73	21	10	28	38	22
99-2000	Syracuse Crunch	AHL	70	4	12	16	59	2	0	0	0	0
2000-01	Kansas City	IHL	67	10	15	25	75	....	....	....	....	....

OHL First All-Star Team (1999)

Signed as a free agent by **Vancouver**, June 16, 1999.

REED, Josh (REED, JAWSH) VAN.

Defense. Shoots right. 6'2", 204 lbs. Born, Vernon, B.C., May 21, 1979.
(Vancouver's 5th choice, 172nd overall, in 1999 Entry Draft).

			Regular Season					Playoffs				
Season	Club	Lea	GP	G	A	TP	PIM	GP	G	A	TP	PIM
1994-95	Vernon Leafs	BCAHA	56	13	41	54	136	....	....	....	....	....
1995-96	Vernon Vikings	BCAHA	50	9	43	52	150	....	....	....	....	....
1996-97	Cowichan Valley	BCJHL	42	3	3	6	61	....	....	....	....	....
1997-98	Cowichan Valley	BCJHL	50	5	20	25	115	....	....	....	....	....
1998-99	Vernon Vipers	BCJHL	54	16	38	54	110	....	....	....	....	....
99-2000	U. Mass-Lowell	H-East	30	2	10	12	24	....	....	....	....	....
2000-01	U. Mass-Lowell	H-East	17	1	6	7	22	....	....	....	....	....

REHNBERG, Henrik (REHN-buhrg, HEHN-rihk) N.J.

Defense. Shoots left. 6'2", 195 lbs. Born, Grava, Sweden, July 20, 1977.
(New Jersey's 6th choice, 96th overall, in 1995 Entry Draft).

			Regular Season					Playoffs				
Season	Club	Lea	GP	G	A	TP	PIM	GP	G	A	TP	PIM
1994-95	Farjestads BK	Swede-Jr.	24	1	2	3	62	....	....	....	....	....
1995-96	Farjestads BK	Swede-Jr.	21	1	4	5	38	....	....	....	....	....
	Farjestads BK	Sweden	4	0	0	0	0	....	....	....	....	....
1996-97	Farjestads BK	Sweden	42	2	3	5	38	14	1	1	2	16
1997-98	Farjestads BK	Sweden	32	0	1	1	24	10	0	0	0	12
	Farjestads BK	EuroHL	6	0	0	0	39	....	....	....	....	....
1998-99	Albany River Rats	AHL	55	1	4	5	49	2	0	0	0	0
99-2000	Farjestads BK	Sweden	46	1	3	4	66	7	0	1	1	18
2000-01	Albany River Rats	AHL	80	1	8	9	78	....	....	....	....	....

REICH, Jeremy (RIGHK, JAIR-eh-MEE) CBJ

Center. Shoots left. 6'1", 190 lbs. Born, Craik, Sask., February 11, 1979.
(Chicago's 3rd choice, 39th overall, in 1997 Entry Draft).

			Regular Season					Playoffs				
Season	Club	Lea	GP	G	A	TP	PIM	GP	G	A	TP	PIM
1993-94	Pilote Butte	SAHA	80	70	65	135	120	....	....	....	....	....
1994-95	Saskatoon AAA	SMHL	35	13	20	33	81	....	....	....	....	....
1995-96	Seattle T-Birds	WHL	65	11	11	22	88	5	0	1	1	10
1996-97	Seattle T-Birds	WHL	62	19	31	50	134	15	2	5	7	36
1997-98	Seattle T-Birds	WHL	43	24	23	47	121	....	....	....	....	....
	Swift Current	WHL	22	8	8	16	47	12	5	6	11	37
1998-99	Swift Current	WHL	67	21	28	49	220	6	0	3	3	26
99-2000	Swift Current	WHL	72	33	58	91	167	12	2	10	12	19
2000-01	Syracuse Crunch	AHL	56	6	9	15	108	5	0	0	0	6

Signed as a free agent by **Columbus**, May 17, 2000.

REID, Brandon (REED, BRAN-duhn) VAN.

Center. Shoots right. 5'8", 165 lbs. Born, Kirkland, Que., March 9, 1981.
(Vancouver's 5th choice, 208th overall, in 2000 Entry Draft).

			Regular Season					Playoffs				
Season	Club	Lea	GP	G	A	TP	PIM	GP	G	A	TP	PIM
1996-97	Lac St-Louis	QAAA	44	17	34	51	....	7	2	3	5	....
1997-98	Halifax	QMJHL	67	13	21	36	6	5	1	0	1	15
1998-99	Halifax	QMJHL	70	32	25	57	33	5	2	2	4	0
99-2000	Halifax	QMJHL	62	44	80	124	10	10	7	11	18	4
2000-01	Val d'Or Foreurs	QMJHL	57	45	81	126	18	21	13	29	42	14

QMJHL Second All-Star Team (2000) • Won George Parsons Trophy (Memorial Cup Tournament Most Sportsmanlike Player) (2000, 2001) • QMJHL First All-Star Team (2001)

Traded to **Val d'Or** by **Halifax** with Jonathan Jolette to complete earlier transaction that sent Benoit Dusablon and Nick Greenough to Halifax (January 7, 2000), June 6, 2000.

REITZ, Erik (RIGHTZ, AIR-ihk) MIN.

Defense. Shoots right. 6', 192 lbs. Born, Detroit, MI, July 29, 1982.
(Minnesota's 5th choice, 170th overall, in 2000 Entgry Draft).

			Regular Season					Playoffs				
Season	Club	Lea	GP	G	A	TP	PIM	GP	G	A	TP	PIM
1998-99	Leamington Flyers	OJHL-B	50	5	10	15	80	....	....	....	....	....
99-2000	Barrie Colts	OHL	63	2	10	12	85	25	0	5	5	44
2000-01	Barrie Colts	OHL	68	5	21	26	178	5	1	0	1	21

Memorial Cup All-Star Team (2000)

RENNETTE, Tyler (REHN-neht, TIGH-luhr) ST.L.

Center. Shoots right. 6'1", 179 lbs. Born, North Bay, Ont., April 16, 1979.
(St. Louis' 1st choice, 40th overall, in 1997 Entry Draft).

			Regular Season					Playoffs				
Season	Club	Lea	GP	G	A	TP	PIM	GP	G	A	TP	PIM
1994-95	North Bay	NOHA	52	24	42	66	72	....	....	....	....	....
1995-96	Waterloo Hawks	OJHL-B	45	27	47	74	64	....	....	....	....	....
1996-97	North Bay	OHL	63	24	34	58	42	....	....	....	....	....
1997-98	North Bay	OHL	31	17	14	31	37	....	....	....	....	....
	Erie Otters	OHL	24	16	17	33	20	6	3	3	6	2
1998-99	Erie Otters	OHL	61	30	37	67	40	5	6	1	7	8
99-2000	Worcester	AHL	55	8	17	25	16	7	2	3	5	4
2000-01	Peoria	ECHL	7	5	1	6	6	14	9	2	11	14
	Worcester	AHL	29	3	8	11	24	....	....	....	....	....

REYNOLDS, Peter (REH-nolds, PEE-tuhr) CAR.

Defense. Shoots right. 6'3", 195 lbs. Born, Waterloo, Ont., April 27, 1981.
(Carolina's 8th choice, 274th overall, in 2001 Entry Draft).

			Regular Season					Playoffs				
Season	Club	Lea	GP	G	A	TP	PIM	GP	G	A	TP	PIM
1996-97	Caledon Canucks	MTJHL	45	1	10	11	69	....	....	....	....	....
1997-98	London Knights	OHL	55	0	8	8	30	16	0	0	0	10
1998-99	London Knights	OHL	59	2	25	27	55	23	2	3	5	24
99-2000	North Bay	OHL	61	3	29	32	53	6	1	3	4	10
2000-01	North Bay	OHL	58	2	27	29	85	4	0	1	1	7
	St. John's Leafs	AHL	2	0	0	0	0	1	0	0	0	0

• Re-entered NHL Entry Draft. Originally Toronto's 2nd choice, 60th overall, in 1999 Entry Draft.

RIAZANTSEV, Alexander (ree-ZAHNT-sehv, al-ehx-AN-duhr) COL.

Defense. Shoots right. 6', 210 lbs. Born, Moscow, USSR, March 15, 1980.
(Colorado's 10th choice, 167th overall, in 1998 Entry Draft).

			Regular Season					Playoffs				
Season	Club	Lea	GP	G	A	TP	PIM	GP	G	A	TP	PIM
1996-97	Krylja Sovetov-2	Russia-3	18	0	0	0	8	....	....	....	....	....
	Krylja Sovetov	Russia	20	1	2	3	4	....	....	....	....	....
1997-98	Krylja Sovetov-2	Russia-3	31	3	8	11	26	....	....	....	....	....
	Victoriaville Tigres	QMJHL	22	6	9	15	14	4	0	0	0	0
1998-99	Victoriaville Tigres	QMJHL	64	17	40	57	57	6	0	3	3	10
	Hershey Bears	AHL	2	0	0	0	0	....	....	....	....	....
99-2000	Victoriaville Tigres	QMJHL	48	17	45	62	45	6	2	5	7	20
	Hershey Bears	AHL	2	0	1	1	2	6	1	1	2	0
2000-01	Hershey Bears	AHL	66	5	18	23	26	11	0	0	0	2

RICHTER, Martin (RIHKH-tuhr, MAHR-tihn) NYR

Defense. Shoots right. 6'1", 196 lbs. Born, Prostejov, Czech., December 6, 1977.
(NY Rangers' 9th choice, 269th overall, in 2000 Entry Draft).

			Regular Season					Playoffs				
Season	Club	Lea	GP	G	A	TP	PIM	GP	G	A	TP	PIM
1995-96	HC Olomouc	Cze-Rep	3	0	0	0	0	1	0	0	0	0
1996-97	HC Olomouc	Cze-Rep	27	1	0	1	26	....	....	....	....	....
1997-98	HC Karlovy Vary	Cze-Rep	42	1	2	3	32	....	....	....	....	....
1998-99	HC Karlovy Vary	Cze-Rep	51	3	6	9	44	....	....	....	....	....
99-2000	HC Karlovy Vary	Cze-Rep	24	0	5	5	18	....	....	....	....	....
	Sai-Lappeenranta	Finland	26	1	3	4	54	....	....	....	....	....
2000-01	Sai-Lappeenranta	Finland	41	4	5	9	80	....	....	....	....	....
	Hartford	AHL	1	0	0	0	0	....	....	....	....	....

RIDDLE, Troy (RIH-duhl, TROI) ST.L.

Center. Shoots right. 6', 172 lbs. Born, Minneapolis, MN, August 24, 1981.
(St. Louis' 5th choice, 129th overall, in 2000 Entry Draft).

			Regular Season					Playoffs				
Season	Club	Lea	GP	G	A	TP	PIM	GP	G	A	TP	PIM
1997-98	St. Margaret's	Hi-School	29	33	35	68	....	....	....	....	....	....
1998-99	St. Margaret's	Hi-School	29	54	45	99	....	....	....	....	....	....
99-2000	Des Moines	USHL	53	36	30	66	95	8	2	2	4	31
2000-01	U. of Minnesota	WCHA	38	16	14	30	49	....	....	....	....	....

USHL Second All-Star Team (2000) • Won USHL Rookie of the Year Award (2000)

RITA, Jani (REETA, YA-nee) EDM.

Left wing. Shoots left. 6'1", 206 lbs. Born, Helsinki, Finland, July 25, 1981.
(Edmonton's 1st choice, 13th overall, in 1999 Entry Draft).

			Regular Season					Playoffs				
Season	Club	Lea	GP	G	A	TP	PIM	GP	G	A	TP	PIM
1994-95	Jokerit Helsinki-C	Finn-Jr.	7	3	0	3	0	6	1	0	1	0
1995-96	Jokerit Helsinki-C	Finn-Jr.	12	10	3	13	2	....	....	....	....	....
	Jokerit Helsinki-B	Finn-Jr.	5	0	0	0	0	....	....	....	....	....
1996-97	Jokerit Helsinki-B	Finn-Jr.	27	22	7	29	4	....	....	....	....	....
1997-98	Jokerit Helsinki-B	Finn-Jr.	7	7	4	11	2	....	....	....	....	....
	Jokerit Helsinki	Finn-Jr.	36	15	9	24	2	8	4	1	5	0
	Jokerit Helsinki	Finland	....	....	....	....	....	1	0	0	0	0
1998-99	Jokerit Helsinki	Finn-Jr.	20	9	13	22	8	....	....	....	....	....
	Jokerit Helsinki	Finland	41	3	2	5	39	....	....	....	....	....
	Jokerit Helsinki	EuroHL	3	0	0	0	0	....	....	....	....	....
99-2000	Jokerit Helsinki	Finn-Jr.	1	1	0	1	0	....	....	....	....	....
	Jokerit Helsinki	Finland	49	6	3	9	10	11	1	0	1	0
2000-01	Jokerit Helsinki	Finn-Jr.	3	3	2	5	0	....	....	....	....	....
	Jokerit Helsinki	Finland	50	5	10	15	18	5	0	0	0	2

RIVA, Danny (REE-vuh, DAN-nee)

Center. Shoots right. 6', 190 lbs. Born, Framingham, MA, September 17, 1975.

			Regular Season					Playoffs				
Season	Club	Lea	GP	G	A	TP	PIM	GP	G	A	TP	PIM
1995-96	RPI Engineers	ECAC	35	3	7	10	30	....	....	....	....	....
1996-97	RPI Engineers	ECAC	36	12	14	26	30	....	....	....	....	....
1997-98	RPI Engineers	ECAC	35	10	18	28	16	....	....	....	....	....
1998-99	RPI Engineers	ECAC	36	*22	*35	*57	35	....	....	....	....	....
	Milwaukee	IHL	8	0	2	2	4	1	0	1	1	0
99-2000	Milwaukee	IHL	67	8	12	20	18	3	0	0	0	2
2000-01	Milwaukee	IHL	75	12	9	21	23	5	0	1	1	2

ECAC First All-Star Team (1999)

Signed as a free agent by **Nashville**, May 4, 1999.

ROBINSON, Darcy (RAW-bihn-suhn, DAHR-see) **PIT.**

Defense. Shoots right. 6'3", 229 lbs. Born, Kamloops, B.C., May 3, 1981.
(Pittsburgh's 10th choice, 233rd overall, in 1999 Entry Draft).

			Regular Season					Playoffs				
Season	Club	Lea	GP	G	A	TP	PIM	GP	G	A	TP	PIM
1996-97	Kamloops	BCAHA	59	18	42	60	188	....	....	....	....	....
1997-98	Saskatoon Blades	WHL	62	1	2	3	84	4	0	0	0	2
1998-99	Saskatoon Blades	WHL	48	3	6	9	86	....	....	....	....	....
99-2000	Saskatoon Blades	WHL	59	5	9	14	91	10	1	3	4	13
2000-01	Saskatoon Blades	WHL	41	2	6	8	80	....	....	....	....	....
	Red Deer Rebels	WHL	30	1	5	6	70	20	1	1	2	20

Traded to **Red Deer** by **Saskatoon** with Martin Erat and Cam Ondrik for Michael Garnett, Justin Wallin, Martin Vymazzal and future considerations, January 11, 2001.

ROBSON, Blake (ROHB-suhn, BLAYK) **ATL.**

Center. Shoots left. 6', 190 lbs. Born, Calgary, Alta., March 31, 1982.
(Atlanta's 5th choice, 108th overall, in 2000 Entry Draft).

			Regular Season					Playoffs				
Season	Club	Lea	GP	G	A	TP	PIM	GP	G	A	TP	PIM
1997-98	Calgary Royals	AMHL	36	21	26	47	74	....	....	....	....	....
	Portland	WHL	2	0	1	1	0	....	....	....	....	....
1998-99	Portland	WHL	61	14	18	32	54	4	0	0	0	4
99-2000	Portland	WHL	70	20	27	47	96	....	....	....	....	....
2000-01	Portland	WHL	9	5	2	7	8	....	....	....	....	....
	Prince George	WHL	58	24	35	59	98	6	1	5	6	2

Traded to **Prince George** by **Portland** with Chad Grisdale for Willy Glover and Joey Hope, October 26, 2000.

ROCHEFORT, Richard (ROHSH-fohr, RIH-chahrd) **N.J.**

Center. Shoots right. 5'10", 195 lbs. Born, North Bay, Ont., January 7, 1977.
(New Jersey's 9th choice, 174th overall, in 1995 Entry Draft).

			Regular Season					Playoffs				
Season	Club	Lea	GP	G	A	TP	PIM	GP	G	A	TP	PIM
1993-94	Waterloo Hawks	OJHL-B	45	21	32	53	41	....	....	....	....	....
1994-95	Sudbury Wolves	OHL	57	21	44	65	26	13	3	7	10	6
1995-96	Sudbury Wolves	OHL	56	25	40	65	38	....	....	....	....	....
1996-97	Sudbury Wolves	OHL	28	18	24	42	40	....	....	....	....	....
	Sarnia Sting	OHL	18	5	23	28	23	12	3	9	12	8
1997-98	Albany River Rats	AHL	59	7	14	21	16	13	1	0	1	4
1998-99	Albany River Rats	AHL	70	16	10	26	26	5	1	0	1	0
99-2000	Albany River Rats	AHL	55	12	12	24	22	5	0	0	0	0
2000-01	Albany River Rats	AHL	75	16	24	40	18	....	....	....	....	....

ROGERS, Brandon (RAW-juhrs, BRAN-duhn) **ANA.**

Defense. Shoots right. 6'1", 190 lbs. Born, Rochester, NH, February 27, 1982.
(Anaheim's 6th choice, 118th overall, in 2001 Entry Draft).

			Regular Season					Playoffs				
Season	Club	Lea	GP	G	A	TP	PIM	GP	G	A	TP	PIM
99-2000	Hotchkiss High	Hi-School	25	9	12	21	35	....	....	....	....	....
2000-01	Hotchkiss High	Hi-School	22	10	13	23	45	....	....	....	....	....

ROHLOFF, Todd (ROH-lawf, TAWD) **WSH.**

Defense. Shoots left. 6'3", 213 lbs. Born, Grand Rapids, IL, January 16, 1974.

			Regular Season					Playoffs				
Season	Club	Lea	GP	G	A	TP	PIM	GP	G	A	TP	PIM
1993-94	St. Paul Vulcans	USHL	47	4	22	26	....	....	....	....	....	....
1994-95	U. of Miami-Ohio	CCHA	38	1	6	7	22	....	....	....	....	....
1995-96	U. of Miami-Ohio	CCHA	23	2	4	6	24	....	....	....	....	....
1996-97	U. of Miami-Ohio	CCHA	38	2	12	14	48	....	....	....	....	....
1997-98	U. of Miami-Ohio	CCHA	17	2	5	7	38	....	....	....	....	....
	Indianapolis Ice	IHL	5	0	1	1	6	1	0	0	0	0
1998-99	Portland Pirates	AHL	58	1	6	7	58	....	....	....	....	....
	Indianapolis Ice	IHL	12	2	0	2	8	5	1	1	2	6
99-2000	Cleveland	IHL	77	1	13	14	88	9	0	0	0	6
2000-01	Portland Pirates	AHL	58	3	8	11	59	3	0	0	0	2

Signed as a free agent by **Chicago**, March 24, 1998. Signed as a free agent by **Washington**, July 21, 2000.

ROSSITER, Kyle (RAWS-ih-tuhr, KIGHL) **FLA.**

Defense. Shoots left. 6'3", 217 lbs. Born, Edmonton, Alta., June 9, 1980.
(Florida's 1st choice, 30th overall, in 1998 Entry Draft).

			Regular Season					Playoffs				
Season	Club	Lea	GP	G	A	TP	PIM	GP	G	A	TP	PIM
1995-96	Edmonton South	AMHL	34	5	19	24	116	....	....	....	....	....
1996-97	Spokane Chiefs	WHL	50	0	2	2	65	9	0	0	0	6
1997-98	Spokane Chiefs	WHL	61	6	16	22	190	15	0	3	3	28
1998-99	Spokane Chiefs	WHL	71	4	17	21	206	....	....	....	....	....
99-2000	Spokane Chiefs	WHL	63	11	22	33	155	15	1	4	5	25
2000-01	Louisville Panthers	AHL	78	2	5	7	110	....	....	....	....	....

Canadian Major Junior Scholastic Player of the Year (1998)

ROSTOV, Sergei (roh-STOHV, SAIR-gay) **TOR.**

Defense. Shoots left. 6'3", 194 lbs. Born, Murmansk, USSR, March 29, 1980.
(Toronto's 10th choice, 236th overall, in 1998 Entry Draft).

			Regular Season					Playoffs				
Season	Club	Lea	GP	G	A	TP	PIM	GP	G	A	TP	PIM
1995-96	Torpedo Yaroslavl	Russia-2	80	1	3	4	60	....	....	....	....	....
1996-97	CSKA Moscow	Russia-Jr.	45	8	10	18	70	....	....	....	....	....
	HC Yaroslavl-2	Russia-3	8	0	0	0	0	....	....	....	....	....
1997-98	Dynamo Moscow	Russia-2	32	1	1	2	51	....	....	....	....	....
1998-99	HC Tverskoi Tver	Russia-2	11	3	1	4	8	....	....	....	....	....
99-2000	Krylja Sovetov-2	Russia-3	2	1	1	2	2	....	....	....	....	....
	Krylja Sovetov	Russia-2	2	0	0	0	0	....	....	....	....	....
2000-01	Krylja Sovetov	Russia-2		STATISTICS NOT AVAILABLE								

ROULEAU, Alexandre (ROO-loh, al-ehx-AHN-druh) **PIT.**

Defense. Shoots left. 6'1", 180 lbs. Born, Mont-Laurier, Que., July 29, 1983.
(Pittsburgh's 4th choice, 96th overall, in 2001 Entry Draft).

			Regular Season					Playoffs				
Season	Club	Lea	GP	G	A	TP	PIM	GP	G	A	TP	PIM
1998-99	Amos Forestiers	QAAA	41	7	6	13	144	....	....	....	....	....
99-2000	Val d'Or Foreurs	QMJHL	41	3	3	6	39	....	....	....	....	....
2000-01	Val d'Or Foreurs	QMJHL	70	8	17	25	124	21	1	0	1	46

ROURKE, Allan (RAWRK, AL-lan) **TOR.**

Defense. Shoots left. 6'1", 214 lbs. Born, Mississauga, Ont., March 6, 1980.
(Toronto's 6th choice, 154th overall, in 1998 Entry Draft).

			Regular Season					Playoffs				
Season	Club	Lea	GP	G	A	TP	PIM	GP	G	A	TP	PIM
1995-96	Mississauga Reps	MTHL	38	15	25	40	173	....	....	....	....	....
1996-97	Kitchener	OHL	25	1	1	2	12	6	0	0	0	0
1997-98	Kitchener	OHL	48	5	17	22	59	6	1	1	2	6
1998-99	Kitchener	OHL	66	11	28	39	79	1	0	0	0	2
99-2000	Kitchener	OHL	67	31	43	74	57	5	0	6	6	13
2000-01	St. John's Leafs	AHL	64	9	19	28	36	....	....	....	....	....

OHL Second All-Star Team (2000)

ROY, Derek (ROI, DEHR-ihk) **BUF.**

Center. Shoots left. 5'8", 187 lbs. Born, Ottawa, Ont., May 4, 1983.
(Buffalo's 2nd choice, 32nd overall, in 2001 Entry Draft).

			Regular Season					Playoffs				
Season	Club	Lea	GP	G	A	TP	PIM	GP	G	A	TP	PIM
1998-99	Ontario East	OMHA	34	61	31	92	42	....	....	....	....	....
99-2000	Kitchener	OHL	66	34	53	87	44	5	4	1	5	6
2000-01	Kitchener	OHL	65	42	39	81	114	....	....	....	....	....

OHL All-Rookie Team (2000) • Won OHL Rookie of the Year Award (2000) • CHL All-Rookie Team (2000) • Won CHL Plus/Minus Award (2000) • Won CHL Most Sportsmanlike Player Award (2000)

ROY, Jimmy (ROI, JIHM-mee)

Center. Shoots right. 5'11", 170 lbs. Born, Sioux Lookout, Ont., September 22, 1975.
(Dallas' 7th choice, 254th overall, in 1994 Entry Draft).

			Regular Season					Playoffs				
Season	Club	Lea	GP	G	A	TP	PIM	GP	G	A	TP	PIM
1993-94	Thunder Bay	USHL	46	21	33	54	101	....	....	....	....	....
1994-95	Michigan Tech	WCHA	38	5	11	16	62	....	....	....	....	....
1995-96	Michigan Tech	WCHA	42	17	17	34	84	....	....	....	....	....
1996-97	Canada	Nat-Team	55	10	17	27	82	....	....	....	....	....
1997-98	Manitoba Moose	IHL	61	8	10	18	133	3	0	0	0	6
1998-99	Manitoba Moose	IHL	78	10	16	26	185	5	0	1	1	6
99-2000	Manitoba Moose	IHL	74	12	9	21	187	1	0	0	0	16
2000-01	Manitoba Moose	IHL	77	18	13	31	150	12	1	1	2	22

ROYER, Gaetan (ROI-ay, GAY-tan) **CGY.**

Right wing. Shoots right. 6'3", 210 lbs. Born, Donnacona, Que., March 13, 1976.

			Regular Season					Playoffs				
Season	Club	Lea	GP	G	A	TP	PIM	GP	G	A	TP	PIM
1994-95	Sherbrooke	QMJHL	65	11	25	36	194	7	0	2	2	6
1995-96	Sherbrooke	QMJHL	36	25	26	51	174	....	....	....	....	....
	Beauport	QMJHL	25	11	10	21	59	19	5	9	14	47
1996-97	Jacksonville	ECHL	28	7	8	15	149	....	....	....	....	....
	Indianapolis Ice	IHL	29	2	4	6	60	....	....	....	....	....
1997-98	Grand Rapids	IHL	52	12	6	18	177	....	....	....	....	....
1998-99	Saint John Flames	AHL	15	1	0	1	36	7	0	1	1	8
99-2000	Michigan K-Wings	IHL	20	6	2	8	64	....	....	....	....	....
2000-01	Saint John Flames	AHL	58	8	4	12	134	14	0	0	0	16

Signed as a free agent by **Calgary**, September 12, 2000.

ROZAKOV, Rail (roh-zah-KAWF, righ-EEL) **CGY.**

Defense. Shoots left. 6'1", 198 lbs. Born, Murmansk, USSR, March 29, 1981.
(Calgary's 4th choice, 106th overall, in 1999 Entry Draft).

			Regular Season					Playoffs				
Season	Club	Lea	GP	G	A	TP	PIM	GP	G	A	TP	PIM
1997-98	Lada Togliatti-2	Russia-3	36	0	2	2	43	....	....	....	....	....
1998-99	Lada Togliatti-2	Russia-4	30	0	0	0	14	....	....	....	....	....
99-2000	Krylja Sovetov	Russia-2	23	0	1	1	41	....	....	....	....	....
2000-01	Ust-Novokuznetsk	Russia	21	0	1	1	10	....	....	....	....	....

RUDENKO, Konstantin (roo-DEHN-koh, KOHN-stan-tihn) **PHI.**

Left wing. Shoots right. 5'11", 180 lbs. Born, Ust-Kamenogorsk, USSR, July 23, 1981.
(Philadelphia's 3rd choice, 160th overall, in 1999 Entry Draft).

			Regular Season					Playoffs				
Season	Club	Lea	GP	G	A	TP	PIM	GP	G	A	TP	PIM
1997-98	VDV Omsk-2	Russia-3	22	7	8	15	4	....	....	....	....	....
1998-99	HC Cherepovets	Russia-2	28	15	9	24	67	....	....	....	....	....
	HC Cherepovets-2	Russia-3	3	0	1	1	4	....	....	....	....	....
99-2000	St. Petersburg	Russia-2	7	2	4	6	2	....	....	....	....	....
	St. Petersburg	Russia	19	1	1	2	10	1	0	0	0	0
2000-01	HC Yaroslavl	Russia	18	2	3	5	28	9	2	1	3	8

RULLIER, Joe (ROO-yay, JOH) **L.A.**

Defense. Shoots right. 6'3", 200 lbs. Born, Montreal, Que., January 28, 1980.
(Los Angeles' 5th choice, 133rd overall, in 1998 Entry Draft).

			Regular Season					Playoffs				
Season	Club	Lea	GP	G	A	TP	PIM	GP	G	A	TP	PIM
1996-97	Montreal Bourassa	QAAA	24	5	10	15	....	....	....	....	....	....
	Rimouski Oceanic	QMJHL	23	0	3	3	87	4	0	0	0	11
1997-98	Rimouski Oceanic	QMJHL	55	1	10	11	176	16	1	4	5	34
1998-99	Rimouski Oceanic	QMJHL	54	7	32	39	202	11	2	3	5	26
99-2000	Rimouski Oceanic	QMJHL	49	3	32	35	161	14	1	8	9	34
2000-01	Lowell	AHL	63	1	1	2	162	4	0	1	1	2

RUPP, Mike (RUHP, MIGHK) **N.J.**

Left wing. Shoots left. 6'5", 225 lbs. Born, Cleveland, OH, January 13, 1980.
(New Jersey's 7th choice, 76th overall, in 2000 Entry Draft).

			Regular Season					Playoffs				
Season	Club	Lea	GP	G	A	TP	PIM	GP	G	A	TP	PIM
1996-97	St. Edwards	HI-School	20	26	24	50	....	....	....	....	....	....
1997-98	Windsor Spitfires	OHL	38	9	8	17	60	....	....	....	....	....
	Erie Otters	OHL	26	7	3	10	57	7	3	1	4	6
1998-99	Erie Otters	OHL	63	22	25	47	102	5	0	2	2	25
99-2000	Erie Otters	OHL	58	32	21	53	134	13	5	5	10	22
2000-01	Albany River Rats	AHL	71	10	10	20	63	....	....	....	....	....

• Re-entered NHL Entry Draft. Originally NY Islanders's 1st choice, 9th overall, in 1998 Entry Draft.

RUUTU, Mikko (ROO-too, MIH-koh) **OTT.**

Left wing. Shoots left. 6'4", 183 lbs. Born, Vantaa, Finland, September 10, 1978.
(Ottawa's 7th choice, 201st overall, in 1999 Entry Draft).

			Regular Season					Playoffs				
Season	**Club**	**Lea**	**GP**	**G**	**A**	**TP**	**PIM**	**GP**	**G**	**A**	**TP**	**PIM**
1997-98	HIFK Helsinki	Finn-Jr.	24	4	2	6	37	....	....	....	....	....
1998-99	HIFK Helsinki	Finn-Jr.	23	13	8	21	30	....	....	....	....	....
	HIFK Helsinki	Finland	31	3	1	4	12	4	0	0	0	2
99-2000	Clarkson Knights	ECAC	33	5	6	11	26	....	....	....	....	....
2000-01	Jokerit Helsinki	Finland	56	5	6	11	38	5	0	1	1	2

RUUTU, Tuomo (ROO-too, TOO-oh-moh) **CHI.**

Center. Shoots left. 6', 201 lbs. Born, Vantaa, Finland, February 16, 1983.
(Chicago's 1st choice, 9th overall, in 2001 Entry Draft).

			Regular Season					Playoffs				
Season	**Club**	**Lea**	**GP**	**G**	**A**	**TP**	**PIM**	**GP**	**G**	**A**	**TP**	**PIM**
1998-99	HIFK Helsinki	Finn-Jr.	25	9	11	20	88	2	1	1	2	2
99-2000	HIFK Helsinki	Finn-Jr.	35	11	16	27	32	3	0	1	1	4
	HIFK Helsinki	Finland	1	0	0	0	2	....	....	....	....	....
2000-01	HIFK Helsinki	Finn-Jr.	2	1	0	1	0	....	....	....	....	....
	Jokerit Helsinki	Finland	47	11	11	22	86	5	0	0	0	4

RYAN, Mike (RIGH-yan) **DAL.**

Center. Shoots left. 6'1", 180 lbs. Born, Milton, MA, May 16, 1980.
(Dallas' 1st choice, 32nd overall, in 1999 Entry Draft).

			Regular Season					Playoffs				
Season	**Club**	**Lea**	**GP**	**G**	**A**	**TP**	**PIM**	**GP**	**G**	**A**	**TP**	**PIM**
1997-98	Boston College	Hi-School	23	22	14	36	28	....	....	....	....	....
1998-99	Boston College	Hi-School	21	20	24	44	22	....	....	....	....	....
99-2000	Northeastern	H-East	32	4	9	13	47	....	....	....	....	....
2000-01	Northeastern	H-East	33	17	12	29	52	....	....	....	....	....

RYBIN, Maxim (ray-bihn, max-EEM) **ANA.**

Left wing. Shoots right. 5'8", 182 lbs. Born, Zhukovsky, USSR, June 15, 1981.
(Anaheim's 4th choice, 141st overall, in 1999 Entry Draft).

			Regular Season					Playoffs				
Season	**Club**	**Lea**	**GP**	**G**	**A**	**TP**	**PIM**	**GP**	**G**	**A**	**TP**	**PIM**
1996-97	Krylja Sovetov-2	Russia-3	5	0	0	0	4	....	....	....	....	....
	Krylja Sovetov	Russia	6	0	0	0	0	....	....	....	....	....
1997-98	Krylja Sovetov-2	Russia-3	25	13	5	18	26	....	....	....	....	....
	Krylja Sovetov	Russia	5	0	0	0	2	....	....	....	....	....
1998-99	Krylja Sovetov	Russia	53	15	12	27	83	....	....	....	....	....
99-2000	Sarnia Sting	OHL	66	29	27	56	47	7	4	1	5	2
2000-01	Sarnia Sting	OHL	67	34	36	70	60	4	0	3	3	2

Won Russian Elite League's Rookie Forward of the Year Award (1999)

RYCROFT, Mark (RIGH-krawft, MAHRK) **ST.L.**

Right wing. Shoots right. 5'11", 197 lbs. Born, Nanaimo, B.C., July 12, 1978.

			Regular Season					Playoffs				
Season	**Club**	**Lea**	**GP**	**G**	**A**	**TP**	**PIM**	**GP**	**G**	**A**	**TP**	**PIM**
1993-94	Penticton	BCAHA	60	47	65	112	100	....	....	....	....	....
1994-95	Penticton	BCAHA	43	33	43	76	90	....	....	....	....	....
1995-96					STATISTICS NOT AVAILABLE							
1996-97	Nanaimo Clippers	BCJHL	58	32	35	67	79	....	....	....	....	....
1997-98	U. of Denver	WCHA	35	15	17	32	28	....	....	....	....	....
1998-99	U. of Denver	WCHA	41	19	18	37	36	....	....	....	....	....
99-2000	U. of Denver	WCHA	41	17	17	34	87	....	....	....	....	....
2000-01	Worcester	AHL	71	24	26	50	68	11	2	5	7	4

WCHA All-Rookie Team (1998) • Signed as a free agent by **St. Louis**, May 15, 2000.

RYDER, Michael (RIGH-duhr, MIGH-kuhl) **MTL.**

Center. Shoots right. 6'1", 191 lbs. Born, St. John's, Nfld., March 31, 1980.
(Montreal's 9th choice, 216th overall, in 1998 Entry Draft).

			Regular Season					Playoffs				
Season	**Club**	**Lea**	**GP**	**G**	**A**	**TP**	**PIM**	**GP**	**G**	**A**	**TP**	**PIM**
1996-97	Bonavista Saints	NFAHA	23	31	17	48	....	....	....	....	....	....
1997-98	Hull Olympiques	QMJHL	69	34	28	62	41	10	4	2	6	4
1998-99	Hull Olympiques	QMJHL	69	44	43	87	65	23	*20	16	36	39
99-2000	Hull Olympiques	QMJHL	63	50	58	108	50	15	11	17	28	28
2000-01	Tallahassee	ECHL	5	4	5	9	6	....	....	....	....	....
	Quebec Citadelles	AHL	61	6	9	15	14	....	....	....	....	....

SAARINEN, Pasi **S.J.**

Defense. Shoots right. 5'11", 194 lbs. Born, Hyvinkaa, Finland, April 17, 1977.
(San Jose's 7th choice, 256th overall, in 2000 Entry Draft).

			Regular Season					Playoffs				
Season	**Club**	**Lea**	**GP**	**G**	**A**	**TP**	**PIM**	**GP**	**G**	**A**	**TP**	**PIM**
1993-94	Ilves Tampere	Finn-Jr.	34	5	4	9	24	6	1	2	3	4
1994-95	Ilves Tampere	Finn-Jr.	24	4	5	9	55	....	....	....	....	....
	Ilves Tampere	Finland	1	0	0	0	0	....	....	....	....	....
1995-96	Ilves Tampere	Finn-Jr.	8	2	2	4	24	....	....	....	....	....
	KooVee Tampere	Finn-2	7	1	1	2	22	....	....	....	....	....
	Ilves Tampere	Finland	7	0	1	1	10	....	....	....	....	....
1996-97	Ilves Tampere	Finn-Jr.	9	3	3	6	22	....	....	....	....	....
	Ilves Tampere	Finland	44	4	3	7	83	6	1	0	1	10
1997-98	Ilves Tampere	Finland	36	11	8	19	73	....	....	....	....	....
1998-99	Ilves Tampere	Finland	45	2	8	10	56	4	1	0	1	8
99-2000	Ilves Tampere	Finland	50	9	19	28	79	3	0	0	0	26
2000-01	Jokerit Helsinki	Finland	52	6	9	15	79	5	2	0	2	4

SACHL, Petr (SAH-khuhl, PEE-tuhr) **NSH.**

Left wing. Shoots right. 6'2", 205 lbs. Born, Jindrivichuk Hradec, Czech., December 2, 1977.
(NY Islanders' 6th choice, 128th overall, in 1996 Entry Draft).

			Regular Season					Playoffs				
Season	**Club**	**Lea**	**GP**	**G**	**A**	**TP**	**PIM**	**GP**	**G**	**A**	**TP**	**PIM**
1994-95	HC Budejovice-Jr.	Cze-Rep	40	6	8	14	....	....	....	....	....	....
1995-96	HC Budejovice-Jr.	Cze-Rep	39	19	17	36	....	....	....	....	....	....
	HC Budejovice	Cze-Rep	....	....	....	....	....	2	0	0	0	....
1996-97	HC Budejovice	Cze-Rep	2	0	0	0	0	....	....	....	....	....
	Tri-City Americans	WHL	63	13	24	37	32	....	....	....	....	....
1997-98	HC Budejovice	Cze-Rep	20	1	3	4	4	....	....	....	....	....
1998-99	HC Budejovice	Cze-Rep	4	0	1	1	2	....	....	....	....	....
99-2000	Tacoma Sabercats	WCHL	1	0	0	0	0	....	....	....	....	....
	Asheville Smoke	UHL	3	0	1	1	4	....	....	....	....	....
	Fort Wayne	UHL	55	30	24	54	28	10	4	7	11	8
2000-01	Milwaukee	IHL	76	12	17	29	33	5	0	0	0	4

Traded to **Nashville** by **NY Islanders** for Nashville's 9th round choice (Tomi Pettinen) in 2000 Entry Draft, March 14, 2000.

SAFRONOV, Kirill (sah-FRAW-nawf, kih-RIHL) **PHX.**

Defense. Shoots left. 6'2", 209 lbs. Born, Leningrad, USSR, February 26, 1981.
(Phoenix's 2nd choice, 19th overall, in 1999 Entry Draft).

			Regular Season					Playoffs				
Season	**Club**	**Lea**	**GP**	**G**	**A**	**TP**	**PIM**	**GP**	**G**	**A**	**TP**	**PIM**
1996-97	St. Petersburg-2	Russia-3	9	0	0	0	6	....	....	....	....	....
	St. Petersburg	Russia	1	0	0	0	0	....	....	....	....	....
1997-98	St. Petersburg-2	Russia-3	34	4	3	7	36	....	....	....	....	....
	St. Petersburg	Russia	9	0	1	1	4	1	0	0	0	0
1998-99	St. Petersburg-2	Russia-4	4	2	1	3	2	....	....	....	....	....
	St. Petersburg	Russia	45	1	3	4	32	....	....	....	....	....
99-2000	Quebec Remparts	QMJHL	55	11	32	43	95	11	2	4	6	14
2000-01	Springfield	AHL	65	5	13	18	77	....	....	....	....	....

SAINOMAA, Teemu (SIGH-noh-muh, TEE-moo) **OTT.**

Left wing. Shoots left. 6'3", 202 lbs. Born, Helsinki, Finland, May 15, 1981.
(Ottawa's 3rd choice, 62nd overall, in 1999 Entry Draft).

			Regular Season					Playoffs				
Season	**Club**	**Lea**	**GP**	**G**	**A**	**TP**	**PIM**	**GP**	**G**	**A**	**TP**	**PIM**
1997-98	Jokerit Helsinki-B	Finn-Jr.	12	3	5	8	8	3	1	1	2	6
1998-99	Jokerit Helsinki	Finn-Jr.	11	4	5	9	0	....	....	....	....	....
99-2000	Jokerit Helsinki	Finn-Jr.	30	6	7	13	59	11	6	2	8	20
	Jokerit Helsinki	Finland	6	0	0	0	0	....	....	....	....	....
2000-01	Jokerit Helsinki	Finland	28	1	3	4	2	4	0	1	1	0

ST. CROIX, Chris (SAINT KWAH, KRIHS) **NYR**

Defense. Shoots right. 6'1", 199 lbs. Born, Voorhees, NJ, May 2, 1979.
(Calgary's 7th choice, 92nd overall, in 1997 Entry Draft).

			Regular Season					Playoffs				
Season	**Club**	**Lea**	**GP**	**G**	**A**	**TP**	**PIM**	**GP**	**G**	**A**	**TP**	**PIM**
1993-94	Winnipeg Blues	MAHA	35	2	40	42	30	....	....	....	....	....
1994-95	Winnipeg Blues	MAHA	40	9	32	41	20	....	....	....	....	....
1995-96	Kamloops Blazers	WHL	61	4	5	9	29	13	0	2	2	4
1996-97	Kamloops Blazers	WHL	67	11	39	50	67	5	0	1	1	2
1997-98	Kamloops Blazers	WHL	46	3	13	16	51	7	1	1	2	6
1998-99	Kamloops Blazers	WHL	64	8	27	35	123	14	0	4	4	16
99-2000	Saint John Flames	AHL	75	5	16	21	51	3	0	1	1	2
2000-01	Saint John Flames	AHL	69	0	4	4	66	5	0	1	1	4

Traded to **NY Rangers** by **Calgary** for Burke Henry, June 23, 2001.

ST. JACQUES, Bruno (SAINT ZHAWK, BREW-noh) **PHI.**

Defense. Shoots left. 6'2", 210 lbs. Born, Montreal, Que., August 22, 1980.
(Philadelphia's 12th choice, 253rd overall, in 1998 Entry Draft).

			Regular Season					Playoffs				
Season	**Club**	**Lea**	**GP**	**G**	**A**	**TP**	**PIM**	**GP**	**G**	**A**	**TP**	**PIM**
1996-97	Mtl-Bourassa	QAAA	40	5	8	13	....	16	0	7	7	....
1997-98	Baie-Comeau	QMJHL	63	1	11	12	140	....	....	....	....	....
1998-99	Baie-Comeau	QMJHL	49	8	13	21	85	....	....	....	....	....
99-2000	Baie-Comeau	QMJHL	60	8	28	36	120	6	0	2	2	10
	Philadelphia	AHL	3	0	1	1	0	1	0	0	0	0
2000-01	Philadelphia	AHL	45	1	16	17	83	10	1	0	1	16

SALMELAINEN, Tony (sal-meh-LIGH-nehn, TOH-nee) **EDM.**

Left wing. Shoots right. 5'9", 176 lbs. Born, Espoo, Finland, August 8, 1981.
(Edmonton's 3rd choice, 41st overall, in 1999 Entry Draft).

			Regular Season					Playoffs				
Season	**Club**	**Lea**	**GP**	**G**	**A**	**TP**	**PIM**	**GP**	**G**	**A**	**TP**	**PIM**
1996-97	Blues Espoo	Finn-Jr.	30	8	5	13	38	....	....	....	....	....
1997-98	Blues Espoo-B	Finn-Jr.	5	2	2	4	10	....	....	....	....	....
	HIFK Helsinki-B	Finn-Jr.	28	23	16	39	30	....	....	....	....	....
	HIFK Helsinki	Finn-Jr.	5	0	0	0	0	....	....	....	....	....
1998-99	HIFK Helsinki-B	Finn-Jr.	21	13	10	23	45	....	....	....	....	....
	HIFK Helsinki	Finn-Jr.	....	....	....	....	....	10	10	8	18	10
99-2000	HIFK Helsinki	Finn-Jr.	1	0	1	1	0	....	....	....	....	....
	HIFK Helsinki	Finland	1	1	0	1	0	....	....	....	....	....
2000-01	HIFK Helsinki	Finn-Jr.	3	3	3	6	0	....	....	....	....	....
	HIFK Helsinki	Finland	19	1	0	1	6	....	....	....	....	....
	Ilves Tampere	Finn-Jr.	3	1	2	3	2	....	....	....	....	....
	Ilves Tampere	Finland	26	3	10	13	4	3	0	0	0	0

SALOMONSSON, Andreas (sal-oh-MAWN-suhn, an-DRAY-uhs) **N.J.**

Center. Shoots left. 6', 185 lbs. Born, Ornskoldsvik, Sweden, December 19, 1973.
(New Jersey's 8th choice, 163rd overall, in 2001 Entry Draft).

			Regular Season					Playoffs				
Season	**Club**	**Lea**	**GP**	**G**	**A**	**TP**	**PIM**	**GP**	**G**	**A**	**TP**	**PIM**
1990-91	MoDo Hockey	Sweden	2	0	0	0	0	....	....	....	....	....
1991-92	MoDo Hockey	Sweden	20	1	1	2	26	....	....	....	....	....
1992-93	MoDo Hockey	Swede-Jr.	10	4	16	20	8	....	....	....	....	....
	MoDo Hockey	Sweden	33	1	1	2	0	....	....	....	....	....
1993-94	MoDo Hockey	Sweden	38	15	8	23	33	11	1	2	3	4
1994-95	MoDo Hockey	Sweden	40	5	9	14	34	....	....	....	....	....
1995-96	MoDo Hockey	Sweden	38	13	6	19	22	7	0	4	4	8
1996-97	MoDo Hockey	Sweden	23	6	6	12	22	....	....	....	....	....
	Ratinger Lowen	DEL	21	5	1	6	49	....	....	....	....	....
1997-98	MoDo Hockey	Sweden	45	6	15	21	69	8	4	3	7	4
1998-99	MoDo Hockey	Sweden	46	13	13	26	60	13	4	5	9	12
99-2000	MoDo Hockey	EuroHL	5	2	2	4	4	3	1	1	2	4
	MoDo Hockey	Sweden	48	9	15	24	38	12	0	4	4	12
2000-01	Djurgardens IF	Sweden	48	10	12	22	46	13	3	4	7	31

SAMOILOV, Igor (sam-OI-lawf, EE-gohr) **PHX.**

Defense. Shoots left. 5'11", 195 lbs. Born, Moscow, USSR, January 23, 1982.
(Phoenix's 6th choice, 217th overall, in 2000 Entry Draft).

			Regular Season					Playoffs				
Season	**Club**	**Lea**	**GP**	**G**	**A**	**TP**	**PIM**	**GP**	**G**	**A**	**TP**	**PIM**
1998-99	HK Yaroslavl-2	Russia-3	16	0	1	1	6	....	....	....	....	....
99-2000	HK Yaroslavl-2	Russia-3	41	1	3	4	50	....	....	....	....	....
2000-01	St. Petersburg	Russia	38	0	2	2	22	....	....	....	....	....

SAMUELSSON, Martin (SAM-yuhl-suhn, MAHR-tihn) BOS.

Right wing. Shoots left. 6'2", 194 lbs. Born, Upplands Vasby, Sweden, January 25, 1982.
(Boston's 2nd choice, 27th overall, in 2000 Entry Draft).

			Regular Season					Playoffs				
Season	**Club**	**Lea**	**GP**	**G**	**A**	**TP**	**PIM**	**GP**	**G**	**A**	**TP**	**PIM**
1996-97	Hammarby IF	Swede-Jr.	6	1	1	2	0	....	....	....	....	....
1997-98	Hammarby IF	Swede-Jr.	20	13	12	25	....	....	....	....	....	....
	Hammarby IF	Swede-2	2	0	0	0	0	....	....	....	....	....
1998-99	MoDo Hockey	Swede-Jr.	31	18	13	31	10	....	....	....	....	....
99-2000	MoDo Hockey-B	Swede-Jr.	6	3	0	3	4	....	....	....	....	....
	MoDo Hockey	Swede-Jr.	19	9	8	17	18	2	1	0	1	2
2000-01	Hammarby IF	Swede-Jr.	1	0	1	1	0	....	....	....	....	....
	Hammarby IF	Sweden	38	15	6	21	28	....	....	....	....	....

SANDSTROM, Jan (SAND-struhm, YAN) ANA.

Defense. Shoots left. 6', 190 lbs. Born, Pitea, Sweden, January 24, 1978.
(Anaheim's 5th choice, 173rd overall, in 1999 Entry Draft).

			Regular Season					Playoffs				
Season	**Club**	**Lea**	**GP**	**G**	**A**	**TP**	**PIM**	**GP**	**G**	**A**	**TP**	**PIM**
1994-95	Pitea HC	Swede-2	12	1	0	1	4	....	....	....	....	....
1995-96	Pitea HC	Swede-2	29	1	11	12	18	....	....	....	....	....
1996-97	Pitea HC	Swede-2	28	3	4	7	28	....	....	....	....	....
1997-98	AIK Solna	Sweden	38	0	2	2	16	....	....	....	....	....
1998-99	AIK Solna	Sweden	47	2	7	9	18	....	....	....	....	....
99-2000	AIK Solna	Sweden	49	2	6	8	22	....	....	....	....	....
2000-01	Skelleftea IK	Swede-2	22	0	5	5	14	....	....	....	....	....
	AIK Solna	Sweden	18	1	3	4	10	....	....	....	....	....

SANTALA, Tommi (SAHN-tah-luh, TAW-mee) ATL.

Center. Shoots right. 6'2", 198 lbs. Born, Helsinki, Finland, June 27, 1979.
(Atlanta's 10th choice, 245th overall, in 1999 Entry Draft).

			Regular Season					Playoffs				
Season	**Club**	**Lea**	**GP**	**G**	**A**	**TP**	**PIM**	**GP**	**G**	**A**	**TP**	**PIM**
1995-96	Jokerit Helsinki	Finn-Jr.	25	8	4	12	12	6	1	2	3	4
1996-97	Jokerit Helsinki	Finn-Jr.	20	0	2	2	10	5	0	0	0	0
1997-98	Jokerit Helsinki	Finn-Jr.	36	10	28	38	48	8	0	1	1	4
1998-99	Jokerit Helsinki	Finn-Jr.	30	20	24	44	20	8	1	3	4	22
	Jokerit Helsinki	Finland	30	0	0	0	14	3	0	0	0	0
99-2000	Jokerit Helsinki	Finn-Jr.	5	6	4	10	4	....	....	....	....	....
	Jokerit Helsinki	Finland	14	0	1	1	0	....	....	....	....	....
	HPK Hameenlinna	Finn-Jr.	2	3	1	4	2	....	....	....	....	....
	HPK Hameenlinna	Finland	38	8	19	27	65	8	3	4	7	10
2000-01	HPK Hameenlinna	Finland	56	16	24	40	90	....	....	....	....	....

SAPOZHNIKOV, Vladimir (suh-POHZH-nih-kahf, vla-DIH-meer) FLA.

Defense. Shoots left. 6'3", 205 lbs. Born, Seversk, USSR, August 2, 1982.
(Florida's 1st choice, 58th overall, in 2000 Entry Draft).

			Regular Season					Playoffs				
Season	**Club**	**Lea**	**GP**	**G**	**A**	**TP**	**PIM**	**GP**	**G**	**A**	**TP**	**PIM**
1997-98	HC Novosibirsk-2	Russia-3	15	0	0	0	2	....	....	....	....	....
1998-99	HC Novokuznetsk	Russia-Jr.		STATISTICS NOT AVAILABLE								
99-2000	Novokuznetsk-2	Russia-3		STATISTICS NOT AVAILABLE								
2000-01	North Bay	OHL	53	0	6	6	70	4	0	0	0	2

SARNO, Peter (SAHR-noh, PEE-tuhr) EDM.

Center. Shoots left. 5'11", 185 lbs. Born, Toronto, Ont., July 26, 1979.
(Edmonton's 6th choice, 141st overall, in 1997 Entry Draft).

			Regular Season					Playoffs				
Season	**Club**	**Lea**	**GP**	**G**	**A**	**TP**	**PIM**	**GP**	**G**	**A**	**TP**	**PIM**
1995-96	North York	MTJHL	52	39	57	96	27	....	....	....	....	....
1996-97	Windsor Spitfires	OHL	66	20	63	83	59	5	0	3	3	6
1997-98	Windsor Spitfires	OHL	64	33	*88	*121	18	....	....	....	....	....
	Hamilton Bulldogs	AHL	8	1	1	2	2	....	....	....	....	....
1998-99	Sarnia Sting	OHL	68	37	*93	*130	49	6	1	7	8	2
99-2000	Hamilton Bulldogs	AHL	67	10	36	46	31	....	....	....	....	....
2000-01	Hamilton Bulldogs	AHL	79	19	46	65	64	....	....	....	....	....

SAUER, Kent (SAW-uhr, KEHNT) NSH.

Defense. Shoots right. 6'2", 231 lbs. Born, St. Cloud, MN, May 10, 1979.
(Nashville's 4th choice, 88th overall, in 1998 Entry Draft).

			Regular Season					Playoffs				
Season	**Club**	**Lea**	**GP**	**G**	**A**	**TP**	**PIM**	**GP**	**G**	**A**	**TP**	**PIM**
1996-97	St. Cloud-Apollo	Hi-School	23	14	15	29	20	....	....	....	....	....
1997-98	North Iowa	USHL	54	4	19	23	99	10	1	2	3	18
1998-99	Minnesota-Duluth	WCHA	38	1	3	4	50	....	....	....	....	....
99-2000	Portland Hawks	WHL	65	12	13	25	116	....	....	....	....	....
	Milwaukee	IHL	6	0	0	0	0	....	....	....	....	....
2000-01	New Orleans	ECHL	46	4	11	15	84	....	....	....	....	....
	Milwaukee	IHL	1	0	0	0	0	....	....	....	....	....

SAUER, Kurt (SAW-uhr, KUHRT) COL.

Defense. Shoots left. 6'4", 220 lbs. Born, St. Cloud, MN, January 16, 1981.
(Colorado's 5th choice, 88th overall, in 2000 Entry Draft).

			Regular Season					Playoffs				
Season	**Club**	**Lea**	**GP**	**G**	**A**	**TP**	**PIM**	**GP**	**G**	**A**	**TP**	**PIM**
1998-99	North Iowa	USHL	52	1	4	5	67	....	....	....	....	....
99-2000	Spokane Chiefs	WHL	71	3	12	15	48	15	2	1	3	8
2000-01	Spokane Chiefs	WHL	48	5	10	15	85	3	1	0	1	2

SAVIELS, Agris (sah-VEE-ehls, AG-rihs) COL.

Defense. Shoots left. 6'2", 200 lbs. Born, Riga, Latvia, January 15, 1982.
(Colorado's 4th choice, 63rd overall, in 2000 Entry Draft).

			Regular Season					Playoffs				
Season	**Club**	**Lea**	**GP**	**G**	**A**	**TP**	**PIM**	**GP**	**G**	**A**	**TP**	**PIM**
1996-97	Dynamo Riga	Latvia-Jr.	15	1	2	3	4	....	....	....	....	....
	HK Lido-Nafta	Latvia	40	4	15	19	40	....	....	....	....	....
1997-98	Dynamo Riga	Latvia-Jr.	15	1	2	3	4	....	....	....	....	....
	HK Lido-Nafta	Latvia	40	7	21	28	30	....	....	....	....	....
1998-99	Notre Dame	SAHA	18	6	9	15	25	....	....	....	....	....
	Notre Dame	SJHL	30	6	13	19	....	....	....	....	....	....
99-2000	Owen Sound	OHL	65	7	25	32	56	....	....	....	....	....
2000-01	Owen Sound	OHL	68	14	37	51	46	5	0	1	1	2

SCHADILOV, Igor (sha-DEE-lahf, EE-gor) WSH.

Defense. Shoots left. 6'2", 189 lbs. Born, Moscow, USSR, June 7, 1980.
(Washington's 10th choice, 249th overall, in 1999 Entry Draft).

			Regular Season					Playoffs				
Season	**Club**	**Lea**	**GP**	**G**	**A**	**TP**	**PIM**	**GP**	**G**	**A**	**TP**	**PIM**
1996-97	Dynamo Moscow	Russia-Jr.	30	3	7	10	30	....	....	....	....	....
1997-98	Dynamo Moscow	Russia-2	38	1	0	1	6	....	....	....	....	....
1998-99	Dynamo Moscow	Russia-2	28	2	9	11	15	....	....	....	....	....
	Dynamo Moscow	Russia	2	0	0	0	0	....	....	....	....	....
	Krylja Sovetov	Russia	9	0	0	0	0	....	....	....	....	....
99-2000	THK Tver	Russia-2	14	0	3	3	6	....	....	....	....	....
	Dynamo Moscow	Russia	26	0	2	2	8	16	0	0	0	2
2000-01	Dynamo Moscow	Russia	34	1	5	6	12	....	....	....	....	....

SCHAUER, Stefan (SHOW-uhr, SHTEH-fuhn) OTT.

Defense. Shoots left. 6'1", 180 lbs. Born, Schongau, Germany, January 12, 1983.
(Ottawa's 6th choice, 162nd overall, in 2001 Entry Draft).

			Regular Season					Playoffs				
Season	**Club**	**Lea**	**GP**	**G**	**A**	**TP**	**PIM**	**GP**	**G**	**A**	**TP**	**PIM**
99-2000	SC Riessersee	DEB-Jr.	30	7	14	21	82	....	....	....	....	....
	SC Riessersee	DEB	3	0	0	0	0	....	....	....	....	....
2000-01	SC Riessersee	DEB	44	1	3	4	4	11	1	7	8	24

SCHEFFELMAIER, Brett (sch-EHFEHL-mai-uhr, BREHT) ST.L.

Defense. Shoots right. 6'5", 200 lbs. Born, Coronation, Alta., March 31, 1981.
(St. Louis' 5th choice, 190th overall, in 2001 Entry Draft).

			Regular Season					Playoffs				
Season	**Club**	**Lea**	**GP**	**G**	**A**	**TP**	**PIM**	**GP**	**G**	**A**	**TP**	**PIM**
1997-98	Red Deer Chiefs	AMHL	13	0	4	4	36	....	....	....	....	....
	Medicine Hat	WHL	25	0	1	1	69	....	....	....	....	....
1998-99	Medicine Hat	WHL	69	3	10	13	252	....	....	....	....	....
99-2000	Medicine Hat	WHL	71	1	9	10	281	....	....	....	....	....
2000-01	Medicine Hat	WHL	62	3	10	13	279	....	....	....	....	....

• Re-entered NHL Entry Draft. Originally Tampa Bay' 3rd choice, 75th overall, in 1999 Entry Draft.

SCHILL, Jonathan (SHIHL, JAWN-ah-thuhn) CBJ

Left wing. Shoots left. 6'1", 201 lbs. Born, Kitchener, Ont., June 28, 1979.

			Regular Season					Playoffs				
Season	**Club**	**Lea**	**GP**	**G**	**A**	**TP**	**PIM**	**GP**	**G**	**A**	**TP**	**PIM**
1995-96	Kitchener Lions	OMHA	30	17	12	29	100	....	....	....	....	....
	Kitchener	OJHL-B	1	0	0	0	0	....	....	....	....	....
1996-97	Kingston	OHL	52	3	7	10	16	4	0	0	0	0
1997-98	Kingston	OHL	64	14	17	31	34	12	1	1	2	4
1998-99	Kingston	OHL	68	32	27	59	93	5	2	1	3	6
99-2000	Kingston	OHL	65	39	48	87	79	3	1	1	2	6
2000-01	Syracuse Crunch	AHL	4	0	1	1	8	....	....	....	....	....
	Dayton Bombers	ECHL	58	18	6	24	153	6	2	3	5	22

Signed as a free agent by **Columbus**, May 8, 2000.

SCHNABEL, Robert (SHNAH-buhl, RAW-buhrt) NSH.

Defense. Shoots left. 6'5", 233 lbs. Born, Prague, Czech., November 10, 1978.
(Phoenix's 7th choice, 129th overall, in 1998 Entry Draft).

			Regular Season					Playoffs				
Season	**Club**	**Lea**	**GP**	**G**	**A**	**TP**	**PIM**	**GP**	**G**	**A**	**TP**	**PIM**
1994-95	Slavia Praha-Jr.	Cze-Rep	35	11	6	17	14	....	....	....	....	....
1995-96	Slavia Praha-Jr.	Cze-Rep	38	3	5	8	....	....	....	....	....	....
1996-97	Slavia Praha-Jr.	Cze-Rep	36	5	2	7	....	....	....	....	....	....
	Slavia Praha	Cze-Rep	4	0	0	0	4	1	0	0	0	0
1997-98	Red Deer Rebels	WHL	61	1	22	23	143	5	0	0	0	16
1998-99	Red Deer Rebels	WHL	1	0	0	0	2	....	....	....	....	....
	Springfield	AHL	77	1	7	8	155	3	1	0	1	4
99-2000	Springfield	AHL	40	2	8	10	133	5	0	0	0	4
2000-01	Springfield	AHL	22	1	2	3	38	....	....	....	....	....
	Timra IK	Sweden	16	0	2	2	72	....	....	....	....	....

• Re-entered NHL Entry Draft. Originally NY Islanders's 5th choice, 79th overall, in 1997 Entry Draft.

Claimed on waivers by **Nashville** from **Phoenix**, January 2, 2001.

SCHNEIDER, Andrew (SHNIGH-duhr, AN-droo) PIT.

Defense. Shoots left. 6', 220 lbs. Born, Grand Forks, ND, July 31, 1981.
(Pittsburgh's 7th choice, 156th overall, in 2001 Entry Draft).

			Regular Season					Playoffs				
Season	**Club**	**Lea**	**GP**	**G**	**A**	**TP**	**PIM**	**GP**	**G**	**A**	**TP**	**PIM**
1998-99	Lincoln Stars	USHL	9	0	4	4	8	4	0	0	0	2
99-2000	Lincoln Stars	USHL	46	7	10	17	102	10	6	4	10	27
2000-01	Lincoln Stars	USHL	54	12	24	36	134	....	....	....	....	....

SCHUBERT, Christoph (SHOO-buhrt, KRIHS-tawf) OTT.

Defense. Shoots left. 6'3", 198 lbs. Born, Munich, West Germany, February 5, 1982.
(Ottawa's 5th choice, 127th overall, in 2001 Entry Draft).

			Regular Season					Playoffs				
Season	**Club**	**Lea**	**GP**	**G**	**A**	**TP**	**PIM**	**GP**	**G**	**A**	**TP**	**PIM**
1998-99	EV Landshut	DEB-Jr.	28	15	20	35	77	....	....	....	....	....
99-2000	EV Landshut	DEB-Jr.	11	14	11	25	51	....	....	....	....	....
	EV Landshut	DEB	55	7	5	12	66	....	....	....	....	....
2000-01	Munich Barons	DEL	55	6	3	9	80	10	0	2	2	27

SCHUELLER, Doug (SHOO-luhr, DUHG)

Defense. Shoots right. 6'1", 210 lbs. Born, Inver Grove Heights, MN, March 30, 1977.
(Florida's 9th choice, 211th overall, in 1997 Entry Draft).

			Regular Season					Playoffs				
Season	**Club**	**Lea**	**GP**	**G**	**A**	**TP**	**PIM**	**GP**	**G**	**A**	**TP**	**PIM**
1994-95	White Bear Lake	Hi-School	25	7	17	24	32	....	....	....	....	....
1995-96	White Bear Lake	Hi-School	5	0	2	2	6	....	....	....	....	....
	Twin Cities	USHL	39	5	13	18	186	....	....	....	....	....
1996-97	Twin Cities	USHL	54	7	29	36	83	5	0	2	2	29
1997-98	Bowling Green	CCHA	36	5	14	19	62	....	....	....	....	....
1998-99	Bowling Green	CCHA	37	7	5	12	54	....	....	....	....	....
99-2000	Bowling Green	CCHA	32	2	5	7	85	....	....	....	....	....
2000-01	Bowling Green	CCHA	33	2	6	8	50	....	....	....	....	....
	Louisville Panthers	AHL	11	1	4	5	11	....	....	....	....	....

SCHULTZ, Nick (SHULTZ, NIHK) MIN.

Defense. Shoots left. 6', 187 lbs. Born, Regina, Sask., August 25, 1982.
(Minnesota's 2nd choice, 33rd overall, in 2000 Entry Draft).

Season	Club	Lea	RS GP	RS G	RS A	RS TP	RS PIM	PO GP	PO G	PO A	PO TP	PO PIM
1997-98	Yorkton Mallers	SMHL	59	10	30	40	74					
1998-99	Prince Albert	WHL	58	5	18	23	37	14	0	7	7	0
99-2000	Prince Albert	WHL	72	11	33	44	38	6	0	3	3	2
2000-01	Prince Albert	WHL	59	17	30	47	120					
	Cleveland	IHL	4	1	1	2	2	3	0	1	1	0

SCISSONS, Jeff (SKIH-zuhns, JEHF) VAN.

Center. Shoots left. 6'1", 190 lbs. Born, Saskatoon, Sask., November 24, 1976.
(Vancouver's 7th choice, 201st overall, in 1996 Entry Draft).

Season	Club	Lea	RS GP	RS G	RS A	RS TP	RS PIM	PO GP	PO G	PO A	PO TP	PO PIM
1992-93	Saskatoon AA	SAHA	35	8	11	19	32					
1993-94	Saskatoon Elites	SMHL	35	20	37	57	42					
1994-95	Vernon Lakers	BCJHL	50	10	20	30						
1995-96	Vernon Vipers	BCJHL	60	26	48	74	28	30	14	18	32	
1996-97	Minnesota-Duluth	WCHA	38	3	14	17	30					
1997-98	Minnesota-Duluth	WCHA	40	17	24	41	50					
1998-99	Minnesota-Duluth	WCHA	38	18	19	37	42					
99-2000	Minnesota-Duluth	WCHA	37	14	19	33	32					
2000-01	Kansas City	IHL	68	5	19	24	24					

WCHA Student Athlete of the Year (2000) • Established **Minnesota-Duluth** record by appearing in 153 consecutive games, March 23, 2000.

SCORSUNE, Matthew (SKOHR-soon, MAT-thew) COL.

Defense. Shoots right. 6'2", 210 lbs. Born, Morristown, NJ, June 27, 1977.
(Colorado's 12th choice, 214th overall, in 1996 Entry Draft).

Season	Club	Lea	RS GP	RS G	RS A	RS TP	RS PIM	PO GP	PO G	PO A	PO TP	PO PIM
1995-96	Hotchkiss High	Hi-School	24	7	22	29	24					
1996-97	Harvard University	ECAC	30	3	8	11	28					
1997-98	Harvard University	ECAC	33	9	10	19	30					
1998-99	Harvard University	ECAC	31	8	9	17	34					
99-2000	Harvard University	ECAC	30	5	8	13	38					
2000-01	Hershey Bears	AHL	57	3	9	12	25					

SCOTT, Richard NYR

Left wing. Shoots left. 6'2", 195 lbs. Born, Orillia, Ont., August 1, 1978.

Season	Club	Lea	RS GP	RS G	RS A	RS TP	RS PIM	PO GP	PO G	PO A	PO TP	PO PIM
1996-97	Orillia Terriers	OPJHL	10	0	0	0	23					
1997-98	Couchiching	OPJHL	45	13	19	32	166					
1998-99	Oshawa Generals	OHL	54	12	12	24	193					
99-2000	Charlotte	ECHL	55	1	5	6	317					
2000-01	Hartford	AHL	64	2	5	7	320	1	0	0	0	0
	Charlotte	ECHL	4	1	1	2	22					

Signed as a free agent by **NY Rangers**, May 8, 2001.

SCUDERI, Rob (SKUD-uhree, RAW-buhrt) PIT.

Defense. Shoots left. 6'2", 194 lbs. Born, Syosset, NY, December 30, 1978.
(Pittsburgh's 5th choice, 134th overall, in 1998 Entry Draft).

Season	Club	Lea	RS GP	RS G	RS A	RS TP	RS PIM	PO GP	PO G	PO A	PO TP	PO PIM
1995-96	NY Apple Core	MJBHL	76	18	60	78						
1996-97	NY Apple Core	MJBHL	82	42	70	112	64					
1997-98	Boston College	H-East	42	0	24	24	12					
1998-99	Boston College	H-East	41	2	8	10	20					
99-2000	Boston College	H-East	42	1	12	13	22					
2000-01	Boston College	H-East	43	4	19	23	42					

NCAA Championship All-Tournament Team (2001)

SEDOV, Pavel (se-DAHF), PAH-vehl) T.B.

Left wing. Shoots left. 6'3", 200 lbs. Born, Voskresensk, USSR, January 12, 1982.
(Tampa Bay's 5th choice, 161st overall, in 2000 Entry Draft).

Season	Club	Lea	RS GP	RS G	RS A	RS TP	RS PIM	PO GP	PO G	PO A	PO TP	PO PIM
99-2000	HC Voskresensk	Russia-2	10	0	0	0	2					
2000-01	HC Voskresensk	Russia-2	38	2	1	3	10					

SEELEY, Richard (SEE-lee, RIH-chahrd) L.A.

Defense. Shoots left. 6'2", 205 lbs. Born, Powell River, B.C., April 30, 1979.
(Los Angeles' 6th choice, 137th overall, in 1997 Entry Draft).

Season	Club	Lea	RS GP	RS G	RS A	RS TP	RS PIM	PO GP	PO G	PO A	PO TP	PO PIM
1995-96	Powell River	BCJHL	44	1	8	9	42					
1996-97	Lethbridge	WHL	3	0	0	0	11					
	Prince Albert	WHL	18	0	1	1	9	4	0	0	0	2
1997-98	Prince Albert	WHL	65	8	21	29	114					
1998-99	Prince Albert	WHL	61	10	48	58	110	14	1	11	12	14
99-2000	Lowell	AHL	36	5	1	6	37					
2000-01	Lowell	AHL	55	2	8	10	102					
	Trenton Titans	ECHL	9	0	2	2	18					

SEIKKULA, Timo (SAY-koo-lah, TEE-moh) PIT.

Center. Shoots left. 6'2", 183 lbs. Born, Kalajoki, Finland, May 27, 1978.
(Pittsburgh's 8th choice, 238th overall, in 1996 Entry Draft).

Season	Club	Lea	RS GP	RS G	RS A	RS TP	RS PIM	PO GP	PO G	PO A	PO TP	PO PIM
1994-95	Junkkarit HT	Finland-2	44	1	2	3	8					
1995-96	Junkkarit HT	Finland-2	41	9	9	18	58					
	Junkkarit HT	Finland-3						5	1	2	3	22
1996-97	TPS Turku	Finn-Jr.	4	1	0	1	4					
	Kiekko-67	Finland-2	43	5	5	10	38					
	Kiekko-67	Finland-3						3	1	0	1	4
1997-98	TPS Turku	Finn-Jr.	12	6	2	8	10	7	3	4	7	12
	TuTo Turku	Finland-2	17	4	4	8	29					
	TPS Turku	Finland	1	0	1	1	0					
1998-99	KalPa Kuopio	Finn-Jr.	1	1	0	1	4					
	KalPa Kuopio	Finland	52	3	8	11	40					
	KalPa Kuopio-B	Finn-Jr.						1	0	0	0	0
	KalPa Kuopio	Finland-2						6	0	0	0	0
99-2000	Hermes Kokkola	Finland-2	48	3	11	14	34	3	1	0	1	2
2000-01	FPS Fossa	Finland-2	22	5	8	13	28					

SEIKOLA, Markus (SAY-koh-la, MAHR-kuhs) TOR.

Defense. Shoots right. 6'1", 194 lbs. Born, Laitila, Finland, June 5, 1982.
(Toronto's 7th choice, 209th overall, in 2000 Entry Draft).

Season	Club	Lea	RS GP	RS G	RS A	RS TP	RS PIM	PO GP	PO G	PO A	PO TP	PO PIM
1997-98	TPS Turku	Finn-Jr.	2	0	0	0	0	1	0	0	0	2
1998-99	TPS Turku	Finn-Jr.	36	2	10	12	24					
99-2000	TPS Turku-B	Finn-Jr.	9	2	1	3	6					
2000-01	TPS Turku	Finn-Jr.	26	13	7	20	6	3	1	0	1	0
	TPS Turku	Finland	23	1	0	1	16					

SELIG, Scott (SEH-lihg, SKAWT) MTL.

Center. Shoots right. 6'3", 178 lbs. Born, Philadelphia, PA, March 2, 1981.
(Montreal's 8th choice, 172nd overall, in 2000 Entry Draft).

Season	Club	Lea	RS GP	RS G	RS A	RS TP	RS PIM	PO GP	PO G	PO A	PO TP	PO PIM
99-2000	Thayer Academy	Hi-School	28	32	25	57	25					
2000-01	Northeastern	H-East	35	7	8	15	34					

SELLARS, Luke (SEHL-lahrs, LEWK) ATL.

Defense. Shoots left. 6'1", 195 lbs. Born, Toronto, Ont., May 21, 1981.
(Atlanta's 2nd choice, 30th overall, in 1999 Entry Draft).

Season	Club	Lea	RS GP	RS G	RS A	RS TP	RS PIM	PO GP	PO G	PO A	PO TP	PO PIM
1997-98	Wexford Raiders	MTJHL	46	2	18	20	155					
1998-99	Ottawa 67's	OHL	56	4	19	23	87	9	1	2	3	7
99-2000	Ottawa 67's	OHL	56	8	34	42	147	11	4	6	10	28
2000-01	Ottawa 67's	OHL	59	9	21	30	136	18	4	10	14	47

SELUYANOV, Alexander (sehl-oo-YA-nahf, al-ehx-AN-duhr) DET.

Defense. Shoots right. 5'11", 172 lbs. Born, Ufa, USSR, March 24, 1982.
(Detroit's 5th choice, 128th overall, in 2000 Entry Draft).

Season	Club	Lea	RS GP	RS G	RS A	RS TP	RS PIM	PO GP	PO G	PO A	PO TP	PO PIM
1997-98	Novoil Ufa-2	Russia-3	19	0	1	1	8					
1998-99	Novoil Ufa-2	Russia-4	20	3	3	6	8					
99-2000	Ufa-Salavat-2	Russia-3	18	3	4	7	10					
	Ufa-Salavat	Russia	13	1	2	3	4					
2000-01	Ufa-Salavat	Russia	30	0	3	3	10					

SEMENOV, Alexei (seh-MEH-nahv, al-EHX-ay) EDM.

Defense. Shoots left. 6'6", 210 lbs. Born, Murmansk, USSR, April 10, 1981.
(Edmonton's 2nd choice, 36th overall, in 1999 Entry Draft).

Season	Club	Lea	RS GP	RS G	RS A	RS TP	RS PIM	PO GP	PO G	PO A	PO TP	PO PIM
1997-98	Krylja Sovetov-2	Russia-3	52	1	2	3	48					
1998-99	St. Petersburg-2	Russia-4	19	0	1	1	20					
	Sudbury Wolves	OHL	28	0	3	3	28	2	0	0	0	4
99-2000	Sudbury Wolves	OHL	65	9	35	44	135	12	1	3	4	23
	Hamilton Bulldogs	AHL						3	0	0	0	0
2000-01	Sudbury Wolves	OHL	65	21	42	63	106	12	4	13	17	17

OHL First All-Star Team (2001)

SEMENOV, Dmitri (seh-MEH-nahv, dih-MEE-tree) DET.

Right wing. Shoots left. 5'10", 178 lbs. Born, Moscow, USSR, April 19, 1982.
(Detroit's 4th choice, 127th overall, in 2000 Entry Draft).

Season	Club	Lea	RS GP	RS G	RS A	RS TP	RS PIM	PO GP	PO G	PO A	PO TP	PO PIM
1997-98	Dynamo Moscow	Russia-2	13	2	1	3	2					
1998-99	D'amo Moscow-2	Russia-3	26	14	4	18	16					
99-2000	HC Tver	Russia-2	16	4	2	6	63					
2000-01	Dynamo Moscow	Russia	12	0	0	0	8					
	HC Yekaterinburg	Russia	24	0	0	0	18					

SEMIN, Dmitri (SEH-min, dih-MEE-tree) ST.L.

Center. Shoots left. 5'10", 165 lbs. Born, Moscow, USSR, August 14, 1983.
(St. Louis' 4th choice, 159th overall, in 2001 Entry Draft).

Season	Club	Lea	RS GP	RS G	RS A	RS TP	RS PIM	PO GP	PO G	PO A	PO TP	PO PIM
99-2000	Krylja Sovetov-2	Russia-3	27	9	10	19	10					
	Krylja Sovetov	Russia-2	1	0	0	0	0					
2000-01	Krylja Sovetov	Russia-2	32	8	6	14	8					

SESSA, Jason (SEH-sa, JAY-suhn) TOR.

Right wing. Shoots right. 6'1", 190 lbs. Born, Long Island, NY, July 17, 1977.
(Toronto's 5th choice, 86th overall, in 1996 Entry Draft).

Season	Club	Lea	RS GP	RS G	RS A	RS TP	RS PIM	PO GP	PO G	PO A	PO TP	PO PIM
1994-95	Rochester	USHL	47	45	22	67	81					
1995-96	Lake Superior	CCHA	30	9	5	14	12					
1996-97	Lake Superior	CCHA	34	22	22	44	91					
1997-98	Lake Superior	CCHA	32	16	13	29	55					
	St. John's Leafs	AHL	5	0	0	0	6					
1998-99	St. John's Leafs	AHL	56	9	4	13	25					
99-2000	St. John's Leafs	AHL	30	7	14	21	54					
	Louisiana Gators	ECHL	17	1	4	5	14					
	South Carolina	ECHL	15	10	8	18	30	7	4	1	5	2
2000-01	South Carolina	ECHL	58	34	30	64	113					
	St. John's Leafs	AHL	9	4	4	8	4	3	1	0	1	6

CCHA Second All-Star Team (1997)

SETZINGER, Oliver (SEHT-zihn-guhr, AW-lih-vuhr) NSH.

Center. Shoots left. 6', 200 lbs. Born, Horn, Austria, July 11, 1983.
(Nashville's 5th choice, 76th overall, in 2001 Entry Draft).

Season	Club	Lea	RS GP	RS G	RS A	RS TP	RS PIM	PO GP	PO G	PO A	PO TP	PO PIM
1998-99	EV Wien	Austria-Jr.	30	25	27	52	30					
99-2000	Ilves Tampere-B	Finn-Jr.	35	6	4	10	65					
	Ilves Tampere	Finn-Jr.	1	0	0	0	2					
	Ilves Tampere	Finland-2	18	16	9	25	38					
2000-01	Ilves Tampere-B	Finn-Jr.	14	0	1	1	10					
	Ilves Tampere	Finn-Jr.	31	8	12	20	74					

SHARP, Patrick (SHAHRP, PAT-rihk) PHI.

Center. Shoots right. 6', 188 lbs. Born, Thunder Bay, Ont., December 27, 1981.
(Philadelphia's 2nd choice, 95th overall, in 2001 Entry Draft).

			Regular Season					Playoffs				
Season	Club	Lea	GP	G	A	TP	PIM	GP	G	A	TP	PIM
1998-99	Thunder Bay	USHL	55	19	24	43	48	3	1	1	2	0
99-2000	Thunder Bay	USHL	56	20	35	55	41	....	....	....	....	....
2000-01	U. of Vermont	ECAC	34	12	15	27	36	....	....	....	....	....

SHASBY, Matt (SHAS-bee, MAT) MTL.

Defense. Shoots left. 6'3", 188 lbs. Born, Sioux Falls, SD, July 2, 1980.
(Montreal's 7th choice, 150th overall, in 1999 Entry Draft).

			Regular Season					Playoffs				
Season	Club	Lea	GP	G	A	TP	PIM	GP	G	A	TP	PIM
1997-98	Lincoln Stars	USHL	43	1	15	16	30	8	0	0	0	2
1998-99	Des Moines	USHL	49	4	22	26	34	11	0	1	1	12
99-2000	Alaska-Anchorage	WCHA	32	1	8	9	36	....	....	....	....	....
2000-01	Alaska-Anchorage	WCHA	35	4	14	18	32	....	....	....	....	....

SHASTIN, Yegor (SHAS-tihn, yeh-GOHR) CGY.

Left wing. Shoots left. 5'9", 172 lbs. Born, Kiev, USSR, September 10, 1982.
(Calgary's 5th choice, 124th overall, in 2001 Entry Draft).

			Regular Season					Playoffs				
Season	Club	Lea	GP	G	A	TP	PIM	GP	G	A	TP	PIM
1997-98	VDV Omsk-2	Russia-3	4	0	1	1	0	....	....	....	....	....
1998-99	VDV Omsk-2	Russia-4	19	11	17	28	30	....	....	....	....	....
	Avangard Omsk	Russia	4	0	0	0	0	4	0	1	1	0
99-2000	VDV Omsk-2	Russia-3	11	6	5	11	20	....	....	....	....	....
	Avangard Omsk	Russia	26	2	4	6	20	7	3	1	4	16
2000-01	VDV Omsk-2	Russia-3	14	13	9	22	62	....	....	....	....	....
	Avangard Omsk	Russia	35	3	11	14	59	9	1	0	1	18

SHEFER, Andrei (SHEH-fuhr, AN-dray) L.A.

Right wing. Shoots left. 6'1", 194 lbs. Born, Sverdlovsk, USSR, July 26, 1981.
(Los Angeles' 1st choice, 43rd overall, in 1999 Entry Draft).

			Regular Season					Playoffs				
Season	Club	Lea	GP	G	A	TP	PIM	GP	G	A	TP	PIM
1997-98	Yekaterinburg-2	Russia-3	16	3	3	6	18	....	....	....	....	....
1998-99	Cherepovets-3	Russia-4	6	2	2	4	18	....	....	....	....	....
	Cherepovets-2	Russia-3	21	6	5	11	20	....	....	....	....	....
	HC Cherepovets	Russia	8	1	0	1	4	....	....	....	....	....
99-2000	Halifax	QMJHL	72	34	42	76	30	10	0	5	5	4
2000-01	St. Petersburg	Russia	11	6	1	7	4	....	....	....	....	....
	HC Cherepovets	Russia	20	1	1	2	10	6	1	0	1	0

SHIELDS, Colin (SHEELDZ, CAW-lihn) PHI.

Right wing. Shoots right. 6', 175 lbs. Born, Glasgow, Scotland, January 27, 1980.
(Philadelphia's 4th choice, 195th overall, in 2000 Entry Draft).

			Regular Season					Playoffs				
Season	Club	Lea	GP	G	A	TP	PIM	GP	G	A	TP	PIM
1998-99	Cleveland Barons	NAJHL	55	30	30	60	131	....	....	....	....	....
99-2000	Cleveland Barons	NAJHL	55	46	*49	*95	40	3	1	3	4	2
2000-01	U. of Maine	H-East	DID NOT PLAY – ACADEMICALLY INELIGIBLE									

NAJHL All-League First All-Star Team (2000) • Signed Letter of Intent to attend University of Maine (H-East), October 26, 1999. • Ruled ineligible to play 2000-01 season by H-East officials due to academic violations while playing U.S. junior hockey, October 10, 2000.

SHIKHANOV, Sergei (shih-KHAHN-ohf, SAIR-gay) CHI.

Right wing. Shoots left. 6'2", 190 lbs. Born, Togliatti, USSR, April 8, 1978.
(Chicago's 10th choice, 204th overall, in 1997 Entry Draft).

			Regular Season					Playoffs				
Season	Club	Lea	GP	G	A	TP	PIM	GP	G	A	TP	PIM
1996-97	Lada Togliatti	Russia	19	4	4	8	20	8	1	0	1	10
	HC Neftekhimik	Russia	5	1	1	2	2	....	....	....	....	....
1997-98	HC Neftekhimik-2	Russia-3	32	9	7	16	14	....	....	....	....	....
	Lada Togliatti	Russia	19	3	0	3	4	....	....	....	....	....
1998-99	Lada Togliatti	Russia	29	4	5	9	65	3	0	0	0	2
	SKA Samara	Russia	11	3	4	7	10	3	1	0	1	2
99-2000	Torpedo Yaroslavl	Russia	31	2	3	5	24	7	0	2	2	4
2000-01	HC Neftekhimik	Russia	24	4	4	8	39	10	1	0	1	4

SHINKAR, Alexander (shihn-KAHR, al-ehx-AN-duhr) TOR.

Right wing. Shoots left. 6', 176 lbs. Born, Ufa, USSR, July 3, 1981.
(Toronto's 9th choice, 254th overall, in 2000 Entry Draft).

			Regular Season					Playoffs				
Season	Club	Lea	GP	G	A	TP	PIM	GP	G	A	TP	PIM
1997-98	Novoil Ufa-2	Russia-3	22	6	2	8	4	....	....	....	....	....
1998-99	HC Cherepovets-2	Russia-3	25	7	2	9	8	....	....	....	....	....
	HC Cherepovets-2	Russia-4	8	0	4	4	4	....	....	....	....	....
99-2000	HC Cherepovets	Russia	18	1	1	2	2	8	0	0	0	0
2000-01	St. Petersburg	Russia	43	7	4	11	50	....	....	....	....	....

SHISHKANOV, Timofei (SHIHSH-kuh-nahv, tee-moh-FAY) NSH.

Left wing. Shoots right. 6', 183 lbs. Born, Moscow, USSR, June 10, 1983.
(Nashville's 2nd choice, 33rd overall, in 2001 Entry Draft).

			Regular Season					Playoffs				
Season	Club	Lea	GP	G	A	TP	PIM	GP	G	A	TP	PIM
99-2000	Krylja Sovetov-2	Russia-3	14	6	5	11	10	....	....	....	....	....
	Krylja Sovetov	Russia-2	14	1	0	1	2	....	....	....	....	....
2000-01	Krylja Sovetov-2	Russia-3	STATISTICS NOT AVAILABLE									
	Krylja Sovetov	Russia-2	12	0	0	0	2	....	....	....	....	....

SHMYR, Jason (SHMEER, JAY-suhn)

Left wing. Shoots left. 6'4", 220 lbs. Born, Fairview, Alta., July 27, 1975.

			Regular Season					Playoffs				
Season	Club	Lea	GP	G	A	TP	PIM	GP	G	A	TP	PIM
1995-96	Bonnyville	AJHL	42	10	22	32	270	....	....	....	....	....
1996-97	Anchorage Aces	WCHL	51	8	12	20	388	9	1	1	2	50
	Pensacola	ECHL	1	0	0	0	2	....	....	....	....	....
1997-98	Anchorage Aces	WCHL	31	4	6	10	177	....	....	....	....	....
	Utah Grizzlies	IHL	3	0	0	0	7	....	....	....	....	....
	San Diego Gulls	WCHL	14	0	3	3	50	11	3	3	6	78
1998-99	Long Beach	IHL	8	0	0	0	35	....	....	....	....	....
	San Diego Gulls	WCHL	2	0	0	0	7	....	....	....	....	....
	Manitoba Moose	IHL	57	1	1	2	227	3	0	0	0	0
99-2000	Portland Pirates	AHL	53	3	4	7	170	2	0	0	0	2
2000-01	Portland Pirates	AHL	32	0	0	0	141	....	....	....	....	....
	Utah Grizzlies	IHL	25	0	1	1	167	....	....	....	....	....

Signed as a free agent by **Washington**, April 27, 1999.

SICAK, Vladimir (SEE-tsak, vla-DEE-mihr) ATL.

Defense. Shoots left. 5'11", 192 lbs. Born, Jindrichuv Hradec, Czech., January 12, 1980.

			Regular Season					Playoffs				
Season	Club	Lea	GP	G	A	TP	PIM	GP	G	A	TP	PIM
1998-99	HC Budejovice	Cze-Rep	25	1	1	2	10	....	....	....	....	....
	Medicine Hat	WHL	35	1	9	10	71	....	....	....	....	....
99-2000	Medicine Hat	WHL	72	7	27	34	73	....	....	....	....	....
2000-01	Greenville Growl	ECHL	34	4	6	10	16	....	....	....	....	....
	Orlando	IHL	33	1	3	4	15	....	....	....	....	....

Signed as a free agent by **Atlanta**, September 24, 1999.

SIDYAKIN, Andrei (sihd-YA-kihn, AN-dray) MTL.

Right wing. Shoots right. 5'11", 169 lbs. Born, Ufa, USSR, January 20, 1979.
(Montreal's 10th choice, 202nd overall, in 1997 Entry Draft).

			Regular Season					Playoffs				
Season	Club	Lea	GP	G	A	TP	PIM	GP	G	A	TP	PIM
1994-95	Ufa-Salavat	CIS	7	0	1	1	0	....	....	....	....	....
1995-96	Ufa-Salavat	CIS	25	1	0	1	4	3	0	0	0	2
1996-97	Ufa-Salavat	Russia	29	3	5	8	4	....	....	....	....	....
1997-98	Ufa-Salavat	Russia	42	5	4	9	32	....	....	....	....	....
1998-99	Ufa-Salavat	Russia	36	6	4	10	14	2	0	0	0	2
99-2000	Ufa-Salavat	Russia	38	7	2	9	32	....	....	....	....	....
2000-01	Ufa-Salavat	Russia	44	10	13	23	42	....	....	....	....	....

SIKLENKA, Mike (sih-KLEHN-kuh, MIGHK) WSH.

Right wing. Shoots right. 6'5", 224 lbs. Born, Meadow Lake, Sask., December 18, 1979.
(Washington's 5th choice, 118th overall, in 1998 Entry Draft).

			Regular Season					Playoffs				
Season	Club	Lea	GP	G	A	TP	PIM	GP	G	A	TP	PIM
1997-98	Lloydminster	SJHL	54	10	17	27	120	....	....	....	....	....
1998-99	Seattle T-Birds	WHL	68	19	13	32	115	11	6	6	12	24
99-2000	Portland Pirates	AHL	9	0	0	0	14	....	....	....	....	....
	Hampton Roads	ECHL	58	7	4	11	62	8	1	0	1	15
2000-01	Richmond	ECHL	65	19	18	37	117	4	0	0	0	34
	Portland Pirates	AHL	3	0	0	0	0	....	....	....	....	....

SIMON, Ben (SIGH-mohn, BEN-ja-mihn) ATL.

Center. Shoots left. 6', 195 lbs. Born, Shaker Heights, OH, June 14, 1978.
(Chicago's 5th choice, 110th overall, in 1997 Entry Draft).

			Regular Season					Playoffs				
Season	Club	Lea	GP	G	A	TP	PIM	GP	G	A	TP	PIM
1992-93	Shaker High	Hi-School	25	15	21	36	....	....	....	....	....	....
1993-94	Shaker High	Hi-School	24	45	41	86	....	....	....	....	....	....
1994-95	Shaker High	Hi-School	25	61	68	129	....	....	....	....	....	....
1995-96	Cleveland Barons	NAJHL	45	38	33	71	....	5	7	13	20	....
1996-97	Notre Dame	CCHA	30	4	15	19	79	....	....	....	....	....
1997-98	Notre Dame	CCHA	37	9	28	37	91	....	....	....	....	....
1998-99	Notre Dame	CCHA	37	18	24	42	65	....	....	....	....	....
99-2000	Notre Dame	CCHA	40	13	19	32	53	....	....	....	....	....
2000-01	Orlando	IHL	77	8	12	20	47	16	6	5	11	20

NAJHL First All-Star Team (1996) • Won NAJHL Rookie of the Year Award (1996) • CCHA Second All-Star Team (1999)

Rights traded to **Atlanta** by **Chicago** for Atlanta's 9th round choice (Peter Flache) in 2000 Entry Draft, June 25, 2000.

SIMONS, Mikael (SIH-mawns, mih-KIGHL) L.A.

Center. Shoots left. 6'2", 194 lbs. Born, Falun, Sweden, January 15, 1978.
(Los Angeles' 4th choice, 84th overall, in 1996 Entry Draft).

			Regular Season					Playoffs				
Season	Club	Lea	GP	G	A	TP	PIM	GP	G	A	TP	PIM
1994-95	Mora IK	Swede-Jr.	26	5	3	8	57	....	....	....	....	....
1995-96	Mora IK	Swede-Jr.	10	4	4	8	12	....	....	....	....	....
	Mora IK	Swede-2	33	6	3	9	22	6	0	2	2	2
1996-97	Mora IK	Swede-Jr.	1	0	0	0	0	....	....	....	....	....
	Mora IK	Swede-2	33	6	3	9	22	6	0	2	2	2
1997-98	Mora IK	Swede-2	30	16	9	25	88	4	3	0	3	2
1998-99	Mora IK	Swede-2	41	14	9	23	36	14	4	3	7	14
99-2000	Mora IK	Swede-2	36	13	10	23	56	5	0	1	1	4
2000-01	Mora IK	Swede-2	34	9	15	24	55	....	....	....	....	....

SIPOTZ, Brian (SIHP-awtz, BRIGH-uhn) ATL.

Defense. Shoots right. 6'6", 225 lbs. Born, South Bend, IN, September 16, 1981.
(Atlanta's 3rd choice, 100th overall, in 2001 Entry Draft).

			Regular Season					Playoffs				
Season	Club	Lea	GP	G	A	TP	PIM	GP	G	A	TP	PIM
99-2000	Culver Academy	Hi-School	45	14	22	36	56	....	....	....	....	....
2000-01	Miami-Ohio	CCHA	32	0	1	1	48	....	....	....	....	....

SIVEK, Michal (sih-VIHK, mee-KHAHL) PIT.

Center. Shoots left. 6'3", 209 lbs. Born, Nachod, Czech., January 21, 1981.
(Washington's 2nd choice, 29th overall, in 1999 Entry Draft).

			Regular Season					Playoffs				
Season	Club	Lea	GP	G	A	TP	PIM	GP	G	A	TP	PIM
1997-98	Sparta Praha-Jr.	Cze-Rep	31	13	8	21	....	....	....	....	....	....
	Sparta Praha	Cze-Rep	25	1	1	2	10	5	1	0	1	0
1998-99	Sparta Praha	Cze-Rep	1	1	0	1	....	....	....	....	....	....
	Velvana Kladno	Cze-Rep	34	3	8	11	24	....	....	....	....	....
99-2000	Prince Albert	WHL	53	23	37	60	65	6	1	4	5	10
2000-01	Sparta Praha	Cze-Rep	32	6	7	13	28	13	4	2	6	8

Traded to **Pittsburgh** by **Washington** with Kris Beech, Ross Lupaschuk and future considerations for Jaromir Jagr and Frantisek Kucera, July 11, 2001.

SJOSTROM, Fredrik (SHAW-strahm, FREHD-rihk) PHX.

Right wing. Shoots left. 6', 194 lbs. Born, Fargelanda, Sweden, May 6, 1983.
(Phoenix's 1st choice, 11th overall, in 2001 Entry Draft).

			Regular Season					Playoffs				
Season	Club	Lea	GP	G	A	TP	PIM	GP	G	A	TP	PIM
99-2000	MoDo Hockey-B	Swede-Jr.	4	0	2	2	6	....	....	....	....	....
	MoDo Hockey	Swede-Jr.	18	4	6	10	8	....	....	....	....	....
2000-01	Vastra Frolunda	Swede-Jr.	11	3	7	10	12	4	1	2	3	6
	Vastra Frolunda	Sweden	31	3	2	5	6	5	0	0	0	2

SKLADANY, Frantisek (sklah-DAH-nee, FRAN-tih-shehk) **COL.**

Left wing. Shoots left. 6', 185 lbs. Born, Martin, Czech., April 22, 1982.
(Colorado's 4th choice, 143rd overall, in 2001 Entry Draft).

			Regular Season					Playoffs				
Season	Club	Lea	GP	G	A	TP	PIM	GP	G	A	TP	PIM
1998-99	HC Martimex	Slovakia	1	0	0	0	0	....	....	....	....	....
99-2000	HC Martimex-Jr	Cze-Rep		STATISTICS NOT AVAILABLE								
	HC Martimex	Slovakia	13	1	4	5	2	....	....	....	....	....
2000-01	Boston University	H-East	35	4	5	9	4	....	....	....	....	....

SKRLAC, Rob (SKUHR-lak, RAWB) **N.J.**

Left wing. Shoots left. 6'5", 245 lbs. Born, Port McNeill, B.C., June 10, 1976.
(Buffalo's 11th choice, 224th overall, in 1995 Entry Draft).

			Regular Season					Playoffs				
Season	Club	Lea	GP	G	A	TP	PIM	GP	G	A	TP	PIM
1993-94	Kamloops BB's	BCAHA	49	44	55	99	56	....	....	....	....	....
1994-95	Kamloops Blazers	WHL	23	0	1	1	177	....	....	....	....	....
1995-96	Kamloops Blazers	WHL	63	1	4	5	216	13	0	0	0	52
1996-97	Kamloops Blazers	WHL	61	8	10	18	278	5	0	0	0	35
1997-98	Albany River Rats	AHL	53	0	2	2	256	....	....	....	....	....
1998-99	Albany River Rats	AHL	61	1	1	2	213	1	0	0	0	0
99-2000	Albany River Rats	AHL	37	0	0	0	115	....	....	....	....	....
2000-01	Albany River Rats	AHL	38	0	0	0	105	....	....	....	....	....

Signed as a free agent by **New Jersey**, June 17, 1997.

SKVARIDLO, Tomas (SHKVAHR-ihd-loh, TOH-mas) **PIT.**

Left wing. Shoots left. 6'1", 180 lbs. Born, Zvolen, Czech., June 19, 1981.
(Pittsburgh's 6th choice, 144th overall, in 1999 Entry Draft).

			Regular Season					Playoffs				
Season	Club	Lea	GP	G	A	TP	PIM	GP	G	A	TP	PIM
1997-98	HKM Zvolen	Slovak-Jr.	51	11	11	22	22	....	....	....	....	....
1998-99	HKM Zvolen	Slovak-Jr.	35	21	11	32	18	6	0	4	4	2
	HKM Zvolen	Slovak-2	9	1	1	2	2	....	....	....	....	....
	HKM Zvolen	Slovakia	1	0	0	0	0	....	....	....	....	....
99-2000	Kingston	OHL	66	19	25	44	14	5	0	0	0	2
2000-01	Kingston	OHL	58	10	19	29	33	4	2	0	2	6

SLOVAK, Tomas (SLOHW-vahk, TAW-mawsh) **NSH.**

Defense. Shoots right. 6', 186 lbs. Born, Kosice, Czech., April 5, 1983.
(Nashville's 3rd choice, 42nd overall, in 2001 Entry Draft).

			Regular Season					Playoffs				
Season	Club	Lea	GP	G	A	TP	PIM	GP	G	A	TP	PIM
99-2000	VSZ Kosice	Slovakia	2	0	0	0	0	....	....	....	....	....
2000-01	VSZ Kosice	Slovakia	43	5	5	10	28	3	1	0	1	2

SMIRNOV, Alexei (smihr-NAHV, al-EHX-ay) **ANA.**

Left wing. Shoots left. 6'3", 207 lbs. Born, Tver, USSR, January 28, 1982.
(Anaheim's 1st choice, 12th overall, in 2000 Entry Draft).

			Regular Season					Playoffs				
Season	Club	Lea	GP	G	A	TP	PIM	GP	G	A	TP	PIM
1997-98	D'amo Moscow-2	Russia-3	11	1	1	2	4	....	....	....	....	....
1998-99	D'amo Moscow-2	Russia-3	27	9	3	12	24	....	....	....	....	....
99-2000	D'amo Moscow-2	Russia-3	12	5	3	8	34	....	....	....	....	....
	THC Tver	Russia-2	35	3	5	8	24	....	....	....	....	....
	Dynamo Moscow	Russia	1	0	0	0	0	....	....	....	....	....
2000-01	Dynamo Moscow	Russia	29	2	0	2	16	....	....	....	....	....

SMIRNOV, Oleg (smihr-NOHF, OH-lehg) **EDM.**

Left wing. Shoots right. 5'11", 176 lbs. Born, Elektrostal, USSR, April 8, 1980.
(Edmonton's 6th choice, 144th overall, in 1998 Entry Draft).

			Regular Season					Playoffs				
Season	Club	Lea	GP	G	A	TP	PIM	GP	G	A	TP	PIM
1996-97	HC Elektrostal-2	Russia-3	38	2	2	4	8	....	....	....	....	....
1997-98	HC Elektrostal-2	Russia-3	10	0	0	0	2	....	....	....	....	....
	Kristall Elektrostal	Russia	6	0	2	2	0	....	....	....	....	....
1998-99	HC Chelyabinsk	Russia	27	0	3	3	6	....	....	....	....	....
	HC Lipetsk	Russia	3	0	0	0	0	....	....	....	....	....
	Krylja Sovetov	Russia	14	4	0	4	4	....	....	....	....	....
99-2000	Krylja Sovetov-2	Russia-3		STATISTICS NOT AVAILABLE								
2000-01	Dynamo Moscow	Russia	18	0	0	0	6	....	....	....	....	....

SMITH, Don (SMIHTH, DAWN) **CAR.**

Center. Shoots left. 6'3", 195 lbs. Born, Buffalo, NY, March 17, 1979.
(Carolina's 7th choice, 184th overall, in 1998 Entry Draft).

			Regular Season					Playoffs				
Season	Club	Lea	GP	G	A	TP	PIM	GP	G	A	TP	PIM
1996-97	Nichols High	Hi-School	31	25	29	54	....	....	....	....	....	....
1997-98	Clarkson Knights	ECAC	30	4	6	10	8	....	....	....	....	....
1998-99	Clarkson Knights	ECAC	37	9	12	21	18	....	....	....	....	....
99-2000	Clarkson Knights	ECAC	35	7	9	16	20	....	....	....	....	....
2000-01	Clarkson Knights	ECAC	31	12	13	25	18	....	....	....	....	....

SMITH, Jarrett (SMIHTH, JAHR-reht) **ANA.**

Center. Shoots left. 6'2", 201 lbs. Born, Edmonton, Alta., June 15, 1979.
(NY Islanders' 4th choice, 59th overall, in 1997 Entry Draft).

			Regular Season					Playoffs				
Season	Club	Lea	GP	G	A	TP	PIM	GP	G	A	TP	PIM
1994-95	Sherwood Park	AMHL	34	21	26	47	45	....	....	....	....	....
1995-96	Prince George	WHL	18	2	0	2	6	....	....	....	....	....
1996-97	Prince George	WHL	67	20	22	42	58	15	2	2	4	5
1997-98	Prince George	WHL	42	12	22	34	21	11	3	1	4	8
1998-99	Prince George	WHL	49	20	37	57	54	3	0	2	2	2
99-2000	Prince Albert	WHL	72	27	32	59	53	6	2	4	6	20
2000-01	Cincinnati Ducks	AHL	46	5	9	14	28	....	....	....	....	....
	Baton Rouge	ECHL	18	4	7	11	16	....	....	....	....	....

Signed as a free agent by **Anaheim**, June 13, 2000.

SMITH, Kenny (SMIHTH, KEHN-nee) **EDM.**

Defense. Shoots right. 6'2", 209 lbs. Born, Stoneham, MA, December 31, 1981.
(Edmonton's 4th choice, 84th overall, in 2001 Entry Draft).

			Regular Season					Playoffs				
Season	Club	Lea	GP	G	A	TP	PIM	GP	G	A	TP	PIM
1998-99	Team USA	USDP-17	29	2	5	7	32	....	....	....	....	....
99-2000	Team USA	USDP	27	4	6	10	77	....	....	....	....	....
2000-01	Harvard University	ECAC	21	0	2	2	37	....	....	....	....	....

SMITH, Kenton (SMIHTH, KEHN-tuhn) **T.B.**

Forward/Defense. Shoots left. 5'11", 177 lbs. Born, Edmonton, AB, September 10, 1979.

			Regular Season					Playoffs				
Season	Club	Lea	GP	G	A	TP	PIM	GP	G	A	TP	PIM
1994-95	Edmonton East	AAHA	33	20	25	45	30	....	....	....	....	....
1995-96	Calgary Hitmen	WHL	53	3	17	20	32	....	....	....	....	....
1996-97	Calgary Hitmen	WHL	72	7	26	33	63	....	....	....	....	....
1997-98	Calgary Hitmen	WHL	69	7	26	33	81	18	1	6	7	26
1998-99	Calgary Hitmen	WHL	69	19	35	54	138	21	1	14	15	34
99-2000	Calgary Hitmen	WHL	71	7	46	53	128	13	3	8	11	25
2000-01	Detroit Vipers	IHL	59	1	3	4	24	....	....	....	....	....
	Johnstown Chiefs	ECHL	13	0	3	3	12	4	0	1	1	2

Signed as a free agent by **Tampa Bay**, March 30, 2000.

SMITH, Nathan (SMIHTH, NAY-thun) **VAN.**

Center. Shoots left. 6'2", 192 lbs. Born, Edmonton, Alta., February 9, 1982.
(Vancouver's 1st choice, 23rd overall, in 2000 Entry Draft).

			Regular Season					Playoffs				
Season	Club	Lea	GP	G	A	TP	PIM	GP	G	A	TP	PIM
1997-98	Sherwood Park	AMHL	35	15	13	28	24	....	....	....	....	....
1998-99	Swift Current	WHL	47	5	8	13	26	....	....	....	....	....
99-2000	Swift Current	WHL	70	21	28	49	72	12	1	6	7	4
2000-01	Swift Current	WHL	67	28	62	90	78	19	4	3	7	20

SMITH, Nick (SMIHTH, NIHK) **FLA.**

Center. Shoots left. 6'2", 196 lbs. Born, Hamilton, Ont., March 23, 1979.
(Florida's 4th choice, 74th overall, in 1997 Entry Draft).

			Regular Season					Playoffs				
Season	Club	Lea	GP	G	A	TP	PIM	GP	G	A	TP	PIM
1995-96	Shelburne Wolves	MTJHL	42	13	18	31	12	....	....	....	....	....
1996-97	Barrie Colts	OHL	63	10	18	28	15	9	3	8	11	13
1997-98	Barrie Colts	OHL	63	13	21	34	21	6	1	2	3	4
1998-99	Barrie Colts	OHL	68	19	34	53	18	12	3	8	11	8
99-2000	Louisville Panthers	AHL	53	8	4	12	8	4	0	0	0	0
	Port Huron	UHL	2	1	1	2	0	....	....	....	....	....
2000-01	Louisville Panthers	AHL	23	1	2	3	25	....	....	....	....	....

• Missed majority of 2000-01 season recovering from knee injury suffered in training camp, September 25, 2000.

SMITH, Tim (SMIHTH, TIHM) **VAN.**

Center. Shoots left. 5'9", 160 lbs. Born, Whitecourt, Alta., July 21, 1981.
(Vancouver's 7th choice, 272nd overall, in 2000 Entry Draft).

			Regular Season					Playoffs				
Season	Club	Lea	GP	G	A	TP	PIM	GP	G	A	TP	PIM
1997-98	Lebret Eagles	SJHL	36	6	7	13	12	....	....	....	....	....
1998-99	Spokane Chiefs	WHL	57	5	20	25	21	....	....	....	....	....
99-2000	Spokane Chiefs	WHL	71	26	70	96	65	15	7	7	14	32
2000-01	Spokane Chiefs	WHL	38	19	37	56	65	....	....	....	....	....
	Swift Current	WHL	30	12	22	34	38	19	10	14	24	38

Traded to **Swift Current** by **Spokane** for Scott Henkleman, Scott Scherger and future considerations, January 15, 2001.

SMITHSON, Jerred (SMIHTH-suhn, JEHR-rehd) **L.A.**

Right wing. Shoots right. 6'2", 190 lbs. Born, Vernon, B.C., February 4, 1979.

			Regular Season					Playoffs				
Season	Club	Lea	GP	G	A	TP	PIM	GP	G	A	TP	PIM
1994-95	Vernon Leafs	BCAHA	64	39	46	85	120	....	....	....	....	....
1995-96	Calgary Hitmen	WHL	60	4	2	6	16	....	....	....	....	....
1996-97	Calgary Hitmen	WHL	65	3	6	9	49	....	....	....	....	....
1997-98	Calgary Hitmen	WHL	65	12	9	21	65	18	0	2	2	25
1998-99	Calgary Hitmen	WHL	63	14	22	36	108	21	3	7	10	17
99-2000	Calgary Hitmen	WHL	66	14	25	39	111	10	1	1	2	16
2000-01	Lowell	AHL	24	1	1	2	10	4	0	0	0	2

Signed as a free agent by **LA Kings**, February 18, 2000.

SNESRUD, Mat (SHEHS-rud, MAT) **ANA.**

Defense. Shoots right. 6'1", 205 lbs. Born, Minneapolis, MN, January 28, 1977.
(Anaheim's 6th choice, 181st overall, in 1997 Entry Draft).

			Regular Season					Playoffs				
Season	Club	Lea	GP	G	A	TP	PIM	GP	G	A	TP	PIM
1995-96	North Iowa	USHL	43	0	6	6	30	....	....	....	....	....
1996-97	North Iowa	USHL	50	12	22	34	76	....	....	....	....	....
1997-98	Michigan Tech	WCHA	39	0	18	18	44	....	....	....	....	....
1998-99	Michigan Tech	WCHA	37	3	8	11	22	....	....	....	....	....
99-2000	Michigan Tech	WCHA	38	3	7	10	44	....	....	....	....	....
2000-01	Michigan Tech	WCHA	32	5	11	16	28	....	....	....	....	....

SOCHOR, Jan (soh-KHAWR, YAN) **TOR.**

Left wing. Shoots right. 6', 198 lbs. Born, Usti nad Labem, Czech., January 17, 1980.
(Toronto's 6th choice, 161st overall, in 1999 Entry Draft).

			Regular Season					Playoffs				
Season	Club	Lea	GP	G	A	TP	PIM	GP	G	A	TP	PIM
1996-97	Slavia Praha-Jr.	Cze-Rep	26	11	12	23	....	....	....	....	....	....
1997-98	Slavia Praha-Jr.	Cze-Rep	33	26	12	38	....	....	....	....	....	....
	Slavia Praha	Cze-Rep	14	1	1	2	2	1	0	0	0	0
1998-99	Slavia Praha-Jr.	Cze-Rep	7	2	1	3	2	....	....	....	....	....
	Slavia Praha	Cze-Rep	47	10	10	20	14	....	....	....	....	....
99-2000	Slavia Praha	Cze-Rep	39	7	11	18	37	....	....	....	....	....
2000-01	Slovnaft Vsetin	Cze-Rep	41	5	4	9	28	3	0	0	0	0

SODERBERG, Anders (SOH-dehr-buhrg, AN-duhrs) **BOS.**

Right wing. Shoots right. 5'6", 161 lbs. Born, Ornskoldsvik, Sweden, October 7, 1975.
(Boston's 10th choice, 234th overall, in 1996 Entry Draft).

			Regular Season					Playoffs				
Season	Club	Lea	GP	G	A	TP	PIM	GP	G	A	TP	PIM
1992-93	MoDo Hockey	Swede-Jr.	13	6	12	18	2	....	....	....	....	....
	MoDo Hockey	Sweden	1	0	0	0	0	....	....	....	....	....
1993-94	MoDo Hockey	Swede-Jr.	9	8	5	13	10	....	....	....	....	....
	MoDo Hockey	Sweden	19	0	0	0	2	9	0	0	0	0
1994-95	MoDo Hockey	Sweden	38	9	14	23	2	....	....	....	....	....
1995-96	MoDo Hockey	Sweden	40	10	18	28	10	8	3	3	6	0
1996-97	MoDo Hockey	Sweden	39	9	13	22	16	....	....	....	....	....
1997-98	MoDo Hockey	Sweden	44	15	10	25	4	9	5	1	6	2
1998-99	MoDo Hockey	Sweden	49	6	15	21	18	13	3	6	9	4
99-2000	MoDo Hockey	Sweden	43	15	10	25	18	9	1	2	3	0
2000-01	MoDo Hockey	Sweden	42	11	4	15	12	6	1	6	7	0

SOIN, Sergei (SOY-ihn, SAIR-gay) COL.

Center. Shoots left. 6', 175 lbs. Born, Moscow, USSR, March 31, 1982.
(Colorado's 3rd choice, 50th overall, in 2000 Entry Draft).

			Regular Season					Playoffs				
Season	Club	Lea	GP	G	A	TP	PIM	GP	G	A	TP	PIM
1997-98	Krylja Sovetov-2	Russia-3	2	0	0	0	0	....	....	....	....	....
1998-99	Krylja Sovetov	Russia	34	1	4	5	12	....	....	....	....	....
99-2000	Krylja Sovetov	Russia-2	33	8	7	5	24	....	....	....	....	....
2000-01	Krylja Sovetov-2	Russia-3	8	2	3	5	12	....	....	....	....	....
	Krylja Sovetov	Russia-2	30	8	5	13	10	....	....	....	....	....

SOMERVUORI, Eero (soh-muhr-VOH-ree, AIR-oh) T.B.

Right wing. Shoots right. 5'10", 167 lbs. Born, Jarvenpaa, Finland, February 7, 1979.
(Tampa Bay's 9th choice, 170th overall, in 1997 Entry Draft).

			Regular Season					Playoffs				
Season	Club	Lea	GP	G	A	TP	PIM	GP	G	A	TP	PIM
1993-94	Jokerit Helsinki-C	Finn-Jr.	29	23	31	54	16	....	....	....	....	....
1994-95	Jokerit Helsinki-C	Finn-Jr.	17	23	16	39	8	6	7	3	10	2
	Jokerit Helsinki-B	Finn-Jr.	15	8	10	18	4	....	....	....	....	....
	Jokerit Helsinki	Finn-Jr.	11	1	2	3	2	....	....	....	....	....
1995-96	Jokerit Helsinki	Finn-Jr.	28	14	12	26	10	9	4	1	5	4
	KJT Jarvenpaa	Finland-2	1	0	0	0	0	....	....	....	....	....
	Jokerit Helsinki	Finland	6	1	2	3	0	....	....	....	....	....
1996-97	Jokerit Helsinki	Finn-Jr.	28	20	19	39	30	5	3	0	3	4
	Jokerit Helsinki	EuroHL	3	0	0	0	0	2	2	0	0	0
	Jokerit Helsinki	Finland	35	1	1	2	2	5	0	0	0	0
1997-98	Jokerit Helsinki	Finn-Jr.	14	4	8	12	2	....	....	....	....	....
	Jokerit Helsinki	Finland	42	3	7	10	46	8	2	1	3	6
	Jokerit Helsinki	EuroHL	5	0	0	0	0	....	....	....	....	....
1998-99	Jokerit Helsinki	Finn-Jr.	4	1	1	2	2	....	....	....	....	....
	Jokerit Helsinki	Finland	50	7	8	15	24	3	1	0	1	6
	Jokerit Helsinki	EuroHL	6	0	0	0	0	1	0	0	0	0
99-2000	Jokerit Helsinki	Finland	54	6	6	12	10	11	1	0	1	0
2000-01	HPK Hameenlinna	Finland	56	14	6	20	35	....	....	....	....	....

SOMIK, Radovan (SAW-mihk, RAH-doh-vahn) PHI.

Right wing. Shoots right. 6'2", 194 lbs. Born, Martin, Czech., May 5, 1977.
(Philadelphia's 3rd choice, 100th overall, in 1995 Entry Draft).

			Regular Season					Playoffs				
Season	Club	Lea	GP	G	A	TP	PIM	GP	G	A	TP	PIM
1993-94	ZTS Martin	Slovakia	1	0	0	0	0	....	....	....	....	....
1994-95	ZTS Martin	Slovakia	25	3	0	3	39	3	1	0	1	2
1995-96	ZTS Martin	Slovakia	25	3	6	9	8	9	1	0	1	....
1996-97	ZTS Martin	Slovakia	35	3	5	8	....	3	0	0	0	....
1997-98	ZTS Martin	Slovakia	26	6	9	15	10	3	0	0	0	0
1998-99	Dukla Trencin	Slovakia	26	1	4	5	6	....	....	....	....	....
99-2000	ZTS Martin	Slovak-2	40	38	28	66	32	....	....	....	....	....
2000-01	HCC Zlin	Cze-Rep	46	15	10	25	22	6	1	0	1	0

SOMMERFELD, Mathew (SUHM-muhr-fehld, MA-thew) FLA.

Left wing. Shoots left. 6'2", 207 lbs. Born, Prince Albert, Sask., April 26, 1982.
(Florida's 8th choice, 253rd overall, in 2000 Entry Draft).

			Regular Season					Playoffs				
Season	Club	Lea	GP	G	A	TP	PIM	GP	G	A	TP	PIM
1998-99	Swift Current	SMHL	35	16	12	28	230	....	....	....	....	....
	Swift Current	WHL	1	0	0	0	0	....	....	....	....	....
99-2000	Swift Current	WHL	67	1	3	4	215	5	0	0	0	15
2000-01	Swift Current	WHL	62	5	5	10	258	15	0	2	2	42

SOUZA, Mike (SOO-zah, MIGHK) CHI.

Left wing. Shoots left. 6'1", 210 lbs. Born, Melrose, MA, January 28, 1978.
(Chicago's 4th choice, 67th overall, in 1997 Entry Draft).

			Regular Season					Playoffs				
Season	Club	Lea	GP	G	A	TP	PIM	GP	G	A	TP	PIM
1992-93	Wakefield High	Hi-School	20	22	13	35	....	....	....	....	....	....
1993-94	Wakefield High	Hi-School	22	28	34	62	....	....	....	....	....	....
1994-95	Wakefield High	Hi-School	21	22	31	53	....	....	....	....	....	....
1995-96	Wakefield High	Hi-School	21	25	31	56	22	....	....	....	....	....
1996-97	New Hampshire	H-East	39	15	11	26	20	....	....	....	....	....
1997-98	New Hampshire	H-East	38	13	12	25	36	....	....	....	....	....
1998-99	New Hampshire	H-East	41	23	42	65	38	....	....	....	....	....
99-2000	New Hampshire	H-East	38	15	25	40	58	....	....	....	....	....
2000-01	Norfolk Admirals	AHL	75	14	17	31	44	3	0	0	0	2

NCAA Championship All-Tournament Team (1999) • Hockey East Second All-Star Team (2000)

SOZINOV, Vadim (SOH-zih-nahf, va-DEEM) TOR.

Center. Shoots left. 6'1", 185 lbs. Born, Ust-Kamenogorsk, USSR, June 17, 1981.
(Toronto's 6th choice, 179th overall, in 2000 Entry Draft).

			Regular Season					Playoffs				
Season	Club	Lea	GP	G	A	TP	PIM	GP	G	A	TP	PIM
1997-98	Novokuznetsk-2	Russia-3	24	3	0	3	0	....	....	....	....	....
1998-99	Novokuznetsk-3	Russia-4	43	7	10	17	16	....	....	....	....	....
99-2000	Kristall Saratov	Russia-2	2	1	0	1	0	....	....	....	....	....
2000-01	Ottawa 67's	OHL	57	21	18	39	57	20	7	8	15	4

SPEZZA, Jason (SPEHT-zah, JAY-suhn) OTT.

Center. Shoots right. 6'2", 214 lbs. Born, Mississauga, Ont., June 13, 1983.
(Ottawa's 1st choice, 2nd overall, in 2001 Entry Draft).

			Regular Season					Playoffs				
Season	Club	Lea	GP	G	A	TP	PIM	GP	G	A	TP	PIM
1997-98	Toronto Wings	MTHL	54	53	61	114	42	....	....	....	....	....
1998-99	Brampton	OHL	67	22	49	71	18	....	....	....	....	....
99-2000	Mississauga	OHL	52	24	37	61	33	....	....	....	....	....
2000-01	Mississauga	OHL	15	7	23	30	11	....	....	....	....	....
	Windsor Spitfires	OHL	41	36	50	86	32	9	4	5	9	10

OHL First All-Rookie Team (1989) • OHL Third All-Star Team (2001)

Traded to **Windsor** by **Mississauga** with Mark Rideout and Mike Jannes for Ryan Courtney and Tyler Eady, November 15, 2000.

SPILLER, Matthew (SPIHL-uhr, MA-thew) PHX.

Defense. Shoots left. 6'5", 210 lbs. Born, Daysland, Alta., February 7, 1983.
(Phoenix's 2nd choice, 31st overall, in 2001 Entry Draft).

			Regular Season					Playoffs				
Season	Club	Lea	GP	G	A	TP	PIM	GP	G	A	TP	PIM
1998-99	East Central	AMHL	36	8	19	27	140	....	....	....	....	....
99-2000	Seattle T-Birds	WHL	60	1	10	11	108	7	0	0	0	25
2000-01	Seattle T-Birds	WHL	71	4	7	11	174	....	....	....	....	....

SPIRIDONOV, Maxim (spih-rih-DAWN-uhv, max-EEM) EDM.

Left wing. Shoots left. 5'10", 185 lbs. Born, Moscow, USSR, April 7, 1978.
(Edmonton's 10th choice, 241st overall, in 1998 Entry Draft).

			Regular Season					Playoffs				
Season	Club	Lea	GP	G	A	TP	PIM	GP	G	A	TP	PIM
1993-94	CSKA Moscow	Russia-Jr.	35	20	20	40	16	....	....	....	....	....
1994-95	CSKA Moscow	Russia-Jr.	68	60	31	91	34	....	....	....	....	....
1995-96	Smiths Falls Bears	OCJHL	51	52	36	88	71	....	....	....	....	....
1996-97	London Knights	OHL	55	31	22	53	99	....	....	....	....	....
1997-98	London Knights	OHL	66	54	44	98	52	16	3	4	7	4
	Grand Rapids	IHL	....	....	....	....	....	3	0	0	0	0
1998-99	Grand Rapids	IHL	41	11	17	28	12	....	....	....	....	....
	Springfield	AHL	23	8	8	16	2	2	0	0	0	2
99-2000	Tallahassee	ECHL	57	22	30	52	67	....	....	....	....	....
	Hamilton Bulldogs	AHL	10	5	2	7	2	4	1	1	2	0
2000-01	Hamilton Bulldogs	AHL	62	15	2	17	62	....	....	....	....	....

OHL Second All-Star Team (1998)

SPRUKTS, Janis (SPRUKTS, YAN-ish) FLA.

Center. Shoots left. 6'3", 224 lbs. Born, Riga, Latvia, January 31, 1982.
(Florida's 7th choice, 234th overall, in 2000 Entry Draft).

			Regular Season					Playoffs				
Season	Club	Lea	GP	G	A	TP	PIM	GP	G	A	TP	PIM
99-2000	Lukko Rauma	Finn-Jr.	26	2	5	7	6	....	....	....	....	....
2000-01	Lukko Rauma	Finland-2	36	15	22	37	24	3	0	0	0	0
	Lukko Rauma	Finland	9	0	0	0	2	....	....	....	....	....

SRDINKO, Jan (suhr-DIHN-koh, YAN) N.J.

Defense. Shoots left. 5'11", 195 lbs. Born, Vsetin, Czech., February 22, 1974.
(New Jersey's 8th choice, 241st overall, in 1997 Entry Draft).

			Regular Season					Playoffs				
Season	Club	Lea	GP	G	A	TP	PIM	GP	G	A	TP	PIM
1995-96	Petra Vsetin	Cze-Rep	31	0	3	3	....	9	0	0	0	....
1996-97	Petra Vsetin	Cze-Rep	49	2	8	10	71	10	0	3	3	29
1997-98	Petra Vsetin	Cze-Rep	47	1	4	5	95	10	0	3	3	4
	Petra Vsetin	EuroHL	9	0	1	1	4	....	....	....	....	....
1998-99	Slovnaft Vsetin	Cze-Rep	50	2	7	9	58	12	0	1	1	....
99-2000	Slovnaft Vsetin	Cze-Rep	48	3	10	13	50	9	2	0	2	29
2000-01	Slovnaft Vsetin	Cze-Rep	47	8	9	17	81	14	1	1	2	24

SRYUBKO, Andrei (SHROOB-koh, AN-dray) CBJ

Defense. Shoots left. 6'3", 205 lbs. Born, Kiev, USSR, October 21, 1975.

			Regular Season					Playoffs				
Season	Club	Lea	GP	G	A	TP	PIM	GP	G	A	TP	PIM
1996-97	Toledo Storm	ECHL	62	0	8	8	238	5	0	0	0	4
1997-98	Toledo Storm	ECHL	50	1	12	13	165	7	0	0	0	8
	Las Vegas	IHL	13	0	0	0	57	....	....	....	....	....
1998-99	Port Huron	UHL	22	2	2	4	78	2	0	0	0	4
	Fort Wayne	IHL	1	0	0	0	0	....	....	....	....	....
	Las Vegas	IHL	51	0	8	8	164	....	....	....	....	....
99-2000	Port Huron	UHL	2	0	0	0	7	....	....	....	....	....
	Utah Grizzlies	IHL	5	1	1	2	32	....	....	....	....	....
	Grand Rapids	IHL	28	0	1	1	109	2	0	0	0	9
2000-01	Syracuse Crunch	AHL	70	1	6	7	169	5	0	0	0	0

Signed as a free agent by **Columbus**, August 3, 2000.

STAAL, Kim (STOHL, KIHM) MTL.

Center. Shoots right. 6', 185 lbs. Born, Herlev, Denmark, March 10, 1978.
(Montreal's 4th choice, 92nd overall, in 1996 Entry Draft).

			Regular Season					Playoffs				
Season	Club	Lea	GP	G	A	TP	PIM	GP	G	A	TP	PIM
1994-95	Malmo IF	Swede-Jr.	17	4	2	6	4	....	....	....	....	....
1995-96	Malmo IF	Swede-Jr.	30	24	20	44	14	....	....	....	....	....
1996-97	Malmo IF	Swede-Jr.	3	6	4	10	2	....	....	....	....	....
	Malmo IF	Sweden	4	0	1	1	2	....	....	....	....	....
1997-98	Malmo IF	Swede-Jr.	20	13	11	24	36	....	....	....	....	....
	Malmo IF	Sweden	13	0	1	1	1	....	....	....	....	....
1998-99	Malmo IF	Sweden	48	1	5	6	14	4	0	0	0	0
99-2000	Malmo IF	Sweden	50	14	10	24	24	6	1	1	2	4
2000-01	Malmo IF	Sweden	48	16	15	31	32	9	4	2	6	4

STAYZER, Blair (STAY-zuhr, BLAIR) CGY.

Left wing. Shoots left. 6'3", 205 lbs. Born, Dunnville, Ont., October 4, 1980.
(Calgary's 9th choice, 190th overall, in 1999 Entry Draft).

			Regular Season					Playoffs				
Season	Club	Lea	GP	G	A	TP	PIM	GP	G	A	TP	PIM
1995-96	Welland Cougars	OJHL-B	41	4	7	11	79	....	....	....	....	....
1996-97	Windsor	OHL	58	3	5	8	54	3	0	0	0	2
1997-98	Windsor	OHL	57	4	8	12	132	....	....	....	....	....
1998-99	Windsor	OHL	62	12	19	31	140	5	2	0	2	14
99-2000	Windsor	OHL	44	14	5	19	100	11	1	3	4	14
2000-01	Johnstown	ECHL	37	1	3	4	104	....	....	....	....	....

STECKEL, Dave (STEH-kuhl, DAYV) L.A.

Center. Shoots left. 6'5", 200 lbs. Born, Milwaukee, WI, March 15, 1982.
(Los Angeles' 2nd choice, 30th overall, in 2001 Entry Draft).

			Regular Season					Playoffs				
Season	Club	Lea	GP	G	A	TP	PIM	GP	G	A	TP	PIM
1998-99	Team USA	USDP-17	51	3	14	17	18	....	....	....	....	....
	Team USA	USDP	2	0	0	0	2	....	....	....	....	....
99-2000	Team USA	USDP	52	13	13	26	94	....	....	....	....	....
2000-01	Ohio State	CCHA	33	17	18	35	80	....	....	....	....	....

CCHA All-Rookie Team (2001)

STEEN, Calle (STEEN, CAL-lee) DET.

Right wing. Shoots left. 5'11", 198 lbs. Born, Stockholm, Sweden, May 16, 1980.
(Detroit's 6th choice, 142nd overall, in 1998 Entry Draft).

			Regular Season					Playoffs				
Season	Club	Lea	GP	G	A	TP	PIM	GP	G	A	TP	PIM
1995-96	Hammarby IF	Swede-Jr.	5	0	0	0	0	....	....	....	....	....
1996-97	Hammarby IF	Swede-Jr.	24	4	9	13	....	....	....	....	....	....
1997-98	Hammarby IF	Swede-2	21	1	3	4	22	....	....	....	....	....
1998-99	Hammarby IF	Swede-2	33	4	16	20	28	5	0	2	2	6
99-2000	Mora IK	Swede-2	32	4	4	8	48	9	0	2	2	10
2000-01	Bofors IK	Swede-2	31	4	7	11	69	....	....	....	....	....
	JyP Jyvaskyla	Finland	5	0	0	0	0	....	....	....	....	....

STEPHENS, Charlie (STEE-vuhns, CHAHR-lee) **COL.**

Center/Right wing. Shoots right. 6'3", 225 lbs. Born, London, Ont., April 5, 1981.
(Colorado's 9th choice, 196th overall, in 2001 Entry Draft).

			Regular Season					Playoffs				
Season	Club	Lea	GP	G	A	TP	PIM	GP	G	A	TP	PIM
1995-96	Elgin-Middlesex	OMHA	60	25	29	54	60	....	....	....	....	....
1996-97	Leamington	OJHL-B	50	26	36	62	103	....	....	....	....	....
1997-98	St. Michael's	OHL	58	9	21	30	38	....	....	....	....	....
1998-99	St. Michael's	OHL	7	2	4	6	8	....	....	....	....	....
	Guelph Storm	OHL	61	24	28	52	72	11	3	5	8	19
99-2000	Guelph Storm	OHL	56	16	34	50	87	6	1	3	4	15
2000-01	Guelph Storm	OHL	67	38	38	76	53	4	0	2	2	2

• Re-entered NHL Entry Draft. Originally Washington's 3rd choice, 31st overall, in 1999 Entry Draft.

STEPP, Joel (STEHP, JOHL) **ANA.**

Center. Shoots left. 6', 185 lbs. Born, Estevan, Sask., February 11, 1983.
(Anaheim's 3rd choice, 69th overall, in 2001 Entry Draft).

			Regular Season					Playoffs				
Season	Club	Lea	GP	G	A	TP	PIM	GP	G	A	TP	PIM
1998-99	Estevan	SAHA	60	65	70	135	120	....	....	....	....	....
	Red Deer Rebels	WHL	2	0	0	0	0	....	....	....	....	....
99-2000	Red Deer Rebels	WHL	65	11	13	24	59	4	1	0	1	8
2000-01	Red Deer Rebels	WHL	70	24	13	37	89	22	6	3	9	24

STIENSTRA, Doug

Left wing. Shoots left. 6'1", 210 lbs. Born, Kelowna, B.C., June 18, 1976.

			Regular Season					Playoffs				
Season	Club	Lea	GP	G	A	TP	PIM	GP	G	A	TP	PIM
1992-93	Columbia Valley	KIJHL	38	30	32	62	20	....	....	....	....	....
1993-94	Prince George	RMJHL	51	15	29	44	16	....	....	....	....	....
1994-95	Cowichan Valley	BCJHL	58	38	33	71	....	....	....	....	....	....
1995-96			STATISTICS NOT AVAILABLE									
1996-97	Cornell Big Red	ECAC	35	6	10	16	35	....	....	....	....	....
1997-98	Cornell Big Red	ECAC	32	13	15	28	56	....	....	....	....	....
1998-99	Cornell Big Red	ECAC	31	12	11	23	30	....	....	....	....	....
99-2000	Cornell Big Red	ECAC	28	15	17	32	44	....	....	....	....	....
2000-01	Adirondack	UHL	72	19	13	32	67	5	0	2	2	2

All-Ivy Second All-StarTeam (2000) • Won ECAC Best Defenseman Award (2000) • Signed as a free agent by **New Jersey**, May 4, 2000. Signed as a free agent by **Bracknell Bees** (Britain), July 27, 2001.

STILLMAN, Cory (STIHL-mahn, KOHR-ee) **NYI**

Center. Shoots left. 6'2", 204 lbs. Born, Lindsay, Ont., March 2, 1983.
(NY Islanders' 1st choice, 101st overall, in 2001 Entry Draft).

			Regular Season					Playoffs				
Season	Club	Lea	GP	G	A	TP	PIM	GP	G	A	TP	PIM
1998-99	Lindsay Muskies	OPJHL	49	16	15	31	12	....	....	....	....	....
99-2000	Kingston	OHL	61	13	10	23	27	5	0	0	0	0
2000-01	Kingston	OHL	68	29	27	56	39	4	2	0	2	0

STOLL, Jarret (STOHL, JEHR-eht) **CGY.**

Center. Shoots right. 6'1", 199 lbs. Born, Melville, Sask., June 25, 1982.
(Calgary's 3rd choice, 46th overall, in 2000 Entry Draft).

			Regular Season					Playoffs				
Season	Club	Lea	GP	G	A	TP	PIM	GP	G	A	TP	PIM
1997-98	Saskatoon Blaze	SMHL	44	45	44	*89	78	....	....	....	....	....
	Edmonton Ice	WHL	8	2	3	5	4	....	....	....	....	....
1998-99	Kootenay Ice	WHL	57	13	21	34	38	4	0	0	0	2
99-2000	Kootenay Ice	WHL	71	37	38	75	64	20	7	9	16	24
2000-01	Kootenay Ice	WHL	62	40	66	106	105	11	5	9	14	22

WHL East First All-Star Team (2001) • Canadian Major Junior First All-Star Team (2001)

STOREY, Ben (STOY-ree, BEHN)

Defense. Shoots left. 6'2", 200 lbs. Born, Ottawa, Ont., June 22, 1977.
(Colorado's 4th choice, 98th overall, in 1996 Entry Draft).

			Regular Season					Playoffs				
Season	Club	Lea	GP	G	A	TP	PIM	GP	G	A	TP	PIM
1993-94	Ottawa Jr. Sens	OCJHL	57	5	30	35	86	....	....	....	....	....
1994-95	Ottawa Jr. Sens	OCJHL	51	6	33	39	83	....	....	....	....	....
1995-96	Harvard University	ECAC	33	2	11	13	44	....	....	....	....	....
1996-97	Harvard University	ECAC	25	0	6	6	40	....	....	....	....	....
1997-98	Harvard University	ECAC	33	9	16	25	56	....	....	....	....	....
1998-99	Harvard University	ECAC	23	4	11	15	30	....	....	....	....	....
	Hershey Bears	AHL	5	0	0	0	0	....	....	....	....	....
99-2000	Hershey Bears	AHL	65	6	18	24	69	14	2	2	4	8
2000-01	Hershey Bears	AHL	58	2	12	14	71	4	1	3	4	2

STREIT, Martin (STRIGHT, MAHR-tihn) **CBJ**

Left wing. Shoots right. 6'2", 191 lbs. Born, Vyskov, Czech., February 2, 1977.
(Philadelphia's 7th choice, 178th overall, in 1995 Entry Draft).

			Regular Season					Playoffs				
Season	Club	Lea	GP	G	A	TP	PIM	GP	G	A	TP	PIM
1995-96	HC Olomouc-Jr.	Cze-Rep	19	10	6	16	....	....	....	....	....	....
	HC Olomouc	Cze-Rep	10	0	0	0	....	....	....	....	....	....
1996-97	HC Olomouc	Cze-Rep	18	1	2	3	14	....	....	....	....	....
1997-98	Karlovy Vary	Cze-Rep	48	5	13	18	24	....	....	....	....	....
1998-99	Karlovy Vary	Cze-Rep	48	9	4	13	34	....	....	....	....	....
99-2000	Karlovy Vary	Cze-Rep	18	0	2	2	20	....	....	....	....	....
	HC Vitkovice	Cze-Rep	31	3	6	9	28	....	....	....	....	....
2000-01	HCF Havirov	Cze-Rep	11	0	0	0	6	....	....	....	....	....
	Karlovy Vary	Cze-Rep	14	0	1	1	12	....	....	....	....	....

Selected by **Columbus** from **Philadelphia** in Expansion Draft, June 23, 2000.

STROM, Peter (STRUHM, PEE-tuhr) **MTL.**

Left wing. Shoots right. 6', 178 lbs. Born, Snotorp, Sweden, January 14, 1975.
(Montreal's 10th choice, 200th overall, in 1994 Entry Draft).

			Regular Season					Playoffs				
Season	Club	Lea	GP	G	A	TP	PIM	GP	G	A	TP	PIM
1993-94	Vastra Frolunda	Sweden	29	0	0	0	8	....	....	....	....	....
1994-95	Vastra Frolunda	Swede-2	12	8	10	18	10	....	....	....	....	....
	Vastra Frolunda	Sweden	16	0	3	3	10	....	....	....	....	....
1995-96	Vastra Frolunda	Sweden	35	7	8	15	10	13	0	3	3	0
1996-97	Vastra Frolunda	Sweden	49	7	16	23	24	3	0	0	0	2
1997-98	Vastra Frolunda	Sweden	46	6	15	21	22	7	0	4	4	0
1998-99	Vastra Frolunda	Sweden	49	17	15	32	18	4	0	2	2	0
99-2000	Vastra Frolunda	Sweden	50	12	26	38	20	5	0	1	1	2
2000-01	Vastra Frolunda	Sweden	50	15	18	33	16	5	0	3	3	6

STUART, Colin (STOO-uhrt, CAW-lihn) **ATL.**

Center. Shoots left. 6'1", 195 lbs. Born, Rochester, MN, July 8, 1982.
(Atlanta's 5th choice, 135th overall, in 2001 Entry Draft).

			Regular Season					Playoffs				
Season	Club	Lea	GP	G	A	TP	PIM	GP	G	A	TP	PIM
1998-99	Lourdes High	Hi-School	23	22	32	54	....	....	....	....	....	....
99-2000	Lincoln Stars	USHL	53	18	19	37	38	....	....	....	....	....
2000-01	Colorado College	WCHA	41	2	7	9	26	....	....	....	....	....

STUART, Mike (STOO-uhrt, MIGHK) **NSH.**

Defense. Shoots right. 6', 200 lbs. Born, Rochester, MN, August 31, 1980.
(Nashville's 6th choice, 137th overall, in 2000 Entry Draft).

			Regular Season					Playoffs				
Season	Club	Lea	GP	G	A	TP	PIM	GP	G	A	TP	PIM
1996-97	Rochester	USHL	46	4	9	13	22	....	....	....	....	....
1997-98	Rochester	USHL	50	4	15	19	40	....	....	....	....	....
1998-99	Colorado College	WCHA	40	2	12	14	44	....	....	....	....	....
99-2000	Colorado College	WCHA	32	2	5	7	26	....	....	....	....	....
2000-01	Colorado College	WCHA	33	1	13	14	36	....	....	....	....	....

USHL All-Rookie Team (1997)

STUSSI, Rene (SHTOO-see, REH-nay) **ANA.**

Center. Shoots right. 5'11", 183 lbs. Born, Muri, Switzerland, December 13, 1978.
(Anaheim's 7th choice, 209th overall, in 1997 Entry Draft).

			Regular Season					Playoffs				
Season	Club	Lea	GP	G	A	TP	PIM	GP	G	A	TP	PIM
1995-96	HC Thurgau	Switz-2	34	2	4	6	10	7	3	0	3	2
1996-97	HC Thurgau	Switz-2	42	20	31	51	24	8	5	4	9	4
1997-98	EHC Kloten	Switz.	38	9	8	17	10	7	1	0	1	4
1998-99	EHC Kloten	Switz.	36	5	5	10	14	....	....	....	....	....
	ZSC Zurich	Switz.	7	1	1	2	6	7	1	1	2	4
99-2000	EV Zug	Switz.	45	7	5	12	13	9	0	1	1	0
2000-01	EHC Chur	Switz.	36	7	7	14	26	11	1	1	2	26

SUBBOTIN, Dmitri (soo-BOH-tihn, DIH-mih-TREE) **CBJ**

Left wing. Shoots left. 6'1", 183 lbs. Born, Tomsk, USSR, October 20, 1977.
(NY Rangers' 3rd choice, 76th overall, in 1996 Entry Draft).

			Regular Season					Playoffs				
Season	Club	Lea	GP	G	A	TP	PIM	GP	G	A	TP	PIM
1993-94	HC Yekaterinburg	CIS	12	0	3	3	4	....	....	....	....	....
1994-95	HC Yekaterinburg	CIS	52	9	6	15	75	2	0	0	0	2
1995-96	CSKA Moscow	CIS	41	6	5	11	62	3	0	0	0	0
1996-97	HC Moscow	Russia-2	8	1	0	1	8	....	....	....	....	....
	CSKA Moscow	Russia	17	5	3	8	22	2	0	0	0	2
1997-98	CSKA Moscow	Russia	16	1	1	2	47	....	....	....	....	....
1998-99	Dynamo Moscow	Russia	1	0	1	1	0	....	....	....	....	....
	Lada Togliatti	Russia	31	8	3	11	47	7	0	0	0	4
99-2000	Lada Togliatti	Russia-2	2	0	1	1	0	....	....	....	....	....
	Lada Togliatti	Russia	27	10	4	14	26	7	1	1	2	4
2000-01	Dynamo Moscow	Russia	39	11	15	26	48	....	....	....	....	....

Selected by **Columbus** from **NY Rangers** in Expansion Draft, June 23, 2000.

SUGDEN, Brandon (SUHG-duhn, BRAN-duhn) **ST.L.**

Defense. Shoots right. 6'2", 178 lbs. Born, Toronto, Ont., June 23, 1978.
(Toronto's 8th choice, 111th overall, in 1996 Entry Draft).

			Regular Season					Playoffs				
Season	Club	Lea	GP	G	A	TP	PIM	GP	G	A	TP	PIM
1994-95	Toronto Wings	MTHL	53	12	24	36	162	....	....	....	....	....
	St. Michael's	MTJHL	15	0	3	3	69	....	....	....	....	....
1995-96	London Knights	OHL	55	2	7	9	*264	....	....	....	....	....
1996-97	London Knights	OHL	31	4	10	14	158	....	....	....	....	....
	Sudbury Wolves	OHL	20	....	4	4	70	....	....	....	....	....
1997-98	Sudbury Wolves	OHL	11	2	3	5	62	....	....	....	....	....
	Barrie Colts	OHL	49	6	21	27	191	6	0	0	0	18
1998-99	Cincinnati	IHL	6	0	2	2	51	....	....	....	....	....
	Dayton Bombers	ECHL	44	0	1	1	233	1	0	0	0	17
99-2000	Dayton Bombers	ECHL	13	0	1	1	110	....	....	....	....	....
2000-01	Worcester	AHL	11	0	0	0	56	....	....	....	....	....
	Tallahassee	ECHL	12	1	0	1	75	....	....	....	....	....
	Peoria	ECHL	1	0	0	0	0	....	....	....	....	....

Signed as a free agent by **St. Louis**, June 29, 1998. • Suspended for life by ECHL for throwing his stick into the crowd during game vs. Dayton (ECHL), January 26, 2001.

SUGLOBOV, Alexander (suh-GLOH-bahf, al-ehx-AN-duhr) **N.J.**

Right wing. Shoots left. 6', 176 lbs. Born, Elektrostal, USSR, January 15, 1982.
(New Jersey's 3rd choice, 56th overall, in 2000 Entry Draft).

			Regular Season					Playoffs				
Season	Club	Lea	GP	G	A	TP	PIM	GP	G	A	TP	PIM
1998-99	Krylja Sovetov-2	Russia-4	1	0	0	0	0	....	....	....	....	....
	Krylja Sovetov	Russia	1	0	0	0	0	....	....	....	....	....
99-2000	HC Yaroslavl-2	Russia-3	38	23	10	33	....	....	....	....	....	....
2000-01	St. Petersburg	Russia	8	1	0	1	6	....	....	....	....	....
	Ufa-Salavat	Russia	6	0	0	0	4	....	....	....	....	....
	HC Yaroslavl	Russia	4	0	0	0	2	11	1	2	3	6

SULLIVAN, Brian (suh-LIH-vuhn, BRIGH-uhn) **DAL.**

Defense. Shoots left. 6'3", 185 lbs. Born, Marshfield, MA, June 27, 1980.
(Dallas' 9th choice, 243rd overall, in 1999 Entry Draft).

			Regular Season					Playoffs				
Season	Club	Lea	GP	G	A	TP	PIM	GP	G	A	TP	PIM
1997-98	Thayer Academy	Hi-School	26	0	5	5	17	....	....	....	....	....
1998-99	Thayer Academy	Hi-School	21	0	7	7	10	....	....	....	....	....
99-2000	Northeastern	H-East	23	0	1	1	8	....	....	....	....	....
2000-01	Northeastern	H-East	34	1	2	3	37	....	....	....	....	....

SULLIVAN, Jeff (SUHL-lih-vahn, JEHF)

Defense. Shoots left. 6'1", 185 lbs. Born, St. John's, Nfld., September 18, 1978.
(Ottawa's 5th choice, 146th overall, in 1997 Entry Draft).

			Regular Season					Playoffs				
Season	Club	Lea	GP	G	A	TP	PIM	GP	G	A	TP	PIM
1994-95	St. John's Caps	NFAHA	40	10	15	25	120	....	....	....	....	....
1995-96	East Hants	MJrHL	52	15	20	35	270	....	....	....	....	....
1996-97	Granby Bisons	QMJHL	25	4	8	12	47	....	....	....	....	....
	Halifax	QMJHL	45	4	23	27	200	18	0	5	5	96
1997-98	Halifax	QMJHL	69	9	27	36	377	5	0	1	1	21
1998-99	Halifax	QMJHL	69	7	30	37	320	5	1	1	2	14
99-2000	Saint John Flames	AHL	9	0	3	3	16	....	....	....	....	....
	Johnstown Chiefs	ECHL	58	2	8	10	181	7	0	2	2	32
2000-01	Johnstown Chiefs	ECHL	69	2	9	11	302	4	0	0	0	9
	Kentucky	AHL	1	0	0	0	4	....	....	....	....	....
	Saint John Flames	AHL	2	0	0	0	0	....	....	....	....	....

SURMA, Damian (SUHR-ma, DAY-mee-an) **CAR.**

Left wing. Shoots left. 5'9", 200 lbs. Born, Lincoln Park, MI, June 22, 1981.
(Carolina's 5th choice, 174th overall, in 1999 Entry Draft).

					Regular Season					Playoffs		
Season	**Club**	**Lea**	**GP**	**G**	**A**	**TP**	**PIM**	**GP**	**G**	**A**	**TP**	**PIM**
1997-98	Det-Compuware	NAJHL	50	12	17	29	50	6	3	1	4	4
1998-99	Plymouth Whalers	OHL	65	17	15	32	62	11	3	6	9	15
99-2000	Plymouth Whalers	OHL	66	34	44	78	114	20	9	8	17	10
2000-01	Plymouth Whalers	OHL	55	26	34	60	62	19	8	9	17	25

SUROVY, Tomas (suh-ROH-vee, TAW-mahsh) **PIT.**

Center. Shoots left. 6'1", 187 lbs. Born, Banska Bystrica, Czech., September 24, 1981.
(Pittsburgh's 5th choice, 120th overall, in 2001 Entry Draft).

					Regular Season					Playoffs		
Season	**Club**	**Lea**	**GP**	**G**	**A**	**TP**	**PIM**	**GP**	**G**	**A**	**TP**	**PIM**
99-2000	Banska Bystrica	Slovak-2	39	25	29	54	4	....	....	....	....	....
2000-01	HC SKP Poprad	Slovakia	53	22	28	50	30	6	2	1	3	14

SUTHERBY, Brian (SUH-thur-bee, BRIGH-uhn) **WSH.**

Center. Shoots left. 6'2", 180 lbs. Born, Edmonton, Alta., March 1, 1982.
(Washington's 1st choice, 26th overall, in 2000 Entry Draft).

					Regular Season					Playoffs		
Season	**Club**	**Lea**	**GP**	**G**	**A**	**TP**	**PIM**	**GP**	**G**	**A**	**TP**	**PIM**
1997-98	CAC Cement	AMHL	36	36	23	59	60	....	....	....	....	....
1998-99	Moose Jaw	WHL	66	9	12	21	47	11	0	1	1	0
99-2000	Moose Jaw	WHL	47	18	17	35	102	4	1	1	2	12
2000-01	Moose Jaw	WHL	59	34	43	77	138	4	2	1	3	10

SUTTER, Shaun (SUH-tuhr, SHAWN)

Center. Shoots right. 6'1", 175 lbs. Born, Red Deer, Alta., June 2, 1980.
(Calgary's 4th choice, 102nd overall, in 1998 Entry Draft).

					Regular Season					Playoffs		
Season	**Club**	**Lea**	**GP**	**G**	**A**	**TP**	**PIM**	**GP**	**G**	**A**	**TP**	**PIM**
1995-96	Red Deer Chiefs	AMHL	23	4	6	10	62	....	....	....	....	....
1996-97	Red Deer Chiefs	AMHL	33	15	24	39	143	....	....	....	....	....
	Lethbridge	WHL	1	0	0	0	0	....	....	....	....	....
1997-98	Lethbridge	WHL	69	11	9	20	146	4	0	0	0	4
1998-99	Lethbridge	WHL	35	8	4	12	43	....	....	....	....	....
	Medicine Hat	WHL	23	9	5	14	38	....	....	....	....	....
99-2000	Medicine Hat	WHL	29	1	7	8	43	....	....	....	....	....
	Calgary Hitmen	WHL	6	0	1	1	8	....	....	....	....	....
2000-01	Calgary Hitmen	WHL	63	29	35	64	102	12	1	2	3	12
	Saint John Flames	AHL	1	0	0	0	0	....	....	....	....	....

SUURSOO, Toivo (SUH-uhr-soh-oh, TOI-voh) **DET.**

Left wing. Shoots right. 6', 175 lbs. Born, Tallinn, USSR, November 23, 1975.
(Detroit's 10th choice, 283rd overall, in 1994 Entry Draft).

					Regular Season					Playoffs		
Season	**Club**	**Lea**	**GP**	**G**	**A**	**TP**	**PIM**	**GP**	**G**	**A**	**TP**	**PIM**
1993-94	Krylja Sovetov	CIS	33	3	0	3	8	....	....	....	....	....
1994-95	Krylja Sovetov	CIS	47	10	5	15	36	4	0	0	0	4
1995-96	Krylja Sovetov	CIS	47	6	4	10	36	....	....	....	....	....
1996-97	TPS Turku	Finland	50	11	8	19	64	12	2	3	5	4
1997-98	TPS Turku	Finland	38	17	5	22	46	4	2	1	3	2
	TPS Turku	EuroHL	4	2	0	2	0	....	....	....	....	....
1998-99	Malmo IF	Sweden	29	8	6	14	57	8	4	3	7	12
	Adirondack	AHL	2	0	0	0	0	....	....	....	....	....
99-2000	Malmo IF	Sweden	32	6	5	11	24	1	0	0	0	0
2000-01	Cincinnati Ducks	AHL	51	14	12	26	37	....	....	....	....	....

SVENSSON, Jimmie (SVEHN-sohn, JIH-mee) **DET.**

Center. Shoots left. 6'1", 183 lbs. Born, Vasteras, Sweden, February 25, 1982.
(Detroit's 9th choice, 228th overall, in 2000 Entry Draft).

					Regular Season					Playoffs		
Season	**Club**	**Lea**	**GP**	**G**	**A**	**TP**	**PIM**	**GP**	**G**	**A**	**TP**	**PIM**
99-2000	Vasteras IK	Swede-Jr.	29	10	2	12	121	....	....	....	....	....
2000-01	Malmo IF	Swede-Jr.	23	3	1	4	74	....	....	....	....	....

SVITOV, Alexander (SVEE-tawf, al-ehx-AN-duhr) **T.B.**

Center. Shoots left. 6'3", 198 lbs. Born, Omsk, USSR, November 3, 1982.
(Tampa Bay's 1st choice, 3rd overall, in 2001 Entry Draft).

					Regular Season					Playoffs		
Season	**Club**	**Lea**	**GP**	**G**	**A**	**TP**	**PIM**	**GP**	**G**	**A**	**TP**	**PIM**
1997-98	Novokuznetsk-2	Russia-3	4	0	0	0	0	....	....	....	....	....
1998-99	VDV Omsk-2	Russia-4	27	15	8	23	20	....	....	....	....	....
	Avangard Omsk	Russia	....	....	....	....	....	1	0	0	0	0
99-2000	VDV Omsk-2	Russia-3	14	13	9	22	62	....	....	....	....	....
	Avangard Omsk	Russia	18	3	3	6	45	6	1	0	1	16
2000-01	Avangard Omsk	Russia	39	8	6	14	115	14	2	1	3	34

SVOBODA, Jaroslav (svah-BOH-duh, YAR-oh-slawf) **CAR.**

Left wing. Shoots left. 6'2", 190 lbs. Born, Cervenka, Czech., June 1, 1980.
(Carolina's 8th choice, 208th overall, in 1998 Entry Draft).

					Regular Season					Playoffs		
Season	**Club**	**Lea**	**GP**	**G**	**A**	**TP**	**PIM**	**GP**	**G**	**A**	**TP**	**PIM**
1995-96	HC Olomouc-Jr.	Cze-Rep	40	13	15	28	....	....	....	....	....	....
1996-97	HC Olomouc-Jr.	Cze-Rep	39	19	14	33	....	....	....	....	....	....
1997-98	HC Olomouc-Jr.	Cze-Rep	36	14	21	35	....	....	....	....	....	....
	HC Olomouc-2	Cze-Rep	13	0	1	1	....	....	....	....	....	....
1998-99	Kootenay Ice	WHL	54	26	33	59	46	7	2	2	4	11
99-2000	Kootenay Ice	WHL	56	23	43	66	97	21	*15	13	*28	51
2000-01	Cincinnati	IHL	52	4	10	14	25	....	....	....	....	....

SZYSKY, Chris (SHIHS-kee, KRIHS)

Right wing. Shoots right. 6', 208 lbs. Born, White City, Sask., June 8, 1976.
(Dallas' 8th choice, 280th overall, in 1994 Entry Draft).

					Regular Season					Playoffs		
Season	**Club**	**Lea**	**GP**	**G**	**A**	**TP**	**PIM**	**GP**	**G**	**A**	**TP**	**PIM**
1992-93	Swift Current	SMHL	35	23	24	47	150	....	....	....	....	....
	Swift Current	WHL	....	....	....	....	....	1	0	0	0	0
1993-94	Swift Current	WHL	60	6	10	16	82	7	0	1	1	12
1994-95	Swift Current	WHL	61	6	6	12	105	6	2	0	2	10
1995-96	Swift Current	WHL	63	19	16	35	115	6	3	2	5	21
1996-97	Swift Current	WHL	66	28	30	58	181	10	5	10	15	18
1997-98	Canada	Nat-Team	50	9	20	29	111	....	....	....	....	....
1998-99	Canada	Nat-Team	41	9	13	22	56	....	....	....	....	....
	Grand Rapids	IHL	6	1	1	2	10	....	....	....	....	....
99-2000	Grand Rapids	IHL	32	5	4	9	44	15	2	3	5	*45
2000-01	Grand Rapids	IHL	70	15	13	28	108	7	0	2	2	13

Signed as a free agent by **Ottawa**, June 20, 1999.

TAFFE, Jeff (TAYF, JEHF) **PHX.**

Center. Shoots left. 6'3", 180 lbs. Born, Hastings, MN, February 19, 1981.
(St. Louis' 1st choice, 30th overall, in 2000 Entry Draft).

					Regular Season					Playoffs		
Season	**Club**	**Lea**	**GP**	**G**	**A**	**TP**	**PIM**	**GP**	**G**	**A**	**TP**	**PIM**
1996-97	Hastings High	Hi-School	25	21	37	58	....	....	....	....	....	....
1997-98	Hastings High	Hi-School	28	37	29	66	....	....	....	....	....	....
1998-99	Hastings High	Hi-School	28	39	51	90	....	....	....	....	....	....
99-2000	U. of Minnesota	WCHA	39	10	10	20	22	....	....	....	....	....
2000-01	U. of Minnesota	WCHA	38	12	23	35	56	....	....	....	....	....

Minnesota High School Player of the Year (1999) • Rights traded to **Phoenix** by **St. Louis** with Michal Handzus, Ladislav Nagy and St. Louis' 1st round choice in 2002 Entry Draft for Keith Tkachuk, March 13, 2001.

TALLINDER, Henrik (tah-LIHN-duhr, HEHN-rihk) **BUF.**

Defense. Shoots left. 6'3", 194 lbs. Born, Stockholm, Sweden, January 10, 1979.
(Buffalo's 2nd choice, 48th overall, in 1997 Entry Draft).

					Regular Season					Playoffs		
Season	**Club**	**Lea**	**GP**	**G**	**A**	**TP**	**PIM**	**GP**	**G**	**A**	**TP**	**PIM**
1996-97	AIK Solna	Swede-Jr.	40	4	13	17	55	....	....	....	....	....
	AIK Solna	Sweden	1	0	0	0	0	....	....	....	....	....
1997-98	AIK Solna	Sweden	34	0	0	0	26	....	....	....	....	....
1998-99	AIK Solna	Sweden	36	0	0	0	30	....	....	....	....	....
99-2000	AIK Solna	Sweden	50	0	2	2	59	....	....	....	....	....
2000-01	TPS Turku	Finland	56	5	9	14	62	10	2	1	3	8

TARATUKHIN, Andrei (tahr-a-TOO-khin, AN-dray) **CGY.**

Center. Shoots left. 6', 198 lbs. Born, Omsk, USSR, February 22, 1983.
(Calgary's 2nd choice, 41st overall, in 2001 Entry Draft).

					Regular Season					Playoffs		
Season	**Club**	**Lea**	**GP**	**G**	**A**	**TP**	**PIM**	**GP**	**G**	**A**	**TP**	**PIM**
1998-99	Avangard Omsk-2	Russia-4	1	0	0	0	0	....	....	....	....	....
99-2000	Avangard Omsk-2	Russia-3	27	10	6	16	16	....	....	....	....	....
	Avangard Omsk	Russia	....	....	....	....	....	1	1	0	1	0
2000-01	Avangard Omsk-2	Russia-3	41	19	28	47	69	....	....	....	....	....

TARVAINEN, Jussi (tahr-VIGH-nehn, YU-see) **EDM.**

Right wing. Shoots right. 6'3", 215 lbs. Born, Lahti, Finland, May 31, 1976.
(Edmonton's 7th choice, 95th overall, in 1994 Entry Draft).

					Regular Season					Playoffs		
Season	**Club**	**Lea**	**GP**	**G**	**A**	**TP**	**PIM**	**GP**	**G**	**A**	**TP**	**PIM**
1992-93	KalPa Kuopio-B	Finn-Jr.	18	13	9	22	38	....	....	....	....	....
	KalPa Kuopio	Finn-Jr.	17	3	6	9	35	....	....	....	....	....
1993-94	KalPa Kuopio	Finn-Jr.	16	9	14	23	12	....	....	....	....	....
	Junkkarit HT	Finland-2	1	0	0	0	0	....	....	....	....	....
	KalPa Kuopio	Finland	42	3	4	7	20	....	....	....	....	....
1994-95	KalPa Kuopio	Finn-Jr.	3	4	0	4	2	....	....	....	....	....
	KalPa Kuopio	Finland	45	10	7	17	34	3	0	0	0	2
1995-96	KalPa Kuopio	Finn-Jr.	3	2	3	5	10	7	3	4	7	12
	KalPa Kuopio	Finland	47	8	11	19	50	....	....	....	....	....
1996-97	KalPa Kuopio	Finland	49	14	26	40	62	....	....	....	....	....
	KalPa Kuopio	Finn-Jr.	....	....	....	....	....	1	0	0	0	2
	KalPa Kuopio	Finland-2	....	....	....	....	....	6	4	3	7	4
1997-98	JyP Jyvaskyla	Finland	43	12	26	38	59	....	....	....	....	....
1998-99	JyP Jyvaskyla	Finland	54	17	24	41	84	3	0	0	0	8
99-2000	Tappara Tampere	Finland	52	20	27	47	91	4	1	0	1	2
2000-01	Tappara Tampere	Finland	56	23	32	55	36	10	*8	2	10	2

TATARINOV, Alexander (ta-TAHR-ee-nahf, al-ehx-AN-duhr) **PHX.**

Right wing. Shoots left. 5'11", 176 lbs. Born, Sverdlovsk, USSR, April 14, 1982.
(Phoenix's 2nd choice, 53rd overall, in 2000 Entry Draft).

					Regular Season					Playoffs		
Season	**Club**	**Lea**	**GP**	**G**	**A**	**TP**	**PIM**	**GP**	**G**	**A**	**TP**	**PIM**
1998-99	Krylja Sovetov	Russia	3	0	0	0	0	....	....	....	....	....
99-2000	HC Yaroslavl-2	Russia-3	35	12	12	24	36	....	....	....	....	....
2000-01	HC Yaroslavl	Russia	2	0	1	1	0	1	0	0	0	0
	Kristall Saratov	Russia-2	24	3	3	6	8	....	....	....	....	....

TERESCHENKO, Alexei (teh-REH-shehn-koh, al-EHX-ay) **DAL.**

Center. Shoots left. 5'11", 176 lbs. Born, Mozhaisk, USSR, December 16, 1980.
(Dallas' 4th choice, 91st overall, in 2000 Entry Draft).

					Regular Season					Playoffs		
Season	**Club**	**Lea**	**GP**	**G**	**A**	**TP**	**PIM**	**GP**	**G**	**A**	**TP**	**PIM**
1996-97	D'amo Moscow-2	Russia-3	9	0	0	0	2	....	....	....	....	....
1997-98	Dynamo Moscow-2	Russia-2	26	6	7	13	30	....	....	....	....	....
1998-99	D'amo Moscow-2	Russia-3	28	4	17	21	20	....	....	....	....	....
	THC Tver	Russia-2	12	3	4	7	4	....	....	....	....	....
	Dynamo Moscow	Russia	1	0	1	1	0	2	0	0	0	0
99-2000	Dynamo Moscow	Russia	27	1	1	2	10	17	1	1	2	8
2000-01	Dynamo Moscow	Russia	40	3	3	6	18	....	....	....	....	....

TERNAVSKY, Artem (tuhr-NAV-skee, ahr-TEHM) **WSH.**

Defense. Shoots left. 6'3", 213 lbs. Born, Magnitogorsk, USSR, June 2, 1983.
(Washington's 4th choice, 160th overall, in 2001 Entry Draft).

					Regular Season					Playoffs		
Season	**Club**	**Lea**	**GP**	**G**	**A**	**TP**	**PIM**	**GP**	**G**	**A**	**TP**	**PIM**
99-2000	CSKA Moscow	Russia-Jr.	2	0	1	1	0	....	....	....	....	....
	HC Moscow-2	Russia-3	25	0	4	4	42	....	....	....	....	....
2000-01	Sherbrooke	QMJHL	65	3	15	18	143	....	....	....	....	....

THEORET, Luc (THEE-ohr-eht, LEWK) **BUF.**

Defense. Shoots left. 6'2", 192 lbs. Born, Winnipeg, Man., July 30, 1979.
(Buffalo's 5th choice, 101st overall, in 1997 Entry Draft).

					Regular Season					Playoffs		
Season	**Club**	**Lea**	**GP**	**G**	**A**	**TP**	**PIM**	**GP**	**G**	**A**	**TP**	**PIM**
1994-95	Winnipeg Braves	MAHA	34	5	31	36	48	....	....	....	....	....
1995-96	Lethbridge	WHL	47	4	13	17	41	4	0	0	0	6
1996-97	Lethbridge	WHL	43	3	7	10	51	19	1	5	6	8
1997-98	Lethbridge	WHL	65	12	37	49	98	4	0	1	1	8
1998-99	Lethbridge	WHL	46	13	39	52	92	....	....	....	....	....
	Portland	WHL	3	0	0	0	10	....	....	....	....	....
99-2000	South Carolina	ECHL	48	9	10	19	74	10	2	2	4	10
2000-01	South Carolina	ECHL	19	4	2	6	19	....	....	....	....	....

THINEL, Marc-Andre (tih-nehl, MAHRK-AWN-dray) **MTL.**

Right wing. Shoots left. 5'10", 178 lbs. Born, St-Jerome, Que., March 24, 1981.
(Montreal's 6th choice, 145th overall, in 1999 Entry Draft).

			Regular Season					Playoffs				
Season	Club	Lea	GP	G	A	TP	PIM	GP	G	A	TP	PIM
1996-97	Laval-Laurentide	QAAA	40	12	10	22	....	13	0	5	5	....
1997-98	Victoriaville Tigres	QMJHL	58	7	10	17	20	6	0	3	3	4
1998-99	Victoriaville Tigres	QMJHL	66	45	58	103	16	6	5	3	8	4
99-2000	Victoriaville Tigres	QMJHL	71	59	73	132	55	6	5	6	11	18
2000-01	Victoriaville Tigres	QMJHL	70	62	88	150	101	13	12	13	25	18

QMJHL First All-Star Team (2000) • QMJHL Second All-Star Team (2001)

THOMPSON, Jamie **ST.L.**

Left wing. Shoots left. 6', 200 lbs. Born, Framingham, MA, March 24, 1974.

			Regular Season					Playoffs				
Season	Club	Lea	GP	G	A	TP	PIM	GP	G	A	TP	PIM
1992-93	U. of Maine	H-East	16	3	1	4	10	....	....	....	....	....
1993-94	Omaha Lancers	USHL	STATISTICS NOT AVAILABLE									
1994-95	U. of Maine	H-East	43	11	15	26	22	....	....	....	....	....
1995-96	U. of Maine	H-East	19	2	9	11	16	....	....	....	....	....
1996-97	RMC Palladins	OUAA	2	0	0	0	0	....	....	....	....	....
	El Paso Buzzards	WPHL	50	34	28	62	65	9	4	8	12	12
1997-98	El Paso Buzzards	WPHL	58	*71	51	122	34	15	*15	11	*26	8
	Utah Grizzlies	IHL	6	1	2	3	2	....	....	....	....	....
1998-99	Peoria Rivermen	ECHL	43	21	22	43	37	2	3	0	3	2
	Worcester	AHL	25	7	3	10	12	1	0	0	0	0
99-2000	Worcester	AHL	64	17	13	30	31	7	3	5	8	6
2000-01	Worcester	AHL	37	8	6	14	35	6	1	2	3	2

• Ruled academically ineligable to play 1993-94 season by U. of Maine. Signed as a free agent by **St. Louis**, September 21, 1999. • Missed majority of 2000-01 season recovering from knee injury originally suffered in game vs. Hartford (AHL), April 29, 2000.

THORBURN, Chris (THOHR-buhrn, KRIHS) **BUF.**

Center. Shoots right. 6'2", 190 lbs. Born, Sault Ste. Marie, Ont., June 3, 1983.
(Buffalo's 3rd choice, 50th overall, in 2001 Entry Draft).

			Regular Season					Playoffs				
Season	Club	Lea	GP	G	A	TP	PIM	GP	G	A	TP	PIM
1998-99	Eliot Lake Vikings	NOJHA	40	21	12	33	28	....	....	....	....	....
99-2000	North Bay	OHL	56	12	8	20	33	6	0	2	2	0
2000-01	North Bay	OHL	66	22	32	54	64	4	0	1	1	9

THORNTON, Shawn (THOHR-tohn, SHAWN) **TOR.**

Right wing. Shoots right. 6'1", 196 lbs. Born, Oshawa, Ont., July 23, 1979.
(Toronto's 6th choice, 190th overall, in 1997 Entry Draft).

			Regular Season					Playoffs				
Season	Club	Lea	GP	G	A	TP	PIM	GP	G	A	TP	PIM
1995-96	Peterborough	OHL	63	4	10	14	192	24	3	0	3	25
1996-97	Peterborough	OHL	61	19	10	29	204	11	2	4	6	20
1997-98	St. John's Leafs	AHL	59	0	3	3	225	....	....	....	....	....
1998-99	St. John's Leafs	AHL	78	8	11	19	354	5	0	0	0	9
99-2000	St. John's Leafs	AHL	60	4	12	16	316	....	....	....	....	....
2000-01	St. John's Leafs	AHL	79	5	12	17	320	3	1	2	3	2

TIILIKAINEN, Jukka (TEE-ee-lee-kigh-nehn, yoo-KUH) **L.A.**

Left wing. Shoots left. 6', 190 lbs. Born, Espoo, Finland, April 4, 1974.
(Los Angeles' 8th choice, 255th overall, in 1992 Entry Draft).

			Regular Season					Playoffs				
Season	Club	Lea	GP	G	A	TP	PIM	GP	G	A	TP	PIM
1992-93	Vantaa HT	Finland-2	18	7	3	10	10	....	....	....	....	....
	Kiekko Espoo	Finland	5	0	0	0	4	....	....	....	....	....
1993-94	Kiekko Espoo	Finland	33	2	4	6	12	....	....	....	....	....
1994-95	TPS Turku	Finland	38	5	4	9	8	11	1	0	1	8
1995-96	TPS Turku	Finland	38	6	13	19	28	10	0	2	2	2
1996-97	Lukko Rauma	Finland	49	15	12	27	42	....	....	....	....	....
1997-98	Assat-Pori	Finland	48	13	13	26	18	3	0	2	2	0
1998-99	Jokerit Helsinki	Finland	51	7	8	15	52	2	0	0	0	4
99-2000	Jokerit Helsinki	Finland	19	1	2	3	31	....	....	....	....	....
	AIK Solna	Sweden	29	8	6	14	22	....	....	....	....	....
2000-01	Blues Espoo	Finland	53	2	12	14	50	....	....	....	....	....

TIMMONS, K.C. (TIHM-mohns, KAY-SEE) **COL.**

Left wing. Shoots left. 6'4", 215 lbs. Born, Victoria, B.C., April 6, 1980.
(Colorado's 9th choice, 141st overall, in 1998 Entry Draft).

			Regular Season					Playoffs				
Season	Club	Lea	GP	G	A	TP	PIM	GP	G	A	TP	PIM
1995-96	Victoria Lions	BCAHA	68	82	101	183	190	....	....	....	....	....
1996-97	Tri-City Americans	WHL	52	0	5	5	27	....	....	....	....	....
1997-98	Tri-City Americans	WHL	72	11	7	18	139	....	....	....	....	....
1998-99	Tri-City Americans	WHL	69	13	11	24	113	12	1	1	2	36
99-2000	Tri-City Americans	WHL	69	24	24	48	193	4	0	0	0	4
	Hershey Bears	AHL	....	....	....	....	....	4	0	0	0	15
2000-01	Hershey Bears	AHL	39	3	9	12	69	....	....	....	....	....

TIMOFEEV, Denis (teh-moh-FAY-ehf, DEH-nihs) **BOS.**

Defense. Shoots left. 6'6", 210 lbs. Born, Moscow, USSR, January 14, 1979.
(Boston's 7th choice, 135th overall, in 1997 Entry Draft).

			Regular Season					Playoffs				
Season	Club	Lea	GP	G	A	TP	PIM	GP	G	A	TP	PIM
1996-97	HC Moscow-2	Russia-3	11	0	0	0	2	....	....	....	....	....
	CSKA Moscow	Russia	41	6	8	14	....	....	....	....	....	....
1997-98	CSKA Moscow	Russia-Jr.	STATISTICS NOT AVAILABLE									
1998-99	CSKA Moscow	Russia-Jr.	31	4	12	16	16	....	....	....	....	....
99-2000	Providence Bruins	AHL	16	0	1	1	14	....	....	....	....	....
	Greenville Growl	ECHL	24	2	3	5	30	10	0	1	1	24
2000-01	Greenville Growl	ECHL	3	0	0	0	8	....	....	....	....	....
	Pensacola	ECHL	20	0	4	4	28	....	....	....	....	....
	New Orleans	ECHL	38	2	6	8	49	3	0	0	0	0

TIMONEN, Jussi (TEEM-oh-nehn, YU-see) **PHI.**

Defense. Shoots left. 6', 200 lbs. Born, Kuopio, Finland, June 29, 1983.
(Philadelphia's 3rd choice, 146th overall, in 2001 Entry Draft).

			Regular Season					Playoffs				
Season	Club	Lea	GP	G	A	TP	PIM	GP	G	A	TP	PIM
99-2000	Kalpa Kuopio	Finn-Jr.	33	4	2	6	16	4	0	0	0	4
2000-01	Kalpa Kuopio-B	Finn-Jr.	38	6	7	13	22	....	....	....	....	....
	Kalpa Kuopio	Finn-Jr.	1	0	1	1	0	....	....	....	....	....

TJARNQVIST, Daniel (TUH-yahrn-kvihst, DAN-yehl) **ATL.**

Defense. Shoots left. 6'2", 195 lbs. Born, Umea, Sweden, October 14, 1976.
(Florida's 5th choice, 88th overall, in 1995 Entry Draft).

			Regular Season					Playoffs				
Season	Club	Lea	GP	G	A	TP	PIM	GP	G	A	TP	PIM
1994-95	Rogle BK	Swede-2	15	2	3	5	0	....	....	....	....	....
	Rogle BK	Sweden	18	0	1	1	2	....	....	....	....	....
1995-96	Rogle BK	Sweden	22	1	7	8	6	....	....	....	....	....
1996-97	Jokerit Helsinki	Finland	44	3	8	11	4	9	0	3	3	4
	Jokerit Helsinki	EuroHL	6	1	1	2	2	....	....	....	....	....
1997-98	Djurgardens IF	Sweden	40	5	9	14	12	15	1	1	2	2
1998-99	Djurgardens IF	Sweden	40	4	3	7	16	4	0	0	0	2
99-2000	Djurgardens IF	Sweden	42	3	16	19	8	5	0	0	0	2
2000-01	Djurgardens IF	Sweden	45	9	17	26	26	16	6	5	11	2

Traded to **Atlanta** by **Florida** with Gord Murphy, Herbert Vasiljevs and Ottawa's 6th round choice (previously acquired, later traded to Dallas - Dallas selected Justin Cox) in 1999 Entry Draft for Trevor Kidd, June 25, 1999.

TJARNQVIST, Mathias (TUH-yahrn-kvihst, MAT-ee-uhs) **DAL.**

Right wing. Shoots left. 6'1", 183 lbs. Born, Umea, Sweden, April 15, 1979.
(Dallas' 3rd choice, 96th overall, in 1999 Entry Draft).

			Regular Season					Playoffs				
Season	Club	Lea	GP	G	A	TP	PIM	GP	G	A	TP	PIM
1995-96	Rogle BK	Swede-Jr.	4	2	0	2	0	....	....	....	....	....
1996-97	Rogle BK	Swede-Jr.	18	5	8	13	....	....	....	....	....	....
	Rogle BK	Swede-2	15	1	4	5	4	....	....	....	....	....
1997-98	Rogle BK	Swede-2	31	12	11	23	30	....	....	....	....	....
1998-99	Rogle BK	Swede-2	34	18	16	34	44	5	4	1	5	4
99-2000	Djurgardens IF	Sweden	50	12	12	24	20	13	3	2	5	16
2000-01	Djurgardens IF	Sweden	47	11	8	19	53	16	1	2	3	6

TOBLER, Ryan (TOH-bluhr, RIGH-uhn)

Left wing. Shoots left. 6'3", 222 lbs. Born, Calgary, Alta., May 13, 1976.

			Regular Season					Playoffs				
Season	Club	Lea	GP	G	A	TP	PIM	GP	G	A	TP	PIM
1993-94	Calgary Royals	AJHL	56	32	17	49	195	....	....	....	....	....
1994-95	Saskatoon Blades	WHL	61	11	19	30	81	10	1	2	3	8
1995-96	Calgary Hitmen	WHL	16	10	3	13	8	....	....	....	....	....
	Swift Current	WHL	25	17	11	28	31	6	1	1	2	2
1996-97	Moose Jaw	WHL	24	6	15	21	16	12	1	6	7	16
	Swift Current	WHL	39	10	17	27	40	....	....	....	....	....
1997-98	Lake Charles	WPHL	66	22	34	56	204	4	2	3	5	18
	Utah Grizzlies	IHL	3	1	0	1	2	....	....	....	....	....
1998-99	Adirondack	AHL	64	9	18	27	157	3	0	0	0	2
99-2000	Milwaukee	IHL	78	19	28	47	293	2	0	0	0	0
2000-01	Hartford	AHL	13	1	5	6	71	5	0	0	0	2
	Milwaukee	IHL	49	7	9	16	196	....	....	....	....	....

Signed as a free agent by **Nashville**, May 1, 2000. Traded to **NY Rangers** by **Nashville** for Bert Robertsson, March 7, 2001.

TOLKUNOV, Dmitri (tohl-ku-NAWF, di-MEE-tree) **CHI.**

Defense. Shoots right. 6'2", 200 lbs. Born, Kiev, USSR, May 5, 1979.

			Regular Season					Playoffs				
Season	Club	Lea	GP	G	A	TP	PIM	GP	G	A	TP	PIM
1996-97	Hull Olympiques	QMJHL	34	3	8	11	99	....	....	....	....	....
	Beauport	QMJHL	27	3	7	10	18	4	0	1	1	4
1997-98	Quebec Rafales	QMJHL	66	10	25	35	81	14	3	9	12	22
1998-99	Quebec Rafales	QMJHL	69	11	57	68	110	13	2	7	9	22
99-2000	Cleveland	IHL	65	3	12	15	54	8	0	0	0	2
2000-01	Norfolk Admirals	AHL	78	5	18	23	93	9	0	1	1	4

QMJHL Second All-Star Team (1999)

Signed as a free agent by **Chicago**, October 8, 1998.

TOLSA, Jari (TOHL-suh, YA-ree) **DET.**

Center. Shoots left. 6', 172 lbs. Born, Goteborg, Sweden, April 20, 1981.
(Detroit's 1st choice, 120th overall, in 1999 Entry Draft).

			Regular Season					Playoffs				
Season	Club	Lea	GP	G	A	TP	PIM	GP	G	A	TP	PIM
1997-98	Vastra Frolunda	Swede-Jr.	26	18	25	43	30	....	....	....	....	....
1998-99	Vastra Frolunda	Swede-Jr.	35	16	21	37	51	....	....	....	....	....
99-2000	Vastra Frolunda	Swede-Jr.	39	16	55	71	76	....	....	....	....	....
	Vastra Frolunda	Sweden	10	0	0	0	0	....	....	....	....	....
2000-01	Vastra Frolunda	Swede-Jr.	12	6	10	16	12	....	....	....	....	....
	Molndals HK	Swede-2	1	0	2	2	0	....	....	....	....	....
	Vastra Frolunda	Sweden	42	2	5	7	18	5	0	0	0	0

TOOTOO, Jordin (TOO-TOO, JOHR-dihn) **NSH.**

Right wing. Shoots right. 5'9", 187 lbs. Born, Churchill, Man., February 2, 1983.
(Nashville's 6th choice, 98th overall, in 2001 Entry Draft).

			Regular Season					Playoffs				
Season	Club	Lea	GP	G	A	TP	PIM	GP	G	A	TP	PIM
1998-99	OCN Blizzard	MJHL	47	16	21	37	251	....	....	....	....	....
99-2000	Brandon	WHL	45	6	10	16	214	....	....	....	....	....
2000-01	Brandon	WHL	60	20	28	48	172	6	2	4	6	18

TORRES, Raffi (TAW-rehs, RA-fee) **NYI**

Left wing. Shoots left. 5'11", 207 lbs. Born, Toronto, Ont., October 8, 1981.
(NY Islanders' 2nd choice, 5th overall, in 2000 Entry Draft).

			Regular Season					Playoffs				
Season	Club	Lea	GP	G	A	TP	PIM	GP	G	A	TP	PIM
1997-98	Thornhill Rattlers	MTJHL	46	17	16	33	90	....	....	....	....	....
1998-99	Brampton	OHL	62	35	27	62	32	....	....	....	....	....
99-2000	Brampton	OHL	68	43	48	91	40	6	5	2	7	23
2000-01	Brampton	OHL	55	33	37	70	76	8	7	4	11	19

OHL All-Rookie Team (1999) • OHL Second All-Star Team (2000, 2001)

TORY, Jeff (TOH-ree, JEHF)

Defense. Shoots right. 5'11", 190 lbs. Born, Burnaby, B.C., May 9, 1973.

			Regular Season					Playoffs				
Season	Club	Lea	GP	G	A	TP	PIM	GP	G	A	TP	PIM
1993-94	U. of Maine	H-East	3	0	0	0	4	....	....	....	....	....
1994-95	U. of Maine	H-East	40	13	42	55	22	....	....	....	....	....
1995-96	U. of Maine	H-East	37	4	36	40	36	....	....	....	....	....
1996-97	Canada	Nat-Team	54	8	37	45	30	....	....	....	....	....
	Kentucky	AHL	3	0	2	2	0	4	0	0	0	2
1997-98	Houston Aeros	IHL	74	11	27	38	35	4	0	1	1	2
1998-99	Houston Aeros	IHL	79	19	36	55	46	18	2	6	8	8
99-2000	Philadelphia	AHL	76	17	41	58	44	5	1	3	4	4
2000-01	Utah Grizzlies	IHL	10	1	3	4	7	....	....	....	....	....
	Houston Aeros	IHL	70	12	23	35	24	7	1	4	5	2

Hockey East First All-Star Team (1995) • NCAA East Second All-American Team (1995) • Hockey East All-Star Team (1996) • NCAA East First All-American Team (1996)

Signed as a free agent by **Philadelphia**, July 27, 1999. Signed as a free agent by **Dallas**, July 26, 2000.

TRAVNICEK, Michal (TRAV-nih-chehk, MEE-khuhl) **TOR.**

Right wing. Shoots left. 6'1", 198 lbs. Born, Decin, Czech., March 14, 1980.
(Toronto's 9th choice, 228th overall, in 1998 Entry Draft).

			Regular Season					Playoffs				
Season	Club	Lea	GP	G	A	TP	PIM	GP	G	A	TP	PIM
1996-97	CHZ Litvinov-Jr.	Cze-Rep	45	35	22	57	....	....	....	....	....	....
1997-98	CHZ Litvinov-Jr.	Cze-Rep	43	18	20	38	....	....	....	....	....	....
1998-99	CHZ Litvinov	Cze-Rep	49	7	7	14	65	....	....	....	....	....
99-2000	CHZ Litvinov	Cze-Rep	51	3	6	9	28	7	0	0	0	0
2000-01	St. John's Leafs	AHL	80	3	21	24	70	4	0	1	1	4

TREILLE, Yorick (TRAYL, YOH-rihk) **CHI.**

Right wing. Shoots right. 6'3", 205 lbs. Born, Cannes, France, July 15, 1980.
(Chicago's 7th choice, 195th overall, in 1999 Entry Draft).

			Regular Season					Playoffs				
Season	Club	Lea	GP	G	A	TP	PIM	GP	G	A	TP	PIM
1997-98	Notre Dame	SJHL	54	18	28	46	42	....	....	....	....	....
1998-99	U. Mass-Lowell	H-East	30	6	5	11	24	....	....	....	....	....
99-2000	U. Mass-Lowell	H-East	33	10	12	22	34	....	....	....	....	....
2000-01	U. Mass-Lowell	H-East	31	10	14	24	35	....	....	....	....	....

TREMBLAY, Didier (TRAHM-blay, DEE-duhr) **ST.L.**

Defense. Shoots left. 6'1", 206 lbs. Born, Laval, Que., May 4, 1979.
(St. Louis' 2nd choice, 86th overall, in 1997 Entry Draft).

			Regular Season					Playoffs				
Season	Club	Lea	GP	G	A	TP	PIM	GP	G	A	TP	PIM
1993-94	Rive-Nord Elks	QAHA	31	11	20	31	44	....	....	....	....	....
1994-95	Laval Regents	QAAA	44	3	22	25	52	....	....	....	....	....
1995-96	Halifax	QMJHL	56	4	10	14	80	6	0	3	3	4
1996-97	Halifax	QMJHL	68	11	26	37	79	12	1	3	4	6
1997-98	Halifax	QMJHL	39	6	19	25	26	....	....	....	....	....
	Val-d'Or Foreurs	QMJHL	31	6	24	30	43	19	5	13	18	8
1998-99	Val-d'Or Foreurs	QMJHL	63	23	51	74	56	6	1	4	5	4
99-2000	Worcester	AHL	27	1	6	7	8	....	....	....	....	....
	Peoria Rivermen	ECHL	36	5	16	21	14	18	6	7	13	18
2000-01	Peoria Rivermen	ECHL	51	5	23	28	63	14	2	3	5	8
	Worcester	AHL	7	1	1	2	2	1	0	0	0	0

TROSCHINSKY, Andrei (troh-SCHIHN-skee, AN-dray) **ST.L.**

Center. Shoots left. 6'5", 187 lbs. Born, Ust-Kamenogorsk, USSR, February 14, 1978.
(St. Louis' 5th choice, 170th overall, in 1998 Entry Draft).

			Regular Season					Playoffs				
Season	Club	Lea	GP	G	A	TP	PIM	GP	G	A	TP	PIM
1996-97	Ust-Kamenogorsk	Russia-2	9	1	1	2	8	....	....	....	....	....
1997-98	Ust-Kamenogorsk	Russia-2	47	10	16	26	34	....	....	....	....	....
1998-99	Kamenogorsk-3	Russia-4	4	4	4	8	6	....	....	....	....	....
	Kamenogorsk-2	Russia-3	42	11	21	32	62	....	....	....	....	....
99-2000	Kamenogorsk-2	Russia-3	50	20	46	66	....	....	....	....	....	....
2000-01	Worcester	AHL	78	17	28	45	32	11	2	2	4	2

TRUBACHEV, Yuri (troo-bah-CHEHV, YOO-ree) **CGY.**

Center. Shoots left. 5'9", 187 lbs. Born, Cherepovets, USSR, March 9, 1983.
(Calgary's 7th choice, 164th overall, in 2001 Entry Draft).

			Regular Season					Playoffs				
Season	Club	Lea	GP	G	A	TP	PIM	GP	G	A	TP	PIM
1997-98	HC Cherepovets-2	Russia-3	1	0	0	0	0	....	....	....	....	....
1998-99	HC Cherepovets-3	Russia-4	9	5	1	6	0	....	....	....	....	....
	HC Cherepovets-2	Russia-3	2	0	0	0	0	....	....	....	....	....
99-2000	HC Cherepovets-2	Russia-3	42	13	19	32	76	....	....	....	....	....
2000-01	St. Petersburg	Russia	34	6	5	11	24	....	....	....	....	....

TSELIOS, Nikos (TSEHL-ee-ohs, NEE-kohs) **CAR.**

Defense. Shoots left. 6'5", 210 lbs. Born, Oak Park, IL, January 20, 1979.
(Carolina's 1st choice, 22nd overall, in 1997 Entry Draft).

			Regular Season					Playoffs				
Season	Club	Lea	GP	G	A	TP	PIM	GP	G	A	TP	PIM
1995-96	Chicago Amerks	MEHL	27	5	8	13	40	....	....	....	....	....
1996-97	Belleville Bulls	OHL	64	9	37	46	61	6	1	1	2	2
1997-98	Belleville Bulls	OHL	20	2	10	12	16	....	....	....	....	....
	Plymouth Whalers	OHL	41	8	20	28	27	15	1	8	9	27
1998-99	Plymouth Whalers	OHL	60	21	39	60	60	11	4	10	14	8
99-2000	Cincinnati	IHL	80	3	19	22	75	10	0	2	2	4
2000-01	Cincinnati	IHL	79	7	18	25	98	5	0	3	3	0

TSYBUK, Yevgeny (tsee-BUHK, YEHV-jeh-nee)

Defense. Shoots left. 6', 196 lbs. Born, Chebarkul, USSR, February 2, 1978.
(Dallas' 5th choice, 113th overall, in 1996 Entry Draft).

			Regular Season					Playoffs				
Season	Club	Lea	GP	G	A	TP	PIM	GP	G	A	TP	PIM
1996-97	Torpedo Yaroslavl	Russia-2	STATISTICS NOT AVAILABLE									
	Lethbridge	WHL	10	0	1	1	13	....	....	....	....	....
1997-98	Lethbridge	WHL	41	5	13	18	129	4	1	1	2	12
1998-99	Michigan K-Wings	IHL	42	1	3	4	69	2	0	0	0	2
99-2000	Michigan K-Wings	IHL	50	0	2	2	82	....	....	....	....	....
	Fort Wayne	UHL	2	0	0	0	0	....	....	....	....	....
2000-01	Utah Grizzlies	IHL	61	4	12	16	157	....	....	....	....	....

TUKIO, Arto (TOO-kee-oh, AHR-toh) **NYI**

Defense. Shoots left. 5'10", 176 lbs. Born, Tampere, Finland, April 4, 1981.
(NY Islanders' 3rd choice, 101st overall, in 2000 Entry Draft).

			Regular Season					Playoffs				
Season	Club	Lea	GP	G	A	TP	PIM	GP	G	A	TP	PIM
1996-97	Ilves Tampere-C	Finn-Jr.	6	1	3	4	4	....	....	....	....	....
	Ilves Tampere-B	Finn-Jr.	20	0	2	2	6	1	1	0	1	0
1997-98	Ilves Tampere-B	Finn-Jr.	39	7	7	14	64	....	....	....	....	....
1998-99	Ilves Tampere-B	Finn-Jr.	10	1	5	6	18	....	....	....	....	....
	Ilves Tampere	Finn-Jr.	18	1	4	5	12	10	0	0	0	2
99-2000	Ilves Tampere	Finn-Jr.	11	2	1	3	24	....	....	....	....	....
	Hermes Kokkola	Finland-2	1	0	0	0	0	....	....	....	....	....
	Ilves Tampere	Finland	42	2	1	3	20	3	0	0	0	0
2000-01	Ilves Tampere	Finland	43	5	10	15	26	7	2	1	3	4

TUOKKO, Marco (too-OH-koh, MAHR-koh) **DAL.**

Center. Shoots left. 6', 185 lbs. Born, Raisio, Finland, March 27, 1979.
(Dallas' 9th choice, 219th overall, in 2000 Entry Draft).

			Regular Season					Playoffs				
Season	Club	Lea	GP	G	A	TP	PIM	GP	G	A	TP	PIM
1995-96	TPS Turku-B	Finn-Jr.	31	9	13	22	49	3	1	0	1	0
	Kiekko-67	Finland-2	1	0	0	0	0	....	....	....	....	....
1996-97	TPS Turku-B	Finn-Jr.	5	1	3	4	0	6	1	6	7	4
	TPS Turku	Finn-Jr.	30	8	7	15	32	....	....	....	....	....
	Kiekko-67	Finland-2	6	3	1	4	31	....	....	....	....	....
1997-98	TPS Turku	Finn-Jr.	26	5	13	18	77	7	1	4	5	14
1998-99	TPS Turku	Finn-Jr.	1	0	0	0	0	....	....	....	....	....
	TPS Turku	Finland	48	5	4	9	24	10	0	1	1	10
99-2000	TPS Turku	Finland	54	10	10	20	73	11	2	2	4	6
2000-01	TPS Turku	Finland	53	5	11	16	54	10	2	2	4	16

TUTIN, Fedor (TYOO-tihn, feh-DUHR) **NYR**

Defense. Shoots left. 6'2", 196 lbs. Born, Izhevsk, USSR, July 19, 1983.
(NY Rangers' 2nd choice, 40th overall, in 2001 Entry Draft).

			Regular Season					Playoffs				
Season	Club	Lea	GP	G	A	TP	PIM	GP	G	A	TP	PIM
1998-99	Magnitororsk-2	Russia-3	7	0	1	1	2	....	....	....	....	....
99-2000	Izhstal Izhevsk-2	Russia-3	38	11	8	19	68	....	....	....	....	....
	Izhstal Izhevsk	Russia-2	10	0	1	1	12	....	....	....	....	....
2000-01	St. Petersburg	Russia	34	2	4	6	20	....	....	....	....	....

TVRDON, Roman (t-vahr-DAWN, ROH-muhn) **WSH.**

Center. Shoots left. 6'1", 189 lbs. Born, Trencin, Czech., January 29, 1981.
(Washington's 6th choice, 132nd overall, in 1999 Entry Draft).

			Regular Season					Playoffs				
Season	Club	Lea	GP	G	A	TP	PIM	GP	G	A	TP	PIM
1997-98	Dukla Trencin	Slovak-Jr.	48	4	12	16	39	....	....	....	....	....
1998-99	Dukla Trencin	Slovak-Jr.	49	23	23	46	20	6	4	4	8	4
99-2000	Spokane Chiefs	WHL	69	26	44	70	40	15	4	7	11	16
2000-01	Spokane Chiefs	WHL	62	28	34	62	55	12	5	11	16	0

UCHEVATOV, Victor (oo-cheh-VA-tawf, VIHK-tohr) **N.J.**

Defense. Shoots left. 6'4", 205 lbs. Born, Angarsk, USSR, February 10, 1983.
(New Jersey's 4th choice, 60th overall, in 2001 Entry Draft).

			Regular Season					Playoffs				
Season	Club	Lea	GP	G	A	TP	PIM	GP	G	A	TP	PIM
2000-01	HC Yaroslavl-2	Russia-3	28	1	1	2	74	....	....	....	....	....

ULMER, Layne (UHL-muhr, LAYN) **NYR**

Center. Shoots left. 6'1", 205 lbs. Born, North Battleford, Sask., September 14, 1980.
(Ottawa's 8th choice, 209th overall, in 1999 Entry Draft).

			Regular Season					Playoffs				
Season	Club	Lea	GP	G	A	TP	PIM	GP	G	A	TP	PIM
1996-97	Swift Current	SMHL	43	35	49	84	31	....	....	....	....	....
1997-98	Swift Current	WHL	50	8	9	17	23	12	3	1	4	0
1998-99	Swift Current	WHL	72	40	35	75	34	6	2	1	3	4
99-2000	Swift Current	WHL	71	50	54	104	66	12	12	6	18	16
2000-01	Swift Current	WHL	68	63	56	119	75	19	7	3	10	20

WHL East First All-Star Team (2000, 2001)

Signed as a free agent by **NY Rangers**, June 13, 2001.

UMBERGER, R.J. (UHM-buhr-guhr, AHR-JAY) **VAN.**

Center. Shoots left. 6'2", 200 lbs. Born, Pittsburgh, PA, May 3, 1982.
(Vancouver's 1st choice, 16th overall, in 2001 Entry Draft).

			Regular Season					Playoffs				
Season	Club	Lea	GP	G	A	TP	PIM	GP	G	A	TP	PIM
1998-99	Team USA	USDP	50	29	29	58	....	....	....	....	....	....
99-2000	Team USA	USDP	57	33	35	68	20	....	....	....	....	....
2000-01	Ohio State	CCHA	32	14	23	37	18	....	....	....	....	....

CCHA All-Rookie Team (2001) • Won CCHA Rookie of the Year Award (2001)

UPPER, Dmitri (OO-puhr, dih-MEE-tree) **NYI**

Center. Shoots right. 6', 185 lbs. Born, Ust-Kamenogorsk, USSR, July 27, 1978.
(NY Islanders' 5th choice, 136th overall, in 2000 Entry Draft).

			Regular Season					Playoffs				
Season	Club	Lea	GP	G	A	TP	PIM	GP	G	A	TP	PIM
1997-98	Ust-Kamenogorsk	Russia-2	47	16	12	28	44	....	....	....	....	....
1998-99	Kamenogorsk-2	Russia-3	29	10	11	21	44	....	....	....	....	....
	Torpedo Nizhny	Russia-2	28	10	16	26	65	....	....	....	....	....
99-2000	Torpedo Nizhny	Russia	36	14	6	20	50	5	1	1	2	4
2000-01	Torpedo Nizhny	Russia	6	0	2	2	4	....	....	....	....	....
	Ak Bars Kazan	Russia	31	7	4	11	6	1	0	0	0	0

URICK, Brian (YOOR-ihk, BRIGH-uhn)

Right wing. Shoots right. 6'1", 195 lbs. Born, Minneapolis, MN, January 25, 1977.
(Edmonton's 5th choice, 114th overall, in 1996 Entry Draft).

			Regular Season					Playoffs				
Season	Club	Lea	GP	G	A	TP	PIM	GP	G	A	TP	PIM
1994-95	Minnetonka High	Hi-School	24	30	29	59	28	....	....	....	....	....
1995-96	Notre Dame	CCHA	36	12	15	27	66	....	....	....	....	....
1996-97	Notre Dame	CCHA	34	13	12	25	88	....	....	....	....	....
1997-98	Notre Dame	CCHA	41	16	18	34	40	....	....	....	....	....
1998-99	Notre Dame	CCHA	35	16	25	41	45	....	....	....	....	....
99-2000	Tallahassee	ECHL	45	21	20	41	14	....	....	....	....	....
	Hamilton Bulldogs	AHL	14	2	1	3	2	6	1	0	1	0
2000-01	Hamilton Bulldogs	AHL	50	11	8	19	22	....	....	....	....	....

USTRNUL, Libor (OOS-tuhr-nuhl, LEE-bohr) ATL.

Defense. Shoots left. 6'4", 220 lbs. Born, Steruberk, Czech., February 20, 1982.
(Atlanta's 3rd choice, 42nd overall, in 2000 Entry Draft).

			Regular Season					Playoffs				
Season	Club	Lea	GP	G	A	TP	PIM	GP	G	A	TP	PIM
1997-98	HC Olomouc-Jr.	Cze-Rep	45	2	11	13	54	....	....	....	....	....
1998-99	Thunder Bay	USHL	52	2	5	7	65	18	1	4	5	95
99-2000	Plymouth Whalers	OHL	68	0	15	15	208	23	0	3	3	29
2000-01	Plymouth Whalers	OHL	35	3	13	16	66	19	1	4	5	19

VALENTINE, Curtis (VAL-lehn-tighn, KUHR-tihs) VAN.

Left wing. Shoots left. 6'5", 195 lbs. Born, Haileybury, Ont., July 22, 1979.
(Vancouver's 11th choice, 219th overall, in 1998 Entry Draft).

			Regular Season					Playoffs				
Season	Club	Lea	GP	G	A	TP	PIM	GP	G	A	TP	PIM
1996-97	Capital District	X-Games	56	53	60	113	28	....	....	....	....	....
1997-98	Bowling Green	CCHA	38	7	8	15	34	....	....	....	....	....
1998-99	Bowling Green	CCHA	38	4	8	12	40	....	....	....	....	....
99-2000	Bowling Green	CCHA	37	5	7	12	24	....	....	....	....	....
2000-01	Bowling Green	CCHA	40	9	7	16	8	....	....	....	....	....
	Pensacola	ECHL	3	1	0	1	0	....	....	....	....	....

VALEYEV, Igor (val-AY-ehv, EE-gohr) ST.L.

Left wing. Shoots left. 5'11", 203 lbs. Born, Snezhinsk, USSR, January 9, 1981.
(St. Louis' 3rd choice, 122nd overall, in 2001 Entry Draft).

			Regular Season					Playoffs				
Season	Club	Lea	GP	G	A	TP	PIM	GP	G	A	TP	PIM
1998-99	Lethbridge	WHL	8	2	3	5	13	....	....	....	....	....
	Saskatoon	WHL	23	2	2	4	36	....	....	....	....	....
99-2000	Swift Current	WHL	36	7	5	12	78	4	0	1	1	22
2000-01	North Bay	OHL	62	17	61	78	175	4	0	1	1	22
	Muskegon Fury	UHL	....	....	....	....	....	3	0	1	1	2

VALTONEN, Tomek (VAL-tuh-nehn, Toh-MEHK) DET.

Left wing. Shoots left. 6'1", 198 lbs. Born, Piotrkow Trybunalski, Poland, January 8, 1980.
(Detroit's 3rd choice, 56th overall, in 1998 Entry Draft).

			Regular Season					Playoffs				
Season	Club	Lea	GP	G	A	TP	PIM	GP	G	A	TP	PIM
1995-96	Ilves Tampere-C	Finn-Jr.	9	3	3	6	24	....	....	....	....	....
	Ilves Tampere-B	Finn-Jr.	11	7	7	14	28	....	....	....	....	....
	Ilves Tampere	Finn-Jr.	....	....	....	....	....	1	0	0	0	0
1996-97	Ilves Tampere-B	Finn-Jr.	26	10	9	19	82	3	0	1	1	6
	Ilves Tampere	Finn-Jr.	1	0	0	0	0	....	....	....	....	....
1997-98	JyP Joensuu	Finn-Jr.	3	0	0	0	12	....	....	....	....	....
	JyP Joensuu	Finland-2	6	1	2	3	39	....	....	....	....	....
	Ilves Tampere	Finn-Jr.	13	3	2	5	36	....	....	....	....	....
	Ilves Tampere	Finland	19	1	0	1	14	3	0	0	0	0
	Ilves Tampere-B	Finn-Jr.	....	....	....	....	....	7	0	2	2	16
1998-99	Plymouth Whalers	OHL	43	8	16	24	53	7	1	0	1	0
99-2000	Jokerit Helsinki	Finland	41	0	3	3	63	9	1	0	1	8
2000-01	Jokerit Helsinki	Finland	45	3	2	5	138	3	0	0	0	0

VAN HOOF, Jeremy (van-HOOF, JAIR-reh-mee) T.B.

Defense. Shoots left. 6'2", 208 lbs. Born, Lindsay, Ont., August 12, 1981.
(Tampa Bay's 9th choice, 222nd overall, in 2001 Entry Draft).

			Regular Season					Playoffs				
Season	Club	Lea	GP	G	A	TP	PIM	GP	G	A	TP	PIM
1997-98	Lindsay Muskies	OPJHL	50	2	8	10	40	....	....	....	....	....
1998-99	Ottawa 67's	OHL	54	0	13	13	46	5	1	0	1	2
99-2000	Ottawa 67's	OHL	66	4	14	18	71	11	1	0	1	12
2000-01	Ottawa 67's	OHL	65	1	14	15	49	20	3	4	7	27

• Re-entered NHL Entry Draft. Originally Pittsburgh's 3rd choice, 57th overall, in 1999 Entry Draft.

VAN LEUSEN, Aaron (VAN LOO-suhn, AIR-ruhn) DET.

Center. Shoots right. 6', 196 lbs. Born, Barrie, Ont., October 28, 1981.
(Detroit's 6th choice, 130th overall, in 2000 Entry Draft).

			Regular Season					Playoffs				
Season	Club	Lea	GP	G	A	TP	PIM	GP	G	A	TP	PIM
1996-97	Barrie Flyers	OMHA	45	46	57	103	....	....	....	....	....	....
1997-98	Barrie Lions	OMHA	50	26	36	62	45	....	....	....	....	....
1998-99	Brampton	OHL	58	7	8	15	15	....	....	....	....	....
99-2000	Brampton	OHL	57	17	20	37	24	6	2	1	3	6
2000-01	Brampton	OHL	68	25	40	65	33	9	3	4	7	4

VAN ACKER, Eric (VAN-akuhr, EH-rihk) BOS.

Defense. Shoots left. 6'5", 246 lbs. Born, St-Jean, Que., March 1, 1979.
(Boston's 11th choice, 218th overall, in 1997 Entry Draft).

			Regular Season					Playoffs				
Season	Club	Lea	GP	G	A	TP	PIM	GP	G	A	TP	PIM
1995-96	Richilieu Regents	QAAA	52	3	7	10	84	....	....	....	....	....
1996-97	Chicoutimi	QMJHL	69	2	5	7	153	16	0	0	0	4
1997-98	Chicoutimi	QMJHL	49	1	5	6	136	6	0	0	0	14
1998-99	Baie-Comeau	QMJHL	65	1	6	7	192	....	....	....	....	....
99-2000	Greenville Growl	ECHL	46	0	8	8	112	13	1	0	1	37
	Providence Bruins	AHL	4	0	0	0	2	....	....	....	....	....
2000-01	Greenville Growl	ECHL	59	1	2	3	149	....	....	....	....	....

VanBUSKIRK, Ryan (van-BUHS-kuhrk, RIGH-uhn) WSH.

Defense. Shoots left. 6'1", 190 lbs. Born, Sault Ste. Marie, MI, January 12, 1980.
(Washington's 4th choice, 121st overall, in 2000 Entry Draft).

			Regular Season					Playoffs				
Season	Club	Lea	GP	G	A	TP	PIM	GP	G	A	TP	PIM
1995-96	Petrolia Jets	OJHL-B	48	6	16	22	124	....	....	....	....	....
1996-97	Petrolia Jets	OJHL-B	43	7	28	35	133	....	....	....	....	....
1997-98	Sarnia Sting	OHL	61	8	17	25	84	5	1	2	3	4
1998-99	Sarnia Sting	OHL	66	15	33	48	85	6	1	2	3	4
99-2000	Sarnia Sting	OHL	45	8	20	28	62	7	1	2	3	16
	Springfield	AHL	1	0	0	0	0	....	....	....	....	....
2000-01	Portland Pirates	AHL	18	0	0	0	16	....	....	....	....	....
	Richmond	ECHL	15	0	2	2	16	3	0	2	2	6

• Re-entered NHL Entry Draft. Originally Phoenix's 4th choice, 100th overall, in 1998 Entry Draft.
• Missed majority of 2000-01 season recovering from shoulder injury suffered in game vs. St. John's (AHL), January 6, 2001.

VANDERMEER, Jim (VAN-duhr-meer, JIHM) PHI.

Defense. Shoots left. 6'1", 208 lbs. Born, Caroline, Alta., February 21, 1980.

			Regular Season					Playoffs				
Season	Club	Lea	GP	G	A	TP	PIM	GP	G	A	TP	PIM
1997-98	Red Deer Chiefs	AMHL	26	4	8	12	51	....	....	....	....	....
	Red Deer Rebels	WHL	35	0	3	3	55	2	0	0	0	0
1998-99	Red Deer Rebels	WHL	70	5	23	28	258	9	0	1	1	24
99-2000	Red Deer Rebels	WHL	71	8	30	38	221	4	0	1	1	16
2000-01	Red Deer Rebels	WHL	65	28	37	65	180	22	3	13	16	43

WHL East First All-Star Team (2001) • Canadian Major Junior Humanitarian Player of the Year (2001)

Signed as a free agent by **Philadelphia**, December 21, 2000.

VANDERMEER, Peter PHI.

Left wing. Shoots left. 6', 195 lbs. Born, Caroline, Alta., October 14, 1975.

			Regular Season					Playoffs				
Season	Club	Lea	GP	G	A	TP	PIM	GP	G	A	TP	PIM
1992-93	Red Deer Chiefs	AMHL	34	26	30	56	172	....	....	....	....	....
	Red Deer Rebels	WHL	2	0	0	0	2	....	....	....	....	....
1993-94	Red Deer Rebels	WHL	54	4	9	13	170	....	....	....	....	....
1994-95	Red Deer Rebels	WHL	61	16	16	32	218	....	....	....	....	....
1995-96	Red Deer Rebels	WHL	63	21	40	61	207	....	....	....	....	....
1996-97	Columbus Chill	ECHL	30	6	11	17	195	7	2	1	3	26
1997-98	Columbus Chill	ECHL	20	4	7	11	78	....	....	....	....	....
	Richmond	ECHL	18	2	5	7	165	....	....	....	....	....
	Rochester	AHL	30	4	2	6	140	4	1	0	1	13
1998-99	B.C. Icemen	UHL	62	15	21	36	390	5	2	2	4	0
	Rochester	AHL	2	1	0	1	16	16	1	0	1	38
99-2000	Richmond	ECHL	58	31	25	56	457	3	0	1	1	20
	Wilkes-Barre	AHL	4	0	0	0	7	....	....	....	....	....
	Providence	AHL	....	....	....	....	....	9	0	3	3	2
2000-01	Providence	AHL	62	19	18	37	240	4	0	0	0	16

Signed as a free agent by **Philadelphia**, July 6, 2001.

VAN OENE, Darren (van OH-uhn, DAIR-rehn) BUF.

Left wing. Shoots left. 6'4", 216 lbs. Born, Edmonton, Alta., January 18, 1978.
(Buffalo's 3rd choice, 33rd overall, in 1996 Entry Draft).

			Regular Season					Playoffs				
Season	Club	Lea	GP	G	A	TP	PIM	GP	G	A	TP	PIM
1993-94	Edmonton SSAC	AMHL	34	15	16	31	121	....	....	....	....	....
1994-95	Brandon	WHL	58	5	13	18	106	18	1	1	2	34
1995-96	Brandon	WHL	47	10	18	28	126	18	1	6	7	*78
1996-97	Brandon	WHL	56	21	27	48	139	6	2	3	5	19
1997-98	Brandon	WHL	51	23	24	47	161	18	6	8	14	51
1998-99	Rochester	AHL	73	11	20	31	143	12	2	4	6	8
99-2000	Rochester	AHL	80	20	18	38	153	21	1	3	4	24
2000-01	Rochester	AHL	64	10	12	22	147	4	1	0	1	4

VAUCLAIR, Julien (voh-KLAIR, JEW-lee-ehn) OTT.

Defense. Shoots left. 6', 198 lbs. Born, Delemont, Switzerland, October 2, 1979.
(Ottawa's 4th choice, 74th overall, in 1998 Entry Draft).

			Regular Season					Playoffs				
Season	Club	Lea	GP	G	A	TP	PIM	GP	G	A	TP	PIM
1995-96	HC Ajoie	Switz-3	20	4	10	14	....	....	....	....	....	....
1996-97	HC Ajoie	Switz-2	40	0	6	6	24	9	0	2	2	8
1997-98	HC Lugano	Switz.	36	1	2	3	12	7	0	0	0	25
1998-99	HC Lugano	Switz.	38	0	3	3	8	....	....	....	....	....
99-2000	HC Lugano	Switz.	45	3	3	6	16	14	0	0	0	0
2000-01	HC Lugano	Switz.	42	3	4	7	57	18	0	1	1	4

VEILLEUX, Stephane (VAY-oo, STEH-fan) MIN.

Right wing. Shoots left. 6'1", 187 lbs. Born, Beauceville, Quebec, November 16, 1981.
(Minnesota's 4th choice, 93rd overall, in 2001 Entry Draft).

			Regular Season					Playoffs				
Season	Club	Lea	GP	G	A	TP	PIM	GP	G	A	TP	PIM
1997-98	Beauce-Amiante	QAAA	21	20	17	37	....	....	....	....	....	....
	Levis Elites	QAAA	14	3	5	8	....	1	0	0	0	0
1998-99	Victoriaville	QMJHL	65	6	13	19	35	6	1	3	4	2
99-2000	Victoriaville	QMJHl	22	1	4	5	17	....	....	....	....	....
	Val d'Or Foreurs	QMJHL	50	14	28	42	100	....	....	....	....	....
2000-01	Val d'or Foreurs	QMJHL	68	48	67	115	90	21	15	18	33	42

VELEBNY, Lubos (vehl-EHB-nee, LOO-bohsh) TOR.

Defense. Shoots left. 6'1", 189 lbs. Born, Zvolen, Czech., February 9, 1982.
(Toronto's 8th choice, 223rd overall, in 2000 Entry Draft).

			Regular Season					Playoffs				
Season	Club	Lea	GP	G	A	TP	PIM	GP	G	A	TP	PIM
1997-98	HKm Zvolen	Slovak-Jr.	45	23	19	42	99	....	....	....	....	....
1998-99	HKm Zvolen	Slovak-Jr.	37	12	17	29	91	....	....	....	....	....
99-2000	HKm Zvolen	Slovak-Jr.	41	6	8	14	11	....	....	....	....	....
	HKm Zvolen	Slovakia	7	0	0	0	0	....	....	....	....	....
2000-01	Waterloo Hawks	USHL	45	11	25	36	179	....	....	....	....	....

VENALAINEN, Sami (veh-na-LIGH-nehn, SA-mee) PHX.

Right wing. Shoots right. 5'11", 183 lbs. Born, Kangasala, Finland, October 14, 1981.
(Phoenix's 7th choice, 249th overall, in 2000 Entry Draft).

			Regular Season					Playoffs				
Season	Club	Lea	GP	G	A	TP	PIM	GP	G	A	TP	PIM
1996-97	HC Tampere-C	Finn-Jr.	32	21	17	38	31	4	2	1	3	0
1997-98	HC Tampere-C	Finn-Jr.	2	2	0	2	6	6	4	5	9	6
	HC Tampere-B	Finn-Jr.	33	18	7	25	12	....	....	....	....	....
1998-99	HC Tampere-B	Finn-Jr.	31	27	17	44	45	....	....	....	....	....
	Tappara Tampere	Finn-Jr.	10	3	2	5	29	....	....	....	....	....
99-2000	Tappara Tampere	Finn-Jr.	37	8	9	17	18	....	....	....	....	....
2000-01	Tappara Tampere	Finn-Jr.	21	6	13	19	12	9	3	1	4	0
	Tappara Tampere	Finland	36	0	1	1	2	1	0	0	0	0

VERCIK, Rudolf (VEHR-chihk, ROO-dawlf) NYR

Left wing. Shoots left. 6'1", 189 lbs. Born, Bratislava, Czech., March 19, 1976.
(NY Rangers' 2nd choice, 52nd overall, in 1994 Entry Draft).

			Regular Season					Playoffs				
Season	Club	Lea	GP	G	A	TP	PIM	GP	G	A	TP	PIM
1993-94	HC Bratislava	Slovakia	17	1	4	5	14	....	....	....	....	....
1994-95	HC Bratislava	Slovakia	33	14	9	23	22	....	....	....	....	....
1995-96	HC Bratislava	Slovakia	28	7	3	10	61	13	1	0	1	....
1996-97	HC Bratislava	Slovakia	40	8	3	11	....	2	0	0	0	....
1997-98	Nova Ves	Slovakia	36	8	5	13	36	3	1	1	2	0
1998-99	HC Bratislava	Slovakia	35	6	7	13	53	7	1	0	1	4
99-2000	HC Bratislava	Slovakia	51	8	15	23	36	3	1	1	2	0
2000-01	HC Bratislava	Slovakia	DID NOT PLAY – INJURED									

VERENIKIN, Sergei (veh-rih-NEE-kihn, SAIR-gay) **OTT.**

Right wing. Shoots left. 5'11", 187 lbs. Born, Yaroslavl, USSR, September 8, 1979.
(Ottawa's 9th choice, 223rd overall, in 1998 Entry Draft).

			Regular Season					Playoffs				
Season	**Club**	**Lea**	**GP**	**G**	**A**	**TP**	**PIM**	**GP**	**G**	**A**	**TP**	**PIM**
1997-98	Torpedo Yaroslavl	Russia-2	44	11	4	15	100	....	....	....	....	....
	Torpedo Yaroslavl	Russia	3	0	0	0	0	....	....	....	....	....
1998-99	Torpedo Yaroslavl	Russia	37	2	5	7	16	8	0	0	0	18
99-2000	Torpedo Yaroslavl	Russia	25	4	1	5	18	4	0	0	0	2
2000-01	Ust-Novokuznetsk	Russia	31	1	0	1	14	....	....	....	....	....

VERMETTE, Antoine (vuhr-MEHT, AN-twuhn) **OTT.**

Center. Shoots left. 6'1", 184 lbs. Born, St-Agapit, Quebec, July 20, 1982.
(Ottawa's 3rd choice, 55th overall, in 2000 Entry Draft).

			Regular Season					Playoffs				
Season	**Club**	**Lea**	**GP**	**G**	**A**	**TP**	**PIM**	**GP**	**G**	**A**	**TP**	**PIM**
1997-98	Quebec City	QAHA	19	11	20	31	36	....	....	....	....	....
	Levis Commanders	QAAA	8	1	1	2	4	1	0	0	0	0
1998-99	Quebec Remparts	QMJHL	57	9	17	26	32	13	0	0	0	2
99-2000	Victoriaville Tigres	QMJHL	71	30	41	71	87	6	0	1	1	6
2000-01	Victoriaville Tigres	QMJHL	71	57	62	119	102	9	4	6	10	14

VERNARSKY, Kris (veh-NAHR-skee, KRIHS) **TOR.**

Center. Shoots left. 6'3", 201 lbs. Born, Detroit, MI, April 5, 1982.
(Toronto's 2nd choice, 51st overall, in 2000 Entry Draft).

			Regular Season					Playoffs				
Season	**Club**	**Lea**	**GP**	**G**	**A**	**TP**	**PIM**	**GP**	**G**	**A**	**TP**	**PIM**
1997-98	Team USA	USDP	69	11	18	29	97	....	....	....	....	....
1998-99	Plymouth Whalers	OHL	45	3	14	17	30	11	0	0	0	2
99-2000	Plymouth Whalers	OHL	64	16	22	38	63	19	3	6	9	24
2000-01	Plymouth Whalers	OHL	60	14	21	35	35	19	7	10	17	19

VEROT, Darcy (vuhr-AWT, DAHR-see) **PIT.**

Left wing. Shoots left. 6', 190 lbs. Born, Radville, Sask., July 13, 1976.

			Regular Season					Playoffs				
Season	**Club**	**Lea**	**GP**	**G**	**A**	**TP**	**PIM**	**GP**	**G**	**A**	**TP**	**PIM**
1994-95	Weyburn Wings	SJHL	57	8	18	26	240	16	5	2	7	50
1995-96	Weyburn Wings	SJHL	64	15	30	45	191	3	1	0	1	20
1996-97	Weyburn Wings	SJHL	61	26	51	77	218	13	3	8	11	24
1997-98	Lake Charles	WPHL	68	11	26	37	269	4	0	1	1	25
1998-99	Lake Charles	WPHL	68	17	23	40	236	9	2	4	6	53
99-2000	Wheeling Nailers	ECHL	44	7	12	19	240	....	....	....	....	....
	Wilkes-Barre	AHL	23	5	5	10	96	....	....	....	....	....
2000-01	Wilkes-Barre	AHL	78	10	15	25	347	21	2	3	5	40

Signed as a free agent by **Wilkes-Barre** (AHL), February 25, 2000. Signed as a free agent by **Pittsburgh**, July 28, 2000.

VERTALA, Timo (vehr-TAH-lah, TEE-moh) **MTL.**

Left wing. Shoots left. 6'1", 180 lbs. Born, Jyvaskyla, Finland, May 2, 1978.
(Montreal's 8th choice, 181st overall, in 1996 Entry Draft).

			Regular Season					Playoffs				
Season	**Club**	**Lea**	**GP**	**G**	**A**	**TP**	**PIM**	**GP**	**G**	**A**	**TP**	**PIM**
1993-94	JyP Jyvaskyla-C	Finn-Jr.	26	24	13	37	60	6	2	4	6	*28
	JyP Jyvaskyla-B	Finn-Jr.	6	0	0	0	0	....	....	....	....	....
1994-95	JyP Jyvaskyla-B	Finn-Jr.	16	3	5	8	46	....	....	....	....	....
	JyP Jyvaskyla	Finn-Jr.	30	2	8	10	18	8	0	1	1	10
1995-96	JyP Jyvaskyla	Finn-Jr.	35	15	10	25	54	6	1	1	2	6
	JyP Jyvaskyla	Finland	3	0	1	1	2	....	....	....	....	....
1996-97	JyP Jyvaskyla	Finn-Jr.	7	4	4	8	12	....	....	....	....	....
	JyP Jyvaskyla	Finland	46	8	5	13	39	4	0	0	0	0
1997-98	JyP Jyvaskyla	Finn-Jr.	2	2	1	3	4	....	....	....	....	....
	JyP Jyvaskyla	Finland	43	4	8	12	34	....	....	....	....	....
1998-99	JyP Jyvaskyla	Finland	48	5	5	10	60	3	0	0	0	2
99-2000	Tappara Tampere	Finland	50	24	18	42	82	4	0	2	2	0
2000-01	Tappara Tampere	Finland	46	17	10	27	78	10	4	2	6	6

VIITANEN, Mikko (vee-EE-tan-ehn, MEE-koh) **COL.**

Defense. Shoots left. 6'3", 220 lbs. Born, Rajamaki, Finland, February 18, 1982.
(Colorado's 6th choice, 149th overall, in 2001 Entry Draft).

			Regular Season					Playoffs				
Season	**Club**	**Lea**	**GP**	**G**	**A**	**TP**	**PIM**	**GP**	**G**	**A**	**TP**	**PIM**
1998-99	HPK Hameenlinna	Finn-Jr.	1	0	0	0	0	....	....	....	....	....
99-2000	Chicago Freeze	NAJHL	53	4	6	10	126	....	....	....	....	....
2000-01	Ahmat Hyvinkaa	Finn-Jr.	9	3	4	7	41	....	....	....	....	....
	Ahmat Hyvinkaa	Finland-2	41	3	9	12	66	3	0	0	0	0

VIKINGSTAD, Tore (VIH-kihng-stahd, TOO-reh) **ST.L.**

Center. Shoots left. 6'4", 200 lbs. Born, Stavenger, Norway, October 8, 1975.
(St. Louis' 5th choice, 180th overall, in 1999 Entry Draft).

			Regular Season					Playoffs				
Season	**Club**	**Lea**	**GP**	**G**	**A**	**TP**	**PIM**	**GP**	**G**	**A**	**TP**	**PIM**
1994-95	Viking IHK	Norway	28	5	3	8	8	....	....	....	....	....
1995-96	Viking IHK	Norway	27	12	11	23	....	....	....	....	....	....
1996-97	IL Stjernen	Norway	42	23	35	58	20	....	....	....	....	....
1997-98	IL Stjernen	Norway	42	26	31	57	18	....	....	....	....	....
1998-99	Farjestads BK	Sweden	49	9	11	20	18	4	2	3	5	0
99-2000	Farjestads BK	Sweden	47	8	19	27	26	7	3	0	3	6
2000-01	Leksands IF	Sweden	41	10	15	25	24	....	....	....	....	....

VIRTA, Tony (VIHR-ta, TON-nee) **MIN.**

Right wing. Shoots left. 5'10", 187 lbs. Born, Hameenlinna, Finland, June 28, 1972.
(Minnesota's 5th choice, 103rd overall, in 2001 Entry Draft).

			Regular Season					Playoffs				
Season	**Club**	**Lea**	**GP**	**G**	**A**	**TP**	**PIM**	**GP**	**G**	**A**	**TP**	**PIM**
1990-91	Hameenlinna-Jr.	Finn-Jr.	28	17	34	51	42	....	....	....	....	....
1991-92	HPK Hameenlinna	Finland	35	24	31	55	114	....	....	....	....	....
1992-93	HPK Hameenlinna	Finn-Jr.	2	1	2	3	2	....	....	....	....	....
	HPK Hameenlinna	Finland	48	9	8	17	35	12	1	0	1	0
1993-94	HPK Hameenlinna	Finland	47	17	16	33	50	....	....	....	....	....
1994-95	HPK Hameenlinna	Finland	43	9	24	33	75	....	....	....	....	....
1995-96	HPK Hameenlinna	Finland	48	15	19	34	12	9	1	3	4	31
1996-97	Frankfurt Lions	DEL	48	13	13	26	40	8	1	2	3	56
1997-98	TPS Turku	EuroHL	6	1	0	1	0	....	....	....	....	....
	TPS Turku	Finland	48	17	15	32	26	3	0	0	0	0
1998-99	TPS Turku	Finland	54	16	27	43	32	10	6	6	12	8
99-2000	TPS Turku	EuroHL	5	1	5	6	2	4	1	2	3	0
	TPS Turku	Finland	53	14	37	51	57	11	2	7	9	6
2000-01	TPS Turku	Finland	56	27	33	60	24	10	2	5	7	6

VLASENKOV, Dmitri (vlah-SEHN-khahf, dih-MEE-tree) **ATL.**

Left wing. Shoots left. 6'1", 200 lbs. Born, Safonovo, USSR, January 1, 1978.
(Calgary's 4th choice, 73rd overall, in 1996 Entry Draft).

			Regular Season					Playoffs				
Season	**Club**	**Lea**	**GP**	**G**	**A**	**TP**	**PIM**	**GP**	**G**	**A**	**TP**	**PIM**
1995-96	Torpedo Yaroslavl	CIS	17	1	1	2	4	1	0	0	0	0
1996-97	HC Yaroslavl-2	Russia-3	18	10	2	12	6	....	....	....	....	....
	Torpedo Yaroslavl	Russia	28	3	2	5	10	8	1	1	2	2
1997-98	Torpedo Yaroslavl	EuroHL	6	0	0	0	2	....	....	....	....	....
	Torpedo Yaroslavl	Russia	44	10	3	13	12	....	....	....	....	....
1998-99	Torpedo Yaroslavl	Russia	41	11	5	16	26	10	1	2	3	6
99-2000	Torpedo Yaroslavl	Russia	38	15	20	35	10	10	3	4	7	6
2000-01	Orlando	IHL	49	5	8	13	10	1	0	0	0	0

Traded to **Atlanta** by **Calgary** with Hnat Domenichelli for Darryl Shannon and Jason Botterill, February 11, 2000.

VLCEK, Ladislav (vuhl-CHEHK, LA-dih-dlav) **DAL.**

Right wing. Shoots left. 5'9", 180 lbs. Born, Kladno, Czech., September 26, 1981.
(Dallas' 8th choice, 192nd overall, in 2000 Entry Draft).

			Regular Season					Playoffs				
Season	**Club**	**Lea**	**GP**	**G**	**A**	**TP**	**PIM**	**GP**	**G**	**A**	**TP**	**PIM**
1998-99	HC Kladno-Jr.	Cze-Rep	46	13	27	40	....	....	....	....	....	....
	Velvana Kladno	Cze-Rep	4	0	1	1	0	....	....	....	....	....
99-2000	HC Kladno-Jr.	Cze-Rep	34	16	15	31	16	....	....	....	....	....
	HC Slany-3	Cze-Rep	4	3	0	3	0	....	....	....	....	....
	HK Kralupy-3	Cze-Rep	1	0	1	1	0	5	2	2	4	4
	Velvana Kladno	Cze-Rep	21	3	2	5	4	....	....	....	....	....
2000-01	HC Kladno	Cze-Rep	45	6	10	16	22	....	....	....	....	....

VOLCHENKOV, Anton (vohl-chen-KAHF, an-TUHN) **OTT.**

Defense. Shoots left. 6', 209 lbs. Born, Moscow, USSR, February 25, 1982.
(Ottawa's 1st choice, 21st overall, in 2000 Entry Draft).

			Regular Season					Playoffs				
Season	**Club**	**Lea**	**GP**	**G**	**A**	**TP**	**PIM**	**GP**	**G**	**A**	**TP**	**PIM**
99-2000	HC Moscow-2	Russia-3	6	0	1	1	10	....	....	....	....	....
	HC Moscow	Russia-2	30	2	9	11	36	....	....	....	....	....
2000-01	Krylya Sovetov	Russia-2	34	3	4	7	56	....	....	....	....	....

VOLRAB, Daniel (VOHL-rab, DAN-yehl) **DAL.**

Center. Shoots left. 6', 178 lbs. Born, Decin, Czech., March 11, 1983.
(Dallas' 4th choice, 126th overall, in 2001 Entry Draft).

			Regular Season					Playoffs				
Season	**Club**	**Lea**	**GP**	**G**	**A**	**TP**	**PIM**	**GP**	**G**	**A**	**TP**	**PIM**
1998-99	CHZ Litvinov-Jr.	Cze-Rep	7	1	1	2	....	....	....	....	....	....
	Sparta Praha-Jr.	Cze-Rep	37	23	20	43	....	....	....	....	....	....
99-2000	Sparta Praha-Jr.	Cze-Rep	39	33	25	58	18	7	4	6	10	2
2000-01	Sparta Praha-Jr.	Cze-Rep	27	9	10	19	30	2	1	0	1	0
	Sparta Praha	Cze-Rep	1	0	0	0	0	....	....	....	....	....

VONDRKA, Michal (VOHND-rah-ka, MEE-khahl) **BUF.**

Left wing. Shoots right. 6', 178 lbs. Born, Ceske Budejovice, Czech., May 17, 1983.
(Buffalo's 5th choice, 155th overall, in 2001 Entry Draft).

			Regular Season					Playoffs				
Season	**Club**	**Lea**	**GP**	**G**	**A**	**TP**	**PIM**	**GP**	**G**	**A**	**TP**	**PIM**
2000-01	HC Budejovice-Jr	Cze-Rep	28	8	13	21	....	....	....	....	....	....

VOROBIEV, Pavel (voh-roh-BEE-ehf, PAH-vehl) **CHI.**

Right wing. Shoots left. 6', 183 lbs. Born, Karaganda, USSR, May 5, 1982.
(Chicago's 2nd choice, 11th overall, in 2000 Entry Draft).

			Regular Season					Playoffs				
Season	**Club**	**Lea**	**GP**	**G**	**A**	**TP**	**PIM**	**GP**	**G**	**A**	**TP**	**PIM**
1997-98	HC Yaroslavl-2	Russia-3	16	2	0	2	6	....	....	....	....	....
1998-99	HC Yaroslavl-2	Russia-3	17	0	1	1	0	....	....	....	....	....
99-2000	HC Yaroslavl-2	Russia-3	40	19	15	34	20	....	....	....	....	....
	Torpedo Yaroslavl	Russia	8	2	0	2	4	10	2	2	4	0
2000-01	HC Yaroslavl	Russia	36	8	8	16	28	10	4	1	5	8

VRBATA, Radim (vuhr-BA-tuh, ra-DEEM) **COL.**

Right wing. Shoots right. 6'1", 185 lbs. Born, Boleslav, Czech., June 13, 1981.
(Colorado's 10th choice, 212th overall, in 1999 Entry Draft).

			Regular Season					Playoffs				
Season	**Club**	**Lea**	**GP**	**G**	**A**	**TP**	**PIM**	**GP**	**G**	**A**	**TP**	**PIM**
1997-98	Mlada Boleslav	Cze-Rep	35	42	31	73	4	....	....	....	....	....
1998-99	Hull Olympiques	QMJHL	54	22	38	60	16	23	6	13	19	6
99-2000	Hull Olympiques	QMJHL	58	29	45	74	26	15	3	9	12	8
2000-01	Shawinigan	QMJHL	55	56	64	120	67	10	4	7	11	4
	Hershey Bears	AHL	....	....	....	....	....	1	0	1	1	2

QMJHL First All-Star Team (2001)

VYDARENY, Rene (vih-DAH-reh-nay, REH-nay) **VAN.**

Defense. Shoots left. 6'1", 198 lbs. Born, Bratislava, Czech., May 6, 1981.
(Vancouver's 3rd choice, 69th overall, in 1999 Entry Draft).

			Regular Season					Playoffs				
Season	**Club**	**Lea**	**GP**	**G**	**A**	**TP**	**PIM**	**GP**	**G**	**A**	**TP**	**PIM**
1997-98	Slovan Bratislava	Slovak-Jr.	50	5	14	19	26	....	....	....	....	....
1998-99	Slovan Bratislava	Slovak-Jr.	42	4	7	11	65	2	0	0	0	2
	HC Trnava	Slovak-2	20	1	6	7	6	....	....	....	....	....
99-2000	Rimouski Oceanic	QMJHL	51	7	23	30	41	14	2	2	4	20
2000-01	Kansas City	IHL	39	0	1	1	25	....	....	....	....	....

• Missed majority of 2000-01 season due to dispute over ownership of playing rights between Vancouver and HC Bratislava (Slovakia), November 28, 2000.

WALBY, Steffon (WAHL-bee, STEH-fohn)

Right wing. Shoots right. 6'1", 198 lbs. Born, Madison, WI, November 22, 1972.

			Regular Season					Playoffs				
Season	Club	Lea	GP	G	A	TP	PIM	GP	G	A	TP	PIM
1990-91	Madison Capitols	USHL	45	23	16	39	89	....	....	....	....	....
1991-92	Kelowna Spartans	BCJHL	24	18	13	31	10	....	....	....	....	....
1992-93	Kelowna Spartans	BCJHL	59	53	68	121	76	....	....	....	....	....
1993-94	St. John's Leafs	AHL	63	15	22	37	79	2	0	0	0	2
1994-95	St. John's Leafs	AHL	70	23	23	46	30	5	1	1	2	4
1995-96	St. John's Leafs	AHL	57	23	31	54	61	4	2	2	4	17
1996-97	Hershey Bears	AHL	74	24	23	47	61	23	9	5	14	38
1997-98	Fort Wayne	IHL	77	28	26	54	53	4	1	1	2	6
1998-99	Rochester	AHL	48	15	13	28	52	....	....	....	....	....
	Kentucky	AHL	11	8	4	12	6	12	3	2	5	14
99-2000	Hershey Bears	AHL	49	19	13	32	50	14	3	9	12	11
2000-01	Hershey Bears	AHL	69	12	21	33	48	12	2	6	8	12

Signed as a free agent by **Toronto**, August 20, 1993. Signed as a free agent by **Buffalo**, August 31, 1998. Signed as a free agent by **Colorado**, September, 1999.

WALKER, Matt (WAHL-kuhr, MAT) ST.L.

Defense. Shoots right. 6'2", 222 lbs. Born, Beaverlodge, Alta., April 7, 1980.
(St. Louis' 3rd choice, 83rd overall, in 1998 Entry Draft).

			Regular Season					Playoffs				
Season	Club	Lea	GP	G	A	TP	PIM	GP	G	A	TP	PIM
1996-97	Grand Prairie	AAHA	68	22	62	74	186	....	....	....	....	....
1997-98	Portland	WHL	64	2	13	15	124	16	0	0	0	21
1998-99	Portland	WHL	64	1	10	11	151	4	0	1	1	6
99-2000	Portland	WHL	38	2	7	9	97	....	....	....	....	....
	Kootenay Ice	WHL	31	4	19	23	53	21	5	13	18	24
2000-01	Peoria Rivermen	ECHL	8	1	0	1	70	....	....	....	....	....
	Worcester	AHL	61	4	8	12	131	11	0	0	0	6

WALLIN, Rickard (WAHL-in, RIH-kahrd) MIN.

Center. Shoots left. 6'2", 185 lbs. Born, Stockholm, Sweden, April 19, 1980.
(Phoenix's 8th choice, 160th overall, in 1998 Entry Draft).

			Regular Season					Playoffs				
Season	Club	Lea	GP	G	A	TP	PIM	GP	G	A	TP	PIM
1996-97	Farjestads BK	Swede-Jr.	26	3	3	6	....	....	....	....	....	....
1997-98	Farjestads BK	Swede-Jr.	29	20	30	50	32	2	1	1	2	2
1998-99	Farjestads BK	Swede-Jr.	21	11	15	26	30	....	....	....	....	....
	Farjestads BK	Sweden	5	0	0	0	0	....	....	....	....	....
99-2000	Troja-Ljungby	Sweden-2	46	15	22	37	54	....	....	....	....	....
2000-01	Farjestads BK	Sweden	47	9	22	31	24	16	11	3	14	4

Rights traded to **Minnesota** by **Phoenix** for Joe Juneau, June 23, 2000.

WALLIN, Viktor (WAHL-in, VIHK-tohr) ANA.

Defense. Shoots left. 6'3", 200 lbs. Born, Jonkoping, Sweden, January 17, 1980.
(Anaheim's 3rd choice, 112th overall, in 1998 Entry Draft).

			Regular Season					Playoffs				
Season	Club	Lea	GP	G	A	TP	PIM	GP	G	A	TP	PIM
1996-97	HV Jonkoping	Swede-Jr.	16	1	2	3	....	....	....	....	....	....
1997-98	HV Jonkoping	Swede-Jr.	28	9	15	24	42	....	....	....	....	....
1998-99	HV Jonkoping	Sweden	23	0	0	0	4	....	....	....	....	....
99-2000	HV Jonkoping	Swede-Jr.	6	3	1	4	2	....	....	....	....	....
	HV Jonkoping	Sweden	43	2	2	4	16	6	1	1	2	4
2000-01	HV Jonkoping	Sweden	5	0	1	1	2	....	....	....	....	....

WALSER, Derrick (WAHL-zuhr, DEHR-rihk)

Defense. Shoots left. 5'10", 190 lbs. Born, New Glasgow, N.S., May 12, 1978.

			Regular Season					Playoffs				
Season	Club	Lea	GP	G	A	TP	PIM	GP	G	A	TP	PIM
1994-95	Beauport	QMJHL	48	4	18	22	34	12	2	5	7	2
1995-96	Beauport	QMJHL	69	9	31	40	56	20	2	11	13	16
1996-97	Beauport	QMJHL	37	13	25	38	26	....	....	....	....	....
	Rimouski Oceanic	QMJHL	31	15	30	45	44	4	2	2	4	6
1997-98	Rimouski Oceanic	QMJHL	70	41	69	110	135	18	10	*26	36	49
1998-99	Saint John Flames	AHL	40	3	7	10	24	....	....	....	....	....
	Johnstown Chiefs	ECHL	24	8	12	20	29	....	....	....	....	....
99-2000	Saint John Flames	AHL	14	2	3	5	10	....	....	....	....	....
	Johnstown Chiefs	ECHL	54	17	26	43	104	7	3	3	6	8
2000-01	Saint John Flames	AHL	76	19	36	55	36	19	7	9	16	14

QMJHL First All-Star Team (1997) • Won Emile Bouchard Trophy (Top Defenseman - QMJHL) (1998) • QMJHL First All-Star Team (1998) • Canadian Major Junior First All-Star Team (1998) • Canadian Major Junior Defenseman of the Year (1998)

Signed as a free agent by **Calgary**, October 16, 1998.

WALSH, Brendan (WAHLSH, BREHN-duhn)

Right wing. Shoots right. 5'9", 181 lbs. Born, Dorchester, MA, October 22, 1974.

			Regular Season					Playoffs				
Season	Club	Lea	GP	G	A	TP	PIM	GP	G	A	TP	PIM
1995-96	Boston University	H-East	38	8	16	24	90	....	....	....	....	....
1996-97	Boston University	H-East	27	5	8	13	83	....	....	....	....	....
1997-98	U. of Maine	H-East	DID NOT PLAY – TRANSFERRED COLLEGES									
1998-99	U. of Maine	H-East	30	7	13	20	58	....	....	....	....	....
99-2000	U. of Maine	H-East	39	9	21	30	*106	....	....	....	....	....
2000-01	Jackson Bandits	ECHL	25	3	6	9	179	....	....	....	....	....
	Cleveland	IHL	10	1	1	2	45	4	0	0	0	11

Signed as a free agent by **Minnesota**, May 18, 2000.

WANVIG, Kyle (WEHN-vihg, KIGHL) MIN.

Right wing. Shoots right. 6'2", 219 lbs. Born, Calgary, Alta., January 29, 1981.
(Minnesota's 2nd choice, 36th overall, in 2001 Entry Draft).

			Regular Season					Playoffs				
Season	Club	Lea	GP	G	A	TP	PIM	GP	G	A	TP	PIM
1996-97	Calgary Blazers	AMHL	26	31	48	79	85	....	....	....	....	....
1997-98	Edmonton Ice	WHL	62	17	12	29	69	....	....	....	....	....
1998-99	Kootenay Ice	WHL	71	12	20	32	119	7	1	3	4	18
99-2000	Kootenay Ice	WHL	6	2	2	4	12	....	....	....	....	....
	Red Deer Rebels	WHL	58	21	18	39	123	4	1	0	1	4
2000-01	Red Deer Rebels	WHL	69	55	46	101	202	22	10	12	22	47

• Re-entered NHL Entry Draft. Originally Boston's 3rd choice, 89th overall, in 1999 Entry Draft.

WHL East Second All-Star Team (2001) • Memorial Cup All-Star Team (2001) • Won Stafford Smythe Memorial Trophy (Memorial Cup Tournament MVP) (2001)

Traded to **Red Deer** by **Kootenay** with future considerations for Zdenek Blatny, October 21, 1999.

WARREN, Morgan (WAWR-ihn, MOHR-gan) TOR.

Right wing. Shoots right. 6'2", 193 lbs. Born, Summerside, P.E.I., March 6, 1980.
(Toronto's 5th choice, 126th overall, in 1998 Entry Draft).

			Regular Season					Playoffs				
Season	Club	Lea	GP	G	A	TP	PIM	GP	G	A	TP	PIM
1996-97	Quinte Hawks	MTJHL	49	32	38	70	65	....	....	....	....	....
1997-98	Moncton Wildcats	QMJHL	58	11	10	21	80	10	2	2	4	2
1998-99	Moncton Wildcats	QMJHL	48	20	16	36	68	1	0	0	0	2
99-2000	Moncton Wildcats	QMJHL	65	29	36	65	53	16	7	5	12	4
2000-01	St. John's Leafs	AHL	57	2	10	12	16	4	0	0	0	0

WATSON, Dan (WAWT-suhn, DAN) CBJ

Defense. Shoots right. 6'2", 221 lbs. Born, Glencoe, Ont., October 5, 1979.

			Regular Season					Playoffs				
Season	Club	Lea	GP	G	A	TP	PIM	GP	G	A	TP	PIM
1995-96	Strathroy	OJHL-B	46	6	13	19	12	....	....	....	....	....
1996-97	Strathroy	OJHL-B	49	5	25	30	33	....	....	....	....	....
	Sarnia Sting	OHL	10	0	2	2	7	....	....	....	....	....
1997-98	Sarnia Sting	OHL	66	6	15	21	19	5	0	1	1	4
1998-99	Sarnia Sting	OHL	68	2	18	20	27	6	0	0	0	4
99-2000	Sarnia Sting	OHL	68	1	15	16	40	7	0	0	0	4
2000-01	Elmira Jackals	UHL	1	0	0	0	0	....	....	....	....	....
	Syracuse Crunch	AHL	59	3	4	7	12	4	0	0	0	6

Signed as a free agent by **Columbus**, May 29, 2000.

WATSON, Greg (WAWT-suhn, GREHG) FLA.

Center. Shoots left. 6'2", 198 lbs. Born, Eastend, Sask., March 2, 1983.
(Florida's 3rd choice, 34th overall, in 2001 Entry Draft).

			Regular Season					Playoffs				
Season	Club	Lea	GP	G	A	TP	PIM	GP	G	A	TP	PIM
1998-99	Calgary Buffaloes	AMHL	71	23	23	46	120	....	....	....	....	....
	Prince Albert	WHL	2	0	0	0	5	....	....	....	....	....
99-2000	Prince Albert	WHL	67	10	5	15	63	6	0	2	2	2
2000-01	Prince Albert	WHL	71	22	28	50	72	....	....	....	....	....

WEAVER, Mike (WEE-vuhr, MIGHK) ATL.

Defense. Shoots right. 5'9", 185 lbs. Born, Bramalea, Ont., May 2, 1978.

			Regular Season					Playoffs				
Season	Club	Lea	GP	G	A	TP	PIM	GP	G	A	TP	PIM
1995-96	Bramalea Blues	OPJHL	48	10	39	49	103	....	....	....	....	....
1996-97	Michigan State	CCHA	39	0	7	7	46	....	....	....	....	....
1997-98	Michigan State	CCHA	44	4	22	26	68	....	....	....	....	....
1998-99	Michigan State	CCHA	42	1	6	7	54	....	....	....	....	....
99-2000	Michigan State	CCHA	26	0	7	7	20	....	....	....	....	....
2000-01	Orlando	IHL	68	0	8	8	34	16	0	2	2	8

Won OPJHL Defenseman of the Year Award (1996) • CCHA All-Tournament Team (1997) • CCHA First All-Star Team (1999, 2000) • NCAA West Second All-American Team (1999, 2000) • Won CCHA Best Defensive Defenseman Award (1999, 2000)

Signed as a free agent by **Atlanta**, June 15, 2000.

WEINHANDL, Mattias (vayn-hanh-duhl, mah-TEE-uhs) NYI

Right wing. Shoots right. 6', 183 lbs. Born, Ljungby, Sweden, June 1, 1980.
(NY Islanders' 5th choice, 78th overall, in 1999 Entry Draft).

			Regular Season					Playoffs				
Season	Club	Lea	GP	G	A	TP	PIM	GP	G	A	TP	PIM
1995-96	Troja-Ljungby	Swede-Jr.	28	38	40	78	....	....	....	....	....	....
1996-97	Troja-Ljungby	Swede-Jr.	48	61	69	130	46	....	....	....	....	....
1997-98	Troja-Ljungby	Swede-2	28	3	2	5	2	5	0	0	0	2
1998-99	Troja-Ljungby	Swede-2	38	20	20	40	30	5	4	3	7	4
99-2000	MoDo Hockey	Swede-Jr.	1	2	2	4	2	....	....	....	....	....
	MoDo Hockey	Sweden	32	15	9	24	6	13	5	3	8	8
2000-01	MoDo Hockey	Sweden	48	16	16	32	14	6	1	3	4	6

WEISS, Stephen (WIGHS, STEEV-ehn) FLA.

Center. Shoots left. 6', 183 lbs. Born, Toronto, Ont., April 3, 1983.
(Florida's 1st choice, 4th overall, in 2001 Entry Draft).

			Regular Season					Playoffs				
Season	Club	Lea	GP	G	A	TP	PIM	GP	G	A	TP	PIM
1997-98	Toronto Nats	MTHL	48	51	58	109	....	....	....	....	....	....
1998-99	North York	OPJHL	35	15	22	37	10	....	....	....	....	....
99-2000	Plymouth Whalers	OHL	64	24	42	66	35	23	8	18	26	18
2000-01	Plymouth Whalers	OHL	62	40	47	87	45	18	7	16	23	10

OHL All-Rookie Team (2000)

WELCH, Dan (WEHLCH, DAN) L.A.

Right wing. Shoots right. 5'10", 199 lbs. Born, Lansing, MI, February 23, 1981.
(Los Angeles' 9th choice, 245th overall, in 2000 Entry Draft).

			Regular Season					Playoffs				
Season	Club	Lea	GP	G	A	TP	PIM	GP	G	A	TP	PIM
1996/99	Hastings High	Hi-School	90	76	123	199	....	....	....	....	....	....
99-2000	U. of Minnesota	WCHA	36	6	8	14	31	....	....	....	....	....
2000-01	Omaha Lancers	USHL	52	30	27	57	103	12	9	13	22	20

• Statistics for **Hastings High School** are career totals for 1996-1999 seaons. • Ruled academically ineligible to play 2000-01 WCHA season by Univerisity of Minnesota.

WELCH, Noah (WEHLCH, NOH-ah) PIT.

Defense. Shoots left. 6'3", 212 lbs. Born, Brighton, MA, August 26, 1982.
(Pittsburgh's 2nd choice, 54th overall, in 2001 Entry Draft).

			Regular Season					Playoffs				
Season	Club	Lea	GP	G	A	TP	PIM	GP	G	A	TP	PIM
99-2000	St. Sebastian's	Hi-School	26	4	11	15	35	....	....	....	....	....
	Eastern Mass	MBHL	4	0	3	3	6	....	....	....	....	....
2000-01	St. Sebastian's	Hi-School	30	11	20	31	37	....	....	....	....	....

WELLER, Craig (WEH-luhr) ST.L.

Defense. Shoots right. 6'3", 195 lbs. Born, Calgary, Alta., January 17, 1981.
(St. Louis' 6th choice, 167th overall, in 2000 Entry Draft).

			Regular Season					Playoffs				
Season	Club	Lea	GP	G	A	TP	PIM	GP	G	A	TP	PIM
1997-98	Calgary Flames	AMHL	33	2	10	12	65	3	0	1	1	2
1998-99	Calgary Canucks	AJHL	49	4	14	18	80	13	0	1	1	10
99-2000	Calgary Canucks	AJHL	53	3	14	17	100	4	0	0	0	4
2000-01	Minnesota-Duluth	WCHA	6	0	1	1	0	....	....	....	....	....
	Kootenay Ice	WHL	30	1	5	6	40	11	0	2	2	26

• Left **University of Minnesota-Duluth** (WCHA) and signed as a free agent by **Kootenay** (WHL), January 7, 2001.

WELLWOOD, Kyle (WEHL-wud, KIGHL) **TOR.**

Center. Shoots right. 5'9", 190 lbs. Born, Windsor, Ont., May 16, 1983.
(Toronto's 6th choice, 134th overall, in 2001 Entry Draft).

			Regular Season					Playoffs				
Season	Club	Lea	GP	G	A	TP	PIM	GP	G	A	TP	PIM
1998-99	Tecumseh Dogs	OJHL-B	51	22	41	63	12	....	....	....	....	....
99-2000	Belleville Bulls	OHL	65	14	37	51	14	16	3	7	10	6
2000-01	Belleville Bulls	OHL	68	35	*83	*118	24	10	3	16	19	4

OHL First All-Star Team (2001)

WENDELL, Erik (WEHN-dehl, AIR-ihk) **WSH.**

Center. Shoots left. 6'1", 197 lbs. Born, Minneapolis, MN, August 23, 1979.
(Washington's 6th choice, 125th overall, in 1998 Entry Draft).

			Regular Season					Playoffs				
Season	Club	Lea	GP	G	A	TP	PIM	GP	G	A	TP	PIM
1997-98	Maple Grove	Hi-School	24	24	23	47	38	....	....	....	....	....
	Twin Cities	USHL	17	7	2	9	64	....	....	....	....	....
1998-99	U. of Minnesota	WCHA	41	7	7	14	46	....	....	....	....	....
99-2000	U. of Minnesota	WCHA	32	4	2	6	26	....	....	....	....	....
2000-01	U. of Minnesota	WCHA	33	5	2	7	38	....	....	....	....	....

WENNERBERG, Mattias (VEH-nuhr-buhrg, MA-tee-uhs) **CHI.**

Center. Shoots left. 5'11", 191 lbs. Born, Uma, Sweden, August 6, 1981.
(Chicago's 6th choice, 194th overall, in 1999 Entry Draft).

			Regular Season					Playoffs				
Season	Club	Lea	GP	G	A	TP	PIM	GP	G	A	TP	PIM
1996-97	Vilhelmina HC	Swede-4	20	7	12	19	14	....	....	....	....	....
1997-98	MoDo Hockey	Swede-Jr.	30	10	17	27	....	....	....	....	....	....
1998-99	MoDo Hockey	Swede-Jr.	43	13	12	25	....	....	....	....	....	....
99-2000	MoDo Hockey	Swede-Jr.	32	14	6	20	102	....	....	....	....	....
2000-01	Boden IK	Swede-2	34	9	4	13	36	....	....	....	....	....

WESTCOTT, Duvie (WEST-coht, DOO-vee) **CBJ**

Defense. Shoots right. 5'11", 180 lbs. Born, Winnipeg, Man., October 30, 1977.

			Regular Season					Playoffs				
Season	Club	Lea	GP	G	A	TP	PIM	GP	G	A	TP	PIM
1996-97	Winnipeg Blues	MJHL	52	12	47	59	....	....	....	....	....	....
1997-98	Alaska-Anchorage	WCHA	25	3	5	8	43	....	....	....	....	....
	Omaha Lancers	USHL	12	3	3	6	31	14	0	8	8	84
1998-99	St. Cloud State	WCHA	DID NOT PLAY – TRANSFERRED COLLEGES									
99-2000	St. Cloud State	WCHA	36	1	18	19	67	....	....	....	....	....
2000-01	St. Cloud State	WCHA	38	10	24	34	116	....	....	....	....	....

WCHA Second All-Star Team (2001)

Signed as a free agent by **Columbus**, May 10, 2001.

WESTRUM, Erik (WEHST-ruhm, AIR-ihk) **PHX.**

Center. Shoots left. 5'11", 194 lbs. Born, Minneapolis, MN, July 26, 1979.
(Phoenix's 9th choice, 187th overall, in 1998 Entry Draft).

			Regular Season					Playoffs				
Season	Club	Lea	GP	G	A	TP	PIM	GP	G	A	TP	PIM
1995/97	Apple Valley High	Hi-School	78	56	84	140	....	....	....	....	....	....
1997-98	U. of Minnesota	WCHA	39	6	12	18	43	....	....	....	....	....
1998-99	U. of Minnesota	WCHA	41	10	26	36	81	....	....	....	....	....
99-2000	U. of Minnesota	WCHA	39	27	26	53	99	....	....	....	....	....
2000-01	U. of Minnesota	WCHA	42	26	35	61	84	....	....	....	....	....

• Statistics for Apple Valley High School are career totals for 1995-1997 seasons. • WCHA Third All-Star Team (2000) • WCHA Second All-Star Team (2001)

WICHSER, Adrian (WIH-shuhr, A-dree-uhn) **FLA.**

Center. Shoots left. 6', 180 lbs. Born, Winterthor, Switz., March 18, 1980.
(Florida's 9th choice, 231st overall, in 1998 Entry Draft).

			Regular Season					Playoffs				
Season	Club	Lea	GP	G	A	TP	PIM	GP	G	A	TP	PIM
1997-98	EHC Kloten	Switz.	35	6	5	11	31	7	0	1	1	8
1998-99	EHC Kloten	Switz.	40	11	14	25	14	9	7	0	7	8
99-2000	EHC Kloten	Switz.	33	8	15	23	12	6	2	1	3	0
2000-01	EHC Kloten	Switz.	31	9	9	18	12	9	2	3	5	0

WIDING, Daniel (VEE-dihng, DAN-yehl) **NSH.**

Right wing. Shoots right. 6'1", 187 lbs. Born, Gavle, Sweden, April 13, 1982.
(Nashville's 2nd choice, 36th overall, in 2000 Entry Draft).

			Regular Season					Playoffs				
Season	Club	Lea	GP	G	A	TP	PIM	GP	G	A	TP	PIM
99-2000	Leksands IF-B	Swede-Jr.	6	2	1	3	20	....	....	....	....	....
	Leksands IF	Swede-Jr.	34	15	12	27	65	2	1	0	1	4
	Leksands IF	Sweden	3	0	0	0	2	....	....	....	....	....
2000-01	Leksands IF	Swede-Jr.	6	2	3	5	31	....	....	....	....	....
	Leksands IF	Sweden	40	6	5	11	18	....	....	....	....	....

WIKSTROM, John (WIHK-strohm, JAWN) **DET.**

Defense. Shoots left. 6'3", 200 lbs. Born, Lulea, Sweden, January 30, 1979.
(Detroit's 4th choice, 129th overall, in 1997 Entry Draft).

			Regular Season					Playoffs				
Season	Club	Lea	GP	G	A	TP	PIM	GP	G	A	TP	PIM
1995-96	Lulea HF	Sweden	9	0	0	0	2	....	....	....	....	....
1996-97	Lulea HF	Sweden	9	0	0	0	0	3	0	0	0	0
1997-98	Lulea HF	Sweden	1	0	0	0	0	....	....	....	....	....
	Lulea HF	EuroHL	1	0	0	0	0	....	....	....	....	....
	Pitea IK	Swede-2	4	0	0	0	0	....	....	....	....	....
1998-99	Morrum IS	Swede-2	23	0	1	1	28	....	....	....	....	....
99-2000	Louisiana Gators	ECHL	10	0	0	0	4	....	....	....	....	....
	Wheeling Nailers	ECHL	48	4	4	8	23	....	....	....	....	....
2000-01	Cincinnati Ducks	AHL	43	3	1	4	35	2	0	0	0	2

WILFORD, Marty (WIHL-fohrd, MAHR-tee) **CHI.**

Defense. Shoots left. 6'1", 216 lbs. Born, Cobourg, Ont., April 17, 1977.
(Chicago's 7th choice, 149th overall, in 1995 Entry Draft).

			Regular Season					Playoffs				
Season	Club	Lea	GP	G	A	TP	PIM	GP	G	A	TP	PIM
1993-94	Peterborough	OPJHL	40	3	19	22	*107	....	....	....	....	....
1994-95	Oshawa Generals	OHL	63	1	6	7	95	7	1	1	2	4
1995-96	Oshawa Generals	OHL	65	3	24	27	107	5	0	1	1	4
1996-97	Oshawa Generals	OHL	62	19	43	62	126	16	2	18	20	28
1997-98	Columbus Chill	ECHL	46	8	27	35	123	....	....	....	....	....
	Indianapolis Ice	IHL	26	0	4	4	16	....	....	....	....	....
1998-99	Indianapolis Ice	IHL	80	3	13	16	116	7	0	1	1	16
99-2000	Cleveland	IHL	7	0	3	3	24	....	....	....	....	....
	Houston Aeros	IHL	45	0	9	9	30	11	2	2	4	18
2000-01	Norfolk Admirals	AHL	80	7	41	48	102	9	1	5	6	8

OHL Second All-Star Team (1997)

WILLIAMS, Jeff (WIHL-lee-ams, JEHF)

Center. Shoots left. 6'1", 200 lbs. Born, Pointe Claire, Que., February 11, 1976.
(New Jersey's 8th choice, 181st overall, in 1994 Entry Draft).

			Regular Season					Playoffs				
Season	Club	Lea	GP	G	A	TP	PIM	GP	G	A	TP	PIM
1991-92	North York	MTHL	56	53	51	104	23	....	....	....	....	....
	Newmarket	OPJHL	4	1	1	2	4	....	....	....	....	....
1992-93	Newmarket	OPJHL	45	28	35	63	18	....	....	....	....	....
1993-94	Newmarket	OPJHL	4	1	1	2	4	....	....	....	....	....
	Guelph Storm	OHL	62	14	12	26	19	9	2	1	3	4
1994-95	Guelph Storm	OHL	52	15	32	47	21	14	5	5	10	0
1995-96	Guelph Storm	OHL	63	15	49	64	42	16	13	15	28	10
1996-97	Raleigh IceCaps	ECHL	20	4	8	12	8	....	....	....	....	....
	Albany River Rats	AHL	46	13	20	33	12	15	1	2	3	15
1997-98	Albany River Rats	AHL	58	13	12	25	20	12	5	6	11	2
1998-99	Albany River Rats	AHL	74	*46	27	73	39	5	1	2	3	0
99-2000	Orlando	IHL	6	2	4	6	0	....	....	....	....	....
	Albany River Rats	AHL	71	29	20	49	24	5	0	0	0	2
2000-01	Syracuse Crunch	AHL	76	22	27	49	36	5	0	1	1	0

Canadian Major Junior Sportsmanlike Player of the Year (1996) • AHL Second All-Star Team (1999)

Claimed by **Atlanta** from **New Jersey** in Waiver Draft, September 27, 1999. Traded to **New Jersey** by **Atlanta** with Sylvain Cloutier and Atlanta's 7th round choice (Ken Magovan) in 2000 Entry Draft for Wes Mason and Eric Bertrand, November 1, 1999. Selected by **Columbus** from **New Jersey** in Expansion Draft, June 23, 2000.

WILLIS, Tyler (WHIL-lihs, TIGH-luhr)

Right wing. Shoots right. 5'9", 171 lbs. Born, Princeton, B.C., April 8, 1977.
(Vancouver's 8th choice, 196th overall, in 1995 Entry Draft).

			Regular Season					Playoffs				
Season	Club	Lea	GP	G	A	TP	PIM	GP	G	A	TP	PIM
1992-93	Merritt Luckies	BCJHL	54	11	22	33	129	....	....	....	....	....
1993-94	Swift Current	WHL	71	19	26	45	263	....	....	....	....	....
1994-95	Swift Current	WHL	71	21	29	50	284	6	0	0	0	20
1995-96	Swift Current	WHL	40	9	38	47	196	....	....	....	....	....
	Seattle T-Birds	WHL	15	1	3	4	71	5	1	5	6	13
1996-97	Seattle T-Birds	WHL	72	12	40	52	302	15	1	7	8	68
1997-98	Worcester	AHL	24	2	1	3	140	....	....	....	....	....
	Baton Rouge	ECHL	21	4	10	14	112	....	....	....	....	....
1998-99	Worcester	AHL	55	8	10	18	227	....	....	....	....	....
99-2000	Worcester	AHL	32	3	10	13	98	9	1	2	3	8
	Peoria Rivermen	ECHL	19	5	6	11	89	....	....	....	....	....
2000-01	Peoria Rivermen	ECHL	58	14	18	32	251	14	1	2	3	45
	Worcester	AHL	16	2	1	3	50	....	....	....	....	....

Signed as a free agent by **St. Louis**, October 3, 1997.

WINCHESTER, Brad (WIHN-chehst-uhr, BRAD) **EDM.**

Left wing. Shoots left. 6'5", 208 lbs. Born, Madison, WI, March 1, 1981.
(Edmonton's 2nd choice, 35th overall, in 2000 Entry Draft).

			Regular Season					Playoffs				
Season	Club	Lea	GP	G	A	TP	PIM	GP	G	A	TP	PIM
1997-98	Team USA	USDP	74	22	23	45	162	....	....	....	....	....
1998-99	Team USA	USDP	65	21	23	44	103	....	....	....	....	....
99-2000	U. of Wisconsin	WCHA	33	9	9	18	48	....	....	....	....	....
2000-01	U. of Wisconsin	WCHA	41	7	9	16	71	....	....	....	....	....

WISEMAN, Chad (WIGHZ-man, CHAD) **S.J.**

Left wing. Shoots left. 6', 190 lbs. Born, Burlington, Ont., March 25, 1981.
(San Jose's 8th choice, 246th overall, in 2000 Entry Draft).

			Regular Season					Playoffs				
Season	Club	Lea	GP	G	A	TP	PIM	GP	G	A	TP	PIM
1997-98	Burlington	OPJHL	50	28	36	64	31	....	....	....	....	....
1998-99	Mississauga	OHL	64	11	25	36	29	....	....	....	....	....
99-2000	Mississauga	OHL	68	23	45	68	53	....	....	....	....	....
2000-01	Mississauga	OHL	30	15	29	44	22	....	....	....	....	....
	Plymouth Whalers	OHL	32	11	16	27	12	19	12	8	20	22

Traded to **Plymouth** by **Mississauga** for Nathan O'Nabigon and Plymouth's 3rd round choice in 2002 OHL Priority Draft, December 28, 2000.

WOODFORD, Mike (WUD-fohrd, MIGHK) **FLA.**

Right wing. Shoots right. 5'11", 183 lbs. Born, Boston, MA, October 4, 1981.
(Florida's 6th choice, 117th overall, in 2001 Entry Draft).

			Regular Season					Playoffs				
Season	Club	Lea	GP	G	A	TP	PIM	GP	G	A	TP	PIM
99-2000	Cushing Academy	Hi-School	31	35	35	70	60	....	....	....	....	....
2000-01	Cushing Academy	Hi-School	36	34	39	73	68	....	....	....	....	....

WOYWITKA, Jeff (WOI-wiht-ka, JEHF) **PHI.**

Defense. Shoots left. 6'2", 209 lbs. Born, Vermilion, B.C., September 1, 1983.
(Philadelphia's 1st choice, 27th overall, in 2001 Entry Draft).

			Regular Season					Playoffs				
Season	Club	Lea	GP	G	A	TP	PIM	GP	G	A	TP	PIM
1998-99	Wainwright Kings	AAHA	26	7	15	22	69	....	....	....	....	....
99-2000	Red Deer Rebels	WHL	67	4	12	16	40	4	0	3	3	2
2000-01	Red Deer Rebels	WHL	72	7	28	35	113	22	2	8	10	25

YAKOUBOV, Mikhail (yuh-KOO-bahf, mih-KIGH-eel) CHI.

Center. Shoots left. 6'3", 208 lbs. Born, Barnaul, USSR, February 16, 1982.
(Chicago's 1st choice, 10th overall, in 2000 Entry Draft).

			Regular Season					Playoffs				
Season	Club	Lea	GP	G	A	TP	PIM	GP	G	A	TP	PIM
1997-98	Lada Togliatti-2	Russia-3	7	0	0	0	0	....	....	....	....	....
1998-99	Lada Togliatti-3	Russia-4	38	11	4	15	32	....	....	....	....	....
99-2000	Lada Togliatti-2	Russia-3	26	12	19	31	14	....	....	....	....	....
2000-01	Lada Togliatti	Russia	25	0	0	0	4	4	0	0	0	0

YERSHOV, Andrei (yuhr-SHAWF, AWN-dray) CHI.

Defense. Shoots left. 6', 216 lbs. Born, Voskresensk, USSR, August 22, 1976.
(Chicago's 9th choice, 240th overall, in 1998 Entry Draft).

			Regular Season					Playoffs				
Season	Club	Lea	GP	G	A	TP	PIM	GP	G	A	TP	PIM
1994-95	HK Khimik	CIS	16	0	0	0	6	....	....	....	....	....
1995-96	HK Khimik	CIS	18	1	0	1	28	....	....	....	....	....
1996-97	HK Khimik	Russia	23	3	1	4	32	2	0	0	0	2
1997-98	HK Khimik	Russia	45	5	8	13	60	....	....	....	....	....
1998-99	HK Khimik	Russia	33	6	6	12	88	....	....	....	....	....
99-2000	Lada Togliatti	Russia	10	0	1	1	12	4	0	0	0	6
2000-01	Vityaz Podolsk	Russia	30	1	5	6	32	....	....	....	....	....

YONKMAN, Nolan (YAWK-man, NOH-lan) WSH.

Defense. Shoots right. 6'5", 218 lbs. Born, Punnicht, Sask., April 1, 1981.
(Washington's 5th choice, 37th overall, in 1999 Entry Draft).

			Regular Season					Playoffs				
Season	Club	Lea	GP	G	A	TP	PIM	GP	G	A	TP	PIM
1996-97	Naicam Vikings	SAHA	64	15	23	38	36	....	....	....	....	....
	Kelowna Rockets	WHL	4	0	0	0	0	....	....	....	....	....
1997-98	Kelowna Rockets	WHL	65	0	2	2	36	7	0	0	0	2
1998-99	Kelowna Rockets	WHL	61	1	6	7	129	6	0	0	0	6
99-2000	Kelowna Rockets	WHL	71	5	7	12	153	5	0	0	0	8
2000-01	Kelowna Rockets	WHL	7	0	1	1	19	....	....	....	....	....
	Brandon	WHL	51	6	10	16	94	6	0	1	1	12

Traded to **Brandon** by **Kelowna** for Bart Rushner and Jan Fadrny, October 12, 2000.

YTFELDT, David (YOOT-fehld, DAY-vihd) VAN.

Defense. Shoots left. 6'1", 187 lbs. Born, Ornskoldsvik, Sweden, September 29, 1979.
(Vancouver's 6th choice, 136th overall, in 1998 Entry Draft).

			Regular Season					Playoffs				
Season	Club	Lea	GP	G	A	TP	PIM	GP	G	A	TP	PIM
1996-97	Leksands IF	Swede-Jr.	25	3	5	8	....	....	....	....	....	....
1997-98	Leksands IF	Swede-Jr.	23	13	10	23	101	....	....	....	....	....
	Leksands IF	Sweden	10	0	0	0	2	....	....	....	....	....
1998-99	Leksands IF	Sweden	39	0	4	4	65	4	0	1	1	4
99-2000	Leksands IF	Sweden	50	3	9	12	72	....	....	....	....	....
2000-01	Vastra Frolunda	Swede-Jr.	2	2	1	3	0	....	....	....	....	....
	JyP Jyvaskyla	Finland	11	0	4	4	26	....	....	....	....	....
	Vastra Frolunda	Sweden	9	0	1	1	8	5	0	1	1	4

• Name when drafted was David Jonsson. His last name was legally changed to Ytfeldt.

ZAINULLIN, Ruslan (zihj-NOO-luhn, roos-LAHN) PHX.

Right wing. Shoots left. 6'2", 202 lbs. Born, Kazan, USSR, February 14, 1982.
(Tampa Bay's 2nd choice, 34th overall, in 2000 Entry Draft).

			Regular Season					Playoffs				
Season	Club	Lea	GP	G	A	TP	PIM	GP	G	A	TP	PIM
1997-98	Ak Bars Kazan-2	Russia-3	27	0	1	1	2	....	....	....	....	....
1998-99	Ak Bars Kazan-2	Russia-4	36	13	8	21	22	....	....	....	....	....
99-2000	Ak Bars Kazan-2	Russia-3	12	13	6	19	....	....	....	....	....	....
	Ak Bars Kazan	Russia	14	1	1	2	4	....	....	....	....	....
2000-01	Ak Bars Kazan	Russia	29	1	3	4	14	1	0	0	0	0

Traded to **Phoenix** by **Tampa Bay** with Mike Johnson, Paul Mara and NY Islanders' 2nd round choice (previously acquired, Phoenix selected Matthew Spiller) in 2001 Entry Draft for Nikolai Khabibulin and Stan Neckar, March 5, 2001.

ZALESAK, Miroslav (zah-LIH-sahk, MEER-oh-slav) S.J.

Right wing. Shoots left. 6', 185 lbs. Born, Skalica, Czech., January 2, 1980.
(San Jose's 5th choice, 104th overall, in 1998 Entry Draft).

			Regular Season					Playoffs				
Season	Club	Lea	GP	G	A	TP	PIM	GP	G	A	TP	PIM
1995-96	MHC Nitra	Slovak-Jr.	49	53	29	82	....	....	....	....	....	....
1996-97	MHC Nitra	Slovak-Jr.	58	51	31	82	....	....	....	....	....	....
1997-98	MHC Nitra	Slovak-Jr.	27	32	29	61	30	....	....	....	....	....
	MHC Nitra	Slovakia	30	8	6	14	0	....	....	....	....	....
1998-99	MHC Nitra	Slovakia	15	4	3	7	10	....	....	....	....	....
	Drummondville	QMJHL	45	24	27	51	18	....	....	....	....	....
99-2000	Drummondville	QMJHL	60	50	61	111	40	16	7	11	18	4
2000-01	Kentucky	AHL	60	14	11	25	26	3	0	1	1	4

ZANON, Greg (ZA-nuhn, GREHG) OTT.

Defense. Shoots left. 5'11", 200 lbs. Born, Burnaby, B.C., June 5, 1980.
(Ottawa's 6th choice, 156th overall, in 2000 Entry Draft).

			Regular Season					Playoffs				
Season	Club	Lea	GP	G	A	TP	PIM	GP	G	A	TP	PIM
1995-96	Burnaby WCC	BCAHA	49	16	27	43	142	....	....	....	....	....
1996-97	Victoria Salsa	BCJHL	53	4	13	17	124	....	....	....	....	....
1997-98	Victoria Salsa	BCJHL	59	11	21	32	108	7	0	2	2	10
1998-99	Surrey Eagles	BCJHL	59	17	54	71	154	....	....	....	....	....
99-2000	Nebraska-Omaha	CCHA	42	3	26	29	56	....	....	....	....	....
2000-01	Nebraska-Omaha	CCHA	39	12	16	28	64	....	....	....	....	....

CCHA First All-Star Team (2001) • NCAA West Second All-American Team (2001)

ZAVORAL, Vaclav (ZA-vohr-uhl, VATS-lahf) TOR.

Defense. Shoots left. 6'3", 207 lbs. Born, Teplice, Czech., May 22, 1981.
(Toronto's 5th choice, 151st overall, in 1999 Entry Draft).

			Regular Season					Playoffs				
Season	Club	Lea	GP	G	A	TP	PIM	GP	G	A	TP	PIM
1997-98	HC Litvinov-Jr.	Cze-Rep	46	0	5	5	....	....	....	....	....	....
1998-99	HC Litvinov-Jr.	Cze-Rep	43	2	10	12	....	....	....	....	....	....
	HC Litvinov	Cze-Rep	1	0	1	1	2	....	....	....	....	....
99-2000	Sault Ste. Marie	OHL	57	3	11	14	89	14	0	2	2	28
2000-01	Sault Ste. Marie	OHL	55	4	6	10	116	....	....	....	....	....

ZETTERBERG, Henrik (ZEH-tuhr-buhrg, HEHN-rihk) DET.

Left wing. Shoots left. 5'11", 176 lbs. Born, Njurunda, Sweden, October 9, 1980.
(Detroit's 4th choice, 210th overall, in 1999 Entry Draft).

			Regular Season					Playoffs				
Season	Club	Lea	GP	G	A	TP	PIM	GP	G	A	TP	PIM
1997-98	Timra IK	Swede-Jr.	18	9	5	14	4	....	....	....	....	....
	Timra IK	Swede-2	16	1	2	3	4	4	0	1	1	0
1998-99	Timra IK	Swede-2	37	15	13	28	2	4	2	1	3	2
99-2000	Timra IK	Swede-2	32	20	14	34	20	10	10	4	14	4
2000-01	Timra IK	Sweden	47	15	31	46	24	....	....	....	....	....

Named Swedish Elite League Rookie-of-the-Year (2001)

ZEVAKHIN, Alexander (zeh-VAH-khin, al-ehx-AN-duhr) PIT.

Right wing. Shoots left. 6', 187 lbs. Born, Perm, USSR, December 30, 1978.
(Pittsburgh's 2nd choice, 54th overall, in 1998 Entry Draft).

			Regular Season					Playoffs				
Season	Club	Lea	GP	G	A	TP	PIM	GP	G	A	TP	PIM
1995-96	CSKA Moscow	Russia-Jr.	65	52	30	82	30	....	....	....	....	....
1996-97	HC Moscow-2	Russia-3	30	15	18	33	10	....	....	....	....	....
	CSKA Moscow	Russia	29	7	3	10	10	....	....	....	....	....
1997-98	HC Moscow-2	Russia-3	32	13	14	27	20	....	....	....	....	....
	CSKA Moscow	Russia	10	1	0	1	0	....	....	....	....	....
1998-99	CSKA Moscow	Russia	42	7	4	11	16	3	0	0	0	0
99-2000	CSKA Moscow	Russia	15	1	0	1	6	....	....	....	....	....
2000-01	Wilkes-Barre	AHL	77	14	11	25	16	21	2	4	6	0

ZIB, Lukas (ZIHB, LOO-kahsh) EDM.

Defense. Shoots right. 6'1", 200 lbs. Born, Ceske Budejovice, Czech., February 24, 1977.
(Edmonton's 3rd choice, 57th overall, in 1995 Entry Draft).

			Regular Season					Playoffs				
Season	Club	Lea	GP	G	A	TP	PIM	GP	G	A	TP	PIM
1994-95	HC Budejovice	Cze-Rep	13	2	0	2	16	9	1	0	1	6
1995-96	HC Budejovice-Jr.	Cze-Rep	11	5	1	6	....	....	....	....	....	....
	HC Budejovice	Cze-Rep	10	1	0	1	....	2	0	0	0	....
1996-97	HC Budejovice	Cze-Rep	13	0	0	0	4	2	0	0	0	0
1997-98	HC Budejovice	Cze-Rep	47	5	6	11	22	....	....	....	....	....
1998-99	HC Budejovice	Cze-Rep	24	1	4	5	18	....	....	....	....	....
99-2000	HC Budejovice	Cze-Rep	38	3	6	9	10	1	0	0	0	0
2000-01	HC Budejovice	Cze-Rep	22	2	3	5	16	....	....	....	....	....
	HCC Zlin	Cze-Rep	19	4	3	7	8	....	....	....	....	....

ZIGOMANIS, Michael (zih-goh-MAN-his, MIGH-kuhl) CAR.

Center. Shoots right. 6'1", 189 lbs. Born, North York, Ont., January 17, 1981.
(Carolina's 2nd choice, 46th overall, in 2001 Entry Draft).

			Regular Season					Playoffs				
Season	Club	Lea	GP	G	A	TP	PIM	GP	G	A	TP	PIM
1996-97	Wexford Hawks	MTHL	40	37	48	85	23	....	....	....	....	....
	Wexford Raiders	MTJHL	8	2	5	7	2	....	....	....	....	....
1997-98	Kingston	OHL	62	23	51	74	30	12	1	6	7	2
1998-99	Kingston	OHL	67	29	56	85	36	5	1	7	8	2
99-2000	Kingston	OHL	59	40	54	94	49	5	0	4	4	0
2000-01	Kingston	OHL	52	40	37	77	44	....	....	....	....	....

• Re-entered NHL Entry Draft. Originally Buffalo's 4th choice, 64th overall, in 1999 Entry Draft.

ZIMAKOV, Sergei (zih-MAH-kahv, SAIR-gay) WSH.

Defense. Shoots left. 6'1", 194 lbs. Born, Moscow, USSR, January 15, 1978.
(Washington's 4th choice, 58th overall, in 1996 Entry Draft).

			Regular Season					Playoffs				
Season	Club	Lea	GP	G	A	TP	PIM	GP	G	A	TP	PIM
1994-95	Omaha Lancers	USHL	48	14	46	60	22	....	....	....	....	....
1995-96	Krylja Sovetov	CIS	49	2	7	9	36	....	....	....	....	....
1996-97	Krylja Sovetov	Russia	39	4	3	7	57	2	0	0	0	0
1997-98	Krylja Sovetov	Russia	42	4	1	5	48	....	....	....	....	....
1998-99	Ak Bars Kazan	Russia	28	1	0	1	6	8	0	1	1	6
99-2000	Molot-Perm	Russia	31	1	2	3	34	3	0	1	1	0
2000-01	CSKA Moscow	Russia	26	1	5	6	28	....	....	....	....	....

ZINGER, Dwayne DET.

Defense. Shoots left. 6'4", 225 lbs. Born, Coronation, Alta., July 5, 1976.

			Regular Season					Playoffs				
Season	Club	Lea	GP	G	A	TP	PIM	GP	G	A	TP	PIM
1995-96	Melville	SJHL	64	7	17	24	....	....	....	....	....	....
1996-97	Alaska-Fairbanks	CCHA	32	1	5	6	45	....	....	....	....	....
1997-98	Alaska-Fairbanks	CCHA	32	1	3	4	91	....	....	....	....	....
1998-99	Alaska-Fairbanks	CCHA	33	4	14	18	42	....	....	....	....	....
99-2000	Alaska-Fairbanks	CCHA	34	10	4	14	34	....	....	....	....	....
	Cincinnati Ducks	AHL	13	0	2	2	33	....	....	....	....	....
2000-01	Cincinnati Ducks	AHL	68	6	9	15	120	4	1	1	2	2

SJHL First All-Star Team (1996)

Signed as a free agent by **Detroit**, March 13, 2000.

ZINGONI, Peter (zihn-GOH-nee, PEE-tuhr) CBJ

Center. Shoots left. 5'11", 180 lbs. Born, Bridgeport, CT, April 28, 1981.
(Columbus' 8th choice, 231st overall, in 2000 Entry Draft).

			Regular Season					Playoffs				
Season	Club	Lea	GP	G	A	TP	PIM	GP	G	A	TP	PIM
1998-99	New England	EJHL	40	26	22	48	....	....	....	....	....	....
99-2000	New England	EJHL	40	39	38	77	85	3	1	1	2	0
2000-01	Providence	H-East	28	2	6	8	38	....	....	....	....	....

ZINOVJEV, Sergei (zih-NOH-vee-ehv, SAIR-gay) BOS.

Center/Left wing. Shoots left. 5'11", 176 lbs. Born, Novokuznetsk, USSR, March 4, 1980.
(Boston's 6th choice, 73rd overall, in 2000 Entry Draft).

			Regular Season					Playoffs				
Season	Club	Lea	GP	G	A	TP	PIM	GP	G	A	TP	PIM
1997-98	Novokuznetsk-2	Russia-3	40	7	7	14	36	....	....	....	....	....
1998-99	Novokuznetsk-2	Russia-3	4	0	1	1	8	....	....	....	....	....
	Ust-Novokuznetsk	Russia	31	2	4	6	14	3	0	0	0	0
99-2000	Ust-Novokuznetsk	Russia	28	0	2	2	16	....	....	....	....	....
2000-01	HC Yaroslavl	Russia	27	2	10	12	36	....	....	....	....	....
	Ufa-Salavat	Russia	8	4	5	9	6	....	....	....	....	....

ZION, Jon (ZIGH-awn, JAWN) TOR.

Defense. Shoots left. 6', 198 lbs. Born, Nepean, Ont., May 21, 1981.
(Toronto's 4th choice, 110th overall, in 1999 Entry Draft).

			Regular Season					Playoffs				
Season	Club	Lea	GP	G	A	TP	PIM	GP	G	A	TP	PIM
1996-97	Nepean Raiders	OCJHL	47	8	26	34	14	....	....	....	....	....
1997-98	Ottawa 67's	OHL	53	4	19	23	20	13	3	12	15	2
1998-99	Ottawa 67's	OHL	60	8	33	41	10	9	2	3	5	8
99-2000	Ottawa 67's	OHL	66	7	52	59	16	11	3	10	13	8
2000-01	Ottawa 67's	OHL	59	22	51	73	38	20	3	*19	22	18

OHL Second All-Star Team (2001)

ZIZKA, Tomas (ZHIHZH-kuh, TAW-mahsh) L.A.

Defense. Shoots left. 6'1", 198 lbs. Born, Sternberk, Czech., October 10, 1979.
(Los Angeles' 6th choice, 163rd overall, in 1998 Entry Draft).

			Regular Season					Playoffs				
Season	Club	Lea	GP	G	A	TP	PIM	GP	G	A	TP	PIM
1994-95	ZPS Zlin-Jr.	Cze-Rep	39	1	10	11	....	....	....	....	....	....
1995-96	ZPS Zlin-Jr.	Cze-Rep	47	2	8	10	....	....	....	....	....	....
1996-97	ZPS Zlin-Jr.	Cze-Rep	14	1	0	1	....	....	....	....	....	....
1997-98	ZPS Zlin-Jr.	Cze-Rep	11	3	4	7	....	....	....	....	....	....
	ZPS Zlin	Cze-Rep	33	0	3	3	2	....	....	....	....	....
1998-99	ZPS Zlin	Cze-Rep	44	3	7	10	14	11	1	2	3	....
99-2000	HC Barum Zlin	Cze-Rep	46	4	6	10	30	4	1	0	1	4
2000-01	HCC Zlin	Cze-Rep	43	2	11	13	16	6	0	0	0	6

ZOTKIN, Alexei (ZOHT-kihn, al-EHX-ay) CHI.

Left wing. Shoots left. 6', 200 lbs. Born, Magnitogorsk, USSR, February 5, 1982.
(Chicago's 7th choice, 119th overall, in 2001 Entry Draft).

			Regular Season					Playoffs				
Season	Club	Lea	GP	G	A	TP	PIM	GP	G	A	TP	PIM
1997-98	Magnitogorsk-2	Russia-3	2	0	1	1	2	....	....	....	....	....
1998-99	Magnitogorsk-3	Russia-4	23	5	1	6	20	....	....	....	....	....
99-2000	Magnitogorsk-2	Russia-3	38	22	27	49	86	....	....	....	....	....
	HC Magnitogorsk	Russia	1	0	0	0	0	....	....	....	....	....
2000-01	Magnitogorsk-2	Russia-3	5	6	2	8	26	....	....	....	....	....
	HC Magnitogorsk	Russia	40	2	3	5	34	12	1	1	2	20

ZULTEK, Matt (ZUHL-tehk, MAT) PHI.

Left wing. Shoots left. 6'4", 222 lbs. Born, Windsor, Ont., March 12, 1979.
(Boston's 2nd choice, 56th overall, in 1999 Entry Draft).

			Regular Season					Playoffs				
Season	Club	Lea	GP	G	A	TP	PIM	GP	G	A	TP	PIM
1994-95	Toronto Marlies	MTHL	94	45	36	81	110	....	....	....	....	....
1995-96	Caledon Canucks	MTJHL	50	19	14	33	40	....	....	....	....	....
1996-97	Ottawa 67's	OHL	63	27	13	40	76	21	7	6	13	27
1997-98	Ottawa 67's	OHL	62	28	28	56	156	13	6	12	18	20
1998-99	Ottawa 67's	OHL	56	33	33	66	71	9	6	2	8	4
99-2000	Ottawa 67's	OHL	28	9	6	15	34	11	3	5	8	12
2000-01	St. Thomas U.	AUAA	17	12	7	19	68	....	....	....	....	....
	Philadelphia	AHL	16	1	4	5	6	9	0	1	1	8

• Re-entered NHL Entry Draft. Originally Los Angeles's 2nd choice, 15th overall, in 1997 Entry Draft.

Rights traded to **Philadelphia** by **Boston** for Philadelphia's 9th round choice (Michael Rodman) in 2001 Entry Draft, February 13, 2001.

Key to Prospect, NHL Player and Goaltender Registers

Demographics: Position, shooting side (catching hand for goaltenders), height, weight, place and date of birth as well as draft information, if any, is located on this line.

Major Junior, NCAA, minor pro, senior European and NHL clubs form a permanent part of each player's data panel. If a player sees action with more than one club in any of the above categories, a separate line is included for each one.

Olympic Team statistics are also listed.

Player's NHL organization as of August 20, 2001. This includes players under contract, unsigned draft choices and other players on reserve lists. Free agents as of August 20, 2001 show a blank here.

The complete career data panels of players with NHL experience who announced their retirement before the start of the 2001-02 season are included in the 2001-02 Player Register. These newly-retired players also show a blank here.

Each NHL club's minor-pro affiliates are listed on page 18.

SAKIC, Joe (SAK-ihk, JOH) **COL.**

Center. Shoots left. 5'11", 185 lbs. Born, Burnaby, B.C., July 7, 1969. Quebec's 2nd choice, 15th overall, in 1987 Entry Draft.

Season	Club	League	GP	G	A	Pts	PIM	PP	SH	GW	S	%	+/-
			Regular Season										
1985-86	Burnaby	BCAHA	80	83	73	156	96	....	....	....	....	....	....
	Lethbridge	WHL	3	0	0	0	0	....	....	....	....	....	....
1986-87	Swift Current	WHL	72	60	73	133	31	....	....	....	....	....	....
1987-88	Swift Current	WHL	64	*78	82	*160	64	....	....	....	....	....	....
1988-89	**Quebec**	**NHL**	**70**	**23**	**39**	**62**	**24**	**10**	**0**	**2**	**148**	**15.5**	**–36**
1989-90	**Quebec**	**NHL**	**80**	**39**	**63**	**102**	**27**	**8**	**1**	**2**	**234**	**16.7**	**–40**
1990-91	**Quebec**	**NHL**	**80**	**48**	**61**	**109**	**24**	**12**	**3**	**7**	**245**	**19.6**	**–26**
1991-92	**Quebec**	**NHL**	**69**	**29**	**65**	**94**	**20**	**6**	**3**	**1**	**217**	**13.4**	**5**
1992-93	**Quebec**	**NHL**	**78**	**48**	**57**	**105**	**40**	**20**	**2**	**4**	**264**	**18.2**	**–3**
1993-94	**Quebec**	**NHL**	**84**	**28**	**64**	**92**	**18**	**10**	**1**	**9**	**279**	**10.0**	**–8**
1994-95	**Quebec**	**NHL**	**47**	**19**	**43**	**62**	**30**	**3**	**2**	**5**	**157**	**12.1**	**7**
1995-96 ♦	**Colorado**	**NHL**	**82**	**51**	**69**	**120**	**44**	**17**	**6**	**7**	**339**	**15.0**	**14**
1996-97	**Colorado**	**NHL**	**65**	**22**	**52**	**74**	**34**	**10**	**2**	**5**	**261**	**8.4**	**–10**
1997-98	**Colorado**	**NHL**	**64**	**27**	**36**	**63**	**50**	**12**	**1**	**2**	**254**	**10.6**	**0**
	Canada	Olympics	4	1	2	3	4	....	....	....	....	....	....
1998-99	**Colorado**	**NHL**	**73**	**41**	**55**	**96**	**29**	**12**	**5**	**6**	**255**	**16.1**	**23**
1999-2000	**Colorado**	**NHL**	**60**	**28**	**53**	**81**	**28**	**5**	**1**	**5**	**242**	**11.6**	**30**
2000-01 ♦	**Colorado**	**NHL**	**82**	**54**	**64**	**118**	**30**	**19**	**3**	**12**	**332**	**16.3**	**45**
	NHL Totals		**934**	**457**	**721**	**1178**	**398**	**144**	**30**	**67**	**3227**	**14.2**	

Season	Club	TF	F%	H	SB	Min	GP	G	A	Pts	PIM	PP	SH	GW
							Playoffs							
1985-86	Burnaby	....	....	....	....	....	....	....	....	....	....	....	....	....
	Lethbridge	....	....	....	....	....	....	....	....	....	....	....	....	....
1986-87	Swift Current	....	....	....	....	....	4	0	1	[illegible]	0	....	....	....
1987-88	Swift Current	....	....	....	....	....	10	11	13	24	12	....	....	....
1988-89	**Quebec**	....	....	....	....	....	....	....	....	....	....	....	....	....
1989-90	**Quebec**	....	....	....	....	....	....	....	....	....	....	....	....	....
1990-91	**Quebec**	....	....	....	....	....	....	....	....	....	....	....	....	....
1991-92	**Quebec**	....	....	....	....	....	....	....	....	....	....	....	....	....
1992-93	**Quebec**	[illegible]	[illegible]	[illegible]	[illegible]	....	**6**	**3**	**3**	**6**	**2**	**1**	**0**	**0**
1993-94	**Quebec**	[illegible]	[illegible]	[illegible]	[illegible]	....	....	....	....	....	....	....	....	....
1994-95	**Quebec**	[illegible]	[illegible]	[illegible]	[illegible]	....	**6**	**4**	**1**	**5**	[illegible]	**1**	**1**	**1**
1995-96 ♦	**Colorado**	[illegible]	[illegible]	[illegible]	[illegible]	....	**22**	***18**	**16**	***34**	**14**	**6**	**0**	**6**
1996-97	**Colorado**	....	....	....	....	....	**17**	**8**	***17**	**25**	**14**	**3**	**0**	**0**
1997-98	**Colorado**	....	....	....	....	....	**6**	**2**	**3**	**5**	**6**	**0**	**1**	**2**
	Canada	....	....	....	....	....	....	....	....	....	....	....	....	....
1998-99	**Colorado**	**1723**	**51.4**	**31**	**47**	**25:35**	[illegible]	**6**	**13**	**19**	**8**	**1**	**1**	**1**
1999-2000	**Colorado**	**1392**	**53.8**	**19**	**26**	**23:16**	[illegible]	**2**	**7**	**9**	**8**	**2**	**0**	**0**
2000-01 ♦	**Colorado**	**2292**	**53.0**	**44**	**54**	**23:01**	**21**	***13**	**13**	***26**	**6**	**5**	**0**	**3**
	NHL Totals	**5407**	**52.7**	**94**	**127**	**23:57**	**114**	**56**	**73**	**129**	**58**	[illegible]	**3**	**13**

WHL East Second All-Star Team (1987) • WHL East First All-Star Team (1988) • Canadian Major Junior Player of the Year (1988) • Shared Bob Clarke Trophy (WHL's Leading Scorer with Theo Fleury) (1988) • Won Conn Smythe Trophy (1996) • NHL First All-Star Team (2001) • Won Lady Byng Trophy (2001) • Won Hart Trophy (2001) • Played in NHL All-Star Game 1990, 1991, 1992, 1993, 1994, 1995, 1998, 2000, 2001)

Transferred to **Colorado** after **Quebec** franchise relocated, June 21, 1995.

Diamond (♦) indicates member of Stanley Cup-winning team.

Asterisk (*) indicates league leader in this statistical category.

Trade and free agent signing dates are based on when the player's contract is filed with NHL Central Registry. This date often differs from the date when the club announces that it has made a trade or come to terms with a free agent.

All-Star Team selections and awards are listed below player's year-by-year data.

NHL All-Star Game appearances are listed above trade notes.

All trades, free agent signings and other transactions involving NHL clubs are listed in chronological order. First draft selection for players who re-enter the NHL Entry Draft is noted here. Other special notes are also listed here. These are highlighted with a bullet (•).

THIS 70TH EDITION OF THE *NHL Official Guide & Record Book* is the third to include additional statistical categories for forwards and defensemen in the National Hockey League. These new categories are, from left to right in the sample panel above, power-play goals (PP), shorthand goals (SH), game-winning goals (GW), shots on goal (S), percentage of shots that score (%), plus-minus rating (+/–), total faceoffs taken (TF), faceoff winning percentage (F%), hits (H), shots blocked (SB) and average time-on-ice per game played (Min).

To integrate this new data, the Player Register has been has been split into two sections. The Prospect Register presents data on players who have yet to play in the NHL. The NHL Player Register, containing more information and a photo of each player, lists all active players who have appeared in an NHL regular-season or playoff game at any time.

Goaltenders, whether prospects or veterans, are included in one register.

Registers (with their starting page) are presented in the following order: Prospects (275), NHL Players (338), Goaltenders (575), Retired Players (601) and Retired Goaltenders (633).

Late additions to the Registers and a list of league abbreviations are found on page 274.

Some information is unavailable at press time. Readers are encouraged to contribute. See page 5 for contact names and addresses.

Pronunciation of Player Names

United Press International phonetic style.

AY	long A as in mate
A	short A as in cat
AI	nasal A as on air
AH	short A as in father
AW	broad A as in talk
EE	long E as in meat
EH	short E as in get
UH	hollow E as in "the"
AY	French long E with acute accent as in Pathe
IH	middle E as in pretty
EW	EW dipthong as in few
IGH	long I as in time
EE	French long I as in machine
IH	short I as in pity
OH	long O as in note
AH	short O as in hot
AW	broad O as in fought
OI	OI dipthong as in noise
OO	long double OO as in fool
UH	short double O as in ouch
OW	OW dipthong as in how
EW	long U as in mule
OO	long U as in rule
U	middle U as in put
UH	short U as in shut or hurt
K	hard C as in cat
S	soft C as in cease
SH	soft CH as in machine
CH	hard CH or TCH as in catch
Z	hard S as in bells
S	soft S as in sun
G	hard G as in gang
J	soft G as in general
ZH	soft J as in French version of Joliet
KH	gutteral CH as in Scottish version of Loch

2001-02 NHL Player Register

Note: The 2001-02 NHL Player Register lists forwards and defensemen only. Goaltenders are listed separately. The NHL Player Register lists every skater who has played in the NHL. Trades and roster changes are current as of August 20, 2001.

Abbreviations: A – assists; **F%** – faceoff winning percentage; **G** – goals; **GP** – games played; **GT** – game-tying goals scored; **GW** – game-winning goals scored; **H** – HITS: any legal contact by one player on an opposing player that impedes the opposing player's progress; **Lea** – league; MIN – average time on ice; **PIM** – penalties in minutes; **+/–** – plus/minus rating; **PP** – powerplay goals scored; **Pts** – points; **S** – shots on goal; **S%** – shooting percentage; **SB** – shots blocked; **SH** – shorthand goal scored; **TF** – Total faceoffs taken; ***** – league-leading total; ♦ – member of Stanley Cup-winning team.

Prospect Register begins on page 275.
Goaltender Register begins on page 575.
League abbreviations are listed on page 274.

AALTO, Antti
(AL-toh, AN-tee)

Center. Shoots left. 6'2", 210 lbs. Born, Lappeenranta, Finland, March 4, 1975. Anaheim's 6th choice, 134th overall, in 1993 Entry Draft.

Season	Club	League	GP	G	A	Pts	PIM	PP	SH	GW	S	%	+/-	TF	F%	H	SB	Min	Playoffs GP	G	A	Pts	PIM	PP	SH	GW
1991-92	Lappeenranta-2	Finn-Jr.	13	7	9	16	38	....	....	....	....	....	....	....	....	....	....	....	6	3	1	4	6	....	....	....
	Sai-Lappeenranta	Finland-2	20	6	6	12	20	....	....	....	....	....	....	....	....	....	....	....	....	....	....	....	....	....	....	....
1992-93	Lappeenranta-B	Finn-Jr.	3	0	1	1	2	....	....	....	....	....	....	....	....	....	....	....	....	....	....	....	....	....	....	....
	Lappeenranta-2	Finn-Jr.	3	4	2	6	2	....	....	....	....	....	....	....	....	....	....	....	....	....	....	....	....	....	....	....
	TPS Turku	Finn-Jr.	14	6	8	14	18	....	....	....	....	....	....	....	....	....	....	....	6	2	2	4	8	....	....	....
	TPS Turku	Finland	1	0	0	0	0	....	....	....	....	....	....	....	....	....	....	....	....	....	....	....	....	....	....	....
	Sai-Lappeenranta	Finland-2	23	6	8	14	14	....	....	....	....	....	....	....	....	....	....	....	....	....	....	....	....	....	....	....
1993-94	TPS Turku	Finn-Jr.	10	3	8	11	14	....	....	....	....	....	....	....	....	....	....	....	5	1	4	5	12	....	....	....
	Kiekko-67 Turku	Finland-2	4	2	2	4	27	....	....	....	....	....	....	....	....	....	....	....	....	....	....	....	....	....	....	....
	TPS Turku	Finland	33	5	9	14	16	....	....	....	....	....	....	....	....	....	....	....	10	1	1	2	4	....	....	....
1994-95	Kiekko-67 Turku	Finn-Jr.	2	1	2	3	2	....	....	....	....	....	....	....	....	....	....	....	....	....	....	....	....	....	....	....
	Kiekko-67 Turku	Finland-2	1	1	0	1	29	....	....	....	....	....	....	....	....	....	....	....	....	....	....	....	....	....	....	....
	TPS Turku	Finland	44	11	7	18	18	....	....	....	....	....	....	....	....	....	....	....	5	0	1	1	2	....	....	....
1995-96	Kiekko-67 Turku	Finland-2	2	0	2	2	2	....	....	....	....	....	....	....	....	....	....	....	....	....	....	....	....	....	....	....
	TPS Turku	Finland	40	15	16	31	22	....	....	....	....	....	....	....	....	....	....	....	11	3	5	8	14	....	....	....
1996-97	TPS Turku	Finland	44	15	19	34	60	....	....	....	....	....	....	....	....	....	....	....	11	5	6	11	31	....	....	....
	TPS Turku	EuroHL	5	3	3	6	2	....	....	....	....	....	....	....	....	....	....	....	2	1	1	2	0	....	....	....
1997-98	**Anaheim**	**NHL**	**3**	**0**	**0**	**0**	**0**	**0**	**0**	**0**	**1**	**0.0**	**–1**	....	....	....	....	....	....	....	....	....	....	....	....	....
	Cincinnati Ducks	AHL	29	4	9	13	30	....	....	....	....	....	....	....	....	....	....	....	....	....	....	....	....	....	....	....
1998-99	**Anaheim**	**NHL**	**73**	**3**	**5**	**8**	**24**	**2**	**0**	**0**	**61**	**4.9**	**–12**	**22**	**22.7**	**64**	**12**	**9:23**	**4**	**0**	**0**	**0**	**2**	**0**	**0**	**0**
99-2000	**Anaheim**	**NHL**	**63**	**7**	**11**	**18**	**26**	**1**	**0**	**1**	**102**	**6.9**	**–13**	**827**	**51.0**	**83**	**12**	**13:11**	....	....	....	....	....	....	....	....
2000-01	**Anaheim**	**NHL**	**12**	**1**	**1**	**2**	**2**	**0**	**0**	**0**	**18**	**5.6**	**1**	**57**	**40.4**	**19**	**1**	**10:37**	....	....	....	....	....	....	....	....
	Cincinnati Ducks	AHL	40	14	26	40	39	....	....	....	....	....	....	....	....	....	....	....	3	2	1	3	2	....	....	....
	NHL Totals		**151**	**11**	**17**	**28**	**52**	**3**	**0**	**1**	**182**	**6.0**		**906**	**49.7**	**166**	**25**	**11:06**	**4**	**0**	**0**	**0**	**2**	**0**	**0**	**0**

ADAMS, Bryan
(A-duhms, BRIGH-uhn) **ATL.**

Left wing. Shoots left. 6', 185 lbs. Born, Fort St. James, B.C., March 20, 1977.

Season	Club	League	GP	G	A	Pts	PIM	PP	SH	GW	S	%	+/-	TF	F%	H	SB	Min	Playoffs GP	G	A	Pts	PIM	PP	SH	GW
1994-95	Prince George	RMJHL	48	37	53	90	....	....	....	....	....	....	....	....	....	....	....	....	....	....	....	....	....	....	....	....
1995-96	Michigan State	CCHA	42	3	8	11	12	....	....	....	....	....	....	....	....	....	....	....	....	....	....	....	....	....	....	....
1996-97	Michigan State	CCHA	29	7	7	14	51	....	....	....	....	....	....	....	....	....	....	....	....	....	....	....	....	....	....	....
1997-98	Michigan State	CCHA	31	9	21	30	39	....	....	....	....	....	....	....	....	....	....	....	....	....	....	....	....	....	....	....
1998-99	Michigan State	CCHA	42	21	16	37	56	....	....	....	....	....	....	....	....	....	....	....	....	....	....	....	....	....	....	....
99-2000	**Atlanta**	**NHL**	**2**	**0**	**0**	**0**	**0**	**0**	**0**	**0**	**1**	**0.0**	**–1**	**0**	**0.0**	**5**	**0**	**10:57**	....	....	....	....	....	....	....	....
	Orlando	IHL	64	16	18	34	27	....	....	....	....	....	....	....	....	....	....	....	4	0	1	1	6	....	....	....
2000-01	**Atlanta**	**NHL**	**9**	**0**	**1**	**1**	**2**	**0**	**0**	**0**	**3**	**0.0**	**–4**	**1**	**0.0**	**8**	**3**	**9:37**	....	....	....	....	....	....	....	....
	Orlando	IHL	61	18	28	46	43	....	....	....	....	....	....	....	....	....	....	....	16	3	4	7	20	....	....	....
	NHL Totals		**11**	**0**	**1**	**1**	**2**	**0**	**0**	**0**	**4**	**0.0**		**1**	**0.0**	**13**	**3**	**9:51**	....	....	....	....	....	....	....	....

Signed as a free agent by **Atlanta**, July 6, 1999.

ADAMS, Craig
(A-duhms, KRAYG) **CAR.**

Right wing. Shoots right. 6', 200 lbs. Born, Brunei, Borneo, April 26, 1977. Hartford's 9th choice, 223rd overall, in 1996 Entry Draft.

Season	Club	League	GP	G	A	Pts	PIM	PP	SH	GW	S	%	+/-	TF	F%	H	SB	Min	Playoffs GP	G	A	Pts	PIM	PP	SH	GW
1994-95	Calgary Canucks	AJHL	STATISTICS NOT AVAILABLE																							
1995-96	Harvard University	ECAC	34	8	9	17	56	....	....	....	....	....	....	....	....	....	....	....	....	....	....	....	....	....	....	....
1996-97	Harvard University	ECAC	32	6	4	10	36	....	....	....	....	....	....	....	....	....	....	....	....	....	....	....	....	....	....	....
1997-98	Harvard University	ECAC	12	6	6	12	12	....	....	....	....	....	....	....	....	....	....	....	....	....	....	....	....	....	....	....
1998-99	Harvard University	ECAC	31	9	14	23	53	....	....	....	....	....	....	....	....	....	....	....	....	....	....	....	....	....	....	....
99-2000	Cincinnati	IHL	73	12	12	24	124	....	....	....	....	....	....	....	....	....	....	....	8	0	1	1	14	....	....	....
2000-01	**Carolina**	**NHL**	**44**	**1**	**0**	**1**	**20**	**0**	**0**	**0**	**15**	**6.7**	**–7**	**4**	**25.0**	**61**	**5**	**4:30**	**3**	**0**	**0**	**0**	**0**	**0**	**0**	**0**
	Cincinnati	IHL	4	0	1	1	9	....	....	....	....	....	....	....	....	....	....	....	1	0	0	0	2	....	....	....
	NHL Totals		**44**	**1**	**0**	**1**	**20**	**0**	**0**	**0**	**15**	**6.7**		**4**	**25.0**	**61**	**5**	**4:30**	**3**	**0**	**0**	**0**	**0**	**0**	**0**	**0**

Rights transferred to **Carolina** after **Hartford** franchise relocated, June 25, 1997. • Missed majority of 1997-98 season recovering from shoulder injury suffered in game vs. University of Wisconsin, December 27, 1997.

ADAMS, Greg
(A-duhms, GREHG)

Left wing. Shoots left. 6'3", 195 lbs. Born, Nelson, B.C., August 15, 1963.

Season	Club	League	GP	G	A	Pts	PIM	PP	SH	GW	S	%	+/-	TF	F%	H	SB	Min	Playoffs GP	G	A	Pts	PIM	PP	SH	GW
1980-81	Kelowna Bucks	BCJHL	48	40	50	90	16	....	....	....	....	....	....	....	....	....	....	....	....	....	....	....	....	....	....	....
1981-82	Kelowna Bucks	BCJHL	45	31	42	73	24	....	....	....	....	....	....	....	....	....	....	....	....	....	....	....	....	....	....	....
1982-83	North-Arizona	ACHA	29	14	21	35	46	....	....	....	....	....	....	....	....	....	....	....	....	....	....	....	....	....	....	....
1983-84	North-Arizona	ACHA	26	44	29	73	24	....	....	....	....	....	....	....	....	....	....	....	....	....	....	....	....	....	....	....
1984-85	**New Jersey**	**NHL**	**36**	**12**	**9**	**21**	**14**	**5**	**0**	**0**	**63**	**19.0**	**–14**	....	....	....	....	....	....	....	....	....	....	....	....	....
	Maine Mariners	AHL	41	15	20	35	12	....	....	....	....	....	....	....	....	....	....	....	11	3	4	7	0	....	....	....
1985-86	**New Jersey**	**NHL**	**78**	**35**	**42**	**77**	**30**	**10**	**0**	**2**	**202**	**17.3**	**–7**	....	....	....	....	....	....	....	....	....	....	....	....	....

			Regular Season																Playoffs							
Season	Club	League	GP	G	A	Pts	PIM	PP	SH	GW	S	%	+/-	TF	F%	H	SB	Min	GP	G	A	Pts	PIM	PP	SH	GW
1986-87	**New Jersey**	**NHL**	**72**	**20**	**27**	**47**	**19**	**6**	**0**	**1**	**143**	**14.0**	**–16**	....	....	....	....	....	....	....	....	....	....	....	....	....
1987-88	**Vancouver**	**NHL**	**80**	**36**	**40**	**76**	**30**	**12**	**0**	**3**	**227**	**15.9**	**–24**	....	....	....	....	....	....	....	....	....	....	....	....	....
1988-89	**Vancouver**	**NHL**	**61**	**19**	**14**	**33**	**24**	**9**	**0**	**2**	**144**	**13.2**	**–21**	....	....	....	....	....	**7**	**2**	**3**	**5**	**2**	**0**	**0**	**0**
1989-90	**Vancouver**	**NHL**	**65**	**30**	**20**	**50**	**18**	**13**	**0**	**1**	**181**	**16.6**	**–8**	....	....	....	....	....	....	....	....	....	....	....	....	....
1990-91	**Vancouver**	**NHL**	**55**	**21**	**24**	**45**	**10**	**5**	**1**	**2**	**148**	**14.2**	**–5**	....	....	....	....	....	**5**	**0**	**0**	**0**	**2**	**0**	**0**	**0**
1991-92	**Vancouver**	**NHL**	**76**	**30**	**27**	**57**	**26**	**13**	**1**	**5**	**184**	**16.3**	**8**	....	....	....	....	....	**6**	**0**	**2**	**2**	**4**	**0**	**0**	**0**
1992-93	**Vancouver**	**NHL**	**53**	**25**	**31**	**56**	**14**	**6**	**1**	**3**	**124**	**20.2**	**31**	....	....	....	....	....	**12**	**7**	**6**	**13**	**6**	**5**	**0**	**1**
1993-94	**Vancouver**	**NHL**	**68**	**13**	**24**	**37**	**20**	**5**	**1**	**2**	**139**	**9.4**	**–1**	....	....	....	....	....	**23**	**6**	**8**	**14**	**2**	**2**	**0**	**2**
1994-95	**Vancouver**	**NHL**	**31**	**5**	**10**	**15**	**12**	**2**	**2**	**0**	**56**	**8.9**	**1**	....	....	....	....	....	....	....	....	....	....	....	....	....
	Dallas	**NHL**	**12**	**3**	**3**	**6**	**4**	**1**	**0**	**0**	**16**	**18.8**	**–4**	....	....	....	....	....	**5**	**2**	**0**	**2**	**0**	**0**	**0**	**0**
1995-96	**Dallas**	**NHL**	**66**	**22**	**21**	**43**	**33**	**11**	**1**	**1**	**140**	**15.7**	**–21**	....	....	....	....	....	....	....	....	....	....	....	....	....
1996-97	**Dallas**	**NHL**	**50**	**21**	**15**	**36**	**2**	**5**	**0**	**4**	**113**	**18.6**	**27**	....	....	....	....	....	**3**	**0**	**1**	**1**	**0**	**0**	**0**	**0**
1997-98	**Dallas**	**NHL**	**49**	**14**	**18**	**32**	**20**	**7**	**0**	**1**	**75**	**18.7**	**11**	....	....	....	....	....	**12**	**2**	**2**	**4**	**0**	**0**	**0**	**2**
1998-99	**Phoenix**	**NHL**	**75**	**19**	**24**	**43**	**26**	**5**	**0**	**3**	**176**	**10.8**	**–1**	**295**	**52.9**	**26**	**15**	**17:22**	**3**	**0**	**1**	**1**	**0**	**0**	**0**	**0**
99-2000	**Phoenix**	**NHL**	**69**	**19**	**27**	**46**	**14**	**5**	**0**	**0**	**129**	**14.7**	**–1**	**141**	**45.4**	**27**	**15**	**16:58**	**5**	**0**	**0**	**0**	**0**	**0**	**0**	**0**
2000-01	**Florida**	**NHL**	**60**	**11**	**12**	**23**	**10**	**2**	**0**	**1**	**66**	**16.7**	**–3**	**26**	**46.2**	**20**	**18**	**14:23**	....	....	....	....	....	....	....	....
	NHL Totals		**1056**	**355**	**388**	**743**	**326**	**122**	**7**	**31**	**2326**	**15.3**		**462**	**50.2**	**73**	**48**	**16:21**	**81**	**19**	**23**	**42**	**16**	**7**	**0**	**5**

Played in NHL All-Star Game (1988) • Family name originally Adamakos

Signed as a free agent by **New Jersey**, June 25, 1984. Traded to **Vancouver** by **New Jersey** with Kirk McLean and New Jersey's 2nd round choice (Leif Rohlin) in 1988 Entry Draft for Patrik Sundstrom and Vancouver's 2nd (Jeff Christian) and 4th (Matt Ruchty) round choices in 1988 Entry Draft, September 15, 1987. Traded to **Dallas** by **Vancouver** with Dan Kesa and Vancouver's 5th round choice (later traded to LA Kings - LA Kings selected Jason Morgan) in 1995 Entry Draft for Russ Courtnall, April 7, 1995. Signed as a free agent by **Phoenix**, September 1, 1998. Signed as a free agent by **Florida**, November 6, 2000.

ADAMS, Kevyn

(A-duhms, KEH-vihn) **FLA.**

Center. Shoots right. 6'1", 195 lbs. Born, Washington, D.C., October 8, 1974. Boston's 1st choice, 25th overall, in 1993 Entry Draft.

1990-91	Niagara Scenics	NAJHL	55	17	20	37	24	....	....	....	....	....	....	....	....	....	....	....	....	....	....	....	....	....	....	....
1991-92	Niagara Scenics	NAJHL	40	25	33	58	51	....	....	....	....	....	....	....	....	....	....	....	....	....	....	....	....	....	....	....
1992-93	U. of Miami-Ohio	CCHA	40	17	15	32	18	....	....	....	....	....	....	....	....	....	....	....	....	....	....	....	....	....	....	....
1993-94	U. of Miami-Ohio	CCHA	36	15	28	43	24	....	....	....	....	....	....	....	....	....	....	....	....	....	....	....	....	....	....	....
1994-95	U. of Miami-Ohio	CCHA	38	20	29	49	30	....	....	....	....	....	....	....	....	....	....	....	....	....	....	....	....	....	....	....
1995-96	U. of Miami-Ohio	CCHA	36	17	30	47	30	....	....	....	....	....	....	....	....	....	....	....	....	....	....	....	....	....	....	....
1996-97	Grand Rapids	IHL	82	22	25	47	47	....	....	....	....	....	....	....	....	....	....	....	5	1	1	2	4	....	....	....
1997-98	**Toronto**	**NHL**	**5**	**0**	**0**	**0**	**7**	**0**	**0**	**0**	**3**	**0.0**	**0**	....	....	....	....	....	....	....	....	....	....	....	....	....
	St. John's Leafs	AHL	59	17	20	37	99	....	....	....	....	....	....	....	....	....	....	....	4	0	0	0	4	....	....	....
1998-99	**Toronto**	**NHL**	**1**	**0**	**0**	**0**	**0**	**0**	**0**	**0**	**1**	**0.0**	**0**	**9**	**44.4**	**2**	**0**	**7:56**	**7**	**0**	**2**	**2**	**14**	**0**	**0**	**0**
	St. John's Leafs	AHL	80	15	35	50	85	....	....	....	....	....	....	....	....	....	....	....	5	2	0	2	4	....	....	....
99-2000	**Toronto**	**NHL**	**52**	**5**	**8**	**13**	**39**	**0**	**0**	**0**	**70**	**7.1**	**–7**	**604**	**56.5**	**78**	**13**	**12:23**	**12**	**1**	**0**	**1**	**7**	**0**	**1**	**0**
	St. John's Leafs	AHL	23	6	11	17	24	....	....	....	....	....	....	....	....	....	....	....	....	....	....	....	....	....	....	....
2000-01	**Columbus**	**NHL**	**66**	**8**	**12**	**20**	**52**	**0**	**0**	**1**	**84**	**9.5**	**–4**	**1152**	**57.4**	**104**	**41**	**15:18**	....	....	....	....	....	....	....	....
	Florida	**NHL**	**12**	**3**	**6**	**9**	**2**	**0**	**0**	**2**	**21**	**14.3**	**7**	**198**	**47.5**	**16**	**5**	**17:25**	....	....	....	....	....	....	....	....
	NHL Totals		**136**	**16**	**26**	**42**	**100**	**0**	**0**	**3**	**179**	**8.9**		**1963**	**56.0**	**200**	**59**	**14:17**	**19**	**1**	**2**	**3**	**21**	**0**	**1**	**0**

CCHA Second All-Star Team (1995)

Signed as a free agent by **Toronto**, August 7, 1997. Selected by **Columbus** from **Toronto** in Expansion Draft, June 23, 2000. Traded to **Florida** by **Columbus** with future considerations for Ray Whitney, March 13, 2001.

AFANASENKOV, Dmitry

(a-fahn-A-sehn-kahv, dih-MEE-tree) **T.B.**

Left wing. Shoots right. 6'2", 200 lbs. Born, Arkhangelsk, USSR, May 12, 1980. Tampa Bay's 3rd choice, 72nd overall, in 1998 Entry Draft.

1995-96	Torpedo Yaroslavl	Russia-Jr.	35	28	16	44	8	....	....	....	....	....	....	....	....	....	....	....	....	....	....	....	....	....	....	....
	Torpedo Yaroslavl	Russia-2	25	10	5	15	10	....	....	....	....	....	....	....	....	....	....	....	....	....	....	....	....	....	....	....
1996-97	HC Yaroslavl-2	Russia-3	45	20	15	35	14	....	....	....	....	....	....	....	....	....	....	....	....	....	....	....	....	....	....	....
1997-98	Torpedo Yaroslavl	Russia-2	48	14	7	21	20	....	....	....	....	....	....	....	....	....	....	....	....	....	....	....	....	....	....	....
1998-99	Moncton Wildcats	QMJHL	15	5	5	10	12	....	....	....	....	....	....	....	....	....	....	....	....	....	....	....	....	....	....	....
	Sherbrooke	QMJHL	51	23	30	53	22	....	....	....	....	....	....	....	....	....	....	....	13	10	6	16	6	....	....	....
99-2000	Sherbrooke	QMJHL	60	56	43	99	70	....	....	....	....	....	....	....	....	....	....	....	5	3	2	5	4	....	....	....
2000-01	**Tampa Bay**	**NHL**	**9**	**1**	**1**	**2**	**4**	**0**	**0**	**0**	**8**	**12.5**	**1**	**7**	**28.6**	**4**	**2**	**11:24**	....	....	....	....	....	....	....	....
	Detroit Vipers	IHL	65	15	22	37	26	....	....	....	....	....	....	....	....	....	....	....	....	....	....	....	....	....	....	....
	NHL Totals		**9**	**1**	**1**	**2**	**4**	**0**	**0**	**0**	**8**	**12.5**		**7**	**28.6**	**4**	**2**	**11:24**	....	....	....	....	....	....	....	....

AFINOGENOV, Maxim

(ah-fihn-ah-GEHN-ahf, mahx-EEM) **BUF.**

Right wing. Shoots left. 6', 195 lbs. Born, Moscow, USSR, September 4, 1979. Buffalo's 3rd choice, 69th overall, in 1997 Entry Draft.

1996-97	Dynamo Moscow	Russia	29	6	5	11	10	....	....	....	....	....	....	....	....	....	....	....	4	0	2	2	0	....	....	....
	Dynamo Moscow	EuroHL	3	0	0	0	0	....	....	....	....	....	....	....	....	....	....	....	3	1	0	1	4	....	....	....
1997-98	Dynamo Moscow	Russia	35	10	5	15	53	....	....	....	....	....	....	....	....	....	....	....	....	....	....	....	....	....	....	....
	Dynamo Moscow	EuroHL	6	3	1	4	27	....	....	....	....	....	....	....	....	....	....	....	....	....	....	....	....	....	....	....
1998-99	Dynamo Moscow	Russia	38	8	13	21	24	....	....	....	....	....	....	....	....	....	....	....	16	*10	6	*16	14	....	....	....
	Dynamo Moscow	EuroHL	5	3	5	8	29	....	....	....	....	....	....	....	....	....	....	....	4	2	1	3	27	....	....	....
99-2000	**Buffalo**	**NHL**	**65**	**16**	**18**	**34**	**41**	**2**	**0**	**2**	**128**	**12.5**	**–4**	**0**	**0.0**	**32**	**10**	**13:09**	**5**	**0**	**1**	**1**	**2**	**0**	**0**	**0**
	Rochester	AHL	15	6	12	18	8	....	....	....	....	....	....	....	....	....	....	....	8	3	1	4	4	....	....	....
2000-01	**Buffalo**	**NHL**	**78**	**14**	**22**	**36**	**40**	**3**	**0**	**5**	**190**	**7.4**	**1**	**2**	**0.0**	**33**	**17**	**14:32**	**11**	**2**	**3**	**5**	**4**	**0**	**0**	**0**
	NHL Totals		**143**	**30**	**40**	**70**	**81**	**5**	**0**	**7**	**318**	**9.4**		**2**	**0.0**	**65**	**27**	**13:54**	**16**	**2**	**4**	**6**	**6**	**0**	**0**	**0**

AITKEN, Johnathan

(ATE-kin, JAWN-uh-thuhn)

Defense. Shoots left. 6'4", 215 lbs. Born, Edmonton, Alta., May 24, 1978. Boston's 1st choice, 8th overall, in 1996 Entry Draft.

1993-94	Sherwood Park	AMHL	31	4	9	13	54	....	....	....	....	....	....	....	....	....	....	....	....	....	....	....	....	....	....	....
1994-95	Medicine Hat	WHL	53	0	5	5	71	....	....	....	....	....	....	....	....	....	....	....	5	0	0	0	0	....	....	....
1995-96	Medicine Hat	WHL	71	6	14	20	131	....	....	....	....	....	....	....	....	....	....	....	5	1	0	1	6	....	....	....
1996-97	Brandon	WHL	65	4	18	22	211	....	....	....	....	....	....	....	....	....	....	....	6	0	0	0	4	....	....	....
1997-98	Brandon	WHL	69	9	25	34	183	....	....	....	....	....	....	....	....	....	....	....	18	0	8	8	67	....	....	....
1998-99	Providence Bruins	AHL	65	2	9	11	92	....	....	....	....	....	....	....	....	....	....	....	13	0	0	0	17	....	....	....
99-2000	**Boston**	**NHL**	**3**	**0**	**0**	**0**	**0**	**0**	**0**	**0**	**2**	**0.0**	**–3**	**0**	**0.0**	**5**	**3**	**18:57**	....	....	....	....	....	....	....	....
	Providence Bruins	AHL	70	2	12	14	121	....	....	....	....	....	....	....	....	....	....	....	11	1	0	1	26	....	....	....
2000-01	Sparta Praha	Cze-Rep	24	0	3	3	62	....	....	....	....	....	....	....	....	....	....	....	....	....	....	....	....	....	....	....
	NHL Totals		**3**	**0**	**0**	**0**	**0**	**0**	**0**	**0**	**2**	**0.0**		**0**	**0.0**	**5**	**3**	**18:57**	....	....	....	....	....	....	....	....

WHL East Second All-Star Team (1998)

ALATALO, Mika

(a-luh-TAH-loh, MEE-kuh)

Left wing. Shoots left. 6', 202 lbs. Born, Oulu, Finland, June 11, 1971. Winnipeg's 11th choice, 203rd overall, in 1990 Entry Draft.

1988-89	KooKoo Kouvola	Finland	34	8	6	14	10	....	....	....	....	....	....	....	....	....	....	....	....	....	....	....	....	....	....	....
1989-90	KooKoo Kouvola	Finland	41	3	5	8	22	....	....	....	....	....	....	....	....	....	....	....	....	....	....	....	....	....	....	....
1990-91	Lukko Rauma	Finland	39	10	1	11	10	....	....	....	....	....	....	....	....	....	....	....	....	....	....	....	....	....	....	....
1991-92	Lukko Rauma	Finland	43	20	17	37	32	....	....	....	....	....	....	....	....	....	....	....	2	0	0	0	0	....	....	....
1992-93	Lukko Rauma	Finland	48	16	19	35	38	....	....	....	....	....	....	....	....	....	....	....	3	0	0	0	0	....	....	....
1993-94	Lukko Rauma	Finland	45	19	15	34	77	....	....	....	....	....	....	....	....	....	....	....	9	2	2	4	4	....	....	....
	Finland	Olympics	7	2	1	3	2	....	....	....	....	....	....	....	....	....	....	....	....	....	....	....	....	....	....	....
1994-95	TPS Turku	Finland	44	23	13	36	79	....	....	....	....	....	....	....	....	....	....	....	13	2	5	7	8	....	....	....
1995-96	TPS Turku	Finland	49	19	18	37	44	....	....	....	....	....	....	....	....	....	....	....	11	3	4	7	8	....	....	....
1996-97	Lulea HF	Sweden	50	19	18	37	54	....	....	....	....	....	....	....	....	....	....	....	10	2	3	5	22	....	....	....
	Lulea HF	EuroHL	6	4	3	7	4	....	....	....	....	....	....	....	....	....	....	....	....	....	....	....	....	....	....	....
1997-98	Lulea HF	Sweden	45	14	10	24	22	....	....	....	....	....	....	....	....	....	....	....	2	0	0	0	0	....	....	....
	Lulea HF	EuroHL	6	2	1	3	6	....	....	....	....	....	....	....	....	....	....	....	....	....	....	....	....	....	....	....
1998-99	TPS Turku	Finland	53	14	23	37	44	....	....	....	....	....	....	....	....	....	....	....	10	6	3	9	6	....	....	....

			Regular Season																Playoffs							
Season	Club	League	GP	G	A	Pts	PIM	PP	SH	GW	S	%	+/-	TF	F%	H	SB	Min	GP	G	A	Pts	PIM	PP	SH	GW
99-2000	Phoenix	NHL	82	10	17	27	36	1	0	1	107	9.3	–3	3	0.0	92	17	12:37	5	0	0	0	2	0	0	0
2000-01	Phoenix	NHL	70	7	12	19	22	0	0	1	64	10.9	1	2	0.0	78	13	10:59								
	NHL Totals		152	17	29	46	58	1	0	2	171	9.9		5	0.0	170	30	11:52	5	0	0	0	2	0	0	0

Rights transferred to **Phoenix** after **Winnipeg** franchise relocated, July 1, 1996.

ALBELIN, Tommy

(AHL-buh-LEEN,TAW-mee) **N.J.**

Defense. Shoots left. 6'1", 195 lbs. Born, Stockholm, Sweden, May 21, 1964. Quebec's 7th choice, 158th overall, in 1983 Entry Draft.

Season	Club	League	GP	G	A	Pts	PIM	PP	SH	GW	S	%	+/-	TF	F%	H	SB	Min	GP	G	A	Pts	PIM	PP	SH	GW
1980-81	Stocksunds IF	Sweden-3	18	6	1	7																				
1981-82	Stocksunds IF	Sweden-3	22	6	2	8																				
1982-83	Djurgardens IF	Sweden	19	2	5	7	4												6	1	0	1	2			
1983-84	Djurgardens IF	Sweden	30	9	5	14	26												4	0	1	1	2			
1984-85	Djurgardens IF	Sweden	32	9	8	17	22												8	2	1	3	4			
1985-86	Djurgardens IF	Sweden	35	4	8	12	26																			
1986-87	Djurgardens IF	Sweden	33	7	5	12	49												2	0	0	0	0			
1987-88	**Quebec**	**NHL**	**60**	**3**	**23**	**26**	**47**	**0**	**0**	**0**	**98**	**3.1**	**–7**													
1988-89	**Quebec**	**NHL**	**14**	**2**	**4**	**6**	**27**	**1**	**0**	**1**	**16**	**12.5**	**–6**													
	Halifax Citadels	AHL	8	2	5	7	4																			
	New Jersey	**NHL**	**46**	**7**	**24**	**31**	**40**	**1**	**1**	**1**	**82**	**8.5**	**18**													
1989-90	**New Jersey**	**NHL**	**68**	**6**	**23**	**29**	**63**	**4**	**0**	**0**	**125**	**4.8**	**–1**													
1990-91	**New Jersey**	**NHL**	**47**	**2**	**12**	**14**	**44**	**1**	**0**	**0**	**66**	**3.0**	**1**						**3**	**0**	**1**	**1**	**2**	**0**	**0**	**0**
	Utica Devils	AHL	14	4	2	6	10																			
1991-92	**New Jersey**	**NHL**	**19**	**0**	**4**	**4**	**4**	**0**	**0**	**0**	**18**	**0.0**	**7**						**1**	**1**	**1**	**2**	**0**	**0**	**0**	**0**
	Utica Devils	AHL	11	4	6	10	4																			
1992-93	**New Jersey**	**NHL**	**36**	**1**	**5**	**6**	**14**	**1**	**0**	**1**	**33**	**3.0**	**0**						**5**	**2**	**0**	**2**	**0**	**1**	**0**	**1**
1993-94	**New Jersey**	**NHL**	**62**	**2**	**17**	**19**	**36**	**1**	**0**	**1**	**62**	**3.2**	**20**						**20**	**2**	**5**	**7**	**14**	**1**	**0**	**1**
	Albany River Rats	AHL	4	0	2	2	17																			
1994-95♦	**New Jersey**	**NHL**	**48**	**5**	**10**	**15**	**20**	**2**	**0**	**0**	**60**	**8.3**	**9**						**20**	**1**	**7**	**8**	**2**	**0**	**0**	**0**
1995-96	**New Jersey**	**NHL**	**53**	**1**	**12**	**13**	**14**	**0**	**0**	**0**	**90**	**1.1**	**0**													
	Calgary	**NHL**	**20**	**0**	**1**	**1**	**4**	**0**	**0**	**0**	**31**	**0.0**	**1**						**4**	**0**	**0**	**0**	**0**	**0**	**0**	**0**
1996-97	**Calgary**	**NHL**	**72**	**4**	**11**	**15**	**14**	**2**	**0**	**0**	**103**	**3.9**	**–8**													
1997-98	**Calgary**	**NHL**	**69**	**2**	**17**	**19**	**32**	**1**	**0**	**2**	**88**	**2.3**	**9**													
	Sweden	Olympics	3	0	0	0	4																			
1998-99	**Calgary**	**NHL**	**60**	**1**	**5**	**6**	**8**	**0**	**0**	**0**	**54**	**1.9**	**–11**	**1**	**0.0**	**34**	**55**	**19:08**								
99-2000	**Calgary**	**NHL**	**41**	**4**	**6**	**10**	**12**	**1**	**1**	**1**	**37**	**10.8**	**–3**	**0**	**0.0**	**21**	**60**	**21:35**								
2000-01	**Calgary**	**NHL**	**77**	**1**	**19**	**20**	**22**	**1**	**0**	**0**	**69**	**1.4**	**2**	**0**	**0.0**	**27**	**69**	**20:53**								
	NHL Totals		**792**	**41**	**193**	**234**	**401**	**16**	**2**	**7**	**1032**	**4.0**		**1**	**0.0**	**82**	**184**	**20:27**	**53**	**6**	**14**	**20**	**18**	**2**	**0**	**2**

Traded to **New Jersey** by **Quebec** for New Jersey's 4th round choice (Niklas Andersson) in 1989 Entry Draft, December 12, 1988. Traded to **Calgary** by **New Jersey** with Cale Hulse and Jocelyn Lemieux for Phil Housley and Dan Keczmer, February 26, 1996. Signed as a free agent by **New Jersey**, July 9, 2001.

ALDRIDGE, Keith

(AHL-drihj, KEETH)

Defense. Shoots right. 5'11", 185 lbs. Born, Detroit, MI, July 20, 1973.

Season	Club	League	GP	G	A	Pts	PIM	PP	SH	GW	S	%	+/-	TF	F%	H	SB	Min	GP	G	A	Pts	PIM	PP	SH	GW
1991-92	Rochester	USHL	STATISTICS NOT AVAILABLE																							
1992-93	Lake Superior	CCHA	37	3	11	14	30																			
1993-94	Lake Superior	CCHA	45	10	24	34	86																			
1994-95	Lake Superior	CCHA	40	10	31	41	89																			
1995-96	Lake Superior	CCHA	38	14	36	50	88																			
	Baltimore Bandits	AHL	7	0	2	2	2																			
1996-97	Baltimore Bandits	AHL	51	4	9	13	92												3	0	0	0	4			
1997-98	Detroit Vipers	IHL	79	13	21	34	89												23	1	9	10	67			
1998-99	Detroit Vipers	IHL	66	15	28	43	130												11	2	7	9	49			
99-2000	**Dallas**	**NHL**	**4**	**0**	**0**	**0**	**0**	**0**	**0**	**0**	**6**	**0.0**	**1**	**1**	**100.0**	**9**	**1**	**11:05**								
	Michigan K-Wings	IHL	55	2	10	12	55																			
2000-01	Frankfurt Lions	DEL	39	9	12	21	141																			
	Grand Rapids	IHL	36	3	8	11	99												10	0	2	2	8			
	NHL Totals		**4**	**0**	**0**	**0**	**0**	**0**	**0**	**0**	**6**	**0.0**		**1**	**100.0**	**9**	**1**	**11:05**								

USHL First All-Star Team (1992) • CCHA Second All-Star Team (1994) • CCHA First All-Star Team (1995, 1996) • NCAA West Second All-American Team (1995) • NCAA West First All-American Team (1996)

Signed as a free agent by **Dallas**, September 1, 1999. Signed as a free agent by **Grand Rapids** (IHL), January 26, 2001. Signed as a free agent by **Eisbaren Berlin** (DEL), July 27, 2001.

ALFREDSSON, Daniel

(AHL-frehd-suhn, DAN-yehl) **OTT.**

Right wing. Shoots right. 5'11", 195 lbs. Born, Gothenburg, Sweden, December 11, 1972. Ottawa's 5th choice, 133rd overall, in 1994 Entry Draft.

Season	Club	League	GP	G	A	Pts	PIM	PP	SH	GW	S	%	+/-	TF	F%	H	SB	Min	GP	G	A	Pts	PIM	PP	SH	GW
1990-91	IF Molndal	Sweden-2	3	0	0	0	2												8	4	4	8	4			
1991-92	IF Molndal	Sweden-2	32	12	8	20	43																			
1992-93	Vastra Frolunda	Sweden	20	1	5	6	8																			
1993-94	Vastra Frolunda	Sweden	39	20	10	30	18												4	1	1	2				
1994-95	Vastra Frolunda	Sweden	22	7	11	18	22																			
1995-96	**Ottawa**	**NHL**	**82**	**26**	**35**	**61**	**28**	**8**	**2**	**3**	**212**	**12.3**	**–18**													
1996-97	**Ottawa**	**NHL**	**76**	**24**	**47**	**71**	**30**	**11**	**1**	**1**	**247**	**9.7**	**5**						**7**	**5**	**2**	**7**	**6**	**3**	**0**	**2**
1997-98	**Ottawa**	**NHL**	**55**	**17**	**28**	**45**	**18**	**7**	**0**	**7**	**149**	**11.4**	**7**						**11**	**7**	**2**	**9**	**20**	**2**	**1**	**1**
	Sweden	Olympics	4	2	3	5	2																			
1998-99	**Ottawa**	**NHL**	**58**	**11**	**22**	**33**	**14**	**3**	**0**	**5**	**163**	**6.7**	**8**	**7**	**57.1**	**67**	**21**	**17:22**	**4**	**1**	**2**	**3**	**4**	**1**	**0**	**0**
99-2000	**Ottawa**	**NHL**	**57**	**21**	**38**	**59**	**28**	**4**	**2**	**0**	**164**	**12.8**	**11**	**3**	**66.7**	**58**	**29**	**18:45**	**6**	**1**	**3**	**4**	**2**	**1**	**0**	**0**
2000-01	**Ottawa**	**NHL**	**68**	**24**	**46**	**70**	**30**	**10**	**0**	**3**	**206**	**11.7**	**11**	**8**	**50.0**	**85**	**26**	**18:47**	**4**	**1**	**0**	**1**	**2**	**0**	**0**	**0**
	NHL Totals		**396**	**123**	**216**	**339**	**148**	**43**	**5**	**19**	**1141**	**10.8**		**18**	**55.6**	**210**	**76**	**18:19**	**32**	**15**	**9**	**24**	**34**	**7**	**1**	**3**

NHL All-Rookie Team (1996) • Won Calder Memorial Trophy (1996) • Played in NHL All-Star Game (1996, 1997, 1998)

ALLEN, Bryan

(AHL-lehn, BRIGH-uhn) **VAN.**

Defense. Shoots left. 6'4", 215 lbs. Born, Kingston, Ont., August 21, 1980. Vancouver's 1st choice, 4th overall, in 1998 Entry Draft.

Season	Club	League	GP	G	A	Pts	PIM	PP	SH	GW	S	%	+/-	TF	F%	H	SB	Min	GP	G	A	Pts	PIM	PP	SH	GW
1995-96	Ernestown Jets	OJHL-C	36	1	16	17	71																			
1996-97	Oshawa Generals	OHL	60	2	4	6	76												18	1	3	4	26			
1997-98	Oshawa Generals	OHL	48	6	13	19	126												5	0	5	5	18			
1998-99	Oshawa Generals	OHL	37	7	15	22	77												15	0	3	3	26			
99-2000	Oshawa Generals	OHL	3	0	2	2	12												3	0	0	0	13			
	Syracuse Crunch	AHL	9	1	1	2	11												2	0	0	0	2			
2000-01	**Vancouver**	**NHL**	**6**	**0**	**0**	**0**	**0**	**0**	**0**	**0**	**2**	**0.0**	**0**	**0**	**0.0**	**9**	**6**	**9:20**	**2**	**0**	**0**	**0**	**2**	**0**	**0**	**0**
	Kansas City	IHL	75	5	20	25	99																			
	NHL Totals		**6**	**0**	**0**	**0**	**0**	**0**	**0**	**0**	**2**	**0.0**		**0**	**0.0**	**9**	**6**	**9:20**	**2**	**0**	**0**	**0**	**2**	**0**	**0**	**0**

OHL First All-Star Team (1999) • Missed majority of 1999-2000 season recovering from knee injury suffered in training camp, September 21, 1999.

ALLISON, Jamie

(AHL-lih-sohn, JAY-mee) **CHI.**

Defense. Shoots left. 6'1", 200 lbs. Born, Lindsay, Ont., May 13, 1975. Calgary's 2nd choice, 44th overall, in 1993 Entry Draft.

Season	Club	League	GP	G	A	Pts	PIM	PP	SH	GW	S	%	+/-	TF	F%	H	SB	Min	GP	G	A	Pts	PIM	PP	SH	GW
1990-91	Waterloo Siskins	OJHL-B	38	3	8	11	91																			
1991-92	Windsor Spitfires	OHL	59	4	8	12	70												4	1	1	2	2			
1992-93	Detroit Jr. Wings	OHL	61	0	13	13	64												15	2	5	7	23			
1993-94	Detroit Jr. Wings	OHL	40	2	22	24	69												17	2	9	11	35			
1994-95	Detroit Jr. Wings	OHL	50	1	14	15	119												18	2	7	9	35			
	Calgary	**NHL**	**1**	**0**	**0**	**0**	**0**	**0**	**0**	**0**	**0**	**0.0**	**0**													
1995-96	Saint John Flames	AHL	71	3	16	19	223												14	0	2	2	16			
1996-97	**Calgary**	**NHL**	**20**	**0**	**0**	**0**	**35**	**0**	**0**	**0**	**8**	**0.0**	**–4**													
	Saint John Flames	AHL	46	3	6	9	139												5	0	1	1	4			
1997-98	**Calgary**	**NHL**	**43**	**3**	**8**	**11**	**104**	**0**	**0**	**1**	**27**	**11.1**	**3**													
	Saint John Flames	AHL	16	0	5	5	49																			

			Regular Season																Playoffs							
Season	Club	League	GP	G	A	Pts	PIM	PP	SH	GW	S	%	+/-	TF	F%	H	SB	Min	GP	G	A	Pts	PIM	PP	SH	GW
1998-99	Saint John Flames	AHL	5	0	0	0	23																			
	Chicago	**NHL**	39	2	2	4	62	0	0	0	24	8.3	0	0	0.0	50	12	14:01								
	Indianapolis Ice	IHL	3	1	0	1	10																			
99-2000	**Chicago**	**NHL**	59	1	3	4	102	0	0	0	24	4.2	–5	0	0.0	87	29	14:14								
2000-01	**Chicago**	**NHL**	44	1	3	4	53	0	0	0	16	6.3	7	1	100.0	57	33	14:33								
	NHL Totals		206	7	16	23	356	0	0	1	99	7.1		1	100.0	194	74	14:16								

Traded to **Chicago** by **Calgary** with Marty McInnis and Erik Andersson for Jeff Shantz and Steve Dubinsky, October 27, 1998.

ALLISON, Jason

(AHL-lih-sohn, JAY-suhn) **BOS.**

Center. Shoots right. 6'3", 215 lbs. Born, North York, Ont., May 29, 1975. Washington's 2nd choice, 17th overall, in 1993 Entry Draft.

Season	Club	League	GP	G	A	Pts	PIM	PP	SH	GW	S	%	+/-	TF	F%	H	SB	Min	GP	G	A	Pts	PIM	PP	SH	GW
1990-91	North York	MTHL	63	53	41	94																				
1991-92	London Knights	OHL	65	11	19	30	15												7	0	0	0	0			
1992-93	London Knights	OHL	66	42	76	118	50												12	7	13	20	8			
1993-94	London Knights	OHL	56	55	87	*142	68												5	2	13	15	13			
	Washington	**NHL**	2	0	1	1	0	0	0	0	5	0.0	1													
	Portland Pirates	AHL																	6	2	1	3	0			
1994-95	London Knights	OHL	15	15	21	36	43																			
	Washington	**NHL**	12	2	1	3	6	2	0	0	9	22.2	–3													
	Portland Pirates	AHL	8	5	4	9	2												7	3	8	11	2			
1995-96	**Washington**	**NHL**	19	0	3	3	2	0	0	0	18	0.0	–3													
	Portland Pirates	AHL	57	28	41	69	42												6	1	6	7	9			
1996-97	**Washington**	**NHL**	53	5	17	22	25	1	0	1	71	7.0	–3													
	Boston	**NHL**	19	3	9	12	9	1	0	0	28	10.7	–3													
1997-98	**Boston**	**NHL**	81	33	50	83	60	5	0	8	158	20.9	33						6	2	6	8	4	1	0	0
1998-99	**Boston**	**NHL**	82	23	53	76	68	5	1	3	158	14.6	5	1760	52.2	91	28	22:23	12	2	9	11	6	1	0	0
99-2000	**Boston**	**NHL**	37	10	18	28	20	3	0	1	66	15.2	5	100	60.0	61	20	21:33								
2000-01	**Boston**	**NHL**	82	36	59	95	85	11	3	6	185	19.5	–8	1897	51.9	108	48	23:21								
	NHL Totals		387	112	211	323	275	28	4	19	698	16.0		3757	52.3	260	96	22:38	18	4	15	19	10	2	0	0

OHL First All-Star Team (1994) • Canadian Major Junior First All-Star Team (1994) • Canadian Major Junior Player of the Year (1994) • Played in NHL All-Star Game (2001)

Traded to **Boston** by **Washington** with Jim Carey, Anson Carter and Washington's 3rd round choice (Lee Goren) in 1997 Entry Draft for Bill Ranford, Adam Oates and Rick Tocchet, March 1, 1997. • Missed majority of 1999-2000 season recovering from thumb injury suffered in game vs. NY Islanders, January 8, 2000.

AMONTE, Tony

(uh-MAHN-tee, TOH-nee) **CHI.**

Right wing. Shoots left. 6', 200 lbs. Born, Hingham, MA, August 2, 1970. NY Rangers' 3rd choice, 68th overall, in 1988 Entry Draft.

Season	Club	League	GP	G	A	Pts	PIM	PP	SH	GW	S	%	+/-	TF	F%	H	SB	Min	GP	G	A	Pts	PIM	PP	SH	GW
1985-86	Thayer Academy	Hi-School	2	0	0	0	0																			
1986-87	Thayer Academy	Hi-School	25	25	32	57																				
1987-88	Thayer Academy	Hi-School	28	30	38	68																				
1988-89	Thayer Academy	Hi-School	25	35	38	73																				
1989-90	Boston University	H-East	41	25	33	58	52																			
1990-91	Boston University	H-East	38	31	37	68	82																			
	NY Rangers	**NHL**																	2	0	2	2	2	0	0	0
1991-92	**NY Rangers**	**NHL**	79	35	34	69	55	9	0	4	234	15.0	12						13	3	6	9	2	2	0	0
1992-93	**NY Rangers**	**NHL**	83	33	43	76	49	13	0	4	270	12.2	0													
1993-94	**NY Rangers**	**NHL**	72	16	22	38	31	3	0	4	179	8.9	5													
	Chicago	**NHL**	7	1	3	4	6	1	0	0	16	6.3	–5						6	4	2	6	4	1	0	1
1994-95	HC Fassa	Alpenliga	14	22	16	38	10																			
	HC Fassa	EuroHL	2	5	1	6	0																			
	Chicago	**NHL**	48	15	20	35	41	6	1	3	105	14.3	7						16	3	3	6	10	0	0	0
1995-96	**Chicago**	**NHL**	81	31	32	63	62	5	4	5	216	14.4	10						7	2	4	6	6	1	0	0
1996-97	**Chicago**	**NHL**	81	41	36	77	64	9	2	4	266	15.4	35						6	4	2	6	8	0	0	0
1997-98	**Chicago**	**NHL**	82	31	42	73	66	7	3	5	296	10.5	21													
	United States	Olympics	4	0	1	1	4																			
1998-99	**Chicago**	**NHL**	82	44	31	75	60	14	3	8	256	17.2	0	8	12.5	55	40	22:12								
99-2000	**Chicago**	**NHL**	82	43	41	84	48	11	5	2	260	16.5	10	22	22.7	34	44	21:54								
2000-01	**Chicago**	**NHL**	82	35	29	64	54	9	1	3	256	13.7	–22	27	40.7	52	39	22:09								
	NHL Totals		779	325	333	658	536	87	19	42	2354	13.8		57	29.8	141	123	22:05	50	16	19	35	32	4	0	1

Hockey East Second All-Star Team (1991) • NCAA Championship All-Tournament Team (1991) • NHL All-Rookie Team (1992) • Played in NHL All-Star Game (1997, 1998, 1999, 2000, 2001)

• Missed majority of 1985-86 season recovering from knee injury, October, 1985. Traded to **Chicago** by **NY Rangers** with the rights to Matt Oates for Stephane Matteau and Brian Noonan, March 21, 1994.

ANDERSSON, Mikael

(AN-duhr-suhn, MIH-kaihl)

Left wing. Shoots left. 5'11", 181 lbs. Born, Malmo, Sweden, May 10, 1966. Buffalo's 1st choice, 18th overall, in 1984 Entry Draft.

Season	Club	League	GP	G	A	Pts	PIM	PP	SH	GW	S	%	+/-	TF	F%	H	SB	Min	GP	G	A	Pts	PIM	PP	SH	GW
1982-83	Vastra Frolunda	Sweden	1	1	0	1	0																			
1983-84	Vastra Frolunda	Sweden	18	0	3	3	6																			
1984-85	Vastra Frolunda	Sweden	30	16	11	27	18												6	3	2	5	2			
1985-86	**Buffalo**	**NHL**	32	1	9	10	4	0	0	0	13	7.7	0													
	Rochester	AHL	20	10	4	14	6																			
1986-87	**Buffalo**	**NHL**	16	0	3	3	0	0	0	0	6	0.0	–2													
	Rochester	AHL	42	6	20	26	14												9	1	2	3	2			
1987-88	**Buffalo**	**NHL**	37	3	20	23	10	0	1	1	34	8.8	7						1	1	0	1	0	0	0	0
	Rochester	AHL	35	12	24	36	16																			
1988-89	**Buffalo**	**NHL**	14	0	1	1	4	0	0	0	12	0.0	–1													
	Rochester	AHL	56	18	33	51	12																			
1989-90	**Hartford**	**NHL**	50	13	24	37	6	1	2	2	86	15.1	0						5	0	3	3	2	0	0	0
1990-91	**Hartford**	**NHL**	41	4	7	11	8	0	0	0	57	7.0	0													
	Springfield	AHL	26	7	22	29	10												18	*10	8	18	12			
1991-92	**Hartford**	**NHL**	74	18	29	47	14	1	3	1	149	12.1	18						7	0	2	2	6	0	0	0
1992-93	**Tampa Bay**	**NHL**	77	16	11	27	14	3	2	4	169	9.5	–14													
1993-94	**Tampa Bay**	**NHL**	76	13	12	25	23	1	1	2	136	9.6	8													
1994-95	Vastra Frolunda	Sweden	7	1	0	1	31																			
	Tampa Bay	**NHL**	36	4	7	11	4	0	0	0	36	11.1	–3													
1995-96	**Tampa Bay**	**NHL**	64	8	11	19	2	0	0	1	104	7.7	0						6	1	1	2	0	0	0	0
1996-97	**Tampa Bay**	**NHL**	70	5	14	19	8	0	3	1	102	4.9	1													
1997-98	**Tampa Bay**	**NHL**	72	6	11	17	29	0	1	1	105	5.7	–4													
	Sweden	Olympics	4	1	1	2	0																			
1998-99	**Tampa Bay**	**NHL**	40	2	3	5	4	0	0	0	40	5.0	–8	38	34.2	10	13	12:39								
	Philadelphia	**NHL**	7	0	1	1	0	0	0	0	11	0.0	1	35	28.6	5	2	12:59	6	0	1	1	2	0	0	0
99-2000	**Philadelphia**	**NHL**	36	2	3	5	0	0	1	0	38	5.3	–2	28	39.3	14	11	10:29								
	NY Islanders	**NHL**	19	0	3	3	4	0	0	0	19	0.0	–1	5	60.0	8	2	9:33								
2000-01	Vastra Frolunda	Sweden	48	10	6	16	12												3	0	0	0	2			
	NHL Totals		761	95	169	264	134	6	14	13	1117	8.5		106	34.9	37	28	11:20	25	2	7	9	10	0	0	0

Claimed by **Hartford** from **Buffalo** in NHL Waiver Draft, October 2, 1989. Signed as a free agent by **Tampa Bay**, June 29, 1992. Traded to **Philadelphia** by **Tampa Bay** with Sandy McCarthy for Colin Forbes and Philadelphia's 4th round choice (Michal Lanicek) in 1999 Entry Draft, March 20, 1999. Traded to **NY Islanders** by **Philadelphia** with Carolina's 5th round choice (previously acquired, NY Islanders selected Kristofer Ottosson) in 2000 Entry Draft for Gino Odjick, February 15, 2000.

ANDERSSON, Niklas

(AN-duhr-suhn, NIHK-las)

Left wing. Shoots left. 5'9", 180 lbs. Born, Kungalv, Sweden, May 20, 1971. Quebec's 5th choice, 68th overall, in 1989 Entry Draft.

Season	Club	League	GP	G	A	Pts	PIM	PP	SH	GW	S	%	+/-	TF	F%	H	SB	Min	GP	G	A	Pts	PIM	PP	SH	GW
1987-88	Vastra Frolunda	Sweden-2	15	5	4	9	6												8	6	4	10	4			
1988-89	Vastra Frolunda	Sweden-2	30	12	24	36	24												10	4	6	10	4			
1989-90	Vastra Frolunda	Sweden	38	10	21	31	14																			
1990-91	Vastra Frolunda	Sweden	39	14	25	39	38												10	6	3	9	24			
1991-92	Halifax Citadels	AHL	57	8	26	34	41																			
1992-93	**Quebec**	**NHL**	3	0	1	1	2	0	0	0	4	0.0	0													
	Halifax Citadels	AHL	76	32	50	82	42																			
1993-94	Cornwall Aces	AHL	42	18	34	52	8																			
1994-95	Denver Grizzlies	IHL	66	22	39	61	28												15	8	13	21	10			

			Regular Season																Playoffs							
Season	Club	League	GP	G	A	Pts	PIM	PP	SH	GW	S	%	+/-	TF	F%	H	SB	Min	GP	G	A	Pts	PIM	PP	SH	GW
1995-96	**NY Islanders**	**NHL**	**47**	**14**	**12**	**26**	**12**	**3**	**2**	**1**	**89**	**15.7**	**–3**	....	....	....	....	....	....	....	....	....	....	....	....	....
	Utah Grizzlies	IHL	30	13	22	35	25	....	....	....	....	....	....	....	....	....	....	....	....	....	....	....	....	....	....	....
1996-97	**NY Islanders**	**NHL**	**74**	**12**	**31**	**43**	**57**	**1**	**1**	**1**	**122**	**9.8**	**4**	....	....	....	....	....	....	....	....	....	....	....	....	....
1997-98	**San Jose**	**NHL**	**5**	**0**	**0**	**0**	**2**	**0**	**0**	**0**	**6**	**0.0**	**–1**	....	....	....	....	....	....	....	....	....	....	....	....	....
	Kentucky	AHL	37	10	28	38	54	....	....	....	....	....	....	....	....	....	....	....	....	....	....	....	....	....	....	....
	Utah Grizzlies	IHL	21	6	20	26	24	....	....	....	....	....	....	....	....	....	....	....	4	3	1	4	4	....	....	....
1998-99	Chicago Wolves	IHL	65	17	47	64	49	....	....	....	....	....	....	....	....	....	....	....	10	2	2	4	10	....	....	....
99-2000	**NY Islanders**	**NHL**	**17**	**3**	**7**	**10**	**8**	**1**	**0**	**0**	**24**	**12.5**	**–3**	**0**	**0.0**	**10**	**4**	**13:19**	....	....	....	....	....	....	....	....
	Chicago Wolves	IHL	52	20	21	41	59	....	....	....	....	....	....	....	....	....	....	....	9	6	1	7	4	....	....	....
	Nashville	**NHL**	**7**	**0**	**1**	**1**	**0**	**0**	**0**	**0**	**7**	**0.0**	**0**	**0**	**0.0**	**1**	**0**	**12:50**	....	....	....	....	....	....	....	....
2000-01	**Calgary**	**NHL**	**11**	**0**	**1**	**1**	**4**	**0**	**0**	**0**	**8**	**0.0**	**0**	**4**	**25.0**	**5**	**2**	**11:10**	....	....	....	....	....	....	....	....
	Chicago Wolves	IHL	66	33	39	72	81	....	....	....	....	....	....	....	....	....	....	....	16	1	*14	15	14	....	....	....
	NHL Totals		**164**	**29**	**53**	**82**	**85**	**5**	**3**	**2**	**260**	**11.2**		**4**	**25.0**	**16**	**6**	**12:33**	....	....	....	....	....	....	....	....

IHL Second All-Star Team (2000) • IHL First All-Star Team (2001)

Signed as a free agent by **NY Islanders**, July 15, 1994. Signed as a free agent by **San Jose**, September 17, 1997. Signed as a free agent by **Toronto**, September 4, 1998. Traded to **NY Islanders** by **Toronto** for Craig Charron, August 17, 1999. Claimed on waivers by **Nashville** from **NY Islanders**, January 20, 2000. Claimed on waivers by **NY Islanders** from **Nashville**, February 19, 2000. Signed as a free agent by **Calgary**, August 29, 2000.

ANDREYCHUK, Dave

(AN-druh-chuhk, DAYV) **T.B.**

Left wing. Shoots right. 6'4", 220 lbs. Born, Hamilton, Ont., September 29, 1963. Buffalo's 3rd choice, 16th overall, in 1982 Entry Draft.

Season	Club	League	GP	G	A	Pts	PIM	PP	SH	GW	S	%	+/-	TF	F%	H	SB	Min	GP	G	A	Pts	PIM	PP	SH	GW
1979-80	Hamilton Hawks	OMHA	21	25	24	49	....	....	....	....	....	....	....	....	....	....	....	....	....	....	....	....	....	....	....	....
1980-81	Oshawa Generals	OMJHL	67	22	22	44	80	....	....	....	....	....	....	....	....	....	....	....	10	3	2	5	20	....	....	....
1981-82	Oshawa Generals	OHL	67	57	43	100	71	....	....	....	....	....	....	....	....	....	....	....	3	1	4	5	16	....	....	....
1982-83	Oshawa Generals	OHL	14	8	24	32	6	....	....	....	....	....	....	....	....	....	....	....	....	....	....	....	....	....	....	....
	Buffalo	**NHL**	**43**	**14**	**23**	**37**	**16**	**3**	**0**	**1**	**66**	**21.2**	**6**	....	....	....	....	....	**4**	**1**	**0**	**1**	**4**	**0**	**0**	**0**
1983-84	**Buffalo**	**NHL**	**78**	**38**	**42**	**80**	**42**	**10**	**0**	**7**	**178**	**21.3**	**20**	....	....	....	....	....	**2**	**0**	**1**	**1**	**2**	**0**	**0**	**0**
1984-85	**Buffalo**	**NHL**	**64**	**31**	**30**	**61**	**54**	**14**	**0**	**2**	**153**	**20.3**	**–4**	....	....	....	....	....	**5**	**4**	**2**	**6**	**4**	**0**	**0**	**2**
1985-86	**Buffalo**	**NHL**	**80**	**36**	**51**	**87**	**61**	**12**	**0**	**3**	**225**	**16.0**	**3**	....	....	....	....	....	....	....	....	....	....	....	....	....
1986-87	**Buffalo**	**NHL**	**77**	**25**	**48**	**73**	**46**	**13**	**0**	**2**	**255**	**9.8**	**2**	....	....	....	....	....	....	....	....	....	....	....	....	....
1987-88	**Buffalo**	**NHL**	**80**	**30**	**48**	**78**	**112**	**15**	**0**	**5**	**253**	**11.9**	**1**	....	....	....	....	....	**6**	**2**	**4**	**6**	**0**	**1**	**0**	**0**
1988-89	**Buffalo**	**NHL**	**56**	**28**	**24**	**52**	**40**	**7**	**0**	**3**	**145**	**19.3**	**0**	....	....	....	....	....	**5**	**0**	**3**	**3**	**0**	**0**	**0**	**0**
1989-90	**Buffalo**	**NHL**	**73**	**40**	**42**	**82**	**42**	**18**	**0**	**3**	**206**	**19.4**	**6**	....	....	....	....	....	**6**	**2**	**5**	**7**	**2**	**1**	**0**	**0**
1990-91	**Buffalo**	**NHL**	**80**	**36**	**33**	**69**	**32**	**13**	**0**	**4**	**234**	**15.4**	**11**	....	....	....	....	....	**6**	**2**	**2**	**4**	**8**	**1**	**0**	**0**
1991-92	**Buffalo**	**NHL**	**80**	**41**	**50**	**91**	**71**	**28**	**0**	**2**	**337**	**12.2**	**–9**	....	....	....	....	....	**7**	**1**	**3**	**4**	**12**	**0**	**0**	**0**
1992-93	**Buffalo**	**NHL**	**52**	**29**	**32**	**61**	**48**	**20**	**0**	**2**	**171**	**17.0**	**–8**	....	....	....	....	....	....	....	....	....	....	....	....	....
	Toronto	**NHL**	**31**	**25**	**13**	**38**	**8**	**12**	**0**	**2**	**139**	**18.0**	**12**	....	....	....	....	....	**21**	**12**	**7**	**19**	**35**	**4**	**0**	**3**
1993-94	**Toronto**	**NHL**	**83**	**53**	**46**	**99**	**98**	**21**	**5**	**8**	**333**	**15.9**	**22**	....	....	....	....	....	**18**	**5**	**5**	**10**	**16**	**3**	**1**	**0**
1994-95	**Toronto**	**NHL**	**48**	**22**	**16**	**38**	**34**	**8**	**0**	**2**	**168**	**13.1**	**–7**	....	....	....	....	....	**7**	**3**	**2**	**5**	**25**	**2**	**0**	**0**
1995-96	**Toronto**	**NHL**	**61**	**20**	**24**	**44**	**54**	**12**	**2**	**3**	**200**	**10.0**	**–11**	....	....	....	....	....	....	....	....	....	....	....	....	....
	New Jersey	**NHL**	**15**	**8**	**5**	**13**	**10**	**2**	**0**	**0**	**41**	**19.5**	**2**	....	....	....	....	....	....	....	....	....	....	....	....	....
1996-97	**New Jersey**	**NHL**	**82**	**27**	**34**	**61**	**48**	**4**	**1**	**2**	**233**	**11.6**	**38**	....	....	....	....	....	**1**	**0**	**0**	**0**	**0**	**0**	**0**	**0**
1997-98	**New Jersey**	**NHL**	**75**	**14**	**34**	**48**	**26**	**4**	**0**	**2**	**180**	**7.8**	**19**	....	....	....	....	....	**6**	**1**	**0**	**1**	**4**	**1**	**0**	**0**
1998-99	**New Jersey**	**NHL**	**52**	**15**	**13**	**28**	**20**	**4**	**0**	**3**	**110**	**13.6**	**1**	**9**	**44.4**	**36**	**17**	**15:32**	**4**	**2**	**0**	**2**	**4**	**0**	**0**	**0**
99-2000	**Boston**	**NHL**	**63**	**19**	**14**	**33**	**28**	**7**	**0**	**2**	**192**	**9.9**	**–11**	**446**	**52.0**	**68**	**66**	**19:50**	....	....	....	....	....	....	....	....
	Colorado	**NHL**	**14**	**1**	**2**	**3**	**2**	**1**	**0**	**1**	**41**	**2.4**	**–9**	**15**	**60.0**	**10**	**9**	**17:16**	**17**	**3**	**2**	**5**	**18**	**2**	**0**	**0**
2000-01	**Buffalo**	**NHL**	**74**	**20**	**13**	**33**	**32**	**8**	**0**	**4**	**119**	**16.8**	**0**	**187**	**49.7**	**36**	**25**	**11:60**	**13**	**1**	**2**	**3**	**4**	**1**	**0**	**0**
	NHL Totals		**1361**	**572**	**637**	**1209**	**924**	**236**	**8**	**63**	**3979**	**14.4**		**657**	**51.4**	**150**	**117**	**15:42**	**128**	**39**	**38**	**77**	**138**	**16**	**1**	**5**

Played in NHL All-Star Game (1990, 1994)

Traded to **Toronto** by **Buffalo** with Daren Puppa and Buffalo's 1st round choice (Kenny Jonsson) in 1993 Entry Draft for Grant Fuhr and Toronto's 5th round choice (Kevin Popp) in 1995 Entry Draft, February 2, 1993. Traded to **New Jersey** by **Toronto** for New Jersey's 2nd round choice (Marek Posmyk) in 1996 Entry Draft and New Jersey's 3rd round choice (later traded back to New Jersey - New Jersey selected Andre Lakos) in 1999 Entry Draft, March 13, 1996. Signed as a free agent by Boston, July 29, 1999. Traded to **Colorado** by **Boston** with Ray Bourque for Brian Rolston, Martin Grenier, Sami Pahlsson and New Jersey's 1st round choice (previously acquired, Boston selected Martin Samuelsson) in 2000 Entry Draft, March 6, 2000. Signed as a free agent by **Buffalo**, July 13, 2000. Signed as a free agent by **Tampa Bay**, July 13, 2001.

ANDRUSAK, Greg

(AN-druh-sak, GREHG)

Defense. Shoots right. 6'1", 195 lbs. Born, Cranbrook, B.C., November 14, 1969. Pittsburgh's 5th choice, 88th overall, in 1988 Entry Draft.

Season	Club	League	GP	G	A	Pts	PIM	PP	SH	GW	S	%	+/-	TF	F%	H	SB	Min	GP	G	A	Pts	PIM	PP	SH	GW
1986-87	Kelowna Packers	BCJHL	45	10	24	34	95	....	....	....	....	....	....	....	....	....	....	....	....	....	....	....	....	....	....	....
1987-88	Minnesota-Duluth	WCHA	37	4	5	9	42	....	....	....	....	....	....	....	....	....	....	....	....	....	....	....	....	....	....	....
1988-89	Minnesota-Duluth	WCHA	35	4	8	12	74	....	....	....	....	....	....	....	....	....	....	....	....	....	....	....	....	....	....	....
1989-90	Minnesota-Duluth	WCHA	35	5	29	34	74	....	....	....	....	....	....	....	....	....	....	....	....	....	....	....	....	....	....	....
1990-91	Canada	Nat-Team	53	4	11	15	34	....	....	....	....	....	....	....	....	....	....	....	....	....	....	....	....	....	....	....
1991-92	Minnesota-Duluth	WCHA	36	7	27	34	125	....	....	....	....	....	....	....	....	....	....	....	....	....	....	....	....	....	....	....
1992-93	Cleveland	IHL	55	3	22	25	78	....	....	....	....	....	....	....	....	....	....	....	2	0	0	0	2	....	....	....
	Muskegon Fury	ColHL	2	0	3	3	7	....	....	....	....	....	....	....	....	....	....	....	....	....	....	....	....	....	....	....
1993-94	**Pittsburgh**	**NHL**	**3**	**0**	**0**	**0**	**2**	**0**	**0**	**0**	**4**	**0.0**	**–1**	....	....	....	....	....	....	....	....	....	....	....	....	....
	Cleveland	IHL	69	13	26	39	109	....	....	....	....	....	....	....	....	....	....	....	....	....	....	....	....	....	....	....
1994-95	Detroit Vipers	IHL	37	5	26	31	50	....	....	....	....	....	....	....	....	....	....	....	....	....	....	....	....	....	....	....
	Pittsburgh	**NHL**	**7**	**0**	**4**	**4**	**6**	**0**	**0**	**0**	**7**	**0.0**	**–1**	....	....	....	....	....	....	....	....	....	....	....	....	....
	Cleveland	IHL	8	0	8	8	14	....	....	....	....	....	....	....	....	....	....	....	....	....	....	....	....	....	....	....
1995-96	**Pittsburgh**	**NHL**	**2**	**0**	**0**	**0**	**0**	**0**	**0**	**0**	**1**	**0.0**	**–1**	....	....	....	....	....	....	....	....	....	....	....	....	....
	Detroit Vipers	IHL	58	6	30	36	128	....	....	....	....	....	....	....	....	....	....	....	....	....	....	....	....	....	....	....
	Minnesota	IHL	5	0	4	4	8	....	....	....	....	....	....	....	....	....	....	....	....	....	....	....	....	....	....	....
1996-97	Eisbaren Berlin	DEL	45	5	17	22	170	....	....	....	....	....	....	....	....	....	....	....	8	1	1	2	20	....	....	....
1997-98	Eisbaren Berlin	DEL	34	3	7	10	65	....	....	....	....	....	....	....	....	....	....	....	9	0	1	1	8	....	....	....
1998-99	Eisbaren Berlin	DEL	19	2	5	7	12	....	....	....	....	....	....	....	....	....	....	....	....	....	....	....	....	....	....	....
	Eisbaren Berlin	EuroHL	5	0	1	1	18	....	....	....	....	....	....	....	....	....	....	....	....	....	....	....	....	....	....	....
	Geneve-Servette	Switz-2	10	3	13	16	....	....	....	....	....	....	....	....	....	....	....	....	....	....	....	....	....	....	....	....
	Houston Aeros	IHL	3	0	1	1	2	....	....	....	....	....	....	....	....	....	....	....	6	1	4	5	16	....	....	....
	Pittsburgh	**NHL**	**7**	**0**	**1**	**1**	**4**	**0**	**0**	**0**	**2**	**0.0**	**4**	**0**	**0.0**	**14**	**3**	**17:42**	**12**	**1**	**0**	**1**	**6**	**0**	**0**	**1**
99-2000	**Toronto**	**NHL**	**9**	**0**	**1**	**1**	**4**	**0**	**0**	**0**	**5**	**0.0**	**1**	**0**	**0.0**	**14**	**2**	**18:25**	**3**	**0**	**0**	**0**	**2**	**0**	**0**	**0**
	Chicago Wolves	IHL	54	2	23	25	50	....	....	....	....	....	....	....	....	....	....	....	11	1	5	6	20	....	....	....
2000-01	Kentucky	AHL	58	5	14	19	63	....	....	....	....	....	....	....	....	....	....	....	2	0	0	0	0	....	....	....
	NHL Totals		**28**	**0**	**6**	**6**	**16**	**0**	**0**	**0**	**19**	**0.0**		**0**	**0.0**	**28**	**5**	**18:06**	**15**	**1**	**0**	**1**	**8**	**0**	**0**	**1**

WCHA First All-Star Team (1992)

Signed as a free agent by **Pittsburgh**, March 19, 1999. Signed as a free agent by **Toronto**, July 19, 1999. Signed as a free agent by **San Jose**, August 14, 2000.

ANTROPOV, Nik

(an-TROH-pahv, NIHK) **TOR.**

Center. Shoots left. 6'5", 203 lbs. Born, Vost, USSR, February 18, 1980. Toronto's 1st choice, 10th overall, in 1998 Entry Draft.

Season	Club	League	GP	G	A	Pts	PIM	PP	SH	GW	S	%	+/-	TF	F%	H	SB	Min	GP	G	A	Pts	PIM	PP	SH	GW
1995-96	Ust-Kamenogorsk	Russia-Jr.	20	18	20	38	30	....	....	....	....	....	....	....	....	....	....	....	....	....	....	....	....	....	....	....
1996-97	Ust-Kamenogorsk	Russia-2	8	2	1	3	6	....	....	....	....	....	....	....	....	....	....	....	....	....	....	....	....	....	....	....
1997-98	Ust-Kamenogorsk	Russia-2	42	15	24	39	62	....	....	....	....	....	....	....	....	....	....	....	....	....	....	....	....	....	....	....
1998-99	Dynamo Moscow	Russia	30	5	9	14	30	....	....	....	....	....	....	....	....	....	....	....	11	0	1	1	4	....	....	....
99-2000	**Toronto**	**NHL**	**66**	**12**	**18**	**30**	**41**	**0**	**0**	**2**	**89**	**13.5**	**14**	**501**	**46.3**	**79**	**22**	**12:48**	**3**	**0**	**0**	**0**	**4**	**0**	**0**	**0**
	St. John's Leafs	AHL	2	0	0	0	4	....	....	....	....	....	....	....	....	....	....	....	....	....	....	....	....	....	....	....
2000-01	**Toronto**	**NHL**	**52**	**6**	**11**	**17**	**30**	**0**	**0**	**1**	**71**	**8.5**	**5**	**431**	**44.3**	**53**	**8**	**10:02**	**9**	**2**	**1**	**3**	**12**	**1**	**0**	**1**
	NHL Totals		**118**	**18**	**29**	**47**	**71**	**0**	**0**	**3**	**160**	**11.3**		**932**	**45.4**	**132**	**30**	**11:35**	**12**	**2**	**1**	**3**	**16**	**1**	**0**	**1**

ARKHIPOV, Denis

(AHR-kih-pahv, DIHN-ihs) **NSH.**

Right wing. Shoots left. 6'3", 210 lbs. Born, Kazan, USSR, May 19, 1979. Nashville's 2nd choice, 60th overall, in 1998 Entry Draft.

Season	Club	League	GP	G	A	Pts	PIM	PP	SH	GW	S	%	+/-	TF	F%	H	SB	Min	GP	G	A	Pts	PIM	PP	SH	GW
1994-95	Ak Bars Kazan	Russia-Jr	40	20	12	32	10	....	....	....	....	....	....	....	....	....	....	....	....	....	....	....	....	....	....	....
1995-96	Ak Bars Kazan	Russia-Jr.	40	15	8	23	30	....	....	....	....	....	....	....	....	....	....	....	....	....	....	....	....	....	....	....
	Ak Bars Kazan	Russia-2	15	10	8	18	10	....	....	....	....	....	....	....	....	....	....	....	....	....	....	....	....	....	....	....
1996-97	Ak Bars Kazan-2	Russia-3	50	17	23	40	20	....	....	....	....	....	....	....	....	....	....	....	....	....	....	....	....	....	....	....
	Ak Bars Kazan	Russia	1	1	0	1	0	....	....	....	....	....	....	....	....	....	....	....	....	....	....	....	....	....	....	....
1997-98	Ak Bars Kazan	Russia	29	2	2	4	2	....	....	....	....	....	....	....	....	....	....	....	....	....	....	....	....	....	....	....

			Regular Season																Playoffs							
Season	**Club**	**League**	**GP**	**G**	**A**	**Pts**	**PIM**	**PP**	**SH**	**GW**	**S**	**%**	**+/-**	**TF**	**F%**	**H**	**SB**	**Min**	**GP**	**G**	**A**	**Pts**	**PIM**	**PP**	**SH**	**GW**
1998-99	Ak Bars Kazan	Russia	34	12	1	13	22												9	2	3	5	6			
	Ak Bars Kazan	EuroHL	4	0	0	0	0												1	0	0	0	0			
99-2000	Ak Bars Kazan	Russia	32	7	9	16	14												18	5	5	10	6			
2000-01	**Nashville**	**NHL**	**40**	**6**	**7**	**13**	**4**	**0**	**0**	**0**	**42**	**14.3**	**0**	**299**	**43.8**	**16**	**10**	**9:56**								
	Milwaukee	IHL	40	9	8	17	11																			
	NHL Totals		**40**	**6**	**7**	**13**	**4**	**0**	**0**	**0**	**42**	**14.3**		**299**	**43.8**	**16**	**10**	**9:56**								

ARMSTRONG, Chris

(ahrm-STRAWNG, KRIHS)

Defense. Shoots left. 6', 205 lbs. Born, Regina, Sask., June 26, 1975. Florida's 3rd choice, 57th overall, in 1993 Entry Draft.

Season	Club	League	GP	G	A	Pts	PIM	PP	SH	GW	S	%	+/-	TF	F%	H	SB	Min	GP	G	A	Pts	PIM	PP	SH	GW
1990-91	Whitewood Mites	SAHA	40	25	30	55	40																			
1991-92	Moose Jaw	WHL	43	2	7	9	19												4	0	0	0	0			
1992-93	Moose Jaw	WHL	67	9	35	44	104																			
1993-94	Moose Jaw	WHL	64	13	55	68	54																			
	Cincinnati	IHL	1	0	0	0	0												10	1	3	4	2			
1994-95	Moose Jaw	WHL	66	17	54	71	61												10	2	12	14	22			
	Cincinnati	IHL																	9	1	3	4	10			
1995-96	Carolina	AHL	78	9	33	42	65																			
1996-97	Carolina	AHL	66	9	23	32	38																			
1997-98	Fort Wayne	IHL	79	8	36	44	66												4	0	2	2	4			
1998-99	Milwaukee	IHL	5	0	3	3	4																			
	Hershey Bears	AHL	65	12	32	44	30												5	0	1	1	0			
99-2000	Kentucky	AHL	78	9	48	57	77												9	1	5	6	4			
2000-01	**Minnesota**	**NHL**	**3**	**0**	**0**	**0**	**0**	**0**	**0**	**0**	**4**	**0.0**	**–3**	**0**	**0.0**	**4**	**2**	**18:06**								
	Cleveland	IHL	77	9	32	41	42												4	0	2	2	2			
	NHL Totals		**3**	**0**	**0**	**0**	**0**	**0**	**0**	**0**	**4**	**0.0**		**0**	**0.0**	**4**	**2**	**18:06**								

WHL East First All-Star Team (1994) • Canadian Major Junior Second All-Star Team (1994) • WHL East Second All-Star Team (1995)

Claimed by **Nashville** from **Florida** in Expansion Draft, June 26, 1998. Signed as a free agent by **San Jose**, September 2, 1999. Selected by **Minnesota** from **San Jose** in Expansion Draft, June 23, 2000.

ARMSTRONG, Derek

(ahrm-STRAWNG, DEHR-ehk)

Center. Shoots right. 5'11", 188 lbs. Born, Ottawa, Ont., April 23, 1973. NY Islanders' 5th choice, 128th overall, in 1992 Entry Draft.

Season	Club	League	GP	G	A	Pts	PIM	PP	SH	GW	S	%	+/-	TF	F%	H	SB	Min	GP	G	A	Pts	PIM	PP	SH	GW
1989-90	Hawkesbury	OCJHL	48	8	10	18	30																			
1990-91	Hawkesbury	OCJHL	54	27	45	72	49																			
	Sudbury Wolves	OHL	2	0	2	2	0																			
1991-92	Sudbury Wolves	OHL	66	31	54	85	22												9	2	2	4	2			
1992-93	Sudbury Wolves	OHL	66	44	62	106	56												14	9	10	19	26			
1993-94	**NY Islanders**	**NHL**	**1**	**0**	**0**	**0**	**0**	**0**	**0**	**0**	**2**	**0.0**	**0**													
	Salt Lake City	IHL	76	23	35	58	61																			
1994-95	Denver Grizzlies	IHL	59	13	18	31	65												6	0	2	2	0			
1995-96	**NY Islanders**	**NHL**	**19**	**1**	**3**	**4**	**14**	**0**	**0**	**0**	**23**	**4.3**	**–6**													
	Worcester	AHL	51	11	15	26	33												4	2	1	3	0			
1996-97	**NY Islanders**	**NHL**	**50**	**6**	**7**	**13**	**33**	**0**	**0**	**2**	**36**	**16.7**	**–8**													
	Utah Grizzlies	IHL	17	4	8	12	10												6	0	4	4	4			
1997-98	**Ottawa**	**NHL**	**9**	**2**	**0**	**2**	**9**	**0**	**0**	**1**	**8**	**25.0**	**1**													
	Detroit Vipers	IHL	10	0	1	1	2																			
	Hartford	AHL	54	16	30	46	40												15	2	6	8	22			
1998-99	**NY Rangers**	**NHL**	**3**	**0**	**0**	**0**	**0**	**0**	**0**	**0**	**1**	**0.0**	**0**	**0**	**0.0**	**0**	**0**	**2:50**								
	Hartford	AHL	59	29	51	80	73												7	5	4	9	10			
99-2000	**NY Rangers**	**NHL**	**1**	**0**	**0**	**0**	**0**	**0**	**0**	**0**	**1**	**0.0**	**0**	**3**	**33.3**	**0**	**0**	**3:10**								
	Hartford	AHL	77	28	54	82	101												23	7	16	23	24			
2000-01	**NY Rangers**	**NHL**	**3**	**0**	**0**	**0**	**0**	**0**	**0**	**0**	**6**	**0.0**	**0**	**30**	**50.0**	**4**	**0**	**11:22**								
	Hartford	AHL	75	32	*69	*101	73												5	0	6	6	6			
	NHL Totals		**86**	**9**	**10**	**19**	**56**	**0**	**0**	**3**	**77**	**11.7**		**33**	**48.5**	**4**	**0**	**6:32**								

AHL Second All-Star Team (2000) • AHL First All-Star Team (2001) • Won John P. Sollenberger Trophy (Top Scorer - AHL) (2001) • Won Les Cunningham Award (MVP - AHL) (2001)

Signed as a free agent by **Ottawa**, July 28, 1997. Signed as a free agent by **NY Rangers**, August 10, 1998. Signed as a free agent by **SC Bern** (Switz.), July 18, 2001.

ARNOTT, Jason

(AHR-nawt, JAY-suhn) **N.J.**

Center. Shoots right. 6'4", 225 lbs. Born, Collingwood, Ont., October 11, 1974. Edmonton's 1st choice, 7th overall, in 1993 Entry Draft.

Season	Club	League	GP	G	A	Pts	PIM	PP	SH	GW	S	%	+/-	TF	F%	H	SB	Min	GP	G	A	Pts	PIM	PP	SH	GW
1989-90	Stayner Siskins	OJHL-C	34	21	31	52	12																			
1990-91	Lindsay Bears	OJHL-B	42	17	44	61	10												8	9	8	17	6			
1991-92	Oshawa Generals	OHL	57	9	15	24	12																			
1992-93	Oshawa Generals	OHL	56	41	57	98	74												13	9	9	18	20			
1993-94	**Edmonton**	**NHL**	**78**	**33**	**35**	**68**	**104**	**10**	**0**	**4**	**194**	**17.0**	**1**													
1994-95	**Edmonton**	**NHL**	**42**	**15**	**22**	**37**	**128**	**7**	**0**	**1**	**156**	**9.6**	**–14**													
1995-96	**Edmonton**	**NHL**	**64**	**28**	**31**	**59**	**87**	**8**	**0**	**5**	**244**	**11.5**	**–6**													
1996-97	**Edmonton**	**NHL**	**67**	**19**	**38**	**57**	**92**	**10**	**1**	**2**	**248**	**7.7**	**–21**						**12**	**3**	**6**	**9**	**18**	**1**	**0**	**0**
1997-98	**Edmonton**	**NHL**	**35**	**5**	**13**	**18**	**78**	**1**	**0**	**0**	**100**	**5.0**	**–16**													
	New Jersey	**NHL**	**35**	**5**	**10**	**15**	**21**	**3**	**0**	**2**	**99**	**5.1**	**–8**						**5**	**0**	**2**	**2**	**0**	**0**	**0**	**0**
1998-99	**New Jersey**	**NHL**	**74**	**27**	**27**	**54**	**79**	**8**	**0**	**3**	**200**	**13.5**	**10**	**872**	**49.3**	**196**	**16**	**15:24**	**7**	**2**	**2**	**4**	**4**	**1**	**0**	**0**
99-2000♦	**New Jersey**	**NHL**	**76**	**22**	**34**	**56**	**51**	**7**	**0**	**4**	**244**	**9.0**	**22**	**1172**	**46.9**	**194**	**18**	**17:05**	**23**	**8**	**12**	**20**	**18**	**3**	**0**	**1**
2000-01	**New Jersey**	**NHL**	**54**	**21**	**34**	**55**	**75**	**8**	**0**	**3**	**138**	**15.2**	**23**	**760**	**49.6**	**108**	**14**	**16:12**	**23**	**8**	**7**	**15**	**16**	**5**	**0**	**0**
	NHL Totals		**525**	**175**	**244**	**419**	**715**	**62**	**1**	**24**	**1623**	**10.8**		**2804**	**48.4**	**498**	**48**	**16:15**	**70**	**21**	**29**	**50**	**56**	**10**	**0**	**1**

NHL All-Rookie Team (1994) • Played in NHL All-Star Game (1997)

Traded to **New Jersey** by **Edmonton** with Bryan Muir for Valeri Zelepukin and Bill Guerin, January 4, 1998.

ARVEDSON, Magnus

(AHR-vehd-suhn, MAGH-nuhs) **OTT.**

Center. Shoots left. 6'2", 198 lbs. Born, Karlstad, Sweden, November 25, 1971. Ottawa's 4th choice, 119th overall, in 1997 Entry Draft.

Season	Club	League	GP	G	A	Pts	PIM	PP	SH	GW	S	%	+/-	TF	F%	H	SB	Min	GP	G	A	Pts	PIM	PP	SH	GW
1990-91	Orebro IK	Sweden-2	29	7	11	18	12												2	0	1	1	2			
1991-92	Orebro IK	Sweden-2	32	12	21	33	30												7	4	4	8	4			
1992-93	Orebro IK	Sweden-2	36	11	18	29	34												6	2	1	3	0			
1993-94	Farjestads BK	Sweden	16	1	7	8	10																			
1994-95	Farjestads BK	Swede-Jr.	1	0	0	0	0																			
	Farjestads BK	Sweden	36	1	6	7	45												4	0	0	0	6			
1995-96	Farjestads BK	Sweden	40	10	14	24	40												8	0	3	3	10			
1996-97	Farjestads BK	Sweden	48	13	11	24	36												14	4	7	11	8			
	Farjestads BK	EuroHL	5	1	0	1	2												2	0	1	1	2			
1997-98	**Ottawa**	**NHL**	**61**	**11**	**15**	**26**	**36**	**0**	**1**	**0**	**90**	**12.2**	**2**						**11**	**0**	**1**	**1**	**6**	**0**	**0**	**0**
1998-99	**Ottawa**	**NHL**	**80**	**21**	**26**	**47**	**50**	**0**	**4**	**6**	**136**	**15.4**	**33**	**25**	**20.0**	**48**	**42**	**17:08**	**3**	**0**	**1**	**1**	**2**	**0**	**0**	**0**
99-2000	**Ottawa**	**NHL**	**47**	**15**	**13**	**28**	**36**	**1**	**1**	**4**	**91**	**16.5**	**4**	**11**	**45.5**	**33**	**43**	**18:04**	**6**	**0**	**0**	**0**	**6**	**0**	**0**	**0**
2000-01	**Ottawa**	**NHL**	**51**	**17**	**16**	**33**	**24**	**1**	**2**	**4**	**79**	**21.5**	**23**	**7**	**28.6**	**36**	**30**	**16:01**	**2**	**0**	**0**	**0**	**0**	**0**	**0**	**0**
	NHL Totals		**239**	**64**	**70**	**134**	**146**	**2**	**8**	**14**	**396**	**16.2**		**43**	**27.9**	**117**	**115**	**17:04**	**22**	**0**	**2**	**2**	**14**	**0**	**0**	**0**

ASHAM, Arron

(ASH-uhm, AIR-ruhn) **MTL.**

Right wing. Shoots right. 5'11", 209 lbs. Born, Portage La Prairie, Man., April 13, 1978. Montreal's 3rd choice, 71st overall, in 1996 Entry Draft.

Season	Club	League	GP	G	A	Pts	PIM	PP	SH	GW	S	%	+/-	TF	F%	H	SB	Min	GP	G	A	Pts	PIM	PP	SH	GW
1993-94	Portage Terriers	MAHA	21	18	19	37	82																			
1994-95	Red Deer Rebels	WHL	62	11	16	27	126																			
1995-96	Red Deer Rebels	WHL	70	32	45	77	174												10	6	3	9	20			
1996-97	Red Deer Rebels	WHL	67	45	51	96	149												16	12	14	26	36			
1997-98	Red Deer Rebels	WHL	67	43	49	92	153												5	0	2	2	8			
	Fredericton	AHL	2	1	1	2	0												2	0	1	1	0			
1998-99	**Montreal**	**NHL**	**7**	**0**	**0**	**0**	**0**	**0**	**0**	**0**	**5**	**0.0**	**–4**	**0**	**0.0**	**8**	**2**	**7:27**								
	Fredericton	AHL	60	16	18	34	118												13	8	6	14	11			
99-2000	**Montreal**	**NHL**	**33**	**4**	**2**	**6**	**24**	**0**	**1**	**1**	**29**	**13.8**	**–7**	**1**	**0.0**	**47**	**10**	**10:14**								
	Quebec Citadelles	AHL	13	4	5	9	32												2	0	0	0	2			

Season	Club	League	GP	G	A	Pts	PIM	PP	SH	GW	S	%	+/-	TF	F%	H	SB	Min	GP	G	A	Pts	PIM	PP	SH	GW
			Regular Season																Playoffs							
2000-01	**Montreal**	**NHL**	**46**	**2**	**3**	**5**	**59**	**0**	**0**	**0**	**32**	**6.3**	**-9**	**3**	**100.0**	**93**	**10**	**8:28**								
	Quebec Citadelles	AHL	15	7	9	16	51												7	1	2	3	2			
	NHL Totals		**86**	**6**	**5**	**11**	**83**	**0**	**1**	**1**	**66**	**9.1**		**4**	**75.0**	**148**	**22**	**9:04**								

ASTASHENKO, Kaspars

(ahs-tuh-SHEHN-koh, KAHS-pars) **T.B.**

Defense/Forward. Shoots left. 6'2", 183 lbs. Born, Riga, Latvia, February 17, 1975. Tampa Bay's 5th choice, 127th overall, in 1999 Entry Draft.

Season	Club	League	GP	G	A	Pts	PIM	PP	SH	GW	S	%	+/-	TF	F%	H	SB	Min	GP	G	A	Pts	PIM	PP	SH	GW
1993-94	Pardaugava Riga	CIS	4	0	0	0	10																			
1994-95	Pardaugava Riga	CIS	25	0	0	0	24																			
1995-96	CSKA Moscow	CIS	26	0	1	1	10																			
1996-97	CSKA Moscow	Russia	41	0	0	0	48												2	0	1	1	4			
1997-98	CSKA Moscow	Russia	25	1	3	4	6																			
1998-99	Cincinnati	IHL	74	3	11	14	166												3	0	2	2	6			
	Dayton Bombers	ECHL	2	0	1	1	4																			
99-2000	**Tampa Bay**	**NHL**	**8**	**0**	**1**	**1**	**4**	**0**	**0**	**0**	**3**	**0.0**	**-2**	**0**	**0.0**	**11**	**6**	**16:48**								
	Detroit Vipers	IHL	51	1	10	11	86																			
	Long Beach	IHL	14	0	3	3	10																			
2000-01	**Tampa Bay**	**NHL**	**15**	**1**	**1**	**2**	**4**	**0**	**0**	**0**	**4**	**25.0**	**-4**	**0**	**0.0**	**16**	**1**	**6:50**								
	Detroit Vipers	IHL	51	6	10	16	58																			
	NHL Totals		**23**	**1**	**2**	**3**	**8**	**0**	**0**	**0**	**7**	**14.3**		**0**	**0.0**	**27**	**7**	**10:18**								

ATCHEYNUM, Blair

(ATCH-uh-num, BLAIR)

Right wing. Shoots right. 6'2", 198 lbs. Born, Estevan, Sask., April 20, 1969. Hartford's 2nd choice, 52nd overall, in 1989 Entry Draft.

Season	Club	League	GP	G	A	Pts	PIM	PP	SH	GW	S	%	+/-	TF	F%	H	SB	Min	GP	G	A	Pts	PIM	PP	SH	GW
1984-85	North Battleford	SAHA	26	25	21	46	106																			
1985-86	North Battleford	SJHL	33	16	14	30	41												6	2	0	2	6			
	Saskatoon Blades	WHL	19	1	4	5	22																			
1986-87	Saskatoon Blades	WHL	21	0	4	4	4																			
	Swift Current	WHL	5	2	1	3	0																			
	Moose Jaw	WHL	12	3	0	3	2																			
1987-88	Moose Jaw	WHL	60	32	16	48	52																			
1988-89	Moose Jaw	WHL	71	70	68	138	70												7	2	5	7	13			
1989-90	Binghamton	AHL	78	20	21	41	45																			
1990-91	Springfield	AHL	72	25	27	52	42												13	0	6	6	6			
1991-92	Springfield	AHL	62	16	21	37	64												6	1	1	2	2			
1992-93	**Ottawa**	**NHL**	**4**	**0**	**1**	**1**	**0**	**0**	**0**	**0**	**2**	**0.0**	**-3**													
	New Haven	AHL	51	16	18	34	47																			
1993-94	Columbus Chill	ECHL	16	15	12	27	10																			
	Portland Pirates	AHL	2	0	0	0	0																			
	Springfield	AHL	40	18	22	40	13												6	0	2	2	0			
1994-95	Minnesota Moose	IHL	17	4	6	10	7																			
	Worcester	AHL	55	17	29	46	26																			
1995-96	Cape Breton	AHL	79	30	42	72	65																			
1996-97	Hershey Bears	AHL	77	42	45	87	57												13	6	11	17	6			
1997-98	**St. Louis**	**NHL**	**61**	**11**	**15**	**26**	**10**	**0**	**1**	**3**	**103**	**10.7**	**5**						**10**	**0**	**0**	**0**	**2**	**0**	**0**	**0**
1998-99	**Nashville**	**NHL**	**53**	**8**	**6**	**14**	**16**	**2**	**0**	**1**	**70**	**11.4**	**-10**	**5**	**40.0**	**28**	**26**	**14:54**								
	St. Louis	**NHL**	**12**	**2**	**2**	**4**	**2**	**0**	**0**	**1**	**23**	**8.7**	**2**	**2**	**0.0**	**12**	**5**	**15:38**	**13**	**1**	**3**	**4**	**6**	**0**	**0**	**0**
99-2000	**Chicago**	**NHL**	**47**	**5**	**7**	**12**	**6**	**0**	**0**	**0**	**48**	**10.4**	**-8**	**23**	**17.4**	**27**	**17**	**12:15**								
2000-01	**Chicago**	**NHL**	**19**	**1**	**2**	**3**	**2**	**0**	**0**	**0**	**18**	**5.6**	**-7**	**31**	**35.5**	**21**	**2**	**9:06**								
	Chicago Wolves	IHL	7	1	0	1	0																			
	Norfolk Admirals	AHL	37	12	8	20	16												4	0	0	0	6			
	NHL Totals		**196**	**27**	**33**	**60**	**36**	**2**	**1**	**5**	**264**	**10.2**		**61**	**27.9**	**88**	**50**	**13:10**	**23**	**1**	**3**	**4**	**8**	**0**	**0**	**0**

WHL First All-Star Team (1989) • AHL First All-Star Team (1997)

Claimed by **Ottawa** from **Hartford** in Expansion Draft, June 18, 1992. Signed as a free agent by **St. Louis**, September 15, 1997. Claimed by **Nashville** from **St. Louis** in Expansion Draft, June 26, 1998. Traded to **St. Louis** by **Nashville** for St. Louis' 6th round choice (Zbynek Irgl) in 2000 Entry Draft, March 23, 1999. Signed as a free agent by **Chicago**, September 30, 1999.

AUBIN, Serge

(oh-BEHN, SAIRZH) **CBJ**

Center. Shoots left. 6'1", 194 lbs. Born, Val d'Or, Que., February 15, 1975. Pittsburgh's 9th choice, 161st overall, in 1994 Entry Draft.

Season	Club	League	GP	G	A	Pts	PIM	PP	SH	GW	S	%	+/-	TF	F%	H	SB	Min	GP	G	A	Pts	PIM	PP	SH	GW
1990-91	Abitibi Forestiers	QAAA	27	2	4	6	10																			
1991-92	Abitibi Forestiers	QAAA	42	28	32	60	36												1	0	1	1	0			
1992-93	Drummondville	QMJHL	65	16	34	50	30												8	0	1	1	16			
1993-94	Granby Bisons	QMJHL	63	42	32	74	80												7	2	3	5	8			
1994-95	Granby Bisons	QMJHL	60	37	73	110	55												11	8	15	23	4			
1995-96	Hampton Roads	ECHL	62	24	62	86	74												3	1	4	5	10			
	Cleveland	IHL	2	0	0	0	0												2	0	0	0	0			
1996-97	Cleveland	IHL	57	9	16	25	38												2	0	0	0	0			
1997-98	Syracuse Crunch	AHL	55	6	14	20	57																			
	Hershey Bears	AHL	5	2	1	3	0												7	1	3	4	6			
1998-99	Hershey Bears	AHL	64	30	39	69	58												3	0	1	1	2			
	Colorado	**NHL**	**1**	**0**	**0**	**0**	**0**	**0**	**0**	**0**	**1**	**0.0**	**0**	**1**	**0.0**	**0**	**0**	**4:16**								
99-2000	**Colorado**	**NHL**	**15**	**2**	**1**	**3**	**6**	**0**	**0**	**1**	**14**	**14.3**	**1**	**79**	**50.6**	**15**	**3**	**6:37**	**17**	**0**	**1**	**1**	**6**	**0**	**0**	**0**
	Hershey Bears	AHL	58	42	38	80	56																			
2000-01	**Columbus**	**NHL**	**81**	**13**	**17**	**30**	**107**	**0**	**0**	**2**	**110**	**11.8**	**-20**	**1346**	**51.3**	**144**	**73**	**16:20**								
	NHL Totals		**97**	**15**	**18**	**33**	**113**	**0**	**0**	**3**	**125**	**12.0**		**1426**	**51.3**	**159**	**76**	**14:43**	**17**	**0**	**1**	**1**	**6**	**0**	**0**	**0**

AHL First All-Star Team (2000)

Signed as a free agent by **Hershey** (AHL), July 24, 1998. Signed as a free agent by **Colorado**, December 22, 1998. Signed as a free agent by **Columbus**, July 11, 2000.

AUCOIN, Adrian

(oh-KOIN, AY-dree-an) **NYI**

Defense. Shoots right. 6'2", 210 lbs. Born, Ottawa, Ont., July 3, 1973. Vancouver's 7th choice, 117th overall, in 1992 Entry Draft.

Season	Club	League	GP	G	A	Pts	PIM	PP	SH	GW	S	%	+/-	TF	F%	H	SB	Min	GP	G	A	Pts	PIM	PP	SH	GW
1989-90	Nepean Raiders	OCJHL	54	2	14	16	95												4	0	1	1				
1990-91	Nepean Raiders	OCJHL	56	17	33	50	125																			
1991-92	Boston University	H-East	32	2	10	12	60																			
1992-93	Canada	Nat-Team	42	8	10	18	71																			
1993-94	Canada	Nat-Team	59	5	12	17	80																			
	Canada	Olympics	4	0	0	0	2																			
	Hamilton Canucks	AHL	13	1	2	3	19												4	0	2	2	6			
1994-95	Syracuse Crunch	AHL	71	13	18	31	52																			
	Vancouver	**NHL**	**1**	**1**	**0**	**1**	**0**	**0**	**0**	**0**	**2**	**50.0**	**1**						**4**	**1**	**0**	**1**	**0**	**1**	**0**	**0**
1995-96	**Vancouver**	**NHL**	**49**	**4**	**14**	**18**	**34**	**2**	**0**	**0**	**85**	**4.7**	**8**						**6**	**0**	**0**	**0**	**2**	**0**	**0**	**0**
	Syracuse Crunch	AHL	29	5	13	18	47																			
1996-97	**Vancouver**	**NHL**	**70**	**5**	**16**	**21**	**63**	**1**	**0**	**0**	**116**	**4.3**	**0**													
1997-98	**Vancouver**	**NHL**	**35**	**3**	**3**	**6**	**21**	**1**	**0**	**1**	**44**	**6.8**	**-4**													
1998-99	**Vancouver**	**NHL**	**82**	**23**	**11**	**34**	**77**	**18**	**2**	**3**	**174**	**13.2**	**-14**	**1**	**100.0**	**208**	**50**	**23:52**								
99-2000	**Vancouver**	**NHL**	**57**	**10**	**14**	**24**	**30**	**4**	**0**	**1**	**126**	**7.9**	**7**	**0**	**0.0**	**123**	**36**	**23:06**								
2000-01	**Vancouver**	**NHL**	**47**	**3**	**13**	**16**	**20**	**1**	**0**	**0**	**99**	**3.0**	**13**	**0**	**0.0**	**62**	**14**	**18:21**								
	Tampa Bay	**NHL**	**26**	**1**	**11**	**12**	**25**	**1**	**0**	**0**	**60**	**1.7**	**-8**	**0**	**0.0**	**43**	**25**	**23:34**								
	NHL Totals		**367**	**50**	**82**	**132**	**270**	**28**	**2**	**5**	**706**	**7.1**		**1**	**100.0**	**436**	**125**	**22:24**	**10**	**1**	**0**	**1**	**2**	**1**	**0**	**0**

• Missed majority of 1997-98 season recovering from ankle injury suffered in game vs. Anaheim (October 4, 1997) and groin injury suffered in game vs. Pittsburgh (November 1, 1997). Traded to **Tampa Bay** by **Vancouver** with Vancouver's 2nd round choice (Alexander Polushin) in 2001 Entry Draft for Dan Cloutier, February 7, 2001. Traded to **NY Islanders** by **Tampa Bay** with Alexander Kharitonov for Mathieu Biron and NY Islanders' 2nd round choice in 2002 Entry Draft, June 22, 2001.

AUDET, Philippe
(aw-DEHT, fihl-EEP)

Left wing. Shoots left. 6'2", 202 lbs. Born, Ottawa, Ont., June 4, 1977. Detroit's 2nd choice, 52nd overall, in 1995 Entry Draft.

			Regular Season																Playoffs							
Season	Club	League	GP	G	A	Pts	PIM	PP	SH	GW	S	%	+/-	TF	F%	H	SB	Min	GP	G	A	Pts	PIM	PP	SH	GW
1992-93	Beauce-Amiante	QAAA	28	21	24	45	75																			
1993-94	Cap-d-Madelaine	QAAA	34	22	21	43	90												4	3	3	6	6			
1994-95	Granby Bisons	QMJHL	62	19	17	36	93												13	2	5	7	10			
1995-96	Granby Bisons	QMJHL	67	40	43	83	162												21	12	18	30	32			
1996-97	Granby Bisons	QMJHL	67	52	56	108	138												4	4	1	5	35			
	Adirondack	AHL	3	1	1	2	0												1	1	0	1	0			
1997-98	Adirondack	AHL	50	7	8	15	43												1	0	0	0	0			
1998-99	**Detroit**	**NHL**	**4**	**0**	**0**	**0**	**0**	**0**	**0**	**0**	**3**	**0.0**	**-2**	**0**	**0.0**	**4**	**1**	**4:19**								
	Adirondack	AHL	70	20	20	40	77												2	1	0	1	4			
99-2000	Cincinnati Ducks	AHL	62	19	22	41	115																			
	Springfield	AHL	14	3	7	10	6												5	3	1	4	14			
2000-01	Springfield	AHL	80	26	31	57	113																			
	NHL Totals		**4**	**0**	**0**	**0**	**0**	**0**	**0**	**0**	**3**	**0.0**		**0**	**0.0**	**4**	**1**	**4:19**								

Memorial Cup All-Star Team (1996) • QMJHL First All-Star Team (1997)

Traded to **Phoenix** by **Detroit** for Todd Gill, March 13, 2000.

AUDETTE, Donald
(aw-DEHT, DAW-nohld) **DAL.**

Right wing. Shoots right. 5'8", 190 lbs. Born, Laval, Que., September 23, 1969. Buffalo's 8th choice, 183rd overall, in 1989 Entry Draft.

Season	Club	League	GP	G	A	Pts	PIM	PP	SH	GW	S	%	+/-	TF	F%	H	SB	Min	GP	G	A	Pts	PIM	PP	SH	GW
1985-86	Laval-Laurentides	QAAA	41	32	38	70	51												8	5	9	14	10			
1986-87	Laval Titan	QMJHL	66	17	22	39	36												14	2	6	8	10			
1987-88	Laval Titan	QMJHL	63	48	61	109	56												14	7	12	19	20			
1988-89	Laval Titan	QMJHL	70	76	85	161	123												17	17	12	29	43			
1989-90	Rochester	AHL	70	42	46	88	78												15	9	8	17	29			
	Buffalo	**NHL**																	**2**	**0**	**0**	**0**	**0**	**0**	**0**	**0**
1990-91	**Buffalo**	**NHL**	**8**	**4**	**3**	**7**	**4**	**2**	**0**	**1**	**17**	**23.5**	**-1**													
	Rochester	AHL	5	4	0	4	2																			
1991-92	**Buffalo**	**NHL**	**63**	**31**	**17**	**48**	**75**	**5**	**0**	**6**	**153**	**20.3**	**-1**													
1992-93	**Buffalo**	**NHL**	**44**	**12**	**7**	**19**	**51**	**2**	**0**	**0**	**92**	**13.0**	**-8**						**8**	**2**	**2**	**4**	**6**	**0**	**0**	**0**
	Rochester	AHL	6	8	4	12	10																			
1993-94	**Buffalo**	**NHL**	**77**	**29**	**30**	**59**	**41**	**16**	**1**	**4**	**207**	**14.0**	**2**						**7**	**0**	**1**	**1**	**6**	**0**	**0**	**0**
1994-95	**Buffalo**	**NHL**	**46**	**24**	**13**	**37**	**27**	**13**	**0**	**7**	**124**	**19.4**	**-3**						**5**	**1**	**1**	**2**	**4**	**1**	**0**	**0**
1995-96	**Buffalo**	**NHL**	**23**	**12**	**13**	**25**	**18**	**8**	**0**	**1**	**92**	**13.0**	**0**													
1996-97	**Buffalo**	**NHL**	**73**	**28**	**22**	**50**	**48**	**8**	**0**	**5**	**182**	**15.4**	**-6**						**11**	**4**	**5**	**9**	**6**	**3**	**0**	**0**
1997-98	**Buffalo**	**NHL**	**75**	**24**	**20**	**44**	**59**	**10**	**0**	**5**	**198**	**12.1**	**10**						**15**	**5**	**8**	**13**	**10**	**3**	**0**	**2**
1998-99	**Los Angeles**	**NHL**	**49**	**18**	**18**	**36**	**51**	**6**	**0**	**2**	**152**	**11.8**	**7**	**4**	**50.0**	**28**	**9**	**16:50**								
99-2000	**Los Angeles**	**NHL**	**49**	**12**	**20**	**32**	**45**	**1**	**0**	**3**	**112**	**10.7**	**6**	**4**	**50.0**	**12**	**8**	**14:56**								
	Atlanta	**NHL**	**14**	**7**	**4**	**11**	**12**	**0**	**1**	**1**	**50**	**14.0**	**-4**	**0**	**0.0**	**8**	**4**	**21:35**								
2000-01	**Atlanta**	**NHL**	**64**	**32**	**39**	**71**	**64**	**13**	**1**	**2**	**187**	**17.1**	**-3**	**7**	**57.1**	**18**	**23**	**20:18**								
	Buffalo	**NHL**	**12**	**2**	**6**	**8**	**12**	**1**	**0**	**1**	**38**	**5.3**	**1**	**1**	**0.0**	**1**	**1**	**17:25**	**13**	**3**	**6**	**9**	**4**	**0**	**0**	**0**
	NHL Totals		**597**	**235**	**212**	**447**	**507**	**85**	**3**	**38**	**1604**	**14.7**		**16**	**50.0**	**67**	**45**	**17:55**	**61**	**15**	**23**	**38**	**36**	**7**	**0**	**2**

QMJHL First All-Star Team (1989) • AHL First All-Star Team (1990) • Won Dudley "Red" Garret Memorial Trophy (Top Rookie - AHL) (1990) • Played in NHL ALL-Star Game (2001)

• Missed majority of 1990-91 season recovering from knee injury originally suffered in game vs. Edmonton, November 16, 1990. • Missed majority of 1995-96 season recovering from knee injury suffered in training camp, September 23, 1995. Traded to **Los Angeles** by **Buffalo** for Los Angeles' 2nd round choice (Milan Bartovic) in 1999 Entry Draft, December 18, 1998. Traded to **Atlanta** by **Los Angeles** with Frantisek Kaberle for Kelly Buchberger and Nelson Emerson, March 13, 2000. Traded to **Buffalo** by **Atlanta** for the rights to Kamil Piros and Buffalo's 4th round choice (later traded to St. Louis - St. Louis selected Igor Valeyev) in 2001 Entry Draft, March 13, 2001. Signed as a free agent by **Dallas**, July 2, 2001.

AUGUSTA, Patrik
(ah-GOOS-tuh, pa-TREEK)

Right wing. Shoots left. 5'10", 170 lbs. Born, Jihlava, Czech., November 13, 1969. Toronto's 8th choice, 149th overall, in 1992 Entry Draft.

Season	Club	League	GP	G	A	Pts	PIM	PP	SH	GW	S	%	+/-	TF	F%	H	SB	Min	GP	G	A	Pts	PIM	PP	SH	GW
1988-89	Dukla Jihlava	Czech.	15	3	1	4	4																			
1989-90	Dukla Jihlava	Czech.	39	9	11	20	....												7	3	1	4	....			
1990-91	Dukla Jihlava	Czech.	51	20	23	43	....																			
1991-92	Dukla Jihlava	Czech.	42	16	16	32	26																			
	Czechoslovakia	Olympics	8	3	2	5	0																			
1992-93	St. John's Leafs	AHL	75	32	45	77	74												8	3	3	6	23			
1993-94	**Toronto**	**NHL**	**2**	**0**	**0**	**0**	**0**	**0**	**0**	**0**	**3**	**0.0**	**0**													
	St. John's Leafs	AHL	77	*53	43	96	105												11	4	8	12	4			
1994-95	St. John's Leafs	AHL	71	37	32	69	98												4	2	0	2	7			
1995-96	Los Angeles	IHL	79	34	51	85	83																			
1996-97	Long Beach	IHL	82	45	42	87	96												18	4	4	8	33			
1997-98	Long Beach	IHL	82	41	40	81	84												17	11	7	18	20			
1998-99	Long Beach	IHL	68	24	35	59	125												8	4	6	10	4			
	Washington	**NHL**	**2**	**0**	**0**	**0**	**0**	**0**	**0**	**0**	**4**	**0.0**	**0**	**0**	**0.0**	**0**	**1**	**13:38**								
99-2000	Schwenningen	DEL	34	14	15	29	52																			
2000-01	Schwenningen	DEL	56	25	25	50	44																			
	NHL Totals		**4**	**0**	**0**	**0**	**0**	**0**	**0**	**0**	**7**	**0.0**		**0**	**0.0**	**0**	**1**	**13:38**								

AHL Second All-Star Team (1994) • IHL Second All-Star Team (1997)

Signed as a free agent by **Washington**, December 11, 1998.

AXELSSON, P.J.
(AHX-ehl-suhn, PAIR, YEW-hahn) **BOS.**

Left wing. Shoots left. 6'1", 175 lbs. Born, Kungalv, Sweden, February 26, 1975. Boston's 7th choice, 177th overall, in 1995 Entry Draft.

Season	Club	League	GP	G	A	Pts	PIM	PP	SH	GW	S	%	+/-	TF	F%	H	SB	Min	GP	G	A	Pts	PIM	PP	SH	GW
1992-93	Vastra Frolunda	Swede-Jr.	16	9	5	14	12																			
	Vastra Frolunda	Sweden-2	1	0	0	0	0																			
1993-94	Vastra Frolunda	Sweden	11	0	0	0	4												4	0	0	0	0			
1994-95	Vastra Frolunda	Swede-Jr.	19	16	9	25	22																			
	Vastra Frolunda	Sweden	11	2	1	3	6												5	0	0	0	0			
1995-96	Vastra Frolunda	Sweden	36	15	5	20	10												13	3	0	3	10			
1996-97	Vastra Frolunda	Sweden	50	19	15	34	34												3	0	2	2	0			
	Vastra Frolunda	EuroHL	3	1	1	2	0												3	0	0	0	2			
1997-98	**Boston**	**NHL**	**82**	**8**	**19**	**27**	**38**	**2**	**0**	**1**	**144**	**5.6**	**-14**						**6**	**1**	**0**	**1**	**0**	**0**	**0**	**0**
1998-99	**Boston**	**NHL**	**77**	**7**	**10**	**17**	**18**	**0**	**0**	**2**	**146**	**4.8**	**-14**	**8**	**75.0**	**66**	**22**	**16:38**	**12**	**1**	**1**	**2**	**4**	**0**	**0**	**0**
99-2000	**Boston**	**NHL**	**81**	**10**	**16**	**26**	**24**	**0**	**0**	**4**	**186**	**5.4**	**1**	**22**	**27.3**	**82**	**22**	**16:43**								
2000-01	**Boston**	**NHL**	**81**	**8**	**15**	**23**	**27**	**0**	**0**	**2**	**146**	**5.5**	**-12**	**41**	**36.6**	**94**	**14**	**12:30**								
	NHL Totals		**321**	**33**	**60**	**93**	**107**	**2**	**0**	**9**	**622**	**5.3**		**71**	**38.0**	**244**	**58**	**15:16**	**18**	**2**	**1**	**3**	**4**	**0**	**0**	**0**

BABENKO, Yuri
(bah-BEHN-koh, EW-ree) **COL.**

Center. Shoots left. 6'1", 200 lbs. Born, Penza, USSR, January 2, 1978. Colorado's 2nd choice, 51st overall, in 1996 Entry Draft.

Season	Club	League	GP	G	A	Pts	PIM	PP	SH	GW	S	%	+/-	TF	F%	H	SB	Min	GP	G	A	Pts	PIM	PP	SH	GW
1995-96	Krylja Sovetov	CIS	21	0	0	0	16																			
1996-97	Krylja Sovetov-2	Russia-3	26	8	10	18	24																			
	HC Moscow	Russia-2	24	3	3	6	12																			
	Krylja Sovetov	Russia	4	1	0	1	4																			
1997-98	Plymouth Whalers	OHL	59	22	34	56	22												15	3	7	10	24			
1998-99	Hershey Bears	AHL	74	11	15	26	47												2	0	1	1	0			
99-2000	Hershey Bears	AHL	75	20	25	45	53												14	4	3	7	37			
2000-01	**Colorado**	**NHL**	**3**	**0**	**0**	**0**	**0**	**0**	**0**	**0**	**2**	**0.0**	**0**	**26**	**23.1**	**4**	**0**	**10:34**								
	Hershey Bears	AHL	71	17	18	35	80												12	2	1	3	6			
	NHL Totals		**3**	**0**	**0**	**0**	**0**	**0**	**0**	**0**	**2**	**0.0**		**26**	**23.1**	**4**	**0**	**10:34**								

BALMOCHNYKH, Maxim
(bahl-MAWCH-nihky, mahx-EEM) **ANA.**

Left wing. Shoots left. 6'1", 180 lbs. Born, Lipetsk, USSR, March 7, 1979. Anaheim's 2nd choice, 45th overall, in 1997 Entry Draft.

			Regular Season																Playoffs							
Season	Club	League	GP	G	A	Pts	PIM	PP	SH	GW	S	%	+/-	TF	F%	H	SB	Min	GP	G	A	Pts	PIM	PP	SH	GW
1994-95	HC Lipetsk	CIS-2	3	0	1	1	4	....	....	....	....	....	....	....	....	....	....	....	....	....	....	....	....	....	....	....
1995-96	HC Lipetsk	CIS-2	40	15	5	20	60	....	....	....	....	....	....	....	....	....	....	....	....	....	....	....	....	....	....	....
1996-97	Lada Togliatti	Russia	18	6	1	7	22	....	....	....	....	....	....	....	....	....	....	....	....	....	....	....	....	....	....	....
1997-98	Lada Togliatti	Russia	37	10	4	14	46	....	....	....	....	....	....	....	....	....	....	....	....	....	....	....	....	....	....	....
	HC Chelyabinsk	Russia	2	0	0	0	2	....	....	....	....	....	....	....	....	....	....	....	....	....	....	....	....	....	....	....
1998-99	Lada Togliatti	Russia	15	2	1	3	10	....	....	....	....	....	....	....	....	....	....	....	4	0	1	1	8	....	....	....
	Quebec Remparts	QMJHL	21	9	22	31	38	....	....	....	....	....	....	....	....	....	....	....	....	....	....	....	....	....	....	....
99-2000	**Anaheim**	**NHL**	**6**	**0**	**1**	**1**	**2**	**0**	**0**	**0**	**6**	**0.0**	**2**	**0**	**0.0**	**5**	**0**	**6:44**	....	....	....	....	....	....	....	....
	Cincinnati Ducks	AHL	40	9	12	21	82	....	....	....	....	....	....	....	....	....	....	....	....	....	....	....	....	....	....	....
2000-01	Cincinnati Ducks	AHL	65	6	9	15	45	....	....	....	....	....	....	....	....	....	....	....	....	....	....	....	....	....	....	....
	NHL Totals		**6**	**0**	**1**	**1**	**2**	**0**	**0**	**0**	**6**	**0.0**		**0**	**0.0**	**5**	**0**	**6:44**	....	....	....	....	....	....	....	....

BANCROFT, Steve
(BAN-crawft, STEEV) **S.J.**

Defense. Shoots left. 6'1", 214 lbs. Born, Toronto, Ont., October 6, 1970. Toronto's 3rd choice, 21st overall, in 1989 Entry Draft.

			Regular Season																Playoffs							
Season	Club	League	GP	G	A	Pts	PIM	PP	SH	GW	S	%	+/-	TF	F%	H	SB	Min	GP	G	A	Pts	PIM	PP	SH	GW
1985-86	Madoc MTM	OJHL-C	7	1	0	1	21	....	....	....	....	....	....	....	....	....	....	....	....	....	....	....	....	....	....	....
	Trenton Bobcats	MTJHL	16	1	5	6	16	....	....	....	....	....	....	....	....	....	....	....	....	....	....	....	....	....	....	....
1986-87	St. Catharines	OJHL-B	11	5	8	13	20	....	....	....	....	....	....	....	....	....	....	....	....	....	....	....	....	....	....	....
	Trenton Bobcats	MTJHL	13	2	3	5	45	....	....	....	....	....	....	....	....	....	....	....	....	....	....	....	....	....	....	....
1987-88	Belleville Bulls	OHL	56	1	8	9	42	....	....	....	....	....	....	....	....	....	....	....	....	....	....	....	....	....	....	....
1988-89	Belleville Bulls	OHL	66	7	30	37	99	....	....	....	....	....	....	....	....	....	....	....	5	0	2	2	10	....	....	....
1989-90	Belleville Bulls	OHL	53	10	33	43	135	....	....	....	....	....	....	....	....	....	....	....	11	3	9	12	38	....	....	....
1990-91	Newmarket	AHL	9	0	3	3	22	....	....	....	....	....	....	....	....	....	....	....	....	....	....	....	....	....	....	....
	Maine Mariners	AHL	53	2	12	14	46	....	....	....	....	....	....	....	....	....	....	....	2	0	0	0	2	....	....	....
1991-92	Maine Mariners	AHL	26	1	3	4	45	....	....	....	....	....	....	....	....	....	....	....	....	....	....	....	....	....	....	....
	Indianapolis Ice	IHL	36	8	23	31	49	....	....	....	....	....	....	....	....	....	....	....	....	....	....	....	....	....	....	....
1992-93	**Chicago**	**NHL**	**1**	**0**	**0**	**0**	**0**	**0**	**0**	**0**	**0**	**0.0**	**0**	....	....	....	....	....	....	....	....	....	....	....	....	....
	Indianapolis Ice	IHL	53	10	35	45	138	....	....	....	....	....	....	....	....	....	....	....	....	....	....	....	....	....	....	....
	Moncton Hawks	AHL	21	3	13	16	16	....	....	....	....	....	....	....	....	....	....	....	5	0	0	0	16	....	....	....
1993-94	Cleveland	IHL	33	2	12	14	58	....	....	....	....	....	....	....	....	....	....	....	....	....	....	....	....	....	....	....
1994-95	Detroit Vipers	IHL	6	1	3	4	0	....	....	....	....	....	....	....	....	....	....	....	....	....	....	....	....	....	....	....
	Fort Wayne	IHL	50	7	17	24	100	....	....	....	....	....	....	....	....	....	....	....	....	....	....	....	....	....	....	....
	St. John's Leafs	AHL	4	2	0	2	2	....	....	....	....	....	....	....	....	....	....	....	5	0	3	3	8	....	....	....
1995-96	Los Angeles	IHL	15	3	10	13	22	....	....	....	....	....	....	....	....	....	....	....	....	....	....	....	....	....	....	....
	Chicago Wolves	IHL	64	9	41	50	91	....	....	....	....	....	....	....	....	....	....	....	9	1	7	8	22	....	....	....
1996-97	Chicago Wolves	IHL	39	6	10	16	66	....	....	....	....	....	....	....	....	....	....	....	....	....	....	....	....	....	....	....
	Las Vegas	IHL	36	9	28	37	64	....	....	....	....	....	....	....	....	....	....	....	3	0	0	0	2	....	....	....
1997-98	Las Vegas	IHL	70	15	44	59	148	....	....	....	....	....	....	....	....	....	....	....	....	....	....	....	....	....	....	....
	Saint John Flames	AHL	9	0	4	4	12	....	....	....	....	....	....	....	....	....	....	....	19	2	11	13	30	....	....	....
1998-99	Saint John Flames	AHL	8	1	4	5	22	....	....	....	....	....	....	....	....	....	....	....	....	....	....	....	....	....	....	....
	Providence Bruins	AHL	62	7	34	41	78	....	....	....	....	....	....	....	....	....	....	....	15	0	6	6	28	....	....	....
99-2000	Cincinnati	IHL	39	6	14	20	37	....	....	....	....	....	....	....	....	....	....	....	....	....	....	....	....	....	....	....
	Houston Aeros	IHL	37	2	18	20	47	....	....	....	....	....	....	....	....	....	....	....	10	2	6	8	40	....	....	....
2000-01	Kentucky	AHL	80	23	50	73	162	....	....	....	....	....	....	....	....	....	....	....	3	0	2	2	8	....	....	....
	NHL Totals		**1**	**0**	**0**	**0**	**0**	**0**	**0**	**0**	**0**	**0.0**		....	....	....	....	....	....	....	....	....	....	....	....	....

AHL First All-Star Team (2001)

Traded to **Boston** by **Toronto** for Rob Cimetta, November 9, 1990. Traded to **Chicago** by **Boston** with Boston's 11th round choice (later traded to Winnipeg - Winnipeg selected Russ Hewson) in 1993 Entry Draft for Chicago's 11th round choice (Evgeny Pavlov) in 1992 Entry Draft, January 8, 1992. Traded to **Winnipeg** by **Chicago** with future considerations for Troy Murray, February 21, 1993. Claimed by **Florida** from **Winnipeg** in Expansion Draft, June 24, 1993. Signed as a free agent by **Pittsburgh**, August 2, 1993. Signed as a free agent by **Carolina**, August 4, 1999. Traded to **Houston** (IHL) by **Cincinnati** (IHL) for Brian Felsner with Carolina retaining his NHL rights, January 19, 2000. Signed as a free agent by **San Jose**, August 10, 2000.

BANHAM, Frank
(BAN-ham, FRANK)

Right wing. Shoots right. 6', 190 lbs. Born, Calahoo, Alta., April 14, 1975. Washington's 4th choice, 147th overall, in 1993 Entry Draft.

			Regular Season																Playoffs							
Season	Club	League	GP	G	A	Pts	PIM	PP	SH	GW	S	%	+/-	TF	F%	H	SB	Min	GP	G	A	Pts	PIM	PP	SH	GW
1991-92	Fernie Ghostriders	RMJHL	47	45	45	90	120	....	....	....	....	....	....	....	....	....	....	....	....	....	....	....	....	....	....	....
1992-93	Saskatoon Blades	WHL	71	29	33	62	55	....	....	....	....	....	....	....	....	....	....	....	9	2	7	9	8	....	....	....
1993-94	Saskatoon Blades	WHL	65	28	39	67	99	....	....	....	....	....	....	....	....	....	....	....	16	8	11	19	36	....	....	....
1994-95	Saskatoon Blades	WHL	70	50	39	89	63	....	....	....	....	....	....	....	....	....	....	....	8	2	6	8	12	....	....	....
1995-96	Saskatoon Blades	WHL	72	*83	69	152	116	....	....	....	....	....	....	....	....	....	....	....	4	6	0	6	2	....	....	....
	Baltimore Bandits	AHL	9	1	4	5	0	....	....	....	....	....	....	....	....	....	....	....	7	1	1	2	2	....	....	....
1996-97	**Anaheim**	**NHL**	**3**	**0**	**0**	**0**	**0**	**0**	**0**	**0**	**1**	**0.0**	**−2**	....	....	....	....	....	....	....	....	....	....	....	....	....
	Baltimore Bandits	AHL	21	11	13	24	4	....	....	....	....	....	....	....	....	....	....	....	....	....	....	....	....	....	....	....
1997-98	**Anaheim**	**NHL**	**21**	**9**	**2**	**11**	**12**	**1**	**0**	**0**	**43**	**20.9**	**−6**	....	....	....	....	....	....	....	....	....	....	....	....	....
	Cincinnati Ducks	AHL	35	7	8	15	39	....	....	....	....	....	....	....	....	....	....	....	....	....	....	....	....	....	....	....
1998-99	Cincinnati Ducks	AHL	66	22	27	49	20	....	....	....	....	....	....	....	....	....	....	....	3	0	1	1	0	....	....	....
99-2000	**Anaheim**	**NHL**	**3**	**0**	**0**	**0**	**2**	**0**	**0**	**0**	**4**	**0.0**	**0**	**5**	**40.0**	**1**	**0**	**6:47**	....	....	....	....	....	....	....	....
	Cincinnati Ducks	AHL	72	19	22	41	58	....	....	....	....	....	....	....	....	....	....	....	....	....	....	....	....	....	....	....
2000-01	Blues Espoo	Finland	56	24	27	51	70	....	....	....	....	....	....	....	....	....	....	....	....	....	....	....	....	....	....	....
	NHL Totals		**27**	**9**	**2**	**11**	**14**	**1**	**0**	**0**	**48**	**18.8**		**5**	**40.0**	**1**	**0**	**6:47**	....	....	....	....	....	....	....	....

WHL East First All-Star Team (1996)

Signed as a free agent by **Anaheim**, January 27, 1996. Signed as a free agent by **Jokerit Helsinki** (Finland), April 24, 2001.

BANNISTER, Drew
(BAN-nihs-stuhr, DREW) **ANA.**

Defense. Shoots right. 6'2", 200 lbs. Born, Belleville, Ont., September 4, 1974. Tampa Bay's 2nd choice, 26th overall, in 1992 Entry Draft.

			Regular Season																Playoffs							
Season	Club	League	GP	G	A	Pts	PIM	PP	SH	GW	S	%	+/-	TF	F%	H	SB	Min	GP	G	A	Pts	PIM	PP	SH	GW
1989-90	Sudbury Legion	NOHA	26	13	14	27	98	....	....	....	....	....	....	....	....	....	....	....	....	....	....	....	....	....	....	....
1990-91	Sault Ste. Marie	OHL	41	2	8	10	51	....	....	....	....	....	....	....	....	....	....	....	4	0	0	0	0	....	....	....
1991-92	Sault Ste. Marie	OHL	64	4	21	25	122	....	....	....	....	....	....	....	....	....	....	....	16	3	10	13	36	....	....	....
1992-93	Sault Ste. Marie	OHL	59	5	28	33	114	....	....	....	....	....	....	....	....	....	....	....	18	2	7	9	12	....	....	....
1993-94	Sault Ste. Marie	OHL	58	7	43	50	108	....	....	....	....	....	....	....	....	....	....	....	14	6	9	15	20	....	....	....
1994-95	Atlanta Knights	IHL	72	5	7	12	74	....	....	....	....	....	....	....	....	....	....	....	5	0	2	2	22	....	....	....
1995-96	**Tampa Bay**	**NHL**	**13**	**0**	**1**	**1**	**4**	**0**	**0**	**0**	**10**	**0.0**	**−1**	....	....	....	....	....	....	....	....	....	....	....	....	....
	Atlanta Knights	IHL	61	3	13	16	105	....	....	....	....	....	....	....	....	....	....	....	3	0	0	0	4	....	....	....
1996-97	**Tampa Bay**	**NHL**	**64**	**4**	**13**	**17**	**44**	**1**	**0**	**0**	**57**	**7.0**	**−21**	....	....	....	....	....	....	....	....	....	....	....	....	....
	Edmonton	**NHL**	**1**	**0**	**1**	**1**	**0**	**0**	**0**	**0**	**2**	**0.0**	**−2**	....	....	....	....	....	**12**	**0**	**0**	**0**	**30**	**0**	**0**	**0**
1997-98	**Edmonton**	**NHL**	**34**	**0**	**2**	**2**	**42**	**0**	**0**	**0**	**27**	**0.0**	**−7**	....	....	....	....	....	....	....	....	....	....	....	....	....
	Anaheim	**NHL**	**27**	**0**	**6**	**6**	**47**	**0**	**0**	**0**	**23**	**0.0**	**−2**	....	....	....	....	....	....	....	....	....	....	....	....	....
1998-99	Las Vegas	IHL	16	2	1	3	73	....	....	....	....	....	....	....	....	....	....	....	....	....	....	....	....	....	....	....
	Tampa Bay	**NHL**	**21**	**1**	**2**	**3**	**24**	**0**	**0**	**0**	**29**	**3.4**	**−4**	**0**	**0.0**	**25**	**11**	**15:49**	....	....	....	....	....	....	....	....
99-2000	Hartford	AHL	44	6	14	20	121	....	....	....	....	....	....	....	....	....	....	....	18	2	9	11	53	....	....	....
2000-01	**NY Rangers**	**NHL**	**3**	**0**	**0**	**0**	**0**	**0**	**0**	**0**	**3**	**0.0**	**−1**	**0**	**0.0**	**3**	**3**	**10:47**	....	....	....	....	....	....	....	....
	Hartford	AHL	73	9	30	39	143	....	....	....	....	....	....	....	....	....	....	....	5	0	2	2	6	....	....	....
	NHL Totals		**163**	**5**	**25**	**30**	**161**	**1**	**0**	**0**	**151**	**3.3**		**0**	**0.0**	**28**	**14**	**15:11**	**12**	**0**	**0**	**0**	**30**	**0**	**0**	**0**

Memorial Cup All-Star Team (1993) • OHL Second All-Star Team (1994)

Traded to **Edmonton** by **Tampa Bay** with Tampa Bay's 6th round choice (Peter Sarno) in 1997 Entry Draft for Jeff Norton, March 18, 1997. Traded to **Anaheim** by **Edmonton** for Bobby Dollas, January 9, 1998. Traded to **Tampa Bay** by **Anaheim** for Tampa Bay's 5th round choice (Peter Podhradsky) in 2000 Entry Draft, December 10, 1998. Signed as a free agent by **NY Rangers**, October 3, 1999. Signed as a free agent by **Anaheim**, July 27, 2001.

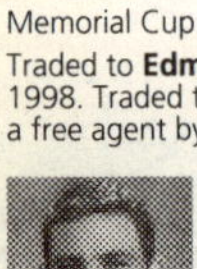

BARNABY, Matthew
(BAHR-na-BEE, MAT-thew) **T.B.**

Right wing. Shoots left. 6', 189 lbs. Born, Ottawa, Ont., May 4, 1973. Buffalo's 5th choice, 83rd overall, in 1992 Entry Draft.

			Regular Season																Playoffs							
Season	Club	League	GP	G	A	Pts	PIM	PP	SH	GW	S	%	+/-	TF	F%	H	SB	Min	GP	G	A	Pts	PIM	PP	SH	GW
1989-90	Hull Frontaliers	QAHA	50	43	50	93	149	....	....	....	....	....	....	....	....	....	....	....	....	....	....	....	....	....	....	....
	L'Outaouais Elans	QAAA	2	0	0	0	0	....	....	....	....	....	....	....	....	....	....	....	....	....	....	....	....	....	....	....
1990-91	Beauport	QMJHL	52	9	5	14	262	....	....	....	....	....	....	....	....	....	....	....	....	....	....	....	....	....	....	....
1991-92	Beauport	QMJHL	63	29	37	66	*476	....	....	....	....	....	....	....	....	....	....	....	....	....	....	....	....	....	....	....
1992-93	Victoriaville Tigres	QMJHL	65	44	67	111	*448	....	....	....	....	....	....	....	....	....	....	....	6	2	4	6	44	....	....	....
	Buffalo	**NHL**	**2**	**1**	**0**	**1**	**10**	**1**	**0**	**0**	**8**	**12.5**	**0**	....	....	....	....	....	**1**	**0**	**1**	**1**	**4**	**0**	**0**	**0**

			Regular Season																Playoffs							
Season	Club	League	GP	G	A	Pts	PIM	PP	SH	GW	S	%	+/-	TF	F%	H	SB	Min	GP	G	A	Pts	PIM	PP	SH	GW
1993-94	Buffalo	NHL	35	2	4	6	106	1	0	0	13	15.4	–7						3	0	0	0	17	0	0	0
	Rochester	AHL	42	10	32	42	153																			
1994-95	Rochester	AHL	56	21	29	50	274																			
	Buffalo	NHL	23	1	1	2	116	0	0	0	27	3.7	–2													
1995-96	Buffalo	NHL	73	15	16	31	*335	0	0	0	131	11.5	–2													
1996-97	Buffalo	NHL	68	19	24	43	249	2	0	1	121	15.7	16						8	0	4	4	36	0	0	0
1997-98	Buffalo	NHL	72	5	20	25	289	0	0	2	96	5.2	8						15	7	6	13	22	3	0	1
1998-99	Buffalo	NHL	44	4	14	18	143	0	0	3	52	7.7	–2	6	16.7	45	8	13:56								
	Pittsburgh	NHL	18	2	2	4	34	1	0	0	27	7.4	–10	3	66.7	40	6	13:33	13	0	0	0	35	0	0	0
99-2000	Pittsburgh	NHL	64	12	12	24	197	0	0	3	80	15.0	3	75	44.0	99	10	12:38	11	0	2	2	29	0	0	0
2000-01	Pittsburgh	NHL	47	1	4	5	*168	0	0	0	38	2.6	–7	15	33.3	55	5	7:49								
	Tampa Bay	NHL	29	4	4	8	*97	1	0	0	29	13.8	–3	1	100.0	32	7	12:34								
	NHL Totals		475	66	101	167	1744	6	0	9	622	10.6		100	42.0	271	36	11:52	51	7	13	20	143	3	0	1

Traded to **Pittsburgh** by **Buffalo** for Stu Barnes, March 11, 1999. Traded to **Tampa Bay** by **Pittsburgh** for Wayne Primeau, February 1, 2001.

BARNES, Stu

(BAHRNZ, STEW) **BUF.**

Center. Shoots right. 5'11", 180 lbs. Born, Spruce Grove, Alta., December 25, 1970. Winnipeg's 1st choice, 4th overall, in 1989 Entry Draft.

1986-87	St. Albert Saints	AJHL	53	41	34	*75	103												19	7	15	22				
1987-88	New Westminster	WHL	71	37	64	101	88												5	2	3	5	6			
1988-89	Tri-City Americans	WHL	70	59	82	141	117												7	6	5	11	10			
1989-90	Tri-City Americans	WHL	63	52	92	144	165												7	1	5	6	26			
1990-91	Canada	Nat-Team	53	22	27	49	68																			
1991-92	Winnipeg	NHL	46	8	9	17	26	4	0	0	75	10.7	–2													
	Moncton Hawks	AHL	30	13	19	32	10												11	3	9	12	6			
1992-93	Winnipeg	NHL	38	12	10	22	10	3	0	3	73	16.4	–3						6	1	3	4	2	0	0	0
	Moncton Hawks	AHL	42	23	31	54	58																			
1993-94	Winnipeg	NHL	18	5	4	9	8	2	0	0	24	20.8	–1													
	Florida	NHL	59	18	20	38	30	6	1	3	148	12.2	5													
1994-95	Florida	NHL	41	10	19	29	8	1	0	2	93	10.8	7													
1995-96	Florida	NHL	72	19	25	44	46	8	0	5	158	12.0	–12						22	6	10	16	4	2	0	2
1996-97	Florida	NHL	19	2	8	10	10	1	0	0	44	4.5	–3													
	Pittsburgh	NHL	62	17	22	39	16	4	0	3	132	12.9	–20						5	0	1	1	0	0	0	0
1997-98	Pittsburgh	NHL	78	30	35	65	30	15	1	5	196	15.3	15						6	3	3	6	2	0	0	1
1998-99	Pittsburgh	NHL	64	20	12	32	20	13	0	3	155	12.9	–12	720	51.9	57	13	17:52								
	Buffalo	NHL	17	0	4	4	10	0	0	0	25	0.0	1	236	51.3	15	4	18:20	21	7	3	10	6	4	0	1
99-2000	Buffalo	NHL	82	20	25	45	16	8	2	2	137	14.6	–3	778	48.5	22	32	17:23	5	3	0	3	2	2	0	1
2000-01	Buffalo	NHL	75	19	24	43	26	3	2	5	160	11.9	–2	1470	48.3	19	35	19:06	13	4	4	8	2	2	0	2
	NHL Totals		671	180	217	397	256	68	6	31	1420	12.7		3204	49.4	113	84	18:07	78	24	24	48	18	10	0	7

WHL West Second All-Star Team (1988, 1989)

Traded to **Florida** by **Winnipeg** with St. Louis' 6th round choice (previously acquired by Winnipeg - later traded to Edmonton - later traded to Winnipeg - Winnipeg selected Chris Kibermanis) in 1994 Entry Draft for Randy Gilhen, November 25, 1993. Traded to **Pittsburgh** by **Florida** with Jason Woolley for Chris Wells, November 19, 1996. Traded to **Buffalo** by **Pittsburgh** for Matthew Barnaby, March 11, 1999.

BARON, Murray

(BAIR-uhn, MUHR-ray) **VAN.**

Defense. Shoots left. 6'3", 215 lbs. Born, Prince George, B.C., June 1, 1967. Philadelphia's 7th choice, 167th overall, in 1986 Entry Draft.

1984-85	Vernon Lakers	BCJHL	37	5	9	14	93												13	5	6	11	107			
1985-86	Vernon Lakers	BCJHL	46	12	32	44	179												7	1	2	3	13			
1986-87	North Dakota	WCHA	41	4	10	14	62																			
1987-88	North Dakota	WCHA	41	1	10	11	95																			
1988-89	North Dakota	WCHA	40	2	6	8	92																			
	Hershey Bears	AHL	9	0	3	3	8																			
1989-90	Philadelphia	NHL	16	2	2	4	12	0	0	0	18	11.1	–1													
	Hershey Bears	AHL	50	0	10	10	101																			
1990-91	Philadelphia	NHL	67	8	8	16	74	3	0	1	86	9.3	–3													
	Hershey Bears	AHL	6	2	3	5	0																			
1991-92	St. Louis	NHL	67	3	8	11	94	0	0	0	55	5.5	–3						2	0	0	0	2	0	0	0
1992-93	St. Louis	NHL	53	2	2	4	59	0	0	1	42	4.8	–5						11	0	0	0	12	0	0	0
1993-94	St. Louis	NHL	77	5	9	14	123	0	0	0	73	6.8	–14						4	0	0	0	10	0	0	0
1994-95	St. Louis	NHL	39	0	5	5	93	0	0	0	28	0.0	9						7	1	1	2	2	0	0	0
1995-96	St. Louis	NHL	82	2	9	11	190	0	0	0	86	2.3	3						13	1	0	1	20	0	1	0
1996-97	St. Louis	NHL	11	0	2	2	11	0	0	0	7	0.0	–4													
	Montreal	NHL	60	1	5	6	107	0	0	0	52	1.9	–16													
	Phoenix	NHL	8	0	0	0	4	0	0	0	5	0.0	0						1	0	0	0	0	0	0	0
1997-98	Phoenix	NHL	45	1	5	6	106	0	0	0	23	4.3	–10						6	0	2	2	6	0	0	0
1998-99	Vancouver	NHL	81	2	6	8	115	0	0	0	53	3.8	–23	0	0.0	192	100	18:14								
99-2000	Vancouver	NHL	81	2	10	12	67	0	0	0	48	4.2	8	2	50.0	187	185	21:36								
2000-01	Vancouver	NHL	82	3	8	11	63	0	0	1	56	5.4	–13	3	66.7	168	170	19:24	4	0	0	0	0	0	0	0
	NHL Totals		769	31	79	110	1118	3	0	3	632	4.9		5	60.0	547	455	19:45	48	2	3	5	52	0	1	0

Traded to **St. Louis** by **Philadelphia** with Ron Sutter for Dan Quinn and Rod Brind'Amour, September 22, 1991. Traded to **Montreal** by **St. Louis** with Shayne Corson and St. Louis' 5th round choice (Gennady Razin) in 1997 Entry Draft for Pierre Turgeon, Rory Fitzpatrick and Craig Conroy, October 29, 1996. Traded to **Phoenix** by **Montreal** with Chris Murray for Dave Manson, March 18, 1997. Signed as a free agent by **Vancouver**, July 14, 1998.

BARRIE, Len

(BAIR-ree, LEHN)

Center. Shoots left. 6', 200 lbs. Born, Kimberley, B.C., June 4, 1969. Edmonton's 7th choice, 124th overall, in 1988 Entry Draft.

1984-85	Kelowna Blazers	BCAHA	20	51	55	106	24																			
1985-86	Calgary Spurs	AJHL	23	7	14	21	86																			
	Calgary Wranglers	WHL	32	3	0	3	18																			
1986-87	Calgary Wranglers	WHL	34	13	13	26	81																			
	Victoria Cougars	WHL	34	7	6	13	92												5	0	1	1	15			
1987-88	Victoria Cougars	WHL	70	37	49	86	192												8	2	0	2	29			
1988-89	Victoria Cougars	WHL	67	39	48	87	157												7	5	2	7	23			
1989-90	Kamloops Blazers	WHL	70	*85	*100	*185	108												17	*14	23	*37	24			
	Philadelphia	NHL	1	0	0	0	0	0	0	0	0	0.0	–2													
1990-91	Hershey Bears	AHL	63	26	32	58	60												7	4	0	4	12			
1991-92	Hershey Bears	AHL	75	42	43	85	78												3	0	2	2	32			
1992-93	Philadelphia	NHL	8	2	2	4	9	0	0	0	14	14.3	2													
	Hershey Bears	AHL	61	31	45	76	162																			
1993-94	Florida	NHL	2	0	0	0	0	0	0	0	0	0.0	–2													
	Cincinnati	IHL	77	45	71	116	246												11	8	13	21	60			
1994-95	Cleveland	IHL	28	13	30	43	137																			
	Pittsburgh	NHL	48	3	11	14	66	0	0	1	37	8.1	–4						4	1	0	1	8	1	0	0
1995-96	Pittsburgh	NHL	5	0	0	0	18	0	0	0	5	0.0	–1													
	Cleveland	IHL	55	29	43	72	178												3	2	3	5	6			
1996-97	San Antonio	IHL	57	26	40	66	196												9	5	5	10	20			
1997-98	San Antonio	IHL	32	7	13	20	90																			
	Frankfurt Lions	DEL	25	11	19	30	32												6	2	3	5	35			
1998-99	Frankfurt Lions	DEL	41	24	35	59	105												8	2	4	6	43			
99-2000	Los Angeles	NHL	46	5	8	13	56	0	0	0	46	10.9	5	322	52.5	66	5	11:52								
	Long Beach	IHL	17	10	10	20	16																			
	Florida	NHL	14	4	6	10	6	0	0	0	15	26.7	4	98	61.2	18	7	13:57	4	0	0	0	0	0	0	0
2000-01	Florida	NHL	60	5	18	23	135	0	1	2	48	10.4	4	528	50.6	45	18	12:34								
	NHL Totals		184	19	45	64	290	0	1	3	165	11.5		948	52.3	129	30	12:28	8	1	0	1	8	1	0	0

WHL West First All-Star Team (1990) • IHL Second All-Star Team (1994)

Signed as a free agent by **Philadelphia**, February 28, 1990. Signed as a free agent by **Florida**, July 20, 1993. Signed as a free agent by **Pittsburgh**, August 15, 1994. Signed as a free agent by **LA Kings**, July 9, 1999. Claimed on waivers by **Florida** from **LA Kings**, March 10, 2000.

BARTECKO, Lubos

(bahr-TESHK-oh, LOO-bohsh) **ATL.**

Left wing. Shoots left. 6'1", 200 lbs. Born, Kezmarok, Czech., July 14, 1976.

			Regular Season																Playoffs							
Season	Club	League	GP	G	A	Pts	PIM	PP	SH	GW	S	%	+/-	TF	F%	H	SB	Min	GP	G	A	Pts	PIM	PP	SH	GW
1994-95	SKP Propad	Slovakia	3	1	0	1	0	....	....	....	....	....	....	....	....	....	....	....	....	....	....	....	....	....	....	....
1995-96	Chicoutimi	QMJHL	70	32	41	73	50	....	....	....	....	....	....	....	....	....	....	....	17	8	15	23	10	....	....	....
1996-97	Drummondville	QMJHL	58	40	51	91	49	....	....	....	....	....	....	....	....	....	....	....	8	1	8	9	4	....	....	....
1997-98	Worcester	AHL	34	10	12	22	24	....	....	....	....	....	....	....	....	....	....	....	10	4	2	6	2	....	....	....
1998-99	SKP Poprad	Slovakia	1	1	0	1	0	....	....	....	....	....	....	....	....	....	....	....	....	....	....	....	....	....	....	....
	St. Louis	**NHL**	**32**	**5**	**11**	**16**	**6**	**0**	**0**	**1**	**37**	**13.5**	**4**	**0**	**0.0**	**34**	**5**	**13:13**	**5**	**0**	**0**	**0**	**2**	**0**	**0**	**0**
	Worcester	AHL	49	14	24	38	22	....	....	....	....	....	....	....	....	....	....	....	....	....	....	....	....	....	....	....
99-2000	**St. Louis**	**NHL**	**67**	**16**	**23**	**39**	**51**	**3**	**0**	**3**	**75**	**21.3**	**24**	**10**	**50.0**	**46**	**12**	**13:33**	**7**	**1**	**1**	**2**	**0**	**0**	**0**	**0**
	Worcester	AHL	12	4	7	11	4	....	....	....	....	....	....	....	....	....	....	....	....	....	....	....	....	....	....	....
2000-01	**St. Louis**	**NHL**	**50**	**5**	**8**	**13**	**12**	**0**	**0**	**3**	**51**	**9.8**	**–1**	**2**	**50.0**	**64**	**5**	**10:25**	....	....	....	....	....	....	....	....
	NHL Totals		**149**	**26**	**42**	**68**	**69**	**3**	**0**	**7**	**163**	**16.0**		**12**	**50.0**	**144**	**22**	**12:26**	**12**	**1**	**1**	**2**	**2**	**0**	**0**	**0**

Signed as a free agent by **St. Louis**, October 3, 1997. Traded to **Atlanta** by **St. Louis** for Buffalo's 4th round choice (previously acquired, St. Louis selected Igor Valeyev) in 2001 Entry Draft, June 23, 2001.

BARTOS, Peter

(bahr-TAWSH, PEE-tuhr) **MIN.**

Left wing. Shoots right. 6', 185 lbs. Born, Martin, Czech., September 5, 1973. Minnesota's 7th choice, 214th overall, in 2000 Entry Draft.

Season	Club	League	GP	G	A	Pts	PIM	PP	SH	GW	S	%	+/-	TF	F%	H	SB	Min	GP	G	A	Pts	PIM	PP	SH	GW
1991-92	HC Martin	Czech-2	33	13	8	21	16	....	....	....	....	....	....	....	....	....	....	....	....	....	....	....	....	....	....	....
1992-93	HC Martin	Czech-2	22	6	5	11	4	....	....	....	....	....	....	....	....	....	....	....	....	....	....	....	....	....	....	....
	Dukla Trencin	Czech.	28	1	2	3	....	....	....	....	....	....	....	....	....	....	....	....	10	1	1	2	....	....	....	....
1993-94	ZTS Martin	Slovakia	36	12	9	21	10	....	....	....	....	....	....	....	....	....	....	....	6	2	1	3	8	....	....	....
1994-95	ZTS Martin	Slovakia	34	14	20	34	20	....	....	....	....	....	....	....	....	....	....	....	3	0	0	0	0	....	....	....
1995-96	ZTS Martin	Slovakia	36	23	16	39	8	....	....	....	....	....	....	....	....	....	....	....	13	4	4	8	4	....	....	....
1996-97	ZTS Martin	Slovakia	46	22	15	37	....	....	....	....	....	....	....	....	....	....	....	....	5	1	5	6	....	....	....	....
1997-98	ZTS Martin	Slovakia	36	20	26	46	20	....	....	....	....	....	....	....	....	....	....	....	3	0	2	2	0	....	....	....
1998-99	HC Budejovice	Cze-Rep	52	22	26	48	24	....	....	....	....	....	....	....	....	....	....	....	3	3	0	3	....	....	....	....
99-2000	HC Budejovice	Cze-Rep	52	23	25	48	24	....	....	....	....	....	....	....	....	....	....	....	3	0	1	1	6	....	....	....
2000-01	**Minnesota**	**NHL**	**13**	**4**	**2**	**6**	**6**	**1**	**0**	**1**	**18**	**22.2**	**2**	**3**	**33.3**	**5**	**4**	**13:50**	....	....	....	....	....	....	....	....
	Cleveland	IHL	60	18	28	46	18	....	....	....	....	....	....	....	....	....	....	....	4	0	1	1	2	....	....	....
	NHL Totals		**13**	**4**	**2**	**6**	**6**	**1**	**0**	**1**	**18**	**22.2**		**3**	**33.3**	**5**	**4**	**13:50**	....	....	....	....	....	....	....	....

BASHKIROV, Andrei

(bahsh-KIHR-ahf, AWN-dray)

Left wing. Shoots left. 6', 215 lbs. Born, Shelekhov, USSR, June 22, 1970. Montreal's 4th choice, 132nd overall, in 1998 Entry Draft.

Season	Club	League	GP	G	A	Pts	PIM	PP	SH	GW	S	%	+/-	TF	F%	H	SB	Min	GP	G	A	Pts	PIM	PP	SH	GW
1991-92	HK Khimik	CIS	11	2	0	2	4	....	....	....	....	....	....	....	....	....	....	....	....	....	....	....	....	....	....	....
1992-93	HK Angarsk-2	CIS-3	STATISTICS NOT AVAILABLE					....	....	....	....	....	....	....	....	....	....	....	....	....	....	....	....	....	....	....
1993-94	Charlotte	ECHL	62	28	42	70	25	....	....	....	....	....	....	....	....	....	....	....	3	1	0	1	0	....	....	....
	Providence Bruins	AHL	1	0	0	0	2	....	....	....	....	....	....	....	....	....	....	....	....	....	....	....	....	....	....	....
1994-95	Charlotte	ECHL	61	19	27	46	20	....	....	....	....	....	....	....	....	....	....	....	3	0	0	0	0	....	....	....
1995-96	Huntington	ECHL	55	19	39	58	35	....	....	....	....	....	....	....	....	....	....	....	....	....	....	....	....	....	....	....
1996-97	Huntington	ECHL	47	29	41	70	12	....	....	....	....	....	....	....	....	....	....	....	....	....	....	....	....	....	....	....
	Detroit Vipers	IHL	2	0	0	0	0	....	....	....	....	....	....	....	....	....	....	....	....	....	....	....	....	....	....	....
	Las Vegas	IHL	27	10	12	22	0	....	....	....	....	....	....	....	....	....	....	....	2	0	0	0	0	....	....	....
1997-98	Las Vegas	IHL	15	2	3	5	5	....	....	....	....	....	....	....	....	....	....	....	....	....	....	....	....	....	....	....
	Port Huron	UHL	3	1	3	4	0	....	....	....	....	....	....	....	....	....	....	....	....	....	....	....	....	....	....	....
	Fort Wayne	IHL	65	28	48	76	16	....	....	....	....	....	....	....	....	....	....	....	4	2	2	4	2	....	....	....
1998-99	**Montreal**	**NHL**	**10**	**0**	**0**	**0**	**0**	**0**	**0**	**0**	**4**	**0.0**	**–3**	**0**	**0.0**	**3**	**3**	**6:57**	....	....	....	....	....	....	....	....
	Fredericton	AHL	13	7	5	12	4	....	....	....	....	....	....	....	....	....	....	....	....	....	....	....	....	....	....	....
	Fort Wayne	IHL	34	11	25	36	10	....	....	....	....	....	....	....	....	....	....	....	....	....	....	....	....	....	....	....
99-2000	**Montreal**	**NHL**	**2**	**0**	**0**	**0**	**0**	**0**	**0**	**0**	**0**	**0.0**	**0**	**0**	**0.0**	**0**	**0**	**5:09**	....	....	....	....	....	....	....	....
	Quebec Citadelles	AHL	78	28	33	61	17	....	....	....	....	....	....	....	....	....	....	....	3	0	3	3	0	....	....	....
2000-01	**Montreal**	**NHL**	**18**	**0**	**3**	**3**	**0**	**0**	**0**	**0**	**22**	**0.0**	**–2**	**3**	**100.0**	**6**	**8**	**11:41**	....	....	....	....	....	....	....	....
	Quebec Citadelles	AHL	53	17	25	42	6	....	....	....	....	....	....	....	....	....	....	....	6	1	1	2	0	....	....	....
	NHL Totals		**30**	**0**	**3**	**3**	**0**	**0**	**0**	**0**	**26**	**0.0**		**3**	**100.0**	**9**	**11**	**9:40**	....	....	....	....	....	....	....	....

• Signed as a free agent by **HC Lusanne** (Switz-2), August 7, 2001.

BAST, Ryan

(BAST, RIGH-yuhn)

Defense. Shoots left. 6'2", 190 lbs. Born, Spruce Grove, Alta., August 27, 1975.

Season	Club	League	GP	G	A	Pts	PIM	PP	SH	GW	S	%	+/-	TF	F%	H	SB	Min	GP	G	A	Pts	PIM	PP	SH	GW
1992-93	St. Albert Raiders	AMHL	35	1	18	19	51	....	....	....	....	....	....	....	....	....	....	....	....	....	....	....	....	....	....	....
1993-94	Portland	WHL	6	0	0	0	4	....	....	....	....	....	....	....	....	....	....	....	....	....	....	....	....	....	....	....
	Prince Albert	WHL	47	2	8	10	139	....	....	....	....	....	....	....	....	....	....	....	....	....	....	....	....	....	....	....
1994-95	Prince Albert	WHL	42	1	10	11	149	....	....	....	....	....	....	....	....	....	....	....	14	0	3	3	13	....	....	....
1995-96	Prince Albert	WHL	44	7	15	22	129	....	....	....	....	....	....	....	....	....	....	....	....	....	....	....	....	....	....	....
	Calgary Hitmen	WHL	3	0	0	0	24	....	....	....	....	....	....	....	....	....	....	....	....	....	....	....	....	....	....	....
	Swift Current	WHL	25	2	3	5	50	....	....	....	....	....	....	....	....	....	....	....	6	1	0	1	21	....	....	....
1996-97	Las Vegas	IHL	49	2	3	5	266	....	....	....	....	....	....	....	....	....	....	....	....	....	....	....	....	....	....	....
	Toledo Storm	ECHL	12	2	2	4	75	....	....	....	....	....	....	....	....	....	....	....	....	....	....	....	....	....	....	....
	Saint John Flames	AHL	12	0	0	0	21	....	....	....	....	....	....	....	....	....	....	....	5	0	0	0	4	....	....	....
1997-98	Saint John Flames	AHL	77	3	8	11	187	....	....	....	....	....	....	....	....	....	....	....	21	0	1	1	55	....	....	....
1998-99	Saint John Flames	AHL	2	0	0	0	5	....	....	....	....	....	....	....	....	....	....	....	....	....	....	....	....	....	....	....
	Philadelphia	**NHL**	**2**	**0**	**1**	**1**	**0**	**0**	**0**	**0**	**1**	**0.0**	**0**	**0**	**0.0**	**0**	**0**	**13:24**	....	....	....	....	....	....	....	....
	Philadelphia	AHL	69	0	11	11	160	....	....	....	....	....	....	....	....	....	....	....	16	0	0	0	30	....	....	....
99-2000	Philadelphia	AHL	71	1	9	10	198	....	....	....	....	....	....	....	....	....	....	....	5	0	0	0	6	....	....	....
2000-01	Hartford	AHL	50	1	1	2	146	....	....	....	....	....	....	....	....	....	....	....	....	....	....	....	....	....	....	....
	NHL Totals		**2**	**0**	**1**	**1**	**0**	**0**	**0**	**0**	**1**	**0.0**		**0**	**0.0**	**0**	**0**	**13:24**	....	....	....	....	....	....	....	....

AHL Second All-Star Team (1998)

Signed as a free agent by **Las Vegas** (IHL), September 30, 1996. Traded to **Saint John** (AHL) by **Las Vegas** (IHL) for loan of Sasha Lakovic, March 20, 1997. Signed as a free agent by **Philadelphia**, May 18, 1998. • Calgary Flames filed official protest contesting Philadelphia's signing of Bast under the contention that he was property of AHL's Saint John Flames, May 20, 1998. • NHL ruled that Bast was not under contract to Calgary since he was never drafted and had no NHL clause in contract, May 22, 1998. NHL also ruled that Bast was not property of Philadelphia because Flyers' contract offer exceeded NHL rookie salary cap, May 22, 1998. A compromise was reached that traded Bast to **Philadelphia** by **Calgary** with Calgary's 8th round choice (David Nystrom) in 1999 Entry Draft for Philadelphia's 3rd round choice (later traded to NY Rangers - NY Rangers selected Patrik Aufiero) in 1999 Entry Draft, October 13, 1998. Signed as a free agent by **Hartford** (AHL), September 18, 2001.

BATES, Shawn

(BAYTS, SHAWN) **NYI**

Center. Shoots right. 5'11", 212 lbs. Born, Melrose, MA, April 3, 1975. Boston's 4th choice, 103rd overall, in 1993 Entry Draft.

Season	Club	League	GP	G	A	Pts	PIM	PP	SH	GW	S	%	+/-	TF	F%	H	SB	Min	GP	G	A	Pts	PIM	PP	SH	GW
1990-91	Medford High	Hi-School	22	18	43	61	6	....	....	....	....	....	....	....	....	....	....	....	....	....	....	....	....	....	....	....
1991-92	Medford High	Hi-School	22	38	41	79	10	....	....	....	....	....	....	....	....	....	....	....	....	....	....	....	....	....	....	....
1992-93	Medford High	Hi-School	25	49	46	95	20	....	....	....	....	....	....	....	....	....	....	....	....	....	....	....	....	....	....	....
1993-94	Boston University	H-East	41	10	19	29	24	....	....	....	....	....	....	....	....	....	....	....	....	....	....	....	....	....	....	....
1994-95	Boston University	H-East	38	18	12	30	48	....	....	....	....	....	....	....	....	....	....	....	....	....	....	....	....	....	....	....
1995-96	Boston University	H-East	40	28	22	50	54	....	....	....	....	....	....	....	....	....	....	....	....	....	....	....	....	....	....	....
1996-97	Boston University	H-East	41	17	18	35	64	....	....	....	....	....	....	....	....	....	....	....	....	....	....	....	....	....	....	....
1997-98	**Boston**	**NHL**	**13**	**2**	**0**	**2**	**2**	**0**	**0**	**0**	**12**	**16.7**	**–3**	....	....	....	....	....	....	....	....	....	....	....	....	....
	Providence Bruins	AHL	50	15	19	34	22	....	....	....	....	....	....	....	....	....	....	....	....	....	....	....	....	....	....	....
1998-99	**Boston**	**NHL**	**33**	**5**	**4**	**9**	**2**	**0**	**0**	**0**	**30**	**16.7**	**3**	**178**	**51.1**	**47**	**5**	**8:35**	**12**	**0**	**0**	**0**	**4**	**0**	**0**	**0**
	Providence Bruins	AHL	37	25	21	46	39	....	....	....	....	....	....	....	....	....	....	....	....	....	....	....	....	....	....	....
99-2000	**Boston**	**NHL**	**44**	**5**	**7**	**12**	**14**	**0**	**0**	**1**	**65**	**7.7**	**–17**	**460**	**47.0**	**76**	**8**	**10:52**	....	....	....	....	....	....	....	....
2000-01	**Boston**	**NHL**	**45**	**2**	**3**	**5**	**26**	**0**	**0**	**0**	**59**	**3.4**	**–12**	**413**	**50.6**	**51**	**8**	**9:19**	....	....	....	....	....	....	....	....
	Providence Bruins	AHL	11	5	8	13	12	....	....	....	....	....	....	....	....	....	....	....	8	2	6	8	8	....	....	....
	NHL Totals		**135**	**14**	**14**	**28**	**44**	**0**	**0**	**1**	**166**	**8.4**		**1051**	**49.1**	**174**	**21**	**9:41**	**12**	**0**	**0**	**0**	**4**	**0**	**0**	**0**

NCAA Championship All-Tournament Team (1995)

Signed as a free agent by **NY Islanders**, July 8, 2001.

			Regular Season																Playoffs							
Season	Club	League	GP	G	A	Pts	PIM	PP	SH	GW	S	%	+/-	TF	F%	H	SB	Min	GP	G	A	Pts	PIM	PP	SH	GW

BATTAGLIA, Bates

(buh-TAG-lee-ah, BAYTS) **CAR.**

Left wing. Shoots left. 6'2", 205 lbs. Born, Chicago, IL, December 13, 1975. Anaheim's 6th choice, 132nd overall, in 1994 Entry Draft.

Season	Club	League	GP	G	A	Pts	PIM	PP	SH	GW	S	%	+/-	TF	F%	H	SB	Min	GP	G	A	Pts	PIM	PP	SH	GW
1992-93	Team Illinois	MEHL	60	42	42	84	68																			
1993-94	Caledon Canucks	MTJHL	44	15	33	48	104																			
1994-95	Lake Superior	CCHA	38	6	14	20	34																			
1995-96	Lake Superior	CCHA	40	13	22	35	48																			
1996-97	Lake Superior	CCHA	38	12	27	39	80																			
1997-98	**Carolina**	**NHL**	**33**	**2**	**4**	**6**	**10**	**0**	**0**	**1**	**21**	**9.5**	**–1**													
	New Haven	AHL	48	15	21	36	48												1	0	0	0	0			
1998-99	**Carolina**	**NHL**	**60**	**7**	**11**	**18**	**97**	**0**	**0**	**0**	**52**	**13.5**	**7**	**144**	**39.6**	**67**	**9**	**9:53**	**6**	**0**	**3**	**3**	**8**	**0**	**0**	**0**
99-2000	**Carolina**	**NHL**	**77**	**16**	**18**	**34**	**39**	**3**	**0**	**3**	**86**	**18.6**	**20**	**23**	**26.1**	**128**	**19**	**15:12**								
2000-01	**Carolina**	**NHL**	**80**	**12**	**15**	**27**	**76**	**2**	**0**	**3**	**133**	**9.0**	**–14**	**5**	**60.0**	**155**	**10**	**14:28**	**6**	**0**	**2**	**2**	**2**	**0**	**0**	**0**
	NHL Totals		**250**	**37**	**48**	**85**	**222**	**5**	**0**	**7**	**292**	**12.7**		**172**	**38.4**	**350**	**38**	**13:28**	**12**	**0**	**5**	**5**	**10**	**0**	**0**	**0**

Traded to **Hartford** by **Anaheim** with Anaheim's 4th round choice (Josef Vasicek) in 1998 Entry Draft for Mark Janssens, March 18, 1997. Rights transferred to **Carolina** after **Hartford** franchise relocated, June 25, 1997.

BAUMGARTNER, Nolan

(BAWM-gahrt-nuhr, NOH-lan) **CHI.**

Defense. Shoots right. 6'2", 205 lbs. Born, Calgary, Alta., March 23, 1976. Washington's 1st choice, 10th overall, in 1994 Entry Draft.

Season	Club	League	GP	G	A	Pts	PIM	PP	SH	GW	S	%	+/-	TF	F%	H	SB	Min	GP	G	A	Pts	PIM	PP	SH	GW
1991-92	Calgary Flames	AMHL	39	11	29	40	40																			
1992-93	Kamloops Blazers	WHL	43	0	5	5	30												11	1	1	2	0			
1993-94	Kamloops Blazers	WHL	69	13	42	55	109												19	3	14	17	33			
1994-95	Kamloops Blazers	WHL	62	8	36	44	71												21	4	13	17	16			
1995-96	Kamloops Blazers	WHL	28	13	15	28	45												16	1	9	10	26			
	Washington	**NHL**	**1**	**0**	**0**	**0**	**0**	**0**	**0**	**0**	**0**	**0.0**	**–1**						**1**	**0**	**0**	**0**	**10**	**0**	**0**	**0**
1996-97	Portland Pirates	AHL	8	2	2	4	4																			
1997-98	**Washington**	**NHL**	**4**	**0**	**1**	**1**	**0**	**0**	**0**	**0**	**4**	**0.0**	**0**													
	Portland Pirates	AHL	70	2	24	26	70												10	1	4	5	10			
1998-99	**Washington**	**NHL**	**5**	**0**	**0**	**0**	**0**	**0**	**0**	**0**	**1**	**0.0**	**–3**	**0**	**0.0**	**1**	**0**	**8:41**								
	Portland Pirates	AHL	38	5	14	19	62																			
99-2000	**Washington**	**NHL**	**8**	**0**	**1**	**1**	**2**	**0**	**0**	**0**	**6**	**0.0**	**1**	**0**	**0.0**	**8**	**2**	**10:31**								
	Portland Pirates	AHL	71	5	18	23	56												4	1	2	3	10			
2000-01	**Chicago**	**NHL**	**8**	**0**	**0**	**0**	**6**	**0**	**0**	**0**	**7**	**0.0**	**–4**	**2**	**50.0**	**6**	**4**	**12:40**								
	Norfolk Admirals	AHL	63	5	28	33	75												9	2	3	5	11			
	NHL Totals		**26**	**0**	**2**	**2**	**8**	**0**	**0**	**0**	**18**	**0.0**		**2**	**50.0**	**15**	**6**	**10:54**	**1**	**0**	**0**	**0**	**10**	**0**	**0**	**0**

Memorial Cup All-Star Team (1994, 1995) • WHL West First All-Star Team (1995, 1996) • Canadian Major Junior First All-Star Team (1995) • Canadian Major Junior Defenseman of the Year (1995)
Traded to **Chicago** by **Washington** for Remi Royer, July 20, 2000.

BEAUFAIT, Mark

(BOH-fayt, MAHRK) **MIN.**

Center. Shoots right. 5'9", 170 lbs. Born, Livonia, MI, May 13, 1970. San Jose's 2nd choice, 7th overall, in 1991 Supplemental Draft.

Season	Club	League	GP	G	A	Pts	PIM	PP	SH	GW	S	%	+/-	TF	F%	H	SB	Min	GP	G	A	Pts	PIM	PP	SH	GW
1987-88	Redford Royals	NAJHL	STATISTICS NOT AVAILABLE																							
1988-89	North-Michigan	WCHA	11	2	1	3	2																			
1989-90	North-Michigan	WCHA	34	10	14	24	12																			
1990-91	North-Michigan	WCHA	47	19	30	49	18																			
1991-92	North-Michigan	WCHA	39	31	44	75	43																			
1992-93	**San Jose**	**NHL**	**5**	**1**	**0**	**1**	**0**	**0**	**0**	**0**	**3**	**33.3**	**–1**													
	Kansas City	IHL	66	19	40	59	22												9	1	1	2	8			
1993-94	United States	Nat-Team	51	22	29	51	36																			
	United States	Olympics	8	1	4	5	2																			
	Kansas City	IHL	21	12	9	21	18																			
1994-95	San Diego Gulls	IHL	68	24	39	63	22												5	2	2	4	2			
1995-96	Orlando	IHL	77	30	79	109	87												22	9	*19	*28	22			
1996-97	Orlando	IHL	80	26	65	91	63												10	5	8	13	18			
1997-98	Orlando	IHL	76	24	61	85	56												17	6	16	22	10			
1998-99	Orlando	IHL	71	28	43	71	38												15	2	12	14	14			
99-2000	Orlando	IHL	78	28	49	77	87												6	2	0	2	4			
2000-01	Orlando	IHL	54	23	42	65	34												9	1	9	10	2			
	NHL Totals		**5**	**1**	**0**	**1**	**0**	**0**	**0**	**0**	**3**	**33.3**														

IHL Second All-Star Team (1997)
Selected by **Orlando** (IHL) from **San Diego** (IHL) in 1995 IHL Expansion Draft, July 13, 1995. Signed as a free agent by **Minnesota**, July, 2001.

BEECH, Kris

(BEECH, KRIHS) **PIT.**

Center. Shoots left. 6'2", 178 lbs. Born, Salmon Arm, B.C., February 5, 1981. Washington's 1st choice, 7th overall, in 1999 Entry Draft.

Season	Club	League	GP	G	A	Pts	PIM	PP	SH	GW	S	%	+/-	TF	F%	H	SB	Min	GP	G	A	Pts	PIM	PP	SH	GW
1996-97	Sicamous Eagles	KIJHL	49	34	36	70	80																			
	Calgary Hitmen	WHL	8	1	1	2	0																			
1997-98	Calgary Hitmen	WHL	58	10	25	35	24												12	4	5	9	32			
1998-99	Calgary Hitmen	WHL	68	26	41	67	103												6	1	4	5	8			
99-2000	Calgary Hitmen	WHL	66	32	54	86	99												5	3	5	8	16			
2000-01	**Washington**	**NHL**	**4**	**0**	**0**	**0**	**2**	**0**	**0**	**0**	**0**	**0.0**	**–2**	**25**	**36.0**	**1**	**0**	**7:29**								
	Calgary Hitmen	WHL	40	22	44	66	103												10	2	8	10	26			
	NHL Totals		**4**	**0**	**0**	**0**	**2**	**0**	**0**	**0**	**0**	**0.0**		**25**	**36.0**	**1**	**0**	**7:29**								

Returned to **Calgary Hitmen** (WHL) by **Washington**, October 24, 2000. Traded to **Pittsburgh** by **Washington** with Michal Sivek, Ross Lupaschuk and future considerations for Jaromir Jagr and Frantisek Kucera, July 11, 2001.

BEGIN, Steve

(bay-ZHIN, STEEV) **CGY.**

Center. Shoots left. 5'11", 190 lbs. Born, Trois-Rivieres, Que., June 14, 1978. Calgary's 3rd choice, 40th overall, in 1996 Entry Draft.

Season	Club	League	GP	G	A	Pts	PIM	PP	SH	GW	S	%	+/-	TF	F%	H	SB	Min	GP	G	A	Pts	PIM	PP	SH	GW
1993-94	Cap-d-Madelaine	QAAA	8	0	1	1	6												2	0	0	0	0			
1994-95	Cap-d-Madelaine	QAAA	35	9	15	24	48												3	0	0	0	2			
1995-96	Val-d'Or Foreurs	QMJHL	64	13	23	36	218												13	1	3	4	33			
1996-97	Val-d'Or Foreurs	QMJHL	58	13	33	46	229												10	0	3	3	8			
	Saint John Flames	AHL																	4	0	2	2	6			
1997-98	Val-d'Or Foreurs	QMJHL	35	18	17	35	73												15	2	12	14	34			
	Calgary	**NHL**	**5**	**0**	**0**	**0**	**23**	**0**	**0**	**0**	**2**	**0.0**	**0**													
1998-99	Saint John Flames	AHL	73	11	9	20	156												7	2	0	2	18			
99-2000	**Calgary**	**NHL**	**13**	**1**	**1**	**2**	**18**	**0**	**0**	**0**	**3**	**33.3**	**–3**	**19**	**47.4**	**23**	**2**	**7:13**								
	Saint John Flames	AHL	47	13	12	25	99																			
2000-01	**Calgary**	**NHL**	**4**	**0**	**0**	**0**	**21**	**0**	**0**	**0**	**3**	**0.0**	**0**	**0**	**0.0**	**7**	**1**	**6:04**								
	Saint John Flames	AHL	58	14	14	28	109												19	10	7	17	18			
	NHL Totals		**22**	**1**	**1**	**2**	**62**	**0**	**0**	**0**	**8**	**12.5**		**19**	**47.4**	**30**	**3**	**6:57**								

Won Jack A. Butterfield Trophy (Playoff MVP - AHL) (2001)

BEKAR, Derek

(BEH-kahr, DAIR-ehk)

Left wing. Shoots left. 6'3", 194 lbs. Born, Burnaby, B.C., September 15, 1975. St. Louis' 7th choice, 205th overall, in 1995 Entry Draft.

Season	Club	League	GP	G	A	Pts	PIM	PP	SH	GW	S	%	+/-	TF	F%	H	SB	Min	GP	G	A	Pts	PIM	PP	SH	GW
1992-93	Notre Dame	AMHL	29	25	24	49	68																			
1993-94	Notre Dame	SJHL	62	20	31	51	77																			
1994-95	Powell River	BCJHL	46	33	29	62	35																			
1995-96	New Hampshire	H-East	34	15	18	33	4																			
1996-97	New Hampshire	H-East	39	18	21	39	34																			
1997-98	New Hampshire	H-East	35	32	28	60	46																			
1998-99	Worcester	AHL	51	16	20	36	6												4	0	0	0	0			
99-2000	**St. Louis**	**NHL**	**1**	**0**	**0**	**0**	**0**	**0**	**0**	**0**	**0**	**0.0**	**0**	**0**	**0.0**	**1**	**0**	**5:14**								
	Worcester	AHL	71	21	19	40	26												7	0	3	3	2			

			Regular Season																Playoffs							
Season	Club	League	GP	G	A	Pts	PIM	PP	SH	GW	S	%	+/-	TF	F%	H	SB	Min	GP	G	A	Pts	PIM	PP	SH	GW
2000-01	Worcester	AHL	18	5	2	7	10																			
	Portland Pirates	AHL	58	19	16	35	49												3	0	0	0	0			
	NHL Totals		**1**	**0**	**0**	**0**	**0**	**0**	**0**	**0**	**0**	**0.0**		**0**	**0.0**	**1**	**0**	**5:14**								

Hockey East Second All-Star Team (1998)

Traded to **Washington** by **St. Louis** with future considerations for Mike Peluso and future considerations, November 29, 2000.

BELAK, Wade

(BEE-lak, WAYD) **TOR.**

Defense. Shoots right. 6'5", 222 lbs. Born, Saskatoon, Sask., July 3, 1976. Quebec's 1st choice, 12th overall, in 1994 Entry Draft.

Season	Club	League	GP	G	A	Pts	PIM	PP	SH	GW	S	%	+/-	TF	F%	H	SB	Min	GP	G	A	Pts	PIM	PP	SH	GW
1991-92	North Battleford	SAHA	57	6	20	26	186																			
1992-93	North Battleford	SJHL	50	5	15	20	146																			
	Saskatoon Blades	WHL	7	0	0	0	23												7	0	0	0	0			
1993-94	Saskatoon Blades	WHL	69	4	13	17	226												16	2	2	4	43			
1994-95	Saskatoon Blades	WHL	72	4	14	18	290												9	0	0	0	36			
	Cornwall Aces	AHL																	11	1	2	3	40			
1995-96	Saskatoon Blades	WHL	63	3	15	18	207												4	0	0	0	9			
	Cornwall Aces	AHL	5	0	0	0	18												2	0	0	0	2			
1996-97	**Colorado**	**NHL**	**5**	**0**	**0**	**0**	**11**	**0**	**0**	**0**	**1**	**0.0**	**-1**													
	Hershey Bears	AHL	65	1	7	8	320												16	0	1	1	61			
1997-98	**Colorado**	**NHL**	**8**	**1**	**1**	**2**	**27**	**0**	**0**	**1**	**2**	**50.0**	**-3**													
	Hershey Bears	AHL	11	0	0	0	30																			
1998-99	**Colorado**	**NHL**	**22**	**0**	**0**	**0**	**71**	**0**	**0**	**0**	**5**	**0.0**	**-2**	**0**	**0.0**	**18**	**10**	**6:48**								
	Hershey Bears	AHL	17	0	1	1	49																			
	Calgary	**NHL**	**9**	**0**	**1**	**1**	**23**	**0**	**0**	**0**	**2**	**0.0**	**3**	**0**	**0.0**	**9**	**7**	**10:46**								
	Saint John Flames	AHL	12	0	2	2	43												6	0	1	1	23			
99-2000	**Calgary**	**NHL**	**40**	**0**	**2**	**2**	**122**	**0**	**0**	**0**	**11**	**0.0**	**-4**	**1**	**0.0**	**41**	**23**	**7:33**								
2000-01	**Calgary**	**NHL**	**23**	**0**	**0**	**0**	**79**	**0**	**0**	**0**	**8**	**0.0**	**-2**	**0**	**0.0**	**26**	**4**	**6:54**								
	Toronto	**NHL**	**16**	**1**	**1**	**2**	**31**	**0**	**0**	**0**	**8**	**12.5**	**-4**	**0**	**0.0**	**32**	**16**	**13:38**								
	NHL Totals		**123**	**2**	**5**	**7**	**364**	**0**	**0**	**1**	**37**	**5.4**		**1**	**0.0**	**126**	**60**	**8:25**								

Rights transferred to **Colorado** after **Quebec** franchise relocated, June 21, 1995. Traded to **Calgary** by **Colorado** with Rene Corbet, Robyn Regehr and Colorado's 2nd round compensatory choice (Jarret Stoll) in 2000 Entry Draft for Theoren Fleury and Chris Dingman, February 28, 1999. • Missed majority of 1999-2000 and 2000-01 seasons recovering from shoulder injury suffered in game vs. Colorado, February 10, 2000. Claimed on waivers by **Toronto** from **Calgary**, February 16, 2001.

BELANGER, Eric

(buh-LAWN-zhay, AIR-ihk) **L.A.**

Center. Shoots left. 6', 185 lbs. Born, Sherbrooke, Que., December 16, 1977. Los Angeles' 5th choice, 96th overall, in 1996 Entry Draft.

Season	Club	League	GP	G	A	Pts	PIM	PP	SH	GW	S	%	+/-	TF	F%	H	SB	Min	GP	G	A	Pts	PIM	PP	SH	GW
1993-94	Magog Elites	QAAA	32	19	24	43	24												13	5	6	11	36			
1994-95	Beauport	QMJHL	71	12	28	40	24												18	5	9	14	25			
1995-96	Beauport	QMJHL	59	35	48	83	18												20	13	14	27	6			
1996-97	Beauport	QMJHL	31	13	37	50	30																			
	Rimouski Oceanic	QMJHL	31	26	41	67	36												4	2	3	5	10			
1997-98	Fredericton	AHL	56	17	34	51	28												4	2	1	3	2			
1998-99	Springfield	AHL	33	8	18	26	10												3	0	1	1	2			
	Long Beach	IHL	1	0	0	0	0																			
99-2000	Lowell	AHL	65	15	25	40	20												7	3	3	6	2			
	Mohawk Valley	UHL	3	0	0	0	0																			
2000-01	**Los Angeles**	**NHL**	**62**	**9**	**12**	**21**	**16**	**1**	**2**	**1**	**80**	**11.3**	**14**	**849**	**56.4**	**136**	**28**	**13:25**	**13**	**1**	**4**	**5**	**2**	**0**	**0**	**1**
	Lowell	AHL	13	8	10	18	4																			
	NHL Totals		**62**	**9**	**12**	**21**	**16**	**1**	**2**	**1**	**80**	**11.3**		**849**	**56.4**	**136**	**28**	**13:25**	**13**	**1**	**4**	**5**	**2**	**0**	**0**	**1**

BELANGER, Francis

(buh-LAWN-zhay, FRAN-sihs) **MTL.**

Left wing. Shoots left. 6'3", 228 lbs. Born, Bellefeuille, Que., January 15, 1978. Philadelphia's 5th choice, 124th overall, in 1998 Entry Draft.

Season	Club	League	GP	G	A	Pts	PIM	PP	SH	GW	S	%	+/-	TF	F%	H	SB	Min	GP	G	A	Pts	PIM	PP	SH	GW
1994-95	Laval Regents	QAAA	25	11	8	19	78																			
1995-96	Hull Olympiques	QMJHL	1	0	0	0	0																			
1996-97	Hull Olympiques	QMJHL	53	13	13	26	134												8	2	2	4	57			
1997-98	Hull Olympiques	QMJHL	33	22	23	45	133																			
	Rimouski Oceanic	QMJHL	30	18	10	28	248												17	14	8	22	61			
1998-99	Philadelphia	AHL	58	13	13	26	242												16	4	3	7	16			
99-2000	Philadelphia	AHL	35	5	6	11	112																			
	Trenton Titans	ECHL	9	1	1	2	29																			
2000-01	Philadelphia	AHL	13	1	3	4	32																			
	Montreal	**NHL**	**10**	**0**	**0**	**0**	**29**	**0**	**0**	**0**	**2**	**0.0**	**-3**	**0**	**0.0**	**13**	**0**	**4:30**								
	Quebec Citadelles	AHL	22	15	4	19	101												9	2	5	7	20			
	NHL Totals		**10**	**0**	**0**	**0**	**29**	**0**	**0**	**0**	**2**	**0.0**		**0**	**0.0**	**13**	**0**	**4:30**								

Signed as a free agent by **Montreal**, February 15, 2001.

BELANGER, Jesse

(buh-LAWN-zhay, JEH-see)

Center. Shoots right. 6'1", 190 lbs. Born, St-Georges-de-Beauce, Que., June 15, 1969.

Season	Club	League	GP	G	A	Pts	PIM	PP	SH	GW	S	%	+/-	TF	F%	H	SB	Min	GP	G	A	Pts	PIM	PP	SH	GW
1987-88	Granby Bisons	QMJHL	69	33	43	76	10												5	3	3	6	0			
1988-89	Granby Bisons	QMJHL	67	40	63	103	26												4	0	5	5	0			
1989-90	Granby Bisons	QMJHL	67	53	54	107	53																			
1990-91	Fredericton	AHL	75	40	58	98	30												6	2	4	6	0			
1991-92	**Montreal**	**NHL**	**4**	**0**	**0**	**0**	**0**	**0**	**0**	**0**	**4**	**0.0**	**-1**													
	Fredericton	AHL	65	30	41	71	26												7	3	3	6	2			
1992-93♦	**Montreal**	**NHL**	**19**	**4**	**2**	**6**	**4**	**0**	**0**	**0**	**24**	**16.7**	**1**						**9**	**0**	**1**	**1**	**0**	**0**	**0**	**0**
	Fredericton	AHL	39	19	32	51	24																			
1993-94	**Florida**	**NHL**	**70**	**17**	**33**	**50**	**16**	**11**	**0**	**3**	**104**	**16.3**	**-4**													
1994-95	**Florida**	**NHL**	**47**	**15**	**14**	**29**	**18**	**6**	**0**	**3**	**89**	**16.9**	**-5**													
1995-96	**Florida**	**NHL**	**63**	**17**	**21**	**38**	**10**	**7**	**0**	**1**	**140**	**12.1**	**-5**													
	Vancouver	**NHL**	**9**	**3**	**0**	**3**	**4**	**1**	**0**	**1**	**11**	**27.3**	**0**						**3**	**0**	**2**	**2**	**2**	**0**	**0**	**0**
1996-97	**Edmonton**	**NHL**	**6**	**0**	**0**	**0**	**0**	**0**	**0**	**0**	**8**	**0.0**	**-3**													
	Hamilton Bulldogs	AHL	6	4	3	7	0																			
	Quebec Rafales	IHL	47	34	28	62	18												9	3	5	8	13			
1997-98	SC Herisau	Switz.	5	4	3	7	4																			
	Las Vegas	IHL	54	32	36	68	20												4	0	1	1	0			
1998-99	Cleveland	IHL	22	9	13	22	10																			
99-2000	**Montreal**	**NHL**	**16**	**3**	**6**	**9**	**2**	**0**	**0**	**0**	**21**	**14.3**	**2**	**177**	**49.2**	**14**	**4**	**10:41**								
	Quebec Citadelles	AHL	36	15	18	33	20												3	0	3	3	4			
2000-01	**NY Islanders**	**NHL**	**12**	**0**	**0**	**0**	**2**	**0**	**0**	**0**	**7**	**0.0**	**-5**	**47**	**59.6**	**13**	**0**	**5:52**								
	Chicago Wolves	IHL	58	17	22	39	28												14	3	4	7	10			
	NHL Totals		**246**	**59**	**76**	**135**	**56**	**25**	**0**	**8**	**408**	**14.5**		**224**	**51.3**	**27**	**4**	**8:37**	**12**	**0**	**3**	**3**	**2**	**0**	**0**	**0**

Signed as a free agent by **Montreal**, October 3, 1990. Claimed by **Florida** from **Montreal** in Expansion Draft, June 24, 1993. Traded to **Vancouver** by **Florida** for Vancouver's 3rd round choice (Oleg Kvasha) in 1996 Entry Draft, March 20, 1996. Signed as a free agent by **Edmonton**, September 16, 1996. Signed as a free agent by **Tampa Bay**, August 18, 1998. Signed as a free agent by **Montreal**, July 23, 1999. Signed as a free agent by **NY Islanders**, July 27, 2000. Signed as a free agent by **HC La Chaux-de-Fonds** (Switz), May 30, 2001.

BELANGER, Ken

(buh-LAWN-zhay, KEHN) **L.A.**

Left wing. Shoots left. 6'4", 225 lbs. Born, Sault Ste. Marie, Ont., May 14, 1974. Hartford's 7th choice, 153rd overall, in 1992 Entry Draft.

Season	Club	League	GP	G	A	Pts	PIM	PP	SH	GW	S	%	+/-	TF	F%	H	SB	Min	GP	G	A	Pts	PIM	PP	SH	GW
1990-91	S.S. Marie Legion	NOHA	43	24	29	53	169																			
1991-92	Ottawa 67's	OHL	51	4	4	8	174												11	0	0	0	24			
1992-93	Ottawa 67's	OHL	34	6	12	18	139																			
	Guelph Storm	OHL	29	10	14	24	86												5	2	1	3	14			
1993-94	Guelph Storm	OHL	55	11	22	33	185												9	2	3	5	30			
1994-95	St. John's Leafs	AHL	47	5	5	10	246												4	0	0	0	30			
	Toronto	**NHL**	**3**	**0**	**0**	**0**	**9**	**0**	**0**	**0**	**1**	**0.0**	**0**													
1995-96	St. John's Leafs	AHL	40	16	14	30	222																			
	NY Islanders	**NHL**	**7**	**0**	**0**	**0**	**27**	**0**	**0**	**0**	**0**	**0.0**	**-2**													

			Regular Season																Playoffs							
Season	Club	League	GP	G	A	Pts	PIM	PP	SH	GW	S	%	+/-	TF	F%	H	SB	Min	GP	G	A	Pts	PIM	PP	SH	GW
1996-97	**NY Islanders**	**NHL**	18	0	2	2	102	0	0	0	5	0.0	–1													
	Kentucky	AHL	38	10	12	22	164												4	0	1	1	27			
1997-98	**NY Islanders**	**NHL**	37	3	1	4	101	0	0	1	10	30.0	1													
1998-99	**NY Islanders**	**NHL**	9	1	1	2	30	0	0	0	3	33.3	1	0	0.0	15	1	5:05								
	Boston	**NHL**	45	1	4	5	152	0	0	0	16	6.3	–2	1	0.0	66	4	4:38	12	1	0	1	16	0	0	0
99-2000	**Boston**	**NHL**	37	2	2	4	44	0	0	0	20	10.0	–4	1	0.0	79	4	5:17								
2000-01	**Boston**	**NHL**	40	2	2	4	121	0	0	1	35	5.7	–6	1	100.0	74	1	7:06								
	Providence Bruins	AHL	10	1	4	5	47												2	0	0	0	4			
	NHL Totals		196	9	12	21	586	0	0	2	90	10.0		3	33.3	234	10	5:36	12	1	0	1	16	0	0	0

Traded to **Toronto** by **Hartford** for Toronto's 9th round choice (Matt Ball) in 1994 Entry Draft, March 18, 1994. Traded to **NY Islanders** by **Toronto** with Damian Rhodes for future considerations (Kirk Muller and Don Beaupre, January 23, 1996), January 23, 1996. Traded to **Boston** by **NY Islanders** for Ted Donato, November 7, 1998. • Missed majority of 1999-2000 season recovering from head injury suffered in game vs. Toronto, November 11, 1999. Signed as a free agent by **LA Kings**, July 2, 2001.

BELL, Mark (BEHL, MAWRK) CHI.

Center. Shoots left. 6'3", 198 lbs. Born, St. Paul's, Ont., August 5, 1980. Chicago's 1st choice, 8th overall, in 1998 Entry Draft.

1995-96	Stratford Cullitons	OJHL-B	47	8	15	23	32																			
1996-97	Ottawa 67's	OHL	65	8	12	20	40												24	4	7	11	13			
1997-98	Ottawa 67's	OHL	55	34	26	60	87												13	6	5	11	14			
1998-99	Ottawa 67's	OHL	44	29	26	55	69												9	6	5	11	8			
99-2000	Ottawa 67's	OHL	48	34	38	72	95												2	0	1	1	0			
2000-01	**Chicago**	**NHL**	13	0	1	1	4	0	0	0	14	0.0	0	141	48.9	16	5	12:00								
	Norfolk Admirals	AHL	61	15	27	42	126												9	4	3	7	10			
	NHL Totals		13	0	1	1	4	0	0	0	14	0.0		141	48.9	16	5	12:00								

BENDA, Jan (BEHN-duh, YAHN) EDM.

Center. Shoots right. 6'3", 215 lbs. Born, Reef, Belgium, March 28, 1972.

1988-89	Henry Carr	MTJHL	18	0	3	3	22																			
1989-90	Oshawa Legion	MTJHL	44	50	80	130	24																			
	Oshawa Generals	OHL	1	0	1	1	0																			
1990-91	Grefrather EC	DEB-2	13	0	0	0	2																			
	Oshawa Generals	OHL	51	4	11	15	64												16	2	4	6	19			
1991-92	Oshawa Generals	OHL	61	12	23	35	68												7	1	1	2	12			
1992-93	EHC Freiburg	DEL	41	6	11	17	49												9	3	3	6	12			
1993-94	ECH Munich	DEL	43	16	11	27	67												10	3	2	5	21			
	Germany	Olympics	8	0	1	1	6																			
1994-95	Binghamton	AHL	4	0	0	0	0																			
	Richmond	ECHL	62	21	39	60	187												17	8	5	13	50			
1995-96	ESC Essen-West	DEB	2	1	0	1	6																			
	Slavia Praha	Cze-Rep	28	8	11	19													7	1	5	6				
1996-97	Sparta Praha	Cze-Rep	49	7	21	28	61												10	1	1	2	12			
	Sparta Praha	EuroHL	5	1	0	1	4												4	0	1	1	2			
1997-98	Sparta Praha	Cze-Rep	1	0	1	1	4																			
	Washington	**NHL**	9	0	3	3	6																			
	Portland Pirates	AHL	62	25	29	54	90												8	0	7	7	6			
	Germany	Olympics	4	3	0	3	8																			
1998-99	Assat-Pori	Finland	52	21	22	43	139																			
99-2000	Jokerit Helsinki	Finland	52	19	28	47	99												11	2	4	6	16			
2000-01	Jokerit Helsinki	Finland	52	18	26	44	56												5	0	1	1	6			
	NHL Totals		9	0	3	3	6																			

Signed as a free agent by **Washington**, October 1, 1997. Signed as a free agent by **Edmonton**, July 17, 2001.

BENYSEK, Ladislav (BEHN-ih-sihk, LAD-ihs-SLAHV) MIN.

Defense. Shoots left. 6'2", 190 lbs. Born, Olomouc, Czech., March 24, 1975. Edmonton's 16th choice, 266th overall, in 1994 Entry Draft.

1992-93	HC Olomouc	Czech.	3	0	0	0	0																			
1993-94	HC Olomouc-Jr	Cze-Rep	STATISTICS NOT AVAILABLE																							
1994-95	Cape Breton	AHL	58	2	7	9	54																			
1995-96	HC Olomouc	Cze-Rep	33	1	4	5													4	0	0	0				
1996-97	HC Olomouc	Cze-Rep	14	0	1	1	8																			
	Sparta Praha	Cze-Rep	36	5	5	10	28												5	0	1	1	2			
	Sparta Praha	EuroHL	3	0	0	0	4												4	0	0	0	0			
1997-98	Sparta Praha	Cze-Rep	1	0	0	0	0																			
	Edmonton	**NHL**	2	0	0	0	0																			
	Hamilton Bulldogs	AHL	53	2	14	16	29												9	1	1	2	2			
1998-99	Sparta Praha	Cze-Rep	52	8	11	19	47												8	0	1	1				
	Sparta Praha	EuroHL	7	0	0	0	2												2	0	0	0	0			
99-2000	Sparta Praha	Cze-Rep	51	1	5	6	45												9	0	0	0	4			
	Sparta Praha	EuroHL	5	1	1	2	6												4	0	0	0	4			
2000-01	**Minnesota**	**NHL**	71	2	5	7	38	1	0	0	48	4.2	–11	0	0.0	122	109	18:25								
	NHL Totals		73	2	5	7	38	1	0	0	48	4.2		0	0.0	122	109	18:25								

Claimed by **Anaheim** from **Edmonton** in Waiver Draft, September 27, 1999. Selected by **Minnesota** from **Anaheim** in Expansion Draft, June 23, 2000.

BERANEK, Josef (buh-RAH-nehk, JOH-sehf)

Left wing/Center. Shoots left. 6'2", 195 lbs. Born, Litvinov, Czech., October 25, 1969. Edmonton's 3rd choice, 78th overall, in 1989 Entry Draft.

1987-88	CHZ Litvinov	Czech.	14	7	4	11	12																			
1988-89	CHZ Litvinov	Czech.	32	18	10	28	47																			
1989-90	Dukla Trencin	Czech.	40	16	21	37													9	3	2	5				
1990-91	CHZ Litvinov	Czech.	58	29	31	60	98																			
1991-92	**Edmonton**	**NHL**	58	12	16	28	18	0	0	1	79	15.2	–2						12	2	1	3	0	1	0	1
1992-93	**Edmonton**	**NHL**	26	2	6	8	28	0	0	0	44	4.5	–7													
	Cape Breton	AHL	6	1	2	3	8																			
	Philadelphia	**NHL**	40	13	12	25	50	1	0	0	86	15.1	–1													
1993-94	**Philadelphia**	**NHL**	80	28	21	49	85	6	0	2	182	15.4	–2													
1994-95	Petra Vsetin	Cze-Rep	16	7	7	14	26																			
	Philadelphia	**NHL**	14	5	5	10	2	1	0	0	39	12.8	3													
	Vancouver	**NHL**	37	8	13	21	28	2	0	0	95	8.4	–10						11	1	1	2	12	0	0	0
1995-96	**Vancouver**	**NHL**	61	6	14	20	60	0	0	1	131	4.6	–11						3	2	1	3	0	0	0	0
1996-97	Petra Vsetin	Cze-Rep	39	19	24	43	115												3	3	2	5	4			
	Pittsburgh	**NHL**	8	3	1	4	4	1	0	0	15	20.0	–1						5	0	0	0	2	0	0	0
1997-98	Petra Vsetin	Cze-Rep	45	24	27	51	92												10	2	8	10	14			
	Petra Vsetin	EuroHL	8	5	4	9	10																			
	Czech-Republic	Olympics	6	1	0	1	4																			
1998-99	**Edmonton**	**NHL**	66	19	30	49	23	7	0	2	160	11.9	6	1261	50.2	47	21	16:25	2	0	0	0	4	0	0	0
99-2000	**Edmonton**	**NHL**	58	9	8	17	39	3	0	1	107	8.4	–6	558	53.4	42	6	13:19								
	Pittsburgh	**NHL**	13	4	4	8	18	1	0	0	32	12.5	–6	73	42.5	13	4	19:46	11	0	3	3	4	0	0	0
2000-01	**Pittsburgh**	**NHL**	70	9	14	23	43	2	0	2	152	5.9	–7	172	44.8	56	19	14:27	13	0	2	2	2	0	0	0
	NHL Totals		531	118	144	262	398	24	0	9	1122	10.5		2064	50.3	158	50	15:05	57	5	8	13	24	1	0	1

Traded to **Philadelphia** by **Edmonton** with Greg Hawgood for Brian Benning, January 16, 1993. Traded to **Vancouver** by **Philadelphia** for Shawn Antoski, February 15, 1995. Traded to **Pittsburgh** by **Vancouver** for future considerations, March 18, 1997. Traded to **Edmonton** by **Pittsburgh** for Bobby Dollas and Tony Hrkac, June 16, 1998. Traded to **Pittsburgh** by **Edmonton** for German Titov, March 14, 2000.

BEREHOWSKY, Drake
(beh-reh-HOW-skee, DRAYK) **VAN.**

Defense. Shoots right. 6'2", 225 lbs. Born, Toronto, Ont., January 3, 1972. Toronto's 1st choice, 10th overall, in 1990 Entry Draft.

			Regular Season																Playoffs							
Season	Club	League	GP	G	A	Pts	PIM	PP	SH	GW	S	%	+/-	TF	F%	H	SB	Min	GP	G	A	Pts	PIM	PP	SH	GW
1987-88	Barrie Colts	OJHL-B	40	10	36	46	81																			
1988-89	Kingston Raiders	OHL	63	7	39	46	85																			
1989-90	Kingston	OHL	9	3	11	14	28																			
1990-91	**Toronto**	**NHL**	**8**	**0**	**1**	**1**	**25**	**0**	**0**	**0**	**4**	**0.0**	**–6**													
	Kingston	OHL	13	5	13	18	38																			
	North Bay	OHL	26	7	23	30	51												10	2	7	9	21			
1991-92	North Bay	OHL	62	19	63	82	147												21	7	24	31	22			
	Toronto	**NHL**	**1**	**0**	**0**	**0**	**0**	**0**	**0**	**0**	**0**	**0.0**	**0**													
	St. John's Leafs	AHL																	6	0	5	5	21			
1992-93	**Toronto**	**NHL**	**41**	**4**	**15**	**19**	**61**	**1**	**0**	**1**	**41**	**9.8**	**1**													
	St. John's Leafs	AHL	28	10	17	27	38																			
1993-94	**Toronto**	**NHL**	**49**	**2**	**8**	**10**	**63**	**2**	**0**	**2**	**29**	**6.9**	**–3**													
	St. John's Leafs	AHL	18	3	12	15	40																			
1994-95	**Toronto**	**NHL**	**25**	**0**	**2**	**2**	**15**	**0**	**0**	**0**	**12**	**0.0**	**–10**													
	Pittsburgh	**NHL**	**4**	**0**	**0**	**0**	**13**	**0**	**0**	**0**	**2**	**0.0**	**1**						**1**	**0**	**0**	**0**	**0**	**0**	**0**	**0**
1995-96	**Pittsburgh**	**NHL**	**1**	**0**	**0**	**0**	**0**	**0**	**0**	**0**	**0**	**0.0**	**1**													
	Cleveland	IHL	74	6	28	34	141												3	0	3	3	6			
1996-97	Carolina	AHL	49	2	15	17	55																			
	San Antonio	IHL	16	3	4	7	36																			
1997-98	**Edmonton**	**NHL**	**67**	**1**	**6**	**7**	**169**	**1**	**0**	**1**	**58**	**1.7**	**1**						**12**	**1**	**2**	**3**	**14**	**0**	**0**	**1**
	Hamilton Bulldogs	AHL	8	2	0	2	21																			
1998-99	**Nashville**	**NHL**	**74**	**2**	**15**	**17**	**140**	**0**	**0**	**0**	**79**	**2.5**	**–9**	**1**	**100.0**	**140**	**109**	**21:43**								
99-2000	**Nashville**	**NHL**	**79**	**12**	**20**	**32**	**87**	**5**	**0**	**1**	**102**	**11.8**	**–4**	**0**	**0.0**	**140**	**110**	**22:39**								
2000-01	**Nashville**	**NHL**	**66**	**6**	**18**	**24**	**100**	**3**	**0**	**1**	**94**	**6.4**	**–9**	**1**	**0.0**	**115**	**56**	**21:38**								
	Vancouver	**NHL**	**14**	**1**	**1**	**2**	**21**	**1**	**0**	**0**	**13**	**7.7**	**0**	**0**	**0.0**	**13**	**16**	**17:10**	**4**	**0**	**0**	**0**	**12**	**0**	**0**	**0**
	NHL Totals		**429**	**28**	**86**	**114**	**694**	**13**	**0**	**6**	**434**	**6.5**		**2**	**50.0**	**408**	**291**	**21:44**	**17**	**1**	**2**	**3**	**26**	**0**	**0**	**1**

OHL First All-Star Team (1992) • Canadian Major Junior Defenseman of the Year (1992)

Traded to **Pittsburgh** by **Toronto** for Grant Jennings, April 7, 1995. Signed as a free agent by **Edmonton**, September 30, 1997. Traded to **Nashville** by **Edmonton** with Eric Fichaud and Greg de Vries for Mikhail Shtalenkov and Jim Dowd, October 1, 1998. Traded to **Vancouver** by **Nashville** for future considerations, March 9, 2001.

BERENZWEIG, Bubba
(BAIR-ehn-zwighg, BUH-buh) **NSH.**

Defense. Shoots left. 6'1", 217 lbs. Born, Arlington Heights, IL, August 8, 1977. NY Islanders' 5th choice, 109th overall, in 1996 Entry Draft.

Season	Club	League	GP	G	A	Pts	PIM	PP	SH	GW	S	%	+/-	TF	F%	H	SB	Min	GP	G	A	Pts	PIM	PP	SH	GW
1992-93	Loomis-Chaffee	Hi-School	22	5	13	18																				
1993-94	Loomis-Chaffee	Hi-School	22	12	27	39																				
1994-95	Loomis-Chaffee	Hi-School	23	19	23	42	10																			
1995-96	U. of Michigan	CCHA	42	4	8	12	4																			
1996-97	U. of Michigan	CCHA	38	7	12	19	49																			
1997-98	U. of Michigan	CCHA	45	8	11	19	32																			
1998-99	U. of Michigan	CCHA	42	7	24	31	38																			
99-2000	**Nashville**	**NHL**	**2**	**0**	**0**	**0**	**0**	**0**	**0**	**0**	**3**	**0.0**	**–1**	**0**	**0.0**	**5**	**4**	**17:31**								
	Milwaukee	IHL	79	4	23	27	48												3	1	2	3	0			
2000-01	**Nashville**	**NHL**	**5**	**0**	**0**	**0**	**0**	**0**	**0**	**0**	**0**	**0.0**	**0**	**0**	**0.0**	**1**	**0**	**11:57**								
	Milwaukee	IHL	72	10	26	36	38												5	0	4	4	4			
	NHL Totals		**7**	**0**	**0**	**0**	**0**	**0**	**0**	**0**	**3**	**0.0**		**0**	**0.0**	**6**	**4**	**13:33**								

CCHA Second All-Star Team (1998) • NCAA Championship All-Tournament Team (1998) • Won Ken McKenzie Trophy (Outstanding US-born Player - IHL) (2000) • IHL Second All-Star Team (2001)

Traded to **Nashville** by **NY Islanders** for Nashville's 4th round choice (Johan Halvardsson) in 1999 Entry Draft, April 14, 1999.

BEREZIN, Sergei
(BEH-reh-zihn, SAIR-gay) **PHX.**

Left wing. Shoots right. 5'10", 200 lbs. Born, Voskresensk, USSR, November 5, 1971. Toronto's 8th choice, 256th overall, in 1994 Entry Draft.

Season	Club	League	GP	G	A	Pts	PIM	PP	SH	GW	S	%	+/-	TF	F%	H	SB	Min	GP	G	A	Pts	PIM	PP	SH	GW
1990-91	HK Khimik	USSR	30	6	2	8	4																			
1991-92	HK Khimik	CIS	36	7	5	12	10																			
1992-93	HK Khimik	CIS	38	9	3	12	12												2	1	0	1	0			
1993-94	HK Khimik	CIS	40	31	10	41	16												3	2	0	2	2			
	Russia	Olympics	8	3	2	5	2																			
1994-95	Kolner Haie	DEL	43	*38	19	57	8												18	*17	8	25	14			
1995-96	Kolner Haie	DEL	45	*49	31	80	8												14	*13	9	22	10			
1996-97	**Toronto**	**NHL**	**73**	**25**	**16**	**41**	**2**	**7**	**0**	**2**	**177**	**14.1**	**–3**													
1997-98	**Toronto**	**NHL**	**68**	**16**	**15**	**31**	**10**	**3**	**0**	**3**	**167**	**9.6**	**–3**													
1998-99	**Toronto**	**NHL**	**76**	**37**	**22**	**59**	**12**	**9**	**1**	**4**	**263**	**14.1**	**16**	**26**	**57.7**	**24**	**11**	**15:32**	**17**	**6**	**6**	**12**	**4**	**2**	**0**	**2**
99-2000	**Toronto**	**NHL**	**61**	**26**	**13**	**39**	**2**	**5**	**0**	**4**	**241**	**10.8**	**8**	**11**	**45.5**	**18**	**9**	**16:52**	**12**	**4**	**4**	**8**	**0**	**0**	**0**	**1**
2000-01	**Toronto**	**NHL**	**79**	**22**	**28**	**50**	**8**	**10**	**0**	**3**	**256**	**8.6**	**2**	**4**	**75.0**	**33**	**10**	**15:41**	**11**	**2**	**5**	**7**	**2**	**0**	**0**	**2**
	NHL Totals		**357**	**126**	**94**	**220**	**34**	**34**	**1**	**16**	**1104**	**11.4**		**41**	**56.1**	**75**	**30**	**15:58**	**40**	**12**	**15**	**27**	**6**	**2**	**0**	**5**

NHL All-Rookie Team (1997)

Traded to **Phoenix** by **Toronto** for Mikael Renberg, June 23, 2001.

BERG, Aki
(BUHRG, AH-kee) **TOR.**

Defense. Shoots left. 6'3", 215 lbs. Born, Turku, Finland, July 28, 1977. Los Angeles' 1st choice, 3rd overall, in 1995 Entry Draft.

Season	Club	League	GP	G	A	Pts	PIM	PP	SH	GW	S	%	+/-	TF	F%	H	SB	Min	GP	G	A	Pts	PIM	PP	SH	GW
1992-93	TPS Turku	Finn-Jr.	39	18	24	42	24																			
1993-94	TPS Turku	Finn-Jr.	21	3	11	14	24												7	0	0	0	10			
	Kiekko-67 Turku	Finland-2	12	1	1	2	16																			
	TPS Turku	Finland	6	0	3	3	4																			
1994-95	TPS Turku	Finn-Jr.	8	1	0	1	30																			
	Kiekko-67 Turku	Finland-2	21	3	9	12	24												7	0	0	0	10			
	TPS Turku	Finland	5	0	0	0	4																			
1995-96	**Los Angeles**	**NHL**	**51**	**0**	**7**	**7**	**29**	**0**	**0**	**0**	**56**	**0.0**	**–13**													
	Phoenix	IHL	20	0	3	3	18												2	0	0	0	4			
1996-97	**Los Angeles**	**NHL**	**41**	**2**	**6**	**8**	**24**	**2**	**0**	**0**	**65**	**3.1**	**–9**													
	Phoenix	IHL	23	1	3	4	21																			
1997-98	**Los Angeles**	**NHL**	**72**	**0**	**8**	**8**	**61**	**0**	**0**	**0**	**58**	**0.0**	**3**						**4**	**0**	**3**	**3**	**0**	**0**	**0**	**0**
	Finland	Olympics	6	0	0	0	6																			
1998-99	TPS Turku	Finland	48	8	7	15	137												9	1	1	2	45			
99-2000	**Los Angeles**	**NHL**	**70**	**3**	**13**	**16**	**45**	**0**	**0**	**0**	**70**	**4.3**	**–1**	**0**	**0.0**	**197**	**83**	**16:39**	**2**	**0**	**0**	**0**	**2**	**0**	**0**	**0**
2000-01	**Los Angeles**	**NHL**	**47**	**0**	**4**	**4**	**43**	**0**	**0**	**0**	**31**	**0.0**	**3**	**0**	**0.0**	**130**	**73**	**14:54**								
	Toronto	**NHL**	**12**	**3**	**0**	**3**	**2**	**3**	**0**	**1**	**12**	**25.0**	**–6**	**0**	**0.0**	**22**	**13**	**18:13**	**11**	**0**	**2**	**2**	**4**	**0**	**0**	**0**
	NHL Totals		**293**	**8**	**38**	**46**	**204**	**5**	**0**	**1**	**292**	**2.7**		**0**	**0.0**	**349**	**169**	**16:09**	**17**	**0**	**5**	**5**	**6**	**0**	**0**	**0**

Traded to **Toronto** by **LA Kings** for Adam Mair and Toronto's 2nd round choice (Mike Cammalleri) in 2001 Entry Draft, March 13, 2001.

BERGEVIN, Marc
(BUHR-zheh-vihn, MAHRK)

Defense. Shoots left. 6'1", 214 lbs. Born, Montreal, Que., August 11, 1965. Chicago's 3rd choice, 60th overall, in 1983 Entry Draft.

Season	Club	League	GP	G	A	Pts	PIM	PP	SH	GW	S	%	+/-	TF	F%	H	SB	Min	GP	G	A	Pts	PIM	PP	SH	GW
1981-82	Mtl-Concordia	QAAA	44	10	20	30	54												5	0	2	2	4			
1982-83	Chicoutimi	QMJHL	64	3	27	30	113																			
1983-84	Chicoutimi	QMJHL	70	10	35	45	125																			
	Springfield	AHL	7	0	1	1	2																			
1984-85	**Chicago**	**NHL**	**60**	**0**	**6**	**6**	**54**	**0**	**0**	**0**	**41**	**0.0**	**–9**						**6**	**0**	**3**	**3**	**2**	**0**	**0**	**0**
	Springfield	AHL																	4	0	0	0	0			
1985-86	**Chicago**	**NHL**	**71**	**7**	**7**	**14**	**60**	**0**	**0**	**1**	**50**	**14.0**	**0**						**3**	**0**	**0**	**0**	**0**	**0**	**0**	**0**
1986-87	**Chicago**	**NHL**	**66**	**4**	**10**	**14**	**66**	**0**	**0**	**0**	**56**	**7.1**	**4**						**3**	**1**	**0**	**1**	**2**	**0**	**0**	**0**
1987-88	**Chicago**	**NHL**	**58**	**1**	**6**	**7**	**85**	**0**	**0**	**0**	**51**	**2.0**	**–19**													
	Saginaw Hawks	IHL	10	2	7	9	20																			
1988-89	**Chicago**	**NHL**	**11**	**0**	**0**	**0**	**18**	**0**	**0**	**0**	**9**	**0.0**	**–3**													
	NY Islanders	**NHL**	**58**	**2**	**13**	**15**	**62**	**1**	**0**	**0**	**56**	**3.6**	**2**													

			Regular Season																Playoffs							
Season	Club	League	GP	G	A	Pts	PIM	PP	SH	GW	S	%	+/-	TF	F%	H	SB	Min	GP	G	A	Pts	PIM	PP	SH	GW
1989-90	NY Islanders	NHL	18	0	4	4	30	0	0	0	12	0.0	-8													
	Springfield	AHL	47	7	16	23	66												17	2	11	13	16			
1990-91	Capital District	AHL	7	0	5	5	6																			
	Hartford	NHL	4	0	0	0	4	0	0	0	2	0.0	-3													
	Springfield	AHL	58	4	23	27	85												18	0	7	7	26			
1991-92	Hartford	NHL	75	7	17	24	64	4	1	1	96	7.3	-13						5	0	0	0	2	0	0	0
1992-93	Tampa Bay	NHL	78	2	12	14	66	0	0	0	69	2.9	-16													
1993-94	Tampa Bay	NHL	83	1	15	16	87	0	0	1	76	1.3	-5													
1994-95	Tampa Bay	NHL	44	2	4	6	51	0	1	0	32	6.3	-6													
1995-96	Detroit	NHL	70	1	9	10	33	0	0	0	26	3.8	7						17	1	0	1	14	1	0	0
1996-97	St. Louis	NHL	82	0	4	4	53	0	0	0	30	0.0	-9						6	1	0	1	8	0	0	0
1997-98	St. Louis	NHL	81	3	7	10	90	0	0	0	40	7.5	-2						10	0	1	1	8	0	0	0
1998-99	St. Louis	NHL	52	1	1	2	99	0	0	0	40	2.5	-14	0	0.0	90	40	16:09								
99-2000	St. Louis	NHL	81	1	8	9	75	0	0	0	54	1.9	27	0	0.0	100	98	21:16	7	0	1	1	6	0	0	0
2000-01	St. Louis	NHL	2	0	0	0	0	0	0	0	1	0.0	1	0	0.0	2	2	14:51								
	Pittsburgh	NHL	36	1	4	5	26	0	0	0	11	9.1	5	0	0.0	56	48	16:57	12	0	1	1	2	0	0	0
	NHL Totals		1030	33	127	160	1023	5	2	3	752	4.4		0	0.0	248	188	18:44	69	3	6	9	44	1	0	0

Traded to **NY Islanders** by **Chicago** with Gary Nylund for Steve Konroyd and Bob Bassen, November 25, 1988. Traded to **Hartford** by **NY Islanders** for Hartford's 5th round choice (Ryan Duthie) in 1992 Entry Draft, October 30, 1990. Signed as a free agent by **Tampa Bay**, July 9, 1992. Traded to **Detroit** by **Tampa Bay** with Ben Hankinson for Shawn Burr and Detroit's 3rd round choice (later traded to Boston - Boston selected Jason Doyle) in 1996 Entry Draft, August 17, 1995. Signed as a free agent by **St. Louis**, July 31, 1996. Traded to **Pittsburgh** by **St. Louis** for Dan Trebil, December 28, 2000. • Missed majority of 2000-01 season recovering from thumb (October 5, 2000 vs. Phoenix) and knee (February 23, 2001 vs. Detroit) injuries.

BERRY, Rick (BAIR-ree, RIHK) COL.

Defense. Shoots left. 6'2", 210 lbs. Born, Birtle, Man., November 4, 1978. Colorado's 3rd choice, 55th overall, in 1997 Entry Draft.

Season	Club	League	GP	G	A	Pts	PIM	PP	SH	GW	S	%	+/-	TF	F%	H	SB	Min	GP	G	A	Pts	PIM	PP	SH	GW
1994-95	Yellowhead Pass	MMHL	33	12	19	31	90																			
1995-96	Seattle T-Birds	WHL	59	4	9	13	103												1	0	0	0	0			
1996-97	Seattle T-Birds	WHL	72	12	21	33	125												15	3	7	10	23			
1997-98	Seattle T-Birds	WHL	37	5	12	17	100																			
	Spokane Chiefs	WHL	22	4	9	13	31												17	1	4	5	26			
1998-99	Hershey Bears	AHL	62	2	6	8	153																			
99-2000	Hershey Bears	AHL	64	9	16	25	148												13	2	3	5	24			
2000-01	Colorado	NHL	19	0	4	4	38	0	0	0	10	0.0	5	0	0.0	29	15	12:08								
	Hershey Bears	AHL	48	6	17	23	87												12	2	2	4	18			
	NHL Totals		19	0	4	4	38	0	0	0	10	0.0		0	0.0	29	15	12:08								

BERTRAND, Eric (BURH-tran, AIR-ihk)

Left wing. Shoots left. 6'1", 205 lbs. Born, St-Ephrem, Que., April 16, 1975. New Jersey's 9th choice, 207th overall, in 1994 Entry Draft.

Season	Club	League	GP	G	A	Pts	PIM	PP	SH	GW	S	%	+/-	TF	F%	H	SB	Min	GP	G	A	Pts	PIM	PP	SH	GW
1991-92	Beauce-Amiante	QAAA	STATISTICS NOT AVAILABLE																							
1992-93	Granby Bisons	QMJHL	64	10	15	25	82																			
1993-94	Granby Bisons	QMJHL	60	11	15	26	151												6	1	0	1	18			
1994-95	Granby Bisons	QMJHL	56	14	26	40	268												13	3	8	11	50			
1995-96	Albany River Rats	AHL	70	16	13	29	199												4	0	0	0	6			
1996-97	Albany River Rats	AHL	77	16	27	43	204												8	3	3	6	15			
1997-98	Albany River Rats	AHL	76	20	29	49	256												13	5	5	10	4			
1998-99	Albany River Rats	AHL	78	34	31	65	160												5	4	2	6	0			
99-2000	New Jersey	NHL	4	0	0	0	0	0	0	0	1	0.0	-1	0	0.0	11	0	7:47								
	Atlanta	NHL	8	0	0	0	4	0	0	0	11	0.0	-5	1	0.0	19	1	9:56								
	Philadelphia	AHL	15	3	6	9	67																			
	Milwaukee	IHL	27	7	9	16	56												3	0	0	0	2			
2000-01	Montreal	NHL	3	0	0	0	0	0	0	0	0	0.0	0	0	0.0	9	1	4:20								
	Quebec Citadelles	AHL	66	21	21	42	113												9	4	2	6	12			
	NHL Totals		15	0	0	0	4	0	0	0	12	0.0		1	0.0	39	2	8:14								

Traded to **Atlanta** by **New Jersey** with Wes Mason for Sylvain Cloutier, Jeff Williams and Atlanta's 7th round choice (Ken Magowan) in 2000 Entry Draft, November 1, 1999. Traded to **Philadelphia** by **Atlanta** for Brian Wesenberg, December 9, 1999. Traded to **Nashville** by **Philadelphia** for future considerations, February 14, 2000. Signed as a free agent by **Montreal**, July 7, 2000.

BERTUZZI, Todd (buhr-TOO-zee, TAWD) VAN.

Center. Shoots left. 6'3", 235 lbs. Born, Sudbury, Ont., February 2, 1975. NY Islanders' 1st choice, 23rd overall, in 1993 Entry Draft.

Season	Club	League	GP	G	A	Pts	PIM	PP	SH	GW	S	%	+/-	TF	F%	H	SB	Min	GP	G	A	Pts	PIM	PP	SH	GW
1990-91	Sudbury Legion	NOHA	48	25	46	71	247																			
	Sudbury Cubs	NOJHA	3	3	2	5	10																			
1991-92	Guelph Storm	OHL	47	7	14	21	145																			
1992-93	Guelph Storm	OHL	59	27	32	59	164												5	2	2	4	6			
1993-94	Guelph Storm	OHL	61	28	54	82	165												9	2	6	8	30			
1994-95	Guelph Storm	OHL	62	54	65	119	58												14	*15	18	33	41			
1995-96	NY Islanders	NHL	76	18	21	39	83	4	0	2	127	14.2	-14													
1996-97	NY Islanders	NHL	64	10	13	23	68	3	0	1	79	12.7	-3													
	Utah Grizzlies	IHL	13	5	5	10	16																			
1997-98	NY Islanders	NHL	52	7	11	18	58	1	0	1	63	11.1	-19													
	Vancouver	NHL	22	6	9	15	63	1	1	1	39	15.4	2													
1998-99	Vancouver	NHL	32	8	8	16	44	1	0	3	72	11.1	-6	191	43.5	53	12	18:28								
99-2000	Vancouver	NHL	80	25	25	50	126	4	0	2	173	14.5	-2	476	46.6	187	16	15:24								
2000-01	Vancouver	NHL	79	25	30	55	93	14	0	3	203	12.3	-18	84	45.2	132	25	17:13	4	2	2	4	8	0	0	0
	NHL Totals		405	99	117	216	535	28	1	13	756	13.1		751	45.7	372	53	16:40	4	2	2	4	8	0	0	0

OHL Second All-Star team (1995)

Traded to **Vancouver** by **NY Islanders** with Bryan McCabe and NY Islanders' 3rd round choice (Jarkko Ruutu) in 1998 Entry Draft for Trevor Linden, February 6, 1998. • Missed majority of 1998-99 season recovering from leg injury suffered in game vs. Washington, November 1, 1998.

BERUBE, Craig (buh-ROO-bee, KRAYG) NYI

Left wing. Shoots left. 6'1", 205 lbs. Born, Calahoo, Alta., December 17, 1965.

Season	Club	League	GP	G	A	Pts	PIM	PP	SH	GW	S	%	+/-	TF	F%	H	SB	Min	GP	G	A	Pts	PIM	PP	SH	GW
1982-83	Williams Lake	PCJHL	33	9	24	33	99																			
	Kamloops Oilers	WHL	4	0	0	0	0																			
1983-84	New Westminster	WHL	70	11	20	31	104												8	1	2	3	5			
1984-85	New Westminster	WHL	70	25	44	69	191												10	3	2	5	4			
1985-86	Kamloops Blazers	WHL	32	17	14	31	119																			
	Medicine Hat	WHL	34	14	16	30	95												25	7	8	15	102			
1986-87	Philadelphia	NHL	7	0	0	0	57	0	0	0	4	0.0	2						5	0	0	0	17	0	0	0
	Hershey Bears	AHL	63	7	17	24	325																			
1987-88	Philadelphia	NHl	27	3	2	5	108	0	0	2	13	23.1	1													
	Hershey Bears	AHL	31	5	9	14	119																			
1988-89	Philadelphia	NHL	53	1	1	2	199	0	0	0	31	3.2	-15						16	0	0	0	56	0	0	0
	Hershey Bears	AHL	7	0	2	2	19																			
1989-90	Philadelphia	NHL	74	4	14	18	291	0	0	0	52	7.7	-7													
1990-91	Philadelphia	NHL	74	8	9	17	293	0	0	0	46	17.4	-6													
1991-92	Toronto	NHL	40	5	7	12	109	1	0	1	42	11.9	-2													
	Calgary	NHL	36	1	4	5	155	0	0	0	27	3.7	-3													
1992-93	Calgary	NHL	77	4	8	12	209	0	0	2	58	6.9	-6						6	0	1	1	21	0	0	0
1993-94	Washington	NHL	84	7	7	14	305	0	0	0	48	14.6	-4						8	0	0	0	21	0	0	0
1994-95	Washington	NHL	43	2	4	6	173	0	0	0	22	9.1	-5						7	0	0	0	29	0	0	0
1995-96	Washington	NHL	50	2	10	12	151	1	0	1	28	7.1	1						2	0	0	0	19	0	0	0
1996-97	Washington	NHL	80	4	3	7	218	0	0	1	55	7.3	-11													
1997-98	Washington	NHL	74	6	9	15	189	0	0	0	68	8.8	-3						21	1	0	1	21	0	0	1
1998-99	Washington	NHL	66	5	4	9	166	0	0	0	45	11.1	-7	14	42.9	85	10	6:47								
	Philadelphia	NHL	11	0	0	0	28	0	0	0	7	0.0	-3	0	0.0	8	1	8:15	6	1	0	1	4	0	0	0
99-2000	Philadelphia	NHL	77	4	8	12	162	0	0	0	63	6.3	3	4	25.0	111	7	8:00	18	1	0	1	23	0	0	1

			Regular Season																Playoffs							
Season	Club	League	GP	G	A	Pts	PIM	PP	SH	GW	S	%	+/-	TF	F%	H	SB	Min	GP	G	A	Pts	PIM	PP	SH	GW
2000-01	Washington	NHL	22	0	1	1	18	0	0	0	8	0.0	–3	0	0.0	11	3	5:34	....	....	....	....	....	....	....	....
	NY Islanders	NHL	38	0	2	2	54	0	0	0	27	0.0	–5	11	45.5	46	4	6:02	....	....	....	....	....	....	....	....
	NHL Totals		933	56	93	149	2885	2	0	7	644	8.7		29	41.4	261	25	7:02	89	3	1	4	211	0	0	2

Signed as a free agent by **Philadelphia**, March 19, 1986. Traded to **Edmonton** by **Philadelphia** with Craig Fisher and Scott Mellanby for Dave Brown, Corey Foster and Jari Kurri, May 30, 1991. Traded to **Toronto** by **Edmonton** with Grant Fuhr and Glenn Anderson for Vincent Damphousse, Peter Ing, Scott Thornton and Luke Richardson, September 19, 1991. Traded to **Calgary** by **Toronto** with Alexander Godynyuk, Gary Leeman, Michel Petit and Jeff Reese for Doug Gilmour, Jamie Macoun, Ric Nattress, Rick Wamsley and Kent Manderville, January 2, 1992. Traded to **Washington** by **Calgary** for Washington's 5th round choice (Darryl Lafrance) in 1993 Entry Draft, June 26, 1993. Traded to **Philadelphia** by **Washington** for cash, March 23, 1999. Signed as a free agent by **Washington**, July 7, 2000. Traded to **NY Islanders** by **Washington** for Vancouver's 9th round choice (previously acquired, Washington selected Robert Muller) in 2001 Entry Draft, January 11, 2001.

BETIK, Karel

(BEH-tihk, KAHR-ehl)

Defense. Shoots left. 6'2", 208 lbs. Born, Karvina, Czech., October 28, 1978. Tampa Bay's 6th choice, 112th overall, in 1997 Entry Draft.

1995-96	HC Vitkovice-Jr.	Cze-Rep	48	3	12	15	88	....	....	....	....	....	....	....	....	....	....	....	....	....	....	....	....	....	....	....
1996-97	Kelowna Rockets	WHL	56	3	10	13	76	....	....	....	....	....	....	....	....	....	....	....	6	1	1	2	2	....	....	....
1997-98	Kelowna Rockets	WHL	61	5	25	30	121	....	....	....	....	....	....	....	....	....	....	....	7	1	2	3	8	....	....	....
1998-99	Tampa Bay	NHL	3	0	2	2	2	0	0	0	2	0.0	–3	0	0.0	2	2	13:28	....	....	....	....	....	....	....	....
	Cleveland	IHL	74	5	11	16	97	....	....	....	....	....	....	....	....	....	....	....	....	....	....	....	....	....	....	....
99-2000	Detroit Vipers	IHL	17	0	0	0	22	....	....	....	....	....	....	....	....	....	....	....	....	....	....	....	....	....	....	....
	Toledo Storm	ECHL	22	0	7	7	42	....	....	....	....	....	....	....	....	....	....	....	....	....	....	....	....	....	....	....
2000-01	Bakersfield	WCHL	62	3	18	21	105	....	....	....	....	....	....	....	....	....	....	....	3	0	1	1	10	....	....	....
	NHL Totals		3	0	2	2	2	0	0	0	2	0.0		0	0.0	2	2	13:28	....	....	....	....	....	....	....	....

BICANEK, Radim

(BEE-chah-nehk, RA-dihm) **CBJ**

Defense. Shoots left. 6'1", 195 lbs. Born, Uherske Hradiste, Czech., January 18, 1975. Ottawa's 2nd choice, 27th overall, in 1993 Entry Draft.

1992-93	Dukla Jihlava	Czech.	43	2	3	5	....	....	....	....	....	....	....	....	....	....	....	....	....	....	....	....	....	....	....	....
1993-94	Belleville Bulls	OHL	63	16	27	43	49	....	....	....	....	....	....	....	....	....	....	....	12	2	8	10	21	....	....	....
1994-95	Belleville Bulls	OHL	49	13	26	39	61	....	....	....	....	....	....	....	....	....	....	....	16	6	5	11	30	....	....	....
	Ottawa	NHL	6	0	0	0	0	0	0	0	6	0.0	3	....	....	....	....	....	....	....	....	....	....	....	....	....
	P.E.I. Senators	AHL	....	....	....	....	....	....	....	....	....	....	....	....	....	....	....	....	3	0	1	1	0	....	....	....
1995-96	P.E.I. Senators	AHL	74	7	19	26	87	....	....	....	....	....	....	....	....	....	....	....	5	0	2	2	6	....	....	....
1996-97	Ottawa	NHL	21	0	1	1	8	0	0	0	27	0.0	–4	....	....	....	....	....	7	0	0	0	8	0	0	0
	Worcester	AHL	44	1	15	16	22	....	....	....	....	....	....	....	....	....	....	....	....	....	....	....	....	....	....	....
1997-98	Ottawa	NHL	1	0	0	0	0	0	0	0	0	0.0	0	....	....	....	....	....	....	....	....	....	....	....	....	....
	Detroit Vipers	IHL	9	1	3	4	16	....	....	....	....	....	....	....	....	....	....	....	....	....	....	....	....	....	....	....
	Manitoba Moose	IHL	42	1	7	8	52	....	....	....	....	....	....	....	....	....	....	....	....	....	....	....	....	....	....	....
1998-99	Ottawa	NHL	7	0	0	0	4	0	0	0	6	0.0	–1	0	0.0	11	4	10:51	....	....	....	....	....	....	....	....
	Grand Rapids	IHL	46	8	17	25	48	....	....	....	....	....	....	....	....	....	....	....	....	....	....	....	....	....	....	....
	Chicago	NHL	7	0	0	0	6	0	0	0	7	0.0	–3	0	0.0	7	8	15:57	....	....	....	....	....	....	....	....
99-2000	Chicago	NHL	11	0	3	3	4	0	0	0	8	0.0	7	0	0.0	22	7	18:27	....	....	....	....	....	....	....	....
	Cleveland	IHL	70	5	27	32	125	....	....	....	....	....	....	....	....	....	....	....	9	2	2	4	8	....	....	....
2000-01	Columbus	NHL	9	0	2	2	6	0	0	0	11	0.0	1	1	100.0	24	6	17:08	....	....	....	....	....	....	....	....
	Syracuse Crunch	AHL	68	22	43	65	124	....	....	....	....	....	....	....	....	....	....	....	5	4	2	6	2	....	....	....
	NHL Totals		62	0	6	6	28	0	0	0	65	0.0		1	100.0	64	25	16:01	7	0	0	0	8	0	0	0

AHL Second All-Star Team (2001)

Traded to **Chicago** by **Ottawa** for Los Angeles' 6th round choice (previously acquired, Ottawa selected Martin Prusek) in 1999 Entry Draft, March 12, 1999. Selected by **Columbus** from **Chicago** in Expansion Draft, June 23, 2000.

BICEK, Jiri

(bee-CHEHK, YEH-ree) **N.J.**

Left wing. Shoots left. 5'10", 190 lbs. Born, Kosice, Czech., December 3, 1978. New Jersey's 4th choice, 131st overall, in 1997 Entry Draft.

1994-95	HC Kosice	Slovak-Jr.	42	38	36	74	18	....	....	....	....	....	....	....	....	....	....	....	....	....	....	....	....	....	....	....
1995-96	HC Kosice	Slovakia	30	10	15	25	16	....	....	....	....	....	....	....	....	....	....	....	9	2	4	6	0	....	....	....
1996-97	HC Kosice	Slovakia	44	11	14	25	20	....	....	....	....	....	....	....	....	....	....	....	7	1	3	4	....	....	....	....
1997-98	Albany River Rats	AHL	50	10	10	20	22	....	....	....	....	....	....	....	....	....	....	....	13	1	6	7	4	....	....	....
1998-99	Albany River Rats	AHL	79	15	45	60	102	....	....	....	....	....	....	....	....	....	....	....	5	2	2	4	2	....	....	....
99-2000	Albany River Rats	AHL	80	7	36	43	51	....	....	....	....	....	....	....	....	....	....	....	4	0	2	2	0	....	....	....
2000-01	New Jersey	NHL	5	1	0	1	4	0	0	0	10	10.0	0	0	0.0	3	1	13:04	....	....	....	....	....	....	....	....
	Albany River Rats	AHL	73	12	29	41	73	....	....	....	....	....	....	....	....	....	....	....	....	....	....	....	....	....	....	....
	NHL Totals		5	1	0	1	4	0	0	0	10	10.0		0	0.0	3	1	13:04	....	....	....	....	....	....	....	....

BIRON, Mathieu

(BEE-rawn, mat-yoo) **T.B.**

Defense. Shoots right. 6'6", 229 lbs. Born, Lac St-Charles, Que., April 29, 1980. Los Angeles' 1st choice, 21st overall, in 1998 Entry Draft.

1996-97	Ste-Foy Governors	QAAA	40	4	22	26	49	....	....	....	....	....	....	....	....	....	....	....	10	3	4	7	....	....	....	....
1997-98	Shawinigan	QMJHL	59	8	28	36	60	....	....	....	....	....	....	....	....	....	....	....	6	0	1	1	10	....	....	....
1998-99	Shawinigan	QMJHL	69	13	32	45	116	....	....	....	....	....	....	....	....	....	....	....	6	0	2	2	6	....	....	....
99-2000	NY Islanders	NHL	60	4	4	8	38	2	0	2	70	5.7	–13	2	0.0	120	65	15:02	....	....	....	....	....	....	....	....
2000-01	NY Islanders	NHL	14	0	1	1	12	0	0	0	10	0.0	2	0	0.0	26	14	12:21	....	....	....	....	....	....	....	....
	Lowell	AHL	22	1	3	4	17	....	....	....	....	....	....	....	....	....	....	....	....	....	....	....	....	....	....	....
	Springfield	AHL	34	0	6	6	18	....	....	....	....	....	....	....	....	....	....	....	....	....	....	....	....	....	....	....
	NHL Totals		74	4	5	9	50	2	0	2	80	5.0		2	0.0	146	79	14:31	....	....	....	....	....	....	....	....

Traded to **NY Islanders** by **LA Kings** with Olli Jokinen, Josh Green and LA Kings' 1st round choice (Taylor Pyatt) in 1999 Entry Draft for Ziggy Palffy, Brian Smolinski, Marcel Cousineau and New Jersey's 4th round choice (previously acquired, LA Kings selected Daniel Johansson) in 1999 Entry Draft, June 20, 1999. Traded to **Tampa Bay** by **NY Islanders** with NY Islanders' 2nd round choice in 2002 Entry Draft for Adrian Aucoin and Alexander Kharitonov, June 22, 2001.

BLACK, James

(BLAK, JAYMS)

Left wing. Shoots left. 6', 202 lbs. Born, Regina, Sask., August 15, 1969. Hartford's 4th choice, 94th overall, in 1989 Entry Draft.

1986-87	Edmonton Mets	AJHL	41	36	48	84	58	....	....	....	....	....	....	....	....	....	....	....	....	....	....	....	....	....	....	....
1987-88	Portland	WHL	72	30	50	80	50	....	....	....	....	....	....	....	....	....	....	....	....	....	....	....	....	....	....	....
1988-89	Portland	WHL	71	45	51	96	57	....	....	....	....	....	....	....	....	....	....	....	19	13	6	19	28	....	....	....
1989-90	Hartford	NHL	1	0	0	0	0	0	0	0	0	0.0	0	....	....	....	....	....	....	....	....	....	....	....	....	....
	Binghamton	AHL	80	37	35	72	34	....	....	....	....	....	....	....	....	....	....	....	....	....	....	....	....	....	....	....
1990-91	Hartford	NHL	1	0	0	0	0	0	0	0	0	0.0	0	....	....	....	....	....	....	....	....	....	....	....	....	....
	Springfield	AHL	79	35	61	96	34	....	....	....	....	....	....	....	....	....	....	....	18	9	9	18	6	....	....	....
1991-92	Hartford	NHL	30	4	6	10	10	1	0	1	54	7.4	–4	....	....	....	....	....	....	....	....	....	....	....	....	....
	Springfield	AHL	47	15	25	40	33	....	....	....	....	....	....	....	....	....	....	....	10	3	2	5	18	....	....	....
1992-93	Minnesota	NHL	10	2	1	3	4	0	0	0	10	20.0	0	....	....	....	....	....	....	....	....	....	....	....	....	....
	Kalamazoo	IHL	63	25	45	70	40	....	....	....	....	....	....	....	....	....	....	....	....	....	....	....	....	....	....	....
1993-94	Dallas	NHL	13	2	3	5	2	2	0	0	16	12.5	–4	....	....	....	....	....	....	....	....	....	....	....	....	....
	Buffalo	NHL	2	0	0	0	0	2	0	0	2	0.0	0	....	....	....	....	....	....	....	....	....	....	....	....	....
	Rochester	AHL	45	19	32	51	28	....	....	....	....	....	....	....	....	....	....	....	4	2	3	5	0	....	....	....
1994-95	Las Vegas	IHL	78	29	44	73	54	....	....	....	....	....	....	....	....	....	....	....	10	1	6	7	4	....	....	....
1995-96	Chicago	NHL	13	3	3	6	16	0	0	1	23	13.0	1	....	....	....	....	....	8	1	0	1	2	0	0	0
	Indianapolis Ice	IHL	67	32	50	82	56	....	....	....	....	....	....	....	....	....	....	....	....	....	....	....	....	....	....	....
1996-97	Chicago	NHL	64	12	11	23	20	0	0	3	122	9.8	6	....	....	....	....	....	5	1	1	2	2	0	0	0
1997-98	Chicago	NHL	52	10	5	15	8	2	1	3	90	11.1	–8	....	....	....	....	....	....	....	....	....	....	....	....	....
1998-99	Chicago Wolves	IHL	5	6	0	6	0	....	....	....	....	....	....	....	....	....	....	....	....	....	....	....	....	....	....	....
	Washington	NHL	75	16	14	30	14	1	1	3	135	11.9	5	10	50.0	42	30	15:04	....	....	....	....	....	....	....	....
99-2000	Washington	NHL	49	8	9	17	6	1	0	1	71	11.3	–1	18	38.9	27	31	12:03	....	....	....	....	....	....	....	....
2000-01	Washington	NHL	42	1	5	6	4	0	0	0	34	2.9	–3	7	57.1	23	13	9:04	....	....	....	....	....	....	....	....
	Portland Pirates	AHL	5	2	3	5	0	....	....	....	....	....	....	....	....	....	....	....	....	....	....	....	....	....	....	....
	NHL Totals		352	58	57	115	84	9	2	12	557	10.4		35	45.7	92	74	12:40	13	2	1	3	4	0	0	0

Traded to **Minnesota** by **Hartford** for Mark Janssens, September 3, 1992. Transferred to **Dallas** after **Minnesota** franchise relocated, June 9, 1993. Traded to **Buffalo** by **Dallas** with Dallas' 7th round choice (Steve Webb) in 1994 Entry Draft for Gord Donnelly, December 15, 1993. Signed as a free agent by **Chicago**, September 18, 1995. Traded to **Washington** by **Chicago** for Washington's 9th round choice (later traded back to Washington - Washington selected Igor Shadilov) in 1999 Entry Draft, October 15, 1998.

			Regular Season																Playoffs							
Season	Club	League	GP	G	A	Pts	PIM	PP	SH	GW	S	%	+/-	TF	F%	H	SB	Min	GP	G	A	Pts	PIM	PP	SH	GW

BLAKE, Jason

(BLAYK, JAY-suhn) **NYI**

Center. Shoots left. 5'10", 185 lbs. Born, Moorhead, MN, September 2, 1973.

1991-92	Moorehead High	Hi-School	25	30	30	60	....																			
1992-93	Waterloo Hawks	USHL	45	24	27	51	107																			
1993-94	Waterloo Hawks	USHL	47	50	50	100	76																			
1994-95	Ferris State	CCHA	36	16	16	32	46																			
1995-96	North Dakota	CCHA	DID NOT PLAY – TRANSFERRED COLLEGES																							
1996-97	North Dakota	WCHA	43	19	32	51	44																			
1997-98	North Dakota	WCHA	38	24	27	51	62																			
1998-99	North Dakota	WCHA	38	*28	*41	*69	49																			
	Los Angeles	**NHL**	**1**	**1**	**0**	**1**	**0**	**0**	**0**	**0**	**5**	**20.0**	**1**	**14**	**35.7**	**1**	**0**	**17:13**								
	Orlando	IHL	5	3	5	8	6												13	3	4	7	20			
99-2000	**Los Angeles**	**NHL**	**64**	**5**	**18**	**23**	**26**	**0**	**0**	**1**	**131**	**3.8**	**4**	**269**	**43.9**	**68**	**14**	**11:17**	**3**	**0**	**0**	**0**	**0**	**0**	**0**	**0**
	Long Beach	IHL	7	3	6	9	2																			
2000-01	**Los Angeles**	**NHL**	**17**	**1**	**3**	**4**	**10**	**0**	**0**	**0**	**27**	**3.7**	**–8**	**13**	**61.5**	**18**	**4**	**10:03**								
	Lowell	AHL	2	0	1	1	2																			
	NY Islanders	**NHL**	**30**	**4**	**8**	**12**	**24**	**1**	**1**	**0**	**73**	**5.5**	**–12**	**118**	**44.1**	**80**	**17**	**15:43**								
	NHL Totals		**112**	**11**	**29**	**40**	**60**	**1**	**1**	**1**	**236**	**4.7**		**414**	**44.2**	**167**	**35**	**12:20**	**3**	**0**	**0**	**0**	**0**	**0**	**0**	**0**

WCHA First All-Star Team (1997, 1998, 1999) • NCAA West Second All-American Team (1998) • NCAA West First All-American Team (1999)

Signed as a free agent by **LA Kings**, April 20, 1999. Traded to **NY Islanders** by **LA Kings** for future considerations, January 3, 2001.

BLAKE, Rob

(BLAYK, RAWB) **COL.**

Defense. Shoots right. 6'4", 225 lbs. Born, Simcoe, Ont., December 10, 1969. Los Angeles' 4th choice, 70th overall, in 1988 Entry Draft.

1985-86	Brantford Classics	OJHL-B	39	3	13	16	43																			
1986-87	Stratford Cullitons	OJHL-B	31	11	20	31	115																			
1987-88	Bowling Green	CCHA	43	5	8	13	88																			
1988-89	Bowling Green	CCHA	46	11	21	32	140																			
1989-90	Bowling Green	CCHA	42	23	36	59	140																			
	Los Angeles	**NHL**	**4**	**0**	**0**	**0**	**4**	**0**	**0**	**0**	**3**	**0.0**	**0**						**8**	**1**	**3**	**4**	**4**	**1**	**0**	**0**
1990-91	**Los Angeles**	**NHL**	**75**	**12**	**34**	**46**	**125**	**9**	**0**	**2**	**150**	**8.0**	**3**						**12**	**1**	**4**	**5**	**26**	**1**	**0**	**0**
1991-92	**Los Angeles**	**NHL**	**57**	**7**	**13**	**20**	**102**	**5**	**0**	**0**	**131**	**5.3**	**–5**						**6**	**2**	**1**	**3**	**12**	**0**	**0**	**0**
1992-93	**Los Angeles**	**NHL**	**76**	**16**	**43**	**59**	**152**	**10**	**0**	**4**	**243**	**6.6**	**18**						**23**	**4**	**6**	**10**	**46**	**1**	**1**	**0**
1993-94	**Los Angeles**	**NHL**	**84**	**20**	**48**	**68**	**137**	**7**	**0**	**6**	**304**	**6.6**	**–7**													
1994-95	**Los Angeles**	**NHL**	**24**	**4**	**7**	**11**	**38**	**4**	**0**	**1**	**76**	**5.3**	**–16**													
1995-96	**Los Angeles**	**NHL**	**6**	**1**	**2**	**3**	**8**	**0**	**0**	**0**	**13**	**7.7**	**0**													
1996-97	**Los Angeles**	**NHL**	**62**	**8**	**23**	**31**	**82**	**4**	**0**	**1**	**169**	**4.7**	**–28**													
1997-98	**Los Angeles**	**NHL**	**81**	**23**	**27**	**50**	**94**	**11**	**0**	**4**	**261**	**8.8**	**–3**						**4**	**0**	**0**	**0**	**6**	**0**	**0**	**0**
	Canada	Olympics	6	1	1	2	2																			
1998-99	**Los Angeles**	**NHL**	**62**	**12**	**23**	**35**	**128**	**5**	**1**	**2**	**216**	**5.6**	**–7**	**0**	**0.0**	**132**	**139**	**24:52**								
99-2000	**Los Angeles**	**NHL**	**77**	**18**	**39**	**57**	**112**	**12**	**0**	**5**	**327**	**5.5**	**10**	**0**	**0.0**	**202**	**181**	**28:30**	**4**	**0**	**2**	**2**	**4**	**0**	**0**	**0**
2000-01	**Los Angeles**	**NHL**	**54**	**17**	**32**	**49**	**69**	**9**	**0**	**1**	**223**	**7.6**	**–8**	**0**	**0.0**	**144**	**132**	**28:11**								
	♦ Colorado	**NHL**	**13**	**2**	**8**	**10**	**8**	**1**	**0**	**1**	**44**	**4.5**	**11**	**0**	**0.0**	**31**	**23**	**26:03**	**23**	**6**	**13**	**19**	**16**	**3**	**0**	**0**
	NHL Totals		**675**	**140**	**299**	**439**	**1059**	**77**	**1**	**27**	**2160**	**6.5**		**0**	**0.0**	**509**	**475**	**27:10**	**80**	**14**	**29**	**43**	**114**	**6**	**1**	**0**

CCHA Second All-Star Team (1989) • CCHA First All-Star Team (1990) • NCAA West First All-American Team (1990) • NHL All-Rookie Team (1991) • NHL First All-Star Team (1998) • Won James Norris Memorial Trophy (1998) • NHL Second All-Star Team (2000, 2001) • Played in NHL All-Star Game (1994, 1999, 2000, 2001)

• Missed majority of 1995-96 season recovering from knee injury suffered in game vs. Washington, October 20, 1995. Traded to **Colorado** by **LA Kings** with Steve Reinprecht for Adam Deadmarsh, Aaron Miller, Colorado's 1st round choice (David Steckel) in 2001 Entry Draft and future considerations (Jared Aulin, March 22, 2001), February 21, 2001.

BLOUIN, Sylvain

(bluh-WHEN, SIHL-veh) **MIN.**

Left wing. Shoots left. 6'2", 207 lbs. Born, Montreal, Que., May 21, 1974. NY Rangers' 5th choice, 104th overall, in 1994 Entry Draft.

1991-92	Laval Titan	QMJHL	28	0	0	0	23												9	0	0	0	35			
1992-93	Laval Titan	QMJHL	68	0	10	10	373												13	1	0	1	*66			
1993-94	Laval Titan	QMJHL	62	18	22	40	*492												21	4	13	17	*177			
1994-95	Chicago Wolves	IHL	1	0	0	0	2																			
	Charlotte	ECHL	50	5	7	12	280												3	0	0	0	6			
	Binghamton	AHL	10	1	0	1	46												2	0	0	0	24			
1995-96	Binghamton	AHL	71	5	8	13	*352												4	0	3	3	4			
1996-97	**NY Rangers**	**NHL**	**6**	**0**	**0**	**0**	**18**	**0**	**0**	**0**	**1**	**0.0**	**–1**													
	Binghamton	AHL	62	13	17	30	301												4	2	1	3	16			
1997-98	**NY Rangers**	**NHL**	**1**	**0**	**0**	**0**	**5**	**0**	**0**	**0**	**0**	**0.0**	**0**													
	Hartford	AHL	53	8	9	17	286												9	0	1	1	63			
1998-99	**Montreal**	**NHL**	**5**	**0**	**0**	**0**	**19**	**0**	**0**	**0**	**1**	**0.0**	**0**	**0**	**0.0**	**2**	**0**	**3:37**								
	Fredericton	AHL	67	6	10	16	333												15	2	0	2	*87			
99-2000	Worcester	AHL	70	16	18	34	337												8	3	5	8	30			
2000-01	**Minnesota**	**NHL**	**41**	**3**	**2**	**5**	**117**	**0**	**0**	**0**	**37**	**8.1**	**–5**	**2**	**100.0**	**118**	**10**	**9:54**								
	NHL Totals		**53**	**3**	**2**	**5**	**159**	**0**	**0**	**0**	**39**	**7.7**		**2**	**100.0**	**120**	**10**	**9:13**								

Traded to **Montreal** by **NY Rangers** with NY Rangers' 6th round choice (later traded to Phoenix - Phoenix selected Erik Lewerstrom) in 1999 Entry Draft for Peter Popovic, June 30, 1998. Signed as a free agent by **St. Louis**, August 25, 1999. Signed as a free agent by **Montreal**, July 7, 2000. Claimed by **Minnesota** from **Montreal** in Waiver Draft, September 29, 2000. • Missed majority of 2000-01 season recovering from shoulder injury suffered in game vs. Chicago, December 7, 2000.

BOGUNIECKI, Eric

(BOH-guhn-ih-kee, AIR-ihk) **ST.L.**

Center. Shoots right. 5'8", 192 lbs. Born, New Haven, CT, May 6, 1975. St. Louis' 6th choice, 193rd overall, in 1993 Entry Draft.

1992-93	Westminster Prep	Hi-School	24	30	24	54	55																			
1993-94	New Hampshire	H-East	40	17	16	33	66																			
1994-95	New Hampshire	H-East	34	12	16	28	62																			
1995-96	New Hampshire	H-East	32	23	28	51	46																			
1996-97	New Hampshire	H-East	36	26	31	57	58																			
1997-98	Dayton Bombers	ECHL	26	19	18	37	36																			
	Fort Wayne	IHL	35	4	8	12	29												4	1	2	3	10			
1998-99	Fort Wayne	IHL	72	32	34	66	100												2	0	1	1	2			
99-2000	**Florida**	**NHL**	**4**	**0**	**0**	**0**	**2**	**0**	**0**	**0**	**5**	**0.0**	**–1**	**25**	**36.0**	**8**	**0**	**8:35**								
	Louisville Panthers	AHL	57	33	42	75	148												4	3	2	5	20			
2000-01	Louisville Panthers	AHL	28	13	12	25	56																			
	St. Louis	**NHL**	**1**	**0**	**0**	**0**	**0**	**0**	**0**	**0**	**1**	**0.0**	**–1**	**0**	**0.0**	**1**	**1**	**13:44**								
	Worcester	AHL	45	17	28	45	100												9	3	2	5	10			
	NHL Totals		**5**	**0**	**0**	**0**	**2**	**0**	**0**	**0**	**6**	**0.0**		**25**	**36.0**	**9**	**1**	**9:37**								

Hockey East Second All-Star Team (1997)

Signed as a free agent by **Florida**, July 7, 1999. Traded to **St. Louis** by **Florida** for Andrei Podkonicky, December 17, 2000.

BOHONOS, Lonny

(boh-HOH-nohz, LAW-nee) **TOR.**

Right wing. Shoots right. 5'11", 190 lbs. Born, Winnipeg, Man., May 20, 1973.

1990-91	Winnipeg Blues	MJHL	46	33	22	55	70																			
1991-92	Winnipeg Blues	MJHL	40	53	36	89	42																			
	Moose Jaw	WHL	8	1	1	2	0																			
1992-93	Seattle T-Birds	WHL	46	13	13	26	27																			
	Portland	WHL	27	20	17	37	16												15	8	13	21	19			
1993-94	Portland	WHL	70	*62	*90	*152	80												10	8	11	19	13			
1994-95	Syracuse Crunch	AHL	67	30	45	75	71																			
1995-96	**Vancouver**	**NHL**	**3**	**0**	**1**	**1**	**0**	**0**	**0**	**0**	**3**	**0.0**	**1**													
	Syracuse Crunch	AHL	74	40	39	79	82												16	14	8	22	16			
1996-97	**Vancouver**	**NHL**	**36**	**11**	**11**	**22**	**10**	**2**	**0**	**1**	**67**	**16.4**	**–3**													
	Syracuse Crunch	AHL	41	22	30	52	28												3	2	2	4	4			

			Regular Season																Playoffs							
Season	Club	League	GP	G	A	Pts	PIM	PP	SH	GW	S	%	+/-	TF	F%	H	SB	Min	GP	G	A	Pts	PIM	PP	SH	GW
1997-98	Vancouver	NHL	31	2	1	3	4	0	0	0	37	5.4	–9													
	Syracuse Crunch	AHL	17	12	12	24	8																			
	Toronto	NHL	6	3	3	6	4	0	0	0	13	23.1	1													
	St. John's Leafs	AHL	11	7	9	16	10												2	1	1	2	2			
1998-99	Toronto	NHL	7	3	0	3	4	0	0	0	13	23.1	3	2	50.0	3	2	13:47	9	3	6	9	2	0	0	0
	St. John's Leafs	AHL	70	34	48	82	40												5	2	4	6	2			
99-2000	Manitoba Moose	IHL	63	18	33	51	45												2	0	0	0	2			
2000-01	HC Davos	Switz.	43	28	32	*60	42												4	0	1	1	2			
	NHL Totals		83	19	16	35	22	2	0	1	133	14.3		2	50.0	3	2	13:47	9	3	6	9	2	0	0	0

WHL West First All-Star Team (1994) • Canadian Major Junior First All-Star Team (1994)

Signed as a free agent by **Vancouver**, May 31, 1994. Traded to **Toronto** by **Vancouver** for Brandon Convery, March 7, 1998. Signed as a free agent by **HC Davos** (Switz.), August 1, 2000.

BOIKOV, Alexandre (bohy-KAHV, al-ehx-AN-duhr) NSH.

Defense. Shoots left. 6', 200 lbs. Born, Chelyabinsk, USSR, February 7, 1975.

Season	Club	League	GP	G	A	Pts	PIM	PP	SH	GW	S	%	+/-	TF	F%	H	SB	Min	GP	G	A	Pts	PIM	PP	SH	GW
1993-94	Victoria Cougars	WHL	70	4	31	35	250																			
1994-95	Prince George	WHL	46	5	23	28	115																			
	Tri-City Americans	WHL	24	3	13	16	63												17	1	7	8	30			
1995-96	Tri-City Americans	WHL	71	3	49	52	230												11	2	4	6	28			
1996-97	Kentucky	AHL	61	1	19	20	182												4	0	1	1	4			
1997-98	Kentucky	AHL	69	5	14	19	153												3	0	1	1	8			
1998-99	Kentucky	AHL	55	5	13	18	116																			
	Rochester	AHL	13	0	1	1	15												17	1	3	4	24			
99-2000	Nashville	NHL	2	0	0	0	2	0	0	0	1	0.0	0	0	0.0	5	0	8:31								
	Milwaukee	IHL	58	1	6	7	120																			
2000-01	Nashville	NHL	8	0	0	0	13	0	0	0	3	0.0	–1	0	0.0	19	3	6:18								
	Milwaukee	IHL	56	2	11	13	147												5	2	1	3	0			
	NHL Totals		10	0	0	0	15	0	0	0	4	0.0		0	0.0	24	3	6:45								

Signed as a free agent by **San Jose**, April 22, 1996. Signed as a free agent by **Nashville**, July 26, 1999.

BOILEAU, Patrick (BWOI-loh, PA-trihk) WSH.

Defense. Shoots right. 6', 202 lbs. Born, Montreal, Que., February 22, 1975. Washington's 3rd choice, 69th overall, in 1993 Entry Draft.

Season	Club	League	GP	G	A	Pts	PIM	PP	SH	GW	S	%	+/-	TF	F%	H	SB	Min	GP	G	A	Pts	PIM	PP	SH	GW
1990-91	Laval Regents	QAAA	3	0	1	1	0																			
1991-92	Laval Regents	QAAA	42	9	36	45	94												12	3	5	8	10			
1992-93	Laval Titan	QMJHL	69	4	19	23	73												13	1	2	3	10			
1993-94	Laval Titan	QMJHL	64	13	57	70	56												21	1	7	8	24			
1994-95	Laval Titan	QMJHL	38	8	25	33	46												20	4	16	20	24			
1995-96	Portland Pirates	AHL	78	10	28	38	41												19	1	3	4	12			
1996-97	Washington	NHL	1	0	0	0	0	0	0	0	0	0.0	0													
	Portland Pirates	AHL	67	16	28	44	63												5	1	1	2	4			
1997-98	Portland Pirates	AHL	47	6	21	27	53												10	0	1	1	8			
1998-99	Washington	NHL	4	0	1	1	2	0	0	0	7	0.0	–4	0	0.0	8	2	15:56								
	Portland Pirates	AHL	52	6	18	24	52																			
	Indianapolis Ice	IHL	29	8	13	21	27												4	0	1	1	2			
99-2000	Portland Pirates	AHL	63	2	15	17	61												4	0	0	0	4			
2000-01	Portland Pirates	AHL	77	6	14	20	50												3	0	0	0	8			
	NHL Totals		5	0	1	1	2	0	0	0	7	0.0		0	0.0	8	2	15:56								

Canadian Major Junior Scholastic Player of the Year (1994)

Loaned to **Indianapolis** (IHL) by **Portland** (AHL), February 4, 1999.

BOMBARDIR, Brad (bawm-bahr-DEER, BRAD) MIN.

Defense. Shoots left. 6'1", 205 lbs. Born, Powell River, B.C., May 5, 1972. New Jersey's 5th choice, 56th overall, in 1990 Entry Draft.

Season	Club	League	GP	G	A	Pts	PIM	PP	SH	GW	S	%	+/-	TF	F%	H	SB	Min	GP	G	A	Pts	PIM	PP	SH	GW
1988-89	Powell River	BCJHL	30	6	5	11	24												6	0	0	0	0			
1989-90	Powell River	BCJHL	60	10	35	45	93												8	2	3	5	4			
1990-91	North Dakota	WCHA	33	3	6	9	18																			
1991-92	North Dakota	WCHA	35	3	14	17	54																			
1992-93	North Dakota	WCHA	38	8	15	23	34																			
1993-94	North Dakota	WCHA	38	5	17	22	38																			
1994-95	Albany River Rats	AHL	77	5	22	27	22												14	0	3	3	6			
1995-96	Albany River Rats	AHL	80	6	25	31	63												3	0	1	1	4			
1996-97	Albany River Rats	AHL	32	0	8	8	6												16	1	3	4	8			
1997-98	New Jersey	NHL	43	1	5	6	8	0	0	0	16	6.3	11													
	Albany River Rats	AHL	5	0	0	0	0																			
1998-99	New Jersey	NHL	56	1	7	8	16	0	0	0	47	2.1	–4	1	0.0	48	57	15:03	5	0	0	0	0	0	0	0
99-2000♦	New Jersey	NHL	32	3	1	4	6	0	0	0	24	12.5	–6	0	0.0	31	37	15:54	1	0	0	0	0	0	0	0
2000-01	Minnesota	NHL	70	0	15	15	42	0	0	0	81	0.0	–6	1	0.0	61	164	20:50								
	NHL Totals		201	5	28	33	72	0	0	0	168	3.0		2	0.0	140	258	17:47	6	0	0	0	0	0	0	0

AHL Second All-Star Team (1996)

• Missed majority of 1999-2000 season recovering from esosopagus injury, October 30, 1999. Traded to **Minnesota** by **New Jersey** for Chris Terreri and Minnesota's 9th round choice (later traded to Tampa Bay - Tampa Bay selected Thomas Ziegler) in 2000 Entry Draft, June 23, 2000.

BONDRA, Peter (BAWN-druh, PEE-tuhr) WSH.

Right wing. Shoots left. 6'1", 205 lbs. Born, Luck, USSR, February 7, 1968. Washington's 9th choice, 156th overall, in 1990 Entry Draft.

Season	Club	League	GP	G	A	Pts	PIM	PP	SH	GW	S	%	+/-	TF	F%	H	SB	Min	GP	G	A	Pts	PIM	PP	SH	GW
1986-87	VSZ Kosice	Czech.	32	4	5	9	24																			
1987-88	VSZ Kosice	Czech.	45	27	11	38	20																			
1988-89	VSZ Kosice	Czech.	40	30	10	40	20																			
1989-90	VSZ Kosice	Czech.	44	29	17	46													5	7	2	9				
1990-91	Washington	NHL	54	12	16	28	47	4	0	1	95	12.6	–10						4	0	1	1	2	0	0	0
1991-92	Washington	NHL	71	28	28	56	42	4	0	3	158	17.7	16						7	6	2	8	4	1	0	0
1992-93	Washington	NHL	83	37	48	85	70	10	0	7	239	15.5	8						6	0	6	6	0	0	0	0
1993-94	Washington	NHL	69	24	19	43	40	4	0	2	200	12.0	22						9	2	4	6	4	0	0	1
1994-95	HC Kosice	Slovakia	2	1	0	1	0																			
	Washington	NHL	47	*34	9	43	24	12	6	3	177	19.2	9						7	5	3	8	10	2	0	1
1995-96	Detroit Vipers	IHL	7	8	1	9	0																			
	Washington	NHL	67	52	28	80	40	11	4	7	322	16.1	18						6	3	2	5	8	2	0	1
1996-97	Washington	NHL	77	46	31	77	72	10	4	3	314	14.6	7													
1997-98	Washington	NHL	76	*52	26	78	44	11	5	13	284	18.3	14						17	7	5	12	12	3	0	2
	Slovakia	Olympics	2	1	0	1	25																			
1998-99	Washington	NHL	66	31	24	55	56	6	3	5	284	10.9	–1	1	0.0	87	22	20:35								
99-2000	Washington	NHL	62	21	17	38	30	5	3	5	187	11.2	5	2	50.0	81	22	18:48	5	1	1	2	4	1	0	0
2000-01	Washington	NHL	82	45	36	81	60	22	4	8	305	14.8	8	2	50.0	131	29	20:48	6	2	0	2	2	2	0	1
	NHL Totals		754	382	282	664	525	99	29	57	2565	14.9		5	40.0	299	73	20:09	67	26	24	50	46	11	0	6

Played in NHL All-Star Game (1993, 1996, 1997, 1998, 1999)

BONIN, Brian (BAWN-ihn, BRIGH-uhn)

Center. Shoots left. 5'10", 186 lbs. Born, St. Paul, MN, November 28, 1973. Pittsburgh's 9th choice, 211th overall, in 1992 Entry Draft.

Season	Club	League	GP	G	A	Pts	PIM	PP	SH	GW	S	%	+/-	TF	F%	H	SB	Min	GP	G	A	Pts	PIM	PP	SH	GW
1991-92	White Bear Lake	Hi-School	23	22	35	57	8																			
1992-93	U. of Minnesota	WCHA	38	10	18	28	10																			
1993-94	U. of Minnesota	WCHA	42	24	20	44	14																			
1994-95	U. of Minnesota	WCHA	44	32	31	*63	28																			
1995-96	U. of Minnesota	WCHA	42	34	*47	*81	30																			
1996-97	Cleveland	IHL	60	13	26	39	18												1	1	0	1	0			
1997-98	Syracuse Crunch	AHL	67	31	38	69	46												5	1	3	4	6			

			Regular Season																Playoffs							
Season	Club	League	GP	G	A	Pts	PIM	PP	SH	GW	S	%	+/-	TF	F%	H	SB	Min	GP	G	A	Pts	PIM	PP	SH	GW
1998-99	Pittsburgh	NHL	5	0	0	0	0	0	0	0	2	0.0	–2	28	39.3	4	2	12:19	3	0	0	0	0	0	0	0
	Kansas City	IHL	19	2	5	7	10																			
	Adirondack	AHL	54	19	16	35	31												2	0	0	0	0			
99-2000	Syracuse Crunch	AHL	67	19	28	47	20												4	0	1	1	0			
2000-01	Minnesota	NHL	7	0	0	0	0	0	0	0	7	0.0	–3	20	50.0	5	2	9:46								
	Cleveland	IHL	72	35	42	77	45												4	2	0	2	0			
	NHL Totals		12	0	0	0	0	0	0	0	9	0.0		48	43.8	9	4	10:50	3	0	0	0	0	0	0	0

Minnesota High School Player of the Year (1992) • WCHA First All-Star Team (1995, 1996) • NCAA West First All-American Team (1995, 1996) • Won Hobey Baker Memorial Award (Top U.S. Collegiate Player) (1996) • IHL Second All-Star Team (2001)

Signed as a free agent by **Vancouver**, September 9, 1999. Signed as a free agent by **Minnesota**, July 6, 2000.

BONK, Radek
(BOHNK, RA-dehk) **OTT.**

Center. Shoots left. 6'3", 210 lbs. Born, Krnov, Czech., January 9, 1976. Ottawa's 1st choice, 3rd overall, in 1994 Entry Draft.

Season	Club	League	GP	G	A	Pts	PIM	PP	SH	GW	S	%	+/-	TF	F%	H	SB	Min	GP	G	A	Pts	PIM	PP	SH	GW
1990-91	HC Opava	Czech-Jr.	35	47	42	89	25																			
1991-92	ZPS Zlin	Czech-Jr.	45	47	36	83	30																			
1992-93	ZPS Zlin	Czech.	30	5	5	10	10																			
1993-94	Las Vegas	IHL	76	42	45	87	208												5	1	2	3	10			
1994-95	Las Vegas	IHL	33	7	13	20	62																			
	Ottawa	NHL	42	3	8	11	28	1	0	0	40	7.5	–5													
	P.E.I. Senators	AHL																	1	0	0	0	0			
1995-96	Ottawa	NHL	76	16	19	35	36	5	0	1	161	9.9	–5													
1996-97	Ottawa	NHL	53	5	13	18	14	0	1	0	82	6.1	–4						7	0	1	1	4	0	0	0
1997-98	Ottawa	NHL	65	7	9	16	16	1	0	0	93	7.5	–13						5	0	0	0	2	0	0	0
1998-99	Ottawa	NHL	81	16	16	32	48	0	1	6	110	14.5	15	1184	50.1	225	30	13:44	4	0	0	0	6	0	0	0
99-2000	HC Pardubice	Cze-Rep	3	1	0	1	4																			
	Ottawa	NHL	80	23	37	60	53	10	0	5	167	13.8	–2	1654	52.0	211	45	18:14	6	0	0	0	8	0	0	0
2000-01	Ottawa	NHL	74	23	36	59	52	5	2	3	139	16.5	27	1506	51.2	136	52	18:16	2	0	0	0	2	0	0	0
	NHL Totals		471	93	138	231	247	22	4	15	792	11.7		4344	51.2	572	127	16:41	24	0	1	1	22	0	0	0

Won Garry F. Longman Memorial Trophy (Top Rookie - IHL) (1994) • Played in NHL All-Star Game (2000, 2001)

BONNI, Ryan
(baw-NEE, RIGH-uhn) **VAN.**

Defense. Shoots left. 6'4", 190 lbs. Born, Winnipeg, Man., February 18, 1979. Vancouver's 2nd choice, 34th overall, in 1997 Entry Draft.

Season	Club	League	GP	G	A	Pts	PIM	PP	SH	GW	S	%	+/-	TF	F%	H	SB	Min	GP	G	A	Pts	PIM	PP	SH	GW
1994-95	Winnipeg Sharks	MMHL	24	3	19	22	59																			
1995-96	Saskatoon Blades	WHL	63	1	7	8	78												3	0	0	0	0			
1996-97	Saskatoon Blades	WHL	69	11	19	30	219																			
1997-98	Saskatoon Blades	WHL	42	5	14	19	100												0	0	0	0	0			
1998-99	Saskatoon Blades	WHL	51	6	26	32	211																			
	Red Deer Rebels	WHL	20	3	10	13	41												9	0	4	4	25			
99-2000	Vancouver	NHL	3	0	0	0	0	0	0	0	1	0.0	–1	0	0.0	1	2	9:37								
	Syracuse Crunch	AHL	71	5	13	18	125												2	0	1	1	2			
2000-01	Kansas City	IHL	80	2	9	11	127																			
	NHL Totals		3	0	0	0	0	0	0	0	1	0.0		0	0.0	1	2	9:37								

BONVIE, Dennis
(BOHN-vee, DEHN-his)

Right wing/Defense. Shoots right. 5'11", 205 lbs. Born, Antigonish, N.S., July 23, 1973.

Season	Club	League	GP	G	A	Pts	PIM	PP	SH	GW	S	%	+/-	TF	F%	H	SB	Min	GP	G	A	Pts	PIM	PP	SH	GW
1989-90	Antigonish	NSMHL	50	15	30	45	52																			
1990-91	Antigonish	MJrHL	40	1	8	9	347																			
1991-92	Kitchener	OHL	7	1	1	2	23																			
	North Bay	OHL	49	0	12	12	261												21	0	1	1	91			
1992-93	North Bay	OHL	64	3	21	24	*316												5	0	0	0	34			
1993-94	Cape Breton	AHL	63	1	10	11	278												4	0	0	0	11			
1994-95	Cape Breton	AHL	74	5	15	20	422																			
	Edmonton	NHL	2	0	0	0	0	0	0	0	0	0.0	0													
1995-96	Edmonton	NHL	8	0	0	0	47	0	0	0	0	0.0	–3													
	Cape Breton	AHL	38	13	14	27	269																			
1996-97	Hamilton Bulldogs	AHL	73	9	20	29	*522												22	3	11	14	*91			
1997-98	Edmonton	NHL	4	0	0	0	27	0	0	0	0	0.0	0													
	Hamilton Bulldogs	AHL	57	11	19	30	295												9	0	5	5	18			
1998-99	Chicago	NHL	11	0	0	0	44	0	0	0	1	0.0	–4	0	0.0	10	0	3:59								
	Portland Pirates	AHL	3	1	0	1	16																			
	Philadelphia	AHL	37	4	10	14	158												14	3	3	6	26			
99-2000	Pittsburgh	NHL	28	0	0	0	80	0	0	0	6	0.0	–2	0	0.0	28	4	3:14								
	Wilkes-Barre	AHL	42	5	26	31	243																			
2000-01	Pittsburgh	NHL	3	0	0	0	0	0	0	0	1	0.0	–1	0	0.0	3	1	3:30								
	Wilkes-Barre	AHL	65	5	18	23	221												21	0	4	4	35			
	NHL Totals		56	0	0	0	198	0	0	0	8	0.0		0	0.0	41	5	3:27								

Signed as a free agent by **Edmonton**, August 25, 1994. Claimed by **Chicago** from **Edmonton** in NHL Waiver Draft, October 5, 1998. Traded to **Philadelphia** by **Chicago** for Frank Bialowas, January 8, 1999. Signed as a free agent by **Pittsburgh**, September 20, 1999.

BORDELEAU, Sebastien
(BOHR-duh-loh, SEH-bas-tyehn) **ST.L.**

Center. Shoots right. 5'11", 185 lbs. Born, Vancouver, B.C., February 15, 1975. Montreal's 3rd choice, 73rd overall, in 1993 Entry Draft.

Season	Club	League	GP	G	A	Pts	PIM	PP	SH	GW	S	%	+/-	TF	F%	H	SB	Min	GP	G	A	Pts	PIM	PP	SH	GW
1990-91	Laval Regents	QAAA	39	27	36	63																				
1991-92	Hull Olympiques	QMJHL	62	26	32	58	91												5	0	3	3	23			
1992-93	Hull Olympiques	QMJHL	60	18	39	57	95												10	3	8	11	20			
1993-94	Hull Olympiques	QMJHL	60	26	57	83	147												17	6	14	20	26			
1994-95	Hull Olympiques	QMJHL	68	52	76	128	142												18	*13	19	*32	25			
	Fredericton	AHL																	1	0	0	0	0			
1995-96	Montreal	NHL	4	0	0	0	0	0	0	0	0	0.0	–1													
	Fredericton	AHL	43	17	29	46	68												7	0	2	2	8			
1996-97	Montreal	NHL	28	2	9	11	2	0	0	0	27	7.4	–3													
	Fredericton	AHL	34	18	22	40	50																			
1997-98	Montreal	NHL	53	6	8	14	36	2	1	0	55	10.9	5						5	0	0	0	2	0	0	0
1998-99	Nashville	NHL	72	16	24	40	26	1	2	3	168	9.5	–14	1368	57.1	76	22	15:18								
99-2000	Nashville	NHL	60	10	13	23	30	0	2	1	127	7.9	–12	942	54.4	43	22	13:56								
2000-01	Nashville	NHL	14	2	3	5	14	0	0	0	20	10.0	–4	192	59.4	11	4	12:40								
	Worcester	AHL	2	0	2	2	9												11	1	7	8	23			
	NHL Totals		231	36	57	93	108	3	5	4	397	9.1		2502	56.2	130	48	14:29	5	0	0	0	2	0	0	0

QMJHL First All-Star Team (1995)

Traded to **Nashville** by **Montreal** for future considerations, June 26, 1998. • Missed majority of 2000-01 season recovering from abdominal injury suffered in game vs. Detroit, November 18, 2000. Claimed on waivers by **St. Louis** from **Nashville**, March 13, 2001.

BOTTERILL, Jason
(BOH-tuhr-ihl, JAY-suhn)

Left wing. Shoots left. 6'4", 220 lbs. Born, Edmonton, Alta., May 19, 1976. Dallas' 1st choice, 20th overall, in 1994 Entry Draft.

Season	Club	League	GP	G	A	Pts	PIM	PP	SH	GW	S	%	+/-	TF	F%	H	SB	Min	GP	G	A	Pts	PIM	PP	SH	GW
1992-93	St. Paul's Prep	Hi-School	22	22	26	48																				
1993-94	U. of Michigan	CCHA	36	20	19	39	94																			
1994-95	U. of Michigan	CCHA	34	14	14	28	117																			
1995-96	U. of Michigan	CCHA	37	*32	25	57	*143																			
1996-97	U. of Michigan	CCHA	42	*37	24	61	129																			
1997-98	Dallas	NHL	4	0	0	0	19	0	0	0	2	0.0	–1													
	Michigan K-Wings	IHL	50	11	11	22	82												4	0	0	0	5			
1998-99	Dallas	NHL	17	0	0	0	23	0	0	0	8	0.0	–2	0	0.0	27	0	8:19								
	Michigan K-Wings	IHL	56	13	25	38	106												5	2	1	3	4			

Season	Club	League	GP	G	A	Pts	PIM	PP	SH	GW	S	%	+/-	TF	F%	H	SB	Min	GP	G	A	Pts	PIM	PP	SH	GW
			Regular Season																Playoffs							
99-2000	Atlanta	NHL	25	1	4	5	17	0	0	1	17	5.9	–7	2	50.0	51	3	11:16								
	Orlando	IHL	17	7	8	15	27																			
	Calgary	NHL	2	0	0	0	0	0	0	0	2	0.0	–4	0	0.0	1	0	8:00								
	Saint John Flames	AHL	21	3	4	7	39												3	0	0	0	19			
2000-01	Saint John Flames	AHL	60	13	20	33	101												19	2	7	9	30			
	NHL Totals		48	1	4	5	59	0	0	1	29	3.4		2	50.0	79	3	9:59								

CCHA Second All-Star Team (1996) • NCAA West Second All-American Team (1997)

Traded to **Atlanta** by **Dallas** for Jamie Pushor, July 15, 1999. Traded to **Calgary** by **Atlanta** with Darryl Shannon for Hnat Domenichelli and Dmitri Vlasenkov, February 11, 2000.

BOUCHARD, Joel

(BOO-shahrd, JOHEL) **PHX.**

Defense. Shoots left. 6'1", 209 lbs. Born, Montreal, Que., January 23, 1974. Calgary's 7th choice, 129th overall, in 1992 Entry Draft.

Season	Club	League	GP	G	A	Pts	PIM	PP	SH	GW	S	%	+/-	TF	F%	H	SB	Min	GP	G	A	Pts	PIM	PP	SH	GW
1989-90	Mtl-Bourassa	QAAA	41	7	17	24	10												1	1	0	1	0			
1990-91	Longueuil	QMJHL	53	3	19	22	34												8	1	0	1	11			
1991-92	Verdun	QMJHL	70	9	20	29	55												19	1	7	8	20			
1992-93	Verdun	QMJHL	60	10	49	59	126												4	0	2	2	4			
1993-94	Verdun	QMJHL	60	15	55	70	62												4	1	0	1	6			
	Saint John Flames	AHL	1	0	0	0	0												2	0	0	0	0			
1994-95	Saint John Flames	AHL	77	6	25	31	63												5	1	0	1	4			
	Calgary	NHL	2	0	0	0	0	0	0	0	0	0.0	0													
1995-96	Calgary	NHL	4	0	0	0	4	0	0	0	0	0.0	0													
	Saint John Flames	AHL	74	8	25	33	104												16	1	4	5	10			
1996-97	Calgary	NHL	76	4	5	9	49	0	1	0	61	6.6	–23													
1997-98	Calgary	NHL	44	5	7	12	57	0	1	1	51	9.8	0													
	Saint John Flames	AHL	3	2	1	3	6																			
1998-99	Nashville	NHL	64	4	11	15	60	0	0	0	78	5.1	–10	0	0.0	109	67	22:34								
99-2000	Nashville	NHL	52	1	4	5	23	0	0	0	60	1.7	–11	0	0.0	88	48	18:41								
	Dallas	NHL	2	0	0	0	2	0	0	0	1	0.0	1	0	0.0	2	2	9:45								
2000-01	Grand Rapids	IHL	19	3	9	12	8																			
	Phoenix	NHL	32	1	2	3	22	0	0	0	26	3.8	–8	0	0.0	32	27	14:28								
	NHL Totals		276	15	29	44	217	0	2	1	277	5.4		0	0.0	231	144	19:19								

QMJHL First All-Star Team (1994)

Claimed by **Nashville** from **Calgary** in Expansion Draft, June 26, 1998. Claimed on waivers by **Dallas** from **Nashville**, March 14, 2000. Signed as a free agent by **Phoenix**, August 31, 2000.

BOUCHER, Philippe

(boo-SHAY, fihl-EEP) **L.A.**

Defense. Shoots right. 6'2", 221 lbs. Born, Ste-Apollinaire, Que., March 24, 1973. Buffalo's 1st choice, 13th overall, in 1991 Entry Draft.

Season	Club	League	GP	G	A	Pts	PIM	PP	SH	GW	S	%	+/-	TF	F%	H	SB	Min	GP	G	A	Pts	PIM	PP	SH	GW
1988-89	Ste-Foy Governors	QAAA	5	0	0	0	2																			
1989-90	Ste-Foy Governors	QAAA	42	26	60	86	76												12	6	*19	25	16			
1990-91	Granby Bisons	QMJHL	69	21	46	67	92																			
1991-92	Granby Bisons	QMJHL	49	22	37	59	47																			
	Laval Titans	QMJHL	16	7	11	18	36												10	5	6	11	8			
1992-93	Laval Titans	QMJHL	16	12	15	27	37												13	6	15	21	12			
	Buffalo	NHL	18	0	4	4	14	0	0	0	28	0.0	1													
	Rochester	AHL	5	4	3	7	8												3	0	1	1	2			
1993-94	Buffalo	NHL	38	6	8	14	29	4	0	1	67	9.0	–1						7	1	1	2	2	1	0	0
	Rochester	AHL	31	10	22	32	51																			
1994-95	Rochester	AHL	43	14	27	41	26																			
	Buffalo	NHL	9	1	4	5	0	0	0	0	15	6.7	6													
	Los Angeles	NHL	6	1	0	1	4	0	0	0	15	6.7	–3													
1995-96	Los Angeles	NHL	53	7	16	23	31	5	0	1	145	4.8	–26													
	Phoenix	IHL	10	4	3	7	4																			
1996-97	Los Angeles	NHL	60	7	18	25	25	2	0	1	159	4.4	0													
1997-98	Los Angeles	NHL	45	6	10	16	49	1	0	0	80	7.5	6													
	Long Beach	IHL	2	0	1	1	4																			
1998-99	Los Angeles	NHL	45	2	6	8	32	1	0	0	87	2.3	–12	0	0.0	58	63	17:51								
99-2000	Los Angeles	NHL	1	0	0	0	0	0	0	0	3	0.0	0	0	0.0	4	3	17:04								
	Long Beach	IHL	14	4	11	15	8												6	0	9	9	8			
2000-01	Los Angeles	NHL	22	2	4	6	20	2	0	0	40	5.0	4	0	0.0	42	24	18:25	13	0	1	1	2	0	0	0
	Manitoba Moose	IHL	45	10	22	32	39																			
	NHL Totals		297	32	70	102	204	15	0	3	639	5.0		0	0.0	104	90	18:01	20	1	2	3	4	1	0	0

QMJHL Second All-Star Team (1991, 1992) • Canadian Major Junior Rookie of the Year (1991)

Traded to **LA Kings** by **Buffalo** with Denis Tsygurov and Grant Fuhr for Alexei Zhitnik, Robb Stauber, Charlie Huddy and LA Kings' 5th round choice (Marian Menhart) in 1995 Entry Draft, February 14, 1995. • Missed majority of 1999-2000 season recovering from foot injury suffered in training camp, September, 1999.

BOUCK, Tyler

(BOWK, TIGH-luhr) **PHX.**

Right wing. Shoots left. 6', 196 lbs. Born, Camrose, Alta., January 13, 1980. Dallas' 2nd choice, 57th overall, in 1998 Entry Draft.

Season	Club	League	GP	G	A	Pts	PIM	PP	SH	GW	S	%	+/-	TF	F%	H	SB	Min	GP	G	A	Pts	PIM	PP	SH	GW
1995-96	Sherwood Park	AMHL	22	10	21	31	58																			
1996-97	Prince George	WHL	12	0	2	2	11																			
1997-98	Prince George	WHL	65	11	26	37	90												11	1	0	1	21			
1998-99	Prince George	WHL	56	22	25	47	178												2	0	2	2	10			
99-2000	Prince George	WHL	57	30	33	63	183												13	6	13	19	36			
2000-01	Dallas	NHL	48	2	5	7	29	0	0	1	41	4.9	–3	1	0.0	81	2	8:59	1	0	0	0	0	0	0	0
	Utah Grizzlies	IHL	24	2	6	8	39																			
	NHL Totals		48	2	5	7	29	0	0	1	41	4.9		1	0.0	81	2	8:59	1	0	0	0	0	0	0	0

WHL West First All-Star Team (2000)

Traded to **Phoenix** by **Dallas** for Jyrki Lumme, June 23, 2001.

BOUGHNER, Bob

(BOOG-nuhr, BAWB) **CGY.**

Defense. Shoots right. 6', 203 lbs. Born, Windsor, Ont., March 8, 1971. Detroit's 2nd choice, 32nd overall, in 1989 Entry Draft.

Season	Club	League	GP	G	A	Pts	PIM	PP	SH	GW	S	%	+/-	TF	F%	H	SB	Min	GP	G	A	Pts	PIM	PP	SH	GW
1986-87	Belle River	OJHL-C	37	3	11	14	88																			
1987-88	St. Mary's	OJHL-B	36	4	18	22	177																			
1988-89	Sault Ste. Marie	OHL	64	6	15	21	182																			
1989-90	Sault Ste. Marie	OHL	49	7	23	30	122																			
1990-91	Sault Ste. Marie	OHL	64	13	33	46	156												14	2	9	11	35			
1991-92	Toledo Storm	ECHL	28	3	10	13	79												5	2	0	2	15			
	Adirondack	AHL	1	0	0	0	7																			
1992-93	Adirondack	AHL	69	1	16	17	190																			
1993-94	Adirondack	AHL	72	8	14	22	292												10	1	1	2	18			
1994-95	Cincinnati	IHL	81	2	14	16	192												10	0	0	0	18			
1995-96	Carolina	AHL	46	2	15	17	127																			
	Buffalo	NHL	31	0	1	1	104	0	0	0	14	0.0	3													
1996-97	Buffalo	NHL	77	1	7	8	225	0	0	0	34	2.9	12						11	0	1	1	9	0	0	0
1997-98	Buffalo	NHL	69	1	3	4	165	0	0	0	26	3.8	5						14	0	4	4	15	0	0	0
1998-99	Nashville	NHL	79	3	10	13	137	0	0	1	59	5.1	–6	0	0.0	233	91	18:31								
99-2000	Nashville	NHL	62	2	4	6	97	0	0	0	32	6.3	–13	0	0.0	207	67	17:20								
	Pittsburgh	NHL	11	1	0	1	69	1	0	1	8	12.5	2	0	0.0	26	14	17:05	11	0	2	2	15	0	0	0
2000-01	Pittsburgh	NHL	58	1	3	4	147	0	0	0	46	2.2	18	0	0.0	171	65	16:30	18	0	1	1	22	0	0	0
	NHL Totals		387	9	28	37	944	1	0	2	219	4.1		0	0.0	637	237	17:32	54	0	8	8	61	0	0	0

Signed as a free agent by **Florida**, July 25, 1994. Traded to **Buffalo** by **Florida** for Buffalo's 3rd round choice (Chris Allen) in 1996 Entry Draft, February 1, 1996. Claimed by **Nashville** from **Buffalo** in Expansion Draft, June 26, 1998. Traded to **Pittsburgh** by **Nashville** for Pavel Skrbek, March 13, 2000. Signed as a free agent by **Calgary**, July 2, 2001.

BOUILLON, Francis
(BOO-liawn, FRAN-sihs) **MTL.**

Defense. Shoots left. 5'8", 190 lbs. Born, New York, NY, October 17, 1975.

			Regular Season																Playoffs							
Season	Club	League	GP	G	A	Pts	PIM	PP	SH	GW	S	%	+/-	TF	F%	H	SB	Min	GP	G	A	Pts	PIM	PP	SH	GW
1991-92	Mtl-Bourassa	QAAA	42	2	5	7	28												9	1	0	1	6			
1992-93	Laval Titan	QMJHL	46	0	7	7	45																			
1993-94	Laval Titan	QMJHL	68	3	15	18	129												19	2	9	11	48			
1994-95	Laval Titan	QMJHL	72	8	25	33	115												20	3	11	14	21			
1995-96	Granby	QMJHL	68	11	35	46	156												21	2	12	14	30			
1996-97	Wheeling Nailers	ECHL	69	10	32	42	77												3	0	2	2	10			
1997-98	Quebec Rafales	IHL	71	8	27	35	76																			
1998-99	Fredericton	AHL	79	19	36	55	174												5	2	1	3	0			
99-2000	**Montreal**	**NHL**	**74**	**3**	**13**	**16**	**38**	**2**	**0**	**1**	**76**	**3.9**	**–7**	**1**	**0.0**	**68**	**52**	**15:52**								
2000-01	**Montreal**	**NHL**	**29**	**0**	**6**	**6**	**26**	**0**	**0**	**0**	**24**	**0.0**	**3**	**0**	**0.0**	**42**	**16**	**13:24**								
	Quebec Citadelles	AHL	4	0	0	0	0																			
	NHL Totals		**103**	**3**	**19**	**22**	**64**	**2**	**0**	**1**	**100**	**3.0**		**1**	**0.0**	**110**	**68**	**15:10**								

Signed as a free agent by **Montreal**, August 18, 1998 • Missed majority of 2000-01 season recovering from ankle injury suffered in game vs. Calgary, December 31, 2000..

BOULTON, Eric
(BOHL-tuhn, AIR-ihk) **BUF.**

Left wing. Shoots left. 6'1", 215 lbs. Born, Halifax, N.S., August 17, 1976. NY Rangers' 12th choice, 234th overall, in 1994 Entry Draft.

Season	Club	League	GP	G	A	Pts	PIM	PP	SH	GW	S	%	+/-	TF	F%	H	SB	Min	GP	G	A	Pts	PIM	PP	SH	GW
1992-93	Cole Harbour	MJrHL	44	12	15	27	212																			
1993-94	Oshawa Generals	OHL	45	4	3	7	149												5	0	0	0	16			
1994-95	Oshawa Generals	OHL	27	7	5	12	125																			
	Sarnia Sting	OHL	24	3	7	10	134												4	0	1	1	10			
1995-96	Sarnia Sting	OHL	66	14	29	43	243												9	0	3	3	29			
1996-97	Binghamton	AHL	23	2	3	5	67												3	0	0	0	4			
	Charlotte	ECHL	44	14	11	25	325												3	0	1	1	6			
1997-98	Charlotte	ECHL	53	11	16	27	202												4	1	0	1	0			
	Fort Wayne	IHL	8	0	2	2	42																			
1998-99	Kentucky	AHL	34	3	3	6	154												10	0	1	1	36			
	Florida Everblades	ECHL	26	9	13	22	143																			
	Houston Aeros	IHL	7	1	0	1	41																			
99-2000	Rochester	AHL	76	2	2	4	276												18	2	1	3	53			
2000-01	**Buffalo**	**NHL**	**35**	**1**	**2**	**3**	**94**	**0**	**0**	**0**	**20**	**5.0**	**–1**	**2**	**0.0**	**44**	**6**	**5:42**								
	NHL Totals		**35**	**1**	**2**	**3**	**94**	**0**	**0**	**0**	**20**	**5.0**		**2**	**0.0**	**44**	**6**	**5:42**								

Signed as a free agent by **Buffalo**, September 14, 1999.

BOURQUE, Raymond
(BOHRK, ray-MAWN)

Defense. Shoots left. 5'11", 219 lbs. Born, Montreal, Que., December 28, 1960. Boston's 1st choice, 8th overall, in 1979 Entry Draft.

Season	Club	League	GP	G	A	Pts	PIM	PP	SH	GW	S	%	+/-	TF	F%	H	SB	Min	GP	G	A	Pts	PIM	PP	SH	GW
1976-77	Sorel Eperviers	QMJHL	69	12	36	48	61																			
1977-78	Verdun Eperviers	QMJHL	72	22	57	79	90												4	2	1	3	0			
1978-79	Verdun Eperviers	QMJHL	63	22	71	93	44												11	3	16	19	18			
1979-80	**Boston**	**NHL**	**80**	**17**	**48**	**65**	**73**	**3**	**2**	**1**	**185**	**9.2**	**52**						**10**	**2**	**9**	**11**	**27**	**0**	**0**	**0**
1980-81	**Boston**	**NHL**	**67**	**27**	**29**	**56**	**96**	**9**	**1**	**6**	**207**	**13.0**	**29**						**3**	**0**	**1**	**1**	**2**	**0**	**0**	**0**
1981-82	**Boston**	**NHL**	**65**	**17**	**49**	**66**	**51**	**4**	**0**	**2**	**211**	**8.1**	**22**						**9**	**1**	**5**	**6**	**16**	**0**	**0**	**1**
1982-83	**Boston**	**NHL**	**65**	**22**	**51**	**73**	**20**	**7**	**0**	**5**	**205**	**10.7**	**49**						**17**	**8**	**15**	**23**	**10**	**2**	**0**	**1**
1983-84	**Boston**	**NHL**	**78**	**31**	**65**	**96**	**57**	**12**	**1**	**5**	**340**	**9.1**	**51**						**3**	**0**	**2**	**2**	**0**	**0**	**0**	**0**
1984-85	**Boston**	**NHL**	**73**	**20**	**66**	**86**	**53**	**10**	**1**	**1**	**333**	**6.0**	**30**						**5**	**0**	**3**	**3**	**4**	**0**	**0**	**0**
1985-86	**Boston**	**NHL**	**74**	**19**	**58**	**77**	**68**	**11**	**0**	**3**	**289**	**6.6**	**17**						**3**	**0**	**0**	**0**	**0**	**0**	**0**	**0**
1986-87	**Boston**	**NHL**	**78**	**23**	**72**	**95**	**36**	**6**	**1**	**3**	**334**	**6.9**	**44**						**4**	**1**	**2**	**3**	**0**	**0**	**0**	**0**
1987-88	**Boston**	**NHL**	**78**	**17**	**64**	**81**	**72**	**7**	**1**	**5**	**344**	**4.9**	**34**						**23**	**3**	**18**	**21**	**26**	**0**	**0**	**1**
1988-89	**Boston**	**NHL**	**60**	**18**	**43**	**61**	**52**	**6**	**0**	**0**	**243**	**7.4**	**20**						**10**	**0**	**4**	**4**	**6**	**0**	**0**	**0**
1989-90	**Boston**	**NHL**	**76**	**19**	**65**	**84**	**50**	**8**	**0**	**3**	**310**	**6.1**	**31**						**17**	**5**	**12**	**17**	**16**	**1**	**0**	**0**
1990-91	**Boston**	**NHL**	**76**	**21**	**73**	**94**	**75**	**7**	**0**	**3**	**323**	**6.5**	**33**						**19**	**7**	**18**	**25**	**12**	**3**	**0**	**0**
1991-92	**Boston**	**NHL**	**80**	**21**	**60**	**81**	**56**	**7**	**1**	**2**	**334**	**6.3**	**11**						**12**	**3**	**6**	**9**	**12**	**2**	**0**	**0**
1992-93	**Boston**	**NHL**	**78**	**19**	**63**	**82**	**40**	**8**	**0**	**7**	**330**	**5.8**	**38**						**4**	**1**	**0**	**1**	**2**	**1**	**0**	**0**
1993-94	**Boston**	**NHL**	**72**	**20**	**71**	**91**	**58**	**10**	**3**	**1**	**386**	**5.2**	**26**						**13**	**2**	**8**	**10**	**0**	**1**	**0**	**0**
1994-95	**Boston**	**NHL**	**46**	**12**	**31**	**43**	**20**	**9**	**0**	**2**	**210**	**5.7**	**3**						**5**	**0**	**3**	**3**	**0**	**0**	**0**	**0**
1995-96	**Boston**	**NHL**	**82**	**20**	**62**	**82**	**58**	**9**	**2**	**2**	**390**	**5.1**	**31**						**5**	**1**	**6**	**7**	**2**	**1**	**0**	**0**
1996-97	**Boston**	**NHL**	**62**	**19**	**31**	**50**	**18**	**8**	**1**	**3**	**230**	**8.3**	**–11**													
1997-98	**Boston**	**NHL**	**82**	**13**	**35**	**48**	**80**	**9**	**0**	**3**	**264**	**4.9**	**2**						**6**	**1**	**4**	**5**	**2**	**1**	**0**	**0**
	Canada	Olympics	6	1	2	3	4																			
1998-99	**Boston**	**NHL**	**81**	**10**	**47**	**57**	**34**	**8**	**0**	**3**	**262**	**3.8**	**–7**	**2**	**0.0**	**173**	**113**	**29:31**	**12**	**1**	**9**	**10**	**14**	**0**	**0**	**0**
99-2000	**Boston**	**NHL**	**65**	**10**	**28**	**38**	**20**	**6**	**0**	**0**	**217**	**4.6**	**–11**	**1**	**0.0**	**132**	**73**	**27:12**								
	Colorado	**NHL**	**14**	**8**	**6**	**14**	**6**	**7**	**0**	**0**	**43**	**18.6**	**9**	**0**	**0.0**	**32**	**21**	**27:08**	**13**	**1**	**8**	**9**	**8**	**0**	**0**	**0**
2000-01♦	**Colorado**	**NHL**	**80**	**7**	**52**	**59**	**48**	**2**	**2**	**0**	**216**	**3.2**	**25**	**0**	**0.0**	**113**	**109**	**26:06**	**21**	**4**	**6**	**10**	**12**	**3**	**0**	**1**
	NHL Totals		**1612**	**410**	**1169**	**1579**	**1141**	**173**	**16**	**60**	**6206**	**6.6**		**3**	**0.0**	**450**	**316**	**27:37**	**214**	**41**	**139**	**180**	**171**	**15**	**0**	**4**

QMJHL First All-Star Team (1978, 1979) • Won Calder Memorial Trophy (1980) • NHL First All-Star Team (1980, 1982, 1984, 1985, 1987, 1988, 1990, 1991, 1992, 1993, 1994, 1996, 2001) • NHL Second All-Star Team (1981, 1983, 1986, 1989, 1995, 1999) • Won James Norris Memorial Trophy (1987, 1988, 1990, 1991, 1994) • Won King Clancy Memorial Trophy (1992) • Played in NHL All-Star Game (1981, 1982, 1983, 1984, 1985, 1986, 1988, 1989, 1990, 1991, 1992, 1993, 1994, 1996, 1997, 1998, 1999, 2000, 2001)

Traded to **Colorado** by **Boston** with Dave Andreychuk for Brian Rolston, Martin Grenier, Sami Pahlsson and New Jersey's 1st round choice (previously acquired, Boston selected Martin Samuelsson) in 2000 Entry Draft, March 6, 2000. • Officially announced retirement, June 26, 2001.

BOWLER, Bill
NSH.

Center. Shoots left. 5'9", 180 lbs. Born, Toronto, Ont., September 25, 1974.

Season	Club	League	GP	G	A	Pts	PIM	PP	SH	GW	S	%	+/-	TF	F%	H	SB	Min	GP	G	A	Pts	PIM	PP	SH	GW
1990-91	Toronto Wings	MTHL	69	58	99	157																				
1991-92	Windsor Spitfires	OHL	66	25	63	88	28												7	2	3	5	13			
1992-93	Windsor Spitfires	OHL	57	44	77	121	41																			
1993-94	Windsor Spitfires	OHL	66	47	76	123	39																			
1994-95	Windsor Spitfires	OHL	61	33	102	135	63												10	7	15	22	13			
	Las Vegas	IHL																	1	0	0	0	0			
1995-96	Las Vegas	IHL	75	31	55	86	26												14	3	5	8	22			
1996-97	Houston Aeros	IHL	78	22	43	65	79												13	2	5	7	6			
1997-98	Hamilton Bulldogs	AHL	46	7	24	31	22																			
	Manitoba Moose	IHL	30	9	26	34	30												3	0	2	2	4			
1998-99	Manitoba Moose	IHL	82	26	67	93	59												5	6	5	11	6			
99-2000	Manitoba Moose	IHL	75	20	42	62	59												2	1	2	3	6			
2000-01	**Columbus**	**NHL**	**9**	**0**	**2**	**2**	**8**	**0**	**0**	**0**	**3**	**0.0**	**–3**	**48**	**47.9**	**1**	**0**	**9:44**								
	Syracuse Crunch	AHL	72	21	58	79	50												4	1	3	4	2			
	NHL Totals		**9**	**0**	**2**	**2**	**8**	**0**	**0**	**0**	**3**	**0.0**		**48**	**47.9**	**1**	**0**	**9:44**								

IHL Second All-Star Team (1999)

Signed as a free agent by **Manitoba** (IHL), August 28, 1998. Signed as a free agent by **Columbus**, August 3, 2000. Claimed on waivers by **Nashville** from **Columbus**, June 1, 2001.

BOYLE, Dan
(BOIL, DAN) **FLA.**

Defense. Shoots right. 5'11", 190 lbs. Born, Ottawa, Ont., July 12, 1976.

Season	Club	League	GP	G	A	Pts	PIM	PP	SH	GW	S	%	+/-	TF	F%	H	SB	Min	GP	G	A	Pts	PIM	PP	SH	GW
1992-93	Gloucester	OCJHL	55	22	51	73	60																			
1993-94	Gloucester	OCJHL	53	27	54	81	155																			
1994-95	U. of Miami-Ohio	CCHA	35	8	18	26	24																			
1995-96	U. of Miami-Ohio	CCHA	36	7	20	27	70																			
1996-97	U. of Miami-Ohio	CCHA	40	11	43	54	52																			
1997-98	U. of Miami-Ohio	CCHA	37	14	26	40	58																			
1998-99	**Florida**	**NHL**	**22**	**3**	**5**	**8**	**6**	**1**	**0**	**1**	**31**	**9.7**	**0**	**1**	**100.0**	**27**	**14**	**18:50**								
	Kentucky	AHL	53	8	34	42	87												12	3	5	8	16			
99-2000	**Florida**	**NHL**	**13**	**0**	**3**	**3**	**4**	**0**	**0**	**0**	**9**	**0.0**	**–2**	**0**	**0.0**	**9**	**12**	**16:57**								
	Louisville Panthers	AHL	58	14	38	52	75												4	0	2	2	8			

			Regular Season																Playoffs							
Season	Club	League	GP	G	A	Pts	PIM	PP	SH	GW	S	%	+/-	TF	F%	H	SB	Min	GP	G	A	Pts	PIM	PP	SH	GW
2000-01	**Florida**	**NHL**	**69**	**4**	**18**	**22**	**28**	1	0	0	83	4.8	–14	0	0.0	95	30	16:56								
	Louisville Panthers	AHL	6	0	5	5	12																			
	NHL Totals		**104**	**7**	**26**	**33**	**38**	2	0	1	123	5.7		1	100.0	131	56	17:20								

CCHA First All-Star Team (1997, 1998) • NCAA West First All-American Team (1997, 1998) • AHL Second All-Star Team (1999, 2000)

Signed as a free agent by **Florida**, March 30, 1998.

BOYNTON, Nick (BOIN-tuhn, NIHK) BOS.

Defense. Shoots right. 6'2", 210 lbs. Born, Nobleton, Ont., January 14, 1979. Boston's 1st choice, 21st overall, in 1999 Entry Draft.

1993-94	Caledon Canucks	MJAHL	4	0	1	1	0																			
1994-95	Caledon Canucks	MJAHL	44	10	35	45	139																			
1995-96	Ottawa 67's	OHL	64	10	14	24	90												4	0	3	3	10			
1996-97	Ottawa 67's	OHL	63	13	51	64	143												24	4	*24	28	38			
1997-98	Ottawa 67's	OHL	40	7	31	38	94												13	0	4	4	24			
1998-99	Ottawa 67's	OHL	51	11	48	59	83												9	1	9	10	18			
99-2000	**Boston**	**NHL**	**5**	**0**	**0**	**0**	**0**	0	0	0	6	0.0	–5	0	0.0	6	8	21:21								
	Providence Bruins	AHL	53	5	14	19	66												12	1	0	1	6			
2000-01	**Boston**	**NHL**	**1**	**0**	**0**	**0**	**0**	0	0	0	1	0.0	–1	0	0.0	2	3	14:27								
	Providence Bruins	AHL	78	6	27	33	105												17	0	2	2	35			
	NHL Totals		**6**	**0**	**0**	**0**	**0**	0	0	0	7	0.0		0	0.0	8	11	20:12								

• Re-entered NHL Entry Draft. Originally Washington's 1st choice, 9th overall, in 1997 Entry Draft.

Memorial Cup All-Star Team (1999) • Won Stafford Smythe Memorial Trophy (Memorial Cup Tournament MVP) (1999)

BRADLEY, Matt (BRAD-lee, MAT) S.J.

Right wing. Shoots right. 6'2", 195 lbs. Born, Stittsville, Ont., June 13, 1978. San Jose's 4th choice, 102nd overall, in 1996 Entry Draft.

1994-95	Cumberland	OCJHL	49	13	20	33	18																			
1995-96	Kingston	OHL	55	10	14	24	17												6	0	1	1	6			
1996-97	Kingston	OHL	65	24	24	48	41												5	0	4	4	2			
	Kentucky	AHL	1	0	1	1	0																			
1997-98	Kingston	OHL	55	33	50	83	24												8	3	4	7	7			
1998-99	Kentucky	AHL	79	23	20	43	57												10	1	4	5	4			
99-2000	Kentucky	AHL	80	22	19	41	81												9	6	3	9	9			
2000-01	Kentucky	AHL	22	5	8	13	16												1	1	0	1	5			
	San Jose	**NHL**	**21**	**1**	**1**	**2**	**19**	0	0	0	16	6.3	0	0	0.0	49	1	6:58								
	NHL Totals		**21**	**1**	**1**	**2**	**19**	0	0	0	16	6.3		0	0.0	49	1	6:58								

Won William Hanley Award (Most Gentlemanly Player - OHL) (1998)

BRASHEAR, Donald (bra-SHEER, DAWN-ohld) VAN.

Left wing. Shoots left. 6'2", 225 lbs. Born, Bedford, IN, January 7, 1972.

1988-89	Ste-Foy Governors	QAAA	10	1	2	3	10																			
1989-90	Longueuil	QMJHL	64	12	14	26	169												7	0	0	0	11			
1990-91	Longueuil	QMJHL	68	12	26	38	195												8	0	3	3	33			
1991-92	Verdun	QMJHL	65	18	24	42	283												18	4	2	6	98			
1992-93	Fredericton	AHL	76	11	3	14	261												5	0	0	0	8			
1993-94	**Montreal**	**NHL**	**14**	**2**	**2**	**4**	**34**	0	0	0	15	13.3	0						**2**	**0**	**0**	**0**	**0**	0	0	0
	Fredericton	AHL	62	38	28	66	250																			
1994-95	Fredericton	AHL	29	10	9	19	182												17	7	5	12	77			
	Montreal	**NHL**	**20**	**1**	**1**	**2**	**63**	0	0	1	10	10.0	–5													
1995-96	**Montreal**	**NHL**	**67**	**0**	**4**	**4**	**223**	0	0	0	25	0.0	–10						**6**	**0**	**0**	**0**	**2**	0	0	0
1996-97	**Montreal**	**NHL**	**10**	**0**	**0**	**0**	**38**	0	0	0	6	0.0	–2													
	Vancouver	**NHL**	**59**	**8**	**5**	**13**	**207**	0	0	2	55	14.5	–6													
1997-98	**Vancouver**	**NHL**	**77**	**9**	**9**	**18**	***372**	0	0	1	64	14.1	–9													
1998-99	**Vancouver**	**NHL**	**82**	**8**	**10**	**18**	**209**	2	0	1	112	7.1	–25	6	16.7	126	20	13:25								
99-2000	**Vancouver**	**NHL**	**60**	**11**	**2**	**13**	**136**	1	0	3	83	13.3	–9	11	36.4	125	18	13:07								
2000-01	**Vancouver**	**NHL**	**79**	**9**	**19**	**28**	**145**	0	0	1	127	7.1	0	6	16.7	183	24	13:27	**4**	**0**	**0**	**0**	**0**	0	0	0
	NHL Totals		**468**	**48**	**52**	**100**	**1427**	3	0	9	497	9.7		23	26.1	434	62	13:21	**12**	**0**	**0**	**0**	**2**	0	0	0

Signed as a free agent by **Montreal**, July 28, 1992. Traded to **Vancouver** by **Montreal** for Jassen Cullimore, November 13, 1996.

BRENNAN, Rich (BREHN-nan, RIHCH) NSH.

Defense. Shoots right. 6'2", 200 lbs. Born, Schenectady, NY, November 26, 1972. Quebec's 3rd choice, 46th overall, in 1991 Entry Draft.

1988-89	Albany Academy	Hi-School	25	17	30	47	57																			
1989-90	Tabor Academy	Hi-School	33	12	14	26	68																			
1990-91	Tabor Academy	Hi-School	34	13	37	50	91																			
1991-92	Boston University	H-East	30	4	13	17	50																			
1992-93	Boston University	H-East	40	9	11	20	68																			
1993-94	Boston University	H-East	41	8	27	35	82																			
1994-95	Boston University	H-East	31	5	22	27	56																			
1995-96	Brantford	ColHL	5	1	2	3	2																			
	Cornwall Aces	AHL	36	4	8	12	61												7	0	0	0	6			
1996-97	**Colorado**	**NHL**	**2**	**0**	**0**	**0**	**0**	0	0	0	0	0.0	0													
	Hershey Bears	AHL	74	11	45	56	88												23	2	*16	18	22			
1997-98	**San Jose**	**NHL**	**11**	**1**	**2**	**3**	**2**	1	0	0	24	4.2	–4													
	Kentucky	AHL	42	11	17	28	71																			
	Hartford	AHL	9	2	4	6	12												15	4	5	9	14			
1998-99	**NY Rangers**	**NHL**	**24**	**1**	**3**	**4**	**23**	0	0	0	36	2.8	–4	0	0.0	40	22	13:02								
	Hartford	AHL	47	4	24	28	42																			
99-2000	Lowell	AHL	67	15	30	45	110												7	1	5	6	0			
2000-01	**Los Angeles**	**NHL**	**2**	**0**	**0**	**0**	**0**	0	0	0	1	0.0	–3	0	0.0	4	2	14:44								
	Lowell	AHL	69	10	31	41	146																			
	NHL Totals		**39**	**2**	**5**	**7**	**25**	1	0	0	61	3.3		0	0.0	44	24	13:10								

Hockey East First All-Star Team (1994) • NCAA East Second All-American Team (1994)

Rights transferred to **Colorado** after **Quebec** franchise relocated, June 21, 1995. Signed as a free agent by **San Jose**, July 9, 1997. Traded to **NY Rangers** by **San Jose** for Jason Muzzatti, March 24, 1998. Signed as a free agent by **Nashville**, September 23, 1999. Claimed by **LA Kings** from **Nashville** in Waiver Draft, September 27, 1999. Signed as a free agent by **Nashville**, August 8, 2001.

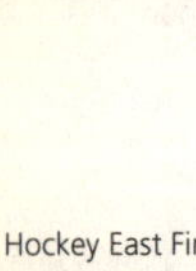

BREWER, Eric (BREW-uhr, AIR-ihk) EDM.

Defense. Shoots left. 6'3", 220 lbs. Born, Vernon, B.C., April 17, 1979. NY Islanders' 2nd choice, 5th overall, in 1997 Entry Draft.

1994-95	Kamloops	BCAHA	40	19	19	38	62																			
1995-96	Prince George	WHL	63	4	10	14	25																			
1996-97	Prince George	WHL	71	5	24	29	81												15	2	4	6	16			
1997-98	Prince George	WHL	34	5	28	33	45												11	4	2	6	19			
1998-99	**NY Islanders**	**NHL**	**63**	**5**	**6**	**11**	**32**	2	0	0	63	7.9	–14	0	0.0	89	32	15:28								
99-2000	**NY Islanders**	**NHL**	**26**	**0**	**2**	**2**	**20**	0	0	0	30	0.0	–11	0	0.0	55	32	18:33								
	Lowell	AHL	25	2	2	4	26												7	0	0	0	0			
2000-01	**Edmonton**	**NHL**	**77**	**7**	**14**	**21**	**53**	2	0	2	91	7.7	15	0	0.0	162	91	18:31	**6**	**1**	**5**	**6**	**2**	1	0	0
	NHL Totals		**166**	**12**	**22**	**34**	**105**	4	0	2	184	6.5		0	0.0	306	155	17:22	**6**	**1**	**5**	**6**	**2**	1	0	0

WHL West Second All-Star Team (1998)

Traded to **Edmonton** by **NY Islanders** with Josh Green and NY Islanders' 2nd round choice (Brad Winchester) in 2000 Entry Draft for Roman Hamrlik, June 24, 2000.

BRIERE, Daniel
(bree-AIR, DAN-yehl) **PHX.**

Center. Shoots right. 5'10", 181 lbs. Born, Gatineau, Que., October 6, 1977. Phoenix's 2nd choice, 24th overall, in 1996 Entry Draft.

Season	Club	League	GP	G	A	Pts	PIM	PP	SH	GW	S	%	+/-	TF	F%	H	SB	Min	Playoffs GP	G	A	Pts	PIM	PP	SH	GW
1992-93	D'Abitibi Regents	QAAA	42	24	30	54	28												3	0	3	3	8			
1993-94	Gatineau Elites	QAAA	44	56	47	103	56																			
1994-95	Drummondville	QMJHL	72	51	72	123	54												4	2	3	5	2			
1995-96	Drummondville	QMJHL	67	*67	*96	*163	84												6	6	12	18	8			
1996-97	Drummondville	QMJHL	59	52	78	130	94												8	7	7	14	14			
1997-98	**Phoenix**	**NHL**	**5**	**1**	**0**	**1**	**2**	**0**	**0**	**0**	**4**	**25.0**	**1**													
	Springfield	AHL	68	36	56	92	42												4	1	2	3	4			
1998-99	**Phoenix**	**NHL**	**64**	**8**	**14**	**22**	**30**	**2**	**0**	**2**	**90**	**8.9**	**-3**	**484**	**47.5**	**15**	**8**	**11:13**								
	Las Vegas	IHL	1	1	1	2	0																			
	Springfield	AHL	13	2	6	8	20												3	0	1	1	2			
99-2000	**Phoenix**	**NHL**	**13**	**1**	**1**	**2**	**0**	**0**	**0**	**0**	**9**	**11.1**	**0**	**65**	**49.2**	**4**	**1**	**7:41**	**1**	**0**	**0**	**0**	**0**	**0**	**0**	**0**
	Springfield	AHL	58	29	42	71	56																			
2000-01	**Phoenix**	**NHL**	**30**	**11**	**4**	**15**	**12**	**9**	**0**	**1**	**43**	**25.6**	**-2**	**210**	**50.0**	**7**	**2**	**10:50**								
	Springfield	AHL	30	21	25	46	30																			
	NHL Totals		**112**	**21**	**19**	**40**	**44**	**11**	**0**	**3**	**146**	**14.4**		**759**	**48.4**	**26**	**11**	**10:41**	**1**	**0**	**0**	**0**	**0**	**0**	**0**	**0**

QMJHL Second All-Star Team (1996, 1997) • AHL First All-Star Team (1998) • Won Dudley "Red" Garrett Memorial Trophy (Top Rookie - AHL) (1998)

BRIGLEY, Travis
(BRIH-glee), TRA-vihs)

Left wing. Shoots left. 6'1", 195 lbs. Born, Coronation, Alta., June 16, 1977. Calgary's 2nd choice, 39th overall, in 1996 Entry Draft.

Season	Club	League	GP	G	A	Pts	PIM	PP	SH	GW	S	%	+/-	TF	F%	H	SB	Min	Playoffs GP	G	A	Pts	PIM	PP	SH	GW
1992-93	Leduc Barons	AMHL	32	36	24	60	56																			
1993-94	Leduc Barons	AMHL	34	29	44	73	141																			
	Lethbridge	WHL	1	0	0	0	0																			
1994-95	Lethbridge	WHL	64	14	18	32	14																			
1995-96	Lethbridge	WHL	69	34	43	77	94												4	2	3	5	8			
1996-97	Lethbridge	WHL	71	43	47	90	56												19	9	9	18	31			
1997-98	**Calgary**	**NHL**	**2**	**0**	**0**	**0**	**2**	**0**	**0**	**0**	**1**	**0.0**	**0**													
	Saint John Flames	AHL	79	17	15	32	28												8	0	0	0	0			
1998-99	Saint John Flames	AHL	74	15	35	50	48												7	3	1	4	2			
99-2000	**Calgary**	**NHL**	**17**	**0**	**2**	**2**	**4**	**0**	**0**	**0**	**17**	**0.0**	**-6**	**2**	**0.0**	**16**	**8**	**14:14**								
	Saint John Flames	AHL	9	3	1	4	4																			
	Detroit Vipers	IHL	29	6	10	16	24																			
	Philadelphia	AHL	15	2	2	4	15												5	1	0	1	4			
2000-01	Knoxville Speed	UHL	4	2	4	6	4																			
	Cardiff Devils	Britain	12	5	9	14	6																			
	Louisville Panthers	AHL	49	14	21	35	34																			
	NHL Totals		**19**	**0**	**2**	**2**	**6**	**0**	**0**	**0**	**18**	**0.0**		**2**	**0.0**	**16**	**8**	**14:14**								

Traded to **Philadelphia** by **Calgary** with Calgary's 6th round choice (Andrei Razin) in 2001 Entry Draft for Marc Bureau, March 6, 2000. Signed as a free agent by **Cardiff Devils** (Britain), November 3, 2000. Signed as a free agent by **Florida**, December 16, 2000.

BRIMANIS, Aris
(brih-MAN-ihs, AR-ihs) **ANA.**

Defense. Shoots right. 6'3", 210 lbs. Born, Cleveland, OH, March 14, 1972. Philadelphia's 3rd choice, 86th overall, in 1991 Entry Draft.

Season	Club	League	GP	G	A	Pts	PIM	PP	SH	GW	S	%	+/-	TF	F%	H	SB	Min	Playoffs GP	G	A	Pts	PIM	PP	SH	GW
1988-89	Culver Academy	Hi-School	38	10	13	23	24																			
1989-90	Culver Academy	Hi-School	37	15	10	25	52																			
1990-91	Bowling Green	CCHA	38	3	6	9	42																			
1991-92	Bowling Green	CCHA	32	2	9	11	38																			
1992-93	Brandon	WHL	71	8	50	58	110												4	2	1	3	7			
1993-94	**Philadelphia**	**NHL**	**1**	**0**	**0**	**0**	**0**	**0**	**0**	**0**	**1**	**0.0**	**-1**													
	Hershey Bears	AHL	75	8	15	23	65												11	2	3	5	12			
1994-95	Hershey Bears	AHL	76	8	17	25	68												6	1	1	2	14			
1995-96	**Philadelphia**	**NHL**	**17**	**0**	**2**	**2**	**12**	**0**	**0**	**0**	**11**	**0.0**	**-1**													
	Hershey Bears	AHL	54	9	22	31	64												5	1	2	3	4			
1996-97	**Philadelphia**	**NHL**	**3**	**0**	**1**	**1**	**0**	**0**	**0**	**0**	**1**	**0.0**	**0**													
	Philadelphia	AHL	65	14	18	32	69												10	2	2	4	13			
1997-98	Philadelphia	AHL	30	1	11	12	26																			
	Michigan K-Wings	IHL	35	3	9	12	24												4	1	0	1	4			
1998-99	Grand Rapids	IHL	66	16	21	37	70																			
	Fredericton	AHL	8	2	4	6	6												15	3	10	13	18			
99-2000	**NY Islanders**	**NHL**	**18**	**2**	**1**	**3**	**6**	**2**	**0**	**0**	**16**	**12.5**	**-5**	**1**	**0.0**	**32**	**28**	**19:60**								
	Kansas City	IHL	46	5	17	22	28																			
	Providence Bruins	AHL	7	0	2	2	2												14	3	4	7	10			
2000-01	**NY Islanders**	**NHL**	**56**	**0**	**8**	**8**	**26**	**0**	**0**	**0**	**66**	**0.0**	**-12**	**0**	**0.0**	**137**	**52**	**15:36**								
	Chicago Wolves	IHL	20	2	2	4	14												16	3	1	4	8			
	NHL Totals		**95**	**2**	**12**	**14**	**44**	**2**	**0**	**0**	**95**	**2.1**		**1**	**0.0**	**169**	**80**	**16:40**								

Signed as a free agent by **NY Islanders**, August 16, 1999. Loaned to **Providence** (AHL) by **NY Islanders**, March 14, 2000. Signed as a free agent by **Anaheim**, August 1, 2001.

BRIND'AMOUR, Rod
(BRIHND-uh-MOHR, RAWD) **CAR.**

Center. Shoots left. 6'1", 202 lbs. Born, Ottawa, Ont., August 9, 1970. St. Louis' 1st choice, 9th overall, in 1988 Entry Draft.

Season	Club	League	GP	G	A	Pts	PIM	PP	SH	GW	S	%	+/-	TF	F%	H	SB	Min	Playoffs GP	G	A	Pts	PIM	PP	SH	GW
1986-87	Notre Dame	AMHL	33	38	50	88	66																			
1987-88	Notre Dame	SJHL	56	46	61	107	136																			
1988-89	Michigan State	CCHA	42	27	32	59	63																			
	St. Louis	**NHL**																	**5**	**2**	**0**	**2**	**4**	**0**	**0**	**0**
1989-90	**St. Louis**	**NHL**	**79**	**26**	**35**	**61**	**46**	**10**	**0**	**1**	**160**	**16.3**	**23**						**12**	**5**	**8**	**13**	**6**	**1**	**0**	**0**
1990-91	**St. Louis**	**NHL**	**78**	**17**	**32**	**49**	**93**	**4**	**0**	**3**	**169**	**10.1**	**2**						**13**	**2**	**5**	**7**	**10**	**1**	**0**	**0**
1991-92	**Philadelphia**	**NHL**	**80**	**33**	**44**	**77**	**100**	**8**	**4**	**5**	**202**	**16.3**	**-3**													
1992-93	**Philadelphia**	**NHL**	**81**	**37**	**49**	**86**	**89**	**13**	**4**	**4**	**206**	**18.0**	**-8**													
1993-94	**Philadelphia**	**NHL**	**84**	**35**	**62**	**97**	**85**	**14**	**1**	**4**	**230**	**15.2**	**-9**													
1994-95	**Philadelphia**	**NHL**	**48**	**12**	**27**	**39**	**33**	**4**	**1**	**2**	**86**	**14.0**	**-4**						**15**	**6**	**9**	**15**	**8**	**2**	**1**	**1**
1995-96	**Philadelphia**	**NHL**	**82**	**26**	**61**	**87**	**110**	**4**	**4**	**5**	**213**	**12.2**	**20**						**12**	**2**	**5**	**7**	**6**	**2**	**1**	**0**
1996-97	**Philadelphia**	**NHL**	**82**	**27**	**32**	**59**	**41**	**8**	**2**	**3**	**205**	**13.2**	**2**						**19**	***13**	**8**	**21**	**10**	**4**	**2**	**1**
1997-98	**Philadelphia**	**NHL**	**82**	**36**	**38**	**74**	**54**	**10**	**2**	**8**	**205**	**17.6**	**-2**						**5**	**2**	**2**	**4**	**7**	**0**	**0**	**0**
	Canada	Olympics	6	1	2	3	0																			
1998-99	**Philadelphia**	**NHL**	**82**	**24**	**50**	**74**	**47**	**10**	**0**	**3**	**191**	**12.6**	**3**	**1773**	**56.5**	**90**	**31**	**21:29**	**6**	**1**	**3**	**4**	**0**	**0**	**0**	**0**
99-2000	**Philadelphia**	**NHL**	**12**	**5**	**3**	**8**	**4**	**4**	**0**	**0**	**26**	**19.2**	**-1**	**291**	**60.5**	**17**	**11**	**20:50**								
	Carolina	**NHL**	**33**	**4**	**10**	**14**	**22**	**0**	**1**	**1**	**61**	**6.6**	**-12**	**704**	**55.5**	**62**	**13**	**20:35**								
2000-01	**Carolina**	**NHL**	**79**	**20**	**36**	**56**	**47**	**5**	**1**	**5**	**163**	**12.3**	**-7**	**1907**	**60.4**	**117**	**51**	**22:07**	**6**	**1**	**3**	**4**	**6**	**0**	**0**	**1**
	NHL Totals		**902**	**302**	**479**	**781**	**771**	**94**	**20**	**44**	**2117**	**14.3**		**4675**	**58.2**	**286**	**106**	**21:33**	**93**	**34**	**43**	**77**	**57**	**9**	**3**	**3**

NHL All-Rookie Team (1990) • Played in NHL All-Star Game (1992)

Traded to **Philadelphia** by **St. Louis** with Dan Quinn for Ron Sutter and Murray Baron, September 22, 1991. Traded to **Carolina** by **Philadelphia** with Jean-Marc Pelletier and Philadelphia's 2nd round choice (later traded to Colorado - Colorado selected Agris Saviels) in 2000 Entry Draft for Keith Primeau and Carolina's 5th round choice (later traded to NY Islanders - NY Islanders selected Kristofer Ottosson) in 2000 Entry Draft, January 23, 2000.

BRISEBOIS, Patrice
(BREES-bwah, pa-TREEZ) **MTL.**

Defense. Shoots right. 6'1", 203 lbs. Born, Montreal, Que., January 27, 1971. Montreal's 2nd choice, 30th overall, in 1989 Entry Draft.

Season	Club	League	GP	G	A	Pts	PIM	PP	SH	GW	S	%	+/-	TF	F%	H	SB	Min	Playoffs GP	G	A	Pts	PIM	PP	SH	GW
1986-87	Mtl-Bourassa	QAAA	39	15	19	34	66																			
1987-88	Laval Titan	QMJHL	48	10	34	44	95												6	0	2	2	2			
1988-89	Laval Titan	QMJHL	50	20	45	65	95												17	8	14	22	45			
1989-90	Laval Titan	QMJHL	56	18	70	88	108												13	7	9	16	26			
1990-91	Drummondville	QMJHL	54	17	44	61	72												14	6	18	24	49			
	Montreal	**NHL**	**10**	**0**	**2**	**2**	**4**	**0**	**0**	**0**	**11**	**0.0**	**1**													
1991-92	**Montreal**	**NHL**	**26**	**2**	**8**	**10**	**20**	**0**	**0**	**1**	**37**	**5.4**	**9**						**11**	**2**	**4**	**6**	**6**	**1**	**0**	**1**
	Fredericton	AHL	53	12	27	39	51																			
1992-93♦	**Montreal**	**NHL**	**70**	**10**	**21**	**31**	**79**	**4**	**0**	**2**	**123**	**8.1**	**6**						**20**	**0**	**4**	**4**	**18**	**0**	**0**	**0**
1993-94	**Montreal**	**NHL**	**53**	**2**	**21**	**23**	**63**	**1**	**0**	**0**	**71**	**2.8**	**5**						**7**	**0**	**4**	**4**	**6**	**0**	**0**	**0**

			Regular Season																Playoffs							
Season	Club	League	GP	G	A	Pts	PIM	PP	SH	GW	S	%	+/-	TF	F%	H	SB	Min	GP	G	A	Pts	PIM	PP	SH	GW
1994-95	Montreal	NHL	35	4	8	12	26	0	0	2	67	6.0	-2	....	....	....	....	....	....	....	....	....	....	....	....	....
1995-96	Montreal	NHL	69	9	27	36	65	3	0	1	127	7.1	10	....	....	....	....	....	6	1	2	3	6	0	0	0
1996-97	Montreal	NHL	49	2	13	15	24	0	0	1	72	2.8	-7	....	....	....	....	....	3	1	1	2	24	0	0	1
1997-98	Montreal	NHL	79	10	27	37	67	5	0	1	125	8.0	16	....	....	....	....	....	10	1	0	1	0	0	0	0
1998-99	Montreal	NHL	54	3	9	12	28	1	0	1	90	3.3	-8	0	0.0	62	80	22:26	....	....	....	....	....	....	....	....
99-2000	Montreal	NHL	54	10	25	35	18	5	0	2	88	11.4	-1	0	0.0	82	79	23:14	....	....	....	....	....	....	....	....
2000-01	Montreal	NHL	77	15	21	36	28	11	0	4	178	8.4	-31	1	100.0	100	122	24:43	....	....	....	....	....	....	....	....
	NHL Totals		576	67	182	249	422	30	0	15	989	6.8		1	100.0	244	281	23:37	57	5	15	20	60	1	0	2

QMJHL Second All-Star Team (1990) • QMJHL First All-Star Team (1991) • Canadian Major Junior Defenseman of the Year (1991) • Memorial Cup All-Star Team (1991)

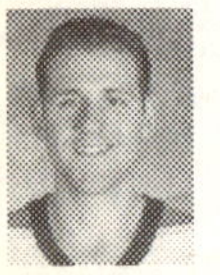

BROUSSEAU, Paul

(BROO-soh, PAWL)

Right wing. Shoots right. 6'2", 203 lbs. Born, Pierrefonds, Que., September 18, 1973. Quebec's 2nd choice, 28th overall, in 1992 Entry Draft.

1988-89	Lac St-Louis	QAAA	37	6	17	23	28	....	....	....	....	....	....	....	....	....	....	....	3	3	1	4	2	....	....	....
1989-90	Chicoutimi	QMJHL	57	17	24	41	32	....	....	....	....	....	....	....	....	....	....	....	7	0	3	3	0	....	....	....
1990-91	Trois-Rivieres	QMJHL	67	30	66	96	48	....	....	....	....	....	....	....	....	....	....	....	6	3	2	5	2	....	....	....
1991-92	Hull Olympiques	QMJHL	57	35	61	96	54	....	....	....	....	....	....	....	....	....	....	....	6	3	5	8	10	....	....	....
1992-93	Hull Olympiques	QMJHL	59	27	48	75	49	....	....	....	....	....	....	....	....	....	....	....	10	7	8	15	6	....	....	....
1993-94	Cornwall Aces	AHL	69	18	26	44	35	....	....	....	....	....	....	....	....	....	....	....	1	0	0	0	0	....	....	....
1994-95	Cornwall Aces	AHL	57	19	17	36	29	....	....	....	....	....	....	....	....	....	....	....	7	2	1	3	10	....	....	....
1995-96	Colorado	NHL	8	1	1	2	2	0	0	0	10	10.0	1	....	....	....	....	....	....	....	....	....	....	....	....	....
	Cornwall Aces	AHL	63	21	22	43	60	....	....	....	....	....	....	....	....	....	....	....	8	4	0	4	2	....	....	....
1996-97	Tampa Bay	NHL	6	0	0	0	0	0	0	0	3	0.0	-4	....	....	....	....	....	....	....	....	....	....	....	....	....
	Adirondack	AHL	66	35	31	66	25	....	....	....	....	....	....	....	....	....	....	....	4	1	2	3	0	....	....	....
1997-98	Tampa Bay	NHL	11	0	2	2	27	0	0	0	6	0.0	0	....	....	....	....	....	....	....	....	....	....	....	....	....
	Adirondack	AHL	67	45	20	65	18	....	....	....	....	....	....	....	....	....	....	....	3	1	1	2	0	....	....	....
1998-99	Milwaukee	IHL	5	1	1	2	2	....	....	....	....	....	....	....	....	....	....	....	....	....	....	....	....	....	....	....
	Hershey Bears	AHL	39	11	21	32	15	....	....	....	....	....	....	....	....	....	....	....	5	1	1	2	0	....	....	....
99-2000	Louisville Panthers	AHL	36	19	24	43	10	....	....	....	....	....	....	....	....	....	....	....	4	1	1	2	12	....	....	....
2000-01	Florida	NHL	1	0	0	0	0	0	0	0	0	0.0	0	0	0.0	0	0	1:39	....	....	....	....	....	....	....	....
	Louisville Panthers	AHL	73	29	39	68	21	....	....	....	....	....	....	....	....	....	....	....	....	....	....	....	....	....	....	....
	NHL Totals		26	1	3	4	29	0	0	0	19	5.3		0	0.0	0	0	1:39	....	....	....	....	....	....	....	....

AHL Second All-Star Team (1998)

Rights transferred to **Colorado** after **Quebec** franchise relocated, June 21, 1995. Signed as a free agent by **Tampa Bay**, September 10, 1996. Claimed by **Nashville** from **Tampa Bay** in Expansion Draft, June 26, 1998. Signed as a free agent by **Florida**, September 20, 1999. • Missed majority of 1999-2000 season recovering from knee injury suffered in game vs. Rochester (AHL), January 8, 2000.

BROWN, Brad

(BROWN, BRAD) **MIN.**

Defense. Shoots right. 6'4", 220 lbs. Born, Baie Verte, Nfld., December 27, 1975. Montreal's 1st choice, 18th overall, in 1994 Entry Draft.

1990-91	Toronto Wings	MTHL	80	15	45	60	105	....	....	....	....	....	....	....	....	....	....	....	....	....	....	....	....	....	....	....
	St. Michael's	MTJHL	2	0	0	0	0	....	....	....	....	....	....	....	....	....	....	....	....	....	....	....	....	....	....	....
1991-92	North Bay	OHL	49	2	9	11	170	....	....	....	....	....	....	....	....	....	....	....	18	0	6	6	43	....	....	....
1992-93	North Bay	OHL	61	4	9	13	228	....	....	....	....	....	....	....	....	....	....	....	2	0	2	2	13	....	....	....
1993-94	North Bay	OHL	66	8	24	32	196	....	....	....	....	....	....	....	....	....	....	....	18	3	12	15	33	....	....	....
1994-95	North Bay	OHL	64	8	38	46	172	....	....	....	....	....	....	....	....	....	....	....	6	1	4	5	8	....	....	....
1995-96	Barrie Colts	OHL	27	3	13	16	82	....	....	....	....	....	....	....	....	....	....	....	....	....	....	....	....	....	....	....
	Fredericton	AHL	38	0	3	3	148	....	....	....	....	....	....	....	....	....	....	....	10	2	1	3	6	....	....	....
1996-97	Montreal	NHL	8	0	0	0	22	0	0	0	0	0.0	-1	....	....	....	....	....	....	....	....	....	....	....	....	....
	Fredericton	AHL	64	3	7	10	368	....	....	....	....	....	....	....	....	....	....	....	....	....	....	....	....	....	....	....
1997-98	Fredericton	AHL	64	1	8	9	297	....	....	....	....	....	....	....	....	....	....	....	4	0	0	0	29	....	....	....
1998-99	Montreal	NHL	5	0	0	0	21	0	0	0	0	0.0	0	0	0.0	1	5	6:02	....	....	....	....	....	....	....	....
	Chicago	NHL	61	1	7	8	184	0	0	0	26	3.8	-4	0	0.0	145	63	15:08	....	....	....	....	....	....	....	....
99-2000	Chicago	NHL	57	0	9	9	134	0	0	0	15	0.0	-1	0	0.0	93	64	14:12	....	....	....	....	....	....	....	....
2000-01	NY Rangers	NHL	48	1	3	4	107	0	0	0	14	7.1	0	0	0.0	98	71	14:31	....	....	....	....	....	....	....	....
	NHL Totals		179	2	19	21	468	0	0	0	55	3.6		0	0.0	337	203	14:23	....	....	....	....	....	....	....	....

Traded to **Chicago** by **Montreal** with Jocelyn Thibault and Dave Manson for Jeff Hackett, Eric Weinrich, Alain Nasreddine and Tampa Bay's 4th round choice (previously acquired, Montreal selected Chris Dyment) in 1999 Entry Draft, November 16, 1998. Traded to **NY Rangers** by **Chicago** with Michael Grosek for future considerations, October 5, 2000. Signed as a free agent by **Minnesota**, July 31, 2001.

BROWN, Curtis

(BROWN, KUHR-tihs) **BUF.**

Center/Left wing. Shoots left. 6', 196 lbs. Born, Unity, Sask., February 12, 1976. Buffalo's 2nd choice, 43rd overall, in 1994 Entry Draft.

1990-91	Unity Bantams	SAHA	60	93	104	197	55	....	....	....	....	....	....	....	....	....	....	....	....	....	....	....	....	....	....	....
1991-92	Moose Jaw	SMHL	36	35	30	65	44	....	....	....	....	....	....	....	....	....	....	....	....	....	....	....	....	....	....	....
1992-93	Moose Jaw	WHL	71	13	16	29	30	....	....	....	....	....	....	....	....	....	....	....	....	....	....	....	....	....	....	....
1993-94	Moose Jaw	WHL	72	27	38	65	82	....	....	....	....	....	....	....	....	....	....	....	....	....	....	....	....	....	....	....
1994-95	Moose Jaw	WHL	70	51	53	104	63	....	....	....	....	....	....	....	....	....	....	....	10	8	7	15	20	....	....	....
	Buffalo	NHL	1	1	1	2	2	0	0	0	4	25.0	2	....	....	....	....	....	....	....	....	....	....	....	....	....
1995-96	Moose Jaw	WHL	25	20	18	38	30	....	....	....	....	....	....	....	....	....	....	....	....	....	....	....	....	....	....	....
	Prince Albert	WHL	19	12	21	33	8	....	....	....	....	....	....	....	....	....	....	....	18	10	15	25	18	....	....	....
	Buffalo	NHL	4	0	0	0	0	0	0	0	1	0.0	0	....	....	....	....	....	....	....	....	....	....	....	....	....
	Rochester	AHL	....	....	....	....	....	....	....	....	....	....	....	....	....	....	....	....	12	0	1	1	2	....	....	....
1996-97	Buffalo	NHL	28	4	3	7	18	0	0	1	31	12.9	4	....	....	....	....	....	....	....	....	....	....	....	....	....
	Rochester	AHL	51	22	21	43	30	....	....	....	....	....	....	....	....	....	....	....	10	4	6	10	4	....	....	....
1997-98	Buffalo	NHL	63	12	12	24	34	1	1	2	91	13.2	11	....	....	....	....	....	13	1	2	3	10	1	0	0
1998-99	Buffalo	NHL	78	16	31	47	56	5	1	3	128	12.5	23	1198	45.0	83	64	17:30	21	7	6	13	10	3	0	3
99-2000	Buffalo	NHL	74	22	29	51	42	5	0	4	149	14.8	19	1318	48.6	48	65	18:11	5	1	3	4	6	1	0	0
2000-01	Buffalo	NHL	70	10	22	32	34	2	1	0	105	9.5	15	1159	50.4	45	62	16:34	13	5	0	5	8	0	2	1
	NHL Totals		318	65	98	163	186	13	3	10	509	12.8		3675	48.0	176	191	17:26	52	14	11	25	34	5	2	4

WHL East First All-Star Team (1995) • WHL East Second All-Star Team (1996)

BROWN, Doug

(BROWN, DUHG)

Right wing. Shoots right. 5'10", 185 lbs. Born, Southborough, MA, June 12, 1964.

1982-83	Boston College	ECAC	22	9	8	17	0	....	....	....	....	....	....	....	....	....	....	....	....	....	....	....	....	....	....	....
1983-84	Boston College	ECAC	38	11	10	21	6	....	....	....	....	....	....	....	....	....	....	....	....	....	....	....	....	....	....	....
1984-85	Boston College	H-East	45	37	31	68	10	....	....	....	....	....	....	....	....	....	....	....	....	....	....	....	....	....	....	....
1985-86	Boston College	H-East	38	16	40	56	16	....	....	....	....	....	....	....	....	....	....	....	....	....	....	....	....	....	....	....
1986-87	New Jersey	NHL	4	0	1	1	0	0	0	0	10	0.0	-4	....	....	....	....	....	....	....	....	....	....	....	....	....
	Maine Mariners	AHL	73	24	34	58	15	....	....	....	....	....	....	....	....	....	....	....	....	....	....	....	....	....	....	....
1987-88	New Jersey	NHL	70	14	11	25	20	1	4	2	112	12.5	7	....	....	....	....	....	19	5	1	6	6	0	1	1
	Utica Devils	AHL	2	0	2	2	2	....	....	....	....	....	....	....	....	....	....	....	....	....	....	....	....	....	....	....
1988-89	New Jersey	NHL	63	15	10	25	15	4	0	2	110	13.6	-7	....	....	....	....	....	....	....	....	....	....	....	....	....
	Utica Devils	AHL	4	1	4	5	0	....	....	....	....	....	....	....	....	....	....	....	....	....	....	....	....	....	....	....
1989-90	New Jersey	NHL	69	14	20	34	16	1	3	3	135	10.4	7	....	....	....	....	....	6	0	1	1	2	0	0	0
1990-91	New Jersey	NHL	58	14	16	30	4	0	2	2	122	11.5	18	....	....	....	....	....	7	2	2	4	2	0	1	0
1991-92	New Jersey	NHL	71	11	17	28	27	1	2	1	140	7.9	17	....	....	....	....	....	....	....	....	....	....	....	....	....
1992-93	New Jersey	NHL	15	0	5	5	2	0	0	0	17	0.0	3	....	....	....	....	....	....	....	....	....	....	....	....	....
	Utica Devils	AHL	25	11	17	28	8	....	....	....	....	....	....	....	....	....	....	....	....	....	....	....	....	....	....	....
1993-94	Pittsburgh	NHL	77	18	37	55	18	2	0	1	152	11.8	19	....	....	....	....	....	6	0	0	0	2	0	0	0
1994-95	Detroit	NHL	45	9	12	21	16	1	1	2	69	13.0	14	....	....	....	....	....	18	4	8	12	2	0	1	1
1995-96	Detroit	NHL	62	12	15	27	4	0	1	1	115	10.4	11	....	....	....	....	....	13	3	3	6	4	0	1	0
1996-97♦	Detroit	NHL	49	6	7	13	8	1	0	0	69	8.7	-3	....	....	....	....	....	14	3	3	6	2	0	0	0
1997-98♦	Detroit	NHL	80	19	23	42	12	6	1	5	145	13.1	17	....	....	....	....	....	9	4	2	6	0	3	0	1
1998-99	Detroit	NHL	80	9	19	28	42	3	1	1	180	5.0	5	235	52.8	33	27	13:47	10	2	2	4	4	1	0	1

Season	Club	League	GP	G	A	Pts	PIM	PP	SH	GW	S	%	+/-	TF	F%	H	SB	Min	GP	G	A	Pts	PIM	PP	SH	GW
			Regular Season																Playoffs							
99-2000	**Detroit**	**NHL**	**51**	**10**	**8**	**18**	**12**	**0**	**1**	**0**	**67**	**14.9**	**8**	**95**	**41.1**	**27**	**15**	**12:53**	**3**	**0**	**1**	**1**	**0**	**0**	**0**	**0**
2000-01	**Detroit**	**NHL**	**60**	**9**	**13**	**22**	**14**	**2**	**1**	**1**	**91**	**9.9**	**0**	**234**	**52.6**	**38**	**24**	**11:14**	**4**	**0**	**0**	**0**	**2**	**0**	**0**	**0**
	NHL Totals		**854**	**160**	**214**	**374**	**210**	**22**	**17**	**21**	**1534**	**10.4**		**564**	**50.7**	**98**	**66**	**12:45**	**109**	**23**	**23**	**46**	**26**	**4**	**4**	**4**

Hockey East Second All-Star Team (1985, 1986)

Signed as a free agent by **New Jersey**, August 6, 1986. Signed as a free agent by **Pittsburgh**, September 28, 1993. Claimed by **Detroit** from **Pittsburgh** in NHL Waiver Draft, January 18, 1995. Claimed by **Nashville** from **Detroit** in Expansion Draft, June 26, 1998. Traded to **Detroit** by **Nashville** for Petr Sykora, Detroit's 3rd round choice (later traded to Edmonton - Edmonton selected Mike Comrie) and 4th round compensatory choice (Alexander Krevsun) in 1999 Entry Draft), July 14, 1998.

BROWN, Kevin

(BROWN, KEH-vihn)

Right wing. Shoots right. 6'1", 212 lbs. Born, Birmingham, England, May 11, 1974. Los Angeles' 3rd choice, 87th overall, in 1992 Entry Draft.

Season	Club	League	GP	G	A	Pts	PIM	PP	SH	GW	S	%	+/-	TF	F%	H	SB	Min	GP	G	A	Pts	PIM	PP	SH	GW
1989-90	Georgetown	OJHL-B	31	3	8	11	59																			
1990-91	Waterloo Hawks	OJHL-B	46	25	33	58	116																			
1991-92	Belleville Bulls	OHL	66	24	24	48	52												5	1	4	5	8			
1992-93	Belleville Bulls	OHL	6	2	5	7	4																			
	Detroit Jr. Wings	OHL	56	48	86	134	76												15	10	18	28	18			
1993-94	Detroit Jr. Wings	OHL	57	54	81	135	85												17	14	*26	*40	28			
1994-95	Phoenix	IHL	48	19	31	50	64																			
	Los Angeles	**NHL**	**23**	**2**	**3**	**5**	**18**	**0**	**0**	**0**	**25**	**8.0**	**−7**													
1995-96	**Los Angeles**	**NHL**	**7**	**1**	**0**	**1**	**4**	**0**	**0**	**0**	**9**	**11.1**	**−2**													
	Phoenix	IHL	45	10	16	26	39																			
	P.E.I. Senators	AHL	8	3	6	9	2												3	1	3	4	0			
1996-97	**Hartford**	**NHL**	**11**	**0**	**4**	**4**	**6**	**0**	**0**	**0**	**12**	**0.0**	**−6**													
	Springfield	AHL	48	32	16	48	45												17	*11	6	17	24			
1997-98	**Carolina**	**NHL**	**4**	**0**	**0**	**0**	**0**	**0**	**0**	**0**	**0**	**0.0**	**−2**													
	New Haven	AHL	67	28	44	72	65												3	0	2	2	0			
1998-99	**Edmonton**	**NHL**	**12**	**4**	**2**	**6**	**0**	**2**	**0**	**0**	**13**	**30.8**	**−2**	**1**	**0.0**	**19**	**3**	**9:11**								
	Hamilton Bulldogs	AHL	32	9	14	23	47																			
	Hartford	AHL	9	3	2	5	14												5	1	3	4	4			
99-2000	Hamilton Bulldogs	AHL	54	21	38	59	53												4	2	2	4	8			
	Edmonton	**NHL**	**7**	**0**	**0**	**0**	**0**	**0**	**0**	**0**	**5**	**0.0**	**0**	**1**	**0.0**	**6**	**1**	**8:21**	**1**	**0**	**0**	**0**	**0**	**0**	**0**	**0**
2000-01	Manchester Storm	Britain	36	17	32	49	118																			
	Phoenix Mustangs	WCHL	13	7	7	14	32																			
	Anchorage Aces	WCHL	10	10	10	20	8												3	2	3	5	20			
	NHL Totals		**64**	**7**	**9**	**16**	**28**	**2**	**0**	**0**	**64**	**10.9**		**2**	**0.0**	**25**	**4**	**8:53**	**1**	**0**	**0**	**0**	**0**	**0**	**0**	**0**

OHL Second All-Star Team (1993) • OHL First All-Star Team (1994) • Canadian Major Junior Second All-Star Team (1994)

Traded to **Ottawa** by **LA Kings** for Jaroslav Modry and Ottawa's 8th round choice (Stephen Valiquette) in 1996 Entry Draft, March 20, 1996. Traded to **Anaheim** by **Ottawa** for Mike Maneluk, July 1, 1996. Traded to **Hartford** by **Anaheim** for the rights to Espen Knutsen, October 1, 1996. Transferred to **Carolina** after **Hartford** franchise relocated, June 25, 1997. Signed as a free agent by **Edmonton**, August 14, 1998. Traded to **NY Rangers** by **Edmonton** for Vladimir Vorobiev, March 23, 1999. Signed as a free agent by **Edmonton**, March 7, 2000. Signed as a free agent by **Manchester** (Britain), September 10, 2000. Signed as a free agent by **Phoenix** (WCHL) after securing release from Manchester, February 16, 2001. Traded to **Anchorage** (WCHL) by **Phoenix** (WCHL) for Derry Minard, March 23, 2001.

BROWN, Mike

(BROWN, MIGHK) **VAN.**

Left wing. Shoots left. 6'5", 185 lbs. Born, Surrey, B.C., April 27, 1979. Florida's 1st choice, 20th overall, in 1997 Entry Draft.

Season	Club	League	GP	G	A	Pts	PIM	PP	SH	GW	S	%	+/-	TF	F%	H	SB	Min	GP	G	A	Pts	PIM	PP	SH	GW
1993-94	Penticton	BCJHL	50	52	48	100	100																			
1994-95	Merritt Luckies	BCJHL	45	3	4	7	145																			
1995-96	Red Deer Rebels	WHL	62	4	5	9	125												10	0	0	0	18			
1996-97	Red Deer Rebels	WHL	70	19	13	32	243												16	1	2	3	47			
1997-98	Kamloops Blazers	WHL	72	23	33	56	305												7	2	1	3	22			
1998-99	Kamloops Blazers	WHL	69	28	16	44	*285												15	3	7	10	*68			
99-2000	Syracuse Crunch	AHL	71	13	18	31	284												4	0	0	0	0			
2000-01	**Vancouver**	**NHL**	**1**	**0**	**0**	**0**	**5**	**0**	**0**	**0**	**1**	**0.0**	**0**	**0**	**0.0**	**1**	**0**	**4:48**								
	Kansas City	IHL	78	14	13	27	214																			
	NHL Totals		**1**	**0**	**0**	**0**	**5**	**0**	**0**	**0**	**1**	**0.0**		**0**	**0.0**	**1**	**0**	**4:48**								

Traded to **Vancouver** by **Florida** with Ed Jovanovski, Dave Gagner, Kevin Weekes and Florida's 1st round choice (Nathan Smith) in 2000 Entry Draft for Pavel Bure, Bret Hedican, Brad Ference and Vancouver's 3rd round choice (Robert Fried) in 2000 Entry Draft, January 17, 1999.

BROWN, Rob

(BROWN, RAWB)

Right wing. Shoots left. 5'10", 177 lbs. Born, Kingston, Ont., April 10, 1968. Pittsburgh's 4th choice, 67th overall, in 1986 Entry Draft.

Season	Club	League	GP	G	A	Pts	PIM	PP	SH	GW	S	%	+/-	TF	F%	H	SB	Min	GP	G	A	Pts	PIM	PP	SH	GW
1982-83	St. Albert Royals	AAHA	61	137	122	259	200																			
1983-84	St. Albert Saints	AJHL	1	0	0	0	0																			
	Kamloops Oilers	WHL	50	16	42	58	80												15	1	2	3	17			
1984-85	Kamloops Blazers	WHL	60	29	50	79	95												15	8	8	26	28			
1985-86	Kamloops Blazers	WHL	69	58	*115	*173	171												16	*18	*28	*46	14			
1986-87	Kamloops Blazers	WHL	63	*76	*136	*212	101												5	6	5	11	6			
1987-88	**Pittsburgh**	**NHL**	**51**	**24**	**20**	**44**	**56**	**13**	**0**	**1**	**80**	**30.0**	**8**													
1988-89	**Pittsburgh**	**NHL**	**68**	**49**	**66**	**115**	**118**	**24**	**0**	**6**	**169**	**29.0**	**27**						**11**	**5**	**3**	**8**	**22**	**1**	**0**	**3**
1989-90	**Pittsburgh**	**NHL**	**80**	**33**	**47**	**80**	**102**	**12**	**0**	**3**	**157**	**21.0**	**−10**													
1990-91	**Pittsburgh**	**NHL**	**25**	**6**	**10**	**16**	**31**	**2**	**0**	**0**	**32**	**18.8**	**0**													
	Hartford	**NHL**	**44**	**18**	**24**	**42**	**101**	**10**	**0**	**2**	**94**	**19.1**	**−7**						**5**	**1**	**0**	**1**	**7**	**1**	**0**	**1**
1991-92	**Hartford**	**NHL**	**42**	**16**	**15**	**31**	**39**	**13**	**0**	**2**	**65**	**24.6**	**−14**													
	Chicago	**NHL**	**25**	**5**	**11**	**16**	**34**	**3**	**0**	**1**	**41**	**12.2**	**−1**						**8**	**2**	**4**	**6**	**4**	**1**	**0**	**0**
1992-93	**Chicago**	**NHL**	**15**	**1**	**6**	**7**	**33**	**0**	**0**	**0**	**16**	**6.3**	**6**													
	Indianapolis Ice	IHL	19	14	19	33	32												2	0	1	1	2			
1993-94	**Dallas**	**NHL**	**1**	**0**	**0**	**0**	**0**	**0**	**0**	**0**	**1**	**0.0**	**−1**													
	Kalamazoo Wings	IHL	79	42	*113	*155	188												5	1	3	4	6			
1994-95	Phoenix	IHL	69	34	73	107	135												9	4	12	16	0			
	Los Angeles	**NHL**	**2**	**0**	**0**	**0**	**0**	**0**	**0**	**0**	**1**	**0.0**	**−2**													
1995-96	Chicago Wolves	IHL	79	52	*91	*143	100												9	4	11	15	6			
1996-97	Chicago Wolves	IHL	76	37	*80	*117	98												4	2	4	6	16			
1997-98	**Pittsburgh**	**NHL**	**82**	**15**	**25**	**40**	**59**	**4**	**0**	**4**	**172**	**8.7**	**−1**						**6**	**1**	**0**	**1**	**4**	**1**	**0**	**0**
1998-99	**Pittsburgh**	**NHL**	**58**	**13**	**11**	**24**	**16**	**9**	**0**	**1**	**78**	**16.7**	**−15**	**18**	**38.9**	**115**	**18**	**12:35**	**13**	**2**	**5**	**7**	**8**	**2**	**0**	**0**
99-2000	**Pittsburgh**	**NHL**	**50**	**10**	**13**	**23**	**10**	**4**	**0**	**3**	**73**	**13.7**	**−13**	**14**	**35.7**	**70**	**6**	**10:37**	**11**	**1**	**2**	**3**	**0**	**0**	**0**	**0**
2000-01	Chicago Wolves	IHL	75	24	53	77	99												16	4	13	17	26			
	NHL Totals		**543**	**190**	**248**	**438**	**599**	**94**	**0**	**23**	**979**	**19.4**		**32**	**21.9**	**185**	**24**	**12:35**	**54**	**12**	**14**	**26**	**45**	**6**	**0**	**4**

WHL West First All-Star Team (1986, 1987) • Canadian Major Junior Player of the Year (1987) • IHL First All-Star Team (1994, 1996, 1997) • Won Leo P. Lamoureux Memorial Trophy (Top Scorer - IHL) (1994, 1996, 1997) • Won James Gatschene Memorial Trophy (MVP - IHL) (1994) • IHL Second All-Star Team (1995) • Played in NHL All-Star Game (1989)

Traded to **Hartford** by **Pittsburgh** for Scott Young, December 21, 1990. Traded to **Chicago** by **Hartford** for Steve Konroyd, January 24, 1992. Signed as a free agent by **Dallas**, August 12, 1993. Signed as a free agent by **LA Kings**, June 14, 1994. Signed as a free agent by **Pittsburgh**, October 1, 1997.

BROWN, Sean

(BROWN, SHAWN) **EDM.**

Defense. Shoots left. 6'3", 205 lbs. Born, Oshawa, Ont., November 5, 1976. Boston's 2nd choice, 21st overall, in 1995 Entry Draft.

Season	Club	League	GP	G	A	Pts	PIM	PP	SH	GW	S	%	+/-	TF	F%	H	SB	Min	GP	G	A	Pts	PIM	PP	SH	GW
1992-93	Oshawa Legion	OMHA	15	0	1	1	9																			
1993-94	Wellington Dukes	MTJHL	32	5	14	19	165																			
	Belleville Bulls	OHL	28	1	2	3	53												8	0	0	0	17			
1994-95	Belleville Bulls	OHL	58	2	16	18	200												16	4	2	6	*67			
1995-96	Belleville Bulls	OHL	37	10	23	33	150																			
	Sarnia Sting	OHL	26	8	17	25	112												10	1	0	1	38			
1996-97	**Edmonton**	**NHL**	**5**	**0**	**0**	**0**	**4**	**0**	**0**	**0**	**2**	**0.0**	**−1**													
	Hamilton Bulldogs	AHL	61	1	7	8	238												19	1	0	1	47			
1997-98	**Edmonton**	**NHL**	**18**	**0**	**1**	**1**	**43**	**0**	**0**	**0**	**9**	**0.0**	**−1**													
	Hamilton Bulldogs	AHL	43	4	6	10	166												6	0	2	2	38			
1998-99	**Edmonton**	**NHL**	**51**	**0**	**7**	**7**	**188**	**0**	**0**	**0**	**27**	**0.0**	**1**	**0**	**0.0**	**104**	**29**	**12:14**	**1**	**0**	**0**	**0**	**10**	**0**	**0**	**0**

			Regular Season																Playoffs							
Season	Club	League	GP	G	A	Pts	PIM	PP	SH	GW	S	%	+/-	TF	F%	H	SB	Min	GP	G	A	Pts	PIM	PP	SH	GW
99-2000	Edmonton	NHL	72	4	8	12	192	0	0	2	36	11.1	1	0	0.0	146	46	12:41	3	0	0	0	23	0	0	0
2000-01	Edmonton	NHL	62	2	3	5	110	0	0	0	30	6.7	2	0	0.0	106	32	11:07	....	....	....	....	....	....	....	....
	NHL Totals		**208**	**6**	**19**	**25**	**537**	**0**	**0**	**2**	**104**	**5.8**		**0**	**0.0**	**356**	**107**	**12:02**	**4**	**0**	**0**	**0**	**33**	**0**	**0**	**0**

OHL Second All-Star Team (1996)

Rights traded to **Edmonton** by **Boston** with Mariusz Czerkawski and Boston's 1st round choice (Matthieu Descoteaux) in 1996 Entry Draft for Bill Ranford, January 11, 1996.

BRULE, Steve (broo-LAY, STEEV) DET.

Right wing. Shoots right. 6', 200 lbs. Born, Montreal, Que., January 15, 1975. New Jersey's 6th choice, 143rd overall, in 1993 Entry Draft.

Season	Club	League	GP	G	A	Pts	PIM	PP	SH	GW	S	%	+/-	TF	F%	H	SB	Min	GP	G	A	Pts	PIM	PP	SH	GW
1990-91	Montreal Etoiles	QAHA	32	25	30	55	20	....	....	....	....	....	....	....	....	....	....	....	....	....	....	....	....	....	....	....
1991-92	Mtl-Bourassa	QAAA	40	33	37	70	46	....	....	....	....	....	....	....	....	....	....	....	9	9	7	16	10	....	....	....
1992-93	St-Jean Lynx	QMJHL	70	33	47	80	46	....	....	....	....	....	....	....	....	....	....	....	4	0	0	0	9	....	....	....
1993-94	St-Jean Lynx	QMJHL	66	41	64	105	46	....	....	....	....	....	....	....	....	....	....	....	5	2	1	3	0	....	....	....
1994-95	St-Jean Lynx	QMJHL	69	44	64	108	42	....	....	....	....	....	....	....	....	....	....	....	7	3	4	7	8	....	....	....
	Albany River Rats	AHL	3	1	4	5	0	....	....	....	....	....	....	....	....	....	....	....	14	9	5	14	4	....	....	....
1995-96	Albany River Rats	AHL	80	30	21	51	37	....	....	....	....	....	....	....	....	....	....	....	4	0	0	0	17	....	....	....
1996-97	Albany River Rats	AHL	79	28	48	76	27	....	....	....	....	....	....	....	....	....	....	....	16	7	7	14	12	....	....	....
1997-98	Albany River Rats	AHL	80	34	43	77	34	....	....	....	....	....	....	....	....	....	....	....	13	8	3	11	4	....	....	....
1998-99	Albany River Rats	AHL	78	32	52	84	35	....	....	....	....	....	....	....	....	....	....	....	5	3	1	4	4	....	....	....
99-2000	Albany River Rats	AHL	75	30	46	76	18	....	....	....	....	....	....	....	....	....	....	....	5	1	2	3	0	....	....	....
	♦ **New Jersey**	**NHL**	....	....	....	....	....	....	....	....	....	....	....	....	....	....	....	....	**1**	**0**	**0**	**0**	**0**	**0**	**0**	**0**
2000-01	Manitoba Moose	IHL	78	21	48	69	22	....	....	....	....	....	....	....	....	....	....	....	13	3	10	13	12	....	....	....
	NHL Totals		....	....	....	....	....	....	....	....	....	....		....	....	....	....	....	**1**	**0**	**0**	**0**	**0**	**0**	**0**	**0**

QMJHL All-Rookie Team (1993) • Won Michel Bergeron Trophy (Top Rookie Forward - QMJHL) (1993) • QMJHL Second All-Star Team (1995)

Signed as a free agent by **Detroit**, July 20, 2000.

BRUNET, Benoit (broo-NAY, BEHN-wah) MTL.

Left wing. Shoots left. 6', 203 lbs. Born, Ste-Anne-de-Bellevue, Que., August 24, 1968. Montreal's 2nd choice, 27th overall, in 1986 Entry Draft.

Season	Club	League	GP	G	A	Pts	PIM	PP	SH	GW	S	%	+/-	TF	F%	H	SB	Min	GP	G	A	Pts	PIM	PP	SH	GW
1985-86	Hull Olympiques	QMJHL	71	33	37	70	81	....	....	....	....	....	....	....	....	....	....	....	....	....	....	....	....	....	....	....
1986-87	Hull Olympiques	QMJHL	60	43	67	110	105	....	....	....	....	....	....	....	....	....	....	....	6	7	5	12	8	....	....	....
1987-88	Hull Olympiques	QMJHL	62	54	89	143	131	....	....	....	....	....	....	....	....	....	....	....	10	3	10	13	11	....	....	....
1988-89	**Montreal**	**NHL**	**2**	**0**	**1**	**1**	**0**	**0**	**0**	**0**	**1**	**0.0**	**0**	....	....	....	....	....	....	....	....	....	....	....	....	....
	Sherbrooke	AHL	73	41	*76	117	95	....	....	....	....	....	....	....	....	....	....	....	6	2	0	2	4	....	....	....
1989-90	Sherbrooke	AHL	72	32	35	67	82	....	....	....	....	....	....	....	....	....	....	....	12	8	7	15	20	....	....	....
1990-91	**Montreal**	**NHL**	**17**	**1**	**3**	**4**	**0**	**0**	**0**	**0**	**12**	**8.3**	**–1**	....	....	....	....	....	....	....	....	....	....	....	....	....
	Fredericton	AHL	24	13	18	31	16	....	....	....	....	....	....	....	....	....	....	....	6	5	6	11	2	....	....	....
1991-92	**Montreal**	**NHL**	**18**	**4**	**6**	**10**	**14**	**0**	**0**	**0**	**37**	**10.8**	**4**	....	....	....	....	....	....	....	....	....	....	....	....	....
	Fredericton	AHL	6	7	9	16	27	....	....	....	....	....	....	....	....	....	....	....	....	....	....	....	....	....	....	....
1992-93 ♦	**Montreal**	**NHL**	**47**	**10**	**15**	**25**	**19**	**0**	**0**	**1**	**71**	**14.1**	**13**	....	....	....	....	....	**20**	**2**	**8**	**10**	**8**	**1**	**0**	**1**
1993-94	**Montreal**	**NHL**	**71**	**10**	**20**	**30**	**20**	**0**	**3**	**1**	**92**	**10.9**	**14**	....	....	....	....	....	**7**	**1**	**4**	**5**	**16**	**0**	**0**	**0**
1994-95	**Montreal**	**NHL**	**45**	**7**	**18**	**25**	**16**	**1**	**1**	**2**	**80**	**8.8**	**7**	....	....	....	....	....	....	....	....	....	....	....	....	....
1995-96	**Montreal**	**NHL**	**26**	**7**	**8**	**15**	**17**	**3**	**1**	**4**	**48**	**14.6**	**–4**	....	....	....	....	....	**3**	**0**	**2**	**2**	**0**	**0**	**0**	**0**
	Fredericton	AHL	3	2	1	3	6	....	....	....	....	....	....	....	....	....	....	....	....	....	....	....	....	....	....	....
1996-97	**Montreal**	**NHL**	**39**	**10**	**13**	**23**	**14**	**2**	**0**	**2**	**63**	**15.9**	**6**	....	....	....	....	....	**4**	**1**	**3**	**4**	**4**	**0**	**1**	**0**
1997-98	**Montreal**	**NHL**	**68**	**12**	**20**	**32**	**61**	**1**	**2**	**2**	**87**	**13.8**	**11**	....	....	....	....	....	**8**	**1**	**0**	**1**	**4**	**0**	**0**	**1**
1998-99	**Montreal**	**NHL**	**60**	**14**	**17**	**31**	**31**	**4**	**2**	**0**	**115**	**12.2**	**–1**	**375**	**41.6**	**27**	**37**	**17:47**	....	....	....	....	....	....	....	....
99-2000	**Montreal**	**NHL**	**50**	**14**	**15**	**29**	**13**	**6**	**1**	**2**	**103**	**13.6**	**3**	**293**	**42.7**	**27**	**22**	**17:59**	....	....	....	....	....	....	....	....
2000-01	**Montreal**	**NHL**	**35**	**3**	**11**	**14**	**12**	**0**	**0**	**0**	**61**	**4.9**	**–4**	**24**	**45.8**	**20**	**21**	**16:40**	....	....	....	....	....	....	....	....
	NHL Totals		**478**	**92**	**147**	**239**	**217**	**17**	**10**	**14**	**770**	**11.9**		**692**	**42.2**	**74**	**80**	**17:35**	**42**	**5**	**17**	**22**	**32**	**1**	**1**	**2**

QMJHL Second All-Star Team (1987) • AHL First All-Star Team (1989)

• Missed majority of 2000-01 season recovering from knee injury suffered in game vs. Pittsburgh, December 16, 2000.

BRUNETTE, Andrew (broo-NEHT, AN-droo) MIN.

Left wing. Shoots left. 6'1", 210 lbs. Born, Sudbury, Ont., August 24, 1973. Washington's 6th choice, 174th overall, in 1993 Entry Draft.

Season	Club	League	GP	G	A	Pts	PIM	PP	SH	GW	S	%	+/-	TF	F%	H	SB	Min	GP	G	A	Pts	PIM	PP	SH	GW
1989-90	Rayside-Balfour	NOHA	32	38	*65	*103	....	....	....	....	....	....	....	....	....	....	....	....	....	....	....	....	....	....	....	....
	Rayside-Balfour	NOJHA	4	1	1	2	0	....	....	....	....	....	....	....	....	....	....	....	....	....	....	....	....	....	....	....
1990-91	Owen Sound	OHL	63	15	20	35	15	....	....	....	....	....	....	....	....	....	....	....	....	....	....	....	....	....	....	....
1991-92	Owen Sound	OHL	66	51	47	98	42	....	....	....	....	....	....	....	....	....	....	....	5	5	0	5	8	....	....	....
1992-93	Owen Sound	OHL	66	*62	*100	*162	91	....	....	....	....	....	....	....	....	....	....	....	8	8	6	14	16	....	....	....
1993-94	Portland Pirates	AHL	23	9	11	20	10	....	....	....	....	....	....	....	....	....	....	....	2	0	1	1	0	....	....	....
	Providence Bruins	AHL	3	0	0	0	0	....	....	....	....	....	....	....	....	....	....	....	....	....	....	....	....	....	....	....
	Hampton Roads	ECHL	20	12	18	30	32	....	....	....	....	....	....	....	....	....	....	....	7	7	6	13	18	....	....	....
1994-95	Portland Pirates	AHL	79	30	50	80	53	....	....	....	....	....	....	....	....	....	....	....	7	3	3	6	10	....	....	....
1995-96	**Washington**	**NHL**	**11**	**3**	**3**	**6**	**0**	**0**	**0**	**1**	**16**	**18.8**	**5**	....	....	....	....	....	**6**	**1**	**3**	**4**	**0**	**0**	**0**	**0**
	Portland Pirates	AHL	69	28	66	94	125	....	....	....	....	....	....	....	....	....	....	....	20	11	18	29	15	....	....	....
1996-97	**Washington**	**NHL**	**23**	**4**	**7**	**11**	**12**	**2**	**0**	**0**	**23**	**17.4**	**–3**	....	....	....	....	....	....	....	....	....	....	....	....	....
	Portland Pirates	AHL	50	22	51	73	48	....	....	....	....	....	....	....	....	....	....	....	5	1	2	3	0	....	....	....
1997-98	**Washington**	**NHL**	**28**	**11**	**12**	**23**	**12**	**4**	**0**	**2**	**42**	**26.2**	**2**	....	....	....	....	....	....	....	....	....	....	....	....	....
	Portland Pirates	AHL	43	21	46	67	64	....	....	....	....	....	....	....	....	....	....	....	10	1	11	12	12	....	....	....
1998-99	**Nashville**	**NHL**	**77**	**11**	**20**	**31**	**26**	**7**	**0**	**1**	**65**	**16.9**	**–10**	**8**	**50.0**	**13**	**10**	**13:13**	....	....	....	....	....	....	....	....
99-2000	**Atlanta**	**NHL**	**81**	**23**	**27**	**50**	**30**	**9**	**0**	**2**	**107**	**21.5**	**–32**	**8**	**25.0**	**45**	**17**	**15:42**	....	....	....	....	....	....	....	....
2000-01	**Atlanta**	**NHL**	**77**	**15**	**44**	**59**	**26**	**6**	**0**	**4**	**104**	**14.4**	**–5**	**11**	**54.6**	**38**	**12**	**16:58**	....	....	....	....	....	....	....	....
	NHL Totals		**297**	**67**	**113**	**180**	**106**	**28**	**0**	**10**	**357**	**18.8**		**27**	**44.4**	**96**	**39**	**15:18**	**6**	**1**	**3**	**4**	**0**	**0**	**0**	**0**

OHL First All-Star Team (1993) • Canadian Major Junior Second All-Star Team (1993) • AHL Second All-Star Team (1995)

Claimed by **Nashville** from **Washington** in Expansion Draft, June 26, 1998. Traded to **Atlanta** by **Nashville** for Atlanta's 5th round choice (Matt Hendricks) in 2000 Entry Draft, June 21, 1999. Signed as a free agent by **Minnesota**, July 17, 2001.

BRYLIN, Sergei (BRIH-lin, SAIR-gay) N.J.

Center. Shoots left. 5'10", 190 lbs. Born, Moscow, USSR, January 13, 1974. New Jersey's 2nd choice, 42nd overall, in 1992 Entry Draft.

Season	Club	League	GP	G	A	Pts	PIM	PP	SH	GW	S	%	+/-	TF	F%	H	SB	Min	GP	G	A	Pts	PIM	PP	SH	GW
1991-92	CSKA Moscow	CIS	44	1	6	7	4	....	....	....	....	....	....	....	....	....	....	....	....	....	....	....	....	....	....	....
1992-93	CSKA Moscow	CIS	42	5	4	9	36	....	....	....	....	....	....	....	....	....	....	....	....	....	....	....	....	....	....	....
1993-94	CSKA Moscow	CIS	39	4	6	10	36	....	....	....	....	....	....	....	....	....	....	....	3	1	0	1	2	....	....	....
	Russian Penguins	IHL	13	4	5	9	18	....	....	....	....	....	....	....	....	....	....	....	....	....	....	....	....	....	....	....
1994-95	Albany River Rats	AHL	63	19	35	54	78	....	....	....	....	....	....	....	....	....	....	....	....	....	....	....	....	....	....	....
	♦ **New Jersey**	**NHL**	**26**	**6**	**8**	**14**	**8**	**0**	**0**	**0**	**41**	**14.6**	**12**	....	....	....	....	....	**12**	**1**	**2**	**3**	**4**	**0**	**0**	**0**
1995-96	**New Jersey**	**NHL**	**50**	**4**	**5**	**9**	**26**	**0**	**0**	**1**	**51**	**7.8**	**–2**	....	....	....	....	....	....	....	....	....	....	....	....	....
1996-97	**New Jersey**	**NHL**	**29**	**2**	**2**	**4**	**20**	**0**	**0**	**0**	**34**	**5.9**	**–13**	....	....	....	....	....	....	....	....	....	....	....	....	....
	Albany River Rats	AHL	43	17	24	41	38	....	....	....	....	....	....	....	....	....	....	....	16	4	8	12	12	....	....	....
1997-98	**New Jersey**	**NHL**	**18**	**2**	**3**	**5**	**0**	**0**	**0**	**0**	**20**	**10.0**	**4**	....	....	....	....	....	....	....	....	....	....	....	....	....
	Albany River Rats	AHL	44	21	22	43	60	....	....	....	....	....	....	....	....	....	....	....	....	....	....	....	....	....	....	....
1998-99	**New Jersey**	**NHL**	**47**	**5**	**10**	**15**	**28**	**3**	**0**	**1**	**51**	**9.8**	**8**	**184**	**50.5**	**61**	**7**	**12:55**	**5**	**3**	**1**	**4**	**4**	**1**	**0**	**1**
99-2000 ♦	**New Jersey**	**NHL**	**64**	**9**	**11**	**20**	**20**	**1**	**0**	**1**	**84**	**10.7**	**0**	**72**	**41.7**	**107**	**21**	**13:23**	**17**	**3**	**5**	**8**	**0**	**0**	**0**	**0**
2000-01	**New Jersey**	**NHL**	**75**	**23**	**29**	**52**	**24**	**3**	**1**	**0**	**130**	**17.7**	**25**	**43**	**44.2**	**108**	**16**	**15:31**	**20**	**3**	**4**	**7**	**6**	**1**	**0**	**1**
	NHL Totals		**309**	**51**	**68**	**119**	**126**	**7**	**1**	**3**	**411**	**12.4**		**299**	**47.5**	**276**	**44**	**14:07**	**54**	**10**	**12**	**22**	**14**	**2**	**0**	**2**

BUCHBERGER, Kelly (BUK-buhr-guhr, KEHL-lee) L.A.

Right wing. Shoots left. 6'2", 210 lbs. Born, Langenburg, Sask., December 2, 1966. Edmonton's 8th choice, 188th overall, in 1985 Entry Draft.

Season	Club	League	GP	G	A	Pts	PIM	PP	SH	GW	S	%	+/-	TF	F%	H	SB	Min	GP	G	A	Pts	PIM	PP	SH	GW
1983-84	Melville	SJHL	60	14	11	25	139	....	....	....	....	....	....	....	....	....	....	....	....	....	....	....	....	....	....	....
1984-85	Moose Jaw	WHL	51	12	17	29	114	....	....	....	....	....	....	....	....	....	....	....	....	....	....	....	....	....	....	....
1985-86	Moose Jaw	WHL	72	14	22	36	206	....	....	....	....	....	....	....	....	....	....	....	13	11	4	15	37	....	....	....
1986-87	Nova Scotia	AHL	70	12	20	32	257	....	....	....	....	....	....	....	....	....	....	....	5	0	1	1	23	....	....	....
	♦ **Edmonton**	**NHL**	....	....	....	....	....	....	....	....	....	....	....	....	....	....	....	....	**3**	**0**	**1**	**1**	**5**	**0**	**0**	**0**
1987-88	**Edmonton**	**NHL**	**19**	**1**	**0**	**1**	**81**	**0**	**0**	**0**	**10**	**10.0**	**–1**	....	....	....	....	....	....	....	....	....	....	....	....	....
	Nova Scotia	AHL	49	21	23	44	206	....	....	....	....	....	....	....	....	....	....	....	2	0	0	0	11	....	....	....

Season	Club	League	Regular Season																Playoffs							
			GP	G	A	Pts	PIM	PP	SH	GW	S	%	+/-	TF	F%	H	SB	Min	GP	G	A	Pts	PIM	PP	SH	GW
1988-89	**Edmonton**	**NHL**	**66**	**5**	**9**	**14**	**234**	**1**	**0**	**1**	**57**	**8.8**	**–14**													
1989-90♦	**Edmonton**	**NHL**	**55**	**2**	**6**	**8**	**168**	**0**	**0**	**2**	**35**	**5.7**	**–8**						**19**	**0**	**5**	**5**	**13**	**0**	**0**	**0**
1990-91	**Edmonton**	**NHL**	**64**	**3**	**1**	**4**	**160**	**0**	**0**	**2**	**54**	**5.6**	**–6**						**12**	**2**	**1**	**3**	**25**	**0**	**0**	**0**
1991-92	**Edmonton**	**NHL**	**79**	**20**	**24**	**44**	**157**	**0**	**4**	**3**	**90**	**22.2**	**9**						**16**	**1**	**4**	**5**	**32**	**0**	**0**	**0**
1992-93	**Edmonton**	**NHL**	**83**	**12**	**18**	**30**	**133**	**1**	**2**	**3**	**92**	**13.0**	**–27**													
1993-94	**Edmonton**	**NHL**	**84**	**3**	**18**	**21**	**199**	**0**	**0**	**0**	**93**	**3.2**	**–20**													
1994-95	**Edmonton**	**NHL**	**48**	**7**	**17**	**24**	**82**	**2**	**1**	**5**	**73**	**9.6**	**0**													
1995-96	**Edmonton**	**NHL**	**82**	**11**	**14**	**25**	**184**	**0**	**2**	**3**	**119**	**9.2**	**–20**													
1996-97	**Edmonton**	**NHL**	**81**	**8**	**30**	**38**	**159**	**0**	**0**	**3**	**78**	**10.3**	**4**						**12**	**5**	**2**	**7**	**16**	**0**	**0**	**1**
1997-98	**Edmonton**	**NHL**	**82**	**6**	**17**	**23**	**122**	**1**	**1**	**1**	**86**	**7.0**	**–10**						**12**	**1**	**2**	**3**	**25**	**0**	**0**	**0**
1998-99	**Edmonton**	**NHL**	**52**	**4**	**4**	**8**	**68**	**0**	**2**	**1**	**29**	**13.8**	**–6**	**23**	**26.1**	**41**	**27**	**11:49**	**4**	**0**	**0**	**0**	**0**	**0**	**0**	**0**
99-2000	**Atlanta**	**NHL**	**68**	**5**	**12**	**17**	**139**	**0**	**0**	**0**	**56**	**8.9**	**–34**	**577**	**45.6**	**137**	**47**	**16:21**								
	Los Angeles	**NHL**	**13**	**2**	**1**	**3**	**13**	**0**	**0**	**0**	**20**	**10.0**	**–2**	**6**	**16.7**	**42**	**5**	**14:43**	**4**	**0**	**0**	**0**	**4**	**0**	**0**	**0**
2000-01	**Los Angeles**	**NHL**	**82**	**6**	**14**	**20**	**75**	**0**	**0**	**1**	**66**	**9.1**	**–10**	**155**	**40.7**	**175**	**52**	**14:26**	**8**	**1**	**0**	**1**	**2**	**0**	**0**	**0**
	NHL Totals		**958**	**95**	**185**	**280**	**1974**	**5**	**12**	**25**	**958**	**9.9**		**761**	**43.8**	**395**	**131**	**14:25**	**90**	**10**	**15**	**25**	**122**	**0**	**0**	**1**

Claimed by **Atlanta** from **Edmonton** in Expansion Draft, June 25, 1999. Traded to **Los Angeles** by **Atlanta** with Nelson Emerson for Donald Audette and Frantisek Kaberle, March 13, 2000.

BULIS, Jan

(BOO-lihs, YAHN) **MTL.**

Center. Shoots left. 6'1", 208 lbs. Born, Pardubice, Czech., March 18, 1978. Washington's 3rd choice, 43rd overall, in 1996 Entry Draft.

Season	Club	League	GP	G	A	Pts	PIM	PP	SH	GW	S	%	+/-	TF	F%	H	SB	Min	Playoffs GP	G	A	Pts	PIM	PP	SH	GW
1993-94	HC Pardubice-Jr.	Cze-Rep	25	16	11	27																				
1994-95	Kelowna Spartans	BCJHL	51	23	25	48	36												17	7	9	16	0			
1995-96	Barrie Colts	OHL	59	29	30	59	22												7	2	3	5	2			
1996-97	Barrie Colts	OHL	64	42	61	103	42												9	3	7	10	10			
1997-98	Kingston	OHL	2	0	1	1	0												12	8	10	18	12			
	Washington	**NHL**	**48**	**5**	**11**	**16**	**18**	**0**	**0**	**0**	**37**	**13.5**	**–5**													
	Portland Pirates	AHL	3	1	4	5	12																			
1998-99	**Washington**	**NHL**	**38**	**7**	**16**	**23**	**6**	**3**	**0**	**3**	**57**	**12.3**	**3**	**599**	**48.9**	**48**	**3**	**14:27**								
	Cincinnati	IHL	10	2	2	4	14																			
99-2000	**Washington**	**NHL**	**56**	**9**	**22**	**31**	**30**	**0**	**0**	**1**	**92**	**9.8**	**7**	**609**	**45.5**	**66**	**14**	**13:55**								
2000-01	**Washington**	**NHL**	**39**	**5**	**13**	**18**	**26**	**1**	**0**	**0**	**41**	**12.2**	**0**	**224**	**46.9**	**34**	**11**	**11:53**								
	Portland Pirates	AHL	4	0	2	2	0																			
	Montreal	**NHL**	**12**	**0**	**5**	**5**	**0**	**0**	**0**	**0**	**20**	**0.0**	**–1**	**230**	**48.3**	**8**	**6**	**18:25**								
	NHL Totals		**193**	**26**	**67**	**93**	**80**	**4**	**0**	**4**	**247**	**10.5**		**1662**	**47.3**	**156**	**34**	**13:53**								

Traded to **Montreal** by **Washington** with Richard Zednik and Washington's 1st round choice (Alexander Perezhogin) in 2001 Entry Draft for Trevor Linden, Dainius Zubrus and New Jersey's 2nd round choice (previously acquired, later traded to Tampa Bay - Tampa Bay selected Andreas Holmqvist) in 2001 Entry Draft, March 13, 2001.

BURE, Pavel

(boo-RAY, PAH-vehl) **FLA.**

Right wing. Shoots left. 5'10", 189 lbs. Born, Moscow, USSR, March 31, 1971. Vancouver's 4th choice, 113th overall, in 1989 Entry Draft.

Season	Club	League	GP	G	A	Pts	PIM	PP	SH	GW	S	%	+/-	TF	F%	H	SB	Min	Playoffs GP	G	A	Pts	PIM	PP	SH	GW
1987-88	CSKA Moscow	USSR	5	1	1	2	0																			
1988-89	CSKA Moscow	USSR	32	17	9	26	8																			
1989-90	CSKA Moscow	USSR	46	14	10	24	20																			
1990-91	CSKA Moscow	USSR	44	35	11	46	24																			
1991-92	**Vancouver**	**NHL**	**65**	**34**	**26**	**60**	**30**	**7**	**3**	**6**	**268**	**12.7**	**0**						**13**	**6**	**4**	**10**	**14**	**0**	**0**	**0**
1992-93	**Vancouver**	**NHL**	**83**	**60**	**50**	**110**	**69**	**13**	**7**	**9**	**407**	**14.7**	**35**						**12**	**5**	**7**	**12**	**8**	**0**	**0**	**1**
1993-94	**Vancouver**	**NHL**	**76**	***60**	**47**	**107**	**86**	**25**	**4**	**9**	**374**	**16.0**	**1**						**24**	***16**	**15**	**31**	**40**	**3**	**0**	**2**
1994-95	EV Landshut	DEL	1	3	0	3	2																			
	Krylja Sovetov	CIS	1	2	0	2	2																			
	Vancouver	**NHL**	**44**	**20**	**23**	**43**	**47**	**6**	**2**	**2**	**198**	**10.1**	**–8**						**11**	**7**	**6**	**13**	**10**	**2**	**2**	**0**
1995-96	**Vancouver**	**NHL**	**15**	**6**	**7**	**13**	**8**	**1**	**1**	**0**	**78**	**7.7**	**–2**													
1996-97	**Vancouver**	**NHL**	**63**	**23**	**32**	**55**	**40**	**4**	**1**	**2**	**265**	**8.7**	**–14**													
1997-98	**Vancouver**	**NHL**	**82**	**51**	**39**	**90**	**48**	**13**	**6**	**4**	**329**	**15.5**	**5**													
	Russia	Olympics	6	*9	0	9	2																			
1998-99	**Florida**	**NHL**	**11**	**13**	**3**	**16**	**4**	**5**	**1**	**0**	**44**	**29.5**	**3**	**1**	**0.0**	**2**	**5**	**21:41**								
99-2000	**Florida**	**NHL**	**74**	***58**	**36**	**94**	**16**	**11**	**2**	**14**	**360**	**16.1**	**25**	**1**	**0.0**	**25**	**12**	**24:23**	**4**	**1**	**3**	**4**	**2**	**1**	**0**	**0**
2000-01	**Florida**	**NHL**	**82**	***59**	**33**	**92**	**58**	**19**	**5**	**8**	**384**	**15.4**	**–2**	**5**	**20.0**	**33**	**22**	**26:52**								
	NHL Totals		**595**	**384**	**296**	**680**	**406**	**104**	**32**	**54**	**2707**	**14.2**		**7**	**14.3**	**60**	**39**	**25:26**	**64**	**35**	**35**	**70**	**74**	**6**	**2**	**3**

Won Calder Memorial Trophy (1992) • NHL First All-Star Team (1994) • Best Forward at Olympic Games (1998) • NHL Second All-Star Team (2000, 2001) • Won Maurice "Rocket" Richard Trophy (2000, 2001) • Played in NHL All-Star Game (1993, 1994, 1997, 1998, 2000, 2001)

Traded to **Florida** by **Vancouver** with Bret Hedican, Brad Ference and Vancouver's 3rd round choice (Robert Fried) in 2000 Entry Draft for Ed Jovanovski, Dave Gagner, Mike Brown, Kevin Weekes and Florida's 1st round choice (Nathan Smith) in 2000 Entry Draft, January 17, 1999. • Missed majority of 1998-99 season after demanding trade (August 10, 1998) and recovering from knee injury suffered in game vs. Pittsburgh, February 5, 1999.

BURE, Valeri

(boo-RAY, VAL-uhr-ee) **FLA.**

Right wing. Shoots right. 5'10", 185 lbs. Born, Moscow, USSR, June 13, 1974. Montreal's 2nd choice, 33rd overall, in 1992 Entry Draft.

Season	Club	League	GP	G	A	Pts	PIM	PP	SH	GW	S	%	+/-	TF	F%	H	SB	Min	Playoffs GP	G	A	Pts	PIM	PP	SH	GW
1990-91	CSKA Moscow	USSR	3	0	0	0	0																			
1991-92	Spokane Chiefs	WHL	53	27	22	49	78												10	11	6	17	10			
1992-93	Spokane Chiefs	WHL	66	68	79	147	49												9	6	11	17	14			
1993-94	Spokane Chiefs	WHL	59	40	62	102	48												3	5	3	8	2			
1994-95	Fredericton	AHL	45	23	25	48	32																			
	Montreal	**NHL**	**24**	**3**	**1**	**4**	**6**	**0**	**0**	**1**	**39**	**7.7**	**–1**													
1995-96	**Montreal**	**NHL**	**77**	**22**	**20**	**42**	**28**	**5**	**0**	**1**	**143**	**15.4**	**10**						**6**	**0**	**1**	**1**	**6**	**0**	**0**	**0**
1996-97	**Montreal**	**NHL**	**64**	**14**	**21**	**35**	**6**	**4**	**0**	**2**	**131**	**10.7**	**4**						**5**	**0**	**1**	**1**	**2**	**0**	**0**	**0**
1997-98	**Montreal**	**NHL**	**50**	**7**	**22**	**29**	**33**	**2**	**0**	**1**	**134**	**5.2**	**–5**													
	Calgary	**NHL**	**16**	**5**	**4**	**9**	**2**	**0**	**0**	**1**	**45**	**11.1**	**0**													
	Russia	Olympics	6	1	0	1	0																			
1998-99	**Calgary**	**NHL**	**80**	**26**	**27**	**53**	**22**	**7**	**0**	**4**	**260**	**10.0**	**0**	**15**	**40.0**	**25**	**8**	**16:11**								
99-2000	**Calgary**	**NHL**	**82**	**35**	**40**	**75**	**50**	**13**	**0**	**6**	**308**	**11.4**	**–7**	**8**	**25.0**	**28**	**23**	**20:58**								
2000-01	**Calgary**	**NHL**	**78**	**27**	**28**	**55**	**26**	**16**	**0**	**2**	**276**	**9.8**	**–21**	**9**	**11.1**	**21**	**16**	**19:01**								
	NHL Totals		**471**	**139**	**163**	**302**	**173**	**47**	**0**	**18**	**1336**	**10.4**		**32**	**28.1**	**74**	**47**	**18:44**	**11**	**0**	**2**	**2**	**8**	**0**	**0**	**0**

WHL West First All-Star Team (1993) • WHL West Second All-Star Team (1994) • Played in NHL All-Star Game (2000)

Traded to **Calgary** by **Montreal** with Montreal's 4th round choice (Shaun Sutter) in 1998 Entry Draft for Jonas Hoglund and Zarley Zalapski, February 1, 1998. Traded to **Florida** by **Calgary** with Jason Wiemer for Rob Neidermayer and Philadelphia's 2nd round choice (previously acquired, Calgary selected Andrei Medvedev) in 2001 Entry Draft, June 24, 2001.

BUREAU, Marc

(BEWR-oh, MAHRK)

Center. Shoots right. 6'1", 203 lbs. Born, Trois-Rivières, Que., May 19, 1966.

Season	Club	League	GP	G	A	Pts	PIM	PP	SH	GW	S	%	+/-	TF	F%	H	SB	Min	Playoffs GP	G	A	Pts	PIM	PP	SH	GW
1982-83	St-Denis Jets	MMJHL	34	29	32	61	8																			
1983-84	Chicoutimi	QMJHL	56	6	16	22	14																			
1984-85	Chicoutimi	QMJHL	41	30	25	55	15																			
	Granby	QMJHL	27	20	45	65	14																			
1985-86	Granby	QMJHL	19	6	17	23	36																			
	Chicoutimi	QMJHL	44	30	45	75	33												9	3	7	10	10			
1986-87	Longueuil	QMJHL	66	54	58	112	68												20	17	20	37	12			
1987-88	Salt Lake City	IHL	69	7	20	27	86												7	0	3	3	8			
1988-89	Salt Lake City	IHL	76	28	36	64	119												14	7	5	12	31			
1989-90	**Calgary**	**NHL**	**5**	**0**	**0**	**0**	**4**	**0**	**0**	**0**	**3**	**0.0**	**–1**													
	Salt Lake City	IHL	67	43	48	91	173												11	4	8	12	0			
1990-91	**Calgary**	**NHL**	**5**	**0**	**0**	**0**	**2**	**0**	**0**	**0**	**4**	**0.0**	**–4**													
	Salt Lake City	IHL	54	40	48	88	101																			
	Minnesota	**NHL**	**9**	**0**	**6**	**6**	**4**	**0**	**0**	**0**	**8**	**0.0**	**–3**						**23**	**3**	**2**	**5**	**20**	**0**	**1**	**0**
1991-92	**Minnesota**	**NHL**	**46**	**6**	**4**	**10**	**50**	**0**	**0**	**0**	**53**	**11.3**	**–5**						**5**	**0**	**0**	**0**	**14**	**0**	**0**	**0**
	Kalamazoo Wings	IHL	7	2	8	10	2																			
1992-93	**Tampa Bay**	**NHL**	**63**	**10**	**21**	**31**	**111**	**1**	**2**	**1**	**132**	**7.6**	**–12**													
1993-94	**Tampa Bay**	**NHL**	**75**	**8**	**7**	**15**	**30**	**0**	**1**	**1**	**110**	**7.3**	**–9**													
1994-95	**Tampa Bay**	**NHL**	**48**	**2**	**12**	**14**	**30**	**0**	**1**	**0**	**72**	**2.8**	**–8**													
1995-96	**Montreal**	**NHL**	**65**	**3**	**7**	**10**	**46**	**0**	**0**	**1**	**43**	**7.0**	**–3**						**6**	**1**	**1**	**2**	**4**	**0**	**0**	**0**
1996-97	**Montreal**	**NHL**	**43**	**6**	**9**	**15**	**16**	**1**	**1**	**2**	**56**	**10.7**	**4**													

			Regular Season																Playoffs							
Season	Club	League	GP	G	A	Pts	PIM	PP	SH	GW	S	%	+/-	TF	F%	H	SB	Min	GP	G	A	Pts	PIM	PP	SH	GW
1997-98	Montreal	NHL	74	13	6	19	12	0	0	2	82	15.9	0	....	....	....	....	....	10	1	2	3	6	0	0	0
1998-99	Philadelphia	NHL	71	4	6	10	10	0	0	0	52	7.7	–2	776	53.5	74	28	11:02	6	0	2	2	2	0	0	0
99-2000	Philadelphia	NHL	54	2	2	4	10	0	1	0	46	4.3	–1	682	56.3	71	25	11:02	....	....	....	....	....	....	....	....
	Calgary	NHL	9	1	3	4	2	0	0	0	5	20.0	–3	72	51.4	18	5	14:13	....	....	....	....	....	....	....	....
2000-01	Saint John Flames	AHL	17	4	7	11	13	....	....	....	....	....	....	....	....	....	....	....	....	....	....	....	....	....	....	....
	NHL Totals		567	55	83	138	327	2	6	7	666	8.3		1530	54.6	163	58	11:15	50	5	7	12	46	0	1	0

IHL Second All-Star Team (1990, 1991)

Signed as a free agent by **Calgary**, May 19, 1987. Traded to **Minnesota** by **Calgary** for Minnesota's 3rd round choice (Sandy McCarthy) in 1991 Entry Draft, March 5, 1991. Claimed on waivers by **Tampa Bay** from **Minnesota**, October 16, 1992. Traded to **Montreal** by **Tampa Bay** for Brian Bellows, June 30, 1995. Signed as a free agent by **Philadelphia**, July 20, 1998. Traded to **Calgary** by **Philadelphia** for Travis Brigley and Calgary's 6th round choice (Andrei Razin) in 2001 Entry Draft, March 6, 2000. • Missed majority of 2000-01 season recovering from back injury suffered in practice, October 20, 2000.

BURT, Adam

(BUHRT, A-duhm) **ATL.**

Defense. Shoots left. 6'2", 205 lbs. Born, Detroit, MI, January 15, 1969. Hartford's 2nd choice, 39th overall, in 1987 Entry Draft.

Season	Club	League	GP	G	A	Pts	PIM	PP	SH	GW	S	%	+/-	TF	F%	H	SB	Min	GP	G	A	Pts	PIM	PP	SH	GW
1983-84	North Bay AA	NOHA	15	5	7	12	48	....	....	....	....	....	....	....	....	....	....	....	....	....	....	....	....	....	....	....
1984-85	Det-Compuware	MNHL	STATISTICS NOT AVAILABLE																							
1985-86	North Bay	OHL	49	0	11	11	81	....	....	....	....	....	....	....	....	....	....	....	10	0	0	0	24	....	....	....
1986-87	North Bay	OHL	57	4	27	31	138	....	....	....	....	....	....	....	....	....	....	....	24	1	6	7	68	....	....	....
1987-88	North Bay	OHL	66	17	53	70	176	....	....	....	....	....	....	....	....	....	....	....	2	0	3	3	6	....	....	....
	Binghamton	AHL	....	....	....	....	....	....	....	....	....	....	....	....	....	....	....	....	2	1	1	2	0	....	....	....
1988-89	North Bay	OHL	23	4	11	15	45	....	....	....	....	....	....	....	....	....	....	....	12	2	12	14	12	....	....	....
	Hartford	NHL	5	0	0	0	6	0	0	0	1	0.0	–1	....	....	....	....	....	....	....	....	....	....	....	....	....
	Binghamton	AHL	5	0	2	2	13	....	....	....	....	....	....	....	....	....	....	....	....	....	....	....	....	....	....	....
1989-90	Hartford	NHL	63	4	8	12	105	1	0	0	83	4.8	3	....	....	....	....	....	2	0	0	0	0	0	0	0
1990-91	Hartford	NHL	42	2	7	9	63	1	0	1	43	4.7	–4	....	....	....	....	....	....	....	....	....	....	....	....	....
	Springfield	AHL	9	1	3	4	22	....	....	....	....	....	....	....	....	....	....	....	....	....	....	....	....	....	....	....
1991-92	Hartford	NHL	66	9	15	24	93	4	0	1	89	10.1	–16	....	....	....	....	....	2	0	0	0	0	0	0	0
1992-93	Hartford	NHL	65	6	14	20	116	0	0	0	81	7.4	–11	....	....	....	....	....	....	....	....	....	....	....	....	....
1993-94	Hartford	NHL	63	1	17	18	75	0	0	0	91	1.1	–4	....	....	....	....	....	....	....	....	....	....	....	....	....
1994-95	Hartford	NHL	46	7	11	18	65	3	0	1	73	9.6	0	....	....	....	....	....	....	....	....	....	....	....	....	....
1995-96	Hartford	NHL	78	4	9	13	121	0	0	1	90	4.4	–4	....	....	....	....	....	....	....	....	....	....	....	....	....
1996-97	Hartford	NHL	71	2	11	13	79	0	0	0	85	2.4	–13	....	....	....	....	....	....	....	....	....	....	....	....	....
1997-98	Carolina	NHL	76	1	11	12	106	0	1	0	51	2.0	–6	....	....	....	....	....	....	....	....	....	....	....	....	....
1998-99	Carolina	NHL	51	0	3	3	46	0	0	0	37	0.0	3	0	0.0	78	60	18:39	....	....	....	....	....	....	....	....
	Philadelphia	NHL	17	0	1	1	14	0	0	0	24	0.0	1	0	0.0	16	16	17:25	6	0	0	0	4	0	0	0
99-2000	Philadelphia	NHL	67	1	6	7	45	0	0	1	49	2.0	–2	0	0.0	92	70	16:19	11	0	1	1	4	0	0	0
2000-01	Atlanta	NHL	27	0	2	2	27	0	0	0	18	0.0	2	0	0.0	55	44	19:05	....	....	....	....	....	....	....	....
	NHL Totals		737	37	115	152	961	9	1	5	815	4.5		0	0.0	241	190	17:38	21	0	1	1	8	0	0	0

OHL Second All-Star Team (1988)

Transferred to **Carolina** after **Hartford** franchise relocated, June 25, 1997. Traded to **Philadelphia** by **Carolina** for Andrei Kovalenko, March 6, 1999. Signed as a free agent by **Atlanta**, July 14, 2000. • Missed majority of 2000-01 season recovering from back injury suffered in game vs. Washington, January 1, 2001.

BUTENSCHON, Sven

(BUH-tehn-shohn, SVEHN) **EDM.**

Defense. Shoots left. 6'4", 215 lbs. Born, Itzehoe, West Germany, March 22, 1976. Pittsburgh's 3rd choice, 57th overall, in 1994 Entry Draft.

Season	Club	League	GP	G	A	Pts	PIM	PP	SH	GW	S	%	+/-	TF	F%	H	SB	Min	GP	G	A	Pts	PIM	PP	SH	GW
1991-92	Eastman Selects	MMHL	36	2	10	12	110	....	....	....	....	....	....	....	....	....	....	....	....	....	....	....	....	....	....	....
1992-93	Eastman Selects	MMHL	35	14	22	36	101	....	....	....	....	....	....	....	....	....	....	....	....	....	....	....	....	....	....	....
1993-94	Brandon	WHL	70	3	19	22	51	....	....	....	....	....	....	....	....	....	....	....	4	0	0	0	6	....	....	....
1994-95	Brandon	WHL	21	1	5	6	44	....	....	....	....	....	....	....	....	....	....	....	18	1	2	3	11	....	....	....
1995-96	Brandon	WHL	70	4	37	41	99	....	....	....	....	....	....	....	....	....	....	....	19	1	12	13	18	....	....	....
1996-97	Cleveland	IHL	75	3	12	15	68	....	....	....	....	....	....	....	....	....	....	....	10	0	1	1	4	....	....	....
1997-98	Pittsburgh	NHL	8	0	0	0	6	0	0	0	4	0.0	–1	....	....	....	....	....	....	....	....	....	....	....	....	....
	Syracuse Crunch	AHL	65	14	23	37	66	....	....	....	....	....	....	....	....	....	....	....	5	1	2	3	0	....	....	....
1998-99	Pittsburgh	NHL	17	0	0	0	6	0	0	0	8	0.0	–7	0	0.0	13	12	13:08	....	....	....	....	....	....	....	....
	Houston Aeros	IHL	57	1	4	5	81	....	....	....	....	....	....	....	....	....	....	....	....	....	....	....	....	....	....	....
99-2000	Pittsburgh	NHL	3	0	0	0	0	0	0	0	2	0.0	3	0	0.0	1	2	16:25	....	....	....	....	....	....	....	....
	Wilkes-Barre	AHL	75	19	21	40	101	....	....	....	....	....	....	....	....	....	....	....	....	....	....	....	....	....	....	....
2000-01	Pittsburgh	NHL	5	0	1	1	2	0	0	0	6	0.0	1	0	0.0	5	6	17:51	....	....	....	....	....	....	....	....
	Wilkes-Barre	AHL	55	7	28	35	85	....	....	....	....	....	....	....	....	....	....	....	....	....	....	....	....	....	....	....
	Edmonton	NHL	7	1	1	2	2	0	0	0	3	33.3	2	0	0.0	5	3	11:07	....	....	....	....	....	....	....	....
	NHL Totals		40	1	2	3	16	0	0	0	23	4.3		0	0.0	24	23	13:44	....	....	....	....	....	....	....	....

Traded to **Edmonton** by **Pittsburgh** for Dan LaCouture, March 13, 2001.

BUTSAYEV, Viacheslav

(boot-SIGH-yehf, VYACH-ih-slav)

Center. Shoots left. 6'2", 228 lbs. Born, Togliatti, USSR, June 13, 1970. Philadelphia's 10th choice, 109th overall, in 1990 Entry Draft.

Season	Club	League	GP	G	A	Pts	PIM	PP	SH	GW	S	%	+/-	TF	F%	H	SB	Min	GP	G	A	Pts	PIM	PP	SH	GW
1987-88	Lada Togliatti	USSR-2	10	1	7	8	....	....	....	....	....	....	....	....	....	....	....	....	....	....	....	....	....	....	....	....
1988-89	Lada Togliatti-2	USSR-3	60	14	7	21	32	....	....	....	....	....	....	....	....	....	....	....	....	....	....	....	....	....	....	....
1989-90	CSKA Moscow	USSR	48	14	4	18	30	....	....	....	....	....	....	....	....	....	....	....	....	....	....	....	....	....	....	....
1990-91	CSKA Moscow	USSR	46	14	9	23	32	....	....	....	....	....	....	....	....	....	....	....	....	....	....	....	....	....	....	....
1991-92	CSKA Moscow	CIS	36	12	13	25	26	....	....	....	....	....	....	....	....	....	....	....	....	....	....	....	....	....	....	....
	Russia	Olympics	8	1	1	2	4	....	....	....	....	....	....	....	....	....	....	....	....	....	....	....	....	....	....	....
1992-93	CSKA Moscow	CIS	5	3	4	7	6	....	....	....	....	....	....	....	....	....	....	....	....	....	....	....	....	....	....	....
	Philadelphia	NHL	52	2	14	16	61	0	0	0	58	3.4	3	....	....	....	....	....	....	....	....	....	....	....	....	....
	Hershey Bears	AHL	24	8	10	18	51	....	....	....	....	....	....	....	....	....	....	....	....	....	....	....	....	....	....	....
1993-94	Philadelphia	NHL	47	12	9	21	58	0	0	3	79	15.2	2	....	....	....	....	....	....	....	....	....	....	....	....	....
	San Jose	NHL	12	0	2	2	10	2	0	0	6	0.0	–2	....	....	....	....	....	....	....	....	....	....	....	....	....
1994-95	Lada Togliatti	CIS	9	2	6	8	6	....	....	....	....	....	....	....	....	....	....	....	....	....	....	....	....	....	....	....
	San Jose	NHL	6	2	0	2	0	0	0	0	6	33.3	–2	....	....	....	....	....	....	....	....	....	....	....	....	....
	Kansas City	IHL	13	3	4	7	12	....	....	....	....	....	....	....	....	....	....	....	3	0	0	0	2	....	....	....
1995-96	Anaheim	NHL	7	1	0	1	0	0	0	0	9	11.1	–4	....	....	....	....	....	....	....	....	....	....	....	....	....
	Baltimore Bandits	AHL	62	23	42	65	70	....	....	....	....	....	....	....	....	....	....	....	12	4	8	12	28	....	....	....
1996-97	Sodertalje SK	Sweden	16	2	4	6	61	....	....	....	....	....	....	....	....	....	....	....	....	....	....	....	....	....	....	....
	Farjestads BK	Sweden	24	4	3	7	47	....	....	....	....	....	....	....	....	....	....	....	8	3	4	7	41	....	....	....
	Farjestads BK	EuroHL	1	0	0	0	0	....	....	....	....	....	....	....	....	....	....	....	....	....	....	....	....	....	....	....
1997-98	Fort Wayne	IHL	76	36	51	87	128	....	....	....	....	....	....	....	....	....	....	....	4	2	2	4	4	....	....	....
1998-99	Florida	NHL	1	0	0	0	2	0	0	0	0	0.0	–1	20	60.0	0	0	16:21	....	....	....	....	....	....	....	....
	Fort Wayne	IHL	71	28	44	72	123	....	....	....	....	....	....	....	....	....	....	....	2	1	0	1	4	....	....	....
	Ottawa	NHL	2	0	1	1	2	0	0	0	5	0.0	0	6	33.3	2	0	11:08	....	....	....	....	....	....	....	....
99-2000	Tampa Bay	NHL	2	0	0	0	0	0	0	0	1	0.0	–2	13	30.8	1	0	8:42	....	....	....	....	....	....	....	....
	Ottawa	NHL	3	0	0	0	0	0	0	0	1	0.0	–2	18	38.9	1	0	9:19	....	....	....	....	....	....	....	....
	Grand Rapids	IHL	68	28	35	63	85	....	....	....	....	....	....	....	....	....	....	....	17	4	*12	16	24	....	....	....
2000-01	Grand Rapids	IHL	75	33	35	68	65	....	....	....	....	....	....	....	....	....	....	....	10	1	5	6	18	....	....	....
	NHL Totals		132	17	26	43	133	2	0	3	165	10.3		57	43.9	4	0	10:30	....	....	....	....	....	....	....	....

IHL Second All-Star Team (1998)

Traded to **San Jose** by **Philadelphia** for Rob Zettler, February 1, 1994. Signed as a free agent by **Anaheim**, October 19, 1995. Signed as a free agent by **Florida**, August 1, 1998. Traded to **Ottawa** by **Florida** for Ottawa's 6th round choice (later traded to Dallas - Dallas selected Justin Cox) in 1999 Entry Draft, March 8, 1999. Claimed by **Tampa Bay** from **Ottawa** in Waiver Draft, September 27, 1999. Claimed on waivers by **Ottawa** from **Tampa Bay**, October 28, 1999.

BUTSAYEV, Yuri

(buht-SIGH-ehv, YOO-ree) **DET.**

Center. Shoots left. 6'1", 183 lbs. Born, Togliatti, USSR, October 11, 1978. Detroit's 1st choice, 49th overall, in 1997 Entry Draft.

Season	Club	League	GP	G	A	Pts	PIM	PP	SH	GW	S	%	+/-	TF	F%	H	SB	Min	GP	G	A	Pts	PIM	PP	SH	GW
1995-96	Lada Togliatti	CIS-2	35	19	7	26	....	....	....	....	....	....	....	....	....	....	....	....	....	....	....	....	....	....	....	....
	Lada Togliatti	CIS	1	0	0	0	0	....	....	....	....	....	....	....	....	....	....	....	....	....	....	....	....	....	....	....
1996-97	Lada Togliatti	Russia	42	13	11	24	38	....	....	....	....	....	....	....	....	....	....	....	11	2	2	4	8	....	....	....
1997-98	Lada Togliatti	Russia	44	8	9	17	63	....	....	....	....	....	....	....	....	....	....	....	....	....	....	....	....	....	....	....
	Lada Togliatti	EuroHL	6	2	0	2	8	....	....	....	....	....	....	....	....	....	....	....	....	....	....	....	....	....	....	....
1998-99	Dynamo Moscow	Russia	1	0	1	1	0	....	....	....	....	....	....	....	....	....	....	....	....	....	....	....	....	....	....	....
	Lada Togliatti	Russia	39	10	7	17	55	....	....	....	....	....	....	....	....	....	....	....	7	1	2	3	14	....	....	....

			Regular Season																Playoffs							
Season	Club	League	GP	G	A	Pts	PIM	PP	SH	GW	S	%	+/-	TF	F%	H	SB	Min	GP	G	A	Pts	PIM	PP	SH	GW
99-2000	**Detroit**	**NHL**	57	5	3	8	12	0	0	0	46	10.9	-6	22	40.9	29	11	9:36								
	Cincinnati Ducks	AHL	9	0	1	1	0																			
2000-01	**Detroit**	**NHL**	15	1	1	2	4	0	0	0	18	5.6	-2	6	33.3	4	1	9:09								
	Cincinnati Ducks	AHL	54	29	17	46	26												4	0	2	2	2			
	NHL Totals		72	6	4	10	16	0	0	0	64	9.4		28	39.3	33	12	9:30								

BUZEK, Petr

(BOO-zehk, PEE-tuhr) **ATL.**

Defense. Shoots left. 6', 210 lbs. Born, Jihlava, Czech., April 26, 1977. Dallas' 3rd choice, 63rd overall, in 1995 Entry Draft.

Season	Club	League	GP	G	A	Pts	PIM	PP	SH	GW	S	%	+/-	TF	F%	H	SB	Min	GP	G	A	Pts	PIM	PP	SH	GW
1993-94	Dukla Jihlava-Jr.	Cze-Rep	3	0	0	0																				
1994-95	Dukla Jihlava	Cze-Rep	43	2	5	7	47												2	0	0	0	2			
1995-96	Michigan K-Wings	IHL	DID NOT PLAY – INJURED																							
1996-97	Michigan K-Wings	IHL	67	4	6	10	48																			
1997-98	**Dallas**	**NHL**	2	0	0	0	2	0	0	0	0	0.0	1													
	Michigan K-Wings	IHL	60	10	15	25	58												2	0	1	1	17			
1998-99	**Dallas**	**NHL**	2	0	0	0	2	0	0	0	0	0.0	0	0	0.0	3	0	13:50								
	Michigan K-Wings	IHL	74	5	14	19	68												5	0	0	0	10			
99-2000	**Atlanta**	**NHL**	63	5	14	19	41	3	0	0	90	5.6	-22	0	0.0	139	76	18:24								
2000-01	**Atlanta**	**NHL**	5	0	0	0	8	0	0	0	11	0.0	2	0	0.0	14	2	17:26								
	NHL Totals		72	5	14	19	53	3	0	0	101	5.0		0	0.0	156	78	18:12								

Played in NHL All-Star Game (2000)

• Missed entire 1995-96 season recovering from injuries suffered in automobile accident, July, 1995. Claimed by **Atlanta** from **Dallas** in Expansion Draft, June 25, 1999. • Missed majority of 2000-01 season recovering from neck injury suffered in game vs. Anaheim, October 17, 2000.

BYLSMA, Dan

(BEEL-smah, DAN) **ANA.**

Right wing. Shoots left. 6'2", 212 lbs. Born, Grand Haven, MI, September 19, 1970. Winnipeg's 7th choice, 109th overall, in 1989 Entry Draft.

Season	Club	League	GP	G	A	Pts	PIM	PP	SH	GW	S	%	+/-	TF	F%	H	SB	Min	GP	G	A	Pts	PIM	PP	SH	GW
1986-87	Oakville Blades	OJHL-B	10	4	9	13	21																			
	St. Mary's Lincolns	OJHL-B	27	14	28	42	21																			
1987-88	St. Mary's Lincolns	OJHL-B	40	30	39	69	33												8	8	18	26				
1988-89	Bowling Green	CCHA	32	3	7	10	10																			
1989-90	Bowling Green	CCHA	44	13	17	30	30																			
1990-91	Bowling Green	CCHA	40	9	12	21	48																			
1991-92	Bowling Green	CCHA	34	11	14	25	24																			
1992-93	Greensboro	ECHL	60	25	35	60	66												1	0	1	1	10			
	Rochester	AHL	2	0	1	1	0																			
1993-94	Greensboro	ECHL	25	14	16	30	52																			
	Albany River Rats	AHL	3	0	1	1	2																			
	Moncton Hawks	AHL	50	12	16	28	25												21	3	4	7	31			
1994-95	Phoenix	IHL	81	19	23	42	41												9	4	4	8	4			
1995-96	**Los Angeles**	**NHL**	4	0	0	0	0	0	0	0	6	0.0	0													
	Phoenix	IHL	78	22	20	42	48												4	1	0	1	2			
1996-97	**Los Angeles**	**NHL**	79	3	6	9	32	0	0	0	86	3.5	-15													
1997-98	**Los Angeles**	**NHL**	65	3	9	12	33	0	0	0	57	5.3	9						2	0	0	0	0	0	0	0
	Long Beach	IHL	8	2	3	5	0																			
1998-99	**Los Angeles**	**NHL**	8	0	0	0	2	0	0	0	3	0.0	-1	0	0.0	15	4	9:51								
	Springfield	AHL	2	0	2	2	2																			
	Long Beach	IHL	58	10	8	18	53												4	0	0	0	8			
99-2000	**Los Angeles**	**NHL**	64	3	6	9	55	0	1	0	43	7.0	-2	62	43.6	168	33	10:23	3	0	0	0	0	0	0	0
	Long Beach	IHL	6	0	3	3	2																			
	Lowell	AHL	2	1	1	2	2																			
2000-01	**Anaheim**	**NHL**	82	1	9	10	22	0	0	0	50	2.0	-12	10	50.0	109	88	11:45								
	NHL Totals		302	10	30	40	144	0	1	0	245	4.1		72	44.4	292	125	11:05	5	0	0	0	0	0	0	0

CCHA All-Academic Team (1991, 1992)

Signed as a free agent by **LA Kings**, July 7, 1994. Signed as a free agent by **Anaheim**, July 13, 2000.

CAIRNS, Eric

(KAIRNZ, AIR-ihk) **NYI**

Defense. Shoots left. 6'6", 230 lbs. Born, Oakville, Ont., June 27, 1974. NY Rangers' 3rd choice, 72nd overall, in 1992 Entry Draft.

Season	Club	League	GP	G	A	Pts	PIM	PP	SH	GW	S	%	+/-	TF	F%	H	SB	Min	GP	G	A	Pts	PIM	PP	SH	GW
1990-91	Burlington	MTJHL	37	5	16	21	120																			
1991-92	Detroit	OHL	64	1	11	12	237												7	0	0	0	31			
1992-93	Detroit Jr. Wings	OHL	64	3	13	16	194												15	0	3	3	24			
1993-94	Detroit Jr. Wings	OHL	59	7	35	42	204												17	0	4	4	46			
1994-95	Birmingham Bulls	ECHL	11	1	3	4	49																			
	Binghamton	AHL	27	0	3	3	134												9	1	1	2	28			
1995-96	Binghamton	AHL	46	1	13	14	192												4	0	0	0	37			
	Charlotte	ECHL	6	0	1	1	34																			
1996-97	**NY Rangers**	**NHL**	40	0	1	1	147	0	0	0	17	0.0	-7						3	0	0	0	0	0	0	0
	Binghamton	AHL	10	1	1	2	96																			
1997-98	**NY Rangers**	**NHL**	39	0	3	3	92	0	0	0	17	0.0	-3													
	Hartford	AHL	7	1	2	3	43																			
1998-99	Hartford	AHL	11	0	2	2	49																			
	NY Islanders	**NHL**	9	0	3	3	23	0	0	0	2	0.0	1	0	0.0	13	5	10:15								
	Lowell	AHL	24	0	0	0	91												3	1	0	1	32			
99-2000	**NY Islanders**	**NHL**	67	2	7	9	196	0	0	0	55	3.6	-5	0	0.0	182	73	17:43								
	Providence Bruins	AHL	4	1	1	2	14																			
2000-01	**NY Islanders**	**NHL**	45	2	2	4	106	0	0	0	21	9.5	-18	1	0.0	71	58	16:24								
	NHL Totals		200	4	16	20	564	0	0	0	112	3.6		1	0.0	266	136	16:40	3	0	0	0	0	0	0	0

Claimed on waivers by **NY Islanders** from **NY Rangers**, December 22, 1998. Loaned to **Providence** (AHL) by **NY Islanders**, October 6, 1999 and recalled October 13, 1999. • Missed most of 2000-01 season recovering from hand injury originally suffered in game vs. Tampa Bay, October 6, 2000.

CALDER, Kyle

(KAWL-dehr, KIGHL) **CHI.**

Center. Shoots left. 5'11", 180 lbs. Born, Mannville, Alta., January 5, 1979. Chicago's 7th choice, 130th overall, in 1997 Entry Draft.

Season	Club	League	GP	G	A	Pts	PIM	PP	SH	GW	S	%	+/-	TF	F%	H	SB	Min	GP	G	A	Pts	PIM	PP	SH	GW
1994-95	Leduc Barons	AAHA	27	25	32	57	22																			
1995-96	Regina Pats	WHL	27	1	7	8	10												11	0	0	0	0			
1996-97	Regina Pats	WHL	62	25	34	59	17												5	3	0	3	6			
1997-98	Regina Pats	WHL	62	27	50	77	58												2	0	1	1	0			
1998-99	Regina Pats	WHL	34	23	28	51	29																			
	Kamloops Blazers	WHL	27	19	18	37	30												15	6	10	16	6			
99-2000	**Chicago**	**NHL**	8	1	1	2	2	0	0	0	5	20.0	-3	2	0.0	5	1	9:59								
	Cleveland	IHL	74	14	22	36	43												9	2	2	4	14			
2000-01	**Chicago**	**NHL**	43	5	10	15	14	0	0	1	63	7.9	-4	2	0.0	31	8	12:43								
	Norfolk Admirals	AHL	37	12	15	27	21												9	2	6	8	2			
	NHL Totals		51	6	11	17	16	0	0	1	68	8.8		4	0.0	36	9	12:17								

CALOUN, Jan

(CHAH-loon, YAHN)

Right wing. Shoots right. 5'10", 190 lbs. Born, Usti-Nad-Labem, Czech., December 20, 1972. San Jose's 4th choice, 75th overall, in 1992 Entry Draft.

Season	Club	League	GP	G	A	Pts	PIM	PP	SH	GW	S	%	+/-	TF	F%	H	SB	Min	GP	G	A	Pts	PIM	PP	SH	GW
1990-91	CHZ Litvinov	Czech.	50	28	19	47	12																			
1991-92	CHZ Litvinov	Czech.	46	39	13	52	24																			
1992-93	CHZ Litvinov	Czech.	36	37	16	53													11	8	6	14				
1993-94	CHZ Litvinov	Cze-Rep	38	25	17	42													4	2	2	4				
1994-95	Kansas City	IHL	76	34	39	73	50												21	13	10	23	18			
1995-96	**San Jose**	**NHL**	11	8	3	11	0	2	0	0	20	40.0	4													
	Kansas City	IHL	61	38	30	68	58												5	0	1	1	6			
1996-97	**San Jose**	**NHL**	2	0	0	0	0	0	0	0	3	0.0	-2													
	Kentucky	AHL	66	43	43	86	68												4	0	1	1	4			

			Regular Season																Playoffs							
Season	**Club**	**League**	**GP**	**G**	**A**	**Pts**	**PIM**	**PP**	**SH**	**GW**	**S**	**%**	**+/-**	**TF**	**F%**	**H**	**SB**	**Min**	**GP**	**G**	**A**	**Pts**	**PIM**	**PP**	**SH**	**GW**
1997-98	HIFK Helsinki	Finland	41	22	26	48	73	....	....	....	....	....	....	....	....	....	....	....	9	6	*11	*17	6	....	....	....
	Czech-Republic	Olympics	3	0	0	0	6	....	....	....	....	....	....	....	....	....	....	....	....	....	....	....	....	....	....	....
1998-99	HIFK Helsinki	Finland	51	24	*57	*81	95	....	....	....	....	....	....	....	....	....	....	....	8	*8	6	*14	31	....	....	....
	HIFK Helsinki	EuroHL	5	4	2	6	26	....	....	....	....	....	....	....	....	....	....	....	3	1	1	2	30	....	....	....
99-2000	HIFK Helsinki	Finland	44	38	34	72	94	....	....	....	....	....	....	....	....	....	....	....	9	3	6	9	10	....	....	....
	HIFK Helsinki	EuroHL	4	1	3	4	6	....	....	....	....	....	....	....	....	....	....	....	1	0	1	1	0	....	....	....
2000-01	**Columbus**	**NHL**	**11**	**0**	**3**	**3**	**2**	**0**	**0**	**0**	**14**	**0.0**	**-8**	**0**	**0.0**	**2**	**3**	**12:40**	....	....	....	....	....	....	....	....
	HIFK Helsinki	Finland	24	8	14	22	42	....	....	....	....	....	....	....	....	....	....	....	....	....	....	....	....	....	....	....
	NHL Totals		**24**	**8**	**6**	**14**	**2**	**2**	**0**	**0**	**37**	**21.6**		**0**	**0.0**	**2**	**3**	**12:40**	....	....	....	....	....	....	....	....

AHL Second All-Star Team (1997)

Traded to **Columbus** by **San Jose** with San Jose's 9th round choice (Martin Paroulek) in 2000 Entry Draft for future considerations, June 12, 2000. Signed as a free agent by **HIFK Helsinki** (Finland) after securing release from **Columbus**, November 28, 2000.

CAMPBELL, Brian

(KAM-behl, BRIGH-uhn) **BUF.**

Defense. Shoots left. 6', 190 lbs. Born, Strathroy, Ont., May 23, 1979. Buffalo's 7th choice, 156th overall, in 1997 Entry Draft.

Season	Club	League	GP	G	A	Pts	PIM	PP	SH	GW	S	%	+/-	TF	F%	H	SB	Min	GP	G	A	Pts	PIM	PP	SH	GW
1994-95	Petrolia Barons	OJHL-B	49	11	27	38	43	....	....	....	....	....	....	....	....	....	....	....	....	....	....	....	....	....	....	....
1995-96	Ottawa 67's	OHL	66	5	22	27	23	....	....	....	....	....	....	....	....	....	....	....	4	0	1	1	2	....	....	....
1996-97	Ottawa 67's	OHL	66	7	36	43	12	....	....	....	....	....	....	....	....	....	....	....	24	2	11	13	8	....	....	....
1997-98	Ottawa 67's	OHL	66	14	39	53	31	....	....	....	....	....	....	....	....	....	....	....	13	1	14	15	0	....	....	....
1998-99	Ottawa 67's	OHL	62	12	75	87	27	....	....	....	....	....	....	....	....	....	....	....	9	2	10	12	6	....	....	....
	Rochester	AHL	....	....	....	....	....	....	....	....	....	....	....	....	....	....	....	....	2	0	0	0	0	....	....	....
99-2000	**Buffalo**	**NHL**	**12**	**1**	**4**	**5**	**4**	**0**	**0**	**0**	**10**	**10.0**	**-2**	**0**	**0.0**	**8**	**3**	**15:48**	....	....	....	....	....	....	....	....
	Rochester	AHL	67	2	24	26	22	....	....	....	....	....	....	....	....	....	....	....	21	0	3	3	0	....	....	....
2000-01	**Buffalo**	**NHL**	**8**	**0**	**0**	**0**	**2**	**0**	**0**	**0**	**7**	**0.0**	**-2**	**0**	**0.0**	**8**	**8**	**15:40**	....	....	....	....	....	....	....	....
	Rochester	AHL	65	7	25	32	24	....	....	....	....	....	....	....	....	....	....	....	4	0	1	1	0	....	....	....
	NHL Totals		**20**	**1**	**4**	**5**	**6**	**0**	**0**	**0**	**17**	**5.9**		**0**	**0.0**	**16**	**11**	**15:45**	....	....	....	....	....	....	....	....

OHL First All-Star Team (1999) • Canadian Major Junior First All-Star Team (1999) • Won George Parsons Trophy (Memorial Cup Tournament Most Sportsmanlike Player) (1999) • Canadian Major Junior Player of the Year (1999)

CAMPBELL, Jim

(KAM-behl, JIHM)

Right wing. Shoots right. 6'2", 205 lbs. Born, Worcester, MA, April 3, 1973. Montreal's 2nd choice, 28th overall, in 1991 Entry Draft.

Season	Club	League	GP	G	A	Pts	PIM	PP	SH	GW	S	%	+/-	TF	F%	H	SB	Min	GP	G	A	Pts	PIM	PP	SH	GW
1988-89	Northwood Prep	Hi-School	12	12	8	20	6	....	....	....	....	....	....	....	....	....	....	....	....	....	....	....	....	....	....	....
1989-90	Northwood Prep	Hi-School	8	14	7	21	8	....	....	....	....	....	....	....	....	....	....	....	....	....	....	....	....	....	....	....
1990-91	Lawrence Prep	Hi-School	26	36	47	83	26	....	....	....	....	....	....	....	....	....	....	....	....	....	....	....	....	....	....	....
1991-92	Hull Olympiques	QMJHL	64	41	44	85	51	....	....	....	....	....	....	....	....	....	....	....	6	7	3	10	8	....	....	....
1992-93	Hull Olympiques	QMJHL	50	42	29	71	66	....	....	....	....	....	....	....	....	....	....	....	8	11	4	15	43	....	....	....
1993-94	United States	Nat-Team	56	24	33	57	59	....	....	....	....	....	....	....	....	....	....	....	....	....	....	....	....	....	....	....
	United States	Olympics	8	0	0	0	6	....	....	....	....	....	....	....	....	....	....	....	....	....	....	....	....	....	....	....
	Fredericton	AHL	19	6	17	23	6	....	....	....	....	....	....	....	....	....	....	....	....	....	....	....	....	....	....	....
1994-95	Fredericton	AHL	77	27	24	51	103	....	....	....	....	....	....	....	....	....	....	....	12	0	7	7	8	....	....	....
1995-96	Fredericton	AHL	44	28	23	51	24	....	....	....	....	....	....	....	....	....	....	....	....	....	....	....	....	....	....	....
	Anaheim	**NHL**	**16**	**2**	**3**	**5**	**36**	**1**	**0**	**0**	**25**	**8.0**	**0**	....	....	....	....	....	....	....	....	....	....	....	....	....
	Baltimore Bandits	AHL	16	13	7	20	8	....	....	....	....	....	....	....	....	....	....	....	12	7	5	12	10	....	....	....
1996-97	**St. Louis**	**NHL**	**68**	**23**	**20**	**43**	**68**	**5**	**0**	**6**	**169**	**13.6**	**3**	....	....	....	....	....	**4**	**1**	**0**	**1**	**6**	**1**	**0**	**0**
1997-98	**St. Louis**	**NHL**	**76**	**22**	**19**	**41**	**55**	**7**	**0**	**6**	**147**	**15.0**	**0**	....	....	....	....	....	**10**	**7**	**3**	**10**	**12**	**4**	**0**	**2**
1998-99	**St. Louis**	**NHL**	**55**	**4**	**21**	**25**	**41**	**1**	**0**	**0**	**99**	**4.0**	**-8**	**7**	**42.9**	**65**	**7**	**13:34**	....	....	....	....	....	....	....	....
99-2000	Manitoba Moose	IHL	10	1	3	4	10	....	....	....	....	....	....	....	....	....	....	....	....	....	....	....	....	....	....	....
	St. Louis	**NHL**	**2**	**0**	**0**	**0**	**9**	**0**	**0**	**0**	**6**	**0.0**	**0**	**0**	**0.0**	**1**	**0**	**15:17**	....	....	....	....	....	....	....	....
	Worcester	AHL	66	31	34	65	88	....	....	....	....	....	....	....	....	....	....	....	9	1	2	3	6	....	....	....
2000-01	**Montreal**	**NHL**	**57**	**9**	**11**	**20**	**53**	**6**	**0**	**1**	**81**	**11.1**	**-3**	**14**	**42.9**	**23**	**10**	**10:19**	....	....	....	....	....	....	....	....
	Quebec Citadelles	AHL	3	5	0	5	6	....	....	....	....	....	....	....	....	....	....	....	....	....	....	....	....	....	....	....
	NHL Totals		**274**	**60**	**74**	**134**	**262**	**20**	**0**	**13**	**527**	**11.4**		**21**	**42.9**	**89**	**17**	**11:58**	**14**	**8**	**3**	**11**	**18**	**5**	**0**	**2**

NHL All-Rookie Team (1997)

Traded to **Anaheim** by **Montreal** for Robert Dirk, January 21, 1996. Signed as a free agent by **St. Louis**, July 11, 1996. Loaned to **Manitoba** (IHL) by **St. Louis**, October 4, 1999 and recalled November 1, 1999. Signed as a free agent by **Montreal**, August 21, 2000.

CARNEY, Keith

(KAHRN-nee, KEETH) **ANA.**

Defense. Shoots left. 6'2", 214 lbs. Born, Providence, RI, February 3, 1970. Buffalo's 3rd choice, 76th overall, in 1988 Entry Draft.

Season	Club	League	GP	G	A	Pts	PIM	PP	SH	GW	S	%	+/-	TF	F%	H	SB	Min	GP	G	A	Pts	PIM	PP	SH	GW
1987-88	Mount St. Charles	Hi-School	23	12	43	55	....	....	....	....	....	....	....	....	....	....	....	....	....	....	....	....	....	....	....	....
1988-89	U. of Maine	H-East	40	4	22	26	24	....	....	....	....	....	....	....	....	....	....	....	....	....	....	....	....	....	....	....
1989-90	U. of Maine	H-East	41	3	41	44	43	....	....	....	....	....	....	....	....	....	....	....	....	....	....	....	....	....	....	....
1990-91	U. of Maine	H-East	40	7	49	56	38	....	....	....	....	....	....	....	....	....	....	....	....	....	....	....	....	....	....	....
1991-92	United States	Nat-Team	49	2	17	19	16	....	....	....	....	....	....	....	....	....	....	....	....	....	....	....	....	....	....	....
	Buffalo	**NHL**	**14**	**1**	**2**	**3**	**18**	**1**	**0**	**0**	**17**	**5.9**	**-3**	....	....	....	....	....	**7**	**0**	**3**	**3**	**0**	**0**	**0**	**0**
	Rochester	AHL	24	1	10	11	2	....	....	....	....	....	....	....	....	....	....	....	2	0	2	2	0	....	....	....
1992-93	**Buffalo**	**NHL**	**30**	**2**	**4**	**6**	**55**	**0**	**0**	**1**	**26**	**7.7**	**3**	....	....	....	....	....	**8**	**0**	**3**	**3**	**6**	**0**	**0**	**0**
	Rochester	AHL	41	5	21	26	32	....	....	....	....	....	....	....	....	....	....	....	....	....	....	....	....	....	....	....
1993-94	**Buffalo**	**NHL**	**7**	**1**	**3**	**4**	**4**	**0**	**0**	**0**	**6**	**16.7**	**-1**	....	....	....	....	....	....	....	....	....	....	....	....	....
	Chicago	**NHL**	**30**	**3**	**5**	**8**	**35**	**0**	**0**	**0**	**31**	**9.7**	**15**	....	....	....	....	....	**6**	**0**	**1**	**1**	**4**	**0**	**0**	**0**
	Indianapolis Ice	IHL	28	0	14	14	20	....	....	....	....	....	....	....	....	....	....	....	....	....	....	....	....	....	....	....
1994-95	**Chicago**	**NHL**	**18**	**1**	**0**	**1**	**11**	**0**	**0**	**1**	**14**	**7.1**	**-1**	....	....	....	....	....	**4**	**0**	**1**	**1**	**0**	**0**	**0**	**0**
1995-96	**Chicago**	**NHL**	**82**	**5**	**14**	**19**	**94**	**1**	**0**	**1**	**69**	**7.2**	**31**	....	....	....	....	....	**10**	**0**	**3**	**3**	**4**	**0**	**0**	**0**
1996-97	**Chicago**	**NHL**	**81**	**3**	**15**	**18**	**62**	**0**	**0**	**1**	**77**	**3.9**	**26**	....	....	....	....	....	**6**	**1**	**1**	**2**	**2**	**0**	**0**	**0**
1997-98	**Chicago**	**NHL**	**60**	**2**	**13**	**15**	**73**	**0**	**1**	**0**	**53**	**3.8**	**-7**	....	....	....	....	....	....	....	....	....	....	....	....	....
	United States	Olympics	4	0	0	0	2	....	....	....	....	....	....	....	....	....	....	....	....	....	....	....	....	....	....	....
	Phoenix	**NHL**	**20**	**1**	**6**	**7**	**18**	**1**	**0**	**0**	**18**	**5.6**	**5**	....	....	....	....	....	**6**	**0**	**0**	**0**	**4**	**0**	**0**	**0**
1998-99	**Phoenix**	**NHL**	**82**	**2**	**14**	**16**	**62**	**0**	**2**	**0**	**62**	**3.2**	**15**	**0**	**0.0**	**133**	**87**	**22:46**	**7**	**1**	**2**	**3**	**10**	**0**	**0**	**0**
99-2000	**Phoenix**	**NHL**	**82**	**4**	**20**	**24**	**87**	**0**	**0**	**1**	**73**	**5.5**	**11**	**0**	**0.0**	**189**	**98**	**21:12**	**5**	**0**	**0**	**0**	**17**	**0**	**0**	**0**
2000-01	**Phoenix**	**NHL**	**82**	**2**	**14**	**16**	**86**	**0**	**0**	**0**	**65**	**3.1**	**15**	**0**	**0.0**	**194**	**94**	**20:53**	....	....	....	....	....	....	....	....
	NHL Totals		**588**	**27**	**110**	**137**	**605**	**3**	**3**	**5**	**511**	**5.3**		**0**	**0.0**	**516**	**279**	**21:49**	**59**	**2**	**14**	**16**	**47**	**0**	**0**	**0**

Hockey East Second All-Star Team (1990) • NCAA East Second All-American Team (1990) • Hockey East First All-Star Team (1991) • NCAA East First All-American Team (1991)

Traded to **Chicago** by **Buffalo** with Buffalo's 6th round choice (Marc Magliarditi) in 1995 Entry Draft for Craig Muni and Chicago's 5th round choice (Daniel Bienvenue) in 1995 Entry Draft, October 26, 1993. Traded to **Phoenix** by **Chicago** with Jim Cummins for Chad Kilger and Jayson More, March 4, 1998. Traded to **Anaheim** by **Phoenix** for Calgary's 2nd round choice (previously acquired, later traded back to Calgary - Calgary selected Andrei Taratukhin) in 2001 Entry Draft, June 19, 2001.

CARTER, Anson

(KAHR-tuhr, AN-sohn) **EDM.**

Right wing. Shoots right. 6'1", 200 lbs. Born, Toronto, Ont., June 6, 1974. Quebec's 11th choice, 220th overall, in 1992 Entry Draft.

Season	Club	League	GP	G	A	Pts	PIM	PP	SH	GW	S	%	+/-	TF	F%	H	SB	Min	GP	G	A	Pts	PIM	PP	SH	GW
1989-90	Don Mills Flyers	MTHL	40	15	47	62	105	....	....	....	....	....	....	....	....	....	....	....	....	....	....	....	....	....	....	....
1990-91	Don Mills Flyers	MTHL	67	69	73	142	43	....	....	....	....	....	....	....	....	....	....	....	....	....	....	....	....	....	....	....
1991-92	Wexford Raiders	MTJHL	42	18	22	40	24	....	....	....	....	....	....	....	....	....	....	....	....	....	....	....	....	....	....	....
1992-93	Michigan State	CCHA	34	15	7	22	20	....	....	....	....	....	....	....	....	....	....	....	....	....	....	....	....	....	....	....
1993-94	Michigan State	CCHA	39	30	24	54	36	....	....	....	....	....	....	....	....	....	....	....	....	....	....	....	....	....	....	....
1994-95	Michigan State	CCHA	39	34	17	51	40	....	....	....	....	....	....	....	....	....	....	....	....	....	....	....	....	....	....	....
1995-96	Michigan State	CCHA	42	23	20	43	36	....	....	....	....	....	....	....	....	....	....	....	....	....	....	....	....	....	....	....
1996-97	**Washington**	**NHL**	**19**	**3**	**2**	**5**	**7**	**1**	**0**	**1**	**28**	**10.7**	**0**	....	....	....	....	....	....	....	....	....	....	....	....	....
	Portland Pirates	AHL	27	19	19	38	11	....	....	....	....	....	....	....	....	....	....	....	....	....	....	....	....	....	....	....
	Boston	**NHL**	**19**	**8**	**5**	**13**	**2**	**1**	**1**	**1**	**51**	**15.7**	**-7**	....	....	....	....	....	....	....	....	....	....	....	....	....
1997-98	**Boston**	**NHL**	**78**	**16**	**27**	**43**	**31**	**6**	**0**	**4**	**179**	**8.9**	**7**	....	....	....	....	....	**6**	**1**	**1**	**2**	**0**	**0**	**0**	**0**
1998-99	Utah Grizzlies	IHL	6	1	1	2	0	....	....	....	....	....	....	....	....	....	....	....	....	....	....	....	....	....	....	....
	Boston	**NHL**	**55**	**24**	**16**	**40**	**22**	**6**	**0**	**6**	**123**	**19.5**	**7**	**172**	**43.0**	**62**	**5**	**18:44**	**12**	**4**	**3**	**7**	**0**	**1**	**0**	**1**

			Regular Season																Playoffs							
Season	Club	League	GP	G	A	Pts	PIM	PP	SH	GW	S	%	+/-	TF	F%	H	SB	Min	GP	G	A	Pts	PIM	PP	SH	GW
99-2000	Boston	NHL	59	22	25	47	14	4	0	1	144	15.3	8	793	48.2	87	9	20:31	....	....	....	....	....	....	....	....
2000-01	Edmonton	NHL	61	16	26	42	23	7	1	4	102	15.7	1	80	47.5	66	11	18:13	6	3	1	4	4	1	0	1
	NHL Totals		291	89	101	190	99	25	2	17	627	14.2		1045	47.3	215	25	19:09	24	8	5	13	4	2	0	2

CCHA First All-Star Team (1994, 1995) • NCAA West Second All-American Team (1995) • CCHA Second All-Star Team (1996)

Rights transferred to **Colorado** after **Quebec** franchise relocated, June 21, 1995. Traded to **Washington** by **Colorado** for Washington's 4th round choice (Ben Storey) in 1996 Entry Draft, April 3, 1996. Traded to **Boston** by **Washington** with Jim Carey, Jason Allison and Washington's 3rd round choice (Lee Goren) in 1997 Entry Draft for Bill Ranford, Adam Oates and Rick Tocchet, March 1, 1997. Traded to **Edmonton** by **Boston** with Boston's 1st (Ales Hemsky) and 2nd (Doug Lynch) round choices in 2001 Entry Draft for Bill Guerin and future considerations, November 15, 2000.

CASSELS, Andrew

(KAS-uhls, AN-droo) **VAN.**

Center. Shoots left. 6'1", 185 lbs. Born, Bramalea, Ont., July 23, 1969. Montreal's 1st choice, 17th overall, in 1987 Entry Draft.

1985-86	Bramalea Blues	MTJHL	33	18	25	43	26	....	....	....	....	....	....	....	....	....	....	....	....	....	....	....	....	....	....	....
1986-87	Ottawa 67's	OHL	66	26	66	92	28	....	....	....	....	....	....	....	....	....	....	....	11	5	9	14	7	....	....	....
1987-88	Ottawa 67's	OHL	61	48	*103	*151	39	....	....	....	....	....	....	....	....	....	....	....	16	8	*24	*32	13	....	....	....
1988-89	Ottawa 67's	OHL	56	37	97	134	66	....	....	....	....	....	....	....	....	....	....	....	12	5	10	15	10	....	....	....
1989-90	Montreal	NHL	6	2	0	2	2	0	0	1	5	40.0	1	....	....	....	....	....	....	....	....	....	....	....	....	....
	Sherbrooke	AHL	55	22	45	67	25	....	....	....	....	....	....	....	....	....	....	....	12	2	11	13	6	....	....	....
1990-91	Montreal	NHL	54	6	19	25	20	1	0	3	55	10.9	2	....	....	....	....	....	8	0	2	2	2	0	0	0
1991-92	Hartford	NHL	67	11	30	41	18	2	2	3	99	11.1	3	....	....	....	....	....	7	2	4	6	6	1	0	0
1992-93	Hartford	NHL	84	21	64	85	62	8	3	1	134	15.7	–11	....	....	....	....	....	....	....	....	....	....	....	....	....
1993-94	Hartford	NHL	79	16	42	58	37	8	1	3	126	12.7	–21	....	....	....	....	....	....	....	....	....	....	....	....	....
1994-95	Hartford	NHL	46	7	30	37	18	1	0	1	74	9.5	–3	....	....	....	....	....	....	....	....	....	....	....	....	....
1995-96	Hartford	NHL	81	20	43	63	39	6	0	1	135	14.8	8	....	....	....	....	....	....	....	....	....	....	....	....	....
1996-97	Hartford	NHL	81	22	44	66	46	8	0	2	142	15.5	–16	....	....	....	....	....	....	....	....	....	....	....	....	....
1997-98	Calgary	NHL	81	17	27	44	32	6	1	2	138	12.3	–7	....	....	....	....	....	....	....	....	....	....	....	....	....
1998-99	Calgary	NHL	70	12	25	37	18	4	1	3	97	12.4	–12	1322	51.1	25	40	18:58	....	....	....	....	....	....	....	....
99-2000	Vancouver	NHL	79	17	45	62	16	6	0	1	109	15.6	8	1127	48.3	45	36	19:19	....	....	....	....	....	....	....	....
2000-01	Vancouver	NHL	66	12	44	56	10	2	0	1	104	11.5	1	1164	49.9	41	31	19:22	....	....	....	....	....	....	....	....
	NHL Totals		794	163	413	576	318	52	8	22	1218	13.4		3613	49.8	111	107	19:13	15	2	6	8	8	1	0	0

OHL First All-Star Team (1988,1989)

Traded to **Hartford** by **Montreal** for Hartford's 2nd round choice (Valeri Bure) in 1992 Entry Draft, September 17, 1991. Transferred to **Carolina** after **Hartford** franchise relocated, June 25, 1997. Traded to **Calgary** by **Carolina** with Jean-Sebastien Giguere for Gary Roberts and Trevor Kidd, August 25, 1997. Signed as a free agent by **Vancouver**, August 19, 1999.

CHARA, Zdeno

(KHAH-rah, ZDEH-noh) **OTT.**

Defense. Shoots left. 6'9", 255 lbs. Born, Trencin, Czech., March 18, 1977. NY Islanders' 3rd choice, 56th overall, in 1996 Entry Draft.

1994-95	Dukla Trencin-B	Slovak-Jr.	30	22	22	44	113	....	....	....	....	....	....	....	....	....	....	....	....	....	....	....	....	....	....	....
	Dukla Trencin	Slovak-Jr.	2	0	0	0	0	....	....	....	....	....	....	....	....	....	....	....	....	....	....	....	....	....	....	....
1995-96	Dukla Trencin	Slovak-Jr.	22	1	13	14	80	....	....	....	....	....	....	....	....	....	....	....	....	....	....	....	....	....	....	....
	HK Piestany	Slovakia-2	10	1	3	4	10	....	....	....	....	....	....	....	....	....	....	....	....	....	....	....	....	....	....	....
	Sparta Praha-Jr.	Cze-Rep	15	1	2	3	42	....	....	....	....	....	....	....	....	....	....	....	....	....	....	....	....	....	....	....
	Sparta Praha	Cze-Rep	1	0	0	0	0	....	....	....	....	....	....	....	....	....	....	....	....	....	....	....	....	....	....	....
1996-97	Prince George	WHL	49	3	19	22	120	....	....	....	....	....	....	....	....	....	....	....	15	1	7	8	45	....	....	....
1997-98	NY Islanders	NHL	25	0	1	1	50	0	0	0	10	0.0	1	....	....	....	....	....	....	....	....	....	....	....	....	....
	Kentucky	AHL	48	4	9	13	125	....	....	....	....	....	....	....	....	....	....	....	1	0	0	0	4	....	....	....
1998-99	NY Islanders	NHL	59	2	6	8	83	0	1	0	56	3.6	–8	0	0.0	214	55	18:54	....	....	....	....	....	....	....	....
	Lowell	AHL	23	2	2	4	47	....	....	....	....	....	....	....	....	....	....	....	....	....	....	....	....	....	....	....
99-2000	NY Islanders	NHL	65	2	9	11	57	0	0	1	47	4.3	–27	0	0.0	309	100	22:52	....	....	....	....	....	....	....	....
2000-01	NY Islanders	NHL	82	2	7	9	157	0	1	0	83	2.4	–27	0	0.0	373	126	22:20	....	....	....	....	....	....	....	....
	NHL Totals		231	6	23	29	347	0	2	1	196	3.1		0	0.0	896	281	21:31	....	....	....	....	....	....	....	....

Traded to **Ottawa** by **NY Islanders** with Bill Muckalt and NY Islanders' 1st round choice (Jason Spezza) in 2001 Entry Draft for Alexei Yashin, June 23, 2001.

CHARRON, Eric

(shah-ROHN, AIR-ihk)

Defense. Shoots left. 6'3", 195 lbs. Born, Verdun, Que., January 14, 1970. Montreal's 1st choice, 20th overall, in 1988 Entry Draft.

1986-87	Lac St-Louis	QAAA	41	1	8	9	92	....	....	....	....	....	....	....	....	....	....	....	2	0	2	2	2	....	....	....
1987-88	Trois-Rivieres	QMJHL	67	3	13	16	135	....	....	....	....	....	....	....	....	....	....	....	....	....	....	....	....	....	....	....
1988-89	Trois-Rivieres	QMJHL	38	2	16	18	111	....	....	....	....	....	....	....	....	....	....	....	....	....	....	....	....	....	....	....
	Verdun	QMJHL	28	2	15	17	66	....	....	....	....	....	....	....	....	....	....	....	....	....	....	....	....	....	....	....
	Sherbrooke	AHL	1	0	0	0	0	....	....	....	....	....	....	....	....	....	....	....	....	....	....	....	....	....	....	....
1989-90	St-Hyacinthe	QMJHL	68	13	38	51	152	....	....	....	....	....	....	....	....	....	....	....	11	3	4	7	67	....	....	....
	Sherbrooke	AHL	....	....	....	....	....	....	....	....	....	....	....	....	....	....	....	....	2	0	0	0	0	....	....	....
1990-91	Fredericton	AHL	71	1	11	12	108	....	....	....	....	....	....	....	....	....	....	....	2	1	0	1	29	....	....	....
1991-92	Fredericton	AHL	59	2	11	13	98	....	....	....	....	....	....	....	....	....	....	....	6	1	0	1	4	....	....	....
1992-93	Montreal	NHL	3	0	0	0	2	0	0	0	0	0.0	0	....	....	....	....	....	....	....	....	....	....	....	....	....
	Fredericton	AHL	54	3	13	16	93	....	....	....	....	....	....	....	....	....	....	....	....	....	....	....	....	....	....	....
	Atlanta Knights	IHL	11	0	2	2	12	....	....	....	....	....	....	....	....	....	....	....	3	0	1	1	6	....	....	....
1993-94	Tampa Bay	NHL	4	0	0	0	2	0	0	0	1	0.0	0	....	....	....	....	....	....	....	....	....	....	....	....	....
	Atlanta Knights	IHL	66	5	18	23	144	....	....	....	....	....	....	....	....	....	....	....	14	1	4	5	28	....	....	....
1994-95	Tampa Bay	NHL	45	1	4	5	26	0	0	0	33	3.0	1	....	....	....	....	....	....	....	....	....	....	....	....	....
1995-96	Tampa Bay	NHL	14	0	0	0	18	0	0	0	11	0.0	–6	....	....	....	....	....	....	....	....	....	....	....	....	....
	Washington	NHL	4	0	1	1	4	0	0	0	2	0.0	3	....	....	....	....	....	6	0	0	0	8	0	0	0
	Portland Pirates	AHL	45	0	8	8	88	....	....	....	....	....	....	....	....	....	....	....	20	1	1	2	33	....	....	....
1996-97	Washington	NHL	25	1	1	2	20	0	0	0	11	9.1	1	....	....	....	....	....	....	....	....	....	....	....	....	....
	Portland Pirates	AHL	29	6	8	14	55	....	....	....	....	....	....	....	....	....	....	....	5	0	3	3	0	....	....	....
1997-98	Calgary	NHL	2	0	0	0	4	0	0	0	1	0.0	0	....	....	....	....	....	....	....	....	....	....	....	....	....
	Saint John Flames	AHL	56	8	20	28	136	....	....	....	....	....	....	....	....	....	....	....	20	1	7	8	55	....	....	....
1998-99	Calgary	NHL	12	0	1	1	14	0	0	0	9	0.0	–6	0	0.0	12	13	13:45	....	....	....	....	....	....	....	....
	Saint John Flames	AHL	50	10	12	22	148	....	....	....	....	....	....	....	....	....	....	....	3	1	0	1	22	....	....	....
99-2000	Calgary	NHL	21	0	0	0	37	0	0	0	8	0.0	–3	0	0.0	17	20	10:29	....	....	....	....	....	....	....	....
	Saint John Flames	AHL	37	2	15	17	82	....	....	....	....	....	....	....	....	....	....	....	....	....	....	....	....	....	....	....
2000-01	Cleveland	IHL	60	9	10	19	99	....	....	....	....	....	....	....	....	....	....	....	....	....	....	....	....	....	....	....
	NHL Totals		130	2	7	9	127	0	0	0	76	2.6		0	0.0	29	33	11:40	6	0	0	0	8	0	0	0

Traded to **Tampa Bay** by **Montreal** with Alain Cote and future considerations (Donald Dufresne, June 18, 1993) for Rob Ramage, March 20, 1993. Traded to **Washington** by **Tampa Bay** for Washington's 7th round choice (Eero Somervuori) in 1997 Entry Draft, November 16, 1995. Traded to **Calgary** by **Washington** for Calgary's 7th round choice (Nathan Forster) in 1998 Entry Draft, September 4, 1997. Signed as a free agent by **Minnesota**, August 31, 2000.

CHARTRAND, Brad

(SHAR-trand, BRAD) **L.A.**

Right wing. Shoots left. 5'11", 191 lbs. Born, Winnipeg, Man., December 14, 1974.

1988-89	Winnipeg Hawks	MAHA	24	30	50	80	40	....	....	....	....	....	....	....	....	....	....	....	....	....	....	....	....	....	....	....
1989-90	Winnipeg Hawks	MAHA	24	26	55	81	40	....	....	....	....	....	....	....	....	....	....	....	....	....	....	....	....	....	....	....
1990-91	Winnipeg Hawks	MAHA	34	26	45	71	40	....	....	....	....	....	....	....	....	....	....	....	....	....	....	....	....	....	....	....
1991-92	St. James	MJHL	STATISTICS NOT AVAILABLE																							
1992-93	Cornell Big Red	ECAC	26	10	6	16	16	....	....	....	....	....	....	....	....	....	....	....	....	....	....	....	....	....	....	....
1993-94	Cornell Big Red	ECAC	30	4	14	18	48	....	....	....	....	....	....	....	....	....	....	....	....	....	....	....	....	....	....	....
1994-95	Cornell Big Red	ECAC	28	9	9	18	10	....	....	....	....	....	....	....	....	....	....	....	....	....	....	....	....	....	....	....
1995-96	Cornell Big Red	ECAC	34	24	19	43	16	....	....	....	....	....	....	....	....	....	....	....	....	....	....	....	....	....	....	....
1996-97	Canada	Nat-Team	54	10	14	24	42	....	....	....	....	....	....	....	....	....	....	....	....	....	....	....	....	....	....	....
1997-98	Canada	Nat-Team	60	24	30	54	47	....	....	....	....	....	....	....	....	....	....	....	....	....	....	....	....	....	....	....
	HC Rapperswil	Switz.	8	2	3	5	4	....	....	....	....	....	....	....	....	....	....	....	....	....	....	....	....	....	....	....
1998-99	St. John's Leafs	AHL	64	16	14	30	48	....	....	....	....	....	....	....	....	....	....	....	5	0	2	2	2	....	....	....
99-2000	Los Angeles	NHL	50	6	6	12	17	0	1	3	51	11.8	4	62	53.2	70	18	11:03	4	0	0	0	6	0	0	0
	Lowell	AHL	16	5	10	15	8	....	....	....	....	....	....	....	....	....	....	....	....	....	....	....	....	....	....	....
	Long Beach	IHL	1	0	0	0	0	....	....	....	....	....	....	....	....	....	....	....	3	0	0	0	0	....	....	....
2000-01	Los Angeles	NHL	4	1	0	1	2	0	0	1	6	16.7	–2	0	0.0	7	0	11:37	....	....	....	....	....	....	....	....
	Lowell	AHL	72	17	34	51	44	....	....	....	....	....	....	....	....	....	....	....	4	0	1	1	8	....	....	....
	NHL Totals		54	7	6	13	19	0	1	4	57	12.3		62	53.2	77	18	11:05	4	0	0	0	6	0	0	0

Signed as a free agent by **LA Kings**, July 15, 1999. Loaned to **Lowell** (AHL) by **LA Kings**, January 26, 2000.

CHEBATURKIN, Vladimir

(cheh-bah-TOOR-kihn)

Defense. Shoots left. 6'2", 226 lbs. Born, Tyumen, USSR, April 23, 1975. NY Islanders' 3rd choice, 66th overall, in 1993 Entry Draft.

			Regular Season																Playoffs							
Season	Club	League	GP	G	A	Pts	PIM	PP	SH	GW	S	%	+/-	TF	F%	H	SB	Min	GP	G	A	Pts	PIM	PP	SH	GW
1993-94	Kristall Elektrostal	CIS-2	42	4	4	8	38	....	....	....	....	....	....	....	....	....	....	....	....	....	....	....	....	....	....	....
1994-95	Kristall Elektrostal	CIS	52	2	6	8	90	....	....	....	....	....	....	....	....	....	....	....	....	....	....	....	....	....	....	....
1995-96	Kristall Elektrostal	CIS	44	1	6	7	30	....	....	....	....	....	....	....	....	....	....	....	1	0	0	0	0	....	....	....
1996-97	Utah Grizzlies	IHL	68	0	4	4	34	....	....	....	....	....	....	....	....	....	....	....	....	....	....	....	....	....	....	....
1997-98	**NY Islanders**	**NHL**	**2**	**0**	**2**	**2**	**0**	**0**	**0**	**0**	**0**	**0.0**	**–1**	....	....	....	....	....	....	....	....	....	....	....	....	....
	Kentucky	AHL	54	6	8	14	52	....	....	....	....	....	....	....	....	....	....	....	2	0	0	0	4	....	....	....
1998-99	**NY Islanders**	**NHL**	**8**	**0**	**0**	**0**	**12**	**0**	**0**	**0**	**4**	**0.0**	**6**	**0**	**0.0**	**27**	**8**	**17:12**	....	....	....	....	....	....	....	....
	Lowell	AHL	69	2	12	14	85	....	....	....	....	....	....	....	....	....	....	....	3	0	0	0	0	....	....	....
99-2000	**NY Islanders**	**NHL**	**17**	**1**	**1**	**2**	**8**	**0**	**0**	**0**	**9**	**11.1**	**–3**	**0**	**0.0**	**58**	**25**	**16:57**	....	....	....	....	....	....	....	....
	Lowell	AHL	63	1	8	9	118	....	....	....	....	....	....	....	....	....	....	....	7	0	4	4	11	....	....	....
2000-01	**St. Louis**	**NHL**	**22**	**1**	**2**	**3**	**26**	**0**	**0**	**0**	**5**	**20.0**	**5**	**0**	**0.0**	**54**	**15**	**13:09**	....	....	....	....	....	....	....	....
	Worcester	AHL	33	0	7	7	73	....	....	....	....	....	....	....	....	....	....	....	10	1	0	1	10	....	....	....
	NHL Totals		**49**	**2**	**5**	**7**	**46**	**0**	**0**	**0**	**18**	**11.1**		**0**	**0.0**	**139**	**48**	**15:13**	....	....	....	....	....	....	....	....

Signed as a free agent by **St. Louis**, June 9, 2000.

CHELIOS, Chris

(CHELL-EE-ohs, KRIHS) **DET.**

Defense. Shoots right. 6'1", 190 lbs. Born, Chicago, IL, January 25, 1962. Montreal's 5th choice, 40th overall, in 1981 Entry Draft.

			Regular Season																Playoffs							
Season	Club	League	GP	G	A	Pts	PIM	PP	SH	GW	S	%	+/-	TF	F%	H	SB	Min	GP	G	A	Pts	PIM	PP	SH	GW
1979-80	Moose Jaw	SJHL	53	12	31	43	118	....	....	....	....	....	....	....	....	....	....	....	....	....	....	....	....	....	....	....
1980-81	Moose Jaw	SJHL	54	23	64	87	175	....	....	....	....	....	....	....	....	....	....	....	....	....	....	....	....	....	....	....
1981-82	U. of Wisconsin	WCHA	43	6	43	49	50	....	....	....	....	....	....	....	....	....	....	....	....	....	....	....	....	....	....	....
1982-83	U. of Wisconsin	WCHA	26	9	17	26	50	....	....	....	....	....	....	....	....	....	....	....	....	....	....	....	....	....	....	....
1983-84	United States	Nat-Team	60	14	35	49	58	....	....	....	....	....	....	....	....	....	....	....	....	....	....	....	....	....	....	....
	United States	Olympics	6	0	4	4	8	....	....	....	....	....	....	....	....	....	....	....	....	....	....	....	....	....	....	....
	Montreal	**NHL**	**12**	**0**	**2**	**2**	**12**	**0**	**0**	**0**	**23**	**0.0**	**–5**	....	....	....	....	....	**15**	**1**	**9**	**10**	**17**	**1**	**0**	**0**
1984-85	**Montreal**	**NHL**	**74**	**9**	**55**	**64**	**87**	**2**	**1**	**0**	**199**	**4.5**	**11**	....	....	....	....	....	**9**	**2**	**8**	**10**	**17**	**2**	**0**	**0**
1985-86♦	**Montreal**	**NHL**	**41**	**8**	**26**	**34**	**67**	**2**	**0**	**0**	**101**	**7.9**	**4**	....	....	....	....	....	**20**	**2**	**9**	**11**	**49**	**1**	**0**	**0**
1986-87	**Montreal**	**NHL**	**71**	**11**	**33**	**44**	**124**	**6**	**0**	**2**	**141**	**7.8**	**–5**	....	....	....	....	....	**17**	**4**	**9**	**13**	**38**	**2**	**1**	**0**
1987-88	**Montreal**	**NHL**	**71**	**20**	**41**	**61**	**172**	**10**	**1**	**5**	**199**	**10.1**	**14**	....	....	....	....	....	**11**	**3**	**1**	**4**	**29**	**1**	**0**	**0**
1988-89	**Montreal**	**NHL**	**80**	**15**	**58**	**73**	**185**	**8**	**0**	**6**	**206**	**7.3**	**35**	....	....	....	....	....	**21**	**4**	**15**	**19**	**28**	**1**	**0**	**2**
1989-90	**Montreal**	**NHL**	**53**	**9**	**22**	**31**	**136**	**1**	**2**	**1**	**123**	**7.3**	**20**	....	....	....	....	....	**5**	**0**	**1**	**1**	**8**	**0**	**0**	**0**
1990-91	**Chicago**	**NHL**	**77**	**12**	**52**	**64**	**192**	**5**	**2**	**2**	**187**	**6.4**	**23**	....	....	....	....	....	**6**	**1**	**7**	**8**	**46**	**1**	**0**	**0**
1991-92	**Chicago**	**NHL**	**80**	**9**	**47**	**56**	**245**	**2**	**2**	**2**	**239**	**3.8**	**24**	....	....	....	....	....	**18**	**6**	**15**	**21**	**37**	**3**	**0**	**1**
1992-93	**Chicago**	**NHL**	**84**	**15**	**58**	**73**	**282**	**8**	**0**	**2**	**290**	**5.2**	**14**	....	....	....	....	....	**4**	**0**	**2**	**2**	**14**	**0**	**0**	**0**
1993-94	**Chicago**	**NHL**	**76**	**16**	**44**	**60**	**212**	**7**	**1**	**2**	**219**	**7.3**	**12**	....	....	....	....	....	**6**	**1**	**1**	**2**	**8**	**1**	**0**	**0**
1994-95	EHC Biel-Bienne	Switz.	3	0	3	3	4	....	....	....	....	....	....	....	....	....	....	....	....	....	....	....	....	....	....	....
	Chicago	**NHL**	**48**	**5**	**33**	**38**	**72**	**3**	**1**	**0**	**166**	**3.0**	**17**	....	....	....	....	....	**16**	**4**	**7**	**11**	**12**	**0**	**1**	**3**
1995-96	**Chicago**	**NHL**	**81**	**14**	**58**	**72**	**140**	**7**	**0**	**3**	**219**	**6.4**	**25**	....	....	....	....	....	**9**	**0**	**3**	**3**	**8**	**0**	**0**	**0**
1996-97	**Chicago**	**NHL**	**72**	**10**	**38**	**48**	**112**	**2**	**0**	**2**	**194**	**5.2**	**16**	....	....	....	....	....	**6**	**0**	**1**	**1**	**8**	**0**	**0**	**0**
1997-98	**Chicago**	**NHL**	**81**	**3**	**39**	**42**	**151**	**1**	**0**	**0**	**205**	**1.5**	**–7**	....	....	....	....	....	....	....	....	....	....	....	....	....
	United States	Olympics	4	2	0	2	2	....	....	....	....	....	....	....	....	....	....	....	....	....	....	....	....	....	....	....
1998-99	**Chicago**	**NHL**	**65**	**8**	**26**	**34**	**89**	**2**	**1**	**0**	**172**	**4.7**	**–4**	**4**	**25.0**	**72**	**109**	**27:19**	....	....	....	....	....	....	....	....
	Detroit	**NHL**	**10**	**1**	**1**	**2**	**4**	**1**	**0**	**1**	**15**	**6.7**	**5**	**0**	**0.0**	**11**	**7**	**22:21**	**10**	**0**	**4**	**4**	**14**	**0**	**0**	**0**
99-2000	**Detroit**	**NHL**	**81**	**3**	**31**	**34**	**103**	**0**	**0**	**0**	**135**	**2.2**	**48**	**0**	**0.0**	**120**	**86**	**25:16**	**9**	**0**	**1**	**1**	**8**	**0**	**0**	**0**
2000-01	**Detroit**	**NHL**	**24**	**0**	**3**	**3**	**45**	**0**	**0**	**0**	**26**	**0.0**	**4**	**0**	**0.0**	**41**	**32**	**22:51**	**5**	**1**	**0**	**1**	**2**	**0**	**0**	**0**
	NHL Totals		**1181**	**168**	**667**	**835**	**2430**	**67**	**11**	**28**	**3059**	**5.5**		**4**	**25.0**	**244**	**234**	**25:31**	**187**	**29**	**93**	**122**	**343**	**13**	**2**	**6**

WCHA Second All-Star Team (1983) • NCAA Championship All-Tournament Team (1983) • NHL All-Rookie Team (1985) • NHL First All-Star Team (1989, 1993, 1995, 1996) • Won James Norris Memorial Trophy (1989, 1993, 1996) • NHL Second All-Star Team (1991, 1997) • Played in NHL All-Star Game (1985, 1990, 1991, 1992, 1993, 1994, 1996, 1997, 1998, 2000)

Traded to **Chicago** by **Montreal** with Montreal's 2nd round choice (Michael Pomichter) in 1991 Entry Draft for Denis Savard, June 29, 1990. Traded to **Detroit** by **Chicago** for Anders Eriksson and Detroit's 1st round choices in 1999 (Steve McCarthy) and 2001 (Adam Munro) Entry Drafts, March 23, 1999. • Missed majority of 2000-01 season recovering from knee injury suffered in game vs. Dallas, November 17, 2000.

CHIMERA, Jason

(chihm-AIR-a, JAY-suhn) **EDM.**

Center. Shoots left. 6', 180 lbs. Born, Edmonton, Alta., May 2, 1979. Edmonton's 5th choice, 121st overall, in 1997 Entry Draft.

			Regular Season																Playoffs							
Season	Club	League	GP	G	A	Pts	PIM	PP	SH	GW	S	%	+/-	TF	F%	H	SB	Min	GP	G	A	Pts	PIM	PP	SH	GW
1994-95	Edmonton Pats	AMHL	33	27	31	58	42	....	....	....	....	....	....	....	....	....	....	....	....	....	....	....	....	....	....	....
1995-96	Edmonton Pats	AMHL	34	23	24	47	44	....	....	....	....	....	....	....	....	....	....	....	....	....	....	....	....	....	....	....
1996-97	Medicine Hat	WHL	71	16	23	39	64	....	....	....	....	....	....	....	....	....	....	....	4	0	1	1	4	....	....	....
1997-98	Medicine Hat	WHL	72	34	32	66	93	....	....	....	....	....	....	....	....	....	....	....	....	....	....	....	....	....	....	....
	Hamilton Bulldogs	AHL	4	0	0	0	8	....	....	....	....	....	....	....	....	....	....	....	....	....	....	....	....	....	....	....
1998-99	Medicine Hat	WHL	37	18	22	40	84	....	....	....	....	....	....	....	....	....	....	....	....	....	....	....	....	....	....	....
	Brandon	WHL	21	14	12	26	32	....	....	....	....	....	....	....	....	....	....	....	5	4	1	5	8	....	....	....
99-2000	Hamilton Bulldogs	AHL	78	15	13	28	77	....	....	....	....	....	....	....	....	....	....	....	10	0	2	2	12	....	....	....
2000-01	**Edmonton**	**NHL**	**1**	**0**	**0**	**0**	**0**	**0**	**0**	**0**	**0**	**0.0**	**0**	**0**	**0.0**	**0**	**0**	**6:58**	....	....	....	....	....	....	....	....
	Hamilton Bulldogs	AHL	78	29	25	54	93	....	....	....	....	....	....	....	....	....	....	....	....	....	....	....	....	....	....	....
	NHL Totals		**1**	**0**	**0**	**0**	**0**	**0**	**0**	**0**	**0**	**0.0**		**0**	**0.0**	**0**	**0**	**6:58**	....	....	....	....	....	....	....	....

CHORSKE, Tom

(CHOHR-skee, TAWM)

Left wing. Shoots right. 6'1", 212 lbs. Born, Minneapolis, MN, September 18, 1966. Montreal's 2nd choice, 16th overall, in 1985 Entry Draft.

			Regular Season																Playoffs							
Season	Club	League	GP	G	A	Pts	PIM	PP	SH	GW	S	%	+/-	TF	F%	H	SB	Min	GP	G	A	Pts	PIM	PP	SH	GW
1984-85	Southwest High	Hi-School	23	44	26	70	....	....	....	....	....	....	....	....	....	....	....	....	....	....	....	....	....	....	....	....
1985-86	U. of Minnesota	WCHA	39	6	4	10	16	....	....	....	....	....	....	....	....	....	....	....	....	....	....	....	....	....	....	....
1986-87	U. of Minnesota	WCHA	47	20	22	42	20	....	....	....	....	....	....	....	....	....	....	....	....	....	....	....	....	....	....	....
1987-88	United States	Nat-Team	36	9	16	25	24	....	....	....	....	....	....	....	....	....	....	....	....	....	....	....	....	....	....	....
1988-89	U. of Minnesota	WCHA	37	25	24	49	28	....	....	....	....	....	....	....	....	....	....	....	....	....	....	....	....	....	....	....
1989-90	**Montreal**	**NHL**	**14**	**3**	**1**	**4**	**2**	**0**	**0**	**0**	**19**	**15.8**	**2**	....	....	....	....	....	....	....	....	....	....	....	....	....
	Sherbrooke	AHL	59	22	24	46	54	....	....	....	....	....	....	....	....	....	....	....	12	4	4	8	8	....	....	....
1990-91	**Montreal**	**NHL**	**57**	**9**	**11**	**20**	**32**	**3**	**0**	**1**	**82**	**11.0**	**–8**	....	....	....	....	....	....	....	....	....	....	....	....	....
1991-92	**New Jersey**	**NHL**	**76**	**19**	**17**	**36**	**32**	**0**	**3**	**2**	**143**	**13.3**	**8**	....	....	....	....	....	**7**	**0**	**3**	**3**	**4**	**0**	**0**	**0**
1992-93	**New Jersey**	**NHL**	**50**	**7**	**12**	**19**	**25**	**0**	**0**	**1**	**63**	**11.1**	**–1**	....	....	....	....	....	**1**	**0**	**0**	**0**	**0**	**0**	**0**	**0**
	Utica Devils	AHL	6	1	4	5	2	....	....	....	....	....	....	....	....	....	....	....	....	....	....	....	....	....	....	....
1993-94	**New Jersey**	**NHL**	**76**	**21**	**20**	**41**	**32**	**1**	**1**	**4**	**131**	**16.0**	**14**	....	....	....	....	....	**20**	**4**	**3**	**7**	**0**	**0**	**0**	**1**
1994-95	HC Milano	Italy	7	11	5	16	6	....	....	....	....	....	....	....	....	....	....	....	....	....	....	....	....	....	....	....
	HC Milano	EuroHL	4	6	7	13	2	....	....	....	....	....	....	....	....	....	....	....	....	....	....	....	....	....	....	....
	♦ New Jersey	**NHL**	**42**	**10**	**8**	**18**	**16**	**0**	**0**	**2**	**59**	**16.9**	**–4**	....	....	....	....	....	**17**	**1**	**5**	**6**	**4**	**0**	**0**	**0**
1995-96	**Ottawa**	**NHL**	**72**	**15**	**14**	**29**	**21**	**0**	**2**	**1**	**118**	**12.7**	**–9**	....	....	....	....	....	....	....	....	....	....	....	....	....
1996-97	**Ottawa**	**NHL**	**68**	**18**	**8**	**26**	**16**	**1**	**1**	**1**	**116**	**15.5**	**–1**	....	....	....	....	....	**5**	**0**	**1**	**1**	**2**	**0**	**0**	**0**
1997-98	**NY Islanders**	**NHL**	**82**	**12**	**23**	**35**	**39**	**1**	**4**	**2**	**132**	**9.1**	**7**	....	....	....	....	....	....	....	....	....	....	....	....	....
1998-99	**NY Islanders**	**NHL**	**2**	**0**	**1**	**1**	**2**	**0**	**0**	**0**	**9**	**0.0**	**1**	**0**	**0.0**	**2**	**0**	**12:54**	....	....	....	....	....	....	....	....
	Washington	**NHL**	**17**	**0**	**2**	**2**	**4**	**0**	**0**	**0**	**22**	**0.0**	**–4**	**4**	**50.0**	**15**	**5**	**11:26**	....	....	....	....	....	....	....	....
	Calgary	**NHL**	**7**	**0**	**0**	**0**	**2**	**0**	**0**	**0**	**0**	**13.0**	**–5**	**7**	**71.4**	**7**	**2**	**13:48**	....	....	....	....	....	....	....	....
99-2000	**Pittsburgh**	**NHL**	**33**	**1**	**5**	**6**	**2**	**0**	**0**	**0**	**14**	**7.1**	**–2**	**18**	**38.9**	**29**	**10**	**7:50**	....	....	....	....	....	....	....	....
2000-01	Houston Aeros	IHL	78	27	25	52	36	....	....	....	....	....	....	....	....	....	....	....	7	3	2	5	4	....	....	....
	NHL Totals		**596**	**115**	**122**	**237**	**225**	**6**	**11**	**14**	**908**	**12.7**		**29**	**48.3**	**53**	**17**	**9:45**	**50**	**5**	**12**	**17**	**10**	**0**	**0**	**1**

Minnesota High School Player of the Year (1985) • WCHA First All-Star Team (1989)

Traded to **New Jersey** by **Montreal** with Stephane Richer for Kirk Muller and Rollie Melanson, September 20, 1991. Claimed on waivers by **Ottawa** from **New Jersey**, October 5, 1995. Claimed by **NY Islanders** from **Ottawa** in NHL Waiver Draft, September 28, 1997. Traded to **Washington** by **NY Islanders** with NY Islanders' 8th round choice (Maxim Orlov) in 1999 Entry Draft for Washington's 6th round choice (Bjorn Melin) in 1999 Entry Draft, October 16, 1998. Traded to **Calgary** by **Washington** for Calgary's 7th round choice (later traded to LA Kings - LA Kings selected Tim Eriksson) in 2000 Entry Draft and Washington's 9th round choice (previously acquired, Washington selected Bjorn Nord) in 2000 Entry Draft, March 22, 1999. Signed as a free agent by **Pittsburgh**, September 2, 1999. • Missed majority of 1999-2000 season recovering from thumb injury suffered in game vs. NY Islanders, February 3, 2000.

Regular Season / Playoffs

CHOUINARD, Eric
(shwee-NAHR, AIR-ihk) **MTL.**

Center. Shoots left. 6'3", 205 lbs. Born, Atlanta, GA, July 8, 1980. Montreal's 1st choice, 16th overall, in 1998 Entry Draft.

Season	Club	League	GP	G	A	Pts	PIM	PP	SH	GW	S	%	+/-	TF	F%	H	SB	Min	GP	G	A	Pts	PIM	PP	SH	GW
1995-96	Magog Selectes	QAHA	22	12	14	26	12																			
	Ste-Foy Governors	QAAA	17	2	5	7													15	7	12	19	12			
1996-97	Ste-Foy Governors	QAAA	40	29	41	70	40												10	14	9	23				
1997-98	Quebec Remparts	QMJHL	68	41	42	83	18												14	7	10	17	6			
1998-99	Quebec Remparts	QMJHL	62	50	59	109	56												13	8	10	18	8			
	Fredericton	AHL																	6	3	2	5	0			
99-2000	Quebec Remparts	QMJHL	50	57	47	104	105												11	14	4	18	8			
2000-01	**Montreal**	**NHL**	**13**	**1**	**3**	**4**	**0**	**1**	**0**	**0**	**11**	**9.1**	**0**	**31**	**54.8**	**5**	**1**	**10:59**								
	Quebec Citadelles	AHL	48	12	21	33	6												9	2	0	2	2			
	NHL Totals		**13**	**1**	**3**	**4**	**0**	**1**	**0**	**0**	**11**	**9.1**		**31**	**54.8**	**5**	**1**	**10:59**								

CHOUINARD, Marc
(shwee-NAHR, MAHRK) **ANA.**

Center. Shoots right. 6'5", 206 lbs. Born, Charlesbourg, Que., May 6, 1977. Winnipeg's 2nd choice, 32nd overall, in 1995 Entry Draft.

Season	Club	League	GP	G	A	Pts	PIM	PP	SH	GW	S	%	+/-	TF	F%	H	SB	Min	GP	G	A	Pts	PIM	PP	SH	GW
1992-93	Beaubourg AA	QAHA	28	26	45	71	42																			
1993-94	Beauport	QMJHL	62	11	19	30	23												13	2	5	7	2			
1994-95	Beauport	QMJHL	68	24	40	64	32												18	1	6	7	4			
1995-96	Beauport	QMJHL	30	14	21	35	19																			
	Halifax	QMJHL	24	6	12	18	17												6	2	1	3	2			
1996-97	Halifax	QMJHL	63	24	49	73	74												18	9	16	25	12			
1997-98	Cincinnati Ducks	AHL	8	1	2	3	4																			
1998-99	Cincinnati Ducks	AHL	69	7	8	15	20												3	0	0	0	4			
99-2000	Cincinnati Ducks	AHL	70	17	16	33	29																			
2000-01	**Anaheim**	**NHL**	**44**	**3**	**4**	**7**	**12**	**0**	**0**	**1**	**26**	**11.5**	**–5**	**414**	**60.9**	**55**	**11**	**7:50**								
	Cincinnati Ducks	AHL	32	10	9	19	4																			
	NHL Totals		**44**	**3**	**4**	**7**	**12**	**0**	**0**	**1**	**26**	**11.5**		**414**	**60.9**	**55**	**11**	**7:50**								

Traded to **Anaheim** by **Winnipeg** with Teemu Selanne and Winnipeg's 4th round choice (later traded to Toronto - later traded to Montreal - Montreal selected Kim Staal) in 1996 Entry Draft for Chad Kilger, Oleg Tverdovsky and Anaheim's 3rd round choice (Per-Anton Ludstrom) in 1996 Entry Draft, February 7, 1996.

CHRISTIAN, Jeff
(KRIHS-tyan, JEHF)

Left wing. Shoots left. 6'2", 210 lbs. Born, Burlington, Ont., July 30, 1970. New Jersey's 2nd choice, 23rd overall, in 1988 Entry Draft.

Season	Club	League	GP	G	A	Pts	PIM	PP	SH	GW	S	%	+/-	TF	F%	H	SB	Min	GP	G	A	Pts	PIM	PP	SH	GW
1986-87	Dundas Blues	OJHL-C	29	20	34	54	42																			
1987-88	London Knights	OHL	64	15	29	44	154												9	1	5	6	27			
1988-89	London Knights	OHL	60	27	30	57	221												20	3	4	7	56			
1989-90	London Knights	OHL	18	14	7	21	64																			
	Owen Sound	OHL	37	19	26	45	145												10	6	7	13	43			
1990-91	Utica Devils	AHL	80	24	42	66	165																			
1991-92	**New Jersey**	**NHL**	**2**	**0**	**0**	**0**	**2**	**0**	**0**	**0**	**1**	**0.0**	**0**													
	Utica Devils	AHL	76	27	24	51	198												4	0	0	0	16			
1992-93	Utica Devils	AHL	22	4	6	10	39																			
	Hamilton Canucks	AHL	11	2	5	7	35																			
	Cincinnati	IHL	36	5	12	17	113																			
1993-94	Albany River Rats	AHL	76	34	43	77	227												5	1	2	3	19			
1994-95	Cleveland	IHL	56	13	24	37	126												2	0	1	1	8			
	Pittsburgh	**NHL**	**1**	**0**	**0**	**0**	**0**	**0**	**0**	**0**	**2**	**0.0**	**0**													
1995-96	**Pittsburgh**	**NHL**	**3**	**0**	**0**	**0**	**2**	**0**	**0**	**0**	**0**	**0.0**	**0**													
	Cleveland	IHL	66	23	32	55	131												3	0	1	1	8			
1996-97	**Pittsburgh**	**NHL**	**11**	**2**	**2**	**4**	**13**	**0**	**0**	**0**	**18**	**11.1**	**–3**													
	Cleveland	IHL	69	40	40	80	262												12	6	8	14	44			
1997-98	**Phoenix**	**NHL**	**1**	**0**	**0**	**0**	**0**	**0**	**0**	**0**	**0**	**0.0**	**–1**													
	Las Vegas	IHL	30	12	15	27	90												4	2	2	4	20			
1998-99	Houston Aeros	IHL	80	45	41	86	252												18	4	12	16	32			
99-2000	Cleveland	IHL	77	29	35	64	202												9	1	4	5	20			
2000-01	Krefeld Pinguine	DEL	51	17	22	39	205																			
	NHL Totals		**18**	**2**	**2**	**4**	**17**	**0**	**0**	**0**	**21**	**9.5**														

Signed as a free agent by **Pittsburgh**, August 2, 1994. Signed as a free agent by **Phoenix**, July 28, 1997. Signed as a free agent by **Chicago**, August 25, 1999.

CHRISTIE, Ryan
(KRIHS-tee, RIGH-yuhn) **CGY.**

Left wing. Shoots left. 6'3", 200 lbs. Born, Beamsville, Ont., July 3, 1978. Dallas' 4th choice, 112th overall, in 1996 Entry Draft.

Season	Club	League	GP	G	A	Pts	PIM	PP	SH	GW	S	%	+/-	TF	F%	H	SB	Min	GP	G	A	Pts	PIM	PP	SH	GW
1994-95	St. Catharines	OJHL-B	40	10	11	21	96																			
1995-96	Owen Sound	OHL	66	29	17	46	93												6	1	1	2	0			
1996-97	Owen Sound	OHL	66	23	29	52	136												4	1	1	2	8			
1997-98	Owen Sound	OHL	66	39	41	80	208												11	3	5	8	13			
1998-99	Michigan K-Wings	IHL	48	4	5	9	74												3	1	1	2	2			
99-2000	**Dallas**	**NHL**	**5**	**0**	**0**	**0**	**0**	**0**	**0**	**0**	**1**	**0.0**	**–1**	**0**	**0.0**	**3**	**0**	**2:29**								
	Michigan K-Wings	IHL	76	24	25	49	140																			
2000-01	Utah Grizzlies	IHL	69	22	16	38	88																			
	NHL Totals		**5**	**0**	**0**	**0**	**0**	**0**	**0**	**0**	**1**	**0.0**		**0**	**0.0**	**3**	**0**	**2:29**								

Signed as a free agent by **Calgary**, July 1, 2001.

CHUBAROV, Artem
(choo-BAH-rahf, AHR-tehm) **VAN.**

Center. Shoots left. 6'1", 189 lbs. Born, Gorky, USSR, December 12, 1979. Vancouver's 2nd choice, 31st overall, in 1998 Entry Draft.

Season	Club	League	GP	G	A	Pts	PIM	PP	SH	GW	S	%	+/-	TF	F%	H	SB	Min	GP	G	A	Pts	PIM	PP	SH	GW
1994-95	Torpedo Nizhny	CIS-Jr.	60	20	30	50	20																			
1995-96	Torpedo Nizhny	CIS-Jr.	60	22	25	47	20																			
1996-97	HC Nizhny-2	Russia-3	40	24	5	29	16																			
	Torpedo Nizhny	Russia-2	15	1	1	2	8																			
1997-98	Dynamo Moscow	Russia	30	1	4	5	4																			
1998-99	Dynamo Moscow	Russia	34	8	2	10	10												12	0	0	0	4			
99-2000	**Vancouver**	**NHL**	**49**	**1**	**8**	**9**	**10**	**0**	**0**	**1**	**53**	**1.9**	**–4**	**488**	**48.0**	**38**	**17**	**11:43**								
	Syracuse Crunch	AHL	14	7	6	13	4												1	0	0	0	0			
2000-01	**Vancouver**	**NHL**	**1**	**0**	**0**	**0**	**0**	**0**	**0**	**0**	**0**	**0.0**	**–1**	**17**	**52.9**	**1**	**0**	**15:08**								
	Kansas City	IHL	10	7	4	11	12																			
	NHL Totals		**50**	**1**	**8**	**9**	**10**	**0**	**0**	**1**	**53**	**1.9**		**505**	**48.1**	**39**	**17**	**11:47**								

• Missed majority of 2000-01 season recovering from shoulder injury suffered in game vs. Manitoba (IHL), November 15, 2000.

CHURCH, Brad
(CHUHRCH, BRAD)

Left wing. Shoots left. 6'1", 210 lbs. Born, Dauphin, Man., November 14, 1976. Washington's 1st choice, 17th overall, in 1995 Entry Draft.

Season	Club	League	GP	G	A	Pts	PIM	PP	SH	GW	S	%	+/-	TF	F%	H	SB	Min	GP	G	A	Pts	PIM	PP	SH	GW
1991-92	Parkland Rangers	MAHA	26	15	17	32	62																			
1992-93	Dauphin Kings	MJHL	45	15	23	38	80																			
1993-94	Prince Albert	WHL	71	33	20	53	197																			
1994-95	Prince Albert	WHL	62	26	24	50	184												15	6	9	15	32			
1995-96	Prince Albert	WHL	69	42	46	88	123												18	15	*20	*35	74			
1996-97	Portland Pirates	AHL	50	4	8	12	92												1	0	0	0	0			
1997-98	**Washington**	**NHL**	**2**	**0**	**0**	**0**	**0**	**0**	**0**	**0**	**4**	**0.0**	**0**													
	Portland Pirates	AHL	59	6	5	11	98												9	2	4	6	14			
1998-99	Portland Pirates	AHL	10	1	3	4	18																			
	Hampton Roads	ECHL	24	10	9	19	129																			
	Hamilton Bulldogs	AHL	9	0	2	2	4																			
	New Orleans	ECHL	5	3	4	7	4												11	1	1	2	22			

			Regular Season																Playoffs							
Season	Club	League	GP	G	A	Pts	PIM	PP	SH	GW	S	%	+/-	TF	F%	H	SB	Min	GP	G	A	Pts	PIM	PP	SH	GW
99-2000	Hampton Roads	ECHL	11	4	3	7	31	....	....	....	....	....	....	....	....	....	....	....	....	....	....	....	....	....	....	....
	Portland Pirates	AHL	56	9	17	26	52	....	....	....	....	....	....	....	....	....	....	....	4	1	1	2	4	....	....	....
2000-01	Portland Pirates	AHL	61	14	18	32	90	....	....	....	....	....	....	....	....	....	....	....	3	1	1	2	18	....	....	....
	NHL Totals		**2**	**0**	**0**	**0**	**0**	**0**	**0**	**0**	**4**	**0.0**		....	....	....	....	....	....	....	....	....	....	....	....	....

Traded to **Edmonton** by **Washington** for the rights to Barrie Moore, February 3, 1999.

CICCONE, Enrico

(CHIH-koh-nee, EHN-ree-KOH)

Defense. Shoots left. 6'5", 220 lbs. Born, Montreal, Que., April 10, 1970. Minnesota's 5th choice, 92nd overall, in 1990 Entry Draft.

1986-87	Lac St-Louis	QAAA	38	10	20	30	172	....	....	....	....	....	....	....	....	....	....	....	....	....	....	....	....	....	....	....
1987-88	Shawinigan	QMJHL	61	2	12	14	324	....	....	....	....	....	....	....	....	....	....	....	....	....	....	....	....	....	....	....
1988-89	Shawinigan	QMJHL	34	7	11	18	132	....	....	....	....	....	....	....	....	....	....	....	....	....	....	....	....	....	....	....
	Trois-Rivieres	QMJHL	24	0	7	7	153	....	....	....	....	....	....	....	....	....	....	....	....	....	....	....	....	....	....	....
1989-90	Trois-Rivieres	QMJHL	40	4	24	28	227	....	....	....	....	....	....	....	....	....	....	....	3	0	0	0	15	....	....	....
1990-91	Kalamazoo Wings	IHL	57	4	9	13	384	....	....	....	....	....	....	....	....	....	....	....	4	0	1	1	32	....	....	....
1991-92	**Minnesota**	**NHL**	**11**	**0**	**0**	**0**	**48**	**0**	**0**	**0**	**2**	**0.0**	**–2**	....	....	....	....	....	....	....	....	....	....	....	....	....
	Kalamazoo Wings	IHL	53	4	16	20	406	....	....	....	....	....	....	....	....	....	....	....	10	0	1	1	58	....	....	....
1992-93	**Minnesota**	**NHL**	**31**	**0**	**1**	**1**	**115**	**0**	**0**	**0**	**13**	**0.0**	**2**	....	....	....	....	....	....	....	....	....	....	....	....	....
	Kalamazoo Wings	IHL	13	1	3	4	50	....	....	....	....	....	....	....	....	....	....	....	....	....	....	....	....	....	....	....
	Hamilton Canucks	AHL	6	1	3	4	44	....	....	....	....	....	....	....	....	....	....	....	....	....	....	....	....	....	....	....
1993-94	**Washington**	**NHL**	**46**	**1**	**1**	**2**	**174**	**0**	**0**	**0**	**23**	**4.3**	**–2**	....	....	....	....	....	....	....	....	....	....	....	....	....
	Portland Pirates	AHL	6	0	0	0	27	....	....	....	....	....	....	....	....	....	....	....	....	....	....	....	....	....	....	....
	Tampa Bay	**NHL**	**11**	**0**	**1**	**1**	**52**	**0**	**0**	**0**	**10**	**0.0**	**–2**	....	....	....	....	....	....	....	....	....	....	....	....	....
1994-95	**Tampa Bay**	**NHL**	**41**	**2**	**4**	**6**	***225**	**0**	**0**	**0**	**43**	**4.7**	**3**	....	....	....	....	....	....	....	....	....	....	....	....	....
1995-96	**Tampa Bay**	**NHL**	**55**	**2**	**3**	**5**	**258**	**0**	**0**	**0**	**48**	**4.2**	**–4**	....	....	....	....	....	....	....	....	....	....	....	....	....
	Chicago	**NHL**	**11**	**0**	**1**	**1**	**48**	**0**	**0**	**0**	**12**	**0.0**	**5**	....	....	....	....	....	**9**	**1**	**0**	**1**	**30**	**0**	**0**	**0**
1996-97	**Chicago**	**NHL**	**67**	**2**	**2**	**4**	**233**	**0**	**0**	**1**	**65**	**3.1**	**–1**	....	....	....	....	....	**4**	**0**	**0**	**0**	**18**	**0**	**0**	**0**
1997-98	**Carolina**	**NHL**	**14**	**0**	**3**	**3**	**83**	**0**	**0**	**0**	**8**	**0.0**	**3**	....	....	....	....	....	....	....	....	....	....	....	....	....
	Vancouver	**NHL**	**13**	**0**	**1**	**1**	**47**	**0**	**0**	**0**	**7**	**0.0**	**–2**	....	....	....	....	....	....	....	....	....	....	....	....	....
	Tampa Bay	**NHL**	**12**	**0**	**0**	**0**	**45**	**0**	**0**	**0**	**7**	**0.0**	**–3**	....	....	....	....	....	....	....	....	....	....	....	....	....
1998-99	**Tampa Bay**	**NHL**	**16**	**1**	**1**	**2**	**24**	**0**	**0**	**0**	**9**	**11.1**	**–1**	**0**	**0.0**	**20**	**7**	**10:18**	....	....	....	....	....	....	....	....
	Cleveland	IHL	6	0	0	0	23	....	....	....	....	....	....	....	....	....	....	....	....	....	....	....	....	....	....	....
	Washington	**NHL**	**43**	**2**	**0**	**2**	**103**	**0**	**0**	**0**	**43**	**4.7**	**–6**	**0**	**0.0**	**58**	**21**	**11:29**	....	....	....	....	....	....	....	....
99-2000	Moskitos Essen	DEL	14	0	4	4	101	....	....	....	....	....	....	....	....	....	....	....	....	....	....	....	....	....	....	....
2000-01	**Montreal**	**NHL**	**3**	**0**	**0**	**0**	**14**	**0**	**0**	**0**	**0**	**0.0**	**–1**	**0**	**0.0**	**2**	**0**	**2:57**	....	....	....	....	....	....	....	....
	Quebec Citadelles	AHL	2	0	0	0	22	....	....	....	....	....	....	....	....	....	....	....	....	....	....	....	....	....	....	....
	NHL Totals		**374**	**10**	**18**	**28**	**1469**	**0**	**0**	**1**	**290**	**3.4**		**0**	**0.0**	**80**	**28**	**10:46**	**13**	**1**	**0**	**1**	**48**	**0**	**0**	**0**

Traded to **Washington** by **Dallas** to complete transaction that sent Paul Cavallini to Dallas (June 20, 1993), June 25, 1993. Traded to **Tampa Bay** by **Washington** with Washington's 3rd round choice (later traded to Anaheim - Anaheim selected Craig Reichert) in 1994 Entry Draft and the return of conditional draft choice transferred in the Pat Elynuik trade for Joe Reekie, March 21, 1994. Traded to **Chicago** by **Tampa Bay** with Tampa Bay's 2nd round choice (Jeff Paul) in 1996 Entry Draft for Patrick Poulin, Igor Ulanov and Chicago's 2nd round choice (later traded to New Jersey - New Jersey selected Pierre Dagenais) in 1996 Entry Draft, March 20, 1996. Traded to **Carolina** by **Chicago** for Ryan Risidore and Carolina's 5th round choice (later traded to Toronto - Toronto selected Morgan Warren) in 1998 Entry Draft, July 25, 1997. Traded to **Vancouver** by **Carolina** with Sean Burke and Geoff Sanderson for Kirk McLean and Martin Gelinas, January 3, 1998. Traded to **Tampa Bay** by **Vancouver** for Jamie Huscroft, March 14, 1998. Traded to **Washington** by **Tampa Bay** for cash, December 28, 1998. Signed as a free agent by **Montreal**, July 7, 2000. • Officially announced retirement, December 8, 2000.

CIERNIK, Ivan

(CHAIR-nihk, ee-VAHN) **OTT.**

Left wing. Shoots left. 6'1", 234 lbs. Born, Levice, Czech., October 30, 1977. Ottawa's 6th choice, 216th overall, in 1996 Entry Draft.

1994-95	MHC Nitra	Slovak-Jr.	30	22	15	37	36	....	....	....	....	....	....	....	....	....	....	....	....	....	....	....	....	....	....	....
	MHC Nitra	Slovakia	7	1	0	1	2	....	....	....	....	....	....	....	....	....	....	....	....	....	....	....	....	....	....	....
1995-96	MHC Nitra	Slovakia	35	9	7	16	36	....	....	....	....	....	....	....	....	....	....	....	8	3	3	6	....	....	....	....
1996 97	MHC Nitra	Slovakia	41	11	19	30	....	....	....	....	....	....	....	....	....	....	....	....	....	....	....	....	....	....	....	....
1997-98	**Ottawa**	**NHL**	**2**	**0**	**0**	**0**	**0**	**0**	**0**	**0**	**0**	**0.0**	**0**	....	....	....	....	....	....	....	....	....	....	....	....	....
	Worcester	AHL	53	9	12	21	38	....	....	....	....	....	....	....	....	....	....	....	1	0	0	0	2	....	....	....
1998-99	Adirondack	AHL	21	1	4	5	4	....	....	....	....	....	....	....	....	....	....	....	....	....	....	....	....	....	....	....
	Cincinnati Ducks	AHL	32	10	3	13	10	....	....	....	....	....	....	....	....	....	....	....	2	0	0	0	2	....	....	....
99-2000	Grand Rapids	IHL	66	13	12	25	64	....	....	....	....	....	....	....	....	....	....	....	6	0	6	6	2	....	....	....
2000-01	**Ottawa**	**NHL**	**4**	**2**	**0**	**2**	**2**	**0**	**0**	**0**	**7**	**28.6**	**2**	**0**	**0.0**	**0**	**0**	**7:41**	....	....	....	....	....	....	....	....
	Grand Rapids	IHL	66	27	38	65	53	....	....	....	....	....	....	....	....	....	....	....	10	5	6	11	26	....	....	....
	NHL Totals		**6**	**2**	**0**	**2**	**2**	**0**	**0**	**0**	**7**	**28.6**		**0**	**0.0**	**0**	**0**	**7:41**	....	....	....	....	....	....	....	....

Loaned to **Cincinnati** (AHL) by **Ottawa** with Ratislav Pavlikovsky and Erich Goldmann, January 12, 1999.

CIERNY, Jozef

(chee-ER-nee, JOH-zehf) **EDM.**

Left wing. Shoots left. 6'2", 185 lbs. Born, Zvolen, Czech., May 13, 1974. Buffalo's 2nd choice, 35th overall, in 1992 Entry Draft.

1991-92	ZTK Zvolen	Czech-2	26	10	3	13	8	....	....	....	....	....	....	....	....	....	....	....	....	....	....	....	....	....	....	....
1992-93	Rochester	AHL	54	27	27	54	36	....	....	....	....	....	....	....	....	....	....	....	....	....	....	....	....	....	....	....
1993-94	**Edmonton**	**NHL**	**1**	**0**	**0**	**0**	**0**	**0**	**0**	**0**	**0**	**0.0**	**–1**	....	....	....	....	....	....	....	....	....	....	....	....	....
	Cape Breton	AHL	73	30	27	57	88	....	....	....	....	....	....	....	....	....	....	....	4	1	1	2	4	....	....	....
1994-95	Cape Breton	AHL	73	28	24	52	58	....	....	....	....	....	....	....	....	....	....	....	....	....	....	....	....	....	....	....
1995-96	Detroit Vipers	IHL	20	2	5	7	16	....	....	....	....	....	....	....	....	....	....	....	....	....	....	....	....	....	....	....
	Los Angeles	IHL	43	23	16	39	36	....	....	....	....	....	....	....	....	....	....	....	....	....	....	....	....	....	....	....
1996-97	Long Beach	IHL	68	27	27	54	106	....	....	....	....	....	....	....	....	....	....	....	16	8	5	13	7	....	....	....
1997-98	EHC Nurnberg	DEL	45	20	22	42	61	....	....	....	....	....	....	....	....	....	....	....	....	....	....	....	....	....	....	....
1998-99	EHC Nurnberg	DEL	47	22	21	43	65	....	....	....	....	....	....	....	....	....	....	....	13	3	2	5	37	....	....	....
99-2000	EHC Nurnberg	DEL	67	19	15	34	68	....	....	....	....	....	....	....	....	....	....	....	....	....	....	....	....	....	....	....
	EHC Nurnberg	EuroHL	5	3	1	4	10	....	....	....	....	....	....	....	....	....	....	....	2	0	0	0	0	....	....	....
2000-01	HKm Zvolen	Slovakia	35	11	5	16	42	....	....	....	....	....	....	....	....	....	....	....	8	1	1	2	6	....	....	....
	NHL Totals		**1**	**0**	**0**	**0**	**0**	**0**	**0**	**0**	**0**	**0.0**		....	....	....	....	....	....	....	....	....	....	....	....	....

Traded to **Edmonton** by **Buffalo** with Buffalo's 4th round choice (Jussi Tarvainen) in 1994 Entry Draft for Craig Simpson, September 1, 1993.

CIGER, Zdeno

(SEE-guhr, ZDEH-noh) **NYR**

Left wing. Shoots left. 6'1", 190 lbs. Born, Martin, Czech., October 19, 1969. New Jersey's 3rd choice, 54th overall, in 1988 Entry Draft.

1987-88	Dukla Trencin	Czech.	8	3	4	7	2	....	....	....	....	....	....	....	....	....	....	....	....	....	....	....	....	....	....	....
1988-89	Dukla Trencin	Czech.	43	18	13	31	18	....	....	....	....	....	....	....	....	....	....	....	....	....	....	....	....	....	....	....
1989-90	Dukla Trencin	Czech.	44	17	24	41	....	....	....	....	....	....	....	....	....	....	....	....	9	1	4	5	....	....	....	....
1990-91	**New Jersey**	**NHL**	**45**	**8**	**17**	**25**	**8**	**2**	**0**	**1**	**82**	**9.8**	**3**	....	....	....	....	....	**6**	**0**	**2**	**2**	**4**	**0**	**0**	**0**
	Utica Devils	AHL	8	5	4	9	2	....	....	....	....	....	....	....	....	....	....	....	....	....	....	....	....	....	....	....
1991-92	**New Jersey**	**NHL**	**20**	**6**	**5**	**11**	**10**	**1**	**0**	**0**	**33**	**18.2**	**–2**	....	....	....	....	....	**7**	**2**	**4**	**6**	**0**	**0**	**0**	**1**
1992-93	**New Jersey**	**NHL**	**27**	**4**	**8**	**12**	**2**	**2**	**0**	**1**	**39**	**10.3**	**–8**	....	....	....	....	....	....	....	....	....	....	....	....	....
	Edmonton	**NHL**	**37**	**9**	**15**	**24**	**6**	**0**	**0**	**1**	**67**	**13.4**	**–5**	....	....	....	....	....	....	....	....	....	....	....	....	....
1993-94	**Edmonton**	**NHL**	**84**	**22**	**35**	**57**	**8**	**8**	**0**	**1**	**158**	**13.9**	**–11**	....	....	....	....	....	....	....	....	....	....	....	....	....
1994-95	Dukla Trencin	Slovakia	34	23	25	48	8	....	....	....	....	....	....	....	....	....	....	....	9	2	9	11	2	....	....	....
	Edmonton	**NHL**	**5**	**2**	**2**	**4**	**0**	**1**	**0**	**1**	**10**	**20.0**	**–1**	....	....	....	....	....	....	....	....	....	....	....	....	....
1995-96	**Edmonton**	**NHL**	**78**	**31**	**39**	**70**	**41**	**12**	**0**	**3**	**184**	**16.8**	**–15**	....	....	....	....	....	....	....	....	....	....	....	....	....
1996-97	HC Bratislava	Slovakia	44	26	27	53	....	....	....	....	....	....	....	....	....	....	....	....	2	1	3	4	....	....	....	....
	HC Bratislava	EuroHL	6	4	5	9	2	....	....	....	....	....	....	....	....	....	....	....	2	1	1	2	2	....	....	....
1997-98	HC Bratislava	Slovakia	36	14	*31	45	2	....	....	....	....	....	....	....	....	....	....	....	11	6	*10	*16	4	....	....	....
	HC Bratislava	EuroHL	8	1	5	6	6	....	....	....	....	....	....	....	....	....	....	....	....	....	....	....	....	....	....	....
	Slovakia	Olympics	4	1	1	2	4	....	....	....	....	....	....	....	....	....	....	....	....	....	....	....	....	....	....	....
1998-99	HC Bratislava	Slovakia	40	26	32	*58	8	....	....	....	....	....	....	....	....	....	....	....	9	3	*10	13	2	....	....	....
	HC Bratislava	EuroHL	6	4	5	9	8	....	....	....	....	....	....	....	....	....	....	....	....	....	....	....	....	....	....	....
99-2000	HC Bratislava	Slovakia	51	23	39	62	48	....	....	....	....	....	....	....	....	....	....	....	8	1	*8	*9	0	....	....	....
	HC Bratislava	EuroHL	6	3	4	7	2	....	....	....	....	....	....	....	....	....	....	....	2	0	2	2	4	....	....	....
2000-01	HC Bratislava	Slovakia	53	17	32	49	22	....	....	....	....	....	....	....	....	....	....	....	8	6	3	9	16	....	....	....
	NHL Totals		**296**	**82**	**121**	**203**	**75**	**26**	**0**	**8**	**573**	**14.3**		....	....	....	....	....	**13**	**2**	**6**	**8**	**4**	**0**	**0**	**1**

Traded to **Edmonton** by **New Jersey** with Kevin Todd for Bernie Nicholls, January 13, 1993. Claimed by **Nashville** from **Edmonton** in Waiver Draft, October 5, 1998. Claimed by **Minnesota** from **Nashville** in Waiver Draft, September 29, 2000.

											Regular Season											Playoffs				
Season	Club	League	GP	G	A	Pts	PIM	PP	SH	GW	S	%	+/-	TF	F%	H	SB	Min	GP	G	A	Pts	PIM	PP	SH	GW

CISAR, Marian

(SIH-sahr, MAIR-eean) **NSH.**

Right wing. Shoots right. 6', 197 lbs. Born, Bratislava, Czech., February 25, 1978. Los Angeles' 2nd choice, 37th overall, in 1996 Entry Draft.

1994-95	Sloven Bratislava	Slovak-Jr.	38	42	28	70	16	....	....	....	....	....	....	....	....	....	....	....	....	....	....	....	....	....	....	....
1995-96	Sloven Bratislava	Slovak-Jr.	16	26	17	43	2	....	....	....	....	....	....	....	....	....	....	....	....	....	....	....	....	....	....	....
	Sloven Bratislava	Slovakia	13	3	3	6	0	....	....	....	....	....	....	....	....	....	....	....	6	3	0	3	0	....	....	....
1996-97	Spokane Chiefs	WHL	70	31	35	66	52	....	....	....	....	....	....	....	....	....	....	....	9	6	2	8	4	....	....	....
1997-98	Spokane Chiefs	WHL	52	33	40	73	34	....	....	....	....	....	....	....	....	....	....	....	18	8	5	13	8	....	....	....
1998-99	Milwaukee	IHL	51	11	17	28	31	....	....	....	....	....	....	....	....	....	....	....	2	0	0	0	12	....	....	....
99-2000	**Nashville**	**NHL**	**3**	**0**	**0**	**0**	**4**	**0**	**0**	**0**	**2**	**0.0**	**–2**	**0**	**0.0**	**1**	**1**	**8:18**	....	....	....	....	....	....	....	....
	Milwaukee	IHL	78	20	32	52	82	....	....	....	....	....	....	....	....	....	....	....	1	0	0	0	0	....	....	....
2000-01	**Nashville**	**NHL**	**60**	**12**	**15**	**27**	**45**	**5**	**0**	**1**	**97**	**12.4**	**–7**	**0**	**0.0**	**50**	**13**	**13:10**	....	....	....	....	....	....	....	....
	Milwaukee	IHL	15	4	7	11	4	....	....	....	....	....	....	....	....	....	....	....	....	....	....	....	....	....	....	....
	NHL Totals		**63**	**12**	**15**	**27**	**49**	**5**	**0**	**1**	**99**	**12.1**		**0**	**0.0**	**51**	**14**	**12:56**	....	....	....	....	....	....	....	....

Traded to **Nashville** by **LA Kings** for future considerations, June 1, 1998.

CLARK, Brett

(KLAHRK, BREHT) **ATL.**

Defense. Shoots left. 6', 185 lbs. Born, Wapella, Sask., December 23, 1976. Montreal's 7th choice, 154th overall, in 1996 Entry Draft.

1994-95	Melville	SJHL	62	19	32	51	77	....	....	....	....	....	....	....	....	....	....	....	....	....	....	....	....	....	....	....
1995-96	U. of Maine	H-East	39	7	31	38	22	....	....	....	....	....	....	....	....	....	....	....	....	....	....	....	....	....	....	....
1996-97	Canada	Nat-Team	57	6	21	27	52	....	....	....	....	....	....	....	....	....	....	....	....	....	....	....	....	....	....	....
1997-98	**Montreal**	**NHL**	**41**	**1**	**0**	**1**	**20**	**0**	**0**	**0**	**26**	**3.8**	**–3**	....	....	....	....	....	....	....	....	....	....	....	....	....
	Fredericton	AHL	20	0	6	6	6	....	....	....	....	....	....	....	....	....	....	....	4	0	1	1	17	....	....	....
1998-99	**Montreal**	**NHL**	**61**	**2**	**2**	**4**	**16**	**0**	**0**	**0**	**36**	**5.6**	**–3**	**0**	**0.0**	**62**	**43**	**13:11**	....	....	....	....	....	....	....	....
	Fredericton	AHL	3	1	0	1	0	....	....	....	....	....	....	....	....	....	....	....	....	....	....	....	....	....	....	....
99-2000	**Atlanta**	**NHL**	**14**	**0**	**1**	**1**	**4**	**0**	**0**	**0**	**13**	**0.0**	**–12**	**0**	**0.0**	**27**	**19**	**16:51**	....	....	....	....	....	....	....	....
	Orlando	IHL	63	9	17	26	31	....	....	....	....	....	....	....	....	....	....	....	6	0	1	1	0	....	....	....
2000-01	**Atlanta**	**NHL**	**28**	**1**	**2**	**3**	**14**	**0**	**0**	**0**	**35**	**2.9**	**–12**	**0**	**0.0**	**42**	**21**	**18:02**	....	....	....	....	....	....	....	....
	Orlando	IHL	43	2	9	11	32	....	....	....	....	....	....	....	....	....	....	....	15	1	6	7	2	....	....	....
	NHL Totals		**144**	**4**	**5**	**9**	**54**	**0**	**0**	**0**	**110**	**3.6**		**0**	**0.0**	**131**	**83**	**15:00**	....	....	....	....	....	....	....	....

Claimed by **Atlanta** from **Montreal** in Expansion Draft, June 25, 1999.

CLARK, Chris

(KLAHRK, KRIHS) **CGY.**

Right wing. Shoots right. 6', 200 lbs. Born, Manchester, CT, March 8, 1976. Calgary's 3rd choice, 77th overall, in 1994 Entry Draft.

1990-91	South Windsor	Hi-School	23	16	15	31	24	....	....	....	....	....	....	....	....	....	....	....	....	....	....	....	....	....	....	....
1991-92	Springfield Pics	EJHL	49	21	29	50	56	....	....	....	....	....	....	....	....	....	....	....	....	....	....	....	....	....	....	....
1992-93	Springfield Pics	EJHL	43	17	60	77	120	....	....	....	....	....	....	....	....	....	....	....	....	....	....	....	....	....	....	....
1993-94	Springfield Pics	EJHL	35	31	26	57	185	....	....	....	....	....	....	....	....	....	....	....	....	....	....	....	....	....	....	....
1994-95	Clarkson Knights	ECAC	32	12	11	23	92	....	....	....	....	....	....	....	....	....	....	....	....	....	....	....	....	....	....	....
1995-96	Clarkson Knights	ECAC	38	10	8	18	108	....	....	....	....	....	....	....	....	....	....	....	....	....	....	....	....	....	....	....
1996-97	Clarkson Knights	ECAC	37	23	25	48	*86	....	....	....	....	....	....	....	....	....	....	....	....	....	....	....	....	....	....	....
1997-98	Clarkson Knights	ECAC	35	18	21	39	*106	....	....	....	....	....	....	....	....	....	....	....	....	....	....	....	....	....	....	....
1998-99	Saint John Flames	AHL	73	13	27	40	123	....	....	....	....	....	....	....	....	....	....	....	7	2	4	6	15	....	....	....
99-2000	**Calgary**	**NHL**	**22**	**0**	**1**	**1**	**14**	**0**	**0**	**0**	**17**	**0.0**	**–3**	**0**	**0.0**	**22**	**3**	**9:02**	....	....	....	....	....	....	....	....
	Saint John Flames	AHL	48	16	17	33	134	....	....	....	....	....	....	....	....	....	....	....	....	....	....	....	....	....	....	....
2000-01	**Calgary**	**NHL**	**29**	**5**	**1**	**6**	**38**	**1**	**0**	**0**	**43**	**11.6**	**0**	**3**	**33.3**	**40**	**10**	**11:56**	....	....	....	....	....	....	....	....
	Saint John Flames	AHL	48	18	17	35	131	....	....	....	....	....	....	....	....	....	....	....	18	4	10	14	49	....	....	....
	NHL Totals		**51**	**5**	**2**	**7**	**52**	**1**	**0**	**0**	**60**	**8.3**		**3**	**33.3**	**62**	**13**	**10:41**	....	....	....	....	....	....	....	....

ECAC Second All-Star Team (1998)

CLARKE, Dale

(KLAHRK, DAIL) **ST.L.**

Defense. Shoots right. 6'2", 193 lbs. Born, Belleville, Ont., March 23, 1978.

1994-95	Wellington Dukes	MTJHL	48	2	13	15	18	....	....	....	....	....	....	....	....	....	....	....	....	....	....	....	....	....	....	....
1995-96	Wellington Dukes	MTJHL	51	6	24	30	78	....	....	....	....	....	....	....	....	....	....	....	....	....	....	....	....	....	....	....
1996-97	St. Lawrence	ECAC	34	1	6	7	20	....	....	....	....	....	....	....	....	....	....	....	....	....	....	....	....	....	....	....
1997-98	St. Lawrence	ECAC	33	1	6	7	66	....	....	....	....	....	....	....	....	....	....	....	....	....	....	....	....	....	....	....
1998-99	St. Lawrence	ECAC	39	3	13	16	44	....	....	....	....	....	....	....	....	....	....	....	....	....	....	....	....	....	....	....
99-2000	St. Lawrence	ECAC	36	6	17	23	24	....	....	....	....	....	....	....	....	....	....	....	....	....	....	....	....	....	....	....
	Worcester	AHL	....	....	....	....	....	....	....	....	....	....	....	....	....	....	....	....	2	0	0	0	0	....	....	....
2000-01	**St. Louis**	**NHL**	**3**	**0**	**0**	**0**	**0**	**0**	**0**	**0**	**5**	**0.0**	**1**	**0**	**0.0**	**3**	**1**	**13:38**	....	....	....	....	....	....	....	....
	Peoria	ECHL	2	1	0	1	0	....	....	....	....	....	....	....	....	....	....	....	....	....	....	....	....	....	....	....
	Worcester	AHL	67	7	25	32	26	....	....	....	....	....	....	....	....	....	....	....	1	0	0	0	0	....	....	....
	NHL Totals		**3**	**0**	**0**	**0**	**0**	**0**	**0**	**0**	**5**	**0.0**		**0**	**0.0**	**3**	**1**	**13:38**	....	....	....	....	....	....	....	....

Signed as a free agent by **St. Louis**, July 24, 1999.

CLASSEN, Greg

(KLAW-sihn, GREHG) **NSH.**

Center. Shoots left. 6'1", 198 lbs. Born, Aylsham, Sask., August 24, 1977.

1997-98	Nipawin Hawks	SJHL	59	32	50	82	50	....	....	....	....	....	....	....	....	....	....	....	14	8	13	21	6	....	....	....
1998-99	Merrimack	H-East	36	14	11	25	28	....	....	....	....	....	....	....	....	....	....	....	....	....	....	....	....	....	....	....
99-2000	Merrimack	H-East	36	14	16	30	16	....	....	....	....	....	....	....	....	....	....	....	....	....	....	....	....	....	....	....
	Milwaukee	IHL	11	1	0	1	2	....	....	....	....	....	....	....	....	....	....	....	2	0	0	0	2	....	....	....
2000-01	**Nashville**	**NHL**	**27**	**2**	**4**	**6**	**14**	**1**	**0**	**0**	**18**	**11.1**	**–4**	**195**	**42.1**	**21**	**4**	**10:16**	....	....	....	....	....	....	....	....
	Milwaukee	IHL	23	5	10	15	31	....	....	....	....	....	....	....	....	....	....	....	5	0	0	0	0	....	....	....
	NHL Totals		**27**	**2**	**4**	**6**	**14**	**1**	**0**	**0**	**18**	**11.1**		**195**	**42.1**	**21**	**4**	**10:16**	....	....	....	....	....	....	....	....

Hockey East All-Rookie Team (1999)

Signed as a free agent by **Nashville**, March 27, 2000.

CLEARY, Daniel

(KLIH-ree, DAN-yehl) **EDM.**

Left wing. Shoots left. 6', 203 lbs. Born, Carbonear, Nfld., December 18, 1978. Chicago's 1st choice, 13th overall, in 1997 Entry Draft.

1993-94	Kingston	MTJHL	41	18	28	46	33	....	....	....	....	....	....	....	....	....	....	....	2	0	1	1	0	....	....	....
1994-95	Belleville Bulls	OHL	62	26	55	81	62	....	....	....	....	....	....	....	....	....	....	....	16	7	10	17	23	....	....	....
1995-96	Belleville Bulls	OHL	64	53	62	115	74	....	....	....	....	....	....	....	....	....	....	....	14	10	17	27	40	....	....	....
1996-97	Belleville Bulls	OHL	64	32	48	80	88	....	....	....	....	....	....	....	....	....	....	....	6	3	4	7	6	....	....	....
1997-98	Belleville Bulls	OHL	30	16	31	47	14	....	....	....	....	....	....	....	....	....	....	....	10	6	*17	*23	10	....	....	....
	Chicago	**NHL**	**6**	**0**	**0**	**0**	**0**	**0**	**0**	**0**	**4**	**0.0**	**–2**	....	....	....	....	....	....	....	....	....	....	....	....	....
	Indianapolis Ice	IHL	4	2	1	3	6	....	....	....	....	....	....	....	....	....	....	....	....	....	....	....	....	....	....	....
1998-99	**Chicago**	**NHL**	**35**	**4**	**5**	**9**	**24**	**0**	**0**	**0**	**49**	**8.2**	**–1**	**13**	**46.2**	**28**	**9**	**14:21**	....	....	....	....	....	....	....	....
	Portland Pirates	AHL	30	9	17	26	74	....	....	....	....	....	....	....	....	....	....	....	....	....	....	....	....	....	....	....
	Hamilton Bulldogs	AHL	9	0	1	1	7	....	....	....	....	....	....	....	....	....	....	....	3	0	0	0	0	....	....	....
99-2000	**Edmonton**	**NHL**	**17**	**3**	**2**	**5**	**8**	**0**	**0**	**1**	**18**	**16.7**	**–1**	**1**	**100.0**	**16**	**2**	**9:44**	**4**	**0**	**1**	**1**	**2**	**0**	**0**	**0**
	Hamilton Bulldogs	AHL	58	22	52	74	108	....	....	....	....	....	....	....	....	....	....	....	5	2	3	5	18	....	....	....
2000-01	**Edmonton**	**NHL**	**81**	**14**	**21**	**35**	**37**	**2**	**0**	**2**	**107**	**13.1**	**5**	**13**	**23.1**	**73**	**26**	**12:58**	**6**	**1**	**1**	**2**	**8**	**1**	**0**	**0**
	NHL Totals		**139**	**21**	**28**	**49**	**69**	**2**	**0**	**3**	**178**	**11.8**		**27**	**37.0**	**117**	**37**	**12:55**	**10**	**1**	**2**	**3**	**10**	**1**	**0**	**0**

OHL First All-Star Team (1996, 1997) • AHL Second All-Star Team (2000)

Traded to **Edmonton** by **Chicago** with Chad Kilger, Ethan Moreau and Christian Laflamme for Boris Mironov, Dean McAmmond and Jonas Elofsson, March 20, 1999.

CLOUTIER, Sylvain
(klootz-YAY, SIHL-vehn) **N.J.**

Center. Shoots left. 6', 200 lbs. Born, Mont-Laurier, Que., February 13, 1974. Detroit's 3rd choice, 70th overall, in 1992 Entry Draft.

			Regular Season																Playoffs							
Season	Club	League	GP	G	A	Pts	PIM	PP	SH	GW	S	%	+/-	TF	F%	H	SB	Min	GP	G	A	Pts	PIM	PP	SH	GW
1990-91	S.S. Marie Legion	NOHA	34	51	40	91	92	....	....	....	....	....	....	....	....	....	....	....	....	....	....	....	....	....	....	....
1991-92	Guelph Storm	OHL	62	35	31	66	74	....	....	....	....	....	....	....	....	....	....	....	....	....	....	....	....	....	....	....
1992-93	Guelph Storm	OHL	44	26	29	55	78	....	....	....	....	....	....	....	....	....	....	....	5	0	5	5	14	....	....	....
1993-94	Guelph Storm	OHL	66	45	71	116	127	....	....	....	....	....	....	....	....	....	....	....	9	7	9	16	32	....	....	....
	Adirondack	AHL	2	0	2	2	2	....	....	....	....	....	....	....	....	....	....	....	....	....	....	....	....	....	....	....
1994-95	Adirondack	AHL	71	7	26	33	144	....	....	....	....	....	....	....	....	....	....	....	....	....	....	....	....	....	....	....
1995-96	Adirondack	AHL	65	11	17	28	118	....	....	....	....	....	....	....	....	....	....	....	3	0	0	0	4	....	....	....
	Toledo Storm	ECHL	6	4	2	6	4	....	....	....	....	....	....	....	....	....	....	....	....	....	....	....	....	....	....	....
1996-97	Adirondack	AHL	77	13	36	49	190	....	....	....	....	....	....	....	....	....	....	....	4	0	2	2	4	....	....	....
1997-98	Adirondack	AHL	72	14	22	36	155	....	....	....	....	....	....	....	....	....	....	....	....	....	....	....	....	....	....	....
	Detroit Vipers	IHL	8	0	1	1	18	....	....	....	....	....	....	....	....	....	....	....	21	7	5	12	31	....	....	....
1998-99	**Chicago**	**NHL**	**7**	**0**	**0**	**0**	**0**	**0**	**0**	**0**	**3**	**0.0**	**-1**	**35**	**51.4**	**4**	**0**	**5:28**	....	....	....	....	....	....	....	....
	Indianapolis Ice	IHL	73	21	33	54	128	....	....	....	....	....	....	....	....	....	....	....	7	3	2	5	12	....	....	....
99-2000	Albany River Rats	AHL	66	15	28	43	127	....	....	....	....	....	....	....	....	....	....	....	5	0	0	0	6	....	....	....
	Orlando	IHL	9	1	1	2	25	....	....	....	....	....	....	....	....	....	....	....	....	....	....	....	....	....	....	....
2000-01	Albany River Rats	AHL	79	16	35	51	115	....	....	....	....	....	....	....	....	....	....	....	....	....	....	....	....	....	....	....
	NHL Totals		**7**	**0**	**0**	**0**	**0**	**0**	**0**	**0**	**3**	**0.0**		**35**	**51.4**	**4**	**0**	**5:28**	....	....	....	....	....	....	....	....

Signed as a free agent by **Chicago**, August 17, 1998. Claimed by **Atlanta** from **Chicago** in Expansion Draft, June 25, 1999. Traded to **New Jersey** by **Atlanta** with Jeff Williams and Atlanta's 7th round choice (Ken Magowan) in 2000 Entry Draft for Wes Mason and Eric Bertrand, November 1, 1999.

CLYMER, Ben
(KLIH-mehr, BEHN) **T.B.**

Left wing. Shoots right. 6'1", 195 lbs. Born, Edina, MN, April 11, 1978. Boston's 3rd choice, 27th overall, in 1997 Entry Draft.

Season	Club	League	GP	G	A	Pts	PIM	PP	SH	GW	S	%	+/-	TF	F%	H	SB	Min	GP	G	A	Pts	PIM	PP	SH	GW
1993-94	Jefferson High	Hi-School	23	3	7	10	20	....	....	....	....	....	....	....	....	....	....	....	....	....	....	....	....	....	....	....
1994-95	Jefferson High	Hi-School	28	11	22	33	36	....	....	....	....	....	....	....	....	....	....	....	....	....	....	....	....	....	....	....
1995-96	Jefferson High	Hi-School	18	12	34	46	34	....	....	....	....	....	....	....	....	....	....	....	5	0	6	6	6	....	....	....
1996-97	U. of Minnesota	WCHA	29	7	13	20	64	....	....	....	....	....	....	....	....	....	....	....	....	....	....	....	....	....	....	....
1997-98	U. of Minnesota	WCHA	1	0	0	0	2	....	....	....	....	....	....	....	....	....	....	....	....	....	....	....	....	....	....	....
1998-99	Seattle T-Birds	WHL	70	12	44	56	93	....	....	....	....	....	....	....	....	....	....	....	11	1	5	6	12	....	....	....
99-2000	**Tampa Bay**	**NHL**	**60**	**2**	**6**	**8**	**87**	**2**	**0**	**0**	**98**	**2.0**	**-26**	**3**	**66.7**	**121**	**41**	**19:37**	....	....	....	....	....	....	....	....
	Detroit Vipers	IHL	19	1	9	10	30	....	....	....	....	....	....	....	....	....	....	....	....	....	....	....	....	....	....	....
2000-01	**Tampa Bay**	**NHL**	**23**	**5**	**1**	**6**	**21**	**3**	**0**	**0**	**25**	**20.0**	**-7**	**8**	**25.0**	**33**	**5**	**13:03**	....	....	....	....	....	....	....	....
	Detroit Vipers	IHL	53	5	8	13	88	....	....	....	....	....	....	....	....	....	....	....	....	....	....	....	....	....	....	....
	NHL Totals		**83**	**7**	**7**	**14**	**108**	**5**	**0**	**0**	**123**	**5.7**		**11**	**36.4**	**154**	**46**	**17:48**	....	....	....	....	....	....	....	....

• Missed majority of 1997-98 season recovering from shoulder injury suffered in game vs. U. of Michigan (CCHA), October 10, 1997. Signed as a free agent by **Tampa Bay**, October 2, 1999.

COFFEY, Paul
(KAW-fee, PAWL)

Defense. Shoots left. 6', 205 lbs. Born, Weston, Ont., June 1, 1961. Edmonton's 1st choice, 6th overall, in 1980 Entry Draft.

Season	Club	League	GP	G	A	Pts	PIM	PP	SH	GW	S	%	+/-	TF	F%	H	SB	Min	GP	G	A	Pts	PIM	PP	SH	GW
1977-78	North York	MTJHL	50	14	33	47	64	....	....	....	....	....	....	....	....	....	....	....	....	....	....	....	....	....	....	....
	Kingston	OMJHL	8	2	2	4	11	....	....	....	....	....	....	....	....	....	....	....	5	0	0	0	0	....	....	....
1978-79	Sault Ste. Marie	OMJHL	68	17	72	89	103	....	....	....	....	....	....	....	....	....	....	....	....	....	....	....	....	....	....	....
1979-80	Sault Ste. Marie	OMJHL	23	10	21	31	63	....	....	....	....	....	....	....	....	....	....	....	....	....	....	....	....	....	....	....
	Kitchener	OMJHL	52	19	52	71	130	....	....	....	....	....	....	....	....	....	....	....	....	....	....	....	....	....	....	....
1980-81	**Edmonton**	**NHL**	**74**	**9**	**23**	**32**	**130**	**2**	**0**	**0**	**113**	**8.0**	**4**	....	....	....	....	....	**9**	**4**	**3**	**7**	**22**	**1**	**0**	**0**
1981-82	**Edmonton**	**NHL**	**80**	**29**	**60**	**89**	**106**	**13**	**0**	**1**	**234**	**12.4**	**35**	....	....	....	....	....	**5**	**1**	**1**	**2**	**6**	**1**	**0**	**0**
1982-83	**Edmonton**	**NHL**	**80**	**29**	**67**	**96**	**87**	**9**	**1**	**2**	**259**	**11.2**	**52**	....	....	....	....	....	**16**	**7**	**7**	**14**	**14**	**2**	**2**	**0**
1983-84♦	**Edmonton**	**NHL**	**80**	**40**	**86**	**126**	**104**	**14**	**1**	**4**	**258**	**15.5**	**52**	....	....	....	....	....	**19**	**8**	**14**	**22**	**21**	**2**	**0**	**1**
1984-85♦	**Edmonton**	**NHL**	**80**	**37**	**84**	**121**	**97**	**12**	**2**	**6**	**284**	**13.0**	**55**	....	....	....	....	....	**18**	**12**	**25**	**37**	**44**	**3**	**1**	**4**
1985-86	**Edmonton**	**NHL**	**79**	**48**	**90**	**138**	**120**	**9**	**9**	**3**	**307**	**15.6**	**61**	....	....	....	....	....	**10**	**1**	**9**	**10**	**30**	**1**	**0**	**0**
1986-87♦	**Edmonton**	**NHL**	**59**	**17**	**50**	**67**	**49**	**10**	**2**	**3**	**165**	**10.3**	**12**	....	....	....	....	....	**17**	**3**	**8**	**11**	**30**	**1**	**0**	**1**
1987-88	**Pittsburgh**	**NHL**	**46**	**15**	**52**	**67**	**93**	**6**	**2**	**2**	**193**	**7.8**	**-1**	....	....	....	....	....	....	....	....	....	....	....	....	....
1988-89	**Pittsburgh**	**NHL**	**75**	**30**	**83**	**113**	**195**	**11**	**0**	**2**	**342**	**8.8**	**-10**	....	....	....	....	....	**11**	**2**	**13**	**15**	**31**	**2**	**0**	**1**
1989-90	**Pittsburgh**	**NHL**	**80**	**29**	**74**	**103**	**95**	**10**	**0**	**3**	**324**	**9.0**	**-25**	....	....	....	....	....	....	....	....	....	....	....	....	....
1990-91♦	**Pittsburgh**	**NHL**	**76**	**24**	**69**	**93**	**128**	**8**	**0**	**3**	**240**	**10.0**	**-18**	....	....	....	....	....	**12**	**2**	**9**	**11**	**6**	**0**	**0**	**0**
1991-92	**Pittsburgh**	**NHL**	**54**	**10**	**54**	**64**	**62**	**5**	**0**	**1**	**207**	**4.8**	**4**	....	....	....	....	....	....	....	....	....	....	....	....	....
	Los Angeles	**NHL**	**10**	**1**	**4**	**5**	**25**	**0**	**0**	**0**	**25**	**4.0**	**-3**	....	....	....	....	....	**6**	**4**	**3**	**7**	**2**	**3**	**0**	**0**
1992-93	**Los Angeles**	**NHL**	**50**	**8**	**49**	**57**	**50**	**2**	**0**	**0**	**182**	**4.4**	**9**	....	....	....	....	....	....	....	....	....	....	....	....	....
	Detroit	**NHL**	**30**	**4**	**26**	**30**	**27**	**3**	**0**	**0**	**72**	**5.6**	**7**	....	....	....	....	....	**7**	**2**	**9**	**11**	**2**	**0**	**0**	**0**
1993-94	**Detroit**	**NHL**	**80**	**14**	**63**	**77**	**106**	**5**	**0**	**3**	**278**	**5.0**	**28**	....	....	....	....	....	**7**	**1**	**6**	**7**	**8**	**0**	**0**	**0**
1994-95	**Detroit**	**NHL**	**45**	**14**	**44**	**58**	**72**	**4**	**1**	**2**	**181**	**7.7**	**18**	....	....	....	....	....	**18**	**6**	**12**	**18**	**10**	**2**	**1**	**0**
1995-96	**Detroit**	**NHL**	**76**	**14**	**60**	**74**	**90**	**3**	**1**	**3**	**234**	**6.0**	**19**	....	....	....	....	....	**17**	**5**	**9**	**14**	**30**	**3**	**2**	**1**
1996-97	**Hartford**	**NHL**	**20**	**3**	**5**	**8**	**18**	**1**	**0**	**1**	**39**	**7.7**	**0**	....	....	....	....	....	....	....	....	....	....	....	....	....
	Philadelphia	**NHL**	**37**	**6**	**20**	**26**	**20**	**0**	**1**	**1**	**71**	**8.5**	**11**	....	....	....	....	....	**17**	**1**	**8**	**9**	**6**	**0**	**0**	**0**
1997-98	**Philadelphia**	**NHL**	**57**	**2**	**27**	**29**	**30**	**1**	**0**	**1**	**107**	**1.9**	**3**	....	....	....	....	....	....	....	....	....	....	....	....	....
1998-99	**Chicago**	**NHL**	**10**	**0**	**4**	**4**	**0**	**0**	**0**	**0**	**8**	**0.0**	**-6**	**0**	**0.0**	**1**	**8**	**15:22**	....	....	....	....	....	....	....	....
	Carolina	**NHL**	**44**	**2**	**8**	**10**	**28**	**1**	**0**	**0**	**79**	**2.5**	**-1**	**0**	**0.0**	**16**	**31**	**19:41**	**5**	**0**	**1**	**1**	**2**	**0**	**0**	**0**
99-2000	**Carolina**	**NHL**	**69**	**11**	**29**	**40**	**40**	**6**	**0**	**3**	**155**	**7.1**	**-6**	**0**	**0.0**	**18**	**70**	**22:35**	....	....	....	....	....	....	....	....
2000-01	**Boston**	**NHL**	**18**	**0**	**4**	**4**	**30**	**0**	**0**	**0**	**28**	**0.0**	**-6**	**0**	**0.0**	**15**	**19**	**18:57**	....	....	....	....	....	....	....	....
	NHL Totals		**1409**	**396**	**1135**	**1531**	**1802**	**135**	**20**	**44**	**4385**	**9.0**		**0**	**0.0**	**50**	**128**	**20:42**	**194**	**59**	**137**	**196**	**264**	**21**	**6**	**8**

OMJHL Second All-Star Team (1980) • NHL Second All-Star Team (1982, 1983, 1984, 1990) • Won James Norris Memorial Trophy (1985, 1986, 1995) • NHL First All-Star Team (1985, 1986, 1989, 1995)
• Played in NHL All-Star Game (1982, 1983, 1984, 1985, 1986, 1988, 1989, 1990, 1991, 1992, 1993, 1994, 1996, 1997)

Traded to **Pittsburgh** by **Edmonton** with Dave Hunter and Wayne Van Dorp for Craig Simpson, Dave Hannan, Moe Mantha and Chris Joseph, November 24, 1987. Traded to **LA Kings** by **Pittsburgh** for Brian Benning, Jeff Chychrun and LA Kings' 1st round choice (later traded to Philadelphia - Philadelphia selected Jason Bowen) in 1992 Entry Draft, February 19, 1992. Traded to **Detroit** by **LA Kings** with Sylvain Couturier and Jim Hiller for Jimmy Carson, Marc Potvin and Gary Shuchuk, January 29, 1993. Traded to **Hartford** by **Detroit** with Keith Primeau and Detroit's 1st round choice (Nikos Tselios) in 1997 Entry Draft for Brendan Shanahan and Brian Glynn, October 9, 1996. Traded to **Philadelphia** by **Hartford** with Hartford-Carolina's 3rd round choice (Kris Mallette) in 1997 Entry Draft for Kevin Haller, Philadelphia's 1st round choice (later traded to San Jose - San Jose selected Scott Hannan) in 1997 Entry Draft and Hartford's 7th round choice (previously acquired, Carolina selected Andrew Merrick) in 1997 Entry Draft, December 15, 1996. Traded to **Chicago** by **Philadelphia** for NY Islanders' 5th round choice (previously acquired, Philadelphia selected Francis Belanger) in 1998 Entry Draft, June 27, 1998. Traded to **Carolina** by **Chicago** for Nelson Emerson, December 29, 1998. Signed as a free agent by **Boston**, July 13, 2000. • Released by **Boston**, December 15, 2000.

COMMODORE, Mike
(KAWM-uh-dohr, MIGHK) **N.J.**

Defense. Shoots right. 6'4", 230 lbs. Born, Fort Saskatchewan, Alta., November 7, 1979. New Jersey's 2nd choice, 42nd overall, in 1999 Entry Draft.

Season	Club	League	GP	G	A	Pts	PIM	PP	SH	GW	S	%	+/-	TF	F%	H	SB	Min	GP	G	A	Pts	PIM	PP	SH	GW
1996-97	Ft-Saskatchewan	AJHL	51	3	8	11	244	....	....	....	....	....	....	....	....	....	....	....	....	....	....	....	....	....	....	....
1997-98	North Dakota	WCHA	29	0	5	5	74	....	....	....	....	....	....	....	....	....	....	....	....	....	....	....	....	....	....	....
1998-99	North Dakota	WCHA	39	5	8	13	154	....	....	....	....	....	....	....	....	....	....	....	....	....	....	....	....	....	....	....
99-2000	North Dakota	WCHA	38	5	7	12	*154	....	....	....	....	....	....	....	....	....	....	....	....	....	....	....	....	....	....	....
2000-01	**New Jersey**	**NHL**	**20**	**1**	**4**	**5**	**14**	**0**	**0**	**0**	**11**	**9.1**	**5**	**0**	**0.0**	**43**	**17**	**12:46**	....	....	....	....	....	....	....	....
	Albany River Rats	AHL	41	2	5	7	59	....	....	....	....	....	....	....	....	....	....	....	....	....	....	....	....	....	....	....
	NHL Totals		**20**	**1**	**4**	**5**	**14**	**0**	**0**	**0**	**11**	**9.1**		**0**	**0.0**	**43**	**17**	**12:46**	....	....	....	....	....	....	....	....

NCAA Championship All-Tournament Team (2000)

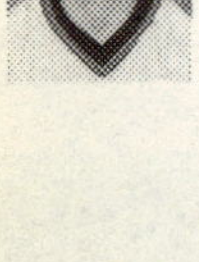

COMRIE, Mike
(KAWM-ree, MIGHK) **EDM.**

Center. Shoots left. 5'9", 172 lbs. Born, Edmonton, Alta., September 11, 1980. Edmonton's 5th choice, 91st overall, in 1999 Entry Draft.

Season	Club	League	GP	G	A	Pts	PIM	PP	SH	GW	S	%	+/-	TF	F%	H	SB	Min	GP	G	A	Pts	PIM	PP	SH	GW
1995-96	Edmonton SSAC	AMHL	33	51	52	103		....	....	....	....	....	....	....	....	....	....	....	....	....	....	....	....	....	....	....
1996-97	St. Albert Saints	AJHL	63	37	41	78	44	....	....	....	....	....	....	....	....	....	....	....	....	....	....	....	....	....	....	....
1997-98	St. Albert Saints	AJHL	58	*60	*78	*138	134	....	....	....	....	....	....	....	....	....	....	....	19	*24	*24	*48	51	....	....	....
1998-99	U. of Michigan	CCHA	42	19	25	44	38	....	....	....	....	....	....	....	....	....	....	....	....	....	....	....	....	....	....	....
99-2000	U. of Michigan	CCHA	40	24	35	59	95	....	....	....	....	....	....	....	....	....	....	....	....	....	....	....	....	....	....	....

			Regular Season																Playoffs							
Season	Club	League	GP	G	A	Pts	PIM	PP	SH	GW	S	%	+/-	TF	F%	H	SB	Min	GP	G	A	Pts	PIM	PP	SH	GW
2000-01	Kootenay Ice	WHL	37	39	40	79	79																			
	Edmonton	**NHL**	**41**	**8**	**14**	**22**	**14**	**3**	**0**	**1**	**62**	**12.9**	**6**	**372**	**43.3**	**12**	**13**	**11:23**	**6**	**1**	**2**	**3**	**0**	**1**	**0**	**1**
	NHL Totals		**41**	**8**	**14**	**22**	**14**	**3**	**0**	**1**	**62**	**12.9**		**372**	**43.3**	**12**	**13**	**11:23**	**6**	**1**	**2**	**3**	**0**	**1**	**0**	**1**

Won AJHL Rookie of the Year Award (1997) • AJHL MVP (1998) • Canadian Junior "A" Player of the Year (1998) • Won CCHA Rookie of the Year Award (1999) • CCHA All-Rookie Team (1999) • CCHA First All-Star Team (1999) • CCHA First All-Star Team (2000) • NCAA West Second All-American Team (2000)

• Left **University of Michigan** and signed as a free agent by **Kootenay** (WHL), August 23, 2000. • Left **Kootenay** (WHL) and signed NHL contract with **Edmonton**, December 30, 2000.

COMRIE, Paul

(KAWM-ree, PAWL) **EDM.**

Center. Shoots left. 5'11", 192 lbs. Born, Edmonton, Alta., February 7, 1977. Tampa Bay's 12th choice, 224th overall, in 1997 Entry Draft.

1993-94	Ft-Saskatchewan	AJHL	55	7	23	30	50												6	0	1	1	2			
1994-95	Ft-Saskatchewan	AJHL	51	30	37	67	121																			
1995-96	U. of Denver	WCHA	38	13	10	23	61																			
1996-97	U. of Denver	WCHA	40	21	28	49	72																			
1997-98	U. of Denver	WCHA	33	17	23	40	72																			
1998-99	U. of Denver	WCHA	40	18	31	49	84																			
	Hamilton Bulldogs	AHL	7	0	1	1	0												8	1	3	4	2			
99-2000	**Edmonton**	**NHL**	**15**	**1**	**2**	**3**	**4**	**0**	**0**	**0**	**11**	**9.1**	**–2**	**4**	**50.0**	**7**	**0**	**10:21**								
	Hamilton Bulldogs	AHL	12	3	3	6	6																			
2000-01	**Edmonton**	**NHL**	DID NOT PLAY – INJURED																							
	NHL Totals		**15**	**1**	**2**	**3**	**4**	**0**	**0**	**0**	**11**	**9.1**		**4**	**50.0**	**7**	**0**	**10:21**								

WCHA First All-Star Team (1999) • NCAA West Second All-American Team (1999)

Traded to **Edmonton** by **Tampa Bay** with Roman Hamrlik for Bryan Marchment, Steve Kelly and Jason Bonsignore, December 30, 1997. • Missed remainder of 1999-2000 and entire 2000-01 seasons recovering from head injury suffered during game vs. Tampa Bay, January 7, 2000.

CONNOLLY, Tim

(KAHN-noh-lee, TIHM) **BUF.**

Center. Shoots right. 6', 186 lbs. Born, Syracuse, NY, May 7, 1981. NY Islanders' 1st choice, 5th overall, in 1999 Entry Draft.

1996-97	Syracuse Crunch	MTJHL	50	42	62	104	34																			
1997-98	Erie Otters	OHL	59	30	32	62	32												7	1	6	7	6			
1998-99	Erie Otters	OHL	46	34	34	68	50																			
99-2000	**NY Islanders**	**NHL**	**81**	**14**	**20**	**34**	**44**	**2**	**1**	**1**	**114**	**12.3**	**–25**	**786**	**36.3**	**51**	**29**	**16:18**								
2000-01	**NY Islanders**	**NHL**	**82**	**10**	**31**	**41**	**42**	**5**	**0**	**0**	**171**	**5.8**	**–14**	**989**	**41.7**	**37**	**47**	**20:02**								
	NHL Totals		**163**	**24**	**51**	**75**	**86**	**7**	**1**	**1**	**285**	**8.4**		**1775**	**39.3**	**88**	**76**	**18:11**								

Traded to **Buffalo** by **NY Islanders** with Taylor Pyatt for Mike Peca, June 24, 2001.

CONROY, Craig

(KAWN-roi, KRAYG) **CGY.**

Center. Shoots right. 6'2", 197 lbs. Born, Potsdam, NY, September 4, 1971. Montreal's 7th choice, 123rd overall, in 1990 Entry Draft.

1989-90	Northwood Prep	Hi-School	31	33	43	76																				
1990-91	Clarkson Knights	ECAC	40	8	21	29	24																			
1991-92	Clarkson Knights	ECAC	31	19	17	36	36																			
1992-93	Clarkson Knights	ECAC	35	10	23	33	26																			
1993-94	Clarkson Knights	ECAC	34	26	*40	*66	46																			
1994-95	Fredericton	AHL	55	26	18	44	29												11	7	3	10	6			
	Montreal	**NHL**	**6**	**1**	**0**	**1**	**0**	**0**	**0**	**0**	**4**	**25.0**	**–1**													
1995-96	**Montreal**	**NHL**	**7**	**0**	**0**	**0**	**2**	**0**	**0**	**0**	**1**	**0.0**	**–4**													
	Fredericton	AHL	67	31	38	69	65												10	5	7	12	6			
1996-97	Fredericton	AHL	9	10	6	16	10																			
	St. Louis	**NHL**	**61**	**6**	**11**	**17**	**43**	**0**	**0**	**1**	**74**	**8.1**	**0**						**6**	**0**	**0**	**0**	**8**	**0**	**0**	**0**
	Worcester	AHL	5	5	6	11	2																			
1997-98	**St. Louis**	**NHL**	**81**	**14**	**29**	**43**	**46**	**0**	**3**	**1**	**118**	**11.9**	**20**						**10**	**1**	**2**	**3**	**8**	**0**	**0**	**1**
1998-99	**St. Louis**	**NHL**	**69**	**14**	**25**	**39**	**38**	**0**	**1**	**1**	**134**	**10.4**	**14**	**1190**	**54.6**	**77**	**35**	**16:39**	**13**	**2**	**1**	**3**	**6**	**0**	**0**	**0**
99-2000	**St. Louis**	**NHL**	**79**	**12**	**15**	**27**	**36**	**1**	**2**	**3**	**98**	**12.2**	**5**	**1339**	**53.6**	**105**	**29**	**14:48**	**7**	**0**	**2**	**2**	**2**	**0**	**0**	**0**
2000-01	**St. Louis**	**NHL**	**69**	**11**	**14**	**25**	**46**	**0**	**3**	**2**	**101**	**10.9**	**2**	**729**	**55.1**	**101**	**30**	**14:01**								
	Calgary	**NHL**	**14**	**3**	**4**	**7**	**14**	**0**	**1**	**0**	**32**	**9.4**	**0**	**264**	**52.7**	**16**	**11**	**18:08**								
	NHL Totals		**386**	**61**	**98**	**159**	**225**	**1**	**10**	**8**	**562**	**10.9**		**3522**	**54.2**	**299**	**105**	**15:19**	**36**	**3**	**5**	**8**	**24**	**0**	**0**	**1**

ECAC First All-Star Team (1994) • NCAA East First All-American Team (1994) • NCAA Final Four All-Tournament Team (1994)

Traded to **St. Louis** by **Montreal** with Pierre Turgeon and Rory Fitzpatrick for Murray Baron, Shayne Corson and St. Louis' 5th round choice (Gennady Razin) in 1997 Entry Draft, October 29, 1996. Traded to **Calgary** by **St. Louis** with St. Louis' 7th round choice (David Moss) in 2001 Entry Draft for Cory Stillman, March 13, 2001.

COOKE, Matt

(KUK, MAT) **VAN.**

Left wing. Shoots left. 5'11", 205 lbs. Born, Belleville, Ont., September 7, 1978. Vancouver's 8th choice, 144th overall, in 1997 Entry Draft.

1994-95	Wellington Dukes	MTJHL	46	9	23	32	62																			
1995-96	Windsor Spitfires	OHL	61	8	11	19	102												7	1	3	4	6			
1996-97	Windsor Spitfires	OHL	65	45	50	95	146												5	5	5	10	10			
1997-98	Windsor Spitfires	OHL	23	14	19	33	50																			
	Kingston	OHL	25	8	13	21	49												12	8	8	16	20			
1998-99	**Vancouver**	**NHL**	**30**	**0**	**2**	**2**	**27**	**0**	**0**	**0**	**22**	**0.0**	**–12**	**189**	**40.2**	**43**	**7**	**8:07**								
	Syracuse Crunch	AHL	37	15	18	33	119																			
99-2000	**Vancouver**	**NHL**	**51**	**5**	**7**	**12**	**39**	**0**	**1**	**1**	**58**	**8.6**	**3**	**71**	**39.4**	**124**	**14**	**11:48**								
	Syracuse Crunch	AHL	18	5	8	13	27																			
2000-01	**Vancouver**	**NHL**	**81**	**14**	**13**	**27**	**94**	**0**	**2**	**0**	**121**	**11.6**	**5**	**321**	**43.0**	**198**	**40**	**14:35**	**4**	**0**	**0**	**0**	**4**	**0**	**0**	**0**
	NHL Totals		**162**	**19**	**22**	**41**	**160**	**0**	**3**	**1**	**201**	**9.5**		**581**	**41.7**	**365**	**61**	**12:30**	**4**	**0**	**0**	**0**	**4**	**0**	**0**	**0**

COOPER, David

(KOO-puhr, DAY-vihd)

Defense. Shoots left. 6'2", 204 lbs. Born, Ottawa, Ont., November 2, 1973. Buffalo's 1st choice, 11th overall, in 1992 Entry Draft.

1988-89	Edmonton Mets	AAHA	32	24	22	46	151																			
1989-90	Medicine Hat	WHL	61	4	11	15	65												3	0	2	2	2			
1990-91	Medicine Hat	WHL	64	12	31	43	66												11	1	3	4	23			
1991-92	Medicine Hat	WHL	72	17	47	64	176												4	1	4	5	8			
1992-93	Medicine Hat	WHL	63	15	50	65	88												10	2	2	4	32			
	Rochester	AHL																	2	0	0	0	2			
1993-94	Rochester	AHL	68	10	25	35	82												4	1	1	2	2			
1994-95	Rochester	AHL	21	2	4	6	48																			
	South Carolina	ECHL	39	9	19	28	90												9	3	8	11	24			
1995-96	Rochester	AHL	67	9	18	27	79												8	0	1	1	12			
1996-97	**Toronto**	**NHL**	**19**	**3**	**3**	**6**	**16**	**2**	**0**	**0**	**23**	**13.0**	**–3**													
	St. John's Leafs	AHL	44	16	19	35	65																			
1997-98	**Toronto**	**NHL**	**9**	**0**	**4**	**4**	**8**	**0**	**0**	**0**	**13**	**0.0**	**2**													
	St. John's Leafs	AHL	60	19	23	42	117												4	0	1	1	6			
1998-99	Saint John Flames	AHL	65	18	24	42	121												7	1	4	5	10			
99-2000	Kassel Huskies	DEL	55	11	13	24	82												6	2	1	3	38			
2000-01	**Toronto**	**NHL**	**2**	**0**	**0**	**0**	**0**	**0**	**0**	**0**	**3**	**0.0**	**–1**	**0**	**0.0**	**2**	**0**	**11:33**								
	St. John's Leafs	AHL	71	16	26	42	117												4	1	1	2	10			
	NHL Totals		**30**	**3**	**7**	**10**	**24**	**2**	**0**	**0**	**39**	**7.7**		**0**	**0.0**	**2**	**0**	**11:33**								

WHL East First All-Star Team (1992) • AHL Second All-Star Team (1998)

Signed as a free agent by **Toronto**, September 26, 1996. Traded to **Calgary** by **Toronto** for Ladislav Kohn, July 2, 1998. Signed as a free agent by **Toronto**, October 16, 2000.

CORBET, Rene

(kohr-BAY, ruh-NAY)

Left wing. Shoots left. 6', 195 lbs. Born, Victoriaville, Que., June 25, 1973. Quebec's 2nd choice, 24th overall, in 1991 Entry Draft.

			Regular Season																Playoffs							
Season	Club	League	GP	G	A	Pts	PIM	PP	SH	GW	S	%	+/-	TF	F%	H	SB	Min	GP	G	A	Pts	PIM	PP	SH	GW
1988-89	Richelieu Riverains	QAAA	3	0	1	1	2	....	....	....	....	....	....	....	....	....	....	....	....	....	....	....	....	....	....	....
1989-90	Richelieu Riverains	QAAA	42	53	63	116	34	....	....	....	....	....	....	....	....	....	....	....	4	4	3	7	4	....	....	....
1990-91	Drummondville	QMJHL	45	25	40	65	34	....	....	....	....	....	....	....	....	....	....	....	14	11	6	17	15	....	....	....
1991-92	Drummondville	QMJHL	56	46	50	96	90	....	....	....	....	....	....	....	....	....	....	....	4	1	2	3	17	....	....	....
1992-93	Drummondville	QMJHL	63	*79	69	*148	143	....	....	....	....	....	....	....	....	....	....	....	10	7	13	20	16	....	....	....
1993-94	**Quebec**	**NHL**	**9**	**1**	**1**	**2**	**0**	**0**	**0**	**0**	**14**	**7.1**	**1**	....	....	....	....	....	....	....	....	....	....	....	....	....
	Cornwall Aces	AHL	68	37	40	77	56	....	....	....	....	....	....	....	....	....	....	....	13	7	2	9	18	....	....	....
1994-95	Cornwall Aces	AHL	65	33	24	57	79	....	....	....	....	....	....	....	....	....	....	....	12	2	8	10	27	....	....	....
	Quebec	**NHL**	**8**	**0**	**3**	**3**	**2**	**0**	**0**	**0**	**4**	**0.0**	**3**	....	....	....	....	....	**2**	**0**	**1**	**1**	**0**	**0**	**0**	**0**
1995-96♦	**Colorado**	**NHL**	**33**	**3**	**6**	**9**	**33**	**0**	**0**	**0**	**35**	**8.6**	**10**	....	....	....	....	....	**8**	**3**	**2**	**5**	**2**	**1**	**0**	**1**
	Cornwall Aces	AHL	9	5	6	11	10	....	....	....	....	....	....	....	....	....	....	....	....	....	....	....	....	....	....	....
1996-97	**Colorado**	**NHL**	**76**	**12**	**15**	**27**	**67**	**1**	**0**	**3**	**128**	**9.4**	**14**	....	....	....	....	....	**17**	**2**	**2**	**4**	**27**	**0**	**0**	**0**
1997-98	**Colorado**	**NHL**	**68**	**16**	**12**	**28**	**133**	**4**	**0**	**4**	**117**	**13.7**	**8**	....	....	....	....	....	**2**	**0**	**0**	**0**	**2**	**0**	**0**	**0**
1998-99	**Colorado**	**NHL**	**53**	**8**	**14**	**22**	**58**	**2**	**0**	**1**	**82**	**9.8**	**3**	**211**	**45.0**	**37**	**16**	**11:39**	....	....	....	....	....	....	....	....
	Calgary	**NHL**	**20**	**5**	**4**	**9**	**10**	**1**	**0**	**0**	**45**	**11.1**	**−2**	**4**	**50.0**	**39**	**6**	**18:05**	....	....	....	....	....	....	....	....
99-2000	**Calgary**	**NHL**	**48**	**4**	**10**	**14**	**60**	**0**	**0**	**0**	**100**	**4.0**	**−7**	**20**	**45.0**	**74**	**24**	**11:46**	....	....	....	....	....	....	....	....
	Pittsburgh	**NHL**	**4**	**1**	**0**	**1**	**0**	**1**	**0**	**0**	**9**	**11.1**	**−4**	**0**	**0.0**	**11**	**1**	**9:55**	**7**	**1**	**1**	**2**	**9**	**0**	**0**	**0**
2000-01	**Pittsburgh**	**NHL**	**43**	**8**	**9**	**17**	**57**	**2**	**0**	**1**	**85**	**9.4**	**−3**	**24**	**45.8**	**48**	**20**	**11:28**	**17**	**1**	**0**	**1**	**12**	**0**	**0**	**1**
	NHL Totals		**362**	**58**	**74**	**132**	**420**	**11**	**0**	**9**	**619**	**9.4**		**259**	**45.2**	**209**	**67**	**12:22**	**53**	**7**	**6**	**13**	**52**	**1**	**0**	**2**

QMJHL First All-Star Team (1993) • Canadian Major Junior First All-Star Team (1993) • Won Dudley "Red" Garrett Memorial Trophy (Top Rookie - AHL) (1994)

Transferred to **Colorado** after **Quebec** franchise relocated, June 21, 1995. Traded to **Calgary** by **Colorado** with Wade Belak, Robyn Regehr and Colorado's 2nd round compensatory choice (Jarret Stoll) in 2000 Entry Draft for Theoren Fleury and Chris Dingman, February 28, 1999. Traded to **Pittsburgh** by **Calgary** with Tyler Moss for Brad Werenka, March 14, 2000. • Missed most of 2000-01 season recovering from foot injury originally suffered in game vs. New Jersey, February 10, 2001.

CORKUM, Bob

(KOHR-kuhm, BAWB) **ATL.**

Center. Shoots right. 6'2", 225 lbs. Born, Salisbury, MA, December 18, 1967. Buffalo's 3rd choice, 47th overall, in 1986 Entry Draft.

Season	Club	League	GP	G	A	Pts	PIM	PP	SH	GW	S	%	+/-	TF	F%	H	SB	Min	GP	G	A	Pts	PIM	PP	SH	GW
1984-85	Triton Regional	Hi-School	18	35	36	71	....	....	....	....	....	....	....	....	....	....	....	....	....	....	....	....	....	....	....	....
1985-86	U. of Maine	H-East	39	7	26	33	53	....	....	....	....	....	....	....	....	....	....	....	....	....	....	....	....	....	....	....
1986-87	U. of Maine	H-East	35	18	11	29	24	....	....	....	....	....	....	....	....	....	....	....	....	....	....	....	....	....	....	....
1987-88	U. of Maine	H-East	40	14	18	32	64	....	....	....	....	....	....	....	....	....	....	....	....	....	....	....	....	....	....	....
1988-89	U. of Maine	H-East	45	17	31	48	64	....	....	....	....	....	....	....	....	....	....	....	....	....	....	....	....	....	....	....
1989-90	**Buffalo**	**NHL**	**8**	**2**	**0**	**2**	**4**	**0**	**0**	**1**	**6**	**33.3**	**2**	....	....	....	....	....	**5**	**1**	**0**	**1**	**4**	**0**	**0**	**0**
	Rochester	AHL	43	8	11	19	45	....	....	....	....	....	....	....	....	....	....	....	12	2	5	7	16	....	....	....
1990-91	Rochester	AHL	69	13	21	34	77	....	....	....	....	....	....	....	....	....	....	....	15	4	4	8	4	....	....	....
1991-92	**Buffalo**	**NHL**	**20**	**2**	**4**	**6**	**21**	**0**	**0**	**0**	**23**	**8.7**	**−9**	....	....	....	....	....	**4**	**1**	**0**	**1**	**0**	**1**	**0**	**0**
	Rochester	AHL	52	16	12	28	47	....	....	....	....	....	....	....	....	....	....	....	8	0	6	6	8	....	....	....
1992-93	**Buffalo**	**NHL**	**68**	**6**	**4**	**10**	**38**	**0**	**1**	**1**	**69**	**8.7**	**−3**	....	....	....	....	....	**5**	**0**	**0**	**0**	**2**	**0**	**0**	**0**
1993-94	**Anaheim**	**NHL**	**76**	**23**	**28**	**51**	**18**	**3**	**3**	**0**	**180**	**12.8**	**4**	....	....	....	....	....	....	....	....	....	....	....	....	....
1994-95	**Anaheim**	**NHL**	**44**	**10**	**9**	**19**	**25**	**0**	**0**	**1**	**100**	**10.0**	**−7**	....	....	....	....	....	....	....	....	....	....	....	....	....
1995-96	**Anaheim**	**NHL**	**48**	**5**	**7**	**12**	**26**	**0**	**0**	**1**	**88**	**5.7**	**0**	....	....	....	....	....	....	....	....	....	....	....	....	....
	Philadelphia	**NHL**	**28**	**4**	**3**	**7**	**8**	**0**	**0**	**2**	**38**	**10.5**	**3**	....	....	....	....	....	**12**	**1**	**2**	**3**	**6**	**0**	**0**	**0**
1996-97	**Phoenix**	**NHL**	**80**	**9**	**11**	**20**	**40**	**0**	**1**	**3**	**119**	**7.6**	**−7**	....	....	....	....	....	**7**	**2**	**2**	**4**	**4**	**0**	**0**	**1**
1997-98	**Phoenix**	**NHL**	**76**	**12**	**9**	**21**	**28**	**0**	**5**	**0**	**105**	**11.4**	**−7**	....	....	....	....	....	**6**	**1**	**0**	**1**	**4**	**0**	**0**	**0**
1998-99	**Phoenix**	**NHL**	**77**	**9**	**10**	**19**	**17**	**0**	**0**	**0**	**146**	**6.2**	**−9**	**1644**	**51.6**	**116**	**28**	**17:15**	**7**	**0**	**1**	**1**	**4**	**0**	**0**	**0**
99-2000	**Los Angeles**	**NHL**	**45**	**5**	**6**	**11**	**14**	**0**	**0**	**0**	**45**	**11.1**	**0**	**910**	**55.3**	**90**	**22**	**14:26**	**4**	**0**	**0**	**0**	**0**	**0**	**0**	**0**
2000-01	**Los Angeles**	**NHL**	**58**	**4**	**6**	**10**	**18**	**1**	**0**	**0**	**47**	**8.5**	**−12**	**1020**	**53.2**	**96**	**40**	**12:59**	....	....	....	....	....	....	....	....
	New Jersey	**NHL**	**17**	**3**	**1**	**4**	**4**	**0**	**0**	**0**	**19**	**15.8**	**4**	**150**	**58.7**	**31**	**3**	**11:19**	**12**	**1**	**2**	**3**	**0**	**0**	**0**	**0**
	NHL Totals		**645**	**94**	**98**	**192**	**261**	**4**	**10**	**9**	**985**	**9.5**		**3724**	**53.2**	**333**	**93**	**14:50**	**62**	**7**	**7**	**14**	**24**	**1**	**0**	**1**

Claimed by **Anaheim** from **Buffalo** in Expansion Draft, June 24, 1993. Traded to **Philadelphia** by **Anaheim** for Chris Herperger and Winnipeg's 7th round choice (previously acquired, Anaheim selected Tony Mohagen) in 1997 Entry Draft, February 6, 1996. Claimed by **Phoenix** from **Philadelphia** in Waiver Draft, September 30, 1996. Signed as a free agent by **LA Kings**, December 28, 1999. Traded to **New Jersey** by **LA Kings** for future considerations (Steve Kelly, February 27, 2001), February 23, 2001. Signed as a free agent by **Atlanta**, July 16, 2001.

CORSO, Daniel

(KOHR-soh, DAN-yehl) **ST.L.**

Center. Shoots left. 5'10", 187 lbs. Born, Montreal, Que., April 3, 1978. St. Louis' 6th choice, 169th overall, in 1996 Entry Draft.

Season	Club	League	GP	G	A	Pts	PIM	PP	SH	GW	S	%	+/-	TF	F%	H	SB	Min	GP	G	A	Pts	PIM	PP	SH	GW
1993-94	Magog Elites	QAAA	36	17	22	39	....	....	....	....	....	....	....	....	....	....	....	....	12	10	12	22	....	....	....	....
1994-95	Victoriaville Tigres	QMJHL	65	27	26	53	6	....	....	....	....	....	....	....	....	....	....	....	4	2	5	7	2	....	....	....
1995-96	Victoriaville Tigres	QMJHL	65	49	65	114	77	....	....	....	....	....	....	....	....	....	....	....	12	6	7	13	4	....	....	....
1996-97	Victoriaville Tigres	QMJHL	54	51	68	119	50	....	....	....	....	....	....	....	....	....	....	....	....	....	....	....	....	....	....	....
1997-98	Victoriaville Tigres	QMJHL	35	24	51	75	20	....	....	....	....	....	....	....	....	....	....	....	3	1	1	2	2	....	....	....
1998-99	Worcester	AHL	63	14	14	28	26	....	....	....	....	....	....	....	....	....	....	....	....	....	....	....	....	....	....	....
99-2000	Worcester	AHL	71	21	34	55	19	....	....	....	....	....	....	....	....	....	....	....	9	2	3	5	10	....	....	....
2000-01	**St. Louis**	**NHL**	**28**	**10**	**3**	**13**	**14**	**5**	**0**	**4**	**42**	**23.8**	**0**	**296**	**56.1**	**21**	**3**	**13:56**	**12**	**0**	**1**	**1**	**0**	**0**	**0**	**0**
	Worcester	AHL	52	19	37	56	47	....	....	....	....	....	....	....	....	....	....	....	....	....	....	....	....	....	....	....
	NHL Totals		**28**	**10**	**3**	**13**	**14**	**5**	**0**	**4**	**42**	**23.8**		**296**	**56.1**	**21**	**3**	**13:56**	**12**	**0**	**1**	**1**	**0**	**0**	**0**	**0**

QMJHL All-Rookie Team (1995) • Won Michel Briere Award (MVP - QMJHL) (1997) • QMJHL First All-Star Team (1997)

CORSON, Shayne

(KOHR-sohn, SHAYN) **TOR.**

Left wing. Shoots left. 6'1", 202 lbs. Born, Barrie, Ont., August 13, 1966. Montreal's 2nd choice, 8th overall, in 1984 Entry Draft.

Season	Club	League	GP	G	A	Pts	PIM	PP	SH	GW	S	%	+/-	TF	F%	H	SB	Min	GP	G	A	Pts	PIM	PP	SH	GW
1982-83	Barrie Colts	OJHL-B	23	13	29	42	87	....	....	....	....	....	....	....	....	....	....	....	....	....	....	....	....	....	....	....
1983-84	Brantford	OHL	66	25	46	71	165	....	....	....	....	....	....	....	....	....	....	....	6	4	1	5	26	....	....	....
1984-85	Hamilton Hawks	OHL	54	27	63	90	154	....	....	....	....	....	....	....	....	....	....	....	11	3	7	10	19	....	....	....
1985-86	Hamilton Hawks	OHL	47	41	57	98	153	....	....	....	....	....	....	....	....	....	....	....	....	....	....	....	....	....	....	....
	Montreal	**NHL**	**3**	**0**	**0**	**0**	**2**	**0**	**0**	**0**	**1**	**0.0**	**−3**	....	....	....	....	....	....	....	....	....	....	....	....	....
1986-87	**Montreal**	**NHL**	**55**	**12**	**11**	**23**	**144**	**0**	**1**	**3**	**69**	**17.4**	**10**	....	....	....	....	....	**17**	**6**	**5**	**11**	**30**	**1**	**1**	**1**
1987-88	**Montreal**	**NHL**	**71**	**12**	**27**	**39**	**152**	**2**	**0**	**2**	**90**	**13.3**	**22**	....	....	....	....	....	**3**	**1**	**0**	**1**	**12**	**0**	**0**	**0**
1988-89	**Montreal**	**NHL**	**80**	**26**	**24**	**50**	**193**	**10**	**0**	**3**	**133**	**19.5**	**−1**	....	....	....	....	....	**21**	**4**	**5**	**9**	**65**	**2**	**0**	**2**
1989-90	**Montreal**	**NHL**	**76**	**31**	**44**	**75**	**144**	**7**	**0**	**6**	**192**	**16.1**	**33**	....	....	....	....	....	**11**	**2**	**8**	**10**	**20**	**0**	**0**	**0**
1990-91	**Montreal**	**NHL**	**71**	**23**	**24**	**47**	**138**	**7**	**0**	**2**	**164**	**14.0**	**9**	....	....	....	....	....	**13**	**9**	**6**	**15**	**36**	**4**	**1**	**3**
1991-92	**Montreal**	**NHL**	**64**	**17**	**36**	**53**	**118**	**3**	**0**	**2**	**165**	**10.3**	**15**	....	....	....	....	....	**10**	**2**	**5**	**7**	**15**	**0**	**0**	**0**
1992-93	**Edmonton**	**NHL**	**80**	**16**	**31**	**47**	**209**	**9**	**2**	**1**	**164**	**9.8**	**−19**	....	....	....	....	....	....	....	....	....	....	....	....	....
1993-94	**Edmonton**	**NHL**	**64**	**25**	**29**	**54**	**118**	**11**	**0**	**3**	**171**	**14.6**	**−8**	....	....	....	....	....	....	....	....	....	....	....	....	....
1994-95	**Edmonton**	**NHL**	**48**	**12**	**24**	**36**	**86**	**2**	**0**	**1**	**131**	**9.2**	**−17**	....	....	....	....	....	....	....	....	....	....	....	....	....
1995-96	**St. Louis**	**NHL**	**77**	**18**	**28**	**46**	**192**	**13**	**0**	**0**	**150**	**12.0**	**3**	....	....	....	....	....	**13**	**8**	**6**	**14**	**22**	**6**	**1**	**1**
1996-97	**St. Louis**	**NHL**	**11**	**2**	**1**	**3**	**24**	**1**	**0**	**0**	**19**	**10.5**	**−4**	....	....	....	....	....	....	....	....	....	....	....	....	....
	Montreal	**NHL**	**47**	**6**	**15**	**21**	**80**	**2**	**0**	**2**	**96**	**6.3**	**−5**	....	....	....	....	....	**5**	**1**	**0**	**1**	**4**	**0**	**1**	**0**
1997-98	**Montreal**	**NHL**	**62**	**21**	**34**	**55**	**108**	**14**	**1**	**1**	**142**	**14.8**	**2**	....	....	....	....	....	**10**	**3**	**6**	**9**	**26**	**1**	**0**	**1**
	Canada	Olympics	6	1	1	2	2	....	....	....	....	....	....	....	....	....	....	....	....	....	....	....	....	....	....	....
1998-99	**Montreal**	**NHL**	**63**	**12**	**20**	**32**	**147**	**7**	**0**	**4**	**142**	**8.5**	**−10**	**184**	**45.1**	**71**	**38**	**20:42**	....	....	....	....	....	....	....	....
99-2000	**Montreal**	**NHL**	**70**	**8**	**20**	**28**	**115**	**2**	**0**	**1**	**121**	**6.6**	**−2**	**445**	**43.4**	**121**	**48**	**19:05**	....	....	....	....	....	....	....	....
2000-01	**Toronto**	**NHL**	**77**	**8**	**18**	**26**	**189**	**0**	**0**	**2**	**102**	**7.8**	**1**	**602**	**48.8**	**151**	**42**	**15:50**	**11**	**1**	**1**	**2**	**14**	**0**	**0**	**0**
	NHL Totals		**1019**	**249**	**386**	**635**	**2159**	**90**	**4**	**33**	**2052**	**12.1**		**1231**	**46.3**	**343**	**128**	**18:23**	**114**	**37**	**42**	**79**	**244**	**14**	**4**	**8**

Played in NHL All-Star Game (1990, 1994, 1998)

Traded to **Edmonton** by **Montreal** with Brent Gilchrist and Vladimir Vujtek for Vincent Damphousse and Edmonton's 4th round choice (Adam Wiesel) in 1993 Entry Draft, August 27, 1992. Signed as a free agent by **St. Louis**, July 28, 1995. Traded to **Montreal** by **St. Louis** with Murray Baron and St. Louis' 5th round choice (Gennady Razin) in 1997 Entry Draft for Pierre Turgeon, Rory Fitzpatrick and Craig Conroy, October 29, 1996. Signed as a free agent by **Toronto**, July 4, 2000.

Season	Club	League	Regular Season GP	G	A	Pts	PIM	PP	SH	GW	S	%	+/-	TF	F%	H	SB	Min	Playoffs GP	G	A	Pts	PIM	PP	SH	GW

COTE, Patrick

(KOH-tay, PA-trihk)

Left wing. Shoots left. 6'3", 220 lbs. Born, LaSalle, Que., January 24, 1975. Dallas' 2nd choice, 37th overall, in 1995 Entry Draft.

Season	Club	League	GP	G	A	Pts	PIM	PP	SH	GW	S	%	+/-	TF	F%	H	SB	Min	GP	G	A	Pts	PIM	PP	SH	GW
1992-93	Etoiles St-Laurent	QAHA	STATISTICS NOT AVAILABLE																							
1993-94	Beauport	QMJHL	48	2	4	6	230												12	1	0	1	61			
1994-95	Beauport	QMJHL	56	20	20	40	314												17	8	8	16	115			
1995-96	**Dallas**	**NHL**	**2**	**0**	**0**	**0**	**5**	**0**	**0**	**0**	**0**	**0.0**	**–2**													
	Michigan K-Wings	IHL	57	4	6	10	239												3	0	0	0	2			
1996-97	**Dallas**	**NHL**	**3**	**0**	**0**	**0**	**27**	**0**	**0**	**0**	**1**	**0.0**	**0**													
	Michigan K-Wings	IHL	58	14	10	24	237												4	2	0	2	6			
1997-98	**Dallas**	**NHL**	**3**	**0**	**0**	**0**	**15**	**0**	**0**	**0**	**3**	**0.0**	**–1**													
	Michigan K-Wings	IHL	4	2	0	2	4																			
1998-99	**Nashville**	**NHL**	**70**	**1**	**2**	**3**	**242**	**0**	**0**	**0**	**21**	**4.8**	**–7**	**0**	**0.0**	**47**	**7**	**4:14**								
99-2000	**Nashville**	**NHL**	**21**	**0**	**0**	**0**	**70**	**0**	**0**	**0**	**8**	**0.0**	**–7**	**0**	**0.0**	**9**	**1**	**5:13**								
2000-01	**Edmonton**	**NHL**	**6**	**0**	**0**	**0**	**18**	**0**	**0**	**0**	**0**	**0.0**	**–2**	**0**	**0.0**	**2**	**0**	**3:07**								
	Hamilton Bulldogs	AHL	16	0	1	1	61																			
	NHL Totals		**105**	**1**	**2**	**3**	**377**	**0**	**0**	**0**	**33**	**3.0**		**0**	**0.0**	**58**	**8**	**4:09**								

Claimed by **Nashville** from **Dallas** in Expansion Draft, June 26, 1998. Traded to **Edmonton** by **Nashville** for Phoenix's 5th round choice (previously acquired, Nashville selected Matt Koalska) in 2000 Entry Draft, June 12, 2000. • Missed majority of 2000-01 season after volunteering to enter NHL/NHLPA Substance Abuse Program, March 26, 2001.

COTE, Sylvain

(KOH-tay, SIHL-vayn) **WSH.**

Defense. Shoots right. 5'11", 190 lbs. Born, Quebec City, Que., January 19, 1966. Hartford's 1st choice, 11th overall, in 1984 Entry Draft.

Season	Club	League	GP	G	A	Pts	PIM	PP	SH	GW	S	%	+/-	TF	F%	H	SB	Min	GP	G	A	Pts	PIM	PP	SH	GW
1981-82	Ste-Foy Governors	QAAA	46	18	29	47	117												5	0	3	3	8			
1982-83	Quebec Remparts	QMJHL	66	10	24	34	50																			
1983-84	Quebec Remparts	QMJHL	66	15	50	65	89												5	1	1	2	0			
1984-85	**Hartford**	**NHL**	**67**	**3**	**9**	**12**	**17**	**1**	**0**	**1**	**90**	**3.3**	**–30**													
1985-86	Hull Olympiques	QMJHL	26	10	33	43	14												13	6	*28	34	22			
	Hartford	**NHL**	**2**	**0**	**0**	**0**	**0**	**0**	**0**	**0**	**0**	**0.0**	**1**													
	Binghamton	AHL	12	2	4	6	0																			
1986-87	**Hartford**	**NHL**	**67**	**2**	**8**	**10**	**20**	**0**	**0**	**0**	**100**	**2.0**	**11**						**2**	**0**	**2**	**2**	**2**	**0**	**0**	**0**
1987-88	**Hartford**	**NHL**	**67**	**7**	**21**	**28**	**30**	**0**	**1**	**0**	**142**	**4.9**	**–8**						**6**	**1**	**1**	**2**	**4**	**1**	**0**	**0**
1988-89	**Hartford**	**NHL**	**78**	**8**	**9**	**17**	**49**	**1**	**0**	**0**	**130**	**6.2**	**–7**						**3**	**0**	**1**	**1**	**4**	**0**	**0**	**0**
1989-90	**Hartford**	**NHL**	**28**	**4**	**2**	**6**	**14**	**1**	**0**	**1**	**50**	**8.0**	**2**						**5**	**0**	**0**	**0**	**2**	**0**	**0**	**0**
1990-91	**Hartford**	**NHL**	**73**	**7**	**12**	**19**	**17**	**1**	**0**	**0**	**154**	**4.5**	**–17**						**6**	**0**	**2**	**2**	**2**	**0**	**0**	**0**
1991-92	**Washington**	**NHL**	**78**	**11**	**29**	**40**	**31**	**6**	**0**	**2**	**151**	**7.3**	**7**						**7**	**1**	**2**	**3**	**4**	**0**	**0**	**0**
1992-93	**Washington**	**NHL**	**77**	**21**	**29**	**50**	**34**	**8**	**2**	**3**	**206**	**10.2**	**28**						**6**	**1**	**1**	**2**	**4**	**0**	**0**	**0**
1993-94	**Washington**	**NHL**	**84**	**16**	**35**	**51**	**66**	**3**	**2**	**2**	**212**	**7.5**	**30**						**9**	**1**	**8**	**9**	**6**	**0**	**0**	**0**
1994-95	**Washington**	**NHL**	**47**	**5**	**14**	**19**	**53**	**1**	**0**	**2**	**124**	**4.0**	**2**						**7**	**1**	**3**	**4**	**2**	**0**	**0**	**0**
1995-96	**Washington**	**NHL**	**81**	**5**	**33**	**38**	**40**	**3**	**0**	**2**	**212**	**2.4**	**5**						**6**	**2**	**0**	**2**	**12**	**1**	**0**	**0**
1996-97	**Washington**	**NHL**	**57**	**6**	**18**	**24**	**28**	**2**	**0**	**0**	**131**	**4.6**	**11**													
1997-98	**Washington**	**NHL**	**59**	**1**	**15**	**16**	**36**	**0**	**0**	**0**	**83**	**1.2**	**–5**													
	Toronto	**NHL**	**12**	**3**	**6**	**9**	**6**	**1**	**0**	**1**	**20**	**15.0**	**2**													
1998-99	**Toronto**	**NHL**	**79**	**5**	**24**	**29**	**28**	**0**	**0**	**1**	**119**	**4.2**	**22**	**1**	**0.0**	**76**	**95**	**21:04**	**17**	**2**	**1**	**3**	**10**	**0**	**0**	**0**
99-2000	**Toronto**	**NHL**	**3**	**0**	**1**	**1**	**0**	**0**	**0**	**0**	**3**	**0.0**	**1**	**0**	**0.0**	**6**	**3**	**21:40**								
	Chicago	**NHL**	**45**	**6**	**18**	**24**	**14**	**5**	**0**	**2**	**78**	**7.7**	**–4**	**1**	**100.0**	**49**	**62**	**23:22**								
	Dallas	**NHL**	**28**	**2**	**8**	**10**	**14**	**0**	**0**	**0**	**47**	**4.3**	**6**	**0**	**0.0**	**33**	**23**	**18:10**	**23**	**2**	**1**	**3**	**8**	**2**	**0**	**0**
2000-01	**Washington**	**NHL**	**68**	**7**	**11**	**18**	**18**	**1**	**1**	**1**	**86**	**8.1**	**–3**	**0**	**0.0**	**125**	**72**	**17:47**	**5**	**0**	**0**	**0**	**2**	**0**	**0**	**0**
	NHL Totals		**1100**	**119**	**302**	**421**	**515**	**34**	**6**	**18**	**2138**	**5.6**		**2**	**50.0**	**289**	**255**	**20:10**	**102**	**11**	**22**	**33**	**62**	**4**	**0**	**0**

QMJHL Second All-Star Team (1984) • QMJHL First All-Star Team (1986)

Traded to **Washington** by **Hartford** for Washington's 2nd round choice (Andrei Nikolishin) in 1992 Entry Draft, September 8, 1991. Traded to **Toronto** by **Washington** for Jeff Brown, March 24, 1998. Traded to **Chicago** by **Toronto** for Chicago's 2nd round choice in 2001 Entry Draft and a conditional choice in 2001 Entry Draft, October 8, 1999. Traded to **Dallas** by **Chicago** with Dave Manson for Kevin Dean, Derek Plante and Dallas' 2nd round choice (Matt Keith) in 2001 Entry Draft, February 8, 2000. Signed as a free agent by **Washington**, July 7, 2000.

COURVILLE, Larry

(KOOR-vihl, LAIR-ree)

Left wing. Shoots left. 6'1", 180 lbs. Born, Timmins, Ont., April 2, 1975. Vancouver's 2nd choice, 61st overall, in 1995 Entry Draft.

Season	Club	League	GP	G	A	Pts	PIM	PP	SH	GW	S	%	+/-	TF	F%	H	SB	Min	GP	G	A	Pts	PIM	PP	SH	GW
1990-91	Waterloo Siskins	OJHL-B	47	20	18	38	144																			
1991-92	Cornwall Royals	OHL	60	8	12	20	80												6	0	0	0	8			
1992-93	Newmarket	OHL	64	21	18	39	181												7	0	6	6	14			
1993-94	Newmarket	OHL	39	20	19	39	134																			
	Moncton Hawks	AHL	8	2	0	2	37												10	2	2	4	27			
1994-95	Sarnia Sting	OHL	16	9	9	18	58																			
	Oshawa Generals	OHL	28	25	30	55	72												7	4	10	14	10			
1995-96	**Vancouver**	**NHL**	**3**	**1**	**0**	**1**	**0**	**0**	**0**	**1**	**2**	**50.0**	**1**													
	Syracuse Crunch	AHL	71	17	32	49	127												14	5	3	8	10			
1996-97	**Vancouver**	**NHL**	**19**	**0**	**2**	**2**	**11**	**0**	**0**	**0**	**11**	**0.0**	**–4**													
	Syracuse Crunch	AHL	54	20	24	44	103												3	0	1	1	20			
1997-98	**Vancouver**	**NHL**	**11**	**0**	**0**	**0**	**5**	**0**	**0**	**0**	**3**	**0.0**	**–7**													
	Syracuse Crunch	AHL	29	6	12	18	84																			
1998-99	Syracuse Crunch	AHL	71	13	28	41	155																			
99-2000	Kentucky	AHL	61	11	12	23	107												9	1	5	6	16			
2000-01	Kentucky	AHL	71	20	16	36	112												3	0	0	0	6			
	NHL Totals		**33**	**1**	**2**	**3**	**16**	**0**	**0**	**1**	**16**	**6.3**														

• Re-entered NHL Entry Draft. Originally Winnipeg's 6th choice, 119th overall, in 1993 Entry Draft.

OHL Second All-Star Team (1995)

Signed as a free agent by **Kentucky** (AHL), September 1, 1999. Signed as a free agent by **San Jose**, September 1, 2000.

COWAN, Jeff

(KOW-an, JEHF) **CGY.**

Left wing. Shoots left. 6'2", 195 lbs. Born, Scarborough, Ont., September 27, 1976.

Season	Club	League	GP	G	A	Pts	PIM	PP	SH	GW	S	%	+/-	TF	F%	H	SB	Min	GP	G	A	Pts	PIM	PP	SH	GW
1992-93	Guelph Platers	OJHL-B	45	8	8	16	22																			
1993-94	Guelph Platers	OJHL-B	43	30	26	56	96																			
	Guelph Storm	OHL	17	1	0	1	5																			
1994-95	Guelph Storm	OHL	51	10	7	17	14												14	1	1	2	0			
1995-96	Barrie Colts	OHL	66	38	14	52	29												5	1	2	3	6			
1996-97	Saint John Flames	AHL	22	5	5	10	8																			
	Roanoke Express	ECHL	47	21	13	34	42																			
1997-98	Saint John Flames	AHL	69	15	13	28	23												13	4	1	5	14			
1998-99	Saint John Flames	AHL	71	7	12	19	117												4	0	1	1	10			
99-2000	**Calgary**	**NHL**	**13**	**4**	**1**	**5**	**16**	**0**	**0**	**0**	**26**	**15.4**	**2**	**0**	**0.0**	**22**	**5**	**10:22**								
	Saint John Flames	AHL	47	15	10	25	77																			
2000-01	**Calgary**	**NHL**	**51**	**9**	**4**	**13**	**74**	**2**	**0**	**1**	**48**	**18.8**	**–8**	**5**	**20.0**	**51**	**8**	**9:06**								
	NHL Totals		**64**	**13**	**5**	**18**	**90**	**2**	**0**	**1**	**74**	**17.6**		**5**	**20.0**	**73**	**13**	**9:22**								

Signed as a free agent by **Calgary**, October 2, 1995.

CRAIG, Mike

(KRAYG, MIGHK) **S.J.**

Right wing. Shoots right. 6'1", 185 lbs. Born, London, Ont., June 6, 1971. Minnesota's 2nd choice, 28th overall, in 1989 Entry Draft.

Season	Club	League	GP	G	A	Pts	PIM	PP	SH	GW	S	%	+/-	TF	F%	H	SB	Min	GP	G	A	Pts	PIM	PP	SH	GW
1986-87	Woodstock Vets	OJHL-C	32	29	19	48	64																			
1987-88	Oshawa Generals	OHL	61	6	10	16	39												7	7	0	1	11			
1988-89	Oshawa Generals	OHL	63	36	36	72	34												6	3	1	4	6			
1989-90	Oshawa Generals	OHL	43	36	40	76	85												17	10	16	26	46			
1990-91	**Minnesota**	**NHL**	**39**	**8**	**4**	**12**	**32**	**1**	**0**	**2**	**59**	**13.6**	**–11**						**10**	**1**	**1**	**2**	**20**	**1**	**0**	**1**
1991-92	**Minnesota**	**NHL**	**67**	**15**	**16**	**31**	**155**	**4**	**0**	**4**	**136**	**11.0**	**–12**						**4**	**1**	**0**	**1**	**7**	**0**	**0**	**0**
1992-93	**Minnesota**	**NHL**	**70**	**15**	**23**	**38**	**106**	**7**	**0**	**0**	**131**	**11.5**	**–11**													
1993-94	**Dallas**	**NHL**	**72**	**13**	**24**	**37**	**139**	**3**	**0**	**2**	**150**	**8.7**	**–14**						**4**	**0**	**0**	**0**	**2**	**0**	**0**	**0**
1994-95	**Toronto**	**NHL**	**37**	**5**	**5**	**10**	**12**	**1**	**0**	**1**	**61**	**8.2**	**–21**						**2**	**0**	**1**	**1**	**2**	**0**	**0**	**0**
1995-96	**Toronto**	**NHL**	**70**	**8**	**12**	**20**	**42**	**1**	**0**	**1**	**108**	**7.4**	**–8**						**6**	**0**	**0**	**0**	**18**	**0**	**0**	**0**

Season	Club	League	GP	G	A	Pts	PIM	PP	SH	GW	S	%	+/-	TF	F%	H	SB	Min	GP	G	A	Pts	PIM	PP	SH	GW
			Regular Season																Playoffs							
1996-97	**Toronto**	**NHL**	**65**	**7**	**13**	**20**	**62**	**1**	**0**	**0**	**128**	**5.5**	**-20**	....	....	....	....	....	....	....	....	....	....	....	....	....
1997-98	San Antonio	IHL	12	4	1	5	18	....	....	....	....	....	....	....	....	....	....	....	....	....	....	....	....	....	....	....
	Kansas City	IHL	59	14	33	47	68	....	....	....	....	....	....	....	....	....	....	....	11	5	5	10	28	....	....	....
1998-99	**San Jose**	**NHL**	**1**	**0**	**0**	**0**	**0**	**0**	**0**	**0**	**1**	**0.0**	**-1**	**0**	**0.0**	**1**	**1**	**11:25**	....	....	....	....	....	....	....	....
	Kentucky	AHL	52	27	17	44	72	....	....	....	....	....	....	....	....	....	....	....	12	5	4	9	18	....	....	....
99-2000	Kentucky	AHL	76	39	39	78	116	....	....	....	....	....	....	....	....	....	....	....	9	5	5	10	14	....	....	....
2000-01	Hershey Bears	AHL	57	21	22	43	73	....	....	....	....	....	....	....	....	....	....	....	12	3	2	5	20	....	....	....
	NHL Totals		**421**	**71**	**97**	**168**	**548**	**18**	**0**	**10**	**774**	**9.2**		**0**	**0.0**	**1**	**1**	**11:25**	**26**	**2**	**2**	**4**	**49**	**1**	**0**	**1**

Transferred to **Dallas** after **Minnesota** franchise relocated, June 9, 1993. Signed as a free agent by **Toronto**, July 29, 1994. Signed as a free agent by **San Jose**, July 13, 1998. Signed as a free agent by **Colorado**, August 2, 2000. Signed as a free agent by **San Jose**, August, 2001.

CROSS, Cory

(KRAWS, KOHR-ee) **TOR.**

Defense. Shoots left. 6'5", 220 lbs. Born, Lloydminster, Alta., January 3, 1971. Tampa Bay's 1st choice, 1st overall, in 1992 Supplemental Draft.

Season	Club	League	GP	G	A	Pts	PIM	PP	SH	GW	S	%	+/-	TF	F%	H	SB	Min	GP	G	A	Pts	PIM	PP	SH	GW
1990-91	U. of Alberta	CWUAA	20	2	5	7	16	....	....	....	....	....	....	....	....	....	....	....	....	....	....	....	....	....	....	....
1991-92	U. of Alberta	CWUAA	41	4	11	15	82	....	....	....	....	....	....	....	....	....	....	....	....	....	....	....	....	....	....	....
1992-93	U. of Alberta	CWUAA	43	11	28	39	105	....	....	....	....	....	....	....	....	....	....	....	....	....	....	....	....	....	....	....
	Atlanta Knights	IHL	7	0	1	1	2	....	....	....	....	....	....	....	....	....	....	....	4	0	0	0	6	....	....	....
1993-94	**Tampa Bay**	**NHL**	**5**	**0**	**0**	**0**	**6**	**0**	**0**	**0**	**5**	**0.0**	**-3**	....	....	....	....	....	....	....	....	....	....	....	....	....
	Atlanta Knights	IHL	70	4	14	18	72	....	....	....	....	....	....	....	....	....	....	....	9	1	2	3	14	....	....	....
1994-95	Atlanta Knights	IHL	41	5	10	15	67	....	....	....	....	....	....	....	....	....	....	....	....	....	....	....	....	....	....	....
	Tampa Bay	**NHL**	**43**	**1**	**5**	**6**	**41**	**0**	**0**	**1**	**35**	**2.9**	**-6**	....	....	....	....	....	....	....	....	....	....	....	....	....
1995-96	**Tampa Bay**	**NHL**	**75**	**2**	**14**	**16**	**66**	**0**	**0**	**0**	**57**	**3.5**	**4**	....	....	....	....	....	**6**	**0**	**0**	**0**	**22**	**0**	**0**	**0**
1996-97	**Tampa Bay**	**NHL**	**72**	**4**	**5**	**9**	**95**	**0**	**0**	**2**	**75**	**5.3**	**6**	....	....	....	....	....	....	....	....	....	....	....	....	....
1997-98	**Tampa Bay**	**NHL**	**74**	**3**	**6**	**9**	**77**	**0**	**1**	**0**	**72**	**4.2**	**-24**	....	....	....	....	....	....	....	....	....	....	....	....	....
1998-99	**Tampa Bay**	**NHL**	**67**	**2**	**16**	**18**	**92**	**0**	**0**	**0**	**96**	**2.1**	**-25**	**0**	**0.0**	**127**	**82**	**22:38**	....	....	....	....	....	....	....	....
99-2000	**Toronto**	**NHL**	**71**	**4**	**11**	**15**	**64**	**0**	**0**	**1**	**60**	**6.7**	**13**	**0**	**0.0**	**154**	**53**	**15:59**	**12**	**0**	**2**	**2**	**2**	**0**	**0**	**0**
2000-01	**Toronto**	**NHL**	**41**	**3**	**5**	**8**	**50**	**1**	**0**	**1**	**34**	**8.8**	**7**	**0**	**0.0**	**109**	**55**	**18:00**	**11**	**2**	**1**	**3**	**10**	**0**	**0**	**1**
	NHL Totals		**448**	**19**	**62**	**81**	**491**	**1**	**1**	**5**	**434**	**4.4**		**0**	**0.0**	**390**	**190**	**18:56**	**29**	**2**	**3**	**5**	**34**	**0**	**0**	**1**

Traded to **Toronto** by **Tampa Bay** with Tampa Bay's 7th round choice (Ivan Kolozvary) in 2001 Entry Draft for Fredrik Modin, October 1, 1999.

CROWE, Phil

(KROH, FIHL)

Left wing. Shoots right. 6'2", 230 lbs. Born, Nanton, Alta., April 4, 1970.

Season	Club	League	GP	G	A	Pts	PIM	PP	SH	GW	S	%	+/-	TF	F%	H	SB	Min	GP	G	A	Pts	PIM	PP	SH	GW
1988-89	Red Deer Rebels	AJHL	41	6	4	10	142	....	....	....	....	....	....	....	....	....	....	....	....	....	....	....	....	....	....	....
1989-90	Olds Grizzlys	AJHL	47	8	21	29	248	....	....	....	....	....	....	....	....	....	....	....	....	....	....	....	....	....	....	....
1990-91	Olds Grizzlys	AJHL	50	16	24	40	290	....	....	....	....	....	....	....	....	....	....	....	....	....	....	....	....	....	....	....
1991-92	Adirondack	AHL	6	1	0	1	29	....	....	....	....	....	....	....	....	....	....	....	....	....	....	....	....	....	....	....
	Columbus Chill	ECHL	32	4	7	11	145	....	....	....	....	....	....	....	....	....	....	....	....	....	....	....	....	....	....	....
	Toledo Storm	ECHL	2	0	0	0	0	....	....	....	....	....	....	....	....	....	....	....	5	0	0	0	58	....	....	....
1992-93	Phoenix	IHL	53	3	3	6	190	....	....	....	....	....	....	....	....	....	....	....	....	....	....	....	....	....	....	....
1993-94	Fort Wayne	IHL	5	0	1	1	26	....	....	....	....	....	....	....	....	....	....	....	....	....	....	....	....	....	....	....
	Los Angeles	**NHL**	**31**	**0**	**2**	**2**	**77**	**0**	**0**	**0**	**5**	**0.0**	**4**	....	....	....	....	....	....	....	....	....	....	....	....	....
	Phoenix	IHL	2	0	0	0	0	....	....	....	....	....	....	....	....	....	....	....	....	....	....	....	....	....	....	....
1994-95	Hershey Bears	AHL	46	11	6	17	132	....	....	....	....	....	....	....	....	....	....	....	6	0	1	1	19	....	....	....
1995-96	**Philadelphia**	**NHL**	**16**	**1**	**1**	**2**	**28**	**0**	**0**	**0**	**6**	**16.7**	**0**	....	....	....	....	....	....	....	....	....	....	....	....	....
	Hershey Bears	AHL	39	6	8	14	105	....	....	....	....	....	....	....	....	....	....	....	5	1	2	3	19	....	....	....
1996-97	**Ottawa**	**NHL**	**26**	**0**	**1**	**1**	**30**	**0**	**0**	**0**	**8**	**0.0**	**0**	....	....	....	....	....	**3**	**0**	**0**	**0**	**16**	**0**	**0**	**0**
	Detroit Vipers	IHL	41	7	7	14	83	....	....	....	....	....	....	....	....	....	....	....	....	....	....	....	....	....	....	....
1997-98	**Ottawa**	**NHL**	**9**	**3**	**0**	**3**	**24**	**0**	**0**	**1**	**6**	**50.0**	**3**	....	....	....	....	....	....	....	....	....	....	....	....	....
	Detroit Vipers	IHL	55	6	13	19	160	....	....	....	....	....	....	....	....	....	....	....	20	5	2	7	48	....	....	....
1998-99	**Ottawa**	**NHL**	**8**	**0**	**1**	**1**	**4**	**0**	**0**	**0**	**2**	**0.0**	**1**	**0**	**0.0**	**5**	**1**	**4:10**	....	....	....	....	....	....	....	....
	Cincinnati	IHL	39	2	6	8	62	....	....	....	....	....	....	....	....	....	....	....	....	....	....	....	....	....	....	....
	Detroit Vipers	IHL	2	0	0	0	9	....	....	....	....	....	....	....	....	....	....	....	....	....	....	....	....	....	....	....
	Las Vegas	IHL	14	1	3	4	18	....	....	....	....	....	....	....	....	....	....	....	....	....	....	....	....	....	....	....
99-2000	**Nashville**	**NHL**	**4**	**0**	**0**	**0**	**10**	**0**	**0**	**0**	**1**	**0.0**	**0**	**0**	**0.0**	**5**	**0**	**4:06**	....	....	....	....	....	....	....	....
	Milwaukee	IHL	20	3	1	4	31	....	....	....	....	....	....	....	....	....	....	....	....	....	....	....	....	....	....	....
2000-01	Detroit Vipers	IHL	4	0	1	1	0	....	....	....	....	....	....	....	....	....	....	....	....	....	....	....	....	....	....	....
	NHL Totals		**94**	**4**	**5**	**9**	**173**	**0**	**0**	**1**	**28**	**14.3**		**0**	**0.0**	**10**	**1**	**4:09**	**3**	**0**	**0**	**0**	**16**	**0**	**0**	**0**

Signed as a free agent by **LA Kings**, November 8, 1993. Signed as a free agent by **Philadelphia**, July 19, 1994. Signed as a free agent by **Ottawa**, July 29, 1996. Claimed by **Atlanta** from **Ottawa** in Expansion Draft, June 25, 1999. Traded to **Nashville** by **Atlanta** for future considerations, June 26, 1999. • Missed majority of 1999-2000 season recovering from knee injury suffered in game vs. Milwaukee (IHL), January 2, 2000. Signed as a free agent by **Detroit Vipers** (IHL), October 25, 2000. Released by **Detroit Vipers** (IHL), November 7, 2000.

CROWLEY, Mike

(KROH-lee, MIGHK) **MIN.**

Defense. Shoots left. 5'11", 190 lbs. Born, Bloomington, MN, July 4, 1975. Philadelphia's 5th choice, 140th overall, in 1993 Entry Draft.

Season	Club	League	GP	G	A	Pts	PIM	PP	SH	GW	S	%	+/-	TF	F%	H	SB	Min	GP	G	A	Pts	PIM	PP	SH	GW
1990-91	Jefferson High	Hi-School	20	3	9	12	2	....	....	....	....	....	....	....	....	....	....	....	....	....	....	....	....	....	....	....
1991-92	Jefferson High	Hi-School	28	5	18	23	8	....	....	....	....	....	....	....	....	....	....	....	....	....	....	....	....	....	....	....
1992-93	Jefferson High	Hi-School	22	10	32	42	18	....	....	....	....	....	....	....	....	....	....	....	....	....	....	....	....	....	....	....
1993-94	Jefferson High	Hi-School	28	23	54	77	26	....	....	....	....	....	....	....	....	....	....	....	....	....	....	....	....	....	....	....
1994-95	U. of Minnesota	WCHA	41	11	27	38	60	....	....	....	....	....	....	....	....	....	....	....	....	....	....	....	....	....	....	....
1995-96	U. of Minnesota	WCHA	42	17	46	63	28	....	....	....	....	....	....	....	....	....	....	....	....	....	....	....	....	....	....	....
1996-97	U. of Minnesota	WCHA	42	9	*47	*56	24	....	....	....	....	....	....	....	....	....	....	....	....	....	....	....	....	....	....	....
1997-98	**Anaheim**	**NHL**	**8**	**2**	**2**	**4**	**8**	**0**	**0**	**1**	**17**	**11.8**	**0**	....	....	....	....	....	....	....	....	....	....	....	....	....
	Cincinnati Ducks	AHL	76	12	26	38	91	....	....	....	....	....	....	....	....	....	....	....	....	....	....	....	....	....	....	....
1998-99	**Anaheim**	**NHL**	**20**	**2**	**3**	**5**	**16**	**1**	**0**	**1**	**41**	**4.9**	**-10**	**0**	**0.0**	**8**	**20**	**16:36**	....	....	....	....	....	....	....	....
	Cincinnati Ducks	AHL	44	5	23	28	42	....	....	....	....	....	....	....	....	....	....	....	3	0	3	3	2	....	....	....
99-2000	Long Beach	IHL	67	9	39	48	35	....	....	....	....	....	....	....	....	....	....	....	4	2	1	3	6	....	....	....
2000-01	**Anaheim**	**NHL**	**39**	**1**	**10**	**11**	**20**	**0**	**0**	**1**	**45**	**2.2**	**-16**	**1**	**0.0**	**30**	**34**	**17:21**	....	....	....	....	....	....	....	....
	Grand Rapids	IHL	22	4	12	16	10	....	....	....	....	....	....	....	....	....	....	....	....	....	....	....	....	....	....	....
	NHL Totals		**67**	**5**	**15**	**20**	**44**	**1**	**0**	**3**	**103**	**4.9**		**1**	**0.0**	**38**	**54**	**17:06**	....	....	....	....	....	....	....	....

Minnesota High School Player of the Year (1994) • WCHA First All-Star Team (1996, 1997) • NCAA West First All-American Team (1996, 1997) • IHL First All-Star Team (2000)

Traded to **Anaheim** by **Philadelphia** with Anatoli Semenov for Brian Wesenberg, March 19, 1996. Signed as a free agent by **Long Beach** (IHL), August 24, 1999. Signed as a free agent by **Anaheim**, December 8, 2000. Signed as a free agent by **Minnesota**, July 25, 2001.

CROZIER, Greg

(KROH-zhuhr, GREHG) **BOS.**

Left wing. Shoots left. 6'3", 200 lbs. Born, Calgary, Alta., July 6, 1976. Pittsburgh's 4th choice, 73rd overall, in 1994 Entry Draft.

Season	Club	League	GP	G	A	Pts	PIM	PP	SH	GW	S	%	+/-	TF	F%	H	SB	Min	GP	G	A	Pts	PIM	PP	SH	GW
1991-92	Amherst	Hi-School	46	61	47	108	47	....	....	....	....	....	....	....	....	....	....	....	....	....	....	....	....	....	....	....
1992-93	Lawrence Prep	Hi-School	22	22	14	36	....	....	....	....	....	....	....	....	....	....	....	....	....	....	....	....	....	....	....	....
1993-94	Lawrence Prep	Hi-School	18	22	26	48	12	....	....	....	....	....	....	....	....	....	....	....	....	....	....	....	....	....	....	....
1994-95	Lawrence Prep	Hi-School	31	45	32	77	22	....	....	....	....	....	....	....	....	....	....	....	....	....	....	....	....	....	....	....
1995-96	U. of Michigan	CCHA	42	14	10	24	46	....	....	....	....	....	....	....	....	....	....	....	....	....	....	....	....	....	....	....
1996-97	U. of Michigan	CCHA	31	5	15	20	45	....	....	....	....	....	....	....	....	....	....	....	....	....	....	....	....	....	....	....
1997-98	U. of Michigan	CCHA	45	12	10	22	26	....	....	....	....	....	....	....	....	....	....	....	....	....	....	....	....	....	....	....
1998-99	U. of Michigan	CCHA	39	7	6	13	63	....	....	....	....	....	....	....	....	....	....	....	....	....	....	....	....	....	....	....
99-2000	Wilkes-Barre	AHL	71	22	22	44	33	....	....	....	....	....	....	....	....	....	....	....	....	....	....	....	....	....	....	....
2000-01	**Pittsburgh**	**NHL**	**1**	**0**	**0**	**0**	**0**	**0**	**0**	**0**	**0**	**0.0**	**0**	**0**	**0.0**	**0**	**0**	**4:10**	....	....	....	....	....	....	....	....
	Wilkes-Barre	AHL	77	24	36	60	81	....	....	....	....	....	....	....	....	....	....	....	21	6	5	11	16	....	....	....
	NHL Totals		**1**	**0**	**0**	**0**	**0**	**0**	**0**	**0**	**0**	**0.0**		**0**	**0.0**	**0**	**0**	**4:10**	....	....	....	....	....	....	....	....

Signed as a free agent by **Boston**, August 8, 2001.

CULLEN, David
(KUH-lehn, DAY-vihd) **PHX.**

Defense. Shoots right. 6'2", 209 lbs. Born, St. Catharines, Ont., December 30, 1976.

Season	Club	League	GP	G	A	Pts	PIM	PP	SH	GW	S	%	+/-	TF	F%	H	SB	Min	Playoffs GP	G	A	Pts	PIM	PP	SH	GW
1992-93	Thorold Hawks	OJHL-B	34	4	6	10	28																			
1993-94	Thorold Hawks	OJHL-B	40	10	35	45	26																			
1994-95	Thorold Hawks	OJHL-B	36	16	30	46	12																			
1995-96	U. of Maine	H-East	34	2	4	6	22																			
1996-97	U. of Maine	H-East	35	5	25	30	8																			
1997-98	U. of Maine	H-East	36	10	27	37	24																			
1998-99	U. of Maine	H-East	41	11	33	44	24																			
99-2000	Springfield	AHL	78	10	21	31	57												2	0	0	0	2			
2000-01	**Phoenix**	**NHL**	**2**	**0**	**0**	**0**	**0**	0	0	0	0	0.0	1	0	0.0	1	0	12:25								
	Springfield	AHL	69	13	29	42	40																			
	NHL Totals		**2**	**0**	**0**	**0**	**0**	**0**	**0**	**0**	**0**	**0.0**		**0**	**0.0**	**1**	**0**	**12:25**								

Hockey East First All-Star Team (1999) • NCAA East First All-American Team (1999) • NCAA Championship All-Tournament Team (1999)

Signed as a free agent by **Phoenix**, April 16, 1999.

CULLEN, Matt
(KUH-lehn, MAT) **ANA.**

Center. Shoots left. 6'1", 204 lbs. Born, Virginia, MN, November 2, 1976. Anaheim's 2nd choice, 35th overall, in 1996 Entry Draft.

Season	Club	League	GP	G	A	Pts	PIM	PP	SH	GW	S	%	+/-	TF	F%	H	SB	Min	Playoffs GP	G	A	Pts	PIM	PP	SH	GW
1994-95	Moorehead High	Hi-School	28	47	42	89	78																			
1995-96	St. Cloud State	WCHA	39	12	29	41	28																			
1996-97	St. Cloud State	WCHA	36	15	30	45	70																			
	Baltimore Bandits	AHL	6	3	3	6	7												3	0	2	2	0			
1997-98	**Anaheim**	**NHL**	**61**	**6**	**21**	**27**	**23**	2	0	0	75	8.0	–4													
	Cincinnati Ducks	AHL	18	15	12	27	2																			
1998-99	**Anaheim**	**NHL**	**75**	**11**	**14**	**25**	**47**	5	1	1	112	9.8	–12	1047	47.7	41	22	15:31	4	0	0	0	0	0	0	0
	Cincinnati Ducks	AHL	3	1	2	3	8																			
99-2000	**Anaheim**	**NHL**	**80**	**13**	**26**	**39**	**24**	1	0	1	137	9.5	5	1247	44.6	74	39	16:54								
2000-01	**Anaheim**	**NHL**	**82**	**10**	**30**	**40**	**38**	4	0	1	159	6.3	–23	1478	48.0	49	37	18:15								
	NHL Totals		**298**	**40**	**91**	**131**	**132**	**12**	**1**	**3**	**483**	**8.3**		**3772**	**46.8**	**164**	**98**	**16:56**	**4**	**0**	**0**	**0**	**0**	**0**	**0**	**0**

WCHA Second All-Star Team (1997)

CULLIMORE, Jassen
(KUHL-ih-mohr, JAY-sehn) **T.B.**

Defense. Shoots left. 6'5", 235 lbs. Born, Simcoe, Ont., December 4, 1972. Vancouver's 2nd choice, 29th overall, in 1991 Entry Draft.

Season	Club	League	GP	G	A	Pts	PIM	PP	SH	GW	S	%	+/-	TF	F%	H	SB	Min	Playoffs GP	G	A	Pts	PIM	PP	SH	GW
1986-87	Caledonia	OJHL-C	18	2	0	2	9																			
1987-88	Simcoe Rams	OJHL-C	35	11	14	25	92																			
1988-89	Peterborough	OJHL-B	29	11	17	28	88																			
	Peterborough	OHL	20	2	1	3	6																			
1989-90	Peterborough	OHL	59	2	6	8	61												11	0	2	2	8			
1990-91	Peterborough	OHL	62	8	16	24	74												4	1	0	1	7			
1991-92	Peterborough	OHL	54	9	37	46	65												10	3	6	9	8			
1992-93	Hamilton Canucks	AHL	56	5	7	12	60																			
1993-94	Hamilton Canucks	AHL	71	8	20	28	86												3	0	1	1	2			
1994-95	Syracuse Crunch	AHL	33	2	7	9	66																			
	Vancouver	**NHL**	**34**	**1**	**2**	**3**	**39**	0	0	0	30	3.3	–2						**11**	**0**	**0**	**0**	**12**	**0**	**0**	**0**
1995-96	**Vancouver**	**NHL**	**27**	**1**	**1**	**2**	**21**	0	0	1	12	8.3	4													
1996-97	**Vancouver**	**NHL**	**3**	**0**	**0**	**0**	**2**	0	0	0	2	0.0	–2													
	Montreal	**NHL**	**49**	**2**	**6**	**8**	**42**	0	1	1	52	3.8	4						**2**	**0**	**0**	**0**	**2**	**0**	**0**	**0**
1997-98	**Montreal**	**NHL**	**3**	**0**	**0**	**0**	**4**	0	0	0	1	0.0	0													
	Fredericton	AHL	5	1	0	1	8																			
	Tampa Bay	**NHL**	**25**	**1**	**2**	**3**	**22**	1	0	0	17	5.9	–4													
1998-99	**Tampa Bay**	**NHL**	**78**	**5**	**12**	**17**	**81**	1	1	1	73	6.8	–22	0	0.0	161	67	20:14								
99-2000	**Tampa Bay**	**NHL**	**46**	**1**	**1**	**2**	**66**	0	0	0	23	4.3	–12	2	0.0	92	45	15:38								
	Providence Bruins	AHL	16	5	10	15	31																			
2000-01	**Tampa Bay**	**NHL**	**74**	**1**	**6**	**7**	**80**	0	0	0	56	1.8	–6	0	0.0	186	114	19:43								
	NHL Totals		**339**	**12**	**30**	**42**	**357**	**2**	**2**	**3**	**266**	**4.5**		**2**	**0.0**	**439**	**226**	**18:58**	**13**	**0**	**0**	**0**	**14**	**0**	**0**	**0**

OHL Second All-Star Team (1992)

Traded to **Montreal** by **Vancouver** for Donald Brashear, November 13, 1996. Claimed on waivers by **Tampa Bay** from **Montreal**, January 22, 1998. Loaned to **Providence** (AHL) by **Tampa Bay**, October 1, 1999.

CUMMINS, Jim
(KUH-mihns, JIHM) **ANA.**

Right wing. Shoots right. 6'2", 212 lbs. Born, Dearborn, MI, May 17, 1970. NY Rangers' 5th choice, 67th overall, in 1989 Entry Draft.

Season	Club	League	GP	G	A	Pts	PIM	PP	SH	GW	S	%	+/-	TF	F%	H	SB	Min	Playoffs GP	G	A	Pts	PIM	PP	SH	GW
1987-88	Det-Compuware	NAJHL	31	11	15	26	146																			
1988-89	Michigan State	CCHA	30	3	8	11	98																			
1989-90	Michigan State	CCHA	41	8	7	15	94																			
1990-91	Michigan State	CCHA	34	9	6	15	110																			
1991-92	**Detroit**	**NHL**	**1**	**0**	**0**	**0**	**7**	0	0	0	0	0.0	0													
	Adirondack	AHL	65	7	13	20	338												5	0	0	0	19			
1992-93	**Detroit**	**NHL**	**7**	**1**	**1**	**2**	**58**	0	0	0	5	20.0	0													
	Adirondack	AHL	43	16	4	20	179												9	3	1	4	4			
1993-94	**Philadelphia**	**NHL**	**22**	**1**	**2**	**3**	**71**	0	0	0	17	5.9	0													
	Hershey Bears	AHL	17	6	6	12	70																			
	Tampa Bay	**NHL**	**4**	**0**	**0**	**0**	**13**	0	0	0	3	0.0	–1													
	Atlanta Knights	IHL	7	4	5	9	14												13	1	2	3	90			
1994-95	**Tampa Bay**	**NHL**	**10**	**1**	**0**	**1**	**41**	0	0	1	3	33.3	–3													
	Chicago	**NHL**	**27**	**3**	**1**	**4**	**117**	0	0	0	20	15.0	–3						**14**	**1**	**1**	**2**	**4**	**0**	**0**	**1**
1995-96	**Chicago**	**NHL**	**52**	**2**	**4**	**6**	**180**	0	0	2	34	5.9	–1						**10**	**0**	**0**	**0**	**2**	**0**	**0**	**0**
1996-97	**Chicago**	**NHL**	**65**	**6**	**6**	**12**	**199**	0	0	0	61	9.8	4						**6**	**0**	**0**	**0**	**24**	**0**	**0**	**0**
1997-98	**Chicago**	**NHL**	**55**	**0**	**2**	**2**	**178**	0	0	0	33	0.0	–9													
	Phoenix	**NHL**	**20**	**0**	**0**	**0**	**47**	0	0	0	10	0.0	–7						**3**	**0**	**0**	**0**	**4**	**0**	**0**	**0**
1998-99	**Phoenix**	**NHL**	**55**	**1**	**7**	**8**	**190**	0	0	0	26	3.8	3	0	0.0	74	7	7:07	**3**	**0**	**1**	**1**	**0**	**0**	**0**	**0**
99-2000	**Montreal**	**NHL**	**47**	**3**	**5**	**8**	**92**	0	0	0	33	9.1	–5	4	25.0	59	12	8:58								
2000-01	**Anaheim**	**NHL**	**79**	**5**	**6**	**11**	**167**	0	0	1	45	11.1	–11	7	28.6	70	12	7:14								
	NHL Totals		**444**	**23**	**34**	**57**	**1360**	**0**	**0**	**4**	**290**	**7.9**		**11**	**27.3**	**203**	**31**	**7:39**	**36**	**1**	**2**	**3**	**34**	**0**	**0**	**1**

Traded to **Detroit** by **NY Rangers** with Kevin Miller and Dennis Vial for Joe Kocur and Per Djoos, March 5, 1991. Traded to **Philadelphia** by **Detroit** with Philadelphia's 4th round choice (previously acquired by Detroit - later traded to Boston - Boston selected Charles Paquette) in 1993 Entry Draft for Greg Johnson and Philadelphia's 5th round choice (Frederic Deschenes) in 1994 Entry Draft, June 20, 1993. Traded to **Tampa Bay** by **Philadelphia** with Philadelphia's 4th round choice (later traded back to Philadelphia - Philadelphia selected Radovan Somik) in 1995 Entry Draft for Rob DiMaio, March 18, 1994. Traded to **Chicago** by **Tampa Bay** with Tom Tilley and Jeff Buchanan for Paul Ysebaert and Rich Sutter, February 22, 1995. Traded to **Phoenix** by **Chicago** with Keith Carney for Chad Kilger and Jayson More, March 4, 1998. Traded to **Montreal** by **Phoenix** for NY Rangers' 6th round choice (previously acquired, Phoenix selected Erik Lewerstrom) in 1999 Entry Draft, June 26, 1999. Signed as a free agent by **Anaheim**, July 5, 2000.

CUTTA, Jakub
(KOO-tuh, YA-kuhb) **WSH.**

Defense. Shoots left. 6'3", 207 lbs. Born, Jablonec nad Nisou, Czech., December 29, 1981. Washington's 3rd choice, 61st overall, in 2000 Entry Draft.

Season	Club	League	GP	G	A	Pts	PIM	PP	SH	GW	S	%	+/-	TF	F%	H	SB	Min	Playoffs GP	G	A	Pts	PIM	PP	SH	GW
1997-98	Stadion Liberec-Jr.	Cze-Rep	29	3	13	16	70																			
1998-99	Swift Current	WHL	59	3	3	6	63																			
99-2000	Swift Current	WHL	71	2	12	14	114												12	0	2	2	24			
2000-01	**Washington**	**NHL**	**3**	**0**	**0**	**0**	**0**	0	0	0	1	0.0	–1	0	0.0	2	0	11:33								
	Swift Current	WHL	47	5	8	13	102												16	1	3	4	32			
	NHL Totals		**3**	**0**	**0**	**0**	**0**	**0**	**0**	**0**	**1**	**0.0**		**0**	**0.0**	**2**	**0**	**11:33**								

Returned to **Swift Current** (WHL) by **Washington**, October 16, 2000.

CZERKAWSKI, Mariusz (chehr-KAWV-skee, MAIR-ee-UHZ) NYI

Right wing. Shoots left. 6', 195 lbs. Born, Radomsko, Poland, April 13, 1972. Boston's 5th choice, 106th overall, in 1991 Entry Draft.

			Regular Season																Playoffs							
Season	Club	League	GP	G	A	Pts	PIM	PP	SH	GW	S	%	+/-	TF	F%	H	SB	Min	GP	G	A	Pts	PIM	PP	SH	GW
1990-91	GKS Tychy	Poland	24	25	15	40																				
1991-92	Djurgardens IF	Sweden	39	8	5	13	4												3	0	0	0	2			
	Poland	Olympics	5	0	1	1	4																			
1992-93	SC Hammarby	Sweden-2	32	*39	30	*69	74												13	*16	7	*23	34			
1993-94	Djurgardens IF	Sweden	39	13	21	34	20												6	3	1	4	2			
	Boston	**NHL**	**4**	**2**	**1**	**3**	**0**	**1**	**0**	**0**	**11**	**18.2**	**-2**						**13**	**3**	**3**	**6**	**4**	**1**	**0**	**0**
1994-95	Kiekko-Espoo	Finland	7	9	3	12	10																			
	Boston	**NHL**	**47**	**12**	**14**	**26**	**31**	**1**	**0**	**2**	**126**	**9.5**	**4**						**5**	**1**	**0**	**1**	**0**	**0**	**0**	**0**
1995-96	**Boston**	**NHL**	**33**	**5**	**6**	**11**	**10**	**1**	**0**	**0**	**63**	**7.9**	**-11**													
	Edmonton	**NHL**	**37**	**12**	**17**	**29**	**8**	**2**	**0**	**1**	**79**	**15.2**	**7**													
1996-97	**Edmonton**	**NHL**	**76**	**26**	**21**	**47**	**16**	**4**	**0**	**3**	**182**	**14.3**	**0**						**12**	**2**	**1**	**3**	**10**	**0**	**0**	**0**
1997-98	**NY Islanders**	**NHL**	**68**	**12**	**13**	**25**	**23**	**2**	**0**	**1**	**136**	**8.8**	**11**													
1998-99	**NY Islanders**	**NHL**	**78**	**21**	**17**	**38**	**14**	**4**	**0**	**1**	**205**	**10.2**	**-10**	**2**	**0.0**	**47**	**14**	**14:18**								
99-2000	**NY Islanders**	**NHL**	**79**	**35**	**35**	**70**	**34**	**16**	**0**	**4**	**276**	**12.7**	**-16**	**4**	**25.0**	**77**	**25**	**17:45**								
2000-01	**NY Islanders**	**NHL**	**82**	**30**	**32**	**62**	**48**	**10**	**1**	**0**	**287**	**10.5**	**-24**	**8**	**50.0**	**86**	**31**	**18:44**								
	NHL Totals		**504**	**155**	**156**	**311**	**184**	**41**	**1**	**12**	**1365**	**11.4**		**14**	**35.7**	**210**	**70**	**16:58**	**30**	**6**	**4**	**10**	**14**	**1**	**0**	**0**

Played in NHL All-Star Game (2000)

Traded to **Edmonton** by **Boston** with Sean Brown and Boston's 1st round choice (Matthieu Descoteaux) in 1996 Entry Draft for Bill Ranford, January 11, 1996. Traded to **NY Islanders** by **Edmonton** for Dan Lacouture, August 25, 1997.

DACKELL, Andreas (DA-kuhl, an-DRAY-uhs) MTL.

Right wing. Shoots right. 5'11", 195 lbs. Born, Gavle, Sweden, December 29, 1972. Ottawa's 3rd choice, 136th overall, in 1996 Entry Draft.

Season	Club	League	GP	G	A	Pts	PIM	PP	SH	GW	S	%	+/-	TF	F%	H	SB	Min	GP	G	A	Pts	PIM	PP	SH	GW
1990-91	Stromsbro HC	Sweden-2	29	21	9	30	12																			
	Brynas IF	Sweden	3	0	1	1	2																			
1991-92	Brynas IF	Sweden-2	26	17	24	41	42												2	3	1	4	2			
	Brynas IF	Sweden	4	0	0	0	2												2	0	1	1	4			
1992-93	Brynas IF	Sweden	40	12	15	27	12												10	4	5	9	2			
1993-94	Brynas IF	Sweden	38	12	17	29	47												7	2	2	4	8			
	Sweden	Olympics	4	0	0	0	0																			
1994-95	Brynas IF	Sweden	39	17	16	33	34												14	3	3	6	14			
1995-96	Brynas IF	Sweden	40	25	22	47	79												10	9	6	15	12			
1996-97	**Ottawa**	**NHL**	**79**	**12**	**19**	**31**	**8**	**2**	**0**	**3**	**79**	**15.2**	**-6**						**7**	**1**	**0**	**1**	**0**	**0**	**0**	**0**
1997-98	**Ottawa**	**NHL**	**82**	**15**	**18**	**33**	**24**	**3**	**2**	**2**	**130**	**11.5**	**-11**						**11**	**1**	**1**	**2**	**2**	**1**	**0**	**0**
1998-99	**Ottawa**	**NHL**	**77**	**15**	**35**	**50**	**30**	**6**	**0**	**3**	**107**	**14.0**	**9**	**5**	**40.0**	**34**	**29**	**17:18**	**4**	**0**	**1**	**1**	**0**	**0**	**0**	**0**
99-2000	**Ottawa**	**NHL**	**82**	**10**	**25**	**35**	**18**	**0**	**0**	**1**	**99**	**10.1**	**5**	**11**	**100.0**	**34**	**35**	**16:17**	**6**	**2**	**1**	**3**	**2**	**0**	**0**	**1**
2000-01	**Ottawa**	**NHL**	**81**	**13**	**18**	**31**	**24**	**1**	**0**	**3**	**72**	**18.1**	**7**	**13**	**15.4**	**29**	**39**	**14:02**	**4**	**0**	**0**	**0**	**0**	**0**	**0**	**0**
	NHL Totals		**401**	**65**	**115**	**180**	**104**	**12**	**2**	**12**	**487**	**13.3**		**19**	**26.3**	**97**	**103**	**15:51**	**32**	**4**	**3**	**7**	**4**	**1**	**0**	**1**

Traded to **Montreal** by **Ottawa** for Montreal's 8th round choice (Neil Petruic) in 2001 Entry Draft, June 24, 2001.

DAGENAIS, Pierre (da-ZHUH-nay, PEE-air) N.J.

Right wing. Shoots left. 6'5", 215 lbs. Born, Blainville, Que., March 4, 1978. New Jersey's 6th choice, 105th overall, in 1998 Entry Draft.

Season	Club	League	GP	G	A	Pts	PIM	PP	SH	GW	S	%	+/-	TF	F%	H	SB	Min	GP	G	A	Pts	PIM	PP	SH	GW
1994-95	Laval Regents	QAAA	34	28	14	42	68												13	10	9	19	32			
1995-96	Moncton Alpines	QMJHL	67	43	25	68	59																			
1996-97	Moncton Wildcats	QMJHL	6	4	2	6	0																			
	Laval Titan	QMJHL	37	16	14	30	40																			
	Rouyn-Noranda	QMJHL	27	21	8	29	22																			
1997-98	Rouyn-Noranda	QMJHL	60	*66	67	133	50												6	6	2	8	2			
1998-99	Albany River Rats	AHL	69	17	13	30	37												4	0	0	0	0			
99-2000	Albany River Rats	AHL	80	35	30	65	47												5	1	0	1	14			
2000-01	**New Jersey**	**NHL**	**9**	**3**	**2**	**5**	**6**	**1**	**0**	**1**	**20**	**15.0**	**1**	**8**	**37.5**	**6**	**2**	**12:22**								
	Albany River Rats	AHL	69	34	28	62	52																			
	NHL Totals		**9**	**3**	**2**	**5**	**6**	**1**	**0**	**1**	**20**	**15.0**		**8**	**37.5**	**6**	**2**	**12:22**								

• Re-entered NHL Entry Draft. Originally New Jersey's 4th choice, 47th overall, in 1996 Entry Draft.

QMJHL Second All-Star Team (1998) • AHL Second All-Star Team (2001)

DAHL, Kevin (DAHL, KEH-vihn)

Defense. Shoots right. 5'11", 190 lbs. Born, Regina, Sask., December 30, 1968. Montreal's 12th choice, 230th overall, in 1988 Entry Draft.

Season	Club	League	GP	G	A	Pts	PIM	PP	SH	GW	S	%	+/-	TF	F%	H	SB	Min	GP	G	A	Pts	PIM	PP	SH	GW
1985-86	Stratford Cullitons	OJHL-B	29	8	15	23	99																			
1986-87	Bowling Green	CCHA	32	2	6	8	54																			
1987-88	Bowling Green	CCHA	44	2	23	25	78																			
1988-89	Bowling Green	CCHA	46	9	26	35	51																			
1989-90	Bowling Green	CCHA	43	8	22	30	74																			
1990-91	Fredericton	AHL	32	1	15	16	45												9	0	1	1	11			
	Winston-Salem	ECHL	36	7	17	24	58																			
1991-92	Canada	Nat-Team	45	2	15	17	44																			
	Canada	Olympics	8	2	0	2	6																			
	Salt Lake City	IHL	13	0	2	2	12												5	0	0	0	13			
1992-93	**Calgary**	**NHL**	**61**	**2**	**9**	**11**	**56**	**1**	**0**	**0**	**40**	**5.0**	**9**						**6**	**0**	**2**	**2**	**8**	**0**	**0**	**0**
1993-94	**Calgary**	**NHL**	**33**	**0**	**3**	**3**	**23**	**0**	**0**	**0**	**20**	**0.0**	**-2**						**6**	**0**	**0**	**0**	**4**	**0**	**0**	**0**
	Saint John Flames	AHL	2	0	0	0	0																			
1994-95	**Calgary**	**NHL**	**34**	**4**	**8**	**12**	**38**	**0**	**0**	**0**	**30**	**13.3**	**8**						**3**	**0**	**0**	**0**	**0**	**0**	**0**	**0**
1995-96	**Calgary**	**NHL**	**32**	**1**	**1**	**2**	**26**	**0**	**0**	**1**	**17**	**5.9**	**-2**						**1**	**0**	**0**	**0**	**0**	**0**	**0**	**0**
	Saint John Flames	AHL	23	4	11	15	37																			
1996-97	**Phoenix**	**NHL**	**2**	**0**	**0**	**0**	**0**	**0**	**0**	**0**	**2**	**0.0**	**0**													
	Las Vegas	IHL	73	10	21	31	101												3	0	0	0	2			
1997-98	**Calgary**	**NHL**	**19**	**0**	**1**	**1**	**6**	**0**	**0**	**0**	**17**	**0.0**	**-3**													
	Chicago Wolves	IHL	45	8	9	17	61												20	1	8	9	32			
1998-99	**Toronto**	**NHL**	**3**	**0**	**0**	**0**	**2**	**0**	**0**	**0**	**0**	**0.0**	**0**	**0**	**0.0**	**6**	**1**	**15:19**								
	Chicago Wolves	IHL	34	3	6	9	61												10	2	3	5	8			
99-2000	Chicago Wolves	IHL	27	1	2	3	44												3	0	1	1	2			
2000-01	**Columbus**	**NHL**	**4**	**0**	**0**	**0**	**2**	**0**	**0**	**0**	**3**	**0.0**	**1**	**0**	**0.0**	**3**	**3**	**10:34**								
	Chicago Wolves	IHL	72	2	6	8	63												16	2	2	4	16			
	NHL Totals		**188**	**7**	**22**	**29**	**153**	**1**	**0**	**1**	**129**	**5.4**		**0**	**0.0**	**9**	**4**	**12:36**	**16**	**0**	**2**	**2**	**12**	**0**	**0**	**0**

Signed as a free agent by **Calgary**, July 27, 1991. Signed as a free agent by **Phoenix**, September 4, 1996. Signed as a free agent by **Calgary**, September 8, 1997. Signed as a free agent by **St. Louis**, September 4, 1998. Claimed by **Toronto** from **St. Louis** in NHL Waiver Draft, October 5, 1998. Signed as a free agent by **NY Islanders**, August 12, 1999. Signed as a free agent by **Columbus**, August 24, 2000.

DAHLEN, Ulf (DAH-lehn, UHLF) WSH.

Right wing. Shoots left. 6'2", 199 lbs. Born, Ostersund, Sweden, January 12, 1967. NY Rangers' 1st choice, 7th overall, in 1985 Entry Draft.

Season	Club	League	GP	G	A	Pts	PIM	PP	SH	GW	S	%	+/-	TF	F%	H	SB	Min	GP	G	A	Pts	PIM	PP	SH	GW
1983-84	Ostersunds IK	Sweden-2	36	15	11	26	10																			
1984-85	Ostersunds IK	Sweden-2	31	27	*26	*53	20												5	6	0	6	4			
1985-86	IF Bjorkloven	Sweden	22	4	3	7	8																			
1986-87	IF Bjorkloven	Sweden	31	9	12	21	20												6	6	2	8	4			
1987-88	**NY Rangers**	**NHL**	**70**	**29**	**23**	**52**	**26**	**11**	**0**	**4**	**159**	**18.2**	**5**													
	Colorado Rangers	IHL	2	2	2	4	0																			
1988-89	**NY Rangers**	**NHL**	**56**	**24**	**19**	**43**	**50**	**8**	**0**	**1**	**147**	**16.3**	**-6**						**4**	**0**	**0**	**0**	**0**	**0**	**0**	**0**
1989-90	**NY Rangers**	**NHL**	**63**	**18**	**18**	**36**	**30**	**13**	**0**	**4**	**111**	**16.2**	**-4**													
	Minnesota	**NHL**	**13**	**2**	**4**	**6**	**0**	**0**	**0**	**0**	**24**	**8.3**	**1**						**7**	**1**	**4**	**5**	**2**	**0**	**0**	**0**
1990-91	**Minnesota**	**NHL**	**66**	**21**	**18**	**39**	**6**	**4**	**0**	**3**	**133**	**15.8**	**7**						**15**	**2**	**6**	**8**	**4**	**0**	**0**	**0**
1991-92	**Minnesota**	**NHL**	**79**	**36**	**30**	**66**	**10**	**16**	**1**	**5**	**216**	**16.7**	**-5**						**7**	**0**	**3**	**3**	**2**	**0**	**0**	**0**
1992-93	**Minnesota**	**NHL**	**83**	**35**	**39**	**74**	**6**	**13**	**0**	**6**	**223**	**15.7**	**-20**													
1993-94	**Dallas**	**NHL**	**65**	**19**	**38**	**57**	**10**	**12**	**0**	**3**	**147**	**12.9**	**-1**													
	San Jose	**NHL**	**13**	**6**	**6**	**12**	**0**	**3**	**0**	**2**	**43**	**14.0**	**0**						**14**	**6**	**2**	**8**	**0**	**3**	**0**	**1**

			Regular Season																Playoffs							
Season	Club	League	GP	G	A	Pts	PIM	PP	SH	GW	S	%	+/-	TF	F%	H	SB	Min	GP	G	A	Pts	PIM	PP	SH	GW
1994-95	**San Jose**	**NHL**	**46**	**11**	**23**	**34**	**11**	**4**	**1**	**4**	**85**	**12.9**	**-2**	....	....	....	....	....	**11**	**5**	**4**	**9**	**0**	**3**	**0**	**1**
1995-96	**San Jose**	**NHL**	**59**	**16**	**12**	**28**	**27**	**5**	**0**	**2**	**103**	**15.5**	**-21**	....	....	....	....	....	....	....	....	....	....	....	....	....
1996-97	**San Jose**	**NHL**	**43**	**8**	**11**	**19**	**8**	**3**	**0**	**1**	**78**	**10.3**	**-11**	....	....	....	....	....	....	....	....	....	....	....	....	....
	Chicago	**NHL**	**30**	**6**	**8**	**14**	**10**	**1**	**0**	**3**	**53**	**11.3**	**9**	....	....	....	....	....	**5**	**0**	**1**	**1**	**0**	**0**	**0**	**0**
1997-98	HV Jonkoping	Sweden	29	9	22	31	16	....	....	....	....	....	....	....	....	....	....	....	5	1	3	4	12	....	....	....
	Sweden	Olympics	4	1	0	1	2	....	....	....	....	....	....	....	....	....	....	....	....	....	....	....	....	....	....	....
1998-99	HV Jonkoping	Sweden	25	14	15	29	4	....	....	....	....	....	....	....	....	....	....	....	....	....	....	....	....	....	....	....
99-2000	**Washington**	**NHL**	**75**	**15**	**23**	**38**	**8**	**5**	**0**	**4**	**106**	**14.2**	**11**	**115**	**48.7**	**59**	**11**	**12:40**	**5**	**0**	**1**	**1**	**2**	**0**	**0**	**0**
2000-01	**Washington**	**NHL**	**73**	**15**	**33**	**48**	**6**	**6**	**0**	**2**	**145**	**10.3**	**11**	**6**	**66.7**	**35**	**13**	**14:48**	**6**	**0**	**1**	**1**	**2**	**0**	**0**	**0**
	NHL Totals		**834**	**261**	**305**	**566**	**208**	**104**	**2**	**44**	**1773**	**14.7**		**121**	**49.6**	**94**	**24**	**13:43**	**74**	**14**	**22**	**36**	**12**	**6**	**0**	**2**

Traded to **Minnesota** by **NY Rangers** with LA Kings' 4th round choice (previously acquired, Minnesota selected Cal McGowan) in 1990 Entry Draft and future considerations for Mike Gartner, March 6, 1990. Transferred to **Dallas** after **Minnesota** franchise relocated, June 9, 1993. Traded to **San Jose** by **Dallas** with Dallas' 7th round choice (Brad Mehalko) in 1995 Entry Draft for Doug Zmolek and Mike Lalor, March 19, 1994. Traded to **Chicago** by **San Jose** with Chris Terreri and Michal Sykora for Ed Belfour, January 25, 1997. Signed as a free agent by **Washington**, August 16, 1999.

DAIGNEAULT, J-J

(DAYN-yoh, JAY-JAY)

Defense. Shoots left. 5'10", 192 lbs. Born, Montreal, Que., October 12, 1965. Vancouver's 1st choice, 10th overall, in 1984 Entry Draft.

1980-81	Mtl-Concordia	QAAA	48	7	48	55	95	....	....	....	....	....	....	....	....	....	....	....	3	3	3	6	4	....	....	....
1981-82	Laval Voisins	QMJHL	64	4	25	29	41	....	....	....	....	....	....	....	....	....	....	....	18	1	3	4	2	....	....	....
1982-83	Longueuil	QMJHL	70	26	58	84	58	....	....	....	....	....	....	....	....	....	....	....	15	4	11	15	35	....	....	....
1983-84	Canada	Nat-Team	55	5	14	19	40	....	....	....	....	....	....	....	....	....	....	....	....	....	....	....	....	....	....	....
	Longueuil	QMJHL	10	2	11	13	6	....	....	....	....	....	....	....	....	....	....	....	14	3	13	16	30	....	....	....
	Canada	Olympics	7	1	1	2	0	....	....	....	....	....	....	....	....	....	....	....	....	....	....	....	....	....	....	....
1984-85	**Vancouver**	**NHL**	**67**	**4**	**23**	**27**	**69**	**2**	**0**	**0**	**93**	**4.3**	**-14**	....	....	....	....	....	....	....	....	....	....	....	....	....
1985-86	**Vancouver**	**NHL**	**64**	**5**	**23**	**28**	**45**	**4**	**0**	**0**	**114**	**4.4**	**-20**	....	....	....	....	....	**3**	**0**	**2**	**2**	**0**	**0**	**0**	**0**
1986-87	**Philadelphia**	**NHL**	**77**	**6**	**16**	**22**	**56**	**0**	**0**	**1**	**82**	**7.3**	**12**	....	....	....	....	....	**9**	**1**	**0**	**1**	**0**	**0**	**0**	**1**
1987-88	**Philadelphia**	**NHL**	**28**	**2**	**2**	**4**	**12**	**2**	**0**	**0**	**20**	**10.0**	**-8**	....	....	....	....	....	....	....	....	....	....	....	....	....
	Hershey Bears	AHL	10	1	5	6	8	....	....	....	....	....	....	....	....	....	....	....	....	....	....	....	....	....	....	....
1988-89	Hershey Bears	AHL	12	0	10	10	13	....	....	....	....	....	....	....	....	....	....	....	....	....	....	....	....	....	....	....
	Sherbrooke	AHL	63	10	33	43	48	....	....	....	....	....	....	....	....	....	....	....	6	1	3	4	2	....	....	....
1989-90	**Montreal**	**NHL**	**36**	**2**	**10**	**12**	**14**	**0**	**0**	**1**	**40**	**5.0**	**11**	....	....	....	....	....	**9**	**0**	**0**	**0**	**2**	**0**	**0**	**0**
	Sherbrooke	AHL	28	8	19	27	18	....	....	....	....	....	....	....	....	....	....	....	....	....	....	....	....	....	....	....
1990-91	**Montreal**	**NHL**	**51**	**3**	**16**	**19**	**31**	**2**	**0**	**0**	**68**	**4.4**	**-2**	....	....	....	....	....	**5**	**0**	**1**	**1**	**0**	**0**	**0**	**0**
1991-92	**Montreal**	**NHL**	**79**	**4**	**14**	**18**	**36**	**2**	**0**	**0**	**108**	**3.7**	**16**	....	....	....	....	....	**11**	**0**	**3**	**3**	**4**	**0**	**0**	**0**
1992-93♦	**Montreal**	**NHL**	**66**	**8**	**10**	**18**	**57**	**0**	**0**	**1**	**68**	**11.8**	**25**	....	....	....	....	....	**20**	**1**	**3**	**4**	**22**	**0**	**0**	**0**
1993-94	**Montreal**	**NHL**	**68**	**2**	**12**	**14**	**73**	**0**	**0**	**1**	**61**	**3.3**	**16**	....	....	....	....	....	**7**	**0**	**1**	**1**	**12**	**0**	**0**	**0**
1994-95	**Montreal**	**NHL**	**45**	**3**	**5**	**8**	**40**	**0**	**0**	**0**	**36**	**8.3**	**2**	....	....	....	....	....	....	....	....	....	....	....	....	....
1995-96	**Montreal**	**NHL**	**7**	**0**	**1**	**1**	**6**	**0**	**0**	**0**	**3**	**0.0**	**0**	....	....	....	....	....	....	....	....	....	....	....	....	....
	St. Louis	**NHL**	**37**	**1**	**3**	**4**	**24**	**0**	**0**	**0**	**45**	**2.2**	**-6**	....	....	....	....	....	....	....	....	....	....	....	....	....
	Worcester	AHL	9	1	10	11	10	....	....	....	....	....	....	....	....	....	....	....	....	....	....	....	....	....	....	....
	Pittsburgh	**NHL**	**13**	**3**	**3**	**6**	**23**	**2**	**0**	**0**	**13**	**23.1**	**0**	....	....	....	....	....	**17**	**1**	**9**	**10**	**36**	**1**	**0**	**1**
1996-97	**Pittsburgh**	**NHL**	**53**	**3**	**14**	**17**	**36**	**0**	**0**	**1**	**49**	**6.1**	**-5**	....	....	....	....	....	....	....	....	....	....	....	....	....
	Anaheim	**NHL**	**13**	**2**	**9**	**11**	**22**	**0**	**0**	**0**	**13**	**15.4**	**5**	....	....	....	....	....	**11**	**2**	**7**	**9**	**16**	**1**	**0**	**1**
1997-98	**Anaheim**	**NHL**	**53**	**2**	**15**	**17**	**28**	**1**	**0**	**1**	**74**	**2.7**	**-10**	....	....	....	....	....	....	....	....	....	....	....	....	....
	NY Islanders	**NHL**	**18**	**0**	**6**	**6**	**21**	**0**	**0**	**0**	**18**	**0.0**	**1**	....	....	....	....	....	....	....	....	....	....	....	....	....
1998-99	**Nashville**	**NHL**	**35**	**2**	**2**	**4**	**38**	**1**	**0**	**1**	**38**	**5.3**	**-4**	**1**	**100.0**	**46**	**29**	**20:47**	....	....	....	....	....	....	....	....
	Phoenix	**NHL**	**35**	**0**	**7**	**7**	**32**	**0**	**0**	**0**	**27**	**0.0**	**-8**	**0**	**0.0**	**58**	**34**	**18:00**	**6**	**0**	**0**	**0**	**8**	**0**	**0**	**0**
99-2000	**Phoenix**	**NHL**	**53**	**1**	**6**	**7**	**22**	**0**	**0**	**0**	**44**	**2.3**	**-16**	**1**	**100.0**	**65**	**65**	**14:12**	**1**	**0**	**0**	**0**	**0**	**0**	**0**	**0**
2000-01	**Minnesota**	**NHL**	**1**	**0**	**0**	**0**	**2**	**0**	**0**	**0**	**0**	**0.0**	**-1**	**0**	**0.0**	**2**	**0**	**11:38**	....	....	....	....	....	....	....	....
	Cleveland	IHL	44	8	9	17	18	....	....	....	....	....	....	....	....	....	....	....	....	....	....	....	....	....	....	....
	NHL Totals		**899**	**53**	**197**	**250**	**687**	**16**	**0**	**7**	**1014**	**5.2**		**2**	**100.0**	**171**	**128**	**16:46**	**99**	**5**	**26**	**31**	**100**	**2**	**0**	**3**

QMJHL First All-Star Team (1983)

Traded to **Philadelphia** by **Vancouver** with Vancouver's 2nd round choice (Kent Hawley) in 1986 Entry Draft and 5th round choice (later traded back to Vancouver - Vancouver selected Sean Fabian) in 1987 Entry Draft for Dave Richter, Rich Sutter and Vancouver's 3rd round choice (previously acquired, Vancouver selected Don Gibson) in 1986 Entry Draft, June 6, 1986. Traded to **Montreal** by **Philadelphia** for Scott Sandelin, November 7, 1988. Traded to **St. Louis** by **Montreal** for Pat Jablonski, November 7, 1995. Traded to **Pittsburgh** by **St. Louis** for Pittsburgh's 6th round choice (Stephen Wagner) in 1996 Entry Draft, March 20, 1996. Traded to **Anaheim** by **Pittsburgh** for Garry Valk, February 21, 1997. Traded to **NY Islanders** by **Anaheim** with Joe Sacco and Mark Janssens for Travis Green, Doug Houda and Tony Tuzzolino, February 6, 1998. Claimed by **Nashville** from **NY Islanders** in Expansion Draft, June 26, 1998. Traded to **Phoenix** by **Nashville** for future considerations, January 13, 1999. Signed as a free agent by **Minnesota**, July 24, 2000.

DAMPHOUSSE, Vincent

(DAHM-fooz, VIHN-seht) **S.J.**

Center. Shoots left. 6'1", 200 lbs. Born, Montreal, Que., December 17, 1967. Toronto's 1st choice, 6th overall, in 1986 Entry Draft.

1982-83	Mtl-Bourassa	QAAA	48	33	45	78	22	....	....	....	....	....	....	....	....	....	....	....	10	4	4	8	12	....	....	....
1983-84	Laval Voisins	QMJHL	66	29	36	65	25	....	....	....	....	....	....	....	....	....	....	....	....	....	....	....	....	....	....	....
1984-85	Laval Voisins	QMJHL	68	35	68	103	62	....	....	....	....	....	....	....	....	....	....	....	....	....	....	....	....	....	....	....
1985-86	Laval Voisins	QMJHL	69	45	110	155	70	....	....	....	....	....	....	....	....	....	....	....	14	9	27	36	12	....	....	....
1986-87	**Toronto**	**NHL**	**80**	**21**	**25**	**46**	**26**	**4**	**0**	**1**	**142**	**14.8**	**-6**	....	....	....	....	....	**12**	**1**	**5**	**6**	**8**	**1**	**0**	**0**
1987-88	**Toronto**	**NHL**	**75**	**12**	**36**	**48**	**40**	**1**	**0**	**2**	**111**	**10.8**	**2**	....	....	....	....	....	**6**	**0**	**1**	**1**	**10**	**0**	**0**	**0**
1988-89	**Toronto**	**NHL**	**80**	**26**	**42**	**68**	**75**	**6**	**0**	**4**	**190**	**13.7**	**-8**	....	....	....	....	....	....	....	....	....	....	....	....	....
1989-90	**Toronto**	**NHL**	**80**	**33**	**61**	**94**	**56**	**9**	**0**	**5**	**229**	**14.4**	**2**	....	....	....	....	....	**5**	**0**	**2**	**2**	**2**	**0**	**0**	**0**
1990-91	**Toronto**	**NHL**	**79**	**26**	**47**	**73**	**65**	**10**	**1**	**4**	**247**	**10.5**	**-31**	....	....	....	....	....	....	....	....	....	....	....	....	....
1991-92	**Edmonton**	**NHL**	**80**	**38**	**51**	**89**	**53**	**12**	**1**	**8**	**247**	**15.4**	**10**	....	....	....	....	....	**16**	**6**	**8**	**14**	**8**	**1**	**0**	**0**
1992-93♦	**Montreal**	**NHL**	**84**	**39**	**58**	**97**	**98**	**9**	**3**	**8**	**287**	**13.6**	**5**	....	....	....	....	....	**20**	**11**	**12**	**23**	**16**	**5**	**0**	**3**
1993-94	**Montreal**	**NHL**	**84**	**40**	**51**	**91**	**75**	**13**	**0**	**10**	**274**	**14.6**	**0**	....	....	....	....	....	**7**	**1**	**2**	**3**	**8**	**0**	**0**	**0**
1994-95	Ratinger-Lowen	DEL	11	5	7	12	24	....	....	....	....	....	....	....	....	....	....	....	....	....	....	....	....	....	....	....
	Montreal	**NHL**	**48**	**10**	**30**	**40**	**42**	**4**	**0**	**4**	**123**	**8.1**	**15**	....	....	....	....	....	....	....	....	....	....	....	....	....
1995-96	**Montreal**	**NHL**	**80**	**38**	**56**	**94**	**158**	**11**	**4**	**3**	**254**	**15.0**	**5**	....	....	....	....	....	**6**	**4**	**4**	**8**	**0**	**0**	**1**	**2**
1996-97	**Montreal**	**NHL**	**82**	**27**	**54**	**81**	**82**	**7**	**2**	**3**	**244**	**11.1**	**-6**	....	....	....	....	....	**5**	**0**	**0**	**0**	**2**	**0**	**0**	**0**
1997-98	**Montreal**	**NHL**	**76**	**18**	**41**	**59**	**58**	**2**	**1**	**5**	**164**	**11.0**	**14**	....	....	....	....	....	**10**	**3**	**6**	**9**	**22**	**1**	**0**	**0**
1998-99	**Montreal**	**NHL**	**65**	**12**	**24**	**36**	**46**	**3**	**2**	**2**	**147**	**8.2**	**-7**	**1425**	**48.4**	**41**	**37**	**20:27**	....	....	....	....	....	....	....	....
	San Jose	**NHL**	**12**	**7**	**6**	**13**	**4**	**3**	**0**	**1**	**43**	**16.3**	**3**	**230**	**51.3**	**9**	**1**	**19:21**	**6**	**3**	**2**	**5**	**6**	**0**	**2**	**0**
99-2000	**San Jose**	**NHL**	**82**	**21**	**49**	**70**	**58**	**3**	**1**	**1**	**204**	**10.3**	**4**	**1642**	**49.0**	**54**	**38**	**20:26**	**12**	**1**	**7**	**8**	**16**	**1**	**0**	**0**
2000-01	**San Jose**	**NHL**	**45**	**9**	**37**	**46**	**62**	**4**	**0**	**3**	**101**	**8.9**	**17**	**1027**	**52.7**	**30**	**17**	**20:49**	**6**	**2**	**1**	**3**	**14**	**0**	**1**	**0**
	NHL Totals		**1132**	**377**	**668**	**1045**	**998**	**101**	**15**	**64**	**3007**	**12.5**		**4324**	**49.8**	**134**	**93**	**20:28**	**111**	**32**	**50**	**82**	**112**	**9**	**4**	**5**

QMJHL Second All-Star Team (1986) • Played in NHL All-Star Game (1991, 1992)

Traded to **Edmonton** by **Toronto** with Peter Ing, Scott Thornton and Luke Richardson for Grant Fuhr, Glenn Anderson and Craig Berube, September 19, 1991. Traded to **Montreal** by **Edmonton** with Edmonton's 4th round choice (Adam Wiesel) in 1993 Entry Draft for Shayne Corson, Brent Gilchrist and Vladimir Vujtek, August 27, 1992. Traded to **San Jose** by **Montreal** for Phoenix's 5th round choice (previously acquired, Montreal selected Marc-Andre Thinel) in 1999 Entry Draft, San Jose's 1st round choice (Marcel Hossa) in 2000 Entry Draft and 2nd round choice (later traded to Columbus - Columbus selected Kiel McLeod) in 2001 Entry Draft, March 23, 1999.

DANDENAULT, Mathieu

(DAHN-deh-noh, MAT-yoo) **DET.**

Right wing/Defense. Shoots right. 6', 200 lbs. Born, Sherbrooke, Que., February 3, 1976. Detroit's 2nd choice, 49th overall, in 1994 Entry Draft.

1990-91	Gloucester	OMHA	44	52	50	102	30	....	....	....	....	....	....	....	....	....	....	....	....	....	....	....	....	....	....	....
1991-92	Vanier Voyageurs	OCJHL	33	27	31	58	20	....	....	....	....	....	....	....	....	....	....	....	....	....	....	....	....	....	....	....
	Gloucester	OCJHL	6	3	4	7	0	....	....	....	....	....	....	....	....	....	....	....	....	....	....	....	....	....	....	....
1992-93	Gloucester	OCJHL	55	11	26	37	64	....	....	....	....	....	....	....	....	....	....	....	....	....	....	....	....	....	....	....
1993-94	Sherbrooke	QMJHL	67	17	36	53	67	....	....	....	....	....	....	....	....	....	....	....	12	4	10	14	12	....	....	....
1994-95	Sherbrooke	QMJHL	67	37	70	107	76	....	....	....	....	....	....	....	....	....	....	....	7	1	7	8	10	....	....	....
1995-96	**Detroit**	**NHL**	**34**	**5**	**7**	**12**	**6**	**1**	**0**	**0**	**32**	**15.6**	**6**	....	....	....	....	....	....	....	....	....	....	....	....	....
	Adirondack	AHL	4	0	0	0	0	....	....	....	....	....	....	....	....	....	....	....	....	....	....	....	....	....	....	....
1996-97♦	**Detroit**	**NHL**	**65**	**3**	**9**	**12**	**28**	**0**	**0**	**0**	**81**	**3.7**	**-10**	....	....	....	....	....	....	....	....	....	....	....	....	....
1997-98♦	**Detroit**	**NHL**	**68**	**5**	**12**	**17**	**43**	**0**	**0**	**0**	**75**	**6.7**	**5**	....	....	....	....	....	**3**	**1**	**0**	**1**	**0**	**1**	**0**	**0**
1998-99	**Detroit**	**NHL**	**75**	**4**	**10**	**14**	**59**	**0**	**0**	**0**	**94**	**4.3**	**17**	**3**	**0.0**	**109**	**37**	**15:10**	**10**	**0**	**1**	**1**	**0**	**0**	**0**	**0**
99-2000	**Detroit**	**NHL**	**81**	**6**	**12**	**18**	**20**	**0**	**0**	**0**	**98**	**6.1**	**-12**	**1**	**100.0**	**108**	**28**	**12:10**	**6**	**0**	**0**	**0**	**2**	**0**	**0**	**0**
2000-01	**Detroit**	**NHL**	**73**	**10**	**15**	**25**	**38**	**2**	**0**	**2**	**95**	**10.5**	**11**	**0**	**0.0**	**90**	**54**	**16:06**	**6**	**0**	**1**	**1**	**0**	**0**	**0**	**0**
	NHL Totals		**396**	**33**	**65**	**98**	**194**	**3**	**0**	**2**	**475**	**6.9**		**4**	**25.0**	**307**	**119**	**14:24**	**25**	**1**	**2**	**3**	**2**	**1**	**0**	**0**

DANEYKO, Ken
(DAN-ee-KOH, KEHN) **N.J.**

Defense. Shoots left. 6'1", 215 lbs. Born, Windsor, Ont., April 17, 1964. New Jersey's 2nd choice, 18th overall, in 1982 Entry Draft.

			Regular Season																Playoffs							
Season	Club	League	GP	G	A	Pts	PIM	PP	SH	GW	S	%	+/-	TF	F%	H	SB	Min	GP	G	A	Pts	PIM	PP	SH	GW
1980-81	St. Albert Saints	AJHL	1	0	0	0	4																			
	Spokane Flyers	WHL	62	6	13	19	140												4	0	0	0	6			
1981-82	Spokane Flyers	WHL	26	1	11	12	147																			
	Seattle Breakers	WHL	38	1	22	23	151												14	1	9	10	49			
1982-83	Seattle Breakers	WHL	69	17	43	60	150												4	1	3	4	14			
1983-84	Kamloops Oilers	WHL	19	6	28	34	52												17	4	9	13	28			
	New Jersey	NHL	11	1	4	5	17	0	0	0	17	5.9	–1													
1984-85	New Jersey	NHL	1	0	0	0	10	0	0	0	1	0.0	–1													
	Maine Mariners	AHL	80	4	9	13	206												11	1	3	4	36			
1985-86	New Jersey	NHL	44	0	10	10	100	0	0	0	48	0.0	0													
	Maine Mariners	AHL	21	3	2	5	75																			
1986-87	New Jersey	NHL	79	2	12	14	183	0	0	0	113	1.8	–13													
1987-88	New Jersey	NHL	80	5	7	12	239	1	0	0	82	6.1	–3						20	1	6	7	83	0	0	1
1988-89	New Jersey	NHL	80	5	5	10	283	1	0	0	108	4.6	–22													
1989-90	New Jersey	NHL	74	6	15	21	219	0	1	1	64	9.4	15						6	2	0	2	21	0	0	0
1990-91	New Jersey	NHL	80	4	16	20	249	1	2	1	106	3.8	–10						7	0	1	1	10	0	0	0
1991-92	New Jersey	NHL	80	1	7	8	170	0	0	0	57	1.8	7						7	0	3	3	16	0	0	0
1992-93	New Jersey	NHL	84	2	11	13	236	0	0	0	71	2.8	4						5	0	0	0	8	0	0	0
1993-94	New Jersey	NHL	78	1	9	10	176	0	0	1	60	1.7	27						20	0	1	1	45	0	0	0
1994-95♦	New Jersey	NHL	25	1	2	3	54	0	0	0	27	3.7	4						20	1	0	1	22	0	0	0
1995-96	New Jersey	NHL	80	2	4	6	115	0	0	0	67	3.0	–10													
1996-97	New Jersey	NHL	77	2	7	9	70	0	0	0	63	3.2	24						10	0	0	0	28	0	0	0
1997-98	New Jersey	NHL	37	0	1	1	57	0	0	0	18	0.0	3						6	0	1	1	10	0	0	0
1998-99	New Jersey	NHL	82	2	9	11	63	0	0	0	63	3.2	27	1	0.0	182	159	20:03	7	0	0	0	8	0	0	0
99-2000♦	New Jersey	NHL	78	0	6	6	98	0	0	0	74	0.0	13	0	0.0	183	161	18:06	23	1	2	3	14	0	0	0
2000-01	New Jersey	NHL	77	0	4	4	87	0	0	0	50	0.0	8	0	0.0	173	122	17:17	25	0	3	3	21	0	0	0
	NHL Totals		1147	34	129	163	2426	3	3	3	1089	3.1		1	0.0	538	442	18:30	156	5	17	22	286	0	0	1

• Missed majority of 1997-98 season after voluntarily entering NHL/NHLPA substance abuse program, November 6, 1997. • Won Bill Masterton Memorial Trophy (2000)

DANIELS, Jeff
(DAN-yehls, JEHF) **CAR.**

Left wing. Shoots left. 6'1", 200 lbs. Born, Oshawa, Ont., June 24, 1968. Pittsburgh's 6th choice, 109th overall, in 1986 Entry Draft.

			Regular Season																Playoffs							
Season	Club	League	GP	G	A	Pts	PIM	PP	SH	GW	S	%	+/-	TF	F%	H	SB	Min	GP	G	A	Pts	PIM	PP	SH	GW
1983-84	Oshawa Legion	OMHA	57	59	72	131	22																			
1984-85	Oshawa Legion	MTJHL	7	7	2	9	11																			
	Oshawa Generals	OHL	59	7	11	18	16																			
1985-86	Oshawa Generals	OHL	62	13	19	32	23												6	0	1	1	0			
1986-87	Oshawa Generals	OHL	54	14	9	23	22												15	3	2	5	5			
1987-88	Oshawa Generals	OHL	64	29	39	68	59												4	2	3	5	0			
1988-89	Muskegon	IHL	58	21	21	42	58												11	3	5	8	11			
1989-90	Muskegon	IHL	80	30	47	77	39												6	1	1	2	7			
1990-91	Pittsburgh	NHL	11	0	2	2	2	0	0	0	6	0.0	0													
	Muskegon	IHL	62	23	29	52	18												5	1	3	4	2			
1991-92	Pittsburgh	NHL	2	0	0	0	0	0	0	0	0	0.0	0													
	Muskegon	IHL	44	19	16	35	38												10	5	4	9	9			
1992-93	Pittsburgh	NHL	58	5	4	9	14	0	0	1	30	16.7	–5						12	3	2	5	0	0	0	1
	Cleveland	IHL	3	2	1	3	0																			
1993-94	Pittsburgh	NHL	63	3	5	8	20	0	0	1	46	6.5	–1													
	Florida	NHL	7	0	0	0	0	0	0	0	6	0.0	0													
1994-95	Florida	NHL	3	0	0	0	0	0	0	0	0	0.0	0													
	Detroit Vipers	IHL	25	8	12	20	6												5	1	0	1	0			
1995-96	Springfield	AHL	72	22	20	42	32												10	3	0	3	2			
1996-97	Hartford	NHL	10	0	2	2	0	0	0	0	6	0.0	2													
	Springfield	AHL	38	18	14	32	19												16	7	3	10	4			
1997-98	Carolina	NHL	2	0	0	0	0	0	0	0	1	0.0	0													
	New Haven	AHL	71	24	27	51	34												3	0	1	1	0			
1998-99	Nashville	NHL	9	1	3	4	2	0	0	0	8	12.5	–1	1	0.0	9	1	10:56								
	Milwaukee	IHL	62	12	31	43	19												2	1	1	2	0			
99-2000	Carolina	NHL	69	3	4	7	10	0	0	0	28	10.7	–8	47	46.8	54	37	7:42								
2000-01	Carolina	NHL	67	1	1	2	15	0	0	0	42	2.4	–3	125	53.6	51	27	7:30	6	0	2	2	2	0	0	0
	NHL Totals		301	13	21	34	63	0	0	2	173	7.5		173	51.4	114	65	7:48	18	3	4	7	2	0	0	1

Traded to **Florida** by **Pittsburgh** for Greg Hawgood, March 19, 1994. Signed as a free agent by **Hartford**, August 18, 1995. Transferred to **Carolina** after **Hartford** franchise relocated, June 25, 1997. Claimed by **Nashville** from **Carolina** in Expansion Draft, June 26, 1998. Signed as a free agent by **Carolina**, August 31, 1999.

DARBY, Craig
(DAHR-bee, KRAYG) **MTL.**

Center. Shoots right. 6'3", 197 lbs. Born, Oneida, NY, September 26, 1972. Montreal's 3rd choice, 43rd overall, in 1991 Entry Draft.

			Regular Season																Playoffs							
Season	Club	League	GP	G	A	Pts	PIM	PP	SH	GW	S	%	+/-	TF	F%	H	SB	Min	GP	G	A	Pts	PIM	PP	SH	GW
1987-88	Albany Academy	Hi-School	29	11	27	38	....																			
1988-89	Albany Academy	Hi-School	29	36	40	*76	....																			
1989-90	Albany Academy	Hi-School	29	32	53	85	....																			
1990-91	Albany Academy	Hi-School	29	33	61	*94	....												4	8	1	9				
1991-92	Providence	H-East	35	17	24	41	47																			
1992-93	Providence	H-East	35	11	21	32	62																			
1993-94	Fredericton	AHL	66	23	33	56	51																			
1994-95	Fredericton	AHL	64	21	47	68	82																			
	Montreal	NHL	10	0	2	2	0	0	0	0	4	0.0	–5													
	NY Islanders	NHL	3	0	0	0	0	0	0	0	1	0.0	–1													
1995-96	NY Islanders	NHL	10	0	2	2	0	0	0	0	1	0.0	–1													
	Worcester	AHL	68	22	28	50	47												4	1	1	2	2			
1996-97	Philadelphia	NHL	9	1	4	5	2	0	1	0	13	7.7	2													
	Philadelphia	AHL	59	26	33	59	24												10	3	6	9	0			
1997-98	Philadelphia	NHL	3	1	0	1	0	0	0	0	3	33.3	0													
	Philadelphia	AHL	77	*42	45	87	34												20	5	9	14	4			
1998-99	Milwaukee	IHL	81	32	22	54	33												2	3	0	3	0			
99-2000	Montreal	NHL	76	7	10	17	14	0	1	2	90	7.8	–14	1068	48.3	46	18	13:45								
2000-01	Montreal	NHL	78	12	16	28	16	0	1	0	97	12.4	–17	1214	46.9	64	33	15:53								
	NHL Totals		189	21	34	55	32	0	3	2	209	10.0		2282	47.5	110	51	14:50								

AHL First All-Star Team (1998)

Traded to **NY Islanders** by **Montreal** with Kirk Muller and Mathieu Schneider for Pierre Turgeon and Vladimir Malakhov, April 5, 1995. Claimed on waivers by **Philadelphia** from **NY Islanders**, June 4, 1996. Claimed by **Nashville** from **Philadelphia** in Expansion Draft, June 26, 1998. Signed as a free agent by **Montreal**, August 4, 1999.

DARCHE, Mathieu
(DAHRSH, MATH-you) **CBJ**

Left wing. Shoots left. 6'1", 225 lbs. Born, St-Laurent, Que., November 26, 1976.

			Regular Season																Playoffs							
Season	Club	League	GP	G	A	Pts	PIM	PP	SH	GW	S	%	+/-	TF	F%	H	SB	Min	GP	G	A	Pts	PIM	PP	SH	GW
1995-96	Choate-Rosemary	Hi-School	STATISTICS NOT AVAILABLE																							
1996-97	McGill University	OUAA	23	1	2	3	27																			
1997-98	McGill University	OUAA	40	28	17	45	69																			
1998-99	McGill University	OUAA	32	16	24	40	60																			
99-2000	McGill University	OUAA	33	31	41	*72	38												5	2	8	10	16			
2000-01	Columbus	NHL	9	0	0	0	0	0	0	0	9	0.0	–4	1	0.0	12	0	10:07								
	Syracuse Crunch	AHL	66	16	24	40	21												5	0	1	1	4			
	NHL Totals		9	0	0	0	0	0	0	0	9	0.0		1	0.0	12	0	10:07								

• Played CIAU Football (1996-97) • OUAA East Second All-Star Team (1998) • OUAA East First All-Star Team (1999) • OUAA First All-Star Team (2000) • CIAU All-Canadian Team (2000) • Won Randy Gregg Trophy (Athletics and Academics) (2000)

Signed as a free agent by **Columbus**, May 16, 2000.

										Regular Season									Playoffs							
Season	Club	League	GP	G	A	Pts	PIM	PP	SH	GW	S	%	+/-	TF	F%	H	SB	Min	GP	G	A	Pts	PIM	PP	SH	GW

DAVIDSON, Matt
(DAY-vihd-SOHN, MAT) **CBJ**

Right wing. Shoots right. 6'2", 190 lbs. Born, Flin Flon, Man., August 9, 1977. Buffalo's 5th choice, 94th overall, in 1995 Entry Draft.

1992-93	Saskatoon AAA	SMHL	36	14	18	32	36	....	....	....	....	....	....	....	....	....	....	....	....	....	....	....	....	....	....	....
1993-94	Portland	WHL	59	4	12	16	18	....	....	....	....	....	....	....	....	....	....	....	10	0	0	0	4	....	....	....
1994-95	Portland	WHL	72	17	20	37	51	....	....	....	....	....	....	....	....	....	....	....	9	1	3	4	0	....	....	....
1995-96	Portland	WHL	70	24	26	50	96	....	....	....	....	....	....	....	....	....	....	....	7	2	2	4	2	....	....	....
1996-97	Portland	WHL	72	44	27	71	47	....	....	....	....	....	....	....	....	....	....	....	6	0	1	1	2	....	....	....
1997-98	Rochester	AHL	72	15	12	27	12	....	....	....	....	....	....	....	....	....	....	....	3	1	0	1	2	....	....	....
1998-99	Rochester	AHL	80	26	15	41	44	....	....	....	....	....	....	....	....	....	....	....	18	2	1	3	6	....	....	....
99-2000	Rochester	AHL	80	12	20	32	30	....	....	....	....	....	....	....	....	....	....	....	19	4	2	6	8	....	....	....
2000-01	**Columbus**	**NHL**	**5**	**0**	**0**	**0**	**0**	**0**	**0**	**0**	**2**	**0.0**	**2**	**0**	**0.0**	**4**	**2**	**7:14**	....	....	....	....	....	....	....	....
	Syracuse Crunch	AHL	72	14	11	25	24	....	....	....	....	....	....	....	....	....	....	....	5	1	2	3	2	....	....	....
	NHL Totals		**5**	**0**	**0**	**0**	**0**	**0**	**0**	**0**	**2**	**0.0**		**0**	**0.0**	**4**	**2**	**7:14**	....	....	....	....	....	....	....	....

Traded to **Columbus** by **Buffalo** with Jean-Luc Grand-Pierre, San Jose's 5th round choice (previously acquired, Columbus selected Tyler Kolarik) in 2000 Entry Draft and Buffalo's 5th round choice (later traded to Calgary - later traded to Detroit - Detroit selected Andreas Jamtin) in 2001 Entry Draft to complete Expansion Draft agreement which had Columbus select Geoff Sanderson and Dwayne Roloson from Buffalo, June 23, 2000.

DAVIDSSON, Johan
(DAH-vihd-suhn, YOH-hahn) **VAN.**

Center. Shoots right. 6'1", 190 lbs. Born, Jonkoping, Sweden, January 6, 1976. Anaheim's 2nd choice, 28th overall, in 1994 Entry Draft.

1992-93	HV Jonkoping	Sweden	8	1	0	1	0	....	....	....	....	....	....	....	....	....	....	....	....	....	....	....	....	....	....	....
1993-94	HV Jonkoping	Swede-Jr.	5	2	3	5	0	....	....	....	....	....	....	....	....	....	....	....	....	....	....	....	....	....	....	....
	HV Jonkoping	Sweden	38	2	5	7	4	....	....	....	....	....	....	....	....	....	....	....	....	....	....	....	....	....	....	....
1994-95	HV Jonkoping	Swede-Jr.	3	4	1	5	0	....	....	....	....	....	....	....	....	....	....	....	....	....	....	....	....	....	....	....
	HV Jonkoping	Sweden	37	4	7	11	20	....	....	....	....	....	....	....	....	....	....	....	13	3	2	5	0	....	....	....
1995-96	HV Jonkoping	Sweden	39	7	11	18	20	....	....	....	....	....	....	....	....	....	....	....	4	0	2	2	0	....	....	....
1996-97	HV Jonkoping	Sweden	50	18	21	39	18	....	....	....	....	....	....	....	....	....	....	....	5	0	3	3	2	....	....	....
1997-98	HIFK Helsinki	Finland	43	10	30	40	8	....	....	....	....	....	....	....	....	....	....	....	9	3	10	13	0	....	....	....
1998-99	**Anaheim**	**NHL**	**64**	**3**	**5**	**8**	**14**	**1**	**0**	**1**	**48**	**6.3**	**–9**	**516**	**37.0**	**34**	**7**	**10:37**	**1**	**0**	**0**	**0**	**0**	**0**	**0**	**0**
	Cincinnati Ducks	AHL	9	1	6	7	2	....	....	....	....	....	....	....	....	....	....	....	....	....	....	....	....	....	....	....
99-2000	**Anaheim**	**NHL**	**5**	**1**	**0**	**1**	**2**	**0**	**0**	**1**	**8**	**12.5**	**0**	**38**	**42.1**	**8**	**0**	**10:42**	....	....	....	....	....	....	....	....
	Cincinnati Ducks	AHL	56	9	31	40	24	....	....	....	....	....	....	....	....	....	....	....	....	....	....	....	....	....	....	....
	NY Islanders	**NHL**	**14**	**2**	**4**	**6**	**0**	**0**	**0**	**0**	**21**	**9.5**	**0**	**130**	**40.0**	**9**	**9**	**11:32**	....	....	....	....	....	....	....	....
2000-01	Blues Espoo	Finland	35	12	17	29	34	....	....	....	....	....	....	....	....	....	....	....	....	....	....	....	....	....	....	....
	NHL Totals		**83**	**6**	**9**	**15**	**16**	**1**	**0**	**2**	**77**	**7.8**		**684**	**37.9**	**51**	**16**	**10:47**	**1**	**0**	**0**	**0**	**0**	**0**	**0**	**0**

Traded to **NY Islanders** by **Anaheim** with future considerations for Jorgen Jonsson, March 11, 2000. Signed as a free agent by **Vancouver**, September 6, 2000.

DAWE, Jason
(DAW, JAY-suhn) **NYR**

Right wing. Shoots left. 5'10", 189 lbs. Born, North York, Ont., May 29, 1973. Buffalo's 2nd choice, 35th overall, in 1991 Entry Draft.

1988-89	Don Mills Flyers	MTHL	44	35	28	63	103	....	....	....	....	....	....	....	....	....	....	....	....	....	....	....	....	....	....	....
1989-90	Peterborough	OHL	50	15	18	33	19	....	....	....	....	....	....	....	....	....	....	....	12	4	7	11	4	....	....	....
1990-91	Peterborough	OHL	66	43	27	70	43	....	....	....	....	....	....	....	....	....	....	....	4	3	1	4	0	....	....	....
1991-92	Peterborough	OHL	66	53	55	108	55	....	....	....	....	....	....	....	....	....	....	....	4	5	0	5	0	....	....	....
1992-93	Peterborough	OHL	59	58	68	126	80	....	....	....	....	....	....	....	....	....	....	....	21	18	33	51	18	....	....	....
	Rochester	AHL	....	....	....	....	....	....	....	....	....	....	....	....	....	....	....	....	3	1	0	1	0	....	....	....
1993-94	**Buffalo**	**NHL**	**32**	**6**	**7**	**13**	**12**	**3**	**0**	**1**	**35**	**17.1**	**1**	....	....	....	....	....	**6**	**0**	**1**	**1**	**6**	**0**	**0**	**0**
	Rochester	AHL	48	22	14	36	44	....	....	....	....	....	....	....	....	....	....	....	....	....	....	....	....	....	....	....
1994-95	Rochester	AHL	44	27	19	46	24	....	....	....	....	....	....	....	....	....	....	....	....	....	....	....	....	....	....	....
	Buffalo	**NHL**	**42**	**7**	**4**	**11**	**19**	**0**	**1**	**2**	**51**	**13.7**	**–6**	....	....	....	....	....	**5**	**2**	**1**	**3**	**6**	**0**	**0**	**0**
1995-96	**Buffalo**	**NHL**	**67**	**25**	**25**	**50**	**33**	**8**	**1**	**0**	**130**	**19.2**	**–8**	....	....	....	....	....	....	....	....	....	....	....	....	....
	Rochester	AHL	7	5	4	9	2	....	....	....	....	....	....	....	....	....	....	....	....	....	....	....	....	....	....	....
1996-97	**Buffalo**	**NHL**	**81**	**22**	**26**	**48**	**32**	**4**	**1**	**3**	**136**	**16.2**	**14**	....	....	....	....	....	**11**	**2**	**1**	**3**	**6**	**0**	**0**	**0**
1997-98	**Buffalo**	**NHL**	**68**	**19**	**17**	**36**	**36**	**4**	**1**	**3**	**115**	**16.5**	**10**	....	....	....	....	....	....	....	....	....	....	....	....	....
	NY Islanders	**NHL**	**13**	**1**	**2**	**3**	**6**	**0**	**0**	**0**	**19**	**5.3**	**–2**	....	....	....	....	....	....	....	....	....	....	....	....	....
1998-99	**NY Islanders**	**NHL**	**22**	**2**	**3**	**5**	**8**	**0**	**0**	**0**	**29**	**6.9**	**0**	**4**	**25.0**	**27**	**5**	**11:55**	....	....	....	....	....	....	....	....
	Montreal	**NHL**	**37**	**4**	**5**	**9**	**14**	**1**	**0**	**1**	**52**	**7.7**	**0**	**4**	**0.0**	**44**	**4**	**11:00**	....	....	....	....	....	....	....	....
99-2000	Milwaukee	IHL	41	11	13	24	24	....	....	....	....	....	....	....	....	....	....	....	....	....	....	....	....	....	....	....
	NY Rangers	**NHL**	**3**	**0**	**1**	**1**	**2**	**0**	**0**	**0**	**8**	**0.0**	**0**	**1**	**100.0**	**3**	**0**	**13:35**	....	....	....	....	....	....	....	....
	Hartford	AHL	27	9	9	18	24	....	....	....	....	....	....	....	....	....	....	....	21	10	7	17	37	....	....	....
2000-01	Hartford	AHL	4	2	0	2	2	....	....	....	....	....	....	....	....	....	....	....	....	....	....	....	....	....	....	....
	NHL Totals		**365**	**86**	**90**	**176**	**162**	**20**	**4**	**10**	**575**	**15.0**		**9**	**22.2**	**74**	**9**	**11:27**	**22**	**4**	**3**	**7**	**18**	**0**	**0**	**0**

OHL First All-Star Team (1993) • Canadian Major Junior Second All-Star Team (1993) • Won George Parsons Trophy (Memorial Cup Tournament Most Sportsmanlike Player) (1993)

Traded to **NY Islanders** by **Buffalo** for Jason Holland and Paul Kruse, March 24, 1998. Claimed on waivers by **Montreal** from **NY Islanders**, December 15, 1998. Signed as a free agent by **Nashville**, October 2, 1999. Traded to **NY Rangers** by **Nashville** for John Namestnikov, February 3, 2000. • Missed majority of 2000-01 season recovering from ankle injury originally suffered in game vs. Springfield (AHL), October 6, 2000.

DAZE, Eric
(dah-ZAY, AIR-ihk) **CHI.**

Left wing. Shoots left. 6'6", 234 lbs. Born, Montreal, Que., July 2, 1975. Chicago's 5th choice, 90th overall, in 1993 Entry Draft.

1990-91	Laval-Laurentide	QAHA	30	25	20	45	30	....	....	....	....	....	....	....	....	....	....	....	....	....	....	....	....	....	....	....
1991-92	Laval Regents	QAAA	35	30	29	59	40	....	....	....	....	....	....	....	....	....	....	....	12	8	10	18	8	....	....	....
1992-93	Beauport	QMJHL	68	19	36	55	24	....	....	....	....	....	....	....	....	....	....	....	....	....	....	....	....	....	....	....
1993-94	Beauport	QMJHL	66	59	48	107	31	....	....	....	....	....	....	....	....	....	....	....	15	16	8	24	2	....	....	....
1994-95	Beauport	QMJHL	57	54	45	99	20	....	....	....	....	....	....	....	....	....	....	....	16	9	12	21	23	....	....	....
	Chicago	**NHL**	**4**	**1**	**1**	**2**	**2**	**0**	**0**	**0**	**1**	**100.0**	**2**	....	....	....	....	....	**16**	**0**	**1**	**1**	**4**	**0**	**0**	**0**
1995-96	**Chicago**	**NHL**	**80**	**30**	**23**	**53**	**18**	**2**	**0**	**2**	**167**	**18.0**	**16**	....	....	....	....	....	**10**	**3**	**5**	**8**	**0**	**0**	**0**	**1**
1996-97	**Chicago**	**NHL**	**71**	**22**	**19**	**41**	**16**	**11**	**0**	**4**	**176**	**12.5**	**–4**	....	....	....	....	....	**6**	**2**	**1**	**3**	**2**	**0**	**0**	**0**
1997-98	**Chicago**	**NHL**	**80**	**31**	**11**	**42**	**22**	**10**	**0**	**7**	**216**	**14.4**	**4**	....	....	....	....	....	....	....	....	....	....	....	....	....
1998-99	**Chicago**	**NHL**	**72**	**22**	**20**	**42**	**22**	**8**	**0**	**2**	**189**	**11.6**	**–13**	**4**	**0.0**	**92**	**22**	**16:16**	....	....	....	....	....	....	....	....
99-2000	**Chicago**	**NHL**	**59**	**23**	**13**	**36**	**28**	**6**	**0**	**1**	**143**	**16.1**	**–16**	**9**	**22.2**	**91**	**29**	**16:15**	....	....	....	....	....	....	....	....
2000-01	**Chicago**	**NHL**	**79**	**33**	**24**	**57**	**16**	**9**	**1**	**8**	**205**	**16.1**	**1**	**3**	**33.3**	**77**	**35**	**17:45**	....	....	....	....	....	....	....	....
	NHL Totals		**445**	**162**	**111**	**273**	**124**	**46**	**1**	**24**	**1097**	**14.8**		**16**	**18.8**	**260**	**86**	**16:49**	**32**	**5**	**7**	**12**	**6**	**0**	**0**	**1**

QMJHL First All-Star Team (1994, 1995) • Canadian Major Junior Most Sportsmanlike Player of the Year (1995) • NHL All-Rookie Team (1996)

DEADMARSH, Adam
(DEHD-mahrsh, A-duhm) **L.A.**

Left wing/Center. Shoots right. 6', 195 lbs. Born, Trail, B.C., May 10, 1975. Quebec's 2nd choice, 14th overall, in 1993 Entry Draft.

1990-91	Beaver Valley	KIJHL	35	28	44	72	95	....	....	....	....	....	....	....	....	....	....	....	....	....	....	....	....	....	....	....
1991-92	Portland	WHL	68	30	30	60	81	....	....	....	....	....	....	....	....	....	....	....	6	3	3	6	13	....	....	....
1992-93	Portland	WHL	58	33	36	69	126	....	....	....	....	....	....	....	....	....	....	....	16	7	8	15	29	....	....	....
1993-94	Portland	WHL	65	43	56	99	212	....	....	....	....	....	....	....	....	....	....	....	10	9	8	17	33	....	....	....
1994-95	Portland	WHL	29	28	20	48	129	....	....	....	....	....	....	....	....	....	....	....	....	....	....	....	....	....	....	....
	Quebec	**NHL**	**48**	**9**	**8**	**17**	**56**	**0**	**0**	**0**	**48**	**18.8**	**16**	....	....	....	....	....	**6**	**0**	**1**	**1**	**0**	**0**	**0**	**0**
1995-96◆	**Colorado**	**NHL**	**78**	**21**	**27**	**48**	**142**	**3**	**0**	**2**	**151**	**13.9**	**20**	....	....	....	....	....	**22**	**5**	**12**	**17**	**25**	**1**	**0**	**0**
1996-97	**Colorado**	**NHL**	**78**	**33**	**27**	**60**	**136**	**10**	**3**	**4**	**198**	**16.7**	**8**	....	....	....	....	....	**17**	**3**	**6**	**9**	**24**	**1**	**0**	**1**
1997-98	**Colorado**	**NHL**	**73**	**22**	**21**	**43**	**125**	**10**	**0**	**6**	**187**	**11.8**	**0**	....	....	....	....	....	**7**	**2**	**0**	**2**	**4**	**1**	**0**	**0**
	United States	Olympics	4	1	0	1	2	....	....	....	....	....	....	....	....	....	....	....	....	....	....	....	....	....	....	....
1998-99	**Colorado**	**NHL**	**66**	**22**	**27**	**49**	**99**	**10**	**0**	**3**	**152**	**14.5**	**–2**	**621**	**45.9**	**121**	**51**	**20:46**	**19**	**8**	**4**	**12**	**20**	**3**	**0**	**0**
99-2000	**Colorado**	**NHL**	**71**	**18**	**27**	**45**	**106**	**5**	**0**	**4**	**153**	**11.8**	**–10**	**430**	**46.5**	**133**	**45**	**20:27**	**17**	**4**	**11**	**15**	**21**	**1**	**0**	**1**
2000-01	**Colorado**	**NHL**	**39**	**13**	**13**	**26**	**59**	**7**	**0**	**2**	**86**	**15.1**	**–9**	**56**	**55.4**	**81**	**10**	**17:38**	....	....	....	....	....	....	....	....
	Los Angeles	**NHL**	**18**	**4**	**2**	**6**	**4**	**0**	**0**	**0**	**40**	**10.0**	**3**	**21**	**57.1**	**49**	**7**	**18:47**	**13**	**3**	**3**	**6**	**4**	**0**	**0**	**2**
	NHL Totals		**471**	**142**	**152**	**294**	**727**	**45**	**3**	**21**	**1015**	**14.0**		**1128**	**46.8**	**384**	**113**	**19:50**	**101**	**25**	**37**	**62**	**98**	**7**	**0**	**4**

Transferred to **Colorado** after **Quebec** franchise relocated, June 21, 1995. Traded to **LA Kings** by **Colorado** with Aaron Miller, Colorado's 1st round choice (David Steckel) in 2001 Entry Draft and future considerations (Jared Aulin, March 22, 2001) for Rob Blake and Steve Reinprecht, February 21, 2001.

DEAN, Kevin
(DEEN, KEH-vihn) **CHI.**

Defense. Shoots left. 6'3", 210 lbs. Born, Madison, WI, April 1, 1969. New Jersey's 4th choice, 86th overall, in 1987 Entry Draft.

Season	Club	League	Regular Season GP	G	A	Pts	PIM	PP	SH	GW	S	%	+/-	TF	F%	H	SB	Min	Playoffs GP	G	A	Pts	PIM	PP	SH	GW
1985-86	Culver Eagles	Hi-School	35	28	44	72	48																			
1986-87	Culver Eagles	Hi-School	25	19	25	44	30																			
1987-88	New Hampshire	H-East	27	1	6	7	34																			
1988-89	New Hampshire	H-East	34	1	12	13	28																			
1989-90	New Hampshire	H-East	39	2	6	8	42																			
1990-91	New Hampshire	H-East	31	10	12	22	22																			
	Utica Devils	AHL	7	0	1	1	2																			
1991-92	Utica Devils	AHL	23	0	3	3	6																			
	Cincinnati	ECHL	30	3	22	25	43												9	1	6	7	8			
1992-93	Cincinnati	IHL	13	2	1	3	15																			
	Utica Devils	AHL	57	2	16	18	76												5	1	0	1	8			
1993-94	Albany River Rats	AHL	70	9	33	42	92												5	0	2	2	7			
1994-95	Albany River Rats	AHL	68	5	37	42	66												8	0	4	4	4			
	♦ New Jersey	**NHL**	**17**	**0**	**1**	**1**	**4**	**0**	**0**	**0**	**11**	**0.0**	**6**						**3**	**0**	**2**	**2**	**0**	**0**	**0**	**0**
1995-96	**New Jersey**	**NHL**	**41**	**0**	**6**	**6**	**28**	**0**	**0**	**0**	**29**	**0.0**	**4**													
	Albany River Rats	AHL	1	1	0	1	2																			
1996-97	**New Jersey**	**NHL**	**28**	**2**	**4**	**6**	**6**	**0**	**0**	**0**	**21**	**9.5**	**2**						**1**	**1**	**0**	**1**	**0**	**0**	**0**	**1**
	Albany River Rats	AHL	2	0	1	1	4																			
1997-98	**New Jersey**	**NHL**	**50**	**1**	**8**	**9**	**12**	**1**	**0**	**0**	**28**	**3.6**	**12**						**5**	**1**	**0**	**1**	**2**	**0**	**0**	**0**
	Albany River Rats	AHL	2	0	1	1	2																			
1998-99	**New Jersey**	**NHL**	**62**	**1**	**10**	**11**	**22**	**1**	**0**	**0**	**51**	**2.0**	**4**	**1**	**0.0**	**77**	**59**	**15:42**	**7**	**0**	**0**	**0**	**0**	**0**	**0**	**0**
99-2000	**Atlanta**	**NHL**	**23**	**1**	**0**	**1**	**14**	**0**	**1**	**0**	**9**	**11.1**	**–5**	**1**	**0.0**	**48**	**39**	**16:53**								
	Dallas	**NHL**	**14**	**0**	**0**	**0**	**10**	**0**	**0**	**0**	**6**	**0.0**	**–1**	**0**	**0.0**	**11**	**15**	**11:19**								
	Chicago	**NHL**	**27**	**2**	**8**	**10**	**12**	**0**	**0**	**0**	**32**	**6.3**	**9**	**0**	**0.0**	**34**	**42**	**18:36**								
2000-01	**Chicago**	**NHL**	**69**	**0**	**11**	**11**	**30**	**0**	**0**	**0**	**75**	**0.0**	**–16**	**0**	**0.0**	**76**	**103**	**19:27**								
	NHL Totals		**331**	**7**	**48**	**55**	**138**	**2**	**1**	**0**	**262**	**2.7**		**1**	**0.0**	**246**	**258**	**17:15**	**16**	**2**	**2**	**4**	**2**	**0**	**0**	**1**

AHL First All-Star Team (1995)

Claimed by **Atlanta** from **New Jersey** in Expansion Draft, June 25, 1999. Traded to **Dallas** by **Atlanta** for Dallas' 9th round choice (Mark McRae) in 2000 Entry Draft, December 15, 1999. Traded to **Chicago** by **Dallas** with Derek Plante and Dallas' 2nd round choice (Matt Keith) in 2001 Entry Draft for Sylvain Cote and Dave Manson, February 8, 2000.

DeBRUSK, Louie
(duh-BRUHSK, LEW-ee)

Left wing. Shoots left. 6'2", 238 lbs. Born, Cambridge, Ont., March 19, 1971. NY Rangers' 4th choice, 49th overall, in 1989 Entry Draft.

Season	Club	League	GP	G	A	Pts	PIM	PP	SH	GW	S	%	+/-	TF	F%	H	SB	Min	GP	G	A	Pts	PIM	PP	SH	GW
1986-87	Port Elgin Huskies	OJHL-C	10	2	1	3	4																			
1987-88	Stratford Cullitons	OJHL-B	45	13	14	27	205																			
1988-89	London Knights	OHL	59	11	11	22	149												19	1	1	2	43			
1989-90	London Knights	OHL	61	21	19	40	198												6	2	2	4	24			
1990-91	London Knights	OHL	61	31	33	64	*223												7	2	2	4	14			
	Binghamton	AHL	2	0	0	0	7												2	0	0	0	9			
1991-92	**Edmonton**	**NHL**	**25**	**2**	**1**	**3**	**124**	**0**	**0**	**1**	**7**	**28.6**	**4**													
	Cape Breton	AHL	28	2	2	4	73																			
1992-93	**Edmonton**	**NHL**	**51**	**8**	**2**	**10**	**205**	**0**	**0**	**1**	**33**	**24.2**	**–16**													
1993-94	**Edmonton**	**NHL**	**48**	**4**	**6**	**10**	**185**	**0**	**0**	**0**	**27**	**14.8**	**–9**													
	Cape Breton	AHL	5	3	1	4	58																			
1994-95	**Edmonton**	**NHL**	**34**	**2**	**0**	**2**	**93**	**0**	**0**	**0**	**14**	**14.3**	**–4**													
1995-96	**Edmonton**	**NHL**	**38**	**1**	**3**	**4**	**96**	**0**	**0**	**0**	**17**	**5.9**	**–7**													
1996-97	**Edmonton**	**NHL**	**32**	**2**	**0**	**2**	**94**	**0**	**0**	**0**	**10**	**20.0**	**–6**						**6**	**0**	**0**	**0**	**4**	**0**	**0**	**0**
1997-98	**Tampa Bay**	**NHL**	**54**	**1**	**2**	**3**	**166**	**0**	**0**	**0**	**14**	**7.1**	**–2**													
	San Antonio	IHL	17	7	4	11	130																			
1998-99	**Phoenix**	**NHL**	**15**	**0**	**0**	**0**	**34**	**0**	**0**	**0**	**6**	**0.0**	**–2**	**0**	**0.0**	**16**	**0**	**5:57**	**6**	**2**	**0**	**2**	**6**	**0**	**0**	**0**
	Las Vegas	IHL	26	3	6	9	160																			
	Springfield	AHL	3	1	0	1	0																			
	Long Beach	IHL	24	5	5	10	134																			
99-2000	**Phoenix**	**NHL**	**61**	**4**	**3**	**7**	**78**	**0**	**0**	**0**	**24**	**16.7**	**1**	**0**	**0.0**	**55**	**4**	**5:21**	**3**	**0**	**0**	**0**	**0**	**0**	**0**	**0**
2000-01	**Phoenix**	**NHL**	**39**	**0**	**0**	**0**	**79**	**0**	**0**	**0**	**12**	**0.0**	**–5**	**0**	**0.0**	**18**	**5**	**4:49**								
	NHL Totals		**397**	**24**	**17**	**41**	**1154**	**0**	**0**	**2**	**164**	**14.6**		**0**	**0.0**	**89**	**9**	**5:15**	**15**	**2**	**0**	**2**	**10**	**0**	**0**	**0**

Traded to **Edmonton** by **NY Rangers** with Bernie Nicholls and Steven Rice for Mark Messier and future considerations (Jeff Beukeboom for David Shaw, November 12, 1991), October 4, 1991. Signed as a free agent by **Tampa Bay**, September 23, 1997. Traded to **Phoenix** by **Tampa Bay** with Tampa Bay's 5th round choice (Jay Leach) in 1998 Entry Draft for Craig Janney, June 11, 1998.

DELISLE, Jonathan
(duh-LIGHL, JAWN-ah-thuhn)

Right wing. Shoots right. 5'10", 180 lbs. Born, Ste-Anne-des-Plaines, Que., June 30, 1977. Montreal's 4th choice, 86th overall, in 1995 Entry Draft.

Season	Club	League	GP	G	A	Pts	PIM	PP	SH	GW	S	%	+/-	TF	F%	H	SB	Min	GP	G	A	Pts	PIM	PP	SH	GW
1992-93	Laval Regents	QAAA	14	3	3	6	12												13	2	5	7	24			
1993-94	Verdun College	QMJHL	61	16	17	33	130												4	0	1	1	14			
1994-95	Hull Olympiques	QMJHL	60	21	38	59	218												19	11	8	19	43			
1995-96	Hull Olympiques	QMJHL	62	31	57	88	193												18	6	13	19	64			
1996-97	Hull Olympiques	QMJHL	61	35	54	89	228												14	11	13	24	46			
1997-98	Fredericton	AHL	78	15	21	36	138												4	0	1	1	7			
1998-99	Fredericton	AHL	78	7	29	36	118												15	3	6	9	39			
	Montreal	**NHL**	**1**	**0**	**0**	**0**	**0**	**0**	**0**	**0**	**0**	**0.0**	**0**	**0**	**0.0**	**1**	**0**	**4:32**								
99-2000	Quebec Citadelles	AHL	62	7	19	26	142												3	0	0	0	4			
2000-01	Quebec Citadelles	AHL	71	6	18	24	201												6	1	0	1	53			
	NHL Totals		**1**	**0**	**0**	**0**	**0**	**0**	**0**	**0**	**0**	**0.0**		**0**	**0.0**	**1**	**0**	**4:32**								

DELISLE, Xavier
(duh-LIGHL, ehx-AY-vee-uhr) **MTL.**

Center. Shoots right. 5'11", 193 lbs. Born, Quebec City, Que., May 24, 1977. Tampa Bay's 5th choice, 157th overall, in 1996 Entry Draft.

Season	Club	League	GP	G	A	Pts	PIM	PP	SH	GW	S	%	+/-	TF	F%	H	SB	Min	GP	G	A	Pts	PIM	PP	SH	GW
1992-93	Ste-Foy Governors	QAAA	41	20	23	43	10												12	8	10	18	2			
1993-94	Granby Bisons	QMJHL	46	11	22	33	25												7	2	0	2	0			
1994-95	Granby Bisons	QMJHL	72	18	36	54	48												13	2	6	8	4			
1995-96	Granby Bisons	QMJHL	67	45	75	120	45												20	13	*27	*40	12			
1996-97	Granby Bisons	QMJHL	59	36	56	92	20												5	1	4	5	6			
1997-98	Adirondack	AHL	76	10	19	29	47												3	0	0	0	0			
1998-99	**Tampa Bay**	**NHL**	**2**	**0**	**0**	**0**	**0**	**0**	**0**	**0**	**1**	**0.0**	**0**	**11**	**45.5**	**1**	**0**	**5:51**								
	Cleveland	IHL	77	15	29	44	36																			
99-2000	Detroit Vipers	IHL	20	2	6	8	18																			
	Toledo Storm	ECHL	2	0	1	1	0																			
	Quebec Citadelles	AHL	42	17	28	45	8												3	1	2	3	0			
2000-01	**Montreal**	**NHL**	**14**	**3**	**2**	**5**	**6**	**1**	**0**	**0**	**15**	**20.0**	**–5**	**3**	**33.3**	**5**	**1**	**10:14**								
	Quebec Citadelles	AHL	62	18	29	47	34												9	1	5	6	2			
	NHL Totals		**16**	**3**	**2**	**5**	**6**	**1**	**0**	**0**	**16**	**18.8**		**14**	**42.9**	**6**	**1**	**9:41**								

QMJHL Second All-Star Team (1996) • Memorial Cup All-Star Team (1996)

Signed as a free agent by **Montreal**, August 8, 2000.

DELMORE, Andy
(DEHL-mohr, AN-dee) **NSH.**

Defense. Shoots right. 6'1", 200 lbs. Born, LaSalle, Ont., December 26, 1976.

Season	Club	League	GP	G	A	Pts	PIM	PP	SH	GW	S	%	+/-	TF	F%	H	SB	Min	GP	G	A	Pts	PIM	PP	SH	GW
1992-93	Chatham	OJHL-B	47	4	21	25	38																			
1993-94	North Bay	OHL	45	2	7	9	33												17	0	0	0	2			
1994-95	North Bay	OHL	40	2	14	16	21																			
	Sarnia Sting	OHL	27	5	13	18	27												3	0	0	0	2			
1995-96	Sarnia Sting	OHL	64	21	38	59	45												10	3	7	10	2			
1996-97	Sarnia Sting	OHL	64	18	60	78	39												12	2	10	12	10			
	Fredericton	AHL	4	0	1	1	0																			
1997-98	Philadelphia	AHL	73	9	30	39	46												18	4	4	8	21			
1998-99	**Philadelphia**	**NHL**	**2**	**0**	**1**	**1**	**0**	**0**	**0**	**0**	**2**	**0.0**	**–1**	**0**	**0.0**	**1**	**1**	**20:42**								
	Philadelphia	AHL	70	5	18	23	51												15	1	4	5	6			

			Regular Season																Playoffs							
Season	Club	League	GP	G	A	Pts	PIM	PP	SH	GW	S	%	+/-	TF	F%	H	SB	Min	GP	G	A	Pts	PIM	PP	SH	GW
99-2000	**Philadelphia**	**NHL**	**27**	**2**	**5**	**7**	**8**	**0**	**0**	**1**	**55**	**3.6**	**–1**	**0**	**0.0**	**24**	**31**	**17:17**	**18**	**5**	**2**	**7**	**14**	**1**	**0**	**1**
	Philadelphia	AHL	39	12	14	26	31																			
2000-01	**Philadelphia**	**NHL**	**66**	**5**	**9**	**14**	**16**	**2**	**0**	**0**	**119**	**4.2**	**2**	**0**	**0.0**	**70**	**65**	**17:39**	**2**	**1**	**0**	**1**	**2**	**0**	**0**	**1**
	NHL Totals		**95**	**7**	**15**	**22**	**24**	**2**	**0**	**1**	**176**	**4.0**		**0**	**0.0**	**95**	**97**	**17:36**	**20**	**6**	**2**	**8**	**16**	**1**	**0**	**2**

OHL First All-Star Team (1997)

Signed as a free agent by **Philadelphia**, June 9, 1997. Traded to **Nashville** by **Philadelphia** for Nashville's 3rd round choice in 2002 Entry Draft, July 31, 2001.

DEMITRA, Pavol

(deh-MEET-rah, PAH-vohl) **ST.L.**

Left wing. Shoots left. 5'11", 203 lbs. Born, Dubnica, Czech., November 29, 1974. Ottawa's 9th choice, 227th overall, in 1993 Entry Draft.

Season	Club	League	GP	G	A	Pts	PIM	PP	SH	GW	S	%	+/-	TF	F%	H	SB	Min	GP	G	A	Pts	PIM	PP	SH	GW
1991-92	Spartak Dubnica	Czech-2	28	13	10	23	12																			
1992-93	Spartak Dubnica	Czech-2	4	3	0	3																				
	Dukla Trencin	Czech.	46	11	17	28	0																			
1993-94	**Ottawa**	**NHL**	**12**	**1**	**1**	**2**	**4**	**1**	**0**	**0**	**10**	**10.0**	**–7**													
	P.E.I. Senators	AHL	41	18	23	41	8																			
1994-95	P.E.I. Senators	AHL	61	26	48	74	23												5	0	7	7	0			
	Ottawa	**NHL**	**16**	**4**	**3**	**7**	**0**	**1**	**0**	**0**	**21**	**19.0**	**–4**													
1995-96	**Ottawa**	**NHL**	**31**	**7**	**10**	**17**	**6**	**2**	**0**	**1**	**66**	**10.6**	**–3**													
	P.E.I. Senators	AHL	48	28	53	81	44																			
1996-97	Dukla Trencin	Slovakia	1	1	1	2																				
	Las Vegas	IHL	22	8	13	21	10																			
	St. Louis	**NHL**	**8**	**3**	**0**	**3**	**2**	**2**	**0**	**1**	**15**	**20.0**	**0**						**6**	**1**	**3**	**4**	**6**	**0**	**0**	**0**
	Grand Rapids	IHL	42	20	30	50	24																			
1997-98	**St. Louis**	**NHL**	**61**	**22**	**30**	**52**	**22**	**4**	**4**	**6**	**147**	**15.0**	**11**						**10**	**3**	**3**	**6**	**2**	**0**	**0**	**0**
1998-99	**St. Louis**	**NHL**	**82**	**37**	**52**	**89**	**16**	**14**	**0**	**10**	**259**	**14.3**	**13**	**250**	**44.0**	**31**	**15**	**20:10**	**13**	**5**	**4**	**9**	**4**	**3**	**0**	**1**
99-2000	**St. Louis**	**NHL**	**71**	**28**	**47**	**75**	**8**	**8**	**0**	**4**	**241**	**11.6**	**34**	**41**	**39.0**	**15**	**15**	**19:13**								
2000-01	**St. Louis**	**NHL**	**44**	**20**	**25**	**45**	**16**	**5**	**0**	**5**	**124**	**16.1**	**27**	**8**	**37.5**	**9**	**5**	**18:03**	**15**	**2**	**4**	**6**	**2**	**0**	**0**	**1**
	NHL Totals		**325**	**122**	**168**	**290**	**74**	**37**	**4**	**27**	**883**	**13.8**		**299**	**43.1**	**55**	**35**	**19:21**	**44**	**11**	**14**	**25**	**14**	**3**	**0**	**2**

Won Lady Byng Trophy (2000) • Played in NHL All-Star Game (1999, 2000)

Traded to **St. Louis** by **Ottawa** for Christer Olsson, November 27, 1996. • Missed most of 2000-01 season recovering from eye (January 1, 2001 vs. Edmonton) and leg (February 1, 2001 vs. Columbus) injuries.

DEMPSEY, Nathan

(DEHMP-see, NAY-thun) **TOR.**

Defense. Shoots right. 6', 190 lbs. Born, Spruce Grove, Alta., July 14, 1974. Toronto's 12th choice, 245th overall, in 1992 Entry Draft.

Season	Club	League	GP	G	A	Pts	PIM	PP	SH	GW	S	%	+/-	TF	F%	H	SB	Min	GP	G	A	Pts	PIM	PP	SH	GW
1990-91	St. Albert Saints	AJHL	34	11	20	31	73																			
1991-92	Regina Pats	WHL	70	4	22	26	72																			
1992-93	Regina Pats	WHL	72	12	29	41	95												13	3	8	11	14			
	St. John's Leafs	AHL																	2	0	0	0	0			
1993-94	Regina Pats	WHL	56	14	36	50	100												4	0	0	0	4			
1994-95	St. John's Leafs	AHL	74	7	30	37	91												5	1	0	1	11			
1995-96	St. John's Leafs	AHL	73	5	15	20	103												4	1	0	1	9			
1996-97	**Toronto**	**NHL**	**14**	**1**	**1**	**2**	**2**	**0**	**0**	**0**	**11**	**9.1**	**–2**													
	St. John's Leafs	AHL	52	8	18	26	108												6	1	0	1	4			
1997-98	St. John's Leafs	AHL	68	12	16	28	85												4	0	0	0	0			
1998-99	St. John's Leafs	AHL	67	2	29	31	70												5	0	1	1	2			
99-2000	**Toronto**	**NHL**	**6**	**0**	**2**	**2**	**2**	**0**	**0**	**0**	**3**	**0.0**	**2**	**1**	**0.0**	**4**	**2**	**13:40**								
	St. John's Leafs	AHL	44	15	12	27	40																			
2000-01	**Toronto**	**NHL**	**25**	**1**	**9**	**10**	**4**	**1**	**0**	**0**	**31**	**3.2**	**13**	**0**	**0.0**	**37**	**18**	**15:53**								
	St. John's Leafs	AHL	55	11	28	39	60												4	0	4	4	8			
	NHL Totals		**45**	**2**	**12**	**14**	**8**	**1**	**0**	**0**	**45**	**4.4**		**1**	**0.0**	**41**	**20**	**15:27**								

WHL East Second All-Star Team (1994)

DESCOTEAUX, Matthieu

(DAY-koh-toh, MAT-yoo) **MTL.**

Defense. Shoots left. 6'4", 208 lbs. Born, Pierreville, Que., September 23, 1977. Edmonton's 2nd choice, 19th overall, in 1996 Entry Draft.

Season	Club	League	GP	G	A	Pts	PIM	PP	SH	GW	S	%	+/-	TF	F%	H	SB	Min	GP	G	A	Pts	PIM	PP	SH	GW
1993-94	Cap-d-Madelaine	QAAA	43	2	5	7	26																			
1994-95	Shawinigan	QMJHL	50	3	2	5	28												15	1	1	2	19			
1995-96	Shawinigan	QMJHL	69	2	13	15	129												6	0	0	0	6			
1996-97	Shawinigan	QMJHL	38	6	18	24	121																			
	Hull Olympiques	QMJHL	32	6	19	25	34												14	1	8	9	29			
1997-98	Hamilton Bulldogs	AHL	67	2	8	10	70												2	0	0	0	0			
1998-99	Hamilton Bulldogs	AHL	74	6	12	18	49												4	0	0	0	0			
99-2000	Hamilton Bulldogs	AHL	49	5	7	12	29																			
	Quebec Citadelles	AHL	12	0	6	6	6												2	0	1	1	0			
2000-01	**Montreal**	**NHL**	**5**	**1**	**1**	**2**	**4**	**1**	**0**	**0**	**6**	**16.7**	**–2**	**0**	**0.0**	**5**	**3**	**15:10**								
	Quebec Citadelles	AHL	73	16	27	43	38												7	0	3	3	4			
	NHL Totals		**5**	**1**	**1**	**2**	**4**	**1**	**0**	**0**	**6**	**16.7**		**0**	**0.0**	**5**	**3**	**15:10**								

Traded to **Montreal** by **Edmonton** with Christian Laflamme for Igor Ulanov and Alain Nasreddine, March 9, 2000.

DESJARDINS, Eric

(deh-ZHAHR-dai, AIR-ihk) **PHI.**

Defense. Shoots right. 6'1", 205 lbs. Born, Rouyn, Que., June 14, 1969. Montreal's 3rd choice, 38th overall, in 1987 Entry Draft.

Season	Club	League	GP	G	A	Pts	PIM	PP	SH	GW	S	%	+/-	TF	F%	H	SB	Min	GP	G	A	Pts	PIM	PP	SH	GW
1985-86	Laval-Laurentide	QAAA	42	6	30	36	54												8	2	10	12	14			
1986-87	Granby Bisons	QMJHL	66	14	24	38	178												8	3	2	5	10			
1987-88	Granby Bisons	QMJHL	62	18	49	67	138												5	0	3	3	10			
	Sherbrooke	AHL	3	0	0	0	6												4	0	2	2	2			
1988-89	**Montreal**	**NHL**	**36**	**2**	**12**	**14**	**26**	**1**	**0**	**0**	**39**	**5.1**	**9**						**14**	**1**	**1**	**2**	**6**	**1**	**0**	**0**
1989-90	**Montreal**	**NHL**	**55**	**3**	**13**	**16**	**51**	**1**	**0**	**0**	**48**	**6.3**	**1**						**6**	**0**	**0**	**0**	**10**	**0**	**0**	**0**
1990-91	**Montreal**	**NHL**	**62**	**7**	**18**	**25**	**27**	**0**	**0**	**1**	**114**	**6.1**	**7**						**13**	**1**	**4**	**5**	**8**	**1**	**0**	**0**
1991-92	**Montreal**	**NHL**	**77**	**6**	**32**	**38**	**50**	**4**	**0**	**2**	**141**	**4.3**	**17**						**11**	**3**	**3**	**6**	**4**	**1**	**0**	**0**
1992-93♦	**Montreal**	**NHL**	**82**	**13**	**32**	**45**	**98**	**7**	**0**	**1**	**163**	**8.0**	**20**						**20**	**4**	**10**	**14**	**23**	**1**	**0**	**1**
1993-94	**Montreal**	**NHL**	**84**	**12**	**23**	**35**	**97**	**6**	**1**	**3**	**193**	**6.2**	**–1**						**7**	**0**	**2**	**2**	**4**	**0**	**0**	**0**
1994-95	**Montreal**	**NHL**	**9**	**0**	**6**	**6**	**2**	**0**	**0**	**0**	**14**	**0.0**	**2**													
	Philadelphia	**NHL**	**34**	**5**	**18**	**23**	**12**	**1**	**0**	**1**	**79**	**6.3**	**10**						**15**	**4**	**4**	**8**	**10**	**1**	**0**	**2**
1995-96	**Philadelphia**	**NHL**	**80**	**7**	**40**	**47**	**45**	**5**	**0**	**2**	**184**	**3.8**	**19**						**12**	**0**	**6**	**6**	**2**	**0**	**0**	**0**
1996-97	**Philadelphia**	**NHL**	**82**	**12**	**34**	**46**	**50**	**5**	**1**	**1**	**183**	**6.6**	**25**						**19**	**2**	**8**	**10**	**12**	**0**	**0**	**0**
1997-98	**Philadelphia**	**NHL**	**77**	**6**	**27**	**33**	**36**	**2**	**1**	**0**	**150**	**4.0**	**11**						**5**	**0**	**1**	**1**	**0**	**0**	**0**	**0**
	Canada	Olympics	6	0	0	0	2																			
1998-99	**Philadelphia**	**NHL**	**68**	**15**	**36**	**51**	**38**	**6**	**0**	**2**	**190**	**7.9**	**18**	**0**	**0.0**	**36**	**108**	**25:48**	**6**	**2**	**2**	**4**	**4**	**1**	**0**	**1**
99-2000	**Philadelphia**	**NHL**	**81**	**14**	**41**	**55**	**32**	**8**	**0**	**4**	**207**	**6.8**	**20**	**1**	**0.0**	**28**	**141**	**27:01**	**18**	**2**	**10**	**12**	**2**	**1**	**0**	**1**
2000-01	**Philadelphia**	**NHL**	**79**	**15**	**33**	**48**	**50**	**6**	**1**	**4**	**187**	**8.0**	**–3**	**3**	**100.0**	**38**	**122**	**26:27**	**6**	**1**	**1**	**2**	**0**	**0**	**0**	**0**
	NHL Totals		**906**	**117**	**365**	**482**	**614**	**52**	**4**	**21**	**1892**	**6.2**		**4**	**75.0**	**102**	**371**	**26:27**	**152**	**20**	**52**	**72**	**85**	**7**	**0**	**5**

QMJHL Second All-Star Team (1987) • QMJHL First All-Star Team (1988) • NHL Second All-Star Team (1999, 2000) • Played in NHL All-Star Game (1992, 1996, 2000)

Traded to **Philadelphia** by **Montreal** with Gilbert Dionne and John LeClair for Mark Recchi and Philadelphia's 3rd round choice (Martin Hohenberger) in 1995 Entry Draft, February 9, 1995.

DEULING, Jarrett

(DEW-lihng, JAIR-uht)

Left wing. Shoots left. 6', 205 lbs. Born, Vernon, B.C., March 4, 1974. NY Islanders' 2nd choice, 56th overall, in 1992 Entry Draft.

Season	Club	League	GP	G	A	Pts	PIM	PP	SH	GW	S	%	+/-	TF	F%	H	SB	Min	GP	G	A	Pts	PIM	PP	SH	GW
1989-90	Whitehorse Bears	AAHL	28	34	48	72	84																			
1990-91	Kamloops Blazers	WHL	48	4	12	16	43												12	5	2	7	7			
1991-92	Kamloops Blazers	WHL	68	28	26	54	79												17	10	6	16	18			
1992-93	Kamloops Blazers	WHL	68	31	32	63	93												13	6	7	13	14			
1993-94	Kamloops Blazers	WHL	70	44	59	103	171												18	*13	8	21	43			
1994-95	Worcester	AHL	63	11	8	19	37																			
1995-96	**NY Islanders**	**NHL**	**14**	**0**	**1**	**1**	**11**	**0**	**0**	**0**	**11**	**0.0**	**–1**													
	Worcester	AHL	57	16	7	23	57												4	1	2	3	2			

			Regular Season																Playoffs							
Season	Club	League	GP	G	A	Pts	PIM	PP	SH	GW	S	%	+/-	TF	F%	H	SB	Min	GP	G	A	Pts	PIM	PP	SH	GW
1996-97	**NY Islanders**	**NHL**	1	0	0	0	0	0	0	0	0	0.0	0	....	....	....	....	....	....	....	....	....	....	....	....	....
	Kentucky	AHL	58	15	31	46	57	....	....	....	....	....	....	....	....	....	....	....	4	3	0	3	8	....	....	....
1997-98	Milwaukee	IHL	64	18	18	36	84	....	....	....	....	....	....	....	....	....	....	....	10	4	3	7	36	....	....	....
1998-99	Kentucky	AHL	60	22	31	53	68	....	....	....	....	....	....	....	....	....	....	....	12	3	6	9	8	....	....	....
99-2000	Kentucky	AHL	75	17	25	42	83	....	....	....	....	....	....	....	....	....	....	....	8	1	1	2	6	....	....	....
2000-01	Kentucky	AHL	54	10	29	39	61	....	....	....	....	....	....	....	....	....	....	....	3	0	0	0	0	....	....	....
	NHL Totals		15	0	1	1	11	0	0	0	11	0.0		....	....	....	....	....	....	....	....	....	....	....	....	....

Signed as a free agent by **San Jose**, August 27, 1998.

DEVEREAUX, Boyd

(DEH-vuhr-oh, BOID) **DET.**

Center. Shoots left. 6'2", 195 lbs. Born, Seaforth, Ont., April 16, 1978. Edmonton's 1st choice, 6th overall, in 1996 Entry Draft.

Season	Club	League	GP	G	A	Pts	PIM	PP	SH	GW	S	%	+/-	TF	F%	H	SB	Min	GP	G	A	Pts	PIM	PP	SH	GW
1992-93	Seaforth Sailors	OJHL-D	34	7	20	27	13	....	....	....	....	....	....	....	....	....	....	....	....	....	....	....	....	....	....	....
1993-94	Stratford Cullitons	OJHL-B	46	12	27	39	8	....	....	....	....	....	....	....	....	....	....	....	....	....	....	....	....	....	....	....
1994-95	Stratford Cullitons	OJHL-B	45	31	74	105	21	....	....	....	....	....	....	....	....	....	....	....	....	....	....	....	....	....	....	....
1995-96	Kitchener	OHL	66	20	38	58	35	....	....	....	....	....	....	....	....	....	....	....	12	3	7	10	4	....	....	....
1996-97	Kitchener	OHL	54	28	41	69	37	....	....	....	....	....	....	....	....	....	....	....	13	4	11	15	8	....	....	....
	Hamilton Bulldogs	AHL	....	....	....	....	....	....	....	....	....	....	....	....	....	....	....	....	1	0	1	1	0	....	....	....
1997-98	**Edmonton**	**NHL**	38	1	4	5	6	0	0	0	27	3.7	–5	....	....	....	....	....	....	....	....	....	....	....	....	....
	Hamilton Bulldogs	AHL	14	5	6	11	6	....	....	....	....	....	....	....	....	....	....	....	9	1	1	2	8	....	....	....
1998-99	**Edmonton**	**NHL**	61	6	8	14	23	0	1	4	39	15.4	2	409	42.8	32	32	10:09	1	0	0	0	0	0	0	0
	Hamilton Bulldogs	AHL	7	4	6	10	2	....	....	....	....	....	....	....	....	....	....	....	8	0	3	3	4	....	....	....
99-2000	**Edmonton**	**NHL**	76	8	19	27	20	0	1	2	108	7.4	7	241	34.9	54	26	12:36	....	....	....	....	....	....	....	....
2000-01	**Detroit**	**NHL**	55	5	6	11	14	0	0	0	66	7.6	1	124	37.1	45	18	10:08	2	0	0	0	0	0	0	0
	NHL Totals		230	20	37	57	63	0	2	6	240	8.3		774	39.4	131	76	11:07	3	0	0	0	0	0	0	0

Canadian Major Junior Scholastic Player of the Year (1996)

Signed as a free agent by **Detroit**, August 23, 2000.

de VRIES, Greg

(deh-VREES, GREHG) **COL.**

Defense. Shoots left. 6'3", 215 lbs. Born, Sundridge, Ont., January 4, 1973.

Season	Club	League	GP	G	A	Pts	PIM	PP	SH	GW	S	%	+/-	TF	F%	H	SB	Min	GP	G	A	Pts	PIM	PP	SH	GW
1988-89	Cortina Astros	OMHA	35	28	40	68	....	....	....	....	....	....	....	....	....	....	....	....	....	....	....	....	....	....	....	....
1989-90	Aurora Eagles	OJHL-B	42	1	16	17	32	....	....	....	....	....	....	....	....	....	....	....	....	....	....	....	....	....	....	....
1990-91	Stratford Cullitons	OJHL-B	40	8	32	40	120	....	....	....	....	....	....	....	....	....	....	....	3	2	1	3	20	....	....	....
1991-92	Thorold Eagles	OJHL-B	3	0	0	0	0	....	....	....	....	....	....	....	....	....	....	....	....	....	....	....	....	....	....	....
	Bowling Green	CCHA	24	0	3	3	20	....	....	....	....	....	....	....	....	....	....	....	....	....	....	....	....	....	....	....
1992-93	Niagara Falls	OHL	62	3	23	26	86	....	....	....	....	....	....	....	....	....	....	....	4	0	1	1	6	....	....	....
1993-94	Niagara Falls	OHL	64	5	40	45	135	....	....	....	....	....	....	....	....	....	....	....	....	....	....	....	....	....	....	....
	Cape Breton	AHL	9	0	0	0	11	....	....	....	....	....	....	....	....	....	....	....	1	0	0	0	0	....	....	....
1994-95	Cape Breton	AHL	77	5	19	24	68	....	....	....	....	....	....	....	....	....	....	....	....	....	....	....	....	....	....	....
1995-96	**Edmonton**	**NHL**	13	1	1	2	12	0	0	0	8	12.5	–2	....	....	....	....	....	....	....	....	....	....	....	....	....
	Cape Breton	AHL	58	9	30	39	174	....	....	....	....	....	....	....	....	....	....	....	....	....	....	....	....	....	....	....
1996-97	**Edmonton**	**NHL**	37	0	4	4	52	0	0	0	31	0.0	–2	....	....	....	....	....	12	0	1	1	8	0	0	0
	Hamilton Bulldogs	AHL	34	4	14	18	26	....	....	....	....	....	....	....	....	....	....	....	....	....	....	....	....	....	....	....
1997-98	**Edmonton**	**NHL**	65	7	4	11	80	1	0	0	53	13.2	–17	....	....	....	....	....	7	0	0	0	21	0	0	0
1998-99	**Nashville**	**NHL**	6	0	0	0	4	0	0	0	1	1.0	–4	0	0.0	12	7	18:11	....	....	....	....	....	....	....	....
	Colorado	**NHL**	67	1	3	4	60	0	0	0	56	56.0	–3	1	100.0	85	69	16:23	19	0	2	2	22	0	0	0
99-2000	**Colorado**	**NHL**	69	2	7	9	73	0	0	0	40	5.0	–7	0	0.0	87	61	14:59	5	0	0	0	4	0	0	0
2000-01♦	**Colorado**	**NHL**	79	5	12	17	51	0	0	0	76	6.6	23	0	0.0	142	93	17:06	23	0	1	1	20	0	0	0
	NHL Totals		336	16	31	47	332	1	0	0	265	6.0		1	100.0	326	230	16:15	66	0	4	4	75	0	0	0

Signed as a free agent by **Edmonton**, March 20, 1994. Traded to **Nashville** by **Edmonton** with Eric Fichaud and Drake Berehowsky for Mikhail Shtalenkov and Jim Dowd, October 1, 1998. Traded to **Colorado** by **Nashville** for Colorado's 2nd round choice (Ed Hill) in 1999 Entry Draft, October 24, 1998.

DIDUCK, Gerald

(DIH-duhk, JAIR-ohld)

Defense. Shoots right. 6'1", 216 lbs. Born, Edmonton, Alta., April 6, 1965. NY Islanders' 2nd choice, 16th overall, in 1983 Entry Draft.

Season	Club	League	GP	G	A	Pts	PIM	PP	SH	GW	S	%	+/-	TF	F%	H	SB	Min	GP	G	A	Pts	PIM	PP	SH	GW
1981-82	Lethbridge	WHL	71	1	15	16	81	....	....	....	....	....	....	....	....	....	....	....	12	0	3	3	27	....	....	....
1982-83	Lethbridge	WHL	67	8	16	24	151	....	....	....	....	....	....	....	....	....	....	....	20	3	12	15	49	....	....	....
1983-84	Lethbridge	WHL	65	10	24	34	133	....	....	....	....	....	....	....	....	....	....	....	5	1	4	5	27	....	....	....
	Indianapolis	CHL	....	....	....	....	....	....	....	....	....	....	....	....	....	....	....	....	10	1	6	7	19	....	....	....
1984-85	**NY Islanders**	**NHL**	65	2	8	10	80	0	0	0	52	3.8	2	....	....	....	....	....	....	....	....	....	....	....	....	....
1985-86	**NY Islanders**	**NHL**	10	1	2	3	2	0	0	0	6	16.7	5	....	....	....	....	....	....	....	....	....	....	....	....	....
	Springfield	AHL	61	6	14	20	173	....	....	....	....	....	....	....	....	....	....	....	....	....	....	....	....	....	....	....
1986-87	**NY Islanders**	**NHL**	30	2	3	5	67	0	0	0	54	3.7	–3	....	....	....	....	....	14	0	1	1	35	0	0	0
	Springfield	AHL	45	6	8	14	120	....	....	....	....	....	....	....	....	....	....	....	....	....	....	....	....	....	....	....
1987-88	**NY Islanders**	**NHL**	68	7	12	19	113	4	0	1	128	5.5	22	....	....	....	....	....	6	1	0	1	42	1	0	0
1988-89	**NY Islanders**	**NHL**	65	11	21	32	155	6	0	0	132	8.3	9	....	....	....	....	....	....	....	....	....	....	....	....	....
1989-90	**NY Islanders**	**NHL**	76	3	17	20	163	1	0	0	102	2.9	2	....	....	....	....	....	5	0	0	0	12	0	0	0
1990-91	**Montreal**	**NHL**	32	1	2	3	39	0	0	0	34	2.9	3	....	....	....	....	....	....	....	....	....	....	....	....	....
	Vancouver	**NHL**	31	3	7	10	66	0	0	1	66	4.5	–8	....	....	....	....	....	6	1	0	1	11	1	0	0
1991-92	**Vancouver**	**NHL**	77	6	21	27	229	2	0	1	128	4.7	–3	....	....	....	....	....	5	0	0	0	10	0	0	0
1992-93	**Vancouver**	**NHL**	80	6	14	20	171	0	1	0	92	6.5	32	....	....	....	....	....	12	4	2	6	12	0	0	0
1993-94	**Vancouver**	**NHL**	55	1	10	11	72	0	0	0	50	2.0	2	....	....	....	....	....	24	1	7	8	22	0	0	0
1994-95	**Vancouver**	**NHL**	22	1	3	4	15	1	0	0	25	4.0	–8	....	....	....	....	....	....	....	....	....	....	....	....	....
	Chicago	**NHL**	13	1	0	1	48	1	0	0	42	2.4	3	....	....	....	....	....	16	1	3	4	22	0	0	0
1995-96	**Hartford**	**NHL**	79	1	9	10	88	0	0	0	93	1.1	7	....	....	....	....	....	....	....	....	....	....	....	....	....
1996-97	**Hartford**	**NHL**	56	1	10	11	40	0	0	1	59	1.7	–9	....	....	....	....	....	....	....	....	....	....	....	....	....
	Phoenix	**NHL**	11	1	2	3	23	1	0	0	21	4.8	2	....	....	....	....	....	7	0	0	0	10	0	0	0
1997-98	**Phoenix**	**NHL**	78	8	10	18	118	1	0	4	104	7.7	14	....	....	....	....	....	6	0	2	2	20	0	0	0
1998-99	**Phoenix**	**NHL**	44	0	2	2	72	0	0	0	39	0.0	9	0	0.0	127	50	18:32	3	0	0	0	2	0	0	0
99-2000	Canada	Nat-Team	12	3	0	3	6	....	....	....	....	....	....	....	....	....	....	....	....	....	....	....	....	....	....	....
	Toronto	**NHL**	26	0	3	3	33	0	0	0	18	0.0	2	0	0.0	84	20	15:25	10	0	1	1	14	0	0	0
2000-01	**Dallas**	**NHL**	14	0	0	0	18	0	0	0	8	0.0	4	0	0.0	32	7	10:44	....	....	....	....	....	....	....	....
	NHL Totals		932	56	156	212	1612	17	1	8	1253	4.5		0	0.0	243	77	16:16	114	8	16	24	212	2	0	0

Traded to **Montreal** by **NY Islanders** for Craig Ludwig, September 4, 1990. Traded to **Vancouver** by **Montreal** for Vancouver's 4th round choice (Vladimir Vujtek) in 1991 Entry Draft, January 12, 1991. Traded to **Chicago** by **Vancouver** for Bogdan Savenko and Hartford's 3rd round choice (previously acquired, Vancouver selected Larry Courville) in 1995 Entry Draft, April 7, 1995. Signed as a free agent by **Hartford**, August 24, 1995. Traded to **Phoenix** by **Hartford** for Chris Murray, March 18, 1997. Signed as a free agent by **Toronto**, February 3, 2000. Traded to **Dallas** by **Toronto** for future considerations, October 29, 2000. • Missed majority of 2000-01 season recovering from ankle injury suffered in game vs. San Jose, December 6, 2000.

DiMAIO, Rob

(duh-MIGH-oh, RAWB) **DAL.**

Center. Shoots right. 5'10", 190 lbs. Born, Calgary, Alta., February 19, 1968. NY Islanders' 6th choice, 118th overall, in 1987 Entry Draft.

Season	Club	League	GP	G	A	Pts	PIM	PP	SH	GW	S	%	+/-	TF	F%	H	SB	Min	GP	G	A	Pts	PIM	PP	SH	GW
1984-85	Kamloops Blazers	WHL	55	9	18	27	29	....	....	....	....	....	....	....	....	....	....	....	7	1	3	4	2	....	....	....
1985-86	Kamloops Blazers	WHL	6	1	0	1	0	....	....	....	....	....	....	....	....	....	....	....	....	....	....	....	....	....	....	....
	Medicine Hat	WHL	55	20	30	50	82	....	....	....	....	....	....	....	....	....	....	....	22	6	6	12	39	....	....	....
1986-87	Medicine Hat	WHL	70	27	43	70	130	....	....	....	....	....	....	....	....	....	....	....	20	7	11	18	46	....	....	....
1987-88	Medicine Hat	WHL	54	47	43	90	120	....	....	....	....	....	....	....	....	....	....	....	14	12	19	*31	59	....	....	....
1988-89	**NY Islanders**	**NHL**	16	1	0	1	30	0	0	1	16	6.3	–6	....	....	....	....	....	....	....	....	....	....	....	....	....
	Springfield	AHL	40	13	18	31	67	....	....	....	....	....	....	....	....	....	....	....	....	....	....	....	....	....	....	....
1989-90	**NY Islanders**	**NHL**	7	0	0	0	2	0	0	0	2	0.0	0	....	....	....	....	....	1	1	0	1	4	0	0	0
	Springfield	AHL	54	25	27	52	69	....	....	....	....	....	....	....	....	....	....	....	16	4	7	11	45	....	....	....
1990-91	**NY Islanders**	**NHL**	1	0	0	0	0	0	0	0	0	0.0	0	....	....	....	....	....	....	....	....	....	....	....	....	....
	Capital District	AHL	12	3	4	7	22	....	....	....	....	....	....	....	....	....	....	....	....	....	....	....	....	....	....	....
1991-92	**NY Islanders**	**NHL**	50	5	2	7	43	0	2	0	43	11.6	–23	....	....	....	....	....	....	....	....	....	....	....	....	....
1992-93	**Tampa Bay**	**NHL**	54	9	15	24	62	2	0	0	75	12.0	0	....	....	....	....	....	....	....	....	....	....	....	....	....
1993-94	**Tampa Bay**	**NHL**	39	8	7	15	40	2	0	1	51	15.7	–5	....	....	....	....	....	....	....	....	....	....	....	....	....
	Philadelphia	**NHL**	14	3	5	8	6	0	0	1	30	10.0	1	....	....	....	....	....	....	....	....	....	....	....	....	....
1994-95	**Philadelphia**	**NHL**	36	3	1	4	53	0	0	0	34	8.8	8	....	....	....	....	....	15	2	4	6	4	0	1	1
1995-96	**Philadelphia**	**NHL**	59	6	15	21	58	1	1	0	49	12.2	0	....	....	....	....	....	3	0	0	0	0	0	0	0
1996-97	**Boston**	**NHL**	72	13	15	28	82	0	3	2	152	8.6	–21	....	....	....	....	....	....	....	....	....	....	....	....	....

			Regular Season																Playoffs							
Season	Club	League	GP	G	A	Pts	PIM	PP	SH	GW	S	%	+/-	TF	F%	H	SB	Min	GP	G	A	Pts	PIM	PP	SH	GW
1997-98	Boston	NHL	79	10	17	27	82	0	0	4	112	8.9	–13						6	1	0	1	8	0	0	0
1998-99	Boston	NHL	71	7	14	21	95	1	0	0	121	5.8	–14	83	45.8	106	26	16:41	12	2	0	2	8	0	0	1
99-2000	Boston	NHL	50	5	16	21	42	0	0	0	93	5.4	–1	278	44.2	103	20	16:47								
	NY Rangers	NHL	12	1	3	4	8	0	0	0	18	5.6	–8	1	0.0	16	6	15:30								
2000-01	Carolina	NHL	74	6	18	24	54	0	2	1	99	6.1	–14	46	43.5	107	31	14:58	6	0	0	0	4	0	0	0
	NHL Totals		634	77	128	205	657	6	8	10	895	8.6		408	44.4	332	83	16:02	43	6	4	10	28	0	1	2

Won Stafford Smythe Memorial Trophy (Memorial Cup Tournament MVP) (1988)

Claimed by **Tampa Bay** from **NY Islanders** in Expansion Draft, June 18, 1992. Traded to **Philadelphia** by **Tampa Bay** for Jim Cummins and Philadelphia's 4th round choice (later traded back to Philadelphia - Philadelphia selected Radovan Somik) in 1995 Entry Draft, March 18, 1994. Claimed by **San Jose** from **Philadelphia** in NHL Waiver Draft, September 30, 1996. Traded to **Boston** by **San Jose** for Boston's 5th round choice (Adam Nittel) in 1997 Entry Draft, September 30, 1996. Traded to **NY Rangers** by **Boston** for Mike Knuble, March 10, 2000. Traded to **Carolina** by **NY Rangers** with Darren Langdon for Sandy McCarthy and Carolina's 4th round choice (Bryce Lampman) in 2001 Entry Draft, August 4, 2000. Signed as a free agent by **Dallas**, July 1, 2001.

DINEEN, Kevin

(DIH-neen, KEH-vihn) **CBJ**

Right wing. Shoots right. 5'11", 190 lbs. Born, Quebec City, Que., October 28, 1963. Hartford's 3rd choice, 56th overall, in 1982 Entry Draft.

Season	Club	League	GP	G	A	Pts	PIM	PP	SH	GW	S	%	+/-	TF	F%	H	SB	Min	GP	G	A	Pts	PIM	PP	SH	GW
1980-81	St. Michael's	MTJHL	40	15	28	43	167																			
1981-82	U. of Denver	WCHA	26	10	10	20	70																			
1982-83	U. of Denver	WCHA	36	16	13	29	108																			
1983-84	Canada	Nat-Team	52	5	11	16	2																			
	Canada	Olympics	7	0	0	0	8																			
1984-85	Hartford	NHL	57	25	16	41	120	8	4	2	141	17.7	–6													
	Binghamton	AHL	25	15	8	23	41																			
1985-86	Hartford	NHL	57	33	35	68	124	6	0	8	167	19.8	16						10	6	7	13	18	1	0	2
1986-87	Hartford	NHL	78	40	39	79	110	11	0	7	234	17.1	7						6	2	1	3	31	1	0	0
1987-88	Hartford	NHL	74	25	25	50	217	5	0	4	223	11.2	–14						6	4	4	8	8	1	0	1
1988-89	Hartford	NHL	79	45	44	89	167	20	1	4	294	15.3	–6						4	1	0	1	10	0	0	0
1989-90	Hartford	NHL	67	25	41	66	164	8	2	2	214	11.7	7						6	3	2	5	18	0	0	1
1990-91	Hartford	NHL	61	17	30	47	104	4	0	2	161	10.6	–15						6	1	0	1	16	0	0	0
1991-92	Hartford	NHL	16	4	2	6	23	1	0	1	28	14.3	–6													
	Philadelphia	NHL	64	26	30	56	130	5	3	4	197	13.2	1													
1992-93	Philadelphia	NHL	83	35	28	63	201	6	3	7	241	14.5	14													
1993-94	Philadelphia	NHL	71	19	23	42	113	5	1	2	156	12.2	–9													
1994-95	Houston Aeros	IHL	17	6	4	10	42																			
	Philadelphia	NHL	40	8	5	13	39	4	0	2	55	14.5	–1						15	6	4	10	18	1	0	1
1995-96	Philadelphia	NHL	26	0	2	2	50	0	0	0	31	0.0	–8													
	Hartford	NHL	20	2	7	9	67	0	0	0	35	5.7	7													
1996-97	Hartford	NHL	78	19	29	48	141	8	0	5	185	10.3	–6													
1997-98	Carolina	NHL	54	7	16	23	105	0	0	1	96	7.3	–7													
1998-99	Carolina	NHL	67	8	10	18	97	0	0	1	86	9.3	5	6	16.7	77	6	9:58	6	0	0	0	8	0	0	0
99-2000	Ottawa	NHL	67	4	8	12	57	0	0	1	71	5.6	2	10	50.0	67	14	9:31								
2000-01	Columbus	NHL	66	8	7	15	126	0	0	3	74	10.8	2	13	30.8	101	18	10:37								
	NHL Totals		1125	350	397	747	2155	91	14	56	2689	13.0		29	34.5	245	38	10:02	59	23	18	41	127	4	0	5

Won Bud Light/NHL Man of the Year Award (1991) • Played in NHL All-Star Game (1988, 1989)

Traded to **Philadelphia** by **Hartford** for Murray Craven and Philadelphia's 4th round choice (Kevin Smyth) in 1992 Entry Draft, November 13, 1991. Traded to **Hartford** by **Philadelphia** for Hartford/Carolina's 3rd (Kris Mallette) and 7th (later traded back to Hartford/Carolina - Carolina selected Andrew Merrick) round choices in 1997 Entry Draft, December 28, 1995. Transferred to **Carolina** after **Hartford** franchise relocated, June 25, 1997. Signed as a free agent by **Ottawa**, September 1, 1999. Selected by **Columbus** from **Ottawa** in Expansion Draft, June 23, 2000.

DINGMAN, Chris

(DIHNG-man, KRIHS) **CAR.**

Left wing. Shoots left. 6'4", 245 lbs. Born, Edmonton, Alta., July 6, 1976. Calgary's 1st choice, 19th overall, in 1994 Entry Draft.

Season	Club	League	GP	G	A	Pts	PIM	PP	SH	GW	S	%	+/-	TF	F%	H	SB	Min	GP	G	A	Pts	PIM	PP	SH	GW
1991-92	Edmonton Mercs	AMHL	36	23	18	41	72																			
1992-93	Brandon	WHL	50	10	17	27	64												4	0	0	0	0			
1993-94	Brandon	WHL	45	21	20	41	77												13	1	7	8	39			
1994-95	Brandon	WHL	66	40	43	83	201												3	1	0	1	9			
1995-96	Brandon	WHL	40	16	29	45	109												19	12	11	23	60			
	Saint John Flames	AHL																	1	0	0	0	0			
1996-97	Saint John Flames	AHL	71	5	6	11	195																			
1997-98	Calgary	NHL	70	3	3	6	149	1	0	0	47	6.4	–11													
1998-99	Calgary	NHL	2	0	0	0	17	0	0	0	1	0.0	–2	0	0.0	3	1	8:11								
	Saint John Flames	AHL	50	5	7	12	140																			
	Colorado	NHL	1	0	0	0	7	0	0	0	0	0.0	0	0	0.0	0	0	0:30								
	Hershey Bears	AHL	17	1	3	4	102												5	0	2	2	6			
99-2000	Colorado	NHL	68	8	3	11	132	2	0	1	54	14.8	–2	2	0.0	73	18	6:29								
2000-01♦	Colorado	NHL	41	1	1	2	108	0	0	0	33	3.0	–3	0	0.0	74	9	6:26	16	0	4	4	14	0	0	0
	NHL Totals		182	12	7	19	413	3	0	1	135	8.9		2	0.0	150	28	6:27	16	0	4	4	14	0	0	0

Traded to **Colorado** by **Calgary** with Theoren Fleury for Rene Corbet, Wade Belak, Robyn Regehr and Colorado's 2nd round compensatory choice (Jarret Stoll) in 2000 Entry Draft, February 28, 1999. • Missed majority of 2000-01 season recovering from knee injury suffered in game vs. Ottawa, November 15, 2000. Traded to **Carolina** by **Colorado** for Carolina's 5th round choice (Mikko Viitanen) in 2001 Entry Draft, June 24, 2001.

DIONNE, Gilbert

(dee-AHN, ZHIHL-bair)

Left wing. Shoots left. 6', 194 lbs. Born, Drummondville, Que., September 19, 1970. Montreal's 5th choice, 81st overall, in 1990 Entry Draft.

Season	Club	League	GP	G	A	Pts	PIM	PP	SH	GW	S	%	+/-	TF	F%	H	SB	Min	GP	G	A	Pts	PIM	PP	SH	GW
1986-87	Niagara Falls	OJHL-B	17	9	6	15	16																			
1987-88	Niagara Falls	OJHL-B	36	36	48	84	60																			
1988-89	Kitchener	OHL	66	11	33	44	13												5	1	1	2	4			
1989-90	Kitchener	OHL	64	48	57	105	85												17	13	10	23	22			
1990-91	Montreal	NHL	2	0	0	0	0	0	0	0	0	0.0	–2													
	Fredericton	AHL	77	40	47	87	62												9	6	5	11	8			
1991-92	Montreal	NHL	39	21	13	34	10	7	0	2	90	23.3	7						11	3	4	7	10	1	0	1
	Fredericton	AHL	29	19	27	46	20																			
1992-93♦	Montreal	NHL	75	20	28	48	63	6	1	2	145	13.8	5						20	6	6	12	20	1	0	1
	Fredericton	AHL	3	4	3	7	0																			
1993-94	Montreal	NHL	74	19	26	45	31	3	0	5	162	11.7	–9						5	1	2	3	0	0	0	0
1994-95	Montreal	NHL	6	0	3	3	2	0	0	0	4	0.0	–3													
	Philadelphia	NHL	20	0	6	6	2	0	0	0	29	0.0	–1						3	0	0	0	4	0	0	0
1995-96	Philadelphia	NHL	2	0	1	1	0	0	0	0	0	0.0	0													
	Florida	NHL	5	1	2	3	0	0	0	0	12	8.3	0													
	Carolina	AHL	55	43	58	101	29																			
1996-97	Carolina	AHL	72	41	47	88	69																			
1997-98	Cincinnati	IHL	76	42	57	99	54												9	3	4	7	28			
1998-99	Cincinnati	IHL	76	35	53	88	123												3	0	2	2	6			
99-2000	Cincinnati	IHL	81	34	49	83	88												11	4	3	7	8			
2000-01	Cincinnati	IHL	80	23	43	66	46												5	0	2	2	0			
	NHL Totals		223	61	79	140	108	16	1	9	442	13.8							39	10	12	22	34	2	0	2

NHL All-Rookie Team (1992) • AHL Second All-Star Team (1996) • IHL First All-Star Team (1998) • IHL Second All-Star Team (2000)

Traded to **Philadelphia** by **Montreal** with Eric Desjardins and John LeClair for Mark Recchi and Philadelphia's 3rd round choice (Martin Hohenberger) in 1995 Entry Draft, February 9, 1995. Signed as a free agent by **Florida**, January 29, 1996. Signed as a free agent by **Cincinnati** (IHL), July 23, 1997. Signed as a free agent by **Carolina**, August 31, 1999.

DIVISEK, Tomas

(DIH-vih-sehk, TOH-mahs) **PHI.**

Center. Shoots left. 6'2", 204 lbs. Born, Most, Czech., July 19, 1979. Philadelphia's 9th choice, 195th overall, in 1998 Entry Draft.

Season	Club	League	GP	G	A	Pts	PIM	PP	SH	GW	S	%	+/-	TF	F%	H	SB	Min	GP	G	A	Pts	PIM	PP	SH	GW
1995-96	Slavia Praha-Jr.	Cze-Rep	36	20	27	47	12																			
1996-97	Slavia Praha-Jr.	Cze-Rep	41	17	25	42	18																			
	Slavia Praha	Cze-Rep	1	0	0	0	0																			
1997-98	Slavia Praha-Jr.	Cze-Rep	27	20	16	36	12																			
	Slavia Praha	Cze-Rep	22	2	0	2	8																			
1998-99	Slavia Praha	Cze-Rep	45	8	4	12	26																			
99-2000	Philadelphia	AHL	59	18	31	49	30												5	0	3	3	2			

			Regular Season																Playoffs							
Season	Club	League	GP	G	A	Pts	PIM	PP	SH	GW	S	%	+/-	TF	F%	H	SB	Min	GP	G	A	Pts	PIM	PP	SH	GW
2000-01	Philadelphia	NHL	2	0	0	0	0	0	0	0	2	0.0	−1	0	0.0	3	0	11:30								
	Philadelphia	AHL	45	10	22	32	33												10	4	9	13	4			
	NHL Totals		2	0	0	0	0	0	0	0	2	0.0		0	0.0	3	0	11:30								

DOAN, Shane

(DOHN, SHAYN) **PHX.**

Right wing. Shoots right. 6'2", 223 lbs. Born, Halkirk, Alta., October 10, 1976. Winnipeg's 1st choice, 7th overall, in 1995 Entry Draft.

1991-92	Killam Selects	AAHA	56	80	84	164	74																			
1992-93	Kamloops Blazers	WHL	51	7	12	19	65												13	0	1	1	8			
1993-94	Kamloops Blazers	WHL	52	24	24	48	88																			
1994-95	Kamloops Blazers	WHL	71	37	57	94	106												21	6	10	16	16			
1995-96	**Winnipeg**	**NHL**	74	7	10	17	101	1	0	3	106	6.6	−9						6	0	0	0	6	0	0	0
1996-97	**Phoenix**	**NHL**	63	4	8	12	49	0	0	0	100	4.0	−3						4	0	0	0	2	0	0	0
1997-98	**Phoenix**	**NHL**	33	5	6	11	35	0	0	3	42	11.9	−3						6	1	0	1	6	0	0	0
	Springfield	AHL	39	21	21	42	64																			
1998-99	**Phoenix**	**NHL**	79	6	16	22	54	0	0	0	156	3.8	−5	6	16.7	161	15	12:42	7	2	2	4	6	0	0	2
99-2000	**Phoenix**	**NHL**	81	26	25	51	66	1	1	4	221	11.8	6	25	36.0	225	11	16:51	4	1	2	3	8	1	0	0
2000-01	**Phoenix**	**NHL**	76	26	37	63	89	6	1	6	220	11.8	0	15	40.0	206	19	19:32								
	NHL Totals		406	74	102	176	394	8	2	16	845	8.8		46	34.8	592	45	16:20	27	4	4	8	28	1	0	2

Memorial Cup All-Star Team (1995) • Won Stafford Smythe Memorial Trophy (Memorial Cup Tournament MVP) (1995)

Transferred to **Phoenix** after **Winnipeg** franchise relocated, July 1, 1996.

DOIG, Jason

(DOIG, JAY-suhn) **OTT.**

Defense. Shoots right. 6'3", 228 lbs. Born, Montreal, Que., January 29, 1977. Winnipeg's 3rd choice, 34th overall, in 1995 Entry Draft.

1990-91	North Shore	QAHA	31	30	33	63	53																			
1991-92	North Shore	QAHA	29	11	11	22	20																			
1992-93	Lac St-Louis	QAAA	35	11	16	27	40												7	5	5	10	16			
1993-94	St-Jean Lynx	QMJHL	63	8	17	25	65												5	0	2	2	2			
1994-95	Laval Titan	QMJHL	55	13	42	55	259												20	4	13	17	39			
1995-96	Laval Titan	QMJHL	5	3	6	9	20																			
	Granby	QMJHL	24	4	30	34	91												20	10	22	32	*110			
	Winnipeg	**NHL**	15	1	1	2	28	0	0	0	7	14.3	−2													
	Springfield	AHL	5	0	0	0	28																			
1996-97	Granby	QMJHL	39	14	33	47	211												5	0	4	4	27			
	Las Vegas	IHL	6	0	1	1	19																			
	Springfield	AHL	5	0	3	3	2												17	1	4	5	37			
1997-98	**Phoenix**	**NHL**	4	0	1	1	12	0	0	0	1	0.0	−4													
	Springfield	AHL	46	2	25	27	153												3	0	0	0	2			
1998-99	**Phoenix**	**NHL**	9	0	1	1	10	0	0	0	0	0.0	2	0	0.0	1	2	5:08								
	Springfield	AHL	32	3	5	8	67																			
	Hartford	AHL	8	1	4	5	40												7	1	1	2	39			
99-2000	**NY Rangers**	**NHL**	7	0	1	1	22	0	0	0	3	0.0	−2	0	0.0	9	6	8:50								
	Hartford	AHL	27	3	11	14	70												21	1	5	6	20			
2000-01	**NY Rangers**	**NHL**	3	0	0	0	0	0	0	0	1	0.0	0	0	0.0	1	2	6:35								
	Hartford	AHL	52	4	20	24	178												5	0	1	1	4			
	NHL Totals		38	1	4	5	72	0	0	0	12	8.3		0	0.0	11	10	6:43								

Memorial Cup All-Star Team (1996)

Transferred to **Phoenix** after **Winnipeg** franchise relocated, July 1, 1996. Traded to **NY Rangers** by **Phoenix** with Phoenix's 6th round choice (Jay Dardis) in 1999 Entry Draft for Stan Neckar, March 23, 1999. Traded to **Ottawa** by **NY Rangers** with Jeff Ulmer for Sean Gagnon, June 29, 2001.

DOLLAS, Bobby

(DAW-luhs, BAW-bee)

Defense. Shoots left. 6'2", 212 lbs. Born, Montreal, Que., January 31, 1965. Winnipeg's 2nd choice, 14th overall, in 1983 Entry Draft.

1980-81	Lac-St-Louis	QAAA	46	9	14	23	34												6	0	1	1	0			
1981-82	Lac St-Louis	QAAA	44	9	31	40	138												11	2	8	10	20			
1982-83	Laval Voisins	QMJHL	63	16	45	61	144												11	5	5	10	23			
1983-84	Laval Voisins	QMJHL	54	12	33	45	80												14	1	8	9	23			
	Winnipeg	**NHL**	1	0	0	0	0	0	0	0	0	0.0	−2													
1984-85	**Winnipeg**	**NHL**	9	0	0	0	0	0	0	0	2	0.0	4													
	Sherbrooke	AHL	8	1	3	4	4												17	3	6	9	17			
1985-86	**Winnipeg**	**NHL**	46	0	5	5	66	0	0	0	50	0.0	−3						3	0	0	0	2	0	0	0
	Sherbrooke	AHL	25	4	7	11	29																			
1986-87	Sherbrooke	AHL	75	6	18	24	87												16	2	4	6	13			
1987-88	**Quebec**	**NHL**	9	0	0	0	2	0	0	0	5	0.0	−4													
	Moncton Hawks	AHL	26	4	10	14	20																			
	Fredericton	AHL	33	4	8	12	27												15	2	2	4	24			
1988-89	**Quebec**	**NHL**	16	0	3	3	16	0	0	0	11	0.0	−11													
	Halifax Citadels	AHL	57	5	19	24	65												4	1	0	1	14			
1989-90	Canada	Nat-Team	68	8	29	37	60																			
1990-91	**Detroit**	**NHL**	56	3	5	8	20	0	0	1	59	5.1	6						7	1	0	1	13	0	0	0
1991-92	**Detroit**	**NHL**	27	3	1	4	20	0	1	0	26	11.5	4						2	0	1	1	0	0	0	0
	Adirondack	AHL	19	1	6	7	33												18	7	4	11	22			
1992-93	**Detroit**	**NHL**	6	0	0	0	2	0	0	0	5	0.0	−1													
	Adirondack	AHL	64	7	36	43	54												11	3	8	11	8			
1993-94	**Anaheim**	**NHL**	77	9	11	20	55	1	0	1	121	7.4	20													
1994-95	**Anaheim**	**NHL**	45	7	13	20	12	3	1	1	70	10.0	−3													
1995-96	**Anaheim**	**NHL**	82	8	22	30	64	0	1	1	117	6.8	9													
1996-97	**Anaheim**	**NHL**	79	4	14	18	55	1	0	1	96	4.2	17						11	0	0	0	4	0	0	0
1997-98	**Anaheim**	**NHL**	22	0	1	1	27	0	0	0	11	0.0	−12													
	Edmonton	**NHL**	30	2	5	7	22	0	0	0	27	7.4	6						11	0	0	0	16	0	0	0
1998-99	**Pittsburgh**	**NHL**	70	2	8	10	60	0	0	0	34	5.9	−3	0	0.0	47	56	15:35	13	1	0	1	6	0	0	0
99-2000	Long Beach	IHL	13	2	4	6	8																			
	Calgary	**NHL**	49	3	7	10	28	1	0	0	36	8.3	4	0	0.0	52	69	20:09								
	Ottawa	**NHL**	1	0	0	0	0	0	0	0	0	0.0	2	0	0.0	1	1	16:10								
2000-01	**San Jose**	**NHL**	16	1	1	2	14	0	0	0	5	20.0	4	0	0.0	9	9	11:15								
	Manitoba Moose	IHL	8	1	2	3	2																			
	Pittsburgh	**NHL**	5	0	0	0	4	0	0	0	6	0.0	0	0	0.0	10	6	18:06								
	NHL Totals		646	42	96	138	467	6	3	5	681	6.2		0	0.0	119	141	16:46	47	2	1	3	41	0	0	0

QMJHL Second All-Star Team (1983) • AHL First All-Star Team (1993) • Won Eddie Shore Award (Top Defenseman - AHL) (1993)

Traded to **Quebec** by **Winnipeg** for Stu Kulak, December 17, 1987. Signed as a free agent by **Detroit**, October 18, 1990. Claimed by **Anaheim** from **Detroit** in Expansion Draft, June 24, 1993. Traded to **Edmonton** by **Anaheim** for Drew Bannister, January 9, 1998. Traded to **Pittsburgh** by **Edmonton** with Tony Hrkac for Josef Beranek, June 16, 1998. Signed as a free agent by **Long Beach**, October 12, 1999. Signed as a free agent by **Ottawa**, November 9, 1999. Claimed on waivers by **Calgary** from **Ottawa**, November 11, 1999. Signed as a free agent by **San Jose**, November 4, 2000. Traded to **Pittsburgh** by **San Jose** with Johan Hedberg for Jeff Norton, March 12, 2001.

DOME, Robert

(doh-MAY, RAW-buhrt) **PIT.**

Right wing. Shoots left. 6', 210 lbs. Born, Skalica, Czech., January 29, 1979. Pittsburgh's 1st choice, 17th overall, in 1997 Entry Draft.

1994-95	HC Dukla	Slovak-Jr.	36	36	43	79	39																			
1995-96	Utah Grizzlies	IHL	56	10	9	19	28																			
1996-97	Long Beach	IHL	13	4	6	10	14																			
	Las Vegas	IHL	43	10	7	17	22																			
1997-98	**Pittsburgh**	**NHL**	30	5	2	7	12	1	0	0	29	17.2	−1													
	Syracuse Crunch	AHL	36	21	25	46	77																			
1998-99	Syracuse Crunch	AHL	48	18	17	35	70																			
	Houston Aeros	IHL	20	2	4	6	24																			
99-2000	**Pittsburgh**	**NHL**	22	2	5	7	0	0	0	0	27	7.4	1	5	40.0	12	6	9:51								
	Wilkes-Barre	AHL	51	12	26	38	83																			

			Regular Season																Playoffs							
Season	Club	League	GP	G	A	Pts	PIM	PP	SH	GW	S	%	+/-	TF	F%	H	SB	Min	GP	G	A	Pts	PIM	PP	SH	GW
2000-01	HCO Trinec	Cze-Rep	5	0	3	3	4																			
	HC Kladno	Cze-Rep	29	9	12	21	57																			
	NHL Totals		**52**	**7**	**7**	**14**	**12**	**1**	**0**	**0**	**56**	**12.5**		**5**	**40.0**	**12**	**6**	**9:51**								

DOMENICHELLI, Hnat

(daw-meh-CHEHL-ee, NAT) **ATL.**

Center. Shoots left. 6', 195 lbs. Born, Edmonton, Alta., February 17, 1976. Hartford's 2nd choice, 83rd overall, in 1994 Entry Draft.

Season	Club	League	GP	G	A	Pts	PIM	PP	SH	GW	S	%	+/-	TF	F%	H	SB	Min	GP	G	A	Pts	PIM	PP	SH	GW
1991-92	Edmonton Freeze	AAHA	34	34	49	83	101																			
1992-93	Kamloops Blazers	WHL	45	12	8	20	15												11	1	1	2	2			
1993-94	Kamloops Blazers	WHL	69	27	40	67	31												19	10	12	22	0			
1994-95	Kamloops Blazers	WHL	72	52	62	114	34												19	9	9	18	9			
1995-96	Kamloops Blazers	WHL	62	59	89	148	37												16	7	9	16	29			
1996-97	**Hartford**	**NHL**	**13**	**2**	**1**	**3**	**7**	**1**	**0**	**0**	**14**	**14.3**	**-4**													
	Springfield	AHL	39	24	24	48	12																			
	Calgary	**NHL**	**10**	**1**	**2**	**3**	**2**	**1**	**0**	**0**	**16**	**6.3**	**1**													
	Saint John Flames	AHL	1	1	1	2	0												5	5	0	5	2			
1997-98	**Calgary**	**NHL**	**31**	**9**	**7**	**16**	**6**	**1**	**0**	**1**	**70**	**12.9**	**4**													
	Saint John Flames	AHL	48	33	13	46	24												19	7	8	15	14			
1998-99	**Calgary**	**NHL**	**23**	**5**	**5**	**10**	**11**	**3**	**0**	**0**	**45**	**11.1**	**-4**	**3**	**0.0**	**27**	**0**	**12:59**								
	Saint John Flames	AHL	51	25	21	46	26												7	4	4	8	2			
99-2000	**Calgary**	**NHL**	**32**	**5**	**9**	**14**	**12**	**1**	**0**	**1**	**57**	**8.8**	**0**	**78**	**46.2**	**37**	**7**	**12:39**								
	Saint John Flames	AHL	12	6	7	13	8																			
	Atlanta	**NHL**	**27**	**6**	**9**	**15**	**4**	**0**	**0**	**0**	**68**	**8.8**	**-21**	**9**	**55.6**	**36**	**3**	**16:55**								
2000-01	**Atlanta**	**NHL**	**63**	**15**	**12**	**27**	**18**	**4**	**0**	**1**	**150**	**10.0**	**-9**	**24**	**37.5**	**70**	**12**	**14:21**								
	NHL Totals		**199**	**43**	**45**	**88**	**60**	**11**	**0**	**3**	**420**	**10.2**		**114**	**43.9**	**170**	**22**	**14:14**								

WHL West Second All-Star Team (1995) • WHL West First All-Star Team (1996) • Canadian Major Junior First All-Star Team (1996) • Canadian Major Junior Most Sportsmanlike Player of the Year (1996)

Traded to **Calgary** by **Hartford** with Glen Featherstone, New Jersey's 2nd round choice (previously acquired, Calgary selected Dimitri Kokorev) in 1997 Entry Draft and Vancouver's 3rd round choice (previously acquired, Calgary selected Paul Manning) in 1998 Entry Draft for Steve Chiasson and Colorado's 3rd round choice (previously acquired, Carolina selected Francis Lessard) in 1997 Entry Draft, March 5, 1997. Traded to **Atlanta** by **Calgary** with Dmitri Vlasenkov for Darryl Shannon and Jason Botterill, February 11, 2000.

DOMI, Tie

(DOH-mee, TIGH) **TOR.**

Right wing. Shoots right. 5'10", 200 lbs. Born, Windsor, Ont., November 1, 1969. Toronto's 2nd choice, 27th overall, in 1988 Entry Draft.

Season	Club	League	GP	G	A	Pts	PIM	PP	SH	GW	S	%	+/-	TF	F%	H	SB	Min	GP	G	A	Pts	PIM	PP	SH	GW
1984-85	Belle River	OJHL-C	28	7	5	12	98																			
1985-86	Windsor Bulldogs	OJHL-B	42	8	17	25	*346																			
1986-87	Peterborough B's	OJHL-B	2	0	0	0	10																			
	Peterborough	OHL	18	1	1	2	79																			
1987-88	Peterborough	OHL	60	22	21	43	*292												12	3	9	12	24			
1988-89	Peterborough	OHL	43	14	16	30	175												17	10	9	19	*70			
1989-90	**Toronto**	**NHL**	**2**	**0**	**0**	**0**	**42**	**0**	**0**	**0**	**0**	**0.0**	**0**													
	Newmarket	AHL	57	14	11	25	285																			
1990-91	**NY Rangers**	**NHL**	**28**	**1**	**0**	**1**	**185**	**0**	**0**	**0**	**5**	**20.0**	**-5**													
	Binghamton	AHL	25	11	6	17	219												7	3	2	5	16			
1991-92	**NY Rangers**	**NHL**	**42**	**2**	**4**	**6**	**246**	**0**	**0**	**1**	**20**	**10.0**	**-4**						**6**	**1**	**1**	**2**	**32**	**0**	**0**	**0**
1992-93	**NY Rangers**	**NHL**	**12**	**2**	**0**	**2**	**95**	**0**	**0**	**0**	**11**	**18.2**	**-1**													
	Winnipeg	**NHL**	**49**	**3**	**10**	**13**	**249**	**0**	**0**	**0**	**29**	**10.3**	**2**						**6**	**1**	**0**	**1**	**23**	**0**	**0**	**0**
1993-94	**Winnipeg**	**NHL**	**81**	**8**	**11**	**19**	***347**	**0**	**0**	**1**	**98**	**8.2**	**-8**													
1994-95	**Winnipeg**	**NHL**	**31**	**4**	**4**	**8**	**128**	**0**	**0**	**0**	**34**	**11.8**	**-6**													
	Toronto	**NHL**	**9**	**0**	**1**	**1**	**31**	**0**	**0**	**0**	**12**	**0.0**	**1**						**7**	**1**	**0**	**1**	**0**	**0**	**0**	**0**
1995-96	**Toronto**	**NHL**	**72**	**7**	**6**	**13**	**297**	**0**	**0**	**1**	**61**	**11.5**	**-3**						**6**	**0**	**2**	**2**	**4**	**0**	**0**	**0**
1996-97	**Toronto**	**NHL**	**80**	**11**	**17**	**28**	**275**	**2**	**0**	**1**	**98**	**11.2**	**-17**													
1997-98	**Toronto**	**NHL**	**80**	**4**	**10**	**14**	**365**	**0**	**0**	**0**	**72**	**5.6**	**-5**													
1998-99	**Toronto**	**NHL**	**72**	**8**	**14**	**22**	**198**	**0**	**0**	**1**	**65**	**12.3**	**5**	**9**	**44.4**	**100**	**3**	**9:42**	**14**	**0**	**2**	**2**	**24**	**0**	**0**	**0**
99-2000	**Toronto**	**NHL**	**70**	**5**	**9**	**14**	**198**	**0**	**0**	**2**	**64**	**7.8**	**-5**	**4**	**25.0**	**85**	**10**	**9:58**	**12**	**0**	**1**	**1**	**20**	**0**	**0**	**0**
2000-01	**Toronto**	**NHL**	**82**	**13**	**7**	**20**	**214**	**1**	**0**	**1**	**60**	**21.7**	**2**	**5**	**80.0**	**129**	**9**	**8:23**	**8**	**0**	**1**	**1**	**20**	**0**	**0**	**0**
	NHL Totals		**710**	**68**	**93**	**161**	**2870**	**3**	**0**	**8**	**629**	**10.8**		**18**	**50.0**	**314**	**22**	**9:18**	**59**	**3**	**7**	**10**	**123**	**0**	**0**	**0**

Traded to **NY Rangers** by **Toronto** with Mark LaForest for Greg Johnston, June 28, 1990. Traded to **Winnipeg** by **NY Rangers** with Kris King for Ed Olczyk, December 28, 1992. Traded to **Toronto** by **Winnipeg** for Mike Eastwood and Toronto's 3rd round choice (Brad Isbister) in 1995 Entry Draft, April 7, 1995.

DONATO, Ted

(duh-NAH-toh, TEHD)

Left wing. Shoots left. 5'10", 178 lbs. Born, Boston, MA, April 28, 1969. Boston's 6th choice, 98th overall, in 1987 Entry Draft.

Season	Club	League	GP	G	A	Pts	PIM	PP	SH	GW	S	%	+/-	TF	F%	H	SB	Min	GP	G	A	Pts	PIM	PP	SH	GW
1986-87	Catholic Memorial	Hi-School	22	29	34	63	30																			
1987-88	Harvard University	ECAC	28	12	14	26	24																			
1988-89	Harvard University	ECAC	34	14	37	51	30																			
1989-90	Harvard University	ECAC	16	5	6	11	34																			
1990-91	Harvard University	ECAC	27	19	*37	56	26																			
1991-92	United States	Nat-Team	52	11	22	33	24																			
	United States	Olympics	8	4	3	7	8																			
	Boston	**NHL**	**10**	**1**	**2**	**3**	**8**	**0**	**0**	**0**	**13**	**7.7**	**-1**						**15**	**3**	**4**	**7**	**4**	**0**	**0**	**1**
1992-93	**Boston**	**NHL**	**82**	**15**	**20**	**35**	**61**	**3**	**2**	**5**	**118**	**12.7**	**2**						**4**	**0**	**1**	**1**	**0**	**0**	**0**	**0**
1993-94	**Boston**	**NHL**	**84**	**22**	**32**	**54**	**59**	**9**	**2**	**1**	**158**	**13.9**	**0**						**13**	**4**	**2**	**6**	**10**	**2**	**0**	**1**
1994-95	TuTo Turku	Finland	14	5	5	10	47																			
	Boston	**NHL**	**47**	**10**	**10**	**20**	**10**	**1**	**0**	**1**	**71**	**14.1**	**3**						**5**	**0**	**0**	**0**	**4**	**0**	**0**	**0**
1995-96	**Boston**	**NHL**	**82**	**23**	**26**	**49**	**46**	**7**	**0**	**1**	**152**	**15.1**	**6**						**5**	**1**	**2**	**3**	**2**	**1**	**0**	**0**
1996-97	**Boston**	**NHL**	**67**	**25**	**26**	**51**	**37**	**6**	**2**	**2**	**172**	**14.5**	**-9**													
1997-98	**Boston**	**NHL**	**79**	**16**	**23**	**39**	**54**	**3**	**0**	**5**	**129**	**12.4**	**6**						**5**	**0**	**0**	**0**	**2**	**0**	**0**	**0**
1998-99	**Boston**	**NHL**	**14**	**1**	**3**	**4**	**4**	**0**	**0**	**0**	**22**	**4.5**	**0**	**18**	**44.4**	**6**	**1**	**15:21**								
	NY Islanders	**NHL**	**55**	**7**	**11**	**18**	**27**	**2**	**0**	**0**	**68**	**10.3**	**-10**	**142**	**45.8**	**23**	**2**	**12:09**								
	Ottawa	**NHL**	**13**	**3**	**2**	**5**	**10**	**1**	**0**	**0**	**16**	**18.8**	**2**	**4**	**25.0**	**7**	**5**	**11:10**	**1**	**0**	**0**	**0**	**0**	**0**	**0**	**0**
99-2000	**Anaheim**	**NHL**	**81**	**11**	**19**	**30**	**26**	**2**	**0**	**3**	**138**	**8.0**	**-3**	**212**	**41.5**	**72**	**23**	**14:35**								
2000-01	**Dallas**	**NHL**	**65**	**8**	**17**	**25**	**26**	**1**	**0**	**3**	**71**	**11.3**	**6**	**16**	**37.5**	**62**	**8**	**10:13**	**8**	**0**	**1**	**1**	**0**	**0**	**0**	**0**
	NHL Totals		**679**	**142**	**191**	**333**	**368**	**35**	**6**	**21**	**1128**	**12.6**		**392**	**42.9**	**170**	**39**	**12:36**	**56**	**8**	**10**	**18**	**22**	**3**	**0**	**2**

NCAA Championship All-Tournament Team (1989) • NCAA Championship Tournament MVP (1989) • ECAC First All-Star Team (1991)

Traded to **NY Islanders** by **Boston** for Ken Belanger, November 7, 1998. Traded to **Ottawa** by **NY Islanders** for Ottawa's 4th round choice (later traded to Phoenix - Phoenix selected Preston Mizzi) in 1999 Entry Draft, March 20, 1999. Traded to **Anaheim** by **Ottawa** with the rights to Antti-Jussi Niemi for Patrick Lalime, June 18, 1999. Signed as a free agent agent by **Dallas**, August 17, 2000.

DONOVAN, Shean

(DAW-nuh-vuhn, SHAWN) **ATL.**

Right wing. Shoots right. 6'3", 210 lbs. Born, Timmins, Ont., January 22, 1975. San Jose's 2nd choice, 28th overall, in 1993 Entry Draft.

Season	Club	League	GP	G	A	Pts	PIM	PP	SH	GW	S	%	+/-	TF	F%	H	SB	Min	GP	G	A	Pts	PIM	PP	SH	GW
1990-91	Kanata Lasers	OCJHL	44	8	5	13	8																			
1991-92	Ottawa 67's	OHL	58	11	8	19	14												11	1	0	1	5			
1992-93	Ottawa 67's	OHL	66	29	23	52	33																			
1993-94	Ottawa 67's	OHL	62	35	49	84	63												17	10	11	21	14			
1994-95	Ottawa 67's	OHL	29	22	19	41	41																			
	San Jose	**NHL**	**14**	**0**	**0**	**0**	**6**	**0**	**0**	**0**	**13**	**0.0**	**-6**						**7**	**0**	**1**	**1**	**6**	**0**	**0**	**0**
	Kansas City	IHL	5	0	2	2	7												14	5	3	8	23			
1995-96	**San Jose**	**NHL**	**74**	**13**	**8**	**21**	**39**	**0**	**1**	**2**	**73**	**17.8**	**-17**													
	Kansas City	IHL	4	0	0	0	8												5	0	0	0	8			
1996-97	**San Jose**	**NHL**	**73**	**9**	**6**	**15**	**42**	**0**	**1**	**0**	**115**	**7.8**	**-18**													
	Kentucky	AHL	3	1	3	4	18																			
1997-98	**San Jose**	**NHL**	**20**	**3**	**3**	**6**	**22**	**0**	**0**	**0**	**24**	**12.5**	**3**													
	Colorado	**NHL**	**47**	**5**	**7**	**12**	**48**	**0**	**0**	**0**	**57**	**8.8**	**3**													
1998-99	**Colorado**	**NHL**	**68**	**7**	**12**	**19**	**37**	**1**	**0**	**1**	**81**	**8.6**	**4**	**9**	**22.2**	**35**	**8**	**8:46**	**5**	**0**	**0**	**0**	**2**	**0**	**0**	**0**

			Regular Season																Playoffs							
Season	Club	League	GP	G	A	Pts	PIM	PP	SH	GW	S	%	+/-	TF	F%	H	SB	Min	GP	G	A	Pts	PIM	PP	SH	GW
99-2000	Colorado	NHL	18	1	0	1	8	0	0	0	13	7.7	–4	1	0.0	7	1	5:20	....	....	....	....	....	....	....	....
	Atlanta	NHL	33	4	7	11	18	1	0	1	53	7.5	–13	22	31.8	36	11	14:19	....	....	....	....	....	....	....	....
2000-01	Atlanta	NHL	63	12	11	23	47	1	3	1	93	12.9	–14	218	45.9	42	20	14:03	....	....	....	....	....	....	....	....
	NHL Totals		410	54	54	108	267	3	5	5	522	10.3		250	43.6	120	40	11:16	12	0	1	1	8	0	0	0

Traded to **Colorado** by **San Jose** with San Jose's 1st round choice (Alex Tanguay) in 1998 Entry Draft for Mike Ricci and Colorado's 2nd round choice (later traded to Buffalo - Buffalo selected Jaroslav Kristek), in 1998 Entry Draft, November 21, 1997. Traded to **Atlanta** by **Colorado** for Rick Tabaracci, December 8, 1999.

DOWD, Jim

(DOWD, JIHM) **MIN.**

Center. Shoots right. 6'1", 190 lbs. Born, Brick, NJ, December 25, 1968. New Jersey's 7th choice, 149th overall, in 1987 Entry Draft.

Season	Club	League	GP	G	A	Pts	PIM	PP	SH	GW	S	%	+/-	TF	F%	H	SB	Min	GP	G	A	Pts	PIM	PP	SH	GW
1983-84	Brick High	Hi-School	20	19	30	49	....	....	....	....	....	....	....	....	....	....	....	....	....	....	....	....	....	....	....	....
1984-85	Brick High	Hi-School	24	58	55	113	....	....	....	....	....	....	....	....	....	....	....	....	....	....	....	....	....	....	....	....
1985-86	Brick High	Hi-School	24	47	51	98	....	....	....	....	....	....	....	....	....	....	....	....	....	....	....	....	....	....	....	....
1986-87	Brick High	Hi-School	24	22	33	55	....	....	....	....	....	....	....	....	....	....	....	....	....	....	....	....	....	....	....	....
1987-88	Lake Superior	CCHA	45	18	27	45	16	....	....	....	....	....	....	....	....	....	....	....	....	....	....	....	....	....	....	....
1988-89	Lake Superior	CCHA	46	24	35	59	40	....	....	....	....	....	....	....	....	....	....	....	....	....	....	....	....	....	....	....
1989-90	Lake Superior	CCHA	46	25	*67	92	30	....	....	....	....	....	....	....	....	....	....	....	....	....	....	....	....	....	....	....
1990-91	Lake Superior	CCHA	44	24	*54	*78	53	....	....	....	....	....	....	....	....	....	....	....	....	....	....	....	....	....	....	....
1991-92	New Jersey	NHL	1	0	0	0	0	0	0	0	0	0.0	0	....	....	....	....	....	....	....	....	....	....	....	....	....
	Utica Devils	AHL	78	17	42	59	47	....	....	....	....	....	....	....	....	....	....	....	4	2	2	4	4	....	....	....
1992-93	New Jersey	NHL	1	0	0	0	0	0	0	0	1	0.0	–1	....	....	....	....	....	....	....	....	....	....	....	....	....
	Utica Devils	AHL	78	27	45	72	62	....	....	....	....	....	....	....	....	....	....	....	5	1	7	8	10	....	....	....
1993-94	New Jersey	NHL	15	5	10	15	0	2	0	0	26	19.2	8	....	....	....	....	....	19	2	6	8	8	0	0	0
	Albany River Rats	AHL	58	26	37	63	76	....	....	....	....	....	....	....	....	....	....	....	....	....	....	....	....	....	....	....
1994-95♦	New Jersey	NHL	10	1	4	5	0	1	0	0	14	7.1	–5	....	....	....	....	....	11	2	1	3	8	0	0	1
1995-96	New Jersey	NHL	28	4	9	13	17	1	0	0	41	9.8	–1	....	....	....	....	....	....	....	....	....	....	....	....	....
	Vancouver	NHL	38	1	6	7	6	0	0	0	35	2.9	–8	....	....	....	....	....	1	0	0	0	0	0	0	0
1996-97	NY Islanders	NHL	3	0	0	0	0	0	0	0	0	0.0	–1	....	....	....	....	....	....	....	....	....	....	....	....	....
	Utah Grizzlies	IHL	48	10	21	31	27	....	....	....	....	....	....	....	....	....	....	....	....	....	....	....	....	....	....	....
	Saint John Flames	AHL	24	5	11	16	18	....	....	....	....	....	....	....	....	....	....	....	5	1	2	3	0	....	....	....
1997-98	Calgary	NHL	48	6	8	14	12	0	1	0	58	10.3	10	....	....	....	....	....	....	....	....	....	....	....	....	....
	Saint John Flames	AHL	35	8	30	38	20	....	....	....	....	....	....	....	....	....	....	....	19	3	13	16	10	....	....	....
1998-99	Edmonton	NHL	1	0	0	0	0	0	0	0	1	0.0	0	7	14.3	1	0	9:47	....	....	....	....	....	....	....	....
	Hamilton Bulldogs	AHL	51	15	29	44	82	....	....	....	....	....	....	....	....	....	....	....	11	3	6	9	8	....	....	....
99-2000	Edmonton	NHL	69	5	18	23	45	2	0	1	103	4.9	10	720	54.0	51	25	13:08	5	2	1	3	4	0	0	0
2000-01	Minnesota	NHL	68	7	22	29	80	0	0	0	92	7.6	–6	1154	50.7	41	39	17:50	....	....	....	....	....	....	....	....
	NHL Totals		282	29	77	106	160	5	1	1	371	7.8		1881	51.8	93	64	15:26	36	6	8	14	20	0	0	1

CCHA Second All-Star Team (1990) • NCAA West Second All-American Team (1990) • CCHA First All-Star Team (1991) • NCAA West First All-American Team (1991)

• Missed majority of 1994-95 season recovering from shoulder injury suffered in game vs. Quebec, February 2, 1995. Traded to **Hartford** by **New Jersey** with New Jersey's 2nd round choice (later traded to Calgary - Calgary selected Dmitri Kokorev) in 1997 Entry Draft for Jocelyn Lemieux and Hartford's 2nd round choice (later traded to Dallas - Dallas selected John Erskine) in 1998 Entry Draft, December 19, 1995. Traded to **Vancouver** by **Hartford** with Frantisek Kucera and Hartford's 2nd round choice (Ryan Bonni) in 1997 Entry Draft for Jeff Brown and Vancouver's 3rd round choice (later traded to Calgary - Calgary selected Paul Manning) in 1998 Entry Draft, December 19, 1995. Claimed by **NY Islanders** from **Vancouver** in NHL Waiver Draft, September 30, 1996. Signed as a free agent by **Calgary**, August, 1997. Traded to **Nashville** by **Calgary** for future considerations, June 26, 1998. Traded to **Edmonton** by **Nashville** with Mikhail Shtalenkov for Eric Fichaud, Drake Berehowsky and Greg de Vries, October 1, 1998. Selected by **Minnesota** from **Edmonton** in Expansion Draft, June 23, 2000.

DOWNEY, Aaron

(DOW-nee, AIR-ruhn) **CHI.**

Right wing. Shoots right. 6'1", 216 lbs. Born, Shelburne, Ont., August 27, 1974.

Season	Club	League	GP	G	A	Pts	PIM	PP	SH	GW	S	%	+/-	TF	F%	H	SB	Min	GP	G	A	Pts	PIM	PP	SH	GW
1990-91	Grand Valley	OJHL-C	27	6	8	14	57	....	....	....	....	....	....	....	....	....	....	....	....	....	....	....	....	....	....	....
1991-92	Collingwood	OJHL-B	40	9	8	17	111	....	....	....	....	....	....	....	....	....	....	....	....	....	....	....	....	....	....	....
1992-93	Guelph Storm	OHL	53	3	3	6	88	....	....	....	....	....	....	....	....	....	....	....	5	1	0	1	0	....	....	....
1993-94	Cole Harbour	MJrHL	35	8	20	28	210	....	....	....	....	....	....	....	....	....	....	....	....	....	....	....	....	....	....	....
1994-95	Cole Harbour	MJrHL	40	10	31	41	320	....	....	....	....	....	....	....	....	....	....	....	....	....	....	....	....	....	....	....
1995-96	Hampton Roads	ECHL	65	12	11	23	354	....	....	....	....	....	....	....	....	....	....	....	....	....	....	....	....	....	....	....
1996-97	Manitoba Moose	IHL	2	0	0	0	17	....	....	....	....	....	....	....	....	....	....	....	....	....	....	....	....	....	....	....
	Portland Pirates	AHL	3	0	0	0	19	....	....	....	....	....	....	....	....	....	....	....	....	....	....	....	....	....	....	....
	Hampton Roads	ECHL	64	8	8	16	338	....	....	....	....	....	....	....	....	....	....	....	9	0	3	3	26	....	....	....
1997-98	Providence Bruins	AHL	78	5	10	15	*407	....	....	....	....	....	....	....	....	....	....	....	....	....	....	....	....	....	....	....
1998-99	Providence Bruins	AHL	75	10	12	22	*401	....	....	....	....	....	....	....	....	....	....	....	19	1	1	2	46	....	....	....
99-2000	Boston	NHL	1	0	0	0	0	0	0	0	0	0.0	0	0	0.0	1	0	8:31	....	....	....	....	....	....	....	....
	Providence Bruins	AHL	47	6	4	10	221	....	....	....	....	....	....	....	....	....	....	....	14	1	0	1	24	....	....	....
2000-01	Chicago	NHL	3	0	0	0	6	0	0	0	2	0.0	–1	0	0.0	3	1	5:30	....	....	....	....	....	....	....	....
	Norfolk Admirals	AHL	67	6	15	21	234	....	....	....	....	....	....	....	....	....	....	....	9	0	0	0	4	....	....	....
	NHL Totals		4	0	0	0	6	0	0	0	2	0.0		0	0.0	4	1	6:16	....	....	....	....	....	....	....	....

Signed as a free agent by **Boston**, January 20, 1998. Signed as a free agent by **Chicago**, August 13, 2000.

DRAKE, Dallas

(DRAYK, DAL-uhs) **ST.L.**

Right wing. Shoots left. 6'1", 187 lbs. Born, Trail, B.C., February 4, 1969. Detroit's 6th choice, 116th overall, in 1989 Entry Draft.

Season	Club	League	GP	G	A	Pts	PIM	PP	SH	GW	S	%	+/-	TF	F%	H	SB	Min	GP	G	A	Pts	PIM	PP	SH	GW
1984-85	Rossland	KIJHL	30	13	37	50	....	....	....	....	....	....	....	....	....	....	....	....	....	....	....	....	....	....	....	....
1985-86	Rossland	KIJHL	41	53	73	126	....	....	....	....	....	....	....	....	....	....	....	....	....	....	....	....	....	....	....	....
1986-87	Rossland	KIJHL	40	55	80	135	....	....	....	....	....	....	....	....	....	....	....	....	....	....	....	....	....	....	....	....
1987-88	Vernon Lakers	BCJHL	47	39	85	124	50	....	....	....	....	....	....	....	....	....	....	....	11	9	17	26	30	....	....	....
1988-89	North-Michigan	WCHA	38	17	22	39	22	....	....	....	....	....	....	....	....	....	....	....	7	1	2	3	4	....	....	....
1989-90	North-Michigan	WCHA	36	13	24	37	42	....	....	....	....	....	....	....	....	....	....	....	....	....	....	....	....	....	....	....
1990-91	North-Michigan	WCHA	44	22	36	58	89	....	....	....	....	....	....	....	....	....	....	....	....	....	....	....	....	....	....	....
1991-92	North-Michigan	WCHA	38	*39	41	*80	46	....	....	....	....	....	....	....	....	....	....	....	....	....	....	....	....	....	....	....
1992-93	Detroit	NHL	72	18	26	44	93	3	2	5	89	20.2	15	....	....	....	....	....	7	3	3	6	6	1	0	0
1993-94	Detroit	NHL	47	10	22	32	37	0	1	2	78	12.8	5	....	....	....	....	....	....	....	....	....	....	....	....	....
	Adirondack	AHL	1	2	0	2	0	....	....	....	....	....	....	....	....	....	....	....	....	....	....	....	....	....	....	....
	Winnipeg	NHL	15	3	5	8	12	1	1	1	34	8.8	–6	....	....	....	....	....	....	....	....	....	....	....	....	....
1994-95	Winnipeg	NHL	43	8	18	26	30	0	0	1	66	12.1	–6	....	....	....	....	....	....	....	....	....	....	....	....	....
1995-96	Winnipeg	NHL	69	19	20	39	36	4	4	2	121	15.7	–7	....	....	....	....	....	3	0	0	0	0	0	0	0
1996-97	Phoenix	NHL	63	17	19	36	52	5	1	1	113	15.0	–11	....	....	....	....	....	7	0	1	1	2	0	0	0
1997-98	Phoenix	NHL	60	11	29	40	71	3	0	2	112	9.8	17	....	....	....	....	....	4	0	1	1	2	0	0	0
1998-99	Phoenix	NHL	53	9	22	31	65	0	0	3	105	8.6	17	5	60.0	105	17	15:38	7	4	3	7	4	2	0	1
99-2000	Phoenix	NHL	79	15	30	45	62	0	2	5	127	11.8	11	4	25.0	176	46	15:48	5	0	1	1	4	0	0	0
2000-01	St. Louis	NHL	82	12	29	41	71	2	0	3	142	8.5	18	11	45.5	163	33	14:44	15	4	2	6	16	0	1	1
	NHL Totals		583	122	220	342	529	18	11	25	987	12.4		20	45.0	444	96	15:21	48	11	11	22	34	3	1	2

WCHA First All-Star Team (1992) • NCAA West First All-American Team (1992)

Traded to **Winnipeg** by **Detroit** with Tim Cheveldae for Bob Essensa and Sergei Bautin, March 8, 1994. Transferred to **Phoenix** after **Winnipeg** franchise relocated, July 1, 1996. Selected by **Minnesota** from **Phoenix** in Expansion Draft, June 23, 2000. Signed as a free agent by **St. Louis**, July 1, 2000.

DRAPER, Kris

(DRAY-puhr, KRIHS) **DET.**

Center. Shoots left. 5'11", 190 lbs. Born, Toronto, Ont., May 24, 1971. Winnipeg's 4th choice, 62nd overall, in 1989 Entry Draft.

Season	Club	League	GP	G	A	Pts	PIM	PP	SH	GW	S	%	+/-	TF	F%	H	SB	Min	GP	G	A	Pts	PIM	PP	SH	GW
1987-88	Don Mills Flyers	MTHL	40	35	32	67	46	....	....	....	....	....	....	....	....	....	....	....	....	....	....	....	....	....	....	....
1988-89	Canada	Nat-Team	60	11	15	26	16	....	....	....	....	....	....	....	....	....	....	....	....	....	....	....	....	....	....	....
1989-90	Canada	Nat-Team	61	12	22	34	44	....	....	....	....	....	....	....	....	....	....	....	....	....	....	....	....	....	....	....
1990-91	Ottawa 67's	OHL	39	19	42	61	35	....	....	....	....	....	....	....	....	....	....	....	17	8	11	19	20	....	....	....
	Winnipeg	NHL	3	1	0	1	5	0	0	0	1	100.0	0	....	....	....	....	....	....	....	....	....	....	....	....	....
	Moncton Hawks	AHL	7	2	1	3	2	....	....	....	....	....	....	....	....	....	....	....	....	....	....	....	....	....	....	....
1991-92	Winnipeg	NHL	10	2	0	2	2	0	0	0	19	10.5	0	....	....	....	....	....	2	0	0	0	0	0	0	0
	Moncton Hawks	AHL	61	11	18	29	113	....	....	....	....	....	....	....	....	....	....	....	4	0	1	1	6	....	....	....
1992-93	Winnipeg	NHL	7	0	0	0	2	0	0	0	5	0.0	–6	....	....	....	....	....	....	....	....	....	....	....	....	....
	Moncton Hawks	AHL	67	12	23	35	40	....	....	....	....	....	....	....	....	....	....	....	5	2	2	4	18	....	....	....
1993-94	Detroit	NHL	39	5	8	13	31	0	1	0	55	9.1	11	....	....	....	....	....	7	2	2	4	4	0	1	0
	Adirondack	AHL	46	20	23	43	49	....	....	....	....	....	....	....	....	....	....	....	....	....	....	....	....	....	....	....
1994-95	Detroit	NHL	36	2	6	8	22	0	0	0	44	4.5	1	....	....	....	....	....	18	4	1	5	12	0	1	1
1995-96	Detroit	NHL	52	7	9	16	32	0	1	0	51	13.7	2	....	....	....	....	....	18	4	2	6	18	0	1	0

			Regular Season																Playoffs							
Season	Club	League	GP	G	A	Pts	PIM	PP	SH	GW	S	%	+/-	TF	F%	H	SB	Min	GP	G	A	Pts	PIM	PP	SH	GW
1996-97♦	**Detroit**	**NHL**	**76**	**8**	**5**	**13**	**73**	**1**	**0**	**1**	**85**	**9.4**	**–11**						**20**	**2**	**4**	**6**	**12**	**0**	**1**	**0**
1997-98♦	**Detroit**	**NHL**	**64**	**13**	**10**	**23**	**45**	**1**	**0**	**4**	**96**	**13.5**	**5**						**19**	**1**	**3**	**4**	**12**	**0**	**0**	**1**
1998-99	**Detroit**	**NHL**	**80**	**4**	**14**	**18**	**79**	**0**	**1**	**1**	**78**	**5.1**	**2**	**887**	**54.6**	**82**	**18**	**12:43**	**10**	**0**	**1**	**1**	**6**	**0**	**0**	**0**
99-2000	**Detroit**	**NHL**	**51**	**5**	**7**	**12**	**28**	**0**	**0**	**3**	**76**	**6.6**	**3**	**380**	**57.6**	**69**	**13**	**13:33**	**9**	**2**	**0**	**2**	**6**	**0**	**0**	**0**
2000-01	**Detroit**	**NHL**	**75**	**8**	**17**	**25**	**38**	**0**	**1**	**1**	**123**	**6.5**	**17**	**997**	**56.5**	**109**	**23**	**13:26**	**6**	**0**	**1**	**1**	**2**	**0**	**0**	**0**
	NHL Totals		**493**	**55**	**76**	**131**	**357**	**2**	**4**	**10**	**633**	**8.7**		**2264**	**55.9**	**260**	**54**	**13:11**	**109**	**15**	**14**	**29**	**72**	**0**	**4**	**2**

Traded to **Detroit** by **Winnipeg** for future considerations, June 30, 1993.

DRUKEN, Harold
(DROO-kehn, HAIR-ohld) **VAN.**

Center. Shoots left. 6', 205 lbs. Born, St. John's, Nfld., January 26, 1979. Vancouver's 3rd choice, 36th overall, in 1997 Entry Draft.

Season	Club	League	GP	G	A	Pts	PIM	PP	SH	GW	S	%	+/-	TF	F%	H	SB	Min	GP	G	A	Pts	PIM	PP	SH	GW
1995-96	Noble High	Hi-School	30	37	28	65	28																			
1996-97	Detroit Whalers	OHL	63	27	31	58	14												5	3	2	5	0			
1997-98	Plymouth Whalers	OHL	64	38	44	82	12												15	9	11	20	4			
1998-99	Plymouth Whalers	OHL	60	*58	45	103	34												11	9	12	21	14			
99-2000	**Vancouver**	**NHL**	**33**	**7**	**9**	**16**	**10**	**2**	**0**	**0**	**69**	**10.1**	**14**	**307**	**47.9**	**13**	**10**	**13:01**								
	Syracuse Crunch	AHL	47	20	25	45	32												4	1	2	3	6			
2000-01	**Vancouver**	**NHL**	**55**	**15**	**15**	**30**	**14**	**6**	**0**	**3**	**82**	**18.3**	**2**	**598**	**43.8**	**16**	**17**	**11:59**	**4**	**0**	**1**	**1**	**0**	**0**	**0**	**0**
	Kansas City	IHL	15	5	9	14	20																			
	NHL Totals		**88**	**22**	**24**	**46**	**24**	**8**	**0**	**3**	**151**	**14.6**		**905**	**45.2**	**29**	**27**	**12:22**	**4**	**0**	**1**	**1**	**0**	**0**	**0**	**0**

OHL Second All-Star Team (1999)

DRULIA, Stan
(DROO-lee-ah, STAN)

Right wing. Shoots right. 5'11", 190 lbs. Born, Elmira, NY, January 5, 1968. Pittsburgh's 11th choice, 214th overall, in 1986 Entry Draft.

Season	Club	League	GP	G	A	Pts	PIM	PP	SH	GW	S	%	+/-	TF	F%	H	SB	Min	GP	G	A	Pts	PIM	PP	SH	GW
1983-84	Fort Erie Meteors	OJHL-B	39	29	36	65	104																			
1984-85	Belleville Bulls	OHL	63	24	31	55	33																			
1985-86	Belleville Bulls	OHL	66	43	36	79	73												24	4	11	15	15			
1986-87	Hamilton Hawks	OHL	55	27	51	78	26												9	4	4	8	2			
1987-88	Hamilton Hawks	OHL	65	52	69	121	44												14	8	16	24	12			
1988-89	Niagara Falls	OHL	47	52	93	145	59												17	11	*26	37	18			
	Maine Mariners	AHL	3	1	1	2	0																			
1989-90	Phoenix	IHL	16	6	3	9	2																			
	Cape Breton	AHL	31	5	7	12	2																			
1990-91	Knoxville	ECHL	64	*63	77	*140	39												3	3	2	5	4			
1991-92	New Haven	AHL	77	49	53	102	46												5	2	4	6	4			
1992-93	**Tampa Bay**	**NHL**	**24**	**2**	**1**	**3**	**10**	**0**	**0**	**1**	**22**	**9.1**	**1**													
	Atlanta Knights	IHL	47	28	26	54	38												3	2	3	5	4			
1993-94	Atlanta Knights	IHL	79	54	60	114	70												14	13	12	25	8			
1994-95	Atlanta Knights	IHL	66	41	49	90	60												5	1	5	6	2			
1995-96	Atlanta Knights	IHL	75	38	56	94	80												3	0	2	2	18			
1996-97	Detroit Vipers	IHL	73	33	38	71	42												21	5	*21	26	14			
1997-98	Detroit Vipers	IHL	58	25	35	60	50												15	2	4	6	16			
1998-99	Detroit Vipers	IHL	82	23	52	75	64												11	5	4	9	10			
99-2000	**Tampa Bay**	**NHL**	**68**	**11**	**22**	**33**	**24**	**1**	**2**	**1**	**94**	**11.7**	**–18**	**11**	**18.2**	**68**	**41**	**16:37**								
2000-01	**Tampa Bay**	**NHL**	**34**	**2**	**4**	**6**	**18**	**1**	**0**	**0**	**20**	**10.0**	**–11**	**9**	**33.3**	**19**	**40**	**10:41**								
	NHL Totals		**126**	**15**	**27**	**42**	**52**	**2**	**2**	**2**	**136**	**11.0**		**20**	**25.0**	**87**	**81**	**14:38**								

OHL First All-Star Team (1989) • ECHL First All-Star Team (1991) • Won ECHL MVP Award (1991) • AHL Second All-Star Team (1992) • IHL First All-Star Team (1994, 1995) • Won "Bud" Poile Trophy (Playoff MVP - IHL) (1994)

Signed as a free agent by **Edmonton**, February 24, 1989. Signed as a free agent by **Tampa Bay**, September 1, 1992. Signed as a free agent by **Tampa Bay**, September 29, 1999. • Missed majority of 2000-01 season recovering from back injury originally suffered in game vs. Detroit, December 2, 2000.

DRURY, Chris
(DROO-ree, KRIHS) **COL.**

Center. Shoots right. 5'10", 180 lbs. Born, Trumbull, CT, August 20, 1976. Quebec's 5th choice, 72nd overall, in 1994 Entry Draft.

Season	Club	League	GP	G	A	Pts	PIM	PP	SH	GW	S	%	+/-	TF	F%	H	SB	Min	GP	G	A	Pts	PIM	PP	SH	GW
1991-92	Fairfield Prep	Hi-School	25	22	27	49																				
1992-93	Fairfield Prep	Hi-School	24	25	32	57	15																			
1993-94	Fairfield Prep	Hi-School	24	37	18	55																				
1994-95	Boston University	H-East	39	12	15	27	38																			
1995-96	Boston University	H-East	37	35	33	*68	46																			
1996-97	Boston University	H-East	41	*38	24	62	64																			
1997-98	Boston University	H-East	38	28	29	57	88																			
1998-99	**Colorado**	**NHL**	**79**	**20**	**24**	**44**	**62**	**6**	**0**	**3**	**138**	**14.5**	**9**	**418**	**46.9**	**88**	**39**	**13:15**	**19**	**6**	**2**	**8**	**4**	**0**	**0**	**4**
99-2000	**Colorado**	**NHL**	**82**	**20**	**47**	**67**	**42**	**7**	**0**	**2**	**213**	**9.4**	**8**	**1321**	**53.1**	**68**	**50**	**18:33**	**17**	**4**	**10**	**14**	**4**	**1**	**0**	**2**
2000-01♦	**Colorado**	**NHL**	**71**	**24**	**41**	**65**	**47**	**11**	**0**	**5**	**204**	**11.8**	**6**	**552**	**55.1**	**65**	**32**	**18:03**	**23**	**11**	**5**	**16**	**4**	**2**	**0**	**2**
	NHL Totals		**232**	**64**	**112**	**176**	**151**	**24**	**0**	**10**	**555**	**11.5**		**2291**	**52.4**	**221**	**121**	**16:36**	**59**	**21**	**17**	**38**	**12**	**3**	**0**	**8**

Hockey East Second All-Star Team (1996, 1997) • NCAA East Second All-American Team (1996) • NCAA East First All-American Team (1997, 1998) • NCAA Championship All-Tournament Team (1997) • Hockey East First All-Star Team (1998) • Won Hobey Baker Memorial Award (Top U.S. Collegiate Player) (1998) • NHL All-Rookie Team (1999) • Won Calder Memorial Trophy (1999)

Rights transferred to **Colorado** after **Quebec** franchise relocated, June 21, 1995.

DRURY, Ted
(DROO-ree, TEHD) **N.J.**

Center. Shoots left. 6'2", 210 lbs. Born, Boston, MA, September 13, 1971. Calgary's 2nd choice, 42nd overall, in 1989 Entry Draft.

Season	Club	League	GP	G	A	Pts	PIM	PP	SH	GW	S	%	+/-	TF	F%	H	SB	Min	GP	G	A	Pts	PIM	PP	SH	GW
1987-88	Fairfield Prep	Hi-School	24	21	28	49																				
1988-89	Fairfield Prep	Hi-School	25	35	31	66																				
1989-90	Harvard University	ECAC	17	9	13	22	10																			
1990-91	Harvard University	ECAC	25	18	18	36	22																			
1991-92	United States	Nat-Team	53	11	23	34	30																			
	United States	Olympics	7	1	1	2	0																			
1992-93	Harvard University	ECAC	31	22	*41	*63	28																			
1993-94	**Calgary**	**NHL**	**34**	**5**	**7**	**12**	**26**	**0**	**1**	**1**	**43**	**11.6**	**–5**													
	United States	Nat-Team	11	1	4	5	11																			
	United States	Olympics	7	1	2	3	2																			
	Hartford	**NHL**	**16**	**1**	**5**	**6**	**10**	**0**	**0**	**0**	**37**	**2.7**	**–10**													
1994-95	**Hartford**	**NHL**	**34**	**3**	**6**	**9**	**21**	**0**	**0**	**0**	**31**	**9.7**	**–3**													
	Springfield	AHL	2	0	1	1	0																			
1995-96	**Ottawa**	**NHL**	**42**	**9**	**7**	**16**	**54**	**1**	**0**	**1**	**80**	**11.3**	**–19**													
1996-97	**Anaheim**	**NHL**	**73**	**9**	**9**	**18**	**54**	**1**	**0**	**2**	**114**	**7.9**	**–9**						**10**	**1**	**0**	**1**	**4**	**0**	**0**	**0**
1997-98	**Anaheim**	**NHL**	**73**	**6**	**10**	**16**	**82**	**0**	**1**	**0**	**110**	**5.5**	**–10**													
1998-99	**Anaheim**	**NHL**	**75**	**5**	**6**	**11**	**83**	**0**	**0**	**0**	**79**	**6.3**	**2**	**449**	**47.9**	**77**	**13**	**8:15**	**4**	**0**	**0**	**0**	**0**	**0**	**0**	**0**
99-2000	**Anaheim**	**NHL**	**11**	**1**	**1**	**2**	**6**	**0**	**0**	**0**	**9**	**11.1**	**–1**	**82**	**41.5**	**12**	**2**	**7:06**								
	NY Islanders	**NHL**	**55**	**2**	**1**	**3**	**31**	**1**	**0**	**0**	**48**	**4.2**	**–8**	**194**	**47.9**	**46**	**15**	**7:27**								
2000-01	**Columbus**	**NHL**	**1**	**0**	**0**	**0**	**0**	**0**	**0**	**0**	**3**	**0.0**	**–3**	**10**	**80.0**	**0**	**1**	**14:44**								
	Chicago Wolves	IHL	68	21	21	42	53												14	5	4	9	4			
	NHL Totals		**414**	**41**	**52**	**93**	**367**	**3**	**2**	**4**	**554**	**7.4**		**735**	**47.6**	**135**	**31**	**7:54**	**14**	**1**	**0**	**1**	**4**	**0**	**0**	**0**

ECAC First All-Star Team (1993) • NCAA East First All-America Team (1993)

Traded to **Hartford** by **Calgary** with Gary Suter and Paul Ranheim for James Patrick, Zarley Zalapski and Michael Nylander, March 10, 1994. Claimed by **Ottawa** from **Hartford** in NHL Waiver Draft, October 2, 1995. Traded to **Anaheim** by **Ottawa** with the rights to Marc Moro for Jason York and Shaun Van Allen, October 1, 1996. Traded to **NY Islanders** by **Anaheim** for Tony Hrkac and Dean Malkoc, October 29, 1999. Selected by **Columbus** from **NY Islanders** in Expansion Draft, June 23, 2000. Signed as a free agent by **New Jersey**, August 20, 2001.

DUBE, Christian

(doo-BAY, KRIHS-tyehn)

Center. Shoots right. 5'11", 170 lbs. Born, Sherbrooke, Que., April 25, 1977. NY Rangers' 1st choice, 39th overall, in 1995 Entry Draft.

			Regular Season																Playoffs							
Season	Club	League	GP	G	A	Pts	PIM	PP	SH	GW	S	%	+/-	TF	F%	H	SB	Min	GP	G	A	Pts	PIM	PP	SH	GW
1992-93	HC Martigny	Switz-2	27	36	40	76	34	....	....	....	....	....	....	....	....	....	....	....	....	....	....	....	....	....	....	....
1993-94	Sherbrooke	QMJHL	72	31	41	72	22	....	....	....	....	....	....	....	....	....	....	....	11	3	2	5	8	....	....	....
1994-95	Sherbrooke	QMJHL	71	36	65	101	43	....	....	....	....	....	....	....	....	....	....	....	7	1	7	8	8	....	....	....
1995-96	Sherbrooke	QMJHL	62	52	93	145	105	....	....	....	....	....	....	....	....	....	....	....	7	5	5	10	6	....	....	....
1996-97	Hull Olympiques	QMJHL	19	15	22	37	37	....	....	....	....	....	....	....	....	....	....	....	14	7	16	23	14	....	....	....
	NY Rangers	**NHL**	**27**	**1**	**1**	**2**	**4**	**1**	**0**	**0**	**14**	**7.1**	**-4**	....	....	....	....	....	**3**	**0**	**0**	**0**	**0**	**0**	**0**	**0**
1997-98	Hartford	AHL	79	11	46	57	46	....	....	....	....	....	....	....	....	....	....	....	9	0	4	4	6	....	....	....
1998-99	**NY Rangers**	**NHL**	**6**	**0**	**0**	**0**	**0**	**0**	**0**	**0**	**0**	**0.0**	**0**	**13**	**38.5**	**2**	**1**	**2:39**	....	....	....	....	....	....	....	....
	Hartford	AHL	58	21	30	51	20	....	....	....	....	....	....	....	....	....	....	....	6	0	3	3	4	....	....	....
99-2000	HC Lugano	Switz.	45	*25	26	51	52	....	....	....	....	....	....	....	....	....	....	....	14	8	*12	*20	14	....	....	....
	HC Lugano	EuroHL	6	2	2	4	2	....	....	....	....	....	....	....	....	....	....	....	4	2	2	4	2	....	....	....
2000-01	HC Lugano	Switz.	44	20	34	54	50	....	....	....	....	....	....	....	....	....	....	....	18	4	*14	*18	22	....	....	....
	NHL Totals		**33**	**1**	**1**	**2**	**4**	**1**	**0**	**0**	**14**	**7.1**		**13**	**38.5**	**2**	**1**	**2:39**	**3**	**0**	**0**	**0**	**0**	**0**	**0**	**0**

QMJHL First All-Star Team (1996) • Canadian Major Junior First All-Star Team (1996) • Canadian Major Junior Player of the Year (1996) • Won Stafford Smythe Memorial Trophy (Memorial Cup Tournament MVP) (1997)

DUBINSKY, Steve

(doo-BIHN-skee, STEEV) **CHI.**

Center. Shoots left. 6', 190 lbs. Born, Montreal, Que., July 9, 1970. Chicago's 9th choice, 226th overall, in 1990 Entry Draft.

1989-90	Clarkson Knights	ECAC	35	7	10	17	24	....	....	....	....	....	....	....	....	....	....	....	....	....	....	....	....	....	....	....
1990-91	Clarkson Knights	ECAC	39	13	23	36	26	....	....	....	....	....	....	....	....	....	....	....	....	....	....	....	....	....	....	....
1991-92	Clarkson Knights	ECAC	32	20	31	51	40	....	....	....	....	....	....	....	....	....	....	....	....	....	....	....	....	....	....	....
1992-93	Clarkson Knights	ECAC	35	18	26	44	58	....	....	....	....	....	....	....	....	....	....	....	....	....	....	....	....	....	....	....
1993-94	**Chicago**	**NHL**	**27**	**2**	**6**	**8**	**16**	**0**	**0**	**0**	**20**	**10.0**	**1**	....	....	....	....	....	**6**	**0**	**0**	**0**	**10**	**0**	**0**	**0**
	Indianapolis Ice	IHL	54	15	25	40	63	....	....	....	....	....	....	....	....	....	....	....	....	....	....	....	....	....	....	....
1994-95	**Chicago**	**NHL**	**16**	**0**	**0**	**0**	**8**	**0**	**0**	**0**	**16**	**0.0**	**-5**	....	....	....	....	....	....	....	....	....	....	....	....	....
	Indianapolis Ice	IHL	62	16	11	27	29	....	....	....	....	....	....	....	....	....	....	....	....	....	....	....	....	....	....	....
1995-96	**Chicago**	**NHL**	**43**	**2**	**3**	**5**	**14**	**0**	**0**	**0**	**33**	**6.1**	**3**	....	....	....	....	....	....	....	....	....	....	....	....	....
	Indianapolis Ice	IHL	16	8	8	16	10	....	....	....	....	....	....	....	....	....	....	....	....	....	....	....	....	....	....	....
1996-97	**Chicago**	**NHL**	**5**	**0**	**0**	**0**	**0**	**0**	**0**	**0**	**4**	**0.0**	**2**	....	....	....	....	....	**4**	**1**	**0**	**1**	**4**	**0**	**0**	**0**
	Indianapolis Ice	IHL	77	32	40	72	53	....	....	....	....	....	....	....	....	....	....	....	1	3	1	4	0	....	....	....
1997-98	**Chicago**	**NHL**	**82**	**5**	**13**	**18**	**57**	**0**	**1**	**0**	**112**	**4.5**	**-6**	....	....	....	....	....	....	....	....	....	....	....	....	....
1998-99	**Chicago**	**NHL**	**1**	**0**	**0**	**0**	**0**	**0**	**0**	**0**	**1**	**0.0**	**0**	**5**	**60.0**	**1**	**0**	**5:11**	....	....	....	....	....	....	....	....
	Calgary	**NHL**	**61**	**4**	**10**	**14**	**14**	**0**	**2**	**0**	**69**	**5.8**	**-7**	**223**	**46.6**	**161**	**75**	**14:38**	....	....	....	....	....	....	....	....
99-2000	**Calgary**	**NHL**	**23**	**0**	**1**	**1**	**4**	**0**	**0**	**0**	**29**	**0.0**	**-12**	**207**	**49.3**	**58**	**26**	**12:05**	....	....	....	....	....	....	....	....
2000-01	**Chicago**	**NHL**	**60**	**6**	**4**	**10**	**33**	**0**	**1**	**0**	**70**	**8.6**	**-4**	**714**	**56.7**	**105**	**36**	**10:60**	....	....	....	....	....	....	....	....
	Norfolk Admirals	AHL	14	6	5	11	4	....	....	....	....	....	....	....	....	....	....	....	....	....	....	....	....	....	....	....
	NHL Totals		**318**	**19**	**37**	**56**	**146**	**0**	**4**	**0**	**354**	**5.4**		**1149**	**53.4**	**325**	**137**	**12:40**	**10**	**1**	**0**	**1**	**14**	**0**	**0**	**0**

Traded to **Calgary** by **Chicago** with Jeff Shantz for Marty McInnis, Jamie Allison and Eric Andersson, October 27, 1998. • Missed remainder of 1999-2000 season recovering from knee injury suffered in game vs. Chicago, December 12, 1999. Signed as a free agent by **Chicago**, August 25, 2000.

DUCHESNE, Steve

(doo-SHAYN, STEEV) **DET.**

Defense. Shoots left. 5'11", 195 lbs. Born, Sept-Iles, Que., June 30, 1965.

1983-84	Wawa Travellers	NOJHA	10	9	23	32	9	....	....	....	....	....	....	....	....	....	....	....	....	....	....	....	....	....	....	....
	Drummondville	QMJHL	67	1	34	35	79	....	....	....	....	....	....	....	....	....	....	....	....	....	....	....	....	....	....	....
1984-85	Drummondville	QMJHL	65	22	54	76	94	....	....	....	....	....	....	....	....	....	....	....	5	4	7	11	8	....	....	....
1985-86	New Haven	AHL	75	14	35	49	76	....	....	....	....	....	....	....	....	....	....	....	5	0	2	2	9	....	....	....
1986-87	**Los Angeles**	**NHL**	**75**	**13**	**25**	**38**	**74**	**5**	**0**	**2**	**113**	**11.5**	**8**	....	....	....	....	....	**5**	**2**	**2**	**4**	**4**	**1**	**0**	**0**
1987-88	**Los Angeles**	**NHL**	**71**	**16**	**39**	**55**	**109**	**5**	**0**	**4**	**190**	**8.4**	**0**	....	....	....	....	....	**5**	**1**	**3**	**4**	**14**	**1**	**0**	**0**
1988-89	**Los Angeles**	**NHL**	**79**	**25**	**50**	**75**	**92**	**8**	**5**	**2**	**215**	**11.6**	**31**	....	....	....	....	....	**11**	**4**	**4**	**8**	**12**	**2**	**0**	**0**
1989-90	**Los Angeles**	**NHL**	**79**	**20**	**42**	**62**	**36**	**6**	**0**	**1**	**224**	**8.9**	**-3**	....	....	....	....	....	**10**	**2**	**9**	**11**	**6**	**1**	**0**	**0**
1990-91	**Los Angeles**	**NHL**	**78**	**21**	**41**	**62**	**66**	**8**	**0**	**3**	**171**	**12.3**	**19**	....	....	....	....	....	**12**	**4**	**8**	**12**	**8**	**1**	**0**	**0**
1991-92	**Philadelphia**	**NHL**	**78**	**18**	**38**	**56**	**86**	**7**	**2**	**3**	**229**	**7.9**	**-7**	....	....	....	....	....	....	....	....	....	....	....	....	....
1992-93	**Quebec**	**NHL**	**82**	**20**	**62**	**82**	**57**	**8**	**0**	**2**	**227**	**8.8**	**15**	....	....	....	....	....	**6**	**0**	**5**	**5**	**6**	**0**	**0**	**0**
1993-94	**St. Louis**	**NHL**	**36**	**12**	**19**	**31**	**14**	**8**	**0**	**1**	**115**	**10.4**	**1**	....	....	....	....	....	**4**	**0**	**2**	**2**	**2**	**0**	**0**	**0**
1994-95	**St. Louis**	**NHL**	**47**	**12**	**26**	**38**	**36**	**1**	**0**	**1**	**116**	**10.3**	**29**	....	....	....	....	....	**7**	**0**	**4**	**4**	**2**	**0**	**0**	**0**
1995-96	**Ottawa**	**NHL**	**62**	**12**	**24**	**36**	**42**	**7**	**0**	**2**	**163**	**7.4**	**-23**	....	....	....	....	....	....	....	....	....	....	....	....	....
1996-97	**Ottawa**	**NHL**	**78**	**19**	**28**	**47**	**38**	**10**	**2**	**3**	**208**	**9.1**	**-9**	....	....	....	....	....	**7**	**1**	**4**	**5**	**0**	**1**	**0**	**1**
1997-98	**St. Louis**	**NHL**	**80**	**14**	**42**	**56**	**32**	**5**	**1**	**1**	**153**	**9.2**	**9**	....	....	....	....	....	**10**	**0**	**4**	**4**	**6**	**0**	**0**	**0**
1998-99	**Los Angeles**	**NHL**	**60**	**4**	**19**	**23**	**22**	**1**	**0**	**1**	**99**	**4.0**	**-6**	**2**	**50.0**	**38**	**95**	**21:11**	....	....	....	....	....	....	....	....
	Philadelphia	**NHL**	**11**	**2**	**5**	**7**	**2**	**1**	**0**	**1**	**19**	**10.5**	**0**	**0**	**0.0**	**5**	**14**	**22:28**	**6**	**0**	**2**	**2**	**2**	**0**	**0**	**0**
99-2000	**Detroit**	**NHL**	**79**	**10**	**31**	**41**	**42**	**1**	**0**	**1**	**154**	**6.5**	**12**	**1**	**0.0**	**41**	**104**	**21:14**	**9**	**0**	**4**	**4**	**10**	**0**	**0**	**0**
2000-01	**Detroit**	**NHL**	**54**	**6**	**19**	**25**	**48**	**2**	**0**	**0**	**76**	**7.9**	**9**	**0**	**0.0**	**40**	**75**	**18:20**	**6**	**2**	**4**	**6**	**0**	**2**	**0**	**0**
	NHL Totals		**1049**	**224**	**510**	**734**	**796**	**83**	**10**	**28**	**2472**	**9.1**		**3**	**33.3**	**124**	**288**	**20:31**	**98**	**16**	**55**	**71**	**72**	**9**	**0**	**1**

QMJHL First All-Star Team (1985) • NHL All-Rookie Team (1987) • Played in NHL All-Star Game (1989, 1990, 1993)

Signed as a free agent by **LA Kings**, October 1, 1984. Traded to **Philadelphia** by **LA Kings** with Steve Kasper and LA Kings' 4th round choice (Aris Brimanis) in 1991 Entry Draft for Jari Kurri and Jeff Chychrun, May 30, 1991. Traded to **Quebec** by **Philadelphia** with Peter Forsberg, Kerry Huffman, Mike Ricci, Ron Hextall, Philadelphia's 1st round choice (Jocelyn Thibault) in 1993 Entry Draft, $15,000,000 and future considerations (Chris Simon and Philadelphia's 1st round choice (later traded to Toronto - later traded to Washington - Washington selected Nolan Baumgartner) in 1994 Entry Draft, July 21, 1992) for Eric Lindros, June 30, 1992. Traded to **St. Louis** by **Quebec** with Denis Chasse for Garth Butcher, Ron Sutter and Bob Bassen, January 23, 1994. Traded to **Ottawa** by **St. Louis** for Ottawa's 2nd round choice (later traded to Buffalo - Buffalo selected Cory Sarich) in 1996 Entry Draft, August 4, 1995. Traded to **St. Louis** by **Ottawa** for Igor Kravchuk, August 25, 1997. Signed as a free agent by **LA Kings**, July 2, 1998. Traded to **Philadelphia** by **Los Angeles** for Dave Babych and Philadelphia's 5th round choice (Nathan Marsters) in 2000 Entry Draft, March 23, 1999. Signed as a free agent by **Detroit**, September 3, 1999.

DUERDEN, Dave

(DEWER-dehn, DAYV) **NYR**

Left wing. Shoots left. 6'2", 200 lbs. Born, Oshawa, Ont., April 11, 1977. Florida's 4th choice, 80th overall, in 1995 Entry Draft.

1991-92	Ajax Knights	OMHA	60	47	48	95	100	....	....	....	....	....	....	....	....	....	....	....	....	....	....	....	....	....	....	....
1992-93	Ajax Knights	OMHA	60	21	48	69	45	....	....	....	....	....	....	....	....	....	....	....	....	....	....	....	....	....	....	....
1993-94	Wexford Raiders	MTJHL	47	17	27	44	26	....	....	....	....	....	....	....	....	....	....	....	....	....	....	....	....	....	....	....
1994-95	Peterborough	OHL	66	20	33	53	21	....	....	....	....	....	....	....	....	....	....	....	11	6	2	8	6	....	....	....
1995-96	Peterborough	OHL	66	35	35	70	47	....	....	....	....	....	....	....	....	....	....	....	24	14	13	27	16	....	....	....
1996-97	Peterborough	OHL	66	36	48	84	34	....	....	....	....	....	....	....	....	....	....	....	4	2	4	6	0	....	....	....
1997-98	Port Huron	UHL	7	0	4	4	10	....	....	....	....	....	....	....	....	....	....	....	....	....	....	....	....	....	....	....
	New Haven	AHL	36	6	7	13	10	....	....	....	....	....	....	....	....	....	....	....	....	....	....	....	....	....	....	....
	Fort Wayne	IHL	7	0	1	1	0	....	....	....	....	....	....	....	....	....	....	....	....	....	....	....	....	....	....	....
1998-99	Miami Matadors	ECHL	13	10	7	17	0	....	....	....	....	....	....	....	....	....	....	....	....	....	....	....	....	....	....	....
	Kentucky	AHL	36	8	9	17	9	....	....	....	....	....	....	....	....	....	....	....	6	0	2	2	0	....	....	....
99-2000	**Florida**	**NHL**	**2**	**0**	**0**	**0**	**0**	**0**	**0**	**0**	**1**	**0.0**	**0**	**0**	**0.0**	**0**	**0**	**1:35**	....	....	....	....	....	....	....	....
	Louisville Panthers	AHL	74	25	38	63	6	....	....	....	....	....	....	....	....	....	....	....	4	0	1	1	0	....	....	....
2000-01	Louisville Panthers	AHL	34	9	14	23	8	....	....	....	....	....	....	....	....	....	....	....	....	....	....	....	....	....	....	....
	Hartford	AHL	43	16	9	25	10	....	....	....	....	....	....	....	....	....	....	....	5	0	2	2	....	....	....	....
	NHL Totals		**2**	**0**	**0**	**0**	**0**	**0**	**0**	**0**	**1**	**0.0**		**0**	**0.0**	**0**	**0**	**1:35**	....	....	....	....	....	....	....	....

OHL Second All-Star Team (1997)

Traded to **NY Rangers** by **Florida** for future considerations, June 29, 2001.

DUMONT, J-P

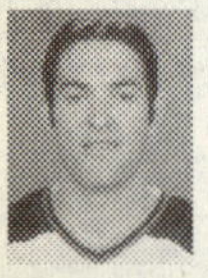

(DOO-mawnt, zhaw-pee-AIR) **BUF.**

Right wing. Shoots left. 6'2", 202 lbs. Born, Montreal, Que., April 1, 1978. NY Islanders' 1st choice, 3rd overall, in 1996 Entry Draft.

1993-94	Mtl-Bourassa	QAAA	44	27	20	47	44	....	....	....	....	....	....	....	....	....	....	....	4	2	3	5	4	....	....	....
1994-95	Val-d'Or Foreurs	QMJHL	48	5	14	19	24	....	....	....	....	....	....	....	....	....	....	....	....	....	....	....	....	....	....	....
1995-96	Val-d'Or Foreurs	QMJHL	66	48	57	105	109	....	....	....	....	....	....	....	....	....	....	....	13	12	8	20	22	....	....	....
1996-97	Val-d'Or Foreurs	QMJHL	62	44	64	108	86	....	....	....	....	....	....	....	....	....	....	....	13	9	7	16	12	....	....	....
1997-98	Val-d'Or Foreurs	QMJHL	55	57	42	99	63	....	....	....	....	....	....	....	....	....	....	....	19	31	15	46	18	....	....	....
1998-99	**Chicago**	**NHL**	**25**	**9**	**6**	**15**	**10**	**0**	**0**	**2**	**42**	**21.4**	**7**	**10**	**50.0**	**22**	**8**	**14:14**	....	....	....	....	....	....	....	....
	Portland Pirates	AHL	50	32	14	46	39	....	....	....	....	....	....	....	....	....	....	....	....	....	....	....	....	....	....	....
	Chicago Wolves	IHL	....	....	....	....	....	....	....	....	....	....	....	....	....	....	....	....	10	4	1	5	6	....	....	....

			Regular Season																Playoffs							
Season	Club	League	GP	G	A	Pts	PIM	PP	SH	GW	S	%	+/-	TF	F%	H	SB	Min	GP	G	A	Pts	PIM	PP	SH	GW
99-2000	Chicago	NHL	47	10	8	18	18	0	0	1	86	11.6	−6	12	33.3	49	7	12:54								
	Cleveland	IHL	7	5	2	7	8																			
	Rochester	AHL	13	7	10	17	18												21	14	7	21	32			
2000-01	Buffalo	NHL	79	23	28	51	54	9	0	5	156	14.7	1	3	33.3	132	20	15:01	13	4	3	7	8	0	0	0
	NHL Totals		151	42	42	84	82	9	0	8	284	14.8		25	40.0	203	35	14:14	13	4	3	7	8	0	0	0

QMJHL Second All-Star Team (1997)

Rights traded to **Chicago** by **NY Islanders** with Chicago's 5th round choice (later traded to Philadelphia - Philadelphia selected Francis Belanger) in 1998 Entry Draft for Dmitri Nabokov, May 30, 1998. Traded to **Buffalo** by **Chicago** with Doug Gilmour and future considerations for Michal Grosek, March 10, 2000.

DUPUIS, Pascal
(doo-PWEE, pas-KAL) **MIN.**

Left wing. Shoots Right. 6', 195 lbs. Born, Laval, Quebec, April 7, 1979.

1995-96	Laval-Laurentide	QAAA	41	10	15	25													14	11	11	22				
1996-97	Rouyn-Noranda	QMJHL	44	9	15	24	20																			
1997-98	Rouyn-Noranda	QMJHL	39	9	17	26	36																			
	Shawinigan	QMJHL	28	7	13	20	10												6	2	0	2	4			
1998-99	Shawinigan	QMJHL	57	30	42	72	118												6	1	8	9	18			
99-2000	Shawinigan	QMJHL	61	50	55	105	99												13	*15	7	22	4			
2000-01	Minnesota	NHL	4	1	0	1	4	1	0	0	8	12.5	0	0	0.0	12	1	15:36								
	Cleveland	IHL	70	19	24	43	37												4	0	0	0	0			
	NHL Totals		4	1	0	1	4	1	0	0	8	12.5		0	0.0	12	1	15:36								

Signed as a free agent by **Minnesota**, August 18, 2000.

DVORAK, Radek
(duh-VOHR-ak, RA-dehk) **NYR**

Right wing. Shoots right. 6'1", 194 lbs. Born, Tabor, Czech., March 9, 1977. Florida's 1st choice, 10th overall, in 1995 Entry Draft.

1992-93	MC Budejovice	Czech-Jr.	35	44	46	90																				
1993-94	MC Budejovice-Jr.	Cze-Rep	20	17	18	35																				
	MC Budejovice	Cze-Rep	8	0	0	0	0																			
1994-95	MC Budejovice	Cze-Rep	10	3	5	8	2												9	5	1	6				
1995-96	Florida	NHL	77	13	14	27	20	0	0	4	126	10.3	5						16	1	3	4	0	0	0	0
1996-97	Florida	NHL	78	18	21	39	30	2	0	1	139	12.9	−2						3	0	0	0	0	0	0	0
1997-98	Florida	NHL	64	12	24	36	33	2	3	0	112	10.7	−1													
1998-99	Florida	NHL	82	19	24	43	29	0	4	0	182	10.4	7	98	46.9	30	33	16:13								
99-2000	Florida	NHL	35	7	10	17	6	0	0	1	67	10.4	5	16	37.5	5	11	15:25								
	NY Rangers	NHL	46	11	22	33	10	2	1	0	90	12.2	0	34	35.3	22	16	18:24								
2000-01	NY Rangers	NHL	82	31	36	67	20	5	2	3	230	13.5	9	20	30.0	29	41	19:04								
	NHL Totals		464	111	151	262	148	11	10	9	946	11.7		168	41.7	86	101	17:28	19	1	3	4	0	0	0	0

Traded to **San Jose** by **Florida** for Mike Vernon, San Jose's 3rd round choice (Sean O'Connor) in 2000 Entry Draft and future considerations, December 30, 1999. Traded to **NY Rangers** by **San Jose** for Todd Harvey and NY Rangers' 4th round choice (Dimitri Patzold) in 2001 Entry Draft, December 30, 1999.

DWYER, Gordie
(DWIGH-uhr, GOHR-dee) **T.B.**

Left wing. Shoots left. 6'3", 216 lbs. Born, Dalhousie, NB, January 25, 1978. Montreal's 5th choice, 152nd overall, in 1998 Entry Draft.

1993-94	Magog Selectes	QAAA	42	7	15	22	62												4	2	1	3	0			
1994-95	Hull Olympiques	QMJHL	57	3	7	10	204												17	1	3	4	54			
1995-96	Hull Olympiques	QMJHL	25	5	9	14	199																			
	Laval Titan	QMJHL	22	5	17	22	72																			
	Beauport	QMJHL	22	4	9	13	87												20	3	5	8	104			
1996-97	Drummondville	QMJHL	66	21	48	69	393												8	6	1	7	39			
1997-98	Quebec Remparts	QMJHL	59	18	27	45	365												14	4	9	13	67			
1998-99	Fredericton	AHL	14	0	0	0	46																			
	New Orleans	ECHL	36	1	3	4	163												11	0	0	0	27			
99-2000	Quebec Citadelles	AHL	7	0	0	0	37																			
	Tampa Bay	NHL	24	0	1	1	135	0	0	0	7	0.0	−6	0	0.0	53	4	4:57								
	Detroit Vipers	IHL	27	0	2	2	147																			
2000-01	Tampa Bay	NHL	28	0	1	1	96	0	0	0	12	0.0	−7	2	50.0	48	2	5:47								
	Detroit Vipers	IHL	24	2	3	5	169																			
	NHL Totals		52	0	2	2	231	0	0	0	19	0.0		2	50.0	101	6	5:24								

• Re-entered NHL Entry Draft. Originally St. Louis's 2nd choice, 67th overall, in 1996 Entry Draft.

Traded to **Tampa Bay** by **Montreal** for Mike McBain, November 26, 1999.

DYKHUIS, Karl
(DIGH-kowz, KAHRL) **MTL.**

Defense. Shoots left. 6'3", 214 lbs. Born, Sept-Iles, Que., July 8, 1972. Chicago's 1st choice, 16th overall, in 1990 Entry Draft.

1987-88	Lac St-Jean	QAAA	37	2	12	14													2	0	1	1	2			
1988-89	Hull Olympiques	QMJHL	63	2	29	31	59												9	1	9	10	6			
1989-90	Hull Olympiques	QMJHL	69	10	46	56	119												11	2	5	7	2			
1990-91	Canada	Nat-Team	37	2	9	11	16																			
	Longueuil College	QMJHL	3	1	4	5	6												8	2	5	7	6			
1991-92	Canada	Nat-Team	19	1	2	3	16																			
	Verdun College	QMJHL	29	5	19	24	55												17	0	12	12	14			
	Chicago	NHL	6	1	3	4	4	1	0	0	12	8.3	−1													
1992-93	Chicago	NHL	12	0	5	5	0	0	0	0	10	0.0	2													
	Indianapolis Ice	IHL	59	5	18	23	76												5	1	1	2	8			
1993-94	Indianapolis Ice	IHL	73	7	25	32	132																			
1994-95	Indianapolis Ice	IHL	52	2	21	23	63																			
	Philadelphia	NHL	33	2	6	8	37	1	0	1	46	4.3	7						15	4	4	8	14	2	0	2
	Hershey Bears	AHL	1	0	0	0	0																			
1995-96	Philadelphia	NHL	82	5	15	20	101	1	0	0	104	4.8	12						12	2	2	4	22	1	0	0
1996-97	Philadelphia	NHL	62	4	15	19	35	2	0	1	101	4.0	6						18	0	3	3	2	0	0	0
1997-98	Tampa Bay	NHL	78	5	9	14	110	0	1	0	91	5.5	−8													
1998-99	Tampa Bay	NHL	33	2	1	3	18	0	0	0	27	7.4	−21	0	0.0	44	39	20:14								
	Philadelphia	NHL	45	2	4	6	32	1	0	0	61	3.3	−2	0	0.0	38	47	18:15	5	1	0	1	4	0	0	0
99-2000	Philadelphia	NHL	5	0	1	1	6	0	0	0	5	0.0	−2	0	0.0	9	3	14:54								
	Montreal	NHL	67	7	12	19	40	3	1	0	64	10.9	−3	0	0.0	97	98	19:53								
2000-01	Montreal	NHL	67	8	9	17	44	2	0	1	66	12.1	9	4	100.0	89	63	15:40								
	NHL Totals		490	36	80	116	427	11	2	3	587	6.1		4	100.0	277	250	18:11	50	7	9	16	42	3	0	2

QMJHL First All-Star Team (1990)

Traded to **Philadelphia** by **Chicago** for Bob Wilkie and Philadelphia's 5th round choice (Kyle Calder) in 1997 Entry Draft, February 16, 1995. Traded to **Tampa Bay** by **Philadelphia** with Mikael Renberg for Philadelphia's 1st round choices (previously acquired by Tampa Bay) in 1998 (Simon Gagne), 1999 (Maxime Ouellet), 2000 (Justin Williams) and 2001 (later traded to Ottawa - Ottawa selected Tim Gleason) Entry Drafts, August 20, 1997. Traded to **Philadelphia** by **Tampa Bay** for Petr Svoboda, December 28, 1998. Traded to **Montreal** by **Philadelphia** for cash, October 20, 1999.

EAKINS, Dallas
(EE-kins, DAL-las) **CGY.**

Defense. Shoots left. 6'2", 195 lbs. Born, Dade City, FL, February 27, 1967. Washington's 11th choice, 208th overall, in 1985 Entry Draft.

1983-84	Peterborough AA	OMHA	29	7	20	27	67																			
	Peterborough	OJHL-B	5	0	3	3	4																			
1984-85	Peterborough	OHL	48	0	8	8	96												7	0	0	0	18			
1985-86	Peterborough	OHL	60	6	16	22	134												16	0	1	1	30			
1986-87	Peterborough	OHL	54	3	11	14	145												12	1	4	5	37			
1987-88	Peterborough	OHL	64	11	27	38	129												12	3	12	15	16			
1988-89	Baltimore	AHL	62	0	10	10	139																			
1989-90	Moncton Hawks	AHL	75	2	11	13	189																			
1990-91	Moncton Hawks	AHL	75	1	12	13	132												9	0	1	1	44			
1991-92	Moncton Hawks	AHL	67	3	13	16	136												11	2	1	3	16			
1992-93	Winnipeg	NHL	14	0	2	2	38	0	0	0	9	0.0	2													
	Moncton Hawks	AHL	55	4	6	10	132																			

			Regular Season																Playoffs							
Season	Club	League	GP	G	A	Pts	PIM	PP	SH	GW	S	%	+/-	TF	F%	H	SB	Min	GP	G	A	Pts	PIM	PP	SH	GW
1993-94	**Florida**	**NHL**	**1**	**0**	**0**	**0**	**0**	**0**	**0**	**0**	**2**	**0.0**	**0**	....	....	....	....	....	....	....	....	....	....	....	....	....
	Cincinnati	IHL	80	1	18	19	143	....	....	....	....	....	....	....	....	....	....	....	8	0	1	1	41	....	....	....
1994-95	Cincinnati	IHL	59	6	12	18	69	....	....	....	....	....	....	....	....	....	....	....	....	....	....	....	....	....	....	....
	Florida	**NHL**	**17**	**0**	**1**	**1**	**35**	**0**	**0**	**0**	**3**	**0.0**	**2**	....	....	....	....	....	....	....	....	....	....	....	....	....
1995-96	**St. Louis**	**NHL**	**16**	**0**	**1**	**1**	**34**	**0**	**0**	**0**	**6**	**0.0**	**−2**	....	....	....	....	....	....	....	....	....	....	....	....	....
	Worcester	AHL	4	0	0	0	12	....	....	....	....	....	....	....	....	....	....	....	....	....	....	....	....	....	....	....
	Winnipeg	**NHL**	**2**	**0**	**0**	**0**	**0**	**0**	**0**	**0**	**0**	**0.0**	**1**	....	....	....	....	....	....	....	....	....	....	....	....	....
1996-97	**Phoenix**	**NHL**	**4**	**0**	**0**	**0**	**10**	**0**	**0**	**0**	**2**	**0.0**	**−3**	....	....	....	....	....	....	....	....	....	....	....	....	....
	Springfield	AHL	38	6	7	13	63	....	....	....	....	....	....	....	....	....	....	....	....	....	....	....	....	....	....	....
	NY Rangers	**NHL**	**3**	**0**	**0**	**0**	**6**	**0**	**0**	**0**	**2**	**0.0**	**−1**	....	....	....	....	....	**4**	**0**	**0**	**0**	**4**	**0**	**0**	**0**
	Binghamton	AHL	19	1	7	8	15	....	....	....	....	....	....	....	....	....	....	....	....	....	....	....	....	....	....	....
1997-98	**Florida**	**NHL**	**23**	**0**	**1**	**1**	**44**	**0**	**0**	**0**	**16**	**0.0**	**1**	....	....	....	....	....	....	....	....	....	....	....	....	....
	New Haven	AHL	4	0	1	1	7	....	....	....	....	....	....	....	....	....	....	....	....	....	....	....	....	....	....	....
1998-99	**Toronto**	**NHL**	**18**	**0**	**2**	**2**	**24**	**0**	**0**	**0**	**11**	**0.0**	**3**	**0**	**0.0**	**20**	**10**	**16:28**	**1**	**0**	**0**	**0**	**0**	**0**	**0**	**0**
	Chicago Wolves	IHL	2	0	0	0	0	....	....	....	....	....	....	....	....	....	....	....	....	....	....	....	....	....	....	....
	St. John's Leafs	AHL	20	3	7	10	16	....	....	....	....	....	....	....	....	....	....	....	5	0	1	1	6	....	....	....
99-2000	**NY Islanders**	**NHL**	**2**	**0**	**1**	**1**	**2**	**0**	**0**	**0**	**4**	**0.0**	**3**	**0**	**0.0**	**2**	**1**	**21:28**	....	....	....	....	....	....	....	....
	Chicago Wolves	IHL	68	5	26	31	99	....	....	....	....	....	....	....	....	....	....	....	16	1	4	5	16	....	....	....
2000-01	**Calgary**	**NHL**	**17**	**0**	**1**	**1**	**11**	**0**	**0**	**0**	**4**	**0.0**	**−1**	**0**	**0.0**	**3**	**11**	**12:18**	....	....	....	....	....	....	....	....
	Chicago Wolves	IHL	64	3	16	19	49	....	....	....	....	....	....	....	....	....	....	....	14	0	0	0	24	....	....	....
	NHL Totals		**117**	**0**	**9**	**9**	**204**	**0**	**0**	**0**	**59**	**0.0**		**0**	**0.0**	**25**	**22**	**14:50**	**5**	**0**	**0**	**0**	**4**	**0**	**0**	**0**

IHL Second All-Star Team (2000)

Signed as a free agent by **Winnipeg**, October 17, 1989. Signed as a free agent by **Florida**, July 8, 1993. Traded to **St. Louis** by **Florida** for St. Louis' 4th round choice (Ivan Novoseltsev) in 1997 Entry Draft, September 28, 1995. Claimed on waivers by **Winnipeg** from **St. Louis**, March 20, 1996. Transferred to **Phoenix** after **Winnipeg** franchise relocated, July 1, 1996. Traded to **NY Rangers** by **Phoenix** with Mike Eastwood for Jayson More, February 6, 1997. Signed as a free agent by **Florida**, July 30, 1997. Signed as a free agent by **Toronto**, July 28, 1998. Signed as a free agent by **NY Islanders**, August 12, 1999. Traded to **Chicago** by **NY Islanders** for future considerations, March 3, 2000. Signed as a free agent by **Calgary**, July 27, 2000.

EASTWOOD, Mike

(EEST-wuhd, MIGHK) **ST.L.**

Center. Shoots right. 6'3", 213 lbs. Born, Ottawa, Ont., July 1, 1967. Toronto's 5th choice, 91st overall, in 1987 Entry Draft.

1984-85	Nepean Raiders	OCJHL	46	10	13	23	18	....	....	....	....	....	....	....	....	....	....	....	....	....	....	....	....	....	....	....
1985-86	Nepean Raiders	OCJHL	7	4	2	6	6	....	....	....	....	....	....	....	....	....	....	....	....	....	....	....	....	....	....	....
1986-87	Pembroke Kings	OCJHL	54	58	45	103	62	....	....	....	....	....	....	....	....	....	....	....	23	36	11	47	32	....	....	....
1987-88	Western Michigan	CCHA	42	5	8	13	14	....	....	....	....	....	....	....	....	....	....	....	....	....	....	....	....	....	....	....
1988-89	Western Michigan	CCHA	40	10	13	23	87	....	....	....	....	....	....	....	....	....	....	....	....	....	....	....	....	....	....	....
1989-90	Western Michigan	CCHA	40	25	27	52	36	....	....	....	....	....	....	....	....	....	....	....	....	....	....	....	....	....	....	....
1990-91	Western Michigan	CCHA	42	29	32	61	84	....	....	....	....	....	....	....	....	....	....	....	....	....	....	....	....	....	....	....
1991-92	**Toronto**	**NHL**	**9**	**0**	**2**	**2**	**4**	**0**	**0**	**0**	**6**	**0.0**	**−4**	....	....	....	....	....	....	....	....	....	....	....	....	....
	St. John's Leafs	AHL	61	18	25	43	28	....	....	....	....	....	....	....	....	....	....	....	16	9	10	19	16	....	....	....
1992-93	**Toronto**	**NHL**	**12**	**1**	**6**	**7**	**21**	**0**	**0**	**0**	**11**	**9.1**	**−2**	....	....	....	....	....	**10**	**1**	**2**	**3**	**8**	**0**	**0**	**0**
	St. John's Leafs	AHL	60	24	35	59	32	....	....	....	....	....	....	....	....	....	....	....	....	....	....	....	....	....	....	....
1993-94	**Toronto**	**NHL**	**54**	**8**	**10**	**18**	**28**	**1**	**0**	**2**	**41**	**19.5**	**2**	....	....	....	....	....	**18**	**3**	**2**	**5**	**12**	**1**	**0**	**1**
1994-95	**Toronto**	**NHL**	**36**	**5**	**5**	**10**	**32**	**0**	**0**	**0**	**38**	**13.2**	**−12**	....	....	....	....	....	....	....	....	....	....	....	....	....
	Winnipeg	**NHL**	**13**	**3**	**6**	**9**	**4**	**0**	**0**	**0**	**17**	**17.6**	**3**	....	....	....	....	....	....	....	....	....	....	....	....	....
1995-96	**Winnipeg**	**NHL**	**80**	**14**	**14**	**28**	**20**	**2**	**0**	**3**	**94**	**14.9**	**−14**	....	....	....	....	....	**6**	**0**	**1**	**1**	**2**	**0**	**0**	**0**
1996-97	**Phoenix**	**NHL**	**33**	**1**	**3**	**4**	**4**	**0**	**0**	**0**	**22**	**4.5**	**−3**	....	....	....	....	....	....	....	....	....	....	....	....	....
	NY Rangers	**NHL**	**27**	**1**	**7**	**8**	**10**	**0**	**0**	**0**	**22**	**4.5**	**2**	....	....	....	....	....	**15**	**1**	**2**	**3**	**22**	**0**	**0**	**0**
1997-98	**NY Rangers**	**NHL**	**48**	**5**	**5**	**10**	**16**	**0**	**0**	**0**	**34**	**14.7**	**−2**	....	....	....	....	....	....	....	....	....	....	....	....	....
	St. Louis	**NHL**	**10**	**1**	**0**	**1**	**6**	**0**	**0**	**1**	**4**	**25.0**	**0**	....	....	....	....	....	**3**	**1**	**0**	**1**	**0**	**0**	**0**	**1**
1998-99	**St. Louis**	**NHL**	**82**	**9**	**21**	**30**	**36**	**0**	**0**	**0**	**76**	**11.8**	**6**	**1235**	**56.6**	**40**	**35**	**14:59**	**13**	**1**	**1**	**2**	**6**	**0**	**0**	**0**
99-2000	**St. Louis**	**NHL**	**79**	**19**	**15**	**34**	**32**	**1**	**3**	**3**	**83**	**22.9**	**5**	**872**	**52.2**	**43**	**37**	**15:08**	**7**	**1**	**1**	**2**	**6**	**0**	**0**	**0**
2000-01	**St. Louis**	**NHL**	**77**	**6**	**17**	**23**	**28**	**0**	**2**	**1**	**51**	**11.8**	**4**	**1230**	**53.4**	**41**	**35**	**14:08**	**15**	**0**	**2**	**2**	**2**	**0**	**0**	**0**
	NHL Totals		**560**	**73**	**111**	**184**	**241**	**4**	**5**	**10**	**499**	**14.6**		**3337**	**54.3**	**124**	**107**	**14:46**	**87**	**8**	**11**	**19**	**58**	**1**	**0**	**2**

CCHA Second All-Star Team (1991)

Traded to **Winnipeg** by **Toronto** with Toronto's 3rd round choice (Brad Isbister) in 1995 Entry Draft for Tie Domi, April 7, 1995. Transferred to **Phoenix** after **Winnipeg** franchise relocated, July 1, 1996. Traded to **NY Rangers** by **Phoenix** with Dallas Eakins for Jayson More, February 6, 1997. Traded to **St. Louis** by **NY Rangers** for Harry York, March 24, 1998.

EATON, Mark

(EE-tohn, MAHRK) **NSH.**

Defense. Shoots left. 6'2", 205 lbs. Born, Wilmington, DE, May 6, 1977.

1995-96	Waterloo Hawks	USHL	50	4	21	25	....	....	....	....	....	....	....	....	....	....	....	....	....	....	....	....	....	....	....	....
1996-97	Waterloo Hawks	USHL	50	6	32	38	62	....	....	....	....	....	....	....	....	....	....	....	....	....	....	....	....	....	....	....
1997-98	Notre Dame	CCHA	41	12	17	29	32	....	....	....	....	....	....	....	....	....	....	....	....	....	....	....	....	....	....	....
1998-99	Philadelphia	AHL	74	9	27	36	38	....	....	....	....	....	....	....	....	....	....	....	16	4	8	12	0	....	....	....
99-2000	**Philadelphia**	**NHL**	**27**	**1**	**1**	**2**	**8**	**0**	**0**	**1**	**25**	**4.0**	**1**	**0**	**0.0**	**21**	**35**	**18:17**	**7**	**0**	**0**	**0**	**0**	**0**	**0**	**0**
	Philadelphia	AHL	47	9	17	26	6	....	....	....	....	....	....	....	....	....	....	....	....	....	....	....	....	....	....	....
2000-01	**Nashville**	**NHL**	**34**	**3**	**8**	**11**	**14**	**1**	**0**	**1**	**32**	**9.4**	**7**	**0**	**0.0**	**29**	**23**	**17:13**	....	....	....	....	....	....	....	....
	Milwaukee	IHL	34	3	12	15	27	....	....	....	....	....	....	....	....	....	....	....	....	....	....	....	....	....	....	....
	NHL Totals		**61**	**4**	**9**	**13**	**22**	**1**	**0**	**2**	**57**	**7.0**		**0**	**0.0**	**50**	**58**	**17:42**	**7**	**0**	**0**	**0**	**0**	**0**	**0**	**0**

Won Curt Hammer Award (Most Gentlemanly Player - USHL) (1997) • USHL Second All-Star Team (1997) • CCHA Rookie of the Year (1998)

Signed as a free agent by **Philadelphia**, August 4, 1998. Traded to **Nashville** by **Philadelphia** for Detroit's 3rd round choice (previously acquired, Philadelphia selected Patrick Sharp) in 2001 Entry Draft, September 29, 2000.

EKMAN, Nils

(EHK-mahn, NIHLS) **NYR**

Left wing. Shoots left. 5'11", 185 lbs. Born, Stockholm, Sweden, March 11, 1976. Calgary's 6th choice, 107th overall, in 1994 Entry Draft.

1993-94	Hammarby IF	Swede-Jr.	11	4	5	9	14	....	....	....	....	....	....	....	....	....	....	....	....	....	....	....	....	....	....	....
	Hammarby IF	Sweden-2	18	7	2	9	4	....	....	....	....	....	....	....	....	....	....	....	....	....	....	....	....	....	....	....
1994-95	Hammarby IF	Swede-Jr.	2	2	1	3	0	....	....	....	....	....	....	....	....	....	....	....	....	....	....	....	....	....	....	....
	Hammarby IF	Sweden-2	32	10	8	18	18	....	....	....	....	....	....	....	....	....	....	....	....	....	....	....	....	....	....	....
1995-96	Hammarby IF	Sweden-2	26	9	7	16	53	....	....	....	....	....	....	....	....	....	....	....	1	0	0	0	0	....	....	....
1996-97	Kiekko-Espoo	Finland	50	24	19	43	60	....	....	....	....	....	....	....	....	....	....	....	4	2	0	2	4	....	....	....
1997-98	Kiekko-Espoo	Finland	43	14	14	28	86	....	....	....	....	....	....	....	....	....	....	....	7	2	2	4	27	....	....	....
	Saint John Flames	AHL	....	....	....	....	....	....	....	....	....	....	....	....	....	....	....	....	1	0	0	0	2	....	....	....
1998-99	Kiekko-Espoo	Finland	52	20	14	34	96	....	....	....	....	....	....	....	....	....	....	....	3	1	1	2	6	....	....	....
99-2000	Detroit Vipers	IHL	10	7	2	9	8	....	....	....	....	....	....	....	....	....	....	....	....	....	....	....	....	....	....	....
	Tampa Bay	**NHL**	**28**	**2**	**2**	**4**	**36**	**1**	**0**	**0**	**42**	**4.8**	**−8**	**3**	**0.0**	**23**	**8**	**11:12**	....	....	....	....	....	....	....	....
	Long Beach	IHL	27	11	12	23	26	....	....	....	....	....	....	....	....	....	....	....	5	3	3	6	4	....	....	....
2000-01	**Tampa Bay**	**NHL**	**43**	**9**	**11**	**20**	**40**	**2**	**1**	**1**	**72**	**12.5**	**−15**	**16**	**37.5**	**21**	**13**	**15:45**	....	....	....	....	....	....	....	....
	Detroit Vipers	IHL	33	22	14	36	63	....	....	....	....	....	....	....	....	....	....	....	....	....	....	....	....	....	....	....
	NHL Totals		**71**	**11**	**13**	**24**	**76**	**3**	**1**	**1**	**114**	**9.6**		**19**	**31.6**	**44**	**21**	**13:57**	....	....	....	....	....	....	....	....

Won Garry F. Longman Memorial Trophy (Top Rookie - IHL) (2000)

Traded to **Tampa Bay** by **Calgary** with Calgary's 4th round choice (later traded to NY Islanders - NY Islanders selected Vladimir Gorbunov) in 2000 Entry Draft for Andreas Johansson, November 20, 1999. Traded to **NY Rangers** by **Tampa Bay** with Kyle Freadrich for Tim Taylor, June 30, 2001.

ELIAS, Patrik

(ehl-EE-ahsh, PA-trihk) **N.J.**

Left wing. Shoots left. 6'1", 195 lbs. Born, Trebic, Czech., April 13, 1976. New Jersey's 2nd choice, 51st overall, in 1994 Entry Draft.

1992-93	Poldi Kladno	Czech.	2	0	0	0	....	....	....	....	....	....	....	....	....	....	....	....	....	....	....	....	....	....	....	....
1993-94	Poldi Kladno	Cze-Rep	15	1	2	3	....	....	....	....	....	....	....	....	....	....	....	....	11	2	2	4	....	....	....	....
1994-95	Poldi Kladno	Cze-Rep	28	4	3	7	37	....	....	....	....	....	....	....	....	....	....	....	7	1	2	3	12	....	....	....
1995-96	**New Jersey**	**NHL**	**1**	**0**	**0**	**0**	**0**	**0**	**0**	**0**	**2**	**0.0**	**−1**	....	....	....	....	....	....	....	....	....	....	....	....	....
	Albany River Rats	AHL	74	27	36	63	83	....	....	....	....	....	....	....	....	....	....	....	4	1	1	2	2	....	....	....
1996-97	**New Jersey**	**NHL**	**17**	**2**	**3**	**5**	**2**	**0**	**0**	**0**	**23**	**8.7**	**−4**	....	....	....	....	....	**8**	**2**	**3**	**5**	**4**	**1**	**0**	**0**
	Albany River Rats	AHL	57	24	43	67	76	....	....	....	....	....	....	....	....	....	....	....	6	1	2	3	8	....	....	....
1997-98	**New Jersey**	**NHL**	**74**	**18**	**19**	**37**	**28**	**5**	**0**	**6**	**147**	**12.2**	**18**	....	....	....	....	....	**4**	**0**	**1**	**1**	**0**	**0**	**0**	**0**
	Albany River Rats	AHL	3	3	0	3	2	....	....	....	....	....	....	....	....	....	....	....	....	....	....	....	....	....	....	....
1998-99	**New Jersey**	**NHL**	**74**	**17**	**33**	**50**	**34**	**3**	**0**	**2**	**157**	**10.8**	**19**	**99**	**38.4**	**86**	**13**	**15:50**	**7**	**0**	**5**	**5**	**6**	**0**	**0**	**0**

			Regular Season															Playoffs							
Season	**Club**	**League**	**GP**	**G**	**A**	**Pts**	**PIM**	**PP**	**SH**	**GW**	**S**	**%**	**+/-**	**TF**	**F%**	**H**	**SB**	**Min**	**GP**	**G**	**A**	**Pts**	**PIM**	**PP**	**SH**	**GW**
99-2000	SK Trebic-2	Cze-Rep	2	2	1	3	2																			
	HC Pardubice	Cze-Rep	5	1	4	5	31																			
	♦ **New Jersey**	**NHL**	**72**	**35**	**37**	**72**	**58**	**9**	**0**	**9**	**183**	**19.1**	**16**	**134**	**45.5**	**112**	**12**	**17:28**	**23**	**7**	***13**	**20**	**9**	**2**	**1**	**1**
2000-01	**New Jersey**	**NHL**	**82**	**40**	**56**	**96**	**51**	**8**	**3**	**6**	**220**	**18.2**	**45**	**155**	**41.3**	**85**	**20**	**18:44**	**25**	**9**	**14**	**23**	**10**	**3**	**1**	**2**
	NHL Totals		**320**	**112**	**148**	**260**	**173**	**25**	**3**	**23**	**732**	**15.3**		**388**	**42.0**	**283**	**45**	**17:23**	**67**	**18**	**36**	**54**	**29**	**6**	**2**	**3**

NHL All-Rookie Team (1998) • NHL First All-Star Team (2001) • Played in NHL All-Star Game (2000)

ELICH, Matt

(EHL-ihch, MAT) **T.B.**

Right wing. Shoots right. 6'3", 196 lbs. Born, Detroit, MI, September 22, 1979. Tampa Bay's 3rd choice, 61st overall, in 1997 Entry Draft.

1993-94	Detroit Caesars	MNHL	40	20	20	40	110																			
1994-95	Detroit Caesars	MNHL	45	31	22	53	170																			
1995-96	Windsor Spitfires	OHL	52	10	2	12	17												5	1	0	1	2			
1996-97	Windsor Spitfires	OHL	58	15	13	28	19												5	0	1	1	6			
1997-98	Windsor Spitfires	OHL	20	9	12	21	8																			
	Kingston	OHL	34	14	4	18	2												12	2	4	6	2			
1998-99	Kingston	OHL	67	44	30	74	32												5	3	5	8	0			
99-2000	**Tampa Bay**	**NHL**	**8**	**1**	**1**	**2**	**0**	**0**	**0**	**0**	**5**	**20.0**	**–1**	**0**	**0.0**	**7**	**0**	**6:07**								
	Detroit Vipers	IHL	48	12	4	16	12																			
2000-01	**Tampa Bay**	**NHL**	**8**	**0**	**0**	**0**	**0**	**0**	**0**	**0**	**7**	**0.0**	**–5**	**0**	**0.0**	**1**	**2**	**8:59**								
	Detroit Vipers	IHL	60	12	16	28	12																			
	NHL Totals		**16**	**1**	**1**	**2**	**0**	**0**	**0**	**0**	**12**	**8.3**		**0**	**0.0**	**8**	**2**	**7:33**								

ELOMO, Miika

(eh-LOH-moh, MEE-ka) **CGY.**

Left wing. Shoots left. 6', 200 lbs. Born, Turku, Finland, April 21, 1977. Washington's 2nd choice, 23rd overall, in 1995 Entry Draft.

1993-94	TPS Turku	Finn-Jr.	30	8	5	13	24												5	1	1	2	2			
1994-95	TPS Turku	Finn-Jr.	14	3	8	11	24																			
	Kiekko-67 Turku	Finland-2	14	9	2	11	39																			
1995-96	TPS Turku	Finn-Jr.	6	0	2	2	18																			
	Kiekko-67 Turku	Finland-2	21	9	6	15	100																			
	TPS Turku	Finland	10	1	1	2	8												3	0	0	0	2			
1996-97	Portland	AHL	52	8	9	17	37																			
1997-98	Portland	AHL	33	1	1	2	54																			
	HIFK Helsinki	Finland	16	4	1	5	6												9	4	3	7	6			
1998-99	TPS Turku	Finland	36	5	10	15	76												10	3	5	8	6			
99-2000	**Washington**	**NHL**	**2**	**0**	**1**	**1**	**2**	**0**	**0**	**0**	**3**	**0.0**	**1**	**4**	**100.0**	**5**	**0**	**11:12**								
	Portland	AHL	59	21	14	35	50																			
2000-01	Saint John Flames	AHL	72	10	21	31	109												6	0	2	2	12			
	NHL Totals		**2**	**0**	**1**	**1**	**2**	**0**	**0**	**0**	**3**	**0.0**		**4**	**100.0**	**5**	**0**	**11:12**								

Traded to **Calgary** by **Washington** with Buffalo's compensatory 4th round choice (previously acquired, Calgary selected Levente Szuper) in 2000 Entry Draft for Anaheim's 2nd round choice (previously acquired, Washington selected Matt Pettinger) in 2000 Entry Draft, June 24, 2000.

ELORANTA, Mikko

(ehl-oh-RAN-tuh, MEE-koh) **BOS.**

Left wing. Shoots left. 6', 190 lbs. Born, Turku, Finland, August 24, 1972. Boston's 9th choice, 247th overall, in 1999 Entry Draft.

1989-90	TPS Turku	Finn-Jr.	2	0	0	0	0																			
1990-91	TPS Turku	Finn-Jr.	35	8	8	16	18																			
1991-92	TPS Turku	Finn-Jr.	19	3	1	4	8												8	0	0	0	0			
1992-93	TPS Turku	Finn-Jr.	31	11	6	17	20												6	0	4	4	6			
1993-94	Kiekko-67 Turku	Finland-2	45	3	4	7	24																			
1994-95	Kiekko-67 Turku	Finland-2	47	18	14	32	52												3	3	0	3	4			
1995-96	Kiekko-67 Turku	Finland-2	8	6	7	13	2																			
	Ilves Tampere	Finland	43	18	15	33	86												3	0	2	2	2			
1996-97	TPS Turku	EuroHL	6	3	1	4	6												1	0	0	0	0			
	TPS Turku	Finland	31	6	15	21	52												10	5	2	7	6			
1997-98	TPS Turku	EuroHL	3	1	0	1	12																			
	TPS Turku	Finland	46	23	14	37	82												2	0	0	0	8			
1998-99	TPS Turku	Finland	52	19	21	40	103												10	1	6	7	26			
99-2000	**Boston**	**NHL**	**50**	**6**	**12**	**18**	**36**	**1**	**0**	**0**	**59**	**10.2**	**–10**	**77**	**35.1**	**74**	**10**	**12:18**								
2000-01	**Boston**	**NHL**	**62**	**12**	**11**	**23**	**38**	**1**	**1**	**2**	**89**	**13.5**	**2**	**82**	**23.2**	**75**	**14**	**10:26**								
	NHL Totals		**112**	**18**	**23**	**41**	**74**	**2**	**1**	**2**	**148**	**12.2**		**159**	**28.9**	**149**	**24**	**11:16**								

EMERSON, Nelson

(EH-muhr-SOHN, NEHL-sohn) **L.A.**

Right wing. Shoots right. 5'11", 180 lbs. Born, Hamilton, Ont., August 17, 1967. St. Louis' 2nd choice, 44th overall, in 1985 Entry Draft.

1984-85	Stratford Cullitons	OJHL-B	40	23	38	61	70																			
1985-86	Stratford Cullitons	OJHL-B	39	*54	58	*112	91																			
1986-87	Bowling Green	CCHA	45	26	35	61	28																			
1987-88	Bowling Green	CCHA	45	34	49	83	54																			
1988-89	Bowling Green	CCHA	44	22	46	68	46																			
1989-90	Bowling Green	CCHA	44	30	52	82	42																			
	Peoria Rivermen	IHL	3	1	1	2	0																			
1990-91	**St. Louis**	**NHL**	**4**	**0**	**3**	**3**	**2**	**0**	**0**	**0**	**3**	**0.0**	**–2**													
	Peoria Rivermen	IHL	73	36	79	115	91												17	9	12	21	16			
1991-92	**St. Louis**	**NHL**	**79**	**23**	**36**	**59**	**66**	**3**	**0**	**2**	**143**	**16.1**	**–5**						**6**	**3**	**3**	**6**	**21**	**2**	**0**	**0**
1992-93	**St. Louis**	**NHL**	**82**	**22**	**51**	**73**	**62**	**5**	**2**	**4**	**196**	**11.2**	**2**						**11**	**1**	**6**	**7**	**6**	**0**	**0**	**0**
1993-94	**Winnipeg**	**NHL**	**83**	**33**	**41**	**74**	**80**	**4**	**5**	**6**	**282**	**11.7**	**–38**													
1994-95	**Winnipeg**	**NHL**	**48**	**14**	**23**	**37**	**26**	**4**	**1**	**1**	**122**	**11.5**	**–12**													
1995-96	**Hartford**	**NHL**	**81**	**29**	**29**	**58**	**78**	**12**	**2**	**5**	**247**	**11.7**	**–7**													
1996-97	**Hartford**	**NHL**	**66**	**9**	**29**	**38**	**34**	**2**	**1**	**2**	**194**	**4.6**	**–21**													
1997-98	**Carolina**	**NHL**	**81**	**21**	**24**	**45**	**50**	**6**	**0**	**4**	**203**	**10.3**	**–17**													
1998-99	**Carolina**	**NHL**	**35**	**8**	**13**	**21**	**36**	**3**	**0**	**0**	**84**	**9.5**	**1**	**7**	**42.9**	**6**	**7**	**14:30**								
	Chicago	**NHL**	**27**	**4**	**10**	**14**	**13**	**0**	**0**	**1**	**94**	**4.3**	**8**	**169**	**41.4**	**8**	**9**	**19:37**								
	Ottawa	**NHL**	**3**	**1**	**1**	**2**	**2**	**0**	**0**	**0**	**10**	**10.0**	**–1**	**5**	**60.0**	**1**	**0**	**17:05**	**4**	**1**	**3**	**4**	**0**	**0**	**0**	**0**
99-2000	**Atlanta**	**NHL**	**58**	**14**	**19**	**33**	**47**	**4**	**0**	**0**	**183**	**7.7**	**–24**	**124**	**39.5**	**27**	**33**	**19:10**								
	Los Angeles	**NHL**	**5**	**1**	**1**	**2**	**0**	**0**	**0**	**0**	**13**	**7.7**	**1**	**0**	**0.0**	**2**	**0**	**14:39**	**1**	**0**	**0**	**0**	**0**	**0**	**0**	**0**
2000-01	**Los Angeles**	**NHL**	**78**	**11**	**11**	**22**	**54**	**0**	**0**	**1**	**157**	**7.0**	**–13**	**28**	**32.1**	**37**	**30**	**13:51**	**13**	**2**	**2**	**4**	**4**	**0**	**0**	**0**
	NHL Totals		**730**	**190**	**291**	**481**	**550**	**43**	**11**	**26**	**1931**	**9.8**		**333**	**40.2**	**81**	**79**	**16:17**	**35**	**7**	**14**	**21**	**31**	**2**	**0**	**0**

NCAA West Second All-American Team (1988) • CCHA First All-Star Team (1988, 1990) • CCHA Second All-Star Team (1989) • NCAA West First All-American Team (1990) • IHL First All-Star Team (1991) • Won Garry F. Longman Memorial Trophy (Top Rookie - IHL) (1991)

Traded to **Winnipeg** by **St. Louis** with Stephane Quintal for Phil Housley, September 24, 1993. Traded to **Hartford** by **Winnipeg** for Darren Turcotte, October 6, 1995. Transferred to **Carolina** after **Hartford** franchise relocated, June 25, 1997. Traded to **Chicago** by **Carolina** for Paul Coffey, December 29, 1998. Traded to **Ottawa** by **Chicago** for Chris Murray, March 23, 1999. Signed as a free agent by **Atlanta**, August 3, 1999. Traded to **Los Angeles** by **Atlanta** with Kelly Buchberger for Donald Audette and Frantisek Kaberle, March 13, 2000.

EMMA, David

(EH-muh, DAY-vihd)

Center. Shoots left. 5'10", 185 lbs. Born, Cranston, RI, January 14, 1969. New Jersey's 6th choice, 110th overall, in 1989 Entry Draft.

1987-88	Boston College	H-East	30	19	16	35	30																			
1988-89	Boston College	H-East	36	20	31	51	36																			
1989-90	Boston College	H-East	42	38	34	*72	46																			
1990-91	Boston College	H-East	39	*35	46	*81	44																			
1991-92	United States	Nat-Team	55	15	16	31	32																			
	United States	Olympics	6	0	1	1	6																			
	Utica Devils	AHL	15	4	7	11	12												4	1	1	2	2			
1992-93	**New Jersey**	**NHL**	**2**	**0**	**0**	**0**	**0**	**0**	**0**	**0**	**2**	**0.0**	**0**													
	Utica Devils	AHL	61	21	40	61	47												5	2	1	3	6			
1993-94	**New Jersey**	**NHL**	**15**	**5**	**5**	**10**	**2**	**1**	**0**	**2**	**24**	**20.8**	**0**													
	Albany River Rats	AHL	56	26	29	55	53												5	1	2	3	8			

Season	Club	League	GP	G	A	Pts	PIM	PP	SH	GW	S	%	+/-	TF	F%	H	SB	Min	GP	G	A	Pts	PIM	PP	SH	GW
			Regular Season																Playoffs							
1994-95	**New Jersey**	**NHL**	**6**	**0**	**1**	**1**	**0**	**0**	**0**	**0**	**4**	**0.0**	**–2**	....	....	....	....	....	....	....	....	....	....	....	....	....
	Albany River Rats	AHL	1	0	0	0	0	....	....	....	....	....	....	....	....	....	....	....	....	....	....	....	....	....	....	....
1995-96	Detroit Vipers	IHL	79	30	32	62	75	....	....	....	....	....	....	....	....	....	....	....	11	5	2	7	2	....	....	....
1996-97	**Boston**	**NHL**	**5**	**0**	**0**	**0**	**0**	**0**	**0**	**0**	**3**	**0.0**	**–1**	....	....	....	....	....	....	....	....	....	....	....	....	....
	Providence Bruins	AHL	53	10	18	28	24	....	....	....	....	....	....	....	....	....	....	....	....	....	....	....	....	....	....	....
	Phoenix	IHL	8	0	4	4	4	....	....	....	....	....	....	....	....	....	....	....	....	....	....	....	....	....	....	....
1997-98	KAC Klagenfurt	Alpenliga	16	6	17	23	....	....	....	....	....	....	....	....	....	....	....	....	....	....	....	....	....	....	....	....
	KAC Klagenfurt	Austria	33	22	22	44	48	....	....	....	....	....	....	....	....	....	....	....	....	....	....	....	....	....	....	....
1998-99	KAC Klagenfurt	Alpenliga	26	15	32	47	49	....	....	....	....	....	....	....	....	....	....	....	....	....	....	....	....	....	....	....
	KAC Klagenfurt	Austria	15	8	7	15	16	....	....	....	....	....	....	....	....	....	....	....	....	....	....	....	....	....	....	....
99-2000	KAC Klagenfurt	IEL	32	26	28	54	28	....	....	....	....	....	....	....	....	....	....	....	....	....	....	....	....	....	....	....
	KAC Klagenfurt	Austria	15	9	6	15	18	....	....	....	....	....	....	....	....	....	....	....	....	....	....	....	....	....	....	....
2000-01	**Florida**	**NHL**	**6**	**0**	**0**	**0**	**0**	**0**	**0**	**0**	**6**	**0.0**	**–1**	**1**	**0.0**	**2**	**4**	**7:23**	....	....	....	....	....	....	....	....
	Louisville Panthers	AHL	55	22	28	50	63	....	....	....	....	....	....	....	....	....	....	....	....	....	....	....	....	....	....	....
	Portland Pirates	AHL	16	2	8	10	6	....	....	....	....	....	....	....	....	....	....	....	2	0	0	0	0	....	....	....
	NHL Totals		**34**	**5**	**6**	**11**	**2**	**1**	**0**	**2**	**39**	**12.8**		**1**	**0.0**	**2**	**4**	**7:23**	....	....	....	....	....	....	....	....

Hockey East Second All-Star Team (1989) • Hockey East First All-Star Team (1990, 1991) • NCAA East First All-American Team (1990, 1991) • Won Hobey Baker Memorial Award (Top U.S. Collegiate Player) (1991)

Signed as a free agent by **Boston**, August 27, 1996. Signed as a free agent by **Florida**, August 1, 2000. Traded to **Washington** by **Florida** for Remi Royer, March 3, 2001.

EMMONS, John

(eh-mohns, JAWN) **BOS.**

Center. Shoots left. 6'1", 203 lbs. Born, San Jose, CA, August 17, 1974. Calgary's 7th choice, 122nd overall, in 1993 Entry Draft.

Season	Club	League	GP	G	A	Pts	PIM	PP	SH	GW	S	%	+/-	TF	F%	H	SB	Min	GP	G	A	Pts	PIM	PP	SH	GW
1990-91	New Canaan	Hi-School	20	19	37	56	20	....	....	....	....	....	....	....	....	....	....	....	....	....	....	....	....	....	....	....
1991-92	New Canaan	Hi-School	22	24	49	73	24	....	....	....	....	....	....	....	....	....	....	....	....	....	....	....	....	....	....	....
1992-93	Yale University	ECAC	28	3	5	8	66	....	....	....	....	....	....	....	....	....	....	....	....	....	....	....	....	....	....	....
1993-94	Yale University	ECAC	25	5	12	17	66	....	....	....	....	....	....	....	....	....	....	....	....	....	....	....	....	....	....	....
1994-95	Yale University	ECAC	28	4	16	20	57	....	....	....	....	....	....	....	....	....	....	....	....	....	....	....	....	....	....	....
1995-96	Yale University	ECAC	31	8	20	28	124	....	....	....	....	....	....	....	....	....	....	....	....	....	....	....	....	....	....	....
1996-97	Dayton Bombers	ECHL	69	20	37	57	62	....	....	....	....	....	....	....	....	....	....	....	4	0	1	1	2	....	....	....
	Fort Wayne	IHL	1	0	0	0	0	....	....	....	....	....	....	....	....	....	....	....	....	....	....	....	....	....	....	....
1997-98	Michigan K-Wings	IHL	81	9	25	34	85	....	....	....	....	....	....	....	....	....	....	....	4	1	1	2	10	....	....	....
1998-99	Detroit Vipers	IHL	75	13	22	35	172	....	....	....	....	....	....	....	....	....	....	....	11	4	5	9	22	....	....	....
99-2000	**Ottawa**	**NHL**	**10**	**0**	**0**	**0**	**6**	**0**	**0**	**0**	**3**	**0.0**	**–2**	**62**	**58.1**	**11**	**2**	**7:27**	....	....	....	....	....	....	....	....
	Grand Rapids	IHL	64	10	16	26	78	....	....	....	....	....	....	....	....	....	....	....	16	1	4	5	28	....	....	....
2000-01	**Ottawa**	**NHL**	**41**	**1**	**1**	**2**	**20**	**0**	**0**	**0**	**28**	**3.6**	**–5**	**315**	**51.4**	**29**	**21**	**7:46**	....	....	....	....	....	....	....	....
	Grand Rapids	IHL	9	1	0	1	4	....	....	....	....	....	....	....	....	....	....	....	....	....	....	....	....	....	....	....
	Tampa Bay	**NHL**	**12**	**1**	**1**	**2**	**22**	**0**	**0**	**0**	**9**	**11.1**	**0**	**160**	**52.5**	**7**	**6**	**13:07**	....	....	....	....	....	....	....	....
	NHL Totals		**63**	**2**	**2**	**4**	**48**	**0**	**0**	**0**	**40**	**5.0**		**537**	**52.5**	**47**	**29**	**8:44**	....	....	....	....	....	....	....	....

Signed as a free agent by **Ottawa**, August 7, 1998. Traded to **Tampa Bay** by **Ottawa** for Craig Millar, March 13, 2001. Signed as a free agent by **Boston**, August 8, 2001.

ERIKSSON, Anders

(AIR-ihk-suhn, AND-uhrs) **TOR.**

Defense. Shoots left. 6'2", 220 lbs. Born, Bollnas, Sweden, January 9, 1975. Detroit's 1st choice, 22nd overall, in 1993 Entry Draft.

Season	Club	League	GP	G	A	Pts	PIM	PP	SH	GW	S	%	+/-	TF	F%	H	SB	Min	GP	G	A	Pts	PIM	PP	SH	GW
1992-93	MoDo AIK	Swede-Jr.	10	5	3	8	14	....	....	....	....	....	....	....	....	....	....	....	....	....	....	....	....	....	....	....
	MoDo AIK	Sweden	20	0	2	2	2	....	....	....	....	....	....	....	....	....	....	....	1	0	0	0	0	....	....	....
1993-94	MoDo AIK	Swede-Jr.	3	1	2	3	34	....	....	....	....	....	....	....	....	....	....	....	....	....	....	....	....	....	....	....
	MoDo AIK	Sweden	38	2	8	10	42	....	....	....	....	....	....	....	....	....	....	....	11	0	0	0	8	....	....	....
1994-95	MoDo AIK	Sweden	39	3	6	9	54	....	....	....	....	....	....	....	....	....	....	....	....	....	....	....	....	....	....	....
1995-96	**Detroit**	**NHL**	**1**	**0**	**0**	**0**	**2**	**0**	**0**	**0**	**0**	**0.0**	**1**	....	....	....	....	....	**3**	**0**	**0**	**0**	**0**	**0**	**0**	**0**
	Adirondack	AHL	75	6	36	42	64	....	....	....	....	....	....	....	....	....	....	....	3	0	0	0	0	....	....	....
1996-97	**Detroit**	**NHL**	**23**	**0**	**6**	**6**	**10**	**0**	**0**	**0**	**27**	**0.0**	**5**	....	....	....	....	....	....	....	....	....	....	....	....	....
	Adirondack	AHL	44	3	25	28	36	....	....	....	....	....	....	....	....	....	....	....	4	0	1	1	4	....	....	....
1997-98♦	**Detroit**	**NHL**	**66**	**7**	**14**	**21**	**32**	**1**	**0**	**2**	**91**	**7.7**	**21**	....	....	....	....	....	**18**	**0**	**5**	**5**	**16**	**0**	**0**	**0**
1998-99	**Detroit**	**NHL**	**61**	**2**	**10**	**12**	**34**	**0**	**0**	**1**	**67**	**3.0**	**5**	**0**	**0.0**	**72**	**60**	**15:54**	....	....	....	....	....	....	....	....
	Chicago	**NHL**	**11**	**0**	**8**	**8**	**0**	**0**	**0**	**0**	**12**	**0.0**	**6**	**0**	**0.0**	**15**	**20**	**22:51**	....	....	....	....	....	....	....	....
99-2000	**Chicago**	**NHL**	**73**	**3**	**25**	**28**	**20**	**0**	**0**	**1**	**86**	**3.5**	**4**	**1**	**100.0**	**86**	**80**	**21:03**	....	....	....	....	....	....	....	....
2000-01	**Chicago**	**NHL**	**13**	**2**	**3**	**5**	**2**	**1**	**0**	**0**	**19**	**10.5**	**–4**	**0**	**0.0**	**9**	**17**	**21:20**	....	....	....	....	....	....	....	....
	Florida	**NHL**	**60**	**0**	**21**	**21**	**28**	**0**	**0**	**0**	**80**	**0.0**	**2**	**1**	**0.0**	**79**	**60**	**21:02**	....	....	....	....	....	....	....	....
	NHL Totals		**308**	**14**	**87**	**101**	**128**	**2**	**0**	**4**	**382**	**3.7**		**2**	**50.0**	**261**	**237**	**19:43**	**21**	**0**	**5**	**5**	**16**	**0**	**0**	**0**

Traded to **Chicago** by **Detroit** with Detroit's 1st round choices in 1999 (Steve McCarthy) and 2001 (Adam Munro) Entry Drafts for Chris Chelios, March 23, 1999. Traded to **Florida** by **Chicago** for Jaroslav Spacek, November 6, 2000. Signed as a free agent by **Toronto**, July 9, 2001.

FAIRCHILD, Kelly

(FAIR-chighld, KEHL-lee) **COL.**

Center. Shoots left. 5'11", 180 lbs. Born, Hibbing, MN, April 9, 1973. Los Angeles' 6th choice, 152nd overall, in 1991 Entry Draft.

Season	Club	League	GP	G	A	Pts	PIM	PP	SH	GW	S	%	+/-	TF	F%	H	SB	Min	GP	G	A	Pts	PIM	PP	SH	GW
1988-89	Hibbing High	Hi-School	22	9	8	17	24	....	....	....	....	....	....	....	....	....	....	....	....	....	....	....	....	....	....	....
1989-90	Grand Rapids	Hi-School	28	12	17	29	73	....	....	....	....	....	....	....	....	....	....	....	....	....	....	....	....	....	....	....
1990-91	Grand Rapids	Hi-School	28	28	45	73	25	....	....	....	....	....	....	....	....	....	....	....	....	....	....	....	....	....	....	....
1991-92	U. of Wisconsin	WCHA	37	11	10	21	45	....	....	....	....	....	....	....	....	....	....	....	....	....	....	....	....	....	....	....
1992-93	U. of Wisconsin	WCHA	42	25	29	54	54	....	....	....	....	....	....	....	....	....	....	....	....	....	....	....	....	....	....	....
1993-94	U. of Wisconsin	WCHA	42	20	44	*64	81	....	....	....	....	....	....	....	....	....	....	....	....	....	....	....	....	....	....	....
1994-95	St. John's Leafs	AHL	53	27	23	50	51	....	....	....	....	....	....	....	....	....	....	....	4	0	2	2	4	....	....	....
1995-96	**Toronto**	**NHL**	**1**	**0**	**1**	**1**	**2**	**0**	**0**	**0**	**1**	**0.0**	**1**	....	....	....	....	....	....	....	....	....	....	....	....	....
	St. John's Leafs	AHL	78	29	49	78	85	....	....	....	....	....	....	....	....	....	....	....	2	0	1	1	4	....	....	....
1996-97	**Toronto**	**NHL**	**22**	**0**	**2**	**2**	**2**	**0**	**0**	**0**	**14**	**0.0**	**–5**	....	....	....	....	....	....	....	....	....	....	....	....	....
	St. John's Leafs	AHL	29	9	22	31	36	....	....	....	....	....	....	....	....	....	....	....	....	....	....	....	....	....	....	....
	Orlando	IHL	25	9	6	15	20	....	....	....	....	....	....	....	....	....	....	....	9	6	5	11	16	....	....	....
1997-98	St. John's Leafs	AHL	17	5	2	7	24	....	....	....	....	....	....	....	....	....	....	....	....	....	....	....	....	....	....	....
	Orlando	IHL	22	2	6	8	20	....	....	....	....	....	....	....	....	....	....	....	....	....	....	....	....	....	....	....
	Milwaukee	IHL	40	20	24	44	32	....	....	....	....	....	....	....	....	....	....	....	10	5	2	7	4	....	....	....
1998-99	**Dallas**	**NHL**	**1**	**0**	**0**	**0**	**0**	**0**	**0**	**0**	**4**	**0.0**	**0**	**12**	**25.0**	**1**	**1**	**12:37**	....	....	....	....	....	....	....	....
	Michigan K-Wings	IHL	74	17	33	50	88	....	....	....	....	....	....	....	....	....	....	....	5	2	2	4	16	....	....	....
99-2000	Michigan K-Wings	IHL	78	21	41	62	89	....	....	....	....	....	....	....	....	....	....	....	....	....	....	....	....	....	....	....
2000-01	Hershey Bears	AHL	70	23	40	63	68	....	....	....	....	....	....	....	....	....	....	....	12	2	9	11	10	....	....	....
	NHL Totals		**24**	**0**	**3**	**3**	**4**	**0**	**0**	**0**	**19**	**0.0**		**12**	**25.0**	**1**	**1**	**12:37**								

WCHA First All-Star Team (1994)

Traded to **Toronto** by **LA Kings** with Dixon Ward, Guy Leveque and Shayne Toporowski for Eric Lacroix, Chris Snell and Toronto's 4th round choice (Eric Belanger) in 1996 Entry Draft, October 3, 1994. Traded to **Milwaukee** (IHL) by **Orlando** (IHL) with Dave McIntyre for Sean McCann and Dave Mackey, January 11, 1998. Signed as a free agent by **Dallas**, July 2, 1998. Signed as a free agent by **Colorado**, August, 2000.

FALLOON, Pat

(fah-LOON, PAT)

Right wing. Shoots right. 5'11", 190 lbs. Born, Foxwarren, Man., September 22, 1972. San Jose's 1st choice, 2nd overall, in 1991 Entry Draft.

Season	Club	League	GP	G	A	Pts	PIM	PP	SH	GW	S	%	+/-	TF	F%	H	SB	Min	GP	G	A	Pts	PIM	PP	SH	GW
1987-88	Yellowhead Pass	AAHA	52	74	69	143	50	....	....	....	....	....	....	....	....	....	....	....	....	....	....	....	....	....	....	....
1988-89	Spokane Chiefs	WHL	72	22	56	78	41	....	....	....	....	....	....	....	....	....	....	....	....	....	....	....	....	....	....	....
1989-90	Spokane Chiefs	WHL	71	60	64	124	48	....	....	....	....	....	....	....	....	....	....	....	6	5	8	13	4	....	....	....
1990-91	Spokane Chiefs	WHL	61	64	74	138	33	....	....	....	....	....	....	....	....	....	....	....	15	10	14	24	10	....	....	....
1991-92	**San Jose**	**NHL**	**79**	**25**	**34**	**59**	**16**	**5**	**0**	**1**	**181**	**13.8**	**–32**	....	....	....	....	....	....	....	....	....	....	....	....	....
1992-93	**San Jose**	**NHL**	**41**	**14**	**14**	**28**	**12**	**5**	**1**	**1**	**131**	**10.7**	**–25**	....	....	....	....	....	....	....	....	....	....	....	....	....
1993-94	**San Jose**	**NHL**	**83**	**22**	**31**	**53**	**18**	**6**	**0**	**1**	**193**	**11.4**	**–3**	....	....	....	....	....	**14**	**1**	**2**	**3**	**6**	**0**	**0**	**0**
1994-95	**San Jose**	**NHL**	**46**	**12**	**7**	**19**	**25**	**0**	**0**	**3**	**91**	**13.2**	**–4**	....	....	....	....	....	**11**	**3**	**1**	**4**	**0**	**0**	**0**	**0**
1995-96	**San Jose**	**NHL**	**9**	**3**	**0**	**3**	**4**	**0**	**0**	**0**	**18**	**16.7**	**–1**	....	....	....	....	....	....	....	....	....	....	....	....	....
	Philadelphia	**NHL**	**62**	**22**	**26**	**48**	**6**	**9**	**0**	**2**	**152**	**14.5**	**15**	....	....	....	....	....	**12**	**3**	**2**	**5**	**2**	**2**	**0**	**0**
1996-97	**Philadelphia**	**NHL**	**52**	**11**	**12**	**23**	**10**	**2**	**0**	**4**	**124**	**8.9**	**–8**	....	....	....	....	....	**14**	**3**	**1**	**4**	**2**	**1**	**0**	**0**
1997-98	**Philadelphia**	**NHL**	**30**	**5**	**7**	**12**	**8**	**1**	**0**	**0**	**63**	**7.9**	**3**	....	....	....	....	....	....	....	....	....	....	....	....	....
	Ottawa	**NHL**	**28**	**3**	**3**	**6**	**8**	**2**	**0**	**0**	**73**	**4.1**	**–11**	....	....	....	....	....	**1**	**0**	**0**	**0**	**0**	**0**	**0**	**0**
1998-99	**Edmonton**	**NHL**	**82**	**17**	**23**	**40**	**20**	**8**	**0**	**2**	**152**	**11.2**	**–4**	**29**	**48.3**	**49**	**11**	**14:42**	**4**	**0**	**1**	**1**	**4**	**0**	**0**	**0**

Season	Club	League	GP	G	A	Pts	PIM	PP	SH	GW	S	%	+/-	TF	F%	H	SB	Min	GP	G	A	Pts	PIM	PP	SH	GW
			Regular Season																Playoffs							
99-2000	**Edmonton**	**NHL**	**33**	**5**	**13**	**18**	**4**	**1**	**0**	**0**	**51**	**9.8**	**6**	**9**	**66.7**	**17**	**4**	**13:19**								
	Pittsburgh	**NHL**	**30**	**4**	**9**	**13**	**10**	**0**	**0**	**0**	**41**	**9.8**	**–2**	**8**	**62.5**	**12**	**2**	**11:13**	**10**	**1**	**0**	**1**	**2**	**0**	**0**	**0**
2000-01	HC Davos	Switz.	43	12	26	38	49												4	1	0	1	2			
	NHL Totals		**575**	**143**	**179**	**322**	**141**	**39**	**1**	**14**	**1270**	**11.3**		**46**	**54.3**	**78**	**17**	**13:40**	**66**	**11**	**7**	**18**	**16**	**3**	**0**	**0**

WHL West Second All-Star Team (1989) • WHL West First All-Star Team (1991) • Canadian Major Junior Most Sportsmanlike Player of the Year (1991) • Memorial Cup All-Star Team (1991) • Won Stafford Smythe Memorial Trophy (Memorial Cup Tournament MVP) (1991)

Traded to **Philadelphia** by **San Jose** for Martin Spanhel, Philadelphia's 1st round choice (later traded to Buffalo - later traded to Phoenix - Phoenix selected Daniel Briere) in 1996 Entry Draft and Philadelphia's 4th round choice (later traded to Buffalo - Buffalo selected Mike Martone), in 1996 Entry Draft, November 16, 1995. Traded to **Ottawa** by **Philadelphia** with Vaclav Prospal and Dallas' 2nd round choice (previously acquired, Ottawa selected Chris Bala) in 1998 Entry Draft for Alexandre Daigle, January 17, 1998. Signed as a free agent by **Edmonton**, August 21, 1998. Claimed on waivers by **Pittsburgh** from **Edmonton**, February 4, 2000. Signed as a free agent by **HC Davos** (Switz.), August 25, 2000.

FARKAS, Jeff
(FAHR-kuhs, JEHF) **TOR.**

Center. Shoots left. 6', 185 lbs. Born, Amherst, MA, January 24, 1978. Toronto's 1st choice, 57th overall, in 1997 Entry Draft.

Season	Club	League	GP	G	A	Pts	PIM	PP	SH	GW	S	%	+/-	TF	F%	H	SB	Min	GP	G	A	Pts	PIM	PP	SH	GW
1993-94	Nichols School	Hi-School	28	27	57	84	25																			
1994-95	Niagara Scenics	EJHL	47	54	55	99	70																			
1995-96	Niagara Scenics	MJAHL	47	42	70	112	75																			
1996-97	Boston College	H-East	35	13	23	36	34																			
1997-98	Boston College	H-East	40	11	28	39	42																			
1998-99	Boston College	H-East	43	32	25	57	56																			
99-2000	Boston College	H-East	41	32	26	*58	61																			
	Toronto	**NHL**																	**3**	**1**	**0**	**1**	**0**	**0**	**0**	**0**
2000-01	**Toronto**	**NHL**	**2**	**0**	**0**	**0**	**2**	**0**	**0**	**0**	**1**	**0.0**	**–1**	**0**	**0.0**	**1**	**2**	**14:09**								
	St. John's Leafs	AHL	77	28	40	68	62												4	1	2	3	4			
	NHL Totals		**2**	**0**	**0**	**0**	**2**	**0**	**0**	**0**	**1**	**0.0**		**0**	**0.0**	**1**	**2**	**14:09**	**3**	**1**	**0**	**1**	**0**	**0**	**0**	**0**

Hockey East First All-Star Team (2000) • NCAA East First All-American Team (2000) • NCAA Championship All-Tournament Team (2000)

FATA, Rico
(FA-tuh, REE-koh) **CGY.**

Center. Shoots left. 5'11", 200 lbs. Born, Sault Ste. Marie, Ont., February 12, 1980. Calgary's 1st choice, 6th overall, in 1998 Entry Draft.

Season	Club	League	GP	G	A	Pts	PIM	PP	SH	GW	S	%	+/-	TF	F%	H	SB	Min	GP	G	A	Pts	PIM	PP	SH	GW
1994-95	S.S. Marie Legion	NOHA	51	52	51	103																				
1995-96	Sault Ste. Marie	OHL	62	11	15	26	52												4	0	0	0	0			
1996-97	London Knights	OHL	59	19	34	53	76																			
1997-98	London Knights	OHL	64	43	33	76	110												16	9	5	14	*49			
1998-99	**Calgary**	**NHL**	**20**	**0**	**1**	**1**	**4**	**0**	**0**	**0**	**13**	**0.0**	**0**	**2**	**50.0**	**10**	**5**	**7:36**								
	London Knights	OHL	23	15	18	33	41												25	10	12	22	42			
99-2000	**Calgary**	**NHL**	**2**	**0**	**0**	**0**	**0**	**0**	**0**	**0**	**0**	**0.0**	**–1**	**0**	**0.0**	**3**	**0**	**10:06**								
	Saint John Flames	AHL	76	29	29	58	65												3	0	0	0	4			
2000-01	**Calgary**	**NHL**	**5**	**0**	**0**	**0**	**6**	**0**	**0**	**0**	**6**	**0.0**	**–3**	**0**	**0.0**	**3**	**0**	**9:25**								
	Saint John Flames	AHL	70	23	29	52	129												19	2	3	5	22			
	NHL Totals		**27**	**0**	**1**	**1**	**10**	**0**	**0**	**0**	**19**	**0.0**		**2**	**50.0**	**16**	**5**	**8:07**								

FEDOROV, Sergei
(FEH-duh-rahf, SAIR-gay) **DET.**

Center. Shoots left. 6'1", 200 lbs. Born, Pskov, USSR, December 13, 1969. Detroit's 4th choice, 74th overall, in 1989 Entry Draft.

Season	Club	League	GP	G	A	Pts	PIM	PP	SH	GW	S	%	+/-	TF	F%	H	SB	Min	GP	G	A	Pts	PIM	PP	SH	GW
1985-86	Dynamo Minsk	USSR	15	6	1	7	10																			
1986-87	CSKA Moscow	USSR	29	6	6	12	12																			
1987-88	CSKA Moscow	USSR	48	7	9	16	20																			
1988-89	CSKA Moscow	USSR	44	9	8	17	35																			
1989-90	CSKA Moscow	USSR	48	19	10	29	22																			
1990-91	**Detroit**	**NHL**	**77**	**31**	**48**	**79**	**66**	**11**	**3**	**5**	**259**	**12.0**	**11**						**7**	**1**	**5**	**6**	**4**	**0**	**0**	**1**
1991-92	**Detroit**	**NHL**	**80**	**32**	**54**	**86**	**72**	**7**	**2**	**5**	**249**	**12.9**	**26**						**11**	**5**	**5**	**10**	**8**	**1**	**2**	**1**
1992-93	**Detroit**	**NHL**	**73**	**34**	**53**	**87**	**72**	**13**	**4**	**3**	**217**	**15.7**	**33**						**7**	**3**	**6**	**9**	**23**	**1**	**1**	**0**
1993-94	**Detroit**	**NHL**	**82**	**56**	**64**	**120**	**34**	**13**	**4**	**10**	**337**	**16.6**	**48**						**7**	**1**	**7**	**8**	**6**	**0**	**0**	**0**
1994-95	**Detroit**	**NHL**	**42**	**20**	**30**	**50**	**24**	**7**	**3**	**5**	**147**	**13.6**	**6**						**17**	**7**	***17**	***24**	**6**	**3**	**0**	**0**
1995-96	**Detroit**	**NHL**	**78**	**39**	**68**	**107**	**48**	**11**	**3**	**11**	**306**	**12.7**	**49**						**19**	**2**	***18**	**20**	**10**	**0**	**0**	**2**
1996-97♦	**Detroit**	**NHL**	**74**	**30**	**33**	**63**	**30**	**9**	**2**	**4**	**273**	**11.0**	**29**						**20**	**8**	**12**	**20**	**12**	**3**	**0**	**4**
1997-98	Russia	Olympics	6	1	5	6	8																			
	♦ Detroit	**NHL**	**21**	**6**	**11**	**17**	**25**	**2**	**0**	**2**	**68**	**8.8**	**10**						**22**	***10**	**10**	**20**	**12**	**2**	**1**	**1**
1998-99	**Detroit**	**NHL**	**77**	**26**	**37**	**63**	**66**	**6**	**2**	**3**	**224**	**11.6**	**9**	**1414**	**51.7**	**77**	**24**	**19:21**	**10**	**1**	**8**	**9**	**8**	**0**	**0**	**0**
99-2000	**Detroit**	**NHL**	**68**	**27**	**35**	**62**	**22**	**4**	**4**	**7**	**263**	**10.3**	**8**	**1274**	**53.8**	**62**	**23**	**20:05**	**9**	**4**	**4**	**8**	**4**	**2**	**0**	**1**
2000-01	**Detroit**	**NHL**	**75**	**32**	**37**	**69**	**40**	**14**	**2**	**7**	**268**	**11.9**	**12**	**1601**	**55.8**	**75**	**34**	**21:05**	**6**	**2**	**5**	**7**	**0**	**1**	**0**	**1**
	NHL Totals		**747**	**333**	**470**	**803**	**499**	**97**	**29**	**62**	**2611**	**12.8**		**4289**	**53.8**	**214**	**81**	**20:10**	**135**	**44**	**97**	**141**	**93**	**13**	**4**	**11**

NHL All-Rookie Team (1991) • NHL First All-Star Team (1994) • Won Frank J. Selke Trophy (1994, 1996) • Won Lester B. Pearson Award (1994) • Won Hart Trophy (1994) • Played in NHL All-Star Game (1992, 1994, 1996, 2001)

• Missed majority of 1997-98 season after failing to come to contract terms with **Detroit**.

FEDORUK, Todd
(FEH-duh-ruhk, TAWD) **PHI.**

Left wing. Shoots left. 6'2", 235 lbs. Born, Redwater, Alta., February 13, 1979. Philadelphia's 6th choice, 164th overall, in 1997 Entry Draft.

Season	Club	League	GP	G	A	Pts	PIM	PP	SH	GW	S	%	+/-	TF	F%	H	SB	Min	GP	G	A	Pts	PIM	PP	SH	GW
1994-95	Ft-Saskatchewan	AAHA	STATISTICS NOT AVAILABLE																							
1995-96	Kelowna Rockets	WHL	44	1	1	2	83												4	0	0	0	6			
1996-97	Kelowna Rockets	WHL	31	1	5	6	87												6	0	0	0	13			
1997-98	Kelowna Rockets	WHL	31	3	5	8	120																			
	Regina Pats	WHL	21	4	3	7	80												9	1	2	3	23			
1998-99	Regina Pats	WHL	39	12	12	24	107																			
	Prince Albert	WHL	28	6	4	10	75												13	1	6	7	49			
99-2000	Trenton Titans	ECHL	18	2	5	7	118																			
	Philadelphia	AHL	19	1	2	3	40												5	0	1	1	2			
2000-01	Philadelphia	AHL	14	0	1	1	49																			
	Philadelphia	**NHL**	**53**	**5**	**5**	**10**	**109**	**0**	**0**	**0**	**28**	**17.9**	**0**	**0**	**0.0**	**65**	**2**	**7:02**	**2**	**0**	**0**	**0**	**20**	**0**	**0**	**0**
	NHL Totals		**53**	**5**	**5**	**10**	**109**	**0**	**0**	**0**	**28**	**17.9**		**0**	**0.0**	**65**	**2**	**7:02**	**2**	**0**	**0**	**0**	**20**	**0**	**0**	**0**

FEDOTENKO, Ruslan
(feh-doh-TEHN-koh, roos-LAHN) **PHI.**

Left wing. Shoots left. 6'2", 195 lbs. Born, Kiev, Ukraine, January 18, 1979.

Season	Club	League	GP	G	A	Pts	PIM	PP	SH	GW	S	%	+/-	TF	F%	H	SB	Min	GP	G	A	Pts	PIM	PP	SH	GW
1997-98	Melfort Mustangs	SJHL	68	35	31	66	55																			
1998-99	Sioux City	USHL	55	43	34	77	139												5	5	1	6	9			
99-2000	Trenton Titans	ECHL	8	5	3	8	9																			
	Philadelphia	AHL	67	16	34	50	42												2	0	0	0	0			
2000-01	**Philadelphia**	**NHL**	**74**	**16**	**20**	**36**	**72**	**3**	**0**	**4**	**119**	**13.4**	**8**	**7**	**71.4**	**94**	**28**	**14:38**	**6**	**0**	**1**	**1**	**4**	**0**	**0**	**0**
	Philadelphia	AHL	8	1	0	1	8																			
	NHL Totals		**74**	**16**	**20**	**36**	**72**	**3**	**0**	**4**	**119**	**13.4**		**7**	**71.4**	**94**	**28**	**14:38**	**6**	**0**	**1**	**1**	**4**	**0**	**0**	**0**

Signed as a free agent by **Philadelphia**, August 3, 1999.

FELSNER, Brian
(FEHLZ-nuhr, BRIGH-uhn)

Left wing. Shoots left. 5'11", 189 lbs. Born, Mt. Clemens, MI, November 11, 1972.

Season	Club	League	GP	G	A	Pts	PIM	PP	SH	GW	S	%	+/-	TF	F%	H	SB	Min	GP	G	A	Pts	PIM	PP	SH	GW
1992-93	Detroit	NAJHL	50	25	35	60																				
1993-94	Lake Superior	CCHA	6	1	1	2	6																			
1994-95	Lake Superior	CCHA	41	24	28	52	51																			
1995-96	Lake Superior	CCHA	38	16	36	52	40																			
1996-97	Orlando	IHL	75	29	41	70	38												7	2	3	5	6			
1997-98	**Chicago**	**NHL**	**12**	**1**	**3**	**4**	**12**	**0**	**0**	**0**	**14**	**7.1**	**0**													
	Indianapolis Ice	IHL	53	17	36	53	36																			
	Milwaukee	IHL	15	7	8	15	20												10	3	9	12	12			
1998-99	Detroit Vipers	IHL	72	20	35	55	49												11	4	6	10	12			

			Regular Season																Playoffs							
Season	Club	League	GP	G	A	Pts	PIM	PP	SH	GW	S	%	+/-	TF	F%	H	SB	Min	GP	G	A	Pts	PIM	PP	SH	GW
99-2000	Houston Aeros	IHL	28	7	16	23	20	....	....	....	....	....	....	....	....	....	....	....	....	....	....	....	....	....	....	....
	Cincinnati	IHL	38	15	17	32	18	....	....	....	....	....	....	....	....	....	....	....	11	4	5	9	20	....	....	....
2000-01	Cincinnati	IHL	73	27	38	65	62	....	....	....	....	....	....	....	....	....	....	....	5	3	2	5	6	....	....	....
	NHL Totals		**12**	**1**	**3**	**4**	**12**	**0**	**0**	**0**	**14**	**7.1**		....	....	....	....	....	....	....	....	....	....	....	....	....

• Played football at Lanse Creuse High School, 1987-1992. • Ruled academically ineligible by NCAA for remainder of 1993-94 season. Signed as a free agent by **Chicago**, September 5, 1997. Traded to **Ottawa** by **Chicago** for Justin Hocking, August 21, 1998. Signed as a free agent by **Houston** (IHL), October 9, 1999. Traded to **Cincinnati** (IHL) by **Houston** (IHL) for Steve Bancroft with Ottawa retaining his NHL rights, January 19, 2000. Signed as a free agent by **Carolina**, July 28, 2000.

FERENCE, Andrew

(fuhr-EHNS, AN-droo) **PIT.**

Defense. Shoots left. 5'10", 190 lbs. Born, Edmonton, Alta., March 17, 1979. Pittsburgh's 8th choice, 208th overall, in 1997 Entry Draft.

Season	Club	League	GP	G	A	Pts	PIM	PP	SH	GW	S	%	+/-	TF	F%	H	SB	Min	GP	G	A	Pts	PIM	PP	SH	GW
1994-95	Sherwood Park	AMHL	31	4	14	18	74	....	....	....	....	....	....	....	....	....	....	....	....	....	....	....	....	....	....	....
	Portland	WHL	2	0	0	0	4	....	....	....	....	....	....	....	....	....	....	....	....	....	....	....	....	....	....	....
1995-96	Portland	WHL	72	9	31	40	159	....	....	....	....	....	....	....	....	....	....	....	7	1	3	4	12	....	....	....
1996-97	Portland	WHL	72	12	32	44	163	....	....	....	....	....	....	....	....	....	....	....	6	1	2	3	12	....	....	....
1997-98	Portland	WHL	72	11	57	68	142	....	....	....	....	....	....	....	....	....	....	....	16	2	18	20	28	....	....	....
1998-99	Portland	WHL	40	11	21	32	104	....	....	....	....	....	....	....	....	....	....	....	4	1	4	5	10	....	....	....
	Kansas City	IHL	5	1	2	3	4	....	....	....	....	....	....	....	....	....	....	....	3	0	0	0	9	....	....	....
99-2000	**Pittsburgh**	**NHL**	**30**	**2**	**4**	**6**	**20**	**0**	**0**	**1**	**26**	**7.7**	**3**	**0**	**0.0**	**61**	**26**	**16:19**	....	....	....	....	....	....	....	....
	Wilkes-Barre	AHL	44	8	20	28	58	....	....	....	....	....	....	....	....	....	....	....	....	....	....	....	....	....	....	....
2000-01	Wilkes-Barre	AHL	43	6	18	24	95	....	....	....	....	....	....	....	....	....	....	....	3	1	0	1	12	....	....	....
	Pittsburgh	**NHL**	**36**	**4**	**11**	**15**	**28**	**1**	**0**	**1**	**47**	**8.5**	**6**	**0**	**0.0**	**82**	**38**	**18:51**	**18**	**3**	**7**	**10**	**16**	**1**	**0**	**1**
	NHL Totals		**66**	**6**	**15**	**21**	**48**	**1**	**0**	**2**	**73**	**8.2**		**0**	**0.0**	**143**	**64**	**17:42**	**18**	**3**	**7**	**10**	**16**	**1**	**0**	**1**

WHL West First All-Star Team (1998) • WHL West Second All-Star Team (1999)

FERENCE, Brad

(FAIR-ehns, BRAD) **FLA.**

Defense. Shoots right. 6'3", 212 lbs. Born, Calgary, Alta., April 2, 1979. Vancouver's 1st choice, 10th overall, in 1997 Entry Draft.

Season	Club	League	GP	G	A	Pts	PIM	PP	SH	GW	S	%	+/-	TF	F%	H	SB	Min	GP	G	A	Pts	PIM	PP	SH	GW
1994-95	Calgary AA Royals	AAHA	60	19	47	66	220	....	....	....	....	....	....	....	....	....	....	....	....	....	....	....	....	....	....	....
1995-96	Calgary Royals	AMHL	22	7	21	28	140	....	....	....	....	....	....	....	....	....	....	....	....	....	....	....	....	....	....	....
	Spokane Chiefs	WHL	5	0	2	2	18	....	....	....	....	....	....	....	....	....	....	....	....	....	....	....	....	....	....	....
1996-97	Spokane Chiefs	WHL	67	6	20	26	324	....	....	....	....	....	....	....	....	....	....	....	9	0	4	4	21	....	....	....
1997-98	Spokane Chiefs	WHL	54	9	30	39	213	....	....	....	....	....	....	....	....	....	....	....	18	0	7	7	59	....	....	....
1998-99	Spokane Chiefs	WHL	31	3	22	25	125	....	....	....	....	....	....	....	....	....	....	....	....	....	....	....	....	....	....	....
	Tri-City Americans	WHL	20	6	15	21	116	....	....	....	....	....	....	....	....	....	....	....	12	1	9	10	63	....	....	....
99-2000	**Florida**	**NHL**	**13**	**0**	**2**	**2**	**46**	**0**	**0**	**0**	**10**	**0.0**	**2**	**0**	**0.0**	**13**	**17**	**13:40**	....	....	....	....	....	....	....	....
	Louisville	AHL	58	2	7	9	231	....	....	....	....	....	....	....	....	....	....	....	2	0	0	0	2	....	....	....
2000-01	**Florida**	**NHL**	**14**	**0**	**1**	**1**	**14**	**0**	**0**	**0**	**5**	**0.0**	**-10**	**0**	**0.0**	**17**	**10**	**13:03**	....	....	....	....	....	....	....	....
	Louisville	AHL	52	3	21	24	200	....	....	....	....	....	....	....	....	....	....	....	....	....	....	....	....	....	....	....
	NHL Totals		**27**	**0**	**3**	**3**	**60**	**0**	**0**	**0**	**15**	**0.0**		**0**	**0.0**	**30**	**27**	**13:21**	....	....	....	....	....	....	....	....

Memorial Cup All-Star Team (1998)

Traded to **Florida** by **Vancouver** with Pavel Bure, Bret Hedican and Vancouver's 3rd round choice (Robert Fried) in 2000 Entry Draft for Ed Jovanovski, Dave Gagner, Mike Brown, Kevin Weekes and Florida's 1st round choice (Nathan Smith) in 2000 Entry Draft, January 17, 1999.

FERGUSON, Craig

(fuhr-GUH-sohn, KRAYG)

Center. Shoots left. 5'11", 190 lbs. Born, Castro Valley, CA, April 8, 1970. Montreal's 6th choice, 146th overall, in 1989 Entry Draft.

Season	Club	League	GP	G	A	Pts	PIM	PP	SH	GW	S	%	+/-	TF	F%	H	SB	Min	GP	G	A	Pts	PIM	PP	SH	GW
1988-89	Yale University	ECAC	24	11	6	17	20	....	....	....	....	....	....	....	....	....	....	....	....	....	....	....	....	....	....	....
1989-90	Yale University	ECAC	28	6	13	19	36	....	....	....	....	....	....	....	....	....	....	....	....	....	....	....	....	....	....	....
1990-91	Yale University	ECAC	29	11	10	21	34	....	....	....	....	....	....	....	....	....	....	....	....	....	....	....	....	....	....	....
1991-92	Yale University	ECAC	27	9	16	25	26	....	....	....	....	....	....	....	....	....	....	....	....	....	....	....	....	....	....	....
1992-93	Fredericton	AHL	55	15	13	28	20	....	....	....	....	....	....	....	....	....	....	....	5	0	1	1	2	....	....	....
	Wheeling	ECHL	9	6	5	11	24	....	....	....	....	....	....	....	....	....	....	....	....	....	....	....	....	....	....	....
1993-94	**Montreal**	**NHL**	**2**	**0**	**1**	**1**	**0**	**0**	**0**	**0**	**0**	**0.0**	**1**	....	....	....	....	....	....	....	....	....	....	....	....	....
	Fredericton	AHL	57	29	32	61	60	....	....	....	....	....	....	....	....	....	....	....	....	....	....	....	....	....	....	....
1994-95	Fredericton	AHL	80	27	35	62	62	....	....	....	....	....	....	....	....	....	....	....	17	6	2	8	6	....	....	....
	Montreal	**NHL**	**1**	**0**	**0**	**0**	**0**	**0**	**0**	**0**	**3**	**0.0**	**0**	....	....	....	....	....	....	....	....	....	....	....	....	....
1995-96	**Montreal**	**NHL**	**10**	**1**	**0**	**1**	**2**	**0**	**0**	**0**	**9**	**11.1**	**-5**	....	....	....	....	....	....	....	....	....	....	....	....	....
	Calgary	**NHL**	**8**	**0**	**0**	**0**	**4**	**0**	**0**	**0**	**11**	**0.0**	**-4**	....	....	....	....	....	....	....	....	....	....	....	....	....
	Saint John Flames	AHL	18	5	13	18	8	....	....	....	....	....	....	....	....	....	....	....	....	....	....	....	....	....	....	....
	Phoenix	IHL	31	6	9	15	25	....	....	....	....	....	....	....	....	....	....	....	4	0	2	2	6	....	....	....
1996-97	**Florida**	**NHL**	**3**	**0**	**0**	**0**	**0**	**0**	**0**	**0**	**5**	**0.0**	**-1**	....	....	....	....	....	....	....	....	....	....	....	....	....
	Carolina	AHL	74	29	41	70	57	....	....	....	....	....	....	....	....	....	....	....	....	....	....	....	....	....	....	....
1997-98	New Haven	AHL	64	24	28	52	41	....	....	....	....	....	....	....	....	....	....	....	3	2	1	3	2	....	....	....
1998-99	New Haven	AHL	61	18	27	45	76	....	....	....	....	....	....	....	....	....	....	....	....	....	....	....	....	....	....	....
99-2000	**Florida**	**NHL**	**3**	**0**	**0**	**0**	**0**	**0**	**0**	**0**	**2**	**0.0**	**-2**	**19**	**47.4**	**0**	**0**	**5:34**	....	....	....	....	....	....	....	....
	Louisville Panthers	AHL	61	29	27	56	28	....	....	....	....	....	....	....	....	....	....	....	4	1	3	4	2	....	....	....
2000-01	Fribourg-Gotteron	Switz.	42	16	22	38	65	....	....	....	....	....	....	....	....	....	....	....	5	0	3	3	18	....	....	....
	NHL Totals		**27**	**1**	**1**	**2**	**6**	**0**	**0**	**0**	**30**	**3.3**		**19**	**47.4**	**0**	**0**	**5:34**	....	....	....	....	....	....	....	....

Traded to **Calgary** by **Montreal** with Yves Sarault for Calgary's 8th round choice (Petr Kubos) in 1997 Entry Draft, November 26, 1995. Traded to **LA Kings** by **Calgary** for Pat Conacher, February 10, 1996. Signed as a free agent by **Florida**, July 24, 1996.

FERGUSON, Scott

(fuhr-GUH-sohn, SKAWT) **EDM.**

Defense. Shoots left. 6'1", 202 lbs. Born, Camrose, Alta., January 6, 1973.

Season	Club	League	GP	G	A	Pts	PIM	PP	SH	GW	S	%	+/-	TF	F%	H	SB	Min	GP	G	A	Pts	PIM	PP	SH	GW
1990-91	Sherwood Park	AJHL	32	2	9	11	91	....	....	....	....	....	....	....	....	....	....	....	....	....	....	....	....	....	....	....
	Kamloops Blazers	WHL	4	0	0	0	0	....	....	....	....	....	....	....	....	....	....	....	....	....	....	....	....	....	....	....
1991-92	Kamloops Blazers	WHL	62	4	10	14	138	....	....	....	....	....	....	....	....	....	....	....	12	0	2	2	21	....	....	....
1992-93	Kamloops Blazers	WHL	71	4	19	23	206	....	....	....	....	....	....	....	....	....	....	....	13	0	2	2	24	....	....	....
1993-94	Kamloops Blazers	WHL	68	5	49	54	180	....	....	....	....	....	....	....	....	....	....	....	19	5	11	16	48	....	....	....
1994-95	Cape Breton	AHL	58	4	6	10	103	....	....	....	....	....	....	....	....	....	....	....	....	....	....	....	....	....	....	....
	Wheeling	ECHL	5	1	5	6	16	....	....	....	....	....	....	....	....	....	....	....	....	....	....	....	....	....	....	....
1995-96	Cape Breton	AHL	80	5	16	21	196	....	....	....	....	....	....	....	....	....	....	....	....	....	....	....	....	....	....	....
1996-97	Hamilton Bulldogs	AHL	74	6	14	20	115	....	....	....	....	....	....	....	....	....	....	....	21	5	7	12	59	....	....	....
1997-98	**Edmonton**	**NHL**	**1**	**0**	**0**	**0**	**0**	**0**	**0**	**0**	**0**	**0.0**	**1**	....	....	....	....	....	....	....	....	....	....	....	....	....
	Hamilton Bulldogs	AHL	77	7	17	24	150	....	....	....	....	....	....	....	....	....	....	....	9	0	3	3	16	....	....	....
1998-99	**Anaheim**	**NHL**	**2**	**0**	**1**	**1**	**0**	**0**	**0**	**0**	**1**	**0.0**	**0**	**0**	**0.0**	**1**	**4**	**15:09**	....	....	....	....	....	....	....	....
	Cincinnati Ducks	AHL	78	4	31	35	59	....	....	....	....	....	....	....	....	....	....	....	3	0	0	0	4	....	....	....
99-2000	Cincinnati Ducks	AHL	77	7	25	32	166	....	....	....	....	....	....	....	....	....	....	....	....	....	....	....	....	....	....	....
2000-01	**Edmonton**	**NHL**	**20**	**0**	**1**	**1**	**13**	**0**	**0**	**0**	**8**	**0.0**	**2**	**0**	**0.0**	**27**	**11**	**10:55**	**6**	**0**	**0**	**0**	**0**	**0**	**0**	**0**
	Hamilton Bulldogs	AHL	42	3	18	21	79	....	....	....	....	....	....	....	....	....	....	....	....	....	....	....	....	....	....	....
	NHL Totals		**23**	**0**	**2**	**2**	**13**	**0**	**0**	**0**	**9**	**0.0**		**0**	**0.0**	**28**	**15**	**11:18**	**6**	**0**	**0**	**0**	**0**	**0**	**0**	**0**

WHL West Second All-Star Team (1994)

Signed as a free agent by **Edmonton**, June 2, 1994. Traded to **Ottawa** by **Edmonton** for Frantisek Musil, March 9, 1998. Signed as a free agent by **Anaheim**, July 27, 1998. Signed as a free agent by **Edmonton**, July 5, 2000.

FERRARO, Chris

(fuh-RAHR-oh, KRIHS) **N.J.**

Center. Shoots right. 5'9", 175 lbs. Born, Port Jefferson, NY, January 24, 1973. NY Rangers' 4th choice, 85th overall, in 1992 Entry Draft.

Season	Club	League	GP	G	A	Pts	PIM	PP	SH	GW	S	%	+/-	TF	F%	H	SB	Min	GP	G	A	Pts	PIM	PP	SH	GW
1990-91	Dubuque Saints	USHL	45	53	44	97	84	....	....	....	....	....	....	....	....	....	....	....	8	3	9	12	12	....	....	....
1991-92	Dubuque Saints	USHL	20	30	19	49	52	....	....	....	....	....	....	....	....	....	....	....	....	....	....	....	....	....	....	....
	Waterloo Hawks	USHL	18	19	31	50	54	....	....	....	....	....	....	....	....	....	....	....	4	5	6	11	14	....	....	....
1992-93	U. of Maine	H-East	39	25	26	51	46	....	....	....	....	....	....	....	....	....	....	....	....	....	....	....	....	....	....	....
1993-94	U. of Maine	H-East	4	0	1	1	8	....	....	....	....	....	....	....	....	....	....	....	....	....	....	....	....	....	....	....
	United States	Nat-Team	48	8	34	42	58	....	....	....	....	....	....	....	....	....	....	....	....	....	....	....	....	....	....	....
1994-95	Atlanta Knights	IHL	54	13	14	27	72	....	....	....	....	....	....	....	....	....	....	....	....	....	....	....	....	....	....	....
	Binghamton	AHL	13	6	4	10	38	....	....	....	....	....	....	....	....	....	....	....	10	2	3	5	16	....	....	....
1995-96	**NY Rangers**	**NHL**	**2**	**1**	**0**	**1**	**0**	**1**	**0**	**0**	**4**	**25.0**	**-3**	....	....	....	....	....	....	....	....	....	....	....	....	....
	Binghamton	AHL	77	32	67	99	208	....	....	....	....	....	....	....	....	....	....	....	4	4	2	6	13	....	....	....

			Regular Season																Playoffs							
Season	Club	League	GP	G	A	Pts	PIM	PP	SH	GW	S	%	+/-	TF	F%	H	SB	Min	GP	G	A	Pts	PIM	PP	SH	GW
1996-97	NY Rangers	NHL	12	1	1	2	6	0	0	0	23	4.3	1													
	Binghamton	AHL	53	29	34	63	94																			
1997-98	Pittsburgh	NHL	46	3	4	7	43	0	0	0	42	7.1	−2													
1998-99	Edmonton	NHL	2	1	0	1	0	0	0	0	1	100.0	1	19	52.6	0	0	8:33								
	Hamilton Bulldogs	AHL	72	35	41	76	104												11	8	5	13	20			
99-2000	NY Islanders	NHL	11	1	3	4	8	0	0	0	15	6.7	1	92	50.0	8	7	9:30								
	Providence Bruins	AHL	21	9	9	18	32																			
	Chicago Wolves	IHL	25	7	18	25	40												16	5	8	13	14			
2000-01	Albany River Rats	AHL	74	24	42	66	111																			
	NHL Totals		73	7	8	15	57	1	0	0	85	8.2		111	50.5	8	7	9:22								

Claimed on waivers by **Pittsburgh** from **NY Rangers**, October 1, 1997. Signed as a free agent by **Edmonton**, August 13, 1998. Signed as a free agent by **NY Islanders**, July 22, 1999. Signed as a free agent by **New Jersey**, July 20, 2000.

FERRARO, Peter

(fuh-RAHR-oh, PEE-tuhr) **WSH.**

Right wing. Shoots right. 5'10", 180 lbs. Born, Port Jefferson, NY, January 24, 1973. NY Rangers' 1st choice, 24th overall, in 1992 Entry Draft.

Season	Club	League	GP	G	A	Pts	PIM	PP	SH	GW	S	%	+/-	TF	F%	H	SB	Min	GP	G	A	Pts	PIM	PP	SH	GW
1990-91	Dubuque Saints	USHL	29	21	31	52	83												8	7	5	12	10			
1991-92	Dubuque Saints	USHL	21	25	25	50	92																			
	Waterloo Hawks	USHL	21	23	28	51	76												4	8	5	13	16			
1992-93	U. of Maine	H-East	36	18	32	50	106																			
1993-94	U. of Maine	H-East	4	3	6	9	16																			
	United States	Nat-Team	60	30	34	64	87																			
	United States	Olympics	8	6	0	6	6																			
1994-95	Atlanta Knights	IHL	61	15	24	39	118																			
	Binghamton	AHL	12	2	6	8	67												11	4	3	7	51			
1995-96	NY Rangers	NHL	5	0	1	1	0	0	0	0	6	0.0	−5													
	Binghamton	AHL	68	48	53	101	157												4	1	6	7	22			
1996-97	NY Rangers	NHL	2	0	0	0	0	0	0	0	3	0.0	0						2	0	0	0	0	0	0	0
	Binghamton	AHL	75	38	39	77	171												4	3	1	4	18			
1997-98	Pittsburgh	NHL	29	3	4	7	12	0	0	0	34	8.8	−2													
	NY Rangers	NHL	1	0	0	0	2	0	0	0	3	0.0	−2													
	Hartford	AHL	36	17	23	40	54												15	8	6	14	59			
1998-99	Boston	NHL	46	6	8	14	44	1	0	1	61	9.8	10	70	37.1	52	21	10:12								
	Providence Bruins	AHL	16	15	10	25	14												19	9	12	21	38			
99-2000	Boston	NHL	5	0	1	1	0	0	0	0	3	0.0	−1	19	47.4	8	1	8:11								
	Providence Bruins	AHL	48	21	25	46	98												13	5	7	12	14			
2000-01	Providence Bruins	AHL	78	26	45	71	109												17	4	5	9	34			
	NHL Totals		88	9	14	23	58	1	0	1	110	8.2		89	39.3	60	22	10:00	2	0	0	0	0	0	0	0

AHL First All-Star Team (1996) • Won Jack A. Butterfield Trophy (Playoff MVP - AHL) (1999)

Claimed on waivers by **Pittsburgh** from **NY Rangers**, October 1, 1997. Claimed on waivers by **NY Rangers** from **Pittsburgh**, January 9, 1998. Signed as a free agent by **Boston**, August 5, 1998. Claimed by **Atlanta** from **Boston** in Expansion Draft, June 25, 1999. Traded to **Boston** by **Atlanta** for Randy Robitaille, June 25, 1999. Signed as a free agent by **Washington**, August 1, 2001.

FERRARO, Ray

(fuh-RAHR-oh, RAY) **ATL.**

Center. Shoots left. 5'9", 200 lbs. Born, Trail, B.C., August 23, 1964. Hartford's 5th choice, 88th overall, in 1982 Entry Draft.

Season	Club	League	GP	G	A	Pts	PIM	PP	SH	GW	S	%	+/-	TF	F%	H	SB	Min	GP	G	A	Pts	PIM	PP	SH	GW
1981-82	Penticton	BCJHL	48	65	70	135	90																			
1982-83	Portland	WHL	50	41	49	90	39												14	14	10	24	13			
1983-84	Brandon	WHL	72	*108	84	*192	84												11	13	15	28	20			
1984-85	Hartford	NHL	44	11	17	28	40	6	0	2	59	18.6	−1													
	Binghamton	AHL	37	20	13	33	29																			
1985-86	Hartford	NHL	76	30	47	77	57	14	0	0	132	22.7	10						10	3	6	9	4	3	0	0
1986-87	Hartford	NHL	80	27	32	59	42	14	0	2	96	28.1	−9						6	1	1	2	8	0	0	0
1987-88	Hartford	NHL	68	21	29	50	81	6	0	2	105	20.0	1						6	1	1	2	6	1	0	0
1988-89	Hartford	NHL	80	41	35	76	86	11	0	7	169	24.3	1						4	2	0	2	4	0	0	0
1989-90	Hartford	NHL	79	25	29	54	109	7	0	4	138	18.1	−15						7	0	3	3	2	0	0	0
1990-91	Hartford	NHL	15	2	5	7	18	1	0	0	18	11.1	−1													
	NY Islanders	NHL	61	19	16	35	52	5	0	1	91	20.9	−11													
1991-92	NY Islanders	NHL	80	40	40	80	92	7	0	4	154	26.0	25													
1992-93	NY Islanders	NHL	46	14	13	27	40	3	0	1	72	19.4	0						18	13	7	20	18	0	0	0
	Capital District	AHL	1	0	2	2	2																			
1993-94	NY Islanders	NHL	82	21	32	53	83	5	0	3	136	15.4	1						4	1	0	1	6	0	0	0
1994-95	NY Islanders	NHL	47	22	21	43	30	2	0	1	94	23.4	1													
1995-96	NY Rangers	NHL	65	25	29	54	82	8	0	4	160	15.6	13													
	Los Angeles	NHL	11	4	2	6	10	1	0	0	18	22.2	−13													
1996-97	Los Angeles	NHL	81	25	21	46	112	11	0	2	152	16.4	−22													
1997-98	Los Angeles	NHL	40	6	9	15	42	0	0	2	45	13.3	−10						3	0	1	1	2	0	0	0
1998-99	Los Angeles	NHL	65	13	18	31	59	4	0	4	84	15.5	0	979	47.8	58	24	14:34								
99-2000	Atlanta	NHL	81	19	25	44	88	10	0	3	170	11.2	−33	1390	51.2	111	26	16:10								
2000-01	Atlanta	NHL	81	29	47	76	91	11	0	2	172	16.9	−11	1705	48.0	78	43	18:19								
	NHL Totals		1182	394	467	861	1214	126	0	44	2065	19.1		4074	49.0	247	93	16:28	58	21	19	40	50	4	0	0

WHL First All-Star Team (1984) • Played in NHL All-Star Game (1992)

Traded to **NY Islanders** by **Hartford** for Doug Crossman, November 13, 1990. Signed as a free agent by **NY Rangers**, August 9, 1995. Traded to **LA Kings** by **NY Rangers** with Ian Laperriere, Mattias Norstrom, Nathan LaFayette and NY Rangers' 4th round choice (Sean Blanchard) in 1997 Entry Draft for Marty McSorley, Jari Kurri and Shane Churla, March 14, 1996. Signed as a free agent by **Atlanta**, August 9, 1999.

FINLEY, Jeff

(FIHN-lee, JEHF) **ST.L.**

Defense. Shoots left. 6'2", 205 lbs. Born, Edmonton, Alta., April 14, 1967. NY Islanders' 4th choice, 55th overall, in 1985 Entry Draft.

Season	Club	League	GP	G	A	Pts	PIM	PP	SH	GW	S	%	+/-	TF	F%	H	SB	Min	GP	G	A	Pts	PIM	PP	SH	GW
1983-84	Summerland	BCJHL	49	0	21	21	14																			
	Portland	WHL	5	0	0	0	5												5	0	1	1	4			
1984-85	Portland	WHL	69	6	44	50	57												6	1	2	3	2			
1985-86	Portland	WHL	70	11	59	70	83												15	1	7	8	16			
1986-87	Portland	WHL	72	13	53	66	113												20	1	*21	22	27			
1987-88	NY Islanders	NHL	10	0	5	5	15	0	0	0	9	0.0	5						1	0	0	0	2	0	0	0
	Springfield	AHL	52	5	18	23	50																			
1988-89	NY Islanders	NHL	4	0	0	0	6	0	0	0	1	0.0	1													
	Springfield	AHL	65	3	16	19	55																			
1989-90	NY Islanders	NHL	11	0	1	1	0	0	0	0	7	0.0	0						5	0	2	2	2	0	0	0
	Springfield	AHL	57	1	15	16	41												13	1	4	5	23			
1990-91	NY Islanders	NHL	11	0	0	0	4	0	0	0	0	0.0	−1													
	Capital District	AHL	67	10	34	44	34																			
1991-92	NY Islanders	NHL	51	1	10	11	26	0	0	0	25	4.0	−6													
	Capital District	AHL	20	1	9	10	6																			
1992-93	Capital District	AHL	61	6	29	35	34												4	0	1	1	0			
1993-94	Philadelphia	NHL	55	1	8	9	24	0	0	0	43	2.3	16													
1994-95	Hershey Bears	AHL	36	2	9	11	33												6	0	1	1	8			
1995-96	Winnipeg	NHL	65	1	5	6	81	0	0	0	27	3.7	−2						6	0	0	0	4	0	0	0
	Springfield	AHL	14	3	12	15	22																			
1996-97	Phoenix	NHL	65	3	7	10	40	1	0	1	38	7.9	−8						1	0	0	0	2	0	0	0
1997-98	NY Rangers	NHL	63	1	6	7	55	0	0	0	32	3.1	−3													
1998-99	NY Rangers	NHL	2	0	0	0	0	0	0	0	0	0.0	−1	0	0.0	2	2	11:40								
	Hartford	AHL	42	2	10	12	28																			
	St. Louis	NHL	30	1	2	3	20	0	0	0	16	6.3	12	0	0.0	35	28	17:36	13	1	2	3	8	0	0	1
99-2000	St. Louis	NHL	74	2	8	10	38	0	0	2	31	6.5	26	1	100.0	121	67	17:49	7	0	2	2	4	0	0	0
2000-01	St. Louis	NHL	72	2	8	10	38	0	0	0	35	5.7	7	1	0.0	85	83	18:53	2	0	0	0	0	0	0	0
	NHL Totals		513	12	60	72	347	1	0	3	264	4.5		2	50.0	243	180	18:08	35	1	6	7	22	0	0	1

Rights traded to **Ottawa** by **NY Islanders** for Chris Luongo, June 30, 1993. Signed as a free agent by **Philadelphia**, July 30, 1993. Traded to **Winnipeg** by **Philadelphia** for Russ Romaniuk, June 27, 1995. Transferred to **Phoenix** after **Winnipeg** franchise relocated, July 1, 1996. Signed as a free agent by **NY Rangers**, August 18, 1997. Traded to **St. Louis** by **NY Rangers** with Geoff Smith for future considerations (Chris Kenady, February 22, 1999), February 13, 1999.

FISCHER, Jiri
(FIH-shuhr, YIH-ree) **DET.**

Defense. Shoots left. 6'5", 225 lbs. Born, Horovice, Czech., July 31, 1980. Detroit's 1st choice, 25th overall, in 1998 Entry Draft.

			Regular Season																Playoffs							
Season	Club	League	GP	G	A	Pts	PIM	PP	SH	GW	S	%	+/-	TF	F%	H	SB	Min	GP	G	A	Pts	PIM	PP	SH	GW
1995-96	Poldi Kladno-Jr.	Cze-Rep	39	6	10	16	....	....	....	....	....	....	....	....	....	....	....	....	....	....	....	....	....	....	....	....
1996-97	Poldi Kladno-Jr.	Cze-Rep	38	7	21	28	....	....	....	....	....	....	....	....	....	....	....	....	....	....	....	....	....	....	....	....
1997-98	Hull Olympiques	QMJHL	70	3	19	22	112	....	....	....	....	....	....	....	....	....	....	....	11	1	4	5	16	....	....	....
1998-99	Hull Olympiques	QMJHL	65	22	56	78	141	....	....	....	....	....	....	....	....	....	....	....	23	6	17	23	44	....	....	....
99-2000	**Detroit**	**NHL**	**52**	**0**	**8**	**8**	**45**	**0**	**0**	**0**	**41**	**0.0**	**1**	**0**	**0.0**	**68**	**25**	**10:51**	....	....	....	....	....	....	....	....
	Cincinnati Ducks	AHL	7	0	2	2	10	....	....	....	....	....	....	....	....	....	....	....	....	....	....	....	....	....	....	....
2000-01	**Detroit**	**NHL**	**55**	**1**	**8**	**9**	**59**	**0**	**0**	**0**	**64**	**1.6**	**3**	**0**	**0.0**	**131**	**37**	**16:46**	**5**	**0**	**0**	**0**	**9**	**0**	**0**	**0**
	Cincinnati Ducks	AHL	18	2	6	8	22	....	....	....	....	....	....	....	....	....	....	....	....	....	....	....	....	....	....	....
	NHL Totals		**107**	**1**	**16**	**17**	**104**	**0**	**0**	**0**	**105**	**1.0**		**0**	**0.0**	**199**	**62**	**13:54**	**5**	**0**	**0**	**0**	**9**	**0**	**0**	**0**

QMJHL First All-Star Team (1999)

FISHER, Mike
(FIH-shuhr, MIGHK) **OTT.**

Center. Shoots right. 6'1", 193 lbs. Born, Peterborough, Ont., June 5, 1980. Ottawa's 2nd choice, 44th overall, in 1998 Entry Draft.

Season	Club	League	GP	G	A	Pts	PIM	PP	SH	GW	S	%	+/-	TF	F%	H	SB	Min	GP	G	A	Pts	PIM	PP	SH	GW
1996-97	Peterborough	OPJHL	51	26	30	56	35	....	....	....	....	....	....	....	....	....	....	....	....	....	....	....	....	....	....	....
1997-98	Sudbury Wolves	OHL	66	24	25	49	65	....	....	....	....	....	....	....	....	....	....	....	9	2	2	4	13	....	....	....
1998-99	Sudbury Wolves	OHL	68	41	65	106	55	....	....	....	....	....	....	....	....	....	....	....	4	2	1	3	4	....	....	....
99-2000	**Ottawa**	**NHL**	**32**	**4**	**5**	**9**	**15**	**0**	**0**	**1**	**49**	**8.2**	**−6**	**356**	**47.8**	**76**	**13**	**12:57**	....	....	....	....	....	....	....	....
2000-01	**Ottawa**	**NHL**	**60**	**7**	**12**	**19**	**46**	**0**	**0**	**3**	**83**	**8.4**	**−1**	**709**	**50.2**	**129**	**32**	**11:38**	**4**	**0**	**1**	**1**	**4**	**0**	**0**	**0**
	NHL Totals		**92**	**11**	**17**	**28**	**61**	**0**	**0**	**4**	**132**	**8.3**		**1065**	**49.4**	**205**	**45**	**12:05**	**4**	**0**	**1**	**1**	**4**	**0**	**0**	**0**

• Missed rmajority of 1999-2000 season recovering from knee injury suffered in game vs. Boston, December 30, 1999.

FITZGERALD, Tom
(FIHTZ-jair-uhld, TAWM) **NSH.**

Right wing/Center. Shoots right. 6', 195 lbs. Born, Billerica, MA, August 28, 1968. NY Islanders' 1st choice, 17th overall, in 1986 Entry Draft.

Season	Club	League	GP	G	A	Pts	PIM	PP	SH	GW	S	%	+/-	TF	F%	H	SB	Min	GP	G	A	Pts	PIM	PP	SH	GW
1984-85	Austin Prep	Hi-School	18	20	21	41	....	....	....	....	....	....	....	....	....	....	....	....	....	....	....	....	....	....	....	....
1985-86	Austin Prep	Hi-School	24	35	38	73	....	....	....	....	....	....	....	....	....	....	....	....	....	....	....	....	....	....	....	....
1986-87	Providence	H-East	27	8	14	22	22	....	....	....	....	....	....	....	....	....	....	....	....	....	....	....	....	....	....	....
1987-88	Providence	H-East	36	19	15	34	50	....	....	....	....	....	....	....	....	....	....	....	....	....	....	....	....	....	....	....
1988-89	**NY Islanders**	**NHL**	**23**	**3**	**5**	**8**	**10**	**0**	**0**	**1**	**24**	**12.5**	**1**	....	....	....	....	....	....	....	....	....	....	....	....	....
	Springfield	AHL	61	24	18	42	43	....	....	....	....	....	....	....	....	....	....	....	....	....	....	....	....	....	....	....
1989-90	**NY Islanders**	**NHL**	**19**	**2**	**5**	**7**	**4**	**0**	**0**	**1**	**24**	**8.3**	**−3**	....	....	....	....	....	**4**	**1**	**0**	**1**	**4**	**0**	**0**	**0**
	Springfield	AHL	53	30	23	53	32	....	....	....	....	....	....	....	....	....	....	....	14	2	9	11	13	....	....	....
1990-91	**NY Islanders**	**NHL**	**41**	**5**	**5**	**10**	**24**	**0**	**0**	**2**	**60**	**8.3**	**−9**	....	....	....	....	....	....	....	....	....	....	....	....	....
	Capital District	AHL	27	7	7	14	50	....	....	....	....	....	....	....	....	....	....	....	....	....	....	....	....	....	....	....
1991-92	**NY Islanders**	**NHL**	**45**	**6**	**11**	**17**	**28**	**0**	**2**	**2**	**71**	**8.5**	**−3**	....	....	....	....	....	....	....	....	....	....	....	....	....
	Capital District	AHL	4	1	1	2	4	....	....	....	....	....	....	....	....	....	....	....	....	....	....	....	....	....	....	....
1992-93	**NY Islanders**	**NHL**	**77**	**9**	**18**	**27**	**34**	**0**	**3**	**1**	**83**	**10.8**	**−2**	....	....	....	....	....	**18**	**2**	**5**	**7**	**18**	**0**	**0**	**0**
1993-94	**Florida**	**NHL**	**83**	**18**	**14**	**32**	**54**	**0**	**3**	**1**	**144**	**12.5**	**−3**	....	....	....	....	....	....	....	....	....	....	....	....	....
1994-95	**Florida**	**NHL**	**48**	**3**	**13**	**16**	**31**	**0**	**0**	**0**	**78**	**3.8**	**−3**	....	....	....	....	....	....	....	....	....	....	....	....	....
1995-96	**Florida**	**NHL**	**82**	**13**	**21**	**34**	**75**	**1**	**6**	**2**	**141**	**9.2**	**−3**	....	....	....	....	....	**22**	**4**	**4**	**8**	**34**	**0**	**0**	**2**
1996-97	**Florida**	**NHL**	**71**	**10**	**14**	**24**	**64**	**0**	**2**	**1**	**135**	**7.4**	**7**	....	....	....	....	....	**5**	**0**	**1**	**1**	**0**	**0**	**0**	**0**
1997-98	**Florida**	**NHL**	**69**	**10**	**5**	**15**	**57**	**0**	**1**	**1**	**105**	**9.5**	**−4**	....	....	....	....	....	....	....	....	....	....	....	....	....
	Colorado	**NHL**	**11**	**2**	**1**	**3**	**22**	**0**	**1**	**0**	**14**	**14.3**	**0**	....	....	....	....	....	**7**	**0**	**1**	**1**	**20**	**0**	**0**	**0**
1998-99	**Nashville**	**NHL**	**80**	**13**	**19**	**32**	**48**	**0**	**0**	**1**	**180**	**7.2**	**−18**	**155**	**52.3**	**70**	**49**	**17:17**	....	....	....	....	....	....	....	....
99-2000	**Nashville**	**NHL**	**82**	**13**	**9**	**22**	**66**	**0**	**3**	**1**	**119**	**10.9**	**−18**	**264**	**51.9**	**75**	**43**	**13:57**	....	....	....	....	....	....	....	....
2000-01	**Nashville**	**NHL**	**82**	**9**	**9**	**18**	**71**	**0**	**2**	**2**	**135**	**6.7**	**−5**	**458**	**54.6**	**96**	**42**	**14:58**	....	....	....	....	....	....	....	....
	NHL Totals		**813**	**116**	**149**	**265**	**588**	**1**	**23**	**16**	**1313**	**8.8**		**877**	**53.4**	**241**	**134**	**15:23**	**56**	**7**	**11**	**18**	**76**	**0**	**0**	**2**

Claimed by **Florida** from **NY Islanders** in Expansion Draft, June 24, 1993. Traded to **Colorado** by **Florida** for the rights to Mark Parrish and Anaheim's 3rd round choice (previously acquired, Florida selected Lance Ward) in 1998 Entry Draft, March 24, 1998. Signed as a free agent by **Nashville**, July 6, 1998.

FITZPATRICK, Rory
(fitz-PA-trihk, ROHR-ee) **BUF.**

Defense. Shoots right. 6'2", 208 lbs. Born, Rochester, NY, January 11, 1975. Montreal's 2nd choice, 47th overall, in 1993 Entry Draft.

Season	Club	League	GP	G	A	Pts	PIM	PP	SH	GW	S	%	+/-	TF	F%	H	SB	Min	GP	G	A	Pts	PIM	PP	SH	GW
1990-91	Rochester	EJHL	40	0	5	5	....	....	....	....	....	....	....	....	....	....	....	....	....	....	....	....	....	....	....	....
1991-92	Rochester	EJHL	28	8	28	36	141	....	....	....	....	....	....	....	....	....	....	....	....	....	....	....	....	....	....	....
1992-93	Sudbury Wolves	OHL	58	4	20	24	68	....	....	....	....	....	....	....	....	....	....	....	14	0	0	0	17	....	....	....
1993-94	Sudbury Wolves	OHL	65	12	34	46	112	....	....	....	....	....	....	....	....	....	....	....	10	2	5	7	10	....	....	....
1994-95	Sudbury Wolves	OHL	56	12	36	48	72	....	....	....	....	....	....	....	....	....	....	....	18	3	15	18	21	....	....	....
	Fredericton	AHL	....	....	....	....	....	....	....	....	....	....	....	....	....	....	....	....	10	1	2	3	5	....	....	....
1995-96	**Montreal**	**NHL**	**42**	**0**	**2**	**2**	**18**	**0**	**0**	**0**	**31**	**0.0**	**−7**	....	....	....	....	....	**6**	**1**	**1**	**2**	**0**	**0**	**0**	**0**
	Fredericton	AHL	18	4	6	10	36	....	....	....	....	....	....	....	....	....	....	....	....	....	....	....	....	....	....	....
1996-97	**Montreal**	**NHL**	**6**	**0**	**1**	**1**	**6**	**0**	**0**	**0**	**5**	**0.0**	**−2**	....	....	....	....	....	....	....	....	....	....	....	....	....
	St. Louis	**NHL**	**2**	**0**	**0**	**0**	**2**	**0**	**0**	**0**	**1**	**0.0**	**−2**	....	....	....	....	....	....	....	....	....	....	....	....	....
	Worcester	AHL	49	4	13	17	78	....	....	....	....	....	....	....	....	....	....	....	5	1	2	3	0	....	....	....
1997-98	Worcester	AHL	62	8	22	30	111	....	....	....	....	....	....	....	....	....	....	....	11	0	3	3	26	....	....	....
1998-99	**St. Louis**	**NHL**	**1**	**0**	**0**	**0**	**2**	**0**	**0**	**0**	**0**	**0.0**	**−3**	**0**	**0.0**	**0**	**0**	**4:49**	....	....	....	....	....	....	....	....
	Worcester	AHL	53	5	16	21	82	....	....	....	....	....	....	....	....	....	....	....	4	0	1	1	17	....	....	....
99-2000	Worcester	AHL	28	0	5	5	48	....	....	....	....	....	....	....	....	....	....	....	....	....	....	....	....	....	....	....
	Milwaukee	IHL	27	2	1	3	27	....	....	....	....	....	....	....	....	....	....	....	3	0	2	2	2	....	....	....
2000-01	**Nashville**	**NHL**	**2**	**0**	**0**	**0**	**2**	**0**	**0**	**0**	**0**	**0.0**	**−2**	**0**	**0.0**	**1**	**0**	**9:47**	....	....	....	....	....	....	....	....
	Milwaukee	IHL	22	0	2	2	32	....	....	....	....	....	....	....	....	....	....	....	....	....	....	....	....	....	....	....
	Hamilton Bulldogs	AHL	34	3	17	20	29	....	....	....	....	....	....	....	....	....	....	....	....	....	....	....	....	....	....	....
	NHL Totals		**53**	**0**	**3**	**3**	**30**	**0**	**0**	**0**	**37**	**0.0**		**0**	**0.0**	**1**	**0**	**8:08**	**6**	**1**	**1**	**2**	**0**	**0**	**0**	**0**

Traded to **St. Louis** by **Montreal** with Pierre Turgeon and Craig Conroy for Murray Baron, Shayne Corson and St. Louis' 5th round choice (Gennady Razin) in 1997 Entry Draft, October 29, 1996. Claimed by **Boston** from **St. Louis** in NHL Waiver Draft, October 5, 1998. Claimed on waivers by **St. Louis** from **Boston**, October 7, 1998. Traded to **Nashville** by **St. Louis** for Dan Keczmer, February 9, 2000. Traded to **Edmonton** by **Nashville** for future considerations, January 12, 2001. Signed as a free agent by **Buffalo**, August 14, 2001.

FLEURY, Theoren
(FLUH-ree, THAIR-ihn) **NYR**

Right wing. Shoots right. 5'6", 180 lbs. Born, Oxbow, Sask., June 29, 1968. Calgary's 9th choice, 166th overall, in 1987 Entry Draft.

Season	Club	League	GP	G	A	Pts	PIM	PP	SH	GW	S	%	+/-	TF	F%	H	SB	Min	GP	G	A	Pts	PIM	PP	SH	GW
1983-84	St. James	MAHA	22	33	31	64	88	....	....	....	....	....	....	....	....	....	....	....	....	....	....	....	....	....	....	....
1984-85	Moose Jaw	WHL	71	29	46	75	82	....	....	....	....	....	....	....	....	....	....	....	....	....	....	....	....	....	....	....
1985-86	Moose Jaw	WHL	72	43	65	108	124	....	....	....	....	....	....	....	....	....	....	....	13	7	13	20	16	....	....	....
1986-87	Moose Jaw	WHL	66	61	68	129	110	....	....	....	....	....	....	....	....	....	....	....	9	7	9	16	34	....	....	....
1987-88	Moose Jaw	WHL	65	68	92	*160	235	....	....	....	....	....	....	....	....	....	....	....	....	....	....	....	....	....	....	....
	Salt Lake	IHL	2	3	4	7	7	....	....	....	....	....	....	....	....	....	....	....	8	11	5	16	16	....	....	....
1988-89♦	**Calgary**	**NHL**	**36**	**14**	**20**	**34**	**46**	**5**	**0**	**3**	**89**	**15.7**	**5**	....	....	....	....	....	**22**	**5**	**6**	**11**	**24**	**3**	**0**	**3**
	Salt Lake	IHL	40	37	37	74	81	....	....	....	....	....	....	....	....	....	....	....	....	....	....	....	....	....	....	....
1989-90	**Calgary**	**NHL**	**80**	**31**	**35**	**66**	**157**	**9**	**3**	**6**	**200**	**15.5**	**22**	....	....	....	....	....	**6**	**2**	**3**	**5**	**10**	**0**	**0**	**0**
1990-91	**Calgary**	**NHL**	**79**	**51**	**53**	**104**	**136**	**9**	**7**	**9**	**249**	**20.5**	**48**	....	....	....	....	....	**7**	**2**	**5**	**7**	**14**	**0**	**0**	**1**
1991-92	**Calgary**	**NHL**	**80**	**33**	**40**	**73**	**133**	**11**	**1**	**6**	**225**	**14.7**	**0**	....	....	....	....	....	....	....	....	....	....	....	....	....
1992-93	**Calgary**	**NHL**	**83**	**34**	**66**	**100**	**88**	**12**	**2**	**4**	**250**	**13.6**	**14**	....	....	....	....	....	**6**	**5**	**7**	**12**	**27**	**3**	**1**	**0**
1993-94	**Calgary**	**NHL**	**83**	**40**	**45**	**85**	**186**	**16**	**1**	**6**	**278**	**14.4**	**30**	....	....	....	....	....	**7**	**6**	**4**	**10**	**5**	**1**	**0**	**2**
1994-95	Tappara Tampere	Finland	10	8	9	17	22	....	....	....	....	....	....	....	....	....	....	....	....	....	....	....	....	....	....	....
	Calgary	**NHL**	**47**	**29**	**29**	**58**	**112**	**9**	**2**	**5**	**173**	**16.8**	**6**	....	....	....	....	....	**7**	**7**	**7**	**14**	**2**	**2**	**1**	**0**
1995-96	**Calgary**	**NHL**	**80**	**46**	**50**	**96**	**112**	**17**	**5**	**4**	**353**	**13.0**	**17**	....	....	....	....	....	**4**	**2**	**1**	**3**	**14**	**0**	**0**	**0**
1996-97	**Calgary**	**NHL**	**81**	**29**	**38**	**67**	**104**	**9**	**2**	**3**	**336**	**8.6**	**−12**	....	....	....	....	....	....	....	....	....	....	....	....	....
1997-98	**Calgary**	**NHL**	**82**	**27**	**51**	**78**	**197**	**3**	**2**	**4**	**282**	**9.6**	**0**	....	....	....	....	....	....	....	....	....	....	....	....	....
	Canada	Olympics	6	1	3	4	2	....	....	....	....	....	....	....	....	....	....	....	....	....	....	....	....	....	....	....
1998-99	**Calgary**	**NHL**	**60**	**30**	**39**	**69**	**68**	**7**	**3**	**3**	**250**	**12.0**	**18**	**517**	**59.2**	**51**	**25**	**23:33**	....	....	....	....	....	....	....	....
	Colorado	**NHL**	**15**	**10**	**14**	**24**	**18**	**1**	**0**	**2**	**51**	**19.6**	**8**	**150**	**58.7**	**12**	**3**	**22:33**	**18**	**5**	**12**	**17**	**20**	**2**	**0**	**0**

Season	Club	League	GP	G	A	Pts	PIM	PP	SH	GW	S	%	+/-	TF	F%	H	SB	Min	GP	G	A	Pts	PIM	PP	SH	GW
			Regular Season																Playoffs							
99-2000	NY Rangers	NHL	80	15	49	64	68	1	0	1	246	6.1	–4	490	56.5	69	31	19:41	....	....	....	....	....	....	....	....
2000-01	NY Rangers	NHL	62	30	44	74	122	8	7	3	238	12.6	0	139	47.5	63	30	21:47	....	....	....	....	....	....	....	....
	NHL Totals		948	419	573	992	1547	117	35	59	3220	13.0		1296	56.9	195	89	21:33	77	34	45	79	116	11	2	6

WHL East Second All-Star Team (1988) • Shared Alka-Seltzer Plus Award with Marty McSorley (1991) • NHL Second All-Star Team (1995) • Played in NHL All-Star Game (1991, 1992, 1996, 1997, 1998, 1999, 2001)

Traded to **Colorado** by **Calgary** with Chris Dingman for Rene Corbet, Wade Belak, Robyn Regehr and Colorado's 2nd round compensatory choice (Jarret Stoll) in 2000 Entry Draft, February 28, 1999. Signed as a free agent by **NY Rangers**, July 8, 1999.

FOOTE, Adam (FUT, A-duhm) COL.

Defense. Shoots right. 6'2", 215 lbs. Born, Toronto, Ont., July 10, 1971. Quebec's 2nd choice, 22nd overall, in 1989 Entry Draft.

Season	Club	League	GP	G	A	Pts	PIM	PP	SH	GW	S	%	+/-	TF	F%	H	SB	Min	GP	G	A	Pts	PIM	PP	SH	GW
1987-88	Brooklin Whitby	OMHA	65	25	43	68	108																			
1988-89	Sault Ste. Marie	OHL	66	7	32	39	120																			
1989-90	Sault Ste. Marie	OHL	61	12	43	55	199																			
1990-91	Sault Ste. Marie	OHL	59	18	51	69	93												14	5	12	17	28			
1991-92	**Quebec**	**NHL**	46	2	5	7	44	0	0	0	55	3.6	–4													
	Halifax Citadels	AHL	6	0	1	1	2																			
1992-93	**Quebec**	**NHL**	81	4	12	16	168	0	1	0	54	7.4	6						6	0	1	1	2	0	0	0
1993-94	**Quebec**	**NHL**	45	2	6	8	67	0	0	0	42	4.8	3													
1994-95	**Quebec**	**NHL**	35	0	7	7	52	0	0	0	24	0.0	17						6	0	1	1	14	0	0	0
1995-96♦	**Colorado**	**NHL**	73	5	11	16	88	1	0	1	49	10.2	27						22	1	3	4	36	0	0	0
1996-97	**Colorado**	**NHL**	78	2	19	21	135	0	0	0	60	3.3	16						17	0	4	4	62	0	0	0
1997-98	**Colorado**	**NHL**	77	3	14	17	124	0	0	1	64	4.7	–3						7	0	0	0	23	0	0	0
	Canada	Olympics	6	0	1	1	4																			
1998-99	**Colorado**	**NHL**	64	5	16	21	92	3	0	0	83	6.0	20	0	0.0	125	93	24:50	19	2	3	5	24	1	0	0
99-2000	**Colorado**	**NHL**	59	5	13	18	98	1	0	2	63	7.9	5	0	0.0	156	87	25:51	16	0	7	7	28	0	0	0
2000-01♦	**Colorado**	**NHL**	35	3	12	15	42	1	1	1	59	5.1	6	0	0.0	96	43	25:22	23	3	4	7	*47	1	0	1
	NHL Totals		593	31	115	146	910	6	2	5	553	5.6		0	0.0	377	223	25:20	116	6	23	29	236	2	0	1

OHL First All-Star Team (1991)

Transferred to **Colorado** after **Quebec** franchise relocated, June 21, 1995. • Missed majority of 2000-01 season recovering from shoulder injury suffered in game vs. Carolina, January 6, 2001.

FORBES, Colin (FOHRBS, COHL-ihn)

Left wing. Shoots left. 6'3", 205 lbs. Born, New Westminster, B.C., February 16, 1976. Philadelphia's 5th choice, 166th overall, in 1994 Entry Draft.

Season	Club	League	GP	G	A	Pts	PIM	PP	SH	GW	S	%	+/-	TF	F%	H	SB	Min	GP	G	A	Pts	PIM	PP	SH	GW
1993-94	Sherwood Park	AJHL	47	18	22	40	76																			
1994-95	Portland	WHL	72	24	31	55	108												9	1	3	4	10			
1995-96	Portland	WHL	72	33	44	77	137												7	2	5	7	14			
	Hershey Bears	AHL	2	1	0	1	2												4	0	2	2	2			
1996-97	**Philadelphia**	**NHL**	3	1	0	1	0	0	0	0	3	33.3	0						3	0	0	0	0	0	0	0
	Philadelphia	AHL	74	21	28	49	108												10	5	5	10	33			
1997-98	**Philadelphia**	**NHL**	63	12	7	19	59	2	0	2	93	12.9	2						5	0	0	0	2	0	0	0
	Philadelphia	AHL	13	7	4	11	22																			
1998-99	**Philadelphia**	**NHL**	66	9	7	16	51	0	0	4	92	9.8	0	2	50.0	46	10	12:35								
	Tampa Bay	**NHL**	14	3	1	4	10	0	1	0	25	12.0	–5	0	0.0	21	4	17:30								
99-2000	**Tampa Bay**	**NHL**	8	0	0	0	18	0	0	0	3	0.0	–4	1	0.0	9	0	8:53								
	Ottawa	**NHL**	45	2	5	7	12	0	0	0	54	3.7	–1	82	47.6	70	6	8:34	5	1	0	1	14	0	0	0
2000-01	**Ottawa**	**NHL**	39	0	1	1	31	0	0	0	26	0.0	–3	10	40.0	60	3	6:10								
	NY Rangers	**NHL**	19	1	4	5	15	0	0	0	20	5.0	–3	1	0.0	28	5	7:52								
	NHL Totals		257	28	25	53	196	2	1	6	316	8.9		96	45.8	234	28	10:04	13	1	0	1	16	0	0	0

Traded to **Tampa Bay** by **Philadelphia** with Philadelphia's 4th round choice (Michal Lanicek) in 1999 Entry Draft for Mikael Andersson and Sandy McCarthy, March 20, 1999. Traded to **Ottawa** by **Tampa Bay** for Bruce Gardiner, November 11, 1999. Traded to **NY Rangers** by **Ottawa** for Eric Lacroix, March 1, 2001.

FORSBERG, Peter (FOHRS-buhrg, PEE-tuhr) COL.

Center. Shoots left. 6', 205 lbs. Born, Ornskoldsvik, Sweden, July 20, 1973. Philadelphia's 1st choice, 6th overall, in 1991 Entry Draft.

Season	Club	League	GP	G	A	Pts	PIM	PP	SH	GW	S	%	+/-	TF	F%	H	SB	Min	GP	G	A	Pts	PIM	PP	SH	GW
1989-90	MoDo AIK	Swede-Jr.	30	15	12	27	42																			
	MoDo AIK	Sweden	1	0	1	1	4																			
1990-91	MoDo AIK	Swede-Jr.	39	38	64	102	56																			
	MoDo AIK	Sweden	23	7	10	17	22																			
1991-92	MoDo AIK	Sweden	39	9	18	27	78																			
1992-93	MoDo AIK	Swede-Jr.	2	0	3	3	4																			
	MoDo AIK	Sweden	39	23	24	47	92												3	4	1	5	0			
1993-94	MoDo AIK	Sweden	39	18	26	44	82												11	9	7	16	14			
	Sweden	Olympics	8	2	6	8	6																			
1994-95	MoDo Hockey	Sweden	11	5	9	14	20																			
	Quebec	**NHL**	47	15	35	50	16	3	0	3	86	17.4	17						6	2	4	6	4	1	0	0
1995-96♦	**Colorado**	**NHL**	82	30	86	116	47	7	3	3	217	13.8	26						22	10	11	21	18	3	0	1
1996-97	**Colorado**	**NHL**	65	28	58	86	73	5	4	4	188	14.9	31						14	5	12	17	10	3	0	0
1997-98	**Colorado**	**NHL**	72	25	66	91	94	7	3	7	202	12.4	6						7	6	5	11	12	2	0	0
	Sweden	Olympics	4	1	4	5	6																			
1998-99	**Colorado**	**NHL**	78	30	67	97	108	9	2	7	217	13.8	27	895	54.4	108	31	23:29	19	8	16	*24	31	1	1	0
99-2000	**Colorado**	**NHL**	49	14	37	51	52	3	0	2	105	13.3	9	519	46.6	70	19	20:55	16	7	8	15	12	2	1	4
2000-01♦	**Colorado**	**NHL**	73	27	62	89	54	12	2	5	178	15.2	23	755	46.6	85	19	20:48	11	4	10	14	6	1	0	2
	NHL Totals		466	169	411	580	444	46	14	31	1193	14.2		2169	49.8	263	69	21:52	95	42	66	108	93	13	2	7

NHL All-Rookie Team (1995) • Won Calder Memorial Trophy (1995) • NHL First All-Star Team (1998, 1999) • Played in NHL All-Star Game (1996, 1998, 1999, 2001)

Traded to **Quebec** by **Philadelphia** with Steve Duchesne, Kerry Huffman, Mike Ricci, Ron Hextall, Philadelphia's 1st round choice (Jocelyn Thibault) in 1993 Entry Draft, $15,000,000 and future considerations (Chris Simon and Philadelphia's 1st round choice (later traded to Toronto - later traded to Washington - Washington selected Nolan Baumgartner) in 1994 Entry Draft, July 21, 1992) for Eric Lindros, June 30, 1992. Transferred to **Colorado** after **Quebec** franchise relocated, June 21, 1995.

FRANCIS, Ron (FRAN-sihs, RAWN) CAR.

Center. Shoots left. 6'3", 200 lbs. Born, Sault Ste. Marie, Ont., March 1, 1963. Hartford's 1st choice, 4th overall, in 1981 Entry Draft.

Season	Club	League	GP	G	A	Pts	PIM	PP	SH	GW	S	%	+/-	TF	F%	H	SB	Min	GP	G	A	Pts	PIM	PP	SH	GW
1979-80	S.S. Marie Legion	NOHA	45	57	92	149	....																			
1980-81	Sault Ste. Marie	OMJHL	64	26	43	69	33												19	7	8	15	34			
1981-82	Sault Ste. Marie	OHL	25	18	30	48	46																			
	Hartford	**NHL**	59	25	43	68	51	12	0	1	163	15.3	–13													
1982-83	**Hartford**	**NHL**	79	31	59	90	60	4	2	4	212	14.6	–25													
1983-84	**Hartford**	**NHL**	72	23	60	83	45	5	0	5	202	11.4	–10													
1984-85	**Hartford**	**NHL**	80	24	57	81	66	4	0	1	195	12.3	–23													
1985-86	**Hartford**	**NHL**	53	24	53	77	24	7	1	4	120	20.0	8						10	1	2	3	4	0	0	0
1986-87	**Hartford**	**NHL**	75	30	63	93	45	7	0	7	189	15.9	10						6	2	2	4	6	1	0	0
1987-88	**Hartford**	**NHL**	80	25	50	75	87	11	1	3	172	14.5	–8						6	2	5	7	2	1	0	0
1988-89	**Hartford**	**NHL**	69	29	48	77	36	8	0	4	156	18.6	4						4	0	2	2	0	0	0	0
1989-90	**Hartford**	**NHL**	80	32	69	101	73	15	1	5	170	18.8	13						7	3	3	6	8	1	0	0
1990-91	**Hartford**	**NHL**	67	21	55	76	51	10	1	6	149	14.1	–2													
	♦ Pittsburgh	**NHL**	14	2	9	11	21	0	0	1	25	8.0	0						24	7	10	17	24	0	0	4
1991-92♦	**Pittsburgh**	**NHL**	70	21	33	54	30	5	1	2	121	17.4	–7						21	8	*19	27	6	2	0	2
1992-93	**Pittsburgh**	**NHL**	84	24	76	100	68	9	2	4	215	11.2	6						12	6	11	17	19	1	0	1
1993-94	**Pittsburgh**	**NHL**	82	27	66	93	62	8	0	2	216	12.5	–3						6	0	2	2	6	0	0	0
1994-95	**Pittsburgh**	**NHL**	44	11	*48	59	18	3	0	1	94	11.7	30						12	6	13	19	4	2	0	0
1995-96	**Pittsburgh**	**NHL**	77	27	*92	119	56	12	1	4	158	17.1	25						11	3	6	9	4	2	0	1
1996-97	**Pittsburgh**	**NHL**	81	27	63	90	20	10	1	2	183	14.8	7						5	1	2	3	2	1	0	0
1997-98	**Pittsburgh**	**NHL**	81	25	62	87	20	7	0	5	189	13.2	12						6	1	5	6	2	0	0	0
1998-99	**Carolina**	**NHL**	82	21	31	52	34	8	0	2	133	15.8	–2	1589	51.5	36	57	21:55	3	0	1	1	0	0	0	0

Season	Club	League	GP	G	A	Pts	PIM	PP	SH	GW	S	%	+/-	TF	F%	H	SB	Min	GP	G	A	Pts	PIM	PP	SH	GW
			Regular Season																Playoffs							
99-2000	Carolina	NHL	78	23	50	73	18	7	0	4	150	15.3	10	1566	53.3	48	53	21:58	....	....	....	....	....	....	....	....
2000-01	Carolina	NHL	82	15	50	65	32	7	0	4	130	11.5	–15	1271	57.5	37	54	20:15	3	0	0	0	0	0	0	0
	NHL Totals		**1489**	**487**	**1137**	**1624**	**917**	**159**	**11**	**71**	**3342**	**14.6**		**4426**	**53.9**	**121**	**164**	**21:22**	**136**	**40**	**83**	**123**	**87**	**11**	**0**	**8**

Won Alka-Seltzer Plus Award (1995) • Won Frank J. Selke Trophy (1995) • Won Lady Byng Trophy (1995, 1998) • Played in NHL All-Star Game (1983, 1985, 1990, 1996)
Traded to **Pittsburgh** by **Hartford** with Grant Jennings and Ulf Samuelsson for John Cullen, Jeff Parker and Zarley Zalapski, March 4, 1991. Signed as a free agent by **Carolina**, July 13, 1998.

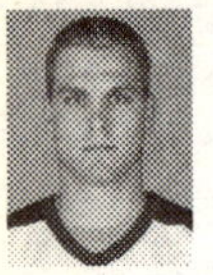

FREADRICH, Kyle
(FREE-drihk, KIGHL) **NYR**

Left wing. Shoots left. 6'7", 260 lbs. Born, Edmonton, Alta., December 28, 1978. Vancouver's 4th choice, 64th overall, in 1997 Entry Draft.

1995-96	Killam Selects	AAHA	37	11	22	33	176	....	....	....	....	....	....	....	....	....	....	....	....	....	....	....	....	....	....	....
1996-97	Prince George	WHL	12	0	0	0	12	....	....	....	....	....	....	....	....	....	....	....	....	....	....	....	....	....	....	....
	Regina Pats	WHL	50	1	3	4	152	....	....	....	....	....	....	....	....	....	....	....	4	0	0	0	8	....	....	....
1997-98	Regina Pats	WHL	62	6	5	11	259	....	....	....	....	....	....	....	....	....	....	....	9	0	1	1	25	....	....	....
1998-99	Regina Pats	WHL	52	2	2	4	215	....	....	....	....	....	....	....	....	....	....	....	....	....	....	....	....	....	....	....
	Syracuse Crunch	AHL	5	0	0	0	20	....	....	....	....	....	....	....	....	....	....	....	....	....	....	....	....	....	....	....
	Louisiana	ECHL	5	0	0	0	17	....	....	....	....	....	....	....	....	....	....	....	4	0	0	0	2	....	....	....
99-2000	**Tampa Bay**	**NHL**	**10**	**0**	**0**	**0**	**39**	**0**	**0**	**0**	**0**	**0.0**	**–1**	**0**	**0.0**	**4**	**1**	**2:19**	....	....	....	....	....	....	....	....
	Louisiana	ECHL	3	0	0	0	17	....	....	....	....	....	....	....	....	....	....	....	....	....	....	....	....	....	....	....
	Detroit Vipers	IHL	45	0	1	1	203	....	....	....	....	....	....	....	....	....	....	....	....	....	....	....	....	....	....	....
2000-01	**Tampa Bay**	**NHL**	**13**	**0**	**1**	**1**	**36**	**0**	**0**	**0**	**3**	**0.0**	**–1**	**0**	**0.0**	**6**	**2**	**3:32**	....	....	....	....	....	....	....	....
	Detroit Vipers	IHL	29	3	3	6	120	....	....	....	....	....	....	....	....	....	....	....	....	....	....	....	....	....	....	....
	NHL Totals		**23**	**0**	**1**	**1**	**75**	**0**	**0**	**0**	**3**	**0.0**		**0**	**0.0**	**10**	**3**	**3:00**	....	....	....	....	....	....	....	....

Signed as a free agent by **Tampa Bay**, July 16, 1999. Traded to **NY Rangers** by **Tampa Bay** with Nils Ekman for Tim Taylor, June 30, 2001.

FRIEDMAN, Doug
(FREED-man, DUHG)

Left wing. Shoots left. 6'1", 200 lbs. Born, Cape Elizabeth, ME, September 1, 1971. Quebec's 13th choice, 222nd overall, in 1991 Entry Draft.

1989-90	Lawrence Prep	Hi-School	20	9	26	35	....	....	....	....	....	....	....	....	....	....	....	....	....	....	....	....	....	....	....	....
1990-91	Boston University	H-East	36	6	6	12	37	....	....	....	....	....	....	....	....	....	....	....	....	....	....	....	....	....	....	....
1991-92	Boston University	H-East	34	11	8	19	42	....	....	....	....	....	....	....	....	....	....	....	....	....	....	....	....	....	....	....
1992-93	Boston University	H-East	38	17	24	41	62	....	....	....	....	....	....	....	....	....	....	....	....	....	....	....	....	....	....	....
1993-94	Boston University	H-East	41	9	23	32	110	....	....	....	....	....	....	....	....	....	....	....	....	....	....	....	....	....	....	....
1994-95	Cornwall Aces	AHL	55	6	9	15	56	....	....	....	....	....	....	....	....	....	....	....	3	0	0	0	0	....	....	....
1995-96	Cornwall Aces	AHL	80	12	22	34	178	....	....	....	....	....	....	....	....	....	....	....	8	1	1	2	17	....	....	....
1996-97	Hershey Bears	AHL	61	12	21	33	245	....	....	....	....	....	....	....	....	....	....	....	23	6	9	15	49	....	....	....
1997-98	**Edmonton**	**NHL**	**16**	**0**	**0**	**0**	**20**	**0**	**0**	**0**	**8**	**0.0**	**0**	....	....	....	....	....	....	....	....	....	....	....	....	....
	Hamilton Bulldogs	AHL	55	19	27	46	235	....	....	....	....	....	....	....	....	....	....	....	9	4	4	8	40	....	....	....
1998-99	**Nashville**	**NHL**	**2**	**0**	**1**	**1**	**14**	**0**	**0**	**0**	**3**	**0.0**	**0**	**0**	**0.0**	**2**	**1**	**6:60**	....	....	....	....	....	....	....	....
	Milwaukee	IHL	69	26	25	51	251	....	....	....	....	....	....	....	....	....	....	....	2	1	2	3	8	....	....	....
99-2000	Kentucky	AHL	73	13	23	36	237	....	....	....	....	....	....	....	....	....	....	....	9	1	3	4	45	....	....	....
2000-01	Worcester	AHL	41	9	10	19	78	....	....	....	....	....	....	....	....	....	....	....	8	2	0	2	22	....	....	....
	NHL Totals		**18**	**0**	**1**	**1**	**34**	**0**	**0**	**0**	**11**	**0.0**		**0**	**0.0**	**2**	**1**	**7:00**	....	....	....	....	....	....	....	....

Rights transferred to **Colorado** after **Quebec** franchise relocated, June 21, 1995. Signed as a free agent by **Edmonton**, July 14, 1997. Claimed by **Nashville** from **Edmonton** in Expansion Draft, June 26, 1998. Signed as a free agent by **San Jose**, August 26, 1999.

FRIESEN, Jeff
(FREE-zuhn, JEHF) **ANA.**

Center. Shoots left. 6', 215 lbs. Born, Meadow Lake, Sask., August 5, 1976. San Jose's 1st choice, 11th overall, in 1994 Entry Draft.

1991-92	Saskatoon	SMHL	35	37	51	88	75	....	....	....	....	....	....	....	....	....	....	....	....	....	....	....	....	....	....	....
	Regina Pats	WHL	4	3	1	4	2	....	....	....	....	....	....	....	....	....	....	....	....	....	....	....	....	....	....	....
1992-93	Regina Pats	WHL	70	45	38	83	23	....	....	....	....	....	....	....	....	....	....	....	13	7	10	17	8	....	....	....
1993-94	Regina Pats	WHL	66	51	67	118	48	....	....	....	....	....	....	....	....	....	....	....	4	3	2	5	2	....	....	....
1994-95	Regina Pats	WHL	25	21	23	44	22	....	....	....	....	....	....	....	....	....	....	....	....	....	....	....	....	....	....	....
	San Jose	**NHL**	**48**	**15**	**10**	**25**	**14**	**5**	**1**	**2**	**86**	**17.4**	**–8**	....	....	....	....	....	**11**	**1**	**5**	**6**	**4**	**0**	**0**	**0**
1995-96	**San Jose**	**NHL**	**79**	**15**	**31**	**46**	**42**	**2**	**0**	**0**	**123**	**12.2**	**–19**	....	....	....	....	....	....	....	....	....	....	....	....	....
1996-97	**San Jose**	**NHL**	**82**	**28**	**34**	**62**	**75**	**6**	**2**	**5**	**200**	**14.0**	**–8**	....	....	....	....	....	....	....	....	....	....	....	....	....
1997-98	**San Jose**	**NHL**	**79**	**31**	**32**	**63**	**40**	**7**	**6**	**7**	**186**	**16.7**	**8**	....	....	....	....	....	**6**	**0**	**1**	**1**	**2**	**0**	**0**	**0**
1998-99	**San Jose**	**NHL**	**78**	**22**	**35**	**57**	**42**	**10**	**1**	**3**	**215**	**10.2**	**3**	**24**	**33.3**	**99**	**22**	**19:25**	**6**	**2**	**2**	**4**	**14**	**1**	**0**	**0**
99-2000	**San Jose**	**NHL**	**82**	**26**	**35**	**61**	**47**	**11**	**3**	**7**	**191**	**13.6**	**–2**	**3**	**66.7**	**110**	**37**	**19:48**	**11**	**2**	**2**	**4**	**10**	**0**	**0**	**0**
2000-01	**San Jose**	**NHL**	**64**	**12**	**24**	**36**	**56**	**2**	**0**	**1**	**120**	**10.0**	**7**	**7**	**28.6**	**107**	**36**	**18:51**	....	....	....	....	....	....	....	....
	Anaheim	**NHL**	**15**	**2**	**10**	**12**	**10**	**2**	**0**	**0**	**29**	**6.9**	**–2**	**43**	**55.8**	**19**	**11**	**21:28**	....	....	....	....	....	....	....	....
	NHL Totals		**527**	**151**	**211**	**362**	**326**	**45**	**13**	**25**	**1150**	**13.1**		**77**	**46.8**	**335**	**106**	**19:31**	**34**	**5**	**10**	**15**	**30**	**1**	**0**	**0**

Canadian Major Junior Rookie of the Year (1993) • NHL All-Rookie Team (1995)
Traded to **Anaheim** by **San Jose** with Steve Shields and future considerations for Teemu Selanne, March 5, 2001.

GABORIK, Marian
(gah-BOHR-ihk, MAIR-ee-uhn) **MIN.**

Left wing. Shoots left. 6'1", 183 lbs. Born, Trencin, Czech., February 14, 1982. Minnesota's 1st choice, 3rd overall, in 2000 Entry Draft.

1997-98	Dukla Trencin	Slovak-Jr.	36	37	22	59	28	....	....	....	....	....	....	....	....	....	....	....	....	....	....	....	....	....	....	....
	Dukla Trencin	Slovakia	1	1	0	1	0	....	....	....	....	....	....	....	....	....	....	....	....	....	....	....	....	....	....	....
1998-99	Dukla Trencin	Slovakia	33	11	9	20	6	....	....	....	....	....	....	....	....	....	....	....	3	1	0	1	2	....	....	....
99-2000	Dukla Trencin	Slovakia	50	25	21	46	34	....	....	....	....	....	....	....	....	....	....	....	5	1	2	3	2	....	....	....
2000-01	**Minnesota**	**NHL**	**71**	**18**	**18**	**36**	**32**	**6**	**0**	**3**	**179**	**10.1**	**–6**	**3**	**33.3**	**25**	**14**	**15:26**	....	....	....	....	....	....	....	....
	NHL Totals		**71**	**18**	**18**	**36**	**32**	**6**	**0**	**3**	**179**	**10.1**		**3**	**33.3**	**25**	**14**	**15:26**	....	....	....	....	....	....	....	....

GAGNE, Simon
(GAH-nyay, SIGH-mohn) **PHI.**

Left wing. Shoots left. 6', 190 lbs. Born, Ste. Foy, Que., February 29, 1980. Philadelphia's 1st choice, 22nd overall, in 1998 Entry Draft.

1995-96	Ste-Foy Governors	QAAA	27	13	9	22	18	....	....	....	....	....	....	....	....	....	....	....	15	7	8	15	8	....	....	....
1996-97	Beauport	QMJHL	51	9	22	31	49	....	....	....	....	....	....	....	....	....	....	....	....	....	....	....	....	....	....	....
1997-98	Quebec Remparts	QMJHL	53	30	39	69	26	....	....	....	....	....	....	....	....	....	....	....	12	11	5	16	23	....	....	....
1998-99	Quebec Remparts	QMJHL	61	50	70	120	42	....	....	....	....	....	....	....	....	....	....	....	13	9	8	17	4	....	....	....
99-2000	**Philadelphia**	**NHL**	**80**	**20**	**28**	**48**	**22**	**8**	**1**	**4**	**159**	**12.6**	**11**	**443**	**42.2**	**46**	**23**	**14:58**	**17**	**5**	**5**	**10**	**2**	**2**	**0**	**1**
2000-01	**Philadelphia**	**NHL**	**69**	**27**	**32**	**59**	**18**	**6**	**0**	**7**	**191**	**14.1**	**24**	**21**	**28.6**	**41**	**17**	**18:05**	**6**	**3**	**0**	**3**	**0**	**2**	**0**	**0**
	NHL Totals		**149**	**47**	**60**	**107**	**40**	**14**	**1**	**11**	**350**	**13.4**		**464**	**41.6**	**87**	**40**	**16:25**	**23**	**8**	**5**	**13**	**2**	**4**	**0**	**1**

QMJHL Second All-Star Team (1999) • NHL All-Rookie Team (2000) • Played in NHL ALL-Star Game (2001)

GAGNON, Sean
(gah-NYAWN, SHAWN) **NYR**

Defense. Shoots left. 6'2", 219 lbs. Born, Sault Ste. Marie, Ont., September 11, 1973.

1990-91	S.S. Marie Elks	NOHA	46	21	26	47	218	....	....	....	....	....	....	....	....	....	....	....	....	....	....	....	....	....	....	....
1991-92	Sudbury	NOJHA	13	10	13	23	34	....	....	....	....	....	....	....	....	....	....	....	....	....	....	....	....	....	....	....
	Sudbury Wolves	OHL	44	3	4	7	60	....	....	....	....	....	....	....	....	....	....	....	5	0	1	1	0	....	....	....
1992-93	Sudbury Wolves	OHL	6	1	1	2	16	....	....	....	....	....	....	....	....	....	....	....	....	....	....	....	....	....	....	....
	Ottawa 67's	OHL	33	2	10	12	68	....	....	....	....	....	....	....	....	....	....	....	....	....	....	....	....	....	....	....
	Sault Ste. Marie	OHL	24	1	5	6	65	....	....	....	....	....	....	....	....	....	....	....	15	2	2	4	25	....	....	....
1993-94	Sault Ste. Marie	OHL	42	4	12	16	147	....	....	....	....	....	....	....	....	....	....	....	14	1	1	2	52	....	....	....
1994-95	Dayton Bombers	ECHL	68	9	23	32	339	....	....	....	....	....	....	....	....	....	....	....	8	0	3	3	69	....	....	....
1995-96	Dayton Bombers	ECHL	68	7	22	29	326	....	....	....	....	....	....	....	....	....	....	....	3	0	1	1	33	....	....	....
1996-97	Fort Wayne	IHL	72	7	7	14	*457	....	....	....	....	....	....	....	....	....	....	....	....	....	....	....	....	....	....	....
1997-98	**Phoenix**	**NHL**	**5**	**0**	**1**	**1**	**14**	**0**	**0**	**0**	**3**	**0.0**	**1**	....	....	....	....	....	....	....	....	....	....	....	....	....
	Springfield	AHL	54	4	13	17	330	....	....	....	....	....	....	....	....	....	....	....	2	0	1	1	17	....	....	....
1998-99	**Phoenix**	**NHL**	**2**	**0**	**0**	**0**	**7**	**0**	**0**	**0**	**1**	**0.0**	**–2**	**0**	**0.0**	**1**	**2**	**7:56**	....	....	....	....	....	....	....	....
	Springfield	AHL	68	8	14	22	331	....	....	....	....	....	....	....	....	....	....	....	3	0	0	0	14	....	....	....
99-2000	Jokerit Helsinki	Finland	42	3	5	8	183	....	....	....	....	....	....	....	....	....	....	....	11	4	1	5	22	....	....	....

			Regular Season																Playoffs							
Season	Club	League	GP	G	A	Pts	PIM	PP	SH	GW	S	%	+/-	TF	F%	H	SB	Min	GP	G	A	Pts	PIM	PP	SH	GW
2000-01	Ottawa	NHL	5	0	0	0	13	0	0	0	0	0.0	0	0	0.0	12	4	10:45	....	....	....	....	....	....	....	....
	Grand Rapids	IHL	70	4	16	20	226	....	....	....	....	....	....	....	....	....	....	....	10	2	3	5	30	....	....	....
	NHL Totals		12	0	1	1	34	0	0	0	4	0.0		0	0.0	13	6	9:57	....	....	....	....	....	....	....	....

Signed as a free agent by **Phoenix**, May 14, 1997. Signed as a free agent by **Ottawa**, July 7, 2000. Traded to **NY Rangers** by **Ottawa** for Jason Doig and Jeff Ulmer, June 29, 2001.

GAINEY, Steve

(GAY-nee, STEEV) **DAL.**

Left wing. Shoots left. 6', 185 lbs. Born, Montreal, Que., January 26, 1979. Dallas' 3rd choice, 77th overall, in 1997 Entry Draft.

Season	Club	League	GP	G	A	Pts	PIM	PP	SH	GW	S	%	+/-	TF	F%	H	SB	Min	GP	G	A	Pts	PIM	PP	SH	GW
1995-96	Kamloops Blazers	WHL	49	1	4	5	40	....	....	....	....	....	....	....	....	....	....	....	3	0	0	0	0	....	....	....
1996-97	Kamloops Blazers	WHL	60	9	18	27	60	....	....	....	....	....	....	....	....	....	....	....	2	0	0	0	9	....	....	....
1997-98	Kamloops Blazers	WHL	68	21	34	55	93	....	....	....	....	....	....	....	....	....	....	....	7	1	7	8	15	....	....	....
1998-99	Kamloops Blazers	WHL	68	30	34	64	155	....	....	....	....	....	....	....	....	....	....	....	15	5	4	9	38	....	....	....
99-2000	Fort Wayne	UHL	1	0	0	0	0	....	....	....	....	....	....	....	....	....	....	....	....	....	....	....	....	....	....	....
	Michigan K-Wings	IHL	58	8	10	18	41	....	....	....	....	....	....	....	....	....	....	....	....	....	....	....	....	....	....	....
2000-01	Dallas	NHL	1	0	0	0	0	0	0	0	0	0.0	0	0	0.0	0	0	2:21	....	....	....	....	....	....	....	....
	Utah Grizzlies	IHL	61	7	7	14	167	....	....	....	....	....	....	....	....	....	....	....	....	....	....	....	....	....	....	....
	NHL Totals		1	0	0	0	0	0	0	0	0	0.0		0	0.0	0	0	2:21	....	....	....	....	....	....	....	....

GALANOV, Maxim

(gah-LAH-nahf, mahx-EEM) **TOR.**

Defense. Shoots left. 6'1", 205 lbs. Born, Krasnoyarsk, USSR, March 13, 1974. NY Rangers' 3rd choice, 61st overall, in 1993 Entry Draft.

Season	Club	League	GP	G	A	Pts	PIM	PP	SH	GW	S	%	+/-	TF	F%	H	SB	Min	GP	G	A	Pts	PIM	PP	SH	GW
1992-93	Lada Togliatti	CIS	41	4	2	6	12	....	....	....	....	....	....	....	....	....	....	....	10	1	1	2	12	....	....	....
1993-94	Lada Togliatti	CIS	7	1	0	1	4	....	....	....	....	....	....	....	....	....	....	....	12	1	0	1	8	....	....	....
1994-95	Lada Togliatti	CIS	45	5	6	11	54	....	....	....	....	....	....	....	....	....	....	....	9	0	1	1	12	....	....	....
1995-96	Binghamton	AHL	72	17	36	53	24	....	....	....	....	....	....	....	....	....	....	....	4	1	1	2	0	....	....	....
1996-97	Binghamton	AHL	73	13	30	43	30	....	....	....	....	....	....	....	....	....	....	....	3	0	0	0	2	....	....	....
1997-98	NY Rangers	NHL	6	0	1	1	2	0	0	0	5	0.0	1	....	....	....	....	....	....	....	....	....	....	....	....	....
	Hartford	AHL	61	6	24	30	22	....	....	....	....	....	....	....	....	....	....	....	13	3	6	9	2	....	....	....
1998-99	Pittsburgh	NHL	51	4	3	7	14	2	0	0	44	9.1	–8	1	0.0	32	49	15:13	1	0	0	0	0	0	0	0
99-2000	Atlanta	NHL	40	4	3	7	20	0	0	0	47	8.5	–12	0	0.0	40	56	21:32	....	....	....	....	....	....	....	....
2000-01	Tampa Bay	NHL	25	0	5	5	8	0	0	0	10	0.0	–5	0	0.0	10	19	16:12	....	....	....	....	....	....	....	....
	Detroit Vipers	IHL	16	0	3	3	6	....	....	....	....	....	....	....	....	....	....	....	....	....	....	....	....	....	....	....
	Louisville Panthers	AHL	9	4	5	9	11	....	....	....	....	....	....	....	....	....	....	....	....	....	....	....	....	....	....	....
	NHL Totals		122	8	12	20	44	2	0	0	106	7.5		1	0.0	82	124	17:36	1	0	0	0	0	0	0	0

Claimed by **Pittsburgh** from **NY Rangers** in NHL Waiver Draft, October 5, 1998. Claimed by **Atlanta** from **Pittsburgh** in Expansion Draft, June 25, 1999. • Missed majority of 1999-2000 season recovering from hand injury suffered in game vs. NY Rangers, October 17, 1999. Signed as a free agent by **Florida**, September, 2000. Claimed on waivers by **Tampa Bay** from **Florida**, November 1, 2000. Traded to **Toronto** by **Tampa Bay** for Konstantin Kalmikov, February 20, 2001.

GALLEY, Garry

(GA-lee, GAHR-ee)

Defense. Shoots left. 6', 202 lbs. Born, Montreal, Que., April 16, 1963. Los Angeles' 4th choice, 103rd overall, in 1983 Entry Draft.

Season	Club	League	GP	G	A	Pts	PIM	PP	SH	GW	S	%	+/-	TF	F%	H	SB	Min	GP	G	A	Pts	PIM	PP	SH	GW
1979-80	Ottawa 79's	OMHA	STATISTICS NOT AVAILABLE																							
	Ottawa Jr. Sens	OCJHL	2	1	0	1	4																			
1980-81	Gloucester	OCJHL	49	18	26	44	103	....	....	....	....	....	....	....	....	....	....	....	....	....	....	....	....	....	....	....
1981-82	Bowling Green	CCHA	42	3	36	39	48	....	....	....	....	....	....	....	....	....	....	....	....	....	....	....	....	....	....	....
1982-83	Bowling Green	CCHA	40	17	29	46	40	....	....	....	....	....	....	....	....	....	....	....	....	....	....	....	....	....	....	....
1983-84	Bowling Green	CCHA	44	15	52	67	61	....	....	....	....	....	....	....	....	....	....	....	....	....	....	....	....	....	....	....
1984-85	Los Angeles	NHL	78	8	30	38	82	1	1	2	131	6.1	3	....	....	....	....	....	3	1	0	1	2	0	0	0
1985-86	Los Angeles	NHL	49	9	13	22	46	1	0	1	57	15.8	–9	....	....	....	....	....	....	....	....	....	....	....	....	....
	New Haven	AHL	4	2	6	8	6	....	....	....	....	....	....	....	....	....	....	....	....	....	....	....	....	....	....	....
1986-87	Los Angeles	NHL	30	5	11	16	57	2	0	1	43	11.6	–9	....	....	....	....	....	....	....	....	....	....	....	....	....
	Washington	NHL	18	1	10	11	10	1	0	0	27	3.7	3	....	....	....	....	....	....	....	....	....	....	....	....	....
1987-88	Washington	NHL	58	7	23	30	44	3	0	0	100	7.0	11	....	....	....	....	....	2	0	0	0	0	0	0	0
1988-89	Boston	NHL	78	8	22	30	80	2	1	0	145	5.5	–7	....	....	....	....	....	13	2	4	6	13	0	0	0
1989-90	Boston	NHL	71	8	27	35	75	1	0	0	142	5.6	2	....	....	....	....	....	9	0	1	1	33	0	0	0
1990-91	Boston	NHL	70	6	21	27	84	1	0	0	128	4.7	0	....	....	....	....	....	21	3	3	6	34	1	0	2
1991-92	Boston	NHL	38	2	12	14	83	1	0	0	51	3.9	–3	....	....	....	....	....	16	1	5	6	17	0	0	0
	Philadelphia	NHL	39	3	15	18	34	2	0	1	74	4.1	1	....	....	....	....	....	....	....	....	....	....	....	....	....
1992-93	Philadelphia	NHL	83	13	49	62	115	4	1	3	231	5.6	18	....	....	....	....	....	....	....	....	....	....	....	....	....
1993-94	Philadelphia	NHL	81	10	60	70	91	5	1	0	186	5.4	–11	....	....	....	....	....	....	....	....	....	....	....	....	....
1994-95	Philadelphia	NHL	33	2	20	22	20	1	0	0	66	3.0	0	....	....	....	....	....	....	....	....	....	....	....	....	....
	Buffalo	NHL	14	1	9	10	10	2	0	0	31	3.2	4	....	....	....	....	....	5	0	3	3	4	0	0	0
1995-96	Buffalo	NHL	78	10	44	54	81	7	1	2	175	5.7	–2	....	....	....	....	....	....	....	....	....	....	....	....	....
1996-97	Buffalo	NHL	71	4	34	38	102	1	1	1	84	4.8	10	....	....	....	....	....	12	0	6	6	14	0	0	0
1997-98	Los Angeles	NHL	74	9	28	37	63	7	0	0	128	7.0	–5	....	....	....	....	....	4	0	1	1	2	0	0	0
1998-99	Los Angeles	NHL	60	4	12	16	30	3	0	0	77	5.2	–9	0	0.0	100	59	17:16	....	....	....	....	....	....	....	....
99-2000	Los Angeles	NHL	70	9	21	30	52	2	0	1	96	9.4	9	0	0.0	152	79	20:15	4	0	0	0	0	0	0	0
2000-01	NY Islanders	NHL	56	6	14	20	59	4	0	0	94	6.4	–4	2	50.0	114	61	20:50	....	....	....	....	....	....	....	....
	NHL Totals		1149	125	475	600	1218	51	6	12	2066	6.1		2	50.0	366	199	19:28	89	7	23	30	119	1	0	2

CCHA First All-Star Team (1983, 1984) • NCAA East First All-American Team (1984) • NCAA Championship All-Tournament Team (1984) • Played in NHL All-Star Game (1991, 1994)

Traded to **Washington** by **LA Kings** for Al Jensen, February 14, 1987. Signed as a free agent by **Boston**, July 8, 1988. Traded to **Philadelphia** by **Boston** with Wes Walz and Boston's 3rd round choice (Milos Holan) in 1993 Entry Draft for Gord Murphy, Brian Dobbin, Philadelphia's 3rd round choice (Sergei Zholtok) in 1992 Entry Draft and 4th round choice (Charles Paquette) in 1993 Entry Draft, January 2, 1992. Traded to **Buffalo** by **Philadelphia** for Petr Svoboda, April 7, 1995. Signed as a free agent by **LA Kings**, July 15, 1997. Signed as a free agent by **NY Islanders**, September 25, 2000.

GARDINER, Bruce

(gahr-DIHN-uhr, BREWS)

Right wing. Shoots right. 6'1", 193 lbs. Born, Barrie, Ont., February 11, 1972. St. Louis' 6th choice, 131st overall, in 1991 Entry Draft.

Season	Club	League	GP	G	A	Pts	PIM	PP	SH	GW	S	%	+/-	TF	F%	H	SB	Min	GP	G	A	Pts	PIM	PP	SH	GW
1988-89	Barrie Colts	OJHL-B	41	17	28	45	29	....	....	....	....	....	....	....	....	....	....	....	....	....	....	....	....	....	....	....
1989-90	Barrie Colts	OJHL-B	40	19	26	45	89	....	....	....	....	....	....	....	....	....	....	....	13	10	11	21	32	....	....	....
1990-91	Colgate	ECAC	27	4	9	13	72	....	....	....	....	....	....	....	....	....	....	....	....	....	....	....	....	....	....	....
1991-92	Colgate	ECAC	23	7	8	15	77	....	....	....	....	....	....	....	....	....	....	....	....	....	....	....	....	....	....	....
1992-93	Colgate	ECAC	33	17	12	29	64	....	....	....	....	....	....	....	....	....	....	....	....	....	....	....	....	....	....	....
1993-94	Colgate	ECAC	33	23	23	46	68	....	....	....	....	....	....	....	....	....	....	....	....	....	....	....	....	....	....	....
	Peoria	IHL	3	0	0	0	0	....	....	....	....	....	....	....	....	....	....	....	....	....	....	....	....	....	....	....
1994-95	P.E.I. Senators	AHL	72	17	20	37	132	....	....	....	....	....	....	....	....	....	....	....	7	4	1	5	4	....	....	....
1995-96	P.E.I. Senators	AHL	38	11	13	24	87	....	....	....	....	....	....	....	....	....	....	....	5	2	4	6	4	....	....	....
1996-97	Ottawa	NHL	67	11	10	21	49	0	1	2	94	11.7	4	....	....	....	....	....	7	0	1	1	2	0	0	0
1997-98	Ottawa	NHL	55	7	11	18	50	0	0	0	64	10.9	2	....	....	....	....	....	11	1	3	4	2	0	0	1
1998-99	Ottawa	NHL	59	4	8	12	43	0	0	1	70	5.7	6	278	45.7	88	17	12:52	3	0	0	0	4	0	0	0
99-2000	Ottawa	NHL	10	0	3	3	4	0	0	0	18	0.0	1	62	59.7	16	2	13:24	....	....	....	....	....	....	....	....
	Tampa Bay	NHL	41	3	6	9	37	0	0	0	30	10.0	–21	330	56.4	52	28	13:36	....	....	....	....	....	....	....	....
2000-01	Columbus	NHL	73	7	15	22	78	0	0	1	60	11.7	–1	505	51.5	143	47	14:36	....	....	....	....	....	....	....	....
	NHL Totals		305	32	53	85	261	0	1	4	336	9.5		1175	51.9	299	94	13:45	21	1	4	5	8	0	0	1

ECAC Second All-Star Team (1994)

Signed as a free agent by **Ottawa**, June 14, 1994. Traded to **Tampa Bay** by **Ottawa** for Colin Forbes, November 11, 1999. Selected by **Columbus** from **Tampa Bay** in Expansion Draft, June 23, 2000.

GARPENLOV, Johan

(GAHR-pehn-LAHV, YOH-hahn)

Left wing. Shoots left. 6', 185 lbs. Born, Stockholm, Sweden, March 21, 1968. Detroit's 5th choice, 85th overall, in 1986 Entry Draft.

Season	Club	League	GP	G	A	Pts	PIM	PP	SH	GW	S	%	+/-	TF	F%	H	SB	Min	GP	G	A	Pts	PIM	PP	SH	GW
1984-85	Nacka HK	Sweden-2	4	1	2	3	2	....	....	....	....	....	....	....	....	....	....	....	....	....	....	....	....	....	....	....
1985-86	Nacka HK	Sweden-2	20	8	12	20	22	....	....	....	....	....	....	....	....	....	....	....	....	....	....	....	....	....	....	....
1986-87	Djurgardens IF	Sweden	29	5	8	13	22	....	....	....	....	....	....	....	....	....	....	....	2	0	0	0	0	....	....	....
1987-88	Djurgardens IF	Sweden	30	7	10	17	12	....	....	....	....	....	....	....	....	....	....	....	3	1	3	4	4	....	....	....
1988-89	Djurgardens IF	Sweden	36	12	19	31	20	....	....	....	....	....	....	....	....	....	....	....	8	3	4	7	10	....	....	....
1989-90	Djurgardens IF	Sweden	39	20	13	33	35	....	....	....	....	....	....	....	....	....	....	....	8	2	4	6	4	....	....	....
1990-91	Detroit	NHL	71	18	22	40	18	2	0	3	91	19.8	–4	....	....	....	....	....	6	0	1	1	4	0	0	0
1991-92	Detroit	NHL	16	1	1	2	4	0	0	0	13	7.7	2	....	....	....	....	....	....	....	....	....	....	....	....	....
	Adirondack	AHL	9	3	3	6	6	....	....	....	....	....	....	....	....	....	....	....	....	....	....	....	....	....	....	....
	San Jose	NHL	12	5	6	11	4	1	0	1	21	23.8	–2	....	....	....	....	....	....	....	....	....	....	....	....	....

			Regular Season																Playoffs							
Season	Club	League	GP	G	A	Pts	PIM	PP	SH	GW	S	%	+/-	TF	F%	H	SB	Min	GP	G	A	Pts	PIM	PP	SH	GW
1992-93	**San Jose**	**NHL**	**79**	**22**	**44**	**66**	**56**	**14**	**0**	**1**	**171**	**12.9**	**–26**	....	....	....	....	....	....	....	....	....	....	....	....	....
1993-94	**San Jose**	**NHL**	**80**	**18**	**35**	**53**	**28**	**7**	**0**	**3**	**125**	**14.4**	**9**	....	....	....	....	....	**14**	**4**	**6**	**10**	**6**	**0**	**0**	**2**
1994-95	**San Jose**	**NHL**	**13**	**1**	**1**	**2**	**2**	**0**	**0**	**0**	**16**	**6.3**	**–3**	....	....	....	....	....	....	....	....	....	....	....	....	....
	Florida	**NHL**	**27**	**3**	**9**	**12**	**0**	**0**	**0**	**0**	**28**	**10.7**	**4**	....	....	....	....	....	....	....	....	....	....	....	....	....
1995-96	**Florida**	**NHL**	**82**	**23**	**28**	**51**	**36**	**8**	**0**	**7**	**130**	**17.7**	**–10**	....	....	....	....	....	**20**	**4**	**2**	**6**	**8**	**0**	**0**	**0**
1996-97	**Florida**	**NHL**	**53**	**11**	**25**	**36**	**47**	**1**	**0**	**1**	**83**	**13.3**	**10**	....	....	....	....	....	**4**	**2**	**0**	**2**	**4**	**2**	**0**	**1**
1997-98	**Florida**	**NHL**	**39**	**2**	**3**	**5**	**8**	**0**	**0**	**0**	**43**	**4.7**	**–6**	....	....	....	....	....	....	....	....	....	....	....	....	....
1998-99	**Florida**	**NHL**	**64**	**8**	**9**	**17**	**42**	**0**	**1**	**0**	**71**	**11.3**	**–9**	**3**	**0.0**	**23**	**13**	**13:14**	....	....	....	....	....	....	....	....
99-2000	**Atlanta**	**NHL**	**73**	**2**	**14**	**16**	**31**	**0**	**0**	**0**	**79**	**2.5**	**–30**	**166**	**41.6**	**111**	**24**	**15:19**	....	....	....	....	....	....	....	....
2000-01	Djurgardens IF	Sweden	29	8	7	15	80	....	....	....	....	....	....	....	....	....	....	....	....	....	....	....	....	....	....	....
	NHL Totals		**609**	**114**	**197**	**311**	**276**	**33**	**1**	**16**	**871**	**13.1**		**169**	**40.8**	**134**	**37**	**14:21**	**44**	**10**	**9**	**19**	**22**	**2**	**0**	**3**

Traded to **San Jose** by **Detroit** for Bob McGill and Vancouver's 8th round choice (previously acquired, Detroit selected C.J. Denomme) in 1992 Entry Draft, March 9, 1992. Traded to **Florida** by **San Jose** for future considerations, March 3, 1995. Claimed by **Atlanta** from **Florida** in Expansion Draft, June 25, 1999.

GAUL, Mike

(GAWL, MIGH-kuhl)

Defense. Shoots right. 6'1", 200 lbs. Born, Lachine, Que., April 22, 1973. Los Angeles' 10th choice, 262nd overall, in 1991 Entry Draft.

1989-90	Lac St-Louis	QAAA	39	5	9	14	46	....	....	....	....	....	....	....	....	....	....	....	2	0	1	1	14	....	....	....
1990-91	St. Lawrence	ECAC	31	1	3	4	46	....	....	....	....	....	....	....	....	....	....	....	....	....	....	....	....	....	....	....
1991-92	Laval Titan	QMJHL	50	6	38	44	44	....	....	....	....	....	....	....	....	....	....	....	10	0	2	2	20	....	....	....
1992-93	Laval Titan	QMJHL	57	16	57	73	66	....	....	....	....	....	....	....	....	....	....	....	13	3	10	13	10	....	....	....
1993-94	Laval Titan	QMJHL	22	10	17	27	24	....	....	....	....	....	....	....	....	....	....	....	21	5	15	20	14	....	....	....
1994-95	Phoenix	IHL	4	0	1	1	2	....	....	....	....	....	....	....	....	....	....	....	....	....	....	....	....	....	....	....
	Knoxville	ECHL	68	13	41	54	51	....	....	....	....	....	....	....	....	....	....	....	4	2	1	3	2	....	....	....
1995-96	Knoxville	ECHL	54	13	48	61	44	....	....	....	....	....	....	....	....	....	....	....	....	....	....	....	....	....	....	....
1996-97	ETC Timmendorf	DEB	51	40	52	92	100	....	....	....	....	....	....	....	....	....	....	....	....	....	....	....	....	....	....	....
1997-98	Hershey Bears	AHL	60	12	47	59	69	....	....	....	....	....	....	....	....	....	....	....	7	0	7	7	6	....	....	....
	Mobile Mysticks	ECHL	5	0	7	7	0	....	....	....	....	....	....	....	....	....	....	....	....	....	....	....	....	....	....	....
1998-99	Lowell	AHL	18	3	5	8	14	....	....	....	....	....	....	....	....	....	....	....	....	....	....	....	....	....	....	....
	Colorado	**NHL**	**1**	**0**	**0**	**0**	**0**	**0**	**0**	**0**	**1**	**0.0**	**0**	**0**	**0.0**	**2**	**0**	**10:46**	....	....	....	....	....	....	....	....
	Hershey Bears	AHL	43	9	31	40	22	....	....	....	....	....	....	....	....	....	....	....	5	1	1	2	6	....	....	....
99-2000	Hershey Bears	AHL	65	12	57	69	52	....	....	....	....	....	....	....	....	....	....	....	12	0	8	8	....	....	....	....
2000-01	**Columbus**	**NHL**	**2**	**0**	**0**	**0**	**4**	**0**	**0**	**0**	**3**	**0.0**	**0**	**0**	**0.0**	**2**	**3**	**13:17**	....	....	....	....	....	....	....	....
	Syracuse Crunch	AHL	70	16	45	61	80	....	....	....	....	....	....	....	....	....	....	....	5	1	2	3	8	....	....	....
	NHL Totals		**3**	**0**	**0**	**0**	**4**	**0**	**0**	**0**	**4**	**0.0**		**0**	**0.0**	**4**	**3**	**12:27**	....	....	....	....	....	....	....	....

AHL Second All-Star Team (2000, 2001)

Signed as a free agent by **NY Islanders**, July 16, 1998. Traded to **Colorado** by **NY Islanders** for Ted Crowley, December 15, 1998. Signed as a free agent by **Columbus**, July 18, 2000.

GAUTHIER, Denis

(GOH-tyay, DEH-nihs) **CGY.**

Defense. Shoots left. 6'2", 210 lbs. Born, Montreal, Que., October 1, 1976. Calgary's 1st choice, 20th overall, in 1995 Entry Draft.

1991-92	St-Jean Richelieu	QAHA	STATISTICS NOT AVAILABLE																							
1992-93	Drummondville	QMJHL	61	1	7	8	136	....	....	....	....	....	....	....	....	....	....	....	10	0	5	5	40	....	....	....
1993-94	Drummondville	QMJHL	60	0	7	7	176	....	....	....	....	....	....	....	....	....	....	....	9	2	0	2	41	....	....	....
1994-95	Drummondville	QMJHL	64	9	31	40	190	....	....	....	....	....	....	....	....	....	....	....	4	0	5	5	12	....	....	....
1995-96	Drummondville	QMJHL	53	25	49	74	140	....	....	....	....	....	....	....	....	....	....	....	6	4	4	8	32	....	....	....
	Saint John Flames	AHL	5	2	0	2	8	....	....	....	....	....	....	....	....	....	....	....	16	1	6	7	20	....	....	....
1996-97	Saint John Flames	AHL	73	3	28	31	74	....	....	....	....	....	....	....	....	....	....	....	5	0	0	0	6	....	....	....
1997-98	**Calgary**	**NHL**	**10**	**0**	**0**	**0**	**16**	**0**	**0**	**0**	**3**	**0.0**	**–5**	....	....	....	....	....	....	....	....	....	....	....	....	....
	Saint John Flames	AHL	68	4	20	24	154	....	....	....	....	....	....	....	....	....	....	....	21	0	4	4	83	....	....	....
1998-99	**Calgary**	**NHL**	**55**	**3**	**4**	**7**	**68**	**0**	**0**	**0**	**40**	**7.5**	**3**	**0**	**0.0**	**162**	**51**	**12:41**	....	....	....	....	....	....	....	....
	Saint John Flames	AHL	16	0	3	3	31	....	....	....	....	....	....	....	....	....	....	....	....	....	....	....	....	....	....	....
99-2000	**Calgary**	**NHL**	**39**	**1**	**1**	**2**	**50**	**0**	**0**	**0**	**29**	**3.4**	**–4**	**0**	**0.0**	**168**	**52**	**19:21**	....	....	....	....	....	....	....	....
2000-01	**Calgary**	**NHL**	**62**	**2**	**6**	**8**	**78**	**0**	**0**	**0**	**33**	**6.1**	**3**	**0**	**0.0**	**252**	**62**	**16:37**	....	....	....	....	....	....	....	....
	NHL Totals		**166**	**6**	**11**	**17**	**212**	**0**	**0**	**0**	**105**	**5.7**		**0**	**0.0**	**582**	**165**	**15:55**	....	....	....	....	....	....	....	....

QMJHL First All-Star Team (1996) • Canadian Major Junior First All-Star Team (1996) • Missed majority of 1999-2000 season recovering from hip injury suffered in game vs. St. Louis, February 1, 2000.

GAVEY, Aaron

(GAY-vee, AIR-ruhn) **MIN.**

Center. Shoots left. 6'2", 200 lbs. Born, Sudbury, Ont., February 22, 1974. Tampa Bay's 4th choice, 74th overall, in 1992 Entry Draft.

1990-91	Peterborough	OPJHL	42	26	30	56	68	....	....	....	....	....	....	....	....	....	....	....	....	....	....	....	....	....	....	....
1991-92	Sault Ste. Marie	OHL	48	7	11	18	27	....	....	....	....	....	....	....	....	....	....	....	19	5	1	6	10	....	....	....
1992-93	Sault Ste. Marie	OHL	62	45	39	84	116	....	....	....	....	....	....	....	....	....	....	....	18	5	9	14	36	....	....	....
1993-94	Sault Ste. Marie	OHL	60	42	60	102	116	....	....	....	....	....	....	....	....	....	....	....	14	11	10	21	22	....	....	....
1994-95	Atlanta Knights	IHL	66	18	17	35	85	....	....	....	....	....	....	....	....	....	....	....	5	0	1	1	9	....	....	....
1995-96	**Tampa Bay**	**NHL**	**73**	**8**	**4**	**12**	**56**	**1**	**1**	**2**	**65**	**12.3**	**–6**	....	....	....	....	....	**6**	**0**	**0**	**0**	**4**	**0**	**0**	**0**
1996-97	**Tampa Bay**	**NHL**	**16**	**1**	**2**	**3**	**12**	**0**	**0**	**0**	**8**	**12.5**	**–1**	....	....	....	....	....	....	....	....	....	....	....	....	....
	Calgary	**NHL**	**41**	**7**	**9**	**16**	**34**	**3**	**0**	**1**	**54**	**13.0**	**–11**	....	....	....	....	....	....	....	....	....	....	....	....	....
1997-98	**Calgary**	**NHL**	**26**	**2**	**3**	**5**	**24**	**0**	**0**	**1**	**27**	**7.4**	**–5**	....	....	....	....	....	....	....	....	....	....	....	....	....
	Saint John Flames	AHL	8	4	3	7	28	....	....	....	....	....	....	....	....	....	....	....	....	....	....	....	....	....	....	....
1998-99	**Dallas**	**NHL**	**7**	**0**	**0**	**0**	**10**	**0**	**0**	**0**	**4**	**0.0**	**–1**	**43**	**48.8**	**13**	**0**	**8:09**	....	....	....	....	....	....	....	....
	Michigan K-Wings	IHL	67	24	33	57	128	....	....	....	....	....	....	....	....	....	....	....	5	2	3	5	4	....	....	....
99-2000	**Dallas**	**NHL**	**41**	**7**	**6**	**13**	**44**	**1**	**0**	**2**	**39**	**17.9**	**0**	**263**	**51.7**	**88**	**12**	**9:55**	**13**	**1**	**2**	**3**	**10**	**0**	**0**	**1**
	Michigan K-Wings	IHL	28	14	15	29	73	....	....	....	....	....	....	....	....	....	....	....	....	....	....	....	....	....	....	....
2000-01	**Minnesota**	**NHL**	**75**	**10**	**14**	**24**	**52**	**1**	**0**	**2**	**100**	**10.0**	**–8**	**584**	**43.5**	**84**	**53**	**14:00**	....	....	....	....	....	....	....	....
	NHL Totals		**279**	**35**	**38**	**73**	**232**	**6**	**1**	**8**	**297**	**11.8**		**890**	**46.2**	**185**	**65**	**12:18**	**19**	**1**	**2**	**3**	**14**	**0**	**0**	**1**

Traded to **Calgary** by **Tampa Bay** for Rick Tabaracci, November 19, 1996. Traded to **Dallas** by **Calgary** for Bob Bassen, July 14, 1998. Traded to **Minnesota** by **Dallas** with Pavel Patera, Dallas' 8th round choice (Eric Johansson) in 2000 Entry Draft and Minnesota's 4th round choice (previously acquired) in 2002 Entry Draft for Brad Lukowich and Minnesota's 3rd (Yared Hagos) and 9th (Dale Sullivan) round choices in 2001 Entry Draft, June 25, 2000.

GELINAS, Martin

(ZHEHL-in-nuh, MAHR-tihn) **CAR.**

Left wing. Shoots left. 5'11", 195 lbs. Born, Shawinigan, Que., June 5, 1970. Los Angeles' 1st choice, 7th overall, in 1988 Entry Draft.

1985-86	Noranda Aces	NOHA	5	1	1	2	0	....	....	....	....	....	....	....	....	....	....	....	....	....	....	....	....	....	....	....
1986-87	Montreal L'est	QAAA	41	36	42	78	36	....	....	....	....	....	....	....	....	....	....	....	7	7	5	12	2	....	....	....
1987-88	Hull Olympiques	QMJHL	65	63	68	131	74	....	....	....	....	....	....	....	....	....	....	....	17	15	18	33	32	....	....	....
1988-89	Hull Olympiques	QMJHL	41	38	39	77	31	....	....	....	....	....	....	....	....	....	....	....	9	5	4	9	14	....	....	....
	Edmonton	**NHL**	**6**	**1**	**2**	**3**	**0**	**0**	**0**	**0**	**14**	**7.1**	**–1**	....	....	....	....	....	....	....	....	....	....	....	....	....
1989-90♦	**Edmonton**	**NHL**	**46**	**17**	**8**	**25**	**30**	**5**	**0**	**2**	**71**	**23.9**	**0**	....	....	....	....	....	**20**	**2**	**3**	**5**	**6**	**0**	**0**	**0**
1990-91	**Edmonton**	**NHL**	**73**	**20**	**20**	**40**	**34**	**4**	**0**	**2**	**124**	**16.1**	**–7**	....	....	....	....	....	**18**	**3**	**6**	**9**	**25**	**0**	**0**	**1**
1991-92	**Edmonton**	**NHL**	**68**	**11**	**18**	**29**	**62**	**1**	**0**	**0**	**94**	**11.7**	**14**	....	....	....	....	....	**15**	**1**	**3**	**4**	**10**	**0**	**0**	**0**
1992-93	**Edmonton**	**NHL**	**65**	**11**	**12**	**23**	**30**	**0**	**0**	**1**	**93**	**11.8**	**3**	....	....	....	....	....	....	....	....	....	....	....	....	....
1993-94	**Quebec**	**NHL**	**31**	**6**	**6**	**12**	**8**	**0**	**0**	**0**	**53**	**11.3**	**–2**	....	....	....	....	....	....	....	....	....	....	....	....	....
	Vancouver	**NHL**	**33**	**8**	**8**	**16**	**26**	**3**	**0**	**1**	**54**	**14.8**	**–6**	....	....	....	....	....	**24**	**5**	**4**	**9**	**14**	**2**	**0**	**1**
1994-95	**Vancouver**	**NHL**	**46**	**13**	**10**	**23**	**36**	**1**	**0**	**4**	**75**	**17.3**	**8**	....	....	....	....	....	**3**	**0**	**1**	**1**	**0**	**0**	**0**	**0**
1995-96	**Vancouver**	**NHL**	**81**	**30**	**26**	**56**	**59**	**3**	**4**	**5**	**181**	**16.6**	**8**	....	....	....	....	....	**6**	**1**	**1**	**2**	**12**	**1**	**0**	**0**
1996-97	**Vancouver**	**NHL**	**74**	**35**	**33**	**68**	**42**	**6**	**1**	**3**	**177**	**19.8**	**6**	....	....	....	....	....	....	....	....	....	....	....	....	....
1997-98	**Vancouver**	**NHL**	**24**	**4**	**4**	**8**	**10**	**1**	**1**	**1**	**49**	**8.2**	**–6**	....	....	....	....	....	....	....	....	....	....	....	....	....
	Carolina	**NHL**	**40**	**12**	**14**	**26**	**30**	**2**	**1**	**4**	**98**	**12.2**	**1**	....	....	....	....	....	....	....	....	....	....	....	....	....
1998-99	**Carolina**	**NHL**	**76**	**13**	**15**	**28**	**67**	**0**	**0**	**2**	**111**	**11.7**	**3**	**6**	**50.0**	**70**	**13**	**13:13**	**6**	**0**	**3**	**3**	**2**	**0**	**0**	**0**
99-2000	**Carolina**	**NHL**	**81**	**14**	**16**	**30**	**40**	**3**	**0**	**0**	**139**	**10.1**	**–10**	**5**	**40.0**	**85**	**31**	**13:39**	....	....	....	....	....	....	....	....
2000-01	**Carolina**	**NHL**	**79**	**23**	**29**	**52**	**59**	**6**	**1**	**4**	**170**	**13.5**	**–4**	**6**	**0.0**	**131**	**54**	**17:54**	**6**	**0**	**1**	**1**	**6**	**0**	**0**	**0**
	NHL Totals		**823**	**218**	**221**	**439**	**533**	**35**	**8**	**29**	**1503**	**14.5**		**17**	**29.4**	**286**	**98**	**14:56**	**98**	**12**	**22**	**34**	**75**	**3**	**0**	**2**

QMJHL First All-Star Team (1988) • Canadian Major Junior Rookie of the Year (1988) • Won George Parsons Trophy (Memorial Cup Tournament Most Sportsmanlike Player) (1988)

Traded to **Edmonton** by **LA Kings** with Jimmy Carson and LA Kings' 1st round choices in 1989 (later traded to New Jersey - New Jersey selected Jason Miller), 1991 (Martin Rucinsky) and 1993 (Nick Stajduhar) Entry Drafts and cash for Wayne Gretzky, Mike Krushelnyski and Marty McSorley, August 9, 1988. Traded to **Quebec** by **Edmonton** with Edmonton's 6th round choice (Nicholas Checco) in 1993 Entry Draft for Scott Pearson, June 20, 1993. Claimed on waivers by **Vancouver** from **Quebec**, January 15, 1994. Traded to **Carolina** by **Vancouver** with Kirk McLean for Sean Burke, Geoff Sanderson and Enrico Ciccone, January 3, 1998.

GERNANDER, Ken (guhr-NAN-duhr, KEHN) **NYR**

Center. Shoots left. 5'10", 175 lbs. Born, Coleraine, MN, June 30, 1969. Winnipeg's 4th choice, 96th overall, in 1987 Entry Draft.

			Regular Season																Playoffs							
Season	Club	League	GP	G	A	Pts	PIM	PP	SH	GW	S	%	+/-	TF	F%	H	SB	Min	GP	G	A	Pts	PIM	PP	SH	GW
1985-86	Greenway High	Hi-School	23	14	23	37																				
1986-87	Greenway High	Hi-School	26	35	34	69																				
1987-88	U. of Minnesota	WCHA	44	14	14	28	14																			
1988-89	U. of Minnesota	WCHA	44	9	11	20	2																			
1989-90	U. of Minnesota	WCHA	44	32	17	49	24																			
1990-91	U. of Minnesota	WCHA	44	23	20	43	24																			
1991-92	Fort Wayne	IHL	13	7	6	13	2																			
	Moncton Hawks	AHL	43	8	18	26	9												8	1	1	2	2			
1992-93	Moncton Hawks	AHL	71	18	29	47	20												5	1	4	5	0			
1993-94	Moncton Hawks	AHL	71	22	25	47	12												19	6	1	7	0			
1994-95	Binghamton	AHL	80	28	25	53	24												11	2	2	4	6			
1995-96	**NY Rangers**	**NHL**	**10**	**2**	**3**	**5**	**4**	**2**	**0**	**0**	**10**	**20.0**	**-3**						**6**	**0**	**0**	**0**	**0**	**0**	**0**	**0**
	Binghamton	AHL	63	44	29	73	38																			
1996-97	Binghamton	AHL	46	13	18	31	30												2	0	1	1	0			
	NY Rangers	**NHL**																	**9**	**0**	**0**	**0**	**0**	**0**	**0**	**0**
1997-98	Hartford	AHL	80	35	28	63	26												12	5	6	11	4			
1998-99	Hartford	AHL	70	23	26	49	32												7	1	2	3	2			
99-2000	Hartford	AHL	79	28	29	57	24												23	5	5	10	0			
2000-01	Hartford	AHL	80	22	27	49	39												2	0	0	0	0			
	NHL Totals		**10**	**2**	**3**	**5**	**4**	**2**	**0**	**0**	**10**	**20.0**							**15**	**0**	**0**	**0**	**0**	**0**	**0**	**0**

Won Fred Hunt Memorial Trophy (Sportsmanship - AHL) (1996)
Signed as a free agent by **NY Rangers**, July 4, 1994.

GILCHRIST, Brent (GIHL-chrihst, BREHNT) **DET.**

Left wing. Shoots left. 5'11", 180 lbs. Born, Moose Jaw, Sask., April 3, 1967. Montreal's 6th choice, 79th overall, in 1985 Entry Draft.

			Regular Season																Playoffs							
Season	Club	League	GP	G	A	Pts	PIM	PP	SH	GW	S	%	+/-	TF	F%	H	SB	Min	GP	G	A	Pts	PIM	PP	SH	GW
1983-84	Kelowna Wings	WHL	69	16	11	27	16																			
1984-85	Kelowna Wings	WHL	51	35	38	73	58												6	5	2	7	8			
1985-86	Spokane Chiefs	WHL	52	45	45	90	57												9	6	7	13	19			
1986-87	Spokane Chiefs	WHL	46	45	55	100	71												5	2	7	9	6			
	Sherbrooke	AHL																	10	2	7	9	2			
1987-88	Sherbrooke	AHL	77	26	48	74	83												6	1	3	4	6			
1988-89	**Montreal**	**NHL**	**49**	**8**	**16**	**24**	**16**	**0**	**0**	**2**	**68**	**11.8**	**9**						**9**	**1**	**1**	**2**	**10**	**0**	**0**	**0**
	Sherbrooke	AHL	7	6	5	11	7																			
1989-90	**Montreal**	**NHL**	**57**	**9**	**15**	**24**	**28**	**1**	**0**	**0**	**80**	**11.3**	**3**						**8**	**2**	**0**	**2**	**2**	**0**	**0**	**0**
1990-91	**Montreal**	**NHL**	**51**	**6**	**9**	**15**	**10**	**1**	**0**	**1**	**81**	**7.4**	**-3**						**13**	**5**	**3**	**8**	**6**	**0**	**0**	**1**
1991-92	**Montreal**	**NHL**	**79**	**23**	**27**	**50**	**57**	**2**	**0**	**3**	**146**	**15.8**	**29**						**11**	**2**	**4**	**6**	**6**	**1**	**0**	**0**
1992-93	**Edmonton**	**NHL**	**60**	**10**	**10**	**20**	**47**	**2**	**0**	**0**	**94**	**10.6**	**-10**													
	Minnesota	**NHL**	**8**	**0**	**1**	**1**	**2**	**0**	**0**	**0**	**12**	**0.0**	**-2**													
1993-94	**Dallas**	**NHL**	**76**	**17**	**14**	**31**	**31**	**3**	**1**	**5**	**103**	**16.5**	**0**						**9**	**3**	**1**	**4**	**2**	**1**	**0**	**0**
1994-95	**Dallas**	**NHL**	**32**	**9**	**4**	**13**	**16**	**1**	**3**	**1**	**70**	**12.9**	**-3**						**5**	**0**	**1**	**1**	**2**	**0**	**0**	**0**
1995-96	**Dallas**	**NHL**	**77**	**20**	**22**	**42**	**36**	**6**	**1**	**2**	**164**	**12.2**	**-11**													
1996-97	**Dallas**	**NHL**	**67**	**10**	**20**	**30**	**24**	**2**	**0**	**2**	**116**	**8.6**	**6**						**6**	**2**	**2**	**4**	**2**	**0**	**0**	**0**
1997-98♦	**Detroit**	**NHL**	**61**	**13**	**14**	**27**	**40**	**5**	**0**	**3**	**124**	**10.5**	**4**						**15**	**2**	**1**	**3**	**12**	**0**	**0**	**0**
1998-99	**Detroit**	**NHL**	**5**	**1**	**0**	**1**	**0**	**0**	**0**	**1**	**4**	**25.0**	**-1**	**28**	**42.9**	**1**	**2**	**11:58**	**3**	**0**	**0**	**0**	**0**	**0**	**0**	**0**
99-2000	**Detroit**	**NHL**	**24**	**4**	**2**	**6**	**24**	**0**	**0**	**0**	**33**	**12.1**	**1**	**180**	**50.0**	**18**	**8**	**11:19**	**6**	**0**	**0**	**0**	**6**	**0**	**0**	**0**
2000-01	**Detroit**	**NHL**	**60**	**1**	**8**	**9**	**41**	**0**	**0**	**0**	**75**	**1.3**	**-8**	**401**	**50.9**	**59**	**15**	**11:41**	**5**	**0**	**1**	**1**	**0**	**0**	**0**	**0**
	NHL Totals		**706**	**131**	**162**	**293**	**372**	**23**	**5**	**20**	**1170**	**11.2**		**609**	**50.2**	**78**	**25**	**11:36**	**90**	**17**	**14**	**31**	**48**	**2**	**0**	**1**

Traded to **Edmonton** by **Montreal** with Shayne Corson and Vladimir Vujtek for Vincent Damphousse and Edmonton's 4th round choice (Adam Wiesel) in 1993 Entry Draft, August 27, 1992. Traded to **Minnesota** by **Edmonton** for Todd Elik, March 5, 1993. Transferred to **Dallas** after **Minnesota** franchise relocated, June 9, 1993. Signed as a free agent by **Detroit**, August 1, 1997. Claimed by **Tampa Bay** from **Detroit** in NHL Waiver Draft, October 5, 1998. Traded to **Detroit** by **Tampa Bay** for future considerations, October 5, 1998. • Missed majority of 1998-99 and 1999-2000 seasons recovering from hernia surgery, September 22, 1998.

GILL, Hal (GIHL, HAL) **BOS.**

Defense. Shoots left. 6'7", 230 lbs. Born, Concord, MA, April 6, 1975. Boston's 8th choice, 207th overall, in 1993 Entry Draft.

			Regular Season																Playoffs							
Season	Club	League	GP	G	A	Pts	PIM	PP	SH	GW	S	%	+/-	TF	F%	H	SB	Min	GP	G	A	Pts	PIM	PP	SH	GW
1992-93	Nashoba High	Hi-School	20	25	25	50																				
1993-94	Providence	H-East	31	1	2	3	26																			
1994-95	Providence	H-East	26	1	3	4	22																			
1995-96	Providence	H-East	39	5	12	17	54																			
1996-97	Providence	H-East	35	5	16	21	52																			
1997-98	**Boston**	**NHL**	**68**	**2**	**4**	**6**	**47**	**0**	**0**	**0**	**56**	**3.6**	**4**						**6**	**0**	**0**	**0**	**4**	**0**	**0**	**0**
	Providence Bruins	AHL	4	1	0	1	23																			
1998-99	**Boston**	**NHL**	**80**	**3**	**7**	**10**	**63**	**0**	**0**	**2**	**102**	**2.9**	**-10**	**1**	**100.0**	**144**	**102**	**20:54**	**12**	**0**	**0**	**0**	**14**	**0**	**0**	**0**
99-2000	**Boston**	**NHL**	**81**	**3**	**9**	**12**	**51**	**0**	**0**	**0**	**120**	**2.5**	**0**	**0**	**0.0**	**245**	**63**	**17:15**								
2000-01	**Boston**	**NHL**	**80**	**1**	**10**	**11**	**71**	**0**	**0**	**0**	**79**	**1.3**	**-2**	**0**	**0.0**	**206**	**62**	**18:21**								
	NHL Totals		**309**	**9**	**30**	**39**	**232**	**0**	**0**	**2**	**357**	**2.5**		**1**	**100.0**	**595**	**227**	**18:50**	**18**	**0**	**0**	**0**	**18**	**0**	**0**	**0**

GILL, Todd (GIHL, TAWD) **COL.**

Defense. Shoots left. 6', 180 lbs. Born, Cardinal, Ont., November 9, 1965. Toronto's 2nd choice, 25th overall, in 1984 Entry Draft.

			Regular Season																Playoffs							
Season	Club	League	GP	G	A	Pts	PIM	PP	SH	GW	S	%	+/-	TF	F%	H	SB	Min	GP	G	A	Pts	PIM	PP	SH	GW
1980-81	Cardinal Broncos	OHA-B	35	10	14	24	65																			
1981-82	Brockville Braves	OJHL-B	48	5	16	21	169																			
1982-83	Windsor Spitfires	OHL	70	12	24	36	108												3	0	0	0	11			
1983-84	Windsor Spitfires	OHL	68	9	48	57	184												3	1	1	2	10			
1984-85	Windsor Spitfires	OHL	53	17	40	57	148												4	0	1	1	14			
	Toronto	**NHL**	**10**	**1**	**0**	**1**	**13**	**0**	**0**	**0**	**9**	**11.1**	**-1**													
1985-86	**Toronto**	**NHL**	**15**	**1**	**2**	**3**	**28**	**0**	**0**	**0**	**9**	**11.1**	**0**						**1**	**0**	**0**	**0**	**0**	**0**	**0**	**0**
	St. Catharines	AHL	58	8	25	33	90												10	1	6	7	17			
1986-87	**Toronto**	**NHL**	**61**	**4**	**27**	**31**	**92**	**1**	**0**	**0**	**51**	**7.8**	**-3**						**13**	**2**	**2**	**4**	**42**	**0**	**0**	**0**
	Newmarket Saints	AHL	11	1	8	9	33																			
1987-88	**Toronto**	**NHL**	**65**	**8**	**17**	**25**	**131**	**1**	**0**	**3**	**109**	**7.3**	**-20**						**6**	**1**	**3**	**4**	**20**	**1**	**0**	**0**
	Newmarket Saints	AHL	2	0	1	1	2																			
1988-89	**Toronto**	**NHL**	**59**	**11**	**14**	**25**	**72**	**0**	**0**	**1**	**92**	**12.0**	**-3**													
1989-90	**Toronto**	**NHL**	**48**	**1**	**14**	**15**	**92**	**0**	**0**	**0**	**44**	**2.3**	**-8**						**5**	**0**	**3**	**3**	**16**	**0**	**0**	**0**
1990-91	**Toronto**	**NHL**	**72**	**2**	**22**	**24**	**113**	**0**	**0**	**0**	**90**	**2.2**	**4**													
1991-92	**Toronto**	**NHL**	**74**	**2**	**15**	**17**	**91**	**1**	**0**	**0**	**82**	**2.4**	**-22**													
1992-93	**Toronto**	**NHL**	**69**	**11**	**32**	**43**	**66**	**5**	**0**	**2**	**113**	**9.7**	**4**						**21**	**1**	**10**	**11**	**26**	**0**	**0**	**0**
1993-94	**Toronto**	**NHL**	**45**	**4**	**24**	**28**	**44**	**2**	**0**	**1**	**74**	**5.4**	**8**						**18**	**1**	**5**	**6**	**37**	**0**	**0**	**1**
1994-95	**Toronto**	**NHL**	**47**	**7**	**25**	**32**	**64**	**3**	**1**	**2**	**82**	**8.5**	**-8**						**7**	**0**	**3**	**3**	**6**	**0**	**0**	**0**
1995-96	**Toronto**	**NHL**	**74**	**7**	**18**	**25**	**116**	**1**	**0**	**2**	**109**	**6.4**	**-15**						**6**	**0**	**0**	**0**	**24**	**0**	**0**	**0**
1996-97	**San Jose**	**NHL**	**79**	**0**	**21**	**21**	**101**	**0**	**0**	**0**	**101**	**0.0**	**-20**													
1997-98	**San Jose**	**NHL**	**64**	**8**	**13**	**21**	**31**	**4**	**0**	**1**	**100**	**8.0**	**-13**													
	St. Louis	**NHL**	**11**	**5**	**4**	**9**	**10**	**3**	**0**	**1**	**22**	**22.7**	**2**						**10**	**2**	**2**	**4**	**10**	**1**	**1**	**0**
1998-99	**St. Louis**	**NHL**	**28**	**2**	**3**	**5**	**16**	**1**	**0**	**0**	**36**	**5.6**	**-6**	**0**	**0.0**	**34**	**16**	**17:36**								
	Detroit	**NHL**	**23**	**2**	**2**	**4**	**11**	**0**	**0**	**1**	**25**	**8.0**	**-4**	**0**	**0.0**	**32**	**13**	**18:45**	**2**	**0**	**1**	**1**	**0**	**0**	**0**	**0**
99-2000	**Phoenix**	**NHL**	**41**	**1**	**6**	**7**	**30**	**0**	**0**	**1**	**41**	**2.4**	**-10**	**0**	**0.0**	**74**	**37**	**16:07**								
	Detroit	**NHL**	**13**	**2**	**0**	**2**	**15**	**0**	**0**	**1**	**20**	**10.0**	**2**	**1**	**100.0**	**12**	**10**	**15:31**	**9**	**0**	**1**	**1**	**4**	**0**	**0**	**0**
2000-01	**Detroit**	**NHL**	**68**	**3**	**8**	**11**	**53**	**0**	**1**	**0**	**66**	**4.5**	**17**	**2**	**0.0**	**103**	**70**	**18:36**	**5**	**0**	**0**	**0**	**8**	**0**	**0**	**0**
	Cincinnati Ducks	AHL	2	0	1	1	2																			
	NHL Totals		**966**	**82**	**267**	**349**	**1189**	**22**	**2**	**16**	**1275**	**6.4**		**3**	**33.3**	**255**	**146**	**17:38**	**103**	**7**	**30**	**37**	**193**	**2**	**1**	**1**

Traded to **San Jose** by **Toronto** for Jamie Baker and San Jose's 5th round choice (Peter Cava) in 1996 Entry Draft, June 14, 1996. Traded to **St. Louis** by **San Jose** for Joe Murphy, March 24, 1998. Claimed on waivers by **Detroit** from **St. Louis**, December 30, 1998. Signed as a free agent by **Phoenix**, July 21, 1999. Traded to **Detroit** by **Phoenix** for Philippe Audet, March 13, 2000. Signed as a free agent by **Colorado**, July 24, 2001.

GILMOUR, Doug

(GIHL-mohr, DUHG)

Center/Left wing. Shoots left. 5'11", 180 lbs. Born, Kingston, Ont., June 25, 1963. St. Louis' 4th choice, 134th overall, in 1982 Entry Draft.

			Regular Season																Playoffs							
Season	Club	League	GP	G	A	Pts	PIM	PP	SH	GW	S	%	+/-	TF	F%	H	SB	Min	GP	G	A	Pts	PIM	PP	SH	GW
1979-80	Kingston	OHA-B	15	2	5	7	26	....	....	....	....	....	....	....	....	....	....	....	....	....	....	....	....	....	....	....
	Belleville Bulls	OPJHL	25	9	14	23	18	....	....	....	....	....	....	....	....	....	....	....	....	....	....	....	....	....	....	....
1980-81	Cornwall Royals	QMJHL	51	12	23	35	35	....	....	....	....	....	....	....	....	....	....	....	....	....	....	....	....	....	....	....
1981-82	Cornwall Royals	OHL	67	46	73	119	42	....	....	....	....	....	....	....	....	....	....	....	5	6	9	15	2	....	....	....
1982-83	Cornwall Royals	OHL	68	70	*107	*177	62	....	....	....	....	....	....	....	....	....	....	....	8	8	10	18	16	....	....	....
1983-84	**St. Louis**	**NHL**	80	25	28	53	57	3	1	1	157	15.9	6	....	....	....	....	....	11	2	9	11	10	1	0	1
1984-85	**St. Louis**	**NHL**	78	21	36	57	49	3	1	3	162	13.0	3	....	....	....	....	....	3	1	1	2	2	0	0	0
1985-86	**St. Louis**	**NHL**	74	25	28	53	41	2	1	5	183	13.7	–3	....	....	....	....	....	19	9	12	*21	25	1	2	2
1986-87	**St. Louis**	**NHL**	80	42	63	105	58	17	1	2	207	20.3	–2	....	....	....	....	....	6	2	2	4	16	1	0	1
1987-88	**St. Louis**	**NHL**	72	36	50	86	59	19	2	4	163	22.1	–13	....	....	....	....	....	10	3	14	17	18	1	0	0
1988-89♦	**Calgary**	**NHL**	72	26	59	85	44	11	0	5	161	16.1	45	....	....	....	....	....	22	11	11	22	20	3	0	3
1989-90	**Calgary**	**NHL**	78	24	67	91	54	12	1	3	152	15.8	20	....	....	....	....	....	6	3	1	4	8	0	0	1
1990-91	**Calgary**	**NHL**	78	20	61	81	144	2	2	5	135	14.8	27	....	....	....	....	....	7	1	1	2	0	0	0	1
1991-92	**Calgary**	**NHL**	38	11	27	38	46	4	1	1	64	17.2	12	....	....	....	....	....	....	....	....	....	....	....	....	....
	Toronto	**NHL**	40	15	34	49	32	6	0	3	104	14.4	13	....	....	....	....	....	....	....	....	....	....	....	....	....
1992-93	**Toronto**	**NHL**	83	32	95	127	100	15	3	2	211	15.2	32	....	....	....	....	....	21	10	*25	35	30	4	0	1
1993-94	**Toronto**	**NHL**	83	27	84	111	105	10	1	3	167	16.2	25	....	....	....	....	....	18	6	22	28	42	5	0	1
1994-95	HC Rapperswil	Switz.	9	2	13	15	16	....	....	....	....	....	....	....	....	....	....	....	....	....	....	....	....	....	....	....
	Toronto	**NHL**	44	10	23	33	26	3	0	1	73	13.7	–5	....	....	....	....	....	7	0	6	6	6	0	0	0
1995-96	**Toronto**	**NHL**	81	32	40	72	77	10	2	3	180	17.8	–5	....	....	....	....	....	6	1	7	8	12	1	0	0
1996-97	**Toronto**	**NHL**	61	15	45	60	46	2	1	1	103	14.6	–5	....	....	....	....	....	....	....	....	....	....	....	....	....
	New Jersey	**NHL**	20	7	15	22	22	2	0	0	40	17.5	7	....	....	....	....	....	10	0	4	4	14	0	0	0
1997-98	**New Jersey**	**NHL**	63	13	40	53	68	3	0	5	94	13.8	10	....	....	....	....	....	6	5	2	7	4	1	0	1
1998-99	**Chicago**	**NHL**	72	16	40	56	56	7	1	4	110	14.5	–16	1619	53.6	37	45	22:29	....	....	....	....	....	....	....	....
99-2000	**Chicago**	**NHL**	63	22	34	56	51	8	0	3	100	22.0	–12	941	53.7	34	31	19:59	....	....	....	....	....	....	....	....
	Buffalo	**NHL**	11	3	14	17	12	2	0	0	13	23.1	3	35	51.4	8	6	18:58	5	0	1	1	0	0	0	0
2000-01	**Buffalo**	**NHL**	71	7	31	38	70	4	0	0	91	7.7	3	429	51.1	51	36	18:02	13	2	4	6	12	1	0	1
	NHL Totals		**1342**	**429**	**914**	**1343**	**1217**	**145**	**18**	**54**	**2670**	**16.1**		**3024**	**53.2**	**130**	**118**	**20:07**	**170**	**56**	**122**	**178**	**219**	**19**	**2**	**13**

OHL First All-Star Team (1983) • Won Frank J. Selke Trophy (1993) • Played in NHL All-Star Game (1993, 1994)

Traded to **Calgary** by **St. Louis** with Mark Hunter, Steve Bozek and Michael Dark for Mike Bullard, Craig Coxe and Tim Corkery, September 6, 1988. Traded to **Toronto** by **Calgary** with Jamie Macoun, Ric Nattress, Kent Manderville and Rick Wamsley for Gary Leeman, Alexander Godynyuk, Jeff Reese, Michel Petit and Craig Berube, January 2, 1992. Traded to **New Jersey** by **Toronto** with Dave Ellett and New Jersey's 3rd round choice (previously acquired, New Jersey selected Andre Lakos) in 1999 Entry Draft for Jason Smith, Steve Sullivan and the rights to Alyn McCauley, February 25, 1997. Signed as a free agent by **Chicago**, July 28, 1998. Traded to **Buffalo** by **Chicago** with J-P Dumont and future considerations for Michal Grosek, March 10, 2000.

GIRARD, Jonathan

(zhih-RAHR, JAWN-ah-thuhn) **BOS.**

Defense. Shoots right. 5'11", 192 lbs. Born, Joliette, Que., May 27, 1980. Boston's 1st choice, 48th overall, in 1998 Entry Draft.

			Regular Season																Playoffs							
Season	Club	League	GP	G	A	Pts	PIM	PP	SH	GW	S	%	+/-	TF	F%	H	SB	Min	GP	G	A	Pts	PIM	PP	SH	GW
1995-96	Laval-Laurentides	QAAA	39	11	22	33	44	....	....	....	....	....	....	....	....	....	....	....	16	4	11	15	16	....	....	....
1996-97	Laval Titan	QMJHL	39	11	23	34	13	....	....	....	....	....	....	....	....	....	....	....	3	0	3	3	0	....	....	....
1997-98	Laval Titan	QMJHL	64	20	47	67	44	....	....	....	....	....	....	....	....	....	....	....	16	2	16	18	13	....	....	....
1998-99	Acadie-Bathurst	QMJHL	50	9	58	67	60	....	....	....	....	....	....	....	....	....	....	....	23	13	18	31	22	....	....	....
	Boston	**NHL**	3	0	0	0	0	0	0	0	3	0.0	1	0	0.0	0	0	9:28	....	....	....	....	....	....	....	....
99-2000	Moncton Wildcats	QMJHL	26	10	25	35	36	....	....	....	....	....	....	....	....	....	....	....	16	3	15	18	36	....	....	....
	Boston	**NHL**	23	1	2	3	2	0	0	0	17	5.9	–1	0	0.0	24	4	9:32	....	....	....	....	....	....	....	....
	Providence Bruins	AHL	5	0	1	1	0	....	....	....	....	....	....	....	....	....	....	....	....	....	....	....	....	....	....	....
2000-01	**Boston**	**NHL**	31	3	13	16	14	2	0	1	42	7.1	2	0	0.0	31	17	16:32	....	....	....	....	....	....	....	....
	Providence Bruins	AHL	39	3	21	24	6	....	....	....	....	....	....	....	....	....	....	....	17	0	5	5	4	....	....	....
	NHL Totals		**57**	**4**	**15**	**19**	**16**	**2**	**0**	**1**	**62**	**6.5**		**0**	**0.0**	**55**	**21**	**13:20**	....	....	....	....	....	....	....	....

QMJHL Second All-Star Team (1998) • QMJHL First All-Star Team (1999, 2000)

GIROUX, Raymond

(zhih-ROO, ray-MAWN) **NYI**

Defense. Shoots left. 6', 180 lbs. Born, North Bay, Ont., July 20, 1976. Philadelphia's 7th choice, 202nd overall, in 1994 Entry Draft.

			Regular Season																Playoffs							
Season	Club	League	GP	G	A	Pts	PIM	PP	SH	GW	S	%	+/-	TF	F%	H	SB	Min	GP	G	A	Pts	PIM	PP	SH	GW
1992-93	Powasson Hawks	NOJHA	45	8	18	26	117	....	....	....	....	....	....	....	....	....	....	....	....	....	....	....	....	....	....	....
1993-94	Powasson Hawks	NOJHA	36	10	40	50	42	....	....	....	....	....	....	....	....	....	....	....	....	....	....	....	....	....	....	....
1994-95	Yale University	ECAC	27	1	3	4	8	....	....	....	....	....	....	....	....	....	....	....	....	....	....	....	....	....	....	....
1995-96	Yale University	ECAC	30	3	16	19	36	....	....	....	....	....	....	....	....	....	....	....	....	....	....	....	....	....	....	....
1996-97	Yale University	ECAC	32	9	12	21	38	....	....	....	....	....	....	....	....	....	....	....	....	....	....	....	....	....	....	....
1997-98	Yale University	ECAC	35	9	*30	39	62	....	....	....	....	....	....	....	....	....	....	....	....	....	....	....	....	....	....	....
1998-99	Lowell	AHL	59	13	19	32	92	....	....	....	....	....	....	....	....	....	....	....	3	1	1	2	0	....	....	....
99-2000	**NY Islanders**	**NHL**	14	0	9	9	10	0	0	0	24	0.0	0	9	22.2	34	5	14:40	....	....	....	....	....	....	....	....
	Lowell	AHL	49	12	21	33	34	....	....	....	....	....	....	....	....	....	....	....	7	0	0	0	2	....	....	....
2000-01	HIFK Helsinki	Finland	22	3	9	12	34	....	....	....	....	....	....	....	....	....	....	....	....	....	....	....	....	....	....	....
	AIK Solna	Sweden	9	0	1	1	16	....	....	....	....	....	....	....	....	....	....	....	....	....	....	....	....	....	....	....
	Jokerit Helsinki	Finland	24	4	9	13	16	....	....	....	....	....	....	....	....	....	....	....	5	0	0	0	0	....	....	....
	NHL Totals		**14**	**0**	**9**	**9**	**10**	**0**	**0**	**0**	**24**	**0.0**		**9**	**22.2**	**34**	**5**	**14:40**	....	....	....	....	....	....	....	....

ECAC First All-Star Team (1998) • NCAA East First All-American Team (1998)

Rights traded to **NY Islanders** by **Philadelphia** for NY Islanders' 6th round choice (later traded to Montreal - Montreal selected Scott Selig) in 2000 Entry Draft, August 25, 1998.

GOC, Sascha

(GAWCH, SA-shah) **N.J.**

Defense. Shoots right. 6'2", 225 lbs. Born, Calw, West Germany, April 17, 1979. New Jersey's 5th choice, 159th overall, in 1997 Entry Draft.

			Regular Season																Playoffs							
Season	Club	League	GP	G	A	Pts	PIM	PP	SH	GW	S	%	+/-	TF	F%	H	SB	Min	GP	G	A	Pts	PIM	PP	SH	GW
1995-96	Schwenningen	DEL-Jr.	11	3	6	9	77	....	....	....	....	....	....	....	....	....	....	....	....	....	....	....	....	....	....	....
	Schwenningen	DEL	1	0	0	0	0	....	....	....	....	....	....	....	....	....	....	....	....	....	....	....	....	....	....	....
1996-97	Schwenningen	DEL	41	3	1	4	28	....	....	....	....	....	....	....	....	....	....	....	5	0	0	0	0	....	....	....
1997-98	Schwenningen	DEL	49	5	5	10	45	....	....	....	....	....	....	....	....	....	....	....	....	....	....	....	....	....	....	....
1998-99	Albany River Rats	AHL	55	1	12	13	24	....	....	....	....	....	....	....	....	....	....	....	2	0	0	0	0	....	....	....
99-2000	Albany River Rats	AHL	64	9	22	31	35	....	....	....	....	....	....	....	....	....	....	....	5	2	0	2	6	....	....	....
2000-01	**New Jersey**	**NHL**	11	0	0	0	4	0	0	0	7	0.0	7	0	0.0	14	13	13:37	....	....	....	....	....	....	....	....
	Albany River Rats	AHL	55	10	29	39	49	....	....	....	....	....	....	....	....	....	....	....	....	....	....	....	....	....	....	....
	NHL Totals		**11**	**0**	**0**	**0**	**4**	**0**	**0**	**0**	**7**	**0.0**		**0**	**0.0**	**14**	**13**	**13:37**	....	....	....	....	....	....	....	....

GOLDMANN, Erich

(GOHLD-mahn, AIR-ihk)

Defense. Shoots left. 6'3", 212 lbs. Born, Dingolfing, West Germany, April 7, 1976. Ottawa's 5th choice, 212th overall, in 1996 Entry Draft.

			Regular Season																Playoffs							
Season	Club	League	GP	G	A	Pts	PIM	PP	SH	GW	S	%	+/-	TF	F%	H	SB	Min	GP	G	A	Pts	PIM	PP	SH	GW
1993-94	EV Landshut	DEL	33	0	0	0	4	....	....	....	....	....	....	....	....	....	....	....	7	0	0	0	0	....	....	....
1994-95	Adler Mannheim	DEL	31	0	0	0	22	....	....	....	....	....	....	....	....	....	....	....	10	1	0	1	2	....	....	....
1995-96	Adler Mannheim	DEL	47	0	3	3	40	....	....	....	....	....	....	....	....	....	....	....	8	0	0	0	4	....	....	....
1996-97	Kaufbeurer Adler	DEL	44	2	4	6	58	....	....	....	....	....	....	....	....	....	....	....	6	1	0	1	2	....	....	....
1997-98	Worcester	AHL	31	0	2	2	40	....	....	....	....	....	....	....	....	....	....	....	....	....	....	....	....	....	....	....
	Germany	Olympics	4	0	1	1	27	....	....	....	....	....	....	....	....	....	....	....	....	....	....	....	....	....	....	....
	Detroit Vipers	IHL	3	0	0	0	2	....	....	....	....	....	....	....	....	....	....	....	....	....	....	....	....	....	....	....
	Dayton Bombers	ECHL	3	0	2	2	5	....	....	....	....	....	....	....	....	....	....	....	5	0	0	0	8	....	....	....
1998-99	Hershey Bears	AHL	21	1	1	2	23	....	....	....	....	....	....	....	....	....	....	....	....	....	....	....	....	....	....	....
	Cincinnati	IHL	5	0	1	1	7	....	....	....	....	....	....	....	....	....	....	....	....	....	....	....	....	....	....	....
	Cincinnati Ducks	AHL	32	0	2	2	18	....	....	....	....	....	....	....	....	....	....	....	3	0	0	0	2	....	....	....
99-2000	**Ottawa**	**NHL**	1	0	0	0	0	0	0	0	0	0.0	0	0	0.0	0	1	9:44	....	....	....	....	....	....	....	....
	Grand Rapids	IHL	26	1	1	2	15	....	....	....	....	....	....	....	....	....	....	....	....	....	....	....	....	....	....	....
	Detroit Vipers	IHL	11	1	0	1	13	....	....	....	....	....	....	....	....	....	....	....	....	....	....	....	....	....	....	....
2000-01	ESC Essen	DEL	58	7	3	10	44	....	....	....	....	....	....	....	....	....	....	....	....	....	....	....	....	....	....	....
	NHL Totals		**1**	**0**	**0**	**0**	**0**	**0**	**0**	**0**	**0**	**0.0**		**0**	**0.0**	**0**	**1**	**9:44**	....	....	....	....	....	....	....	....

Loaned to **Cincinnati** (AHL) by **Ottawa** with Ratislav Pavlikovsky and Ivan Ciernik, January 12, 1999.

GOLUBOVSKY, Yan

(goh-luh-BOHV-skee, YAN)

Defense. Shoots right. 6'3", 183 lbs. Born, Novosibirsk, USSR, March 9, 1976. Detroit's 1st choice, 23rd overall, in 1994 Entry Draft.

			Regular Season																Playoffs							
Season	Club	League	GP	G	A	Pts	PIM	PP	SH	GW	S	%	+/-	TF	F%	H	SB	Min	GP	G	A	Pts	PIM	PP	SH	GW
1993-94	D'amo Moscow-2	CIS-3	10	0	1	1	....	....	....	....	....	....	....	....	....	....	....	....	....	....	....	....	....	....	....	....
	Russian Penguins	IHL	8	0	0	0	23	....	....	....	....	....	....	....	....	....	....	....	....	....	....	....	....	....	....	....
1994-95	Adirondack	AHL	57	4	2	6	39	....	....	....	....	....	....	....	....	....	....	....	....	....	....	....	....	....	....	....
1995-96	Adirondack	AHL	71	5	16	21	97	....	....	....	....	....	....	....	....	....	....	....	3	0	0	0	2	....	....	....
1996-97	Adirondack	AHL	62	2	11	13	67	....	....	....	....	....	....	....	....	....	....	....	4	0	0	0	0	....	....	....
1997-98	**Detroit**	**NHL**	**12**	**0**	**2**	**2**	**6**	**0**	**0**	**0**	**9**	**0.0**	**1**	....	....	....	....	....	....	....	....	....	....	....	....	....
	Adirondack	AHL	52	1	15	16	57	....	....	....	....	....	....	....	....	....	....	....	3	0	0	0	2	....	....	....
1998-99	**Detroit**	**NHL**	**17**	**0**	**1**	**1**	**16**	**0**	**0**	**0**	**10**	**0.0**	**4**	**0**	**0.0**	**9**	**4**	**9:39**	....	....	....	....	....	....	....	....
	Adirondack	AHL	43	2	2	4	32	....	....	....	....	....	....	....	....	....	....	....	2	0	0	0	4	....	....	....
99-2000	**Detroit**	**NHL**	**21**	**1**	**2**	**3**	**8**	**0**	**0**	**0**	**7**	**14.3**	**3**	**0**	**0.0**	**13**	**23**	**8:54**	....	....	....	....	....	....	....	....
2000-01	Cincinnati Ducks	AHL	28	4	4	8	16	....	....	....	....	....	....	....	....	....	....	....	....	....	....	....	....	....	....	....
	Florida	**NHL**	**6**	**0**	**2**	**2**	**2**	**0**	**0**	**0**	**4**	**0.0**	**3**	**0**	**0.0**	**6**	**6**	**16:38**	....	....	....	....	....	....	....	....
	Louisville Panthers	AHL	30	1	12	13	36	....	....	....	....	....	....	....	....	....	....	....	....	....	....	....	....	....	....	....
	NHL Totals		**56**	**1**	**7**	**8**	**32**	**0**	**0**	**0**	**30**	**3.3**		**0**	**0.0**	**28**	**33**	**10:15**	....	....	....	....	....	....	....	....

Traded to **Florida** by **Detroit** for Igor Larionov, December 28, 2000.

GOMEZ, Scott

(GOH-mehz, SKAWT) **N.J.**

Center. Shoots left. 5'11", 200 lbs. Born, Anchorage, AK, December 23, 1979. New Jersey's 2nd choice, 27th overall, in 1998 Entry Draft.

Season	Club	League	GP	G	A	Pts	PIM	PP	SH	GW	S	%	+/-	TF	F%	H	SB	Min	GP	G	A	Pts	PIM	PP	SH	GW
1994-95	East High T-Birds	Hi-School	28	30	48	78	....	....	....	....	....	....	....	....	....	....	....	....	....	....	....	....	....	....	....	....
1995-96	East High T-Birds	Hi-School	27	*56	49	*101	....	....	....	....	....	....	....	....	....	....	....	....	....	....	....	....	....	....	....	....
	Anchorage Stars	AAHL	40	*70	*67	*137	44	....	....	....	....	....	....	....	....	....	....	....	....	....	....	....	....	....	....	....
1996-97	South Surrey	BCJHL	56	48	76	124	94	....	....	....	....	....	....	....	....	....	....	....	21	18	23	41	57	....	....	....
1997-98	Tri-City Americans	WHL	45	12	37	49	57	....	....	....	....	....	....	....	....	....	....	....	....	....	....	....	....	....	....	....
1998-99	Tri-City Americans	WHL	58	30	*78	108	55	....	....	....	....	....	....	....	....	....	....	....	10	6	13	19	31	....	....	....
99-2000♦	**New Jersey**	**NHL**	**82**	**19**	**51**	**70**	**78**	**7**	**0**	**1**	**204**	**9.3**	**14**	**341**	**44.6**	**49**	**12**	**16:21**	**23**	**4**	**6**	**10**	**4**	**1**	**0**	**2**
2000-01	**New Jersey**	**NHL**	**76**	**14**	**49**	**63**	**46**	**2**	**0**	**4**	**155**	**9.0**	**–1**	**1010**	**44.6**	**36**	**15**	**15:46**	**25**	**5**	**9**	**14**	**24**	**0**	**0**	**0**
	NHL Totals		**158**	**33**	**100**	**133**	**124**	**9**	**0**	**5**	**359**	**9.2**		**1351**	**44.6**	**85**	**27**	**16:04**	**48**	**9**	**15**	**24**	**28**	**1**	**0**	**2**

BCJHL All-Rookie Team (1997) • WHL West First All-Star Team (1999) • NHL All-Rookie Team (2000) • Won Calder Memorial Trophy (2000) • Played in NHL All-Star Game (2000)

GONCHAR, Sergei

(gohn-CHAR, SAIR-gay) **WSH.**

Defense. Shoots left. 6'2", 212 lbs. Born, Chelyabinsk, USSR, April 13, 1974. Washington's 1st choice, 14th overall, in 1992 Entry Draft.

Season	Club	League	GP	G	A	Pts	PIM	PP	SH	GW	S	%	+/-	TF	F%	H	SB	Min	GP	G	A	Pts	PIM	PP	SH	GW
1991-92	HC Chelyabinsk	CIS	31	1	0	1	6	....	....	....	....	....	....	....	....	....	....	....	....	....	....	....	....	....	....	....
1992-93	Dynamo Moscow	CIS	31	1	3	4	70	....	....	....	....	....	....	....	....	....	....	....	10	0	0	0	12	....	....	....
1993-94	Dynamo Moscow	CIS	44	4	5	9	36	....	....	....	....	....	....	....	....	....	....	....	10	0	3	3	14	....	....	....
	Portland Pirates	AHL	....	....	....	....	....	....	....	....	....	....	....	....	....	....	....	....	2	0	0	0	0	....	....	....
1994-95	Portland Pirates	AHL	61	10	32	42	67	....	....	....	....	....	....	....	....	....	....	....	....	....	....	....	....	....	....	....
	Washington	**NHL**	**31**	**2**	**5**	**7**	**22**	**0**	**0**	**0**	**38**	**5.3**	**4**	....	....	....	....	....	**7**	**2**	**2**	**4**	**2**	**0**	**0**	**1**
1995-96	**Washington**	**NHL**	**78**	**15**	**26**	**41**	**60**	**4**	**0**	**4**	**139**	**10.8**	**25**	....	....	....	....	....	**6**	**2**	**4**	**6**	**4**	**1**	**0**	**0**
1996-97	**Washington**	**NHL**	**57**	**13**	**17**	**30**	**36**	**3**	**0**	**3**	**129**	**10.1**	**–11**	....	....	....	....	....	....	....	....	....	....	....	....	....
1997-98	Lada Togliatti	Russia	7	3	2	5	4	....	....	....	....	....	....	....	....	....	....	....	....	....	....	....	....	....	....	....
	Lada Togliatti	EuroHL	1	1	0	1	2	....	....	....	....	....	....	....	....	....	....	....	....	....	....	....	....	....	....	....
	Washington	**NHL**	**72**	**5**	**16**	**21**	**66**	**2**	**0**	**0**	**134**	**3.7**	**2**	....	....	....	....	....	**21**	**7**	**4**	**11**	**30**	**3**	**1**	**2**
	Russia	Olympics	6	0	2	2	0	....	....	....	....	....	....	....	....	....	....	....	....	....	....	....	....	....	....	....
1998-99	**Washington**	**NHL**	**53**	**21**	**10**	**31**	**57**	**13**	**1**	**3**	**180**	**11.7**	**1**	**0**	**0.0**	**72**	**31**	**23:55**	....	....	....	....	....	....	....	....
99-2000	**Washington**	**NHL**	**73**	**18**	**36**	**54**	**52**	**5**	**0**	**3**	**181**	**9.9**	**26**	**0**	**0.0**	**97**	**44**	**21:46**	**5**	**1**	**0**	**1**	**6**	**0**	**0**	**0**
2000-01	**Washington**	**NHL**	**76**	**19**	**38**	**57**	**70**	**8**	**0**	**2**	**241**	**7.9**	**12**	**1**	**100.0**	**88**	**53**	**22:26**	**6**	**1**	**3**	**4**	**2**	**1**	**0**	**0**
	NHL Totals		**440**	**93**	**148**	**241**	**363**	**35**	**1**	**15**	**1042**	**8.9**		**1**	**100.0**	**257**	**128**	**22:35**	**45**	**13**	**13**	**26**	**44**	**5**	**1**	**3**

Played in NHL All-Star Game (2001)

GONEAU, Daniel

(guh-NOH, DAN-yehl)

Left wing. Shoots left. 6', 195 lbs. Born, Montreal, Que., January 16, 1976. NY Rangers' 2nd choice, 48th overall, in 1996 Entry Draft.

Season	Club	League	GP	G	A	Pts	PIM	PP	SH	GW	S	%	+/-	TF	F%	H	SB	Min	GP	G	A	Pts	PIM	PP	SH	GW
1990-91	Laval Leafs	QAHA	32	16	18	34	20	....	....	....	....	....	....	....	....	....	....	....	....	....	....	....	....	....	....	....
1991-92	Lac St-Louis	QAAA	42	21	14	35	52	....	....	....	....	....	....	....	....	....	....	....	14	1	4	5	6	....	....	....
1992-93	Laval Titan	QMJHL	62	16	25	41	44	....	....	....	....	....	....	....	....	....	....	....	13	0	4	4	4	....	....	....
1993-94	Laval Titan	QMJHL	68	29	57	86	81	....	....	....	....	....	....	....	....	....	....	....	19	8	21	29	45	....	....	....
1994-95	Laval Titan	QMJHL	56	16	31	47	78	....	....	....	....	....	....	....	....	....	....	....	20	5	10	15	33	....	....	....
1995-96	Granby Bisons	QMJHL	67	54	51	105	115	....	....	....	....	....	....	....	....	....	....	....	21	11	22	33	40	....	....	....
1996-97	**NY Rangers**	**NHL**	**41**	**10**	**3**	**13**	**10**	**3**	**0**	**2**	**44**	**22.7**	**–5**	....	....	....	....	....	....	....	....	....	....	....	....	....
	Binghamton	AHL	39	15	15	30	10	....	....	....	....	....	....	....	....	....	....	....	....	....	....	....	....	....	....	....
1997-98	**NY Rangers**	**NHL**	**11**	**2**	**0**	**2**	**4**	**0**	**0**	**1**	**13**	**15.4**	**–4**	....	....	....	....	....	....	....	....	....	....	....	....	....
	Hartford	AHL	66	21	26	47	44	....	....	....	....	....	....	....	....	....	....	....	13	1	4	5	18	....	....	....
1998-99	Hartford	AHL	72	20	19	39	56	....	....	....	....	....	....	....	....	....	....	....	2	1	0	1	0	....	....	....
99-2000	**NY Rangers**	**NHL**	**1**	**0**	**0**	**0**	**0**	**0**	**0**	**0**	**3**	**0.0**	**–1**	**0**	**0.0**	**0**	**1**	**14:26**	....	....	....	....	....	....	....	....
	Hartford	AHL	51	15	17	32	48	....	....	....	....	....	....	....	....	....	....	....	22	1	2	3	6	....	....	....
2000-01	Manitoba Moose	IHL	58	10	14	24	26	....	....	....	....	....	....	....	....	....	....	....	....	....	....	....	....	....	....	....
	Detroit Vipers	IHL	15	6	4	10	8	....	....	....	....	....	....	....	....	....	....	....	....	....	....	....	....	....	....	....
	NHL Totals		**53**	**12**	**3**	**15**	**14**	**3**	**0**	**3**	**60**	**20.0**		**0**	**0.0**	**0**	**1**	**14:26**	....	....	....	....	....	....	....	....

• Re-entered NHL Entry Draft. Originally Boston' 2nd choice, 47th overall, in 1994 Entry Draft.
QMJHL First All-Star Team (1996)

GOREN, Lee

(GOH-rehn, LEE) **BOS.**

Right wing. Shoots right. 6'3", 205 lbs. Born, Winnipeg, Man., December 26, 1977. Boston's 5th choice, 63rd overall, in 1997 Entry Draft.

Season	Club	League	GP	G	A	Pts	PIM	PP	SH	GW	S	%	+/-	TF	F%	H	SB	Min	GP	G	A	Pts	PIM	PP	SH	GW
1994-95	Winnipeg	MMHL	31	19	31	50	50	....	....	....	....	....	....	....	....	....	....	....	....	....	....	....	....	....	....	....
1995-96	Minot Top Guns	SJHL	56	25	35	61	....	....	....	....	....	....	....	....	....	....	....	....	12	5	20	25	....	....	....	....
	Saskatoon Blades	WHL	2	0	0	0	2	....	....	....	....	....	....	....	....	....	....	....	....	....	....	....	....	....	....	....
1996-97	North Dakota	WCHA	DID NOT PLAY – FRESHMAN																....	....	....	....	....	....	....	....
1997-98	North Dakota	WCHA	29	3	13	16	26	....	....	....	....	....	....	....	....	....	....	....	....	....	....	....	....	....	....	....
1998-99	North Dakota	WCHA	38	26	19	45	20	....	....	....	....	....	....	....	....	....	....	....	....	....	....	....	....	....	....	....
99-2000	North Dakota	WCHA	44	*34	29	63	42	....	....	....	....	....	....	....	....	....	....	....	....	....	....	....	....	....	....	....
2000-01	**Boston**	**NHL**	**21**	**2**	**0**	**2**	**7**	**1**	**0**	**0**	**9**	**22.2**	**–3**	**21**	**38.1**	**15**	**0**	**4:24**	....	....	....	....	....	....	....	....
	Providence Bruins	AHL	54	15	18	33	72	....	....	....	....	....	....	....	....	....	....	....	17	5	2	7	11	....	....	....
	NHL Totals		**21**	**2**	**0**	**2**	**7**	**1**	**0**	**0**	**9**	**22.2**		**21**	**38.1**	**15**	**0**	**4:24**	....	....	....	....	....	....	....	....

WCHA Second All-Star Team (2000) • NCAA West Second All-American Team (2000) • NCAA Championship All-Tournament Team (2000) • NCAA Championship Tournament MVP (2000)
• Ruled ineligible to play during 1996-97 season by NCAA due to appearance with Saskatoon (WHL) in 1995-96 season.

GOSSELIN, David

(GAH-sih-lihn, DAY-vihd) **NSH.**

Right wing. Shoots right. 6'1", 205 lbs. Born, Levis, Que., June 22, 1977. New Jersey's 4th choice, 78th overall, in 1995 Entry Draft.

Season	Club	League	GP	G	A	Pts	PIM	PP	SH	GW	S	%	+/-	TF	F%	H	SB	Min	GP	G	A	Pts	PIM	PP	SH	GW
1992-93	Richelieu Riverains	QAAA	40	5	12	17	24	....	....	....	....	....	....	....	....	....	....	....	4	0	0	0	2	....	....	....
1993-94	Richelieu Riverains	QAAA	44	26	19	45	62	....	....	....	....	....	....	....	....	....	....	....	4	2	1	3	0	....	....	....
1994-95	Sherbrooke	QMJHL	58	8	8	16	36	....	....	....	....	....	....	....	....	....	....	....	7	0	0	0	2	....	....	....
1995-96	Sherbrooke	QMJHL	55	24	24	48	147	....	....	....	....	....	....	....	....	....	....	....	7	2	2	4	4	....	....	....
1996-97	Sherbrooke	QMJHL	23	11	15	26	52	....	....	....	....	....	....	....	....	....	....	....	....	....	....	....	....	....	....	....
	Chicoutimi	QMJHL	28	16	33	49	65	....	....	....	....	....	....	....	....	....	....	....	12	9	7	16	16	....	....	....
1997-98	Chicoutimi	QMJHL	69	46	64	110	139	....	....	....	....	....	....	....	....	....	....	....	6	1	4	5	8	....	....	....
1998-99	Milwaukee	IHL	74	17	11	28	78	....	....	....	....	....	....	....	....	....	....	....	2	0	2	2	2	....	....	....
99-2000	**Nashville**	**NHL**	**10**	**2**	**1**	**3**	**6**	**0**	**0**	**0**	**14**	**14.3**	**–4**	**0**	**0.0**	**7**	**1**	**9:16**	....	....	....	....	....	....	....	....
	Milwaukee	IHL	70	21	20	41	118	....	....	....	....	....	....	....	....	....	....	....	3	0	0	0	10	....	....	....
2000-01	Milwaukee	IHL	32	5	9	14	56	....	....	....	....	....	....	....	....	....	....	....	....	....	....	....	....	....	....	....
	NHL Totals		**10**	**2**	**1**	**3**	**6**	**0**	**0**	**0**	**14**	**14.3**		**0**	**0.0**	**7**	**1**	**9:16**	....	....	....	....	....	....	....	....

Signed as a free agent by **Nashville**, July 1, 1998. • Missed majority of 2000-01 season recovering from knee injury suffered in game vs. Grand Rapids (IHL), December 28, 2000.

GRANATO, Tony

(gruh-NA-toh, TOH-nee) **S.J.**

Right wing. Shoots right. 5'10", 185 lbs. Born, Downers Grove, IL, July 25, 1964. NY Rangers' 5th choice, 120th overall, in 1982 Entry Draft.

			Regular Season																Playoffs							
Season	Club	League	GP	G	A	Pts	PIM	PP	SH	GW	S	%	+/-	TF	F%	H	SB	Min	GP	G	A	Pts	PIM	PP	SH	GW
1982-83	Northwood Prep	Hi-School	34	32	60	92	....	....	....	....	....	....	....	....	....	....	....	....	....	....	....	....	....	....	....	....
1983-84	U. of Wisconsin	WCHA	35	14	17	31	48	....	....	....	....	....	....	....	....	....	....	....	....	....	....	....	....	....	....	....
1984-85	U. of Wisconsin	WCHA	42	33	34	67	94	....	....	....	....	....	....	....	....	....	....	....	....	....	....	....	....	....	....	....
1985-86	U. of Wisconsin	WCHA	33	25	24	49	36	....	....	....	....	....	....	....	....	....	....	....	....	....	....	....	....	....	....	....
1986-87	U. of Wisconsin	WCHA	42	28	45	73	64	....	....	....	....	....	....	....	....	....	....	....	....	....	....	....	....	....	....	....
1987-88	United States	Nat-Team	49	40	31	71	55	....	....	....	....	....	....	....	....	....	....	....	....	....	....	....	....	....	....	....
	United States	Olympics	6	1	7	8	4	....	....	....	....	....	....	....	....	....	....	....	....	....	....	....	....	....	....	....
	Colorado Rangers	IHL	22	13	14	27	36	....	....	....	....	....	....	....	....	....	....	....	8	9	4	13	16	....	....	....
1988-89	**NY Rangers**	**NHL**	**78**	**36**	**27**	**63**	**140**	**4**	**4**	**3**	**234**	**15.4**	**17**	....	....	....	....	....	**4**	**1**	**1**	**2**	**21**	**0**	**0**	**0**
1989-90	**NY Rangers**	**NHL**	**37**	**7**	**18**	**25**	**77**	**1**	**0**	**0**	**79**	**8.9**	**1**	....	....	....	....	....	....	....	....	....	....	....	....	....
	Los Angeles	**NHL**	**19**	**5**	**6**	**11**	**45**	**1**	**0**	**0**	**41**	**12.2**	**–2**	....	....	....	....	....	**10**	**5**	**4**	**9**	**12**	**2**	**1**	**2**
1990-91	**Los Angeles**	**NHL**	**68**	**30**	**34**	**64**	**154**	**11**	**1**	**3**	**197**	**15.2**	**22**	....	....	....	....	....	**12**	**1**	**4**	**5**	**28**	**0**	**0**	**0**
1991-92	**Los Angeles**	**NHL**	**80**	**39**	**29**	**68**	**187**	**7**	**2**	**8**	**223**	**17.5**	**4**	....	....	....	....	....	**6**	**1**	**5**	**6**	**10**	**0**	**0**	**0**
1992-93	**Los Angeles**	**NHL**	**81**	**37**	**45**	**82**	**171**	**14**	**2**	**6**	**247**	**15.0**	**–1**	....	....	....	....	....	**24**	**6**	**11**	**17**	**50**	**1**	**0**	**1**
1993-94	**Los Angeles**	**NHL**	**50**	**7**	**14**	**21**	**150**	**2**	**0**	**0**	**117**	**6.0**	**–2**	....	....	....	....	....	....	....	....	....	....	....	....	....
1994-95	**Los Angeles**	**NHL**	**33**	**13**	**11**	**24**	**68**	**2**	**0**	**3**	**106**	**12.3**	**9**	....	....	....	....	....	....	....	....	....	....	....	....	....
1995-96	**Los Angeles**	**NHL**	**49**	**17**	**18**	**35**	**46**	**5**	**0**	**1**	**156**	**10.9**	**–5**	....	....	....	....	....	....	....	....	....	....	....	....	....
1996-97	**San Jose**	**NHL**	**76**	**25**	**15**	**40**	**159**	**5**	**1**	**4**	**231**	**10.8**	**–7**	....	....	....	....	....	....	....	....	....	....	....	....	....
1997-98	**San Jose**	**NHL**	**59**	**16**	**9**	**25**	**70**	**3**	**0**	**2**	**119**	**13.4**	**3**	....	....	....	....	....	**1**	**0**	**0**	**0**	**0**	**0**	**0**	**0**
1998-99	**San Jose**	**NHL**	**35**	**6**	**6**	**12**	**54**	**0**	**1**	**1**	**65**	**9.2**	**4**	**3**	**100.0**	**31**	**4**	**10:29**	**6**	**1**	**1**	**2**	**2**	**0**	**0**	**0**
99-2000	**San Jose**	**NHL**	**48**	**6**	**7**	**13**	**39**	**1**	**0**	**0**	**67**	**9.0**	**2**	**4**	**50.0**	**47**	**6**	**9:05**	**12**	**0**	**1**	**1**	**14**	**0**	**0**	**0**
2000-01	**San Jose**	**NHL**	**60**	**4**	**5**	**9**	**65**	**1**	**0**	**1**	**85**	**4.7**	**–1**	**5**	**40.0**	**80**	**4**	**8:25**	**4**	**1**	**0**	**1**	**4**	**0**	**0**	**0**
	NHL Totals		**773**	**248**	**244**	**492**	**1425**	**57**	**11**	**32**	**1967**	**12.6**		**12**	**58.3**	**158**	**14**	**9:09**	**79**	**16**	**27**	**43**	**141**	**3**	**1**	**3**

WCHA Second All-Star Team (1985, 1987) • NCAA West Second All-American Team (1985, 1987) • NHL All-Rookie Team (1989) • Won Bill Masterton Memorial Trophy (1997) • Played in NHL All-Star Game (1997)

Traded to **LA Kings** by **NY Rangers** with Tomas Sandstrom for Bernie Nicholls, January 20, 1990. Signed as a free agent by **San Jose**, August 15, 1996.

GRAND-PIERRE, Jean-Luc

(GRAHN pee-AIR, ZHAHN-LOOK) **CBJ**

Defense. Shoots right. 6'3", 207 lbs. Born, Montreal, Que., February 2, 1977. St. Louis' 6th choice, 179th overall, in 1995 Entry Draft.

Season	Club	League	GP	G	A	Pts	PIM	PP	SH	GW	S	%	+/-	TF	F%	H	SB	Min	GP	G	A	Pts	PIM	PP	SH	GW
1992-93	Lac St-Louis	QAAA	1	0	0	0	2	....	....	....	....	....	....	....	....	....	....	....	....	....	....	....	....	....	....	....
1993-94	Beauport	QMJHL	46	1	4	5	27	....	....	....	....	....	....	....	....	....	....	....	1	0	0	0	0	....	....	....
1994-95	Val-d'Or Foreurs	QMJHL	59	10	13	23	126	....	....	....	....	....	....	....	....	....	....	....	....	....	....	....	....	....	....	....
1995-96	Val-d'Or Foreurs	QMJHL	67	13	21	34	209	....	....	....	....	....	....	....	....	....	....	....	13	1	4	5	47	....	....	....
1996-97	Val-d'Or Foreurs	QMJHL	58	9	24	33	186	....	....	....	....	....	....	....	....	....	....	....	13	5	8	13	46	....	....	....
1997-98	Rochester	AHL	75	4	6	10	211	....	....	....	....	....	....	....	....	....	....	....	4	0	0	0	2	....	....	....
1998-99	**Buffalo**	**NHL**	**16**	**0**	**1**	**1**	**17**	**0**	**0**	**0**	**11**	**0.0**	**0**	**0**	**0.0**	**46**	**13**	**13:36**	....	....	....	....	....	....	....	....
	Rochester	AHL	55	5	4	9	90	....	....	....	....	....	....	....	....	....	....	....	....	....	....	....	....	....	....	....
99-2000	**Buffalo**	**NHL**	**11**	**0**	**0**	**0**	**15**	**0**	**0**	**0**	**11**	**0.0**	**–1**	**0**	**0.0**	**29**	**8**	**15:11**	**4**	**0**	**0**	**0**	**4**	**0**	**0**	**0**
	Rochester	AHL	62	5	8	13	124	....	....	....	....	....	....	....	....	....	....	....	17	0	1	1	40	....	....	....
2000-01	**Columbus**	**NHL**	**64**	**1**	**4**	**5**	**73**	**0**	**0**	**0**	**33**	**3.0**	**–6**	**0**	**0.0**	**112**	**53**	**12:51**	....	....	....	....	....	....	....	....
	NHL Totals		**91**	**1**	**5**	**6**	**105**	**0**	**0**	**0**	**55**	**1.8**		**0**	**0.0**	**187**	**74**	**13:16**	**4**	**0**	**0**	**0**	**4**	**0**	**0**	**0**

Traded to **Buffalo** by **St. Louis** with Ottawa's 2nd round choice (previously acquired, Buffalo selected Cory Sarich) in 1996 Entry Draft and St. Louis' 3rd round choice (Maxim Afinogenov) in 1997 Entry Draft for Yuri Khmylev and Buffalo's 8th round choice (Andrei Podkonicky) in 1996 Entry Draft, March 20, 1996. Traded to **Columbus** by **Buffalo** with Matt Davidson, San Jose's 5th round choice (previously acquired, Columbus selected Tyler Kolarik) in 2000 Entry Draft and Buffalo's 5th round choice (later traded to Calgary - later traded to Detroit - Detroit selected Andreas Jamtin) in 2001 Entry Draft to complete Expansion Draft agreement which had Columbus select Geoff Sanderson and Dwayne Roloson from Buffalo, June 23, 2000.

GRATTON, Benoit

(grah-TOHN, BEHN-wah) **MTL.**

Left wing. Shoots left. 5'11", 194 lbs. Born, Montreal, Que., December 28, 1976. Washington's 6th choice, 105th overall, in 1995 Entry Draft.

Season	Club	League	GP	G	A	Pts	PIM	PP	SH	GW	S	%	+/-	TF	F%	H	SB	Min	GP	G	A	Pts	PIM	PP	SH	GW
1992-93	Laval Regents	QAAA	40	19	38	57	74	....	....	....	....	....	....	....	....	....	....	....	13	1	9	10	27	....	....	....
1993-94	Laval Titan	QMJHL	51	9	14	23	70	....	....	....	....	....	....	....	....	....	....	....	20	2	1	3	19	....	....	....
1994-95	Laval Titan	QMJHL	71	30	58	88	199	....	....	....	....	....	....	....	....	....	....	....	20	8	*21	29	42	....	....	....
1995-96	Laval Titan	QMJHL	38	21	39	60	130	....	....	....	....	....	....	....	....	....	....	....	....	....	....	....	....	....	....	....
	Granby Bisons	QMJHL	27	12	46	58	97	....	....	....	....	....	....	....	....	....	....	....	21	13	26	39	68	....	....	....
1996-97	Portland Pirates	AHL	76	6	40	46	140	....	....	....	....	....	....	....	....	....	....	....	5	2	1	3	14	....	....	....
1997-98	**Washington**	**NHL**	**6**	**0**	**1**	**1**	**6**	**0**	**0**	**0**	**5**	**0.0**	**1**	....	....	....	....	....	....	....	....	....	....	....	....	....
	Portland Pirates	AHL	58	19	31	50	137	....	....	....	....	....	....	....	....	....	....	....	8	4	2	6	24	....	....	....
1998-99	**Washington**	**NHL**	**16**	**4**	**3**	**7**	**16**	**0**	**0**	**0**	**24**	**16.7**	**–1**	**136**	**54.4**	**26**	**7**	**13:28**	....	....	....	....	....	....	....	....
	Portland Pirates	AHL	64	18	42	60	135	....	....	....	....	....	....	....	....	....	....	....	....	....	....	....	....	....	....	....
99-2000	**Calgary**	**NHL**	**10**	**0**	**2**	**2**	**10**	**0**	**0**	**0**	**4**	**0.0**	**1**	**68**	**63.2**	**8**	**2**	**8:15**	....	....	....	....	....	....	....	....
	Saint John Flames	AHL	65	17	49	66	137	....	....	....	....	....	....	....	....	....	....	....	3	0	1	1	4	....	....	....
2000-01	**Calgary**	**NHL**	**14**	**1**	**3**	**4**	**14**	**0**	**0**	**0**	**13**	**7.7**	**0**	**105**	**63.8**	**13**	**3**	**9:11**	....	....	....	....	....	....	....	....
	Saint John Flames	AHL	53	10	36	46	153	....	....	....	....	....	....	....	....	....	....	....	....	....	....	....	....	....	....	....
	NHL Totals		**46**	**5**	**9**	**14**	**46**	**0**	**0**	**0**	**46**	**10.9**		**309**	**59.5**	**47**	**12**	**10:40**	....	....	....	....	....	....	....	....

Traded to **Calgary** by **Washington** for Steve Shirreffs, August 18, 1999. Claimed on waivers by **Montreal** from **Calgary**, April 11, 2001.

GRATTON, Chris

(GRA-tuhn, KRIHS) **BUF.**

Center. Shoots left. 6'4", 226 lbs. Born, Brantford, Ont., July 5, 1975. Tampa Bay's 1st choice, 3rd overall, in 1993 Entry Draft.

Season	Club	League	GP	G	A	Pts	PIM	PP	SH	GW	S	%	+/-	TF	F%	H	SB	Min	GP	G	A	Pts	PIM	PP	SH	GW
1989-90	Brantford	OJHL-B	1	0	2	2	2	....	....	....	....	....	....	....	....	....	....	....	....	....	....	....	....	....	....	....
1990-91	Brantford	OJHL-B	31	30	30	60	28	....	....	....	....	....	....	....	....	....	....	....	....	....	....	....	....	....	....	....
1991-92	Kingston	OHL	62	27	39	66	37	....	....	....	....	....	....	....	....	....	....	....	....	....	....	....	....	....	....	....
1992-93	Kingston	OHL	58	55	54	109	125	....	....	....	....	....	....	....	....	....	....	....	16	11	18	29	42	....	....	....
1993-94	**Tampa Bay**	**NHL**	**84**	**13**	**29**	**42**	**123**	**5**	**1**	**2**	**161**	**8.1**	**–25**	....	....	....	....	....	....	....	....	....	....	....	....	....
1994-95	**Tampa Bay**	**NHL**	**46**	**7**	**20**	**27**	**89**	**2**	**0**	**0**	**91**	**7.7**	**–2**	....	....	....	....	....	....	....	....	....	....	....	....	....
1995-96	**Tampa Bay**	**NHL**	**82**	**17**	**21**	**38**	**105**	**7**	**0**	**3**	**183**	**9.3**	**–13**	....	....	....	....	....	**6**	**0**	**2**	**2**	**27**	**0**	**0**	**0**
1996-97	**Tampa Bay**	**NHL**	**82**	**30**	**32**	**62**	**201**	**9**	**0**	**4**	**230**	**13.0**	**–28**	....	....	....	....	....	....	....	....	....	....	....	....	....
1997-98	**Philadelphia**	**NHL**	**82**	**22**	**40**	**62**	**159**	**5**	**0**	**2**	**182**	**12.1**	**11**	....	....	....	....	....	**5**	**2**	**0**	**2**	**10**	**0**	**0**	**0**
1998-99	**Philadelphia**	**NHL**	**26**	**1**	**7**	**8**	**41**	**0**	**0**	**0**	**54**	**1.9**	**–8**	**38**	**42.1**	**35**	**0**	**14:25**	....	....	....	....	....	....	....	....
	Tampa Bay	**NHL**	**52**	**7**	**19**	**26**	**102**	**1**	**0**	**1**	**127**	**5.5**	**–20**	**1032**	**53.9**	**74**	**12**	**18:20**	....	....	....	....	....	....	....	....
99-2000	**Tampa Bay**	**NHL**	**58**	**14**	**27**	**41**	**121**	**4**	**0**	**1**	**168**	**8.3**	**–24**	**1341**	**55.9**	**120**	**13**	**20:03**	....	....	....	....	....	....	....	....
	Buffalo	**NHL**	**14**	**1**	**7**	**8**	**15**	**0**	**0**	**0**	**34**	**2.9**	**1**	**256**	**54.3**	**27**	**8**	**16:40**	**5**	**0**	**1**	**1**	**4**	**0**	**0**	**0**
2000-01	**Buffalo**	**NHL**	**82**	**19**	**21**	**40**	**102**	**5**	**0**	**5**	**156**	**12.2**	**0**	**1161**	**57.3**	**118**	**34**	**14:37**	**13**	**6**	**4**	**10**	**14**	**2**	**0**	**1**
	NHL Totals		**608**	**131**	**223**	**354**	**1058**	**38**	**1**	**18**	**1386**	**9.5**		**3828**	**55.5**	**374**	**67**	**16:55**	**29**	**8**	**7**	**15**	**55**	**2**	**0**	**1**

Signed as a free agent by **Philadelphia**, August 14, 1997. Traded to **Tampa Bay** by **Philadelphia** with Mike Sillinger for Mikael Renberg and Daymond Langkow, December 12, 1998. Traded to **Buffalo** by **Tampa Bay** with Tampa Bay's 2nd round choice (Derek Roy) in 2001 Entry Draft for Cory Sarich, Wayne Primeau, Brian Holzinger and Buffalo's 3rd round choice (Alexander Kharitonov) in 2000 Entry Draft, March 9, 2000.

GRAVES, Adam

(GRAYVS, A-duhm) **S.J.**

Center. Shoots left. 6', 205 lbs. Born, Toronto, Ont., April 12, 1968. Detroit's 2nd choice, 22nd overall, in 1986 Entry Draft.

Season	Club	League	GP	G	A	Pts	PIM	PP	SH	GW	S	%	+/-	TF	F%	H	SB	Min	GP	G	A	Pts	PIM	PP	SH	GW
1984-85	King City Dukes	OJHL-B	25	23	33	56	29	....	....	....	....	....	....	....	....	....	....	....	....	....	....	....	....	....	....	....
1985-86	Windsor Spitfires	OHL	62	27	37	64	35	....	....	....	....	....	....	....	....	....	....	....	16	5	11	16	10	....	....	....
1986-87	Windsor Spitfires	OHL	66	45	55	100	70	....	....	....	....	....	....	....	....	....	....	....	14	9	8	17	32	....	....	....
	Adirondack	AHL	....	....	....	....	....	....	....	....	....	....	....	....	....	....	....	....	5	0	1	1	0	....	....	....
1987-88	Windsor Spitfires	OHL	37	28	32	60	107	....	....	....	....	....	....	....	....	....	....	....	12	14	18	*32	16	....	....	....
	Detroit	**NHL**	**9**	**0**	**1**	**1**	**8**	**0**	**0**	**0**	**9**	**0.0**	**–2**	....	....	....	....	....	....	....	....	....	....	....	....	....
1988-89	**Detroit**	**NHL**	**56**	**7**	**5**	**12**	**60**	**0**	**0**	**1**	**60**	**11.7**	**–5**	....	....	....	....	....	**5**	**0**	**0**	**0**	**4**	**0**	**0**	**0**
	Adirondack	AHL	14	10	11	21	28	....	....	....	....	....	....	....	....	....	....	....	14	11	7	18	17	....	....	....
1989-90	**Detroit**	**NHL**	**13**	**0**	**1**	**1**	**13**	**0**	**0**	**0**	**10**	**0.0**	**–5**	....	....	....	....	....	....	....	....	....	....	....	....	....
	♦ Edmonton	**NHL**	**63**	**9**	**12**	**21**	**123**	**1**	**0**	**1**	**84**	**10.7**	**5**	....	....	....	....	....	**22**	**5**	**6**	**11**	**17**	**0**	**0**	**1**
1990-91	**Edmonton**	**NHL**	**76**	**7**	**18**	**25**	**127**	**2**	**0**	**1**	**126**	**5.6**	**–21**	....	....	....	....	....	**18**	**2**	**4**	**6**	**22**	**0**	**0**	**0**
1991-92	**NY Rangers**	**NHL**	**80**	**26**	**33**	**59**	**139**	**4**	**4**	**4**	**228**	**11.4**	**19**	....	....	....	....	....	**10**	**5**	**3**	**8**	**22**	**1**	**0**	**1**
1992-93	**NY Rangers**	**NHL**	**84**	**36**	**29**	**65**	**148**	**12**	**1**	**6**	**275**	**13.1**	**–4**	....	....	....	....	....	....	....	....	....	....	....	....	....
1993-94♦	**NY Rangers**	**NHL**	**84**	**52**	**27**	**79**	**127**	**20**	**4**	**4**	**291**	**17.9**	**27**	....	....	....	....	....	**23**	**10**	**7**	**17**	**24**	**3**	**0**	**0**
1994-95	**NY Rangers**	**NHL**	**47**	**17**	**14**	**31**	**51**	**9**	**0**	**3**	**185**	**9.2**	**9**	....	....	....	....	....	**10**	**4**	**4**	**8**	**8**	**2**	**0**	**0**

			Regular Season																Playoffs							
Season	Club	League	GP	G	A	Pts	PIM	PP	SH	GW	S	%	+/-	TF	F%	H	SB	Min	GP	G	A	Pts	PIM	PP	SH	GW
1995-96	NY Rangers	NHL	82	22	36	58	100	9	1	2	266	8.3	18	....	....	....	....	....	10	7	1	8	4	6	0	2
1996-97	NY Rangers	NHL	82	33	28	61	66	10	4	3	269	12.3	10	....	....	....	....	....	15	2	1	3	12	1	0	2
1997-98	NY Rangers	NHL	72	23	12	35	41	10	0	2	226	10.2	−30	....	....	....	....	....	....	....	....	....	....	....	....	....
1998-99	NY Rangers	NHL	82	38	15	53	47	14	2	7	239	15.9	−12	347	51.3	162	28	20:33	....	....	....	....	....	....	....	....
99-2000	NY Rangers	NHL	77	23	17	40	14	11	0	4	194	11.9	−15	51	49.0	166	27	18:46	....	....	....	....	....	....	....	....
2000-01	NY Rangers	NHL	82	10	16	26	77	1	0	1	136	7.4	−16	98	55.1	186	23	15:44	....	....	....	....	....	....	....	....
	NHL Totals		989	303	264	567	1141	103	16	39	2598	11.7		496	51.8	514	78	18:20	113	35	26	61	113	13	0	6

NHL Second All-Star Team (1994) • Won King Clancy Memorial Trophy (1994) • Won Bill Masterton Memorial Trophy (2001) • Played in NHL All-Star Game (1994)

Traded to **Edmonton** by **Detroit** with Petr Klima, Joe Murphy and Jeff Sharples for Jimmy Carson, Kevin McClelland and Edmonton's 5th round choice (later traded to Montreal - Montreal selected Brad Layzell) in 1991 Entry Draft, November 2, 1989. Signed as a free agent by **NY Rangers**, September 3, 1991. Traded to **San Jose** by **NY Rangers** with future considerations for Mikael Samuelsson and Christian Gosselin, June 24, 2001.

GREEN, Josh

(GREEN, JAWSH) **EDM.**

Left wing. Shoots left. 6'4", 212 lbs. Born, Camrose, Alta., November 16, 1977. Los Angeles' 1st choice, 30th overall, in 1996 Entry Draft.

Season	Club	League	GP	G	A	Pts	PIM	PP	SH	GW	S	%	+/-	TF	F%	H	SB	Min	GP	G	A	Pts	PIM	PP	SH	GW
1992-93	Camrose Kodiaks	AAHA	60	55	45	100	80	....	....	....	....	....	....	....	....	....	....	....	....	....	....	....	....	....	....	....
1993-94	Medicine Hat	WHL	63	22	22	44	43	....	....	....	....	....	....	....	....	....	....	....	3	0	0	0	4	....	....	....
1994-95	Medicine Hat	WHL	68	32	23	55	64	....	....	....	....	....	....	....	....	....	....	....	5	5	1	6	2	....	....	....
1995-96	Medicine Hat	WHL	46	18	25	43	55	....	....	....	....	....	....	....	....	....	....	....	5	2	2	4	4	....	....	....
1996-97	Medicine Hat	WHL	51	25	32	57	61	....	....	....	....	....	....	....	....	....	....	....	....	....	....	....	....	....	....	....
	Swift Current	WHL	23	10	15	25	33	....	....	....	....	....	....	....	....	....	....	....	10	9	7	16	19	....	....	....
1997-98	Swift Current	WHL	5	9	1	10	9	....	....	....	....	....	....	....	....	....	....	....	....	....	....	....	....	....	....	....
	Portland	WHL	26	26	18	44	27	....	....	....	....	....	....	....	....	....	....	....	....	....	....	....	....	....	....	....
	Fredericton	AHL	43	16	15	31	14	....	....	....	....	....	....	....	....	....	....	....	4	1	3	4	6	....	....	....
1998-99	Los Angeles	NHL	27	1	3	4	8	1	0	0	35	2.9	−5	2	50.0	30	1	11:44	....	....	....	....	....	....	....	....
	Springfield	AHL	41	15	15	30	29	....	....	....	....	....	....	....	....	....	....	....	....	....	....	....	....	....	....	....
99-2000	NY Islanders	NHL	49	12	14	26	41	2	0	3	109	11.0	−7	12	50.0	105	8	13:36	....	....	....	....	....	....	....	....
	Lowell	AHL	17	6	2	8	19	....	....	....	....	....	....	....	....	....	....	....	....	....	....	....	....	....	....	....
2000-01	Hamilton Bulldogs	AHL	2	2	0	2	2	....	....	....	....	....	....	....	....	....	....	....	....	....	....	....	....	....	....	....
	Edmonton	NHL	....	....	....	....	....	....	....	....	....	....	....	....	....	....	....	....	3	0	0	0	0	0	0	0
	NHL Totals		76	13	17	30	49	3	0	3	144	9.0		14	50.0	135	9	12:56	3	0	0	0	0	0	0	0

Traded to **NY Islanders** by **LA Kings** with Olli Jokinen, Mathieu Biron and LA Kings' 1st round choice (Taylor Pyatt) in 1999 Entry Draft for Ziggy Palffy, Brian Smolinski, Marcel Cousineau and New Jersey's 4th round choice (previously acquired, LA Kings selected Daniel Johansson) in 1999 Entry Draft, June 20, 1999. Traded to **Edmonton** by **NY Islanders** with Eric Brewer and NY Islanders' 2nd round choice (Brad Winchester) in 2000 Entry Draft for Roman Hamrlik, June 24, 2000. • Missed majority of 2000-01 season recovering from shoulder injury suffered in game vs. Detroit, October 10, 2000.

GREEN, Travis

(GREEN, TRA-vihs) **TOR.**

Center. Shoots right. 6'2", 200 lbs. Born, Castlegar, B.C., December 20, 1970. NY Islanders' 2nd choice, 23rd overall, in 1989 Entry Draft.

Season	Club	League	GP	G	A	Pts	PIM	PP	SH	GW	S	%	+/-	TF	F%	H	SB	Min	GP	G	A	Pts	PIM	PP	SH	GW
1985-86	Castlegar Rebels	KIJHL	35	30	40	70	41	....	....	....	....	....	....	....	....	....	....	....	....	....	....	....	....	....	....	....
1986-87	Spokane Chiefs	WHL	64	8	17	25	27	....	....	....	....	....	....	....	....	....	....	....	3	0	0	0	0	....	....	....
1987-88	Spokane Chiefs	WHL	72	33	54	87	42	....	....	....	....	....	....	....	....	....	....	....	15	10	10	20	13	....	....	....
1988-89	Spokane Chiefs	WHL	75	51	51	102	79	....	....	....	....	....	....	....	....	....	....	....	....	....	....	....	....	....	....	....
1989-90	Spokane Chiefs	WHL	50	45	44	89	80	....	....	....	....	....	....	....	....	....	....	....	....	....	....	....	....	....	....	....
	Medicine Hat	WHL	25	15	24	39	19	....	....	....	....	....	....	....	....	....	....	....	3	0	0	0	2	....	....	....
1990-91	Capital District	AHL	73	21	34	55	26	....	....	....	....	....	....	....	....	....	....	....	....	....	....	....	....	....	....	....
1991-92	Capital District	AHL	71	23	27	50	10	....	....	....	....	....	....	....	....	....	....	....	7	0	4	4	21	....	....	....
1992-93	NY Islanders	NHL	61	7	18	25	43	1	0	0	115	6.1	4	....	....	....	....	....	12	3	1	4	6	0	0	0
	Capital District	AHL	20	12	11	23	39	....	....	....	....	....	....	....	....	....	....	....	....	....	....	....	....	....	....	....
1993-94	NY Islanders	NHL	83	18	22	40	44	1	0	2	164	11.0	16	....	....	....	....	....	4	0	0	0	2	0	0	0
1994-95	NY Islanders	NHL	42	5	7	12	25	0	0	0	59	8.5	−10	....	....	....	....	....	....	....	....	....	....	....	....	....
1995-96	NY Islanders	NHL	69	25	45	70	42	14	1	2	186	13.4	−20	....	....	....	....	....	....	....	....	....	....	....	....	....
1996-97	NY Islanders	NHL	79	23	41	64	38	10	0	3	177	13.0	−5	....	....	....	....	....	....	....	....	....	....	....	....	....
1997-98	NY Islanders	NHL	54	14	12	26	66	8	0	2	99	14.1	−19	....	....	....	....	....	....	....	....	....	....	....	....	....
	Anaheim	NHL	22	5	11	16	16	1	0	0	42	11.9	−10	....	....	....	....	....	....	....	....	....	....	....	....	....
1998-99	Anaheim	NHL	79	13	17	30	81	3	1	2	165	7.9	−7	1325	52.8	97	24	17:17	4	0	1	1	4	0	0	0
99-2000	Phoenix	NHL	78	25	21	46	45	6	0	2	157	15.9	−4	1322	55.6	120	11	16:36	5	2	1	3	2	0	0	0
2000-01	Phoenix	NHL	69	13	15	28	63	3	0	0	113	11.5	−11	1135	54.9	83	16	16:05	....	....	....	....	....	....	....	....
	NHL Totals		636	148	209	357	463	47	2	13	1277	11.6		3782	54.4	300	51	16:41	25	5	3	8	14	0	0	0

Traded to **Anaheim** by **NY Islanders** with Doug Houda and Tony Tuzzolino for Joe Sacco, J-J Daigneault and Mark Janssens, February 6, 1998. Traded to **Phoenix** by **Anaheim** with Anaheim's 1st round choice (Scott Kelman) in 1999 Entry Draft for Oleg Tverdovsky, June 26, 1999. Traded to **Toronto** by **Phoenix** with Robert Reichel and Craig Mills for Danny Markov, June 12, 2001.

GREIG, Mark

(GREG, MAHRK) **PHI.**

Right wing. Shoots right. 5'11", 190 lbs. Born, High River, Alta., January 25, 1970. Hartford's 1st choice, 15th overall, in 1990 Entry Draft.

Season	Club	League	GP	G	A	Pts	PIM	PP	SH	GW	S	%	+/-	TF	F%	H	SB	Min	GP	G	A	Pts	PIM	PP	SH	GW
1985-86	Blackie Bisons	AAHA	31	12	43	55	44	....	....	....	....	....	....	....	....	....	....	....	....	....	....	....	....	....	....	....
1986-87	Calgary Stars	AMHL	18	9	28	37	30	....	....	....	....	....	....	....	....	....	....	....	....	....	....	....	....	....	....	....
	Calgary Wranglers	WHL	5	0	0	0	0	....	....	....	....	....	....	....	....	....	....	....	....	....	....	....	....	....	....	....
1987-88	Lethbridge	WHL	65	9	18	27	38	....	....	....	....	....	....	....	....	....	....	....	....	....	....	....	....	....	....	....
1988-89	Lethbridge	WHL	71	36	72	108	113	....	....	....	....	....	....	....	....	....	....	....	8	5	5	10	16	....	....	....
1989-90	Lethbridge	WHL	65	55	80	135	149	....	....	....	....	....	....	....	....	....	....	....	18	11	21	32	35	....	....	....
1990-91	Hartford	NHL	4	0	0	0	0	0	0	0	1	0.0	−1	....	....	....	....	....	....	....	....	....	....	....	....	....
	Springfield	AHL	73	32	55	87	73	....	....	....	....	....	....	....	....	....	....	....	17	2	6	8	22	....	....	....
1991-92	Hartford	NHL	17	0	5	5	6	0	0	0	18	0.0	7	....	....	....	....	....	....	....	....	....	....	....	....	....
	Springfield	AHL	50	20	27	47	38	....	....	....	....	....	....	....	....	....	....	....	9	1	1	2	20	....	....	....
1992-93	Hartford	NHL	22	1	7	8	27	0	0	0	16	6.3	−11	....	....	....	....	....	....	....	....	....	....	....	....	....
	Springfield	AHL	55	20	38	58	86	....	....	....	....	....	....	....	....	....	....	....	....	....	....	....	....	....	....	....
1993-94	Hartford	NHL	31	4	5	9	31	0	0	0	41	9.8	−6	....	....	....	....	....	....	....	....	....	....	....	....	....
	Springfield	AHL	4	0	4	4	21	....	....	....	....	....	....	....	....	....	....	....	....	....	....	....	....	....	....	....
	Toronto	NHL	13	2	2	4	10	0	0	0	14	14.3	1	....	....	....	....	....	....	....	....	....	....	....	....	....
	St. John's Leafs	AHL	9	4	6	10	0	....	....	....	....	....	....	....	....	....	....	....	11	4	2	6	26	....	....	....
1994-95	Saint John Flames	AHL	67	31	50	81	82	....	....	....	....	....	....	....	....	....	....	....	2	0	1	1	0	....	....	....
	Calgary	NHL	8	1	1	2	2	0	0	0	5	20.0	1	....	....	....	....	....	....	....	....	....	....	....	....	....
1995-96	Atlanta Knights	IHL	71	25	48	73	104	....	....	....	....	....	....	....	....	....	....	....	3	2	1	3	4	....	....	....
1996-97	Quebec Rafales	IHL	5	1	2	3	0	....	....	....	....	....	....	....	....	....	....	....	....	....	....	....	....	....	....	....
	Houston Aeros	IHL	59	12	30	42	59	....	....	....	....	....	....	....	....	....	....	....	13	5	8	13	2	....	....	....
1997-98	Grand Rapids	IHL	69	26	36	62	103	....	....	....	....	....	....	....	....	....	....	....	3	0	4	4	4	....	....	....
1998-99	Philadelphia	NHL	7	1	3	4	2	0	0	0	9	11.1	1	0	0.0	5	3	9:55	2	0	1	1	0	0	0	0
	Philadelphia	AHL	67	23	46	69	102	....	....	....	....	....	....	....	....	....	....	....	7	1	5	6	14	....	....	....
99-2000	Philadelphia	NHL	11	3	2	5	6	0	0	1	14	21.4	0	1	0.0	7	1	11:19	3	0	0	0	0	0	0	0
	Philadelphia	AHL	68	34	48	82	116	....	....	....	....	....	....	....	....	....	....	....	5	3	2	5	6	....	....	....
2000-01	Philadelphia	NHL	7	1	1	2	4	0	0	0	7	14.3	−2	0	0.0	2	0	14:23	....	....	....	....	....	....	....	....
	Philadelphia	AHL	74	31	57	88	98	....	....	....	....	....	....	....	....	....	....	....	10	6	5	11	4	....	....	....
	NHL Totals		120	13	26	39	88	0	0	1	125	10.4		1	0.0	14	4	11:47	5	0	1	1	0	0	0	0

WHL East First All-Star Team (1990) • AHL First All-Star Team (2001)

Traded to **Toronto** by **Hartford** with Hartford's 6th round choice (Doug Bonner) in 1995 Entry Draft for Ted Crowley, January 25, 1994. Signed as a free agent by **Calgary**, August 9, 1994. Signed as a free agent by **Philadelphia**, July 28, 1998.

GRIER, Mike

(GREER, MIGHK) **EDM.**

Right wing. Shoots right. 6'1", 227 lbs. Born, Detroit, MI, January 5, 1975. St. Louis' 7th choice, 219th overall, in 1993 Entry Draft.

Season	Club	League	GP	G	A	Pts	PIM	PP	SH	GW	S	%	+/-	TF	F%	H	SB	Min	GP	G	A	Pts	PIM	PP	SH	GW
1992-93	St. Sebastian's	Hi-School	22	16	27	43	32	....	....	....	....	....	....	....	....	....	....	....	....	....	....	....	....	....	....	....
1993-94	Boston University	H-East	39	9	9	18	56	....	....	....	....	....	....	....	....	....	....	....	....	....	....	....	....	....	....	....
1994-95	Boston University	H-East	37	*29	26	55	85	....	....	....	....	....	....	....	....	....	....	....	....	....	....	....	....	....	....	....
1995-96	Boston University	H-East	38	21	25	46	82	....	....	....	....	....	....	....	....	....	....	....	....	....	....	....	....	....	....	....
1996-97	Edmonton	NHL	79	15	17	32	45	4	0	2	89	16.9	7	....	....	....	....	....	12	3	1	4	4	1	0	1
1997-98	Edmonton	NHL	66	9	6	15	73	1	0	1	90	10.0	−3	....	....	....	....	....	12	2	2	4	13	0	0	1
1998-99	Edmonton	NHL	82	20	24	44	54	3	2	1	143	14.0	5	34	20.6	188	49	15:57	4	1	1	2	6	0	0	0

			Regular Season																Playoffs							
Season	Club	League	GP	G	A	Pts	PIM	PP	SH	GW	S	%	+/-	TF	F%	H	SB	Min	GP	G	A	Pts	PIM	PP	SH	GW
99-2000	Edmonton	NHL	65	9	22	31	68	0	3	2	115	7.8	9	32	46.8	174	38	15:45	....	....	....	....	....	....	....	....
2000-01	Edmonton	NHL	74	20	16	36	20	2	3	2	124	16.1	11	36	38.9	144	51	16:44	6	0	0	0	8	0	0	0
	NHL Totals		366	73	85	158	260	10	8	8	561	13.0		102	20.6	506	138	16:19	34	6	4	10	31	1	0	2

Hockey East First All-Star Team (1995) • NCAA East First All-American Team (1995)

Rights traded to **Edmonton** by **St. Louis** with Curtis Joseph for St. Louis' 1st round choices in 1966 (previously acquired, St. Louis selected Marty Reasoner) and 1997 (later traded to LA Kings - LA Kings selected Matt Zultek) Entry Drafts, August 4, 1995.

GRIMSON, Stu (GRIHM-suhn, STOO) NSH.

Left wing. Shoots left. 6'4", 240 lbs. Born, Kamloops, B.C., May 20, 1965. Calgary's 8th choice, 143rd overall, in 1985 Entry Draft.

1982-83	Regina Pats	WHL	48	0	1	1	105	....	....	....	....	....	....	....	....	....	....	....	5	0	0	0	14	....	....	....
1983-84	Regina Pats	WHL	63	8	8	16	131	....	....	....	....	....	....	....	....	....	....	....	21	0	1	1	29	....	....	....
1984-85	Regina Pats	WHL	71	24	32	56	248	....	....	....	....	....	....	....	....	....	....	....	8	1	2	3	14	....	....	....
1985-86	U. of Manitoba	CWUAA	12	7	4	11	113	....	....	....	....	....	....	....	....	....	....	....	8	1	1	2	24	....	....	....
1986-87	U. of Manitoba	CWUAA	29	8	8	16	67	....	....	....	....	....	....	....	....	....	....	....	14	4	2	6	28	....	....	....
1987-88	Salt Lake City	IHL	38	9	5	14	268	....	....	....	....	....	....	....	....	....	....	....	....	....	....	....	....	....	....	....
1988-89	**Calgary**	**NHL**	**1**	**0**	**0**	**0**	**5**	**0**	**0**	**0**	**0**	**0.0**	**0**	....	....	....	....	....	....	....	....	....	....	....	....	....
	Salt Lake City	IHL	72	9	18	27	397	....	....	....	....	....	....	....	....	....	....	....	14	2	3	5	86	....	....	....
1989-90	**Calgary**	**NHL**	**3**	**0**	**0**	**0**	**17**	**0**	**0**	**0**	**0**	**0.0**	**–1**	....	....	....	....	....	....	....	....	....	....	....	....	....
	Salt Lake City	IHL	62	8	8	16	319	....	....	....	....	....	....	....	....	....	....	....	4	0	0	0	8	....	....	....
1990-91	**Chicago**	**NHL**	**35**	**0**	**1**	**1**	**183**	**0**	**0**	**0**	**14**	**0.0**	**–3**	....	....	....	....	....	**5**	**0**	**0**	**0**	**46**	**0**	**0**	**0**
1991-92	**Chicago**	**NHL**	**54**	**2**	**2**	**4**	**234**	**0**	**0**	**0**	**23**	**8.7**	**–2**	....	....	....	....	....	**14**	**0**	**1**	**1**	**10**	**0**	**0**	**0**
	Indianapolis Ice	IHL	5	1	1	2	17	....	....	....	....	....	....	....	....	....	....	....	....	....	....	....	....	....	....	....
1992-93	**Chicago**	**NHL**	**78**	**1**	**1**	**2**	**193**	**1**	**0**	**0**	**14**	**7.1**	**2**	....	....	....	....	....	**2**	**0**	**0**	**0**	**4**	**0**	**0**	**0**
1993-94	**Anaheim**	**NHL**	**77**	**1**	**5**	**6**	**199**	**0**	**0**	**0**	**34**	**2.9**	**–6**	....	....	....	....	....	....	....	....	....	....	....	....	....
1994-95	**Anaheim**	**NHL**	**31**	**0**	**1**	**1**	**110**	**0**	**0**	**0**	**14**	**0.0**	**–7**	....	....	....	....	....	....	....	....	....	....	....	....	....
	Detroit	**NHL**	**11**	**0**	**0**	**0**	**37**	**0**	**0**	**0**	**4**	**0.0**	**–4**	....	....	....	....	....	**11**	**1**	**0**	**1**	**26**	**0**	**0**	**0**
1995-96	**Detroit**	**NHL**	**56**	**0**	**1**	**1**	**128**	**0**	**0**	**0**	**19**	**0.0**	**–10**	....	....	....	....	....	**2**	**0**	**0**	**0**	**0**	**0**	**0**	**0**
1996-97	**Detroit**	**NHL**	**1**	**0**	**0**	**0**	**0**	**0**	**0**	**0**	**0**	**0.0**	**–1**	....	....	....	....	....	....	....	....	....	....	....	....	....
	Hartford	**NHL**	**75**	**2**	**2**	**4**	**218**	**0**	**0**	**0**	**17**	**11.8**	**–7**	....	....	....	....	....	....	....	....	....	....	....	....	....
1997-98	**Carolina**	**NHL**	**82**	**3**	**4**	**7**	**204**	**0**	**0**	**1**	**17**	**17.6**	**0**	....	....	....	....	....	....	....	....	....	....	....	....	....
1998-99	**Anaheim**	**NHL**	**73**	**3**	**0**	**3**	**158**	**0**	**0**	**1**	**10**	**30.0**	**0**	**0**	**0.0**	**25**	**4**	**3:25**	**3**	**0**	**0**	**0**	**30**	**0**	**0**	**0**
99-2000	**Anaheim**	**NHL**	**50**	**1**	**2**	**3**	**116**	**0**	**0**	**0**	**14**	**7.1**	**0**	**0**	**0.0**	**55**	**2**	**5:13**	....	....	....	....	....	....	....	....
2000-01	**Los Angeles**	**NHL**	**72**	**3**	**2**	**5**	**235**	**0**	**0**	**1**	**26**	**11.5**	**–2**	**0**	**0.0**	**79**	**1**	**5:60**	**5**	**0**	**0**	**0**	**4**	**0**	**0**	**0**
	NHL Totals		**699**	**16**	**21**	**37**	**2037**	**1**	**0**	**3**	**206**	**7.8**		**0**	**0.0**	**159**	**7**	**4:50**	**42**	**1**	**1**	**2**	**120**	**0**	**0**	**0**

• Re-entered NHL Entry Draft. Originally Detroit's 11th choice, 193rd overall, in 1983 Entry Draft.

Claimed on waivers by **Chicago** from **Calgary**, October 1, 1990. Claimed by **Anaheim** from **Chicago** in Expansion Draft, June 24, 1993. Traded to **Detroit** by **Anaheim** with Mark Ferner and Anaheim's 6th round choice (Magnus Nilsson) in 1996 Entry Draft for Mike Sillinger and Jason York, April 4, 1995. Claimed on waivers by **Hartford** from **Detroit**, October 13, 1996. Transferred to **Carolina** after **Hartford** franchise relocated, June 25, 1997. Traded to **Anaheim** by **Carolina** with Kevin Haller for David Karpa and Anaheim's 4th round choice (later traded to Atlanta - Atlanta selected Blake Robson) in 2000 Entry Draft, August 11, 1998. Signed as a free agent by **LA Kings**, July 6, 2000. Signed as a free agent by **Nashville**, July 2, 2001.

GROLEAU, Francois (groh-LOH, FRAN-swuh)

Defense. Shoots left. 6', 197 lbs. Born, Longueuil, Que., January 23, 1973. Calgary's 2nd choice, 41st overall, in 1991 Entry Draft.

1988-89	Ste-Foy Governors	QAAA	42	3	24	27	42	....	....	....	....	....	....	....	....	....	....	....	13	1	7	8	28	....	....	....
1989-90	Shawinigan	QMJHL	65	11	54	65	80	....	....	....	....	....	....	....	....	....	....	....	6	0	1	1	12	....	....	....
1990-91	Shawinigan	QMJHL	70	9	60	69	70	....	....	....	....	....	....	....	....	....	....	....	6	0	3	3	2	....	....	....
1991-92	Shawinigan	QMJHL	65	8	70	78	74	....	....	....	....	....	....	....	....	....	....	....	10	5	15	20	8	....	....	....
1992-93	St-Jean Lynx	QMJHL	48	7	38	45	66	....	....	....	....	....	....	....	....	....	....	....	4	0	1	1	14	....	....	....
1993-94	Saint John Flames	AHL	73	8	14	22	49	....	....	....	....	....	....	....	....	....	....	....	7	0	1	1	2	....	....	....
1994-95	Saint John Flames	AHL	65	6	34	40	28	....	....	....	....	....	....	....	....	....	....	....	....	....	....	....	....	....	....	....
	Cornwall Aces	AHL	8	1	2	3	7	....	....	....	....	....	....	....	....	....	....	....	14	2	7	9	16	....	....	....
1995-96	**Montreal**	**NHL**	**2**	**0**	**1**	**1**	**2**	**0**	**0**	**0**	**1**	**0.0**	**2**	....	....	....	....	....	....	....	....	....	....	....	....	....
	San Francisco	IHL	63	6	26	32	60	....	....	....	....	....	....	....	....	....	....	....	....	....	....	....	....	....	....	....
	Fredericton	AHL	12	3	5	8	10	....	....	....	....	....	....	....	....	....	....	....	10	1	6	7	14	....	....	....
1996-97	**Montreal**	**NHL**	**5**	**0**	**0**	**0**	**4**	**0**	**0**	**0**	**3**	**0.0**	**0**	....	....	....	....	....	....	....	....	....	....	....	....	....
	Fredericton	AHL	47	8	24	32	43	....	....	....	....	....	....	....	....	....	....	....	....	....	....	....	....	....	....	....
1997-98	**Montreal**	**NHL**	**1**	**0**	**0**	**0**	**0**	**0**	**0**	**0**	**3**	**0.0**	**1**	....	....	....	....	....	....	....	....	....	....	....	....	....
	Fredericton	AHL	63	14	26	40	70	....	....	....	....	....	....	....	....	....	....	....	4	0	2	2	4	....	....	....
1998-99	Augsburger EV	DEL	52	9	21	30	67	....	....	....	....	....	....	....	....	....	....	....	5	0	4	4	4	....	....	....
99-2000	Quebec Citadelles	AHL	63	7	24	31	48	....	....	....	....	....	....	....	....	....	....	....	3	0	2	2	0	....	....	....
2000-01	Adler Mannheim	DEL	59	2	16	18	52	....	....	....	....	....	....	....	....	....	....	....	4	0	0	0	2	....	....	....
	NHL Totals		**8**	**0**	**1**	**1**	**6**	**0**	**0**	**0**	**7**	**0.0**							....	....	....	....	....	....	....	....

QMJHL Second All-Star Team (1990) • QMJHL First All-Star Team (1992)

Traded to **Quebec** by **Calgary** for Ed Ward, March 23, 1995. Signed as a free agent by **Montreal**, June 17, 1995.

GRON, Stanislav (GRAHN, Stan-ih-slav) N.J.

Right wing. Shoots left. 6'2", 205 lbs. Born, Bratislava, Czech., October 28, 1978. New Jersey's 2nd choice, 38th overall, in 1997 Entry Draft.

1994-95	Slovan Bratislava	Slovak-Jr.	40	49	26	75	20	....	....	....	....	....	....	....	....	....	....	....	....	....	....	....	....	....	....	....
1995-96	Slovan Bratislava	Slovak-Jr.	43	33	25	58	14	....	....	....	....	....	....	....	....	....	....	....	....	....	....	....	....	....	....	....
	Slovan Bratislava	Slovakia	....	....	....	....	....	....	....	....	....	....	....	....	....	....	....	....	1	0	0	0	0	....	....	....
1996-97	Slovan Bratislava	Slovak-Jr.	22	20	16	36	....	....	....	....	....	....	....	....	....	....	....	....	....	....	....	....	....	....	....	....
	Slovan Bratislava	Slovakia	7	0	0	0	....	....	....	....	....	....	....	....	....	....	....	....	....	....	....	....	....	....	....	....
1997-98	Seattle T-Birds	WHL	61	9	29	38	21	....	....	....	....	....	....	....	....	....	....	....	5	1	5	6	0	....	....	....
1998-99	Kootenay Ice	WHL	49	28	18	46	18	....	....	....	....	....	....	....	....	....	....	....	7	3	8	11	12	....	....	....
	Utah Grizzlies	IHL	4	0	3	3	0	....	....	....	....	....	....	....	....	....	....	....	....	....	....	....	....	....	....	....
99-2000	Albany River Rats	AHL	65	19	10	29	17	....	....	....	....	....	....	....	....	....	....	....	5	1	1	2	2	....	....	....
2000-01	**New Jersey**	**NHL**	**1**	**0**	**0**	**0**	**0**	**0**	**0**	**0**	**2**	**0.0**	**1**	**2**	**0.0**	**2**	**0**	**9:55**	....	....	....	....	....	....	....	....
	Albany River Rats	AHL	61	16	9	25	19	....	....	....	....	....	....	....	....	....	....	....	....	....	....	....	....	....	....	....
	NHL Totals		**1**	**0**	**0**	**0**	**0**	**0**	**0**	**0**	**2**	**0.0**		**2**	**0.0**	**2**	**0**	**9:55**	....	....	....	....	....	....	....	....

GROSEK, Michal (GROH-shehk, MIHK-al) NYR

Left wing. Shoots right. 6'2", 207 lbs. Born, Vyskov, Czech., June 1, 1975. Winnipeg's 7th choice, 145th overall, in 1993 Entry Draft.

1992-93	Skoda Zlin	Czech.	17	1	3	4	....	....	....	....	....	....	....	....	....	....	....	....	....	....	....	....	....	....	....	....
1993-94	Tacoma Rockets	WHL	30	25	20	45	106	....	....	....	....	....	....	....	....	....	....	....	7	2	2	4	30	....	....	....
	Winnipeg	**NHL**	**3**	**1**	**0**	**1**	**0**	**0**	**0**	**0**	**4**	**25.0**	**–1**	....	....	....	....	....	....	....	....	....	....	....	....	....
	Moncton Hawks	AHL	20	1	2	3	47	....	....	....	....	....	....	....	....	....	....	....	2	0	0	0	0	....	....	....
1994-95	Springfield	AHL	45	10	22	32	98	....	....	....	....	....	....	....	....	....	....	....	....	....	....	....	....	....	....	....
	Winnipeg	**NHL**	**24**	**2**	**2**	**4**	**21**	**0**	**0**	**1**	**27**	**7.4**	**–3**	....	....	....	....	....	....	....	....	....	....	....	....	....
1995-96	**Winnipeg**	**NHL**	**1**	**0**	**0**	**0**	**0**	**0**	**0**	**0**	**1**	**0.0**	**–1**	....	....	....	....	....	....	....	....	....	....	....	....	....
	Springfield	AHL	39	16	19	35	68	....	....	....	....	....	....	....	....	....	....	....	....	....	....	....	....	....	....	....
	Buffalo	**NHL**	**22**	**6**	**4**	**10**	**31**	**2**	**0**	**1**	**33**	**18.2**	**0**	....	....	....	....	....	....	....	....	....	....	....	....	....
1996-97	**Buffalo**	**NHL**	**82**	**15**	**21**	**36**	**71**	**1**	**0**	**2**	**117**	**12.8**	**25**	....	....	....	....	....	**12**	**3**	**3**	**6**	**8**	**0**	**0**	**0**
1997-98	**Buffalo**	**NHL**	**67**	**10**	**20**	**30**	**60**	**2**	**0**	**1**	**114**	**8.8**	**9**	....	....	....	....	....	**15**	**6**	**4**	**10**	**28**	**2**	**0**	**3**
1998-99	**Buffalo**	**NHL**	**76**	**20**	**30**	**50**	**102**	**4**	**0**	**3**	**140**	**14.3**	**21**	**5**	**60.0**	**98**	**20**	**17:14**	**13**	**0**	**4**	**4**	**28**	**0**	**0**	**0**
99-2000	**Buffalo**	**NHL**	**61**	**11**	**23**	**34**	**35**	**2**	**0**	**2**	**96**	**11.5**	**12**	**8**	**25.0**	**58**	**13**	**16:17**	....	....	....	....	....	....	....	....
	Chicago	**NHL**	**14**	**2**	**4**	**6**	**12**	**1**	**0**	**0**	**18**	**11.1**	**–1**	**1**	**0.0**	**28**	**1**	**13:06**	....	....	....	....	....	....	....	....
2000-01	**NY Rangers**	**NHL**	**65**	**9**	**11**	**20**	**61**	**2**	**0**	**0**	**84**	**10.7**	**–10**	**14**	**28.6**	**99**	**13**	**11:05**	....	....	....	....	....	....	....	....
	Hartford	AHL	12	8	7	15	12	....	....	....	....	....	....	....	....	....	....	....	....	....	....	....	....	....	....	....
	NHL Totals		**415**	**76**	**115**	**191**	**393**	**14**	**0**	**10**	**634**	**12.0**		**28**	**32.1**	**283**	**47**	**14:51**	**40**	**9**	**11**	**20**	**64**	**2**	**0**	**3**

Traded to **Buffalo** by **Winnipeg** with Darryl Shannon for Craig Muni, February 15, 1996. Traded to **Chicago** by **Buffalo** for Doug Gilmour, J-P Dumont and future considerations, March 10, 2000. Traded to **NY Rangers** by **Chicago** with Brad Brown for future considerations, October 5, 2000.

Regular Season: GP–Min; Playoffs: second GP–GW

GRUDEN, John

(GROO-duhn, JAWN) **OTT.**

Defense. Shoots left. 6', 203 lbs. Born, Virginia, MN, June 4, 1970. Boston's 7th choice, 168th overall, in 1990 Entry Draft.

Season	Club	League	GP	G	A	Pts	PIM	PP	SH	GW	S	%	+/-	TF	F%	H	SB	Min	GP	G	A	Pts	PIM	PP	SH	GW
1989-90	Waterloo Hawks	USHL	47	7	39	46	35																			
1990-91	Ferris State	CCHA	37	4	11	15	27																			
1991-92	Ferris State	CCHA	37	9	14	23	24																			
1992-93	Ferris State	CCHA	41	16	14	30	58																			
1993-94	Ferris State	CCHA	38	11	25	36	52																			
	Boston	**NHL**	**7**	**0**	**1**	**1**	**2**	**0**	**0**	**0**	**8**	**0.0**	**–3**													
1994-95	**Boston**	**NHL**	**38**	**0**	**6**	**6**	**22**	**0**	**0**	**0**	**30**	**0.0**	**3**													
	Providence Bruins	AHL	1	0	1	1	0																			
1995-96	**Boston**	**NHL**	**14**	**0**	**0**	**0**	**4**	**0**	**0**	**0**	**12**	**0.0**	**–3**						**3**	**0**	**1**	**1**	**0**	**0**	**0**	**0**
	Providence Bruins	AHL	39	5	19	24	29																			
1996-97	Providence Bruins	AHL	78	18	27	45	52												10	3	6	9	4			
1997-98	Detroit Vipers	IHL	76	13	42	55	74												21	1	8	9	14			
1998-99	**Ottawa**	**NHL**	**13**	**0**	**1**	**1**	**8**	**0**	**0**	**0**	**10**	**0.0**	**0**	**0**	**0.0**	**16**	**4**	**13:07**								
	Detroit Vipers	IHL	59	10	28	38	52												10	0	1	1	6			
99-2000	**Ottawa**	**NHL**	**9**	**0**	**0**	**0**	**4**	**0**	**0**	**0**	**3**	**0.0**	**0**	**0**	**0.0**	**6**	**6**	**16:29**								
	Grand Rapids	IHL	50	5	17	22	24												12	1	4	5	8			
2000-01	Grand Rapids	IHL	34	2	6	8	18												10	1	4	5	8			
	NHL Totals		**81**	**0**	**8**	**8**	**40**	**0**	**0**	**0**	**63**	**0.0**		**0**	**0.0**	**22**	**10**	**14:30**	**3**	**0**	**1**	**1**	**0**	**0**	**0**	**0**

CCHA First All-Star Team (1994) • NCAA West First All-American Team (1994) • IHL Second All-Star Team (1998)

Signed as a free agent by **Ottawa**, August 7, 1998. • Missed majority of 2000-01 season recovering from shoulder injury suffered in training camp, October 1, 2000.

GUERIN, Bill

(GAIR-ihn, BIHL) **BOS.**

Right wing. Shoots right. 6'2", 210 lbs. Born, Worcester, MA, November 9, 1970. New Jersey's 1st choice, 5th overall, in 1989 Entry Draft.

Season	Club	League	GP	G	A	Pts	PIM	PP	SH	GW	S	%	+/-	TF	F%	H	SB	Min	GP	G	A	Pts	PIM	PP	SH	GW
1985-86	Springfield	NEJHL	48	26	19	45	71																			
1986-87	Springfield	NEJHL	32	34	20	54	40																			
1987-88	Springfield	NEJHL	38	31	44	75	146																			
1988-89	Springfield	NEJHL	31	32	35	67	90																			
1989-90	Boston College	H-East	39	14	11	25	54																			
1990-91	Boston College	H-East	38	26	19	45	102																			
	United States	Nat-Team	46	12	15	27	67																			
1991-92	**New Jersey**	**NHL**	**5**	**0**	**1**	**1**	**9**	**0**	**0**	**0**	**8**	**0.0**	**1**						**6**	**3**	**0**	**3**	**4**	**0**	**0**	**0**
	Utica Devils	AHL	22	13	10	23	6												4	1	3	4	14			
1992-93	**New Jersey**	**NHL**	**65**	**14**	**20**	**34**	**63**	**0**	**0**	**2**	**123**	**11.4**	**14**						**5**	**1**	**1**	**2**	**4**	**0**	**0**	**0**
	Utica Devils	AHL	18	10	7	17	47																			
1993-94	**New Jersey**	**NHL**	**81**	**25**	**19**	**44**	**101**	**2**	**0**	**3**	**195**	**12.8**	**14**						**17**	**2**	**1**	**3**	**35**	**0**	**0**	**1**
1994-95♦	**New Jersey**	**NHL**	**48**	**12**	**13**	**25**	**72**	**4**	**0**	**3**	**96**	**12.5**	**6**						**20**	**3**	**8**	**11**	**30**	**1**	**0**	**0**
1995-96	**New Jersey**	**NHL**	**80**	**23**	**30**	**53**	**116**	**8**	**0**	**6**	**216**	**10.6**	**7**													
1996-97	**New Jersey**	**NHL**	**82**	**29**	**18**	**47**	**95**	**7**	**0**	**9**	**177**	**16.4**	**–2**						**8**	**2**	**1**	**3**	**18**	**1**	**0**	**1**
1997-98	**New Jersey**	**NHL**	**19**	**5**	**5**	**10**	**13**	**1**	**0**	**2**	**48**	**10.4**	**0**													
	Edmonton	**NHL**	**40**	**13**	**16**	**29**	**80**	**8**	**0**	**2**	**130**	**10.0**	**1**						**12**	**7**	**1**	**8**	**17**	**4**	**0**	**0**
	United States	Olympics	4	0	3	3	2																			
1998-99	**Edmonton**	**NHL**	**80**	**30**	**34**	**64**	**133**	**13**	**0**	**2**	**261**	**11.5**	**7**	**74**	**40.5**	**131**	**20**	**19:42**	**3**	**0**	**2**	**2**	**2**	**0**	**0**	**0**
99-2000	**Edmonton**	**NHL**	**70**	**24**	**22**	**46**	**123**	**11**	**0**	**2**	**188**	**12.8**	**4**	**13**	**46.2**	**101**	**33**	**18:01**	**5**	**3**	**2**	**5**	**9**	**1**	**0**	**0**
2000-01	**Edmonton**	**NHL**	**21**	**12**	**10**	**22**	**18**	**4**	**0**	**1**	**64**	**18.8**	**11**	**0**	**0.0**	**35**	**9**	**19:49**								
	Boston	**NHL**	**64**	**28**	**35**	**63**	**122**	**7**	**1**	**4**	**225**	**12.4**	**–4**	**36**	**41.7**	**118**	**51**	**22:43**								
	NHL Totals		**655**	**215**	**223**	**438**	**945**	**65**	**1**	**36**	**1731**	**12.4**		**123**	**41.5**	**385**	**113**	**20:02**	**76**	**21**	**16**	**37**	**119**	**7**	**0**	**2**

Played in NHL All-Star Game (2001)

Traded to **Edmonton** by **New Jersey** with Valeri Zelepukin for Jason Arnott and Bryan Muir, January 4, 1998. Traded to **Boston** by **Edmonton** for Anson Carter, Boston's 1st (Ales Hemsky) and 2nd (Doug Lynch) round choices in 2001 Entry Draft and future considerations, November 15, 2000.

GUOLLA, Stephen

(GUH-wah-lah, STEEV-vuhn)

Left wing. Shoots left. 6', 190 lbs. Born, Scarborough, Ont., March 15, 1973. Ottawa's 1st choice, 3rd overall, in 1994 Supplemental Draft.

Season	Club	League	GP	G	A	Pts	PIM	PP	SH	GW	S	%	+/-	TF	F%	H	SB	Min	GP	G	A	Pts	PIM	PP	SH	GW
1988-89	Toronto Wings	MTHL	25	14	20	34	....																			
1989-90	Toronto Wings	MTHL	40	42	47	89	....																			
1990-91	Wexford Raiders	MTJHL	44	34	44	78	34												12	12	16	28	....			
1991-92	Michigan State	CCHA	33	4	9	13	8																			
1992-93	Michigan State	CCHA	39	19	35	54	6																			
1993-94	Michigan State	CCHA	41	23	46	69	16																			
1994-95	Michigan State	CCHA	40	16	35	51	16																			
1995-96	P.E.I. Senators	AHL	72	32	48	80	28												3	0	0	0	0			
1996-97	**San Jose**	**NHL**	**43**	**13**	**8**	**21**	**14**	**2**	**0**	**1**	**81**	**16.0**	**–10**													
	Kentucky	AHL	34	22	22	44	10												4	2	1	3	0			
1997-98	**San Jose**	**NHL**	**7**	**1**	**1**	**2**	**0**	**0**	**0**	**0**	**9**	**11.1**	**–2**													
	Kentucky	AHL	69	37	63	100	45												3	0	0	0	0			
1998-99	**San Jose**	**NHL**	**14**	**2**	**2**	**4**	**6**	**0**	**0**	**1**	**22**	**9.1**	**3**	**172**	**36.6**	**19**	**6**	**13:54**								
	Kentucky	AHL	53	29	47	76	33																			
99-2000	**Tampa Bay**	**NHL**	**46**	**6**	**10**	**16**	**11**	**2**	**0**	**0**	**52**	**11.5**	**2**	**155**	**45.8**	**33**	**8**	**11:26**								
	Atlanta	**NHL**	**20**	**4**	**9**	**13**	**4**	**2**	**0**	**0**	**34**	**11.8**	**–13**	**345**	**42.6**	**19**	**9**	**17:47**								
2000-01	**Atlanta**	**NHL**	**63**	**12**	**16**	**28**	**23**	**2**	**0**	**3**	**96**	**12.5**	**–6**	**859**	**47.7**	**63**	**22**	**14:41**								
	NHL Totals		**193**	**38**	**46**	**84**	**58**	**8**	**0**	**5**	**294**	**12.9**		**1531**	**45.1**	**134**	**45**	**13:60**								

CCHA Second All-Star Team (1994) • NCAA West Second All-American Team (1994) • AHL Second All-Star Team (1998, 1999) • Won Les Cunningham Award (MVP - AHL) (1998)

Signed as a free agent by **San Jose**, August 22, 1996. Traded to **Tampa Bay** by **San Jose** with Bill Houlder, Shawn Burr and Andrei Zyuzin for Niklas Sundstrom and NY Rangers' 3rd round choice (previously acquired, later traded to Chicago - Chicago selected Igor Radulov) in 2000 Entry Draft, August 4, 1999. Claimed on waivers by **Atlanta** from **Tampa Bay**, March 1, 2000.

GUREN, Miloslav

(GOO-rihn, MEER-oh-slahf) **MTL.**

Defense. Shoots left. 6'2", 215 lbs. Born, Uherske Hradiste, Czech., September 24, 1976. Montreal's 2nd choice, 60th overall, in 1995 Entry Draft.

Season	Club	League	GP	G	A	Pts	PIM	PP	SH	GW	S	%	+/-	TF	F%	H	SB	Min	GP	G	A	Pts	PIM	PP	SH	GW
1993-94	ZPS Zlin	Cze-Rep	22	1	5	6	....												3	0	0	0	....			
1994-95	ZPS Zlin	Cze-Rep	32	3	7	10	10												12	1	0	1	6			
1995-96	ZPS Zlin	Cze-Rep	28	1	2	3	....												7	1	0	1	....			
1996-97	Fredericton	AHL	79	6	26	32	26																			
1997-98	Fredericton	AHL	78	15	36	51	36												4	1	2	3	0			
1998-99	**Montreal**	**NHL**	**12**	**0**	**1**	**1**	**4**	**0**	**0**	**0**	**11**	**0.0**	**–1**	**0**	**0.0**	**4**	**10**	**12:02**								
	Fredericton	AHL	63	5	16	21	24												15	4	7	11	10			
99-2000	**Montreal**	**NHL**	**24**	**1**	**2**	**3**	**12**	**1**	**0**	**0**	**20**	**5.0**	**–5**	**0**	**0.0**	**20**	**26**	**15:14**								
	Quebec Citadelles	AHL	29	5	12	17	16												3	0	0	0	2			
2000-01	Quebec Citadelles	AHL	75	11	40	51	24												8	4	2	6	6			
	NHL Totals		**36**	**1**	**3**	**4**	**16**	**1**	**0**	**0**	**31**	**3.2**		**0**	**0.0**	**24**	**36**	**14:10**								

GUSAROV, Alexei

(goo-SAH-rahf, al-EXE-ay)

Defense. Shoots left. 6'3", 185 lbs. Born, Leningrad, USSR, July 8, 1964. Quebec's 11th choice, 213th overall, in 1988 Entry Draft.

Season	Club	League	GP	G	A	Pts	PIM	PP	SH	GW	S	%	+/-	TF	F%	H	SB	Min	GP	G	A	Pts	PIM	PP	SH	GW
1981-82	SKA Leningrad	USSR	20	1	2	3	16																			
1982-83	SKA Leningrad	USSR	42	2	1	3	32																			
1983-84	SKA Leningrad	USSR	43	2	3	5	32																			
1984-85	CSKA Moscow	USSR	36	3	2	5	26																			
1985-86	CSKA Moscow	USSR	40	3	5	8	30																			
1986-87	CSKA Moscow	USSR	38	4	7	11	24																			
1987-88	CSKA Moscow	USSR	39	3	2	5	28																			
	Soviet Union	Olympics	8	1	3	4	6																			
1988-89	CSKA Moscow	USSR	42	5	4	9	37																			
1989-90	CSKA Moscow	USSR	42	4	7	11	42																			
1990-91	CSKA Moscow	USSR	15	0	0	0	12																			
	Quebec	**NHL**	**36**	**3**	**9**	**12**	**12**	**1**	**0**	**0**	**36**	**8.3**	**–4**													
	Halifax Citadels	AHL	2	0	3	3	2																			

			Regular Season																Playoffs							
Season	Club	League	GP	G	A	Pts	PIM	PP	SH	GW	S	%	+/-	TF	F%	H	SB	Min	GP	G	A	Pts	PIM	PP	SH	GW
1991-92	Quebec	NHL	68	5	18	23	22	3	0	1	66	7.6	−9	....	....	....	....	....	....	....	....	....	....	....	....	....
	Halifax Citadels	AHL	3	0	0	0	0	....	....	....	....	....	....	....	....	....	....	....	....	....	....	....	....	....	....	....
1992-93	Quebec	NHL	79	8	22	30	57	0	2	1	60	13.3	18	....	....	....	....	....	5	0	1	1	0	0	0	0
1993-94	Quebec	NHL	76	5	20	25	38	0	1	0	84	6.0	3	....	....	....	....	....	....	....	....	....	....	....	....	....
1994-95	Quebec	NHL	14	1	2	3	6	0	0	1	7	14.3	−1	....	....	....	....	....	....	....	....	....	....	....	....	....
1995-96♦	Colorado	NHL	65	5	15	20	56	0	0	0	42	11.9	29	....	....	....	....	....	21	0	9	9	12	0	0	0
1996-97	Colorado	NHL	58	2	12	14	28	0	0	0	33	6.1	4	....	....	....	....	....	17	0	3	3	14	0	0	0
1997-98	Colorado	NHL	72	4	10	14	42	0	1	1	47	8.5	9	....	....	....	....	....	7	0	1	1	6	0	0	0
	Russia	Olympics	6	0	1	1	8	....	....	....	....	....	....	....	....	....	....	....	....	....	....	....	....	....	....	....
1998-99	Colorado	NHL	54	3	10	13	24	1	0	0	28	10.7	12	1	0.0	22	65	19:57	5	0	0	0	2	0	0	0
99-2000	Colorado	NHL	34	2	2	4	10	0	0	0	16	12.5	−8	0	0.0	13	45	19:27	....	....	....	....	....	....	....	....
2000-01	Colorado	NHL	9	0	1	1	6	0	0	0	4	0.0	2	0	0.0	4	4	14:59	....	....	....	....	....	....	....	....
	NY Rangers	NHL	26	1	3	4	6	0	0	0	21	4.8	−2	0	0.0	11	45	19:33	....	....	....	....	....	....	....	....
	St. Louis	NHL	16	0	4	4	6	0	0	0	10	0.0	−3	0	0.0	7	21	21:11	13	0	0	0	4	0	0	0
	NHL Totals		**607**	**39**	**128**	**167**	**313**	**5**	**4**	**4**	**454**	**8.6**		**1**	**0.0**	**57**	**180**	**19:34**	**68**	**0**	**14**	**14**	**38**	**0**	**0**	**0**

Transferred to **Colorado** after **Quebec** franchise relocated, June 21, 1995. • Missed majority of 1999-2000 season recovering from leg injury suffered in game vs. Dallas, February 27, 2000. Traded to **NY Rangers** by **Colorado** for NY Rangers' 5th round choice (Frantisek Skladany) in 2001 Entry Draft, December 28, 2000. Traded to **St. Louis** by **NY Rangers** for Peter Smrek, March 5, 2001.

GUSEV, Sergey

(GOO-sehv, SAIR-gay)

Defense. Shoots left. 6'1", 205 lbs. Born, Nizhny Tagil, USSR, July 31, 1975. Dallas' 4th choice, 69th overall, in 1995 Entry Draft.

1994-95	CSK Samara	CIS	50	3	5	8	58	....	....	....	....	....	....	....	....	....	....	....	....	....	....	....	....	....	....	....
1995-96	Michigan K-Wings	IHL	73	11	17	28	76	....	....	....	....	....	....	....	....	....	....	....	....	....	....	....	....	....	....	....
1996-97	Michigan K-Wings	IHL	51	7	8	15	44	....	....	....	....	....	....	....	....	....	....	....	4	0	4	4	6	....	....	....
1997-98	Dallas	NHL	9	0	0	0	2	0	0	0	5	0.0	−5	....	....	....	....	....	....	....	....	....	....	....	....	....
	Michigan K-Wings	IHL	36	3	6	9	36	....	....	....	....	....	....	....	....	....	....	....	4	0	2	2	6	....	....	....
1998-99	Dallas	NHL	22	1	4	5	6	0	0	1	30	3.3	5	0	0.0	12	16	12:04	....	....	....	....	....	....	....	....
	Michigan K-Wings	IHL	12	0	6	6	14	....	....	....	....	....	....	....	....	....	....	....	....	....	....	....	....	....	....	....
	Tampa Bay	NHL	14	0	3	3	10	0	0	0	16	0.0	−8	0	0.0	13	28	21:30	....	....	....	....	....	....	....	....
99-2000	Tampa Bay	NHL	28	2	3	5	6	1	0	0	23	8.7	−9	0	0.0	35	46	17:34	....	....	....	....	....	....	....	....
2000-01	Tampa Bay	NHL	16	1	0	1	10	0	0	0	13	7.7	−3	0	0.0	8	22	13:23	....	....	....	....	....	....	....	....
	Detroit Vipers	IHL	13	1	4	5	10	....	....	....	....	....	....	....	....	....	....	....	....	....	....	....	....	....	....	....
	NHL Totals		**89**	**4**	**10**	**14**	**34**	**1**	**0**	**1**	**87**	**4.6**		**0**	**0.0**	**68**	**112**	**15:55**	....	....	....	....	....	....	....	....

Traded to **Tampa Bay** by **Dallas** for Benoit Hogue and Tampa Bay's 6th round choice (Michal Blazek) in 2001 Entry Draft, March 21, 1999. • Missed majority of 1999-2000 season recovering from knee injury suffered in game vs. NY Rangers, December 19, 1999. • Missed majority of 2000-01 season recovering from knee injury originally suffered in game vs. NY Islanders, October 10, 2000.

GUSMANOV, Ravil

(goos-MAN-ohv, ra-VIHL) **MIN.**

Left wing. Shoots left. 6'3", 185 lbs. Born, Naberezhnye Chelny, USSR, July 25, 1972. Winnipeg's 5th choice, 93rd overall, in 1993 Entry Draft.

1990-91	HC Chelyabinsk	USSR	15	0	0	0	10	....	....	....	....	....	....	....	....	....	....	....	....	....	....	....	....	....	....	....
1991-92	HC Chelyabinsk	CIS	38	4	4	8	20	....	....	....	....	....	....	....	....	....	....	....	....	....	....	....	....	....	....	....
1992-93	HC Chelyabinsk	CIS	39	15	8	23	30	....	....	....	....	....	....	....	....	....	....	....	8	4	0	4	2	....	....	....
1993-94	HC Chelyabinsk	CIS	43	18	9	27	51	....	....	....	....	....	....	....	....	....	....	....	6	4	3	7	10	....	....	....
	Russia	Olympics	8	3	1	4	0	....	....	....	....	....	....	....	....	....	....	....	....	....	....	....	....	....	....	....
1994-95	Springfield	AHL	72	18	15	33	14	....	....	....	....	....	....	....	....	....	....	....	....	....	....	....	....	....	....	....
1995-96	Winnipeg	NHL	4	0	0	0	0	0	0	0	6	0.0	−3	....	....	....	....	....	....	....	....	....	....	....	....	....
	Springfield	AHL	60	36	32	68	20	....	....	....	....	....	....	....	....	....	....	....	....	....	....	....	....	....	....	....
	Indianapolis Ice	IHL	11	6	10	16	4	....	....	....	....	....	....	....	....	....	....	....	5	2	3	5	4	....	....	....
1996-97	Indianapolis Ice	IHL	60	21	27	48	14	....	....	....	....	....	....	....	....	....	....	....	....	....	....	....	....	....	....	....
	Saint John Flames	AHL	12	4	4	8	2	....	....	....	....	....	....	....	....	....	....	....	3	0	1	1	2	....	....	....
1997-98	Chicago Wolves	IHL	56	27	28	55	26	....	....	....	....	....	....	....	....	....	....	....	11	1	3	4	19	....	....	....
1998-99	HC Magnitogorsk	Russia	42	14	24	38	28	....	....	....	....	....	....	....	....	....	....	....	16	2	8	10	16	....	....	....
	HC Magnitogorsk	EuroHL	6	3	3	6	4	....	....	....	....	....	....	....	....	....	....	....	6	0	2	2	0	....	....	....
99-2000	HC Magnitogorsk	Russia	37	12	13	25	30	....	....	....	....	....	....	....	....	....	....	....	11	3	5	8	6	....	....	....
	HC Magnitogorsk	EuroHL	6	2	0	2	0	....	....	....	....	....	....	....	....	....	....	....	5	0	1	1	6	....	....	....
2000-01	HC Magnitogorsk	Russia	43	6	19	25	20	....	....	....	....	....	....	....	....	....	....	....	12	1	9	10	10	....	....	....
	NHL Totals		**4**	**0**	**0**	**0**	**0**	**0**	**0**	**0**	**6**	**0.0**		....	....	....	....	....	....	....	....	....	....	....	....	....

Traded to **Chicago** by **Winnipeg** for Chicago's 4th round choice (later traded to Toronto - Toronto selected Vladimir Antipov) in 1996 Entry Draft, March 20, 1996. Traded to **Calgary** by **Chicago** for Marc Hussey, March 18, 1997. Signed as a free agent by **Minnesota**, June 21, 2001.

HAGGERTY, Sean

(HA-guhr-tee, SHAWN)

Left wing. Shoots left. 6'1", 186 lbs. Born, Rye, NY, February 11, 1976. Toronto's 2nd choice, 48th overall, in 1994 Entry Draft.

1990-91	Westminster High	Hi-School	25	20	22	42	....	....	....	....	....	....	....	....	....	....	....	....	....	....	....	....	....	....	....	....
1991-92	Westminster High	Hi-School	25	24	36	60	....	....	....	....	....	....	....	....	....	....	....	....	....	....	....	....	....	....	....	....
1992-93	Boston Bruins	MBHL	72	70	111	181	80	....	....	....	....	....	....	....	....	....	....	....	....	....	....	....	....	....	....	....
1993-94	Detroit Jr. Wings	OHL	60	31	32	63	21	....	....	....	....	....	....	....	....	....	....	....	17	9	10	19	11	....	....	....
1994-95	Detroit Jr. Wings	OHL	61	40	49	89	37	....	....	....	....	....	....	....	....	....	....	....	21	13	24	37	18	....	....	....
1995-96	Detroit Whalers	OHL	66	*60	51	111	78	....	....	....	....	....	....	....	....	....	....	....	17	15	9	24	30	....	....	....
	Toronto	NHL	1	0	0	0	0	0	0	0	0	0.0	0	....	....	....	....	....	....	....	....	....	....	....	....	....
	Worcester	AHL	....	....	....	....	....	....	....	....	....	....	....	....	....	....	....	....	1	0	0	0	2	....	....	....
1996-97	Kentucky	AHL	77	13	22	35	60	....	....	....	....	....	....	....	....	....	....	....	4	1	0	1	4	....	....	....
1997-98	NY Islanders	NHL	5	0	0	0	0	0	0	0	2	0.0	−3	....	....	....	....	....	....	....	....	....	....	....	....	....
	Kentucky	AHL	63	33	20	53	64	....	....	....	....	....	....	....	....	....	....	....	3	0	2	2	4	....	....	....
1998-99	Lowell	AHL	77	19	27	46	40	....	....	....	....	....	....	....	....	....	....	....	3	0	1	1	0	....	....	....
99-2000	NY Islanders	NHL	5	1	1	2	4	0	0	0	2	50.0	3	0	0.0	6	3	9:38	....	....	....	....	....	....	....	....
	Kansas City	IHL	76	27	33	60	94	....	....	....	....	....	....	....	....	....	....	....	....	....	....	....	....	....	....	....
2000-01	Nashville	NHL	3	0	1	1	0	0	0	0	2	0.0	1	0	0.0	4	1	8:35	....	....	....	....	....	....	....	....
	Milwaukee	IHL	76	27	23	50	59	....	....	....	....	....	....	....	....	....	....	....	5	0	1	1	8	....	....	....
	NHL Totals		**14**	**1**	**2**	**3**	**4**	**0**	**0**	**0**	**6**	**16.7**		**0**	**0.0**	**10**	**4**	**9:15**	....	....	....	....	....	....	....	....

Memorial Cup All-Star Team (1995) • OHL Second All-Star Team (1996) • AHL Second All-Star Team (1998)

Traded to **NY Islanders** by **Toronto** with Darby Hendrickson, Kenny Jonsson and Toronto's 1st round choice (Roberto Luongo) in 1997 Entry Draft for Wendel Clark, Mathieu Schneider and D.J. Smith, March 13, 1996. Claimed on waivers by **Nashville** from **NY Islanders**, May 23, 2000.

HAJT, Chris

(HIGHT, KRIHS) **EDM.**

Defense. Shoots left. 6'3", 206 lbs. Born, Saskatoon, Sask., July 5, 1978. Edmonton's 3rd choice, 32nd overall, in 1996 Entry Draft.

1993-94	Amherst Knights	WNYHA	38	8	20	28	16	....	....	....	....	....	....	....	....	....	....	....	....	....	....	....	....	....	....	....
1994-95	Guelph Storm	OHL	57	1	7	8	35	....	....	....	....	....	....	....	....	....	....	....	14	0	2	2	9	....	....	....
1995-96	Guelph Storm	OHL	63	8	27	35	69	....	....	....	....	....	....	....	....	....	....	....	16	0	6	6	13	....	....	....
1996-97	Guelph Storm	OHL	58	11	15	26	62	....	....	....	....	....	....	....	....	....	....	....	18	0	8	8	25	....	....	....
1997-98	Guelph Storm	OHL	44	2	21	23	46	....	....	....	....	....	....	....	....	....	....	....	12	1	5	6	11	....	....	....
1998-99	Hamilton Bulldogs	AHL	64	0	4	4	36	....	....	....	....	....	....	....	....	....	....	....	....	....	....	....	....	....	....	....
99-2000	Hamilton Bulldogs	AHL	54	0	8	8	30	....	....	....	....	....	....	....	....	....	....	....	10	0	2	2	0	....	....	....
2000-01	Edmonton	NHL	1	0	0	0	0	0	0	0	0	0.0	−1	0	0.0	1	1	7:38	....	....	....	....	....	....	....	....
	Hamilton Bulldogs	AHL	70	0	10	10	48	....	....	....	....	....	....	....	....	....	....	....	....	....	....	....	....	....	....	....
	NHL Totals		**1**	**0**	**0**	**0**	**0**	**0**	**0**	**0**	**0**	**0.0**		**0**	**0.0**	**1**	**1**	**7:38**	....	....	....	....	....	....	....	....

OHL Second All-Star Team (1998)

HALKO, Steven

(HAL-koh, STEE-vehn) **CAR.**

Defense. Shoots right. 6'1", 200 lbs. Born, Etobicoke, Ont., March 8, 1974. Hartford's 10th choice, 225th overall, in 1992 Entry Draft.

1989-90	Newmarket 87's	OJHL-B	30	3	5	8	16	....	....	....	....	....	....	....	....	....	....	....	....	....	....	....	....	....	....	....
1990-91	Newmarket 87's	OJHL-B	35	2	13	15	37	....	....	....	....	....	....	....	....	....	....	....	....	....	....	....	....	....	....	....
	Markham	OJHL-B	8	4	3	7	2	....	....	....	....	....	....	....	....	....	....	....	....	....	....	....	....	....	....	....
1991-92	Thornhill Islanders	MTJHL	44	15	46	61	43	....	....	....	....	....	....	....	....	....	....	....	....	....	....	....	....	....	....	....
1992-93	U. of Michigan	CCHA	39	1	12	13	12	....	....	....	....	....	....	....	....	....	....	....	....	....	....	....	....	....	....	....
1993-94	U. of Michigan	CCHA	41	2	13	15	32	....	....	....	....	....	....	....	....	....	....	....	....	....	....	....	....	....	....	....
1994-95	U. of Michigan	CCHA	39	2	14	16	20	....	....	....	....	....	....	....	....	....	....	....	....	....	....	....	....	....	....	....

Season	Club	League	GP	G	A	Pts	PIM	PP	SH	GW	S	%	+/-	TF	F%	H	SB	Min	GP	G	A	Pts	PIM	PP	SH	GW
			Regular Season																Playoffs							
1995-96	U. of Michigan	CCHA	43	4	16	20	32																			
1996-97	Springfield	AHL	70	1	5	6	37												11	0	2	2	8			
1997-98	**Carolina**	**NHL**	**18**	**0**	**2**	**2**	**10**	**0**	**0**	**0**	**7**	**0.0**	**–1**													
	New Haven	AHL	65	1	19	20	44												1	0	0	0	0			
1998-99	**Carolina**	**NHL**	**20**	**0**	**3**	**3**	**24**	**0**	**0**	**0**	**6**	**0.0**	**5**	**0**	**0.0**	**32**	**11**	**15:57**	**4**	**0**	**0**	**0**	**2**	**0**	**0**	**0**
	New Haven	AHL	42	2	7	9	58																			
99-2000	**Carolina**	**NHL**	**58**	**0**	**8**	**8**	**25**	**0**	**0**	**0**	**54**	**0.0**	**0**	**1**	**100.0**	**85**	**60**	**16:43**								
2000-01	**Carolina**	**NHL**	**48**	**0**	**1**	**1**	**6**	**0**	**0**	**0**	**24**	**0.0**	**–10**	**0**	**0.0**	**67**	**36**	**13:27**								
	NHL Totals		**144**	**0**	**14**	**14**	**65**	**0**	**0**	**0**	**91**	**0.0**		**1**	**100.0**	**184**	**107**	**15:21**	**4**	**0**	**0**	**0**	**2**	**0**	**0**	**0**

CCHA Second All-Star Team (1995, 1996) • NCAA Championship All-Tournament Team (1996)

Transferred to **Carolina** after **Hartford** franchise relocated, June 25, 1997.

HALLER, Kevin

(HAHL-her, KEH-vihn) **NYI**

Defense. Shoots left. 6'2", 199 lbs. Born, Trochu, Alta., December 5, 1970. Buffalo's 1st choice, 14th overall, in 1989 Entry Draft.

Season	Club	League	GP	G	A	Pts	PIM	PP	SH	GW	S	%	+/-	TF	F%	H	SB	Min	GP	G	A	Pts	PIM	PP	SH	GW
1986-87	Three Hills Braves	AAHA	12	10	11	21	8																			
1987-88	Olds Grizzlys	AJHL	51	13	31	44	58																			
	Regina Pats	WHL	5	0	1	1	2												4	1	1	2	2			
1988-89	Regina Pats	WHL	72	10	31	41	99																			
1989-90	Regina Pats	WHL	58	16	37	53	93												11	2	9	11	16			
	Buffalo	**NHL**	**2**	**0**	**0**	**0**	**0**	**0**	**0**	**0**	**1**	**0.0**	**0**													
1990-91	**Buffalo**	**NHL**	**21**	**1**	**8**	**9**	**20**	**1**	**0**	**0**	**42**	**2.4**	**9**						**6**	**1**	**4**	**5**	**10**	**0**	**0**	**0**
	Rochester	AHL	52	2	8	10	53												10	2	1	3	6			
1991-92	**Buffalo**	**NHL**	**58**	**6**	**15**	**21**	**75**	**2**	**0**	**1**	**76**	**7.9**	**–13**													
	Rochester	AHL	4	0	0	0	18																			
	Montreal	**NHL**	**8**	**2**	**2**	**4**	**17**	**1**	**0**	**0**	**9**	**22.2**	**4**						**9**	**0**	**0**	**0**	**6**	**0**	**0**	**0**
1992-93♦	**Montreal**	**NHL**	**73**	**11**	**14**	**25**	**117**	**6**	**0**	**1**	**126**	**8.7**	**7**						**17**	**1**	**6**	**7**	**16**	**1**	**0**	**0**
1993-94	**Montreal**	**NHL**	**68**	**4**	**9**	**13**	**118**	**0**	**0**	**1**	**72**	**5.6**	**3**						**7**	**1**	**1**	**2**	**19**	**0**	**0**	**0**
1994-95	**Philadelphia**	**NHL**	**36**	**2**	**8**	**10**	**48**	**0**	**0**	**0**	**26**	**7.7**	**16**						**15**	**4**	**4**	**8**	**10**	**0**	**1**	**1**
1995-96	**Philadelphia**	**NHL**	**69**	**5**	**9**	**14**	**92**	**0**	**2**	**2**	**89**	**5.6**	**18**						**6**	**0**	**1**	**1**	**8**	**0**	**0**	**0**
1996-97	**Philadelphia**	**NHL**	**27**	**0**	**5**	**5**	**37**	**0**	**0**	**0**	**34**	**0.0**	**–1**													
	Hartford	**NHL**	**35**	**2**	**6**	**8**	**48**	**0**	**0**	**0**	**43**	**4.7**	**–11**													
1997-98	**Carolina**	**NHL**	**65**	**3**	**5**	**8**	**94**	**0**	**0**	**0**	**67**	**4.5**	**–5**													
1998-99	**Anaheim**	**NHL**	**82**	**1**	**6**	**7**	**122**	**0**	**0**	**0**	**64**	**1.6**	**–1**	**0**	**0.0**	**95**	**110**	**20:39**	**4**	**0**	**0**	**0**	**2**	**0**	**0**	**0**
99-2000	**Anaheim**	**NHL**	**67**	**3**	**5**	**8**	**61**	**0**	**0**	**2**	**50**	**6.0**	**–8**	**1**	**100.0**	**107**	**83**	**18:10**								
2000-01	**NY Islanders**	**NHL**	**30**	**1**	**5**	**6**	**56**	**0**	**0**	**0**	**19**	**5.3**	**5**	**0**	**0.0**	**75**	**30**	**19:07**								
	NHL Totals		**641**	**41**	**97**	**138**	**905**	**10**	**2**	**7**	**718**	**5.7**		**1**	**100.0**	**277**	**223**	**19:28**	**64**	**7**	**16**	**23**	**71**	**1**	**1**	**1**

WHL East First All-Star Team (1990)

Traded to **Montreal** by **Buffalo** for Petr Svoboda, March 10, 1992. Traded to **Philadelphia** by **Montreal** for Yves Racine, June 29, 1994. Traded to **Hartford** by **Philadelphia** with Philadelphia's 1st round choice (later traded to San Jose - San Jose selected Scott Hannan) in 1997 Entry Draft and Hartford/Carolina's 7th round choice (previously acquired, Carolina selected Andrew Merrick) in 1997 Entry Draft for Paul Coffey and Hartford/Carolina's 3rd round choice (Kris Mallette) in 1997 Entry Draft, December 15, 1996. Transferred to **Carolina** after **Hartford** franchise relocated, June 25, 1997. Traded to **Anaheim** by **Carolina** with Stu Grimson for David Karpa and Anaheim's 4th round choice (later traded to Atlanta - Atlanta selected Blake Robson) in 2000 Entry Draft, August 11, 1998. Signed as a free agent by **NY Islanders**, July 3, 2000. • Missed majority of 2000-01 season recovering from hernia injury suffered in game vs. Ottawa, December 16, 2000.

HALPERN, Jeff

(HAL-pehrn, JEHF) **WSH.**

Center. Shoots right. 5'11", 195 lbs. Born, Potomac, MD, May 3, 1976.

Season	Club	League	GP	G	A	Pts	PIM	PP	SH	GW	S	%	+/-	TF	F%	H	SB	Min	GP	G	A	Pts	PIM	PP	SH	GW
1994-95	Stratford Cullitons	OJHL-B	44	29	54	83	43																			
1995-96	Princeton	ECAC	29	3	11	14	30																			
1996-97	Princeton	ECAC	33	7	24	31	35																			
1997-98	Princeton	ECAC	36	*28	25	*53	46																			
1998-99	Princeton	ECAC	33	*22	22	44	32																			
	Portland Pirates	AHL	6	2	1	3	4																			
99-2000	**Washington**	**NHL**	**79**	**18**	**11**	**29**	**39**	**4**	**4**	**1**	**108**	**16.7**	**21**	**812**	**51.1**	**84**	**44**	**13:14**	**5**	**2**	**1**	**3**	**0**	**1**	**0**	**1**
2000-01	**Washington**	**NHL**	**80**	**21**	**21**	**42**	**60**	**2**	**1**	**5**	**110**	**19.1**	**13**	**1293**	**52.4**	**92**	**49**	**16:08**	**6**	**2**	**3**	**5**	**17**	**1**	**0**	**1**
	NHL Totals		**159**	**39**	**32**	**71**	**99**	**6**	**5**	**6**	**218**	**17.9**		**2105**	**51.9**	**176**	**93**	**14:42**	**11**	**4**	**4**	**8**	**17**	**2**	**0**	**2**

ECAC Second All-Star Team (1998, 1999)

Signed as a free agent by **Washington**, March 29, 1999.

HAMEL, Denis

(ha-MEHL, deh-NEE) **BUF.**

Left wing. Shoots left. 6'2", 200 lbs. Born, Lachute, Que., May 10, 1977. St. Louis' 5th choice, 153rd overall, in 1995 Entry Draft.

Season	Club	League	GP	G	A	Pts	PIM	PP	SH	GW	S	%	+/-	TF	F%	H	SB	Min	GP	G	A	Pts	PIM	PP	SH	GW
1992-93	Lachute Regents	QAAA	32	18	24	42																				
1993-94	Lac St-Louis	QAAA	28	10	11	21	50																			
	Abitibi Forestiers	QAAA	15	5	7	12	29												5	0	3	3	16			
1994-95	Chicoutimi	QMJHL	66	15	12	27	155												12	2	0	2	27			
1995-96	Chicoutimi	QMJHL	65	40	49	89	199												17	10	14	24	64			
1996-97	Chicoutimi	QMJHL	70	50	50	100	357												20	15	10	25	58			
1997-98	Rochester	AHL	74	10	15	25	98												4	1	2	3	0			
1998-99	Rochester	AHL	74	16	17	33	121												20	3	4	7	10			
99-2000	**Buffalo**	**NHL**	**3**	**1**	**0**	**1**	**0**	**0**	**0**	**0**	**3**	**33.3**	**–1**	**0**	**0.0**	**10**	**0**	**9:45**								
	Rochester	AHL	76	34	24	58	122												21	6	7	13	49			
2000-01	**Buffalo**	**NHL**	**41**	**8**	**3**	**11**	**22**	**1**	**1**	**3**	**55**	**14.5**	**–2**	**171**	**33.9**	**78**	**18**	**10:58**								
	NHL Totals		**44**	**9**	**3**	**12**	**22**	**1**	**1**	**3**	**58**	**15.5**		**171**	**33.9**	**88**	**18**	**10:53**								

Traded to **Buffalo** by **St. Louis** for Charlie Huddy and Buffalo's 7th round choice (Daniel Corso) in 1996 Entry Draft, March 19, 1996. • Missed majority of 2000-01 season recovering from knee injury suffered in game vs. NY Islanders, January 27, 2001.

HAMRLIK, Roman

(HAHM-reh-lik, ROH-muhn) **NYI**

Defense. Shoots left. 6'2", 215 lbs. Born, Gottwaldov, Czech., April 12, 1974. Tampa Bay's 1st choice, 1st overall, in 1992 Entry Draft.

Season	Club	League	GP	G	A	Pts	PIM	PP	SH	GW	S	%	+/-	TF	F%	H	SB	Min	GP	G	A	Pts	PIM	PP	SH	GW
1990-91	ZPS Zlin	Czech.	14	2	2	4	18																			
1991-92	ZPS Zlin	Czech.	34	5	5	10	50																			
1992-93	**Tampa Bay**	**NHL**	**67**	**6**	**15**	**21**	**71**	**1**	**0**	**1**	**113**	**5.3**	**–21**													
	Atlanta Knights	IHL	2	1	1	2	2																			
1993-94	**Tampa Bay**	**NHL**	**64**	**3**	**18**	**21**	**135**	**0**	**0**	**0**	**158**	**1.9**	**–14**													
1994-95	ZPS Zlin	Cze-Rep	2	1	0	1	10																			
	Tampa Bay	**NHL**	**48**	**12**	**11**	**23**	**86**	**7**	**1**	**2**	**134**	**9.0**	**–18**													
1995-96	**Tampa Bay**	**NHL**	**82**	**16**	**49**	**65**	**103**	**12**	**0**	**2**	**281**	**5.7**	**–24**						**5**	**0**	**1**	**1**	**4**	**0**	**0**	**0**
1996-97	**Tampa Bay**	**NHL**	**79**	**12**	**28**	**40**	**57**	**6**	**0**	**0**	**238**	**5.0**	**–29**													
1997-98	**Tampa Bay**	**NHL**	**37**	**3**	**12**	**15**	**22**	**1**	**0**	**0**	**86**	**3.5**	**–18**													
	Edmonton	**NHL**	**41**	**6**	**20**	**26**	**48**	**4**	**1**	**3**	**112**	**5.4**	**3**						**12**	**0**	**6**	**6**	**12**	**0**	**0**	**0**
	Czech-Republic	Olympics	6	1	0	1	2																			
1998-99	**Edmonton**	**NHL**	**75**	**8**	**24**	**32**	**70**	**3**	**0**	**0**	**172**	**4.7**	**9**	**0**	**0.0**	**144**	**121**	**23:49**	**3**	**0**	**0**	**0**	**2**	**0**	**0**	**0**
99-2000	Barum Zlin	Cze-Rep	6	0	3	3	4																			
	Edmonton	**NHL**	**80**	**8**	**37**	**45**	**68**	**5**	**0**	**0**	**180**	**4.4**	**1**	**0**	**0.0**	**122**	**99**	**25:18**	**5**	**0**	**1**	**1**	**4**	**0**	**0**	**0**
2000-01	**NY Islanders**	**NHL**	**76**	**16**	**30**	**46**	**92**	**5**	**1**	**4**	**232**	**6.9**	**–20**	**1**	**100.0**	**156**	**119**	**25:12**								
	NHL Totals		**649**	**90**	**244**	**334**	**752**	**44**	**3**	**12**	**1706**	**5.3**		**1**	**100.0**	**422**	**339**	**24:47**	**25**	**0**	**8**	**8**	**22**	**0**	**0**	**0**

Played in NHL All-Star Game (1996, 1999)

Traded to **Edmonton** by **Tampa Bay** with Paul Comrie for Bryan Marchment, Steve Kelly and Jason Bonsignore, December 30, 1997. Traded to **NY Islanders** by **Edmonton** for Eric Brewer, Josh Green and NY Islanders' 2nd round choice (Brad Winchester) in 2000 Entry Draft, June 24, 2000.

Regular Season / Playoffs

HANDZUS, Michal
(HAHND-zuhs, MEE-chal) **PHX.**

Center. Shoots left. 6'5", 210 lbs. Born, Banska Bystrica, Czech., March 11, 1977. St. Louis' 3rd choice, 101st overall, in 1995 Entry Draft.

Season	Club	League	GP	G	A	Pts	PIM	PP	SH	GW	S	%	+/-	TF	F%	H	SB	Min	GP	G	A	Pts	PIM	PP	SH	GW
1993-94	Banska Bystrica	Slovak-Jr.	40	23	36	59	....	....	....	....	....	....	....	....	....	....	....	....	....	....	....	....	....	....	....	....
1994-95	Banska Bystrica	Slovak-2	22	15	14	29	10	....	....	....	....	....	....	....	....	....	....	....	....	....	....	....	....	....	....	....
1995-96	Banska Bystrica	Slovakia	19	3	1	4	8	....	....	....	....	....	....	....	....	....	....	....	....	....	....	....	....	....	....	....
1996-97	SKP Poprad	Slovakia	44	15	18	33	....	....	....	....	....	....	....	....	....	....	....	....	....	....	....	....	....	....	....	....
1997-98	Worcester	AHL	69	27	36	63	54	....	....	....	....	....	....	....	....	....	....	....	11	2	6	8	10	....	....	....
1998-99	**St. Louis**	**NHL**	**66**	**4**	**12**	**16**	**30**	**0**	**0**	**0**	**78**	**5.1**	**–9**	**794**	**49.9**	**56**	**38**	**14:48**	**11**	**0**	**2**	**2**	**8**	**0**	**0**	**0**
99-2000	**St. Louis**	**NHL**	**81**	**25**	**28**	**53**	**44**	**3**	**4**	**5**	**166**	**15.1**	**19**	**1243**	**51.5**	**50**	**31**	**17:43**	**7**	**0**	**3**	**3**	**6**	**0**	**0**	**0**
2000-01	**St. Louis**	**NHL**	**36**	**10**	**14**	**24**	**12**	**3**	**2**	**2**	**58**	**17.2**	**11**	**581**	**50.6**	**34**	**17**	**17:60**	....	....	....	....	....	....	....	....
	Phoenix	**NHL**	**10**	**4**	**4**	**8**	**21**	**0**	**1**	**0**	**14**	**28.6**	**5**	**111**	**60.4**	**6**	**1**	**15:26**	....	....	....	....	....	....	....	....
	NHL Totals		**193**	**43**	**58**	**101**	**107**	**6**	**7**	**7**	**316**	**13.6**		**2729**	**51.2**	**146**	**87**	**16:39**	**18**	**0**	**5**	**5**	**14**	**0**	**0**	**0**

Traded to **Phoenix** by **St. Louis** with Ladislav Nagy, the rights to Jeff Taffe and St. Louis' 1st round choice in 2002 Entry Draft for Keith Tkachuk, March 13, 2001.

HANKINSON, Casey
(HAN-kihn-suhn, KAY-see) **CHI.**

Left wing. Shoots left. 6'1", 187 lbs. Born, Edina, MN, May 8, 1976. Chicago's 9th choice, 201st overall, in 1995 Entry Draft.

Season	Club	League	GP	G	A	Pts	PIM	PP	SH	GW	S	%	+/-	TF	F%	H	SB	Min	GP	G	A	Pts	PIM	PP	SH	GW
1992-93	Edina High	Hi-School	25	20	26	46	....	....	....	....	....	....	....	....	....	....	....	....	....	....	....	....	....	....	....	....
1993-94	Edina High	Hi-School	24	21	20	41	50	....	....	....	....	....	....	....	....	....	....	....	....	....	....	....	....	....	....	....
1994-95	U. of Minnesota	WCHA	33	7	1	8	86	....	....	....	....	....	....	....	....	....	....	....	....	....	....	....	....	....	....	....
1995-96	U. of Minnesota	WCHA	39	16	19	35	101	....	....	....	....	....	....	....	....	....	....	....	....	....	....	....	....	....	....	....
1996-97	U. of Minnesota	WCHA	42	17	24	41	79	....	....	....	....	....	....	....	....	....	....	....	....	....	....	....	....	....	....	....
1997-98	U. of Minnesota	WCHA	35	10	12	22	81	....	....	....	....	....	....	....	....	....	....	....	....	....	....	....	....	....	....	....
1998-99	Portland Pirates	AHL	72	10	13	23	106	....	....	....	....	....	....	....	....	....	....	....	....	....	....	....	....	....	....	....
99-2000	Cleveland	IHL	82	7	22	29	140	....	....	....	....	....	....	....	....	....	....	....	2	0	0	0	2	....	....	....
2000-01	**Chicago**	**NHL**	**11**	**0**	**1**	**1**	**9**	**0**	**0**	**0**	**15**	**0.0**	**–3**	**0**	**0.0**	**30**	**3**	**9:46**	....	....	....	....	....	....	....	....
	Norfolk Admirals	AHL	69	30	21	51	74	....	....	....	....	....	....	....	....	....	....	....	9	5	4	9	2	....	....	....
	NHL Totals		**11**	**0**	**1**	**1**	**9**	**0**	**0**	**0**	**15**	**0.0**		**0**	**0.0**	**30**	**3**	**9:46**	....	....	....	....	....	....	....	....

HANNAN, Scott
(HAN-nan, SKAWT) **S.J.**

Defense. Shoots left. 6'2", 220 lbs. Born, Richmond, B.C., January 23, 1979. San Jose's 2nd choice, 23rd overall, in 1997 Entry Draft.

Season	Club	League	GP	G	A	Pts	PIM	PP	SH	GW	S	%	+/-	TF	F%	H	SB	Min	GP	G	A	Pts	PIM	PP	SH	GW
1994-95	Surrey Wolves	BCAHA	70	54	54	108	200	....	....	....	....	....	....	....	....	....	....	....	....	....	....	....	....	....	....	....
	Tacoma Rockets	WHL	2	0	0	0	0	....	....	....	....	....	....	....	....	....	....	....	....	....	....	....	....	....	....	....
1995-96	Kelowna Rockets	WHL	69	4	5	9	76	....	....	....	....	....	....	....	....	....	....	....	6	0	1	1	4	....	....	....
1996-97	Kelowna Rockets	WHL	70	17	26	43	101	....	....	....	....	....	....	....	....	....	....	....	6	0	0	0	8	....	....	....
1997-98	Kelowna Rockets	WHL	47	10	30	40	70	....	....	....	....	....	....	....	....	....	....	....	7	2	7	9	14	....	....	....
1998-99	**San Jose**	**NHL**	**5**	**0**	**2**	**2**	**6**	**0**	**0**	**0**	**4**	**0.0**	**0**	**0**	**0.0**	**2**	**0**	**7:15**	....	....	....	....	....	....	....	....
	Kelowna Rockets	WHL	47	15	30	45	92	....	....	....	....	....	....	....	....	....	....	....	6	1	2	3	14	....	....	....
	Kentucky	AHL	2	0	0	0	2	....	....	....	....	....	....	....	....	....	....	....	12	0	2	2	10	....	....	....
99-2000	**San Jose**	**NHL**	**30**	**1**	**2**	**3**	**10**	**0**	**0**	**0**	**28**	**3.6**	**7**	**1**	**0.0**	**27**	**9**	**17:09**	**1**	**0**	**1**	**1**	**0**	**0**	**0**	**0**
	Kentucky	AHL	41	5	12	17	40	....	....	....	....	....	....	....	....	....	....	....	....	....	....	....	....	....	....	....
2000-01	**San Jose**	**NHL**	**75**	**3**	**14**	**17**	**51**	**0**	**0**	**1**	**96**	**3.1**	**10**	**0**	**0.0**	**109**	**67**	**19:02**	**6**	**0**	**1**	**1**	**6**	**0**	**0**	**0**
	NHL Totals		**110**	**4**	**18**	**22**	**67**	**0**	**0**	**1**	**128**	**3.1**		**1**	**0.0**	**138**	**76**	**17:59**	**7**	**0**	**2**	**2**	**6**	**0**	**0**	**0**

WHL West First All-Star Team (1999)

HANSEN, Tavis
(HAN-sehn, TA-vihs)

Center. Shoots right. 6'1", 205 lbs. Born, Prince Albert, Sask., June 17, 1975. Winnipeg's 3rd choice, 58th overall, in 1994 Entry Draft.

Season	Club	League	GP	G	A	Pts	PIM	PP	SH	GW	S	%	+/-	TF	F%	H	SB	Min	GP	G	A	Pts	PIM	PP	SH	GW
1992-93	Shellbrook	SAHA	42	42	63	105	107	....	....	....	....	....	....	....	....	....	....	....	....	....	....	....	....	....	....	....
1993-94	Tacoma Rockets	WHL	71	23	31	54	122	....	....	....	....	....	....	....	....	....	....	....	8	1	3	4	17	....	....	....
1994-95	Tacoma Rockets	WHL	71	32	41	73	142	....	....	....	....	....	....	....	....	....	....	....	4	1	1	2	8	....	....	....
	Winnipeg	**NHL**	**1**	**0**	**0**	**0**	**0**	**0**	**0**	**0**	**0**	**0.0**	**0**	....	....	....	....	....	....	....	....	....	....	....	....	....
1995-96	Springfield	AHL	67	6	16	22	85	....	....	....	....	....	....	....	....	....	....	....	5	1	2	3	2	....	....	....
1996-97	**Phoenix**	**NHL**	**1**	**0**	**0**	**0**	**0**	**0**	**0**	**0**	**0**	**0.0**	**0**	....	....	....	....	....	....	....	....	....	....	....	....	....
	Springfield	AHL	12	3	1	4	23	....	....	....	....	....	....	....	....	....	....	....	....	....	....	....	....	....	....	....
1997-98	Springfield	AHL	73	20	14	34	70	....	....	....	....	....	....	....	....	....	....	....	4	1	2	3	18	....	....	....
1998-99	**Phoenix**	**NHL**	**20**	**2**	**1**	**3**	**12**	**0**	**0**	**0**	**14**	**14.3**	**–4**	**5**	**80.0**	**26**	**3**	**8:07**	**2**	**0**	**0**	**0**	**0**	**0**	**0**	**0**
	Springfield	AHL	63	23	11	34	85	....	....	....	....	....	....	....	....	....	....	....	3	0	1	1	5	....	....	....
99-2000	**Phoenix**	**NHL**	**5**	**0**	**0**	**0**	**0**	**0**	**0**	**0**	**2**	**0.0**	**0**	**0**	**0.0**	**2**	**1**	**4:17**	....	....	....	....	....	....	....	....
	Springfield	AHL	59	21	27	48	164	....	....	....	....	....	....	....	....	....	....	....	5	2	1	3	4	....	....	....
2000-01	**Phoenix**	**NHL**	**7**	**0**	**0**	**0**	**4**	**0**	**0**	**0**	**2**	**0.0**	**–1**	**1**	**100.0**	**9**	**1**	**5:05**	....	....	....	....	....	....	....	....
	Springfield	AHL	24	6	10	16	81	....	....	....	....	....	....	....	....	....	....	....	....	....	....	....	....	....	....	....
	NHL Totals		**34**	**2**	**1**	**3**	**16**	**0**	**0**	**0**	**18**	**11.1**		**6**	**83.3**	**37**	**5**	**6:51**	**2**	**0**	**0**	**0**	**0**	**0**	**0**	**0**

Transferred to **Phoenix** after **Winnipeg** franchise relocated, July 1, 1996. • Missed majority of 2000-01 season recovering from arm injury suffered in game vs. Hershey (AHL), February 3, 2001.

HARKINS, Brett
(HAHR-kihns, BREHT) **CBJ**

Left wing. Shoots left. 6'1", 185 lbs. Born, North Ridgeville, OH, July 2, 1970. NY Islanders' 9th choice, 133rd overall, in 1989 Entry Draft.

Season	Club	League	GP	G	A	Pts	PIM	PP	SH	GW	S	%	+/-	TF	F%	H	SB	Min	GP	G	A	Pts	PIM	PP	SH	GW
1986-87	St. Andrews	Hi-School	30	47	60	107	....	....	....	....	....	....	....	....	....	....	....	....	....	....	....	....	....	....	....	....
1987-88	Brockville Braves	OCJHL	55	21	55	76	36	....	....	....	....	....	....	....	....	....	....	....	....	....	....	....	....	....	....	....
1988-89	Det-Compuware	NAJHL	38	23	46	69	94	....	....	....	....	....	....	....	....	....	....	....	....	....	....	....	....	....	....	....
1989-90	Bowling Green	CCHA	41	11	43	54	45	....	....	....	....	....	....	....	....	....	....	....	....	....	....	....	....	....	....	....
1990-91	Bowling Green	CCHA	40	22	38	60	30	....	....	....	....	....	....	....	....	....	....	....	....	....	....	....	....	....	....	....
1991-92	Bowling Green	CCHA	34	8	39	47	32	....	....	....	....	....	....	....	....	....	....	....	....	....	....	....	....	....	....	....
1992-93	Bowling Green	CCHA	35	19	28	47	28	....	....	....	....	....	....	....	....	....	....	....	....	....	....	....	....	....	....	....
1993-94	Adirondack	AHL	80	22	47	69	23	....	....	....	....	....	....	....	....	....	....	....	10	1	5	6	4	....	....	....
1994-95	Providence Bruins	AHL	80	23	*69	92	32	....	....	....	....	....	....	....	....	....	....	....	13	8	14	22	4	....	....	....
	Boston	**NHL**	**1**	**0**	**1**	**1**	**0**	**0**	**0**	**0**	**1**	**0.0**	**0**	....	....	....	....	....	....	....	....	....	....	....	....	....
1995-96	**Florida**	**NHL**	**8**	**0**	**3**	**3**	**6**	**0**	**0**	**0**	**4**	**0.0**	**–2**	....	....	....	....	....	....	....	....	....	....	....	....	....
	Carolina	AHL	55	23	*71	94	44	....	....	....	....	....	....	....	....	....	....	....	....	....	....	....	....	....	....	....
1996-97	**Boston**	**NHL**	**44**	**4**	**14**	**18**	**8**	**3**	**0**	**2**	**52**	**7.7**	**–3**	....	....	....	....	....	....	....	....	....	....	....	....	....
	Providence Bruins	AHL	28	9	31	40	32	....	....	....	....	....	....	....	....	....	....	....	10	2	10	12	0	....	....	....
1997-98	Cleveland	IHL	80	32	62	94	82	....	....	....	....	....	....	....	....	....	....	....	10	4	13	17	14	....	....	....
1998-99	Cleveland	IHL	74	20	67	87	84	....	....	....	....	....	....	....	....	....	....	....	....	....	....	....	....	....	....	....
99-2000	Cleveland	IHL	76	20	50	70	79	....	....	....	....	....	....	....	....	....	....	....	9	2	8	10	6	....	....	....
2000-01	Houston Aeros	IHL	81	16	*64	80	51	....	....	....	....	....	....	....	....	....	....	....	7	0	3	3	8	....	....	....
	NHL Totals		**53**	**4**	**18**	**22**	**14**	**3**	**0**	**2**	**57**	**7.0**		....	....	....	....	....	....	....	....	....	....	....	....	....

Signed as a free agent by **Boston**, July 1, 1994. Signed as a free agent by **Florida**, July 24, 1995. Signed as a free agent by **Boston**, September 4, 1996. Signed as a free agent by **Columbus**, May 29, 2001.

HARLOCK, David
(HAHR-lahk, DAY-vihd) **ATL.**

Defense. Shoots left. 6'2", 215 lbs. Born, Toronto, Ont., March 16, 1971. New Jersey's 2nd choice, 24th overall, in 1990 Entry Draft.

Season	Club	League	GP	G	A	Pts	PIM	PP	SH	GW	S	%	+/-	TF	F%	H	SB	Min	GP	G	A	Pts	PIM	PP	SH	GW
1986-87	Toronto Wings	MTHL	86	17	55	72	60	....	....	....	....	....	....	....	....	....	....	....	....	....	....	....	....	....	....	....
1987-88	Toronto Wings	MTHL	70	16	56	72	100	....	....	....	....	....	....	....	....	....	....	....	....	....	....	....	....	....	....	....
	Henry Carr	MTJHL	3	0	0	0	4	....	....	....	....	....	....	....	....	....	....	....	....	....	....	....	....	....	....	....
1988-89	St. Michael's	MTJHL	25	4	16	20	34	....	....	....	....	....	....	....	....	....	....	....	27	3	12	15	14	....	....	....
1989-90	U. of Michigan	CCHA	42	2	13	15	44	....	....	....	....	....	....	....	....	....	....	....	....	....	....	....	....	....	....	....
1990-91	U. of Michigan	CCHA	39	2	8	10	70	....	....	....	....	....	....	....	....	....	....	....	....	....	....	....	....	....	....	....
1991-92	U. of Michigan	CCHA	44	1	6	7	80	....	....	....	....	....	....	....	....	....	....	....	....	....	....	....	....	....	....	....
1992-93	U. of Michigan	CCHA	38	3	9	12	58	....	....	....	....	....	....	....	....	....	....	....	....	....	....	....	....	....	....	....
1993-94	Canada	Nat-Team	41	0	3	3	28	....	....	....	....	....	....	....	....	....	....	....	....	....	....	....	....	....	....	....
	Canada	Olympics	8	0	0	0	8	....	....	....	....	....	....	....	....	....	....	....	....	....	....	....	....	....	....	....
	Toronto	**NHL**	**6**	**0**	**0**	**0**	**0**	**0**	**0**	**0**	**2**	**0.0**	**–2**	....	....	....	....	....	....	....	....	....	....	....	....	....
	St. John's Leafs	AHL	10	0	3	3	2	....	....	....	....	....	....	....	....	....	....	....	9	0	0	0	6	....	....	....
1994-95	St. John's Leafs	AHL	58	0	6	6	44	....	....	....	....	....	....	....	....	....	....	....	5	0	0	0	0	....	....	....
	Toronto	**NHL**	**1**	**0**	**0**	**0**	**0**	**0**	**0**	**0**	**0**	**0.0**	**–1**	....	....	....	....	....	....	....	....	....	....	....	....	....

			Regular Season																	Playoffs							
Season	Club	League	GP	G	A	Pts	PIM	PP	SH	GW	S	%	+/-	TF	F%	H	SB	Min	GP	G	A	Pts	PIM	PP	SH	GW
1995-96	Toronto	NHL	1	0	0	0	0	0	0	0	0	0.0	0	....	....	....	....	....	....	....	....	....	....	....	....	....
	St. John's Leafs	AHL	77	0	12	12	92	....	....	....	....	....	....	....	....	....	....	....	4	0	1	1	2	....	....	....
1996-97	San Antonio	IHL	69	3	10	13	82	....	....	....	....	....	....	....	....	....	....	....	9	0	0	0	10	....	....	....
1997-98	Washington	NHL	6	0	0	0	4	0	0	0	2	0.0	2	....	....	....	....	....	....	....	....	....	....	....	....	....
	Portland Pirates	AHL	71	3	15	18	66	....	....	....	....	....	....	....	....	....	....	....	10	2	2	4	6	....	....	....
1998-99	NY Islanders	NHL	70	2	6	8	68	0	0	0	35	5.7	–16	0	0.0	172	65	18:15	....	....	....	....	....	....	....	....
99-2000	Atlanta	NHL	44	0	6	6	36	0	0	0	29	0.0	–8	0	0.0	166	55	19:41	....	....	....	....	....	....	....	....
2000-01	Atlanta	NHL	65	0	1	1	62	0	0	0	26	0.0	–28	0	0.0	186	87	17:04	....	....	....	....	....	....	....	....
	NHL Totals		193	2	13	15	170	0	0	0	94	2.1		0	0.0	524	207	18:10	....	....	....	....	....	....	....	....

Signed as a free agent by **Toronto**, August 20, 1993. Signed as a free agent by **Washington**, August 20, 1997. Signed as a free agent by **NY Islanders**, August 24, 1998. Claimed by **Atlanta** from **NY Islanders** in Expansion Draft, June 25, 1999.

HARTNELL, Scott

(HAHRT-nuhl, SKAWT) **NSH.**

Left wing. Shoots left. 6'2", 208 lbs. Born, Regina, Sask., April 18, 1982. Nashville's 1st choice, 6th overall, in 2000 Entry Draft.

1997-98	Lloydminster	AJHL	56	9	25	34	82	....	....	....	....	....	....	....	....	....	....	....	4	2	1	3	8	....	....	....
	Prince Albert	WHL	1	0	1	1	2	....	....	....	....	....	....	....	....	....	....	....	....	....	....	....	....	....	....	....
1998-99	Prince Albert	WHL	65	10	34	44	104	....	....	....	....	....	....	....	....	....	....	....	14	0	5	5	22	....	....	....
99-2000	Prince Albert	WHL	62	27	55	82	124	....	....	....	....	....	....	....	....	....	....	....	6	3	2	5	6	....	....	....
2000-01	Nashville	NHL	75	2	14	16	48	0	0	0	92	2.2	–8	3	33.3	100	22	10:54	....	....	....	....	....	....	....	....
	NHL Totals		75	2	14	16	48	0	0	0	92	2.2		3	33.3	100	22	10:54	....	....	....	....	....	....	....	....

HARVEY, Todd

(HAHR-vee, TAWD) **S.J.**

Center. Shoots right. 6', 200 lbs. Born, Hamilton, Ont., February 17, 1975. Dallas' 1st choice, 9th overall, in 1993 Entry Draft.

1989-90	Cambridge Hawks	OJHL-B	41	35	27	62	213	....	....	....	....	....	....	....	....	....	....	....	....	....	....	....	....	....	....	....
1990-91	Cambridge Hawks	OJHL-B	35	32	39	71	174	....	....	....	....	....	....	....	....	....	....	....	....	....	....	....	....	....	....	....
1991-92	Detroit	OHL	58	21	43	64	141	....	....	....	....	....	....	....	....	....	....	....	7	3	5	8	30	....	....	....
1992-93	Detroit Jr. Wings	OHL	55	50	50	100	83	....	....	....	....	....	....	....	....	....	....	....	15	9	12	21	39	....	....	....
1993-94	Detroit Jr. Wings	OHL	49	34	51	85	75	....	....	....	....	....	....	....	....	....	....	....	17	10	12	22	26	....	....	....
1994-95	Detroit Jr. Wings	OHL	11	8	14	22	12	....	....	....	....	....	....	....	....	....	....	....	....	....	....	....	....	....	....	....
	Dallas	NHL	40	11	9	20	67	2	0	1	64	17.2	–3	....	....	....	....	....	5	0	0	0	8	0	0	0
1995-96	Dallas	NHL	69	9	20	29	136	3	0	1	101	8.9	–13	....	....	....	....	....	....	....	....	....	....	....	....	....
	Michigan K-Wings	IHL	5	1	3	4	8	....	....	....	....	....	....	....	....	....	....	....	....	....	....	....	....	....	....	....
1996-97	Dallas	NHL	71	9	22	31	142	1	0	2	99	9.1	19	....	....	....	....	....	7	0	1	1	10	0	0	0
1997-98	Dallas	NHL	59	9	10	19	104	0	0	1	88	10.2	5	....	....	....	....	....	....	....	....	....	....	....	....	....
1998-99	NY Rangers	NHL	37	11	17	28	72	6	0	2	58	19.0	–1	175	50.3	126	22	17:19	....	....	....	....	....	....	....	....
99-2000	NY Rangers	NHL	31	3	3	6	62	0	0	0	31	9.7	–9	173	49.1	94	20	12:21	....	....	....	....	....	....	....	....
	San Jose	NHL	40	8	4	12	78	2	0	0	59	13.6	–2	44	43.2	94	9	12:55	12	1	0	1	8	1	0	0
2000-01	San Jose	NHL	69	10	11	21	72	1	0	2	66	15.2	6	98	40.8	178	7	11:05	6	0	0	0	8	0	0	0
	NHL Totals		416	70	96	166	733	15	0	9	566	12.4		490	47.3	492	58	13:01	30	1	1	2	34	1	0	0

Traded to **NY Rangers** by **Dallas** with Bob Errey and Dallas' 4th round choice (Boyd Kane) in 1998 Entry Draft for Brian Skrudland, Mike Keane and NY Rangers' 6th round choice (Pavel Patera) in 1998 Entry Draft, March 24, 1998. Traded to **San Jose** by **NY Rangers** with NY Rangers' 4th round choice (Dimitri Patzold) in 2001 Entry Draft for Radek Dvorak, December 30, 1999.

HATCHER, Derian

(HAT-chuhr, DAIR-ee-an) **DAL.**

Defense. Shoots left. 6'5", 230 lbs. Born, Sterling Heights, MI, June 4, 1972. Minnesota's 1st choice, 8th overall, in 1990 Entry Draft.

1987-88	Detroit G.P.D.	MNHL	25	5	13	18	52	....	....	....	....	....	....	....	....	....	....	....	....	....	....	....	....	....	....	....
1988-89	Detroit G.P.D.	MNHL	51	19	35	54	100	....	....	....	....	....	....	....	....	....	....	....	....	....	....	....	....	....	....	....
1989-90	North Bay	OHL	64	14	38	52	81	....	....	....	....	....	....	....	....	....	....	....	5	2	3	5	8	....	....	....
1990-91	North Bay	OHL	64	13	49	62	163	....	....	....	....	....	....	....	....	....	....	....	10	2	10	12	28	....	....	....
1991-92	Minnesota	NHL	43	8	4	12	88	0	0	2	51	15.7	7	....	....	....	....	....	5	0	2	2	8	0	0	0
1992-93	Minnesota	NHL	67	4	15	19	178	0	0	1	73	5.5	–27	....	....	....	....	....	....	....	....	....	....	....	....	....
	Kalamazoo	IHL	2	1	2	3	21	....	....	....	....	....	....	....	....	....	....	....	....	....	....	....	....	....	....	....
1993-94	Dallas	NHL	83	12	19	31	211	2	1	2	132	9.1	19	....	....	....	....	....	9	0	2	2	14	0	0	0
1994-95	Dallas	NHL	43	5	11	16	105	2	0	2	74	6.8	3	....	....	....	....	....	....	....	....	....	....	....	....	....
1995-96	Dallas	NHL	79	8	23	31	129	2	0	1	125	6.4	–12	....	....	....	....	....	....	....	....	....	....	....	....	....
1996-97	Dallas	NHL	63	3	19	22	97	0	0	0	96	3.1	8	....	....	....	....	....	7	0	2	2	20	0	0	0
1997-98	Dallas	NHL	70	6	25	31	132	3	0	2	74	8.1	9	....	....	....	....	....	17	3	3	6	39	2	0	0
	United States	Olympics	4	0	0	0	0	....	....	....	....	....	....	....	....	....	....	....	....	....	....	....	....	....	....	....
1998-99♦	Dallas	NHL	80	9	21	30	102	3	0	2	125	7.2	21	0	0.0	204	97	24:44	18	1	6	7	24	0	0	0
99-2000	Dallas	NHL	57	2	22	24	68	0	0	0	90	2.2	6	0	0.0	179	82	27:33	23	1	3	4	29	0	0	0
2000-01	Dallas	NHL	80	2	21	23	77	1	0	2	97	2.1	5	0	0.0	250	114	25:53	10	0	1	1	16	0	0	0
	NHL Totals		665	59	180	239	1187	13	1	14	937	6.3		0	0.0	633	293	25:54	89	5	19	24	150	2	0	0

Played in NHL All-Star Game (1997)

Transferred to **Dallas** after **Minnesota** franchise relocated, June 9, 1993.

HATCHER, Kevin

(HAT-chuhr, KEH-vihn)

Defense. Shoots right. 6'3", 230 lbs. Born, Detroit, MI, September 9, 1966. Washington's 1st choice, 17th overall, in 1984 Entry Draft.

1982-83	Det-Compuware	MNHL	75	30	45	75	120	....	....	....	....	....	....	....	....	....	....	....	....	....	....	....	....	....	....	....
1983-84	North Bay	OHL	67	10	39	49	61	....	....	....	....	....	....	....	....	....	....	....	4	2	2	4	11	....	....	....
1984-85	North Bay	OHL	58	26	37	63	75	....	....	....	....	....	....	....	....	....	....	....	8	3	8	11	9	....	....	....
	Washington	NHL	2	1	0	1	0	0	1	0	3	33.3	1	....	....	....	....	....	1	0	0	0	0	0	0	0
1985-86	Washington	NHL	79	9	10	19	119	1	0	1	132	6.8	6	....	....	....	....	....	9	1	1	2	19	0	0	0
1986-87	Washington	NHL	78	8	16	24	144	1	0	2	100	8.0	–29	....	....	....	....	....	7	1	0	1	20	0	0	0
1987-88	Washington	NHL	71	14	27	41	137	5	0	3	181	7.7	1	....	....	....	....	....	14	5	7	12	55	1	0	1
1988-89	Washington	NHL	62	13	27	40	101	3	0	2	148	8.8	19	....	....	....	....	....	6	1	4	5	20	1	0	0
1989-90	Washington	NHL	80	13	41	54	102	4	0	2	240	5.4	4	....	....	....	....	....	11	0	8	8	32	0	0	0
1990-91	Washington	NHL	79	24	50	74	69	9	2	3	267	9.0	–10	....	....	....	....	....	11	3	3	6	8	2	0	0
1991-92	Washington	NHL	79	17	37	54	105	8	1	2	246	6.9	18	....	....	....	....	....	7	2	4	6	19	0	1	0
1992-93	Washington	NHL	83	34	45	79	114	13	1	6	329	10.3	–7	....	....	....	....	....	6	0	1	1	14	0	0	0
1993-94	Washington	NHL	72	16	24	40	108	6	0	3	217	7.4	–13	....	....	....	....	....	11	3	4	7	37	0	1	0
1994-95	Dallas	NHL	47	10	19	29	66	3	0	2	138	7.2	–4	....	....	....	....	....	5	2	1	3	2	1	0	1
1995-96	Dallas	NHL	74	15	26	41	58	7	0	3	237	6.3	–24	....	....	....	....	....	....	....	....	....	....	....	....	....
1996-97	Pittsburgh	NHL	80	15	39	54	103	9	0	1	199	7.5	11	....	....	....	....	....	5	1	1	2	4	1	0	0
1997-98	Pittsburgh	NHL	74	19	29	48	66	13	1	3	169	11.2	–3	....	....	....	....	....	6	1	0	1	12	1	0	0
	United States	Olympics	3	0	2	2	0	....	....	....	....	....	....	....	....	....	....	....	....	....	....	....	....	....	....	....
1998-99	Pittsburgh	NHL	66	11	27	38	24	4	2	3	131	8.4	11	2	50.0	87	102	24:38	13	2	3	5	4	1	0	0
99-2000	NY Rangers	NHL	74	4	19	23	38	2	0	0	112	3.6	–10	0	0.0	135	123	21:11	....	....	....	....	....	....	....	....
2000-01	Carolina	NHL	57	4	14	18	38	3	0	1	98	4.1	2	0	0.0	60	99	23:23	6	0	0	0	6	0	0	0
	NHL Totals		1157	227	450	677	1392	91	8	37	2947	7.7		2	50.0	282	324	22:59	118	22	37	59	252	8	2	2

OHL Second All-Star Team (1985) • Played in NHL All-Star Game (1990, 1991, 1992, 1996, 1997)

Traded to **Dallas** by **Washington** for Mark Tinordi and Rick Mrozik, January 18, 1995. Traded to **Pittsburgh** by **Dallas** for Sergei Zubov, June 22, 1996. Traded to **NY Rangers** by **Pittsburgh** for Peter Popovic, September 30, 1999. Signed as a free agent by **Carolina**, July 31, 2000.

HAUER, Brett

(HOW-uhr, BREHT) **L.A.**

Defense. Shoots right. 6'2", 210 lbs. Born, Richfield, MN, July 11, 1971. Vancouver's 3rd choice, 71st overall, in 1989 Entry Draft.

1987-88	Richfield Spartans	Hi-School	24	3	3	6		....	....	....	....	....	....	....	....	....	....	....	....	....	....	....	....	....	....	....
1988-89	Richfield Spartans	Hi-School	24	8	15	23	70	....	....	....	....	....	....	....	....	....	....	....	....	....	....	....	....	....	....	....
1989-90	Minnesota-Duluth	WCHA	37	2	6	8	44	....	....	....	....	....	....	....	....	....	....	....	....	....	....	....	....	....	....	....
1990-91	Minnesota-Duluth	WCHA	30	1	7	8	54	....	....	....	....	....	....	....	....	....	....	....	....	....	....	....	....	....	....	....
1991-92	Minnesota-Duluth	WCHA	33	8	14	22	40	....	....	....	....	....	....	....	....	....	....	....	....	....	....	....	....	....	....	....
1992-93	Minnesota-Duluth	WCHA	40	10	46	56	52	....	....	....	....	....	....	....	....	....	....	....	....	....	....	....	....	....	....	....
1993-94	United States	Nat-Team	57	6	14	20	88	....	....	....	....	....	....	....	....	....	....	....	....	....	....	....	....	....	....	....
	United States	Olympics	8	0	0	0	10	....	....	....	....	....	....	....	....	....	....	....	....	....	....	....	....	....	....	....
	Las Vegas	IHL	21	0	7	7	8	....	....	....	....	....	....	....	....	....	....	....	1	0	0	0	0	....	....	....

			Regular Season																Playoffs							
Season	Club	League	GP	G	A	Pts	PIM	PP	SH	GW	S	%	+/-	TF	F%	H	SB	Min	GP	G	A	Pts	PIM	PP	SH	GW
1994-95	AIK Solna	Sweden	37	1	3	4	38																			
1995-96	**Edmonton**	**NHL**	**29**	**4**	**2**	**6**	**30**	**2**	**0**	**1**	**53**	**7.5**	**-11**													
	Cape Breton	AHL	17	3	5	8	29																			
1996-97	Chicago Wolves	IHL	81	10	30	40	50												4	2	0	2	4			
1997-98	Manitoba Moose	IHL	82	13	48	61	58												3	0	0	0	2			
1998-99	Manitoba Moose	IHL	81	15	56	71	66												5	0	5	5	4			
99-2000	**Edmonton**	**NHL**	**5**	**0**	**2**	**2**	**2**	**0**	**0**	**0**	**8**	**0.0**	**-2**	**0**	**0.0**	**10**	**2**	**14:48**								
	Manitoba Moose	IHL	77	13	47	60	92												2	0	1	1	2			
2000-01	Manitoba Moose	IHL	82	17	42	59	52												13	1	9	10	12			
	NHL Totals		**34**	**4**	**4**	**8**	**32**	**2**	**0**	**1**	**61**	**6.6**		**0**	**0.0**	**10**	**2**	**14:48**								

WCHA First All-Star Team (1993) • NCAA West First All-American Team (1993) • IHL First All-Star Team (1999, 2000, 2001) • Won Govenors' Trophy (Top Defenseman - IHL) (2000, 2001)

Traded to **Edmonton** by **Vancouver** for Edmonton's 7th round choice (Larry Shapley) in 1997 Entry Draft, August 24, 1995. Signed as a free agent by **Manitoba** (IHL), September 15, 1997. Signed as a free agent by **LA Kings**, July 8, 2001.

HAVELID, Niclas
(HAHV-lihd, NIHK-lahs) **ANA.**

Defense. Shoots left. 5'11", 196 lbs. Born, Stockholm, Sweden, April 12, 1973. Anaheim's 2nd choice, 83rd overall, in 1999 Entry Draft.

Season	Club	League	GP	G	A	Pts	PIM	PP	SH	GW	S	%	+/-	TF	F%	H	SB	Min	GP	G	A	Pts	PIM	PP	SH	GW
1988-89	Enkopings SK	Sweden-3	7	0	1	1	0																			
1989-90	Enkopings SK	Sweden-3	24	1	2	3	28																			
1990-91	RA-73	Sweden-2	30	2	3	5	22																			
1991-92	AIK Solna	Sweden	10	0	0	0	2																			
1992-93	AIK Solna	Sweden	30	1	2	3	22												3	0	0	0	2			
1993-94	AIK Solna	Sweden-2	22	3	9	12	14																			
1994-95	AIK Solna	Sweden	40	3	7	10	38																			
1995-96	AIK Solna	Sweden	40	5	6	11	30																			
1996-97	AIK Solna	Sweden	49	3	6	9	42												7	1	2	3	8			
1997-98	AIK Solna	Sweden	43	8	4	12	42												10	1	3	4	39			
1998-99	Malmo IF	Sweden	50	10	12	22	42												8	0	4	4	10			
99-2000	**Anaheim**	**NHL**	**50**	**2**	**7**	**9**	**20**	**0**	**0**	**2**	**70**	**2.9**	**0**	**1**	**0.0**	**103**	**66**	**19:10**								
	Cincinnati Ducks	AHL	2	0	0	0	0																			
2000-01	**Anaheim**	**NHL**	**47**	**4**	**10**	**14**	**34**	**2**	**0**	**1**	**69**	**5.8**	**-6**	**4**	**0.0**	**101**	**54**	**21:51**								
	NHL Totals		**97**	**6**	**17**	**23**	**54**	**2**	**0**	**3**	**139**	**4.3**		**5**	**0.0**	**204**	**120**	**20:28**								

HAVLAT, Martin
(HAHV-lat, MAHR-tihn) **OTT.**

Center. Shoots left. 6'1", 190 lbs. Born, Mlada Boleslav, Czech., April 19, 1981. Ottawa's 1st choice, 26th overall, in 1999 Entry Draft.

Season	Club	League	GP	G	A	Pts	PIM	PP	SH	GW	S	%	+/-	TF	F%	H	SB	Min	GP	G	A	Pts	PIM	PP	SH	GW
1997-98	Ytong Brno-Jr.	Cze-Rep	32	38	29	67	....																			
1998-99	HC Trinec-Jr.	Cze-Rep	31	28	23	51	....																			
	HC Trinec	Cze-Rep	24	2	3	5	4												8	0	0	0	....			
99-2000	HC Trinec	Cze-Rep	46	13	29	42	42												4	0	2	2	8			
2000-01	**Ottawa**	**NHL**	**73**	**19**	**23**	**42**	**20**	**7**	**0**	**5**	**133**	**14.3**	**8**	**40**	**30.0**	**68**	**9**	**13:47**	**4**	**0**	**0**	**0**	**2**	**0**	**0**	**0**
	NHL Totals		**73**	**19**	**23**	**42**	**20**	**7**	**0**	**5**	**133**	**14.3**		**40**	**30.0**	**68**	**9**	**13:47**	**4**	**0**	**0**	**0**	**2**	**0**	**0**	**0**

NHL All-Rookie Team (2001)

HAWGOOD, Greg
(HAW-guhd, GREHG) **DAL.**

Defense. Shoots left. 5'10", 190 lbs. Born, Edmonton, Alta., August 10, 1968. Boston's 9th choice, 202nd overall, in 1986 Entry Draft.

Season	Club	League	GP	G	A	Pts	PIM	PP	SH	GW	S	%	+/-	TF	F%	H	SB	Min	GP	G	A	Pts	PIM	PP	SH	GW
1983-84	Kamloops Blazers	WHL	49	10	23	33	39												6	0	2	2	2			
1984-85	Kamloops Blazers	WHL	66	25	40	65	72												15	3	15	18	15			
1985-86	Kamloops Blazers	WHL	71	34	85	119	86												16	9	22	31	16			
1986-87	Kamloops Blazers	WHL	61	30	93	123	139												13	7	16	23	18			
1987-88	Kamloops Blazers	WHL	63	48	85	133	142												16	10	16	26	33			
	Boston	**NHL**	**1**	**0**	**0**	**0**	**0**	**0**	**0**	**0**	**1**	**0.0**	**-1**						**3**	**1**	**0**	**1**	**0**	**0**	**0**	**0**
1988-89	**Boston**	**NHL**	**56**	**16**	**24**	**40**	**84**	**5**	**0**	**0**	**132**	**12.1**	**4**						**10**	**0**	**2**	**2**	**2**	**0**	**0**	**0**
	Maine Mariners	AHL	21	2	9	11	41																			
1989-90	**Boston**	**NHL**	**77**	**11**	**27**	**38**	**76**	**2**	**0**	**1**	**127**	**8.7**	**12**						**15**	**1**	**3**	**4**	**12**	**1**	**0**	**0**
1990-91	HC Asiago	Italy	2	3	0	3	9																			
	Maine Mariners	AHL	5	0	1	1	13																			
	Edmonton	**NHL**	**6**	**0**	**1**	**1**	**6**	**0**	**0**	**0**	**9**	**0.0**	**-2**													
	Cape Breton	AHL	55	10	32	42	73												4	0	3	3	23			
1991-92	**Edmonton**	**NHL**	**20**	**2**	**11**	**13**	**22**	**0**	**0**	**0**	**24**	**8.3**	**19**						**13**	**0**	**3**	**3**	**23**	**0**	**0**	**0**
	Cape Breton	AHL	56	20	55	75	26												3	2	2	4	0			
1992-93	**Edmonton**	**NHL**	**29**	**5**	**13**	**18**	**35**	**2**	**0**	**0**	**47**	**10.6**	**-1**													
	Philadelphia	**NHL**	**40**	**6**	**22**	**28**	**39**	**5**	**0**	**1**	**91**	**6.6**	**-7**													
1993-94	**Philadelphia**	**NHL**	**19**	**3**	**12**	**15**	**19**	**3**	**0**	**0**	**37**	**8.1**	**2**													
	Florida	**NHL**	**33**	**2**	**14**	**16**	**9**	**0**	**0**	**1**	**55**	**3.6**	**8**													
	Pittsburgh	**NHL**	**12**	**1**	**2**	**3**	**8**	**1**	**0**	**1**	**20**	**5.0**	**-1**						**1**	**0**	**0**	**0**	**0**	**0**	**0**	**0**
1994-95	**Pittsburgh**	**NHL**	**21**	**1**	**4**	**5**	**25**	**1**	**0**	**0**	**17**	**5.9**	**2**													
	Cleveland	IHL	....	....	....	....	....												3	1	0	1	4			
1995-96	Las Vegas	IHL	78	20	65	85	101												15	5	11	16	24			
1996-97	**San Jose**	**NHL**	**63**	**6**	**12**	**18**	**69**	**3**	**0**	**0**	**83**	**7.2**	**-22**													
1997-98	Kolner Haie	DEL	4	0	1	1	16																			
	Kolner Haie	EuroHL	1	0	0	0	2																			
	Houston Aeros	IHL	81	19	52	71	75												4	0	4	4	0			
1998-99	Houston Aeros	IHL	76	17	57	74	90												19	4	8	12	24			
99-2000	**Vancouver**	**NHL**	**79**	**5**	**17**	**22**	**26**	**2**	**0**	**0**	**70**	**7.1**	**5**	**2**	**50.0**	**64**	**57**	**17:11**								
2000-01	**Vancouver**	**NHL**	**16**	**2**	**5**	**7**	**6**	**1**	**0**	**1**	**16**	**12.5**	**8**	**1**	**0.0**	**16**	**5**	**14:55**								
	Kansas City	IHL	46	6	16	22	21																			
	NHL Totals		**472**	**60**	**164**	**224**	**424**	**25**	**0**	**5**	**729**	**8.2**		**3**	**33.3**	**80**	**62**	**16:48**	**42**	**2**	**8**	**10**	**37**	**1**	**0**	**0**

WHL West First All-Star Team (1986, 1987, 1988) • Canadian Major Junior Defenseman of the Year (1988) • AHL First All-Star Team (1992) • Won Eddie Shore Award (Top Defenseman - AHL) (1992) • IHL First All-Star Team (1996, 1998, 1999) • Won Governors' Trophy (Top Defenseman - IHL) (1996, 1999)

Traded to **Edmonton** by **Boston** for Vladimir Ruzicka, October 22, 1990. Traded to **Philadelphia** by **Edmonton** with Josef Beranek for Brian Benning, January 16, 1993. Traded to **Florida** by **Philadelphia** for cash, November 30, 1993. Traded to **Pittsburgh** by **Florida** for Jeff Daniels, March 19, 1994. Signed as a free agent by **San Jose**, September 25, 1996. Signed as a free agent by **Vancouver**, September 30, 1999. Signed as a free agent by **Dallas**, July 17, 2001.

HAY, Dwayne
(HAY, DWAYN) **CGY.**

Left wing. Shoots left. 6'1", 203 lbs. Born, London, Ont., February 11, 1977. Washington's 3rd choice, 43rd overall, in 1995 Entry Draft.

Season	Club	League	GP	G	A	Pts	PIM	PP	SH	GW	S	%	+/-	TF	F%	H	SB	Min	GP	G	A	Pts	PIM	PP	SH	GW
1991-92	London Travellers	OMHA	86	70	56	126	104																			
1992-93	Listowel Cyclones	OJHL-B	50	19	33	52	40																			
1993-94	Listowel Cyclones	OJHL-B	48	10	24	34	56																			
1994-95	Guelph Storm	OHL	65	26	28	54	37												14	5	7	12	6			
1995-96	Guelph Storm	OHL	60	28	30	58	49												16	4	9	13	18			
1996-97	Guelph Storm	OHL	32	17	17	34	21												11	4	6	10	0			
1997-98	**Washington**	**NHL**	**2**	**0**	**0**	**0**	**2**	**0**	**0**	**0**	**1**	**0.0**	**0**													
	Portland Pirates	AHL	58	6	7	13	35																			
	New Haven	AHL	10	3	2	5	4												2	0	0	0	0			
1998-99	**Florida**	**NHL**	**9**	**0**	**0**	**0**	**0**	**0**	**0**	**0**	**3**	**0.0**	**-1**	**1**	**0.0**	**5**	**0**	**6:35**								
	New Haven	AHL	46	18	17	35	22																			
99-2000	**Florida**	**NHL**	**6**	**0**	**0**	**0**	**2**	**0**	**0**	**0**	**3**	**0.0**	**-2**	**0**	**0.0**	**3**	**1**	**6:36**								
	Louisville Panthers	AHL	41	11	20	31	18																			
	Tampa Bay	**NHL**	**13**	**1**	**1**	**2**	**2**	**0**	**0**	**0**	**11**	**9.1**	**0**	**1**	**0.0**	**15**	**1**	**6:04**								
2000-01	**Calgary**	**NHL**	**49**	**1**	**3**	**4**	**16**	**0**	**0**	**0**	**39**	**2.6**	**-4**	**6**	**16.7**	**92**	**9**	**8:24**								
	NHL Totals		**79**	**2**	**4**	**6**	**22**	**0**	**0**	**0**	**57**	**3.5**		**8**	**12.5**	**115**	**11**	**7:39**								

Traded to **Florida** by **Washington** with future considerations for Esa Tikkanen, March 9, 1998. Traded to **Tampa Bay** by **Florida** with Ryan Johnson for Mike Sillinger, March 14, 2000. Claimed on waivers by **Calgary** from **Tampa Bay**, October 3, 2000.

HEALEY, Paul (HEE-lee, PAWL) TOR.

Right wing. Shoots right. 6'2", 185 lbs. Born, Edmonton, Alta., March 20, 1975. Philadelphia's 7th choice, 192nd overall, in 1993 Entry Draft.

Season	Club	League	GP	G	A	Pts	PIM	PP	SH	GW	S	%	+/-	TF	F%	H	SB	Min	GP	G	A	Pts	PIM	PP	SH	GW
			Regular Season																Playoffs							
1991-92	Ft-Saskatchewan	AJHL	52	11	19	30	40	....	....	....	....	....	....	....	....	....	....	....	....	....	....	....	....	....	....	....
1992-93	Prince Albert	WHL	72	12	20	32	66	....	....	....	....	....	....	....	....	....	....	....	....	....	....	....	....	....	....	....
1993-94	Prince Albert	WHL	63	23	26	49	70	....	....	....	....	....	....	....	....	....	....	....	....	....	....	....	....	....	....	....
1994-95	Prince Albert	WHL	71	43	50	93	67	....	....	....	....	....	....	....	....	....	....	....	12	3	4	7	2	....	....	....
1995-96	Hershey Bears	AHL	60	7	15	22	35	....	....	....	....	....	....	....	....	....	....	....	....	....	....	....	....	....	....	....
1996-97	**Philadelphia**	**NHL**	**2**	**0**	**0**	**0**	**0**	**0**	**0**	**0**	**0**	**0.0**	**0**	....	....	....	....	....	....	....	....	....	....	....	....	....
	Philadelphia	AHL	64	21	19	40	56	....	....	....	....	....	....	....	....	....	....	....	10	4	1	5	10	....	....	....
1997-98	**Philadelphia**	**NHL**	**4**	**0**	**0**	**0**	**12**	**0**	**0**	**0**	**0**	**0.0**	**0**	....	....	....	....	....	....	....	....	....	....	....	....	....
	Philadelphia	AHL	71	34	18	52	48	....	....	....	....	....	....	....	....	....	....	....	20	6	2	8	4	....	....	....
1998-99	Philadelphia	AHL	72	26	20	46	39	....	....	....	....	....	....	....	....	....	....	....	15	4	6	10	11	....	....	....
99-2000	Milwaukee	IHL	76	21	18	39	28	....	....	....	....	....	....	....	....	....	....	....	3	1	2	3	0	....	....	....
2000-01	Hamilton Bulldogs	AHL	79	39	32	71	34	....	....	....	....	....	....	....	....	....	....	....	....	....	....	....	....	....	....	....
	NHL Totals		**6**	**0**	**0**	**0**	**12**	**0**	**0**	**0**	**0**	**0.0**		....	....	....	....	....	....	....	....	....	....	....	....	....

WHL East Second All-Star Team (1995)

Traded to **Nashville** by **Philadelphia** for Matt Henderson, September 27, 1999. Signed as a free agent by **Edmonton**, August 31, 2000. Signed as a free agent by **Toronto**, July 24, 2001.

HECHT, Jochen (HEHKHT, yoh-HEHN) EDM.

Center. Shoots left. 6'3", 196 lbs. Born, Mannheim, West Germany, June 21, 1977. St. Louis' 1st choice, 49th overall, in 1995 Entry Draft.

Season	Club	League	GP	G	A	Pts	PIM	PP	SH	GW	S	%	+/-	TF	F%	H	SB	Min	GP	G	A	Pts	PIM	PP	SH	GW
1994-95	Adler Mannheim	DEL	43	11	12	23	68	....	....	....	....	....	....	....	....	....	....	....	10	5	4	9	12	....	....	....
1995-96	Adler Mannheim	DEL	44	12	16	28	68	....	....	....	....	....	....	....	....	....	....	....	8	3	2	5	6	....	....	....
1996-97	Adler Mannheim	DEL	46	21	21	42	36	....	....	....	....	....	....	....	....	....	....	....	9	3	3	6	4	....	....	....
1997-98	Adler Mannheim	DEL	44	7	19	26	42	....	....	....	....	....	....	....	....	....	....	....	10	1	1	2	14	....	....	....
	Adler Mannheim	EuroHL	5	0	4	4	8	....	....	....	....	....	....	....	....	....	....	....	....	....	....	....	....	....	....	....
	Germany	Olympics	4	1	0	1	6	....	....	....	....	....	....	....	....	....	....	....	....	....	....	....	....	....	....	....
1998-99	**St. Louis**	**NHL**	**3**	**0**	**0**	**0**	**0**	**0**	**0**	**0**	**4**	**0.0**	**-2**	**19**	**21.1**	**1**	**0**	**13:16**	**5**	**2**	**0**	**2**	**0**	**0**	**0**	**0**
	Worcester	AHL	74	21	35	56	48	....	....	....	....	....	....	....	....	....	....	....	4	1	1	2	2	....	....	....
99-2000	**St. Louis**	**NHL**	**63**	**13**	**21**	**34**	**28**	**5**	**0**	**1**	**140**	**9.3**	**20**	**75**	**49.3**	**36**	**6**	**15:25**	**7**	**4**	**6**	**10**	**2**	**1**	**0**	**1**
2000-01	**St. Louis**	**NHL**	**72**	**19**	**25**	**44**	**48**	**8**	**3**	**1**	**208**	**9.1**	**11**	**160**	**43.8**	**48**	**18**	**17:56**	**15**	**2**	**4**	**6**	**4**	**0**	**0**	**0**
	NHL Totals		**138**	**32**	**46**	**78**	**76**	**13**	**3**	**2**	**352**	**9.1**		**254**	**43.7**	**85**	**24**	**16:41**	**27**	**8**	**10**	**18**	**6**	**1**	**0**	**1**

Traded to **Edmonton** by **St. Louis** with Marty Reasoner and Jan Horacek for Doug Weight and Michel Riesen, July 1, 2001.

HEDICAN, Bret (HEH-dih-kan, BREHT) FLA.

Defense. Shoots left. 6'2", 205 lbs. Born, St. Paul, MN, August 10, 1970. St. Louis' 10th choice, 198th overall, in 1988 Entry Draft.

Season	Club	League	GP	G	A	Pts	PIM	PP	SH	GW	S	%	+/-	TF	F%	H	SB	Min	GP	G	A	Pts	PIM	PP	SH	GW
1987-88	North St. Paul	Hi-School	23	15	19	34	16	....	....	....	....	....	....	....	....	....	....	....	....	....	....	....	....	....	....	....
1988-89	St. Cloud State	NCAA	28	5	3	8	28	....	....	....	....	....	....	....	....	....	....	....	....	....	....	....	....	....	....	....
1989-90	St. Cloud State	NCAA	36	4	17	21	37	....	....	....	....	....	....	....	....	....	....	....	....	....	....	....	....	....	....	....
1990-91	St. Cloud State	WCHA	41	21	26	47	26	....	....	....	....	....	....	....	....	....	....	....	....	....	....	....	....	....	....	....
1991-92	United States	Nat-Team	54	1	8	9	59	....	....	....	....	....	....	....	....	....	....	....	....	....	....	....	....	....	....	....
	United States	Olympics	8	0	0	0	4	....	....	....	....	....	....	....	....	....	....	....	....	....	....	....	....	....	....	....
	St. Louis	**NHL**	**4**	**1**	**0**	**1**	**0**	**0**	**0**	**0**	**1**	**100.0**	**1**	....	....	....	....	....	**5**	**0**	**0**	**0**	**0**	**0**	**0**	**0**
1992-93	**St. Louis**	**NHL**	**42**	**0**	**8**	**8**	**30**	**0**	**0**	**0**	**40**	**0.0**	**-2**	....	....	....	....	....	**10**	**0**	**0**	**0**	**14**	**0**	**0**	**0**
	Peoria Rivermen	IHL	19	0	8	8	10	....	....	....	....	....	....	....	....	....	....	....	....	....	....	....	....	....	....	....
1993-94	**St. Louis**	**NHL**	**61**	**0**	**11**	**11**	**64**	**0**	**0**	**0**	**78**	**0.0**	**-8**	....	....	....	....	....	....	....	....	....	....	....	....	....
	Vancouver	**NHL**	**8**	**0**	**1**	**1**	**0**	**0**	**0**	**0**	**10**	**0.0**	**1**	....	....	....	....	....	**24**	**1**	**6**	**7**	**16**	**0**	**0**	**0**
1994-95	**Vancouver**	**NHL**	**45**	**2**	**11**	**13**	**34**	**0**	**0**	**0**	**56**	**3.6**	**-3**	....	....	....	....	....	**11**	**0**	**2**	**2**	**6**	**0**	**0**	**0**
1995-96	**Vancouver**	**NHL**	**77**	**6**	**23**	**29**	**83**	**1**	**0**	**0**	**113**	**5.3**	**8**	....	....	....	....	....	**6**	**0**	**1**	**1**	**10**	**0**	**0**	**0**
1996-97	**Vancouver**	**NHL**	**67**	**4**	**15**	**19**	**51**	**2**	**0**	**1**	**93**	**4.3**	**-3**	....	....	....	....	....	....	....	....	....	....	....	....	....
1997-98	**Vancouver**	**NHL**	**71**	**3**	**24**	**27**	**79**	**1**	**0**	**0**	**84**	**3.6**	**3**	....	....	....	....	....	....	....	....	....	....	....	....	....
1998-99	**Vancouver**	**NHL**	**42**	**2**	**11**	**13**	**34**	**0**	**2**	**0**	**52**	**3.8**	**7**	**0**	**0.0**	**60**	**32**	**18:40**	....	....	....	....	....	....	....	....
	Florida	**NHL**	**25**	**3**	**7**	**10**	**17**	**0**	**0**	**1**	**38**	**7.9**	**-2**	**0**	**0.0**	**46**	**42**	**22:24**	....	....	....	....	....	....	....	....
99-2000	**Florida**	**NHL**	**76**	**6**	**19**	**25**	**68**	**2**	**0**	**1**	**58**	**10.3**	**4**	**0**	**0.0**	**128**	**89**	**19:36**	**4**	**0**	**0**	**0**	**0**	**0**	**0**	**0**
2000-01	**Florida**	**NHL**	**70**	**5**	**15**	**20**	**72**	**4**	**0**	**1**	**104**	**4.8**	**-7**	**0**	**0.0**	**144**	**80**	**21:49**	....	....	....	....	....	....	....	....
	NHL Totals		**588**	**32**	**145**	**177**	**532**	**10**	**2**	**4**	**727**	**4.4**		**0**	**0.0**	**378**	**243**	**20:28**	**60**	**1**	**9**	**10**	**46**	**0**	**0**	**0**

WCHA First All-Star Team (1991)

Traded to **Vancouver** by **St. Louis** with Jeff Brown and Nathan Lafayette for Craig Janney, March 21, 1994. Traded to **Florida** by **Vancouver** with Pavel Bure, Brad Ference and Vancouver's 3rd round choice (Robert Fried) in 2000 Entry Draft for Ed Jovanovski, Dave Gagner, Mike Brown, Kevin Weekes and Florida's 1st round choice (Nathan Smith) in 2000 Entry Draft, January 17, 1999.

HEINS, Shawn (HIGHNS, SHAWN) S.J.

Defense. Shoots left. 6'4", 210 lbs. Born, Eganville, Ont., December 24, 1973.

Season	Club	League	GP	G	A	Pts	PIM	PP	SH	GW	S	%	+/-	TF	F%	H	SB	Min	GP	G	A	Pts	PIM	PP	SH	GW
1991-92	Peterborough	OHL	49	1	1	2	73	....	....	....	....	....	....	....	....	....	....	....	7	0	0	0	5	....	....	....
1992-93	Peterborough	OHL	5	0	0	0	10	....	....	....	....	....	....	....	....	....	....	....	....	....	....	....	....	....	....	....
	Windsor Spitfires	OHL	53	7	10	17	107	....	....	....	....	....	....	....	....	....	....	....	....	....	....	....	....	....	....	....
1993-94	Renfrew T-Wolves	NOJHA	32	16	34	50	250	....	....	....	....	....	....	....	....	....	....	....	....	....	....	....	....	....	....	....
1994-95	Renfrew T-Wolves	NOJHA	35	30	49	79	188	....	....	....	....	....	....	....	....	....	....	....	....	....	....	....	....	....	....	....
1995-96	Mobile Mysticks	ECHL	62	7	20	27	152	....	....	....	....	....	....	....	....	....	....	....	....	....	....	....	....	....	....	....
	Cape Breton	AHL	1	0	0	0	0	....	....	....	....	....	....	....	....	....	....	....	....	....	....	....	....	....	....	....
1996-97	Mobile Mysticks	ECHL	56	6	17	23	253	....	....	....	....	....	....	....	....	....	....	....	3	0	2	2	2	....	....	....
	Kansas City	IHL	6	0	0	0	9	....	....	....	....	....	....	....	....	....	....	....	....	....	....	....	....	....	....	....
1997-98	Kansas City	IHL	82	22	28	50	303	....	....	....	....	....	....	....	....	....	....	....	11	1	0	1	49	....	....	....
1998-99	Canada	Nat-Team	36	5	16	21	66	....	....	....	....	....	....	....	....	....	....	....	....	....	....	....	....	....	....	....
	San Jose	**NHL**	**5**	**0**	**0**	**0**	**13**	**0**	**0**	**0**	**4**	**0.0**	**0**	**0**	**0.0**	**4**	**1**	**13:38**	....	....	....	....	....	....	....	....
	Kentucky	AHL	18	2	2	4	108	....	....	....	....	....	....	....	....	....	....	....	12	2	7	9	10	....	....	....
99-2000	**San Jose**	**NHL**	**1**	**0**	**0**	**0**	**2**	**0**	**0**	**0**	**1**	**0.0**	**-1**	**0**	**0.0**	**1**	**2**	**10:57**	....	....	....	....	....	....	....	....
	Kentucky	AHL	69	11	52	63	238	....	....	....	....	....	....	....	....	....	....	....	9	3	3	6	44	....	....	....
2000-01	**San Jose**	**NHL**	**38**	**3**	**4**	**7**	**57**	**2**	**0**	**0**	**45**	**6.7**	**2**	**0**	**0.0**	**54**	**13**	**10:15**	**2**	**0**	**0**	**0**	**0**	**0**	**0**	**0**
	NHL Totals		**44**	**3**	**4**	**7**	**72**	**2**	**0**	**0**	**50**	**6.0**		**0**	**0.0**	**59**	**16**	**10:39**	**2**	**0**	**0**	**0**	**0**	**0**	**0**	**0**

AHL First All-Star Team (2000)

Signed as a free agent by **San Jose**, January 5, 1997. • Missed majority of 2000-01 season recovering from head injury suffered in game vs. Chicago, February 14, 2001.

HEINZE, Steve (HIGHNS, STEEV) L.A.

Right wing. Shoots right. 5'11", 202 lbs. Born, Lawrence, MA, January 30, 1970. Boston's 2nd choice, 60th overall, in 1988 Entry Draft.

Season	Club	League	GP	G	A	Pts	PIM	PP	SH	GW	S	%	+/-	TF	F%	H	SB	Min	GP	G	A	Pts	PIM	PP	SH	GW
1986-87	Lawrence Prep	Hi-School	23	26	24	50	....	....	....	....	....	....	....	....	....	....	....	....	....	....	....	....	....	....	....	....
1987-88	Lawrence Prep	Hi-School	23	30	25	55	....	....	....	....	....	....	....	....	....	....	....	....	....	....	....	....	....	....	....	....
1988-89	Boston College	H-East	36	26	23	49	26	....	....	....	....	....	....	....	....	....	....	....	....	....	....	....	....	....	....	....
1989-90	Boston College	H-East	40	27	36	63	41	....	....	....	....	....	....	....	....	....	....	....	....	....	....	....	....	....	....	....
1990-91	Boston College	H-East	35	21	26	47	35	....	....	....	....	....	....	....	....	....	....	....	....	....	....	....	....	....	....	....
1991-92	United States	Nat-Team	49	18	15	33	38	....	....	....	....	....	....	....	....	....	....	....	....	....	....	....	....	....	....	....
	United States	Olympics	8	1	3	4	8	....	....	....	....	....	....	....	....	....	....	....	....	....	....	....	....	....	....	....
	Boston	**NHL**	**14**	**3**	**4**	**7**	**6**	**0**	**0**	**2**	**29**	**10.3**	**-1**	....	....	....	....	....	**7**	**0**	**3**	**3**	**17**	**0**	**0**	**0**
1992-93	**Boston**	**NHL**	**73**	**18**	**13**	**31**	**24**	**0**	**2**	**4**	**146**	**12.3**	**20**	....	....	....	....	....	**4**	**1**	**1**	**2**	**2**	**0**	**0**	**0**
1993-94	**Boston**	**NHL**	**77**	**10**	**11**	**21**	**32**	**0**	**2**	**1**	**183**	**5.5**	**-2**	....	....	....	....	....	**13**	**2**	**3**	**5**	**7**	**0**	**0**	**0**
1994-95	**Boston**	**NHL**	**36**	**7**	**9**	**16**	**23**	**0**	**1**	**0**	**70**	**10.0**	**0**	....	....	....	....	....	**5**	**0**	**0**	**0**	**0**	**0**	**0**	**0**
1995-96	**Boston**	**NHL**	**76**	**16**	**12**	**28**	**43**	**0**	**1**	**3**	**129**	**12.4**	**-3**	....	....	....	....	....	**5**	**1**	**1**	**2**	**4**	**0**	**1**	**0**
1996-97	**Boston**	**NHL**	**30**	**17**	**8**	**25**	**27**	**4**	**2**	**2**	**96**	**17.7**	**-8**	....	....	....	....	....	....	....	....	....	....	....	....	....
1997-98	**Boston**	**NHL**	**61**	**26**	**20**	**46**	**54**	**9**	**0**	**6**	**160**	**16.3**	**8**	....	....	....	....	....	**6**	**0**	**0**	**0**	**6**	**0**	**0**	**0**
1998-99	**Boston**	**NHL**	**73**	**22**	**18**	**40**	**30**	**9**	**0**	**3**	**146**	**15.1**	**7**	**2**	**0.0**	**91**	**13**	**15:48**	**12**	**4**	**3**	**7**	**0**	**2**	**0**	**0**
99-2000	**Boston**	**NHL**	**75**	**12**	**13**	**25**	**36**	**2**	**0**	**2**	**145**	**8.3**	**-8**	**8**	**12.5**	**129**	**10**	**14:57**	....	....	....	....	....	....	....	....

			Regular Season																Playoffs							
Season	Club	League	GP	G	A	Pts	PIM	PP	SH	GW	S	%	+/-	TF	F%	H	SB	Min	GP	G	A	Pts	PIM	PP	SH	GW
2000-01	**Columbus**	**NHL**	**65**	**22**	**20**	**42**	**38**	**14**	**0**	**3**	**125**	**17.6**	**–19**	**38**	**29.0**	**71**	**12**	**18:49**	....	....	....	....	....	....	....	....
	Buffalo	**NHL**	**14**	**5**	**7**	**12**	**8**	**1**	**0**	**1**	**19**	**26.3**	**6**	**0**	**0.0**	**20**	**3**	**15:24**	**13**	**3**	**4**	**7**	**10**	**3**	**0**	**0**
	NHL Totals		**594**	**158**	**135**	**293**	**321**	**39**	**8**	**27**	**1248**	**12.7**		**48**	**25.0**	**311**	**38**	**16:21**	**65**	**11**	**15**	**26**	**46**	**5**	**1**	**0**

Hockey East First All-Star Team (1990) • NCAA East First All-American Team (1990)

Selected by **Columbus** from **Boston** in Expansion Draft, June 23, 2000. Traded to **Buffalo** by **Columbus** for Buffalo's 3rd round choice (Per Mars) in 2001 Entry Draft, March 13, 2001. Signed as a free agent by **LA Kings**, July 4, 2001.

HEJDUK, Milan (HAY-dook, MEE-lan) COL.

Right wing. Shoots right. 5'11", 185 lbs. Born, Usti-nad-Labem, Czech., February 14, 1976. Quebec's 6th choice, 87th overall, in 1994 Entry Draft.

1993-94	HC Pardubice	Cze-Rep	22	6	3	9	....	....	....	....	....	....	....	....	....	....	....	....	10	5	1	6	....	....	....	....
1994-95	HC Pardubice	Cze-Rep	43	11	13	24	6	....	....	....	....	....	....	....	....	....	....	....	6	3	1	4	0	....	....	....
1995-96	HC Pardubice	Cze-Rep	37	13	7	20	....	....	....	....	....	....	....	....	....	....	....	....	....	....	....	....	....	....	....	....
1996-97	HC Pardubice	Cze-Rep	51	27	11	38	10	....	....	....	....	....	....	....	....	....	....	....	10	6	0	6	27	....	....	....
1997-98	HC Pardubice	Cze-Rep	48	26	19	45	20	....	....	....	....	....	....	....	....	....	....	....	3	0	0	0	2	....	....	....
	Czech-Republic	Olympics	4	0	0	0	2	....	....	....	....	....	....	....	....	....	....	....	....	....	....	....	....	....	....	....
1998-99	**Colorado**	**NHL**	**82**	**14**	**34**	**48**	**26**	**4**	**0**	**5**	**178**	**7.9**	**8**	**2**	**50.0**	**50**	**30**	**15:45**	**16**	**6**	**6**	**12**	**4**	**1**	**0**	**3**
99-2000	**Colorado**	**NHL**	**82**	**36**	**36**	**72**	**16**	**13**	**0**	**9**	**228**	**15.8**	**14**	**3**	**100.0**	**46**	**40**	**19:58**	**17**	**5**	**4**	**9**	**6**	**3**	**0**	**1**
2000-01♦	**Colorado**	**NHL**	**80**	**41**	**38**	**79**	**36**	**12**	**1**	**9**	**213**	**19.2**	**32**	**3**	**33.3**	**88**	**33**	**19:52**	**23**	**7**	***16**	**23**	**6**	**4**	**0**	**1**
	NHL Totals		**244**	**91**	**108**	**199**	**78**	**29**	**1**	**23**	**619**	**14.7**		**8**	**62.5**	**184**	**103**	**18:31**	**56**	**18**	**26**	**44**	**16**	**8**	**0**	**5**

NHL All-Rookie Team (1999) • Played in NHL All-Star Game (2000, 2001)

Rights transferred to **Colorado** after **Quebec** franchise relocated, June 21, 1995.

HELENIUS, Sami (huh-LEHN-ee-uhs, SA-mee) DAL.

Defense. Shoots left. 6'6", 230 lbs. Born, Helsinki, Finland, January 22, 1974. Calgary's 5th choice, 102nd overall, in 1992 Entry Draft.

1990-91	Jokerit Helsinki	Finn-Jr.	2	0	0	0	6	....	....	....	....	....	....	....	....	....	....	....	....	....	....	....	....	....	....	....
1991-92	Jokerit Helsinki	Finn-Jr.	14	3	3	6	24	....	....	....	....	....	....	....	....	....	....	....	....	....	....	....	....	....	....	....
	Jokerit Helsinki	Finland-2	13	4	4	8	24	....	....	....	....	....	....	....	....	....	....	....	....	....	....	....	....	....	....	....
1992-93	Jokerit Helsinki	Finn-Jr.	13	2	3	5	18	....	....	....	....	....	....	....	....	....	....	....	....	....	....	....	....	....	....	....
	Vantaa HT	Finland-2	21	3	2	5	50	....	....	....	....	....	....	....	....	....	....	....	....	....	....	....	....	....	....	....
	Jokerit Helsinki	Finland	1	0	0	0	0	....	....	....	....	....	....	....	....	....	....	....	....	....	....	....	....	....	....	....
1993-94	Reipas Lahti	Finn-Jr.	11	3	4	7	48	....	....	....	....	....	....	....	....	....	....	....	....	....	....	....	....	....	....	....
	Reipas Lahti	Finland	37	2	3	5	46	....	....	....	....	....	....	....	....	....	....	....	....	....	....	....	....	....	....	....
1994-95	Saint John Flames	AHL	69	2	5	7	217	....	....	....	....	....	....	....	....	....	....	....	....	....	....	....	....	....	....	....
1995-96	Saint John Flames	AHL	68	0	3	3	231	....	....	....	....	....	....	....	....	....	....	....	10	0	0	0	9	....	....	....
1996-97	**Calgary**	**NHL**	**3**	**0**	**1**	**1**	**0**	**0**	**0**	**0**	**1**	**0.0**	**1**	....	....	....	....	....	....	....	....	....	....	....	....	....
	Saint John Flames	AHL	72	5	10	15	218	....	....	....	....	....	....	....	....	....	....	....	2	0	0	0	0	....	....	....
1997-98	Saint John Flames	AHL	63	1	2	3	185	....	....	....	....	....	....	....	....	....	....	....	....	....	....	....	....	....	....	....
	Las Vegas	IHL	10	0	1	1	19	....	....	....	....	....	....	....	....	....	....	....	4	0	0	0	25	....	....	....
1998-99	**Calgary**	**NHL**	**4**	**0**	**0**	**0**	**8**	**0**	**0**	**0**	**1**	**0.0**	**–2**	**0**	**0.0**	**6**	**6**	**10:16**	....	....	....	....	....	....	....	....
	Las Vegas	IHL	42	2	3	5	193	....	....	....	....	....	....	....	....	....	....	....	....	....	....	....	....	....	....	....
	Tampa Bay	**NHL**	**4**	**1**	**0**	**1**	**15**	**0**	**1**	**0**	**3**	**33.3**	**–3**	**0**	**0.0**	**6**	**3**	**16:53**	....	....	....	....	....	....	....	....
	Chicago Wolves	IHL	4	0	0	0	11	....	....	....	....	....	....	....	....	....	....	....	....	....	....	....	....	....	....	....
	Hershey Bears	AHL	8	0	0	0	29	....	....	....	....	....	....	....	....	....	....	....	5	0	0	0	16	....	....	....
99-2000	**Colorado**	**NHL**	**33**	**0**	**0**	**0**	**46**	**0**	**0**	**0**	**6**	**0.0**	**–5**	**0**	**0.0**	**34**	**19**	**7:04**	....	....	....	....	....	....	....	....
	Hershey Bears	AHL	12	0	1	1	31	....	....	....	....	....	....	....	....	....	....	....	9	0	0	0	40	....	....	....
2000-01	**Dallas**	**NHL**	**57**	**1**	**2**	**3**	**99**	**0**	**0**	**0**	**18**	**5.6**	**1**	**0**	**0.0**	**84**	**25**	**10:39**	**1**	**0**	**0**	**0**	**0**	**0**	**0**	**0**
	NHL Totals		**101**	**2**	**3**	**5**	**168**	**0**	**1**	**0**	**29**	**6.9**		**0**	**0.0**	**130**	**53**	**9:41**	**1**	**0**	**0**	**0**	**0**	**0**	**0**	**0**

Traded to **Tampa Bay** by **Calgary** for future considerations, January 29, 1999. Traded to **Colorado** by **Tampa Bay** for future considerations, March 23, 1999. Signed as a free agent by **Dallas**, July 12, 2000.

HELMER, Bryan (HEHL-muhr, BRIGH-uhn) VAN.

Defense. Shoots right. 6'1", 200 lbs. Born, Sault Ste. Marie, Ont., July 15, 1972.

1989-90	Wellington Dukes	MTJHL	44	4	20	24	204	....	....	....	....	....	....	....	....	....	....	....	....	....	....	....	....	....	....	....
	Belleville Bulls	OHL	6	0	1	1	0	....	....	....	....	....	....	....	....	....	....	....	....	....	....	....	....	....	....	....
1990-91	Wellington Dukes	MTJHL	50	11	14	25	109	....	....	....	....	....	....	....	....	....	....	....	....	....	....	....	....	....	....	....
1991-92	Wellington Dukes	MTJHL	42	17	31	48	66	....	....	....	....	....	....	....	....	....	....	....	3	2	1	3	0	....	....	....
1992-93	Wellington Dukes	MTJHL	48	21	54	75	84	....	....	....	....	....	....	....	....	....	....	....	9	4	8	12	22	....	....	....
1993-94	Albany River Rats	AHL	65	4	19	23	79	....	....	....	....	....	....	....	....	....	....	....	5	0	0	0	9	....	....	....
1994-95	Albany River Rats	AHL	77	7	36	43	101	....	....	....	....	....	....	....	....	....	....	....	7	1	0	1	0	....	....	....
1995-96	Albany River Rats	AHL	80	14	30	44	107	....	....	....	....	....	....	....	....	....	....	....	4	2	0	2	6	....	....	....
1996-97	Albany River Rats	AHL	77	12	27	39	113	....	....	....	....	....	....	....	....	....	....	....	16	1	7	8	10	....	....	....
1997-98	Albany River Rats	AHL	80	14	49	63	101	....	....	....	....	....	....	....	....	....	....	....	13	4	9	13	18	....	....	....
1998-99	**Phoenix**	**NHL**	**11**	**0**	**0**	**0**	**23**	**0**	**0**	**0**	**11**	**0.0**	**2**	**0**	**0.0**	**1**	**2**	**7:43**	....	....	....	....	....	....	....	....
	Las Vegas	IHL	8	1	3	4	28	....	....	....	....	....	....	....	....	....	....	....	....	....	....	....	....	....	....	....
	St. Louis	**NHL**	**29**	**0**	**4**	**4**	**19**	**0**	**0**	**0**	**38**	**0.0**	**3**	**1**	**100.0**	**34**	**28**	**19:08**	....	....	....	....	....	....	....	....
	Worcester	AHL	16	7	8	15	18	....	....	....	....	....	....	....	....	....	....	....	4	0	0	0	12	....	....	....
99-2000	**St. Louis**	**NHL**	**15**	**1**	**1**	**2**	**10**	**1**	**0**	**1**	**19**	**5.3**	**–3**	**0**	**0.0**	**16**	**8**	**16:15**	....	....	....	....	....	....	....	....
	Worcester	AHL	54	10	25	35	124	....	....	....	....	....	....	....	....	....	....	....	9	1	4	5	10	....	....	....
2000-01	**Vancouver**	**NHL**	**20**	**2**	**4**	**6**	**18**	**0**	**0**	**0**	**28**	**7.1**	**0**	**0**	**0.0**	**16**	**21**	**16:51**	....	....	....	....	....	....	....	....
	Kansas City	IHL	42	4	15	19	76	....	....	....	....	....	....	....	....	....	....	....	....	....	....	....	....	....	....	....
	NHL Totals		**75**	**3**	**9**	**12**	**70**	**1**	**0**	**1**	**96**	**3.1**		**1**	**100.0**	**67**	**59**	**16:16**	....	....	....	....	....	....	....	....

AHL First All-Star Team (1998)

Signed as a free agent by **New Jersey**, July 10, 1994. Signed as a free agent by **Phoenix**, July 17, 1998. Claimed on waivers by **St. Louis** from **Phoenix**, December 19, 1998. Signed as a free agent by **Vancouver**, August 21, 2000.

HENDERSON, Jay (HEHN-duhr-SOHN, JAY) BOS.

Left wing. Shoots left. 5'11", 190 lbs. Born, Edmonton, Alta., September 17, 1978. Boston's 12th choice, 246th overall, in 1997 Entry Draft.

1993-94	Sherwood Park	AAHA	31	12	21	33	36	....	....	....	....	....	....	....	....	....	....	....	....	....	....	....	....	....	....	....
1994-95	Red Deer Rebels	WHL	54	3	9	12	80	....	....	....	....	....	....	....	....	....	....	....	....	....	....	....	....	....	....	....
1995-96	Red Deer Rebels	WHL	71	15	13	28	139	....	....	....	....	....	....	....	....	....	....	....	10	1	1	2	11	....	....	....
1996-97	Edmonton Ice	WHL	66	28	32	60	127	....	....	....	....	....	....	....	....	....	....	....	....	....	....	....	....	....	....	....
1997-98	Edmonton Ice	WHL	72	49	45	94	130	....	....	....	....	....	....	....	....	....	....	....	....	....	....	....	....	....	....	....
	Providence Bruins	AHL	11	3	1	4	11	....	....	....	....	....	....	....	....	....	....	....	....	....	....	....	....	....	....	....
1998-99	**Boston**	**NHL**	**4**	**0**	**0**	**0**	**2**	**0**	**0**	**0**	**4**	**0.0**	**–1**	**0**	**0.0**	**1**	**1**	**5:39**	....	....	....	....	....	....	....	....
	Providence Bruins	AHL	55	7	9	16	172	....	....	....	....	....	....	....	....	....	....	....	2	0	0	0	2	....	....	....
99-2000	**Boston**	**NHL**	**16**	**1**	**3**	**4**	**9**	**0**	**0**	**0**	**18**	**5.6**	**1**	**2**	**0.0**	**16**	**2**	**5:22**	....	....	....	....	....	....	....	....
	Providence Bruins	AHL	60	18	27	45	200	....	....	....	....	....	....	....	....	....	....	....	14	1	2	3	16	....	....	....
2000-01	**Boston**	**NHL**	**13**	**0**	**0**	**0**	**26**	**0**	**0**	**0**	**12**	**0.0**	**–1**	**3**	**100.0**	**9**	**2**	**6:58**	....	....	....	....	....	....	....	....
	Providence Bruins	AHL	41	9	7	16	121	....	....	....	....	....	....	....	....	....	....	....	1	0	0	0	2	....	....	....
	NHL Totals		**33**	**1**	**3**	**4**	**37**	**0**	**0**	**0**	**34**	**2.9**		**5**	**60.0**	**26**	**5**	**6:02**	....	....	....	....	....	....	....	....

HENDERSON, Matt (HEHN-duhr-SOHN, MAT)

Right wing. Shoots left. 6'1", 200 lbs. Born, White Bear Lake, MN, June 22, 1974.

1993-94	St. Paul Vulcans	USHL	48	27	24	51	....	....	....	....	....	....	....	....	....	....	....	....	....	....	....	....	....	....	....	....
1994-95	North Dakota	WCHA	19	1	3	4	16	....	....	....	....	....	....	....	....	....	....	....	....	....	....	....	....	....	....	....
1995-96	North Dakota	WCHA	36	9	10	19	34	....	....	....	....	....	....	....	....	....	....	....	2	0	1	1	0	....	....	....
1996-97	North Dakota	WCHA	42	14	17	31	71	....	....	....	....	....	....	....	....	....	....	....	7	5	4	9	10	....	....	....
1997-98	North Dakota	WCHA	38	24	14	38	74	....	....	....	....	....	....	....	....	....	....	....	5	2	2	4	4	....	....	....
1998-99	**Nashville**	**NHL**	**2**	**0**	**0**	**0**	**2**	**0**	**0**	**0**	**0**	**0.0**	**–1**	**0**	**0.0**	**4**	**0**	**6:23**	....	....	....	....	....	....	....	....
	Milwaukee	IHL	77	19	19	38	117	....	....	....	....	....	....	....	....	....	....	....	2	0	0	0	0	....	....	....

			Regular Season																Playoffs							
Season	Club	League	GP	G	A	Pts	PIM	PP	SH	GW	S	%	+/-	TF	F%	H	SB	Min	GP	G	A	Pts	PIM	PP	SH	GW
99-2000	Philadelphia	AHL	51	4	8	12	37												5	0	0	0	4			
	Trenton Titans	ECHL	16	2	4	6	47																			
2000-01	Norfolk Admirals	AHL	78	14	24	38	80												9	1	1	2	16			
	NHL Totals		**2**	**0**	**0**	**0**	**2**	**0**	**0**	**0**	**0**	**0.0**		**0**	**0.0**	**4**	**0**	**6:23**								

NCAA Championship All-Tournament Team (1997) • NCAA Championship Tournament MVP (1997)

Signed as a free agent by **Nashville**, July 14, 1998. Traded to **Philadelphia** by **Nashville** for Paul Healey, September 27, 1999.

HENDRICKSON, Darby (HEHN-drihk-SOHN, DAHR-bee) MIN.

Center. Shoots left. 6'1", 195 lbs. Born, Richfield, MN, August 28, 1972. Toronto's 3rd choice, 73rd overall, in 1990 Entry Draft.

Season	Club	League	GP	G	A	Pts	PIM	PP	SH	GW	S	%	+/-	TF	F%	H	SB	Min	GP	G	A	Pts	PIM	PP	SH	GW
1987-88	Richfield Spartans	Hi-School	22	12	9	21	10																			
1988-89	Richfield Spartans	Hi-School	22	22	20	42	12																			
1989-90	Richfield Spartans	Hi-School	24	23	27	50	49																			
1990-91	Richfield Spartans	Hi-School	27	32	29	61																				
1991-92	U. of Minnesota	WCHA	41	25	28	53	61																			
1992-93	U. of Minnesota	WCHA	31	12	15	27	35																			
1993-94	United States	Nat-Team	59	12	16	28	30																			
	United States	Olympics	8	0	0	0	6																			
	Toronto	**NHL**																	**2**	**0**	**0**	**0**	**0**	**0**	**0**	**0**
	St. John's Leafs	AHL	6	4	1	5	4												3	1	1	2	0			
1994-95	St. John's Leafs	AHL	59	16	20	36	48																			
	Toronto	**NHL**	**8**	**0**	**1**	**1**	**4**	**0**	**0**	**0**	**4**	**0.0**	**0**													
1995-96	**Toronto**	**NHL**	**46**	**6**	**6**	**12**	**47**	**0**	**0**	**0**	**43**	**14.0**	**–2**													
	NY Islanders	**NHL**	**16**	**1**	**4**	**5**	**33**	**0**	**0**	**1**	**30**	**3.3**	**–6**													
1996-97	**Toronto**	**NHL**	**64**	**11**	**6**	**17**	**47**	**0**	**1**	**0**	**105**	**10.5**	**–20**													
	St. John's Leafs	AHL	12	5	4	9	21																			
1997-98	**Toronto**	**NHL**	**80**	**8**	**4**	**12**	**67**	**0**	**0**	**0**	**115**	**7.0**	**–20**													
1998-99	**Toronto**	**NHL**	**35**	**2**	**3**	**5**	**30**	**0**	**0**	**0**	**34**	**5.9**	**–4**	**278**	**46.0**	**35**	**8**	**10:16**								
	Vancouver	**NHL**	**27**	**2**	**2**	**4**	**22**	**1**	**0**	**0**	**36**	**5.6**	**–15**	**427**	**46.8**	**24**	**23**	**17:15**								
99-2000	**Vancouver**	**NHL**	**40**	**5**	**4**	**9**	**14**	**0**	**1**	**1**	**39**	**12.8**	**–3**	**407**	**46.2**	**26**	**27**	**11:32**								
	Syracuse Crunch	AHL	20	5	8	13	16																			
2000-01	**Minnesota**	**NHL**	**72**	**18**	**11**	**29**	**36**	**3**	**1**	**1**	**114**	**15.8**	**1**	**1119**	**45.2**	**44**	**44**	**15:50**								
	NHL Totals		**388**	**53**	**41**	**94**	**300**	**4**	**3**	**3**	**520**	**10.2**		**2231**	**45.8**	**129**	**102**	**13:57**	**2**	**0**	**0**	**0**	**0**	**0**	**0**	**0**

Minnesota High School Player of the Year (1991)

Traded to **NY Islanders** by **Toronto** with Sean Haggerty, Kenny Jonsson and Toronto's 1st round choice (Roberto Luongo) in 1997 Entry Draft for Wendel Clark, Mathieu Schneider and D.J. Smith, March 13, 1996. Traded to **Toronto** by **NY Islanders** for a conditional choice in 1998 Entry Draft, October 11, 1996. Traded to **Vancouver** by **Toronto** for Chris McAllister, February 16, 1999. Selected by **Minnesota** from **Vancouver** in Expansion Draft, June 23, 2000.

HERBERS, Ian (HEHR-buhrs, EE-an)

Defense. Shoots left. 6'4", 225 lbs. Born, Jasper, Alta., July 18, 1967. Buffalo's 11th choice, 190th overall, in 1987 Entry Draft.

Season	Club	League	GP	G	A	Pts	PIM	PP	SH	GW	S	%	+/-	TF	F%	H	SB	Min	GP	G	A	Pts	PIM	PP	SH	GW
1984-85	Kelowna Wings	WHL	68	3	14	17	120												6	0	1	1	9			
1985-86	Spokane Chiefs	WHL	29	1	6	7	85																			
	Lethbridge	WHL	32	1	4	5	109												10	1	0	1	37			
1986-87	Swift Current	WHL	72	5	8	13	230												4	1	1	2	12			
1987-88	Swift Current	WHL	56	5	14	19	238												4	0	2	2	4			
1988-89	U. of Alberta	CWUAA	47	4	22	26	137																			
1989-90	U. of Alberta	CWUAA	45	5	31	36	83																			
1990-91	U. of Alberta	CWUAA	45	6	24	30	87																			
1991-92	U. of Alberta	CWUAA	43	14	34	48	86																			
1992-93	Cape Breton	AHL	77	7	15	22	129												10	0	1	1	16			
1993-94	**Edmonton**	**NHL**	**22**	**0**	**2**	**2**	**32**	**0**	**0**	**0**	**16**	**0.0**	**–6**													
	Cape Breton	AHL	53	7	16	23	122												5	0	3	3	12			
1994-95	Cape Breton	AHL	36	1	11	12	104																			
	Detroit Vipers	IHL	37	1	5	6	46												5	1	1	2	6			
1995-96	Detroit Vipers	IHL	73	3	11	14	140												12	3	5	8	29			
1996-97	Detroit Vipers	IHL	67	3	16	19	129												21	0	4	4	34			
1997-98	Detroit Vipers	IHL	70	6	6	12	100												23	0	3	3	54			
1998-99	Detroit Vipers	IHL	82	8	16	24	142												11	1	3	4	18			
99-2000	**Tampa Bay**	**NHL**	**37**	**0**	**0**	**0**	**45**	**0**	**0**	**0**	**11**	**0.0**	**–12**	**0**	**0.0**	**38**	**46**	**15:06**								
	Detroit Vipers	IHL	13	1	4	5	22																			
	NY Islanders	**NHL**	**6**	**0**	**3**	**3**	**2**	**0**	**0**	**0**	**3**	**0.0**	**6**	**0**	**0.0**	**5**	**10**	**15:29**								
2000-01	Cleveland	IHL	78	3	7	10	179												4	0	1	1	10			
	NHL Totals		**65**	**0**	**5**	**5**	**79**	**0**	**0**	**0**	**30**	**0.0**		**0**	**0.0**	**43**	**56**	**15:09**								

CIAU All-Canadian Team (1991, 1992)

Signed as a free agent by **Edmonton**, September 9, 1992. Signed as a free agent by **Tampa Bay**, September, 1999. Traded to **NY Islanders** by **Tampa Bay** for NY Islanders' 7th round choice (later traded back to NY Islanders - NY Islanders selected Ryan Caldwell) in 2000 Entry Draft, March 9, 2000. Selected by **Minnesota** from **NY Islanders** in Expansion Draft, June 23, 2000.

HERPERGER, Chris (HUHR-puhr-GEHR, KRIHS) OTT.

Left wing. Shoots left. 6', 190 lbs. Born, Esterhazy, Sask., February 24, 1974. Philadelphia's 9th choice, 223rd overall, in 1992 Entry Draft.

Season	Club	League	GP	G	A	Pts	PIM	PP	SH	GW	S	%	+/-	TF	F%	H	SB	Min	GP	G	A	Pts	PIM	PP	SH	GW
1990-91	Swift Current	SMHL	STATISTICS NOT AVAILABLE																							
	Swift Current	WHL	10	0	1	1	5																			
1991-92	Swift Current	WHL	72	14	19	33	44												8	0	1	1	9			
1992-93	Swift Current	WHL	20	9	7	16	31																			
	Seattle T-Birds	WHL	46	20	11	31	30												5	1	1	2	6			
1993-94	Seattle T-Birds	WHL	71	44	51	95	110												9	12	10	22	12			
1994-95	Seattle T-Birds	WHL	59	49	52	101	106												4	4	0	4	6			
	Hershey Bears	AHL	4	0	0	0	0																			
1995-96	Hershey Bears	AHL	46	8	12	20	36																			
	Baltimore Bandits	AHL	21	2	3	5	17												9	2	3	5	6			
1996-97	Baltimore Bandits	AHL	67	19	22	41	88												3	0	0	0	0			
1997-98	Canada	Nat-Team	63	20	30	50	102																			
1998-99	Indianapolis Ice	IHL	79	19	29	48	81												7	0	4	4	4			
99-2000	**Chicago**	**NHL**	**9**	**0**	**0**	**0**	**5**	**0**	**0**	**0**	**2**	**0.0**	**–2**	**52**	**55.8**	**7**	**1**	**7:39**								
	Cleveland	IHL	73	22	26	48	122												9	3	3	6	8			
2000-01	**Chicago**	**NHL**	**61**	**10**	**15**	**25**	**20**	**0**	**1**	**3**	**76**	**13.2**	**0**	**678**	**56.2**	**28**	**21**	**13:07**								
	Norfolk Admirals	AHL	9	1	4	5	9																			
	NHL Totals		**70**	**10**	**15**	**25**	**25**	**0**	**1**	**3**	**78**	**12.8**		**730**	**56.2**	**35**	**22**	**12:25**								

WHL West Second All-Star Team (1995)

Traded to **Anaheim** by **Philadelphia** with Winnipeg/Phoenix's 7th round choice (previously acquired, Anaheim selected Tony Mohagen) in 1997 Entry Draft for Bob Corkum, February 6, 1996. Signed as a free agent by **Chicago**, September 2, 1998. Signed as a free agent by **Ottawa**, July 13, 2001.

HERR, Matt (HUHR, MAT)

Center. Shoots left. 6'2", 204 lbs. Born, Hackensack, NJ, May 26, 1976. Washington's 4th choice, 93rd overall, in 1994 Entry Draft.

Season	Club	League	GP	G	A	Pts	PIM	PP	SH	GW	S	%	+/-	TF	F%	H	SB	Min	GP	G	A	Pts	PIM	PP	SH	GW
1990-91	Hotchkiss Prep	Hi-School	26	9	5	14																				
1991-92	Hotchkiss Prep	Hi-School	25	17	16	33																				
1992-93	Hotchkiss Prep	Hi-School	24	48	30	78																				
1993-94	Hotchkiss Prep	Hi-School	24	28	19	47																				
1994-95	U. of Michigan	CCHA	37	11	8	19	51												3	1	0	1	4			
1995-96	U. of Michigan	CCHA	40	18	13	31	55												7	0	4	4	0			
1996-97	U. of Michigan	CCHA	43	29	23	52	67												6	2	2	4	8			
1997-98	U. of Michigan	CCHA	31	14	17	31	62																			
1998-99	**Washington**	**NHL**	**30**	**2**	**2**	**4**	**8**	**1**	**0**	**0**	**40**	**5.0**	**–7**	**176**	**52.8**	**42**	**10**	**11:05**								
	Portland Pirates	AHL	46	15	14	29	29																			
99-2000	Portland Pirates	AHL	77	22	21	43	51												4	1	1	2	4			

			Regular Season																Playoffs							
Season	Club	League	GP	G	A	Pts	PIM	PP	SH	GW	S	%	+/-	TF	F%	H	SB	Min	GP	G	A	Pts	PIM	PP	SH	GW
2000-01	**Washington**	**NHL**	**22**	**2**	**3**	**5**	**17**	**0**	**0**	**1**	**20**	**10.0**	**3**	**21**	**100.0**	**30**	**1**	**8:09**	....	....	....	....	....	....	....	....
	Portland Pirates	AHL	40	21	13	34	58	....	....	....	....	....	....	....	....	....	....	....	....	....	....	....	....	....	....	....
	Philadelphia	AHL	11	2	4	6	18	....	....	....	....	....	....	....	....	....	....	....	9	2	1	3	8	....	....	....
	NHL Totals		**52**	**4**	**5**	**9**	**25**	**1**	**0**	**1**	**60**	**6.7**		**178**	**53.4**	**72**	**11**	**9:50**	....	....	....	....	....	....	....	....

Traded to **Philadelphia** by **Washington** for Dean Melanson, March 13, 2001.

HEWARD, Jamie

(HEW-uhrd, JAY-mee) **CBJ**

Defense. Shoots right. 6'2", 207 lbs. Born, Regina, Sask., March 30, 1971. Pittsburgh's 1st choice, 16th overall, in 1989 Entry Draft.

Season	Club	League	GP	G	A	Pts	PIM	PP	SH	GW	S	%	+/-	TF	F%	H	SB	Min	GP	G	A	Pts	PIM	PP	SH	GW
1987-88	Regina Pats	WHL	68	10	17	27	17	....	....	....	....	....	....	....	....	....	....	....	4	1	1	2	2	....	....	....
1988-89	Regina Pats	WHL	52	31	28	59	29	....	....	....	....	....	....	....	....	....	....	....	....	....	....	....	....	....	....	....
1989-90	Regina Pats	WHL	72	14	44	58	42	....	....	....	....	....	....	....	....	....	....	....	11	2	2	4	10	....	....	....
1990-91	Regina Pats	WHL	71	23	61	84	41	....	....	....	....	....	....	....	....	....	....	....	8	2	9	11	6	....	....	....
1991-92	Muskegon	IHL	54	6	21	27	37	....	....	....	....	....	....	....	....	....	....	....	14	1	4	5	4	....	....	....
1992-93	Cleveland	IHL	58	9	18	27	64	....	....	....	....	....	....	....	....	....	....	....	....	....	....	....	....	....	....	....
1993-94	Cleveland	IHL	73	8	16	24	72	....	....	....	....	....	....	....	....	....	....	....	....	....	....	....	....	....	....	....
1994-95	Canada	Nat-Team	51	11	35	46	32	....	....	....	....	....	....	....	....	....	....	....	....	....	....	....	....	....	....	....
1995-96	**Toronto**	**NHL**	**5**	**0**	**0**	**0**	**0**	**0**	**0**	**0**	**8**	**0.0**	**-1**	....	....	....	....	....	....	....	....	....	....	....	....	....
	St. John's Leafs	AHL	73	22	34	56	33	....	....	....	....	....	....	....	....	....	....	....	3	1	1	2	6	....	....	....
1996-97	**Toronto**	**NHL**	**20**	**1**	**4**	**5**	**6**	**0**	**0**	**0**	**23**	**4.3**	**-6**	....	....	....	....	....	....	....	....	....	....	....	....	....
	St. John's Leafs	AHL	27	8	19	27	26	....	....	....	....	....	....	....	....	....	....	....	9	1	3	4	6	....	....	....
1997-98	Philadelphia	AHL	72	17	48	65	54	....	....	....	....	....	....	....	....	....	....	....	20	3	16	19	10	....	....	....
1998-99	**Nashville**	**NHL**	**63**	**6**	**12**	**18**	**44**	**4**	**0**	**1**	**124**	**4.8**	**-24**	**0**	**0.0**	**80**	**35**	**16:12**	....	....	....	....	....	....	....	....
99-2000	**NY Islanders**	**NHL**	**54**	**6**	**11**	**17**	**26**	**2**	**0**	**1**	**92**	**6.5**	**-9**	**0**	**0.0**	**54**	**74**	**19:58**	....	....	....	....	....	....	....	....
2000-01	**Columbus**	**NHL**	**69**	**11**	**16**	**27**	**33**	**9**	**0**	**1**	**108**	**10.2**	**3**	**0**	**0.0**	**53**	**38**	**14:21**	....	....	....	....	....	....	....	....
	NHL Totals		**211**	**24**	**43**	**67**	**109**	**15**	**0**	**3**	**355**	**6.8**		**0**	**0.0**	**187**	**147**	**16:37**	....	....	....	....	....	....	....	....

WHL East First All-Star Team (1991) • AHL First All-Star Team (1996, 1998) • Won Eddie Shore Award (Top Defenseman - AHL) (1998)

Signed as a free agent by **Toronto**, May 4, 1995. Signed as a free agent by **Philadelphia**, July 31, 1997. Signed as a free agent by **Nashville**, August 10, 1998. Signed as a free agent by **NY Islanders**, July 27, 1999. Claimed on waivers by **Columbus** from **NY Islanders**, May 26, 2000.

HICKS, Alex

(HIHKS, AL-ehx)

Left wing. Shoots left. 6', 190 lbs. Born, Calgary, Alta., September 4, 1969.

Season	Club	League	GP	G	A	Pts	PIM	PP	SH	GW	S	%	+/-	TF	F%	H	SB	Min	GP	G	A	Pts	PIM	PP	SH	GW
1986-87	Calgary Spurs	AJHL	53	40	47	87	117	....	....	....	....	....	....	....	....	....	....	....	....	....	....	....	....	....	....	....
1987-88	Calgary Spurs	AJHL	56	37	58	95	185	....	....	....	....	....	....	....	....	....	....	....	....	....	....	....	....	....	....	....
1988-89	Wisc-Eau Claire	NCHA	30	21	26	47	42	....	....	....	....	....	....	....	....	....	....	....	....	....	....	....	....	....	....	....
1989-90	Wisc-Eau Claire	NCHA	34	31	48	79	30	....	....	....	....	....	....	....	....	....	....	....	....	....	....	....	....	....	....	....
1990-91	Wisc-Eau Claire	NCHA	26	22	35	57	43	....	....	....	....	....	....	....	....	....	....	....	....	....	....	....	....	....	....	....
1991-92	Wisc-Eau Claire	NCHA	26	24	42	66	63	....	....	....	....	....	....	....	....	....	....	....	....	....	....	....	....	....	....	....
1992-93	Toledo Storm	ECHL	50	26	34	60	100	....	....	....	....	....	....	....	....	....	....	....	16	5	10	15	79	....	....	....
	Adirondack	AHL	3	0	0	0	0	....	....	....	....	....	....	....	....	....	....	....	....	....	....	....	....	....	....	....
1993-94	Toledo Storm	ECHL	60	31	49	80	240	....	....	....	....	....	....	....	....	....	....	....	14	10	10	20	56	....	....	....
	Adirondack	AHL	8	1	3	4	2	....	....	....	....	....	....	....	....	....	....	....	5	0	2	2	2	....	....	....
1994-95	Las Vegas	IHL	79	24	42	66	212	....	....	....	....	....	....	....	....	....	....	....	9	2	4	6	47	....	....	....
1995-96	**Anaheim**	**NHL**	**64**	**10**	**11**	**21**	**37**	**0**	**0**	**2**	**83**	**12.0**	**11**	....	....	....	....	....	....	....	....	....	....	....	....	....
	Baltimore Bandits	AHL	13	2	10	12	23	....	....	....	....	....	....	....	....	....	....	....	....	....	....	....	....	....	....	....
1996-97	**Anaheim**	**NHL**	**18**	**2**	**6**	**8**	**14**	**0**	**0**	**0**	**21**	**9.5**	**1**	....	....	....	....	....	....	....	....	....	....	....	....	....
	Pittsburgh	**NHL**	**55**	**5**	**15**	**20**	**76**	**0**	**0**	**3**	**57**	**8.8**	**-6**	....	....	....	....	....	**5**	**0**	**1**	**1**	**2**	**0**	**0**	**0**
1997-98	**Pittsburgh**	**NHL**	**58**	**7**	**13**	**20**	**54**	**0**	**0**	**1**	**78**	**9.0**	**4**	....	....	....	....	....	**6**	**0**	**0**	**0**	**2**	**0**	**0**	**0**
1998-99	**San Jose**	**NHL**	**4**	**0**	**1**	**1**	**4**	**0**	**0**	**0**	**4**	**0.0**	**-1**	**0**	**0.0**	**3**	**0**	**4:33**	....	....	....	....	....	....	....	....
	Florida	**NHL**	**51**	**0**	**6**	**6**	**58**	**0**	**0**	**0**	**47**	**0.0**	**-4**	**33**	**42.4**	**89**	**17**	**10:21**	....	....	....	....	....	....	....	....
99-2000	**Florida**	**NHL**	**8**	**1**	**2**	**3**	**4**	**0**	**0**	**0**	**6**	**16.7**	**3**	**1**	**0.0**	**13**	**1**	**8:39**	**4**	**0**	**1**	**1**	**4**	**0**	**0**	**0**
	Louisville Panthers	AHL	17	6	5	11	23	....	....	....	....	....	....	....	....	....	....	....	....	....	....	....	....	....	....	....
2000-01	Eisbaren Berlin	DEL	56	27	31	58	189	....	....	....	....	....	....	....	....	....	....	....	....	....	....	....	....	....	....	....
	NHL Totals		**258**	**25**	**54**	**79**	**247**	**0**	**0**	**6**	**296**	**8.4**		**34**	**41.2**	**105**	**18**	**9:46**	**15**	**0**	**2**	**2**	**8**	**0**	**0**	**0**

NCHA West First All-American Team (1991, 1992)

Signed as a free agent by **Anaheim**, August 17, 1995. Traded to **Pittsburgh** by **Anaheim** with Fredrik Olausson for Shawn Antoski and Dmitri Mironov, November 19, 1996. Signed as a free agent by **San Jose**, October, 1998. Traded to **Florida** by **San Jose** with San Jose's 5th round choice (later traded to NY Islanders - NY Islanders selected Adam Johnson) in 1999 Entry Draft for Jeff Norton, November 11, 1998. • Missed majority of 1999-2000 season recovering from knee injury suffered in training camp after being re-assigned to minors, September 28, 1999.

HIGGINS, Matt

(HIH-gihns, MAT)

Center. Shoots left. 6'2", 190 lbs. Born, Calgary, Alta., October 29, 1977. Montreal's 1st choice, 18th overall, in 1996 Entry Draft.

Season	Club	League	GP	G	A	Pts	PIM	PP	SH	GW	S	%	+/-	TF	F%	H	SB	Min	GP	G	A	Pts	PIM	PP	SH	GW
1992-93	Vernon Lakers	BCAHA	70	53	76	129	54	....	....	....	....	....	....	....	....	....	....	....	....	....	....	....	....	....	....	....
1993-94	Moose Jaw	WHL	64	6	10	16	10	....	....	....	....	....	....	....	....	....	....	....	....	....	....	....	....	....	....	....
1994-95	Moose Jaw	WHL	72	36	34	70	26	....	....	....	....	....	....	....	....	....	....	....	10	1	2	3	2	....	....	....
1995-96	Moose Jaw	WHL	67	30	33	63	43	....	....	....	....	....	....	....	....	....	....	....	....	....	....	....	....	....	....	....
1996-97	Moose Jaw	WHL	71	33	57	90	51	....	....	....	....	....	....	....	....	....	....	....	12	3	5	8	2	....	....	....
1997-98	**Montreal**	**NHL**	**1**	**0**	**0**	**0**	**0**	**0**	**0**	**0**	**1**	**0.0**	**-1**	....	....	....	....	....	....	....	....	....	....	....	....	....
	Fredericton	AHL	50	5	22	27	12	....	....	....	....	....	....	....	....	....	....	....	4	1	2	3	2	....	....	....
1998-99	**Montreal**	**NHL**	**25**	**1**	**0**	**1**	**0**	**0**	**0**	**0**	**12**	**8.3**	**-2**	**108**	**45.4**	**9**	**4**	**5:41**	....	....	....	....	....	....	....	....
	Fredericton	AHL	11	3	4	7	6	....	....	....	....	....	....	....	....	....	....	....	5	0	2	2	0	....	....	....
99-2000	**Montreal**	**NHL**	**25**	**0**	**2**	**2**	**4**	**0**	**0**	**0**	**9**	**0.0**	**-6**	**145**	**48.3**	**12**	**13**	**7:57**	....	....	....	....	....	....	....	....
	Quebec Citadelles	AHL	29	1	15	16	21	....	....	....	....	....	....	....	....	....	....	....	....	....	....	....	....	....	....	....
2000-01	**Montreal**	**NHL**	**6**	**0**	**0**	**0**	**2**	**0**	**0**	**0**	**3**	**0.0**	**-2**	**40**	**47.5**	**5**	**3**	**9:27**	....	....	....	....	....	....	....	....
	Quebec Citadelles	AHL	66	10	18	28	18	....	....	....	....	....	....	....	....	....	....	....	8	0	1	1	4	....	....	....
	NHL Totals		**57**	**1**	**2**	**3**	**6**	**0**	**0**	**0**	**25**	**4.0**		**293**	**47.1**	**26**	**20**	**7:06**	....	....	....	....	....	....	....	....

HILL, Sean

(HIHL, SHAWN) **ST.L.**

Defense. Shoots right. 6', 203 lbs. Born, Duluth, MN, February 14, 1970. Montreal's 9th choice, 167th overall, in 1988 Entry Draft.

Season	Club	League	GP	G	A	Pts	PIM	PP	SH	GW	S	%	+/-	TF	F%	H	SB	Min	GP	G	A	Pts	PIM	PP	SH	GW
1986-87	Lakefield Chiefs	OJHL-C	3	1	1	2	14	....	....	....	....	....	....	....	....	....	....	....	....	....	....	....	....	....	....	....
1987-88	East Duluth	Hi-School	24	10	17	27	....	....	....	....	....	....	....	....	....	....	....	....	....	....	....	....	....	....	....	....
1988-89	U. of Wisconsin	WCHA	45	2	23	25	69	....	....	....	....	....	....	....	....	....	....	....	....	....	....	....	....	....	....	....
1989-90	U. of Wisconsin	WCHA	42	14	39	53	78	....	....	....	....	....	....	....	....	....	....	....	....	....	....	....	....	....	....	....
1990-91	U. of Wisconsin	WCHA	37	19	32	51	122	....	....	....	....	....	....	....	....	....	....	....	....	....	....	....	....	....	....	....
	Montreal	**NHL**	....	....	....	....	....	....	....	....	....	....	....	....	....	....	....	....	**1**	**0**	**0**	**0**	**0**	**0**	**0**	**0**
	Fredericton	AHL	....	....	....	....	....	....	....	....	....	....	....	....	....	....	....	....	3	0	2	2	2	....	....	....
1991-92	Fredericton	AHL	42	7	20	27	65	....	....	....	....	....	....	....	....	....	....	....	7	1	3	4	6	....	....	....
	Team USA	Nat-Team	12	4	3	7	16	....	....	....	....	....	....	....	....	....	....	....	....	....	....	....	....	....	....	....
	United States	Olympics	8	2	0	2	6	....	....	....	....	....	....	....	....	....	....	....	....	....	....	....	....	....	....	....
	Montreal	**NHL**	....	....	....	....	....	....	....	....	....	....	....	....	....	....	....	....	**4**	**1**	**0**	**1**	**2**	**0**	**0**	**0**
1992-93♦	**Montreal**	**NHL**	**31**	**2**	**6**	**8**	**54**	**1**	**0**	**1**	**37**	**5.4**	**-5**	....	....	....	....	....	**3**	**0**	**0**	**0**	**4**	**0**	**0**	**0**
	Fredericton	AHL	6	1	3	4	10	....	....	....	....	....	....	....	....	....	....	....	....	....	....	....	....	....	....	....
1993-94	**Anaheim**	**NHL**	**68**	**7**	**20**	**27**	**78**	**2**	**1**	**1**	**165**	**4.2**	**-12**	....	....	....	....	....	....	....	....	....	....	....	....	....
1994-95	**Ottawa**	**NHL**	**45**	**1**	**14**	**15**	**30**	**0**	**0**	**0**	**107**	**0.9**	**-11**	....	....	....	....	....	....	....	....	....	....	....	....	....
1995-96	**Ottawa**	**NHL**	**80**	**7**	**14**	**21**	**94**	**2**	**0**	**2**	**157**	**4.5**	**-26**	....	....	....	....	....	....	....	....	....	....	....	....	....
1996-97	**Ottawa**	**NHL**	**5**	**0**	**0**	**0**	**4**	**0**	**0**	**0**	**9**	**0.0**	**1**	....	....	....	....	....	....	....	....	....	....	....	....	....
1997-98	**Ottawa**	**NHL**	**13**	**1**	**1**	**2**	**6**	**0**	**0**	**0**	**16**	**6.3**	**-3**	....	....	....	....	....	....	....	....	....	....	....	....	....
	Carolina	**NHL**	**42**	**0**	**5**	**5**	**48**	**0**	**0**	**0**	**37**	**0.0**	**-2**	....	....	....	....	....	....	....	....	....	....	....	....	....
1998-99	**Carolina**	**NHL**	**54**	**0**	**10**	**10**	**48**	**0**	**0**	**0**	**44**	**0.0**	**9**	**0**	**0.0**	**194**	**79**	**19:02**	....	....	....	....	....	....	....	....
99-2000	**Carolina**	**NHL**	**62**	**13**	**31**	**44**	**59**	**8**	**0**	**2**	**150**	**8.7**	**3**	**1**	**0.0**	**246**	**94**	**24:31**	....	....	....	....	....	....	....	....
2000-01	**St. Louis**	**NHL**	**48**	**1**	**10**	**11**	**51**	**0**	**0**	**0**	**47**	**2.1**	**5**	**1**	**0.0**	**111**	**49**	**17:23**	**15**	**0**	**1**	**1**	**12**	**0**	**0**	**0**
	NHL Totals		**448**	**32**	**111**	**143**	**472**	**13**	**1**	**6**	**769**	**4.2**		**2**	**0.0**	**551**	**222**	**20:38**	**23**	**1**	**1**	**2**	**18**	**0**	**0**	**0**

WCHA Second All-Star Team (1990, 1991) • NCAA West Second All-American Team (1991)

Claimed by **Anaheim** from **Montreal** in Expansion Draft, June 24, 1993. Traded to **Ottawa** by **Anaheim** with Anaheim's 9th round choice (Frederic Cassivi) in 1994 Entry Draft for Ottawa's 3rd round choice (later traded to Tampa Bay - Tampa Bay selected Vadim Epanchintsev) in 1994 Entry Draft, June 29, 1994. Traded to **Carolina** by **Ottawa** for Chris Murray, November 18, 1997. Signed as a free agent by **St. Louis**, July 1, 2000.

HINOTE, Dan
(HIGH-noht, DAN) **COL.**

Right wing. Shoots right. 6', 190 lbs. Born, Leesburg, FL, January 30, 1977. Colorado's 9th choice, 167th overall, in 1996 Entry Draft.

			Regular Season																	Playoffs							
Season	Club	League	GP	G	A	Pts	PIM	PP	SH	GW	S	%	+/-	TF	F%	H	SB	Min	GP	G	A	Pts	PIM	PP	SH	GW
1994-95	Army Academy	NCAA	33	20	24	44	20	....	....	....	....	....	....	....	....	....	....	....	....	....	....	....	....	....	....	....
1995-96	Army Academy	NCAA	34	21	24	45	22	....	....	....	....	....	....	....	....	....	....	....	....	....	....	....	....	....	....	....
1996-97	Oshawa Generals	OHL	60	15	13	28	58	....	....	....	....	....	....	....	....	....	....	....	18	4	5	9	8	....	....	....
1997-98	Oshawa Generals	OHL	35	12	15	27	39	....	....	....	....	....	....	....	....	....	....	....	5	2	2	4	7	....	....	....
	Hershey Bears	AHL	24	1	4	5	25	....	....	....	....	....	....	....	....	....	....	....	....	....	....	....	....	....	....	....
1998-99	Hershey Bears	AHL	65	4	16	20	95	....	....	....	....	....	....	....	....	....	....	....	5	3	1	4	6	....	....	....
99-2000	**Colorado**	**NHL**	**27**	**1**	**3**	**4**	**10**	**0**	**0**	**0**	**14**	**7.1**	**0**	**132**	**51.5**	**47**	**8**	**7:51**	....	....	....	....	....	....	....	....
	Hershey Bears	AHL	55	28	31	59	96	....	....	....	....	....	....	....	....	....	....	....	14	4	5	9	19	....	....	....
2000-01♦	**Colorado**	**NHL**	**76**	**5**	**10**	**15**	**51**	**1**	**0**	**1**	**69**	**7.2**	**1**	**506**	**49.8**	**199**	**38**	**10:21**	**23**	**2**	**4**	**6**	**21**	**0**	**0**	**0**
	NHL Totals		**103**	**6**	**13**	**19**	**61**	**1**	**0**	**1**	**83**	**7.2**		**638**	**50.2**	**246**	**46**	**9:42**	**23**	**2**	**4**	**6**	**21**	**0**	**0**	**0**

HLAVAC, Jan
(huh-LAH-vahch, YAHN) **PHI.**

Left wing. Shoots left. 6', 185 lbs. Born, Prague, Czech., September 20, 1976. NY Islanders' 2nd choice, 28th overall, in 1995 Entry Draft.

Season	Club	League	GP	G	A	Pts	PIM	PP	SH	GW	S	%	+/-	TF	F%	H	SB	Min	GP	G	A	Pts	PIM	PP	SH	GW
1993-94	Sparta Praha-Jr.	Cze-Rep.	27	12	15	27		....	....	....	....	....	....	....	....	....	....	....	....	....	....	....	....	....	....	....
	Sparta Praha	Cze-Rep	9	1	1	2	....	....	....	....	....	....	....	....	....	....	....	....	....	....	....	....	....	....	....	....
1994-95	Sparta Praha	Cze-Rep	38	7	6	13	18	....	....	....	....	....	....	....	....	....	....	....	5	0	2	2	0	....	....	....
1995-96	Sparta Praha	Cze-Rep	34	8	5	13	....	....	....	....	....	....	....	....	....	....	....	....	12	1	2	3	....	....	....	....
1996-97	Sparta Praha	Cze-Rep	38	8	13	21	24	....	....	....	....	....	....	....	....	....	....	....	10	5	2	7	2	....	....	....
	Sparta Praha	EuroHL	3	4	0	4	6	....	....	....	....	....	....	....	....	....	....	....	....	....	....	....	....	....	....	....
1997-98	Sparta Praha	Cze-Rep	48	17	30	47	40	....	....	....	....	....	....	....	....	....	....	....	5	1	0	1	2	....	....	....
	Sparta Praha	EuroHL	5	0	3	3	4	....	....	....	....	....	....	....	....	....	....	....	....	....	....	....	....	....	....	....
1998-99	Sparta Praha	Cze-Rep	49	*33	20	53	52	....	....	....	....	....	....	....	....	....	....	....	6	1	3	4	....	....	....	....
	Sparta Praha	EuroHL	5	4	2	6	0	....	....	....	....	....	....	....	....	....	....	....	1	1	1	2	0	....	....	....
99-2000	**NY Rangers**	**NHL**	**67**	**19**	**23**	**42**	**16**	**6**	**0**	**2**	**134**	**14.2**	**3**	**6**	**33.3**	**39**	**17**	**15:09**	....	....	....	....	....	....	....	....
	Hartford	AHL	3	1	0	1	0	....	....	....	....	....	....	....	....	....	....	....	....	....	....	....	....	....	....	....
2000-01	**NY Rangers**	**NHL**	**79**	**28**	**36**	**64**	**20**	**5**	**0**	**6**	**195**	**14.4**	**3**	**0**	**0.0**	**68**	**25**	**16:38**	....	....	....	....	....	....	....	....
	NHL Totals		**146**	**47**	**59**	**106**	**36**	**11**	**0**	**8**	**329**	**14.3**		**6**	**33.3**	**107**	**42**	**15:57**	....	....	....	....	....	....	....	....

Traded to **Calgary** by **NY Islanders** for Jorgen Jonsson, July 14, 1998. Rights traded to **NY Rangers** by **Calgary** with Calgary's 1st (Jamie Lundmark) and 3rd (later traded back to Calgary - Calgary selected Craig Andersson) round choices in 1999 Entry Draft for Marc Savard and NY Rangers' 1st round choice (Oleg Saprykin) in 1999 Entry Draft, June 26, 1999. Traded to **Philadelphia** by **NY Rangers** with Pavel Brendl, Kim Johnsson and NY Rangers' 3rd round choice in 2003 Entry Draft for the rights to Eric Lindros and a conditional 1st round choice in 2003 Entry Draft, August 20, 2001.

HLUSHKO, Todd
(huh-LUSH-koh, TAWD)

Center. Shoots left. 5'11", 185 lbs. Born, Toronto, Ont., February 7, 1970. Washington's 14th choice, 240th overall, in 1990 Entry Draft.

Season	Club	League	GP	G	A	Pts	PIM	PP	SH	GW	S	%	+/-	TF	F%	H	SB	Min	GP	G	A	Pts	PIM	PP	SH	GW
1987-88	Guelph Jr. B's	OJHL-B	44	36	47	83	94	....	....	....	....	....	....	....	....	....	....	....	....	....	....	....	....	....	....	....
1988-89	Guelph Platers	OHL	66	28	18	46	71	....	....	....	....	....	....	....	....	....	....	....	7	5	3	8	18	....	....	....
1989-90	Owen Sound	OHL	25	9	17	26	31	....	....	....	....	....	....	....	....	....	....	....	....	....	....	....	....	....	....	....
	London Knights	OHL	40	27	17	44	39	....	....	....	....	....	....	....	....	....	....	....	6	2	4	6	10	....	....	....
1990-91	Baltimore	AHL	66	9	14	23	55	....	....	....	....	....	....	....	....	....	....	....	....	....	....	....	....	....	....	....
1991-92	Baltimore	AHL	74	16	35	51	113	....	....	....	....	....	....	....	....	....	....	....	....	....	....	....	....	....	....	....
1992-93	Canada	Nat-Team	58	22	26	48	10	....	....	....	....	....	....	....	....	....	....	....	....	....	....	....	....	....	....	....
1993-94	Canada	Nat-Team	55	22	6	28	61	....	....	....	....	....	....	....	....	....	....	....	....	....	....	....	....	....	....	....
	Canada	Olympics	8	5	0	5	6	....	....	....	....	....	....	....	....	....	....	....	....	....	....	....	....	....	....	....
	Philadelphia	**NHL**	**2**	**1**	**0**	**1**	**0**	**0**	**0**	**0**	**2**	**50.0**	**1**	....	....	....	....	....	....	....	....	....	....	....	....	....
	Hershey Bears	AHL	9	6	0	6	4	....	....	....	....	....	....	....	....	....	....	....	6	2	1	3	4	....	....	....
1994-95	Saint John Flames	AHL	46	22	10	32	36	....	....	....	....	....	....	....	....	....	....	....	4	2	2	4	22	....	....	....
	Calgary	**NHL**	**2**	**0**	**1**	**1**	**2**	**0**	**0**	**0**	**3**	**0.0**	**1**	....	....	....	....	....	**1**	**0**	**0**	**0**	**2**	**0**	**0**	**0**
1995-96	**Calgary**	**NHL**	**4**	**0**	**0**	**0**	**6**	**0**	**0**	**0**	**6**	**0.0**	**0**	....	....	....	....	....	....	....	....	....	....	....	....	....
	Saint John Flames	AHL	35	14	13	27	70	....	....	....	....	....	....	....	....	....	....	....	16	8	1	9	26	....	....	....
1996-97	**Calgary**	**NHL**	**58**	**7**	**11**	**18**	**49**	**0**	**0**	**0**	**76**	**9.2**	**–2**	....	....	....	....	....	....	....	....	....	....	....	....	....
1997-98	**Calgary**	**NHL**	**13**	**0**	**1**	**1**	**27**	**0**	**0**	**0**	**7**	**0.0**	**0**	....	....	....	....	....	....	....	....	....	....	....	....	....
	Saint John Flames	AHL	33	10	14	24	48	....	....	....	....	....	....	....	....	....	....	....	21	*13	4	17	61	....	....	....
1998-99	Grand Rapids	IHL	82	24	26	50	78	....	....	....	....	....	....	....	....	....	....	....	....	....	....	....	....	....	....	....
	Pittsburgh	**NHL**	....	....	....	....	....	....	....	....	....	....	....	....	....	....	....	....	**2**	**0**	**0**	**0**	**0**	**0**	**0**	**0**
99-2000	Kolner Haie	DEL	55	13	28	41	78	....	....	....	....	....	....	....	....	....	....	....	10	5	2	7	20	....	....	....
2000-01	Adler Mannheim	DEL	54	18	19	37	126	....	....	....	....	....	....	....	....	....	....	....	10	1	1	2	16	....	....	....
	NHL Totals		**79**	**8**	**13**	**21**	**84**	**0**	**0**	**0**	**94**	**8.5**		....	....	....	....	....	**3**	**0**	**0**	**0**	**2**	**0**	**0**	**0**

Signed as a free agent by **Philadelphia**, March 7, 1994. Signed as a free agent by **Calgary**, June 17, 1994. Traded to **Pittsburgh** by **Calgary** with German Titov for Ken Wregget and Dave Roche, June 17, 1998.

HNIDY, Shane
(NIGH-dee, SHAYN) **OTT.**

Defense. Shoots right. 6'2", 210 lbs. Born, Neepawa, Man., November 8, 1975. Buffalo's 7th choice, 173rd overall, in 1994 Entry Draft.

Season	Club	League	GP	G	A	Pts	PIM	PP	SH	GW	S	%	+/-	TF	F%	H	SB	Min	GP	G	A	Pts	PIM	PP	SH	GW
1990-91	Yellowhead Pass	MAHA	36	9	11	20	92	....	....	....	....	....	....	....	....	....	....	....	....	....	....	....	....	....	....	....
1991-92	Swift Current	WHL	56	1	3	4	11	....	....	....	....	....	....	....	....	....	....	....	4	0	0	0	0	....	....	....
1992-93	Swift Current	WHL	45	5	12	17	62	....	....	....	....	....	....	....	....	....	....	....	....	....	....	....	....	....	....	....
	Prince Albert	WHL	27	2	10	12	43	....	....	....	....	....	....	....	....	....	....	....	....	....	....	....	....	....	....	....
1993-94	Prince Albert	WHL	69	7	26	33	113	....	....	....	....	....	....	....	....	....	....	....	....	....	....	....	....	....	....	....
1994-95	Prince Albert	WHL	72	5	29	34	169	....	....	....	....	....	....	....	....	....	....	....	15	4	7	11	29	....	....	....
1995-96	Prince Albert	WHL	58	11	42	53	100	....	....	....	....	....	....	....	....	....	....	....	18	4	11	15	34	....	....	....
1996-97	Baton Rouge	ECHL	21	3	10	13	50	....	....	....	....	....	....	....	....	....	....	....	....	....	....	....	....	....	....	....
	Saint John Flames	AHL	44	2	12	14	112	....	....	....	....	....	....	....	....	....	....	....	....	....	....	....	....	....	....	....
1997-98	Grand Rapids	IHL	77	6	12	18	210	....	....	....	....	....	....	....	....	....	....	....	3	0	2	2	23	....	....	....
1998-99	Adirondack	AHL	68	9	20	29	121	....	....	....	....	....	....	....	....	....	....	....	3	0	1	1	0	....	....	....
99-2000	Cincinnati Ducks	AHL	68	9	19	28	153	....	....	....	....	....	....	....	....	....	....	....	....	....	....	....	....	....	....	....
2000-01	**Ottawa**	**NHL**	**52**	**3**	**2**	**5**	**84**	**0**	**0**	**1**	**47**	**6.4**	**8**	**0**	**0.0**	**90**	**44**	**13:05**	**1**	**0**	**0**	**0**	**0**	**0**	**0**	**0**
	Grand Rapids	IHL	2	0	0	0	2	....	....	....	....	....	....	....	....	....	....	....	....	....	....	....	....	....	....	....
	NHL Totals		**52**	**3**	**2**	**5**	**84**	**0**	**0**	**1**	**47**	**6.4**		**0**	**0.0**	**90**	**44**	**13:05**	**1**	**0**	**0**	**0**	**0**	**0**	**0**	**0**

Signed as a free agent by **Detroit**, August 6, 1998. Traded to **Ottawa** by **Detroit** for Ottawa's 8th round choice (Todd Jackson) in 2000 Entry Draft, June 25, 2000.

HOCKING, Justin
(HAWK-ihng, JUHS-tihn)

Defense. Shoots right. 6'4", 215 lbs. Born, Stettler, Alta., January 9, 1974. Los Angeles' 1st choice, 39th overall, in 1992 Entry Draft.

Season	Club	League	GP	G	A	Pts	PIM	PP	SH	GW	S	%	+/-	TF	F%	H	SB	Min	GP	G	A	Pts	PIM	PP	SH	GW
1990-91	Ft-Saskatchewan	AJHL	38	4	6	10	84	....	....	....	....	....	....	....	....	....	....	....	....	....	....	....	....	....	....	....
1991-92	Spokane Chiefs	WHL	71	4	6	10	309	....	....	....	....	....	....	....	....	....	....	....	10	0	3	3	28	....	....	....
1992-93	Spokane Chiefs	WHL	16	0	1	1	75	....	....	....	....	....	....	....	....	....	....	....	....	....	....	....	....	....	....	....
	Medicine Hat	WHL	54	1	9	10	119	....	....	....	....	....	....	....	....	....	....	....	10	0	1	1	13	....	....	....
1993-94	Medicine Hat	WHL	68	7	26	33	236	....	....	....	....	....	....	....	....	....	....	....	3	0	0	0	6	....	....	....
	Los Angeles	**NHL**	**1**	**0**	**0**	**0**	**0**	**0**	**0**	**0**	**0**	**0.0**	**0**	....	....	....	....	....	....	....	....	....	....	....	....	....
	Phoenix	IHL	3	0	0	0	15	....	....	....	....	....	....	....	....	....	....	....	....	....	....	....	....	....	....	....
1994-95	Syracuse Crunch	AHL	7	0	0	0	24	....	....	....	....	....	....	....	....	....	....	....	....	....	....	....	....	....	....	....
	Portland Pirates	AHL	9	0	1	1	34	....	....	....	....	....	....	....	....	....	....	....	....	....	....	....	....	....	....	....
	Knoxville	ECHL	20	0	6	6	70	....	....	....	....	....	....	....	....	....	....	....	4	0	0	0	26	....	....	....
	Phoenix	IHL	20	1	1	2	50	....	....	....	....	....	....	....	....	....	....	....	1	0	0	0	0	....	....	....
1995-96	P.E.I. Senators	AHL	74	4	8	12	251	....	....	....	....	....	....	....	....	....	....	....	4	0	2	2	5	....	....	....
1996-97	Worcester	AHL	68	1	10	11	198	....	....	....	....	....	....	....	....	....	....	....	5	0	3	3	2	....	....	....
1997-98	Worcester	AHL	79	5	12	17	198	....	....	....	....	....	....	....	....	....	....	....	11	1	2	3	19	....	....	....
1998-99	Indianapolis Ice	IHL	34	2	4	6	111	....	....	....	....	....	....	....	....	....	....	....	....	....	....	....	....	....	....	....
	St. John's Leafs	AHL	44	4	6	10	99	....	....	....	....	....	....	....	....	....	....	....	5	0	0	0	2	....	....	....
99-2000	St. John's Leafs	AHL	68	4	9	13	175	....	....	....	....	....	....	....	....	....	....	....	....	....	....	....	....	....	....	....
2000-01	Springfield	AHL	60	0	7	7	114	....	....	....	....	....	....	....	....	....	....	....	....	....	....	....	....	....	....	....
	Grand Rapids	IHL	6	0	0	0	12	....	....	....	....	....	....	....	....	....	....	....	....	....	....	....	....	....	....	....
	NHL Totals		**1**	**0**	**0**	**0**	**0**	**0**	**0**	**0**	**0**	**0.0**		....	....	....	....	....	....	....	....	....	....	....	....	....

WHL East Second All-Star Team (1994)

Claimed by **Ottawa** from **LA Kings** in Waiver Draft, October 2, 1995. Traded to **Chicago** by **Ottawa** for Brian Felsner, August 21, 1998. Signed as a free agent by **Toronto**, July 23, 1999. Signed as a free agent by **Phoenix**, August 1, 2000.

HOGLUND, Jonas

(HOHG-lund, YOH-nuhs) **TOR.**

Right wing. Shoots right. 6'3", 215 lbs. Born, Hammaro, Swe., August 29, 1972. Calgary's 11th choice, 222nd overall, in 1992 Entry Draft.

			Regular Season																Playoffs							
Season	Club	League	GP	G	A	Pts	PIM	PP	SH	GW	S	%	+/-	TF	F%	H	SB	Min	GP	G	A	Pts	PIM	PP	SH	GW
1990-91	Farjestads BK	Sweden	40	5	5	10	4	....	....	....	....	....	....	....	....	....	....	....	8	1	0	1	0	....	....	....
1991-92	Farjestads BK	Sweden	40	14	11	25	6	....	....	....	....	....	....	....	....	....	....	....	6	2	4	6	2	....	....	....
1992-93	Farjestads BK	Sweden	40	13	13	26	14	....	....	....	....	....	....	....	....	....	....	....	3	1	0	1	0	....	....	....
1993-94	Farjestads BK	Sweden	22	7	2	9	10	....	....	....	....	....	....	....	....	....	....	....	....	....	....	....	....	....	....	....
1994-95	Farjestads BK	Sweden	40	14	12	26	16	....	....	....	....	....	....	....	....	....	....	....	4	3	2	5	0	....	....	....
1995-96	Farjestads BK	Sweden	40	32	11	43	18	....	....	....	....	....	....	....	....	....	....	....	8	2	1	3	6	....	....	....
1996-97	**Calgary**	**NHL**	**68**	**19**	**16**	**35**	**12**	**3**	**0**	**6**	**189**	**10.1**	**–4**	....	....	....	....	....	....	....	....	....	....	....	....	....
1997-98	**Calgary**	**NHL**	**50**	**6**	**8**	**14**	**16**	**0**	**0**	**0**	**124**	**4.8**	**–9**	....	....	....	....	....	....	....	....	....	....	....	....	....
	Montreal	**NHL**	**28**	**6**	**5**	**11**	**6**	**4**	**0**	**0**	**62**	**9.7**	**2**	....	....	....	....	....	**10**	**2**	**0**	**2**	**0**	**0**	**0**	**0**
1998-99	**Montreal**	**NHL**	**74**	**8**	**10**	**18**	**16**	**1**	**0**	**0**	**122**	**6.6**	**–5**	**17**	**29.4**	**41**	**15**	**11:50**	....	....	....	....	....	....	....	....
99-2000	**Toronto**	**NHL**	**82**	**29**	**27**	**56**	**10**	**9**	**1**	**3**	**215**	**13.5**	**–2**	**4**	**50.0**	**55**	**24**	**17:10**	**12**	**2**	**4**	**6**	**2**	**0**	**0**	**0**
2000-01	**Toronto**	**NHL**	**82**	**23**	**26**	**49**	**14**	**5**	**0**	**5**	**196**	**11.7**	**1**	**4**	**50.0**	**53**	**23**	**15:08**	**10**	**0**	**0**	**0**	**4**	**0**	**0**	**0**
	NHL Totals		**384**	**91**	**92**	**183**	**74**	**22**	**1**	**14**	**908**	**10.0**		**25**	**36.0**	**149**	**62**	**14:48**	**32**	**4**	**4**	**8**	**6**	**0**	**0**	**0**

Traded to **Montreal** by **Calgary** with Zarley Zalapski for Valeri Bure and Montreal's 4th round choice (Shaun Sutter) in 1998 Entry Draft, February 1, 1998. Signed as a free agent by **Toronto**, July 13, 1999.

HOGUE, Benoit

(HOHG, BEHN-wah) **DAL.**

Center. Shoots left. 5'10", 194 lbs. Born, Repentigny, Que., October 28, 1966. Buffalo's 2nd choice, 35th overall, in 1985 Entry Draft.

			Regular Season																Playoffs							
Season	Club	League	GP	G	A	Pts	PIM	PP	SH	GW	S	%	+/-	TF	F%	H	SB	Min	GP	G	A	Pts	PIM	PP	SH	GW
1982-83	Mtl-Bourassa	QAAA	40	20	20	40	34	....	....	....	....	....	....	....	....	....	....	....	10	2	1	3	4	....	....	....
1983-84	St-Jean Castors	QMJHL	59	14	11	25	42	....	....	....	....	....	....	....	....	....	....	....	....	....	....	....	....	....	....	....
1984-85	St-Jean Castors	QMJHL	63	46	44	90	92	....	....	....	....	....	....	....	....	....	....	....	....	....	....	....	....	....	....	....
1985-86	St-Jean Castors	QMJHL	65	54	54	108	115	....	....	....	....	....	....	....	....	....	....	....	9	6	4	10	26	....	....	....
1986-87	Rochester	AHL	52	14	20	34	52	....	....	....	....	....	....	....	....	....	....	....	12	5	4	9	8	....	....	....
1987-88	**Buffalo**	**NHL**	**3**	**1**	**1**	**2**	**0**	**0**	**0**	**1**	**3**	**33.3**	**3**	....	....	....	....	....	....	....	....	....	....	....	....	....
	Rochester	AHL	62	24	31	55	141	....	....	....	....	....	....	....	....	....	....	....	7	6	1	7	46	....	....	....
1988-89	**Buffalo**	**NHL**	**69**	**14**	**30**	**44**	**120**	**1**	**2**	**0**	**114**	**12.3**	**–5**	....	....	....	....	....	**5**	**0**	**0**	**0**	**17**	**0**	**0**	**0**
1989-90	**Buffalo**	**NHL**	**45**	**11**	**7**	**18**	**79**	**1**	**0**	**1**	**73**	**15.1**	**0**	....	....	....	....	....	**3**	**0**	**0**	**0**	**10**	**0**	**0**	**0**
1990-91	**Buffalo**	**NHL**	**76**	**19**	**28**	**47**	**76**	**1**	**0**	**2**	**134**	**14.2**	**–8**	....	....	....	....	....	**5**	**3**	**1**	**4**	**10**	**0**	**0**	**0**
1991-92	**Buffalo**	**NHL**	**3**	**0**	**1**	**1**	**0**	**0**	**0**	**0**	**6**	**0.0**	**0**	....	....	....	....	....	....	....	....	....	....	....	....	....
	NY Islanders	**NHL**	**72**	**30**	**45**	**75**	**67**	**8**	**0**	**5**	**143**	**21.0**	**30**	....	....	....	....	....	....	....	....	....	....	....	....	....
1992-93	**NY Islanders**	**NHL**	**70**	**33**	**42**	**75**	**108**	**5**	**3**	**5**	**147**	**22.4**	**13**	....	....	....	....	....	**18**	**6**	**6**	**12**	**31**	**0**	**0**	**0**
1993-94	**NY Islanders**	**NHL**	**83**	**36**	**33**	**69**	**73**	**9**	**5**	**3**	**218**	**16.5**	**–7**	....	....	....	....	....	**4**	**0**	**1**	**1**	**4**	**0**	**0**	**0**
1994-95	**NY Islanders**	**NHL**	**33**	**6**	**4**	**10**	**34**	**1**	**0**	**1**	**50**	**12.0**	**0**	....	....	....	....	....	....	....	....	....	....	....	....	....
	Toronto	**NHL**	**12**	**3**	**3**	**6**	**0**	**1**	**0**	**1**	**16**	**18.8**	**0**	....	....	....	....	....	**7**	**0**	**0**	**0**	**6**	**0**	**0**	**0**
1995-96	**Toronto**	**NHL**	**44**	**12**	**25**	**37**	**68**	**3**	**0**	**5**	**94**	**12.8**	**6**	....	....	....	....	....	....	....	....	....	....	....	....	....
	Dallas	**NHL**	**34**	**7**	**20**	**27**	**36**	**2**	**0**	**0**	**61**	**11.5**	**4**	....	....	....	....	....	....	....	....	....	....	....	....	....
1996-97	**Dallas**	**NHL**	**73**	**19**	**24**	**43**	**54**	**5**	**0**	**5**	**131**	**14.5**	**8**	....	....	....	....	....	**7**	**2**	**2**	**4**	**6**	**1**	**0**	**0**
1997-98	**Dallas**	**NHL**	**53**	**6**	**16**	**22**	**35**	**3**	**0**	**1**	**55**	**10.9**	**7**	....	....	....	....	....	**17**	**4**	**2**	**6**	**16**	**1**	**0**	**2**
1998-99	**Tampa Bay**	**NHL**	**62**	**11**	**14**	**25**	**50**	**2**	**0**	**3**	**101**	**10.9**	**–12**	**63**	**42.9**	**89**	**24**	**16:23**	....	....	....	....	....	....	....	....
	♦ **Dallas**	**NHL**	**12**	**1**	**3**	**4**	**4**	**0**	**0**	**0**	**20**	**5.0**	**2**	**52**	**46.2**	**31**	**4**	**15:04**	**14**	**0**	**2**	**2**	**16**	**0**	**0**	**0**
99-2000	**Phoenix**	**NHL**	**27**	**3**	**10**	**13**	**10**	**0**	**0**	**0**	**39**	**7.7**	**–1**	**24**	**37.5**	**56**	**11**	**15:45**	**5**	**1**	**2**	**3**	**2**	**0**	**0**	**0**
2000-01	**Dallas**	**NHL**	**34**	**3**	**7**	**10**	**26**	**0**	**0**	**0**	**35**	**8.6**	**–1**	**143**	**44.8**	**70**	**5**	**12:28**	**7**	**1**	**0**	**1**	**6**	**0**	**0**	**1**
	NHL Totals		**805**	**215**	**313**	**528**	**840**	**42**	**10**	**33**	**1440**	**14.9**		**282**	**44.0**	**246**	**44**	**15:09**	**92**	**17**	**16**	**33**	**124**	**2**	**0**	**3**

Traded to **NY Islanders** by **Buffalo** with Pierre Turgeon, Uwe Krupp and Dave McLlwain for Pat LaFontaine, Randy Hillier, Randy Wood and NY Islanders' 4th round choice (Dean Melanson) in 1992 Entry Draft, October 25, 1991. Traded to **Toronto** by **NY Islanders** with NY Islanders' 3rd round choice (Ryan Pepperall) in 1995 Entry Draft and 5th round choice (Brandon Sugden) in 1996 Entry Draft for Eric Fichaud, April 6, 1995. Traded to **Dallas** by **Toronto** with Randy Wood for Dave Gagner and Dallas' 6th round choice (Dmitri Yakushin) in 1996 Entry Draft, January 29, 1996. Signed as a free agent by **Tampa Bay**, August 19, 1998. Traded to **Dallas** by **Tampa Bay** with Tampa Bay's 6th round choice (Michal Blazek) in 2001 Entry Draft for Sergey Gusev, March 21, 1999. Signed as a free agent by **Phoenix**, February 3, 2000. Signed as a free agent by **Dallas**, January 5, 2001.

HOLDEN, Josh

(HOHL-dehn, JAWSH) **VAN.**

Center. Shoots left. 6', 190 lbs. Born, Calgary, Alta., January 18, 1978. Vancouver's 1st choice, 12th overall, in 1996 Entry Draft.

			Regular Season																Playoffs							
Season	Club	League	GP	G	A	Pts	PIM	PP	SH	GW	S	%	+/-	TF	F%	H	SB	Min	GP	G	A	Pts	PIM	PP	SH	GW
1993-94	Calgary Buffaloes	AMHL	34	14	15	29	82	....	....	....	....	....	....	....	....	....	....	....	....	....	....	....	....	....	....	....
1994-95	Regina Pats	WHL	62	20	23	43	45	....	....	....	....	....	....	....	....	....	....	....	4	3	1	4	0	....	....	....
1995-96	Regina Pats	WHL	70	57	55	112	105	....	....	....	....	....	....	....	....	....	....	....	11	4	5	9	23	....	....	....
1996-97	Regina Pats	WHL	58	49	49	98	148	....	....	....	....	....	....	....	....	....	....	....	5	3	2	5	10	....	....	....
1997-98	Regina Pats	WHL	56	41	58	99	134	....	....	....	....	....	....	....	....	....	....	....	2	2	2	4	10	....	....	....
1998-99	**Vancouver**	**NHL**	**30**	**2**	**4**	**6**	**10**	**1**	**0**	**0**	**44**	**4.5**	**–10**	**269**	**39.0**	**38**	**6**	**12:44**	....	....	....	....	....	....	....	....
	Syracuse Crunch	AHL	38	14	15	29	48	....	....	....	....	....	....	....	....	....	....	....	....	....	....	....	....	....	....	....
99-2000	**Vancouver**	**NHL**	**6**	**1**	**5**	**6**	**2**	**0**	**0**	**0**	**5**	**20.0**	**2**	**42**	**42.9**	**14**	**2**	**10:25**	....	....	....	....	....	....	....	....
	Syracuse Crunch	AHL	45	19	32	51	113	....	....	....	....	....	....	....	....	....	....	....	4	1	0	1	10	....	....	....
2000-01	Kansas City	IHL	60	27	26	53	136	....	....	....	....	....	....	....	....	....	....	....	....	....	....	....	....	....	....	....
	Vancouver	**NHL**	**10**	**1**	**0**	**1**	**0**	**0**	**0**	**0**	**12**	**8.3**	**0**	**85**	**35.3**	**21**	**2**	**9:27**	....	....	....	....	....	....	....	....
	NHL Totals		**46**	**4**	**9**	**13**	**12**	**1**	**0**	**0**	**61**	**6.6**		**396**	**38.6**	**73**	**10**	**11:43**	....	....	....	....	....	....	....	....

WHL East Second All-Star Team (1998)

HOLIK, Bobby

(HOH-leek, BAWB-ee) **N.J.**

Center. Shoots right. 6'4", 230 lbs. Born, Jihlava, Czech., January 1, 1971. Hartford's 1st choice, 10th overall, in 1989 Entry Draft.

			Regular Season																Playoffs							
Season	Club	League	GP	G	A	Pts	PIM	PP	SH	GW	S	%	+/-	TF	F%	H	SB	Min	GP	G	A	Pts	PIM	PP	SH	GW
1987-88	Dukla Jihlava	Czech.	31	5	9	14	16	....	....	....	....	....	....	....	....	....	....	....	....	....	....	....	....	....	....	....
1988-89	Dukla Jihlava	Czech.	24	7	10	17	32	....	....	....	....	....	....	....	....	....	....	....	....	....	....	....	....	....	....	....
1989-90	Dukla Jihlava	Czech.	42	15	26	41	....	....	....	....	....	....	....	....	....	....	....	....	....	....	....	....	....	....	....	....
1990-91	**Hartford**	**NHL**	**78**	**21**	**22**	**43**	**113**	**8**	**0**	**3**	**173**	**12.1**	**–3**	....	....	....	....	....	**6**	**0**	**0**	**0**	**7**	**0**	**0**	**0**
1991-92	**Hartford**	**NHL**	**76**	**21**	**24**	**45**	**44**	**1**	**0**	**2**	**207**	**10.1**	**4**	....	....	....	....	....	**7**	**0**	**1**	**1**	**6**	**0**	**0**	**0**
1992-93	**New Jersey**	**NHL**	**61**	**20**	**19**	**39**	**76**	**7**	**0**	**4**	**180**	**11.1**	**–6**	....	....	....	....	....	**5**	**1**	**1**	**2**	**6**	**0**	**0**	**0**
	Utica Devils	AHL	1	0	0	0	2	....	....	....	....	....	....	....	....	....	....	....	....	....	....	....	....	....	....	....
1993-94	**New Jersey**	**NHL**	**70**	**13**	**20**	**33**	**72**	**2**	**0**	**3**	**130**	**10.0**	**28**	....	....	....	....	....	**20**	**0**	**3**	**3**	**6**	**0**	**0**	**0**
1994-95♦	**New Jersey**	**NHL**	**48**	**10**	**10**	**20**	**18**	**0**	**0**	**2**	**84**	**11.9**	**9**	....	....	....	....	....	**20**	**4**	**4**	**8**	**22**	**2**	**0**	**1**
1995-96	**New Jersey**	**NHL**	**63**	**13**	**17**	**30**	**58**	**1**	**0**	**1**	**157**	**8.3**	**9**	....	....	....	....	....	....	....	....	....	....	....	....	....
1996-97	**New Jersey**	**NHL**	**82**	**23**	**39**	**62**	**54**	**5**	**0**	**6**	**192**	**12.0**	**24**	....	....	....	....	....	**10**	**2**	**3**	**5**	**4**	**1**	**0**	**0**
1997-98	**New Jersey**	**NHL**	**82**	**29**	**36**	**65**	**100**	**8**	**0**	**8**	**238**	**12.2**	**23**	....	....	....	....	....	**5**	**0**	**0**	**0**	**8**	**0**	**0**	**0**
1998-99	**New Jersey**	**NHL**	**78**	**27**	**37**	**64**	**119**	**5**	**0**	**8**	**253**	**10.7**	**16**	**1350**	**53.6**	**217**	**24**	**17:34**	**7**	**0**	**7**	**7**	**6**	**0**	**0**	**0**
99-2000♦	**New Jersey**	**NHL**	**79**	**23**	**23**	**46**	**106**	**7**	**0**	**4**	**257**	**8.9**	**7**	**1390**	**55.6**	**139**	**17**	**16:53**	**23**	**3**	**7**	**10**	**14**	**0**	**0**	**1**
2000-01	**New Jersey**	**NHL**	**80**	**15**	**35**	**50**	**97**	**3**	**0**	**3**	**206**	**7.3**	**19**	**1365**	**56.0**	**213**	**20**	**15:49**	**25**	**6**	**10**	**16**	**37**	**1**	**0**	**3**
	NHL Totals		**797**	**215**	**282**	**497**	**857**	**47**	**0**	**44**	**2077**	**10.4**		**4105**	**55.1**	**569**	**61**	**16:45**	**128**	**16**	**36**	**52**	**116**	**4**	**0**	**5**

Played in NHL All-Star Game (1998, 1999)

Traded to **New Jersey** by **Hartford** with Hartford's 2nd round choice (Jay Pandolfo) in 1993 Entry Draft for Sean Burke and Eric Weinrich, August 28, 1992.

HOLLAND, Jason

(HAWL-land, JAY-suhn)

Defense. Shoots right. 6'3", 209 lbs. Born, Morinville, Alta., April 30, 1976. NY Islanders' 2nd choice, 38th overall, in 1994 Entry Draft.

			Regular Season																Playoffs							
Season	Club	League	GP	G	A	Pts	PIM	PP	SH	GW	S	%	+/-	TF	F%	H	SB	Min	GP	G	A	Pts	PIM	PP	SH	GW
1991-92	St. Albert Eagles	AMHL	38	9	29	38	94	....	....	....	....	....	....	....	....	....	....	....	....	....	....	....	....	....	....	....
1992-93	St. Albert Eagles	AMHL	31	11	25	36	36	....	....	....	....	....	....	....	....	....	....	....	....	....	....	....	....	....	....	....
	Kamloops Blazers	WHL	4	0	0	0	2	....	....	....	....	....	....	....	....	....	....	....	....	....	....	....	....	....	....	....
1993-94	Kamloops Blazers	WHL	59	14	15	29	80	....	....	....	....	....	....	....	....	....	....	....	18	2	3	5	4	....	....	....
1994-95	Kamloops Blazers	WHL	71	9	32	41	65	....	....	....	....	....	....	....	....	....	....	....	21	2	7	9	9	....	....	....
1995-96	Kamloops Blazers	WHL	63	24	33	57	98	....	....	....	....	....	....	....	....	....	....	....	16	4	9	13	22	....	....	....
1996-97	**NY Islanders**	**NHL**	**4**	**1**	**0**	**1**	**0**	**0**	**0**	**0**	**3**	**33.3**	**1**	....	....	....	....	....	....	....	....	....	....	....	....	....
	Kentucky	AHL	72	14	25	39	46	....	....	....	....	....	....	....	....	....	....	....	4	0	2	2	0	....	....	....
1997-98	**NY Islanders**	**NHL**	**8**	**0**	**0**	**0**	**4**	**0**	**0**	**0**	**6**	**0.0**	**–4**	....	....	....	....	....	....	....	....	....	....	....	....	....
	Kentucky	AHL	50	10	16	26	29	....	....	....	....	....	....	....	....	....	....	....	....	....	....	....	....	....	....	....
	Rochester	AHL	9	0	4	4	10	....	....	....	....	....	....	....	....	....	....	....	4	0	3	3	4	....	....	....
1998-99	**Buffalo**	**NHL**	**3**	**0**	**0**	**0**	**8**	**0**	**0**	**0**	**2**	**0.0**	**–1**	**0**	**0.0**	**0**	**2**	**10:58**	....	....	....	....	....	....	....	....
	Rochester	AHL	74	4	25	29	36	....	....	....	....	....	....	....	....	....	....	....	20	2	5	7	8	....	....	....

			Regular Season																Playoffs							
Season	Club	League	GP	G	A	Pts	PIM	PP	SH	GW	S	%	+/-	TF	F%	H	SB	Min	GP	G	A	Pts	PIM	PP	SH	GW
99-2000	**Buffalo**	**NHL**	**9**	**0**	**1**	**1**	**0**	**0**	**0**	**0**	**8**	**0.0**	**0**	**0**	**0.0**	**5**	**3**	**15:31**	**1**	**0**	**0**	**0**	**0**	**0**	**0**	**0**
	Rochester	AHL	54	3	15	18	24	....	....	....	....	....	....	....	....	....	....	....	12	1	0	1	2	....	....	....
2000-01	Rochester	AHL	63	4	19	23	45	....	....	....	....	....	....	....	....	....	....	....	4	1	0	1	0	....	....	....
	NHL Totals		**24**	**1**	**1**	**2**	**12**	**0**	**0**	**0**	**19**	**5.3**		**0**	**0.0**	**5**	**5**	**14:23**	**1**	**0**	**0**	**0**	**0**	**0**	**0**	**0**

Won Warwick Trophy (MVP - AMHL) (1993) • WHL West First All-Star Team (1996)

Traded to **Buffalo** by **NY Islanders** with Paul Kruse for Jason Dawe, March 24, 1998.

HOLLINGER, Terry
(HAWL-lihn-GUHR, TAIR-ree)

Defense. Shoots left. 6'1", 200 lbs. Born, Regina, Sask., February 24, 1971. St. Louis' 7th choice, 153rd overall, in 1991 Entry Draft.

1986-87	Regina Cougars	SAHA	31	37	36	73	59	....	....	....	....	....	....	....	....	....	....	....	....	....	....	....	....	....	....	....
1987-88	Regina Canucks	SMHL	30	13	36	49	74	....	....	....	....	....	....	....	....	....	....	....	....	....	....	....	....	....	....	....
	Regina Pats	WHL	7	1	1	2	4	....	....	....	....	....	....	....	....	....	....	....	....	....	....	....	....	....	....	....
1988-89	Regina Pats	WHL	65	2	27	29	49	....	....	....	....	....	....	....	....	....	....	....	....	....	....	....	....	....	....	....
1989-90	Regina Pats	WHL	70	14	43	57	40	....	....	....	....	....	....	....	....	....	....	....	11	1	3	4	10	....	....	....
1990-91	Regina Pats	WHL	8	1	6	7	6	....	....	....	....	....	....	....	....	....	....	....	....	....	....	....	....	....	....	....
	Lethbridge	WHL	62	9	32	41	113	....	....	....	....	....	....	....	....	....	....	....	16	3	14	17	22	....	....	....
1991-92	Lethbridge	WHL	65	23	62	85	155	....	....	....	....	....	....	....	....	....	....	....	5	1	2	3	13	....	....	....
	Peoria Rivermen	IHL	1	0	2	2	0	....	....	....	....	....	....	....	....	....	....	....	5	0	1	1	0	....	....	....
1992-93	Peoria Rivermen	IHL	72	2	28	30	67	....	....	....	....	....	....	....	....	....	....	....	4	1	1	2	0	....	....	....
1993-94	**St. Louis**	**NHL**	**2**	**0**	**0**	**0**	**0**	**0**	**0**	**0**	**0**	**0.0**	**1**	....	....	....	....	....	....	....	....	....	....	....	....	....
	Peoria Rivermen	IHL	78	12	31	43	96	....	....	....	....	....	....	....	....	....	....	....	6	0	3	3	31	....	....	....
1994-95	Peoria Rivermen	IHL	69	7	25	32	137	....	....	....	....	....	....	....	....	....	....	....	4	2	4	6	8	....	....	....
	St. Louis	**NHL**	**5**	**0**	**0**	**0**	**2**	**0**	**0**	**0**	**1**	**0.0**	**–1**	....	....	....	....	....	....	....	....	....	....	....	....	....
1995-96	Rochester	AHL	62	5	50	55	71	....	....	....	....	....	....	....	....	....	....	....	19	3	11	14	12	....	....	....
1996-97	Rochester	AHL	73	12	51	63	54	....	....	....	....	....	....	....	....	....	....	....	10	2	7	9	27	....	....	....
1997-98	Worcester	AHL	55	8	24	32	34	....	....	....	....	....	....	....	....	....	....	....	....	....	....	....	....	....	....	....
	Houston Aeros	IHL	8	1	1	2	6	....	....	....	....	....	....	....	....	....	....	....	4	1	2	3	11	....	....	....
1998-99	Utah Grizzlies	IHL	58	4	19	23	40	....	....	....	....	....	....	....	....	....	....	....	....	....	....	....	....	....	....	....
	Orlando	IHL	21	9	9	18	18	....	....	....	....	....	....	....	....	....	....	....	17	3	5	8	14	....	....	....
99-2000	Orlando	IHL	20	4	4	8	13	....	....	....	....	....	....	....	....	....	....	....	....	....	....	....	....	....	....	....
	Manitoba Moose	IHL	18	3	10	13	4	....	....	....	....	....	....	....	....	....	....	....	....	....	....	....	....	....	....	....
	Providence Bruins	AHL	4	0	3	3	2	....	....	....	....	....	....	....	....	....	....	....	10	1	4	5	6	....	....	....
2000-01	Providence Bruins	AHL	70	8	14	22	73	....	....	....	....	....	....	....	....	....	....	....	17	2	5	7	24	....	....	....
	NHL Totals		**7**	**0**	**0**	**0**	**2**	**0**	**0**	**0**	**1**	**0.0**		....	....	....	....	....	....	....	....	....	....	....	....	....

AHL Second All-Star Team (1996) • AHL First All-Star Team (1997)

Signed as a free agent by **Buffalo**, August 23, 1995. Signed as a free agent by **St. Louis**, July 28, 1997. Traded to **Orlando** (IHL) by **Utah** (IHL) for Rob Bonneau and Mike Nicholishen, March 1, 1999. Traded to **Manitoba** (IHL) by **Orlando** (IHL) for Jason McDonald, January 10, 2000. Traded to **Providence** (AHL) by **Manitoba** (IHL) for Sean Pronger and Keith McCambridge, March 16, 2000.

HOLMSTROM, Tomas
(HOHLM-struhm, TAW-mas) **DET.**

Left wing. Shoots left. 6', 200 lbs. Born, Pitea, Sweden, January 23, 1973. Detroit's 9th choice, 257th overall, in 1994 Entry Draft.

1989-90	Pitea HC	Sweden-2	9	1	0	1	4	....	....	....	....	....	....	....	....	....	....	....	....	....	....	....	....	....	....	....
1990-91	Pitea HC	Sweden-2	26	5	4	9	16	....	....	....	....	....	....	....	....	....	....	....	....	....	....	....	....	....	....	....
1991-92	Pitea HC	Sweden-2	31	15	12	27	44	....	....	....	....	....	....	....	....	....	....	....	....	....	....	....	....	....	....	....
1992-93	Pitea HC	Sweden-2	32	17	15	32	30	....	....	....	....	....	....	....	....	....	....	....	....	....	....	....	....	....	....	....
1993-94	Bodens IK	Sweden-2	34	23	16	39	86	....	....	....	....	....	....	....	....	....	....	....	9	3	3	6	24	....	....	....
1994-95	Lulea HF	Sweden	40	14	14	28	56	....	....	....	....	....	....	....	....	....	....	....	8	1	2	3	20	....	....	....
1995-96	Lulea HF	Sweden	34	12	11	23	78	....	....	....	....	....	....	....	....	....	....	....	11	6	2	8	22	....	....	....
1996-97♦	**Detroit**	**NHL**	**47**	**6**	**3**	**9**	**33**	**3**	**0**	**0**	**53**	**11.3**	**–10**	....	....	....	....	....	**1**	**0**	**0**	**0**	**0**	**0**	**0**	**0**
	Adirondack	AHL	6	3	1	4	7	....	....	....	....	....	....	....	....	....	....	....	....	....	....	....	....	....	....	....
1997-98♦	**Detroit**	**NHL**	**57**	**5**	**17**	**22**	**44**	**1**	**0**	**1**	**48**	**10.4**	**6**	....	....	....	....	....	**22**	**7**	**12**	**19**	**16**	**2**	**0**	**0**
1998-99	**Detroit**	**NHL**	**82**	**13**	**21**	**34**	**69**	**5**	**0**	**4**	**100**	**13.0**	**–11**	**0**	**0.0**	**94**	**9**	**12:22**	**10**	**4**	**3**	**7**	**4**	**2**	**0**	**1**
99-2000	**Detroit**	**NHL**	**72**	**13**	**22**	**35**	**43**	**4**	**0**	**1**	**71**	**18.3**	**4**	**0**	**0.0**	**68**	**9**	**12:06**	**9**	**3**	**1**	**4**	**16**	**1**	**0**	**1**
2000-01	**Detroit**	**NHL**	**73**	**16**	**24**	**40**	**40**	**9**	**0**	**2**	**74**	**21.6**	**–12**	**2**	**50.0**	**75**	**8**	**11:41**	**6**	**1**	**3**	**4**	**8**	**1**	**0**	**0**
	NHL Totals		**331**	**53**	**87**	**140**	**229**	**22**	**0**	**8**	**346**	**15.3**		**2**	**50.0**	**237**	**26**	**12:04**	**48**	**15**	**19**	**34**	**44**	**6**	**0**	**2**

HOLZINGER, Brian
(HOHL-zihn-guhr, BRIGH-uhn) **T.B.**

Center. Shoots right. 5'11", 190 lbs. Born, Parma, OH, October 10, 1972. Buffalo's 7th choice, 124th overall, in 1991 Entry Draft.

1988-89	Padua High	Hi-School	35	73	65	138	....	....	....	....	....	....	....	....	....	....	....	....	....	....	....	....	....	....	....	....
1989-90	Det-Compuware	NAJHL	44	36	37	73	....	....	....	....	....	....	....	....	....	....	....	....	....	....	....	....	....	....	....	....
1990-91	Det-Compuware	NAJHL	37	45	41	86	16	....	....	....	....	....	....	....	....	....	....	....	....	....	....	....	....	....	....	....
1991-92	Bowling Green	CCHA	30	14	8	22	36	....	....	....	....	....	....	....	....	....	....	....	....	....	....	....	....	....	....	....
1992-93	Bowling Green	CCHA	41	31	26	57	44	....	....	....	....	....	....	....	....	....	....	....	....	....	....	....	....	....	....	....
1993-94	Bowling Green	CCHA	38	22	15	37	24	....	....	....	....	....	....	....	....	....	....	....	....	....	....	....	....	....	....	....
1994-95	Bowling Green	CCHA	38	35	33	68	42	....	....	....	....	....	....	....	....	....	....	....	....	....	....	....	....	....	....	....
	Buffalo	**NHL**	**4**	**0**	**3**	**3**	**0**	**0**	**0**	**0**	**3**	**0.0**	**2**	....	....	....	....	....	**4**	**2**	**1**	**3**	**2**	**1**	**0**	**0**
1995-96	**Buffalo**	**NHL**	**58**	**10**	**10**	**20**	**37**	**5**	**0**	**1**	**71**	**14.1**	**–21**	....	....	....	....	....	....	....	....	....	....	....	....	....
	Rochester	AHL	17	10	11	21	14	....	....	....	....	....	....	....	....	....	....	....	19	10	14	24	10	....	....	....
1996-97	**Buffalo**	**NHL**	**81**	**22**	**29**	**51**	**54**	**2**	**2**	**6**	**142**	**15.5**	**9**	....	....	....	....	....	**12**	**2**	**5**	**7**	**8**	**0**	**1**	**0**
1997-98	**Buffalo**	**NHL**	**69**	**14**	**21**	**35**	**36**	**4**	**2**	**1**	**116**	**12.1**	**–2**	....	....	....	....	....	**15**	**4**	**7**	**11**	**18**	**1**	**1**	**0**
1998-99	**Buffalo**	**NHL**	**81**	**17**	**17**	**34**	**45**	**5**	**0**	**2**	**143**	**11.9**	**2**	**852**	**50.4**	**72**	**23**	**16:31**	**21**	**3**	**5**	**8**	**33**	**1**	**0**	**0**
99-2000	**Buffalo**	**NHL**	**59**	**7**	**17**	**24**	**30**	**0**	**1**	**2**	**81**	**8.6**	**4**	**839**	**45.7**	**60**	**18**	**14:38**	....	....	....	....	....	....	....	....
	Tampa Bay	**NHL**	**14**	**3**	**3**	**6**	**21**	**1**	**1**	**0**	**23**	**13.0**	**–7**	**119**	**46.2**	**16**	**3**	**16:10**	....	....	....	....	....	....	....	....
2000-01	**Tampa Bay**	**NHL**	**70**	**11**	**25**	**36**	**64**	**3**	**0**	**2**	**87**	**12.6**	**–9**	**775**	**47.4**	**40**	**40**	**16:03**	....	....	....	....	....	....	....	....
	NHL Totals		**436**	**84**	**125**	**209**	**287**	**20**	**6**	**14**	**666**	**12.6**		**2585**	**47.7**	**188**	**84**	**15:51**	**52**	**11**	**18**	**29**	**61**	**3**	**2**	**0**

CCHA Second All-Star Team (1993) • CCHA First All-Star Team (1995) • NCAA West First All-American Team (1995) • Won Hobey Baker Memorial Award (Top U.S. Collegiate Player) (1995)

Traded to **Tampa Bay** by **Buffalo** with Cory Sarich, Wayne Primeau and Buffalo's 3rd round choice (Alexander Kharitonov) in 2000 Entry Draft for Chris Gratton and Tampa Bay's 2nd round choice (Derek Roy) in 2001 Entry Draft, March 9, 2000.

HORCOFF, Shawn
(HOHR-cuhf, SHAWN) **EDM.**

Center. Shoots left. 6'1", 202 lbs. Born, Trail, B.C., September 17, 1978. Edmonton's 3rd choice, 99th overall, in 1998 Entry Draft.

1995-96	Chilliwack Chiefs	BCJHL	58	49	96	*146	44	....	....	....	....	....	....	....	....	....	....	....	....	....	....	....	....	....	....	....
1996-97	Michigan State	CCHA	40	10	13	23	20	....	....	....	....	....	....	....	....	....	....	....	....	....	....	....	....	....	....	....
1997-98	Michigan State	CCHA	34	14	13	27	50	....	....	....	....	....	....	....	....	....	....	....	....	....	....	....	....	....	....	....
1998-99	Michigan State	CCHA	39	12	25	37	70	....	....	....	....	....	....	....	....	....	....	....	....	....	....	....	....	....	....	....
99-2000	Michigan State	CCHA	42	14	*51	*65	50	....	....	....	....	....	....	....	....	....	....	....	....	....	....	....	....	....	....	....
2000-01	**Edmonton**	**NHL**	**49**	**9**	**7**	**16**	**10**	**0**	**0**	**2**	**42**	**21.4**	**8**	**122**	**41.8**	**9**	**4**	**9:14**	**5**	**0**	**0**	**0**	**0**	**0**	**0**	**0**
	Hamilton Bulldogs	AHL	24	10	18	28	19	....	....	....	....	....	....	....	....	....	....	....	....	....	....	....	....	....	....	....
	NHL Totals		**49**	**9**	**7**	**16**	**10**	**0**	**0**	**2**	**42**	**21.4**		**122**	**41.8**	**9**	**4**	**9:14**	**5**	**0**	**0**	**0**	**0**	**0**	**0**	**0**

BCJHL Player of the Year (1996) • Won Brett Hull Trophy (Top Scorer - BCJHL) (1996) • BCJHL First All-Star Team (1996) • CCHA First All-Star Team (2000) • NCAA West First All-American Team (2000)

HORDICHUK, Darcy
(HOHR-dih-chuhk, DAHR-see) **ATL.**

Left wing. Shoots left. 6'1", 215 lbs. Born, Kamsack, Sask., August 10, 1980. Atlanta's 9th choice, 180th overall, in 2000 Entry Draft.

1996-97	Yorkton Mallers	SMHL	57	6	15	21	230	....	....	....	....	....	....	....	....	....	....	....	....	....	....	....	....	....	....	....
	Calgary Hitmen	WHL	3	0	0	0	2	....	....	....	....	....	....	....	....	....	....	....	....	....	....	....	....	....	....	....
1997-98	Dauphin Kings	MJHL	58	12	21	33	279	....	....	....	....	....	....	....	....	....	....	....	....	....	....	....	....	....	....	....
1998-99	Saskatoon	WHL	66	3	2	5	246	....	....	....	....	....	....	....	....	....	....	....	....	....	....	....	....	....	....	....
99-2000	Saskatoon	WHL	63	6	8	14	269	....	....	....	....	....	....	....	....	....	....	....	11	4	2	6	43	....	....	....
2000-01	**Atlanta**	**NHL**	**11**	**0**	**0**	**0**	**38**	**0**	**0**	**0**	**6**	**0.0**	**–3**	**0**	**0.0**	**34**	**2**	**7:18**	....	....	....	....	....	....	....	....
	Orlando	IHL	69	7	3	10	*369	....	....	....	....	....	....	....	....	....	....	....	16	3	3	6	*41	....	....	....
	NHL Totals		**11**	**0**	**0**	**0**	**38**	**0**	**0**	**0**	**6**	**0.0**		**0**	**0.0**	**34**	**2**	**7:18**	....	....	....	....	....	....	....	....

HOSSA, Marian

(HOH-sah, MAIR-ee-an) **OTT.**

Wing. Shoots left. 6'1", 199 lbs. Born, Stara Lubovna, Czech., January 12, 1979. Ottawa's 1st choice, 12th overall, in 1997 Entry Draft.

			Regular Season																Playoffs							
Season	Club	League	GP	G	A	Pts	PIM	PP	SH	GW	S	%	+/-	TF	F%	H	SB	Min	GP	G	A	Pts	PIM	PP	SH	GW
1995-96	Dukla Trencin	Slovak-Jr.	53	42	49	91	26																			
1996-97	Dukla Trencin	Slovakia	46	25	19	44	33												7	5	5	10				
1997-98	Portland	WHL	53	45	40	85	50												16	13	6	19	6			
	Ottawa	**NHL**	**7**	**0**	**1**	**1**	**0**	**0**	**0**	**0**	**10**	**0.0**	**–1**													
1998-99	**Ottawa**	**NHL**	**60**	**15**	**15**	**30**	**37**	**1**	**0**	**2**	**124**	**12.1**	**18**	**4**	**25.0**	**59**	**6**	**13:59**	**4**	**0**	**2**	**2**	**4**	**0**	**0**	**0**
99-2000	**Ottawa**	**NHL**	**78**	**29**	**27**	**56**	**32**	**5**	**0**	**4**	**240**	**12.1**	**5**	**7**	**57.1**	**100**	**18**	**17:12**	**6**	**0**	**0**	**0**	**2**	**0**	**0**	**0**
2000-01	**Ottawa**	**NHL**	**81**	**32**	**43**	**75**	**44**	**11**	**2**	**7**	**249**	**12.9**	**19**	**14**	**42.9**	**97**	**32**	**18:01**	**4**	**1**	**1**	**2**	**4**	**0**	**0**	**0**
	NHL Totals		**226**	**76**	**86**	**162**	**113**	**17**	**2**	**13**	**623**	**12.2**		**25**	**44.0**	**256**	**56**	**16:37**	**14**	**1**	**3**	**4**	**10**	**0**	**0**	**0**

WHL West First All-Star Team (1998) • Canadian Major Junior First All-Star Team (1998) • Memorial Cup All-Star Team (1998) • NHL All-Rookie Team (1999) • Played in NHL All-Star Game (2001)

HOUDA, Doug

(HOO-duh, DUHG) **BUF.**

Defense. Shoots right. 6'2", 209 lbs. Born, Blairmore, Alta., June 3, 1966. Detroit's 2nd choice, 28th overall, in 1984 Entry Draft.

			Regular Season																Playoffs							
Season	Club	League	GP	G	A	Pts	PIM	PP	SH	GW	S	%	+/-	TF	F%	H	SB	Min	GP	G	A	Pts	PIM	PP	SH	GW
1982-83	Calgary Wranglers	WHL	71	5	23	28	99												16	1	3	4	44			
1983-84	Calgary Wranglers	WHL	69	6	30	36	195												4	0	0	0	7			
1984-85	Calgary Wranglers	WHL	65	20	54	74	182												8	3	4	7	29			
	Kalamazoo Wings	IHL																	7	0	2	2	10			
1985-86	Calgary Wranglers	WHL	16	4	10	14	60																			
	Medicine Hat	WHL	35	9	23	32	80												25	4	19	23	64			
	Detroit	**NHL**	**6**	**0**	**0**	**0**	**4**	**0**	**0**	**0**	**5**	**0.0**	**–7**													
1986-87	Adirondack	AHL	77	6	23	29	142												11	1	8	9	50			
1987-88	**Detroit**	**NHL**	**11**	**1**	**1**	**2**	**10**	**0**	**0**	**0**	**10**	**10.0**	**0**													
	Adirondack	AHL	71	10	32	42	169												11	0	3	3	44			
1988-89	**Detroit**	**NHL**	**57**	**2**	**11**	**13**	**67**	**0**	**0**	**0**	**38**	**5.3**	**17**						**6**	**0**	**1**	**1**	**0**	**0**	**0**	**0**
	Adirondack	AHL	7	0	3	3	8																			
1989-90	**Detroit**	**NHL**	**73**	**2**	**9**	**11**	**127**	**0**	**0**	**0**	**59**	**3.4**	**–5**													
1990-91	**Detroit**	**NHL**	**22**	**0**	**4**	**4**	**43**	**0**	**0**	**0**	**21**	**0.0**	**–2**													
	Adirondack	AHL	38	9	17	26	67																			
	Hartford	**NHL**	**19**	**1**	**2**	**3**	**41**	**0**	**0**	**0**	**21**	**4.8**	**–3**						**6**	**0**	**0**	**0**	**8**	**0**	**0**	**0**
1991-92	**Hartford**	**NHL**	**56**	**3**	**6**	**9**	**125**	**1**	**0**	**1**	**40**	**7.5**	**–2**						**6**	**0**	**2**	**2**	**13**	**0**	**0**	**0**
1992-93	**Hartford**	**NHL**	**60**	**2**	**6**	**8**	**167**	**0**	**0**	**0**	**43**	**4.7**	**–19**													
1993-94	**Hartford**	**NHL**	**7**	**0**	**0**	**0**	**23**	**0**	**0**	**0**	**1**	**0.0**	**–4**													
	Los Angeles	**NHL**	**54**	**2**	**6**	**8**	**165**	**0**	**0**	**0**	**31**	**6.5**	**–15**													
1994-95	**Buffalo**	**NHL**	**28**	**1**	**2**	**3**	**68**	**0**	**0**	**0**	**21**	**4.8**	**1**													
1995-96	**Buffalo**	**NHL**	**38**	**1**	**3**	**4**	**52**	**0**	**0**	**0**	**21**	**4.8**	**3**													
	Rochester	AHL	21	1	6	7	41												19	3	5	8	30			
1996-97	**NY Islanders**	**NHL**	**70**	**2**	**8**	**10**	**99**	**0**	**0**	**0**	**29**	**6.9**	**1**													
	Utah Grizzlies	IHL	3	0	0	0	7																			
1997-98	**NY Islanders**	**NHL**	**31**	**1**	**2**	**3**	**47**	**0**	**0**	**0**	**15**	**6.7**	**–6**													
	Anaheim	**NHL**	**24**	**1**	**2**	**3**	**52**	**0**	**1**	**0**	**9**	**11.1**	**–5**													
1998-99	**Detroit**	**NHL**	**3**	**0**	**1**	**1**	**0**	**0**	**0**	**0**	**1**	**0.0**	**–2**	**0**	**0.0**	**4**	**1**	**6:51**								
	Adirondack	AHL	73	7	21	28	122												3	0	1	1	4			
99-2000	**Buffalo**	**NHL**	**1**	**0**	**0**	**0**	**12**	**0**	**0**	**0**	**0**	**0.0**	**0**	**0**	**0.0**	**5**	**0**	**9:10**								
	Rochester	AHL	79	7	17	24	175												21	1	8	9	39			
2000-01	Rochester	AHL	43	6	20	26	106												4	0	0	0	4			
	NHL Totals		**560**	**19**	**63**	**82**	**1102**	**1**	**1**	**1**	**365**	**5.2**		**0**	**0.0**	**9**	**1**	**7:26**	**18**	**0**	**3**	**3**	**21**	**0**	**0**	**0**

WHL East Second All-Star Team (1985) • AHL First All-Star Team (1988)

Traded to **Hartford** by **Detroit** for Doug Crossman, February 20, 1991. Traded to **LA Kings** by **Hartford** for Marc Potvin, November 3, 1993. Traded to **Buffalo** by **LA Kings** for Sean O'Donnell, July 26, 1994. Signed as a free agent by **NY Islanders**, October 26, 1996. Traded to **Anaheim** by **NY Islanders** with Travis Green and Tony Tuzzolino for Joe Sacco, J.J. Daigneault and Mark Janssens, February 6, 1998. Traded to **Detroit** by **Anaheim** for future considerations, October 9, 1998. Signed as a free agent by **Buffalo**, July 13, 1999.

HOUDE, Eric

(OOD, AIR-ihk)

Center. Shoots left. 5'11", 191 lbs. Born, Montreal, Que., December 19, 1976. Montreal's 9th choice, 216th overall, in 1995 Entry Draft.

			Regular Season																Playoffs							
Season	Club	League	GP	G	A	Pts	PIM	PP	SH	GW	S	%	+/-	TF	F%	H	SB	Min	GP	G	A	Pts	PIM	PP	SH	GW
1992-93	St-Hubert Selects	QAHA	35	45	40	85																				
	Richelieu Riverains	QAAA	14	3	2	5	0																			
1993-94	St-Jean Lynx	QMJHL	71	16	16	32	14												5	1	1	2	4			
1994-95	St-Jean Lynx	QMJHL	40	10	13	23	23																			
	Halifax	QMJHL	28	13	23	36	8												3	2	1	3	4			
1995-96	Halifax	QMJHL	69	40	48	88	35												6	3	4	7	2			
1996-97	**Montreal**	**NHL**	**13**	**0**	**2**	**2**	**2**	**0**	**0**	**0**	**1**	**0.0**	**1**													
	Fredericton	AHL	66	30	36	66	20																			
1997-98	**Montreal**	**NHL**	**9**	**1**	**0**	**1**	**0**	**0**	**0**	**1**	**4**	**25.0**	**–3**													
	Fredericton	AHL	71	28	42	70	24												4	5	2	7	4			
1998-99	**Montreal**	**NHL**	**8**	**1**	**1**	**2**	**2**	**0**	**0**	**1**	**4**	**25.0**	**–2**	**41**	**46.3**	**4**	**0**	**7:11**								
	Fredericton	AHL	69	27	37	64	32												14	2	7	9	4			
99-2000	Hamilton Bulldogs	AHL	18	3	4	7	10																			
	Springfield	AHL	57	28	34	62	43												5	2	2	4	2			
2000-01	Utah Grizzlies	IHL	34	2	13	15	18																			
	Chicago Wolves	IHL	30	2	4	6	10												1	0	0	0	0			
	NHL Totals		**30**	**2**	**3**	**5**	**4**	**0**	**0**	**2**	**9**	**22.2**		**41**	**46.3**	**4**	**0**	**7:11**								

Signed as a free agent by **Edmonton**, August 11, 1999. Traded to **Phoenix** by **Edmonton** for Rob Murray, November 30, 1999. Signed as a free agent by **Dallas**, July 28, 2000. Signed as a free agent by **HC Asiago** (Italy), August 18, 2001.

HOULDER, Bill

(HOHL-duhr, BIHL) **NSH.**

Defense. Shoots left. 6'2", 217 lbs. Born, Thunder Bay, Ont., March 11, 1967. Washington's 4th choice, 82nd overall, in 1985 Entry Draft.

			Regular Season																Playoffs							
Season	Club	League	GP	G	A	Pts	PIM	PP	SH	GW	S	%	+/-	TF	F%	H	SB	Min	GP	G	A	Pts	PIM	PP	SH	GW
1983-84	Thunder Bay	TBJHL	23	4	18	22	37																			
1984-85	North Bay	OHL	66	4	20	24	37												8	0	0	0	2			
1985-86	North Bay	OHL	59	5	30	35	97												10	1	6	7	12			
1986-87	North Bay	OHL	62	17	51	68	68												22	4	19	23	20			
1987-88	**Washington**	**NHL**	**30**	**1**	**2**	**3**	**10**	**0**	**0**	**0**	**20**	**5.0**	**–2**													
	Fort Wayne	IHL	43	10	14	24	32																			
1988-89	**Washington**	**NHL**	**8**	**0**	**3**	**3**	**4**	**0**	**0**	**0**	**5**	**0.0**	**7**													
	Baltimore	AHL	65	10	36	46	50																			
1989-90	**Washington**	**NHL**	**41**	**1**	**11**	**12**	**28**	**0**	**0**	**0**	**49**	**2.0**	**8**													
	Baltimore	AHL	26	3	7	10	12												7	0	2	2	2			
1990-91	**Buffalo**	**NHL**	**7**	**0**	**2**	**2**	**4**	**0**	**0**	**0**	**7**	**0.0**	**–2**													
	Rochester	AHL	69	13	53	66	28												15	5	13	18	4			
1991-92	**Buffalo**	**NHL**	**10**	**1**	**0**	**1**	**8**	**0**	**0**	**0**	**18**	**5.6**	**–2**													
	Rochester	AHL	42	8	26	34	16												16	5	6	11	4			
1992-93	**Buffalo**	**NHL**	**15**	**3**	**5**	**8**	**6**	**0**	**0**	**0**	**29**	**10.3**	**5**						**8**	**0**	**2**	**2**	**4**	**0**	**0**	**0**
	San Diego Gulls	IHL	64	24	48	72	39																			
1993-94	**Anaheim**	**NHL**	**80**	**14**	**25**	**39**	**40**	**3**	**0**	**3**	**187**	**7.5**	**–18**													
1994-95	**St. Louis**	**NHL**	**41**	**5**	**13**	**18**	**20**	**1**	**0**	**0**	**59**	**8.5**	**16**						**4**	**1**	**1**	**2**	**0**	**0**	**0**	**0**
1995-96	**Tampa Bay**	**NHL**	**61**	**5**	**23**	**28**	**22**	**3**	**0**	**0**	**90**	**5.6**	**1**						**6**	**0**	**1**	**1**	**4**	**0**	**0**	**0**
1996-97	**Tampa Bay**	**NHL**	**79**	**4**	**21**	**25**	**30**	**0**	**0**	**2**	**116**	**3.4**	**16**													
1997-98	**San Jose**	**NHL**	**82**	**7**	**25**	**32**	**48**	**4**	**0**	**2**	**102**	**6.9**	**13**						**6**	**1**	**2**	**3**	**2**	**0**	**0**	**0**
1998-99	**San Jose**	**NHL**	**76**	**9**	**23**	**32**	**40**	**7**	**0**	**5**	**115**	**7.8**	**8**	**0**	**0.0**	**70**	**83**	**22:08**	**6**	**3**	**0**	**3**	**4**	**3**	**0**	**0**

			Regular Season																Playoffs							
Season	Club	League	GP	G	A	Pts	PIM	PP	SH	GW	S	%	+/-	TF	F%	H	SB	Min	GP	G	A	Pts	PIM	PP	SH	GW
99-2000	Tampa Bay	NHL	14	1	2	3	2	1	0	0	21	4.8	–3	1	100.0	12	26	21:29								
	Nashville	NHL	57	2	12	14	24	1	0	1	68	2.9	–6	1	100.0	56	71	22:36								
2000-01	Nashville	NHL	81	4	12	16	40	0	1	1	78	5.1	–7	2	0.0	66	76	21:12								
	NHL Totals		682	57	179	236	326	20	1	14	964	5.9		4	50.0	204	256	21:53	30	5	6	11	14	3	0	0

AHL First All-Star Team (1991) • Won Governor's Trophy (Top Defenseman - IHL) (1993) • IHL First All-Star Team (1993)

Traded to **Buffalo** by **Washington** for Shawn Anderson, September 30, 1990. Claimed by **Anaheim** from **Buffalo** in Expansion Draft, June 24, 1993. Traded to **St. Louis** by **Anaheim** for Jason Marshall, August 29, 1994. Signed as a free agent by **Tampa Bay**, July 26, 1995. Signed as a free agent by **San Jose**, July 16, 1997. Traded to **Tampa Bay** by **San Jose** with Andrei Zyuzin, Shawn Burr and Steve Guolla for Niklas Sundstrom and NY Rangers' 3rd round choice (previously acquired, later traded to Chicago - Chicago selected Igor Radulov) in 2000 Entry Draft, August 4, 1999. Claimed on waivers by **Nashville** from **Tampa Bay**, November 10, 1999.

HOUSLEY, Phil

(HOWZ-lee, FIHL) **CGY.**

Defense. Shoots left. 5'10", 185 lbs. Born, St. Paul, MN, March 9, 1964. Buffalo's 1st choice, 6th overall, in 1982 Entry Draft.

1980-81	St. Paul Vulcans	USHL	6	7	7	14	6												10	5	5	10	0			
1981-82	South St. Paul	Hi-School	22	31	34	65	18																			
1982-83	Buffalo	NHL	77	19	47	66	39	11	0	2	183	10.4	–4						10	3	4	7	2	1	0	0
1983-84	Buffalo	NHL	75	31	46	77	33	13	2	6	234	13.2	3						3	0	0	0	6	0	0	0
1984-85	Buffalo	NHL	73	16	53	69	28	3	0	4	188	8.5	15						5	3	2	5	2	0	0	0
1985-86	Buffalo	NHL	79	15	47	62	54	7	0	2	180	8.3	–9													
1986-87	Buffalo	NHL	78	21	46	67	57	8	1	2	202	10.4	–2													
1987-88	Buffalo	NHL	74	29	37	66	96	6	0	1	231	12.6	–17						6	2	4	6	6	1	0	0
1988-89	Buffalo	NHL	72	26	44	70	47	5	0	3	178	14.6	6						5	1	3	4	2	0	0	0
1989-90	Buffalo	NHL	80	21	60	81	32	8	1	4	201	10.4	11						6	1	4	5	4	1	0	0
1990-91	Winnipeg	NHL	78	23	53	76	24	12	1	3	206	11.2	–13													
1991-92	Winnipeg	NHL	74	23	63	86	92	11	0	4	234	9.8	–5						7	1	4	5	0	1	0	1
1992-93	Winnipeg	NHL	80	18	79	97	52	6	0	2	249	7.2	–14						6	0	7	7	2	0	0	0
1993-94	St. Louis	NHL	26	7	15	22	12	4	0	1	60	11.7	–5						4	2	1	3	4	2	0	0
1994-95	ZSC Zurich	Switz.	10	6	8	14	34																			
	Calgary	NHL	43	8	35	43	18	3	0	0	135	5.9	17						7	0	9	9	0	0	0	0
1995-96	Calgary	NHL	59	16	36	52	22	6	0	1	155	10.3	–2													
	New Jersey	NHL	22	1	15	16	8	0	0	0	50	2.0	–4													
1996-97	Washington	NHL	77	11	29	40	24	3	1	2	167	6.6	–10													
1997-98	Washington	NHL	64	6	25	31	24	4	1	0	116	5.2	–10						18	0	4	4	4	0	0	0
1998-99	Calgary	NHL	79	11	43	54	52	4	0	1	193	5.7	14	0	0.0	21	52	20:52								
99-2000	Calgary	NHL	78	11	44	55	24	5	0	2	176	6.3	–12	1	0.0	23	50	23:29								
2000-01	Calgary	NHL	69	4	30	34	24	0	0	0	115	3.5	–15	0	0.0	25	40	18:10								
	NHL Totals		1357	317	847	1164	762	119	7	40	3453	9.2		1	0.0	69	142	20:57	77	13	42	55	32	6	0	1

NHL All-Rookie Team (1983) • NHL Second All-Star Team (1992) • Played in NHL All-Star Game (1984, 1989, 1990, 1991, 1992, 1993, 2000)

Traded to **Winnipeg** by **Buffalo** with Scott Arniel, Jeff Parker and Buffalo's 1st round choice (Keith Tkachuk) in 1990 Entry Draft for Dale Hawerchuk and Winnipeg's 1st round choice (Brad May) in 1990 Entry Draft, June 16, 1990. Traded to **St. Louis** by **Winnipeg** for Nelson Emerson and Stephane Quintal, September 24, 1993. Traded to **Calgary** by **St. Louis** with St. Louis' 2nd round choices in 1996 (Steve Begin) and 1997 (John Tripp) Entry Drafts for Al MacInnis and Calgary's 4th round choice (Didier Tremblay) in 1997 Entry Draft, July 4, 1994. Traded to **New Jersey** by **Calgary** with Dan Keczmer for Tommy Albelin, Cale Hulse and Jocelyn Lemieux, February 26, 1996. Signed as a free agent by **Washington**, July 22, 1996. Claimed on waivers by **Calgary** from **Washington**, July 21, 1998.

HRDINA, Jan

(huhr-DEE-nah, YAN) **PIT.**

Center. Shoots right. 6', 200 lbs. Born, Hradec Kralove, Czech., February 5, 1976. Pittsburgh's 4th choice, 128th overall, in 1995 Entry Draft.

1993-94	HC Stadion-Jr.	Cze-Rep	10	1	6	7	0																			
	HC Stadion	Cze-Rep	23	1	5	6													4	0	1	1				
1994-95	Seattle T-Birds	WHL	69	41	59	100	79												4	0	1	1	8			
1995-96	Seattle T-Birds	WHL	30	19	28	47	37																			
	Spokane Chiefs	WHL	18	10	16	26	25												18	5	14	19	49			
1996-97	Cleveland	IHL	68	23	31	54	82												13	1	2	3	8			
1997-98	Syracuse Crunch	AHL	72	20	24	44	82												5	1	3	4	10			
1998-99	Pittsburgh	NHL	82	13	29	42	40	3	0	2	94	13.8	–2	1461	56.7	104	26	16:26	13	4	1	5	12	1	0	1
99-2000	Pittsburgh	NHL	70	13	33	46	43	3	0	1	84	15.5	13	1392	53.7	57	24	18:47	9	4	8	12	2	1	0	0
2000-01	Pittsburgh	NHL	78	15	28	43	48	3	0	1	89	16.9	19	1067	53.8	47	24	15:56	18	2	5	7	8	0	0	0
	NHL Totals		230	41	90	131	131	9	0	4	267	15.4		3920	54.8	208	74	16:59	40	10	14	24	22	2	0	1

HRKAC, Tony

(HUHR-kuhz, TOH-nee) **ATL.**

Center. Shoots left. 5'11", 190 lbs. Born, Thunder Bay, Ont., July 7, 1966. St. Louis' 2nd choice, 32nd overall, in 1984 Entry Draft.

1983-84	Orillia Travelways	OPJHL	42	*52	54	*106	20																			
1984-85	North Dakota	WCHA	36	18	36	54	16																			
1985-86	Canada	Nat-Team	62	19	30	49	36																			
1986-87	North Dakota	WCHA	48	46	70	116	48																			
	St. Louis	NHL																	3	0	0	0	0	0	0	0
1987-88	St. Louis	NHL	67	11	37	48	22	2	1	3	86	12.8	5						10	6	1	7	4	3	1	1
1988-89	St. Louis	NHL	70	17	28	45	8	5	0	1	133	12.8	–10						4	1	1	2	0	0	0	1
1989-90	St. Louis	NHL	28	5	12	17	8	1	0	0	41	12.2	1													
	Quebec	NHL	22	4	8	12	2	2	0	0	29	13.8	–5													
	Halifax Citadels	AHL	20	12	21	33	4												6	5	9	14	4			
1990-91	Quebec	NHL	70	16	32	48	16	6	0	0	122	13.1	–22													
	Halifax Citadels	AHL	3	4	1	5	2																			
1991-92	San Jose	NHL	22	2	10	12	4	0	0	0	31	6.5	–2													
	Chicago	NHL	18	1	2	3	6	0	0	0	22	4.5	4						3	0	0	0	2	0	0	0
1992-93	Indianapolis Ice	IHL	80	45	*87	*132	70												5	0	2	2	2			
1993-94	St. Louis	NHL	36	6	5	11	8	1	1	1	43	14.0	–11						4	0	0	0	0	0	0	0
	Peoria Rivermen	IHL	45	30	51	81	25												1	1	2	3	0			
1994-95	Milwaukee	IHL	71	24	67	91	26												15	4	9	13	16			
1995-96	Milwaukee	IHL	43	14	28	42	18												5	1	3	4	4			
1996-97	Milwaukee	IHL	81	27	61	88	20												3	1	1	2	2			
1997-98	Dallas	NHL	13	5	3	8	0	3	0	0	14	35.7	0													
	Michigan K-Wings	IHL	20	7	15	22	6																			
	Edmonton	NHL	36	8	11	19	10	4	0	1	43	18.6	3						12	0	3	3	2	0	0	0
1998-99♦	Dallas	NHL	69	13	14	27	26	2	0	2	67	19.4	2	666	48.0	49	13	12:02	5	0	2	2	4	0	0	0
99-2000	NY Islanders	NHL	7	0	2	2	0	0	0	0	2	0.0	–1	34	35.3	2	0	11:22								
	Anaheim	NHL	60	4	7	11	8	1	0	0	37	10.8	–2	536	50.8	22	11	9:04								
2000-01	Anaheim	NHL	80	13	25	38	29	0	0	1	88	14.8	0	1072	50.7	22	17	13:46								
	NHL Totals		598	105	196	301	147	27	2	9	758	13.9		2308	49.7	95	41	11:50	41	7	7	14	12	3	1	2

WCHA First All-Star Team (1987) • NCAA West First All-American Team (1987) • NCAA Championship All-Tournament Team (1987) • NCAA Championship Tournament MVP (1987) • Won 1987 Hobey Baker Memorial Award (Top U.S. Collegiate Player) (1987) • Won James Gatschene Memorial Trophy (MVP - IHL) (1993) • Won Leo P. Lamoureux Memorial Trophy (Top Scorer - IHL) (1993) • IHL First All-Star Team (1993)

Traded to **Quebec** by **St. Louis** with Greg Millen for Jeff Brown, December 13, 1989. Traded to **San Jose** by **Quebec** for Greg Paslawski, May 31, 1991. Traded to **Chicago** by **San Jose** for Chicago's 6th round choice (Fredrik Oduya) in 1993 Entry Draft, February 7, 1992. Signed as a free agent by **St. Louis**, July 30, 1993. Signed as a free agent by **Dallas**, August 12, 1997. Claimed on waivers by **Edmonton** from **Dallas**, January 6, 1998. Traded to **Pittsburgh** by **Edmonton** with Bobby Dollas for Josef Beranek, June 16, 1998. Claimed by **Nashville** from **Pittsburgh** in Expansion Draft, June 26, 1998. Traded to **Dallas** by **Nashville** for future considerations, July 9, 1998. Signed as a free agent by **NY Islanders**, July 29, 1999. Traded to **Anaheim** by **NY Islanders** with Dean Malkoc for Ted Drury, October 29, 1999. Signed as a free agent by **Atlanta**, July 25, 2001.

HUARD, Bill

(HEW-ahrd, BIHL)

Left wing. Shoots left. 6'1", 215 lbs. Born, Welland, Ont., June 24, 1967.

1984-85	Fort Erie Meteors	OJHL-B	41	4	9	13	114																			
1985-86	Welland Cougars	OJHL-B	28	8	17	25	123																			
	Peterborough	OHL	7	1	1	2	2																			
1986-87	Peterborough	OHL	61	14	11	25	61												12	5	2	7	19			
1987-88	Peterborough	OHL	66	28	33	61	132												12	7	8	15	33			
1988-89	Carolina	ECHL	40	27	21	48	177												10	7	2	9	70			
	Flint Spirits	IHL	1	0	0	0	2																			
1989-90	Utica Devils	AHL	27	1	7	8	67												5	0	1	1	33			
	Nashville Knights	ECHL	34	24	27	51	212																			

Season	Club	League	GP	G	A	Pts	PIM	PP	SH	GW	S	%	+/-	TF	F%	H	SB	Min
			Regular Season															
1990-91	Utica Devils	AHL	72	11	16	27	359	....	....	....	....	....	....	....	....	....	....	....
1991-92	Utica Devils	AHL	62	9	11	20	233	....	....	....	....	....	....	....	....	....	....	....
1992-93	**Boston**	**NHL**	**2**	**0**	**0**	**0**	**0**	**0**	**0**	**0**	**0**	**0.0**	**0**	....	....	....	....	....
	Providence Bruins	AHL	72	18	19	37	302	....	....	....	....	....	....	....	....	....	....	....
1993-94	**Ottawa**	**NHL**	**63**	**2**	**2**	**4**	**162**	**0**	**0**	**0**	**24**	**8.3**	**−19**	....	....	....	....	....
1994-95	**Ottawa**	**NHL**	**26**	**1**	**1**	**2**	**64**	**0**	**0**	**0**	**15**	**6.7**	**−2**	....	....	....	....	....
	Quebec	**NHL**	**7**	**2**	**2**	**4**	**13**	**0**	**0**	**0**	**6**	**33.3**	**2**	....	....	....	....	....
1995-96	**Dallas**	**NHL**	**51**	**6**	**6**	**12**	**176**	**0**	**0**	**0**	**34**	**17.6**	**3**	....	....	....	....	....
	Michigan K-Wings	IHL	12	1	1	2	74	....	....	....	....	....	....	....	....	....	....	....
1996-97	**Dallas**	**NHL**	**40**	**5**	**6**	**11**	**105**	**0**	**0**	**0**	**34**	**14.7**	**5**	....	....	....	....	....
1997-98	**Edmonton**	**NHL**	**30**	**0**	**1**	**1**	**72**	**0**	**0**	**0**	**12**	**0.0**	**−5**	....	....	....	....	....
1998-99	**Edmonton**	**NHL**	**3**	**0**	**0**	**0**	**0**	**0**	**0**	**0**	**2**	**0.0**	**0**	**1**	**100.0**	**5**	**0**	**5:36**
	Houston Aeros	IHL	38	9	5	14	201	....	....	....	....	....	....	....	....	....	....	....
99-2000	**Los Angeles**	**NHL**	**1**	**0**	**0**	**0**	**2**	**0**	**0**	**0**	**0**	**0.0**	**0**	**0**	**0.0**	**1**	**0**	**2:14**
	Lowell	AHL	13	2	2	4	65	....	....	....	....	....	....	....	....	....	....	....
	Orlando	IHL	19	4	2	6	85	....	....	....	....	....	....	....	....	....	....	....
2000-01	London Knights	Britain	1	1	1	2	4	....	....	....	....	....	....	....	....	....	....	....
	NHL Totals		**223**	**16**	**18**	**34**	**594**	**0**	**0**	**0**	**127**	**12.6**		**1**	**100.0**	**6**	**0**	**4:46**

Season	Club	League	GP	G	A	Pts	PIM	PP	SH	GW
			Playoffs							
1990-91	Utica Devils	AHL	....	....	....	....	....	....	....	....
1991-92	Utica Devils	AHL	4	1	1	2	4	....	....	....
1992-93	**Boston**	**NHL**	....	....	....	....	....	....	....	....
	Providence Bruins	AHL	6	3	0	3	9	....	....	....
1993-94	**Ottawa**	**NHL**	....	....	....	....	....	....	....	....
1994-95	**Ottawa**	**NHL**	....	....	....	....	....	....	....	....
	Quebec	**NHL**	**1**	**0**	**0**	**0**	**0**	**0**	**0**	**0**
1995-96	**Dallas**	**NHL**	....	....	....	....	....	....	....	....
	Michigan K-Wings	IHL	....	....	....	....	....	....	....	....
1996-97	**Dallas**	**NHL**	....	....	....	....	....	....	....	....
1997-98	**Edmonton**	**NHL**	**4**	**0**	**0**	**0**	**2**	**0**	**0**	**0**
1998-99	**Edmonton**	**NHL**	....	....	....	....	....	....	....	....
	Houston Aeros	IHL	10	0	0	0	8	....	....	....
99-2000	**Los Angeles**	**NHL**	....	....	....	....	....	....	....	....
	Lowell	AHL	....	....	....	....	....	....	....	....
	Orlando	IHL	3	0	0	0	10	....	....	....
2000-01	London Knights	Britain	....	....	....	....	....	....	....	....
	NHL Totals		**5**	**0**	**0**	**0**	**2**	**0**	**0**	**0**

Signed as a free agent by **New Jersey**, October 1, 1989. Signed as a free agent by **Boston**, December 4, 1992. Signed as a free agent by **Ottawa**, June 30, 1993. Traded to **Quebec** by **Ottawa** for the rights to Mika Stromberg and Quebec's 4th round choice (Kevin Boyd) in 1995 Entry Draft, April 7, 1995. Transferred to **Colorado** after **Quebec** franchise relocated, July 1, 1995. Claimed by **Dallas** from **Colorado** in NHL Waiver Draft, October 2, 1995. Signed as a free agent by **Edmonton**, July 22, 1997. Signed as a free agent by **Houston** (IHL), January 23, 1999. Signed as a free agent by **LA Kings**, July 19, 1999. Traded to **Atlanta** by **LA Kings** for future considerations, January 25, 2000. Signed as a free agent by **London** (Britain), September 28, 2000. • Granted leave of absence from **London** (Britain) for personal reasons, October 4, 2000.

HUBACEK, Petr

(HOO-buh-chehk, PEE-tuhr) **PHI.**

Center. Shoots right. 6'2", 183 lbs. Born, Brno, Czech., September 2, 1979. Philadelphia's 11th choice, 243rd overall, in 1998 Entry Draft.

1997-98	HC Brno-Jr.	Cze-Rep	17	9	5	14	....	....	....	....	....	....	....	....	....	....	....	....
	Zetor Brno-Jr.	Cze-Rep	48	6	10	16	....	....	....	....	....	....	....	....	....	....	....	....
1998-99	HC Vitkovice	Cze-Rep	25	0	4	4	2	....	....	....	....	....	....	....	....	....	....	....
99-2000	HC Vitkovice	Cze-Rep	48	11	12	23	81	....	....	....	....	....	....	....	....	....	....	....
2000-01	**Philadelphia**	**NHL**	**6**	**1**	**0**	**1**	**2**	**0**	**0**	**0**	**5**	**20.0**	**−1**	**39**	**25.6**	**1**	**3**	**11:20**
	Philadelphia	AHL	62	3	9	12	29	....	....	....	....	....	....	....	....	....	....	....
	NHL Totals		**6**	**1**	**0**	**1**	**2**	**0**	**0**	**0**	**5**	**20.0**		**39**	**25.6**	**1**	**3**	**11:20**

1997-98	HC Brno-Jr.	Cze-Rep	....	....	....	....	....	....	....	....
	Zetor Brno-Jr.	Cze-Rep	....	....	....	....	....	....	....	....
1998-99	HC Vitkovice	Cze-Rep	4	0	0	0	....	....	....	....
99-2000	HC Vitkovice	Cze-Rep	....	....	....	....	....	....	....	....
2000-01	**Philadelphia**	**NHL**	....	....	....	....	....	....	....	....
	Philadelphia	AHL	9	0	1	1	6	....	....	....
	NHL Totals		....	....	....	....	....	....	....	....

HULBIG, Joe

(HUHL-bihg, JOH)

Left wing. Shoots left. 6'3", 215 lbs. Born, Norwood, MA, September 29, 1973. Edmonton's 1st choice, 13th overall, in 1992 Entry Draft.

1989-90	St. Sebastian's	Hi-School	30	13	12	25	....	....	....	....	....	....	....	....	....	....	....	....
1990-91	St. Sebastian's	Hi-School	30	23	19	42	....	....	....	....	....	....	....	....	....	....	....	....
1991-92	St. Sebastian's	Hi-School	17	19	24	43	30	....	....	....	....	....	....	....	....	....	....	....
1992-93	Providence	H-East	26	3	13	16	22	....	....	....	....	....	....	....	....	....	....	....
1993-94	Providence	H-East	28	6	4	10	36	....	....	....	....	....	....	....	....	....	....	....
1994-95	Providence	H-East	37	14	21	35	36	....	....	....	....	....	....	....	....	....	....	....
1995-96	Providence	H-East	31	14	22	36	56	....	....	....	....	....	....	....	....	....	....	....
1996-97	**Edmonton**	**NHL**	**6**	**0**	**0**	**0**	**0**	**0**	**0**	**0**	**4**	**0.0**	**−1**	....	....	....	....	....
	Hamilton Bulldogs	AHL	73	18	28	46	59	....	....	....	....	....	....	....	....	....	....	....
1997-98	**Edmonton**	**NHL**	**17**	**2**	**2**	**4**	**2**	**0**	**0**	**1**	**8**	**25.0**	**−1**	....	....	....	....	....
	Hamilton Bulldogs	AHL	46	15	16	31	52	....	....	....	....	....	....	....	....	....	....	....
1998-99	**Edmonton**	**NHL**	**1**	**0**	**0**	**0**	**2**	**0**	**0**	**0**	**2**	**0.0**	**1**	**0**	**0.0**	**0**	**1**	**8:20**
	Hamilton Bulldogs	AHL	76	22	24	46	68	....	....	....	....	....	....	....	....	....	....	....
99-2000	**Boston**	**NHL**	**24**	**2**	**2**	**4**	**8**	**0**	**0**	**0**	**15**	**13.3**	**−8**	**2**	**0.0**	**52**	**4**	**8:18**
	Providence Bruins	AHL	15	4	5	9	17	....	....	....	....	....	....	....	....	....	....	....
2000-01	**Boston**	**NHL**	**7**	**0**	**0**	**0**	**4**	**0**	**0**	**0**	**0**	**0.0**	**−3**	**0**	**0.0**	**15**	**0**	**5:28**
	Providence Bruins	AHL	36	4	11	15	19	....	....	....	....	....	....	....	....	....	....	....
	NHL Totals		**55**	**4**	**4**	**8**	**16**	**0**	**0**	**1**	**29**	**13.8**		**2**	**0.0**	**67**	**5**	**7:41**

1989-90	St. Sebastian's	Hi-School	....	....	....	....	....	....	....	....
1990-91	St. Sebastian's	Hi-School	....	....	....	....	....	....	....	....
1991-92	St. Sebastian's	Hi-School	....	....	....	....	....	....	....	....
1992-93	Providence	H-East	....	....	....	....	....	....	....	....
1993-94	Providence	H-East	....	....	....	....	....	....	....	....
1994-95	Providence	H-East	....	....	....	....	....	....	....	....
1995-96	Providence	H-East	....	....	....	....	....	....	....	....
1996-97	**Edmonton**	**NHL**	**6**	**0**	**1**	**1**	**2**	**0**	**0**	**0**
	Hamilton Bulldogs	AHL	16	6	10	16	6	....	....	....
1997-98	**Edmonton**	**NHL**	....	....	....	....	....	....	....	....
	Hamilton Bulldogs	AHL	3	0	1	1	2	....	....	....
1998-99	**Edmonton**	**NHL**	....	....	....	....	....	....	....	....
	Hamilton Bulldogs	AHL	11	4	2	6	18	....	....	....
99-2000	**Boston**	**NHL**	....	....	....	....	....	....	....	....
	Providence Bruins	AHL	....	....	....	....	....	....	....	....
2000-01	**Boston**	**NHL**	....	....	....	....	....	....	....	....
	Providence Bruins	AHL	15	2	2	4	20	....	....	....
	NHL Totals		**6**	**0**	**1**	**1**	**2**	**0**	**0**	**0**

Signed as a free agent by **Boston**, July 23, 1999. • Missed majority of 2000-01 season recovering from head injury suffered in game vs. Ottawa, November 9, 2000.

HULL, Brett

(HUHL, BREHT)

Right wing. Shoots right. 5'11", 203 lbs. Born, Belleville, Ont., August 9, 1964. Calgary's 6th choice, 117th overall, in 1984 Entry Draft.

1982-83	Penticton Knights	BCJHL	50	48	56	104	27	....	....	....	....	....	....	....	....	....	....	....
1983-84	Penticton Knights	BCJHL	56	*105	83	*188	20	....	....	....	....	....	....	....	....	....	....	....
1984-85	Minnesota-Duluth	WCHA	48	32	28	60	24	....	....	....	....	....	....	....	....	....	....	....
1985-86	Minnesota-Duluth	WCHA	42	52	32	84	46	....	....	....	....	....	....	....	....	....	....	....
	Calgary	**NHL**	....	....	....	....	....	....	....	....	....	....	....	....	....	....	....	....
1986-87	**Calgary**	**NHL**	**5**	**1**	**0**	**1**	**0**	**0**	**0**	**1**	**5**	**20.0**	**−1**	....	....	....	....	....
	Moncton Flames	AHL	67	50	42	92	16	....	....	....	....	....	....	....	....	....	....	....
1987-88	**Calgary**	**NHL**	**52**	**26**	**24**	**50**	**12**	**4**	**0**	**3**	**153**	**17.0**	**10**	....	....	....	....	....
	St. Louis	**NHL**	**13**	**6**	**8**	**14**	**4**	**2**	**0**	**0**	**58**	**10.3**	**4**	....	....	....	....	....
1988-89	**St. Louis**	**NHL**	**78**	**41**	**43**	**84**	**33**	**16**	**0**	**6**	**305**	**13.4**	**−17**	....	....	....	....	....
1989-90	**St. Louis**	**NHL**	**80**	***72**	**41**	**113**	**24**	**27**	**0**	**12**	**385**	**18.7**	**−1**	....	....	....	....	....
1990-91	**St. Louis**	**NHL**	**78**	***86**	**45**	**131**	**22**	**29**	**0**	**11**	**389**	**22.1**	**23**	....	....	....	....	....
1991-92	**St. Louis**	**NHL**	**73**	***70**	**39**	**109**	**48**	**20**	**5**	**9**	**408**	**17.2**	**−2**	....	....	....	....	....
1992-93	**St. Louis**	**NHL**	**80**	**54**	**47**	**101**	**41**	**29**	**0**	**2**	**390**	**13.8**	**−27**	....	....	....	....	....
1993-94	**St. Louis**	**NHL**	**81**	**57**	**40**	**97**	**38**	**25**	**3**	**6**	**392**	**14.5**	**−3**	....	....	....	....	....
1994-95	**St. Louis**	**NHL**	**48**	**29**	**21**	**50**	**10**	**9**	**3**	**6**	**200**	**14.5**	**13**	....	....	....	....	....
1995-96	**St. Louis**	**NHL**	**70**	**43**	**40**	**83**	**30**	**16**	**5**	**6**	**327**	**13.1**	**4**	....	....	....	....	....
1996-97	**St. Louis**	**NHL**	**77**	**42**	**40**	**82**	**10**	**12**	**2**	**6**	**302**	**13.9**	**−9**	....	....	....	....	....
1997-98	**St. Louis**	**NHL**	**66**	**27**	**45**	**72**	**26**	**10**	**0**	**6**	**211**	**12.8**	**−1**	....	....	....	....	....
	United States	Olympics	4	2	1	3	0	....	....	....	....	....	....	....	....	....	....	....
1998-99♦	**Dallas**	**NHL**	**60**	**32**	**26**	**58**	**30**	**15**	**0**	**11**	**192**	**16.7**	**19**	**12**	**50.0**	**9**	**18**	**17:24**
99-2000	**Dallas**	**NHL**	**79**	**24**	**35**	**59**	**43**	**11**	**0**	**3**	**223**	**10.8**	**−21**	**10**	**40.0**	**27**	**18**	**18:37**
2000-01	**Dallas**	**NHL**	**79**	**39**	**40**	**79**	**18**	**11**	**0**	**8**	**219**	**17.8**	**10**	**10**	**30.0**	**31**	**20**	**17:53**
	NHL Totals		**1019**	**649**	**534**	**1183**	**389**	**236**	**18**	**96**	**4159**	**15.6**		**32**	**40.6**	**67**	**56**	**18:01**

1982-83	Penticton Knights	BCJHL	....	....	....	....	....	....	....	....
1983-84	Penticton Knights	BCJHL	....	....	....	....	....	....	....	....
1984-85	Minnesota-Duluth	WCHA	....	....	....	....	....	....	....	....
1985-86	Minnesota-Duluth	WCHA	....	....	....	....	....	....	....	....
	Calgary	**NHL**	**2**	**0**	**0**	**0**	**0**	**0**	**0**	**0**
1986-87	**Calgary**	**NHL**	**4**	**2**	**1**	**3**	**0**	**0**	**0**	**0**
	Moncton Flames	AHL	3	2	2	4	2	....	....	....
1987-88	**Calgary**	**NHL**	....	....	....	....	....	....	....	....
	St. Louis	**NHL**	**10**	**7**	**2**	**9**	**4**	**4**	**0**	**3**
1988-89	**St. Louis**	**NHL**	**10**	**5**	**5**	**10**	**6**	**1**	**0**	**2**
1989-90	**St. Louis**	**NHL**	**12**	**13**	**8**	**21**	**17**	**7**	**0**	**3**
1990-91	**St. Louis**	**NHL**	**13**	**11**	**8**	**19**	**4**	**3**	**0**	**2**
1991-92	**St. Louis**	**NHL**	**6**	**4**	**4**	**8**	**4**	**1**	**1**	**1**
1992-93	**St. Louis**	**NHL**	**11**	**8**	**5**	**13**	**2**	**5**	**0**	**2**
1993-94	**St. Louis**	**NHL**	**4**	**2**	**1**	**3**	**0**	**1**	**0**	**0**
1994-95	**St. Louis**	**NHL**	**7**	**6**	**2**	**8**	**0**	**2**	**0**	**0**
1995-96	**St. Louis**	**NHL**	**13**	**6**	**5**	**11**	**10**	**2**	**1**	**1**
1996-97	**St. Louis**	**NHL**	**6**	**2**	**7**	**9**	**2**	**0**	**0**	**0**
1997-98	**St. Louis**	**NHL**	**10**	**3**	**3**	**6**	**2**	**1**	**0**	**1**
	United States	Olympics	....	....	....	....	....	....	....	....
1998-99♦	**Dallas**	**NHL**	**22**	**8**	**7**	**15**	**4**	**3**	**0**	**2**
99-2000	**Dallas**	**NHL**	**23**	***11**	***13**	***24**	**4**	**3**	**0**	**4**
2000-01	**Dallas**	**NHL**	**10**	**2**	**5**	**7**	**6**	**1**	**0**	**0**
	NHL Totals		**163**	**90**	**76**	**166**	**65**	**34**	**2**	**21**

WCHA First All-Star Team (1986) • AHL First All-Star Team (1987) • Won Dudley "Red" Garrett Memorial Trophy (Top Rookie - AHL) (1987) • NHL First All-Star Team (1990, 1991, 1992) • Won Lady Byng Trophy (1990) • Won Dodge Ram Tough Award (1990, 1991) • Won Hart Memorial Trophy (1991) • Won Lester B. Pearson Award (1991) • Won ProSet/NHL Player of the Year Award (1991) • Played in NHL All-Star Game (1989, 1990, 1992, 1993, 1994, 1996, 1997, 2001)

Traded to **St. Louis** by **Calgary** with Steve Bozek for Rob Ramage and Rick Wamsley, March 7, 1988. Signed as a free agent by **Dallas**, July 3, 1998.

HULL, Jody

(HUHL, JOH-dee)

Right wing. Shoots right. 6'2", 200 lbs. Born, Petrolia, Ont., February 2, 1969. Hartford's 1st choice, 18th overall, in 1987 Entry Draft.

1984-85	Cambridge Hawks	OJHL-B	38	13	17	30	39	....	....	....	....	....	....	....	....	....	....	....
1985-86	Peterborough	OHL	61	20	22	42	29	....	....	....	....	....	....	....	....	....	....	....
1986-87	Peterborough	OHL	49	18	34	52	22	....	....	....	....	....	....	....	....	....	....	....
1987-88	Peterborough	OHL	60	50	44	94	33	....	....	....	....	....	....	....	....	....	....	....
1988-89	**Hartford**	**NHL**	**60**	**16**	**18**	**34**	**10**	**6**	**0**	**2**	**82**	**19.5**	**6**	....	....	....	....	....
1989-90	**Hartford**	**NHL**	**38**	**7**	**10**	**17**	**21**	**2**	**0**	**0**	**46**	**15.2**	**−6**	....	....	....	....	....
	Binghamton	AHL	21	7	10	17	6	....	....	....	....	....	....	....	....	....	....	....
1990-91	**NY Rangers**	**NHL**	**47**	**5**	**8**	**13**	**10**	**0**	**0**	**0**	**57**	**8.8**	**2**	....	....	....	....	....
1991-92	**NY Rangers**	**NHL**	**3**	**0**	**0**	**0**	**2**	**0**	**0**	**0**	**4**	**0.0**	**−4**	....	....	....	....	....
	Binghamton	AHL	69	34	31	65	28	....	....	....	....	....	....	....	....	....	....	....
1992-93	**Ottawa**	**NHL**	**69**	**13**	**21**	**34**	**14**	**5**	**1**	**0**	**134**	**9.7**	**−24**	....	....	....	....	....
1993-94	**Florida**	**NHL**	**69**	**13**	**13**	**26**	**8**	**0**	**1**	**5**	**100**	**13.0**	**6**	....	....	....	....	....
1994-95	**Florida**	**NHL**	**46**	**11**	**8**	**19**	**8**	**0**	**0**	**4**	**63**	**17.5**	**−1**	....	....	....	....	....
1995-96	**Florida**	**NHL**	**78**	**20**	**17**	**37**	**25**	**2**	**0**	**3**	**120**	**16.7**	**5**	....	....	....	....	....
1996-97	**Florida**	**NHL**	**67**	**10**	**6**	**16**	**4**	**0**	**1**	**2**	**92**	**10.9**	**1**	....	....	....	....	....
1997-98	**Florida**	**NHL**	**21**	**2**	**0**	**2**	**4**	**0**	**1**	**0**	**23**	**8.7**	**1**	....	....	....	....	....
	Tampa Bay	**NHL**	**28**	**2**	**4**	**6**	**4**	**0**	**0**	**2**	**28**	**7.1**	**2**	....	....	....	....	....
1998-99	**Philadelphia**	**NHL**	**72**	**3**	**11**	**14**	**12**	**0**	**0**	**1**	**73**	**4.1**	**−2**	**15**	**53.3**	**34**	**28**	**12:59**

1984-85	Cambridge Hawks	OJHL-B	....	....	....	....	....	....	....	....
1985-86	Peterborough	OHL	16	1	5	6	4	....	....	....
1986-87	Peterborough	OHL	12	4	9	13	14	....	....	....
1987-88	Peterborough	OHL	12	10	8	18	8	....	....	....
1988-89	**Hartford**	**NHL**	**1**	**0**	**0**	**0**	**2**	**0**	**0**	**0**
1989-90	**Hartford**	**NHL**	**5**	**0**	**1**	**1**	**2**	**0**	**0**	**0**
	Binghamton	AHL	....	....	....	....	....	....	....	....
1990-91	**NY Rangers**	**NHL**	....	....	....	....	....	....	....	....
1991-92	**NY Rangers**	**NHL**	....	....	....	....	....	....	....	....
	Binghamton	AHL	11	5	2	7	4	....	....	....
1992-93	**Ottawa**	**NHL**	....	....	....	....	....	....	....	....
1993-94	**Florida**	**NHL**	....	....	....	....	....	....	....	....
1994-95	**Florida**	**NHL**	....	....	....	....	....	....	....	....
1995-96	**Florida**	**NHL**	**14**	**3**	**2**	**5**	**0**	**0**	**0**	**0**
1996-97	**Florida**	**NHL**	**5**	**0**	**0**	**0**	**0**	**0**	**0**	**0**
1997-98	**Florida**	**NHL**	....	....	....	....	....	....	....	....
	Tampa Bay	**NHL**	....	....	....	....	....	....	....	....
1998-99	**Philadelphia**	**NHL**	**6**	**0**	**0**	**0**	**4**	**0**	**0**	**0**

Season	Club	League	GP	G	A	Pts	PIM	PP	SH	GW	S	%	+/-	TF	F%	H	SB	Min	GP	G	A	Pts	PIM	PP	SH	GW
			Regular Season																Playoffs							
99-2000	Orlando	IHL	1	0	0	0	0																			
	Philadelphia	**NHL**	**67**	**10**	**3**	**13**	**4**	**0**	**2**	**2**	**63**	**15.9**	**8**	**36**	**41.7**	**28**	**44**	**11:58**	**18**	**0**	**1**	**1**	**0**	**0**	**0**	**0**
2000-01	**Philadelphia**	**NHL**	**71**	**7**	**8**	**15**	**10**	**0**	**2**	**2**	**78**	**9.0**	**–1**	**83**	**36.1**	**41**	**34**	**13:13**	**6**	**0**	**0**	**0**	**4**	**0**	**0**	**0**
	NHL Totals		**736**	**119**	**127**	**246**	**136**	**15**	**8**	**23**	**963**	**12.4**		**134**	**39.6**	**103**	**106**	**12:44**	**55**	**3**	**4**	**7**	**12**	**0**	**0**	**0**

OHL Second All-Star Team (1988)

Traded to **NY Rangers** by **Hartford** for Carey Wilson and NY Rangers' 3rd round choice (Michael Nylander) in the 1991 Entry Draft, July 9, 1990. Traded to **Ottawa** by **NY Rangers** for future considerations, July 28, 1992. Signed as a free agent by **Florida**, August 10, 1993. Traded to **Tampa Bay** by **Florida** with Mark Fitzpatrick for Dino Ciccarelli and Jeff Norton, January 15, 1998. Signed as a free agent by **Philadelphia**, October 7, 1998. Claimed by **Atlanta** from **Philadelphia** in Expansion Draft, June 25, 1999. Traded to **Philadelphia** by **Atlanta** for cash, October 15, 1999.

HULSE, Cale

(HUHLS, KAYL) **NSH.**

Defense. Shoots right. 6'3", 220 lbs. Born, Edmonton, Alta., November 10, 1973. New Jersey's 3rd choice, 66th overall, in 1992 Entry Draft.

Season	Club	League	GP	G	A	Pts	PIM	PP	SH	GW	S	%	+/-	TF	F%	H	SB	Min	GP	G	A	Pts	PIM	PP	SH	GW
1990-91	Calgary Royals	AJHL	49	3	23	26	220																			
1991-92	Portland	WHL	70	4	18	22	230												6	0	2	2	27			
1992-93	Portland	WHL	72	10	26	36	284												16	4	4	8	65			
1993-94	Albany River Rats	AHL	79	7	14	21	186												5	0	3	3	11			
1994-95	Albany River Rats	AHL	77	5	13	18	215												12	1	1	2	17			
1995-96	**New Jersey**	**NHL**	**8**	**0**	**0**	**0**	**15**	**0**	**0**	**0**	**5**	**0.0**	**–2**													
	Albany River Rats	AHL	42	4	23	27	107																			
	Calgary	**NHL**	**3**	**0**	**0**	**0**	**5**	**0**	**0**	**0**	**4**	**0.0**	**3**						**1**	**0**	**0**	**0**	**0**	**0**	**0**	**0**
	Saint John Flames	AHL	13	2	7	9	39																			
1996-97	**Calgary**	**NHL**	**63**	**1**	**6**	**7**	**91**	**0**	**1**	**0**	**58**	**1.7**	**–2**													
1997-98	**Calgary**	**NHL**	**79**	**5**	**22**	**27**	**169**	**1**	**1**	**0**	**117**	**4.3**	**1**													
1998-99	**Calgary**	**NHL**	**73**	**3**	**9**	**12**	**117**	**0**	**0**	**0**	**83**	**3.6**	**–8**	**1**	**0.0**	**113**	**74**	**16:38**								
99-2000	**Calgary**	**NHL**	**47**	**1**	**6**	**7**	**47**	**0**	**0**	**0**	**41**	**2.4**	**–11**	**1**	**100.0**	**85**	**37**	**12:38**								
2000-01	**Nashville**	**NHL**	**82**	**1**	**7**	**8**	**128**	**0**	**0**	**1**	**93**	**1.1**	**–5**	**0**	**0.0**	**232**	**71**	**20:05**								
	NHL Totals		**355**	**11**	**50**	**61**	**572**	**1**	**2**	**1**	**401**	**2.7**		**2**	**50.0**	**430**	**182**	**17:06**	**1**	**0**	**0**	**0**	**0**	**0**	**0**	**0**

Traded to **Calgary** by **New Jersey** with Tommy Albelin and Jocelyn Lemieux for Phil Housley and Dan Keczmer, February 26, 1996. Traded to **Nashville** by **Calgary** with Calgary's 3rd round choice (Denis Platonov) in 2001 Entry Draft for Sergei Krivokrasov, March 14, 2000.

HURLBUT, Mike

(HUHRL-buht, MIGHK)

Defense. Shoots left. 6'2", 206 lbs. Born, Massena, NY, October 7, 1966. NY Rangers' 1st choice, 5th overall, in 1988 Supplemental Draft.

Season	Club	League	GP	G	A	Pts	PIM	PP	SH	GW	S	%	+/-	TF	F%	H	SB	Min	GP	G	A	Pts	PIM	PP	SH	GW
1983-84	Massena High	Hi-School	27	22	31	53	15																			
1984-85	Northwood Prep	Hi-School	34	20	27	47	30																			
1985-86	St. Lawrence	ECAC	25	2	10	12	40																			
1986-87	St. Lawrence	ECAC	35	8	15	23	44																			
1987-88	St. Lawrence	ECAC	38	6	12	18	18																			
1988-89	St. Lawrence	ECAC	36	8	25	33	30																			
	Denver Rangers	IHL	8	0	2	2	13												4	1	2	3	2			
1989-90	Flint Spirits	IHL	74	3	34	37	38												3	0	1	1	2			
1990-91	San Diego Gulls	IHL	2	1	0	1	0																			
	Binghamton	AHL	33	2	11	13	27												3	0	1	1	0			
1991-92	Binghamton	AHL	79	16	39	55	64												11	2	7	9	8			
1992-93	**NY Rangers**	**NHL**	**23**	**1**	**8**	**9**	**16**	**1**	**0**	**0**	**26**	**3.8**	**4**													
	Binghamton	AHL	45	11	25	36	46												14	2	5	7	12			
1993-94	**Quebec**	**NHL**	**1**	**0**	**0**	**0**	**0**	**0**	**0**	**0**	**1**	**0.0**	**–1**													
	Cornwall Aces	AHL	77	13	33	46	100												13	3	7	10	12			
1994-95	Cornwall Aces	AHL	74	11	49	60	69												3	1	0	1	15			
1995-96	Minnesota Moose	IHL	22	1	4	5	22																			
	Houston Aeros	IHL	38	3	12	15	33																			
1996-97	Houston Aeros	IHL	70	11	24	35	62												13	5	8	13	12			
1997-98	**Buffalo**	**NHL**	**3**	**0**	**0**	**0**	**2**	**0**	**0**	**0**	**3**	**0.0**	**–1**													
	Rochester	AHL	45	10	20	30	48												4	1	1	2	2			
1998-99	**Buffalo**	**NHL**	**1**	**0**	**0**	**0**	**0**	**0**	**0**	**0**	**2**	**0.0**	**2**	**0**	**0.0**	**1**	**2**	**17:53**								
	Rochester	AHL	72	15	39	54	46												20	4	5	9	12			
99-2000	**Buffalo**	**NHL**	**1**	**0**	**0**	**0**	**2**	**0**	**0**	**0**	**1**	**0.0**	**1**	**0**	**0.0**	**0**	**1**	**12:25**								
	Rochester	AHL	74	10	29	39	83												21	5	6	11	14			
2000-01	Rochester	AHL	53	6	26	32	36												4	1	0	1	6			
	NHL Totals		**29**	**1**	**8**	**9**	**20**	**1**	**0**	**0**	**33**	**3.0**		**0**	**0.0**	**1**	**3**	**15:09**								

ECAC First All-Star Team (1989) • NCAA East First All-American Team (1989) • AHL Second All-Star Team (1995)

Traded to **Quebec** by **NY Rangers** for Alexander Karpovtsev, September 7, 1993. Signed as a free agent by **Buffalo**, September 9, 1997.

HUSCROFT, Jamie

(HUHS-krawft, JAY-mee)

Defense. Shoots right. 6'3", 210 lbs. Born, Creston, B.C., January 9, 1967. New Jersey's 9th choice, 171st overall, in 1985 Entry Draft.

Season	Club	League	GP	G	A	Pts	PIM	PP	SH	GW	S	%	+/-	TF	F%	H	SB	Min	GP	G	A	Pts	PIM	PP	SH	GW
1983-84	Portland	WHL	18	0	5	5	15																			
	Seattle Breakers	WHL	45	0	7	7	62												5	0	0	0	15			
1984-85	Seattle Breakers	WHL	69	3	13	16	273																			
1985-86	Seattle T-Birds	WHL	66	6	20	26	394												5	0	1	1	18			
1986-87	Seattle T-Birds	WHL	21	1	18	19	99																			
	Medicine Hat	WHL	14	3	3	6	71												20	0	3	3	*125			
1987-88	Utica Devils	AHL	71	5	7	12	316																			
	Flint Spirits	IHL	3	1	0	1	2												16	0	1	1	110			
1988-89	**New Jersey**	**NHL**	**15**	**0**	**2**	**2**	**51**	**0**	**0**	**0**	**9**	**0.0**	**–3**													
	Utica Devils	AHL	41	2	10	12	215												5	0	0	0	40			
1989-90	**New Jersey**	**NHL**	**42**	**2**	**3**	**5**	**149**	**0**	**0**	**0**	**19**	**10.5**	**–2**						**5**	**0**	**0**	**0**	**16**	**0**	**0**	**0**
	Utica Devils	AHL	22	3	6	9	122																			
1990-91	**New Jersey**	**NHL**	**8**	**0**	**1**	**1**	**27**	**0**	**0**	**0**	**3**	**0.0**	**1**						**3**	**0**	**0**	**0**	**6**	**0**	**0**	**0**
	Utica Devils	AHL	59	3	15	18	339																			
1991-92	Utica Devils	AHL	50	4	7	11	224																			
1992-93	Providence Bruins	AHL	69	2	15	17	257												2	0	1	1	6			
1993-94	**Boston**	**NHL**	**36**	**0**	**1**	**1**	**144**	**0**	**0**	**0**	**13**	**0.0**	**–2**						**4**	**0**	**0**	**0**	**9**	**0**	**0**	**0**
	Providence Bruins	AHL	32	1	10	11	157																			
1994-95	Fresno Falcons	SunHL	3	1	1	2	7																			
	Boston	**NHL**	**34**	**0**	**6**	**6**	**103**	**0**	**0**	**0**	**30**	**0.0**	**–3**						**5**	**0**	**0**	**0**	**11**	**0**	**0**	**0**
1995-96	**Calgary**	**NHL**	**70**	**3**	**9**	**12**	**162**	**0**	**0**	**1**	**57**	**5.3**	**14**						**4**	**0**	**1**	**1**	**4**	**0**	**0**	**0**
1996-97	**Calgary**	**NHL**	**39**	**0**	**4**	**4**	**117**	**0**	**0**	**0**	**33**	**0.0**	**2**													
	Tampa Bay	**NHL**	**13**	**0**	**1**	**1**	**34**	**0**	**0**	**0**	**7**	**0.0**	**–4**													
1997-98	**Tampa Bay**	**NHL**	**44**	**0**	**3**	**3**	**122**	**0**	**0**	**0**	**21**	**0.0**	**–4**													
	Vancouver	**NHL**	**7**	**0**	**1**	**1**	**55**	**0**	**0**	**0**	**5**	**0.0**	**2**													
1998-99	**Vancouver**	**NHL**	**26**	**0**	**1**	**1**	**63**	**0**	**0**	**0**	**20**	**0.0**	**–3**	**0**	**0.0**	**36**	**15**	**8:54**								
	Phoenix	**NHL**	**11**	**0**	**1**	**1**	**27**	**0**	**0**	**0**	**7**	**0.0**	**–1**	**0**	**0.0**	**27**	**3**	**11:02**								
99-2000	**Washington**	**NHL**	**7**	**0**	**0**	**0**	**11**	**0**	**0**	**0**	**4**	**0.0**	**–5**	**0**	**0.0**	**15**	**4**	**10:37**								
	Portland Pirates	AHL	56	0	12	12	154												4	0	0	0	14			
2000-01	Portland Pirates	AHL	6	0	1	1	12																			
	NHL Totals		**352**	**5**	**33**	**38**	**1065**	**0**	**0**	**1**	**228**	**2.2**		**0**	**0.0**	**78**	**22**	**9:42**	**21**	**0**	**1**	**1**	**46**	**0**	**0**	**0**

Signed as a free agent by **Boston**, July 23, 1992. Signed as a free agent by **Calgary**, August 22, 1995. Traded to **Tampa Bay** by **Calgary** for Tyler Moss, March 18, 1997. Traded to **Vancouver** by **Tampa Bay** for Enrico Ciccone, March 14, 1998. Traded to **Phoenix** by **Vancouver** for future considerations, March 8, 1999. Signed as a free agent by **Washington**, August 9, 1999. • Missed majority of 2000-01 season recovering from head injury suffered in game vs. Albany (AHL), October 13, 2000.

IGINLA, Jarome

(ih-GIHN-lah, jah-ROHM) **CGY.**

Right wing. Shoots right. 6'1", 200 lbs. Born, Edmonton, Alta., July 1, 1977. Dallas' 1st choice, 11th overall, in 1995 Entry Draft.

Season	Club	League	GP	G	A	Pts	PIM	PP	SH	GW	S	%	+/-	TF	F%	H	SB	Min	GP	G	A	Pts	PIM	PP	SH	GW
1991-92	St. Albert Eagles	AAHA	36	26	30	56	22																			
1992-93	St. Albert Raiders	AMHL	36	34	53	87	20																			
1993-94	Kamloops Blazers	WHL	48	6	23	29	33												19	3	6	9	10			
1994-95	Kamloops Blazers	WHL	72	33	38	71	111												21	7	11	18	34			
1995-96	Kamloops Blazers	WHL	63	63	73	136	120												16	16	13	29	44			
	Calgary	**NHL**																	**2**	**1**	**1**	**2**	**0**	**0**	**0**	**0**

			Regular Season																Playoffs							
Season	Club	League	GP	G	A	Pts	PIM	PP	SH	GW	S	%	+/-	TF	F%	H	SB	Min	GP	G	A	Pts	PIM	PP	SH	GW
1996-97	**Calgary**	**NHL**	82	21	29	50	37	8	1	3	169	12.4	–4													
1997-98	**Calgary**	**NHL**	70	13	19	32	29	0	2	1	154	8.4	–10													
1998-99	**Calgary**	**NHL**	82	28	23	51	58	7	0	4	211	13.3	1	111	51.4	119	25	16:30								
99-2000	**Calgary**	**NHL**	77	29	34	63	26	12	0	4	256	11.3	0	278	52.9	133	29	18:24								
2000-01	**Calgary**	**NHL**	77	31	40	71	62	10	0	4	229	13.5	–2	638	51.7	99	34	19:58								
	NHL Totals		388	122	145	267	212	37	3	16	1019	12.0		1027	52.0	351	88	18:15	2	1	1	2	0	0	0	0

Won George Parsons Trophy (Memorial Cup Tournament Most Sportsmanlike Player) (1995) • WHL West First All-Star Team (1996) • Canadian Major Junior First All-Star Team (1996) • NHL All-Rookie Team (1997)

Traded to **Calgary** by **Dallas** with Corey Millen for Joe Nieuwendyk, December 19, 1995.

IGNATJEV, Victor

(ihg-NYAT-ee-ehv, VIHK-tohr)

Defense. Shoots left. 6'4", 215 lbs. Born, Riga, USSR, April 26, 1970. San Jose's 11th choice, 243rd overall, in 1992 Entry Draft.

1989-90	Dynamo Riga	USSR	40	0	0	0	26																			
1990-91	Dynamo Riga	USSR	10	0	0	0	2																			
1991-92	Dynamo Riga	CIS	22	4	5	9	22																			
1992-93	Kansas City	IHL	64	5	16	21	68												4	1	2	3	24			
1993-94	Kansas City	IHL	67	1	24	25	123																			
1994-95	Oklahoma City	CHL	47	11	35	46	66																			
	Denver Grizzlies	IHL	23	2	11	13	4												17	3	8	11	8			
1995-96	Utah Grizzlies	IHL	73	9	29	38	67												21	3	8	11	22			
1996-97	Long Beach	IHL	82	16	53	69	112												16	3	4	7	26			
1997-98	Long Beach	IHL	71	12	33	45	102												17	3	11	14	16			
1998-99	**Pittsburgh**	**NHL**	11	0	1	1	6	0	0	0	15	0.0	–3	0	0.0	10	6	12:14	1	0	0	0	2	0	0	0
99-2000	EHC Nurnberg	DEL	60	3	15	18	56																			
	EHC Nurnberg	EuroHL	4	0	3	3	22												2	0	0	0	6			
2000-01	Leksands IF	Sweden	39	0	1	1	32																			
	NHL Totals		11	0	1	1	6	0	0	0	15	0.0		0	0.0	10	6	12:14	1	0	0	0	2	0	0	0

IHL Second All-Star Team (1997)

Signed as a free agent by **Pittsburgh**, August 11, 1998. • Missed majority of 1998-99 season recovering from shoulder surgery, November, 1998.

ISBISTER, Brad

(IHZ-bihs-tuhr, BRAD) **NYI**

Left wing. Shoots right. 6'4", 227 lbs. Born, Edmonton, Alta., May 7, 1977. Winnipeg's 4th choice, 67th overall, in 1995 Entry Draft.

1992-93	Calgary Canucks	AAHA	35	24	25	49	74																			
1993-94	Portland	WHL	64	7	10	17	45												10	0	2	2	0			
1994-95	Portland	WHL	67	16	20	36	123																			
1995-96	Portland	WHL	71	45	44	89	184												7	2	4	6	20			
1996-97	Portland	WHL	24	15	18	33	45												6	2	1	3	16			
	Springfield	AHL	7	3	1	4	14												9	1	2	3	10			
1997-98	**Phoenix**	**NHL**	66	9	8	17	102	1	0	1	115	7.8	4						5	0	0	0	2	0	0	0
	Springfield	AHL	9	8	2	10	36																			
1998-99	**Phoenix**	**NHL**	32	4	4	8	46	0	0	2	48	8.3	1	3	0.0	39	3	11:33								
	Springfield	AHL	4	1	1	2	12																			
	Las Vegas	IHL	2	0	0	0	9																			
99-2000	**NY Islanders**	**NHL**	64	22	20	42	100	9	0	1	135	16.3	–18	55	54.6	134	15	16:58								
2000-01	**NY Islanders**	**NHL**	51	18	14	32	59	7	1	4	129	14.0	–19	255	45.9	119	16	19:26								
	NHL Totals		213	53	46	99	307	17	1	8	427	12.4		313	47.0	292	34	16:38	5	0	0	0	2	0	0	0

WHL West Second All-Star Team (1997)

Rights transferred to **Phoenix** after **Winnipeg** franchise relocated, July 1, 1996. Traded to **NY Islanders** by **Phoenix** with Phoenix's 3rd round choice (Brian Collins) in 1999 Entry Draft for Robert Reichel, NY Islanders' 3rd round choice (Jason Jaspers) in 1999 Entry Draft and Ottawa's 4th round choice (previously acquired, Phoenix selected Preston Mizzi) in 1999 Entry Draft, March 20, 1999.

JACKMAN, Richard

(JAK-man, RIH-chuhrd) **BOS.**

Defense. Shoots right. 6'2", 192 lbs. Born, Toronto, Ont., June 28, 1978. Dallas' 1st choice, 5th overall, in 1996 Entry Draft.

1993-94	Mississauga Sens	MTHL	81	35	53	88	156																			
1994-95	Mississauga Sens	MTHL	53	20	37	57	120																			
	Richmond Hill	MTJHL	10	2	9	11	16																			
1995-96	Sault Ste. Marie	OHL	66	13	29	42	97												4	1	0	1	15			
1996-97	Sault Ste. Marie	OHL	53	13	34	47	116												10	2	6	8	24			
1997-98	Sault Ste. Marie	OHL	60	33	40	73	111																			
	Michigan K-Wings	IHL	14	1	5	6	10												4	0	0	0	10			
1998-99	Michigan K-Wings	IHL	71	13	17	30	106												5	0	4	4	6			
99-2000	**Dallas**	**NHL**	22	1	2	3	6	1	0	0	16	6.3	–1	0	0.0	18	10	8:06								
	Michigan K-Wings	IHL	50	3	16	19	51																			
2000-01	**Dallas**	**NHL**	16	0	0	0	18	0	0	0	10	0.0	–6	0	0.0	23	8	8:51								
	Utah Grizzlies	IHL	57	9	19	28	24																			
	NHL Totals		38	1	2	3	24	1	0	0	26	3.8		0	0.0	41	18	8:25								

OHL Second All-Star Team (1998)

Traded to **Boston** by **Dallas** for Cameron Mann, June 23, 2001.

JACKSON, Dane

(JAK-sohn, DAYN)

Right wing. Shoots right. 6'1", 200 lbs. Born, Castlegar, B.C., May 17, 1970. Vancouver's 3rd choice, 44th overall, in 1988 Entry Draft.

1987-88	Vernon Lakers	BCJHL	49	24	30	54	95												13	7	10	17	49			
1988-89	North Dakota	WCHA	30	4	5	9	33																			
1989-90	North Dakota	WCHA	44	15	11	26	56																			
1990-91	North Dakota	WCHA	37	17	9	26	79																			
1991-92	North Dakota	WCHA	39	23	19	42	81																			
1992-93	Hamilton Canucks	AHL	68	23	20	43	59																			
1993-94	**Vancouver**	**NHL**	12	5	1	6	9	0	0	0	18	27.8	3													
	Hamilton Canucks	AHL	60	25	35	60	75												4	2	2	4	16			
1994-95	Syracuse Crunch	AHL	78	30	28	58	162																			
	Vancouver	**NHL**	3	1	0	1	4	0	0	0	6	16.7	0						6	0	0	0	10	0	0	0
1995-96	**Buffalo**	**NHL**	22	5	4	9	41	0	0	1	20	25.0	3													
	Rochester	AHL	50	27	19	46	132												19	4	6	10	53			
1996-97	Rochester	AHL	78	24	34	58	111												10	7	4	11	14			
1997-98	**NY Islanders**	**NHL**	8	1	1	2	4	0	0	1	5	20.0	1													
	Rochester	AHL	28	10	13	23	55												3	2	2	4	4			
1998-99	Lowell	AHL	80	16	27	43	103												3	0	1	1	16			
99-2000	Rochester	AHL	21	6	9	15	8																			
2000-01	Rochester	AHL	69	16	12	28	104												4	1	1	2	4			
	NHL Totals		45	12	6	18	58	0	0	2	49	24.5							6	0	0	0	10	0	0	0

Signed as a free agent by **Buffalo**, September 20, 1995. Signed as a free agent by **NY Islanders**, July 21, 1997. Signed as a free agent by **Rochester** (AHL), August 29, 1999. • Missed majority of 1999-2000 season recovering from knee injury suffered in game vs. Springfield (AHL), January 21, 2000.

JAGR, Jaromir

(YAH-guhr, YAIR-oh-MEER) **WSH.**

Right wing. Shoots left. 6'2", 234 lbs. Born, Kladno, Czech., February 15, 1972. Pittsburgh's 1st choice, 5th overall, in 1990 Entry Draft.

1984-85	Poldi Kladno	Czech-Jr.	34	24	17	41																				
1985-86	Poldi Kladno	Czech-Jr.	36	41	29	70																				
1986-87	Poldi Kladno	Czech-Jr.	30	35	35	70																				
1987-88	Poldi Kladno	Czech-Jr.	35	57	27	84																				
1988-89	Poldi Kladno	Czech.	29	3	3	6	4												10	5	7	12	0			
1989-90	Poldi Kladno	Czech.	42	22	28	50													9	*8	2	10				
1990-91♦	**Pittsburgh**	**NHL**	80	27	30	57	42	7	0	4	136	19.9	–4						24	3	10	13	6	1	0	1
1991-92♦	**Pittsburgh**	**NHL**	70	32	37	69	34	4	0	4	194	16.5	12						21	11	13	24	6	2	0	4
1992-93	**Pittsburgh**	**NHL**	81	34	60	94	61	10	1	9	242	14.0	30						12	5	4	9	23	1	0	1

			Regular Season																Playoffs							
Season	Club	League	GP	G	A	Pts	PIM	PP	SH	GW	S	%	+/-	TF	F%	H	SB	Min	GP	G	A	Pts	PIM	PP	SH	GW
1993-94	**Pittsburgh**	**NHL**	**80**	**32**	**67**	**99**	**61**	**9**	**0**	**6**	**298**	**10.7**	**15**						**6**	**2**	**4**	**6**	**16**	**0**	**0**	**1**
1994-95	Poldi Kladno	Cze-Rep	11	8	14	22	10																			
	HC Bolzano	Alpenliga	5	8	8	16	4																			
	HC Bolzano	Italy	1	0	0	0	0																			
	EHC Schalke	DEB-3	1	1	10	11	0																			
	Pittsburgh	**NHL**	**48**	**32**	**38**	***70**	**37**	**8**	**3**	**7**	**192**	**16.7**	**23**						**12**	**10**	**5**	**15**	**6**	**2**	**1**	**1**
1995-96	**Pittsburgh**	**NHL**	**82**	**62**	**87**	**149**	**96**	**20**	**1**	**12**	**403**	**15.4**	**31**						**18**	**11**	**12**	**23**	**18**	**5**	**1**	**1**
1996-97	**Pittsburgh**	**NHL**	**63**	**47**	**48**	**95**	**40**	**11**	**2**	**6**	**234**	**20.1**	**22**						**5**	**4**	**4**	**8**	**4**	**2**	**0**	**0**
1997-98	**Pittsburgh**	**NHL**	**77**	**35**	***67**	***102**	**64**	**7**	**0**	**8**	**262**	**13.4**	**17**						**6**	**4**	**5**	**9**	**2**	**1**	**0**	**0**
	Czech-Republic	Olympics	6	1	4	5	2																			
1998-99	**Pittsburgh**	**NHL**	**81**	**44**	***83**	***127**	**66**	**10**	**1**	**7**	**343**	**12.8**	**17**	**4**	**50.0**	**27**	**23**	**25:51**	**9**	**5**	**7**	**12**	**16**	**1**	**0**	**1**
99-2000	**Pittsburgh**	**NHL**	**63**	**42**	**54**	***96**	**50**	**10**	**0**	**5**	**290**	**14.5**	**25**	**9**	**22.2**	**19**	**12**	**23:12**	**11**	**8**	**8**	**16**	**6**	**2**	**0**	**4**
2000-01	**Pittsburgh**	**NHL**	**81**	**52**	***69**	***121**	**42**	**14**	**1**	**10**	**317**	**16.4**	**19**	**2**	**0.0**	**25**	**27**	**23:19**	**16**	**2**	**10**	**12**	**18**	**2**	**0**	**0**
	NHL Totals		**806**	**439**	**640**	**1079**	**593**	**110**	**9**	**78**	**2911**	**15.1**		**15**	**26.7**	**71**	**62**	**24:12**	**140**	**65**	**82**	**147**	**121**	**19**	**2**	**14**

NHL All-Rookie Team (1991) • NHL First All-Star Team (1995, 1996, 1998, 1999, 2000, 2001) • Won Art Ross Trophy (1995, 1998, 1999, 2000, 2001) • NHL Second All-Star Team (1997) • Won Lester B. Pearson Award (1999, 2000) • Won Hart Trophy (1999) • Played in NHL All-Star Game (1992, 1993, 1996, 1998, 1999, 2000)

Traded to **Washington** by **Pittsburgh** with Frantisek Kucera for Kris Beech, Michal Sivek, Ross Lupaschuk and future considerations, July 11, 2001.

JAKOPIN, John

(JA-koh-pihn, JAWN) **FLA.**

Defense. Shoots right. 6'5", 239 lbs. Born, Toronto, Ont., May 16, 1975. Detroit's 4th choice, 97th overall, in 1993 Entry Draft.

1992-93	St. Michael's	MTJHL	45	9	21	30	42												13	3	2	5	4			
1993-94	Merrimack	H-East	36	2	8	10	64																			
1994-95	Merrimack	H-East	37	4	10	14	42																			
1995-96	Merrimack	H-East	32	10	15	25	68																			
1996-97	Merrimack	H-East	31	4	12	16	68																			
	Adirondack	AHL	3	0	0	0	9																			
1997-98	**Florida**	**NHL**	**2**	**0**	**0**	**0**	**4**	**0**	**0**	**0**	**1**	**0.0**	**–3**													
	New Haven	AHL	60	2	18	20	151												3	0	0	0	0			
1998-99	**Florida**	**NHL**	**3**	**0**	**0**	**0**	**0**	**0**	**0**	**0**	**0**	**0.0**	**–1**	**0**	**0.0**	**8**	**2**	**13:32**								
	New Haven	AHL	60	2	7	9	154																			
99-2000	**Florida**	**NHL**	**17**	**0**	**0**	**0**	**26**	**0**	**0**	**0**	**1**	**0.0**	**–2**	**0**	**0.0**	**37**	**10**	**11:58**								
	Louisville Panthers	AHL	23	4	6	10	47																			
2000-01	**Florida**	**NHL**	**60**	**1**	**2**	**3**	**62**	**0**	**0**	**0**	**23**	**4.3**	**–4**	**2**	**50.0**	**181**	**46**	**12:54**								
	Louisville Panthers	AHL	8	0	1	1	21																			
	NHL Totals		**82**	**1**	**2**	**3**	**92**	**0**	**0**	**0**	**25**	**4.0**		**2**	**50.0**	**226**	**58**	**12:44**								

Signed as a free agent by **Florida**, May 14, 1997. • Missed majority of 1999-2000 season recovering from groin injury suffered in game vs. Carolina, February 1, 2000.

JANSSENS, Mark

(JAN-sehns, MAHRK)

Center. Shoots left. 6'3", 212 lbs. Born, Surrey, B.C., May 19, 1968. NY Rangers' 4th choice, 72nd overall, in 1986 Entry Draft.

1983-84	Surrey Eagles	BCAHA	40	40	58	98	64																			
1984-85	Regina Pats	WHL	70	8	22	30	51												5	1	1	2	0			
1985-86	Regina Pats	WHL	71	25	38	63	146												9	0	2	2	17			
1986-87	Regina Pats	WHL	68	24	38	62	209												3	0	1	1	14			
1987-88	Regina Pats	WHL	71	39	51	90	202												4	3	4	7	6			
	NY Rangers	**NHL**	**1**	**0**	**0**	**0**	**0**	**0**	**0**	**0**	**0**	**0.0**	**0**													
	Colorado Rangers	IHL	6	2	2	4	24												12	3	2	5	20			
1988-89	**NY Rangers**	**NHL**	**5**	**0**	**0**	**0**	**0**	**0**	**0**	**0**	**4**	**0.0**	**–4**													
	Denver Rangers	IHL	38	19	19	38	104												4	3	0	3	18			
1989-90	**NY Rangers**	**NHL**	**80**	**5**	**8**	**13**	**161**	**0**	**0**	**0**	**61**	**8.2**	**–26**						**9**	**2**	**1**	**3**	**10**	**0**	**0**	**1**
1990-91	**NY Rangers**	**NHL**	**67**	**9**	**7**	**16**	**172**	**0**	**0**	**1**	**45**	**20.0**	**–1**						**6**	**3**	**0**	**3**	**6**	**0**	**0**	**0**
1991-92	**NY Rangers**	**NHL**	**4**	**0**	**0**	**0**	**5**	**0**	**0**	**0**	**0**	**0.0**	**–1**													
	Binghamton	AHL	55	10	23	33	109																			
	Minnesota	**NHL**	**3**	**0**	**0**	**0**	**0**	**0**	**0**	**0**	**1**	**0.0**	**–1**													
	Kalamazoo Wings	IHL	2	0	0	0	2												11	1	2	3	22			
1992-93	**Hartford**	**NHL**	**76**	**12**	**17**	**29**	**237**	**0**	**0**	**1**	**63**	**19.0**	**–15**													
1993-94	**Hartford**	**NHL**	**84**	**2**	**10**	**12**	**137**	**0**	**0**	**0**	**52**	**3.8**	**–13**													
1994-95	**Hartford**	**NHL**	**46**	**2**	**5**	**7**	**93**	**0**	**0**	**0**	**33**	**6.1**	**–8**													
1995-96	**Hartford**	**NHL**	**81**	**2**	**7**	**9**	**155**	**0**	**0**	**0**	**63**	**3.2**	**–13**													
1996-97	**Hartford**	**NHL**	**54**	**2**	**4**	**6**	**90**	**0**	**0**	**0**	**30**	**6.7**	**–10**													
	Anaheim	**NHL**	**12**	**0**	**2**	**2**	**47**	**0**	**0**	**0**	**9**	**0.0**	**–3**						**11**	**0**	**0**	**0**	**15**	**0**	**0**	**0**
1997-98	**Anaheim**	**NHL**	**55**	**4**	**5**	**9**	**116**	**0**	**0**	**1**	**43**	**9.3**	**–22**													
	NY Islanders	**NHL**	**12**	**0**	**0**	**0**	**34**	**0**	**0**	**0**	**4**	**0.0**	**–3**													
	Phoenix	**NHL**	**7**	**1**	**2**	**3**	**4**	**0**	**0**	**0**	**6**	**16.7**	**4**						**1**	**0**	**0**	**0**	**2**	**0**	**0**	**0**
1998-99	**Chicago**	**NHL**	**60**	**1**	**0**	**1**	**65**	**0**	**0**	**0**	**27**	**3.7**	**–11**	**594**	**57.9**	**34**	**19**	**8:17**								
99-2000	**Chicago**	**NHL**	**36**	**0**	**6**	**6**	**73**	**0**	**0**	**0**	**14**	**0.0**	**–2**	**127**	**51.2**	**15**	**10**	**7:12**								
2000-01	**Chicago**	**NHL**	**28**	**0**	**0**	**0**	**33**	**0**	**0**	**0**	**15**	**0.0**	**–8**	**290**	**57.9**	**27**	**9**	**10:27**								
	Norfolk Admirals	AHL	28	3	9	12	41																			
	Houston Aeros	IHL	4	2	1	3	2																			
	NHL Totals		**711**	**40**	**73**	**113**	**1422**	**0**	**0**	**3**	**470**	**8.5**		**1011**	**57.1**	**76**	**38**	**8:28**	**27**	**5**	**1**	**6**	**33**	**0**	**0**	**1**

Traded to **Minnesota** by **NY Rangers** for Mario Thyer and Minnesota's 3rd round choice (Maxim Galanov) in 1993 Entry Draft, March 10, 1992. Traded to **Hartford** by **Minnesota** for James Black, September 3, 1992. Traded to **Anaheim** by **Hartford** for Bates Battaglia and Anaheim's 4th round choice (Carolina selected Josef Vasicek) in 1998 Entry Draft, March 18, 1997. Traded to **NY Islanders** by **Anaheim** with Joe Sacco and J.J. Daigneault for Travis Green, Doug Houda and Tony Tuzzolino, February 6, 1998. Traded to **Phoenix** by **NY Islanders** for Phoenix's 9th round choice (Jason Doyle) in 1998 Entry Draft, March 24, 1998. Signed as a free agent by **Chicago**, July 28, 1998. • Missed majority of 1999-2000 season recovering from back injury suffered in game vs. Edmonton, December 3, 1999. Traded to **Philadelphia** by **Chicago** for Philadelphia's 9th round choice (Arne Ramholt) in 2000 Entry Draft, June 12, 2000. Claimed on waivers by **Chicago** from **Philadelphia**, July 6, 2000.

JEFFERSON, Mike

(JEH-fuhr-suhn, MIGHK) **N.J.**

Center. Shoots right. 5'9", 180 lbs. Born, Brampton, Ont., October 21, 1980. New Jersey's 8th choice, 135th overall, in 2000 Entry Draft.

1996-97	Quinte Hawks	MTJHL	35	10	18	28	281																			
1997-98	Sarnia Sting	OHL	12	6	1	7	37																			
	St. Michael's	OHL	18	4	6	10	77																			
1998-99	St. Michael's	OHL	27	18	22	40	116																			
	Barrie Colts	OHL	26	15	20	35	62												9	6	5	11	38			
99-2000	Barrie Colts	OHL	58	34	53	87	203												25	7	16	23	*107			
2000-01	**New Jersey**	**NHL**	**2**	**0**	**0**	**0**	**6**	**0**	**0**	**0**	**3**	**0.0**	**0**	**6**	**50.0**	**8**	**0**	**7:52**								
	Albany River Rats	AHL	69	19	15	34	195																			
	NHL Totals		**2**	**0**	**0**	**0**	**6**	**0**	**0**	**0**	**3**	**0.0**		**6**	**50.0**	**8**	**0**	**7:52**								

JOHANSSON, Andreas

(yoh-HAHN-suhn, ahn-DRAY-uhs) **NYR**

Center. Shoots left. 6', 202 lbs. Born, Hofors, Sweden, May 19, 1973. NY Islanders' 7th choice, 136th overall, in 1991 Entry Draft.

1987-88	Bofors HC	Sweden-3	1	0	0	0	0																			
1988-89	Bofors HC	Sweden-3	28	19	11	30	....																			
1989-90	Falu IF	Sweden-2	21	3	1	4	14																			
1990-91	Falu IF	Sweden-2	31	12	10	22	38																			
1991-92	Farjestads BK	Sweden	30	3	1	4	10												6	0	0	0	4			
1992-93	Farjestads BK	Sweden	38	4	7	11	38												2	0	0	0	0			
1993-94	Farjestads BK	Sweden	37	11	16	27	24												3	1	4	5	2			
1994-95	Farjestads BK	Sweden	36	9	10	19	42												4	0	0	0	10			
1995-96	**NY Islanders**	**NHL**	**3**	**0**	**1**	**1**	**0**	**0**	**0**	**0**	**6**	**0.0**	**1**													
	Worcester	AHL	29	5	5	10	32																			
	Utah Grizzlies	IHL	22	4	13	17	28												12	0	5	5	6			
1996-97	**NY Islanders**	**NHL**	**15**	**2**	**2**	**4**	**0**	**1**	**0**	**0**	**21**	**9.5**	**–6**													
	Pittsburgh	**NHL**	**27**	**2**	**7**	**9**	**20**	**0**	**0**	**0**	**38**	**5.3**	**–6**													
	Cleveland	IHL	10	2	4	6	42												11	1	5	6	8			
1997-98	**Pittsburgh**	**NHL**	**50**	**5**	**10**	**15**	**20**	**0**	**1**	**0**	**49**	**10.2**	**4**						**1**	**0**	**0**	**0**	**0**	**0**	**0**	**0**
	Sweden	Olympics	3	0	0	0	2																			
1998-99	**Ottawa**	**NHL**	**69**	**21**	**16**	**37**	**34**	**7**	**0**	**6**	**144**	**14.6**	**1**	**9**	**22.2**	**48**	**8**	**14:39**	**2**	**0**	**0**	**0**	**0**	**0**	**0**	**0**

			Regular Season															Playoffs							
Season	Club	League	GP	G	A	Pts	PIM	PP	SH	GW	S	%	+/-	TF	F%	H	SB	Min	GP	G	A	Pts	PIM	PP	SH	GW
99-2000	Tampa Bay	NHL	12	2	3	5	8	0	0	0	11	18.2	1	0	0.0	8	2	10:50	....	....	....	....	....	....	....	....
	Calgary	NHL	28	3	7	10	14	1	0	0	47	6.4	–3	5	20.0	22	8	13:33	....	....	....	....	....	....	....	....
2000-01	SC Bern	Switz.	40	15	29	44	94	....	....	....	....	....	....	....	....	....	....	....	7	5	4	9	0	....	....	....
	NHL Totals		204	35	46	81	96	9	1	6	316	11.1		14	21.4	78	18	13:57	3	0	0	0	0	0	0	0

Traded to **Pittsburgh** by **NY Islanders** with Darius Kasparaitis for Bryan Smolinski, November 17, 1996. Signed as a free agent by **Ottawa**, September 29, 1998. Traded to **Tampa Bay** by **Ottawa** for Rob Zamuner and future considerations, June 29, 1999. Traded to **Calgary** by **Tampa Bay** for Nils Ekman and Calgary's 4th round choice (later traded to NY Islanders - NY Islanders selected Vladimir Gorbunov) in 2000 Entry Draft, November 13, 1999. • Missed majority of 1999-2000 season recovering from back injury suffered in game vs. Vancouver, January 2, 2000. Claimed by **NY Rangers** from **Calgary** in Waiver Draft, September 29, 2000.

JOHANSSON, Calle

(yoh-HAHN-suhn, KAL-ee) **WSH.**

Defense. Shoots left. 5'11", 208 lbs. Born, Goteborg, Sweden, February 14, 1967. Buffalo's 1st choice, 14th overall, in 1985 Entry Draft.

Season	Club	League	GP	G	A	Pts	PIM	PP	SH	GW	S	%	+/-	TF	F%	H	SB	Min	GP	G	A	Pts	PIM	PP	SH	GW
1981-82	KBA-67	Sweden-3	27	3	3	6	....	....	....	....	....	....	....	....	....	....	....	....	....	....	....	....	....	....	....	....
1982-83	KBA-67	Sweden-3	29	12	11	23	....	....	....	....	....	....	....	....	....	....	....	....	....	....	....	....	....	....	....	....
1983-84	Vastra Frolunda	Sweden	28	4	4	8	10	....	....	....	....	....	....	....	....	....	....	....	....	....	....	....	....	....	....	....
1984-85	Vastra Frolunda	Sweden-2	30	8	13	21	16	....	....	....	....	....	....	....	....	....	....	....	....	....	....	....	....	....	....	....
1985-86	Bjorkloven	Sweden	17	1	2	3	4	....	....	....	....	....	....	....	....	....	....	....	....	....	....	....	....	....	....	....
1986-87	Bjorkloven	Sweden	30	2	13	15	20	....	....	....	....	....	....	....	....	....	....	....	6	1	3	4	6	....	....	....
1987-88	Buffalo	NHL	71	4	38	42	37	2	0	0	93	4.3	12	....	....	....	....	....	6	0	1	1	0	0	0	0
1988-89	Buffalo	NHL	47	2	11	13	33	0	0	1	53	3.8	–7	....	....	....	....	....	....	....	....	....	....	....	....	....
	Washington	NHL	12	1	7	8	4	1	0	0	22	4.5	1	....	....	....	....	....	6	1	2	3	0	1	0	0
1989-90	Washington	NHL	70	8	31	39	25	4	0	2	103	7.8	7	....	....	....	....	....	15	1	6	7	4	0	0	0
1990-91	Washington	NHL	80	11	41	52	23	2	1	2	128	8.6	–2	....	....	....	....	....	10	2	7	9	8	1	0	0
1991-92	Washington	NHL	80	14	42	56	49	5	2	2	119	11.8	2	....	....	....	....	....	7	0	5	5	4	0	0	0
1992-93	Washington	NHL	77	7	38	45	56	6	0	0	133	5.3	3	....	....	....	....	....	6	0	5	5	4	0	0	0
1993-94	Washington	NHL	84	9	33	42	59	4	0	1	141	6.4	3	....	....	....	....	....	6	1	3	4	4	0	0	1
1994-95	EHC Kloten	Switz.	5	1	2	3	8	....	....	....	....	....	....	....	....	....	....	....	....	....	....	....	....	....	....	....
	Washington	NHL	46	5	26	31	35	4	0	2	112	4.5	–6	....	....	....	....	....	7	3	1	4	0	1	0	0
1995-96	Washington	NHL	78	10	25	35	50	4	0	0	182	5.5	13	....	....	....	....	....	....	....	....	....	....	....	....	....
1996-97	Washington	NHL	65	6	11	17	16	2	0	0	133	4.5	–2	....	....	....	....	....	....	....	....	....	....	....	....	....
1997-98	Washington	NHL	73	15	20	35	30	10	1	1	163	9.2	–11	....	....	....	....	....	21	2	8	10	16	0	0	0
	Sweden	Olympics	4	0	0	0	2	....	....	....	....	....	....	....	....	....	....	....	....	....	....	....	....	....	....	....
1998-99	Washington	NHL	67	8	21	29	22	2	0	2	145	5.5	10	0	0.0	51	140	23:58	....	....	....	....	....	....	....	....
99-2000	Washington	NHL	82	7	25	32	24	1	0	3	138	5.1	13	0	0.0	67	161	23:55	5	1	2	3	0	1	0	0
2000-01	Washington	NHL	76	7	29	36	26	5	0	0	154	4.5	11	0	0.0	41	136	23:44	6	1	2	3	2	0	0	0
	NHL Totals		1008	114	398	512	489	52	4	16	1819	6.3		0	0.0	159	437	23:52	95	12	42	54	42	4	0	1

NHL All-Rookie Team (1988)

Traded to **Washington** by **Buffalo** with Buffalo's 2nd round choice (Byron Dafoe) in 1989 Entry Draft for Clint Malarchuk, Grant Ledyard and Washington's 6th round choice (Brian Holzinger) in 1991 Entry Draft, March 7, 1989.

JOHNSON, Craig

(JAWN-suhn, KRAYG) **L.A.**

Left wing. Shoots left. 6'2", 200 lbs. Born, St. Paul, MN, March 18, 1972. St. Louis' 1st choice, 33rd overall, in 1990 Entry Draft.

Season	Club	League	GP	G	A	Pts	PIM	PP	SH	GW	S	%	+/-	TF	F%	H	SB	Min	GP	G	A	Pts	PIM	PP	SH	GW
1987-88	Hill-Murray	Hi-School	28	14	20	34	4	....	....	....	....	....	....	....	....	....	....	....	....	....	....	....	....	....	....	....
1988-89	Hill-Murray	Hi-School	24	22	30	52	10	....	....	....	....	....	....	....	....	....	....	....	....	....	....	....	....	....	....	....
1989-90	Hill-Murray	Hi-School	23	15	36	51	0	....	....	....	....	....	....	....	....	....	....	....	....	....	....	....	....	....	....	....
1990-91	U. of Minnesota	WCHA	33	13	18	31	34	....	....	....	....	....	....	....	....	....	....	....	....	....	....	....	....	....	....	....
1991-92	U. of Minnesota	WCHA	41	17	38	55	66	....	....	....	....	....	....	....	....	....	....	....	....	....	....	....	....	....	....	....
1992-93	U. of Minnesota	WCHA	42	22	24	46	70	....	....	....	....	....	....	....	....	....	....	....	....	....	....	....	....	....	....	....
	Jacksonville	SunHL	23	2	9	11	38	....	....	....	....	....	....	....	....	....	....	....	....	....	....	....	....	....	....	....
1993-94	United States	Nat-Team	54	25	26	51	64	....	....	....	....	....	....	....	....	....	....	....	....	....	....	....	....	....	....	....
	United States	Olympics	8	0	4	4	4	....	....	....	....	....	....	....	....	....	....	....	....	....	....	....	....	....	....	....
1994-95	St. Louis	NHL	15	3	3	6	6	0	0	0	19	15.8	4	....	....	....	....	....	1	0	0	0	2	0	0	0
	Peoria Rivermen	IHL	16	2	6	8	25	....	....	....	....	....	....	....	....	....	....	....	9	0	4	4	10	....	....	....
1995-96	St. Louis	NHL	49	8	7	15	30	1	0	0	69	11.6	–4	....	....	....	....	....	....	....	....	....	....	....	....	....
	Worcester	AHL	5	3	0	3	2	....	....	....	....	....	....	....	....	....	....	....	....	....	....	....	....	....	....	....
	Los Angeles	NHL	11	5	4	9	6	3	0	0	28	17.9	–4	....	....	....	....	....	....	....	....	....	....	....	....	....
1996-97	Los Angeles	NHL	31	4	3	7	26	1	0	0	30	13.3	–7	....	....	....	....	....	....	....	....	....	....	....	....	....
1997-98	Los Angeles	NHL	74	17	21	38	42	6	0	2	125	13.6	9	....	....	....	....	....	4	1	0	1	4	0	0	0
1998-99	Los Angeles	NHL	69	7	12	19	32	2	0	2	94	7.4	–12	2	50.0	70	11	12:02	....	....	....	....	....	....	....	....
99-2000	Los Angeles	NHL	76	9	14	23	28	1	0	1	106	8.5	–10	9	55.6	82	18	13:56	4	1	0	1	2	0	0	0
2000-01	Los Angeles	NHL	26	4	5	9	16	0	0	0	36	11.1	0	2	100.0	26	3	10:40	....	....	....	....	....	....	....	....
	NHL Totals		351	57	69	126	186	14	0	5	507	11.2		13	61.5	178	32	12:40	9	2	0	2	8	0	0	0

Traded to **LA Kings** by **St. Louis** with Patrice Tardif, Roman Vopat, St. Louis 5th round choice (Peter Hogan) in 1996 Entry Draft and 1st round choice (Matt Zultek) in 1997 Entry Draft for Wayne Gretzky, February 27, 1996. • Missed majority of 2000-01 season recovering from ankle injury suffered in game vs. San Jose, December 26, 2000.

JOHNSON, Greg

(JAWN-suhn, GREHG) **NSH.**

Center. Shoots left. 5'11", 202 lbs. Born, Thunder Bay, Ont., March 16, 1971. Philadelphia's 1st choice, 33rd overall, in 1989 Entry Draft.

Season	Club	League	GP	G	A	Pts	PIM	PP	SH	GW	S	%	+/-	TF	F%	H	SB	Min	GP	G	A	Pts	PIM	PP	SH	GW
1988-89	Thunder Bay	USHL	47	32	64	96	4	....	....	....	....	....	....	....	....	....	....	....	12	5	13	18	0	....	....	....
1989-90	North Dakota	WCHA	44	17	38	55	11	....	....	....	....	....	....	....	....	....	....	....	....	....	....	....	....	....	....	....
1990-91	North Dakota	WCHA	38	18	*61	79	6	....	....	....	....	....	....	....	....	....	....	....	....	....	....	....	....	....	....	....
1991-92	North Dakota	WCHA	39	20	*54	74	8	....	....	....	....	....	....	....	....	....	....	....	....	....	....	....	....	....	....	....
1992-93	North Dakota	WCHA	34	19	45	64	18	....	....	....	....	....	....	....	....	....	....	....	....	....	....	....	....	....	....	....
	Canada	Nat-Team	23	6	14	20	2	....	....	....	....	....	....	....	....	....	....	....	....	....	....	....	....	....	....	....
1993-94	Detroit	NHL	52	6	11	17	22	1	1	0	48	12.5	–7	....	....	....	....	....	7	2	2	4	2	1	0	0
	Adirondack	AHL	3	2	4	6	0	....	....	....	....	....	....	....	....	....	....	....	4	0	4	4	2	....	....	....
	Canada	Olympics	8	0	3	3	0	....	....	....	....	....	....	....	....	....	....	....	....	....	....	....	....	....	....	....
1994-95	Detroit	NHL	22	3	5	8	14	2	0	0	32	9.4	1	....	....	....	....	....	1	0	0	0	0	0	0	0
1995-96	Detroit	NHL	60	18	22	40	30	5	0	2	87	20.7	6	....	....	....	....	....	13	3	1	4	8	0	0	0
1996-97	Detroit	NHL	43	6	10	16	12	0	0	0	56	10.7	–5	....	....	....	....	....	....	....	....	....	....	....	....	....
	Pittsburgh	NHL	32	7	9	16	14	1	0	0	52	13.5	–13	....	....	....	....	....	5	1	0	1	2	0	0	0
1997-98	Pittsburgh	NHL	5	1	0	1	2	0	0	0	4	25.0	0	....	....	....	....	....	....	....	....	....	....	....	....	....
	Chicago	NHL	69	11	22	33	38	4	0	3	85	12.9	–2	....	....	....	....	....	....	....	....	....	....	....	....	....
1998-99	Nashville	NHL	68	16	34	50	24	2	3	0	120	13.3	–8	1441	53.6	28	36	19:26	....	....	....	....	....	....	....	....
99-2000	Nashville	NHL	82	11	33	44	40	2	0	1	133	8.3	–15	1684	50.8	17	41	19:13	....	....	....	....	....	....	....	....
2000-01	Nashville	NHL	82	15	17	32	46	1	0	4	97	15.5	–6	1583	51.8	27	32	17:49	....	....	....	....	....	....	....	....
	NHL Totals		515	94	163	257	242	18	4	10	714	13.2		4708	52.0	72	109	18:47	26	6	3	9	12	1	0	0

WCHA First All-Star Team (1991, 1992, 1993) • NCAA West First All-American Team (1991, 1993) • NCAA West Second All-American Team (1992)

Traded to **Detroit** by **Philadelphia** with Philadelphia's 5th round choice (Frederic Deschenes) in 1994 Entry Draft for Jim Cummins and Philadelphia's 4th round choice (previously acquired by Detroit - later traded to Boston - Boston selected Charles Paquette) in 1993 Entry Draft, June 20, 1993. Traded to **Pittsburgh** by **Detroit** for Tomas Sandstrom, January 27, 1997. Traded to **Chicago** by **Pittsburgh** for Tuomas Gronman, October 27, 1997. Claimed by **Nashville** from **Chicago** in Expansion Draft, June 26, 1998.

JOHNSON, Matt

(JAWN-suhn, MAT) **MIN.**

Left wing. Shoots left. 6'5", 232 lbs. Born, Welland, Ont., November 23, 1975. Los Angeles' 2nd choice, 33rd overall, in 1994 Entry Draft.

Season	Club	League	GP	G	A	Pts	PIM	PP	SH	GW	S	%	+/-	TF	F%	H	SB	Min	GP	G	A	Pts	PIM	PP	SH	GW
1991-92	Welland Aerostars	OJHL-B	38	6	19	25	214	....	....	....	....	....	....	....	....	....	....	....	....	....	....	....	....	....	....	....
	Ajax Axemen	MTJHL	1	0	0	0	0	....	....	....	....	....	....	....	....	....	....	....	....	....	....	....	....	....	....	....
1992-93	Peterborough	OHL	66	8	17	25	211	....	....	....	....	....	....	....	....	....	....	....	16	1	1	2	56	....	....	....
1993-94	Peterborough	OHL	50	13	24	37	233	....	....	....	....	....	....	....	....	....	....	....	....	....	....	....	....	....	....	....
1994-95	Peterborough	OHL	14	1	2	3	43	....	....	....	....	....	....	....	....	....	....	....	....	....	....	....	....	....	....	....
	Los Angeles	NHL	14	1	0	1	102	0	0	0	4	25.0	0	....	....	....	....	....	....	....	....	....	....	....	....	....
1995-96	Los Angeles	NHL	1	0	0	0	5	0	0	0	1	0.0	0	....	....	....	....	....	....	....	....	....	....	....	....	....
	Phoenix	IHL	29	4	4	8	87	....	....	....	....	....	....	....	....	....	....	....	....	....	....	....	....	....	....	....
1996-97	Los Angeles	NHL	52	1	3	4	194	0	0	0	20	5.0	–4	....	....	....	....	....	....	....	....	....	....	....	....	....
1997-98	Los Angeles	NHL	66	2	4	6	249	0	0	0	18	11.1	–8	....	....	....	....	....	4	0	0	0	6	0	0	0
1998-99	Los Angeles	NHL	49	2	1	3	131	0	0	0	14	14.3	–5	1	0.0	62	4	5:55	....	....	....	....	....	....	....	....

Season	Club	League	GP	G	A	Pts	PIM	PP	SH	GW	S	%	+/-	TF	F%	H	SB	Min	GP	G	A	Pts	PIM	PP	SH	GW
			Regular Season																Playoffs							
99-2000	**Atlanta**	**NHL**	**64**	**2**	**5**	**7**	**144**	**0**	**0**	**0**	**54**	**3.7**	**-11**	**1**	**100.0**	**133**	**8**	**8:25**								
2000-01	**Minnesota**	**NHL**	**50**	**1**	**1**	**2**	**137**	**0**	**0**	**0**	**21**	**4.8**	**-6**	**1**	**100.0**	**103**	**8**	**7:43**								
	NHL Totals		**296**	**9**	**14**	**23**	**962**	**0**	**0**	**0**	**132**	**6.8**		**3**	**66.7**	**298**	**20**	**7:27**	**4**	**0**	**0**	**0**	**6**	**0**	**0**	**0**

Claimed by **Atlanta** from **Los Angeles** in Expansion Draft, June 25, 1999. Traded to **Minnesota** by **Atlanta** for San Jose's 3rd round choice (previously acquired, later traded to Pittsburgh - later traded to Columbus - Columbus selected Aaron Johnson) in 2001 Entry Draft, September 29, 2000.

JOHNSON, Mike

(JAWN-suhn, MIGHK) **PHX.**

Right wing. Shoots right. 6'2", 200 lbs. Born, Scarborough, Ont., October 3, 1974.

Season	Club	League	GP	G	A	Pts	PIM	PP	SH	GW	S	%	+/-	TF	F%	H	SB	Min	GP	G	A	Pts	PIM	PP	SH	GW
1991-92	Hillcrest Summits	MTHL	45	43	66	109													20	10	19	29				
1992-93	Aurora Eagles	MTJHL	48	25	40	65	18												7	7	15	22				
1993-94	Bowling Green	CCHA	38	6	14	20	18																			
1994-95	Bowling Green	CCHA	37	16	33	49	35																			
1995-96	Bowling Green	CCHA	30	12	19	31	22																			
1996-97	Bowling Green	CCHA	38	30	32	62	46																			
	Toronto	**NHL**	**13**	**2**	**2**	**4**	**4**	**0**	**1**	**1**	**27**	**7.4**	**-2**													
1997-98	**Toronto**	**NHL**	**82**	**15**	**32**	**47**	**24**	**5**	**0**	**0**	**143**	**10.5**	**-4**													
1998-99	**Toronto**	**NHL**	**79**	**20**	**24**	**44**	**35**	**5**	**3**	**2**	**149**	**13.4**	**13**	**15**	**53.3**	**70**	**17**	**16:16**	**17**	**3**	**2**	**5**	**4**	**0**	**0**	**1**
99-2000	**Toronto**	**NHL**	**52**	**11**	**14**	**25**	**23**	**2**	**1**	**3**	**89**	**12.4**	**8**	**2**	**50.0**	**58**	**6**	**15:22**								
	Tampa Bay	**NHL**	**28**	**10**	**12**	**22**	**4**	**4**	**0**	**0**	**43**	**23.3**	**-2**	**5**	**60.0**	**26**	**11**	**20:33**								
2000-01	**Tampa Bay**	**NHL**	**64**	**11**	**27**	**38**	**38**	**3**	**1**	**0**	**107**	**10.3**	**-10**	**2**	**0.0**	**67**	**22**	**18:13**								
	Phoenix	**NHL**	**12**	**2**	**3**	**5**	**4**	**1**	**0**	**0**	**17**	**11.8**	**0**	**0**	**0.0**	**14**	**1**	**12:12**								
	NHL Totals		**330**	**71**	**114**	**185**	**132**	**20**	**6**	**6**	**575**	**12.3**		**24**	**50.0**	**235**	**57**	**16:54**	**17**	**3**	**2**	**5**	**4**	**0**	**0**	**1**

NHL All-Rookie Team (1998)

Signed as a free agent by **Toronto**, March 16, 1997. Traded to **Tampa Bay** by **Toronto** with Marek Posmyk, Toronto's 5th (Pavel Sedov) and 6th (Aaron Gionet) round choices in 2000 Entry Draft and future considerations for Darcy Tucker, Tampa Bay's 4th round choice (Miguel Delisle) in 2000 Entry Draft and future considerations, February 9, 2000. Traded to **Phoenix** by **Tampa Bay** with Paul Mara, Ruslan Zainullin and NY Islanders' 2nd round choice (previously acquired, Phoenix selected Matthew Spiller) in 2001 Entry Draft for Nikolai Khabibulin and Stan Neckar, March 5, 2001.

JOHNSON, Ryan

(JAWN-suhn, RIGH-yuhn) **FLA.**

Center. Shoots left. 6'1", 200 lbs. Born, Thunder Bay, Ont., June 14, 1976. Florida's 4th choice, 36th overall, in 1994 Entry Draft.

Season	Club	League	GP	G	A	Pts	PIM	PP	SH	GW	S	%	+/-	TF	F%	H	SB	Min	GP	G	A	Pts	PIM	PP	SH	GW
1992-93	Thunder Bay	TBAHA	60	25	33	58																				
1993-94	Thunder Bay	USHL	48	14	36	50	28																			
1994-95	North Dakota	WCHA	38	6	22	28	39																			
1995-96	North Dakota	WCHA	21	2	17	19	14																			
	Canada	Nat-Team	28	5	12	17	14																			
1996-97	Carolina	AHL	79	18	24	42	28																			
1997-98	**Florida**	**NHL**	**10**	**0**	**2**	**2**	**0**	**0**	**0**	**0**	**6**	**0.0**	**-4**													
	New Haven	AHL	64	19	48	67	12												3	0	1	1	0			
1998-99	**Florida**	**NHL**	**1**	**1**	**0**	**1**	**0**	**0**	**0**	**0**	**1**	**100.0**	**0**	**16**	**37.5**	**1**	**0**	**15:26**								
	New Haven	AHL	37	8	19	27	18																			
99-2000	**Florida**	**NHL**	**66**	**4**	**12**	**16**	**14**	**0**	**0**	**0**	**44**	**9.1**	**1**	**684**	**51.8**	**127**	**29**	**11:47**								
	Tampa Bay	**NHL**	**14**	**0**	**2**	**2**	**2**	**0**	**0**	**0**	**5**	**0.0**	**-9**	**117**	**53.0**	**28**	**6**	**11:02**								
2000-01	**Tampa Bay**	**NHL**	**80**	**7**	**14**	**21**	**44**	**1**	**0**	**0**	**71**	**9.9**	**-20**	**951**	**48.9**	**177**	**68**	**15:47**								
	NHL Totals		**171**	**12**	**30**	**42**	**60**	**1**	**0**	**0**	**127**	**9.4**		**1768**	**50.2**	**333**	**103**	**13:43**								

Traded to **Tampa Bay** by **Florida** with Dwayne Hay for Mike Sillinger, March 14, 2000. Traded to **Florida** by **Tampa Bay** with Tampa Bay's 6th round choice in 2003 Entry Draft for Vaclav Prospal, July 10, 2001.

JOHNSSON, Kim

(YAWN-suhn, KIHM) **PHI.**

Defense. Shoots left. 6'1", 178 lbs. Born, Malmo, Sweden, March 16, 1976. NY Rangers' 15th choice, 286th overall, in 1994 Entry Draft.

Season	Club	League	GP	G	A	Pts	PIM	PP	SH	GW	S	%	+/-	TF	F%	H	SB	Min	GP	G	A	Pts	PIM	PP	SH	GW
1993-94	Malmo IF	Swede-Jr.	14	5	3	8	14																			
	Malmo IF	Sweden	2	0	0	0	0																			
1994-95	Malmo IF	Swede-Jr.	29	6	15	21	40																			
	Malmo IF	Sweden	13	0	0	0	4												1	0	0	0	0			
1995-96	Malmo IF	Sweden	38	2	0	2	30												4	0	1	1	8			
1996-97	Malmo IF	Sweden	49	4	9	13	42												4	0	0	0	2			
1997-98	Malmo IF	Sweden	45	5	9	14	29																			
1998-99	Malmo IF	Sweden	49	9	8	17	76												8	2	3	5	12			
99-2000	**NY Rangers**	**NHL**	**76**	**6**	**15**	**21**	**46**	**1**	**0**	**1**	**101**	**5.9**	**-13**	**0**	**0.0**	**61**	**116**	**18:06**								
2000-01	**NY Rangers**	**NHL**	**75**	**5**	**21**	**26**	**40**	**4**	**0**	**0**	**104**	**4.8**	**-3**	**0**	**0.0**	**68**	**122**	**21:16**								
	NHL Totals		**151**	**11**	**36**	**47**	**86**	**5**	**0**	**1**	**205**	**5.4**		**0**	**0.0**	**129**	**238**	**19:40**								

Traded to **Philadelphia** by **NY Rangers** with Pavel Brendl, Jan Hlavac and NY Rangers' 3rd round choice in 2003 Entry Draft for the rights to Eric Lindros and a conditional 1st round choice in 2003 Entry Draft, August 20, 2001.

JOKINEN, Olli

(YOH-kih-nihn, OH-lee) **FLA.**

Center. Shoots left. 6'3", 208 lbs. Born, Kuopio, Finland, December 5, 1978. Los Angeles' 1st choice, 3rd overall, in 1997 Entry Draft.

Season	Club	League	GP	G	A	Pts	PIM	PP	SH	GW	S	%	+/-	TF	F%	H	SB	Min	GP	G	A	Pts	PIM	PP	SH	GW
1992-93	KalPa Kuopio-C	Finn-Jr.	14	8	3	11	12																			
1993-94	KalPa Kuopio-C	Finn-Jr.	31	27	25	52	62																			
1994-95	KalPa Kuopio-B	Finn-Jr.	12	9	14	23	46																			
	KaiPa Kuopio	Finn-Jr.	6	0	1	1	6																			
1995-96	KalPa Kuopio	Finn-Jr.	25	20	14	34	47												7	4	4	8	20			
	KalPa Kuopio	Finland	15	1	1	2	2																			
1996-97	HIFK Helsinki	Finn-Jr.	2	1	0	1	6																			
	HIFK Helsinki	Finland	50	14	27	41	88																			
1997-98	**Los Angeles**	**NHL**	**8**	**0**	**0**	**0**	**6**	**0**	**0**	**0**	**12**	**0.0**	**-5**													
	HIFK Helsinki	Finland	30	11	28	39	8												9	*7	2	9	2			
1998-99	**Los Angeles**	**NHL**	**66**	**9**	**12**	**21**	**44**	**3**	**1**	**1**	**87**	**10.3**	**-10**	**779**	**43.9**	**109**	**26**	**14:42**								
	Springfield	AHL	9	3	6	9	6																			
99-2000	**NY Islanders**	**NHL**	**82**	**11**	**10**	**21**	**80**	**1**	**2**	**3**	**138**	**8.0**	**0**	**841**	**46.1**	**156**	**27**	**16:15**								
2000-01	**Florida**	**NHL**	**78**	**6**	**10**	**16**	**106**	**0**	**0**	**0**	**121**	**5.0**	**-22**	**638**	**42.3**	**98**	**21**	**13:23**								
	NHL Totals		**234**	**26**	**32**	**58**	**236**	**4**	**3**	**4**	**358**	**7.3**		**2258**	**44.3**	**363**	**74**	**14:48**								

Traded to **NY Islanders** by **LA Kings** with Josh Green, Mathieu Biron and LA Kings' 1st round choice (Taylor Pyatt) in 1999 Entry Draft for Ziggy Palffy, Brian Smolinski, Marcel Cousineau and New Jersey's 4th round choice (previously acquired, LA Kings selected Daniel Johansson) in 1999 Entry Draft, June 20, 1999. Traded to **Florida** by **NY Islanders** with Roberto Luongo for Mark Parrish and Oleg Kvasha, June 24, 2000.

JOMPHE, Jean-Francois

(ZHAWMF, ZHAWN-fran-SWUH)

Center. Shoots left. 6'1", 195 lbs. Born, Harve St-Pierre, Que., December 28, 1972.

Season	Club	League	GP	G	A	Pts	PIM	PP	SH	GW	S	%	+/-	TF	F%	H	SB	Min	GP	G	A	Pts	PIM	PP	SH	GW
1990-91	Shawinigan	QMJHL	42	17	22	39	14												6	2	1	3	2			
1991-92	Shawinigan	QMJHL	44	28	33	61	69												10	6	10	16	10			
1992-93	Sherbrooke	QMJHL	60	43	43	86	86												15	10	13	23	18			
1993-94	San Diego Gulls	IHL	29	2	3	5	12																			
	Greensboro	ECHL	25	9	9	18	41												1	1	0	1	0			
1994-95	Canada	Nat-Team	52	33	25	58	85																			
1995-96	**Anaheim**	**NHL**	**31**	**2**	**12**	**14**	**39**	**2**	**0**	**0**	**46**	**4.3**	**7**													
	Baltimore Bandits	AHL	47	21	34	55	75																			
1996-97	**Anaheim**	**NHL**	**64**	**7**	**14**	**21**	**53**	**0**	**1**	**0**	**81**	**8.6**	**-9**													
1997-98	**Anaheim**	**NHL**	**9**	**1**	**3**	**4**	**8**	**0**	**0**	**0**	**8**	**12.5**	**1**													
	Cincinnati Ducks	AHL	38	9	19	28	32																			
	Quebec Rafales	IHL	17	6	4	10	24																			
1998-99	**Phoenix**	**NHL**	**1**	**0**	**0**	**0**	**2**	**0**	**0**	**0**	**0**	**0.0**	**0**	**3**	**66.7**	**3**	**0**	**7:36**								
	Springfield	AHL	29	10	18	28	36																			
	Las Vegas	IHL	32	6	14	20	63																			
	Montreal	**NHL**	**6**	**0**	**0**	**0**	**0**	**0**	**0**	**0**	**4**	**0.0**	**0**	**41**	**48.8**	**10**	**1**	**9:01**								
	Fredericton	AHL	3	1	3	4	6												15	5	11	16	49			

Season	Club	League	GP	G	A	Pts	PIM	PP	SH	GW	S	%	+/-	TF	F%	H	SB	Min	GP	G	A	Pts	PIM	PP	SH	GW
			Regular Season																Playoffs							
99-2000	Krefeld Pinguine	DEL	47	12	33	45	109												4	0	1	1	6			
2000-01	Adler Mannheim	DEL	47	11	16	27	178												11	5	5	10	22			
	NHL Totals		**111**	**10**	**29**	**39**	**102**	**2**	**1**	**0**	**139**	**7.2**		**44**	**50.0**	**13**	**1**	**8:49**								

Signed as a free agent by **Anaheim**, September 7, 1993. Traded to **Phoenix** by **Anaheim** for Jim McKenzie, June 18, 1998. Traded to **Montreal** by **Phoenix** for cash, March 23, 1999.

JONES, Keith

(JOHNS, KEETH)

Right wing. Shoots left. 6'2", 200 lbs. Born, Brantford, Ont., November 8, 1968. Washington's 7th choice, 141st overall, in 1988 Entry Draft.

Season	Club	League	GP	G	A	Pts	PIM	PP	SH	GW	S	%	+/-	TF	F%	H	SB	Min	GP	G	A	Pts	PIM	PP	SH	GW
1985-86	Paris Mounties	OJHL-C	30	26	13	39	61																			
1986-87	Paris Mounties	OJHL-C	30	39	38	77	136																			
1987-88	Niagara Falls	OJHL-B	40	50	80	130	113																			
1988-89	Western Michigan	CCHA	37	9	12	21	51																			
1989-90	Western Michigan	CCHA	40	19	18	37	82																			
1990-91	Western Michigan	CCHA	41	30	19	49	106																			
1991-92	Western Michigan	CCHA	35	25	31	56	77																			
	Baltimore	AHL	6	2	4	6	0																			
1992-93	**Washington**	**NHL**	**71**	**12**	**14**	**26**	**124**	**0**	**0**	**3**	**73**	**16.4**	**18**						**6**	**0**	**0**	**0**	**10**	**0**	**0**	**0**
	Baltimore	AHL	8	7	3	10	4																			
1993-94	**Washington**	**NHL**	**68**	**16**	**19**	**35**	**149**	**5**	**0**	**1**	**97**	**16.5**	**4**						**11**	**0**	**1**	**1**	**36**	**0**	**0**	**0**
	Portland Pirates	AHL	6	5	7	12	4																			
1994-95	**Washington**	**NHL**	**40**	**14**	**6**	**20**	**65**	**1**	**0**	**4**	**85**	**16.5**	**−2**						**7**	**4**	**4**	**8**	**22**	**1**	**0**	**0**
1995-96	**Washington**	**NHL**	**68**	**18**	**23**	**41**	**103**	**5**	**0**	**2**	**155**	**11.6**	**8**						**2**	**0**	**0**	**0**	**7**	**0**	**0**	**0**
1996-97	**Washington**	**NHL**	**11**	**2**	**3**	**5**	**13**	**1**	**0**	**0**	**12**	**16.7**	**−2**													
	Colorado	**NHL**	**67**	**23**	**20**	**43**	**105**	**13**	**1**	**7**	**158**	**14.6**	**5**						**6**	**3**	**3**	**6**	**4**	**1**	**0**	**0**
1997-98	**Colorado**	**NHL**	**23**	**3**	**7**	**10**	**22**	**1**	**0**	**2**	**31**	**9.7**	**−4**						**7**	**0**	**0**	**0**	**13**	**0**	**0**	**0**
	Hershey Bears	AHL	4	2	1	3	2																			
1998-99	**Colorado**	**NHL**	**12**	**2**	**2**	**4**	**20**	**1**	**0**	**0**	**11**	**18.2**	**−6**	**2**	**100.0**	**16**	**2**	**13:48**								
	Philadelphia	**NHL**	**66**	**18**	**31**	**49**	**78**	**2**	**0**	**3**	**124**	**14.5**	**29**	**78**	**44.9**	**40**	**18**	**16:59**	**6**	**2**	**1**	**3**	**14**	**0**	**0**	**0**
99-2000	**Philadelphia**	**NHL**	**57**	**9**	**16**	**25**	**82**	**1**	**0**	**0**	**92**	**9.8**	**8**	**28**	**32.1**	**28**	**11**	**13:38**	**18**	**3**	**3**	**6**	**14**	**1**	**0**	**0**
2000-01	**Philadelphia**	**NHL**	**8**	**0**	**0**	**0**	**4**	**0**	**0**	**0**	**11**	**0.0**	**−5**	**2**	**50.0**	**5**	**1**	**11:00**								
	NHL Totals		**491**	**117**	**141**	**258**	**765**	**30**	**1**	**22**	**849**	**13.8**		**110**	**42.7**	**89**	**32**	**15:03**	**63**	**12**	**12**	**24**	**120**	**3**	**0**	**0**

CCHA First All-Star Team (1992)

Traded to **Colorado** by **Washington** with Washington's 1st (Scott Parker) and 4th (later traded back to Washington - Washington selected Krys Barch) in 1998 Entry Draft for Curtis Leschyshyn and Chris Simon, November 2, 1996. • Missed remainder of 1996-97 and majority of 1997-98 seasons recovering from knee injury suffered in game vs. Chicago, May 13, 1996. Traded to **Philadelphia** by **Colorado** for Shjon Podein, November 12, 1998. • Officially announced retirement, November 21, 2000.

JONES, Ty

(JOHNS, TIGH) **CHI.**

Right wing. Shoots right. 6'3", 218 lbs. Born, Richland, WA, February 22, 1979. Chicago's 2nd choice, 16th overall, in 1997 Entry Draft.

Season	Club	League	GP	G	A	Pts	PIM	PP	SH	GW	S	%	+/-	TF	F%	H	SB	Min	GP	G	A	Pts	PIM	PP	SH	GW
1993-94	Alaska All-Stars	AAHL	64	84	104	188	126																			
1994-95	Alaska All-Stars	AAHL	42	33	35	68	98																			
1995-96	Spokane Chiefs	WHL	34	1	0	1	77												3	0	0	0	6			
1996-97	Spokane Chiefs	WHL	67	20	34	54	202												9	2	4	6	10			
1997-98	Spokane Chiefs	WHL	60	36	48	84	161												18	2	14	16	35			
1998-99	Spokane Chiefs	WHL	26	15	12	27	98																			
	Kamloops Blazers	WHL	20	3	16	19	84												14	5	3	8	22			
	Chicago	**NHL**	**8**	**0**	**0**	**0**	**12**	**0**	**0**	**0**	**3**	**0.0**	**−1**	**0**	**0.0**	**5**	**1**	**7:53**								
99-2000	Cleveland	IHL	10	1	1	2	34																			
	Florida Everblades	ECHL	48	11	26	37	81												5	1	1	2	17			
2000-01	Norfolk Admirals	AHL	64	11	17	28	114																			
	NHL Totals		**8**	**0**	**0**	**0**	**12**	**0**	**0**	**0**	**3**	**0.0**		**0**	**0.0**	**5**	**1**	**7:53**								

JONSSON, Hans

(YAWN-suhn, HANS) **PIT.**

Defense. Shoots left. 6'1", 202 lbs. Born, Jarved, Sweden, August 2, 1973. Pittsburgh's 11th choice, 286th overall, in 1993 Entry Draft.

Season	Club	League	GP	G	A	Pts	PIM	PP	SH	GW	S	%	+/-	TF	F%	H	SB	Min	GP	G	A	Pts	PIM	PP	SH	GW
1991-92	Hasums IF	Swede-2	13	4	6	10	10																			
	MoDo AIK	Sweden	6	0	1	1	4																			
1992-93	MoDo AIK	Sweden	40	2	2	4	24												3	0	1	1	2			
1993-94	MoDo Hockey	Sweden	23	4	1	5	18												10	0	1	1	12			
1994-95	MoDo Hockey	Sweden	39	4	6	10	30																			
1995-96	MoDo Hockey	Sweden	36	10	6	16	30												8	2	1	3	24			
1996-97	MoDo Hockey	Sweden	27	7	5	12	18																			
1997-98	MoDo Hockey	Sweden	40	8	6	14	40												8	1	1	2	12			
1998-99	MoDo Hockey	Sweden	41	3	4	7	40												13	2	4	6	22			
99-2000	**Pittsburgh**	**NHL**	**68**	**3**	**11**	**14**	**12**	**0**	**1**	**1**	**49**	**6.1**	**−5**	**0**	**0.0**	**79**	**97**	**18:34**	**11**	**0**	**1**	**1**	**6**	**0**	**0**	**0**
2000-01	**Pittsburgh**	**NHL**	**58**	**4**	**18**	**22**	**22**	**2**	**0**	**0**	**44**	**9.1**	**11**	**0**	**0.0**	**72**	**96**	**18:27**	**16**	**0**	**0**	**0**	**8**	**0**	**0**	**0**
	NHL Totals		**126**	**7**	**29**	**36**	**34**	**2**	**1**	**1**	**93**	**7.5**		**0**	**0.0**	**151**	**193**	**18:31**	**27**	**0**	**1**	**1**	**14**	**0**	**0**	**0**

JONSSON, Jorgen

(YAWN-suhn, YOHR-gahn)

Left wing. Shoots left. 6', 185 lbs. Born, Angelholm, Sweden, September 29, 1972. Calgary's 11th choice, 227th overall, in 1994 Entry Draft.

Season	Club	League	GP	G	A	Pts	PIM	PP	SH	GW	S	%	+/-	TF	F%	H	SB	Min	GP	G	A	Pts	PIM	PP	SH	GW
1989-90	Rogle BK	Sweden-2	1	0	0	0	0												4	0	0	0	0			
1990-91	Rogle BK	Sweden-2	21	4	2	6	2												12	2	1	3	2			
1991-92	Rogle BK	Sweden-2	27	1	8	9	6												5	0	0	0	0			
1992-93	Rogle BK	Sweden	40	17	11	28	28																			
1993-94	Rogle BK	Sweden	40	17	14	31	46																			
	Sweden	Olympics	6	0	0	0	0																			
1994-95	Rogle BK	Sweden	22	4	6	10	18																			
1995-96	Farjestads BK	Sweden	39	11	15	26	36												8	0	4	4	6			
1996-97	Farjestads BK	Sweden	49	12	21	33	58												14	9	5	14	14			
	Farjestads BK	EuroHL	4	2	1	3	2																			
1997-98	Farjestads BK	Sweden	45	22	25	47	53												12	2	*9	11	12			
	Farjestads BK	EuroHL	7	2	4	6	6																			
	Sweden	Olympics	1	0	0	0	0																			
1998-99	Farjestads BK	Sweden	48	17	24	41	44												4	0	2	2	4			
	Farjestads BK	EuroHL	5	2	4	6	4												2	1	0	1	4			
99-2000	**NY Islanders**	**NHL**	**68**	**11**	**17**	**28**	**16**	**1**	**2**	**0**	**95**	**11.6**	**−6**	**642**	**44.2**	**72**	**37**	**16:07**								
	Anaheim	**NHL**	**13**	**1**	**2**	**3**	**0**	**0**	**0**	**1**	**21**	**4.8**	**−2**	**118**	**35.6**	**15**	**8**	**12:51**								
2000-01	Farjestads BK	Sweden	50	20	26	46	32												15	5	12	17	12			
	NHL Totals		**81**	**12**	**19**	**31**	**16**	**1**	**2**	**1**	**116**	**10.3**		**760**	**42.9**	**87**	**45**	**15:35**								

Traded to **NY Islanders** by **Calgary** for Jan Hlavac, July 14, 1998. Traded to **Anaheim** by **NY Islanders** for Johan Davidsson and future considerations, March 11, 2000.

JONSSON, Kenny

(YAWN-suhn, KEHN-nee) **NYI**

Defense. Shoots left. 6'3", 195 lbs. Born, Angelholm, Sweden, October 6, 1974. Toronto's 1st choice, 12th overall, in 1993 Entry Draft.

Season	Club	League	GP	G	A	Pts	PIM	PP	SH	GW	S	%	+/-	TF	F%	H	SB	Min	GP	G	A	Pts	PIM	PP	SH	GW
1991-92	Rogle BK	Sweden-2	30	4	11	15	24												5	0	0	0	0			
1992-93	Rogle BK	Swede-Jr.	2	1	2	3	25																			
	Rogle BK	Sweden	39	3	10	13	42																			
1993-94	Rogle BK	Sweden	36	4	13	17	40												3	1	1	2	2			
	Sweden	Olympics	3	1	0	1	0																			
1994-95	Rogle BK	Sweden	8	3	1	4	20																			
	St. John's Leafs	AHL	10	2	5	7	2																			
	Toronto	**NHL**	**39**	**2**	**7**	**9**	**16**	**0**	**0**	**1**	**50**	**4.0**	**−8**						**4**	**0**	**0**	**0**	**0**	**0**	**0**	**0**
1995-96	**Toronto**	**NHL**	**50**	**4**	**22**	**26**	**22**	**3**	**0**	**1**	**90**	**4.4**	**12**													
	NY Islanders	**NHL**	**16**	**0**	**4**	**4**	**10**	**0**	**0**	**0**	**40**	**0.0**	**−5**													
1996-97	**NY Islanders**	**NHL**	**81**	**3**	**18**	**21**	**24**	**1**	**0**	**0**	**92**	**3.3**	**10**													
1997-98	**NY Islanders**	**NHL**	**81**	**14**	**26**	**40**	**58**	**6**	**0**	**2**	**108**	**13.0**	**−2**													
1998-99	**NY Islanders**	**NHL**	**63**	**8**	**18**	**26**	**34**	**6**	**0**	**0**	**91**	**8.8**	**−18**	**0**	**0.0**	**57**	**90**	**24:59**								

			Regular Season																Playoffs							
Season	Club	League	GP	G	A	Pts	PIM	PP	SH	GW	S	%	+/-	TF	F%	H	SB	Min	GP	G	A	Pts	PIM	PP	SH	GW
99-2000	NY Islanders	NHL	65	1	24	25	32	1	0	0	84	1.2	−15	0	0.0	51	113	24:29	....	....	....	....	....	....	....	....
2000-01	NY Islanders	NHL	65	8	21	29	30	5	0	0	91	8.8	−22	0	0.0	47	114	24:04	....	....	....	....	....	....	....	....
	NHL Totals		**460**	**40**	**140**	**180**	**226**	**22**	**0**	**4**	**646**	**6.2**		**0**	**0.0**	**155**	**317**	**24:30**	**4**	**0**	**0**	**0**	**0**	**0**	**0**	**0**

• NHL All-Rookie Team (1995)

Traded to **NY Islanders** by **Toronto** with Sean Haggerty, Darby Hendrickson and Toronto's 1st round choice (Roberto Luongo) in 1997 Entry Draft for Wendel Clark, Mathieu Schneider and D.J. Smith, March 13, 1996.

JOSEPH, Chris

(JOH-sehf, KRIHS)

Defense. Shoots right. 6'3", 212 lbs. Born, Burnaby, B.C., September 10, 1969. Pittsburgh's 1st choice, 5th overall, in 1987 Entry Draft.

1984-85	Burnaby Beavers	BCAHA	52	18	48	66	52	....	....	....	....	....	....	....	....	....	....	....	....	....	....	....	....	....	....	....
1985-86	Seattle T-Birds	WHL	72	4	8	12	50	....	....	....	....	....	....	....	....	....	....	....	5	0	3	3	12	....	....	....
1986-87	Seattle T-Birds	WHL	67	13	45	58	155	....	....	....	....	....	....	....	....	....	....	....	....	....	....	....	....	....	....	....
1987-88	**Pittsburgh**	**NHL**	**17**	**0**	**4**	**4**	**12**	**0**	**0**	**0**	**13**	**0.0**	**2**	....	....	....	....	....	....	....	....	....	....	....	....	....
	Edmonton	**NHL**	**7**	**0**	**4**	**4**	**6**	**0**	**0**	**0**	**1**	**0.0**	**−3**	....	....	....	....	....	....	....	....	....	....	....	....	....
	Seattle T-Birds	WHL	23	5	14	19	49	....	....	....	....	....	....	....	....	....	....	....	....	....	....	....	....	....	....	....
	Nova Scotia	AHL	8	0	2	2	8	....	....	....	....	....	....	....	....	....	....	....	4	0	0	0	9	....	....	....
1988-89	**Edmonton**	**NHL**	**44**	**4**	**5**	**9**	**54**	**0**	**0**	**0**	**36**	**11.1**	**−9**	....	....	....	....	....	....	....	....	....	....	....	....	....
	Cape Breton	AHL	5	1	1	2	18	....	....	....	....	....	....	....	....	....	....	....	....	....	....	....	....	....	....	....
1989-90	**Edmonton**	**NHL**	**4**	**0**	**2**	**2**	**2**	**0**	**0**	**0**	**5**	**0.0**	**−2**	....	....	....	....	....	....	....	....	....	....	....	....	....
	Cape Breton	AHL	61	10	20	30	69	....	....	....	....	....	....	....	....	....	....	....	6	2	1	3	4	....	....	....
1990-91	**Edmonton**	**NHL**	**49**	**5**	**17**	**22**	**59**	**2**	**0**	**0**	**74**	**6.8**	**3**	....	....	....	....	....	....	....	....	....	....	....	....	....
1991-92	**Edmonton**	**NHL**	**7**	**0**	**0**	**0**	**8**	**0**	**0**	**0**	**5**	**0.0**	**−1**	....	....	....	....	....	**5**	**1**	**3**	**4**	**2**	**0**	**0**	**0**
	Cape Breton	AHL	63	14	29	43	72	....	....	....	....	....	....	....	....	....	....	....	5	0	2	2	8	....	....	....
1992-93	**Edmonton**	**NHL**	**33**	**2**	**10**	**12**	**48**	**1**	**0**	**0**	**49**	**4.1**	**−9**	....	....	....	....	....	....	....	....	....	....	....	....	....
1993-94	**Edmonton**	**NHL**	**10**	**1**	**1**	**2**	**28**	**1**	**0**	**0**	**25**	**4.0**	**−8**	....	....	....	....	....	....	....	....	....	....	....	....	....
	Tampa Bay	**NHL**	**66**	**10**	**19**	**29**	**108**	**7**	**0**	**0**	**154**	**6.5**	**−13**	....	....	....	....	....	....	....	....	....	....	....	....	....
1994-95	**Pittsburgh**	**NHL**	**33**	**5**	**10**	**15**	**46**	**3**	**0**	**0**	**73**	**6.8**	**3**	....	....	....	....	....	**10**	**1**	**1**	**2**	**12**	**0**	**0**	**0**
1995-96	**Pittsburgh**	**NHL**	**70**	**5**	**14**	**19**	**71**	**0**	**0**	**1**	**94**	**5.3**	**6**	....	....	....	....	....	**15**	**1**	**0**	**1**	**8**	**0**	**0**	**0**
1996-97	**Vancouver**	**NHL**	**63**	**3**	**13**	**16**	**62**	**2**	**0**	**1**	**99**	**3.0**	**−21**	....	....	....	....	....	....	....	....	....	....	....	....	....
1997-98	**Philadelphia**	**NHL**	**15**	**1**	**0**	**1**	**19**	**0**	**0**	**1**	**20**	**5.0**	**1**	....	....	....	....	....	**1**	**0**	**0**	**0**	**2**	**0**	**0**	**0**
	Philadelphia	AHL	6	2	3	5	2	....	....	....	....	....	....	....	....	....	....	....	....	....	....	....	....	....	....	....
1998-99	**Philadelphia**	**NHL**	**2**	**0**	**0**	**0**	**2**	**0**	**0**	**0**	**1**	**0.0**	**0**	**0**	**0.0**	**0**	**0**	**9:36**	....	....	....	....	....	....	....	....
	Cincinnati	IHL	27	11	19	30	38	....	....	....	....	....	....	....	....	....	....	....	....	....	....	....	....	....	....	....
	Philadelphia	AHL	51	9	29	38	26	....	....	....	....	....	....	....	....	....	....	....	16	3	10	13	8	....	....	....
99-2000	**Vancouver**	**NHL**	**38**	**2**	**9**	**11**	**6**	**1**	**0**	**0**	**73**	**2.7**	**−4**	**0**	**0.0**	**17**	**24**	**17:14**	....	....	....	....	....	....	....	....
	Phoenix	**NHL**	**9**	**0**	**0**	**0**	**0**	**0**	**0**	**0**	**13**	**0.0**	**−5**	**0**	**0.0**	**8**	**9**	**13:20**	....	....	....	....	....	....	....	....
2000-01	**Phoenix**	**NHL**	**24**	**1**	**1**	**2**	**16**	**0**	**1**	**0**	**33**	**3.0**	**−4**	**0**	**0.0**	**11**	**20**	**12:59**	....	....	....	....	....	....	....	....
	Atlanta	**NHL**	**19**	**0**	**3**	**3**	**20**	**0**	**0**	**0**	**25**	**0.0**	**−7**	**0**	**0.0**	**33**	**26**	**20:48**	....	....	....	....	....	....	....	....
	NHL Totals		**510**	**39**	**112**	**151**	**567**	**17**	**1**	**3**	**793**	**4.9**		**0**	**0.0**	**69**	**79**	**16:19**	**31**	**3**	**4**	**7**	**24**	**0**	**0**	**0**

WHL West Second All-Star Team (1987)

Traded to **Edmonton** by **Pittsburgh** with Craig Simpson, Dave Hannan and Moe Mantha for Paul Coffey, Dave Hunter and Wayne Van Dorp, November 24, 1987. Traded to **Tampa Bay** by **Edmonton** for Bob Beers, November 11, 1993. Claimed by **Pittsburgh** from **Tampa Bay** in Waiver Draft, January 18, 1995. Claimed by **Vancouver** from **Pittsburgh** in Waiver Draft, September 30, 1996. Signed as a free agent by **Philadelphia**, September 11, 1997. Signed as a free agent by **Ottawa**, August 18, 1999. Claimed by **Vancouver** from **Ottawa** in Waiver Draft, September 27, 1999. Claimed on waivers by **Phoenix** from **Vancouver**, March 14, 2000. Claimed on waivers by **Atlanta** from **Phoenix**, February 14, 2001.

JOVANOVSKI, Ed

(joh-van-OHV-skee, EHD) **VAN.**

Defense. Shoots left. 6'2", 210 lbs. Born, Windsor, Ont., June 26, 1976. Florida's 1st choice, 1st overall, in 1994 Entry Draft.

1991-92	Windsor Bulldogs	OMHA	50	25	40	65	88	....	....	....	....	....	....	....	....	....	....	....	....	....	....	....	....	....	....	....
1992-93	Windsor Bulldogs	OJHL-B	48	7	46	53	88	....	....	....	....	....	....	....	....	....	....	....	....	....	....	....	....	....	....	....
1993-94	Windsor Spitfires	OHL	62	15	36	51	221	....	....	....	....	....	....	....	....	....	....	....	4	0	0	0	15	....	....	....
1994-95	Windsor Spitfires	OHL	50	23	42	65	198	....	....	....	....	....	....	....	....	....	....	....	9	2	7	9	39	....	....	....
1995-96	**Florida**	**NHL**	**70**	**10**	**11**	**21**	**137**	**2**	**0**	**2**	**116**	**8.6**	**−3**	....	....	....	....	....	**22**	**1**	**8**	**9**	**52**	**0**	**0**	**0**
1996-97	**Florida**	**NHL**	**61**	**7**	**16**	**23**	**172**	**3**	**0**	**1**	**80**	**8.8**	**−1**	....	....	....	....	....	**5**	**0**	**0**	**0**	**4**	**0**	**0**	**0**
1997-98	**Florida**	**NHL**	**81**	**9**	**14**	**23**	**158**	**2**	**1**	**3**	**142**	**6.3**	**−12**	....	....	....	....	....	....	....	....	....	....	....	....	....
1998-99	**Florida**	**NHL**	**41**	**3**	**13**	**16**	**82**	**1**	**0**	**1**	**68**	**4.4**	**−4**	**0**	**0.0**	**88**	**36**	**22:35**	....	....	....	....	....	....	....	....
	Vancouver	**NHL**	**31**	**2**	**9**	**11**	**44**	**0**	**0**	**1**	**41**	**4.9**	**−5**	**0**	**0.0**	**68**	**35**	**21:16**	....	....	....	....	....	....	....	....
99-2000	**Vancouver**	**NHL**	**75**	**5**	**21**	**26**	**54**	**1**	**0**	**1**	**109**	**4.6**	**−3**	**0**	**0.0**	**167**	**104**	**24:03**	....	....	....	....	....	....	....	....
2000-01	**Vancouver**	**NHL**	**79**	**12**	**35**	**47**	**102**	**4**	**0**	**2**	**193**	**6.2**	**−1**	**0**	**0.0**	**172**	**122**	**24:57**	**4**	**1**	**1**	**2**	**0**	**0**	**0**	**0**
	NHL Totals		**438**	**48**	**119**	**167**	**749**	**13**	**1**	**10**	**749**	**6.4**		**0**	**0.0**	**495**	**297**	**23:43**	**31**	**2**	**9**	**11**	**56**	**0**	**0**	**0**

OHL Second All-Star Team (1994) • OHL First All-Star Team (1995) • NHL All-Rookie Team (1996) • Played in NHL All-Star Game (2001)

Traded to **Vancouver** by **Florida** with Dave Gagner, Mike Brown, Kevin Weekes and Florida's 1st round choice (Nathan Smith) in 2000 Entry Draft for Pavel Bure, Bret Hedican, Brad Ference and Vancouver's 3rd round choice (Robert Fried) in 2000 Entry Draft, January 17, 1999.

JUNEAU, Joe

(ZHOO-noh, JOH) **MTL.**

Center. Shoots left. 6', 198 lbs. Born, Pont-Rouge, Que., January 5, 1968. Boston's 3rd choice, 81st overall, in 1988 Entry Draft.

1983-84	Ste-Foy Governors	QAAA	30	3	7	10	24	....	....	....	....	....	....	....	....	....	....	....	12	3	11	14	4	....	....	....
1984-85	Ste-Foy Governors	QAAA	41	25	46	71	60	....	....	....	....	....	....	....	....	....	....	....	13	9	15	24	20	....	....	....
1985-86	Levis-Lauzon	CEGEP	STATISTICS NOT AVAILABLE																							
1986-87	Levis-Lauzon	CEGEP	38	27	57	84	....	....	....	....	....	....	....	....	....	....	....	....	....	....	....	....	....	....	....	....
1987-88	RPI Engineers	ECAC	31	16	29	45	18	....	....	....	....	....	....	....	....	....	....	....	....	....	....	....	....	....	....	....
1988-89	RPI Engineers	ECAC	30	12	23	35	40	....	....	....	....	....	....	....	....	....	....	....	....	....	....	....	....	....	....	....
1989-90	RPI Engineers	ECAC	34	18	*52	*70	31	....	....	....	....	....	....	....	....	....	....	....	....	....	....	....	....	....	....	....
1990-91	RPI Engineers	ECAC	29	23	40	63	68	....	....	....	....	....	....	....	....	....	....	....	....	....	....	....	....	....	....	....
1991-92	Canada	Nat-Team	60	20	49	69	35	....	....	....	....	....	....	....	....	....	....	....	....	....	....	....	....	....	....	....
	Canada	Olympics	8	6	*9	*15	4	....	....	....	....	....	....	....	....	....	....	....	....	....	....	....	....	....	....	....
	Boston	**NHL**	**14**	**5**	**14**	**19**	**4**	**2**	**0**	**0**	**38**	**13.2**	**6**	....	....	....	....	....	**15**	**4**	**8**	**12**	**21**	**2**	**0**	**0**
1992-93	**Boston**	**NHL**	**84**	**32**	**70**	**102**	**33**	**9**	**0**	**3**	**229**	**14.0**	**23**	....	....	....	....	....	**4**	**2**	**4**	**6**	**6**	**2**	**0**	**0**
1993-94	**Boston**	**NHL**	**63**	**14**	**58**	**72**	**35**	**4**	**0**	**2**	**142**	**9.9**	**11**	....	....	....	....	....	....	....	....	....	....	....	....	....
	Washington	**NHL**	**11**	**5**	**8**	**13**	**6**	**2**	**0**	**0**	**22**	**22.7**	**0**	....	....	....	....	....	**11**	**4**	**5**	**9**	**6**	**2**	**0**	**1**
1994-95	**Washington**	**NHL**	**44**	**5**	**38**	**43**	**8**	**3**	**0**	**0**	**70**	**7.1**	**−1**	....	....	....	....	....	**7**	**2**	**6**	**8**	**2**	**0**	**0**	**0**
1995-96	**Washington**	**NHL**	**80**	**14**	**50**	**64**	**30**	**7**	**2**	**2**	**176**	**8.0**	**−3**	....	....	....	....	....	**5**	**0**	**7**	**7**	**6**	**0**	**0**	**0**
1996-97	**Washington**	**NHL**	**58**	**15**	**27**	**42**	**8**	**9**	**1**	**3**	**124**	**12.1**	**−11**	....	....	....	....	....	....	....	....	....	....	....	....	....
1997-98	**Washington**	**NHL**	**56**	**9**	**22**	**31**	**26**	**4**	**1**	**1**	**87**	**10.3**	**−8**	....	....	....	....	....	**21**	**7**	**10**	**17**	**8**	**1**	**1**	**4**
1998-99	**Washington**	**NHL**	**63**	**14**	**27**	**41**	**20**	**2**	**1**	**3**	**142**	**9.9**	**−3**	**437**	**48.1**	**34**	**26**	**19:28**	....	....	....	....	....	....	....	....
	Buffalo	**NHL**	**9**	**1**	**1**	**2**	**2**	**0**	**0**	**0**	**8**	**12.5**	**−1**	**8**	**12.5**	**3**	**2**	**17:11**	**20**	**3**	**8**	**11**	**10**	**0**	**1**	**0**
99-2000	**Ottawa**	**NHL**	**65**	**13**	**24**	**37**	**22**	**2**	**0**	**2**	**126**	**10.3**	**3**	**830**	**51.6**	**27**	**25**	**18.28**	**6**	**2**	**1**	**3**	**0**	**0**	**0**	**0**
2000-01	**Phoenix**	**NHL**	**69**	**10**	**23**	**33**	**28**	**5**	**0**	**3**	**100**	**10.0**	**−2**	**210**	**50.5**	**27**	**14**	**17:25**	....	....	....	....	....	....	....	....
	NHL Totals		**616**	**137**	**362**	**499**	**222**	**49**	**5**	**19**	**1264**	**10.8**		**1485**	**50.2**	**91**	**67**	**18:22**	**89**	**24**	**49**	**73**	**59**	**7**	**2**	**5**

NCAA East First All-American Team (1990) • ECAC Second All-Star Team (1991) • NCAA East Second All-American Team (1991) • NHL All-Rookie Team (1993)

Traded to **Washington** by **Boston** for Al Iafrate, March 21, 1994. Traded to **Buffalo** by **Washington** with Washington's 3rd round choice (Tim Preston) in 1999 Entry Draft for Alexei Tezikov and Buffalo's 4th round compensatory choice (later traded to Calgary - Calgary selected Levente Szuper) in 2000 Entry Draft, March 22, 1999. Signed as a free agent by **Ottawa**, October 25, 1999. Selected by **Minnesota** from **Ottawa** in Expansion Draft, June 23, 2000. Traded to **Phoenix** by **Minnesota** for the rights to Rickard Wallin, June 23, 2000. Traded to **Montreal** by **Phoenix** for future considerations, June 15, 2001.

KABERLE, Frantisek

(KA-buhr-lay, FRAN-tih-sehk) **ATL.**

Defense. Shoots left. 6', 185 lbs. Born, Kladno, Czech., November 8, 1973. Los Angeles' 3rd choice, 76th overall, in 1999 Entry Draft.

1991-92	Poldi Kladno	Czech.	37	1	4	5	8	....	....	....	....	....	....	....	....	....	....	....	8	0	1	1	0	....	....	....
1992-93	Poldi Kladno	Czech.	40	4	5	9	....	....	....	....	....	....	....	....	....	....	....	....	9	2	4	6	....	....	....	....
1993-94	HC Kladno	Cze-Rep	41	4	16	20	....	....	....	....	....	....	....	....	....	....	....	....	11	1	1	2	....	....	....	....
1994-95	HC Kladno	Cze-Rep	40	7	17	24	20	....	....	....	....	....	....	....	....	....	....	....	8	0	3	3	12	....	....	....
1995-96	MoDo Hockey	Sweden	40	5	7	12	34	....	....	....	....	....	....	....	....	....	....	....	8	0	1	1	0	....	....	....
1996-97	MoDo Hockey	Sweden	50	3	11	14	28	....	....	....	....	....	....	....	....	....	....	....	....	....	....	....	....	....	....	....
1997-98	MoDo Hockey	Sweden	46	5	4	9	22	....	....	....	....	....	....	....	....	....	....	....	9	1	1	2	4	....	....	....
1998-99	MoDo Hockey	Sweden	45	15	18	33	4	....	....	....	....	....	....	....	....	....	....	....	13	2	5	7	8	....	....	....

			Regular Season															Playoffs							
Season	Club	League	GP	G	A	Pts	PIM	PP	SH	GW	S	%	+/-	TF	F%	H	SB	Min	GP	G	A	Pts	PIM	PP	SH	GW
99-2000	**Los Angeles**	**NHL**	**37**	**0**	**9**	**9**	**4**	**0**	**0**	**0**	**41**	**0.0**	**3**	**0**	**0.0**	**29**	**31**	**17:04**	....	....	....	....	....	....	....	....
	Long Beach	IHL	18	2	8	10	8	....	....	....	....	....	....	....	....	....	....	....	....	....	....	....	....	....	....	....
	Atlanta	**NHL**	**14**	**1**	**6**	**7**	**6**	**0**	**1**	**0**	**35**	**2.9**	**–13**	**0**	**0.0**	**25**	**23**	**24:39**	....	....	....	....	....	....	....	....
	Lowell	AHL	4	0	2	2	0	....	....	....	....	....	....	....	....	....	....	....	....	....	....	....	....	....	....	....
2000-01	**Atlanta**	**NHL**	**51**	**4**	**11**	**15**	**18**	**1**	**0**	**1**	**99**	**4.0**	**11**	**1**	**0.0**	**35**	**62**	**22:17**	....	....	....	....	....	....	....	....
	NHL Totals		**102**	**5**	**26**	**31**	**28**	**1**	**1**	**1**	**175**	**2.9**		**1**	**0.0**	**89**	**116**	**20:43**	....	....	....	....	....	....	....	....

Traded to **Atlanta** by **Los Angeles** with Donald Audette for Kelly Buchberger and Nelson Emerson, March 13, 2000.

KABERLE, Tomas

(KA-buhr-lay, TAW-mas) **TOR.**

Defense. Shoots left. 6'2", 190 lbs. Born, Rakovnik, Czech., March 2, 1978. Toronto's 13th choice, 204th overall, in 1996 Entry Draft.

Season	Club	League	GP	G	A	Pts	PIM	PP	SH	GW	S	%	+/-	TF	F%	H	SB	Min	GP	G	A	Pts	PIM	PP	SH	GW
1994-95	Poldi Kladno-Jr.	Cze-Rep	37	7	10	17	....	....	....	....	....	....	....	....	....	....	....	....	....	....	....	....	....	....	....	....
	Poldi Kladno	Cze-Rep	4	0	1	1	0	....	....	....	....	....	....	....	....	....	....	....	....	....	....	....	....	....	....	....
1995-96	Poldi Kladno-Jr.	Cze-Rep	23	6	13	19	....	....	....	....	....	....	....	....	....	....	....	....	....	....	....	....	....	....	....	....
	Poldi Kladno	Cze-Rep	23	0	1	1	2	....	....	....	....	....	....	....	....	....	....	....	2	0	0	0	0			
1996-97	Poldi Kladno	Cze-Rep	49	0	5	5	26	....	....	....	....	....	....	....	....	....	....	....	3	0	0	0	0			
1997-98	Poldi Kladno	Cze-Rep	47	4	19	23	12	....	....	....	....	....	....	....	....	....	....	....	....	....	....	....	....	....	....	....
	St. John's Leafs	AHL	2	0	0	0	0	....	....	....	....	....	....	....	....	....	....	....	....	....	....	....	....	....	....	....
1998-99	**Toronto**	**NHL**	**57**	**4**	**18**	**22**	**12**	**0**	**0**	**2**	**71**	**5.6**	**3**	**0**	**0.0**	**27**	**46**	**18:42**	**14**	**0**	**3**	**3**	**2**	**0**	**0**	**0**
99-2000	**Toronto**	**NHL**	**82**	**7**	**33**	**40**	**24**	**2**	**0**	**0**	**82**	**8.5**	**3**	**0**	**0.0**	**86**	**106**	**22:55**	**12**	**1**	**4**	**5**	**0**	**0**	**0**	**1**
2000-01	**Toronto**	**NHL**	**82**	**6**	**39**	**45**	**24**	**0**	**0**	**1**	**96**	**6.3**	**10**	**2**	**0.0**	**57**	**124**	**22:41**	**11**	**1**	**3**	**4**	**0**	**0**	**0**	**1**
	NHL Totals		**221**	**17**	**90**	**107**	**60**	**2**	**0**	**3**	**249**	**6.8**		**2**	**0.0**	**170**	**276**	**21:44**	**37**	**2**	**10**	**12**	**2**	**0**	**0**	**2**

KALININ, Dmitri

(kah-LIHN-ihn, DIH-mih-TREE) **BUF.**

Defense. Shoots left. 6'2", 206 lbs. Born, Chelyabinsk, USSR, July 22, 1980. Buffalo's 1st choice, 18th overall, in 1998 Entry Draft.

Season	Club	League	GP	G	A	Pts	PIM	PP	SH	GW	S	%	+/-	TF	F%	H	SB	Min	GP	G	A	Pts	PIM	PP	SH	GW
1995-96	HC Chelyabinsk	Russia-Jr.	30	10	10	20	60	....	....	....	....	....	....	....	....	....	....	....	....	....	....	....	....	....	....	....
	HC Chelyabinsk	Russia-2	20	0	3	3	10	....	....	....	....	....	....	....	....	....	....	....	....	....	....	....	....	....	....	....
1996-97	HC Chelyabinsk-2	Russia-3	20	0	0	0	10	....	....	....	....	....	....	....	....	....	....	....	....	....	....	....	....	....	....	....
	HC Chelyabinsk	Russia	2	0	0	0	0	....	....	....	....	....	....	....	....	....	....	....	2	0	0	0	0			
1997-98	HC Chelyabinsk	Russia	26	0	2	2	24	....	....	....	....	....	....	....	....	....	....	....	....	....	....	....	....	....	....	....
1998-99	Moncton Wildcats	QMJHL	39	7	18	25	44	....	....	....	....	....	....	....	....	....	....	....	4	1	1	2	0			
	Rochester	AHL	3	0	1	1	14	....	....	....	....	....	....	....	....	....	....	....	7	0	0	0	6			
99-2000	**Buffalo**	**NHL**	**4**	**0**	**0**	**0**	**4**	**0**	**0**	**0**	**3**	**0.0**	**0**	**0**	**0.0**	**2**	**0**	**16:53**								
	Rochester	AHL	75	2	19	21	52	....	....	....	....	....	....	....	....	....	....	....	21	2	9	11	8			
2000-01	**Buffalo**	**NHL**	**79**	**4**	**18**	**22**	**38**	**2**	**0**	**0**	**88**	**4.5**	**–2**	**1**	**100.0**	**88**	**101**	**19:50**	**13**	**0**	**2**	**2**	**4**	**0**	**0**	**0**
	NHL Totals		**83**	**4**	**18**	**22**	**42**	**2**	**0**	**0**	**91**	**4.4**		**1**	**100.0**	**90**	**101**	**19:50**	**13**	**0**	**2**	**2**	**4**	**0**	**0**	**0**

KALLIO, Tomi

(KAL-ee-oh, TAW-mee) **ATL.**

Left wing. Shoots left. 6', 190 lbs. Born, Turku, Finland, January 27, 1977. Colorado's 4th choice, 81st overall, in 1995 Entry Draft.

Season	Club	League	GP	G	A	Pts	PIM	PP	SH	GW	S	%	+/-	TF	F%	H	SB	Min	GP	G	A	Pts	PIM	PP	SH	GW
1992-93	TPS Turku-C	Finn-Jr.	39	39	34	73	18	....	....	....	....	....	....	....	....	....	....	....	....	....	....	....	....	....	....	....
1993-94	TPS Turku-B	Finn-Jr.	10	5	6	11	14	....	....	....	....	....	....	....	....	....	....	....	1	0	1	1	0			
	TPS Turku	Finn-Jr.	33	9	7	16	16	....	....	....	....	....	....	....	....	....	....	....	6	0	1	1	2			
1994-95	TPS Turku	Finn-Jr.	14	5	12	17	24	....	....	....	....	....	....	....	....	....	....	....	....	....	....	....	....	....	....	....
	TPS Turku-B	Finn-Jr.	1	2	0	2	0	....	....	....	....	....	....	....	....	....	....	....	....	....	....	....	....	....	....	....
	Kiekko-67	Finland-2	25	8	5	13	16	....	....	....	....	....	....	....	....	....	....	....	7	3	1	4	6			
1995-96	TPS Turku	Finn-Jr.	8	8	3	11	14	....	....	....	....	....	....	....	....	....	....	....	....	....	....	....	....	....	....	....
	Kiekko-67	Finland-2	29	10	11	21	28	....	....	....	....	....	....	....	....	....	....	....	....	....	....	....	....	....	....	....
	TPS Turku	Finland	8	2	3	5	10	....	....	....	....	....	....	....	....	....	....	....	4	0	0	0	2			
1996-97	TPS Turku	Finland	47	9	10	19	18	....	....	....	....	....	....	....	....	....	....	....	8	2	0	2	2			
	TPS Turku	EuroHL	6	2	0	2	25	....	....	....	....	....	....	....	....	....	....	....	4	0	0	0	0			
1997-98	TPS Turku	Finland	47	10	10	20	8	....	....	....	....	....	....	....	....	....	....	....	4	0	2	2	0			
	TPS Turku	EuroHL	6	0	1	1	2	....	....	....	....	....	....	....	....	....	....	....	....	....	....	....	....	....	....	....
1998-99	TPS Turku	Finland	54	15	21	36	20	....	....	....	....	....	....	....	....	....	....	....	10	3	4	7	6			
99-2000	TPS Turku	Finland	50	26	27	53	40	....	....	....	....	....	....	....	....	....	....	....	11	4	*9	13	4			
	TPS Turku	EuroHL	5	2	1	3	0	....	....	....	....	....	....	....	....	....	....	....	5	5	3	8	2			
2000-01	**Atlanta**	**NHL**	**56**	**14**	**13**	**27**	**22**	**2**	**0**	**2**	**115**	**12.2**	**–3**	**8**	**12.5**	**45**	**10**	**16:17**	....	....	....	....	....	....	....	....
	NHL Totals		**56**	**14**	**13**	**27**	**22**	**2**	**0**	**2**	**115**	**12.2**		**8**	**12.5**	**45**	**10**	**16:17**	....	....	....	....	....	....	....	....

Claimed by **Atlanta** from **Colorado** in Expansion Draft, June 25, 1999.

KAMENSKY, Valeri

(kah-MEHN-skee, VAL-uhr-ee) **DAL.**

Left wing. Shoots right. 6'2", 198 lbs. Born, Voskresensk, USSR, April 18, 1966. Quebec's 8th choice, 129th overall, in 1988 Entry Draft.

Season	Club	League	GP	G	A	Pts	PIM	PP	SH	GW	S	%	+/-	TF	F%	H	SB	Min	GP	G	A	Pts	PIM	PP	SH	GW
1982-83	HK Khimik	USSR	5	0	0	0	0	....	....	....	....	....	....	....	....	....	....	....	....	....	....	....	....	....	....	....
1983-84	HK Khimik	USSR	20	2	2	4	6	....	....	....	....	....	....	....	....	....	....	....	....	....	....	....	....	....	....	....
1984-85	HK Khimik	USSR	45	9	3	12	24	....	....	....	....	....	....	....	....	....	....	....	....	....	....	....	....	....	....	....
1985-86	CSKA Moscow	USSR	40	15	9	24	8	....	....	....	....	....	....	....	....	....	....	....	....	....	....	....	....	....	....	....
1986-87	CSKA Moscow	USSR	37	13	8	21	16	....	....	....	....	....	....	....	....	....	....	....	....	....	....	....	....	....	....	....
1987-88	CSKA Moscow	USSR	51	26	20	46	40	....	....	....	....	....	....	....	....	....	....	....	....	....	....	....	....	....	....	....
	Soviet Union	Olympics	8	4	2	6	4	....	....	....	....	....	....	....	....	....	....	....	....	....	....	....	....	....	....	....
1988-89	CSKA Moscow	USSR	40	18	10	28	30	....	....	....	....	....	....	....	....	....	....	....	....	....	....	....	....	....	....	....
1989-90	CSKA Moscow	USSR	45	19	18	37	40	....	....	....	....	....	....	....	....	....	....	....	....	....	....	....	....	....	....	....
1990-91	CSKA Moscow	USSR	46	20	26	46	66	....	....	....	....	....	....	....	....	....	....	....	....	....	....	....	....	....	....	....
1991-92	**Quebec**	**NHL**	**23**	**7**	**14**	**21**	**14**	**2**	**0**	**1**	**42**	**16.7**	**–1**	....	....	....	....	....	....	....	....	....	....	....	....	....
1992-93	**Quebec**	**NHL**	**32**	**15**	**22**	**37**	**14**	**2**	**3**	**0**	**94**	**16.0**	**13**	....	....	....	....	....	**6**	**0**	**1**	**1**	**6**	**0**	**0**	**0**
1993-94	**Quebec**	**NHL**	**76**	**28**	**37**	**65**	**42**	**6**	**0**	**1**	**170**	**16.5**	**12**	....	....	....	....	....	....	....	....	....	....	....	....	....
1994-95	Ambri-Piotta	Switz.	12	13	6	19	2	....	....	....	....	....	....	....	....	....	....	....	....	....	....	....	....	....	....	....
	Quebec	**NHL**	**40**	**10**	**20**	**30**	**22**	**5**	**1**	**5**	**70**	**14.3**	**3**	....	....	....	....	....	**2**	**1**	**0**	**1**	**0**	**0**	**0**	**0**
1995-96◆	**Colorado**	**NHL**	**81**	**38**	**47**	**85**	**85**	**18**	**1**	**5**	**220**	**17.3**	**14**	....	....	....	....	....	**22**	**10**	**12**	**22**	**28**	**3**	**0**	**2**
1996-97	**Colorado**	**NHL**	**68**	**28**	**38**	**66**	**38**	**8**	**0**	**4**	**165**	**17.0**	**5**	....	....	....	....	....	**17**	**8**	**14**	**22**	**16**	**5**	**0**	**2**
1997-98	**Colorado**	**NHL**	**75**	**26**	**40**	**66**	**60**	**8**	**0**	**4**	**173**	**15.0**	**–2**	....	....	....	....	....	**7**	**2**	**3**	**5**	**18**	**1**	**0**	**0**
	Russia	Olympics	6	1	2	3	0	....	....	....	....	....	....	....	....	....	....	....	....	....	....	....	....	....	....	....
1998-99	**Colorado**	**NHL**	**65**	**14**	**30**	**44**	**28**	**2**	**0**	**2**	**123**	**11.4**	**1**	**4**	**25.0**	**32**	**9**	**17:35**	**10**	**4**	**5**	**9**	**4**	**1**	**0**	**1**
99-2000	**NY Rangers**	**NHL**	**58**	**13**	**19**	**32**	**24**	**3**	**0**	**1**	**88**	**14.8**	**–13**	**5**	**0.0**	**32**	**14**	**14:57**	....	....	....	....	....	....	....	....
2000-01	**NY Rangers**	**NHL**	**65**	**14**	**20**	**34**	**36**	**6**	**0**	**1**	**129**	**10.9**	**–18**	**2**	**50.0**	**49**	**15**	**15:19**	....	....	....	....	....	....	....	....
	NHL Totals		**583**	**193**	**287**	**480**	**363**	**60**	**5**	**24**	**1274**	**15.1**		**11**	**18.2**	**113**	**38**	**15:59**	**64**	**25**	**35**	**60**	**72**	**10**	**0**	**5**

• Played in NHL All-Star Game (1998)

• Missed majority of 1991-92 season recovering from ankle injury suffered in game vs. Tampa Bay, October 27, 1991. Transferred to **Colorado** after **Quebec** franchise relocated, June 21, 1995. Signed as a free agent by **NY Rangers**, July 7, 1999. Signed as a free agent by **Dallas**, July 5, 2001.

KAPANEN, Sami

(KA-pah-nehn, SA-mee) **CAR.**

Left wing. Shoots left. 5'10", 195 lbs. Born, Vantaa, Finland, June 14, 1973. Hartford's 4th choice, 87th overall, in 1995 Entry Draft.

Season	Club	League	GP	G	A	Pts	PIM	PP	SH	GW	S	%	+/-	TF	F%	H	SB	Min	GP	G	A	Pts	PIM	PP	SH	GW
1989-90	KalPa Kuopio	Finn-Jr.	30	14	13	27	4	....	....	....	....	....	....	....	....	....	....	....	....	....	....	....	....	....	....	....
1990-91	KalPa Kuopio	Finn-Jr.	31	9	27	36	10	....	....	....	....	....	....	....	....	....	....	....	....	....	....	....	....	....	....	....
	KalPa Kuopio	Finland	14	1	2	3	2	....	....	....	....	....	....	....	....	....	....	....	8	2	1	3	2			
1991-92	KalPa Kuopio	Finn-Jr.	8	1	3	4	12	....	....	....	....	....	....	....	....	....	....	....	....	....	....	....	....	....	....	....
	KalPa Kuopio	Finland	42	15	10	25	8	....	....	....	....	....	....	....	....	....	....	....	....	....	....	....	....	....	....	....
1992-93	KalPa Kuopio	Finn-Jr.	7	11	14	25	2	....	....	....	....	....	....	....	....	....	....	....	....	....	....	....	....	....	....	....
	KalPa Kuopio	Finland	37	4	17	21	12	....	....	....	....	....	....	....	....	....	....	....	....	....	....	....	....	....	....	....
1993-94	KalPa Kuopio	Finland	48	23	32	55	16	....	....	....	....	....	....	....	....	....	....	....	....	....	....	....	....	....	....	....
	Finland	Olympics	8	1	0	1	2	....	....	....	....	....	....	....	....	....	....	....	....	....	....	....	....	....	....	....
1994-95	HIFK Helsinki	Finland	49	14	28	42	42	....	....	....	....	....	....	....	....	....	....	....	3	0	0	0	0			
1995-96	**Hartford**	**NHL**	**35**	**5**	**4**	**9**	**6**	**0**	**0**	**0**	**46**	**10.9**	**0**	....	....	....	....	....	....	....	....	....	....	....	....	....
	Springfield	AHL	28	14	17	31	4	....	....	....	....	....	....	....	....	....	....	....	3	1	2	3	0			
1996-97	**Hartford**	**NHL**	**45**	**13**	**12**	**25**	**2**	**3**	**0**	**2**	**82**	**15.9**	**6**	....	....	....	....	....	....	....	....	....	....	....	....	....

			Regular Season																Playoffs							
Season	Club	League	GP	G	A	Pts	PIM	PP	SH	GW	S	%	+/-	TF	F%	H	SB	Min	GP	G	A	Pts	PIM	PP	SH	GW
1997-98	Carolina	NHL	81	26	37	63	16	4	0	5	190	13.7	9													
	Finland	Olympics	6	0	1	1	0																			
1998-99	Carolina	NHL	81	24	35	59	10	5	0	7	254	9.4	-1	10	50.0	123	28	19:25	5	1	1	2	0	0	0	0
99-2000	Carolina	NHL	76	24	24	48	12	7	0	5	229	10.5	10	2	50.0	91	33	19:53								
2000-01	Carolina	NHL	82	20	37	57	24	7	0	4	223	9.0	-12	6	16.7	155	38	18:56	6	2	3	5	0	1	0	0
	NHL Totals		400	112	149	261	70	26	0	23	1024	10.9		18	38.9	369	99	19:24	11	3	4	7	0	1	0	0

Played in NHL All-Star Game (2000)

Transferred to **Carolina** after **Hartford** franchise relocated, June 25, 1997.

KARALAHTI, Jere

(kar-ah-LAHKH-tee, YEH-reh) **L.A.**

Defense. Shoots right. 6'2", 210 lbs. Born, Helsinki, Finland, March 25, 1975. Los Angeles' 7th choice, 146th overall, in 1993 Entry Draft.

1991-92	HIFK Helsinki	Finn-Jr.	30	12	5	17	36												1	0	0	0	2			
1992-93	HIFK Helsinki-B	Finn-Jr.	7	3	1	4	4																			
	HIFK Helsinki	Finn-Jr.	30	2	13	15	49												2	0	0	0	0			
1993-94	HIFK Helsinki	Finn-Jr.	3	0	0	0	0																			
	HIFK Helsinki	Finland	46	1	10	11	36												3	0	0	0	6			
1994-95	HIFK Helsinki	Finn-Jr.	1	0	0	0	8																			
	HIFK Helsinki	Finland	37	1	7	8	42												3	0	0	0	0			
1995-96	HIFK Helsinki	Finn-Jr.	3	1	2	3	2																			
	HIFK Helsinki	Finland	36	4	6	10	102												3	0	0	0	4			
1996-97	HIFK Helsinki	Finland	18	3	5	8	20																			
1997-98	HIFK Helsinki	Finland	43	14	16	30	32												9	2	0	2	8			
1998-99	HIFK Helsinki	Finland	49	11	22	33	65												11	1	1	2	10			
	HIFK Helsinki	EuroHL	6	2	1	3	2												4	....	2	....				
99-2000	HIFK Helsinki	Finland	13	2	2	4	55																			
	Los Angeles	NHL	48	6	10	16	18	4	0	1	69	8.7	3	0	0.0	108	28	17:05	4	0	1	1	2	0	0	0
	Long Beach	IHL	10	0	3	3	4																			
2000-01	Los Angeles	NHL	56	2	7	9	38	0	0	0	26	7.7	8	0	0.0	159	65	17:04	13	0	0	0	18	0	0	0
	NHL Totals		104	8	17	25	56	4	0	1	95	8.4		0	0.0	267	93	17:05	17	0	1	1	20	0	0	0

KARIYA, Paul

(kah-REE-ah, PAWL) **ANA.**

Left wing. Shoots left. 5'10", 173 lbs. Born, Vancouver, B.C., October 16, 1974. Anaheim's 1st choice, 4th overall, in 1993 Entry Draft.

1990-91	Penticton	BCJHL	54	45	67	112	8																			
1991-92	Penticton	BCJHL	40	46	86	132	18																			
1992-93	U. of Maine	H-East	39	25	*75	*100	12																			
1993-94	U. of Maine	H-East	12	8	16	24	4																			
	Canada	Nat-Team	23	7	34	41	2																			
	Canada	Olympics	8	3	4	7	2																			
1994-95	Anaheim	NHL	47	18	21	39	4	7	1	3	134	13.4	-17													
1995-96	Anaheim	NHL	82	50	58	108	20	20	3	9	349	14.3	9													
1996-97	Anaheim	NHL	69	44	55	99	6	15	3	10	340	12.9	36						11	7	6	13	4	4	0	1
1997-98	Anaheim	NHL	22	17	14	31	23	3	0	2	103	16.5	12													
1998-99	Anaheim	NHL	82	39	62	101	40	11	2	4	429	9.1	17	91	48.4	35	65	25:32	3	1	3	4	0	0	0	0
99-2000	Anaheim	NHL	74	42	44	86	24	11	3	3	324	13.0	22	99	39.4	23	39	24:22								
2000-01	Anaheim	NHL	66	33	34	67	20	18	3	3	230	14.3	-9	149	44.3	19	29	23:02								
	NHL Totals		442	243	288	531	137	85	15	34	1909	12.7		339	44.0	77	133	24:24	14	8	9	17	4	4	0	1

Hockey East First All-Star Team (1993) • NCAA East First All-American Team (1993) • NCAA Championship All-Tournament Team (1993) • Won Hobey Baker Memorial Award (Top U.S. Collegiate Player) (1993) • NHL All-Rookie Team (1995) • Won Lady Byng Trophy (1996, 1997) • NHL First All-Star Team (1996, 1997, 1999) • NHL Second All-Star Team (2000) • Played in NHL All-Star Game (1996, 1997, 1999, 2000, 2001)

KARIYA, Steve

(kah-REE-ah, STEEV) **VAN.**

Left wing. Shoots right. 5'8", 170 lbs. Born, North Vancouver, B.C., December 22, 1977.

1994-95	Nanaimo Clippers	BCJHL	60	36	60	96	4																			
1995-96	U. of Maine	H-East	39	7	16	23	8																			
1996-97	U. of Maine	H-East	35	19	31	50	10																			
1997-98	U. of Maine	H-East	35	25	25	50	22																			
1998-99	U. of Maine	H-East	41	27	38	65	24																			
99-2000	Vancouver	NHL	45	8	11	19	22	0	0	0	41	19.5	9	4	50.0	29	4	12:38								
	Syracuse Crunch	AHL	29	18	23	41	22												4	2	1	3	0			
2000-01	Vancouver	NHL	17	1	6	7	8	1	0	0	22	4.5	-1	0	0.0	5	2	11:42								
	Kansas City	IHL	43	15	29	44	51																			
	NHL Totals		62	9	17	26	30	1	0	0	63	14.3		4	50.0	34	6	12:23								

BCJHL First Team All-Star (1995) • BCJHL Most Sportsmanlike Player (1995) • Hockey East First All-Star Team (1999) • NCAA East First All-American Team (1999)

Signed as a free agent by **Vancouver**, April 21, 1999.

KARLSSON, Andreas

(KARLS-uhn, AN-dray-uhs) **ATL.**

Center. Shoots left. 6'3", 210 lbs. Born, Ludvika, Sweden, August 19, 1975. Calgary's 8th choice, 148th overall, in 1993 Entry Draft.

1992-93	Leksands IF	Sweden	13	0	0	0	6																			
1993-94	Leksands IF	Sweden	21	0	0	0	10												3	0	0	0	0			
1994-95	Leksands IF	Swede-Jr.	3	3	3	6	0																			
	Leksands IF	Sweden	24	7	8	15	0												4	0	1	1	0			
1995-96	Leksands IF	Swede-Jr.	2	4	1	5	6																			
	Leksands IF	Sweden	40	10	13	23	10																			
1996-97	Leksands IF	Sweden	49	13	11	24	39												9	2	0	2	2			
1997-98	Leksands IF	Sweden	33	9	14	23	20												4	1	0	1	0			
	Leksands IF	EuroHL	6	2	3	5	2																			
1998-99	Leksands IF	Sweden	49	18	15	33	18												4	1	0	1	6			
	Leksands IF	EuroHL	6	1	3	4	2												2	1	1	2	2			
99-2000	Atlanta	NHL	51	5	9	14	14	1	0	0	74	6.8	-17	552	46.7	52	17	12:60								
	Orlando	IHL	18	5	5	10	6																			
2000-01	Atlanta	NHL	60	5	11	16	16	0	1	0	83	6.0	-2	743	48.6	47	28	12:54								
	NHL Totals		111	10	20	30	30	1	1	0	157	6.4		1295	47.8	99	45	12:57								

Traded to **Atlanta** by **Calgary** for future considerations, June 25, 1999.

KARPA, Dave

(KAHR-puh, DAYV) **NYR**

Defense. Shoots right. 6'1", 210 lbs. Born, Regina, Sask., May 7, 1971. Quebec's 4th choice, 68th overall, in 1991 Entry Draft.

1988-89	Notre Dame	SJHL	41	16	37	53																				
1989-90	Notre Dame	SJHL	43	9	19	28	271																			
1990-91	Ferris State	CCHA	41	6	19	25	109																			
1991-92	Ferris State	CCHA	34	7	12	19	124																			
	Quebec	NHL	4	0	0	0	14	0	0	0	2	0.0	2													
	Halifax Citadels	AHL	2	0	0	0	4																			
1992-93	Quebec	NHL	12	0	1	1	13	0	0	0	2	0.0	-6						3	0	0	0	0	0	0	0
	Halifax Citadels	AHL	71	4	27	31	167																			
1993-94	Quebec	NHL	60	5	12	17	148	2	0	0	48	10.4	0													
	Cornwall Aces	AHL	1	0	0	0	0												12	2	2	4	27			
1994-95	Cornwall Aces	AHL	6	0	2	2	19																			
	Quebec	NHL	2	0	0	0	0	0	0	0	1	0.0	-1													
	Anaheim	NHL	26	1	5	6	91	0	0	0	32	3.1	0													
1995-96	Anaheim	NHL	72	3	16	19	270	0	1	1	62	4.8	-3													
1996-97	Anaheim	NHL	69	2	11	13	210	0	1	1	90	2.2	11						8	1	1	2	20	0	0	1
1997-98	Anaheim	NHL	78	1	11	12	217	0	0	0	64	1.6	-3													
1998-99	Carolina	NHL	33	0	2	2	55	0	0	0	21	0.0	1	0	0.0	62	45	16:55	2	0	0	0	2	0	0	0

			Regular Season																Playoffs							
Season	Club	League	GP	G	A	Pts	PIM	PP	SH	GW	S	%	+/-	TF	F%	H	SB	Min	GP	G	A	Pts	PIM	PP	SH	GW
99-2000	**Carolina**	**NHL**	**27**	**1**	**4**	**5**	**52**	**0**	**0**	**0**	**24**	**4.2**	**9**	**0**	**0.0**	**68**	**33**	**17:21**	....	....	....	....	....	....	....	....
	Cincinnati	IHL	39	1	8	9	147	....	....	....	....	....	....	....	....	....	....	....	....	....	....	....	....	....	....	....
2000-01	**Carolina**	**NHL**	**80**	**4**	**6**	**10**	**159**	**2**	**0**	**0**	**69**	**5.8**	**–19**	**0**	**0.0**	**193**	**188**	**20:01**	**6**	**0**	**0**	**0**	**17**	**0**	**0**	**0**
	NHL Totals		**463**	**17**	**68**	**85**	**1229**	**4**	**1**	**2**	**415**	**4.1**		**0**	**0.0**	**323**	**266**	**18:46**	**19**	**1**	**1**	**2**	**39**	**0**	**0**	**1**

Traded to **Anaheim** by **Quebec** for Anaheim's 4th round choice (later traded to St. Louis - St. Louis selected Jan Horacek) in 1997 Entry Draft, March 9, 1995. Traded to **Carolina** by **Anaheim** with Anaheim's 4th round choice (later traded to Atlanta - Atlanta selected Blake Robson) in 2000 Entry Draft for Stu Grimson and Kevin Haller, August 11, 1998. Signed as a free agent by **NY Rangers**, July 1, 2001.

KARPOVTSEV, Alexander
(kar-POHV-tzehv, al-ehx-AN-duhr) **CHI.**

Defense. Shoots right. 6'3", 215 lbs. Born, Moscow, USSR, April 7, 1970. Quebec's 7th choice, 158th overall, in 1990 Entry Draft.

Season	Club	League	GP	G	A	Pts	PIM	PP	SH	GW	S	%	+/-	TF	F%	H	SB	Min	GP	G	A	Pts	PIM	PP	SH	GW
1989-90	Dynamo Moscow	USSR	35	1	1	2	27	....	....	....	....	....	....	....	....	....	....	....	....	....	....	....	....	....	....	....
1990-91	Dynamo Moscow	USSR	40	0	5	5	15	....	....	....	....	....	....	....	....	....	....	....	....	....	....	....	....	....	....	....
1991-92	Dynamo Moscow	CIS	35	4	2	6	26	....	....	....	....	....	....	....	....	....	....	....	....	....	....	....	....	....	....	....
1992-93	Dynamo Moscow	CIS	36	3	11	14	100	....	....	....	....	....	....	....	....	....	....	....	7	2	1	3	0	....	....	....
1993-94♦	**NY Rangers**	**NHL**	**67**	**3**	**15**	**18**	**58**	**1**	**0**	**1**	**78**	**3.8**	**12**	....	....	....	....	....	**17**	**0**	**4**	**4**	**12**	**0**	**0**	**0**
1994-95	Dynamo Moscow	CIS	13	0	2	2	10	....	....	....	....	....	....	....	....	....	....	....	....	....	....	....	....	....	....	....
	NY Rangers	**NHL**	**47**	**4**	**8**	**12**	**30**	**1**	**0**	**1**	**82**	**4.9**	**–4**	....	....	....	....	....	**8**	**1**	**0**	**1**	**0**	**0**	**0**	**0**
1995-96	**NY Rangers**	**NHL**	**40**	**2**	**16**	**18**	**26**	**1**	**0**	**1**	**71**	**2.8**	**12**	....	....	....	....	....	**6**	**0**	**1**	**1**	**4**	**0**	**0**	**0**
1996-97	**NY Rangers**	**NHL**	**77**	**9**	**29**	**38**	**59**	**6**	**1**	**0**	**84**	**10.7**	**1**	....	....	....	....	....	**13**	**1**	**3**	**4**	**20**	**1**	**0**	**0**
1997-98	**NY Rangers**	**NHL**	**47**	**3**	**7**	**10**	**38**	**1**	**0**	**1**	**46**	**6.5**	**–1**	....	....	....	....	....	....	....	....	....	....	....	....	....
1998-99	**NY Rangers**	**NHL**	**2**	**1**	**0**	**1**	**0**	**0**	**0**	**0**	**4**	**25.0**	**1**	**0**	**0.0**	**2**	**3**	**22:38**	....	....	....	....	....	....	....	....
	Toronto	**NHL**	**56**	**2**	**25**	**27**	**52**	**1**	**0**	**1**	**61**	**3.3**	**38**	**0**	**0.0**	**79**	**103**	**20:58**	**14**	**1**	**3**	**4**	**12**	**1**	**0**	**0**
99-2000	**Toronto**	**NHL**	**69**	**3**	**14**	**17**	**54**	**3**	**0**	**0**	**51**	**5.9**	**9**	**2**	**0.0**	**88**	**129**	**20:14**	**11**	**0**	**3**	**3**	**4**	**0**	**0**	**0**
2000-01	Dynamo Moscow	Russia	5	0	1	1	0	....	....	....	....	....	....	....	....	....	....	....	....	....	....	....	....	....	....	....
	Chicago	**NHL**	**53**	**2**	**13**	**15**	**39**	**1**	**0**	**0**	**52**	**3.8**	**–4**	**0**	**0.0**	**47**	**110**	**20:28**	....	....	....	....	....	....	....	....
	NHL Totals		**458**	**29**	**127**	**156**	**356**	**15**	**1**	**5**	**529**	**5.5**		**2**	**0.0**	**216**	**345**	**20:33**	**69**	**3**	**14**	**17**	**52**	**2**	**0**	**0**

Traded to **NY Rangers** by **Quebec** for Mike Hurlbut, September 7, 1993. Traded to **Toronto** by **NY Rangers** with NY Rangers' 4th round choice (Mirko Murovic) in 1999 Entry Draft for Mathieu Schneider, October 14, 1998. Traded to **Chicago** by **Toronto** with Toronto's 4th round choice (Vladimir Gusev) in 2001 Entry Draft for Bryan McCabe, October 2, 2000.

KASPARAITIS, Darius
(KAZ-puhr-IGH-tihz, DAIR-ee-uhs) **PIT.**

Defense. Shoots left. 5'11", 212 lbs. Born, Elektrenai, USSR, October 16, 1972. NY Islanders' 1st choice, 5th overall, in 1992 Entry Draft.

Season	Club	League	GP	G	A	Pts	PIM	PP	SH	GW	S	%	+/-	TF	F%	H	SB	Min	GP	G	A	Pts	PIM	PP	SH	GW
1988-89	Dynamo Moscow	USSR	3	0	0	0	0	....	....	....	....	....	....	....	....	....	....	....	....	....	....	....	....	....	....	....
1989-90	Dynamo Moscow	USSR	1	0	0	0	0	....	....	....	....	....	....	....	....	....	....	....	....	....	....	....	....	....	....	....
1990-91	Dynamo Moscow	USSR	17	0	1	1	10	....	....	....	....	....	....	....	....	....	....	....	....	....	....	....	....	....	....	....
1991-92	Dynamo Moscow	CIS	31	2	10	12	14	....	....	....	....	....	....	....	....	....	....	....	....	....	....	....	....	....	....	....
1992-93	Dynamo Moscow	CIS	7	1	3	4	8	....	....	....	....	....	....	....	....	....	....	....	....	....	....	....	....	....	....	....
	NY Islanders	**NHL**	**79**	**4**	**17**	**21**	**166**	**0**	**0**	**0**	**92**	**4.3**	**15**	....	....	....	....	....	**18**	**0**	**5**	**5**	**31**	**0**	**0**	**0**
1993-94	**NY Islanders**	**NHL**	**76**	**1**	**10**	**11**	**142**	**0**	**0**	**0**	**81**	**1.2**	**–6**	....	....	....	....	....	**4**	**0**	**0**	**0**	**8**	**0**	**0**	**0**
1994-95	**NY Islanders**	**NHL**	**13**	**0**	**1**	**1**	**22**	**0**	**0**	**0**	**8**	**0.0**	**–11**	....	....	....	....	....	....	....	....	....	....	....	....	....
1995-96	**NY Islanders**	**NHL**	**46**	**1**	**7**	**8**	**93**	**0**	**0**	**0**	**34**	**2.9**	**–12**	....	....	....	....	....	....	....	....	....	....	....	....	....
1996-97	**NY Islanders**	**NHL**	**18**	**0**	**5**	**5**	**16**	**0**	**0**	**0**	**12**	**0.0**	**–7**	....	....	....	....	....	....	....	....	....	....	....	....	....
	Pittsburgh	**NHL**	**57**	**2**	**16**	**18**	**84**	**0**	**0**	**0**	**46**	**4.3**	**24**	....	....	....	....	....	**5**	**0**	**0**	**0**	**6**	**0**	**0**	**0**
1997-98	**Pittsburgh**	**NHL**	**81**	**4**	**8**	**12**	**127**	**0**	**2**	**0**	**71**	**5.6**	**3**	....	....	....	....	....	**5**	**0**	**0**	**0**	**8**	**0**	**0**	**0**
	Russia	Olympics	6	0	2	2	6	....	....	....	....	....	....	....	....	....	....	....	....	....	....	....	....	....	....	....
1998-99	**Pittsburgh**	**NHL**	**48**	**1**	**4**	**5**	**70**	**0**	**0**	**0**	**32**	**3.1**	**12**	**0**	**0.0**	**173**	**48**	**16:01**	....	....	....	....	....	....	....	....
99-2000	**Pittsburgh**	**NHL**	**73**	**3**	**12**	**15**	**146**	**1**	**0**	**1**	**76**	**3.9**	**–12**	**0**	**0.0**	**261**	**119**	**18:07**	**11**	**1**	**1**	**2**	**10**	**0**	**0**	**0**
2000-01	**Pittsburgh**	**NHL**	**77**	**3**	**16**	**19**	**111**	**1**	**0**	**0**	**81**	**3.7**	**11**	**0**	**0.0**	**351**	**124**	**19:14**	**17**	**1**	**1**	**2**	**26**	**0**	**0**	**1**
	NHL Totals		**568**	**19**	**96**	**115**	**977**	**2**	**2**	**1**	**533**	**3.6**		**0**	**0.0**	**785**	**291**	**18:03**	**60**	**2**	**7**	**9**	**89**	**0**	**0**	**1**

Traded to **Pittsburgh** by **NY Islanders** with Andreas Johansson for Bryan Smolinski, November 17, 1996.

KAVANAGH, Pat
(KA-vuh-naw, PAT) **VAN.**

Right wing. Shoots right. 6'3", 192 lbs. Born, Ottawa, Ont., March 14, 1979. Philadelphia's 2nd choice, 50th overall, in 1997 Entry Draft.

Season	Club	League	GP	G	A	Pts	PIM	PP	SH	GW	S	%	+/-	TF	F%	H	SB	Min	GP	G	A	Pts	PIM	PP	SH	GW
1995-96	Kanata Lasers	OCJHL	54	19	16	35	99	....	....	....	....	....	....	....	....	....	....	....	....	....	....	....	....	....	....	....
1996-97	Peterborough	OHL	43	6	8	14	53	....	....	....	....	....	....	....	....	....	....	....	11	1	1	2	12	....	....	....
1997-98	Peterborough	OHL	66	10	16	26	85	....	....	....	....	....	....	....	....	....	....	....	4	1	0	1	6	....	....	....
1998-99	Peterborough	OHL	68	26	43	69	118	....	....	....	....	....	....	....	....	....	....	....	5	0	5	5	10	....	....	....
99-2000	Syracuse Crunch	AHL	68	12	8	20	56	....	....	....	....	....	....	....	....	....	....	....	4	0	0	0	0	....	....	....
2000-01	Kansas City	IHL	78	26	15	41	86	....	....	....	....	....	....	....	....	....	....	....	....	....	....	....	....	....	....	....
	Vancouver	**NHL**	....	....	....	....	....	....	....	....	....	....	....	....	....	....	....	....	**3**	**0**	**0**	**0**	**2**	**0**	**0**	**0**
	NHL Totals		....	....	....	....	....	....	....	....	....	....		....	....	....	....	....	**3**	**0**	**0**	**0**	**2**	**0**	**0**	**0**

Traded to **Vancouver** by **Philadelphia** for Vancouver's 6th round choice (Konstantin Rudenko) in 1999 Entry Draft, June 1, 1999.

KEANE, Mike
(KEEN, MIGHK) **ST.L.**

Right wing. Shoots right. 6', 185 lbs. Born, Winnipeg, Man., May 29, 1967.

Season	Club	League	GP	G	A	Pts	PIM	PP	SH	GW	S	%	+/-	TF	F%	H	SB	Min	GP	G	A	Pts	PIM	PP	SH	GW
1983-84	Winnipeg	MAHA	21	17	19	36	59	....	....	....	....	....	....	....	....	....	....	....	....	....	....	....	....	....	....	....
	Winnipeg	WHL	1	0	0	0	0	....	....	....	....	....	....	....	....	....	....	....	....	....	....	....	....	....	....	....
1984-85	Moose Jaw	WHL	65	17	26	43	141	....	....	....	....	....	....	....	....	....	....	....	....	....	....	....	....	....	....	....
1985-86	Moose Jaw	WHL	67	34	49	83	162	....	....	....	....	....	....	....	....	....	....	....	13	6	8	14	9	....	....	....
1986-87	Moose Jaw	WHL	53	25	45	70	107	....	....	....	....	....	....	....	....	....	....	....	9	3	9	12	11	....	....	....
	Sherbrooke	AHL	....	....	....	....	....	....	....	....	....	....	....	....	....	....	....	....	9	2	2	4	16	....	....	....
1987-88	Sherbrooke	AHL	78	25	43	68	70	....	....	....	....	....	....	....	....	....	....	....	6	1	1	2	18	....	....	....
1988-89	**Montreal**	**NHL**	**69**	**16**	**19**	**35**	**69**	**5**	**0**	**1**	**90**	**17.8**	**9**	....	....	....	....	....	**21**	**4**	**3**	**7**	**17**	**2**	**0**	**0**
1989-90	**Montreal**	**NHL**	**74**	**9**	**15**	**24**	**78**	**1**	**0**	**1**	**92**	**9.8**	**0**	....	....	....	....	....	**11**	**0**	**1**	**1**	**8**	**0**	**0**	**0**
1990-91	**Montreal**	**NHL**	**73**	**13**	**23**	**36**	**50**	**2**	**1**	**2**	**109**	**11.9**	**6**	....	....	....	....	....	**12**	**3**	**2**	**5**	**6**	**0**	**0**	**0**
1991-92	**Montreal**	**NHL**	**67**	**11**	**30**	**41**	**64**	**2**	**0**	**2**	**116**	**9.5**	**16**	....	....	....	....	....	**8**	**1**	**1**	**2**	**16**	**0**	**0**	**0**
1992-93♦	**Montreal**	**NHL**	**77**	**15**	**45**	**60**	**95**	**0**	**0**	**1**	**120**	**12.5**	**29**	....	....	....	....	....	**19**	**2**	**13**	**15**	**6**	**0**	**0**	**0**
1993-94	**Montreal**	**NHL**	**80**	**16**	**30**	**46**	**119**	**6**	**2**	**2**	**129**	**12.4**	**6**	....	....	....	....	....	**6**	**3**	**1**	**4**	**4**	**0**	**0**	**0**
1994-95	**Montreal**	**NHL**	**48**	**10**	**10**	**20**	**15**	**1**	**0**	**0**	**75**	**13.3**	**5**	....	....	....	....	....	....	....	....	....	....	....	....	....
1995-96	**Montreal**	**NHL**	**18**	**0**	**7**	**7**	**6**	**0**	**0**	**0**	**17**	**0.0**	**–6**	....	....	....	....	....	....	....	....	....	....	....	....	....
	♦ Colorado	**NHL**	**55**	**10**	**10**	**20**	**40**	**0**	**2**	**2**	**67**	**14.9**	**1**	....	....	....	....	....	**22**	**3**	**2**	**5**	**16**	**0**	**0**	**1**
1996-97	**Colorado**	**NHL**	**81**	**10**	**17**	**27**	**63**	**0**	**1**	**1**	**91**	**11.0**	**2**	....	....	....	....	....	**17**	**3**	**1**	**4**	**24**	**0**	**0**	**1**
1997-98	**NY Rangers**	**NHL**	**70**	**8**	**10**	**18**	**47**	**2**	**0**	**0**	**113**	**7.1**	**–12**	....	....	....	....	....	....	....	....	....	....	....	....	....
	Dallas	**NHL**	**13**	**2**	**3**	**5**	**5**	**0**	**0**	**1**	**15**	**13.3**	**0**	....	....	....	....	....	**17**	**4**	**4**	**8**	**0**	**0**	**1**	**1**
1998-99♦	**Dallas**	**NHL**	**81**	**6**	**23**	**29**	**62**	**1**	**1**	**1**	**106**	**5.7**	**–2**	**11**	**27.3**	**126**	**36**	**13:57**	**23**	**5**	**2**	**7**	**6**	**0**	**1**	**1**
99-2000	**Dallas**	**NHL**	**81**	**13**	**21**	**34**	**41**	**0**	**4**	**3**	**85**	**15.3**	**9**	**10**	**50.0**	**163**	**54**	**16:10**	**23**	**2**	**4**	**6**	**14**	**0**	**0**	**0**
2000-01	**Dallas**	**NHL**	**67**	**10**	**14**	**24**	**35**	**1**	**0**	**1**	**64**	**15.6**	**4**	**25**	**60.0**	**90**	**41**	**15:28**	**10**	**3**	**2**	**5**	**4**	**0**	**0**	**0**
	NHL Totals		**954**	**149**	**277**	**426**	**789**	**21**	**11**	**18**	**1289**	**11.6**		**46**	**50.0**	**379**	**131**	**15:11**	**189**	**33**	**36**	**69**	**121**	**2**	**2**	**4**

Signed as a free agent by **Montreal**, September 25, 1985. Traded to **Colorado** by **Montreal** with Patrick Roy for Andrei Kovalenko, Martin Rucinsky and Jocelyn Thibault, December 6, 1995. Signed as a free agent by **NY Rangers**, July 30, 1997. Traded to **Dallas** by **NY Rangers** with Brian Skrudland and NY Rangers' 6th round choice (Pavel Patera) in 1998 Entry Draft for Todd Harvey, Bob Errey and Dallas' 4th round choice (Boyd Kane) in 1998 Entry Draft, March 24, 1998. Signed as a free agent by **St. Louis**, July 10, 2001.

KEEFE, Sheldon
(KEEF, SHEHL-duhn) **T.B.**

Right wing. Shoots right. 5'11", 185 lbs. Born, Brampton, Ont., September 17, 1980. Tampa Bay's 1st choice, 47th overall, in 1999 Entry Draft.

Season	Club	League	GP	G	A	Pts	PIM	PP	SH	GW	S	%	+/-	TF	F%	H	SB	Min	GP	G	A	Pts	PIM	PP	SH	GW
1995-96	Toronto Nats	MTHL	45	66	71	137	....	....	....	....	....	....	....	....	....	....	....	....	....	....	....	....	....	....	....	....
1996-97	Quinte Hawks	MTJHL	44	21	23	44	41	....	....	....	....	....	....	....	....	....	....	....	....	....	....	....	....	....	....	....
	Bramalea Blues	OPJHL	8	0	3	3	4	....	....	....	....	....	....	....	....	....	....	....	....	....	....	....	....	....	....	....
1997-98	Caledon Canucks	MTJHL	43	41	40	81	117	....	....	....	....	....	....	....	....	....	....	....	13	15	8	23	....	....	....	....
1998-99	St. Michael's	OHL	38	37	37	74	80	....	....	....	....	....	....	....	....	....	....	....	....	....	....	....	....	....	....	....
	Barrie Colts	OHL	28	14	28	42	60	....	....	....	....	....	....	....	....	....	....	....	10	5	5	10	31	....	....	....
99-2000	Barrie Colts	OHL	66	48	*73	*121	95	....	....	....	....	....	....	....	....	....	....	....	25	10	13	23	41	....	....	....

			Regular Season															Playoffs							
Season	Club	League	GP	G	A	Pts	PIM	PP	SH	GW	S	%	+/-	TF	F%	H	SB	Min	GP	G	A	Pts	PIM	PP	SH	GW
2000-01	**Tampa Bay**	**NHL**	**49**	**4**	**0**	**4**	**38**	**0**	**0**	**0**	**32**	**12.5**	**–13**	**1**	**0.0**	**77**	**8**	**8:00**								
	Detroit Vipers	IHL	13	7	5	12	23																			
	NHL Totals		**49**	**4**	**0**	**4**	**38**	**0**	**0**	**0**	**32**	**12.5**		**1**	**0.0**	**77**	**8**	**8:00**								

Won Emms Family Award (Top Rookie - OHL) (1999) • Won Eddie Powers Memorial Trophy (Top Scorer - OHL) (2000) • OHL Second All-Star Team (2000) • CHL First All-Star Team (2000) • Memorial Cup All-Star Team (2000)

KELLY, Steve

(KEHL-lee, STEEV) **L.A.**

Center. Shoots left. 6'2", 210 lbs. Born, Vancouver, B.C., October 26, 1976. Edmonton's 1st choice, 6th overall, in 1995 Entry Draft.

Season	Club	League	GP	G	A	Pts	PIM	PP	SH	GW	S	%	+/-	TF	F%	H	SB	Min	GP	G	A	Pts	PIM	PP	SH	GW
1991-92	Westbank West	BCAHA	30	25	60	85	75																			
1992-93	Prince Albert	WHL	65	11	9	20	75																			
1993-94	Prince Albert	WHL	65	19	42	61	106																			
1994-95	Prince Albert	WHL	68	31	41	72	153												15	7	9	16	35			
1995-96	Prince Albert	WHL	70	27	74	101	203												18	13	18	31	47			
1996-97	**Edmonton**	**NHL**	**8**	**1**	**0**	**1**	**6**	**0**	**0**	**1**	**6**	**16.7**	**–1**						**6**	**0**	**0**	**0**	**2**	**0**	**0**	**0**
	Hamilton Bulldogs	AHL	48	9	29	38	111												11	3	3	6	24			
1997-98	**Edmonton**	**NHL**	**19**	**0**	**2**	**2**	**8**	**0**	**0**	**0**	**5**	**0.0**	**–4**													
	Hamilton Bulldogs	AHL	11	2	8	10	18																			
	Tampa Bay	**NHL**	**24**	**2**	**1**	**3**	**15**	**1**	**0**	**0**	**17**	**11.8**	**–9**													
	Milwaukee	IHL	5	0	1	1	19																			
	Cleveland	IHL	5	1	1	2	29												1	0	1	1	0			
1998-99	**Tampa Bay**	**NHL**	**34**	**1**	**3**	**4**	**27**	**0**	**0**	**1**	**15**	**6.7**	**–15**	**11**	**54.5**	**12**	**13**	**10:51**								
	Cleveland	IHL	18	6	7	13	36																			
99-2000	Detroit Vipers	IHL	1	0	0	0	4																			
	♦ **New Jersey**	**NHL**	**1**	**0**	**0**	**0**	**0**	**0**	**0**	**0**	**0**	**0.0**	**0**	**0**	**0.0**	**0**	**0**	**4:28**	**10**	**0**	**0**	**0**	**4**	**0**	**0**	**0**
	Albany River Rats	AHL	76	21	36	57	131												3	1	1	2	2			
2000-01	**New Jersey**	**NHL**	**24**	**2**	**2**	**4**	**21**	**0**	**0**	**0**	**18**	**11.1**	**0**	**87**	**48.3**	**21**	**10**	**9:58**								
	Los Angeles	**NHL**	**11**	**1**	**0**	**1**	**4**	**0**	**0**	**0**	**4**	**25.0**	**0**	**51**	**39.2**	**8**	**5**	**6:44**	**8**	**0**	**0**	**0**	**2**	**0**	**0**	**0**
	NHL Totals		**121**	**7**	**8**	**15**	**81**	**1**	**0**	**2**	**65**	**10.8**		**149**	**45.6**	**41**	**28**	**9:49**	**24**	**0**	**0**	**0**	**8**	**0**	**0**	**0**

Traded to **Tampa Bay** by **Edmonton** with Bryan Marchment and Jason Bonsignore for Roman Hamrlik and Paul Comrie, December 30, 1997. Traded to **New Jersey** by **Tampa Bay** for New Jersey's 7th round choice (Brian Eklund) in 2000 Entry Draft, October 7, 1999. Traded to **LA Kings** by **New Jersey** to complete transaction that sent Bob Corkum to New Jersey (February 23, 2001), February 27, 2001. • Was a healthy scratch for majority of 2000-01 season.

KENADY, Chris

(KEHN-a-dee, KRIHS)

Right wing. Shoots right. 6'2", 195 lbs. Born, Mound, MN, April 10, 1973. St. Louis' 8th choice, 175th overall, in 1991 Entry Draft.

Season	Club	League	GP	G	A	Pts	PIM	PP	SH	GW	S	%	+/-	TF	F%	H	SB	Min	GP	G	A	Pts	PIM	PP	SH	GW
1990-91	St. Paul Vulcans	USHL	45	16	20	36	57																			
1991-92	U. of Denver	WCHA	36	8	5	13	56																			
1992-93	U. of Denver	WCHA	38	8	16	24	95																			
1993-94	U. of Denver	WCHA	37	14	11	25	125																			
1994-95	U. of Denver	WCHA	39	21	17	38	113																			
1995-96	Worcester	AHL	43	9	10	19	58												2	0	0	0	0			
1996-97	Worcester	AHL	73	23	26	49	131												5	0	1	1	2			
1997-98	**St. Louis**	**NHL**	**5**	**0**	**2**	**2**	**0**	**0**	**0**	**0**	**3**	**0.0**	**1**													
	Worcester	AHL	63	23	22	45	84												11	1	5	6	26			
1998-99	Utah Grizzlies	IHL	35	7	6	13	68																			
	Long Beach	IHL	19	1	6	7	47																			
	Hartford	AHL	22	2	6	8	52												2	0	1	1	6			
99-2000	**NY Rangers**	**NHL**	**2**	**0**	**0**	**0**	**0**	**0**	**0**	**0**	**1**	**0.0**	**–1**	**0**	**0.0**	**6**	**0**	**7:27**								
	Hartford	AHL	71	15	16	31	196												21	8	3	11	40			
2000-01	Louisville	AHL	20	2	1	3	36																			
	Hartford	AHL	42	5	12	17	58												5	2	0	2	7			
	NHL Totals		**7**	**0**	**2**	**2**	**0**	**0**	**0**	**0**	**4**	**0.0**		**0**	**0.0**	**6**	**0**	**7:27**								

Traded to **NY Rangers** by **St. Louis** to complete transaction that sent Jeff Finley and Geoff Smith to St. Louis (February 13, 1999), February 22, 1999.

KENNEDY, Mike

(KEHN-a-dee, MIGHK)

Center. Shoots right. 6'1", 195 lbs. Born, Vancouver, B.C., April 13, 1972. Minnesota's 3rd choice, 97th overall, in 1991 Entry Draft.

Season	Club	League	GP	G	A	Pts	PIM	PP	SH	GW	S	%	+/-	TF	F%	H	SB	Min	GP	G	A	Pts	PIM	PP	SH	GW
1989-90	U.B.C. T-Birds	CWUAA	9	5	7	12	0																			
1990-91	U.B.C. T-Birds	CWUAA	28	17	17	34	18																			
1991-92	Seattle T-Birds	WHL	71	42	47	89	134												15	11	6	17	20			
1992-93	Kalamazoo Wings	IHL	77	21	30	51	39																			
1993-94	Kalamazoo Wings	IHL	63	20	18	38	42												3	1	2	3	2			
1994-95	Kalamazoo Wings	IHL	42	20	28	48	29																			
	Dallas	**NHL**	**44**	**6**	**12**	**18**	**33**	**2**	**0**	**0**	**76**	**7.9**	**4**						**5**	**0**	**0**	**0**	**9**	**0**	**0**	**0**
1995-96	**Dallas**	**NHL**	**61**	**9**	**17**	**26**	**48**	**4**	**0**	**1**	**111**	**8.1**	**–7**													
1996-97	**Dallas**	**NHL**	**24**	**1**	**6**	**7**	**13**	**0**	**0**	**1**	**26**	**3.8**	**3**													
	Michigan K-Wings	IHL	2	0	1	1	2																			
1997-98	**Toronto**	**NHL**	**13**	**0**	**1**	**1**	**14**	**0**	**0**	**0**	**12**	**0.0**	**–2**													
	St. John's Leafs	AHL	49	11	17	28	86																			
	Dallas	**NHL**	**2**	**0**	**0**	**0**	**2**	**0**	**0**	**0**	**0**	**0.0**	**1**													
1998-99	**NY Islanders**	**NHL**	**1**	**0**	**0**	**0**	**2**	**0**	**0**	**0**	**0**	**0.0**	**0**	**0**	**0.0**	**4**	**0**	**10:50**								
	Lowell	AHL	62	14	26	40	52												3	1	0	1	0			
99-2000	Munich Barons	DEL	13	2	5	7	6												12	4	4	8	28			
2000-01	Munich Barons	DEL	44	14	17	31	67												11	5	5	10	12			
	NHL Totals		**145**	**16**	**36**	**52**	**112**	**6**	**0**	**2**	**225**	**7.1**		**0**	**0.0**	**4**	**0**	**10:50**	**5**	**0**	**0**	**0**	**9**	**0**	**0**	**0**

WHL West Second All-Star Team (1992)

Rights transferred to **Dallas** after **Minnesota** franchise relocated, June 9, 1993. Signed as a free agent by **Toronto**, July 2, 1997. Traded to **Dallas** by **Toronto** for Dallas' 8th round choice (Michal Travnicek) in 1998 Entry Draft, March 24, 1998. Signed as a free agent by **NY Islanders**, July 1, 1998. • Missed majority of 1999-2000 season recovering from ankle injury suffered in game vs. Moskitos Essen (DEL), September 17, 1999.

KESA, Dan

(KEH-suh, DAN)

Right wing. Shoots right. 6', 198 lbs. Born, Vancouver, B.C., November 23, 1971. Vancouver's 4th choice, 95th overall, in 1991 Entry Draft.

Season	Club	League	GP	G	A	Pts	PIM	PP	SH	GW	S	%	+/-	TF	F%	H	SB	Min	GP	G	A	Pts	PIM	PP	SH	GW
1988-89	Richmond	BCJHL	44	21	21	42	71																			
1989-90	Richmond	BCJHL	54	39	38	77	103																			
1990-91	Prince Albert	WHL	69	30	23	53	116												3	1	1	2	0			
1991-92	Prince Albert	WHL	62	46	51	97	201												10	9	10	19	27			
1992-93	Hamilton Canucks	AHL	62	16	24	40	76																			
1993-94	**Vancouver**	**NHL**	**19**	**2**	**4**	**6**	**18**	**1**	**0**	**1**	**18**	**11.1**	**–3**													
	Hamilton Canucks	AHL	53	37	33	70	33												4	1	4	5	4			
1994-95	Syracuse Crunch	AHL	70	34	44	78	81																			
1995-96	**Dallas**	**NHL**	**3**	**0**	**0**	**0**	**0**	**0**	**0**	**0**	**0**	**0.0**	**–1**													
	Michigan K-Wings	IHL	15	4	11	15	33																			
	Springfield	AHL	22	10	5	15	13																			
	Detroit Vipers	IHL	27	9	6	15	22												12	6	4	10	4			
1996-97	Detroit Vipers	IHL	60	22	21	43	19												20	7	5	12	20			
1997-98	Detroit Vipers	IHL	76	40	37	77	40												20	*13	5	18	14			
1998-99	**Pittsburgh**	**NHL**	**67**	**2**	**8**	**10**	**27**	**0**	**0**	**0**	**33**	**6.1**	**–9**	**392**	**48.2**	**91**	**46**	**10:07**	**13**	**1**	**0**	**1**	**0**	**1**	**0**	**1**
	Detroit Vipers	IHL	8	3	5	8	12																			
99-2000	**Tampa Bay**	**NHL**	**50**	**4**	**10**	**14**	**21**	**0**	**1**	**1**	**55**	**7.3**	**–11**	**234**	**43.6**	**112**	**22**	**13:34**								
	Manitoba Moose	IHL	1	0	0	0	0																			
	Detroit Vipers	IHL	5	3	0	3	2																			
2000-01	Manitoba Moose	IHL	79	16	31	47	48												13	2	3	5	12			
	NHL Totals		**139**	**8**	**22**	**30**	**66**	**1**	**1**	**2**	**106**	**7.5**		**626**	**46.5**	**203**	**68**	**11:36**	**13**	**1**	**0**	**1**	**0**	**1**	**0**	**1**

Traded to **Dallas** by **Vancouver** with Greg Adams and Vancouver's 5th round choice (later traded to LA Kings - LA Kings selected Jason Morgan) in 1995 Entry Draft for Russ Courtnall, April 7, 1995. Traded to **Hartford** by **Dallas** for Robert Petrovicky, November 29, 1995. Signed as a free agent by **Pittsburgh**, August 20, 1998. Signed as a free agent by **Tampa Bay**, September 6, 1999. Signed as a free agent by **Avangard Omsk** (Russia), August 3, 2001.

KHARITONOV, Alexander
(khar-ih-TOH-nahf, al-ehx-AN-duhr) **NYI**

Left wing. Shoots right. 5'9", 169 lbs. Born, Moscow, USSR, March 30, 1976. Tampa Bay's 3rd choice, 81st overall, in 2000 Entry Draft.

			Regular Season																Playoffs							
Season	Club	League	GP	G	A	Pts	PIM	PP	SH	GW	S	%	+/-	TF	F%	H	SB	Min	GP	G	A	Pts	PIM	PP	SH	GW
1993-94	Vyatich Ryazan	CIS-2	44	19	8	27	10																			
1994-95	Dynamo Moscow	CIS	10	0	0	0	4																			
1995-96	D'amo Moscow-2	CIS-3	3	1	3	4	4																			
	HC Lipetsk	CIS-2	64	30	22	52	44																			
1996-97	D'amo Moscow-2	Russia-3	3	1	1	2	0																			
	Dynamo Moscow	Russia	36	11	9	20	12												4	2	0	2	2			
	Dynamo Moscow	EuroHL	6	0	1	1	4												4	2	1	3	2			
1997-98	Dynamo Moscow	Russia	44	19	16	35	20																			
	Dynamo Moscow	EuroHL	6	5	4	9	2												2	0	0	0	0			
1998-99	Dynamo Moscow	Russia	42	8	6	14	24												16	4	3	7	2			
	Dynamo Moscow	EuroHL	5	0	1	1	2												6	0	0	0	4			
99-2000	Dynamo Moscow	Russia	35	14	20	34	26												17	*8	4	12	10			
2000-01	**Tampa Bay**	**NHL**	**66**	**7**	**15**	**22**	**8**	**0**	**0**	**0**	**103**	**6.8**	**-9**	**1**	**100.0**	**20**	**12**	**11:40**								
	NHL Totals		**66**	**7**	**15**	**22**	**8**	**0**	**0**	**0**	**103**	**6.8**		**1**	**100.0**	**20**	**12**	**11:40**								

Traded to **NY Islanders** by **Tampa Bay** with Adrian Aucoin for Mathieu Biron and NY Islanders' 2nd round choice in 2002 Entry Draft, June 22, 2001.

KHAVANOV, Alexander
(khuh-VAN-ahf, al-ehx-AN-duhr) **ST.L.**

Defense. Shoots left. 6', 187 lbs. Born, Ryazan, USSR, January 30, 1972. St. Louis' 8th choice, 232nd overall, in 1999 Entry Draft.

Season	Club	League	GP	G	A	Pts	PIM	PP	SH	GW	S	%	+/-	TF	F%	H	SB	Min	GP	G	A	Pts	PIM	PP	SH	GW
1992-93	Birmingham Bulls	ECHL	19	0	3	3	14																			
	Raleigh Icecaps	ECHL	17	0	6	6	8																			
1993-94	St. Petersburg	CIS	41	1	2	3	24																			
1994-95	St. Petersburg	CIS	49	7	0	7	32												3	0	0	0	0			
1995-96	St. Petersburg	CIS	32	1	5	6	41																			
	HPK Hameenlinna	Finland	16	0	2	2	4												9	0	0	0	0			
1996-97	HK Cherepovets	Russia	39	3	8	11	56												3	1	0	1	4			
1997-98	HK Cherepovets	Russia	44	3	5	8	46																			
1998-99	Dynamo Moscow	Russia	40	2	7	9	14												16	1	5	6	35			
	Dynamo Moscow	EuroHL	5	0	1	1	2												6	0	0	0	4			
99-2000	Dynamo Moscow	Russia	38	5	12	17	49												17	0	3	3	4			
	Dynamo Moscow	EuroHL	6	2	0	2	0																			
2000-01	**St. Louis**	**NHL**	**74**	**7**	**16**	**23**	**52**	**2**	**0**	**0**	**92**	**7.6**	**16**	**0**	**0.0**	**122**	**89**	**20:54**	**15**	**3**	**2**	**5**	**14**	**1**	**0**	**0**
	NHL Totals		**74**	**7**	**16**	**23**	**52**	**2**	**0**	**0**	**92**	**7.6**		**0**	**0.0**	**122**	**89**	**20:54**	**15**	**3**	**2**	**5**	**14**	**1**	**0**	**0**

KHRISTICH, Dmitri
(KRIH-stihch, dih-MEE-tree) **WSH.**

Left wing/Center. Shoots right. 6'2", 195 lbs. Born, Kiev, USSR, July 23, 1969. Washington's 6th choice, 120th overall, in 1988 Entry Draft.

Season	Club	League	GP	G	A	Pts	PIM	PP	SH	GW	S	%	+/-	TF	F%	H	SB	Min	GP	G	A	Pts	PIM	PP	SH	GW
1985-86	Sokol Kiev	USSR	4	0	0	0	0																			
1986-87	Sokol Kiev	USSR	20	3	0	3	4																			
1987-88	Sokol Kiev	USSR	37	9	1	10	18																			
1988-89	Sokol Kiev	USSR	42	17	10	27	15																			
1989-90	Sokol Kiev	USSR	47	14	22	36	32																			
1990-91	Sokol Kiev	USSR	28	10	12	22	20																			
	Washington	**NHL**	**40**	**13**	**14**	**27**	**21**	**1**	**0**	**0**	**77**	**16.9**	**-1**						**11**	**1**	**3**	**4**	**6**	**0**	**0**	**0**
	Baltimore	AHL	3	0	0	0	0																			
1991-92	**Washington**	**NHL**	**80**	**36**	**37**	**73**	**35**	**14**	**1**	**7**	**188**	**19.1**	**24**						**7**	**3**	**2**	**5**	**15**	**3**	**0**	**1**
1992-93	**Washington**	**NHL**	**64**	**31**	**35**	**66**	**28**	**9**	**1**	**1**	**127**	**24.4**	**29**						**6**	**2**	**5**	**7**	**2**	**1**	**0**	**0**
1993-94	**Washington**	**NHL**	**83**	**29**	**29**	**58**	**73**	**10**	**0**	**4**	**195**	**14.9**	**-2**						**11**	**2**	**3**	**5**	**10**	**0**	**0**	**0**
1994-95	**Washington**	**NHL**	**48**	**12**	**14**	**26**	**41**	**8**	**0**	**2**	**92**	**13.0**	**0**						**7**	**1**	**4**	**5**	**0**	**0**	**0**	**0**
1995-96	**Los Angeles**	**NHL**	**76**	**27**	**37**	**64**	**44**	**12**	**0**	**3**	**204**	**13.2**	**0**													
1996-97	**Los Angeles**	**NHL**	**75**	**19**	**37**	**56**	**38**	**3**	**0**	**2**	**135**	**14.1**	**8**													
1997-98	**Boston**	**NHL**	**82**	**29**	**37**	**66**	**42**	**13**	**2**	**1**	**144**	**20.1**	**25**						**6**	**2**	**2**	**4**	**2**	**2**	**0**	**0**
1998-99	**Boston**	**NHL**	**79**	**29**	**42**	**71**	**48**	**13**	**1**	**6**	**144**	**20.1**	**11**	**76**	**44.7**	**80**	**39**	**19:46**	**12**	**3**	**4**	**7**	**6**	**0**	**0**	**1**
99-2000	**Toronto**	**NHL**	**53**	**12**	**18**	**30**	**24**	**3**	**0**	**0**	**79**	**15.2**	**8**	**84**	**45.2**	**52**	**19**	**16:10**	**12**	**1**	**2**	**3**	**0**	**1**	**0**	**0**
2000-01	**Toronto**	**NHL**	**27**	**3**	**6**	**9**	**8**	**2**	**0**	**0**	**23**	**13.0**	**8**	**129**	**41.9**	**21**	**8**	**15:01**								
	Washington	**NHL**	**43**	**10**	**19**	**29**	**8**	**4**	**0**	**4**	**54**	**18.5**	**-8**	**3**	**33.3**	**25**	**19**	**14:53**	**3**	**0**	**0**	**0**	**0**	**0**	**0**	**0**
	NHL Totals		**750**	**250**	**325**	**575**	**410**	**92**	**5**	**30**	**1462**	**17.1**		**292**	**43.5**	**178**	**85**	**17:09**	**75**	**15**	**25**	**40**	**41**	**7**	**0**	**2**

Played in NHL All-Star Game (1997, 1999)

Traded to **LA Kings** by **Washington** with Byron Dafoe for LA Kings' 1st round choice (Alexandre Volchkov) and Dallas' 4th round choice (previously acquired, Washington selected Justin Davis) in 1996 Entry Draft, July 8, 1995. Traded to **Boston** by **LA Kings** with Byron Dafoe for Jozef Stumpel, Sandy Moger and Boston's 4th round choice (later traded to New Jersey - New Jersey selected Pierre Dagenais) in 1998 Entry Draft, August 29, 1997. Traded to **Toronto** by **Boston** for Toronto's 2nd round choice (Ivan Huml) in 2000 Entry Draft, October 20, 1999. Traded to **Washington** by **Toronto** for Tampa Bay's 3rd round choice (previously acquired, Toronto selected Brendan Bell) in 2001 Entry Draft, December 11, 2000.

KILGER, Chad
(KIHL-guhr, CHAD) **MTL.**

Center. Shoots left. 6'3", 215 lbs. Born, Cornwall, Ont., November 27, 1976. Anaheim's 1st choice, 4th overall, in 1995 Entry Draft.

Season	Club	League	GP	G	A	Pts	PIM	PP	SH	GW	S	%	+/-	TF	F%	H	SB	Min	GP	G	A	Pts	PIM	PP	SH	GW
1992-93	Cornwall Colts	OCJHL	55	30	36	66	26												6	0	0	0	0			
1993-94	Kingston	OHL	66	17	35	52	23												6	7	2	9	8			
1994-95	Kingston	OHL	65	42	53	95	95												6	5	2	7	10			
1995-96	**Anaheim**	**NHL**	**45**	**5**	**7**	**12**	**22**	**0**	**0**	**1**	**38**	**13.2**	**-2**													
	Winnipeg	**NHL**	**29**	**2**	**3**	**5**	**12**	**0**	**0**	**0**	**19**	**10.5**	**-2**						**4**	**1**	**0**	**1**	**0**	**0**	**0**	**1**
1996-97	**Phoenix**	**NHL**	**24**	**4**	**3**	**7**	**13**	**1**	**0**	**0**	**30**	**13.3**	**-5**													
	Springfield	AHL	52	17	28	45	36												16	5	7	12	56			
1997-98	**Phoenix**	**NHL**	**10**	**0**	**1**	**1**	**4**	**0**	**0**	**0**	**9**	**0.0**	**-2**													
	Springfield	AHL	35	14	14	28	33																			
	Chicago	**NHL**	**22**	**3**	**8**	**11**	**6**	**2**	**0**	**1**	**23**	**13.0**	**2**													
1998-99	**Chicago**	**NHL**	**64**	**14**	**11**	**25**	**30**	**2**	**1**	**1**	**68**	**20.6**	**-1**	**488**	**56.6**	**124**	**27**	**14:03**								
	Edmonton	**NHL**	**13**	**1**	**1**	**2**	**4**	**0**	**0**	**0**	**13**	**7.7**	**-3**	**82**	**53.7**	**33**	**3**	**11:22**	**4**	**0**	**0**	**0**	**4**	**0**	**0**	**0**
99-2000	**Edmonton**	**NHL**	**40**	**3**	**2**	**5**	**18**	**0**	**0**	**0**	**32**	**9.4**	**-6**	**269**	**48.0**	**60**	**7**	**8:33**	**3**	**0**	**0**	**0**	**0**	**0**	**0**	**0**
	Hamilton Bulldogs	AHL	7	4	2	6	4																			
2000-01	**Edmonton**	**NHL**	**34**	**5**	**2**	**7**	**17**	**1**	**0**	**0**	**28**	**17.9**	**-7**	**391**	**53.5**	**53**	**12**	**8:18**								
	Montreal	**NHL**	**43**	**9**	**16**	**25**	**34**	**1**	**1**	**1**	**75**	**12.0**	**-1**	**319**	**52.4**	**148**	**26**	**17:57**								
	NHL Totals		**324**	**46**	**54**	**100**	**160**	**7**	**2**	**4**	**335**	**13.7**		**1549**	**53.3**	**418**	**75**	**12:36**	**11**	**1**	**0**	**1**	**4**	**0**	**0**	**1**

Traded to **Winnipeg** by **Anaheim** with Oleg Tverdovsky and Anaheim's 3rd round choice (Per-Anton Lundstrom) in 1996 Entry Draft for Teemu Selanne, Marc Chouinard and Winnipeg's 4th round choice (later traded to Toronto - later traded to Montreal - Montreal selected Kim Staal) in 1996 Entry Draft, February 7, 1996. Transferred to **Phoenix** after **Winnipeg** franchise relocated, July 1, 1996. Traded to **Chicago** by **Phoenix** with Jayson More for Keith Carney and Jim Cummins, March 4, 1998. Traded to **Edmonton** by **Chicago** with Daniel Cleary, Ethan Moreau and Christian Laflamme for Boris Mironov, Dean McAmmond and Jonas Elofsson, March 20, 1999. Traded to **Montreal** by **Edmonton** for Sergei Zholtok, December 18, 2000.

KING, Derek
(KIHNG, DAIR-ehk)

Left wing. Shoots left. 6'1", 203 lbs. Born, Hamilton, Ont., February 11, 1967. NY Islanders' 2nd choice, 13th overall, in 1985 Entry Draft.

Season	Club	League	GP	G	A	Pts	PIM	PP	SH	GW	S	%	+/-	TF	F%	H	SB	Min	GP	G	A	Pts	PIM	PP	SH	GW
1982-83	Hamilton A's	OPJHL	8	1	2	3	0																			
1983-84	Hamilton A's	OPJHL	37	10	14	24	142																			
1984-85	Sault Ste. Marie	OHL	63	35	38	73	106												16	3	13	16	11			
1985-86	Sault Ste. Marie	OHL	25	12	17	29	33																			
	Oshawa Generals	OHL	19	8	13	21	15												6	3	2	5	13			
1986-87	Oshawa Generals	OHL	57	53	53	106	74												17	14	10	24	40			
	NY Islanders	**NHL**	**2**	**0**	**0**	**0**	**0**	**0**	**0**	**0**	**5**	**0.0**	**0**													
1987-88	**NY Islanders**	**NHL**	**55**	**12**	**24**	**36**	**30**	**1**	**0**	**4**	**94**	**12.8**	**7**						**5**	**0**	**2**	**2**	**2**	**0**	**0**	**0**
	Springfield	AHL	10	7	6	13	6																			
1988-89	**NY Islanders**	**NHL**	**60**	**14**	**29**	**43**	**14**	**4**	**0**	**0**	**103**	**13.6**	**10**													
	Springfield	AHL	4	4	0	4	0																			
1989-90	**NY Islanders**	**NHL**	**46**	**13**	**27**	**40**	**20**	**5**	**0**	**1**	**91**	**14.3**	**2**						**4**	**0**	**0**	**0**	**4**	**0**	**0**	**0**
	Springfield	AHL	21	11	12	23	33																			
1990-91	**NY Islanders**	**NHL**	**66**	**19**	**26**	**45**	**44**	**2**	**0**	**2**	**130**	**14.6**	**1**													
1991-92	**NY Islanders**	**NHL**	**80**	**40**	**38**	**78**	**46**	**21**	**0**	**6**	**189**	**21.2**	**-10**													

			Regular Season																Playoffs							
Season	Club	League	GP	G	A	Pts	PIM	PP	SH	GW	S	%	+/-	TF	F%	H	SB	Min	GP	G	A	Pts	PIM	PP	SH	GW
1992-93	**NY Islanders**	**NHL**	**77**	**38**	**38**	**76**	**47**	**21**	**0**	**7**	**201**	**18.9**	**-4**						**18**	**3**	**11**	**14**	**14**	**0**	**0**	**0**
1993-94	**NY Islanders**	**NHL**	**78**	**30**	**40**	**70**	**59**	**10**	**0**	**7**	**171**	**17.5**	**18**						**4**	**0**	**1**	**1**	**0**	**0**	**0**	**0**
1994-95	**NY Islanders**	**NHL**	**43**	**10**	**16**	**26**	**41**	**7**	**0**	**0**	**118**	**8.5**	**-5**													
1995-96	**NY Islanders**	**NHL**	**61**	**12**	**20**	**32**	**23**	**5**	**1**	**0**	**154**	**7.8**	**-10**													
1996-97	**NY Islanders**	**NHL**	**70**	**23**	**30**	**53**	**20**	**5**	**0**	**3**	**153**	**15.0**	**-6**													
	Hartford	**NHL**	**12**	**3**	**3**	**6**	**2**	**1**	**0**	**0**	**28**	**10.7**	**0**													
1997-98	**Toronto**	**NHL**	**77**	**21**	**25**	**46**	**43**	**4**	**0**	**3**	**166**	**12.7**	**-7**													
1998-99	**Toronto**	**NHL**	**81**	**24**	**28**	**52**	**20**	**8**	**0**	**4**	**150**	**16.0**	**15**	**1**	**0.0**	**36**	**20**	**14:02**	**16**	**1**	**3**	**4**	**4**	**0**	**0**	**0**
99-2000	**Toronto**	**NHL**	**3**	**0**	**0**	**0**	**2**	**0**	**0**	**0**	**4**	**0.0**	**-2**	**0**	**0.0**	**3**	**0**	**11:29**								
	St. Louis	**NHL**	**19**	**2**	**7**	**9**	**6**	**1**	**0**	**0**	**29**	**6.9**	**0**	**0**	**0.0**	**5**	**11**	**12:44**								
	Grand Rapids	IHL	52	19	30	49	25												17	7	8	15	8			
2000-01	Grand Rapids	IHL	76	32	51	*83	19												10	5	5	10	4			
	NHL Totals		**830**	**261**	**351**	**612**	**417**	**95**	**1**	**37**	**1786**	**14.6**		**1**	**0.0**	**44**	**31**	**13:43**	**47**	**4**	**17**	**21**	**24**	**0**	**0**	**0**

OHL First All-Star Team (1987) • IHL Second All-Star Team (2001) • Shared Leo P. Lamoureux Memorial Trophy (Top Scorer - IHL) with Steve Larouche (2001)

Traded to **Hartford** by **NY Islanders** for Hartford's 5th round choice (Adam Edinger) in 1997 Entry Draft, March 18, 1997. Signed as a free agent by **Toronto**, July 4, 1997. Traded to **St. Louis** by **Toronto** for Tyler Harlton and future considerations, October 20, 1999. Signed as a free agent by **Ottawa**, August 10, 2000. Signed as a free agent with **Munich Barons** (DEL), July 13, 2001.

KING, Kris

(KIHNG, KRIHS)

Left wing. Shoots left. 5'11", 208 lbs. Born, Bracebridge, Ont., February 18, 1966. Washington's 4th choice, 80th overall, in 1984 Entry Draft.

Season	Club	League	GP	G	A	Pts	PIM	PP	SH	GW	S	%	+/-	TF	F%	H	SB	Min	GP	G	A	Pts	PIM	PP	SH	GW
1982-83	Gravenhurst	OJHL-C	32	*72	53	*125	115																			
1983-84	Peterborough	OHL	62	13	18	31	168												8	3	3	6	14			
1984-85	Peterborough	OHL	61	18	35	53	222												16	2	8	10	28			
1985-86	Peterborough	OHL	58	19	40	59	254												8	4	0	4	21			
1986-87	Peterborough	OHL	46	23	33	56	160												12	5	8	13	41			
	Binghamton	AHL	7	0	0	0	18																			
1987-88	**Detroit**	**NHL**	**3**	**1**	**0**	**1**	**2**	**0**	**0**	**0**	**3**	**33.3**	**1**													
	Adirondack	AHL	76	21	32	53	337												10	4	4	8	53			
1988-89	**Detroit**	**NHL**	**55**	**2**	**3**	**5**	**168**	**0**	**0**	**0**	**34**	**5.9**	**-7**						**2**	**0**	**0**	**0**	**2**	**0**	**0**	**0**
1989-90	**NY Rangers**	**NHL**	**68**	**6**	**7**	**13**	**286**	**0**	**0**	**0**	**49**	**12.2**	**2**						**10**	**0**	**1**	**1**	**38**	**0**	**0**	**0**
1990-91	**NY Rangers**	**NHL**	**72**	**11**	**14**	**25**	**154**	**0**	**0**	**0**	**107**	**10.3**	**-1**						**6**	**2**	**0**	**2**	**36**	**0**	**0**	**1**
1991-92	**NY Rangers**	**NHL**	**79**	**10**	**9**	**19**	**224**	**0**	**0**	**2**	**97**	**10.3**	**13**						**13**	**4**	**1**	**5**	**14**	**0**	**0**	**3**
1992-93	**NY Rangers**	**NHL**	**30**	**0**	**3**	**3**	**67**	**0**	**0**	**0**	**23**	**0.0**	**-1**													
	Winnipeg	**NHL**	**48**	**8**	**8**	**16**	**136**	**0**	**0**	**1**	**51**	**15.7**	**5**						**6**	**1**	**1**	**2**	**4**	**0**	**0**	**0**
1993-94	**Winnipeg**	**NHL**	**83**	**4**	**8**	**12**	**205**	**0**	**0**	**1**	**86**	**4.7**	**-22**													
1994-95	**Winnipeg**	**NHL**	**48**	**4**	**2**	**6**	**85**	**0**	**0**	**0**	**58**	**6.9**	**0**													
1995-96	**Winnipeg**	**NHL**	**81**	**9**	**11**	**20**	**151**	**0**	**1**	**2**	**89**	**10.1**	**-7**						**5**	**0**	**1**	**1**	**4**	**0**	**0**	**0**
1996-97	**Phoenix**	**NHL**	**81**	**3**	**11**	**14**	**185**	**0**	**0**	**0**	**57**	**5.3**	**-7**						**7**	**0**	**0**	**0**	**17**	**0**	**0**	**0**
1997-98	**Toronto**	**NHL**	**82**	**3**	**3**	**6**	**199**	**0**	**0**	**2**	**53**	**5.7**	**-13**													
1998-99	**Toronto**	**NHL**	**67**	**2**	**2**	**4**	**105**	**0**	**1**	**1**	**34**	**5.9**	**-16**	**6**	**50.0**	**116**	**14**	**9:22**	**17**	**1**	**1**	**2**	**25**	**0**	**0**	**0**
99-2000	**Toronto**	**NHL**	**39**	**2**	**4**	**6**	**55**	**0**	**0**	**0**	**24**	**8.3**	**4**	**0**	**0.0**	**60**	**7**	**8:31**	**1**	**0**	**0**	**0**	**2**	**0**	**0**	**0**
	Chicago Wolves	IHL	15	2	4	6	19																			
2000-01	**Chicago**	**NHL**	**13**	**1**	**0**	**1**	**8**	**0**	**0**	**0**	**12**	**8.3**	**-3**	**1**	**0.0**	**25**	**2**	**9:60**								
	NHL Totals		**849**	**66**	**85**	**151**	**2030**	**0**	**2**	**9**	**777**	**8.5**		**7**	**42.9**	**201**	**23**	**9:09**	**67**	**8**	**5**	**13**	**142**	**0**	**0**	**4**

Won King Clancy Memorial Trophy (1996)

Signed as a free agent by **Detroit**, March 23, 1987. Traded to **NY Rangers** by **Detroit** for Chris McRae and Detroit's 5th round choice (previously acquired, Detroit selected Tony Burns) in 1990 Entry Draft, September 7, 1989. Traded to **Winnipeg** by **NY Rangers** with Tie Domi for Ed Olczyk, December 28, 1992. Transferred to **Phoenix** after **Winnipeg** franchise relocated, July 1, 1996. Signed as a free agent by **Toronto**, July 23, 1997. Signed as a free agent by **Chicago**, October 9, 2000. • Officially announced retirement, December 3, 2000.

KJELLBERG, Patric

(SHEHL-buhrg, PA-trihk) **NSH.**

Right wing. Shoots left. 6'2", 210 lbs. Born, Trelleborg, Sweden, June 17, 1969. Montreal's 4th choice, 83rd overall, in 1988 Entry Draft.

Season	Club	League	GP	G	A	Pts	PIM	PP	SH	GW	S	%	+/-	TF	F%	H	SB	Min	GP	G	A	Pts	PIM	PP	SH	GW
1985-86	Falun IF	Sweden-2	5	0	2	2	0																			
1986-87	Falun IF	Sweden-2	32	11	13	24	16																			
1987-88	Falun IF	Sweden-2	29	15	10	25	6																			
1988-89	AIK Solna	Sweden	25	7	9	16	8																			
1989-90	AIK Solna	Sweden	33	8	16	24	6												3	1	0	1	0			
1990-91	AIK Solna	Sweden	38	4	11	15	18																			
1991-92	AIK Solna	Sweden	40	20	13	33	14												3	1	0	1	2			
	Sweden	Olympics	8	1	3	4	0																			
1992-93	**Montreal**	**NHL**	**7**	**0**	**0**	**0**	**2**	**0**	**0**	**0**	**7**	**0.0**	**-3**													
	Fredericton	AHL	41	10	27	37	14												5	2	2	4	0			
1993-94	HV Jonkoping	Sweden	40	11	17	28	18																			
	Sweden	Olympics	8	0	1	1	2																			
1994-95	HV Jonkoping	Sweden	29	5	15	20	12																			
1995-96	Djurgardens IF	Sweden	40	9	7	16	10												4	0	2	2	2			
1996-97	Djurgardens IF	Sweden	49	29	11	40	18												4	2	3	5	4			
1997-98	Djurgardens IF	Sweden	46	*30	18	48	16												15	7	3	10	12			
1998-99	**Nashville**	**NHL**	**71**	**11**	**20**	**31**	**24**	**2**	**0**	**2**	**103**	**10.7**	**-13**	**83**	**37.3**	**44**	**18**	**17:41**								
99-2000	**Nashville**	**NHL**	**82**	**23**	**23**	**46**	**14**	**9**	**0**	**3**	**129**	**17.8**	**-11**	**22**	**31.8**	**44**	**24**	**18:12**								
2000-01	**Nashville**	**NHL**	**81**	**14**	**31**	**45**	**12**	**5**	**0**	**2**	**139**	**10.1**	**-2**	**9**	**33.3**	**21**	**20**	**17:39**								
	NHL Totals		**241**	**48**	**74**	**122**	**52**	**16**	**0**	**7**	**378**	**12.7**		**114**	**36.0**	**109**	**62**	**17:51**								

Signed as a free agent by **Nashville**, June 27, 1998.

KLATT, Trent

(KLAT, TREHNT) **VAN.**

Right wing. Shoots right. 6'1", 210 lbs. Born, Robbinsdale, MN, January 30, 1971. Washington's 5th choice, 82nd overall, in 1989 Entry Draft.

Season	Club	League	GP	G	A	Pts	PIM	PP	SH	GW	S	%	+/-	TF	F%	H	SB	Min	GP	G	A	Pts	PIM	PP	SH	GW
1986-87	Osseo High	Hi-School	22	9	27	36	....																			
1987-88	Osseo High	Hi-School	22	19	17	36																				
1988-89	Osseo High	Hi-School	22	24	39	63																				
1989-90	U. of Minnesota	WCHA	38	22	14	36	16																			
1990-91	U. of Minnesota	WCHA	39	16	28	44	58																			
1991-92	U. of Minnesota	WCHA	41	27	36	63	76																			
	Minnesota	**NHL**	**1**	**0**	**0**	**0**	**0**	**0**	**0**	**0**	**1**	**0.0**	**0**						**6**	**0**	**0**	**0**	**2**	**0**	**0**	**0**
1992-93	**Minnesota**	**NHL**	**47**	**4**	**19**	**23**	**38**	**1**	**0**	**0**	**69**	**5.8**	**2**													
	Kalamazoo Wings	IHL	31	8	11	19	18																			
1993-94	**Dallas**	**NHL**	**61**	**14**	**24**	**38**	**30**	**3**	**0**	**2**	**86**	**16.3**	**13**						**9**	**2**	**1**	**3**	**4**	**1**	**0**	**0**
	Kalamazoo Wings	IHL	6	3	2	5	4																			
1994-95	**Dallas**	**NHl**	**47**	**12**	**10**	**22**	**26**	**5**	**0**	**3**	**91**	**13.2**	**-2**						**5**	**1**	**0**	**1**	**0**	**1**	**0**	**0**
1995-96	**Dallas**	**NHL**	**22**	**4**	**4**	**8**	**23**	**0**	**0**	**1**	**37**	**10.8**	**0**													
	Michigan K-Wings	IHL	2	1	2	3	5																			
	Philadelphia	**NHL**	**49**	**3**	**8**	**11**	**21**	**0**	**0**	**1**	**64**	**4.7**	**2**						**12**	**4**	**1**	**5**	**0**	**0**	**0**	**0**
1996-97	**Philadelphia**	**NHL**	**76**	**24**	**21**	**45**	**20**	**5**	**5**	**5**	**131**	**18.3**	**9**						**19**	**4**	**3**	**7**	**12**	**0**	**0**	**2**
1997-98	**Philadelphia**	**NHL**	**82**	**14**	**28**	**42**	**16**	**5**	**0**	**3**	**143**	**9.8**	**2**						**5**	**0**	**0**	**0**	**0**	**0**	**0**	**0**
1998-99	**Philadelphia**	**NHL**	**2**	**0**	**0**	**0**	**0**	**0**	**0**	**0**	**2**	**0.0**	**0**	**0**	**0.0**	**3**	**2**	**11:11**								
	Vancouver	**NHL**	**73**	**4**	**10**	**14**	**12**	**0**	**0**	**0**	**58**	**6.9**	**-3**	**37**	**32.4**	**73**	**29**	**11:21**								
99-2000	**Vancouver**	**NHL**	**47**	**10**	**10**	**20**	**26**	**8**	**0**	**0**	**100**	**10.0**	**-8**	**19**	**63.2**	**129**	**14**	**16:04**								
	Syracuse Crunch	AHL	24	13	10	23	6																			
2000-01	**Vancouver**	**NHL**	**77**	**13**	**20**	**33**	**31**	**3**	**0**	**1**	**140**	**9.3**	**8**	**75**	**50.7**	**148**	**26**	**13:33**	**4**	**3**	**0**	**3**	**0**	**2**	**0**	**0**
	NHL Totals		**584**	**102**	**154**	**256**	**243**	**30**	**5**	**16**	**922**	**11.1**		**131**	**47.3**	**353**	**71**	**13:19**	**60**	**14**	**5**	**19**	**18**	**4**	**0**	**2**

Minnesota High School Player of the Year (1989)

Traded to **Minnesota** by **Washington** with Steve Maltais for Shawn Chambers, June 21, 1991. Transferred to **Dallas** after **Minnesota** franchise relocated, June 9, 1993. Traded to **Philadelphia** by **Dallas** for Brent Fedyk, December 13, 1995. Traded to **Vancouver** by **Philadelphia** for Vancouver's 6th round choice (later traded to Atlanta - Atlanta selected Jeff Dwyer) in 2000 Entry Draft, October 19, 1998.

KLEE, Ken
(KLEE, KEHN) **WSH.**

Defense. Shoots right. 6'1", 212 lbs. Born, Indianapolis, IN, April 24, 1971. Washington's 11th choice, 177th overall, in 1990 Entry Draft.

Season	Club	League	Regular Season GP	G	A	Pts	PIM	PP	SH	GW	S	%	+/-	TF	F%	H	SB	Min	Playoffs GP	G	A	Pts	PIM	PP	SH	GW
1988-89	St. Michael's	MTJHL	40	9	23	32	64	....	....	....	....	....	....	....	....	....	....	....	27	5	12	17	54	....	....	....
1989-90	Bowling Green	CCHA	39	0	5	5	52	....	....	....	....	....	....	....	....	....	....	....	....	....	....	....	....	....	....	....
1990-91	Bowling Green	CCHA	37	7	28	35	50	....	....	....	....	....	....	....	....	....	....	....	....	....	....	....	....	....	....	....
1991-92	Bowling Green	CCHA	10	0	1	1	14	....	....	....	....	....	....	....	....	....	....	....	....	....	....	....	....	....	....	....
1992-93	Baltimore	AHL	77	4	14	18	93	....	....	....	....	....	....	....	....	....	....	....	7	0	1	1	15	....	....	....
1993-94	Portland Pirates	AHL	65	2	9	11	87	....	....	....	....	....	....	....	....	....	....	....	17	1	2	3	14	....	....	....
1994-95	Portland Pirates	AHL	49	5	7	12	89	....	....	....	....	....	....	....	....	....	....	....	....	....	....	....	....	....	....	....
	Washington	NHL	23	3	1	4	41	0	0	0	18	16.7	2	....	....	....	....	....	7	0	0	0	4	0	0	0
1995-96	Washington	NHL	66	8	3	11	60	0	1	2	76	10.5	−1	....	....	....	....	....	1	0	0	0	0	0	0	0
1996-97	Washington	NHL	80	3	8	11	115	0	0	2	108	2.8	−5	....	....	....	....	....	....	....	....	....	....	....	....	....
1997-98	Washington	NHL	51	4	2	6	46	0	0	1	44	9.1	−3	....	....	....	....	....	9	1	0	1	10	0	0	0
1998-99	Washington	NHL	78	7	13	20	80	0	0	1	132	5.3	−9	0	0.0	248	71	19:07	....	....	....	....	....	....	....	....
99-2000	Washington	NHL	80	7	13	20	79	0	0	2	113	6.2	8	0	0.0	307	134	20:29	5	0	1	1	10	0	0	0
2000-01	Washington	NHL	54	2	4	6	60	0	0	0	58	3.4	−5	0	0.0	127	40	17:15	6	0	1	1	8	0	0	0
	NHL Totals		432	34	44	78	481	0	1	8	549	6.2		0	0.0	682	245	19:09	28	1	2	3	32	0	0	0

KLEMM, Jon
(KLEHM, JAWN) **CHI.**

Defense. Shoots right. 6'2", 200 lbs. Born, Cranbrook, B.C., January 8, 1970.

Season	Club	League	Regular Season GP	G	A	Pts	PIM	PP	SH	GW	S	%	+/-	TF	F%	H	SB	Min	Playoffs GP	G	A	Pts	PIM	PP	SH	GW
1986-87	Cranbrook Colts	KIJHL	59	20	51	71	54	....	....	....	....	....	....	....	....	....	....	....	....	....	....	....	....	....	....	....
1987-88	Seattle T-Birds	WHL	68	6	7	13	24	....	....	....	....	....	....	....	....	....	....	....	....	....	....	....	....	....	....	....
1988-89	Seattle T-Birds	WHL	2	1	1	2	0	....	....	....	....	....	....	....	....	....	....	....	....	....	....	....	....	....	....	....
	Spokane Chiefs	WHL	66	6	34	40	42	....	....	....	....	....	....	....	....	....	....	....	....	....	....	....	....	....	....	....
1989-90	Spokane Chiefs	WHL	66	3	28	31	100	....	....	....	....	....	....	....	....	....	....	....	6	1	1	2	5	....	....	....
1990-91	Spokane Chiefs	WHL	72	7	58	65	65	....	....	....	....	....	....	....	....	....	....	....	15	3	6	9	8	....	....	....
1991-92	Quebec	NHL	4	0	1	1	0	0	0	0	2	0.0	2	....	....	....	....	....	....	....	....	....	....	....	....	....
	Halifax Citadels	AHL	70	6	13	19	40	....	....	....	....	....	....	....	....	....	....	....	....	....	....	....	....	....	....	....
1992-93	Halifax Citadels	AHL	80	3	20	23	32	....	....	....	....	....	....	....	....	....	....	....	....	....	....	....	....	....	....	....
1993-94	Quebec	NHL	7	0	0	0	4	0	0	0	11	0.0	−1	....	....	....	....	....	....	....	....	....	....	....	....	....
	Cornwall Aces	AHL	66	4	26	30	78	....	....	....	....	....	....	....	....	....	....	....	13	1	2	3	6	....	....	....
1994-95	Cornwall Aces	AHL	65	6	13	19	84	....	....	....	....	....	....	....	....	....	....	....	....	....	....	....	....	....	....	....
	Quebec	NHL	4	1	0	1	2	0	0	0	5	20.0	3	....	....	....	....	....	....	....	....	....	....	....	....	....
1995-96♦	Colorado	NHL	56	3	12	15	20	0	1	1	61	4.9	12	....	....	....	....	....	15	2	1	3	0	1	0	0
1996-97	Colorado	NHL	80	9	15	24	37	1	2	1	103	8.7	12	....	....	....	....	....	17	1	1	2	6	0	0	0
1997-98	Colorado	NHL	67	6	8	14	30	0	0	0	60	10.0	−3	....	....	....	....	....	4	0	0	0	0	0	0	0
1998-99	Colorado	NHL	39	1	2	3	31	0	0	0	28	3.6	4	14	35.7	38	21	13:43	19	0	1	1	10	0	0	0
99-2000	Colorado	NHL	73	5	7	12	34	0	0	0	64	7.8	26	17	47.1	129	80	17:22	17	2	1	3	9	0	0	0
2000-01♦	Colorado	NHL	78	4	11	15	54	2	0	2	97	4.1	22	1	100.0	175	92	19:56	22	1	2	3	16	0	0	1
	NHL Totals		408	29	56	85	212	3	3	4	431	6.7		32	43.8	342	193	17:40	94	6	6	12	41	1	0	1

WHL West Second All-Star Team (1991)

Signed as a free agent by **Quebec**, May 14, 1991. Transferred to **Colorado** after **Quebec** franchise relocated, June 21, 1995. • Missed majority of 1998-99 season recovering from knee injury suffered in game vs. Phoenix, November 10, 1998. Signed as a free agent by **Chicago**, July 1, 2001.

KLESLA, Rostislav
(KLEHS-luh, RAHS-tih-slav) **CBJ**

Defense. Shoots left. 6'2", 198 lbs. Born, Novy Jicin, Czech., March 21, 1982. Columbus' 1st choice, 4th overall, in 2000 Entry Draft.

Season	Club	League	Regular Season GP	G	A	Pts	PIM	PP	SH	GW	S	%	+/-	TF	F%	H	SB	Min	Playoffs GP	G	A	Pts	PIM	PP	SH	GW
1997-98	HC Opava-Jr.	Cze-Rep	38	11	18	29	87	....	....	....	....	....	....	....	....	....	....	....	8	2	2	4	0	....	....	....
1998-99	Sioux City	USHL	54	4	12	16	100	....	....	....	....	....	....	....	....	....	....	....	5	2	0	2	2	....	....	....
99-2000	Brampton	OHL	67	16	29	45	174	....	....	....	....	....	....	....	....	....	....	....	6	1	1	2	21	....	....	....
2000-01	Columbus	NHL	8	2	0	2	6	0	0	0	10	20.0	−1	0	0.0	7	9	18:25	....	....	....	....	....	....	....	....
	Brampton	OHL	45	18	36	54	59	....	....	....	....	....	....	....	....	....	....	....	9	2	9	11	26	....	....	....
	NHL Totals		8	2	0	2	6	0	0	0	10	20.0		0	0.0	7	9	18:25	....	....	....	....	....	....	....	....

OHL All-Rookie Team (2000) • Canadian Major Junior All-Rookie Team (2000) • OHL First All-Star Team (2001)

Returned to **Brampton** (OHL) by **Columbus**, October 28, 2000.

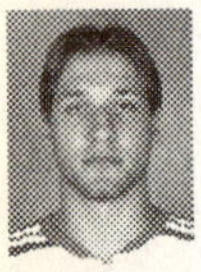

KLOUCEK, Tomas
(KLOH-chehk, TAW-mahsh) **NYR**

Defense. Shoots left. 6'3", 203 lbs. Born, Prague, Czech., March 7, 1980. NY Rangers' 6th choice, 131st overall, in 1998 Entry Draft.

Season	Club	League	Regular Season GP	G	A	Pts	PIM	PP	SH	GW	S	%	+/-	TF	F%	H	SB	Min	Playoffs GP	G	A	Pts	PIM	PP	SH	GW
1995-96	Slavia Praha-Jr.	Cze-Rep	40	2	8	10	....	....	....	....	....	....	....	....	....	....	....	....	....	....	....	....	....	....	....	....
1996-97	Slavia Praha-Jr.	Cze-Rep	43	4	14	18	44	....	....	....	....	....	....	....	....	....	....	....	....	....	....	....	....	....	....	....
1997-98	Slavia Praha-Jr.	Cze-Rep	43	1	9	10	....	....	....	....	....	....	....	....	....	....	....	....	....	....	....	....	....	....	....	....
1998-99	Cape Breton	QMJHL	59	4	17	21	162	....	....	....	....	....	....	....	....	....	....	....	2	0	0	0	4	....	....	....
99-2000	Hartford	AHL	73	2	8	10	113	....	....	....	....	....	....	....	....	....	....	....	23	0	4	4	18	....	....	....
2000-01	NY Rangers	NHL	43	1	4	5	74	0	0	0	22	4.5	−3	0	0.0	127	53	16:43	....	....	....	....	....	....	....	....
	Hartford	AHL	21	0	2	2	44	....	....	....	....	....	....	....	....	....	....	....	....	....	....	....	....	....	....	....
	NHL Totals		43	1	4	5	74	0	0	0	22	4.5		0	0.0	127	53	16:43								

KNUBLE, Mike
(kuh-NOO-buhl, MIGHK) **BOS.**

Right wing. Shoots right. 6'3", 208 lbs. Born, Toronto, Ont., July 4, 1972. Detroit's 4th choice, 76th overall, in 1991 Entry Draft.

Season	Club	League	Regular Season GP	G	A	Pts	PIM	PP	SH	GW	S	%	+/-	TF	F%	H	SB	Min	Playoffs GP	G	A	Pts	PIM	PP	SH	GW
1988-89	East Kentwood	Hi-School	28	52	37	89	60	....	....	....	....	....	....	....	....	....	....	....	....	....	....	....	....	....	....	....
1989-90	East Kentwood	Hi-School	29	63	40	103	40	....	....	....	....	....	....	....	....	....	....	....	....	....	....	....	....	....	....	....
1990-91	Kalamazoo	NAJHL	36	18	24	42	30	....	....	....	....	....	....	....	....	....	....	....	....	....	....	....	....	....	....	....
1991-92	U. of Michigan	CCHA	43	7	8	15	48	....	....	....	....	....	....	....	....	....	....	....	....	....	....	....	....	....	....	....
1992-93	U. of Michigan	CCHA	39	26	16	42	57	....	....	....	....	....	....	....	....	....	....	....	....	....	....	....	....	....	....	....
1993-94	U. of Michigan	CCHA	41	32	26	58	71	....	....	....	....	....	....	....	....	....	....	....	....	....	....	....	....	....	....	....
1994-95	U. of Michigan	CCHA	34	*38	22	60	62	....	....	....	....	....	....	....	....	....	....	....	....	....	....	....	....	....	....	....
	Adirondack	AHL	....	....	....	....	....	....	....	....	....	....	....	....	....	....	....	....	3	0	0	0	0	....	....	....
1995-96	Adirondack	AHL	80	22	23	45	59	....	....	....	....	....	....	....	....	....	....	....	3	1	0	1	0	....	....	....
1996-97	Detroit	NHL	9	1	0	1	0	0	0	0	10	10.0	−1	....	....	....	....	....	....	....	....	....	....	....	....	....
	Adirondack	AHL	68	28	35	63	54	....	....	....	....	....	....	....	....	....	....	....	....	....	....	....	....	....	....	....
1997-98♦	Detroit	NHL	53	7	6	13	16	0	0	0	54	13.0	2	....	....	....	....	....	3	0	1	1	0	0	0	0
1998-99	NY Rangers	NHL	82	15	20	35	26	3	0	1	113	13.3	−7	1	100.0	180	32	14:52	....	....	....	....	....	....	....	....
99-2000	NY Rangers	NHL	59	9	5	14	18	1	0	1	50	18.0	−5	9	55.6	101	18	10:39	....	....	....	....	....	....	....	....
	Boston	NHL	14	3	3	6	8	1	0	1	28	10.7	−2	3	0.0	25	8	19:29	....	....	....	....	....	....	....	....
2000-01	Boston	NHL	82	7	13	20	37	0	1	1	92	7.6	0	115	31.3	167	28	10:34	....	....	....	....	....	....	....	....
	NHL Totals		299	42	47	89	105	5	1	4	347	12.1		128	32.8	473	86	12:36	3	0	1	1	0	0	0	0

CCHA Second All-Star Team (1994, 1995) • NCAA West Second All-American Team (1995)

Traded to **NY Rangers** by **Detroit** for NY Rangers' 2nd round choice (Tomas Kopecky) in 2000 Entry Draft, October 1, 1998. Traded to **Boston** by **NY Rangers** for Rob DiMaio, March 10, 2000.

KNUTSEN, Espen
(kuh-NOOT-suhn, EHS-pehn) **CBJ**

Center. Shoots left. 5'11", 180 lbs. Born, Oslo, Norway, January 12, 1972. Hartford's 9th choice, 204th overall, in 1990 Entry Draft.

Season	Club	League	Regular Season GP	G	A	Pts	PIM	PP	SH	GW	S	%	+/-	TF	F%	H	SB	Min	Playoffs GP	G	A	Pts	PIM	PP	SH	GW
1988-89	Valerengen IF	Norge-Jr.	36	14	7	21	18	....	....	....	....	....	....	....	....	....	....	....	....	....	....	....	....	....	....	....
1989-90	Valerengen IF	Norway	40	25	28	53	44	....	....	....	....	....	....	....	....	....	....	....	....	....	....	....	....	....	....	....
1990-91	Valerengen IF	Norway	31	30	24	54	42	....	....	....	....	....	....	....	....	....	....	....	5	3	4	7	....	....	....	....
1991-92	Valerengen IF	Norway	30	28	26	54	37	....	....	....	....	....	....	....	....	....	....	....	8	7	8	15	....	....	....	....
1992-93	Valerengen IF	Norway	13	11	13	24	4	....	....	....	....	....	....	....	....	....	....	....	....	....	....	....	....	....	....	....
1993-94	Valerengen IF	Norway	38	32	26	58	20	....	....	....	....	....	....	....	....	....	....	....	....	....	....	....	....	....	....	....
	Norway	Olympics	7	1	3	4	2	....	....	....	....	....	....	....	....	....	....	....	....	....	....	....	....	....	....	....
1994-95	Djurgardens IF	Sweden	30	6	14	20	18	....	....	....	....	....	....	....	....	....	....	....	3	0	1	1	0	....	....	....
1995-96	Djurgardens IF	Sweden	32	10	23	33	50	....	....	....	....	....	....	....	....	....	....	....	4	1	0	1	2	....	....	....
1996-97	Djurgardens IF	Sweden	39	16	33	49	20	....	....	....	....	....	....	....	....	....	....	....	4	2	4	6	6	....	....	....
1997-98	Anaheim	NHL	19	3	0	3	6	1	0	0	21	14.3	−10	....	....	....	....	....	....	....	....	....	....	....	....	....
	Cincinnati Ducks	AHL	41	4	13	17	18	....	....	....	....	....	....	....	....	....	....	....	....	....	....	....	....	....	....	....

			Regular Season																Playoffs							
Season	Club	League	GP	G	A	Pts	PIM	PP	SH	GW	S	%	+/-	TF	F%	H	SB	Min	GP	G	A	Pts	PIM	PP	SH	GW
1998-99	Djurgardens IF	Sweden	39	18	24	42	32												4	0	1	1	2			
	Djurgardens IF	EuroHL	4	2	2	4	2																			
99-2000	Djurgardens IF	Sweden	48	18	35	53	65												13	5	*16	*21	2			
2000-01	**Columbus**	**NHL**	**66**	**11**	**42**	**53**	**30**	**2**	**0**	**0**	**62**	**17.7**	**–3**	**125**	**52.8**	**57**	**27**	**15:59**								
	NHL Totals		**85**	**14**	**42**	**56**	**36**	**3**	**0**	**0**	**83**	**16.9**		**125**	**52.8**	**57**	**27**	**15:59**								

Rights traded to **Anaheim** by **Hartford** for Kevin Brown, October 1, 1996. Traded to **Columbus** by **Anaheim** for Columbus' 4th round choice (Anaheim selected Vladmir Korsunov) in 2001 Entry Draft, May 25, 2000.

KOEHLER, Greg

(KOH-luhr, GREHG) **CAR.**

Center. Shoots left. 6'2", 195 lbs. Born, Scarborough, Ont., February 27, 1975.

Season	Club	League	GP	G	A	Pts	PIM	PP	SH	GW	S	%	+/-	TF	F%	H	SB	Min	GP	G	A	Pts	PIM	PP	SH	GW
1992-93	Niagara Falls	OJHL-B	40	24	19	43	125																			
1993-94	North York	MTJHL	49	27	47	74	179																			
1994-95	North York	MTJHL	47	28	43	71	126																			
1995-96	Brampton	MTJHL	49	33	64	97	87																			
1996-97	U. Mass-Lowell	H-East	37	16	20	36	49																			
1997-98	U. Mass-Lowell	H-East	33	20	17	37	62																			
	New Haven	AHL	3	0	0	0	2																			
1998-99	New Haven	AHL	26	4	0	4	29																			
	Florida Everblades	ECHL	29	13	14	27	62												6	2	3	5	12			
99-2000	Cincinnati	IHL	74	12	13	25	157												8	0	3	3	14			
2000-01	Cincinnati	IHL	80	35	36	71	122												5	2	2	4	6			
	Carolina	**NHL**	**1**	**0**	**0**	**0**	**0**	**0**	**0**	**0**	**0**	**0.0**	**0**	**0**	**0.0**	**0**	**0**	**0:46**								
	NHL Totals		**1**	**0**	**0**	**0**	**0**	**0**	**0**	**0**	**0**	**0.0**		**0**	**0.0**	**0**	**0**	**0:46**								

Hockey East Rookie of the Year (1997) • Hockey East All-Rookie Team (1997) • IHL Second All-Star Team (2001)

Signed as a free agent by **Carolina**, March 31, 1998.

KOHN, Ladislav

(KOHN, LA-dih-slahf)

Right wing. Shoots left. 5'11", 194 lbs. Born, Uherske Hradiste, Czech., March 4, 1975. Calgary's 9th choice, 175th overall, in 1994 Entry Draft.

Season	Club	League	GP	G	A	Pts	PIM	PP	SH	GW	S	%	+/-	TF	F%	H	SB	Min	GP	G	A	Pts	PIM	PP	SH	GW
1993-94	Brandon	WHL	2	0	0	0	0																			
	Swift Current	WHL	69	33	35	68	68												7	5	4	9	8			
1994-95	Swift Current	WHL	65	32	60	92	122												6	2	6	8	14			
	Saint John Flames	AHL	1	0	0	0	0																			
1995-96	**Calgary**	**NHL**	**5**	**1**	**0**	**1**	**2**	**0**	**0**	**0**	**8**	**12.5**	**–1**													
	Saint John Flames	AHL	73	28	45	73	97												16	6	5	11	12			
1996-97	Saint John Flames	AHL	76	28	29	57	81												5	0	0	0	0			
1997-98	**Calgary**	**NHL**	**4**	**0**	**1**	**1**	**0**	**0**	**0**	**0**	**2**	**0.0**	**2**													
	Saint John Flames	AHL	65	25	31	56	90												21	14	6	20	20			
1998-99	**Toronto**	**NHL**	**16**	**1**	**3**	**4**	**4**	**0**	**0**	**0**	**23**	**4.3**	**1**	**16**	**18.8**	**15**	**3**	**12:34**	**2**	**0**	**0**	**0**	**5**	**0**	**0**	**0**
	St. John's Leafs	AHL	61	27	42	69	90																			
99-2000	**Anaheim**	**NHL**	**77**	**5**	**16**	**21**	**27**	**1**	**0**	**1**	**123**	**4.1**	**–17**	**15**	**33.3**	**121**	**16**	**12:06**								
2000-01	**Anaheim**	**NHL**	**51**	**4**	**3**	**7**	**42**	**0**	**1**	**0**	**86**	**4.7**	**–15**	**45**	**26.7**	**68**	**18**	**10:59**								
	Atlanta	**NHL**	**26**	**3**	**4**	**7**	**44**	**0**	**1**	**0**	**43**	**7.0**	**–12**	**16**	**37.5**	**33**	**14**	**13:38**								
	NHL Totals		**179**	**14**	**27**	**41**	**119**	**1**	**2**	**1**	**285**	**4.9**		**92**	**28.3**	**237**	**51**	**12:03**	**2**	**0**	**0**	**0**	**5**	**0**	**0**	**0**

Traded to **Toronto** by **Calgary** for David Cooper, July 2, 1998. Claimed by **Atlanta** from **Toronto** in Waiver Draft, September 27, 1999. Traded to **Anaheim** by **Atlanta** for Anaheim's 8th round choice (Evan Nielsen) in 2000 Entry Draft, September 27, 1999. Traded to **Atlanta** by **Anaheim** for Sergei Vyshedkevich and Scott Langkow, February 9, 2001.

KOIVU, Saku

(KOI-voo, SA-koo) **MTL.**

Center. Shoots left. 5'10", 180 lbs. Born, Turku, Finland, November 23, 1974. Montreal's 1st choice, 21st overall, in 1993 Entry Draft.

Season	Club	League	GP	G	A	Pts	PIM	PP	SH	GW	S	%	+/-	TF	F%	H	SB	Min	GP	G	A	Pts	PIM	PP	SH	GW
1990-91	TPS Turku-B	Finn-Jr.	24	20	28	48	26																			
1991-92	TPS Turku-B	Finn-Jr.	12	3	7	10	6																			
	TPS Turku	Finn-Jr.	34	25	28	53	57												8	5	*9	*14	6			
1992-93	TPS Turku	Finland	46	3	7	10	28												11	3	2	5	2			
1993-94	TPS Turku	Finland	47	23	30	53	42												11	4	8	12	16			
	Finland	Olympics	8	4	3	7	12																			
1994-95	TPS Turku	Finland	45	27	*47	*74	73												13	*7	10	17	16			
1995-96	**Montreal**	**NHL**	**82**	**20**	**25**	**45**	**40**	**8**	**3**	**2**	**136**	**14.7**	**–7**						**6**	**3**	**1**	**4**	**8**	**0**	**0**	**0**
1996-97	**Montreal**	**NHL**	**50**	**17**	**39**	**56**	**38**	**5**	**0**	**3**	**135**	**12.6**	**7**						**5**	**1**	**3**	**4**	**10**	**0**	**0**	**0**
1997-98	**Montreal**	**NHL**	**69**	**14**	**43**	**57**	**48**	**2**	**2**	**3**	**145**	**9.7**	**8**						**6**	**2**	**3**	**5**	**2**	**1**	**0**	**0**
	Finland	Olympics	6	2	*8	*10	4																			
1998-99	**Montreal**	**NHL**	**65**	**14**	**30**	**44**	**38**	**4**	**2**	**0**	**145**	**9.7**	**–7**	**1427**	**52.6**	**53**	**12**	**20:02**								
99-2000	**Montreal**	**NHL**	**24**	**3**	**18**	**21**	**14**	**1**	**0**	**0**	**53**	**5.7**	**7**	**495**	**52.9**	**21**	**3**	**19:13**								
2000-01	**Montreal**	**NHL**	**54**	**17**	**30**	**47**	**40**	**7**	**0**	**3**	**113**	**15.0**	**2**	**1092**	**47.6**	**44**	**12**	**21:23**								
	NHL Totals		**344**	**85**	**185**	**270**	**218**	**27**	**7**	**11**	**727**	**11.7**		**3014**	**50.9**	**118**	**27**	**20:24**	**17**	**6**	**7**	**13**	**20**	**1**	**0**	**0**

Played in NHL All-Star Game (1998) • Missed majority of 1999-2000 season recovering from shoulder injury suffered in game vs. NY Rangers, October 30, 1999.

KOLARIK, Pavel

(koh-LAHR-ihk, PAH-vehl) **BOS.**

Defense. Shoots left. 6'1", 207 lbs. Born, Vyskov, Czech., October 24, 1972. Boston's 11th choice, 268th overall, in 2000 Entry Draft.

Season	Club	League	GP	G	A	Pts	PIM	PP	SH	GW	S	%	+/-	TF	F%	H	SB	Min	GP	G	A	Pts	PIM	PP	SH	GW
1994-95	HC Beroun-2	Cze-Rep	STATISTICS NOT AVAILABLE																							
	HC Poldi Kladno	Cze-Rep																	1	0	0	0	0			
1996-97	Slavia Praha	Cze-Rep	27	1	2	3	10												3	0	0	0	2			
1997-98	Slavia Praha	Cze-Rep	51	0	4	4	24												5	0	0	0	2			
1998-99	Slavia Praha	Cze-Rep	51	1	8	9	44																			
99-2000	Slavia Praha	Cze-Rep	52	5	3	8	38																			
2000-01	**Boston**	**NHL**	**10**	**0**	**0**	**0**	**4**	**0**	**0**	**0**	**1**	**0.0**	**–2**	**0**	**0.0**	**7**	**3**	**8:49**								
	Providence Bruins	AHL	51	5	6	11	14												17	0	4	4	4			
	NHL Totals		**10**	**0**	**0**	**0**	**4**	**0**	**0**	**0**	**1**	**0.0**		**0**	**0.0**	**7**	**3**	**8:49**								

KOLNIK, Juraj

(KOHL-nihk, YEW-igh) **NYI**

Right wing. Shoots right. 5'10", 182 lbs. Born, Nitra, Czech., November 13, 1980. NY Islanders' 7th choice, 101st overall, in 1999 Entry Draft.

Season	Club	League	GP	G	A	Pts	PIM	PP	SH	GW	S	%	+/-	TF	F%	H	SB	Min	GP	G	A	Pts	PIM	PP	SH	GW
1997-98	MHC Nitra	Slovak-Jr.	26	28	16	44	50																			
	MHC Nitra	Slovakia	28	1	3	4	6																			
1998-99	Quebec Remparts	QMJHL	12	6	5	11	6																			
	Rimouski Oceanic	QMJHL	50	36	37	73	34												11	9	6	15	6			
99-2000	Rimouski Oceanic	QMJHL	47	53	53	106	53												14	10	17	27	16			
2000-01	Lowell	AHL	25	2	6	8	18																			
	NY Islanders	**NHL**	**29**	**4**	**3**	**7**	**12**	**0**	**0**	**0**	**38**	**10.5**	**–8**	**1**	**100.0**	**49**	**6**	**10:28**								
	Springfield	AHL	29	15	20	35	20																			
	NHL Totals		**29**	**4**	**3**	**7**	**12**	**0**	**0**	**0**	**38**	**10.5**		**1**	**100.0**	**49**	**6**	**10:28**								

Memorial Cup All-Star Team (2000)

KOMARNISKI, Zenith

(KOH-mahr-NIHS-kee, ZEE-nihth) **VAN.**

Defense. Shoots left. 6', 200 lbs. Born, Edmonton, Alta., August 13, 1978. Vancouver's 2nd choice, 75th overall, in 1996 Entry Draft.

Season	Club	League	GP	G	A	Pts	PIM	PP	SH	GW	S	%	+/-	TF	F%	H	SB	Min	GP	G	A	Pts	PIM	PP	SH	GW
1993-94	Ft-Saskatchewan	AAHA	32	14	32	46	42																			
1994-95	Tri-City Americans	WHL	66	5	19	24	110												17	1	2	3	47			
1995-96	Tri-City Americans	WHL	42	5	21	26	85																			
1996-97	Tri-City Americans	WHL	58	12	44	56	112																			
1997-98	Tri-City Americans	WHL	3	0	4	4	18																			
	Spokane Chiefs	WHL	43	7	20	27	90												18	4	6	10	49			
1998-99	Syracuse Crunch	AHL	58	9	19	28	89																			

			Regular Season																Playoffs							
Season	Club	League	GP	G	A	Pts	PIM	PP	SH	GW	S	%	+/-	TF	F%	H	SB	Min	GP	G	A	Pts	PIM	PP	SH	GW
99-2000	**Vancouver**	**NHL**	**18**	**1**	**1**	**2**	**8**	**0**	**0**	**0**	**21**	**4.8**	**–1**	**0**	**0.0**	**40**	**29**	**16:11**	....	....	....	....	....	....	....	....
	Syracuse Crunch	AHL	42	4	12	16	130	....	....	....	....	....	....	....	....	....	....	....	4	2	0	2	6	....	....	....
2000-01	Kansas City	IHL	70	7	22	29	191	....	....	....	....	....	....	....	....	....	....	....	....	....	....	....	....	....	....	....
	NHL Totals		**18**	**1**	**1**	**2**	**8**	**0**	**0**	**0**	**21**	**4.8**		**0**	**0.0**	**40**	**29**	**16:11**	....	....	....	....	....	....	....	....

WHL West First All-Star Team (1997)

KONOWALCHUK, Steve (kahn-uh-WAHL-chuhk, STEEV) WSH.

Center. Shoots left. 6'1", 207 lbs. Born, Salt Lake City, UT, November 11, 1972. Washington's 5th choice, 58th overall, in 1991 Entry Draft.

1989-90	Prince Albert	SMHL	36	30	28	58	22	....	....	....	....	....	....	....	....	....	....	....	....	....	....	....	....	....	....	....
1990-91	Portland	WHL	72	43	49	92	78	....	....	....	....	....	....	....	....	....	....	....	....	....	....	....	....	....	....	....
1991-92	Portland	WHL	64	51	53	104	95	....	....	....	....	....	....	....	....	....	....	....	6	3	6	9	12	....	....	....
	Washington	**NHL**	**1**	**0**	**0**	**0**	**0**	**0**	**0**	**0**	**1**	**0.0**	**0**	....	....	....	....	....	....	....	....	....	....	....	....	....
	Baltimore	AHL	3	1	1	2	0	....	....	....	....	....	....	....	....	....	....	....	....	....	....	....	....	....	....	....
1992-93	**Washington**	**NHL**	**36**	**4**	**7**	**11**	**16**	**1**	**0**	**1**	**34**	**11.8**	**4**	....	....	....	....	....	**2**	**0**	**1**	**1**	**0**	**0**	**0**	**0**
	Baltimore	AHL	37	18	28	46	74	....	....	....	....	....	....	....	....	....	....	....	....	....	....	....	....	....	....	....
1993-94	**Washington**	**NHL**	**62**	**12**	**14**	**26**	**33**	**0**	**0**	**0**	**63**	**19.0**	**9**	....	....	....	....	....	**11**	**0**	**1**	**1**	**10**	**0**	**0**	**0**
	Portland Pirates	AHL	8	11	4	15	4	....	....	....	....	....	....	....	....	....	....	....	....	....	....	....	....	....	....	....
1994-95	**Washington**	**NHL**	**46**	**11**	**14**	**25**	**44**	**3**	**3**	**3**	**88**	**12.5**	**7**	....	....	....	....	....	**7**	**2**	**5**	**7**	**12**	**0**	**1**	**0**
1995-96	**Washington**	**NHL**	**70**	**23**	**22**	**45**	**92**	**7**	**1**	**3**	**197**	**11.7**	**13**	....	....	....	....	....	**2**	**0**	**2**	**2**	**0**	**0**	**0**	**0**
1996-97	**Washington**	**NHL**	**78**	**17**	**25**	**42**	**67**	**2**	**1**	**3**	**155**	**11.0**	**–3**	....	....	....	....	....	....	....	....	....	....	....	....	....
1997-98	**Washington**	**NHL**	**80**	**10**	**24**	**34**	**80**	**2**	**0**	**2**	**131**	**7.6**	**9**	....	....	....	....	....	....	....	....	....	....	....	....	....
1998-99	**Washington**	**NHL**	**45**	**12**	**12**	**24**	**26**	**4**	**1**	**2**	**98**	**12.2**	**0**	**124**	**51.6**	**125**	**13**	**17:50**	....	....	....	....	....	....	....	....
99-2000	**Washington**	**NHL**	**82**	**16**	**27**	**43**	**80**	**3**	**0**	**1**	**146**	**11.0**	**19**	**147**	**49.7**	**245**	**39**	**17:36**	**5**	**1**	**0**	**1**	**2**	**0**	**1**	**0**
2000-01	**Washington**	**NHL**	**82**	**24**	**23**	**47**	**87**	**6**	**0**	**5**	**163**	**14.7**	**8**	**91**	**55.0**	**203**	**35**	**17:04**	**6**	**2**	**3**	**5**	**14**	**2**	**0**	**0**
	NHL Totals		**582**	**129**	**168**	**297**	**525**	**28**	**6**	**20**	**1076**	**12.0**		**362**	**51.7**	**573**	**87**	**17:27**	**33**	**5**	**12**	**17**	**38**	**2**	**2**	**0**

WHL First All-Star Team (1992)

KOROLEV, Evgeny (KOH-roh-lehv, ehv-GEHN-ee) NYI

Defense. Shoots left. 6'1", 186 lbs. Born, Moscow, USSR, July 24, 1978. NY Islanders' 6th choice, 182nd overall, in 1998 Entry Draft.

1995-96	Peterborough	OHL	60	2	12	14	60	....	....	....	....	....	....	....	....	....	....	....	6	0	0	0	2	....	....	....
1996-97	Peterborough	OHL	64	5	17	22	60	....	....	....	....	....	....	....	....	....	....	....	11	1	1	2	8	....	....	....
1997-98	Peterborough	OHL	37	5	21	26	39	....	....	....	....	....	....	....	....	....	....	....	....	....	....	....	....	....	....	....
	London Knights	OHL	27	4	10	14	36	....	....	....	....	....	....	....	....	....	....	....	15	2	7	9	29	....	....	....
1998-99	Roanoke	ECHL	2	0	1	1	0	....	....	....	....	....	....	....	....	....	....	....	....	....	....	....	....	....	....	....
	Lowell	AHL	54	2	6	8	48	....	....	....	....	....	....	....	....	....	....	....	2	0	1	1	0	....	....	....
99-2000	**NY Islanders**	**NHL**	**17**	**1**	**2**	**3**	**8**	**0**	**0**	**0**	**7**	**14.3**	**–10**	**0**	**0.0**	**34**	**19**	**16:12**	....	....	....	....	....	....	....	....
	Lowell	AHL	57	1	10	11	61	....	....	....	....	....	....	....	....	....	....	....	6	0	0	0	4	....	....	....
2000-01	**NY Islanders**	**NHL**	**8**	**0**	**0**	**0**	**6**	**0**	**0**	**0**	**11**	**0.0**	**0**	**0**	**0.0**	**17**	**11**	**16:40**	....	....	....	....	....	....	....	....
	Chicago Wolves	IHL	4	0	1	1	0	....	....	....	....	....	....	....	....	....	....	....	....	....	....	....	....	....	....	....
	Louisville Panthers	AHL	36	2	14	16	68	....	....	....	....	....	....	....	....	....	....	....	....	....	....	....	....	....	....	....
	NHL Totals		**25**	**1**	**2**	**3**	**14**	**0**	**0**	**0**	**18**	**5.6**		**0**	**0.0**	**51**	**30**	**16:21**	....	....	....	....	....	....	....	....

• Re-entered NHL Entry Draft. Originally NY Islanders' 9th choice, 192nd overall, in 1996 Entry Draft.

KOROLEV, Igor (KOH-roh-lehv, EE-gohr) CHI.

Center/Left wing. Shoots left. 6'1", 190 lbs. Born, Moscow, USSR, September 6, 1970. St. Louis' 1st choice, 38th overall, in 1992 Entry Draft.

1988-89	Dynamo Moscow	USSR	1	0	0	0	2	....	....	....	....	....	....	....	....	....	....	....	....	....	....	....	....	....	....	....
1989-90	Dynamo Moscow	USSR	17	3	2	5	2	....	....	....	....	....	....	....	....	....	....	....	....	....	....	....	....	....	....	....
1990-91	Dynamo Moscow	USSR	38	12	4	16	12	....	....	....	....	....	....	....	....	....	....	....	....	....	....	....	....	....	....	....
1991-92	Dynamo Moscow	CIS	39	15	12	27	16	....	....	....	....	....	....	....	....	....	....	....	....	....	....	....	....	....	....	....
1992-93	Dynamo Moscow	CIS	5	1	2	3	4	....	....	....	....	....	....	....	....	....	....	....	....	....	....	....	....	....	....	....
	St. Louis	**NHL**	**74**	**4**	**23**	**27**	**20**	**2**	**0**	**0**	**76**	**5.3**	**–1**	....	....	....	....	....	**3**	**0**	**0**	**0**	**0**	**0**	**0**	**0**
1993-94	**St. Louis**	**NHL**	**73**	**6**	**10**	**16**	**40**	**0**	**0**	**1**	**93**	**6.5**	**–12**	....	....	....	....	....	**2**	**0**	**0**	**0**	**0**	**0**	**0**	**0**
1994-95	Dynamo Moscow	CIS	13	4	6	10	18	....	....	....	....	....	....	....	....	....	....	....	....	....	....	....	....	....	....	....
	Winnipeg	**NHL**	**45**	**8**	**22**	**30**	**10**	**1**	**0**	**1**	**85**	**9.4**	**1**	....	....	....	....	....	....	....	....	....	....	....	....	....
1995-96	**Winnipeg**	**NHL**	**73**	**22**	**29**	**51**	**42**	**8**	**0**	**5**	**165**	**13.3**	**1**	....	....	....	....	....	**6**	**0**	**3**	**3**	**0**	**0**	**0**	**0**
1996-97	**Phoenix**	**NHL**	**41**	**3**	**7**	**10**	**28**	**2**	**0**	**0**	**41**	**7.3**	**–5**	....	....	....	....	....	**1**	**0**	**0**	**0**	**0**	**0**	**0**	**0**
	Michigan K-Wings	IHL	4	2	2	4	0	....	....	....	....	....	....	....	....	....	....	....	....	....	....	....	....	....	....	....
	Phoenix	IHL	4	2	6	8	4	....	....	....	....	....	....	....	....	....	....	....	....	....	....	....	....	....	....	....
1997-98	**Toronto**	**NHL**	**78**	**17**	**22**	**39**	**22**	**6**	**3**	**5**	**97**	**17.5**	**–18**	....	....	....	....	....	....	....	....	....	....	....	....	....
1998-99	**Toronto**	**NHL**	**66**	**13**	**34**	**47**	**46**	**1**	**0**	**2**	**99**	**13.1**	**11**	**973**	**42.0**	**23**	**13**	**18:06**	**1**	**0**	**0**	**0**	**0**	**0**	**0**	**0**
99-2000	**Toronto**	**NHL**	**80**	**20**	**26**	**46**	**22**	**5**	**3**	**4**	**101**	**19.8**	**12**	**964**	**41.3**	**42**	**26**	**17:56**	**12**	**0**	**4**	**4**	**6**	**0**	**0**	**0**
2000-01	**Toronto**	**NHL**	**73**	**10**	**19**	**29**	**28**	**2**	**0**	**0**	**78**	**12.8**	**3**	**569**	**42.5**	**30**	**19**	**15:41**	**11**	**0**	**0**	**0**	**0**	**0**	**0**	**0**
	NHL Totals		**603**	**103**	**192**	**295**	**258**	**27**	**6**	**18**	**835**	**12.3**		**2506**	**41.9**	**95**	**58**	**17:14**	**36**	**0**	**7**	**7**	**6**	**0**	**0**	**0**

Claimed by **Winnipeg** from **St. Louis** in NHL Waiver Draft, January 18, 1995. Transferred to **Phoenix** after **Winnipeg** franchise relocated, July 1, 1996. Signed as a free agent by **Toronto**, September 29, 1997. Traded to **Chicago** by **Toronto** for Philadelphia's 3rd round choice (previously acquired, Toronto selected Nicolas Corbeil) in 2001 Entry Draft, June 23, 2001.

KOROLYUK, Alexander (koh-roh-LYUHK, al-ehx-AN-duhr) S.J.

Right wing. Shoots left. 5'9", 195 lbs. Born, Moscow, USSR, January 15, 1976. San Jose's 6th choice, 141st overall, in 1994 Entry Draft.

1993-94	Krylja Sovetov	CIS	22	4	4	8	20	....	....	....	....	....	....	....	....	....	....	....	3	1	0	1	4	....	....	....
1994-95	Krylja Sovetov	CIS	52	16	13	29	62	....	....	....	....	....	....	....	....	....	....	....	4	1	2	3	4	....	....	....
1995-96	Krylja Sovetov	CIS	50	30	19	49	77	....	....	....	....	....	....	....	....	....	....	....	....	....	....	....	....	....	....	....
1996-97	Krylja Sovetov	Russia	17	8	5	13	46	....	....	....	....	....	....	....	....	....	....	....	....	....	....	....	....	....	....	....
	Manitoba Moose	IHL	42	20	16	36	71	....	....	....	....	....	....	....	....	....	....	....	....	....	....	....	....	....	....	....
1997-98	**San Jose**	**NHL**	**19**	**2**	**3**	**5**	**6**	**1**	**0**	**0**	**23**	**8.7**	**–5**	....	....	....	....	....	....	....	....	....	....	....	....	....
	Kentucky	AHL	44	16	23	39	96	....	....	....	....	....	....	....	....	....	....	....	3	0	0	0	0	....	....	....
1998-99	**San Jose**	**NHL**	**55**	**12**	**18**	**30**	**26**	**2**	**0**	**0**	**96**	**12.5**	**3**	**4**	**50.0**	**66**	**7**	**13:53**	**6**	**1**	**3**	**4**	**2**	**0**	**0**	**1**
	Kentucky	AHL	23	9	13	22	16	....	....	....	....	....	....	....	....	....	....	....	....	....	....	....	....	....	....	....
99-2000	**San Jose**	**NHL**	**57**	**14**	**21**	**35**	**35**	**3**	**0**	**1**	**124**	**11.3**	**4**	**1**	**100.0**	**47**	**12**	**13:36**	**9**	**0**	**3**	**3**	**6**	**0**	**0**	**0**
2000-01	Ak Bars Kazan	Russia	6	0	5	5	4	....	....	....	....	....	....	....	....	....	....	....	....	....	....	....	....	....	....	....
	San Jose	**NHL**	**70**	**12**	**13**	**25**	**41**	**3**	**0**	**1**	**140**	**8.6**	**2**	**30**	**33.3**	**49**	**10**	**11:56**	**2**	**0**	**0**	**0**	**0**	**0**	**0**	**0**
	NHL Totals		**201**	**40**	**55**	**95**	**108**	**9**	**0**	**2**	**383**	**10.4**		**35**	**37.1**	**162**	**29**	**13:03**	**17**	**1**	**6**	**7**	**8**	**0**	**0**	**1**

KOVALENKO, Andrei (koh-vah-LEHN-koh, AWN-dray)

Right wing. Shoots left. 5'10", 200 lbs. Born, Balakovo, USSR, June 7, 1970. Quebec's 6th choice, 148th overall, in 1990 Entry Draft.

1987-88	Torpedo Gorky	USSR	2	1	0	1	0	....	....	....	....	....	....	....	....	....	....	....	....	....	....	....	....	....	....	....
1988-89	SKA Kalinin	USSR-2	30	8	7	15	29	....	....	....	....	....	....	....	....	....	....	....	....	....	....	....	....	....	....	....
	CSKA Moscow	USSR	10	1	0	1	0	....	....	....	....	....	....	....	....	....	....	....	....	....	....	....	....	....	....	....
1989-90	CSKA Moscow	USSR	48	8	5	13	20	....	....	....	....	....	....	....	....	....	....	....	....	....	....	....	....	....	....	....
1990-91	CSKA Moscow	USSR	45	13	8	21	26	....	....	....	....	....	....	....	....	....	....	....	....	....	....	....	....	....	....	....
1991-92	CSKA Moscow	CIS	44	19	13	32	32	....	....	....	....	....	....	....	....	....	....	....	....	....	....	....	....	....	....	....
	Russia	Olympics	8	1	1	2	2	....	....	....	....	....	....	....	....	....	....	....	....	....	....	....	....	....	....	....
1992-93	CSKA Moscow	CIS	3	3	1	4	4	....	....	....	....	....	....	....	....	....	....	....	....	....	....	....	....	....	....	....
	Quebec	**NHL**	**81**	**27**	**41**	**68**	**57**	**8**	**1**	**4**	**153**	**17.6**	**13**	....	....	....	....	....	**4**	**1**	**0**	**1**	**2**	**0**	**0**	**0**
1993-94	**Quebec**	**NHL**	**58**	**16**	**17**	**33**	**46**	**5**	**0**	**4**	**92**	**17.4**	**–5**	....	....	....	....	....	....	....	....	....	....	....	....	....
1994-95	Lada Togliatti	CIS	11	9	2	11	14	....	....	....	....	....	....	....	....	....	....	....	....	....	....	....	....	....	....	....
	Quebec	**NHL**	**45**	**14**	**10**	**24**	**31**	**1**	**0**	**3**	**63**	**22.2**	**–4**	....	....	....	....	....	**6**	**0**	**1**	**1**	**2**	**0**	**0**	**0**
1995-96	**Colorado**	**NHL**	**26**	**11**	**11**	**22**	**16**	**3**	**0**	**3**	**46**	**23.9**	**11**	....	....	....	....	....	....	....	....	....	....	....	....	....
	Montreal	**NHL**	**51**	**17**	**17**	**34**	**33**	**3**	**0**	**3**	**85**	**20.0**	**9**	....	....	....	....	....	**6**	**0**	**0**	**0**	**6**	**0**	**0**	**0**
1996-97	**Edmonton**	**NHL**	**74**	**32**	**27**	**59**	**81**	**14**	**0**	**2**	**163**	**19.6**	**–5**	....	....	....	....	....	**12**	**4**	**3**	**7**	**6**	**3**	**0**	**0**
1997-98	**Edmonton**	**NHL**	**59**	**6**	**17**	**23**	**28**	**1**	**0**	**2**	**89**	**6.7**	**–14**	....	....	....	....	....	**1**	**0**	**0**	**0**	**2**	**0**	**0**	**0**
	Russia	Olympics	6	4	1	5	14	....	....	....	....	....	....	....	....	....	....	....	....	....	....	....	....	....	....	....
1998-99	**Edmonton**	**NHL**	**43**	**13**	**14**	**27**	**30**	**2**	**0**	**3**	**75**	**17.3**	**–4**	**0**	**0.0**	**40**	**7**	**16:19**	....	....	....	....	....	....	....	....
	Philadelphia	**NHL**	**13**	**0**	**1**	**1**	**2**	**0**	**0**	**0**	**8**	**0.0**	**–5**	**0**	**0.0**	**12**	**1**	**8:02**	....	....	....	....	....	....	....	....
	Carolina	**NHL**	**18**	**6**	**6**	**12**	**0**	**1**	**0**	**1**	**21**	**28.6**	**3**	**1**	**0.0**	**40**	**2**	**13:53**	**4**	**0**	**2**	**2**	**2**	**0**	**0**	**0**

			Regular Season																Playoffs							
Season	Club	League	GP	G	A	Pts	PIM	PP	SH	GW	S	%	+/-	TF	F%	H	SB	Min	GP	G	A	Pts	PIM	PP	SH	GW
99-2000	Carolina	NHL	76	15	24	39	38	2	0	3	114	13.2	–13	4	75.0	143	21	14:59	....	....	....	....	....	....	....	....
2000-01	Boston	NHL	76	16	21	37	27	7	1	3	119	13.4	–14	17	29.4	123	20	15:27	....	....	....	....	....	....	....	....
	NHL Totals		620	173	206	379	389	47	2	31	1028	16.8		22	36.4	358	51	14:54	33	5	6	11	20	3	0	0

Transferred to **Colorado** after **Quebec** franchise relocated, June 21, 1995. Traded to **Montreal** by **Colorado** with Martin Rucinsky and Jocelyn Thibault for Patrick Roy and Mike Keane, December 6, 1995. Traded to **Edmonton** by **Montreal** for Scott Thornton, September 6, 1996. Traded to **Philadelphia** by **Edmonton** for Alexandre Daigle, January 29, 1999. Traded to **Carolina** by **Philadelphia** for Adam Burt, March 6, 1999. Signed as a free agent by **Boston**, July 25, 2000.

KOVALEV, Alexei (koh-VAH-lehv, al-EHX-ay) PIT.

Right wing. Shoots left. 6'1", 215 lbs. Born, Togliatti, USSR, February 24, 1973. NY Rangers' 1st choice, 15th overall, in 1991 Entry Draft.

1989-90	Dynamo Moscow	USSR	1	0	0	0	0	....	....	....	....	....	....	....	....	....	....	....	....	....	....	....	....	....	....	....
1990-91	Dynamo Moscow	USSR	18	1	2	3	4	....	....	....	....	....	....	....	....	....	....	....	....	....	....	....	....	....	....	....
1991-92	Dynamo Moscow	CIS	33	16	9	25	20	....	....	....	....	....	....	....	....	....	....	....	....	....	....	....	....	....	....	....
	Russia	Olympics	8	1	2	3	14	....	....	....	....	....	....	....	....	....	....	....	....	....	....	....	....	....	....	....
1992-93	**NY Rangers**	**NHL**	65	20	18	38	79	3	0	3	134	14.9	–10	....	....	....	....	....	....	....	....	....	....	....	....	....
	Binghamton	AHL	13	13	11	24	35	....	....	....	....	....	....	....	....	....	....	....	9	3	5	8	14	....	....	....
1993-94♦	**NY Rangers**	**NHL**	76	23	33	56	154	7	0	3	184	12.5	18	....	....	....	....	....	23	9	12	21	18	5	0	2
1994-95	Lada Togliatti	CIS	12	8	8	16	49	....	....	....	....	....	....	....	....	....	....	....	....	....	....	....	....	....	....	....
	NY Rangers	**NHL**	48	13	15	28	30	1	1	1	103	12.6	–6	....	....	....	....	....	10	4	7	11	10	0	0	0
1995-96	**NY Rangers**	**NHL**	81	24	34	58	98	8	1	7	206	11.7	5	....	....	....	....	....	11	3	4	7	14	0	0	1
1996-97	**NY Rangers**	**NHL**	45	13	22	35	42	1	0	0	110	11.8	11	....	....	....	....	....	....	....	....	....	....	....	....	....
1997-98	**NY Rangers**	**NHL**	73	23	30	53	44	8	0	3	173	13.3	–22	....	....	....	....	....	....	....	....	....	....	....	....	....
1998-99	**NY Rangers**	**NHL**	14	3	4	7	12	1	0	1	35	8.6	–6	18	44.4	13	5	19:53	....	....	....	....	....	....	....	....
	Pittsburgh	**NHL**	63	20	26	46	37	5	1	4	156	12.8	8	226	43.4	82	40	20:30	10	5	7	12	14	0	0	1
99-2000	**Pittsburgh**	**NHL**	82	26	40	66	94	9	2	4	254	10.2	–3	306	47.4	90	25	22:53	11	1	5	6	10	0	0	0
2000-01	**Pittsburgh**	**NHL**	79	44	51	95	96	12	2	9	307	14.3	12	255	40.0	104	27	23:35	18	5	5	10	16	1	0	0
	NHL Totals		626	209	273	482	686	55	7	35	1662	12.6		805	43.9	289	97	22:18	83	27	40	67	82	6	0	4

Played in NHL All-Star Game (2001)

Traded to **Pittsburgh** by **NY Rangers** with Harry York for Petr Nedved, Chris Tamer and Sean Pronger, November 25, 1998.

KOZLOV, Viktor (KAHS-lahf, VIHK-tohr) FLA.

Center. Shoots right. 6'5", 220 lbs. Born, Togliatti, USSR, February 14, 1975. San Jose's 1st choice, 6th overall, in 1993 Entry Draft.

1990-91	Lada Togliatti	USSR-2	2	2	0	2	0	....	....	....	....	....	....	....	....	....	....	....	....	....	....	....	....	....	....	....
1991-92	Lada Togliatti	CIS	3	0	0	0	0	....	....	....	....	....	....	....	....	....	....	....	....	....	....	....	....	....	....	....
1992-93	Dynamo Moscow	CIS	30	6	5	11	4	....	....	....	....	....	....	....	....	....	....	....	10	3	0	3	0	....	....	....
1993-94	Dynamo Moscow	CIS	42	16	9	25	14	....	....	....	....	....	....	....	....	....	....	....	7	3	2	5	0	....	....	....
1994-95	Dynamo Moscow	CIS	3	1	1	2	2	....	....	....	....	....	....	....	....	....	....	....	....	....	....	....	....	....	....	....
	San Jose	**NHL**	16	2	0	2	2	0	0	0	23	8.7	–5	....	....	....	....	....	....	....	....	....	....	....	....	....
	Kansas City	IHL	4	1	1	2	0	....	....	....	....	....	....	....	....	....	....	....	13	4	5	9	12	....	....	....
1995-96	**San Jose**	**NHL**	62	6	13	19	6	1	0	0	107	5.6	–15	....	....	....	....	....	....	....	....	....	....	....	....	....
	Kansas City	IHL	15	4	7	11	12	....	....	....	....	....	....	....	....	....	....	....	....	....	....	....	....	....	....	....
1996-97	**San Jose**	**NHL**	78	16	25	41	40	4	0	4	184	8.7	–16	....	....	....	....	....	....	....	....	....	....	....	....	....
1997-98	**San Jose**	**NHL**	18	5	2	7	2	2	0	0	51	9.8	–2	....	....	....	....	....	....	....	....	....	....	....	....	....
	Florida	**NHL**	46	12	11	23	14	3	2	0	114	10.5	–1	....	....	....	....	....	....	....	....	....	....	....	....	....
1998-99	**Florida**	**NHL**	65	16	35	51	24	5	1	1	209	7.7	13	985	41.2	32	30	19:03	....	....	....	....	....	....	....	....
99-2000	**Florida**	**NHL**	80	17	53	70	16	6	0	2	223	7.6	24	1616	42.9	62	33	19:27	4	0	1	1	0	0	0	0
2000-01	**Florida**	**NHL**	51	14	23	37	10	6	0	2	139	10.1	–4	817	41.6	50	22	18:23	....	....	....	....	....	....	....	....
	NHL Totals		416	88	162	250	114	27	3	9	1050	8.4		3418	42.1	144	85	19:02	4	0	1	1	0	0	0	0

Played in NHL All-Star Game (2000)

Traded to **Florida** by **San Jose** with Florida's 5th round choice (previously acquired, Florida selected Jaroslav Spacek) in 1998 Entry Draft for Dave Lowry and Florida's 1st round choice (later traded to Tampa Bay - Tampa Bay selected Vincent Lecavalier) in 1998 Entry Draft, November 13, 1997.

KOZLOV, Vyacheslav (KAHS-lahf, VYACH-ih-slav) BUF.

Center. Shoots left. 5'10", 180 lbs. Born, Voskresensk, USSR, May 3, 1972. Detroit's 2nd choice, 45th overall, in 1990 Entry Draft.

1987-88	HK Khimik	USSR	2	0	0	0	0	....	....	....	....	....	....	....	....	....	....	....	....	....	....	....	....	....	....	....
1988-89	HK Khimik	USSR	14	0	1	1	2	....	....	....	....	....	....	....	....	....	....	....	....	....	....	....	....	....	....	....
1989-90	HK Khimik	USSR	45	14	12	26	38	....	....	....	....	....	....	....	....	....	....	....	....	....	....	....	....	....	....	....
1990-91	HK Khimik	USSR	45	11	13	24	46	....	....	....	....	....	....	....	....	....	....	....	....	....	....	....	....	....	....	....
1991-92	CSKA Moscow	CIS	11	6	5	11	12	....	....	....	....	....	....	....	....	....	....	....	....	....	....	....	....	....	....	....
	Detroit	**NHL**	7	0	2	2	2	0	0	0	9	0.0	–2	....	....	....	....	....	....	....	....	....	....	....	....	....
1992-93	**Detroit**	**NHL**	17	4	1	5	14	0	0	0	26	15.4	–1	....	....	....	....	....	4	0	2	2	2	0	0	0
	Adirondack	AHL	45	23	36	59	54	....	....	....	....	....	....	....	....	....	....	....	4	1	1	2	4	....	....	....
1993-94	**Detroit**	**NHL**	77	34	39	73	50	8	2	6	202	16.8	27	....	....	....	....	....	7	2	5	7	12	0	0	0
	Adirondack	AHL	3	0	1	1	15	....	....	....	....	....	....	....	....	....	....	....	....	....	....	....	....	....	....	....
1994-95	CSKA Moscow	CIS	10	3	4	7	14	....	....	....	....	....	....	....	....	....	....	....	....	....	....	....	....	....	....	....
	Detroit	**NHL**	46	13	20	33	45	5	0	3	97	13.4	12	....	....	....	....	....	18	9	7	16	10	1	0	4
1995-96	**Detroit**	**NHL**	82	36	37	73	70	9	0	7	237	15.2	33	....	....	....	....	....	19	5	7	12	10	2	0	1
1996-97♦	**Detroit**	**NHL**	75	23	22	45	46	3	0	6	211	10.9	21	....	....	....	....	....	20	8	5	13	14	4	0	2
1997-98♦	**Detroit**	**NHL**	80	25	27	52	46	6	0	1	221	11.3	14	....	....	....	....	....	22	6	8	14	10	1	0	4
1998-99	**Detroit**	**NHL**	79	29	29	58	45	6	1	4	209	13.9	10	38	36.8	41	20	16:02	10	6	1	7	4	3	0	0
99-2000	**Detroit**	**NHL**	72	18	18	36	28	4	0	3	165	10.9	11	28	35.7	35	20	15:30	8	2	1	3	12	1	0	1
2000-01	**Detroit**	**NHL**	72	20	18	38	30	4	0	5	187	10.7	9	51	47.1	50	19	14:43	6	4	1	5	2	2	0	0
	NHL Totals		607	202	213	415	376	45	3	35	1564	12.9		117	41.0	126	59	15:26	114	42	37	79	76	14	0	12

Traded to **Buffalo** by **Detroit** with Detroit's 1st round choice in 2002 Entry Draft and future considerations for Dominik Hasek, July 1, 2001.

KRAFT, Milan (KRAFT, MIH-lan) PIT.

Center. Shoots right. 6'3", 195 lbs. Born, Plzen, Czech., January 17, 1980. Pittsburgh's 1st choice, 23rd overall, in 1998 Entry Draft.

1995-96	ZKZ Plzen-Jr.	Cze-Rep	49	54	41	95	....	....	....	....	....	....	....	....	....	....	....	....	....	....	....	....	....	....	....	....
1996-97	ZKZ Plzen-Jr.	Cze-Rep	29	24	12	36	....	....	....	....	....	....	....	....	....	....	....	....	....	....	....	....	....	....	....	....
	ZKZ Plzen	Cze-Rep	9	0	1	1	2	....	....	....	....	....	....	....	....	....	....	....	....	....	....	....	....	....	....	....
1997-98	Keramika Plzen	Cze-Rep	24	22	21	43	12	....	....	....	....	....	....	....	....	....	....	....	....	....	....	....	....	....	....	....
	Keramika Plzen	Cze-Rep	16	0	5	5	0	....	....	....	....	....	....	....	....	....	....	....	1	0	0	0	0	....	....	....
1998-99	Prince Albert	WHL	68	40	46	86	32	....	....	....	....	....	....	....	....	....	....	....	14	7	13	20	6	....	....	....
99-2000	Prince Albert	WHL	56	34	35	69	42	....	....	....	....	....	....	....	....	....	....	....	6	4	1	5	4	....	....	....
2000-01	**Pittsburgh**	**NHL**	42	7	7	14	8	1	1	1	63	11.1	–6	427	37.9	10	3	11:41	8	0	0	0	2	0	0	0
	Wilkes-Barre	AHL	40	21	23	44	27	....	....	....	....	....	....	....	....	....	....	....	14	12	7	19	6	....	....	....
	NHL Totals		42	7	7	14	8	1	1	1	63	11.1		427	37.9	10	3	11:41	8	0	0	0	2	0	0	0

KRAVCHUK, Igor (krahv-CHOOK, EE-gohr) CGY.

Defense. Shoots left. 6'1", 218 lbs. Born, Ufa, USSR, September 13, 1966. Chicago's 5th choice, 71st overall, in 1991 Entry Draft.

1984-85	Salavat Yulayev	USSR-2	50	3	2	5	22	....	....	....	....	....	....	....	....	....	....	....	....	....	....	....	....	....	....	....
1985-86	Salavat Yulayev	USSR	21	2	2	4	6	....	....	....	....	....	....	....	....	....	....	....	....	....	....	....	....	....	....	....
1986-87	Salavat Yulayev	USSR	22	0	1	1	8	....	....	....	....	....	....	....	....	....	....	....	....	....	....	....	....	....	....	....
1987-88	CSKA Moscow	USSR	48	1	8	9	12	....	....	....	....	....	....	....	....	....	....	....	....	....	....	....	....	....	....	....
	Soviet Union	Olympics	6	1	0	1	0	....	....	....	....	....	....	....	....	....	....	....	....	....	....	....	....	....	....	....
1988-89	CSKA Moscow	USSR	22	3	3	6	2	....	....	....	....	....	....	....	....	....	....	....	....	....	....	....	....	....	....	....
1989-90	CSKA Moscow	USSR	48	1	3	4	16	....	....	....	....	....	....	....	....	....	....	....	....	....	....	....	....	....	....	....
1990-91	CSKA Moscow	USSR	41	6	5	11	16	....	....	....	....	....	....	....	....	....	....	....	....	....	....	....	....	....	....	....
1991-92	CSKA Moscow	CIS	30	3	8	11	6	....	....	....	....	....	....	....	....	....	....	....	....	....	....	....	....	....	....	....
	Russia	Olympics	8	3	2	5	6	....	....	....	....	....	....	....	....	....	....	....	....	....	....	....	....	....	....	....
	Chicago	**NHL**	18	1	8	9	4	0	0	1	40	2.5	–3	....	....	....	....	....	18	2	6	8	8	1	0	0
1992-93	**Chicago**	**NHL**	38	6	9	15	30	3	0	0	101	5.9	11	....	....	....	....	....	....	....	....	....	....	....	....	....
	Edmonton	**NHL**	17	4	8	12	2	1	0	0	42	9.5	–8	....	....	....	....	....	....	....	....	....	....	....	....	....

			Regular Season																Playoffs							
Season	Club	League	GP	G	A	Pts	PIM	PP	SH	GW	S	%	+/-	TF	F%	H	SB	Min	GP	G	A	Pts	PIM	PP	SH	GW
1993-94	**Edmonton**	**NHL**	**81**	**12**	**38**	**50**	**16**	**5**	**0**	**2**	**197**	**6.1**	**–12**	....	....	....	....	....	....	....	....	....	....	....	....	....
1994-95	**Edmonton**	**NHL**	**36**	**7**	**11**	**18**	**29**	**3**	**1**	**0**	**93**	**7.5**	**–15**	....	....	....	....	....	....	....	....	....	....	....	....	....
1995-96	**Edmonton**	**NHL**	**26**	**4**	**4**	**8**	**10**	**3**	**0**	**0**	**59**	**6.8**	**–13**	....	....	....	....	....	....	....	....	....	....	....	....	....
	St. Louis	**NHL**	**40**	**3**	**12**	**15**	**24**	**0**	**0**	**1**	**114**	**2.6**	**–6**	....	....	....	....	....	**10**	**1**	**5**	**6**	**4**	**0**	**0**	**1**
1996-97	**St. Louis**	**NHL**	**82**	**4**	**24**	**28**	**35**	**1**	**0**	**0**	**142**	**2.8**	**7**	....	....	....	....	....	**2**	**0**	**0**	**0**	**2**	**0**	**0**	**0**
1997-98	**Ottawa**	**NHL**	**81**	**8**	**27**	**35**	**8**	**3**	**1**	**1**	**191**	**4.2**	**–19**	....	....	....	....	....	**11**	**2**	**3**	**5**	**4**	**0**	**0**	**0**
	Russia	Olympics	6	0	2	2	2	....	....	....	....	....	....	....	....	....	....	....	....	....	....	....	....	....	....	....
1998-99	**Ottawa**	**NHL**	**79**	**4**	**21**	**25**	**32**	**3**	**0**	**0**	**171**	**2.3**	**14**	**0**	**0.0**	**89**	**115**	**23:51**	**4**	**0**	**0**	**0**	**0**	**0**	**0**	**0**
99-2000	**Ottawa**	**NHL**	**64**	**6**	**12**	**18**	**20**	**5**	**0**	**1**	**126**	**4.8**	**–5**	**0**	**0.0**	**57**	**78**	**20:41**	**6**	**1**	**1**	**2**	**0**	**0**	**0**	**0**
2000-01	**Ottawa**	**NHL**	**15**	**1**	**5**	**6**	**14**	**0**	**0**	**1**	**13**	**7.7**	**4**	**0**	**0.0**	**11**	**14**	**20:41**	....	....	....	....	....	....	....	....
	Calgary	**NHL**	**37**	**0**	**8**	**8**	**4**	**0**	**0**	**0**	**54**	**0.0**	**–12**	**0**	**0.0**	**23**	**49**	**23:43**	....	....	....	....	....	....	....	....
	NHL Totals		**614**	**60**	**187**	**247**	**228**	**27**	**2**	**7**	**1343**	**4.5**		**0**	**0.0**	**180**	**256**	**22:33**	**51**	**6**	**15**	**21**	**18**	**1**	**0**	**1**

Played in NHL All-Star Game (1999)

Traded to **Edmonton** by **Chicago** with Dean McAmmond for Joe Murphy, February 24, 1993. Traded to **St. Louis** by **Edmonton** with Ken Sutton for Jeff Norton and Donald Dufresne, January 4, 1996. Traded to **Ottawa** by **St. Louis** for Steve Duchesne, August 25, 1997. Claimed on waivers by **Calgary** from **Ottawa**, November 10, 2000.

KRIVOKRASOV, Sergei

(krih-vuh-KRA-sahf, SAIR-gay)

Right wing. Shoots left. 5'11", 185 lbs. Born, Angarsk, USSR, April 15, 1974. Chicago's 1st choice, 12th overall, in 1992 Entry Draft.

1990-91	CSKA Moscow	USSR	41	4	0	4	8	....	....	....	....	....	....	....	....	....	....	....	....	....	....	....	....	....	....	....
1991-92	CSKA Moscow	CIS	42	10	8	18	35	....	....	....	....	....	....	....	....	....	....	....	....	....	....	....	....	....	....	....
1992-93	**Chicago**	**NHL**	**4**	**0**	**0**	**0**	**2**	**0**	**0**	**0**	**0**	**0.0**	**–2**	....	....	....	....	....	....	....	....	....	....	....	....	....
	Indianapolis Ice	IHL	78	36	33	69	157	....	....	....	....	....	....	....	....	....	....	....	5	3	1	4	2	....	....	....
1993-94	**Chicago**	**NHL**	**9**	**1**	**0**	**1**	**4**	**0**	**0**	**0**	**7**	**14.3**	**–2**	....	....	....	....	....	....	....	....	....	....	....	....	....
	Indianapolis Ice	IHL	53	19	26	45	145	....	....	....	....	....	....	....	....	....	....	....	....	....	....	....	....	....	....	....
1994-95	Indianapolis Ice	IHL	29	12	15	27	41	....	....	....	....	....	....	....	....	....	....	....	....	....	....	....	....	....	....	....
	Chicago	**NHL**	**41**	**12**	**7**	**19**	**33**	**6**	**0**	**2**	**72**	**16.7**	**9**	....	....	....	....	....	**10**	**0**	**0**	**0**	**8**	**0**	**0**	**0**
1995-96	**Chicago**	**NHL**	**46**	**6**	**10**	**16**	**32**	**0**	**0**	**1**	**52**	**11.5**	**10**	....	....	....	....	....	**5**	**1**	**0**	**1**	**2**	**0**	**0**	**1**
	Indianapolis Ice	IHL	9	4	5	9	28	....	....	....	....	....	....	....	....	....	....	....	....	....	....	....	....	....	....	....
1996-97	**Chicago**	**NHL**	**67**	**13**	**11**	**24**	**42**	**2**	**0**	**3**	**104**	**12.5**	**–1**	....	....	....	....	....	**6**	**1**	**0**	**1**	**4**	**0**	**0**	**0**
1997-98	**Chicago**	**NHL**	**58**	**10**	**13**	**23**	**33**	**1**	**0**	**2**	**127**	**7.9**	**–1**	....	....	....	....	....	....	....	....	....	....	....	....	....
	Russia	Olympics	6	0	0	0	4	....	....	....	....	....	....	....	....	....	....	....	....	....	....	....	....	....	....	....
1998-99	**Nashville**	**NHL**	**70**	**25**	**23**	**48**	**42**	**10**	**0**	**6**	**208**	**12.0**	**–5**	**0**	**0.0**	**19**	**7**	**16:08**	....	....	....	....	....	....	....	....
99-2000	**Nashville**	**NHL**	**63**	**9**	**17**	**26**	**40**	**3**	**0**	**2**	**132**	**6.8**	**–7**	**1**	**0.0**	**24**	**5**	**13:08**	....	....	....	....	....	....	....	....
	Calgary	**NHL**	**12**	**1**	**10**	**11**	**4**	**0**	**0**	**0**	**27**	**3.7**	**2**	**0**	**0.0**	**3**	**2**	**13:22**	....	....	....	....	....	....	....	....
2000-01	**Minnesota**	**NHL**	**54**	**7**	**15**	**22**	**20**	**2**	**0**	**1**	**107**	**6.5**	**–1**	**3**	**0.0**	**37**	**13**	**13:05**	....	....	....	....	....	....	....	....
	NHL Totals		**424**	**84**	**106**	**190**	**252**	**24**	**0**	**17**	**836**	**10.0**		**4**	**0.0**	**83**	**27**	**14:11**	**21**	**2**	**0**	**2**	**14**	**0**	**0**	**1**

Played in NHL All-Star Game (1999)

Traded to **Nashville** by **Chicago** for future considerations, June 26, 1998. Traded to **Calgary** by **Nashville** for Cale Hulse and Calgary's 3rd round choice (Denis Platonov) in 2001 Entry Draft, March 14, 2000. Selected by **Minnesota** from **Calgary** in Expansion Draft, June 23, 2000.

KROG, Jason

(KRAWG, JAY-suhn) **NYI**

Center. Shoots right. 5'11", 191 lbs. Born, Fernie, B.C., October 9, 1975.

1992-93	Chilliwack Chiefs	BCJHL	52	30	27	57	52	....	....	....	....	....	....	....	....	....	....	....	....	....	....	....	....	....	....	....
1993-94	Chilliwack Chiefs	BCJHL	42	19	36	55	20	....	....	....	....	....	....	....	....	....	....	....	....	....	....	....	....	....	....	....
1994-95	Chilliwack Chiefs	BCJHL	60	47	81	128	36	....	....	....	....	....	....	....	....	....	....	....	....	....	....	....	....	....	....	....
1995-96	New Hampshire	H-East	34	4	16	20	20	....	....	....	....	....	....	....	....	....	....	....	....	....	....	....	....	....	....	....
1996-97	New Hampshire	H-East	39	23	*44	*67	28	....	....	....	....	....	....	....	....	....	....	....	....	....	....	....	....	....	....	....
1997-98	New Hampshire	H-East	38	*33	33	66	44	....	....	....	....	....	....	....	....	....	....	....	....	....	....	....	....	....	....	....
1998-99	New Hampshire	H-East	41	*34	*51	*85	38	....	....	....	....	....	....	....	....	....	....	....	....	....	....	....	....	....	....	....
99-2000	**NY Islanders**	**NHL**	**17**	**2**	**4**	**6**	**6**	**1**	**0**	**0**	**22**	**9.1**	**–1**	**81**	**53.1**	**15**	**6**	**10:03**	....	....	....	....	....	....	....	....
	Lowell	AHL	45	6	21	27	22	....	....	....	....	....	....	....	....	....	....	....	....	....	....	....	....	....	....	....
	Providence Bruins	AHL	11	9	8	17	4	....	....	....	....	....	....	....	....	....	....	....	6	2	2	4	0	....	....	....
2000-01	**NY Islanders**	**NHL**	**9**	**0**	**3**	**3**	**0**	**0**	**0**	**0**	**7**	**0.0**	**4**	**60**	**48.3**	**6**	**4**	**10:32**	....	....	....	....	....	....	....	....
	Lowell	AHL	26	11	16	27	6	....	....	....	....	....	....	....	....	....	....	....	....	....	....	....	....	....	....	....
	Springfield	AHL	24	7	23	30	4	....	....	....	....	....	....	....	....	....	....	....	....	....	....	....	....	....	....	....
	NHL Totals		**26**	**2**	**7**	**9**	**6**	**1**	**0**	**0**	**29**	**6.9**		**141**	**51.1**	**21**	**10**	**10:13**								

Hockey East All-Star Team (1997) • NCAA East Second All-American Team (1997) • Hockey East First All-Star Team (1998, 1999) • NCAA East First All-American Team (1999) • NCAA Championship All-Tournament Team (1999) • Won Hobey Baker Memorial Award (Top U.S. Collegiate Player) (1999)

Signed as a free agent by **NY Islanders**, May 14, 1999. Loaned to **Providence** (AHL) by **NY Islanders**, March 1, 2000.

KRON, Robert

(KROHN, RAW-buhrt) **CBJ**

Left wing. Shoots left. 5'11", 185 lbs. Born, Brno, Czech., February 27, 1967. Vancouver's 5th choice, 88th overall, in 1985 Entry Draft.

1983-84	Ingstav Brno	Czech-2	3	0	1	1	0	....	....	....	....	....	....	....	....	....	....	....	....	....	....	....	....	....	....	....
1984-85	Zetor Brno	Czech.	40	6	8	14	6	....	....	....	....	....	....	....	....	....	....	....	....	....	....	....	....	....	....	....
1985-86	Zetor Brno	Czech.	44	5	6	11	....	....	....	....	....	....	....	....	....	....	....	....	....	....	....	....	....	....	....	....
1986-87	Zetor Brno	Czech.	34	18	11	29	10	....	....	....	....	....	....	....	....	....	....	....	....	....	....	....	....	....	....	....
1987-88	Zetor Brno	Czech.	44	14	7	21	30	....	....	....	....	....	....	....	....	....	....	....	....	....	....	....	....	....	....	....
1988-89	Dukla Trencin	Czech.	43	28	19	47	26	....	....	....	....	....	....	....	....	....	....	....	....	....	....	....	....	....	....	....
1989-90	Dukla Trencin	Czech.	39	22	22	44	....	....	....	....	....	....	....	....	....	....	....	....	....	....	....	....	....	....	....	....
1990-91	**Vancouver**	**NHL**	**76**	**12**	**20**	**32**	**21**	**2**	**3**	**0**	**124**	**9.7**	**–11**	....	....	....	....	....	....	....	....	....	....	....	....	....
1991-92	**Vancouver**	**NHL**	**36**	**2**	**2**	**4**	**2**	**0**	**0**	**0**	**49**	**4.1**	**–9**	....	....	....	....	....	**11**	**1**	**2**	**3**	**2**	**0**	**1**	**0**
1992-93	**Vancouver**	**NHL**	**32**	**10**	**11**	**21**	**14**	**2**	**2**	**2**	**60**	**16.7**	**10**	....	....	....	....	....	....	....	....	....	....	....	....	....
	Hartford	**NHL**	**13**	**4**	**2**	**6**	**4**	**2**	**0**	**0**	**37**	**10.8**	**–5**	....	....	....	....	....	....	....	....	....	....	....	....	....
1993-94	**Hartford**	**NHL**	**77**	**24**	**26**	**50**	**8**	**2**	**1**	**3**	**194**	**12.4**	**0**	....	....	....	....	....	....	....	....	....	....	....	....	....
1994-95	**Hartford**	**NHL**	**37**	**10**	**8**	**18**	**10**	**3**	**1**	**1**	**88**	**11.4**	**–3**	....	....	....	....	....	....	....	....	....	....	....	....	....
1995-96	**Hartford**	**NHL**	**77**	**22**	**28**	**50**	**6**	**8**	**1**	**3**	**203**	**10.8**	**–1**	....	....	....	....	....	....	....	....	....	....	....	....	....
1996-97	**Hartford**	**NHL**	**68**	**10**	**12**	**22**	**10**	**2**	**0**	**4**	**182**	**5.5**	**–18**	....	....	....	....	....	....	....	....	....	....	....	....	....
1997-98	**Carolina**	**NHL**	**81**	**16**	**20**	**36**	**12**	**4**	**0**	**2**	**175**	**9.1**	**–8**	....	....	....	....	....	....	....	....	....	....	....	....	....
1998-99	**Carolina**	**NHL**	**75**	**9**	**16**	**25**	**10**	**3**	**1**	**2**	**134**	**6.7**	**–13**	**244**	**38.9**	**88**	**27**	**16:14**	**5**	**2**	**0**	**2**	**0**	**0**	**0**	**1**
99-2000	**Carolina**	**NHL**	**81**	**13**	**27**	**40**	**8**	**2**	**1**	**3**	**134**	**9.7**	**–4**	**717**	**43.0**	**48**	**21**	**15:14**	....	....	....	....	....	....	....	....
2000-01	**Columbus**	**NHL**	**59**	**8**	**11**	**19**	**10**	**0**	**1**	**1**	**134**	**6.0**	**4**	**264**	**43.9**	**34**	**22**	**17:08**	....	....	....	....	....	....	....	....
	NHL Totals		**712**	**140**	**183**	**323**	**115**	**30**	**11**	**21**	**1514**	**9.2**		**1225**	**42.4**	**170**	**70**	**16:06**	**16**	**3**	**2**	**5**	**2**	**0**	**1**	**1**

Traded to **Hartford** by **Vancouver** with Vancouver's 3rd round choice (Marek Malik) in 1993 Entry Draft and future considerations (Jim Sandlak, May 17, 1993) for Murray Craven and Vancouver's 5th round choice (previously acquired, Vancouver selected Scott Walker) in 1993 Entry Draft, March 22, 1993. Transferred to **Carolina** after **Hartford** franchise relocated, June 25, 1997. Selected by **Columbus** from **Carolina** in Expansion Draft, June 23, 2000.

KRUSE, Paul

(KROOZ, PAWL)

Left wing. Shoots left. 6'1", 215 lbs. Born, Merritt, B.C., March 15, 1970. Calgary's 6th choice, 83rd overall, in 1990 Entry Draft.

1986-87	Merritt	BCJHL	35	8	15	23	120	....	....	....	....	....	....	....	....	....	....	....	....	....	....	....	....	....	....	....
1987-88	Merritt	BCJHL	44	12	32	44	223	....	....	....	....	....	....	....	....	....	....	....	4	1	4	5	18	....	....	....
	Moose Jaw	WHL	1	0	0	0	0	....	....	....	....	....	....	....	....	....	....	....	....	....	....	....	....	....	....	....
1988-89	Kamloops Blazers	WHL	68	8	15	23	209	....	....	....	....	....	....	....	....	....	....	....	16	0	0	0	36	....	....	....
1989-90	Kamloops Blazers	WHL	67	22	23	45	291	....	....	....	....	....	....	....	....	....	....	....	17	3	5	8	79	....	....	....
1990-91	**Calgary**	**NHL**	**1**	**0**	**0**	**0**	**7**	**0**	**0**	**0**	**0**	**0.0**	**–1**	....	....	....	....	....	....	....	....	....	....	....	....	....
	Salt Lake City	IHL	83	24	20	44	313	....	....	....	....	....	....	....	....	....	....	....	4	1	1	2	4	....	....	....
1991-92	**Calgary**	**NHL**	**16**	**3**	**1**	**4**	**65**	**0**	**0**	**0**	**12**	**25.0**	**1**	....	....	....	....	....	....	....	....	....	....	....	....	....
	Salt Lake City	IHL	57	14	15	29	267	....	....	....	....	....	....	....	....	....	....	....	5	1	2	3	19	....	....	....
1992-93	**Calgary**	**NHL**	**27**	**2**	**3**	**5**	**41**	**0**	**0**	**0**	**17**	**11.8**	**2**	....	....	....	....	....	....	....	....	....	....	....	....	....
	Salt Lake City	IHL	35	1	4	5	206	....	....	....	....	....	....	....	....	....	....	....	....	....	....	....	....	....	....	....
1993-94	**Calgary**	**NHL**	**68**	**3**	**8**	**11**	**185**	**0**	**0**	**0**	**52**	**5.8**	**–6**	....	....	....	....	....	**7**	**0**	**0**	**0**	**14**	**0**	**0**	**0**
1994-95	**Calgary**	**NHL**	**45**	**11**	**5**	**16**	**141**	**0**	**0**	**2**	**52**	**21.2**	**13**	....	....	....	....	....	**7**	**4**	**2**	**6**	**10**	**0**	**1**	**0**
1995-96	**Calgary**	**NHL**	**75**	**3**	**12**	**15**	**145**	**0**	**0**	**0**	**83**	**3.6**	**–5**	....	....	....	....	....	**3**	**0**	**0**	**0**	**4**	**0**	**0**	**0**
1996-97	**Calgary**	**NHL**	**14**	**2**	**0**	**2**	**30**	**0**	**0**	**1**	**10**	**20.0**	**–4**	....	....	....	....	....	....	....	....	....	....	....	....	....
	NY Islanders	**NHL**	**48**	**4**	**2**	**6**	**111**	**0**	**0**	**0**	**39**	**10.3**	**–5**	....	....	....	....	....	....	....	....	....	....	....	....	....
1997-98	**NY Islanders**	**NHL**	**62**	**6**	**1**	**7**	**138**	**0**	**0**	**2**	**44**	**13.6**	**–12**	....	....	....	....	....	....	....	....	....	....	....	....	....
	Buffalo	**NHL**	**12**	**1**	**1**	**2**	**49**	**0**	**0**	**0**	**8**	**12.5**	**1**	....	....	....	....	....	**1**	**1**	**0**	**1**	**4**	**0**	**0**	**0**

			Regular Season																Playoffs							
Season	Club	League	GP	G	A	Pts	PIM	PP	SH	GW	S	%	+/-	TF	F%	H	SB	Min	GP	G	A	Pts	PIM	PP	SH	GW
1998-99	**Buffalo**	**NHL**	**43**	**3**	**0**	**3**	**114**	**0**	**0**	**0**	**33**	**9.1**	**0**	**3**	**33.3**	**56**	**8**	**6:24**	**10**	**0**	**0**	**0**	**4**	**0**	**0**	**0**
99-2000	**Buffalo**	**NHL**	**11**	**0**	**0**	**0**	**43**	**0**	**0**	**0**	**7**	**0.0**	**–2**	**0**	**0.0**	**13**	**2**	**6:15**								
	Utah Grizzlies	IHL	44	10	13	23	71												5	0	3	3	28			
2000-01	**San Jose**	**NHL**	**1**	**0**	**0**	**0**	**5**	**0**	**0**	**0**	**0**	**0.0**	**0**	**0**	**0.0**	**1**	**0**	**3:32**								
	Chicago Wolves	IHL	71	8	12	20	180												16	2	3	5	22			
	NHL Totals		**423**	**38**	**33**	**71**	**1074**	**0**	**0**	**5**	**357**	**10.6**		**3**	**33.3**	**70**	**10**	**6:19**	**28**	**5**	**2**	**7**	**36**	**0**	**1**	**0**

Traded to **NY Islanders** by **Calgary** for Colorado's 3rd round choice (previously acquired by NY Islanders - later traded to Hartford - Hartford selected Francis Lessard) in 1997 Entry Draft, November 27, 1996. Traded to **Buffalo** by **NY Islanders** with Jason Holland for Jason Dawe, March 24, 1998. Loaned to **Utah** (IHL) by **Buffalo** after clearing NHL waivers, January 11, 2000. Signed as a free agent by **San Jose**, September 10, 2000.

KUBA, Filip
(KOO-bah, FIHL-ihp) **MIN.**

Defense. Shoots left. 6'3", 205 lbs. Born, Ostrava, Czech., December 29, 1976. Florida's 8th choice, 192nd overall, in 1995 Entry Draft.

Season	Club	League	GP	G	A	Pts	PIM	PP	SH	GW	S	%	+/-	TF	F%	H	SB	Min	GP	G	A	Pts	PIM	PP	SH	GW
1994-95	HC Vitkovice-Jr.	Cze-Rep	35	10	15	25																				
	HC Vitkovice	Cze-Rep																	4	0	0	0	2			
1995-96	HC Vitkovice	Cze-Rep	19	0	1	1																				
1996-97	Carolina	AHL	51	0	12	12	38																			
1997-98	New Haven	AHL	77	4	13	17	58												3	1	1	2	0			
1998-99	**Florida**	**NHL**	**5**	**0**	**1**	**1**	**0**	**0**	**0**	**0**	**5**	**0.0**	**2**	**0**	**0.0**	**7**	**6**	**22:29**								
	Kentucky	AHL	45	2	8	10	33												10	0	1	1	4			
99-2000	**Florida**	**NHL**	**13**	**1**	**5**	**6**	**2**	**1**	**0**	**1**	**16**	**6.3**	**–3**	**0**	**0.0**	**10**	**13**	**13:52**								
	Houston Aeros	IHL	27	3	6	9	13												11	1	2	3	4			
2000-01	**Minnesota**	**NHL**	**75**	**9**	**21**	**30**	**28**	**4**	**0**	**4**	**141**	**6.4**	**–6**	**1**	**0.0**	**81**	**139**	**24:16**								
	NHL Totals		**93**	**10**	**27**	**37**	**30**	**5**	**0**	**5**	**162**	**6.2**		**1**	**0.0**	**98**	**158**	**22:43**								

Traded to **Calgary** by **Florida** for Rocky Thompson, March 16, 2000. Selected by **Minnesota** from **Calgary** in Expansion Draft, June 23, 2000.

KUBINA, Pavel
(koo-BEE-nuh, PAH-vehl) **T.B.**

Defense. Shoots right. 6'4", 230 lbs. Born, Celadna, Czech., April 15, 1977. Tampa Bay's 6th choice, 179th overall, in 1996 Entry Draft.

Season	Club	League	GP	G	A	Pts	PIM	PP	SH	GW	S	%	+/-	TF	F%	H	SB	Min	GP	G	A	Pts	PIM	PP	SH	GW
1993-94	HC Vitkovice-Jr.	Cze-Rep	35	4	3	7																				
	HC Vitkovice	Cze-Rep	1	0	0	0																				
1994-95	HC Vitkovice-Jr.	Cze-Rep	20	6	10	16																				
	HC Vitkovice	Cze-Rep	8	2	0	2	10												4	0	0	0	0			
1995-96	HC Vitkovice-Jr.	Cze-Rep	16	5	10	15																				
	HC Vitkovice	Cze-Rep	33	3	4	7	32												4	0	0	0	0			
1996-97	HC Vitkovice	Cze-Rep	1	0	0	0	0																			
	Moose Jaw	WHL	61	12	32	44	116												11	2	5	7	27			
1997-98	**Tampa Bay**	**NHL**	**10**	**1**	**2**	**3**	**22**	**0**	**0**	**0**	**8**	**12.5**	**–1**													
	Adirondack	AHL	55	4	8	12	86												1	1	0	1	14			
1998-99	**Tampa Bay**	**NHL**	**68**	**9**	**12**	**21**	**80**	**3**	**1**	**1**	**119**	**7.6**	**–33**	**2**	**0.0**	**156**	**82**	**22:47**								
	Cleveland	IHL	6	2	2	4	16																			
99-2000	**Tampa Bay**	**NHL**	**69**	**8**	**18**	**26**	**93**	**6**	**0**	**3**	**128**	**6.3**	**–19**	**0**	**0.0**	**121**	**78**	**22:32**								
2000-01	**Tampa Bay**	**NHL**	**70**	**11**	**19**	**30**	**103**	**6**	**1**	**1**	**128**	**8.6**	**–14**	**2**	**0.0**	**105**	**131**	**24:06**								
	NHL Totals		**217**	**29**	**51**	**80**	**298**	**15**	**2**	**5**	**383**	**7.6**		**4**	**0.0**	**382**	**291**	**23:09**								

KUCERA, Frantisek
(koo-CHAIR-uh, FRAN-tih-sehk) **WSH.**

Defense. Shoots right. 6'2", 205 lbs. Born, Prague, Czech., February 3, 1968. Chicago's 3rd choice, 77th overall, in 1986 Entry Draft.

Season	Club	League	GP	G	A	Pts	PIM	PP	SH	GW	S	%	+/-	TF	F%	H	SB	Min	GP	G	A	Pts	PIM	PP	SH	GW
1985-86	Sparta Praha	Czech.	15	0	0	0																				
1986-87	Sparta Praha	Czech.	40	5	2	7	14																			
1987-88	Sparta Praha	Czech.	46	7	2	9	30																			
1988-89	Dukla Jihlava	Czech.	45	10	9	19	28																			
1989-90	Dukla Jihlava	Czech.	42	8	10	18													1	1	0	1				
1990-91	**Chicago**	**NHL**	**40**	**2**	**12**	**14**	**32**	**1**	**0**	**0**	**65**	**3.1**	**3**													
	Indianapolis Ice	IHL	35	8	19	27	23												7	0	1	1	15			
1991-92	**Chicago**	**NHL**	**61**	**3**	**10**	**13**	**36**	**1**	**0**	**1**	**82**	**3.7**	**3**						**6**	**0**	**0**	**0**	**0**	**0**	**0**	**0**
	Indianapolis Ice	IHL	7	1	2	3	4																			
1992-93	**Chicago**	**NHL**	**71**	**5**	**14**	**19**	**59**	**1**	**0**	**1**	**117**	**4.3**	**7**													
1993-94	**Chicago**	**NHL**	**60**	**4**	**13**	**17**	**34**	**2**	**0**	**0**	**90**	**4.4**	**9**													
	Hartford	**NHL**	**16**	**1**	**3**	**4**	**14**	**1**	**0**	**0**	**32**	**3.1**	**–12**													
1994-95	Sparta Praha	Cze-Rep	16	1	2	3	14																			
	Hartford	**NHL**	**48**	**3**	**17**	**20**	**30**	**0**	**0**	**1**	**73**	**4.1**	**3**													
1995-96	**Hartford**	**NHL**	**30**	**2**	**6**	**8**	**10**	**0**	**0**	**1**	**43**	**4.7**	**–3**													
	Vancouver	**NHL**	**24**	**1**	**0**	**1**	**10**	**0**	**0**	**0**	**34**	**2.9**	**5**						**6**	**0**	**1**	**1**	**0**	**0**	**0**	**0**
1996-97	**Vancouver**	**NHL**	**2**	**0**	**0**	**0**	**0**	**0**	**0**	**0**	**3**	**0.0**	**0**													
	Syracuse Crunch	AHL	42	6	29	35	36																			
	Houston Aeros	IHL	12	0	3	3	20																			
	Philadelphia	**NHL**	**2**	**0**	**0**	**0**	**2**	**0**	**0**	**0**	**2**	**0.0**	**–2**													
	Philadelphia	AHL	9	1	5	6	2												10	1	6	7	20			
1997-98	Sparta Praha	Cze-Rep	43	8	12	20	49												9	3	1	4	*53			
	Sparta Praha	EuroHL	4	0	1	1	2																			
	Czech-Republic	Olympics	6	0	0	0	0																			
1998-99	Sparta Praha	Cze-Rep	42	3	12	15	92												8	0	2	2				
	Sparta Praha	EuroHL	6	0	2	2	10												2	0	0	0	2			
99-2000	Sparta Praha	Cze-Rep	51	7	26	33	40												9	1	9	10	4			
	Sparta Praha	EuroHL	6	0	2	2	4												4	0	1	1	2			
2000-01	**Columbus**	**NHL**	**48**	**2**	**5**	**7**	**12**	**0**	**0**	**0**	**51**	**3.9**	**–5**	**0**	**0.0**	**43**	**69**	**17:42**								
	Pittsburgh	**NHL**	**7**	**0**	**2**	**2**	**0**	**0**	**0**	**0**	**9**	**0.0**	**–2**	**0**	**0.0**	**10**	**10**	**16:28**								
	NHL Totals		**409**	**23**	**82**	**105**	**239**	**6**	**0**	**4**	**601**	**3.8**		**0**	**0.0**	**53**	**79**	**17:33**	**12**	**0**	**1**	**1**	**0**	**0**	**0**	**0**

Traded to **Hartford** by **Chicago** with Jocelyn Lemieux for Gary Suter, Randy Cunneyworth and Hartford's 3rd round choice (later traded to Vancouver - Vancouver selected Larry Courville) in 1995 Entry Draft, March 11, 1994. Traded to **Vancouver** by **Hartford** with Jim Dowd and Hartford's 2nd round choice (Ryan Bonni) in 1997 Entry Draft for Jeff Brown and Vancouver's 3rd round choice (later traded to Calgary - Calgary selected Paul Manning) in 1998 Entry Draft, December 19, 1995. Traded to **Philadelphia** by **Vancouver** for future considerations, March 18, 1997. Signed as a free agent by **Columbus**, July 7, 2000. Traded to **Pittsburgh** by **Columbus** for Pittsburgh's 6th round choice (Columbus selected Scott Horvath) in 2001 Entry Draft, March 13, 2001. Traded to **Washington** by **Pittsburgh** with Jaromir Jagr for Kris Beech, Michal Sivek, Ross Lupaschuk and future considerations, July 11, 2001.

KUDROC, Kristian
(KOO-drawch, KRIHS-tan) **T.B.**

Defense. Shoots right. 6'6", 240 lbs. Born, Michalovce, Czech., May 21, 1981. NY Islanders' 4th choice, 28th overall, in 1999 Entry Draft.

Season	Club	League	GP	G	A	Pts	PIM	PP	SH	GW	S	%	+/-	TF	F%	H	SB	Min	GP	G	A	Pts	PIM	PP	SH	GW
1997-98	HK Michalovce	Slovak-Jr.	47	7	4	11	66																			
	HK Michalovce	Slovak-2	4	0	0	0	0																			
1998-99	HK Michalovce	Slovak-2	17	0	3	3	12																			
99-2000	Quebec Remparts	QMJHL	57	9	22	31	172												11	2	5	7	29			
2000-01	**Tampa Bay**	**NHL**	**22**	**2**	**2**	**4**	**36**	**0**	**0**	**1**	**12**	**16.7**	**0**	**0**	**0.0**	**44**	**11**	**9:09**								
	Detroit Vipers	IHL	44	4	3	7	80																			
	NHL Totals		**22**	**2**	**2**	**4**	**36**	**0**	**0**	**1**	**12**	**16.7**		**0**	**0.0**	**44**	**11**	**9:09**								

Traded to **Tampa Bay** by **NY Islanders** with Kevin Weekes and NY Islanders' 2nd round choice (later traded to Phoenix - Phoenix selected Matthew Spiller) in 2001 Entry Draft for Tampa Bay's 1st round choice (Raffi Torres) in 2000 Entry Draft, Calgary's 4th round choice (previously acquired, NY Islanders selected Vladimir Gorbunov) in 2000 Entry Draft and NY Islanders' 7th round choice (previously acquired, NY Islanders selected Ryan Caldwell) in 2000 Entry Draft, June 24, 2000.

KULTANEN, Jarno
(kuhl-TAH-nuhn, YAR-noh) **BOS.**

Defense. Shoots left. 6'2", 198 lbs. Born, Luumaki, Finland, January 8, 1973. Boston's 8th choice, 174th overall, in 2000 Entry Draft.

Season	Club	League	GP	G	A	Pts	PIM	PP	SH	GW	S	%	+/-	TF	F%	H	SB	Min	GP	G	A	Pts	PIM	PP	SH	GW
1991-92	KooKoo Kouvola	Finn-Jr.	22	7	17	24	28																			
	KooKoo Kouvola	Finland-2	1	0	0	0	0																			
1992-93	KooKoo Kouvola	Finn-Jr.	11	6	5	11	8																			
	KooKoo Kouvola	Finland-2	27	1	1	2	33																			
	Center Pietarssari	Finland-2	1	1	0	1	0																			
1993-94	KooKoo Kouvola	Finn-Jr.	3	1	0	1	2																			
	KooKoo Kouvola	Finland-2	45	7	10	17	42																			

			Regular Season																Playoffs							
Season	Club	League	GP	G	A	Pts	PIM	PP	SH	GW	S	%	+/-	TF	F%	H	SB	Min	GP	G	A	Pts	PIM	PP	SH	GW
1994-95	KalPa Kuopio	Finland	47	5	12	17	26	....	....	....	....	....	....	....	....	....	....	....	3	0	0	0	8	....	....	....
1995-96	KalPa Kuopio	Finland	49	4	10	14	42	....	....	....	....	....	....	....	....	....	....	....	....	....	....	....	....	....	....	....
1996-97	HIFK Helsinki	Finland	24	1	3	4	6	....	....	....	....	....	....	....	....	....	....	....	....	....	....	....	....	....	....	....
1997-98	HIFK Helsinki	Finland	25	0	1	1	20	....	....	....	....	....	....	....	....	....	....	....	8	0	1	1	2	....	....	....
1998-99	HIFK Helsinki	Finland	51	6	6	12	53	....	....	....	....	....	....	....	....	....	....	....	10	1	0	1	27	....	....	....
	HIFK Helsinki	EuroHL	5	1	0	1	4	....	....	....	....	....	....	....	....	....	....	....	4	0	1	1	2	....	....	....
99-2000	HIFK Helsinki	Finland	46	6	8	14	51	....	....	....	....	....	....	....	....	....	....	....	9	0	0	0	6	....	....	....
	HIFK Helsinki	EuroHL	5	2	2	4	31	....	....	....	....	....	....	....	....	....	....	....	2	0	0	0	2	....	....	....
2000-01	**Boston**	**NHL**	**62**	**2**	**8**	**10**	**26**	**0**	**0**	**1**	**76**	**2.6**	**-3**	**0**	**0.0**	**87**	**53**	**19:29**	....	....	....	....	....	....	....	....
	NHL Totals		**62**	**2**	**8**	**10**	**26**	**0**	**0**	**1**	**76**	**2.6**		**0**	**0.0**	**87**	**53**	**19:29**	....	....	....	....	....	....	....	....

KUTLAK, Zdenek

(KUHT-lak, zuh-DEHN-ehk) **BOS.**

Defense. Shoots left. 6'3", 207 lbs. Born, Budejovice, Czech., February 13, 1980. Boston's 10th choice, 237th overall, in 2000 Entry Draft.

Season	Club	League	GP	G	A	Pts	PIM	PP	SH	GW	S	%	+/-	TF	F%	H	SB	Min	GP	G	A	Pts	PIM	PP	SH	GW
1996-97	HC Budejovice-Jr.	Cze-Rep	45	8	11	19	20	....	....	....	....	....	....	....	....	....	....	....	....	....	....	....	....	....	....	....
1997-98	HC Budejovice-Jr.	Cze-Rep	43	1	6	7	30	....	....	....	....	....	....	....	....	....	....	....	....	....	....	....	....	....	....	....
1998-99	HC Budejovice-Jr.	Cze-Rep	31	6	14	20	20	....	....	....	....	....	....	....	....	....	....	....	....	....	....	....	....	....	....	....
	HC Budejovice	Cze-Rep	22	1	3	4	4	....	....	....	....	....	....	....	....	....	....	....	3	0	0	0	0	....	....	....
99-2000	HC Budejovice-Jr.	Cze-Rep	8	4	2	6	26	....	....	....	....	....	....	....	....	....	....	....	....	....	....	....	....	....	....	....
	SHC Hradec-2	Cze-Rep	4	1	1	2	0	....	....	....	....	....	....	....	....	....	....	....	....	....	....	....	....	....	....	....
	IHC Pisek-2	Cze-Rep	3	1	0	1	0	....	....	....	....	....	....	....	....	....	....	....	2	0	0	0	2	....	....	....
	HC Budejovice	Cze-Rep	28	1	0	1	2	....	....	....	....	....	....	....	....	....	....	....	1	0	0	0	0	....	....	....
2000-01	**Boston**	**NHL**	**10**	**0**	**2**	**2**	**4**	**0**	**0**	**0**	**7**	**0.0**	**-3**	**0**	**0.0**	**9**	**4**	**16:05**	....	....	....	....	....	....	....	....
	Providence Bruins	AHL	62	4	5	9	16	....	....	....	....	....	....	....	....	....	....	....	....	....	....	....	....	....	....	....
	NHL Totals		**10**	**0**	**2**	**2**	**4**	**0**	**0**	**0**	**7**	**0.0**		**0**	**0.0**	**9**	**4**	**16:05**	....	....	....	....	....	....	....	....

KUZNETSOV, Maxim

(kooz-NEHT-zahv, MAX-ihm) **DET.**

Defense. Shoots left. 6'5", 198 lbs. Born, Pavlodar, USSR, March 24, 1977. Detroit's 1st choice, 26th overall, in 1995 Entry Draft.

Season	Club	League	GP	G	A	Pts	PIM	PP	SH	GW	S	%	+/-	TF	F%	H	SB	Min	GP	G	A	Pts	PIM	PP	SH	GW
1994-95	Dynamo Moscow	CIS	11	0	0	0	8	....	....	....	....	....	....	....	....	....	....	....	....	....	....	....	....	....	....	....
1995-96	Dynamo Moscow	CIS	9	1	1	2	22	....	....	....	....	....	....	....	....	....	....	....	4	0	0	0	0	....	....	....
1996-97	Dynamo Moscow	Russia	23	0	2	2	16	....	....	....	....	....	....	....	....	....	....	....	....	....	....	....	....	....	....	....
	Adirondack	AHL	2	0	1	1	6	....	....	....	....	....	....	....	....	....	....	....	2	0	0	0	0	....	....	....
1997-98	Adirondack	AHL	51	5	5	10	43	....	....	....	....	....	....	....	....	....	....	....	3	0	1	1	4	....	....	....
1998-99	Adirondack	AHL	60	0	4	4	30	....	....	....	....	....	....	....	....	....	....	....	3	0	0	0	0	....	....	....
99-2000	Cincinnati Ducks	AHL	47	2	9	11	36	....	....	....	....	....	....	....	....	....	....	....	....	....	....	....	....	....	....	....
2000-01	**Detroit**	**NHL**	**25**	**1**	**2**	**3**	**23**	**0**	**0**	**0**	**17**	**5.9**	**-1**	**1**	**0.0**	**54**	**7**	**9:28**	....	....	....	....	....	....	....	....
	NHL Totals		**25**	**1**	**2**	**3**	**23**	**0**	**0**	**0**	**17**	**5.9**		**1**	**0.0**	**54**	**7**	**9:28**	....	....	....	....	....	....	....	....

• Missed majority of 2000-01 season recovering from knee injury originally suffered in game vs. Vancouver, November 24, 2000.

KUZNIK, Greg

(kooz-NIHK, GREHG) **CAR.**

Defense. Shoots left. 6', 185 lbs. Born, Prince George, B.C., June 12, 1978. Hartford's 7th choice, 171st overall, in 1996 Entry Draft.

Season	Club	League	GP	G	A	Pts	PIM	PP	SH	GW	S	%	+/-	TF	F%	H	SB	Min	GP	G	A	Pts	PIM	PP	SH	GW
1994-95	Royal City	BCJHL	45	2	13	15	83	....	....	....	....	....	....	....	....	....	....	....	....	....	....	....	....	....	....	....
1995-96	Seattle T-Birds	WHL	70	2	13	15	149	....	....	....	....	....	....	....	....	....	....	....	5	0	0	0	6	....	....	....
1996-97	Seattle T-Birds	WHL	70	4	9	13	161	....	....	....	....	....	....	....	....	....	....	....	14	0	2	2	26	....	....	....
1997-98	Seattle T-Birds	WHL	72	5	12	17	197	....	....	....	....	....	....	....	....	....	....	....	5	0	0	0	4	....	....	....
1998-99	New Haven	AHL	27	1	0	1	33	....	....	....	....	....	....	....	....	....	....	....	....	....	....	....	....	....	....	....
	Florida Everblades	ECHL	50	6	8	14	110	....	....	....	....	....	....	....	....	....	....	....	5	1	0	1	0	....	....	....
99-2000	Cincinnati	IHL	46	0	3	3	53	....	....	....	....	....	....	....	....	....	....	....	4	0	0	0	4	....	....	....
	Dayton Bombers	ECHL	7	1	0	1	16	....	....	....	....	....	....	....	....	....	....	....	....	....	....	....	....	....	....	....
	Florida Everblades	ECHL	9	1	4	5	6	....	....	....	....	....	....	....	....	....	....	....	3	0	0	0	2	....	....	....
2000-01	**Carolina**	**NHL**	**1**	**0**	**0**	**0**	**0**	**0**	**0**	**0**	**0**	**0.0**	**0**	**0**	**0.0**	**0**	**1**	**7:32**	....	....	....	....	....	....	....	....
	Cincinnati	IHL	73	0	7	7	72	....	....	....	....	....	....	....	....	....	....	....	5	0	1	1	4	....	....	....
	NHL Totals		**1**	**0**	**0**	**0**	**0**	**0**	**0**	**0**	**0**	**0.0**		**0**	**0.0**	**0**	**1**	**7:32**	....	....	....	....	....	....	....	....

Transferred to **Carolina** after **Hartford** franchise relocated, June 25, 1997.

KVASHA, Oleg

(kuh-VAH-shah, OH-lehg) **NYI**

Center/Left wing. Shoots right. 6'5", 215 lbs. Born, Moscow, USSR, July 26, 1978. Florida's 3rd choice, 65th overall, in 1996 Entry Draft.

Season	Club	League	GP	G	A	Pts	PIM	PP	SH	GW	S	%	+/-	TF	F%	H	SB	Min	GP	G	A	Pts	PIM	PP	SH	GW
1995-96	CSKA Moscow	CIS	38	2	3	5	14	....	....	....	....	....	....	....	....	....	....	....	2	0	0	0	0	....	....	....
1996-97	CSKA Moscow	Russia	44	20	22	42	115	....	....	....	....	....	....	....	....	....	....	....	....	....	....	....	....	....	....	....
1997-98	New Haven	AHL	57	13	16	29	46	....	....	....	....	....	....	....	....	....	....	....	3	2	1	3	0	....	....	....
1998-99	**Florida**	**NHL**	**68**	**12**	**13**	**25**	**45**	**4**	**0**	**2**	**138**	**8.7**	**5**	**373**	**28.4**	**21**	**13**	**12:48**	....	....	....	....	....	....	....	....
99-2000	**Florida**	**NHL**	**78**	**5**	**20**	**25**	**34**	**2**	**0**	**0**	**110**	**4.5**	**3**	**553**	**34.9**	**22**	**22**	**11:24**	**4**	**0**	**0**	**0**	**0**	**0**	**0**	**0**
2000-01	**NY Islanders**	**NHL**	**62**	**11**	**9**	**20**	**46**	**0**	**0**	**0**	**118**	**9.3**	**-15**	**627**	**43.7**	**33**	**22**	**14:56**	....	....	....	....	....	....	....	....
	NHL Totals		**208**	**28**	**42**	**70**	**125**	**6**	**0**	**2**	**366**	**7.7**		**1553**	**36.9**	**76**	**57**	**12:55**	**4**	**0**	**0**	**0**	**0**	**0**	**0**	**0**

Traded to **NY Islanders** by **Florida** with Mark Parrish for Roberto Luongo and Olli Jokinen, June 24, 2000.

KWIATKOWSKI, Joel

(KWEE-at-KOW-skee, JOHL) **OTT.**

Defense. Shoots left. 6'2", 210 lbs. Born, Kindersley, Sask., March 22, 1977. Dallas' 7th choice, 194th overall, in 1996 Entry Draft.

Season	Club	League	GP	G	A	Pts	PIM	PP	SH	GW	S	%	+/-	TF	F%	H	SB	Min	GP	G	A	Pts	PIM	PP	SH	GW
1994-95	North Battleford	SJHL	51	3	14	17	89	....	....	....	....	....	....	....	....	....	....	....	....	....	....	....	....	....	....	....
	Tacoma Rockets	WHL	70	4	13	17	66	....	....	....	....	....	....	....	....	....	....	....	4	0	0	0	2	....	....	....
1995-96	Kelowna Rockets	WHL	40	6	17	23	85	....	....	....	....	....	....	....	....	....	....	....	....	....	....	....	....	....	....	....
	Prince George	WHL	32	6	11	17	48	....	....	....	....	....	....	....	....	....	....	....	....	....	....	....	....	....	....	....
1996-97	Prince George	WHL	72	15	37	52	94	....	....	....	....	....	....	....	....	....	....	....	15	4	2	6	24	....	....	....
1997-98	Prince George	WHL	62	21	43	64	65	....	....	....	....	....	....	....	....	....	....	....	11	3	6	9	6	....	....	....
1998-99	Cincinnati Ducks	AHL	80	12	21	33	48	....	....	....	....	....	....	....	....	....	....	....	3	2	0	2	0	....	....	....
99-2000	Cincinnati Ducks	AHL	70	4	22	26	28	....	....	....	....	....	....	....	....	....	....	....	....	....	....	....	....	....	....	....
2000-01	**Ottawa**	**NHL**	**4**	**1**	**0**	**1**	**0**	**0**	**0**	**0**	**2**	**50.0**	**1**	**0**	**0.0**	**3**	**4**	**12:04**	....	....	....	....	....	....	....	....
	Grand Rapids	IHL	77	4	17	21	58	....	....	....	....	....	....	....	....	....	....	....	10	1	0	1	4	....	....	....
	NHL Totals		**4**	**1**	**0**	**1**	**0**	**0**	**0**	**0**	**2**	**50.0**		**0**	**0.0**	**3**	**4**	**12:04**	....	....	....	....	....	....	....	....

WHL West Second All-Star Team (1997) • WHL West First All-Star Team (1998)

Signed as a free agent by **Anaheim**, June 18, 1998. Traded to **Ottawa** by **Anaheim** for Patrick Traverse, June 12, 2000.

LAAKSONEN, Antti

(lah-AHK-soh-nehn, AHN-tee) **MIN.**

Left wing. Shoots left. 6', 180 lbs. Born, Tammela, Finland, October 3, 1973. Boston's 10th choice, 191st overall, in 1997 Entry Draft.

Season	Club	League	GP	G	A	Pts	PIM	PP	SH	GW	S	%	+/-	TF	F%	H	SB	Min	GP	G	A	Pts	PIM	PP	SH	GW
1991-92	FoPS Forssa	Finn-Jr.	24	19	23	42	22	....	....	....	....	....	....	....	....	....	....	....	....	....	....	....	....	....	....	....
	FoPS Forssa	Finland-2	41	16	15	31	8	....	....	....	....	....	....	....	....	....	....	....	....	....	....	....	....	....	....	....
1992-93	FoPS Forssa	Finn-Jr.	9	5	3	8	10	....	....	....	....	....	....	....	....	....	....	....	....	....	....	....	....	....	....	....
	FoPS Forssa	Finland-2	34	11	19	30	36	....	....	....	....	....	....	....	....	....	....	....	....	....	....	....	....	....	....	....
	HPK Hameenlinna	Finn-Jr.	1	1	1	2	0	....	....	....	....	....	....	....	....	....	....	....	....	....	....	....	....	....	....	....
	HPK Hameenlinna	Finland	2	0	0	0	0	....	....	....	....	....	....	....	....	....	....	....	....	....	....	....	....	....	....	....
1993-94	U. of Denver	WCHA	36	12	9	21	38	....	....	....	....	....	....	....	....	....	....	....	....	....	....	....	....	....	....	....
1994-95	U. of Denver	WCHA	40	17	18	35	42	....	....	....	....	....	....	....	....	....	....	....	....	....	....	....	....	....	....	....
1995-96	U. of Denver	WCHA	39	25	28	53	71	....	....	....	....	....	....	....	....	....	....	....	....	....	....	....	....	....	....	....
1996-97	U. of Denver	WCHA	39	21	17	38	63	....	....	....	....	....	....	....	....	....	....	....	....	....	....	....	....	....	....	....
1997-98	Providence Bruins	AHL	38	3	2	5	14	....	....	....	....	....	....	....	....	....	....	....	....	....	....	....	....	....	....	....
	Charlotte	ECHL	15	4	3	7	12	....	....	....	....	....	....	....	....	....	....	....	6	0	3	3	0	....	....	....
1998-99	**Boston**	**NHL**	**11**	**1**	**2**	**3**	**2**	**0**	**0**	**0**	**8**	**12.5**	**-1**	**0**	**0.0**	**5**	**3**	**9:20**	....	....	....	....	....	....	....	....
	Providence Bruins	AHL	66	25	33	58	52	....	....	....	....	....	....	....	....	....	....	....	19	7	2	9	28	....	....	....

			Regular Season															Playoffs							
Season	Club	League	GP	G	A	Pts	PIM	PP	SH	GW	S	%	+/-	TF	F%	H	SB	Min	GP	G	A	Pts	PIM	PP	SH	GW
99-2000	**Boston**	**NHL**	**27**	**6**	**3**	**9**	**2**	**0**	**0**	**1**	**23**	**26.1**	**3**	**3**	**66.7**	**22**	**2**	**7:50**	....	....	....	....	....	....	....	....
	Providence Bruins	AHL	40	10	12	22	57	....	....	....	....	....	....	....	....	....	....	....	14	5	4	9	4	....	....	....
2000-01	**Minnesota**	**NHL**	**82**	**12**	**16**	**28**	**24**	**0**	**2**	**1**	**129**	**9.3**	**−7**	**15**	**26.7**	**106**	**32**	**16:27**	....	....	....	....	....	....	....	....
	NHL Totals		**120**	**19**	**21**	**40**	**28**	**0**	**2**	**2**	**160**	**11.9**		**18**	**33.3**	**133**	**37**	**13:51**	....	....	....	....	....	....	....	....

WCHA Second All-Star Team (1996)

Signed as a free agent by **Minnesota**, July 14, 2000.

LACHANCE, Scott

(lah-CHANTS, SKAWT) **VAN.**

Defense. Shoots left. 6'1", 209 lbs. Born, Charlottesville, VA, October 22, 1972. NY Islanders' 1st choice, 4th overall, in 1991 Entry Draft.

Season	Club	League	GP	G	A	Pts	PIM	PP	SH	GW	S	%	+/-	TF	F%	H	SB	Min	GP	G	A	Pts	PIM	PP	SH	GW
1988-89	Springfield Blues	NEJHL	36	8	28	36	20	....	....	....	....	....	....	....	....	....	....	....	....	....	....	....	....	....	....	....
1989-90	Springfield Blues	NEJHL	34	25	41	66	62	....	....	....	....	....	....	....	....	....	....	....	....	....	....	....	....	....	....	....
1990-91	Boston University	H-East	31	5	19	24	48	....	....	....	....	....	....	....	....	....	....	....	....	....	....	....	....	....	....	....
1991-92	United States	Nat-Team	36	1	10	11	34	....	....	....	....	....	....	....	....	....	....	....	....	....	....	....	....	....	....	....
	United States	Olympics	8	0	1	1	6	....	....	....	....	....	....	....	....	....	....	....	....	....	....	....	....	....	....	....
	NY Islanders	**NHL**	**17**	**1**	**4**	**5**	**9**	**0**	**0**	**0**	**20**	**5.0**	**13**	....	....	....	....	....	....	....	....	....	....	....	....	....
1992-93	**NY Islanders**	**NHL**	**75**	**7**	**17**	**24**	**67**	**0**	**1**	**2**	**62**	**11.3**	**−1**	....	....	....	....	....	....	....	....	....	....	....	....	....
1993-94	**NY Islanders**	**NHL**	**74**	**3**	**11**	**14**	**70**	**0**	**0**	**1**	**59**	**5.1**	**−5**	....	....	....	....	....	**3**	**0**	**0**	**0**	**0**	**0**	**0**	**0**
1994-95	**NY Islanders**	**NHL**	**26**	**6**	**7**	**13**	**26**	**3**	**0**	**0**	**56**	**10.7**	**2**	....	....	....	....	....	....	....	....	....	....	....	....	....
1995-96	**NY Islanders**	**NHL**	**55**	**3**	**10**	**13**	**54**	**1**	**0**	**0**	**81**	**3.7**	**−19**	....	....	....	....	....	....	....	....	....	....	....	....	....
1996-97	**NY Islanders**	**NHL**	**81**	**3**	**11**	**14**	**47**	**1**	**0**	**0**	**97**	**3.1**	**−7**	....	....	....	....	....	....	....	....	....	....	....	....	....
1997-98	**NY Islanders**	**NHL**	**63**	**2**	**11**	**13**	**45**	**1**	**0**	**0**	**62**	**3.2**	**−11**	....	....	....	....	....	....	....	....	....	....	....	....	....
1998-99	**NY Islanders**	**NHL**	**59**	**1**	**8**	**9**	**30**	**1**	**0**	**0**	**37**	**2.7**	**−19**	**0**	**0.0**	**67**	**92**	**21:34**	....	....	....	....	....	....	....	....
	Montreal	**NHL**	**17**	**1**	**1**	**2**	**11**	**0**	**0**	**0**	**22**	**4.5**	**−2**	**0**	**0.0**	**19**	**47**	**22:29**	....	....	....	....	....	....	....	....
99-2000	**Montreal**	**NHL**	**57**	**0**	**6**	**6**	**22**	**0**	**0**	**0**	**41**	**0.0**	**−4**	**0**	**0.0**	**95**	**86**	**17:47**	....	....	....	....	....	....	....	....
2000-01	**Vancouver**	**NHL**	**76**	**3**	**11**	**14**	**46**	**0**	**0**	**0**	**55**	**5.5**	**5**	**0**	**0.0**	**139**	**136**	**19:26**	**2**	**0**	**1**	**1**	**2**	**0**	**0**	**0**
	NHL Totals		**600**	**30**	**97**	**127**	**427**	**7**	**1**	**3**	**592**	**5.1**		**0**	**0.0**	**320**	**361**	**19:50**	**5**	**0**	**1**	**1**	**2**	**0**	**0**	**0**

Played in NHL All-Star Game (1997)

Traded to **Montreal** by **NY Islanders** for Montreal's 3rd round choice (Mattias Weinhandl) in 1999 Entry Draft, March 9, 1999. Signed as a free agent by **Vancouver**, August 13, 2000.

LaCOUTURE, Dan

(LA-koo-TUHR, DAN) **PIT.**

Left wing. Shoots left. 6'3", 210 lbs. Born, Hyannis, MA, April 18, 1977. NY Islanders' 2nd choice, 29th overall, in 1996 Entry Draft.

Season	Club	League	GP	G	A	Pts	PIM	PP	SH	GW	S	%	+/-	TF	F%	H	SB	Min	GP	G	A	Pts	PIM	PP	SH	GW
1992-93	Natick Academy	Hi-School	20	38	34	72	46	....	....	....	....	....	....	....	....	....	....	....	....	....	....	....	....	....	....	....
1993-94	Natick Academy	Hi-School	21	52	49	101	58	....	....	....	....	....	....	....	....	....	....	....	....	....	....	....	....	....	....	....
1994-95	Springfield Pics	IJHL	52	44	56	100	98	....	....	....	....	....	....	....	....	....	....	....	....	....	....	....	....	....	....	....
1995-96	Springfield	NAJHL	41	36	41	77	87	....	....	....	....	....	....	....	....	....	....	....	13	12	13	25	23	....	....	....
1996-97	Boston University	H-East	31	13	12	25	18	....	....	....	....	....	....	....	....	....	....	....	....	....	....	....	....	....	....	....
1997-98	Hamilton Bulldogs	AHL	77	15	10	25	31	....	....	....	....	....	....	....	....	....	....	....	5	1	0	1	0	....	....	....
1998-99	**Edmonton**	**NHL**	**3**	**0**	**0**	**0**	**0**	**0**	**0**	**0**	**0**	**0.0**	**1**	**0**	**0.0**	**3**	**0**	**6:30**	....	....	....	....	....	....	....	....
	Hamilton Bulldogs	AHL	72	17	14	31	73	....	....	....	....	....	....	....	....	....	....	....	9	2	1	3	2	....	....	....
99-2000	**Edmonton**	**NHL**	**5**	**0**	**0**	**0**	**10**	**0**	**0**	**0**	**2**	**0.0**	**0**	**0**	**0.0**	**7**	**1**	**7:02**	**1**	**0**	**0**	**0**	**0**	**0**	**0**	**0**
	Hamilton Bulldogs	AHL	70	23	17	40	85	....	....	....	....	....	....	....	....	....	....	....	6	2	1	3	0	....	....	....
2000-01	**Edmonton**	**NHL**	**37**	**2**	**4**	**6**	**29**	**0**	**0**	**1**	**22**	**9.1**	**−2**	**5**	**20.0**	**44**	**5**	**7:06**	....	....	....	....	....	....	....	....
	Pittsburgh	**NHL**	**11**	**0**	**0**	**0**	**14**	**0**	**0**	**0**	**1**	**0.0**	**0**	**1**	**100.0**	**14**	**2**	**5:57**	**5**	**0**	**0**	**0**	**2**	**0**	**0**	**0**
	NHL Totals		**56**	**2**	**4**	**6**	**53**	**0**	**0**	**1**	**25**	**8.0**	**0**	**6**	**33.3**	**68**	**8**	**6:50**	**6**	**0**	**0**	**0**	**2**	**0**	**0**	**0**

Traded to **Edmonton** by **NY Islanders** for Mariusz Czerkawski, August 25, 1997. Traded to **Pittsburgh** by **Edmonton** for Sven Butenschon, March 13, 2001.

LACROIX, Daniel

(luh-KWAH, DAN-yehl)

Left wing. Shoots left. 6'2", 205 lbs. Born, Montreal, Que., March 11, 1969. NY Rangers' 2nd choice, 31st overall, in 1987 Entry Draft.

Season	Club	League	GP	G	A	Pts	PIM	PP	SH	GW	S	%	+/-	TF	F%	H	SB	Min	GP	G	A	Pts	PIM	PP	SH	GW
1985-86	L'Outaouais	QAAA	37	10	13	23	46	....	....	....	....	....	....	....	....	....	....	....	....	....	....	....	....	....	....	....
1986-87	Granby Bisons	QMJHL	54	9	16	25	311	....	....	....	....	....	....	....	....	....	....	....	8	1	2	3	22	....	....	....
1987-88	Granby Bisons	QMJHL	58	24	50	74	468	....	....	....	....	....	....	....	....	....	....	....	5	0	4	4	12	....	....	....
1988-89	Granby Bisons	QMJHL	70	45	49	94	320	....	....	....	....	....	....	....	....	....	....	....	4	1	1	2	57	....	....	....
	Denver Rangers	IHL	2	0	1	1	0	....	....	....	....	....	....	....	....	....	....	....	2	0	1	1	0	....	....	....
1989-90	Flint Spirits	IHL	61	12	16	28	128	....	....	....	....	....	....	....	....	....	....	....	4	2	0	2	24	....	....	....
1990-91	Binghamton	AHL	54	7	12	19	237	....	....	....	....	....	....	....	....	....	....	....	5	1	0	1	24	....	....	....
1991-92	Binghamton	AHL	52	12	20	32	149	....	....	....	....	....	....	....	....	....	....	....	11	2	4	6	28	....	....	....
1992-93	Binghamton	AHL	73	21	22	43	255	....	....	....	....	....	....	....	....	....	....	....	....	....	....	....	....	....	....	....
1993-94	**NY Rangers**	**NHL**	**4**	**0**	**0**	**0**	**0**	**0**	**0**	**0**	**0**	**0.0**	**0**	....	....	....	....	....	....	....	....	....	....	....	....	....
	Binghamton	AHL	59	20	23	43	278	....	....	....	....	....	....	....	....	....	....	....	....	....	....	....	....	....	....	....
1994-95	Providence Bruins	AHL	40	15	11	26	266	....	....	....	....	....	....	....	....	....	....	....	....	....	....	....	....	....	....	....
	Boston	**NHL**	**23**	**1**	**0**	**1**	**38**	**0**	**0**	**0**	**14**	**7.1**	**−2**	....	....	....	....	....	....	....	....	....	....	....	....	....
	NY Rangers	**NHL**	**1**	**0**	**0**	**0**	**0**	**0**	**0**	**0**	**0**	**0.0**	**0**	....	....	....	....	....	....	....	....	....	....	....	....	....
1995-96	**NY Rangers**	**NHL**	**25**	**2**	**2**	**4**	**30**	**0**	**0**	**0**	**14**	**14.3**	**−1**	....	....	....	....	....	....	....	....	....	....	....	....	....
	Binghamton	AHL	26	12	15	27	155	....	....	....	....	....	....	....	....	....	....	....	....	....	....	....	....	....	....	....
1996-97	**Philadelphia**	**NHL**	**74**	**7**	**1**	**8**	**163**	**1**	**0**	**0**	**54**	**13.0**	**−1**	....	....	....	....	....	**12**	**0**	**1**	**1**	**22**	**0**	**0**	**0**
1997-98	**Philadelphia**	**NHL**	**56**	**1**	**4**	**5**	**135**	**0**	**0**	**0**	**28**	**3.6**	**0**	....	....	....	....	....	**4**	**0**	**0**	**0**	**4**	**0**	**0**	**0**
1998-99	**Edmonton**	**NHL**	**4**	**0**	**0**	**0**	**13**	**0**	**0**	**0**	**5**	**0.0**	**0**	**10**	**40.0**	**5**	**0**	**6:22**	....	....	....	....	....	....	....	....
	Hamilton Bulldogs	AHL	46	13	9	22	260	....	....	....	....	....	....	....	....	....	....	....	11	3	1	4	65	....	....	....
99-2000	**NY Islanders**	**NHL**	**1**	**0**	**0**	**0**	**0**	**0**	**0**	**0**	**0**	**0.0**	**−1**	**0**	**0.0**	**3**	**0**	**10:40**	....	....	....	....	....	....	....	....
	Chicago Wolves	IHL	61	3	10	13	194	....	....	....	....	....	....	....	....	....	....	....	7	0	0	0	28	....	....	....
2000-01	Newcastle Jesters	Britain	42	8	11	19	140	....	....	....	....	....	....	....	....	....	....	....	....	....	....	....	....	....	....	....
	NHL Totals		**188**	**11**	**7**	**18**	**379**	**1**	**0**	**0**	**115**	**9.6**		**10**	**40.0**	**8**	**0**	**7:14**	**16**	**0**	**1**	**1**	**26**	**0**	**0**	**0**

Traded to **Boston** by **NY Rangers** for Glen Featherstone, August 19, 1994. Claimed on waivers by **NY Rangers** from **Boston**, March 23, 1995. Signed as a free agent by **Philadelphia**, July 18, 1996. Traded to **Edmonton** by **Philadelphia** for Valeri Zelepukin, October 5, 1998. Signed as a free agent by **NY Islanders**, August 11, 1999. Signed as a free agent by **Newcastle** (Britain), December 9, 2000.

LACROIX, Eric

(luh-KWAH, AIR-ihk)

Left wing. Shoots left. 6'1", 210 lbs. Born, Montreal, Que., July 15, 1971. Toronto's 6th choice, 136th overall, in 1990 Entry Draft.

Season	Club	League	GP	G	A	Pts	PIM	PP	SH	GW	S	%	+/-	TF	F%	H	SB	Min	GP	G	A	Pts	PIM	PP	SH	GW
1989-90	Dummer Prep	Hi-School	25	23	18	41	....	....	....	....	....	....	....	....	....	....	....	....	....	....	....	....	....	....	....	....
1990-91	St. Lawrence	ECAC	35	13	11	24	35	....	....	....	....	....	....	....	....	....	....	....	....	....	....	....	....	....	....	....
1991-92	St. Lawrence	ECAC	34	11	20	31	40	....	....	....	....	....	....	....	....	....	....	....	....	....	....	....	....	....	....	....
1992-93	St. John's Leafs	AHL	76	15	19	34	59	....	....	....	....	....	....	....	....	....	....	....	9	5	3	8	4	....	....	....
1993-94	**Toronto**	**NHL**	**3**	**0**	**0**	**0**	**2**	**0**	**0**	**0**	**3**	**0.0**	**0**	....	....	....	....	....	**2**	**0**	**0**	**0**	**0**	**0**	**0**	**0**
	St. John's Leafs	AHL	59	17	22	39	69	....	....	....	....	....	....	....	....	....	....	....	11	5	3	8	6	....	....	....
1994-95	St. John's Leafs	AHL	1	0	0	0	2	....	....	....	....	....	....	....	....	....	....	....	....	....	....	....	....	....	....	....
	Phoenix	IHL	25	7	1	8	31	....	....	....	....	....	....	....	....	....	....	....	....	....	....	....	....	....	....	....
	Los Angeles	**NHL**	**45**	**9**	**7**	**16**	**54**	**2**	**1**	**1**	**64**	**14.1**	**2**	....	....	....	....	....	....	....	....	....	....	....	....	....
1995-96	**Los Angeles**	**NHL**	**72**	**16**	**16**	**32**	**110**	**3**	**0**	**1**	**107**	**15.0**	**−11**	....	....	....	....	....	....	....	....	....	....	....	....	....
1996-97	**Colorado**	**NHL**	**81**	**18**	**18**	**36**	**26**	**2**	**0**	**4**	**141**	**12.8**	**16**	....	....	....	....	....	**17**	**1**	**4**	**5**	**19**	**0**	**0**	**0**
1997-98	**Colorado**	**NHL**	**82**	**16**	**15**	**31**	**84**	**5**	**0**	**6**	**126**	**12.7**	**0**	....	....	....	....	....	**7**	**0**	**0**	**0**	**6**	**0**	**0**	**0**
1998-99	**Colorado**	**NHL**	**7**	**0**	**0**	**0**	**2**	**0**	**0**	**0**	**4**	**0.0**	**−2**	**1**	**0.0**	**14**	**5**	**11:58**	....	....	....	....	....	....	....	....
	Los Angeles	**NHL**	**27**	**0**	**1**	**1**	**12**	**0**	**0**	**0**	**17**	**0.0**	**−5**	**2**	**50.0**	**82**	**10**	**8:37**	....	....	....	....	....	....	....	....
	NY Rangers	**NHL**	**30**	**2**	**1**	**3**	**4**	**0**	**0**	**1**	**17**	**11.8**	**−5**	**14**	**100.0**	**49**	**12**	**4:05**	....	....	....	....	....	....	....	....
99-2000	**NY Rangers**	**NHL**	**70**	**4**	**8**	**12**	**24**	**0**	**0**	**1**	**46**	**8.7**	**−12**	**4**	**25.0**	**142**	**48**	**10:02**	....	....	....	....	....	....	....	....
2000-01	**NY Rangers**	**NHL**	**46**	**2**	**3**	**5**	**39**	**0**	**0**	**0**	**22**	**9.1**	**−6**	**4**	**0.0**	**67**	**21**	**6:19**	....	....	....	....	....	....	....	....
	Ottawa	**NHL**	**9**	**0**	**1**	**1**	**4**	**0**	**0**	**0**	**10**	**0.0**	**0**	**1**	**0.0**	**23**	**4**	**8:05**	**4**	**0**	**1**	**1**	**0**	**0**	**0**	**0**
	NHL Totals		**472**	**67**	**70**	**137**	**361**	**12**	**1**	**14**	**557**	**12.0**		**26**	**61.5**	**377**	**100**	**7:58**	**30**	**1**	**5**	**6**	**25**	**0**	**0**	**0**

Traded to **LA Kings** by **Toronto** with Chris Snell and Toronto's 4th round choice (Eric Belanger) in 1996 Entry Draft for Dixon Ward, Guy Leveque, Kelly Fairchild and Shayne Toporowski, October 3, 1994. Traded to **Colorado** by **LA Kings** with LA Kings' 1st round choice (Martin Skoula) in 1998 Entry Draft for Stephane Fiset and Colorado's 1st round choice (Mathieu Biron) in 1998 Entry Draft, June 20, 1996. Traded to **LA Kings** by **Colorado** for Roman Vopat and Los Angeles' 6th round choice (later traded to Ottawa - Ottawa selected Martin Prusek) in 1999 Entry Draft, October 29, 1998. Traded to **NY Rangers** by **LA Kings** for Sean Pronger, February 12, 1999. Traded to **Ottawa** by **NY Rangers** for Colin Forbes, March 1, 2001.

LAFLAMME, Christian

(lah-FLAM, KRIHS-tan)

Defense. Shoots right. 6'1", 210 lbs. Born, St-Charles, Que., November 24, 1976. Chicago's 2nd choice, 45th overall, in 1995 Entry Draft.

			Regular Season																Playoffs							
Season	Club	League	GP	G	A	Pts	PIM	PP	SH	GW	S	%	+/-	TF	F%	H	SB	Min	GP	G	A	Pts	PIM	PP	SH	GW
1991-92	Ste-Foy Governors	QAAA	42	5	27	32	100	....	....	....	....	....	....	....	....	....	....	....	8	1	2	3	14	....	....	....
1992-93	Verdun College	QMJHL	69	2	17	19	85	....	....	....	....	....	....	....	....	....	....	....	3	0	2	2	6	....	....	....
1993-94	Verdun College	QMJHL	72	4	34	38	85	....	....	....	....	....	....	....	....	....	....	....	4	0	3	3	4	....	....	....
1994-95	Beauport	QMJHL	67	6	41	47	82	....	....	....	....	....	....	....	....	....	....	....	8	1	4	5	6	....	....	....
1995-96	Beauport	QMJHL	41	13	23	36	63	....	....	....	....	....	....	....	....	....	....	....	20	7	17	24	32	....	....	....
1996-97	**Chicago**	**NHL**	**4**	**0**	**1**	**1**	**2**	**0**	**0**	**0**	**3**	**0.0**	**3**	....	....	....	....	....	....	....	....	....	....	....	....	....
	Indianapolis Ice	IHL	62	5	15	20	60	....	....	....	....	....	....	....	....	....	....	....	4	1	1	2	16	....	....	....
1997-98	**Chicago**	**NHL**	**72**	**0**	**11**	**11**	**59**	**0**	**0**	**0**	**75**	**0.**[illegible]	**4**	....	....	....	....	....	....	....	....	....	....	....	....	....
1998-99	**Chicago**	**NHL**	**62**	**2**	**11**	**13**	**70**	**0**	**0**	**0**	**53**	**3.**[illegible]	[illegible]	**0**	**0.0**	**154**	**58**	**18:51**	....	....	....	....	....	....	....	....
	Portland Pirates	AHL	2	0	1	1	2	....	....	....	....	....	[illegible]	[illegible]	[illegible]	....	....	....	....	....	....	....	....	....	....	....
	Edmonton	**NHL**	**11**	**0**	**1**	**1**	**0**	**0**	**0**	**0**	**15**	**0.**[illegible]	[illegible]	[illegible]	**0.0**	**22**	**14**	**16:33**	**4**	**0**	**1**	**1**	**2**	**0**	**0**	**0**
99-2000	**Edmonton**	**NHL**	**50**	**0**	**5**	**5**	**32**	**0**	**0**	**0**	**18**	**0.**[illegible]	[illegible]	[illegible]	[illegible]**.0**	**113**	**33**	**13:40**	....	....	....	....	....	....	....	....
	Montreal	**NHL**	**15**	**0**	**2**	**2**	**8**	**0**	**0**	**0**	**6**	[illegible]	[illegible]	[illegible]	[illegible]	**28**	**11**	**14:32**	....	....	....	....	....	....	....	....
2000-01	**Montreal**	**NHL**	**39**	**0**	**3**	**3**	**42**	**0**	**0**	**0**	**16**	[illegible]	[illegible]	[illegible]	[illegible]	**74**	**27**	**12:04**	....	....	....	....	....	....	....	....
	NHL Totals		**253**	**2**	**34**	**36**	**213**	**0**	**0**	**0**	**186**	[illegible]	[illegible]	[illegible]	[illegible]	**391**	**143**	**15:23**	**4**	**0**	**1**	**1**	**2**	**0**	**0**	**0**

QMJHL Second All-Star Team (1995)

Traded to **Edmonton** by **Chicago** with Daniel Cleary, Ethan Moreau and Chad Kilger for Boris Mironov, Dean M[illegible]son, March 20, 1999. Traded to **Montreal** by **Edmonton** with Matthieu Descoteaux for Igor Ulanov and Alain Nasreddine, March 9, 2000. • Missed majority of 2000-01 season [illegible]ury suffered in game vs. Calgary, December 13, 2000.

LAKOVIC, Sasha

(LA-koh-vik, SA-shuh)

Right wing. Shoots left. 6', 220 lbs. Born, Vancouver, B.C., September 7, 1971.

Season	Club	League	GP	G	A	Pts	PIM	PP	SH	GW	S	%	+/-	TF	F%	H	SB	Min	GP	G	A	Pts	PIM	PP	SH	GW
1991-92	Kelowna Spartans	BCJHL	4	1	0	1	14	....	....	....	....	....	....	....	....	....	....	....	....	....	....	....	....	....	....	....
	Bellingham Hawks	BCJHL	24	8	3	11	67	....	....	....	....	....	....	....	....	....	....	....	....	....	....	....	....	....	....	....
1992-93	Chatham Wheels	ColHL	28	7	5	12	235	....	....	....	....	....	....	....	....	....	....	....	....	....	....	....	....	....	....	....
	Columbus Chill	ECHL	27	7	9	16	162	....	....	....	....	....	....	....	....	....	....	....	....	....	....	....	....	....	....	....
	Binghamton	AHL	3	0	0	0	0	....	....	....	....	....	....	....	....	....	....	....	....	....	....	....	....	....	....	....
	Brantford Smoke	ColHL	....	....	....	....	....	....	....	....	....	....	....	....	....	....	....	....	5	2	1	3	66	....	....	....
1993-94	Toledo Storm	ECHL	24	5	10	15	198	....	....	....	....	....	....	....	....	....	....	....	....	....	....	....	....	....	....	....
	Chatham Wheels	ColHL	13	11	7	18	61	....	....	....	....	....	....	....	....	....	....	....	....	....	....	....	....	....	....	....
1994-95	Tulsa Oilers	CHL	40	20	24	44	214	....	....	....	....	....	....	....	....	....	....	....	5	1	3	4	88	....	....	....
1995-96	Las Vegas	IHL	49	1	2	3	416	....	....	....	....	....	....	....	....	....	....	....	13	1	1	2	*57	....	....	....
1996-97	**Calgary**	**NHL**	**19**	**0**	**1**	**1**	**54**	**0**	**0**	**0**	**10**	**0.0**	**–1**	....	....	....	....	....	....	....	....	....	....	....	....	....
	Saint John Flames	AHL	18	1	8	9	182	....	....	....	....	....	....	....	....	....	....	....	....	....	....	....	....	....	....	....
	Las Vegas	IHL	10	0	0	0	81	....	....	....	....	....	....	....	....	....	....	....	2	0	0	0	14	....	....	....
1997-98	**New Jersey**	**NHL**	**2**	**0**	**0**	**0**	**5**	**0**	**0**	**0**	**2**	**0.0**	**0**	....	....	....	....	....	....	....	....	....	....	....	....	....
	Albany River Rats	AHL	30	7	6	13	158	....	....	....	....	....	....	....	....	....	....	....	13	3	4	7	*84	....	....	....
1998-99	**New Jersey**	**NHL**	**16**	**0**	**3**	**3**	**59**	**0**	**0**	**0**	**10**	**0.0**	**0**	**0**	**0.0**	**41**	**1**	**6:20**	....	....	....	....	....	....	....	....
	Albany River Rats	AHL	10	1	1	2	93	....	....	....	....	....	....	....	....	....	....	....	....	....	....	....	....	....	....	....
99-2000	Albany River Rats	AHL	51	10	16	26	144	....	....	....	....	....	....	....	....	....	....	....	5	0	0	0	14	....	....	....
2000-01	Rochester	AHL	51	3	9	12	161	....	....	....	....	....	....	....	....	....	....	....	4	1	1	2	32	....	....	....
	Long Beach	WCHL	8	3	6	9	29	....	....	....	....	....	....	....	....	....	....	....	....	....	....	....	....	....	....	....
	NHL Totals		**37**	**0**	**4**	**4**	**118**	**0**	**0**	**0**	**22**	**0.0**		**0**	**0.0**	**41**	**1**	**6:20**	....	....	....	....	....	....	....	....

Signed as a free agent by **Calgary**, October 10, 1996. Signed as a free agent by **New Jersey**, September 24, 1997.

LAMBERT, Denny

(lahm-BAIR, DEH-nee) **ANA.**

Left wing. Shoots left. 5'10", 215 lbs. Born, Wawa, Ont., January 7, 1970.

Season	Club	League	GP	G	A	Pts	PIM	PP	SH	GW	S	%	+/-	TF	F%	H	SB	Min	GP	G	A	Pts	PIM	PP	SH	GW
1986-87	S.S. Marie Legion	NOHA	22	8	13	21	129	....	....	....	....	....	....	....	....	....	....	....	....	....	....	....	....	....	....	....
1987-88	S.S. Marie T-Birds	NOJHA	32	25	27	52	184	....	....	....	....	....	....	....	....	....	....	....	....	....	....	....	....	....	....	....
1988-89	Sault Ste. Marie	OHL	61	14	15	29	203	....	....	....	....	....	....	....	....	....	....	....	....	....	....	....	....	....	....	....
1989-90	Sault Ste. Marie	OHL	61	23	29	52	276	....	....	....	....	....	....	....	....	....	....	....	....	....	....	....	....	....	....	....
1990-91	Sault Ste. Marie	OHL	59	28	39	67	169	....	....	....	....	....	....	....	....	....	....	....	14	7	9	16	48	....	....	....
1991-92	San Diego Gulls	IHL	71	17	14	31	229	....	....	....	....	....	....	....	....	....	....	....	3	0	0	0	10	....	....	....
	St. Thomas	ColHL	5	2	6	8	9	....	....	....	....	....	....	....	....	....	....	....	....	....	....	....	....	....	....	....
1992-93	San Diego Gulls	IHL	56	18	12	30	277	....	....	....	....	....	....	....	....	....	....	....	14	1	1	2	44	....	....	....
1993-94	San Diego Gulls	IHL	79	13	14	27	314	....	....	....	....	....	....	....	....	....	....	....	6	1	0	1	55	....	....	....
1994-95	San Diego Gulls	IHL	75	25	35	60	222	....	....	....	....	....	....	....	....	....	....	....	....	....	....	....	....	....	....	....
	Anaheim	**NHL**	**13**	**1**	**3**	**4**	**4**	**0**	**0**	**0**	**14**	**7.1**	**3**	....	....	....	....	....	....	....	....	....	....	....	....	....
1995-96	**Anaheim**	**NHL**	**33**	**0**	**8**	**8**	**55**	**0**	**0**	**0**	**28**	**0.0**	**–2**	....	....	....	....	....	....	....	....	....	....	....	....	....
	Baltimore Bandits	AHL	44	14	28	42	126	....	....	....	....	....	....	....	....	....	....	....	12	3	9	12	39	....	....	....
1996-97	**Ottawa**	**NHL**	**80**	**4**	**16**	**20**	**217**	**0**	**0**	**1**	**58**	**6.9**	**–4**	....	....	....	....	....	**6**	**0**	**1**	**1**	**9**	**0**	**0**	**0**
1997-98	**Ottawa**	**NHL**	**72**	**9**	**10**	**19**	**250**	**0**	**0**	**1**	**76**	**11.8**	**4**	....	....	....	....	....	**11**	**0**	**0**	**0**	**19**	**0**	**0**	**0**
1998-99	**Nashville**	**NHL**	**76**	**5**	**11**	**16**	**218**	**1**	**0**	**0**	**66**	**7.6**	**–3**	**1**	**100.0**	**57**	**17**	**10:20**	....	....	....	....	....	....	....	....
99-2000	**Atlanta**	**NHL**	**73**	**5**	**6**	**11**	***219**	**2**	**0**	**0**	**83**	**6.0**	**–17**	**5**	**0.0**	**127**	**22**	**11:39**	....	....	....	....	....	....	....	....
2000-01	**Atlanta**	**NHL**	**67**	**1**	**7**	**8**	**215**	**0**	**0**	**0**	**44**	**2.3**	**–5**	**18**	**38.9**	**79**	**11**	**9:08**	....	....	....	....	....	....	....	....
	NHL Totals		**414**	**25**	**61**	**86**	**1178**	**3**	**0**	**2**	**369**	**6.8**		**24**	**33.3**	**263**	**50**	**10:24**	**17**	**0**	**1**	**1**	**28**	**0**	**0**	**0**

Signed as a free agent by **Anaheim**, August 16, 1993. Signed as a free agent by **Ottawa**, July 29, 1996. Claimed by **Nashville** from **Ottawa** in Expansion Draft, June 26, 1998. Traded to **Atlanta** by **Nashville** for the rights to Randy Robitaille, August 16, 1999. Traded to **Anaheim** by **Atlanta** for future considerations, July 2, 2001.

LANDRY, Eric

(LAN-dree, AIR-ihk) **MTL.**

Center. Shoots left. 5'10", 182 lbs. Born, Gatineau, Que., January 20, 1975.

Season	Club	League	GP	G	A	Pts	PIM	PP	SH	GW	S	%	+/-	TF	F%	H	SB	Min	GP	G	A	Pts	PIM	PP	SH	GW
1992-93	Abitibi Foresters	QAAA	40	15	11	26	98	....	....	....	....	....	....	....	....	....	....	....	1	0	0	0	19	....	....	....
1993-94	St-Hyacinthe	QMJHL	69	42	34	76	128	....	....	....	....	....	....	....	....	....	....	....	7	4	2	6	13	....	....	....
1994-95	St-Hyacinthe	QMJHL	68	38	36	74	249	....	....	....	....	....	....	....	....	....	....	....	5	2	1	3	10	....	....	....
1995-96	Cape Breton	AHL	74	19	33	52	187	....	....	....	....	....	....	....	....	....	....	....	....	....	....	....	....	....	....	....
1996-97	Hamilton Bulldogs	AHL	74	15	17	32	139	....	....	....	....	....	....	....	....	....	....	....	22	6	7	13	43	....	....	....
1997-98	**Calgary**	**NHL**	**12**	**1**	**0**	**1**	**4**	**0**	**0**	**0**	**7**	**14.3**	**–2**	....	....	....	....	....	....	....	....	....	....	....	....	....
	Saint John Flames	AHL	61	17	21	38	194	....	....	....	....	....	....	....	....	....	....	....	20	4	6	10	58	....	....	....
1998-99	**Calgary**	**NHL**	**3**	**0**	**1**	**1**	**0**	**0**	**0**	**0**	**1**	**0.0**	**1**	**15**	**46.7**	**8**	**0**	**9:54**	....	....	....	....	....	....	....	....
	Saint John Flames	AHL	56	19	22	41	158	....	....	....	....	....	....	....	....	....	....	....	7	2	5	7	12	....	....	....
99-2000	Kentucky	AHL	79	35	31	66	170	....	....	....	....	....	....	....	....	....	....	....	9	3	6	9	2	....	....	....
2000-01	**Montreal**	**NHL**	**51**	**4**	**7**	**11**	**43**	**2**	**0**	**0**	**54**	**7.4**	**–9**	**510**	**52.8**	**94**	**10**	**9:19**	....	....	....	....	....	....	....	....
	Quebec Citadelles	AHL	27	14	18	32	90	....	....	....	....	....	....	....	....	....	....	....	9	4	4	8	35	....	....	....
	NHL Totals		**66**	**5**	**8**	**13**	**47**	**2**	**0**	**0**	**62**	**8.1**		**525**	**52.6**	**102**	**10**	**9:21**	....	....	....	....	....	....	....	....

Signed as a free agent by **Calgary**, August 20, 1997. Traded to **San Jose** by **Calgary** for Fredrik Oduya, July 12, 1999. Signed as a free agent by **Montreal**, July 7, 2000.

LANG, Robert

(LANG, RAW-buhrt) **PIT.**

Center. Shoots right. 6'2", 216 lbs. Born, Teplice, Czech., December 19, 1970. Los Angeles' 6th choice, 133rd overall, in 1990 Entry Draft.

Season	Club	League	GP	G	A	Pts	PIM	PP	SH	GW	S	%	+/-	TF	F%	H	SB	Min	GP	G	A	Pts	PIM	PP	SH	GW
1988-89	CHZ Litvinov	Czech.	7	3	2	5	0	....	....	....	....	....	....	....	....	....	....	....	....	....	....	....	....	....	....	....
1989-90	CHZ Litvinov	Czech.	32	8	7	15		....	....	....	....	....	....	....	....	....	....	....	8	3	3	6	....	....	....	....
1990-91	CHZ Litvinov	Czech.	56	26	26	52	38	....	....	....	....	....	....	....	....	....	....	....	....	....	....	....	....	....	....	....
1991-92	CHZ Litvinov	Czech.	43	12	31	43	34	....	....	....	....	....	....	....	....	....	....	....	....	....	....	....	....	....	....	....
	Czechoslovakia	Olympics	8	5	8	13	8	....	....	....	....	....	....	....	....	....	....	....	....	....	....	....	....	....	....	....
1992-93	**Los Angeles**	**NHL**	**11**	**0**	**5**	**5**	**2**	**0**	**0**	**0**	**3**	**0.0**	**–3**	....	....	....	....	....	....	....	....	....	....	....	....	....
	Phoenix	IHL	38	9	21	30	20	....	....	....	....	....	....	....	....	....	....	....	....	....	....	....	....	....	....	....
1993-94	**Los Angeles**	**NHL**	**32**	**9**	**10**	**19**	**10**	**0**	**0**	**0**	**41**	**22.0**	**7**	....	....	....	....	....	....	....	....	....	....	....	....	....
	Phoenix	IHL	44	11	24	35	34	....	....	....	....	....	....	....	....	....	....	....	....	....	....	....	....	....	....	....
1994-95	CHZ Litvinov	Cze-Rep	16	4	19	23	28	....	....	....	....	....	....	....	....	....	....	....	....	....	....	....	....	....	....	....
	Los Angeles	**NHL**	**36**	**4**	**8**	**12**	**4**	**0**	**0**	**0**	**38**	**10.5**	**–7**	....	....	....	....	....	....	....	....	....	....	....	....	....
1995-96	**Los Angeles**	**NHL**	**68**	**6**	**16**	**22**	**10**	**0**	**2**	**0**	**71**	**8.5**	**–15**	....	....	....	....	....	....	....	....	....	....	....	....	....
1996-97	Sparta Praha	Cze-Rep	38	14	27	41	30	....	....	....	....	....	....	....	....	....	....	....	5	1	2	3	4	....	....	....
	Sparta Praha	EuroHL	4	2	2	4	0	....	....	....	....	....	....	....	....	....	....	....	4	2	1	3	2	....	....	....

			Regular Season																Playoffs							
Season	Club	League	GP	G	A	Pts	PIM	PP	SH	GW	S	%	+/-	TF	F%	H	SB	Min	GP	G	A	Pts	PIM	PP	SH	GW
1997-98	**Boston**	**NHL**	**3**	**0**	**0**	**0**	**2**	**0**	**0**	**0**	**2**	**0.0**	**1**	....	....	....	....	....	....	....	....	....	....	....	....	....
	Pittsburgh	**NHL**	**51**	**9**	**13**	**22**	**14**	**1**	**1**	**2**	**64**	**14.1**	**6**	....	....	....	....	....	**6**	**0**	**3**	**3**	**2**	**0**	**0**	**0**
	Czech-Republic	Olympics	6	0	3	3	0	....	....	....	....	....	....	....	....	....	....	....	....	....	....	....	....	....	....	....
	Houston Aeros	IHL	9	1	7	8	4	....	....	....	....	....	....	....	....	....	....	....	....	....	....	....	....	....	....	....
1998-99	**Pittsburgh**	**NHL**	**72**	**21**	**23**	**44**	**24**	**7**	**0**	**3**	**137**	**15.3**	**–10**	**964**	**44.8**	**84**	**22**	**16:24**	**12**	**0**	**2**	**2**	**0**	**0**	**0**	**0**
99-2000	**Pittsburgh**	**NHL**	**78**	**23**	**42**	**65**	**14**	**13**	**0**	**5**	**142**	**16.2**	**–9**	**1433**	**50.7**	**60**	**51**	**19:22**	**11**	**3**	**3**	**6**	**0**	**2**	**0**	**0**
2000-01	**Pittsburgh**	**NHL**	**82**	**32**	**48**	**80**	**28**	**10**	**0**	**2**	**177**	**18.1**	**20**	**1348**	**43.9**	**51**	**38**	**20:24**	**16**	**4**	**4**	**8**	**4**	**0**	**0**	**0**
	NHL Totals		**433**	**104**	**165**	**269**	**108**	**31**	**3**	**12**	**675**	**15.4**		**3745**	**46.7**	**195**	**111**	**18:49**	**45**	**7**	**12**	**19**	**6**	**2**	**0**	**0**

Signed as a free agent by **Pittsburgh**, September 2, 1997. Claimed by **Boston** from **Pittsburgh** in NHL Waiver Draft, September 28, 1997. Claimed on waivers by **Pittsburgh** from **Boston**, October 25, 1997.

LANGDON, Darren

(LAING-duhn, DAIR-uhn) **CAR.**

Left wing. Shoots left. 6'1", 205 lbs. Born, Deer Lake, Nfld., January 8, 1971.

1991-92	Summerside	MJrHL	44	34	49	83	441	....	....	....	....	....	....	....	....	....	....	....	....	....	....	....	....	....	....	....
1992-93	Binghamton	AHL	18	3	4	7	115	....	....	....	....	....	....	....	....	....	....	....	8	0	1	1	14	....	....	....
	Dayton Bombers	ECHL	54	23	22	45	429	....	....	....	....	....	....	....	....	....	....	....	3	0	1	1	40	....	....	....
1993-94	Binghamton	AHL	54	2	7	9	327	....	....	....	....	....	....	....	....	....	....	....	....	....	....	....	....	....	....	....
1994-95	Binghamton	AHL	55	6	14	20	296	....	....	....	....	....	....	....	....	....	....	....	11	1	3	4	*84	....	....	....
	NY Rangers	**NHL**	**18**	**1**	**1**	**2**	**62**	**0**	**0**	**0**	**6**	**16.7**	**0**	....	....	....	....	....	....	....	....	....	....	....	....	....
1995-96	**NY Rangers**	**NHL**	**64**	**7**	**4**	**11**	**175**	**0**	**0**	**1**	**29**	**24.1**	**2**	....	....	....	....	....	**2**	**0**	**0**	**0**	**0**	**0**	**0**	**0**
	Binghamton	AHL	1	0	0	0	12	....	....	....	....	....	....	....	....	....	....	....	....	....	....	....	....	....	....	....
1996-97	**NY Rangers**	**NHL**	**60**	**3**	**6**	**9**	**195**	**0**	**0**	**1**	**24**	**12.5**	**–1**	....	....	....	....	....	**10**	**0**	**0**	**0**	**2**	**0**	**0**	**0**
1997-98	**NY Rangers**	**NHL**	**70**	**3**	**3**	**6**	**197**	**0**	**0**	**0**	**15**	**20.0**	**0**	....	....	....	....	....	....	....	....	....	....	....	....	....
1998-99	**NY Rangers**	**NHL**	**44**	**0**	**0**	**0**	**80**	**0**	**0**	**0**	**8**	**0.0**	**–3**	**0**	**0.0**	**37**	**5**	**3:33**	....	....	....	....	....	....	....	....
99-2000	**NY Rangers**	**NHL**	**21**	**0**	**1**	**1**	**26**	**0**	**0**	**0**	**13**	**0.0**	**–2**	**0**	**0.0**	**22**	**2**	**5:36**	....	....	....	....	....	....	....	....
2000-01	**Carolina**	**NHL**	**54**	**0**	**2**	**2**	**94**	**0**	**0**	**0**	**6**	**0.0**	**–4**	**2**	**100.0**	**36**	**6**	**3:21**	**4**	**0**	**0**	**0**	**12**	**0**	**0**	**0**
	NHL Totals		**331**	**14**	**17**	**31**	**829**	**0**	**0**	**2**	**101**	**13.9**		**2**	**100.0**	**95**	**13**	**3:49**	**16**	**0**	**0**	**0**	**14**	**0**	**0**	**0**

Signed as a free agent by **NY Rangers**, August 16, 1993. • Missed majority of 1999-2000 season recovering from hernia injury suffered in game vs. New Jersey, December 1, 1999. Traded to **Carolina** by **NY Rangers** with Rob DiMaio for Sandy McCarthy and Carolina's 4th round choice (Bryce Lampman) in 2001 Entry Draft, August 4, 2000.

LANGENBRUNNER, Jamie

(lan-gehn-BRUH-nuhr, JAY-mee) **DAL.**

Center. Shoots right. 6'1", 200 lbs. Born, Duluth, MN, July 24, 1975. Dallas' 2nd choice, 35th overall, in 1993 Entry Draft.

1990-91	Cloquet High	Hi-School	20	6	16	22	8	....	....	....	....	....	....	....	....	....	....	....	....	....	....	....	....	....	....	....
1991-92	Cloquet High	Hi-School	23	16	23	39	24	....	....	....	....	....	....	....	....	....	....	....	....	....	....	....	....	....	....	....
1992-93	Cloquet High	Hi-School	27	27	62	89	18	....	....	....	....	....	....	....	....	....	....	....	....	....	....	....	....	....	....	....
1993-94	Peterborough	OHL	62	33	58	91	53	....	....	....	....	....	....	....	....	....	....	....	7	4	6	10	2	....	....	....
1994-95	Peterborough	OHL	62	42	57	99	84	....	....	....	....	....	....	....	....	....	....	....	11	8	14	22	12	....	....	....
	Dallas	**NHL**	**2**	**0**	**0**	**0**	**2**	**0**	**0**	**0**	**1**	**0.0**	**0**	....	....	....	....	....	....	....	....	....	....	....	....	....
	Kalamazoo Wings	IHL	....	....	....	....	....	....	....	....	....	....	....	....	....	....	....	....	11	1	3	4	2	....	....	....
1995-96	**Dallas**	**NHL**	**12**	**2**	**2**	**4**	**6**	**1**	**0**	**0**	**15**	**13.3**	**–2**	....	....	....	....	....	....	....	....	....	....	....	....	....
	Michigan K-Wings	IHL	59	25	40	65	129	....	....	....	....	....	....	....	....	....	....	....	10	3	10	13	8	....	....	....
1996-97	**Dallas**	**NHL**	**76**	**13**	**26**	**39**	**51**	**3**	**0**	**3**	**112**	**11.6**	**–2**	....	....	....	....	....	**5**	**1**	**1**	**2**	**14**	**0**	**0**	**1**
1997-98	**Dallas**	**NHL**	**81**	**23**	**29**	**52**	**61**	**8**	**0**	**6**	**159**	**14.5**	**9**	....	....	....	....	....	**16**	**1**	**4**	**5**	**14**	**0**	**0**	**1**
	United States	Olympics	3	0	0	0	4	....	....	....	....	....	....	....	....	....	....	....	....	....	....	....	....	....	....	....
1998-99♦	**Dallas**	**NHL**	**75**	**12**	**33**	**45**	**62**	**4**	**0**	**1**	**145**	**8.3**	**10**	**217**	**46.1**	**129**	**21**	**15:51**	**23**	**10**	**7**	**17**	**16**	**4**	**0**	**3**
99-2000	**Dallas**	**NHL**	**65**	**18**	**21**	**39**	**68**	**4**	**2**	**6**	**153**	**11.8**	**16**	**40**	**50.0**	**117**	**10**	**17:33**	**15**	**1**	**7**	**8**	**18**	**1**	**0**	**0**
2000-01	**Dallas**	**NHL**	**53**	**12**	**18**	**30**	**57**	**3**	**2**	**4**	**104**	**11.5**	**4**	**316**	**45.3**	**78**	**26**	**16:30**	**10**	**2**	**2**	**4**	**6**	**0**	**0**	**1**
	NHL Totals		**364**	**80**	**129**	**209**	**307**	**23**	**4**	**20**	**689**	**11.6**		**573**	**45.9**	**324**	**57**	**16:36**	**69**	**15**	**21**	**36**	**68**	**5**	**0**	**6**

LANGKOW, Daymond

(LAING-kow, DAY-muhn) **PHX.**

Center. Shoots left. 5'11", 180 lbs. Born, Edmonton, Alta, September 27, 1976. Tampa Bay's 1st choice, 5th overall, in 1995 Entry Draft.

1991-92	Edmonton Pats	AMHL	35	36	45	81	100	....	....	....	....	....	....	....	....	....	....	....	....	....	....	....	....	....	....	....
	Tri-City Americans	WHL	1	0	0	0	0	....	....	....	....	....	....	....	....	....	....	....	....	....	....	....	....	....	....	....
1992-93	Tri-City Americans	WHL	64	22	42	64	100	....	....	....	....	....	....	....	....	....	....	....	4	1	0	1	4	....	....	....
1993-94	Tri-City Americans	WHL	61	40	43	83	174	....	....	....	....	....	....	....	....	....	....	....	4	2	2	4	15	....	....	....
1994-95	Tri-City Americans	WHL	72	*67	73	*140	142	....	....	....	....	....	....	....	....	....	....	....	17	12	15	27	52	....	....	....
1995-96	Tri-City Americans	WHL	48	30	61	91	103	....	....	....	....	....	....	....	....	....	....	....	11	14	13	27	20	....	....	....
	Tampa Bay	**NHL**	**4**	**0**	**1**	**1**	**0**	**0**	**0**	**0**	**4**	**0.0**	**–1**	....	....	....	....	....	....	....	....	....	....	....	....	....
1996-97	**Tampa Bay**	**NHL**	**79**	**15**	**13**	**28**	**35**	**3**	**1**	**1**	**170**	**8.8**	**1**	....	....	....	....	....	....	....	....	....	....	....	....	....
	Adirondack	AHL	2	1	1	2	0	....	....	....	....	....	....	....	....	....	....	....	....	....	....	....	....	....	....	....
1997-98	**Tampa Bay**	**NHL**	**68**	**8**	**14**	**22**	**62**	**2**	**0**	**1**	**156**	**5.1**	**–9**	....	....	....	....	....	....	....	....	....	....	....	....	....
1998-99	**Tampa Bay**	**NHL**	**22**	**4**	**6**	**10**	**15**	**1**	**0**	**1**	**40**	**10.0**	**0**	**399**	**48.4**	**20**	**8**	**17:10**	....	....	....	....	....	....	....	....
	Cleveland	IHL	4	1	1	2	18	....	....	....	....	....	....	....	....	....	....	....	....	....	....	....	....	....	....	....
	Philadelphia	**NHL**	**56**	**10**	**13**	**23**	**24**	**3**	**1**	**1**	**109**	**9.2**	**–8**	**738**	**48.0**	**35**	**12**	**15:12**	**6**	**0**	**2**	**2**	**2**	**0**	**0**	**0**
99-2000	**Philadelphia**	**NHL**	**82**	**18**	**32**	**50**	**56**	**5**	**0**	**7**	**222**	**8.1**	**1**	**1263**	**45.1**	**78**	**41**	**16:57**	**16**	**5**	**5**	**10**	**23**	**1**	**1**	**2**
2000-01	**Philadelphia**	**NHL**	**71**	**13**	**41**	**54**	**50**	**3**	**0**	**2**	**190**	**6.8**	**12**	**1181**	**47.2**	**61**	**32**	**18:38**	**6**	**2**	**4**	**6**	**2**	**1**	**0**	**0**
	NHL Totals		**382**	**68**	**120**	**188**	**242**	**17**	**2**	**13**	**891**	**7.6**		**3581**	**46.7**	**194**	**93**	**17:04**	**28**	**7**	**11**	**18**	**27**	**2**	**1**	**2**

WHL West First All-Star Team (1995) • Canadian Major Junior First All-Star Team (1995) • WHL West Second All-Star Team (1996)

Traded to **Philadelphia** by **Tampa Bay** with Mikael Renberg for Chris Gratton and Mike Sillinger, December 12, 1998. Traded to **Phoenix** by **Philadelphia** for future considerations, July 2, 2001.

LAPERRIERE, Ian

(luh-PAIR-ee-YAIR, EE-ihn) **L.A.**

Center. Shoots right. 6'1", 201 lbs. Born, Montreal, Que., January 19, 1974. St. Louis' 6th choice, 158th overall, in 1992 Entry Draft.

1989-90	Mtl-Bourassa	QAAA	22	4	10	14	10	....	....	....	....	....	....	....	....	....	....	....	3	0	1	1	6	....	....	....
1990-91	Drummondville	QMJHL	65	19	29	48	117	....	....	....	....	....	....	....	....	....	....	....	14	2	9	11	48	....	....	....
1991-92	Drummondville	QMJHL	70	28	49	77	160	....	....	....	....	....	....	....	....	....	....	....	4	2	2	4	9	....	....	....
1992-93	Drummondville	QMJHL	60	44	*96	140	188	....	....	....	....	....	....	....	....	....	....	....	10	6	13	19	20	....	....	....
1993-94	Drummondville	QMJHL	62	41	72	113	150	....	....	....	....	....	....	....	....	....	....	....	9	4	6	10	35	....	....	....
	St. Louis	**NHL**	**1**	**0**	**0**	**0**	**0**	**0**	**0**	**0**	**1**	**0.0**	**0**	....	....	....	....	....	....	....	....	....	....	....	....	....
	Peoria Rivermen	IHL	....	....	....	....	....	....	....	....	....	....	....	....	....	....	....	....	5	1	3	4	2	....	....	....
1994-95	Peoria Rivermen	IHL	51	16	32	48	111	....	....	....	....	....	....	....	....	....	....	....	....	....	....	....	....	....	....	....
	St. Louis	**NHL**	**37**	**13**	**14**	**27**	**85**	**1**	**0**	**1**	**53**	**24.5**	**12**	....	....	....	....	....	**7**	**0**	**4**	**4**	**21**	**0**	**0**	**0**
1995-96	**St. Louis**	**NHL**	**33**	**3**	**6**	**9**	**87**	**1**	**0**	**1**	**31**	**9.7**	**–4**	....	....	....	....	....	....	....	....	....	....	....	....	....
	Worcester	AHL	3	2	1	3	22	....	....	....	....	....	....	....	....	....	....	....	....	....	....	....	....	....	....	....
	NY Rangers	**NHL**	**28**	**1**	**2**	**3**	**53**	**0**	**0**	**0**	**21**	**4.8**	**–5**	....	....	....	....	....	....	....	....	....	....	....	....	....
	Los Angeles	**NHL**	**10**	**2**	**3**	**5**	**15**	**0**	**0**	**0**	**18**	**11.1**	**–2**	....	....	....	....	....	....	....	....	....	....	....	....	....
1996-97	**Los Angeles**	**NHL**	**62**	**8**	**15**	**23**	**102**	**0**	**1**	**2**	**84**	**9.5**	**–25**	....	....	....	....	....	....	....	....	....	....	....	....	....
1997-98	**Los Angeles**	**NHL**	**77**	**6**	**15**	**21**	**131**	**0**	**1**	**1**	**74**	**8.1**	**0**	....	....	....	....	....	**4**	**1**	**0**	**1**	**6**	**0**	**0**	**0**
1998-99	**Los Angeles**	**NHL**	**72**	**3**	**10**	**13**	**138**	**0**	**0**	**1**	**62**	**4.8**	**–5**	**643**	**47.3**	**149**	**60**	**11:47**	....	....	....	....	....	....	....	....
99-2000	**Los Angeles**	**NHL**	**79**	**9**	**13**	**22**	**185**	**0**	**0**	**1**	**87**	**10.3**	**–14**	**1111**	**53.7**	**181**	**60**	**13:15**	**4**	**0**	**0**	**0**	**2**	**0**	**0**	**0**
2000-01	**Los Angeles**	**NHL**	**79**	**8**	**10**	**18**	**141**	**0**	**0**	**0**	**60**	**13.3**	**5**	**297**	**51.9**	**209**	**29**	**12:02**	**13**	**1**	**2**	**3**	**12**	**0**	**0**	**0**
	NHL Totals		**478**	**53**	**88**	**141**	**937**	**2**	**2**	**7**	**491**	**10.8**		**2051**	**51.4**	**539**	**149**	**12:23**	**28**	**2**	**6**	**8**	**41**	**0**	**0**	**0**

QMJHL Second All-Star Team (1993)

Traded to **NY Rangers** by **St. Louis** for Stephane Matteau, December 28, 1995. Traded to **LA Kings** by **NY Rangers** with Ray Ferraro, Mattias Norstrom, Nathan Lafayette and NY Rangers' 4th round choice (Sean Blanchard) in 1997 Entry Draft for Marty McSorley, Jari Kurri and Shane Churla, March 14, 1996.

LAPLANTE, Darryl

(LA-plawnt, DAIR-ihl) **MIN.**

Center. Shoots left. 6', 198 lbs. Born, Calgary, Alta., March 28, 1977. Detroit's 3rd choice, 58th overall, in 1995 Entry Draft.

1992-93	Calgary AA Royals	AAHA	32	20	26	46	60	....	....	....	....	....	....	....	....	....	....	....	....	....	....	....	....	....	....	....
1993-94	Calgary Royals	AMHL	35	24	27	51	50	....	....	....	....	....	....	....	....	....	....	....	....	....	....	....	....	....	....	....
1994-95	Moose Jaw	WHL	71	22	24	46	66	....	....	....	....	....	....	....	....	....	....	....	10	2	2	4	7	....	....	....
1995-96	Moose Jaw	WHL	72	42	40	82	76	....	....	....	....	....	....	....	....	....	....	....	....	....	....	....	....	....	....	....
1996-97	Moose Jaw	WHL	69	38	42	80	79	....	....	....	....	....	....	....	....	....	....	....	12	2	4	6	15	....	....	....
1997-98	**Detroit**	**NHL**	**2**	**0**	**0**	**0**	**0**	**0**	**0**	**0**	**2**	**0.0**	**0**	....	....	....	....	....	....	....	....	....	....	....	....	....
	Adirondack	AHL	77	15	10	25	51	....	....	....	....	....	....	....	....	....	....	....	3	0	1	1	4	....	....	....

			Regular Season																Playoffs							
Season	Club	League	GP	G	A	Pts	PIM	PP	SH	GW	S	%	+/-	TF	F%	H	SB	Min	GP	G	A	Pts	PIM	PP	SH	GW
1998-99	**Detroit**	**NHL**	**3**	**0**	**0**	**0**	**0**	**0**	**0**	**0**	**0**	**0.0**	**0**	**0**	**0.0**	**0**	**1**	**1:59**	....	....	....	....	....	....	....	....
	Adirondack	AHL	71	17	15	32	96	....	....	....	....	....	....	....	....	....	....	....	3	0	1	1	0	....	....	....
99-2000	**Detroit**	**NHL**	**30**	**0**	**6**	**6**	**10**	**0**	**0**	**0**	**19**	**0.0**	**–2**	**58**	**53.5**	**44**	**9**	**9:35**	....	....	....	....	....	....	....	....
	Cincinnati Ducks	AHL	35	13	9	22	47	....	....	....	....	....	....	....	....	....	....	....	....	....	....	....	....	....	....	....
2000-01	Cleveland	IHL	67	6	19	25	43	....	....	....	....	....	....	....	....	....	....	....	4	0	1	1	6	....	....	....
	NHL Totals		**35**	**0**	**6**	**6**	**10**	**0**	**0**	**0**	**21**	**0.0**		**58**	**53.4**	**44**	**10**	**8:53**	....	....	....	....	....	....	....	....

Selected by **Minnesota** from **Detroit** in Expansion Draft, June 23, 2000.

LAPOINTE, Claude

(luh-PWAH, KLOHD) **NYI**

Center. Shoots left. 5'9", 181 lbs. Born, Lachine, Que., October 11, 1968. Quebec's 12th choice, 234th overall, in 1988 Entry Draft.

Season	Club	League	GP	G	A	Pts	PIM	PP	SH	GW	S	%	+/-	TF	F%	H	SB	Min	GP	G	A	Pts	PIM	PP	SH	GW
1983-84	Lac St-Louis	QAAA	42	28	29	57	42	....	....	....	....	....	....	....	....	....	....	....	8	3	7	10	8	....	....	....
1984-85	Lac St-Louis	QAAA	42	20	32	52	66	....	....	....	....	....	....	....	....	....	....	....	11	4	8	12	16	....	....	....
1985-86	Trois-Rivieres	QMJHL	63	14	32	46	70	....	....	....	....	....	....	....	....	....	....	....	9	5	6	11	4	....	....	....
1986-87	Trois-Rivieres	QMJHL	70	47	57	104	123	....	....	....	....	....	....	....	....	....	....	....	....	....	....	....	....	....	....	....
1987-88	Laval Titan	QMJHL	69	37	83	120	143	....	....	....	....	....	....	....	....	....	....	....	13	2	17	19	53	....	....	....
1988-89	Laval Titan	QMJHL	63	32	72	104	158	....	....	....	....	....	....	....	....	....	....	....	17	5	14	19	66	....	....	....
1989-90	Halifax Citadels	AHL	63	18	19	37	51	....	....	....	....	....	....	....	....	....	....	....	6	1	1	2	34	....	....	....
1990-91	**Quebec**	**NHL**	**13**	**2**	**2**	**4**	**4**	**0**	**0**	**0**	**7**	**28.6**	**3**	....	....	....	....	....	....	....	....	....	....	....	....	....
	Halifax Citadels	AHL	43	17	17	34	46	....	....	....	....	....	....	....	....	....	....	....	....	....	....	....	....	....	....	....
1991-92	**Quebec**	**NHL**	**78**	**13**	**20**	**33**	**86**	**0**	**2**	**2**	**95**	**13.7**	**–8**	....	....	....	....	....	....	....	....	....	....	....	....	....
1992-93	**Quebec**	**NHL**	**74**	**10**	**26**	**36**	**98**	**0**	**0**	**1**	**91**	**11.0**	**5**	....	....	....	....	....	**6**	**2**	**4**	**6**	**8**	**0**	**0**	**0**
1993-94	**Quebec**	**NHL**	**59**	**11**	**17**	**28**	**70**	**1**	**1**	**1**	**73**	**15.1**	**2**	....	....	....	....	....	....	....	....	....	....	....	....	....
1994-95	**Quebec**	**NHL**	**29**	**4**	**8**	**12**	**41**	**0**	**0**	**0**	**40**	**10.0**	**5**	....	....	....	....	....	**5**	**0**	**0**	**0**	**8**	**0**	**0**	**0**
1995-96	**Colorado**	**NHL**	**3**	**0**	**0**	**0**	**0**	**0**	**0**	**0**	**0**	**0.0**	**–1**	....	....	....	....	....	....	....	....	....	....	....	....	....
	Calgary	**NHL**	**32**	**4**	**5**	**9**	**20**	**0**	**2**	**1**	**44**	**9.1**	**2**	....	....	....	....	....	**2**	**0**	**0**	**0**	**0**	**0**	**0**	**0**
	Saint John Flames	AHL	12	5	3	8	10	....	....	....	....	....	....	....	....	....	....	....	....	....	....	....	....	....	....	....
1996-97	**NY Islanders**	**NHL**	**73**	**13**	**5**	**18**	**49**	**0**	**3**	**3**	**80**	**16.3**	**–12**	....	....	....	....	....	....	....	....	....	....	....	....	....
	Utah Grizzlies	IHL	9	7	6	13	14	....	....	....	....	....	....	....	....	....	....	....	....	....	....	....	....	....	....	....
1997-98	**NY Islanders**	**NHL**	**78**	**10**	**10**	**20**	**47**	**0**	**1**	**3**	**82**	**12.2**	**–9**	....	....	....	....	....	....	....	....	....	....	....	....	....
1998-99	**NY Islanders**	**NHL**	**82**	**14**	**23**	**37**	**62**	**2**	**2**	**1**	**134**	**10.4**	**–19**	**1218**	**56.6**	**168**	**60**	**19:21**	....	....	....	....	....	....	....	....
99-2000	**NY Islanders**	**NHL**	**76**	**15**	**16**	**31**	**60**	**2**	**1**	**3**	**129**	**11.6**	**–22**	**1284**	**54.0**	**147**	**71**	**19:39**	....	....	....	....	....	....	....	....
2000-01	**NY Islanders**	**NHL**	**80**	**9**	**23**	**32**	**56**	**1**	**1**	**1**	**94**	**9.6**	**–2**	**1074**	**50.4**	**133**	**79**	**18:40**	....	....	....	....	....	....	....	....
	NHL Totals		**677**	**105**	**155**	**260**	**593**	**6**	**13**	**16**	**869**	**12.1**		**3576**	**53.8**	**448**	**210**	**19:13**	**13**	**2**	**4**	**6**	**16**	**0**	**0**	**0**

Transferred to **Colorado** after **Quebec** franchise relocated, June 21, 1995. Traded to **Calgary** by **Colorado** for Calgary's 7th round choice (Samual Pahlsson) in 1996 Entry Draft, November 1, 1995. Signed as a free agent by **NY Islanders**, August 14, 1996.

LAPOINTE, Martin

(luh-POYNT, MAHR-tihn) **BOS.**

Right wing. Shoots right. 5'11", 200 lbs. Born, Ville St-Pierre, Que., September 12, 1973. Detroit's 1st choice, 10th overall, in 1991 Entry Draft.

Season	Club	League	GP	G	A	Pts	PIM	PP	SH	GW	S	%	+/-	TF	F%	H	SB	Min	GP	G	A	Pts	PIM	PP	SH	GW
1988-89	Lac St-Louis	QAAA	42	39	45	84	46	....	....	....	....	....	....	....	....	....	....	....	3	6	2	8	4	....	....	....
1989-90	Laval Titan	QMJHL	65	42	54	96	77	....	....	....	....	....	....	....	....	....	....	....	14	8	17	25	54	....	....	....
1990-91	Laval Titan	QMJHL	64	44	54	98	66	....	....	....	....	....	....	....	....	....	....	....	13	7	14	21	26	....	....	....
1991-92	Laval Titan	QMJHL	31	25	30	55	84	....	....	....	....	....	....	....	....	....	....	....	10	4	10	14	32	....	....	....
	Detroit	**NHL**	**4**	**0**	**1**	**1**	**5**	**0**	**0**	**0**	**2**	**0.0**	**2**	....	....	....	....	....	**3**	**0**	**1**	**1**	**4**	**0**	**0**	**0**
	Adirondack	AHL	....	....	....	....	....	....	....	....	....	....	....	....	....	....	....	....	8	2	2	4	4	....	....	....
1992-93	Laval Titan	QMJHL	35	38	51	89	41	....	....	....	....	....	....	....	....	....	....	....	13	*13	*17	*30	22	....	....	....
	Detroit	**NHL**	**3**	**0**	**0**	**0**	**0**	**0**	**0**	**0**	**2**	**0.0**	**–2**	....	....	....	....	....	....	....	....	....	....	....	....	....
	Adirondack	AHL	8	1	2	3	9	....	....	....	....	....	....	....	....	....	....	....	....	....	....	....	....	....	....	....
1993-94	**Detroit**	**NHL**	**50**	**8**	**8**	**16**	**55**	**2**	**0**	**0**	**45**	**17.8**	**7**	....	....	....	....	....	**4**	**0**	**0**	**0**	**6**	**0**	**0**	**0**
	Adirondack	AHL	28	25	21	46	47	....	....	....	....	....	....	....	....	....	....	....	4	1	1	2	8	....	....	....
1994-95	Adirondack	AHL	39	29	16	45	80	....	....	....	....	....	....	....	....	....	....	....	....	....	....	....	....	....	....	....
	Detroit	**NHL**	**39**	**4**	**6**	**10**	**73**	**0**	**0**	**1**	**46**	**8.7**	**1**	....	....	....	....	....	**2**	**0**	**1**	**1**	**8**	**0**	**0**	**0**
1995-96	**Detroit**	**NHL**	**58**	**6**	**3**	**9**	**93**	**1**	**0**	**0**	**76**	**7.9**	**0**	....	....	....	....	....	**11**	**1**	**2**	**3**	**12**	**0**	**0**	**0**
1996-97♦	**Detroit**	**NHL**	**78**	**16**	**17**	**33**	**167**	**5**	**1**	**1**	**149**	**10.7**	**–14**	....	....	....	....	....	**20**	**4**	**8**	**12**	**60**	**1**	**0**	**1**
1997-98♦	**Detroit**	**NHL**	**79**	**15**	**19**	**34**	**106**	**4**	**0**	**3**	**154**	**9.7**	**0**	....	....	....	....	....	**21**	**9**	**6**	**15**	**20**	**2**	**1**	**1**
1998-99	**Detroit**	**NHL**	**77**	**16**	**13**	**29**	**141**	**7**	**1**	**4**	**153**	**10.5**	**7**	**217**	**47.9**	**167**	**16**	**15:06**	**10**	**0**	**2**	**2**	**20**	**0**	**0**	**0**
99-2000	**Detroit**	**NHL**	**82**	**16**	**25**	**41**	**121**	**1**	**1**	**2**	**127**	**12.6**	**17**	**287**	**54.4**	**207**	**19**	**14:43**	**9**	**3**	**1**	**4**	**20**	**2**	**0**	**1**
2000-01	**Detroit**	**NHL**	**82**	**27**	**30**	**57**	**127**	**13**	**0**	**8**	**181**	**14.9**	**3**	**461**	**53.2**	**259**	**17**	**16:06**	**6**	**0**	**1**	**1**	**8**	**0**	**0**	**0**
	NHL Totals		**552**	**108**	**122**	**230**	**888**	**33**	**3**	**19**	**935**	**11.6**		**965**	**52.3**	**633**	**52**	**15:19**	**86**	**17**	**22**	**39**	**158**	**5**	**1**	**3**

QMJHL First All-Star Team (1990, 1993) • QMJHL Second All-Star Team (1991) • Memorial Cup All-Star Team (1993)

Signed as a free agent by **Boston**, July 2, 2001.

LARAQUE, Georges

(luh-RAK, zhawrzh) **EDM.**

Right wing. Shoots right. 6'3", 240 lbs. Born, Montreal, Que., December 7, 1976. Edmonton's 2nd choice, 31st overall, in 1995 Entry Draft.

Season	Club	League	GP	G	A	Pts	PIM	PP	SH	GW	S	%	+/-	TF	F%	H	SB	Min	GP	G	A	Pts	PIM	PP	SH	GW
1991-92	Mtl-Bourassa "B"	QAHA	28	20	20	40	30	....	....	....	....	....	....	....	....	....	....	....	....	....	....	....	....	....	....	....
1992-93	Mtl-Bourassa	QAAA	37	8	20	28	50	....	....	....	....	....	....	....	....	....	....	....	3	1	2	3	2	....	....	....
1993-94	St-Jean Lynx	QMJHL	70	11	11	22	142	....	....	....	....	....	....	....	....	....	....	....	4	0	0	0	7	....	....	....
1994-95	St-Jean Lynx	QMJHL	62	19	22	41	259	....	....	....	....	....	....	....	....	....	....	....	7	1	1	2	42	....	....	....
1995-96	Laval Titan	QMJHL	11	8	13	21	76	....	....	....	....	....	....	....	....	....	....	....	....	....	....	....	....	....	....	....
	St-Hyacinthe	QMJHL	8	3	4	7	59	....	....	....	....	....	....	....	....	....	....	....	....	....	....	....	....	....	....	....
	Granby Bisons	QMJHL	22	9	7	16	125	....	....	....	....	....	....	....	....	....	....	....	18	7	6	13	104	....	....	....
1996-97	Hamilton Bulldogs	AHL	73	14	20	34	179	....	....	....	....	....	....	....	....	....	....	....	15	1	3	4	12	....	....	....
1997-98	**Edmonton**	**NHL**	**11**	**0**	**0**	**0**	**59**	**0**	**0**	**0**	**4**	**0.0**	**–4**	....	....	....	....	....	....	....	....	....	....	....	....	....
	Hamilton Bulldogs	AHL	46	10	20	30	154	....	....	....	....	....	....	....	....	....	....	....	3	0	0	0	11	....	....	....
1998-99	**Edmonton**	**NHL**	**39**	**3**	**2**	**5**	**57**	**0**	**0**	**0**	**17**	**17.6**	**–1**	**0**	**0.0**	**32**	**4**	**5:31**	**4**	**0**	**0**	**0**	**2**	**0**	**0**	**0**
	Hamilton Bulldogs	AHL	25	6	8	14	93	....	....	....	....	....	....	....	....	....	....	....	....	....	....	....	....	....	....	....
99-2000	**Edmonton**	**NHL**	**76**	**8**	**8**	**16**	**123**	**0**	**0**	**0**	**56**	**14.3**	**5**	**0**	**0.0**	**84**	**21**	**8:28**	**5**	**0**	**1**	**1**	**6**	**0**	**0**	**0**
2000-01	**Edmonton**	**NHL**	**82**	**13**	**16**	**29**	**148**	**1**	**0**	**1**	**73**	**17.8**	**5**	**0**	**0.0**	**95**	**19**	**9:03**	**6**	**1**	**1**	**2**	**8**	**0**	**0**	**0**
	NHL Totals		**208**	**24**	**26**	**50**	**387**	**1**	**0**	**1**	**150**	**16.0**		**0**	**0.0**	**211**	**44**	**8:08**	**15**	**1**	**2**	**3**	**16**	**0**	**0**	**0**

LARIONOV, Igor

(LAIR-ee-AH-nohv, EE-gohr) **DET.**

Center. Shoots left. 5'9", 170 lbs. Born, Voskresensk, USSR, December 3, 1960. Vancouver's 11th choice, 214th overall, in 1985 Entry Draft.

Season	Club	League	GP	G	A	Pts	PIM	PP	SH	GW	S	%	+/-	TF	F%	H	SB	Min	GP	G	A	Pts	PIM	PP	SH	GW
1977-78	HK Khimik	USSR	6	3	0	3	4	....	....	....	....	....	....	....	....	....	....	....	....	....	....	....	....	....	....	....
1978-79	HK Khimik	USSR	32	3	4	7	12	....	....	....	....	....	....	....	....	....	....	....	....	....	....	....	....	....	....	....
1979-80	HK Khimik	USSR	42	11	7	18	24	....	....	....	....	....	....	....	....	....	....	....	....	....	....	....	....	....	....	....
1980-81	HK Khimik	USSR	43	22	23	45	36	....	....	....	....	....	....	....	....	....	....	....	....	....	....	....	....	....	....	....
1981-82	CSKA Moscow	USSR	46	31	22	53	6	....	....	....	....	....	....	....	....	....	....	....	....	....	....	....	....	....	....	....
1982-83	CSKA Moscow	USSR	44	20	19	39	20	....	....	....	....	....	....	....	....	....	....	....	....	....	....	....	....	....	....	....
1983-84	CSKA Moscow	USSR	43	15	26	41	30	....	....	....	....	....	....	....	....	....	....	....	....	....	....	....	....	....	....	....
	Soviet Union	Olympics	6	1	4	5	6	....	....	....	....	....	....	....	....	....	....	....	....	....	....	....	....	....	....	....
1984-85	CSKA Moscow	USSR	40	18	28	46	20	....	....	....	....	....	....	....	....	....	....	....	....	....	....	....	....	....	....	....
1985-86	CSKA Moscow	USSR	40	21	31	52	33	....	....	....	....	....	....	....	....	....	....	....	....	....	....	....	....	....	....	....
1986-87	CSKA Moscow	USSR	39	20	26	46	34	....	....	....	....	....	....	....	....	....	....	....	....	....	....	....	....	....	....	....
1987-88	CSKA Moscow	USSR	51	25	32	57	54	....	....	....	....	....	....	....	....	....	....	....	....	....	....	....	....	....	....	....
	Soviet Union	Olympics	8	4	*9	13	4	....	....	....	....	....	....	....	....	....	....	....	....	....	....	....	....	....	....	....
1988-89	CSKA Moscow	USSR	31	15	12	27	22	....	....	....	....	....	....	....	....	....	....	....	....	....	....	....	....	....	....	....
1989-90	**Vancouver**	**NHL**	**74**	**17**	**27**	**44**	**20**	**8**	**0**	**2**	**118**	**14.4**	**–5**	....	....	....	....	....	....	....	....	....	....	....	....	....
1990-91	**Vancouver**	**NHL**	**64**	**13**	**21**	**34**	**14**	**1**	**1**	**0**	**66**	**19.7**	**–3**	....	....	....	....	....	**6**	**1**	**0**	**1**	**6**	**0**	**0**	**0**
1991-92	**Vancouver**	**NHL**	**72**	**21**	**44**	**65**	**54**	**10**	**3**	**4**	**97**	**21.6**	**7**	....	....	....	....	....	**13**	**3**	**7**	**10**	**4**	**1**	**0**	**0**
1992-93	HC Lugano	Switz.	24	10	19	29	44	....	....	....	....	....	....	....	....	....	....	....	8	3	15	18	0	....	....	....
1993-94	**San Jose**	**NHL**	**60**	**18**	**38**	**56**	**40**	**3**	**2**	**2**	**72**	**25.0**	**20**	....	....	....	....	....	**14**	**5**	**13**	**18**	**10**	**0**	**0**	**0**
1994-95	**San Jose**	**NHL**	**33**	**4**	**20**	**24**	**14**	**0**	**0**	**1**	**69**	**5.8**	**–3**	....	....	....	....	....	**11**	**1**	**8**	**9**	**2**	**0**	**0**	**0**
1995-96	**San Jose**	**NHL**	**4**	**1**	**1**	**2**	**0**	**1**	**0**	**0**	**5**	**20.0**	**–6**	....	....	....	....	....	....	....	....	....	....	....	....	....
	Detroit	**NHL**	**69**	**21**	**50**	**71**	**34**	**9**	**1**	**5**	**108**	**19.4**	**37**	....	....	....	....	....	**19**	**6**	**7**	**13**	**6**	**3**	**0**	**2**
1996-97♦	**Detroit**	**NHL**	**64**	**12**	**42**	**54**	**26**	**2**	**1**	**4**	**95**	**12.6**	**31**	....	....	....	....	....	**20**	**4**	**8**	**12**	**8**	**3**	**0**	**1**
1997-98♦	**Detroit**	**NHL**	**69**	**8**	**39**	**47**	**40**	**3**	**0**	**2**	**93**	**8.6**	**14**	....	....	....	....	....	**22**	**3**	**10**	**13**	**12**	**0**	**0**	**0**
1998-99	**Detroit**	**NHL**	**75**	**14**	**49**	**63**	**48**	**4**	**2**	**2**	**83**	**16.9**	**13**	**867**	**49.8**	**13**	**16**	**17:20**	**7**	**0**	**2**	**2**	**0**	**0**	**0**	**0**
99-2000	**Detroit**	**NHL**	**79**	**9**	**38**	**47**	**28**	**3**	**0**	**4**	**69**	**13.0**	**13**	**729**	**43.6**	**22**	**18**	**16:05**	**9**	**1**	**2**	**3**	**6**	**1**	**0**	**0**

Season	Club	League	GP	G	A	Pts	PIM	PP	SH	GW	S	%	+/-	TF	F%	H	SB	Min	GP	G	A	Pts	PIM	PP	SH	GW
			Regular Season																Playoffs							
2000-01	**Florida**	**NHL**	**26**	**5**	**6**	**11**	**10**	**2**	**0**	**0**	**15**	**33.3**	**–11**	**299**	**48.8**	**7**	**8**	**16:33**								
	Detroit	**NHL**	**39**	**4**	**25**	**29**	**28**	**2**	**0**	**1**	**31**	**12.9**	**6**	**311**	**44.4**	**8**	**6**	**16:36**	**6**	**1**	**3**	**4**	**2**	**1**	**0**	**0**
	NHL Totals		**728**	**147**	**400**	**547**	**356**	**48**	**10**	**27**	**921**	**16.0**		**2206**	**46.9**	**50**	**48**	**16:39**	**127**	**25**	**60**	**85**	**56**	**9**	**0**	**3**

Played in NHL All-Star Game (1998)

Claimed by **San Jose** from **Vancouver** in NHL Waiver Draft, October 4, 1992. Traded to **Detroit** by **San Jose** with future considerations for Ray Sheppard, October 24, 1995. Signed as a free agent by **Florida**, July 1, 2000. Traded to **Detroit** by **Florida** for Yan Golubovsky, December 28, 2000.

LAROCQUE, Mario (luh-RAWK, MAIR-ee-oh) BUF.

Defense. Shoots left. 6'2", 182 lbs. Born, Montreal, Que., April 24, 1978. Tampa Bay's 1st choice, 16th overall, in 1996 Entry Draft.

Season	Club	League	GP	G	A	Pts	PIM	PP	SH	GW	S	%	+/-	TF	F%	H	SB	Min	GP	G	A	Pts	PIM	PP	SH	GW
1994-95	Mtl-Bourassa	QAAA	43	0	6	6	153																			
1995-96	Hull Olympiques	QMJHL	68	7	19	26	196												14	2	5	7	16			
1996-97	Hull Olympiques	QMJHL	64	14	36	50	155												14	2	6	8	36			
1997-98	Sherbrooke	QMJHL	28	6	10	16	125																			
1998-99	**Tampa Bay**	**NHL**	**5**	**0**	**0**	**0**	**16**	**0**	**0**	**0**	**3**	**0.0**	**–4**	**0**	**0.0**	**8**	**1**	**12:33**								
	Cleveland	IHL	59	5	7	12	202																			
99-2000	Detroit Vipers	IHL	60	0	5	5	234																			
2000-01	Detroit Vipers	IHL	71	2	1	3	233																			
	NHL Totals		**5**	**0**	**0**	**0**	**16**	**0**	**0**	**0**	**3**	**0.0**		**0**	**0.0**	**8**	**1**	**12:33**								

Signed as a free agent by **Buffalo**, August 7, 2001.

LAROUCHE, Steve (luh-ROOSH, STEEV)

Center. Shoots right. 6', 180 lbs. Born, Rouyn, Que., April 14, 1971. Montreal's 3rd choice, 41st overall, in 1989 Entry Draft.

Season	Club	League	GP	G	A	Pts	PIM	PP	SH	GW	S	%	+/-	TF	F%	H	SB	Min	GP	G	A	Pts	PIM	PP	SH	GW
1986-87	Richelieu Regents	QAAA	42	25	35	60													9	3	7	10	2			
1987-88	Trois-Rivieres	QMJHL	66	11	29	40	25																			
1988-89	Trois-Rivieres	QMJHL	70	51	102	153	53												4	4	2	6	6			
1989-90	Trois-Rivieres	QMJHL	60	55	90	145	40												7	3	5	8	8			
1990-91	Chicoutimi	QMJHL	45	35	41	76	64												17	*13	*20	*33	20			
1991-92	Fredericton	AHL	74	21	35	56	41												7	1	0	1	0			
1992-93	Fredericton	AHL	77	27	65	92	52												5	2	5	7	6			
1993-94	Atlanta Knights	IHL	80	43	53	96	73												14	*16	10	*26	16			
1994-95	P.E.I. Senators	AHL	70	*53	48	101	54												2	1	0	1	0			
	Ottawa	**NHL**	**18**	**8**	**7**	**15**	**6**	**2**	**0**	**2**	**38**	**21.1**	**–5**													
1995-96	**NY Rangers**	**NHL**	**1**	**0**	**0**	**0**	**0**	**0**	**0**	**0**	**1**	**0.0**	**0**													
	Binghamton	AHL	39	20	46	66	47																			
	Los Angeles	**NHL**	**7**	**1**	**2**	**3**	**4**	**1**	**0**	**0**	**13**	**7.7**	**0**													
	Phoenix	IHL	33	19	17	36	14												4	0	1	1	8			
1996-97	Quebec Rafales	IHL	79	49	53	102	78												9	3	10	13	18			
1997-98	Quebec Rafales	IHL	68	23	44	67	40																			
	Chicago Wolves	IHL	13	9	10	19	20												22	9	11	20	14			
1998-99	Chicago Wolves	IHL	33	13	25	38	18																			
99-2000	Chicago Wolves	IHL	82	31	*57	88	52												16	6	8	14	22			
2000-01	Chicago Wolves	IHL	75	31	52	*83	78												15	*12	6	*18	6			
	NHL Totals		**26**	**9**	**9**	**18**	**10**	**3**	**0**	**2**	**52**	**17.3**														

QMJHL Second All-Star Team (1990) • AHL First All-Star Team (1995) • Won Fred Hunt Memorial Trophy (Sportsmanship - AHL) (1995) • Won Les Cunningham Award (MVP - AHL) (1995) • IHL First All-Star Team (1997, 2000, 2001) • Shared Leo P. Lamoureux Memorial Trophy (Top Scorer - IHL) with Derek King (2001)

Signed as a free agent by **Ottawa**, September 11, 1994. Traded to **NY Rangers** by **Ottawa** for Jean-Yves Roy, October 5, 1995. Traded to **LA Kings** by **NY Rangers** for Chris Snell, January 14, 1996. Traded to **Chicago Wolves** (IHL) by **Quebec** (IHL) for cash, March 19, 1998. • Missed majority of 1998-99 season recovering from knee injury suffered in game vs. Detroit (IHL), December 29, 1998. Signed as a free agent by **EHC Berlin** (DEL), April 17, 2001.

LARSEN, Brad (LARH-sehn, BRAD) COL.

Left wing. Shoots left. 6', 200 lbs. Born, Nakusp, B.C., June 28, 1977. Colorado's 5th choice, 87th overall, in 1997 Entry Draft.

Season	Club	League	GP	G	A	Pts	PIM	PP	SH	GW	S	%	+/-	TF	F%	H	SB	Min	GP	G	A	Pts	PIM	PP	SH	GW
1992-93	Nelson Leafs	RMJHL	42	31	37	68	164																			
1993-94	Swift Current	WHL	64	15	18	33	32												7	1	2	3	4			
1994-95	Swift Current	WHL	62	24	33	57	73												6	0	1	1	2			
1995-96	Swift Current	WHL	51	30	47	77	67												6	3	2	5	13			
1996-97	Swift Current	WHL	61	36	46	82	61																			
1997-98	**Colorado**	**NHL**	**1**	**0**	**0**	**0**	**0**	**0**	**0**	**0**	**0**	**0.0**	**0**													
	Hershey Bears	AHL	65	12	10	22	80												7	3	2	5	2			
1998-99	Hershey Bears	AHL	18	3	4	7	11												5	0	1	1	6			
99-2000	Hershey Bears	AHL	52	13	26	39	66												14	5	2	7	29			
2000-01	**Colorado**	**NHL**	**9**	**0**	**0**	**0**	**0**	**0**	**0**	**0**	**3**	**0.0**	**1**	**14**	**57.1**	**19**	**4**	**9:17**								
	Hershey Bears	AHL	67	21	25	46	93												10	1	3	4	6			
	NHL Totals		**10**	**0**	**0**	**0**	**0**	**0**	**0**	**0**	**3**	**0.0**		**14**	**57.1**	**19**	**4**	**9:17**								

• Re-entered NHL Entry Draft. Originally Ottawa's 3rd choice, 53rd overall, in 1995 Entry Draft.

WHL East Second All-Star Team (1997)

Rights traded to **Colorado** by **Ottawa** for Janne Laukkanen, January 26, 1996. • Missed majority of 1998-99 season recovering from abdominal injury suffered in game vs. Albany (AHL), November 20, 1998.

LAUER, Brad (LOW-er, BRAD)

Left wing. Shoots left. 6', 195 lbs. Born, Humboldt, Sask., October 27, 1966. NY Islanders' 3rd choice, 34th overall, in 1985 Entry Draft.

Season	Club	League	GP	G	A	Pts	PIM	PP	SH	GW	S	%	+/-	TF	F%	H	SB	Min	GP	G	A	Pts	PIM	PP	SH	GW
1983-84	Regina Pats	WHL	60	5	7	12	51												16	0	1	1	24			
1984-85	Regina Pats	WHL	72	33	46	79	57												8	6	6	12	9			
1985-86	Regina Pats	WHL	57	36	38	74	69												10	4	5	9	2			
1986-87	**NY Islanders**	**NHL**	**61**	**7**	**14**	**21**	**65**	**1**	**0**	**1**	**75**	**9.3**	**0**						**6**	**2**	**0**	**2**	**4**	**0**	**0**	**0**
1987-88	**NY Islanders**	**NHL**	**69**	**17**	**18**	**35**	**67**	**3**	**0**	**4**	**94**	**18.1**	**13**						**5**	**3**	**1**	**4**	**4**	**0**	**0**	**0**
1988-89	**NY Islanders**	**NHL**	**14**	**3**	**2**	**5**	**2**	**0**	**0**	**0**	**21**	**14.3**	**–2**													
	Springfield	AHL	8	1	5	6	0																			
1989-90	**NY Islanders**	**NHL**	**63**	**6**	**18**	**24**	**19**	**0**	**0**	**2**	**86**	**7.0**	**5**						**4**	**0**	**2**	**2**	**10**	**0**	**0**	**0**
	Springfield	AHL	7	4	2	6	0																			
1990-91	**NY Islanders**	**NHL**	**44**	**4**	**8**	**12**	**45**	**0**	**1**	**0**	**70**	**5.7**	**–6**													
	Capital District	AHL	11	5	11	16	14																			
1991-92	**NY Islanders**	**NHL**	**8**	**1**	**0**	**1**	**2**	**0**	**1**	**0**	**12**	**8.3**	**–2**													
	Chicago	**NHL**	**6**	**0**	**0**	**0**	**4**	**0**	**0**	**0**	**6**	**0.0**	**–3**						**7**	**1**	**1**	**2**	**2**	**0**	**0**	**0**
	Indianapolis Ice	IHL	57	24	30	54	46																			
1992-93	**Chicago**	**NHL**	**7**	**0**	**1**	**1**	**2**	**0**	**0**	**0**	**8**	**0.0**	**–1**													
	Indianapolis Ice	IHL	62	*50	41	91	80												5	3	1	4	6			
1993-94	**Ottawa**	**NHL**	**30**	**2**	**5**	**7**	**6**	**0**	**1**	**0**	**45**	**4.4**	**–15**													
	Las Vegas	IHL	32	21	21	42	30												4	1	0	1	2			
1994-95	Cleveland	IHL	51	32	27	59	48												4	4	2	6	6			
1995-96	**Pittsburgh**	**NHL**	**21**	**4**	**1**	**5**	**6**	**1**	**0**	**1**	**29**	**13.8**	**–5**						**12**	**1**	**1**	**2**	**4**	**0**	**0**	**0**
	Cleveland	IHL	53	25	27	52	44																			
1996-97	Cleveland	IHL	64	27	21	48	61												14	4	6	10	8			
1997-98	Cleveland	IHL	68	22	33	55	74												10	0	3	3	12			
1998-99	Utah Grizzlies	IHL	78	31	30	61	68																			
99-2000	Utah Grizzlies	IHL	71	26	22	48	73												5	0	1	1	2			
2000-01	Utah Grizzlies	IHL	73	15	23	38	70																			
	NHL Totals		**323**	**44**	**67**	**111**	**218**	**5**	**3**	**8**	**446**	**9.9**							**34**	**7**	**5**	**12**	**24**	**0**	**0**	**0**

IHL First All-Star Team (1993)

• Missed majority of 1988-89 season recovering from knee injury suffered in training camp, October, 1988. Traded to **Chicago** by **NY Islanders** with Brent Sutter for Adam Creighton and Steve Thomas, October 25, 1991. Signed as a free agent by **Ottawa**, January 3, 1994. Signed as a free agent by **Pittsburgh**, August 10, 1995.

LAUKKANEN, Janne
(LOW-kah-nehn, YAN-nee) **PIT.**

Defense. Shoots left. 6'1", 194 lbs. Born, Lahti, Finland, March 19, 1970. Quebec's 8th choice, 156th overall, in 1991 Entry Draft.

			Regular Season																Playoffs							
Season	Club	League	GP	G	A	Pts	PIM	PP	SH	GW	S	%	+/-	TF	F%	H	SB	Min	GP	G	A	Pts	PIM	PP	SH	GW
1986-87	Kiekko Lahti	Finn-Jr.	1	0	0	0	0																			
1987-88	Kiekko Lahti-B	Finn-Jr.	20	5	5	10	48																			
1988-89	Sport Academy	Finn-Jr.	6	0	1	1	6																			
	Kiekko Lahti	Finland-2	33	1	7	8	24																			
1989-90	Reipas Lahti	Finn-Jr.	2	2	2	4	2																			
	Reipas Lahti	Finland-2	44	8	22	30	60																			
1990-91	Reipas Lahti	Finland	44	8	14	22	56																			
1991-92	HPK Hameenlinna	Finland	43	5	14	19	62																			
	Finland	Olympics	8	0	1	1	6																			
1992-93	HPK Hameenlinna	Finland	47	8	21	29	76												12	1	4	5	10			
1993-94	HPK Hameenlinna	Finland	48	5	24	29	46																			
	Finland	Olympics	8	0	2	2	12																			
	MC Budejovice	Cze-Rep																	3	0	1	1	0			
1994-95	Cornwall Aces	AHL	55	8	26	34	41																			
	Quebec	**NHL**	**11**	**0**	**3**	**3**	**4**	**0**	**0**	**0**	**12**	**0.0**	**3**						**6**	**1**	**0**	**1**	**2**	**0**	**0**	**0**
1995-96	**Colorado**	**NHL**	**3**	**1**	**0**	**1**	**0**	**1**	**0**	**0**	**4**	**25.0**	**-1**													
	Cornwall Aces	AHL	35	7	20	27	60																			
	Ottawa	**NHL**	**20**	**0**	**2**	**2**	**14**	**0**	**0**	**0**	**31**	**0.0**	**0**													
1996-97	**Ottawa**	**NHL**	**76**	**3**	**18**	**21**	**76**	**2**	**0**	**0**	**109**	**2.8**	**-14**						**7**	**0**	**1**	**1**	**6**	**0**	**0**	**0**
1997-98	**Ottawa**	**NHL**	**60**	**4**	**17**	**21**	**64**	**2**	**0**	**2**	**69**	**5.8**	**-15**						**11**	**2**	**2**	**4**	**8**	**1**	**0**	**1**
	Finland	Olympics	6	0	0	0	4																			
1998-99	**Ottawa**	**NHL**	**50**	**1**	**11**	**12**	**40**	**0**	**0**	**0**	**46**	**2.2**	**18**	**0**	**0.0**	**87**	**80**	**18:37**	**4**	**0**	**0**	**0**	**4**	**0**	**0**	**0**
99-2000	**Ottawa**	**NHL**	**60**	**1**	**11**	**12**	**55**	**0**	**0**	**0**	**62**	**1.6**	**14**	**0**	**0.0**	**108**	**108**	**19:47**								
	Pittsburgh	**NHL**	**11**	**1**	**7**	**8**	**12**	**1**	**0**	**0**	**19**	**5.3**	**3**	**0**	**0.0**	**20**	**9**	**16:55**	**11**	**2**	**4**	**6**	**10**	**1**	**0**	**1**
2000-01	**Pittsburgh**	**NHL**	**50**	**3**	**17**	**20**	**34**	**0**	**0**	**0**	**58**	**5.2**	**9**	**0**	**0.0**	**96**	**64**	**18:28**	**18**	**2**	**2**	**4**	**14**	**1**	**0**	**0**
	NHL Totals		**341**	**14**	**86**	**100**	**299**	**6**	**0**	**2**	**410**	**3.4**		**0**	**0.0**	**311**	**261**	**18:52**	**57**	**7**	**9**	**16**	**44**	**3**	**0**	**2**

Transferred to **Colorado** after **Quebec** franchise relocated, June 21, 1995. Traded to **Ottawa** by **Colorado** for the rights to Brad Larsen, January 26, 1996. Traded to **Pittsburgh** by **Ottawa** with Ron Tugnutt for Tom Barrasso, March 14, 2000.

LAUS, Paul
(LOWZ, PAWL) **FLA.**

Defense. Shoots right. 6'1", 212 lbs. Born, Beamsville, Ont., September 26, 1970. Pittsburgh's 2nd choice, 37th overall, in 1989 Entry Draft.

1986-87	St. Catharines	OJHL-B	40	1	8	9	56																			
1987-88	Hamilton Hawks	OHL	56	1	9	10	171												14	0	0	0	28			
1988-89	Niagara Falls	OHL	49	1	10	11	225												15	0	5	5	56			
1989-90	Niagara Falls	OHL	60	13	35	48	231												16	6	16	22	71			
1990-91	Albany Choppers	IHL	7	0	0	0	7																			
	Knoxville	ECHL	20	6	12	18	83																			
	Muskegon	IHL	35	3	4	7	103												4	0	0	0	13			
1991-92	Muskegon	IHL	75	0	21	21	248												14	2	5	7	70			
1992-93	Cleveland	IHL	76	8	18	26	427												4	1	0	1	27			
1993-94	**Florida**	**NHL**	**39**	**2**	**0**	**2**	**109**	**0**	**0**	**1**	**15**	**13.3**	**9**													
1994-95	**Florida**	**NHL**	**37**	**0**	**7**	**7**	**138**	**0**	**0**	**0**	**18**	**0.0**	**12**													
1995-96	**Florida**	**NHL**	**78**	**3**	**6**	**9**	**236**	**0**	**0**	**0**	**45**	**6.7**	**-2**						**21**	**2**	**6**	**8**	***62**	**0**	**0**	**0**
1996-97	**Florida**	**NHL**	**77**	**0**	**12**	**12**	**313**	**0**	**0**	**0**	**63**	**0.0**	**13**						**5**	**0**	**1**	**1**	**4**	**0**	**0**	**0**
1997-98	**Florida**	**NHL**	**77**	**0**	**11**	**11**	**293**	**0**	**0**	**0**	**64**	**0.0**	**-5**													
1998-99	**Florida**	**NHL**	**75**	**1**	**9**	**10**	**218**	**0**	**0**	**0**	**54**	**1.9**	**-1**	**0**	**0.0**	**93**	**20**	**11:09**								
99-2000	**Florida**	**NHL**	**77**	**3**	**8**	**11**	**172**	**0**	**0**	**0**	**44**	**6.8**	**-1**	**1**	**0.0**	**106**	**15**	**7:37**	**4**	**0**	**0**	**0**	**8**	**0**	**0**	**0**
2000-01	**Florida**	**NHL**	**25**	**1**	**2**	**3**	**66**	**0**	**0**	**0**	**18**	**5.6**	**5**	**0**	**0.0**	**63**	**13**	**14:22**								
	NHL Totals		**485**	**10**	**55**	**65**	**1545**	**0**	**0**	**1**	**321**	**3.1**		**1**	**0.0**	**262**	**48**	**10:04**	**30**	**2**	**7**	**9**	**74**	**0**	**0**	**0**

Claimed by **Florida** from **Pittsburgh** in Expansion Draft, June 24, 1993. • Missed majority of 2000-01 season recovering from hernia injury suffered in game vs. Carolina, November 15, 2000.

LAW, Kirby
(LAW, KUHR-bee) **PHI.**

Right wing. Shoots right. 6'1", 185 lbs. Born, McCreary, Man., March 11, 1977.

1991-92	McCreary Macs	MAHA	60	89	103	192	60																			
1992-93	Dauphin Kings	MJHL	48	20	15	35	8																			
1993-94	Saskatoon Blades	WHL	66	9	11	20	39												16	0	0	0	6			
1994-95	Saskatoon Blades	WHL	46	10	15	25	44																			
	Lethbridge	WHL	24	4	10	14	38																			
1995-96	Lethbridge	WHL	71	17	45	62	133												4	0	0	0	12			
1996-97	Lethbridge	WHL	72	39	52	91	200												19	4	14	18	60			
1997-98	Brandon	WHL	49	34	44	78	153												9	3	3	6	41			
1998-99	Orlando	IHL	67	18	13	31	136																			
	Adirondack	AHL	11	2	3	5	40												3	1	0	1	2			
99-2000	Louisville Panthers	AHL	66	31	21	52	173																			
	Orlando	IHL	1	1	0	1	0																			
	Philadelphia	AHL	12	1	4	5	6												5	2	0	2	2			
2000-01	**Philadelphia**	**NHL**	**1**	**0**	**0**	**0**	**0**	**0**	**0**	**0**	**0**	**0.0**	**-1**	**0**	**0.0**	**0**	**0**	**3:23**								
	Philadelphia	AHL	78	27	34	61	150												10	1	6	7	16			
	NHL Totals		**1**	**0**	**0**	**0**	**0**	**0**	**0**	**0**	**0**	**0.0**		**0**	**0.0**	**0**	**0**	**3:23**								

Signed as a free agent by **Atlanta**, July 27, 1999. Traded to **Philadelphia** by **Atlanta** for Vancouver's 6th round choice (previously acquired, Atlanta selected Jeff Dwyer) in 2000 Entry Draft and Philadelphia's 6th round choice (Pasi Nurminen) in 2001 Entry Draft, March 14, 2000.

LAWRENCE, Mark
(LAW-rehns, MAHRK) **NYI**

Right wing. Shoots right. 6'4", 215 lbs. Born, Burlington, Ont., January 27, 1972. Minnesota's 4th choice, 118th overall, in 1991 Entry Draft.

1987-88	Burlington	OJHL-B	40	11	12	23	90																			
1988-89	Niagara Falls	OHL	63	9	27	36	142																			
1989-90	Niagara Falls	OHL	54	15	18	33	123												16	2	5	7	42			
1990-91	Detroit	OHL	66	27	38	65	53																			
1991-92	Detroit	OHL	28	19	26	45	54																			
	North Bay	OHL	24	13	14	27	21												21	*23	12	35	36			
1992-93	Dayton Bombers	ECHL	20	8	14	22	46																			
	Kalamazoo Wings	IHL	57	22	13	35	47																			
1993-94	Kalamazoo Wings	IHL	64	17	20	37	90																			
1994-95	Kalamazoo Wings	IHL	77	21	29	50	92												16	3	7	10	28			
	Dallas	**NHL**	**2**	**0**	**0**	**0**	**0**	**0**	**0**	**0**	**3**	**0.0**	**0**													
1995-96	**Dallas**	**NHL**	**13**	**0**	**1**	**1**	**17**	**0**	**0**	**0**	**13**	**0.0**	**0**													
	Michigan K-Wings	IHL	55	15	14	29	92												10	3	4	7	30			
1996-97	Michigan K-Wings	IHL	68	15	21	36	141												4	0	0	0	18			
1997-98	**NY Islanders**	**NHL**	**2**	**0**	**0**	**0**	**2**	**0**	**0**	**0**	**4**	**0.0**	**0**													
	Utah Grizzlies	IHL	80	36	28	64	102												4	1	1	2	4			
1998-99	**NY Islanders**	**NHL**	**60**	**14**	**16**	**30**	**38**	**4**	**0**	**2**	**88**	**15.9**	**-8**	**0**	**0.0**	**99**	**10**	**14:08**								
	Lowell	AHL	21	10	6	16	28																			
99-2000	**NY Islanders**	**NHL**	**29**	**1**	**5**	**6**	**26**	**0**	**0**	**0**	**33**	**3.0**	**-13**	**0**	**0.0**	**55**	**6**	**13:57**								
	Chicago Wolves	IHL	16	4	6	10	32																			
	Lowell	AHL	18	4	4	8	8												7	2	2	4	10			
2000-01	**NY Islanders**	**NHL**	**36**	**3**	**4**	**7**	**32**	**1**	**0**	**0**	**32**	**9.4**	**-9**	**2**	**50.0**	**63**	**13**	**9:52**								
	Chicago Wolves	IHL	32	8	6	14	26												2	0	0	0	0			
	NHL Totals		**142**	**18**	**26**	**44**	**115**	**5**	**0**	**2**	**173**	**10.4**		**2**	**50.0**	**217**	**29**	**12:52**								

Rights transferred to **Dallas** after **Minnesota** franchise relocated, June 9, 1993. Signed as a free agent by **NY Islanders**, August 25, 1997.

LEACH, Stephen
(LEECH, STEEV-ehn)

Right wing. Shoots right. 5'11", 197 lbs. Born, Cambridge, MA, January 16, 1966. Washington's 2nd choice, 34th overall, in 1984 Entry Draft.

			Regular Season																Playoffs							
Season	Club	League	GP	G	A	Pts	PIM	PP	SH	GW	S	%	+/-	TF	F%	H	SB	Min	GP	G	A	Pts	PIM	PP	SH	GW
1982-83	Matignon High	Hi-School	23	17	21	38	....	....	....	....	....	....	....	....	....	....	....	....	....	....	....	....	....	....	....	....
1983-84	Matignon High	Hi-School	21	27	22	49	49	....	....	....	....	....	....	....	....	....	....	....	....	....	....	....	....	....	....	....
1984-85	New Hampshire	H-East	41	12	25	37	53	....	....	....	....	....	....	....	....	....	....	....	....	....	....	....	....	....	....	....
1985-86	New Hampshire	H-East	25	22	6	28	30	....	....	....	....	....	....	....	....	....	....	....	....	....	....	....	....	....	....	....
	Washington	NHL	11	1	1	2	2	0	0	0	4	25.0	0	....	....	....	....	....	6	0	1	1	0	0	0	0
1986-87	Washington	NHL	15	1	0	1	6	0	0	0	17	5.9	–4	....	....	....	....	....	....	....	....	....	....	....	....	....
	Binghamton	AHL	54	18	21	39	39	....	....	....	....	....	....	....	....	....	....	....	13	3	1	4	6	....	....	....
1987-88	United States	Nat-Team	49	26	20	46	30	....	....	....	....	....	....	....	....	....	....	....	....	....	....	....	....	....	....	....
	United States	Olympics	6	1	2	3	0	....	....	....	....	....	....	....	....	....	....	....	....	....	....	....	....	....	....	....
	Washington	NHL	8	1	1	2	17	0	0	1	5	20.0	2	....	....	....	....	....	9	2	1	3	0	0	0	1
1988-89	Washington	NHL	74	11	19	30	94	4	0	0	145	7.6	–4	....	....	....	....	....	6	1	0	1	12	1	0	0
1989-90	Washington	NHL	70	18	14	32	104	0	0	2	122	14.8	10	....	....	....	....	....	14	2	2	4	8	0	0	0
1990-91	Washington	NHL	68	11	19	30	99	4	0	1	134	8.2	–9	....	....	....	....	....	9	1	2	3	8	0	0	0
1991-92	Boston	NHL	78	31	29	60	147	12	0	4	243	12.8	–8	....	....	....	....	....	15	4	0	4	10	0	0	1
1992-93	Boston	NHL	79	26	25	51	126	9	0	4	256	10.2	–6	....	....	....	....	....	4	1	1	2	2	0	0	0
1993-94	Boston	NHL	42	5	10	15	74	1	0	1	89	5.6	–10	....	....	....	....	....	5	0	1	1	2	0	0	0
1994-95	Boston	NHL	35	5	6	11	68	1	0	1	82	6.1	–3	....	....	....	....	....	....	....	....	....	....	....	....	....
1995-96	Boston	NHL	59	9	13	22	86	1	0	2	124	7.3	–4	....	....	....	....	....	....	....	....	....	....	....	....	....
	St. Louis	NHL	14	2	4	6	22	0	0	0	33	6.1	–3	....	....	....	....	....	11	3	2	5	10	1	0	1
1996-97	St. Louis	NHL	17	2	1	3	24	0	0	0	33	6.1	–2	....	....	....	....	....	6	0	0	0	33	0	0	0
1997-98	Carolina	NHL	45	4	5	9	42	1	1	2	60	6.7	–19	....	....	....	....	....	....	....	....	....	....	....	....	....
1998-99	Ottawa	NHL	9	0	2	2	6	0	0	0	4	0.0	–1	2	50.0	10	0	11:00	....	....	....	....	....	....	....	....
	Detroit Vipers	IHL	4	0	0	0	2	....	....	....	....	....	....	....	....	....	....	....	....	....	....	....	....	....	....	....
	Phoenix	NHL	22	1	1	2	37	0	0	0	23	4.3	–6	0	0.0	17	4	7:18	7	1	1	2	2	0	0	0
	Springfield	AHL	13	5	3	8	10	....	....	....	....	....	....	....	....	....	....	....	....	....	....	....	....	....	....	....
99-2000	Pittsburgh	NHL	56	2	3	5	24	0	0	1	41	4.9	–11	15	20.0	45	9	6:39	....	....	....	....	....	....	....	....
	Wilkes-Barre	AHL	4	2	3	5	4	....	....	....	....	....	....	....	....	....	....	....	....	....	....	....	....	....	....	....
2000-01	Louisville Panthers	AHL	2	0	1	1	0	....	....	....	....	....	....	....	....	....	....	....	....	....	....	....	....	....	....	....
	NHL Totals		702	130	153	283	978	33	1	19	1415	9.2		17	23.5	72	13	7:16	92	15	11	26	87	2	0	3

Traded to **Boston** by **Washington** for Randy Burridge, June 21, 1991. Traded to **St. Louis** by **Boston** for Kevin Sawyer and Steve Staios, March 8, 1996. Traded to **Carolina** by **St. Louis** for Alexander Godynyuk and Carolina's 6th round choice (Brad Voth) in 1998 Entry Draft, June 27, 1997. Signed as a free agent by **Ottawa**, October 4, 1998. Signed as a free agent by **Phoenix**, December 3, 1998. Signed as a free agent by **Pittsburgh**, October 19, 1999. Signed as a free agent by **Louisville** (AHL), November 15, 2000.

LEBEAU, Patrick
(leh-BOH, PA-trihk)

Left wing. Shoots left. 5'10", 172 lbs. Born, St-Jerome, Que., March 17, 1970. Montreal's 8th choice, 167th overall, in 1989 Entry Draft.

Season	Club	League	GP	G	A	Pts	PIM	PP	SH	GW	S	%	+/-	TF	F%	H	SB	Min	GP	G	A	Pts	PIM	PP	SH	GW
1984-85	Montreal L'est	QAAA	38	16	19	35	....	....	....	....	....	....	....	....	....	....	....	....	....	....	....	....	....	....	....	....
1985-86	Montreal L'est	QAAA	42	43	47	90	....	....	....	....	....	....	....	....	....	....	....	....	....	....	....	....	....	....	....	....
1986-87	Shawinigan	QMJHL	66	26	52	78	90	....	....	....	....	....	....	....	....	....	....	....	13	2	6	8	17	....	....	....
1987-88	Shawinigan	QMJHL	53	43	56	99	116	....	....	....	....	....	....	....	....	....	....	....	11	3	9	12	16	....	....	....
1988-89	Shawinigan	QMJHL	17	19	17	36	18	....	....	....	....	....	....	....	....	....	....	....	....	....	....	....	....	....	....	....
	St-Jean	QMJHL	49	43	70	113	71	....	....	....	....	....	....	....	....	....	....	....	4	4	3	7	6	....	....	....
1989-90	Victoriaville	QMJHL	72	68	*106	*174	109	....	....	....	....	....	....	....	....	....	....	....	16	7	15	22	12	....	....	....
1990-91	Montreal	NHL	2	1	1	2	0	0	0	0	3	33.3	0	....	....	....	....	....	....	....	....	....	....	....	....	....
	Fredericton	AHL	69	50	51	101	32	....	....	....	....	....	....	....	....	....	....	....	9	4	7	11	8	....	....	....
1991-92	Fredericton	AHL	55	33	38	71	48	....	....	....	....	....	....	....	....	....	....	....	7	4	5	9	10	....	....	....
	Canada	Olympics	8	1	3	4	4	....	....	....	....	....	....	....	....	....	....	....	....	....	....	....	....	....	....	....
1992-93	Calgary	NHL	1	0	0	0	0	0	0	0	0	0.0	0	....	....	....	....	....	....	....	....	....	....	....	....	....
	Salt Lake	IHL	75	40	60	100	65	....	....	....	....	....	....	....	....	....	....	....	....	....	....	....	....	....	....	....
1993-94	Florida	NHL	4	1	1	2	4	1	0	0	4	25.0	0	....	....	....	....	....	....	....	....	....	....	....	....	....
	Cincinnati	IHL	74	47	42	89	90	....	....	....	....	....	....	....	....	....	....	....	11	4	8	12	14	....	....	....
1994-95	ZSC Zurich	Switz.	36	27	25	52	22	....	....	....	....	....	....	....	....	....	....	....	5	4	6	10	6	....	....	....
1995-96	ZSC Zurich	Switz.	11	6	8	14	0	....	....	....	....	....	....	....	....	....	....	....	....	....	....	....	....	....	....	....
	Dusseldorfer EG	Germany	17	13	8	21	18	....	....	....	....	....	....	....	....	....	....	....	13	11	5	16	14	....	....	....
1996-97	ZSC Zurich	Switz.	38	27	19	46	26	....	....	....	....	....	....	....	....	....	....	....	4	1	0	1	25	....	....	....
1997-98	Chaux-de-Fonds	Switz.	40	17	45	62	32	....	....	....	....	....	....	....	....	....	....	....	....	....	....	....	....	....	....	....
1998-99	Pittsburgh	NHL	8	1	0	1	2	0	0	0	4	25.0	–2	0	0.0	11	3	9:32	....	....	....	....	....	....	....	....
99-2000	Ambri-Piotta	Switz.	44	*25	38	63	32	....	....	....	....	....	....	....	....	....	....	....	9	5	5	10	8	....	....	....
2000-01	ZSC Zurich	Switz.	22	9	10	19	31	....	....	....	....	....	....	....	....	....	....	....	13	4	4	8	4	....	....	....
	NHL Totals		15	3	2	5	6	1	0	0	11	27.3		0	0.0	11	3	9:32	....	....	....	....	....	....	....	....

QMJHL First All-Star Team (1990) • AHL Second All-Star Team (1991) • Won Dudley "Red" Garrett Memorial Award (Top Rookie - AHL) (1991)

Traded to **Calgary** by **Montreal** for future considerations, September 27, 1986. Signed as a free agent by **Florida**, July 26, 1993. Signed as a free agent by **Pittsburgh**, October 18, 1998.

LeBOUTILLIER, Peter
(lih-BOO-tihl-eer, PEE-tuhr)

Right wing. Shoots right. 6'1", 190 lbs. Born, Minnedosa, Man., January 11, 1975. Anaheim's 5th choice, 133rd overall, in 1995 Entry Draft.

Season	Club	League	GP	G	A	Pts	PIM	PP	SH	GW	S	%	+/-	TF	F%	H	SB	Min	GP	G	A	Pts	PIM	PP	SH	GW
1989-90	Souris South	MAHA	55	91	109	200	64	....	....	....	....	....	....	....	....	....	....	....	....	....	....	....	....	....	....	....
1990-91	Souris South	MAHA	10	7	12	19	6	....	....	....	....	....	....	....	....	....	....	....	....	....	....	....	....	....	....	....
1991-92	Neepawa Natives	MJHL	35	11	14	25	99	....	....	....	....	....	....	....	....	....	....	....	....	....	....	....	....	....	....	....
	Brandon	WHL	2	0	0	0	5	....	....	....	....	....	....	....	....	....	....	....	....	....	....	....	....	....	....	....
1992-93	Red Deer Rebels	WHL	67	8	26	34	284	....	....	....	....	....	....	....	....	....	....	....	2	0	1	1	5	....	....	....
1993-94	Red Deer Rebels	WHL	66	19	20	39	300	....	....	....	....	....	....	....	....	....	....	....	2	0	1	1	4	....	....	....
1994-95	Red Deer Rebels	WHL	59	27	16	43	159	....	....	....	....	....	....	....	....	....	....	....	....	....	....	....	....	....	....	....
1995-96	Baltimore Bandits	AHL	68	7	9	16	228	....	....	....	....	....	....	....	....	....	....	....	11	0	0	0	33	....	....	....
1996-97	Anaheim	NHL	23	1	0	1	121	0	0	0	5	20.0	0	....	....	....	....	....	....	....	....	....	....	....	....	....
	Baltimore Bandits	AHL	47	6	12	18	175	....	....	....	....	....	....	....	....	....	....	....	....	....	....	....	....	....	....	....
1997-98	Anaheim	NHL	12	1	1	2	55	0	0	0	6	16.7	–1	....	....	....	....	....	....	....	....	....	....	....	....	....
	Cincinnati Ducks	AHL	51	9	11	20	143	....	....	....	....	....	....	....	....	....	....	....	....	....	....	....	....	....	....	....
1998-99	Cincinnati Ducks	AHL	63	12	12	24	189	....	....	....	....	....	....	....	....	....	....	....	3	0	0	0	2	....	....	....
99-2000	Cincinnati Ducks	AHL	19	2	1	3	69	....	....	....	....	....	....	....	....	....	....	....	....	....	....	....	....	....	....	....
2000-01	Lowell	AHL	70	6	13	19	175	....	....	....	....	....	....	....	....	....	....	....	4	0	1	1	2	....	....	....
	NHL Totals		35	2	1	3	176	0	0	0	11	18.2		....	....	....	....	....	....	....	....	....	....	....	....	....

• Re-entered NHL Entry Draft. Originally NY Islanders's 6th choice, 144th overall, in 1993 Entry Draft.

Signed as a free agent by **LA Kings**, August 11, 2000.

LECAVALIER, Vincent
(luh-KAV-uhl-YAY, VIHN-sihnt) **T.B.**

Center. Shoots left. 6'4", 205 lbs. Born, Ile Bizard, Que., April 21, 1980. Tampa Bay's 1st choice, 1st overall, in 1998 Entry Draft.

Season	Club	League	GP	G	A	Pts	PIM	PP	SH	GW	S	%	+/-	TF	F%	H	SB	Min	GP	G	A	Pts	PIM	PP	SH	GW
1995-96	Notre Dame	SAHA	22	52	52	104	....	....	....	....	....	....	....	....	....	....	....	....	....	....	....	....	....	....	....	....
1996-97	Rimouski Oceanic	QMJHL	64	42	61	103	38	....	....	....	....	....	....	....	....	....	....	....	4	4	3	7	2	....	....	....
1997-98	Rimouski Oceanic	QMJHL	58	44	71	115	117	....	....	....	....	....	....	....	....	....	....	....	18	*15	*26	*41	46	....	....	....
1998-99	Tampa Bay	NHL	82	13	15	28	23	2	0	2	125	10.4	–19	953	40.3	52	15	13:40	....	....	....	....	....	....	....	....
99-2000	Tampa Bay	NHL	80	25	42	67	43	6	0	3	166	15.1	–25	1288	44.4	116	19	19:18	....	....	....	....	....	....	....	....
2000-01	Tampa Bay	NHL	68	23	28	51	66	7	0	3	165	13.9	–26	1278	44.9	72	22	19:57	....	....	....	....	....	....	....	....
	NHL Totals		230	61	85	146	132	15	0	8	456	13.4		3519	43.5	240	56	17:29	....	....	....	....	....	....	....	....

QMJHL First All-Star Team (1998) • Canadian Major Junior First All-Star Team (1998) • Canadian Major Junior Rookie of the Year (1997)

LeCLAIR, John
(luh-KLAIR, JAWN) **PHI.**

Left wing. Shoots left. 6'3", 226 lbs. Born, St. Albans, VT, July 5, 1969. Montreal's 2nd choice, 33rd overall, in 1987 Entry Draft.

Season	Club	League	GP	G	A	Pts	PIM	PP	SH	GW	S	%	+/-	TF	F%	H	SB	Min	GP	G	A	Pts	PIM	PP	SH	GW
1985-86	Bellows Academy	Hi-School	22	41	28	69	14	....	....	....	....	....	....	....	....	....	....	....	....	....	....	....	....	....	....	....
1986-87	Bellows Academy	Hi-School	23	44	40	84	14	....	....	....	....	....	....	....	....	....	....	....	....	....	....	....	....	....	....	....
1987-88	U. of Vermont	ECAC	31	12	22	34	62	....	....	....	....	....	....	....	....	....	....	....	....	....	....	....	....	....	....	....
1988-89	U. of Vermont	ECAC	18	9	12	21	40	....	....	....	....	....	....	....	....	....	....	....	....	....	....	....	....	....	....	....
1989-90	U. of Vermont	ECAC	10	10	6	16	38	....	....	....	....	....	....	....	....	....	....	....	....	....	....	....	....	....	....	....
1990-91	U. of Vermont	ECAC	33	25	20	45	58	....	....	....	....	....	....	....	....	....	....	....	....	....	....	....	....	....	....	....
	Montreal	NHL	10	2	5	7	2	0	0	1	12	16.7	1	....	....	....	....	....	3	0	0	0	0	0	0	0

			Regular Season																Playoffs							
Season	Club	League	GP	G	A	Pts	PIM	PP	SH	GW	S	%	+/-	TF	F%	H	SB	Min	GP	G	A	Pts	PIM	PP	SH	GW
1991-92	**Montreal**	**NHL**	**59**	**8**	**11**	**19**	**14**	**3**	**0**	**0**	**73**	**11.0**	**5**	....	....	....	....	....	**8**	**1**	**1**	**2**	**4**	**0**	**0**	**0**
	Fredericton	AHL	8	7	7	14	10	....	....	....	....	....	....	....	....	....	....	....	2	0	0	0	4	....	....	....
1992-93♦	**Montreal**	**NHL**	**72**	**19**	**25**	**44**	**33**	**2**	**0**	**2**	**139**	**13.7**	**11**	....	....	....	....	....	**20**	**4**	**6**	**10**	**14**	**0**	**0**	**3**
1993-94	**Montreal**	**NHL**	**74**	**19**	**24**	**43**	**32**	**1**	**0**	**1**	**153**	**12.4**	**17**	....	....	....	....	....	**7**	**2**	**1**	**3**	**8**	**1**	**0**	**0**
1994-95	**Montreal**	**NHL**	**9**	**1**	**4**	**5**	**10**	**1**	**0**	**0**	**18**	**5.6**	**–1**	....	....	....	....	....	....	....	....	....	....	....	....	....
	Philadelphia	**NHL**	**37**	**25**	**24**	**49**	**20**	**5**	**0**	**7**	**113**	**22.1**	**21**	....	....	....	....	....	**15**	**5**	**7**	**12**	**4**	**1**	**0**	**1**
1995-96	**Philadelphia**	**NHL**	**82**	**51**	**46**	**97**	**64**	**19**	**0**	**10**	**270**	**18.9**	**21**	....	....	....	....	....	**11**	**6**	**5**	**11**	**6**	**4**	**0**	**1**
1996-97	**Philadelphia**	**NHL**	**82**	**50**	**47**	**97**	**58**	**10**	**0**	**5**	**324**	**15.4**	**44**	....	....	....	....	....	**19**	**9**	**12**	**21**	**10**	**4**	**0**	**3**
1997-98	**Philadelphia**	**NHL**	**82**	**51**	**36**	**87**	**32**	**16**	**0**	**9**	**303**	**16.8**	**30**	....	....	....	....	....	**5**	**1**	**1**	**2**	**8**	**1**	**0**	**1**
	United States	Olympics	4	0	1	1	0	....	....	....	....	....	....	....	....	....	....	....	....	....	....	....	....	....	....	....
1998-99	**Philadelphia**	**NHL**	**76**	**43**	**47**	**90**	**30**	**16**	**0**	**7**	**246**	**17.5**	**36**	**7**	**14.3**	**86**	**10**	**21:03**	**6**	**3**	**0**	**3**	**12**	**2**	**0**	**0**
99-2000	**Philadelphia**	**NHL**	**82**	**40**	**37**	**77**	**36**	**13**	**0**	**7**	**249**	**16.1**	**8**	**7**	**28.6**	**106**	**26**	**20:18**	**18**	**6**	**7**	**13**	**6**	**4**	**0**	**2**
2000-01	**Philadelphia**	**NHL**	**16**	**7**	**5**	**12**	**0**	**3**	**0**	**2**	**48**	**14.6**	**2**	**0**	**0.0**	**15**	**3**	**19:06**	**6**	**1**	**2**	**3**	**2**	**0**	**0**	**0**
	NHL Totals		**681**	**316**	**311**	**627**	**331**	**89**	**0**	**51**	**1948**	**16.2**		**14**	**21.4**	**207**	**39**	**20:31**	**118**	**38**	**42**	**80**	**74**	**17**	**0**	**11**

ECAC Second All-Star Team (1991) • NHL First All-Star Team (1995, 1998) • NHL Second All-Star Team (1996, 1997, 1999) • Won Bud Light Plus/Minus Award (1997) • Won Bud Ice Plus/Minus Award (1999) • Played in NHL All-Star Game (1996, 1997, 1998, 1999, 2000)

• Missed majority of 1989-90 season recovering from knee surgery, January 20, 1990. Traded to **Philadelphia** by **Montreal** with Eric Desjardins and Gilbert Dionne for Mark Recchi and Philadelphia's 3rd round choice (Martin Hohenberger) in 1995 Entry Draft, February 9, 1995. • Missed majority of 2000-01 season recovering from back injury suffered in game vs. Boston, October 7, 2000.

LECLERC, Mike

(luh-KLUHRK, MIGHK) **ANA.**

Left wing. Shoots left. 6'2", 204 lbs. Born, Winnipeg, Man., November 10, 1976. Anaheim's 3rd choice, 55th overall, in 1995 Entry Draft.

Season	Club	League	GP	G	A	Pts	PIM	PP	SH	GW	S	%	+/-	TF	F%	H	SB	Min	GP	G	A	Pts	PIM	PP	SH	GW
1991-92	St. Boniface	MJHL	43	16	12	28	25	....	....	....	....	....	....	....	....	....	....	....	....	....	....	....	....	....	....	....
	Victoria Cougars	WHL	2	0	0	0	0	....	....	....	....	....	....	....	....	....	....	....	....	....	....	....	....	....	....	....
1992-93	Victoria Cougars	WHL	70	4	11	15	118	....	....	....	....	....	....	....	....	....	....	....	....	....	....	....	....	....	....	....
1993-94	Victoria Cougars	WHL	68	29	11	40	112	....	....	....	....	....	....	....	....	....	....	....	....	....	....	....	....	....	....	....
1994-95	Prince George	WHL	43	20	36	56	78	....	....	....	....	....	....	....	....	....	....	....	....	....	....	....	....	....	....	....
	Brandon	WHL	23	5	8	13	50	....	....	....	....	....	....	....	....	....	....	....	18	10	6	16	33	....	....	....
1995-96	Brandon	WHL	71	58	53	111	161	....	....	....	....	....	....	....	....	....	....	....	19	6	19	25	25	....	....	....
1996-97	**Anaheim**	**NHL**	**5**	**1**	**1**	**2**	**0**	**0**	**0**	**1**	**3**	**33.3**	**2**	....	....	....	....	....	**1**	**0**	**0**	**0**	**0**	**0**	**0**	**0**
	Baltimore Bandits	AHL	71	29	27	56	134	....	....	....	....	....	....	....	....	....	....	....	....	....	....	....	....	....	....	....
1997-98	**Anaheim**	**NHL**	**7**	**0**	**0**	**0**	**6**	**0**	**0**	**0**	**11**	**0.0**	**–6**	....	....	....	....	....	....	....	....	....	....	....	....	....
	Cincinnati Ducks	AHL	48	18	22	40	83	....	....	....	....	....	....	....	....	....	....	....	....	....	....	....	....	....	....	....
1998-99	**Anaheim**	**NHL**	**7**	**0**	**0**	**0**	**4**	**0**	**0**	**0**	**1**	**0.0**	**–2**	**0**	**0.0**	**9**	**2**	**5:52**	**1**	**0**	**0**	**0**	**0**	**0**	**0**	**0**
	Cincinnati Ducks	AHL	65	25	28	53	153	....	....	....	....	....	....	....	....	....	....	....	3	0	1	1	19	....	....	....
99-2000	**Anaheim**	**NHL**	**69**	**8**	**11**	**19**	**70**	**0**	**0**	**2**	**105**	**7.6**	**–15**	**1**	**0.0**	**145**	**11**	**12:08**	....	....	....	....	....	....	....	....
2000-01	**Anaheim**	**NHL**	**54**	**15**	**20**	**35**	**26**	**3**	**0**	**3**	**130**	**11.5**	**–1**	**5**	**20.0**	**87**	**23**	**17:35**	....	....	....	....	....	....	....	....
	NHL Totals		**142**	**24**	**32**	**56**	**106**	**3**	**0**	**6**	**250**	**9.6**		**6**	**16.7**	**241**	**36**	**14:04**	**2**	**0**	**0**	**0**	**0**	**0**	**0**	**0**

WHL East Second All-Star Team (1996)

LEDYARD, Grant

(LEHD-yahrd, GRANT) **T.B.**

Defense. Shoots left. 6'2", 195 lbs. Born, Winnipeg, Man., November 19, 1961.

Season	Club	League	GP	G	A	Pts	PIM	PP	SH	GW	S	%	+/-	TF	F%	H	SB	Min	GP	G	A	Pts	PIM	PP	SH	GW
1979-80	Fort Garry Blues	MJHL	49	13	24	37	90	....	....	....	....	....	....	....	....	....	....	....	....	....	....	....	....	....	....	....
1980-81	Saskatoon Blades	WHL	71	9	28	37	148	....	....	....	....	....	....	....	....	....	....	....	....	....	....	....	....	....	....	....
1981-82	Fort Garry Blues	MJHL	63	25	45	70	150	....	....	....	....	....	....	....	....	....	....	....	....	....	....	....	....	....	....	....
1982-83	Tulsa Oilers	CHL	80	13	29	42	115	....	....	....	....	....	....	....	....	....	....	....	....	....	....	....	....	....	....	....
1983-84	Tulsa Oilers	CHL	58	9	17	26	71	....	....	....	....	....	....	....	....	....	....	....	9	5	4	9	10	....	....	....
1984-85	**NY Rangers**	**NHL**	**42**	**8**	**12**	**20**	**53**	**1**	**0**	**1**	**91**	**8.8**	**8**	....	....	....	....	....	**3**	**0**	**2**	**2**	**4**	**0**	**0**	**0**
	New Haven	AHL	36	6	20	26	18	....	....	....	....	....	....	....	....	....	....	....	....	....	....	....	....	....	....	....
1985-86	**NY Rangers**	**NHL**	**27**	**2**	**9**	**11**	**20**	**0**	**0**	**0**	**57**	**3.5**	**–7**	....	....	....	....	....	....	....	....	....	....	....	....	....
	Los Angeles	**NHL**	**52**	**7**	**18**	**25**	**78**	**4**	**0**	**2**	**113**	**6.2**	**–22**	....	....	....	....	....	....	....	....	....	....	....	....	....
1986-87	**Los Angeles**	**NHL**	**67**	**14**	**23**	**37**	**93**	**5**	**0**	**1**	**144**	**9.7**	**–40**	....	....	....	....	....	**5**	**0**	**0**	**0**	**10**	**0**	**0**	**0**
1987-88	**Los Angeles**	**NHL**	**23**	**1**	**7**	**8**	**52**	**1**	**0**	**0**	**40**	**2.5**	**–7**	....	....	....	....	....	....	....	....	....	....	....	....	....
	New Haven	AHL	3	2	1	3	4	....	....	....	....	....	....	....	....	....	....	....	....	....	....	....	....	....	....	....
	Washington	**NHL**	**21**	**4**	**3**	**7**	**14**	**1**	**0**	**1**	**41**	**9.8**	**–4**	....	....	....	....	....	**14**	**1**	**0**	**1**	**30**	**0**	**0**	**0**
1988-89	**Washington**	**NHL**	**61**	**3**	**11**	**14**	**43**	**1**	**0**	**1**	**81**	**3.7**	**1**	....	....	....	....	....	....	....	....	....	....	....	....	....
	Buffalo	**NHL**	**13**	**1**	**5**	**6**	**8**	**0**	**0**	**1**	**25**	**4.0**	**1**	....	....	....	....	....	**5**	**1**	**2**	**3**	**2**	**0**	**0**	**0**
1989-90	**Buffalo**	**NHL**	**67**	**2**	**13**	**15**	**37**	**0**	**0**	**1**	**91**	**2.2**	**2**	....	....	....	....	....	....	....	....	....	....	....	....	....
1990-91	**Buffalo**	**NHL**	**60**	**8**	**23**	**31**	**46**	**2**	**1**	**1**	**118**	**6.8**	**13**	....	....	....	....	....	**6**	**3**	**3**	**6**	**10**	**0**	**0**	**0**
1991-92	**Buffalo**	**NHL**	**50**	**5**	**16**	**21**	**45**	**0**	**0**	**0**	**87**	**5.7**	**–4**	....	....	....	....	....	....	....	....	....	....	....	....	....
1992-93	**Buffalo**	**NHL**	**50**	**2**	**14**	**16**	**45**	**1**	**0**	**0**	**79**	**2.5**	**–2**	....	....	....	....	....	**8**	**0**	**0**	**0**	**8**	**0**	**0**	**0**
	Rochester	AHL	5	0	2	2	8	....	....	....	....	....	....	....	....	....	....	....	....	....	....	....	....	....	....	....
1993-94	**Dallas**	**NHL**	**84**	**9**	**37**	**46**	**42**	**6**	**0**	**1**	**177**	**5.1**	**7**	....	....	....	....	....	**9**	**1**	**2**	**3**	**6**	**0**	**0**	**1**
1994-95	**Dallas**	**NHL**	**38**	**5**	**13**	**18**	**20**	**4**	**0**	**0**	**79**	**6.3**	**6**	....	....	....	....	....	**3**	**0**	**0**	**0**	**2**	**0**	**0**	**0**
1995-96	**Dallas**	**NHL**	**73**	**5**	**19**	**24**	**20**	**2**	**0**	**1**	**123**	**4.1**	**–15**	....	....	....	....	....	....	....	....	....	....	....	....	....
1996-97	**Dallas**	**NHL**	**67**	**1**	**15**	**16**	**61**	**0**	**0**	**0**	**99**	**1.0**	**31**	....	....	....	....	....	**7**	**0**	**2**	**2**	**0**	**0**	**0**	**0**
1997-98	**Vancouver**	**NHL**	**49**	**2**	**13**	**15**	**14**	**1**	**0**	**0**	**57**	**3.5**	**–2**	....	....	....	....	....	....	....	....	....	....	....	....	....
	Boston	**NHL**	**22**	**2**	**7**	**9**	**6**	**1**	**0**	**0**	**33**	**6.1**	**–2**	....	....	....	....	....	**6**	**0**	**0**	**0**	**2**	**0**	**0**	**0**
1998-99	**Boston**	**NHL**	**47**	**4**	**8**	**12**	**33**	**1**	**0**	**2**	**47**	**8.5**	**–8**	**1**	**0.0**	**65**	**49**	**17:31**	**2**	**0**	**0**	**0**	**2**	**0**	**0**	**0**
99-2000	**Ottawa**	**NHL**	**40**	**2**	**4**	**6**	**8**	**0**	**0**	**1**	**42**	**4.8**	**–3**	**0**	**0.0**	**58**	**31**	**14:45**	**6**	**0**	**0**	**0**	**16**	**0**	**0**	**0**
2000-01	**Tampa Bay**	**NHL**	**14**	**2**	**2**	**4**	**12**	**0**	**0**	**0**	**12**	**16.7**	**–5**	**0**	**0.0**	**20**	**14**	**18:15**	....	....	....	....	....	....	....	....
	Dallas	**NHL**	**8**	**0**	**1**	**1**	**4**	**0**	**0**	**0**	**7**	**0.0**	**3**	**0**	**0.0**	**12**	**3**	**15:26**	**9**	**0**	**1**	**1**	**4**	**0**	**0**	**0**
	NHL Totals		**975**	**89**	**273**	**362**	**754**	**31**	**1**	**14**	**1643**	**5.4**		**1**	**0.0**	**155**	**97**	**16:27**	**83**	**6**	**12**	**18**	**96**	**0**	**0**	**1**

Won Bob Gassoff Trophy (Most Improved Defenseman - CHL) (1984)

Signed as a free agent by **NY Rangers**, July 7, 1982. Traded to **LA Kings** by **NY Rangers** with Rollie Melanson for LA Kings' 4th round choice (Mike Sullivan) in 1987 Entry Draft and Brian MacLellan, December 9, 1985. Traded to **Washington** by **LA Kings** for Craig Laughlin, February 9, 1988. Traded to **Buffalo** by **Washington** with Clint Malarchuk and Washington's 6th round choice (Brian Holzinger) in 1991 Entry Draft for Calle Johansson and Buffalo's 2nd round choice (Byron Dafoe) in 1989 Entry Draft, March 7, 1989. Signed as a free agent by **Dallas**, August 12, 1993. Signed as a free agent by **Vancouver**, July 17, 1997. Traded to **Boston** by **Vancouver** for Boston's 8th round choice (Curtis Valentine) in 1998 Entry Draft, March 3, 1998. Signed as a free agent by **Ottawa**, November 16, 1999. Signed as a free agent by **Tampa Bay**, January 31, 2001. Traded to **Dallas** by **Tampa Bay** for Dallas' 7th round choice (Tampa Bay selected Jeremy Van Hoof) in 2001 Entry Draft, March 13, 2001. Signed as a free agent by **Tampa Bay**, July 13, 2001.

LEEB, Brad

(LEEB, BRAD) **VAN.**

Right wing. Shoots right. 5'11", 180 lbs. Born, Red Deer, Alta., August 27, 1979.

Season	Club	League	GP	G	A	Pts	PIM	PP	SH	GW	S	%	+/-	TF	F%	H	SB	Min	GP	G	A	Pts	PIM	PP	SH	GW
1994-95	Red Deer Chiefs	AMHL	36	31	14	45	93	....	....	....	....	....	....	....	....	....	....	....	....	....	....	....	....	....	....	....
	Red Deer Rebels	WHL	3	0	0	0	4	....	....	....	....	....	....	....	....	....	....	....	....	....	....	....	....	....	....	....
1995-96	Red Deer Rebels	WHL	38	3	6	9	30	....	....	....	....	....	....	....	....	....	....	....	10	2	0	2	11	....	....	....
1996-97	Red Deer Rebels	WHL	70	15	20	35	76	....	....	....	....	....	....	....	....	....	....	....	16	3	3	6	6	....	....	....
1997-98	Red Deer Rebels	WHL	63	23	23	46	88	....	....	....	....	....	....	....	....	....	....	....	3	2	0	2	2	....	....	....
1998-99	Red Deer Rebels	WHL	64	32	47	79	84	....	....	....	....	....	....	....	....	....	....	....	9	5	9	14	10	....	....	....
99-2000	**Vancouver**	**NHL**	**2**	**0**	**0**	**0**	**2**	**0**	**0**	**0**	**3**	**0.0**	**–2**	**0**	**0.0**	**2**	**1**	**12:07**	....	....	....	....	....	....	....	....
	Syracuse Crunch	AHL	61	19	18	37	50	....	....	....	....	....	....	....	....	....	....	....	4	0	0	0	6	....	....	....
2000-01	Kansas City	IHL	53	18	16	34	53	....	....	....	....	....	....	....	....	....	....	....	....	....	....	....	....	....	....	....
	NHL Totals		**2**	**0**	**0**	**0**	**2**	**0**	**0**	**0**	**3**	**0.0**		**0**	**0.0**	**2**	**1**	....	....	....	....	....	....	....	....	....

WHL East Second All-Star Team (1999)

Signed as a free agent by **Vancouver**, October 8, 1999.

LEEB, Greg

(LEEB, GREHG) **EDM.**

Center. Shoots left. 5'9", 165 lbs. Born, Red Deer, Alta., May 31, 1977.

Season	Club	League	GP	G	A	Pts	PIM	PP	SH	GW	S	%	+/-	TF	F%	H	SB	Min	GP	G	A	Pts	PIM	PP	SH	GW
1993-94	Red Deer Royals	AMHL	36	19	30	49	24	....	....	....	....	....	....	....	....	....	....	....	....	....	....	....	....	....	....	....
1994-95	Spokane Chiefs	WHL	72	21	34	55	48	....	....	....	....	....	....	....	....	....	....	....	11	5	10	15	10	....	....	....
1995-96	Spokane Chiefs	WHL	64	33	21	54	54	....	....	....	....	....	....	....	....	....	....	....	18	1	7	8	16	....	....	....
1996-97	Spokane Chiefs	WHL	72	27	59	86	69	....	....	....	....	....	....	....	....	....	....	....	9	3	3	6	4	....	....	....
1997-98	Spokane Chiefs	WHL	68	46	50	96	54	....	....	....	....	....	....	....	....	....	....	....	18	10	10	20	10	....	....	....
1998-99	Michigan K-Wings	IHL	77	16	27	43	18	....	....	....	....	....	....	....	....	....	....	....	5	0	3	3	4	....	....	....
99-2000	Michigan K-Wings	IHL	73	9	17	26	76	....	....	....	....	....	....	....	....	....	....	....	....	....	....	....	....	....	....	....

Season	Club	League	GP	G	A	Pts	PIM	PP	SH	GW	S	%	+/-	TF	F%	H	SB	Min	GP	G	A	Pts	PIM	PP	SH	GW
			Regular Season																Playoffs							
2000-01	Dallas	NHL	2	0	0	0	0	0	0	0	4	0.0	–1	17	47.1	2	0	6:56	....	....	....	....	....	....	....	....
	Utah Grizzlies	IHL	78	25	40	65	36	....	....	....	....	....	....	....	....	....	....	....	....	....	....	....	....	....	....	....
	NHL Totals		2	0	0	0	0	0	0	0	4	0.0		17	47.1	2	0	6:56	....	....	....	....	....	....	....	....

WHL West Second All-Star Team (1998)

Signed as a free agent by **Dallas**, July 24, 1998. Signed as a free agent by **Edmonton**, July 17, 2001.

LEETCH, Brian (LEECH, BRIGH-uhn) NYR

Defense. Shoots left. 6'1", 190 lbs. Born, Corpus Christi, TX, March 3, 1968. NY Rangers' 1st choice, 9th overall, in 1986 Entry Draft.

Season	Club	League	GP	G	A	Pts	PIM	PP	SH	GW	S	%	+/-	TF	F%	H	SB	Min	GP	G	A	Pts	PIM	PP	SH	GW
1983-84	Avon Old Farms	Hi-School	28	52	49	101	24	....	....	....	....	....	....	....	....	....	....	....	....	....	....	....	....	....	....	....
1984-85	Avon Old Farms	Hi-School	26	30	46	76	15	....	....	....	....	....	....	....	....	....	....	....	....	....	....	....	....	....	....	....
1985-86	Avon Old Farms	Hi-School	28	40	44	84	18	....	....	....	....	....	....	....	....	....	....	....	....	....	....	....	....	....	....	....
1986-87	Boston College	H-East	37	9	38	47	10	....	....	....	....	....	....	....	....	....	....	....	....	....	....	....	....	....	....	....
1987-88	United States	Nat-Team	50	13	61	74	38	....	....	....	....	....	....	....	....	....	....	....	....	....	....	....	....	....	....	....
	United States	Olympics	6	1	5	6	4	....	....	....	....	....	....	....	....	....	....	....	....	....	....	....	....	....	....	....
	NY Rangers	NHL	17	2	12	14	0	1	0	1	40	5.0	5	....	....	....	....	....	....	....	....	....	....	....	....	....
1988-89	NY Rangers	NHL	68	23	48	71	50	8	3	1	268	8.6	8	....	....	....	....	....	4	3	2	5	2	2	0	0
1989-90	NY Rangers	NHL	72	11	45	56	26	5	0	2	222	5.0	–18	....	....	....	....	....	....	....	....	....	....	....	....	....
1990-91	NY Rangers	NHL	80	16	72	88	42	6	0	4	206	7.8	2	....	....	....	....	....	6	1	3	4	0	0	0	0
1991-92	NY Rangers	NHL	80	22	80	102	26	10	1	3	245	9.0	25	....	....	....	....	....	13	4	11	15	4	1	1	0
1992-93	NY Rangers	NHL	36	6	30	36	26	2	1	1	150	4.0	2	....	....	....	....	....	....	....	....	....	....	....	....	....
1993-94♦	NY Rangers	NHL	84	23	56	79	67	17	1	4	328	7.0	28	....	....	....	....	....	23	11	*23	*34	6	4	0	4
1994-95	NY Rangers	NHL	48	9	32	41	18	3	0	2	182	4.9	0	....	....	....	....	....	10	6	8	14	8	3	0	1
1995-96	NY Rangers	NHL	82	15	70	85	30	7	0	3	276	5.4	12	....	....	....	....	....	11	1	6	7	4	1	0	0
1996-97	NY Rangers	NHL	82	20	58	78	40	9	0	2	256	7.8	31	....	....	....	....	....	15	2	8	10	6	1	0	1
1997-98	NY Rangers	NHL	76	17	33	50	32	11	0	2	230	7.4	–36	....	....	....	....	....	....	....	....	....	....	....	....	....
	United States	Olympics	4	1	1	2	0	....	....	....	....	....	....	....	....	....	....	....	....	....	....	....	....	....	....	....
1998-99	NY Rangers	NHL	82	13	42	55	42	4	0	1	184	7.1	–7	0	0.0	173	212	29:52	....	....	....	....	....	....	....	....
99-2000	NY Rangers	NHL	50	7	19	26	20	3	0	2	124	5.6	–16	0	0.0	82	94	26:57	....	....	....	....	....	....	....	....
2000-01	NY Rangers	NHL	82	21	58	79	34	10	1	3	241	8.7	–18	0	0.0	112	177	29:21	....	....	....	....	....	....	....	....
	NHL Totals		939	205	655	860	453	96	7	31	2952	6.9		0	0.0	367	483	28:59	82	28	61	89	30	12	1	6

Hockey East First All-Star Team (1987) • NCAA East First All-American Team (1987) • NHL All-Rookie Team (1989) • Won Calder Memorial Trophy (1989) • NHL Second All-Star Team (1991, 1994, 1996) • Won James Norris Memorial Trophy (1992, 1997) • NHL First All-Star Team (1992, 1997) • Won Conn Smythe Trophy (1994) • Played in NHL All-Star Game (1990, 1991, 1992, 1994, 1996, 1997, 1998, 2001)

LEFEBVRE, Sylvain (luh-FAYV, SIHL-veh) NYR

Defense. Shoots left. 6'2", 205 lbs. Born, Richmond, Que., October 14, 1967.

Season	Club	League	GP	G	A	Pts	PIM	PP	SH	GW	S	%	+/-	TF	F%	H	SB	Min	GP	G	A	Pts	PIM	PP	SH	GW
1983-84	Cantons de l'Est	QAAA	1	0	0	0	0	....	....	....	....	....	....	....	....	....	....	....	2	1	0	1	2	....	....	....
1984-85	Laval Titan	QMJHL	66	7	5	12	31	....	....	....	....	....	....	....	....	....	....	....	....	....	....	....	....	....	....	....
1985-86	Laval Titan	QMJHL	71	8	17	25	48	....	....	....	....	....	....	....	....	....	....	....	14	1	0	1	25	....	....	....
1986-87	Laval Titan	QMJHL	70	10	36	46	44	....	....	....	....	....	....	....	....	....	....	....	15	1	6	7	12	....	....	....
1987-88	Sherbrooke	AHL	79	3	24	27	73	....	....	....	....	....	....	....	....	....	....	....	6	2	3	5	4	....	....	....
1988-89	Sherbrooke	AHL	77	15	32	47	119	....	....	....	....	....	....	....	....	....	....	....	6	1	3	4	4	....	....	....
1989-90	Montreal	NHL	68	3	10	13	61	0	0	0	89	3.4	18	....	....	....	....	....	6	0	0	0	2	0	0	0
1990-91	Montreal	NHL	63	5	18	23	30	1	0	1	76	6.6	–11	....	....	....	....	....	11	1	0	1	6	0	0	0
1991-92	Montreal	NHL	69	3	14	17	91	0	0	0	85	3.5	9	....	....	....	....	....	2	0	0	0	2	0	0	0
1992-93	Toronto	NHL	81	2	12	14	90	0	0	0	81	2.5	8	....	....	....	....	....	21	3	3	6	20	0	0	0
1993-94	Toronto	NHL	84	2	9	11	79	0	0	0	96	2.1	33	....	....	....	....	....	18	0	3	3	16	0	0	0
1994-95	Quebec	NHL	48	2	11	13	17	0	0	0	81	2.5	13	....	....	....	....	....	6	0	2	2	2	0	0	0
1995-96♦	Colorado	NHL	75	5	11	16	49	2	0	0	115	4.3	26	....	....	....	....	....	22	0	5	5	12	0	0	0
1996-97	Colorado	NHL	71	2	11	13	30	1	0	0	77	2.6	12	....	....	....	....	....	17	0	0	0	25	0	0	0
1997-98	Colorado	NHL	81	0	10	10	48	0	0	0	66	0.0	2	....	....	....	....	....	7	0	0	0	4	0	0	0
1998-99	Colorado	NHL	76	2	18	20	48	0	0	0	64	3.1	18	0	0.0	120	79	20:56	19	0	1	1	12	0	0	0
99-2000	NY Rangers	NHL	82	2	10	12	43	0	0	0	67	3.0	–13	0	0.0	181	142	18:36	....	....	....	....	....	....	....	....
2000-01	NY Rangers	NHL	71	2	13	15	55	0	0	0	39	5.1	3	0	0.0	200	103	18:10	....	....	....	....	....	....	....	....
	NHL Totals		869	30	147	177	641	4	0	1	936	3.2		0	0.0	501	324	19:14	129	4	14	18	101	0	0	0

AHL Second All-Star Team (1989)

Signed as a free agent by **Montreal**, September 24, 1986. Traded to **Toronto** by **Montreal** for Toronto's 3rd round choice (Martin Belanger) in 1994 Entry Draft, August 20, 1992. Traded to **Quebec** by **Toronto** with Wendel Clark, Landon Wilson and Toronto's 1st round choice (Jeffrey Kealty) in 1994 Entry Draft for Mats Sundin, Garth Butcher, Todd Warriner and Philadelphia's 1st round choice (previously acquired by Quebec - later traded to Washington - Washington selected Nolan Baumgartner) in 1994 Entry Draft, June 28, 1994. Transferred to **Colorado** after **Quebec** franchise relocated, June 21, 1995. Signed as a free agent by **NY Rangers**, July 22, 1999.

LEGWAND, David (LEHG-wuhnd, DAY-vihd) NSH.

Center. Shoots left. 6'2", 190 lbs. Born, Detroit, MI, August 17, 1980. Nashville's 1st choice, 2nd overall, in 1998 Entry Draft.

Season	Club	League	GP	G	A	Pts	PIM	PP	SH	GW	S	%	+/-	TF	F%	H	SB	Min	GP	G	A	Pts	PIM	PP	SH	GW
1996-97	Det-Compuware	MNHL	44	21	41	62	58	....	....	....	....	....	....	....	....	....	....	....	....	....	....	....	....	....	....	....
1997-98	Plymouth Whalers	OHL	59	54	51	105	56	....	....	....	....	....	....	....	....	....	....	....	15	8	12	20	24	....	....	....
1998-99	Plymouth Whalers	OHL	55	31	49	80	65	....	....	....	....	....	....	....	....	....	....	....	11	3	8	11	8	....	....	....
	Nashville	NHL	1	0	0	0	0	0	0	0	2	0.0	0	9	55.6	0	1	12:50	....	....	....	....	....	....	....	....
99-2000	Nashville	NHL	71	13	15	28	30	4	0	2	111	11.7	–6	637	41.6	48	27	14:43	....	....	....	....	....	....	....	....
2000-01	Nashville	NHL	81	13	28	41	38	3	0	3	172	7.6	1	888	40.3	50	23	15:14	....	....	....	....	....	....	....	....
	NHL Totals		153	26	43	69	68	7	0	5	285	9.1		1534	40.9	98	51	14:59	....	....	....	....	....	....	....	....

OHL First All-Star Team (1998) • Canadian Major Junior Rookie of the Year (1998)

LEHTINEN, Jere (lehkh-TIH-nehn, YUH-ree) DAL.

Right wing. Shoots right. 6', 200 lbs. Born, Espoo, Finland, June 24, 1973. Minnesota's 3rd choice, 88th overall, in 1992 Entry Draft.

Season	Club	League	GP	G	A	Pts	PIM	PP	SH	GW	S	%	+/-	TF	F%	H	SB	Min	GP	G	A	Pts	PIM	PP	SH	GW
1989-90	Kiekoo-67 Turku	Finn-Jr.	32	23	23	46	6	....	....	....	....	....	....	....	....	....	....	....	5	0	3	3	0	....	....	....
1990-91	Kiekko-Espoo	Finn-Jr.	3	3	1	4	0	....	....	....	....	....	....	....	....	....	....	....	....	....	....	....	....	....	....	....
	Kiekko-Espoo	Finland-2	32	15	9	24	12	....	....	....	....	....	....	....	....	....	....	....	....	....	....	....	....	....	....	....
1991-92	Kiekoo-67 Turku	Finn-Jr.	8	5	4	9	2	....	....	....	....	....	....	....	....	....	....	....	....	....	....	....	....	....	....	....
	Kiekko-Espoo	Finland-2	43	32	17	49	6	....	....	....	....	....	....	....	....	....	....	....	....	....	....	....	....	....	....	....
1992-93	Kiekoo-67 Turku	Finn-Jr.	4	5	3	8	8	....	....	....	....	....	....	....	....	....	....	....	....	....	....	....	....	....	....	....
	Kiekko-Espoo	Finland	45	13	14	27	6	....	....	....	....	....	....	....	....	....	....	....	....	....	....	....	....	....	....	....
1993-94	TPS Turku	Finland	42	19	20	39	6	....	....	....	....	....	....	....	....	....	....	....	11	*11	2	13	*2	....	....	....
	Finland	Olympics	8	3	0	3	0	....	....	....	....	....	....	....	....	....	....	....	....	....	....	....	....	....	....	....
1994-95	TPS Turku	Finland	39	19	23	42	33	....	....	....	....	....	....	....	....	....	....	....	13	*8	6	14	4	....	....	....
1995-96	Dallas	NHL	57	6	22	28	16	0	0	1	109	5.5	5	....	....	....	....	....	....	....	....	....	....	....	....	....
	Michigan K-Wings	IHL	1	1	0	1	0	....	....	....	....	....	....	....	....	....	....	....	....	....	....	....	....	....	....	....
1996-97	Dallas	NHL	63	16	27	43	2	3	1	2	134	11.9	26	....	....	....	....	....	7	2	2	4	0	0	0	0
1997-98	Dallas	NHL	72	23	19	42	20	7	2	6	201	11.4	19	....	....	....	....	....	12	3	5	8	2	1	0	0
	Finland	Olympics	6	4	2	6	2	....	....	....	....	....	....	....	....	....	....	....	....	....	....	....	....	....	....	....
1998-99♦	Dallas	NHL	74	20	32	52	18	7	1	2	173	11.6	29	9	33.3	72	47	19:36	23	10	3	13	2	1	1	0
99-2000	Dallas	NHL	17	3	5	8	0	0	0	1	29	10.3	1	0	0.0	17	6	17:31	13	1	5	6	2	0	0	0
2000-01	Dallas	NHL	74	20	25	45	24	7	0	1	148	13.5	14	7	28.6	94	41	19:17	10	1	0	1	2	0	0	0
	NHL Totals		357	88	130	218	80	24	4	13	794	11.1		16	31.3	183	94	19:15	65	17	15	32	8	2	1	0

Won Frank J. Selke Trophy (1998, 1999) • Played in NHL All-Star Game (1998)

Rights transferred to **Dallas** after **Minnesota** franchise relocated, June 9, 1993. • Missed majority of 1999-2000 season recovering from leg injury suffered in game vs. Nashville, October 16, 1999.

LEMIEUX, Claude
(lehm-YOO, KLOHD) **PHX.**

Right wing. Shoots right. 6'1", 226 lbs. Born, Buckingham, Que., July 16, 1965. Montreal's 2nd choice, 26th overall, in 1983 Entry Draft.

			Regular Season																Playoffs							
Season	Club	League	GP	G	A	Pts	PIM	PP	SH	GW	S	%	+/-	TF	F%	H	SB	Min	GP	G	A	Pts	PIM	PP	SH	GW
1981-82	Richelieu Regents	QAAA	48	24	48	72	96												8	10	13	23	14			
1982-83	Trois-Rivieres	QMJHL	62	28	38	66	187												4	1	0	1	30			
1983-84	Verdun Juniors	QMJHL	51	41	45	86	225												9	8	12	20	63			
	Montreal	**NHL**	**8**	**1**	**1**	**2**	**12**	**0**	**0**	**0**	**7**	**14.3**	**–2**													
	Nova Scotia	AHL																	2	1	0	1	0			
1984-85	Verdun	QMJHL	52	58	66	124	152												14	23	17	40	38			
	Montreal	**NHL**	**1**	**0**	**1**	**1**	**7**	**0**	**0**	**0**	**0**	**0.0**	**1**													
1985-86♦	**Montreal**	**NHL**	**10**	**1**	**2**	**3**	**22**	**1**	**0**	**0**	**16**	**6.3**	**–6**						**20**	**10**	**6**	**16**	**68**	**4**	**0**	**4**
	Sherbrooke	AHL	58	21	32	53	145																			
1986-87	**Montreal**	**NHL**	**76**	**27**	**26**	**53**	**156**	**5**	**0**	**1**	**184**	**14.7**	**0**						**17**	**4**	**9**	**13**	**41**	**2**	**0**	**0**
1987-88	**Montreal**	**NHL**	**78**	**31**	**30**	**61**	**137**	**6**	**0**	**3**	**241**	**12.9**	**16**						**11**	**3**	**2**	**5**	**20**	**0**	**0**	**2**
1988-89	**Montreal**	**NHL**	**69**	**29**	**22**	**51**	**136**	**7**	**0**	**3**	**220**	**13.2**	**14**						**18**	**4**	**3**	**7**	**58**	**0**	**0**	**1**
1989-90	**Montreal**	**NHL**	**39**	**8**	**10**	**18**	**106**	**3**	**0**	**1**	**104**	**7.7**	**–8**						**11**	**1**	**3**	**4**	**38**	**0**	**0**	**1**
1990-91	**New Jersey**	**NHL**	**78**	**30**	**17**	**47**	**105**	**10**	**0**	**2**	**271**	**11.1**	**–8**						**7**	**4**	**0**	**4**	**34**	**2**	**0**	**1**
1991-92	**New Jersey**	**NHL**	**74**	**41**	**27**	**68**	**109**	**13**	**1**	**8**	**296**	**13.9**	**9**						**7**	**4**	**3**	**7**	**26**	**1**	**0**	**0**
1992-93	**New Jersey**	**NHL**	**77**	**30**	**51**	**81**	**155**	**13**	**0**	**3**	**311**	**9.6**	**3**						**5**	**2**	**0**	**2**	**19**	**1**	**0**	**0**
1993-94	**New Jersey**	**NHL**	**79**	**18**	**26**	**44**	**86**	**5**	**0**	**5**	**181**	**9.9**	**13**						**20**	**7**	**11**	**18**	**44**	**0**	**0**	**2**
1994-95♦	**New Jersey**	**NHL**	**45**	**6**	**13**	**19**	**86**	**1**	**0**	**1**	**117**	**5.1**	**2**						**20**	***13**	**3**	**16**	**20**	**0**	**0**	**3**
1995-96♦	**Colorado**	**NHL**	**79**	**39**	**32**	**71**	**117**	**9**	**2**	**10**	**315**	**12.4**	**14**						**19**	**5**	**7**	**12**	**55**	**3**	**0**	**0**
1996-97	**Colorado**	**NHL**	**45**	**11**	**17**	**28**	**43**	**5**	**0**	**4**	**168**	**6.5**	**–4**						**17**	***13**	**10**	**23**	**32**	**4**	**0**	**4**
1997-98	**Colorado**	**NHL**	**78**	**26**	**27**	**53**	**115**	**11**	**1**	**1**	**261**	**10.0**	**–7**						**7**	**3**	**3**	**6**	**8**	**1**	**0**	**1**
1998-99	**Colorado**	**NHL**	**82**	**27**	**24**	**51**	**102**	**11**	**0**	**8**	**292**	**9.2**	**0**	**43**	**41.9**	**110**	**26**	**21:14**	**19**	**3**	**11**	**14**	**26**	**1**	**0**	**0**
99-2000	**Colorado**	**NHL**	**13**	**3**	**6**	**9**	**4**	**0**	**0**	**0**	**36**	**8.3**	**0**	**2**	**50.0**	**20**	**2**	**18:40**								
	♦ New Jersey	**NHL**	**70**	**17**	**21**	**38**	**86**	**7**	**0**	**3**	**221**	**7.7**	**–3**	**49**	**28.6**	**116**	**15**	**17:55**	**23**	**4**	**6**	**10**	**28**	**1**	**0**	**0**
2000-01	**Phoenix**	**NHL**	**46**	**10**	**16**	**26**	**58**	**2**	**0**	**1**	**99**	**10.1**	**1**	**28**	**21.4**	**68**	**11**	**17:12**								
	NHL Totals		**1047**	**355**	**369**	**724**	**1642**	**109**	**4**	**54**	**3340**	**10.6**		**122**	**32.0**	**314**	**54**	**19:06**	**221**	**80**	**77**	**157**	**517**	**20**	**0**	**19**

QMJHL Second All-Star Team (1984) • QMJHL First All-Star Team (1985) • Won Conn Smythe Trophy (1995)

• Missed majority of 1989-90 season recovering from abdominal injury suffered in game vs. Boston, October 9, 1989. Traded to **New Jersey** by **Montreal** for Sylvain Turgeon, September 4, 1990. Traded to **NY Islanders** by **New Jersey** for Steve Thomas, October 3, 1995. Traded to **Colorado** by **NY Islanders** for Wendel Clark, October 3, 1995. Traded to **New Jersey** by **Colorado** with Colorado's 1st (David Hale) and 2nd (Matt DeMarchi) round choices in 2000 Entry Draft for Brian Rolston and New Jersey's 1st round choice (later traded to Boston - Boston selected Martin Samuelsson) in 2000 Entry Draft, November 3, 1999. Signed as a free agent by **Phoenix**, December 5, 2000.

LEMIEUX, Mario
(lehm-YOO, MAHR-ee-oh) **PIT.**

Center. Shoots right. 6'4", 225 lbs. Born, Montreal, Que., October 5, 1965. Pittsburgh's 1st choice, 1st overall, in 1984 Entry Draft.

			Regular Season																Playoffs							
Season	Club	League	GP	G	A	Pts	PIM	PP	SH	GW	S	%	+/-	TF	F%	H	SB	Min	GP	G	A	Pts	PIM	PP	SH	GW
1980-81	Montreal	QAAA	47	62	62	124	127												3	2	5	7	8			
1981-82	Laval Titan	QMJHL	64	30	66	96	22												18	5	9	14	31			
1982-83	Laval Titan	QMJHL	66	84	100	184	76												12	14	18	32	18			
1983-84	Laval Titan	QMJHL	70	*133	*149	*282	92												14	*29	*23	*52	29			
1984-85	**Pittsburgh**	**NHL**	**73**	**43**	**57**	**100**	**54**	**11**	**0**	**2**	**209**	**20.6**	**–35**													
1985-86	**Pittsburgh**	**NHL**	**79**	**48**	**93**	**141**	**43**	**17**	**0**	**4**	**276**	**17.4**	**–6**													
1986-87	**Pittsburgh**	**NHL**	**63**	**54**	**53**	**107**	**57**	**19**	**0**	**4**	**267**	**20.2**	**13**													
1987-88	**Pittsburgh**	**NHL**	**77**	***70**	**98**	***168**	**92**	**22**	**10**	**7**	**382**	**18.3**	**23**													
1988-89	**Pittsburgh**	**NHL**	**76**	***85**	***114**	***199**	**100**	**31**	**13**	**8**	**313**	**27.2**	**41**						**11**	**12**	**7**	**19**	**16**	**7**	**1**	**0**
1989-90	**Pittsburgh**	**NHL**	**59**	**45**	**78**	**123**	**78**	**14**	**3**	**4**	**226**	**19.9**	**–18**													
1990-91♦	**Pittsburgh**	**NHL**	**26**	**19**	**26**	**45**	**30**	**6**	**1**	**2**	**89**	**21.3**	**8**						**23**	**16**	***28**	***44**	**16**	**6**	**2**	**0**
1991-92♦	**Pittsburgh**	**NHL**	**64**	**44**	**87**	***131**	**94**	**12**	**4**	**5**	**249**	**17.7**	**27**						**15**	***16**	**18**	***34**	**2**	**8**	**2**	**5**
1992-93	**Pittsburgh**	**NHL**	**60**	**69**	**91**	***160**	**38**	**16**	**6**	**10**	**286**	**24.1**	**55**						**11**	**8**	**10**	**18**	**10**	**3**	**1**	**1**
1993-94	**Pittsburgh**	**NHL**	**22**	**17**	**20**	**37**	**32**	**7**	**0**	**4**	**92**	**18.5**	**–2**						**6**	**4**	**3**	**7**	**2**	**1**	**0**	**0**
1994-95	**Pittsburgh**	**NHL**	DID NOT PLAY																							
1995-96	**Pittsburgh**	**NHL**	**70**	***69**	***92**	***161**	**54**	**31**	**8**	**8**	**338**	**20.4**	**10**						**18**	**11**	**16**	**27**	**33**	**3**	**1**	**2**
1996-97	**Pittsburgh**	**NHL**	**76**	**50**	***72**	***122**	**65**	**15**	**3**	**7**	**327**	**15.3**	**27**						**5**	**3**	**3**	**6**	**4**	**0**	**0**	**0**
1997-98			OUT OF HOCKEY – RETIRED																							
1998-99			OUT OF HOCKEY – RETIRED																							
99-2000			OUT OF HOCKEY – RETIRED																							
2000-01	**Pittsburgh**	**NHL**	**43**	**35**	**41**	**76**	**18**	**16**	**1**	**5**	**171**	**20.5**	**15**	**852**	**52.1**	**29**	**23**	**24:20**	**18**	**6**	**11**	**17**	**4**	**1**	**0**	**3**
	NHL Totals		**788**	**648**	**922**	**1570**	**755**	**217**	**49**	**70**	**3225**	**20.1**		**852**	**52.1**	**29**	**23**	**24:20**	**107**	**76**	**96**	**172**	**87**	**29**	**7**	**11**

• Inducted into Hockey Hall of Fame (1997)

QMJHL Second All-Star Team (1983) • QMJHL First All-Star Team (1984) • Canadian Major Junior Player of the Year (1984) • NHL All-Rookie Team (1985) • Won Calder Memorial Trophy (1985) • NHL Second All-Star Team (1986, 1987, 1992, 2001) • Won Lester B. Pearson Award (1986, 1988, 1993, 1996) • Canada Cup All-Star Team (1987) • NHL First All-Star Team (1988, 1989, 1993, 1996, 1997) • Won Dodge Performance of the Year Award (1988) • Won Dodge Performer of the Year Award (1988, 1989) • Won Art Ross Trophy (1988, 1989, 1992, 1993, 1996, 1997) • Won Hart Trophy (1988, 1993, 1996) • Won Dodge Ram Tough Award (1989) • Won Conn Smythe Trophy (1991, 1992) • Won ProSet/NHL Player of the Year Award (1992) • Won Alka-Seltzer Plus Award (1993) • Won Bill Masterton Memorial Trophy (1993) • Won Lester Patrick Trophy (2000) • Played in NHL All-Star Game (1985, 1986, 1988, 1989, 1990, 1992, 1996, 1997, 2001)

• Missed remainder of 1989-90 and majority of 1990-91 seasons recovering from back injury suffered in game vs. NY Rangers, February 14, 1989. • Missed most of 1992-93 season after being diagnosed with Hodgkin's Disease, January 12, 1993. • Missed majority of 1993-94 season recovering from back injury originally suffered in game vs. Chicago, November 11, 1993. • Missed entire 1994-95 season recovering from effects of treatment for Hodgkin's Disease and back injury suffered in game vs. NY Rangers, March 12, 1994. • Became third player (Gordie Howe, Guy Lafleur) to appear in NHL game after being inducted into Hockey Hall of Fame, December 27, 2000.

LEROUX, Francois
(leh-ROO, FRAN-swuh)

Defense. Shoots left. 6'6", 247 lbs. Born, Ste-Adele, Que., April 18, 1970. Edmonton's 1st choice, 19th overall, in 1988 Entry Draft.

			Regular Season																Playoffs							
Season	Club	League	GP	G	A	Pts	PIM	PP	SH	GW	S	%	+/-	TF	F%	H	SB	Min	GP	G	A	Pts	PIM	PP	SH	GW
1986-87	Laval Laurentide	QAAA	42	5	11	16	76												8	0	1	1	12			
1987-88	St-Jean Lynx	QMJHL	58	3	8	11	143												7	2	0	2	21			
1988-89	St-Jean Lynx	QMJHL	57	8	34	42	185																			
	Edmonton	**NHL**	**2**	**0**	**0**	**0**	**0**	**0**	**0**	**0**	**0**	**0.0**	**1**													
1989-90	Victoriaville Tigres	QMJHL	54	4	33	37	169																			
	Edmonton	**NHL**	**3**	**0**	**1**	**1**	**0**	**0**	**0**	**0**	**0**	**0.0**	**–2**													
1990-91	**Edmonton**	**NHL**	**1**	**0**	**2**	**2**	**0**	**0**	**0**	**0**	**1**	**0.0**	**1**													
	Cape Breton	AHL	71	2	7	9	124												4	0	1	1	19			
1991-92	**Edmonton**	**NHL**	**4**	**0**	**0**	**0**	**7**	**0**	**0**	**0**	**0**	**0.0**	**–1**													
	Cape Breton	AHL	61	7	22	29	114												5	0	0	0	8			
1992-93	**Edmonton**	**NHL**	**1**	**0**	**0**	**0**	**4**	**0**	**0**	**0**	**0**	**0.0**	**0**													
	Cape Breton	AHL	55	10	24	34	139												16	0	5	5	29			
1993-94	**Ottawa**	**NHL**	**23**	**0**	**1**	**1**	**70**	**0**	**0**	**0**	**8**	**0.0**	**–4**													
	P.E.I. Senators	AHL	25	4	6	10	52																			
1994-95	P.E.I. Senators	AHL	45	4	14	18	137																			
	Pittsburgh	**NHL**	**40**	**0**	**2**	**2**	**114**	**0**	**0**	**0**	**19**	**0.0**	**7**						**12**	**0**	**2**	**2**	**14**	**0**	**0**	**0**
1995-96	**Pittsburgh**	**NHL**	**66**	**2**	**9**	**11**	**161**	**0**	**0**	**0**	**43**	**4.7**	**2**						**18**	**1**	**1**	**2**	**20**	**0**	**0**	**1**
1996-97	**Pittsburgh**	**NHL**	**59**	**0**	**3**	**3**	**81**	**0**	**0**	**0**	**5**	**0.0**	**–3**						**3**	**0**	**0**	**0**	**0**	**0**	**0**	**0**
1997-98	**Colorado**	**NHL**	**50**	**1**	**2**	**3**	**140**	**0**	**0**	**0**	**14**	**7.1**	**–3**													
1998-99	Grand Rapids	IHL	13	1	1	2	22																			
99-2000	Springfield	AHL	64	3	6	9	162												5	0	0	0	2			
2000-01	Springfield	AHL	65	4	6	10	180																			
	NHL Totals		**249**	**3**	**20**	**23**	**577**	**0**	**0**	**0**	**90**	**3.3**							**33**	**1**	**3**	**4**	**34**	**0**	**0**	**1**

Claimed on waivers by **Ottawa** from **Edmonton**, October 6, 1993. Claimed by **Pittsburgh** from **Ottawa** in Waiver Draft, January 18, 1995. Traded to **Colorado** by **Pittsburgh** for Colorado's 3rd round choice (David Cameron) in 1998 Entry Draft, September 28, 1997. Signed as a free agent by **Grand Rapids** (IHL), February 18, 1999. Signed as a free agent by **Phoenix**, July 20, 1999. Signed as a free agent by **Berlin Capitals** (DEL), July 17, 2001.

LEROUX, Jean-Yves
(leh-ROO, ZHAWN-EEV) **CHI.**

Left wing. Shoots left. 6'2", 211 lbs. Born, Montreal, Que., June 24, 1976. Chicago's 2nd choice, 40th overall, in 1994 Entry Draft.

			Regular Season																Playoffs							
Season	Club	League	GP	G	A	Pts	PIM	PP	SH	GW	S	%	+/-	TF	F%	H	SB	Min	GP	G	A	Pts	PIM	PP	SH	GW
1991-92	Mtl-Bourassa	QAAA	35	14	31	45	62												7	1	3	4	8			
1992-93	Beauport	QMJHL	62	20	25	45	33																			
1993-94	Beauport	QMJHL	45	14	25	39	43												15	7	6	13	33			
1994-95	Beauport	QMJHL	59	19	33	52	125												17	4	6	10	39			
1995-96	Beauport	QMJHL	54	41	41	82	176												20	5	18	23	20			

Season	Club	League	GP	G	A	Pts	PIM	PP	SH	GW	S	%	+/-	TF	F%	H	SB	Min	Playoffs GP	G	A	Pts	PIM	PP	SH	GW
1996-97	**Chicago**	**NHL**	**1**	**0**	**1**	**1**	**5**	**0**	**0**	**0**	**0**	**0.0**	**1**													
	Indianapolis Ice	IHL	69	14	17	31	112												4	1	0	1	2			
1997-98	**Chicago**	**NHL**	**66**	**6**	**7**	**13**	**55**	**0**	**0**	**0**	**57**	**10.5**	**–2**													
1998-99	**Chicago**	**NHL**	**40**	**3**	**5**	**8**	**21**	**0**	**0**	**0**	**47**	**6.4**	**–7**	**10**	**50.0**	**98**	**8**	**12:43**								
	Chicago Wolves	IHL																	10	1	1	2	18			
99-2000	**Chicago**	**NHL**	**54**	**3**	**5**	**8**	**43**	**0**	**0**	**1**	**36**	**8.3**	**–10**	**7**	**0.0**	**96**	**9**	**10:44**								
2000-01	**Chicago**	**NHL**	**59**	**4**	**4**	**8**	**22**	**1**	**0**	**0**	**60**	**6.7**	**–9**	**1**	**0.0**	**98**	**11**	**10:11**								
	NHL Totals		**220**	**16**	**22**	**38**	**146**	**1**	**0**	**1**	**200**	**8.0**		**18**	**27.8**	**292**	**28**	**11:02**								

QMJHL Second All-Star Team (1994)

LESCHYSHYN, Curtis

(luh-SIH-shuhn, KUHR-tihs) **OTT.**

Defense. Shoots left. 6'1", 220 lbs. Born, Thompson, Man., September 21, 1969. Quebec's 1st choice, 3rd overall, in 1988 Entry Draft.

Season	Club	League	GP	G	A	Pts	PIM	PP	SH	GW	S	%	+/-	TF	F%	H	SB	Min	Playoffs GP	G	A	Pts	PIM	PP	SH	GW
1985-86	Saskatoon Blaze	SMHL	34	9	34	43	52																			
	Saskatoon Blades	WHL	1	0	0	0	0																			
1986-87	Saskatoon Blades	WHL	70	14	26	40	107												11	1	5	6	14			
1987-88	Saskatoon Blades	WHL	56	14	41	55	86												10	2	5	7	16			
1988-89	**Quebec**	**NHL**	**71**	**4**	**9**	**13**	**71**	**1**	**1**	**0**	**58**	**6.9**	**–32**													
1989-90	**Quebec**	**NHL**	**68**	**2**	**6**	**8**	**44**	**1**	**0**	**0**	**42**	**4.8**	**–41**													
1990-91	**Quebec**	**NHL**	**55**	**3**	**7**	**10**	**49**	**2**	**0**	**1**	**57**	**5.3**	**–19**													
1991-92	**Quebec**	**NHL**	**42**	**5**	**12**	**17**	**42**	**3**	**0**	**1**	**61**	**8.2**	**–28**													
	Halifax Citadels	AHL	6	0	2	2	4																			
1992-93	**Quebec**	**NHL**	**82**	**9**	**23**	**32**	**61**	**4**	**0**	**2**	**73**	**12.3**	**25**						**6**	**1**	**1**	**2**	**6**	**1**	**0**	**0**
1993-94	**Quebec**	**NHL**	**72**	**5**	**17**	**22**	**65**	**3**	**0**	**2**	**97**	**5.2**	**–2**													
1994-95	**Quebec**	**NHL**	**44**	**2**	**13**	**15**	**20**	**0**	**0**	**0**	**43**	**4.7**	**29**						**3**	**0**	**1**	**1**	**4**	**0**	**0**	**0**
1995-96♦	**Colorado**	**NHL**	**77**	**4**	**15**	**19**	**73**	**0**	**0**	**1**	**76**	**5.3**	**32**						**17**	**1**	**2**	**3**	**8**	**0**	**0**	**0**
1996-97	**Colorado**	**NHL**	**11**	**0**	**5**	**5**	**6**	**0**	**0**	**0**	**8**	**0.0**	**1**													
	Washington	**NHL**	**2**	**0**	**0**	**0**	**2**	**0**	**0**	**0**	**0**	**0.0**	**0**													
	Hartford	**NHL**	**64**	**4**	**13**	**17**	**30**	**1**	**1**	**1**	**94**	**4.3**	**–19**													
1997-98	**Carolina**	**NHL**	**73**	**2**	**10**	**12**	**45**	**1**	**0**	**1**	**53**	**3.8**	**–2**													
1998-99	**Carolina**	**NHL**	**65**	**2**	**7**	**9**	**50**	**0**	**0**	**0**	**35**	**5.7**	**–1**	**0**	**0.0**	**208**	**103**	**19:18**	**6**	**0**	**0**	**0**	**6**	**0**	**0**	**0**
99-2000	**Carolina**	**NHL**	**53**	**0**	**2**	**2**	**14**	**0**	**0**	**0**	**31**	**0.0**	**–19**	**0**	**0.0**	**164**	**85**	**17:47**								
2000-01	**Minnesota**	**NHL**	**54**	**2**	**3**	**5**	**19**	**1**	**0**	**1**	**43**	**4.7**	**–2**	**0**	**0.0**	**160**	**93**	**19:31**								
	Ottawa	**NHL**	**11**	**0**	**4**	**4**	**0**	**0**	**0**	**0**	**8**	**0.0**	**7**	**0**	**0.0**	**32**	**14**	**19:04**	**4**	**0**	**0**	**0**	**0**	**0**	**0**	**0**
	NHL Totals		**844**	**44**	**146**	**190**	**591**	**17**	**2**	**10**	**779**	**5.6**		**0**	**0.0**	**564**	**295**	**18:55**	**36**	**2**	**4**	**6**	**24**	**1**	**0**	**0**

Transferred to **Colorado** after **Quebec** franchise relcoated, June 21, 1995. Traded to **Washington** by **Colorado** with Chris Simon for Keith Jones, Washington's 1st (Scott Parker) and 4th (later traded back to Washington - Washington selected Krys Barch) round choices in 1998 Entry Draft, November 2, 1996. Traded to **Hartford** by **Washington** for Andrei Nikolishin, November 9, 1996. Transferred to **Carolina** after **Hartford** franchise relocated, June 25, 1997. Selected by **Minnesota** from **Carolina** in Expansion Draft, June 23, 2000. Traded to **Ottawa** by **Minnesota** for Ottawa's 3rd round choice (Stephane Veilleux) in 2001 Entry Draft and future considerations, March 13, 2001.

LETANG, Alan

(leh-TANG, A-luhn)

Defense. Shoots left. 6', 205 lbs. Born, Renfrew, Ont., September 4, 1975. Montreal's 10th choice, 203rd overall, in 1993 Entry Draft.

Season	Club	League	GP	G	A	Pts	PIM	PP	SH	GW	S	%	+/-	TF	F%	H	SB	Min	Playoffs GP	G	A	Pts	PIM	PP	SH	GW
1990-91	Ottawa Valley	OMHA	32	3	26	29	16																			
1991-92	Cornwall Royals	OHL	47	1	4	5	16												6	0	0	0	2			
1992-93	Newmarket	OHL	66	1	25	26	14												6	0	3	3	2			
1993-94	Newmarket	OHL	58	3	21	24	30																			
1994-95	Sarnia Sting	OHL	62	5	36	41	35												4	2	2	4	6			
1995-96	Fredericton	AHL	71	0	26	26	40												10	0	3	3	4			
1996-97	Fredericton	AHL	60	2	9	11	8																			
1997-98	ESV Kaufbeuren	DEL	15	1	5	6	8																			
	SC Langnau	Switz-2	11	4	3	7	6																			
	Augsburger EV	DEL	17	0	1	1	4																			
1998-99	Canada	Nat-Team	41	3	9	12	20																			
	EV Zug	Switz.																	9	0	4	4	4			
	Michigan K-Wings	IHL	12	3	3	6	0												5	0	2	2	0			
99-2000	**Dallas**	**NHL**	**8**	**0**	**0**	**0**	**2**	**0**	**0**	**0**	**1**	**0.0**	**–5**	**0**	**0.0**	**2**	**4**	**9:57**								
	Michigan K-Wings	IHL	51	1	12	13	30																			
2000-01	Utah Grizzlies	IHL	79	6	24	30	26																			
	NHL Totals		**8**	**0**	**0**	**0**	**2**	**0**	**0**	**0**	**1**	**0.0**		**0**	**0.0**	**2**	**4**	**9:57**								

Signed as a free agent by **Dallas**, March 22, 1999.

LETOWSKI, Trevor

(leh-TOW-skee, TREH-vuhr) **PHX.**

Center. Shoots right. 5'10", 176 lbs. Born, Thunder Bay, Ont., April 5, 1977. Phoenix's 6th choice, 174th overall, in 1996 Entry Draft.

Season	Club	League	GP	G	A	Pts	PIM	PP	SH	GW	S	%	+/-	TF	F%	H	SB	Min	Playoffs GP	G	A	Pts	PIM	PP	SH	GW
1993-94	Thunder Bay	TBMHL	64	41	60	101	48																			
1994-95	Sarnia Sting	OHL	66	22	19	41	33												4	0	1	1	9			
1995-96	Sarnia Sting	OHL	66	36	63	99	66												10	9	5	14	10			
1996-97	Sarnia Sting	OHL	55	35	73	108	51												12	9	12	21	20			
1997-98	Springfield	AHL	75	11	20	31	26												4	1	0	1	2			
1998-99	**Phoenix**	**NHL**	**14**	**2**	**2**	**4**	**2**	**0**	**0**	**0**	**8**	**25.0**	**1**	**49**	**55.1**	**4**	**3**	**6:01**								
	Springfield	AHL	67	32	35	67	46												3	1	0	1	2			
99-2000	**Phoenix**	**NHL**	**82**	**19**	**20**	**39**	**20**	**3**	**4**	**3**	**125**	**15.2**	**2**	**692**	**47.7**	**24**	**33**	**16:03**	**5**	**1**	**1**	**2**	**4**	**0**	**0**	**0**
2000-01	**Phoenix**	**NHL**	**77**	**7**	**15**	**22**	**32**	**0**	**1**	**3**	**110**	**6.4**	**–2**	**726**	**46.1**	**24**	**35**	**16:20**								
	NHL Totals		**173**	**28**	**37**	**65**	**54**	**3**	**5**	**6**	**243**	**11.5**		**1467**	**47.2**	**52**	**71**	**15:22**	**5**	**1**	**1**	**2**	**4**	**0**	**0**	**0**

LIDSTROM, Nicklas

(LID-struhm, NIHK-las) **DET.**

Defense. Shoots left. 6'2", 185 lbs. Born, Vasteras, Sweden, April 28, 1970. Detroit's 3rd choice, 53rd overall, in 1989 Entry Draft.

Season	Club	League	GP	G	A	Pts	PIM	PP	SH	GW	S	%	+/-	TF	F%	H	SB	Min	Playoffs GP	G	A	Pts	PIM	PP	SH	GW
1987-88	Vasteras IK	Sweden-2	3	0	0	0	0												5	0	0	0	6			
1988-89	Vasteras IK	Sweden	34	1	6	7	4												5	0	2	2	0			
1989-90	Vasteras IK	Sweden	39	8	8	16	14												2	0	1	1	2			
1990-91	Vasteras IK	Sweden	38	4	19	23	2												4	0	0	0	4			
1991-92	**Detroit**	**NHL**	**80**	**11**	**49**	**60**	**22**	**5**	**0**	**1**	**168**	**6.5**	**36**						**11**	**1**	**2**	**3**	**0**	**1**	**0**	**0**
1992-93	**Detroit**	**NHL**	**84**	**7**	**34**	**41**	**28**	**3**	**0**	**2**	**156**	**4.5**	**7**						**7**	**1**	**0**	**1**	**0**	**1**	**0**	**0**
1993-94	**Detroit**	**NHL**	**84**	**10**	**46**	**56**	**26**	**4**	**0**	**3**	**200**	**5.0**	**43**						**7**	**3**	**2**	**5**	**0**	**1**	**1**	**0**
1994-95	Vasteras IK	Sweden	13	2	10	12	4																			
	Detroit	**NHL**	**43**	**10**	**16**	**26**	**6**	**7**	**0**	**0**	**90**	**11.1**	**15**						**18**	**4**	**12**	**16**	**8**	**3**	**0**	**2**
1995-96	**Detroit**	**NHL**	**81**	**17**	**50**	**67**	**20**	**8**	**1**	**1**	**211**	**8.1**	**29**						**19**	**5**	**9**	**14**	**10**	**1**	**0**	**0**
1996-97♦	**Detroit**	**NHL**	**79**	**15**	**42**	**57**	**30**	**8**	**0**	**1**	**214**	**7.0**	**11**						**20**	**2**	**6**	**8**	**2**	**0**	**0**	**0**
1997-98♦	**Detroit**	**NHL**	**80**	**17**	**42**	**59**	**18**	**7**	**1**	**1**	**205**	**8.3**	**22**						**22**	**6**	**13**	**19**	**8**	**2**	**0**	**2**
1998-99	**Detroit**	**NHL**	**81**	**14**	**43**	**57**	**14**	**6**	**2**	**3**	**205**	**6.8**	**14**	**0**	**0.0**	**53**	**88**	**26:31**	**10**	**2**	**9**	**11**	**4**	**2**	**0**	**0**
99-2000	**Detroit**	**NHL**	**81**	**20**	**53**	**73**	**18**	**9**	**4**	**3**	**218**	**9.2**	**19**	**0**	**0.0**	**59**	**95**	**28:45**	**9**	**2**	**4**	**6**	**4**	**1**	**0**	**0**
2000-01	**Detroit**	**NHL**	**82**	**15**	**56**	**71**	**18**	**8**	**0**	**0**	**272**	**5.5**	**9**	**0**	**0.0**	**65**	**94**	**28:27**	**6**	**1**	**7**	**8**	**0**	**0**	**0**	**0**
	NHL Totals		**775**	**136**	**431**	**567**	**200**	**65**	**8**	**15**	**1939**	**7.0**		**0**	**0.0**	**177**	**277**	**27:54**	**129**	**27**	**64**	**91**	**36**	**12**	**1**	**4**

NHL All-Rookie Team (1992) • NHL First All-Star Team (1998, 1999, 2000, 2001) • Won James Norris Memorial Trophy (2001) • Played in NHL All-Star Game (1996, 1998, 1999, 2000, 2001)

LILJA, Andreas

(LIHL-yuh, an-DRAY-uhs) **L.A.**

Defense. Shoots left. 6'3", 222 lbs. Born, Landskrona, Sweden, July 13, 1975. Los Angeles' 2nd choice, 54th overall, in 2000 Entry Draft.

Season	Club	League	GP	G	A	Pts	PIM	PP	SH	GW	S	%	+/-	TF	F%	H	SB	Min	Playoffs GP	G	A	Pts	PIM	PP	SH	GW
1993-94	Malmo IF	Swede-Jr.	14	3	7	10	38																			
1994-95	Malmo IF	Swede-Jr.	30	7	13	20	82																			
	Malmo IF	Sweden	3	0	0	0	2																			
1995-96	Malmo IF	Swede-Jr.	3	0	1	1	6																			
	Malmo IF	Sweden	40	1	5	6	63												5	0	1	1	2			
1996-97	Malmo IF	Sweden	47	1	0	1	22												4	0	0	0	10			
1997-98	Malmo IF	Sweden-2	11	6	5	11	24																			
	Malmo IF	Sweden	10	0	0	0	0																			
	Mora IK	Sweden	13	1	4	5	30												4	1	0	1	14			
1998-99	Malmo IF	Sweden	41	0	3	3	44												1	0	0	0	4			

Season	Club	League	GP	G	A	Pts	PIM	PP	SH	GW	S	%	+/-	TF	F%	H	SB	Min	GP	G	A	Pts	PIM	PP	SH	GW
			Regular Season																Playoffs							
99-2000	Malmo IF	Sweden	49	8	11	19	88	....	....	....	....	....	....	....	....	....	....	....	6	0	0	0	8	....	....	....
2000-01	**Los Angeles**	**NHL**	**2**	**0**	**0**	**0**	**4**	**0**	**0**	**0**	**1**	**0.0**	**–2**	**0**	**0.0**	**6**	**0**	**12:22**	**1**	**0**	**0**	**0**	**0**	**0**	**0**	**0**
	Lowell	AHL	61	7	29	36	149	....	....	....	....	....	....	....	....	....	....	....	4	0	6	6	6	....	....	....
	NHL Totals		**2**	**0**	**0**	**0**	**4**	**0**	**0**	**0**	**1**	**0.0**		**0**	**0.0**	**6**	**0**	**12:22**	**1**	**0**	**0**	**0**	**0**	**0**	**0**	**0**

LIND, Juha

(LIHND, YOO-huh)

Center. Shoots left. 5'11", 185 lbs. Born, Helsinki, Finland, January 2, 1974. Minnesota's 6th choice, 178th overall, in 1992 Entry Draft.

Season	Club	League	GP	G	A	Pts	PIM	PP	SH	GW	S	%	+/-	TF	F%	H	SB	Min	GP	G	A	Pts	PIM	PP	SH	GW
1990-91	Jokerit Helsinki	Finn-Jr.	8	1	1	2	0	....	....	....	....	....	....	....	....	....	....	....	....	....	....	....	....	....	....	....
1991-92	Jokerit Helsinki-B	Finn-Jr.	14	9	16	25	2	....	....	....	....	....	....	....	....	....	....	....	14	7	8	15	8	....	....	....
1992-93	Vantaa HT	Finland-2	25	8	12	20	8	....	....	....	....	....	....	....	....	....	....	....	....	....	....	....	....	....	....	....
	Jokerit Helsinki	Finland-2	3	2	4	6	2	....	....	....	....	....	....	....	....	....	....	....	....	....	....	....	....	....	....	....
	Jokerit Helsinki	Finland	6	0	0	0	2	....	....	....	....	....	....	....	....	....	....	....	1	0	0	0	0	....	....	....
1993-94	Jokerit Helsinki	Finland-2	11	6	7	13	4	....	....	....	....	....	....	....	....	....	....	....	....	....	....	....	....	....	....	....
	Jokerit Helsinki	Finland	47	17	11	28	37	....	....	....	....	....	....	....	....	....	....	....	11	2	5	7	4	....	....	....
1994-95	Jokerit Helsinki	Finn-Jr.	3	2	1	3	2	....	....	....	....	....	....	....	....	....	....	....	....	....	....	....	....	....	....	....
	Jokerit Helsinki	Finland	50	10	8	18	12	....	....	....	....	....	....	....	....	....	....	....	11	1	2	3	6	....	....	....
1995-96	Jokerit Helsinki	Finland	50	15	22	37	32	....	....	....	....	....	....	....	....	....	....	....	11	4	5	9	4	....	....	....
1996-97	Jokerit Helsinki	Finland	50	16	22	38	28	....	....	....	....	....	....	....	....	....	....	....	9	5	3	8	0	....	....	....
	Jokerit Helsinki	EuroHL	6	4	1	5	6	....	....	....	....	....	....	....	....	....	....	....	2	1	0	1	0	....	....	....
1997-98	**Dallas**	**NHL**	**39**	**2**	**3**	**5**	**6**	**0**	**0**	**0**	**27**	**7.4**	**4**	....	....	....	....	....	**15**	**2**	**2**	**4**	**8**	**0**	**0**	**1**
	Michigan K-Wings	IHL	8	2	2	4	2	....	....	....	....	....	....	....	....	....	....	....	....	....	....	....	....	....	....	....
	Finland	Olympics	6	0	1	1	6	....	....	....	....	....	....	....	....	....	....	....	....	....	....	....	....	....	....	....
1998-99	Jokerit Helsinki	Finland	50	20	19	39	22	....	....	....	....	....	....	....	....	....	....	....	3	3	1	4	2	....	....	....
	Jokerit Helsinki	EuroHL	6	6	2	8	14	....	....	....	....	....	....	....	....	....	....	....	2	0	2	2	0	....	....	....
99-2000	**Dallas**	**NHL**	**34**	**3**	**4**	**7**	**6**	**0**	**0**	**0**	**36**	**8.3**	**–1**	**8**	**50.0**	**52**	**4**	**10:49**	....	....	....	....	....	....	....	....
	Montreal	**NHL**	**13**	**1**	**2**	**3**	**4**	**0**	**0**	**0**	**6**	**16.7**	**–2**	**0**	**0.0**	**18**	**3**	**9:37**	....	....	....	....	....	....	....	....
2000-01	**Montreal**	**NHL**	**47**	**3**	**4**	**7**	**4**	**0**	**0**	**2**	**36**	**8.3**	**–4**	**13**	**46.2**	**37**	**19**	**7:49**	....	....	....	....	....	....	....	....
	Quebec Citadelles	AHL	3	1	1	2	0	....	....	....	....	....	....	....	....	....	....	....	....	....	....	....	....	....	....	....
	NHL Totals		**133**	**9**	**13**	**22**	**20**	**0**	**0**	**2**	**105**	**8.6**		**21**	**47.6**	**107**	**26**	**9:09**	**15**	**2**	**2**	**4**	**8**	**0**	**0**	**1**

Rights transferred to **Dallas** after **Minnesota** franchise relocated, June 9, 1993. Traded to **Montreal** by **Dallas** for Scott Thornton, January 22, 2000.

LINDEN, Trevor

(LIHND-dehn, TREH-vohr) **WSH.**

Center/Right wing. Shoots right. 6'4", 215 lbs. Born, Medicine Hat, Alta., April 11, 1970. Vancouver's 1st choice, 2nd overall, in 1988 Entry Draft.

Season	Club	League	GP	G	A	Pts	PIM	PP	SH	GW	S	%	+/-	TF	F%	H	SB	Min	GP	G	A	Pts	PIM	PP	SH	GW
1985-86	Medicine Hat	AMHL	40	14	22	36	14	....	....	....	....	....	....	....	....	....	....	....	....	....	....	....	....	....	....	....
	Medicine Hat	WHL	5	2	0	2	0	....	....	....	....	....	....	....	....	....	....	....	....	....	....	....	....	....	....	....
1986-87	Medicine Hat	WHL	72	14	22	36	59	....	....	....	....	....	....	....	....	....	....	....	20	5	4	9	17	....	....	....
1987-88	Medicine Hat	WHL	67	46	64	110	76	....	....	....	....	....	....	....	....	....	....	....	16	*13	12	25	19	....	....	....
1988-89	**Vancouver**	**NHL**	**80**	**30**	**29**	**59**	**41**	**10**	**1**	**2**	**186**	**16.1**	**–10**	....	....	....	....	....	**7**	**3**	**4**	**7**	**8**	**2**	**1**	**0**
1989-90	**Vancouver**	**NHL**	**73**	**21**	**30**	**51**	**43**	**6**	**2**	**3**	**171**	**12.3**	**–17**	....	....	....	....	....	....	....	....	....	....	....	....	....
1990-91	**Vancouver**	**NHL**	**80**	**33**	**37**	**70**	**65**	**16**	**2**	**4**	**229**	**14.4**	**–25**	....	....	....	....	....	**6**	**0**	**7**	**7**	**2**	**0**	**0**	**0**
1991-92	**Vancouver**	**NHL**	**80**	**31**	**44**	**75**	**101**	**6**	**1**	**6**	**201**	**15.4**	**3**	....	....	....	....	....	**13**	**4**	**8**	**12**	**6**	**2**	**0**	**1**
1992-93	**Vancouver**	**NHL**	**84**	**33**	**39**	**72**	**64**	**8**	**0**	**3**	**209**	**15.8**	**19**	....	....	....	....	....	**12**	**5**	**8**	**13**	**16**	**2**	**0**	**1**
1993-94	**Vancouver**	**NHL**	**84**	**32**	**29**	**61**	**73**	**10**	**2**	**3**	**234**	**13.7**	**6**	....	....	....	....	....	**24**	**12**	**13**	**25**	**18**	**5**	**1**	**1**
1994-95	**Vancouver**	**NHL**	**48**	**18**	**22**	**40**	**40**	**9**	**0**	**1**	**129**	**14.0**	**–5**	....	....	....	....	....	**11**	**2**	**6**	**8**	**12**	**1**	**0**	**0**
1995-96	**Vancouver**	**NHL**	**82**	**33**	**47**	**80**	**42**	**12**	**1**	**2**	**202**	**16.3**	**6**	....	....	....	....	....	**6**	**4**	**4**	**8**	**6**	**2**	**0**	**0**
1996-97	**Vancouver**	**NHL**	**49**	**9**	**31**	**40**	**27**	**2**	**2**	**2**	**84**	**10.7**	**5**	....	....	....	....	....	....	....	....	....	....	....	....	....
1997-98	**Vancouver**	**NHL**	**42**	**7**	**14**	**21**	**49**	**2**	**0**	**1**	**74**	**9.5**	**–13**	....	....	....	....	....	....	....	....	....	....	....	....	....
	NY Islanders	**NHL**	**25**	**10**	**7**	**17**	**33**	**3**	**2**	**1**	**59**	**16.9**	**–1**	....	....	....	....	....	....	....	....	....	....	....	....	....
	Canada	Olympics	6	1	0	1	10	....	....	....	....	....	....	....	....	....	....	....	....	....	....	....	....	....	....	....
1998-99	**NY Islanders**	**NHL**	**82**	**18**	**29**	**47**	**32**	**8**	**1**	**1**	**167**	**10.8**	**–14**	**261**	**50.2**	**144**	**47**	**21:29**	....	....	....	....	....	....	....	....
99-2000	**Montreal**	**NHL**	**50**	**13**	**17**	**30**	**34**	**4**	**0**	**3**	**87**	**14.9**	**–3**	**860**	**56.3**	**88**	**29**	**17:51**	....	....	....	....	....	....	....	....
2000-01	**Montreal**	**NHL**	**57**	**12**	**21**	**33**	**52**	**6**	**0**	**3**	**96**	**12.5**	**–2**	**1142**	**52.7**	**93**	**37**	**20:47**	....	....	....	....	....	....	....	....
	Washington	**NHL**	**12**	**3**	**1**	**4**	**8**	**0**	**0**	**0**	**30**	**10.0**	**2**	**75**	**60.0**	**14**	**7**	**18:03**	**6**	**0**	**4**	**4**	**14**	**0**	**0**	**0**
	NHL Totals		**928**	**303**	**397**	**700**	**704**	**102**	**14**	**35**	**2158**	**14.0**		**2338**	**54.0**	**339**	**120**	**20:11**	**85**	**30**	**54**	**84**	**82**	**14**	**2**	**3**

WHL East Second All-Star Team (1988) • NHL All-Rookie Team (1989) • Won King Clancy Memorial Trophy (1997) • Played in NHL All-Star Game (1991, 1992)

Traded to **NY Islanders** by **Vancouver** for Todd Bertuzzi, Bryan McCabe and NY Islanders' 3rd round choice (Jarkko Ruutu) in 1998 Entry Draft, February 6, 1998. Traded to **Montreal** by **NY Islanders** for Montreal's 1st round choice (Branislav Mezei) in 1999 Entry Draft, May 29, 1999. Traded to **Washington** by **Montreal** with Dainius Zubrus and New Jersey's 2nd round choice (previously acquired, later traded to Tampa Bay - Tampa Bay selected Andreas Holmqvist) in 2001 Entry Draft for Richard Zednik, Jan Bulis and Washington's 1st round choice (Alexander Perezhogin) in 2001 Entry Draft, March 13, 2001.

LINDGREN, Mats

(LIHND-gruhn, MAHTS) **NYI**

Center/Left Wing. Shoots left. 6'2", 202 lbs. Born, Skelleftea, Sweden, October 1, 1974. Winnipeg's 1st choice, 15th overall, in 1993 Entry Draft.

Season	Club	League	GP	G	A	Pts	PIM	PP	SH	GW	S	%	+/-	TF	F%	H	SB	Min	GP	G	A	Pts	PIM	PP	SH	GW
1990-91	Skelleftea AIK	Sweden-2	10	0	1	1	0	....	....	....	....	....	....	....	....	....	....	....	....	....	....	....	....	....	....	....
1991-92	Skelleftea AIK	Sweden-2	29	14	18	32	12	....	....	....	....	....	....	....	....	....	....	....	3	3	2	5	2	....	....	....
1992-93	Skelleftea AIK	Sweden-2	32	20	18	38	18	....	....	....	....	....	....	....	....	....	....	....	3	0	0	0	2	....	....	....
1993-94	Farjestads BK	Sweden	22	11	6	17	26	....	....	....	....	....	....	....	....	....	....	....	....	....	....	....	....	....	....	....
1994-95	Farjestads BK	Sweden	37	17	15	32	20	....	....	....	....	....	....	....	....	....	....	....	3	0	0	0	4	....	....	....
1995-96	Cape Breton	AHL	13	7	5	12	6	....	....	....	....	....	....	....	....	....	....	....	....	....	....	....	....	....	....	....
1996-97	**Edmonton**	**NHL**	**69**	**11**	**14**	**25**	**12**	**2**	**3**	**1**	**71**	**15.5**	**–7**	....	....	....	....	....	**12**	**0**	**4**	**4**	**0**	**0**	**0**	**0**
	Hamilton Bulldogs	AHL	9	6	7	13	6	....	....	....	....	....	....	....	....	....	....	....	....	....	....	....	....	....	....	....
1997-98	**Edmonton**	**NHL**	**82**	**13**	**13**	**26**	**42**	**1**	**3**	**3**	**131**	**9.9**	**0**	....	....	....	....	....	**12**	**1**	**1**	**2**	**10**	**0**	**0**	**0**
	Sweden	Olympics	4	0	0	0	2	....	....	....	....	....	....	....	....	....	....	....	....	....	....	....	....	....	....	....
1998-99	**Edmonton**	**NHL**	**48**	**5**	**12**	**17**	**22**	**0**	**1**	**0**	**53**	**9.4**	**4**	**363**	**47.9**	**44**	**16**	**11:31**	....	....	....	....	....	....	....	....
	NY Islanders	**NHL**	**12**	**5**	**3**	**8**	**2**	**3**	**0**	**1**	**30**	**16.7**	**2**	**180**	**48.9**	**18**	**4**	**20:08**	....	....	....	....	....	....	....	....
99-2000	**NY Islanders**	**NHL**	**43**	**9**	**7**	**16**	**24**	**1**	**0**	**1**	**68**	**13.2**	**0**	**551**	**49.2**	**54**	**25**	**19:17**	....	....	....	....	....	....	....	....
2000-01	**NY Islanders**	**NHL**	**20**	**3**	**4**	**7**	**10**	**0**	**2**	**0**	**34**	**8.8**	**4**	**176**	**48.3**	**35**	**3**	**15:14**	....	....	....	....	....	....	....	....
	NHL Totals		**274**	**46**	**53**	**99**	**112**	**7**	**9**	**6**	**387**	**11.9**		**1270**	**48.7**	**151**	**48**	**15:41**	**24**	**1**	**5**	**6**	**10**	**0**	**0**	**0**

Traded to **Edmonton** by **Winnipeg** with Boris Mironov, Winnipeg's 1st round choice (Jason Bonsignore) in 1994 Entry Draft and Florida's 4th round choice (previously acquired, Edmonton selected Adam Copeland) in 1994 Entry Draft for Dave Manson and St. Louis' 6th round choice (previously acquired, Winnipeg selected Chris Kibermanis) in 1994 Entry Draft, March 15, 1994. Traded to **NY Islanders** by **Edmonton** with Edmonton's 8th round choice (Radek Martinek) in 1999 Entry Draft for Tommy Salo, March 20, 1999. • Missed majority of 2000-01 season recovering from shoulder injury suffered in game vs. Anaheim, November 25, 2000.

LINDQUIST, Fredrik

(LIHND-kvihst, FREHD-rihk)

Center. Shoots left. 6', 190 lbs. Born, Stockholm, Sweden, June 21, 1973. New Jersey's 4th choice, 55th overall, in 1991 Entry Draft.

Season	Club	League	GP	G	A	Pts	PIM	PP	SH	GW	S	%	+/-	TF	F%	H	SB	Min	GP	G	A	Pts	PIM	PP	SH	GW
1989-90	Huddinge IF	Sweden-2	2	0	0	0	0	....	....	....	....	....	....	....	....	....	....	....	....	....	....	....	....	....	....	....
1990-91	Djurgardens IF	Sweden	28	6	4	10	0	....	....	....	....	....	....	....	....	....	....	....	7	1	0	1	2	....	....	....
	Nacka IK	Sweden-2	7	1	4	5	8	....	....	....	....	....	....	....	....	....	....	....	....	....	....	....	....	....	....	....
1991-92	Djurgardens IF	Sweden	39	9	6	15	14	....	....	....	....	....	....	....	....	....	....	....	10	1	1	2	2	....	....	....
1992-93	Djurgardens IF	Sweden	39	9	11	20	8	....	....	....	....	....	....	....	....	....	....	....	4	1	2	3	2	....	....	....
1993-94	Djurgardens IF	Swede-Jr.	1	0	1	1	0	....	....	....	....	....	....	....	....	....	....	....	....	....	....	....	....	....	....	....
	Djurgardens IF	Sweden	25	5	8	13	8	....	....	....	....	....	....	....	....	....	....	....	6	2	1	3	2	....	....	....
1994-95	Djurgardens IF	Sweden	40	11	16	27	14	....	....	....	....	....	....	....	....	....	....	....	3	0	0	0	2	....	....	....
1995-96	Djurgardens IF	Sweden	33	12	19	31	16	....	....	....	....	....	....	....	....	....	....	....	1	0	0	0	0	....	....	....
1996-97	Djurgardens IF	Sweden	44	19	28	47	20	....	....	....	....	....	....	....	....	....	....	....	4	0	3	3	2	....	....	....
1997-98	Djurgardens IF	Sweden	42	10	*32	42	30	....	....	....	....	....	....	....	....	....	....	....	13	3	6	9	4	....	....	....
1998-99	**Edmonton**	**NHL**	**8**	**0**	**0**	**0**	**2**	**0**	**0**	**0**	**6**	**0.0**	**–2**	**0**	**0.0**	**1**	**1**	**12:18**	....	....	....	....	....	....	....	....
	Hamilton Bulldogs	AHL	57	18	36	54	20	....	....	....	....	....	....	....	....	....	....	....	11	2	2	4	2	....	....	....
99-2000	HC Davos	Switz.	44	14	27	41	20	....	....	....	....	....	....	....	....	....	....	....	5	2	3	5	4	....	....	....
2000-01	Malmo IF	Sweden	42	10	12	22	10	....	....	....	....	....	....	....	....	....	....	....	9	4	3	7	2	....	....	....
	NHL Totals		**8**	**0**	**0**	**0**	**2**	**0**	**0**	**0**	**6**	**0.0**		**0**	**0.0**	**1**	**1**	**12:18**	....	....	....	....	....	....	....	....

Traded to **Edmonton** by **New Jersey** with New Jersey's 4th (Kristian Antila) and 5th (Oleg Smirnov) round choices in 1998 Entry Draft for Pittsburgh's 3rd round choice (previously acquired, New Jersey selected Brian Gionta) in 1998 Entry Draft, June 27, 1998.

LINDROS, Eric

(LIHND-rahz, AIR-ihk) **NYR**

Center. Shoots right. 6'4", 236 lbs. Born, London, Ont., February 28, 1973. Quebec's 1st choice, 1st overall, in 1991 Entry Draft.

			Regular Season																Playoffs							
Season	Club	League	GP	G	A	Pts	PIM	PP	SH	GW	S	%	+/-	TF	F%	H	SB	Min	GP	G	A	Pts	PIM	PP	SH	GW
1988-89	St. Michael's	MTJHL	37	24	43	67	193	....	....	....	....	....	....	....	....	....	....	....	27	23	25	48	155	....	....	....
1989-90	Det-Compuware	NAJHL	14	23	29	52	123	....	....	....	....	....	....	....	....	....	....	....	....	....	....	....	....	....	....	....
	Oshawa Generals	OHL	25	17	19	36	61	....	....	....	....	....	....	....	....	....	....	....	17	18	18	36	76	....	....	....
1990-91	Oshawa Generals	OHL	57	*71	78	*149	189	....	....	....	....	....	....	....	....	....	....	....	16	*18	20	*38	*93	....	....	....
1991-92	Oshawa Generals	OHL	13	9	22	31	54	....	....	....	....	....	....	....	....	....	....	....	....	....	....	....	....	....	....	....
	Canada	Nat-Team	24	19	16	35	34	....	....	....	....	....	....	....	....	....	....	....	....	....	....	....	....	....	....	....
	Canada	Olympics	8	5	6	11	5	....	....	....	....	....	....	....	....	....	....	....	....	....	....	....	....	....	....	....
1992-93	**Philadelphia**	**NHL**	61	41	34	75	147	8	1	5	180	22.8	28	....	....	....	....	....	....	....	....	....	....	....	....	....
1993-94	**Philadelphia**	**NHL**	65	44	53	97	103	13	2	9	197	22.3	16	....	....	....	....	....	....	....	....	....	....	....	....	....
1994-95	**Philadelphia**	**NHL**	46	29	41	*70	60	7	0	4	144	20.1	27	....	....	....	....	....	12	4	11	15	18	0	0	1
1995-96	**Philadelphia**	**NHL**	73	47	68	115	163	15	0	4	294	16.0	26	....	....	....	....	....	12	6	6	12	43	3	0	2
1996-97	**Philadelphia**	**NHL**	52	32	47	79	136	9	0	7	198	16.2	31	....	....	....	....	....	19	12	14	*26	40	4	0	1
1997-98	**Philadelphia**	**NHL**	63	30	41	71	134	10	1	4	202	14.9	14	....	....	....	....	....	5	1	2	3	17	0	0	0
	Canada	Olympics	6	2	3	5	2	....	....	....	....	....	....	....	....	....	....	....	....	....	....	....	....	....	....	....
1998-99	**Philadelphia**	**NHL**	71	40	53	93	120	10	1	2	242	16.5	35	1529	60.0	117	17	22:56	....	....	....	....	....	....	....	....
99-2000	**Philadelphia**	**NHL**	55	27	32	59	83	10	1	2	187	14.4	11	1318	57.8	130	29	22:02	2	1	0	1	0	0	0	0
2000-01	**Philadelphia**	**NHL**	DID NOT PLAY																							
	NHL Totals		**486**	**290**	**369**	**659**	**946**	**82**	**6**	**37**	**1644**	**17.6**		**2847**	**59.0**	**247**	**46**	**22:32**	**50**	**24**	**33**	**57**	**118**	**7**	**0**	**4**

Memorial Cup All-Star Team (1990) • OHL First All-Star Team (1991) • Canadian Major Junior Player of the Year (1991) • NHL All-Rookie Team (1993) • NHL First All-Star Team (1995) • Won Lester B. Pearson Award (1995) • Won Hart Trophy (1995) • NHL Second All-Star Team (1996) • Played in NHL All-Star Game (1994, 1996, 1997, 1998, 1999, 2000)

Rights traded to **Oshawa** by **Sault Ste. Marie** for Mike DeCoff, Jason Denomme, Mike Lenarduzzi and Oshawa's 2nd round choice in 1991 and 4th round choice (Joe Vanvolsen) in 1992 OHL Priority Draft, December 17, 1989. Traded to **Philadelphia** by **Quebec** for Peter Forsberg, Steve Duchesne, Kerry Huffman, Mike Ricci, Ron Hextall, Philadelphia's 1st round choice (Jocelyn Thibault) in 1993 Entry Draft, $15,000,000 and future considerations (Chris Simon and Philadelphia's 1st round choice (later traded to Toronto - later traded to Washington - Washington selected Nolan Baumgartner) in 1994 Entry Draft, July 21, 1992), June 30, 1992. • Missed entire 2000-01 season recovering from head injury suffered in game vs. New Jersey, May 26, 2000 and contract dispute with Philadelphia Flyers management. Rights traded to **NY Rangers** by **Philadelphia** with a conditional 1st round choice in 2003 Entry Draft for Pavel Brendl, Jan Hlavac, Kim Johnsson and NY Rangers' 3rd round choice in 2003 Entry Draft, August 20, 2001.

LINDSAY, Bill

(LIHND-see, BIHL)

Left wing. Shoots left. 6', 195 lbs. Born, Big Fork, MT, May 17, 1971. Quebec's 6th choice, 103rd overall, in 1991 Entry Draft.

1988-89	Vernon Lakers	BCJHL	56	24	29	53	166	....	....	....	....	....	....	....	....	....	....	....	....	....	....	....	....	....	....	....
1989-90	Tri-City Americans	WHL	72	40	45	85	84	....	....	....	....	....	....	....	....	....	....	....	7	3	0	3	17	....	....	....
1990-91	Tri-City Americans	WHL	63	46	47	93	151	....	....	....	....	....	....	....	....	....	....	....	5	3	6	9	10	....	....	....
1991-92	Tri-City Americans	WHL	42	34	59	93	81	....	....	....	....	....	....	....	....	....	....	....	3	2	3	5	16	....	....	....
	Quebec	**NHL**	23	2	4	6	14	0	0	1	35	5.7	–6	....	....	....	....	....	....	....	....	....	....	....	....	....
1992-93	**Quebec**	**NHL**	44	4	9	13	16	0	0	0	58	6.9	0	....	....	....	....	....	....	....	....	....	....	....	....	....
	Halifax Citadels	AHL	20	11	13	24	18	....	....	....	....	....	....	....	....	....	....	....	....	....	....	....	....	....	....	....
1993-94	**Florida**	**NHL**	84	6	6	12	97	0	0	0	90	6.7	–2	....	....	....	....	....	....	....	....	....	....	....	....	....
1994-95	**Florida**	**NHL**	48	10	9	19	46	0	1	0	63	15.9	1	....	....	....	....	....	....	....	....	....	....	....	....	....
1995-96	**Florida**	**NHL**	73	12	22	34	57	0	3	2	118	10.2	13	....	....	....	....	....	22	5	5	10	18	0	1	1
1996-97	**Florida**	**NHL**	81	11	23	34	120	0	1	3	168	6.5	1	....	....	....	....	....	3	0	1	1	8	0	0	0
1997-98	**Florida**	**NHL**	82	12	16	28	80	0	2	5	150	8.0	–2	....	....	....	....	....	....	....	....	....	....	....	....	....
1998-99	**Florida**	**NHL**	75	12	15	27	92	0	1	2	135	8.9	–1	57	40.4	149	20	13:37	....	....	....	....	....	....	....	....
99-2000	**Calgary**	**NHL**	80	8	12	20	86	0	0	2	147	5.4	–7	28	39.3	122	50	12:55	....	....	....	....	....	....	....	....
2000-01	**Calgary**	**NHL**	52	1	9	10	97	0	0	0	57	1.8	–8	9	55.6	105	6	10:32	....	....	....	....	....	....	....	....
	San Jose	**NHL**	16	0	4	4	29	0	0	0	14	0.0	2	2	0.0	49	5	9:16	6	0	0	0	16	0	0	0
	NHL Totals		**658**	**78**	**129**	**207**	**734**	**0**	**8**	**15**	**1035**	**7.5**		**96**	**40.6**	**425**	**81**	**12:20**	**31**	**5**	**6**	**11**	**42**	**0**	**1**	**1**

WHL West Second All-Star Team (1992)

Claimed by **Florida** from **Quebec** in Expansion Draft, June 24, 1993. Traded to **Calgary** by **Florida** for Todd Simpson, September 30, 1999. Traded to **San Jose** by **Calgary** for Minnesota's 8th round choice (previously acquired, Calgary selected Joe Campbell) in 2001 Entry Draft, March 6, 2001.

LING, David

(LIHNG, DAY-vihd) **CBJ**

Right wing. Shoots right. 5'9", 185 lbs. Born, Halifax, N.S., January 9, 1975. Quebec's 9th choice, 179th overall, in 1993 Entry Draft.

1991-92	Charlottetown	MJrHL	30	33	42	75	270	....	....	....	....	....	....	....	....	....	....	....	....	....	....	....	....	....	....	....
	St. Michael's	MTJHL	8	5	14	19	25	....	....	....	....	....	....	....	....	....	....	....	....	....	....	....	....	....	....	....
1992-93	Kingston	OHL	64	17	46	63	275	....	....	....	....	....	....	....	....	....	....	....	16	3	12	15	*72	....	....	....
1993-94	Kingston	OHL	61	37	40	77	*254	....	....	....	....	....	....	....	....	....	....	....	6	4	2	6	16	....	....	....
1994-95	Kingston	OHL	62	*61	74	135	136	....	....	....	....	....	....	....	....	....	....	....	6	7	8	15	12	....	....	....
1995-96	Saint John Flames	AHL	75	24	32	56	179	....	....	....	....	....	....	....	....	....	....	....	9	0	5	5	12	....	....	....
1996-97	Saint John Flames	AHL	5	0	2	2	19	....	....	....	....	....	....	....	....	....	....	....	....	....	....	....	....	....	....	....
	Montreal	**NHL**	2	0	0	0	0	0	0	0	0	0.0	0	....	....	....	....	....	....	....	....	....	....	....	....	....
	Fredericton	AHL	48	22	36	58	229	....	....	....	....	....	....	....	....	....	....	....	....	....	....	....	....	....	....	....
1997-98	**Montreal**	**NHL**	1	0	0	0	0	0	0	0	1	0.0	–1	....	....	....	....	....	....	....	....	....	....	....	....	....
	Fredericton	AHL	67	25	41	66	148	....	....	....	....	....	....	....	....	....	....	....	....	....	....	....	....	....	....	....
	Indianapolis Ice	IHL	12	8	6	14	30	....	....	....	....	....	....	....	....	....	....	....	5	4	1	5	31	....	....	....
1998-99	Kansas City	IHL	82	30	42	72	112	....	....	....	....	....	....	....	....	....	....	....	3	1	0	1	20	....	....	....
99-2000	Kansas City	IHL	82	35	48	83	210	....	....	....	....	....	....	....	....	....	....	....	....	....	....	....	....	....	....	....
2000-01	Utah Grizzlies	IHL	79	15	28	43	202	....	....	....	....	....	....	....	....	....	....	....	....	....	....	....	....	....	....	....
	NHL Totals		**3**	**0**	**0**	**0**	**0**	**0**	**0**	**0**	**1**	**0.0**		....	....	....	....	....	....	....	....	....	....	....	....	....

OHL First All-Star Team (1995) • Canadian Major Junior First All-Star Team (1995) • Canadian Junior Player of the Year (1995) • IHL First All-Star Team (2000)

Rights transferred to **Colorado** after **Quebec** franchise relocated, June 21, 1995. Traded to **Calgary** by **Colorado** with Colorado's 9th round choice (Steve Shirreffs) in 1995 Entry Draft for Calgary's 9th round choice (Chris George) in 1995 Entry Draft, July 7, 1995. Traded to **Montreal** by **Calgary** with Calgary's 6th round choice (Gordie Dwyer) in 1998 Entry Draft for Scott Fraser, October 24, 1996. Traded to **Chicago** by **Montreal** for Martin Gendron, March 14, 1998. Signed as a free agent by **Kansas City** (IHL) with Chicago retaining NHL rights, September 3, 1998. Traded to **Dallas** by **Chicago** for future considerations, August 11, 2000. Signed as a free agent by **Columbus**, July 7, 2001.

LINTNER, Richard

(LIHNT-nuhr, RIH-chahrd) **NSH.**

Defense. Shoots right. 6'3", 212 lbs. Born, Trencin, Czech., November 15, 1977. Phoenix's 4th choice, 119th overall, in 1996 Entry Draft.

1994-95	Dukla Trencin	Slovak-Jr.	42	12	13	25	20	....	....	....	....	....	....	....	....	....	....	....	....	....	....	....	....	....	....	....
1995-96	Dukla Trencin	Slovak-Jr.	30	15	17	32	210	....	....	....	....	....	....	....	....	....	....	....	....	....	....	....	....	....	....	....
	Dukla Trencin	Slovakia	2	0	0	0	0	....	....	....	....	....	....	....	....	....	....	....	....	....	....	....	....	....	....	....
1996-97	Spisska Nova	Slovakia	35	2	1	3	....	....	....	....	....	....	....	....	....	....	....	....	....	....	....	....	....	....	....	....
1997-98	Springfield	AHL	71	6	9	15	61	....	....	....	....	....	....	....	....	....	....	....	3	1	1	2	4	....	....	....
1998-99	Springfield	AHL	8	0	1	1	16	....	....	....	....	....	....	....	....	....	....	....	....	....	....	....	....	....	....	....
	Milwaukee	IHL	66	9	16	25	75	....	....	....	....	....	....	....	....	....	....	....	....	....	....	....	....	....	....	....
99-2000	**Nashville**	**NHL**	33	1	5	6	22	0	0	0	58	1.7	–6	0	0.0	44	15	14:51	....	....	....	....	....	....	....	....
	Milwaukee	IHL	31	13	8	21	37	....	....	....	....	....	....	....	....	....	....	....	....	....	....	....	....	....	....	....
2000-01	**Nashville**	**NHL**	50	3	5	8	22	1	0	0	81	3.7	2	0	0.0	48	26	13:05	....	....	....	....	....	....	....	....
	NHL Totals		**83**	**4**	**10**	**14**	**44**	**1**	**0**	**0**	**139**	**2.9**		**0**	**0.0**	**92**	**41**	**13:47**	....	....	....	....	....	....	....	....

Traded to **Nashville** by **Phoenix** with Cliff Ronning for future considerations, October 31, 1998.

LOW, Reed

(LOH, REED) **ST.L.**

Right wing. Shoots right. 6'3", 222 lbs. Born, Moose Jaw, Sask., June 21, 1976. St. Louis' 7th choice, 177th overall, in 1996 Entry Draft.

1994-95	Minot Top Guns	SJHL	STATISTICS NOT AVAILABLE																							
	Regina Pats	WHL	2	0	0	0	5	....	....	....	....	....	....	....	....	....	....	....	....	....	....	....	....	....	....	....
1995-96	Moose Jaw	WHL	61	12	7	19	221	....	....	....	....	....	....	....	....	....	....	....	....	....	....	....	....	....	....	....
1996-97	Moose Jaw	WHL	62	16	11	27	228	....	....	....	....	....	....	....	....	....	....	....	12	2	1	3	50	....	....	....
1997-98	Worcester	AHL	17	1	1	2	75	....	....	....	....	....	....	....	....	....	....	....	3	0	0	0	0	....	....	....
	Baton Rouge	ECHL	39	4	2	6	145	....	....	....	....	....	....	....	....	....	....	....	....	....	....	....	....	....	....	....
1998-99	Worcester	AHL	77	5	6	11	239	....	....	....	....	....	....	....	....	....	....	....	4	0	0	0	2	....	....	....
99-2000	Worcester	AHL	80	12	16	28	203	....	....	....	....	....	....	....	....	....	....	....	9	1	3	4	16	....	....	....
2000-01	**St. Louis**	**NHL**	56	1	5	6	159	0	0	0	31	3.2	4	2	50.0	71	4	6:17	....	....	....	....	....	....	....	....
	NHL Totals		**56**	**1**	**5**	**6**	**159**	**0**	**0**	**0**	**31**	**3.2**		**2**	**50.0**	**71**	**4**	**6:17**	....	....	....	....	....	....	....	....

LOWRY, Dave (LOW-ree, DAYV) CGY.

Left wing. Shoots left. 6'1", 200 lbs. Born, Sudbury, Ont., February 14, 1965. Vancouver's 6th choice, 114th overall, in 1983 Entry Draft.

			Regular Season																Playoffs							
Season	Club	League	GP	G	A	Pts	PIM	PP	SH	GW	S	%	+/-	TF	F%	H	SB	Min	GP	G	A	Pts	PIM	PP	SH	GW
1981-82	Nepean Raiders	OMHA	60	50	64	114	46																			
1982-83	London Knights	OHL	42	11	16	27	48												3	0	0	0	14			
1983-84	London Knights	OHL	66	29	47	76	125												8	6	6	12	41			
1984-85	London Knights	OHL	61	60	60	120	94												8	6	5	11	10			
1985-86	Vancouver	NHL	73	10	8	18	143	1	0	1	66	15.2	-21						3	0	0	0	0	0	0	0
1986-87	Vancouver	NHL	70	8	10	18	176	0	0	1	74	10.8	-23													
1987-88	Vancouver	NHL	22	1	3	4	38	0	0	0	14	7.1	-2													
	Fredericton	AHL	46	18	27	45	59												14	7	3	10	72			
1988-89	St. Louis	NHL	21	3	3	6	11	0	1	0	22	13.6	1						10	0	5	5	4	0	0	0
	Peoria Rivermen	IHL	58	31	35	66	45																			
1989-90	St. Louis	NHL	78	19	6	25	75	0	2	1	98	19.4	1						12	2	1	3	39	0	0	0
1990-91	St. Louis	NHL	79	19	21	40	168	0	2	5	123	15.4	19						13	1	4	5	35	0	0	0
1991-92	St. Louis	NHL	75	7	13	20	77	0	0	1	85	8.2	-11						6	0	1	1	20	0	0	0
1992-93	St. Louis	NHL	58	5	8	13	101	0	0	0	59	8.5	-18						11	2	0	2	14	0	1	0
1993-94	Florida	NHL	80	15	22	37	64	3	0	3	122	12.3	-4													
1994-95	Florida	NHL	45	10	10	20	25	2	0	3	70	14.3	-3													
1995-96	Florida	NHL	63	10	14	24	36	0	0	1	83	12.0	-2						22	10	7	17	39	4	0	2
1996-97	Florida	NHL	77	15	14	29	51	2	0	2	96	15.6	2						5	0	0	0	0	0	0	0
1997-98	Florida	NHL	7	0	0	0	2	0	0	0	4	0.0	-1													
	San Jose	NHL	50	4	4	8	51	0	0	1	47	8.5	0						6	0	0	0	18	0	0	0
1998-99	San Jose	NHL	61	6	9	15	24	2	0	0	58	10.3	-5	6	50.0	70	7	9:14	1	0	0	0	0	0	0	0
99-2000	San Jose	NHL	32	1	4	5	18	0	0	0	25	4.0	1	1	100.0	81	3	9:11	12	1	2	3	6	0	0	0
2000-01	Calgary	NHL	79	18	17	35	47	5	0	5	108	16.7	-2	20	20.0	121	35	15:57								
	NHL Totals		970	151	166	317	1107	15	5	24	1154	13.1		27	29.6	272	45	12:18	101	16	20	36	175	4	1	2

OHL First All-Star Team (1985)

Traded to **St. Louis** by **Vancouver** for Ernie Vargas, September 29, 1988. Claimed by **Florida** from **St. Louis** in Expansion Draft, June 24, 1993. Traded to **San Jose** by **Florida** with Florida's 1st round choice (later traded to Tampa Bay - Tampa Bay selected Vincent Lecavalier) in 1998 Entry Draft for Viktor Kozlov and Florida's 5th round choice (previously acquired, Florida selected Jaroslav Spacek) in 1998 Entry Draft, November 13, 1997. • Missed majority of 1999-2000 season recovering from shoulder injury suffered in game vs. Montreal, November 23, 1999. Signed as a free agent by **Calgary**, July 24, 2000.

LUKOWICH, Brad (loo-KUH-which, BRAD) DAL.

Defense. Shoots left. 6'1", 200 lbs. Born, Cranbrook, B.C., August 12, 1976. NY Islanders' 4th choice, 90th overall, in 1994 Entry Draft.

			Regular Season																Playoffs							
Season	Club	League	GP	G	A	Pts	PIM	PP	SH	GW	S	%	+/-	TF	F%	H	SB	Min	GP	G	A	Pts	PIM	PP	SH	GW
1992-93	Cranbrook Colts	KIJHL	54	21	41	62	162																			
	Kamloops Blazers	WHL	1	0	0	0	0																			
1993-94	Kamloops Blazers	WHL	42	5	11	16	166												16	0	1	1	35			
1994-95	Kamloops Blazers	WHL	63	10	35	45	125												18	0	7	7	21			
1995-96	Kamloops Blazers	WHL	65	14	55	69	114												13	2	10	12	29			
1996-97	Michigan K-Wings	IHL	69	2	6	8	77												4	0	1	1	2			
1997-98	Dallas	NHL	4	0	1	1	2	0	0	0	2	0.0	-2													
	Michigan K-Wings	IHL	60	6	27	33	104												4	0	4	4	14			
1998-99	Dallas	NHL	14	1	2	3	19	0	0	0	8	12.5	3	0	0.0	32	12	16:18	8	0	1	1	4	0	0	0
	Michigan K-Wings	IHL	67	8	21	29	95																			
99-2000	Dallas	NHL	60	3	1	4	50	0	0	1	33	9.1	-14	1	0.0	96	42	11:44								
2000-01	Dallas	NHL	80	4	10	14	76	0	0	2	43	9.3	28	1	100.0	204	70	14:48	10	1	0	1	4	0	0	0
	NHL Totals		158	8	14	22	147	0	0	3	86	9.3		2	50.0	332	124	13:45	18	1	1	2	8	0	0	0

Traded to **Dallas** by **NY Islanders** for Dallas' 3rd round choice (Robert Schnabel) in 1997 Entry Draft, June 1, 1996. Traded to **Minnesota** by **Dallas** with Manny Fernandez for Minnesota's 3rd round choice (Joel Lundqvist) in 2000 Entry Draft and 4th round choice (later traded back to Minnesota) in 2002 Entry Draft, June 12, 2000. Traded to **Dallas** by **Minnesota** with Minnesota's 3rd (Yared Hagos) and 9th (Dale Sullivan) round choices in 2001 Entry Draft for Aaron Gavey, Pavel Patera, Dallas' 8th round choice (Eric Johansson) in 2000 Entry Draft and Minnesota's 4th round choice (previously acquired) in 2002 Entry Draft, June 25, 2000.

LUMME, Jyrki (LOO-may, YUHR-kee) DAL.

Defense. Shoots left. 6'1", 209 lbs. Born, Tampere, Finland, July 16, 1966. Montreal's 3rd choice, 57th overall, in 1986 Entry Draft.

			Regular Season																Playoffs							
Season	Club	League	GP	G	A	Pts	PIM	PP	SH	GW	S	%	+/-	TF	F%	H	SB	Min	GP	G	A	Pts	PIM	PP	SH	GW
1983-84	KooVee Tampere	Finn-Jr.	28	5	4	9	61																			
1984-85	KooVee Tampere	Finland-3	30	6	4	10	44																			
1985-86	Ilves Tampere	Finn-Jr.	6	3	3	6	6												4	0	0	0	8			
	Ilves Tampere	Finland	31	1	4	5	4																			
1986-87	Ilves Tampere	Finn-Jr.	1	0	1	1	6												1	1	0	1	6			
	Ilves Tampere	Finland	43	12	12	24	52												4	0	1	1	2			
1987-88	Ilves Tampere	Finland	43	8	22	30	75																			
	Finland	Olympics	6	0	1	1	2																			
1988-89	Montreal	NHL	21	1	3	4	10	1	0	0	18	5.6	3													
	Sherbrooke	AHL	26	4	11	15	10												6	1	3	4	4			
1989-90	Montreal	NHL	54	1	19	20	41	0	0	0	79	1.3	17													
	Vancouver	NHL	11	3	7	10	8	0	0	1	30	10.0	0													
1990-91	Vancouver	NHL	80	5	27	32	59	1	0	0	157	3.2	-15						6	2	3	5	0	1	1	0
1991-92	Vancouver	NHL	75	12	32	44	65	3	1	1	106	11.3	25						13	2	3	5	4	1	0	1
1992-93	Vancouver	NHL	74	8	36	44	55	3	2	1	123	6.5	30						12	0	5	5	6	0	0	0
1993-94	Vancouver	NHL	83	13	42	55	50	1	3	3	161	8.1	3						24	2	11	13	16	2	0	1
1994-95	Ilves Tampere	Finland	12	4	4	8	24																			
	Vancouver	NHL	36	5	12	17	26	3	0	1	78	6.4	4						11	2	6	8	8	1	0	0
1995-96	Vancouver	NHL	80	17	37	54	50	8	0	2	192	8.9	-9						6	1	3	4	2	1	0	0
1996-97	Vancouver	NHL	66	11	24	35	32	5	0	2	107	10.3	8													
1997-98	Vancouver	NHL	74	9	21	30	34	4	0	1	117	7.7	-25													
	Finland	Olympics	6	1	0	1	16																			
1998-99	Phoenix	NHL	60	7	21	28	34	1	0	4	121	5.8	5	0	0.0	26	71	23:20	7	0	1	1	6	0	0	0
99-2000	Phoenix	NHL	74	8	32	40	44	4	0	3	142	5.6	9	0	0.0	51	105	23:36	5	0	1	1	2	0	0	0
2000-01	Phoenix	NHL	58	4	21	25	44	0	0	0	77	5.2	3	0	0.0	35	78	21:44								
	NHL Totals		846	104	334	438	552	34	6	19	1508	6.9		0	0.0	112	254	22:57	84	9	33	42	44	6	1	2

Traded to **Vancouver** by **Montreal** for St. Louis' 2nd round choice (previously acquired, Montreal selected Craig Darby) in 1991 Entry Draft, March 6, 1990. Signed as a free agent by **Phoenix**, July 3, 1998. Traded to **Dallas** by **Phoenix** for Tyler Bouck, June 23, 2001.

LYASHENKO, Roman (LIGH-a-SHEHN-koh, ROH-muhn) DAL.

Center. Shoots right. 6', 189 lbs. Born, Murmansk, Russia, May 2, 1979. Dallas' 2nd choice, 52nd overall, in 1997 Entry Draft.

			Regular Season																Playoffs							
Season	Club	League	GP	G	A	Pts	PIM	PP	SH	GW	S	%	+/-	TF	F%	H	SB	Min	GP	G	A	Pts	PIM	PP	SH	GW
1995-96	Torpedo Yaroslavl	CIS-2	60	7	10	17	12																			
1996-97	HC Yaroslavl-2	Russia-3	2	1	1	2	8																			
	Torpedo Yaroslavl	Russia	42	5	7	12	16												9	3	0	3	6			
1997-98	Torpedo Yaroslavl	Russia	46	7	6	13	28																			
	Torpedo Yaroslavl	EuroHL	10	1	1	2	2																			
1998-99	Torpedo Yaroslavl	Russia	42	10	9	19	51												9	0	4	4	8			
99-2000	Dallas	NHL	58	6	6	12	10	0	0	1	51	11.8	-2	339	45.7	46	15	10:56	16	2	1	3	0	0	0	2
	Michigan K-Wings	IHL	9	3	2	5	8																			
2000-01	Dallas	NHL	60	6	3	9	45	0	0	1	48	12.5	-1	418	43.3	54	10	9:35	1	0	0	0	0	0	0	0
	Utah Grizzlies	IHL	6	0	1	1	2																			
	NHL Totals		118	12	9	21	55	0	0	2	99	12.1		757	44.4	100	25	10:15	17	2	1	3	0	0	0	2

LYDMAN, Toni (LEED-man, TOH-nee) CGY.

Defense. Shoots left. 6'1", 200 lbs. Born, Lahti, Finland, September 25, 1977. Calgary's 5th choice, 89th overall, in 1996 Entry Draft.

			Regular Season																Playoffs							
Season	Club	League	GP	G	A	Pts	PIM	PP	SH	GW	S	%	+/-	TF	F%	H	SB	Min	GP	G	A	Pts	PIM	PP	SH	GW
1992-93	Kiekko Reipas-C	Finn-Jr.	36	10	9	19	22																			
1993-94	Kiekko Reipas-B	Finn-Jr.	9	3	1	4	4																			
	Reipas Lahti	Finn-Jr.	1	0	0	0	0																			
1994-95	Kiekko Reipas-B	Finn-Jr.	9	7	4	11	12																			
	Reipas Lahti-B	Finn-Jr.	26	6	4	10	10																			

			Regular Season																Playoffs							
Season	Club	League	GP	G	A	Pts	PIM	PP	SH	GW	S	%	+/-	TF	F%	H	SB	Min	GP	G	A	Pts	PIM	PP	SH	GW
1995-96	Reipas Lahti	Finn-Jr.	9	2	2	4	6	....	....	....	....	....	....	....	....	....	....	....	....	....	....	....	....	....	....	....
	Reipas Lahti	Finland	39	5	2	7	30	....	....	....	....	....	....	....	....	....	....	....	3	0	1	1	0	....	....	....
1996-97	Tappara Tampere	Finland	49	1	2	3	65	....	....	....	....	....	....	....	....	....	....	....	3	0	0	0	6	....	....	....
1997-98	Tappara Tampere	Finland	48	4	10	14	48	....	....	....	....	....	....	....	....	....	....	....	4	0	2	2	0	....	....	....
1998-99	HIFK Helsinki	Finland	42	4	7	11	36	....	....	....	....	....	....	....	....	....	....	....	11	0	3	3	2	....	....	....
	HIFK Finland	EuroHL	6	0	2	2	29	....	....	....	....	....	....	....	....	....	....	....	4	1	....	....	....	....	....	....
99-2000	HIFK Helsinki	Finland	46	4	18	22	36	....	....	....	....	....	....	....	....	....	....	....	9	0	4	4	6	....	....	....
2000-01	**Calgary**	**NHL**	**62**	**3**	**16**	**19**	**30**	**1**	**0**	**0**	**80**	**3.8**	**–7**	**0**	**0.0**	**60**	**61**	**20:36**	....	....	....	....	....	....	....	....
	NHL Totals		**62**	**3**	**16**	**19**	**30**	**1**	**0**	**0**	**80**	**3.8**		**0**	**0.0**	**60**	**61**	**20:36**	....	....	....	....	....	....	....	....

MacDONALD, Craig

(MAK-DAWN-uhld, KRAYG) **CAR.**

Center. Shoots left. 6'2", 195 lbs. Born, Antigonish, N.S., April 7, 1977. Hartford's 3rd choice, 88th overall, in 1996 Entry Draft.

Season	Club	League	GP	G	A	Pts	PIM	PP	SH	GW	S	%	+/-	TF	F%	H	SB	Min	GP	G	A	Pts	PIM	PP	SH	GW
1994-95	Lawrence Prep	Hi-School	30	25	52	77	10	....	....	....	....	....	....	....	....	....	....	....	....	....	....	....	....	....	....	....
1995-96	Harvard University	ECAC	34	7	10	17	10	....	....	....	....	....	....	....	....	....	....	....	....	....	....	....	....	....	....	....
1996-97	Harvard University	ECAC	32	6	10	16	20	....	....	....	....	....	....	....	....	....	....	....	....	....	....	....	....	....	....	....
1997-98	Canada	Nat-Team	58	18	29	47	38	....	....	....	....	....	....	....	....	....	....	....	....	....	....	....	....	....	....	....
1998-99	**Carolina**	**NHL**	**11**	**0**	**0**	**0**	**0**	**0**	**0**	**0**	**5**	**0.0**	**0**	**2**	**100.0**	**6**	**1**	**2:29**	**1**	**0**	**0**	**0**	**0**	**0**	**0**	**0**
	New Haven	AHL	62	17	31	48	77	....	....	....	....	....	....	....	....	....	....	....	....	....	....	....	....	....	....	....
99-2000	Cincinnati	IHL	78	12	24	36	76	....	....	....	....	....	....	....	....	....	....	....	11	4	1	5	8	....	....	....
2000-01	Cincinnati	IHL	82	20	28	48	104	....	....	....	....	....	....	....	....	....	....	....	5	0	1	1	6	....	....	....
	NHL Totals		**11**	**0**	**0**	**0**	**0**	**0**	**0**	**0**	**5**	**0.0**		**2**	**100.0**	**6**	**1**	**2:29**	**1**	**0**	**0**	**0**	**0**	**0**	**0**	**0**

Rights transferred to **Carolina** after **Hartford** franchise relocated, June 25, 1997

MacINNIS, Al

(MAK-IHN-his, AL) **ST.L.**

Defense. Shoots right. 6'2", 209 lbs. Born, Inverness, N.S., July 11, 1963. Calgary's 1st choice, 15th overall, in 1981 Entry Draft.

Season	Club	League	GP	G	A	Pts	PIM	PP	SH	GW	S	%	+/-	TF	F%	H	SB	Min	GP	G	A	Pts	PIM	PP	SH	GW
1979-80	Regina Blues	SJHL	59	20	28	48	110	....	....	....	....	....	....	....	....	....	....	....	....	....	....	....	....	....	....	....
1980-81	Kitchener	OMJHL	47	11	28	39	59	....	....	....	....	....	....	....	....	....	....	....	18	4	12	16	20	....	....	....
1981-82	Kitchener	OHL	59	25	50	75	145	....	....	....	....	....	....	....	....	....	....	....	15	5	10	15	44	....	....	....
	Calgary	**NHL**	**2**	**0**	**0**	**0**	**0**	**0**	**0**	**0**	**2**	**0.0**	**0**	....	....	....	....	....	....	....	....	....	....	....	....	....
1982-83	Kitchener	OHL	51	38	46	84	67	....	....	....	....	....	....	....	....	....	....	....	8	3	8	11	9	....	....	....
	Calgary	**NHL**	**14**	**1**	**3**	**4**	**9**	**0**	**0**	**0**	**7**	**14.3**	**0**	....	....	....	....	....	....	....	....	....	....	....	....	....
1983-84	**Calgary**	**NHL**	**51**	**11**	**34**	**45**	**42**	**7**	**0**	**2**	**160**	**6.9**	**0**	....	....	....	....	....	**11**	**2**	**12**	**14**	**13**	**2**	**0**	**1**
	Colorado Flames	CHL	19	5	14	19	22	....	....	....	....	....	....	....	....	....	....	....	....	....	....	....	....	....	....	....
1984-85	**Calgary**	**NHL**	**67**	**14**	**52**	**66**	**75**	**8**	**0**	**0**	**259**	**5.4**	**7**	....	....	....	....	....	**4**	**1**	**2**	**3**	**8**	**1**	**0**	**0**
1985-86	**Calgary**	**NHL**	**77**	**11**	**57**	**68**	**76**	**4**	**0**	**0**	**241**	**4.6**	**38**	....	....	....	....	....	**21**	**4**	***15**	**19**	**30**	**2**	**0**	**0**
1986-87	**Calgary**	**NHL**	**79**	**20**	**56**	**76**	**97**	**7**	**0**	**2**	**262**	**7.6**	**20**	....	....	....	....	....	**4**	**1**	**0**	**1**	**0**	**1**	**0**	**0**
1987-88	**Calgary**	**NHL**	**80**	**25**	**58**	**83**	**114**	**7**	**2**	**2**	**245**	**10.2**	**13**	....	....	....	....	....	**7**	**3**	**6**	**9**	**18**	**2**	**0**	**0**
1988-89♦	**Calgary**	**NHL**	**79**	**16**	**58**	**74**	**126**	**8**	**0**	**3**	**277**	**5.8**	**38**	....	....	....	....	....	**22**	**7**	***24**	***31**	**46**	**5**	**0**	**4**
1989-90	**Calgary**	**NHL**	**79**	**28**	**62**	**90**	**82**	**14**	**1**	**3**	**304**	**9.2**	**20**	....	....	....	....	....	**6**	**2**	**3**	**5**	**8**	**1**	**0**	**0**
1990-91	**Calgary**	**NHL**	**78**	**28**	**75**	**103**	**90**	**17**	**0**	**1**	**305**	**9.2**	**42**	....	....	....	....	....	**7**	**2**	**3**	**5**	**8**	**2**	**0**	**0**
1991-92	**Calgary**	**NHL**	**72**	**20**	**57**	**77**	**83**	**11**	**0**	**0**	**304**	**6.6**	**13**	....	....	....	....	....	....	....	....	....	....	....	....	....
1992-93	**Calgary**	**NHL**	**50**	**11**	**43**	**54**	**61**	**7**	**0**	**4**	**201**	**5.5**	**15**	....	....	....	....	....	**6**	**1**	**6**	**7**	**10**	**1**	**0**	**0**
1993-94	**Calgary**	**NHL**	**75**	**28**	**54**	**82**	**95**	**12**	**1**	**5**	**324**	**8.6**	**35**	....	....	....	....	....	**7**	**2**	**6**	**8**	**12**	**1**	**0**	**0**
1994-95	**St. Louis**	**NHL**	**32**	**8**	**20**	**28**	**43**	**2**	**0**	**0**	**110**	**7.3**	**19**	....	....	....	....	....	**7**	**1**	**5**	**6**	**10**	**0**	**0**	**0**
1995-96	**St. Louis**	**NHL**	**82**	**17**	**44**	**61**	**88**	**9**	**1**	**1**	**317**	**5.4**	**5**	....	....	....	....	....	**13**	**3**	**4**	**7**	**20**	**1**	**0**	**0**
1996-97	**St. Louis**	**NHL**	**72**	**13**	**30**	**43**	**65**	**6**	**1**	**1**	**296**	**4.4**	**2**	....	....	....	....	....	**6**	**1**	**2**	**3**	**4**	**1**	**0**	**0**
1997-98	**St. Louis**	**NHL**	**71**	**19**	**30**	**49**	**80**	**9**	**1**	**2**	**227**	**8.4**	**6**	....	....	....	....	....	**8**	**2**	**6**	**8**	**12**	**1**	**0**	**0**
	Canada	Olympics	6	2	0	2	2	....	....	....	....	....	....	....	....	....	....	....	....	....	....	....	....	....	....	....
1998-99	**St. Louis**	**NHL**	**82**	**20**	**42**	**62**	**70**	**11**	**1**	**2**	**314**	**6.4**	**33**	**0**	**0.0**	**56**	**128**	**29:07**	**13**	**4**	**8**	**12**	**20**	**2**	**0**	**0**
99-2000	**St. Louis**	**NHL**	**61**	**11**	**28**	**39**	**34**	**6**	**0**	**7**	**245**	**4.5**	**20**	**0**	**0.0**	**44**	**72**	**26:07**	**7**	**1**	**3**	**4**	**14**	**1**	**0**	**0**
2000-01	**St. Louis**	**NHL**	**59**	**12**	**42**	**54**	**52**	**6**	**1**	**3**	**218**	**5.5**	**23**	**0**	**0.0**	**40**	**73**	**26:32**	**15**	**2**	**8**	**10**	**18**	**2**	**0**	**0**
	NHL Totals		**1262**	**313**	**845**	**1158**	**1382**	**151**	**9**	**38**	**4618**	**6.8**		**0**	**0.0**	**140**	**273**	**27:27**	**164**	**39**	**113**	**152**	**251**	**26**	**0**	**5**

OHL First All-Star Team (1982, 1983) • NHL Second All-Star Team (1987, 1989, 1994) • Won Conn Smythe Trophy (1989) • NHL First All-Star Team (1990, 1991, 1999) • Won James Norris Memorial Trophy (1999) • Played in NHL All-Star Game (1985, 1988, 1990, 1991, 1992, 1994, 1996, 1997, 1998, 1999, 2000)

Traded to **St. Louis** by **Calgary** with Calgary's 4th round choice (Didier Tremblay) in 1997 Entry Draft for Phil Housley and St. Louis' 2nd round choices in 1996 (Steve Begin) and 1997 (John Tripp) Entry Drafts, July 4, 1994.

MacLEAN, Don

(MAK-layn, DAWN) **TOR.**

Center. Shoots left. 6'2", 199 lbs. Born, Sydney, N.S., January 14, 1977. Los Angeles' 2nd choice, 33rd overall, in 1995 Entry Draft.

Season	Club	League	GP	G	A	Pts	PIM	PP	SH	GW	S	%	+/-	TF	F%	H	SB	Min	GP	G	A	Pts	PIM	PP	SH	GW
1992-93	Halifax Hawks	NSMHL	27	15	25	40	34	....	....	....	....	....	....	....	....	....	....	....	....	....	....	....	....	....	....	....
1993-94	Halifax Hawks	NSMHL	25	35	35	70	151	....	....	....	....	....	....	....	....	....	....	....	....	....	....	....	....	....	....	....
1994-95	Beauport	QMJHL	64	15	27	42	37	....	....	....	....	....	....	....	....	....	....	....	17	4	4	8	6	....	....	....
1995-96	Beauport	QMJHL	1	0	1	1	0	....	....	....	....	....	....	....	....	....	....	....	....	....	....	....	....	....	....	....
	Laval Titan	QMJHL	21	17	11	28	29	....	....	....	....	....	....	....	....	....	....	....	....	....	....	....	....	....	....	....
	Hull Olympiques	QMJHL	39	26	34	60	44	....	....	....	....	....	....	....	....	....	....	....	17	6	7	13	14	....	....	....
1996-97	Hull Olympiques	QMJHL	69	34	47	81	67	....	....	....	....	....	....	....	....	....	....	....	14	11	10	21	39	....	....	....
1997-98	**Los Angeles**	**NHL**	**22**	**5**	**2**	**7**	**4**	**2**	**0**	**0**	**25**	**20.0**	**–1**	....	....	....	....	....	....	....	....	....	....	....	....	....
	Fredericton	AHL	39	9	5	14	32	....	....	....	....	....	....	....	....	....	....	....	4	1	3	4	2	....	....	....
1998-99	Springfield	AHL	41	5	14	19	31	....	....	....	....	....	....	....	....	....	....	....	....	....	....	....	....	....	....	....
	Grand Rapids	IHL	28	6	13	19	8	....	....	....	....	....	....	....	....	....	....	....	....	....	....	....	....	....	....	....
99-2000	Lowell	AHL	40	11	17	28	18	....	....	....	....	....	....	....	....	....	....	....	....	....	....	....	....	....	....	....
	St. John's Leafs	AHL	21	14	12	26	8	....	....	....	....	....	....	....	....	....	....	....	....	....	....	....	....	....	....	....
2000-01	**Toronto**	**NHL**	**3**	**0**	**1**	**1**	**2**	**0**	**0**	**0**	**2**	**0.0**	**–2**	**33**	**54.6**	**3**	**1**	**9:48**	....	....	....	....	....	....	....	....
	St. John's Leafs	AHL	61	26	34	60	48	....	....	....	....	....	....	....	....	....	....	....	4	2	1	3	2	....	....	....
	NHL Totals		**25**	**5**	**3**	**8**	**6**	**2**	**0**	**0**	**27**	**18.5**		**33**	**54.5**	**3**	**1**	**9:48**	....	....	....	....	....	....	....	....

Traded to **Toronto** by **Los Angeles** for Craig Charron, February 23, 2000.

MacLEAN, John

(MAK-layn, JAWN)

Right wing. Shoots right. 6', 200 lbs. Born, Oshawa, Ont., November 20, 1964. New Jersey's 1st choice, 6th overall, in 1983 Entry Draft.

Season	Club	League	GP	G	A	Pts	PIM	PP	SH	GW	S	%	+/-	TF	F%	H	SB	Min	GP	G	A	Pts	PIM	PP	SH	GW
1980-81	Oshawa Legion	MTJHL	41	35	35	70	151	....	....	....	....	....	....	....	....	....	....	....	....	....	....	....	....	....	....	....
1981-82	Oshawa Generals	OHL	67	17	22	39	197	....	....	....	....	....	....	....	....	....	....	....	12	3	6	9	63	....	....	....
1982-83	Oshawa Generals	OHL	66	47	51	98	138	....	....	....	....	....	....	....	....	....	....	....	17	*18	20	*38	35	....	....	....
1983-84	Oshawa Generals	OHL	30	23	36	59	58	....	....	....	....	....	....	....	....	....	....	....	7	2	5	7	18	....	....	....
	New Jersey	**NHL**	**23**	**1**	**0**	**1**	**10**	**0**	**0**	**0**	**22**	**4.5**	**–7**	....	....	....	....	....	....	....	....	....	....	....	....	....
1984-85	**New Jersey**	**NHL**	**61**	**13**	**20**	**33**	**44**	**1**	**0**	**4**	**92**	**14.1**	**–11**	....	....	....	....	....	....	....	....	....	....	....	....	....
1985-86	**New Jersey**	**NHL**	**74**	**21**	**36**	**57**	**112**	**1**	**0**	**4**	**139**	**15.1**	**–3**	....	....	....	....	....	....	....	....	....	....	....	....	....
1986-87	**New Jersey**	**NHL**	**80**	**31**	**36**	**67**	**120**	**9**	**0**	**4**	**197**	**15.7**	**–23**	....	....	....	....	....	....	....	....	....	....	....	....	....
1987-88	**New Jersey**	**NHL**	**76**	**23**	**16**	**39**	**147**	**12**	**0**	**4**	**204**	**11.3**	**–10**	....	....	....	....	....	**20**	**7**	**11**	**18**	**60**	**2**	**0**	**2**
1988-89	**New Jersey**	**NHL**	**74**	**42**	**45**	**87**	**122**	**14**	**0**	**4**	**266**	**15.8**	**26**	....	....	....	....	....	....	....	....	....	....	....	....	....
1989-90	**New Jersey**	**NHL**	**80**	**41**	**38**	**79**	**80**	**10**	**3**	**11**	**322**	**12.7**	**17**	....	....	....	....	....	**6**	**4**	**1**	**5**	**12**	**2**	**1**	**0**
1990-91	**New Jersey**	**NHL**	**78**	**45**	**33**	**78**	**150**	**19**	**2**	**7**	**292**	**15.4**	**8**	....	....	....	....	....	**7**	**5**	**3**	**8**	**20**	**1**	**0**	**0**
1991-92	**New Jersey**	**NHL**	DID NOT PLAY – INJURED																							
1992-93	**New Jersey**	**NHL**	**80**	**24**	**24**	**48**	**102**	**7**	**1**	**3**	**195**	**12.3**	**–6**	....	....	....	....	....	**5**	**0**	**1**	**1**	**10**	**0**	**0**	**0**
1993-94	**New Jersey**	**NHL**	**80**	**37**	**33**	**70**	**95**	**8**	**0**	**4**	**277**	**13.4**	**30**	....	....	....	....	....	**20**	**6**	**10**	**16**	**22**	**2**	**0**	**1**
1994-95♦	**New Jersey**	**NHL**	**46**	**17**	**12**	**29**	**32**	**2**	**1**	**0**	**139**	**12.2**	**13**	....	....	....	....	....	**20**	**5**	**13**	**18**	**14**	**2**	**0**	**0**
1995-96	**New Jersey**	**NHL**	**76**	**20**	**28**	**48**	**91**	**3**	**3**	**3**	**237**	**8.4**	**3**	....	....	....	....	....	....	....	....	....	....	....	....	....
1996-97	**New Jersey**	**NHL**	**80**	**29**	**25**	**54**	**49**	**5**	**0**	**6**	**254**	**11.4**	**11**	....	....	....	....	....	**10**	**4**	**5**	**9**	**4**	**2**	**1**	**1**
1997-98	**New Jersey**	**NHL**	**26**	**3**	**8**	**11**	**14**	**1**	**0**	**1**	**74**	**4.1**	**–6**	....	....	....	....	....	....	....	....	....	....	....	....	....
	San Jose	**NHL**	**51**	**13**	**19**	**32**	**28**	**5**	**0**	**2**	**139**	**9.4**	**0**	....	....	....	....	....	**6**	**2**	**3**	**5**	**4**	**1**	**0**	**0**
1998-99	**NY Rangers**	**NHL**	**82**	**28**	**27**	**55**	**46**	**11**	**1**	**2**	**231**	**12.1**	**5**	**20**	**35.0**	**120**	**30**	**20:43**	....	....	....	....	....	....	....	....
99-2000	**NY Rangers**	**NHL**	**77**	**18**	**24**	**42**	**52**	**6**	**2**	**3**	**158**	**11.4**	**–2**	**40**	**55.0**	**48**	**43**	**14:44**	....	....	....	....	....	....	....	....

			Regular Season																Playoffs							
Season	Club	League	GP	G	A	Pts	PIM	PP	SH	GW	S	%	+/-	TF	F%	H	SB	Min	GP	G	A	Pts	PIM	PP	SH	GW
2000-01	NY Rangers	NHL	2	0	0	0	0	0	0	0	0	0.0	–2	1	0.0	2	0	10:14	....	....	....	....	....	....	....	....
	Manitoba Moose	IHL	32	6	12	18	28	....	....	....	....	....	....	....	....	....	....	....	....	....	....	....	....	....	....	....
	Dallas	NHL	28	4	2	6	17	1	0	0	41	9.8	0	1	100.0	34	11	12:45	10	2	1	3	6	0	0	0
	NHL Totals		1174	410	426	836	1311	115	13	62	3279	12.5		62	48.4	204	84	16:59	104	35	48	83	152	12	2	4

Memorial Cup All-Star Team (1983) • Played in NHL All-Star Game (1989, 1991)

• Missed entire 1991-92 season recovering from knee surgery, June, 1991. Traded to **San Jose** by **New Jersey** with Ken Sutton for Doug Bodger and Dody Wood, December 7, 1997. Signed as a free agent by **NY Rangers**, July 22, 1998. Traded to **Dallas** by **NY Rangers** for future considerations, February 5, 2001.

MADDEN, John

(MA-dehn, JAWN) **N.J.**

Left wing. Shoots left. 5'11", 195 lbs. Born, Barrie, Ont., May 4, 1973.

Season	Club	League	GP	G	A	Pts	PIM	PP	SH	GW	S	%	+/-	TF	F%	H	SB	Min	GP	G	A	Pts	PIM	PP	SH	GW
1989-90	Alliston Hornets	OJHL-C	31	24	25	49	26	....	....	....	....	....	....	....	....	....	....	....	....	....	....	....	....	....	....	....
1990-91	Alliston Hornets	OJHL-C	14	15	21	36	10	....	....	....	....	....	....	....	....	....	....	....	....	....	....	....	....	....	....	....
	Barrie Colts	OJHL-B	1	0	0	0	0	....	....	....	....	....	....	....	....	....	....	....	....	....	....	....	....	....	....	....
1991-92	Barrie Colts	OJHL-B	42	50	54	104	46	....	....	....	....	....	....	....	....	....	....	....	13	10	9	19	14	....	....	....
1992-93	Barrie Colts	COJHL	43	49	75	124	62	....	....	....	....	....	....	....	....	....	....	....	....	....	....	....	....	....	....	....
1993-94	U. of Michigan	CCHA	36	6	11	17	14	....	....	....	....	....	....	....	....	....	....	....	....	....	....	....	....	....	....	....
1994-95	U. of Michigan	CCHA	39	21	22	43	8	....	....	....	....	....	....	....	....	....	....	....	....	....	....	....	....	....	....	....
1995-96	U. of Michigan	CCHA	43	27	30	57	45	....	....	....	....	....	....	....	....	....	....	....	....	....	....	....	....	....	....	....
1996-97	U. of Michigan	CCHA	42	26	37	63	56	....	....	....	....	....	....	....	....	....	....	....	....	....	....	....	....	....	....	....
1997-98	Albany River Rats	AHL	74	20	36	56	40	....	....	....	....	....	....	....	....	....	....	....	13	3	13	16	14	....	....	....
1998-99	New Jersey	NHL	4	0	1	1	0	0	0	0	4	0.0	–2	0	0.0	3	1	9:13	....	....	....	....	....	....	....	....
	Albany River Rats	AHL	75	38	60	98	44	....	....	....	....	....	....	....	....	....	....	....	5	2	2	4	6	....	....	....
99-2000♦	New Jersey	NHL	74	16	9	25	6	0	6	3	115	13.9	7	770	47.5	92	25	11:40	20	3	4	7	0	0	1	2
2000-01	New Jersey	NHL	80	23	15	38	12	0	3	4	163	14.1	24	974	46.6	69	39	15:35	25	4	3	7	6	0	0	0
	NHL Totals		158	39	25	64	18	0	9	7	282	13.8		1744	47.0	164	65	13:35	45	7	7	14	6	0	1	2

CCHA First All-Star Team (1997) • NCAA West First All-American Team (1997) • Won Frank J. Selke Trophy (2001)

Signed as a free agent by **New Jersey**, June 26, 1997.

MAIR, Adam

(MAIR, A-duhm) **L.A.**

Center. Shoots right. 6'2", 200 lbs. Born, Hamilton, Ont., February 15, 1979. Toronto's 2nd choice, 84th overall, in 1997 Entry Draft.

Season	Club	League	GP	G	A	Pts	PIM	PP	SH	GW	S	%	+/-	TF	F%	H	SB	Min	GP	G	A	Pts	PIM	PP	SH	GW
1994-95	Ohsweken Eagles	OJHL-B	39	21	23	44	91	....	....	....	....	....	....	....	....	....	....	....	....	....	....	....	....	....	....	....
1995-96	Owen Sound	OHL	62	12	15	27	63	....	....	....	....	....	....	....	....	....	....	....	6	0	0	0	2	....	....	....
1996-97	Owen Sound	OHL	65	16	35	51	113	....	....	....	....	....	....	....	....	....	....	....	4	1	0	1	2	....	....	....
1997-98	Owen Sound	OHL	56	25	27	52	179	....	....	....	....	....	....	....	....	....	....	....	11	6	3	9	31	....	....	....
1998-99	Owen Sound	OHL	43	23	41	64	109	....	....	....	....	....	....	....	....	....	....	....	16	10	10	20	*47	....	....	....
	St. John's Leafs	AHL	....	....	....	....	....	....	....	....	....	....	....	....	....	....	....	....	3	1	0	1	6	....	....	....
	Toronto	NHL	....	....	....	....	....	....	....	....	....	....	....	....	....	....	....	....	5	1	0	1	14	0	0	0
99-2000	Toronto	NHL	8	1	0	1	6	0	0	0	7	14.3	–1	9	33.3	14	1	11:33	5	0	0	0	8	0	0	0
	St. John's Leafs	AHL	66	22	27	49	124	....	....	....	....	....	....	....	....	....	....	....	....	....	....	....	....	....	....	....
2000-01	Toronto	NHL	16	0	2	2	14	0	0	0	17	0.0	3	56	51.8	25	0	9:00	....	....	....	....	....	....	....	....
	St. John's Leafs	AHL	47	18	27	45	69	....	....	....	....	....	....	....	....	....	....	....	....	....	....	....	....	....	....	....
	Los Angeles	NHL	10	0	0	0	6	0	0	0	5	0.0	–3	21	61.9	21	4	6:14	....	....	....	....	....	....	....	....
	NHL Totals		34	1	2	3	26	0	0	0	29	3.4		86	52.3	60	5	8:48	10	1	0	1	22	0	0	0

Traded to **LA Kings** by **Toronto** with Toronto's 2nd round choice (Mike Cammalleri) in 2001 Entry Draft for Aki Berg, March 13, 2001.

MALAKHOV, Vladimir

(mah-LAH-kahf, vla-DIH-meer) **NYR**

Defense. Shoots left. 6'4", 230 lbs. Born, Ekaterinburg, USSR, August 30, 1968. NY Islanders' 12th choice, 191st overall, in 1989 Entry Draft.

Season	Club	League	GP	G	A	Pts	PIM	PP	SH	GW	S	%	+/-	TF	F%	H	SB	Min	GP	G	A	Pts	PIM	PP	SH	GW
1986-87	Krylja Sovetov	USSR	22	0	1	1	12	....	....	....	....	....	....	....	....	....	....	....	....	....	....	....	....	....	....	....
1987-88	Krylja Sovetov	USSR	28	2	2	4	26	....	....	....	....	....	....	....	....	....	....	....	....	....	....	....	....	....	....	....
1988-89	CSKA Moscow	USSR	34	6	2	8	16	....	....	....	....	....	....	....	....	....	....	....	....	....	....	....	....	....	....	....
1989-90	CSKA Moscow	USSR	48	2	10	12	34	....	....	....	....	....	....	....	....	....	....	....	....	....	....	....	....	....	....	....
1990-91	CSKA Moscow	USSR	46	5	13	18	22	....	....	....	....	....	....	....	....	....	....	....	....	....	....	....	....	....	....	....
1991-92	CSKA Moscow	CIS	40	1	9	10	12	....	....	....	....	....	....	....	....	....	....	....	....	....	....	....	....	....	....	....
	Russia	Olympics	8	3	0	3	4	....	....	....	....	....	....	....	....	....	....	....	....	....	....	....	....	....	....	....
1992-93	NY Islanders	NHL	64	14	38	52	59	7	0	0	178	7.9	14	....	....	....	....	....	17	3	6	9	12	0	0	0
	Capital District	AHL	3	2	1	3	11	....	....	....	....	....	....	....	....	....	....	....	....	....	....	....	....	....	....	....
1993-94	NY Islanders	NHL	76	10	47	57	80	4	0	2	235	4.3	29	....	....	....	....	....	4	0	0	0	6	0	0	0
1994-95	NY Islanders	NHL	26	3	13	16	32	1	0	0	61	4.9	–1	....	....	....	....	....	....	....	....	....	....	....	....	....
	Montreal	NHL	14	1	4	5	14	0	0	0	30	3.3	–2	....	....	....	....	....	....	....	....	....	....	....	....	....
1995-96	Montreal	NHL	61	5	23	28	79	2	0	0	122	4.1	7	....	....	....	....	....	....	....	....	....	....	....	....	....
1996-97	Montreal	NHL	65	10	20	30	43	5	0	1	177	5.6	3	....	....	....	....	....	5	0	0	0	6	0	0	0
1997-98	Montreal	NHL	74	13	31	44	70	8	0	2	166	7.8	16	....	....	....	....	....	9	3	4	7	10	2	0	0
1998-99	Montreal	NHL	62	13	21	34	77	8	0	3	143	9.1	–7	0	0.0	74	88	23:29	....	....	....	....	....	....	....	....
99-2000	Montreal	NHL	7	0	0	0	4	0	0	0	7	0.0	0	0	0.0	6	9	21:20	....	....	....	....	....	....	....	....
	♦ New Jersey	NHL	17	1	4	5	19	1	0	1	11	9.1	1	0	0.0	20	13	20:18	23	1	4	5	18	1	0	0
2000-01	NY Rangers	NHL	3	0	2	2	4	0	0	0	6	0.0	0	0	0.0	4	7	19:07	....	....	....	....	....	....	....	....
	NHL Totals		469	70	203	273	481	36	0	9	1136	6.2		0	0.0	104	117	22:34	58	7	14	21	52	3	0	0

NHL All-Rookie Team (1993)

Traded to **Montreal** by **NY Islanders** with Pierre Turgeon for Kirk Muller, Mathieu Schneider and Craig Darby, April 5, 1995. • Missed majority of 1999-2000 season recovering from knee injury suffered in exhibition game vs. Boston, September 27, 1999. Traded to **New Jersey** by **Montreal** for Sheldon Souray, Josh DeWolf and New Jersey's 2nd round choice (later traded to Washington - later traded to Tampa Bay - Tampa Bay selected Andreas Holmqvist) in 2001 Entry Draft, March 1, 2000. Signed as a free agent by **NY Rangers**, July 10, 2000. • Missed majority of 2000-01 season recovering from knee injury suffered in game vs. Montreal, November 11, 2000.

MALGUNAS, Stewart

(mal-GOO-nuhs, STEW-ahrt)

Defense. Shoots left. 6', 200 lbs. Born, Prince George, B.C., April 21, 1970. Detroit's 3rd choice, 66th overall, in 1990 Entry Draft.

Season	Club	League	GP	G	A	Pts	PIM	PP	SH	GW	S	%	+/-	TF	F%	H	SB	Min	GP	G	A	Pts	PIM	PP	SH	GW
1985-86	Prince George	BCAHA	49	10	25	35	85	....	....	....	....	....	....	....	....	....	....	....	....	....	....	....	....	....	....	....
1986-87	Prince George	BCAHA	50	11	31	42	102	....	....	....	....	....	....	....	....	....	....	....	....	....	....	....	....	....	....	....
1987-88	Prince George	BCJHL	48	12	34	46	99	....	....	....	....	....	....	....	....	....	....	....	....	....	....	....	....	....	....	....
	New Westminster	WHL	6	0	0	0	0	....	....	....	....	....	....	....	....	....	....	....	....	....	....	....	....	....	....	....
1988-89	Seattle T-Birds	WHL	72	11	41	52	51	....	....	....	....	....	....	....	....	....	....	....	....	....	....	....	....	....	....	....
1989-90	Seattle T-Birds	WHL	63	15	48	63	116	....	....	....	....	....	....	....	....	....	....	....	13	2	9	11	32	....	....	....
1990-91	Adirondack	AHL	78	5	19	24	70	....	....	....	....	....	....	....	....	....	....	....	2	0	0	0	4	....	....	....
1991-92	Adirondack	AHL	69	4	28	32	82	....	....	....	....	....	....	....	....	....	....	....	18	2	6	8	28	....	....	....
1992-93	Adirondack	AHL	45	3	12	15	39	....	....	....	....	....	....	....	....	....	....	....	11	3	3	6	8	....	....	....
1993-94	Philadelphia	NHL	67	1	3	4	86	0	0	0	54	1.9	2	....	....	....	....	....	....	....	....	....	....	....	....	....
1994-95	Philadelphia	NHL	4	0	0	0	4	0	0	0	1	0.0	–1	....	....	....	....	....	....	....	....	....	....	....	....	....
	Hershey Bears	AHL	32	3	5	8	28	....	....	....	....	....	....	....	....	....	....	....	6	2	1	3	31	....	....	....
1995-96	Winnipeg	NHL	29	0	1	1	32	0	0	0	13	0.0	–10	....	....	....	....	....	....	....	....	....	....	....	....	....
	Washington	NHL	1	0	0	0	0	0	0	0	0	0.0	0	....	....	....	....	....	....	....	....	....	....	....	....	....
	Portland Pirates	AHL	16	2	5	7	18	....	....	....	....	....	....	....	....	....	....	....	13	1	3	4	19	....	....	....
1996-97	Washington	NHL	6	0	0	0	2	0	0	0	3	0.0	2	....	....	....	....	....	....	....	....	....	....	....	....	....
	Portland Pirates	AHL	68	6	12	18	59	....	....	....	....	....	....	....	....	....	....	....	5	0	0	0	8	....	....	....
1997-98	Washington	NHL	8	0	0	0	12	0	0	0	5	0.0	1	....	....	....	....	....	....	....	....	....	....	....	....	....
	Portland Pirates	AHL	69	14	25	39	73	....	....	....	....	....	....	....	....	....	....	....	9	1	1	2	19	....	....	....
1998-99	Washington	NHL	10	0	0	0	6	0	0	0	2	0.0	–5	0	0.0	12	9	9:02	....	....	....	....	....	....	....	....
	Portland Pirates	AHL	33	2	10	12	49	....	....	....	....	....	....	....	....	....	....	....	....	....	....	....	....	....	....	....
	Detroit Vipers	IHL	9	0	2	2	10	....	....	....	....	....	....	....	....	....	....	....	11	0	1	1	21	....	....	....

Season	Club	League	GP	G	A	Pts	PIM	PP	SH	GW	S	%	+/-	TF	F%	H	SB	Min	Playoffs GP	G	A	Pts	PIM	PP	SH	GW
99-2000	Utah Grizzlies	IHL	34	4	9	13	55																			
	Calgary	NHL	4	0	1	1	2	0	0	0	0	0.0	1	0	0.0	7	4	12:57								
2000-01	Hershey Bears	AHL	25	0	2	2	39												11	0	1	1	14			
	NHL Totals		129	1	5	6	144	0	0	0	78	1.3		0	0.0	19	13	10:09								

WHL West First All-Star Team (1990)

Traded to **Philadelphia** by **Detroit** for Philadelphia's 5th round choice (David Arsenault) in 1995 Entry Draft, September 9, 1993. Signed as a free agent by **Winnipeg**, August 9, 1995. Traded to **Washington** by **Winnipeg** for Denis Chasse, February 15, 1996. Traded to **Nashville** by **Washington** for future considerations, February 2, 2000. Claimed on waivers by **Calgary** from **Nashville**, February 3, 2000. • Missed majority of 1999-2000 season recovering from head injury suffered in game vs. Los Angeles, February 14, 2000. Signed as a free agent by **Colorado**, August, 2000. Signed as a free agent by **Frankfurt Lions** (DEL), March 24, 2001.

MALHOTRA, Manny

(mal-HOH-truh, MAHN-ee) **NYR**

Center. Shoots left. 6'2", 210 lbs. Born, Mississauga, Ont., May 18, 1980. NY Rangers' 1st choice, 7th overall, in 1998 Entry Draft.

Season	Club	League	GP	G	A	Pts	PIM	PP	SH	GW	S	%	+/-	TF	F%	H	SB	Min	Playoffs GP	G	A	Pts	PIM	PP	SH	GW
1995-96	Mississauga Reps	MTHL	54	27	44	71	62																			
1996-97	Guelph Storm	OHL	61	16	28	44	26												18	7	7	14	11			
1997-98	Guelph Storm	OHL	57	16	35	51	29												12	7	6	13	8			
1998-99	NY Rangers	NHL	73	8	8	16	13	1	0	2	61	13.1	-2	588	43.9	115	17	8:36								
99-2000	NY Rangers	NHL	27	0	0	0	4	0	0	0	18	0.0	-6	132	44.7	37	7	6:42								
	Guelph Storm	OHL	5	2	2	4	4												6	0	2	2	4			
	Hartford	AHL	12	1	5	6	2												23	1	2	3	10			
2000-01	NY Rangers	NHL	50	4	8	12	31	0	0	2	46	8.7	-10	248	44.4	73	17	9:03								
	Hartford	AHL	28	5	6	11	69												5	0	0	0	0			
	NHL Totals		150	12	16	28	48	1	0	4	125	9.6		968	44.1	225	41	8:25								

Memorial Cup All-Star Team (1998) • Won George Parsons Trophy (Memorial Cup Tournament Most Sportsmanlike Player) (1998)

MALIK, Marek

(MAW-leck, MAIR-ehk) **CAR.**

Defense. Shoots left. 6'5", 215 lbs. Born, Ostrava, Czech., June 24, 1975. Hartford's 2nd choice, 72nd overall, in 1993 Entry Draft.

Season	Club	League	GP	G	A	Pts	PIM	PP	SH	GW	S	%	+/-	TF	F%	H	SB	Min	Playoffs GP	G	A	Pts	PIM	PP	SH	GW
1992-93	TJ Vitkovice	Czech-Jr.	20	5	10	15	16																			
1993-94	HC Vitkovice	Cze-Rep	38	3	3	6	0												3	0	1	1	0			
1994-95	Springfield	AHL	58	11	30	41	91																			
	Hartford	NHL	1	0	1	1	0	0	0	0	0	0.0	1													
1995-96	Hartford	NHL	7	0	0	0	4	0	0	0	2	0.0	-3													
	Springfield	AHL	68	8	14	22	135												8	1	3	4	20			
1996-97	Hartford	NHL	47	1	5	6	50	0	0	1	33	3.0	5													
	Springfield	AHL	3	0	3	3	4																			
1997-98	Malmo IF	Sweden	37	1	5	6	21																			
1998-99	HC Vitkovice	Cze-Rep	1	1	0	1	6																			
	Carolina	NHL	52	2	9	11	36	1	0	0	36	5.6	-6	0	0.0	101	76	21:14	4	0	0	0	4	0	0	0
	New Haven	AHL	21	2	8	10	28																			
99-2000	Carolina	NHL	57	4	10	14	63	0	0	1	57	7.0	13	0	0.0	44	64	18:00								
2000-01	Carolina	NHL	61	6	14	20	34	1	0	1	72	8.3	-4	0	0.0	75	87	19:36	3	0	0	0	6	0	0	0
	NHL Totals		225	13	39	52	187	2	0	3	200	6.5		0	0.0	220	227	19:34	7	0	0	0	10	0	0	0

Transferred to **Carolina** after **Hartford** franchise relocated, June 25, 1997.

MALKOC, Dean

(mal-KAWK, DEEN)

Defense. Shoots left. 6'3", 215 lbs. Born, Vancouver, B.C., January 26, 1970. New Jersey's 7th choice, 95th overall, in 1990 Entry Draft.

Season	Club	League	GP	G	A	Pts	PIM	PP	SH	GW	S	%	+/-	TF	F%	H	SB	Min	Playoffs GP	G	A	Pts	PIM	PP	SH	GW
1987-88	Williams Lake	PCJHL	55	6	32	38	215																			
1988-89	Powell River	BCJHL	55	10	32	42	370																			
1989-90	Kamloops Blazers	WHL	48	3	18	21	209												17	0	3	3	56			
1990-91	Kamloops Blazers	WHL	8	1	4	5	47																			
	Swift Current	WHL	56	10	23	33	248												3	0	2	2	5			
	Utica Devils	AHL	1	0	0	0	0																			
1991-92	Utica Devils	AHL	66	1	11	12	274												4	0	2	2	6			
1992-93	Utica Devils	AHL	73	5	19	24	255												5	0	1	1	8			
1993-94	Albany River Rats	AHL	79	0	9	9	296												5	0	0	0	21			
1994-95	Albany River Rats	AHL	9	0	1	1	52																			
	Indianapolis Ice	IHL	62	1	3	4	193																			
1995-96	Vancouver	NHL	41	0	2	2	136	0	0	0	8	0.0	-10													
1996-97	Boston	NHL	33	0	0	0	70	0	0	0	7	0.0	-14													
	Providence Bruins	AHL	4	0	2	2	28																			
1997-98	Boston	NHL	40	1	0	1	86	0	0	0	15	6.7	-12													
1998-99	NY Islanders	NHL	2	0	1	1	7	0	0	0	1	0.0	3	0	0.0	2	6	15:22								
	Lowell	AHL	61	2	8	10	193												3	0	0	0	8			
99-2000	Chicago Wolves	IHL	62	2	8	10	130												1	0	0	0	0			
2000-01	Cincinnati Ducks	AHL	65	1	4	5	232												4	0	0	0	6			
	NHL Totals		116	1	3	4	299	0	0	0	31	3.2		0	0.0	2	6	15:22								

Traded to **Chicago** by **New Jersey** for Rob Conn, January 30, 1995. Signed as a free agent by **Vancouver**, September 8, 1995. Claimed by **Boston** from **Vancouver** in NHL Waiver Draft, September 30, 1996. Signed as a free agent by **NY Islanders**, August 19, 1998. Traded to **Anaheim** by **NY Islanders** with Tony Hrkac for Ted Drury, October 29, 1999.

MALTAIS, Steve

(MAHL-tay, STEEV)

Left wing. Shoots left. 6'2", 205 lbs. Born, Arvida, Que., January 25, 1969. Washington's 2nd choice, 57th overall, in 1987 Entry Draft.

Season	Club	League	GP	G	A	Pts	PIM	PP	SH	GW	S	%	+/-	TF	F%	H	SB	Min	Playoffs GP	G	A	Pts	PIM	PP	SH	GW
1985-86	Wexford Hawks	MTHL	33	35	19	54	38																			
	Wexford Raiders	MTJHL	1	1	0	1	0																			
1986-87	Cornwall Royals	OHL	65	32	12	44	29												5	0	0	0	2			
1987-88	Cornwall Royals	OHL	59	39	46	85	30												11	9	6	15	33			
1988-89	Cornwall Royals	OHL	58	53	70	123	67												18	14	16	30	16			
	Fort Wayne	IHL																	4	2	1	3	0			
1989-90	Washington	NHL	8	0	0	0	2	0	0	0	11	0.0	-2						1	0	0	0	0	0	0	0
	Baltimore	AHL	67	29	37	66	54												12	6	10	16	6			
1990-91	Washington	NHL	7	0	0	0	2	0	0	0	3	0.0	-1													
	Baltimore	AHL	73	36	43	79	97												6	1	4	5	10			
1991-92	Minnesota	NHL	12	2	1	3	2	0	0	0	6	33.3	-1													
	Kalamazoo Wings	IHL	48	25	31	56	51																			
	Halifax Citadels	AHL	10	3	3	6	0																			
1992-93	Tampa Bay	NHL	63	7	13	20	35	4	0	1	96	7.3	-20													
	Atlanta Knights	IHL	16	14	10	24	22																			
1993-94	Detroit	NHL	4	0	1	1	0	0	0	0	2	0.0	-1													
	Adirondack	AHL	73	35	49	84	79												12	5	11	16	14			
1994-95	Chicago Wolves	IHL	79	*57	40	97	145												3	1	1	2	0			
1995-96	Chicago Wolves	IHL	81	56	66	122	161												9	7	7	14	20			
1996-97	Chicago Wolves	IHL	81	*60	54	114	62												4	2	0	2	4			
1997-98	Chicago Wolves	IHL	82	*46	57	103	120												22	8	11	19	28			
1998-99	Chicago Wolves	IHL	82	*56	44	100	164												10	4	6	10	2			
99-2000	Chicago Wolves	IHL	82	*44	46	*90	78												16	9	4	13	14			
2000-01	Columbus	NHL	26	0	3	3	12	0	0	0	30	0.0	-9	2	0.0	24	6	11:57								
	Chicago Wolves	IHL	50	25	26	51	57												16	7	10	17	2			
	NHL Totals		120	9	18	27	53	4	0	1	148	6.1		2	0.0	24	6	11:57	1	0	0	0	0	0	0	0

OHL Second All-Star Team (1989) • IHL First All-Star Team (1995, 1999, 2000) • IHL Second All-Star Team (1996, 1997) • Won Leo P. Lamoureux Memorial Trophy (Top Scorer - IHL) (2000)

Traded to **Minnesota** by **Washington** with Trent Klatt for Shawn Chambers, June 21, 1991. Traded to **Quebec** by **Minnesota** for Kip Miller, March 8, 1992. Claimed by **Tampa Bay** from **Quebec** in Expansion Draft, June 18, 1992. Traded to **Detroit** by **Tampa Bay** for Dennis Vial, June 8, 1993. Signed as a free agent by **Chicago Wolves** (IHL), August 25, 1998. Signed as a free agent by **Columbus**, October 6, 2000.

MALTBY, Kirk

(MAHLT-bee, KUHRK) **DET.**

Right wing. Shoots right. 6', 180 lbs. Born, Guelph, Ont., December 22, 1972. Edmonton's 4th choice, 65th overall, in 1992 Entry Draft.

			Regular Season																Playoffs							
Season	Club	League	GP	G	A	Pts	PIM	PP	SH	GW	S	%	+/-	TF	F%	H	SB	Min	GP	G	A	Pts	PIM	PP	SH	GW
1988-89	Cambridge Hawks	OJHL-B	48	28	18	46	138																			
1989-90	Owen Sound	OHL	61	12	15	27	90												12	1	6	7	15			
1990-91	Owen Sound	OHL	66	34	32	66	100																			
1991-92	Owen Sound	OHL	66	50	41	91	99												5	3	3	6	18			
1992-93	Cape Breton	AHL	73	22	23	45	130												16	3	3	6	45			
1993-94	**Edmonton**	**NHL**	**68**	**11**	**8**	**19**	**74**	**0**	**1**	**1**	**89**	**12.4**	**-2**													
1994-95	**Edmonton**	**NHL**	**47**	**8**	**3**	**11**	**49**	**0**	**2**	**1**	**73**	**11.0**	**-11**													
1995-96	**Edmonton**	**NHL**	**49**	**2**	**6**	**8**	**61**	**0**	**0**	**1**	**51**	**3.9**	**-16**													
	Cape Breton	AHL	4	1	2	3	6																			
	Detroit	**NHL**	**6**	**1**	**0**	**1**	**6**	**0**	**0**	**0**	**4**	**25.0**	**0**						**8**	**0**	**1**	**1**	**4**	**0**	**0**	**0**
1996-97♦	**Detroit**	**NHL**	**66**	**3**	**5**	**8**	**75**	**0**	**0**	**0**	**62**	**4.8**	**3**						**20**	**5**	**2**	**7**	**24**	**0**	**1**	**1**
1997-98♦	**Detroit**	**NHL**	**65**	**14**	**9**	**23**	**89**	**2**	**1**	**3**	**106**	**13.2**	**11**						**22**	**3**	**1**	**4**	**30**	**0**	**1**	**0**
1998-99	**Detroit**	**NHL**	**53**	**8**	**6**	**14**	**34**	**0**	**1**	**2**	**76**	**10.5**	**-6**	**10**	**40.0**	**129**	**33**	**13:13**	**10**	**1**	**0**	**1**	**8**	**0**	**0**	**1**
99-2000	**Detroit**	**NHL**	**41**	**6**	**8**	**14**	**24**	**0**	**2**	**1**	**71**	**8.5**	**1**	**2**	**50.0**	**90**	**34**	**13:30**	**8**	**0**	**1**	**1**	**4**	**0**	**0**	**0**
2000-01	**Detroit**	**NHL**	**79**	**12**	**7**	**19**	**22**	**1**	**3**	**3**	**119**	**10.1**	**16**	**14**	**35.7**	**217**	**54**	**14:17**	**6**	**0**	**0**	**0**	**6**	**0**	**0**	**0**
	NHL Totals		**474**	**65**	**52**	**117**	**434**	**3**	**10**	**12**	**651**	**10.0**		**26**	**38.5**	**436**	**121**	**13:46**	**74**	**9**	**5**	**14**	**76**	**0**	**2**	**2**

Traded to **Detroit** by **Edmonton** for Dan McGillis, March 20, 1996. • Missed majority of 1999-2000 season recovering from hernia injury suffered in game vs. Dallas, October 5, 1999.

MANDERVILLE, Kent

(MAN-duhr-VIHL, KEHNT) **PHI.**

Center. Shoots left. 6'3", 200 lbs. Born, Edmonton, Alta., April 12, 1971. Calgary's 1st choice, 24th overall, in 1989 Entry Draft.

Season	Club	League	GP	G	A	Pts	PIM	PP	SH	GW	S	%	+/-	TF	F%	H	SB	Min	GP	G	A	Pts	PIM	PP	SH	GW
1987-88	Notre Dame	SMHL	32	22	18	40	42																			
1988-89	Notre Dame	SJHL	58	39	36	75	165																			
1989-90	Cornell Big Red	ECAC	26	11	15	26	28																			
1990-91	Cornell Big Red	ECAC	28	17	14	31	60																			
1991-92	Canada	Nat-Team	63	16	24	40	78																			
	Canada	Olympics	8	1	2	3	0																			
	Toronto	**NHL**	**15**	**0**	**4**	**4**	**0**	**0**	**0**	**0**	**14**	**0.0**	**1**													
	St. John's Leafs	AHL																	12	5	9	14	14			
1992-93	**Toronto**	**NHL**	**18**	**1**	**1**	**2**	**17**	**0**	**0**	**1**	**15**	**6.7**	**-9**						**18**	**1**	**0**	**1**	**8**	**0**	**0**	**0**
	St. John's Leafs	AHL	56	19	28	47	86												2	0	2	2	0			
1993-94	**Toronto**	**NHL**	**67**	**7**	**9**	**16**	**63**	**0**	**0**	**1**	**81**	**8.6**	**5**						**12**	**1**	**0**	**1**	**4**	**0**	**1**	**0**
1994-95	**Toronto**	**NHL**	**36**	**0**	**1**	**1**	**22**	**0**	**0**	**0**	**43**	**0.0**	**-2**						**7**	**0**	**0**	**0**	**6**	**0**	**0**	**0**
1995-96	**Edmonton**	**NHL**	**37**	**3**	**5**	**8**	**38**	**0**	**2**	**0**	**63**	**4.8**	**-5**													
	St. John's Leafs	AHL	27	16	12	28	26																			
1996-97	**Hartford**	**NHL**	**44**	**6**	**5**	**11**	**18**	**0**	**0**	**1**	**51**	**11.8**	**3**													
	Springfield	AHL	23	5	20	25	18																			
1997-98	**Carolina**	**NHL**	**77**	**4**	**4**	**8**	**31**	**0**	**0**	**0**	**80**	**5.0**	**-6**													
1998-99	**Carolina**	**NHL**	**81**	**5**	**11**	**16**	**38**	**0**	**0**	**0**	**71**	**7.0**	**9**	**609**	**46.3**	**140**	**28**	**8:07**	**6**	**0**	**0**	**0**	**2**	**0**	**0**	**0**
99-2000	**Carolina**	**NHL**	**56**	**1**	**4**	**5**	**12**	**0**	**0**	**1**	**45**	**2.2**	**-8**	**399**	**47.1**	**96**	**26**	**8:15**								
	Philadelphia	**NHL**	**13**	**0**	**3**	**3**	**4**	**0**	**0**	**0**	**17**	**0.0**	**2**	**148**	**54.1**	**21**	**2**	**11:56**	**18**	**0**	**1**	**1**	**22**	**0**	**0**	**0**
2000-01	**Philadelphia**	**NHL**	**82**	**5**	**10**	**15**	**47**	**0**	**3**	**2**	**136**	**3.7**	**-2**	**813**	**47.9**	**108**	**42**	**12:38**	**6**	**1**	**2**	**3**	**2**	**0**	**0**	**0**
	NHL Totals		**526**	**32**	**57**	**89**	**290**	**0**	**5**	**6**	**616**	**5.2**		**1969**	**47.7**	**365**	**98**	**9:57**	**67**	**3**	**3**	**6**	**44**	**0**	**1**	**0**

Traded to **Toronto** by **Calgary** with Doug Gilmour, Jamie Macoun, Rick Wamsley and Ric Nattress for Gary Leeman, Alexander Godynyuk, Jeff Reese, Michel Petit and Craig Berube, January 2, 1992. Traded to **Edmonton** by **Toronto** for Peter White and Edmonton's 4th round choice (Jason Sessa) in 1996 Entry Draft, December 4, 1995. Signed as a free agent by **Hartford**, October 2, 1996. Transferred to **Carolina** after **Hartford** franchise relocated, June 25, 1997. Traded to **Philadelphia** by **Carolina** for Sandy McCarthy, March 14, 2000.

MANELUK, Mike

(MAN-uh-luhk, MIGHK)

Left wing. Shoots right. 5'11", 190 lbs. Born, Winnipeg, Man., October 1, 1973.

Season	Club	League	GP	G	A	Pts	PIM	PP	SH	GW	S	%	+/-	TF	F%	H	SB	Min	GP	G	A	Pts	PIM	PP	SH	GW
1989-90	Winnipeg Hawks	MMHL	40	49	38	87	92																			
1990-91	St. Boniface	MJHL	45	29	41	70	199																			
1991-92	Brandon	WHL	68	23	30	53	102																			
1992-93	Brandon	WHL	72	36	51	87	75												4	2	1	3	2			
1993-94	Brandon	WHL	63	50	47	97	112												13	11	3	14	23			
	San Diego Gulls	IHL																	1	0	0	0	0			
1994-95	Canada	Nat-Team	44	36	24	60	34																			
	San Diego Gulls	IHL	10	0	1	1	4																			
1995-96	Baltimore Bandits	AHL	74	33	38	71	73												6	4	3	7	14			
1996-97	Worcester	AHL	70	27	27	54	89												5	1	2	3	14			
1997-98	Worcester	AHL	5	3	3	6	4																			
	Philadelphia	AHL	66	27	35	62	62												20	*13	*21	*34	30			
1998-99	**Philadelphia**	**NHL**	**13**	**2**	**6**	**8**	**8**	**0**	**0**	**0**	**23**	**8.7**	**4**	**0**	**0.0**	**8**	**1**	**14:02**								
	Chicago	**NHL**	**28**	**4**	**3**	**7**	**8**	**1**	**0**	**0**	**3**	**13.8**	**2**	**0**	**0.0**	**19**	**7**	**11:28**								
	NY Rangers	**NHL**	**4**	**0**	**0**	**0**	**4**	**0**	**0**	**0**	**3**	**0.0**	**-1**	**0**	**0.0**	**3**	**0**	**7:18**								
99-2000	**Philadelphia**	**NHL**	**1**	**0**	**0**	**0**	**4**	**0**	**0**	**0**	**2**	**0.0**	**0**	**0**	**0.0**	**0**	**0**	**7:34**								
	Philadelphia	AHL	73	*47	40	87	158												4	1	2	3	4			
2000-01	**Columbus**	**NHL**	**39**	**5**	**1**	**6**	**33**	**2**	**0**	**2**	**31**	**16.1**	**-11**	**10**	**60.0**	**29**	**8**	**11:45**								
	Chicago Wolves	IHL	10	2	2	4	11																			
	NHL Totals		**85**	**11**	**10**	**21**	**57**	**3**	**0**	**2**	**62**	**17.7**		**10**	**60.0**	**59**	**16**	**10:18**								

Won Jack A. Butterfield Trophy (Playoff MVP - AHL) (1998) • AHL First All-Star Team (2000)

Signed as a free agent by **Anaheim**, January 28, 1994. Traded to **Ottawa** by **Anaheim** for Kevin Brown, July 1, 1996. Traded to **Philadelphia** by **Ottawa** for future considerations, October 21, 1997. Traded to **Chicago** by **Philadelphia** for Roman Vopat, November 17, 1998. Claimed on waivers by **NY Rangers** from **Chicago**, March 4, 1999. Signed as a free agent by **Philadelphia**, August 2, 1999. Signed as a free agent by **Columbus**, August 24, 2000. Signed as a free agent by **HC Bern** (Switz), July 7, 2001.

MANLOW, Eric

(MAN-low, AIR-ihk) **BOS.**

Center. Shoots left. 6', 190 lbs. Born, Belleville, Ont., April 7, 1975. Chicago's 2nd choice, 50th overall, in 1993 Entry Draft.

Season	Club	League	GP	G	A	Pts	PIM	PP	SH	GW	S	%	+/-	TF	F%	H	SB	Min	GP	G	A	Pts	PIM	PP	SH	GW
1990-91	Peterborough	OMHA	59	67	51	118	90																			
	Peterborough	OJHL-B	1	0	0	0	0																			
1991-92	Kitchener	OHL	59	12	20	32	17												14	2	5	7	10			
1992-93	Kitchener	OHL	53	26	21	47	31												4	0	1	1	2			
1993-94	Kitchener	OHL	49	28	32	60	25												3	0	1	1	4			
1994-95	Kitchener	OHL	44	25	29	54	26																			
	Detroit Whalers	OHL	16	4	16	20	11												21	11	10	21	18			
1995-96	Indianapolis Ice	IHL	75	6	11	17	32												4	0	1	1	4			
1996-97	Baltimore Bandits	AHL	36	6	6	12	13												3	0	0	0	0			
	Columbus Chill	ECHL	32	18	18	36	20																			
1997-98	Indianapolis Ice	IHL	60	8	11	19	25												3	1	0	1	0			
1998-99	Florida Everblades	ECHL	18	8	15	23	11																			
	Long Beach	IHL	51	9	19	28	30												8	0	0	0	8			
99-2000	Florida Everblades	ECHL	26	14	24	38	24																			
	Providence Bruins	AHL	46	17	16	33	14												14	6	8	14	8			
2000-01	**Boston**	**NHL**	**8**	**0**	**1**	**1**	**2**	**0**	**0**	**0**	**3**	**0.0**	**0**	**61**	**50.8**	**3**	**1**	**7:26**								
	Providence Bruins	AHL	60	16	51	67	18												17	6	7	13	6			
	NHL Totals		**8**	**0**	**1**	**1**	**2**	**0**	**0**	**0**	**3**	**0.0**		**61**	**50.8**	**3**	**1**	**7:26**								

Signed as a free agent by **Providence** (AHL), January 24, 2000. Signed as a free agent by **Boston**, July 11, 2000.

MANN, Cameron

(MAN, CAM-uhr-ROHN) **DAL.**

Right wing. Shoots right. 6', 195 lbs. Born, Thompson, Man., April 20, 1977. Boston's 5th choice, 99th overall, in 1995 Entry Draft.

Season	Club	League	GP	G	A	Pts	PIM	PP	SH	GW	S	%	+/-	TF	F%	H	SB	Min	GP	G	A	Pts	PIM	PP	SH	GW
1992-93	Kenora Thistles	NOJHA	35	23	24	47	49																			
1993-94	Peterborough	OPJHL	16	3	14	17	23																			
	Peterborough	OHL	49	8	17	25	18												7	1	1	2	2			
1994-95	Peterborough	OHL	64	19	24	43	40												11	3	8	11	4			
1995-96	Peterborough	OHL	66	42	60	102	108												24	*27	16	*43	33			
1996-97	Peterborough	OHL	51	33	50	83	91												11	10	18	28	16			

			Regular Season																Playoffs							
Season	Club	League	GP	G	A	Pts	PIM	PP	SH	GW	S	%	+/-	TF	F%	H	SB	Min	GP	G	A	Pts	PIM	PP	SH	GW
1997-98	Boston	NHL	9	0	1	1	4	0	0	0	6	0.0	1													
	Providence Bruins	AHL	71	21	26	47	99																			
1998-99	Boston	NHL	33	5	2	7	17	1	0	1	42	11.9	0	22	36.4	28	4	10:40	1	0	0	0	0	0	0	0
	Providence Bruins	AHL	43	21	25	46	65												11	7	7	14	4			
99-2000	Boston	NHL	32	8	4	12	13	1	0	0	48	16.7	-6	16	25.0	28	2	12:50								
	Providence Bruins	AHL	29	7	12	19	45												11	6	7	13	0			
2000-01	Boston	NHL	15	1	3	4	6	0	0	0	17	5.9	0	1	0.0	11	0	8:29								
	Providence Bruins	AHL	39	24	23	47	59																			
	NHL Totals		89	14	10	24	40	2	0	1	113	12.4		39	30.8	67	6	11:08	1	0	0	0	0	0	0	0

OHL First All-Star Team (1996, 1997) • Memorial Cup All-Star Team (1996) • Won Stafford Smythe Memorial Trophy (Memorial Cup Tournament MVP) (1996)

Traded to **Dallas** by **Boston** for Richard Jackman, June 23, 2001.

MANSON, Dave (MAN-suhn, DAIV) TOR.

Defense. Shoots left. 6'2", 200 lbs. Born, Prince Albert, Sask., January 27, 1967. Chicago's 1st choice, 11th overall, in 1985 Entry Draft.

Season	Club	League	GP	G	A	Pts	PIM	PP	SH	GW	S	%	+/-	TF	F%	H	SB	Min	GP	G	A	Pts	PIM	PP	SH	GW
1982-83	Prince Albert	SMHL	28	11	11	22	170																			
	Prince Albert	WHL	6	0	1	1	9																			
1983-84	Prince Albert	WHL	70	2	7	9	233												5	0	0	0	4			
1984-85	Prince Albert	WHL	72	8	30	38	247												13	1	0	1	34			
1985-86	Prince Albert	WHL	70	14	34	48	177												20	1	8	9	63			
1986-87	Chicago	NHL	63	1	8	9	146	0	0	0	42	2.4	-2						3	0	0	0	10	0	0	0
1987-88	Chicago	NHL	54	1	6	7	185	0	0	0	47	2.1	-12						5	0	0	0	27	0	0	0
	Saginaw Hawks	IHL	6	0	3	3	37																			
1988-89	Chicago	NHL	79	18	36	54	352	8	1	0	224	8.0	5						16	0	8	8	84	0	0	0
1989-90	Chicago	NHL	59	5	23	28	301	1	0	1	126	4.0	4						20	2	4	6	46	1	0	0
1990-91	Chicago	NHL	75	14	15	29	191	6	1	2	154	9.1	20						6	0	1	1	36	0	0	0
1991-92	Edmonton	NHL	79	15	32	47	220	7	0	2	206	7.3	9						16	3	9	12	44	1	0	0
1992-93	Edmonton	NHL	83	15	30	45	210	9	1	1	244	6.1	-28													
1993-94	Edmonton	NHL	57	3	13	16	140	0	0	0	144	2.1	-4													
	Winnipeg	NHL	13	1	4	5	51	1	0	0	36	2.8	-10													
1994-95	Winnipeg	NHL	44	3	15	18	139	2	0	1	104	2.9	-20													
1995-96	Winnipeg	NHL	82	7	23	30	205	3	0	0	189	3.7	8						6	2	1	3	30	0	0	1
1996-97	Phoenix	NHL	66	3	17	20	164	2	0	0	153	2.0	-25													
	Montreal	NHL	9	1	1	2	23	0	0	0	22	4.5	-1						5	0	0	0	17	0	0	0
1997-98	Montreal	NHL	81	4	30	34	122	2	0	0	148	2.7	22						10	0	1	1	14	0	0	0
1998-99	Montreal	NHL	11	0	2	2	48	0	0	0	11	0.0	-3	0	0.0	14	8	17:19								
	Chicago	NHL	64	6	15	21	107	2	0	0	134	4.5	4	0	0.0	127	51	22:37								
99-2000	Chicago	NHL	37	0	7	7	40	0	0	0	45	0.0	2	0	0.0	46	27	17:29								
	Dallas	NHL	26	1	2	3	22	0	0	0	21	4.8	10	0	0.0	34	6	13:16	23	0	0	0	33	0	0	0
2000-01	Toronto	NHL	74	4	7	11	93	0	0	0	70	5.7	13	0	0.0	124	61	15:48	2	0	0	0	2	0	0	0
	NHL Totals		1056	102	286	388	2759	43	3	7	2120	4.8		0	0.0	345	153	17:55	112	7	24	31	343	2	0	1

WHL East Second All-Star Team (1986) • Played in NHL All-Star Game (1989, 1993)

Traded to **Edmonton** by **Chicago** with Chicago's 3rd round choice (Kirk Maltby) in 1992 Entry Draft for Steve Smith, October 2, 1991. Traded to **Winnipeg** by **Edmonton** with St. Louis' 6th round choice (previously acquired, Winnipeg selected Chris Kibermanis) in 1994 Entry Draft for Boris Mironov, Mats Lindgren, Winnipeg's 1st round choice (Jason Bonsignore) in 1994 Entry Draft and Florida's 4th round choice (previously acquired, Edmonton selected Adam Copeland) in 1994 Entry Draft, March 15, 1994. Transferred to **Phoenix** after **Winnipeg** franchise relocated, July 1, 1996. Traded to **Montreal** by **Phoenix** for Murray Baron and Chris Murray, March 18, 1997. Traded to **Chicago** by **Montreal** with Jocelyn Thibault and Brad Brown for Jeff Hackett, Eric Weinrich, Alain Nasreddine and Tampa Bay's 4th round choice (previously acquired, Montreal selected Chris Dyment) in 1999 Entry Draft, November 16, 1998. Traded to **Dallas** by **Chicago** with Sylvain Cote for Kevin Dean, Derek Plante and Dallas' 2nd round choice (Matt Keith) in 2001 Entry Draft, February 8, 2000. Signed as a free agent by **Toronto**, August 16, 2000.

MARA, Paul (MAIR-uh, PAWL) PHX.

Defense. Shoots left. 6'4", 210 lbs. Born, Ridgewood, NJ, September 7, 1979. Tampa Bay's 1st choice, 7th overall, in 1997 Entry Draft.

Season	Club	League	GP	G	A	Pts	PIM	PP	SH	GW	S	%	+/-	TF	F%	H	SB	Min	GP	G	A	Pts	PIM	PP	SH	GW
1994-95	Belmont Hill	Hi-School	28	5	17	22	28																			
1995-96	Belmont Hill	Hi-School	28	18	20	38	40																			
1996-97	Sudbury Wolves	OHL	44	9	34	43	61																			
1997-98	Sudbury Wolves	OHL	25	8	18	26	79																			
	Plymouth Whalers	OHL	25	8	15	23	30												15	3	14	17	30			
1998-99	Plymouth Whalers	OHL	52	13	41	54	95												11	5	7	12	28			
	Tampa Bay	NHL	1	1	1	2	0	1	0	0	1	100.0	-3	0	0.0	1	3	19:34								
99-2000	Tampa Bay	NHL	54	7	11	18	73	4	0	1	78	9.0	-27	0	0.0	62	49	22:13								
	Detroit Vipers	IHL	15	3	5	8	22																			
2000-01	Tampa Bay	NHL	46	6	10	16	40	2	0	1	58	10.3	-17	0	0.0	45	56	23:06								
	Detroit Vipers	IHL	10	3	3	6	22																			
	Phoenix	NHL	16	0	4	4	14	0	0	0	20	0.0	1	0	0.0	17	10	19:22								
	NHL Totals		117	14	26	40	127	7	0	2	157	8.9		0	0.0	125	118	22:09								

Traded to **Phoenix** by **Tampa Bay** with Mike Johnson, Ruslan Zainullin and NY Islanders' 2nd round choice (previously acquired, Phoenix selected Matthew Spiller) in 2001 Entry Draft for Nikolai Khabibulin and Stan Neckar, March 5, 2001.

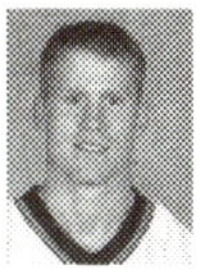

MARCHANT, Todd (mahr-SHAHNT, TAWD) EDM.

Center. Shoots left. 5'10", 178 lbs. Born, Buffalo, NY, August 12, 1973. NY Rangers' 8th choice, 164th overall, in 1993 Entry Draft.

Season	Club	League	GP	G	A	Pts	PIM	PP	SH	GW	S	%	+/-	TF	F%	H	SB	Min	GP	G	A	Pts	PIM	PP	SH	GW
1990-91	Niagara Scenics	NAJHL	37	31	47	78																				
1991-92	Clarkson Knights	ECAC	32	20	12	32	32																			
1992-93	Clarkson Knights	ECAC	33	18	28	46	38																			
1993-94	United States	Nat-Team	59	28	39	67	48																			
	United States	Olympics	8	1	1	2	6																			
	NY Rangers	NHL	1	0	0	0	0	0	0	0	1	0.0	-1													
	Binghamton	AHL	8	2	7	9	6																			
	Edmonton	NHL	3	0	1	1	2	0	0	0	5	0.0	-1													
	Cape Breton	AHL	3	1	4	5	2												5	1	1	2	0			
1994-95	Cape Breton	AHL	38	22	25	47	25																			
	Edmonton	NHL	45	13	14	27	32	3	2	2	95	13.7	-3													
1995-96	Edmonton	NHL	81	19	19	38	66	2	3	2	221	8.6	-19													
1996-97	Edmonton	NHL	79	14	19	33	44	0	4	3	202	6.9	11						12	4	2	6	12	0	3	1
1997-98	Edmonton	NHL	76	14	21	35	71	2	1	3	194	7.2	9						12	1	1	2	10	0	0	0
1998-99	Edmonton	NHL	82	14	22	36	65	3	1	2	183	7.7	3	1449	50.0	133	57	16:47	4	1	1	2	12	0	0	0
99-2000	Edmonton	NHL	82	17	23	40	70	0	1	0	170	10.0	7	1593	52.9	97	58	17:08	3	1	0	1	2	0	0	0
2000-01	Edmonton	NHL	71	13	26	39	51	0	4	2	113	11.5	1	1549	53.8	85	73	17:54	6	0	0	0	4	0	0	0
	NHL Totals		520	104	145	249	401	10	16	14	1184	8.8		4591	52.3	310	188	17:15	37	7	4	11	40	0	3	1

ECAC Second All-Star Team (1993)

Traded to **Edmonton** by **NY Rangers** for Craig MacTavish, March 21, 1994.

MARCHMENT, Bryan (MAHRCH-mehnt, BRIGH-uhn) S.J.

Defense. Shoots left. 6'1", 200 lbs. Born, Scarborough, Ont., May 1, 1969. Winnipeg's 1st choice, 16th overall, in 1987 Entry Draft.

Season	Club	League	GP	G	A	Pts	PIM	PP	SH	GW	S	%	+/-	TF	F%	H	SB	Min	GP	G	A	Pts	PIM	PP	SH	GW
1984-85	Toronto Nats	MTHL	69	14	35	49	229																			
1985-86	Belleville Bulls	OHL	57	5	15	20	225												21	0	7	7	83			
1986-87	Belleville Bulls	OHL	52	6	38	44	238												6	0	4	4	17			
1987-88	Belleville Bulls	OHL	56	7	51	58	200												6	1	3	4	19			
1988-89	Belleville Bulls	OHL	43	14	36	50	118												5	0	1	1	12			
	Winnipeg	NHL	2	0	0	0	2	0	0	0	1	0.0	0													
1989-90	Winnipeg	NHL	7	0	2	2	28	0	0	0	5	0.0	0													
	Moncton Hawks	AHL	56	4	19	23	217																			
1990-91	Winnipeg	NHL	28	2	2	4	91	0	0	0	24	8.3	-5													
	Moncton Hawks	AHL	33	2	11	13	101																			
1991-92	Chicago	NHL	58	5	10	15	168	2	0	0	55	9.1	-4						16	1	0	1	36	0	0	0
1992-93	Chicago	NHL	78	5	15	20	313	1	0	1	75	6.7	15						4	0	0	0	12	0	0	0
1993-94	Chicago	NHL	13	1	4	5	42	0	0	0	18	5.6	-2													
	Hartford	NHL	42	3	7	10	124	0	1	1	74	4.1	-12													
1994-95	Edmonton	NHL	40	1	5	6	184	0	0	0	57	1.8	-11													

Season	Club	League	GP	G	A	Pts	PIM	PP	SH	GW	S	%	+/-	TF	F%	H	SB	Min	GP	G	A	Pts	PIM	PP	SH	GW
			Regular Season																Playoffs							
1995-96	**Edmonton**	**NHL**	**78**	**3**	**15**	**18**	**202**	**0**	**0**	**0**	**96**	**3.1**	**-7**	....	....	....	....	....	....	....	....	....	....	....	....	....
1996-97	**Edmonton**	**NHL**	**71**	**3**	**13**	**16**	**132**	**1**	**0**	**0**	**89**	**3.4**	**13**	....	....	....	....	....	**3**	**0**	**0**	**0**	**4**	**0**	**0**	**0**
1997-98	**Edmonton**	**NHL**	**27**	**0**	**4**	**4**	**58**	**0**	**0**	**0**	**23**	**0.0**	**-2**	....	....	....	....	....	....	....	....	....	....	....	....	....
	Tampa Bay	**NHL**	**22**	**2**	**4**	**6**	**43**	**0**	**0**	**0**	**20**	**10.0**	**-3**	....	....	....	....	....	....	....	....	....	....	....	....	....
	San Jose	**NHL**	**12**	**0**	**3**	**3**	**43**	**0**	**0**	**0**	**13**	**0.0**	**2**	....	....	....	....	....	**6**	**0**	**0**	**0**	**10**	**0**	**0**	**0**
1998-99	**San Jose**	**NHL**	**59**	**2**	**6**	**8**	**101**	**0**	**0**	**0**	**49**	**4.1**	**-7**	**0**	**0.0**	**108**	**64**	**17:43**	**6**	**0**	**0**	**0**	**4**	**0**	**0**	**0**
99-2000	**San Jose**	**NHL**	**49**	**0**	**4**	**4**	**72**	**0**	**0**	**0**	**51**	**0.0**	**3**	**0**	**0.0**	**127**	**51**	**18:55**	**11**	**2**	**1**	**3**	**12**	**0**	**0**	**0**
2000-01	**San Jose**	**NHL**	**75**	**7**	**11**	**18**	**204**	**0**	**1**	**3**	**73**	**9.6**	**15**	**1**	**100.0**	**229**	**90**	**18:12**	**5**	**0**	**1**	**1**	**2**	**0**	**0**	**0**
	NHL Totals		**661**	**34**	**105**	**139**	**1807**	**4**	**2**	**5**	**723**	**4.7**		**1**	**100.0**	**464**	**205**	**18:14**	**51**	**3**	**2**	**5**	**80**	**0**	**0**	**0**

OHL Second All-Star Team (1989)

Traded to **Chicago** by **Winnipeg** with Chris Norton for Troy Murray and Warren Rychel, July 22, 1991. Traded to **Hartford** by **Chicago** with Steve Larmer for Eric Weinrich and Patrick Poulin, November 2, 1993. Transferred to **Edmonton** from **Hartford** as compensation for Hartford's signing of free agent Steven Rice, August 30, 1994. Traded to **Tampa Bay** by **Edmonton** with Steve Kelly and Jason Bonsignore for Roman Hamrlik and Paul Comrie, December 30, 1997. Traded to **San Jose** by **Tampa Bay** with David Shaw and Tampa Bay's 1st round choice (later traded to Nashville - Nashville selected David Legwand) in 1998 Entry Draft for Andrei Nazarov and Florida's 1st round choice (previously acquired, Tampa Bay selected Vincent Lecavallier) in 1998 Entry Draft, March 24, 1998.

MARHA, Josef

(MAHR-hah, JOH-sehf) **CHI.**

Center. Shoots left. 6', 176 lbs. Born, Havlickuv, Czech., June 2, 1976. Quebec's 3rd choice, 35th overall, in 1994 Entry Draft.

Season	Club	League	GP	G	A	Pts	PIM	PP	SH	GW	S	%	+/-	TF	F%	H	SB	Min	GP	G	A	Pts	PIM	PP	SH	GW
1991-92	Dukla Jihlava	Czech-Jr.	25	12	13	25	0	....	....	....	....	....	....	....	....	....	....	....	....	....	....	....	....	....	....	....
1992-93	Dukla Jihlava	Czech.	7	2	2	4	....	....	....	....	....	....	....	....	....	....	....	....	....	....	....	....	....	....	....	....
1993-94	Dukla Jihlava	Cze-Rep	41	7	2	9	....	....	....	....	....	....	....	....	....	....	....	....	3	0	1	1	....	....	....	....
1994-95	Dukla Jihlava	Cze-Rep	35	3	7	10	6	....	....	....	....	....	....	....	....	....	....	....	....	....	....	....	....	....	....	....
1995-96	**Colorado**	**NHL**	**2**	**0**	**1**	**1**	**0**	**0**	**0**	**0**	**2**	**0.0**	**1**	....	....	....	....	....	....	....	....	....	....	....	....	....
	Cornwall Aces	AHL	74	18	30	48	30	....	....	....	....	....	....	....	....	....	....	....	8	1	2	3	10	....	....	....
1996-97	**Colorado**	**NHL**	**6**	**0**	**1**	**1**	**0**	**0**	**0**	**0**	**6**	**0.0**	**0**	....	....	....	....	....	....	....	....	....	....	....	....	....
	Hershey Bears	AHL	67	23	49	72	44	....	....	....	....	....	....	....	....	....	....	....	19	6	*16	*22	10	....	....	....
1997-98	**Colorado**	**NHL**	**11**	**2**	**5**	**7**	**4**	**0**	**0**	**0**	**10**	**20.0**	**0**	....	....	....	....	....	....	....	....	....	....	....	....	....
	Hershey Bears	AHL	55	6	46	52	30	....	....	....	....	....	....	....	....	....	....	....	....	....	....	....	....	....	....	....
	Anaheim	**NHL**	**12**	**7**	**4**	**11**	**0**	**3**	**0**	**0**	**21**	**33.3**	**4**	....	....	....	....	....	....	....	....	....	....	....	....	....
1998-99	**Anaheim**	**NHL**	**10**	**0**	**1**	**1**	**0**	**0**	**0**	**0**	**13**	**0.0**	**-4**	**107**	**40.2**	**3**	**1**	**12:02**	....	....	....	....	....	....	....	....
	Cincinnati Ducks	AHL	3	1	0	1	4	....	....	....	....	....	....	....	....	....	....	....	....	....	....	....	....	....	....	....
	Chicago	**NHL**	**22**	**2**	**5**	**7**	**4**	**1**	**0**	**1**	**32**	**6.3**	**5**	**275**	**50.9**	**6**	**10**	**14:37**	....	....	....	....	....	....	....	....
	Portland Pirates	AHL	8	0	8	8	2	....	....	....	....	....	....	....	....	....	....	....	....	....	....	....	....	....	....	....
99-2000	**Chicago**	**NHL**	**81**	**10**	**12**	**22**	**18**	**2**	**1**	**3**	**91**	**11.0**	**-10**	**1110**	**46.3**	**26**	**31**	**13:20**	....	....	....	....	....	....	....	....
2000-01	**Chicago**	**NHL**	**15**	**0**	**3**	**3**	**6**	**0**	**0**	**0**	**17**	**0.0**	**-4**	**196**	**50.0**	**2**	**3**	**12:46**	....	....	....	....	....	....	....	....
	Norfolk Admirals	AHL	60	18	28	46	44	....	....	....	....	....	....	....	....	....	....	....	9	1	8	9	6	....	....	....
	NHL Totals		**159**	**21**	**32**	**53**	**32**	**6**	**1**	**4**	**192**	**10.9**		**1688**	**47.1**	**37**	**45**	**13:23**	....	....	....	....	....	....	....	....

Rights transferred to **Colorado** after **Quebec** franchise relocated, June 21, 1995. Traded to **Anaheim** by **Colorado** for Warren Rychel and Anaheim's 4th round choice (Sanny Lindstrom) in 1999 Entry Draft, March 24, 1998. Traded to **Chicago** by **Anaheim** for Chicago's 4th round choice (Alexandr Chagodayev) in 1999 Entry Draft, January 28, 1999. Signed as a free agent by **HC Davos** (Switz) with **Chicago** retaining NHL rights, June 13, 2001.

MARKOV, Andrei

(MAHR-kahf, AHN-dray) **MTL.**

Defense. Shoots left. 6', 203 lbs. Born, Voskresensk, USSR, December 20, 1978. Montreal's 6th choice, 162nd overall, in 1998 Entry Draft.

Season	Club	League	GP	G	A	Pts	PIM	PP	SH	GW	S	%	+/-	TF	F%	H	SB	Min	GP	G	A	Pts	PIM	PP	SH	GW
1995-96	HK Khimik	CIS	38	0	0	0	14	....	....	....	....	....	....	....	....	....	....	....	....	....	....	....	....	....	....	....
1996-97	HK Khimik	Russia	43	8	4	12	32	....	....	....	....	....	....	....	....	....	....	....	2	1	1	2	0	....	....	....
1997-98	HK Khimik	Russia	43	10	5	15	83	....	....	....	....	....	....	....	....	....	....	....	....	....	....	....	....	....	....	....
1998-99	Dynamo Moscow	Russia	38	10	11	21	32	....	....	....	....	....	....	....	....	....	....	....	16	3	6	9	6	....	....	....
	Dynamo Moscow	EuroHL	12	7	5	12	12	....	....	....	....	....	....	....	....	....	....	....	6	2	2	4	4	....	....	....
99-2000	Dynamo Moscow	Russia	29	11	12	23	28	....	....	....	....	....	....	....	....	....	....	....	17	4	3	7	8	....	....	....
2000-01	**Montreal**	**NHL**	**63**	**6**	**17**	**23**	**18**	**2**	**0**	**0**	**82**	**7.3**	**-6**	**2**	**50.0**	**38**	**55**	**16:53**	....	....	....	....	....	....	....	....
	Quebec Citadelles	AHL	14	0	5	5	4	....	....	....	....	....	....	....	....	....	....	....	7	1	1	2	2	....	....	....
	NHL Totals		**63**	**6**	**17**	**23**	**18**	**2**	**0**	**0**	**82**	**7.3**		**2**	**50.0**	**38**	**55**	**16:53**	....	....	....	....	....	....	....	....

MARKOV, Danny

(MAHR-kahf, DA-nee) **PHX.**

Defense. Shoots left. 6'1", 190 lbs. Born, Moscow, USSR, July 11, 1976. Toronto's 7th choice, 223rd overall, in 1995 Entry Draft.

Season	Club	League	GP	G	A	Pts	PIM	PP	SH	GW	S	%	+/-	TF	F%	H	SB	Min	GP	G	A	Pts	PIM	PP	SH	GW
1993-94	Krylja Sovetov	CIS	13	1	0	1	6	....	....	....	....	....	....	....	....	....	....	....	1	0	0	0	0	....	....	....
1994-95	Krylja Sovetov	CIS	39	0	1	1	36	....	....	....	....	....	....	....	....	....	....	....	....	....	....	....	....	....	....	....
1995-96	Krylja Sovetov	CIS	38	2	0	2	12	....	....	....	....	....	....	....	....	....	....	....	2	0	0	0	2	....	....	....
1996-97	Krylja Sovetov	Russia	39	3	6	9	41	....	....	....	....	....	....	....	....	....	....	....	....	....	....	....	....	....	....	....
	St. John's Leafs	AHL	10	2	4	6	18	....	....	....	....	....	....	....	....	....	....	....	11	2	6	8	14	....	....	....
1997-98	**Toronto**	**NHL**	**25**	**2**	**5**	**7**	**28**	**1**	**0**	**0**	**15**	**13.3**	**0**	....	....	....	....	....	....	....	....	....	....	....	....	....
	St. John's Leafs	AHL	52	3	23	26	124	....	....	....	....	....	....	....	....	....	....	....	2	0	1	1	0	....	....	....
1998-99	**Toronto**	**NHL**	**57**	**4**	**8**	**12**	**47**	**0**	**0**	**0**	**34**	**11.8**	**5**	**0**	**0.0**	**92**	**66**	**18:41**	**17**	**0**	**6**	**6**	**18**	**0**	**0**	**0**
99-2000	**Toronto**	**NHL**	**59**	**0**	**10**	**10**	**28**	**0**	**0**	**0**	**38**	**0.0**	**13**	**1**	**0.0**	**97**	**100**	**20:08**	**12**	**0**	**3**	**3**	**10**	**0**	**0**	**0**
2000-01	**Toronto**	**NHL**	**59**	**3**	**13**	**16**	**34**	**1**	**0**	**2**	**49**	**6.1**	**6**	**0**	**0.0**	**123**	**73**	**19:02**	**11**	**1**	**1**	**2**	**12**	**0**	**0**	**0**
	NHL Totals		**200**	**9**	**36**	**45**	**137**	**2**	**0**	**2**	**136**	**6.6**		**1**	**0.0**	**312**	**239**	**19:17**	**40**	**1**	**10**	**11**	**40**	**0**	**0**	**0**

Traded to **Phoenix** by **Toronto** for Robert Reichel, Travis Green and Craig Mills, June 12, 2001.

MARLEAU, Patrick

(mahr-LOH, PAT-rihk) **S.J.**

Center. Shoots left. 6'2", 210 lbs. Born, Aneroid, Sask., September 15, 1979. San Jose's 1st choice, 2nd overall, in 1997 Entry Draft.

Season	Club	League	GP	G	A	Pts	PIM	PP	SH	GW	S	%	+/-	TF	F%	H	SB	Min	GP	G	A	Pts	PIM	PP	SH	GW
1993-94	Swift Current AA	SAHA	53	72	95	167		....	....	....	....	....	....	....	....	....	....	....	....	....	....	....	....	....	....	....
1994-95	Swift Current	SMHL	31	30	22	52	18	....	....	....	....	....	....	....	....	....	....	....	....	....	....	....	....	....	....	....
1995-96	Seattle T-Birds	WHL	72	32	42	74	22	....	....	....	....	....	....	....	....	....	....	....	5	3	4	7	4	....	....	....
1996-97	Seattle T-Birds	WHL	71	51	74	125	37	....	....	....	....	....	....	....	....	....	....	....	15	7	16	23	12	....	....	....
1997-98	**San Jose**	**NHL**	**74**	**13**	**19**	**32**	**14**	**1**	**0**	**2**	**90**	**14.4**	**5**	....	....	....	....	....	**5**	**0**	**1**	**1**	**0**	**0**	**0**	**0**
1998-99	**San Jose**	**NHL**	**81**	**21**	**24**	**45**	**24**	**4**	**0**	**4**	**134**	**15.7**	**10**	**1121**	**43.4**	**59**	**15**	**15:11**	**6**	**2**	**1**	**3**	**4**	**2**	**0**	**0**
99-2000	**San Jose**	**NHL**	**81**	**17**	**23**	**40**	**36**	**3**	**0**	**3**	**161**	**10.6**	**-9**	**851**	**42.0**	**74**	**13**	**14:11**	**5**	**1**	**1**	**2**	**2**	**1**	**0**	**0**
2000-01	**San Jose**	**NHL**	**81**	**25**	**27**	**52**	**22**	**5**	**0**	**6**	**146**	**17.1**	**7**	**1088**	**44.8**	**85**	**15**	**16:17**	**6**	**2**	**0**	**2**	**4**	**0**	**0**	**0**
	NHL Totals		**317**	**76**	**93**	**169**	**96**	**13**	**0**	**15**	**531**	**14.3**		**3060**	**43.5**	**218**	**43**	**15:13**	**22**	**5**	**3**	**8**	**10**	**3**	**0**	**0**

WHL West First All-Star Team (1997)

MARSHALL, Grant

(MAHR-shahl, GRANT) **DAL.**

Right wing. Shoots right. 6'1", 200 lbs. Born, Mississauga, Ont., June 9, 1973. Toronto's 2nd choice, 23rd overall, in 1992 Entry Draft.

Season	Club	League	GP	G	A	Pts	PIM	PP	SH	GW	S	%	+/-	TF	F%	H	SB	Min	GP	G	A	Pts	PIM	PP	SH	GW
1989-90	Toronto Nats	MTHL	39	15	28	43	56	....	....	....	....	....	....	....	....	....	....	....	....	....	....	....	....	....	....	....
1990-91	Ottawa 67's	OHL	26	6	11	17	25	....	....	....	....	....	....	....	....	....	....	....	1	0	0	0	0	....	....	....
1991-92	Ottawa 67's	OHL	61	32	51	83	132	....	....	....	....	....	....	....	....	....	....	....	11	6	11	17	11	....	....	....
1992-93	Ottawa 67's	OHL	30	14	29	43	83	....	....	....	....	....	....	....	....	....	....	....	....	....	....	....	....	....	....	....
	Newmarket	OHL	31	11	25	36	89	....	....	....	....	....	....	....	....	....	....	....	7	4	7	11	20	....	....	....
	St. John's Leafs	AHL	2	0	0	0	0	....	....	....	....	....	....	....	....	....	....	....	2	0	0	0	2	....	....	....
1993-94	St. John's Leafs	AHL	67	11	29	40	155	....	....	....	....	....	....	....	....	....	....	....	11	1	5	6	17	....	....	....
1994-95	Kalamazoo Wings	IHL	61	17	29	46	96	....	....	....	....	....	....	....	....	....	....	....	16	9	3	12	27	....	....	....
	Dallas	**NHL**	**2**	**0**	**1**	**1**	**0**	**0**	**0**	**0**	**0**	**0.0**	**1**	....	....	....	....	....	....	....	....	....	....	....	....	....
1995-96	**Dallas**	**NHL**	**70**	**9**	**19**	**28**	**111**	**0**	**0**	**0**	**62**	**14.5**	**0**	....	....	....	....	....	....	....	....	....	....	....	....	....
1996-97	**Dallas**	**NHL**	**56**	**6**	**4**	**10**	**98**	**0**	**0**	**0**	**0**	**0.0**	**5**	....	....	....	....	....	**5**	**0**	**2**	**2**	**8**	**0**	**0**	**0**
1997-98	**Dallas**	**NHL**	**72**	**9**	**10**	**19**	**96**	**3**	**0**	**1**	**91**	**9.9**	**-2**	....	....	....	....	....	**17**	**0**	**2**	**2**	***47**	**0**	**0**	**0**
1998-99♦	**Dallas**	**NHL**	**82**	**13**	**18**	**31**	**85**	**2**	**0**	**4**	**112**	**11.6**	**1**	**2**	**50.0**	**172**	**12**	**12:39**	**14**	**0**	**3**	**3**	**20**	**0**	**0**	**0**
99-2000	**Dallas**	**NHL**	**45**	**2**	**6**	**8**	**38**	**1**	**0**	**0**	**43**	**4.7**	**-5**	**3**	**0.0**	**111**	**6**	**11:19**	**14**	**0**	**1**	**1**	**4**	**0**	**0**	**0**
2000-01	**Dallas**	**NHL**	**75**	**13**	**24**	**37**	**64**	**4**	**0**	**1**	**93**	**14.0**	**1**	**16**	**56.3**	**186**	**13**	**11:05**	**9**	**0**	**0**	**0**	**0**	**0**	**0**	**0**
	NHL Totals		**402**	**52**	**82**	**134**	**492**	**10**	**0**	**6**	**401**	**13.0**		**21**	**47.6**	**469**	**31**	**11:46**	**59**	**0**	**8**	**8**	**79**	**0**	**0**	**0**

• Missed majority of 1990-91 season recovering from neck injury suffered in game vs. Sudbury (OHL), December 4, 1990. Transferred to **Dallas** from **Toronto** with Peter Zezel as compensation for Toronto's signing of free agent Mike Craig, August 10, 1994.

MARSHALL, Jason
(MAHR-shahl, JAY-suhn) **MIN.**

Defense. Shoots right. 6'2", 200 lbs. Born, Cranbrook, B.C., February 22, 1971. St. Louis' 1st choice, 9th overall, in 1989 Entry Draft.

			Regular Season																Playoffs							
Season	Club	League	GP	G	A	Pts	PIM	PP	SH	GW	S	%	+/-	TF	F%	H	SB	Min	GP	G	A	Pts	PIM	PP	SH	GW
1987-88	Columbia Valley	RMJHL	40	4	28	32	150																			
1988-89	Vernon Lakers	BCJHL	48	10	30	40	197												31	6	6	12	14			
1989-90	Canada	Nat-Team	73	1	11	12	57																			
1990-91	Tri-City Americans	WHL	59	10	34	44	236												7	1	2	3	20			
	Peoria Rivermen	IHL																	18	0	1	1	48			
1991-92	**St. Louis**	**NHL**	**2**	**1**	**0**	**1**	**4**	0	0	0	2	50.0	0													
	Peoria Rivermen	IHL	78	4	18	22	178												10	0	1	1	16			
1992-93	Peoria Rivermen	IHL	77	4	16	20	229												4	0	0	0	20			
1993-94	Canada	Nat-Team	41	3	10	13	60																			
	Peoria Rivermen	IHL	20	1	1	2	72												3	2	0	2	2			
1994-95	San Diego Gulls	IHL	80	7	18	25	218												5	0	1	1	8			
	Anaheim	**NHL**	**1**	**0**	**0**	**0**	**0**	0	0	0	1	0.0	-2													
1995-96	**Anaheim**	**NHL**	**24**	**0**	**1**	**1**	**42**	0	0	0	9	0.0	3													
	Baltimore Bandits	AHL	57	1	13	14	150																			
1996-97	**Anaheim**	**NHL**	**73**	**1**	**9**	**10**	**140**	0	0	0	34	2.9	6						7	0	1	1	4	0	0	0
1997-98	**Anaheim**	**NHL**	**72**	**3**	**6**	**9**	**189**	1	0	0	68	4.4	-8													
1998-99	**Anaheim**	**NHL**	**72**	**1**	**7**	**8**	**142**	0	0	0	63	1.6	-5	0	0.0	150	95	19:06	4	1	0	1	10	1	0	0
99-2000	**Anaheim**	**NHL**	**55**	**0**	**3**	**3**	**88**	0	0	0	41	0.0	-10	2	50.0	143	57	16:33								
2000-01	**Anaheim**	**NHL**	**50**	**3**	**4**	**7**	**105**	2	1	1	38	7.9	-12	1	0.0	122	39	14:36								
	Washington	**NHL**	**5**	**0**	**0**	**0**	**17**	0	0	0	5	0.0	-1	0	0.0	16	4	11:48								
	NHL Totals		**354**	**9**	**30**	**39**	**727**	3	1	1	261	3.4		3	33.3	431	195	16:54	11	1	1	2	14	1	0	0

Traded to **Anaheim** by **St. Louis** for Bill Houlder, August 29, 1994. Traded to **Washington** by **Anaheim** for Alexei Tezikov and Edmonton's 4th round choice (previously acquired, Anaheim selected Brandon Rogers) in 2001 Entry Draft, March 13, 2001. Signed as a free agent by **Minnesota**, July 2, 2001.

MARTINS, Steve
(MAHR-tihns, STEEV) **NYI**

Center. Shoots left. 5'9", 175 lbs. Born, Gatineau, Que., April 13, 1972. Hartford's 1st choice, 5th overall, in 1994 Supplemental Draft.

1988-89	L'Outaoais Elites	QAAA	38	18	33	51	70																			
1989-90	Choate-Rosemary	Hi-School	STATISTICS NOT AVAILABLE																							
1990-91	Choate-Rosemary	Hi-School	STATISTICS NOT AVAILABLE																							
1991-92	Harvard University	ECAC	20	13	14	27	26																			
1992-93	Harvard University	ECAC	18	6	8	14	40																			
1993-94	Harvard University	ECAC	32	25	35	60	*93																			
1994-95	Harvard University	ECAC	28	15	23	38	93																			
1995-96	**Hartford**	**NHL**	**23**	**1**	**3**	**4**	**8**	0	0	0	27	3.7	-3													
	Springfield	AHL	30	9	20	29	10																			
1996-97	**Hartford**	**NHL**	**2**	**0**	**1**	**1**	**0**	0	0	0	2	0.0	0													
	Springfield	AHL	63	12	31	43	78												17	1	3	4	26			
1997-98	**Carolina**	**NHL**	**3**	**0**	**0**	**0**	**0**	0	0	0	0	0.0	0													
	Chicago Wolves	IHL	78	20	41	61	122												21	6	14	20	28			
1998-99	**Ottawa**	**NHL**	**36**	**4**	**3**	**7**	**10**	1	0	1	27	14.8	4	191	56.0	23	2	8:28								
	Detroit Vipers	IHL	4	1	6	7	16																			
99-2000	**Ottawa**	**NHL**	**2**	**1**	**0**	**1**	**0**	0	0	0	3	33.3	-1	3	0.0	2	2	11:10								
	Tampa Bay	**NHL**	**57**	**5**	**7**	**12**	**37**	0	1	1	62	8.1	-11	806	50.9	56	36	13:27								
2000-01	**Tampa Bay**	**NHL**	**20**	**1**	**1**	**2**	**13**	0	0	0	18	5.6	-9	184	52.2	19	3	9:35								
	Detroit Vipers	IHL	8	5	4	9	4																			
	NY Islanders	**NHL**	**39**	**1**	**3**	**4**	**20**	0	1	0	28	3.6	-7	302	58.0	22	17	9:41								
	Chicago Wolves	IHL	5	1	2	3	0												16	1	6	7	22			
	NHL Totals		**182**	**13**	**18**	**31**	**88**	1	2	2	167	7.8		1486	53.0	122	60	10:48								

ECAC First All-Star Team (1994) • NCAA East First All-American Team (1994) • NCAA Final Four All-Tournament Team (1994)

Transferred to **Carolina** after **Hartford** franchise relocated, June 25, 1997. Signed as a free agent by **Ottawa**, July 20, 1998. Claimed on waivers by **Tampa Bay** from **Ottawa**, October 29, 1999. Traded to **NY Islanders** by **Tampa Bay** for a conditional choice in 2001 Entry Draft, January 3, 2001.

MATHIEU, Marquis
(MA-thew, MAHR-kihs)

Center. Shoots right. 5'11", 190 lbs. Born, Hartford, CT, May 31, 1973.

1990-91	Hawkesbury	OCJHL	20	6	8	14	62																			
	Beauport	QMJHL	26	4	13	17	73																			
1991-92	St-Jean Lynx	QMJHL	70	20	36	56	166																			
1992-93	St-Jean Lynx	QMJHL	61	31	36	67	115												2	1	0	1	33			
1993-94	Wheeling	ECHL	42	12	11	23	75												9	1	3	4	23			
	Fredericton	AHL	22	4	6	10	28																			
1994-95	Toledo Storm	ECHL	33	13	22	35	168																			
	Raleigh Icecaps	ECHL	33	15	17	32	181																			
	Worcester	AHL	2	0	0	0	0																			
1995-96	Johnstown Chiefs	ECHL	25	4	17	21	89																			
	Worcester	AHL	17	3	10	13	26																			
	Houston Aeros	IHL	2	1	0	1	9																			
	Birmingham Bulls	ECHL	18	5	7	12	87																			
1996-97	Worcester	AHL	30	8	16	24	88												1	0	0	0	0			
1997-98	Wheeling Nailers	ECHL	58	26	29	55	276												15	1	10	11	38			
1998-99	**Boston**	**NHL**	**9**	**0**	**0**	**0**	**8**	0	0	0	4	0.0	-1	84	63.1	9	1	7:20								
	Providence Bruins	AHL	64	15	15	30	166												19	4	7	11	30			
99-2000	**Boston**	**NHL**	**6**	**0**	**2**	**2**	**4**	0	0	0	3	0.0	-2	48	60.4	12	2	6:04								
	Providence Bruins	AHL	18	3	3	6	45																			
2000-01	**Boston**	**NHL**	**1**	**0**	**0**	**0**	**2**	0	0	0	0	0.0	0	9	44.4	3	1	7:04								
	Providence Bruins	AHL	57	10	7	17	205												17	3	2	5	64			
	NHL Totals		**16**	**0**	**2**	**2**	**14**	0	0	0	7	0.0		141	61.0	24	4	6:50								

Signed as a free agent by **Boston**, October 26, 1998. • Missed majority of 1999-2000 season recovering from hip surgery, June, 1999.

MATTE, Christian
(MA-tay, KRIH-stan) **BUF.**

Right wing. Shoots right. 6', 190 lbs. Born, Hull, Que., January 20, 1975. Quebec's 8th choice, 153rd overall, in 1993 Entry Draft.

1991-92	Abitibi Foresters	QAAA	42	18	27	45	30												4	1	0	1	0			
1992-93	Granby Bisons	QMJHL	68	17	36	53	59																			
1993-94	Granby Bisons	QMJHL	59	50	47	97	103												7	5	5	10	12			
	Cornwall Aces	AHL	1	0	0	0	0																			
1994-95	Granby Bisons	QMJHL	66	50	66	116	86												13	11	7	18	12			
	Cornwall Aces	AHL																	3	0	1	1	2			
1995-96	Cornwall Aces	AHL	64	20	32	52	51												7	1	1	2	6			
1996-97	**Colorado**	**NHL**	**5**	**1**	**1**	**2**	**0**	0	0	0	6	16.7	1													
	Hershey Bears	AHL	49	18	18	36	78												22	8	3	11	25			
1997-98	**Colorado**	**NHL**	**5**	**0**	**0**	**0**	**6**	0	0	0	5	0.0	0													
	Hershey Bears	AHL	71	33	40	73	109												7	3	2	5	4			
1998-99	**Colorado**	**NHL**	**7**	**1**	**1**	**2**	**0**	0	0	0	9	11.1	-2	13	30.8	4	1	7:45								
	Hershey Bears	AHL	60	31	47	78	48												5	2	1	3	8			
99-2000	**Colorado**	**NHL**	**5**	**0**	**1**	**1**	**4**	0	0	0	1	0.0	-2	2	0.0	6	1	8:37								
	Hershey Bears	AHL	73	43	*61	*104	85												14	8	6	14	10			
2000-01	**Minnesota**	**NHL**	**3**	**0**	**0**	**0**	**2**	0	0	0	8	0.0	0	0	0.0	2	0	13:21								
	Cleveland	IHL	58	*38	29	67	59												4	1	1	2	0			
	NHL Totals		**25**	**2**	**3**	**5**	**12**	0	0	0	29	6.9		15	26.7	12	2	9:09								

QMJHL Second All-Star Team (1994) • AHL First All-Star Team (2000) • Won John P. Sollenberger Trophy (Top Scorer - AHL) (2000)

Rights transferred to **Colorado** after **Quebec** franchise relocated, June 21, 1995. Signed as a free agent by **Minnesota**, July 11, 2000. Signed as a free agent by **Buffalo**, August 2, 2001.

MATTEAU, Stephane

(mah-TOH, STEH-fan) **S.J.**

Left wing. Shoots left. 6'4", 215 lbs. Born, Rouyn-Noranda, Que., September 2, 1969. Calgary's 2nd choice, 25th overall, in 1987 Entry Draft.

			Regular Season																Playoffs							
Season	Club	League	GP	G	A	Pts	PIM	PP	SH	GW	S	%	+/-	TF	F%	H	SB	Min	GP	G	A	Pts	PIM	PP	SH	GW
1985-86	Hull Olympiques	QMJHL	60	6	8	14	19												4	0	0	0	0			
1986-87	Hull Olympiques	QMJHL	69	27	48	75	113												8	3	7	10	8			
1987-88	Hull Olympiques	QMJHL	57	17	40	57	179												18	5	14	19	94			
1988-89	Hull Olympiques	QMJHL	59	44	45	89	202												9	8	6	14	30			
	Salt Lake City	IHL	....	....	....	....	....												9	0	4	4	13			
1989-90	Salt Lake City	IHL	81	23	35	58	130												10	6	3	9	38			
1990-91	**Calgary**	**NHL**	**78**	**15**	**19**	**34**	**93**	**0**	**1**	**1**	**114**	**13.2**	**17**						**5**	**0**	**1**	**1**	**0**	**0**	**0**	**0**
1991-92	**Calgary**	**NHL**	**4**	**1**	**0**	**1**	**19**	**0**	**0**	**0**	**7**	**14.3**	**2**													
	Chicago	**NHL**	**20**	**5**	**8**	**13**	**45**	**1**	**0**	**0**	**31**	**16.1**	**3**						**18**	**4**	**6**	**10**	**24**	**1**	**1**	**0**
1992-93	**Chicago**	**NHL**	**79**	**15**	**18**	**33**	**98**	**2**	**0**	**4**	**95**	**15.8**	**6**						**3**	**0**	**1**	**1**	**2**	**0**	**0**	**0**
1993-94	**Chicago**	**NHL**	**65**	**15**	**16**	**31**	**55**	**2**	**0**	**2**	**113**	**13.3**	**10**													
	♦ NY Rangers	**NHL**	**12**	**4**	**3**	**7**	**2**	**1**	**0**	**0**	**22**	**18.2**	**5**						**23**	**6**	**3**	**9**	**20**	**1**	**0**	**2**
1994-95	**NY Rangers**	**NHL**	**41**	**3**	**5**	**8**	**25**	**0**	**0**	**0**	**37**	**8.1**	**–8**						**9**	**0**	**1**	**1**	**10**	**0**	**0**	**0**
1995-96	**NY Rangers**	**NHL**	**32**	**4**	**2**	**6**	**22**	**1**	**0**	**0**	**39**	**10.3**	**–4**													
	St. Louis	**NHL**	**46**	**7**	**13**	**20**	**65**	**3**	**0**	**2**	**70**	**10.0**	**–4**						**11**	**0**	**2**	**2**	**8**	**0**	**0**	**0**
1996-97	**St. Louis**	**NHL**	**74**	**16**	**20**	**36**	**50**	**1**	**2**	**2**	**98**	**16.3**	**11**						**5**	**0**	**0**	**0**	**0**	**0**	**0**	**0**
1997-98	**San Jose**	**NHL**	**73**	**15**	**14**	**29**	**60**	**1**	**0**	**2**	**79**	**19.0**	**4**						**4**	**0**	**1**	**1**	**0**	**0**	**0**	**0**
1998-99	**San Jose**	**NHL**	**68**	**8**	**15**	**23**	**73**	**0**	**0**	**0**	**72**	**11.1**	**2**	13	38.5	58	20	13:34	**5**	**0**	**0**	**0**	**6**	**0**	**0**	**0**
99-2000	**San Jose**	**NHL**	**69**	**12**	**12**	**24**	**61**	**0**	**0**	**3**	**73**	**16.4**	**–3**	8	50.0	83	14	11:52	**10**	**0**	**2**	**2**	**8**	**0**	**0**	**0**
2000-01	**San Jose**	**NHL**	**80**	**13**	**19**	**32**	**32**	**1**	**0**	**3**	**81**	**16.0**	**5**	61	37.7	94	24	10:55	**6**	**1**	**3**	**4**	**0**	**0**	**0**	**0**
	NHL Totals		**741**	**133**	**164**	**297**	**700**	**13**	**3**	**19**	**931**	**14.3**		**82**	**39.0**	**235**	**58**	**12:03**	**99**	**11**	**20**	**31**	**78**	**2**	**1**	**2**

• Missed majority of 1991-92 season recovering from thigh injury suffered in game vs. LA Kings, October 10, 1991. Traded to **Chicago** by **Calgary** for Trent Yawney, December 16, 1991. Traded to **NY Rangers** by **Chicago** with Brian Noonan for Tony Amonte and the rights to Matt Oates, March 21, 1994. Traded to **St. Louis** by **NY Rangers** for Ian Laperriere, December 28, 1995. Traded to **San Jose** by **St. Louis** for Darren Turcotte, July 24, 1997.

MATTEUCCI, Mike

(ma-TEW-chee, MIGHK) **MIN.**

Defense. Shoots left. 6'2", 210 lbs. Born, Trail, B.C., December 27, 1971.

Season	Club	League	GP	G	A	Pts	PIM	PP	SH	GW	S	%	+/-	TF	F%	H	SB	Min	GP	G	A	Pts	PIM	PP	SH	GW
1991-92	Estevan Bruins	SJHL	STATISTICS NOT AVAILABLE																							
1992-93	Lake Superior	CCHA	19	1	3	4	16																			
1993-94	Lake Superior	CCHA	45	6	11	17	64																			
1994-95	Lake Superior	CCHA	38	3	11	14	52																			
1995-96	Lake Superior	CCHA	40	3	13	16	82																			
	Los Angeles	IHL	4	0	0	0	7																			
1996-97	Long Beach	IHL	81	4	4	8	254												18	0	1	1	42			
1997-98	Long Beach	IHL	79	1	7	8	258												17	0	2	2	57			
1998-99	Long Beach	IHL	79	3	9	12	253												8	0	1	1	12			
99-2000	Long Beach	IHL	64	0	4	4	170												6	0	0	0	16			
2000-01	**Minnesota**	**NHL**	**3**	**0**	**0**	**0**	**2**	**0**	**0**	**0**	**3**	**0.0**	**–2**	1	100.0	6	0	11:29								
	Cleveland	IHL	69	0	7	7	189												4	0	0	0	15			
	NHL Totals		**3**	**0**	**0**	**0**	**2**	**0**	**0**	**0**	**3**	**0.0**		**1**	**100.0**	**6**	**0**	**11:29**								

Signed as a free agent by **Edmonton**, September 10, 1998. Traded to **Boston** by **Edmonton** for Kay Whitmore, December 29, 1999. Signed as a free agent by **Minnesota**, July 20, 2000.

MATVICHUK, Richard

(MAT-vih-chuhk, RIH-chahrd) **DAL.**

Defense. Shoots left. 6'2", 215 lbs. Born, Edmonton, Alta., February 5, 1973. Minnesota's 1st choice, 8th overall, in 1991 Entry Draft.

Season	Club	League	GP	G	A	Pts	PIM	PP	SH	GW	S	%	+/-	TF	F%	H	SB	Min	GP	G	A	Pts	PIM	PP	SH	GW
1988-89	Ft-Saskatchewan	AJHL	58	7	36	43	147																			
1989-90	Saskatoon Blades	WHL	56	8	24	32	126												10	2	8	10	16			
1990-91	Saskatoon Blades	WHL	68	13	36	49	117																			
1991-92	Saskatoon Blades	WHL	58	14	40	54	126												22	1	9	10	61			
1992-93	**Minnesota**	**NHL**	**53**	**2**	**3**	**5**	**26**	**1**	**0**	**0**	**51**	**3.9**	**–8**													
	Kalamazoo Wings	IHL	3	0	1	1	6																			
1993-94	**Dallas**	**NHL**	**25**	**0**	**3**	**3**	**22**	**0**	**0**	**0**	**18**	**0.0**	**1**						**7**	**1**	**1**	**2**	**12**	**1**	**0**	**0**
	Kalamazoo Wings	IHL	43	8	17	25	84																			
1994-95	**Dallas**	**NHL**	**14**	**0**	**2**	**2**	**14**	**0**	**0**	**0**	**21**	**0.0**	**–7**						**5**	**0**	**2**	**2**	**4**	**0**	**0**	**0**
	Kalamazoo Wings	IHL	17	0	6	6	16																			
1995-96	**Dallas**	**NHL**	**73**	**6**	**16**	**22**	**71**	**0**	**0**	**1**	**81**	**7.4**	**4**													
1996-97	**Dallas**	**NHL**	**57**	**5**	**7**	**12**	**87**	**0**	**2**	**0**	**83**	**6.0**	**1**						**7**	**0**	**1**	**1**	**20**	**0**	**0**	**0**
1997-98	**Dallas**	**NHL**	**74**	**3**	**15**	**18**	**63**	**0**	**0**	**0**	**71**	**4.2**	**7**						**16**	**1**	**1**	**2**	**14**	**0**	**0**	**0**
1998-99♦	**Dallas**	**NHL**	**64**	**3**	**9**	**12**	**51**	**1**	**0**	**0**	**54**	**5.6**	**23**	0	0.0	186	153	21:19	**22**	**1**	**5**	**6**	**20**	**0**	**0**	**0**
99-2000	**Dallas**	**NHL**	**70**	**4**	**21**	**25**	**42**	**0**	**0**	**1**	**73**	**5.5**	**7**	0	0.0	208	150	24:27	**23**	**2**	**5**	**7**	**14**	**0**	**0**	**0**
2000-01	**Dallas**	**NHL**	**78**	**4**	**16**	**20**	**62**	**2**	**0**	**1**	**85**	**4.7**	**5**	1	100.0	233	145	22:53	**10**	**0**	**0**	**0**	**14**	**0**	**0**	**0**
	NHL Totals		**508**	**27**	**92**	**119**	**438**	**4**	**2**	**3**	**537**	**5.0**		**1**	**100.0**	**627**	**448**	**22:56**	**90**	**5**	**15**	**20**	**98**	**1**	**0**	**0**

WHL East First All-Star Team (1992)

Transferred to **Dallas** after **Minnesota** franchise relocated, June 9, 1993.

MAY, Brad

(MAY, BRAD) **PHX.**

Left wing. Shoots left. 6'1", 209 lbs. Born, Toronto, Ont., November 29, 1971. Buffalo's 1st choice, 14th overall, in 1990 Entry Draft.

Season	Club	League	GP	G	A	Pts	PIM	PP	SH	GW	S	%	+/-	TF	F%	H	SB	Min	GP	G	A	Pts	PIM	PP	SH	GW
1987-88	Markham Selects	OMHA	31	22	37	59	58																			
	Markham	MTJHL	6	1	1	2	21																			
1988-89	Niagara Falls	OHL	65	8	14	22	304												17	0	1	1	55			
1989-90	Niagara Falls	OHL	61	32	58	90	223												16	9	13	22	64			
1990-91	Niagara Falls	OHL	34	37	32	69	93												14	11	14	25	53			
1991-92	**Buffalo**	**NHL**	**69**	**11**	**6**	**17**	**309**	**1**	**0**	**3**	**82**	**13.4**	**–12**						**7**	**1**	**4**	**5**	**2**	**0**	**0**	**1**
1992-93	**Buffalo**	**NHL**	**82**	**13**	**13**	**26**	**242**	**0**	**0**	**1**	**114**	**11.4**	**3**						**8**	**1**	**1**	**2**	**14**	**0**	**0**	**1**
1993-94	**Buffalo**	**NHL**	**84**	**18**	**27**	**45**	**171**	**3**	**0**	**3**	**166**	**10.8**	**–6**						**7**	**0**	**2**	**2**	**9**	**0**	**0**	**0**
1994-95	**Buffalo**	**NHL**	**33**	**3**	**3**	**6**	**87**	**1**	**0**	**0**	**42**	**7.1**	**5**						**4**	**0**	**0**	**0**	**2**	**0**	**0**	**0**
1995-96	**Buffalo**	**NHL**	**79**	**15**	**29**	**44**	**295**	**3**	**0**	**4**	**168**	**8.9**	**6**													
1996-97	**Buffalo**	**NHL**	**42**	**3**	**4**	**7**	**106**	**1**	**0**	**1**	**75**	**4.0**	**–8**						**10**	**1**	**1**	**2**	**32**	**0**	**0**	**0**
1997-98	**Buffalo**	**NHL**	**36**	**4**	**7**	**11**	**113**	**0**	**0**	**0**	**41**	**9.8**	**2**													
	Vancouver	**NHL**	**27**	**9**	**3**	**12**	**41**	**4**	**0**	**2**	**56**	**16.1**	**0**													
1998-99	**Vancouver**	**NHL**	**66**	**6**	**11**	**17**	**102**	**1**	**0**	**1**	**91**	**6.6**	**–14**	8	12.5	109	14	13:04								
99-2000	**Vancouver**	**NHL**	**59**	**9**	**7**	**16**	**90**	**0**	**0**	**3**	**66**	**13.6**	**–2**	3	0.0	117	10	10:24								
2000-01	**Phoenix**	**NHL**	**62**	**11**	**14**	**25**	**107**	**0**	**0**	**0**	**83**	**13.3**	**10**	3	33.3	146	11	11:11								
	NHL Totals		**639**	**102**	**124**	**226**	**1663**	**14**	**0**	**18**	**984**	**10.4**		**14**	**14.3**	**372**	**35**	**11:36**	**36**	**3**	**8**	**11**	**59**	**0**	**0**	**2**

OHL Second All-Star Team (1990, 1991)

• Missed majority of 1990-91 season recovering from knee injury suffered at Team Canada Juniors evaluation camp, August 21, 1990. Traded to **Vancouver** by **Buffalo** with Buffalo's 3rd round choice (later traded to Tampa Bay - Tampa Bay selected Jimmie Olvestad) in 1999 Entry Draft for Geoff Sanderson, February 4, 1998. Traded to **Phoenix** by **Vancouver** for future considerations, June 24, 2000.

MAYERS, Jamal

(MAI-uhrz, JUH-MAHL) **ST.L.**

Center. Shoots right. 6'1", 212 lbs. Born, Toronto, Ont., October 24, 1974. St. Louis' 3rd choice, 89th overall, in 1993 Entry Draft.

Season	Club	League	GP	G	A	Pts	PIM	PP	SH	GW	S	%	+/-	TF	F%	H	SB	Min	GP	G	A	Pts	PIM	PP	SH	GW
1990-91	Thornhill Rattlers	OJHL-B	44	12	24	36	78																			
1991-92	Thornhill Rattlers	OJHL-B	56	38	69	107	36																			
1992-93	Western Michigan	CCHA	38	8	17	25	26																			
1993-94	Western Michigan	CCHA	40	17	32	49	40																			
1994-95	Western Michigan	CCHA	39	13	32	45	40																			
1995-96	Western Michigan	CCHA	38	17	22	39	75																			
1996-97	**St. Louis**	**NHL**	**6**	**0**	**1**	**1**	**2**	**0**	**0**	**0**	**7**	**0.0**	**–3**													
	Worcester	AHL	62	12	14	26	104												5	4	5	9	4			
1997-98	Worcester	AHL	61	19	24	43	117												11	3	4	7	10			
1998-99	**St. Louis**	**NHL**	**34**	**4**	**5**	**9**	**40**	**0**	**0**	**0**	**48**	**8.3**	**–3**	2	50.0	56	3	8:08	**11**	**0**	**1**	**1**	**8**	**0**	**0**	**0**
	Worcester	AHL	20	9	7	16	34																			

			Regular Season																Playoffs							
Season	Club	League	GP	G	A	Pts	PIM	PP	SH	GW	S	%	+/-	TF	F%	H	SB	Min	GP	G	A	Pts	PIM	PP	SH	GW
99-2000	St. Louis	NHL	79	7	10	17	90	0	0	0	99	7.1	0	77	52.0	150	11	9:46	7	0	4	4	2	0	0	0
2000-01	St. Louis	NHL	77	8	13	21	117	0	0	0	132	6.1	–3	273	51.3	126	7	11:04	15	2	3	5	8	0	0	0
	NHL Totals		196	19	29	48	249	0	0	0	286	6.6		352	51.4	332	21	10:00	33	2	8	10	18	0	0	0

McALLISTER, Chris
(mih-KAL-ihs-tuhr, KRIHS) **PHI.**

Defense. Shoots left. 6'8", 240 lbs. Born, Saskatoon, Sask., June 16, 1975. Vancouver's 1st choice, 40th overall, in 1995 Entry Draft.

Season	Club	League	GP	G	A	Pts	PIM	PP	SH	GW	S	%	+/-	TF	F%	H	SB	Min	GP	G	A	Pts	PIM	PP	SH	GW
1992-93	Saskatoon Royals	NSJHL	40	14	14	28	224																			
	Saskatoon Blades	WHL	4	0	0	0	2																			
1993-94	Humboldt	SJHL	50	3	5	8	150																			
	Saskatoon Blades	WHL	2	0	0	0	5																			
1994-95	Saskatoon Blades	WHL	65	2	8	10	134												10	0	0	0	28			
1995-96	Syracuse Crunch	AHL	68	0	2	2	142												16	0	0	0	34			
1996-97	Syracuse Crunch	AHL	43	3	1	4	108												3	0	0	0	6			
1997-98	Vancouver	NHL	36	1	2	3	106	0	0	0	15	6.7	–12													
	Syracuse Crunch	AHL	23	0	1	1	71												5	0	0	0	21			
1998-99	Vancouver	NHL	28	1	1	2	63	0	0	0	6	16.7	–7	0	0.0	19	5	5:53								
	Syracuse Crunch	AHL	5	0	0	0	24																			
	Toronto	NHL	20	0	2	2	39	0	0	0	12	0.0	4	0	0.0	37	17	13:59	6	0	1	1	4	0	0	0
99-2000	Toronto	NHL	36	0	3	3	68	0	0	0	12	0.0	–4	0	0.0	65	26	12:02								
2000-01	Philadelphia	NHL	60	2	2	4	124	0	0	0	33	6.1	1	0	0.0	80	74	11:36	2	0	0	0	0	0	0	0
	NHL Totals		180	4	10	14	400	0	0	0	78	5.1		0	0.0	201	122	10:56	8	0	1	1	4	0	0	0

Traded to **Toronto** by **Vancouver** for Darby Hendrickson, February 16, 1999. Traded to **Philadelphia** by **Toronto** for the rights to Regan Kelly, September 26, 2000.

McALPINE, Chris
(mih-KAL-pighn, KRIHS) **CHI.**

Defense. Shoots right. 6', 210 lbs. Born, Roseville, MN, December 1, 1971. New Jersey's 10th choice, 137th overall, in 1990 Entry Draft.

Season	Club	League	GP	G	A	Pts	PIM	PP	SH	GW	S	%	+/-	TF	F%	H	SB	Min	GP	G	A	Pts	PIM	PP	SH	GW
1989-90	Roseville High	Hi-School	25	15	13	28																				
1990-91	U. of Minnesota	WCHA	38	7	9	16	112																			
1991-92	U. of Minnesota	WCHA	39	3	9	12	126																			
1992-93	U. of Minnesota	WCHA	41	14	9	23	82																			
1993-94	U. of Minnesota	WCHA	36	12	18	30	121																			
1994-95	Albany River Rats	AHL	48	4	18	22	49																			
	♦ New Jersey	NHL	24	0	3	3	17	0	0	0	19	0.0	4													
1995-96	Albany River Rats	AHL	57	5	14	19	72												4	0	0	0	13			
1996-97	Albany River Rats	AHL	44	1	9	10	48																			
	St. Louis	NHL	15	0	0	0	24	0	0	0	3	0.0	–2						4	0	1	1	0	0	0	0
1997-98	St. Louis	NHL	54	3	7	10	36	0	0	0	35	8.6	14						10	0	0	0	16	0	0	0
1998-99	St. Louis	NHL	51	1	1	2	50	0	0	0	56	1.8	–10	0	0.0	75	42	12:51	13	0	0	0	2	0	0	0
99-2000	St. Louis	NHL	21	1	1	2	14	0	0	0	25	4.0	1	0	0.0	28	14	11:41								
	Worcester	AHL	10	1	4	5	4																			
	Tampa Bay	NHL	10	1	1	2	10	0	0	0	5	20.0	–5	0	0.0	15	12	18:23								
	Detroit Vipers	IHL	8	0	0	0	6																			
	Atlanta	NHL	3	0	0	0	2	0	0	0	4	0.0	–4	0	0.0	7	4	19:40								
2000-01	Chicago	NHL	50	0	6	6	32	0	0	0	61	0.0	5	2	50.0	74	60	17:41								
	Norfolk Admirals	AHL	13	4	7	11	6																			
	NHL Totals		228	6	19	25	185	0	0	0	208	2.9		2	50.0	199	132	15:01	27	0	1	1	18	0	0	0

WCHA First All-Star Team (1994) • NCAA West Second All-American Team (1994)

Traded to **St. Louis** by **New Jersey** with New Jersey's 9th round choice (James Desmarais) in 1999 Entry Draft for Peter Zezel, February 11, 1997. Traded to **Tampa Bay** by **St. Louis** with Rich Parent for Stephane Richer, January 13, 2000. Traded to **Atlanta** by **Tampa Bay** for Mikko Kuparinen, March 11, 2000. Signed as a free agent by **Chicago**, July 27, 2000.

McAMMOND, Dean
(MIHK-AM-uhnd, DEEN) **CGY.**

Center. Shoots left. 5'11", 200 lbs. Born, Grand Cache, Alta., June 15, 1973. Chicago's 1st choice, 22nd overall, in 1991 Entry Draft.

Season	Club	League	GP	G	A	Pts	PIM	PP	SH	GW	S	%	+/-	TF	F%	H	SB	Min	GP	G	A	Pts	PIM	PP	SH	GW
1988-89	St. Albert Raiders	AMHL	36	33	44	77	132																			
1989-90	Prince Albert	WHL	53	11	11	22	49												14	2	3	5	18			
1990-91	Prince Albert	WHL	71	33	35	68	108												2	0	1	1	6			
1991-92	Prince Albert	WHL	63	37	54	91	189												10	12	11	23	26			
	Chicago	NHL	5	0	2	2	0	0	0	0	4	0.0	–2						3	0	0	0	2	0	0	0
1992-93	Prince Albert	WHL	30	19	29	48	44																			
	Swift Current	WHL	18	10	13	23	24												17	*16	19	35	20			
1993-94	Edmonton	NHL	45	6	21	27	16	2	0	0	52	11.5	12													
	Cape Breton	AHL	28	9	12	21	38																			
1994-95	Edmonton	NHL	6	0	0	0	0	0	0	0	3	0.0	–1													
1995-96	Edmonton	NHL	53	15	15	30	23	4	0	0	79	19.0	6													
	Cape Breton	AHL	22	9	15	24	55																			
1996-97	Edmonton	NHL	57	12	17	29	28	4	0	6	106	11.3	–15													
1997-98	Edmonton	NHL	77	19	31	50	46	8	0	3	128	14.8	9						12	1	4	5	12	0	0	0
1998-99	Edmonton	NHL	65	9	16	25	36	1	0	0	122	7.4	5	26	38.5	116	21	14:15								
	Chicago	NHL	12	1	4	5	2	0	0	1	16	6.3	3	37	48.6	22	4	15:43								
99-2000	Chicago	NHL	76	14	18	32	72	1	0	1	118	11.9	11	257	39.7	121	35	16:25								
2000-01	Chicago	NHL	61	10	16	26	43	1	0	1	95	10.5	4	23	43.5	105	20	15:30								
	Philadelphia	NHL	10	1	1	2	0	1	0	0	17	5.9	–1	65	46.2	12	2	11:60	4	0	0	0	2	0	0	0
	NHL Totals		467	87	141	228	266	22	0	12	740	11.8		408	41.7	376	82	15:18	19	1	4	5	16	0	0	0

Traded to **Edmonton** by **Chicago** with Igor Kravchuk for Joe Murphy, February 24, 1993. Traded to **Chicago** by **Edmonton** with Boris Mironov and Jonas Elofsson for Chad Kilger, Daniel Cleary, Ethan Moreau and Christian Laflamme, March 20, 1999. Traded to **Philadelphia** by **Chicago** for Philadelphia's 3rd round choice (later traded to Toronto - Toronto selected Nicolas Corbeil) in 2001 Entry Draft, March 13, 2001. Traded to **Calgary** by **Philadelphia** for Calgary's 4th round choice in 2002 Entry Draft, June 24, 2001.

McBAIN, Mike
(MIHK-BAYN, MIGHK)

Defense. Shoots left. 6'2", 195 lbs. Born, Kimberley, B.C., January 12, 1977. Tampa Bay's 2nd choice, 30th overall, in 1995 Entry Draft.

Season	Club	League	GP	G	A	Pts	PIM	PP	SH	GW	S	%	+/-	TF	F%	H	SB	Min	GP	G	A	Pts	PIM	PP	SH	GW
1991-92	Kimberley	BCAHA	35	25	62	87	39																			
1992-93	Kimberley	RMJHL	35	0	4	4	48																			
1993-94	Red Deer Rebels	WHL	58	4	13	17	41												4	0	0	0	0			
1994-95	Red Deer Rebels	WHL	68	6	28	34	55																			
1995-96	Red Deer Rebels	WHL	68	7	34	41	68												10	1	7	8	10			
1996-97	Red Deer Rebels	WHL	59	14	35	49	55												15	1	6	7	9			
1997-98	Tampa Bay	NHL	27	0	1	1	8	0	0	0	17	0.0	–10													
	Adirondack	AHL	42	2	13	15	28																			
1998-99	Tampa Bay	NHL	37	0	6	6	14	0	0	0	22	0.0	–11	0	0.0	22	30	14:49								
	Cleveland	IHL	28	2	4	6	15																			
99-2000	Detroit Vipers	IHL	16	0	3	3	4																			
	Quebec Citadelles	AHL	53	5	7	12	34												3	0	0	0	2			
2000-01	Quebec Citadelles	AHL	50	0	2	2	31																			
	Chicago Wolves	IHL	13	0	1	1	2												3	0	0	0	0			
	NHL Totals		64	0	7	7	22	0	0	0	39	0.0		0	0.0	22	30	14:49								

Traded to **Montreal** by **Tampa Bay** for Gordie Dwyer, November 26, 1999.

McCABE, Bryan
(mih-KAYB, BRIGH-uhn) **TOR.**

Defense. Shoots left. 6'1", 210 lbs. Born, St. Catharines, Ont., June 8, 1975. NY Islanders' 2nd choice, 40th overall, in 1993 Entry Draft.

Season	Club	League	GP	G	A	Pts	PIM	PP	SH	GW	S	%	+/-	TF	F%	H	SB	Min	GP	G	A	Pts	PIM	PP	SH	GW
1990-91	Calgary Canucks	AMHL	33	14	34	48	55																			
1991-92	Medicine Hat	WHL	68	6	24	30	157												4	0	0	0	6			
1992-93	Medicine Hat	WHL	14	0	13	13	83																			
	Spokane Chiefs	WHL	46	3	44	47	134												6	1	5	6	28			
1993-94	Spokane Chiefs	WHL	64	22	62	84	218												3	0	4	4	4			
1994-95	Spokane Chiefs	WHL	42	14	39	53	115																			
	Brandon	WHL	20	6	10	16	38												18	4	13	17	59			
1995-96	NY Islanders	NHL	82	7	16	23	156	3	0	1	130	5.4	–24													

			Regular Season																Playoffs							
Season	Club	League	GP	G	A	Pts	PIM	PP	SH	GW	S	%	+/-	TF	F%	H	SB	Min	GP	G	A	Pts	PIM	PP	SH	GW
1996-97	NY Islanders	NHL	82	8	20	28	165	2	1	2	117	6.8	-2	....	....	....	....	....	....	....	....	....	....	....	....	....
1997-98	NY Islanders	NHL	56	3	9	12	145	1	0	0	81	3.7	9	....	....	....	....	....	....	....	....	....	....	....	....	....
	Vancouver	NHL	26	1	11	12	64	0	1	0	42	2.4	10	....	....	....	....	....	....	....	....	....	....	....	....	....
1998-99	Vancouver	NHL	69	7	14	21	120	1	2	0	98	7.1	-11	1	0.0	107	117	24:13	....	....	....	....	....	....	....	....
99-2000	Chicago	NHL	79	6	19	25	139	2	0	2	119	5.0	-8	1	0.0	196	109	23:23	....	....	....	....	....	....	....	....
2000-01	Toronto	NHL	82	5	24	29	123	3	0	2	159	3.1	16	0	0.0	202	110	23:49	11	2	3	5	16	1	0	0
	NHL Totals		476	37	113	150	912	12	4	7	746	5.0		2	0.0	505	336	23:47	11	2	3	5	16	1	0	0

WHL West Second All-Star Team (1993) • WHL West First All-Star Team (1994) • WHL East First All-Star Team (1995) • Memorial Cup All-Star Team (1995)

Traded to **Vancouver** by **NY Islanders** with Todd Bertuzzi and NY Islanders' 3rd round choice (Jarkko Ruutu) in 1998 Entry Draft for Trevor Linden, February 6, 1998. Traded to **Chicago** by **Vancouver** with Vancouver's 1st round choice (Pavel Vorobiev) in 2000 Entry Draft for Chicago's 1st round choice (later traded to Tampa Bay - later traded to NY Rangers - NY Rangers selected Pavel Brendl) in 1999 Entry Draft, June 25, 1999. Traded to **Toronto** by **Chicago** for Alexander Karpovtsev and Toronto's 4th round choice (Vladimir Gusev) in 2001 Entry Draft, October 2, 2000.

McCARTHY, Sandy

(mih-KAHR-thee, SAN-dee) **NYR**

Right wing. Shoots right. 6'3", 225 lbs. Born, Toronto, Ont., June 15, 1972. Calgary's 3rd choice, 52nd overall, in 1991 Entry Draft.

Season	Club	League	GP	G	A	Pts	PIM	PP	SH	GW	S	%	+/-	TF	F%	H	SB	Min	GP	G	A	Pts	PIM	PP	SH	GW
1987-88	Midland	OJHL-C	18	2	1	3	70	....	....	....	....	....	....	....	....	....	....	....	....	....	....	....	....	....	....	....
1988-89	Hawkesbury	OCJHL	42	4	11	15	139	....	....	....	....	....	....	....	....	....	....	....	....	....	....	....	....	....	....	....
1989-90	Laval Titan	QMJHL	65	10	11	21	269	....	....	....	....	....	....	....	....	....	....	....	14	3	3	6	60	....	....	....
1990-91	Laval Titan	QMJHL	68	21	19	40	297	....	....	....	....	....	....	....	....	....	....	....	13	6	5	11	67	....	....	....
1991-92	Laval Titan	QMJHL	62	39	51	90	326	....	....	....	....	....	....	....	....	....	....	....	8	4	5	9	81	....	....	....
1992-93	Salt Lake City	IHL	77	18	20	38	220	....	....	....	....	....	....	....	....	....	....	....	....	....	....	....	....	....	....	....
1993-94	Calgary	NHL	79	5	5	10	173	0	0	0	39	12.8	-3	....	....	....	....	....	7	0	0	0	34	0	0	0
1994-95	Calgary	NHL	37	5	3	8	101	0	0	2	29	17.2	1	....	....	....	....	....	6	0	1	1	17	0	0	0
1995-96	Calgary	NHL	75	9	7	16	173	3	0	1	98	9.2	-8	....	....	....	....	....	4	0	0	0	10	0	0	0
1996-97	Calgary	NHL	33	3	5	8	113	1	0	1	38	7.9	-8	....	....	....	....	....	....	....	....	....	....	....	....	....
1997-98	Calgary	NHL	52	8	5	13	170	1	0	1	68	11.8	-18	....	....	....	....	....	....	....	....	....	....	....	....	....
	Tampa Bay	NHL	14	0	5	5	71	0	0	0	26	0.0	-1	....	....	....	....	....	....	....	....	....	....	....	....	....
1998-99	Tampa Bay	NHL	67	5	7	12	135	1	0	0	89	5.6	-22	0	0.0	118	13	11:02	....	....	....	....	....	....	....	....
	Philadelphia	NHL	13	0	1	1	25	0	0	0	18	0.0	-2	2	50.0	26	2	11:09	6	0	1	1	0	0	0	0
99-2000	Philadelphia	NHL	58	6	5	11	111	1	0	0	68	8.8	-5	4	0.0	121	5	10:27	....	....	....	....	....	....	....	....
	Carolina	NHL	13	0	0	0	9	0	0	0	12	0.0	2	0	0.0	20	1	7:24	....	....	....	....	....	....	....	....
2000-01	NY Rangers	NHL	81	11	10	21	171	0	0	2	95	11.6	3	4	0.0	206	29	10:25	....	....	....	....	....	....	....	....
	NHL Totals		522	52	53	105	1252	7	0	7	580	9.0		10	10.0	491	50	10:28	23	0	2	2	61	0	0	0

Traded to **Tampa Bay** by **Calgary** with Calgary's 3rd (Brad Richards) and 5th (Curtis Rich) round choices in 1998 Entry Draft for Jason Wiemer, March 24, 1998. Traded to **Philadelphia** by **Tampa Bay** with Mikael Andersson for Colin Forbes and Philadelphia's 4th round choice (Michal Lanicek) in 1999 Entry Draft, March 20, 1999. Traded to **Carolina** by **Philadelphia** for Kent Manderville, March 14, 2000. Traded to **NY Rangers** by **Carolina** with Carolina's' 4th round choice (Bryce Lampman) in 2001 Entry Draft for Darren Langdon and Rob DiMaio, August 4, 2000.

McCARTHY, Steve

(mih-KAHR-thee, STEEV) **CHI.**

Defense. Shoots left. 6', 197 lbs. Born, Trail, B.C., February 3, 1981. Chicago's 1st choice, 23rd overall, in 1999 Entry Draft.

Season	Club	League	GP	G	A	Pts	PIM	PP	SH	GW	S	%	+/-	TF	F%	H	SB	Min	GP	G	A	Pts	PIM	PP	SH	GW
1996-97	B.C. River Rats	BCAHA	57	25	52	77	81	....	....	....	....	....	....	....	....	....	....	....	....	....	....	....	....	....	....	....
	Edmonton Ice	WHL	2	0	0	0	0	....	....	....	....	....	....	....	....	....	....	....	....	....	....	....	....	....	....	....
1997-98	Edmonton Ice	WHL	58	11	29	40	59	....	....	....	....	....	....	....	....	....	....	....	....	....	....	....	....	....	....	....
1998-99	Kootenay Ice	WHL	57	19	33	52	79	....	....	....	....	....	....	....	....	....	....	....	6	0	5	5	8	....	....	....
99-2000	Chicago	NHL	5	1	1	2	4	1	0	0	4	25.0	0	0	0.0	4	2	15:09	....	....	....	....	....	....	....	....
	Kootenay Ice	WHL	37	13	23	36	36	....	....	....	....	....	....	....	....	....	....	....	....	....	....	....	....	....	....	....
2000-01	Chicago	NHL	44	0	5	5	8	0	0	0	32	0.0	-7	0	0.0	33	42	14:47	....	....	....	....	....	....	....	....
	Norfolk Admirals	AHL	7	0	4	4	2	....	....	....	....	....	....	....	....	....	....	....	....	....	....	....	....	....	....	....
	NHL Totals		49	1	6	7	12	1	0	0	36	2.8		0	0.0	37	44	14:49	....	....	....	....	....	....	....	....

Returned to **Kootenay** (WHL) by **Chicago**, October 22, 1999.

McCARTY, Darren

(mih-KAHR-tee, DAIR-ehn) **DET.**

Right wing. Shoots right. 6'1", 210 lbs. Born, Burnaby, B.C., April 1, 1972. Detroit's 2nd choice, 46th overall, in 1992 Entry Draft.

Season	Club	League	GP	G	A	Pts	PIM	PP	SH	GW	S	%	+/-	TF	F%	H	SB	Min	GP	G	A	Pts	PIM	PP	SH	GW
1988-89	Peterborough B's	OJHL-B	34	18	17	35	135	....	....	....	....	....	....	....	....	....	....	....	....	....	....	....	....	....	....	....
1989-90	Belleville Bulls	OHL	63	12	15	27	142	....	....	....	....	....	....	....	....	....	....	....	11	1	1	2	21	....	....	....
1990-91	Belleville Bulls	OHL	60	30	37	67	151	....	....	....	....	....	....	....	....	....	....	....	6	2	2	4	13	....	....	....
1991-92	Belleville Bulls	OHL	65	*55	72	127	177	....	....	....	....	....	....	....	....	....	....	....	5	1	4	5	13	....	....	....
1992-93	Adirondack	AHL	73	17	19	36	278	....	....	....	....	....	....	....	....	....	....	....	11	0	1	1	33	....	....	....
1993-94	Detroit	NHL	67	9	17	26	181	0	0	2	81	11.1	12	....	....	....	....	....	7	2	2	4	8	0	0	0
1994-95	Detroit	NHL	31	5	8	13	88	1	0	2	27	18.5	5	....	....	....	....	....	18	3	2	5	14	0	0	0
1995-96	Detroit	NHL	63	15	14	29	158	8	0	1	102	14.7	14	....	....	....	....	....	19	3	2	5	20	0	0	1
1996-97♦	Detroit	NHL	68	19	30	49	126	5	0	6	171	11.1	14	....	....	....	....	....	20	3	4	7	34	0	0	2
1997-98♦	Detroit	NHL	71	15	22	37	157	5	1	2	166	9.0	0	....	....	....	....	....	22	3	8	11	34	0	0	1
1998-99	Detroit	NHL	69	14	26	40	108	6	0	1	140	10.0	10	15	33.3	217	34	17:04	10	1	1	2	23	0	0	0
99-2000	Detroit	NHL	24	6	6	12	48	0	0	1	40	15.0	1	1	0.0	129	7	13:40	9	0	1	1	12	0	0	0
2000-01	Detroit	NHL	72	12	10	22	123	1	1	3	118	10.2	-5	26	53.9	235	24	13:26	6	1	0	1	2	0	0	0
	NHL Totals		465	95	133	228	989	26	2	18	845	11.2		42	45.2	581	65	14:59	111	16	20	36	147	0	0	4

OHL First All-Star Team (1992)

• Missed majority of 1999-2000 season recovering from hernia injury suffered in game vs. Dallas, November 10, 1999.

McCAULEY, Alyn

(mih-KAW-lee, AL-ihn) **TOR.**

Center. Shoots left. 5'11", 190 lbs. Born, Brockville, Ont., May 29, 1977. New Jersey's 5th choice, 79th overall, in 1995 Entry Draft.

Season	Club	League	GP	G	A	Pts	PIM	PP	SH	GW	S	%	+/-	TF	F%	H	SB	Min	GP	G	A	Pts	PIM	PP	SH	GW
1991-92	Kingston	OCJHL	37	5	17	22	6	....	....	....	....	....	....	....	....	....	....	....	....	....	....	....	....	....	....	....
1992-93	Kingston	OCJHL	38	31	29	60	18	....	....	....	....	....	....	....	....	....	....	....	....	....	....	....	....	....	....	....
1993-94	Ottawa 67's	OHL	38	13	23	36	10	....	....	....	....	....	....	....	....	....	....	....	13	5	14	19	4	....	....	....
1994-95	Ottawa 67's	OHL	65	16	38	54	20	....	....	....	....	....	....	....	....	....	....	....	....	....	....	....	....	....	....	....
1995-96	Ottawa 67's	OHL	55	34	48	82	24	....	....	....	....	....	....	....	....	....	....	....	2	0	0	0	0	....	....	....
1996-97	Ottawa 67's	OHL	50	*56	56	112	16	....	....	....	....	....	....	....	....	....	....	....	22	14	22	36	14	....	....	....
	St. John's Leafs	AHL	....	....	....	....	....	....	....	....	....	....	....	....	....	....	....	....	3	0	1	1	0	....	....	....
1997-98	Toronto	NHL	60	6	10	16	6	0	0	1	77	7.8	-7	....	....	....	....	....	....	....	....	....	....	....	....	....
1998-99	Toronto	NHL	39	9	15	24	2	1	0	1	76	11.8	7	591	46.4	10	4	15:10	....	....	....	....	....	....	....	....
99-2000	St. John's Leafs	AHL	5	1	1	2	0	....	....	....	....	....	....	....	....	....	....	....	....	....	....	....	....	....	....	....
	Toronto	NHL	45	5	5	10	10	1	0	0	41	12.2	-6	450	47.8	22	11	10:46	5	0	0	0	6	0	0	0
2000-01	Toronto	NHL	14	1	0	1	0	0	0	0	13	7.7	0	139	46.8	5	3	10:28	10	0	0	0	2	0	0	0
	St. John's Leafs	AHL	47	16	28	44	12	....	....	....	....	....	....	....	....	....	....	....	....	....	....	....	....	....	....	....
	NHL Totals		158	21	30	51	18	2	0	2	207	10.1		1180	46.9	37	18	12:29	15	0	0	0	8	0	0	0

OHL First All-Star Team (1996, 1997) • Canadian Major Junior First All-Star Team (1997) • Canadian Major Junior Player of the Year (1997)

Rights traded to **Toronto** by **New Jersey** with Jason Smith and Steve Sullivan for Doug Gilmour, Dave Ellett and New Jersey's 3rd round choice (previously acquired, New Jersey selected Andre Lakos) in 1999 Entry Draft, February 25, 1997.

McDONALD, Andy

(mihk-DAW-nuhld, AN-dee) **ANA.**

Center. Shoots left. 5'10", 173 lbs. Born, Strathroy, Ont., August 25, 1977.

Season	Club	League	GP	G	A	Pts	PIM	PP	SH	GW	S	%	+/-	TF	F%	H	SB	Min	GP	G	A	Pts	PIM	PP	SH	GW
1993-94	Strathroy Rockets	OJHL-B	7	2	2	4	0	....	....	....	....	....	....	....	....	....	....	....	....	....	....	....	....	....	....	....
1994-95	Strathroy Rockets	OJHL-B	50	32	41	73	24	....	....	....	....	....	....	....	....	....	....	....	....	....	....	....	....	....	....	....
1995-96	Strathroy Rockets	OJHL-B	52	31	56	87	103	....	....	....	....	....	....	....	....	....	....	....	....	....	....	....	....	....	....	....
1996-97	Colgate	ECAC	33	9	10	19	16	....	....	....	....	....	....	....	....	....	....	....	....	....	....	....	....	....	....	....
1997-98	Colgate	ECAC	35	13	19	32	26	....	....	....	....	....	....	....	....	....	....	....	....	....	....	....	....	....	....	....
1998-99	Colgate	ECAC	35	20	26	46	42	....	....	....	....	....	....	....	....	....	....	....	....	....	....	....	....	....	....	....
99-2000	Colgate	ECAC	34	25	*33	*58	49	....	....	....	....	....	....	....	....	....	....	....	....	....	....	....	....	....	....	....
2000-01	Anaheim	NHL	16	1	0	1	6	0	0	0	21	4.8	0	139	48.9	13	4	11:11	....	....	....	....	....	....	....	....
	Cincinnati Ducks	AHL	46	15	25	40	21	....	....	....	....	....	....	....	....	....	....	....	3	0	1	1	2	....	....	....
	NHL Totals		16	1	0	1	6	0	0	0	21	4.8		139	48.9	13	4	11:11	....	....	....	....	....	....	....	....

OJHL-B Player of the Year (1996) • ECAC Second All-Star Team (1999) • ECAC First All-Star Team (2000) • NCAA East First All-American Team (2000)

Signed as a free agent by **Anaheim**, April 3, 2000.

McEACHERN, Shawn
(muh-GEH-kruhn, SHAWN) **OTT.**

Left wing. Shoots left. 5'11", 193 lbs. Born, Waltham, MA, February 28, 1969. Pittsburgh's 6th choice, 110th overall, in 1987 Entry Draft.

			Regular Season																Playoffs							
Season	Club	League	GP	G	A	Pts	PIM	PP	SH	GW	S	%	+/-	TF	F%	H	SB	Min	GP	G	A	Pts	PIM	PP	SH	GW
1985-86	Matignon High	Hi-School	20	32	20	52																				
1986-87	Matignon High	Hi-School	16	29	28	57																				
1987-88	Matignon High	Hi-School	22	52	40	92																				
1988-89	Boston University	H-East	36	20	28	48	32																			
1989-90	Boston University	H-East	43	25	31	56	78																			
1990-91	Boston University	H-East	41	34	48	82	43																			
1991-92	United States	Nat-Team	57	26	23	49	38																			
	United States	Olympics	8	1	0	1	10																			
	♦ Pittsburgh	NHL	15	0	4	4	0	0	0	0	14	0.0	1						19	2	7	9	4	0	0	0
1992-93	Pittsburgh	NHL	84	28	33	61	46	7	0	6	196	14.3	21						12	3	2	5	10	0	0	1
1993-94	Los Angeles	NHL	49	8	13	21	24	0	3	0	81	9.9	1													
	Pittsburgh	NHL	27	12	9	21	10	0	2	1	78	15.4	13						6	1	0	1	2	0	0	0
1994-95	Kiekko-Espoo	Finland	8	1	3	4	6																			
	Pittsburgh	NHL	44	13	13	26	22	1	2	1	97	13.4	4						11	0	2	2	8	0	0	0
1995-96	Boston	NHL	82	24	29	53	34	3	2	3	238	10.1	-5						5	2	1	3	8	0	0	0
1996-97	Ottawa	NHL	65	11	20	31	18	0	1	2	150	7.3	-5						7	2	0	2	8	1	0	0
1997-98	Ottawa	NHL	81	24	24	48	42	8	2	4	229	10.5	1						11	0	4	4	8	0	0	0
1998-99	Ottawa	NHL	77	31	25	56	46	7	0	4	223	13.9	8	441	48.5	37	23	18:45	4	2	0	2	6	1	0	0
99-2000	Ottawa	NHL	69	29	22	51	24	10	0	4	219	13.2	2	54	50.0	45	13	17:50	6	0	3	3	4	0	0	0
2000-01	Ottawa	NHL	82	32	40	72	62	9	0	1	231	13.9	10	420	48.8	82	23	18:25	4	0	2	2	2	0	0	0
	NHL Totals		675	212	232	444	328	45	12	26	1756	12.1		915	48.7	164	59	18:21	85	12	21	33	60	2	0	1

Hockey East Second All-Star Team (1990) • Hockey East First All-Star Team (1991) • NCAA East First All-American Team (1991)

Traded to **LA Kings** by **Pittsburgh** for Marty McSorley, August 27, 1993. Traded to **Pittsburgh** by **LA Kings** with Tomas Sandstrom for Marty McSorley and Jim Paek, February 16, 1994. Traded to **Boston** by **Pittsburgh** with Kevin Stevens for Glen Murray, Bryan Smolinski and Boston's 3rd round choice (Boyd Kane) in 1996 Entry Draft, August 2, 1995. Traded to **Ottawa** by **Boston** for Trent McCleary and Ottawa's 3rd round choice (Eric Naud) in 1996 Entry Draft, June 22, 1996.

McGILLIS, Dan
(MIHK-gihl-his, DAN) **PHI.**

Defense. Shoots left. 6'2", 230 lbs. Born, Hawkesbury, Ont., July 1, 1972. Detroit's 10th choice, 238th overall, in 1992 Entry Draft.

Season	Club	League	GP	G	A	Pts	PIM	PP	SH	GW	S	%	+/-	TF	F%	H	SB	Min	GP	G	A	Pts	PIM	PP	SH	GW
1989-90	Hawkesbury	OCJHL	55	2	1	3	52																			
1990-91	Hawkesbury	OCJHL	56	8	22	30	92																			
1991-92	Hawkesbury	OCJHL	36	5	19	24	106																			
1992-93	Northeastern	H-East	35	5	12	17	42																			
1993-94	Northeastern	H-East	38	4	25	29	82																			
1994-95	Northeastern	H-East	34	9	22	31	70																			
1995-96	Northeastern	H-East	34	12	24	36	50																			
1996-97	Edmonton	NHL	73	6	16	22	52	2	1	2	139	4.3	2						12	0	5	5	24	0	0	0
1997-98	Edmonton	NHL	67	10	15	25	74	5	0	3	119	8.4	-17													
	Philadelphia	NHL	13	1	5	6	35	1	0	0	18	5.6	-4						5	1	2	3	10	1	0	0
1998-99	Philadelphia	NHL	78	8	37	45	61	6	0	4	164	4.9	16	0	0.0	220	71	21:41	6	0	1	1	12	0	0	0
99-2000	Philadelphia	NHL	68	4	14	18	55	3	0	1	128	3.1	16	0	0.0	264	63	20:04	18	2	6	8	12	0	0	0
2000-01	Philadelphia	NHL	82	14	35	49	86	4	0	4	207	6.8	13	1	0.0	292	127	23:23	6	1	0	1	6	0	1	0
	NHL Totals		381	43	122	165	363	21	1	14	775	5.5		1	0.0	776	261	21:49	47	4	14	18	64	1	1	0

Hockey East First All-Star Team (1995, 1996) • NCAA East First All-American Team (1996)

Traded to **Edmonton** by **Detroit** for Kirk Maltby, March 20, 1996. Traded to **Philadelphia** by **Edmonton** with Edmonton's 2nd round choice (Jason Beckett) in 1998 Entry Draft for Janne Niinimaa, March 24, 1998.

McINNIS, Marty
(MAK-ih-nihs, MAHR-tee) **ANA.**

Left wing. Shoots right. 5'11", 187 lbs. Born, Weymouth, MA, June 2, 1970. NY Islanders' 10th choice, 163rd overall, in 1988 Entry Draft.

Season	Club	League	GP	G	A	Pts	PIM	PP	SH	GW	S	%	+/-	TF	F%	H	SB	Min	GP	G	A	Pts	PIM	PP	SH	GW
1986-87	Milton Academy	Hi-School	25	21	19	40																				
1987-88	Milton Academy	Hi-School	25	26	25	51																				
1988-89	Boston College	H-East	39	13	19	32	8																			
1989-90	Boston College	H-East	41	24	29	53	43																			
1990-91	Boston College	H-East	38	21	36	57	40																			
1991-92	United States	Nat-Team	54	15	19	34	20																			
	United States	Olympics	8	5	2	7	4																			
	NY Islanders	NHL	15	3	5	8	0	0	0	0	24	12.5	6													
1992-93	NY Islanders	NHL	56	10	20	30	24	0	1	0	60	16.7	7						3	0	1	1	0	0	0	0
	Capital District	AHL	10	4	12	16	2																			
1993-94	NY Islanders	NHL	81	25	31	56	24	3	5	3	136	18.4	31						4	0	0	0	0	0	0	0
1994-95	NY Islanders	NHL	41	9	7	16	8	0	0	1	68	13.2	-1													
1995-96	NY Islanders	NHL	74	12	34	46	39	2	0	1	167	7.2	-11													
1996-97	NY Islanders	NHL	70	20	22	42	20	4	1	4	163	12.3	-7													
	Calgary	NHL	10	3	4	7	2	1	0	0	19	15.8	-1													
1997-98	Calgary	NHL	75	19	25	44	34	5	4	0	128	14.8	1													
1998-99	Calgary	NHL	6	1	1	2	6	0	0	0	7	14.3	-1	28	32.1	5	0	13:51								
	Anaheim	NHL	75	18	34	52	36	11	1	5	139	12.9	-14	390	46.9	52	15	18:59	4	2	0	2	2	2	0	0
99-2000	Anaheim	NHL	62	10	18	28	26	2	1	2	129	7.8	-4	355	50.1	60	9	19:04								
2000-01	Anaheim	NHL	75	20	22	42	40	10	0	1	136	14.7	-21	605	47.1	57	17	18:30								
	NHL Totals		640	150	223	373	259	38	13	17	1176	12.8		1378	47.5	174	41	18:42	11	2	1	3	2	2	0	0

Traded to **Calgary** by **NY Islanders** with Tyrone Garner and Calgary's 6th round choice (previously acquired, Calgary selected Ilja Demidov) in 1997 Entry Draft for Robert Reichel, March 18, 1997. Traded to **Chicago** by **Calgary** with Eric Andersson and Jamie Allison for Jeff Shantz and Steve Dubinsky, October 27, 1998. Traded to **Anaheim** by **Chicago** for Toronto's 4th round choice (previously acquired, later traded to Washington - Washington selected Ryan Vanbuskirk) in 2000 Entry Draft, October 27, 1998.

McKAY, Randy
(mih-KAY, RAN-dee) **N.J.**

Right wing. Shoots right. 6'2", 210 lbs. Born, Montreal, Que., January 25, 1967. Detroit's 6th choice, 113th overall, in 1985 Entry Draft.

Season	Club	League	GP	G	A	Pts	PIM	PP	SH	GW	S	%	+/-	TF	F%	H	SB	Min	GP	G	A	Pts	PIM	PP	SH	GW
1983-84	Lac St-Louis	QAAA	38	18	28	46	62												11	6	10	16	8			
1984-85	Michigan Tech	WCHA	25	4	5	9	32																			
1985-86	Michigan Tech	WCHA	40	12	22	34	46																			
1986-87	Michigan Tech	WCHA	39	5	11	16	46																			
1987-88	Michigan Tech	WCHA	41	17	24	41	70																			
	Adirondack	AHL	10	0	3	3	12												6	0	4	4	0			
1988-89	Detroit	NHL	3	0	0	0	0	0	0	0	2	0.0	-1						2	0	0	0	2	0	0	0
	Adirondack	AHL	58	29	34	63	170												14	4	7	11	60			
1989-90	Detroit	NHL	33	3	6	9	51	0	0	0	33	9.1	1													
	Adirondack	AHL	36	16	23	39	99												6	3	0	3	35			
1990-91	Detroit	NHL	47	1	7	8	183	0	0	0	22	4.5	-15						5	0	1	1	41	0	0	0
1991-92	New Jersey	NHL	80	17	16	33	246	2	0	1	111	15.3	6						7	1	3	4	10	1	0	0
1992-93	New Jersey	NHL	73	11	11	22	206	1	0	2	94	11.7	0						5	0	0	0	16	0	0	0
1993-94	New Jersey	NHL	78	12	15	27	244	0	0	1	77	15.6	24						20	1	2	3	24	0	0	0
1994-95♦	New Jersey	NHL	33	5	7	12	44	0	0	0	44	11.4	10						19	8	4	12	11	2	0	2
1995-96	New Jersey	NHL	76	11	10	21	145	3	0	3	97	11.3	7													
1996-97	New Jersey	NHL	77	9	18	27	109	0	0	2	92	9.8	15						10	1	1	2	0	0	0	0
1997-98	New Jersey	NHL	74	24	24	48	86	8	0	5	141	17.0	30						6	0	1	1	0	0	0	0
1998-99	New Jersey	NHL	70	17	20	37	143	3	0	5	136	12.5	10	1	0.0	124	11	16:06	7	3	2	5	2	0	0	1
99-2000♦	New Jersey	NHL	67	16	23	39	80	3	0	4	116	13.8	8	2	0.0	144	16	15:39	23	0	6	6	9	0	0	0
2000-01	New Jersey	NHL	77	23	20	43	50	12	0	5	120	19.2	3	2	50.0	114	15	13:58	19	6	3	9	8	2	0	1
	NHL Totals		788	149	177	326	1587	32	0	28	1085	13.7		5	20.0	382	42	15:12	123	20	23	43	123	5	0	4

Transferred to **New Jersey** by **Detroit** with Dave Barr as compensation for Detroit's signing of free agent Troy Crowder, September 9, 1991.

McKEE, Jay

(mih-KEE, JAY) **BUF.**

Defense. Shoots left. 6'4", 201 lbs. Born, Kingston, Ont., September 8, 1977. Buffalo's 1st choice, 14th overall, in 1995 Entry Draft.

			Regular Season																Playoffs							
Season	Club	League	GP	G	A	Pts	PIM	PP	SH	GW	S	%	+/-	TF	F%	H	SB	Min	GP	G	A	Pts	PIM	PP	SH	GW
1991-92	Mimico Monarchs	MTJHL	39	7	9	16	67																			
	Kingston	MTJHL	1	0	0	0	0																			
1992-93	Ernestown Jets	OJHL-C	36	0	17	17	37																			
	Kingston	MTJHL	2	0	0	0	0																			
1993-94	Sudbury Wolves	OHL	51	0	1	1	51												3	0	0	0	0			
1994-95	Sudbury Wolves	OHL	39	6	6	12	91																			
	Niagara Falls	OHL	26	3	13	16	60												6	2	3	5	10			
1995-96	Niagara Falls	OHL	64	5	41	46	129												10	1	5	6	16			
	Buffalo	**NHL**	**1**	**0**	**1**	**1**	**2**	**0**	**0**	**0**	**2**	**0.0**	**1**													
	Rochester	AHL	4	0	1	1	15																			
1996-97	**Buffalo**	**NHL**	**43**	**1**	**9**	**10**	**35**	**0**	**0**	**0**	**29**	**3.4**	**3**						**3**	**0**	**0**	**0**	**0**	**0**	**0**	**0**
	Rochester	AHL	7	2	5	7	4																			
1997-98	**Buffalo**	**NHL**	**56**	**1**	**13**	**14**	**42**	**0**	**0**	**0**	**55**	**1.8**	**−1**						**1**	**0**	**0**	**0**	**0**	**0**	**0**	**0**
	Rochester	AHL	13	1	7	8	11																			
1998-99	**Buffalo**	**NHL**	**72**	**0**	**6**	**6**	**75**	**0**	**0**	**0**	**57**	**0.0**	**20**	**0**	**0.0**	**204**	**129**	**20:28**	**21**	**0**	**3**	**3**	**24**	**0**	**0**	**0**
99-2000	**Buffalo**	**NHL**	**78**	**5**	**12**	**17**	**50**	**1**	**0**	**1**	**84**	**6.0**	**5**	**0**	**0.0**	**153**	**170**	**20:58**	**1**	**0**	**0**	**0**	**0**	**0**	**0**	**0**
2000-01	**Buffalo**	**NHL**	**74**	**1**	**10**	**11**	**76**	**0**	**0**	**0**	**62**	**1.6**	**9**	**2**	**0.0**	**190**	**133**	**19:24**	**8**	**1**	**0**	**1**	**6**	**0**	**0**	**1**
	NHL Totals		**324**	**8**	**51**	**59**	**280**	**1**	**0**	**1**	**289**	**2.8**		**2**	**0.0**	**547**	**432**	**20:17**	**34**	**1**	**3**	**4**	**30**	**0**	**0**	**1**

OHL Second All-Star Team (1996)

McKENNA, Steve

(mih-KEHN-ah, STEEV)

Left wing. Shoots left. 6'8", 255 lbs. Born, Toronto, Ont., August 21, 1973.

Season	Club	League	GP	G	A	Pts	PIM	PP	SH	GW	S	%	+/-	TF	F%	H	SB	Min	GP	G	A	Pts	PIM	PP	SH	GW
1991-92	Cambridge Hawks	OJHL-B	48	21	23	44	173																			
1992-93	Notre Dame	SJHL	STATISTICS NOT AVAILABLE																							
1993-94	Merrimack	H-East	37	1	2	3	74																			
1994-95	Merrimack	H-East	37	1	9	10	74																			
1995-96	Merrimack	H-East	33	3	11	14	67																			
1996-97	**Los Angeles**	**NHL**	**9**	**0**	**0**	**0**	**37**	**0**	**0**	**0**	**6**	**0.0**	**1**													
	Phoenix	IHL	66	6	5	11	187																			
1997-98	**Los Angeles**	**NHL**	**62**	**4**	**4**	**8**	**150**	**1**	**0**	**0**	**42**	**9.5**	**−9**						**3**	**0**	**1**	**1**	**8**	**0**	**0**	**0**
	Fredericton	AHL	6	2	1	3	48																			
1998-99	**Los Angeles**	**NHL**	**20**	**1**	**0**	**1**	**36**	**0**	**0**	**0**	**12**	**8.3**	**−3**	**0**	**0.0**	**35**	**4**	**8:24**								
99-2000	**Los Angeles**	**NHL**	**46**	**0**	**5**	**5**	**125**	**0**	**0**	**0**	**14**	**0.0**	**3**	**1**	**0.0**	**39**	**5**	**4:53**								
2000-01	**Minnesota**	**NHL**	**20**	**1**	**1**	**2**	**19**	**0**	**0**	**0**	**12**	**8.3**	**0**	**0**	**0.0**	**26**	**5**	**7:59**								
	Pittsburgh	**NHL**	**34**	**0**	**0**	**0**	**100**	**0**	**0**	**0**	**7**	**0.0**	**−4**	**0**	**0.0**	**20**	**2**	**3:16**								
	NHL Totals		**191**	**6**	**10**	**16**	**467**	**1**	**0**	**0**	**93**	**6.5**		**1**	**0.0**	**120**	**16**	**5:32**	**3**	**0**	**1**	**1**	**8**	**0**	**0**	**0**

Signed as a free agent by **LA Kings**, May 23, 1996. Selected by **Minnesota** from **LA Kings** in Expansion Draft, June 23, 2000. Traded to **Pittsburgh** by **Minnesota** for Roman Simicek, January 13, 2001.

McKENZIE, Jim

(MIHK-ehn-zee, JIHM) **N.J.**

Left wing. Shoots left. 6'4", 230 lbs. Born, Gull Lake, Sask., November 3, 1969. Hartford's 3rd choice, 73rd overall, in 1989 Entry Draft.

Season	Club	League	GP	G	A	Pts	PIM	PP	SH	GW	S	%	+/-	TF	F%	H	SB	Min	GP	G	A	Pts	PIM	PP	SH	GW
1985-86	Moose Jaw	SMHL	36	18	26	44	89																			
	Moose Jaw	WHL	3	0	2	2	0																			
1986-87	Moose Jaw	WHL	65	5	3	8	125												9	0	0	0	7			
1987-88	Moose Jaw	WHL	62	1	17	18	134																			
1988-89	Victoria Cougars	WHL	67	15	27	42	176												8	1	4	5	30			
1989-90	**Hartford**	**NHL**	**5**	**0**	**0**	**0**	**4**	**0**	**0**	**0**	**0**	**0.0**	**0**													
	Binghamton	AHL	56	4	12	16	149																			
1990-91	**Hartford**	**NHL**	**41**	**4**	**3**	**7**	**108**	**0**	**0**	**0**	**16**	**25.0**	**−7**						**6**	**0**	**0**	**0**	**8**	**0**	**0**	**0**
	Springfield	AHL	24	3	4	7	102																			
1991-92	**Hartford**	**NHL**	**67**	**5**	**1**	**6**	**87**	**0**	**0**	**0**	**34**	**14.7**	**−6**													
1992-93	**Hartford**	**NHL**	**64**	**3**	**6**	**9**	**202**	**0**	**0**	**0**	**36**	**8.3**	**−10**													
1993-94	**Hartford**	**NHL**	**26**	**1**	**2**	**3**	**67**	**0**	**0**	**0**	**9**	**11.1**	**−6**													
	Dallas	**NHL**	**34**	**2**	**3**	**5**	**63**	**0**	**0**	**1**	**18**	**11.1**	**4**													
	Pittsburgh	**NHL**	**11**	**0**	**0**	**0**	**16**	**0**	**0**	**0**	**6**	**0.0**	**−5**						**3**	**0**	**0**	**0**	**0**	**0**	**0**	**0**
1994-95	**Pittsburgh**	**NHL**	**39**	**2**	**1**	**3**	**63**	**0**	**0**	**1**	**16**	**12.5**	**−7**						**5**	**0**	**0**	**0**	**4**	**0**	**0**	**0**
1995-96	**Winnipeg**	**NHL**	**73**	**4**	**2**	**6**	**202**	**0**	**0**	**0**	**28**	**14.3**	**−4**						**1**	**0**	**0**	**0**	**2**	**0**	**0**	**0**
1996-97	**Phoenix**	**NHL**	**65**	**5**	**3**	**8**	**200**	**0**	**0**	**1**	**38**	**13.2**	**−5**						**7**	**0**	**0**	**0**	**2**	**0**	**0**	**0**
1997-98	**Phoenix**	**NHL**	**64**	**3**	**4**	**7**	**146**	**0**	**0**	**0**	**35**	**8.6**	**−7**						**1**	**0**	**0**	**0**	**0**	**0**	**0**	**0**
1998-99	**Anaheim**	**NHL**	**73**	**5**	**4**	**9**	**99**	**1**	**0**	**1**	**59**	**8.5**	**−18**	**8**	**50.0**	**85**	**8**	**10:22**	**4**	**0**	**0**	**0**	**4**	**0**	**0**	**0**
99-2000	**Anaheim**	**NHL**	**31**	**3**	**3**	**6**	**48**	**0**	**0**	**0**	**22**	**13.6**	**−5**	**2**	**0.0**	**50**	**2**	**10:26**								
	Washington	**NHL**	**30**	**1**	**2**	**3**	**16**	**0**	**0**	**0**	**10**	**10.0**	**0**	**0**	**0.0**	**27**	**5**	**6:22**	**1**	**0**	**0**	**0**	**0**	**0**	**0**	**0**
2000-01	**New Jersey**	**NHL**	**53**	**2**	**2**	**4**	**119**	**0**	**0**	**0**	**32**	**6.3**	**0**	**0**	**0.0**	**64**	**4**	**7:56**	**3**	**0**	**0**	**0**	**2**	**0**	**0**	**0**
	NHL Totals		**676**	**40**	**36**	**76**	**1440**	**1**	**0**	**4**	**359**	**11.1**		**10**	**40.0**	**226**	**19**	**9:03**	**31**	**0**	**0**	**0**	**22**	**0**	**0**	**0**

Traded to **Florida** by **Hartford** for Alexander Godynyuk, December 16, 1993. Traded to **Dallas** by **Florida** for Dallas' 4th round choice (later traded to Ottawa - Ottawa selected Kevin Bolibruck) in 1995 Entry Draft, December 16, 1993. Traded to **Pittsburgh** by **Dallas** for Mike Needham, March 21, 1994. Signed as a free agent by **NY Islanders**, August 2, 1995. Claimed by **Winnipeg** from **NY Islanders** in NHL Waiver Draft, October 2, 1995. Transferred to **Phoenix** after **Winnipeg** franchise relocated, July 1, 1996. Traded to **Anaheim** by **Phoenix** for J-F Jomphe, June 18, 1998. Claimed on waivers by **Washington** from **Anaheim**, January 20, 2000. Signed as a free agent by **New Jersey**, July 3, 2000.

McLAREN, Kyle

(mih-KLAIR-uhn, KIGHL) **BOS.**

Defense. Shoots left. 6'4", 230 lbs. Born, Humboldt, Sask., June 18, 1977. Boston's 1st choice, 9th overall, in 1995 Entry Draft.

Season	Club	League	GP	G	A	Pts	PIM	PP	SH	GW	S	%	+/-	TF	F%	H	SB	Min	GP	G	A	Pts	PIM	PP	SH	GW
1992-93	Lethbridge Y's	AMHL	60	28	28	56	84																			
1993-94	Tacoma Rockets	WHL	62	1	9	10	53												6	1	4	5	6			
1994-95	Tacoma Rockets	WHL	47	13	19	32	68												4	1	1	2	4			
1995-96	**Boston**	**NHL**	**74**	**5**	**12**	**17**	**73**	**0**	**0**	**0**	**74**	**6.8**	**16**						**5**	**0**	**0**	**0**	**14**	**0**	**0**	**0**
1996-97	**Boston**	**NHL**	**58**	**5**	**9**	**14**	**54**	**0**	**0**	**1**	**68**	**7.4**	**−9**													
1997-98	**Boston**	**NHL**	**66**	**5**	**20**	**25**	**56**	**2**	**0**	**0**	**101**	**5.0**	**13**						**6**	**1**	**0**	**1**	**4**	**1**	**0**	**0**
1998-99	**Boston**	**NHL**	**52**	**6**	**18**	**24**	**48**	**3**	**0**	**0**	**97**	**6.2**	**1**	**0**	**0.0**	**205**	**69**	**23:25**	**12**	**0**	**3**	**3**	**10**	**0**	**0**	**0**
99-2000	**Boston**	**NHL**	**71**	**8**	**11**	**19**	**67**	**2**	**0**	**3**	**142**	**5.6**	**−4**	**5**	**40.0**	**282**	**155**	**23:18**								
2000-01	**Boston**	**NHL**	**58**	**5**	**12**	**17**	**53**	**2**	**0**	**0**	**91**	**5.5**	**−5**	**4**	**50.0**	**156**	**131**	**24:14**								
	NHL Totals		**379**	**34**	**82**	**116**	**351**	**9**	**0**	**4**	**573**	**5.9**		**9**	**44.4**	**643**	**355**	**23:38**	**23**	**1**	**3**	**4**	**28**	**1**	**0**	**0**

NHL All-Rookie Team (1996)

McSORLEY, Marty

(MIHK-SOHR-lee, MAHR-tee)

Defense. Shoots right. 6'1", 235 lbs. Born, Hamilton, Ont., May 18, 1963.

Season	Club	League	GP	G	A	Pts	PIM	PP	SH	GW	S	%	+/-	TF	F%	H	SB	Min	GP	G	A	Pts	PIM	PP	SH	GW
1979-80	Cayuga Wings	OHA-D	27	8	18	26	92																			
1980-81	Hamilton Kilty B's	OHA-B	40	16	17	33	72																			
1981-82	Belleville Bulls	OHL	58	6	13	19	234																			
1982-83	Belleville Bulls	OHL	70	10	41	51	183												4	0	0	0	7			
	Baltimore	AHL	2	0	0	0	22																			
1983-84	**Pittsburgh**	**NHL**	**72**	**2**	**7**	**9**	**224**	**0**	**0**	**0**	**75**	**2.7**	**−39**													
1984-85	**Pittsburgh**	**NHL**	**15**	**0**	**0**	**0**	**15**	**0**	**0**	**0**	**11**	**0.0**	**−3**													
	Baltimore	AHL	58	6	24	30	154												14	0	7	7	47			
1985-86	**Edmonton**	**NHL**	**59**	**11**	**12**	**23**	**265**	**0**	**0**	**2**	**72**	**15.3**	**9**						**8**	**0**	**2**	**2**	**50**	**0**	**0**	**0**
	Nova Scotia	AHL	9	2	4	6	34																			
1986-87♦	**Edmonton**	**NHL**	**41**	**2**	**4**	**6**	**159**	**0**	**0**	**0**	**32**	**6.3**	**−4**						**21**	**4**	**3**	**7**	**65**	**0**	**0**	**1**
	Nova Scotia	AHL	7	2	2	4	48																			
1987-88♦	**Edmonton**	**NHL**	**60**	**9**	**17**	**26**	**223**	**0**	**0**	**1**	**66**	**13.6**	**23**						**16**	**0**	**3**	**3**	**67**	**0**	**0**	**0**
1988-89	**Los Angeles**	**NHL**	**66**	**10**	**17**	**27**	**350**	**2**	**0**	**1**	**87**	**11.5**	**3**						**11**	**0**	**2**	**2**	**33**	**0**	**0**	**0**
1989-90	**Los Angeles**	**NHL**	**75**	**15**	**21**	**36**	**322**	**2**	**1**	**0**	**127**	**11.8**	**2**						**10**	**1**	**3**	**4**	**18**	**1**	**0**	**0**
1990-91	**Los Angeles**	**NHL**	**61**	**7**	**32**	**39**	**221**	**1**	**1**	**1**	**100**	**7.0**	**48**						**12**	**0**	**0**	**0**	**58**	**0**	**0**	**0**
1991-92	**Los Angeles**	**NHL**	**71**	**7**	**22**	**29**	**268**	**2**	**1**	**0**	**119**	**5.9**	**−13**						**6**	**1**	**0**	**1**	**21**	**0**	**0**	**0**
1992-93	**Los Angeles**	**NHL**	**81**	**15**	**26**	**41**	***399**	**3**	**3**	**0**	**197**	**7.6**	**1**						**24**	**4**	**6**	**10**	***60**	**2**	**0**	**1**

			Regular Season																Playoffs							
Season	Club	League	GP	G	A	Pts	PIM	PP	SH	GW	S	%	+/-	TF	F%	H	SB	Min	GP	G	A	Pts	PIM	PP	SH	GW
1993-94	**Pittsburgh**	**NHL**	**47**	**3**	**18**	**21**	**139**	**0**	**0**	**0**	**122**	**2.5**	**–9**	....	....	....	....	....	....	....	....	....	....	....	....	....
	Los Angeles	**NHL**	**18**	**4**	**6**	**10**	**55**	**1**	**0**	**1**	**38**	**10.5**	**–3**	....	....	....	....	....	....	....	....	....	....	....	....	....
1994-95	**Los Angeles**	**NHL**	**41**	**3**	**18**	**21**	**83**	**1**	**0**	**0**	**75**	**4.0**	**–14**	....	....	....	....	....	....	....	....	....	....	....	....	....
1995-96	**Los Angeles**	**NHL**	**59**	**10**	**21**	**31**	**148**	**1**	**1**	**1**	**118**	**8.5**	**–14**	....	....	....	....	....	....	....	....	....	....	....	....	....
	NY Rangers	**NHL**	**9**	**0**	**2**	**2**	**21**	**0**	**0**	**0**	**12**	**0.0**	**–6**	....	....	....	....	....	**4**	**0**	**0**	**0**	**0**	**0**	**0**	**0**
1996-97	**San Jose**	**NHL**	**57**	**4**	**12**	**16**	**186**	**0**	**1**	**1**	**74**	**5.4**	**–6**	....	....	....	....	....	....	....	....	....	....	....	....	....
1997-98	**San Jose**	**NHL**	**56**	**2**	**10**	**12**	**140**	**0**	**0**	**0**	**46**	**4.3**	**10**	....	....	....	....	....	....	....	....	....	....	....	....	....
1998-99	**Edmonton**	**NHL**	**46**	**2**	**3**	**5**	**101**	**0**	**0**	**0**	**29**	**6.9**	**–5**	**0**	**0.0**	**47**	**55**	**16:58**	**3**	**0**	**0**	**0**	**2**	**0**	**0**	**0**
99-2000	**Boston**	**NHL**	**27**	**2**	**3**	**5**	**62**	**0**	**0**	**0**	**24**	**8.3**	**2**	**0**	**0.0**	**35**	**11**	**14:01**	....	....	....	....	....	....	....	....
2000-01	Grand Rapids	IHL	14	0	2	2	36	....	....	....	....	....	....	....	....	....	....	....	....	....	....	....	....	....	....	....
	NHL Totals		**961**	**108**	**251**	**359**	**3381**	**13**	**8**	**8**	**1424**	**7.6**		**0**	**0.0**	**82**	**66**	**15:53**	**115**	**10**	**19**	**29**	**374**	**3**	**0**	**2**

Shared Alka-Seltzer Plus Award with Theoren Fleury (1991)

Signed as a free agent by **Pittsburgh**, July 30, 1982. Traded to **Edmonton** by **Pittsburgh** with Tim Hrynewich and future considerations (Craig Muni, October 6, 1986) for Gilles Meloche, September 11, 1985. Traded to **LA Kings** by **Edmonton** with Wayne Gretzky and Mike Krushelnyski for Jimmy Carson, Martin Gelinas, LA Kings' 1st round choices in 1989 (later traded to New Jersey - New Jersey selected Jason Miller), 1991 (Martin Rucinsky) and 1993 (Nick Stajduhar) Entry Drafts and cash, August 9, 1988. Traded to **Pittsburgh** by **LA Kings**, for Shawn McEachern, August 27, 1993. Traded to **LA Kings** by **Pittsburgh** with Jim Paek for Tomas Sandstrom and Shawn McEachern, February 16, 1994. Traded to **NY Rangers** by **LA Kings** with Jari Kurri and Shane Churla for Ray Ferraro, Ian Laperriere, Mattias Norstrom, Nathan Lafayette and NY Rangers' 4th round choice (Sean Blanchard) in 1997 Entry Draft, March 14, 1996. Traded to **San Jose** by **NY Rangers** for Jayson More, Brian Swanson and San Jose's 4th round choice (later traded back to San Jose - San Jose selected Adam Colagiacomo) in 1997 Entry Draft, August 20, 1996. Signed as a free agent by **Edmonton**, October 1, 1998. Signed as a free agent by **Boston**, December 9, 1999. • Suspended by NHL until February 21, 2001 for stick assault on Donald Brashear in game vs. Vancouver, February 21, 2000.

MELANSON, Dean

(meh-LAHN-suhn, DEEN) **WSH.**

Defense. Shoots right. 5'11", 190 lbs. Born, Antigonish, N.S., November 19, 1973. Buffalo's 4th choice, 80th overall, in 1992 Entry Draft.

Season	Club	League	GP	G	A	Pts	PIM	PP	SH	GW	S	%	+/-	TF	F%	H	SB	Min	GP	G	A	Pts	PIM	PP	SH	GW
1989-90	Antigonish	MJrHL	STATISTICS NOT AVAILABLE																							
1990-91	St-Hyacinthe	QMJHL	69	10	17	27	110	....	....	....	....	....	....	....	....	....	....	....	4	0	1	1	2	....	....	....
1991-92	St-Hyacinthe	QMJHL	42	8	19	27	158	....	....	....	....	....	....	....	....	....	....	....	6	1	2	3	25	....	....	....
1992-93	St-Hyacinthe	QMJHL	57	13	29	42	253	....	....	....	....	....	....	....	....	....	....	....	....	....	....	....	....	....	....	....
	Rochester	AHL	8	0	1	1	6	....	....	....	....	....	....	....	....	....	....	....	14	1	6	7	18	....	....	....
1993-94	Rochester	AHL	80	1	21	22	138	....	....	....	....	....	....	....	....	....	....	....	4	0	1	1	2	....	....	....
1994-95	Rochester	AHL	43	4	7	11	84	....	....	....	....	....	....	....	....	....	....	....	....	....	....	....	....	....	....	....
	Buffalo	**NHL**	**5**	**0**	**0**	**0**	**4**	**0**	**0**	**0**	**1**	**0.0**	**–1**	....	....	....	....	....	....	....	....	....	....	....	....	....
1995-96	Rochester	AHL	70	3	13	16	204	....	....	....	....	....	....	....	....	....	....	....	14	3	3	6	22	....	....	....
1996-97	Quebec Rafales	IHL	72	3	21	24	95	....	....	....	....	....	....	....	....	....	....	....	7	0	2	2	12	....	....	....
1997-98	Rochester	AHL	73	7	9	16	228	....	....	....	....	....	....	....	....	....	....	....	4	0	2	2	0	....	....	....
1998-99	Rochester	AHL	79	7	27	34	192	....	....	....	....	....	....	....	....	....	....	....	17	3	2	5	32	....	....	....
99-2000	Philadelphia	AHL	58	11	25	36	178	....	....	....	....	....	....	....	....	....	....	....	4	2	3	5	10	....	....	....
2000-01	Philadelphia	AHL	15	1	4	5	48	....	....	....	....	....	....	....	....	....	....	....	....	....	....	....	....	....	....	....
	Chicago Wolves	IHL	42	1	7	8	80	....	....	....	....	....	....	....	....	....	....	....	....	....	....	....	....	....	....	....
	Portland Pirates	AHL	13	1	4	5	14	....	....	....	....	....	....	....	....	....	....	....	2	0	0	0	10	....	....	....
	NHL Totals		**5**	**0**	**0**	**0**	**4**	**0**	**0**	**0**	**1**	**0.0**		....	....	....	....	....	....	....	....	....	....	....	....	....

Signed as a free agent by **Philadelphia**, July 22, 1999. Traded to **Washington** by **Philadelphia** for Matt Herr, March 13, 2001.

MELICHAR, Josef

(mehl-ee-KHAHR, YOH-sehf) **PIT.**

Defense. Shoots left. 6'2", 214 lbs. Born, Ceske Budejovice, Czech., January 20, 1979. Pittsburgh's 3rd choice, 71st overall, in 1997 Entry Draft.

Season	Club	League	GP	G	A	Pts	PIM	PP	SH	GW	S	%	+/-	TF	F%	H	SB	Min	GP	G	A	Pts	PIM	PP	SH	GW
1995-96	HC Budejovice-Jr.	Cze-Rep	38	3	4	7	....	....	....	....	....	....	....	....	....	....	....	....	....	....	....	....	....	....	....	....
1996-97	HC Budejovice-Jr.	Cze-Rep	41	2	3	5	10	....	....	....	....	....	....	....	....	....	....	....	....	....	....	....	....	....	....	....
1997-98	Tri-City Americans	WHL	67	9	24	33	154	....	....	....	....	....	....	....	....	....	....	....	....	....	....	....	....	....	....	....
1998-99	Tri-City Americans	WHL	65	8	28	36	125	....	....	....	....	....	....	....	....	....	....	....	11	1	0	1	15	....	....	....
99-2000	Wilkes-Barre	AHL	80	3	9	12	126	....	....	....	....	....	....	....	....	....	....	....	....	....	....	....	....	....	....	....
2000-01	**Pittsburgh**	**NHL**	**18**	**0**	**2**	**2**	**21**	**0**	**0**	**0**	**9**	**0.0**	**–5**	**0**	**0.0**	**33**	**12**	**14:54**	....	....	....	....	....	....	....	....
	Wilkes-Barre	AHL	46	2	5	7	69	....	....	....	....	....	....	....	....	....	....	....	21	0	5	5	6	....	....	....
	NHL Totals		**18**	**0**	**2**	**2**	**21**	**0**	**0**	**0**	**9**	**0.0**		**0**	**0.0**	**33**	**12**	**14:54**	....	....	....	....	....	....	....	....

MELLANBY, Scott

(MEH-lihn-bee, SKAWT) **ST.L.**

Right wing. Shoots right. 6'1", 205 lbs. Born, Montreal, Que., June 11, 1966. Philadelphia's 2nd choice, 27th overall, in 1984 Entry Draft.

Season	Club	League	GP	G	A	Pts	PIM	PP	SH	GW	S	%	+/-	TF	F%	H	SB	Min	GP	G	A	Pts	PIM	PP	SH	GW
1982-83	Don Mills Flyers	MTHL	72	66	52	118	38	....	....	....	....	....	....	....	....	....	....	....	....	....	....	....	....	....	....	....
1983-84	Henry Carr	MTJHL	39	37	37	74	97	....	....	....	....	....	....	....	....	....	....	....	....	....	....	....	....	....	....	....
1984-85	U. of Wisconsin	WCHA	40	14	24	38	60	....	....	....	....	....	....	....	....	....	....	....	....	....	....	....	....	....	....	....
1985-86	U. of Wisconsin	WCHA	32	21	23	44	89	....	....	....	....	....	....	....	....	....	....	....	....	....	....	....	....	....	....	....
	Philadelphia	**NHL**	**2**	**0**	**0**	**0**	**0**	**0**	**0**	**0**	**0**	**0.0**	**–1**	....	....	....	....	....	....	....	....	....	....	....	....	....
1986-87	**Philadelphia**	**NHL**	**71**	**11**	**21**	**32**	**94**	**1**	**0**	**0**	**118**	**9.3**	**8**	....	....	....	....	....	**24**	**5**	**5**	**10**	**46**	**0**	**0**	**1**
1987-88	**Philadelphia**	**NHL**	**75**	**25**	**26**	**51**	**185**	**7**	**0**	**2**	**190**	**13.2**	**–7**	....	....	....	....	....	**7**	**0**	**1**	**1**	**16**	**0**	**0**	**0**
1988-89	**Philadelphia**	**NHL**	**76**	**21**	**29**	**50**	**183**	**11**	**0**	**3**	**202**	**10.4**	**–13**	....	....	....	....	....	**19**	**4**	**5**	**9**	**28**	**0**	**0**	**0**
1989-90	**Philadelphia**	**NHL**	**57**	**6**	**17**	**23**	**77**	**0**	**0**	**1**	**104**	**5.8**	**–4**	....	....	....	....	....	....	....	....	....	....	....	....	....
1990-91	**Philadelphia**	**NHL**	**74**	**20**	**21**	**41**	**155**	**5**	**0**	**6**	**165**	**12.1**	**8**	....	....	....	....	....	....	....	....	....	....	....	....	....
1991-92	**Edmonton**	**NHL**	**80**	**23**	**27**	**50**	**197**	**7**	**0**	**5**	**159**	**14.5**	**5**	....	....	....	....	....	**16**	**2**	**1**	**3**	**29**	**1**	**0**	**1**
1992-93	**Edmonton**	**NHL**	**69**	**15**	**17**	**32**	**147**	**6**	**0**	**3**	**114**	**13.2**	**–4**	....	....	....	....	....	....	....	....	....	....	....	....	....
1993-94	**Florida**	**NHL**	**80**	**30**	**30**	**60**	**149**	**17**	**0**	**4**	**204**	**14.7**	**0**	....	....	....	....	....	....	....	....	....	....	....	....	....
1994-95	**Florida**	**NHL**	**48**	**13**	**12**	**25**	**90**	**4**	**0**	**5**	**130**	**10.0**	**–16**	....	....	....	....	....	....	....	....	....	....	....	....	....
1995-96	**Florida**	**NHL**	**79**	**32**	**38**	**70**	**160**	**19**	**0**	**3**	**225**	**14.2**	**4**	....	....	....	....	....	**22**	**3**	**6**	**9**	**44**	**2**	**0**	**0**
1996-97	**Florida**	**NHL**	**82**	**27**	**29**	**56**	**170**	**9**	**1**	**4**	**221**	**12.2**	**7**	....	....	....	....	....	**5**	**0**	**2**	**2**	**4**	**0**	**0**	**0**
1997-98	**Florida**	**NHL**	**79**	**15**	**24**	**39**	**127**	**6**	**0**	**1**	**188**	**8.0**	**–14**	....	....	....	....	....	....	....	....	....	....	....	....	....
1998-99	**Florida**	**NHL**	**67**	**18**	**27**	**45**	**85**	**4**	**0**	**3**	**136**	**13.2**	**5**	**11**	**27.3**	**64**	**15**	**16:14**	....	....	....	....	....	....	....	....
99-2000	**Florida**	**NHL**	**77**	**18**	**28**	**46**	**126**	**6**	**0**	**2**	**134**	**13.4**	**14**	**20**	**60.0**	**80**	**25**	**14:51**	**4**	**0**	**1**	**1**	**2**	**0**	**0**	**0**
2000-01	**Florida**	**NHL**	**40**	**4**	**9**	**13**	**46**	**1**	**0**	**0**	**58**	**6.9**	**–13**	**4**	**50.0**	**36**	**11**	**14:59**	....	....	....	....	....	....	....	....
	St. Louis	**NHL**	**23**	**7**	**1**	**8**	**25**	**2**	**0**	**0**	**37**	**18.9**	**0**	**1**	**0.0**	**26**	**4**	**15:00**	**15**	**3**	**3**	**6**	**17**	**2**	**0**	**0**
	NHL Totals		**1079**	**285**	**356**	**641**	**2016**	**105**	**1**	**42**	**2385**	**11.9**		**36**	**47.2**	**206**	**55**	**15:21**	**112**	**17**	**24**	**41**	**186**	**5**	**0**	**2**

Played in NHL All-Star Game (1996)

Traded to **Edmonton** by **Philadelphia** with Craig Fisher and Craig Berube for Dave Brown, Corey Foster and Jari Kurri, May 30, 1991. Claimed by **Florida** from **Edmonton** in Expansion Draft, June 24, 1993. Traded to **St. Louis** by **Florida** for Dave Morisset and future considerations, February 9, 2001.

MESSIER, Eric

(MEHS-see-ay, AIR-ihk) **COL.**

Left wing. Shoots left. 6'2", 200 lbs. Born, Drummondville, Que., October 29, 1973.

Season	Club	League	GP	G	A	Pts	PIM	PP	SH	GW	S	%	+/-	TF	F%	H	SB	Min	GP	G	A	Pts	PIM	PP	SH	GW
1990-91	Swift Textile	QAHA	STATISTICS NOT AVAILABLE																							
	Mtl-Bourassa	QAAA	3	0	1	1	0	....	....	....	....	....	....	....	....	....	....	....	2	0	0	0	0	....	....	....
1991-92	Trois-Rivieres	QMJHL	58	2	10	12	28	....	....	....	....	....	....	....	....	....	....	....	15	2	2	4	13	....	....	....
1992-93	Sherbrooke	QMJHL	51	4	17	21	82	....	....	....	....	....	....	....	....	....	....	....	15	0	4	4	18	....	....	....
1993-94	Sherbrooke	QMJHL	67	4	24	28	69	....	....	....	....	....	....	....	....	....	....	....	12	1	7	8	14	....	....	....
1994-95	U. of Quebec	OUAA	13	8	5	13	20	....	....	....	....	....	....	....	....	....	....	....	4	0	3	3	8	....	....	....
1995-96	Cornwall Aces	AHL	72	5	9	14	111	....	....	....	....	....	....	....	....	....	....	....	8	1	1	2	20	....	....	....
1996-97	**Colorado**	**NHL**	**21**	**0**	**0**	**0**	**4**	**0**	**0**	**0**	**11**	**0.0**	**7**	....	....	....	....	....	**6**	**0**	**0**	**0**	**4**	**0**	**0**	**0**
	Hershey Bears	AHL	55	16	26	42	69	....	....	....	....	....	....	....	....	....	....	....	9	3	8	11	14	....	....	....
1997-98	**Colorado**	**NHL**	**62**	**4**	**12**	**16**	**20**	**0**	**0**	**0**	**66**	**6.1**	**4**	....	....	....	....	....	....	....	....	....	....	....	....	....
1998-99	**Colorado**	**NHL**	**31**	**4**	**2**	**6**	**14**	**1**	**0**	**1**	**30**	**13.3**	**0**	**0**	**0.0**	**29**	**22**	**13:43**	**3**	**0**	**0**	**0**	**0**	**0**	**0**	**0**
	Hershey Bears	AHL	6	1	3	4	4	....	....	....	....	....	....	....	....	....	....	....	....	....	....	....	....	....	....	....
99-2000	**Colorado**	**NHL**	**61**	**3**	**6**	**9**	**24**	**1**	**0**	**0**	**28**	**10.7**	**0**	**4**	**25.0**	**52**	**26**	**10:27**	**14**	**0**	**1**	**1**	**4**	**0**	**0**	**0**
2000-01♦	**Colorado**	**NHL**	**64**	**5**	**7**	**12**	**26**	**0**	**0**	**1**	**60**	**8.3**	**–3**	**9**	**44.4**	**142**	**27**	**12:16**	**23**	**2**	**2**	**4**	**14**	**0**	**0**	**0**
	NHL Totals		**239**	**16**	**27**	**43**	**88**	**2**	**0**	**2**	**195**	**8.2**		**13**	**38.5**	**223**	**75**	**11:51**	**46**	**2**	**3**	**5**	**22**	**0**	**0**	**0**

QMJHL Second All-Star Team (1994)

Signed as a free agent by **Colorado**, June 14, 1995. • Missed majority of 1998-99 season recovering from elbow injury suffered in game vs. Ottawa, October 10, 1998.

MESSIER, Mark
(MEHS-see-ay, MAHRK) **NYR**

Center. Shoots left. 6'1", 210 lbs. Born, Edmonton, Alta., January 18, 1961. Edmonton's 2nd choice, 48th overall, in 1979 Entry Draft.

Season	Club	League	GP	G	A	Pts	PIM	PP	SH	GW	S	%	+/-	TF	F%	H	SB	Min	Playoffs GP	G	A	Pts	PIM	PP	SH	GW
1976-77	Spruce Grove	AJHL	57	27	39	66	91																			
1977-78	St. Albert Saints	AJHL	54	25	49	74	194																			
	Portland	WHL																	7	4	1	5	2			
1978-79	St. Albert Saints	AJHL	17	15	18	33	64																			
	Indianapolis	WHA	5	0	0	0	0																			
	Cincinnati Sting	WHA	47	1	10	11	58																			
1979-80	Edmonton	NHL	75	12	21	33	120	1	1	1	113	10.6	–10						3	1	2	3	2	0	1	0
	Houston Apollos	CHL	4	0	3	3	4																			
1980-81	Edmonton	NHL	72	23	40	63	102	4	0	1	179	12.8	–12						9	2	5	7	13	0	0	0
1981-82	Edmonton	NHL	78	50	38	88	119	10	0	3	235	21.3	21						5	1	2	3	8	0	0	0
1982-83	Edmonton	NHL	77	48	58	106	72	12	1	2	237	20.3	19						15	15	6	21	14	4	2	0
1983-84♦	Edmonton	NHL	73	37	64	101	165	7	4	7	219	16.9	40						19	8	18	26	19	1	1	2
1984-85♦	Edmonton	NHL	55	23	31	54	57	4	5	1	136	16.9	8						18	12	13	25	12	1	1	1
1985-86	Edmonton	NHL	63	35	49	84	68	10	5	7	201	17.4	36						10	4	6	10	18	0	2	0
1986-87♦	Edmonton	NHL	77	37	70	107	73	7	4	5	208	17.8	21						21	12	16	28	16	1	2	1
1987-88♦	Edmonton	NHL	77	37	74	111	103	12	3	7	182	20.3	21						19	11	23	34	29	7	1	0
1988-89	Edmonton	NHL	72	33	61	94	130	6	6	4	164	20.1	–5						7	1	11	12	8	0	0	0
1989-90♦	Edmonton	NHL	79	45	84	129	79	13	6	3	211	21.3	19						22	9	*22	*31	20	1	1	1
1990-91	Edmonton	NHL	53	12	52	64	34	3	1	2	109	11.0	15						18	4	11	15	16	1	0	0
1991-92	NY Rangers	NHL	79	35	72	107	76	12	4	6	212	16.5	31						11	7	7	14	6	2	2	0
1992-93	NY Rangers	NHL	75	25	66	91	72	7	2	2	215	11.6	–6													
1993-94♦	NY Rangers	NHL	76	26	58	84	76	6	2	5	216	12.0	25						23	12	18	30	33	2	1	4
1994-95	NY Rangers	NHL	46	14	39	53	40	3	3	2	126	11.1	8						10	3	10	13	8	2	0	1
1995-96	NY Rangers	NHL	74	47	52	99	122	14	1	5	241	19.5	29						11	4	7	11	16	2	0	1
1996-97	NY Rangers	NHL	71	36	48	84	88	7	5	9	227	15.9	12						15	3	9	12	6	0	0	1
1997-98	Vancouver	NHL	82	22	38	60	58	8	2	2	139	15.8	–10													
1998-99	Vancouver	NHL	59	13	35	48	33	4	2	2	97	13.4	–12	1536	53.9	29	35	22:36								
99-2000	Vancouver	NHL	66	17	37	54	30	6	0	4	131	13.0	–15	1684	56.8	50	26	21:12								
2000-01	NY Rangers	NHL	82	24	43	67	89	12	3	2	131	18.3	–25	1879	55.5	78	47	19:14								
	NHL Totals		1561	651	1130	1781	1806	168	60	82	3929	16.6		5099	55.4	157	108	20:49	236	109	186	295	244	24	14	12

NHL First All-Star Team (1982, 1983, 1990, 1992) • NHL Second All-Star Team (1984) • Won Conn Smythe Trophy (1984) • Won Lester B. Pearson Award (1990, 1992) • Won Hart Trophy (1990, 1992) • Played in NHL All-Star Game (1982, 1983, 1984, 1986, 1988, 1989, 1990, 1991, 1992, 1994, 1996, 1997, 1998, 2000)

Signed as an underage free agent by **Indianapolis** (WHA) to a 10-game tryout contract, November 5, 1978. Signed as a free agent by **Cincinnati** (WHA) after **Indianapolis** (WHA) franchise folded, December, 1978. Traded to **NY Rangers** by **Edmonton** with future considerations (Jeff Beukeboom for David Shaw, November 12, 1991) for Bernie Nicholls, Steven Rice and Louie DeBrusk, October 4, 1991. Signed as a free agent by **Vancouver**, July 30, 1997. Signed as a free agent by **NY Rangers**, July 13, 2000.

METROPOLIT, Glen
(MEH-troh-poh-LIHT, GLEHN) **WSH.**

Right wing. Shoots right. 5'10", 200 lbs. Born, Toronto, Ont., June 25, 1974.

Season	Club	League	GP	G	A	Pts	PIM	PP	SH	GW	S	%	+/-	TF	F%	H	SB	Min	Playoffs GP	G	A	Pts	PIM	PP	SH	GW
1992-93	Richmond Hill	MTJHL	43	27	36	63	36																			
1993-94	Richmond Hill	MTJHL	49	38	62	100	83																			
1994-95	Vernon Lakers	BCJHL	60	43	74	117	92																			
1995-96	Nashville Knights	ECHL	58	30	31	61	62												5	3	8	11	2			
	Atlanta Knights	IHL	1	0	0	0	0																			
1996-97	Pensacola	ECHL	54	35	47	82	45												12	9	16	25	28			
	Quebec Rafales	IHL	22	5	4	9	14												5	0	0	0	2			
1997-98	Grand Rapids	IHL	79	20	35	55	90												3	1	1	2	0			
1998-99	Grand Rapids	IHL	77	28	53	81	92																			
99-2000	Washington	NHL	30	6	13	19	4	1	0	1	57	10.5	5	37	46.0	48	7	13:17	2	0	0	0	2	0	0	0
	Portland Pirates	AHL	48	18	42	60	73												1	1	0	1	0			
2000-01	Washington	NHL	15	1	5	6	10	0	0	0	20	5.0	–2	3	33.3	13	0	11:50	1	0	0	0	0	0	0	0
	Portland Pirates	AHL	51	25	42	67	59																			
	NHL Totals		45	7	18	25	14	1	0	1	77	9.1		40	45.0	61	7	12:48	3	0	0	0	2	0	0	0

Signed as a free agent by **Washington**, July 19, 1999.

MEZEI, Branislav
(MEH-tzay, BRAN-ih-slav) **NYI**

Defense. Shoots left. 6'4", 221 lbs. Born, Nitra, Czech., October 8, 1980. NY Islanders' 3rd choice, 10th overall, in 1999 Entry Draft.

Season	Club	League	GP	G	A	Pts	PIM	PP	SH	GW	S	%	+/-	TF	F%	H	SB	Min	Playoffs GP	G	A	Pts	PIM	PP	SH	GW
1996-97	MHC Nitra	Slovak-Jr.	40	8	17	25	42																			
1997-98	Belleville Bulls	OHL	53	3	5	8	58												8	0	2	2	8			
1998-99	Belleville Bulls	OHL	60	5	18	23	90												18	0	4	4	29			
99-2000	Belleville Bulls	OHL	58	7	21	28	99												6	0	3	3	10			
2000-01	NY Islanders	NHL	42	1	4	5	53	0	0	0	29	3.4	–5	0	0.0	127	31	14:48								
	Lowell	AHL	20	0	3	3	28																			
	NHL Totals		42	1	4	5	53	0	0	0	29	3.4		0	0.0	127	31	14:48								

OHL First All-Star Team (2000)

MIKA, Petr
(MEE-kah, PEE-tuhr) **NYI**

Left wing. Shoots right. 6'4", 194 lbs. Born, Prague, Czech., February 12, 1979. NY Islanders' 6th choice, 85th overall, in 1997 Entry Draft.

Season	Club	League	GP	G	A	Pts	PIM	PP	SH	GW	S	%	+/-	TF	F%	H	SB	Min	Playoffs GP	G	A	Pts	PIM	PP	SH	GW
1995-96	Slavia Praha-Jr.	Cze-Rep	26	5	12	17																				
	Slavia Praha	Cze-Rep	1	0	0	0	0																			
1996-97	HC Beroun-2	Cze-Rep	9	1	0	1																				
	Slavia Praha-2	Cze-Rep	20	1	2	3	6																			
	Slavia Praha	Cze-Rep	15	8	0	8																				
1997-98	Ottawa 67's	OHL	41	10	8	18	28																			
1998-99	Slavia Praha	Cze-Rep	49	6	5	11	57																			
99-2000	NY Islanders	NHL	3	0	0	0	0	0	0	0	1	0.0	–1	0	0.0	3	2	4:30								
	Lowell	AHL	50	8	9	17	20												6	0	0	0	0			
2000-01	Lowell	AHL	13	0	1	1	7																			
	Springfield	AHL	27	0	2	2	8																			
	NHL Totals		3	0	0	0	0	0	0	0	1	0.0		0	0.0	3	2	4:30								

MILLAR, Craig
(MIHL-uhr, KRAYG)

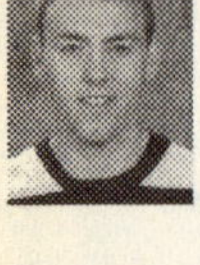

Defense. Shoots left. 6'2", 212 lbs. Born, Winnipeg, Man., July 12, 1976. Buffalo's 10th choice, 225th overall, in 1994 Entry Draft.

Season	Club	League	GP	G	A	Pts	PIM	PP	SH	GW	S	%	+/-	TF	F%	H	SB	Min	Playoffs GP	G	A	Pts	PIM	PP	SH	GW
1991-92	Winnipeg Mavs	MAHA	STATISTICS NOT AVAILABLE																							
1992-93	Swift Current	WHL	43	2	1	3	8																			
1993-94	Swift Current	WHL	66	2	9	11	53												7	0	3	3	4			
1994-95	Swift Current	WHL	72	8	42	50	80												6	1	1	2	10			
1995-96	Swift Current	WHL	72	31	46	77	151												6	1	0	1	22			
1996-97	Rochester	AHL	64	7	18	25	65																			
	Edmonton	NHL	1	0	0	0	2	0	0	0	1	0.0	0													
	Hamilton Bulldogs	AHL	10	1	3	4	10												22	4	4	8	21			
1997-98	Edmonton	NHL	11	4	0	4	8	1	0	0	10	40.0	–3													
	Hamilton Bulldogs	AHL	60	10	22	32	113												9	3	1	4	22			
1998-99	Edmonton	NHL	24	0	2	2	19	0	0	0	18	0.0	–6	0	0.0	23	24	15:09								
	Hamilton Bulldogs	AHL	43	3	17	20	38												11	1	5	6	18			
99-2000	Nashville	NHL	57	3	11	14	28	0	0	1	50	6.0	–6	1	0.0	56	38	16:53								
	Milwaukee	IHL	8	1	5	6	6																			

			Regular Season																Playoffs							
Season	Club	League	GP	G	A	Pts	PIM	PP	SH	GW	S	%	+/-	TF	F%	H	SB	Min	GP	G	A	Pts	PIM	PP	SH	GW
2000-01	Nashville	NHL	5	0	0	0	6	0	0	0	2	0.0	1	0	0.0	6	1	12:04	....	....	....	....	....	....	....	....
	Grand Rapids	IHL	12	1	2	3	2	....	....	....	....	....	....	....	....	....	....	....	....	....	....	....	....	....	....	....
	Tampa Bay	NHL	16	1	1	2	10	0	0	1	10	10.0	–8	0	0.0	4	13	15:01	....	....	....	....	....	....	....	....
	Detroit Vipers	IHL	11	0	2	2	32	....	....	....	....	....	....	....	....	....	....	....	....	....	....	....	....	....	....	....
	NHL Totals		114	8	14	22	73	1	0	2	91	8.8		1	0.0	89	76	15:57	....	....	....	....	....	....	....	....

WHL East First All-Star Team (1996)

Traded to **Edmonton** by **Buffalo** with Barrie Moore for Miroslav Satan, March 18, 1997. Traded to **Nashville** by **Edmonton** for Detroit's 3rd round choice (previously acquired, Edmonton selected Mike Comrie) in 1999 Entry Draft, June 26, 1999. Claimed on waivers by **Tampa Bay** from **Nashville**, October 25, 2000. Traded to **Ottawa** by **Tampa Bay** for John Emmons, March 13, 2001.

MILLER, Aaron

(MIHL-luhr, AIR-ruhn) **L.A.**

Defense. Shoots right. 6'3", 200 lbs. Born, Buffalo, NY, August 11, 1971. NY Rangers' 6th choice, 88th overall, in 1989 Entry Draft.

Season	Club	League	GP	G	A	Pts	PIM	PP	SH	GW	S	%	+/-	TF	F%	H	SB	Min	GP	G	A	Pts	PIM	PP	SH	GW
1987-88	Niagara Scenics	NAJHL	30	4	9	13	2	....	....	....	....	....	....	....	....	....	....	....	....	....	....	....	....	....	....	....
1988-89	Niagara Scenics	NAJHL	59	24	38	62	60	....	....	....	....	....	....	....	....	....	....	....	....	....	....	....	....	....	....	....
1989-90	U. of Vermont	ECAC	31	1	15	16	24	....	....	....	....	....	....	....	....	....	....	....	....	....	....	....	....	....	....	....
1990-91	U. of Vermont	ECAC	30	3	7	10	22	....	....	....	....	....	....	....	....	....	....	....	....	....	....	....	....	....	....	....
1991-92	U. of Vermont	ECAC	31	3	16	19	28	....	....	....	....	....	....	....	....	....	....	....	....	....	....	....	....	....	....	....
1992-93	U. of Vermont	ECAC	30	4	13	17	16	....	....	....	....	....	....	....	....	....	....	....	....	....	....	....	....	....	....	....
1993-94	Quebec	NHL	1	0	0	0	0	0	0	0	0	0.0	–1	....	....	....	....	....	....	....	....	....	....	....	....	....
	Cornwall Aces	AHL	64	4	10	14	49	....	....	....	....	....	....	....	....	....	....	....	13	0	2	2	10	....	....	....
1994-95	Cornwall Aces	AHL	76	4	18	22	69	....	....	....	....	....	....	....	....	....	....	....	....	....	....	....	....	....	....	....
	Quebec	NHL	9	0	3	3	6	0	0	0	12	0.0	2	....	....	....	....	....	....	....	....	....	....	....	....	....
1995-96	Colorado	NHL	5	0	0	0	0	0	0	0	2	0.0	0	....	....	....	....	....	....	....	....	....	....	....	....	....
	Cornwall Aces	AHL	62	4	23	27	77	....	....	....	....	....	....	....	....	....	....	....	8	0	1	1	6	....	....	....
1996-97	Colorado	NHL	56	5	12	17	15	0	0	3	47	10.6	15	....	....	....	....	....	17	1	2	3	10	0	0	0
1997-98	Colorado	NHL	55	2	2	4	51	0	0	0	29	6.9	0	....	....	....	....	....	7	0	0	0	8	0	0	0
1998-99	Colorado	NHL	76	5	13	18	42	1	0	2	87	5.7	3	0	0.0	115	128	21:49	19	1	5	6	10	0	0	0
99-2000	Colorado	NHL	53	1	7	8	36	0	0	0	44	2.3	3	0	0.0	64	76	19:05	17	1	1	2	6	0	0	0
2000-01	Colorado	NHL	56	4	9	13	29	0	0	0	49	8.2	19	0	0.0	69	62	18:25	....	....	....	....	....	....	....	....
	Los Angeles	NHL	13	0	5	5	14	0	0	0	10	0.0	3	1	0.0	41	26	22:44	13	0	1	1	6	0	0	0
	NHL Totals		324	17	51	68	193	1	0	5	280	6.1		1	0.0	289	292	20:11	73	3	9	12	40	0	0	0

ECAC First All-Star Team (1993) • NCAA East Second All-American Team (1993)

Traded to **Quebec** by **NY Rangers** with NY Rangers' 5th round choice (Bill Lindsay) in 1991 Entry Draft for Joe Cirella, January 17, 1991. Transferred to **Colorado** after **Quebec** franchise relocated, June 21, 1995. Traded to **LA Kings** by **Colorado** with Adam Deadmarsh, Colorado's 1st round choice (David Steckel) in 2001 Entry Draft and future considerations (Jared Aulin, March 22, 2001) for Rob Blake and Steve Reinprecht, February 21, 2001.

MILLER, Kevin

(MIHL-luhr, KEH-vihn)

Center. Shoots right. 5'11", 184 lbs. Born, Lansing, MI, September 2, 1965. NY Rangers' 10th choice, 202nd overall, in 1984 Entry Draft.

Season	Club	League	GP	G	A	Pts	PIM	PP	SH	GW	S	%	+/-	TF	F%	H	SB	Min	GP	G	A	Pts	PIM	PP	SH	GW
1983-84	Redford Royals	GLJHL	44	28	57	85	....	....	....	....	....	....	....	....	....	....	....	....	....	....	....	....	....	....	....	....
1984-85	Michigan State	CCHA	44	11	29	40	84	....	....	....	....	....	....	....	....	....	....	....	....	....	....	....	....	....	....	....
1985-86	Michigan State	CCHA	45	19	52	71	112	....	....	....	....	....	....	....	....	....	....	....	....	....	....	....	....	....	....	....
1986-87	Michigan State	CCHA	42	25	56	81	63	....	....	....	....	....	....	....	....	....	....	....	....	....	....	....	....	....	....	....
1987-88	Michigan State	CCHA	9	6	3	9	18	....	....	....	....	....	....	....	....	....	....	....	....	....	....	....	....	....	....	....
	United States	Nat-Team	48	31	32	63	33	....	....	....	....	....	....	....	....	....	....	....	....	....	....	....	....	....	....	....
	United States	Olympics	5	1	3	4	4	....	....	....	....	....	....	....	....	....	....	....	....	....	....	....	....	....	....	....
1988-89	NY Rangers	NHL	24	3	5	8	2	0	0	1	40	7.5	–1	....	....	....	....	....	....	....	....	....	....	....	....	....
	Denver Rangers	IHL	55	29	47	76	19	....	....	....	....	....	....	....	....	....	....	....	4	2	1	3	2	....	....	....
1989-90	NY Rangers	NHL	16	0	5	5	2	0	0	0	9	0.0	–1	....	....	....	....	....	1	0	0	0	0	0	0	0
	Flint Spirits	IHL	48	19	23	42	41	....	....	....	....	....	....	....	....	....	....	....	....	....	....	....	....	....	....	....
1990-91	NY Rangers	NHL	63	17	27	44	63	1	2	3	113	15.0	1	....	....	....	....	....	....	....	....	....	....	....	....	....
	Detroit	NHL	11	5	2	7	4	0	1	0	23	21.7	–4	....	....	....	....	....	7	3	2	5	20	0	1	0
1991-92	Detroit	NHL	80	20	26	46	53	3	1	4	130	15.4	6	....	....	....	....	....	9	0	2	2	4	0	0	0
1992-93	Washington	NHL	10	0	3	3	35	0	0	0	10	0.0	–4	....	....	....	....	....	....	....	....	....	....	....	....	....
	St. Louis	NHL	72	24	22	46	65	8	3	4	153	15.7	6	....	....	....	....	....	10	0	3	3	11	0	0	0
1993-94	St. Louis	NHL	75	23	25	48	83	6	3	5	154	14.9	6	....	....	....	....	....	3	1	0	1	4	0	1	0
1994-95	St. Louis	NHL	15	2	5	7	0	0	0	0	19	10.5	4	....	....	....	....	....	....	....	....	....	....	....	....	....
	San Jose	NHL	21	6	7	13	13	1	1	2	41	14.6	0	....	....	....	....	....	6	0	0	0	2	0	0	0
1995-96	San Jose	NHL	68	22	20	42	41	2	2	2	146	15.1	–8	....	....	....	....	....	....	....	....	....	....	....	....	....
	Pittsburgh	NHL	13	6	5	11	4	1	0	0	33	18.2	4	....	....	....	....	....	18	3	2	5	8	0	0	0
1996-97	Chicago	NHL	69	14	17	31	41	5	1	2	139	10.1	–10	....	....	....	....	....	6	0	1	1	0	0	0	0
1997-98	Chicago	NHL	37	4	7	11	8	0	0	1	37	10.8	–4	....	....	....	....	....	....	....	....	....	....	....	....	....
	Indianapolis Ice	IHL	26	11	11	22	41	....	....	....	....	....	....	....	....	....	....	....	2	1	1	2	0	....	....	....
1998-99	NY Islanders	NHL	33	1	5	6	13	0	0	0	37	2.7	–5	114	49.1	42	11	10:19	....	....	....	....	....	....	....	....
	Chicago Wolves	IHL	30	11	20	31	8	....	....	....	....	....	....	....	....	....	....	....	10	2	7	9	22	....	....	....
99-2000	Ottawa	NHL	9	3	2	5	2	1	0	2	11	27.3	1	34	41.2	9	2	8:10	1	0	0	0	0	0	0	0
	Grand Rapids	IHL	63	20	34	54	51	....	....	....	....	....	....	....	....	....	....	....	17	*11	7	*18	30	....	....	....
2000-01	HC Davos	Switz.	36	*29	27	56	61	....	....	....	....	....	....	....	....	....	....	....	4	3	0	3	2	....	....	....
	NHL Totals		616	150	183	333	429	28	14	26	1095	13.7		148	47.3	51	13	9:51	61	7	10	17	49	0	2	0

Traded to **Detroit** by **NY Rangers** with Jim Cummins and Dennis Vial for Joe Kocur and Per Djoos, March 5, 1991. Traded to **Washington** by **Detroit** for Dino Ciccarelli, June 20, 1992. Traded to **St. Louis** by **Washington** for Paul Cavallini, November 2, 1992. Traded to **San Jose** by **St. Louis** for Todd Elik, March 23, 1995. Traded to **Pittsburgh** by **San Jose** for Pittsburgh's 5th round choice (later traded to Boston - Boston selected Elias Abrahamsson) in 1996 Entry Draft , March 20, 1996. Signed as a free agent by **Chicago**, July 18, 1996. Signed as a free agent by **NY Islanders**, October 9, 1998. Signed as a free agent by **Ottawa**, August 24, 1999. Signed as a free agent by **HC Davos** (Switz.), July 26, 2000.

MILLER, Kip

(MIHL-luhr, KIHP)

Center. Shoots left. 5'10", 190 lbs. Born, Lansing, MI, June 11, 1969. Quebec's 4th choice, 72nd overall, in 1987 Entry Draft.

Season	Club	League	GP	G	A	Pts	PIM	PP	SH	GW	S	%	+/-	TF	F%	H	SB	Min	GP	G	A	Pts	PIM	PP	SH	GW
1984-85	Det-Compuware	MNHL	65	69	63	132	....	....	....	....	....	....	....	....	....	....	....	....	....	....	....	....	....	....	....	....
1985-86	Det-Compuware	GLJHL	30	25	28	53	....	....	....	....	....	....	....	....	....	....	....	....	....	....	....	....	....	....	....	....
1986-87	Michigan State	CCHA	41	20	19	39	92	....	....	....	....	....	....	....	....	....	....	....	....	....	....	....	....	....	....	....
1987-88	Michigan State	CCHA	39	16	25	41	51	....	....	....	....	....	....	....	....	....	....	....	....	....	....	....	....	....	....	....
1988-89	Michigan State	CCHA	47	32	45	77	94	....	....	....	....	....	....	....	....	....	....	....	....	....	....	....	....	....	....	....
1989-90	Michigan State	CCHA	45	*48	53	*101	60	....	....	....	....	....	....	....	....	....	....	....	....	....	....	....	....	....	....	....
1990-91	Quebec	NHL	13	4	3	7	7	0	0	0	16	25.0	–1	....	....	....	....	....	....	....	....	....	....	....	....	....
	Halifax Citadels	AHL	66	36	33	69	40	....	....	....	....	....	....	....	....	....	....	....	....	....	....	....	....	....	....	....
1991-92	Quebec	NHL	36	5	10	15	12	1	0	2	46	10.9	–21	....	....	....	....	....	....	....	....	....	....	....	....	....
	Halifax Citadels	AHL	24	9	17	26	8	....	....	....	....	....	....	....	....	....	....	....	....	....	....	....	....	....	....	....
	Minnesota	NHL	3	1	2	3	2	1	0	0	3	33.3	–1	....	....	....	....	....	....	....	....	....	....	....	....	....
	Kalamazoo	IHL	6	1	8	9	4	....	....	....	....	....	....	....	....	....	....	....	12	3	9	12	12	....	....	....
1992-93	Kalamazoo	IHL	61	17	39	56	59	....	....	....	....	....	....	....	....	....	....	....	....	....	....	....	....	....	....	....
1993-94	San Jose	NHL	11	2	2	4	6	0	0	0	21	9.5	–1	....	....	....	....	....	....	....	....	....	....	....	....	....
	Kansas City	IHL	71	38	54	92	51	....	....	....	....	....	....	....	....	....	....	....	....	....	....	....	....	....	....	....
1994-95	Denver Grizzlies	IHL	71	46	60	106	54	....	....	....	....	....	....	....	....	....	....	....	17	*15	14	29	8	....	....	....
	NY Islanders	NHL	8	0	1	1	0	0	0	0	11	0.0	1	....	....	....	....	....	....	....	....	....	....	....	....	....
1995-96	Chicago	NHL	10	1	4	5	2	0	0	0	12	8.3	1	....	....	....	....	....	....	....	....	....	....	....	....	....
	Indianapolis Ice	IHL	73	32	59	91	46	....	....	....	....	....	....	....	....	....	....	....	5	2	6	8	2	....	....	....
1996-97	Chicago Wolves	IHL	43	11	41	52	32	....	....	....	....	....	....	....	....	....	....	....	....	....	....	....	....	....	....	....
	Indianapolis Ice	IHL	37	17	24	41	18	....	....	....	....	....	....	....	....	....	....	....	4	2	2	4	2	....	....	....
1997-98	Utah Grizzlies	IHL	72	38	59	97	30	....	....	....	....	....	....	....	....	....	....	....	4	3	2	5	10	....	....	....
	NY Islanders	NHL	9	1	3	4	2	0	0	0	11	9.1	–2	....	....	....	....	....	....	....	....	....	....	....	....	....
1998-99	Pittsburgh	NHL	77	19	23	42	22	1	0	4	125	15.2	1	150	44.7	67	25	16:55	13	2	7	9	19	1	0	0
99-2000	Pittsburgh	NHL	44	4	15	19	10	0	0	1	50	8.0	–1	132	40.2	23	13	14:18	....	....	....	....	....	....	....	....
	Anaheim	NHL	30	6	17	23	4	2	0	1	32	18.8	1	7	42.9	28	1	13:44	....	....	....	....	....	....	....	....
2000-01	Pittsburgh	NHL	33	3	8	11	6	1	0	0	38	7.9	0	61	50.8	18	6	9:46	....	....	....	....	....	....	....	....
	Grand Rapids	IHL	34	16	19	35	12	....	....	....	....	....	....	....	....	....	....	....	10	5	8	13	2	....	....	....
	NHL Totals		274	46	88	134	73	6	0	8	365	12.6		350	44.0	136	45	14:30	13	2	7	9	19	1	0	0

CCHA First All-Star Team (1989, 1990) • NCAA West First All-American Team (1989, 1990) • Won Hobey Baker Memorial Award (Top U.S. Collegiate Player) (1990)

Traded to **Minnesota** by **Quebec** for Steve Maltais, March 8, 1992. Signed as a free agent by **San Jose**, August 10, 1993. Signed as a free agent by **NY Islanders**, July 7, 1994. Signed as a free agent by **Chicago**, July 21, 1995. Signed as a free agent by **NY Islanders**, November 26, 1997. Claimed by **Pittsburgh** from **NY Islanders** in NHL Waiver Draft, October 5, 1998. Traded to **Anaheim** by **Pittsburgh** for Anaheim's 9th round choice (Roman Simicek) in 2000 Entry Draft, January 29, 2000. Signed as a free agent by **Pittsburgh**, September 24, 2000.

MILLS, Craig
(MIHLS, KRAYG) **TOR.**

Right wing. Shoots right. 6', 190 lbs. Born, Toronto, Ont., August 27, 1976. Winnipeg's 5th choice, 108th overall, in 1994 Entry Draft.

Season	Club	League	GP	G	A	Pts	PIM	PP	SH	GW	S	%	+/-	TF	F%	H	SB	Min	GP	G	A	Pts	PIM	PP	SH	GW
			Regular Season																Playoffs							
1992-93	St. Michael's	MTJHL	44	9	21	30	42												15	1	6	7	8			
1993-94	Belleville Bulls	OHL	63	15	18	33	88												12	2	1	3	11			
1994-95	Belleville Bulls	OHL	62	39	41	80	104												13	7	9	16	8			
1995-96	Belleville Bulls	OHL	48	10	19	29	113												14	4	5	9	32			
	Winnipeg	NHL	4	0	2	2	0	0	0	0	0	0.0	0						1	0	0	0	0	0	0	0
	Springfield	AHL																	2	0	0	0	0			
1996-97	Indianapolis Ice	IHL	80	12	7	19	199												4	0	0	0	4			
1997-98	Chicago	NHL	20	0	3	3	34	0	0	0	5	0.0	1													
	Indianapolis Ice	IHL	42	8	11	19	119												5	0	0	0	27			
1998-99	Chicago	NHL	7	0	0	0	2	0	0	0	1	0.0	-2	0	0.0	4	0	5:48								
	Chicago Wolves	IHL	5	0	0	0	14																			
	Portland Pirates	AHL	48	7	11	18	59																			
	Indianapolis Ice	IHL	12	2	3	5	14												6	1	0	1	5			
99-2000	Springfield	AHL	78	10	13	23	151												5	2	1	3	6			
2000-01	Springfield	AHL	64	8	5	13	131																			
	NHL Totals		31	0	5	5	36	0	0	0	6	0.0		0	0.0	4	0	5:48	1	0	0	0	0	0	0	0

Canadian Major Junior Humanitarian Player of the Year (1996)

Rights transferred to **Phoenix** after **Winnipeg** franchise relocated, July 1, 1996. Traded to **Chicago** by **Phoenix** with Alexei Zhamnov and Phoenix's 1st round choice (Ty Jones) in 1997 Entry Draft for Jeremy Roenick, August 16, 1996. Traded to **Phoenix** by **Chicago** for cash, September 11, 1999. Traded to **Toronto** by **Phoenix** with Robert Reichel and Travis Green for Danny Markov, June 12, 2001.

MIRONOV, Boris
(mih-RAWN-ohv, BOHR-ihs) **CHI.**

Defense. Shoots right. 6'3", 223 lbs. Born, Moscow, USSR, March 21, 1972. Winnipeg's 2nd choice, 27th overall, in 1992 Entry Draft.

Season	Club	League	GP	G	A	Pts	PIM	PP	SH	GW	S	%	+/-	TF	F%	H	SB	Min	GP	G	A	Pts	PIM	PP	SH	GW
1988-89	CSKA Moscow	USSR	1	0	0	0	0																			
1989-90	CSKA Moscow	USSR	7	0	0	0	0																			
1990-91	CSKA Moscow	USSR	36	1	5	6	16																			
1991-92	CSKA Moscow	CIS	36	2	1	3	22																			
1992-93	CSKA Moscow	CIS	19	0	5	5	20																			
1993-94	Winnipeg	NHL	65	7	22	29	96	5	0	0	122	5.7	-29													
	Edmonton	NHL	14	0	2	2	14	0	0	0	23	0.0	-4													
1994-95	Edmonton	NHL	29	1	7	8	40	0	0	0	48	2.1	-9													
	Cape Breton	AHL	4	2	5	7	23																			
1995-96	Edmonton	NHL	78	8	24	32	101	7	0	1	158	5.1	-23													
1996-97	Edmonton	NHL	55	6	26	32	85	2	0	1	147	4.1	2						12	2	8	10	16	2	0	0
1997-98	Edmonton	NHL	81	16	30	46	100	10	1	1	203	7.9	-8						12	3	3	6	27	1	0	1
	Russia	Olympics	6	0	2	2	2																			
1998-99	Edmonton	NHL	63	11	29	40	104	5	0	4	138	8.0	6	0	0.0	142	103	25:55								
	Chicago	NHL	12	0	9	9	27	0	0	0	35	0.0	7	0	0.0	32	17	24:17								
99-2000	Chicago	NHL	58	9	28	37	72	4	2	1	144	6.3	-3	1	100.0	121	60	24:53								
2000-01	Chicago	NHL	66	5	17	22	42	3	0	0	143	3.5	-14	0	0.0	105	78	22:05								
	NHL Totals		521	63	194	257	681	36	3	8	1161	5.4		1	100.0	400	258	24:15	24	5	11	16	43	3	0	1

NHL All-Rookie Team (1994)

Traded to **Edmonton** by **Winnipeg** with Mats Lindgren, Winnipeg's 1st round choice (Jason Bonsignore) in 1994 Entry Draft and Florida's 4th round choice (previously acquired, Edmonton selected Adam Copeland) in 1994 Entry Draft for Dave Manson and St. Louis' 6th round choice (previously acquired, Winnipeg selected Chris Kibermanis) in 1994 Entry Draft, March 15, 1994. Traded to **Chicago** by **Edmonton** with Dean McAmmond and Jonas Elofsson for Chad Kilger, Daniel Cleary, Ethan Moreau and Christian Laflamme, March 20, 1999.

MIRONOV, Dmitri
(mih-RAWN-ohv, dih-MEE-tree) **WSH.**

Defense. Shoots right. 6'4", 224 lbs. Born, Moscow, USSR, December 25, 1965. Toronto's 7th choice, 160th overall, in 1991 Entry Draft.

Season	Club	League	GP	G	A	Pts	PIM	PP	SH	GW	S	%	+/-	TF	F%	H	SB	Min	GP	G	A	Pts	PIM	PP	SH	GW
1985-86	CSKA Moscow	USSR	9	0	1	1	8																			
1986-87	CSKA Moscow	USSR	20	1	3	4	10																			
1987-88	Krylja Sovetov	USSR	44	12	6	18	30																			
1988-89	Krylja Sovetov	USSR	44	5	6	11	44																			
1989-90	Krylja Sovetov	USSR	45	4	11	15	34																			
1990-91	Krylja Sovetov	USSR	45	16	12	28	22																			
1991-92	Krylja Sovetov	CIS	35	15	16	31	62																			
	Toronto	NHL	7	1	0	1	0	0	0	1	7	14.3	-4													
	Russia	Olympics	8	3	1	4	6																			
1992-93	Toronto	NHL	59	7	24	31	40	4	0	1	105	6.7	-1						14	1	2	3	2	1	0	0
1993-94	Toronto	NHL	76	9	27	36	78	3	0	0	147	6.1	5						18	6	9	15	6	6	0	0
1994-95	Toronto	NHL	33	5	12	17	28	2	0	0	68	7.4	6						6	2	1	3	2	1	0	0
1995-96	Pittsburgh	NHL	72	3	31	34	88	1	0	1	86	3.5	19						15	0	1	1	10	0	0	0
1996-97	Pittsburgh	NHL	15	1	5	6	24	0	0	1	19	5.3	-4													
	Anaheim	NHL	62	12	34	46	77	3	1	1	158	7.6	20						11	1	10	11	10	1	0	0
1997-98	Anaheim	NHL	66	6	30	36	115	2	0	1	142	4.2	-7													
	Russia	Olympics	6	0	3	3	0																			
	♦ Detroit	NHL	11	2	5	7	4	1	0	0	28	7.1	0						7	0	3	3	14	0	0	0
1998-99	Washington	NHL	46	2	14	16	80	2	0	0	86	2.3	-5	0	0.0	47	37	19:51								
99-2000	Washington	NHL	73	3	19	22	28	1	0	0	99	3.0	7	1	0.0	93	52	20:22	4	0	0	0	4	0	0	0
2000-01	Washington	NHL	36	3	5	8	6	1	0	1	33	9.1	-7	1	0.0	26	32	16:32								
	Houston Aeros	IHL	3	2	0	2	2																			
	NHL Totals		556	54	206	260	568	20	1	7	978	5.5		2	0.0	166	121	19:19	75	10	26	36	48	9	0	0

Played in NHL All-Star Game (1998)

Traded to **Pittsburgh** by **Toronto** with Toronto's 2nd round choice (later traded to New Jersey - New Jersey selected Joshua DeWolf) in 1996 Entry Draft for Larry Murphy, July 8, 1995. Traded to **Anaheim** by **Pittsburgh** with Shawn Antoski for Alex Hicks and Fredrik Olausson, November 19, 1996. Traded to **Detroit** by **Anaheim** for Jamie Pushor and Detroit's 4th round choice (Viktor Wallin) in 1998 Entry Draft, March 24, 1998. Signed as a free agent by **Washington**, July 29, 1998. • Missed majority of 2000-01 season recovering from back injury suffered in game vs. Tampa Bay, January 23, 2001.

MITCHELL, Willie
(MIHT-chehl, WIHL-lee) **MIN.**

Defense. Shoots left. 6'3", 205 lbs. Born, Port McNeill, B.C., April 23, 1977. New Jersey's 12th choice, 199th overall, in 1996 Entry Draft.

Season	Club	League	GP	G	A	Pts	PIM	PP	SH	GW	S	%	+/-	TF	F%	H	SB	Min	GP	G	A	Pts	PIM	PP	SH	GW
1993-94	Notre Dame	SMHL	31	4	11	15	81																			
1994-95	Kelowna Spartans	BCJHL	STATISTICS NOT AVAILABLE																							
1995-96	Melfort Mustangs	SJHL	19	2	6	8	....												14	0	2	2	12			
1996-97	Melfort Mustangs	SJHL	64	14	42	56	227												4	0	1	1	23			
1997-98	Clarkson Knights	ECAC	34	9	17	26	105																			
1998-99	Clarkson Knights	ECAC	34	10	19	29	40																			
	Albany River Rats	AHL	6	1	3	4	29																			
99-2000	New Jersey	NHL	2	0	0	0	0	0	0	0	2	0.0	1	0	0.0	1	3	16:04								
	Albany River Rats	AHL	63	5	14	19	71												5	1	2	3	4			
2000-01	New Jersey	NHL	16	0	2	2	29	0	0	0	14	0.0	0	0	0.0	12	16	14:52								
	Albany River Rats	AHL	41	3	13	16	94																			
	Minnesota	NHL	17	1	7	8	11	0	0	0	16	6.3	4	0	0.0	32	24	20:49								
	NHL Totals		35	1	9	10	40	0	0	0	32	3.1		0	0.0	45	43	17:49								

SJHL First All-Star Team (1997) • Won SJHL Top Defenseman Award (1997) • Shared ECAC Rookie of the Year Award with Eric Cole (1998) • ECAC Second All-Star Team (1998) • ECAC First All-Star Team (1999) • NCAA East Second All-American Team (1999)

Traded to **Minnesota** by **New Jersey** for Sean O'Donnell, March 4, 2001.

MODANO, Mike
(moh-DA-noh, MIGHK) **DAL.**

Center. Shoots left. 6'3", 205 lbs. Born, Livonia, MI, June 7, 1970. Minnesota's 1st choice, 1st overall, in 1988 Entry Draft.

Season	Club	League	GP	G	A	Pts	PIM	PP	SH	GW	S	%	+/-	TF	F%	H	SB	Min	GP	G	A	Pts	PIM	PP	SH	GW
1985-86	Det-Compuware	MNHL	69	66	65	131	32																			
1986-87	Prince Albert	WHL	70	32	30	62	96												8	1	4	5	4			
1987-88	Prince Albert	WHL	65	47	80	127	80												9	7	11	18	18			
1988-89	Prince Albert	WHL	41	39	66	105	74																			
	Minnesota	NHL																	2	0	0	0	0	0	0	0
1989-90	Minnesota	NHL	80	29	46	75	63	12	0	2	172	16.9	-7						7	1	1	2	12	0	0	0

								Regular Season											Playoffs							
Season	Club	League	GP	G	A	Pts	PIM	PP	SH	GW	S	%	+/-	TF	F%	H	SB	Min	GP	G	A	Pts	PIM	PP	SH	GW
1990-91	**Minnesota**	**NHL**	**79**	**28**	**36**	**64**	**65**	**9**	**0**	**2**	**232**	**12.1**	**2**	....	....	....	....	....	**23**	**8**	**12**	**20**	**16**	**3**	**0**	**1**
1991-92	**Minnesota**	**NHL**	**76**	**33**	**44**	**77**	**46**	**5**	**0**	**8**	**256**	**12.9**	**−9**	....	....	....	....	....	**7**	**3**	**2**	**5**	**4**	**1**	**0**	**0**
1992-93	**Minnesota**	**NHL**	**82**	**33**	**60**	**93**	**83**	**9**	**0**	**7**	**307**	**10.7**	**−7**	....	....	....	....	....	....	....	....	....	....	....	....	....
1993-94	**Dallas**	**NHL**	**76**	**50**	**43**	**93**	**54**	**18**	**0**	**4**	**281**	**17.8**	**−8**	....	....	....	....	....	**9**	**7**	**3**	**10**	**16**	**2**	**0**	**2**
1994-95	**Dallas**	**NHL**	**30**	**12**	**17**	**29**	**8**	**4**	**1**	**0**	**100**	**12.0**	**7**	....	....	....	....	....	....	....	....	....	....	....	....	....
1995-96	**Dallas**	**NHL**	**78**	**36**	**45**	**81**	**63**	**8**	**4**	**4**	**320**	**11.3**	**−12**	....	....	....	....	....	....	....	....	....	....	....	....	....
1996-97	**Dallas**	**NHL**	**80**	**35**	**48**	**83**	**42**	**9**	**5**	**9**	**291**	**12.0**	**43**	....	....	....	....	....	**7**	**4**	**1**	**5**	**0**	**1**	**1**	**2**
1997-98	**Dallas**	**NHL**	**52**	**21**	**38**	**59**	**32**	**7**	**5**	**2**	**191**	**11.0**	**25**	....	....	....	....	....	**17**	**4**	**10**	**14**	**12**	**1**	**0**	**1**
	United States	Olympics	4	2	0	2	0	....	....	....	....	....	....	....	....	....	....	....	....	....	....	....	....	....	....	....
1998-99♦	**Dallas**	**NHL**	**77**	**34**	**47**	**81**	**44**	**6**	**4**	**7**	**224**	**15.2**	**29**	**1572**	**51.1**	**15**	**33**	**20:50**	**23**	**5**	***18**	**23**	**16**	**1**	**1**	**1**
99-2000	**Dallas**	**NHL**	**77**	**38**	**43**	**81**	**48**	**11**	**1**	**8**	**188**	**20.2**	**0**	**1763**	**51.4**	**16**	**43**	**22:55**	**23**	**10**	***13**	**23**	**10**	**4**	**0**	**2**
2000-01	**Dallas**	**NHL**	**81**	**33**	**51**	**84**	**52**	**8**	**3**	**7**	**208**	**15.9**	**26**	**1791**	**52.0**	**27**	**36**	**22:24**	**9**	**3**	**4**	**7**	**0**	**2**	**0**	**0**
	NHL Totals		**868**	**382**	**518**	**900**	**600**	**106**	**23**	**60**	**2770**	**13.8**		**5126**	**51.5**	**58**	**112**	**22:03**	**127**	**45**	**64**	**109**	**86**	**15**	**2**	**9**

WHL East All-Star Team (1989) • NHL All-Rookie Team (1990) • NHL Second All-Star Team (2000) • Played in NHL All-Star Game (1993, 1998, 1999, 2000)

Transferred to **Dallas** after **Minnesota** franchise relocated, June 9, 1993.

MODIN, Fredrik

(moh-DEEN, FREHD-rihk) **T.B.**

Left wing. Shoots left. 6'4", 220 lbs. Born, Sundsvall, Sweden, October 8, 1974. Toronto's 3rd choice, 64th overall, in 1994 Entry Draft.

1991-92	Timra IF	Sweden-2	11	1	0	1	0	....	....	....	....	....	....	....	....	....	....	....	....	....	....	....	....	....	....	....
1992-93	Timra IF	Sweden-2	30	5	7	12	12	....	....	....	....	....	....	....	....	....	....	....	5	1	0	1	0	....	....	....
1993-94	Timra IF	Sweden-2	30	16	15	31	36	....	....	....	....	....	....	....	....	....	....	....	2	0	1	1	6	....	....	....
1994-95	Brynas IF	Sweden	38	9	10	19	33	....	....	....	....	....	....	....	....	....	....	....	14	4	4	8	6	....	....	....
1995-96	Brynas IF	Sweden	22	4	8	12	22	....	....	....	....	....	....	....	....	....	....	....	....	....	....	....	....	....	....	....
1996-97	**Toronto**	**NHL**	**76**	**6**	**7**	**13**	**24**	**0**	**0**	**0**	**85**	**7.1**	**−14**	....	....	....	....	....	....	....	....	....	....	....	....	....
1997-98	**Toronto**	**NHL**	**74**	**16**	**16**	**32**	**32**	**1**	**0**	**4**	**137**	**11.7**	**−5**	....	....	....	....	....	....	....	....	....	....	....	....	....
1998-99	**Toronto**	**NHL**	**67**	**16**	**15**	**31**	**35**	**1**	**0**	**3**	**108**	**14.8**	**14**	**2**	**50.0**	**77**	**12**	**13:34**	**8**	**0**	**0**	**0**	**6**	**0**	**0**	**0**
99-2000	**Tampa Bay**	**NHL**	**80**	**22**	**26**	**48**	**18**	**3**	**0**	**5**	**167**	**13.2**	**−26**	**6**	**50.0**	**123**	**25**	**15:32**	....	....	....	....	....	....	....	....
2000-01	**Tampa Bay**	**NHL**	**76**	**32**	**24**	**56**	**48**	**8**	**0**	**4**	**217**	**14.7**	**−1**	**21**	**42.9**	**65**	**32**	**17:15**	....	....	....	....	....	....	....	....
	NHL Totals		**373**	**92**	**88**	**180**	**157**	**13**	**0**	**16**	**714**	**12.9**		**29**	**44.8**	**265**	**69**	**15:32**	**8**	**0**	**0**	**0**	**6**	**0**	**0**	**0**

Played in NHL All-Star Game (2001)

Traded to **Tampa Bay** by **Toronto** for Cory Cross and Tampa Bay's 7th round choice (Ivan Kolozvary) in 2001 Entry Draft, October 1, 1999.

MODRY, Jaroslav

(MOH-dree, YAHRO-slahv) **L.A.**

Defense. Shoots left. 6'2", 215 lbs. Born, Ceske-Budejovice, Czech., February 27, 1971. New Jersey's 11th choice, 179th overall, in 1990 Entry Draft.

1987-88	MC Budejovice	Czech.	3	0	0	0	0	....	....	....	....	....	....	....	....	....	....	....	....	....	....	....	....	....	....	....
1988-89	MC Budejovice	Czech.	28	0	1	1	8	....	....	....	....	....	....	....	....	....	....	....	....	....	....	....	....	....	....	....
1989-90	MC Budejovice	Czech.	41	2	2	4	....	....	....	....	....	....	....	....	....	....	....	....	....	....	....	....	....	....	....	....
1990-91	Dukla Trencin	Czech.	33	1	9	10	6	....	....	....	....	....	....	....	....	....	....	....	....	....	....	....	....	....	....	....
1991-92	MC Budejovice	Czech-2	14	4	10	14	....	....	....	....	....	....	....	....	....	....	....	....	....	....	....	....	....	....	....	....
	Dukla Trencin	Czech.	18	0	4	4	6	....	....	....	....	....	....	....	....	....	....	....	....	....	....	....	....	....	....	....
1992-93	Utica Devils	AHL	80	7	35	42	62	....	....	....	....	....	....	....	....	....	....	....	5	0	2	2	2	....	....	....
1993-94	**New Jersey**	**NHL**	**41**	**2**	**15**	**17**	**18**	**2**	**0**	**0**	**35**	**5.7**	**10**	....	....	....	....	....	....	....	....	....	....	....	....	....
	Albany River Rats	AHL	19	1	5	6	25	....	....	....	....	....	....	....	....	....	....	....	....	....	....	....	....	....	....	....
1994-95	HC Budejovice	Cze-Rep	19	1	3	4	30	....	....	....	....	....	....	....	....	....	....	....	....	....	....	....	....	....	....	....
	New Jersey	**NHL**	**11**	**0**	**0**	**0**	**0**	**0**	**0**	**0**	**10**	**0.0**	**−1**	....	....	....	....	....	....	....	....	....	....	....	....	....
	Albany River Rats	AHL	18	5	6	11	14	....	....	....	....	....	....	....	....	....	....	....	14	3	3	6	4	....	....	....
1995-96	**Ottawa**	**NHL**	**64**	**4**	**14**	**18**	**38**	**1**	**0**	**1**	**89**	**4.5**	**−17**	....	....	....	....	....	....	....	....	....	....	....	....	....
	Los Angeles	**NHL**	**9**	**0**	**3**	**3**	**6**	**0**	**0**	**0**	**17**	**0.0**	**−4**	....	....	....	....	....	....	....	....	....	....	....	....	....
1996-97	**Los Angeles**	**NHL**	**30**	**3**	**3**	**6**	**25**	**1**	**1**	**0**	**32**	**9.4**	**−13**	....	....	....	....	....	....	....	....	....	....	....	....	....
	Phoenix	IHL	23	3	12	15	17	....	....	....	....	....	....	....	....	....	....	....	....	....	....	....	....	....	....	....
	Utah Grizzlies	IHL	11	1	4	5	20	....	....	....	....	....	....	....	....	....	....	....	7	0	1	1	6	....	....	....
1997-98	Utah Grizzlies	IHL	74	12	21	33	72	....	....	....	....	....	....	....	....	....	....	....	4	0	2	2	6	....	....	....
1998-99	**Los Angeles**	**NHL**	**5**	**0**	**1**	**1**	**0**	**0**	**0**	**0**	**11**	**0.0**	**1**	**0**	**0.0**	**6**	**7**	**26:00**	....	....	....	....	....	....	....	....
	Long Beach	IHL	64	6	29	35	44	....	....	....	....	....	....	....	....	....	....	....	8	4	2	6	4	....	....	....
99-2000	**Los Angeles**	**NHL**	**26**	**5**	**4**	**9**	**18**	**5**	**0**	**1**	**32**	**15.6**	**−2**	**0**	**0.0**	**20**	**24**	**19:13**	**2**	**0**	**0**	**0**	**2**	**0**	**0**	**0**
	Long Beach	IHL	11	2	4	6	8	....	....	....	....	....	....	....	....	....	....	....	....	....	....	....	....	....	....	....
2000-01	**Los Angeles**	**NHL**	**63**	**4**	**15**	**19**	**48**	**0**	**0**	**0**	**72**	**5.6**	**16**	**0**	**0.0**	**63**	**62**	**18:22**	**10**	**1**	**0**	**1**	**4**	**1**	**0**	**1**
	NHL Totals		**249**	**18**	**55**	**73**	**153**	**9**	**1**	**2**	**298**	**6.0**		**0**	**0.0**	**89**	**93**	**19:01**	**12**	**1**	**0**	**1**	**6**	**1**	**0**	**1**

Traded to **Ottawa** by **New Jersey** for Ottawa's 4th round choice (Alyn McCauley) in 1995 Entry Draft, July 8, 1995. Traded to **LA Kings** by **Ottawa** with Ottawa's 8th round choice (Stephen Valiquette) in 1996 Entry Draft for Kevin Brown, March 20, 1996.

MOGER, Sandy

(MOH-guhr, SAN-dee)

Center. Shoots right. 6'4", 220 lbs. Born, 100 Mile House, B.C., March 21, 1969. Vancouver's 7th choice, 176th overall, in 1989 Entry Draft.

1986-87	Vernon Lakers	BCJHL	13	5	4	9	10	....	....	....	....	....	....	....	....	....	....	....	....	....	....	....	....	....	....	....
1987-88	Yorkton Terriers	SJHL	60	39	41	80	144	....	....	....	....	....	....	....	....	....	....	....	16	7	6	13	....	....	....	....
1988-89	Lake Superior	CCHA	21	3	5	8	26	....	....	....	....	....	....	....	....	....	....	....	....	....	....	....	....	....	....	....
1989-90	Lake Superior	CCHA	46	17	15	32	76	....	....	....	....	....	....	....	....	....	....	....	....	....	....	....	....	....	....	....
1990-91	Lake Superior	CCHA	45	27	21	48	*172	....	....	....	....	....	....	....	....	....	....	....	....	....	....	....	....	....	....	....
1991-92	Lake Superior	CCHA	38	24	24	48	93	....	....	....	....	....	....	....	....	....	....	....	....	....	....	....	....	....	....	....
1992-93	Hamilton Canucks	AHL	78	23	26	49	57	....	....	....	....	....	....	....	....	....	....	....	....	....	....	....	....	....	....	....
1993-94	Hamilton Canucks	AHL	29	9	8	17	41	....	....	....	....	....	....	....	....	....	....	....	....	....	....	....	....	....	....	....
1994-95	Providence Bruins	AHL	63	32	29	61	105	....	....	....	....	....	....	....	....	....	....	....	....	....	....	....	....	....	....	....
	Boston	**NHL**	**18**	**2**	**6**	**8**	**6**	**2**	**0**	**0**	**32**	**6.3**	**−1**	....	....	....	....	....	....	....	....	....	....	....	....	....
1995-96	**Boston**	**NHL**	**80**	**15**	**14**	**29**	**65**	**4**	**0**	**6**	**103**	**14.6**	**−9**	....	....	....	....	....	**5**	**2**	**2**	**4**	**12**	**1**	**0**	**0**
1996-97	**Boston**	**NHL**	**34**	**10**	**3**	**13**	**45**	**3**	**0**	**0**	**54**	**18.5**	**−12**	....	....	....	....	....	....	....	....	....	....	....	....	....
	Providence Bruins	AHL	3	0	2	2	19	....	....	....	....	....	....	....	....	....	....	....	....	....	....	....	....	....	....	....
1997-98	**Los Angeles**	**NHL**	**62**	**11**	**13**	**24**	**70**	**1**	**0**	**2**	**89**	**12.4**	**4**	....	....	....	....	....	....	....	....	....	....	....	....	....
1998-99	**Los Angeles**	**NHL**	**42**	**3**	**2**	**5**	**26**	**0**	**0**	**2**	**28**	**10.7**	**−9**	**2**	**50.0**	**80**	**5**	**10:19**	....	....	....	....	....	....	....	....
99-2000	Houston Aeros	IHL	45	13	10	23	43	....	....	....	....	....	....	....	....	....	....	....	2	1	1	2	4	....	....	....
2000-01	Houston Aeros	IHL	63	18	24	42	58	....	....	....	....	....	....	....	....	....	....	....	7	5	0	5	2	....	....	....
	NHL Totals		**236**	**41**	**38**	**79**	**212**	**10**	**0**	**10**	**306**	**13.4**		**2**	**50.0**	**80**	**5**	**10:19**	**5**	**2**	**2**	**4**	**12**	**1**	**0**	**0**

CCHA Second All-Star Team (1992)

Signed as a free agent by **Boston**, June 22, 1994. • Missed majority of 1996-97 season recovering from elbow injury suffered in game vs. Buffalo, December 14, 1996. Traded to **LA Kings** by **Boston** with Jozef Stumpel and Boston's 4th round choice (later traded to New Jersey - New Jersey selected Pierre Dagenais) in 1998 Entry Draft for Dmitri Khristich and Byron Dafoe, August 29, 1997. Signed as a free agent by **Houston** (IHL), September 6, 1999. Signed as a free agent by **Assat Pori** (Finland), August 16, 2001.

MOGILNY, Alexander

(moh-GIHL-nee, al-ehx-AN-duhr) **TOR.**

Right wing. Shoots left. 5'11", 200 lbs. Born, Khabarovsk, USSR, February 18, 1969. Buffalo's 4th choice, 89th overall, in 1988 Entry Draft.

1986-87	CSKA Moscow	USSR	28	15	1	16	4	....	....	....	....	....	....	....	....	....	....	....	....	....	....	....	....	....	....	....
1987-88	CSKA Moscow	USSR	39	12	8	20	14	....	....	....	....	....	....	....	....	....	....	....	....	....	....	....	....	....	....	....
	Soviet Union	Olympics	6	3	2	5	2	....	....	....	....	....	....	....	....	....	....	....	....	....	....	....	....	....	....	....
1988-89	CSKA Moscow	USSR	31	11	11	22	24	....	....	....	....	....	....	....	....	....	....	....	....	....	....	....	....	....	....	....
1989-90	**Buffalo**	**NHL**	**65**	**15**	**28**	**43**	**16**	**4**	**0**	**2**	**130**	**11.5**	**8**	....	....	....	....	....	**4**	**0**	**1**	**1**	**2**	**0**	**0**	**0**
1990-91	**Buffalo**	**NHL**	**62**	**30**	**34**	**64**	**16**	**3**	**3**	**5**	**201**	**14.9**	**14**	....	....	....	....	....	**6**	**0**	**6**	**6**	**2**	**0**	**0**	**0**
1991-92	**Buffalo**	**NHL**	**67**	**39**	**45**	**84**	**73**	**15**	**0**	**2**	**236**	**16.5**	**7**	....	....	....	....	....	**2**	**0**	**2**	**2**	**0**	**0**	**0**	**0**
1992-93	**Buffalo**	**NHL**	**77**	***76**	**51**	**127**	**40**	**27**	**0**	**11**	**360**	**21.1**	**7**	....	....	....	....	....	**7**	**7**	**3**	**10**	**6**	**2**	**0**	**0**
1993-94	**Buffalo**	**NHL**	**66**	**32**	**47**	**79**	**22**	**17**	**0**	**7**	**258**	**12.4**	**8**	....	....	....	....	....	**7**	**4**	**2**	**6**	**6**	**1**	**0**	**0**
1994-95	Krylja Sovetov	CIS	1	0	1	1	0	....	....	....	....	....	....	....	....	....	....	....	....	....	....	....	....	....	....	....
	Buffalo	**NHL**	**44**	**19**	**28**	**47**	**36**	**12**	**0**	**2**	**148**	**12.8**	**0**	....	....	....	....	....	**5**	**3**	**2**	**5**	**2**	**0**	**0**	**0**
1995-96	**Vancouver**	**NHL**	**79**	**55**	**52**	**107**	**16**	**10**	**5**	**6**	**292**	**18.8**	**14**	....	....	....	....	....	**6**	**1**	**8**	**9**	**8**	**0**	**0**	**0**
1996-97	**Vancouver**	**NHL**	**76**	**31**	**42**	**73**	**18**	**7**	**1**	**4**	**174**	**17.8**	**9**	....	....	....	....	....	....	....	....	....	....	....	....	....
1997-98	**Vancouver**	**NHL**	**51**	**18**	**27**	**45**	**36**	**5**	**4**	**1**	**118**	**15.3**	**−6**	....	....	....	....	....	....	....	....	....	....	....	....	....
1998-99	**Vancouver**	**NHL**	**59**	**14**	**31**	**45**	**58**	**3**	**2**	**1**	**110**	**12.7**	**0**	**47**	**23.4**	**34**	**10**	**20:35**	....	....	....	....	....	....	....	....

			Regular Season																Playoffs							
Season	Club	League	GP	G	A	Pts	PIM	PP	SH	GW	S	%	+/-	TF	F%	H	SB	Min	GP	G	A	Pts	PIM	PP	SH	GW
99-2000	Vancouver	NHL	47	21	17	38	16	3	1	1	126	16.7	7	9	11.1	37	12	19:34	....	....	....	....	....	....	....	....
	♦ New Jersey	NHL	12	3	3	6	4	2	0	0	35	8.6	–4	0	0.0	4	3	17:04	23	4	3	7	4	2	0	1
2000-01	New Jersey	NHL	75	43	40	83	43	12	0	7	240	17.9	10	11	36.4	86	8	16:53	25	5	11	16	8	1	0	2
	NHL Totals		**780**	**396**	**445**	**841**	**394**	**120**	**16**	**49**	**2428**	**16.3**		**67**	**23.9**	**161**	**33**	**18:41**	**85**	**24**	**38**	**62**	**38**	**6**	**0**	**3**

NHL Second All-Star Team (1993, 1996) • Played in NHL All-Star Game (1992, 1993, 1994, 1996)

Traded to **Vancouver** by **Buffalo** with Buffalo's 5th round choice (Todd Norman) in 1995 Entry Draft for Mike Peca, Mike Wilson and Vancouver's 1st round choice (Jay McKee) in 1995 Entry Draft, July 8, 1995. Traded to **New Jersey** by **Vancouver** for Brendan Morrison and Denis Pederson, March 14, 2000. Signed as a free agent by **Toronto**, July 3, 2001.

MONTGOMERY, Jim
(mawnt-GUHM-uhr-ee, JIHM) **DAL.**

Center. Shoots right. 5'10", 180 lbs. Born, Montreal, Que., June 30, 1969.

1988-89	Pembroke Kings	OCJHL	50	53	*101	154	112	....	....	....	....	....	....	....	....	....	....	....	....	....	....	....	....	....	....	....
1989-90	U. of Maine	H-East	45	26	34	60	35	....	....	....	....	....	....	....	....	....	....	....	....	....	....	....	....	....	....	....
1990-91	U. of Maine	H-East	43	24	*57	81	44	....	....	....	....	....	....	....	....	....	....	....	....	....	....	....	....	....	....	....
1991-92	U. of Maine	H-East	37	21	44	65	46	....	....	....	....	....	....	....	....	....	....	....	....	....	....	....	....	....	....	....
1992-93	U. of Maine	H-East	45	32	63	95	40	....	....	....	....	....	....	....	....	....	....	....	....	....	....	....	....	....	....	....
1993-94	**St. Louis**	**NHL**	**67**	**6**	**14**	**20**	**44**	**0**	**0**	**1**	**67**	**9.0**	**–1**	....	....	....	....	....	....	....	....	....	....	....	....	....
	Peoria Rivermen	IHL	12	7	8	15	10	....	....	....	....	....	....	....	....	....	....	....	....	....	....	....	....	....	....	....
1994-95	**Montreal**	**NHL**	**5**	**0**	**0**	**0**	**2**	**0**	**0**	**0**	**3**	**0.0**	**–2**	....	....	....	....	....	....	....	....	....	....	....	....	....
	Philadelphia	**NHL**	**8**	**1**	**1**	**2**	**6**	**0**	**0**	**0**	**10**	**10.0**	**–2**	....	....	....	....	....	**7**	**1**	**0**	**1**	**2**	**0**	**0**	**0**
	Hershey Bears	AHL	16	8	6	14	14	....	....	....	....	....	....	....	....	....	....	....	6	3	2	5	25	....	....	....
1995-96	**Philadelphia**	**NHL**	**5**	**1**	**2**	**3**	**9**	**0**	**0**	**0**	**4**	**25.0**	**1**	....	....	....	....	....	**1**	**0**	**0**	**0**	**0**	**0**	**0**	**0**
	Hershey Bears	AHL	78	34	*71	105	95	....	....	....	....	....	....	....	....	....	....	....	4	3	2	5	6	....	....	....
1996-97	Kolner Haie	DEL	50	12	35	47	111	....	....	....	....	....	....	....	....	....	....	....	4	0	1	1	6	....	....	....
	Kolner Haie	EuroHL	6	0	1	1	16	....	....	....	....	....	....	....	....	....	....	....	....	....	....	....	....	....	....	....
1997-98	Philadelphia	AHL	68	19	43	62	75	....	....	....	....	....	....	....	....	....	....	....	20	*13	16	29	55	....	....	....
1998-99	Philadelphia	AHL	78	29	58	87	89	....	....	....	....	....	....	....	....	....	....	....	16	4	11	15	20	....	....	....
99-2000	Philadelphia	AHL	13	3	9	12	22	....	....	....	....	....	....	....	....	....	....	....	....	....	....	....	....	....	....	....
	Manitoba Moose	IHL	67	18	28	46	111	....	....	....	....	....	....	....	....	....	....	....	....	....	....	....	....	....	....	....
2000-01	**San Jose**	**NHL**	**28**	**1**	**6**	**7**	**19**	**1**	**0**	**0**	**17**	**5.9**	....	**0**	**0.0**	**0**	**0**	**0:00**	....	....	....	....	....	....	....	....
	Kentucky	AHL	55	22	52	74	44	....	....	....	....	....	....	....	....	....	....	....	3	1	2	3	5	....	....	....
	NHL Totals		**113**	**9**	**23**	**32**	**80**	**1**	**0**	**1**	**101**	**8.9**		**0**	**0.0**	**0**	**0**	....	**8**	**1**	**0**	**1**	**2**	**0**	**0**	**0**

Hockey East Second All-Star Team (1991, 1992) • Hockey East First All-Star Team (1993) • NCAA East Second All-American Team (1993) • NCAA Championship All-Tournament Team (1993) • NCAA Championship Tournament MVP (1993) • AHL Second All-Star Team (1996)

Signed as a free agent by **St. Louis**, June 2, 1993. Traded to **Montreal** by **St. Louis** for Guy Carbonneau, August 19, 1994. Claimed on waivers by **Philadelphia** from **Montreal**, February 10, 1995. Signed as a free agent by **San Jose**, August 15, 2000. Signed as a free agent by **Dallas**, July 24, 2001.

MOORE, Barrie
(MOOR, BAIR-ee)

Left wing. Shoots left. 5'11", 198 lbs. Born, London, Ont., May 22, 1975. Buffalo's 7th choice, 220th overall, in 1993 Entry Draft.

1990-91	Strathroy Rockets	OJHL-B	24	9	10	19	14	....	....	....	....	....	....	....	....	....	....	....	....	....	....	....	....	....	....	....
1991-92	Sudbury Wolves	OHL	62	15	38	53	57	....	....	....	....	....	....	....	....	....	....	....	11	0	7	7	12	....	....	....
1992-93	Sudbury Wolves	OHL	57	13	26	39	71	....	....	....	....	....	....	....	....	....	....	....	14	4	3	7	19	....	....	....
1993-94	Sudbury Wolves	OHL	65	36	49	85	69	....	....	....	....	....	....	....	....	....	....	....	10	3	5	8	14	....	....	....
1994-95	Sudbury Wolves	OHL	60	47	42	89	67	....	....	....	....	....	....	....	....	....	....	....	18	*15	14	29	24	....	....	....
1995-96	**Buffalo**	**NHL**	**3**	**0**	**0**	**0**	**0**	**0**	**0**	**0**	**3**	**0.0**	**0**	....	....	....	....	....	....	....	....	....	....	....	....	....
	Rochester	AHL	64	26	30	56	40	....	....	....	....	....	....	....	....	....	....	....	18	3	6	9	18	....	....	....
1996-97	**Buffalo**	**NHL**	**31**	**2**	**6**	**8**	**18**	**1**	**0**	**0**	**42**	**4.8**	**1**	....	....	....	....	....	....	....	....	....	....	....	....	....
	Rochester	AHL	32	14	15	29	14	....	....	....	....	....	....	....	....	....	....	....	....	....	....	....	....	....	....	....
	Edmonton	**NHL**	**4**	**0**	**0**	**0**	**0**	**0**	**0**	**0**	**1**	**0.0**	**0**	....	....	....	....	....	....	....	....	....	....	....	....	....
	Hamilton Bulldogs	AHL	9	5	2	7	0	....	....	....	....	....	....	....	....	....	....	....	22	2	6	8	15	....	....	....
1997-98	Hamilton Bulldogs	AHL	70	22	29	51	64	....	....	....	....	....	....	....	....	....	....	....	8	0	1	1	4	....	....	....
1998-99	Indianapolis Ice	IHL	43	9	10	19	18	....	....	....	....	....	....	....	....	....	....	....	....	....	....	....	....	....	....	....
	Portland Pirates	AHL	23	3	7	10	4	....	....	....	....	....	....	....	....	....	....	....	....	....	....	....	....	....	....	....
99-2000	**Washington**	**NHL**	**1**	**0**	**0**	**0**	**0**	**0**	**0**	**0**	**2**	**0.0**	**0**	**0**	**0.0**	**0**	**0**	**9:50**	....	....	....	....	....	....	....	....
	Portland Pirates	AHL	80	18	33	51	50	....	....	....	....	....	....	....	....	....	....	....	4	0	0	0	6	....	....	....
2000-01	Manitoba Moose	IHL	2	0	0	0	0	....	....	....	....	....	....	....	....	....	....	....	....	....	....	....	....	....	....	....
	Manchester Storm	Britain	32	11	16	27	26	....	....	....	....	....	....	....	....	....	....	....	6	3	3	6	2	....	....	....
	NHL Totals		**39**	**2**	**6**	**8**	**18**	**1**	**0**	**0**	**48**	**4.2**		**0**	**0.0**	**0**	**0**	**9:50**	....	....	....	....	....	....	....	....

Traded to **Edmonton** by **Buffalo** with Craig Millar for Miroslav Satan, March 18, 1997. Rights traded to **Washington** by **Edmonton** for Brad Church, February 3, 1999. Selected by **Columbus** from **Washington** in Expansion Draft, June 23, 2000.

MORAN, Ian
(moh-RAN, EE-an) **PIT.**

Right wing. Shoots right. 6', 206 lbs. Born, Cleveland, OH, August 24, 1972. Pittsburgh's 5th choice, 107th overall, in 1990 Entry Draft.

1987-88	Belmont Hill	Hi-School	25	3	13	16	15	....	....	....	....	....	....	....	....	....	....	....	....	....	....	....	....	....	....	....
1988-89	Belmont Hill	Hi-School	23	7	25	32	8	....	....	....	....	....	....	....	....	....	....	....	....	....	....	....	....	....	....	....
1989-90	Belmont Hill	Hi-School	23	10	36	46	....	....	....	....	....	....	....	....	....	....	....	....	....	....	....	....	....	....	....	....
1990-91	Belmont Hill	Hi-School	23	7	44	51	12	....	....	....	....	....	....	....	....	....	....	....	....	....	....	....	....	....	....	....
1991-92	Boston College	H-East	30	2	16	18	44	....	....	....	....	....	....	....	....	....	....	....	....	....	....	....	....	....	....	....
1992-93	Boston College	H-East	31	8	12	20	32	....	....	....	....	....	....	....	....	....	....	....	....	....	....	....	....	....	....	....
1993-94	United States	Nat-Team	50	8	15	23	69	....	....	....	....	....	....	....	....	....	....	....	....	....	....	....	....	....	....	....
	Cleveland	IHL	33	5	13	18	39	....	....	....	....	....	....	....	....	....	....	....	....	....	....	....	....	....	....	....
1994-95	Cleveland	IHL	64	7	31	38	94	....	....	....	....	....	....	....	....	....	....	....	4	0	1	1	2	....	....	....
	Pittsburgh	**NHL**	....	....	....	....	....	....	....	....	....	....	....	....	....	....	....	....	**8**	**0**	**0**	**0**	**0**	**0**	**0**	**0**
1995-96	**Pittsburgh**	**NHL**	**51**	**1**	**1**	**2**	**47**	**0**	**0**	**0**	**44**	**2.3**	**–1**	....	....	....	....	....	....	....	....	....	....	....	....	....
1996-97	**Pittsburgh**	**NHL**	**36**	**4**	**5**	**9**	**22**	**0**	**0**	**0**	**50**	**8.0**	**–11**	....	....	....	....	....	**5**	**1**	**2**	**3**	**4**	**0**	**0**	**0**
	Cleveland	IHL	36	6	23	29	26	....	....	....	....	....	....	....	....	....	....	....	....	....	....	....	....	....	....	....
1997-98	**Pittsburgh**	**NHL**	**37**	**1**	**6**	**7**	**19**	**0**	**0**	**1**	**33**	**3.0**	**0**	....	....	....	....	....	**6**	**0**	**0**	**0**	**2**	**0**	**0**	**0**
1998-99	**Pittsburgh**	**NHL**	**62**	**4**	**5**	**9**	**37**	**0**	**1**	**0**	**65**	**6.2**	**1**	**32**	**34.4**	**48**	**98**	**16:34**	**13**	**0**	**2**	**2**	**8**	**0**	**0**	**0**
99-2000	**Pittsburgh**	**NHL**	**73**	**4**	**8**	**12**	**28**	**0**	**0**	**0**	**58**	**6.9**	**–10**	**210**	**33.8**	**48**	**62**	**11:21**	**11**	**0**	**1**	**1**	**2**	**0**	**0**	**0**
2000-01	**Pittsburgh**	**NHL**	**40**	**3**	**4**	**7**	**28**	**0**	**0**	**1**	**73**	**4.1**	**5**	**4**	**25.0**	**74**	**34**	**17:42**	**18**	**0**	**1**	**1**	**4**	**0**	**0**	**0**
	NHL Totals		**299**	**17**	**29**	**46**	**181**	**0**	**1**	**2**	**323**	**5.3**		**246**	**33.7**	**170**	**194**	**14:39**	**61**	**1**	**6**	**7**	**20**	**0**	**0**	**0**

Hockey East Rookie of the Year (1992) • Hockey East All-Rookie Team (1992)

• Missed majority of 1997-98 season recovering from knee injury suffered in training camp, September 30, 1997. • Missed majority of 2000-01 season recovering from hand injury originally suffered in game vs. Edmonton, November 11, 2000.

MORAVEC, David
(muh-RAHV-ehts, DAY-vihd) **BUF.**

Right wing. Shoots left. 6', 180 lbs. Born, Vitkovice, Czech., March 24, 1973. Buffalo's 9th choice, 218th overall, in 1998 Entry Draft.

1994-95	HC Vitkovice	Cze-Rep	38	4	13	17	12	....	....	....	....	....	....	....	....	....	....	....	6	1	7	8	0	....	....	....
1995-96	HC Vitkovice	Cze-Rep	37	6	5	11	14	....	....	....	....	....	....	....	....	....	....	....	4	0	0	0	4	....	....	....
1996-97	HC Vitkovice	Cze-Rep	52	18	22	40	30	....	....	....	....	....	....	....	....	....	....	....	9	6	3	9	0	....	....	....
1997-98	HC Vitkovice	Cze-Rep	51	*38	26	64	28	....	....	....	....	....	....	....	....	....	....	....	11	6	9	15	8	....	....	....
1998-99	HC Vitkovice	Cze-Rep	50	21	22	43	44	....	....	....	....	....	....	....	....	....	....	....	4	1	1	2		....	....	....
99-2000	HC Vitkovice	Cze-Rep	38	11	18	29	34	....	....	....	....	....	....	....	....	....	....	....	....	....	....	....	....	....	....	....
	Buffalo	**NHL**	**1**	**0**	**0**	**0**	**0**	**0**	**0**	**0**	**2**	**0.0**	**–1**	**2**	**50.0**	**0**	**0**	**15:15**	....	....	....	....	....	....	....	....
2000-01	HC Vitkovice	Cze-Rep	51	15	20	35	34	....	....	....	....	....	....	....	....	....	....	....	10	4	6	10	4	....	....	....
	NHL Totals		**1**	**0**	**0**	**0**	**0**	**0**	**0**	**0**	**2**	**0.0**		**2**	**50.0**	**0**	**0**	**15:15**	....	....	....	....	....	....	....	....

MOREAU, Ethan
(moh-ROH, EE-than) **EDM.**

Left wing. Shoots left. 6'2", 211 lbs. Born, Huntsville, Ont., September 22, 1975. Chicago's 1st choice, 14th overall, in 1994 Entry Draft.

1990-91	Orillia Terriers	OJHL-B	42	17	22	39	26	....	....	....	....	....	....	....	....	....	....	....	12	6	6	12	18	....	....	....
1991-92	Niagara Falls	OHL	62	20	35	55	39	....	....	....	....	....	....	....	....	....	....	....	17	4	6	10	4	....	....	....
1992-93	Niagara Falls	OHL	65	32	41	73	69	....	....	....	....	....	....	....	....	....	....	....	4	0	3	3	4	....	....	....
1993-94	Niagara Falls	OHL	59	44	54	98	100	....	....	....	....	....	....	....	....	....	....	....	....	....	....	....	....	....	....	....
1994-95	Niagara Falls	OHL	39	25	41	66	69	....	....	....	....	....	....	....	....	....	....	....	....	....	....	....	....	....	....	....
	Sudbury Wolves	OHL	23	13	17	30	22	....	....	....	....	....	....	....	....	....	....	....	18	6	12	18	26	....	....	....

			Regular Season																Playoffs							
Season	**Club**	**League**	**GP**	**G**	**A**	**Pts**	**PIM**	**PP**	**SH**	**GW**	**S**	**%**	**+/-**	**TF**	**F%**	**H**	**SB**	**Min**	**GP**	**G**	**A**	**Pts**	**PIM**	**PP**	**SH**	**GW**
1995-96	**Chicago**	**NHL**	**8**	**0**	**1**	**1**	**4**	**0**	**0**	**0**	**1**	**0.0**	**1**	....	....	....	....	....	....	....	....	....	....	....	....	....
	Indianapolis Ice	IHL	71	21	20	41	126	....	....	....	....	....	....	....	....	....	....	....	5	4	0	4	8	....	....	....
1996-97	**Chicago**	**NHL**	**82**	**15**	**16**	**31**	**123**	**0**	**0**	**1**	**114**	**13.2**	**13**	....	....	....	....	....	**6**	**1**	**0**	**1**	**9**	**0**	**0**	**0**
1997-98	**Chicago**	**NHL**	**54**	**9**	**9**	**18**	**73**	**2**	**0**	**0**	**87**	**10.3**	**0**	....	....	....	....	....	....	....	....	....	....	....	....	....
1998-99	**Chicago**	**NHL**	**66**	**9**	**6**	**15**	**84**	**0**	**0**	**1**	**80**	**11.3**	**-5**	**3**	**33.3**	**113**	**15**	**12:30**	....	....	....	....	....	....	....	....
	Edmonton	**NHL**	**14**	**1**	**5**	**6**	**8**	**0**	**0**	**1**	**16**	**6.3**	**2**	**1**	**0.0**	**26**	**9**	**11:47**	**4**	**0**	**3**	**3**	**6**	**0**	**0**	**0**
99-2000	**Edmonton**	**NHL**	**73**	**17**	**10**	**27**	**62**	**1**	**0**	**3**	**106**	**16.0**	**8**	**8**	**62.5**	**158**	**35**	**15:07**	**5**	**0**	**1**	**1**	**0**	**0**	**0**	**0**
2000-01	**Edmonton**	**NHL**	**68**	**9**	**10**	**19**	**90**	**0**	**1**	**3**	**97**	**9.3**	**-6**	**2**	**0.0**	**148**	**46**	**14:11**	**4**	**0**	**0**	**0**	**2**	**0**	**0**	**0**
	NHL Totals		**365**	**60**	**57**	**117**	**444**	**3**	**1**	**9**	**501**	**12.0**		**14**	**42.9**	**445**	**105**	**13:50**	**19**	**1**	**4**	**5**	**17**	**0**	**0**	**0**

Traded to **Edmonton** by **Chicago** with Daniel Cleary, Chad Kilger and Christian Laflamme for Boris Mironov, Dean McAmmond and Jonas Elofsson, March 20, 1999.

MORGAN, Jason
(MOHR-gan, JAY-son)

Center. Shoots left. 6'1", 200 lbs. Born, St. John's, Nfld., October 9, 1976. Los Angeles' 5th choice, 118th overall, in 1995 Entry Draft.

Season	Club	League	GP	G	A	Pts	PIM	PP	SH	GW	S	%	+/-	TF	F%	H	SB	Min	GP	G	A	Pts	PIM	PP	SH	GW
1992-93	Kitchener	OMHA	69	44	40	84	85	....	....	....	....	....	....	....	....	....	....	....	....	....	....	....	....	....	....	....
1993-94	Kitchener	OHL	65	6	15	21	16	....	....	....	....	....	....	....	....	....	....	....	5	1	0	1	0	....	....	....
1994-95	Kitchener	OHL	35	3	15	18	25	....	....	....	....	....	....	....	....	....	....	....	....	....	....	....	....	....	....	....
	Kingston	OHL	20	0	3	3	14	....	....	....	....	....	....	....	....	....	....	....	6	0	2	2	0	....	....	....
1995-96	Kingston	OHL	66	16	38	54	50	....	....	....	....	....	....	....	....	....	....	....	6	1	2	3	0	....	....	....
1996-97	**Los Angeles**	**NHL**	**3**	**0**	**0**	**0**	**0**	**0**	**0**	**0**	**4**	**0.0**	**-3**	....	....	....	....	....	....	....	....	....	....	....	....	....
	Phoenix	IHL	57	3	6	9	29	....	....	....	....	....	....	....	....	....	....	....	....	....	....	....	....	....	....	....
	Mississippi	ECHL	6	3	0	3	0	....	....	....	....	....	....	....	....	....	....	....	3	1	1	2	6	....	....	....
1997-98	**Los Angeles**	**NHL**	**11**	**1**	**0**	**1**	**4**	**0**	**0**	**0**	**5**	**20.0**	**-7**	....	....	....	....	....	....	....	....	....	....	....	....	....
	Springfield	AHL	58	13	22	35	66	....	....	....	....	....	....	....	....	....	....	....	3	1	0	1	18	....	....	....
1998-99	Long Beach	IHL	13	4	6	10	18	....	....	....	....	....	....	....	....	....	....	....	....	....	....	....	....	....	....	....
	Springfield	AHL	46	6	16	22	51	....	....	....	....	....	....	....	....	....	....	....	3	0	0	0	6	....	....	....
99-2000	Cincinnati	IHL	15	1	3	4	14	....	....	....	....	....	....	....	....	....	....	....	....	....	....	....	....	....	....	....
	Florida Everblades	ECHL	48	14	25	39	79	....	....	....	....	....	....	....	....	....	....	....	5	2	2	4	16	....	....	....
2000-01	Florida Everblades	ECHL	37	15	22	37	41	....	....	....	....	....	....	....	....	....	....	....	5	2	3	5	17	....	....	....
	Hamilton Bulldogs	AHL	11	2	0	2	10	....	....	....	....	....	....	....	....	....	....	....	....	....	....	....	....	....	....	....
	Springfield	AHL	16	1	4	5	19	....	....	....	....	....	....	....	....	....	....	....	....	....	....	....	....	....	....	....
	Saint John Flames	AHL	....	....	....	....	....	....	....	....	....	....	....	....	....	....	....	....	6	0	1	1	2	....	....	....
	NHL Totals		**14**	**1**	**0**	**1**	**4**	**0**	**0**	**0**	**9**	**11.1**		....	....	....	....	....	....	....	....	....	....	....	....	....

MORISSETTE, Dave
(MOH-rih-seht, DAYV)

Left wing. Shoots left. 6'1", 224 lbs. Born, Baie Comeau, Que., December 24, 1971. Washington's 7th choice, 146th overall, in 1991 Entry Draft.

Season	Club	League	GP	G	A	Pts	PIM	PP	SH	GW	S	%	+/-	TF	F%	H	SB	Min	GP	G	A	Pts	PIM	PP	SH	GW
1987-88	Lac St-Jean	QAAA	41	11	25	36	134	....	....	....	....	....	....	....	....	....	....	....	2	2	1	3	2	....	....	....
1988-89	Shawinigan	QMJHL	66	4	11	15	298	....	....	....	....	....	....	....	....	....	....	....	....	....	....	....	....	....	....	....
1989-90	Shawinigan	QMJHL	66	2	9	11	269	....	....	....	....	....	....	....	....	....	....	....	....	....	....	....	....	....	....	....
1990-91	Shawinigan	QMJHL	64	20	26	46	224	....	....	....	....	....	....	....	....	....	....	....	6	1	1	2	17	....	....	....
1991-92	Hampton Roads	ECHL	47	6	10	16	293	....	....	....	....	....	....	....	....	....	....	....	13	1	3	4	74	....	....	....
	Baltimore	AHL	2	0	0	0	6	....	....	....	....	....	....	....	....	....	....	....	....	....	....	....	....	....	....	....
1992-93	Hampton Roads	ECHL	54	9	13	22	226	....	....	....	....	....	....	....	....	....	....	....	2	0	0	0	2	....	....	....
1993-94	Roanoke Express	ECHL	45	8	10	18	278	....	....	....	....	....	....	....	....	....	....	....	2	0	1	1	4	....	....	....
1994-95	Minnesota Moose	IHL	50	1	4	5	174	....	....	....	....	....	....	....	....	....	....	....	....	....	....	....	....	....	....	....
1995-96	Minnesota Moose	IHL	33	3	2	5	104	....	....	....	....	....	....	....	....	....	....	....	....	....	....	....	....	....	....	....
1996-97	Houston Aeros	IHL	59	2	1	3	214	....	....	....	....	....	....	....	....	....	....	....	2	0	0	0	0	....	....	....
	Austin Ice Bats	WPHL	5	2	3	5	10	....	....	....	....	....	....	....	....	....	....	....	....	....	....	....	....	....	....	....
1997-98	Houston Aeros	IHL	67	4	4	8	254	....	....	....	....	....	....	....	....	....	....	....	2	0	0	0	2	....	....	....
1998-99	**Montreal**	**NHL**	**10**	**0**	**0**	**0**	**52**	**0**	**0**	**0**	**2**	**0.0**	**1**	**0**	**0.0**	**5**	**2**	**2:13**	....	....	....	....	....	....	....	....
	Fredericton	AHL	39	4	4	8	152	....	....	....	....	....	....	....	....	....	....	....	12	0	1	1	31	....	....	....
99-2000	**Montreal**	**NHL**	**1**	**0**	**0**	**0**	**5**	**0**	**0**	**0**	**0**	**0.0**	**0**	**0**	**0.0**	**2**	**1**	**3:50**	....	....	....	....	....	....	....	....
	Quebec Citadelles	AHL	47	2	4	6	231	....	....	....	....	....	....	....	....	....	....	....	2	0	0	0	0	....	....	....
2000-01	Lake Charles	WPHL	5	0	2	2	36	....	....	....	....	....	....	....	....	....	....	....	....	....	....	....	....	....	....	....
	London Knights	Britain	13	2	1	3	117	....	....	....	....	....	....	....	....	....	....	....	....	....	....	....	....	....	....	....
	NHL Totals		**11**	**0**	**0**	**0**	**57**	**0**	**0**	**0**	**2**	**0.0**		**0**	**0.0**	**7**	**3**	**2:22**	....	....	....	....	....	....	....	....

Signed as a free agent by **Montreal**, June 10, 1998. Signed as a free agent by **London Knights** (Britain), November 17, 2000.

MORO, Marc
(MOH-roh, MAHRK) **NSH.**

Defense. Shoots left. 6'1", 220 lbs. Born, Toronto, Ont., July 17, 1977. Ottawa's 2nd choice, 27th overall, in 1995 Entry Draft.

Season	Club	League	GP	G	A	Pts	PIM	PP	SH	GW	S	%	+/-	TF	F%	H	SB	Min	GP	G	A	Pts	PIM	PP	SH	GW
1992-93	Mississauga Reps	MTHL	42	9	18	27	56	....	....	....	....	....	....	....	....	....	....	....	....	....	....	....	....	....	....	....
	Mississauga Sens	MTJHL	2	0	0	0	0	....	....	....	....	....	....	....	....	....	....	....	....	....	....	....	....	....	....	....
1993-94	Kingston	MTJHL	12	0	2	2	10	....	....	....	....	....	....	....	....	....	....	....	....	....	....	....	....	....	....	....
	Kingston	OHL	43	0	3	3	81	....	....	....	....	....	....	....	....	....	....	....	....	....	....	....	....	....	....	....
1994-95	Kingston	OHL	64	4	12	16	255	....	....	....	....	....	....	....	....	....	....	....	6	0	0	0	23	....	....	....
1995-96	Kingston	OHL	66	4	17	21	261	....	....	....	....	....	....	....	....	....	....	....	6	0	0	0	12	....	....	....
	P.E.I. Senators	AHL	2	0	0	0	7	....	....	....	....	....	....	....	....	....	....	....	2	0	0	0	4	....	....	....
1996-97	Kingston	OHL	37	4	8	12	97	....	....	....	....	....	....	....	....	....	....	....	....	....	....	....	....	....	....	....
	Sault Ste. Marie	OHL	26	0	5	5	74	....	....	....	....	....	....	....	....	....	....	....	11	1	6	7	38	....	....	....
1997-98	**Anaheim**	**NHL**	**1**	**0**	**0**	**0**	**0**	**0**	**0**	**0**	**0**	**0.0**	**0**	....	....	....	....	....	....	....	....	....	....	....	....	....
	Cincinnati Ducks	AHL	74	1	6	7	181	....	....	....	....	....	....	....	....	....	....	....	....	....	....	....	....	....	....	....
1998-99	Milwaukee	IHL	80	0	5	5	264	....	....	....	....	....	....	....	....	....	....	....	2	0	0	0	4	....	....	....
99-2000	**Nashville**	**NHL**	**8**	**0**	**0**	**0**	**40**	**0**	**0**	**0**	**3**	**0.0**	**-3**	**0**	**0.0**	**19**	**2**	**10:55**	....	....	....	....	....	....	....	....
	Milwaukee	IHL	64	5	5	10	203	....	....	....	....	....	....	....	....	....	....	....	....	....	....	....	....	....	....	....
2000-01	**Nashville**	**NHL**	**6**	**0**	**0**	**0**	**12**	**0**	**0**	**0**	**1**	**0.0**	**1**	**0**	**0.0**	**7**	**0**	**3:34**	....	....	....	....	....	....	....	....
	Milwaukee	IHL	68	2	9	11	190	....	....	....	....	....	....	....	....	....	....	....	5	1	0	1	10	....	....	....
	NHL Totals		**15**	**0**	**0**	**0**	**52**	**0**	**0**	**0**	**4**	**0.0**		**0**	**0.0**	**26**	**2**	**7:46**	....	....	....	....	....	....	....	....

Rights traded to **Anaheim** by **Ottawa** with Ted Drury for Jason York and Shaun Van Allen, October 1, 1996. Traded to **Nashville** by **Anaheim** with Chris Mason for Dominic Roussel, October 5, 1998.

MOROZOV, Aleksey
(moh-ROH-zohv, ah-LEHK-see) **PIT.**

Right wing. Shoots left. 6'1", 196 lbs. Born, Moscow, USSR, February 16, 1977. Pittsburgh's 1st choice, 24th overall, in 1995 Entry Draft.

Season	Club	League	GP	G	A	Pts	PIM	PP	SH	GW	S	%	+/-	TF	F%	H	SB	Min	GP	G	A	Pts	PIM	PP	SH	GW
1993-94	Krylja Sovetov	CIS	7	0	0	0	0	....	....	....	....	....	....	....	....	....	....	....	3	0	0	0	2	....	....	....
1994-95	Krylja Sovetov	CIS	48	15	12	27	53	....	....	....	....	....	....	....	....	....	....	....	4	0	3	3	0	....	....	....
1995-96	Krylja Sovetov	CIS	47	13	9	22	26	....	....	....	....	....	....	....	....	....	....	....	....	....	....	....	....	....	....	....
1996-97	Krylja Sovetov	Russia	44	21	11	32	32	....	....	....	....	....	....	....	....	....	....	....	2	0	1	1	2	....	....	....
1997-98	Krylja Sovetov	Russia	6	2	1	3	4	....	....	....	....	....	....	....	....	....	....	....	....	....	....	....	....	....	....	....
	Pittsburgh	**NHL**	**76**	**13**	**13**	**26**	**8**	**2**	**0**	**3**	**80**	**16.3**	**-4**	....	....	....	....	....	**6**	**0**	**1**	**1**	**2**	**0**	**0**	**0**
	Russia	Olympics	6	2	2	4	0	....	....	....	....	....	....	....	....	....	....	....	....	....	....	....	....	....	....	....
1998-99	**Pittsburgh**	**NHL**	**67**	**9**	**10**	**19**	**14**	**0**	**0**	**0**	**75**	**12.0**	**5**	**7**	**42.9**	**44**	**33**	**11:50**	**10**	**1**	**1**	**2**	**0**	**0**	**0**	**0**
99-2000	**Pittsburgh**	**NHL**	**68**	**12**	**19**	**31**	**14**	**0**	**1**	**0**	**101**	**11.9**	**12**	**27**	**33.3**	**33**	**20**	**13:51**	**5**	**0**	**0**	**0**	**0**	**0**	**0**	**0**
2000-01	**Pittsburgh**	**NHL**	**66**	**5**	**14**	**19**	**6**	**0**	**0**	**1**	**72**	**6.9**	**-8**	**19**	**42.1**	**23**	**25**	**10:41**	**18**	**3**	**3**	**6**	**6**	**0**	**1**	**0**
	NHL Totals		**277**	**39**	**56**	**95**	**42**	**2**	**1**	**4**	**328**	**11.9**		**53**	**37.7**	**100**	**78**	**12:08**	**39**	**4**	**5**	**9**	**8**	**0**	**1**	**0**

MORRIS, Derek
(MOH-rihs, DAIR-ihk) **CGY.**

Defense. Shoots right. 5'11", 200 lbs. Born, Edmonton, Alta., August 24, 1978. Calgary's 1st choice, 13th overall, in 1996 Entry Draft.

Season	Club	League	GP	G	A	Pts	PIM	PP	SH	GW	S	%	+/-	TF	F%	H	SB	Min	GP	G	A	Pts	PIM	PP	SH	GW
1994-95	Red Deer Chiefs	AMHL	31	6	35	41	74	....	....	....	....	....	....	....	....	....	....	....	....	....	....	....	....	....	....	....
1995-96	Regina Pats	WHL	67	8	44	52	70	....	....	....	....	....	....	....	....	....	....	....	11	1	7	8	26	....	....	....
1996-97	Regina Pats	WHL	67	18	57	75	180	....	....	....	....	....	....	....	....	....	....	....	5	0	3	3	9	....	....	....
	Saint John Flames	AHL	7	0	3	3	7	....	....	....	....	....	....	....	....	....	....	....	5	0	3	3	7	....	....	....
1997-98	**Calgary**	**NHL**	**82**	**9**	**20**	**29**	**88**	**5**	**1**	**1**	**120**	**7.5**	**1**	....	....	....	....	....	....	....	....	....	....	....	....	....
1998-99	**Calgary**	**NHL**	**71**	**7**	**27**	**34**	**73**	**3**	**0**	**2**	**150**	**4.7**	**4**	**0**	**0.0**	**93**	**78**	**20:44**	....	....	....	....	....	....	....	....
99-2000	**Calgary**	**NHL**	**78**	**9**	**29**	**38**	**80**	**3**	**0**	**2**	**193**	**4.7**	**2**	**0**	**0.0**	**127**	**119**	**24:51**	....	....	....	....	....	....	....	....

			Regular Season																Playoffs							
Season	Club	League	GP	G	A	Pts	PIM	PP	SH	GW	S	%	+/-	TF	F%	H	SB	Min	GP	G	A	Pts	PIM	PP	SH	GW
2000-01	**Calgary**	**NHL**	**51**	**5**	**23**	**28**	**56**	**3**	**1**	**4**	**142**	**3.5**	**–15**	**0**	**0.0**	**52**	**79**	**25:51**								
	Saint John Flames	AHL	3	1	2	3	2																			
	NHL Totals		**282**	**30**	**99**	**129**	**297**	**14**	**2**	**9**	**605**	**5.0**		**0**	**0.0**	**272**	**276**	**23:38**								

WHL East First All-Star Team (1997) • NHL All-Rookie Team (1998)

MORRISON, Brendan (MOHR-ih-suhn, BREHN-duhn) VAN.

Center. Shoots left. 5'11", 190 lbs. Born, Pitt Meadows, B.C., August 15, 1975. New Jersey's 3rd choice, 39th overall, in 1993 Entry Draft.

Season	Club	League	GP	G	A	Pts	PIM	PP	SH	GW	S	%	+/-	TF	F%	H	SB	Min	GP	G	A	Pts	PIM	PP	SH	GW
1990-91	Ridge Meadows	BCAHA	77	126	127	253	88																			
1991-92	Ridge Meadows	BCAHA	55	56	111	167	56																			
1992-93	Penticton	BCJHL	56	35	59	94	45																			
1993-94	U. of Michigan	CCHA	38	20	28	48	24												5	2	7	9	2			
1994-95	U. of Michigan	CCHA	39	23	*53	*76	42												5	1	11	12	6			
1995-96	U. of Michigan	CCHA	35	28	44	*72	41												7	6	9	15	4			
1996-97	U. of Michigan	CCHA	43	31	*57	*88	52												6	6	8	14	8			
1997-98	**New Jersey**	**NHL**	**11**	**5**	**4**	**9**	**0**	**0**	**0**	**1**	**19**	**26.3**	**3**						**3**	**0**	**1**	**1**	**0**	**0**	**0**	**0**
	Albany River Rats	AHL	72	35	49	84	44												8	3	4	7	19			
1998-99	**New Jersey**	**NHL**	**76**	**13**	**33**	**46**	**18**	**5**	**0**	**2**	**111**	**11.7**	**–4**	**920**	**51.1**	**63**	**19**	**13:55**	**7**	**0**	**2**	**2**	**0**	**0**	**0**	**0**
99-2000	SK Trebic-2	Cze-Rep	2	0	0	0	0																			
	HC Pardubice	Cze-Rep	6	5	2	7	2																			
	New Jersey	**NHL**	**44**	**5**	**21**	**26**	**8**	**2**	**0**	**1**	**79**	**6.3**	**8**	**572**	**51.1**	**53**	**18**	**16:09**								
	Vancouver	**NHL**	**12**	**2**	**7**	**9**	**10**	**0**	**0**	**0**	**17**	**11.8**	**4**	**48**	**54.2**	**11**	**3**	**14:41**								
2000-01	**Vancouver**	**NHL**	**82**	**16**	**38**	**54**	**42**	**3**	**2**	**3**	**179**	**8.9**	**2**	**1685**	**50.1**	**40**	**41**	**18:22**	**4**	**1**	**2**	**3**	**0**	**1**	**0**	**0**
	NHL Totals		**225**	**41**	**103**	**144**	**78**	**10**	**2**	**7**	**405**	**10.1**		**3225**	**50.6**	**167**	**81**	**16:07**	**14**	**1**	**5**	**6**	**0**	**1**	**0**	**0**

CCHA First All-Star Team (1995, 1996, 1997) • NCAA West First All-American Team (1995, 1996, 1997) • NCAA Championship All-Tournament Team (1996) • NCAA Championship Tournament MVP (1996) • Won Hobey Baker Memorial Award (Top U.S. Collegiate Player) (1997)

Traded to **Vancouver** by **New Jersey** with Denis Pederson for Alexander Mogilny, March 14, 2000.

MORROW, Brenden (MOHR-rohw, BREHN-dehn) DAL.

Left wing. Shoots left. 5'11", 200 lbs. Born, Carlyle, Sask., January 16, 1979. Dallas' 1st choice, 25th overall, in 1997 Entry Draft.

Season	Club	League	GP	G	A	Pts	PIM	PP	SH	GW	S	%	+/-	TF	F%	H	SB	Min	GP	G	A	Pts	PIM	PP	SH	GW
1994-95	Estevan Bruins	SAHA	60	117	72	189	45																			
1995-96	Portland	WHL	65	13	12	25	61												7	0	0	0	8			
1996-97	Portland	WHL	71	39	49	88	178												6	2	1	3	4			
1997-98	Portland	WHL	68	34	52	86	184												16	10	8	18	65			
1998-99	Portland	WHL	61	41	44	85	248												4	0	4	4	18			
99-2000	**Dallas**	**NHL**	**64**	**14**	**19**	**33**	**81**	**3**	**0**	**3**	**113**	**12.4**	**8**	**25**	**48.0**	**170**	**24**	**15:51**	**21**	**2**	**4**	**6**	**22**	**1**	**0**	**0**
	Michigan K-Wings	IHL	9	2	0	2	18																			
2000-01	**Dallas**	**NHL**	**82**	**20**	**24**	**44**	**128**	**7**	**0**	**6**	**121**	**16.5**	**18**	**22**	**45.5**	**230**	**20**	**15:29**	**10**	**0**	**3**	**3**	**12**	**0**	**0**	**0**
	NHL Totals		**146**	**34**	**43**	**77**	**209**	**10**	**0**	**9**	**234**	**14.5**		**47**	**46.8**	**400**	**44**	**15:39**	**31**	**2**	**7**	**9**	**34**	**1**	**0**	**0**

WHL West First All-Star Team (1999)

MOTTAU, Mike (MAW-tuh, MIGHK) NYR

Defense. Shoots left. 6', 192 lbs. Born, Quincy, MA, March 19, 1978. NY Rangers' 10th choice, 182nd overall, in 1997 Entry Draft.

Season	Club	League	GP	G	A	Pts	PIM	PP	SH	GW	S	%	+/-	TF	F%	H	SB	Min	GP	G	A	Pts	PIM	PP	SH	GW
1994-95	Thayer Academy	Hi-School	29	7	19	26																				
1995-96	Thayer Academy	Hi-School	31	6	20	26	14																			
1996-97	Boston College	H-East	38	5	18	23	77																			
1997-98	Boston College	H-East	40	13	36	49	50																			
1998-99	Boston College	H-East	43	3	39	42	44																			
99-2000	Boston College	H-East	42	6	37	43	61																			
2000-01	**NY Rangers**	**NHL**	**18**	**0**	**3**	**3**	**13**	**0**	**0**	**0**	**17**	**0.0**	**–6**	**0**	**0.0**	**19**	**17**	**15:18**								
	Hartford	AHL	61	10	33	43	45												5	0	1	1	19			
	NHL Totals		**18**	**0**	**3**	**3**	**13**	**0**	**0**	**0**	**17**	**0.0**		**0**	**0.0**	**19**	**17**	**15:18**								

Hockey East First All-Star Team (1998, 2000) • NCAA East Second All-American Team (1998) • NCAA Championship All-Tournament Team (1998, 2000) • Hockey East Second All-Star Team (1999) • NCAA East First All-American Team (1999, 2000) • Won Hobey Baker Memorial Award (Top U.S. Collegiate Player) (2000)

MOWERS, Mark (MAHW-uhrs, MAHRK) NSH.

Center. Shoots right. 5'11", 187 lbs. Born, Whitesboro, NY, February 16, 1974.

Season	Club	League	GP	G	A	Pts	PIM	PP	SH	GW	S	%	+/-	TF	F%	H	SB	Min	GP	G	A	Pts	PIM	PP	SH	GW
1992-93	Saginaw Gears	NAJHL	39	31	39	70																				
1993-94	Dubuque Saints	USHL	47	51	31	82	80																			
1994-95	New Hampshire	H-East	36	13	23	36	16																			
1995-96	New Hampshire	H-East	34	21	26	47	18																			
1996-97	New Hampshire	H-East	39	26	32	58	52																			
1997-98	New Hampshire	H-East	35	25	31	56	32																			
1998-99	**Nashville**	**NHL**	**30**	**0**	**6**	**6**	**4**	**0**	**0**	**0**	**24**	**0.0**	**–4**	**241**	**49.0**	**19**	**2**	**9:22**								
	Milwaukee	IHL	51	14	22	36	24												1	0	0	0	0			
99-2000	**Nashville**	**NHL**	**41**	**4**	**5**	**9**	**10**	**0**	**0**	**0**	**50**	**8.0**	**0**	**312**	**45.2**	**30**	**11**	**10:58**								
	Milwaukee	IHL	23	11	15	26	34																			
2000-01	Milwaukee	IHL	63	25	25	50	54												5	1	2	3	2			
	NHL Totals		**71**	**4**	**11**	**15**	**14**	**0**	**0**	**0**	**74**	**5.4**		**553**	**46.8**	**49**	**13**	**10:17**								

Hockey East Second All-Star Team (1998) • NCAA East First All-American Team (1998)

Signed as a free agent by **Nashville**, June 11, 1998.

MUCKALT, Bill (MUH-kawlt, BIHL) OTT.

Right wing. Shoots right. 6'1", 200 lbs. Born, Surrey, B.C., July 15, 1974. Vancouver's 9th choice, 221st overall, in 1994 Entry Draft.

Season	Club	League	GP	G	A	Pts	PIM	PP	SH	GW	S	%	+/-	TF	F%	H	SB	Min	GP	G	A	Pts	PIM	PP	SH	GW
1991-92	Merritt	BCJHL	55	14	11	25	75																			
1992-93	Merritt	BCJHL	59	31	43	74	80																			
1993-94	Merritt	BCJHL	43	58	51	109	99																			
	Kelowna Spartans	BCJHL	15	12	10	22	20																			
1994-95	U. of Michigan	CCHA	39	19	18	37	42												5	1	1	2	6			
1995-96	U. of Michigan	CCHA	41	28	30	58	34												7	5	6	11	6			
1996-97	U. of Michigan	CCHA	36	26	38	64	69												6	5	9	14	2			
1997-98	U. of Michigan	CCHA	46	32	*35	*67	94																			
1998-99	**Vancouver**	**NHL**	**73**	**16**	**20**	**36**	**98**	**4**	**2**	**1**	**119**	**13.4**	**–9**	**68**	**55.9**	**66**	**23**	**15:24**								
99-2000	**Vancouver**	**NHL**	**33**	**4**	**8**	**12**	**17**	**1**	**0**	**1**	**53**	**7.5**	**6**	**6**	**50.0**	**38**	**6**	**14:34**								
	NY Islanders	**NHL**	**12**	**4**	**3**	**7**	**4**	**0**	**0**	**0**	**26**	**15.4**	**5**	**8**	**50.0**	**20**	**1**	**12:23**								
2000-01	**NY Islanders**	**NHL**	**60**	**11**	**15**	**26**	**33**	**1**	**0**	**2**	**90**	**12.2**	**–4**	**7**	**14.3**	**94**	**9**	**13:43**								
	NHL Totals		**178**	**35**	**46**	**81**	**152**	**6**	**2**	**4**	**288**	**12.2**		**89**	**51.7**	**218**	**39**	**14:28**								

CCHA First All-Star Team (1998) • NCAA West First All-American Team (1998)

Traded to **NY Islanders** by **Vancouver** with Kevin Weekes and Dave Scatchard for Felix Potvin and NY Islanders' compensatory 2nd (later traded to New Jersey - New Jersey selected Teemu Laine) and 3rd (Thatcher Bell) round choices in 2000 Entry Draft, December 19, 1999. • Missed majority of 1999-2000 season recovering from shoulder injury suffered in game vs. Tampa Bay, January 13, 2000. Traded to **Ottawa** by **NY Islanders** with Zdeno Chara and NY Islanders' 1st round choice (Jason Spezza) in 2001 Entry Draft for Alexei Yashin, June 23, 2001.

MUIR, Bryan (MEWR, BRIGH-uhn) COL.

Defense. Shoots left. 6'4", 220 lbs. Born, Winnipeg, Man., June 8, 1973.

Season	Club	League	GP	G	A	Pts	PIM	PP	SH	GW	S	%	+/-	TF	F%	H	SB	Min	GP	G	A	Pts	PIM	PP	SH	GW
1991-92	Wexford Raiders	MTJHL	44	3	19	22	35																			
1992-93	New Hampshire	H-East	26	1	2	3	24																			
1993-94	New Hampshire	H-East	40	0	4	4	48																			
1994-95	New Hampshire	H-East	28	9	9	18	46																			
1995-96	Canada	Nat-Team	42	6	12	18	38																			
	Edmonton	**NHL**	**5**	**0**	**0**	**0**	**6**	**0**	**0**	**0**	**4**	**0.0**	**–4**													
1996-97	Hamilton Bulldogs	AHL	75	8	16	24	80												14	0	5	5	12			
	Edmonton	**NHL**																	**5**	**0**	**0**	**0**	**4**	**0**	**0**	**0**

			Regular Season																Playoffs							
Season	Club	League	GP	G	A	Pts	PIM	PP	SH	GW	S	%	+/-	TF	F%	H	SB	Min	GP	G	A	Pts	PIM	PP	SH	GW
1997-98	Edmonton	NHL	7	0	0	0	17	0	0	0	6	0.0	0	....	....	....	....	....	....	....	....	....	....	....	....	....
	Hamilton Bulldogs	AHL	28	3	10	13	62	....	....	....	....	....	....	....	....	....	....	....	....	....	....	....	....	....	....	....
	Albany River Rats	AHL	41	3	10	13	67	....	....	....	....	....	....	....	....	....	....	....	13	3	0	3	12	....	....	....
1998-99	New Jersey	NHL	1	0	0	0	0	0	0	0	4	0.0	0	0	0.0	0	0	9:54	....	....	....	....	....	....	....	....
	Albany River Rats	AHL	10	0	0	0	29	....	....	....	....	....	....	....	....	....	....	....	....	....	....	....	....	....	....	....
	Chicago	NHL	53	1	4	5	50	0	0	0	78	1.3	1	0	0.0	82	59	18:49	....	....	....	....	....	....	....	....
	Portland Pirates	AHL	2	1	1	2	2	....	....	....	....	....	....	....	....	....	....	....	....	....	....	....	....	....	....	....
99-2000	Chicago	NHL	11	2	3	5	13	0	1	0	19	10.5	–1	0	0.0	17	18	17:54	....	....	....	....	....	....	....	....
	Tampa Bay	NHL	30	1	1	2	32	0	0	0	32	3.1	–8	1	100.0	41	28	19:29	....	....	....	....	....	....	....	....
2000-01	Tampa Bay	NHL	10	0	3	3	15	0	0	0	14	0.0	–7	1	0.0	16	24	18:34	....	....	....	....	....	....	....	....
	Detroit Vipers	IHL	21	5	7	12	36	....	....	....	....	....	....	....	....	....	....	....	....	....	....	....	....	....	....	....
	♦ Colorado	NHL	8	0	0	0	4	0	0	0	3	0.0	0	0	0.0	5	4	8:14	3	0	0	0	0	0	0	0
	Hershey Bears	AHL	26	5	8	13	50	....	....	....	....	....	....	....	....	....	....	....	....	....	....	....	....	....	....	....
	NHL Totals		125	4	11	15	137	0	1	0	160	2.5		2	50.0	161	133	18:03	8	0	0	0	4	0	0	0

Signed to five-game amateur try-out contract by **Edmonton**, February 29, 1996. Signed as a free agent by **Edmonton**, April 30, 1996. Traded to **New Jersey** by **Edmonton** with Jason Arnott for Valeri Zelepukin and Bill Guerin, January 4, 1998. Traded to **Chicago** by **New Jersey** for Chicago's 3rd round choice (Michael Rupp) in 2000 Entry Draft, November 13, 1998. Traded to **Tampa Bay** by **Chicago** with Reid Simpson for Michael Nylander, November 12, 1999. • Missed majority of 1999-2000 season recovering from leg injury suffered in game vs. Atlanta, November 17, 1999. Traded to **Colorado** by **Tampa Bay** for Colorado's 8th round choice (Dmitri Bezrukov) in 2001 Entry Draft, January 23, 2001.

MULLER, Kirk

(MUHL-luhr, KUHRK) **DAL.**

Left wing. Shoots left. 6', 205 lbs. Born, Kingston, Ont., February 8, 1966. New Jersey's 1st choice, 2nd overall, in 1984 Entry Draft.

Season	Club	League	GP	G	A	Pts	PIM	PP	SH	GW	S	%	+/-	TF	F%	H	SB	Min	GP	G	A	Pts	PIM	PP	SH	GW
1980-81	Kingston	OHA-B	42	17	37	54	5	....	....	....	....	....	....	....	....	....	....	....	....	....	....	....	....	....	....	....
	Kingston	OMJHL	2	0	0	0	0	....	....	....	....	....	....	....	....	....	....	....	....	....	....	....	....	....	....	....
1981-82	Kingston	OHL	67	12	39	51	27	....	....	....	....	....	....	....	....	....	....	....	4	5	1	6	4	....	....	....
1982-83	Guelph Platers	OHL	66	52	60	112	41	....	....	....	....	....	....	....	....	....	....	....	....	....	....	....	....	....	....	....
1983-84	Guelph Platers	OHL	49	31	63	94	27	....	....	....	....	....	....	....	....	....	....	....	....	....	....	....	....	....	....	....
	Canada	Olympics	6	2	1	3	0	....	....	....	....	....	....	....	....	....	....	....	....	....	....	....	....	....	....	....
1984-85	New Jersey	NHL	80	17	37	54	69	9	1	0	157	10.8	–31	....	....	....	....	....	....	....	....	....	....	....	....	....
1985-86	New Jersey	NHL	77	25	41	66	45	5	1	1	168	14.9	–20	....	....	....	....	....	....	....	....	....	....	....	....	....
1986-87	New Jersey	NHL	79	26	50	76	75	10	1	4	193	13.5	–7	....	....	....	....	....	....	....	....	....	....	....	....	....
1987-88	New Jersey	NHL	80	37	57	94	114	17	2	1	215	17.2	19	....	....	....	....	....	20	4	8	12	37	0	0	0
1988-89	New Jersey	NHL	80	31	43	74	119	12	1	4	182	17.0	–23	....	....	....	....	....	....	....	....	....	....	....	....	....
1989-90	New Jersey	NHL	80	30	56	86	74	9	0	6	200	15.0	–1	....	....	....	....	....	6	1	3	4	11	0	0	0
1990-91	New Jersey	NHL	80	19	51	70	76	7	0	3	221	8.6	1	....	....	....	....	....	7	0	2	2	10	0	0	0
1991-92	Montreal	NHL	78	36	41	77	86	15	1	7	191	18.8	15	....	....	....	....	....	11	4	3	7	31	2	1	1
1992-93♦	Montreal	NHL	80	37	57	94	77	12	0	4	231	16.0	8	....	....	....	....	....	20	10	7	17	18	3	0	3
1993-94	Montreal	NHL	76	23	34	57	96	9	2	3	168	13.7	–1	....	....	....	....	....	7	6	2	8	4	3	0	2
1994-95	Montreal	NHL	33	8	11	19	33	3	0	1	81	9.9	–21	....	....	....	....	....	....	....	....	....	....	....	....	....
	NY Islanders	NHL	12	3	5	8	14	1	1	1	16	18.8	3	....	....	....	....	....	....	....	....	....	....	....	....	....
1995-96	NY Islanders	NHL	15	4	3	7	15	0	0	0	23	17.4	–10	....	....	....	....	....	....	....	....	....	....	....	....	....
	Toronto	NHL	36	9	16	25	42	7	0	1	79	11.4	–3	....	....	....	....	....	6	3	2	5	0	2	0	0
1996-97	Toronto	NHL	66	20	17	37	85	9	1	3	153	13.1	–23	....	....	....	....	....	....	....	....	....	....	....	....	....
	Florida	NHL	10	1	2	3	4	1	0	1	21	4.8	–2	....	....	....	....	....	5	1	2	3	4	1	0	0
1997-98	Florida	NHL	70	8	21	29	54	1	0	3	115	7.0	–14	....	....	....	....	....	....	....	....	....	....	....	....	....
1998-99	Florida	NHL	82	4	11	15	49	0	0	1	107	3.7	–11	1157	49.1	68	39	14:28	....	....	....	....	....	....	....	....
99-2000	Dallas	NHL	47	7	15	22	24	3	0	2	57	12.3	–3	443	48.5	77	19	16:24	23	2	3	5	18	0	0	1
2000-01	Dallas	NHL	55	1	9	10	26	0	0	0	54	1.9	–4	539	50.8	102	14	12:22	10	1	3	4	12	0	0	1
	NHL Totals		1216	346	577	923	1177	130	11	46	2632	13.1		2139	49.4	247	72	14:20	115	32	35	67	145	11	1	8

Played in NHL All-Star Game (1985, 1986, 1988, 1990, 1992, 1993)

Traded to **Montreal** by **New Jersey** with Rollie Melanson for Stephane Richer and Tom Chorske, September 20, 1991. Traded to **NY Islanders** by **Montreal** with Mathieu Schneider and Craig Darby for Pierre Turgeon and Vladimir Malakhov, April 5, 1995. Traded to **Toronto** by **NY Islanders** with Don Beaupre to complete transaction that sent Damian Rhodes and Ken Belanger to NY Islanders (January 23, 1996), January 23, 1996. Traded to **Florida** by **Toronto** for Jason Podollan, March 18, 1997. Signed as a free agent by **Dallas**, December 15, 1999.

MURPHY, Gord

(MUHR-fee, GOHRD)

Defense. Shoots right. 6'2", 195 lbs. Born, Willowdale, Ont., March 23, 1967. Philadelphia's 10th choice, 189th overall, in 1985 Entry Draft.

Season	Club	League	GP	G	A	Pts	PIM	PP	SH	GW	S	%	+/-	TF	F%	H	SB	Min	GP	G	A	Pts	PIM	PP	SH	GW
1983-84	Don Mills Flyers	MTHL	65	24	42	66	130	....	....	....	....	....	....	....	....	....	....	....	....	....	....	....	....	....	....	....
1984-85	Oshawa Generals	OHL	59	3	12	15	25	....	....	....	....	....	....	....	....	....	....	....	....	....	....	....	....	....	....	....
1985-86	Oshawa Generals	OHL	64	7	15	22	56	....	....	....	....	....	....	....	....	....	....	....	6	1	1	2	6	....	....	....
1986-87	Oshawa Generals	OHL	56	7	30	37	95	....	....	....	....	....	....	....	....	....	....	....	24	6	16	22	22	....	....	....
1987-88	Hershey Bears	AHL	62	8	20	28	44	....	....	....	....	....	....	....	....	....	....	....	12	0	8	8	12	....	....	....
1988-89	Philadelphia	NHL	75	4	31	35	68	3	0	1	116	3.4	–3	....	....	....	....	....	19	2	7	9	13	1	0	1
1989-90	Philadelphia	NHL	75	14	27	41	95	4	0	1	160	8.8	–7	....	....	....	....	....	....	....	....	....	....	....	....	....
1990-91	Philadelphia	NHL	80	11	31	42	58	6	0	2	203	5.4	–7	....	....	....	....	....	....	....	....	....	....	....	....	....
1991-92	Philadelphia	NHL	31	2	8	10	33	0	0	0	50	4.0	–4	....	....	....	....	....	....	....	....	....	....	....	....	....
	Boston	NHL	42	3	6	9	51	0	0	0	82	3.7	2	....	....	....	....	....	15	1	0	1	12	0	0	0
1992-93	Boston	NHL	49	5	12	17	62	3	0	2	68	7.4	–13	....	....	....	....	....	....	....	....	....	....	....	....	....
	Providence Bruins	AHL	2	1	3	4	2	....	....	....	....	....	....	....	....	....	....	....	....	....	....	....	....	....	....	....
1993-94	Florida	NHL	84	14	29	43	71	9	0	2	172	8.1	–11	....	....	....	....	....	....	....	....	....	....	....	....	....
1994-95	Florida	NHL	46	6	16	22	24	5	0	0	94	6.4	–14	....	....	....	....	....	....	....	....	....	....	....	....	....
1995-96	Florida	NHL	70	8	22	30	30	4	0	0	125	6.4	5	....	....	....	....	....	14	0	4	4	6	0	0	0
1996-97	Florida	NHL	80	8	15	23	51	2	0	0	137	5.8	3	....	....	....	....	....	5	0	5	5	4	0	0	0
1997-98	Florida	NHL	79	6	11	17	46	3	0	0	123	4.9	–3	....	....	....	....	....	....	....	....	....	....	....	....	....
1998-99	Florida	NHL	51	0	7	7	16	0	0	0	56	0.0	4	1	0.0	44	58	19:57	....	....	....	....	....	....	....	....
99-2000	Atlanta	NHL	58	1	10	11	38	0	0	0	74	1.4	–26	0	0.0	96	132	22:41	....	....	....	....	....	....	....	....
2000-01	Atlanta	NHL	27	3	11	14	12	2	0	0	44	6.8	–11	0	0.0	22	47	20:44	....	....	....	....	....	....	....	....
	NHL Totals		847	85	236	321	655	41	0	8	1504	5.7		1	0.0	162	237	21:16	53	3	16	19	35	1	0	1

Traded to **Boston** by **Philadelphia** with Brian Dobbin, Philadelphia's 3rd round choice (Sergei Zholtok) in 1992 Entry Draft and 4th round choice (Charles Paquette) in 1993 Entry Draft, for Garry Galley, Wes Walz and Boston's 3rd round choice (Milos Holan) in 1993 Entry Draft, January 2, 1992. Traded to **Dallas** by **Boston** for future considerations (Jon Casey to Boston for Andy Moog, June 25, 1993), June 20, 1993. Claimed by **Florida** from **Dallas** in Expansion Draft, June 24, 1993. Traded to **Atlanta** by **Florida** with Herbert Vasiljevs, Daniel Tjarnqvist and Ottawa's 6th round choice (previously acquired, later traded to Dallas - Dallas selected Justin Cox) in 1999 Entry Draft for Trevor Kidd, June 25, 1999. • Missed majority of 2000-01 season recovering from shoulder injury suffered in game vs. NY Rangers, October 7, 2000.

MURPHY, Joe

(MUHR-fee, JOH)

Right wing. Shoots left. 6', 190 lbs. Born, London, Ont., October 16, 1967. Detroit's 1st choice, 1st overall, in 1986 Entry Draft.

Season	Club	League	GP	G	A	Pts	PIM	PP	SH	GW	S	%	+/-	TF	F%	H	SB	Min	GP	G	A	Pts	PIM	PP	SH	GW
1984-85	Penticton	BCJHL	51	68	84	*152	92	....	....	....	....	....	....	....	....	....	....	....	....	....	....	....	....	....	....	....
1985-86	Michigan State	CCHA	35	24	37	61	50	....	....	....	....	....	....	....	....	....	....	....	....	....	....	....	....	....	....	....
1986-87	Detroit	NHL	5	0	1	1	2	0	0	0	3	0.0	0	....	....	....	....	....	....	....	....	....	....	....	....	....
	Adirondack	AHL	71	21	38	59	61	....	....	....	....	....	....	....	....	....	....	....	10	2	1	3	33	....	....	....
1987-88	Detroit	NHL	50	10	9	19	37	1	0	2	82	12.2	–4	....	....	....	....	....	8	0	1	1	6	0	0	0
	Adirondack	AHL	6	5	6	11	4	....	....	....	....	....	....	....	....	....	....	....	....	....	....	....	....	....	....	....
1988-89	Detroit	NHL	26	1	7	8	28	0	0	0	29	3.4	–7	....	....	....	....	....	....	....	....	....	....	....	....	....
	Adirondack	AHL	47	31	35	66	66	....	....	....	....	....	....	....	....	....	....	....	16	6	11	17	17	....	....	....
1989-90	Detroit	NHL	9	3	1	4	4	0	0	1	16	18.8	4	....	....	....	....	....	....	....	....	....	....	....	....	....
	♦ Edmonton	NHL	62	7	18	25	56	2	0	0	101	6.9	1	....	....	....	....	....	22	6	8	14	16	0	0	2
1990-91	Edmonton	NHL	80	27	35	62	35	4	1	4	141	19.1	2	....	....	....	....	....	15	2	5	7	14	1	0	1
1991-92	Edmonton	NHL	80	35	47	82	52	10	2	2	193	18.1	17	....	....	....	....	....	16	8	16	24	12	4	0	2
1992-93	Chicago	NHL	19	7	10	17	18	5	0	1	43	16.3	–3	....	....	....	....	....	4	0	0	0	8	0	0	0
1993-94	Chicago	NHL	81	31	39	70	111	7	4	4	222	14.0	1	....	....	....	....	....	6	1	3	4	25	0	0	0
1994-95	Chicago	NHL	40	23	18	41	89	7	0	3	120	19.2	7	....	....	....	....	....	16	9	3	12	29	3	0	3
1995-96	Chicago	NHL	70	22	29	51	86	8	0	3	212	10.4	–3	....	....	....	....	....	10	6	2	8	33	0	0	2
1996-97	St. Louis	NHL	75	20	25	45	69	4	1	2	151	13.2	–1	....	....	....	....	....	6	1	1	2	10	1	0	0
1997-98	St. Louis	NHL	27	4	9	13	22	2	0	0	52	7.7	8	....	....	....	....	....	....	....	....	....	....	....	....	....
	San Jose	NHL	10	5	4	9	14	2	0	0	29	17.2	1	....	....	....	....	....	6	1	1	2	20	1	0	0
1998-99	San Jose	NHL	76	25	23	48	73	7	0	2	176	14.2	10	15	40.0	29	9	14:45	6	0	3	3	4	0	0	0
99-2000	Boston	NHL	26	7	7	14	41	3	0	0	68	10.3	–7	2	50.0	39	5	15:13	....	....	....	....	....	....	....	....
	Washington	NHL	29	5	8	13	53	1	0	2	50	10.0	8	3	0.0	29	9	14:27	5	0	0	0	8	0	0	0

			Regular Season																Playoffs							
Season	Club	League	GP	G	A	Pts	PIM	PP	SH	GW	S	%	+/-	TF	F%	H	SB	Min	GP	G	A	Pts	PIM	PP	SH	GW
2000-01	Washington	NHL	14	1	5	6	20	1	0	0	22	4.5	–5	1	100.0	21	5	12:31	....	....	....	....	....	....	....	....
	Rochester	AHL	74	20	15	35	43	....	....	....	....	....	....	....	....	....	....	....	4	0	1	1	4	....	....	....
	NHL Totals		779	233	295	528	810	64	8	26	1710	13.6		21	38.1	118	28	14:33	120	34	43	77	185	10	0	10

Traded to **Edmonton** by **Detroit** with Petr Klima, Adam Graves and Jeff Sharples for Jimmy Carson, Kevin McClelland and Edmonton's 5th round choice (later traded to Montreal - Montreal selected Brad Layzell) in 1991 Entry Draft, November 2, 1989. • Missed majority of 1992-93 season after failing to come to contract terms with **Edmonton**. Traded to **Chicago** by **Edmonton** for Igor Kravchuk and Dean McAmmond, February 24, 1993. Signed as a free agent by **St. Louis**, July 8, 1996. Traded to **San Jose** by **St. Louis** for Todd Gill, March 24, 1998. Signed as a free agent by **Boston**, November 12, 1999. Claimed on waivers by **Washington** from **Boston**, February 10, 2000.

MURPHY, Larry

(MUHR-fee, LAIR-ree)

Defense. Shoots right. 6'2", 210 lbs. Born, Scarborough, Ont., March 8, 1961. Los Angeles' 1st choice, 4th overall, in 1980 Entry Draft.

1977-78	Toronto Nats	MTJHL	36	10	20	30	25	....	....	....	....	....	....	....	....	....	....	....	....	....	....	....	....	....	....	....
1978-79	Peterborough	OMJHL	66	6	21	27	82	....	....	....	....	....	....	....	....	....	....	....	19	1	9	10	42	....	....	....
1979-80	Peterborough	OMJHL	68	21	68	89	88	....	....	....	....	....	....	....	....	....	....	....	14	4	13	17	20	....	....	....
1980-81	Los Angeles	NHL	80	16	60	76	79	5	1	1	153	10.5	17	....	....	....	....	....	4	3	0	3	2	1	0	0
1981-82	Los Angeles	NHL	79	22	44	66	95	8	1	2	191	11.5	–13	....	....	....	....	....	10	2	8	10	12	1	0	0
1982-83	Los Angeles	NHL	77	14	48	62	81	9	0	2	172	8.1	2	....	....	....	....	....	....	....	....	....	....	....	....	....
1983-84	Los Angeles	NHL	6	0	3	3	0	0	0	0	11	0.0	–4	....	....	....	....	....	....	....	....	....	....	....	....	....
	Washington	NHL	72	13	33	46	50	2	0	2	138	9.4	12	....	....	....	....	....	8	0	3	3	6	0	0	0
1984-85	Washington	NHL	79	13	42	55	51	3	0	0	153	8.5	21	....	....	....	....	....	5	2	3	5	0	2	0	0
1985-86	Washington	NHL	78	21	44	65	50	8	1	2	180	11.7	2	....	....	....	....	....	9	1	5	6	6	1	0	0
1986-87	Washington	NHL	80	23	58	81	39	8	0	4	226	10.2	25	....	....	....	....	....	7	2	2	4	6	0	0	1
1987-88	Washington	NHL	79	8	53	61	72	7	0	1	201	4.0	2	....	....	....	....	....	13	4	4	8	33	2	0	1
1988-89	Washington	NHL	65	7	29	36	70	3	0	0	129	5.4	–5	....	....	....	....	....	....	....	....	....	....	....	....	....
	Minnesota	NHL	13	4	6	10	12	3	0	1	31	12.9	5	....	....	....	....	....	5	0	2	2	8	0	0	0
1989-90	Minnesota	NHL	77	10	58	68	44	4	0	1	173	5.8	–13	....	....	....	....	....	7	1	2	3	31	0	0	1
1990-91	Minnesota	NHL	31	4	11	15	38	1	0	2	103	3.9	–8	....	....	....	....	....	....	....	....	....	....	....	....	....
	♦ Pittsburgh	NHL	44	5	23	28	30	2	0	0	85	5.9	2	....	....	....	....	....	23	5	18	23	44	4	0	0
1991-92	♦ Pittsburgh	NHL	77	21	56	77	48	7	2	3	206	10.2	33	....	....	....	....	....	21	6	10	16	19	3	0	1
1992-93	Pittsburgh	NHL	83	22	63	85	73	6	2	2	230	9.6	45	....	....	....	....	....	12	2	11	13	10	2	0	1
1993-94	Pittsburgh	NHL	84	17	56	73	44	7	0	4	236	7.2	10	....	....	....	....	....	6	0	5	5	0	0	0	0
1994-95	Pittsburgh	NHL	48	13	25	38	18	4	0	3	124	10.5	12	....	....	....	....	....	12	2	13	15	0	1	0	0
1995-96	Toronto	NHL	82	12	49	61	34	8	0	1	182	6.6	–2	....	....	....	....	....	6	0	2	2	4	0	0	0
1996-97	Toronto	NHL	69	7	32	39	20	4	0	0	137	5.1	1	....	....	....	....	....	....	....	....	....	....	....	....	....
	♦ Detroit	NHL	12	2	4	6	0	1	0	1	21	9.5	2	....	....	....	....	....	20	2	9	11	8	1	0	1
1997-98	♦ Detroit	NHL	82	11	41	52	37	2	1	2	129	8.5	35	....	....	....	....	....	22	3	12	15	2	1	2	1
1998-99	Detroit	NHL	80	10	42	52	42	5	1	2	168	6.0	21	0	0.0	36	100	24:15	10	0	2	2	8	0	0	0
99-2000	Detroit	NHL	81	10	30	40	45	7	0	0	146	6.8	4	1	100.0	38	92	21:50	9	2	3	5	2	1	1	0
2000-01	Detroit	NHL	57	2	19	21	12	0	0	1	81	2.5	–6	1	100.0	28	60	19:00	6	0	1	1	0	0	0	0
	NHL Totals		1615	287	929	1216	1084	114	9	37	3606	8.0		2	100.0	102	252	21:59	215	37	115	152	201	20	3	7

OMJHL First All-Star Team (1980) • NHL Second All-Star Team (1987, 1993, 1995) • Played in NHL All-Star Game (1994, 1996, 1999)

Traded to **Washington** by **LA Kings** for Ken Houston and Brian Engblom, October 18, 1983. Traded to **Minnesota** by **Washington** with Mike Gartner for Dino Ciccarelli and Bob Rouse, March 7, 1989. Traded to **Pittsburgh** by **Minnesota** with Peter Taglianetti for Chris Dahlquist and Jim Johnson, December 11, 1990. Traded to **Toronto** by **Pittsburgh** for Dmitri Mironov and Toronto's 2nd round choice (later traded to New Jersey - New Jersey selected Joshua DeWolf) in 1996 Entry Draft, July 8, 1995. Traded to **Detroit** by **Toronto** for future considerations, March 18, 1997.

MURRAY, Chris

(MUHR-ray, KRIHS) **TOR.**

Right wing. Shoots right. 6'2", 213 lbs. Born, Port Hardy, B.C., October 25, 1974. Montreal's 3rd choice, 54th overall, in 1994 Entry Draft.

1990-91	Bellingham Hawks	BCJHL	54	5	8	13	150	....	....	....	....	....	....	....	....	....	....	....	....	....	....	....	....	....	....	....
1991-92	Kamloops Blazers	WHL	33	1	1	2	218	....	....	....	....	....	....	....	....	....	....	....	5	0	0	0	10	....	....	....
1992-93	Kamloops Blazers	WHL	62	6	10	16	217	....	....	....	....	....	....	....	....	....	....	....	13	0	4	4	34	....	....	....
1993-94	Kamloops Blazers	WHL	59	14	16	30	260	....	....	....	....	....	....	....	....	....	....	....	15	4	2	6	*107	....	....	....
1994-95	Fredericton	AHL	55	6	12	18	234	....	....	....	....	....	....	....	....	....	....	....	12	1	1	2	50	....	....	....
	Montreal	NHL	3	0	0	0	4	0	0	0	0	0.0	0	....	....	....	....	....	....	....	....	....	....	....	....	....
1995-96	Montreal	NHL	48	3	4	7	163	0	0	1	32	9.4	5	....	....	....	....	....	4	0	0	0	4	0	0	0
	Fredericton	AHL	30	13	13	26	217	....	....	....	....	....	....	....	....	....	....	....	....	....	....	....	....	....	....	....
1996-97	Montreal	NHL	56	4	2	6	114	0	0	0	32	12.5	–8	....	....	....	....	....	....	....	....	....	....	....	....	....
	Hartford	NHL	8	1	1	2	10	0	0	0	9	11.1	1	....	....	....	....	....	....	....	....	....	....	....	....	....
1997-98	Carolina	NHL	7	0	1	1	22	0	0	0	3	0.0	2	....	....	....	....	....	....	....	....	....	....	....	....	....
	Ottawa	NHL	46	5	3	8	96	0	0	2	48	10.4	1	....	....	....	....	....	11	1	0	1	8	0	0	0
1998-99	Ottawa	NHL	38	1	6	7	65	0	0	0	33	3.0	–2	1	100.0	30	5	7:06	....	....	....	....	....	....	....	....
	Chicago	NHL	4	0	0	0	14	0	0	0	4	0.0	0	1	100.0	3	0	7:20	....	....	....	....	....	....	....	....
99-2000	Dallas	NHL	32	2	1	3	62	0	0	0	25	8.0	–7	0	0.0	25	2	5:19	....	....	....	....	....	....	....	....
	Michigan K-Wings	IHL	31	5	2	7	78	....	....	....	....	....	....	....	....	....	....	....	....	....	....	....	....	....	....	....
2000-01	Worcester	AHL	21	9	8	17	60	....	....	....	....	....	....	....	....	....	....	....	....	....	....	....	....	....	....	....
	NHL Totals		242	16	18	34	550	0	0	3	186	8.6		2	100.0	58	7	6:20	15	1	0	1	12	0	0	0

Traded to **Phoenix** by **Montreal** with Murray Baron for Dave Manson, March 18, 1997. Traded to **Hartford** by **Phoenix** for Gerald Diduck, March 18, 1997. Transferred to **Carolina** after **Hartford** franchise relocated, June 25, 1997. Traded to **Ottawa** by **Carolina** for Sean Hill, November 18, 1997. Traded to **Chicago** by **Ottawa** for Nelson Emerson, March 23, 1999. Claimed by **Dallas** from **Chicago** in Waiver Draft, September 30, 1999. Signed as a free agent by **St. Louis**, July 27, 2000. Signed as a free agent by **Toronto**, August 7, 2001.

MURRAY, Glen

(MUHR-ray, GLEHN) **L.A.**

Right wing. Shoots right. 6'3", 225 lbs. Born, Halifax, N.S., November 1, 1972. Boston's 1st choice, 18th overall, in 1991 Entry Draft.

1988-89	Bridgewater	NSMHL	45	50	56	106	62	....	....	....	....	....	....	....	....	....	....	....	....	....	....	....	....	....	....	....
1989-90	Sudbury Wolves	OHL	62	8	28	36	17	....	....	....	....	....	....	....	....	....	....	....	7	0	0	0	4	....	....	....
1990-91	Sudbury Wolves	OHL	66	27	38	65	82	....	....	....	....	....	....	....	....	....	....	....	5	8	4	12	10	....	....	....
1991-92	Sudbury Wolves	OHL	54	37	47	84	93	....	....	....	....	....	....	....	....	....	....	....	11	7	4	11	18	....	....	....
	Boston	NHL	5	3	1	4	0	1	0	0	20	15.0	2	....	....	....	....	....	15	4	2	6	10	1	0	0
1992-93	Boston	NHL	27	3	4	7	8	2	0	1	28	10.7	–6	....	....	....	....	....	....	....	....	....	....	....	....	....
	Providence Bruins	AHL	48	30	26	56	42	....	....	....	....	....	....	....	....	....	....	....	6	1	4	5	4	....	....	....
1993-94	Boston	NHL	81	18	13	31	48	0	0	4	114	15.8	–1	....	....	....	....	....	13	4	5	9	14	0	0	0
1994-95	Boston	NHL	35	5	2	7	46	0	0	2	64	7.8	–11	....	....	....	....	....	2	0	0	0	2	0	0	0
1995-96	Pittsburgh	NHL	69	14	15	29	57	0	0	2	100	14.0	4	....	....	....	....	....	18	2	6	8	10	0	0	1
1996-97	Pittsburgh	NHL	66	11	11	22	24	3	0	1	127	8.7	–19	....	....	....	....	....	....	....	....	....	....	....	....	....
	Los Angeles	NHL	11	5	3	8	8	0	0	0	26	19.2	–2	....	....	....	....	....	....	....	....	....	....	....	....	....
1997-98	Los Angeles	NHL	81	29	31	60	54	7	3	7	193	15.0	6	....	....	....	....	....	4	2	0	2	6	0	0	0
1998-99	Los Angeles	NHL	61	16	15	31	36	3	3	3	173	9.2	–14	12	25.0	63	15	20:33	....	....	....	....	....	....	....	....
99-2000	Los Angeles	NHL	78	29	33	62	60	10	1	2	202	14.4	13	15	80.0	85	24	18:30	4	0	0	0	2	0	0	0
2000-01	Los Angeles	NHL	64	18	21	39	32	3	1	1	138	13.0	9	7	42.9	88	16	18:12	13	4	3	7	4	1	0	1
	NHL Totals		578	151	149	300	373	29	8	23	1185	12.7		34	52.9	236	55	19:01	69	16	16	32	48	2	0	2

Traded to **Pittsburgh** by **Boston** with Bryan Smolinski and Boston's 3rd round choice (Boyd Kane) in 1996 Entry Draft for Kevin Stevens and Shawn McEachern, August 2, 1995. Traded to **LA Kings** by **Pittsburgh** for Ed Olczyk, March 18, 1997.

MURRAY, Marty

(MUHR-ray, MAHR-tee) **PHI.**

Center. Shoots left. 5'9", 180 lbs. Born, Deloraine, Man., February 16, 1975. Calgary's 5th choice, 96th overall, in 1993 Entry Draft.

1990-91	S-W Cougars	MMHL	36	46	47	93	50	....	....	....	....	....	....	....	....	....	....	....	....	....	....	....	....	....	....	....
1991-92	Brandon	WHL	68	20	36	56	22	....	....	....	....	....	....	....	....	....	....	....	....	....	....	....	....	....	....	....
1992-93	Brandon	WHL	67	29	65	94	50	....	....	....	....	....	....	....	....	....	....	....	4	1	3	4	0	....	....	....
1993-94	Brandon	WHL	64	43	71	114	33	....	....	....	....	....	....	....	....	....	....	....	14	6	14	20	14	....	....	....
1994-95	Brandon	WHL	65	40	*88	128	53	....	....	....	....	....	....	....	....	....	....	....	18	9	*20	29	16	....	....	....
1995-96	Calgary	NHL	15	3	3	6	0	2	0	0	22	13.6	–4	....	....	....	....	....	....	....	....	....	....	....	....	....
	Saint John Flames	AHL	58	25	31	56	20	....	....	....	....	....	....	....	....	....	....	....	14	2	4	6	4	....	....	....
1996-97	Calgary	NHL	2	0	0	0	4	0	0	0	2	0.0	0	....	....	....	....	....	....	....	....	....	....	....	....	....
	Saint John Flames	AHL	67	19	39	58	40	....	....	....	....	....	....	....	....	....	....	....	5	2	3	5	4	....	....	....
1997-98	Calgary	NHL	2	0	0	0	2	0	0	0	2	0.0	1	....	....	....	....	....	....	....	....	....	....	....	....	....
	Saint John Flames	AHL	41	10	30	40	16	....	....	....	....	....	....	....	....	....	....	....	21	10	10	20	12	....	....	....
1998-99	VSV Villach	Alpenliga	33	26	41	67	12	....	....	....	....	....	....	....	....	....	....	....	....	....	....	....	....	....	....	....
	VSV Villach	Austria	17	13	17	30	6	....	....	....	....	....	....	....	....	....	....	....	6	1	4	5	0	....	....	....
99-2000	Kolner Haie	DEL	56	12	47	59	28	....	....	....	....	....	....	....	....	....	....	....	10	4	3	7	2	....	....	....

Season	Club	League	GP	G	A	Pts	PIM	PP	SH	GW	S	%	+/-	TF	F%	H	SB	Min	GP	G	A	Pts	PIM	PP	SH	GW
			Regular Season																Playoffs							
2000-01	**Calgary**	**NHL**	**7**	**0**	**0**	**0**	**0**	**0**	**0**	**0**	**6**	**0.0**	**–2**	**88**	**55.7**	**5**	**4**	**14:28**								
	Saint John Flames	AHL	56	24	52	76	36												19	4	16	20	18			
	NHL Totals		**26**	**3**	**3**	**6**	**6**	**2**	**0**	**0**	**32**	**9.4**		**88**	**55.7**	**5**	**4**	**14:28**								

WHL East First All-Star Team (1994, 1995) • Canadian Major Junior Second All-Star Team (1994)
Signed as a free agent by **Philadelphia**, July 9, 2001.

MURRAY, Rem
(MUHR-ray, REHM) **EDM.**

Center/Left wing. Shoots left. 6'2", 195 lbs. Born, Stratford, Ont., October 9, 1972. Los Angeles' 5th choice, 135th overall, in 1992 Entry Draft.

Season	Club	League	GP	G	A	Pts	PIM	PP	SH	GW	S	%	+/-	TF	F%	H	SB	Min	GP	G	A	Pts	PIM	PP	SH	GW
1989-90	Stratford Cullitons	OJHL-B	46	19	32	51	48																			
1990-91	Stratford Cullitons	OJHL-B	48	39	59	98	39																			
1991-92	Michigan State	CCHA	41	12	36	48	16																			
1992-93	Michigan State	CCHA	40	22	35	57	24																			
1993-94	Michigan State	CCHA	41	16	38	54	18																			
1994-95	Michigan State	CCHA	40	20	36	56	21																			
1995-96	Cape Breton	AHL	79	31	59	90	40																			
1996-97	**Edmonton**	**NHL**	**82**	**11**	**20**	**31**	**16**	**1**	**0**	**2**	**85**	**12.9**	**9**						**12**	**1**	**2**	**3**	**4**	**0**	**0**	**0**
1997-98	**Edmonton**	**NHL**	**61**	**9**	**9**	**18**	**39**	**2**	**2**	**0**	**59**	**15.3**	**–9**						**11**	**1**	**4**	**5**	**2**	**0**	**0**	**0**
1998-99	**Edmonton**	**NHL**	**78**	**21**	**18**	**39**	**20**	**4**	**1**	**4**	**116**	**18.1**	**4**	**1013**	**48.1**	**68**	**30**	**15:50**	**4**	**1**	**1**	**2**	**2**	**0**	**0**	**0**
99-2000	**Edmonton**	**NHL**	**44**	**9**	**5**	**14**	**8**	**2**	**0**	**3**	**65**	**13.8**	**–2**	**303**	**50.5**	**22**	**14**	**14:16**	**5**	**0**	**1**	**1**	**2**	**0**	**0**	**0**
2000-01	**Edmonton**	**NHL**	**82**	**15**	**21**	**36**	**24**	**1**	**3**	**3**	**122**	**12.3**	**5**	**694**	**49.3**	**42**	**29**	**15:21**	**6**	**2**	**0**	**2**	**6**	**1**	**0**	**0**
	NHL Totals		**347**	**65**	**73**	**138**	**107**	**10**	**6**	**12**	**447**	**14.5**		**2010**	**48.9**	**132**	**73**	**15:18**	**38**	**5**	**8**	**13**	**16**	**1**	**0**	**0**

CCHA Second All-Star Team (1995)
Signed as a free agent by **Edmonton**, September 19, 1995.

MURRAY, Rob
(MUHR-ray, RAWB) **CGY.**

Center. Shoots right. 6'1", 180 lbs. Born, Toronto, Ont., April 4, 1967. Washington's 3rd choice, 61st overall, in 1985 Entry Draft.

Season	Club	League	GP	G	A	Pts	PIM	PP	SH	GW	S	%	+/-	TF	F%	H	SB	Min	GP	G	A	Pts	PIM	PP	SH	GW
1983-84	Mississauga Reps	MTHL	35	18	36	54	32																			
1984-85	Peterborough	OHL	63	12	9	21	155												17	2	7	9	45			
1985-86	Peterborough	OHL	52	14	18	32	125												16	1	2	3	50			
1986-87	Peterborough	OHL	62	17	37	54	204												3	1	4	5	8			
1987-88	Fort Wayne	IHL	80	12	21	33	139												6	0	2	2	16			
1988-89	Baltimore	AHL	80	11	23	34	235																			
1989-90	**Washington**	**NHL**	**41**	**2**	**7**	**9**	**58**	**0**	**0**	**0**	**29**	**6.9**	**–10**						**9**	**0**	**0**	**0**	**18**	**0**	**0**	**0**
	Baltimore	AHL	23	5	4	9	63																			
1990-91	**Washington**	**NHL**	**17**	**0**	**3**	**3**	**19**	**0**	**0**	**0**	**8**	**0.0**	**0**													
	Baltimore	AHL	48	6	20	26	177												4	0	0	0	12			
1991-92	**Winnipeg**	**NHL**	**9**	**0**	**1**	**1**	**18**	**0**	**0**	**0**	**2**	**0.0**	**–2**													
	Moncton Hawks	AHL	60	16	15	31	247												8	0	1	1	56			
1992-93	**Winnipeg**	**NHL**	**10**	**1**	**0**	**1**	**6**	**0**	**0**	**1**	**4**	**25.0**	**0**													
	Moncton Hawks	AHL	56	16	21	37	147												3	0	0	0	6			
1993-94	**Winnipeg**	**NHL**	**6**	**0**	**0**	**0**	**2**	**0**	**0**	**0**	**1**	**0.0**	**0**													
	Moncton Hawks	AHL	69	25	32	57	280												21	2	3	5	60			
1994-95	Springfield	AHL	78	16	38	54	373																			
	Winnipeg	**NHL**	**10**	**0**	**2**	**2**	**2**	**0**	**0**	**0**	**5**	**0.0**	**1**													
1995-96	**Winnipeg**	**NHL**	**1**	**0**	**0**	**0**	**2**	**0**	**0**	**0**	**1**	**0.0**	**–1**													
	Springfield	AHL	74	10	28	38	263												10	1	6	7	32			
1996-97	Springfield	AHL	78	16	27	43	234												17	2	3	5	66			
1997-98	Springfield	AHL	80	7	30	37	255												4	0	2	2	2			
1998-99	**Phoenix**	**NHL**	**13**	**1**	**2**	**3**	**4**	**0**	**0**	**0**	**11**	**9.1**	**2**	**28**	**46.4**	**11**	**9**	**8:18**								
	Springfield	AHL	68	6	19	25	197												3	0	0	0	4			
99-2000	Springfield	AHL	22	1	3	4	70																			
	Hamilton Bulldogs	AHL	55	11	20	31	100												10	2	3	5	4			
2000-01	Philadelphia	AHL	46	3	6	9	65																			
	Springfield	AHL	30	3	2	5	43																			
	NHL Totals		**107**	**4**	**15**	**19**	**111**	**0**	**0**	**1**	**61**	**6.6**		**28**	**46.4**	**11**	**9**	**8:18**	**9**	**0**	**0**	**0**	**18**	**0**	**0**	**0**

Claimed by **Minnesota** from **Washington** in Expansion Draft, May 30, 1991. Traded to **Winnipeg** by **Minnesota** with future considerations for Winnipeg's 7th round choice (Geoff Finch) in 1991 Entry Draft and future considerations, May 31, 1991. Transferred to **Phoenix** after **Winnipeg** franchise relocated, July 1, 1996. Traded to **Edmonton** by **Phoenix** for Eric Houde, November 30, 1999. Signed as a free agent by **Philadelphia**, July 24, 2000. Signed as a free agent by **Calgary**, August 2, 2001.

MUSIL, Frantisek
(moo-SIHL, FRAN-tih-sehk)

Defense. Shoots left. 6'3", 215 lbs. Born, Pardubice, Czech., December 17, 1964. Minnesota's 3rd choice, 38th overall, in 1983 Entry Draft.

Season	Club	League	GP	G	A	Pts	PIM	PP	SH	GW	S	%	+/-	TF	F%	H	SB	Min	GP	G	A	Pts	PIM	PP	SH	GW
1980-81	HC Pardubice	Czech.	2	0	0	0	2																			
1981-82	HC Pardubice	Czech.	35	1	3	4	34																			
1982-83	HC Pardubice	Czech.	33	1	2	3	44																			
1983-84	HC Pardubice	Czech.	37	4	8	12	72																			
1984-85	Dukla Jihlava	Czech.	44	4	6	10	76																			
1985-86	Dukla Jihlava	Czech.	34	4	7	11	42																			
1986-87	**Minnesota**	**NHL**	**72**	**2**	**9**	**11**	**148**	**0**	**0**	**0**	**83**	**2.4**	**0**													
1987-88	**Minnesota**	**NHL**	**80**	**9**	**8**	**17**	**213**	**1**	**1**	**0**	**78**	**11.5**	**–2**													
1988-89	**Minnesota**	**NHL**	**55**	**1**	**19**	**20**	**54**	**0**	**0**	**1**	**78**	**1.3**	**4**						**5**	**1**	**1**	**2**	**4**	**0**	**0**	**0**
1989-90	**Minnesota**	**NHL**	**56**	**2**	**8**	**10**	**109**	**0**	**0**	**1**	**78**	**2.6**	**0**						**4**	**0**	**0**	**0**	**14**	**0**	**0**	**0**
1990-91	**Minnesota**	**NHL**	**8**	**0**	**2**	**2**	**23**	**0**	**0**	**0**	**5**	**0.0**	**0**													
	Calgary	**NHL**	**67**	**7**	**14**	**21**	**160**	**2**	**0**	**1**	**68**	**10.3**	**12**						**7**	**0**	**0**	**0**	**10**	**0**	**0**	**0**
1991-92	**Calgary**	**NHL**	**78**	**4**	**8**	**12**	**103**	**1**	**1**	**0**	**71**	**5.6**	**12**													
1992-93	**Calgary**	**NHL**	**80**	**6**	**10**	**16**	**131**	**0**	**0**	**1**	**87**	**6.9**	**28**						**6**	**1**	**1**	**2**	**7**	**0**	**0**	**0**
1993-94	**Calgary**	**NHL**	**75**	**1**	**8**	**9**	**50**	**0**	**0**	**0**	**65**	**1.5**	**38**						**7**	**0**	**1**	**1**	**4**	**0**	**0**	**0**
1994-95	Sparta Praha	Cze-Rep	19	1	4	5	50																			
	HC Saxonia	DEL	1	0	0	0	2																			
	Calgary	**NHL**	**35**	**0**	**5**	**5**	**61**	**0**	**0**	**0**	**18**	**0.0**	**6**						**5**	**0**	**1**	**1**	**0**	**0**	**0**	**0**
1995-96	Karlovy Vary-2	Cze-Rep	16	7	4	11	16																			
	Ottawa	**NHL**	**65**	**1**	**3**	**4**	**85**	**0**	**0**	**0**	**37**	**2.7**	**–10**													
1996-97	**Ottawa**	**NHL**	**57**	**0**	**5**	**5**	**58**	**0**	**0**	**0**	**24**	**0.0**	**6**													
1997-98	Indianapolis Ice	IHL	52	5	8	13	122																			
	Detroit Vipers	IHL	9	0	0	0	6																			
	Edmonton	**NHL**	**17**	**1**	**2**	**3**	**8**	**0**	**1**	**1**	**8**	**12.5**	**1**						**7**	**0**	**0**	**0**	**6**	**0**	**0**	**0**
1998-99	**Edmonton**	**NHL**	**39**	**0**	**3**	**3**	**34**	**0**	**0**	**0**	**9**	**0.0**	**0**	**0**	**0.0**	**60**	**56**	**14:21**	**1**	**0**	**0**	**0**	**2**	**0**	**0**	**0**
99-2000	**Edmonton**	**NHL**	DID NOT PLAY – INJURED																							
2000-01	**Edmonton**	**NHL**	**13**	**0**	**2**	**2**	**4**	**0**	**0**	**0**	**0**	**0.0**	**–2**	**0**	**0.0**	**9**	**17**	**11:09**								
	NHL Totals		**797**	**34**	**106**	**140**	**1241**	**4**	**3**	**5**	**709**	**4.8**		**0**	**0.0**	**69**	**73**	**13:33**	**42**	**2**	**4**	**6**	**47**	**0**	**0**	**0**

Traded to **Calgary** by **Minnesota** for Brian Glynn, October 26, 1990. Traded to **Ottawa** by **Calgary** for Ottawa's 4th round choice (Chris St. Croix) in 1997 Entry Draft, October 7, 1995. Traded to **Edmonton** by **Ottawa** for Scott Ferguson, March 9, 1998. • Missed entire 1999-2000 season and start of 2000-01 season recovering from spinal cord injury suffered in practice, October 2, 1999. • Missed majority of 2000-01 season recovering from neck injury suffered in game vs. Columbus, January 7, 2001.

MYHRES, Brantt
(MIGH-uhrs, BRANT)

Right wing. Shoots right. 6'3", 220 lbs. Born, Edmonton, Alta., March 18, 1974. Tampa Bay's 5th choice, 97th overall, in 1992 Entry Draft.

Season	Club	League	GP	G	A	Pts	PIM	PP	SH	GW	S	%	+/-	TF	F%	H	SB	Min	GP	G	A	Pts	PIM	PP	SH	GW
1989-90	Bonnyville Barons	AMHL	60	40	62	102	195																			
1990-91	Portland	WHL	59	2	7	9	125																			
1991-92	Portland	WHL	4	0	2	2	22																			
	Lethbridge	WHL	53	4	11	15	359												5	0	0	0	36			
1992-93	Lethbridge	WHL	64	13	35	48	277												3	0	0	0	11			
1993-94	Lethbridge	WHL	34	10	21	31	103																			
	Spokane Chiefs	WHL	27	10	22	32	139												3	1	4	5	7			
	Atlanta Knights	IHL	2	0	0	0	17																			
1994-95	Atlanta Knights	IHL	40	5	5	10	213																			
	Tampa Bay	**NHL**	**15**	**2**	**0**	**2**	**81**	**0**	**0**	**1**	**4**	**50.0**	**–2**													
1995-96	Atlanta Knights	IHL	12	0	2	2	58																			

			Regular Season																Playoffs							
Season	Club	League	GP	G	A	Pts	PIM	PP	SH	GW	S	%	+/-	TF	F%	H	SB	Min	GP	G	A	Pts	PIM	PP	SH	GW
1996-97	**Tampa Bay**	**NHL**	**47**	**3**	**1**	**4**	**136**	0	0	1	13	23.1	1	....	....	....	....	....	....	....	....	....	....	....	....	....
	San Antonio	IHL	12	0	0	0	98	....	....	....	....	....	....	....	....	....	....	....	....	....	....	....	....	....	....	....
1997-98	**Philadelphia**	**NHL**	**23**	**0**	**0**	**0**	**169**	0	0	0	0	0.0	–1	....	....	....	....	....	....	....	....	....	....	....	....	....
	Philadelphia	AHL	18	4	4	8	67	....	....	....	....	....	....	....	....	....	....	....	....	....	....	....	....	....	....	....
1998-99	**San Jose**	**NHL**	**30**	**1**	**0**	**1**	**116**	0	0	0	7	14.3	–2	1	0.0	15	2	4:47	....	....	....	....	....	....	....	....
	Kentucky	AHL	4	0	0	0	16	....	....	....	....	....	....	....	....	....	....	....	....	....	....	....	....	....	....	....
99-2000	**San Jose**	**NHL**	**13**	**0**	**1**	**1**	**97**	0	0	0	2	0.0	0	1	0.0	9	1	3:03	....	....	....	....	....	....	....	....
	Kentucky	AHL	10	1	5	6	18	....	....	....	....	....	....	....	....	....	....	....	7	0	1	1	21	....	....	....
2000-01	**Nashville**	**NHL**	**20**	**0**	**0**	**0**	**28**	0	0	0	1	0.0	–5	0	0.0	8	0	3:48	....	....	....	....	....	....	....	....
	Milwaukee	IHL	6	0	1	1	10	....	....	....	....	....	....	....	....	....	....	....	....	....	....	....	....	....	....	....
	Washington	**NHL**	**5**	**0**	**0**	**0**	**29**	0	0	0	0	0.0	0	0	0.0	3	1	3:36	....	....	....	....	....	....	....	....
	Portland Pirates	AHL	9	1	0	1	53	....	....	....	....	....	....	....	....	....	....	....	....	....	....	....	....	....	....	....
	NHL Totals		**153**	**6**	**2**	**8**	**656**	0	0	2	27	22.2		2	0.0	35	4	4:04	....	....	....	....	....	....	....	....

Traded to **Edmonton** by **Tampa Bay** with Toronto's 3rd round choice (previously acquired, Edmonton selected Alex Henry) in 1998 Entry Draft for Vladimir Vujtek and Edmonton's 3rd round choice (Dmitry Afanasenkov) in 1998 Entry Draft, July 16, 1997. Traded to **Philadelphia** by **Edmonton** for Jason Bowen, October 15, 1997. Signed as a free agent by **San Jose**, September 11, 1998. Signed as a free agent by **Nashville**, August 15, 2000. Traded to **Washington** by **Nashville** for future considerations, February 1, 2001.

MYRVOLD, Anders

(MYOOR-vohld, AN-duhrs) **NYI**

Defense. Shoots left. 6'2", 200 lbs. Born, Lorenskog, Norway, August 12, 1975. Quebec's 6th choice, 127th overall, in 1993 Entry Draft.

Season	Club	League	GP	G	A	Pts	PIM	PP	SH	GW	S	%	+/-	TF	F%	H	SB	Min	GP	G	A	Pts	PIM	PP	SH	GW
1991-92	Storhamr IL	Norway	1	0	0	0	4	....	....	....	....	....	....	....	....	....	....	....	....	....	....	....	....	....	....	....
1992-93	Farjestads BK	Sweden	2	0	0	0	0	....	....	....	....	....	....	....	....	....	....	....	....	....	....	....	....	....	....	....
1993-94	Grums HC	Sweden-2	24	1	0	1	59	....	....	....	....	....	....	....	....	....	....	....	2	1	0	1	5	....	....	....
1994-95	Laval Titan	QMJHL	64	14	50	64	173	....	....	....	....	....	....	....	....	....	....	....	20	4	10	14	68	....	....	....
	Cornwall Aces	AHL	....	....	....	....	....	....	....	....	....	....	....	....	....	....	....	....	3	0	1	1	2	....	....	....
1995-96	**Colorado**	**NHL**	**4**	**0**	**1**	**1**	**6**	0	0	0	4	0.0	–2	....	....	....	....	....	....	....	....	....	....	....	....	....
	Cornwall Aces	AHL	70	5	24	29	125	....	....	....	....	....	....	....	....	....	....	....	5	1	0	1	19	....	....	....
1996-97	Hershey Bears	AHL	20	0	3	3	16	....	....	....	....	....	....	....	....	....	....	....	....	....	....	....	....	....	....	....
	Boston	**NHL**	**9**	**0**	**2**	**2**	**4**	0	0	0	8	0.0	–1	....	....	....	....	....	....	....	....	....	....	....	....	....
	Providence Bruins	AHL	53	6	15	21	107	....	....	....	....	....	....	....	....	....	....	....	10	0	1	1	6	....	....	....
1997-98	Providence Bruins	AHL	75	4	21	25	91	....	....	....	....	....	....	....	....	....	....	....	....	....	....	....	....	....	....	....
1998-99	Djurgardens IF	Sweden	29	3	4	7	52	....	....	....	....	....	....	....	....	....	....	....	....	....	....	....	....	....	....	....
	Djurgardens IF	EuroHL	3	0	1	1	4	....	....	....	....	....	....	....	....	....	....	....	....	....	....	....	....	....	....	....
	AIK Solna	Sweden	19	1	3	4	24	....	....	....	....	....	....	....	....	....	....	....	....	....	....	....	....	....	....	....
99-2000	AIK Solna	Sweden	49	1	3	4	87	....	....	....	....	....	....	....	....	....	....	....	....	....	....	....	....	....	....	....
2000-01	**NY Islanders**	**NHL**	**12**	**0**	**1**	**1**	**0**	0	0	0	8	0.0	–2	0	0.0	10	4	9:26	....	....	....	....	....	....	....	....
	Springfield	AHL	69	5	25	30	129	....	....	....	....	....	....	....	....	....	....	....	....	....	....	....	....	....	....	....
	NHL Totals		**25**	**0**	**4**	**4**	**10**	0	0	0	20	0.0		0	0.0	10	4	9:26	....	....	....	....	....	....	....	....

Rights transferred to **Colorado** after **Quebec** franchise relocated, June 21, 1995. Traded to **Boston** by **Colorado** with Landon Wilson for Boston's 1st round choice (Robyn Regehr) in 1998 Entry Draft, November 22, 1996. Signed as a free agent by **NY Islanders**, August 28, 2000.

NABOKOV, Dmitri

(na-BAW-kahv, dih-MEE-tree) **NYI**

Center/Left Wing. Shoots right. 6'2", 209 lbs. Born, Novosibirsk, USSR, January 4, 1977. Chicago's 1st choice, 19th overall, in 1995 Entry Draft.

Season	Club	League	GP	G	A	Pts	PIM	PP	SH	GW	S	%	+/-	TF	F%	H	SB	Min	GP	G	A	Pts	PIM	PP	SH	GW
1993-94	Krylja Sovetov	CIS	17	0	2	2	6	....	....	....	....	....	....	....	....	....	....	....	3	0	0	0	0	....	....	....
1994-95	Krylja Sovetov	CIS	49	15	12	27	32	....	....	....	....	....	....	....	....	....	....	....	4	5	0	5	6	....	....	....
1995-96	Krylja Sovetov	CIS	50	12	14	26	51	....	....	....	....	....	....	....	....	....	....	....	....	....	....	....	....	....	....	....
1996-97	Krylja Sovetov	Russia	1	0	0	0	0	....	....	....	....	....	....	....	....	....	....	....	....	....	....	....	....	....	....	....
	Regina Pats	WHL	50	39	56	95	61	....	....	....	....	....	....	....	....	....	....	....	5	2	3	5	2	....	....	....
	Indianapolis Ice	IHL	2	0	0	0	0	....	....	....	....	....	....	....	....	....	....	....	....	....	....	....	....	....	....	....
1997-98	**Chicago**	**NHL**	**25**	**7**	**4**	**11**	**10**	3	0	2	34	20.6	–1	....	....	....	....	....	....	....	....	....	....	....	....	....
	Indianapolis Ice	IHL	46	6	15	21	16	....	....	....	....	....	....	....	....	....	....	....	5	2	1	3	0	....	....	....
1998-99	**NY Islanders**	**NHL**	**4**	**0**	**2**	**2**	**2**	0	0	0	4	0.0	4	0	0.0	3	0	11:38	....	....	....	....	....	....	....	....
	Lowell	AHL	73	17	25	42	46	....	....	....	....	....	....	....	....	....	....	....	3	0	1	1	0	....	....	....
99-2000	**NY Islanders**	**NHL**	**26**	**4**	**7**	**11**	**16**	0	0	0	40	10.0	–8	12	25.0	36	10	13:33	....	....	....	....	....	....	....	....
	Lowell	AHL	51	8	26	34	42	....	....	....	....	....	....	....	....	....	....	....	6	1	2	3	2	....	....	....
2000-01	Lada Togliatti	Russia	24	8	5	13	40	....	....	....	....	....	....	....	....	....	....	....	5	0	0	0	10	....	....	....
	NHL Totals		**55**	**11**	**13**	**24**	**28**	3	0	2	78	14.1		12	25.0	39	10	13:18	....	....	....	....	....	....	....	....

WHL East Second All-Star Team (1997)

Traded to **NY Islanders** by **Chicago** for J-P Dumont and Chicago's 5th round choice (later traded to Philadelphia - Philadelphia selected Francis Belanger) in 1998 Entry Draft, June 1, 1998.

NAGY, Ladislav

(NA-gee, LA-dih-slahv) **PHX.**

Center. Shoots left. 5'11", 194 lbs. Born, Saca, Czech., June 1, 1979. St. Louis' 6th choice, 177th overall, in 1997 Entry Draft.

Season	Club	League	GP	G	A	Pts	PIM	PP	SH	GW	S	%	+/-	TF	F%	H	SB	Min	GP	G	A	Pts	PIM	PP	SH	GW
1996-97	HC Kosice	Slovak-Jr.	45	29	30	59	105	....	....	....	....	....	....	....	....	....	....	....	....	....	....	....	....	....	....	....
	Dragon Presov	Slovakia-2	11	6	5	11	....	....	....	....	....	....	....	....	....	....	....	....	....	....	....	....	....	....	....	....
1997-98	HC Kosice	Slovakia	29	19	15	34	41	....	....	....	....	....	....	....	....	....	....	....	11	2	4	6	6	....	....	....
1998-99	Halifax	QMJHL	63	71	55	126	148	....	....	....	....	....	....	....	....	....	....	....	5	3	3	6	18	....	....	....
	Worcester	AHL	....	....	....	....	....	....	....	....	....	....	....	....	....	....	....	....	3	2	2	4	0	....	....	....
99-2000	**St. Louis**	**NHL**	**11**	**2**	**4**	**6**	**2**	1	0	0	15	13.3	2	6	33.3	6	3	12:19	**6**	**1**	**1**	**2**	**0**	**0**	**0**	**0**
	Worcester	AHL	69	23	28	51	67	....	....	....	....	....	....	....	....	....	....	....	2	1	0	1	0	....	....	....
2000-01	**St. Louis**	**NHL**	**40**	**8**	**8**	**16**	**20**	2	0	2	59	13.6	–2	28	50.0	20	5	13:03	....	....	....	....	....	....	....	....
	Worcester	AHL	20	6	14	20	36	....	....	....	....	....	....	....	....	....	....	....	....	....	....	....	....	....	....	....
	Phoenix	**NHL**	**6**	**0**	**1**	**1**	**2**	0	0	0	5	0.0	0	0	0.0	4	0	12:38	....	....	....	....	....	....	....	....
	NHL Totals		**57**	**10**	**13**	**23**	**24**	3	0	2	79	12.7		34	47.1	30	8	12:52	**6**	**1**	**1**	**2**	**0**	**0**	**0**	**0**

Traded to **Phoenix** by **St. Louis** with Michal Handzus, the rights to Jeff Taffe and St. Louis' 1st round choice in 2002 Entry Draft for Keith Tkachuk, March 13, 2001.

NAMESTNIKOV, John

(nah-MEST-nih-kov, JAWN)

Defense. Shoots right. 5'11", 190 lbs. Born, Arzamis-Ig, USSR, October 9, 1971. Vancouver's 5th choice, 117th overall, in 1991 Entry Draft.

Season	Club	League	GP	G	A	Pts	PIM	PP	SH	GW	S	%	+/-	TF	F%	H	SB	Min	GP	G	A	Pts	PIM	PP	SH	GW
1988-89	Torpedo Gorky	USSR	2	0	0	0	2	....	....	....	....	....	....	....	....	....	....	....	....	....	....	....	....	....	....	....
1989-90	Torpedo Gorky	USSR	23	0	0	0	25	....	....	....	....	....	....	....	....	....	....	....	....	....	....	....	....	....	....	....
1990-91	Torpedo Nizhny	USSR	42	1	2	3	49	....	....	....	....	....	....	....	....	....	....	....	....	....	....	....	....	....	....	....
1991-92	CSKA Moscow	CIS	42	1	1	2	47	....	....	....	....	....	....	....	....	....	....	....	....	....	....	....	....	....	....	....
1992-93	CSKA Moscow	CIS	42	5	5	10	68	....	....	....	....	....	....	....	....	....	....	....	....	....	....	....	....	....	....	....
1993-94	**Vancouver**	**NHL**	**17**	**0**	**5**	**5**	**10**	0	0	0	11	0.0	–2	....	....	....	....	....	....	....	....	....	....	....	....	....
	Hamilton Canucks	AHL	59	7	27	34	97	....	....	....	....	....	....	....	....	....	....	....	4	0	2	2	19	....	....	....
1994-95	Syracuse Crunch	AHL	59	11	22	33	59	....	....	....	....	....	....	....	....	....	....	....	....	....	....	....	....	....	....	....
	Vancouver	**NHL**	**16**	**0**	**3**	**3**	**4**	0	0	0	18	0.0	2	....	....	....	....	....	**1**	**0**	**0**	**0**	**2**	**0**	**0**	**0**
1995-96	Syracuse Crunch	AHL	59	13	34	47	85	....	....	....	....	....	....	....	....	....	....	....	15	1	8	9	16	....	....	....
	Vancouver	**NHL**	....	....	....	....	....	....	....	....	....	....	....	....	....	....	....	....	**1**	**0**	**0**	**0**	**0**	**0**	**0**	**0**
1996-97	**Vancouver**	**NHL**	**2**	**0**	**0**	**0**	**4**	0	0	0	1	0.0	–1	....	....	....	....	....	....	....	....	....	....	....	....	....
	Syracuse Crunch	AHL	55	9	37	46	73	....	....	....	....	....	....	....	....	....	....	....	3	2	0	2	0	....	....	....
1997-98	**NY Islanders**	**NHL**	**6**	**0**	**1**	**1**	**4**	0	0	0	2	0.0	–1	....	....	....	....	....	....	....	....	....	....	....	....	....
	Utah Grizzlies	IHL	62	6	19	25	48	....	....	....	....	....	....	....	....	....	....	....	4	1	0	1	2	....	....	....
1998-99	Lowell	AHL	42	12	14	26	42	....	....	....	....	....	....	....	....	....	....	....	....	....	....	....	....	....	....	....
99-2000	Hartford	AHL	33	1	9	10	14	....	....	....	....	....	....	....	....	....	....	....	....	....	....	....	....	....	....	....
	Nashville	**NHL**	**2**	**0**	**0**	**0**	**2**	0	0	0	3	0.0	0	0	0.0	5	2	15:48	....	....	....	....	....	....	....	....
	Milwaukee	IHL	12	2	3	5	17	....	....	....	....	....	....	....	....	....	....	....	3	0	0	0	0	....	....	....
2000-01	Milwaukee	IHL	56	7	22	29	36	....	....	....	....	....	....	....	....	....	....	....	3	0	1	1	0	....	....	....
	NHL Totals		**43**	**0**	**9**	**9**	**24**	0	0	0	35	0.0		0	0.0	5	2	....	**2**	**0**	**0**	**0**	**2**	**0**	**0**	**0**

Signed as a free agent by **NY Islanders**, July 21, 1997. Signed as a free agent by **NY Rangers**, August 9, 1999. Claimed by **Vancouver** from **NY Rangers** in Waiver Draft, September 27, 1999. Claimed on waivers by **NY Rangers** from **Vancouver**, October 5, 1999. Traded to **Nashville** by **NY Rangers** for Jason Dawe, February 3, 2000.

NASH, Tyson
(NASH, TIGH-sohn) **ST.L.**

Left wing. Shoots left. 6', 185 lbs. Born, Edmonton, Alta., March 11, 1975. Vancouver's 10th choice, 247th overall, in 1994 Entry Draft.

			Regular Season																Playoffs							
Season	Club	League	GP	G	A	Pts	PIM	PP	SH	GW	S	%	+/-	TF	F%	H	SB	Min	GP	G	A	Pts	PIM	PP	SH	GW
1990-91	Sherwood Park	AMHL	40	17	28	43	63	....	....	....	....	....	....	....	....	....	....	....	....	....	....	....	....	....	....	....
1991-92	Kamloops Blazers	WHL	33	1	6	7	62	....	....	....	....	....	....	....	....	....	....	....	4	0	0	0	0	....	....	....
1992-93	Kamloops Blazers	WHL	61	10	16	26	78	....	....	....	....	....	....	....	....	....	....	....	13	3	2	5	32	....	....	....
1993-94	Kamloops Blazers	WHL	65	20	36	56	135	....	....	....	....	....	....	....	....	....	....	....	16	3	4	7	12	....	....	....
1994-95	Kamloops Blazers	WHL	63	34	41	75	70	....	....	....	....	....	....	....	....	....	....	....	21	10	7	17	30	....	....	....
1995-96	Syracuse Crunch	AHL	50	4	7	11	58	....	....	....	....	....	....	....	....	....	....	....	4	0	0	0	11	....	....	....
	Raleigh IceCaps	ECHL	6	1	1	2	8	....	....	....	....	....	....	....	....	....	....	....	....	....	....	....	....	....	....	....
1996-97	Syracuse Crunch	AHL	77	17	17	34	105	....	....	....	....	....	....	....	....	....	....	....	3	0	2	2	0	....	....	....
1997-98	Syracuse Crunch	AHL	74	20	20	40	184	....	....	....	....	....	....	....	....	....	....	....	5	0	2	2	28	....	....	....
1998-99	**St. Louis**	**NHL**	**2**	**0**	**0**	**0**	**5**	**0**	**0**	**0**	**1**	**0.0**	**–1**	**0**	**0.0**	**8**	**0**	**7:44**	**1**	**0**	**0**	**0**	**2**	**0**	**0**	**0**
	Worcester	AHL	55	14	22	36	143	....	....	....	....	....	....	....	....	....	....	....	4	4	1	5	27	....	....	....
99-2000	**St. Louis**	**NHL**	**66**	**4**	**9**	**13**	**150**	**0**	**1**	**1**	**68**	**5.9**	**6**	**0**	**0.0**	**193**	**7**	**8:35**	**6**	**1**	**0**	**1**	**24**	**0**	**0**	**0**
2000-01	**St. Louis**	**NHL**	**57**	**8**	**7**	**15**	**110**	**0**	**1**	**0**	**113**	**7.1**	**8**	**2**	**50.0**	**149**	**10**	**12:29**	....	....	....	....	....	....	....	....
	NHL Totals		**125**	**12**	**16**	**28**	**265**	**0**	**2**	**1**	**182**	**6.6**		**2**	**50.0**	**350**	**17**	**10:21**	**7**	**1**	**0**	**1**	**26**	**0**	**0**	**0**

Signed as a free agent by **St. Louis**, July 14, 1998.

NASLUND, Markus
(NAZ-luhnd, MAHR-kuhs) **VAN.**

Right wing. Shoots left. 5'11", 195 lbs. Born, Ornskoldsvik, Sweden, July 30, 1973. Pittsburgh's 1st choice, 16th overall, in 1991 Entry Draft.

			Regular Season																Playoffs							
Season	Club	League	GP	G	A	Pts	PIM	PP	SH	GW	S	%	+/-	TF	F%	H	SB	Min	GP	G	A	Pts	PIM	PP	SH	GW
1988-89	Ornskoldsviks IF	Sweden-3	14	7	6	13		....	....	....	....	....	....	....	....	....	....	....	....	....	....	....	....	....	....	....
1989-90	MoDo AIK	Swede-Jr.	33	43	35	78	20	....	....	....	....	....	....	....	....	....	....	....	....	....	....	....	....	....	....	....
1990-91	MoDo AIK	Sweden	32	10	9	19	14	....	....	....	....	....	....	....	....	....	....	....	....	....	....	....	....	....	....	....
1991-92	MoDo AIK	Sweden	39	22	18	40	54	....	....	....	....	....	....	....	....	....	....	....	....	....	....	....	....	....	....	....
1992-93	MoDo AIK	Swede-Jr.	2	4	1	5	2	....	....	....	....	....	....	....	....	....	....	....	....	....	....	....	....	....	....	....
	MoDo AIK	Sweden	39	22	17	39	67	....	....	....	....	....	....	....	....	....	....	....	3	3	2	5	0	....	....	....
1993-94	**Pittsburgh**	**NHL**	**71**	**4**	**7**	**11**	**27**	**1**	**0**	**0**	**80**	**5.0**	**–3**	....	....	....	....	....	....	....	....	....	....	....	....	....
	Cleveland	IHL	5	1	6	7	4	....	....	....	....	....	....	....	....	....	....	....	....	....	....	....	....	....	....	....
1994-95	**Pittsburgh**	**NHL**	**14**	**2**	**2**	**4**	**2**	**0**	**0**	**0**	**13**	**15.4**	**0**	....	....	....	....	....	....	....	....	....	....	....	....	....
	Cleveland	IHL	7	3	4	7	6	....	....	....	....	....	....	....	....	....	....	....	4	1	3	4	8	....	....	....
1995-96	**Pittsburgh**	**NHL**	**66**	**19**	**33**	**52**	**36**	**3**	**0**	**4**	**125**	**15.2**	**17**	....	....	....	....	....	....	....	....	....	....	....	....	....
	Vancouver	**NHL**	**10**	**3**	**0**	**3**	**6**	**1**	**0**	**1**	**19**	**15.8**	**3**	....	....	....	....	....	**6**	**1**	**2**	**3**	**8**	**1**	**0**	**0**
1996-97	**Vancouver**	**NHL**	**78**	**21**	**20**	**41**	**30**	**4**	**0**	**4**	**120**	**17.5**	**–15**	....	....	....	....	....	....	....	....	....	....	....	....	....
1997-98	**Vancouver**	**NHL**	**76**	**14**	**20**	**34**	**56**	**2**	**1**	**0**	**106**	**13.2**	**5**	....	....	....	....	....	....	....	....	....	....	....	....	....
1998-99	**Vancouver**	**NHL**	**80**	**36**	**30**	**66**	**74**	**15**	**2**	**3**	**205**	**17.6**	**–13**	**14**	**57.1**	**40**	**20**	**19:57**	....	....	....	....	....	....	....	....
99-2000	**Vancouver**	**NHL**	**82**	**27**	**38**	**65**	**64**	**6**	**2**	**3**	**271**	**10.0**	**–5**	**13**	**46.2**	**50**	**28**	**20:13**	....	....	....	....	....	....	....	....
2000-01	**Vancouver**	**NHL**	**72**	**41**	**34**	**75**	**58**	**18**	**1**	**5**	**277**	**14.8**	**–2**	**6**	**50.0**	**37**	**11**	**19:03**	....	....	....	....	....	....	....	....
	NHL Totals		**549**	**167**	**184**	**351**	**353**	**50**	**6**	**20**	**1216**	**13.7**		**33**	**51.5**	**127**	**59**	**19:46**	**6**	**1**	**2**	**3**	**8**	**1**	**0**	**0**

Played in NHL All-Star Game (1999, 2001)

Traded to **Vancouver** by **Pittsburgh** for Alek Stojanov, March 20, 1996.

NASREDDINE, Alain
(NAS-ruh-deen, AL-eh) **EDM.**

Defense. Shoots left. 6'1", 201 lbs. Born, Montreal, Que., July 10, 1975. Florida's 8th choice, 135th overall, in 1993 Entry Draft.

			Regular Season																Playoffs							
Season	Club	League	GP	G	A	Pts	PIM	PP	SH	GW	S	%	+/-	TF	F%	H	SB	Min	GP	G	A	Pts	PIM	PP	SH	GW
1990-91	Mtl-Bourassa	QAAA	35	10	25	35	50	....	....	....	....	....	....	....	....	....	....	....	....	....	....	....	....	....	....	....
1991-92	Drummondville	QMJHL	61	1	9	10	78	....	....	....	....	....	....	....	....	....	....	....	4	0	0	0	17	....	....	....
1992-93	Drummondville	QMJHL	64	0	14	14	137	....	....	....	....	....	....	....	....	....	....	....	10	0	1	1	36	....	....	....
1993-94	Chicoutimi	QMJHL	60	3	24	27	218	....	....	....	....	....	....	....	....	....	....	....	26	2	10	12	118	....	....	....
1994-95	Chicoutimi	QMJHL	67	8	31	39	342	....	....	....	....	....	....	....	....	....	....	....	13	3	5	8	40	....	....	....
1995-96	Carolina	AHL	63	0	5	5	245	....	....	....	....	....	....	....	....	....	....	....	....	....	....	....	....	....	....	....
1996-97	Carolina	AHL	26	0	4	4	109	....	....	....	....	....	....	....	....	....	....	....	....	....	....	....	....	....	....	....
	Indianapolis Ice	IHL	49	0	2	2	248	....	....	....	....	....	....	....	....	....	....	....	4	1	1	2	27	....	....	....
1997-98	Indianapolis Ice	IHL	75	1	12	13	258	....	....	....	....	....	....	....	....	....	....	....	5	0	2	2	12	....	....	....
1998-99	**Chicago**	**NHL**	**7**	**0**	**0**	**0**	**19**	**0**	**0**	**0**	**2**	**0.0**	**–2**	**0**	**0.0**	**5**	**1**	**12:11**	....	....	....	....	....	....	....	....
	Portland Pirates	AHL	7	0	1	1	36	....	....	....	....	....	....	....	....	....	....	....	....	....	....	....	....	....	....	....
	Montreal	**NHL**	**8**	**0**	**0**	**0**	**33**	**0**	**0**	**0**	**1**	**0.0**	**1**	**0**	**0.0**	**7**	**1**	**8:12**	....	....	....	....	....	....	....	....
	Fredericton	AHL	38	0	10	10	108	....	....	....	....	....	....	....	....	....	....	....	15	0	3	3	39	....	....	....
99-2000	Quebec Citadelles	AHL	59	1	6	7	178	....	....	....	....	....	....	....	....	....	....	....	....	....	....	....	....	....	....	....
	Hamilton Bulldogs	AHL	11	0	0	0	12	....	....	....	....	....	....	....	....	....	....	....	10	1	1	2	14	....	....	....
2000-01	Hamilton Bulldogs	AHL	74	4	14	18	164	....	....	....	....	....	....	....	....	....	....	....	....	....	....	....	....	....	....	....
	NHL Totals		**15**	**0**	**0**	**0**	**52**	**0**	**0**	**0**	**3**	**0.0**		**0**	**0.0**	**12**	**2**	**10:04**	....	....	....	....	....	....	....	....

QMJHL Second All-Star Team (1995)

Traded to **Chicago** by **Florida** for Ivan Droppa, December 18, 1996. Traded to **Montreal** by **Chicago** with Jeff Hackett, Eric Weinrich and Tampa Bay's 4th round choice (previously acquired, Montreal selected Chris Dyment) in 1999 Entry Draft for Jocelyn Thibault, Dave Manson and Brad Brown, November 16, 1998. Traded to **Edmonton** by **Montreal** with Igor Ulanov for Christian Laflamme and Matthieu Descoteaux, March 9, 2000.

NAZAROV, Andrei
(nah-ZAH-rohv, AWN-dray) **BOS.**

Left wing. Shoots right. 6'5", 230 lbs. Born, Chelyabinsk, USSR, May 22, 1974. San Jose's 2nd choice, 10th overall, in 1992 Entry Draft.

			Regular Season																Playoffs							
Season	Club	League	GP	G	A	Pts	PIM	PP	SH	GW	S	%	+/-	TF	F%	H	SB	Min	GP	G	A	Pts	PIM	PP	SH	GW
1991-92	Dynamo Moscow	CIS	2	1	0	1	2	....	....	....	....	....	....	....	....	....	....	....	....	....	....	....	....	....	....	....
1992-93	Dynamo Moscow	CIS	42	8	2	10	79	....	....	....	....	....	....	....	....	....	....	....	10	1	1	2	8	....	....	....
1993-94	Dynamo Moscow	CIS	6	2	2	4	0	....	....	....	....	....	....	....	....	....	....	....	....	....	....	....	....	....	....	....
	San Jose	**NHL**	**1**	**0**	**0**	**0**	**0**	**0**	**0**	**0**	**0**	**0.0**	**0**	....	....	....	....	....	....	....	....	....	....	....	....	....
	Kansas City	IHL	71	15	18	33	64	....	....	....	....	....	....	....	....	....	....	....	....	....	....	....	....	....	....	....
1994-95	Kansas City	IHL	43	15	10	25	55	....	....	....	....	....	....	....	....	....	....	....	....	....	....	....	....	....	....	....
	San Jose	**NHL**	**26**	**3**	**5**	**8**	**94**	**0**	**0**	**0**	**19**	**15.8**	**–1**	....	....	....	....	....	**6**	**0**	**0**	**0**	**9**	**0**	**0**	**0**
1995-96	**San Jose**	**NHL**	**42**	**7**	**7**	**14**	**62**	**2**	**0**	**1**	**55**	**12.7**	**–15**	....	....	....	....	....	....	....	....	....	....	....	....	....
	Kansas City	IHL	27	4	6	10	118	....	....	....	....	....	....	....	....	....	....	....	2	0	0	0	2	....	....	....
1996-97	**San Jose**	**NHL**	**60**	**12**	**15**	**27**	**222**	**1**	**0**	**1**	**116**	**10.3**	**–4**	....	....	....	....	....	....	....	....	....	....	....	....	....
	Kentucky	AHL	3	1	2	3	4	....	....	....	....	....	....	....	....	....	....	....	....	....	....	....	....	....	....	....
1997-98	**San Jose**	**NHL**	**40**	**1**	**1**	**2**	**112**	**0**	**0**	**0**	**31**	**3.2**	**–4**	....	....	....	....	....	....	....	....	....	....	....	....	....
	Tampa Bay	**NHL**	**14**	**1**	**1**	**2**	**58**	**0**	**0**	**0**	**19**	**5.3**	**–9**	....	....	....	....	....	....	....	....	....	....	....	....	....
1998-99	**Tampa Bay**	**NHL**	**26**	**2**	**0**	**2**	**43**	**0**	**0**	**0**	**18**	**11.1**	**–5**	**4**	**50.0**	**26**	**2**	**8:13**	....	....	....	....	....	....	....	....
	Calgary	**NHL**	**36**	**5**	**9**	**14**	**30**	**0**	**0**	**2**	**53**	**9.4**	**1**	**0**	**0.0**	**38**	**10**	**14:31**	....	....	....	....	....	....	....	....
99-2000	**Calgary**	**NHL**	**76**	**10**	**22**	**32**	**78**	**1**	**0**	**1**	**110**	**9.1**	**3**	**2**	**100.0**	**79**	**16**	**11:44**	....	....	....	....	....	....	....	....
2000-01	**Anaheim**	**NHL**	**16**	**1**	**0**	**1**	**29**	**0**	**0**	**0**	**13**	**7.7**	**–9**	**2**	**50.0**	**19**	**3**	**8:42**	....	....	....	....	....	....	....	....
	Boston	**NHL**	**63**	**1**	**4**	**5**	**200**	**0**	**0**	**0**	**50**	**2.0**	**–14**	**14**	**21.4**	**94**	**13**	**8:12**	....	....	....	....	....	....	....	....
	NHL Totals		**400**	**43**	**64**	**107**	**928**	**4**	**0**	**5**	**484**	**8.9**		**22**	**36.4**	**256**	**44**	**10:31**	**6**	**0**	**0**	**0**	**9**	**0**	**0**	**0**

Traded to **Tampa Bay** by **San Jose** with Florida's 1st round choice (previously acquired, Tampa Bay selected Vincent Lecavalier) in 1998 Entry Draft for Bryan Marchment, David Shaw and Tampa Bay's 1st round choice (later traded to Nashville - Nashville selected David Legwand) in 1998 Entry Draft, March 24, 1998. Traded to **Calgary** by **Tampa Bay** for Michael Nylander, January 19, 1999. Traded to **Anaheim** by **Calgary** with Calgary's 2nd round choice (later traded to Phoenix - later traded back to Calgary - Calgary selected Andrei Taratukhin) in 2001 Entry Draft for Jordan Leopold, September 26, 2000. Traded to **Boston** by **Anaheim** with Patrick Traverse for Sami Pahlsson, November 18, 2000.

NDUR, Rumun
(nih-DOOR, ROO-muhn)

Defense. Shoots left. 6'2", 222 lbs. Born, Zaria, Nigeria, July 7, 1975. Buffalo's 3rd choice, 69th overall, in 1994 Entry Draft.

			Regular Season																Playoffs							
Season	Club	League	GP	G	A	Pts	PIM	PP	SH	GW	S	%	+/-	TF	F%	H	SB	Min	GP	G	A	Pts	PIM	PP	SH	GW
1990-91	Belmont Bombers	OJHL-D	36	3	11	14	70	....	....	....	....	....	....	....	....	....	....	....	....	....	....	....	....	....	....	....
1991-92	Sarnia Bees	OJHL-B	30	2	5	7	46	....	....	....	....	....	....	....	....	....	....	....	....	....	....	....	....	....	....	....
	Clearwater	OJHL-C	4	0	4	4	4	....	....	....	....	....	....	....	....	....	....	....	....	....	....	....	....	....	....	....
1992-93	Guelph Platers	OJHL-B	24	7	8	15	202	....	....	....	....	....	....	....	....	....	....	....	....	....	....	....	....	....	....	....
	Guelph Storm	OHL	22	1	3	4	30	....	....	....	....	....	....	....	....	....	....	....	4	0	1	1	4	....	....	....
1993-94	Guelph Storm	OHL	61	6	33	39	176	....	....	....	....	....	....	....	....	....	....	....	9	4	1	5	24	....	....	....
1994-95	Guelph Storm	OHL	63	10	21	31	187	....	....	....	....	....	....	....	....	....	....	....	14	0	4	4	28	....	....	....
1995-96	Rochester	AHL	73	2	12	14	306	....	....	....	....	....	....	....	....	....	....	....	17	1	2	3	33	....	....	....
1996-97	**Buffalo**	**NHL**	**2**	**0**	**0**	**0**	**2**	**0**	**0**	**0**	**0**	**0.0**	**1**	....	....	....	....	....	....	....	....	....	....	....	....	....
	Rochester	AHL	68	5	11	16	282	....	....	....	....	....	....	....	....	....	....	....	10	3	1	4	21	....	....	....
1997-98	**Buffalo**	**NHL**	**1**	**0**	**0**	**0**	**2**	**0**	**0**	**0**	**0**	**0.0**	**–1**	....	....	....	....	....	....	....	....	....	....	....	....	....
	Rochester	AHL	50	1	12	13	207	....	....	....	....	....	....	....	....	....	....	....	4	0	2	2	16	....	....	....

			Regular Season																Playoffs							
Season	Club	League	GP	G	A	Pts	PIM	PP	SH	GW	S	%	+/-	TF	F%	H	SB	Min	GP	G	A	Pts	PIM	PP	SH	GW
1998-99	**Buffalo**	**NHL**	8	0	0	0	16	0	0	0	1	0.0	1	0	0.0	11	2	10:58	....	....	....	....	....	....	....	....
	NY Rangers	**NHL**	31	1	3	4	46	0	0	0	21	4.8	–2	0	0.0	58	11	11:58	....	....	....	....	....	....	....	....
	Hartford	AHL	6	0	1	1	4	....	....	....	....	....	....	....	....	....	....	....	....	....	....	....	....	....	....	....
99-2000	Hartford	AHL	2	0	0	0	0	....	....	....	....	....	....	....	....	....	....	....	....	....	....	....	....	....	....	....
	Atlanta	**NHL**	27	1	0	1	71	0	0	0	6	16.7	–17	0	0.0	64	18	13:12	....	....	....	....	....	....	....	....
2000-01	Orlando	IHL	16	0	0	0	50	....	....	....	....	....	....	....	....	....	....	....	....	....	....	....	....	....	....	....
	Norfolk Admirals	AHL	21	1	2	3	93	....	....	....	....	....	....	....	....	....	....	....	9	1	0	1	26	....	....	....
	NHL Totals		69	2	3	5	137	0	0	0	28	7.1		0	0.0	133	31	12:21	....	....	....	....	....	....	....	....

Claimed on waivers by **NY Rangers** from **Buffalo**, December 18, 1998. Claimed on waivers by **Atlanta** from **NY Rangers**, December 11, 1999.

NECKAR, Stan

(NEHTS-kahzh, STAN) **T.B.**

Defense. Shoots left. 6'1", 214 lbs. Born, Ceske Budejovice, Czech., December 22, 1975. Ottawa's 2nd choice, 29th overall, in 1994 Entry Draft.

1991-92	MC Budejovice	Czech-Jr.	18	1	3	4	....	....	....	....	....	....	....	....	....	....	....	....	....	....	....	....	....	....	....	....
1992-93	MC Budejovice	Czech.	42	2	9	11	12	....	....	....	....	....	....	....	....	....	....	....	....	....	....	....	....	....	....	....
1993-94	HC Budejovice	Cze-Rep	12	3	2	5	2	....	....	....	....	....	....	....	....	....	....	....	3	0	0	0	....	....	....	....
1994-95	Detroit Vipers	IHL	15	2	2	4	15	....	....	....	....	....	....	....	....	....	....	....	....	....	....	....	....	....	....	....
	Ottawa	**NHL**	48	1	3	4	37	0	0	0	34	2.9	–20	....	....	....	....	....	....	....	....	....	....	....	....	....
1995-96	**Ottawa**	**NHL**	82	3	9	12	54	1	0	0	57	5.3	–16	....	....	....	....	....	....	....	....	....	....	....	....	....
1996-97	**Ottawa**	**NHL**	5	0	0	0	2	0	0	0	3	0.0	2	....	....	....	....	....	....	....	....	....	....	....	....	....
1997-98	**Ottawa**	**NHL**	60	2	2	4	31	0	0	0	43	4.7	–14	....	....	....	....	....	9	0	0	0	2	0	0	0
1998-99	**Ottawa**	**NHL**	3	0	2	2	0	0	0	0	2	0.0	–1	0	0.0	6	3	15:53	....	....	....	....	....	....	....	....
	NY Rangers	**NHL**	18	0	0	0	8	0	0	0	8	0.0	–1	0	0.0	30	27	13:46	....	....	....	....	....	....	....	....
	Phoenix	**NHL**	11	0	1	1	10	0	0	0	6	0.0	3	0	0.0	26	10	15:08	6	0	1	1	4	0	0	0
99-2000	**Phoenix**	**NHL**	66	2	8	10	36	0	0	0	34	5.9	1	0	0.0	119	54	14:27	5	0	0	0	0	0	0	0
2000-01	**Phoenix**	**NHL**	53	2	2	4	63	0	0	1	16	12.5	–2	0	0.0	75	56	15:26	....	....	....	....	....	....	....	....
	Tampa Bay	**NHL**	16	0	2	2	8	0	0	0	10	0.0	–1	0	0.0	27	15	18:33	....	....	....	....	....	....	....	....
	NHL Totals		362	10	29	39	249	1	0	1	213	4.7		0	0.0	283	165	15:09	20	0	1	1	6	0	0	0

Traded to **NY Rangers** by **Ottawa** for Bill Berg and NY Rangers' 2nd round choice (later traded to Anaheim - Anaheim selected Jordan Leopold) in 1999 Entry Draft, November 27, 1998. Traded to **Phoenix** by **NY Rangers** for Jason Doig and Phoenix's 6th round choice (Jay Dardis) in 1999 Entry Draft, March 23, 1999. Traded to **Tampa Bay** by **Phoenix** with Nikolai Khabibulin for Mike Johnson, Paul Mara, Ruslan Zainullin and NY Islanders' 2nd round choice (previously acquired, Phoenix selected Matthew Spiller) in 2001 Entry Draft, March 5, 2001.

NEDVED, Petr

(NEHD-VEHD, PEE-tuhr) **NYR**

Center. Shoots left. 6'3", 195 lbs. Born, Liberec, Czech., December 9, 1971. Vancouver's 1st choice, 2nd overall, in 1990 Entry Draft.

1988-89	CHZ Litvinov	Czech-Jr.	20	32	19	51	12	....	....	....	....	....	....	....	....	....	....	....	....	....	....	....	....	....	....	....
1989-90	Seattle T-Birds	WHL	71	65	80	145	80	....	....	....	....	....	....	....	....	....	....	....	11	4	9	13	2	....	....	....
1990-91	**Vancouver**	**NHL**	61	10	6	16	20	1	0	0	97	10.3	–21	....	....	....	....	....	6	0	1	1	0	0	0	0
1991-92	**Vancouver**	**NHL**	77	15	22	37	36	5	0	1	99	15.2	–3	....	....	....	....	....	10	1	4	5	16	0	0	0
1992-93	**Vancouver**	**NHL**	84	38	33	71	96	2	1	3	149	25.5	20	....	....	....	....	....	12	2	3	5	2	0	0	0
1993-94	Canada	Nat-Team	17	19	12	31	16	....	....	....	....	....	....	....	....	....	....	....	....	....	....	....	....	....	....	....
	Canada	Olympics	8	5	1	6	6	....	....	....	....	....	....	....	....	....	....	....	....	....	....	....	....	....	....	....
	St. Louis	**NHL**	19	6	14	20	8	2	0	0	63	9.5	2	....	....	....	....	....	4	0	1	1	4	0	0	0
1994-95	**NY Rangers**	**NHL**	46	11	12	23	26	1	0	3	123	8.9	–1	....	....	....	....	....	10	3	2	5	6	2	0	0
1995-96	**Pittsburgh**	**NHL**	80	45	54	99	68	8	1	5	204	22.1	37	....	....	....	....	....	18	10	10	20	16	4	0	2
1996-97	**Pittsburgh**	**NHL**	74	33	38	71	66	12	3	4	189	17.5	–2	....	....	....	....	....	5	1	2	3	12	0	1	0
1997-98	HC Liberec-2	Cze-Rep	2	0	3	3	....	....	....	....	....	....	....	....	....	....	....	....	....	....	....	....	....	....	....	....
	Novy Jicin-3	Cze-Rep	7	9	16	25	....	....	....	....	....	....	....	....	....	....	....	....	....	....	....	....	....	....	....	....
	Sparta Praha	Cze-Rep	5	2	3	5	8	....	....	....	....	....	....	....	....	....	....	....	....	....	....	....	....	....	....	....
	Las Vegas	IHL	3	3	3	6	4	....	....	....	....	....	....	....	....	....	....	....	6	0	2	2	52	....	....	....
1998-99	Las Vegas	IHL	13	8	10	18	32	....	....	....	....	....	....	....	....	....	....	....	....	....	....	....	....	....	....	....
	NY Rangers	**NHL**	56	20	27	47	50	9	1	3	153	13.1	–6	1069	52.5	58	34	20:31	....	....	....	....	....	....	....	....
99-2000	**NY Rangers**	**NHL**	76	24	44	68	40	6	2	4	201	11.9	2	1354	54.0	55	33	19:54	....	....	....	....	....	....	....	....
2000-01	**NY Rangers**	**NHL**	79	32	46	78	54	9	1	5	230	13.9	10	1349	49.7	48	40	20:16	....	....	....	....	....	....	....	....
	NHL Totals		652	234	296	530	464	55	9	28	1508	15.5		3772	52.0	161	107	20:12	65	17	23	40	56	6	1	2

Canadian Major Junior Rookie of the Year (1990)

Signed as a free agent by **St. Louis**, March 5, 1994. Traded to **NY Rangers** by **St. Louis** for Esa Tikkanen and Doug Lidster, July 24, 1994. Traded to **Pittsburgh** by **NY Rangers** with Sergei Zubov for Luc Robitaille and Ulf Samuelsson, August 31, 1995. Traded to **NY Rangers** by **Pittsburgh** with Chris Tamer and Sean Pronger for Alexei Kovalev and Harry York, November 25, 1998.

NELSON, Jeff

(NEHL-sohn, JEHF)

Center. Shoots left. 5'11", 190 lbs. Born, Prince Albert, Sask., December 18, 1972. Washington's 4th choice, 36th overall, in 1991 Entry Draft.

1987-88	Prince Albert	AMHL	31	24	32	56	32	....	....	....	....	....	....	....	....	....	....	....	....	....	....	....	....	....	....	....
1988-89	Prince Albert	WHL	71	30	57	87	74	....	....	....	....	....	....	....	....	....	....	....	4	0	3	3	4	....	....	....
1989-90	Prince Albert	WHL	72	28	69	97	79	....	....	....	....	....	....	....	....	....	....	....	14	2	11	13	10	....	....	....
1990-91	Prince Albert	WHL	72	46	74	120	58	....	....	....	....	....	....	....	....	....	....	....	3	1	1	2	4	....	....	....
1991-92	Prince Albert	WHL	64	48	65	113	84	....	....	....	....	....	....	....	....	....	....	....	9	7	14	21	18	....	....	....
1992-93	Baltimore	AHL	72	14	38	52	12	....	....	....	....	....	....	....	....	....	....	....	7	1	3	4	2	....	....	....
1993-94	Portland Pirates	AHL	80	34	73	107	92	....	....	....	....	....	....	....	....	....	....	....	17	10	5	15	20	....	....	....
1994-95	Portland Pirates	AHL	64	33	50	83	57	....	....	....	....	....	....	....	....	....	....	....	7	1	4	5	8	....	....	....
	Washington	**NHL**	10	1	0	1	2	0	0	0	4	25.0	–2	....	....	....	....	....	....	....	....	....	....	....	....	....
1995-96	**Washington**	**NHL**	33	0	7	7	16	0	0	0	21	0.0	3	....	....	....	....	....	3	0	0	0	4	0	0	0
	Portland Pirates	AHL	39	15	32	47	62	....	....	....	....	....	....	....	....	....	....	....	....	....	....	....	....	....	....	....
1996-97	Grand Rapids	IHL	82	34	55	89	85	....	....	....	....	....	....	....	....	....	....	....	5	0	4	4	4	....	....	....
1997-98	Milwaukee	IHL	52	20	34	54	30	....	....	....	....	....	....	....	....	....	....	....	10	2	7	9	15	....	....	....
1998-99	**Nashville**	**NHL**	9	2	1	3	2	0	0	0	8	25.0	–1	138	55.1	4	8	16:09	....	....	....	....	....	....	....	....
	Milwaukee	IHL	70	20	31	51	66	....	....	....	....	....	....	....	....	....	....	....	2	0	0	0	0	....	....	....
99-2000	Portland Pirates	AHL	73	24	30	54	38	....	....	....	....	....	....	....	....	....	....	....	1	0	0	0	0	....	....	....
2000-01	Portland Pirates	AHL	80	18	37	55	63	....	....	....	....	....	....	....	....	....	....	....	3	0	2	2	6	....	....	....
	NHL Totals		52	3	8	11	20	0	0	0	33	9.1		138	55.1	4	8	16:09	3	0	0	0	4	0	0	0

Canadian Major Junior Scholastic Player of the Year (1989, 1990) • WHL East Second All-Star Team (1991, 1992)

Signed as a free agent by **Nashville**, August 19, 1998. Traded to **Washington** by **Nashville** for cash, June 21, 1999. Signed as a free agent by **Schwenningen** (DEL), July 17, 2001.

NEMCHINOV, Sergei

(nehm-CHEE-nahf, SAIR-gay) **N.J.**

Left wing. Shoots left. 6'1", 205 lbs. Born, Moscow, USSR, January 14, 1964. NY Rangers' 14th choice, 244th overall, in 1990 Entry Draft.

1981-82	Krylja Sovetov	USSR	15	1	0	1	0	....	....	....	....	....	....	....	....	....	....	....	....	....	....	....	....	....	....	....
1982-83	CSKA Moscow	USSR	11	0	0	0	2	....	....	....	....	....	....	....	....	....	....	....	....	....	....	....	....	....	....	....
1983-84	CSKA Moscow	USSR	20	6	5	11	4	....	....	....	....	....	....	....	....	....	....	....	....	....	....	....	....	....	....	....
1984-85	CSKA Moscow	USSR	31	2	4	6	4	....	....	....	....	....	....	....	....	....	....	....	....	....	....	....	....	....	....	....
1985-86	Krylja Sovetov	USSR	39	7	12	19	28	....	....	....	....	....	....	....	....	....	....	....	....	....	....	....	....	....	....	....
1986-87	Krylja Sovetov	USSR	40	13	9	22	24	....	....	....	....	....	....	....	....	....	....	....	....	....	....	....	....	....	....	....
1987-88	Krylja Sovetov	USSR	48	17	11	28	26	....	....	....	....	....	....	....	....	....	....	....	....	....	....	....	....	....	....	....
1988-89	Krylja Sovetov	USSR	43	15	14	29	28	....	....	....	....	....	....	....	....	....	....	....	....	....	....	....	....	....	....	....
1989-90	Krylja Sovetov	USSR	48	17	16	33	34	....	....	....	....	....	....	....	....	....	....	....	....	....	....	....	....	....	....	....
1990-91	Krylja Sovetov	USSR	46	21	24	45	30	....	....	....	....	....	....	....	....	....	....	....	....	....	....	....	....	....	....	....
1991-92	**NY Rangers**	**NHL**	73	30	28	58	15	2	0	5	124	24.2	19	....	....	....	....	....	13	1	4	5	8	0	0	0
1992-93	**NY Rangers**	**NHL**	81	23	31	54	34	0	1	3	144	16.0	15	....	....	....	....	....	....	....	....	....	....	....	....	....
1993-94♦	**NY Rangers**	**NHL**	76	22	27	49	36	4	0	6	144	15.3	13	....	....	....	....	....	23	2	5	7	6	0	0	0
1994-95	**NY Rangers**	**NHL**	47	7	6	13	16	0	0	3	67	10.4	–6	....	....	....	....	....	10	4	5	9	2	0	0	1
1995-96	**NY Rangers**	**NHL**	78	17	15	32	38	0	0	2	118	14.4	9	....	....	....	....	....	6	0	1	1	2	0	0	0
1996-97	**NY Rangers**	**NHL**	63	6	13	19	12	1	0	1	90	6.7	5	....	....	....	....	....	....	....	....	....	....	....	....	....
	Vancouver	**NHL**	6	2	3	5	4	0	0	1	7	28.6	4	....	....	....	....	....	....	....	....	....	....	....	....	....
1997-98	**NY Islanders**	**NHL**	74	10	19	29	24	2	1	1	94	10.6	3	....	....	....	....	....	....	....	....	....	....	....	....	....
	Russia	Olympics	6	1	0	1	0	....	....	....	....	....	....	....	....	....	....	....	....	....	....	....	....	....	....	....
1998-99	**NY Islanders**	**NHL**	67	8	8	16	22	1	0	0	61	13.1	–17	606	42.4	52	44	14:21	....	....	....	....	....	....	....	....
	New Jersey	**NHL**	10	4	0	4	6	1	0	1	13	30.8	4	38	52.6	13	0	15:36	4	0	0	0	0	0	0	0

Season	Club	League	GP	G	A	Pts	PIM	PP	SH	GW	S	%	+/-	TF	F%	H	SB	Min	GP	G	A	Pts	PIM	PP	SH	GW
			Regular Season																Playoffs							
99-2000♦	**New Jersey**	**NHL**	**53**	**10**	**16**	**26**	**18**	**0**	**1**	**1**	**55**	**18.2**	**1**	**453**	**45.7**	**47**	**19**	**13:42**	**21**	**3**	**2**	**5**	**2**	**1**	**0**	**0**
2000-01	**New Jersey**	**NHL**	**65**	**8**	**22**	**30**	**16**	**1**	**0**	**2**	**70**	**11.4**	**11**	**649**	**48.1**	**57**	**16**	**13:13**	**25**	**1**	**3**	**4**	**4**	**0**	**0**	**0**
	NHL Totals		**693**	**147**	**188**	**335**	**241**	**12**	**3**	**26**	**987**	**14.9**		**1746**	**45.6**	**169**	**79**	**13:52**	**102**	**11**	**20**	**31**	**24**	**1**	**0**	**1**

Traded to **Vancouver** by **NY Rangers** with Brian Noonan for Esa Tikkanen and Russ Courtnall, March 8, 1997. Signed as a free agent by **NY Islanders**, July 10, 1997. Traded to **New Jersey** by **NY Islanders** for New Jersey's 4th round choice (later traded to Los Angeles - Los Angeles selected Daniel Johansson) in 1999 Entry Draft, March 22, 1999.

NEMECEK, Jan

(NEHM-eh-chehk, YAHN) **L.A.**

Defense. Shoots Left. 6'1", 220 lbs. Born, Pisek, Czech., February 14, 1976. Los Angeles' 7th choice, 215th overall, in 1994 Entry Draft.

Season	Club	League	GP	G	A	Pts	PIM	PP	SH	GW	S	%	+/-	TF	F%	H	SB	Min	GP	G	A	Pts	PIM	PP	SH	GW
1992-93	MC Budejovice	Czech.	15	0	0	0	....	....	....	....	....	....	....	....	....	....	....	....	....	....	....	....	....	....	....	....
1993-94	MC Budejovice	Cze-Rep	16	0	1	1	16	....	....	....	....	....	....	....	....	....	....	....	....	....	....	....	....	....	....	....
1994-95	Hull Olympiques	QMJHL	49	10	16	26	48	....	....	....	....	....	....	....	....	....	....	....	21	5	9	14	10	....	....	....
1995-96	Hull Olympiques	QMJHL	57	17	49	66	58	....	....	....	....	....	....	....	....	....	....	....	17	2	13	15	10	....	....	....
1996-97	Mississippi	ECHL	20	3	9	12	16	....	....	....	....	....	....	....	....	....	....	....	3	0	0	0	4	....	....	....
	Phoenix	IHL	24	1	1	2	2	....	....	....	....	....	....	....	....	....	....	....	....	....	....	....	....	....	....	....
1997-98	Fredericton	AHL	65	7	24	31	43	....	....	....	....	....	....	....	....	....	....	....	2	0	0	0	0	....	....	....
1998-99	**Los Angeles**	**NHL**	**6**	**1**	**0**	**1**	**4**	**0**	**0**	**1**	**8**	**12.5**	**-1**	**0**	**0.0**	**2**	**4**	**16:42**	....	....	....	....	....	....	....	....
	Long Beach	IHL	66	5	16	21	42	....	....	....	....	....	....	....	....	....	....	....	....	....	....	....	....	....	....	....
99-2000	**Los Angeles**	**NHL**	**1**	**0**	**0**	**0**	**0**	**0**	**0**	**0**	**0**	**0.0**	**0**	**0**	**0.0**	**0**	**0**	**9:36**	....	....	....	....	....	....	....	....
	Long Beach	IHL	71	9	15	24	22	....	....	....	....	....	....	....	....	....	....	....	6	1	0	1	4	....	....	....
2000-01	Nurnberg Tigers	DEL	60	5	16	21	18	....	....	....	....	....	....	....	....	....	....	....	4	1	0	1	0	....	....	....
	NHL Totals		**7**	**1**	**0**	**1**	**4**	**0**	**0**	**1**	**8**	**12.5**		**0**	**0.0**	**2**	**4**	**15:41**	....	....	....	....	....	....	....	....

QMJHL Second All-Star Team (1996)

NEMIROVSKY, David

(neh-mih-ROHV-skee, DAY-vihd) **TOR.**

Right wing. Shoots right. 6'2", 205 lbs. Born, Toronto, Ont., August 1, 1976. Florida's 5th choice, 84th overall, in 1994 Entry Draft.

Season	Club	League	GP	G	A	Pts	PIM	PP	SH	GW	S	%	+/-	TF	F%	H	SB	Min	GP	G	A	Pts	PIM	PP	SH	GW
1991-92	Pickering	MTJHL	14	3	10	13	5	....	....	....	....	....	....	....	....	....	....	....	....	....	....	....	....	....	....	....
	Weston Dukes	MTJHL	23	6	13	19	2	....	....	....	....	....	....	....	....	....	....	....	....	....	....	....	....	....	....	....
1992-93	Weston Dukes	MTJHL	2	0	3	3	0	....	....	....	....	....	....	....	....	....	....	....	....	....	....	....	....	....	....	....
	North York	MTJHL	40	19	23	42	27	....	....	....	....	....	....	....	....	....	....	....	....	....	....	....	....	....	....	....
1993-94	Ottawa 67's	OHL	64	21	31	52	18	....	....	....	....	....	....	....	....	....	....	....	17	10	10	20	2	....	....	....
1994-95	Ottawa 67's	OHL	59	27	29	56	25	....	....	....	....	....	....	....	....	....	....	....	....	....	....	....	....	....	....	....
1995-96	Sarnia Sting	OHL	26	18	27	45	14	....	....	....	....	....	....	....	....	....	....	....	10	8	8	16	6	....	....	....
	Florida	**NHL**	**9**	**0**	**2**	**2**	**2**	**0**	**0**	**0**	**6**	**0.0**	**-1**	....	....	....	....	....	....	....	....	....	....	....	....	....
	Carolina	AHL	5	1	2	3	0	....	....	....	....	....	....	....	....	....	....	....	....	....	....	....	....	....	....	....
1996-97	**Florida**	**NHL**	**39**	**7**	**7**	**14**	**32**	**1**	**0**	**0**	**53**	**13.2**	**1**	....	....	....	....	....	**3**	**1**	**0**	**1**	**0**	**0**	**0**	**0**
	Carolina	AHL	34	21	21	42	18	....	....	....	....	....	....	....	....	....	....	....	....	....	....	....	....	....	....	....
1997-98	**Florida**	**NHL**	**41**	**9**	**12**	**21**	**8**	**2**	**0**	**1**	**62**	**14.5**	**-3**	....	....	....	....	....	....	....	....	....	....	....	....	....
	New Haven	AHL	29	10	15	25	10	....	....	....	....	....	....	....	....	....	....	....	1	1	0	1	0	....	....	....
1998-99	**Florida**	**NHL**	**2**	**0**	**1**	**1**	**0**	**0**	**0**	**0**	**2**	**0.0**	**1**	**0**	**0.0**	**0**	**0**	**8:58**	....	....	....	....	....	....	....	....
	Fort Wayne	IHL	44	22	13	35	24	....	....	....	....	....	....	....	....	....	....	....	....	....	....	....	....	....	....	....
	St. John's Leafs	AHL	22	3	9	12	18	....	....	....	....	....	....	....	....	....	....	....	5	4	1	5	0	....	....	....
99-2000	St. John's Leafs	AHL	57	18	25	43	69	....	....	....	....	....	....	....	....	....	....	....	....	....	....	....	....	....	....	....
2000-01	St. John's Leafs	AHL	9	1	2	3	10	....	....	....	....	....	....	....	....	....	....	....	....	....	....	....	....	....	....	....
	HV Jonkoping	Sweden	26	7	11	18	45	....	....	....	....	....	....	....	....	....	....	....	....	....	....	....	....	....	....	....
	NHL Totals		**91**	**16**	**22**	**38**	**42**	**3**	**0**	**1**	**123**	**13.0**		**0**	**0.0**	**0**	**0**	**8:58**	**3**	**1**	**0**	**1**	**0**	**0**	**0**	**0**

Traded to **Toronto** by **Florida** for Jeff Ware, February 17, 1999.

NICHOL, Scott

(NIH-KOHL, SKAWT) **CGY.**

Center. Shoots right. 5'8", 160 lbs. Born, Edmonton, Alta., December 31, 1974. Buffalo's 9th choice, 272nd overall, in 1993 Entry Draft.

Season	Club	League	GP	G	A	Pts	PIM	PP	SH	GW	S	%	+/-	TF	F%	H	SB	Min	GP	G	A	Pts	PIM	PP	SH	GW
1991-92	Calgary Flames	AMHL	23	26	16	42	132	....	....	....	....	....	....	....	....	....	....	....	....	....	....	....	....	....	....	....
1992-93	Portland	WHL	67	31	33	64	146	....	....	....	....	....	....	....	....	....	....	....	16	8	8	16	41	....	....	....
1993-94	Portland	WHL	65	40	53	93	144	....	....	....	....	....	....	....	....	....	....	....	10	3	8	11	16	....	....	....
1994-95	Rochester	AHL	71	11	16	27	136	....	....	....	....	....	....	....	....	....	....	....	5	0	3	3	14	....	....	....
1995-96	**Buffalo**	**NHL**	**2**	**0**	**0**	**0**	**10**	**0**	**0**	**0**	**4**	**0.0**	**0**	....	....	....	....	....	....	....	....	....	....	....	....	....
	Rochester	AHL	62	14	18	32	170	....	....	....	....	....	....	....	....	....	....	....	19	7	6	13	36	....	....	....
1996-97	Rochester	AHL	68	22	21	43	133	....	....	....	....	....	....	....	....	....	....	....	10	2	1	3	26	....	....	....
1997-98	**Buffalo**	**NHL**	**3**	**0**	**0**	**0**	**4**	**0**	**0**	**0**	**5**	**0.0**	**0**	....	....	....	....	....	....	....	....	....	....	....	....	....
	Rochester	AHL	35	13	7	20	113	....	....	....	....	....	....	....	....	....	....	....	....	....	....	....	....	....	....	....
1998-99	Rochester	AHL	52	13	20	33	120	....	....	....	....	....	....	....	....	....	....	....	....	....	....	....	....	....	....	....
99-2000	Rochester	AHL	37	7	11	18	141	....	....	....	....	....	....	....	....	....	....	....	....	....	....	....	....	....	....	....
2000-01	Detroit Vipers	IHL	67	7	24	31	198	....	....	....	....	....	....	....	....	....	....	....	....	....	....	....	....	....	....	....
	NHL Totals		**5**	**0**	**0**	**0**	**14**	**0**	**0**	**0**	**9**	**0.0**		....	....	....	....	....	....	....	....	....	....	....	....	....

• Missed majority of 1999-2000 season recovering from knee injury suffered in game vs. Saint John (AHL), February 16, 2000. Signed as a free agent by **Calgary**, July 1, 2001.

NICKULAS, Eric

(NICK-luhs, AIR-ihk)

Center. Shoots right. 5'11", 200 lbs. Born, Hyannis, MA, March 25, 1975. Boston's 3rd choice, 99th overall, in 1994 Entry Draft.

Season	Club	League	GP	G	A	Pts	PIM	PP	SH	GW	S	%	+/-	TF	F%	H	SB	Min	GP	G	A	Pts	PIM	PP	SH	GW
1991-92	Barnstable High	Hi-School	24	30	25	55	....	....	....	....	....	....	....	....	....	....	....	....	....	....	....	....	....	....	....	....
1992-93	Tabor Academy	Hi-School	28	25	25	50	....	....	....	....	....	....	....	....	....	....	....	....	....	....	....	....	....	....	....	....
1993-94	Cushing Academy	Hi-School	25	46	36	82	....	....	....	....	....	....	....	....	....	....	....	....	....	....	....	....	....	....	....	....
1994-95	New Hampshire	H-East	33	15	9	24	32	....	....	....	....	....	....	....	....	....	....	....	....	....	....	....	....	....	....	....
1995-96	New Hampshire	H-East	34	26	12	38	66	....	....	....	....	....	....	....	....	....	....	....	....	....	....	....	....	....	....	....
1996-97	New Hampshire	H-East	39	29	22	51	80	....	....	....	....	....	....	....	....	....	....	....	....	....	....	....	....	....	....	....
1997-98	Orlando	IHL	76	22	9	31	77	....	....	....	....	....	....	....	....	....	....	....	6	0	0	0	10	....	....	....
1998-99	**Boston**	**NHL**	**2**	**0**	**0**	**0**	**0**	**0**	**0**	**0**	**0**	**0.0**	**0**	**0**	**0.0**	**0**	**0**	**3:27**	**1**	**0**	**0**	**0**	**2**	**0**	**0**	**0**
	Providence Bruins	AHL	75	31	27	58	83	....	....	....	....	....	....	....	....	....	....	....	18	8	12	20	33	....	....	....
99-2000	**Boston**	**NHL**	**20**	**5**	**6**	**11**	**12**	**1**	**0**	**0**	**28**	**17.9**	**-1**	**4**	**50.0**	**31**	**3**	**11:13**	....	....	....	....	....	....	....	....
	Providence Bruins	AHL	40	6	6	12	37	....	....	....	....	....	....	....	....	....	....	....	12	2	3	5	20	....	....	....
2000-01	**Boston**	**NHL**	**7**	**0**	**0**	**0**	**4**	**0**	**0**	**0**	**6**	**0.0**	**-2**	**1**	**100.0**	**17**	**0**	**7:07**	....	....	....	....	....	....	....	....
	Providence Bruins	AHL	62	20	23	43	100	....	....	....	....	....	....	....	....	....	....	....	12	4	4	8	24	....	....	....
	NHL Totals		**29**	**5**	**6**	**11**	**16**	**1**	**0**	**0**	**34**	**14.7**		**5**	**60.0**	**48**	**3**	**9:41**	**1**	**0**	**0**	**0**	**2**	**0**	**0**	**0**

NIEDERMAYER, Rob

(NEE-duhr-MIGH-uhr, RAWB) **CGY.**

Center. Shoots left. 6'2", 204 lbs. Born, Cassiar, B.C., December 28, 1974. Florida's 1st choice, 5th overall, in 1993 Entry Draft.

Season	Club	League	GP	G	A	Pts	PIM	PP	SH	GW	S	%	+/-	TF	F%	H	SB	Min	GP	G	A	Pts	PIM	PP	SH	GW
1989-90	Cranbrook Royals	BCAHA	35	42	40	82	30			....	....	....	....	....	....	....	....	....	....	....	....	....	....	....	....	....
1990-91	Medicine Hat	WHL	71	24	26	50	8	....	....	....	....	....	....	....	....	....	....	....	12	3	7	10	2	....	....	....
1991-92	Medicine Hat	WHL	71	32	46	78	77	....	....	....	....	....	....	....	....	....	....	....	4	2	3	5	2	....	....	....
1992-93	Medicine Hat	WHL	52	43	34	77	67	....	....	....	....	....	....	....	....	....	....	....	....	....	....	....	....	....	....	....
1993-94	**Florida**	**NHL**	**65**	**9**	**17**	**26**	**51**	**3**	**0**	**2**	**67**	**13.4**	**-11**	....	....	....	....	....	....	....	....	....	....	....	....	....
1994-95	Medicine Hat	WHL	13	9	15	24	14	....	....	....	....	....	....	....	....	....	....	....	....	....	....	....	....	....	....	....
	Florida	**NHL**	**48**	**4**	**6**	**10**	**36**	**1**	**0**	**0**	**58**	**6.9**	**-13**	....	....	....	....	....	....	....	....	....	....	....	....	....
1995-96	**Florida**	**NHL**	**82**	**26**	**35**	**61**	**107**	**11**	**0**	**6**	**155**	**16.8**	**1**	....	....	....	....	....	**22**	**5**	**3**	**8**	**12**	**2**	**0**	**2**
1996-97	**Florida**	**NHL**	**60**	**14**	**24**	**38**	**54**	**3**	**0**	**2**	**136**	**10.3**	**4**	....	....	....	....	....	**5**	**2**	**1**	**3**	**6**	**1**	**0**	**0**
1997-98	**Florida**	**NHL**	**33**	**8**	**7**	**15**	**41**	**5**	**0**	**2**	**64**	**12.5**	**-9**	....	....	....	....	....	....	....	....	....	....	....	....	....
1998-99	**Florida**	**NHL**	**82**	**18**	**33**	**51**	**50**	**6**	**1**	**3**	**142**	**12.7**	**-13**	**1895**	**47.1**	**152**	**38**	**21:17**	....	....	....	....	....	....	....	....
99-2000	**Florida**	**NHL**	**81**	**10**	**23**	**33**	**46**	**1**	**0**	**4**	**135**	**7.4**	**-5**	**1632**	**47.9**	**211**	**40**	**19:04**	**4**	**1**	**0**	**1**	**6**	**0**	**0**	**0**
2000-01	**Florida**	**NHL**	**67**	**12**	**20**	**32**	**50**	**3**	**1**	**0**	**115**	**10.4**	**-12**	**997**	**45.0**	**149**	**49**	**20:30**	....	....	....	....	....	....	....	....
	NHL Totals		**518**	**101**	**165**	**266**	**435**	**33**	**2**	**19**	**872**	**11.6**		**4524**	**46.9**	**512**	**127**	**20:17**	**31**	**8**	**4**	**12**	**24**	**3**	**0**	**2**

WHL East First All-Star Team (1993)

• Missed majority of 1997-98 season recovering from thumb (vs. Boston, November 26, 1997) and head (vs. Buffalo, March 19, 1998) injuries. Traded to **Calgary** by **Florida** with Philadelphia's 2nd round choice (previously acquired, Calgary selected Andrei Medvedev) in 2001 Entry Draft for Valeri Bure and Jason Wiemer, June 23, 2001.

NIEDERMAYER, Scott
(NEE-duhr-MIGH-uhr, SKAWT) **N.J.**

Defense. Shoots left. 6'1", 200 lbs. Born, Edmonton, Alta., August 31, 1973. New Jersey's 1st choice, 3rd overall, in 1991 Entry Draft.

			Regular Season																Playoffs							
Season	Club	League	GP	G	A	Pts	PIM	PP	SH	GW	S	%	+/-	TF	F%	H	SB	Min	GP	G	A	Pts	PIM	PP	SH	GW
1988-89	Cranbrook Blaze	BCAHA	62	55	37	92	100	....	....	....	....	....	....	....	....	....	....	....	....	....	....	....	....	....	....	....
1989-90	Kamloops Blazers	WHL	64	14	55	69	64	....	....	....	....	....	....	....	....	....	....	....	17	2	14	16	35	....	....	....
1990-91	Kamloops Blazers	WHL	57	26	56	82	52	....	....	....	....	....	....	....	....	....	....	....	....	....	....	....	....	....	....	....
1991-92	Kamloops Blazers	WHL	35	7	32	39	61	....	....	....	....	....	....	....	....	....	....	....	17	9	14	23	28	....	....	....
	New Jersey	**NHL**	**4**	**0**	**1**	**1**	**2**	**0**	**0**	**0**	**4**	**0.0**	**1**	....	....	....	....	....	....	....	....	....	....	....	....	....
1992-93	**New Jersey**	**NHL**	**80**	**11**	**29**	**40**	**47**	**5**	**0**	**0**	**131**	**8.4**	**8**	....	....	....	....	....	**5**	**0**	**3**	**3**	**2**	**0**	**0**	**0**
1993-94	**New Jersey**	**NHL**	**81**	**10**	**36**	**46**	**42**	**5**	**0**	**2**	**135**	**7.4**	**34**	....	....	....	....	....	**20**	**2**	**2**	**4**	**8**	**1**	**0**	**0**
1994-95♦	**New Jersey**	**NHL**	**48**	**4**	**15**	**19**	**18**	**4**	**0**	**0**	**52**	**7.7**	**19**	....	....	....	....	....	**20**	**4**	**7**	**11**	**10**	**2**	**0**	**1**
1995-96	**New Jersey**	**NHL**	**79**	**8**	**25**	**33**	**46**	**6**	**0**	**0**	**179**	**4.5**	**5**	....	....	....	....	....	....	....	....	....	....	....	....	....
1996-97	**New Jersey**	**NHL**	**81**	**5**	**30**	**35**	**64**	**3**	**0**	**3**	**159**	**3.1**	**–4**	....	....	....	....	....	**10**	**2**	**4**	**6**	**6**	**2**	**0**	**1**
1997-98	**New Jersey**	**NHL**	**81**	**14**	**43**	**57**	**27**	**11**	**0**	**1**	**175**	**8.0**	**5**	....	....	....	....	....	**6**	**0**	**2**	**2**	**4**	**0**	**0**	**0**
1998-99	Utah Grizzlies	IHL	5	0	2	2	0	....	....	....	....	....	....	....	....	....	....	....	....	....	....	....	....	....	....	....
	New Jersey	**NHL**	**72**	**11**	**35**	**46**	**26**	**1**	**1**	**3**	**161**	**6.8**	**16**	**13**	**15.4**	**99**	**49**	**24:40**	**7**	**1**	**3**	**4**	**18**	**1**	**0**	**0**
99-2000♦	**New Jersey**	**NHL**	**71**	**7**	**31**	**38**	**48**	**1**	**0**	**0**	**109**	**6.4**	**19**	**8**	**37.5**	**105**	**82**	**24:21**	**22**	**5**	**2**	**7**	**10**	**0**	**2**	**1**
2000-01	**New Jersey**	**NHL**	**57**	**6**	**29**	**35**	**22**	**1**	**0**	**5**	**87**	**6.9**	**14**	**5**	**0.0**	**61**	**56**	**23:19**	**21**	**0**	**6**	**6**	**14**	**0**	**0**	**0**
	NHL Totals		**654**	**76**	**274**	**350**	**342**	**37**	**1**	**14**	**1192**	**6.4**		**26**	**19.2**	**265**	**187**	**24:10**	**111**	**14**	**29**	**43**	**72**	**6**	**2**	**3**

WHL West First All-Star Team (1991, 1992) • Canadian Major Junior Scholastic Player of the Year (1991) • Memorial Cup All-Star Team (1992) • Won Stafford Smythe Memorial Trophy (Memorial Cup Tournament MVP) (1992) • NHL All-Rookie Team (1993) • NHL Second All-Star Team (1998) • Played in NHL All-Star Game (1998, 2001)

Signed to 25-game try-out contract by **Utah** (IHL) with **New Jersey** retaining NHL rights, October 19, 1998.

NIELSEN, Chris
(NEEL-sehn, KRIHS) **CBJ**

Center. Shoots right. 6'1", 190 lbs. Born, Moshi, Tanzania, February 16, 1980. NY Islanders' 2nd choice, 36th overall, in 1998 Entry Draft.

			Regular Season																Playoffs							
Season	Club	League	GP	G	A	Pts	PIM	PP	SH	GW	S	%	+/-	TF	F%	H	SB	Min	GP	G	A	Pts	PIM	PP	SH	GW
1995-96	S-W Cougars	MMHL	39	37	35	72	59	....	....	....	....	....	....	....	....	....	....	....	....	....	....	....	....	....	....	....
	Calgary Hitmen	WHL	6	0	0	0	0	....	....	....	....	....	....	....	....	....	....	....	....	....	....	....	....	....	....	....
1996-97	Calgary Hitmen	WHL	62	11	19	30	39	....	....	....	....	....	....	....	....	....	....	....	....	....	....	....	....	....	....	....
1997-98	Calgary Hitmen	WHL	68	22	29	51	31	....	....	....	....	....	....	....	....	....	....	....	18	2	4	6	10	....	....	....
1998-99	Calgary Hitmen	WHL	70	22	24	46	45	....	....	....	....	....	....	....	....	....	....	....	21	11	5	16	28	....	....	....
99-2000	Calgary Hitmen	WHL	62	38	31	69	86	....	....	....	....	....	....	....	....	....	....	....	13	14	9	23	20	....	....	....
2000-01	**Columbus**	**NHL**	**29**	**4**	**5**	**9**	**4**	**0**	**0**	**1**	**36**	**11.1**	**4**	**18**	**55.6**	**33**	**3**	**10:30**	....	....	....	....	....	....	....	....
	Syracuse Crunch	AHL	47	10	11	21	24	....	....	....	....	....	....	....	....	....	....	....	5	2	2	4	4	....	....	....
	NHL Totals		**29**	**4**	**5**	**9**	**4**	**0**	**0**	**1**	**36**	**11.1**		**18**	**55.6**	**33**	**3**	**10:30**	....	....	....	....	....	....	....	....

Traded to **Columbus** by **NY Islanders** for Columbus' 4th (later traded to Anaheim - Anaheim selected Jonas Ronnqvist) and 9th (Dmitri Altarev) round choices in 2000 Entry Draft, May 11, 2000.

NIELSEN, Jeff
(NEEL-sehn, JEHF)

Right wing. Shoots left. 6', 200 lbs. Born, Grand Rapids, MN, September 20, 1971. NY Rangers' 4th choice, 69th overall, in 1990 Entry Draft.

			Regular Season																Playoffs							
Season	Club	League	GP	G	A	Pts	PIM	PP	SH	GW	S	%	+/-	TF	F%	H	SB	Min	GP	G	A	Pts	PIM	PP	SH	GW
1987-88	Grand Rapids	Hi-School	21	9	11	20	14	....	....	....	....	....	....	....	....	....	....	....	....	....	....	....	....	....	....	....
1988-89	Grand Rapids	Hi-School	25	13	17	30	26	....	....	....	....	....	....	....	....	....	....	....	....	....	....	....	....	....	....	....
1989-90	Grand Rapids	Hi-School	28	32	25	*57	....	....	....	....	....	....	....	....	....	....	....	....	....	....	....	....	....	....	....	....
1990-91	U. of Minnesota	WCHA	45	11	14	25	50	....	....	....	....	....	....	....	....	....	....	....	....	....	....	....	....	....	....	....
1991-92	U. of Minnesota	WCHA	41	14	14	28	70	....	....	....	....	....	....	....	....	....	....	....	....	....	....	....	....	....	....	....
1992-93	U. of Minnesota	WCHA	42	21	20	41	80	....	....	....	....	....	....	....	....	....	....	....	....	....	....	....	....	....	....	....
1993-94	U. of Minnesota	WCHA	41	29	16	45	94	....	....	....	....	....	....	....	....	....	....	....	....	....	....	....	....	....	....	....
1994-95	Binghamton	AHL	76	24	13	37	139	....	....	....	....	....	....	....	....	....	....	....	7	0	0	0	22	....	....	....
1995-96	Binghamton	AHL	64	22	20	42	56	....	....	....	....	....	....	....	....	....	....	....	4	1	1	2	4	....	....	....
1996-97	**NY Rangers**	**NHL**	**2**	**0**	**0**	**0**	**2**	**0**	**0**	**0**	**1**	**0.0**	**–1**	....	....	....	....	....	....	....	....	....	....	....	....	....
	Binghamton	AHL	76	27	26	53	71	....	....	....	....	....	....	....	....	....	....	....	4	0	0	0	7	....	....	....
1997-98	**Anaheim**	**NHL**	**32**	**4**	**5**	**9**	**16**	**0**	**0**	**0**	**36**	**11.1**	**–1**	....	....	....	....	....	....	....	....	....	....	....	....	....
	Cincinnati Ducks	AHL	18	4	8	12	37	....	....	....	....	....	....	....	....	....	....	....	....	....	....	....	....	....	....	....
1998-99	**Anaheim**	**NHL**	**80**	**5**	**4**	**9**	**34**	**0**	**0**	**2**	**94**	**5.3**	**–12**	**9**	**44.4**	**84**	**38**	**10:16**	**4**	**0**	**0**	**0**	**2**	**0**	**0**	**0**
99-2000	**Anaheim**	**NHL**	**79**	**8**	**10**	**18**	**14**	**1**	**0**	**0**	**113**	**7.1**	**4**	**4**	**50.0**	**113**	**39**	**11:59**	....	....	....	....	....	....	....	....
2000-01	**Minnesota**	**NHL**	**59**	**3**	**8**	**11**	**4**	**1**	**0**	**1**	**82**	**3.7**	**–16**	**1**	**100.0**	**29**	**36**	**13:33**	....	....	....	....	....	....	....	....
	NHL Totals		**252**	**20**	**27**	**47**	**70**	**2**	**0**	**3**	**326**	**6.1**		**14**	**50.0**	**226**	**113**	**11:47**	**4**	**0**	**0**	**0**	**2**	**0**	**0**	**0**

WCHA Second All-Star Team (1994)

Signed as a free agent by **Anaheim**, August 18, 1997. Selected by **Minnesota** from **Anaheim** in Expansion Draft, June 23, 2000.

NIEMI, Antti-Jussi
(nee-mee, AN-tee-YOO-see) **ANA.**

Defense. Shoots left. 6'1", 193 lbs. Born, Vantaa, Finland, September 22, 1977. Ottawa's 2nd choice, 81st overall, in 1996 Entry Draft.

			Regular Season																Playoffs							
Season	Club	League	GP	G	A	Pts	PIM	PP	SH	GW	S	%	+/-	TF	F%	H	SB	Min	GP	G	A	Pts	PIM	PP	SH	GW
1992-93	Jokerit Helsinki-C	Finn-Jr.	38	9	23	32	54	....	....	....	....	....	....	....	....	....	....	....	....	....	....	....	....	....	....	....
	Jokerit Helsinki-B	Finn-Jr.	2	0	0	0	2	....	....	....	....	....	....	....	....	....	....	....	....	....	....	....	....	....	....	....
1993-94	Jokerit Helsinki-B	Finn-Jr.	13	1	1	2	8	....	....	....	....	....	....	....	....	....	....	....	....	....	....	....	....	....	....	....
	Jokerit Helsinki	Finn-Jr.	33	0	3	3	26	....	....	....	....	....	....	....	....	....	....	....	....	....	....	....	....	....	....	....
1994-95	Jokerit Helsinki-B	Finn-Jr.	10	3	5	8	42	....	....	....	....	....	....	....	....	....	....	....	....	....	....	....	....	....	....	....
	Jokerit Helsinki	Finn-Jr.	24	4	8	12	74	....	....	....	....	....	....	....	....	....	....	....	....	....	....	....	....	....	....	....
1995-96	Jokerit Helsinki	Finn-Jr.	34	11	18	29	56	....	....	....	....	....	....	....	....	....	....	....	8	0	4	4	39	....	....	....
	Jarvenpaa HT	Finland-2	4	0	2	2	8	....	....	....	....	....	....	....	....	....	....	....	....	....	....	....	....	....	....	....
	Jokerit Helsinki	Finland	6	0	2	2	6	....	....	....	....	....	....	....	....	....	....	....	1	0	0	0	0	....	....	....
1996-97	Jokerit Helsinki	Finland	44	2	9	11	38	....	....	....	....	....	....	....	....	....	....	....	9	0	2	2	2	....	....	....
1997-98	Jokerit Helsinki	Finland	46	2	6	8	24	....	....	....	....	....	....	....	....	....	....	....	8	0	1	1	0	....	....	....
	Jokerit Helsinki	EuroHL	6	0	1	1	6	....	....	....	....	....	....	....	....	....	....	....	....	....	....	....	....	....	....	....
1998-99	Jokerit Helsinki	Finland	53	3	7	10	107	....	....	....	....	....	....	....	....	....	....	....	3	0	0	0	2	....	....	....
	Jokerit Helsinki	EuroHL	6	2	2	4	4	....	....	....	....	....	....	....	....	....	....	....	2	0	1	1	0	....	....	....
99-2000	Jokerit Helsinki	Finland	53	8	8	16	79	....	....	....	....	....	....	....	....	....	....	....	11	0	3	3	6	....	....	....
2000-01	**Anaheim**	**NHL**	**28**	**1**	**1**	**2**	**22**	**0**	**0**	**0**	**18**	**5.6**	**–6**	**0**	**0.0**	**50**	**32**	**15:56**	....	....	....	....	....	....	....	....
	Cincinnati Ducks	AHL	36	3	8	11	26	....	....	....	....	....	....	....	....	....	....	....	....	....	....	....	....	....	....	....
	NHL Totals		**28**	**1**	**1**	**2**	**22**	**0**	**0**	**0**	**18**	**5.6**		**0**	**0.0**	**50**	**32**	**15:56**	....	....	....	....	....	....	....	....

Rights traded to **Anaheim** by **Ottawa** with Ted Donato for Patrick Lalime, June 18, 1999.

NIEMINEN, Ville
(nee-EHM-ih-nehn, VIHL-ee) **COL.**

Left wing. Shoots left. 6', 200 lbs. Born, Tampere, Finland, April 6, 1977. Colorado's 4th choice, 78th overall, in 1997 Entry Draft.

			Regular Season																Playoffs							
Season	Club	League	GP	G	A	Pts	PIM	PP	SH	GW	S	%	+/-	TF	F%	H	SB	Min	GP	G	A	Pts	PIM	PP	SH	GW
1994-95	Tappara Tampere	Finn-Jr.	16	11	21	32	47	....	....	....	....	....	....	....	....	....	....	....	....	....	....	....	....	....	....	....
	Tappara Tampere	Finland	16	0	0	0	0	....	....	....	....	....	....	....	....	....	....	....	....	....	....	....	....	....	....	....
1995-96	Tappara Tampere	Finn-Jr.	20	20	23	43	63	....	....	....	....	....	....	....	....	....	....	....	....	....	....	....	....	....	....	....
	KooVee Kouvola	Finland-2	7	2	1	3	4	....	....	....	....	....	....	....	....	....	....	....	....	....	....	....	....	....	....	....
	Tappara Tampere	Finland	4	0	1	1	8	....	....	....	....	....	....	....	....	....	....	....	....	....	....	....	....	....	....	....
1996-97	Tappara Tampere	Finland	49	10	13	23	120	....	....	....	....	....	....	....	....	....	....	....	3	1	0	1	8	....	....	....
1997-98	Hershey Bears	AHL	74	14	22	36	85	....	....	....	....	....	....	....	....	....	....	....	....	....	....	....	....	....	....	....
1998-99	Hershey Bears	AHL	67	24	19	43	127	....	....	....	....	....	....	....	....	....	....	....	3	0	1	1	0	....	....	....
99-2000	**Colorado**	**NHL**	**1**	**0**	**0**	**0**	**0**	**0**	**0**	**0**	**2**	**0.0**	**0**	**0**	**0.0**	**0**	**0**	**10:12**	....	....	....	....	....	....	....	....
	Hershey Bears	AHL	74	21	30	51	54	....	....	....	....	....	....	....	....	....	....	....	9	2	4	6	6	....	....	....
2000-01♦	**Colorado**	**NHL**	**50**	**14**	**8**	**22**	**38**	**2**	**0**	**3**	**68**	**20.6**	**8**	**3**	**33.3**	**62**	**14**	**12:26**	**23**	**4**	**6**	**10**	**20**	**3**	**0**	**1**
	Hershey Bears	AHL	28	10	11	21	48	....	....	....	....	....	....	....	....	....	....	....	....	....	....	....	....	....	....	....
	NHL Totals		**51**	**14**	**8**	**22**	**38**	**2**	**0**	**3**	**70**	**20.0**		**3**	**33.3**	**62**	**14**	**12:23**	**23**	**4**	**6**	**10**	**20**	**3**	**0**	**1**

NIEUWENDYK, Joe
(NOO-ihn-DIGHK, JOH) **DAL.**

Center. Shoots left. 6'1", 205 lbs. Born, Oshawa, Ont., September 10, 1966. Calgary's 2nd choice, 27th overall, in 1985 Entry Draft.

			Regular Season																Playoffs							
Season	Club	League	GP	G	A	Pts	PIM	PP	SH	GW	S	%	+/-	TF	F%	H	SB	Min	GP	G	A	Pts	PIM	PP	SH	GW
1983-84	Pickering	MTJHL	38	30	28	58	35	....	....	....	....	....	....	....	....	....	....	....	....	....	....	....	....	....	....	....
1984-85	Cornell Big Red	ECAC	29	21	24	45	30	....	....	....	....	....	....	....	....	....	....	....	....	....	....	....	....	....	....	....
1985-86	Cornell Big Red	ECAC	29	26	28	54	67	....	....	....	....	....	....	....	....	....	....	....	....	....	....	....	....	....	....	....
1986-87	Cornell Big Red	ECAC	23	26	26	52	26	....	....	....	....	....	....	....	....	....	....	....	....	....	....	....	....	....	....	....
	Calgary	**NHL**	**9**	**5**	**1**	**6**	**0**	**2**	**0**	**1**	**16**	**31.3**	**0**	....	....	....	....	....	**6**	**2**	**2**	**4**	**0**	**0**	**0**	**0**
1987-88	**Calgary**	**NHL**	**75**	**51**	**41**	**92**	**23**	**31**	**3**	**8**	**212**	**24.1**	**20**	....	....	....	....	....	**8**	**3**	**4**	**7**	**2**	**1**	**0**	**0**

			Regular Season																Playoffs							
Season	Club	League	GP	G	A	Pts	PIM	PP	SH	GW	S	%	+/-	TF	F%	H	SB	Min	GP	G	A	Pts	PIM	PP	SH	GW
1988-89♦	Calgary	NHL	77	51	31	82	40	19	3	11	215	23.7	26	....	....	....	....	....	22	10	4	14	10	6	0	1
1989-90	Calgary	NHL	79	45	50	95	40	18	0	3	226	19.9	32	....	....	....	....	....	6	4	6	10	4	1	0	0
1990-91	Calgary	NHL	79	45	40	85	36	22	4	1	222	20.3	19	....	....	....	....	....	7	4	1	5	10	2	0	0
1991-92	Calgary	NHL	69	22	34	56	55	7	0	2	137	16.1	−1	....	....	....	....	....	....	....	....	....	....	....	....	....
1992-93	Calgary	NHL	79	38	37	75	52	14	0	6	208	18.3	9	....	....	....	....	....	6	3	6	9	10	1	0	0
1993-94	Calgary	NHL	64	36	39	75	51	14	1	7	191	18.8	19	....	....	....	....	....	6	2	2	4	0	1	0	0
1994-95	Calgary	NHL	46	21	29	50	33	3	0	4	122	17.2	11	....	....	....	....	....	5	4	3	7	0	2	0	1
1995-96	Dallas	NHL	52	14	18	32	41	8	0	3	138	10.1	−17	....	....	....	....	....	....	....	....	....	....	....	....	....
1996-97	Dallas	NHL	66	30	21	51	32	8	0	2	173	17.3	−5	....	....	....	....	....	7	2	2	4	6	0	0	0
1997-98	Dallas	NHL	73	39	30	69	30	14	0	11	203	19.2	16	....	....	....	....	....	1	1	0	1	0	0	0	0
	Canada	Olympics	6	2	3	5	2	....	....	....	....	....	....	....	....	....	....	....	....	....	....	....	....	....	....	....
1998-99♦	Dallas	NHL	67	28	27	55	34	8	0	8	157	17.8	11	1170	63.2	42	9	15:33	23	*11	10	21	19	3	0	6
99-2000	Dallas	NHL	48	15	19	34	26	7	0	2	110	13.6	−1	924	59.1	17	8	16:15	23	7	3	10	18	3	0	2
2000-01	Dallas	NHL	69	29	23	52	30	12	0	4	166	17.5	5	1262	57.2	34	21	16:11	7	4	0	4	4	1	0	1
	NHL Totals		952	469	440	909	523	187	11	73	2496	18.8		3356	59.8	93	38	15:58	127	57	43	100	83	21	0	11

ECAC First All-Star Team (1986, 1987) • NCAA East First All-American Team (1986, 1987) • Won Calder Memorial Trophy (1988) • NHL All-Rookie Team (1988) • Won Dodge Ram Tough Award (1988) • Won King Clancy Memorial Trophy (1995) • Won Conn Smythe Trophy (1999) • Played in NHL All-Star Game (1988, 1989, 1990, 1994)

Traded to **Dallas** by **Calgary** for Corey Millen and Jarome Iginla, December 19, 1995.

NIINIMAA, Janne
(nihn-EE-mah, YAH-nee) **EDM.**

Defense. Shoots left. 6'1", 220 lbs. Born, Raahe, Finland, May 22, 1975. Philadelphia's 1st choice, 36th overall, in 1993 Entry Draft.

1990-91	Karpat Oulu	Finn-Jr.	3	1	0	1	2	....	....	....	....	....	....	....	....	....	....	....	....	....	....	....	....	....	....	....
1991-92	Karpat Oulu	Finn-Jr.	3	0	0	0	4	....	....	....	....	....	....	....	....	....	....	....	....	....	....	....	....	....	....	....
	Karpat Oulu	Finland-2	41	2	11	13	49	....	....	....	....	....	....	....	....	....	....	....	....	....	....	....	....	....	....	....
1992-93	Karpat Oulu	Finn-Jr.	10	3	9	12	16	....	....	....	....	....	....	....	....	....	....	....	....	....	....	....	....	....	....	....
	KKP Kiiminki	Finland-3	1	0	2	2	4	....	....	....	....	....	....	....	....	....	....	....	....	....	....	....	....	....	....	....
	Karpat Oulu	Finland-2	29	2	3	5	14	....	....	....	....	....	....	....	....	....	....	....	....	....	....	....	....	....	....	....
1993-94	Jokerit Helsinki	Finn-Jr.	10	2	6	8	41	....	....	....	....	....	....	....	....	....	....	....	....	....	....	....	....	....	....	....
	Jokerit Helsinki	Finland	45	3	8	11	24	....	....	....	....	....	....	....	....	....	....	....	12	1	1	2	4	....	....	....
1994-95	Jokerit Helsinki	Finn-Jr.	3	1	2	3	4	....	....	....	....	....	....	....	....	....	....	....	....	....	....	....	....	....	....	....
	Jokerit Helsinki	Finland	42	7	10	17	36	....	....	....	....	....	....	....	....	....	....	....	10	1	4	5	35	....	....	....
1995-96	Jokerit Helsinki	Finland	49	5	15	20	79	....	....	....	....	....	....	....	....	....	....	....	11	0	2	2	12	....	....	....
	Jokerit Helsinki	Finn-Jr.	....	....	....	....	....	....	....	....	....	....	....	....	....	....	....	....	2	3	4	7	6	....	....	....
1996-97	Philadelphia	NHL	77	4	40	44	58	1	0	2	141	2.8	12	....	....	....	....	....	19	1	12	13	16	1	0	1
1997-98	Philadelphia	NHL	66	3	31	34	56	2	0	1	115	2.6	6	....	....	....	....	....	....	....	....	....	....	....	....	....
	Finland	Olympics	6	0	3	3	8	....	....	....	....	....	....	....	....	....	....	....	....	....	....	....	....	....	....	....
	Edmonton	NHL	11	1	8	9	6	1	0	0	19	5.3	7	....	....	....	....	....	11	1	1	2	12	0	0	1
1998-99	Edmonton	NHL	81	4	24	28	88	2	0	1	142	2.8	7	1	0.0	144	122	23:54	4	0	0	0	2	0	0	0
99-2000	Edmonton	NHL	81	8	25	33	89	2	2	0	133	6.0	14	0	0.0	124	107	24:28	5	0	2	2	2	0	0	0
2000-01	Edmonton	NHL	82	12	34	46	90	8	0	1	122	9.8	6	0	0.0	137	129	25:20	6	0	2	2	6	0	0	0
	NHL Totals		398	32	162	194	387	16	2	5	672	4.8		1	0.0	405	358	24:34	45	2	17	19	38	1	0	2

NHL All-Rookie Team (1997) • Played in NHL All-Star Game (2001)

Traded to **Edmonton** by **Philadelphia** for Dan McGillis and Edmonton's 2nd round choice (Jason Beckett) in 1998 Entry Draft, March 24, 1998.

NIKOLISHIN, Andrei
(nee-koh-LEE-shin, AWN-dray) **WSH.**

Left wing. Shoots left. 6', 206 lbs. Born, Vorkuta, USSR, March 25, 1973. Hartford's 2nd choice, 47th overall, in 1992 Entry Draft.

1990-91	Dynamo Moscow	USSR	2	0	0	0	0	....	....	....	....	....	....	....	....	....	....	....	....	....	....	....	....	....	....	....
1991-92	Dynamo Moscow	CIS	18	1	0	1	4	....	....	....	....	....	....	....	....	....	....	....	....	....	....	....	....	....	....	....
1992-93	Dynamo Moscow	CIS	42	5	7	12	30	....	....	....	....	....	....	....	....	....	....	....	10	2	1	3	8	....	....	....
1993-94	Dynamo Moscow	CIS	41	8	12	20	30	....	....	....	....	....	....	....	....	....	....	....	9	1	3	4	4	....	....	....
	Russia	Olympics	8	2	5	7	6	....	....	....	....	....	....	....	....	....	....	....	....	....	....	....	....	....	....	....
1994-95	Dynamo Moscow	CIS	12	7	2	9	6	....	....	....	....	....	....	....	....	....	....	....	....	....	....	....	....	....	....	....
	Hartford	NHL	39	8	10	18	10	1	1	0	57	14.0	7	....	....	....	....	....	....	....	....	....	....	....	....	....
1995-96	Hartford	NHL	61	14	37	51	34	4	1	3	83	16.9	−2	....	....	....	....	....	....	....	....	....	....	....	....	....
1996-97	Hartford	NHL	12	2	5	7	2	0	0	0	25	8.0	−2	....	....	....	....	....	....	....	....	....	....	....	....	....
	Washington	NHL	59	7	14	21	30	1	0	0	73	9.6	5	....	....	....	....	....	....	....	....	....	....	....	....	....
1997-98	Washington	NHL	38	6	10	16	14	1	0	1	40	15.0	1	....	....	....	....	....	21	1	13	14	12	1	0	0
	Portland Pirates	AHL	2	0	0	0	2	....	....	....	....	....	....	....	....	....	....	....	....	....	....	....	....	....	....	....
1998-99	Dynamo Moscow	Russia	4	0	0	0	0	....	....	....	....	....	....	....	....	....	....	....	....	....	....	....	....	....	....	....
	Washington	NHL	73	8	27	35	28	0	1	1	121	6.6	0	1354	52.5	70	31	17:34	....	....	....	....	....	....	....	....
99-2000	Washington	NHL	76	11	14	25	28	0	2	2	98	11.2	6	1190	54.7	61	39	15:44	5	0	2	2	4	0	0	0
2000-01	Washington	NHL	81	13	25	38	34	4	0	2	145	9.0	9	1214	55.4	45	32	15:32	6	0	0	0	2	0	0	0
	NHL Totals		439	69	142	211	180	11	5	9	642	10.7		3758	54.1	176	102	16:15	32	1	15	16	18	1	0	0

Traded to **Washington** by **Hartford** for Curtis Leschyshyn, November 9, 1996.

NILSON, Marcus
(NIHL-suhn, MAHR-kuhs) **FLA.**

Right wing. Shoots right. 6'2", 193 lbs. Born, Balsta, Sweden, March 1, 1978. Florida's 1st choice, 20th overall, in 1996 Entry Draft.

1994-95	Djurgardens IF	Swede-Jr.	24	7	8	15	22	....	....	....	....	....	....	....	....	....	....	....	....	....	....	....	....	....	....	....
1995-96	Djurgardens IF	Swede-Jr.	25	19	17	36	46	....	....	....	....	....	....	....	....	....	....	....	2	1	1	2	12	....	....	....
	Djurgardens IF	Sweden	12	0	0	0	0	....	....	....	....	....	....	....	....	....	....	....	1	0	0	0	0	....	....	....
1996-97	Djurgardens IF	Sweden	37	0	3	3	33	....	....	....	....	....	....	....	....	....	....	....	4	0	0	0	0	....	....	....
1997-98	Djurgardens IF	Sweden	41	4	7	11	18	....	....	....	....	....	....	....	....	....	....	....	15	2	1	3	16	....	....	....
1998-99	Florida	NHL	8	1	1	2	5	0	0	1	7	14.3	2	6	50.0	6	3	12:24	....	....	....	....	....	....	....	....
	New Haven	AHL	69	8	25	33	10	....	....	....	....	....	....	....	....	....	....	....	....	....	....	....	....	....	....	....
99-2000	Florida	NHL	9	0	2	2	2	0	0	0	6	0.0	2	14	64.3	5	3	7:56	....	....	....	....	....	....	....	....
	Louisville Panthers	AHL	64	9	23	32	52	....	....	....	....	....	....	....	....	....	....	....	4	0	0	0	2	....	....	....
2000-01	Florida	NHL	78	12	24	36	74	0	0	2	141	8.5	−3	169	40.8	67	29	15:46	....	....	....	....	....	....	....	....
	NHL Totals		95	13	27	40	81	0	0	3	154	8.4		189	42.9	78	35	14:45	....	....	....	....	....	....	....	....

NOLAN, Owen
(NOH-lan, OH-wehn) **S.J.**

Right wing. Shoots right. 6'1", 210 lbs. Born, Belfast, Ireland, February 12, 1972. Quebec's 1st choice, 1st overall, in 1990 Entry Draft.

1987-88	Thorold Hawks	OMHA	28	53	32	85	24	....	....	....	....	....	....	....	....	....	....	....	....	....	....	....	....	....	....	....
	Thorold Hawks	OJHL-B	3	1	0	1	2	....	....	....	....	....	....	....	....	....	....	....	....	....	....	....	....	....	....	....
1988-89	Cornwall Royals	OHL	62	34	25	59	213	....	....	....	....	....	....	....	....	....	....	....	18	5	11	16	41	....	....	....
1989-90	Cornwall Royals	OHL	58	51	59	110	240	....	....	....	....	....	....	....	....	....	....	....	6	7	5	12	26	....	....	....
1990-91	Quebec	NHL	59	3	10	13	109	0	0	0	54	5.6	−19	....	....	....	....	....	....	....	....	....	....	....	....	....
	Halifax Citadels	AHL	6	4	4	8	11	....	....	....	....	....	....	....	....	....	....	....	....	....	....	....	....	....	....	....
1991-92	Quebec	NHL	75	42	31	73	183	17	0	0	190	22.1	−9	....	....	....	....	....	....	....	....	....	....	....	....	....
1992-93	Quebec	NHL	73	36	41	77	185	15	0	4	241	14.9	−1	....	....	....	....	....	5	1	0	1	2	0	0	0
1993-94	Quebec	NHL	6	2	2	4	8	0	0	0	15	13.3	2	....	....	....	....	....	....	....	....	....	....	....	....	....
1994-95	Quebec	NHL	46	30	19	49	46	13	2	8	137	21.9	21	....	....	....	....	....	6	2	3	5	6	0	0	0
1995-96	Colorado	NHL	9	4	4	8	9	4	0	0	23	17.4	−3	....	....	....	....	....	....	....	....	....	....	....	....	....
	San Jose	NHL	72	29	32	61	137	12	1	2	184	15.8	−30	....	....	....	....	....	....	....	....	....	....	....	....	....
1996-97	San Jose	NHL	72	31	32	63	155	10	0	3	225	13.8	−19	....	....	....	....	....	....	....	....	....	....	....	....	....
1997-98	San Jose	NHL	75	14	27	41	144	3	1	1	192	7.3	−2	....	....	....	....	....	6	2	2	4	26	2	0	1
1998-99	San Jose	NHL	78	19	26	45	129	6	2	3	207	9.2	16	657	49.3	174	15	19:09	6	1	1	2	6	0	0	0
99-2000	San Jose	NHL	78	44	40	84	110	18	4	6	261	16.9	−1	357	50.7	209	29	21:07	10	8	2	10	6	2	2	3
2000-01	San Jose	NHL	57	24	25	49	75	10	1	4	191	12.6	0	407	46.9	116	30	21:49	6	1	1	2	8	0	0	1
	NHL Totals		700	278	289	567	1290	108	11	31	1920	14.5		1421	49.0	499	74	20:35	39	15	9	24	54	4	2	5

OHL First All-Star Team (1990) • Played in NHL All-Star Game (1992, 1996, 1997, 2000)

• Missed majority of 1993-94 season recovering from shoulder injury suffered in game vs. Tampa Bay, November 13, 1993. Transferred to **Colorado** after **Quebec** franchise relocated, June 21, 1995. Traded to **San Jose** by **Colorado** for Sandis Ozolinsh, October 26, 1995.

			Regular Season																Playoffs							
Season	Club	League	GP	G	A	Pts	PIM	PP	SH	GW	S	%	+/-	TF	F%	H	SB	Min	GP	G	A	Pts	PIM	PP	SH	GW

NOONAN, Brian

(NOO-nuhn, BRIGH-uhn)

Right wing. Shoots right. 6'1", 200 lbs. Born, Boston, MA, May 29, 1965. Chicago's 10th choice, 186th overall, in 1983 Entry Draft.

Season	Club	League	GP	G	A	Pts	PIM	PP	SH	GW	S	%	+/-	TF	F%	H	SB	Min	GP	G	A	Pts	PIM	PP	SH	GW
1982-83	Bishop Williams	Hi-School	21	26	17	43	....	....	....	....	....	....	....	....	....	....	....	....	....	....	....	....	....	....	....	....
1983-84	Bishop Williams	Hi-School	17	14	23	37	....	....	....	....	....	....	....	....	....	....	....	....	....	....	....	....	....	....	....	....
1984-85	New Westminster	WHL	72	50	66	116	76	....	....	....	....	....	....	....	....	....	....	....	11	8	7	15	4	....	....	....
1985-86	Nova Scotia	AHL	2	0	0	0	0	....	....	....	....	....	....	....	....	....	....	....	....	....	....	....	....	....	....	....
	Saginaw Generals	IHL	76	39	39	78	69	....	....	....	....	....	....	....	....	....	....	....	11	6	3	9	6	....	....	....
1986-87	Nova Scotia	AHL	70	25	26	51	30	....	....	....	....	....	....	....	....	....	....	....	5	3	1	4	4	....	....	....
1987-88	**Chicago**	**NHL**	**77**	**10**	**20**	**30**	**44**	**3**	**0**	**2**	**87**	**11.5**	**–27**	....	....	....	....	....	**3**	**0**	**0**	**0**	**4**	**0**	**0**	**0**
1988-89	**Chicago**	**NHL**	**45**	**4**	**12**	**16**	**28**	**2**	**0**	**0**	**84**	**4.8**	**–2**	....	....	....	....	....	**1**	**0**	**0**	**0**	**0**	**0**	**0**	**0**
	Saginaw Hawks	IHL	19	18	13	31	36	....	....	....	....	....	....	....	....	....	....	....	1	0	0	0	0	....	....	....
1989-90	**Chicago**	**NHL**	**8**	**0**	**2**	**2**	**6**	**0**	**0**	**0**	**13**	**0.0**	**0**	....	....	....	....	....	....	....	....	....	....	....	....	....
	Indianapolis Ice	IHL	56	40	36	76	85	....	....	....	....	....	....	....	....	....	....	....	14	6	9	15	20	....	....	....
1990-91	**Chicago**	**NHL**	**7**	**0**	**4**	**4**	**2**	**0**	**0**	**0**	**12**	**0.0**	**–1**	....	....	....	....	....	....	....	....	....	....	....	....	....
	Indianapolis Ice	IHL	59	38	53	91	67	....	....	....	....	....	....	....	....	....	....	....	7	6	4	10	18	....	....	....
1991-92	**Chicago**	**NHL**	**65**	**19**	**12**	**31**	**81**	**4**	**0**	**0**	**154**	**12.3**	**9**	....	....	....	....	....	**18**	**6**	**9**	**15**	**30**	**3**	**0**	**1**
1992-93	**Chicago**	**NHL**	**63**	**16**	**14**	**30**	**82**	**5**	**0**	**3**	**129**	**12.4**	**3**	....	....	....	....	....	**4**	**3**	**0**	**3**	**4**	**1**	**0**	**0**
1993-94	**Chicago**	**NHL**	**64**	**14**	**21**	**35**	**57**	**8**	**0**	**3**	**134**	**10.4**	**2**	....	....	....	....	....	....	....	....	....	....	....	....	....
	♦ **NY Rangers**	**NHL**	**12**	**4**	**2**	**6**	**12**	**2**	**0**	**3**	**26**	**15.4**	**5**	....	....	....	....	....	**22**	**4**	**7**	**11**	**17**	**2**	**0**	**1**
1994-95	**NY Rangers**	**NHL**	**45**	**14**	**13**	**27**	**26**	**7**	**0**	**1**	**95**	**14.7**	**–3**	....	....	....	....	....	**5**	**0**	**0**	**0**	**8**	**0**	**0**	**0**
1995-96	**St. Louis**	**NHL**	**81**	**13**	**22**	**35**	**84**	**3**	**1**	**6**	**131**	**9.9**	**2**	....	....	....	....	....	**13**	**4**	**1**	**5**	**10**	**0**	**0**	**0**
1996-97	**St. Louis**	**NHL**	**13**	**2**	**5**	**7**	**0**	**0**	**0**	**0**	**13**	**15.4**	**2**	....	....	....	....	....	....	....	....	....	....	....	....	....
	NY Rangers	**NHL**	**44**	**6**	**9**	**15**	**28**	**3**	**0**	**1**	**62**	**9.7**	**–7**	....	....	....	....	....	....	....	....	....	....	....	....	....
	Vancouver	**NHL**	**16**	**4**	**8**	**12**	**6**	**0**	**1**	**0**	**25**	**16.0**	**2**	....	....	....	....	....	....	....	....	....	....	....	....	....
1997-98	**Vancouver**	**NHL**	**82**	**10**	**15**	**25**	**62**	**1**	**0**	**2**	**87**	**11.5**	**–19**	....	....	....	....	....	....	....	....	....	....	....	....	....
1998-99	Indianapolis Ice	IHL	65	19	44	63	128	....	....	....	....	....	....	....	....	....	....	....	....	....	....	....	....	....	....	....
	Phoenix	**NHL**	**7**	**0**	**0**	**0**	**0**	**0**	**0**	**0**	**1**	**0.0**	**–3**	**1**	**0.0**	**7**	**1**	**8:16**	**5**	**0**	**2**	**2**	**4**	**0**	**0**	**0**
99-2000	Chicago Wolves	IHL	80	30	32	62	80	....	....	....	....	....	....	....	....	....	....	....	16	4	7	11	10	....	....	....
2000-01	Chicago Wolves	IHL	82	21	32	53	103	....	....	....	....	....	....	....	....	....	....	....	16	1	6	7	38	....	....	....
	NHL Totals		**629**	**116**	**159**	**275**	**518**	**38**	**2**	**21**	**1053**	**11.0**		**1**	**0.0**	**7**	**1**	**8:16**	**71**	**17**	**19**	**36**	**77**	**6**	**0**	**2**

IHL Second All-Star Team (1990) • IHL First All-Star Team (1991)

Traded to **NY Rangers** by **Chicago** with Stephane Matteau for Tony Amonte and the rights to Matt Oates, March 21, 1994. Signed as a free agent by **St. Louis**, July 24, 1995. Traded to **NY Rangers** by **St. Louis** for Sergio Momesso, November 13, 1996. Traded to **Vancouver** by **NY Rangers** with Sergei Nemchinov for Esa Tikkanen and Russ Courtnall, March 8, 1997. Signed as a free agent by **Phoenix**, March 17, 1999. Signed as a free agent by **Chicago Wolves** (IHL), September 14, 1999.

NORDSTROM, Peter

(NOHRD-struhm, PEE-tuhr) **BOS.**

Center. Shoots left. 6'1", 200 lbs. Born, Munkfors, Sweden, July 26, 1974. Boston's 3rd choice, 78th overall, in 1998 Entry Draft.

Season	Club	League	GP	G	A	Pts	PIM	PP	SH	GW	S	%	+/-	TF	F%	H	SB	Min	GP	G	A	Pts	PIM	PP	SH	GW
1989-90	IFK Munkfors	Sweden-3	21	2	1	3	8	....	....	....	....	....	....	....	....	....	....	....	....	....	....	....	....	....	....	....
1990-91	IFK Munkfors	Sweden-3	32	10	18	28	20	....	....	....	....	....	....	....	....	....	....	....	....	....	....	....	....	....	....	....
1991-92	IFK Munkfors	Sweden-3	31	12	20	32	42	....	....	....	....	....	....	....	....	....	....	....	....	....	....	....	....	....	....	....
1992-93	IFK Munkfors	Sweden-3	35	19	11	30	44	....	....	....	....	....	....	....	....	....	....	....	....	....	....	....	....	....	....	....
1993-94	IFK Munkfors	Sweden-3	31	17	26	43	87	....	....	....	....	....	....	....	....	....	....	....	....	....	....	....	....	....	....	....
1994-95	IFK Munkfors	Sweden-2	21	8	17	25	30	....	....	....	....	....	....	....	....	....	....	....	....	....	....	....	....	....	....	....
	Leksands IF	Sweden	13	1	0	1	0	....	....	....	....	....	....	....	....	....	....	....	....	....	....	....	....	....	....	....
1995-96	Farjestads BK	Sweden	40	6	5	11	36	....	....	....	....	....	....	....	....	....	....	....	8	0	3	3	12	....	....	....
1996-97	Farjestads BK	Sweden	44	9	5	14	32	....	....	....	....	....	....	....	....	....	....	....	14	1	2	3	6	....	....	....
1997-98	Farjestads BK	Sweden	45	6	19	25	46	....	....	....	....	....	....	....	....	....	....	....	12	5	7	*12	8	....	....	....
1998-99	Farjestads BK	Sweden	21	4	4	8	14	....	....	....	....	....	....	....	....	....	....	....	4	1	1	2	2	....	....	....
	Farjestads BK	EuroHL	2	1	0	1	2	....	....	....	....	....	....	....	....	....	....	....	....	....	....	....	....	....	....	....
	Boston	**NHL**	**2**	**0**	**0**	**0**	**0**	**0**	**0**	**0**	**0**	**0.0**	**–1**	**0**	**0.0**	**1**	**0**	**8:04**	....	....	....	....	....	....	....	....
	Providence Bruins	AHL	13	2	1	3	2	....	....	....	....	....	....	....	....	....	....	....	....	....	....	....	....	....	....	....
99-2000	Farjestads BK	Sweden	45	8	14	22	48	....	....	....	....	....	....	....	....	....	....	....	7	0	3	3	2	....	....	....
2000-01	Farjestads BK	Sweden	49	7	15	22	59	....	....	....	....	....	....	....	....	....	....	....	16	2	6	8	30	....	....	....
	NHL Totals		**2**	**0**	**0**	**0**	**0**	**0**	**0**	**0**	**0**	**0.0**		**0**	**0.0**	**1**	**0**	**8:04**	....	....	....	....	....	....	....	....

NORSTROM, Mattias

(NOHR-struhm, MAT-tee-ahs) **L.A.**

Defense. Shoots left. 6'2", 201 lbs. Born, Stockholm, Sweden, January 2, 1972. NY Rangers' 2nd choice, 48th overall, in 1992 Entry Draft.

Season	Club	League	GP	G	A	Pts	PIM	PP	SH	GW	S	%	+/-	TF	F%	H	SB	Min	GP	G	A	Pts	PIM	PP	SH	GW
1990-91	Mora IK	Sweden-2	9	1	1	2	6	....	....	....	....	....	....	....	....	....	....	....	1	0	0	0	2	....	....	....
1991-92	AIK Solna	Sweden	39	4	3	7	28	....	....	....	....	....	....	....	....	....	....	....	3	0	2	2	2	....	....	....
1992-93	AIK Solna	Sweden	22	0	1	1	16	....	....	....	....	....	....	....	....	....	....	....	....	....	....	....	....	....	....	....
1993-94	**NY Rangers**	**NHL**	**9**	**0**	**2**	**2**	**6**	**0**	**0**	**0**	**3**	**0.0**	**0**	....	....	....	....	....	....	....	....	....	....	....	....	....
	Binghamton	AHL	55	1	9	10	70	....	....	....	....	....	....	....	....	....	....	....	....	....	....	....	....	....	....	....
1994-95	Binghamton	AHL	63	9	10	19	91	....	....	....	....	....	....	....	....	....	....	....	....	....	....	....	....	....	....	....
	NY Rangers	**NHL**	**9**	**0**	**3**	**3**	**2**	**0**	**0**	**0**	**4**	**0.0**	**2**	....	....	....	....	....	**3**	**0**	**0**	**0**	**0**	**0**	**0**	**0**
1995-96	**NY Rangers**	**NHL**	**25**	**2**	**1**	**3**	**22**	**0**	**0**	**0**	**17**	**11.8**	**5**	....	....	....	....	....	....	....	....	....	....	....	....	....
	Los Angeles	**NHL**	**11**	**0**	**1**	**1**	**18**	**0**	**0**	**0**	**17**	**0.0**	**–8**	....	....	....	....	....	....	....	....	....	....	....	....	....
1996-97	**Los Angeles**	**NHL**	**80**	**1**	**21**	**22**	**84**	**0**	**0**	**0**	**106**	**0.9**	**–4**	....	....	....	....	....	....	....	....	....	....	....	....	....
1997-98	**Los Angeles**	**NHL**	**73**	**1**	**12**	**13**	**90**	**0**	**0**	**0**	**61**	**1.6**	**14**	....	....	....	....	....	**4**	**0**	**0**	**0**	**2**	**0**	**0**	**0**
	Sweden	Olympics	4	0	1	1	2	....	....	....	....	....	....	....	....	....	....	....	....	....	....	....	....	....	....	....
1998-99	**Los Angeles**	**NHL**	**78**	**2**	**5**	**7**	**36**	**0**	**1**	**0**	**61**	**3.3**	**–10**	**1**	**0.0**	**236**	**157**	**20:20**	....	....	....	....	....	....	....	....
99-2000	**Los Angeles**	**NHL**	**82**	**1**	**13**	**14**	**66**	**0**	**0**	**0**	**62**	**1.6**	**22**	**0**	**0.0**	**261**	**127**	**21:49**	**4**	**0**	**0**	**0**	**6**	**0**	**0**	**0**
2000-01	**Los Angeles**	**NHL**	**82**	**0**	**18**	**18**	**60**	**0**	**0**	**0**	**59**	**0.0**	**10**	**2**	**0.0**	**249**	**137**	**21:50**	**13**	**0**	**2**	**2**	**18**	**0**	**0**	**0**
	NHL Totals		**449**	**7**	**76**	**83**	**384**	**0**	**1**	**0**	**390**	**1.8**		**3**	**0.0**	**746**	**421**	**21:20**	**24**	**0**	**2**	**2**	**26**	**0**	**0**	**0**

Played in NHL All-Star Game (1999)

Traded to **LA Kings** by **NY Rangers** with Ray Ferraro, Ian Laperriere, Nathan Lafayette and NY Rangers' 4th round choice (Sean Blanchard) in 1997 Entry Draft for Marty McSorley, Jari Kurri and Shane Churla, March 14, 1996.

NORTON, Jeff

(NOHR-tohn, JEHF) **FLA.**

Defense. Shoots left. 6'2", 195 lbs. Born, Acton, MA, November 25, 1965. NY Islanders' 3rd choice, 62nd overall, in 1984 Entry Draft.

Season	Club	League	GP	G	A	Pts	PIM	PP	SH	GW	S	%	+/-	TF	F%	H	SB	Min	GP	G	A	Pts	PIM	PP	SH	GW
1983-84	Cushing Penguins	Hi-School	21	22	33	55	....	....	....	....	....	....	....	....	....	....	....	....	....	....	....	....	....	....	....	....
1984-85	U. of Michigan	CCHA	37	8	16	24	103	....	....	....	....	....	....	....	....	....	....	....	....	....	....	....	....	....	....	....
1985-86	U. of Michigan	CCHA	37	15	30	45	99	....	....	....	....	....	....	....	....	....	....	....	....	....	....	....	....	....	....	....
1986-87	U. of Michigan	CCHA	39	12	36	48	92	....	....	....	....	....	....	....	....	....	....	....	....	....	....	....	....	....	....	....
1987-88	United States	Nat-Team	54	7	22	29	52	....	....	....	....	....	....	....	....	....	....	....	....	....	....	....	....	....	....	....
	United States	Olympics	6	0	4	4	4	....	....	....	....	....	....	....	....	....	....	....	....	....	....	....	....	....	....	....
	NY Islanders	**NHL**	**15**	**1**	**6**	**7**	**14**	**1**	**0**	**1**	**18**	**5.6**	**3**	....	....	....	....	....	**3**	**0**	**2**	**2**	**13**	**0**	**0**	**0**
1988-89	**NY Islanders**	**NHL**	**69**	**1**	**30**	**31**	**74**	**1**	**0**	**0**	**126**	**0.8**	**–24**	....	....	....	....	....	....	....	....	....	....	....	....	....
1989-90	**NY Islanders**	**NHL**	**60**	**4**	**49**	**53**	**65**	**4**	**0**	**0**	**104**	**3.8**	**–9**	....	....	....	....	....	**4**	**1**	**3**	**4**	**17**	**0**	**0**	**0**
1990-91	**NY Islanders**	**NHL**	**44**	**3**	**25**	**28**	**16**	**2**	**1**	**0**	**87**	**3.4**	**–13**	....	....	....	....	....	....	....	....	....	....	....	....	....
1991-92	**NY Islanders**	**NHL**	**28**	**1**	**18**	**19**	**18**	**0**	**1**	**0**	**34**	**2.9**	**2**	....	....	....	....	....	....	....	....	....	....	....	....	....
1992-93	**NY Islanders**	**NHL**	**66**	**12**	**38**	**50**	**45**	**5**	**0**	**0**	**127**	**9.4**	**–3**	....	....	....	....	....	**10**	**1**	**1**	**2**	**4**	**0**	**0**	**0**
1993-94	**San Jose**	**NHL**	**64**	**7**	**33**	**40**	**36**	**1**	**0**	**0**	**92**	**7.6**	**16**	....	....	....	....	....	**14**	**1**	**5**	**6**	**20**	**0**	**0**	**0**
1994-95	**San Jose**	**NHL**	**20**	**1**	**9**	**10**	**39**	**0**	**0**	**0**	**21**	**4.8**	**1**	....	....	....	....	....	....	....	....	....	....	....	....	....
	St. Louis	**NHL**	**28**	**2**	**18**	**20**	**33**	**0**	**0**	**1**	**27**	**7.4**	**21**	....	....	....	....	....	**7**	**1**	**1**	**2**	**11**	**0**	**0**	**0**
1995-96	**St. Louis**	**NHL**	**36**	**4**	**7**	**11**	**26**	**0**	**0**	**1**	**33**	**12.1**	**4**	....	....	....	....	....	....	....	....	....	....	....	....	....
	Edmonton	**NHL**	**30**	**4**	**16**	**20**	**16**	**1**	**0**	**1**	**52**	**7.7**	**5**	....	....	....	....	....	....	....	....	....	....	....	....	....
1996-97	**Edmonton**	**NHL**	**62**	**2**	**11**	**13**	**42**	**1**	**0**	**0**	**68**	**2.9**	**–7**	....	....	....	....	....	....	....	....	....	....	....	....	....
	Tampa Bay	**NHL**	**13**	**0**	**5**	**5**	**16**	**0**	**0**	**0**	**13**	**0.0**	**0**	....	....	....	....	....	....	....	....	....	....	....	....	....
1997-98	**Tampa Bay**	**NHL**	**37**	**4**	**6**	**10**	**26**	**4**	**0**	**0**	**41**	**9.8**	**–25**	....	....	....	....	....	....	....	....	....	....	....	....	....
	Florida	**NHL**	**19**	**0**	**7**	**7**	**18**	**0**	**0**	**0**	**20**	**0.0**	**–7**	....	....	....	....	....	....	....	....	....	....	....	....	....
1998-99	**Florida**	**NHL**	**3**	**0**	**0**	**0**	**2**	**0**	**0**	**0**	**2**	**0.0**	**0**	**0**	**0.0**	**1**	**3**	**17:26**	....	....	....	....	....	....	....	....
	San Jose	**NHL**	**69**	**4**	**18**	**22**	**42**	**2**	**0**	**1**	**68**	**5.9**	**2**	**0**	**0.0**	**37**	**86**	**20:55**	**6**	**0**	**7**	**7**	**10**	**0**	**0**	**0**
99-2000	**San Jose**	**NHL**	**62**	**0**	**20**	**20**	**49**	**0**	**0**	**0**	**45**	**0.0**	**–2**	**0**	**0.0**	**29**	**74**	**19:32**	**12**	**0**	**1**	**1**	**7**	**0**	**0**	**0**

			Regular Season																Playoffs							
Season	Club	League	GP	G	A	Pts	PIM	PP	SH	GW	S	%	+/-	TF	F%	H	SB	Min	GP	G	A	Pts	PIM	PP	SH	GW
2000-01	**Pittsburgh**	**NHL**	**32**	**2**	**10**	**12**	**20**	**1**	**0**	**1**	**17**	**11.8**	**8**	**0**	**0.0**	**12**	**51**	**18:30**								
	San Jose	**NHL**	**10**	**0**	**1**	**1**	**8**	**0**	**0**	**0**	**5**	**0.0**	**4**	**0**	**0.0**	**5**	**14**	**19:18**	**6**	**0**	**1**	**1**	**2**	**0**	**0**	**0**
	NHL Totals		**767**	**52**	**327**	**379**	**605**	**22**	**2**	**6**	**1000**	**5.2**		**0**	**0.0**	**84**	**228**	**19:50**	**62**	**4**	**21**	**25**	**84**	**0**	**0**	**0**

CCHA Second All-Star Team (1987)

• Missed majority of 1991-92 season recovering from wrist injury suffered in game vs. Buffalo, January 3, 1992. Traded to **San Jose** by **NY Islanders** for San Jose's 3rd round choice (Jason Strudwick) in 1994 Entry Draft, June 20, 1993. Traded to **St. Louis** by **San Jose** with San Jose's 3rd round choice (later traded to Colorado - Colorado selected Rick Berry) in 1997 Entry Draft for Craig Janney and cash, March 6, 1995. Traded to **Edmonton** by **St. Louis** with Donald Dufresne for Igor Kravchuk and Ken Sutton, January 4, 1996. Traded to **Tampa Bay** by **Edmonton** for Drew Bannister and Tampa Bay's 6th round choice (Peter Sarno) in 1997 Entry Draft, March 18, 1997. Traded to **Florida** by **Tampa Bay** with Dino Ciccarelli for Mark Fitzpatrick and Jody Hull, January 15, 1998. Traded to **San Jose** by **Florida** for Alex Hicks and San Jose's 5th round choice (later traded to NY Islanders - NY Islanders selected Adam Johnson) in 1999 Entry Draft, November 11, 1998. Signed as a free agent by **Pittsburgh**, November 14, 2000. Traded to **San Jose** by **Pittsburgh** for Bobby Dollas and Johan Hedberg, March 12, 2001. Signed as a free agent by **Florida**, July 18, 2001.

NOVOSELTSEV, Ivan

(noh-voh-SEHLT-sehv, ee-VAHN) **FLA.**

Left wing. Shoots left. 6'1", 202 lbs. Born, Golitsino, USSR, January 23, 1979. Florida's 5th choice, 95th overall, in 1997 Entry Draft.

Season	Club	League	GP	G	A	Pts	PIM	PP	SH	GW	S	%	+/-	TF	F%	H	SB	Min	GP	G	A	Pts	PIM	PP	SH	GW
1995-96	Krylja Sovetov	CIS	1	0	0	0	2																			
1996-97	Krylja Sovetov	Russia-3	19	5	3	8	39																			
	Krylja Sovetov	Russia	30	0	3	3	18												2	0	0	0	4			
1997-98	Sarnia Sting	OHL	53	26	22	48	41												5	1	1	2	8			
1998-99	Sarnia Sting	OHL	68	57	39	96	45												5	2	4	6	6			
99-2000	**Florida**	**NHL**	**14**	**2**	**1**	**3**	**8**	**2**	**0**	**0**	**8**	**25.0**	**–3**	**1**	**100.0**	**3**	**3**	**10:29**								
	Louisville Panthers	AHL	47	14	21	35	22												4	1	0	1	6			
2000-01	**Florida**	**NHL**	**38**	**3**	**6**	**9**	**16**	**0**	**0**	**0**	**34**	**8.8**	**–5**	**1**	**0.0**	**27**	**4**	**10:44**								
	Louisville Panthers	AHL	34	2	10	12	8																			
	NHL Totals		**52**	**5**	**7**	**12**	**24**	**2**	**0**	**0**	**42**	**11.9**		**2**	**50.0**	**30**	**7**	**10:40**								

OHL First All-Star Team (1999)

NUMMELIN, Petteri

(NOO-muh-lihn, PEH-tuh-ree) **CBJ**

Defense. Shoots left. 5'10", 196 lbs. Born, Turku, Finland, November 25, 1972. Columbus' 3rd choice, 133rd overall, in 2000 Entry Draft.

Season	Club	League	GP	G	A	Pts	PIM	PP	SH	GW	S	%	+/-	TF	F%	H	SB	Min	GP	G	A	Pts	PIM	PP	SH	GW
1988-89	TPS Turku	Finn-Jr.	11	2	3	5	2																			
1989-90	TPS Turku	Finn-Jr.	33	6	14	20	45																			
1990-91	TPS Turku	Finn-Jr.	35	20	16	36	28																			
	Kiekko-67	Finland-2	2	0	2	2	4																			
1991-92	Kiekko-67	FinnJr.	13	16	15	31	28																			
	Kiekko-67	Finland-2	41	12	24	36	36																			
1992-93	TPS Turku	Finn-Jr.	1	1	0	1	0																			
	TPS Turku	Finland	3	0	0	0	8																			
	Reipas Lahti	Finland	20	5	8	13	20																			
	Kiekko-67	Finland-2	28	14	15	29	18																			
1993-94	TPS Turku	Finland	44	14	24	38	20												11	0	3	3	4			
1994-95	TPS Turku	Finland	48	10	17	27	32												11	4	3	7	0			
1995-96	Vastra Frolunda	Sweden	32	7	11	18	26												12	2	7	9	4			
1996-97	Vastra Frolunda	Sweden	44	20	14	34	39												2	0	1	1	0			
1997-98	HC Davos	Switz.	33	13	17	30	24												17	8	14	22	2			
1998-99	HC Davos	Switz.	44	11	42	53	22												4	0	2	2	2			
99-2000	HC Davos	Switz.	40	15	23	38	20												5	0	3	3	0			
2000-01	**Columbus**	**NHL**	**61**	**4**	**12**	**16**	**10**	**2**	**0**	**0**	**99**	**4.0**	**–11**	**1**	**0.0**	**14**	**39**	**17:14**								
	NHL Totals		**61**	**4**	**12**	**16**	**10**	**2**	**0**	**0**	**99**	**4.0**		**1**	**0.0**	**14**	**39**	**17:14**								

NUMMINEN, Teppo

(NOO-mih-nehn, TEH-poh) **PHX.**

Defense. Shoots right. 6'2", 199 lbs. Born, Tampere, Finland, July 3, 1968. Winnipeg's 2nd choice, 29th overall, in 1986 Entry Draft.

Season	Club	League	GP	G	A	Pts	PIM	PP	SH	GW	S	%	+/-	TF	F%	H	SB	Min	GP	G	A	Pts	PIM	PP	SH	GW
1984-85	Tappara Tampere	Finn-Jr.	30	14	17	31	10																			
	Whitby Lawmen	OPJHL	16	3	9	12	0																			
1985-86	Tappara Tampere	Finn-Jr.	2	0	0	0	0												3	0	1	1	2			
	Tappara Tampere	Finland	31	2	4	6	6												8	0	0	0	0			
1986-87	Tappara Tampere	Finland	44	9	9	18	16												9	4	1	5	4			
1987-88	Tappara Tampere	Finland	40	10	10	20	29												10	6	6	12	6			
	Finland	Olympics	6	1	4	5	0																			
1988-89	**Winnipeg**	**NHL**	**69**	**1**	**14**	**15**	**36**	**0**	**1**	**0**	**85**	**1.2**	**–11**													
1989-90	**Winnipeg**	**NHL**	**79**	**11**	**32**	**43**	**20**	**1**	**0**	**1**	**105**	**10.5**	**–4**						**7**	**1**	**2**	**3**	**10**	**0**	**0**	**0**
1990-91	**Winnipeg**	**NHL**	**80**	**8**	**25**	**33**	**28**	**3**	**0**	**1**	**151**	**5.3**	**–15**													
1991-92	**Winnipeg**	**NHL**	**80**	**5**	**34**	**39**	**32**	**4**	**0**	**1**	**143**	**3.5**	**15**						**7**	**0**	**0**	**0**	**0**	**0**	**0**	**0**
1992-93	**Winnipeg**	**NHL**	**66**	**7**	**30**	**37**	**33**	**3**	**1**	**0**	**103**	**6.8**	**4**						**6**	**1**	**1**	**2**	**2**	**1**	**0**	**0**
1993-94	**Winnipeg**	**NHL**	**57**	**5**	**18**	**23**	**28**	**4**	**0**	**1**	**89**	**5.6**	**–23**													
1994-95	TuTo Turku	Finland	12	3	8	11	4																			
	Winnipeg	**NHL**	**42**	**5**	**16**	**21**	**16**	**2**	**0**	**0**	**86**	**5.8**	**12**													
1995-96	**Winnipeg**	**NHL**	**74**	**11**	**43**	**54**	**22**	**6**	**0**	**3**	**165**	**6.7**	**–4**						**6**	**0**	**0**	**0**	**2**	**0**	**0**	**0**
1996-97	**Phoenix**	**NHL**	**82**	**2**	**25**	**27**	**28**	**0**	**0**	**0**	**135**	**1.5**	**–3**						**7**	**3**	**3**	**6**	**0**	**1**	**0**	**1**
1997-98	**Phoenix**	**NHL**	**82**	**11**	**40**	**51**	**30**	**6**	**0**	**2**	**126**	**8.7**	**25**						**1**	**0**	**0**	**0**	**0**	**0**	**0**	**0**
	Finland	Olympics	6	1	1	2	2																			
1998-99	**Phoenix**	**NHL**	**82**	**10**	**30**	**40**	**30**	**1**	**0**	**0**	**156**	**6.4**	**3**	**2**	**0.0**	**73**	**99**	**24:26**	**7**	**2**	**1**	**3**	**4**	**2**	**0**	**0**
99-2000	**Phoenix**	**NHL**	**79**	**8**	**34**	**42**	**16**	**2**	**0**	**2**	**126**	**6.3**	**21**	**1**	**0.0**	**75**	**96**	**23:37**	**5**	**1**	**1**	**2**	**0**	**0**	**0**	**0**
2000-01	**Phoenix**	**NHL**	**72**	**5**	**26**	**31**	**36**	**1**	**0**	**2**	**109**	**4.6**	**9**	**0**	**0.0**	**42**	**102**	**24:28**								
	NHL Totals		**944**	**89**	**367**	**456**	**355**	**33**	**2**	**12**	**1579**	**5.6**		**3**	**0.0**	**190**	**297**	**24:10**	**46**	**8**	**8**	**16**	**18**	**4**	**0**	**1**

Played in NHL All-Star Game (1999, 2000, 2001)

Transferred to **Phoenix** after **Winnipeg** franchise relocated, July 1, 1996.

NURMINEN, Kai

(NUHR-mih-nehn, KIGH)

Left wing. Shoots left. 6'1", 190 lbs. Born, Turku, Finland, March 29, 1969. Los Angeles' 9th choice, 193rd overall, in 1996 Entry Draft.

Season	Club	League	GP	G	A	Pts	PIM	PP	SH	GW	S	%	+/-	TF	F%	H	SB	Min	GP	G	A	Pts	PIM	PP	SH	GW
1986-87	TPS Turku	Finn-Jr.	2	0	1	1	0																			
1987-88	TPS Turku	Finn-Jr.	32	9	7	16	16																			
1988-89	TPS Turku	Finn-Jr.	22	13	10	23	14																			
1989-90	TPS Turku	Finn-Jr.	22	13	10	23	14																			
1990-91	TuTo Turku	Finland-2	33	26	20	46	14																			
1991-92	Kiekko-67 Turku	Finland-2	44	44	19	63	34																			
1992-93	Kiekko-67 Turku	Finland-2	8	6	4	10	2																			
	TPS Turku	Finland	31	4	6	10	13												7	1	2	3	0			
1993-94	TPS Turku	Finland	45	23	12	35	20												11	0	3	3	4			
1994-95	HPK Hameenlinna	Finland	49	*30	25	55	40																			
1995-96	HV Jonkoping	Sweden	40	31	24	55	30												4	3	1	4	8			
1996-97	**Los Angeles**	**NHL**	**67**	**16**	**11**	**27**	**22**	**4**	**0**	**1**	**112**	**14.3**	**–3**													
1997-98	Vasteras Frolunda	Sweden	23	9	7	16	24																			
	Jokerit Helsinki	Finland	20	7	9	16	30												8	5	3	8	4			
1998-99	HC Davos	Switz.	42	26	14	40	26																			
99-2000	TPS Turku	Finland	54	*41	37	*78	40												10	5	*9	*14	0			
2000-01	**Minnesota**	**NHL**	**2**	**1**	**0**	**1**	**2**	**0**	**0**	**0**	**1**	**100.0**	**–1**	**0**	**0.0**	**1**	**0**	**15:34**								
	Cleveland	IHL	74	28	46	74	34												1	0	0	0	0			
	NHL Totals		**69**	**17**	**11**	**28**	**24**	**4**	**0**	**1**	**113**	**15.0**		**0**	**0.0**	**1**	**0**	**15:34**								

Signed as a free agent by **Minnesota**, May 24, 2000.

NYLANDER, Michael

(NEE-lan-duhr, mihk-AIL) **CHI.**

Center. Shoots left. 6'1", 195 lbs. Born, Stockholm, Sweden, October 3, 1972. Hartford's 4th choice, 59th overall, in 1991 Entry Draft.

			Regular Season																Playoffs							
Season	Club	League	GP	G	A	Pts	PIM	PP	SH	GW	S	%	+/-	TF	F%	H	SB	Min	GP	G	A	Pts	PIM	PP	SH	GW
1989-90	Huddinge IK	Sweden-2	31	7	15	22	4												5	3	0	3	0			
1990-91	Huddinge IK	Sweden-2	33	14	20	34	10												2	0	0	0	0			
1991-92	AIK Solna	Sweden	40	11	17	28	30												3	1	4	5	4			
1992-93	Hartford	NHL	59	11	22	33	36	3	0	1	85	12.9	–7													
	Springfield	AHL																	3	3	3	6	2			
1993-94	Hartford	NHL	58	11	33	44	24	4	0	1	74	14.9	–2													
	Springfield	AHL	4	0	9	9	0																			
	Calgary	NHL	15	2	9	11	6	0	0	0	21	9.5	10						3	0	0	0	0	0	0	0
1994-95	JyP Jyvaskyla	Finland	16	11	19	30	63																			
	Calgary	NHL	6	0	1	1	2	0	0	0	2	0.0	1						6	0	6	6	2	0	0	0
1995-96	Calgary	NHL	73	17	38	55	20	4	0	6	163	10.4	0						4	0	0	0	0	0	0	0
1996-97	HC Lugano	Switz.	36	12	43	55	28												8	3	8	11	8			
1997-98	Calgary	NHL	65	13	23	36	24	0	0	2	117	11.1	10													
	Sweden	Olympics	4	0	0	0	6																			
1998-99	Calgary	NHL	9	2	3	5	2	1	0	0	7	28.6	1	25	60.0	1	0	11:10								
	Tampa Bay	NHL	24	2	7	9	6	0	0	0	26	7.7	–10	75	44.0	4	6	13:29								
99-2000	Tampa Bay	NHL	11	1	2	3	4	1	0	0	10	10.0	–3	35	57.1	0	0	10:32								
	Chicago	NHL	66	23	28	51	26	4	0	2	112	20.5	9	561	46.9	9	11	16:39								
2000-01	Chicago	NHL	82	25	39	64	32	4	0	5	176	14.2	7	1036	48.3	12	22	18:52								
	NHL Totals		468	107	205	312	182	21	0	17	793	13.5		1732	48.0	26	39	16:35	13	0	6	6	2	0	0	0

Traded to **Calgary** by **Hartford** with James Patrick and Zarley Zalapski for Gary Suter, Paul Ranheim and Ted Drury, March 10, 1994. • Missed majority of 1994-95 season recovering from wrist injury suffered in game vs. St. Louis, January 24, 1995. Traded to **Tampa Bay** by **Calgary** for Andrei Nazarov, January 19, 1999. Traded to **Chicago** by **Tampa Bay** for Bryan Muir and Reid Simpson, November 12, 1999.

OATES, Adam

(OHTS, A-duhm) **WSH.**

Center. Shoots right. 5'11", 188 lbs. Born, Weston, Ont., August 27, 1962.

			Regular Season																Playoffs							
Season	Club	League	GP	G	A	Pts	PIM	PP	SH	GW	S	%	+/-	TF	F%	H	SB	Min	GP	G	A	Pts	PIM	PP	SH	GW
1979-80	Port Credit Titans	OHA-B	34	30	36	66	41																			
	Markham Waxers	MTJHL	9	1	6	7	2																			
1980-81	Markham Waxers	MTJHL	43	36	53	89	89																			
1981-82	Markham Waxers	MTJHL	40	59	110	169																				
1982-83	RPI Engineers	ECAC	22	9	33	42	8																			
1983-84	RPI Engineers	ECAC	38	26	57	83	15																			
1984-85	RPI Engineers	ECAC	38	31	60	91	29																			
1985-86	Detroit	NHL	38	9	11	20	10	1	0	1	49	18.4	–24													
	Adirondack	AHL	34	18	28	46	4												17	7	14	21	4			
1986-87	Detroit	NHL	76	15	32	47	21	4	0	1	138	10.9	0						16	4	7	11	6	0	0	1
1987-88	Detroit	NHL	63	14	40	54	20	3	0	3	111	12.6	16						16	8	12	20	6	4	0	1
1988-89	Detroit	NHL	69	16	62	78	14	2	0	1	127	12.6	–1						6	0	8	8	2	0	0	0
1989-90	St. Louis	NHL	80	23	79	102	30	6	2	3	168	13.7	9						12	2	12	14	4	1	0	0
1990-91	St. Louis	NHL	61	25	90	115	29	3	1	3	139	18.0	15						13	7	13	20	10	2	0	1
1991-92	St. Louis	NHL	54	10	59	69	12	3	0	3	118	8.5	–4													
	Boston	NHL	26	10	20	30	10	3	0	1	73	13.7	–5						15	5	14	19	4	3	0	2
1992-93	Boston	NHL	84	45	*97	142	32	24	1	11	254	17.7	15						4	0	9	9	4	0	0	0
1993-94	Boston	NHL	77	32	80	112	45	16	2	3	197	16.2	10						13	3	9	12	8	2	0	0
1994-95	Boston	NHL	48	12	41	53	8	4	1	2	109	11.0	–11						5	1	0	1	2	1	0	0
1995-96	Boston	NHL	70	25	67	92	18	7	1	2	183	13.7	16						5	2	5	7	2	0	1	0
1996-97	Boston	NHL	63	18	52	70	10	2	2	4	138	13.0	–3													
	Washington	NHL	17	4	8	12	4	1	0	1	22	18.2	–2													
1997-98	Washington	NHL	82	18	58	76	36	3	2	3	121	14.9	6						21	6	11	17	8	1	1	1
1998-99	Washington	NHL	59	12	42	54	22	3	0	0	79	15.2	–1	1330	59.2	17	22	20:34								
99-2000	Washington	NHL	82	15	56	71	14	5	0	6	93	16.1	13	2176	56.8	19	45	22:20	5	0	3	3	4	0	0	0
2000-01	Washington	NHL	81	13	*69	82	28	5	0	4	72	18.1	–9	1836	58.9	16	49	20:60	6	0	0	0	0	0	0	0
	NHL Totals		1130	316	963	1279	363	95	12	52	2191	14.4		5342	58.1	52	116	21:23	137	38	103	141	60	14	2	6

ECAC Second All-Star Team (1984) • NCAA East First All-American Team (1984, 1985) • ECAC First All-Star Team (1985) • NCAA Championship All-Tournament Team (1985) • NHL Second All-Star Team (1991) • Played in NHL All-Star Game (1991, 1992, 1993, 1994, 1997)

Signed as a free agent by **Detroit,** June 28, 1985. Traded to **St. Louis** by **Detroit** with Paul MacLean for Bernie Federko and Tony McKegney, June 15, 1989. Traded to **Boston** by **St. Louis** for Craig Janney and Stephane Quintal, February 7, 1992. Traded to **Washington** by **Boston** with Bill Ranford and Rick Tocchet for Jim Carey, Anson Carter, Jason Allison and Washington's 3rd round choice (Lee Goren) in 1997 Entry Draft, March 1, 1997.

OBSUT, Jaroslav

(OHB-suht, YAHR-oh-slahv) **COL.**

Defense. Shoots left. 6'1", 200 lbs. Born, Presov, Czech., September 3, 1976. Winnipeg's 9th choice, 188th overall, in 1995 Entry Draft.

			Regular Season																Playoffs							
Season	Club	League	GP	G	A	Pts	PIM	PP	SH	GW	S	%	+/-	TF	F%	H	SB	Min	GP	G	A	Pts	PIM	PP	SH	GW
1994-95	North Battleford	SJHL	55	21	30	51	126																			
1995-96	Swift Current	WHL	72	10	11	21	57												6	0	0	0	2			
1996-97	Edmonton Ice	WHL	13	2	9	11	4																			
	Medicine Hat	WHL	50	8	26	34	42												4	0	2	2	2			
	Toledo Storm	ECHL	3	1	0	1	0												5	0	1	1	6			
1997-98	Raleigh Icecaps	ECHL	60	6	26	32	46																			
	Syracuse Crunch	AHL	4	0	1	1	4																			
1998-99	Augusta Lynx	ECHL	41	11	25	36	42																			
	Manitoba Moose	IHL	2	0	0	0	0																			
	Worcester	AHL	31	2	8	10	14												4	0	1	1	2			
99-2000	Worcester	AHL	7	0	2	2	4																			
2000-01	St. Louis	NHL	4	0	0	0	2	0	0	0	3	0.0	1	0	0.0	6	4	18:31								
	Peoria Rivermen	ECHL	3	0	4	4	2																			
	Worcester	AHL	47	9	12	21	20												7	0	1	1	4			
	NHL Totals		4	0	0	0	2	0	0	0	3	0.0		0	0.0	6	4	18:31								

Signed as a free agent by **St. Louis**, April 26, 1999. • Missed majority of 1999-2000 season recovering from knee injury suffered in practice, October, 1999. Signed as a free agent by **Colorado**, August 11, 2001.

ODELEIN, Lyle

(OH-duh-LIGHN, LIGHL) **CBJ**

Defense. Shoots right. 5'11", 210 lbs. Born, Quill Lake, Sask., July 21, 1968. Montreal's 8th choice, 141st overall, in 1986 Entry Draft.

			Regular Season																Playoffs							
Season	Club	League	GP	G	A	Pts	PIM	PP	SH	GW	S	%	+/-	TF	F%	H	SB	Min	GP	G	A	Pts	PIM	PP	SH	GW
1984-85	Regina Canucks	AMHL	26	12	13	25	30																			
1985-86	Moose Jaw	WHL	67	9	37	46	117												13	1	6	7	34			
1986-87	Moose Jaw	WHL	59	9	50	59	70												9	2	5	7	26			
1987-88	Moose Jaw	WHL	63	15	43	58	166																			
1988-89	Sherbrooke	AHL	33	3	4	7	120												3	0	2	2	5			
	Peoria Rivermen	IHL	36	2	8	10	116																			
1989-90	Montreal	NHL	8	0	2	2	33	0	0	0	1	0.0	–1													
	Sherbrooke	AHL	68	7	24	31	265												12	6	5	11	79			
1990-91	Montreal	NHL	52	0	2	2	259	0	0	0	25	0.0	7						12	0	0	0	54	0	0	0
1991-92	Montreal	NHL	71	1	7	8	212	0	0	0	43	2.3	15						7	0	0	0	11	0	0	0
1992-93♦	Montreal	NHL	83	2	14	16	205	0	0	0	79	2.5	35						20	1	5	6	30	0	0	0
1993-94	Montreal	NHL	79	11	29	40	276	6	0	2	116	9.5	8						7	0	0	0	17	0	0	0
1994-95	Montreal	NHL	48	3	7	10	152	0	0	0	74	4.1	–13													
1995-96	Montreal	NHL	79	3	14	17	230	0	1	0	74	4.1	8						6	1	1	2	6	0	1	0
1996-97	New Jersey	NHL	79	3	13	16	110	1	0	2	93	3.2	16						10	2	2	4	19	1	0	0
1997-98	New Jersey	NHL	79	4	19	23	171	1	0	0	76	5.3	11						6	1	1	2	21	1	0	1
1998-99	New Jersey	NHL	70	5	26	31	114	1	0	0	101	5.0	6	0	0.0	51	71	19:53	7	0	3	3	10	0	0	0

Season	Club	League	GP	G	A	Pts	PIM	PP	SH	GW	S	%	+/-	TF	F%	H	SB	Min	GP	G	A	Pts	PIM	PP	SH	GW
			Regular Season																Playoffs							
99-2000	New Jersey	NHL	57	1	15	16	104	0	0	1	59	1.7	−10	0	0.0	44	63	16:42								
	Phoenix	NHL	16	1	7	8	19	1	0	0	30	3.3	1	0	0.0	13	28	21:45	5	0	0	0	16	0	0	0
2000-01	Columbus	NHL	81	3	14	17	118	1	0	0	104	2.9	−16	0	0.0	80	142	21:31								
	NHL Totals		802	37	169	206	2003	11	1	5	875	4.2		0	0.0	188	304	19:48	80	5	12	17	184	2	1	1

Traded to **New Jersey** by **Montreal** for Stephane Richer, August 22, 1996. Traded to **Phoenix** by **New Jersey** for Deron Quint and Phoenix's 3rd round choice (later traded back to Phoenix - Phoenix selected Beat Forster) in 2001 Entry Draft, March 7, 2000. Selected by **Columbus** from **Phoenix** in Expansion Draft, June 23, 2000.

ODGERS, Jeff (AWD-juhrs, JEHF) ATL.

Right wing. Shoots right. 6', 200 lbs. Born, Spy Hill, Sask., May 31, 1969.

Season	Club	League	GP	G	A	Pts	PIM	PP	SH	GW	S	%	+/-	TF	F%	H	SB	Min	GP	G	A	Pts	PIM	PP	SH	GW
1985-86	Saskatoon Blaze	SMHL	36	27	29	56	74																			
1986-87	Brandon	WHL	70	7	14	21	150																			
1987-88	Brandon	WHL	70	17	18	35	202												4	1	1	2	14			
1988-89	Brandon	WHL	71	31	29	60	277																			
1989-90	Brandon	WHL	64	37	28	65	209																			
1990-91	Kansas City	IHL	77	12	19	31	318																			
1991-92	San Jose	NHL	61	7	4	11	217	0	0	0	64	10.9	−21													
	Kansas City	IHL	12	2	2	4	56												4	2	1	3	0			
1992-93	San Jose	NHL	66	12	15	27	253	6	0	0	100	12.0	−26													
1993-94	San Jose	NHL	81	13	8	21	222	7	0	0	73	17.8	−13						11	0	0	0	11	0	0	0
1994-95	San Jose	NHL	48	4	3	7	117	0	0	1	47	8.5	−8						11	1	1	2	23	0	0	0
1995-96	San Jose	NHL	78	12	4	16	192	0	0	1	84	14.3	−4													
1996-97	Boston	NHL	80	7	8	15	197	1	0	1	84	8.3	−15													
1997-98	Providence Bruins	AHL	4	0	0	0	31																			
	Colorado	NHL	68	5	8	13	213	0	0	0	47	10.6	5						6	0	0	0	25	0	0	0
1998-99	Colorado	NHL	75	2	3	5	259	1	0	0	39	5.1	−3	8	37.5	56	6	5:07	15	1	0	1	14	0	0	1
99-2000	Colorado	NHL	62	1	2	3	162	0	0	1	29	3.4	−7	2	50.0	64	8	5:23	4	0	0	0	0	0	0	0
2000-01	Atlanta	NHL	82	6	7	13	226	0	0	1	67	9.0	−8	2	50.0	109	31	8:39								
	NHL Totals		701	69	62	131	2058	15	0	5	634	10.9		12	41.7	229	45	6:31	47	2	1	3	73	0	0	1

Signed as a free agent by **San Jose**, September 3, 1991. Traded to **Boston** by **San Jose** with Pittsburgh's 5th round choice (previously acquired, Boston selected Elias Abrahamsson) in 1996 Entry Draft for Al Iafrate, June 21, 1996. Signed as a free agent by **Colorado**, October 24, 1997. Selected by **Minnesota** from **Colorado** in Expansion Draft, June 23, 2000. Claimed by **Atlanta** from **Minnesota** in Waiver Draft, September 29, 2000.

ODJICK, Gino (OH-jihk, GEE-noh) MTL.

Left wing. Shoots left. 6'3", 217 lbs. Born, Maniwaki, Que., September 7, 1970. Vancouver's 5th choice, 86th overall, in 1990 Entry Draft.

Season	Club	League	GP	G	A	Pts	PIM	PP	SH	GW	S	%	+/-	TF	F%	H	SB	Min	GP	G	A	Pts	PIM	PP	SH	GW
1987-88	Hawkesbury	OCJHL	40	2	4	6	167																			
1988-89	Laval Titan	QMJHL	50	9	15	24	278												16	0	9	9	129			
1989-90	Laval Titan	QMJHL	51	12	26	38	280												13	6	5	11	110			
1990-91	Vancouver	NHL	45	7	1	8	296	0	0	0	39	17.9	−6						6	0	0	0	18	0	0	0
	Milwaukee	IHL	17	7	3	10	102																			
1991-92	Vancouver	NHL	65	4	6	10	348	0	0	0	68	5.9	−1						4	0	0	0	6	0	0	0
1992-93	Vancouver	NHL	75	4	13	17	370	0	0	1	79	5.1	3						1	0	0	0	0	0	0	0
1993-94	Vancouver	NHL	76	16	13	29	271	4	0	5	121	13.2	13						10	0	0	0	18	0	0	0
1994-95	Vancouver	NHL	23	4	5	9	109	0	0	0	35	11.4	−3						5	0	0	0	47	0	0	0
1995-96	Vancouver	NHL	55	3	4	7	181	0	0	0	59	5.1	−16						6	3	1	4	6	0	0	2
1996-97	Vancouver	NHL	70	5	8	13	*371	1	0	0	85	5.9	−5													
1997-98	Vancouver	NHL	35	3	2	5	181	0	0	1	36	8.3	−3													
	NY Islanders	NHL	13	0	0	0	31	0	0	0	16	0.0	1													
1998-99	NY Islanders	NHL	23	4	3	7	133	1	0	2	28	14.3	−2	2	0.0	20	2	9:51								
99-2000	NY Islanders	NHL	46	5	10	15	90	0	0	3	91	5.5	−7	3	33.3	56	8	12:10								
	Philadelphia	NHL	13	3	1	4	10	0	0	1	24	12.5	2	0	0.0	11	2	9:03								
2000-01	Philadelphia	NHL	17	1	3	4	28	0	0	0	21	4.8	0	3	0.0	12	3	8:33								
	Montreal	NHL	13	1	0	1	44	0	0	0	11	9.1	0	3	66.7	13	3	7:04								
	NHL Totals		569	60	69	129	2463	6	0	13	713	8.4		11	27.3	112	18	10:12	32	3	1	4	95	0	0	2

Traded to **NY Islanders** by **Vancouver** for Jason Strudwick, March 23, 1998. Traded to **Philadelphia** by **NY Islanders** for Mikael Andersson and Carolina's 5th round choice (previously acquired, NY Islanders selected Kristofer Ottosson) in 2000 Entry Draft, February 15, 2000. Traded to **Montreal** by **Philadelphia** for P.J. Stock and Montreal's 6th round choice (Dennis Seidenberg) in 2001 Entry Draft, December 7, 2000. • Missed majority of 200-01 season recovering from wrist injury suffered in game vs. Carolina, January 16, 2001.

O'DONNELL, Sean (oh-DOHN-ehl, SHAWN) BOS.

Defense. Shoots left. 6'3", 230 lbs. Born, Ottawa, Ont., October 13, 1971. Buffalo's 6th choice, 123rd overall, in 1991 Entry Draft.

Season	Club	League	GP	G	A	Pts	PIM	PP	SH	GW	S	%	+/-	TF	F%	H	SB	Min	GP	G	A	Pts	PIM	PP	SH	GW
1987-88	Kanata Valley	OCJHL	54	4	25	29	96																			
1988-89	Sudbury Wolves	OHL	56	1	9	10	49																			
1989-90	Sudbury Wolves	OHL	64	7	19	26	84												7	1	2	3	8			
1990-91	Sudbury Wolves	OHL	66	8	23	31	114												5	1	4	5	10			
1991-92	Rochester	AHL	73	4	9	13	193												16	1	2	3	21			
1992-93	Rochester	AHL	74	3	18	21	203												17	1	6	7	38			
1993-94	Rochester	AHL	64	2	10	12	242												4	0	1	1	21			
1994-95	Phoenix	IHL	61	2	18	20	132												9	0	1	1	21			
	Los Angeles	NHL	15	0	2	2	49	0	0	0	12	0.0	−2													
1995-96	Los Angeles	NHL	71	2	5	7	127	0	0	0	65	3.1	3													
1996-97	Los Angeles	NHL	55	5	12	17	144	2	0	0	68	7.4	−13													
1997-98	Los Angeles	NHL	80	2	15	17	179	0	0	1	71	2.8	7						4	1	0	1	36	0	0	0
1998-99	Los Angeles	NHL	80	1	13	14	186	0	0	0	64	1.6	1	0	0.0	133	71	19:10								
99-2000	Los Angeles	NHL	80	2	12	14	114	0	0	1	51	3.9	4	0	0.0	154	80	17:41	4	1	0	1	4	0	0	0
2000-01	Minnesota	NHL	63	4	12	16	128	1	0	2	58	6.9	−2	12	50.0	81	72	23:00								
	New Jersey	NHL	17	0	1	1	33	0	0	0	9	0.0	2	0	0.0	14	13	16:27	23	1	2	3	41	0	0	0
	NHL Totals		461	16	72	88	960	3	0	4	398	4.0		12	50.0	382	236	19:29	31	3	2	5	81	0	0	0

Traded to **LA Kings** by **Buffalo** for Doug Houda, July 26, 1994. Selected by **Minnesota** from **LA Kings** in Expansion Draft, June 23, 2000. Traded to **New Jersey** by **Minnesota** for Willie Mitchell, March 4, 2001. Signed as a free agent by **Boston**, July 2, 2001.

OHLUND, Mattias (OH-luhnd, MAT-tee-ahs) VAN.

Defense. Shoots left. 6'2", 220 lbs. Born, Pitea, Sweden, September 9, 1976. Vancouver's 1st choice, 13th overall, in 1994 Entry Draft.

Season	Club	League	GP	G	A	Pts	PIM	PP	SH	GW	S	%	+/-	TF	F%	H	SB	Min	GP	G	A	Pts	PIM	PP	SH	GW
1992-93	Pitea IK	Sweden-2	22	0	6	6	16																			
1993-94	Pitea IK	Sweden-2	28	7	10	17	62																			
1994-95	Lulea HF	Sweden	34	6	10	16	34												9	4	0	4	16			
1995-96	Lulea HF	Sweden	38	4	10	14	26												13	1	0	1	47			
1996-97	Lulea HF	Sweden	47	7	9	16	38												10	1	2	3	8			
	Lulea HF	EuroHL	6	0	3	3	0																			
1997-98	Vancouver	NHL	77	7	23	30	76	1	0	0	172	4.1	3													
	Sweden	Olympics	4	0	1	1	4																			
1998-99	Vancouver	NHL	74	9	26	35	83	2	1	1	129	7.0	−19	0	0.0	133	154	26:04								
99-2000	Vancouver	NHL	42	4	16	20	24	2	1	1	63	6.3	6	0	0.0	91	95	27:41								
2000-01	Vancouver	NHL	65	8	20	28	46	1	1	4	136	5.9	−16	0	0.0	125	146	25:00	4	1	3	4	6	1	0	0
	NHL Totals		258	28	85	113	229	6	3	6	500	5.6		0	0.0	349	385	26:04	4	1	3	4	6	1	0	0

NHL All-Rookie Team (1998) • Played in NHL All-Star Game (1999)

OLAUSSON, Fredrik (OHL-ah-suhn, FREHD-rihk) DET.

Defense. Shoots right. 6'2", 198 lbs. Born, Dadesjo, Sweden, October 5, 1966. Winnipeg's 4th choice, 81st overall, in 1985 Entry Draft.

Season	Club	League	GP	G	A	Pts	PIM	PP	SH	GW	S	%	+/-	TF	F%	H	SB	Min	GP	G	A	Pts	PIM	PP	SH	GW
1982-83	Nybro SK	Sweden-2	31	4	4	8	12																			
1983-84	Nybro SK	Sweden-2	28	8	14	22	32																			
1984-85	Farjestads BK	Sweden	29	5	12	17	22												3	1	0	1	0			
1985-86	Farjestads BK	Sweden	33	4	12	16	22												8	3	2	5	6			
1986-87	Winnipeg	NHL	72	7	29	36	24	1	0	2	119	5.9	−3						10	2	3	5	4	1	0	0
1987-88	Winnipeg	NHL	38	5	10	15	18	2	0	2	65	7.7	3						5	1	1	2	0	0	0	0
1988-89	Winnipeg	NHL	75	15	47	62	32	4	0	1	178	8.4	6													
1989-90	Winnipeg	NHL	77	9	46	55	32	3	0	0	147	6.1	−1						7	0	2	2	2	0	0	0

			Regular Season																Playoffs							
Season	Club	League	GP	G	A	Pts	PIM	PP	SH	GW	S	%	+/-	TF	F%	H	SB	Min	GP	G	A	Pts	PIM	PP	SH	GW
1990-91	Winnipeg	NHL	71	12	29	41	24	5	0	0	168	7.1	–22	....	....	....	....	....	....	....	....	....	....	....	....	....
1991-92	Winnipeg	NHL	77	20	42	62	34	13	1	2	227	8.8	–31	....	....	....	....	....	7	1	5	6	4	1	0	0
1992-93	Winnipeg	NHL	68	16	41	57	22	11	0	3	165	9.7	–4	....	....	....	....	....	6	0	2	2	2	0	0	0
1993-94	Winnipeg	NHL	18	2	5	7	10	1	0	0	41	4.9	–3	....	....	....	....	....	....	....	....	....	....	....	....	....
	Edmonton	NHL	55	9	19	28	20	6	0	1	85	10.6	–4	....	....	....	....	....	....	....	....	....	....	....	....	....
1994-95	EV Ehrwald	Austria-2	10	4	3	7	8	....	....	....	....	....	....	....	....	....	....	....	....	....	....	....	....	....	....	....
	Edmonton	NHL	33	0	10	10	20	0	0	0	52	0.0	–4	....	....	....	....	....	....	....	....	....	....	....	....	....
1995-96	Edmonton	NHL	20	0	6	6	14	0	0	0	20	0.0	–14	....	....	....	....	....	....	....	....	....	....	....	....	....
	Anaheim	NHL	36	2	16	18	24	1	0	0	63	3.2	7	....	....	....	....	....	....	....	....	....	....	....	....	....
1996-97	Anaheim	NHL	20	2	9	11	8	1	0	0	35	5.7	–5	....	....	....	....	....	....	....	....	....	....	....	....	....
	Pittsburgh	NHL	51	7	20	27	24	2	0	3	75	9.3	21	....	....	....	....	....	4	0	1	1	0	0	0	0
1997-98	Pittsburgh	NHL	76	6	27	33	42	2	0	1	89	6.7	13	....	....	....	....	....	6	0	3	3	2	0	0	0
1998-99	Anaheim	NHL	74	16	40	56	30	10	0	2	121	13.2	17	0	0.0	41	56	19:47	4	0	2	2	4	0	0	0
99-2000	Anaheim	NHL	70	15	19	34	28	8	0	1	120	12.5	–13	0	0.0	62	45	20:01	....	....	....	....	....	....	....	....
2000-01	SC Bern	Switz.	43	12	15	27	28	....	....	....	....	....	....	....	....	....	....	....	4	1	4	5	0	....	....	....
	NHL Totals		931	143	415	558	406	70	1	18	1770	8.1		0	0.0	103	101	19:54	49	4	19	23	18	2	0	0

Traded to **Edmonton** by **Winnipeg** with Winnipeg's 7th round choice (Curtis Sheptak) in 1994 Entry Draft for Edmonton's 3rd round choice (Tavis Hansen) in 1994 Entry Draft, December 6, 1993. Claimed on waivers by **Anaheim** from **Edmonton**, January 16, 1996. Traded to **Pittsburgh** by **Anaheim** with Alex Hicks for Shawn Antoski and Dmitri Mironov, November 19, 1996. Signed as a free agent by **Anaheim**, August 28, 1998. Signed as a free agent by **Detroit**, May 24, 2001.

OLIVER, David

(AWL-ih-vuhr, DAY-vihd)

Right wing. Shoots right. 6', 190 lbs. Born, Sechelt, B.C., April 17, 1971. Edmonton's 7th choice, 144th overall, in 1991 Entry Draft.

1988-89	Vernon Lakers	BCJHL	58	41	38	79	38	....	....	....	....	....	....	....	....	....	....	....	....	....	....	....	....	....	....	....
1989-90	Vernon Lakers	BCJHL	58	51	48	99	22	....	....	....	....	....	....	....	....	....	....	....	....	....	....	....	....	....	....	....
1990-91	U. of Michigan	CCHA	27	13	11	24	34	....	....	....	....	....	....	....	....	....	....	....	....	....	....	....	....	....	....	....
1991-92	U. of Michigan	CCHA	44	31	27	58	32	....	....	....	....	....	....	....	....	....	....	....	....	....	....	....	....	....	....	....
1992-93	U. of Michigan	CCHA	40	35	20	55	18	....	....	....	....	....	....	....	....	....	....	....	....	....	....	....	....	....	....	....
1993-94	U. of Michigan	CCHA	41	28	40	68	16	....	....	....	....	....	....	....	....	....	....	....	....	....	....	....	....	....	....	....
1994-95	Cape Breton	AHL	32	11	18	29	8	....	....	....	....	....	....	....	....	....	....	....	....	....	....	....	....	....	....	....
	Edmonton	NHL	44	16	14	30	20	10	0	0	79	20.3	–11	....	....	....	....	....	....	....	....	....	....	....	....	....
1995-96	Edmonton	NHL	80	20	19	39	34	14	0	0	131	15.3	–22	....	....	....	....	....	....	....	....	....	....	....	....	....
1996-97	Edmonton	NHL	17	1	2	3	4	0	0	0	22	4.5	–8	....	....	....	....	....	....	....	....	....	....	....	....	....
	NY Rangers	NHL	14	2	1	3	4	0	0	0	13	15.4	3	....	....	....	....	....	3	0	0	0	0	0	0	0
1997-98	Houston Aeros	IHL	78	38	27	65	60	....	....	....	....	....	....	....	....	....	....	....	4	3	0	3	4	....	....	....
1998-99	Ottawa	NHL	17	2	5	7	4	0	0	0	18	11.1	1	3	33.3	8	2	10:34	....	....	....	....	....	....	....	....
	Houston Aeros	IHL	37	18	17	35	30	....	....	....	....	....	....	....	....	....	....	....	19	10	6	16	22	....	....	....
99-2000	Phoenix	NHL	9	1	0	1	2	1	0	0	6	16.7	0	0	0.0	11	1	7:38	....	....	....	....	....	....	....	....
	Houston Aeros	IHL	45	16	11	27	40	....	....	....	....	....	....	....	....	....	....	....	11	3	4	7	8	....	....	....
2000-01	Ottawa	NHL	7	0	0	0	2	0	0	0	2	0.0	0	0	0.0	8	0	5:37	....	....	....	....	....	....	....	....
	Grand Rapids	IHL	51	14	17	31	35	....	....	....	....	....	....	....	....	....	....	....	10	6	2	8	8	....	....	....
	NHL Totals		188	42	41	83	70	25	0	0	271	15.5		3	33.3	27	3	8:43	3	0	0	0	0	0	0	0

CCHA Second All-Star Team (1993) • CCHA First All-Star Team (1994) • NCAA West First All-American Team (1994)

Claimed on waivers by **NY Rangers** from **Edmonton**, February 21, 1997. Signed as a free agent by **Ottawa**, July 2, 1998. Signed as a free agent by **Phoenix**, July 20, 1999. Signed as a free agent by **Ottawa**, August 2, 2000.

OLIWA, Krzysztof

(oh-LEE-vuh, KHRIH-stahf) **PIT.**

Left wing. Shoots left. 6'5", 235 lbs. Born, Tychy, Poland, April 12, 1973. New Jersey's 4th choice, 65th overall, in 1993 Entry Draft.

1990-91	GKS Katowski	Poland-Jr.	5	4	4	8	10	....	....	....	....	....	....	....	....	....	....	....	....	....	....	....	....	....	....	....
1991-92	GKS Tychy	Poland	10	3	7	10	6	....	....	....	....	....	....	....	....	....	....	....	....	....	....	....	....	....	....	....
1992-93	Welland Cougars	OJHL-B	30	13	21	34	127	....	....	....	....	....	....	....	....	....	....	....	....	....	....	....	....	....	....	....
1993-94	Albany River Rats	AHL	33	2	4	6	151	....	....	....	....	....	....	....	....	....	....	....	....	....	....	....	....	....	....	....
	Raleigh IceCaps	ECHL	15	0	2	2	65	....	....	....	....	....	....	....	....	....	....	....	9	0	0	0	35	....	....	....
1994-95	Albany River Rats	AHL	20	1	1	2	77	....	....	....	....	....	....	....	....	....	....	....	....	....	....	....	....	....	....	....
	Saint John Flames	AHL	14	1	4	5	79	....	....	....	....	....	....	....	....	....	....	....	....	....	....	....	....	....	....	....
	Raleigh IceCaps	ECHL	5	0	2	2	32	....	....	....	....	....	....	....	....	....	....	....	....	....	....	....	....	....	....	....
	Detroit Vipers	IHL	4	0	1	1	24	....	....	....	....	....	....	....	....	....	....	....	....	....	....	....	....	....	....	....
1995-96	Albany River Rats	AHL	51	5	11	16	217	....	....	....	....	....	....	....	....	....	....	....	....	....	....	....	....	....	....	....
	Raleigh IceCaps	ECHL	9	1	0	1	53	....	....	....	....	....	....	....	....	....	....	....	....	....	....	....	....	....	....	....
1996-97	New Jersey	NHL	1	0	0	0	5	0	0	0	0	0.0	–1	....	....	....	....	....	....	....	....	....	....	....	....	....
	Albany River Rats	AHL	60	13	14	27	322	....	....	....	....	....	....	....	....	....	....	....	15	7	1	8	49	....	....	....
1997-98	New Jersey	NHL	73	2	3	5	295	0	0	2	53	3.8	3	....	....	....	....	....	6	0	0	0	23	0	0	0
1998-99	New Jersey	NHL	64	5	7	12	240	0	0	1	59	8.5	4	1	0.0	117	9	7:02	1	0	0	0	2	0	0	0
99-2000♦	New Jersey	NHL	69	6	10	16	184	1	0	2	61	9.8	–2	3	66.7	84	4	6:45	....	....	....	....	....	....	....	....
2000-01	Columbus	NHL	10	0	2	2	34	0	0	0	5	0.0	1	0	0.0	10	0	5:17	....	....	....	....	....	....	....	....
	Pittsburgh	NHL	26	1	2	3	131	0	0	0	17	5.9	–4	1	100.0	13	4	4:58	5	0	0	0	16	0	0	0
	NHL Totals		243	14	24	38	889	1	0	5	195	7.2		5	60.0	224	17	6:30	12	0	0	0	41	0	0	0

• Born Krzystof Graboski • Traded to **Columbus** by **New Jersey** with future considerations (Deron Quint, June 23, 2000) for Columbus' 3rd round choice (Brandon Nolan) in 2001 Entry Draft and future considerations (Turner Stevenson, June 23, 2000), June 12, 2000. • Missed majority of 2000-2001 season recovering from arm injury originally suffered in game vs. Detroit, October 28, 2000. Traded to **Pittsburgh** by **Columbus** for San Jose's 3rd round choice (previously acquired, Columbus selected Aaron Johnson) in 2001 Entry Draft, January 14, 2001.

O'NEILL, Jeff

(OH-NEEL, JEHF) **CAR.**

Center. Shoots right. 6'1", 190 lbs. Born, Richmond Hill, Ont., February 23, 1976. Hartford's 1st choice, 5th overall, in 1994 Entry Draft.

1990-91	Richmond Hill	OMHA	78	56	134	190	....	....	....	....	....	....	....	....	....	....	....	....	....	....	....	....	....	....	....	....
1991-92	Thornhill T-Birds	MTJHL	43	27	*53	80	48	....	....	....	....	....	....	....	....	....	....	....	....	....	....	....	....	....	....	....
1992-93	Guelph Storm	OHL	65	32	47	79	88	....	....	....	....	....	....	....	....	....	....	....	5	2	2	4	6	....	....	....
1993-94	Guelph Storm	OHL	66	45	81	126	95	....	....	....	....	....	....	....	....	....	....	....	9	2	11	13	31	....	....	....
1994-95	Guelph Storm	OHL	57	43	81	124	56	....	....	....	....	....	....	....	....	....	....	....	14	8	18	26	34	....	....	....
1995-96	Hartford	NHL	65	8	19	27	40	1	0	1	65	12.3	–3	....	....	....	....	....	....	....	....	....	....	....	....	....
1996-97	Hartford	NHL	72	14	16	30	40	2	1	2	101	13.9	–24	....	....	....	....	....	....	....	....	....	....	....	....	....
	Springfield	AHL	1	0	0	0	0	....	....	....	....	....	....	....	....	....	....	....	....	....	....	....	....	....	....	....
1997-98	Carolina	NHL	74	19	20	39	67	7	1	4	114	16.7	–8	....	....	....	....	....	....	....	....	....	....	....	....	....
1998-99	Carolina	NHL	75	16	15	31	66	4	0	2	121	13.2	3	941	45.6	207	19	16:44	6	0	1	1	0	0	0	0
99-2000	Carolina	NHL	80	25	38	63	72	4	0	7	189	13.2	–9	1337	49.5	165	33	19:20	....	....	....	....	....	....	....	....
2000-01	Carolina	NHL	82	41	26	67	106	17	0	5	242	16.9	–18	726	50.0	263	16	18:20	6	1	2	3	10	0	0	1
	NHL Totals		448	123	134	257	391	35	2	21	832	14.8		3004	48.4	635	68	18:10	12	1	3	4	10	0	0	1

OHL First All-Star Team (1995)

Transferred to **Carolina** after **Hartford** franchise relocated, June 25, 1997.

ORSZAGH, Vladimir

(OHR-sahk, VLAD-ih-meer) **NSH.**

Right wing. Shoots left. 5'11", 173 lbs. Born, Banska Bystrica, Czech., May 24, 1977. NY Islanders' 4th choice, 106th overall, in 1995 Entry Draft.

1993-94	Banska Bystrica	Slovak-Jr.	38	38	27	65	....	....	....	....	....	....	....	....	....	....	....	....	....	....	....	....	....	....	....	....
1994-95	Banska Bystrica	Slovak-2	38	18	12	30	....	....	....	....	....	....	....	....	....	....	....	....	....	....	....	....	....	....	....	....
1995-96	Banska Bystrica	Slovakia	31	9	5	14	22	....	....	....	....	....	....	....	....	....	....	....	....	....	....	....	....	....	....	....
1996-97	Utah Grizzlies	IHL	68	12	15	27	30	....	....	....	....	....	....	....	....	....	....	....	3	0	1	1	4	....	....	....
1997-98	NY Islanders	NHL	11	0	1	1	2	0	0	0	9	0.0	–3	....	....	....	....	....	....	....	....	....	....	....	....	....
	Utah Grizzlies	IHL	62	13	10	23	60	....	....	....	....	....	....	....	....	....	....	....	4	2	0	2	0	....	....	....
1998-99	NY Islanders	NHL	12	1	0	1	6	0	0	0	4	20.0	2	0	0.0	8	2	6:36	....	....	....	....	....	....	....	....
	Lowell	AHL	68	18	23	41	57	....	....	....	....	....	....	....	....	....	....	....	3	2	2	4	2	....	....	....
99-2000	NY Islanders	NHL	11	2	1	3	4	0	0	0	16	12.5	1	0	0.0	16	6	11:54	....	....	....	....	....	....	....	....
	Lowell	AHL	55	8	12	20	22	....	....	....	....	....	....	....	....	....	....	....	7	3	3	6	2	....	....	....
2000-01	Djurgardens IF	Sweden	50	23	13	36	62	....	....	....	....	....	....	....	....	....	....	....	16	*7	3	10	20	....	....	....
	NHL Totals		34	3	2	5	12	0	0	0	29	10.3		0	0.0	24	8	11:55	....	....	....	....	....	....	....	....

Signed as a free agent by **Nashville**, May 30, 2001.

O'SULLIVAN, Chris
(oh-SUHL-lih-van, KRIHS)

Defense. Shoots left. 6'2", 205 lbs. Born, Dorchester, MA, May 15, 1974. Calgary's 2nd choice, 30th overall, in 1992 Entry Draft.

			Regular Season																Playoffs							
Season	Club	League	GP	G	A	Pts	PIM	PP	SH	GW	S	%	+/-	TF	F%	H	SB	Min	GP	G	A	Pts	PIM	PP	SH	GW
1991-92	Catholic Memorial	Hi-School	26	26	23	49	65																			
1992-93	Boston University	H-East	5	0	2	2	4																			
1993-94	Boston University	H-East	32	5	18	23	25																			
1994-95	Boston University	H-East	40	23	33	56	48																			
1995-96	Boston University	H-East	37	12	35	47	50																			
1996-97	**Calgary**	**NHL**	**27**	**2**	**8**	**10**	**2**	**1**	**0**	**1**	**41**	**4.9**	**0**													
	Saint John Flames	AHL	29	3	8	11	17												5	0	4	4	0			
1997-98	**Calgary**	**NHL**	**12**	**0**	**2**	**2**	**10**	**0**	**0**	**0**	**12**	**0.0**	**4**													
	Saint John Flames	AHL	32	4	10	14	2												21	2	17	19	18			
1998-99	**Calgary**	**NHL**	**10**	**0**	**1**	**1**	**2**	**0**	**0**	**0**	**10**	**0.0**	**–1**	**1**	**0.0**	**4**	**1**	**9:07**								
	Saint John Flames	AHL	41	7	29	36	24																			
	Hartford	AHL	10	1	4	5	0												7	1	3	4	11			
99-2000	**Vancouver**	**NHL**	**11**	**0**	**5**	**5**	**2**	**0**	**0**	**0**	**16**	**0.0**	**2**	**0**	**0.0**	**4**	**2**	**17:47**								
	Syracuse Crunch	AHL	59	18	47	65	24												4	0	1	1	0			
2000-01	Cincinnati Ducks	AHL	60	9	40	49	31												4	0	3	3	0			
	NHL Totals		**60**	**2**	**16**	**18**	**16**	**1**	**0**	**1**	**79**	**2.5**		**1**	**0.0**	**8**	**3**	**13:39**								

Hockey East First All-Star Team (1995) • NCAA East Second All-American Team (1995) • NCAA Championship All-Tournament Team (1995) • NCAA Championship Tournament MVP (1995)

• Missed majority of 1992-93 season recovering from neck injury suffered in game vs. Boston College, November 11, 1992. Traded to **NY Rangers** by **Calgary** for Lee Sorochan, March 23, 1999. Signed as a free agent by **Vancouver**, August 20, 1999. Signed as a free agent by **Anaheim**, July 20, 2000. Signed as a free agent by **EHC Kloten** (Switz), June 22, 2001.

OZOLINSH, Sandis
(OH-zoh-LIHNCH, SAN-dihz) **CAR.**

Defense. Shoots left. 6'3", 205 lbs. Born, Riga, Latvia, August 3, 1972. San Jose's 3rd choice, 30th overall, in 1991 Entry Draft.

Season	Club	League	GP	G	A	Pts	PIM	PP	SH	GW	S	%	+/-	TF	F%	H	SB	Min	GP	G	A	Pts	PIM	PP	SH	GW
1990-91	Dynamo Riga	USSR	44	0	3	3	51																			
1991-92	Dynamo Riga	CIS	30	6	0	6	42																			
	Kansas City	IHL	34	6	9	15	20												15	2	5	7	22			
1992-93	**San Jose**	**NHL**	**37**	**7**	**16**	**23**	**40**	**2**	**0**	**0**	**83**	**8.4**	**–9**													
1993-94	**San Jose**	**NHL**	**81**	**26**	**38**	**64**	**24**	**4**	**0**	**3**	**157**	**16.6**	**16**						**14**	**0**	**10**	**10**	**8**	**0**	**0**	**0**
1994-95	**San Jose**	**NHL**	**48**	**9**	**16**	**25**	**30**	**3**	**1**	**2**	**83**	**10.8**	**–6**						**11**	**3**	**2**	**5**	**6**	**1**	**0**	**0**
1995-96	San Francisco	IHL	2	1	0	1	0																			
	San Jose	**NHL**	**7**	**1**	**3**	**4**	**4**	**1**	**0**	**0**	**21**	**4.8**	**2**													
	♦ **Colorado**	**NHL**	**66**	**13**	**37**	**50**	**50**	**7**	**1**	**1**	**145**	**9.0**	**0**						**22**	**5**	**14**	**19**	**16**	**2**	**0**	**1**
1996-97	**Colorado**	**NHL**	**80**	**23**	**45**	**68**	**88**	**13**	**0**	**4**	**232**	**9.9**	**4**						**17**	**4**	**13**	**17**	**24**	**2**	**0**	**1**
1997-98	**Colorado**	**NHL**	**66**	**13**	**38**	**51**	**65**	**9**	**0**	**2**	**135**	**9.6**	**–12**						**7**	**0**	**7**	**7**	**14**	**0**	**0**	**0**
1998-99	**Colorado**	**NHL**	**39**	**7**	**25**	**32**	**22**	**4**	**0**	**3**	**81**	**8.6**	**10**	**0**	**0.0**	**34**	**23**	**22:06**	**19**	**4**	**8**	**12**	**22**	**3**	**0**	**1**
99-2000	**Colorado**	**NHL**	**82**	**16**	**36**	**52**	**46**	**6**	**0**	**1**	**210**	**7.6**	**17**	**0**	**0.0**	**71**	**47**	**22:41**	**17**	**5**	**5**	**10**	**20**	**3**	**0**	**1**
2000-01	**Carolina**	**NHL**	**72**	**12**	**32**	**44**	**71**	**4**	**2**	**2**	**145**	**8.3**	**–25**	**0**	**0.0**	**84**	**71**	**22:12**	**6**	**0**	**2**	**2**	**5**	**0**	**0**	**0**
	NHL Totals		**578**	**127**	**286**	**413**	**440**	**53**	**4**	**18**	**1292**	**9.8**		**0**	**0.0**	**189**	**141**	**22:23**	**113**	**21**	**61**	**82**	**115**	**11**	**0**	**4**

NHL First All-Star Team (1997) • Played in NHL All-Star Game (1994, 1997, 1998, 2000, 2001)

• Missed majority of 1992-93 season recovering from knee injury suffered in game vs. Philadelphia, December 30, 1992. Traded to **Colorado** by **San Jose** for Owen Nolan, October 26, 1995. Traded to **Carolina** by **Colorado** with Columbus' 2nd round choice (previously acquired, Carolina selected Tomas Kurka) in 2000 Entry Draft for Nolan Pratt, Carolina's 1st (Vaclav Nedorost) and 2nd (Jared Aulin) round choices in 2000 Entry Draft and Philadelphia's 2nd round choice (previously acquired, Colorado selected Agris Saviels) in 2000 Entry Draft, June 24, 2000.

PAHLSSON, Sami
(PAWL-suhn, SAM-ee) **ANA.**

Center. Shoots left. 5'11", 190 lbs. Born, Ornskoldsvik, Sweden, December 17, 1977. Colorado's 10th choice, 176th overall, in 1996 Entry Draft.

Season	Club	League	GP	G	A	Pts	PIM	PP	SH	GW	S	%	+/-	TF	F%	H	SB	Min	GP	G	A	Pts	PIM	PP	SH	GW
1992-93	Ange IK	Sweden-4	9	0	0	0	0																			
1993-94	MoDo Hockey	Sweden-2	STATISTICS NOT AVAILABLE																							
1994-95	MoDo Hockey	Swede-Jr.	30	10	11	21	26																			
	MoDo Hockey	Sweden	1	0	0	0	0																			
1995-96	MoDo Hockey	Swede-Jr.	5	2	6	8	2																			
	MoDo Hockey	Sweden	36	1	3	4	8												4	0	0	0	0			
1996-97	MoDo Hockey	Sweden	49	8	9	17	83																			
1997-98	MoDo Hockey	Sweden	23	6	11	17	24												9	3	0	3	6			
1998-99	MoDo Hockey	Sweden	50	17	17	34	44												13	3	3	6	10			
99-2000	MoDo Hockey	Sweden	47	16	11	27	67												13	3	3	6	8			
	MoDo Hockey	EuroHL	4	1	0	1	0												3	1	1	2	2			
2000-01	**Boston**	**NHL**	**17**	**1**	**1**	**2**	**6**	**0**	**0**	**0**	**13**	**7.7**	**–5**	**239**	**40.2**	**33**	**4**	**14:19**								
	Anaheim	**NHL**	**59**	**3**	**4**	**7**	**14**	**1**	**1**	**1**	**46**	**6.5**	**–9**	**867**	**45.1**	**65**	**25**	**14:14**								
	NHL Totals		**76**	**4**	**5**	**9**	**20**	**1**	**1**	**1**	**59**	**6.8**		**1106**	**44.0**	**98**	**29**	**14:15**								

Traded to **Boston** by **Colorado** with Brian Rolston, Martin Grenier and New Jersey's 1st round choice (previously acquired, Boston selected Martin Samuelsson) in 2000 Entry Draft for Ray Bourque and Dave Andreychuk, March 6, 2000. Traded to **Anaheim** by **Boston** for Patrick Traverse and Andrei Nazarov, November 18, 2000.

PALFFY, Ziggy
(PAHL-fee, ZIHG-gee) **L.A.**

Right wing. Shoots left. 5'10", 183 lbs. Born, Skalica, Czech., May 5, 1972. NY Islanders' 2nd choice, 26th overall, in 1991 Entry Draft.

Season	Club	League	GP	G	A	Pts	PIM	PP	SH	GW	S	%	+/-	TF	F%	H	SB	Min	GP	G	A	Pts	PIM	PP	SH	GW
1990-91	AC Nitra	Czech.	50	34	16	50	18																			
1991-92	Dukla Trencin	Czech.	45	41	33	74	36																			
1992-93	Dukla Trencin	Czech.	43	38	41	79																				
1993-94	**NY Islanders**	**NHL**	**5**	**0**	**0**	**0**	**0**	**0**	**0**	**0**	**5**	**0.0**	**–6**													
	Salt Lake City	IHL	57	25	32	57	83																			
	Slovakia	Olympics	8	3	*7	*10	8																			
1994-95	Denver Grizzlies	IHL	33	20	23	43	40																			
	NY Islanders	**NHL**	**33**	**10**	**7**	**17**	**6**	**1**	**0**	**1**	**75**	**13.3**	**3**													
1995-96	**NY Islanders**	**NHL**	**81**	**43**	**44**	**87**	**56**	**17**	**1**	**6**	**257**	**16.7**	**–17**													
1996-97	Dukla Trencin	Slovakia	1	0	0	0																				
	NY Islanders	**NHL**	**80**	**48**	**42**	**90**	**43**	**6**	**4**	**6**	**292**	**16.4**	**21**													
1997-98	**NY Islanders**	**NHL**	**82**	**45**	**42**	**87**	**34**	**17**	**2**	**5**	**277**	**16.2**	**–2**													
1998-99	HK-36 Skalica	Slovakia	9	11	8	19	6																			
	NY Islanders	**NHL**	**50**	**22**	**28**	**50**	**34**	**5**	**2**	**1**	**168**	**13.1**	**–6**	**1**	**100.0**	**28**	**34**	**22:04**								
99-2000	**Los Angeles**	**NHL**	**64**	**27**	**39**	**66**	**32**	**4**	**0**	**3**	**186**	**14.5**	**18**	**7**	**42.9**	**63**	**19**	**19:39**	**4**	**2**	**0**	**2**	**0**	**0**	**0**	**0**
2000-01	**Los Angeles**	**NHL**	**73**	**38**	**51**	**89**	**20**	**12**	**4**	**8**	**217**	**17.5**	**22**	**5**	**80.0**	**54**	**34**	**19:46**	**13**	**3**	**5**	**8**	**8**	**0**	**0**	**0**
	NHL Totals		**468**	**233**	**253**	**486**	**225**	**62**	**13**	**30**	**1477**	**15.8**		**13**	**61.5**	**145**	**87**	**20:21**	**17**	**5**	**5**	**10**	**8**	**0**	**0**	**0**

Played in NHL All-Star Game (1998, 2001)

Traded to **LA Kings** by **NY Islanders** with Brian Smolinski, Marcel Cousineau and New Jersey's 4th round choice (previously acquired, LA Kings selected Daniel Johansson) in 1999 Entry Draft for Olli Jokinen, Josh Green, Mathieu Biron and LA Kings' 1st round choice (Taylor Pyatt) in 1999 Entry Draft, June 20, 1999.

PANDOLFO, Jay
(pan-DAHL-foh, JAY) **N.J.**

Left wing. Shoots left. 6'1", 190 lbs. Born, Winchester, MA, December 27, 1974. New Jersey's 2nd choice, 32nd overall, in 1993 Entry Draft.

Season	Club	League	GP	G	A	Pts	PIM	PP	SH	GW	S	%	+/-	TF	F%	H	SB	Min	GP	G	A	Pts	PIM	PP	SH	GW
1989-90	Burlington Prep	Hi-School	23	33	30	63	18																			
1990-91	Burlington Prep	Hi-School	20	19	27	46	10																			
1991-92	Burlington Prep	Hi-School	20	35	34	69	14																			
1992-93	Boston University	H-East	37	16	22	38	16																			
1993-94	Boston University	H-East	37	17	25	42	27																			
1994-95	Boston University	H-East	20	7	13	20	6																			
1995-96	Boston University	H-East	39	*38	29	67	6																			
	Albany River Rats	AHL	5	3	1	4	0												3	0	0	0	0			
1996-97	**New Jersey**	**NHL**	**46**	**6**	**8**	**14**	**6**	**0**	**0**	**1**	**61**	**9.8**	**–1**						**6**	**0**	**1**	**1**	**0**	**0**	**0**	**0**
	Albany River Rats	AHL	12	3	9	12	0																			
1997-98	**New Jersey**	**NHL**	**23**	**1**	**3**	**4**	**4**	**0**	**0**	**0**	**23**	**4.3**	**–4**						**3**	**0**	**2**	**2**	**0**	**0**	**0**	**0**
	Albany River Rats	AHL	51	18	19	37	24																			
1998-99	**New Jersey**	**NHL**	**70**	**14**	**13**	**27**	**10**	**1**	**1**	**4**	**100**	**14.0**	**3**	**10**	**40.0**	**103**	**39**	**15:13**	**7**	**1**	**0**	**1**	**0**	**0**	**0**	**0**

			Regular Season																Playoffs							
Season	Club	League	GP	G	A	Pts	PIM	PP	SH	GW	S	%	+/-	TF	F%	H	SB	Min	GP	G	A	Pts	PIM	PP	SH	GW
99-2000♦	**New Jersey**	**NHL**	**71**	**7**	**8**	**15**	**4**	**0**	**0**	**0**	**86**	**8.1**	**0**	**19**	**47.4**	**91**	**22**	**13:25**	**23**	**0**	**5**	**5**	**0**	**0**	**0**	**0**
2000-01	**New Jersey**	**NHL**	**63**	**4**	**12**	**16**	**16**	**0**	**0**	**0**	**57**	**7.0**	**3**	**15**	**53.3**	**77**	**16**	**14:05**	**25**	**1**	**4**	**5**	**4**	**0**	**0**	**0**
	NHL Totals		**273**	**32**	**44**	**76**	**40**	**1**	**1**	**5**	**327**	**9.8**		**44**	**47.7**	**271**	**77**	**14:14**	**64**	**2**	**12**	**14**	**4**	**0**	**0**	**0**

Hockey East First All-Star Team (1996) • NCAA East First All-American Team (1996)

PANKEWICZ, Greg

(PAN-kuh-wihts, GREHG)

Right wing. Shoots right. 6', 185 lbs. Born, Drayton Valley, Alta., November 6, 1970.

Season	Club	League	GP	G	A	Pts	PIM	PP	SH	GW	S	%	+/-	TF	F%	H	SB	Min	GP	G	A	Pts	PIM	PP	SH	GW
1988-89	Sherwood Park	AJHL	53	26	18	44	307	....	....	....	....	....	....	....	....	....	....	....	....	....	....	....	....	....	....	....
1989-90	Regina Pats	WHL	63	14	24	38	136	....	....	....	....	....	....	....	....	....	....	....	10	1	3	4	19	....	....	....
1990-91	Regina Pats	WHL	72	39	41	80	134	....	....	....	....	....	....	....	....	....	....	....	8	4	7	11	12	....	....	....
1991-92	Knoxville	ECHL	59	41	39	80	214	....	....	....	....	....	....	....	....	....	....	....	....	....	....	....	....	....	....	....
1992-93	New Haven	AHL	62	23	20	43	163	....	....	....	....	....	....	....	....	....	....	....	....	....	....	....	....	....	....	....
1993-94	**Ottawa**	**NHL**	**3**	**0**	**0**	**0**	**2**	**0**	**0**	**0**	**3**	**0.0**	**–1**	....	....	....	....	....	....	....	....	....	....	....	....	....
	P.E.I. Senators	AHL	69	33	29	62	241	....	....	....	....	....	....	....	....	....	....	....	....	....	....	....	....	....	....	....
1994-95	P.E.I. Senators	AHL	75	37	30	67	161	....	....	....	....	....	....	....	....	....	....	....	6	1	1	2	24	....	....	....
1995-96	Portland Pirates	AHL	28	9	12	21	99	....	....	....	....	....	....	....	....	....	....	....	....	....	....	....	....	....	....	....
	Chicago Wolves	IHL	45	9	16	25	164	....	....	....	....	....	....	....	....	....	....	....	5	4	0	4	8	....	....	....
1996-97	Manitoba Moose	IHL	79	32	34	66	222	....	....	....	....	....	....	....	....	....	....	....	....	....	....	....	....	....	....	....
1997-98	Manitoba Moose	IHL	76	42	34	76	246	....	....	....	....	....	....	....	....	....	....	....	3	0	0	0	6	....	....	....
1998-99	**Calgary**	**NHL**	**18**	**0**	**3**	**3**	**20**	**0**	**0**	**0**	**10**	**0.0**	**0**	**3**	**66.7**	**17**	**2**	**7:26**	....	....	....	....	....	....	....	....
	Saint John Flames	AHL	30	10	14	24	84	....	....	....	....	....	....	....	....	....	....	....	....	....	....	....	....	....	....	....
	Kentucky	AHL	10	2	3	5	7	....	....	....	....	....	....	....	....	....	....	....	11	4	1	5	10	....	....	....
99-2000	Houston Aeros	IHL	62	22	19	41	134	....	....	....	....	....	....	....	....	....	....	....	5	2	1	3	18	....	....	....
2000-01	Houston Aeros	IHL	74	22	24	46	231	....	....	....	....	....	....	....	....	....	....	....	7	1	1	2	10	....	....	....
	NHL Totals		**21**	**0**	**3**	**3**	**22**	**0**	**0**	**0**	**13**	**0.0**		**3**	**66.7**	**17**	**2**	**7:26**	....	....	....	....	....	....	....	....

Signed as a free agent by **Ottawa**, May 27, 1993. Signed as a free agent by **Calgary**, September 1, 1998. Traded to **San Jose** by **Calgary** for cash, March 23, 1999. Signed as a free agent by **Houston** (IHL), August 31, 2000.

PARK, Richard

(PAHRK, RIH-chahrd) **MIN.**

Center. Shoots right. 5'11", 190 lbs. Born, Seoul, S. Korea, May 27, 1976. Pittsburgh's 2nd choice, 50th overall, in 1994 Entry Draft.

Season	Club	League	GP	G	A	Pts	PIM	PP	SH	GW	S	%	+/-	TF	F%	H	SB	Min	GP	G	A	Pts	PIM	PP	SH	GW
1991-92	Toronto Nats	MTHL	76	49	58	107	91	....	....	....	....	....	....	....	....	....	....	....	....	....	....	....	....	....	....	....
1992-93	Belleville Bulls	OHL	66	23	38	61	38	....	....	....	....	....	....	....	....	....	....	....	5	0	0	0	14	....	....	....
1993-94	Belleville Bulls	OHL	59	27	49	76	70	....	....	....	....	....	....	....	....	....	....	....	12	3	5	8	18	....	....	....
1994-95	Belleville Bulls	OHL	45	28	51	79	35	....	....	....	....	....	....	....	....	....	....	....	16	9	18	27	12	....	....	....
	Pittsburgh	**NHL**	**1**	**0**	**1**	**1**	**2**	**0**	**0**	**0**	**4**	**0.0**	**1**	....	....	....	....	....	**3**	**0**	**0**	**0**	**2**	**0**	**0**	**0**
1995-96	Belleville Bulls	OHL	6	7	6	13	2	....	....	....	....	....	....	....	....	....	....	....	14	18	12	30	10	....	....	....
	Pittsburgh	**NHL**	**56**	**4**	**6**	**10**	**36**	**0**	**1**	**1**	**62**	**6.5**	**3**	....	....	....	....	....	**1**	**0**	**0**	**0**	**0**	**0**	**0**	**0**
1996-97	**Pittsburgh**	**NHL**	**1**	**0**	**0**	**0**	**0**	**0**	**0**	**0**	**1**	**0.0**	**–1**	....	....	....	....	....	....	....	....	....	....	....	....	....
	Cleveland	IHL	50	12	15	27	30	....	....	....	....	....	....	....	....	....	....	....	....	....	....	....	....	....	....	....
	Anaheim	**NHL**	**11**	**1**	**1**	**2**	**10**	**0**	**0**	**0**	**9**	**11.1**	**0**	....	....	....	....	....	**11**	**0**	**1**	**1**	**2**	**0**	**0**	**0**
1997-98	**Anaheim**	**NHL**	**15**	**0**	**2**	**2**	**8**	**0**	**0**	**0**	**14**	**0.0**	**–3**	....	....	....	....	....	....	....	....	....	....	....	....	....
	Cincinnati Ducks	AHL	56	17	26	43	36	....	....	....	....	....	....	....	....	....	....	....	....	....	....	....	....	....	....	....
1998-99	**Philadelphia**	**NHL**	**7**	**0**	**0**	**0**	**0**	**0**	**0**	**0**	**5**	**0.0**	**–1**	**15**	**53.3**	**2**	**0**	**9:21**	....	....	....	....	....	....	....	....
	Philadelphia	AHL	75	41	42	83	33	....	....	....	....	....	....	....	....	....	....	....	16	9	6	15	4	....	....	....
99-2000	Utah Grizzlies	IHL	82	28	32	60	36	....	....	....	....	....	....	....	....	....	....	....	5	1	0	1	0	....	....	....
2000-01	Cleveland	IHL	75	27	21	48	29	....	....	....	....	....	....	....	....	....	....	....	4	0	2	2	4	....	....	....
	NHL Totals		**91**	**5**	**10**	**15**	**56**	**0**	**1**	**1**	**95**	**5.3**		**15**	**53.3**	**2**	**0**	**9:21**	**15**	**0**	**1**	**1**	**4**	**0**	**0**	**0**

AHL Second All-Star Team (1999)

Traded to **Anaheim** by **Pittsburgh** for Roman Oksiuta, March 18, 1997. Signed as a free agent by **Philadelphia**, August 24, 1998. Signed as a free agent by **Utah** (IHL), September 22, 1999. Signed as a free agent by **Minnesota**, June 6, 2000.

PARKER, Scott

(PAR-kuhr, SKAWT) **COL.**

Right wing. Shoots right. 6'5", 230 lbs. Born, Hanford, CA, January 29, 1978. Colorado's 4th choice, 20th overall, in 1998 Entry Draft.

Season	Club	League	GP	G	A	Pts	PIM	PP	SH	GW	S	%	+/-	TF	F%	H	SB	Min	GP	G	A	Pts	PIM	PP	SH	GW
1993-94	Alaska Arctic Ice	AAHL	34	8	12	20	86	....	....	....	....	....	....	....	....	....	....	....	....	....	....	....	....	....	....	....
1994-95	Spokane Braves	KIJHL	43	7	21	28	128	....	....	....	....	....	....	....	....	....	....	....	....	....	....	....	....	....	....	....
1995-96	Kelowna Rockets	WHL	64	3	4	7	159	....	....	....	....	....	....	....	....	....	....	....	6	0	0	0	12	....	....	....
1996-97	Kelowna Rockets	WHL	68	18	8	26	*330	....	....	....	....	....	....	....	....	....	....	....	6	0	2	2	4	....	....	....
1997-98	Kelowna Rockets	WHL	71	30	22	52	243	....	....	....	....	....	....	....	....	....	....	....	7	6	0	6	23	....	....	....
1998-99	**Colorado**	**NHL**	**27**	**0**	**0**	**0**	**71**	**0**	**0**	**0**	**3**	**0.0**	**–3**	**1**	**0.0**	**10**	**0**	**1:37**	....	....	....	....	....	....	....	....
	Hershey Bears	AHL	32	4	3	7	143	....	....	....	....	....	....	....	....	....	....	....	4	0	0	0	6	....	....	....
99-2000	Hershey Bears	AHL	68	12	7	19	206	....	....	....	....	....	....	....	....	....	....	....	11	1	1	2	56	....	....	....
2000-01♦	**Colorado**	**NHL**	**69**	**2**	**3**	**5**	**155**	**0**	**0**	**1**	**35**	**5.7**	**–2**	**2**	**0.0**	**104**	**5**	**5:42**	**4**	**0**	**0**	**0**	**2**	**0**	**0**	**0**
	NHL Totals		**96**	**2**	**3**	**5**	**226**	**0**	**0**	**1**	**38**	**5.3**		**3**	**0.0**	**114**	**5**	**4:33**	**4**	**0**	**0**	**0**	**2**	**0**	**0**	**0**

• Re-entered NHL Entry Draft. Originally New Jersey's 6th choice, 63rd overall, in 1996 Entry Draft.

PARRISH, Mark

(PAIR-ihsh, MAHRK) **NYI**

Right wing. Shoots right. 5'11", 191 lbs. Born, Edina, MN, February 2, 1977. Colorado's 3rd choice, 79th overall, in 1996 Entry Draft.

Season	Club	League	GP	G	A	Pts	PIM	PP	SH	GW	S	%	+/-	TF	F%	H	SB	Min	GP	G	A	Pts	PIM	PP	SH	GW
1994-95	Jefferson High	Hi-School	27	40	20	60	42	....	....	....	....	....	....	....	....	....	....	....	....	....	....	....	....	....	....	....
1995-96	St. Cloud State	WCHA	39	15	13	28	30	....	....	....	....	....	....	....	....	....	....	....	....	....	....	....	....	....	....	....
1996-97	St. Cloud State	WCHA	35	*27	15	42	60	....	....	....	....	....	....	....	....	....	....	....	....	....	....	....	....	....	....	....
1997-98	Seattle T-Birds	WHL	54	54	38	92	29	....	....	....	....	....	....	....	....	....	....	....	5	2	3	5	2	....	....	....
	New Haven	AHL	1	1	0	1	2	....	....	....	....	....	....	....	....	....	....	....	....	....	....	....	....	....	....	....
1998-99	**Florida**	**NHL**	**73**	**24**	**13**	**37**	**25**	**5**	**0**	**5**	**129**	**18.6**	**–6**	**1**	**0.0**	**56**	**5**	**13:59**	....	....	....	....	....	....	....	....
	New Haven	AHL	2	1	0	1	0	....	....	....	....	....	....	....	....	....	....	....	....	....	....	....	....	....	....	....
99-2000	**Florida**	**NHL**	**81**	**26**	**18**	**44**	**39**	**6**	**0**	**3**	**152**	**17.1**	**1**	**8**	**75.0**	**113**	**8**	**14:04**	**4**	**0**	**1**	**1**	**0**	**0**	**0**	**0**
2000-01	**NY Islanders**	**NHL**	**70**	**17**	**13**	**30**	**28**	**6**	**0**	**3**	**123**	**13.8**	**–27**	**3**	**33.3**	**176**	**13**	**15:27**	....	....	....	....	....	....	....	....
	NHL Totals		**224**	**67**	**44**	**111**	**92**	**17**	**0**	**11**	**404**	**16.6**		**12**	**58.3**	**345**	**26**	**14:28**	**4**	**0**	**1**	**1**	**0**	**0**	**0**	**0**

NCAA West Second All-American Team (1997) • WHL West First All-Star Team (1998)

Rights traded to **Florida** by **Colorado** with Anaheim's 3rd round choice (previously acquired, Florida selected Lance Ward) in 1998 Entry Draft for Tom Fitzgerald, March 24, 1998. Traded to **NY Islanders** by **Florida** with Oleg Kvasha for Roberto Luongo and Olli Jokinen, June 24, 2000.

PATERA, Pavel

(puh-TEHR-uh, PAH-vehl) **MIN.**

Center. Shoots left. 6'1", 172 lbs. Born, Kladno, Czech., September 6, 1971. Dallas' 4th choice, 153rd overall, in 1998 Entry Draft.

Season	Club	League	GP	G	A	Pts	PIM	PP	SH	GW	S	%	+/-	TF	F%	H	SB	Min	GP	G	A	Pts	PIM	PP	SH	GW
1990-91	Poldi Kladno	Czech.	3	0	0	0	....	....	....	....	....	....	....	....	....	....	....	....	....	....	....	....	....	....	....	....
1991-92	Poldi Kladno	Czech.	38	12	13	25	26	....	....	....	....	....	....	....	....	....	....	....	8	8	4	12	0	....	....	....
1992-93	Poldi Kladno	Czech.	42	9	23	32	....	....	....	....	....	....	....	....	....	....	....	....	....	....	....	....	....	....	....	....
1993-94	Poldi Kladno	Cze-Rep	43	21	39	60	....	....	....	....	....	....	....	....	....	....	....	....	11	5	10	15	....	....	....	....
1994-95	Poldi Kladno	Cze-Rep	43	26	49	75	24	....	....	....	....	....	....	....	....	....	....	....	11	5	7	12	6	....	....	....
1995-96	Poldi Kladno	Cze-Rep	40	24	31	55	38	....	....	....	....	....	....	....	....	....	....	....	8	3	1	4	34	....	....	....
1996-97	AIK Solna	Sweden	50	19	24	43	44	....	....	....	....	....	....	....	....	....	....	....	7	2	3	5	6	....	....	....
1997-98	AIK Solna	Sweden	46	8	17	25	50	....	....	....	....	....	....	....	....	....	....	....	....	....	....	....	....	....	....	....
1998-99	HC Vsetin	Cze-Rep	52	16	37	53	58	....	....	....	....	....	....	....	....	....	....	....	12	5	*10	15	....	....	....	....
99-2000	**Dallas**	**NHL**	**12**	**1**	**4**	**5**	**4**	**0**	**0**	**0**	**18**	**5.6**	**–1**	**61**	**49.2**	**2**	**1**	**14:04**	....	....	....	....	....	....	....	....
	Slovnaft Vsetin	Cze-Rep	29	8	14	22	36	....	....	....	....	....	....	....	....	....	....	....	9	3	4	7	8	....	....	....
2000-01	**Minnesota**	**NHL**	**20**	**1**	**3**	**4**	**4**	**0**	**0**	**0**	**14**	**7.1**	**–8**	**184**	**44.0**	**7**	**15**	**14:27**	....	....	....	....	....	....	....	....
	Cleveland	IHL	54	8	44	52	22	....	....	....	....	....	....	....	....	....	....	....	....	....	....	....	....	....	....	....
	NHL Totals		**32**	**2**	**7**	**9**	**8**	**0**	**0**	**0**	**32**	**6.3**		**245**	**45.3**	**9**	**16**	**14:19**	....	....	....	....	....	....	....	....

Traded to **Minnesota** by **Dallas** with Aaron Gavey, Dallas' 8th round choice (Eric Johansson) in 2000 Entry Draft and Minnesota's 4th round choice (previously acquired) in 2002 Entry Draft for Brad Lukowich and Minnesota's 3rd (Yared Hagos) and 9th (Dale Sullivan) round choices in 2001 Entry Draft, June 25, 2000.

PATRICK, James
(PAT-rihk, JAYMS) **BUF.**

Defense. Shoots right. 6'3", 201 lbs. Born, Winnipeg, Man., June 14, 1963. NY Rangers' 1st choice, 9th overall, in 1981 Entry Draft.

Season	Club	League	GP	G	A	Pts	PIM	PP	SH	GW	S	%	+/-	TF	F%	H	SB	Min	GP	G	A	Pts	PIM	PP	SH	GW
			Regular Season																Playoffs							
1980-81	Prince Albert	SJHL	59	21	61	82	162																			
1981-82	North Dakota	WCHA	42	5	24	29	26																			
1982-83	North Dakota	WCHA	36	12	36	48	29																			
1983-84	Canada	Nat-Team	63	7	24	31	52																			
	Canada	Olympics	7	0	3	3	4																			
	NY Rangers	NHL	12	1	7	8	2	0	0	0	15	6.7	6						5	0	3	3	2	0	0	0
1984-85	NY Rangers	NHL	75	8	28	36	71	4	1	1	101	7.9	–17						3	0	0	0	4	0	0	0
1985-86	NY Rangers	NHL	75	14	29	43	88	2	1	1	131	10.7	14						16	1	5	6	34	0	0	0
1986-87	NY Rangers	NHL	78	10	45	55	62	5	0	0	143	7.0	13						6	1	2	3	2	1	0	1
1987-88	NY Rangers	NHL	70	17	45	62	52	9	0	1	187	9.1	16													
1988-89	NY Rangers	NHL	68	11	36	47	41	6	0	2	147	7.5	3						4	0	1	1	2	0	0	0
1989-90	NY Rangers	NHL	73	14	43	57	50	9	0	0	136	10.3	4						10	3	8	11	0	2	0	1
1990-91	NY Rangers	NHL	74	10	49	59	58	6	0	2	138	7.2	–5						6	0	0	0	6	0	0	0
1991-92	NY Rangers	NHL	80	14	57	71	54	6	0	1	148	9.5	34						13	0	7	7	12	0	0	0
1992-93	NY Rangers	NHL	60	5	21	26	61	3	0	0	99	5.1	1													
1993-94	NY Rangers	NHL	6	0	3	3	2	0	0	0	6	0.0	1													
	Hartford	NHL	47	8	20	28	32	4	1	2	65	12.3	–12													
	Calgary	NHL	15	2	2	4	6	1	0	0	20	10.0	6						7	0	1	1	6	0	0	0
1994-95	Calgary	NHL	43	0	10	10	14	0	0	0	43	0.0	–3						5	0	1	1	0	0	0	0
1995-96	Calgary	NHL	80	3	32	35	30	1	0	0	116	2.6	3						4	0	0	0	2	0	0	0
1996-97	Calgary	NHL	19	3	1	4	6	1	0	0	22	13.6	2													
1997-98	Calgary	NHL	60	6	11	17	26	1	0	1	57	10.5	–2													
1998-99	Buffalo	NHL	45	1	7	8	16	0	0	0	31	3.2	12	0	0.0	23	38	14:45	20	0	1	1	12	0	0	0
99-2000	Buffalo	NHL	66	5	8	13	22	0	0	3	40	12.5	8	0	0.0	44	61	15:59	5	0	1	1	2	0	0	0
2000-01	Buffalo	NHL	54	4	9	13	12	1	0	0	48	8.3	9	0	0.0	28	64	17:16	13	1	2	3	2	0	0	0
	NHL Totals		1100	136	463	599	705	59	3	14	1693	8.0		0	0.0	95	163	16:04	117	6	32	38	86	3	0	2

WCHA Second All-Star Team (1982) • NCAA Chamionship All-Tournament Team (1982) • WCHA First All-Star Team (1983) • NCAA West All American Team (1983)

Traded to **Hartford** by **NY Rangers** with Darren Turcotte for Steve Larmer, Nick Kypreos, Barry Richter and Hartford's 6th round choice (Yuri Litvinov) in 1994 Entry Draft, November 2, 1993. Traded to **Calgary** by **Hartford** with Zarley Zalapski and Michael Nylander for Gary Suter, Paul Ranheim and Ted Drury, March 10, 1994. • Missed majority of 1996-97 season recovering from knee injury originally suffered in game vs. Pittsburgh, October 24, 1996. Signed as a free agent by **Buffalo**, October 7, 1998.

PATTERSON, Ed
(PAT-uhr-SOHN, EHD)

Right wing. Shoots right. 6'2", 213 lbs. Born, Delta, B.C., November 14, 1972. Pittsburgh's 7th choice, 148th overall, in 1991 Entry Draft.

Season	Club	League	GP	G	A	Pts	PIM	PP	SH	GW	S	%	+/-	TF	F%	H	SB	Min	GP	G	A	Pts	PIM	PP	SH	GW
1987-88	South Delta	BCAHA	50	40	70	110	60																			
1988-89	Seattle T-Birds	WHL	46	4	6	10	55																			
1989-90	Seattle T-Birds	WHL	18	9	2	11	19																			
	Swift Current	WHL	15	1	3	4	0												4	0	0	0	2			
1990-91	Swift Current	WHL	7	2	7	9	0																			
	Kamloops Blazers	WHL	55	14	33	47	134												5	0	0	0	7			
1991-92	Kamloops Blazers	WHL	38	19	25	44	100												1	0	0	0	0			
1992-93	Cleveland	IHL	63	4	16	20	131												3	1	1	2	2			
1993-94	Pittsburgh	NHL	27	3	1	4	10	0	0	0	15	20.0	–5													
	Cleveland	IHL	55	21	32	53	73																			
1994-95	Cleveland	IHL	58	13	17	30	93												4	1	2	3	6			
1995-96	Pittsburgh	NHL	35	0	2	2	38	0	0	0	17	0.0	–5													
1996-97	Pittsburgh	NHL	6	0	0	0	8	0	0	0	2	0.0	0													
	Cleveland	IHL	40	6	12	18	75												13	2	4	6	61			
1997-98	Grand Rapids	IHL	81	12	31	43	226												3	2	1	3	8			
1998-99	Cincinnati	IHL	73	8	25	33	227												3	1	0	1	4			
99-2000	Grand Rapids	IHL	74	20	21	41	141												5	4	0	4	2			
2000-01	Grand Rapids	IHL	70	19	23	42	90												10	1	4	5	17			
	NHL Totals		68	3	3	6	56	0	0	0	34	8.8														

Signed as a free agent by **Grand Rapids** (IHL), September 14, 1999. Signed as a free agent by **EHC Berlin** (DEL), June 12, 2001.

PAYER, Serge
(pie-YAY, SAIRZH) **FLA.**

Center. Shoots left. 6', 203 lbs. Born, Rockland, Ont., May 7, 1979.

Season	Club	League	GP	G	A	Pts	PIM	PP	SH	GW	S	%	+/-	TF	F%	H	SB	Min	GP	G	A	Pts	PIM	PP	SH	GW
1994-95	Cumberland Colts	OMHA	42	37	46	83	55																			
1995-96	Kitchener Rangers	OHL	66	8	16	24	18												12	0	2	2	2			
1996-97	Kitchener Rangers	OHL	63	7	16	23	27												13	1	3	4	2			
1997-98	Kitchener Rangers	OHL	44	20	21	41	51												6	3	0	3	7			
1998-99	Kitchener Rangers	OHL	40	18	19	37	22																			
99-2000	Kitchener Rangers	OHL	44	10	26	36	53												5	0	3	3	6			
2000-01	Florida	NHL	43	5	1	6	21	0	1	0	34	14.7	0	97	42.3	26	9	7:27								
	Louisville Panthers	AHL	32	6	6	12	15																			
	NHL Totals		43	5	1	6	21	0	1	0	34	14.7		97	42.3	26	9	7:27								

Signed as a free agent by **Florida**, September 30, 1997.

PEARSON, Scott
(PEER-sohn, SKAWT)

Left wing. Shoots left. 6'1", 205 lbs. Born, Cornwall, Ont., December 19, 1969. Toronto's 1st choice, 6th overall, in 1988 Entry Draft.

Season	Club	League	GP	G	A	Pts	PIM	PP	SH	GW	S	%	+/-	TF	F%	H	SB	Min	GP	G	A	Pts	PIM	PP	SH	GW
1984-85	Cornwall Royals	OMHA	60	40	40	80	60																			
1985-86	Kingston	OHL	63	16	23	39	56																			
1986-87	Kingston	OHL	62	30	24	54	101												9	3	3	6	42			
1987-88	Kingston	OHL	46	26	32	58	117																			
1988-89	Kingston Raiders	OHL	13	9	8	17	34																			
	Niagara Falls	OHL	32	26	34	60	90												17	14	10	24	53			
	Toronto	NHL	9	0	1	1	2	0	0	0	6	0.0	0													
1989-90	Toronto	NHL	41	5	10	15	90	0	0	1	66	7.6	–7						2	2	0	2	10	0	0	0
	Newmarket	AHL	18	12	11	23	64																			
1990-91	Toronto	NHL	12	0	0	0	20	0	0	0	13	0.0	–5													
	Quebec	NHL	35	11	4	15	86	0	0	0	61	18.0	–4													
	Halifax Citadels	AHL	24	12	15	27	44																			
1991-92	Quebec	NHL	10	1	2	3	14	0	0	0	14	7.1	–5													
	Halifax Citadels	AHL	5	2	1	3	4																			
1992-93	Quebec	NHL	41	13	1	14	95	0	0	1	45	28.9	3						3	0	0	0	0	0	0	0
	Halifax Citadels	AHL	5	3	1	4	25																			
1993-94	Edmonton	NHL	72	19	18	37	165	3	0	7	160	11.9	–4													
1994-95	Edmonton	NHL	28	1	4	5	54	0	0	0	21	4.8	–11													
	Buffalo	NHL	14	2	1	3	20	0	0	0	19	10.5	–3						5	0	0	0	4	0	0	0
1995-96	Buffalo	NHL	27	4	0	4	67	0	0	1	26	15.4	–4													
	Rochester	AHL	26	8	8	16	113																			
1996-97	Toronto	NHL	1	0	0	0	2	0	0	0	0	0.0	0													
	St. John's Leafs	AHL	14	5	2	7	26												9	5	2	7	14			
1997-98	Chicago Wolves	IHL	78	34	17	51	225												22	12	6	18	50			
1998-99	Chicago Wolves	IHL	62	23	13	36	154												8	4	1	5	*50			
99-2000	NY Islanders	NHL	2	0	1	1	0	0	0	0	5	0.0	1	0	0.0	6	0	13:15								
	Chicago Wolves	IHL	77	19	14	33	124												16	5	5	10	28			
2000-01	ESC Essen	DEL	51	21	13	34	*225																			
	NHL Totals		292	56	42	98	615	3	0	10	436	12.8		0	0.0	6	0	13:15	10	2	0	2	14	0	0	0

Traded to **Quebec** by **Toronto** with Toronto's 2nd round choices in 1991 (later traded to Washington - Washington selected Eric Lavigne) and 1992 (Tuomas Gronman) Entry Drafts for Aaron Broten, Lucien Deblois and Michel Petit, November 17, 1990. Traded to **Edmonton** by **Quebec** for Martin Gelinas and Edmonton's 6th round choice (Nicholas Checco) in 1993 Entry Draft, June 20, 1993. Traded to **Buffalo** by **Edmonton** for Ken Sutton, April 7, 1995. Signed as a free agent by **Toronto**, July 24, 1996. • Missed majority of 1996-97 season recovering from abdominal surgery, November, 1996. Signed as a free agent by **NY Islanders**, August 9, 1999.

PECA, Michael

(PEH-kuh, MIGHK-uhl) **NYI**

Center. Shoots right. 5'11", 190 lbs. Born, Toronto, Ont., March 26, 1974. Vancouver's 2nd choice, 40th overall, in 1992 Entry Draft.

			Regular Season															Playoffs							
Season	Club	League	GP	G	A	Pts	PIM	PP	SH	GW	S	%	+/-	TF	F%	H	SB	Min	GP	G	A	Pts	PIM	PP	SH	GW
1989-90	Toronto Nats	MTHL	39	42	53	95	40	....	....	....	....	....	....	....	....	....	....	....	....	....	....	....	....	....	....	....
1990-91	Sudbury Wolves	OHL	62	14	27	41	24	....	....	....	....	....	....	....	....	....	....	....	5	1	0	1	7	....	....	....
1991-92	Sudbury Wolves	OHL	39	16	34	50	61	....	....	....	....	....	....	....	....	....	....	....	....	....	....	....	....	....	....	....
	Ottawa 67's	OHL	27	8	17	25	32	....	....	....	....	....	....	....	....	....	....	....	11	6	10	16	6	....	....	....
1992-93	Ottawa 67's	OHL	55	38	64	102	80	....	....	....	....	....	....	....	....	....	....	....	....	....	....	....	....	....	....	....
	Hamilton Canucks	AHL	9	6	3	9	11	....	....	....	....	....	....	....	....	....	....	....	....	....	....	....	....	....	....	....
1993-94	Ottawa 67's	OHL	55	50	63	113	101	....	....	....	....	....	....	....	....	....	....	....	17	7	22	29	30	....	....	....
	Vancouver	**NHL**	**4**	**0**	**0**	**0**	**2**	**0**	**0**	**0**	**5**	**0.0**	**–1**	....	....	....	....	....	....	....	....	....	....	....	....	....
1994-95	Syracuse Crunch	AHL	35	10	24	34	75	....	....	....	....	....	....	....	....	....	....	....	....	....	....	....	....	....	....	....
	Vancouver	**NHL**	**33**	**6**	**6**	**12**	**30**	**2**	**0**	**1**	**46**	**13.0**	**–6**	....	....	....	....	....	**5**	**0**	**1**	**1**	**8**	**0**	**0**	**0**
1995-96	**Buffalo**	**NHL**	**68**	**11**	**20**	**31**	**67**	**4**	**3**	**1**	**109**	**10.1**	**–1**	....	....	....	....	....	....	....	....	....	....	....	....	....
1996-97	**Buffalo**	**NHL**	**79**	**20**	**29**	**49**	**80**	**5**	**6**	**4**	**137**	**14.6**	**26**	....	....	....	....	....	**10**	**0**	**2**	**2**	**8**	**0**	**0**	**0**
1997-98	**Buffalo**	**NHL**	**61**	**18**	**22**	**40**	**57**	**6**	**5**	**1**	**132**	**13.6**	**12**	....	....	....	....	....	**13**	**3**	**2**	**5**	**8**	**0**	**0**	**1**
1998-99	**Buffalo**	**NHL**	**82**	**27**	**29**	**56**	**81**	**10**	**0**	**8**	**199**	**13.6**	**7**	**1855**	**49.4**	**181**	**64**	**20:44**	**21**	**5**	**8**	**13**	**18**	**2**	**1**	**0**
99-2000	**Buffalo**	**NHL**	**73**	**20**	**21**	**41**	**67**	**2**	**0**	**3**	**144**	**13.9**	**6**	**1604**	**48.6**	**132**	**76**	**19:57**	**5**	**0**	**1**	**1**	**4**	**0**	**0**	**0**
2000-01	**Buffalo**	**NHL**	DID NOT PLAY																							
	NHL Totals		**400**	**102**	**127**	**229**	**384**	**29**	**14**	**18**	**772**	**13.2**		**3459**	**49.0**	**313**	**140**	**20:22**	**54**	**8**	**14**	**22**	**46**	**2**	**1**	**1**

Won Frank J. Selke Trophy (1997)

Traded to **Buffalo** by **Vancouver** with Mike Wilson and Vancouver's 1st round choice (Jay McKee) in 1995 Entry Draft for Alexander Mogilny and Buffalo's 5th round choice (Todd Norman) in 1995 Entry Draft, July 8, 1995. • Missed entire 2000-01 season after failing to come to contract terms with **Buffalo**. Rights traded to **NY Islanders** by **Buffalo** for Tim Connolly and Taylor Pyatt, June 24, 2001.

PEDERSON, Denis

(PEE-duhr-suhn, DEH-nihs) **VAN.**

Center. Shoots right. 6'2", 205 lbs. Born, Prince Albert, Sask., September 10, 1975. New Jersey's 1st choice, 13th overall, in 1993 Entry Draft.

			Regular Season															Playoffs							
Season	Club	League	GP	G	A	Pts	PIM	PP	SH	GW	S	%	+/-	TF	F%	H	SB	Min	GP	G	A	Pts	PIM	PP	SH	GW
1990-91	Prince Albert	AMHL	30	25	17	42	84	....	....	....	....	....	....	....	....	....	....	....	....	....	....	....	....	....	....	....
1991-92	Prince Albert	AMHL	21	33	25	58	40	....	....	....	....	....	....	....	....	....	....	....	....	....	....	....	....	....	....	....
	Prince Albert	WHL	10	0	0	0	6	....	....	....	....	....	....	....	....	....	....	....	7	0	1	1	13	....	....	....
1992-93	Prince Albert	WHL	72	33	40	73	134	....	....	....	....	....	....	....	....	....	....	....	....	....	....	....	....	....	....	....
1993-94	Prince Albert	WHL	71	53	45	98	157	....	....	....	....	....	....	....	....	....	....	....	....	....	....	....	....	....	....	....
1994-95	Prince Albert	WHL	63	30	38	68	122	....	....	....	....	....	....	....	....	....	....	....	15	11	14	25	14	....	....	....
	Albany River Rats	AHL	....	....	....	....	....	....	....	....	....	....	....	....	....	....	....	....	3	0	0	0	2	....	....	....
1995-96	**New Jersey**	**NHL**	**10**	**3**	**1**	**4**	**0**	**1**	**0**	**2**	**6**	**50.0**	**–1**	....	....	....	....	....	....	....	....	....	....	....	....	....
	Albany River Rats	AHL	68	28	43	71	104	....	....	....	....	....	....	....	....	....	....	....	4	1	2	3	0	....	....	....
1996-97	**New Jersey**	**NHL**	**70**	**12**	**20**	**32**	**62**	**3**	**0**	**3**	**106**	**11.3**	**7**	....	....	....	....	....	**9**	**0**	**0**	**0**	**2**	**0**	**0**	**0**
	Albany River Rats	AHL	3	1	3	4	7	....	....	....	....	....	....	....	....	....	....	....	....	....	....	....	....	....	....	....
1997-98	**New Jersey**	**NHL**	**80**	**15**	**13**	**28**	**97**	**7**	**0**	**1**	**135**	**11.1**	**–6**	....	....	....	....	....	**6**	**1**	**1**	**2**	**2**	**0**	**1**	**0**
1998-99	**New Jersey**	**NHL**	**76**	**11**	**12**	**23**	**66**	**3**	**0**	**1**	**145**	**7.6**	**–10**	**540**	**42.8**	**105**	**39**	**15:19**	**3**	**0**	**1**	**1**	**0**	**0**	**0**	**0**
99-2000	**New Jersey**	**NHL**	**35**	**3**	**3**	**6**	**16**	**0**	**0**	**0**	**41**	**7.3**	**–7**	**125**	**48.8**	**41**	**9**	**10:42**	....	....	....	....	....	....	....	....
	Vancouver	**NHL**	**12**	**3**	**2**	**5**	**2**	**0**	**0**	**1**	**15**	**20.0**	**1**	**70**	**45.7**	**15**	**3**	**12:41**	....	....	....	....	....	....	....	....
2000-01	**Vancouver**	**NHL**	**61**	**4**	**8**	**12**	**65**	**0**	**1**	**3**	**70**	**5.7**	**0**	**351**	**42.7**	**71**	**24**	**11:42**	**4**	**0**	**1**	**1**	**4**	**0**	**0**	**0**
	NHL Totals		**344**	**51**	**59**	**110**	**308**	**14**	**1**	**11**	**518**	**9.8**		**1086**	**43.6**	**232**	**75**	**13:04**	**22**	**1**	**3**	**4**	**8**	**0**	**1**	**0**

WHL East Second All-Star Team (1994)

Traded to **Vancouver** by **New Jersey** with Brendan Morrison for Alexander Mogilny, March 14, 2000.

PELLERIN, Scott

(PEHL-ih-rihn, SKAWT) **BOS.**

Left wing. Shoots left. 5'11", 190 lbs. Born, Shediac, N.B., January 9, 1970. New Jersey's 4th choice, 47th overall, in 1989 Entry Draft.

			Regular Season															Playoffs							
Season	Club	League	GP	G	A	Pts	PIM	PP	SH	GW	S	%	+/-	TF	F%	H	SB	Min	GP	G	A	Pts	PIM	PP	SH	GW
1985-86	Moncton Flyers	NBAHA	45	65	34	99	34	....	....	....	....	....	....	....	....	....	....	....	....	....	....	....	....	....	....	....
1986-87	Notre Dame	SMHL	72	62	68	130	98	....	....	....	....	....	....	....	....	....	....	....	....	....	....	....	....	....	....	....
1987-88	Notre Dame	SJHL	57	37	49	86	139	....	....	....	....	....	....	....	....	....	....	....	....	....	....	....	....	....	....	....
1988-89	U. of Maine	H-East	45	29	33	62	92	....	....	....	....	....	....	....	....	....	....	....	....	....	....	....	....	....	....	....
1989-90	U. of Maine	H-East	42	22	34	56	68	....	....	....	....	....	....	....	....	....	....	....	....	....	....	....	....	....	....	....
1990-91	U. of Maine	H-East	43	23	25	48	60	....	....	....	....	....	....	....	....	....	....	....	....	....	....	....	....	....	....	....
1991-92	U. of Maine	H-East	37	*32	25	57	54	....	....	....	....	....	....	....	....	....	....	....	....	....	....	....	....	....	....	....
	Utica Devils	AHL	....	....	....	....	....	....	....	....	....	....	....	....	....	....	....	....	3	1	0	1	0	....	....	....
1992-93	**New Jersey**	**NHL**	**45**	**10**	**11**	**21**	**41**	**1**	**2**	**0**	**60**	**16.7**	**–1**	....	....	....	....	....	....	....	....	....	....	....	....	....
	Utica Devils	AHL	27	15	18	33	33	....	....	....	....	....	....	....	....	....	....	....	2	0	1	1	0	....	....	....
1993-94	**New Jersey**	**NHL**	**1**	**0**	**0**	**0**	**2**	**0**	**0**	**0**	**0**	**0.0**	**0**	....	....	....	....	....	....	....	....	....	....	....	....	....
	Albany River Rats	AHL	73	28	46	74	84	....	....	....	....	....	....	....	....	....	....	....	5	2	1	3	11	....	....	....
1994-95	Albany River Rats	AHL	74	23	33	56	95	....	....	....	....	....	....	....	....	....	....	....	14	6	4	10	8	....	....	....
1995-96	**New Jersey**	**NHL**	**6**	**2**	**1**	**3**	**0**	**0**	**0**	**0**	**9**	**22.2**	**1**	....	....	....	....	....	....	....	....	....	....	....	....	....
	Albany River Rats	AHL	75	35	47	82	142	....	....	....	....	....	....	....	....	....	....	....	4	0	3	3	10	....	....	....
1996-97	**St. Louis**	**NHL**	**54**	**8**	**10**	**18**	**35**	**0**	**2**	**2**	**76**	**10.5**	**12**	....	....	....	....	....	**6**	**0**	**0**	**0**	**6**	**0**	**0**	**0**
	Worcester	AHL	24	10	16	26	37	....	....	....	....	....	....	....	....	....	....	....	....	....	....	....	....	....	....	....
1997-98	**St. Louis**	**NHL**	**80**	**8**	**21**	**29**	**62**	**1**	**1**	**0**	**96**	**8.3**	**14**	....	....	....	....	....	**10**	**0**	**2**	**2**	**10**	**0**	**0**	**0**
1998-99	**St. Louis**	**NHL**	**80**	**20**	**21**	**41**	**42**	**0**	**5**	**4**	**138**	**14.5**	**1**	**6**	**66.7**	**90**	**50**	**17:18**	**8**	**1**	**0**	**1**	**4**	**0**	**0**	**0**
99-2000	**St. Louis**	**NHL**	**80**	**8**	**15**	**23**	**48**	**0**	**2**	**2**	**120**	**6.7**	**9**	**6**	**16.7**	**132**	**33**	**14:47**	**7**	**0**	**0**	**0**	**2**	**0**	**0**	**0**
2000-01	**Minnesota**	**NHL**	**58**	**11**	**28**	**39**	**45**	**2**	**2**	**2**	**117**	**9.4**	**6**	**47**	**31.9**	**111**	**36**	**18:40**	....	....	....	....	....	....	....	....
	Carolina	**NHL**	**19**	**0**	**5**	**5**	**6**	**0**	**0**	**0**	**21**	**0.0**	**–4**	**52**	**44.2**	**66**	**6**	**14:14**	**6**	**0**	**0**	**0**	**4**	**0**	**0**	**0**
	NHL Totals		**423**	**67**	**112**	**179**	**281**	**4**	**14**	**10**	**637**	**10.5**		**111**	**38.7**	**399**	**125**	**16:32**	**37**	**1**	**2**	**3**	**26**	**0**	**0**	**0**

Hockey East First All-Star Team (1992) • NCAA East First All-American Team (1992) • Won Hobey Baker Memorial Award (Top U.S. Collegiate Player) (1992)

Signed as a free agent by **St. Louis**, July 10, 1996. Selected by **Minnesota** from **St. Louis** in Expansion Draft, June 23, 2000. Traded to **Carolina** by **Minnesota** for Askhat Rakhmatullin, Carolina's 3rd round choice (later traded to NY Rangers - NY Rangers selected Garth Murray) in 2001 Entry Draft and future considerations, March 1, 2001. Signed as a free agent by **Boston**, July 26, 2001.

PELTONEN, Ville

(PEHL-TOH-nen, VIHL)

Left wing. Shoots left. 5'11", 188 lbs. Born, Vantaa, Finland, May 24, 1973. San Jose's 4th choice, 58th overall, in 1993 Entry Draft.

			Regular Season															Playoffs							
Season	Club	League	GP	G	A	Pts	PIM	PP	SH	GW	S	%	+/-	TF	F%	H	SB	Min	GP	G	A	Pts	PIM	PP	SH	GW
1990-91	HIFK Helsinki	Finn-Jr.	36	21	16	37	16	....	....	....	....	....	....	....	....	....	....	....	7	2	3	5	10	....	....	....
1991-92	HIFK Helsinki	Finn-Jr.	37	28	23	51	28	....	....	....	....	....	....	....	....	....	....	....	4	0	2	2	0	....	....	....
	HIFK Helsinki	Finland	6	0	0	0	0	....	....	....	....	....	....	....	....	....	....	....	....	....	....	....	....	....	....	....
1992-93	HIFK Helsinki	Finn-Jr.	2	4	2	6	4	....	....	....	....	....	....	....	....	....	....	....	....	....	....	....	....	....	....	....
	HIFK Helsinki	Finland	46	13	24	37	16	....	....	....	....	....	....	....	....	....	....	....	4	0	2	2	2	....	....	....
1993-94	HIFK Helsinki	Finland	43	16	22	38	14	....	....	....	....	....	....	....	....	....	....	....	3	0	0	0	2	....	....	....
	Finland	Olympics	8	4	3	7	0	....	....	....	....	....	....	....	....	....	....	....	....	....	....	....	....	....	....	....
1994-95	HIFK Helsinki	Finland	45	20	16	36	16	....	....	....	....	....	....	....	....	....	....	....	3	0	0	0	0	....	....	....
1995-96	**San Jose**	**NHL**	**31**	**2**	**11**	**13**	**14**	**0**	**0**	**0**	**58**	**3.4**	**–7**	....	....	....	....	....	....	....	....	....	....	....	....	....
	Kansas City	IHL	29	5	13	18	8	....	....	....	....	....	....	....	....	....	....	....	....	....	....	....	....	....	....	....
1996-97	**San Jose**	**NHL**	**28**	**2**	**3**	**5**	**0**	**1**	**0**	**0**	**35**	**5.7**	**–8**	....	....	....	....	....	....	....	....	....	....	....	....	....
	Kentucky	AHL	40	22	30	52	21	....	....	....	....	....	....	....	....	....	....	....	....	....	....	....	....	....	....	....
1997-98	Vastra Frolunda	Sweden	45	22	29	*51	44	....	....	....	....	....	....	....	....	....	....	....	7	4	2	6	0	....	....	....
	Finland	Olympics	6	2	1	3	6	....	....	....	....	....	....	....	....	....	....	....	....	....	....	....	....	....	....	....
1998-99	**Nashville**	**NHL**	**14**	**5**	**5**	**10**	**2**	**1**	**0**	**0**	**31**	**16.1**	**1**	**0**	**0.0**	**4**	**4**	**15:54**	....	....	....	....	....	....	....	....
99-2000	**Nashville**	**NHL**	**79**	**6**	**22**	**28**	**22**	**2**	**0**	**2**	**125**	**4.8**	**–1**	**1**	**100.0**	**41**	**14**	**14:41**	....	....	....	....	....	....	....	....
2000-01	**Nashville**	**NHL**	**23**	**3**	**1**	**4**	**2**	**0**	**0**	**0**	**38**	**7.9**	**–7**	**2**	**0.0**	**13**	**6**	**11:40**	....	....	....	....	....	....	....	....
	Milwaukee	IHL	53	27	33	60	26	....	....	....	....	....	....	....	....	....	....	....	5	2	1	3	6	....	....	....
	NHL Totals		**175**	**18**	**42**	**60**	**40**	**4**	**0**	**2**	**287**	**6.3**		**3**	**33.3**	**58**	**24**	**14:14**	....	....	....	....	....	....	....	....

• IHL Second All-Star Team (2001)

Traded to **Nashville** by **San Jose** for Nashville's 5th round choice (later traded to Phoenix - Phoenix selected Josh Blackburn) in 1998 Entry Draft, June 26, 1998. • Missed majority of 1998-99 season recovering from shoulder surgery, December 10, 1998.

PERREAULT, Yanic (puh-ROH, YAH-nihk) MTL.

Center. Shoots left. 5'10", 185 lbs. Born, Sherbrooke, Que., April 4, 1971. Toronto's 1st choice, 47th overall, in 1991 Entry Draft.

			Regular Season																Playoffs							
Season	Club	League	GP	G	A	Pts	PIM	PP	SH	GW	S	%	+/-	TF	F%	H	SB	Min	GP	G	A	Pts	PIM	PP	SH	GW
1987-88	Montreal L'est	QAAA	42	*70	57	*127	14												8	12	10	22	6			
1988-89	Trois-Rivieres	QMJHL	70	53	55	108	48																			
1989-90	Trois-Rivieres	QMJHL	63	51	63	114	75												7	6	5	11	19			
1990-91	Trois-Rivieres	QMJHL	67	*87	98	*185	103												6	4	7	11	6			
1991-92	St. John's Leafs	AHL	62	38	38	76	19												16	7	8	15	4			
1992-93	St. John's Leafs	AHL	79	49	46	95	56												9	4	5	9	2			
1993-94	**Toronto**	**NHL**	**13**	**3**	**3**	**6**	**0**	**2**	**0**	**0**	**24**	**12.5**	**1**													
	St. John's Leafs	AHL	62	45	60	105	38												11	*12	6	18	14			
1994-95	Phoenix	IHL	68	51	48	99	52																			
	Los Angeles	**NHL**	**26**	**2**	**5**	**7**	**20**	**0**	**0**	**1**	**43**	**4.7**	**3**													
1995-96	**Los Angeles**	**NHL**	**78**	**25**	**24**	**49**	**16**	**8**	**3**	**7**	**175**	**14.3**	**-11**													
1996-97	**Los Angeles**	**NHL**	**41**	**11**	**14**	**25**	**20**	**1**	**1**	**0**	**98**	**11.2**	**0**													
1997-98	**Los Angeles**	**NHL**	**79**	**28**	**20**	**48**	**32**	**3**	**2**	**3**	**206**	**13.6**	**6**						**4**	**1**	**2**	**3**	**6**	**1**	**0**	**0**
1998-99	**Los Angeles**	**NHL**	**64**	**10**	**17**	**27**	**30**	**2**	**2**	**1**	**113**	**8.8**	**-3**	**1024**	**56.5**	**35**	**33**	**15:24**								
	Toronto	**NHL**	**12**	**7**	**8**	**15**	**12**	**2**	**1**	**2**	**28**	**25.0**	**10**	**164**	**62.8**	**9**	**1**	**13:20**	**17**	**3**	**6**	**9**	**6**	**0**	**0**	**2**
99-2000	**Toronto**	**NHL**	**58**	**18**	**27**	**45**	**22**	**5**	**0**	**4**	**114**	**15.8**	**3**	**987**	**61.8**	**23**	**10**	**15:18**	**1**	**0**	**1**	**1**	**0**	**0**	**0**	**0**
2000-01	**Toronto**	**NHL**	**76**	**24**	**28**	**52**	**52**	**5**	**0**	**2**	**134**	**17.9**	**0**	**1055**	**62.7**	**22**	**21**	**14:01**	**11**	**2**	**3**	**5**	**4**	**1**	**0**	**1**
	NHL Totals		**447**	**128**	**146**	**274**	**204**	**28**	**9**	**20**	**935**	**13.7**		**3230**	**60.5**	**89**	**65**	**14:45**	**33**	**6**	**12**	**18**	**16**	**2**	**0**	**3**

Canadian Major Junior Rookie of the Year (1989) • QMJHL First All-Star Team (1991)

Traded to **LA Kings** by **Toronto** for LA Kings' 4th round choice (later traded to Philadelphia - later traded to LA Kings - LA Kings selected Mikael Simons) in 1996 Entry Draft, July 11, 1994. Traded to **Toronto** by **Los Angeles** for Jason Podollan and Toronto's 3rd round choice (Cory Campbell) in 1999 Entry Draft, March 23, 1999. Signed as a free agent by **Montreal**, July 4, 2001.

PERSSON, Ricard (PAIR-suhn, RIH-kahrd) OTT.

Defense. Shoots left. 6'1", 201 lbs. Born, Ostersund, Sweden, August 24, 1969. New Jersey's 2nd choice, 23rd overall, in 1987 Entry Draft.

Season	Club	League	GP	G	A	Pts	PIM	PP	SH	GW	S	%	+/-	TF	F%	H	SB	Min	GP	G	A	Pts	PIM	PP	SH	GW
1984-85	Ostersunds IK	Sweden-2	13	0	3	3	6																			
1985-86	Ostersunds IK	Sweden-2	24	2	2	4	16																			
1986-87	Ostersunds IK	Sweden-2	31	10	11	21	28																			
1987-88	Leksands IF	Sweden	31	2	0	2	8												2	0	1	1	2			
1988-89	Leksands IF	Sweden	33	2	4	6	28												9	0	1	1	6			
1989-90	Leksands IF	Sweden	43	9	10	19	62												3	0	0	0	6			
1990-91	Leksands IF	Sweden	37	6	9	15	42																			
1991-92	Leksands IF	Sweden	21	0	7	7	28																			
1992-93	Leksands IF	Sweden	36	7	15	22	63												2	0	2	2	0			
1993-94	Malmo IF	Sweden	40	11	9	20	38												11	2	0	2	12			
1994-95	Malmo IF	Sweden	31	3	13	16	38												9	0	2	2	8			
	Albany River Rats	AHL	3	0	0	0	0												9	3	5	8	7			
1995-96	**New Jersey**	**NHL**	**12**	**2**	**1**	**3**	**8**	**1**	**0**	**0**	**41**	**4.9**	**5**													
	Albany River Rats	AHL	67	15	31	46	59												4	0	0	0	7			
1996-97	**New Jersey**	**NHL**	**1**	**0**	**0**	**0**	**0**	**0**	**0**	**0**	**2**	**0.0**	**0**													
	Albany River Rats	AHL	13	1	4	5	8																			
	St. Louis	**NHL**	**53**	**4**	**8**	**12**	**45**	**1**	**0**	**0**	**68**	**5.9**	**-2**						**6**	**0**	**0**	**0**	**27**	**0**	**0**	**0**
1997-98	**St. Louis**	**NHL**	**1**	**0**	**0**	**0**	**0**	**0**	**0**	**0**	**0**	**0.0**	**0**													
	Worcester	AHL	32	2	16	18	58												10	3	7	10	24			
1998-99	**St. Louis**	**NHL**	**54**	**1**	**12**	**13**	**94**	**0**	**0**	**0**	**52**	**1.9**	**4**	**1**	**100.0**	**33**	**81**	**19:58**	**13**	**0**	**3**	**3**	**17**	**0**	**0**	**0**
	Worcester	AHL	19	6	4	10	42																			
99-2000	**St. Louis**	**NHL**	**41**	**0**	**8**	**8**	**38**	**0**	**0**	**0**	**30**	**0.0**	**-2**	**0**	**0.0**	**17**	**32**	**12:24**	**3**	**1**	**0**	**1**	**0**	**0**	**0**	**0**
	Worcester	AHL	2	0	1	1	0																			
2000-01	**Ottawa**	**NHL**	**33**	**1**	**8**	**9**	**35**	**0**	**0**	**1**	**43**	**2.3**	**8**	**0**	**0.0**	**26**	**60**	**17:06**	**2**	**0**	**0**	**0**	**0**	**0**	**0**	**0**
	NHL Totals		**195**	**8**	**37**	**45**	**220**	**2**	**0**	**1**	**236**	**3.4**		**1**	**100.0**	**76**	**173**	**16:48**	**24**	**1**	**3**	**4**	**44**	**0**	**0**	**0**

Traded to **St. Louis** by **New Jersey** with Mike Peluso for Ken Sutton and St. Louis' 2nd round choice (Brett Clouthier) in 1999 Entry Draft, November 26, 1996. Signed as a free agent by **Ottawa**, July 12, 2000. • Missed majority of 2000-01 season recovering from ankle injury originally suffered in game vs. Pittsburgh, October 25, 2001.

PETERSEN, Toby (PEE-tuhr-sohn, TOH-bee) PIT.

Center. Shoots left. 5'10", 196 lbs. Born, Minneapolis, MN, October 27, 1978. Pittsburgh's 9th choice, 244th overall, in 1998 Entry Draft.

Season	Club	League	GP	G	A	Pts	PIM	PP	SH	GW	S	%	+/-	TF	F%	H	SB	Min	GP	G	A	Pts	PIM	PP	SH	GW
1995-96	Jefferson High	Hi-School	25	29	30	59																				
1996-97	Colorado College	WCHA	40	17	21	38	18																			
1997-98	Colorado College	WCHA	40	16	17	33	34																			
1998-99	Colorado College	WCHA	21	12	12	24	2																			
99-2000	Colorado College	WCHA	37	14	19	33	8																			
2000-01	**Pittsburgh**	**NHL**	**12**	**2**	**6**	**8**	**4**	**0**	**0**	**1**	**25**	**8.0**	**3**	**39**	**35.9**	**5**	**2**	**13:22**								
	Wilkes-Barre	AHL	73	26	41	67	22												21	7	6	13	4			
	NHL Totals		**12**	**2**	**6**	**8**	**4**	**0**	**0**	**1**	**25**	**8.0**		**39**	**35.9**	**5**	**2**	**13:22**								

Minnesota High School All-State, All-Metro and All-Conference Player of the Year (1996) • WCHA All-Rookie Team (1997)

PETERSON, Brent (PEE-tuhr-sohn, BREHNT)

Left wing. Shoots left. 6'3", 200 lbs. Born, Calgary, Alta., July 20, 1972. Tampa Bay's 1st choice, 3rd overall, in 1993 Supplemental Draft.

Season	Club	League	GP	G	A	Pts	PIM	PP	SH	GW	S	%	+/-	TF	F%	H	SB	Min	GP	G	A	Pts	PIM	PP	SH	GW
1990-91	Thunder Bay	USHL	48	27	40	67	10												10	8	9	17	4			
1991-92	Michigan Tech	WCHA	39	11	9	20	18																			
1992-93	Michigan Tech	WCHA	37	24	18	42	32																			
1993-94	Michigan Tech	WCHA	43	25	21	46	30																			
1994-95	Michigan Tech	WCHA	39	20	16	36	27																			
1995-96	Atlanta Knights	IHL	69	9	19	28	33												3	0	0	0	0			
1996-97	**Tampa Bay**	**NHL**	**17**	**2**	**0**	**2**	**4**	**0**	**0**	**0**	**11**	**18.2**	**-4**													
	Adirondack	AHL	52	22	23	45	56												4	3	1	4	2			
1997-98	**Tampa Bay**	**NHL**	**19**	**5**	**0**	**5**	**2**	**0**	**0**	**0**	**15**	**33.3**	**-2**													
	Milwaukee	IHL	63	20	39	59	48												8	5	3	8	22			
1998-99	**Tampa Bay**	**NHL**	**20**	**2**	**1**	**3**	**0**	**0**	**0**	**0**	**16**	**12.5**	**-2**	**1**	**100.0**	**14**	**3**	**8:58**								
	Cleveland	IHL	18	6	7	13	31																			
	Grand Rapids	IHL	17	7	5	12	14																			
99-2000	Milwaukee	IHL	66	8	24	32	62												3	3	2	5	4			
2000-01	SC Langnau	Switz.	10	3	2	5	8																			
	Kassel Huskies	DEL	28	7	14	21	40												8	2	2	4	8			
	NHL Totals		**56**	**9**	**1**	**10**	**6**	**0**	**0**	**0**	**42**	**21.4**		**1**	**100.0**	**14**	**3**	**8:58**								

Traded to **Pittsburgh** by **Tampa Bay** for cash, March 18, 1999. Signed as a free agent by **Nashville**, July 24, 1999.

PETROV, Oleg (PEH-trahf, OH-lehg) MTL.

Right wing. Shoots left. 5'9", 171 lbs. Born, Moscow, USSR, April 18, 1971. Montreal's 9th choice, 127th overall, in 1991 Entry Draft.

Season	Club	League	GP	G	A	Pts	PIM	PP	SH	GW	S	%	+/-	TF	F%	H	SB	Min	GP	G	A	Pts	PIM	PP	SH	GW
1989-90	CSKA Moscow	USSR	30	4	7	11	4																			
1990-91	CSKA Moscow	USSR	43	7	4	11	8																			
1991-92	CSKA Moscow	CIS	42	10	16	26	8																			
1992-93	**Montreal**	**NHL**	**9**	**2**	**1**	**3**	**10**	**0**	**0**	**1**	**20**	**10.0**	**2**						**1**	**0**	**0**	**0**	**0**	**0**	**0**	**0**
	Fredericton	AHL	55	26	29	55	36												5	4	1	5	0			
1993-94	**Montreal**	**NHL**	**55**	**12**	**15**	**27**	**2**	**1**	**0**	**1**	**107**	**11.2**	**7**						**2**	**0**	**0**	**0**	**0**	**0**	**0**	**0**
	Fredericton	AHL	23	8	20	28	18																			
1994-95	**Montreal**	**NHL**	**12**	**2**	**3**	**5**	**4**	**0**	**0**	**0**	**26**	**7.7**	**-7**													
	Fredericton	AHL	17	7	11	18	12												17	5	6	11	10			
1995-96	**Montreal**	**NHL**	**36**	**4**	**7**	**11**	**23**	**0**	**0**	**2**	**44**	**9.1**	**-9**						**5**	**0**	**1**	**1**	**0**	**0**	**0**	**0**
	Fredericton	AHL	22	12	18	30	71												6	2	6	8	0			
1996-97	Ambri-Piotta	Switz.	45	24	28	52	44																			
	HC Meran	Italy	12	5	12	17	4																			
1997-98	Ambri-Piotta	Switz.	40	30	*63	*93	60												14	11	11	22	40			
1998-99	Ambri-Piotta	Switz.	45	35	*52	*87	52												15	9	11	*20	32			

			Regular Season																Playoffs							
Season	Club	League	GP	G	A	Pts	PIM	PP	SH	GW	S	%	+/-	TF	F%	H	SB	Min	GP	G	A	Pts	PIM	PP	SH	GW
99-2000	**Montreal**	**NHL**	**44**	**2**	**24**	**26**	**8**	**1**	**0**	**0**	**96**	**2.1**	**10**	**9**	**33.3**	**36**	**10**	**15:51**	....	....	....	....	....	....	....	....
	Quebec Citadelles	AHL	16	7	7	14	4	....	....	....	....	....	....	....	....	....	....	....	....	....	....	....	....	....	....	....
2000-01	**Montreal**	**NHL**	**81**	**17**	**30**	**47**	**24**	**4**	**2**	**1**	**158**	**10.8**	**–11**	**8**	**25.0**	**81**	**27**	**18:33**	....	....	....	....	....	....	....	....
	NHL Totals		**237**	**39**	**80**	**119**	**71**	**6**	**2**	**5**	**451**	**8.6**		**17**	**29.4**	**117**	**37**	**17:36**	**8**	**0**	**1**	**1**	**0**	**0**	**0**	**0**

NHL All-Rookie Team (1994)

Signed as a free agent by **Montreal**, July 15, 1999.

PETROVICKY, Robert (PEHT-roh-vih-kee, RAW-buhrt) NYI

Center. Shoots left. 5'11", 172 lbs. Born, Kosice, Czech., October 26, 1973. Hartford's 1st choice, 9th overall, in 1992 Entry Draft.

Season	Club	League	GP	G	A	Pts	PIM	PP	SH	GW	S	%	+/-	TF	F%	H	SB	Min	GP	G	A	Pts	PIM	PP	SH	GW
1990-91	Dukla Trencin	Czech.	33	9	14	23	12	....	....	....	....	....	....	....	....	....	....	....	....	....	....	....	....	....	....	....
1991-92	Dukla Trencin	Czech.	46	25	36	61	28	....	....	....	....	....	....	....	....	....	....	....	....	....	....	....	....	....	....	....
1992-93	**Hartford**	**NHL**	**42**	**3**	**6**	**9**	**45**	**0**	**0**	**0**	**41**	**7.3**	**–10**	....	....	....	....	....	....	....	....	....	....	....	....	....
	Springfield	AHL	16	5	3	8	39	....	....	....	....	....	....	....	....	....	....	....	15	5	6	11	14	....	....	....
1993-94	Dukla Trencin	Slovakia	1	0	0	0	0	....	....	....	....	....	....	....	....	....	....	....	....	....	....	....	....	....	....	....
	Hartford	**NHL**	**33**	**6**	**5**	**11**	**39**	**1**	**0**	**0**	**33**	**18.2**	**–1**	....	....	....	....	....	....	....	....	....	....	....	....	....
	Springfield	AHL	30	16	8	24	39	....	....	....	....	....	....	....	....	....	....	....	4	0	2	2	4	....	....	....
	Slovakia	Olympics	8	1	6	7	18	....	....	....	....	....	....	....	....	....	....	....	....	....	....	....	....	....	....	....
1994-95	Springfield	AHL	74	30	52	82	121	....	....	....	....	....	....	....	....	....	....	....	....	....	....	....	....	....	....	....
	Hartford	**NHL**	**2**	**0**	**0**	**0**	**0**	**0**	**0**	**0**	**1**	**0.0**	**0**	....	....	....	....	....	....	....	....	....	....	....	....	....
1995-96	Springfield	AHL	9	4	8	12	18	....	....	....	....	....	....	....	....	....	....	....	....	....	....	....	....	....	....	....
	Detroit Vipers	IHL	12	5	3	8	16	....	....	....	....	....	....	....	....	....	....	....	....	....	....	....	....	....	....	....
	Dallas	**NHL**	**5**	**1**	**1**	**2**	**0**	**1**	**0**	**1**	**3**	**33.3**	**1**	....	....	....	....	....	....	....	....	....	....	....	....	....
	Michigan	IHL	50	23	23	46	63	....	....	....	....	....	....	....	....	....	....	....	7	3	1	4	16	....	....	....
1996-97	**St. Louis**	**NHL**	**44**	**7**	**12**	**19**	**10**	**0**	**0**	**1**	**54**	**13.0**	**2**	....	....	....	....	....	**2**	**0**	**0**	**0**	**0**	**0**	**0**	**0**
	Worcester	AHL	12	5	4	9	19	....	....	....	....	....	....	....	....	....	....	....	....	....	....	....	....	....	....	....
1997-98	Worcester	AHL	65	27	34	61	97	....	....	....	....	....	....	....	....	....	....	....	10	3	4	7	12	....	....	....
	Slovakia	Olympics	4	2	1	3	0	....	....	....	....	....	....	....	....	....	....	....	....	....	....	....	....	....	....	....
1998-99	**Tampa Bay**	**NHL**	**28**	**3**	**4**	**7**	**6**	**0**	**0**	**0**	**32**	**9.4**	**–8**	**35**	**34.3**	**21**	**8**	**10:33**	....	....	....	....	....	....	....	....
	Grand Rapids	IHL	49	26	32	58	87	....	....	....	....	....	....	....	....	....	....	....	....	....	....	....	....	....	....	....
99-2000	**Tampa Bay**	**NHL**	**43**	**7**	**10**	**17**	**14**	**1**	**0**	**0**	**50**	**14.0**	**2**	**38**	**47.4**	**32**	**5**	**10:05**	....	....	....	....	....	....	....	....
	Grand Rapids	IHL	7	5	3	8	4	....	....	....	....	....	....	....	....	....	....	....	....	....	....	....	....	....	....	....
2000-01	**NY Islanders**	**NHL**	**11**	**0**	**0**	**0**	**4**	**0**	**0**	**0**	**3**	**0.0**	**–1**	**15**	**46.7**	**1**	**0**	**3:26**	....	....	....	....	....	....	....	....
	Chicago Wolves	IHL	23	13	10	23	22	....	....	....	....	....	....	....	....	....	....	....	....	....	....	....	....	....	....	....
	MoDo Hockey	Sweden	7	3	2	5	10	....	....	....	....	....	....	....	....	....	....	....	7	1	1	2	6	....	....	....
	NHL Totals		**208**	**27**	**38**	**65**	**118**	**3**	**0**	**2**	**217**	**12.4**		**88**	**42.0**	**54**	**13**	**9:21**	**2**	**0**	**0**	**0**	**0**	**0**	**0**	**0**

Traded to **Dallas** by **Hartford** for Dan Kesa, November 29, 1995. Signed as a free agent by **St. Louis**, September 6, 1996. Signed as a free agent by **Tampa Bay**, February 15, 1999. Signed as a free agent by **NY Islanders**, July 28, 2000.

PETROVICKY, Ronald (PEHT-roh-vih-kee, RAW-nohld) CGY.

Right wing. Shoots right. 5'11", 190 lbs. Born, Zilina, Czech., February 15, 1977. Calgary's 9th choice, 228th overall, in 1996 Entry Draft.

Season	Club	League	GP	G	A	Pts	PIM	PP	SH	GW	S	%	+/-	TF	F%	H	SB	Min	GP	G	A	Pts	PIM	PP	SH	GW
1993-94	Dukla Trencin	Slovak-Jr.	36	28	27	55	42	....	....	....	....	....	....	....	....	....	....	....	....	....	....	....	....	....	....	....
	Dukla Trencin	Slovakia	1	0	0	0	0	....	....	....	....	....	....	....	....	....	....	....	....	....	....	....	....	....	....	....
1994-95	Tri-City Americans	WHL	39	4	11	15	86	....	....	....	....	....	....	....	....	....	....	....	....	....	....	....	....	....	....	....
	Prince George	WHL	21	4	6	10	37	....	....	....	....	....	....	....	....	....	....	....	....	....	....	....	....	....	....	....
1995-96	Prince George	WHL	39	19	21	40	61	....	....	....	....	....	....	....	....	....	....	....	....	....	....	....	....	....	....	....
1996-97	Prince George	WHL	72	32	37	69	119	....	....	....	....	....	....	....	....	....	....	....	15	4	9	13	31	....	....	....
1997-98	Regina Pats	WHL	71	64	49	113	168	....	....	....	....	....	....	....	....	....	....	....	9	2	4	6	11	....	....	....
1998-99	Saint John Flames	AHL	78	12	21	33	114	....	....	....	....	....	....	....	....	....	....	....	7	1	2	3	19	....	....	....
99-2000	Saint John Flames	AHL	67	23	33	56	131	....	....	....	....	....	....	....	....	....	....	....	3	1	1	2	6	....	....	....
2000-01	**Calgary**	**NHL**	**30**	**4**	**5**	**9**	**54**	**1**	**0**	**1**	**30**	**13.3**	**0**	**7**	**42.9**	**68**	**11**	**11:33**	....	....	....	....	....	....	....	....
	NHL Totals		**30**	**4**	**5**	**9**	**54**	**1**	**0**	**1**	**30**	**13.3**		**7**	**42.9**	**68**	**11**	**11:33**	....	....	....	....	....	....	....	....

WHL East Second All-Star Team (1998)

• Missed majority of 2000-01 season recovering from wrist injury suffered in game vs. Detroit, October 5, 2000.

PETTINGER, Matt (PEH-tihn-juhr, MAT) WSH.

Left wing. Shoots left. 6'1", 205 lbs. Born, Edmonton, Alta, October 22, 1980. Washington's 2nd choice, 43rd overall, in 2000 Entry Draft.

Season	Club	League	GP	G	A	Pts	PIM	PP	SH	GW	S	%	+/-	TF	F%	H	SB	Min	GP	G	A	Pts	PIM	PP	SH	GW
1996-97	Victoria Salsa	BCJHL	49	22	14	36	31	....	....	....	....	....	....	....	....	....	....	....	....	....	....	....	....	....	....	....
1997-98	Victoria Salsa	BCJHL	55	22	20	42	56	....	....	....	....	....	....	....	....	....	....	....	7	5	1	6	8	....	....	....
1998-99	U. of Denver	WCHA	33	6	14	20	44	....	....	....	....	....	....	....	....	....	....	....	....	....	....	....	....	....	....	....
99-2000	U. of Denver	WCHA	19	2	6	8	49	....	....	....	....	....	....	....	....	....	....	....	....	....	....	....	....	....	....	....
	Calgary Hitmen	WHL	27	14	6	20	41	....	....	....	....	....	....	....	....	....	....	....	11	2	6	8	30	....	....	....
2000-01	**Washington**	**NHL**	**10**	**0**	**0**	**0**	**2**	**0**	**0**	**0**	**6**	**0.0**	**–1**	**2**	**50.0**	**13**	**1**	**7:47**	....	....	....	....	....	....	....	....
	Portland Pirates	AHL	64	19	17	36	92	....	....	....	....	....	....	....	....	....	....	....	2	0	0	0	4	....	....	....
	NHL Totals		**10**	**0**	**0**	**0**	**2**	**0**	**0**	**0**	**6**	**0.0**		**2**	**50.0**	**13**	**1**	**7:47**	....	....	....	....	....	....	....	....

PHILLIPS, Chris (FIHL-ihps, KRIHS) OTT.

Defense. Shoots left. 6'3", 215 lbs. Born, Calgary, Alta., March 9, 1978. Ottawa's 1st choice, 1st overall, in 1996 Entry Draft.

Season	Club	League	GP	G	A	Pts	PIM	PP	SH	GW	S	%	+/-	TF	F%	H	SB	Min	GP	G	A	Pts	PIM	PP	SH	GW
1993-94	Fort McMurray	AJHL	56	6	16	22	72	....	....	....	....	....	....	....	....	....	....	....	10	0	3	3	16	....	....	....
1994-95	Fort McMurray	AJHL	48	16	32	48	127	....	....	....	....	....	....	....	....	....	....	....	11	4	2	6	10	....	....	....
1995-96	Prince Albert	WHL	61	10	30	40	97	....	....	....	....	....	....	....	....	....	....	....	18	2	12	14	30	....	....	....
1996-97	Prince Albert	WHL	32	3	23	26	58	....	....	....	....	....	....	....	....	....	....	....	....	....	....	....	....	....	....	....
	Lethbridge	WHL	26	4	18	22	28	....	....	....	....	....	....	....	....	....	....	....	19	4	*21	25	20	....	....	....
1997-98	**Ottawa**	**NHL**	**72**	**5**	**11**	**16**	**38**	**2**	**0**	**2**	**107**	**4.7**	**2**	....	....	....	....	....	**11**	**0**	**2**	**2**	**2**	**0**	**0**	**0**
1998-99	**Ottawa**	**NHL**	**34**	**3**	**3**	**6**	**32**	**2**	**0**	**0**	**51**	**5.9**	**–5**	**0**	**0.0**	**53**	**28**	**18:06**	**3**	**0**	**0**	**0**	**0**	**0**	**0**	**0**
99-2000	**Ottawa**	**NHL**	**65**	**5**	**14**	**19**	**39**	**0**	**0**	**1**	**96**	**5.2**	**12**	**0**	**0.0**	**143**	**50**	**16:50**	**6**	**0**	**1**	**1**	**4**	**0**	**0**	**0**
2000-01	**Ottawa**	**NHL**	**73**	**2**	**12**	**14**	**31**	**2**	**0**	**0**	**77**	**2.6**	**8**	**1**	**0.0**	**136**	**102**	**21:28**	**1**	**1**	**0**	**1**	**0**	**0**	**0**	**0**
	NHL Totals		**244**	**15**	**40**	**55**	**140**	**6**	**0**	**3**	**331**	**4.5**		**1**	**0.0**	**332**	**180**	**19:03**	**21**	**1**	**3**	**4**	**6**	**0**	**0**	**0**

WHL East First All-Star Team (1997) • Canadian Major Junior First All-Star Team (1997)

• Missed majority of 1998-99 season recovering from ankle injury suffered in game vs. Buffalo, December 30, 1998.

PICARD, Michel (PEE-cahr, mih-SHEHL)

Left wing. Shoots left. 5'11", 190 lbs. Born, Beauport, Que., November 7, 1969. Hartford's 8th choice, 178th overall, in 1989 Entry Draft.

Season	Club	League	GP	G	A	Pts	PIM	PP	SH	GW	S	%	+/-	TF	F%	H	SB	Min	GP	G	A	Pts	PIM	PP	SH	GW
1985-86	Ste-Foy Governors	QAAA	42	53	34	87	....	....	....	....	....	....	....	....	....	....	....	....	....	....	....	....	....	....	....	....
1986-87	Trois-Rivieres	QMJHL	66	33	35	68	53	....	....	....	....	....	....	....	....	....	....	....	....	....	....	....	....	....	....	....
1987-88	Trois-Rivieres	QMJHL	69	40	55	95	71	....	....	....	....	....	....	....	....	....	....	....	....	....	....	....	....	....	....	....
1988-89	Trois-Rivieres	QMJHL	66	59	81	140	170	....	....	....	....	....	....	....	....	....	....	....	4	1	3	4	2	....	....	....
1989-90	Binghamton	AHL	67	16	24	40	98	....	....	....	....	....	....	....	....	....	....	....	....	....	....	....	....	....	....	....
1990-91	**Hartford**	**NHL**	**5**	**1**	**0**	**1**	**2**	**0**	**0**	**0**	**7**	**14.3**	**–2**	....	....	....	....	....	....	....	....	....	....	....	....	....
	Springfield	AHL	77	*56	40	96	61	....	....	....	....	....	....	....	....	....	....	....	18	8	13	21	18	....	....	....
1991-92	**Hartford**	**NHL**	**25**	**3**	**5**	**8**	**6**	**1**	**0**	**0**	**41**	**7.3**	**–2**	....	....	....	....	....	....	....	....	....	....	....	....	....
	Springfield	AHL	40	21	17	38	44	....	....	....	....	....	....	....	....	....	....	....	11	2	0	2	34	....	....	....
1992-93	**San Jose**	**NHL**	**25**	**4**	**0**	**4**	**24**	**2**	**0**	**0**	**32**	**12.5**	**–17**	....	....	....	....	....	....	....	....	....	....	....	....	....
	Kansas City	IHL	33	7	10	17	51	....	....	....	....	....	....	....	....	....	....	....	12	3	2	5	20	....	....	....
1993-94	Portland Pirates	AHL	61	41	44	85	99	....	....	....	....	....	....	....	....	....	....	....	17	11	10	21	22	....	....	....
1994-95	P.E.I. Senators	AHL	57	32	57	89	58	....	....	....	....	....	....	....	....	....	....	....	8	4	4	8	6	....	....	....
	Ottawa	**NHL**	**24**	**5**	**8**	**13**	**14**	**1**	**0**	**0**	**33**	**15.2**	**–1**	....	....	....	....	....	....	....	....	....	....	....	....	....
1995-96	**Ottawa**	**NHL**	**17**	**2**	**6**	**8**	**10**	**0**	**0**	**1**	**21**	**9.5**	**–1**	....	....	....	....	....	....	....	....	....	....	....	....	....
	P.E.I. Senators	AHL	55	37	45	82	79	....	....	....	....	....	....	....	....	....	....	....	5	5	1	6	2	....	....	....
1996-97	Vastra Frolunda	Sweden	3	0	1	1	0	....	....	....	....	....	....	....	....	....	....	....	....	....	....	....	....	....	....	....
	Grand Rapids	IHL	82	46	55	101	58	....	....	....	....	....	....	....	....	....	....	....	5	2	0	2	10	....	....	....
1997-98	Grand Rapids	IHL	58	28	41	69	42	....	....	....	....	....	....	....	....	....	....	....	....	....	....	....	....	....	....	....
	St. Louis	**NHL**	**16**	**1**	**8**	**9**	**29**	**0**	**0**	**0**	**19**	**5.3**	**3**	....	....	....	....	....	....	....	....	....	....	....	....	....

			Regular Season																Playoffs							
Season	Club	League	GP	G	A	Pts	PIM	PP	SH	GW	S	%	+/-	TF	F%	H	SB	Min	GP	G	A	Pts	PIM	PP	SH	GW
1998-99	**St. Louis**	**NHL**	**45**	**11**	**11**	**22**	**16**	**0**	**0**	**2**	**69**	**15.9**	**5**	**1**	**100.0**	**9**	**6**	**14:20**	**5**	**0**	**0**	**0**	**2**	**0**	**0**	**0**
	Grand Rapids	IHL	6	2	2	4	2																			
99-2000	**Edmonton**	**NHL**	**2**	**0**	**0**	**0**	**2**	**0**	**0**	**0**	**2**	**0.0**	**0**	**0**	**0.0**	**4**	**0**	**9:56**								
	Grand Rapids	IHL	65	33	35	68	50												17	8	10	*18	4			
2000-01	**Philadelphia**	**NHL**	**7**	**1**	**4**	**5**	**0**	**1**	**0**	**0**	**12**	**8.3**	**6**	**0**	**0.0**	**4**	**2**	**14:14**								
	Philadelphia	AHL	72	31	39	70	22												10	4	5	9	4			
	NHL Totals		**166**	**28**	**42**	**70**	**103**	**5**	**0**	**3**	**236**	**11.9**		**1**	**100.0**	**17**	**8**	**14:09**	**5**	**0**	**0**	**0**	**2**	**0**	**0**	**0**

QMJHL Second All-Star Team (1989) • AHL First All-Star Team (1991, 1995) • AHL Second All-Star Team (1994) • IHL First All-Star Team (1997)

Traded to **San Jose** by **Hartford** for future considerations (Yvon Corriveau, January 21, 1993), October 9, 1992. Signed as a free agent by **Ottawa**, June 16, 1994. Traded to **Washington** by **Ottawa** for cash, May 21, 1996. Signed as a free agent by **St. Louis**, January 5, 1998. Signed as a free agent by **Edmonton**, December 2, 1999. Signed as a free agent by **Philadelphia**, August 14, 2000.

PILON, Rich

(PEE-lahn, RITCH) **ST.L.**

Defense. Shoots left. 6'2", 220 lbs. Born, Saskatoon, Sask., April 30, 1968. NY Islanders' 9th choice, 143rd overall, in 1986 Entry Draft.

Season	Club	League	GP	G	A	Pts	PIM	PP	SH	GW	S	%	+/-	TF	F%	H	SB	Min	GP	G	A	Pts	PIM	PP	SH	GW
1984-85	Prince Albert	SAHA	26	3	11	14	41																			
1985-86	Prince Albert	SAHA	35	3	28	31	142																			
	Prince Albert	WHL	6	0	0	0	0																			
1986-87	Prince Albert	WHL	68	4	21	25	192												7	1	6	7	17			
1987-88	Prince Albert	WHL	65	13	34	47	177												9	0	6	6	38			
1988-89	**NY Islanders**	**NHL**	**62**	**0**	**14**	**14**	**242**	**0**	**0**	**0**	**47**	**0.0**	**-9**													
1989-90	**NY Islanders**	**NHL**	**14**	**0**	**2**	**2**	**31**	**0**	**0**	**0**	**5**	**0.0**	**2**													
1990-91	**NY Islanders**	**NHL**	**60**	**1**	**4**	**5**	**126**	**0**	**0**	**0**	**33**	**3.0**	**-12**													
1991-92	**NY Islanders**	**NHL**	**65**	**1**	**6**	**7**	**183**	**0**	**0**	**0**	**27**	**3.7**	**-1**													
1992-93	**NY Islanders**	**NHL**	**44**	**1**	**3**	**4**	**164**	**0**	**0**	**0**	**20**	**5.0**	**-4**						**15**	**0**	**0**	**0**	**50**	**0**	**0**	**0**
	Capital District	AHL	6	0	1	1	8																			
1993-94	**NY Islanders**	**NHL**	**28**	**1**	**4**	**5**	**75**	**0**	**0**	**0**	**20**	**5.0**	**-4**													
	Salt Lake City	IHL	2	0	0	0	8																			
1994-95	**NY Islanders**	**NHL**	**20**	**1**	**1**	**2**	**40**	**0**	**0**	**0**	**11**	**9.1**	**-3**													
1995-96	**NY Islanders**	**NHL**	**27**	**0**	**3**	**3**	**72**	**0**	**0**	**0**	**7**	**0.0**	**-9**													
1996-97	**NY Islanders**	**NHL**	**52**	**1**	**4**	**5**	**179**	**0**	**0**	**0**	**17**	**5.9**	**4**													
1997-98	**NY Islanders**	**NHL**	**76**	**0**	**7**	**7**	**291**	**0**	**0**	**0**	**37**	**0.0**	**1**													
1998-99	**NY Islanders**	**NHL**	**52**	**0**	**4**	**4**	**88**	**0**	**0**	**0**	**27**	**0.0**	**-8**	**0**	**0.0**	**155**	**49**	**16:35**								
99-2000	**NY Islanders**	**NHL**	**9**	**0**	**2**	**2**	**34**	**0**	**0**	**0**	**0**	**0.0**	**-2**	**0**	**0.0**	**22**	**17**	**16:21**								
	NY Rangers	**NHL**	**45**	**0**	**4**	**4**	**36**	**0**	**0**	**0**	**16**	**0.0**	**0**	**0**	**0.0**	**135**	**67**	**16:29**								
2000-01	**NY Rangers**	**NHL**	**69**	**2**	**9**	**11**	**175**	**0**	**0**	**0**	**24**	**8.3**	**-2**	**0**	**0.0**	**247**	**135**	**16:52**								
	NHL Totals		**623**	**8**	**67**	**75**	**1736**	**0**	**0**	**0**	**291**	**2.7**		**0**	**0.0**	**559**	**268**	**16:40**	**15**	**0**	**0**	**0**	**50**	**0**	**0**	**0**

WHL East Second All-Star Team (1988)

• Missed majority of 1989-90 season recovering from eye injury suffered in game vs. Detroit, November 4, 1989. • Missed majority of 1993-94 season recovering from shoulder injury originally suffered in game vs. Boston, November 13, 1993. • Missed majority of 1994-95 and 1995-96 seasons recovering from wrist injury suffered in game vs. Quebec, April 18, 1995. Claimed on waivers by **NY Rangers** from **NY Islanders**, December 1, 1999. Signed as a free agent by **St. Louis**, July 10, 2001.

PITLICK, Lance

(PIHT-lihk, LANS) **FLA.**

Defense. Shoots right. 6', 205 lbs. Born, Minneapolis, MN, November 5, 1967. Minnesota's 10th choice, 180th overall, in 1986 Entry Draft.

Season	Club	League	GP	G	A	Pts	PIM	PP	SH	GW	S	%	+/-	TF	F%	H	SB	Min	GP	G	A	Pts	PIM	PP	SH	GW
1984-85	Cooper Hawks	Hi-School	23	8	4	12	....																			
1985-86	Cooper Hawks	Hi-School	21	17	8	25	247																			
1986-87	U. of Minnesota	WCHA	45	0	9	9	88																			
1987-88	U. of Minnesota	WCHA	38	3	9	12	76																			
1988-89	U. of Minnesota	WCHA	47	4	9	13	95																			
1989-90	U. of Minnesota	WCHA	14	3	2	5	26																			
1990-91	Hershey Bears	AHL	64	6	15	21	75												3	0	0	0	9			
1991-92	Hershey Bears	AHL	4	0	0	0	6												3	0	0	0	4			
1992-93	Hershey Bears	AHL	53	5	10	15	77																			
1993-94	Hershey Bears	AHL	58	4	13	17	93												11	1	0	1	11			
1994-95	P.E.I. Senators	AHL	61	8	19	27	55												11	1	4	5	10			
	Ottawa	**NHL**	**15**	**0**	**1**	**1**	**6**	**0**	**0**	**0**	**11**	**0.0**	**-5**													
1995-96	**Ottawa**	**NHL**	**28**	**1**	**6**	**7**	**20**	**0**	**0**	**0**	**13**	**7.7**	**-8**													
	P.E.I. Senators	AHL	29	4	10	14	39												5	0	0	0	0			
1996-97	**Ottawa**	**NHL**	**66**	**5**	**5**	**10**	**91**	**0**	**0**	**1**	**54**	**9.3**	**2**						**7**	**0**	**0**	**0**	**4**	**0**	**0**	**0**
1997-98	**Ottawa**	**NHL**	**69**	**2**	**7**	**9**	**50**	**0**	**0**	**0**	**66**	**3.0**	**8**						**11**	**0**	**1**	**1**	**17**	**0**	**0**	**0**
1998-99	**Ottawa**	**NHL**	**50**	**3**	**6**	**9**	**33**	**0**	**0**	**0**	**34**	**8.8**	**7**	**0**	**0.0**	**120**	**64**	**16:39**	**2**	**0**	**0**	**0**	**0**	**0**	**0**	**0**
99-2000	**Florida**	**NHL**	**62**	**3**	**5**	**8**	**44**	**0**	**0**	**1**	**26**	**11.5**	**7**	**0**	**0.0**	**142**	**91**	**16:33**	**4**	**0**	**1**	**1**	**0**	**0**	**0**	**0**
2000-01	**Florida**	**NHL**	**68**	**1**	**2**	**3**	**42**	**0**	**0**	**0**	**24**	**4.2**	**-5**	**0**	**0.0**	**161**	**64**	**13:35**								
	NHL Totals		**358**	**15**	**32**	**47**	**286**	**0**	**0**	**2**	**228**	**6.6**		**0**	**0.0**	**423**	**219**	**15:28**	**24**	**0**	**2**	**2**	**21**	**0**	**0**	**0**

Signed as a free agent by **Philadelphia**, September 5, 1990. Signed as a free agent by **Ottawa**, June 22, 1994. Signed as a free agent by **Florida**, July 21, 1999.

PITTIS, Domenic

(PIH-THIS, DOHM-eh-nihk) **EDM.**

Center. Shoots left. 5'11", 190 lbs. Born, Calgary, Alta., October 1, 1974. Pittsburgh's 2nd choice, 52nd overall, in 1993 Entry Draft.

Season	Club	League	GP	G	A	Pts	PIM	PP	SH	GW	S	%	+/-	TF	F%	H	SB	Min	GP	G	A	Pts	PIM	PP	SH	GW
1990-91	Calgary Flames	AMHL	35	23	54	77	43																			
1991-92	Lethbridge	WHL	65	6	17	23	18												5	0	2	2	4			
1992-93	Lethbridge	WHL	66	46	73	119	69												4	3	3	6	8			
1993-94	Lethbridge	WHL	72	58	69	127	93												8	4	11	15	16			
1994-95	Cleveland	IHL	62	18	32	50	66												3	0	2	2	2			
1995-96	Cleveland	IHL	74	10	28	38	100												3	0	0	0	2			
1996-97	**Pittsburgh**	**NHL**	**1**	**0**	**0**	**0**	**0**	**0**	**0**	**0**	**0**	**0.0**	**-1**													
	Long Beach	IHL	65	23	43	66	91												18	5	9	14	26			
1997-98	Syracuse Crunch	AHL	75	23	41	64	90												5	1	3	4	4			
1998-99	**Buffalo**	**NHL**	**3**	**0**	**0**	**0**	**2**	**0**	**0**	**0**	**1**	**0.0**	**0**	**19**	**42.1**	**4**	**1**	**8:35**								
	Rochester	AHL	76	38	66	*104	108												20	7	*14	*21	40			
99-2000	**Buffalo**	**NHL**	**7**	**1**	**0**	**1**	**6**	**0**	**0**	**0**	**6**	**16.7**	**1**	**65**	**44.6**	**7**	**0**	**11:27**								
	Rochester	AHL	53	17	48	65	85												21	4	*26	*30	28			
2000-01	**Edmonton**	**NHL**	**47**	**4**	**5**	**9**	**49**	**0**	**0**	**2**	**42**	**9.5**	**-5**	**367**	**54.8**	**57**	**23**	**10:46**	**3**	**0**	**0**	**0**	**2**	**0**	**0**	**0**
	NHL Totals		**58**	**5**	**5**	**10**	**57**	**0**	**0**	**2**	**49**	**10.2**		**451**	**52.8**	**68**	**24**	**10:44**	**3**	**0**	**0**	**0**	**2**	**0**	**0**	**0**

WHL East Second All-Star Team (1994) • Won John P. Sollenberger Trophy (Top Scorer - AHL) (1999)

Signed as a free agent by **Buffalo**, August 10, 1998. Signed as a free agent by **Edmonton**, July 25, 2000.

PLANTE, Dan

(PLAHNT, DAN)

Right wing. Shoots right. 5'11", 202 lbs. Born, Hayward, WI, October 5, 1971. NY Islanders' 3rd choice, 48th overall, in 1990 Entry Draft.

Season	Club	League	GP	G	A	Pts	PIM	PP	SH	GW	S	%	+/-	TF	F%	H	SB	Min	GP	G	A	Pts	PIM	PP	SH	GW
1988-89	Edina High	Hi-School	27	10	26	36	23																			
1989-90	Edina High	Hi-School	24	8	18	26	12																			
1990-91	U. of Wisconsin	WCHA	33	1	2	3	54																			
1991-92	U. of Wisconsin	WCHA	36	13	13	26	107																			
1992-93	U. of Wisconsin	WCHA	42	26	31	57	142																			
1993-94	**NY Islanders**	**NHL**	**12**	**0**	**1**	**1**	**4**	**0**	**0**	**0**	**9**	**0.0**	**-2**						**1**	**1**	**0**	**1**	**2**	**0**	**0**	**0**
	Salt Lake City	IHL	66	7	17	24	148																			
1994-95	Denver Grizzlies	IHL	2	0	0	0	4																			
1995-96	**NY Islanders**	**NHL**	**73**	**5**	**3**	**8**	**50**	**0**	**2**	**0**	**103**	**4.9**	**-22**													
1996-97	**NY Islanders**	**NHL**	**67**	**4**	**9**	**13**	**75**	**0**	**2**	**0**	**61**	**6.6**	**-6**													
1997-98	**NY Islanders**	**NHL**	**7**	**0**	**1**	**1**	**6**	**0**	**0**	**0**	**7**	**0.0**	**-1**													
	Utah Grizzlies	IHL	73	22	27	49	125												4	0	2	2	14			
1998-99	Chicago Wolves	IHL	81	21	12	33	119												10	1	5	6	10			
99-2000	Chicago Wolves	IHL	79	11	11	22	71												16	3	5	8	14			
2000-01	Chicago Wolves	IHL	76	15	11	26	58												16	1	0	1	27			
	NHL Totals		**159**	**9**	**14**	**23**	**135**	**0**	**4**	**0**	**180**	**5.0**							**1**	**1**	**0**	**1**	**2**	**0**	**0**	**0**

• Missed majority of 1994-95 season recovering from knee injury suffered in game vs. Houston (IHL), October 2, 1994. Signed as a free agent by **Chicago** (IHL), July 21, 1999.

PLANTE, Derek
(PLAHNT, DAIR-ehk)

Center. Shoots left. 5'11", 181 lbs. Born, Cloquet, MN, January 17, 1971. Buffalo's 7th choice, 161st overall, in 1989 Entry Draft.

			Regular Season																Playoffs							
Season	Club	League	GP	G	A	Pts	PIM	PP	SH	GW	S	%	+/-	TF	F%	H	SB	Min	GP	G	A	Pts	PIM	PP	SH	GW
1987-88	Cloquet High	Hi-School	23	16	25	41	....	....	....	....	....	....	....	....	....	....	....	....	....	....	....	....	....	....	....	....
1988-89	Cloquet High	Hi-School	24	30	33	63	....	....	....	....	....	....	....	....	....	....	....	....	....	....	....	....	....	....	....	....
1989-90	Minnesota-Duluth	WCHA	28	10	11	21	12	....	....	....	....	....	....	....	....	....	....	....	....	....	....	....	....	....	....	....
1990-91	Minnesota-Duluth	WCHA	36	23	20	43	6	....	....	....	....	....	....	....	....	....	....	....	....	....	....	....	....	....	....	....
1991-92	Minnesota-Duluth	WCHA	37	27	36	63	28	....	....	....	....	....	....	....	....	....	....	....	....	....	....	....	....	....	....	....
1992-93	Minnesota-Duluth	WCHA	37	*36	*56	*92	30	....	....	....	....	....	....	....	....	....	....	....	....	....	....	....	....	....	....	....
1993-94	Buffalo	NHL	77	21	35	56	24	8	1	2	147	14.3	4	....	....	....	....	....	7	1	0	1	0	0	0	0
1994-95	Buffalo	NHL	47	3	19	22	12	2	0	0	94	3.2	–4	....	....	....	....	....	....	....	....	....	....	....	....	....
1995-96	Buffalo	NHL	76	23	33	56	28	4	0	5	203	11.3	–4	....	....	....	....	....	....	....	....	....	....	....	....	....
1996-97	Buffalo	NHL	82	27	26	53	24	5	0	6	191	14.1	14	....	....	....	....	....	12	4	6	10	4	1	0	2
1997-98	Buffalo	NHL	72	13	21	34	26	5	0	1	150	8.7	8	....	....	....	....	....	11	0	3	3	10	0	0	0
1998-99	Buffalo	NHL	41	4	11	15	12	0	0	0	66	6.1	3	598	46.2	10	24	15:31	....	....	....	....	....	....	....	....
	♦ Dallas	NHL	10	2	3	5	4	1	0	0	24	8.3	1	113	58.4	9	4	13:42	6	1	0	1	4	0	0	0
99-2000	Dallas	NHL	16	1	1	2	2	1	0	0	17	5.9	–4	119	51.3	5	7	10:05	....	....	....	....	....	....	....	....
	Michigan K-Wings	IHL	13	0	4	4	2	....	....	....	....	....	....	....	....	....	....	....	....	....	....	....	....	....	....	....
	Chicago	NHL	17	1	1	2	2	0	0	0	14	7.1	–1	98	38.8	6	3	7:48	....	....	....	....	....	....	....	....
	Chicago Wolves	IHL	4	2	1	3	2	....	....	....	....	....	....	....	....	....	....	....	8	3	1	4	6	....	....	....
2000-01	Philadelphia	NHL	12	1	2	3	4	0	0	0	20	5.0	0	177	48.6	2	10	16:30	5	0	1	1	0	0	0	0
	Philadelphia	AHL	57	18	35	53	19	....	....	....	....	....	....	....	....	....	....	....	....	....	....	....	....	....	....	....
	NHL Totals		450	96	152	248	138	26	1	14	926	10.4		1105	47.7	32	48	13:11	41	6	10	16	18	1	0	2

WCHA Second All-Star Team (1992) • WCHA First All-Star Team (1993) • NCAA West First All-American Team (1993)

Traded to **Dallas** by **Buffalo** for Dallas' 2nd round choice (Michael Zigomanis) in 1999 Entry Draft, March 23, 1999. Traded to **Chicago** by **Dallas** with Kevin Dean and Dallas' 2nd round choice (Matt Keith) in 2001 Entry Draft for Sylvain Cote and Dave Manson, February 8, 2000. Signed as a free agent by **Philadelphia**, July 26, 2000.

POAPST, Steve
(POHPST, STEEV) **CHI.**

Defense. Shoots left. 6', 200 lbs. Born, Cornwall, Ont., January 3, 1969.

Season	Club	League	GP	G	A	Pts	PIM	PP	SH	GW	S	%	+/-	TF	F%	H	SB	Min	GP	G	A	Pts	PIM	PP	SH	GW
1986-87	Smith Falls Bears	OCJHL	54	10	27	37	94	....	....	....	....	....	....	....	....	....	....	....	....	....	....	....	....	....	....	....
1987-88	Colgate University	ECAC	32	3	13	16	22	....	....	....	....	....	....	....	....	....	....	....	....	....	....	....	....	....	....	....
1988-89	Colgate University	ECAC	30	0	5	5	38	....	....	....	....	....	....	....	....	....	....	....	....	....	....	....	....	....	....	....
1989-90	Colgate University	ECAC	38	4	15	19	54	....	....	....	....	....	....	....	....	....	....	....	....	....	....	....	....	....	....	....
1990-91	Colgate University	ECAC	32	6	15	21	43	....	....	....	....	....	....	....	....	....	....	....	....	....	....	....	....	....	....	....
1991-92	Hampton Roads	ECHL	55	8	20	28	29	....	....	....	....	....	....	....	....	....	....	....	14	1	4	5	12	....	....	....
1992-93	Hampton Roads	ECHL	63	10	35	45	57	....	....	....	....	....	....	....	....	....	....	....	4	0	1	1	4	....	....	....
	Baltimore	AHL	7	0	1	1	4	....	....	....	....	....	....	....	....	....	....	....	7	0	3	3	6	....	....	....
1993-94	Portland Pirates	AHL	78	14	21	35	47	....	....	....	....	....	....	....	....	....	....	....	12	0	3	3	8	....	....	....
1994-95	Portland Pirates	AHL	71	8	22	30	60	....	....	....	....	....	....	....	....	....	....	....	7	0	1	1	16	....	....	....
1995-96	Washington	NHL	3	1	0	1	0	0	0	1	2	50.0	–1	....	....	....	....	....	6	0	0	0	0	0	0	0
	Portland Pirates	AHL	70	10	24	34	79	....	....	....	....	....	....	....	....	....	....	....	20	2	6	8	16	....	....	....
1996-97	Portland Pirates	AHL	47	1	20	21	34	....	....	....	....	....	....	....	....	....	....	....	5	0	1	1	6	....	....	....
1997-98	Portland Pirates	AHL	76	8	29	37	46	....	....	....	....	....	....	....	....	....	....	....	10	2	3	5	8	....	....	....
1998-99	Washington	NHL	22	0	0	0	8	0	0	0	11	0.0	–8	0	0.0	48	6	12:26	....	....	....	....	....	....	....	....
	Portland Pirates	AHL	54	3	21	24	36	....	....	....	....	....	....	....	....	....	....	....	....	....	....	....	....	....	....	....
99-2000	Portland Pirates	AHL	58	0	14	14	20	....	....	....	....	....	....	....	....	....	....	....	3	1	0	1	2	....	....	....
2000-01	Chicago	NHL	36	2	3	5	12	0	0	0	27	7.4	3	0	0.0	57	48	17:03	....	....	....	....	....	....	....	....
	Norfolk Admirals	AHL	37	1	8	9	14	....	....	....	....	....	....	....	....	....	....	....	....	....	....	....	....	....	....	....
	NHL Totals		61	3	3	6	20	0	0	1	40	7.5		0	0.0	105	54	15:18	6	0	0	0	0	0	0	0

ECHL First All-Star Team (1993)

Signed as a free agent by **Washington**, February 4, 1995. Signed as a free agent by **Chicago**, July 27, 2000.

PODEIN, Shjon
(poh-DEEN, SHAWN) **COL.**

Left wing. Shoots left. 6'2", 200 lbs. Born, Rochester, MN, March 5, 1968. Edmonton's 9th choice, 166th overall, in 1988 Entry Draft.

Season	Club	League	GP	G	A	Pts	PIM	PP	SH	GW	S	%	+/-	TF	F%	H	SB	Min	GP	G	A	Pts	PIM	PP	SH	GW
1985-86	John Marshall	Hi-School	25	34	30	64	....	....	....	....	....	....	....	....	....	....	....	....	....	....	....	....	....	....	....	....
1986-87	U.S. International	NCAA-2	6	0	1	1	0	....	....	....	....	....	....	....	....	....	....	....	....	....	....	....	....	....	....	....
1987-88	Minnesota-Duluth	WCHA	30	4	4	8	48	....	....	....	....	....	....	....	....	....	....	....	....	....	....	....	....	....	....	....
1988-89	Minnesota-Duluth	WCHA	36	7	5	12	46	....	....	....	....	....	....	....	....	....	....	....	....	....	....	....	....	....	....	....
1989-90	Minnesota-Duluth	WCHA	35	21	18	39	36	....	....	....	....	....	....	....	....	....	....	....	....	....	....	....	....	....	....	....
1990-91	Cape Breton	AHL	63	14	15	29	65	....	....	....	....	....	....	....	....	....	....	....	4	0	0	0	5	....	....	....
1991-92	Cape Breton	AHL	80	30	24	54	46	....	....	....	....	....	....	....	....	....	....	....	5	3	1	4	2	....	....	....
1992-93	Edmonton	NHL	40	13	6	19	25	2	1	1	64	20.3	–2	....	....	....	....	....	....	....	....	....	....	....	....	....
	Cape Breton	AHL	38	18	21	39	32	....	....	....	....	....	....	....	....	....	....	....	9	2	2	4	29	....	....	....
1993-94	Edmonton	NHL	28	3	5	8	8	0	0	0	26	11.5	3	....	....	....	....	....	....	....	....	....	....	....	....	....
	Cape Breton	AHL	5	4	4	8	4	....	....	....	....	....	....	....	....	....	....	....	....	....	....	....	....	....	....	....
1994-95	Philadelphia	NHL	44	3	7	10	33	0	0	1	48	6.3	–2	....	....	....	....	....	15	1	3	4	10	0	0	0
1995-96	Philadelphia	NHL	79	15	10	25	89	0	4	4	115	13.0	25	....	....	....	....	....	12	1	2	3	50	0	0	1
1996-97	Philadelphia	NHL	82	14	18	32	41	0	0	4	153	9.2	7	....	....	....	....	....	19	4	3	7	16	0	0	1
1997-98	Philadelphia	NHL	82	11	13	24	53	1	1	2	126	8.7	8	....	....	....	....	....	5	0	0	0	10	0	0	0
1998-99	Philadelphia	NHL	14	1	0	1	0	0	0	0	26	3.8	–2	2	50.0	13	4	11:52	....	....	....	....	....	....	....	....
	Colorado	NHL	41	2	6	8	24	0	0	0	49	4.1	–3	21	42.9	41	24	11:49	19	1	1	2	12	0	0	0
99-2000	Colorado	NHL	75	11	8	19	29	0	1	3	104	10.6	12	17	64.7	84	60	13:31	17	5	0	5	8	0	0	1
2000-01 ♦	Colorado	NHL	82	15	17	32	68	0	0	3	137	10.9	7	69	44.9	116	47	14:23	23	2	3	5	14	0	0	1
	NHL Totals		567	88	90	178	370	3	7	18	848	10.4		109	47.7	254	135	13:25	110	14	12	26	120	0	0	4

Won King Clancy Memorial Trophy (2001)

Signed as a free agent by **Philadelphia**, July 27, 1994. Traded to **Colorado** by **Philadelphia** for Keith Jones, November 12, 1998.

PODKONICKY, Andrej
(pohd-koh-NIHTZ-kee, AWN-dray)

Center. Shoots left. 6'2", 202 lbs. Born, Zvolen, Czech., May 9, 1978. St. Louis' 8th choice, 196th overall, in 1996 Entry Draft.

Season	Club	League	GP	G	A	Pts	PIM	PP	SH	GW	S	%	+/-	TF	F%	H	SB	Min	GP	G	A	Pts	PIM	PP	SH	GW
1994-95	ZTK Zvolen	Slovakia-2	17	0	4	4	6	....	....	....	....	....	....	....	....	....	....	....	....	....	....	....	....	....	....	....
1995-96	ZTK Zvolen	Slovakia-2	38	18	12	30	18	....	....	....	....	....	....	....	....	....	....	....	....	....	....	....	....	....	....	....
1996-97	Portland	WHL	71	25	46	71	127	....	....	....	....	....	....	....	....	....	....	....	6	1	1	2	8	....	....	....
1997-98	Portland	WHL	64	30	44	74	81	....	....	....	....	....	....	....	....	....	....	....	16	4	12	16	20	....	....	....
1998-99	Worcester	AHL	61	19	24	43	52	....	....	....	....	....	....	....	....	....	....	....	4	0	0	0	4	....	....	....
99-2000	Worcester	AHL	77	16	25	41	68	....	....	....	....	....	....	....	....	....	....	....	9	2	5	7	6	....	....	....
2000-01	Worcester	AHL	16	2	3	5	15	....	....	....	....	....	....	....	....	....	....	....	....	....	....	....	....	....	....	....
	Florida	NHL	6	1	0	1	2	0	0	0	5	20.0	0	34	55.9	7	1	6:04	....	....	....	....	....	....	....	....
	Louisville Panthers	AHL	41	6	10	16	31	....	....	....	....	....	....	....	....	....	....	....	....	....	....	....	....	....	....	....
	NHL Totals		6	1	0	1	2	0	0	0	5	20.0		34	55.9	7	1	6:04	....	....	....	....	....	....	....	....

Memorial Cup All-Star Team (1998) • Won Ed Chynoweth Award (Memorial Cup Tournament Top Scorer) (1998)

Traded to **Florida** by **St. Louis** for Eric Boguniecki, December 17, 2000. Signed as a free agent by **HIFK Helsinki** (Finland), August 14, 2001.

PODOLLAN, Jason
(poh-DOH-luhn, JAY-suhn)

Right wing. Shoots right. 6'1", 198 lbs. Born, Vernon, B.C., February 18, 1976. Florida's 3rd choice, 31st overall, in 1994 Entry Draft.

Season	Club	League	GP	G	A	Pts	PIM	PP	SH	GW	S	%	+/-	TF	F%	H	SB	Min	GP	G	A	Pts	PIM	PP	SH	GW
1990-91	Sherwood Park	AAHA	61	105	111	216	133	....	....	....	....	....	....	....	....	....	....	....	....	....	....	....	....	....	....	....
1991-92	Penticton	BCJHL	59	20	26	46	66	....	....	....	....	....	....	....	....	....	....	....	....	....	....	....	....	....	....	....
	Spokane Chiefs	WHL	2	0	0	0	2	....	....	....	....	....	....	....	....	....	....	....	10	3	1	4	16	....	....	....
1992-93	Spokane Chiefs	WHL	72	36	33	69	108	....	....	....	....	....	....	....	....	....	....	....	10	4	4	8	14	....	....	....
1993-94	Spokane Chiefs	WHL	69	29	37	66	108	....	....	....	....	....	....	....	....	....	....	....	3	3	0	3	2	....	....	....
1994-95	Spokane Chiefs	WHL	72	43	41	84	102	....	....	....	....	....	....	....	....	....	....	....	11	5	7	12	18	....	....	....
	Cincinnati	IHL	....	....	....	....	....	....	....	....	....	....	....	....	....	....	....	....	3	0	0	0	2	....	....	....
1995-96	Spokane Chiefs	WHL	56	37	25	62	103	....	....	....	....	....	....	....	....	....	....	....	18	*21	12	33	28	....	....	....

			Regular Season																Playoffs							
Season	Club	League	GP	G	A	Pts	PIM	PP	SH	GW	S	%	+/-	TF	F%	H	SB	Min	GP	G	A	Pts	PIM	PP	SH	GW
1996-97	**Florida**	**NHL**	**19**	**1**	**1**	**2**	**4**	**1**	**0**	**0**	**20**	**5.0**	**–3**													
	Carolina	AHL	39	21	25	46	36																			
	Toronto	**NHL**	**10**	**0**	**3**	**3**	**6**	**0**	**0**	**0**	**10**	**0.0**	**–2**													
	St. John's Leafs	AHL																	11	2	3	5	6			
1997-98	St. John's Leafs	AHL	70	30	31	61	116												4	1	0	1	10			
1998-99	**Toronto**	**NHL**	**4**	**0**	**0**	**0**	**0**	**0**	**0**	**0**	**2**	**0.0**	**0**	**0**	**0.0**	**5**	**0**	**6:29**								
	St. John's Leafs	AHL	68	42	26	68	65																			
	Los Angeles	**NHL**	**6**	**0**	**0**	**0**	**5**	**0**	**0**	**0**	**7**	**0.0**	**–3**	**0**	**0.0**	**13**	**1**	**10:15**								
	Long Beach	IHL	8	5	3	8	2												6	1	2	3	4			
99-2000	**Los Angeles**	**NHL**	**1**	**0**	**1**	**1**	**2**	**0**	**0**	**0**	**2**	**0.0**	**0**	**0**	**0.0**	**3**	**0**	**16:13**								
	Lowell	AHL	71	29	26	55	91												4	0	0	0	4			
2000-01	Detroit Vipers	IHL	63	15	16	31	98																			
	Manitoba Moose	IHL	16	5	2	7	10												4	0	0	0	2			
	NHL Totals		**40**	**1**	**5**	**6**	**17**	**1**	**0**	**0**	**41**	**2.4**		**0**	**0.0**	**21**	**1**	**9:25**								

WHL West Second All-Star Team (1996)

Traded to **Toronto** by **Florida** for Kirk Muller, March 18, 1997. Traded to **Los Angeles** by **Toronto** with Toronto's 3rd round choice (Cory Campbell) in 1999 Entry Draft for Yanic Perreault, March 23, 1999. Claimed by **Tampa Bay** from **LA Kings** in Waiver Draft, September 29, 2000.

POESCHEK, Rudy

(POH-shehk, REW-dee)

Right wing/Defense. Shoots right. 6'2", 218 lbs. Born, Kamloops, B.C., September 29, 1966. NY Rangers' 12th choice, 238th overall, in 1985 Entry Draft.

Season	Club	League	GP	G	A	Pts	PIM	PP	SH	GW	S	%	+/-	TF	F%	H	SB	Min	GP	G	A	Pts	PIM	PP	SH	GW
1982-83	Vernon Lakers	BCJHL	54	4	10	14	100																			
1983-84	Revelstoke	BCJHL	22	5	21	26	107																			
	Kamloops Blazers	WHL	47	3	9	12	93												8	0	2	2	7			
1984-85	Kamloops Blazers	WHL	34	6	7	13	100												15	0	3	3	56			
1985-86	Kamloops Blazers	WHL	32	3	13	16	92												16	3	7	10	40			
1986-87	Kamloops Blazers	WHL	54	13	18	31	153												15	2	4	6	37			
1987-88	**NY Rangers**	**NHL**	**1**	**0**	**0**	**0**	**2**	**0**	**0**	**0**	**1**	**0.0**	**0**													
	Colorado	IHL	82	7	31	38	210												12	2	2	4	31			
1988-89	**NY Rangers**	**NHL**	**52**	**0**	**2**	**2**	**199**	**0**	**0**	**0**	**17**	**0.0**	**–8**													
	Colorado	IHL	2	0	0	0	6																			
1989-90	**NY Rangers**	**NHL**	**15**	**0**	**0**	**0**	**55**	**0**	**0**	**0**	**1**	**0.0**	**–1**													
	Flint Spirits	IHL	38	8	13	21	109												4	0	0	0	16			
1990-91	Binghamton	AHL	38	1	3	4	162																			
	Winnipeg	**NHL**	**1**	**0**	**0**	**0**	**5**	**0**	**0**	**0**	**0**	**0.0**	**0**													
	Moncton Hawks	AHL	23	2	4	6	67												9	1	1	2	41			
1991-92	**Winnipeg**	**NHL**	**4**	**0**	**0**	**0**	**17**	**0**	**0**	**0**	**1**	**0.0**	**–5**													
	Moncton Hawks	AHL	63	4	18	22	170												11	0	2	2	48			
1992-93	St. John's Leafs	AHL	78	7	24	31	189												9	0	4	4	13			
1993-94	**Tampa Bay**	**NHL**	**71**	**3**	**6**	**9**	**118**	**0**	**0**	**1**	**46**	**6.5**	**3**													
1994-95	**Tampa Bay**	**NHL**	**25**	**1**	**1**	**2**	**92**	**0**	**0**	**0**	**14**	**7.1**	**0**													
1995-96	**Tampa Bay**	**NHL**	**57**	**1**	**3**	**4**	**88**	**0**	**0**	**0**	**36**	**2.8**	**–2**						**3**	**0**	**0**	**0**	**12**	**0**	**0**	**0**
1996-97	**Tampa Bay**	**NHL**	**60**	**0**	**6**	**6**	**120**	**0**	**0**	**0**	**30**	**0.0**	**–3**													
1997-98	**St. Louis**	**NHL**	**50**	**1**	**7**	**8**	**64**	**0**	**0**	**0**	**29**	**3.4**	**–5**						**2**	**0**	**0**	**0**	**6**	**0**	**0**	**0**
1998-99	**St. Louis**	**NHL**	**16**	**0**	**0**	**0**	**33**	**0**	**0**	**0**	**8**	**0.0**	**0**	**0**	**0.0**	**8**	**5**	**10:14**								
99-2000	**St. Louis**	**NHL**	**12**	**0**	**0**	**0**	**24**	**0**	**0**	**0**	**8**	**0.0**	**–3**	**0**	**0.0**	**13**	**11**	**11:15**								
	Worcester	AHL	5	0	0	0	4																			
	Houston Aeros	IHL	32	2	6	8	51																			
2000-01	Houston Aeros	IHL	67	3	13	16	66												7	0	0	0	8			
	NHL Totals		**364**	**6**	**25**	**31**	**817**	**0**	**0**	**1**	**191**	**3.1**		**0**	**0.0**	**21**	**16**	**10:40**	**5**	**0**	**0**	**0**	**18**	**0**	**0**	**0**

Traded to **Winnipeg** by **NY Rangers** for Guy Larose, January 22, 1991. Signed as a free agent by **Toronto**, July 8, 1992. Signed as a free agent by **Tampa Bay**, August 10, 1993. Signed as a free agent by **St. Louis**, July 31, 1997. Loaned to **Houston** (IHL) by **St. Louis**, November 11, 1999.

PONIKAROVSKY, Alexei

(poh-NIH-kahr-ohv-skee, al-EHX-ay) **TOR.**

Right wing. Shoots left. 6'4", 196 lbs. Born, Kiev, USSR, April 9, 1980. Toronto's 4th choice, 87th overall, in 1998 Entry Draft.

Season	Club	League	GP	G	A	Pts	PIM	PP	SH	GW	S	%	+/-	TF	F%	H	SB	Min	GP	G	A	Pts	PIM	PP	SH	GW
1995-96	Dynamo Moscow	Russia-Jr.	70	14	10	24	20																			
1996-97	Dynamo Moscow	Russia-Jr.	60	12	15	27	30																			
	D'amo Moscow-2	Russia-3	2	0	0	0	2																			
1997-98	Dynamo Moscow	Russia-2	24	1	2	3	30																			
1998-99	Krylja Sovetov	Russia	13	2	1	3	2																			
	Dynamo Moscow	Russia																	3	0	0	0	2			
99-2000	THK Tver	Russia-2	29	8	14	22	26																			
	Dynamo Moscow	Russia	19	1	0	1	8												1	0	0	0	0			
	Dynamo Moscow	EuroHL	2	0	2	2	0																			
2000-01	**Toronto**	**NHL**	**22**	**1**	**3**	**4**	**14**	**0**	**0**	**0**	**21**	**4.8**	**–1**	**7**	**28.6**	**18**	**7**	**8:32**								
	St. John's Leafs	AHL	49	12	24	36	44												4	0	0	0	4			
	NHL Totals		**22**	**1**	**3**	**4**	**14**	**0**	**0**	**0**	**21**	**4.8**		**7**	**28.6**	**18**	**7**	**8:32**								

POPOVIC, Peter

(puh-PUH-vihch, PEE-tuhr)

Defense. Shoots left. 6'6", 243 lbs. Born, Koping, Sweden, February 10, 1968. Montreal's 5th choice, 93rd overall, in 1988 Entry Draft.

Season	Club	League	GP	G	A	Pts	PIM	PP	SH	GW	S	%	+/-	TF	F%	H	SB	Min	GP	G	A	Pts	PIM	PP	SH	GW
1986-87	Vasteras IK	Sweden-2	10	0	1	1	2																			
	Vasteras IK	Sweden-2	24	1	2	3	10												12	2	8	10	6			
1987-88	Vasteras IK	Sweden-2	28	3	17	20	16												15	1	4	5	20			
1988-89	Vasteras IK	Sweden	22	1	4	5	32																			
	Vasteras IK	Sweden	39	3	7	10	52												5	0	1	1	16			
1989-90	Vasteras IK	Sweden	30	2	10	12	24												2	0	1	1	2			
1990-91	Vasteras IK	Sweden	40	3	2	5	62												4	0	0	0	4			
1991-92	Vasteras IK	Sweden	34	7	10	17	30																			
1992-93	Vasteras IK	Sweden	39	6	12	18	46												3	0	1	1	2			
1993-94	**Montreal**	**NHL**	**47**	**2**	**12**	**14**	**26**	**1**	**0**	**0**	**58**	**3.4**	**10**						**6**	**0**	**1**	**1**	**0**	**0**	**0**	**0**
1994-95	Vasteras IK	Sweden	11	0	3	3	10																			
	Montreal	**NHL**	**33**	**0**	**5**	**5**	**8**	**0**	**0**	**0**	**23**	**0.0**	**–10**													
1995-96	**Montreal**	**NHL**	**76**	**2**	**12**	**14**	**69**	**0**	**0**	**0**	**59**	**3.4**	**21**						**6**	**0**	**2**	**2**	**4**	**0**	**0**	**0**
1996-97	**Montreal**	**NHL**	**78**	**1**	**13**	**14**	**32**	**0**	**0**	**0**	**82**	**1.2**	**9**						**3**	**0**	**0**	**0**	**2**	**0**	**0**	**0**
1997-98	**Montreal**	**NHL**	**69**	**2**	**6**	**8**	**38**	**0**	**0**	**0**	**40**	**5.0**	**–6**						**10**	**1**	**1**	**2**	**2**	**0**	**0**	**0**
1998-99	**NY Rangers**	**NHL**	**68**	**1**	**4**	**5**	**40**	**0**	**0**	**0**	**64**	**1.6**	**–12**	**2**	**0.0**	**112**	**178**	**20:41**								
99-2000	**Pittsburgh**	**NHL**	**54**	**1**	**5**	**6**	**30**	**0**	**0**	**0**	**23**	**4.3**	**–8**	**2**	**0.0**	**59**	**85**	**16:12**	**10**	**0**	**0**	**0**	**10**	**0**	**0**	**0**
2000-01	**Boston**	**NHL**	**60**	**1**	**6**	**7**	**48**	**0**	**0**	**0**	**34**	**2.9**	**–5**	**1**	**0.0**	**104**	**102**	**18:41**								
	NHL Totals		**485**	**10**	**63**	**73**	**291**	**1**	**0**	**0**	**383**	**2.6**		**5**	**0.0**	**275**	**365**	**18:42**	**35**	**1**	**4**	**5**	**18**	**0**	**0**	**0**

Traded to **NY Rangers** by **Montreal** for Sylvain Blouin and NY Rangers' 6th round choice (later traded to Phoenix - Phoenix selected Erik Lewerstrom) in 1999 Entry Draft, June 30, 1998. Traded to **Pittsburgh** by **NY Rangers** for Kevin Hatcher, September 30, 1999. Signed as a free agent by **Boston**, July 2, 2000.

POSMYK, Marek

(PAWZ-mihk, MAHR-ehk) **T.B.**

Defense. Shoots right. 6'5", 228 lbs. Born, Jihlava, Czech., September 15, 1978. Toronto's 1st choice, 36th overall, in 1996 Entry Draft.

Season	Club	League	GP	G	A	Pts	PIM	PP	SH	GW	S	%	+/-	TF	F%	H	SB	Min	GP	G	A	Pts	PIM	PP	SH	GW
1994-95	Dukla Jihlava-Jr.	Cze-Rep	16	1	3	4																				
1995-96	Dukla Jihlava-Jr.	Cze-Rep	16	6	5	11																				
	Dukla Jihlava	Cze-Rep	18	1	2	3													1	0	0	0				
1996-97	Dukla Jihlava	Cze-Rep	24	1	7	8	44																			
	St. John's Leafs	AHL	2	0	0	0	2																			
1997-98	Sarnia Sting	OHL	48	8	16	24	94												5	0	2	2	6			
	St. John's Leafs	AHL	3	0	0	0	4																			
1998-99	St. John's Leafs	AHL	41	1	0	1	36																			
99-2000	St. John's Leafs	AHL	38	1	6	7	57																			
	Tampa Bay	**NHL**	**18**	**1**	**2**	**3**	**20**	**0**	**0**	**0**	**22**	**4.5**	**1**	**1**	**100.0**	**21**	**13**	**13:12**								
	Detroit Vipers	IHL	1	0	1	1	0																			

			Regular Season																Playoffs							
Season	Club	League	GP	G	A	Pts	PIM	PP	SH	GW	S	%	+/-	TF	F%	H	SB	Min	GP	G	A	Pts	PIM	PP	SH	GW
2000-01	Tampa Bay	NHL	1	0	0	0	0	0	0	0	0	0.0	–1	0	0.0	0	0	13:27	....	....	....	....	....	....	....	....
	Detroit Vipers	IHL	49	7	14	21	58	....	....	....	....	....	....	....	....	....	....	....	....	....	....	....	....	....	....	....
	NHL Totals		19	1	2	3	20	0	0	0	22	4.5		1	100.0	21	13	13:12	....	....	....	....	....	....	....	....

Traded to **Tampa Bay** by **Toronto** with Mike Johnson, Toronto's 5th (Pavel Sedov) and 6th (Aaron Gionet) round choices in 2000 Entry Draft and future considerations for Darcy Tucker, Tampa Bay's 4th round choice (Miguel Delisle) in 2000 Entry Draft and future considerations, February 9, 2000. Signed as a free agent by **Continental Zlin** (Czech-Rep), August 12, 2001.

POTHIER, Brian

(PAW-tee-ay, BRIGH-uhn) **ATL.**

Defense. Shoots right. 6', 195 lbs. Born, New Bedford, MA, April 15, 1977.

1995-96	Northfield High	Hi-School	27	11	22	33	36	....	....	....	....	....	....	....	....	....	....	....	....	....	....	....	....	....	....	....
1996-97	RPI Engineers	ECAC	34	1	11	12	42	....	....	....	....	....	....	....	....	....	....	....	....	....	....	....	....	....	....	....
1997-98	RPI Engineers	ECAC	35	2	9	11	28	....	....	....	....	....	....	....	....	....	....	....	....	....	....	....	....	....	....	....
1998-99	RPI Engineers	ECAC	37	5	13	18	36	....	....	....	....	....	....	....	....	....	....	....	....	....	....	....	....	....	....	....
99-2000	RPI Engineers	ECAC	36	9	24	33	44	....	....	....	....	....	....	....	....	....	....	....	....	....	....	....	....	....	....	....
2000-01	Atlanta	NHL	3	0	0	0	2	0	0	0	0	0.0	4	0	0.0	2	6	20:38	....	....	....	....	....	....	....	....
	Orlando	IHL	76	12	29	41	69	....	....	....	....	....	....	....	....	....	....	....	16	3	5	8	11	....	....	....
	NHL Totals		3	0	0	0	2	0	0	0	0	0.0		0	0.0	2	6	20:38	....	....	....	....	....	....	....	....

ECAC Second All-Star Team (2000) • ECAC All-Tournament Team (2000) • NCAA East Second All-American Team (2000) • Won Garry F. Longman Memorial Trophy (Top Rookie - IHL) (2001)

Signed as a free agent by **Atlanta**, March 27, 2000.

POTI, Tom

(POH-tee, TAWM) **EDM.**

Defense. Shoots left. 6'3", 215 lbs. Born, Worcester, MA, March 22, 1977. Edmonton's 4th choice, 59th overall, in 1996 Entry Draft.

1992-93	St. Peter's	Hi-School	55	25	46	71	....	....	....	....	....	....	....	....	....	....	....	....	....	....	....	....	....	....	....	....
1993-94	Cushing Academy	Hi-School	30	10	35	45	....	....	....	....	....	....	....	....	....	....	....	....	....	....	....	....	....	....	....	....
1994-95	Cushing Academy	Hi-School	36	17	54	71	35	....	....	....	....	....	....	....	....	....	....	....	....	....	....	....	....	....	....	....
	Central-Mass	MBHL	8	8	10	18	....	....	....	....	....	....	....	....	....	....	....	....	....	....	....	....	....	....	....	....
1995-96	Cushing Academy	Hi-School	29	14	59	73	18	....	....	....	....	....	....	....	....	....	....	....	....	....	....	....	....	....	....	....
1996-97	Boston University	H-East	38	4	17	21	54	....	....	....	....	....	....	....	....	....	....	....	....	....	....	....	....	....	....	....
1997-98	Boston University	H-East	38	13	29	42	60	....	....	....	....	....	....	....	....	....	....	....	....	....	....	....	....	....	....	....
1998-99	Edmonton	NHL	73	5	16	21	42	2	0	3	94	5.3	10	0	0.0	35	82	19:33	4	0	1	1	2	0	0	0
99-2000	Edmonton	NHL	76	9	26	35	65	2	1	1	125	7.2	8	0	0.0	38	119	24:10	5	0	1	1	0	0	0	0
2000-01	Edmonton	NHL	81	12	20	32	60	6	0	3	161	7.5	–4	0	0.0	37	114	22:44	6	0	2	2	2	0	0	0
	NHL Totals		230	26	62	88	167	10	1	7	380	6.8		0	0.0	110	315	22:12	15	0	4	4	4	0	0	0

NCAA Championship All-Tournament Team (1997) • Hockey East First All-Star Team (1998) • NCAA East First All-American Team (1998) • NHL All-Rookie Team (1999)

POULIN, Patrick

(poo-LIHN, PAT-rihk) **MTL.**

Center. Shoots left. 6'1", 216 lbs. Born, Vanier, Que., April 23, 1973. Hartford's 1st choice, 9th overall, in 1991 Entry Draft.

1988-89	Ste-Foy Governors	QAAA	42	28	42	70	44	....	....	....	....	....	....	....	....	....	....	....	13	*13	23	*36	24	....	....	....
1989-90	St-Hyacinthe	QMJHL	60	25	26	51	55	....	....	....	....	....	....	....	....	....	....	....	12	1	9	10	5	....	....	....
1990-91	St-Hyacinthe	QMJHL	56	32	38	70	82	....	....	....	....	....	....	....	....	....	....	....	4	0	2	2	23	....	....	....
1991-92	St-Hyacinthe	QMJHL	56	52	86	*138	58	....	....	....	....	....	....	....	....	....	....	....	5	2	2	4	4	....	....	....
	Hartford	NHL	1	0	0	0	2	0	0	0	0	0.0	–1	....	....	....	....	....	7	2	1	3	0	1	0	0
	Springfield	AHL	....	....	....	....	....	....	....	....	....	....	....	....	....	....	....	....	1	0	0	0	0	....	....	....
1992-93	Hartford	NHL	81	20	31	51	37	4	0	2	160	12.5	–19	....	....	....	....	....	....	....	....	....	....	....	....	....
1993-94	Hartford	NHL	9	2	1	3	11	1	0	0	13	15.4	–8	....	....	....	....	....	....	....	....	....	....	....	....	....
	Chicago	NHL	58	12	13	25	40	1	0	3	83	14.5	0	....	....	....	....	....	4	0	0	0	0	0	0	0
1994-95	Chicago	NHL	45	15	15	30	53	4	0	2	77	19.5	13	....	....	....	....	....	16	4	1	5	8	1	0	0
1995-96	Chicago	NHL	38	7	8	15	16	1	0	0	40	17.5	7	....	....	....	....	....	....	....	....	....	....	....	....	....
	Indianapolis Ice	IHL	1	0	1	1	0	....	....	....	....	....	....	....	....	....	....	....	....	....	....	....	....	....	....	....
	Tampa Bay	NHL	8	0	1	1	0	0	0	0	11	0.0	0	....	....	....	....	....	2	0	0	0	0	0	0	0
1996-97	Tampa Bay	NHL	73	12	14	26	56	2	3	1	124	9.7	–16	....	....	....	....	....	....	....	....	....	....	....	....	....
1997-98	Tampa Bay	NHL	44	2	7	9	19	0	0	0	49	4.1	–3	....	....	....	....	....	....	....	....	....	....	....	....	....
	Montreal	NHL	34	4	6	10	8	0	1	1	39	10.3	–1	....	....	....	....	....	3	0	0	0	0	0	0	0
1998-99	Montreal	NHL	81	8	17	25	21	0	1	1	87	9.2	6	112	30.4	92	29	13:30	....	....	....	....	....	....	....	....
99-2000	Montreal	NHL	82	10	5	15	17	0	1	2	82	12.2	–15	35	34.3	79	38	12:34	....	....	....	....	....	....	....	....
2000-01	Montreal	NHL	52	9	11	20	13	0	0	4	65	13.8	1	11	9.1	77	34	13:16	....	....	....	....	....	....	....	....
	NHL Totals		606	101	129	230	293	13	6	16	830	12.2		158	29.7	248	101	13:05	32	6	2	8	8	2	0	0

QMJHL First All-Star Team (1992) • Canadian Major Junior Player of the Year (1992)

Traded to **Chicago** by **Hartford** with Eric Weinrich for Steve Larmer and Bryan Marchment, November 2, 1993. Traded to **Tampa Bay** by **Chicago** with Igor Ulanov and Chicago's 2nd round choice (later traded to New Jersey - New Jersey selected Pierre Dagenais) in 1996 Entry Draft for Enrico Ciccone and Tampa Bay's 2nd round choice (Jeff Paul) in 1996 Entry Draft, March 20, 1996. Traded to **Montreal** by **Tampa Bay** with Mick Vukota and Igor Ulanov for Stephane Richer, Darcy Tucker and David Wilkie, January 15, 1998.

PRATT, Nolan

(PRAT, NOH-lan) **T.B.**

Defense. Shoots left. 6'3", 200 lbs. Born, Fort McMurray, Alta., August 14, 1975. Hartford's 4th choice, 115th overall, in 1993 Entry Draft.

1991-92	Bonnyville	AJHL	33	3	7	10	57	....	....	....	....	....	....	....	....	....	....	....	....	....	....	....	....	....	....	....
	Portland	WHL	22	2	9	11	13	....	....	....	....	....	....	....	....	....	....	....	6	1	3	4	12	....	....	....
1992-93	Portland	WHL	70	4	19	23	97	....	....	....	....	....	....	....	....	....	....	....	16	2	7	9	31	....	....	....
1993-94	Portland	WHL	72	4	32	36	105	....	....	....	....	....	....	....	....	....	....	....	10	1	2	3	14	....	....	....
1994-95	Portland	WHL	72	6	37	43	196	....	....	....	....	....	....	....	....	....	....	....	9	1	6	7	10	....	....	....
1995-96	Springfield	AHL	62	2	6	8	72	....	....	....	....	....	....	....	....	....	....	....	2	0	0	0	0	....	....	....
	Richmond	ECHL	4	1	0	1	2	....	....	....	....	....	....	....	....	....	....	....	....	....	....	....	....	....	....	....
1996-97	Hartford	NHL	9	0	2	2	6	0	0	0	4	0.0	0	....	....	....	....	....	....	....	....	....	....	....	....	....
	Springfield	AHL	66	1	18	19	127	....	....	....	....	....	....	....	....	....	....	....	17	0	3	3	18	....	....	....
1997-98	Carolina	NHL	23	0	2	2	44	0	0	0	11	0.0	–2	....	....	....	....	....	....	....	....	....	....	....	....	....
	New Haven	AHL	54	3	15	18	135	....	....	....	....	....	....	....	....	....	....	....	....	....	....	....	....	....	....	....
1998-99	Carolina	NHL	61	1	14	15	95	0	0	1	46	2.2	15	0	0.0	121	59	16:45	3	0	0	0	2	0	0	0
99-2000	Carolina	NHL	64	3	1	4	90	0	0	1	47	6.4	–22	0	0.0	155	74	19:10	....	....	....	....	....	....	....	....
2000-01 ♦	Colorado	NHL	46	1	2	3	40	0	0	1	26	3.8	2	1	0.0	41	33	9:50	....	....	....	....	....	....	....	....
	NHL Totals		203	5	21	26	275	0	0	3	134	3.7		1	0.0	317	166	15:48	3	0	0	0	2	0	0	0

Transferred to **Carolina** after **Hartford** franchise relocated, June 25, 1997. Traded to **Colorado** by **Carolina** with Carolina's 1st (Vaclav Nedorost) and 2nd (Jared Aulin) round choices in 2000 Entry Draft and Philadelphia's 2nd round choice (previously acquired, Colorado selected Agris Saviels) in 2000 Entry Draft for Sandis Ozolinsh and Columbus' 2nd round choice (previously acquired, Carolina selected Tomas Kurka) in 2000 Entry Draft, June 24, 2000. Traded to **Tampa Bay** by **Colorado** for LA Kings' 6th round choice (previously acquired, Colorado selected Scott Horvath) in 2001 Entry Draft, June 24, 2001.

PRIMEAU, Keith

(PREE-moh, KEETH) **PHI.**

Center. Shoots left. 6'5", 220 lbs. Born, Toronto, Ont., November 24, 1971. Detroit's 1st choice, 3rd overall, in 1990 Entry Draft.

1986-87	Whitby Flyers	OMHA	65	69	80	149	116	....	....	....	....	....	....	....	....	....	....	....	....	....	....	....	....	....	....	....
1987-88	Hamilton Kilty B's	OJHL-B	19	19	17	36	16	....	....	....	....	....	....	....	....	....	....	....	....	....	....	....	....	....	....	....
	Hamilton Hawks	OHL	47	6	6	12	69	....	....	....	....	....	....	....	....	....	....	....	11	0	2	2	2	....	....	....
1988-89	Niagara Falls	OHL	48	20	35	55	56	....	....	....	....	....	....	....	....	....	....	....	17	9	16	25	12	....	....	....
1989-90	Niagara Falls	OHL	65	*57	70	*127	97	....	....	....	....	....	....	....	....	....	....	....	16	*16	17	*33	49	....	....	....
1990-91	Detroit	NHL	58	3	12	15	106	0	0	1	33	9.1	–12	....	....	....	....	....	5	1	1	2	25	0	0	0
	Adirondack	AHL	6	3	5	8	8	....	....	....	....	....	....	....	....	....	....	....	....	....	....	....	....	....	....	....
1991-92	Detroit	NHL	35	6	10	16	83	0	0	0	27	22.2	9	....	....	....	....	....	11	0	0	0	14	0	0	0
	Adirondack	AHL	42	21	24	45	89	....	....	....	....	....	....	....	....	....	....	....	9	1	7	8	27	....	....	....
1992-93	Detroit	NHL	73	15	17	32	152	4	1	2	75	20.0	–6	....	....	....	....	....	7	0	2	2	26	0	0	0
1993-94	Detroit	NHL	78	31	42	73	173	7	3	4	155	20.0	34	....	....	....	....	....	7	0	2	2	6	0	0	0
1994-95	Detroit	NHL	45	15	27	42	99	1	0	3	96	15.6	17	....	....	....	....	....	17	4	5	9	45	2	0	0
1995-96	Detroit	NHL	74	27	25	52	168	6	2	7	150	18.0	19	....	....	....	....	....	17	1	4	5	28	0	0	0
1996-97	Hartford	NHL	75	26	25	51	161	6	3	2	169	15.4	–3	....	....	....	....	....	....	....	....	....	....	....	....	....
1997-98	Carolina	NHL	81	26	37	63	110	7	3	2	180	14.4	19	....	....	....	....	....	....	....	....	....	....	....	....	....
	Canada	Olympics	6	2	1	3	4	....	....	....	....	....	....	....	....	....	....	....	....	....	....	....	....	....	....	....
1998-99	Carolina	NHL	78	30	32	62	75	9	1	5	178	16.9	8	1823	53.5	231	62	21:21	6	0	3	3	6	0	0	0

Season	Club	League	Regular Season GP	G	A	Pts	PIM	PP	SH	GW	S	%	+/-	TF	F%	H	SB	Min	Playoffs GP	G	A	Pts	PIM	PP	SH	GW
99-2000	**Philadelphia**	**NHL**	**23**	**7**	**10**	**17**	**31**	**1**	**0**	**1**	**51**	**13.7**	**10**	**478**	**54.2**	**37**	**18**	**17:38**	**18**	**2**	**11**	**13**	**13**	**0**	**0**	**1**
2000-01	**Philadelphia**	**NHL**	**71**	**34**	**39**	**73**	**76**	**11**	**0**	**4**	**165**	**20.6**	**17**	**1811**	**53.5**	**151**	**27**	**19:58**	**4**	**0**	**3**	**3**	**8**	**0**	**0**	**0**
	NHL Totals		**691**	**220**	**276**	**496**	**1234**	**52**	**13**	**31**	**1279**	**17.2**		**4112**	**53.6**	**419**	**107**	**20:17**	**92**	**8**	**31**	**39**	**171**	**2**	**0**	**1**

OHL Second All-Star Team (1990) • Played in NHL All-Star Game (1999)

Traded to **Hartford** by **Detroit** with Paul Coffey and Detroit's 1st round choice (Nikos Tselios) in 1997 Entry Draft for Brendan Shanahan and Brian Glynn, October 9, 1996. Transferred to **Carolina** after **Hartford** franchise relocated, June 25, 1997. • Missed majority of 1999-2000 season after failing to come to contract terms with **Carolina**. Traded to **Philadelphia** by **Carolina** with Carolina's 5th round choice (later traded to NY Islanders - NY Islanders selected Kristofer Ottosson) in 2000 Entry Draft for Rod Brind'Amour, Jean-Marc Pelletier and Philadelphia's 2nd round choice (later traded to Colorado - Colorado selected Agris Saviels) in 2000 Entry Draft, January 23, 2000.

PRIMEAU, Wayne (PREE-moh, WAYN) PIT.

Center. Shoots left. 6'3", 220 lbs. Born, Scarborough, Ont., June 4, 1976. Buffalo's 1st choice, 17th overall, in 1994 Entry Draft.

1991-92	Whitby Flyers	OMHA	63	36	50	86	96	....	....	....	....	....	....	....	....	....	....	....	....	....	....	....	....	....	....	....
1992-93	Owen Sound	OHL	66	10	27	37	108	....	....	....	....	....	....	....	....	....	....	....	8	1	4	5	0	....	....	....
1993-94	Owen Sound	OHL	65	25	50	75	75	....	....	....	....	....	....	....	....	....	....	....	9	1	6	7	8	....	....	....
1994-95	Owen Sound	OHL	66	34	62	96	84	....	....	....	....	....	....	....	....	....	....	....	10	4	9	13	15	....	....	....
	Buffalo	**NHL**	**1**	**1**	**0**	**1**	**0**	**0**	**0**	**1**	**2**	**50.0**	**-2**	....	....	....	....	....	....	....	....	....	....	....	....	....
1995-96	Owen Sound	OHL	28	15	29	44	52	....	....	....	....	....	....	....	....	....	....	....	....	....	....	....	....	....	....	....
	Oshawa Generals	OHL	24	12	13	25	33	....	....	....	....	....	....	....	....	....	....	....	3	2	3	5	2	....	....	....
	Buffalo	**NHL**	**2**	**0**	**0**	**0**	**0**	**0**	**0**	**0**	**0**	**0.0**	**0**	....	....	....	....	....	....	....	....	....	....	....	....	....
	Rochester	AHL	8	2	3	5	6	....	....	....	....	....	....	....	....	....	....	....	17	3	1	4	11	....	....	....
1996-97	**Buffalo**	**NHL**	**45**	**2**	**4**	**6**	**64**	**1**	**0**	**0**	**25**	**8.0**	**-2**	....	....	....	....	....	**9**	**0**	**0**	**0**	**6**	**0**	**0**	**0**
	Rochester	AHL	24	9	5	14	27	....	....	....	....	....	....	....	....	....	....	....	1	0	0	0	0	....	....	....
1997-98	**Buffalo**	**NHL**	**69**	**6**	**6**	**12**	**87**	**2**	**0**	**1**	**51**	**11.8**	**9**	....	....	....	....	....	**14**	**1**	**3**	**4**	**6**	**0**	**0**	**0**
1998-99	**Buffalo**	**NHL**	**67**	**5**	**8**	**13**	**38**	**0**	**0**	**0**	**55**	**9.1**	**-6**	**529**	**48.6**	**74**	**15**	**10:19**	**19**	**3**	**4**	**7**	**6**	**1**	**0**	**0**
99-2000	**Buffalo**	**NHL**	**41**	**5**	**7**	**12**	**38**	**2**	**0**	**1**	**40**	**12.5**	**-8**	**430**	**45.6**	**47**	**8**	**11:03**	....	....	....	....	....	....	....	....
	Tampa Bay	**NHL**	**17**	**2**	**3**	**5**	**25**	**0**	**0**	**0**	**35**	**5.7**	**-4**	**290**	**45.5**	**26**	**9**	**14:21**	....	....	....	....	....	....	....	....
2000-01	**Tampa Bay**	**NHL**	**47**	**2**	**13**	**15**	**77**	**0**	**0**	**0**	**47**	**4.3**	**-17**	**630**	**52.2**	**75**	**21**	**14:11**	....	....	....	....	....	....	....	....
	Pittsburgh	**NHL**	**28**	**1**	**6**	**7**	**54**	**0**	**0**	**0**	**30**	**3.3**	**0**	**318**	**51.3**	**39**	**17**	**12:45**	**18**	**1**	**3**	**4**	**2**	**0**	**0**	**0**
	NHL Totals		**317**	**24**	**47**	**71**	**383**	**5**	**0**	**3**	**285**	**8.4**		**2197**	**49.0**	**261**	**70**	**12:04**	**60**	**5**	**10**	**15**	**20**	**1**	**0**	**0**

Traded to **Tampa Bay** by **Buffalo** with Cory Sarich, Brian Holzinger and Buffalo's 3rd round choice (Alexander Kharitonov) in 2000 Entry Draft for Chris Gratton and Tampa Bay's 2nd round choice (Derek Roy) in 2001 Entry Draft, March 9, 2000. Traded to **Pittsburgh** by **Tampa Bay** for Matthew Barnaby, February 1, 2001.

PROBERT, Bob (PROH-buhrt, BAWB) CHI.

Left wing. Shoots left. 6'3", 225 lbs. Born, Windsor, Ont., June 5, 1965. Detroit's 3rd choice, 46th overall, in 1983 Entry Draft.

1981-82	Windsor 240	OMHA	55	60	40	100	40	....	....	....	....	....	....	....	....	....	....	....	....	....	....	....	....	....	....	....
1982-83	Brantford	OHL	51	12	16	28	133	....	....	....	....	....	....	....	....	....	....	....	8	2	2	4	23	....	....	....
1983-84	Brantford	OHL	65	35	28	63	189	....	....	....	....	....	....	....	....	....	....	....	6	0	3	3	16	....	....	....
1984-85	Hamilton Hawks	OHL	4	0	1	1	21	....	....	....	....	....	....	....	....	....	....	....	....	....	....	....	....	....	....	....
	Sault Ste. Marie	OHL	44	20	52	72	172	....	....	....	....	....	....	....	....	....	....	....	15	6	11	17	60	....	....	....
1985-86	**Detroit**	**NHL**	**44**	**8**	**13**	**21**	**186**	**3**	**0**	**0**	**46**	**17.4**	**-14**	....	....	....	....	....	....	....	....	....	....	....	....	....
	Adirondack	AHL	32	12	15	27	152	....	....	....	....	....	....	....	....	....	....	....	10	2	3	5	68	....	....	....
1986-87	**Detroit**	**NHL**	**63**	**13**	**11**	**24**	**221**	**2**	**0**	**0**	**56**	**23.2**	**-6**	....	....	....	....	....	**16**	**3**	**4**	**7**	**63**	**1**	**0**	**1**
	Adirondack	AHL	7	1	4	5	15	....	....	....	....	....	....	....	....	....	....	....	....	....	....	....	....	....	....	....
1987-88	**Detroit**	**NHL**	**74**	**29**	**33**	**62**	***398**	**15**	**0**	**5**	**126**	**23.0**	**16**	....	....	....	....	....	**16**	**8**	**13**	**21**	**51**	**5**	**0**	**1**
1988-89	**Detroit**	**NHL**	**25**	**4**	**2**	**6**	**106**	**1**	**0**	**0**	**23**	**17.4**	**-11**	....	....	....	....	....	....	....	....	....	....	....	....	....
1989-90	**Detroit**	**NHL**	**4**	**3**	**0**	**3**	**21**	**0**	**0**	**1**	**12**	**25.0**	**0**	....	....	....	....	....	....	....	....	....	....	....	....	....
1990-91	**Detroit**	**NHL**	**55**	**16**	**23**	**39**	**315**	**4**	**0**	**3**	**88**	**18.2**	**-3**	....	....	....	....	....	**6**	**1**	**2**	**3**	**50**	**0**	**0**	**0**
1991-92	**Detroit**	**NHL**	**63**	**20**	**24**	**44**	**276**	**8**	**0**	**1**	**96**	**20.8**	**16**	....	....	....	....	....	**11**	**1**	**6**	**7**	**28**	**0**	**0**	**0**
1992-93	**Detroit**	**NHL**	**80**	**14**	**29**	**43**	**292**	**6**	**0**	**3**	**128**	**10.9**	**-9**	....	....	....	....	....	**7**	**0**	**3**	**3**	**10**	**0**	**0**	**0**
1993-94	**Detroit**	**NHL**	**66**	**7**	**10**	**17**	**275**	**1**	**0**	**3**	**105**	**6.7**	**-1**	....	....	....	....	....	**7**	**1**	**1**	**2**	**8**	**0**	**0**	**0**
1994-95	**Chicago**	**NHL**	DID NOT PLAY – SUSPENDED																							
1995-96	**Chicago**	**NHL**	**78**	**19**	**21**	**40**	**237**	**1**	**0**	**3**	**97**	**19.6**	**15**	....	....	....	....	....	**10**	**0**	**2**	**2**	**23**	**0**	**0**	**0**
1996-97	**Chicago**	**NHL**	**82**	**9**	**14**	**23**	**326**	**1**	**0**	**3**	**111**	**8.1**	**-3**	....	....	....	....	....	**6**	**2**	**1**	**3**	**41**	**0**	**0**	**0**
1997-98	**Chicago**	**NHL**	**14**	**2**	**1**	**3**	**48**	**2**	**0**	**0**	**18**	**11.1**	**-7**	....	....	....	....	....	....	....	....	....	....	....	....	....
1998-99	**Chicago**	**NHL**	**78**	**7**	**14**	**21**	**206**	**0**	**0**	**3**	**87**	**8.0**	**-11**	**45**	**51.1**	**105**	**12**	**10:38**	....	....	....	....	....	....	....	....
99-2000	**Chicago**	**NHL**	**69**	**4**	**11**	**15**	**114**	**0**	**0**	**0**	**38**	**10.5**	**10**	**32**	**40.6**	**87**	**15**	**10:28**	....	....	....	....	....	....	....	....
2000-01	**Chicago**	**NHL**	**79**	**7**	**12**	**19**	**103**	**1**	**0**	**0**	**45**	**15.6**	**-13**	**2**	**0.0**	**117**	**13**	**10:50**	....	....	....	....	....	....	....	....
	NHL Totals		**874**	**162**	**218**	**380**	**3124**	**45**	**0**	**22**	**1076**	**15.1**		**79**	**45.6**	**309**	**40**	**10:39**	**79**	**16**	**32**	**48**	**274**	**6**	**0**	**2**

Played in NHL All-Star Game (1988)

Signed as a free agent by **Chicago**, July 23, 1994. • Suspended for entire 1994-95 season for violating NHL substance abuse policy, September 2, 1994. • Missed majority of 1997-98 season recovering from rotator cuff injury suffered in game vs. Detroit, November 16, 1997.

PROCHAZKA, Martin (pro-HAHS-kah, MAHR-tihn)

Right wing. Shoots right. 5'11", 180 lbs. Born, Slany, Czech., March 3, 1972. Toronto's 6th choice, 135th overall, in 1991 Entry Draft.

1989-90	Poldi Kladno	Czech.	49	18	12	30	....	....	....	....	....	....	....	....	....	....	....	....	....	....	....	....	....	....	....	....
1990-91	Poldi Kladno	Czech.	50	19	10	29	21	....	....	....	....	....	....	....	....	....	....	....	....	....	....	....	....	....	....	....
1991-92	Dukla Jihlava	Czech.	44	18	11	29	2	....	....	....	....	....	....	....	....	....	....	....	....	....	....	....	....	....	....	....
1992-93	Poldi Kladno	Czech.	46	26	12	38	....	....	....	....	....	....	....	....	....	....	....	....	....	....	....	....	....	....	....	....
1993-94	Poldi Kladno	Cze-Rep	43	24	16	40	0	....	....	....	....	....	....	....	....	....	....	....	2	2	0	2	....	....	....	....
1994-95	Poldi Kladno	Cze-Rep	41	25	33	58	18	....	....	....	....	....	....	....	....	....	....	....	11	8	4	12	4	....	....	....
1995-96	Poldi Kladno	Cze-Rep	37	15	27	42	....	....	....	....	....	....	....	....	....	....	....	....	8	2	4	6	....	....	....	....
1996-97	AIK Solna	Sweden	49	16	23	39	38	....	....	....	....	....	....	....	....	....	....	....	7	2	3	5	8	....	....	....
1997-98	**Toronto**	**NHL**	**29**	**2**	**4**	**6**	**8**	**0**	**0**	**0**	**40**	**5.0**	**-1**	....	....	....	....	....	....	....	....	....	....	....	....	....
	Czech-Republic	Olympics	6	1	1	2	0	....	....	....	....	....	....	....	....	....	....	....	....	....	....	....	....	....	....	....
1998-99	Petra Vsetin	Cze-Rep	47	20	29	49	12	....	....	....	....	....	....	....	....	....	....	....	12	*10	9	*19	....	....	....	....
99-2000	**Atlanta**	**NHL**	**3**	**0**	**1**	**1**	**0**	**0**	**0**	**0**	**5**	**0.0**	**-1**	**0**	**0.0**	**2**	**2**	**16:37**	....	....	....	....	....	....	....	....
	Slovnaft Vsetin	Cze-Rep	31	10	10	20	16	....	....	....	....	....	....	....	....	....	....	....	9	2	0	2	0	....	....	....
2000-01	HC Vitkovice	Cze-Rep	32	15	16	31	12	....	....	....	....	....	....	....	....	....	....	....	10	4	2	6	0	....	....	....
	NHL Totals		**32**	**2**	**5**	**7**	**8**	**0**	**0**	**0**	**45**	**4.4**		**0**	**0.0**	**2**	**2**	**16:37**	....	....	....	....	....	....	....	....

Traded to **Atlanta** by **Toronto** for Atlanta's 6th round choice (Maxim Kondratjev) in 2001 Entry Draft, July 15, 1999.

PRONGER, Chris (PRAHN-guhr, KRIHS) ST.L.

Defense. Shoots left. 6'6", 220 lbs. Born, Dryden, Ont., October 10, 1974. Hartford's 1st choice, 2nd overall, in 1993 Entry Draft.

1990-91	Stratford Cullitons	OJHL-B	48	15	37	52	132	....	....	....	....	....	....	....	....	....	....	....	....	....	....	....	....	....	....	....
1991-92	Peterborough	OHL	63	17	45	62	90	....	....	....	....	....	....	....	....	....	....	....	10	1	8	9	28	....	....	....
1992-93	Peterborough	OHL	61	15	62	77	108	....	....	....	....	....	....	....	....	....	....	....	21	15	25	40	51	....	....	....
1993-94	**Hartford**	**NHL**	**81**	**5**	**25**	**30**	**113**	**2**	**0**	**0**	**174**	**2.9**	**-3**	....	....	....	....	....	....	....	....	....	....	....	....	....
1994-95	**Hartford**	**NHL**	**43**	**5**	**9**	**14**	**54**	**3**	**0**	**1**	**94**	**5.3**	**-12**	....	....	....	....	....	....	....	....	....	....	....	....	....
1995-96	**St. Louis**	**NHL**	**78**	**7**	**18**	**25**	**110**	**3**	**1**	**1**	**138**	**5.1**	**-18**	....	....	....	....	....	**13**	**1**	**5**	**6**	**16**	**0**	**0**	**0**
1996-97	**St. Louis**	**NHL**	**79**	**11**	**24**	**35**	**143**	**4**	**0**	**0**	**147**	**7.5**	**15**	....	....	....	....	....	**6**	**1**	**1**	**2**	**22**	**0**	**0**	**0**
1997-98	**St. Louis**	**NHL**	**81**	**9**	**27**	**36**	**180**	**1**	**0**	**2**	**145**	**6.2**	**47**	....	....	....	....	....	**10**	**1**	**9**	**10**	**26**	**0**	**0**	**0**
	Canada	Olympics	6	0	0	0	4	....	....	....	....	....	....	....	....	....	....	....	....	....	....	....	....	....	....	....
1998-99	**St. Louis**	**NHL**	**67**	**13**	**33**	**46**	**113**	**8**	**0**	**0**	**172**	**7.6**	**3**	**0**	**0.0**	**132**	**119**	**30:36**	**13**	**1**	**4**	**5**	**28**	**1**	**0**	**0**
99-2000	**St. Louis**	**NHL**	**79**	**14**	**48**	**62**	**92**	**8**	**0**	**3**	**192**	**7.3**	**52**	**1**	**0.0**	**106**	**185**	**30:14**	**7**	**3**	**4**	**7**	**32**	**2**	**0**	**2**
2000-01	**St. Louis**	**NHL**	**51**	**8**	**39**	**47**	**75**	**4**	**0**	**0**	**121**	**6.6**	**21**	**0**	**0.0**	**56**	**80**	**27:45**	**15**	**1**	**7**	**8**	**32**	**0**	**0**	**0**
	NHL Totals		**559**	**72**	**223**	**295**	**880**	**33**	**1**	**7**	**1183**	**6.1**		**1**	**0.0**	**294**	**384**	**29:43**	**64**	**8**	**30**	**38**	**156**	**3**	**0**	**2**

OHL First All-Star Team (1993) • Canadian Major Junior First All-Star Team (1993) • Canadian Major Junior Defenseman of the Year (1993) • NHL All-Rookie Team (1994) • NHL Second All-Star Team (1998) • Won Bud Ice Plus/Minus Award (1998) • NHL First All-Star Team (2000) • Won Bud Light Plus/Minus Award (2000) • Won James Norris Memorial Trophy (2000) • Won Hart Trophy (2000) • Played in NHL All-Star Game (1999, 2000)

Traded to **St. Louis** by **Hartford** for Brendan Shanahan, July 27, 1995.

PRONGER, Sean
(PRAHN-guhr, SHAWN) **CBJ**

Center. Shoots left. 6'2", 205 lbs. Born, Dryden, Ont., November 30, 1972. Vancouver's 3rd choice, 51st overall, in 1991 Entry Draft.

Season	Club	League	GP	G	A	Pts	PIM	PP	SH	GW	S	%	+/-	TF	F%	H	SB	Min	Playoffs GP	G	A	Pts	PIM	PP	SH	GW
1988-89	Kenora Boise	NOJHA	33	38	30	68																				
1989-90	Thunder Bay	USHL	48	18	34	52	61																			
1990-91	Bowling Green	CCHA	40	3	7	10	30																			
1991-92	Bowling Green	CCHA	34	9	7	16	28																			
1992-93	Bowling Green	CCHA	39	23	23	46	35																			
1993-94	Bowling Green	CCHA	38	17	17	34	38																			
1994-95	Knoxville	ECHL	34	18	23	41	55																			
	Greensboro	ECHL	2	0	2	2	0																			
	San Diego Gulls	IHL	8	0	0	0	2																			
1995-96	**Anaheim**	**NHL**	**7**	**0**	**1**	**1**	**6**	**0**	**0**	**0**	**3**	**0.0**	**0**													
	Baltimore Bandits	AHL	72	16	17	33	61												12	3	7	10	16			
1996-97	**Anaheim**	**NHL**	**39**	**7**	**7**	**14**	**20**	**1**	**0**	**1**	**43**	**16.3**	**6**						**9**	**0**	**2**	**2**	**4**	**0**	**0**	**0**
	Baltimore Bandits	AHL	41	26	17	43	17																			
1997-98	**Anaheim**	**NHL**	**62**	**5**	**15**	**20**	**30**	**1**	**0**	**2**	**68**	**7.4**	**-9**													
	Pittsburgh	**NHL**	**5**	**1**	**0**	**1**	**2**	**0**	**0**	**1**	**5**	**20.0**	**-1**						**5**	**0**	**0**	**0**	**4**	**0**	**0**	**0**
1998-99	**Pittsburgh**	**NHL**	**2**	**0**	**0**	**0**	**0**	**0**	**0**	**0**	**3**	**0.0**	**0**	**4**	**75.0**	**2**	**0**	**8:48**								
	Houston Aeros	IHL	16	11	7	18	32																			
	NY Rangers	**NHL**	**14**	**0**	**3**	**3**	**4**	**0**	**0**	**0**	**3**	**0.0**	**-3**	**15**	**20.0**	**12**	**1**	**6:28**								
	Los Angeles	**NHL**	**13**	**0**	**1**	**1**	**4**	**0**	**0**	**0**	**8**	**0.0**	**2**	**20**	**35.0**	**13**	**5**	**11:00**								
99-2000	**Boston**	**NHL**	**11**	**0**	**1**	**1**	**13**	**0**	**0**	**0**	**7**	**0.0**	**-4**	**116**	**46.6**	**28**	**3**	**10:47**								
	Providence Bruins	AHL	51	11	18	29	26																			
	Manitoba Moose	IHL	14	3	5	8	21												2	0	1	1	2			
2000-01	Manitoba Moose	IHL	82	18	21	39	85												13	3	6	9	2			
	NHL Totals		**153**	**13**	**28**	**41**	**79**	**2**	**0**	**4**	**140**	**9.3**		**155**	**43.2**	**55**	**9**	**9:15**	**14**	**0**	**2**	**2**	**8**	**0**	**0**	**0**

Signed as a free agent by **Anaheim**, February 14, 1995. Traded to **Pittsburgh** by **Anaheim** for the rights to Patrick Lalime, March 24, 1998. Traded to **NY Rangers** by **Pittsburgh** with Chris Tamer and Petr Nedved for Alexei Kovalev and Harry York, November 25, 1998. Traded to **Los Angeles** by **NY Rangers** for Eric Lacroix, February 12, 1999. Signed as a free agent by **Boston**, August 25, 1999. Traded to **Manitoba** (IHL) by **Providence** (AHL) with Keith McCambridge for Terry Hollinger, March 16, 2000 with Boston retaining Pronger's NHL rights. Traded to **NY Islanders** by **Boston** for future considerations, December 5, 2000. Claimed on waivers by **Columbus** from **NY Islanders**, May 18, 2001.

PROSPAL, Vaclav
(PRAWS-pahl, VAHT-slahv) **T.B.**

Center. Shoots left. 6'2", 195 lbs. Born, Ceske-Budejovice, Czech., February 17, 1975. Philadelphia's 2nd choice, 71st overall, in 1993 Entry Draft.

Season	Club	League	GP	G	A	Pts	PIM	PP	SH	GW	S	%	+/-	TF	F%	H	SB	Min	Playoffs GP	G	A	Pts	PIM	PP	SH	GW
1991-92	MC Budjevoice	Czech-Jr.	36	16	16	32	12																			
1992-93	MC Budejovice	Czech-Jr.	32	26	31	57	24																			
1993-94	Hershey Bears	AHL	55	14	21	35	38												2	0	0	0	2			
1994-95	Hershey Bears	AHL	69	13	32	45	36												2	1	0	1	4			
1995-96	Hershey Bears	AHL	68	15	36	51	59												5	2	4	6	2			
1996-97	**Philadelphia**	**NHL**	**18**	**5**	**10**	**15**	**4**	**0**	**0**	**0**	**35**	**14.3**	**3**						**5**	**1**	**3**	**4**	**4**	**0**	**0**	**0**
	Philadelphia	AHL	63	32	63	95	70																			
1997-98	**Philadelphia**	**NHL**	**41**	**5**	**13**	**18**	**17**	**4**	**0**	**0**	**60**	**8.3**	**-10**													
	Ottawa	**NHL**	**15**	**1**	**6**	**7**	**4**	**0**	**0**	**0**	**28**	**3.6**	**-1**						**6**	**0**	**0**	**0**	**0**	**0**	**0**	**0**
1998-99	**Ottawa**	**NHL**	**79**	**10**	**26**	**36**	**58**	**2**	**0**	**3**	**114**	**8.8**	**8**	**997**	**56.2**	**202**	**20**	**13:03**	**4**	**0**	**0**	**0**	**0**	**0**	**0**	**0**
99-2000	**Ottawa**	**NHL**	**79**	**22**	**33**	**55**	**40**	**5**	**0**	**4**	**204**	**10.8**	**-2**	**1331**	**49.6**	**92**	**26**	**16:26**	**6**	**0**	**4**	**4**	**4**	**0**	**0**	**0**
2000-01	**Ottawa**	**NHL**	**40**	**1**	**12**	**13**	**12**	**0**	**0**	**0**	**68**	**1.5**	**1**	**501**	**50.1**	**37**	**9**	**12:57**								
	Florida	**NHL**	**34**	**4**	**12**	**16**	**10**	**1**	**0**	**0**	**68**	**5.9**	**-2**	**487**	**54.6**	**58**	**14**	**16:36**								
	NHL Totals		**306**	**48**	**112**	**160**	**145**	**12**	**0**	**7**	**577**	**8.3**		**3316**	**52.4**	**389**	**69**	**14:42**	**21**	**1**	**7**	**8**	**8**	**0**	**0**	**0**

AHL First All-Star Team (1997)

Traded to **Ottawa** by **Philadelphia** with Pat Falloon and Dallas' 2nd round choice (previously acquired, Ottawa selected Chris Bala) in 1998 Entry Draft for Alexandre Daigle, January 17, 1998. Traded to **Florida** by **Ottawa** for future considerations, January 20, 2001. Traded to **Tampa Bay** by **Florida** for Ryan Johnson and Tampa Bay's 6th round choice in 2003 Entry Draft, July 10, 2001.

PRPIC, Joel
(puhr-PIHCH, JOHL) **S.J.**

Center. Shoots left. 6'6", 225 lbs. Born, Sudbury, Ont., September 25, 1974. Boston's 9th choice, 233rd overall, in 1993 Entry Draft.

Season	Club	League	GP	G	A	Pts	PIM	PP	SH	GW	S	%	+/-	TF	F%	H	SB	Min	Playoffs GP	G	A	Pts	PIM	PP	SH	GW
1992-93	Waterloo Siskins	OJHL-B	45	17	43	60	160																			
1993-94	St. Lawrence	ECAC	31	2	4	6	90																			
1994-95	St. Lawrence	ECAC	32	7	10	17	62																			
1995-96	St. Lawrence	ECAC	32	3	10	13	77																			
1996-97	St. Lawrence	ECAC	34	10	8	18	57																			
1997-98	**Boston**	**NHL**	**1**	**0**	**0**	**0**	**2**	**0**	**0**	**0**	**0**	**0.0**	**0**													
	Providence Bruins	AHL	73	17	18	35	53																			
1998-99	Providence Bruins	AHL	75	14	16	30	163												18	4	6	10	48			
99-2000	**Boston**	**NHL**	**14**	**0**	**3**	**3**	**0**	**0**	**0**	**0**	**13**	**0.0**	**-6**	**117**	**52.1**	**10**	**2**	**6:47**								
	Providence Bruins	AHL	70	9	20	29	143												14	3	4	7	58			
2000-01	**Colorado**	**NHL**	**3**	**0**	**0**	**0**	**2**	**0**	**0**	**0**	**0**	**0.0**	**0**	**20**	**60.0**	**7**	**1**	**9:47**								
	Hershey Bears	AHL	74	16	23	39	128												12	1	1	2	26			
	NHL Totals		**18**	**0**	**3**	**3**	**4**	**0**	**0**	**0**	**13**	**0.0**		**137**	**53.3**	**17**	**3**	**7:19**								

Signed as a free agent by **Colorado**, August, 2000. Signed as a free agent by **San Jose**, August 15, 2001.

PURINTON, Dale
(PUHR-ihn-TOHN, DAYL) **NYR**

Defense. Shoots left. 6'3", 214 lbs. Born, Fort Wayne, IN, October 11, 1976. NY Rangers' 5th choice, 117th overall, in 1995 Entry Draft.

Season	Club	League	GP	G	A	Pts	PIM	PP	SH	GW	S	%	+/-	TF	F%	H	SB	Min	Playoffs GP	G	A	Pts	PIM	PP	SH	GW
1992-93	Moose Jaw	SMHL	34	1	16	17	107																			
	Moose Jaw	WHL	2	0	0	0	2																			
1993-94	Vernon Lakers	BCJHL	42	1	6	7	194																			
1994-95	Tacoma Rockets	WHL	65	0	8	8	291												3	0	0	0	13			
1995-96	Kelowna Rockets	WHL	22	1	4	5	88																			
	Lethbridge	WHL	37	3	6	9	144												4	1	1	2	25			
1996-97	Lethbridge	WHL	51	6	26	32	254												18	3	5	8	*88			
1997-98	Hartford	AHL	17	0	0	0	95																			
	Charlotte	ECHL	34	3	5	8	186																			
1998-99	Hartford	AHL	45	1	3	4	306												7	0	2	2	24			
99-2000	**NY Rangers**	**NHL**	**1**	**0**	**0**	**0**	**7**	**0**	**0**	**0**	**1**	**0.0**	**-1**	**0**	**0.0**	**1**	**1**	**12:45**								
	Hartford	AHL	62	4	4	8	415												23	0	3	3	*87			
2000-01	**NY Rangers**	**NHL**	**42**	**0**	**2**	**2**	**180**	**0**	**0**	**0**	**13**	**0.0**	**5**	**0**	**0.0**	**46**	**30**	**9:33**								
	Hartford	AHL	11	0	1	1	75																			
	NHL Totals		**43**	**0**	**2**	**2**	**187**	**0**	**0**	**0**	**14**	**0.0**		**0**	**0.0**	**47**	**31**	**9:38**								

PUSHOR, Jamie
(PUH-shohr, JAY-mee) **CBJ**

Defense. Shoots right. 6'3", 218 lbs. Born, Lethbridge, Alta., February 11, 1973. Detroit's 2nd choice, 32nd overall, in 1991 Entry Draft.

Season	Club	League	GP	G	A	Pts	PIM	PP	SH	GW	S	%	+/-	TF	F%	H	SB	Min	Playoffs GP	G	A	Pts	PIM	PP	SH	GW
1988-89	Lethbridge Y's	AMHL	37	1	8	9	20																			
	Lethbridge	WHL	2	0	0	0	0																			
1989-90	Lethbridge Y's	AMHL	35	6	27	33	92																			
	Lethbridge	WHL	10	0	2	2	2												16	0	0	0	63			
1990-91	Lethbridge	WHL	71	1	13	14	202																			
1991-92	Lethbridge	WHL	49	2	15	17	232												5	0	0	0	33			
1992-93	Lethbridge	WHL	72	6	22	28	200												4	0	1	1	9			
1993-94	Adirondack	AHL	73	1	17	18	124												12	0	0	0	22			
1994-95	Adirondack	AHL	58	2	11	13	129												4	0	1	1	0			
1995-96	**Detroit**	**NHL**	**5**	**0**	**1**	**1**	**17**	**0**	**0**	**0**	**6**	**0.0**	**2**													
	Adirondack	AHL	65	2	16	18	126												3	0	0	0	5			
1996-97♦	**Detroit**	**NHL**	**75**	**4**	**7**	**11**	**129**	**0**	**0**	**0**	**63**	**6.3**	**1**						**5**	**0**	**1**	**1**	**5**	**0**	**0**	**0**
1997-98	**Detroit**	**NHL**	**54**	**2**	**5**	**7**	**71**	**0**	**0**	**0**	**43**	**4.7**	**2**													
	Anaheim	**NHL**	**10**	**0**	**2**	**2**	**10**	**0**	**0**	**0**	**8**	**0.0**	**1**													
1998-99	**Anaheim**	**NHL**	**70**	**1**	**2**	**3**	**112**	**0**	**0**	**0**	**75**	**1.3**	**-20**	**0**	**0.0**	**110**	**153**	**19:16**	**4**	**0**	**0**	**0**	**6**	**0**	**0**	**0**

Season	Club	League	GP	G	A	Pts	PIM	PP	SH	GW	S	%	+/-	TF	F%	H	SB	Min	Playoffs GP	G	A	Pts	PIM	PP	SH	GW
99-2000	**Dallas**	**NHL**	**62**	**0**	**8**	**8**	**53**	**0**	**0**	**0**	**27**	**0.0**	**0**	**0**	**0.0**	**99**	**43**	**11:36**	**5**	**0**	**0**	**0**	**5**	**0**	**0**	**0**
2000-01	**Columbus**	**NHL**	**75**	**3**	**10**	**13**	**94**	**0**	**1**	**0**	**64**	**4.7**	**7**	**0**	**0.0**	**133**	**156**	**20:48**								
	NHL Totals		**351**	**10**	**35**	**45**	**486**	**0**	**1**	**0**	**286**	**3.5**		**0**	**0.0**	**342**	**352**	**17:32**	**14**	**0**	**1**	**1**	**16**	**0**	**0**	**0**

Traded to **Anaheim** by **Detroit** with Detroit's 4th round choice (Viktor Wallin) in 1998 Entry Draft for Dmitri Mironov, March 24, 1998. Claimed by **Atlanta** from **Anaheim** in Expansion Draft, June 25, 1999. Traded to **Dallas** by **Atlanta** for Jason Botterill, July 15, 1999. Selected by **Columbus** from **Dallas** in Expansion Draft, June 23, 2000.

PYATT, Taylor
(PIGH-at, TAY-lohr) **BUF.**

Left wing. Shoots left. 6'4", 220 lbs. Born, Thunder Bay, Ont., August 19, 1981. NY Islanders' 2nd choice, 8th overall, in 1999 Entry Draft.

Season	Club	League	GP	G	A	Pts	PIM	PP	SH	GW	S	%	+/-	TF	F%	H	SB	Min	Playoffs GP	G	A	Pts	PIM	PP	SH	GW
1996-97	Thunder Bay	TBAHA	60	52	61	113	72																			
1997-98	Sudbury Wolves	OHL	58	14	17	31	104												10	3	1	4	8			
1998-99	Sudbury Wolves	OHL	68	37	38	75	95												4	0	4	4	6			
99-2000	Sudbury Wolves	OHL	68	40	49	89	98												12	8	7	15	25			
2000-01	**NY Islanders**	**NHL**	**78**	**4**	**14**	**18**	**39**	**1**	**0**	**2**	**86**	**4.7**	**-17**	**1**	**0.0**	**116**	**28**	**12:14**								
	NHL Totals		**78**	**4**	**14**	**18**	**39**	**1**	**0**	**2**	**86**	**4.7**		**1**	**0.0**	**116**	**28**	**12:14**								

OHL First All-Star Team (2000)

Traded to **Buffalo** by **NY Islanders** with Tim Connolly for Mike Peca, June 24, 2001.

QUINT, Deron
(KWIHNT, DAIR-ohn) **CBJ**

Defense. Shoots left. 6'2", 219 lbs. Born, Durham, NH, March 12, 1976. Winnipeg's 1st choice, 30th overall, in 1994 Entry Draft.

Season	Club	League	GP	G	A	Pts	PIM	PP	SH	GW	S	%	+/-	TF	F%	H	SB	Min	Playoffs GP	G	A	Pts	PIM	PP	SH	GW
1990-91	Cardigan High	Hi-School	31	67	54	121																				
1991-92	Cardigan High	Hi-School	21	111	58	169																				
1992-93	Tabor Academy	Hi-School	28	15	26	41	30												1	0	2	2	0			
1993-94	Seattle T-Birds	WHL	63	15	29	44	47												9	4	12	16	8			
1994-95	Seattle T-Birds	WHL	65	29	60	89	82												3	1	2	3	6			
1995-96	**Winnipeg**	**NHL**	**51**	**5**	**13**	**18**	**22**	**2**	**0**	**0**	**97**	**5.2**	**-2**													
	Springfield	AHL	11	2	3	5	4												10	2	3	5	6			
	Seattle T-Birds	WHL																	5	4	1	5	6			
1996-97	**Phoenix**	**NHL**	**27**	**3**	**11**	**14**	**4**	**1**	**0**	**0**	**63**	**4.8**	**-4**						**7**	**0**	**2**	**2**	**0**	**0**	**0**	**0**
	Springfield	AHL	43	6	18	24	20												12	2	7	9	4			
1997-98	**Phoenix**	**NHL**	**32**	**4**	**7**	**11**	**16**	**1**	**0**	**1**	**61**	**6.6**	**-6**													
	Springfield	AHL	8	1	7	8	10												1	0	0	0	0			
1998-99	**Phoenix**	**NHL**	**60**	**5**	**8**	**13**	**20**	**2**	**0**	**0**	**94**	**5.3**	**-10**	**0**	**0.0**	**53**	**32**	**16:12**								
99-2000	**Phoenix**	**NHL**	**50**	**3**	**7**	**10**	**22**	**0**	**0**	**1**	**88**	**3.4**	**0**	**0**	**0.0**	**61**	**31**	**16:39**								
	New Jersey	**NHL**	**4**	**1**	**0**	**1**	**2**	**0**	**0**	**0**	**6**	**16.7**	**-2**	**0**	**0.0**	**6**	**3**	**16:26**								
2000-01	**Columbus**	**NHL**	**57**	**7**	**16**	**23**	**16**	**3**	**0**	**0**	**148**	**4.7**	**-19**	**1**	**100.0**	**37**	**68**	**24:06**								
	Syracuse Crunch	AHL	21	5	15	20	30																			
	NHL Totals		**281**	**28**	**62**	**90**	**102**	**9**	**0**	**2**	**557**	**5.0**		**1**	**100.0**	**157**	**134**	**18:58**	**7**	**0**	**2**	**2**	**0**	**0**	**0**	**0**

WHL West First All-Star Team (1995)

Transferred to **Phoenix** after **Winnipeg** franchise relocated, July 1, 1996. Traded to **New Jersey** by **Phoenix** with Phoenix's 3rd round choice (later traded back to Phoenix - Phoenix selected Beat Forster) in 2001 Entry Draft for Lyle Odelein, March 7, 2000. Traded to **Columbus** by **New Jersey** to complete transaction that sent Krzysztof Oliwa to Columbus (June 12, 2000) and Turner Stevenson to New Jersey (June 23, 2000), June 23, 2000.

QUINTAL, Stephane
(KAYN-tahl, STEH-fan) **MTL.**

Defense. Shoots right. 6'3", 228 lbs. Born, Boucherville, Que., October 22, 1968. Boston's 2nd choice, 14th overall, in 1987 Entry Draft.

Season	Club	League	GP	G	A	Pts	PIM	PP	SH	GW	S	%	+/-	TF	F%	H	SB	Min	Playoffs GP	G	A	Pts	PIM	PP	SH	GW
1984-85	Richelieu Regents	QAAA	41	1	10	11	68												9	0	5	5	27			
1985-86	Granby Bisons	QMJHL	67	2	17	19	144																			
1986-87	Granby Bisons	QMJHL	67	13	41	54	178												8	0	9	9	10			
1987-88	Hull Olympiques	QMJHL	38	13	23	36	138												19	7	12	19	30			
1988-89	**Boston**	**NHL**	**26**	**0**	**1**	**1**	**29**	**0**	**0**	**0**	**23**	**0.0**	**-5**													
	Maine Mariners	AHL	16	4	10	14	28																			
1989-90	**Boston**	**NHL**	**38**	**2**	**2**	**4**	**22**	**0**	**0**	**0**	**43**	**4.7**	**-11**													
	Maine Mariners	AHL	37	4	16	20	27																			
1990-91	**Boston**	**NHL**	**45**	**2**	**6**	**8**	**89**	**1**	**0**	**0**	**54**	**3.7**	**2**						**3**	**0**	**1**	**1**	**7**	**0**	**0**	**0**
	Maine Mariners	AHL	23	1	5	6	30																			
1991-92	**Boston**	**NHL**	**49**	**4**	**10**	**14**	**77**	**0**	**0**	**0**	**52**	**7.7**	**-8**													
	St. Louis	**NHL**	**26**	**0**	**6**	**6**	**32**	**0**	**0**	**0**	**19**	**0.0**	**-3**						**4**	**1**	**2**	**3**	**6**	**1**	**0**	**0**
1992-93	**St. Louis**	**NHL**	**75**	**1**	**10**	**11**	**100**	**0**	**1**	**0**	**81**	**1.2**	**-6**						**9**	**0**	**0**	**0**	**8**	**0**	**0**	**0**
1993-94	**Winnipeg**	**NHL**	**81**	**8**	**18**	**26**	**119**	**1**	**1**	**1**	**154**	**5.2**	**-25**													
1994-95	**Winnipeg**	**NHL**	**43**	**6**	**17**	**23**	**78**	**3**	**0**	**2**	**107**	**5.6**	**0**													
1995-96	**Montreal**	**NHL**	**68**	**2**	**14**	**16**	**117**	**0**	**1**	**1**	**104**	**1.9**	**-4**						**6**	**0**	**1**	**1**	**6**	**0**	**0**	**0**
1996-97	**Montreal**	**NHL**	**71**	**7**	**15**	**22**	**100**	**1**	**0**	**0**	**139**	**5.0**	**1**						**5**	**0**	**1**	**1**	**6**	**0**	**0**	**0**
1997-98	**Montreal**	**NHL**	**71**	**6**	**10**	**16**	**97**	**0**	**0**	**0**	**88**	**6.8**	**13**						**9**	**0**	**2**	**2**	**4**	**0**	**0**	**0**
1998-99	**Montreal**	**NHL**	**82**	**8**	**19**	**27**	**84**	**1**	**1**	**4**	**159**	**5.0**	**-23**	**0**	**0.0**	**98**	**125**	**22:06**								
99-2000	**NY Rangers**	**NHL**	**75**	**2**	**14**	**16**	**77**	**0**	**0**	**1**	**102**	**2.0**	**-10**	**0**	**0.0**	**133**	**125**	**19:04**								
2000-01	**Chicago**	**NHL**	**72**	**1**	**18**	**19**	**60**	**0**	**0**	**0**	**109**	**0.9**	**-9**	**0**	**0.0**	**85**	**90**	**22:30**								
	NHL Totals		**822**	**49**	**160**	**209**	**1081**	**7**	**4**	**9**	**1234**	**4.0**		**0**	**0.0**	**316**	**340**	**21:14**	**36**	**1**	**7**	**8**	**37**	**1**	**0**	**0**

QMJHL First All-Star Team (1987)

Traded to **St. Louis** by **Boston** with Craig Janney for Adam Oates, February 7, 1992. Traded to **Winnipeg** by **St. Louis** with Nelson Emerson for Phil Housley, September 24, 1993. Traded to **Montreal** by **Winnipeg** for Montreal's 2nd round choice (Jason Doig) in 1995 Entry Draft, July 8, 1995. Signed as a free agent by **NY Rangers**, July 13, 1999. Claimed on waivers by **Chicago** from **NY Rangers**, October 5, 2000. Traded to **Montreal** by **Chicago** for Montreal's 4th round choice (Brent MacLellan) in 2001 Entry Draft, June 23, 2001.

RACHUNEK, Karel
(ra-KHOO-nehk, KAH-rehl) **OTT.**

Defense. Shoots right. 6'2", 202 lbs. Born, Gottwaldov, Czech., August 27, 1979. Ottawa's 8th choice, 229th overall, in 1997 Entry Draft.

Season	Club	League	GP	G	A	Pts	PIM	PP	SH	GW	S	%	+/-	TF	F%	H	SB	Min	Playoffs GP	G	A	Pts	PIM	PP	SH	GW
1995-96	ZPS Zlin-Jr.	Cze-Rep	38	8	11	19																				
1996-97	ZPS Zlin-Jr.	Cze-Rep	27	2	11	13																				
1997-98	ZPS Zlin	Cze-Rep	27	1	2	3	16																			
1998-99	ZPS Zlin	Cze-Rep	39	3	9	12	88												6	0	0	0				
99-2000	**Ottawa**	**NHL**	**6**	**0**	**0**	**0**	**2**	**0**	**0**	**0**	**3**	**0.0**	**0**	**0**	**0.0**	**10**	**5**	**8:03**								
	Grand Rapids	IHL	62	6	20	26	64												9	0	5	5	6			
2000-01	**Ottawa**	**NHL**	**71**	**3**	**30**	**33**	**60**	**3**	**0**	**0**	**77**	**3.9**	**17**	**0**	**0.0**	**173**	**98**	**20:54**	**3**	**0**	**0**	**0**	**0**	**0**	**0**	**0**
	NHL Totals		**77**	**3**	**30**	**33**	**62**	**3**	**0**	**0**	**80**	**3.8**		**0**	**0.0**	**183**	**103**	**19:54**	**3**	**0**	**0**	**0**	**0**	**0**	**0**	**0**

RAFALSKI, Brian
(ra-FAWL-skee, BRIGH-uhn) **N.J.**

Defense. Shoots right. 5'9", 195 lbs. Born, Dearborn, MI, September 28, 1973.

Season	Club	League	GP	G	A	Pts	PIM	PP	SH	GW	S	%	+/-	TF	F%	H	SB	Min	Playoffs GP	G	A	Pts	PIM	PP	SH	GW
1990-91	Madison Capitols	USHL	47	12	11	23	28																			
1991-92	U. of Wisconsin	WCHA	34	3	14	17	34																			
1992-93	U. of Wisconsin	WCHA	32	0	13	13	10																			
1993-94	U. of Wisconsin	WCHA	37	6	17	23	26																			
1994-95	U. of Wisconsin	WCHA	43	11	34	45	48																			
1995-96	Brynas IF	Sweden	40	4	14	18	26												9	0	1	1	2			
1996-97	HK Hameenlinna	Finland	49	11	24	35	26												10	6	5	11	4			
1997-98	HIFK Helsinki	Finland	40	13	10	23	20												9	5	6	11	0			
1998-99	HIFK Helsinki	Finland	53	19	34	53	18												11	5	*9	*14	4			
	HIFK Helsinki	EuroHL	6	4	6	10	10												4	1	0	1	2			
99-2000♦	**New Jersey**	**NHL**	**75**	**5**	**27**	**32**	**28**	**1**	**0**	**1**	**128**	**3.9**	**21**	**1**	**0.0**	**102**	**68**	**18:51**	**23**	**2**	**6**	**8**	**8**	**0**	**0**	**1**
2000-01	**New Jersey**	**NHL**	**78**	**9**	**43**	**52**	**26**	**6**	**0**	**1**	**142**	**6.3**	**36**	**2**	**100.0**	**82**	**55**	**21:41**	**25**	**7**	**11**	**18**	**7**	**1**	**0**	**3**
	NHL Totals		**153**	**14**	**70**	**84**	**54**	**7**	**0**	**2**	**270**	**5.2**		**3**	**66.7**	**184**	**123**	**20:17**	**48**	**9**	**17**	**26**	**15**	**1**	**0**	**4**

WCHA First All-Star Team (1995) • NCAA West First All-American Team (1995) • NHL All-Rookie Team (2000)

Signed as a free agent by **New Jersey**, May 7, 1999.

RAGNARSSON, Marcus
(RAG-nahr-suhn, MAHR-kuhs) **S.J.**

Defense. Shoots left. 6'1", 215 lbs. Born, Ostervala, Sweden, August 13, 1971. San Jose's 5th choice, 99th overall, in 1992 Entry Draft.

Season	Club	League	GP	G	A	Pts	PIM	PP	SH	GW	S	%	+/-	TF	F%	H	SB	Min	Playoffs GP	G	A	Pts	PIM	PP	SH	GW
1986-87	Ostervala IF	Sweden-3	28	1	6	7	....	....	....	....	....	....	....	....	....	....	....	....	....	....	....	....	....	....	....	....
1987-88	Ostervala IF	Sweden-3	25	3	12	15	....	....	....	....	....	....	....	....	....	....	....	....	....	....	....	....	....	....	....	....
1988-89	Ostervala IF	Sweden-3	30	15	14	29	....	....	....	....	....	....	....	....	....	....	....	....	....	....	....	....	....	....	....	....
1989-90	Nacka HK	Sweden-2	9	2	3	5	4	....	....	....	....	....	....	....	....	....	....	....	....	....	....	....	....	....	....	....
	Djurgardens IF	Sweden	13	0	2	2	0	....	....	....	....	....	....	....	....	....	....	....	1	0	0	0	0	....	....	....
1990-91	Djurgardens IF	Sweden	35	4	1	5	12	....	....	....	....	....	....	....	....	....	....	....	7	0	0	0	6	....	....	....
1991-92	Djurgardens IF	Sweden	40	8	5	13	14	....	....	....	....	....	....	....	....	....	....	....	10	0	1	1	4	....	....	....
1992-93	Djurgardens IF	Sweden	35	3	3	6	53	....	....	....	....	....	....	....	....	....	....	....	6	0	3	3	8	....	....	....
1993-94	Djurgardens IF	Sweden	19	0	4	4	24	....	....	....	....	....	....	....	....	....	....	....	....	....	....	....	....	....	....	....
1994-95	Djurgardens IF	Sweden	38	7	9	16	20	....	....	....	....	....	....	....	....	....	....	....	3	0	0	0	4	....	....	....
1995-96	**San Jose**	**NHL**	**71**	**8**	**31**	**39**	**42**	**4**	**0**	**0**	**94**	**8.5**	**-24**	....	....	....	....	....	....	....	....	....	....	....	....	....
1996-97	**San Jose**	**NHL**	**69**	**3**	**14**	**17**	**63**	**2**	**0**	**0**	**57**	**5.3**	**-18**	....	....	....	....	....	....	....	....	....	....	....	....	....
1997-98	**San Jose**	**NHL**	**79**	**5**	**20**	**25**	**65**	**3**	**0**	**2**	**91**	**5.5**	**-11**	....	....	....	....	....	**6**	**0**	**0**	**0**	**4**	**0**	**0**	**0**
	Sweden	Olympics	3	0	1	1	0	....	....	....	....	....	....	....	....	....	....	....	....	....	....	....	....	....	....	....
1998-99	**San Jose**	**NHL**	**74**	**0**	**13**	**13**	**66**	**0**	**0**	**0**	**87**	**0.0**	**7**	**3**	**66.7**	**99**	**66**	**21:55**	**6**	**0**	**1**	**1**	**6**	**0**	**0**	**0**
99-2000	**San Jose**	**NHL**	**63**	**3**	**13**	**16**	**38**	**0**	**0**	**0**	**60**	**5.0**	**13**	**0**	**0.0**	**92**	**76**	**22:52**	**12**	**0**	**3**	**3**	**10**	**0**	**0**	**0**
2000-01	**San Jose**	**NHL**	**68**	**3**	**12**	**15**	**44**	**1**	**0**	**0**	**74**	**4.1**	**2**	**0**	**0.0**	**168**	**60**	**23:36**	**5**	**0**	**1**	**1**	**8**	**0**	**0**	**0**
	NHL Totals		**424**	**22**	**103**	**125**	**318**	**10**	**0**	**2**	**463**	**4.8**		**3**	**66.7**	**359**	**202**	**22:46**	**29**	**0**	**5**	**5**	**28**	**0**	**0**	**0**

Played in NHL All-Star Game (2001)

RALPH, Brad
(RALF, BRAD) **PHX.**

Left wing. Shoots left. 6'2", 206 lbs. Born, Ottawa, Ont., October 17, 1980. Phoenix's 3rd choice, 53rd overall, in 1999 Entry Draft.

Season	Club	League	GP	G	A	Pts	PIM	PP	SH	GW	S	%	+/-	TF	F%	H	SB	Min	Playoffs GP	G	A	Pts	PIM	PP	SH	GW
1995-96	Kanata Valley	OCJHL	19	6	1	7	19	....	....	....	....	....	....	....	....	....	....	....	....	....	....	....	....	....	....	....
1996-97	Kanata Valley	OCJHL	44	13	13	26	63	....	....	....	....	....	....	....	....	....	....	....	....	....	....	....	....	....	....	....
1997-98	Oshawa Generals	OHL	59	20	17	37	45	....	....	....	....	....	....	....	....	....	....	....	7	2	1	3	8	....	....	....
1998-99	Oshawa Generals	OHL	67	31	44	75	93	....	....	....	....	....	....	....	....	....	....	....	14	7	7	14	10	....	....	....
99-2000	Oshawa Generals	OHL	56	28	35	63	68	....	....	....	....	....	....	....	....	....	....	....	5	1	1	2	4	....	....	....
2000-01	**Phoenix**	**NHL**	**1**	**0**	**0**	**0**	**0**	**0**	**0**	**0**	**0**	**0.0**	**0**	**0**	**0.0**	**1**	**0**	**5:16**	....	....	....	....	....	....	....	....
	Springfield	AHL	50	5	13	18	23	....	....	....	....	....	....	....	....	....	....	....	....	....	....	....	....	....	....	....
	NHL Totals		**1**	**0**	**0**	**0**	**0**	**0**	**0**	**0**	**0**	**0.0**		**0**	**0.0**	**1**	**0**	**5:16**	....	....	....	....	....	....	....	....

RANHEIM, Paul
(RAN-highm, PAWL) **PHI.**

Left wing. Shoots right. 6'1", 210 lbs. Born, St. Louis, MO, January 25, 1966. Calgary's 3rd choice, 38th overall, in 1984 Entry Draft.

Season	Club	League	GP	G	A	Pts	PIM	PP	SH	GW	S	%	+/-	TF	F%	H	SB	Min	Playoffs GP	G	A	Pts	PIM	PP	SH	GW
1982-83	Edina High	Hi-School	26	12	25	37	4	....	....	....	....	....	....	....	....	....	....	....	....	....	....	....	....	....	....	....
1983-84	Edina High	Hi-School	26	16	24	40	6	....	....	....	....	....	....	....	....	....	....	....	....	....	....	....	....	....	....	....
1984-85	U. of Wisconsin	WCHA	42	11	11	22	40	....	....	....	....	....	....	....	....	....	....	....	....	....	....	....	....	....	....	....
1985-86	U. of Wisconsin	WCHA	33	17	17	34	34	....	....	....	....	....	....	....	....	....	....	....	....	....	....	....	....	....	....	....
1986-87	U. of Wisconsin	WCHA	42	24	35	59	54	....	....	....	....	....	....	....	....	....	....	....	....	....	....	....	....	....	....	....
1987-88	U. of Wisconsin	WCHA	44	36	26	62	63	....	....	....	....	....	....	....	....	....	....	....	....	....	....	....	....	....	....	....
1988-89	**Calgary**	**NHL**	**5**	**0**	**0**	**0**	**0**	**0**	**0**	**0**	**4**	**0.0**	**-3**	....	....	....	....	....	....	....	....	....	....	....	....	....
	Salt Lake City	IHL	75	*68	29	97	16	....	....	....	....	....	....	....	....	....	....	....	14	5	5	10	8	....	....	....
1989-90	**Calgary**	**NHL**	**80**	**26**	**28**	**54**	**23**	**1**	**3**	**4**	**197**	**13.2**	**27**	....	....	....	....	....	**6**	**1**	**3**	**4**	**2**	**0**	**0**	**0**
1990-91	**Calgary**	**NHL**	**39**	**14**	**16**	**30**	**4**	**2**	**0**	**2**	**108**	**13.0**	**20**	....	....	....	....	....	**7**	**2**	**2**	**4**	**0**	**0**	**0**	**0**
1991-92	**Calgary**	**NHL**	**80**	**23**	**20**	**43**	**32**	**1**	**3**	**3**	**159**	**14.5**	**16**	....	....	....	....	....	....	....	....	....	....	....	....	....
1992-93	**Calgary**	**NHL**	**83**	**21**	**22**	**43**	**26**	**3**	**4**	**1**	**179**	**11.7**	**-4**	....	....	....	....	....	**6**	**0**	**1**	**1**	**0**	**0**	**0**	**0**
1993-94	**Calgary**	**NHL**	**67**	**10**	**14**	**24**	**20**	**0**	**2**	**2**	**110**	**9.1**	**-7**	....	....	....	....	....	....	....	....	....	....	....	....	....
	Hartford	**NHL**	**15**	**0**	**3**	**3**	**2**	**0**	**0**	**0**	**21**	**0.0**	**-11**	....	....	....	....	....	....	....	....	....	....	....	....	....
1994-95	**Hartford**	**NHL**	**47**	**6**	**14**	**20**	**10**	**0**	**0**	**1**	**73**	**8.2**	**-3**	....	....	....	....	....	....	....	....	....	....	....	....	....
1995-96	**Hartford**	**NHL**	**73**	**10**	**20**	**30**	**14**	**0**	**1**	**1**	**126**	**7.9**	**-2**	....	....	....	....	....	....	....	....	....	....	....	....	....
1996-97	**Hartford**	**NHL**	**67**	**10**	**11**	**21**	**18**	**0**	**3**	**1**	**96**	**10.4**	**-13**	....	....	....	....	....	....	....	....	....	....	....	....	....
1997-98	**Carolina**	**NHL**	**73**	**5**	**9**	**14**	**28**	**0**	**1**	**2**	**77**	**6.5**	**-11**	....	....	....	....	....	....	....	....	....	....	....	....	....
1998-99	**Carolina**	**NHL**	**78**	**9**	**10**	**19**	**39**	**0**	**2**	**1**	**67**	**13.4**	**4**	**10**	**50.0**	**72**	**32**	**9:02**	**6**	**0**	**0**	**0**	**2**	**0**	**0**	**0**
99-2000	**Carolina**	**NHL**	**79**	**9**	**13**	**22**	**6**	**0**	**0**	**2**	**98**	**9.2**	**-14**	**78**	**46.2**	**107**	**31**	**11:19**	....	....	....	....	....	....	....	....
2000-01	**Philadelphia**	**NHL**	**80**	**10**	**7**	**17**	**14**	**0**	**2**	**0**	**123**	**8.1**	**2**	**18**	**55.6**	**51**	**38**	**12:57**	**6**	**0**	**2**	**2**	**2**	**0**	**0**	**0**
	NHL Totals		**866**	**153**	**187**	**340**	**236**	**7**	**21**	**20**	**1438**	**10.6**		**106**	**48.1**	**230**	**101**	**11:07**	**31**	**3**	**8**	**11**	**6**	**0**	**0**	**0**

WCHA Second All-Star Team (1987) • WCHA First All-Star Team (1988) • NCAA West First All-American Team (1988) • IHL Second All-Star Team (1989) • Won Garry F. Longman Memorial Trophy (Top Rookie - IHL) (1989)

• Missed majority of 1990-91 season recovering from ankle injury suffered in game vs. Minnesota, December 11, 1990. Traded to **Hartford** by **Calgary** with Gary Suter and Ted Drury for James Patrick, Zarley Zalapski and Michael Nylander, March 10, 1994. Transferred to **Carolina** after **Hartford** franchise relocated, June 25, 1997. Traded to **Philadelphia** by **Carolina** for Philadelphia's 8th round choice in 2002 Entry Draft, May 31, 2000.

RASMUSSEN, Erik
(RAS-moo-suhn, AIR-ihk) **BUF.**

Center/Left wing. Shoots left. 6'3", 208 lbs. Born, Minneapolis, MN, March 28, 1977. Buffalo's 1st choice, 7th overall, in 1996 Entry Draft.

Season	Club	League	GP	G	A	Pts	PIM	PP	SH	GW	S	%	+/-	TF	F%	H	SB	Min	Playoffs GP	G	A	Pts	PIM	PP	SH	GW
1992-93	St. Louis High	Hi-School	23	16	24	40	50	....	....	....	....	....	....	....	....	....	....	....	....	....	....	....	....	....	....	....
1993-94	St. Louis High	Hi-School	18	25	18	43	80	....	....	....	....	....	....	....	....	....	....	....	....	....	....	....	....	....	....	....
1994-95	St. Louis High	Hi-School	23	19	33	52	80	....	....	....	....	....	....	....	....	....	....	....	....	....	....	....	....	....	....	....
1995-96	U. of Minnesota	WCHA	40	16	32	48	55	....	....	....	....	....	....	....	....	....	....	....	....	....	....	....	....	....	....	....
1996-97	U. of Minnesota	WCHA	34	15	12	27	*123	....	....	....	....	....	....	....	....	....	....	....	....	....	....	....	....	....	....	....
1997-98	**Buffalo**	**NHL**	**21**	**2**	**3**	**5**	**14**	**0**	**0**	**0**	**28**	**7.1**	**2**	....	....	....	....	....	....	....	....	....	....	....	....	....
	Rochester	AHL	53	9	14	23	83	....	....	....	....	....	....	....	....	....	....	....	1	0	0	0	5	....	....	....
1998-99	**Buffalo**	**NHL**	**42**	**3**	**7**	**10**	**37**	**0**	**0**	**0**	**40**	**7.5**	**6**	**67**	**40.3**	**104**	**18**	**12:22**	**21**	**2**	**4**	**6**	**18**	**0**	**0**	**1**
	Rochester	AHL	37	12	14	26	47	....	....	....	....	....	....	....	....	....	....	....	....	....	....	....	....	....	....	....
99-2000	**Buffalo**	**NHL**	**67**	**8**	**6**	**14**	**43**	**0**	**0**	**2**	**76**	**10.5**	**1**	**130**	**44.6**	**175**	**12**	**11:27**	**3**	**0**	**0**	**0**	**4**	**0**	**0**	**0**
2000-01	**Buffalo**	**NHL**	**82**	**12**	**19**	**31**	**51**	**1**	**0**	**3**	**95**	**12.6**	**0**	**565**	**43.7**	**207**	**36**	**13:47**	**3**	**0**	**1**	**1**	**0**	**0**	**0**	**0**
	NHL Totals		**212**	**25**	**35**	**60**	**145**	**1**	**0**	**5**	**239**	**10.5**		**762**	**43.6**	**486**	**66**	**12:39**	**27**	**2**	**5**	**7**	**22**	**0**	**0**	**1**

Minnesota High School Player of the Year (1995)

RATCHUK, Peter
(RAT-chuhk, PEE-tuhr) **PIT.**

Defense. Shoots left. 6'1", 185 lbs. Born, Buffalo, NY, September 10, 1977. Colorado's 1st choice, 25th overall, in 1996 Entry Draft.

Season	Club	League	GP	G	A	Pts	PIM	PP	SH	GW	S	%	+/-	TF	F%	H	SB	Min	Playoffs GP	G	A	Pts	PIM	PP	SH	GW
1994-95	Lawrence Prep	Hi-School	31	8	15	23	18	....	....	....	....	....	....	....	....	....	....	....	....	....	....	....	....	....	....	....
1995-96	Shattuck-St. Mary	Hi-School	35	22	28	50	24	....	....	....	....	....	....	....	....	....	....	....	....	....	....	....	....	....	....	....
1996-97	Bowling Green	CCHA	35	9	12	21	14	....	....	....	....	....	....	....	....	....	....	....	....	....	....	....	....	....	....	....
1997-98	Hull Olympiques	QMJHL	60	23	31	54	34	....	....	....	....	....	....	....	....	....	....	....	11	3	6	9	8	....	....	....
1998-99	**Florida**	**NHL**	**24**	**1**	**1**	**2**	**10**	**0**	**0**	**0**	**34**	**2.9**	**-1**	**0**	**0.0**	**16**	**14**	**13:55**	....	....	....	....	....	....	....	....
	New Haven	AHL	53	7	20	27	44	....	....	....	....	....	....	....	....	....	....	....	....	....	....	....	....	....	....	....
99-2000	Louisville Panthers	AHL	76	9	17	26	64	....	....	....	....	....	....	....	....	....	....	....	4	1	2	3	0	....	....	....
2000-01	**Florida**	**NHL**	**8**	**0**	**0**	**0**	**0**	**0**	**0**	**0**	**11**	**0.0**	**-1**	**1**	**100.0**	**9**	**1**	**13:09**	....	....	....	....	....	....	....	....
	Louisville Panthers	AHL	64	5	13	18	85	....	....	....	....	....	....	....	....	....	....	....	....	....	....	....	....	....	....	....
	NHL Totals		**32**	**1**	**1**	**2**	**10**	**0**	**0**	**0**	**45**	**2.2**		**1**	**100.0**	**25**	**15**	**13:43**	....	....	....	....	....	....	....	....

Signed as a free agent by **Florida**, June 15, 1998. Signed as a free agent by **Pittsburgh**, August 14, 2001.

RATHJE, Mike
(RATH-jee, MIGHK) **S.J.**

Defense. Shoots left. 6'5", 245 lbs. Born, Mannville, Alta., May 11, 1974. San Jose's 1st choice, 3rd overall, in 1992 Entry Draft.

Season	Club	League	GP	G	A	Pts	PIM	PP	SH	GW	S	%	+/-	TF	F%	H	SB	Min	Playoffs GP	G	A	Pts	PIM	PP	SH	GW
1989-90	Sherwood Park	AMHL	33	6	11	17	30	....	....	....	....	....	....	....	....	....	....	....	6	1	1	2	2	....	....	....
1990-91	Medicine Hat	WHL	64	1	16	17	28	....	....	....	....	....	....	....	....	....	....	....	12	0	4	4	2	....	....	....
1991-92	Medicine Hat	WHL	67	11	23	34	99	....	....	....	....	....	....	....	....	....	....	....	4	0	1	1	2	....	....	....
1992-93	Medicine Hat	WHL	57	12	37	49	103	....	....	....	....	....	....	....	....	....	....	....	10	3	3	6	12	....	....	....
	Kansas City	IHL	....	....	....	....	....	....	....	....	....	....	....	....	....	....	....	....	5	0	0	0	12	....	....	....
1993-94	**San Jose**	**NHL**	**47**	**1**	**9**	**10**	**59**	**1**	**0**	**0**	**30**	**3.3**	**-9**	....	....	....	....	....	**1**	**0**	**0**	**0**	**0**	**0**	**0**	**0**
	Kansas City	IHL	6	0	2	2	0	....	....	....	....	....	....	....	....	....	....	....	....	....	....	....	....	....	....	....

			Regular Season																Playoffs							
Season	Club	League	GP	G	A	Pts	PIM	PP	SH	GW	S	%	+/-	TF	F%	H	SB	Min	GP	G	A	Pts	PIM	PP	SH	GW
1994-95	Kansas City	IHL	6	0	1	1	7																			
	San Jose	**NHL**	42	2	7	9	29	0	0	0	38	5.3	-1						11	5	2	7	4	5	0	0
1995-96	**San Jose**	**NHL**	27	0	7	7	14	0	0	0	26	0.0	-16													
	Kansas City	IHL	36	6	11	17	34																			
1996-97	**San Jose**	**NHL**	31	0	8	8	21	0	0	0	22	0.0	-1													
1997-98	**San Jose**	**NHL**	81	3	12	15	59	1	0	0	61	4.9	-4						6	1	0	1	6	1	0	0
1998-99	**San Jose**	**NHL**	82	5	9	14	36	2	0	1	67	7.5	15	0	0.0	100	64	20:07	6	0	0	0	4	0	0	0
99-2000	**San Jose**	**NHL**	66	2	14	16	31	0	0	0	46	4.3	-2	0	0.0	82	54	22:11	12	1	3	4	8	0	0	0
2000-01	**San Jose**	**NHL**	81	0	11	11	48	0	0	0	89	0.0	7	0	0.0	144	98	22:20	6	0	1	1	4	0	0	0
	NHL Totals		457	13	77	90	297	4	0	1	379	3.4		0	0.0	326	216	21:30	42	7	6	13	26	6	0	0

WHL East Second All-Star Team (1992, 1993)

• Missed majority of 1996-97 season recovering from groin injury suffered in game vs. Dallas, November 8, 1996.

RAY, Rob

(RAY, RAWB) **BUF.**

Right wing. Shoots left. 6', 216 lbs. Born, Stirling, Ont., June 8, 1968. Buffalo's 5th choice, 97th overall, in 1988 Entry Draft.

Season	Club	League	GP	G	A	Pts	PIM	PP	SH	GW	S	%	+/-	TF	F%	H	SB	Min	GP	G	A	Pts	PIM	PP	SH	GW
1983-84	Trenton Bobcats	OJHL-B	40	11	10	21	57																			
1984-85	Whitby Lawmen	MTJHL	35	5	10	15	318																			
1985-86	Cornwall Royals	OHL	53	6	13	19	253												6	0	0	0	26			
1986-87	Cornwall Royals	OHL	46	17	20	37	158												5	1	1	2	16			
1987-88	Cornwall Royals	OHL	61	11	41	52	179												11	2	3	5	33			
1988-89	Rochester	AHL	74	11	18	29	*446																			
1989-90	**Buffalo**	**NHL**	27	2	1	3	99	0	0	0	20	10.0	-2													
	Rochester	AHL	43	2	13	15	335												17	1	3	4	115			
1990-91	**Buffalo**	**NHL**	66	8	8	16	*350	0	0	1	54	14.8	-11						6	1	1	2	56	0	0	1
	Rochester	AHL	8	1	1	2	15																			
1991-92	**Buffalo**	**NHL**	63	5	3	8	354	0	0	0	29	17.2	-9						7	0	0	0	2	0	0	0
1992-93	**Buffalo**	**NHL**	68	3	2	5	211	1	0	0	28	10.7	-3													
1993-94	**Buffalo**	**NHL**	82	3	4	7	274	0	0	0	34	8.8	2						7	1	0	1	43	0	0	0
1994-95	**Buffalo**	**NHL**	47	0	3	3	173	0	0	0	7	0.0	-4						5	0	0	0	14	0	0	0
1995-96	**Buffalo**	**NHL**	71	3	6	9	287	0	0	0	21	14.3	-8													
1996-97	**Buffalo**	**NHL**	82	7	3	10	286	0	0	1	45	15.6	3						12	0	1	1	28	0	0	0
1997-98	**Buffalo**	**NHL**	63	2	4	6	234	1	0	1	19	10.5	2						10	0	0	0	24	0	0	0
1998-99	**Buffalo**	**NHL**	76	0	4	4	*261	0	0	0	23	0.0	-2	0	0.0	60	4	5:11	5	1	0	1	0	0	0	1
99-2000	**Buffalo**	**NHL**	69	1	3	4	158	0	0	0	17	5.9	0	0	0.0	55	4	4:13								
2000-01	**Buffalo**	**NHL**	63	4	6	10	210	0	0	1	33	12.1	2	1	100.0	83	4	5:38	3	0	0	0	2	0	0	0
	NHL Totals		777	38	47	85	2897	2	0	4	330	11.5		1	100.0	198	12	4:60	55	3	2	5	169	0	0	2

Won King Clancy Memorial Trophy (1999)

REASONER, Marty

(REE-sohn-uhr, MAHR-tee) **EDM.**

Center. Shoots left. 6'1", 203 lbs. Born, Rochester, NY, February 26, 1977. St. Louis' 1st choice, 14th overall, in 1996 Entry Draft.

Season	Club	League	GP	G	A	Pts	PIM	PP	SH	GW	S	%	+/-	TF	F%	H	SB	Min	GP	G	A	Pts	PIM	PP	SH	GW
1993-94	Deerfield Prep	Hi-School	22	27	25	52																				
1994-95	Deerfield Prep	Hi-School	26	25	32	57	14																			
1995-96	Boston College	H-East	34	16	29	45	32																			
1996-97	Boston College	H-East	35	20	24	44	31																			
1997-98	Boston College	H-East	42	*33	40	*73	56																			
1998-99	**St. Louis**	**NHL**	22	3	7	10	8	1	0	0	33	9.1	2	224	53.6	19	1	13:55								
	Worcester	AHL	44	17	22	39	24												4	2	1	3	6			
99-2000	**St. Louis**	**NHL**	32	10	14	24	20	3	0	0	51	19.6	9	379	49.6	26	5	15:20	7	2	1	3	4	1	0	0
	Worcester	AHL	44	23	28	51	39																			
2000-01	**St. Louis**	**NHL**	41	4	9	13	14	0	0	0	65	6.2	-5	454	53.1	31	14	14:00	10	3	1	4	0	0	0	1
	Worcester	AHL	34	17	18	35	25																			
	NHL Totals		95	17	30	47	42	4	0	0	149	11.4		1057	51.9	76	20	14:26	17	5	2	7	4	1	0	1

Hockey East First All-Star Team (1997, 1998) • NCAA East First All-American Team (1998) • NCAA Championship All-Tournament Team (1998)

Traded to **Edmonton** by **St. Louis** with Jochen Hecht and Jan Horacek for Doug Weight and Michel Riesen, July 1, 2001.

RECCHI, Mark

(REH-kee, MAHRK) **PHI.**

Right wing. Shoots left. 5'10", 185 lbs. Born, Kamloops, B.C., February 1, 1968. Pittsburgh's 4th choice, 67th overall, in 1988 Entry Draft.

Season	Club	League	GP	G	A	Pts	PIM	PP	SH	GW	S	%	+/-	TF	F%	H	SB	Min	GP	G	A	Pts	PIM	PP	SH	GW
1984-85	Langley Eagles	BCJHL	51	26	39	65	39																			
	New Westminster	WHL	4	1	0	1	0																			
1985-86	New Westminster	WHL	72	21	40	61	55																			
1986-87	Kamloops Blazers	WHL	40	26	50	76	63												13	3	16	19	17			
1987-88	Kamloops Blazers	WHL	62	61	*93	154	75												17	10	*21	*31	18			
1988-89	**Pittsburgh**	**NHL**	15	1	1	2	0	0	0	0	11	9.1	-2													
	Muskegon	IHL	63	50	49	99	86												14	7	*14	*21	28			
1989-90	**Pittsburgh**	**NHL**	74	30	37	67	44	6	2	4	143	21.0	6													
	Muskegon	IHL	4	7	4	11	2																			
1990-91♦	**Pittsburgh**	**NHL**	78	40	73	113	48	12	0	9	184	21.7	0						24	10	24	34	33	5	0	2
1991-92	**Pittsburgh**	**NHL**	58	33	37	70	78	16	1	4	156	21.2	-16													
	Philadelphia	**NHL**	22	10	17	27	18	4	0	1	54	18.5	-5													
1992-93	**Philadelphia**	**NHL**	84	53	70	123	95	15	4	6	274	19.3	1													
1993-94	**Philadelphia**	**NHL**	84	40	67	107	46	11	0	5	217	18.4	-2													
1994-95	**Philadelphia**	**NHL**	10	2	3	5	12	1	0	2	17	11.8	-6													
	Montreal	**NHL**	39	14	29	43	16	8	0	1	104	13.5	-3													
1995-96	**Montreal**	**NHL**	82	28	50	78	69	11	2	6	191	14.7	20						6	3	3	6	0	3	0	0
1996-97	**Montreal**	**NHL**	82	34	46	80	58	7	2	3	202	16.8	-1						5	4	2	6	2	0	0	0
1997-98	**Montreal**	**NHL**	82	32	42	74	51	9	1	6	216	14.8	11						10	4	8	12	6	0	0	2
	Canada	Olympics	5	0	2	2	0																			
1998-99	**Montreal**	**NHL**	61	12	35	47	28	3	0	2	152	7.9	-4	239	44.8	76	23	20:37								
	Philadelphia	**NHL**	10	4	2	6	6	0	0	0	19	21.1	-3	4	25.0	21	1	19:30	6	0	1	1	2	0	0	0
99-2000	**Philadelphia**	**NHL**	82	28	*63	91	50	7	1	5	223	12.6	20	353	49.6	95	39	21:43	18	6	12	18	6	2	0	1
2000-01	**Philadelphia**	**NHL**	69	27	50	77	33	7	1	8	191	14.1	15	138	42.8	76	18	21:40	6	2	2	4	2	1	0	1
	NHL Totals		932	388	622	1010	652	117	14	62	2354	16.5		734	46.6	268	81	21:18	75	29	52	81	51	11	0	6

WHL West All-Star Team (1988) • IHL Second All-Star Team (1989) • NHL Second All-Star Team (1992) • Played in NHL All-Star Game (1991, 1993, 1994, 1997, 1998, 1999, 2000)

Traded to **Philadelphia** by **Pittsburgh** with Brian Benning and LA Kings' 1st round choice (previously acquired, Philadelphia selected Jason Bowen) in 1992 Entry Draft for Rick Tocchet, Kjell Samuelsson, Ken Wregget and Philadelphia's 3rd round choice (Dave Roche) in 1993 Entry Draft, February 19, 1992. Traded to **Montreal** by **Philadelphia** with Philadelphia's 3rd round choice (Martin Hohenberger) in 1995 Entry Draft for Eric Desjardins, Gilbert Dionne and John LeClair, February 9, 1995. Traded to **Philadelphia** by **Montreal** for Danius Zubrus, Philadelphia's 2nd round choice (Matt Carkner) in 1999 Entry Draft and NY Islanders' 6th round choice (previously acquired, Montreal selected Scott Selig) in 2000 Entry Draft, March 10, 1999.

REDDEN, Wade

(REH-duhn, WAYD) **OTT.**

Defense. Shoots left. 6'2", 205 lbs. Born, Lloydminster, Sask., June 12, 1977. NY Islanders' 1st choice, 2nd overall, in 1995 Entry Draft.

Season	Club	League	GP	G	A	Pts	PIM	PP	SH	GW	S	%	+/-	TF	F%	H	SB	Min	GP	G	A	Pts	PIM	PP	SH	GW
1992-93	Lloydminster	SJHL	34	4	11	15	64																			
1993-94	Brandon	WHL	63	4	35	39	98												14	2	4	6	10			
1994-95	Brandon	WHL	64	14	46	60	83												18	5	10	15	8			
1995-96	Brandon	WHL	51	9	45	54	55												19	5	10	15	19			
1996-97	**Ottawa**	**NHL**	82	6	24	30	41	2	0	1	102	5.9	1						7	1	3	4	2	0	0	0
1997-98	**Ottawa**	**NHL**	80	8	14	22	27	3	0	2	103	7.8	17						9	0	2	2	2	0	0	0
1998-99	**Ottawa**	**NHL**	72	8	21	29	54	3	0	1	127	6.3	7	0	0.0	83	73	23:27	4	1	2	3	2	1	0	0
99-2000	**Ottawa**	**NHL**	81	10	26	36	49	3	0	2	163	6.3	-1	0	0.0	119	103	23:43								
2000-01	**Ottawa**	**NHL**	78	10	37	47	49	4	0	0	159	6.3	22	0	0.0	149	120	25:17	4	0	0	0	0	0	0	0
	NHL Totals		393	42	122	164	220	15	0	6	654	6.4		0	0.0	351	296	24:10	24	2	7	9	6	1	0	0

WHL East Second All-Star Team (1995) • WHL East First All-Star Team (1996) • Memorial Cup All-Star Team (1996)

Traded to **Ottawa** by **NY Islanders** with Damian Rhodes for Don Beaupre, Martin Straka and Bryan Berard, January 23, 1996.

REEKIE, Joe (REE-kee, JOH) WSH.

Defense. Shoots left. 6'3", 220 lbs. Born, Victoria, B.C., February 22, 1965. Buffalo's 6th choice, 119th overall, in 1985 Entry Draft.

Season	Club	League	GP	G	A	Pts	PIM	PP	SH	GW	S	%	+/-	TF	F%	H	SB	Min	GP	G	A	Pts	PIM	PP	SH	GW
			Regular Season																Playoffs							
1981-82	Nepean Raiders	OCJHL	16	2	5	7	4	....	....	....	....	....	....	....	....	....	....	....	....	....	....	....	....	....	....	....
1982-83	Pembroke	OCJHL	7	2	1	3	16	....	....	....	....	....	....	....	....	....	....	....	....	....	....	....	....	....	....	....
	North Bay	OHL	59	2	9	11	49	....	....	....	....	....	....	....	....	....	....	....	8	0	1	1	11	....	....	....
1983-84	North Bay	OHL	9	1	0	1	18	....	....	....	....	....	....	....	....	....	....	....	....	....	....	....	....	....	....	....
	Cornwall Royals	OHL	53	6	27	33	166	....	....	....	....	....	....	....	....	....	....	....	3	0	0	0	4	....	....	....
1984-85	Cornwall Royals	OHL	65	19	63	82	134	....	....	....	....	....	....	....	....	....	....	....	9	4	13	17	18	....	....	....
1985-86	**Buffalo**	**NHL**	**3**	**0**	**0**	**0**	**14**	**0**	**0**	**0**	**1**	**0.0**	**-2**	....	....	....	....	....	....	....	....	....	....	....	....	....
	Rochester	AHL	77	3	25	28	178	....	....	....	....	....	....	....	....	....	....	....	....	....	....	....	....	....	....	....
1986-87	**Buffalo**	**NHL**	**56**	**1**	**8**	**9**	**82**	**0**	**0**	**0**	**56**	**1.8**	**6**	....	....	....	....	....	....	....	....	....	....	....	....	....
	Rochester	AHL	22	0	6	6	52	....	....	....	....	....	....	....	....	....	....	....	....	....	....	....	....	....	....	....
1987-88	**Buffalo**	**NHL**	**30**	**1**	**4**	**5**	**68**	**0**	**0**	**0**	**23**	**4.3**	**-3**	....	....	....	....	....	**2**	**0**	**0**	**0**	**4**	**0**	**0**	**0**
1988-89	**Buffalo**	**NHL**	**15**	**1**	**3**	**4**	**26**	**1**	**0**	**0**	**14**	**7.1**	**6**	....	....	....	....	....	....	....	....	....	....	....	....	....
	Rochester	AHL	21	1	2	3	56	....	....	....	....	....	....	....	....	....	....	....	....	....	....	....	....	....	....	....
1989-90	**NY Islanders**	**NHL**	**31**	**1**	**8**	**9**	**43**	**0**	**0**	**1**	**22**	**4.5**	**13**	....	....	....	....	....	....	....	....	....	....	....	....	....
	Springfield	AHL	15	1	4	5	24	....	....	....	....	....	....	....	....	....	....	....	....	....	....	....	....	....	....	....
1990-91	**NY Islanders**	**NHL**	**66**	**3**	**16**	**19**	**96**	**0**	**0**	**2**	**70**	**4.3**	**17**	....	....	....	....	....	....	....	....	....	....	....	....	....
	Capital District	AHL	2	1	0	1	0	....	....	....	....	....	....	....	....	....	....	....	....	....	....	....	....	....	....	....
1991-92	**NY Islanders**	**NHL**	**54**	**4**	**12**	**16**	**85**	**0**	**0**	**0**	**59**	**6.8**	**15**	....	....	....	....	....	....	....	....	....	....	....	....	....
	Capital District	AHL	3	2	2	4	2	....	....	....	....	....	....	....	....	....	....	....	....	....	....	....	....	....	....	....
1992-93	**Tampa Bay**	**NHL**	**42**	**2**	**11**	**13**	**69**	**0**	**0**	**0**	**53**	**3.8**	**2**	....	....	....	....	....	....	....	....	....	....	....	....	....
1993-94	**Tampa Bay**	**NHL**	**73**	**1**	**11**	**12**	**127**	**0**	**0**	**0**	**88**	**1.1**	**8**	....	....	....	....	....	....	....	....	....	....	....	....	....
	Washington	**NHL**	**12**	**0**	**5**	**5**	**29**	**0**	**0**	**0**	**10**	**0.0**	**7**	....	....	....	....	....	**11**	**2**	**1**	**3**	**29**	**0**	**1**	**1**
1994-95	**Washington**	**NHL**	**48**	**1**	**6**	**7**	**97**	**0**	**0**	**0**	**52**	**1.9**	**10**	....	....	....	....	....	**7**	**0**	**0**	**0**	**2**	**0**	**0**	**0**
1995-96	**Washington**	**NHL**	**78**	**3**	**7**	**10**	**149**	**0**	**0**	**0**	**52**	**5.8**	**7**	....	....	....	....	....	....	....	....	....	....	....	....	....
1996-97	**Washington**	**NHL**	**65**	**1**	**8**	**9**	**107**	**0**	**0**	**0**	**65**	**1.5**	**8**	....	....	....	....	....	....	....	....	....	....	....	....	....
1997-98	**Washington**	**NHL**	**68**	**2**	**8**	**10**	**70**	**0**	**0**	**1**	**59**	**3.4**	**15**	....	....	....	....	....	**21**	**1**	**2**	**3**	**20**	**0**	**0**	**0**
1998-99	**Washington**	**NHL**	**73**	**0**	**10**	**10**	**68**	**0**	**0**	**0**	**81**	**0.0**	**11**	**0**	**0.0**	**182**	**101**	**21:53**	....	....	....	....	....	....	....	....
99-2000	**Washington**	**NHL**	**59**	**0**	**7**	**7**	**50**	**0**	**0**	**0**	**32**	**0.0**	**21**	**0**	**0.0**	**99**	**77**	**17:32**	**5**	**0**	**1**	**1**	**2**	**0**	**0**	**0**
2000-01	**Washington**	**NHL**	**74**	**2**	**9**	**11**	**77**	**0**	**0**	**1**	**59**	**3.4**	**14**	**1**	**0.0**	**122**	**88**	**18:49**	**4**	**0**	**0**	**0**	**4**	**0**	**0**	**0**
	NHL Totals		**847**	**23**	**133**	**156**	**1257**	**1**	**0**	**5**	**796**	**2.9**		**1**	**0.0**	**403**	**266**	**19:32**	**50**	**3**	**4**	**7**	**61**	**0**	**1**	**1**

• Re-entered NHL Entry Draft. Originally Hartford's 8th choice, 128th overall, in 1983 Entry Draft.

• Missed majority of 1987-88 and 1988-89 seasons recovering from knee injury originally suffered in game vs. Toronto, November 11, 1987. Traded to **NY Islanders** by **Buffalo** for NY Islanders' 6th round choice (Bill Pye) in 1989 Entry Draft, June 17, 1989. Claimed by **Tampa Bay** from **NY Islanders** in Expansion Draft, June 18, 1992. Traded to **Washington** by **Tampa Bay** for Enrico Ciccone, Washington's 3rd round choice (later traded to Anaheim - Anaheim selected Craig Reichert) in 1994 Entry Draft and the return of conditional draft choice transferred in the Pat Elynuik trade, March 21, 1994.

REGEHR, Robyn (reh-GUHR, RAW-bihn) CGY.

Defense. Shoots left. 6'2", 210 lbs. Born, Recife, Brazil, April 19, 1980. Colorado's 3rd choice, 19th overall, in 1998 Entry Draft.

Season	Club	League	GP	G	A	Pts	PIM	PP	SH	GW	S	%	+/-	TF	F%	H	SB	Min	GP	G	A	Pts	PIM	PP	SH	GW
1995-96	Prince Albert	SMHL	59	8	24	32	157	....	....	....	....	....	....	....	....	....	....	....	....	....	....	....	....	....	....	....
1996-97	Kamloops Blazers	WHL	64	4	19	23	96	....	....	....	....	....	....	....	....	....	....	....	5	0	1	1	18	....	....	....
1997-98	Kamloops Blazers	WHL	65	4	10	14	120	....	....	....	....	....	....	....	....	....	....	....	5	0	3	3	8	....	....	....
1998-99	Kamloops Blazers	WHL	54	12	20	32	130	....	....	....	....	....	....	....	....	....	....	....	12	1	4	5	21	....	....	....
99-2000	**Calgary**	**NHL**	**57**	**5**	**7**	**12**	**46**	**2**	**0**	**0**	**64**	**7.8**	**-2**	**0**	**0.0**	**135**	**62**	**18:24**	....	....	....	....	....	....	....	....
	Saint John Flames	AHL	5	0	0	0	0	....	....	....	....	....	....	....	....	....	....	....	....	....	....	....	....	....	....	....
2000-01	**Calgary**	**NHL**	**71**	**1**	**3**	**4**	**70**	**0**	**0**	**0**	**62**	**1.6**	**-7**	**1**	**0.0**	**171**	**104**	**19:43**	....	....	....	....	....	....	....	....
	NHL Totals		**128**	**6**	**10**	**16**	**116**	**2**	**0**	**0**	**126**	**4.8**		**1**	**0.0**	**306**	**166**	**19:08**	....	....	....	....	....	....	....	....

WHL West First All-Star Team (1999)

Traded to **Calgary** by **Colorado** with Rene Corbet, Wade Belak and Colorado's 2nd round compensatory choice (Jarret Stoll) in 2000 Entry Draft for Theoren Fleury and Chris Dingman, February 28, 1999.

REICHEL, Robert (RIGH-khul, RAW-buhrt) TOR.

Center. Shoots left. 5'10", 185 lbs. Born, Litvinov, Czech., June 25, 1971. Calgary's 5th choice, 70th overall, in 1989 Entry Draft.

Season	Club	League	GP	G	A	Pts	PIM	PP	SH	GW	S	%	+/-	TF	F%	H	SB	Min	GP	G	A	Pts	PIM	PP	SH	GW
1987-88	CHZ Litvinov	Czech.	36	17	10	27	8	....	....	....	....	....	....	....	....	....	....	....	....	....	....	....	....	....	....	....
1988-89	CHZ Litvinov	Czech.	44	23	25	48	32	....	....	....	....	....	....	....	....	....	....	....	....	....	....	....	....	....	....	....
1989-90	CHZ Litvinov	Czech.	44	*43	28	*71	....	....	....	....	....	....	....	....	....	....	....	....	8	6	6	12	....	....	....	....
1990-91	**Calgary**	**NHL**	**66**	**19**	**22**	**41**	**22**	**3**	**0**	**3**	**131**	**14.5**	**17**	....	....	....	....	....	**6**	**1**	**1**	**2**	**0**	**1**	**0**	**0**
1991-92	**Calgary**	**NHL**	**77**	**20**	**34**	**54**	**32**	**8**	**0**	**3**	**181**	**11.0**	**1**	....	....	....	....	....	....	....	....	....	....	....	....	....
1992-93	**Calgary**	**NHL**	**80**	**40**	**48**	**88**	**54**	**12**	**0**	**5**	**238**	**16.8**	**25**	....	....	....	....	....	**6**	**2**	**4**	**6**	**2**	**2**	**0**	**0**
1993-94	**Calgary**	**NHL**	**84**	**40**	**53**	**93**	**58**	**14**	**0**	**6**	**249**	**16.1**	**20**	....	....	....	....	....	**7**	**0**	**5**	**5**	**0**	**0**	**0**	**0**
1994-95	Frankfurt Lions	DEL	21	19	24	43	41	....	....	....	....	....	....	....	....	....	....	....	....	....	....	....	....	....	....	....
	Calgary	**NHL**	**48**	**18**	**17**	**35**	**28**	**5**	**0**	**2**	**160**	**11.3**	**-2**	....	....	....	....	....	**7**	**2**	**4**	**6**	**4**	**0**	**0**	**1**
1995-96	Frankfurt Lions	DEL	46	47	54	101	84	....	....	....	....	....	....	....	....	....	....	....	3	1	3	4	0	....	....	....
1996-97	**Calgary**	**NHL**	**70**	**16**	**27**	**43**	**22**	**6**	**0**	**3**	**181**	**8.8**	**-2**	....	....	....	....	....	....	....	....	....	....	....	....	....
	NY Islanders	**NHL**	**12**	**5**	**14**	**19**	**4**	**0**	**1**	**0**	**33**	**15.2**	**7**	....	....	....	....	....	....	....	....	....	....	....	....	....
1997-98	**NY Islanders**	**NHL**	**82**	**25**	**40**	**65**	**32**	**8**	**0**	**2**	**201**	**12.4**	**-11**	....	....	....	....	....	....	....	....	....	....	....	....	....
	Czech-Republic	Olympics	6	3	0	3	0	....	....	....	....	....	....	....	....	....	....	....	....	....	....	....	....	....	....	....
1998-99	**NY Islanders**	**NHL**	**70**	**19**	**37**	**56**	**50**	**5**	**1**	**1**	**186**	**10.2**	**-15**	**1241**	**51.7**	**52**	**19**	**19:36**	....	....	....	....	....	....	....	....
	Phoenix	**NHL**	**13**	**7**	**6**	**13**	**4**	**3**	**0**	**3**	**50**	**14.0**	**2**	**241**	**48.5**	**10**	**4**	**20:03**	**7**	**1**	**3**	**4**	**2**	**0**	**0**	**0**
99-2000	CHZ Litvinov	Cze-Rep	45	25	32	57	24	....	....	....	....	....	....	....	....	....	....	....	7	3	4	7	2	....	....	....
2000-01	CHZ Litvinov	Cze-Rep	49	23	33	56	72	....	....	....	....	....	....	....	....	....	....	....	5	1	2	3	4	....	....	....
	NHL Totals		**602**	**209**	**298**	**507**	**306**	**64**	**2**	**28**	**1610**	**13.0**		**1482**	**51.2**	**62**	**23**	**19:40**	**33**	**6**	**17**	**23**	**8**	**3**	**0**	**1**

Traded to **NY Islanders** by **Calgary** for Marty McInnis, Tyrone Garner and Calgary's 6th round choice (previously acquired, Calgary selected Ilja Demidov) in 1997 Entry Draft, March 18, 1997. Traded to **Phoenix** by **NY Islanders** with NY Islanders' 3rd round choice (Jason Jaspers) in 1999 Entry Draft and Ottawa's 4th round choice (previously acquired, Phoenix selected Preston Mizzi) in 1999 Entry Draft for Brad Isbister and Phoenix's 3rd round choice (Brian Collins) in 1999 Entry Draft, March 20, 1999. Traded to **Toronto** by **Phoenix** with Travis Green and Craig Mills for Danny Markov, June 12, 2001.

REICHERT, Craig (RIGH-kuhrt, KRAYG) EDM.

Right wing. Shoots right. 6'1", 200 lbs. Born, Winnipeg, Man., May 11, 1974. Anaheim's 3rd choice, 67th overall, in 1994 Entry Draft.

Season	Club	League	GP	G	A	Pts	PIM	PP	SH	GW	S	%	+/-	TF	F%	H	SB	Min	GP	G	A	Pts	PIM	PP	SH	GW
1990-91	Calgary Buffaloes	AMHL	47	32	36	68	54	....	....	....	....	....	....	....	....	....	....	....	13	13	28	41	27	....	....	....
1991-92	Spokane Chiefs	WHL	68	13	20	33	56	....	....	....	....	....	....	....	....	....	....	....	4	1	0	1	4	....	....	....
1992-93	Red Deer Rebels	WHL	66	32	33	65	62	....	....	....	....	....	....	....	....	....	....	....	4	3	1	4	2	....	....	....
1993-94	Red Deer Rebels	WHL	72	52	67	119	153	....	....	....	....	....	....	....	....	....	....	....	4	2	2	4	8	....	....	....
1994-95	San Diego Gulls	IHL	49	4	12	16	28	....	....	....	....	....	....	....	....	....	....	....	....	....	....	....	....	....	....	....
1995-96	Baltimore Bandits	AHL	68	10	17	27	50	....	....	....	....	....	....	....	....	....	....	....	1	0	0	0	0	....	....	....
1996-97	**Anaheim**	**NHL**	**3**	**0**	**0**	**0**	**0**	**0**	**0**	**0**	**3**	**0.0**	**-2**	....	....	....	....	....	....	....	....	....	....	....	....	....
	Baltimore Bandits	AHL	77	22	53	75	54	....	....	....	....	....	....	....	....	....	....	....	3	0	2	2	0	....	....	....
1997-98	Cincinnati Ducks	AHL	78	28	59	87	28	....	....	....	....	....	....	....	....	....	....	....	....	....	....	....	....	....	....	....
1998-99	Cincinnati Ducks	AHL	72	28	41	69	56	....	....	....	....	....	....	....	....	....	....	....	3	2	0	2	0	....	....	....
99-2000	Louisville Panthers	AHL	72	16	42	58	41	....	....	....	....	....	....	....	....	....	....	....	4	1	1	2	2	....	....	....
2000-01	Dusseldorfer EG	DEL	60	12	23	35	76	....	....	....	....	....	....	....	....	....	....	....	....	....	....	....	....	....	....	....
	NHL Totals		**3**	**0**	**0**	**0**	**0**	**0**	**0**	**0**	**3**	**0.0**		....	....	....	....	....	....	....	....	....	....	....	....	....

Signed as a free agent by **Florida**, July 21, 1999. Signed as a free agent by **Edmonton**, June 11, 2001.

REID, Dave (REED, DAYV)

Left wing. Shoots left. 6'1", 217 lbs. Born, Toronto, Ont., May 15, 1964. Boston's 4th choice, 60th overall, in 1982 Entry Draft.

Season	Club	League	GP	G	A	Pts	PIM	PP	SH	GW	S	%	+/-	TF	F%	H	SB	Min	GP	G	A	Pts	PIM	PP	SH	GW
1979-80	Royal York Royals	MTJHL	41	4	7	11	93	....	....	....	....	....	....	....	....	....	....	....	....	....	....	....	....	....	....	....
1980-81	Mississauga Reps	MTHL	39	21	28	49	....	....	....	....	....	....	....	....	....	....	....	....	....	....	....	....	....	....	....	....
	Dixie Beehives	OHA-B	4	2	3	5	0	....	....	....	....	....	....	....	....	....	....	....	....	....	....	....	....	....	....	....
1981-82	Peterborough	OHL	68	10	32	42	41	....	....	....	....	....	....	....	....	....	....	....	9	2	3	5	11	....	....	....
1982-83	Peterborough	OHL	70	23	34	57	33	....	....	....	....	....	....	....	....	....	....	....	4	3	1	4	0	....	....	....
1983-84	Peterborough	OHL	60	33	64	97	12	....	....	....	....	....	....	....	....	....	....	....	....	....	....	....	....	....	....	....
	Boston	**NHL**	**8**	**1**	**0**	**1**	**2**	**0**	**0**	**0**	**4**	**25.0**	**1**	....	....	....	....	....	....	....	....	....	....	....	....	....
1984-85	**Boston**	**NHL**	**35**	**14**	**13**	**27**	**27**	**2**	**0**	**5**	**52**	**26.9**	**-1**	....	....	....	....	....	**5**	**1**	**0**	**1**	**0**	**0**	**0**	**0**
	Hershey Bears	AHL	43	10	14	24	6	....	....	....	....	....	....	....	....	....	....	....	....	....	....	....	....	....	....	....

			Regular Season																Playoffs							
Season	Club	League	GP	G	A	Pts	PIM	PP	SH	GW	S	%	+/-	TF	F%	H	SB	Min	GP	G	A	Pts	PIM	PP	SH	GW
1985-86	Boston	NHL	37	10	10	20	10	4	0	1	53	18.9	2													
	Moncton Flames	AHL	26	14	18	32	4																			
1986-87	Boston	NHL	12	3	3	6	0	0	0	0	19	15.8	−1						2	0	0	0	0	0	0	0
	Moncton Flames	AHL	40	12	22	34	23												5	0	1	1	0			
1987-88	Boston	NHL	3	0	0	0	0	0	0	0	2	0.0	0													
	Maine Mariners	AHL	63	21	37	58	40												10	6	7	13	0			
1988-89	Toronto	NHL	77	9	21	30	22	1	1	0	87	10.3	12													
1989-90	Toronto	NHL	70	9	19	28	9	0	4	1	97	9.3	−8						3	0	0	0	0	0	0	0
1990-91	Toronto	NHL	69	15	13	28	18	1	8	0	110	13.6	−10													
1991-92	Boston	NHL	43	7	7	14	27	2	1	0	70	10.0	5						15	2	5	7	4	0	0	1
	Maine Mariners	AHL	12	1	5	6	4																			
1992-93	Boston	NHL	65	20	16	36	10	1	5	2	116	17.2	12													
1993-94	Boston	NHL	83	6	17	23	25	0	2	1	145	4.1	10						13	2	1	3	2	0	1	0
1994-95	Boston	NHL	38	5	5	10	10	0	0	0	47	10.6	8						5	0	0	0	0	0	0	0
	Providence Bruins	AHL	7	3	0	3	0																			
1995-96	Boston	NHL	63	23	21	44	4	1	6	3	160	14.4	14						5	0	2	2	2	0	0	0
1996-97	Dallas	NHL	82	19	20	39	10	1	1	4	135	14.1	12						7	1	0	1	4	0	0	0
1997-98	Dallas	NHL	65	6	12	18	14	3	0	1	90	6.7	−15						5	0	3	3	2	0	0	0
1998-99♦	Dallas	NHL	73	6	11	17	16	1	0	1	81	7.4	0	39	41.0	45	34	11:34	23	2	8	10	14	0	0	0
99-2000	Colorado	NHL	65	11	7	18	28	0	0	3	86	12.8	12	46	34.8	30	41	14:57	17	1	3	4	0	0	0	0
2000-01♦	Colorado	NHL	73	1	9	10	21	0	0	0	66	1.5	1	352	40.3	32	39	9:53	18	0	4	4	6	0	0	0
	NHL Totals		961	165	204	369	253	17	28	22	1420	11.6		437	39.8	107	114	12:01	118	9	26	35	34	0	1	1

Signed as a free agent by **Toronto**, June 23, 1988. Signed as a free agent by **Boston**, December 1, 1991. Signed as a free agent by **Dallas**, July 11, 1996. Signed as a free agent by **Colorado**, October 6, 1999.

REINPRECHT, Steve

(REIGHN-prehkt, STEEV) **COL.**

Center. Shoots left. 6', 190 lbs. Born, Edmonton, AB, May 7, 1976.

1993-94	Edmonton SSA	AMHL	71	48	77	125																				
1994-95	St. Albert Saints	AJHL	56	35	44	79	14																			
1995-96	St. Albert Saints	AJHL	32	24	36	60																				
1996-97	U. of Wisconsin	WCHA	38	11	9	20	12																			
1997-98	U. of Wisconsin	WCHA	41	19	24	43	18																			
1998-99	U. of Wisconsin	WCHA	38	16	17	33	14																			
99-2000	U. of Wisconsin	WCHA	37	26	40	*66	14																			
	Los Angeles	NHL	1	0	0	0	2	0	0	0	0	0.0	0	6	50.0	0	0	6:01								
2000-01	Los Angeles	NHL	59	12	17	29	12	3	2	3	72	16.7	11	676	41.4	65	34	12:39								
	♦ Colorado	NHL	21	3	4	7	2	0	0	0	28	10.7	−1	209	51.2	23	14	15:38	22	2	3	5	2	0	0	0
	NHL Totals		81	15	21	36	16	3	2	3	100	15.0		891	43.8	88	48	13:21	22	2	3	5	2	0	0	0

WCHA Second All-Star Team (1998) • WCHA First All-Star Team (2000) • NCAA West First All-American Team (2000)

Signed as a free agent by **LA Kings**, March 31, 2000. Traded to **Colorado** by **LA Kings** with Rob Blake for Adam Deadmarsh, Aaron Miller, Colorado's 1st round choice (David Steckel) in 2001 Entry Draft and future considerations (Jared Aulin, March 22, 2001), February 21, 2001.

REIRDEN, Todd

(REER-dehn, TAWD) **ATL.**

Defense. Shoots left. 6'5", 225 lbs. Born, Deerfield, IL, June 25, 1971. New Jersey's 14th choice, 242nd overall, in 1990 Entry Draft.

1987-88	Deerfield High	Hi-School	22	19	32	51																				
1988-89	Tabor Academy	Hi-School	22	6	16	22																				
1989-90	Tabor Academy	Hi-School	22	10	28	38																				
1990-91	Bowling Green	CCHA	28	1	5	6	22																			
1991-92	Bowling Green	CCHA	33	8	7	15	34																			
1992-93	Bowling Green	CCHA	41	8	17	25	48																			
1993-94	Bowling Green	CCHA	38	7	23	30	56																			
1994-95	Albany River Rats	AHL	2	0	1	1	2																			
	Raleigh Icecaps	ECHL	26	2	13	15	33																			
	Tallahassee	ECHL	43	5	25	30	61												13	2	5	7	40			
1995-96	Tallahassee	ECHL	7	1	3	4	10																			
	Jacksonville	ECHL	15	1	10	11	41												1	0	2	2	4			
	Chicago Wolves	IHL	31	0	2	2	39												9	0	2	2	16			
1996-97	Chicago Wolves	IHL	57	3	10	13	108																			
	San Antonio	IHL	23	2	5	7	51												9	0	1	1	17			
1997-98	San Antonio	IHL	70	5	14	19	132																			
	Fort Wayne	IHL	11	2	2	4	16												4	0	2	2	4			
1998-99	Edmonton	NHL	17	2	3	5	20	0	0	0	26	7.7	−1	0	0.0	18	18	17:17								
	Hamilton Bulldogs	AHL	58	9	25	34	84												11	0	5	5	6			
99-2000	St. Louis	NHL	56	4	21	25	32	0	0	1	77	5.2	18	1	0.0	59	49	18:18	4	0	1	1	0	0	0	0
2000-01	St. Louis	NHL	38	2	4	6	43	1	0	0	58	3.4	−2	2	50.0	48	46	16:50	1	0	0	0	0	0	0	0
	Worcester	AHL	7	2	6	8	20																			
	NHL Totals		111	8	28	36	95	1	0	1	161	5.0		3	33.3	125	113	17:39	5	0	1	1	0	0	0	0

Signed as a free agent by **Edmonton**, September 17, 1998. Claimed on waivers by **St. Louis** from **Edmonton**, September 30, 1999. Signed as a free agent by **Atlanta**, July 16, 2001.

RENBERG, Mikael

(REHN-buhrg, MIHK-al) **TOR.**

Right wing. Shoots left. 6'2", 218 lbs. Born, Pitea, Sweden, May 5, 1972. Philadelphia's 3rd choice, 40th overall, in 1990 Entry Draft.

1988-89	Pitea HC	Sweden-2	12	6	3	9																				
1989-90	Pitea HC	Sweden-2	29	15	19	34																				
1990-91	Lulea HF	Sweden	29	11	6	17	12												5	1	1	2	4			
1991-92	Lulea HF	Sweden	38	8	15	23	20												2	0	0	0	0			
1992-93	Lulea HF	Sweden	39	19	13	32	61												11	4	4	8	4			
1993-94	Philadelphia	NHL	83	38	44	82	36	9	0	1	195	19.5	8													
1994-95	Lulea HF	Sweden	10	9	4	13	16																			
	Philadelphia	NHL	47	26	31	57	20	8	0	4	143	18.2	20						15	6	7	13	6	2	0	0
1995-96	Philadelphia	NHL	51	23	20	43	45	9	0	4	198	11.6	8						11	3	6	9	14	1	0	0
1996-97	Philadelphia	NHL	77	22	37	59	65	1	0	4	249	8.8	36						18	5	6	11	4	2	0	0
1997-98	Tampa Bay	NHL	68	16	22	38	34	6	3	0	175	9.1	−37													
	Sweden	Olympics	4	1	2	3	4																			
1998-99	Tampa Bay	NHL	20	4	8	12	4	2	0	0	42	9.5	−2	2	100.0	1	4	15:32								
	Philadelphia	NHL	46	11	15	26	14	4	0	2	112	9.8	7	1	0.0	8	5	16:00	6	0	1	1	0	0	0	0
99-2000	Philadelphia	NHL	62	8	21	29	30	3	0	1	106	7.5	−1	3	33.3	23	10	13:27								
	Phoenix	NHL	10	2	4	6	2	0	0	0	16	12.5	0	0	0.0	2	1	15:31	5	1	2	3	4	0	0	1
2000-01	Lulea HF	Sweden	48	22	32	54	36												11	6	5	11	35			
	NHL Totals		464	150	202	352	250	42	3	16	1236	12.1		6	50.0	34	20	14:45	55	15	22	37	28	5	0	1

NHL All-Rookie Team (1994)

Traded to **Tampa Bay** by **Philadelphia** with Karl Dykhuis for Philadelphia's 1st round choices in 1998 (previously acquired, Tampa Bay selected Simon Gagne), 1999 (Maxime Ouellet), 2000 (Justin Williams) and 2001 (later traded to Ottawa - Ottawa selected Tim Gleason) Entry Drafts, August 20, 1997. Traded to **Philadelphia** by **Tampa Bay** with Daymond Langkow for Chris Gratton and Mike Sillinger, December 12, 1998. Traded to **Phoenix** by **Philadelphia** for Rick Tocchet, March 8, 2000. Traded to **Toronto** by **Phoenix** for Sergei Berezin, June 23, 2001.

RHEAUME, Pascal

(RAY-awm, PAS-kal) **CHI.**

Left wing. Shoots left. 6'1", 209 lbs. Born, Quebec, Que., June 21, 1973.

1990-91	Ste-Foy Governors	QAAA	37	20	38	58	25												7	7	1	8	6			
1991-92	Trois-Rivieres	QMJHL	65	17	20	37	84												14	5	4	9	23			
1992-93	Sherbrooke	QMJHL	65	28	34	62	88												14	6	5	11	31			
1993-94	Albany River Rats	AHL	55	17	18	35	43												5	0	1	1	0			
1994-95	Albany River Rats	AHL	78	19	25	44	46												14	3	6	9	19			
1995-96	Albany River Rats	AHL	68	26	42	68	50												4	1	2	3	2			
1996-97	New Jersey	NHL	2	1	0	1	0	0	0	0	5	20.0	1													
	Albany River Rats	AHL	51	22	23	45	40												16	2	8	10	16			
1997-98	St. Louis	NHL	48	6	9	15	35	1	0	0	45	13.3	4						10	1	3	4	8	1	0	0
1998-99	St. Louis	NHL	60	9	18	27	24	2	0	0	85	10.6	10	21	71.4	105	14	13:19	5	1	0	1	4	0	0	0

			Regular Season																Playoffs							
Season	Club	League	GP	G	A	Pts	PIM	PP	SH	GW	S	%	+/-	TF	F%	H	SB	Min	GP	G	A	Pts	PIM	PP	SH	GW
99-2000	**St. Louis**	**NHL**	**7**	**1**	**1**	**2**	**6**	**0**	**0**	**0**	**5**	**20.0**	**−2**	**2**	**0.0**	**9**	**1**	**10:08**								
	Worcester	AHL	7	1	1	2	4																			
2000-01	**St. Louis**	**NHL**	**8**	**2**	**0**	**2**	**5**	**2**	**0**	**0**	**16**	**12.5**	**−1**	**7**	**42.9**	**24**	**0**	**11:56**	**3**	**0**	**1**	**1**	**0**	**0**	**0**	**0**
	Worcester	AHL	56	23	35	58	63												11	2	4	6	2			
	NHL Totals		**125**	**19**	**28**	**47**	**70**	**5**	**0**	**0**	**156**	**12.2**		**30**	**60.0**	**138**	**15**	**12:52**	**18**	**2**	**4**	**6**	**12**	**1**	**0**	**0**

Signed as a free agent by **New Jersey**, October 1, 1993. Claimed by **St. Louis** from **New Jersey** in NHL Waiver Draft, September 28, 1997. • Missed majority of 1999-2000 season recovering from shoulder surgery, August, 1999. Signed as a free agent by **Chicago**, July 31, 2001.

RIBEIRO, Mike

(rih-bee-AIR-roh, MIGHK) **MTL.**

Center. Shoots left. 6', 177 lbs. Born, Montreal, Que., February 10, 1980. Montreal's 2nd choice, 45th overall, in 1998 Entry Draft.

1996-97	Mtl-Bourassa	QAAA	43	32	57	89	48												16	15	23	38	14			
1997-98	Rouyn Noranda	QMJHL	67	40	*85	125	55												6	3	1	4	0			
1998-99	Rouyn-Noranda	QMJHL	69	*67	*100	*167	137												11	5	11	16	12			
	Fredericton	AHL																	5	0	1	1	2			
99-2000	**Montreal**	**NHL**	**19**	**1**	**1**	**2**	**2**	**1**	**0**	**0**	**18**	**5.6**	**−6**	**95**	**34.7**	**15**	**5**	**10:40**								
	Quebec Citadelles	AHL	3	0	0	0	2																			
	Rouyn-Noranda	QMJHL	2	1	3	4	0																			
	Quebec Remparts	QMJHL	21	17	28	45	30												11	3	20	23	38			
2000-01	**Montreal**	**NHL**	**2**	**0**	**0**	**0**	**2**	**0**	**0**	**0**	**3**	**0.0**	**0**	**11**	**18.2**	**2**	**0**	**10:38**								
	Quebec Citadelles	AHL	74	26	40	66	44												9	1	5	6	23			
	NHL Totals		**21**	**1**	**1**	**2**	**4**	**1**	**0**	**0**	**21**	**4.8**		**106**	**33.0**	**17**	**5**	**10:40**								

QMJHL Second All-Star Team (1998) • QMJHL First All-Star Team (1999) • Canadian Major Junior First All-Star Team (1999)

Assigned to **Rouyn-Noranda** (QMJHL) by **Montreal**, January 5, 2000. Traded to **Quebec** by **Rouyn-Noranda** for Guillaume Lefebvre and future considerations, January 9, 2000.

RICCI, Mike

(REE-CHEE, MIGHK) **S.J.**

Center. Shoots left. 6', 185 lbs. Born, Scarborough, Ont., October 27, 1971. Philadelphia's 1st choice, 4th overall, in 1990 Entry Draft.

1986-87	Toronto Marlies	MTHL	38	39	42	81	27																			
1987-88	Peterborough	OHL	41	24	37	61	20												8	5	5	10	4			
1988-89	Peterborough	OHL	60	54	52	106	43												17	19	16	35	18			
1989-90	Peterborough	OHL	60	52	64	116	39												12	5	7	12	26			
1990-91	**Philadelphia**	**NHL**	**68**	**21**	**20**	**41**	**64**	**9**	**0**	**4**	**121**	**17.4**	**−8**													
1991-92	**Philadelphia**	**NHL**	**78**	**20**	**36**	**56**	**93**	**11**	**2**	**0**	**149**	**13.4**	**−10**													
1992-93	**Quebec**	**NHL**	**77**	**27**	**51**	**78**	**123**	**12**	**1**	**10**	**142**	**19.0**	**8**						**6**	**0**	**6**	**6**	**8**	**0**	**0**	**0**
1993-94	**Quebec**	**NHL**	**83**	**30**	**21**	**51**	**113**	**13**	**3**	**6**	**138**	**21.7**	**−9**													
1994-95	**Quebec**	**NHL**	**48**	**15**	**21**	**36**	**40**	**9**	**0**	**1**	**73**	**20.5**	**5**						**6**	**1**	**3**	**4**	**8**	**0**	**0**	**0**
1995-96♦	**Colorado**	**NHL**	**62**	**6**	**21**	**27**	**52**	**3**	**0**	**1**	**73**	**8.2**	**1**						**22**	**6**	**11**	**17**	**18**	**3**	**0**	**1**
1996-97	**Colorado**	**NHL**	**63**	**13**	**19**	**32**	**59**	**5**	**0**	**3**	**74**	**17.6**	**−3**						**17**	**2**	**4**	**6**	**17**	**0**	**0**	**1**
1997-98	**Colorado**	**NHL**	**6**	**0**	**4**	**4**	**2**	**0**	**0**	**0**	**5**	**0.0**	**0**													
	San Jose	**NHL**	**59**	**9**	**14**	**23**	**30**	**5**	**0**	**2**	**86**	**10.5**	**−4**						**6**	**1**	**3**	**4**	**6**	**0**	**0**	**0**
1998-99	**San Jose**	**NHL**	**82**	**13**	**26**	**39**	**68**	**2**	**1**	**2**	**98**	**13.3**	**1**	**1465**	**49.6**	**73**	**41**	**15:23**	**6**	**2**	**3**	**5**	**10**	**1**	**0**	**0**
99-2000	**San Jose**	**NHL**	**82**	**20**	**24**	**44**	**60**	**10**	**0**	**5**	**134**	**14.9**	**14**	**1522**	**50.7**	**94**	**52**	**16:52**	**12**	**5**	**1**	**6**	**2**	**3**	**0**	**1**
2000-01	**San Jose**	**NHL**	**81**	**22**	**22**	**44**	**60**	**9**	**2**	**4**	**141**	**15.6**	**3**	**1631**	**51.4**	**107**	**46**	**17:60**	**6**	**0**	**3**	**3**	**0**	**0**	**0**	**0**
	NHL Totals		**789**	**196**	**279**	**475**	**764**	**88**	**9**	**38**	**1234**	**15.9**		**4618**	**50.6**	**274**	**139**	**16:45**	**81**	**17**	**34**	**51**	**69**	**7**	**0**	**3**

OHL Second All-Star Team (1989) • Canadian Major Junior Player of the Year (1990) • OHL First All-Star Team (1990)

Traded to **Quebec** by **Philadelphia** with Steve Duchesne, Peter Forsberg, Kerry Huffman, Ron Hextall, Philadelphia's 1st round choice (Jocelyn Thibault) in 1993 Entry Draft, $15,000,000 and future considerations (Chris Simon and Philadelphia's 1st round choice (later traded to Toronto - later traded to Washington - Washington selected Nolan Baumgartner) in 1994 Entry Draft, July 21, 1992) for Eric Lindros, June 30, 1992. Transferred to **Colorado** after **Quebec** franchise relocated, June 21, 1995. Traded to **San Jose** by **Colorado** with Colorado's 2nd round choice (later traded to Buffalo - Buffalo selected Jaroslav Kristek) in 1998 Entry Draft for Shean Donovan and San Jose's 1st round choice (Alex Tanguay) in 1998 Entry Draft, November 21, 1997.

RICHARDS, Brad

(RIH-chahrds, BRAD) **T.B.**

Left wing. Shoots left. 6'1", 198 lbs. Born, Montague, P.E.I., May 2, 1980. Tampa Bay's 2nd choice, 64th overall, in 1998 Entry Draft.

1996-97	Notre Dame	SJHL	63	39	48	87	73																			
1997-98	Rimouski Oceanic	QMJHL	68	33	82	115	44												19	8	24	32	2			
1998-99	Rimouski Oceanic	QMJHL	59	39	92	131	55												11	9	12	21	6			
99-2000	Rimouski Oceanic	QMJHL	63	*71	*115	*186	69												12	13	*24	*37	16			
2000-01	**Tampa Bay**	**NHL**	**82**	**21**	**41**	**62**	**14**	**7**	**0**	**3**	**179**	**11.7**	**−10**	**955**	**41.4**	**14**	**28**	**16:54**								
	NHL Totals		**82**	**21**	**41**	**62**	**14**	**7**	**0**	**3**	**179**	**11.7**		**955**	**41.4**	**14**	**28**	**16:54**								

SJHL Rookie of the Year (1997) • QMJHL First All-Star Team (2000) • Canadian Major Junior First All-Star Team (2000) • Canadian Major Junior Player of the Year (2000) • Memorial Cup All-Star Team (2000) • Won Stafford Smythe Memorial Trophy (Memorial Cup Tournament MVP) (2000) • NHL All-Rookie Team (2001)

RICHARDS, Travis

(RIH-chuhrds, TRA-vihs) **OTT.**

Defense. Shoots left. 6'1", 195 lbs. Born, Crystal, MN, March 22, 1970. Minnesota's 6th choice, 169th overall, in 1988 Entry Draft.

1986-87	Armstrong High	Hi-School	22	6	16	22	20																			
1987-88	Armstrong High	Hi-School	24	14	14	28	....																			
1988-89	Armstrong High	Hi-School	STATISTICS NOT AVAILABLE																							
1989-90	U. of Minnesota	WCHA	45	4	24	28	38																			
1990-91	U. of Minnesota	WCHA	45	9	25	34	28																			
1991-92	U. of Minnesota	WCHA	41	10	22	32	65																			
1992-93	U. of Minnesota	WCHA	42	12	26	38	52																			
1993-94	United States	Nat-Team	51	1	11	12	38																			
	United States	Olympics	8	0	0	0	2																			
	Kalamazoo	IHL	19	2	10	12	20												4	1	1	2	0			
1994-95	Kalamazoo	IHL	63	4	16	20	53												15	1	5	6	12			
	Dallas	**NHL**	**2**	**0**	**0**	**0**	**0**	**0**	**0**	**0**	**1**	**0.0**	**0**													
1995-96	**Dallas**	**NHL**	**1**	**0**	**0**	**0**	**2**	**0**	**0**	**0**	**0**	**0.0**	**−1**													
	Michigan	IHL	65	8	15	23	55																			
1996-97	Grand Rapids	IHL	77	10	13	23	83												9	2	2	4	4			
1997-98	Grand Rapids	IHL	81	12	20	32	70												5	1	3	4	2			
1998-99	Grand Rapids	IHL	82	9	23	32	84												3	1	1	2	4			
99-2000	Grand Rapids	IHL	71	5	23	28	47												17	1	7	8	18			
2000-01	Grand Rapids	IHL	75	5	30	35	42												10	0	5	5	8			
	NHL Totals		**3**	**0**	**0**	**0**	**2**	**0**	**0**	**0**	**1**	**0.0**														

WCHA Second All-Star Team (1992, 1993) • IHL First All-Star Team (1995, 1996) • Won Governors' Trophy (Outstanding Defenseman - IHL) (1995) • IHL Second All-Star Team (2001)

Rights transferred to **Dallas** after **Minnesota** franchise relocated, June 9, 1993. Signed as a free agent by **Ottawa**, July 13, 2001.

RICHARDSON, Luke

(RIH-chahrd-sohn, LEWK) **PHI.**

Defense. Shoots left. 6'4", 210 lbs. Born, Ottawa, Ont., March 26, 1969. Toronto's 1st choice, 7th overall, in 1987 Entry Draft.

1984-85	Ottawa Knights	OMHL	35	5	26	31	72																			
1985-86	Peterborough	OHL	63	6	18	24	57												16	2	1	3	50			
1986-87	Peterborough	OHL	59	13	32	45	70												12	0	5	5	24			
1987-88	**Toronto**	**NHL**	**78**	**4**	**6**	**10**	**90**	**0**	**0**	**0**	**49**	**8.2**	**−25**						**2**	**0**	**0**	**0**	**0**	**0**	**0**	**0**
1988-89	**Toronto**	**NHL**	**55**	**2**	**7**	**9**	**106**	**0**	**0**	**0**	**59**	**3.4**	**−15**													
1989-90	**Toronto**	**NHL**	**67**	**4**	**14**	**18**	**122**	**0**	**0**	**0**	**80**	**5.0**	**−1**						**5**	**0**	**0**	**0**	**22**	**0**	**0**	**0**
1990-91	**Toronto**	**NHL**	**78**	**1**	**9**	**10**	**238**	**0**	**0**	**0**	**68**	**1.5**	**−28**													
1991-92	**Edmonton**	**NHL**	**75**	**2**	**19**	**21**	**118**	**0**	**0**	**0**	**85**	**2.4**	**−9**						**16**	**0**	**5**	**5**	**45**	**0**	**0**	**0**
1992-93	**Edmonton**	**NHL**	**82**	**3**	**10**	**13**	**142**	**0**	**2**	**0**	**78**	**3.8**	**−18**													
1993-94	**Edmonton**	**NHL**	**69**	**2**	**6**	**8**	**131**	**0**	**0**	**0**	**92**	**2.2**	**−13**													
1994-95	**Edmonton**	**NHL**	**46**	**3**	**10**	**13**	**40**	**1**	**1**	**1**	**51**	**5.9**	**−6**													
1995-96	**Edmonton**	**NHL**	**82**	**2**	**9**	**11**	**108**	**0**	**0**	**0**	**61**	**3.3**	**−27**													
1996-97	**Edmonton**	**NHL**	**82**	**1**	**11**	**12**	**91**	**0**	**0**	**0**	**67**	**1.5**	**9**						**12**	**0**	**2**	**2**	**14**	**0**	**0**	**0**
1997-98	**Philadelphia**	**NHL**	**81**	**2**	**3**	**5**	**139**	**2**	**0**	**0**	**57**	**3.5**	**7**						**5**	**0**	**0**	**0**	**0**	**0**	**0**	**0**
1998-99	**Philadelphia**	**NHL**	**78**	**0**	**6**	**6**	**106**	**0**	**0**	**0**	**49**	**0.0**	**−3**	**0**	**0.0**	**116**	**94**	**16:33**								

			Regular Season																Playoffs							
Season	Club	League	GP	G	A	Pts	PIM	PP	SH	GW	S	%	+/-	TF	F%	H	SB	Min	GP	G	A	Pts	PIM	PP	SH	GW
99-2000	Philadelphia	NHL	74	2	5	7	140	0	0	1	50	4.0	14	0	0.0	125	109	16:11	18	0	1	1	41	0	0	0
2000-01	Philadelphia	NHL	82	2	6	8	131	0	1	0	75	2.7	23	1	0.0	148	125	20:42	6	0	0	0	4	0	0	0
	NHL Totals		1029	30	121	151	1702	3	4	2	921	3.3		1	0.0	389	328	17:53	64	0	8	8	126	0	0	0

Traded to **Edmonton** by **Toronto** with Vincent Damphousse, Peter Ing and Scott Thornton for Grant Fuhr, Glenn Anderson and Craig Berube, September 19, 1991. Signed as a free agent by **Philadelphia**, July 23, 1997.

RICHER, Stephane

(REE-shay, STEH-fan) **PIT.**

Right wing. Shoots right. 6'2", 215 lbs. Born, Ripon, Que., June 7, 1966. Montreal's 3rd choice, 29th overall, in 1984 Entry Draft.

Season	Club	League	GP	G	A	Pts	PIM	PP	SH	GW	S	%	+/-	TF	F%	H	SB	Min	GP	G	A	Pts	PIM	PP	SH	GW
1982-83	Laval Insulaires	QAAA	48	47	54	101	86	....	....	....	....	....	....	....	....	....	....	....	....	....	....	....	....	....	....	....
1983-84	Granby Bisons	QMJHL	67	39	37	76	58	....	....	....	....	....	....	....	....	....	....	....	3	1	1	2	4	....	....	....
1984-85	Granby Bisons	QMJHL	30	30	27	57	31	....	....	....	....	....	....	....	....	....	....	....	....	....	....	....	....	....	....	....
	Chicoutimi	QMJHL	27	31	32	63	40	....	....	....	....	....	....	....	....	....	....	....	12	13	13	26	25	....	....	....
	Montreal	**NHL**	**1**	**0**	**0**	**0**	**0**	**0**	**0**	**0**	**0**	**0.0**	**0**	....	....	....	....	....	....	....	....	....	....	....	....	....
	Sherbrooke	AHL	....	....	....	....	....	....	....	....	....	....	....	....	....	....	....	....	9	6	3	9	10	....	....	....
1985-86♦	**Montreal**	**NHL**	**65**	**21**	**16**	**37**	**50**	**5**	**0**	**2**	**112**	**18.8**	**1**	....	....	....	....	....	**16**	**4**	**1**	**5**	**23**	**3**	**0**	**1**
1986-87	**Montreal**	**NHL**	**57**	**20**	**19**	**39**	**80**	**4**	**0**	**3**	**109**	**18.3**	**11**	....	....	....	....	....	**5**	**3**	**2**	**5**	**0**	**0**	**0**	**1**
	Sherbrooke	AHL	12	10	4	14	11	....	....	....	....	....	....	....	....	....	....	....	....	....	....	....	....	....	....	....
1987-88	**Montreal**	**NHL**	**72**	**50**	**28**	**78**	**72**	**16**	**0**	**11**	**263**	**19.0**	**12**	....	....	....	....	....	**8**	**7**	**5**	**12**	**6**	**1**	**0**	**2**
1988-89	**Montreal**	**NHL**	**68**	**25**	**35**	**60**	**61**	**11**	**0**	**6**	**214**	**11.7**	**4**	....	....	....	....	....	**21**	**6**	**5**	**11**	**14**	**2**	**0**	**3**
1989-90	**Montreal**	**NHL**	**75**	**51**	**40**	**91**	**46**	**9**	**0**	**8**	**269**	**19.0**	**35**	....	....	....	....	....	**9**	**7**	**3**	**10**	**2**	**1**	**0**	**1**
1990-91	**Montreal**	**NHL**	**75**	**31**	**30**	**61**	**53**	**9**	**0**	**4**	**221**	**14.0**	**0**	....	....	....	....	....	**13**	**9**	**5**	**14**	**6**	**1**	**0**	**1**
1991-92	**New Jersey**	**NHL**	**74**	**29**	**35**	**64**	**25**	**5**	**1**	**6**	**240**	**12.1**	**–1**	....	....	....	....	....	**7**	**1**	**2**	**3**	**0**	**0**	**0**	**0**
1992-93	**New Jersey**	**NHL**	**78**	**38**	**35**	**73**	**44**	**7**	**1**	**7**	**286**	**13.3**	**–1**	....	....	....	....	....	**5**	**2**	**2**	**4**	**2**	**1**	**0**	**0**
1993-94	**New Jersey**	**NHL**	**80**	**36**	**36**	**72**	**16**	**7**	**3**	**9**	**217**	**16.6**	**31**	....	....	....	....	....	**20**	**7**	**5**	**12**	**6**	**3**	**0**	**2**
1994-95♦	**New Jersey**	**NHL**	**45**	**23**	**16**	**39**	**10**	**1**	**2**	**5**	**133**	**17.3**	**8**	....	....	....	....	....	**19**	**6**	**15**	**21**	**2**	**3**	**1**	**2**
1995-96	**New Jersey**	**NHL**	**73**	**20**	**12**	**32**	**30**	**3**	**4**	**3**	**192**	**10.4**	**–8**	....	....	....	....	....	....	....	....	....	....	....	....	....
1996-97	**Montreal**	**NHL**	**63**	**22**	**24**	**46**	**32**	**2**	**0**	**2**	**126**	**17.5**	**0**	....	....	....	....	....	**5**	**0**	**0**	**0**	**0**	**0**	**0**	**0**
1997-98	**Montreal**	**NHL**	**14**	**5**	**4**	**9**	**5**	**2**	**0**	**0**	**24**	**20.8**	**1**	....	....	....	....	....	....	....	....	....	....	....	....	....
	Tampa Bay	**NHL**	**26**	**9**	**11**	**20**	**36**	**3**	**0**	**2**	**71**	**12.7**	**–7**	....	....	....	....	....	....	....	....	....	....	....	....	....
1998-99	**Tampa Bay**	**NHL**	**64**	**12**	**21**	**33**	**22**	**3**	**2**	**1**	**139**	**8.6**	**–10**	**67**	**31.3**	**32**	**11**	**16:47**	....	....	....	....	....	....	....	....
99-2000	**Tampa Bay**	**NHL**	**20**	**7**	**5**	**12**	**4**	**1**	**0**	**0**	**47**	**14.9**	**2**	**7**	**57.1**	**14**	**6**	**14:31**	....	....	....	....	....	....	....	....
	Detroit Vipers	IHL	2	0	0	0	0	....	....	....	....	....	....	....	....	....	....	....	....	....	....	....	....	....	....	....
	St. Louis	**NHL**	**36**	**8**	**17**	**25**	**14**	**4**	**0**	**1**	**63**	**12.7**	**7**	**0**	**0.0**	**21**	**3**	**13:27**	**3**	**1**	**0**	**1**	**0**	**0**	**0**	**0**
2000-01			DID NOT PLAY																							
	NHL Totals		**986**	**407**	**384**	**791**	**600**	**92**	**13**	**70**	**2726**	**14.9**		**74**	**33.8**	**67**	**20**	**15:24**	**131**	**53**	**45**	**98**	**61**	**15**	**1**	**13**

QMJHL Rookie of the Year (1984) • QMJHL Second All-Star Team (1985) • Played in NHL All-Star Game (1990)

Traded to **New Jersey** by **Montreal** with Tom Chorske for Kirk Muller and Rollie Melanson, September 20, 1991. Traded to **Montreal** by **New Jersey** for Lyle Odelein, August 22, 1996. Traded to **Tampa Bay** by **Montreal** with Darcy Tucker and David Wilkie for Patrick Poulin, Mick Vukota and Igor Ulanov, January 15, 1998. Traded to **St. Louis** by **Tampa Bay** for Rich Parent and Chris McAlpine, January 13, 2000. Signed as a free agent by **Washington**, August 25, 2000. • Accepted invitation to training camp with **Pittsburgh**, August 9, 2001.

RICHTER, Barry

(RIHK-tuhr, BAIR-ree)

Defense. Shoots left. 6'2", 200 lbs. Born, Madison, WI, September 11, 1970. Hartford's 2nd choice, 32nd overall, in 1988 Entry Draft.

Season	Club	League	GP	G	A	Pts	PIM	PP	SH	GW	S	%	+/-	TF	F%	H	SB	Min	GP	G	A	Pts	PIM	PP	SH	GW
1986-87	Culver Academy	Hi-School	39	15	30	45	....	....	....	....	....	....	....	....	....	....	....	....	....	....	....	....	....	....	....	....
1987-88	Culver Academy	Hi-School	35	24	29	53	18	....	....	....	....	....	....	....	....	....	....	....	....	....	....	....	....	....	....	....
1988-89	Culver Academy	Hi-School	19	21	29	50	16	....	....	....	....	....	....	....	....	....	....	....	....	....	....	....	....	....	....	....
1989-90	U. of Wisconsin	WCHA	42	13	23	36	36	....	....	....	....	....	....	....	....	....	....	....	....	....	....	....	....	....	....	....
1990-91	U. of Wisconsin	WCHA	43	15	20	35	42	....	....	....	....	....	....	....	....	....	....	....	....	....	....	....	....	....	....	....
1991-92	U. of Wisconsin	WCHA	39	10	25	35	62	....	....	....	....	....	....	....	....	....	....	....	....	....	....	....	....	....	....	....
1992-93	U. of Wisconsin	WCHA	42	14	32	46	74	....	....	....	....	....	....	....	....	....	....	....	....	....	....	....	....	....	....	....
1993-94	United States	Nat-Team	56	7	16	23	50	....	....	....	....	....	....	....	....	....	....	....	....	....	....	....	....	....	....	....
	United States	Olympics	8	0	3	3	4	....	....	....	....	....	....	....	....	....	....	....	....	....	....	....	....	....	....	....
	Binghamton	AHL	21	0	9	9	12	....	....	....	....	....	....	....	....	....	....	....	....	....	....	....	....	....	....	....
1994-95	Binghamton	AHL	73	15	41	56	54	....	....	....	....	....	....	....	....	....	....	....	11	4	5	9	12	....	....	....
1995-96	**NY Rangers**	**NHL**	**4**	**0**	**1**	**1**	**0**	**0**	**0**	**0**	**3**	**0.0**	**2**	....	....	....	....	....	....	....	....	....	....	....	....	....
	Binghamton	AHL	69	20	61	81	64	....	....	....	....	....	....	....	....	....	....	....	3	0	3	3	0	....	....	....
1996-97	**Boston**	**NHL**	**50**	**5**	**13**	**18**	**32**	**1**	**0**	**0**	**79**	**6.3**	**–7**	....	....	....	....	....	....	....	....	....	....	....	....	....
	Providence Bruins	AHL	19	2	6	8	4	....	....	....	....	....	....	....	....	....	....	....	10	4	4	8	4	....	....	....
1997-98	Providence Bruins	AHL	75	16	29	45	47	....	....	....	....	....	....	....	....	....	....	....	....	....	....	....	....	....	....	....
1998-99	**NY Islanders**	**NHL**	**72**	**6**	**18**	**24**	**34**	**0**	**0**	**2**	**111**	**5.4**	**–4**	**0**	**0.0**	**52**	**49**	**21:08**	....	....	....	....	....	....	....	....
99-2000	**Montreal**	**NHL**	**23**	**0**	**2**	**2**	**8**	**0**	**0**	**0**	**13**	**0.0**	**–5**	**1**	**100.0**	**20**	**13**	**12:15**	....	....	....	....	....	....	....	....
	Quebec Citadelles	AHL	2	0	0	0	0	....	....	....	....	....	....	....	....	....	....	....	....	....	....	....	....	....	....	....
	Manitoba Moose	IHL	19	5	4	9	6	....	....	....	....	....	....	....	....	....	....	....	2	1	1	2	0	....	....	....
2000-01	**Montreal**	**NHL**	**2**	**0**	**0**	**0**	**2**	**0**	**0**	**0**	**0**	**0.0**	**–1**	**0**	**0.0**	**0**	**0**	**10:44**	....	....	....	....	....	....	....	....
	Quebec Citadelles	AHL	68	4	47	51	45	....	....	....	....	....	....	....	....	....	....	....	6	0	3	3	2	....	....	....
	NHL Totals		**151**	**11**	**34**	**45**	**76**	**1**	**0**	**2**	**206**	**5.3**		**1**	**100.0**	**72**	**62**	**18:49**	....	....	....	....	....	....	....	....

NCAA Championship All-Tournament Team (1992) • WCHA First All-Star Team (1993) • NCAA West First All-American Team (1993) • AHL First All-Star Team (1996) • Won Eddie Shore Award (Top Defenseman - AHL) (1996)

Traded to **NY Rangers** by **Hartford** with Steve Larmer, Nick Kypreos and Hartford's 6th round choice (Yuri Litvinov) in 1994 Entry Draft for Darren Turcotte and James Patrick, November 2, 1993. Signed as a free agent by **Boston**, July 19, 1996. Signed as a free agent by **NY Islanders**, August 17, 1998. Signed as a free agent by **Montreal**, August 20, 1999. Loaned to **Manitoba** (IHL) by **Montreal** for loan of Patrice Tardif to **Quebec** (AHL), March 3, 2000.

RIESEN, Michel

(REE-sehn, MEE-shehl) **ST.L.**

Right wing. Shoots right. 6'2", 190 lbs. Born, Oberbalm, Switzerland, April 11, 1979. Edmonton's 1st choice, 14th overall, in 1997 Entry Draft.

Season	Club	League	GP	G	A	Pts	PIM	PP	SH	GW	S	%	+/-	TF	F%	H	SB	Min	GP	G	A	Pts	PIM	PP	SH	GW
1994-95	EHC Biel-Bienne	Switz.	12	0	2	2	0	....	....	....	....	....	....	....	....	....	....	....	6	2	0	2	0	....	....	....
1995-96	EHC Biel-Bienne	Switz-2	34	9	6	15	2	....	....	....	....	....	....	....	....	....	....	....	3	1	0	1	0	....	....	....
1996-97	EHC Biel-Bienne	Switz-2	38	16	16	32	49	....	....	....	....	....	....	....	....	....	....	....	....	....	....	....	....	....	....	....
1997-98	HC Davos	Switz.	32	16	9	25	8	....	....	....	....	....	....	....	....	....	....	....	18	5	5	10	4	....	....	....
1998-99	Hamilton Bulldogs	AHL	60	6	17	23	6	....	....	....	....	....	....	....	....	....	....	....	3	0	0	0	0	....	....	....
99-2000	Hamilton Bulldogs	AHL	73	29	31	60	20	....	....	....	....	....	....	....	....	....	....	....	10	3	5	8	4	....	....	....
2000-01	**Edmonton**	**NHL**	**12**	**0**	**1**	**1**	**4**	**0**	**0**	**0**	**16**	**0.0**	**2**	**0**	**0.0**	**1**	**1**	**9:54**	....	....	....	....	....	....	....	....
	Hamilton Bulldogs	AHL	69	26	28	54	14	....	....	....	....	....	....	....	....	....	....	....	....	....	....	....	....	....	....	....
	NHL Totals		**12**	**0**	**1**	**1**	**4**	**0**	**0**	**0**	**16**	**0.0**		**0**	**0.0**	**1**	**1**	**9:54**	....	....	....	....	....	....	....	....

Traded to **St. Louis** by **Edmonton** with Doug Weight for Marty Reasoner, Jochen Hecht and Jan Horacek, July 1, 2001.

RITCHIE, Byron

(RIHT-chee, BIGH-rohn) **CAR.**

Center. Shoots left. 5'10", 185 lbs. Born, Burnaby, B.C., April 24, 1977. Hartford's 6th choice, 165th overall, in 1995 Entry Draft.

Season	Club	League	GP	G	A	Pts	PIM	PP	SH	GW	S	%	+/-	TF	F%	H	SB	Min	GP	G	A	Pts	PIM	PP	SH	GW
1992-93	North Delta	BCAHA	60	102	151	253	147	....	....	....	....	....	....	....	....	....	....	....	....	....	....	....	....	....	....	....
1993-94	Lethbridge	WHL	44	4	11	15	44	....	....	....	....	....	....	....	....	....	....	....	6	0	0	0	14	....	....	....
1994-95	Lethbridge	WHL	58	22	28	50	132	....	....	....	....	....	....	....	....	....	....	....	....	....	....	....	....	....	....	....
1995-96	Lethbridge	WHL	66	55	51	106	163	....	....	....	....	....	....	....	....	....	....	....	4	0	2	2	4	....	....	....
	Springfield	AHL	6	2	1	3	4	....	....	....	....	....	....	....	....	....	....	....	8	0	3	3	0	....	....	....
1996-97	Lethbridge	WHL	63	50	76	126	115	....	....	....	....	....	....	....	....	....	....	....	18	*16	12	*28	28	....	....	....
1997-98	New Haven	AHL	65	13	18	31	97	....	....	....	....	....	....	....	....	....	....	....	....	....	....	....	....	....	....	....
1998-99	**Carolina**	**NHL**	**3**	**0**	**0**	**0**	**0**	**0**	**0**	**0**	**0**	**0.0**	**0**	**5**	**20.0**	**1**	**0**	**3:25**	....	....	....	....	....	....	....	....
	New Haven	AHL	66	24	33	57	139	....	....	....	....	....	....	....	....	....	....	....	....	....	....	....	....	....	....	....
99-2000	**Carolina**	**NHL**	**26**	**0**	**2**	**2**	**17**	**0**	**0**	**0**	**13**	**0.0**	**–10**	**155**	**49.7**	**33**	**7**	**7:24**	....	....	....	....	....	....	....	....
	Cincinnati	IHL	34	8	13	21	81	....	....	....	....	....	....	....	....	....	....	....	10	1	6	7	32	....	....	....
2000-01	Cincinnati	IHL	77	31	35	66	166	....	....	....	....	....	....	....	....	....	....	....	5	3	2	5	10	....	....	....
	NHL Totals		**29**	**0**	**2**	**2**	**17**	**0**	**0**	**0**	**13**	**0.0**		**160**	**48.8**	**34**	**7**	**6:60**	....	....	....	....	....	....	....	....

WHL East Second All-Star Team (1996, 1997)

Rights transferred to **Carolina** after **Hartford** franchise relocated, June 25, 1997.

RIVERS, Jamie

(RIH-vuhrs, JAY-mee) **OTT.**

Defense. Shoots left. 6'1", 200 lbs. Born, Ottawa, Ont., March 16, 1975. St. Louis' 2nd choice, 63rd overall, in 1993 Entry Draft.

			Regular Season																Playoffs							
Season	Club	League	GP	G	A	Pts	PIM	PP	SH	GW	S	%	+/-	TF	F%	H	SB	Min	GP	G	A	Pts	PIM	PP	SH	GW
1989-90	Ottawa South	OMHA	50	26	46	72	46	....	....	....	....	....	....	....	....	....	....	....	....	....	....	....	....	....	....	....
1990-91	Ottawa Jr. Sens	OCJHL	55	4	30	34	74	....	....	....	....	....	....	....	....	....	....	....	....	....	....	....	....	....	....	....
1991-92	Sudbury Wolves	OHL	55	3	13	16	20	....	....	....	....	....	....	....	....	....	....	....	8	0	0	0	0	....	....	....
1992-93	Sudbury Wolves	OHL	62	12	43	55	20	....	....	....	....	....	....	....	....	....	....	....	14	7	19	26	4	....	....	....
1993-94	Sudbury Wolves	OHL	65	32	*89	121	58	....	....	....	....	....	....	....	....	....	....	....	10	1	9	10	14	....	....	....
1994-95	Sudbury Wolves	OHL	46	9	56	65	30	....	....	....	....	....	....	....	....	....	....	....	18	7	26	33	22	....	....	....
1995-96	**St. Louis**	**NHL**	**3**	**0**	**0**	**0**	**2**	**0**	**0**	**0**	**5**	**0.0**	**–1**	....	....	....	....	....	....	....	....	....	....	....	....	....
	Worcester	AHL	75	7	45	52	130	....	....	....	....	....	....	....	....	....	....	....	4	0	1	1	4	....	....	....
1996-97	**St. Louis**	**NHL**	**15**	**2**	**5**	**7**	**6**	**1**	**0**	**0**	**9**	**22.2**	**–4**	....	....	....	....	....	....	....	....	....	....	....	....	....
	Worcester	AHL	63	8	35	43	83	....	....	....	....	....	....	....	....	....	....	....	5	1	2	3	14	....	....	....
1997-98	**St. Louis**	**NHL**	**59**	**2**	**4**	**6**	**36**	**1**	**0**	**1**	**53**	**3.8**	**5**	....	....	....	....	....	....	....	....	....	....	....	....	....
1998-99	**St. Louis**	**NHL**	**76**	**2**	**5**	**7**	**47**	**1**	**0**	**0**	**78**	**2.6**	**–3**	**0**	**0.0**	**131**	**63**	**14:10**	**9**	**1**	**1**	**2**	**2**	**1**	**0**	**1**
99-2000	**NY Islanders**	**NHL**	**75**	**1**	**16**	**17**	**84**	**1**	**0**	**0**	**95**	**1.1**	**–4**	**0**	**0.0**	**219**	**112**	**19:39**	....	....	....	....	....	....	....	....
2000-01	Grand Rapids	IHL	2	0	0	0	2	....	....	....	....	....	....	....	....	....	....	....	....	....	....	....	....	....	....	....
	Ottawa	**NHL**	**45**	**2**	**4**	**6**	**44**	**0**	**0**	**0**	**41**	**4.9**	**6**	**0**	**0.0**	**115**	**41**	**14:01**	**1**	**0**	**0**	**0**	**4**	**0**	**0**	**0**
	NHL Totals		**273**	**9**	**34**	**43**	**219**	**4**	**0**	**1**	**281**	**3.2**		**0**	**0.0**	**465**	**216**	**16:14**	**10**	**1**	**1**	**2**	**6**	**1**	**0**	**1**

OHL First All-Star Team (1994) • Canadian Major Junior Second All-Star Team (1994) • OHL Second All-Star Team (1995) • AHL Second All-Star Team (1997)

Claimed by **NY Islanders** from **St. Louis** in Waiver Draft, September 27, 1999. Signed as a free agent by **Ottawa**, November 30, 2000.

RIVET, Craig

(rih-VAY, KRAYG) **MTL.**

Defense. Shoots right. 6'2", 207 lbs. Born, North Bay, Ont., September 13, 1974. Montreal's 4th choice, 68th overall, in 1992 Entry Draft.

			Regular Season																Playoffs							
Season	Club	League	GP	G	A	Pts	PIM	PP	SH	GW	S	%	+/-	TF	F%	H	SB	Min	GP	G	A	Pts	PIM	PP	SH	GW
1990-91	Barrie Colts	OJHL-B	42	9	17	26	55	....	....	....	....	....	....	....	....	....	....	....	....	....	....	....	....	....	....	....
1991-92	Kingston	OHL	66	5	21	26	97	....	....	....	....	....	....	....	....	....	....	....	....	....	....	....	....	....	....	....
1992-93	Kingston	OHL	64	19	55	74	117	....	....	....	....	....	....	....	....	....	....	....	16	5	7	12	39	....	....	....
1993-94	Kingston	OHL	61	12	52	64	100	....	....	....	....	....	....	....	....	....	....	....	6	0	3	3	6	....	....	....
	Fredericton	AHL	4	0	2	2	2	....	....	....	....	....	....	....	....	....	....	....	....	....	....	....	....	....	....	....
1994-95	Fredericton	AHL	78	5	27	32	126	....	....	....	....	....	....	....	....	....	....	....	12	0	4	4	17	....	....	....
	Montreal	**NHL**	**5**	**0**	**1**	**1**	**5**	**0**	**0**	**0**	**2**	**0.0**	**2**	....	....	....	....	....	....	....	....	....	....	....	....	....
1995-96	**Montreal**	**NHL**	**19**	**1**	**4**	**5**	**54**	**0**	**0**	**0**	**9**	**11.1**	**4**	....	....	....	....	....	....	....	....	....	....	....	....	....
	Fredericton	AHL	49	5	18	23	189	....	....	....	....	....	....	....	....	....	....	....	6	0	0	0	12	....	....	....
1996-97	**Montreal**	**NHL**	**35**	**0**	**4**	**4**	**54**	**0**	**0**	**0**	**24**	**0.0**	**7**	....	....	....	....	....	**5**	**0**	**1**	**1**	**14**	**0**	**0**	**0**
	Fredericton	AHL	23	3	12	15	99	....	....	....	....	....	....	....	....	....	....	....	....	....	....	....	....	....	....	....
1997-98	**Montreal**	**NHL**	**61**	**0**	**2**	**2**	**93**	**0**	**0**	**0**	**26**	**0.0**	**–3**	....	....	....	....	....	**5**	**0**	**0**	**0**	**2**	**0**	**0**	**0**
1998-99	**Montreal**	**NHL**	**66**	**2**	**8**	**10**	**66**	**0**	**0**	**0**	**39**	**5.1**	**–3**	**0**	**0.0**	**78**	**40**	**14:20**	....	....	....	....	....	....	....	....
99-2000	**Montreal**	**NHL**	**61**	**3**	**14**	**17**	**76**	**0**	**0**	**1**	**71**	**4.2**	**11**	**0**	**0.0**	**80**	**59**	**19:03**	....	....	....	....	....	....	....	....
2000-01	**Montreal**	**NHL**	**26**	**1**	**2**	**3**	**36**	**0**	**0**	**0**	**22**	**4.5**	**–8**	**0**	**0.0**	**38**	**31**	**19:04**	....	....	....	....	....	....	....	....
	NHL Totals		**273**	**7**	**35**	**42**	**384**	**0**	**0**	**1**	**193**	**3.6**		**0**	**0.0**	**196**	**130**	**17:01**	**10**	**0**	**1**	**1**	**16**	**0**	**0**	**0**

• Missed majority of 2000-01 season recovering from shoulder injury suffered in game vs. Vancouver, October 30, 2000.

ROBERTS, Gary

(RAW-buhrts, GAIR-ree) **TOR.**

Left wing. Shoots left. 6'1", 190 lbs. Born, North York, Ont., May 23, 1966. Calgary's 1st choice, 12th overall, in 1984 Entry Draft.

			Regular Season																Playoffs							
Season	Club	League	GP	G	A	Pts	PIM	PP	SH	GW	S	%	+/-	TF	F%	H	SB	Min	GP	G	A	Pts	PIM	PP	SH	GW
1980-81	Hamilton Kilty B's	OHA-B	3	0	1	1	0	....	....	....	....	....	....	....	....	....	....	....	....	....	....	....	....	....	....	....
1981-82	Whitby Selects	OMHA	44	55	31	86	133	....	....	....	....	....	....	....	....	....	....	....	....	....	....	....	....	....	....	....
1982-83	Ottawa 67's	OHL	53	12	8	20	83	....	....	....	....	....	....	....	....	....	....	....	5	1	0	1	19	....	....	....
1983-84	Ottawa 67's	OHL	48	27	30	57	144	....	....	....	....	....	....	....	....	....	....	....	13	10	7	17	62	....	....	....
1984-85	Ottawa 67's	OHL	59	44	62	106	186	....	....	....	....	....	....	....	....	....	....	....	5	2	8	10	10	....	....	....
	Moncton Flames	AHL	7	4	2	6	7	....	....	....	....	....	....	....	....	....	....	....	....	....	....	....	....	....	....	....
1985-86	Ottawa 67's	OHL	24	26	25	51	83	....	....	....	....	....	....	....	....	....	....	....	....	....	....	....	....	....	....	....
	Guelph Platers	OHL	23	18	15	33	65	....	....	....	....	....	....	....	....	....	....	....	20	18	13	31	43	....	....	....
1986-87	**Calgary**	**NHL**	**32**	**5**	**10**	**15**	**85**	**0**	**0**	**0**	**38**	**13.2**	**6**	....	....	....	....	....	**2**	**0**	**0**	**0**	**4**	**0**	**0**	**0**
	Moncton Flames	AHL	38	20	18	38	72	....	....	....	....	....	....	....	....	....	....	....	....	....	....	....	....	....	....	....
1987-88	**Calgary**	**NHL**	**74**	**13**	**15**	**28**	**282**	**0**	**0**	**1**	**118**	**11.0**	**24**	....	....	....	....	....	**9**	**2**	**3**	**5**	**29**	**0**	**0**	**0**
1988-89♦	**Calgary**	**NHL**	**71**	**22**	**16**	**38**	**250**	**0**	**1**	**2**	**123**	**17.9**	**32**	....	....	....	....	....	**22**	**5**	**7**	**12**	**57**	**0**	**0**	**0**
1989-90	**Calgary**	**NHL**	**78**	**39**	**33**	**72**	**222**	**5**	**0**	**5**	**175**	**22.3**	**31**	....	....	....	....	....	**6**	**2**	**5**	**7**	**41**	**0**	**0**	**0**
1990-91	**Calgary**	**NHL**	**80**	**22**	**31**	**53**	**252**	**0**	**0**	**3**	**132**	**16.7**	**15**	....	....	....	....	....	**7**	**1**	**3**	**4**	**18**	**0**	**0**	**0**
1991-92	**Calgary**	**NHL**	**76**	**53**	**37**	**90**	**207**	**15**	**0**	**2**	**196**	**27.0**	**32**	....	....	....	....	....	....	....	....	....	....	....	....	....
1992-93	**Calgary**	**NHL**	**58**	**38**	**41**	**79**	**172**	**8**	**3**	**4**	**166**	**22.9**	**32**	....	....	....	....	....	**5**	**1**	**6**	**7**	**43**	**1**	**0**	**0**
1993-94	**Calgary**	**NHL**	**73**	**41**	**43**	**84**	**145**	**12**	**3**	**5**	**202**	**20.3**	**37**	....	....	....	....	....	**7**	**2**	**6**	**8**	**24**	**1**	**0**	**1**
1994-95	**Calgary**	**NHL**	**8**	**2**	**2**	**4**	**43**	**2**	**0**	**0**	**20**	**10.0**	**1**	....	....	....	....	....	....	....	....	....	....	....	....	....
1995-96	**Calgary**	**NHL**	**35**	**22**	**20**	**42**	**78**	**9**	**0**	**5**	**84**	**26.2**	**15**	....	....	....	....	....	....	....	....	....	....	....	....	....
1996-97	**Calgary**	**NHL**	DID NOT PLAY – INJURED																							
1997-98	**Carolina**	**NHL**	**61**	**20**	**29**	**49**	**103**	**4**	**0**	**2**	**106**	**18.9**	**3**	....	....	....	....	....	....	....	....	....	....	....	....	....
1998-99	**Carolina**	**NHL**	**77**	**14**	**28**	**42**	**178**	**1**	**1**	**4**	**138**	**10.1**	**2**	**15**	**46.7**	**260**	**16**	**19:36**	**6**	**1**	**1**	**2**	**8**	**0**	**0**	**0**
99-2000	**Carolina**	**NHL**	**69**	**23**	**30**	**53**	**62**	**12**	**0**	**1**	**150**	**15.3**	**–10**	**7**	**28.6**	**212**	**27**	**18:31**	....	....	....	....	....	....	....	....
2000-01	**Toronto**	**NHL**	**82**	**29**	**24**	**53**	**109**	**8**	**2**	**3**	**138**	**21.0**	**16**	**13**	**46.2**	**206**	**17**	**17:08**	**11**	**2**	**9**	**11**	**0**	**0**	**0**	**0**
	NHL Totals		**874**	**343**	**359**	**702**	**2188**	**76**	**10**	**37**	**1786**	**19.2**		**35**	**42.9**	**678**	**60**	**18:23**	**75**	**16**	**40**	**56**	**224**	**2**	**0**	**1**

OHL Second All-Star Team (1985, 1986) • Won Bill Masterton Memorial Trophy (1996) • Played in NHL All-Star Game (1992, 1993)

• Missed remainder of 1994-95 and majority of 1995-96 seasons recovering from neck injury suffered in game vs. Toronto, February 4, 1995. • Missed remainder of 1995-96 and entire 1996-97 seasons recovering from neck injury suffered in game vs. Vancouver, April 3, 1996. Traded to **Carolina** by **Calgary** with Trevor Kidd for Andrew Cassels and Jean-Sebastien Giguere, August 25, 1997. Signed as a free agent by **Toronto**, July 4, 2000.

ROBERTSSON, Bert

(ROH-behrt-suhn, BUHRT) **NSH.**

Defense. Shoots left. 6'3", 205 lbs. Born, Sodertalje, Sweden, June 30, 1974. Vancouver's 8th choice, 254th overall, in 1993 Entry Draft.

			Regular Season																Playoffs							
Season	Club	League	GP	G	A	Pts	PIM	PP	SH	GW	S	%	+/-	TF	F%	H	SB	Min	GP	G	A	Pts	PIM	PP	SH	GW
1992-93	Sodertalje SK	Swede-Jr.	12	1	5	6	20	....	....	....	....	....	....	....	....	....	....	....	....	....	....	....	....	....	....	....
	Sodertalje SK	Sweden-2	23	2	1	3	24	....	....	....	....	....	....	....	....	....	....	....	2	0	0	0	0	....	....	....
1993-94	Sodertalje SK	Sweden-2	28	0	1	1	12	....	....	....	....	....	....	....	....	....	....	....	1	0	0	0	0	....	....	....
1994-95	Sodertalje SK	Swede-Jr.	11	2	3	5	4	....	....	....	....	....	....	....	....	....	....	....	....	....	....	....	....	....	....	....
	Sodertalje SK	Sweden-2	23	1	2	3	24	....	....	....	....	....	....	....	....	....	....	....	3	0	1	1	2	....	....	....
1995-96	Syracuse Crunch	AHL	65	1	7	8	109	....	....	....	....	....	....	....	....	....	....	....	16	0	1	1	26	....	....	....
1996-97	Syracuse Crunch	AHL	80	4	9	13	132	....	....	....	....	....	....	....	....	....	....	....	3	1	0	1	4	....	....	....
1997-98	**Vancouver**	**NHL**	**30**	**2**	**4**	**6**	**24**	**0**	**0**	**0**	**19**	**10.5**	**2**	....	....	....	....	....	....	....	....	....	....	....	....	....
	Syracuse Crunch	AHL	42	5	9	14	87	....	....	....	....	....	....	....	....	....	....	....	3	0	0	0	6	....	....	....
1998-99	**Vancouver**	**NHL**	**39**	**2**	**2**	**4**	**13**	**0**	**0**	**0**	**13**	**15.4**	**–7**	**0**	**0.0**	**28**	**6**	**7:26**	....	....	....	....	....	....	....	....
	Syracuse Crunch	AHL	8	1	0	1	21	....	....	....	....	....	....	....	....	....	....	....	....	....	....	....	....	....	....	....
99-2000	**Edmonton**	**NHL**	**52**	**0**	**4**	**4**	**34**	**0**	**0**	**0**	**31**	**0.0**	**–3**	**3**	**0.0**	**62**	**28**	**10:49**	**5**	**0**	**0**	**0**	**0**	**0**	**0**	**0**
	Hamilton Bulldogs	AHL	6	0	3	3	12	....	....	....	....	....	....	....	....	....	....	....	....	....	....	....	....	....	....	....
2000-01	**NY Rangers**	**NHL**	**2**	**0**	**0**	**0**	**4**	**0**	**0**	**0**	**0**	**0.0**	**–1**	**0**	**0.0**	**4**	**0**	**5:37**	....	....	....	....	....	....	....	....
	Hartford	AHL	27	7	5	12	27	....	....	....	....	....	....	....	....	....	....	....	....	....	....	....	....	....	....	....
	Houston Aeros	IHL	14	0	0	0	26	....	....	....	....	....	....	....	....	....	....	....	....	....	....	....	....	....	....	....
	Milwaukee	IHL	10	0	0	0	0	....	....	....	....	....	....	....	....	....	....	....	5	0	1	1	2	....	....	....
	NHL Totals		**123**	**4**	**10**	**14**	**75**	**0**	**0**	**0**	**63**	**6.3**		**3**	**0.0**	**94**	**34**	**9:17**	**5**	**0**	**0**	**0**	**0**	**0**	**0**	**0**

Signed as a free agent by **Edmonton**, August 19, 1999. Selected by **Columbus** from **Edmonton** in Expansion Draft, June 23, 2000. Traded to **NY Rangers** by **Columbus** for Jean-Francois Labbe, November 9, 2000. Traded to **Nashville** by **NY Rangers** for Ryan Tobler, March 7, 2001.

ROBIDAS, Stephane

(ROH-bih-dah, STEH-fan) **MTL.**

Defense. Shoots right. 5'11", 189 lbs. Born, Sherbrooke, Que., March 3, 1977. Montreal's 7th choice, 164th overall, in 1995 Entry Draft.

			Regular Season																Playoffs							
Season	Club	League	GP	G	A	Pts	PIM	PP	SH	GW	S	%	+/-	TF	F%	H	SB	Min	GP	G	A	Pts	PIM	PP	SH	GW
1992-93	Magog Selectes	QAAA	41	3	12	15	16	....	....	....	....	....	....	....	....	....	....	....	5	1	1	2	2	....	....	....
1993-94	Shawinigan	QMJHL	67	3	18	21	33	....	....	....	....	....	....	....	....	....	....	....	1	0	0	0	0	....	....	....
1994-95	Shawinigan	QMJHL	71	13	56	69	44	....	....	....	....	....	....	....	....	....	....	....	15	7	12	19	4	....	....	....
1995-96	Shawinigan	QMJHL	67	23	56	79	53	....	....	....	....	....	....	....	....	....	....	....	6	1	5	6	10	....	....	....
1996-97	Shawinigan	QMJHL	67	24	51	75	59	....	....	....	....	....	....	....	....	....	....	....	7	4	6	10	14	....	....	....
1997-98	Fredericton	AHL	79	10	21	31	50	....	....	....	....	....	....	....	....	....	....	....	4	0	2	2	0	....	....	....
1998-99	Fredericton	AHL	79	8	33	41	59	....	....	....	....	....	....	....	....	....	....	....	15	1	5	6	10	....	....	....

Season	Club	League	GP	G	A	Pts	PIM	PP	SH	GW	S	%	+/-	TF	F%	H	SB	Min	Playoffs GP	G	A	Pts	PIM	PP	SH	GW
99-2000	Montreal	NHL	1	0	0	0	0	0	0	0	0	0.0	0	0	0.0	1	1	15:54	....	....	....	....	....	....	....	....
	Quebec Citadelles	AHL	76	14	31	45	36	....	....	....	....	....	....	....	....	....	....	....	3	0	1	1	0	....	....	....
2000-01	Montreal	NHL	65	6	6	12	14	1	0	0	77	7.8	0	1	100.0	115	83	20:44	....	....	....	....	....	....	....	....
	NHL Totals		66	6	6	12	14	1	0	0	77	7.8		1	100.0	116	84	20:40	....	....	....	....	....	....	....	....

QMJHL First All-Star Team (1996, 1997)

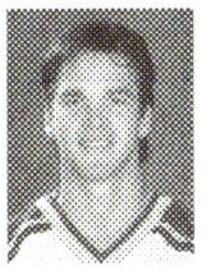

ROBITAILLE, Luc

(ROH-buh-tigh, LEWK) **DET.**

Left wing. Shoots left. 6'1", 215 lbs. Born, Montreal, Que., February 17, 1966. Los Angeles' 9th choice, 171st overall, in 1984 Entry Draft.

Season	Club	League	GP	G	A	Pts	PIM	PP	SH	GW	S	%	+/-	TF	F%	H	SB	Min	Playoffs GP	G	A	Pts	PIM	PP	SH	GW
1982-83	Mtl-Bourassa	QAAA	48	36	57	93	28	....	....	....	....	....	....	....	....	....	....	....	7	9	6	15	14	....	....	....
1983-84	Hull Olympiques	QMJHL	70	32	53	85	48	....	....	....	....	....	....	....	....	....	....	....	....	....	....	....	....	....	....	....
1984-85	Hull Olympiques	QMJHL	64	55	94	149	115	....	....	....	....	....	....	....	....	....	....	....	5	4	2	6	27	....	....	....
1985-86	Hull Olympiques	QMJHL	63	68	123	191	91	....	....	....	....	....	....	....	....	....	....	....	15	17	27	44	28	....	....	....
1986-87	Los Angeles	NHL	79	45	39	84	28	18	0	3	199	22.6	–18	....	....	....	....	....	5	1	4	5	2	0	0	0
1987-88	Los Angeles	NHL	80	53	58	111	82	17	0	6	220	24.1	–9	....	....	....	....	....	5	2	5	7	18	2	0	1
1988-89	Los Angeles	NHL	78	46	52	98	65	10	0	4	237	19.4	5	....	....	....	....	....	11	2	6	8	10	0	0	1
1989-90	Los Angeles	NHL	80	52	49	101	38	20	0	7	210	24.8	8	....	....	....	....	....	10	5	5	10	10	1	0	1
1990-91	Los Angeles	NHL	76	45	46	91	68	11	0	5	229	19.7	28	....	....	....	....	....	12	12	4	16	22	5	0	2
1991-92	Los Angeles	NHL	80	44	63	107	95	26	0	6	240	18.3	–4	....	....	....	....	....	6	3	4	7	12	1	0	1
1992-93	Los Angeles	NHL	84	63	62	125	100	24	2	8	265	23.8	18	....	....	....	....	....	24	9	13	22	28	4	0	2
1993-94	Los Angeles	NHL	83	44	42	86	86	24	0	3	267	16.5	–20	....	....	....	....	....	....	....	....	....	....	....	....	....
1994-95	Pittsburgh	NHL	46	23	19	42	37	5	0	3	109	21.1	10	....	....	....	....	....	12	7	4	11	26	0	0	2
1995-96	NY Rangers	NHL	77	23	46	69	80	11	0	4	223	10.3	13	....	....	....	....	....	11	1	5	6	8	0	0	0
1996-97	NY Rangers	NHL	69	24	24	48	48	5	0	4	200	12.0	16	....	....	....	....	....	15	4	7	11	4	0	0	0
1997-98	Los Angeles	NHL	57	16	24	40	66	5	0	7	130	12.3	5	....	....	....	....	....	4	1	2	3	6	0	0	0
1998-99	Los Angeles	NHL	82	39	35	74	54	11	0	7	292	13.4	–1	7	57.1	40	22	19:11	....	....	....	....	....	....	....	....
99-2000	Los Angeles	NHL	71	36	38	74	68	13	0	7	221	16.3	11	10	30.0	29	12	18:34	4	2	2	4	6	0	0	0
2000-01	Los Angeles	NHL	82	37	51	88	66	16	1	4	235	15.7	10	12	33.3	42	11	18:42	13	4	3	7	10	1	0	1
	NHL Totals		1124	590	648	1238	981	216	3	78	3277	18.0		29	37.9	111	45	18:50	132	53	64	117	162	14	0	11

QMJHL Second All-Star Team (1985) • QMJHL First All-Star Team (1986) • Canadian Major Junior Player of the Year (1986) • NHL All-Rookie Team (1987) • NHL Second All-Star Team (1987, 1992, 2001) • Won Calder Memorial Trophy (1987) • NHL First All-Star Team (1988, 1989, 1990, 1991, 1993) • Played in NHL All-Star Game (1988, 1989, 1990, 1991, 1992, 1993, 1999, 2001)

Traded to **Pittsburgh** by **LA Kings** for Rick Tocchet and Pittsburgh's 2nd round choice (Pavel Rosa) in 1995 Entry Draft, July 29, 1994. Traded to **NY Rangers** by **Pittsburgh** with Ulf Samuelsson for Petr Nedved and Sergei Zubov, August 31, 1995. Traded to **LA Kings** by **NY Rangers** for Kevin Stevens, August 28, 1997. Signed as a free agent by **Detroit**, July 5, 2001.

ROBITAILLE, Randy

(ROH-buh-tigh, RAN-dee) **L.A.**

Center. Shoots left. 5'11", 196 lbs. Born, Ottawa, Ont., October 12, 1975.

Season	Club	League	GP	G	A	Pts	PIM	PP	SH	GW	S	%	+/-	TF	F%	H	SB	Min	Playoffs GP	G	A	Pts	PIM	PP	SH	GW
1993-94	Ottawa Jr. Sens	OCJHL	57	33	55	88	31	....	....	....	....	....	....	....	....	....	....	....	....	....	....	....	....	....	....	....
1994-95	Ottawa Jr. Sens	OCJHL	54	48	77	*125	111	....	....	....	....	....	....	....	....	....	....	....	....	....	....	....	....	....	....	....
1995-96	U. of Miami-Ohio	OCJHL	36	14	31	45	26	....	....	....	....	....	....	....	....	....	....	....	....	....	....	....	....	....	....	....
1996-97	U. of Miami-Ohio	CCHA	39	27	34	61	44	....	....	....	....	....	....	....	....	....	....	....	....	....	....	....	....	....	....	....
	Boston	NHL	1	0	0	0	0	0	0	0	0	0.0	0	....	....	....	....	....	....	....	....	....	....	....	....	....
1997-98	Boston	NHL	4	0	0	0	0	0	0	0	5	0.0	–2	....	....	....	....	....	....	....	....	....	....	....	....	....
	Providence Bruins	AHL	48	15	29	44	16	....	....	....	....	....	....	....	....	....	....	....	....	....	....	....	....	....	....	....
1998-99	Boston	NHL	4	0	2	2	0	0	0	0	5	0.0	–1	24	25.0	0	0	10:11	1	0	0	0	0	0	0	0
	Providence Bruins	AHL	74	28	*74	102	34	....	....	....	....	....	....	....	....	....	....	....	19	6	*14	20	20	....	....	....
99-2000	Nashville	NHL	69	11	14	25	10	2	0	1	113	9.7	–13	528	51.5	30	14	12:52	....	....	....	....	....	....	....	....
2000-01	Nashville	NHL	62	9	17	26	12	5	0	0	121	7.4	–11	481	48.4	30	13	14:10	....	....	....	....	....	....	....	....
	Milwaukee	IHL	19	10	23	33	4	....	....	....	....	....	....	....	....	....	....	....	....	....	....	....	....	....	....	....
	NHL Totals		140	20	33	53	22	7	0	1	244	8.2		1033	49.5	60	27	13:23	1	0	0	0	0	0	0	0

OCJHL First All-Star Team (1995) • CCHA First All-Star Team (1997) • NCAA West First All-American Team (1997) • AHL First All-Star Team (1999) • Won Les Cunningham Award (MVP - AHL) (1999)

Signed as a free agent by **Boston**, March 27, 1997. Traded to **Atlanta** by **Boston** for Peter Ferraro, June 25, 1999. Traded to **Nashville** by **Atlanta** for Denny Lambert, August 16, 1999. Signed as a free agent by **LA Kings**, July 6, 2001.

ROCHE, Dave

(ROHSH, DAYV)

Center. Shoots left. 6'4", 230 lbs. Born, Lindsay, Ont., June 13, 1975. Pittsburgh's 3rd choice, 62nd overall, in 1993 Entry Draft.

Season	Club	League	GP	G	A	Pts	PIM	PP	SH	GW	S	%	+/-	TF	F%	H	SB	Min	Playoffs GP	G	A	Pts	PIM	PP	SH	GW
1990-91	Peterborough	OJHL-B	40	22	17	39	86	....	....	....	....	....	....	....	....	....	....	....	....	....	....	....	....	....	....	....
1991-92	Peterborough	OHL	62	10	17	27	134	....	....	....	....	....	....	....	....	....	....	....	10	0	0	0	34	....	....	....
1992-93	Peterborough	OHL	56	40	60	100	105	....	....	....	....	....	....	....	....	....	....	....	21	14	15	29	42	....	....	....
1993-94	Peterborough	OHL	34	15	22	37	127	....	....	....	....	....	....	....	....	....	....	....	....	....	....	....	....	....	....	....
	Windsor Spitfires	OHL	29	14	20	34	73	....	....	....	....	....	....	....	....	....	....	....	4	1	1	2	15	....	....	....
1994-95	Windsor Spitfires	OHL	66	55	59	114	180	....	....	....	....	....	....	....	....	....	....	....	10	9	6	15	16	....	....	....
1995-96	Pittsburgh	NHL	71	7	7	14	130	0	0	1	65	10.8	–5	....	....	....	....	....	16	2	7	9	26	0	0	0
1996-97	Pittsburgh	NHL	61	5	5	10	155	2	0	0	53	9.4	–13	....	....	....	....	....	....	....	....	....	....	....	....	....
	Cleveland	IHL	18	5	5	10	25	....	....	....	....	....	....	....	....	....	....	....	13	6	3	9	*87	....	....	....
1997-98	Syracuse Crunch	AHL	73	12	20	32	307	....	....	....	....	....	....	....	....	....	....	....	5	2	0	2	10	....	....	....
1998-99	Calgary	NHL	36	3	3	6	44	1	0	2	30	10.0	–1	0	0.0	35	9	7:15	....	....	....	....	....	....	....	....
	Saint John Flames	AHL	7	0	3	3	6	....	....	....	....	....	....	....	....	....	....	....	....	....	....	....	....	....	....	....
99-2000	Calgary	NHL	2	0	0	0	5	0	0	0	3	0.0	–1	0	0.0	5	0	8:33	....	....	....	....	....	....	....	....
	Saint John Flames	AHL	67	22	21	43	130	....	....	....	....	....	....	....	....	....	....	....	3	0	1	1	8	....	....	....
2000-01	Saint John Flames	AHL	79	32	26	58	179	....	....	....	....	....	....	....	....	....	....	....	19	3	6	9	43	....	....	....
	NHL Totals		170	15	15	30	334	3	0	3	151	9.9		0	0.0	40	9	7:19	16	2	7	9	26	0	0	0

OHL First All-Star Team (1995)

Traded to **Calgary** by **Pittsburgh** with Ken Wregget for German Titov and Todd Hlushko, June 17, 1998.

ROCHE, Travis

(ROHSH, TRA-vihs) **MIN.**

Defense. Shoots right. 6'1", 190 lbs. Born, Grand Cache, Alta, June 17, 1978.

Season	Club	League	GP	G	A	Pts	PIM	PP	SH	GW	S	%	+/-	TF	F%	H	SB	Min	Playoffs GP	G	A	Pts	PIM	PP	SH	GW
1996-97	Trail Smokies	BCJHL	49	17	40	57	159	....	....	....	....	....	....	....	....	....	....	....	....	....	....	....	....	....	....	....
1997-98	Trail Smokies	BCJHL	38	11	31	42	104	....	....	....	....	....	....	....	....	....	....	....	11	0	8	8	21	....	....	....
1998-99	North Dakota	WCHA	DID NOT PLAY – FRESHMAN																							
99-2000	North Dakota	WCHA	42	6	22	28	60	....	....	....	....	....	....	....	....	....	....	....	....	....	....	....	....	....	....	....
2000-01	North Dakota	WCHA	42	11	38	49	42	....	....	....	....	....	....	....	....	....	....	....	....	....	....	....	....	....	....	....
	Minnesota	NHL	1	0	0	0	0	0	0	0	0	0.0	0	0	0.0	0	1	15:22	....	....	....	....	....	....	....	....
	NHL Totals		1	0	0	0	0	0	0	0	0	0.0		0	0.0	0	1	15:22	....	....	....	....	....	....	....	....

BCJHL Second All-Star Team (1997) • Won BCJHL Rookie of the Year Award (1997) • Won BCJHL Playoff MVP Award (1997) • BCJHL First All-Star Team (1998) • Won BCJHL Best Defenseman Award (1998) • WCHA All-Rookie Team (2000) • WCHA First All-Star Team (2001) • NCAA West First All-American Team (2001) • NCAA Championship All-Tournament Team (2001)

Left **University of North Dakota** and signed as a free agent by **Minnesota**, April 8, 2001.

RODGERS, Marc

(RAWD-juhrs, MAHRK) **DET.**

Right wing. Shoots right. 5'9", 185 lbs. Born, Shawville, Que., March 16, 1972.

Season	Club	League	GP	G	A	Pts	PIM	PP	SH	GW	S	%	+/-	TF	F%	H	SB	Min	Playoffs GP	G	A	Pts	PIM	PP	SH	GW
1986-87	L'Outaouais	QAAA	42	16	18	34	....	....	....	....	....	....	....	....	....	....	....	....	3	0	2	2	6	....	....	....
1987-88	L'Outaouais	QAAA	38	30	37	67	87	....	....	....	....	....	....	....	....	....	....	....	....	....	....	....	....	....	....	....
1988-89	Granby Bisons	QMJHL	65	11	21	32	70	....	....	....	....	....	....	....	....	....	....	....	4	0	2	2	44	....	....	....
1989-90	Granby Bisons	QMJHL	61	24	31	55	155	....	....	....	....	....	....	....	....	....	....	....	....	....	....	....	....	....	....	....
1990-91	Granby Bisons	QMJHL	64	28	49	77	41	....	....	....	....	....	....	....	....	....	....	....	....	....	....	....	....	....	....	....
1991-92	Granby Bisons	QMJHL	36	30	57	87	49	....	....	....	....	....	....	....	....	....	....	....	....	....	....	....	....	....	....	....
	Verdun College	QMJHL	29	14	19	33	0	....	....	....	....	....	....	....	....	....	....	....	18	3	13	16	26	....	....	....
1992-93	Wheeling	ECHL	64	23	40	63	91	....	....	....	....	....	....	....	....	....	....	....	6	1	1	2	8	....	....	....
1993-94	Knoxville	ECHL	27	12	18	30	83	....	....	....	....	....	....	....	....	....	....	....	....	....	....	....	....	....	....	....
	Las Vegas	IHL	40	7	7	14	110	....	....	....	....	....	....	....	....	....	....	....	4	0	2	2	17	....	....	....
1994-95	Las Vegas	IHL	58	17	19	36	131	....	....	....	....	....	....	....	....	....	....	....	10	2	6	8	25	....	....	....
1995-96	Las Vegas	IHL	51	13	16	29	65	....	....	....	....	....	....	....	....	....	....	....	....	....	....	....	....	....	....	....
	Utah Grizzlies	IHL	31	6	14	20	51	....	....	....	....	....	....	....	....	....	....	....	21	4	4	8	16	....	....	....
1996-97	Utah Grizzlies	IHL	5	2	2	4	10	....	....	....	....	....	....	....	....	....	....	....	....	....	....	....	....	....	....	....
	Quebec Rafales	IHL	70	25	42	67	115	....	....	....	....	....	....	....	....	....	....	....	9	1	9	10	14	....	....	....

			Regular Season																Playoffs							
Season	Club	League	GP	G	A	Pts	PIM	PP	SH	GW	S	%	+/-	TF	F%	H	SB	Min	GP	G	A	Pts	PIM	PP	SH	GW
1997-98	Quebec Rafales	IHL	61	20	22	42	61	....	....	....	....	....	....	....	....	....	....	....	....	....	....	....	....	....	....	....
	Chicago Wolves	IHL	11	5	5	10	22	....	....	....	....	....	....	....	....	....	....	....	22	9	9	18	10	....	....	....
1998-99	Adirondack	AHL	80	19	38	57	66	....	....	....	....	....	....	....	....	....	....	....	3	0	0	0	10	....	....	....
99-2000	**Detroit**	**NHL**	**21**	**1**	**1**	**2**	**10**	**0**	**0**	**0**	**17**	**5.9**	**–3**	**2100.0**		**48**	**3**	**7:55**	....	....	....	....	....	....	....	....
	Manitoba Moose	IHL	34	8	10	18	77	....	....	....	....	....	....	....	....	....	....	....	2	1	0	1	6	....	....	....
2000-01	Cincinnati Ducks	AHL	32	7	5	12	53	....	....	....	....	....	....	....	....	....	....	....	4	1	1	2	8	....	....	....
	NHL Totals		**21**	**1**	**1**	**2**	**10**	**0**	**0**	**0**	**17**	**5.9**		**2100.0**		**48**	**3**	**7:55**	....	....	....	....	....	....	....	....

Signed as a free agent by **Detroit**, August 3, 1998.

ROENICK, Jeremy

(ROH-nihk, JAIR-eh-mee) **PHI.**

Center. Shoots right. 6'1", 207 lbs. Born, Boston, MA, January 17, 1970. Chicago's 1st choice, 8th overall, in 1988 Entry Draft.

1986-87	Thayer Academy	Hi-School	24	31	34	65	....	....	....	....	....	....	....	....	....	....	....	....	....	....	....	....	....	....	....	....
1987-88	Thayer Academy	Hi-School	24	34	50	84	....	....	....	....	....	....	....	....	....	....	....	....	....	....	....	....	....	....	....	....
1988-89	Hull Olympiques	QMJHL	28	34	36	70	14	....	....	....	....	....	....	....	....	....	....	....	....	....	....	....	....	....	....	....
	Chicago	**NHL**	**20**	**9**	**9**	**18**	**4**	**2**	**0**	**0**	**52**	**17.3**	**4**	....	....	....	....	....	**10**	**1**	**3**	**4**	**7**	**1**	**0**	**1**
1989-90	**Chicago**	**NHL**	**78**	**26**	**40**	**66**	**54**	**6**	**0**	**4**	**173**	**15.0**	**2**	....	....	....	....	....	**20**	**11**	**7**	**18**	**8**	**4**	**0**	**1**
1990-91	**Chicago**	**NHL**	**79**	**41**	**53**	**94**	**80**	**15**	**4**	**10**	**194**	**21.1**	**38**	....	....	....	....	....	**6**	**3**	**5**	**8**	**4**	**1**	**0**	**1**
1991-92	**Chicago**	**NHL**	**80**	**53**	**50**	**103**	**98**	**22**	**3**	**13**	**234**	**22.6**	**23**	....	....	....	....	....	**18**	**12**	**10**	**22**	**12**	**4**	**0**	**3**
1992-93	**Chicago**	**NHL**	**84**	**50**	**57**	**107**	**86**	**22**	**3**	**3**	**255**	**19.6**	**15**	....	....	....	....	....	**4**	**1**	**2**	**3**	**2**	**0**	**0**	**0**
1993-94	**Chicago**	**NHL**	**84**	**46**	**61**	**107**	**125**	**24**	**5**	**5**	**281**	**16.4**	**21**	....	....	....	....	....	**6**	**1**	**6**	**7**	**2**	**0**	**0**	**1**
1994-95	Kolner Haie	DEL	3	3	1	4	2	....	....	....	....	....	....	....	....	....	....	....	....	....	....	....	....	....	....	....
	Chicago	**NHL**	**33**	**10**	**24**	**34**	**14**	**5**	**0**	**1**	**93**	**10.8**	**5**	....	....	....	....	....	**8**	**1**	**2**	**3**	**16**	**0**	**0**	**0**
1995-96	**Chicago**	**NHL**	**66**	**32**	**35**	**67**	**109**	**12**	**4**	**2**	**171**	**18.7**	**9**	....	....	....	....	....	**10**	**5**	**7**	**12**	**2**	**1**	**0**	**1**
1996-97	**Phoenix**	**NHL**	**72**	**29**	**40**	**69**	**115**	**10**	**3**	**7**	**228**	**12.7**	**–7**	....	....	....	....	....	**6**	**2**	**4**	**6**	**4**	**0**	**0**	**0**
1997-98	**Phoenix**	**NHL**	**79**	**24**	**32**	**56**	**103**	**6**	**1**	**3**	**182**	**13.2**	**5**	....	....	....	....	....	**6**	**5**	**3**	**8**	**4**	**2**	**2**	**2**
	United States	Olympics	4	0	1	1	6	....	....	....	....	....	....	....	....	....	....	....	....	....	....	....	....	....	....	....
1998-99	**Phoenix**	**NHL**	**78**	**24**	**48**	**72**	**130**	**4**	**0**	**3**	**203**	**11.8**	**7**	**956**	**47.6**	**154**	**30**	**20:10**	**1**	**0**	**0**	**0**	**0**	**0**	**0**	**0**
99-2000	**Phoenix**	**NHL**	**75**	**34**	**44**	**78**	**102**	**6**	**3**	**12**	**192**	**17.7**	**11**	**925**	**50.1**	**125**	**28**	**20:51**	**5**	**2**	**2**	**4**	**10**	**1**	**0**	**0**
2000-01	**Phoenix**	**NHL**	**80**	**30**	**46**	**76**	**114**	**13**	**0**	**7**	**192**	**15.6**	**–1**	**888**	**49.1**	**135**	**25**	**20:60**	....	....	....	....	....	....	....	....
	NHL Totals		**908**	**408**	**539**	**947**	**1134**	**147**	**26**	**70**	**2450**	**16.7**		**2769**	**48.9**	**414**	**83**	**20:40**	**100**	**44**	**51**	**95**	**71**	**14**	**2**	**10**

• QMJHL Second All-Star Team (1989) • Played in NHL All-Star Game (1991, 1992, 1993, 1994, 1999, 2000)

Traded to **Phoenix** by **Chicago** for Alexei Zhamnov, Craig Mills and Phoenix's 1st round choice (Ty Jones) in 1997 Entry Draft, August 16, 1996. Signed as a free agent by **Philadelphia**, July 2, 2001.

ROEST, Stacy

(ROOST, STAY-see) **MIN.**

Center. Shoots right. 5'9", 185 lbs. Born, Lethbridge, Alta., March 15, 1974.

1990-91	Lethbridge	AMHL	34	22	50	72	38	....	....	....	....	....	....	....	....	....	....	....	....	....	....	....	....	....	....	....
	Medicine Hat	WHL	5	1	2	3	0	....	....	....	....	....	....	....	....	....	....	....	12	5	5	10	4	....	....	....
1991-92	Medicine Hat	WHL	72	22	43	65	20	....	....	....	....	....	....	....	....	....	....	....	4	2	1	3	0	....	....	....
1992-93	Medicine Hat	WHL	72	33	73	106	30	....	....	....	....	....	....	....	....	....	....	....	10	3	10	13	6	....	....	....
1993-94	Medicine Hat	WHL	72	48	72	120	48	....	....	....	....	....	....	....	....	....	....	....	3	1	0	1	4	....	....	....
1994-95	Medicine Hat	WHL	69	37	78	115	32	....	....	....	....	....	....	....	....	....	....	....	5	2	7	9	2	....	....	....
	Adirondack	AHL	3	0	0	0	0	....	....	....	....	....	....	....	....	....	....	....	....	....	....	....	....	....	....	....
1995-96	Adirondack	AHL	76	16	39	55	40	....	....	....	....	....	....	....	....	....	....	....	3	0	0	0	0	....	....	....
1996-97	Adirondack	AHL	78	25	41	66	30	....	....	....	....	....	....	....	....	....	....	....	4	1	1	2	0	....	....	....
1997-98	Adirondack	AHL	80	34	58	92	30	....	....	....	....	....	....	....	....	....	....	....	3	2	1	3	6	....	....	....
1998-99	**Detroit**	**NHL**	**59**	**4**	**8**	**12**	**14**	**0**	**0**	**1**	**50**	**8.0**	**–7**	**234**	**57.3**	**72**	**7**	**8:04**	....	....	....	....	....	....	....	....
	Adirondack	AHL	2	0	1	1	0	....	....	....	....	....	....	....	....	....	....	....	....	....	....	....	....	....	....	....
99-2000	**Detroit**	**NHL**	**49**	**7**	**9**	**16**	**12**	**1**	**0**	**1**	**56**	**12.5**	**–1**	**397**	**55.4**	**54**	**12**	**9:56**	**3**	**0**	**0**	**0**	**0**	**0**	**0**	**0**
2000-01	**Minnesota**	**NHL**	**76**	**7**	**20**	**27**	**20**	**1**	**0**	**1**	**125**	**5.6**	**3**	**731**	**57.1**	**51**	**16**	**14:01**	....	....	....	....	....	....	....	....
	NHL Totals		**184**	**18**	**37**	**55**	**46**	**2**	**0**	**3**	**231**	**7.8**		**1362**	**56.6**	**177**	**35**	**11:01**	**3**	**0**	**0**	**0**	**0**	**0**	**0**	**0**

WHL East First All-Star Team (1994) • WHL East Second All-Star Team (1995)

Signed as a free agent by **Detroit**, June 9, 1997. Selected by **Minnesota** from **Detroit** in Expansion Draft, June 23, 2000.

ROHLOFF, Jon

(ROH-lawf, JAWN)

Defense. Shoots right. 5'11", 220 lbs. Born, Mankato, MN, October 3, 1969. Boston's 7th choice, 186th overall, in 1988 Entry Draft.

1986-87	Grand Rapids	Hi-School	21	12	23	35	16	....	....	....	....	....	....	....	....	....	....	....	....	....	....	....	....	....	....	....
1987-88	Grand Rapids	Hi-School	28	10	13	23	....	....	....	....	....	....	....	....	....	....	....	....	....	....	....	....	....	....	....	....
1988-89	Minnesota-Duluth	WCHA	39	1	2	3	44	....	....	....	....	....	....	....	....	....	....	....	....	....	....	....	....	....	....	....
1989-90	Minnesota-Duluth	WCHA	5	0	1	1	6	....	....	....	....	....	....	....	....	....	....	....	....	....	....	....	....	....	....	....
1990-91	Minnesota-Duluth	WCHA	32	6	11	17	38	....	....	....	....	....	....	....	....	....	....	....	....	....	....	....	....	....	....	....
1991-92	Minnesota-Duluth	WCHA	27	9	9	18	48	....	....	....	....	....	....	....	....	....	....	....	....	....	....	....	....	....	....	....
1992-93	Minnesota-Duluth	WCHA	36	15	20	35	87	....	....	....	....	....	....	....	....	....	....	....	....	....	....	....	....	....	....	....
1993-94	Providence Bruins	AHL	55	12	23	35	59	....	....	....	....	....	....	....	....	....	....	....	....	....	....	....	....	....	....	....
1994-95	Providence Bruins	AHL	4	2	1	3	6	....	....	....	....	....	....	....	....	....	....	....	....	....	....	....	....	....	....	....
	Boston	**NHL**	**34**	**3**	**8**	**11**	**39**	**0**	**0**	**1**	**51**	**5.9**	**1**	....	....	....	....	....	**5**	**0**	**0**	**0**	**6**	**0**	**0**	**0**
1995-96	**Boston**	**NHL**	**79**	**1**	**12**	**13**	**59**	**1**	**0**	**0**	**106**	**0.9**	**–8**	....	....	....	....	....	**5**	**1**	**2**	**3**	**2**	**1**	**0**	**0**
1996-97	**Boston**	**NHL**	**37**	**3**	**5**	**8**	**31**	**1**	**0**	**0**	**69**	**4.3**	**–14**	....	....	....	....	....	....	....	....	....	....	....	....	....
	Providence Bruins	AHL	3	1	1	2	0	....	....	....	....	....	....	....	....	....	....	....	....	....	....	....	....	....	....	....
1997-98	Providence Bruins	AHL	58	6	17	23	46	....	....	....	....	....	....	....	....	....	....	....	....	....	....	....	....	....	....	....
1998-99	Kentucky	AHL	12	0	1	1	8	....	....	....	....	....	....	....	....	....	....	....	....	....	....	....	....	....	....	....
	Kansas City	IHL	41	5	13	18	42	....	....	....	....	....	....	....	....	....	....	....	3	0	0	0	18	....	....	....
99-2000	Kansas City	IHL	44	5	18	23	38	....	....	....	....	....	....	....	....	....	....	....	....	....	....	....	....	....	....	....
2000-01	Cincinnati	IHL	66	2	17	19	62	....	....	....	....	....	....	....	....	....	....	....	4	0	0	0	6	....	....	....
	NHL Totals		**150**	**7**	**25**	**32**	**129**	**2**	**0**	**1**	**226**	**3.1**		....	....	....	....	....	**10**	**1**	**2**	**3**	**8**	**1**	**0**	**0**

WCHA Second All-Star Team (1993)

Signed as a free agent by **San Jose**, July 23, 1998. Signed as a free agent by **Carolina**, August 1, 2000.

ROLSTON, Brian

(ROHL-stuhn, BRIGH-uhn) **BOS.**

Center. Shoots left. 6'2", 205 lbs. Born, Flint, MI, February 21, 1973. New Jersey's 2nd choice, 11th overall, in 1991 Entry Draft.

1989-90	Det-Compuware	NAJHL	40	36	37	73	57	....	....	....	....	....	....	....	....	....	....	....	....	....	....	....	....	....	....	....
1990-91	Det-Compuware	NAJHL	36	49	46	95	14	....	....	....	....	....	....	....	....	....	....	....	....	....	....	....	....	....	....	....
1991-92	Lake Superior	CCHA	37	14	23	37	14	....	....	....	....	....	....	....	....	....	....	....	....	....	....	....	....	....	....	....
1992-93	Lake Superior	CCHA	39	33	31	64	20	....	....	....	....	....	....	....	....	....	....	....	....	....	....	....	....	....	....	....
1993-94	United States	Nat-Team	41	20	28	48	36	....	....	....	....	....	....	....	....	....	....	....	....	....	....	....	....	....	....	....
	United States	Olympics	8	7	0	7	8	....	....	....	....	....	....	....	....	....	....	....	....	....	....	....	....	....	....	....
	Albany River Rats	AHL	17	5	5	10	8	....	....	....	....	....	....	....	....	....	....	....	5	1	2	3	0	....	....	....
1994-95	Albany River Rats	AHL	18	9	11	20	10	....	....	....	....	....	....	....	....	....	....	....	....	....	....	....	....	....	....	....
	♦ New Jersey	**NHL**	**40**	**7**	**11**	**18**	**17**	**2**	**0**	**3**	**92**	**7.6**	**5**	....	....	....	....	....	**6**	**2**	**1**	**3**	**4**	**1**	**0**	**0**
1995-96	**New Jersey**	**NHL**	**58**	**13**	**11**	**24**	**8**	**3**	**1**	**4**	**139**	**9.4**	**9**	....	....	....	....	....	....	....	....	....	....	....	....	....
1996-97	**New Jersey**	**NHL**	**81**	**18**	**27**	**45**	**20**	**2**	**2**	**3**	**237**	**7.6**	**6**	....	....	....	....	....	**10**	**4**	**1**	**5**	**6**	**1**	**2**	**0**
1997-98	**New Jersey**	**NHL**	**76**	**16**	**14**	**30**	**16**	**0**	**2**	**1**	**185**	**8.6**	**7**	....	....	....	....	....	**6**	**1**	**0**	**1**	**2**	**0**	**1**	**0**
1998-99	**New Jersey**	**NHL**	**82**	**24**	**33**	**57**	**14**	**5**	**5**	**3**	**210**	**11.4**	**11**	**51**	**45.1**	**70**	**20**	**18:49**	**7**	**1**	**0**	**1**	**2**	**0**	**1**	**0**
99-2000	**New Jersey**	**NHL**	**11**	**3**	**1**	**4**	**0**	**1**	**0**	**2**	**33**	**9.1**	**–2**	**37**	**37.8**	**13**	**2**	**19:09**	....	....	....	....	....	....	....	....
	Colorado	**NHL**	**50**	**8**	**10**	**18**	**12**	**1**	**0**	**3**	**107**	**7.5**	**–6**	**65**	**41.5**	**28**	**19**	**16:18**	....	....	....	....	....	....	....	....
	Boston	**NHL**	**16**	**5**	**4**	**9**	**6**	**3**	**0**	**1**	**66**	**7.6**	**–4**	**265**	**41.1**	**22**	**11**	**22:13**	....	....	....	....	....	....	....	....
2000-01	**Boston**	**NHL**	**77**	**19**	**39**	**58**	**28**	**5**	**0**	**4**	**286**	**6.6**	**6**	**666**	**45.7**	**71**	**31**	**19:19**	....	....	....	....	....	....	....	....
	NHL Totals		**491**	**113**	**150**	**263**	**121**	**22**	**10**	**24**	**1355**	**8.3**		**1084**	**44.0**	**204**	**83**	**18:42**	**29**	**8**	**2**	**10**	**14**	**2**	**4**	**0**

NCAA Championship All-Tournament Team (1992, 1993) • CCHA First All-Star Team (1993) • NCAA West Second All-American Team (1993)

Traded to **Colorado** by **New Jersey** with New Jersey's 1st round choice (later traded to Boston - Boston selected Martin Samuelsson) in 2000 Entry Draft for Claude Lemieux and Colorado's 1st (David Hale) and 2nd (Matt DeMarchi) round choices in 2000 Entry Draft, November 3, 1999. Traded to **Boston** by **Colorado** with Martin Grenier, Sami Pahlsson and New Jersey's 1st round choice (previously acquired, Boston selected Martin Samuelsson) in 2000 Entry Draft for Ray Bourque and Dave Andreychuk, March 6, 2000.

ROMINSKI, Dale
(ROH-mihn-SKEE, DAYL)

Right wing. Shoots right. 6'2", 200 lbs. Born, Farmington Hills, MI, October 1, 1975.

Season	Club	League	GP	G	A	Pts	PIM	PP	SH	GW	S	%	+/-	TF	F%	H	SB	Min	GP	G	A	Pts	PIM	PP	SH	GW
			Regular Season																Playoffs							
1993-94	Brother Rice	Hi-School	25	25	20	45	....																			
1994-95	Det-Compuware	NAJHL	40	21	21	42	30																			
1995-96	U. of Michigan	CCHA	35	8	7	15	37																			
1996-97	U. of Michigan	CCHA	38	6	7	13	58																			
1997-98	U. of Michigan	CCHA	46	10	14	24	102																			
1998-99	U. of Michigan	CCHA	41	15	8	23	80																			
99-2000	**Tampa Bay**	**NHL**	**3**	**0**	**1**	**1**	**2**	**0**	**0**	**0**	**0**	**0.0**	**1**	**0**	**0.0**	**5**	**0**	**8:23**								
	Detroit Vipers	IHL	78	14	15	29	68																			
2000-01	Detroit Vipers	IHL	65	6	6	12	52																			
	NHL Totals		**3**	**0**	**1**	**1**	**2**	**0**	**0**	**0**	**0**	**0.0**		**0**	**0.0**	**5**	**0**	**8:23**								

Signed as a free agent by **Tampa Bay**, August 31, 1999.

RONNING, Cliff
(RAWN-ihng, KLIHF) **NSH.**

Center. Shoots left. 5'8", 165 lbs. Born, Burnaby, B.C., October 1, 1965. St. Louis' 9th choice, 134th overall, in 1984 Entry Draft.

Season	Club	League	GP	G	A	Pts	PIM	PP	SH	GW	S	%	+/-	TF	F%	H	SB	Min	GP	G	A	Pts	PIM	PP	SH	GW
1982-83	New Westminster	BCJHL	52	83	68	151	22																			
1983-84	New Westminster	WHL	71	69	67	136	10												9	8	13	21	10			
1984-85	New Westminster	WHL	70	*89	108	*197	20												11	10	14	24	4			
1985-86	Canada	Nat-Team	71	*55	*63	*118	53																			
	St. Louis	**NHL**																	**5**	**1**	**1**	**2**	**2**	**1**	**0**	**0**
1986-87	Canada	Nat-Team	26	17	16	33	12																			
	St. Louis	**NHL**	**42**	**11**	**14**	**25**	**6**	**2**	**0**	**2**	**68**	**16.2**	**-1**						**4**	**0**	**1**	**1**	**0**	**0**	**0**	**0**
1987-88	**St. Louis**	**NHL**	**26**	**5**	**8**	**13**	**12**	**1**	**0**	**1**	**38**	**13.2**	**6**													
1988-89	**St. Louis**	**NHL**	**64**	**24**	**31**	**55**	**18**	**16**	**0**	**1**	**150**	**16.0**	**3**						**7**	**1**	**3**	**4**	**0**	**1**	**0**	**0**
	Peoria Rivermen	IHL	12	11	20	31	8																			
1989-90	HC Asiago	Italy	36	67	49	116	25												6	7	12	19	4			
1990-91	**St. Louis**	**NHL**	**48**	**14**	**18**	**32**	**10**	**5**	**0**	**2**	**81**	**17.3**	**2**													
	Vancouver	**NHL**	**11**	**6**	**6**	**12**	**0**	**2**	**0**	**0**	**32**	**18.8**	**-2**						**6**	**6**	**3**	**9**	**12**	**2**	**0**	**2**
1991-92	**Vancouver**	**NHL**	**80**	**24**	**47**	**71**	**42**	**6**	**0**	**2**	**216**	**11.1**	**18**						**13**	**8**	**5**	**13**	**6**	**1**	**0**	**1**
1992-93	**Vancouver**	**NHL**	**79**	**29**	**56**	**85**	**30**	**10**	**0**	**2**	**209**	**13.9**	**19**						**12**	**2**	**9**	**11**	**6**	**0**	**0**	**0**
1993-94	**Vancouver**	**NHL**	**76**	**25**	**43**	**68**	**42**	**10**	**0**	**4**	**197**	**12.7**	**7**						**24**	**5**	**10**	**15**	**16**	**2**	**0**	**2**
1994-95	**Vancouver**	**NHL**	**41**	**6**	**19**	**25**	**27**	**3**	**0**	**2**	**93**	**6.5**	**-4**						**11**	**3**	**5**	**8**	**2**	**1**	**0**	**2**
1995-96	**Vancouver**	**NHL**	**79**	**22**	**45**	**67**	**42**	**5**	**0**	**1**	**187**	**11.8**	**16**						**6**	**0**	**2**	**2**	**6**	**0**	**0**	**0**
1996-97	**Phoenix**	**NHL**	**69**	**19**	**32**	**51**	**26**	**8**	**0**	**2**	**171**	**11.1**	**-9**						**7**	**0**	**7**	**7**	**12**	**0**	**0**	**0**
1997-98	**Phoenix**	**NHL**	**80**	**11**	**44**	**55**	**36**	**3**	**0**	**0**	**197**	**5.6**	**5**						**6**	**1**	**3**	**4**	**4**	**0**	**0**	**0**
1998-99	**Phoenix**	**NHL**	**7**	**2**	**5**	**7**	**2**	**2**	**0**	**1**	**18**	**11.1**	**3**	**81**	**51.9**	**0**	**1**	**15:22**								
	Nashville	**NHL**	**72**	**18**	**35**	**53**	**40**	**8**	**0**	**3**	**239**	**7.5**	**-6**	**1129**	**47.7**	**11**	**35**	**19:42**								
99-2000	**Nashville**	**NHL**	**82**	**26**	**36**	**62**	**34**	**7**	**0**	**2**	**248**	**10.5**	**-13**	**611**	**45.7**	**8**	**20**	**18:11**								
2000-01	**Nashville**	**NHL**	**80**	**19**	**43**	**62**	**28**	**6**	**0**	**4**	**237**	**8.0**	**4**	**331**	**45.0**	**13**	**13**	**17:23**								
	NHL Totals		**936**	**261**	**482**	**743**	**395**	**94**	**0**	**29**	**2381**	**11.0**		**2152**	**46.9**	**32**	**69**	**18:17**	**101**	**27**	**49**	**76**	**66**	**8**	**0**	**7**

WHL First All-Star Team (1985)

Traded to **Vancouver** by **St. Louis** with Geoff Courtnall, Robert Dirk, Sergio Momesso and St. Louis' 5th round choice (Brian Loney) in 1992 Entry Draft for Dan Quinn and Garth Butcher, March 5, 1991. Signed as a free agent by **Phoenix**, July 1, 1996. Traded to **Nashville** by **Phoenix** with Richard Lintner for future considerations, October 31, 1998.

RONNQVIST, Jonas
(RAWN-kvihst, YOH-nuhs) **ANA.**

Right wing. Shoots right. 6'2", 200 lbs. Born, Kalix, Sweden, August 22, 1973. Anaheim's 3rd choice, 98th overall, in 2000 Entry Draft.

Season	Club	League	GP	G	A	Pts	PIM	PP	SH	GW	S	%	+/-	TF	F%	H	SB	Min	GP	G	A	Pts	PIM	PP	SH	GW
1991-92	Bodens IK	Sweden-2	6	1	1	2	2												1	0	0	0	0			
1992-93	Bodens IK	Sweden-2	35	10	4	14	16																			
1993-94	Bodens IK	Sweden-2	34	15	10	25	24												9	1	1	2	6			
1994-95	Bodens IK	Sweden-2	35	10	15	5	48												8	1	0	1	0			
1995-96	Bodens IK	Sweden-2	26	12	10	22	26																			
1996-97	Bodens IK	Sweden-2	32	15	14	29	48																			
1997-98	Lulea HF	Sweden	40	6	8	14	24												3	0	0	0	2			
	Lulea HF	EuroHL	5	0	1	1	0																			
1998-99	Lulea HF	Sweden	41	5	8	13	30												3	0	2	2	29			
99-2000	Lulea HF	Sweden	49	15	24	39	42												8	3	3	6	4			
2000-01	**Anaheim**	**NHL**	**38**	**0**	**4**	**4**	**14**	**0**	**0**	**0**	**30**	**0.0**	**-7**	**101**	**44.6**	**19**	**6**	**10:37**								
	Cincinnati Ducks	AHL	13	3	2	5	6																			
	NHL Totals		**38**	**0**	**4**	**4**	**14**	**0**	**0**	**0**	**30**	**0.0**		**101**	**44.6**	**19**	**6**	**10:37**								

ROSA, Pavel
(ROHZA, PAH-vehl) **L.A.**

Right wing. Shoots right. 6', 195 lbs. Born, Most, Czech., June 7, 1977. Los Angeles' 3rd choice, 50th overall, in 1995 Entry Draft.

Season	Club	League	GP	G	A	Pts	PIM	PP	SH	GW	S	%	+/-	TF	F%	H	SB	Min	GP	G	A	Pts	PIM	PP	SH	GW
1994-95	HC Litvinov-Jr.	Cze-Rep	40	56	42	98	....																			
	HC Litvinov	Cze-Rep	2	0	0	0	0												1	0	0	0	0			
1995-96	Hull Olympiques	QMJHL	61	46	70	116	39												18	14	22	36	25			
1996-97	Hull Olympiques	QMJHL	68	*63	*90	*153	66												14	18	13	31	16			
1997-98	Fredericton	AHL	1	0	0	0	0																			
	Long Beach	IHL	2	0	1	1	0												1	1	1	2	0			
1998-99	**Los Angeles**	**NHL**	**29**	**4**	**12**	**16**	**6**	**0**	**0**	**0**	**61**	**6.6**	**0**	**0**	**0.0**	**24**	**6**	**13:34**								
	Long Beach	IHL	31	17	13	30	28												6	1	2	3	0			
99-2000	**Los Angeles**	**NHL**	**3**	**0**	**0**	**0**	**0**	**0**	**0**	**0**	**1**	**0.0**	**-1**	**0**	**0.0**	**6**	**1**	**11:21**								
	Long Beach	IHL	74	22	31	53	76												6	2	2	4	4			
2000-01	HPK Hameenlinna	Finland	54	25	25	50	53																			
	NHL Totals		**32**	**4**	**12**	**16**	**6**	**0**	**0**	**0**	**62**	**6.5**		**0**	**0.0**	**30**	**7**	**13:22**								

QMJHL First All-Star Team (1997) • Canadian Major Junior First All-Star Team (1997)

• Missed majority of 1997-98 season recovering from head injury originally suffered in training camp, September, 1997.

ROY, Andre
(WAH, AHN-dray) **OTT.**

Left wing. Shoots left. 6'4", 213 lbs. Born, Port Chester, NY, February 8, 1975. Boston's 5th choice, 151st overall, in 1994 Entry Draft.

Season	Club	League	GP	G	A	Pts	PIM	PP	SH	GW	S	%	+/-	TF	F%	H	SB	Min	GP	G	A	Pts	PIM	PP	SH	GW
1991-92	Carleton Place	OCJHL	38	9	12	21	96																			
1992-93	Carleton Place	OCJHL	40	16	15	31	80																			
1993-94	Goulbourn Royals	OJHL-C	9	9	13	22	98																			
	Beauport	QMJHL	33	6	7	13	125																			
	Chicoutimi	QMJHL	32	4	14	18	152												25	3	6	9	94			
1994-95	Chicoutimi	QMJHL	20	15	8	23	90																			
	Drummondville	QMJHL	34	18	13	31	233												4	2	0	2	34			
1995-96	**Boston**	**NHL**	**3**	**0**	**0**	**0**	**0**	**0**	**0**	**0**	**0**	**0.0**	**0**													
	Providence Bruins	AHL	58	7	8	15	167												1	0	0	0	10			
1996-97	**Boston**	**NHL**	**10**	**0**	**2**	**2**	**12**	**0**	**0**	**0**	**12**	**0.0**	**-5**													
	Providence Bruins	AHL	50	17	11	28	234																			
1997-98	Providence Bruins	AHL	36	3	11	14	154																			
	Charlotte	ECHL	27	10	8	18	132												7	2	3	5	34			
1998-99	Fort Wayne	IHL	65	15	6	21	*395												2	0	0	0	11			
99-2000	**Ottawa**	**NHL**	**73**	**4**	**3**	**7**	**145**	**0**	**0**	**1**	**39**	**10.3**	**3**	**3**	**33.3**	**109**	**5**	**6:29**	**5**	**0**	**0**	**0**	**2**	**0**	**0**	**0**
2000-01	**Ottawa**	**NHL**	**64**	**3**	**5**	**8**	**169**	**0**	**0**	**0**	**33**	**9.1**	**1**	**2**	**50.0**	**96**	**3**	**4:36**	**2**	**0**	**0**	**0**	**16**	**0**	**0**	**0**
	NHL Totals		**150**	**7**	**10**	**17**	**326**	**0**	**0**	**1**	**84**	**8.3**		**5**	**40.0**	**205**	**8**	**5:36**	**7**	**0**	**0**	**0**	**18**	**0**	**0**	**0**

Signed as a free agent by **Ottawa**, April 28, 1999.

ROYER, Remi

(ROI-ay, REH-mee)

Defense. Shoots right. 6'2", 200 lbs. Born, Donnacona, Que., February 12, 1978. Chicago's 1st choice, 31st overall, in 1996 Entry Draft.

			Regular Season																Playoffs							
Season	Club	League	GP	G	A	Pts	PIM	PP	SH	GW	S	%	+/-	TF	F%	H	SB	Min	GP	G	A	Pts	PIM	PP	SH	GW
1993-94	Ste-Foy Governors	QAAA	44	8	24	32	86												8	3	3	6	16			
1994-95	Victoriaville Tigres	QMJHL	57	3	17	20	144												4	0	1	1	7			
1995-96	Victoriaville Tigres	QMJHL	43	12	14	26	209																			
	St-Hyacinthe	QMJHL	19	10	9	19	80												12	1	4	5	29			
1996-97	Rouyn-Noranda	QMJHL	29	3	12	15	85																			
	Indianapolis Ice	IHL	10	0	1	1	17																			
1997-98	Rouyn-Noranda	QMJHL	66	20	48	68	205												6	1	3	4	8			
	Indianapolis Ice	IHL	5	0	2	2	4												5	1	2	3	12			
1998-99	Chicago	NHL	18	0	0	0	67	0	0	0	24	0.0	-10	0	0.0	25	11	13:37								
	Indianapolis Ice	IHL	54	4	15	19	164												7	0	0	0	44			
	Portland Pirates	AHL	2	0	1	1	2																			
99-2000	Cleveland	IHL	57	3	13	16	204												8	1	1	2	12			
2000-01	Portland Pirates	AHL	40	1	7	8	140																			
	Louisville Panthers	AHL	18	1	1	2	50																			
	NHL Totals		**18**	**0**	**0**	**0**	**67**	**0**	**0**	**0**	**24**	**0.0**		**0**	**0.0**	**25**	**11**	**13:37**								

QMJHL First All-Star Team (1998)

Traded to **Washington** by **Chicago** for Nolan Baumgartner, July 20, 2000. Traded to **Florida** by **Washington** for David Emma, March 3, 2001.

ROZSIVAL, Michal

(roh-ZIH-vahl, mee-KHUHL) **PIT.**

Defense. Shoots right. 6'1", 208 lbs. Born, Vlasim, Czech., September 3, 1978. Pittsburgh's 5th choice, 105th overall, in 1996 Entry Draft.

			Regular Season																Playoffs							
Season	Club	League	GP	G	A	Pts	PIM	PP	SH	GW	S	%	+/-	TF	F%	H	SB	Min	GP	G	A	Pts	PIM	PP	SH	GW
1994-95	Dukla Jihlava-Jr.	Cze-Rep	31	8	13	21																				
1995-96	Dukla Jihlava	Cze-Rep	36	3	4	7																				
1996-97	Swift Current	WHL	63	8	31	39	80												10	0	6	6	15			
1997-98	Swift Current	WHL	71	14	55	69	122												12	0	5	5	33			
1998-99	Syracuse Crunch	AHL	49	3	22	25	72																			
99-2000	Pittsburgh	NHL	75	4	17	21	48	1	0	1	73	5.5	11	1	0.0	124	72	19:01	2	0	0	0	4	0	0	0
2000-01	Pittsburgh	NHL	30	1	4	5	26	0	0	0	17	5.9	3	1	100.0	37	38	17:06								
	Wilkes-Barre	AHL	29	8	8	16	32												21	3	*19	22	23			
	NHL Totals		**105**	**5**	**21**	**26**	**74**	**1**	**0**	**1**	**90**	**5.6**		**2**	**50.0**	**161**	**110**	**18:28**	**2**	**0**	**0**	**0**	**4**	**0**	**0**	**0**

WHL East First All-Star Team (1998)

RUCCHIN, Steve

(ROO-chihn, STEEV) **ANA.**

Center. Shoots left. 6'3", 212 lbs. Born, Thunder Bay, Ont., July 4, 1971. Anaheim's 1st choice, 2nd overall, in 1994 Supplemental Draft.

			Regular Season																Playoffs							
Season	Club	League	GP	G	A	Pts	PIM	PP	SH	GW	S	%	+/-	TF	F%	H	SB	Min	GP	G	A	Pts	PIM	PP	SH	GW
1989-90	Banting High	Hi-School	STATISTICS NOT AVAILABLE																							
	Thamesford	OJHL-D	2	1	2	3	0																			
1990-91	Western Ontario	OUAA	34	13	16	29	14																			
1991-92	Western Ontario	OUAA	37	28	34	62	36																			
1992-93	Western Ontario	OUAA	34	22	26	48	16																			
1993-94	Western Ontario	OUAA	35	30	23	53	30																			
1994-95	San Diego Gulls	IHL	41	11	15	26	14																			
	Anaheim	NHL	43	6	11	17	23	0	0	1	59	10.2	7													
1995-96	Anaheim	NHL	64	19	25	44	12	8	1	4	113	16.8	3													
1996-97	Anaheim	NHL	79	19	48	67	24	6	1	2	153	12.4	26						8	1	2	3	10	0	0	0
1997-98	Anaheim	NHL	72	17	36	53	13	8	1	3	131	13.0	8													
1998-99	Anaheim	NHL	69	23	39	62	22	5	1	5	145	15.9	11	1845	52.3	43	72	22:33	4	0	3	3	0	0	0	0
99-2000	Anaheim	NHL	71	19	38	57	16	10	0	2	131	14.5	9	1996	53.4	69	69	22:12								
2000-01	Anaheim	NHL	16	3	5	8	0	2	0	0	19	15.8	-5	289	51.6	13	5	18:47								
	NHL Totals		**414**	**106**	**202**	**308**	**110**	**39**	**4**	**17**	**751**	**14.1**		**4130**	**52.8**	**125**	**146**	**22:00**	**12**	**1**	**5**	**6**	**10**	**0**	**0**	**0**

• Missed majority of 2000-01 season recovering from jaw injury originally suffered in game vs. Colorado, November 15, 2000.

RUCINSKI, Mike

(roo-SIHN-skee, MIGHK) **CAR.**

Defense. Shoots left. 5'11", 179 lbs. Born, Trenton, MI, March 30, 1975. Hartford's 8th choice, 217th overall, in 1995 Entry Draft.

			Regular Season																Playoffs							
Season	Club	League	GP	G	A	Pts	PIM	PP	SH	GW	S	%	+/-	TF	F%	H	SB	Min	GP	G	A	Pts	PIM	PP	SH	GW
1991-92	Detroit Caesars	MNHL	29	4	15	19	38																			
1992-93	Detroit Jr. Wings	OHL	66	6	13	19	59												15	0	4	4	12			
1993-94	Detroit Jr. Wings	OHL	66	2	26	28	58												17	0	7	7	15			
1994-95	Detroit Jr. Wings	OHL	64	9	18	27	61												21	3	3	6	8			
1995-96	Detroit Whalers	OHL	51	10	26	36	65												11	2	4	6	14			
1996-97	Richmond	ECHL	61	20	23	43	85												8	2	6	8	18			
	Springfield	AHL	6	0	1	1	0																			
1997-98	Carolina	NHL	9	0	1	1	2	0	0	0	3	0.0	0													
	New Haven	AHL	65	5	17	22	50												1	0	0	0	0			
	Cleveland	IHL	2	0	0	0	4																			
1998-99	Carolina	NHL	15	0	1	1	8	0	0	0	8	0.0	1	0	0.0	8	4	10:29								
	New Haven	AHL	23	2	6	8	27																			
	Florida Everblades	ECHL	16	2	5	7	13																			
	Charlotte	ECHL	16	6	10	16	4																			
99-2000	Cincinnati	IHL	66	3	10	13	34												11	0	0	0	28			
2000-01	Carolina	NHL	2	0	0	0	0	0	0	0	2	0.0	0	0	0.0	1	1	13:18								
	Cincinnati	IHL	79	1	22	23	46												5	0	0	0	2			
	NHL Totals		**26**	**0**	**2**	**2**	**10**	**0**	**0**	**0**	**13**	**0.0**		**0**	**0.0**	**9**	**5**	**10:49**								

Rights transferred to **Carolina** after **Hartford** franchise relocated, June 25, 1997.

RUCINSKY, Martin

(roo-SHIHN-skee, MAHR-tihn) **MTL.**

Left wing. Shoots left. 6'1", 205 lbs. Born, Most, Czech., March 11, 1971. Edmonton's 2nd choice, 20th overall, in 1991 Entry Draft.

			Regular Season																Playoffs							
Season	Club	League	GP	G	A	Pts	PIM	PP	SH	GW	S	%	+/-	TF	F%	H	SB	Min	GP	G	A	Pts	PIM	PP	SH	GW
1988-89	CHZ Litvinov	Czech.	3	1	0	1	2																			
1989-90	CHZ Litvinov	Czech.	39	12	6	18													8	5	3	8				
1990-91	CHZ Litvinov	Czech.	56	24	20	44	69																			
1991-92	Edmonton	NHL	2	0	0	0	0	0	0	0	1	0.0	-3													
	Cape Breton	AHL	35	11	12	23	34																			
	Quebec	NHL	4	1	1	2	2	0	0	0	4	25.0	1													
	Halifax Citadels	AHL	7	1	1	2	6																			
1992-93	Quebec	NHL	77	18	30	48	51	4	0	1	133	13.5	16						6	1	1	2	4	1	0	0
1993-94	Quebec	NHL	60	9	23	32	58	4	0	1	96	9.4	4													
1994-95	CHZ Litvinov	Cze-Rep	13	12	10	22	54																			
	Quebec	NHL	20	3	6	9	14	0	0	0	32	9.4	5													
1995-96	HC Vsetin	Cze-Rep	1	1	1	2	0																			
	Colorado	NHL	22	4	11	15	14	0	0	1	39	10.3	10													
	Montreal	NHL	56	25	35	60	54	9	2	3	142	17.6	8													
1996-97	Montreal	NHL	70	28	27	55	62	6	3	3	172	16.3	1						5	0	0	0	4	0	0	0
1997-98	Montreal	NHL	78	21	32	53	84	5	3	3	192	10.9	13						10	3	0	3	4	1	0	0
	Czech-Republic	Olympics	6	3	1	4	4																			
1998-99	CHZ Litvinov	Cze-Rep	3	2	2	4	0																			
	Montreal	NHL	73	17	17	34	50	5	0	1	180	9.4	-25	12	50.0	75	18	18:12								
99-2000	Montreal	NHL	80	25	24	49	70	7	1	4	242	10.3	1	31	54.8	116	21	18:54								
2000-01	Montreal	NHL	57	16	22	38	66	5	1	4	141	11.3	-5	5	40.0	82	18	19:11								
	NHL Totals		**599**	**167**	**228**	**395**	**525**	**45**	**10**	**21**	**1374**	**12.2**		**48**	**52.1**	**273**	**57**	**18:44**	**21**	**4**	**1**	**5**	**12**	**2**	**0**	**0**

Played in NHL All-Star Game (2000)

Traded to **Quebec** by **Edmonton** for Ron Tugnutt and Brad Zavisha, March 10, 1992. Transferred to **Colorado** after **Quebec** franchise relocated, June 21, 1995. Traded to **Montreal** by **Colorado** with Andrei Kovalenko and Jocelyn Thibault for Patrick Roy and Mike Keane, December 6, 1995.

			Regular Season																Playoffs							
Season	Club	League	GP	G	A	Pts	PIM	PP	SH	GW	S	%	+/-	TF	F%	H	SB	Min	GP	G	A	Pts	PIM	PP	SH	GW

RUMBLE, Darren

(RUHM-buhl, DAIR-rehn) **ST.L.**

Defense. Shoots left. 6'1", 200 lbs. Born, Barrie, Ont., January 23, 1969. Philadelphia's 1st choice, 20th overall, in 1987 Entry Draft.

Season	Club	League	GP	G	A	Pts	PIM	PP	SH	GW	S	%	+/-	TF	F%	H	SB	Min	GP	G	A	Pts	PIM	PP	SH	GW
1985-86	Barrie Colts	OJHL-B	46	14	32	46	91																			
1986-87	Kitchener	OHL	64	11	32	43	44												4	0	1	1	9			
1987-88	Kitchener	OHL	55	15	50	65	64																			
1988-89	Kitchener	OHL	46	11	28	39	25												5	1	0	1	2			
1989-90	Hershey Bears	AHL	57	2	13	15	31																			
1990-91	**Philadelphia**	**NHL**	**3**	**1**	**0**	**1**	**0**	**0**	**0**	**0**	**2**	**50.0**	**1**													
	Hershey Bears	AHL	73	6	35	41	48												3	0	5	5	2			
1991-92	Hershey Bears	AHL	79	12	54	66	118												6	0	3	3	2			
1992-93	**Ottawa**	**NHL**	**69**	**3**	**13**	**16**	**61**	**0**	**0**	**0**	**92**	**3.3**	**–24**													
	New Haven	AHL	2	1	0	1	0																			
1993-94	**Ottawa**	**NHL**	**70**	**6**	**9**	**15**	**116**	**0**	**0**	**0**	**95**	**6.3**	**–50**													
	P.E.I. Senators	AHL	3	2	0	2	0																			
1994-95	P.E.I. Senators	AHL	70	7	46	53	77												11	0	6	6	4			
1995-96	**Philadelphia**	**NHL**	**5**	**0**	**0**	**0**	**4**	**0**	**0**	**0**	**7**	**0.0**	**0**													
	Hershey Bears	AHL	58	13	37	50	83												5	0	0	0	6			
1996-97	**Philadelphia**	**NHL**	**10**	**0**	**0**	**0**	**0**	**0**	**0**	**0**	**9**	**0.0**	**–2**													
	Philadelphia	AHL	72	18	44	62	83												7	0	3	3	19			
1997-98	Adler Mannheim	DEL	21	2	7	9	18																			
	Adler Mannheim	EuroHL	4	0	1	1	4																			
	San Antonio	IHL	46	7	22	29	47																			
1998-99	Utah Grizzlies	IHL	10	1	4	5	10																			
	Grand Rapids	IHL	53	6	22	28	44																			
99-2000	Grand Rapids	IHL	29	3	10	13	20																			
	Worcester	AHL	39	0	17	17	31												9	0	2	2	6			
2000-01	Worcester	AHL	53	6	24	30	65												8	0	1	1	10			
	St. Louis	**NHL**	**12**	**0**	**4**	**4**	**27**	**0**	**0**	**0**	**11**	**0.0**	**7**	**0**	**0.0**	**25**	**11**	**18:12**								
	NHL Totals		**169**	**10**	**26**	**36**	**208**	**0**	**0**	**0**	**216**	**4.6**		**0**	**0.0**	**25**	**11**	**18:12**								

AHL Second All-Star Team (1995) • AHL First All-Star Team (1997) • Won Eddie Shore Award (Top Defenseman - AHL) (1997)

Claimed by **Ottawa** from **Philadelphia** in Expansion Draft, June 18, 1992. Signed as a free agent by **Philadelphia**, July 31, 1995. Signed as a free agent by **St. Louis**, February 1, 2000.

RUUTU, Jarkko

(ROO-too, YAHR-koh) **VAN.**

Left wing. Shoots left. 6'2", 194 lbs. Born, Vantaa, Finland, August 23, 1975. Vancouver's 3rd choice, 68th overall, in 1998 Entry Draft.

Season	Club	League	GP	G	A	Pts	PIM	PP	SH	GW	S	%	+/-	TF	F%	H	SB	Min	GP	G	A	Pts	PIM	PP	SH	GW
1991-92	HIFK Helsinki	Finn-Jr.	1	0	0	0	0																			
1992-93	HIFK Helsinki-B	Finn-Jr.	33	26	21	47	53																			
	HIFK Helsinki	Finn-Jr.	1	0	0	0	0																			
1993-94	HIFK Helsinki	Finn-Jr.	19	9	12	21	44																			
1994-95	HIFK Helsinki	Finn-Jr.	35	26	22	48	117																			
1995-96	Michigan Tech	WCHA	39	12	10	22	96																			
1996-97	HIFK Helsinki	Finland	48	11	10	21	*155																			
1997-98	HIFK Helsinki	Finland	37	10	10	20	87												8	*7	4	11	10			
1998-99	HIFK Helsinki	Finland	25	10	4	14	136												9	0	2	2	43			
	HIFK Helsinki	EuroHL	5	1	2	3	8																			
99-2000	**Vancouver**	**NHL**	**8**	**0**	**1**	**1**	**6**	**0**	**0**	**0**	**4**	**0.0**	**–1**	**0**	**0.0**	**14**	**0**	**8:47**								
	Syracuse Crunch	AHL	65	26	32	58	164												4	3	1	4	8			
2000-01	**Vancouver**	**NHL**	**21**	**3**	**3**	**6**	**32**	**0**	**1**	**0**	**23**	**13.0**	**1**	**0**	**0.0**	**65**	**7**	**10:39**	**4**	**0**	**1**	**1**	**8**	**0**	**0**	**0**
	Kansas City	IHL	46	11	18	29	111																			
	NHL Totals		**29**	**3**	**4**	**7**	**38**	**0**	**1**	**0**	**27**	**11.1**		**0**	**0.0**	**79**	**7**	**10:08**	**4**	**0**	**1**	**1**	**8**	**0**	**0**	**0**

RYAN, Terry

(RIGH-yuhn, TAIR-ee)

Left wing. Shoots left. 6'1", 202 lbs. Born, St. John's, Nfld., January 14, 1977. Montreal's 1st choice, 8th overall, in 1995 Entry Draft.

Season	Club	League	GP	G	A	Pts	PIM	PP	SH	GW	S	%	+/-	TF	F%	H	SB	Min	GP	G	A	Pts	PIM	PP	SH	GW
1991-92	Quesnel	RMJHL	49	26	41	67	217																			
1992-93	Quesnel	RMJHL	29	31	25	56	222																			
	Vernon Lakers	BCJHL	9	5	6	11	15																			
	Tri-City Americans	WHL	1	0	0	0	0												1	0	1	1	5			
1993-94	Tri-City Americans	WHL	61	16	17	33	176												4	0	1	1	25			
1994-95	Tri-City Americans	WHL	70	50	60	110	207												17	12	15	27	36			
1995-96	Tri-City Americans	WHL	59	32	37	69	133												5	0	0	0	4			
	Fredericton	AHL																	3	0	0	0	2			
1996-97	Red Deer Rebels	WHL	16	13	22	35	10												16	18	6	24	32			
	Montreal	**NHL**	**3**	**0**	**0**	**0**	**0**	**0**	**0**	**0**	**0**	**0.0**	**0**													
1997-98	**Montreal**	**NHL**	**4**	**0**	**0**	**0**	**31**	**0**	**0**	**0**	**0**	**0.0**	**0**													
	Fredericton	AHL	71	21	18	39	256												3	1	1	2	0			
1998-99	**Montreal**	**NHL**	**1**	**0**	**0**	**0**	**5**	**0**	**0**	**0**	**0**	**0.0**	**0**	**0**	**0.0**	**0**	**0**	**3:09**								
	Fredericton	AHL	55	16	27	43	189												11	1	3	4	10			
99-2000	Utah Grizzlies	IHL	6	0	3	3	24																			
	Long Beach	IHL	1	0	0	0	4																			
	St. John's Leafs	AHL	50	7	17	24	176																			
2000-01	Colorado Kings	WCHL	31	15	25	40	140												8	6	4	10	34			
	Hershey Bears	AHL	8	0	1	1	36																			
	NHL Totals		**8**	**0**	**0**	**0**	**36**	**0**	**0**	**0**	**0**	**0.0**		**0**	**0.0**	**0**	**0**	**3:09**								

WHL West Second All-Star Team (1995)

Signed as a free agent by **Utah** (IHL) with **Montreal** retaining NHL rights, October 15, 1999. Signed as a free agent by **St. John's** (AHL) following release by **Utah** (IHL) with **Montreal** retaining NHL rights, November 12, 1999.

SACCO, Joe

(SAK-oh, JOH) **WSH.**

Right wing. Shoots left. 6'1", 190 lbs. Born, Medford, MA, February 4, 1969. Toronto's 4th choice, 71st overall, in 1987 Entry Draft.

Season	Club	League	GP	G	A	Pts	PIM	PP	SH	GW	S	%	+/-	TF	F%	H	SB	Min	GP	G	A	Pts	PIM	PP	SH	GW
1985-86	Medford Prep	Hi-School	20	30	30	60	....																			
1986-87	Medford Prep	Hi-School	21	22	32	54	....																			
1987-88	Boston University	H-East	34	16	20	36	40																			
1988-89	Boston University	H-East	33	21	19	40	66																			
1989-90	Boston University	H-East	44	28	24	52	70																			
1990-91	**Toronto**	**NHL**	**20**	**0**	**5**	**5**	**2**	**0**	**0**	**0**	**20**	**0.0**	**–5**													
	Newmarket	AHL	49	18	17	35	24																			
1991-92	United States	Nat-Team	50	11	26	37	61																			
	United States	Olympics	8	0	2	2	0																			
	Toronto	**NHL**	**17**	**7**	**4**	**11**	**4**	**0**	**0**	**1**	**40**	**17.5**	**8**													
	St. John's Leafs	AHL																	1	1	1	2	0			
1992-93	**Toronto**	**NHL**	**23**	**4**	**4**	**8**	**8**	**0**	**0**	**0**	**38**	**10.5**	**–4**													
	St. John's Leafs	AHL	37	14	16	30	45												7	6	4	10	2			
1993-94	**Anaheim**	**NHL**	**84**	**19**	**18**	**37**	**61**	**3**	**1**	**2**	**206**	**9.2**	**–11**													
1994-95	**Anaheim**	**NHL**	**41**	**10**	**8**	**18**	**23**	**2**	**0**	**0**	**77**	**13.0**	**–8**													
1995-96	**Anaheim**	**NHL**	**76**	**13**	**14**	**27**	**40**																			
1996-97	**Anaheim**	**NHL**	**77**	**12**	**17**	**29**	**35**	**1**	**1**	**2**	**131**	**9.2**	**1**						**11**	**2**	**0**	**2**	**2**	**0**	**0**	**0**
1997-98	**Anaheim**	**NHL**	**55**	**8**	**11**	**19**	**24**	**0**	**2**	**2**	**90**	**8.9**	**–1**													
	NY Islanders	**NHL**	**25**	**3**	**3**	**6**	**10**	**0**	**0**	**0**	**32**	**9.4**	**1**													
1998-99	**NY Islanders**	**NHL**	**73**	**3**	**0**	**3**	**45**	**0**	**1**	**2**	**84**	**3.6**	**–24**	**32**	**56.3**	**58**	**27**	**9:59**								
99-2000	**Washington**	**NHL**	**79**	**7**	**16**	**23**	**50**	**0**	**0**	**1**	**117**	**6.0**	**7**	**9**	**33.3**	**146**	**40**	**11:51**	**5**	**0**	**0**	**0**	**4**	**0**	**0**	**0**
2000-01	**Washington**	**NHL**	**69**	**7**	**7**	**14**	**48**	**0**	**0**	**0**	**81**	**8.6**	**4**	**1**	**100.0**	**97**	**41**	**11:10**	**6**	**0**	**0**	**0**	**2**	**0**	**0**	**0**
	NHL Totals		**639**	**93**	**107**	**200**	**350**	**6**	**5**	**10**	**916**	**10.2**		**42**	**52.4**	**301**	**108**	**11:01**	**22**	**2**	**0**	**2**	**8**	**0**	**0**	**0**

Claimed by **Anaheim** from **Toronto** in Expansion Draft, June 24, 1993. Traded to **NY Islanders** by **Anaheim** with J-J Daigneault and Mark Janssens for Travis Green, Doug Houda and Tony Tuzzolino, February 6, 1998. Signed as a free agent by **Washington**, August 9, 1999.

SAKIC, Joe
(SAK-ihk, JOH) **COL.**

Center. Shoots left. 5'11", 195 lbs. Born, Burnaby, B.C., July 7, 1969. Quebec's 2nd choice, 15th overall, in 1987 Entry Draft.

			Regular Season																Playoffs							
Season	Club	League	GP	G	A	Pts	PIM	PP	SH	GW	S	%	+/-	TF	F%	H	SB	Min	GP	G	A	Pts	PIM	PP	SH	GW
1985-86	Burnaby	BCAHA	80	83	73	156	96																			
	Lethbridge	WHL	3	0	0	0	0																			
1986-87	Swift Current	WHL	72	60	73	133	31												4	0	1	1	0			
1987-88	Swift Current	WHL	64	*78	82	*160	64												10	11	13	24	12			
1988-89	**Quebec**	**NHL**	70	23	39	62	24	10	0	2	148	15.5	-36													
1989-90	**Quebec**	**NHL**	80	39	63	102	27	8	1	2	234	16.7	-40													
1990-91	**Quebec**	**NHL**	80	48	61	109	24	12	3	7	245	19.6	-26													
1991-92	**Quebec**	**NHL**	69	29	65	94	20	6	3	1	217	13.4	5													
1992-93	**Quebec**	**NHL**	78	48	57	105	40	20	2	4	264	18.2	-3						6	3	3	6	2	1	0	0
1993-94	**Quebec**	**NHL**	84	28	64	92	18	10	1	9	279	10.0	-8													
1994-95	**Quebec**	**NHL**	47	19	43	62	30	3	2	5	157	12.1	7						6	4	1	5	0	1	1	1
1995-96♦	**Colorado**	**NHL**	82	51	69	120	44	17	6	7	339	15.0	14						22	*18	16	*34	14	6	0	6
1996-97	**Colorado**	**NHL**	65	22	52	74	34	10	2	5	261	8.4	-10						17	8	*17	25	14	3	0	0
1997-98	**Colorado**	**NHL**	64	27	36	63	50	12	1	2	254	10.6	0						6	2	3	5	6	0	1	2
	Canada	Olympics	4	1	2	3	4																			
1998-99	**Colorado**	**NHL**	73	41	55	96	29	12	5	6	255	16.1	23	1723	51.4	31	47	25:35	19	6	13	19	8	1	1	1
99-2000	**Colorado**	**NHL**	60	28	53	81	28	5	1	5	242	11.6	30	1392	53.8	19	26	23:16	17	2	7	9	8	2	0	0
2000-01♦	**Colorado**	**NHL**	82	54	64	118	30	19	3	12	332	16.3	45	2292	53.0	44	54	23:01	21	*13	13	*26	6	5	0	3
	NHL Totals		934	457	721	1178	398	144	30	67	3227	14.2		5407	52.7	94	127	23:57	114	56	73	129	58	19	3	13

WHL East Second All-Star Team (1987) • WHL East First All-Star Team (1988) • Canadian Major Junior Player of the Year (1988) • Shared Bob Clarke Trophy (Top Scoroer - WHL) with Theo Fleury (1988) • Won Conn Smythe Trophy (1996) • NHL First All-Star Team (2001) • Won Lady Byng Trophy (2001) • Won Hart Trophy (2001) • Won Lester B. Pearson Award (2001) • Played in NHL All-Star Game (1990, 1991, 1992, 1993, 1994, 1996, 1998, 2000, 2001)

Transferred to **Colorado** after **Quebec** franchise relocated, June 21, 1995.

SALEI, Ruslan
(sah-LAY, roos-LAHN) **ANA.**

Defense. Shoots left. 6'1", 207 lbs. Born, Minsk, USSR, November 2, 1974. Anaheim's 1st choice, 9th overall, in 1996 Entry Draft.

			Regular Season																Playoffs							
Season	Club	League	GP	G	A	Pts	PIM	PP	SH	GW	S	%	+/-	TF	F%	H	SB	Min	GP	G	A	Pts	PIM	PP	SH	GW
1992-93	Dynamo Minsk	CIS	9	1	0	1	10																			
1993-94	Tivali Minsk	CIS	39	2	3	5	50																			
1994-95	Tivali Minsk	CIS	51	4	2	6	44																			
1995-96	Las Vegas	IHL	76	7	23	30	123												15	3	7	10	18			
1996-97	**Anaheim**	**NHL**	30	0	1	1	37	0	0	0	14	0.0	-8													
	Baltimore Bandits	AHL	12	1	4	5	12																			
	Las Vegas	IHL	8	0	2	2	24												3	2	1	3	6			
1997-98	**Anaheim**	**NHL**	66	5	10	15	70	1	0	0	104	4.8	7													
	Cincinnati Ducks	AHL	6	3	6	9	14																			
	Belarus	Olympics	7	1	0	1	4																			
1998-99	**Anaheim**	**NHL**	74	2	14	16	65	1	0	0	123	1.6	1	0	0.0	154	105	22:03	3	0	0	0	4	0	0	0
99-2000	**Anaheim**	**NHL**	71	5	5	10	94	1	0	0	116	4.3	3	0	0.0	205	107	20:21								
2000-01	**Anaheim**	**NHL**	50	1	5	6	70	0	0	0	73	1.4	-14	0	0.0	146	78	20:40								
	NHL Totals		291	13	35	48	336	3	0	0	430	3.0		0	0.0	505	290	21:04	3	0	0	0	4	0	0	0

SALO, Sami
(SA-loh, SA-mee) **OTT.**

Defense. Shoots right. 6'3", 215 lbs. Born, Turku, Finland, September 2, 1974. Ottawa's 7th choice, 239th overall, in 1996 Entry Draft.

			Regular Season																Playoffs							
Season	Club	League	GP	G	A	Pts	PIM	PP	SH	GW	S	%	+/-	TF	F%	H	SB	Min	GP	G	A	Pts	PIM	PP	SH	GW
1991-92	Kiekko Turku	Finn-Jr.	23	4	5	9	26																			
1992-93	Kiekko Turku-2	Finn-Jr.	21	9	4	13	4																			
	Kiekko-67 Turku	Finn-Jr.	13	6	2	8	2																			
1993-94	TPS Turku	Finn-Jr.	36	7	13	20	16												7	0	1	1	10			
1994-95	TPS Turku	Finn-Jr.	14	1	3	4	6																			
	Kiekko-67 Turku	Finland-2	19	4	2	6	4																			
	TPS Turku	Finland	7	1	2	3	8												1	0	0	0	0			
1995-96	TPS Turku	Finland	47	7	14	21	32												11	1	3	4	8			
1996-97	TPS Turku	Finland	48	9	6	15	10												10	2	3	5	4			
	TPS Turku	EuroHL	6	0	2	2	6												2	0	0	0	2			
1997-98	Jokerit Helsinki	Finland	35	3	5	8	10												8	0	1	1	2			
	Jokerit Helsinki	EuroHL	6	1	1	2	2																			
1998-99	**Ottawa**	**NHL**	61	7	12	19	24	2	0	1	106	6.6	20	0	0.0	90	58	19:42	4	0	0	0	0	0	0	0
	Detroit Vipers	IHL	5	0	2	2	0																			
99-2000	**Ottawa**	**NHL**	37	6	8	14	2	3	0	1	85	7.1	6	0	0.0	52	29	20:18	6	1	1	2	0	1	0	0
2000-01	**Ottawa**	**NHL**	31	2	16	18	10	1	0	0	61	3.3	9	0	0.0	57	42	19:44	4	0	0	0	0	0	0	0
	NHL Totals		129	15	36	51	36	6	0	2	252	6.0		0	0.0	199	129	19:53	14	1	1	2	0	1	0	0

NHL All-Rookie Team (1999) • Missed majority of 1999-2000 season recovering from wrist injury originally suffered in game vs. Philadelphia, November 28, 1999. • Missed majority of 2000-01 season recovering from shoulder injury suffered in game vs. Atlanta, December 14, 2000.

SALVADOR, Bryce
(SAL-vuh-dohr, BRIGHS) **ST.L.**

Defense. Shoots left. 6'2", 215 lbs. Born, Brandon, Man., February 11, 1976. Tampa Bay's 6th choice, 138th overall, in 1994 Entry Draft.

			Regular Season																Playoffs							
Season	Club	League	GP	G	A	Pts	PIM	PP	SH	GW	S	%	+/-	TF	F%	H	SB	Min	GP	G	A	Pts	PIM	PP	SH	GW
1991-92	Brandon Kings	MAHA	52	6	23	29	38																			
1992-93	Lethbridge	WHL	64	1	4	5	29												4	0	0	0	0			
1993-94	Lethbridge	WHL	61	4	14	18	36												9	0	1	1	2			
1994-95	Lethbridge	WHL	67	1	9	10	88																			
1995-96	Lethbridge	WHL	56	4	12	16	75												3	0	1	1	2			
1996-97	Lethbridge	WHL	63	8	32	40	81												19	0	7	7	14			
1997-98	Worcester	AHL	46	2	8	10	74												11	0	1	1	45			
1998-99	Worcester	AHL	69	5	13	18	129												4	0	1	1	2			
99-2000	Worcester	AHL	55	0	13	13	53												9	0	1	1	2			
2000-01	**St. Louis**	**NHL**	75	2	8	10	69	0	0	1	60	3.3	-4	1	0.0	142	87	16:38	14	2	0	2	18	0	0	1
	NHL Totals		75	2	8	10	69	0	0	1	60	3.3		1	0.0	142	87	16:38	14	2	0	2	18	0	0	1

Signed as a free agent by **St. Louis**, December 16, 1996.

SAMSONOV, Sergei
(sam-SAWN-nahf, SAIR-gay) **BOS.**

Left wing. Shoots right. 5'8", 180 lbs. Born, Moscow, USSR, October 27, 1978. Boston's 2nd choice, 8th overall, in 1997 Entry Draft.

			Regular Season																Playoffs							
Season	Club	League	GP	G	A	Pts	PIM	PP	SH	GW	S	%	+/-	TF	F%	H	SB	Min	GP	G	A	Pts	PIM	PP	SH	GW
1994-95	CSKA Moscow	CIS-Jr.	50	110	72	182	....																			
	CSKA Moscow	CIS	13	2	2	4	14												2	0	0	0	0			
1995-96	CSKA Moscow	CIS	51	21	17	38	12												3	1	1	2	4			
1996-97	Detroit Vipers	IHL	73	29	35	64	18												19	8	4	12	12			
1997-98	**Boston**	**NHL**	81	22	25	47	8	7	0	3	159	13.8	9						6	2	5	7	0	0	0	1
1998-99	**Boston**	**NHL**	79	25	26	51	18	6	0	8	160	15.6	-6	0	0.0	39	10	16:23	11	3	1	4	0	0	0	0
99-2000	**Boston**	**NHL**	77	19	26	45	4	6	0	3	145	13.1	-6	3	0.0	29	9	16:32								
2000-01	**Boston**	**NHL**	82	29	46	75	18	3	0	3	215	13.5	6	14	42.9	41	19	19:23								
	NHL Totals		319	95	123	218	48	22	0	17	679	14.0		17	35.3	109	38	17:28	17	5	6	11	0	0	0	1

Won Garry F. Longman Memorial Trophy (Top Rookie - IHL) (1997) • NHL All-Rookie Team (1998) • Won Calder Memorial Trophy (1998) • Played in NHL All-Star Game (2001)

SAMUELSSON, Mikael
(SAM-yuhl-suhn, MIH-kigh-ehl) **NYR**

Right wing. Shoots left. 6'1", 195 lbs. Born, Mariefred, Sweden, December 23, 1976. San Jose's 7th choice, 145th overall, in 1998 Entry Draft.

			Regular Season																Playoffs							
Season	Club	League	GP	G	A	Pts	PIM	PP	SH	GW	S	%	+/-	TF	F%	H	SB	Min	GP	G	A	Pts	PIM	PP	SH	GW
1994-95	Sodertalje SK	Swede-Jr.	30	8	6	14	12																			
1995-96	Sodertalje SK	Swede-Jr.	22	13	12	25	20																			
	Sodertalje SK	Sweden-2	18	5	1	6	0												4	0	0	0	0			
1996-97	Sodertalje SK	Swede-Jr.	2	2	1	3	....																			
	Sodertalje SK	Sweden	29	3	2	5	10												10	0	0	0	4			
1997-98	IK Nykopings	Sweden-2	10	5	1	6	14																			
	Sodertalje SK	Sweden	41	11	9	20	66																			

			Regular Season																Playoffs							
Season	Club	League	GP	G	A	Pts	PIM	PP	SH	GW	S	%	+/-	TF	F%	H	SB	Min	GP	G	A	Pts	PIM	PP	SH	GW
1998-99	Sodertalje SK	Sweden-2	18	13	10	23	26												10	2	2	4	12			
	Vastra Frolunda	Sweden	27	0	5	5	10																			
99-2000	Brynas IF	Sweden	40	4	3	7	76												11	7	2	9	6			
	Brynas IF	EuroHL	4	0	2	2	4																			
2000-01	**San Jose**	**NHL**	**4**	**0**	**0**	**0**	**0**	**0**	**0**	**0**	**3**	**0.0**	**0**	**0**	**0.0**	**2**	**0**	**4:41**								
	Kentucky	AHL	66	32	46	78	58												3	1	0	1	0			
	NHL Totals		**4**	**0**	**0**	**0**	**0**	**0**	**0**	**0**	**3**	**0.0**		**0**	**0.0**	**2**	**0**	**4:41**								

Traded to **NY Rangers** by **San Jose** with Christian Gosselin for Adam Graves and future considerations, June 24, 2001.

SANDERSON, Geoff

(SAN-duhr-sohn, JEHF) **CBJ**

Left wing. Shoots left. 6', 190 lbs. Born, Hay River, N.W.T., February 1, 1972. Hartford's 2nd choice, 36th overall, in 1990 Entry Draft.

Season	Club	League	GP	G	A	Pts	PIM	PP	SH	GW	S	%	+/-	TF	F%	H	SB	Min	GP	G	A	Pts	PIM	PP	SH	GW
1987-88	St. Albert Royals	AMHL	45	65	55	120	175																			
1988-89	Swift Current	WHL	58	17	11	28	16												12	3	5	8	6			
1989-90	Swift Current	WHL	70	32	62	94	56												4	1	4	5	8			
1990-91	Swift Current	WHL	70	62	50	112	57												3	1	2	3	4			
	Hartford	**NHL**	**2**	**1**	**0**	**1**	**0**	**0**	**0**	**0**	**2**	**50.0**	**–2**						**3**	**0**	**0**	**0**	**0**	**0**	**0**	**0**
	Springfield	AHL																	1	0	0	0	2			
1991-92	**Hartford**	**NHL**	**64**	**13**	**18**	**31**	**18**	**2**	**0**	**1**	**98**	**13.3**	**5**						**7**	**1**	**0**	**1**	**2**	**0**	**0**	**0**
1992-93	**Hartford**	**NHL**	**82**	**46**	**43**	**89**	**28**	**21**	**2**	**4**	**271**	**17.0**	**–21**													
1993-94	**Hartford**	**NHL**	**82**	**41**	**26**	**67**	**42**	**15**	**1**	**6**	**266**	**15.4**	**–13**													
1994-95	HPK Hameenlinna	Finland	12	6	4	10	24																			
	Hartford	**NHL**	**46**	**18**	**14**	**32**	**24**	**4**	**0**	**4**	**170**	**10.6**	**–10**													
1995-96	**Hartford**	**NHL**	**81**	**34**	**31**	**65**	**40**	**6**	**0**	**7**	**314**	**10.8**	**0**													
1996-97	**Hartford**	**NHL**	**82**	**36**	**31**	**67**	**29**	**12**	**1**	**4**	**297**	**12.1**	**–9**													
1997-98	**Carolina**	**NHL**	**40**	**7**	**10**	**17**	**14**	**2**	**0**	**0**	**96**	**7.3**	**–4**													
	Vancouver	**NHL**	**9**	**0**	**3**	**3**	**4**	**0**	**0**	**0**	**29**	**0.0**	**–1**													
	Buffalo	**NHL**	**26**	**4**	**5**	**9**	**20**	**0**	**0**	**2**	**72**	**5.6**	**6**						**14**	**3**	**1**	**4**	**4**	**1**	**0**	**1**
1998-99	**Buffalo**	**NHL**	**75**	**12**	**18**	**30**	**22**	**1**	**0**	**1**	**155**	**7.7**	**8**	**4**	**50.0**	**43**	**9**	**12:55**	**19**	**4**	**6**	**10**	**14**	**0**	**0**	**1**
99-2000	**Buffalo**	**NHL**	**67**	**13**	**13**	**26**	**22**	**4**	**0**	**3**	**136**	**9.6**	**4**	**3**	**100.0**	**38**	**17**	**12:54**	**5**	**0**	**2**	**2**	**8**	**0**	**0**	**0**
2000-01	**Columbus**	**NHL**	**68**	**30**	**26**	**56**	**46**	**9**	**0**	**7**	**199**	**15.1**	**4**	**726**	**49.0**	**56**	**17**	**16:37**								
	NHL Totals		**724**	**255**	**238**	**493**	**309**	**76**	**4**	**39**	**2105**	**12.1**		**733**	**49.2**	**137**	**43**	**14:07**	**48**	**8**	**9**	**17**	**28**	**1**	**0**	**2**

Played in NHL All-Star Game (1994, 1997)

Transferred to **Carolina** after **Hartford** franchise relocated, June 25, 1997. Traded to **Vancouver** by **Carolina** with Sean Burke and Enrico Ciccone for Kirk McLean and Martin Gelinas, January 3, 1998. Traded to **Buffalo** by **Vancouver** for Brad May and Buffalo's 3rd round choice (later traded to Tampa Bay - Tampa Bay selected Jimmie Olvestad) in 1999 Entry Draft, February 4, 1998. Selected by **Columbus** from **Buffalo** in Expansion Draft, June 23, 2000.

SANDSTROM, Tomas

(SAND-struhm, TOH-mas)

Right wing. Shoots left. 6'2", 205 lbs. Born, Jakobstad, Finland, September 4, 1964. NY Rangers' 2nd choice, 36th overall, in 1982 Entry Draft.

Season	Club	League	GP	G	A	Pts	PIM	PP	SH	GW	S	%	+/-	TF	F%	H	SB	Min	GP	G	A	Pts	PIM	PP	SH	GW
1979-80	Fagersta HK	Sweden-2	6	1	1	2	0																			
1980-81	Fagersta HK	Sweden-2	20	23	5	28																				
1981-82	Fagersta HK	Sweden-2	32	28	11	39	74																			
1982-83	Brynas IF	Sweden	36	23	14	37	50																			
1983-84	Brynas IF	Sweden	34	19	10	29	81																			
	Sweden	Olympics	7	2	1	3	6																			
1984-85	**NY Rangers**	**NHL**	**74**	**29**	**29**	**58**	**51**	**5**	**0**	**3**	**190**	**15.3**	**3**						**3**	**0**	**2**	**2**	**0**	**0**	**0**	**0**
1985-86	**NY Rangers**	**NHL**	**73**	**25**	**29**	**54**	**109**	**8**	**2**	**1**	**238**	**10.5**	**–4**						**16**	**4**	**6**	**10**	**20**	**0**	**0**	**1**
1986-87	**NY Rangers**	**NHL**	**64**	**40**	**34**	**74**	**60**	**13**	**0**	**5**	**240**	**16.7**	**8**						**6**	**1**	**2**	**3**	**20**	**0**	**0**	**0**
1987-88	**NY Rangers**	**NHL**	**69**	**28**	**40**	**68**	**95**	**11**	**0**	**3**	**204**	**13.7**	**–6**													
1988-89	**NY Rangers**	**NHL**	**79**	**32**	**56**	**88**	**148**	**11**	**2**	**4**	**240**	**13.3**	**5**						**4**	**3**	**2**	**5**	**12**	**2**	**0**	**0**
1989-90	**NY Rangers**	**NHL**	**48**	**19**	**19**	**38**	**100**	**6**	**0**	**3**	**166**	**11.4**	**–10**													
	Los Angeles	**NHL**	**28**	**13**	**20**	**33**	**28**	**1**	**1**	**0**	**83**	**15.7**	**–1**						**10**	**5**	**4**	**9**	**19**	**0**	**0**	**0**
1990-91	**Los Angeles**	**NHL**	**68**	**45**	**44**	**89**	**106**	**16**	**0**	**6**	**221**	**20.4**	**27**						**10**	**4**	**4**	**8**	**14**	**3**	**0**	**0**
1991-92	**Los Angeles**	**NHL**	**49**	**17**	**22**	**39**	**70**	**5**	**0**	**4**	**147**	**11.6**	**–2**						**6**	**0**	**3**	**3**	**8**	**0**	**0**	**0**
1992-93	**Los Angeles**	**NHL**	**39**	**25**	**27**	**52**	**57**	**8**	**0**	**3**	**134**	**18.7**	**12**						**24**	**8**	**17**	**25**	**12**	**2**	**0**	**2**
1993-94	**Los Angeles**	**NHL**	**51**	**17**	**24**	**41**	**59**	**4**	**0**	**2**	**121**	**14.0**	**–12**													
	Pittsburgh	**NHL**	**27**	**6**	**11**	**17**	**24**	**0**	**0**	**1**	**72**	**8.3**	**5**						**6**	**0**	**0**	**0**	**4**	**0**	**0**	**0**
1994-95	Malmo IF	Sweden	12	10	5	15	14																			
	Pittsburgh	**NHL**	**47**	**21**	**23**	**44**	**42**	**4**	**1**	**3**	**116**	**18.1**	**1**						**12**	**3**	**3**	**6**	**16**	**2**	**0**	**0**
1995-96	**Pittsburgh**	**NHL**	**58**	**35**	**35**	**70**	**69**	**17**	**1**	**2**	**187**	**18.7**	**4**						**18**	**4**	**2**	**6**	**30**	**0**	**0**	**1**
1996-97	**Pittsburgh**	**NHL**	**40**	**9**	**15**	**24**	**33**	**1**	**1**	**0**	**73**	**12.3**	**4**													
	♦ **Detroit**	**NHL**	**34**	**9**	**9**	**18**	**36**	**0**	**1**	**2**	**66**	**13.6**	**2**						**20**	**0**	**4**	**4**	**24**	**0**	**0**	**0**
1997-98	**Anaheim**	**NHL**	**77**	**9**	**8**	**17**	**64**	**2**	**1**	**0**	**136**	**6.6**	**–25**													
	Sweden	Olympics	4	0	1	1	0																			
1998-99	**Anaheim**	**NHL**	**58**	**15**	**17**	**32**	**42**	**7**	**0**	**2**	**107**	**14.0**	**–5**	**8**	**25.0**	**47**	**11**	**17:22**	**4**	**0**	**0**	**0**	**4**	**0**	**0**	**0**
99-2000	Malmo IF	Sweden	42	16	13	29	28												6	3	2	5	10			
2000-01	Malmo IF	Sweden	50	17	9	26	90												8	3	3	6	*60			
	NHL Totals		**983**	**394**	**462**	**856**	**1193**	**119**	**10**	**44**	**2741**	**14.4**		**8**	**25.0**	**47**	**11**	**17:22**	**139**	**32**	**49**	**81**	**183**	**9**	**0**	**4**

NHL All-Rookie Team (1985) • Played in NHL All-Star Game (1988, 1991)

Traded to **LA Kings** by **NY Rangers** with Tony Granato for Bernie Nicholls, January 20, 1990. Traded to **Pittsburgh** by **LA Kings** with Shawn McEachern for Marty McSorley and Jim Paek, February 16, 1994. Traded to **Detroit** by **Pittsburgh** for Greg Johnson, January 27, 1997. Signed as a free agent by **Anaheim**, October 20, 1997.

SANDWITH, Terran

(SAND-wihth, TAIR-ran)

Defense. Shoots left. 6'4", 210 lbs. Born, Edmonton, Alta., April 17, 1972. Philadelphia's 4th choice, 42nd overall, in 1990 NHL Entry Draft.

Season	Club	League	GP	G	A	Pts	PIM	PP	SH	GW	S	%	+/-	TF	F%	H	SB	Min	GP	G	A	Pts	PIM	PP	SH	GW
1987-88	Hobbema Hawks	AJHL	58	5	8	13	106																			
1988-89	Tri-City Americans	WHL	31	0	0	0	29												6	0	0	0	4			
1989-90	Tri-City Americans	WHL	70	4	14	18	92												7	0	2	2	14			
1990-91	Tri-City Americans	WHL	46	5	17	22	132												7	1	0	1	14			
1991-92	Brandon	WHL	41	6	14	20	115																			
	Saskatoon Blades	WHL	18	2	5	7	53												18	2	1	3	28			
1992-93	Hershey Bears	AHL	61	1	12	13	140																			
1993-94	Hershey Bears	AHL	62	3	5	8	169												2	0	1	1	4			
1994-95	Hershey Bears	AHL	11	1	1	2	32																			
	Kansas City	IHL	25	0	3	3	73																			
1995-96	Canada	Nat-Team	47	3	12	15	63																			
	Cape Breton	AHL	5	0	2	2	4																			
1996-97	Hamilton Bulldogs	AHL	78	3	6	9	213												22	0	2	2	27			
1997-98	**Edmonton**	**NHL**	**8**	**0**	**0**	**0**	**6**	**0**	**0**	**0**	**4**	**0.0**	**–4**													
	Hamilton Bulldogs	AHL	54	4	8	12	131												9	0	0	0	10			
1998-99	Cincinnati Ducks	AHL	40	0	6	6	77																			
99-2000	St. John's Leafs	AHL	78	1	10	11	155																			
2000-01	Hamilton Bulldogs	AHL	59	1	12	13	154																			
	Houston Aeros	IHL	14	0	0	0	17												5	0	0	0	6			
	NHL Totals		**8**	**0**	**0**	**0**	**6**	**0**	**0**	**0**	**4**	**0.0**														

Signed as a free agent by **Edmonton**, April 10, 1996. Signed as a free agent by **Anaheim**, July 13, 1998. Signed as a free agent by **Toronto**, July 2, 1999. Signed as a free agent by **Edmonton**, July 19, 2000.

SAPRYKIN, Oleg

(sah-PRIH-kihn, OH-lehg) **CGY.**

Center. Shoots left. 6', 195 lbs. Born, Moscow, USSR, February 12, 1981. Calgary's 1st choice, 11th overall, in 1999 Entry Draft.

Season	Club	League	GP	G	A	Pts	PIM	PP	SH	GW	S	%	+/-	TF	F%	H	SB	Min	GP	G	A	Pts	PIM	PP	SH	GW
1997-98	HC Moscow-2	Russia-2	15	0	3	3	6																			
	CSKA Moscow	Russia	20	0	2	2	8																			
1998-99	Seattle T-Birds	WHL	66	47	46	93	107												11	5	11	16	36			

			Regular Season																Playoffs							
Season	Club	League	GP	G	A	Pts	PIM	PP	SH	GW	S	%	+/-	TF	F%	H	SB	Min	GP	G	A	Pts	PIM	PP	SH	GW
99-2000	Seattle T-Birds	WHL	48	30	36	66	91	....	....	....	....	....	....	....	....	....	....	....	6	3	3	6	37	....	....	....
	Calgary	**NHL**	**4**	**0**	**1**	**1**	**2**	**0**	**0**	**0**	**2**	**0.0**	**–4**	**0**	**0.0**	**7**	**2**	**12:35**	....	....	....	....	....	....	....	....
2000-01	**Calgary**	**NHL**	**59**	**9**	**14**	**23**	**43**	**2**	**0**	**0**	**95**	**9.5**	**4**	**2**	**50.0**	**34**	**12**	**12:10**	....	....	....	....	....	....	....	....
	NHL Totals		**63**	**9**	**15**	**24**	**45**	**2**	**0**	**0**	**97**	**9.3**		**2**	**50.0**	**41**	**14**	**12:12**	....	....	....	....	....	....	....	....

WHL West Second All-Star Team (1999, 2000)

SARAULT, Yves

(sah-ROH, EEV) **NSH.**

Left wing. Shoots left. 6'1", 190 lbs. Born, Valleyfield, Que., December 23, 1972. Montreal's 4th choice, 61st overall, in 1991 Entry Draft.

Season	Club	League	GP	G	A	Pts	PIM	PP	SH	GW	S	%	+/-	TF	F%	H	SB	Min	GP	G	A	Pts	PIM	PP	SH	GW
1987-88	Lac St-Louis	QAAA	4	0	0	0	4	....	....	....	....	....	....	....	....	....	....	....	....	....	....	....	....	....	....	....
1988-89	Lac St-Louis	QAAA	42	23	30	53	64	....	....	....	....	....	....	....	....	....	....	....	3	2	3	5	4	....	....	....
1989-90	Victoriaville Tigres	QMJHL	70	12	28	40	140	....	....	....	....	....	....	....	....	....	....	....	16	0	3	3	26	....	....	....
1990-91	St-Jean Lynx	QMJHL	56	22	24	46	113	....	....	....	....	....	....	....	....	....	....	....	....	....	....	....	....	....	....	....
1991-92	St-Jean Lynx	QMJHL	50	28	38	66	96	....	....	....	....	....	....	....	....	....	....	....	....	....	....	....	....	....	....	....
	Trois-Rivieres	QMJHL	18	15	14	29	12	....	....	....	....	....	....	....	....	....	....	....	15	10	10	20	18	....	....	....
1992-93	Fredericton	AHL	59	14	17	31	41	....	....	....	....	....	....	....	....	....	....	....	3	0	1	1	2	....	....	....
	Wheeling	ECHL	2	1	3	4	0	....	....	....	....	....	....	....	....	....	....	....	....	....	....	....	....	....	....	....
1993-94	Fredericton	AHL	60	13	14	27	72	....	....	....	....	....	....	....	....	....	....	....	....	....	....	....	....	....	....	....
1994-95	Fredericton	AHL	69	24	21	45	96	....	....	....	....	....	....	....	....	....	....	....	13	2	1	3	33	....	....	....
	Montreal	**NHL**	**8**	**0**	**1**	**1**	**0**	**0**	**0**	**0**	**9**	**0.0**	**–1**	....	....	....	....	....	....	....	....	....	....	....	....	....
1995-96	**Montreal**	**NHL**	**14**	**0**	**0**	**0**	**4**	**0**	**0**	**0**	**14**	**0.0**	**–7**	....	....	....	....	....	....	....	....	....	....	....	....	....
	Calgary	**NHL**	**11**	**2**	**1**	**3**	**4**	**0**	**0**	**1**	**12**	**16.7**	**–2**	....	....	....	....	....	....	....	....	....	....	....	....	....
	Saint John Flames	AHL	26	10	12	22	34	....	....	....	....	....	....	....	....	....	....	....	16	6	2	8	33	....	....	....
1996-97	**Colorado**	**NHL**	**28**	**2**	**1**	**3**	**6**	**0**	**0**	**0**	**41**	**4.9**	**0**	....	....	....	....	....	**5**	**0**	**0**	**0**	**2**	**0**	**0**	**0**
	Hershey Bears	AHL	6	2	3	5	8	....	....	....	....	....	....	....	....	....	....	....	....	....	....	....	....	....	....	....
1997-98	**Colorado**	**NHL**	**2**	**1**	**0**	**1**	**0**	**0**	**0**	**0**	**1**	**100.0**	**1**	....	....	....	....	....	....	....	....	....	....	....	....	....
	Hershey Bears	AHL	63	23	36	59	43	....	....	....	....	....	....	....	....	....	....	....	7	1	2	3	14	....	....	....
1998-99	**Ottawa**	**NHL**	**11**	**0**	**1**	**1**	**4**	**0**	**0**	**0**	**7**	**0.0**	**1**	**0**	**0.0**	**15**	**1**	**7:15**	....	....	....	....	....	....	....	....
	Detroit Vipers	IHL	36	11	12	23	52	....	....	....	....	....	....	....	....	....	....	....	11	7	2	9	40	....	....	....
99-2000	**Ottawa**	**NHL**	**11**	**0**	**2**	**2**	**7**	**0**	**0**	**0**	**13**	**0.0**	**–3**	**1**	**0.0**	**5**	**1**	**9:03**	....	....	....	....	....	....	....	....
	Grand Rapids	IHL	62	17	26	43	77	....	....	....	....	....	....	....	....	....	....	....	17	7	4	11	32	....	....	....
2000-01	**Atlanta**	**NHL**	**20**	**5**	**4**	**9**	**26**	**2**	**0**	**0**	**44**	**11.4**	**–9**	**2**	**50.0**	**30**	**4**	**13:08**	....	....	....	....	....	....	....	....
	Orlando	IHL	35	17	17	34	42	....	....	....	....	....	....	....	....	....	....	....	....	....	....	....	....	....	....	....
	NHL Totals		**105**	**10**	**10**	**20**	**51**	**2**	**0**	**1**	**141**	**7.1**		**3**	**33.3**	**50**	**6**	**10:32**	**5**	**0**	**0**	**0**	**2**	**0**	**0**	**0**

QMJHL Second All-Star Team (1992)

Traded to **Calgary** by **Montreal** with Craig Ferguson for Calgary's 8th round choice (Petr Kubos) in 1997 Entry Draft, November 26, 1995. Signed as a free agent by **Colorado**, September 13, 1996. Signed as a free agent by **Ottawa**, August 7, 1998. Signed as a free agent by **Atlanta**, July 20, 2000. Claimed on waivers by **Nashville** from **Atlanta**, June 19, 2001.

SARICH, Cory

(SAHR-ihch, KOH-ree) **T.B.**

Defense. Shoots right. 6'3", 193 lbs. Born, Saskatoon, Sask., August 16, 1978. Buffalo's 2nd choice, 27th overall, in 1996 Entry Draft.

Season	Club	League	GP	G	A	Pts	PIM	PP	SH	GW	S	%	+/-	TF	F%	H	SB	Min	GP	G	A	Pts	PIM	PP	SH	GW
1994-95	Saskatoon	SMHL	31	5	22	27	99	....	....	....	....	....	....	....	....	....	....	....	....	....	....	....	....	....	....	....
	Saskatoon Blades	WHL	6	0	0	0	4	....	....	....	....	....	....	....	....	....	....	....	3	0	1	1	0	....	....	....
1995-96	Saskatoon Blades	WHL	59	5	18	23	54	....	....	....	....	....	....	....	....	....	....	....	3	0	0	0	4	....	....	....
1996-97	Saskatoon Blades	WHL	58	6	27	33	158	....	....	....	....	....	....	....	....	....	....	....	....	....	....	....	....	....	....	....
1997-98	Saskatoon Blades	WHL	33	5	24	29	90	....	....	....	....	....	....	....	....	....	....	....	....	....	....	....	....	....	....	....
	Seattle T-Birds	WHL	13	3	16	19	47	....	....	....	....	....	....	....	....	....	....	....	0	0	0	0	0	....	....	....
1998-99	**Buffalo**	**NHL**	**4**	**0**	**0**	**0**	**0**	**0**	**0**	**0**	**2**	**0.0**	**3**	**0**	**0.0**	**7**	**0**	**13:11**	....	....	....	....	....	....	....	....
	Rochester	AHL	77	3	26	29	82	....	....	....	....	....	....	....	....	....	....	....	20	2	4	6	14	....	....	....
99-2000	**Buffalo**	**NHL**	**42**	**0**	**4**	**4**	**35**	**0**	**0**	**0**	**49**	**0.0**	**2**	**0**	**0.0**	**108**	**31**	**17:42**	....	....	....	....	....	....	....	....
	Rochester	AHL	15	0	6	6	44	....	....	....	....	....	....	....	....	....	....	....	....	....	....	....	....	....	....	....
	Tampa Bay	**NHL**	**17**	**0**	**2**	**2**	**42**	**0**	**0**	**0**	**20**	**0.0**	**–8**	**0**	**0.0**	**44**	**12**	**20:42**	....	....	....	....	....	....	....	....
2000-01	**Tampa Bay**	**NHL**	**73**	**1**	**8**	**9**	**106**	**0**	**0**	**1**	**66**	**1.5**	**–25**	**3**	**0.0**	**139**	**84**	**18:44**	....	....	....	....	....	....	....	....
	Detroit Vipers	IHL	3	0	2	2	2	....	....	....	....	....	....	....	....	....	....	....	....	....	....	....	....	....	....	....
	NHL Totals		**136**	**1**	**14**	**15**	**183**	**0**	**0**	**1**	**137**	**0.7**		**3**	**0.0**	**298**	**127**	**18:30**	....	....	....	....	....	....	....	....

WHL West Second All-Star Team (1998)

Traded to **Tampa Bay** by **Buffalo** with Wayne Primeau, Brian Holzinger and Buffalo's 3rd round choice (Alexander Kharitonov) in 2000 Entry Draft for Chris Gratton and Tampa Bay's 2nd round choice (Derek Roy) in 2001 Entry Draft, March 9, 2000.

SATAN, Miroslav

(SHA-tuhn, MEER-oh-slahv) **BUF.**

Wing. Shoots left. 6'3", 192 lbs. Born, Topolcany, Czech., October 22, 1974. Edmonton's 6th choice, 111th overall, in 1993 Entry Draft.

Season	Club	League	GP	G	A	Pts	PIM	PP	SH	GW	S	%	+/-	TF	F%	H	SB	Min	GP	G	A	Pts	PIM	PP	SH	GW
1991-92	HC Topocalny	Czech-Jr.	31	30	22	52	....	....	....	....	....	....	....	....	....	....	....	....	....	....	....	....	....	....	....	....
	HC Topocalny	Czech-2	9	2	1	3	6	....	....	....	....	....	....	....	....	....	....	....	....	....	....	....	....	....	....	....
1992-93	Dukla Trencin	Czech.	38	11	6	17	....	....	....	....	....	....	....	....	....	....	....	....	....	....	....	....	....	....	....	....
1993-94	Dukla Trencin	Slovakia	30	32	16	48	16	....	....	....	....	....	....	....	....	....	....	....	....	....	....	....	....	....	....	....
	Slovakia	Olympics	8	*9	0	9	0	....	....	....	....	....	....	....	....	....	....	....	....	....	....	....	....	....	....	....
1994-95	Cape Breton	AHL	25	24	16	40	15	....	....	....	....	....	....	....	....	....	....	....	....	....	....	....	....	....	....	....
	Detroit Vipers	IHL	8	1	3	4	4	....	....	....	....	....	....	....	....	....	....	....	....	....	....	....	....	....	....	....
	San Diego Gulls	IHL	6	0	2	2	6	....	....	....	....	....	....	....	....	....	....	....	....	....	....	....	....	....	....	....
1995-96	**Edmonton**	**NHL**	**62**	**18**	**17**	**35**	**22**	**6**	**0**	**4**	**113**	**15.9**	**0**	....	....	....	....	....	....	....	....	....	....	....	....	....
1996-97	**Edmonton**	**NHL**	**64**	**17**	**11**	**28**	**22**	**5**	**0**	**2**	**90**	**18.9**	**–4**	....	....	....	....	....	....	....	....	....	....	....	....	....
	Buffalo	**NHL**	**12**	**8**	**2**	**10**	**4**	**2**	**0**	**1**	**29**	**27.6**	**1**	....	....	....	....	....	**7**	**0**	**0**	**0**	**0**	**0**	**0**	**0**
1997-98	**Buffalo**	**NHL**	**79**	**22**	**24**	**46**	**34**	**9**	**0**	**4**	**139**	**15.8**	**2**	....	....	....	....	....	**14**	**5**	**4**	**9**	**4**	**4**	**0**	**1**
1998-99	**Buffalo**	**NHL**	**81**	**40**	**26**	**66**	**44**	**13**	**3**	**6**	**208**	**19.2**	**24**	**9**	**55.6**	**42**	**24**	**20:49**	**12**	**3**	**5**	**8**	**2**	**1**	**0**	**1**
99-2000	Dukla Trencin	Slovakia	3	2	8	10	2	....	....	....	....	....	....	....	....	....	....	....	....	....	....	....	....	....	....	....
	Buffalo	**NHL**	**81**	**33**	**34**	**67**	**32**	**5**	**3**	**5**	**265**	**12.5**	**16**	**7**	**14.3**	**45**	**28**	**20:35**	**5**	**3**	**2**	**5**	**0**	**0**	**0**	**0**
2000-01	**Buffalo**	**NHL**	**82**	**29**	**33**	**62**	**36**	**8**	**2**	**4**	**206**	**14.1**	**5**	**11**	**36.4**	**36**	**30**	**19:56**	**13**	**3**	**10**	**13**	**8**	**1**	**0**	**0**
	NHL Totals		**461**	**167**	**147**	**314**	**194**	**48**	**8**	**26**	**1050**	**15.9**		**27**	**37.0**	**123**	**82**	**20:26**	**51**	**14**	**21**	**35**	**14**	**6**	**0**	**2**

Played in NHL All-Star Game (2000)

Traded to **Buffalo** by **Edmonton** for Barrie Moore and Craig Millar, March 18, 1997.

SAVAGE, Andre

(SA-vahj, AWN-dray) **VAN.**

Center. Shoots right. 6', 195 lbs. Born, Ottawa, Ont., May 27, 1975.

Season	Club	League	GP	G	A	Pts	PIM	PP	SH	GW	S	%	+/-	TF	F%	H	SB	Min	GP	G	A	Pts	PIM	PP	SH	GW
1992-93	Gloucester	OCJHL	54	34	34	68	38	....	....	....	....	....	....	....	....	....	....	....	....	....	....	....	....	....	....	....
1993-94	Gloucester	OCJHL	57	43	74	117	44	....	....	....	....	....	....	....	....	....	....	....	....	....	....	....	....	....	....	....
1994-95	Michigan Tech	WCHA	39	7	17	24	56	....	....	....	....	....	....	....	....	....	....	....	....	....	....	....	....	....	....	....
1995-96	Michigan Tech	WCHA	38	13	27	40	42	....	....	....	....	....	....	....	....	....	....	....	....	....	....	....	....	....	....	....
1996-97	Michigan Tech	WCHA	37	18	20	38	34	....	....	....	....	....	....	....	....	....	....	....	....	....	....	....	....	....	....	....
1997-98	Michigan Tech	WCHA	33	14	27	41	34	....	....	....	....	....	....	....	....	....	....	....	....	....	....	....	....	....	....	....
1998-99	**Boston**	**NHL**	**6**	**1**	**0**	**1**	**0**	**0**	**0**	**0**	**8**	**12.5**	**2**	**32**	**65.6**	**3**	**1**	**9:31**	....	....	....	....	....	....	....	....
	Providence Bruins	AHL	63	27	42	69	54	....	....	....	....	....	....	....	....	....	....	....	5	0	1	1	0	....	....	....
99-2000	**Boston**	**NHL**	**43**	**7**	**13**	**20**	**10**	**2**	**0**	**1**	**70**	**10.0**	**–8**	**619**	**55.1**	**50**	**10**	**14:40**	....	....	....	....	....	....	....	....
	Providence Bruins	AHL	30	15	17	32	22	....	....	....	....	....	....	....	....	....	....	....	14	6	7	13	22	....	....	....
2000-01	**Boston**	**NHL**	**1**	**0**	**0**	**0**	**0**	**0**	**0**	**0**	**1**	**0.0**	**0**	**3**	**100.0**	**0**	**0**	**4:38**	....	....	....	....	....	....	....	....
	Providence Bruins	AHL	35	13	15	28	47	....	....	....	....	....	....	....	....	....	....	....	17	3	4	7	18	....	....	....
	NHL Totals		**50**	**8**	**13**	**21**	**10**	**2**	**0**	**1**	**79**	**10.1**		**654**	**55.8**	**53**	**11**	**13:51**	....	....	....	....	....	....	....	....

WCHA First All-Star Team (1998)

Signed as a free agent by **Boston**, June 18, 1998. Signed as a free agent by **Vancouver**, August 2, 2001.

SAVAGE, Brian
(SA-vuhj, BRIGH-uhn) **MTL.**

Right wing. Shoots left. 6'1", 192 lbs. Born, Sudbury, Ont., February 24, 1971. Montreal's 11th choice, 171st overall, in 1991 Entry Draft.

Season	Club	League	GP	G	A	Pts	PIM	PP	SH	GW	S	%	+/-	TF	F%	H	SB	Min	Playoffs GP	G	A	Pts	PIM	PP	SH	GW
1989-90	Sudbury Cubs	NOJHA	32	45	40	85	61																			
1990-91	U. of Miami-Ohio	CCHA	28	5	6	11	26																			
1991-92	U. of Miami-Ohio	CCHA	40	24	16	40	43																			
1992-93	U. of Miami-Ohio	CCHA	38	*37	21	58	44																			
1993-94	Canada	Nat-Team	51	20	26	46	38																			
	Canada	Olympics	8	2	2	4	6																			
	Montreal	NHL	3	1	0	1	0	0	0	0	3	33.3	0						3	0	2	2	0	0	0	0
	Fredericton	AHL	17	12	15	27	4																			
1994-95	Montreal	NHL	37	12	7	19	27	0	0	0	64	18.8	5													
1995-96	Montreal	NHL	75	25	8	33	28	4	0	4	150	16.7	-8						6	0	2	2	2	0	0	0
1996-97	Montreal	NHL	81	23	37	60	39	5	0	2	219	10.5	-14						5	1	1	2	0	0	0	0
1997-98	Montreal	NHL	64	26	17	43	36	8	0	7	152	17.1	11						9	0	2	2	6	0	0	0
1998-99	Montreal	NHL	54	16	10	26	20	5	0	4	124	12.9	-14	70	44.3	57	14	16:30								
99-2000	Montreal	NHL	38	17	12	29	19	6	1	5	107	15.9	-4	67	47.8	27	12	17:56								
2000-01	Montreal	NHL	62	21	24	45	26	12	0	1	172	12.2	-13	30	56.7	70	9	18:50								
	NHL Totals		414	141	115	256	195	40	1	23	991	14.2		167	47.9	154	35	17:48	23	1	7	8	8	0	0	0

CCHA First All-Star Team (1993) • NCAA West Second All-American Team (1993)

• Missed majority of 1999-2000 season recovering from neck injury suffered in game vs. LA Kings, November 20, 1999.

SAVAGE, Reggie
(SA-vuhj, REH-jee)

Center. Shoots left. 5'10", 197 lbs. Born, Montreal, Que., May 1, 1970. Washington's 1st choice, 15th overall, in 1988 Entry Draft.

Season	Club	League	GP	G	A	Pts	PIM	PP	SH	GW	S	%	+/-	TF	F%	H	SB	Min	Playoffs GP	G	A	Pts	PIM	PP	SH	GW
1985-86	Richelieu Elites	QAAA	40	38	26	64													7	10	1	11				
1986-87	Richelieu Elites	QAAA	42	82	57	139	44												9	10	9	19	10			
1987-88	Victoriaville Tigres	QMJHL	68	68	54	122	77												5	2	3	5	8			
1988-89	Victoriaville Tigres	QMJHL	54	58	55	113	178												16	15	13	28	52			
1989-90	Victoriaville Tigres	QMJHL	63	51	43	94	79												16	13	10	23	40			
1990-91	Washington	NHL	1	0	0	0	0	0	0	0	2	0.0	-1													
	Baltimore	AHL	62	32	29	61	10												6	1	1	2	6			
1991-92	Baltimore	AHL	77	42	28	70	51																			
1992-93	Washington	NHL	16	2	3	5	12	2	0	0	20	10.0	-4													
	Baltimore	AHL	40	37	18	55	28																			
1993-94	Quebec	NHL	17	3	4	7	16	1	0	0	25	12.0	3													
	Cornwall Aces	AHL	33	21	13	34	56																			
1994-95	Cornwall Aces	AHL	34	13	7	20	56												14	5	6	11	40			
1995-96	Atlanta Knights	IHL	66	22	14	36	118																			
	Syracuse Crunch	AHL	10	9	5	14	28												16	9	6	15	54			
1996-97	Springfield	AHL	68	32	25	57	103												17	6	7	13	24			
1997-98	Kansas City	IHL	51	6	10	16	60																			
	San Antonio	IHL	22	6	12	18	24																			
	Orlando	IHL	10	5	5	10	18												17	2	9	11	60			
1998-99	HC Asiago	Alpenliga	27	25	27	52	69																			
	HC Asiago	Italy	16	18	15	33	8												2	1	0	1	22			
99-2000	Syracuse Crunch	AHL	78	36	34	70	135												4	0	0	0	8			
2000-01	Syracuse Crunch	AHL	78	37	24	61	90												5	0	2	2	16			
	NHL Totals		34	5	7	12	28	3	0	0	47	10.6														

Traded to **Quebec** by **Washington** with Paul MacDermid for Mike Hough, June 20, 1993. Signed as a free agent by **Phoenix**, August 28, 1996. Signed as a free agent by **Vancouver**, June 17, 1999. Signed as a free agent by **Columbus**, June 2, 2000. Signed as a free agent by **HC Biel-Bienne** (Switz-2), June 21, 2001.

SAVARD, Marc
(sa-VAHR, MAHRK) **CGY.**

Center. Shoots left. 5'10", 185 lbs. Born, Ottawa, Ont., July 17, 1977. NY Rangers' 3rd choice, 91st overall, in 1995 Entry Draft.

Season	Club	League	GP	G	A	Pts	PIM	PP	SH	GW	S	%	+/-	TF	F%	H	SB	Min	Playoffs GP	G	A	Pts	PIM	PP	SH	GW
1992-93	Metcalfe Jets	OJHL-B	36	*44	55	*99	38																			
1993-94	Oshawa Generals	OHL	61	18	39	57	20												5	4	3	7	8			
1994-95	Oshawa Generals	OHL	66	43	96	*139	78												7	5	6	11	8			
1995-96	Oshawa Generals	OHL	48	28	59	87	77												5	4	5	9	6			
1996-97	Oshawa Generals	OHL	64	43	*87	*130	94												18	13	*24	*37	20			
1997-98	NY Rangers	NHL	28	1	5	6	4	0	0	0	32	3.1	-4													
	Hartford	AHL	58	21	53	74	66												15	8	19	27	24			
1998-99	NY Rangers	NHL	70	9	36	45	38	4	0	1	116	7.8	-7	956	48.4	30	18	14:35								
	Hartford	AHL	9	3	10	13	16												7	1	12	13	16			
99-2000	Calgary	NHL	78	22	31	53	56	4	0	3	184	12.0	-2	1021	49.6	44	33	16:36								
2000-01	Calgary	NHL	77	23	42	65	46	10	1	5	197	11.7	-12	1050	53.1	48	19	19:13								
	NHL Totals		253	55	114	169	144	18	1	9	529	10.4		3027	50.4	122	70	16:52								

OHL Second All-Star Team (1995)

Traded to **Calgary** by **NY Rangers** with NY Rangers 1st round choice (Oleg Saprykin) in 1999 Entry Draft for the rights to Jan Hlavac and Calgary's 1st (Jamie Lundmark) and 3rd (later traded back to Calgary - Calgary selected Craig Andersson) round choices in 1999 Entry Draft, June 26, 1999.

SAWYER, Kevin
(SOI-yuhr, KEH-vihn) **ANA.**

Left wing. Shoots left. 6'2", 205 lbs. Born, Christina Lake, B.C., February 21, 1974.

Season	Club	League	GP	G	A	Pts	PIM	PP	SH	GW	S	%	+/-	TF	F%	H	SB	Min	Playoffs GP	G	A	Pts	PIM	PP	SH	GW
1991-92	Grand Forks	KIJHL	24	9	11	20	200																			
	Kelowna Spartans	BCJHL	3	0	0	0	9																			
	Vernon Lakers	BCJHL	12	0	1	1	18																			
	Penticton	BCJHL	3	0	0	0	13																			
1992-93	Spokane Chiefs	WHL	62	4	3	7	274												8	1	1	2	13			
1993-94	Spokane Chiefs	WHL	60	10	15	25	350												3	0	1	1	6			
1994-95	Spokane Chiefs	WHL	54	7	9	16	365												11	2	0	2	58			
	Peoria Rivermen	IHL																	2	0	0	0	12			
1995-96	St. Louis	NHL	6	0	0	0	23	0	0	0	1	0.0	-2													
	Worcester	AHL	41	3	4	7	268																			
	Boston	NHL	2	0	0	0	5	0	0	0	0	0.0	1													
	Providence Bruins	AHL	4	0	0	0	29												4	0	1	1	9			
1996-97	Boston	NHL	2	0	0	0	0	0	0	0	0	0.0	0													
	Providence Bruins	AHL	60	8	9	17	367												6	0	0	0	32			
1997-98	Michigan K-Wings	IHL	60	2	5	7	*398												3	0	0	0	23			
1998-99	Worcester	AHL	70	8	14	22	299												4	0	1	1	4			
99-2000	Phoenix	NHL	3	0	0	0	12	0	0	0	0	0.0	1	0	0.0	4	0	2:20								
	Springfield	AHL	56	4	8	12	321												4	0	0	0	6			
2000-01	Anaheim	NHL	9	0	1	1	27	0	0	0	6	0.0	-1	0	0.0	12	0	6:31								
	Cincinnati Ducks	AHL	41	2	12	14	211																			
	NHL Totals		22	0	1	1	67	0	0	0	7	0.0		0	0.0	16	0	5:28								

Signed as a free agent by **St. Louis**, February 28, 1995. Traded to **Boston** by **St. Louis** with Steve Staios for Steve Leach, March 8, 1996. Signed as a free agent by **Dallas**, August 19, 1997. Signed as a free agent by **St. Louis**, September 4, 1998. Signed as a free agent by **Phoenix**, August 15, 1999. Signed as a free agent by **Anaheim**, July 13, 2000.

SCATCHARD, Dave
(SKAT-chuhrd, DAYV) **NYI**

Center. Shoots right. 6'2", 220 lbs. Born, Hinton, Alta., February 20, 1976. Vancouver's 3rd choice, 42nd overall, in 1994 Entry Draft.

Season	Club	League	GP	G	A	Pts	PIM	PP	SH	GW	S	%	+/-	TF	F%	H	SB	Min	Playoffs GP	G	A	Pts	PIM	PP	SH	GW
1991-92	Salmon Arm	BCAHA	65	98	100	198	167																			
1992-93	Kimberley	RMJHL	51	20	23	43	61																			
1993-94	Portland	WHL	47	9	11	20	46												10	2	1	3	4			
1994-95	Portland	WHL	71	20	30	50	148												8	0	3	3	21			
1995-96	Portland	WHL	59	19	28	47	146												7	1	8	9	14			
	Syracuse Crunch	AHL	1	0	0	0	0												15	2	5	7	29			
1996-97	Syracuse Crunch	AHL	26	8	7	15	65																			
1997-98	Vancouver	NHL	76	13	11	24	165	0	0	1	85	15.3	-4													
1998-99	Vancouver	NHL	82	13	13	26	140	0	2	2	130	10.0	-12	1007	56.3	147	33	13:46								

			Regular Season																Playoffs							
Season	Club	League	GP	G	A	Pts	PIM	PP	SH	GW	S	%	+/-	TF	F%	H	SB	Min	GP	G	A	Pts	PIM	PP	SH	GW
99-2000	**Vancouver**	**NHL**	**21**	**0**	**4**	**4**	**24**	**0**	**0**	**0**	**25**	**0.0**	**-3**	**190**	**59.5**	**40**	**6**	**10:12**	....	....	....	....	....	....	....	....
	NY Islanders	**NHL**	**44**	**12**	**14**	**26**	**93**	**0**	**1**	**1**	**103**	**11.7**	**0**	**710**	**55.8**	**123**	**21**	**13:42**	....	....	....	....	....	....	....	....
2000-01	**NY Islanders**	**NHL**	**81**	**21**	**24**	**45**	**114**	**4**	**0**	**5**	**176**	**11.9**	**-9**	**1322**	**55.1**	**199**	**22**	**16:50**	....	....	....	....	....	....	....	....
	NHL Totals		**304**	**59**	**66**	**125**	**536**	**4**	**3**	**9**	**519**	**11.4**		**3229**	**55.9**	**509**	**82**	**14:31**	....	....	....	....	....	....	....	....

Traded to **NY Islanders** by **Vancouver** with Kevin Weekes and Bill Muckalt for Felix Potvin and NY Islanders' compensatory 2nd (later traded to New Jersey - New Jersey selected Teemu Laine) and 3rd (Thatcher Bell) round choices in 2000 Entry Draft, December 19, 1999.

SCHAEFER, Peter (SHAY-fuhr, PEE-tuhr) VAN.

Left wing. Shoots left. 5'11", 195 lbs. Born, Yellow Grass, Sask., July 12, 1977. Vancouver's 3rd choice, 66th overall, in 1995 Entry Draft.

1993-94	Yorkton Mallers	SMHL	32	27	14	41	133	....	....	....	....	....	....	....	....	....	....	....	....	....	....	....	....	....	....	....
	Brandon	WHL	2	1	0	1	0	....	....	....	....	....	....	....	....	....	....	....	....	....	....	....	....	....	....	....
1994-95	Brandon	WHL	68	27	32	59	34	....	....	....	....	....	....	....	....	....	....	....	18	5	3	8	18	....	....	....
1995-96	Brandon	WHL	69	47	61	108	53	....	....	....	....	....	....	....	....	....	....	....	19	10	13	23	5	....	....	....
1996-97	Brandon	WHL	61	49	74	123	85	....	....	....	....	....	....	....	....	....	....	....	6	1	4	5	4	....	....	....
	Syracuse Crunch	AHL	5	0	3	3	0	....	....	....	....	....	....	....	....	....	....	....	3	1	3	4	14	....	....	....
1997-98	Syracuse Crunch	AHL	73	19	44	63	41	....	....	....	....	....	....	....	....	....	....	....	5	2	1	3	2	....	....	....
1998-99	**Vancouver**	**NHL**	**25**	**4**	**4**	**8**	**8**	**1**	**0**	**1**	**24**	**16.7**	**-1**	**6**	**0.0**	**27**	**6**	**13:21**	....	....	....	....	....	....	....	....
	Syracuse Crunch	AHL	41	10	19	29	66	....	....	....	....	....	....	....	....	....	....	....	....	....	....	....	....	....	....	....
99-2000	**Vancouver**	**NHL**	**71**	**16**	**15**	**31**	**20**	**2**	**2**	**4**	**101**	**15.8**	**0**	**21**	**19.1**	**56**	**32**	**15:28**	....	....	....	....	....	....	....	....
	Syracuse Crunch	AHL	2	0	0	0	2	....	....	....	....	....	....	....	....	....	....	....	....	....	....	....	....	....	....	....
2000-01	**Vancouver**	**NHL**	**82**	**16**	**20**	**36**	**22**	**3**	**4**	**2**	**163**	**9.8**	**4**	**25**	**32.0**	**64**	**46**	**16:18**	**3**	**0**	**0**	**0**	**0**	**0**	**0**	**0**
	NHL Totals		**178**	**36**	**39**	**75**	**50**	**6**	**6**	**7**	**288**	**12.5**		**52**	**23.1**	**147**	**84**	**15:33**	**3**	**0**	**0**	**0**	**0**	**0**	**0**	**0**

WHL East First All-Star Team (1996, 1997) • Canadian Major Junior First All-Star Team (1997)

SCHASTLIVY, Petr (schust-LEE-vee, PEH-tuhr) OTT.

Left wing. Shoots left. 6'1", 204 lbs. Born, Angarsk, USSR, April 18, 1979. Ottawa's 5th choice, 101st overall, in 1998 Entry Draft.

1997-98	Torpedo Yaroslavl	Russia-2	47	15	9	24	34	....	....	....	....	....	....	....	....	....	....	....	....	....	....	....	....	....	....	....
	Torpedo Yaroslavl	Russia	4	0	0	0	0	....	....	....	....	....	....	....	....	....	....	....	....	....	....	....	....	....	....	....
1998-99	Torpedo Yaroslavl	Russia	40	6	1	7	28	....	....	....	....	....	....	....	....	....	....	....	6	0	0	0	2	....	....	....
99-2000	**Ottawa**	**NHL**	**13**	**2**	**5**	**7**	**2**	**1**	**0**	**1**	**22**	**9.1**	**4**	**0**	**0.0**	**2**	**2**	**12:18**	**1**	**0**	**0**	**0**	**0**	**0**	**0**	**0**
	Grand Rapids	IHL	46	16	12	28	10	....	....	....	....	....	....	....	....	....	....	....	17	8	7	15	6	....	....	....
2000-01	**Ottawa**	**NHL**	**17**	**3**	**2**	**5**	**6**	**0**	**0**	**0**	**32**	**9.4**	**-1**	**0**	**0.0**	**4**	**2**	**11:20**	....	....	....	....	....	....	....	....
	Grand Rapids	IHL	43	10	14	24	10	....	....	....	....	....	....	....	....	....	....	....	7	4	4	8	0	....	....	....
	NHL Totals		**30**	**5**	**7**	**12**	**8**	**1**	**0**	**1**	**54**	**9.3**		**0**	**0.0**	**6**	**4**	**11:45**	**1**	**0**	**0**	**0**	**0**	**0**	**0**	**0**

SCHNEIDER, Mathieu (SHNIGH-duhr, MA-thew) L.A.

Defense. Shoots left. 5'10", 192 lbs. Born, New York, NY, June 12, 1969. Montreal's 4th choice, 44th overall, in 1987 Entry Draft.

1985-86	Mount St. Charles	Hi-School	19	3	27	30		....	....	....	....	....	....	....	....	....	....	....	....	....	....	....	....	....	....	....
1986-87	Cornwall Royals	OHL	63	7	29	36	75	....	....	....	....	....	....	....	....	....	....	....	5	0	0	0	22	....	....	....
1987-88	Cornwall Royals	OHL	48	21	40	61	83	....	....	....	....	....	....	....	....	....	....	....	11	2	6	8	14	....	....	....
	Montreal	**NHL**	**4**	**0**	**0**	**0**	**2**	**0**	**0**	**0**	**2**	**0.0**	**-1**	....	....	....	....	....	....	....	....	....	....	....	....	....
	Sherbrooke	AHL	....	....	....	....	....	....	....	....	....	....	....	....	....	....	....	....	3	0	3	3	12	....	....	....
1988-89	Cornwall Royals	OHL	59	16	57	73	96	....	....	....	....	....	....	....	....	....	....	....	18	7	20	27	30	....	....	....
1989-90	**Montreal**	**NHL**	**44**	**7**	**14**	**21**	**25**	**5**	**0**	**1**	**84**	**8.3**	**2**	....	....	....	....	....	**9**	**1**	**3**	**4**	**31**	**1**	**0**	**0**
	Sherbrooke	AHL	28	6	13	19	20	....	....	....	....	....	....	....	....	....	....	....	....	....	....	....	....	....	....	....
1990-91	**Montreal**	**NHL**	**69**	**10**	**20**	**30**	**63**	**5**	**0**	**3**	**164**	**6.1**	**7**	....	....	....	....	....	**13**	**2**	**7**	**9**	**18**	**1**	**0**	**0**
1991-92	**Montreal**	**NHL**	**78**	**8**	**24**	**32**	**72**	**2**	**0**	**1**	**194**	**4.1**	**10**	....	....	....	....	....	**10**	**1**	**4**	**5**	**6**	**1**	**0**	**0**
1992-93♦	**Montreal**	**NHL**	**60**	**13**	**31**	**44**	**91**	**3**	**0**	**2**	**169**	**7.7**	**8**	....	....	....	....	....	**11**	**1**	**2**	**3**	**16**	**0**	**0**	**0**
1993-94	**Montreal**	**NHL**	**75**	**20**	**32**	**52**	**62**	**11**	**0**	**4**	**193**	**10.4**	**15**	....	....	....	....	....	**1**	**0**	**0**	**0**	**0**	**0**	**0**	**0**
1994-95	**Montreal**	**NHL**	**30**	**5**	**15**	**20**	**49**	**2**	**0**	**0**	**82**	**6.1**	**-3**	....	....	....	....	....	....	....	....	....	....	....	....	....
	NY Islanders	**NHL**	**13**	**3**	**6**	**9**	**30**	**1**	**0**	**2**	**36**	**8.3**	**-5**	....	....	....	....	....	....	....	....	....	....	....	....	....
1995-96	**NY Islanders**	**NHL**	**65**	**11**	**36**	**47**	**93**	**7**	**0**	**1**	**155**	**7.1**	**-18**	....	....	....	....	....	....	....	....	....	....	....	....	....
	Toronto	**NHL**	**13**	**2**	**5**	**7**	**10**	**0**	**0**	**0**	**36**	**5.6**	**-2**	....	....	....	....	....	**6**	**0**	**4**	**4**	**8**	**0**	**0**	**0**
1996-97	**Toronto**	**NHL**	**26**	**5**	**7**	**12**	**20**	**1**	**0**	**1**	**63**	**7.9**	**3**	....	....	....	....	....	....	....	....	....	....	....	....	....
1997-98	**Toronto**	**NHL**	**76**	**11**	**26**	**37**	**44**	**4**	**1**	**1**	**181**	**6.1**	**-12**	....	....	....	....	....	....	....	....	....	....	....	....	....
	United States	Olympics	4	0	0	0	6	....	....	....	....	....	....	....	....	....	....	....	....	....	....	....	....	....	....	....
1998-99	**NY Rangers**	**NHL**	**75**	**10**	**24**	**34**	**71**	**5**	**0**	**2**	**159**	**6.3**	**-19**	**0**	**0.0**	**182**	**149**	**24:35**	....	....	....	....	....	....	....	....
99-2000	**NY Rangers**	**NHL**	**80**	**10**	**20**	**30**	**78**	**3**	**0**	**1**	**228**	**4.4**	**-6**	**0**	**0.0**	**178**	**183**	**22:31**	....	....	....	....	....	....	....	....
2000-01	**Los Angeles**	**NHL**	**73**	**16**	**35**	**51**	**56**	**7**	**1**	**2**	**183**	**8.7**	**0**	**0**	**0.0**	**179**	**137**	**23:04**	**13**	**0**	**9**	**9**	**10**	**0**	**0**	**0**
	NHL Totals		**781**	**131**	**295**	**426**	**766**	**56**	**2**	**21**	**1929**	**6.8**		**0**	**0.0**	**539**	**469**	**23:22**	**63**	**5**	**29**	**34**	**89**	**3**	**0**	**0**

OHL First All-Star Team (1988, 1989) • Played in NHL All-Star Game (1996)

Traded to **NY Islanders** by **Montreal** with Kirk Muller and Craig Darby for Pierre Turgeon and Vladimir Malakhov, April 5, 1995. Traded to **Toronto** by **NY Islanders** with Wendel Clark and D.J. Smith for Darby Hendrickson, Sean Haggerty, Kenny Jonsson and Toronto's 1st round choice (Roberto Luongo) in 1997 Entry Draft, March 13, 1996. • Missed majority of 1996-97 season recovering from groin injury suffered in game vs. St. Louis, December 27, 1996. Rights traded to **NY Rangers** by **Toronto** for Alexander Karpovtsev and NY Rangers' 4th round choice (Mirko Murovic) in 1999 Entry Draft, October 14, 1998. Selected by **Columbus** from **NY Rangers** in Expansion Draft, June 23, 2000. Signed as a free agent by **LA Kings**, August 14, 2000.

SCHULTZ, Ray (SHUHLTZ, RAY) NYI

Defense. Shoots left. 6'2", 200 lbs. Born, Red Deer, Alta., November 14, 1976. Ottawa's 8th choice, 184th overall, in 1995 Entry Draft.

1993-94	Edmonton SSA	AMHL	31	3	24	27	94	....	....	....	....	....	....	....	....	....	....	....	....	....	....	....	....	....	....	....
	Tri-City Americans	WHL	3	0	0	0	11	....	....	....	....	....	....	....	....	....	....	....	....	....	....	....	....	....	....	....
1994-95	Tri-City Americans	WHL	63	1	8	9	209	....	....	....	....	....	....	....	....	....	....	....	11	0	0	0	16	....	....	....
1995-96	Calgary Hitmen	WHL	66	3	17	20	282	....	....	....	....	....	....	....	....	....	....	....	....	....	....	....	....	....	....	....
1996-97	Calgary Hitmen	WHL	32	3	17	20	141	....	....	....	....	....	....	....	....	....	....	....	....	....	....	....	....	....	....	....
	Kelowna Rockets	WHL	23	3	11	14	63	....	....	....	....	....	....	....	....	....	....	....	6	0	2	2	12	....	....	....
1997-98	**NY Islanders**	**NHL**	**13**	**0**	**1**	**1**	**45**	**0**	**0**	**0**	**4**	**0.0**	**3**	....	....	....	....	....	....	....	....	....	....	....	....	....
	Kentucky	AHL	51	2	4	6	179	....	....	....	....	....	....	....	....	....	....	....	1	0	0	0	25	....	....	....
1998-99	**NY Islanders**	**NHL**	**4**	**0**	**0**	**0**	**7**	**0**	**0**	**0**	**2**	**0.0**	**-2**	**1**	**0.0**	**5**	**1**	**15:21**	....	....	....	....	....	....	....	....
	Lowell	AHL	54	0	3	3	184	....	....	....	....	....	....	....	....	....	....	....	1	0	0	0	4	....	....	....
99-2000	**NY Islanders**	**NHL**	**9**	**0**	**1**	**1**	**30**	**0**	**0**	**0**	**2**	**0.0**	**1**	**0**	**0.0**	**21**	**5**	**14:18**	....	....	....	....	....	....	....	....
	Kansas City	IHL	65	5	5	10	208	....	....	....	....	....	....	....	....	....	....	....	....	....	....	....	....	....	....	....
2000-01	**NY Islanders**	**NHL**	**13**	**0**	**2**	**2**	**40**	**0**	**0**	**0**	**3**	**0.0**	**-1**	**0**	**0.0**	**27**	**9**	**10:50**	....	....	....	....	....	....	....	....
	Lowell	AHL	13	0	1	1	33	....	....	....	....	....	....	....	....	....	....	....	....	....	....	....	....	....	....	....
	Cleveland	IHL	44	3	5	8	127	....	....	....	....	....	....	....	....	....	....	....	3	1	0	1	16	....	....	....
	NHL Totals		**39**	**0**	**4**	**4**	**122**	**0**	**0**	**0**	**11**	**0.0**		**1**	**0.0**	**53**	**15**	**12:44**	....	....	....	....	....	....	....	....

Signed as a free agent by **NY Islanders**, June 9, 1997.

SCOVILLE, Darryl (SKO-vihl, DAIR-uhl) CBJ

Defense. Shoots left. 6'3", 215 lbs. Born, Swift Current, Sask., October 13, 1975.

1994-95	Lebret Eagles	SJHL	STATISTICS NOT AVAILABLE																							
1995-96	Merrimack	H-East	34	6	20	26	54	....	....	....	....	....	....	....	....	....	....	....	....	....	....	....	....	....	....	....
1996-97	Merrimack	H-East	35	7	16	23	71	....	....	....	....	....	....	....	....	....	....	....	....	....	....	....	....	....	....	....
1997-98	Merrimack	H-East	38	4	26	30	84	....	....	....	....	....	....	....	....	....	....	....	....	....	....	....	....	....	....	....
1998-99	Saint John Flames	AHL	61	1	7	8	66	....	....	....	....	....	....	....	....	....	....	....	7	1	2	3	13	....	....	....
99-2000	**Calgary**	**NHL**	**6**	**0**	**0**	**0**	**2**	**0**	**0**	**0**	**1**	**0.0**	**1**	**0**	**0.0**	**11**	**1**	**9:18**	....	....	....	....	....	....	....	....
	Saint John Flames	AHL	64	11	25	36	99	....	....	....	....	....	....	....	....	....	....	....	3	1	2	3	0	....	....	....
2000-01	Saint John Flames	AHL	76	11	32	47	125	....	....	....	....	....	....	....	....	....	....	....	11	2	6	8	8	....	....	....
	NHL Totals		**6**	**0**	**0**	**0**	**2**	**0**	**0**	**0**	**1**	**0.0**		**0**	**0.0**	**11**	**1**	**9:18**	....	....	....	....	....	....	....	....

Hockey East All-Rookie Team (1996) • Signed as a free agent by **Calgary**, June 12, 1998. Signed as a free agent by **Columbus**, July 10, 2001.

SEDIN, Daniel

(suh-DEEN, DAN-yehl) **VAN.**

Left wing. Shoots left. 6'1", 200 lbs. Born, Ornskoldsvik, Sweden, September 26, 1980. Vancouver's 1st choice, 2nd overall, in 1999 Entry Draft.

			Regular Season																Playoffs							
Season	Club	League	GP	G	A	Pts	PIM	PP	SH	GW	S	%	+/-	TF	F%	H	SB	Min	GP	G	A	Pts	PIM	PP	SH	GW
1996-97	MoDo Hockey	Swede-Jr.	26	26	14	40	....	....	....	....	....	....	....	....	....	....	....	....	....	....	....	....	....	....	....	....
1997-98	MoDo Hockey	Swede-Jr.	4	3	3	6	4	....	....	....	....	....	....	....	....	....	....	....	....	....	....	....	....	....	....	....
	MoDo Hockey	Sweden	45	4	8	12	26	....	....	....	....	....	....	....	....	....	....	....	9	0	0	0	2	....	....	....
1998-99	MoDo Hockey	Sweden	50	21	21	42	20	....	....	....	....	....	....	....	....	....	....	....	13	4	8	12	14	....	....	....
99-2000	MoDo Hockey	Sweden	50	19	26	45	28	....	....	....	....	....	....	....	....	....	....	....	13	*8	6	14	18	....	....	....
	MoDo Hockey	EuroHL	4	3	3	6	0	....	....	....	....	....	....	....	....	....	....	....	2	0	0	0	0	....	....	....
2000-01	**Vancouver**	**NHL**	**75**	**20**	**14**	**34**	**24**	**10**	**0**	**3**	**127**	**15.7**	**–3**	**10**	**60.0**	**22**	**7**	**12:60**	**4**	**1**	**2**	**3**	**0**	**0**	**0**	**0**
	NHL Totals		**75**	**20**	**14**	**34**	**24**	**10**	**0**	**3**	**127**	**15.7**		**10**	**60.0**	**22**	**7**	**12:60**	**4**	**1**	**2**	**3**	**0**	**0**	**0**	**0**

SEDIN, Henrik

(suh-DEEN, HEHN-rihk) **VAN.**

Center. Shoots left. 6'2", 200 lbs. Born, Ornskoldsvik, Sweden, September 26, 1980. Vancouver's 2nd choice, 3rd overall, in 1999 Entry Draft.

			Regular Season																Playoffs							
Season	Club	League	GP	G	A	Pts	PIM	PP	SH	GW	S	%	+/-	TF	F%	H	SB	Min	GP	G	A	Pts	PIM	PP	SH	GW
1996-97	MoDo Hockey	Swede-Jr.	26	14	22	36	....	....	....	....	....	....	....	....	....	....	....	....	....	....	....	....	....	....	....	....
1997-98	MoDo Hockey	Swede-Jr.	8	4	7	11	6	....	....	....	....	....	....	....	....	....	....	....	....	....	....	....	....	....	....	....
	MoDo Hockey	Sweden	39	1	4	5	8	....	....	....	....	....	....	....	....	....	....	....	7	0	0	0	0	....	....	....
1998-99	MoDo Hockey	Sweden	49	12	22	34	32	....	....	....	....	....	....	....	....	....	....	....	13	2	8	10	6	....	....	....
99-2000	MoDo Hockey	Sweden	50	9	38	47	22	....	....	....	....	....	....	....	....	....	....	....	13	5	9	14	2	....	....	....
2000-01	**Vancouver**	**NHL**	**82**	**9**	**20**	**29**	**38**	**2**	**0**	**1**	**98**	**9.2**	**–2**	**1020**	**44.1**	**21**	**11**	**13:31**	**4**	**0**	**4**	**4**	**0**	**0**	**0**	**0**
	NHL Totals		**82**	**9**	**20**	**29**	**38**	**2**	**0**	**1**	**98**	**9.2**		**1020**	**44.1**	**21**	**11**	**13:31**	**4**	**0**	**4**	**4**	**0**	**0**	**0**	**0**

SEKERAS, Lubomir

(SHE-kuhr-ahsh, LOO-boh-mihr) **MIN.**

Defense. Shoots left. 6', 183 lbs. Born, Trencin, Czech., November 18, 1968. Minnesota's 8th choice, 232nd overall, in 2000 Entry Draft.

			Regular Season																Playoffs							
Season	Club	League	GP	G	A	Pts	PIM	PP	SH	GW	S	%	+/-	TF	F%	H	SB	Min	GP	G	A	Pts	PIM	PP	SH	GW
1987-88	Dukla Trencin	Czech-Jr.	STATISTICS NOT AVAILABLE																							
	Dukla Trencin	Czech.	....	....	....	....	....	....	....	....	....	....	....	....	....	....	....	....	9	0	0	0	0	....	....	....
1988-89	Dukla Trencin	Czech.	16	2	5	7	22	....	....	....	....	....	....	....	....	....	....	....	11	0	4	4	0	....	....	....
1989-90	Dukla Trencin	Czech.	44	6	8	14	....	....	....	....	....	....	....	....	....	....	....	....	9	0	2	2	....	....	....	....
1990-91	Dukla Trencin	Czech.	52	6	16	22	....	....	....	....	....	....	....	....	....	....	....	....	6	0	1	1	....	....	....	....
1991-92	Dukla Trencin	Czech.	30	2	6	8	32	....	....	....	....	....	....	....	....	....	....	....	13	1	1	2	0	....	....	....
1992-93	Dukla Trencin	Czech.	40	5	19	24	48	....	....	....	....	....	....	....	....	....	....	....	11	4	9	13	0	....	....	....
1993-94	Dukla Trencin	Slovakia	36	9	12	21	46	....	....	....	....	....	....	....	....	....	....	....	9	2	4	6	10	....	....	....
1994-95	Dukla Trencin	Slovakia	36	11	11	22	24	....	....	....	....	....	....	....	....	....	....	....	9	2	7	9	8	....	....	....
1995-96	HC Trinec	Cze-Rep	40	11	13	24	44	....	....	....	....	....	....	....	....	....	....	....	3	0	0	0	0	....	....	....
1996-97	HC Trinec	Cze-Rep	52	14	21	35	56	....	....	....	....	....	....	....	....	....	....	....	4	1	0	1	2	....	....	....
1997-98	HC Trinec	Cze-Rep	50	11	33	44	42	....	....	....	....	....	....	....	....	....	....	....	13	2	10	12	4	....	....	....
1998-99	HC Trinec	Cze-Rep	50	8	15	23	38	....	....	....	....	....	....	....	....	....	....	....	10	2	6	8	....	....	....	....
99-2000	HC Trinec	Cze-Rep	52	7	24	31	36	....	....	....	....	....	....	....	....	....	....	....	4	0	2	2	2	....	....	....
2000-01	**Minnesota**	**NHL**	**80**	**11**	**23**	**34**	**52**	**4**	**0**	**2**	**102**	**10.8**	**–8**	**0**	**0.0**	**59**	**70**	**21:13**	....	....	....	....	....	....	....	....
	NHL Totals		**80**	**11**	**23**	**34**	**52**	**4**	**0**	**2**	**102**	**10.8**		**0**	**0.0**	**59**	**70**	**21:13**	....	....	....	....	....	....	....	....

SELANNE, Teemu

(SEH-lahn-nay, TEE-moo) **S.J.**

Right wing. Shoots right. 6', 204 lbs. Born, Helsinki, Finland, July 3, 1970. Winnipeg's 1st choice, 10th overall, in 1988 Entry Draft.

			Regular Season																Playoffs							
Season	Club	League	GP	G	A	Pts	PIM	PP	SH	GW	S	%	+/-	TF	F%	H	SB	Min	GP	G	A	Pts	PIM	PP	SH	GW
1986-87	Jokerit Helsinki	Finn-Jr.	33	10	12	22	8	....	....	....	....	....	....	....	....	....	....	....	....	....	....	....	....	....	....	....
1987-88	Jokerit Helsinki	Finn-Jr.	33	*43	23	*66	18	....	....	....	....	....	....	....	....	....	....	....	5	4	3	7	2	....	....	....
	Jokerit Helsinki	Finland-2	5	1	1	2	0	....	....	....	....	....	....	....	....	....	....	....	....	....	....	....	....	....	....	....
1988-89	Army Sports	Finn-Jr.	3	3	1	4	2	....	....	....	....	....	....	....	....	....	....	....	....	....	....	....	....	....	....	....
	Jokerit Helsinki	Finn-Jr.	3	8	8	16	4	....	....	....	....	....	....	....	....	....	....	....	....	....	....	....	....	....	....	....
	Jokerit Helsinki	Finland-2	34	35	33	68	12	....	....	....	....	....	....	....	....	....	....	....	5	7	3	10	4	....	....	....
1989-90	Jokerit Helsinki	Finland	11	4	8	12	0	....	....	....	....	....	....	....	....	....	....	....	....	....	....	....	....	....	....	....
1990-91	Jokerit Helsinki	Finn-Jr.	1	0	0	0	0	....	....	....	....	....	....	....	....	....	....	....	....	....	....	....	....	....	....	....
	Jokerit Helsinki	Finland	42	33	25	58	12	....	....	....	....	....	....	....	....	....	....	....	....	....	....	....	....	....	....	....
1991-92	Jokerit Helsinki	Finland	44	*39	23	62	20	....	....	....	....	....	....	....	....	....	....	....	10	*10	7	*17	18	....	....	....
	Finland	Olympics	8	7	4	11	6	....	....	....	....	....	....	....	....	....	....	....	....	....	....	....	....	....	....	....
1992-93	**Winnipeg**	**NHL**	**84**	***76**	**56**	**132**	**45**	**24**	**0**	**7**	**387**	**19.6**	**8**	....	....	....	....	....	**6**	**4**	**2**	**6**	**2**	**2**	**0**	**2**
1993-94	**Winnipeg**	**NHL**	**51**	**25**	**29**	**54**	**22**	**11**	**0**	**2**	**191**	**13.1**	**–23**	....	....	....	....	....	....	....	....	....	....	....	....	....
1994-95	Jokerit Helsinki	Finland	20	7	12	19	6	....	....	....	....	....	....	....	....	....	....	....	....	....	....	....	....	....	....	....
	Winnipeg	**NHL**	**45**	**22**	**26**	**48**	**2**	**8**	**2**	**1**	**167**	**13.2**	**1**	....	....	....	....	....	....	....	....	....	....	....	....	....
1995-96	**Winnipeg**	**NHL**	**51**	**24**	**48**	**72**	**18**	**6**	**1**	**4**	**163**	**14.7**	**3**	....	....	....	....	....	....	....	....	....	....	....	....	....
	Anaheim	**NHL**	**28**	**16**	**20**	**36**	**4**	**3**	**0**	**1**	**104**	**15.4**	**2**	....	....	....	....	....	....	....	....	....	....	....	....	....
1996-97	**Anaheim**	**NHL**	**78**	**51**	**58**	**109**	**34**	**11**	**1**	**8**	**273**	**18.7**	**28**	....	....	....	....	....	**11**	**7**	**3**	**10**	**4**	**3**	**0**	**1**
1997-98	**Anaheim**	**NHL**	**73**	***52**	**34**	**86**	**30**	**10**	**1**	**10**	**268**	**19.4**	**12**	....	....	....	....	....	....	....	....	....	....	....	....	....
	Finland	Olympics	5	4	6	*10	8	....	....	....	....	....	....	....	....	....	....	....	....	....	....	....	....	....	....	....
1998-99	**Anaheim**	**NHL**	**75**	***47**	**60**	**107**	**30**	**25**	**0**	**7**	**281**	**16.7**	**18**	**5**	**20.0**	**27**	**16**	**22:47**	**4**	**2**	**2**	**4**	**2**	**1**	**0**	**0**
99-2000	**Anaheim**	**NHL**	**79**	**33**	**52**	**85**	**12**	**8**	**0**	**6**	**236**	**14.0**	**6**	**13**	**23.1**	**43**	**19**	**22:44**	....	....	....	....	....	....	....	....
2000-01	**Anaheim**	**NHL**	**61**	**26**	**33**	**59**	**36**	**10**	**0**	**5**	**202**	**12.9**	**–8**	**4**	**50.0**	**36**	**10**	**21:51**	....	....	....	....	....	....	....	....
	San Jose	**NHL**	**12**	**7**	**6**	**13**	**0**	**2**	**0**	**2**	**31**	**22.6**	**1**	**4**	**75.0**	**2**	**0**	**18:14**	**6**	**0**	**2**	**2**	**2**	**0**	**0**	**0**
	NHL Totals		**637**	**379**	**422**	**801**	**233**	**118**	**5**	**53**	**2303**	**16.5**		**26**	**34.6**	**108**	**45**	**22:16**	**27**	**13**	**9**	**22**	**10**	**6**	**0**	**3**

Won Calder Memorial Trophy (1993) • NHL First All-Star Team (1993, 1997) • NHL All-Rookie Team (1993) • NHL Second All-Star Team (1998, 1999) • Won Maurice "Rocket" Richard Trophy (1999) • Played in NHL All-Star Game (1993, 1994, 1996, 1997, 1998, 1999, 2000)

• Missed majority of 1989-90 season recovering from leg injury suffered in game vs. HIFK Helsinki, October 19, 1989. Traded to **Anaheim** by **Winnipeg** with Marc Chouinard and Winnipeg's 4th round choice (later traded to Toronto - later traded to Montreal - Montreal selected Kim Staal) in 1996 Entry Draft for Chad Kilger, Oleg Tverdovsky and Anaheim's 3rd round choice (Per-Anton Lundstrom) in 1996 Entry Draft, February 7, 1996. Traded to **San Jose** by **Anaheim** for Jeff Friesen, Steve Shields and future considerations, March 5, 2001.

SELIVANOV, Alex

(seh-lih-VAH-nohv, AL-ehx)

Right wing. Shoots left. 6', 208 lbs. Born, Moscow, USSR, March 23, 1971. Philadelphia's 4th choice, 140th overall, in 1994 Entry Draft.

			Regular Season																Playoffs							
Season	Club	League	GP	G	A	Pts	PIM	PP	SH	GW	S	%	+/-	TF	F%	H	SB	Min	GP	G	A	Pts	PIM	PP	SH	GW
1988-89	Krylja Sovetov	USSR	1	0	0	0	0	....	....	....	....	....	....	....	....	....	....	....	....	....	....	....	....	....	....	....
1989-90	Krylja Sovetov	USSR	4	0	0	0	0	....	....	....	....	....	....	....	....	....	....	....	....	....	....	....	....	....	....	....
1990-91	Krylja Sovetov	USSR	21	3	1	4	6	....	....	....	....	....	....	....	....	....	....	....	....	....	....	....	....	....	....	....
1991-92	Krylja Sovetov	CIS	31	6	7	13	16	....	....	....	....	....	....	....	....	....	....	....	....	....	....	....	....	....	....	....
1992-93	Krylja Sovetov	CIS	42	12	19	31	66	....	....	....	....	....	....	....	....	....	....	....	3	2	0	2	2	....	....	....
1993-94	Krylja Sovetov	CIS	45	30	11	41	50	....	....	....	....	....	....	....	....	....	....	....	6	5	1	6	2	....	....	....
1994-95	Atlanta Knights	IHL	4	0	3	3	2	....	....	....	....	....	....	....	....	....	....	....	....	....	....	....	....	....	....	....
	Chicago Wolves	IHL	14	4	1	5	8	....	....	....	....	....	....	....	....	....	....	....	....	....	....	....	....	....	....	....
	Tampa Bay	**NHL**	**43**	**10**	**6**	**16**	**14**	**4**	**0**	**3**	**94**	**10.6**	**–2**	....	....	....	....	....	....	....	....	....	....	....	....	....
1995-96	**Tampa Bay**	**NHL**	**79**	**31**	**21**	**52**	**93**	**13**	**0**	**5**	**215**	**14.4**	**3**	....	....	....	....	....	**6**	**2**	**2**	**4**	**6**	**0**	**0**	**1**
1996-97	**Tampa Bay**	**NHL**	**69**	**15**	**18**	**33**	**61**	**3**	**0**	**4**	**187**	**8.0**	**–3**	....	....	....	....	....	....	....	....	....	....	....	....	....
1997-98	**Tampa Bay**	**NHL**	**70**	**16**	**19**	**35**	**85**	**4**	**0**	**3**	**206**	**7.8**	**–38**	....	....	....	....	....	....	....	....	....	....	....	....	....
1998-99	**Tampa Bay**	**NHL**	**43**	**6**	**13**	**19**	**18**	**1**	**0**	**0**	**120**	**5.0**	**–8**	**0**	**0.0**	**40**	**5**	**15:44**	....	....	....	....	....	....	....	....
	Cleveland	IHL	2	0	1	1	4	....	....	....	....	....	....	....	....	....	....	....	....	....	....	....	....	....	....	....
	Edmonton	**NHL**	**29**	**8**	**6**	**14**	**24**	**1**	**0**	**1**	**57**	**14.0**	**0**	**5**	**60.0**	**20**	**5**	**13:28**	**2**	**0**	**1**	**1**	**2**	**0**	**0**	**0**
99-2000	**Edmonton**	**NHL**	**67**	**27**	**20**	**47**	**46**	**10**	**0**	**5**	**122**	**22.1**	**2**	**5**	**0.0**	**29**	**6**	**14:28**	**5**	**0**	**0**	**0**	**8**	**0**	**0**	**0**
2000-01	**Columbus**	**NHL**	**59**	**8**	**11**	**19**	**38**	**5**	**0**	**2**	**104**	**7.7**	**–11**	**13**	**30.8**	**34**	**9**	**14:06**	....	....	....	....	....	....	....	....
	NHL Totals		**459**	**121**	**114**	**235**	**379**	**41**	**0**	**23**	**1105**	**11.0**		**23**	**30.4**	**123**	**25**	**14:29**	**13**	**2**	**3**	**5**	**16**	**0**	**0**	**1**

Traded to **Tampa Bay** by **Philadelphia** for Philadelphia's 4th round choice (previously acquired, Philadelphia selected Radovan Somik) in 1995 Entry Draft, September 6, 1994. Traded to **Edmonton** by **Tampa Bay** for Alexandre Daigle, January 29, 1999. Signed as a free agent by **Columbus**, November 27, 2000. Signed as a free agent by **Frankfurt Lions** (DEL), August 16, 2001.

			Regular Season																Playoffs							
Season	Club	League	GP	G	A	Pts	PIM	PP	SH	GW	S	%	+/-	TF	F%	H	SB	Min	GP	G	A	Pts	PIM	PP	SH	GW

SELMSER, Sean

(SEHLM-suhr, SHAWN)

Left wing. Shoots left. 6'1", 195 lbs. Born, Calgary, Alta., November 10, 1974. Pittsburgh's 7th choice, 182nd overall, in 1993 Entry Draft.

Season	Club	League	GP	G	A	Pts	PIM	PP	SH	GW	S	%	+/-	TF	F%	H	SB	Min	GP	G	A	Pts	PIM	PP	SH	GW
1991-92	Calgary Buffaloes	AMHL	32	21	24	45	131																			
1992-93	Red Deer Rebels	WHL	70	13	27	40	216												4	0	0	0	10			
1993-94	Red Deer Rebels	WHL	71	25	25	50	201												4	1	0	1	14			
1994-95	Red Deer Rebels	WHL	33	11	17	28	65																			
1995-96	Hampton Roads	ECHL	70	23	31	54	211												3	2	0	2	8			
	Portland Pirates	AHL	6	4	1	5	28												5	2	3	5	11			
1996-97	Canada	Nat-Team	59	20	18	38	150																			
	Manitoba Moose	IHL	4	0	2	2	12																			
1997-98	Canada	Nat-Team	52	8	22	30	122																			
	Portland Pirates	AHL																	1	0	1	1	0			
1998-99	Fort Wayne	IHL	80	9	15	24	200												2	0	0	0	2			
99-2000	Hamilton Bulldogs	AHL	72	14	12	26	151												10	3	4	7	10			
2000-01	**Columbus**	**NHL**	**1**	**0**	**0**	**0**	**5**	**0**	**0**	**0**	**2**	**0.0**	**0**	**0**	**0.0**	**1**	**0**	**11:03**								
	Syracuse Crunch	AHL	75	11	15	26	151												5	0	0	0	14			
	NHL Totals		**1**	**0**	**0**	**0**	**5**	**0**	**0**	**0**	**2**	**0.0**		**0**	**0.0**	**1**	**0**	**11:03**								

Signed as a free agent by **Columbus**, August 3, 2000.

SEVERYN, Brent

(SEH-vuh-rihn, BREHNT)

Left wing. Shoots left. 6'2", 211 lbs. Born, Vegreville, Alta., February 22, 1966. Winnipeg's 5th choice, 99th overall, in 1984 Entry Draft.

Season	Club	League	GP	G	A	Pts	PIM	PP	SH	GW	S	%	+/-	TF	F%	H	SB	Min	GP	G	A	Pts	PIM	PP	SH	GW
1982-83	Vegreville Rangers	AJHL	21	20	22	42	10																			
1983-84	Seattle T-Birds	WHL	72	14	22	36	49												5	2	1	3	2			
1984-85	Seattle T-Birds	WHL	26	7	16	23	57																			
	Brandon	WHL	41	8	32	40	54																			
1985-86	Saskatoon Blades	WHL	9	1	4	5	38																			
	Seattle T-Birds	WHL	33	11	20	31	164												5	0	4	4	4			
1986-87	U. of Alberta	CWUAA	43	7	19	26	171																			
1987-88	U. of Alberta	CWUAA	46	21	29	50	178																			
1988-89	Halifax Citadels	AHL	47	2	12	14	141																			
1989-90	**Quebec**	**NHL**	**35**	**0**	**2**	**2**	**42**	**0**	**0**	**0**	**28**	**0.0**	**-19**													
	Halifax Citadels	AHL	43	6	9	15	105												6	1	2	3	49			
1990-91	Halifax Citadels	AHL	50	7	26	33	202																			
1991-92	Utica Devils	AHL	80	11	33	44	211												4	0	1	1	4			
1992-93	Utica Devils	AHL	77	20	32	52	240												5	0	0	0	35			
1993-94	**Florida**	**NHL**	**67**	**4**	**7**	**11**	**156**	**1**	**0**	**1**	**93**	**4.3**	**-1**													
1994-95	**Florida**	**NHL**	**9**	**1**	**1**	**2**	**37**	**1**	**0**	**0**	**10**	**10.0**	**-3**													
	NY Islanders	**NHL**	**19**	**1**	**3**	**4**	**34**	**0**	**0**	**0**	**22**	**4.5**	**1**													
1995-96	**NY Islanders**	**NHL**	**65**	**1**	**8**	**9**	**180**	**0**	**0**	**0**	**40**	**2.5**	**3**													
1996-97	**Colorado**	**NHL**	**66**	**1**	**4**	**5**	**193**	**0**	**0**	**0**	**55**	**1.8**	**-6**						**8**	**0**	**0**	**0**	**12**	**0**	**0**	**0**
1997-98	**Anaheim**	**NHL**	**37**	**1**	**3**	**4**	**133**	**0**	**0**	**0**	**27**	**3.7**	**-3**													
1998-99	**Dallas**	**NHL**	**30**	**1**	**2**	**3**	**50**	**0**	**0**	**0**	**22**	**4.5**	**-2**	**0**	**0.0**	**20**	**0**	**5:07**								
	Michigan K-Wings	IHL	3	0	0	0	0																			
99-2000	Munich Barons	DEL	18	2	6	8	42												12	0	3	3	14			
2000-01	Krefeld Pinguine	DEL	56	6	12	18	113																			
	NHL Totals		**328**	**10**	**30**	**40**	**825**	**2**	**0**	**1**	**297**	**3.4**		**0**	**0.0**	**20**	**0**	**5:07**	**8**	**0**	**0**	**0**	**12**	**0**	**0**	**0**

AHL First All-Star Team (1993)

Signed as a free agent by **Quebec**, July 15, 1988. Traded to **New Jersey** by **Quebec** for Dave Marcinyshyn, June 3, 1991. Traded to **Winnipeg** by **New Jersey** for Winnipeg's 6th round choice (Ryan Smart) in 1994 Entry Draft, September 30, 1993. Traded to **Florida** by **Winnipeg** for Milan Tichy, October 3, 1993. Traded to **NY Islanders** by **Florida** for NY Islanders' 4th round choice (Dave Duerden) in 1995 Entry Draft, March 3, 1995. Traded to **Colorado** by **NY Islanders** for Colorado's 3rd round choice (later traded to Calgary - later traded to Hartford/Carolina - Carolina selected Francis Lessard) in 1997 Entry Draft, September 4, 1996. Claimed by **Anaheim** from **Colorado** in NHL Waiver Draft, September 28, 1997. • Missed majority of 1997-98 season recovering from back injury suffered in game vs. Detroit, October 22, 1997. Signed as a free agent by **Dallas**, August 26, 1998.

SEVIGNY, Pierre

(seh-VIH-nee, PEE-air)

Left wing. Shoots left. 6', 195 lbs. Born, Trois-Rivières, Que., September 8, 1971. Montreal's 4th choice, 51st overall, in 1989 Entry Draft.

Season	Club	League	GP	G	A	Pts	PIM	PP	SH	GW	S	%	+/-	TF	F%	H	SB	Min	GP	G	A	Pts	PIM	PP	SH	GW
1987-88	Montreal L'est	QAAA	40	43	78	121	72												8	8	9	17	26			
1988-89	Verdun Canucks	QMJHL	67	27	43	70	88																			
1989-90	St-Hyacinthe	QMJHL	67	47	72	119	205												12	8	8	16	42			
1990-91	St-Hyacinthe	QMJHL	60	36	46	82	203																			
1991-92	Fredericton	AHL	74	22	37	59	145												7	1	1	2	26			
1992-93	Fredericton	AHL	80	36	40	76	113												5	1	1	2	2			
1993-94	**Montreal**	**NHL**	**43**	**4**	**5**	**9**	**42**	**1**	**0**	**1**	**19**	**21.1**	**6**						**3**	**0**	**1**	**1**	**0**	**0**	**0**	**0**
1994-95	**Montreal**	**NHL**	**19**	**0**	**0**	**0**	**15**	**0**	**0**	**0**	**6**	**0.0**	**-5**													
1995-96	Fredericton	AHL	76	39	42	81	188												10	5	9	14	20			
1996-97	**Montreal**	**NHL**	**13**	**0**	**0**	**0**	**5**	**0**	**0**	**0**	**1**	**0.0**	**0**													
	Fredericton	AHL	32	9	17	26	58																			
1997-98	**NY Rangers**	**NHL**	**3**	**0**	**0**	**0**	**2**	**0**	**0**	**0**	**1**	**0.0**	**0**													
	Hartford	AHL	40	18	13	31	94												12	3	5	8	14			
1998-99	Long Beach	IHL	6	1	3	4	7																			
	Orlando	IHL	43	11	21	32	44												15	4	5	9	32			
99-2000	Quebec Citadelles	AHL	78	24	43	67	154												3	3	0	3	17			
2000-01	Quebec Citadelles	AHL	74	29	37	66	138												8	0	1	1	17			
	NHL Totals		**78**	**4**	**5**	**9**	**64**	**1**	**0**	**1**	**27**	**14.8**							**3**	**0**	**1**	**1**	**0**	**0**	**0**	**0**

QMJHL First All-Star Team (1981) • QMJHL Second All-Star Team (1990, 1991)

Signed as a free agent by **NY Rangers**, August 26, 1997

SHANAHAN, Brendan

(SHAN-na-HAN, BREHN-duhn) **DET.**

Left wing. Shoots right. 6'3", 218 lbs. Born, Mimico, Ont., January 23, 1969. New Jersey's 1st choice, 2nd overall, in 1987 Entry Draft.

Season	Club	League	GP	G	A	Pts	PIM	PP	SH	GW	S	%	+/-	TF	F%	H	SB	Min	GP	G	A	Pts	PIM	PP	SH	GW
1984-85	Mississauga Reps	MTHL	36	20	21	41	26																			
	Dixie Beehives	MTJHL	1	0	0	0	0																			
1985-86	London Knights	OHL	59	28	34	62	70												5	5	5	10	5			
1986-87	London Knights	OHL	56	39	53	92	92																			
1987-88	**New Jersey**	**NHL**	**65**	**7**	**19**	**26**	**131**	**2**	**0**	**2**	**72**	**9.7**	**-20**						**12**	**2**	**1**	**3**	**44**	**1**	**0**	**0**
1988-89	**New Jersey**	**NHL**	**68**	**22**	**28**	**50**	**115**	**9**	**0**	**0**	**152**	**14.5**	**2**													
1989-90	**New Jersey**	**NHL**	**73**	**30**	**42**	**72**	**137**	**8**	**0**	**5**	**196**	**15.3**	**15**						**6**	**3**	**3**	**6**	**20**	**1**	**0**	**1**
1990-91	**New Jersey**	**NHL**	**75**	**29**	**37**	**66**	**141**	**7**	**0**	**2**	**195**	**14.9**	**4**						**7**	**3**	**5**	**8**	**12**	**2**	**0**	**0**
1991-92	**St. Louis**	**NHL**	**80**	**33**	**36**	**69**	**171**	**13**	**0**	**2**	**215**	**15.3**	**-3**						**6**	**2**	**3**	**5**	**14**	**1**	**0**	**0**
1992-93	**St. Louis**	**NHL**	**71**	**51**	**43**	**94**	**174**	**18**	**0**	**8**	**232**	**22.0**	**10**						**11**	**4**	**3**	**7**	**18**	**2**	**0**	**0**
1993-94	**St. Louis**	**NHL**	**81**	**52**	**50**	**102**	**211**	**15**	**7**	**8**	**397**	**13.1**	**-9**						**4**	**2**	**5**	**7**	**4**	**0**	**0**	**0**
1994-95	Dusseldorfer EG	DEL	3	5	3	8	4																			
	St. Louis	**NHL**	**45**	**20**	**21**	**41**	**136**	**6**	**2**	**6**	**153**	**13.1**	**7**						**5**	**4**	**5**	**9**	**14**	**1**	**0**	**1**
1995-96	**Hartford**	**NHL**	**74**	**44**	**34**	**78**	**125**	**17**	**2**	**6**	**280**	**15.7**	**2**													
1996-97	**Hartford**	**NHL**	**2**	**1**	**0**	**1**	**0**	**0**	**1**	**0**	**13**	**7.7**	**1**													
	♦ Detroit	**NHL**	**79**	**46**	**41**	**87**	**131**	**20**	**2**	**7**	**323**	**14.2**	**31**						**20**	**9**	**8**	**17**	**43**	**2**	**0**	**2**
1997-98	**♦ Detroit**	**NHL**	**75**	**28**	**29**	**57**	**154**	**15**	**1**	**9**	**266**	**10.5**	**6**						**20**	**5**	**4**	**9**	**22**	**3**	**0**	**2**
	Canada	Olympics	6	2	0	2	0																			
1998-99	**Detroit**	**NHL**	**81**	**31**	**27**	**58**	**123**	**5**	**0**	**5**	**288**	**10.8**	**2**	**18**	**44.4**	**119**	**35**	**17:31**	**10**	**3**	**7**	**10**	**6**	**1**	**0**	**1**
99-2000	**Detroit**	**NHL**	**78**	**41**	**37**	**78**	**105**	**13**	**1**	**9**	**283**	**14.5**	**24**	**24**	**50.0**	**104**	**34**	**18:35**	**9**	**3**	**2**	**5**	**10**	**0**	**0**	**0**
2000-01	**Detroit**	**NHL**	**81**	**31**	**45**	**76**	**81**	**15**	**1**	**7**	**278**	**11.2**	**9**	**115**	**43.5**	**105**	**24**	**18:22**	**2**	**2**	**2**	**4**	**0**	**0**	**0**	**1**
	NHL Totals		**1028**	**466**	**489**	**955**	**1935**	**163**	**17**	**76**	**3343**	**13.9**		**157**	**44.6**	**328**	**93**	**18:09**	**112**	**42**	**48**	**90**	**207**	**14**	**0**	**8**

NHL First All-Star Team (1994, 2000) • Played in NHL All-Star Game (1994, 1996, 1997, 1998, 1999, 2000)

Signed as a free agent by **St. Louis**, July 25, 1991. Traded to **Hartford** by **St. Louis** for Chris Pronger, July 27, 1995. Traded to **Detroit** by **Hartford** with Brian Glynn for Paul Coffey, Keith Primeau and Detroit's 1st round choice (Nikos Tselios) in 1997 Entry Draft, October 9, 1996.

SHANNON, Darryl
(SHA-nohn, DAIR-ihl)

Defense. Shoots left. 6'2", 208 lbs. Born, Barrie, Ont., June 21, 1968. Toronto's 2nd choice, 36th overall, in 1986 Entry Draft.

			Regular Season																Playoffs							
Season	Club	League	GP	G	A	Pts	PIM	PP	SH	GW	S	%	+/-	TF	F%	H	SB	Min	GP	G	A	Pts	PIM	PP	SH	GW
1983-84	Alliston Hornets	OJHL-C	30	18	22	40	70																			
1984-85	Richmond Hill	OJHL	1	0	0	0	0																			
	Barrie Colts	OJHL-B	39	5	23	28	50																			
1985-86	Windsor Spitfires	OHL	57	6	21	27	52												16	5	6	11	22			
1986-87	Windsor Spitfires	OHL	64	23	27	50	83												14	4	8	12	18			
1987-88	Windsor Spitfires	OHL	60	16	67	83	116												12	3	8	11	17			
1988-89	**Toronto**	**NHL**	**14**	**1**	**3**	**4**	**6**	**0**	**0**	**0**	**16**	**6.3**	**5**													
	Newmarket	AHL	61	5	24	29	37												5	0	3	3	10			
1989-90	**Toronto**	**NHL**	**10**	**0**	**1**	**1**	**12**	**0**	**0**	**0**	**16**	**0.0**	**–10**													
	Newmarket	AHL	47	4	15	19	58																			
1990-91	**Toronto**	**NHL**	**10**	**0**	**1**	**1**	**0**	**0**	**0**	**0**	**3**	**0.0**	**1**													
	Newmarket	AHL	47	2	14	16	51																			
1991-92	**Toronto**	**NHL**	**48**	**2**	**8**	**10**	**23**	**1**	**0**	**0**	**50**	**4.0**	**–17**													
1992-93	**Toronto**	**NHL**	**16**	**0**	**0**	**0**	**11**	**0**	**0**	**0**	**10**	**0.0**	**–5**													
	St. John's Leafs	AHL	7	1	1	2	4																			
1993-94	**Winnipeg**	**NHL**	**20**	**0**	**4**	**4**	**18**	**0**	**0**	**0**	**14**	**0.0**	**–6**													
	Moncton Hawks	AHL	37	1	10	11	62												20	1	7	8	32			
1994-95	**Winnipeg**	**NHL**	**40**	**5**	**9**	**14**	**48**	**0**	**1**	**0**	**42**	**11.9**	**1**													
1995-96	**Winnipeg**	**NHL**	**48**	**2**	**7**	**9**	**72**	**0**	**0**	**0**	**34**	**5.9**	**5**													
	Buffalo	**NHL**	**26**	**2**	**6**	**8**	**20**	**0**	**0**	**0**	**25**	**8.0**	**10**													
1996-97	**Buffalo**	**NHL**	**82**	**4**	**19**	**23**	**112**	**1**	**0**	**1**	**94**	**4.3**	**23**						**12**	**2**	**3**	**5**	**8**	**1**	**0**	**0**
1997-98	**Buffalo**	**NHL**	**76**	**3**	**19**	**22**	**56**	**1**	**0**	**1**	**85**	**3.5**	**26**						**15**	**2**	**4**	**6**	**8**	**0**	**1**	**0**
1998-99	**Buffalo**	**NHL**	**71**	**3**	**12**	**15**	**52**	**1**	**0**	**0**	**80**	**3.8**	**28**	**1**	**0.0**	**103**	**111**	**20:10**	**2**	**0**	**0**	**0**	**0**	**0**	**0**	**0**
99-2000	**Atlanta**	**NHL**	**49**	**5**	**13**	**18**	**65**	**1**	**0**	**1**	**66**	**7.6**	**–14**	**1**	**0.0**	**86**	**84**	**21:21**								
	Calgary	**NHL**	**27**	**1**	**8**	**9**	**22**	**0**	**0**	**0**	**46**	**2.2**	**–13**	**0**	**0.0**	**32**	**44**	**23:33**								
2000-01	**Montreal**	**NHL**	**7**	**0**	**1**	**1**	**6**	**0**	**0**	**0**	**6**	**0.0**	**–4**	**0**	**0.0**	**11**	**13**	**18:03**								
	Quebec Citadelles	AHL	4	0	1	1	4																			
	NHL Totals		**544**	**28**	**111**	**139**	**523**	**5**	**1**	**3**	**587**	**4.8**		**2**	**0.0**	**232**	**252**	**21:03**	**29**	**4**	**7**	**11**	**16**	**1**	**1**	**0**

OHL Second All-Star Team (1987) • OHL First All-Star Team (1988)

Signed as a free agent by **Winnipeg**, June 30, 1993. Traded to **Buffalo** by **Winnipeg** with Michal Grosek for Craig Muni, February 15, 1996. Claimed by **Atlanta** from **Buffalo** in Expansion Draft, June 25, 1999. Traded to **Calgary** by **Atlanta** with Jason Botterill for Hnat Domenichelli and Dmitri Vlasenkov, February 11, 2000. Signed as a free agent by **Montreal**, September 25, 2000. • Officially announced retirement, November 25, 2000.

SHANTZ, Jeff
(SHAWNTS, JEHF) **CGY.**

Center. Shoots right. 6', 195 lbs. Born, Duchess, Alta., October 10, 1973. Chicago's 2nd choice, 36th overall, in 1992 Entry Draft.

			Regular Season																Playoffs							
Season	Club	League	GP	G	A	Pts	PIM	PP	SH	GW	S	%	+/-	TF	F%	H	SB	Min	GP	G	A	Pts	PIM	PP	SH	GW
1989-90	Medicine Hat	AMHL	36	18	31	49	30																			
	Regina Pats	WHL	1	0	0	0	0																			
1990-91	Regina Pats	WHL	69	16	21	37	22												8	2	2	4	2			
1991-92	Regina Pats	WHL	72	39	50	89	35																			
1992-93	Regina Pats	WHL	64	29	54	83	75												13	2	12	14	14			
1993-94	**Chicago**	**NHL**	**52**	**3**	**13**	**16**	**30**	**0**	**0**	**0**	**56**	**5.4**	**–14**						**6**	**0**	**0**	**0**	**6**	**0**	**0**	**0**
	Indianapolis Ice	IHL	19	5	9	14	20																			
1994-95	Indianapolis Ice	IHL	32	9	15	24	20																			
	Chicago	**NHL**	**45**	**6**	**12**	**18**	**33**	**0**	**2**	**0**	**58**	**10.3**	**11**						**16**	**3**	**1**	**4**	**2**	**0**	**0**	**0**
1995-96	**Chicago**	**NHL**	**78**	**6**	**14**	**20**	**24**	**1**	**2**	**0**	**72**	**8.3**	**12**						**10**	**2**	**3**	**5**	**6**	**0**	**0**	**0**
1996-97	**Chicago**	**NHL**	**69**	**9**	**21**	**30**	**28**	**0**	**1**	**1**	**86**	**10.5**	**11**						**6**	**0**	**4**	**4**	**6**	**0**	**0**	**0**
1997-98	**Chicago**	**NHL**	**61**	**11**	**20**	**31**	**36**	**1**	**2**	**2**	**69**	**15.9**	**0**													
1998-99	**Chicago**	**NHL**	**7**	**1**	**0**	**1**	**4**	**0**	**0**	**0**	**5**	**20.0**	**–1**	**72**	**38.9**	**16**	**1**	**15:14**								
	Calgary	**NHL**	**69**	**12**	**17**	**29**	**40**	**1**	**1**	**3**	**77**	**15.6**	**15**	**1112**	**48.4**	**83**	**35**	**16:47**								
99-2000	**Calgary**	**NHL**	**74**	**13**	**18**	**31**	**30**	**6**	**0**	**1**	**112**	**11.6**	**–13**	**1576**	**51.1**	**43**	**71**	**18:15**								
2000-01	**Calgary**	**NHL**	**73**	**5**	**15**	**20**	**58**	**0**	**0**	**0**	**88**	**5.7**	**–7**	**876**	**53.5**	**59**	**38**	**14:51**								
	NHL Totals		**528**	**66**	**130**	**196**	**283**	**9**	**8**	**7**	**623**	**10.6**		**3636**	**50.6**	**201**	**145**	**16:35**	**38**	**5**	**8**	**13**	**20**	**0**	**0**	**0**

WHL East First All-Star Team (1993)

Traded to **Calgary** by **Chicago** with Steve Dubinsky for Marty McInnis, Jamie Allison and Eric Andersson, October 27, 1998.

SHARIFIJANOV, Vadim
(shah-rih-FYAH-nohv, VA-dihm) **VAN.**

Right wing. Shoots left. 6', 205 lbs. Born, Ufa, USSR, December 23, 1975. New Jersey's 1st choice, 25th overall, in 1994 Entry Draft.

			Regular Season																Playoffs							
Season	Club	League	GP	G	A	Pts	PIM	PP	SH	GW	S	%	+/-	TF	F%	H	SB	Min	GP	G	A	Pts	PIM	PP	SH	GW
1992-93	Ufa Salavat	CIS	37	6	4	10	16												2	1	0	1	0			
1993-94	Ufa Salavat	CIS	46	10	6	16	36												5	3	0	3	4			
1994-95	CSKA Moscow	CIS	34	7	3	10	26												2	0	0	0	0			
	Albany River Rats	AHL	1	1	1	2	0												9	3	3	6	10			
1995-96	Albany River Rats	AHL	69	14	28	42	28																			
1996-97	**New Jersey**	**NHL**	**2**	**0**	**0**	**0**	**0**	**0**	**0**	**0**	**4**	**0.0**	**0**													
	Albany River Rats	AHL	70	14	27	41	89												10	3	3	6	6			
1997-98	Albany River Rats	AHL	72	23	27	50	69												12	4	9	13	6			
1998-99	**New Jersey**	**NHL**	**53**	**11**	**16**	**27**	**28**	**1**	**0**	**2**	**71**	**15.5**	**11**	**2**	**50.0**	**43**	**10**	**13:39**	**4**	**0**	**0**	**0**	**0**	**0**	**0**	**0**
	Albany River Rats	AHL	2	1	1	2	0																			
99-2000	**New Jersey**	**NHL**	**20**	**3**	**4**	**7**	**8**	**0**	**0**	**0**	**20**	**15.0**	**–6**	**0**	**0.0**	**19**	**0**	**10:58**								
	Vancouver	**NHL**	**17**	**2**	**1**	**3**	**14**	**1**	**0**	**0**	**26**	**7.7**	**–7**	**3**	**33.3**	**13**	**0**	**13:11**								
2000-01	Kansas City	IHL	70	20	43	63	48																			
	NHL Totals		**92**	**16**	**21**	**37**	**50**	**2**	**0**	**2**	**121**	**13.2**		**5**	**40.0**	**75**	**10**	**12:58**	**4**	**0**	**0**	**0**	**0**	**0**	**0**	**0**

Traded to **Vancouver** by **New Jersey** with New Jersey's 3rd round choice (Tim Branham) in 2000 Entry Draft for NY Islanders' compensatory 2nd round choice (previously acquired, New Jersey selected Teemu Laine) in 2000 Entry Draft and Atlanta's 3rd round choice (previously acquired, New Jersey selected Max Birbraer) in 2000 Entry Draft, January 14, 2000.

SHEARER, Rob
(SHEER-uhr, RAWB)

Center. Shoots right. 5'10", 190 lbs. Born, Kitchener, Ont., October 19, 1976.

			Regular Season																Playoffs							
Season	Club	League	GP	G	A	Pts	PIM	PP	SH	GW	S	%	+/-	TF	F%	H	SB	Min	GP	G	A	Pts	PIM	PP	SH	GW
1992-93	Kitchener Lions	OMHA	27	27	24	51																				
1993-94	Windsor Spitfires	OHL	66	17	25	42	46												4	0	2	2	6			
1994-95	Windsor Spitfires	OHL	59	28	28	56	48												10	4	4	8	10			
1995-96	Windsor Spitfires	OHL	63	40	53	93	74												7	6	3	9	8			
1996-97	Hershey Bears	AHL	78	12	16	28	88												23	0	4	4	9			
1997-98	Hershey Bears	AHL	79	30	30	60	44												7	0	5	5	6			
1998-99	Hershey Bears	AHL	77	24	42	66	43												3	0	0	0	6			
99-2000	Hershey Bears	AHL	70	21	46	67	55												14	1	7	8	10			
2000-01	**Colorado**	**NHL**	**2**	**0**	**0**	**0**	**0**	**0**	**0**	**0**	**0**	**0.0**	**–2**	**12**	**41.7**	**3**	**2**	**6:45**								
	Hershey Bears	AHL	73	18	34	52	64												12	1	3	4	0			
	NHL Totals		**2**	**0**	**0**	**0**	**0**	**0**	**0**	**0**	**0**	**0.0**		**12**	**41.7**	**3**	**2**	**6:45**								

Signed as a free agent by **Colorado**, October 5, 1995.

SHELLEY, Jody
(SHEH-lee, JOH-dee) **CBJ**

Left wing. Shoots left. 6'3", 228 lbs. Born, Yarmouth, N.S., February 7, 1976.

			Regular Season																Playoffs							
Season	Club	League	GP	G	A	Pts	PIM	PP	SH	GW	S	%	+/-	TF	F%	H	SB	Min	GP	G	A	Pts	PIM	PP	SH	GW
1994-95	Halifax	QMJHL	72	10	12	22	194												7	0	1	1	12			
1995-96	Halifax	QMJHL	50	13	19	32	319												6	0	2	2	36			
1996-97	Halifax	QMJHL	58	25	19	44	*448												17	6	6	12	*123			
1997-98	Dalhousie Tigers	AUAA	19	6	11	17	145																			
	Saint John Flames	AHL	18	1	1	2	50																			
1998-99	Saint John Flames	AHL	8	0	0	0	46																			
	Johnstown Chiefs	ECHL	52	12	17	29	325																			
99-2000	Johnstown Chiefs	ECHL	36	9	17	26	256																			
	Saint John Flames	AHL	22	1	4	5	93												3	0	0	0	2			

			Regular Season																Playoffs							
Season	Club	League	GP	G	A	Pts	PIM	PP	SH	GW	S	%	+/-	TF	F%	H	SB	Min	GP	G	A	Pts	PIM	PP	SH	GW
2000-01	Columbus	NHL	1	0	0	0	10	0	0	0	0	0.0	0	0	0.0	0	0	1:33	....	....	....	....	....	....	....	....
	Syracuse Crunch	AHL	69	1	7	8	*357	....	....	....	....	....	....	....	....	....	....	....	5	0	0	0	21	....	....	....
	NHL Totals		1	0	0	0	10	0	0	0	0	0.0		0	0.0	0	0	1:33	....	....	....	....	....	....	....	....

Signed as a free agent by **Calgary**, September 1, 1998. Signed as a free agent by **Syracuse** (AHL), September 15, 2000. Signed as a free agent by **Columbus**, January 31, 2001.

SHEPPARD, Ray (SHEH-pahrd, RAY)

Right wing. Shoots right. 6'1", 195 lbs. Born, Pembroke, Ont., May 27, 1966. Buffalo's 3rd choice, 60th overall, in 1984 Entry Draft.

Season	Club	League	GP	G	A	Pts	PIM	PP	SH	GW	S	%	+/-	TF	F%	H	SB	Min	GP	G	A	Pts	PIM	PP	SH	GW
1982-83	Brockville Braves	OCJHL	48	27	36	63	81	....	....	....	....	....	....	....	....	....	....	....	....	....	....	....	....	....	....	....
1983-84	Cornwall Royals	OHL	68	44	36	80	69	....	....	....	....	....	....	....	....	....	....	....	....	....	....	....	....	....	....	....
1984-85	Cornwall Royals	OHL	49	25	33	58	51	....	....	....	....	....	....	....	....	....	....	....	9	2	12	14	4	....	....	....
1985-86	Cornwall Royals	OHL	63	*81	61	*142	25	....	....	....	....	....	....	....	....	....	....	....	6	7	4	11	0	....	....	....
1986-87	Rochester	AHL	55	18	13	31	11	....	....	....	....	....	....	....	....	....	....	....	15	12	3	15	2	....	....	....
1987-88	Buffalo	NHL	74	38	27	65	14	15	0	5	173	22.0	–6	....	....	....	....	....	6	1	1	2	2	1	0	0
1988-89	Buffalo	NHL	67	22	21	43	15	7	0	4	147	15.0	–7	....	....	....	....	....	1	0	1	1	0	0	0	0
1989-90	Buffalo	NHL	18	4	2	6	0	1	0	1	31	12.9	3	....	....	....	....	....	....	....	....	....	....	....	....	....
	Rochester	AHL	5	3	5	8	2	....	....	....	....	....	....	....	....	....	....	....	17	8	7	15	9	....	....	....
1990-91	NY Rangers	NHL	59	24	23	47	21	7	0	5	129	18.6	8	....	....	....	....	....	....	....	....	....	....	....	....	....
1991-92	Detroit	NHL	74	36	26	62	27	11	1	4	178	20.2	7	....	....	....	....	....	11	6	2	8	4	3	0	0
1992-93	Detroit	NHL	70	32	34	66	29	10	0	1	183	17.5	7	....	....	....	....	....	7	2	3	5	0	2	0	0
1993-94	Detroit	NHL	82	52	41	93	26	19	0	5	260	20.0	13	....	....	....	....	....	7	2	1	3	4	0	0	0
1994-95	Detroit	NHL	43	30	10	40	17	11	0	5	125	24.0	11	....	....	....	....	....	17	4	3	7	5	2	0	0
1995-96	Detroit	NHL	5	2	2	4	2	0	0	1	9	22.2	0	....	....	....	....	....	....	....	....	....	....	....	....	....
	San Jose	NHL	51	27	19	46	10	12	0	4	170	15.9	–19	....	....	....	....	....	....	....	....	....	....	....	....	....
	Florida	NHL	14	8	2	10	4	2	0	2	52	15.4	0	....	....	....	....	....	21	8	8	16	4	3	0	0
1996-97	Florida	NHL	68	29	31	60	4	13	0	7	226	12.8	4	....	....	....	....	....	5	2	0	2	0	1	0	0
1997-98	Florida	NHL	61	14	17	31	21	5	0	1	136	10.3	–13	....	....	....	....	....	....	....	....	....	....	....	....	....
	Carolina	NHL	10	4	2	6	2	2	0	1	33	12.1	2	....	....	....	....	....	....	....	....	....	....	....	....	....
1998-99	Carolina	NHL	74	25	33	58	16	5	0	4	188	13.3	4	7	71.4	20	6	18:12	6	5	1	6	2	1	0	1
99-2000	Florida	NHL	47	10	10	20	4	5	0	2	74	13.5	–4	4	0.0	7	5	13:38	....	....	....	....	....	....	....	....
2000-01	SC Langnau	Switz.	13	13	4	17	0	....	....	....	....	....	....	....	....	....	....	....	4	3	3	6	2	....	....	....
	NHL Totals		817	357	300	657	212	125	1	52	2114	16.9		11	45.5	27	11	16:25	81	30	20	50	21	13	0	1

OHL First All-Star Team (1986) • NHL All-Rookie Team (1988)

• Missed majority of 1989-90 season recovering from ankle injury suffered in game vs. Quebec, January 31, 1990. Traded to **NY Rangers** by **Buffalo** for cash and future considerations, July 9, 1990. Signed as a free agent by **Detroit**, August 5, 1991. Traded to **San Jose** by **Detroit** for Igor Larionov and future considerations, October 24, 1995. Traded to **Florida** by **San Jose** with San Jose's 4th round choice (Joey Tetarenko) in 1996 Entry Draft for Florida's 2nd (later traded to Chicago - Chicago selected Geoff Peters) and 4th (Matt Bradley) round choices in 1996 Entry Draft, March 16, 1996. Traded to **Carolina** by **Florida** for Kirk McLean, March 24, 1998. Signed as a free agent by **Florida**, November 15, 1999.

SHVIDKI, Denis (SHVIHD-kee, DEH-nihs) FLA.

Right wing. Shoots left. 6'2", 213 lbs. Born, Kharkov, USSR, November 21, 1980. Florida's 1st choice, 12th overall, in 1999 Entry Draft.

Season	Club	League	GP	G	A	Pts	PIM	PP	SH	GW	S	%	+/-	TF	F%	H	SB	Min	GP	G	A	Pts	PIM	PP	SH	GW
1996-97	HC Yaroslavl-2	Russia-3	35	21	12	33	32	....	....	....	....	....	....	....	....	....	....	....	....	....	....	....	....	....	....	....
	Torpedo Yaroslavl	Russia	17	3	2	5	6	....	....	....	....	....	....	....	....	....	....	....	....	....	....	....	....	....	....	....
1997-98	Torpedo Yaroslavl	Russia-2	32	20	13	33	20	....	....	....	....	....	....	....	....	....	....	....	....	....	....	....	....	....	....	....
	Torpedo Yaroslavl	Russia	15	1	1	2	2	....	....	....	....	....	....	....	....	....	....	....	....	....	....	....	....	....	....	....
1998-99	Barrie Colts	OHL	61	35	59	94	8	....	....	....	....	....	....	....	....	....	....	....	12	7	9	16	2	....	....	....
99-2000	Barrie Colts	OHL	61	41	65	106	55	....	....	....	....	....	....	....	....	....	....	....	9	3	1	4	2	....	....	....
2000-01	Florida	NHL	43	6	10	16	16	0	0	1	28	21.4	6	4	50.0	22	8	10:21	....	....	....	....	....	....	....	....
	Louisville Panthers	AHL	34	15	11	26	20	....	....	....	....	....	....	....	....	....	....	....	....	....	....	....	....	....	....	....
	NHL Totals		43	6	10	16	16	0	0	1	28	21.4		4	50.0	22	8	10:21	....	....	....	....	....	....	....	....

OHL Second All-Star Team (1999)

SILLINGER, Mike (sih-LIHN-juhr, MIGHK) CBJ

Center. Shoots right. 5'10", 191 lbs. Born, Regina, Sask., June 29, 1971. Detroit's 1st choice, 11th overall, in 1989 Entry Draft.

Season	Club	League	GP	G	A	Pts	PIM	PP	SH	GW	S	%	+/-	TF	F%	H	SB	Min	GP	G	A	Pts	PIM	PP	SH	GW
1986-87	Regina Kings	SAHA	31	83	51	134	....	....	....	....	....	....	....	....	....	....	....	....	....	....	....	....	....	....	....	....
1987-88	Regina Pats	WHL	67	18	25	43	17	....	....	....	....	....	....	....	....	....	....	....	4	2	2	4	0	....	....	....
1988-89	Regina Pats	WHL	72	53	78	131	52	....	....	....	....	....	....	....	....	....	....	....	....	....	....	....	....	....	....	....
1989-90	Regina Pats	WHL	70	57	72	129	41	....	....	....	....	....	....	....	....	....	....	....	11	12	10	22	2	....	....	....
	Adirondack	AHL	....	....	....	....	....	....	....	....	....	....	....	....	....	....	....	....	1	0	0	0	0	....	....	....
1990-91	Regina Pats	WHL	57	50	66	116	42	....	....	....	....	....	....	....	....	....	....	....	8	6	9	15	4	....	....	....
	Detroit	NHL	3	0	1	1	0	0	0	0	6	0.0	–2	....	....	....	....	....	3	0	1	1	0	0	0	0
1991-92	Adirondack	AHL	64	25	41	66	26	....	....	....	....	....	....	....	....	....	....	....	15	9	*19	*28	12	....	....	....
	Detroit	NHL	....	....	....	....	....	....	....	....	....	....	....	....	....	....	....	....	8	2	2	4	2	0	0	0
1992-93	Detroit	NHL	51	4	17	21	16	0	0	0	47	8.5	0	....	....	....	....	....	....	....	....	....	....	....	....	....
	Adirondack	AHL	15	10	20	30	31	....	....	....	....	....	....	....	....	....	....	....	11	5	13	18	10	....	....	....
1993-94	Detroit	NHL	62	8	21	29	10	0	1	1	91	8.8	2	....	....	....	....	....	....	....	....	....	....	....	....	....
1994-95	WEV Wien	Austria	13	13	14	27	10	....	....	....	....	....	....	....	....	....	....	....	....	....	....	....	....	....	....	....
	Detroit	NHL	13	2	6	8	2	0	0	0	11	18.2	3	....	....	....	....	....	....	....	....	....	....	....	....	....
	Anaheim	NHL	15	2	5	7	6	2	0	0	28	7.1	1	....	....	....	....	....	....	....	....	....	....	....	....	....
1995-96	Anaheim	NHL	62	13	21	34	32	7	0	2	143	9.1	–20	....	....	....	....	....	....	....	....	....	....	....	....	....
	Vancouver	NHL	12	1	3	4	6	0	1	0	16	6.3	2	....	....	....	....	....	6	0	0	0	2	0	0	0
1996-97	Vancouver	NHL	78	17	20	37	25	3	3	2	112	15.2	–3	....	....	....	....	....	....	....	....	....	....	....	....	....
1997-98	Vancouver	NHL	48	10	9	19	34	1	2	1	56	17.9	–14	....	....	....	....	....	....	....	....	....	....	....	....	....
	Philadelphia	NHL	27	11	11	22	16	1	2	0	40	27.5	3	....	....	....	....	....	3	1	0	1	0	0	0	0
1998-99	Philadelphia	NHL	25	0	3	3	8	0	0	0	23	0.0	–9	229	62.9	12	5	10:42	....	....	....	....	....	....	....	....
	Tampa Bay	NHL	54	8	2	10	28	0	2	0	69	11.6	–20	320	57.8	70	35	13:57	....	....	....	....	....	....	....	....
99-2000	Tampa Bay	NHL	67	19	25	44	86	6	3	1	126	15.1	–29	493	56.0	69	39	19:42	....	....	....	....	....	....	....	....
	Florida	NHL	13	4	4	8	16	2	0	1	20	20.0	–1	248	61.3	15	14	19:33	4	2	1	3	2	0	0	0
2000-01	Florida	NHL	55	13	21	34	44	1	0	2	100	13.0	–12	1028	59.7	74	29	18:52	....	....	....	....	....	....	....	....
	Ottawa	NHL	13	3	4	7	4	0	0	0	19	15.8	1	215	63.3	14	3	14:31	4	0	0	0	2	0	0	0
	NHL Totals		598	115	173	288	333	23	14	10	907	12.7		2533	59.5	254	125	16:50	28	5	4	9	8	0	0	0

WHL East Second All-Star Team (1990) • WHL East First All-Star Team (1991)

Traded to **Anaheim** by **Detroit** with Jason York for Stu Grimson, Mark Ferner and Anaheim's 6th round choice (Magnus Nilsson) in 1996 Entry Draft, April 4, 1995. Traded to **Vancouver** by **Anaheim** for Roman Oksiuta, March 15, 1996. Traded to **Philadelphia** by **Vancouver** for Philadelphia's 5th round choice (later traded back to Philadelphia - Philadelphia selected Garrett Prosofsky) in 1998 Entry Draft, February 5, 1998. Traded to **Tampa Bay** by **Philadelphia** with Chris Gratton for Mikael Renberg and Daymond Langkow, December 12, 1998. Traded to **Florida** by **Tampa Bay** for Ryan Johnson and Dwayne Hay, March 14, 2000. Traded to **Ottawa** by **Florida** for future considerations, March 13, 2001. Signed as a free agent by **Columbus**, July 7, 2001.

SIM, Jonathan (SIHM, JAWN-ah-thuhn) DAL.

Center. Shoots left. 5'10", 184 lbs. Born, New Glasgow, N.S., September 29, 1977. Dallas' 2nd choice, 70th overall, in 1996 Entry Draft.

Season	Club	League	GP	G	A	Pts	PIM	PP	SH	GW	S	%	+/-	TF	F%	H	SB	Min	GP	G	A	Pts	PIM	PP	SH	GW
1994-95	Laval Titan	QMJHL	9	0	1	1	6	....	....	....	....	....	....	....	....	....	....	....	....	....	....	....	....	....	....	....
	Sarnia Sting	OHL	25	9	12	21	19	....	....	....	....	....	....	....	....	....	....	....	4	3	2	5	2	....	....	....
1995-96	Sarnia Sting	OHL	63	56	46	102	130	....	....	....	....	....	....	....	....	....	....	....	10	8	7	15	26	....	....	....
1996-97	Sarnia Sting	OHL	64	*56	39	95	109	....	....	....	....	....	....	....	....	....	....	....	12	9	5	14	32	....	....	....
1997-98	Sarnia Sting	OHL	59	44	50	94	95	....	....	....	....	....	....	....	....	....	....	....	5	1	4	5	14	....	....	....
1998-99♦	Dallas	NHL	7	1	0	1	12	0	0	0	8	12.5	1	6	50.0	15	0	11:26	4	0	0	0	0	0	0	0
	Michigan K-Wings	IHL	68	24	27	51	91	....	....	....	....	....	....	....	....	....	....	....	5	3	1	4	18	....	....	....
99-2000	Dallas	NHL	25	5	3	8	10	2	0	1	44	11.4	4	4	75.0	29	2	10:51	7	1	0	1	6	0	0	0
	Michigan K-Wings	IHL	35	14	16	30	65	....	....	....	....	....	....	....	....	....	....	....	....	....	....	....	....	....	....	....
2000-01	Dallas	NHL	15	0	3	3	6	0	0	0	18	0.0	–2	1	100.0	28	0	8:47	....	....	....	....	....	....	....	....
	Utah Grizzlies	IHL	39	16	13	29	44	....	....	....	....	....	....	....	....	....	....	....	....	....	....	....	....	....	....	....
	NHL Totals		47	6	6	12	28	2	0	1	70	8.6		11	63.6	72	2	10:16	11	1	0	1	6	0	0	0

OHL Second All-Star Team (1998)

			Regular Season																Playoffs							
Season	Club	League	GP	G	A	Pts	PIM	PP	SH	GW	S	%	+/-	TF	F%	H	SB	Min	GP	G	A	Pts	PIM	PP	SH	GW

SIMICEK, Roman (SIH-mih-chehk, ROH-muhn) MIN.

Center. Shoots left. 6'1", 190 lbs. Born, Ostrava, Czech., November 4, 1971. Pittsburgh's 9th choice, 273rd overall, in 2000 Entry Draft.

1990-91	TJ Vitkovice	Czech.	35	2	4	6	....	....	....	....	....	....	....	....	....	....	....	....	....	....	....	....	....	....	....	....
1991-92	TJ Vitkovice	Czech.	33	6	12	18	34	....	....	....	....	....	....	....	....	....	....	....	12	2	7	9	....	....	....	....
1992-93	TJ Vitkovice	Czech.	38	8	11	19	52	....	....	....	....	....	....	....	....	....	....	....	14	5	8	13	....	....	....	....
1993-94	HC Vitkovice	Cze-Rep	40	18	16	34	78	....	....	....	....	....	....	....	....	....	....	....	5	0	2	2	....	....	....	....
1994-95	HC Vitkovice	Cze-Rep	41	11	14	25	100	....	....	....	....	....	....	....	....	....	....	....	6	1	3	4	8	....	....	....
1995-96	HC Vitkovice	Cze-Rep	39	9	11	20	38	....	....	....	....	....	....	....	....	....	....	....	4	2	0	2	8	....	....	....
1996-97	HC Vitkovice	Cze-Rep	49	18	19	37	48	....	....	....	....	....	....	....	....	....	....	....	9	4	4	8	22	....	....	....
1997-98	HC Vitkovice	Cze-Rep	40	16	27	43	71	....	....	....	....	....	....	....	....	....	....	....	9	2	4	6	6	....	....	....
	HC Vitkovice	EuroHL	4	1	2	3	4	....	....	....	....	....	....	....	....	....	....	....	....	....	....	....	....	....	....	....
1998-99	HPK Hameenlinna	Finland	49	24	27	51	75	....	....	....	....	....	....	....	....	....	....	....	8	2	5	7	18	....	....	....
99-2000	HPK Hameenlinna	Finland	23	10	17	27	50	....	....	....	....	....	....	....	....	....	....	....	8	2	4	6	10	....	....	....
2000-01	**Pittsburgh**	**NHL**	**29**	**3**	**6**	**9**	**30**	**1**	**0**	**1**	**19**	**15.8**	**–5**	**203**	**45.8**	**12**	**2**	**9:28**	....	....	....	....	....	....	....	....
	Minnesota	**NHL**	**28**	**2**	**4**	**6**	**21**	**2**	**0**	**0**	**14**	**14.3**	**–4**	**4**	**0.0**	**26**	**2**	**12:40**	....	....	....	....	....	....	....	....
	NHL Totals		**57**	**5**	**10**	**15**	**51**	**3**	**0**	**1**	**33**	**15.2**		**207**	**44.9**	**38**	**4**	**11:02**	....	....	....	....	....	....	....	....

Traded to **Minnesota** by **Pittsburgh** for Steve McKenna, January 13, 2001.

SIMON, Chris (SIGH-mohn, KRIHS) WSH.

Left wing. Shoots left. 6'4", 235 lbs. Born, Wawa, Ont., January 30, 1972. Philadelphia's 2nd choice, 25th overall, in 1990 Entry Draft.

1986-87	Wawa Flyers	NOHA	36	12	20	32	108	....	....	....	....	....	....	....	....	....	....	....	....	....	....	....	....	....	....	....
1987-88	S.S. Marie T-Birds	NOJHA	55	42	36	78	172	....	....	....	....	....	....	....	....	....	....	....	....	....	....	....	....	....	....	....
1988-89	Ottawa 67's	OHL	36	4	2	6	31	....	....	....	....	....	....	....	....	....	....	....	....	....	....	....	....	....	....	....
1989-90	Ottawa 67's	OHL	57	36	38	74	146	....	....	....	....	....	....	....	....	....	....	....	3	2	1	3	4	....	....	....
1990-91	Ottawa 67's	OHL	20	16	6	22	69	....	....	....	....	....	....	....	....	....	....	....	17	5	9	14	59	....	....	....
1991-92	Ottawa 67's	OHL	2	1	1	2	24	....	....	....	....	....	....	....	....	....	....	....	....	....	....	....	....	....	....	....
	Sault Ste. Marie	OHL	31	19	25	44	143	....	....	....	....	....	....	....	....	....	....	....	11	5	8	13	49	....	....	....
1992-93	**Quebec**	**NHL**	**16**	**1**	**1**	**2**	**67**	**0**	**0**	**1**	**15**	**6.7**	**–2**	....	....	....	....	....	**5**	**0**	**0**	**0**	**26**	**0**	**0**	**0**
	Halifax Citadels	AHL	36	12	6	18	131	....	....	....	....	....	....	....	....	....	....	....	....	....	....	....	....	....	....	....
1993-94	**Quebec**	**NHL**	**37**	**4**	**4**	**8**	**132**	**0**	**0**	**1**	**39**	**10.3**	**–2**	....	....	....	....	....	....	....	....	....	....	....	....	....
1994-95	**Quebec**	**NHL**	**29**	**3**	**9**	**12**	**106**	**0**	**0**	**0**	**33**	**9.1**	**14**	....	....	....	....	....	**6**	**1**	**1**	**2**	**19**	**0**	**0**	**1**
1995-96♦	**Colorado**	**NHL**	**64**	**16**	**18**	**34**	**250**	**4**	**0**	**1**	**105**	**15.2**	**10**	....	....	....	....	....	**12**	**1**	**2**	**3**	**11**	**0**	**0**	**0**
1996-97	**Washington**	**NHL**	**42**	**9**	**13**	**22**	**165**	**3**	**0**	**1**	**89**	**10.1**	**–1**	....	....	....	....	....	....	....	....	....	....	....	....	....
1997-98	**Washington**	**NHL**	**28**	**7**	**10**	**17**	**38**	**4**	**0**	**1**	**71**	**9.9**	**–1**	....	....	....	....	....	**18**	**1**	**0**	**1**	**26**	**0**	**0**	**0**
1998-99	**Washington**	**NHL**	**23**	**3**	**7**	**10**	**48**	**0**	**0**	**0**	**29**	**10.3**	**–4**	**2**	**50.0**	**53**	**5**	**12:08**	....	....	....	....	....	....	....	....
99-2000	**Washington**	**NHL**	**75**	**29**	**20**	**49**	**146**	**7**	**0**	**5**	**201**	**14.4**	**11**	**7**	**28.6**	**141**	**19**	**15:32**	**4**	**2**	**0**	**2**	**24**	**0**	**0**	**0**
2000-01	**Washington**	**NHL**	**60**	**10**	**10**	**20**	**109**	**4**	**0**	**2**	**123**	**8.1**	**–12**	**3**	**33.3**	**69**	**9**	**14:34**	**6**	**0**	**1**	**1**	**4**	**0**	**0**	**0**
	NHL Totals		**374**	**82**	**92**	**174**	**1061**	**22**	**0**	**12**	**705**	**11.6**		**12**	**33.3**	**263**	**33**	**14:40**	**51**	**5**	**4**	**9**	**110**	**0**	**0**	**1**

• Missed majority of 1990-91 season recovering from shoulder surgery, October, 1990. Traded to **Quebec** by **Philadelphia** with Philadelphia's 1st round choice (later traded to Toronto - later traded to Washington - Washington selected Nolan Baumgartner) in 1994 Entry Draft to complete transaction that sent Eric Lindros to Philadelphia (June 30, 1992), July 21, 1992. Transferred to **Colorado** after **Quebec** franchise relocated, June 21, 1995. Traded to **Washington** by **Colorado** with Curtis Leschyshyn for Keith Jones and Washington's 1st (Scott Parker) and 4th (later traded back to Washington - Washington selected Krys Barch) round choices in 1998 Entry Drarft, November 2, 1996.

SIMPSON, Reid (SIHMP-sohn, REED) ST.L.

Left wing. Shoots left. 6'2", 216 lbs. Born, Flin Flon, Man., May 21, 1969. Philadelphia's 3rd choice, 72nd overall, in 1989 Entry Draft.

1984-85	Flin Flon Selects	MMHL	50	60	70	130	100	....	....	....	....	....	....	....	....	....	....	....	....	....	....	....	....	....	....	....
1985-86	Flin Flon Bombers	MJHL	40	20	21	41	200	....	....	....	....	....	....	....	....	....	....	....	....	....	....	....	....	....	....	....
	New Westminster	WHL	2	0	0	0	0	....	....	....	....	....	....	....	....	....	....	....	....	....	....	....	....	....	....	....
1986-87	Prince Albert	WHL	47	3	8	11	105	....	....	....	....	....	....	....	....	....	....	....	8	2	3	5	13	....	....	....
1987-88	Prince Albert	WHL	72	13	14	27	164	....	....	....	....	....	....	....	....	....	....	....	10	1	0	1	43	....	....	....
1988-89	Prince Albert	WHL	59	26	29	55	264	....	....	....	....	....	....	....	....	....	....	....	4	2	1	3	30	....	....	....
1989-90	Prince Albert	WHL	29	15	17	32	121	....	....	....	....	....	....	....	....	....	....	....	14	4	7	11	34	....	....	....
	Hershey Bears	AHL	28	2	2	4	175	....	....	....	....	....	....	....	....	....	....	....	....	....	....	....	....	....	....	....
1990-91	Hershey Bears	AHL	54	9	15	24	183	....	....	....	....	....	....	....	....	....	....	....	1	0	0	0	0	....	....	....
1991-92	**Philadelphia**	**NHL**	**1**	**0**	**0**	**0**	**0**	**0**	**0**	**0**	**0**	**0.0**	**0**	....	....	....	....	....	....	....	....	....	....	....	....	....
	Hershey Bears	AHL	60	11	7	18	145	....	....	....	....	....	....	....	....	....	....	....	....	....	....	....	....	....	....	....
1992-93	**Minnesota**	**NHL**	**1**	**0**	**0**	**0**	**5**	**0**	**0**	**0**	**0**	**0.0**	**0**	....	....	....	....	....	....	....	....	....	....	....	....	....
	Kalamazoo Wings	IHL	45	5	5	10	193	....	....	....	....	....	....	....	....	....	....	....	....	....	....	....	....	....	....	....
1993-94	Kalamazoo Wings	IHL	5	0	0	0	16	....	....	....	....	....	....	....	....	....	....	....	....	....	....	....	....	....	....	....
	Albany River Rats	AHL	37	9	5	14	135	....	....	....	....	....	....	....	....	....	....	....	5	1	1	2	18	....	....	....
1994-95	Albany River Rats	AHL	70	18	25	43	268	....	....	....	....	....	....	....	....	....	....	....	14	1	8	9	13	....	....	....
	New Jersey	**NHL**	**9**	**0**	**0**	**0**	**27**	**0**	**0**	**0**	**5**	**0.0**	**–1**	....	....	....	....	....	....	....	....	....	....	....	....	....
1995-96	**New Jersey**	**NHL**	**23**	**1**	**5**	**6**	**79**	**0**	**0**	**0**	**8**	**12.5**	**2**	....	....	....	....	....	....	....	....	....	....	....	....	....
	Albany River Rats	AHL	6	1	3	4	17	....	....	....	....	....	....	....	....	....	....	....	....	....	....	....	....	....	....	....
1996-97	**New Jersey**	**NHL**	**27**	**0**	**4**	**4**	**60**	**0**	**0**	**0**	**17**	**0.0**	**0**	....	....	....	....	....	**5**	**0**	**0**	**0**	**29**	**0**	**0**	**0**
	Albany River Rats	AHL	3	0	0	0	10	....	....	....	....	....	....	....	....	....	....	....	....	....	....	....	....	....	....	....
1997-98	**New Jersey**	**NHL**	**6**	**0**	**0**	**0**	**16**	**0**	**0**	**0**	**5**	**0.0**	**–2**	....	....	....	....	....	....	....	....	....	....	....	....	....
	Chicago	**NHL**	**38**	**3**	**2**	**5**	**102**	**1**	**0**	**0**	**19**	**15.8**	**–1**	....	....	....	....	....	....	....	....	....	....	....	....	....
1998-99	**Chicago**	**NHL**	**53**	**5**	**4**	**9**	**145**	**1**	**0**	**0**	**23**	**21.7**	**2**	**5**	**40.0**	**37**	**1**	**5:56**	....	....	....	....	....	....	....	....
99-2000	Cleveland	IHL	12	2	2	4	56	....	....	....	....	....	....	....	....	....	....	....	....	....	....	....	....	....	....	....
	Tampa Bay	**NHL**	**26**	**1**	**0**	**1**	**103**	**0**	**0**	**0**	**13**	**7.7**	**–3**	**1**	**100.0**	**30**	**5**	**4:33**	....	....	....	....	....	....	....	....
2000-01	**St. Louis**	**NHL**	**38**	**2**	**1**	**3**	**96**	**0**	**0**	**1**	**23**	**8.7**	**–3**	**1**	**0.0**	**48**	**5**	**6:57**	**5**	**0**	**0**	**0**	**2**	**0**	**0**	**0**
	NHL Totals		**222**	**12**	**16**	**28**	**633**	**2**	**0**	**1**	**113**	**10.6**		**7**	**42.9**	**115**	**11**	**5:57**	**10**	**0**	**0**	**0**	**31**	**0**	**0**	**0**

Signed as a free agent by **Minnesota**, December 14, 1992. Transferred to **Dallas** after **Minnesota** franchise relocated, June 9, 1993. Traded to **New Jersey** by **Dallas** with Roy Mitchell for future considerations, March 21, 1994. Traded to **Chicago** by **New Jersey** for Chicago's 4th round choice (Mikko Jokela) in 1998 Entry Draft and future considerations, January 8, 1998. Traded to **Tampa Bay** by **Chicago** with Bryan Muir for Michael Nylander, November 12, 1999. • Missed majority of 1999-2000 season recovering from jaw injury suffered in game vs. NY Islanders, January 13, 2000. Signed as a free agent by **St. Louis**, August 24, 2000. • Missed majority of 2000-01 season recovering from groin injury originally suffered in game vs. Nashville, November 24, 2000.

SIMPSON, Todd (SIHMP-sohn, TAWD) PHX.

Defense. Shoots left. 6'3", 215 lbs. Born, North Vancouver, B.C., May 28, 1973.

1989-90	Don Mills Flyers	MTHL	42	36	48	84	36	....	....	....	....	....	....	....	....	....	....	....	....	....	....	....	....	....	....	....
1990-91	Port Colborne	OJHL-B	45	40	43	83	120	....	....	....	....	....	....	....	....	....	....	....	....	....	....	....	....	....	....	....
1991-92	Brown University	ECAC	18	1	4	5	38	....	....	....	....	....	....	....	....	....	....	....	....	....	....	....	....	....	....	....
1992-93	Tri-City Americans	WHL	69	5	18	23	196	....	....	....	....	....	....	....	....	....	....	....	4	0	0	0	13	....	....	....
1993-94	Tri-City Americans	WHL	12	2	3	5	32	....	....	....	....	....	....	....	....	....	....	....	....	....	....	....	....	....	....	....
	Saskatoon Blades	WHL	51	7	19	26	175	....	....	....	....	....	....	....	....	....	....	....	16	1	5	6	42	....	....	....
1994-95	Saint John Flames	AHL	80	3	10	13	321	....	....	....	....	....	....	....	....	....	....	....	5	0	0	0	4	....	....	....
1995-96	**Calgary**	**NHL**	**6**	**0**	**0**	**0**	**32**	**0**	**0**	**0**	**3**	**0.0**	**0**	....	....	....	....	....	....	....	....	....	....	....	....	....
	Saint John Flames	AHL	66	4	13	17	277	....	....	....	....	....	....	....	....	....	....	....	16	2	3	5	32	....	....	....
1996-97	**Calgary**	**NHL**	**82**	**1**	**13**	**14**	**208**	**0**	**0**	**0**	**85**	**1.2**	**–14**	....	....	....	....	....	....	....	....	....	....	....	....	....
1997-98	**Calgary**	**NHL**	**53**	**1**	**5**	**6**	**109**	**0**	**0**	**1**	**51**	**2.0**	**–10**	....	....	....	....	....	....	....	....	....	....	....	....	....
1998-99	**Calgary**	**NHL**	**73**	**2**	**8**	**10**	**151**	**0**	**0**	**0**	**52**	**3.8**	**18**	**1**	**100.0**	**91**	**62**	**17:19**	....	....	....	....	....	....	....	....
99-2000	**Florida**	**NHL**	**82**	**1**	**6**	**7**	**202**	**0**	**0**	**0**	**50**	**2.0**	**5**	**0**	**0.0**	**112**	**77**	**16:35**	**4**	**0**	**0**	**0**	**4**	**0**	**0**	**0**
2000-01	**Florida**	**NHL**	**25**	**1**	**3**	**4**	**74**	**0**	**0**	**1**	**26**	**3.8**	**0**	**0**	**0.0**	**40**	**17**	**16:29**	....	....	....	....	....	....	....	....
	Phoenix	**NHL**	**13**	**0**	**1**	**1**	**12**	**0**	**0**	**0**	**9**	**0.0**	**–4**	**0**	**0.0**	**9**	**5**	**13:56**	....	....	....	....	....	....	....	....
	NHL Totals		**334**	**6**	**36**	**42**	**788**	**0**	**0**	**2**	**276**	**2.2**		**1**	**100.0**	**252**	**161**	**16:40**	**4**	**0**	**0**	**0**	**4**	**0**	**0**	**0**

Signed as free agent by **Calgary**, July 6, 1994. Traded to **Florida** by **Calgary** for Bill Lindsay, September 30, 1999. • Missed majority of 2000-01 season recovering from head injury suffered in game vs. NY Islanders, December 6, 2000. Traded to **Phoenix** by **Florida** for Phoenix's 2nd round choice in 2001 Entry Draft, March 13, 2001.

SKALDE, Jarrod

(SKAHL-dee, JAIR-ruhd) **ATL.**

Center. Shoots left. 6', 185 lbs. Born, Niagara Falls, Ont., February 26, 1971. New Jersey's 3rd choice, 26th overall, in 1989 Entry Draft.

			Regular Season																Playoffs							
Season	Club	League	GP	G	A	Pts	PIM	PP	SH	GW	S	%	+/-	TF	F%	H	SB	Min	GP	G	A	Pts	PIM	PP	SH	GW
1986-87	Fort Erie Meteors	OJHL-B	41	27	34	61	36	....	....	....	....	....	....	....	....	....	....	....	....	....	....	....	....	....	....	....
1987-88	Oshawa Generals	OHL	60	12	16	28	24	....	....	....	....	....	....	....	....	....	....	....	7	2	1	3	2	....	....	....
1988-89	Oshawa Generals	OHL	65	38	38	76	36	....	....	....	....	....	....	....	....	....	....	....	6	1	5	6	2	....	....	....
1989-90	Oshawa Generals	OHL	62	40	52	92	66	....	....	....	....	....	....	....	....	....	....	....	17	10	7	17	6	....	....	....
1990-91	Oshawa Generals	OHL	15	8	14	22	14	....	....	....	....	....	....	....	....	....	....	....	....	....	....	....	....	....	....	....
	Belleville Bulls	OHL	40	30	52	82	21	....	....	....	....	....	....	....	....	....	....	....	6	9	6	15	10	....	....	....
	New Jersey	**NHL**	**1**	**0**	**1**	**1**	**0**	**0**	**0**	**0**	**2**	**0.0**	**0**	....	....	....	....	....	....	....	....	....	....	....	....	....
	Utica Devils	AHL	3	3	2	5	0	....	....	....	....	....	....	....	....	....	....	....	....	....	....	....	....	....	....	....
1991-92	**New Jersey**	**NHL**	**15**	**2**	**4**	**6**	**4**	**0**	**0**	**2**	**25**	**8.0**	**–1**	....	....	....	....	....	....	....	....	....	....	....	....	....
	Utica Devils	AHL	62	20	20	40	56	....	....	....	....	....	....	....	....	....	....	....	4	3	1	4	8	....	....	....
1992-93	**New Jersey**	**NHL**	**11**	**0**	**2**	**2**	**4**	**0**	**0**	**0**	**11**	**0.0**	**–3**	....	....	....	....	....	....	....	....	....	....	....	....	....
	Utica Devils	AHL	59	21	39	60	76	....	....	....	....	....	....	....	....	....	....	....	5	0	2	2	19	....	....	....
	Cincinnati	IHL	4	1	2	3	4	....	....	....	....	....	....	....	....	....	....	....	....	....	....	....	....	....	....	....
1993-94	**Anaheim**	**NHL**	**20**	**5**	**4**	**9**	**10**	**2**	**0**	**2**	**25**	**20.0**	**–3**	....	....	....	....	....	....	....	....	....	....	....	....	....
	San Diego Gulls	IHL	57	25	38	63	79	....	....	....	....	....	....	....	....	....	....	....	9	3	12	15	10	....	....	....
1994-95	Las Vegas	IHL	74	34	41	75	103	....	....	....	....	....	....	....	....	....	....	....	9	2	4	6	8	....	....	....
1995-96	Baltimore Bandits	AHL	11	2	6	8	55	....	....	....	....	....	....	....	....	....	....	....	....	....	....	....	....	....	....	....
	Calgary	**NHL**	**1**	**0**	**0**	**0**	**0**	**0**	**0**	**0**	**0**	**0.0**	**0**	....	....	....	....	....	....	....	....	....	....	....	....	....
	Saint John Flames	AHL	68	27	40	67	98	....	....	....	....	....	....	....	....	....	....	....	16	4	9	13	6	....	....	....
1996-97	Saint John Flames	AHL	65	32	36	68	94	....	....	....	....	....	....	....	....	....	....	....	3	0	0	0	14	....	....	....
1997-98	**San Jose**	**NHL**	**22**	**4**	**6**	**10**	**14**	**0**	**0**	**0**	**30**	**13.3**	**–2**	....	....	....	....	....	....	....	....	....	....	....	....	....
	Kentucky	AHL	6	2	6	8	10	....	....	....	....	....	....	....	....	....	....	....	....	....	....	....	....	....	....	....
	Chicago	**NHL**	**4**	**0**	**1**	**1**	**2**	**0**	**0**	**0**	**4**	**0.0**	**0**	....	....	....	....	....	....	....	....	....	....	....	....	....
	Indianapolis Ice	IHL	2	0	2	2	0	....	....	....	....	....	....	....	....	....	....	....	....	....	....	....	....	....	....	....
	Dallas	**NHL**	**1**	**0**	**0**	**0**	**0**	**0**	**0**	**0**	**0**	**0.0**	**0**	....	....	....	....	....	....	....	....	....	....	....	....	....
	Chicago	**NHL**	**3**	**0**	**0**	**0**	**2**	**0**	**0**	**0**	**0**	**0.0**	**0**	....	....	....	....	....	....	....	....	....	....	....	....	....
	Kentucky	AHL	17	3	9	12	38	....	....	....	....	....	....	....	....	....	....	....	3	3	0	3	6	....	....	....
1998-99	**San Jose**	**NHL**	**17**	**1**	**1**	**2**	**4**	**0**	**0**	**0**	**17**	**5.9**	**–6**	**191**	**52.4**	**17**	**1**	**10:07**	....	....	....	....	....	....	....	....
	Kentucky	AHL	54	17	40	57	75	....	....	....	....	....	....	....	....	....	....	....	12	4	5	9	16	....	....	....
99-2000	Utah Grizzlies	IHL	77	25	54	79	98	....	....	....	....	....	....	....	....	....	....	....	5	0	1	1	10	....	....	....
2000-01	**Atlanta**	**NHL**	**19**	**1**	**2**	**3**	**20**	**0**	**0**	**0**	**24**	**4.2**	**–8**	**291**	**47.1**	**22**	**5**	**13:57**	....	....	....	....	....	....	....	....
	Orlando	IHL	60	14	40	54	56	....	....	....	....	....	....	....	....	....	....	....	15	3	6	9	20	....	....	....
	NHL Totals		**114**	**13**	**21**	**34**	**60**	**2**	**0**	**4**	**138**	**9.4**		**482**	**49.2**	**39**	**6**	**12:08**	....	....	....	....	....	....	....	....

OHL Second All-Star Team (1991) • IHL First All-Star Team (2000)

Claimed by **Anaheim** from **New Jersey** in Expansion Draft, June 24, 1993. Traded to **Calgary** by **Anaheim** for Bobby Marshall, October 30, 1995. Signed as a free agent by **San Jose**, August 14, 1997. Claimed on waivers by **Chicago** from **San Jose**, January 8, 1998. Claimed on waivers by **San Jose** from **Chicago**, January 23, 1998. Claimed on waivers by **Dallas** from **San Jose**, January 27, 1998. Claimed on waivers by **Chicago** from **Dallas**, February 10, 1998. Claimed on waivers by **San Jose** from **Chicago**, March 6, 1998. Signed as a free agent by **Atlanta**, July 21, 2000.

SKOPINTSEV, Andrei

(skuh-PIHN-sehf, AWN-dray)

Defense. Shoots right. 6', 185 lbs. Born, Elekrostal, USSR, September 28, 1971. Tampa Bay's 7th choice, 153rd overall, in 1997 Entry Draft.

			Regular Season																Playoffs							
Season	Club	League	GP	G	A	Pts	PIM	PP	SH	GW	S	%	+/-	TF	F%	H	SB	Min	GP	G	A	Pts	PIM	PP	SH	GW
1989-90	Krylja Sovetov	USSR	20	0	0	0	10	....	....	....	....	....	....	....	....	....	....	....	....	....	....	....	....	....	....	....
1990-91	Krylja Sovetov	USSR	16	0	1	1	2	....	....	....	....	....	....	....	....	....	....	....	....	....	....	....	....	....	....	....
1991-92	Krylja Sovetov	CIS	36	1	1	2	14	....	....	....	....	....	....	....	....	....	....	....	....	....	....	....	....	....	....	....
1992-93	Krylja Sovetov	CIS	12	1	0	1	4	....	....	....	....	....	....	....	....	....	....	....	7	1	0	1	2	....	....	....
1993-94	Krylja Sovetov	CIS	43	4	8	12	14	....	....	....	....	....	....	....	....	....	....	....	3	1	0	1	0	....	....	....
1994-95	Krylja Sovetov	CIS	52	8	12	20	55	....	....	....	....	....	....	....	....	....	....	....	4	1	1	2	0	....	....	....
1995-96	Augsburger EV	DEL	46	10	20	30	32	....	....	....	....	....	....	....	....	....	....	....	7	3	2	5	22	....	....	....
1996-97	TPS Turku	Finland	46	3	6	9	80	....	....	....	....	....	....	....	....	....	....	....	10	1	1	2	4	....	....	....
	TPS Turku	EuroHL	5	0	1	1	4	....	....	....	....	....	....	....	....	....	....	....	....	....	....	....	....	....	....	....
1997-98	TPS Turku	Finland	48	2	9	11	8	....	....	....	....	....	....	....	....	....	....	....	4	0	1	1	4	....	....	....
	TPS Turku	EuroHL	5	0	1	1	4	....	....	....	....	....	....	....	....	....	....	....	....	....	....	....	....	....	....	....
1998-99	**Tampa Bay**	**NHL**	**19**	**1**	**1**	**2**	**10**	**0**	**0**	**0**	**17**	**5.9**	**1**	**0**	**0.0**	**13**	**15**	**16:05**	....	....	....	....	....	....	....	....
	Cleveland	IHL	19	3	2	5	8	....	....	....	....	....	....	....	....	....	....	....	....	....	....	....	....	....	....	....
99-2000	**Tampa Bay**	**NHL**	**4**	**0**	**0**	**0**	**6**	**0**	**0**	**0**	**0**	**0.0**	**–4**	**0**	**0.0**	**8**	**7**	**14:07**	....	....	....	....	....	....	....	....
	Detroit Vipers	IHL	51	4	15	19	44	....	....	....	....	....	....	....	....	....	....	....	....	....	....	....	....	....	....	....
2000-01	**Atlanta**	**NHL**	**17**	**1**	**3**	**4**	**16**	**0**	**0**	**1**	**10**	**10.0**	**–7**	**0**	**0.0**	**21**	**33**	**18:13**	....	....	....	....	....	....	....	....
	Orlando	IHL	25	0	6	6	22	....	....	....	....	....	....	....	....	....	....	....	....	....	....	....	....	....	....	....
	NHL Totals		**40**	**2**	**4**	**6**	**32**	**0**	**0**	**1**	**27**	**7.4**		**0**	**0.0**	**42**	**55**	**16:48**	....	....	....	....	....	....	....	....

Signed as a free agent by **Atlanta**, September 7, 2000. • Missed majority of 2000-01 season recovering from abdominal injury suffered in game vs. NY Islanders, December 29, 2000. Signed as a free agent by **Dynamo Moscow** (Russia), July 2, 2001.

SKOULA, Martin

(SHKOH-la, MAHR-tihn) **COL.**

Defense. Shoots left. 6'2", 195 lbs. Born, Litomerice, Czech., October 28, 1979. Colorado's 2nd choice, 17th overall, in 1998 Entry Draft.

			Regular Season																Playoffs							
Season	Club	League	GP	G	A	Pts	PIM	PP	SH	GW	S	%	+/-	TF	F%	H	SB	Min	GP	G	A	Pts	PIM	PP	SH	GW
1995-96	CHZ Litvinov-Jr.	Cze-Rep	38	0	4	4	....	....	....	....	....	....	....	....	....	....	....	....	....	....	....	....	....	....	....	....
	CHZ Litvinov	Cze-Rep	....	....	....	....	....	....	....	....	....	....	....	....	....	....	....	....	1	0	0	0	0	....	....	....
1996-97	CHZ Litvinov-Jr.	Cze-Rep	38	2	9	11	....	....	....	....	....	....	....	....	....	....	....	....	....	....	....	....	....	....	....	....
	CHZ Litvinov	Cze-Rep	1	0	0	0	0	....	....	....	....	....	....	....	....	....	....	....	....	....	....	....	....	....	....	....
1997-98	Barrie Colts	OHL	66	8	36	44	36	....	....	....	....	....	....	....	....	....	....	....	6	1	3	4	4	....	....	....
1998-99	Barrie Colts	OHL	67	13	46	59	46	....	....	....	....	....	....	....	....	....	....	....	12	3	10	13	13	....	....	....
	Hershey Bears	AHL	....	....	....	....	....	....	....	....	....	....	....	....	....	....	....	....	1	0	0	0	0	....	....	....
99-2000	**Colorado**	**NHL**	**80**	**3**	**13**	**16**	**20**	**2**	**0**	**0**	**66**	**4.5**	**5**	**0**	**0.0**	**100**	**45**	**18:15**	**17**	**0**	**2**	**2**	**4**	**0**	**0**	**0**
2000-01♦	**Colorado**	**NHL**	**82**	**8**	**17**	**25**	**38**	**3**	**0**	**2**	**108**	**7.4**	**8**	**1**	**100.0**	**113**	**52**	**20:41**	**23**	**1**	**4**	**5**	**8**	**0**	**0**	**0**
	NHL Totals		**162**	**11**	**30**	**41**	**58**	**5**	**0**	**2**	**174**	**6.3**		**1**	**100.0**	**213**	**97**	**19:29**	**40**	**1**	**6**	**7**	**12**	**0**	**0**	**0**

OHL Second All-Star Team (1999)

SKRASTINS, Karlis

(SKRAS-tinsh, kar-LIHS) **NSH.**

Defense. Shoots left. 6'1", 208 lbs. Born, Riga, USSR, July 19, 1974. Nashville's 8th choice, 230th overall, in 1998 Entry Draft.

			Regular Season																Playoffs							
Season	Club	League	GP	G	A	Pts	PIM	PP	SH	GW	S	%	+/-	TF	F%	H	SB	Min	GP	G	A	Pts	PIM	PP	SH	GW
1992-93	Pardaugava Riga	CIS	40	3	5	8	16	....	....	....	....	....	....	....	....	....	....	....	2	0	0	0	0	....	....	....
1993-94	Pardaugava Riga	CIS	42	7	5	12	18	....	....	....	....	....	....	....	....	....	....	....	2	1	0	1	4	....	....	....
1994-95	Pardaugava Riga	CIS	52	4	14	18	69	....	....	....	....	....	....	....	....	....	....	....	....	....	....	....	....	....	....	....
1995-96	TPS Turku	Finland	50	4	11	15	32	....	....	....	....	....	....	....	....	....	....	....	11	2	2	4	10	....	....	....
1996-97	TPS Turku	Finland	50	2	8	10	20	....	....	....	....	....	....	....	....	....	....	....	12	0	4	4	2	....	....	....
	TPS Turku	EuroHL	6	0	1	1	4	....	....	....	....	....	....	....	....	....	....	....	4	0	0	0	14	....	....	....
1997-98	TPS Turku	Finland	48	4	15	19	67	....	....	....	....	....	....	....	....	....	....	....	4	0	0	0	0	....	....	....
	TPS Turku	EuroHL	6	0	1	1	6	....	....	....	....	....	....	....	....	....	....	....	....	....	....	....	....	....	....	....
1998-99	**Nashville**	**NHL**	**2**	**0**	**1**	**1**	**0**	**0**	**0**	**0**	**0**	**0.0**	**0**	**0**	**0.0**	**1**	**1**	**11:47**	....	....	....	....	....	....	....	....
	Milwaukee	IHL	75	8	36	44	47	....	....	....	....	....	....	....	....	....	....	....	2	0	1	1	2	....	....	....
99-2000	**Nashville**	**NHL**	**59**	**5**	**6**	**11**	**20**	**1**	**0**	**2**	**51**	**9.8**	**–7**	**0**	**0.0**	**104**	**110**	**20:51**	....	....	....	....	....	....	....	....
	Milwaukee	IHL	19	3	8	11	10	....	....	....	....	....	....	....	....	....	....	....	....	....	....	....	....	....	....	....
2000-01	**Nashville**	**NHL**	**82**	**1**	**11**	**12**	**30**	**0**	**0**	**1**	**66**	**1.5**	**–12**	**0**	**0.0**	**146**	**160**	**19:12**	....	....	....	....	....	....	....	....
	NHL Totals		**143**	**6**	**18**	**24**	**50**	**1**	**0**	**3**	**117**	**5.1**		**0**	**0.0**	**251**	**271**	**19:47**								

SKRBEK, Pavel

(skuhr-BEHK, PAH-vehl) **NSH.**

Defense. Shoots left. 6'3", 217 lbs. Born, Kladno, Czech., August 9, 1978. Pittsburgh's 2nd choice, 28th overall, in 1996 Entry Draft.

			Regular Season																Playoffs							
Season	Club	League	GP	G	A	Pts	PIM	PP	SH	GW	S	%	+/-	TF	F%	H	SB	Min	GP	G	A	Pts	PIM	PP	SH	GW
1994-95	Poldi Kladno-Jr.	Cze-Rep	29	7	6	13	....	....	....	....	....	....	....	....	....	....	....	....	....	....	....	....	....	....	....	....
1995-96	Poldi Kladno-Jr.	Cze-Rep	29	10	12	22	....	....	....	....	....	....	....	....	....	....	....	....	....	....	....	....	....	....	....	....
	Poldi Kladno	Cze-Rep	13	0	1	1	....	....	....	....	....	....	....	....	....	....	....	....	5	0	0	0	....	....	....	....
1996-97	Poldi Kladno	Cze-Rep	35	1	5	6	26	....	....	....	....	....	....	....	....	....	....	....	3	0	0	0	4	....	....	....
1997-98	Poldi Kladno	Cze-Rep	47	4	10	14	126	....	....	....	....	....	....	....	....	....	....	....	....	....	....	....	....	....	....	....
1998-99	**Pittsburgh**	**NHL**	**4**	**0**	**0**	**0**	**2**	**0**	**0**	**0**	**1**	**0.0**	**2**	**0**	**0.0**	**6**	**3**	**14:21**	....	....	....	....	....	....	....	....
	Syracuse Crunch	AHL	64	6	16	22	38	....	....	....	....	....	....	....	....	....	....	....	....	....	....	....	....	....	....	....
99-2000	Wilkes-Barre	AHL	51	7	16	23	50	....	....	....	....	....	....	....	....	....	....	....	....	....	....	....	....	....	....	....
	Milwaukee	IHL	6	0	0	0	0	....	....	....	....	....	....	....	....	....	....	....	....	....	....	....	....	....	....	....

			Regular Season																Playoffs							
Season	Club	League	GP	G	A	Pts	PIM	PP	SH	GW	S	%	+/-	TF	F%	H	SB	Min	GP	G	A	Pts	PIM	PP	SH	GW
2000-01	**Nashville**	**NHL**	**5**	**0**	**0**	**0**	**4**	0	0	0	2	0.0	1	0	0.0	2	5	11:44	....	....	....	....	....	....	....	....
	Milwaukee	IHL	54	2	22	24	55	....	....	....	....	....	....	....	....	....	....	....	5	0	0	0	2	....	....	....
	NHL Totals		**9**	**0**	**0**	**0**	**6**	0	0	0	3	0.0		0	0.0	8	8	12:54	....	....	....	....	....	....	....	....

Traded to **Nashville** by **Pittsburgh** for Bob Boughner, March 13, 2000.

SLANEY, John (SLAY-nee, JAWN) PHI.

Defense. Shoots left. 6', 189 lbs. Born, St. John's, Nfld., February 2, 1972. Washington's 1st choice, 9th overall, in 1990 Entry Draft.

Season	Club	League	GP	G	A	Pts	PIM	PP	SH	GW	S	%	+/-	TF	F%	H	SB	Min	GP	G	A	Pts	PIM	PP	SH	GW
1987-88	St. John's Caps	NFAHA	65	41	69	110	70	....	....	....	....	....	....	....	....	....	....	....	....	....	....	....	....	....	....	....
1988-89	Cornwall Royals	OHL	66	16	43	59	23	....	....	....	....	....	....	....	....	....	....	....	18	8	16	24	10	....	....	....
1989-90	Cornwall Royals	OHL	64	38	59	97	68	....	....	....	....	....	....	....	....	....	....	....	6	0	8	8	11	....	....	....
1990-91	Cornwall Royals	OHL	34	21	25	46	28	....	....	....	....	....	....	....	....	....	....	....	....	....	....	....	....	....	....	....
1991-92	Cornwall Royals	OHL	34	19	41	60	43	....	....	....	....	....	....	....	....	....	....	....	6	3	8	11	0	....	....	....
	Baltimore	AHL	6	2	4	6	0	....	....	....	....	....	....	....	....	....	....	....	....	....	....	....	....	....	....	....
1992-93	Baltimore	AHL	79	20	46	66	60	....	....	....	....	....	....	....	....	....	....	....	7	0	7	7	8	....	....	....
1993-94	**Washington**	**NHL**	**47**	**7**	**9**	**16**	**27**	3	0	1	70	10.0	3	....	....	....	....	....	**11**	**1**	**1**	**2**	**2**	1	0	0
	Portland Pirates	AHL	29	14	13	27	17	....	....	....	....	....	....	....	....	....	....	....	....	....	....	....	....	....	....	....
1994-95	**Washington**	**NHL**	**16**	**0**	**3**	**3**	**6**	0	0	0	21	0.0	-3	....	....	....	....	....	....	....	....	....	....	....	....	....
	Portland Pirates	AHL	8	3	10	13	4	....	....	....	....	....	....	....	....	....	....	....	7	1	3	4	4	....	....	....
1995-96	**Colorado**	**NHL**	**7**	**0**	**3**	**3**	**4**	0	0	0	12	0.0	2	....	....	....	....	....	....	....	....	....	....	....	....	....
	Cornwall Aces	AHL	5	0	4	4	2	....	....	....	....	....	....	....	....	....	....	....	....	....	....	....	....	....	....	....
	Los Angeles	**NHL**	**31**	**6**	**11**	**17**	**10**	3	1	0	63	9.5	5	....	....	....	....	....	....	....	....	....	....	....	....	....
1996-97	**Los Angeles**	**NHL**	**32**	**3**	**11**	**14**	**4**	1	0	1	60	5.0	-10	....	....	....	....	....	....	....	....	....	....	....	....	....
	Phoenix	IHL	35	9	25	34	8	....	....	....	....	....	....	....	....	....	....	....	....	....	....	....	....	....	....	....
1997-98	**Phoenix**	**NHL**	**55**	**3**	**14**	**17**	**24**	1	0	1	74	4.1	-3	....	....	....	....	....	....	....	....	....	....	....	....	....
	Las Vegas	IHL	5	2	2	4	10	....	....	....	....	....	....	....	....	....	....	....	....	....	....	....	....	....	....	....
1998-99	**Nashville**	**NHL**	**46**	**2**	**12**	**14**	**14**	0	0	1	84	2.4	-12	0	0.0	54	49	20:39	....	....	....	....	....	....	....	....
	Milwaukee	IHL	7	0	1	1	0	....	....	....	....	....	....	....	....	....	....	....	....	....	....	....	....	....	....	....
99-2000	**Pittsburgh**	**NHL**	**29**	**1**	**4**	**5**	**10**	1	0	0	27	3.7	-10	35	40.0	22	8	12:13	**2**	**1**	**0**	**1**	**2**	1	0	0
	Wilkes-Barre	AHL	49	30	30	60	25	....	....	....	....	....	....	....	....	....	....	....	....	....	....	....	....	....	....	....
2000-01	Wilkes-Barre	AHL	40	12	38	50	4	....	....	....	....	....	....	....	....	....	....	....	....	....	....	....	....	....	....	....
	Philadelphia	AHL	25	6	11	17	10	....	....	....	....	....	....	....	....	....	....	....	10	2	6	8	6	....	....	....
	NHL Totals		**263**	**22**	**67**	**89**	**99**	9	1	4	411	5.4		35	40.0	76	57	17:23	**13**	**2**	**1**	**3**	**4**	2	0	0

OHL First All-Star Team (1990) • Canadian Major Junior Defenseman of the Year (1990) • OHL Second All-Star Team (1991) • AHL First All-Star Team (2001) • Won Eddie Shore Award (Top Defenseman - AHL) (2001)

Traded to **Colorado** by **Washington** for Philadelphia's 3rd round choice (previously acquired, Washington selected Shawn McNeil) in 1996 Entry Draft, July 12, 1995. Traded to **LA Kings** by **Colorado** for Winnipeg's 6th round choice (previously acquired, Colorado selected Brian Willsie) in 1996 Entry Draft, December 28, 1995. Signed as a free agent by **Phoenix**, August 19, 1997. Claimed by **Nashville** from **Phoenix** in Expansion Draft, June 26, 1998. Signed as a free agent by **Pittsburgh**, September 30, 1999. Traded to **Philadelphia** by **Pittsburgh** for Kevin Stevens, January 14, 2001.

SLEGR, Jiri (SLAY-guhr, YEE-ree) ATL.

Defense. Shoots left. 6', 216 lbs. Born, Jihlava, Czech., May 30, 1971. Vancouver's 3rd choice, 23rd overall, in 1990 Entry Draft.

Season	Club	League	GP	G	A	Pts	PIM	PP	SH	GW	S	%	+/-	TF	F%	H	SB	Min	GP	G	A	Pts	PIM	PP	SH	GW
1987-88	CHZ Litvinov	Czech.	4	1	1	2	0	....	....	....	....	....	....	....	....	....	....	....	....	....	....	....	....	....	....	....
1988-89	CHZ Litvinov	Czech.	8	0	0	0	4	....	....	....	....	....	....	....	....	....	....	....	....	....	....	....	....	....	....	....
1989-90	CHZ Litvinov	Czech.	51	4	15	19	....	....	....	....	....	....	....	....	....	....	....	....	....	....	....	....	....	....	....	....
1990-91	CHZ Litvinov	Czech.	47	11	36	47	26	....	....	....	....	....	....	....	....	....	....	....	....	....	....	....	....	....	....	....
1991-92	CHZ Litvinov	Czech.	42	9	23	32	38	....	....	....	....	....	....	....	....	....	....	....	....	....	....	....	....	....	....	....
	Czechoslovakia	Olympics	8	1	1	2	14	....	....	....	....	....	....	....	....	....	....	....	....	....	....	....	....	....	....	....
1992-93	**Vancouver**	**NHL**	**41**	**4**	**22**	**26**	**109**	2	0	0	89	4.5	16	....	....	....	....	....	**5**	**0**	**3**	**3**	**4**	0	0	0
	Hamilton Canucks	AHL	21	4	14	18	42	....	....	....	....	....	....	....	....	....	....	....	....	....	....	....	....	....	....	....
1993-94	**Vancouver**	**NHL**	**78**	**5**	**33**	**38**	**86**	1	0	0	160	3.1	0	....	....	....	....	....	....	....	....	....	....	....	....	....
1994-95	CHZ Litvinov	Cze-Rep	11	3	10	13	80	....	....	....	....	....	....	....	....	....	....	....	....	....	....	....	....	....	....	....
	Vancouver	**NHL**	**19**	**1**	**5**	**6**	**32**	0	0	1	42	2.4	0	....	....	....	....	....	....	....	....	....	....	....	....	....
	Edmonton	**NHL**	**12**	**1**	**5**	**6**	**14**	1	0	0	27	3.7	-5	....	....	....	....	....	....	....	....	....	....	....	....	....
1995-96	**Edmonton**	**NHL**	**57**	**4**	**13**	**17**	**74**	0	1	1	91	4.4	-1	....	....	....	....	....	....	....	....	....	....	....	....	....
	Cape Breton	AHL	4	1	2	3	4	....	....	....	....	....	....	....	....	....	....	....	....	....	....	....	....	....	....	....
1996-97	CHZ Litvinov	Cze-Rep	1	0	0	0	0	....	....	....	....	....	....	....	....	....	....	....	....	....	....	....	....	....	....	....
	Sodertalje SK	Sweden	30	4	14	18	62	....	....	....	....	....	....	....	....	....	....	....	10	4	2	6	32	....	....	....
1997-98	**Pittsburgh**	**NHL**	**73**	**5**	**12**	**17**	**109**	1	1	0	131	3.8	10	....	....	....	....	....	**6**	**0**	**4**	**4**	**2**	0	0	0
	Czech-Republic	Olympics	6	1	0	1	8	....	....	....	....	....	....	....	....	....	....	....	....	....	....	....	....	....	....	....
1998-99	**Pittsburgh**	**NHL**	**63**	**3**	**20**	**23**	**86**	1	0	0	91	3.3	13	2	0.0	78	59	18:42	**13**	**1**	**3**	**4**	**12**	0	0	1
99-2000	**Pittsburgh**	**NHL**	**74**	**11**	**20**	**31**	**82**	0	0	2	144	7.6	20	3	66.7	106	66	21:22	**10**	**2**	**3**	**5**	**19**	0	0	1
2000-01	**Pittsburgh**	**NHL**	**42**	**5**	**10**	**15**	**60**	0	1	1	67	7.5	-9	0	0.0	63	29	17:37	....	....	....	....	....	....	....	....
	Atlanta	**NHL**	**33**	**3**	**16**	**19**	**36**	2	0	0	78	3.8	-1	1	0.0	49	32	21:34	....	....	....	....	....	....	....	....
	NHL Totals		**492**	**42**	**156**	**198**	**688**	8	3	5	920	4.6		6	33.3	296	186	19:52	**34**	**3**	**13**	**16**	**37**	0	0	2

Traded to **Edmonton** by **Vancouver** for Roman Oksiuta, April 7, 1995. Traded to **Pittsburgh** by **Edmonton** for Pittsburgh's 3rd round choice (later traded to New Jersey - New Jersey selected Brian Gionta) in 1998 Entry Draft, August 12, 1997. Traded to **Atlanta** by **Pittsburgh** for San Jose's 3rd round choice (previously acquired, later traded to Columbus - Columbus selected Aaron Johnson) in 2001 Entry Draft, January 14, 2001.

SLOAN, Blake (SLOHN, BLAYK) CBJ

Right wing. Shoots right. 5'10", 196 lbs. Born, Park Ridge, IL, July 27, 1975.

Season	Club	League	GP	G	A	Pts	PIM	PP	SH	GW	S	%	+/-	TF	F%	H	SB	Min	GP	G	A	Pts	PIM	PP	SH	GW
1992-93	Tabor Academy	Hi-School	33	7	15	22	....	....	....	....	....	....	....	....	....	....	....	....	....	....	....	....	....	....	....	....
1993-94	U. of Michigan	CCHA	38	2	4	6	48	....	....	....	....	....	....	....	....	....	....	....	....	....	....	....	....	....	....	....
1994-95	U. of Michigan	CCHA	39	2	15	17	60	....	....	....	....	....	....	....	....	....	....	....	....	....	....	....	....	....	....	....
1995-96	U. of Michigan	CCHA	41	6	24	30	55	....	....	....	....	....	....	....	....	....	....	....	....	....	....	....	....	....	....	....
1996-97	U. of Michigan	CCHA	41	2	15	17	52	....	....	....	....	....	....	....	....	....	....	....	....	....	....	....	....	....	....	....
1997-98	Houston Aeros	IHL	70	2	13	15	86	....	....	....	....	....	....	....	....	....	....	....	2	0	0	0	0	....	....	....
1998-99♦	**Dallas**	**NHL**	**14**	**0**	**0**	**0**	**10**	0	0	0	7	0.0	-1	0	0.0	27	3	9:01	**19**	**0**	**2**	**2**	**8**	0	0	0
	Houston Aeros	IHL	62	8	10	18	76	....	....	....	....	....	....	....	....	....	....	....	....	....	....	....	....	....	....	....
99-2000	**Dallas**	**NHL**	**67**	**4**	**13**	**17**	**50**	0	0	1	78	5.1	11	2	50.0	165	25	13:30	**16**	**0**	**0**	**0**	**12**	0	0	0
2000-01	**Dallas**	**NHL**	**33**	**2**	**2**	**4**	**4**	0	0	1	29	6.9	-2	4	25.0	79	13	9:56	....	....	....	....	....	....	....	....
	Houston Aeros	IHL	20	7	4	11	18	....	....	....	....	....	....	....	....	....	....	....	....	....	....	....	....	....	....	....
	Columbus	**NHL**	**14**	**1**	**0**	**1**	**13**	0	0	0	16	6.3	-2	7	28.6	40	12	13:19	....	....	....	....	....	....	....	....
	NHL Totals		**128**	**7**	**15**	**22**	**77**	0	0	2	130	5.4		13	30.8	311	53	12:04	**35**	**0**	**2**	**2**	**20**	0	0	0

Signed as a free agent by **Dallas**, March 10, 1998. Claimed on waivers by **Columbus** from **Dallas**, March 13, 2001.

SMEHLIK, Richard (SHMEH-lihk, RIH-chahrd) BUF.

Defense. Shoots left. 6'4", 222 lbs. Born, Ostrava, Czech., January 23, 1970. Buffalo's 3rd choice, 97th overall, in 1990 Entry Draft.

Season	Club	League	GP	G	A	Pts	PIM	PP	SH	GW	S	%	+/-	TF	F%	H	SB	Min	GP	G	A	Pts	PIM	PP	SH	GW
1988-89	TJ Vitkovice	Czech.	38	2	5	7	12	....	....	....	....	....	....	....	....	....	....	....	....	....	....	....	....	....	....	....
1989-90	TJ Vitkovice	Czech.	44	4	3	7	....	....	....	....	....	....	....	....	....	....	....	....	7	1	1	2	....	....	....	....
1990-91	Dukla Jihlava	Czech.	58	4	3	7	22	....	....	....	....	....	....	....	....	....	....	....	....	....	....	....	....	....	....	....
1991-92	TJ Vitkovice	Czech.	47	9	10	19	42	....	....	....	....	....	....	....	....	....	....	....	....	....	....	....	....	....	....	....
	Czechoslovakia	Olympics	8	0	1	1	2	....	....	....	....	....	....	....	....	....	....	....	....	....	....	....	....	....	....	....
1992-93	**Buffalo**	**NHL**	**80**	**4**	**27**	**31**	**59**	0	0	0	82	4.9	9	....	....	....	....	....	**8**	**0**	**4**	**4**	**2**	0	0	0
1993-94	**Buffalo**	**NHL**	**84**	**14**	**27**	**41**	**69**	3	3	1	106	13.2	22	....	....	....	....	....	**7**	**0**	**2**	**2**	**10**	0	0	0
1994-95	HC Vitkovice	Cze-Rep	13	5	2	7	12	....	....	....	....	....	....	....	....	....	....	....	....	....	....	....	....	....	....	....
	Buffalo	**NHL**	**39**	**4**	**7**	**11**	**46**	0	1	1	49	8.2	5	....	....	....	....	....	**5**	**0**	**0**	**0**	**2**	0	0	0
1995-96	**Buffalo**	**NHL**	DID NOT PLAY – INJURED																							
1996-97	**Buffalo**	**NHL**	**62**	**11**	**19**	**30**	**43**	2	0	1	100	11.0	19	....	....	....	....	....	**12**	**0**	**2**	**2**	**4**	0	0	0
1997-98	**Buffalo**	**NHL**	**72**	**3**	**17**	**20**	**62**	0	1	0	90	3.3	11	....	....	....	....	....	**15**	**0**	**2**	**2**	**6**	0	0	0
	Czech-Republic	Olympics	6	0	1	1	4	....	....	....	....	....	....	....	....	....	....	....	....	....	....	....	....	....	....	....
1998-99	**Buffalo**	**NHL**	**72**	**3**	**11**	**14**	**44**	0	0	0	61	4.9	-9	0	0.0	107	87	21:50	**21**	**0**	**3**	**3**	**10**	0	0	0
99-2000	**Buffalo**	**NHL**	**64**	**2**	**9**	**11**	**50**	0	0	0	67	3.0	13	0	0.0	65	52	21:04	**5**	**1**	**0**	**1**	**0**	0	0	0
2000-01	**Buffalo**	**NHL**	**56**	**3**	**12**	**15**	**4**	0	0	1	40	7.5	6	0	0.0	86	60	19:25	**10**	**0**	**1**	**1**	**4**	0	0	0
	NHL Totals		**529**	**44**	**129**	**173**	**377**	5	5	4	595	7.4		0	0.0	258	199	20:53	**83**	**1**	**14**	**15**	**38**	0	0	0

• Missed entire 1995-96 season recovering from knee surgery, August 11, 1995.

SMITH, Brandon

(SMIHTH, BRAN-duhn) **S.J.**

Defense. Shoots left. 6'1", 198 lbs. Born, Hazelton, B.C., February 25, 1973.

			Regular Season																Playoffs							
Season	Club	League	GP	G	A	Pts	PIM	PP	SH	GW	S	%	+/-	TF	F%	H	SB	Min	GP	G	A	Pts	PIM	PP	SH	GW
1989-90	Portland	WHL	59	2	17	19	16	....	....	....	....	....	....	....	....	....	....	....	....	....	....	....	....	....	....	....
1990-91	Portland	WHL	17	8	5	13	8	....	....	....	....	....	....	....	....	....	....	....	....	....	....	....	....	....	....	....
1991-92	Portland	WHL	70	12	32	44	63	....	....	....	....	....	....	....	....	....	....	....	....	....	....	....	....	....	....	....
1992-93	Portland	WHL	72	20	54	74	38	....	....	....	....	....	....	....	....	....	....	....	16	4	9	13	6	....	....	....
1993-94	Portland	WHL	72	19	63	82	47	....	....	....	....	....	....	....	....	....	....	....	10	2	10	12	8	....	....	....
1994-95	Dayton Bombers	ECHL	60	16	49	65	57	....	....	....	....	....	....	....	....	....	....	....	4	2	3	5	0	....	....	....
	Minnesota Moose	IHL	1	0	0	0	0	....	....	....	....	....	....	....	....	....	....	....	....	....	....	....	....	....	....	....
	Adirondack	AHL	14	1	2	3	7	....	....	....	....	....	....	....	....	....	....	....	3	0	0	0	2	....	....	....
1995-96	Adirondack	AHL	48	4	13	17	22	....	....	....	....	....	....	....	....	....	....	....	3	0	1	1	2	....	....	....
1996-97	Adirondack	AHL	80	8	26	34	30	....	....	....	....	....	....	....	....	....	....	....	4	0	0	0	0	....	....	....
1997-98	Adirondack	AHL	64	9	27	36	26	....	....	....	....	....	....	....	....	....	....	....	1	0	1	1	0	....	....	....
1998-99	**Boston**	**NHL**	**5**	**0**	**0**	**0**	**0**	**0**	**0**	**0**	**2**	**0.0**	**2**	**0**	**0.0**	**9**	**2**	**9:38**	....	....	....	....	....	....	....	....
	Providence Bruins	AHL	72	16	46	62	32	....	....	....	....	....	....	....	....	....	....	....	19	1	9	10	12	....	....	....
99-2000	**Boston**	**NHL**	**22**	**2**	**4**	**6**	**10**	**0**	**0**	**0**	**24**	**8.3**	**-4**	**0**	**0.0**	**28**	**25**	**19:29**	....	....	....	....	....	....	....	....
	Providence Bruins	AHL	55	8	30	38	20	....	....	....	....	....	....	....	....	....	....	....	14	1	11	12	2	....	....	....
2000-01	**Boston**	**NHL**	**3**	**1**	**0**	**1**	**0**	**1**	**0**	**0**	**2**	**50.0**	**-1**	**0**	**0.0**	**1**	**1**	**6:46**	....	....	....	....	....	....	....	....
	Providence Bruins	AHL	63	11	28	39	30	....	....	....	....	....	....	....	....	....	....	....	17	0	5	5	6	....	....	....
	NHL Totals		**30**	**3**	**4**	**7**	**10**	**1**	**0**	**0**	**28**	**10.7**		**0**	**0.0**	**38**	**28**	**16:34**	....	....	....	....	....	....	....	....

WHL West Second All-Star Team (1993, 1994) • ECHL First All-Star Team (1995) • Won ECHL Top Defenseman Award (1995) • AHL First All-Star Team (1999)

Signed as a free agent by **Detroit**, July 22, 1997. Signed as a free agent by **Boston**, August 5, 1998. Signed as a free agent by **San Jose**, July 23, 2001.

SMITH, D.J.

(SMIHTH, DEE-JAY) **TOR.**

Defense. Shoots left. 6'2", 205 lbs. Born, Windsor, Ont., May 13, 1977. NY Islanders' 3rd choice, 41st overall, in 1995 Entry Draft.

			Regular Season																Playoffs							
Season	Club	League	GP	G	A	Pts	PIM	PP	SH	GW	S	%	+/-	TF	F%	H	SB	Min	GP	G	A	Pts	PIM	PP	SH	GW
1992-93	Belle River	OJHL-C	40	5	18	23	39	....	....	....	....	....	....	....	....	....	....	....	....	....	....	....	....	....	....	....
	Windsor Bulldogs	OJHL-B	1	0	0	0	0	....	....	....	....	....	....	....	....	....	....	....	....	....	....	....	....	....	....	....
1993-94	Windsor Bulldogs	OJHL-B	51	8	34	42	267	....	....	....	....	....	....	....	....	....	....	....	....	....	....	....	....	....	....	....
1994-95	Windsor Spitfires	OHL	61	4	13	17	201	....	....	....	....	....	....	....	....	....	....	....	10	1	3	4	41	....	....	....
1995-96	Windsor Spitfires	OHL	64	14	45	59	260	....	....	....	....	....	....	....	....	....	....	....	7	1	7	8	23	....	....	....
	St. John's Leafs	AHL	1	0	0	0	0	....	....	....	....	....	....	....	....	....	....	....	....	....	....	....	....	....	....	....
1996-97	Windsor Spitfires	OHL	63	15	52	67	190	....	....	....	....	....	....	....	....	....	....	....	5	1	7	8	11	....	....	....
	Toronto	**NHL**	**8**	**0**	**1**	**1**	**7**	**0**	**0**	**0**	**4**	**0.0**	**-5**	....	....	....	....	....	....	....	....	....	....	....	....	....
	St. John's Leafs	AHL	....	....	....	....	....	....	....	....	....	....	....	....	....	....	....	....	1	0	0	0	0	....	....	....
1997-98	St. John's Leafs	AHL	65	4	11	15	237	....	....	....	....	....	....	....	....	....	....	....	4	0	0	0	4	....	....	....
1998-99	St. John's Leafs	AHL	79	7	28	35	216	....	....	....	....	....	....	....	....	....	....	....	5	0	1	1	0	....	....	....
99-2000	**Toronto**	**NHL**	**3**	**0**	**0**	**0**	**5**	**0**	**0**	**0**	**2**	**0.0**	**-1**	**0**	**0.0**	**7**	**1**	**12:37**	....	....	....	....	....	....	....	....
	St. John's Leafs	AHL	74	6	22	28	197	....	....	....	....	....	....	....	....	....	....	....	....	....	....	....	....	....	....	....
2000-01	St. John's Leafs	AHL	59	7	12	19	106	....	....	....	....	....	....	....	....	....	....	....	4	0	0	0	11	....	....	....
	NHL Totals		**11**	**0**	**1**	**1**	**12**	**0**	**0**	**0**	**6**	**0.0**		**0**	**0.0**	**7**	**1**	**12:37**	....	....	....	....	....	....	....	....

OHL Second All-Star Team (1997)

Traded to **Toronto** by **NY Islanders** with Wendel Clark and Mathieu Schneider for Darby Hendrickson, Sean Haggerty, Kenny Jonsson and Toronto's 1st round choice (Roberto Luongo) in 1997 Entry Draft, March 13, 1996.

SMITH, Dan

(SMIHTH, DAN)

Defense. Shoots left. 6'2", 200 lbs. Born, Fernie, B.C., October 19, 1976. Colorado's 7th choice, 181st overall, in 1995 Entry Draft.

			Regular Season																Playoffs							
Season	Club	League	GP	G	A	Pts	PIM	PP	SH	GW	S	%	+/-	TF	F%	H	SB	Min	GP	G	A	Pts	PIM	PP	SH	GW
1994-95	U.B.C. T-Birds	CWUAA	28	1	3	4	26	....	....	....	....	....	....	....	....	....	....	....	....	....	....	....	....	....	....	....
1995-96	Tri-City Americans	WHL	58	1	21	22	70	....	....	....	....	....	....	....	....	....	....	....	11	1	3	4	14	....	....	....
1996-97	Tri-City Americans	WHL	72	5	19	24	174	....	....	....	....	....	....	....	....	....	....	....	....	....	....	....	....	....	....	....
	Hershey Bears	AHL	8	0	1	1	6	....	....	....	....	....	....	....	....	....	....	....	15	0	1	1	25	....	....	....
1997-98	Hershey Bears	AHL	50	1	2	3	71	....	....	....	....	....	....	....	....	....	....	....	6	0	0	0	4	....	....	....
1998-99	**Colorado**	**NHL**	**12**	**0**	**0**	**0**	**9**	**0**	**0**	**0**	**6**	**0.0**	**5**	**0**	**0.0**	**3**	**11**	**12:14**	....	....	....	....	....	....	....	....
	Hershey Bears	AHL	54	5	7	12	72	....	....	....	....	....	....	....	....	....	....	....	5	0	1	1	0	....	....	....
99-2000	**Colorado**	**NHL**	**3**	**0**	**0**	**0**	**0**	**0**	**0**	**0**	**0**	**0.0**	**2**	**0**	**0.0**	**1**	**1**	**11:03**	....	....	....	....	....	....	....	....
	Hershey Bears	AHL	49	7	15	22	56	....	....	....	....	....	....	....	....	....	....	....	....	....	....	....	....	....	....	....
2000-01	Hershey Bears	AHL	58	2	12	14	34	....	....	....	....	....	....	....	....	....	....	....	12	0	1	1	4	....	....	....
	NHL Totals		**15**	**0**	**0**	**0**	**9**	**0**	**0**	**0**	**6**	**0.0**		**0**	**0.0**	**4**	**12**	**11:60**	....	....	....	....	....	....	....	....

SMITH, Jason

(SMIHTH, JAY-suhn) **EDM.**

Defense. Shoots right. 6'3", 210 lbs. Born, Calgary, Alta., November 2, 1973. New Jersey's 1st choice, 18th overall, in 1992 Entry Draft.

			Regular Season																Playoffs							
Season	Club	League	GP	G	A	Pts	PIM	PP	SH	GW	S	%	+/-	TF	F%	H	SB	Min	GP	G	A	Pts	PIM	PP	SH	GW
1990-91	Calgary Canucks	AJHL	45	3	15	18	69	....	....	....	....	....	....	....	....	....	....	....	....	....	....	....	....	....	....	....
	Regina Pats	WHL	2	0	0	0	7	....	....	....	....	....	....	....	....	....	....	....	4	0	0	0	2	....	....	....
1991-92	Regina Pats	WHL	62	9	29	38	138	....	....	....	....	....	....	....	....	....	....	....	....	....	....	....	....	....	....	....
1992-93	Regina Pats	WHL	64	14	52	66	175	....	....	....	....	....	....	....	....	....	....	....	13	4	8	12	39	....	....	....
	Utica Devils	AHL	....	....	....	....	....	....	....	....	....	....	....	....	....	....	....	....	1	0	0	0	2	....	....	....
1993-94	**New Jersey**	**NHL**	**41**	**0**	**5**	**5**	**43**	**0**	**0**	**0**	**47**	**0.0**	**7**	....	....	....	....	....	**6**	**0**	**0**	**0**	**7**	**0**	**0**	**0**
	Albany River Rats	AHL	20	6	3	9	31	....	....	....	....	....	....	....	....	....	....	....	....	....	....	....	....	....	....	....
1994-95	Albany River Rats	AHL	7	0	2	2	15	....	....	....	....	....	....	....	....	....	....	....	11	2	2	4	19	....	....	....
	New Jersey	**NHL**	**2**	**0**	**0**	**0**	**0**	**0**	**0**	**0**	**5**	**0.0**	**-3**	....	....	....	....	....	....	....	....	....	....	....	....	....
1995-96	**New Jersey**	**NHL**	**64**	**2**	**1**	**3**	**86**	**0**	**0**	**0**	**52**	**3.8**	**5**	....	....	....	....	....	....	....	....	....	....	....	....	....
1996-97	**New Jersey**	**NHL**	**57**	**1**	**2**	**3**	**38**	**0**	**0**	**0**	**48**	**2.1**	**-8**	....	....	....	....	....	....	....	....	....	....	....	....	....
	Toronto	**NHL**	**21**	**0**	**5**	**5**	**16**	**0**	**0**	**0**	**26**	**0.0**	**-4**	....	....	....	....	....	....	....	....	....	....	....	....	....
1997-98	**Toronto**	**NHL**	**81**	**3**	**13**	**16**	**100**	**0**	**0**	**0**	**97**	**3.1**	**-5**	....	....	....	....	....	....	....	....	....	....	....	....	....
1998-99	**Toronto**	**NHL**	**60**	**2**	**11**	**13**	**40**	**0**	**0**	**0**	**53**	**3.8**	**-9**	**0**	**0.0**	**113**	**67**	**17:31**	....	....	....	....	....	....	....	....
	Edmonton	**NHL**	**12**	**1**	**1**	**2**	**11**	**0**	**0**	**0**	**15**	**6.7**	**0**	**0**	**0.0**	**35**	**26**	**20:26**	**4**	**0**	**1**	**1**	**4**	**0**	**0**	**0**
99-2000	**Edmonton**	**NHL**	**80**	**3**	**11**	**14**	**60**	**0**	**0**	**1**	**96**	**3.1**	**16**	**1**	**100.0**	**260**	**167**	**21:15**	**5**	**0**	**1**	**1**	**4**	**0**	**0**	**0**
2000-01	**Edmonton**	**NHL**	**82**	**5**	**15**	**20**	**120**	**1**	**1**	**0**	**140**	**3.6**	**14**	**1**	**0.0**	**254**	**210**	**21:40**	**6**	**0**	**2**	**2**	**6**	**0**	**0**	**0**
	NHL Totals		**500**	**17**	**64**	**81**	**514**	**1**	**1**	**1**	**579**	**2.9**		**2**	**50.0**	**662**	**470**	**20:24**	**21**	**0**	**4**	**4**	**21**	**0**	**0**	**0**

WHL East First All-Star Team (1993) • Canadian Major Junior First All-Star Team (1993)

• Missed majority of 1994-95 season recovering from knee injury suffered in practice, November 5, 1994. Traded to **Toronto** by **New Jersey** with Steve Sullivan and the rights to Alyn McCauley for Doug Gilmour, Dave Ellett and New Jersey's 4th round choice (previously acquired, New Jersey selected Andre Lakos) in 1999 Entry Draft, February 25, 1997. Traded to **Edmonton** by **Toronto** for Edmonton's 4th round choice (Jonathon Zion) in 1999 Entry Draft and 2nd round choice (Kris Vernarsky) in 2000 Entry Draft, March 23, 1999.

SMITH, Mark

(SMIHTH, MAHRK) **S.J.**

Center. Shoots left. 5'10", 205 lbs. Born, Edmonton, Alta., October 24, 1977. San Jose's 7th choice, 219th overall, in 1997 Entry Draft.

			Regular Season																Playoffs							
Season	Club	League	GP	G	A	Pts	PIM	PP	SH	GW	S	%	+/-	TF	F%	H	SB	Min	GP	G	A	Pts	PIM	PP	SH	GW
1993-94	Nipawin Hawks	SJHL	62	14	12	26	44	....	....	....	....	....	....	....	....	....	....	....	....	....	....	....	....	....	....	....
1994-95	Lethbridge	WHL	49	3	4	7	25	....	....	....	....	....	....	....	....	....	....	....	....	....	....	....	....	....	....	....
1995-96	Lethbridge	WHL	71	11	24	35	59	....	....	....	....	....	....	....	....	....	....	....	4	2	0	2	2	....	....	....
1996-97	Lethbridge	WHL	62	19	38	57	125	....	....	....	....	....	....	....	....	....	....	....	19	7	13	20	51	....	....	....
1997-98	Lethbridge	WHL	70	42	67	109	206	....	....	....	....	....	....	....	....	....	....	....	3	0	2	2	18	....	....	....
	Kentucky	AHL	2	0	0	0	0	....	....	....	....	....	....	....	....	....	....	....	....	....	....	....	....	....	....	....
1998-99	Kentucky	AHL	78	18	21	39	101	....	....	....	....	....	....	....	....	....	....	....	12	2	7	9	16	....	....	....
99-2000	Kentucky	AHL	79	21	45	66	153	....	....	....	....	....	....	....	....	....	....	....	9	0	5	5	22	....	....	....
2000-01	**San Jose**	**NHL**	**42**	**2**	**2**	**4**	**51**	**0**	**0**	**0**	**39**	**5.1**	**2**	**308**	**52.9**	**52**	**12**	**8:48**	....	....	....	....	....	....	....	....
	Kentucky	AHL	6	2	6	8	23	....	....	....	....	....	....	....	....	....	....	....	....	....	....	....	....	....	....	....
	NHL Totals		**42**	**2**	**2**	**4**	**51**	**0**	**0**	**0**	**39**	**5.1**		**308**	**52.9**	**52**	**12**	**8:48**	....	....	....	....	....	....	....	....

WHL East Second All-Star Team (1998)

SMITH, Steve
(SMIHTH, STEEV)

Defense. Shoots left. 6'4", 215 lbs. Born, Glasgow, Scotland, April 30, 1963. Edmonton's 5th choice, 111th overall, in 1981 Entry Draft.

Season	Club	League	Regular Season																Playoffs							
			GP	G	A	Pts	PIM	PP	SH	GW	S	%	+/-	TF	F%	H	SB	Min	GP	G	A	Pts	PIM	PP	SH	GW
1979-80	Fergus Green	OHA-D	23	10	14	24	40																			
1980-81	London Knights	OMJHL	62	4	12	16	141																			
1981-82	London Knights	OHL	58	10	36	46	207												4	1	2	3	13			
1982-83	London Knights	OHL	50	6	35	41	133												3	1	0	1	10			
	Moncton Alpines	AHL	2	0	0	0	0																			
1983-84	Brantford	OHL	7	1	1	2	0																			
	Moncton Alpines	AHL	64	1	8	9	176																			
1984-85	**Edmonton**	**NHL**	**2**	**0**	**0**	**0**	**2**	**0**	**0**	**0**	**3**	**0.0**	**-2**													
	Nova Scotia	AHL	68	2	28	30	161												5	0	3	3	40			
1985-86	**Edmonton**	**NHL**	**55**	**4**	**20**	**24**	**166**	**1**	**0**	**1**	**74**	**5.4**	**30**						**6**	**0**	**1**	**1**	**14**	**0**	**0**	**0**
	Nova Scotia	AHL	4	0	2	2	11																			
1986-87♦	**Edmonton**	**NHL**	**62**	**7**	**15**	**22**	**165**	**2**	**0**	**1**	**71**	**9.9**	**11**						**15**	**1**	**3**	**4**	**45**	**0**	**0**	**0**
1987-88♦	**Edmonton**	**NHL**	**79**	**12**	**43**	**55**	**286**	**5**	**0**	**1**	**116**	**10.3**	**40**						**19**	**1**	**11**	**12**	**55**	**1**	**0**	**0**
1988-89	**Edmonton**	**NHL**	**35**	**3**	**19**	**22**	**97**	**0**	**0**	**0**	**47**	**6.4**	**5**						**7**	**2**	**2**	**4**	**20**	**0**	**0**	**1**
1989-90♦	**Edmonton**	**NHL**	**75**	**7**	**34**	**41**	**171**	**3**	**0**	**1**	**125**	**5.6**	**6**						**22**	**5**	**10**	**15**	**37**	**0**	**1**	**1**
1990-91	**Edmonton**	**NHL**	**77**	**13**	**41**	**54**	**193**	**4**	**0**	**2**	**114**	**11.4**	**14**						**18**	**1**	**2**	**3**	**45**	**1**	**0**	**0**
1991-92	**Chicago**	**NHL**	**76**	**9**	**21**	**30**	**304**	**3**	**0**	**1**	**153**	**5.9**	**23**						**18**	**1**	**11**	**12**	**16**	**1**	**0**	**0**
1992-93	**Chicago**	**NHL**	**78**	**10**	**47**	**57**	**214**	**7**	**1**	**2**	**212**	**4.7**	**12**						**4**	**0**	**0**	**0**	**10**	**0**	**0**	**0**
1993-94	**Chicago**	**NHL**	**57**	**5**	**22**	**27**	**174**	**1**	**0**	**1**	**89**	**5.6**	**-5**													
1994-95	**Chicago**	**NHL**	**48**	**1**	**12**	**13**	**128**	**0**	**0**	**0**	**43**	**2.3**	**6**						**16**	**0**	**1**	**1**	**26**	**0**	**0**	**0**
1995-96	**Chicago**	**NHL**	**37**	**0**	**9**	**9**	**71**	**0**	**0**	**0**	**17**	**0.0**	**12**						**6**	**0**	**0**	**0**	**16**	**0**	**0**	**0**
1996-97	**Chicago**	**NHL**	**21**	**0**	**0**	**0**	**29**	**0**	**0**	**0**	**7**	**0.0**	**4**						**3**	**0**	**0**	**0**	**4**	**0**	**0**	**0**
1998-99	**Calgary**	**NHL**	**69**	**1**	**14**	**15**	**80**	**0**	**0**	**0**	**42**	**2.4**	**3**	**0**	**0.0**	**93**	**98**	**22:33**								
99-2000	**Calgary**	**NHL**	**20**	**0**	**4**	**4**	**42**	**0**	**0**	**0**	**10**	**0.0**	**-13**	**0**	**0.0**	**39**	**33**	**21:07**								
2000-01	**Calgary**	**NHL**	**13**	**0**	**2**	**2**	**17**	**0**	**0**	**0**	**3**	**0.0**	**-2**	**0**	**0.0**	**15**	**19**	**18:60**								
	NHL Totals		**804**	**72**	**303**	**375**	**2139**	**26**	**1**	**10**	**1126**	**6.4**		**0**	**0.0**	**147**	**150**	**21:49**	**134**	**11**	**41**	**52**	**288**	**3**	**1**	**2**

Played in NHL All-Star Game (1991)

Traded to **Chicago** by **Edmonton** for Dave Manson and Chicago's 3rd round choice (Kirk Maltby) in 1992 Entry Draft, October 2, 1991. Signed as a free agent by **Calgary**, August 17, 1998. • Missed majority of 1999-2000 season recovering from neck injury suffered in game vs. Los Angeles, January 12, 2000. • Officially announced retirement, December 7, 2000.

SMITH, Wyatt
(SMIHTH, WIGH-uht) **PHX.**

Center. Shoots left. 5'11", 208 lbs. Born, Thief River Falls, MN, February 13, 1977. Phoenix's 6th choice, 233rd overall, in 1997 Entry Draft.

Season	Club	League	GP	G	A	Pts	PIM	PP	SH	GW	S	%	+/-	TF	F%	H	SB	Min	GP	G	A	Pts	PIM	PP	SH	GW
1994-95	Warroad High	Hi-School	28	29	31	60	28																			
1995-96	U. of Minnesota	WCHA	32	4	5	9	32																			
1996-97	U. of Minnesota	WCHA	38	16	14	30	44																			
1997-98	U. of Minnesota	WCHA	39	24	23	47	62																			
1998-99	U. of Minnesota	WCHA	43	23	20	43	37																			
99-2000	**Phoenix**	**NHL**	**2**	**0**	**0**	**0**	**0**	**0**	**0**	**0**	**0**	**0.0**	**-2**	**20**	**30.0**	**1**	**1**	**11:39**								
	Springfield	AHL	60	14	26	40	26												5	2	3	5	13			
2000-01	**Phoenix**	**NHL**	**42**	**3**	**7**	**10**	**13**	**0**	**1**	**0**	**40**	**7.5**	**7**	**335**	**40.9**	**15**	**29**	**12:20**								
	Springfield	AHL	18	5	7	12	11																			
	NHL Totals		**44**	**3**	**7**	**10**	**13**	**0**	**1**	**0**	**40**	**7.5**		**355**	**40.3**	**16**	**30**	**12:18**								

SMOLINSKI, Bryan
(smoh-LIHN-skee, BRIGH-uhn) **L.A.**

Center/Right wing. Shoots right. 6'1", 208 lbs. Born, Toledo, OH, December 27, 1971. Boston's 1st choice, 21st overall, in 1990 Entry Draft.

Season	Club	League	GP	G	A	Pts	PIM	PP	SH	GW	S	%	+/-	TF	F%	H	SB	Min	GP	G	A	Pts	PIM	PP	SH	GW
1987-88	Detroit Caesars	MNHL	80	43	77	120	....																			
1988-89	Stratford Cullitons	OJHL-B	46	32	62	94	132																			
1989-90	Michigan State	CCHA	35	9	13	22	34																			
1990-91	Michigan State	CCHA	35	9	12	21	24																			
1991-92	Michigan State	CCHA	41	28	33	61	55																			
1992-93	Michigan State	CCHA	40	31	37	*68	93																			
	Boston	**NHL**	**9**	**1**	**3**	**4**	**0**	**0**	**0**	**0**	**10**	**10.0**	**3**						**4**	**1**	**0**	**1**	**2**	**0**	**0**	**0**
1993-94	**Boston**	**NHL**	**83**	**31**	**20**	**51**	**82**	**4**	**3**	**5**	**179**	**17.3**	**4**						**13**	**5**	**4**	**9**	**4**	**2**	**0**	**0**
1994-95	**Boston**	**NHL**	**44**	**18**	**13**	**31**	**31**	**6**	**0**	**5**	**121**	**14.9**	**-3**						**5**	**0**	**1**	**1**	**4**	**0**	**0**	**0**
1995-96	**Pittsburgh**	**NHL**	**81**	**24**	**40**	**64**	**69**	**8**	**2**	**1**	**229**	**10.5**	**6**						**18**	**5**	**4**	**9**	**10**	**0**	**0**	**1**
1996-97	Detroit Vipers	IHL	6	5	7	12	10																			
	NY Islanders	**NHL**	**64**	**28**	**28**	**56**	**25**	**9**	**0**	**1**	**183**	**15.3**	**9**													
1997-98	**NY Islanders**	**NHL**	**81**	**13**	**30**	**43**	**34**	**3**	**0**	**4**	**203**	**6.4**	**-16**													
1998-99	**NY Islanders**	**NHL**	**82**	**16**	**24**	**40**	**49**	**7**	**0**	**3**	**223**	**7.2**	**-7**	**1011**	**48.3**	**105**	**50**	**19:19**								
99-2000	**Los Angeles**	**NHL**	**79**	**20**	**36**	**56**	**48**	**2**	**0**	**0**	**160**	**12.5**	**2**	**1545**	**50.9**	**129**	**58**	**18:35**	**4**	**0**	**0**	**0**	**2**	**0**	**0**	**0**
2000-01	**Los Angeles**	**NHL**	**78**	**27**	**32**	**59**	**40**	**5**	**3**	**5**	**183**	**14.8**	**10**	**952**	**48.7**	**155**	**54**	**18:32**	**13**	**1**	**5**	**6**	**14**	**0**	**0**	**0**
	NHL Totals		**601**	**178**	**226**	**404**	**378**	**44**	**8**	**24**	**1491**	**11.9**		**3508**	**49.5**	**389**	**162**	**18:49**	**57**	**12**	**14**	**26**	**36**	**2**	**0**	**1**

CCHA First All-Star Team (1993) • NCAA West First All-American Team (1993)

Traded to **Pittsburgh** by **Boston** with Glen Murray and Boston's 3rd round choice (Boyd Kane) in 1996 Entry Draft for Kevin Stevens and Shawn McEachern, August 2, 1995. Traded to **NY Islanders** by **Pittsburgh** for Darius Kasparaitis and Andreas Johansson, November 17, 1996. Traded to **LA Kings** by **NY Islanders** with Ziggy Palffy, Marcel Cousineau and New Jersey's 4th round choice (previously acquired, LA Kings selected Daniel Johansson) in 1999 Entry Draft for Olli Jokinen, Josh Green, Mathieu Biron and LA Kings' 1st round choice (Taylor Pyatt) in 1999 Entry Draft, June 20, 1999.

SMREK, Peter
(SMUHR-ehk, PEE-tuhr) **NYR**

Defense. Shoots left. 6'1", 215 lbs. Born, Martin, Czech., February 16, 1979. St. Louis' 2nd choice, 85th overall, in 1999 Entry Draft.

Season	Club	League	GP	G	A	Pts	PIM	PP	SH	GW	S	%	+/-	TF	F%	H	SB	Min	GP	G	A	Pts	PIM	PP	SH	GW
1996-97	ZTS Martin	Slovakia	12	1	0	1	....												3	0	0	0	....			
1997-98	ZTS Martin	Slovak-Jr.	19	7	6	13	32																			
	ZTS Martin	Slovakia	23	0	5	5	24												1	0	0	0	0			
1998-99	Des Moines	USHL	52	6	26	32	59												14	2	7	9	8			
99-2000	Peoria Rivermen	ECHL	4	1	1	2	2																			
	Worcester	AHL	64	5	19	24	26												2	0	0	0	4			
2000-01	**St. Louis**	**NHL**	**6**	**2**	**0**	**2**	**2**	**0**	**0**	**1**	**5**	**40.0**	**1**	**0**	**0.0**	**9**	**4**	**13:01**								
	Worcester	AHL	50	2	7	9	71																			
	NY Rangers	**NHL**	**14**	**0**	**3**	**3**	**12**	**0**	**0**	**0**	**9**	**0.0**	**1**	**0**	**0.0**	**18**	**24**	**16:47**								
	Hartford	AHL	....	....	....	....	....												5	0	2	2	2			
	NHL Totals		**20**	**2**	**3**	**5**	**14**	**0**	**0**	**1**	**14**	**14.3**		**0**	**0.0**	**27**	**28**	**15:39**								

Traded to **NY Rangers** by **St. Louis** for Alexei Gusarov, March 5, 2001.

SMYTH, Brad
(SMIHTH, BRAD) **NYR**

Right wing. Shoots right. 6', 195 lbs. Born, Ottawa, Ont., March 13, 1973.

Season	Club	League	GP	G	A	Pts	PIM	PP	SH	GW	S	%	+/-	TF	F%	H	SB	Min	GP	G	A	Pts	PIM	PP	SH	GW
1989-90	Nepean Raiders	OMHA	55	53	36	89	105																			
1990-91	London Knights	OHL	29	2	6	8	22																			
1991-92	London Knights	OHL	58	17	18	35	93												10	2	0	2	8			
1992-93	London Knights	OHL	66	54	55	109	118												12	7	8	15	25			
1993-94	Cincinnati	IHL	30	7	3	10	54																			
	Birmingham Bulls	ECHL	29	26	30	56	38												10	8	8	16	19			
1994-95	Springfield	AHL	3	0	0	0	7																			
	Birmingham Bulls	ECHL	36	33	35	68	52												3	5	2	7	0			
	Cincinnati	IHL	26	2	11	13	34												1	0	0	0	2			
1995-96	**Florida**	**NHL**	**7**	**1**	**1**	**2**	**4**	**1**	**0**	**0**	**12**	**8.3**	**-3**													
	Carolina	AHL	68	*68	58	*126	80																			
1996-97	**Florida**	**NHL**	**8**	**1**	**0**	**1**	**2**	**0**	**0**	**0**	**10**	**10.0**	**-3**													
	Los Angeles	**NHL**	**44**	**8**	**8**	**16**	**74**	**0**	**0**	**1**	**74**	**10.8**	**-7**													
	Phoenix	IHL	3	5	2	7	0																			
1997-98	**Los Angeles**	**NHL**	**9**	**1**	**3**	**4**	**4**	**0**	**0**	**0**	**12**	**8.3**	**-1**													
	NY Rangers	**NHL**	**1**	**0**	**0**	**0**	**0**	**0**	**0**	**0**	**1**	**0.0**	**0**													
	Hartford	AHL	57	29	33	62	79												15	12	8	20	11			

			Regular Season																Playoffs							
Season	Club	League	GP	G	A	Pts	PIM	PP	SH	GW	S	%	+/-	TF	F%	H	SB	Min	GP	G	A	Pts	PIM	PP	SH	GW
1998-99	**Nashville**	**NHL**	**3**	**0**	**0**	**0**	**6**	**0**	**0**	**0**	**5**	**0.0**	**−1**	**0**	**0.0**	**1**	**0**	**9:54**	....	....	....	....	....	....	....	....
	Milwaukee	IHL	34	11	16	27	21	....	....	....	....	....	....	....	....	....	....	....	....	....	....	....	....	....	....	....
	Hartford	AHL	36	25	19	44	48	....	....	....	....	....	....	....	....	....	....	....	7	6	0	6	14	....	....	....
99-2000	Hartford	AHL	80	39	37	76	62	....	....	....	....	....	....	....	....	....	....	....	23	*13	10	23	8	....	....	....
2000-01	**NY Rangers**	**NHL**	**4**	**1**	**0**	**1**	**4**	**0**	**0**	**0**	**10**	**10.0**	**0**	**0**	**0.0**	**2**	**0**	**13:57**	....	....	....	....	....	....	....	....
	Hartford	AHL	77	*50	29	79	110	....	....	....	....	....	....	....	....	....	....	....	5	2	3	5	8	....	....	....
	NHL Totals		**76**	**12**	**12**	**24**	**94**	**1**	**0**	**1**	**124**	**9.7**		**0**	**0.0**	**3**	**0**	**12:13**	....	....	....	....	....	....	....	....

AHL First All-Star Team (1996, 2001) • Won John B. Sollenberger Trophy (Top Scorer - AHL) (1996) • Won Les Cunningham Award (MVP - AHL) (1996)

Signed as a free agent by **Florida**, October 4, 1993. Traded to **LA Kings** by **Florida** for LA Kings' 3rd round choice (Vratislav Cech) in 1997 Entry Draft, November 28, 1996. Traded to **NY Rangers** by **LA Kings** for future considerations, November 14, 1997. Signed as a free agent by **Nashville**, July 16, 1998. Traded to **NY Rangers** by **Nashville** for future considerations, May 3, 1999.

SMYTH, Ryan — (SMIHTH, RIGH-uhn) — EDM.

Left wing. Shoots left. 6'1", 195 lbs. Born, Banff, Alta., February 21, 1976. Edmonton's 2nd choice, 6th overall, in 1994 Entry Draft.

1990-91	Banff Blazers	AAHA	25	100	50	150	....	....	....	....	....	....	....	....	....	....	....	....	....	....	....	....	....	....	....	....
	Lethbridge Y-Men	AMHL	34	8	21	29	....	....	....	....	....	....	....	....	....	....	....	....	....	....	....	....	....	....	....	....
1991-92	Caronport	SMHL	35	55	61	116	98	....	....	....	....	....	....	....	....	....	....	....	....	....	....	....	....	....	....	....
	Moose Jaw	WHL	2	0	0	0	0	....	....	....	....	....	....	....	....	....	....	....	....	....	....	....	....	....	....	....
1992-93	Moose Jaw	WHL	64	19	14	33	59	....	....	....	....	....	....	....	....	....	....	....	....	....	....	....	....	....	....	....
1993-94	Moose Jaw	WHL	72	50	55	105	88	....	....	....	....	....	....	....	....	....	....	....	....	....	....	....	....	....	....	....
1994-95	Moose Jaw	WHL	50	41	45	86	66	....	....	....	....	....	....	....	....	....	....	....	10	6	9	15	22	....	....	....
	Edmonton	**NHL**	**3**	**0**	**0**	**0**	**0**	**0**	**0**	**0**	**2**	**0.0**	**−1**	....	....	....	....	....	....	....	....	....	....	....	....	....
1995-96	**Edmonton**	**NHL**	**48**	**2**	**9**	**11**	**28**	**1**	**0**	**0**	**65**	**3.1**	**−10**	....	....	....	....	....	....	....	....	....	....	....	....	....
	Cape Breton	AHL	9	6	5	11	4	....	....	....	....	....	....	....	....	....	....	....	....	....	....	....	....	....	....	....
1996-97	**Edmonton**	**NHL**	**82**	**39**	**22**	**61**	**76**	**20**	**0**	**4**	**265**	**14.7**	**−7**	....	....	....	....	....	**12**	**5**	**5**	**10**	**12**	**1**	**0**	**2**
1997-98	**Edmonton**	**NHL**	**65**	**20**	**13**	**33**	**44**	**10**	**0**	**2**	**205**	**9.8**	**−24**	....	....	....	....	....	**12**	**1**	**3**	**4**	**16**	**1**	**0**	**0**
1998-99	**Edmonton**	**NHL**	**71**	**13**	**18**	**31**	**62**	**6**	**0**	**2**	**161**	**8.1**	**0**	**5**	**20.0**	**84**	**20**	**14:26**	**3**	**3**	**0**	**3**	**0**	**2**	**0**	**0**
99-2000	**Edmonton**	**NHL**	**82**	**28**	**26**	**54**	**58**	**11**	**0**	**4**	**238**	**11.8**	**−2**	**24**	**54.2**	**84**	**34**	**19:12**	**5**	**1**	**0**	**1**	**6**	**0**	**1**	**0**
2000-01	**Edmonton**	**NHL**	**82**	**31**	**39**	**70**	**58**	**11**	**0**	**6**	**245**	**12.7**	**10**	**17**	**35.3**	**89**	**35**	**19:58**	**6**	**3**	**4**	**7**	**4**	**0**	**0**	**0**
	NHL Totals		**433**	**133**	**127**	**260**	**326**	**59**	**0**	**18**	**1181**	**11.3**		**46**	**43.5**	**257**	**89**	**18:02**	**38**	**13**	**12**	**25**	**38**	**4**	**1**	**2**

WHL East Second All-Star Team (1995)

SNYDER, Dan — (SHNIGH-duhr, DAN) — ATL.

Center. Shoots left. 6', 185 lbs. Born, Elmira, Ont., February 23, 1978.

1994-95	Elmira Kings	OJHL-B	43	8	17	25	46	....	....	....	....	....	....	....	....	....	....	....	....	....	....	....	....	....	....	....
1995-96	Owen Sound	OHL	63	8	17	25	78	....	....	....	....	....	....	....	....	....	....	....	6	1	2	3	4	....	....	....
1996-97	Owen Sound	OHL	57	17	29	46	96	....	....	....	....	....	....	....	....	....	....	....	4	2	3	5	8	....	....	....
1997-98	Owen Sound	OHL	46	23	33	56	74	....	....	....	....	....	....	....	....	....	....	....	10	2	3	5	16	....	....	....
1998-99	Owen Sound	OHL	64	27	67	94	110	....	....	....	....	....	....	....	....	....	....	....	16	8	5	13	30	....	....	....
99-2000	Orlando Bears	IHL	71	12	13	25	123	....	....	....	....	....	....	....	....	....	....	....	6	1	2	3	4	....	....	....
2000-01	**Atlanta**	**NHL**	**2**	**0**	**0**	**0**	**0**	**0**	**0**	**0**	**2**	**0.0**	**0**	**12**	**50.0**	**6**	**1**	**6:55**	....	....	....	....	....	....	....	....
	Orlando	IHL	78	13	30	43	127	....	....	....	....	....	....	....	....	....	....	....	16	7	3	10	20	....	....	....
	NHL Totals		**2**	**0**	**0**	**0**	**0**	**0**	**0**	**0**	**2**	**0.0**		**12**	**50.0**	**6**	**1**	**6:55**	....	....	....	....	....	....	....	....

Signed as a free agent by **Atlanta**, June 28, 1999.

SONNENBERG, Martin — (SOHN-nehn-BUHRG, MAHR-tihn) — PIT.

Left wing. Shoots left. 6', 184 lbs. Born, Wetaskiwin, Alta., January 23, 1978.

1994-95	Leduc Oil Kings	AMHL	35	28	40	68	34	....	....	....	....	....	....	....	....	....	....	....	....	....	....	....	....	....	....	....
1995-96	Saskatoon Blades	WHL	58	8	7	15	24	....	....	....	....	....	....	....	....	....	....	....	3	0	0	0	2	....	....	....
1996-97	Saskatoon Blades	WHL	72	38	26	64	79	....	....	....	....	....	....	....	....	....	....	....	....	....	....	....	....	....	....	....
1997-98	Saskatoon Blades	WHL	72	40	52	92	87	....	....	....	....	....	....	....	....	....	....	....	6	1	3	4	9	....	....	....
1998-99	**Pittsburgh**	**NHL**	**44**	**1**	**1**	**2**	**19**	**0**	**0**	**0**	**12**	**8.3**	**−2**	**2**	**0.0**	**33**	**5**	**4:00**	**7**	**0**	**0**	**0**	**0**	**0**	**0**	**0**
	Syracuse Crunch	AHL	36	15	9	24	31	....	....	....	....	....	....	....	....	....	....	....	....	....	....	....	....	....	....	....
99-2000	**Pittsburgh**	**NHL**	**14**	**1**	**2**	**3**	**0**	**1**	**0**	**0**	**19**	**5.3**	**0**	**7**	**28.6**	**10**	**7**	**7:26**	....	....	....	....	....	....	....	....
	Wilkes-Barre	AHL	62	20	33	53	109	....	....	....	....	....	....	....	....	....	....	....	....	....	....	....	....	....	....	....
2000-01	Wilkes-Barre	AHL	73	14	18	32	89	....	....	....	....	....	....	....	....	....	....	....	21	4	3	7	6	....	....	....
	NHL Totals		**58**	**2**	**3**	**5**	**19**	**1**	**0**	**0**	**31**	**6.5**		**9**	**22.2**	**43**	**12**	**4:50**	**7**	**0**	**0**	**0**	**0**	**0**	**0**	**0**

Signed as a free agent by **Pittsburgh**, October 9, 1998.

SOPEL, Brent — (SOH-puhl, BREHNT) — VAN.

Defense. Shoots right. 6'1", 205 lbs. Born, Calgary, Alta., January 7, 1977. Vancouver's 6th choice, 144th overall, in 1995 Entry Draft.

1992-93	Saskatoon Legion	SAHA	36	7	17	24	95	....	....	....	....	....	....	....	....	....	....	....	....	....	....	....	....	....	....	....
1993-94	Saskatoon Blaze	SMHL	34	9	30	39	180	....	....	....	....	....	....	....	....	....	....	....	....	....	....	....	....	....	....	....
	Saskatoon Blades	WHL	11	2	2	4	2	....	....	....	....	....	....	....	....	....	....	....	....	....	....	....	....	....	....	....
1994-95	Saskatoon Blades	WHL	22	1	10	11	31	....	....	....	....	....	....	....	....	....	....	....	....	....	....	....	....	....	....	....
	Swift Current	WHL	41	4	19	23	50	....	....	....	....	....	....	....	....	....	....	....	3	0	3	3	0	....	....	....
1995-96	Swift Current	WHL	71	13	48	61	87	....	....	....	....	....	....	....	....	....	....	....	6	1	2	3	4	....	....	....
	Syracuse Crunch	AHL	1	0	0	0	0	....	....	....	....	....	....	....	....	....	....	....	....	....	....	....	....	....	....	....
1996-97	Swift Current	WHL	62	15	41	56	109	....	....	....	....	....	....	....	....	....	....	....	10	5	11	16	32	....	....	....
	Syracuse Crunch	AHL	2	0	0	0	0	....	....	....	....	....	....	....	....	....	....	....	3	0	0	0	0	....	....	....
1997-98	Syracuse Crunch	AHL	76	10	33	43	70	....	....	....	....	....	....	....	....	....	....	....	5	0	7	7	12	....	....	....
1998-99	**Vancouver**	**NHL**	**5**	**1**	**0**	**1**	**4**	**1**	**0**	**0**	**5**	**20.0**	**−1**	**0**	**0.0**	**4**	**1**	**11:58**	....	....	....	....	....	....	....	....
	Syracuse Crunch	AHL	53	10	21	31	59	....	....	....	....	....	....	....	....	....	....	....	....	....	....	....	....	....	....	....
99-2000	**Vancouver**	**NHL**	**18**	**2**	**4**	**6**	**12**	**0**	**0**	**1**	**11**	**18.2**	**9**	**0**	**0.0**	**29**	**13**	**10:31**	....	....	....	....	....	....	....	....
	Syracuse Crunch	AHL	50	6	25	31	67	....	....	....	....	....	....	....	....	....	....	....	4	0	2	2	8	....	....	....
2000-01	**Vancouver**	**NHL**	**52**	**4**	**10**	**14**	**10**	**0**	**0**	**1**	**57**	**7.0**	**4**	**0**	**0.0**	**93**	**44**	**16:01**	**4**	**0**	**0**	**0**	**2**	**0**	**0**	**0**
	Kansas City	IHL	4	0	1	1	0	....	....	....	....	....	....	....	....	....	....	....	....	....	....	....	....	....	....	....
	NHL Totals		**75**	**7**	**14**	**21**	**26**	**1**	**0**	**2**	**73**	**9.6**		**0**	**0.0**	**126**	**58**	**14:25**	**4**	**0**	**0**	**0**	**2**	**0**	**0**	**0**

SOROCHAN, Lee — (soh-RAW-kihn, LEE)

Defense. Shoots left. 5'11", 210 lbs. Born, Edmonton, Alta., September 9, 1975. NY Rangers' 2nd choice, 34th overall, in 1993 Entry Draft.

1990-91	Sherwood Park	AMHL	34	10	17	27	46	....	....	....	....	....	....	....	....	....	....	....	....	....	....	....	....	....	....	....
1991-92	Lethbridge	WHL	67	2	9	11	105	....	....	....	....	....	....	....	....	....	....	....	5	0	2	2	6	....	....	....
1992-93	Lethbridge	WHL	69	8	32	40	208	....	....	....	....	....	....	....	....	....	....	....	4	0	1	1	12	....	....	....
1993-94	Lethbridge	WHL	46	5	27	32	123	....	....	....	....	....	....	....	....	....	....	....	9	4	3	7	16	....	....	....
1994-95	Lethbridge	WHL	29	4	15	19	93	....	....	....	....	....	....	....	....	....	....	....	....	....	....	....	....	....	....	....
	Saskatoon Blades	WHL	24	5	13	18	63	....	....	....	....	....	....	....	....	....	....	....	10	3	6	9	34	....	....	....
	Binghamton	AHL	....	....	....	....	....	....	....	....	....	....	....	....	....	....	....	....	8	0	0	0	11	....	....	....
1995-96	Binghamton	AHL	45	2	8	10	26	....	....	....	....	....	....	....	....	....	....	....	1	0	0	0	0	....	....	....
1996-97	Binghamton	AHL	77	4	27	31	160	....	....	....	....	....	....	....	....	....	....	....	4	0	2	2	18	....	....	....
1997-98	Hartford	AHL	73	7	11	18	197	....	....	....	....	....	....	....	....	....	....	....	13	0	2	2	51	....	....	....
1998-99	Fort Wayne	IHL	45	0	10	10	204	....	....	....	....	....	....	....	....	....	....	....	....	....	....	....	....	....	....	....
	Hartford	AHL	16	0	2	2	33	....	....	....	....	....	....	....	....	....	....	....	....	....	....	....	....	....	....	....
	Calgary	**NHL**	**2**	**0**	**0**	**0**	**0**	**0**	**0**	**0**	**5**	**0.0**	**−3**	**0**	**0.0**	**3**	**3**	**15:43**	....	....	....	....	....	....	....	....
	Saint John Flames	AHL	3	1	3	4	4	....	....	....	....	....	....	....	....	....	....	....	7	3	3	6	29	....	....	....
99-2000	**Calgary**	**NHL**	**1**	**0**	**0**	**0**	**0**	**0**	**0**	**0**	**0**	**0.0**	**0**	**0**	**0.0**	**2**	**0**	**3:40**	....	....	....	....	....	....	....	....
	Saint John Flames	AHL	60	4	37	41	124	....	....	....	....	....	....	....	....	....	....	....	3	2	1	3	12	....	....	....
2000-01	London Knights	Britain	8	1	3	4	48	....	....	....	....	....	....	....	....	....	....	....	....	....	....	....	....	....	....	....
	Jokerit Helsinki	Finland	16	0	0	0	18	....	....	....	....	....	....	....	....	....	....	....	....	....	....	....	....	....	....	....
	NHL Totals		**3**	**0**	**0**	**0**	**0**	**0**	**0**	**0**	**5**	**0.0**		**0**	**0.0**	**5**	**3**	**11:42**	....	....	....	....	....	....	....	....

Traded to **Calgary** by **NY Rangers** for Chris O'Sullivan, March 23, 1999. Signed as a free agent by **London Knights** (Britain), October 18, 2000.

SOURAY, Sheldon

(SUHR-ee, SHEHL-dohn) **MTL.**

Defense. Shoots left. 6'4", 223 lbs. Born, Elk Point, Alta., July 13, 1976. New Jersey's 3rd choice, 71st overall, in 1994 Entry Draft.

Season	Club	League	GP	G	A	Pts	PIM	PP	SH	GW	S	%	+/-	TF	F%	H	SB	Min	GP	G	A	Pts	PIM	PP	SH	GW
			Regular Season																Playoffs							
1990-91	Bonnyville Sabres	AAHA	30	15	20	35	100	....	....	....	....	....	....	....	....	....	....	....	....	....	....	....	....	....	....	....
1991-92	Quesnel	BCAHA	20	5	15	20	200	....	....	....	....	....	....	....	....	....	....	....	....	....	....	....	....	....	....	....
	Alberta Cycle	AMHL	11	0	5	5	67	....	....	....	....	....	....	....	....	....	....	....	....	....	....	....	....	....	....	....
1992-93	Ft-Saskatchewan	AJHL	35	0	12	12	125	....	....	....	....	....	....	....	....	....	....	....	....	....	....	....	....	....	....	....
	Tri-City Americans	WHL	2	0	0	0	0	....	....	....	....	....	....	....	....	....	....	....	....	....	....	....	....	....	....	....
1993-94	Tri-City Americans	WHL	42	3	6	9	122	....	....	....	....	....	....	....	....	....	....	....	....	....	....	....	....	....	....	....
1994-95	Tri-City Americans	WHL	40	2	24	26	140	....	....	....	....	....	....	....	....	....	....	....	....	....	....	....	....	....	....	....
	Prince George	WHL	11	2	3	5	23	....	....	....	....	....	....	....	....	....	....	....	....	....	....	....	....	....	....	....
	Albany River Rats	AHL	7	0	2	2	8	....	....	....	....	....	....	....	....	....	....	....	....	....	....	....	....	....	....	....
1995-96	Prince George	WHL	32	9	18	27	91	....	....	....	....	....	....	....	....	....	....	....	....	....	....	....	....	....	....	....
	Kelowna Rockets	WHL	27	7	20	27	94	....	....	....	....	....	....	....	....	....	....	....	6	0	5	5	2	....	....	....
	Albany River Rats	AHL	6	0	2	2	12	....	....	....	....	....	....	....	....	....	....	....	4	0	1	1	4	....	....	....
1996-97	Albany River Rats	AHL	70	2	11	13	160	....	....	....	....	....	....	....	....	....	....	....	16	2	3	5	47	....	....	....
1997-98	**New Jersey**	**NHL**	**60**	**3**	**7**	**10**	**85**	**0**	**0**	**1**	**74**	**4.1**	**18**	....	....	....	....	....	**3**	**0**	**1**	**1**	**2**	**0**	**0**	**0**
	Albany River Rats	AHL	6	0	0	0	8	....	....	....	....	....	....	....	....	....	....	....	....	....	....	....	....	....	....	....
1998-99	**New Jersey**	**NHL**	**70**	**1**	**7**	**8**	**110**	**0**	**0**	**0**	**101**	**1.0**	**5**	**0**	**0.0**	**109**	**57**	**14:56**	**2**	**0**	**1**	**1**	**0**	**0**	**0**	**0**
99-2000	**New Jersey**	**NHL**	**52**	**0**	**8**	**8**	**70**	**0**	**0**	**0**	**74**	**0.0**	**-6**	**0**	**0.0**	**97**	**51**	**17:12**	....	....	....	....	....	....	....	....
	Montreal	**NHL**	**19**	**3**	**0**	**3**	**44**	**0**	**0**	**0**	**39**	**7.7**	**7**	**0**	**0.0**	**23**	**34**	**19:18**	....	....	....	....	....	....	....	....
2000-01	**Montreal**	**NHL**	**52**	**3**	**8**	**11**	**95**	**0**	**0**	**2**	**103**	**2.9**	**-11**	**0**	**0.0**	**72**	**78**	**20:36**	....	....	....	....	....	....	....	....
	NHL Totals		**253**	**10**	**30**	**40**	**404**	**0**	**0**	**3**	**391**	**2.6**		**0**	**0.0**	**301**	**220**	**17:30**	**5**	**0**	**2**	**2**	**2**	**0**	**0**	**0**

WHL West Second All-Star Team (1996)

Traded to **Montreal** by **New Jersey** with Josh DeWolf and New Jersey's 2nd round choice (later traded to Washington - later traded to Tampa Bay - Tampa Bay selected Andreas Holmqvist) in 2001 Entry Draft for Vladimir Malakhov, March 1, 2000.

SPACEK, Jaroslav

(SPAH-chehk, YA-roh-slahv) **CHI.**

Defense. Shoots left. 5'11", 198 lbs. Born, Rokycany, Czech., February 11, 1974. Florida's 5th choice, 117th overall, in 1998 Entry Draft.

Season	Club	League	GP	G	A	Pts	PIM	PP	SH	GW	S	%	+/-	TF	F%	H	SB	Min	GP	G	A	Pts	PIM	PP	SH	GW
			Regular Season																Playoffs							
1992-93	Skoda Plzen	Czech.	16	1	3	4	....	....	....	....	....	....	....	....	....	....	....	....	....	....	....	....	....	....	....	....
1993-94	ZKZ Plzen	Cze-Rep	34	2	6	8	....	....	....	....	....	....	....	....	....	....	....	....	....	....	....	....	....	....	....	....
1994-95	ZKZ Plzen	Cze-Rep	38	4	8	12	14	....	....	....	....	....	....	....	....	....	....	....	3	1	0	1	2	....	....	....
1995-96	ZKZ Plzen	Cze-Rep	40	3	10	13	42	....	....	....	....	....	....	....	....	....	....	....	3	0	1	1	4	....	....	....
1996-97	ZKZ Plzen	Cze-Rep	52	9	29	38	44	....	....	....	....	....	....	....	....	....	....	....	....	....	....	....	....	....	....	....
1997-98	Farjestads BK	Sweden	45	10	16	26	63	....	....	....	....	....	....	....	....	....	....	....	12	2	5	7	14	....	....	....
	Farjestads BK	EuroHL	6	2	3	5	2	....	....	....	....	....	....	....	....	....	....	....	....	....	....	....	....	....	....	....
1998-99	**Florida**	**NHL**	**63**	**3**	**12**	**15**	**28**	**2**	**1**	**0**	**92**	**3.3**	**15**	**1**	**100.0**	**78**	**41**	**19:27**	....	....	....	....	....	....	....	....
	New Haven	AHL	14	4	8	12	15	....	....	....	....	....	....	....	....	....	....	....	....	....	....	....	....	....	....	....
99-2000	**Florida**	**NHL**	**82**	**10**	**26**	**36**	**53**	**4**	**0**	**1**	**111**	**9.0**	**7**	**1**	**0.0**	**122**	**98**	**22:40**	**4**	**0**	**0**	**0**	**0**	**0**	**0**	**0**
2000-01	**Florida**	**NHL**	**12**	**2**	**1**	**3**	**8**	**1**	**0**	**0**	**21**	**9.5**	**-4**	**0**	**0.0**	**23**	**11**	**19:12**	....	....	....	....	....	....	....	....
	Chicago	**NHL**	**50**	**5**	**18**	**23**	**20**	**2**	**0**	**1**	**85**	**5.9**	**7**	**0**	**0.0**	**63**	**65**	**21:31**	....	....	....	....	....	....	....	....
	NHL Totals		**207**	**20**	**57**	**77**	**109**	**9**	**1**	**2**	**309**	**6.5**		**2**	**50.0**	**286**	**215**	**21:12**	**4**	**0**	**0**	**0**	**0**	**0**	**0**	**0**

Traded to **Chicago** by **Florida** for Anders Eriksson, November 6, 2000.

SPANHEL, Martin

(SHPAN-hehl, MAHR-tihn) **CBJ**

Right wing. Shoots left. 6'2", 202 lbs. Born, Zlin, Czech., July 1, 1977. Philadelphia's 6th choice, 152nd overall, in 1995 Entry Draft.

Season	Club	League	GP	G	A	Pts	PIM	PP	SH	GW	S	%	+/-	TF	F%	H	SB	Min	GP	G	A	Pts	PIM	PP	SH	GW
			Regular Season																Playoffs							
1994-95	ZPS Zlin-Jr.	Cze-Rep	33	25	16	41	0	....	....	....	....	....	....	....	....	....	....	....	....	....	....	....	....	....	....	....
	ZPS Zlin	Cze-Rep	1	0	0	0	0	....	....	....	....	....	....	....	....	....	....	....	....	....	....	....	....	....	....	....
1995-96	Lethbridge	WHL	6	1	0	1	0	....	....	....	....	....	....	....	....	....	....	....	....	....	....	....	....	....	....	....
	Moose Jaw	WHL	61	4	12	16	33	....	....	....	....	....	....	....	....	....	....	....	....	....	....	....	....	....	....	....
1996-97	ZPS Zlin	Cze-Rep	22	3	6	9	20	....	....	....	....	....	....	....	....	....	....	....	....	....	....	....	....	....	....	....
1997-98	ZPS Zlin	Cze-Rep	40	7	9	16	70	....	....	....	....	....	....	....	....	....	....	....	....	....	....	....	....	....	....	....
1998-99	ZKZ Plzen	Cze-Rep	49	12	12	24	60	....	....	....	....	....	....	....	....	....	....	....	5	2	1	3	27	....	....	....
99-2000	ZKZ Plzen	Cze-Rep	52	21	27	48	86	....	....	....	....	....	....	....	....	....	....	....	7	1	4	5	12	....	....	....
2000-01	**Columbus**	**NHL**	**6**	**1**	**0**	**1**	**2**	**0**	**0**	**0**	**8**	**12.5**	**-1**	**1**	**0.0**	**8**	**0**	**12:29**	....	....	....	....	....	....	....	....
	Syracuse Crunch	AHL	67	11	13	24	75	....	....	....	....	....	....	....	....	....	....	....	2	0	0	0	8	....	....	....
	NHL Totals		**6**	**1**	**0**	**1**	**2**	**0**	**0**	**0**	**8**	**12.5**		**1**	**0.0**	**8**	**0**	**12:29**	....	....	....	....	....	....	....	....

Traded to **San Jose** by **Philadelphia** with Philadelphia's 1st round choice (later traded to Buffalo - later traded to Phoenix - Phoenix selected Daniel Briere) in 1996 Entry Draft and Philadelphia's 4th round choice (later traded to Buffalo - Buffalo selected Mike Martone) in 1996 Entry Draft for Pat Falloon, November 16, 1995. Traded to **Buffalo** by **San Jose** with Vaclav Varada and Philadelphia's 1st (previously acquired by San Jose - later traded to Phoenix - Phoenix selected Daniel Briere) and 4th (previously acquired, Buffalo selected Mike Martone) round choices in 1996 Entry Draft for Doug Bodger, November 16, 1995. Signed as a free agent by **Columbus**, May 30, 2000.

STAIOS, Steve

(STAY-uhs, STEEV) **EDM.**

Defense. Shoots right. 6'1", 200 lbs. Born, Hamilton, Ont., July 28, 1973. St. Louis' 1st choice, 27th overall, in 1991 Entry Draft.

Season	Club	League	GP	G	A	Pts	PIM	PP	SH	GW	S	%	+/-	TF	F%	H	SB	Min	GP	G	A	Pts	PIM	PP	SH	GW
			Regular Season																Playoffs							
1988-89	Hamilton Huskies	OMHA	58	13	39	52	78	....	....	....	....	....	....	....	....	....	....	....	....	....	....	....	....	....	....	....
1989-90	Hamilton Kilty B's	OJHL-B	40	9	27	36	66	....	....	....	....	....	....	....	....	....	....	....	....	....	....	....	....	....	....	....
1990-91	Niagara Falls	OHL	66	17	29	46	115	....	....	....	....	....	....	....	....	....	....	....	12	2	3	5	10	....	....	....
1991-92	Niagara Falls	OHL	65	11	42	53	122	....	....	....	....	....	....	....	....	....	....	....	17	7	8	15	27	....	....	....
1992-93	Niagara Falls	OHL	12	4	14	18	30	....	....	....	....	....	....	....	....	....	....	....	....	....	....	....	....	....	....	....
	Sudbury Wolves	OHL	53	13	44	57	67	....	....	....	....	....	....	....	....	....	....	....	11	5	6	11	22	....	....	....
1993-94	Peoria Rivermen	IHL	38	3	9	12	42	....	....	....	....	....	....	....	....	....	....	....	....	....	....	....	....	....	....	....
1994-95	Peoria Rivermen	IHL	60	3	13	16	64	....	....	....	....	....	....	....	....	....	....	....	6	0	0	0	10	....	....	....
1995-96	Peoria Rivermen	IHL	6	0	1	1	14	....	....	....	....	....	....	....	....	....	....	....	....	....	....	....	....	....	....	....
	Worcester	AHL	57	1	11	12	114	....	....	....	....	....	....	....	....	....	....	....	....	....	....	....	....	....	....	....
	Boston	**NHL**	**12**	**0**	**0**	**0**	**4**	**0**	**0**	**0**	**4**	**0.0**	**-5**	....	....	....	....	....	**3**	**0**	**0**	**0**	**0**	**0**	**0**	**0**
	Providence Bruins	AHL	7	1	4	5	8	....	....	....	....	....	....	....	....	....	....	....	....	....	....	....	....	....	....	....
1996-97	**Boston**	**NHL**	**54**	**3**	**8**	**11**	**71**	**0**	**0**	**0**	**56**	**5.4**	**-26**	....	....	....	....	....	....	....	....	....	....	....	....	....
	Vancouver	**NHL**	**9**	**0**	**6**	**6**	**20**	**0**	**0**	**0**	**10**	**0.0**	**2**	....	....	....	....	....	....	....	....	....	....	....	....	....
1997-98	**Vancouver**	**NHL**	**77**	**3**	**4**	**7**	**134**	**0**	**0**	**1**	**45**	**6.7**	**-3**	....	....	....	....	....	....	....	....	....	....	....	....	....
1998-99	**Vancouver**	**NHL**	**57**	**0**	**2**	**2**	**54**	**0**	**0**	**0**	**33**	**0.0**	**-12**	**4**	**25.0**	**58**	**8**	**6:53**	....	....	....	....	....	....	....	....
99-2000	**Atlanta**	**NHL**	**27**	**2**	**3**	**5**	**66**	**0**	**0**	**0**	**38**	**5.3**	**-5**	**2**	**50.0**	**60**	**14**	**13:01**	....	....	....	....	....	....	....	....
2000-01	**Atlanta**	**NHL**	**70**	**9**	**13**	**22**	**137**	**4**	**0**	**0**	**156**	**5.8**	**-23**	**1**	**0.0**	**102**	**108**	**21:45**	....	....	....	....	....	....	....	....
	NHL Totals		**306**	**17**	**36**	**53**	**486**	**4**	**0**	**1**	**342**	**5.0**		**7**	**28.6**	**220**	**130**	**14:43**	**3**	**0**	**0**	**0**	**0**	**0**	**0**	**0**

Traded to **Boston** by **St. Louis** with Kevin Sawyer for Steve Leach, March 8, 1996. Claimed on waivers by **Vancouver** from **Boston**, March 18, 1997. Claimed by **Atlanta** from **Vancouver** in Expansion Draft, June 25, 1999. • Missed majority of 1999-2000 season recovering from knee injury originally suffered in game vs. Colorado, October 23, 1999. Traded to **New Jersey** by **Atlanta** for New Jersey's 9th round choice (Simon Gamache) in 2000 Entry Draft, June 12, 2000. Traded to **Atlanta** by **New Jersey** for future considerations, July 10, 2000. Signed as a free agent by **Edmonton**, July 12, 2001.

STAPLETON, Mike

(STAY-puhl-TOHN, MIGHK)

Center. Shoots right. 5'10", 183 lbs. Born, Sarnia, Ont., May 5, 1966. Chicago's 7th choice, 132nd overall, in 1984 Entry Draft.

Season	Club	League	GP	G	A	Pts	PIM	PP	SH	GW	S	%	+/-	TF	F%	H	SB	Min	GP	G	A	Pts	PIM	PP	SH	GW
			Regular Season																Playoffs							
1982-83	Strathroy Blades	OJHL-B	40	39	38	77	99	....	....	....	....	....	....	....	....	....	....	....	3	1	2	3	4	....	....	....
1983-84	Cornwall Royals	OHL	70	24	45	69	94	....	....	....	....	....	....	....	....	....	....	....	3	1	2	3	4	....	....	....
1984-85	Cornwall Royals	OHL	56	41	44	85	68	....	....	....	....	....	....	....	....	....	....	....	9	2	4	6	23	....	....	....
1985-86	Cornwall Royals	OHL	56	39	64	103	74	....	....	....	....	....	....	....	....	....	....	....	6	2	3	5	2	....	....	....
1986-87	Canada	Nat-Team	21	2	4	6	4	....	....	....	....	....	....	....	....	....	....	....	....	....	....	....	....	....	....	....
	Chicago	**NHL**	**39**	**3**	**6**	**9**	**6**	**0**	**0**	**0**	**54**	**5.6**	**-9**	....	....	....	....	....	**4**	**0**	**0**	**0**	**2**	**0**	**0**	**0**
1987-88	**Chicago**	**NHL**	**53**	**2**	**9**	**11**	**59**	**0**	**0**	**1**	**50**	**4.0**	**-10**	....	....	....	....	....	....	....	....	....	....	....	....	....
	Saginaw Hawks	IHL	31	11	19	30	52	....	....	....	....	....	....	....	....	....	....	....	10	5	6	11	10	....	....	....
1988-89	**Chicago**	**NHL**	**7**	**0**	**1**	**1**	**7**	**0**	**0**	**0**	**6**	**0.0**	**-1**	....	....	....	....	....	....	....	....	....	....	....	....	....
	Saginaw Hawks	IHL	69	21	47	68	162	....	....	....	....	....	....	....	....	....	....	....	6	1	3	4	4	....	....	....
1989-90	Arvika IF	Sweden-3	30	15	18	33	....	....	....	....	....	....	....	....	....	....	....	....	....	....	....	....	....	....	....	....
	Indianapolis Ice	IHL	16	5	10	15	6	....	....	....	....	....	....	....	....	....	....	....	13	9	10	19	38	....	....	....
1990-91	**Chicago**	**NHL**	**7**	**0**	**1**	**1**	**2**	**0**	**0**	**0**	**6**	**0.0**	**0**	....	....	....	....	....	....	....	....	....	....	....	....	....
	Indianapolis Ice	IHL	75	29	52	81	76	....	....	....	....	....	....	....	....	....	....	....	7	1	4	5	0	....	....	....
1991-92	**Chicago**	**NHL**	**19**	**4**	**4**	**8**	**8**	**1**	**0**	**0**	**32**	**12.5**	**0**	....	....	....	....	....	....	....	....	....	....	....	....	....
	Indianapolis Ice	IHL	59	18	40	58	65	....	....	....	....	....	....	....	....	....	....	....	....	....	....	....	....	....	....	....
1992-93	**Pittsburgh**	**NHL**	**78**	**4**	**9**	**13**	**10**	**0**	**1**	**1**	**78**	**5.1**	**-8**	....	....	....	....	....	**4**	**0**	**0**	**0**	**0**	**0**	**0**	**0**

			Regular Season																Playoffs							
Season	Club	League	GP	G	A	Pts	PIM	PP	SH	GW	S	%	+/-	TF	F%	H	SB	Min	GP	G	A	Pts	PIM	PP	SH	GW
1993-94	**Pittsburgh**	**NHL**	**58**	**7**	**4**	**11**	**18**	**3**	**0**	**0**	**59**	**11.9**	**–4**													
	Edmonton	**NHL**	**23**	**5**	**9**	**14**	**28**	**1**	**0**	**0**	**43**	**11.6**	**–1**													
1994-95	**Edmonton**	**NHL**	**46**	**6**	**11**	**17**	**21**	**3**	**0**	**2**	**59**	**10.2**	**–12**													
1995-96	**Winnipeg**	**NHL**	**58**	**10**	**14**	**24**	**37**	**3**	**1**	**0**	**91**	**11.0**	**–4**						**6**	**0**	**0**	**0**	**21**	**0**	**0**	**0**
1996-97	**Phoenix**	**NHL**	**55**	**4**	**11**	**15**	**36**	**2**	**0**	**1**	**74**	**5.4**	**–4**						**7**	**0**	**0**	**0**	**14**	**0**	**0**	**0**
1997-98	**Phoenix**	**NHL**	**64**	**5**	**5**	**10**	**36**	**1**	**1**	**1**	**69**	**7.2**	**–4**						**6**	**0**	**0**	**0**	**2**	**0**	**0**	**0**
1998-99	**Phoenix**	**NHL**	**76**	**9**	**9**	**18**	**34**	**0**	**2**	**2**	**106**	**8.5**	**–6**	**345**	**46.1**	**67**	**40**	**13:40**	**7**	**1**	**0**	**1**	**0**	**0**	**0**	**0**
99-2000	**Atlanta**	**NHL**	**62**	**10**	**12**	**22**	**30**	**4**	**0**	**1**	**146**	**6.8**	**–29**	**717**	**48.0**	**72**	**44**	**17:18**								
2000-01	**NY Islanders**	**NHL**	**34**	**1**	**4**	**5**	**2**	**0**	**0**	**0**	**22**	**4.5**	**–5**	**192**	**45.3**	**32**	**13**	**9:09**								
	Vancouver	**NHL**	**18**	**1**	**2**	**3**	**8**	**1**	**0**	**0**	**9**	**11.1**	**–6**	**104**	**41.4**	**13**	**4**	**9:58**								
	NHL Totals		**697**	**71**	**111**	**182**	**342**	**19**	**5**	**9**	**904**	**7.9**		**1358**	**46.6**	**184**	**101**	**13:42**	**34**	**1**	**0**	**1**	**39**	**0**	**0**	**0**

Signed as a free agent by **Pittsburgh**, September 30, 1992. Claimed on waivers by **Edmonton** from **Pittsburgh**, February 19, 1994. Signed as a free agent by **Winnipeg**, August 18, 1995. Transferred to **Phoenix** after **Winnipeg** franchise relocated, July 1, 1996. Claimed by **Atlanta** from **Phoenix** in Expansion Draft, June 25, 1999. Signed as a free agent by **NY Islanders**, July 3, 2000. Traded to **Vancouver** by **NY Islanders** for Vancouver's 9th round choice (later traded to Washington - Washington selected Robert Muller) in 2001 Entry Draft, December 28, 2000.

STEFAN, Patrik

(SHTEH-fan, PAT-rihk) **ATL.**

Center. Shoots left. 6'3", 205 lbs. Born, Pribram, Czech., September 16, 1980. Atlanta's 1st choice, 1st overall, in 1999 Entry Draft.

Season	Club	League	GP	G	A	Pts	PIM	PP	SH	GW	S	%	+/-	TF	F%	H	SB	Min	GP	G	A	Pts	PIM	PP	SH	GW
1996-97	Sparta Praha	Cze-Rep	5	0	1	1	2												7	1	0	1	0			
1997-98	Sparta Praha	Cze-Rep	27	2	6	8	16																			
	Long Beach	IHL	25	5	10	15	10												10	1	1	2	2			
1998-99	Long Beach	IHL	33	11	24	35	26																			
99-2000	**Atlanta**	**NHL**	**72**	**5**	**20**	**25**	**30**	**1**	**0**	**0**	**117**	**4.3**	**–20**	**988**	**41.4**	**58**	**22**	**14:49**								
2000-01	**Atlanta**	**NHL**	**66**	**10**	**21**	**31**	**22**	**0**	**0**	**1**	**93**	**10.8**	**–3**	**834**	**42.9**	**32**	**35**	**14:07**								
	NHL Totals		**138**	**15**	**41**	**56**	**52**	**1**	**0**	**1**	**210**	**7.1**		**1822**	**42.1**	**90**	**57**	**14:29**								

STEVENS, Kevin

(STEE-vehns, KEH-vihn) **PIT.**

Left wing. Shoots left. 6'3", 230 lbs. Born, Brockton, MA, April 15, 1965. Los Angeles' 6th choice, 112th overall, in 1983 Entry Draft.

Season	Club	League	GP	G	A	Pts	PIM	PP	SH	GW	S	%	+/-	TF	F%	H	SB	Min	GP	G	A	Pts	PIM	PP	SH	GW
1982-83	Silver Lake	Hi-School	18	24	27	51	....																			
1983-84	Boston College	ECAC	37	6	14	20	36																			
1984-85	Boston College	H-East	40	13	23	36	36																			
1985-86	Boston College	H-East	42	17	27	44	56																			
1986-87	Boston College	H-East	39	35	35	70	54																			
1987-88	United States	Nat-Team	44	22	23	45	52																			
	United States	Olympics	5	1	3	4	2																			
	Pittsburgh	**NHL**	**16**	**5**	**2**	**7**	**8**	**2**	**0**	**0**	**22**	**22.7**	**–6**													
1988-89	**Pittsburgh**	**NHL**	**24**	**12**	**3**	**15**	**19**	**4**	**0**	**3**	**52**	**23.1**	**–8**						**11**	**3**	**7**	**10**	**16**	**0**	**0**	**0**
	Muskegon	IHL	45	24	41	65	113																			
1989-90	**Pittsburgh**	**NHL**	**76**	**29**	**41**	**70**	**171**	**12**	**0**	**1**	**179**	**16.2**	**–13**													
1990-91♦	**Pittsburgh**	**NHL**	**80**	**40**	**46**	**86**	**133**	**18**	**0**	**6**	**253**	**15.8**	**–1**						**24**	***17**	**16**	**33**	**53**	**7**	**0**	**4**
1991-92♦	**Pittsburgh**	**NHL**	**80**	**54**	**69**	**123**	**254**	**19**	**0**	**4**	**325**	**16.6**	**8**						**21**	**13**	**15**	**28**	**28**	**4**	**0**	**3**
1992-93	**Pittsburgh**	**NHL**	**72**	**55**	**56**	**111**	**177**	**26**	**0**	**5**	**326**	**16.9**	**17**						**12**	**5**	**11**	**16**	**22**	**4**	**0**	**0**
1993-94	**Pittsburgh**	**NHL**	**83**	**41**	**47**	**88**	**155**	**21**	**0**	**4**	**284**	**14.4**	**–24**						**6**	**1**	**1**	**2**	**10**	**0**	**0**	**0**
1994-95	**Pittsburgh**	**NHL**	**27**	**15**	**12**	**27**	**51**	**6**	**0**	**4**	**80**	**18.8**	**0**						**12**	**4**	**7**	**11**	**21**	**3**	**0**	**1**
1995-96	**Boston**	**NHL**	**41**	**10**	**13**	**23**	**49**	**3**	**0**	**1**	**101**	**9.9**	**1**													
	Los Angeles	**NHL**	**20**	**3**	**10**	**13**	**22**	**3**	**0**	**0**	**69**	**4.3**	**–11**													
1996-97	**Los Angeles**	**NHL**	**69**	**14**	**20**	**34**	**96**	**4**	**0**	**1**	**175**	**8.0**	**–27**													
1997-98	**NY Rangers**	**NHL**	**80**	**14**	**27**	**41**	**130**	**5**	**0**	**3**	**144**	**9.7**	**–7**													
1998-99	**NY Rangers**	**NHL**	**81**	**23**	**20**	**43**	**64**	**8**	**0**	**3**	**136**	**16.9**	**–10**	**11**	**45.5**	**176**	**27**	**15:12**								
99-2000	**NY Rangers**	**NHL**	**38**	**3**	**5**	**8**	**43**	**1**	**0**	**0**	**44**	**6.8**	**–7**	**11**	**54.6**	**78**	**20**	**12:29**								
2000-01	**Philadelphia**	**NHL**	**23**	**2**	**7**	**9**	**18**	**0**	**0**	**0**	**31**	**6.5**	**–2**	**0**	**0.0**	**45**	**5**	**12:43**								
	Pittsburgh	**NHL**	**32**	**8**	**15**	**23**	**55**	**2**	**0**	**0**	**76**	**10.5**	**–4**	**5**	**20.0**	**73**	**5**	**18:15**	**17**	**3**	**3**	**6**	**20**	**2**	**0**	**1**
	NHL Totals		**842**	**328**	**393**	**721**	**1445**	**134**	**0**	**35**	**2297**	**14.3**		**27**	**44.4**	**372**	**57**	**14:51**	**103**	**46**	**60**	**106**	**170**	**20**	**0**	**9**

Hockey East First All-Star Team (1987) • NCAA East Second All-American Team (1987) • NHL Second All-Star Team (1991, 1993) • NHL First All-Star Team (1992) • Played in NHL All-Star Game (1991, 1992, 1993)

Rights traded to **Pittsburgh** by **LA Kings** for Anders Hakansson, September 9, 1983. Traded to **Boston** by **Pittsburgh** with Shawn McEachern for Glen Murray, Bryan Smolinski and Boston's 3rd round choice (Boyd Kane) in 1996 Entry Draft, August 2, 1995. Traded to **LA Kings** by **Boston** for Rick Tocchet, January 25, 1996. Traded to **NY Rangers** by **LA Kings** for Luc Robitaille, August 28, 1997. • Missed majority of 1999-2000 season after entering NHL/NHLPA substance abuse program, January 23, 2000. Signed as a free agent by **Philadelphia**, July 7, 2000. Traded to **Pittsburgh** by **Philadelphia** for John Slaney, January 14, 2001.

STEVENS, Scott

(STEE-vehns, SKAWT) **N.J.**

Defense. Shoots left. 6'2", 215 lbs. Born, Kitchener, Ont., April 1, 1964. Washington's 1st choice, 5th overall, in 1982 Entry Draft.

Season	Club	League	GP	G	A	Pts	PIM	PP	SH	GW	S	%	+/-	TF	F%	H	SB	Min	GP	G	A	Pts	PIM	PP	SH	GW
1980-81	Kitchener	OHA-B	39	7	33	40	82																			
	Kitchener	OMJHL	1	0	0	0	0																			
1981-82	Kitchener	OHL	68	6	36	42	158												15	1	10	11	71			
1982-83	**Washington**	**NHL**	**77**	**9**	**16**	**25**	**195**	**0**	**0**	**0**	**121**	**7.4**	**14**						**4**	**1**	**0**	**1**	**26**	**0**	**0**	**0**
1983-84	**Washington**	**NHL**	**78**	**13**	**32**	**45**	**201**	**7**	**0**	**2**	**155**	**8.4**	**26**						**8**	**1**	**8**	**9**	**21**	**1**	**0**	**0**
1984-85	**Washington**	**NHL**	**80**	**21**	**44**	**65**	**221**	**16**	**0**	**5**	**170**	**12.4**	**19**						**5**	**0**	**1**	**1**	**20**	**0**	**0**	**0**
1985-86	**Washington**	**NHL**	**73**	**15**	**38**	**53**	**165**	**3**	**0**	**2**	**121**	**12.4**	**0**						**9**	**3**	**8**	**11**	**12**	**2**	**0**	**2**
1986-87	**Washington**	**NHL**	**77**	**10**	**51**	**61**	**283**	**2**	**0**	**0**	**165**	**6.1**	**13**						**7**	**0**	**5**	**5**	**19**	**0**	**0**	**0**
1987-88	**Washington**	**NHL**	**80**	**12**	**60**	**72**	**184**	**5**	**1**	**2**	**231**	**5.2**	**14**						**13**	**1**	**11**	**12**	**46**	**0**	**0**	**0**
1988-89	**Washington**	**NHL**	**80**	**7**	**61**	**68**	**225**	**6**	**0**	**3**	**195**	**3.6**	**1**						**6**	**1**	**4**	**5**	**11**	**0**	**0**	**0**
1989-90	**Washington**	**NHL**	**56**	**11**	**29**	**40**	**154**	**7**	**0**	**0**	**143**	**7.7**	**1**						**15**	**2**	**7**	**9**	**25**	**1**	**0**	**0**
1990-91	**St. Louis**	**NHL**	**78**	**5**	**44**	**49**	**150**	**1**	**0**	**1**	**160**	**3.1**	**23**						**13**	**0**	**3**	**3**	**36**	**0**	**0**	**0**
1991-92	**New Jersey**	**NHL**	**68**	**17**	**42**	**59**	**124**	**7**	**1**	**2**	**156**	**10.9**	**24**						**7**	**2**	**1**	**3**	**29**	**2**	**0**	**1**
1992-93	**New Jersey**	**NHL**	**81**	**12**	**45**	**57**	**120**	**8**	**0**	**1**	**146**	**8.2**	**14**						**5**	**2**	**2**	**4**	**10**	**1**	**0**	**0**
1993-94	**New Jersey**	**NHL**	**83**	**18**	**60**	**78**	**112**	**5**	**1**	**4**	**215**	**8.4**	**53**						**20**	**2**	**9**	**11**	**42**	**2**	**0**	**1**
1994-95♦	**New Jersey**	**NHL**	**48**	**2**	**20**	**22**	**56**	**1**	**0**	**1**	**111**	**1.8**	**4**						**20**	**1**	**7**	**8**	**24**	**0**	**0**	**1**
1995-96	**New Jersey**	**NHL**	**82**	**5**	**23**	**28**	**100**	**2**	**1**	**1**	**174**	**2.9**	**7**													
1996-97	**New Jersey**	**NHL**	**79**	**5**	**19**	**24**	**70**	**0**	**0**	**1**	**166**	**3.0**	**26**						**10**	**0**	**4**	**4**	**2**	**0**	**0**	**0**
1997-98	**New Jersey**	**NHL**	**80**	**4**	**22**	**26**	**80**	**1**	**0**	**1**	**94**	**4.3**	**19**						**6**	**1**	**0**	**1**	**8**	**0**	**0**	**0**
	Canada	Olympics	6	0	0	0	2																			
1998-99	**New Jersey**	**NHL**	**75**	**5**	**22**	**27**	**64**	**0**	**0**	**1**	**111**	**4.5**	**29**	**1**	**0.0**	**187**	**149**	**24:11**	**7**	**2**	**1**	**3**	**10**	**2**	**0**	**0**
99-2000♦	**New Jersey**	**NHL**	**78**	**8**	**21**	**29**	**103**	**0**	**1**	**1**	**133**	**6.0**	**30**	**0**	**0.0**	**169**	**130**	**23:23**	**23**	**3**	**8**	**11**	**6**	**0**	**0**	**2**
2000-01	**New Jersey**	**NHL**	**81**	**9**	**22**	**31**	**71**	**3**	**0**	**2**	**171**	**5.3**	**40**	**0**	**0.0**	**175**	**142**	**24:37**	**25**	**1**	**7**	**8**	**37**	**0**	**0**	**0**
	NHL Totals		**1434**	**188**	**671**	**859**	**2678**	**74**	**5**	**30**	**2938**	**6.4**		**1**	**0.0**	**531**	**421**	**24:04**	**203**	**23**	**86**	**109**	**384**	**11**	**0**	**7**

NHL All-Rookie Team (1983) • NHL First All-Star Team (1988, 1994) • NHL Second All-Star Team (1992, 1997, 2001) • Won Alka-Seltzer Plus Award (1994) • Won Conn Smythe Trophy (2000) • Played in NHL All-Star Game (1985, 1989, 1991, 1992, 1993, 1994, 1996, 1997, 1998, 1999, 2000, 2001)

Signed as a free agent by **St. Louis**, July 16, 1990. Transferred to **New Jersey** from **St. Louis** as compensation for St. Louis' signing of free agent Brendan Shanahan, September 3, 1991.

STEVENSON, Jeremy

(STEE-vehn-sohn, JAIR-eh-mee) **NSH.**

Left wing. Shoots left. 6'2", 218 lbs. Born, San Bernardino, CA, July 28, 1974. Anaheim's 10th choice, 262nd overall, in 1994 Entry Draft.

Season	Club	League	GP	G	A	Pts	PIM	PP	SH	GW	S	%	+/-	TF	F%	H	SB	Min	GP	G	A	Pts	PIM	PP	SH	GW
1989-90	Elliot Lake Vikings	NOHA	61	39	26	65	203																			
1990-91	Cornwall Royals	OHL	58	13	20	33	124																			
1991-92	Cornwall Royals	OHL	63	15	23	38	176												6	3	1	4	4			
1992-93	Newmarket Royals	OHL	54	28	28	56	144												5	5	1	6	28			
1993-94	Newmarket Royals	OHL	9	2	4	6	27																			
	Sault Ste. Marie	OHL	48	18	19	37	183												14	1	1	2	23			
1994-95	Greensboro	ECHL	43	14	13	27	231												17	6	11	17	64			
1995-96	**Anaheim**	**NHL**	**3**	**0**	**1**	**1**	**12**	**0**	**0**	**0**	**1**	**0.0**	**1**													
	Baltimore Bandits	AHL	60	11	10	21	295												12	4	2	6	23			
1996-97	**Anaheim**	**NHL**	**5**	**0**	**0**	**0**	**14**	**0**	**0**	**0**	**1**	**0.0**	**–1**													
	Baltimore Bandits	AHL	25	8	8	16	125												3	0	0	0	8			
1997-98	**Anaheim**	**NHL**	**45**	**3**	**5**	**8**	**101**	**0**	**0**	**1**	**43**	**7.0**	**–4**													
	Cincinnati Ducks	AHL	10	5	0	5	34																			
1998-99	Cincinnati Ducks	AHL	22	4	4	8	83												3	1	0	1	2			

Season	Club	League	GP	G	A	Pts	PIM	PP	SH	GW	S	%	+/-	TF	F%	H	SB	Min	GP	G	A	Pts	PIM	PP	SH	GW
			Regular Season																Playoffs							
99-2000	**Anaheim**	**NHL**	**3**	**0**	**0**	**0**	**7**	**0**	**0**	**0**	**2**	**0.0**	**–1**	**0**	**0.0**	**4**	**1**	**6:50**								
	Cincinnati Ducks	AHL	41	11	14	25	100																			
2000-01	**Nashville**	**NHL**	**8**	**1**	**0**	**1**	**39**	**0**	**0**	**0**	**6**	**16.7**	**–1**	**0**	**0.0**	**8**	**1**	**6:24**								
	Milwaukee	IHL	60	16	13	29	262												5	2	0	2	12			
	NHL Totals		**64**	**4**	**6**	**10**	**173**	**0**	**0**	**1**	**53**	**7.5**		**0**	**0.0**	**12**	**2**	**6:31**								

• Re-entered NHL Entry Draft. Originally Winnipeg's 3rd choice, 60th overall, in 1992 Entry Draft.

Signed as a free agent by **Nashville**, September 25, 2000.

STEVENSON, Turner (STEE-vehn-sohn, TUHR-nuhr) N.J.

Right wing. Shoots right. 6'3", 225 lbs. Born, Prince George, B.C., May 18, 1972. Montreal's 1st choice, 12th overall, in 1990 Entry Draft.

Season	Club	League	GP	G	A	Pts	PIM	PP	SH	GW	S	%	+/-	TF	F%	H	SB	Min	GP	G	A	Pts	PIM	PP	SH	GW
1987-88	Prince George	BCAHA	53	45	46	91	127																			
1988-89	Seattle T-Birds	WHL	69	15	12	27	84																			
1989-90	Seattle T-Birds	WHL	62	29	32	61	276												13	3	2	5	35			
1990-91	Seattle T-Birds	WHL	57	36	27	63	222												6	1	5	6	15			
	Fredericton	AHL																	4	0	0	0	5			
1991-92	Seattle T-Birds	WHL	58	20	32	52	264												15	9	3	12	55			
1992-93	**Montreal**	**NHL**	**1**	**0**	**0**	**0**	**0**	**0**	**0**	**0**	**1**	**0.0**	**–1**													
	Fredericton	AHL	79	25	34	59	102												5	2	3	5	11			
1993-94	**Montreal**	**NHL**	**2**	**0**	**0**	**0**	**2**	**0**	**0**	**0**	**0**	**0.0**	**–2**						**3**	**0**	**2**	**2**	**0**	**0**	**0**	**0**
	Fredericton	AHL	66	19	28	47	155																			
1994-95	Fredericton	AHL	37	12	12	24	109																			
	Montreal	**NHL**	**41**	**6**	**1**	**7**	**86**	**0**	**0**	**1**	**35**	**17.1**	**0**													
1995-96	**Montreal**	**NHL**	**80**	**9**	**16**	**25**	**167**	**0**	**0**	**2**	**101**	**8.9**	**–2**						**6**	**0**	**1**	**1**	**2**	**0**	**0**	**0**
1996-97	**Montreal**	**NHL**	**65**	**8**	**13**	**21**	**97**	**1**	**0**	**0**	**76**	**10.5**	**–14**						**5**	**1**	**1**	**2**	**2**	**0**	**0**	**0**
1997-98	**Montreal**	**NHL**	**63**	**4**	**6**	**10**	**110**	**1**	**0**	**0**	**43**	**9.3**	**–8**						**10**	**3**	**4**	**7**	**12**	**0**	**0**	**0**
1998-99	**Montreal**	**NHL**	**69**	**10**	**17**	**27**	**88**	**0**	**0**	**2**	**102**	**9.8**	**6**	**29**	**37.9**	**142**	**20**	**12:57**								
99-2000	**Montreal**	**NHL**	**64**	**8**	**13**	**21**	**61**	**0**	**0**	**2**	**94**	**8.5**	**–1**	**5**	**20.0**	**160**	**18**	**13:10**								
2000-01	**New Jersey**	**NHL**	**69**	**8**	**18**	**26**	**97**	**2**	**0**	**1**	**92**	**8.7**	**11**	**0**	**0.0**	**141**	**13**	**11:00**	**23**	**1**	**3**	**4**	**20**	**0**	**0**	**1**
	NHL Totals		**454**	**53**	**84**	**137**	**708**	**4**	**0**	**8**	**544**	**9.7**		**34**	**35.3**	**443**	**51**	**12:21**	**47**	**5**	**11**	**16**	**36**	**0**	**0**	**1**

WHL West First All-Star Team (1992) • Memorial Cup All-Star Team (1992).

Selected by **Columbus** from **Montreal** in Expansion Draft, June 23, 2000. Traded to **New Jersey** by **Columbus** to complete transaction that sent Krzysztof Oliwa (June 12, 2000) and Deron Quint (June 23, 2000) to **Columbus**, June 23, 2000.

STEWART, Cam (STEW-ahrt, KAM) MIN.

Left wing. Shoots right. 5'11", 196 lbs. Born, Kitchener, Ont., September 18, 1971. Boston's 2nd choice, 63rd overall, in 1990 Entry Draft.

Season	Club	League	GP	G	A	Pts	PIM	PP	SH	GW	S	%	+/-	TF	F%	H	SB	Min	GP	G	A	Pts	PIM	PP	SH	GW
1987-88	Woolrich Regents	OMHA	21	25	32	57	65																			
1988-89	Elmira Kings	OJHL-B	43	38	50	88	138																			
1989-90	Elmira Kings	OJHL-B	46	43	95	138	174																			
1990-91	U. of Michigan	CCHA	44	8	24	32	122																			
1991-92	U. of Michigan	CCHA	44	13	15	28	106																			
1992-93	U. of Michigan	CCHA	39	20	39	59	69																			
1993-94	**Boston**	**NHL**	**57**	**3**	**6**	**9**	**66**	**0**	**0**	**1**	**55**	**5.5**	**–6**						**8**	**0**	**3**	**3**	**7**	**0**	**0**	**0**
	Providence Bruins	AHL	14	3	2	5	5																			
1994-95	**Boston**	**NHL**	**5**	**0**	**0**	**0**	**2**	**0**	**0**	**0**	**2**	**0.0**	**0**													
	Providence Bruins	AHL	31	13	11	24	38												9	2	5	7	0			
1995-96	**Boston**	**NHL**	**6**	**0**	**0**	**0**	**0**	**0**	**0**	**0**	**2**	**0.0**	**–2**						**5**	**1**	**0**	**1**	**2**	**0**	**0**	**0**
	Providence Bruins	AHL	54	17	25	42	39																			
1996-97	**Boston**	**NHL**	**15**	**0**	**1**	**1**	**4**	**0**	**0**	**0**	**21**	**0.0**	**–2**													
	Providence Bruins	AHL	18	4	3	7	37																			
	Cincinnati	IHL	7	3	2	5	8												1	0	0	0	0			
1997-98	Houston Aeros	IHL	63	18	27	45	51												4	0	1	1	18			
1998-99	Houston Aeros	IHL	61	36	26	62	75												19	10	5	15	26			
99-2000	**Florida**	**NHL**	**65**	**9**	**7**	**16**	**30**	**0**	**0**	**3**	**52**	**17.3**	**–2**	**13**	**7.7**	**78**	**11**	**9:04**								
2000-01	**Minnesota**	**NHL**	**54**	**4**	**9**	**13**	**18**	**0**	**1**	**0**	**61**	**6.6**	**–3**	**9**	**22.2**	**105**	**14**	**13:12**								
	NHL Totals		**202**	**16**	**23**	**39**	**120**	**0**	**1**	**4**	**193**	**8.3**		**22**	**13.6**	**183**	**25**	**10:57**	**13**	**1**	**3**	**4**	**9**	**0**	**0**	**0**

Signed as a free agent by **Florida**, July 21, 1999. Selected by **Minnesota** from **Florida** in Expansion Draft, June 23, 2000.

STILLMAN, Cory (STIHL-mahn, KOHR-ee) ST.L.

Center. Shoots left. 6', 194 lbs. Born, Peterborough, Ont., December 20, 1973. Calgary's 1st choice, 6th overall, in 1992 Entry Draft.

Season	Club	League	GP	G	A	Pts	PIM	PP	SH	GW	S	%	+/-	TF	F%	H	SB	Min	GP	G	A	Pts	PIM	PP	SH	GW
1989-90	Peterborough	OPJHL	41	30	*54	84	76																			
1990-91	Windsor Spitfires	OHL	64	31	70	101	31												11	3	6	9	8			
1991-92	Windsor Spitfires	OHL	53	29	61	90	59												7	2	4	6	8			
1992-93	Peterborough	OHL	61	25	55	80	55												18	3	8	11	18			
1993-94	Saint John Flames	AHL	79	35	48	83	52												7	2	4	6	16			
1994-95	Saint John Flames	AHL	63	28	53	81	70												5	0	2	2	2			
	Calgary	**NHL**	**10**	**0**	**2**	**2**	**2**	**0**	**0**	**0**	**7**	**0.0**	**1**													
1995-96	**Calgary**	**NHL**	**74**	**16**	**19**	**35**	**41**	**4**	**1**	**3**	**132**	**12.1**	**–5**						**2**	**1**	**1**	**2**	**0**	**0**	**0**	**0**
1996-97	**Calgary**	**NHL**	**58**	**6**	**20**	**26**	**14**	**2**	**0**	**0**	**112**	**5.4**	**–6**													
1997-98	**Calgary**	**NHL**	**72**	**27**	**22**	**49**	**40**	**9**	**4**	**1**	**178**	**15.2**	**–9**													
1998-99	**Calgary**	**NHL**	**76**	**27**	**30**	**57**	**38**	**9**	**3**	**5**	**175**	**15.4**	**7**	**535**	**46.5**	**128**	**33**	**16:19**								
99-2000	**Calgary**	**NHL**	**37**	**12**	**9**	**21**	**12**	**6**	**0**	**3**	**59**	**20.3**	**–9**	**283**	**54.4**	**39**	**27**	**17:45**								
2000-01	**Calgary**	**NHL**	**66**	**21**	**24**	**45**	**45**	**7**	**0**	**4**	**148**	**14.2**	**–6**	**346**	**43.9**	**62**	**35**	**18:50**								
	St. Louis	**NHL**	**12**	**3**	**4**	**7**	**6**	**3**	**0**	**0**	**26**	**11.5**	**–2**	**36**	**61.1**	**16**	**2**	**18:37**	**15**	**3**	**5**	**8**	**8**	**1**	**0**	**1**
	NHL Totals		**405**	**112**	**130**	**242**	**198**	**40**	**8**	**16**	**837**	**13.4**		**1200**	**48.1**	**245**	**97**	**17:37**	**17**	**4**	**6**	**10**	**8**	**1**	**0**	**1**

• Missed majority of 1999-2000 season recovering from shoulder injury suffered in game vs. Philadelphia, December 27, 1999. Traded to **St. Louis by Calgary** for Craig Conroy and St. Louis' 7th round choice (David Moss) in 2001 Entry Draft, March 13, 2001.

ST-LOUIS, Martin (sehn-loo-EE, mahr-TEHN) T.B.

Right wing. Shoots left. 5'9", 185 lbs. Born, Laval, Que., June 18, 1975.

Season	Club	League	GP	G	A	Pts	PIM	PP	SH	GW	S	%	+/-	TF	F%	H	SB	Min	GP	G	A	Pts	PIM	PP	SH	GW
1991-92	Laval-Laurentides	QAAA	42	29	*74	*103	38												12	7	15	22	16			
1992-93	Hawkesbury	OCJHL	31	37	50	87	70																			
1993-94	U. of Vermont	ECAC	33	15	36	51	24																			
1994-95	U. of Vermont	ECAC	35	23	48	71	36																			
1995-96	U. of Vermont	ECAC	35	29	56	85	38																			
1996-97	U. of Vermont	ECAC	36	24	*36	60	65																			
1997-98	Cleveland	IHL	56	16	34	50	24																			
	Saint John Flames	AHL	25	15	11	26	20												20	5	15	20	16			
1998-99	**Calgary**	**NHL**	**13**	**1**	**1**	**2**	**10**	**0**	**0**	**0**	**14**	**7.1**	**–2**	**0**	**0.0**	**8**	**4**	**8:15**								
	Saint John Flames	AHL	53	28	34	62	30												7	4	4	8	2			
99-2000	**Calgary**	**NHL**	**56**	**3**	**15**	**18**	**22**	**0**	**0**	**1**	**73**	**4.1**	**–5**	**3**	**0.0**	**47**	**45**	**14:41**								
	Saint John Flames	AHL	17	15	11	26	14																			
2000-01	**Tampa Bay**	**NHL**	**78**	**18**	**22**	**40**	**12**	**3**	**3**	**4**	**141**	**12.8**	**–4**	**48**	**41.7**	**45**	**53**	**15:14**								
	NHL Totals		**147**	**22**	**38**	**60**	**44**	**3**	**3**	**5**	**228**	**9.6**		**51**	**39.2**	**100**	**102**	**14:25**								

ECAC First All-Star Team (1995, 1996, 1997) • NCAA East First All-American Team (1995, 1996, 1997) • NCAA Championship All-Tournament Team (1996)

Signed as a free agent by **Calgary**, February 19, 1998. Signed as a free agent by **Tampa Bay**, July 31, 2000.

STOCK, P.J.

(STAWK, PEE-JAY)

Left wing. Shoots left. 5'10", 190 lbs. Born, Victoriaville, Que., May 26, 1975.

			Regular Season																Playoffs							
Season	Club	League	GP	G	A	Pts	PIM	PP	SH	GW	S	%	+/-	TF	F%	H	SB	Min	GP	G	A	Pts	PIM	PP	SH	GW
1992-93	Pembroke Kings	OCJHL	55	10	38	48	189	....	....	....	....	....	....	....	....	....	....	....	....	....	....	....	....	....	....	....
1993-94	Pembroke Kings	OCJHL	52	25	48	73	262	....	....	....	....	....	....	....	....	....	....	....	....	....	....	....	....	....	....	....
1994-95	Victoriaville Tigres	QMJHL	70	9	46	55	386	....	....	....	....	....	....	....	....	....	....	....	4	0	0	0	60	....	....	....
1995-96	Victoriaville Tigres	QMJHL	67	19	43	62	432	....	....	....	....	....	....	....	....	....	....	....	12	5	4	9	79	....	....	....
1996-97	St. FX University	AUAA	27	11	20	31	110	....	....	....	....	....	....	....	....	....	....	....	3	0	4	4	14	....	....	....
1997-98	Hartford	AHL	41	8	8	16	202	....	....	....	....	....	....	....	....	....	....	....	11	1	3	4	79	....	....	....
	NY Rangers	**NHL**	**38**	**2**	**3**	**5**	**114**	**0**	**0**	**1**	**9**	**22.2**	**4**	....	....	....	....	....	....	....	....	....	....	....	....	....
1998-99	**NY Rangers**	**NHL**	**5**	**0**	**0**	**0**	**6**	**0**	**0**	**0**	**0**	**0.0**	**–1**	**8**	**50.0**	**8**	**0**	**2:42**	....	....	....	....	....	....	....	....
	Hartford	AHL	55	4	14	18	250	....	....	....	....	....	....	....	....	....	....	....	6	0	1	1	35	....	....	....
99-2000	**NY Rangers**	**NHL**	**11**	**0**	**1**	**1**	**11**	**0**	**0**	**0**	**2**	**0.0**	**1**	**63**	**31.8**	**14**	**1**	**6:13**	....	....	....	....	....	....	....	....
	Hartford	AHL	64	13	23	36	290	....	....	....	....	....	....	....	....	....	....	....	23	1	11	12	69	....	....	....
2000-01	**Montreal**	**NHL**	**20**	**1**	**2**	**3**	**32**	**0**	**0**	**0**	**9**	**11.1**	**–1**	**83**	**53.0**	**19**	**4**	**5:31**	....	....	....	....	....	....	....	....
	Philadelphia	**NHL**	**31**	**1**	**3**	**4**	**78**	**0**	**0**	**0**	**18**	**5.6**	**–2**	**12**	**50.0**	**37**	**0**	**7:48**	**2**	**0**	**0**	**0**	**0**	**0**	**0**	**0**
	Philadelphia	AHL	9	1	2	3	37	....	....	....	....	....	....	....	....	....	....	....	....	....	....	....	....	....	....	....
	NHL Totals		**105**	**4**	**9**	**13**	**241**	**0**	**0**	**1**	**38**	**10.5**		**166**	**44.6**	**78**	**5**	**6:29**	**2**	**0**	**0**	**0**	**0**	**0**	**0**	**0**

Signed as a free agent by **NY Rangers**, November 18, 1997. Signed as a free agent by **Montreal**, July 7, 2000. Traded to **Philadelphia** by **Montreal** with Montreal's 6th round choice (Dennis Seidenberg) in 2001 Entry Draft for Gino Odjick, December 7, 2000.

STRAKA, Martin

(STRAH-kuh, MAHR-tihn) **PIT.**

Center. Shoots left. 5'9", 176 lbs. Born, Plzen, Czech., September 3, 1972. Pittsburgh's 1st choice, 19th overall, in 1992 Entry Draft.

Season	Club	League	GP	G	A	Pts	PIM	PP	SH	GW	S	%	+/-	TF	F%	H	SB	Min	GP	G	A	Pts	PIM	PP	SH	GW
1989-90	Skoda Plzen	Czech.	1	0	3	3	....	....	....	....	....	....	....	....	....	....	....	....	....	....	....	....	....	....	....	....
1990-91	Skoda Plzen	Czech.	47	7	24	31	6	....	....	....	....	....	....	....	....	....	....	....	....	....	....	....	....	....	....	....
1991-92	Skoda Plzen	Czech.	50	27	28	55	20	....	....	....	....	....	....	....	....	....	....	....	....	....	....	....	....	....	....	....
1992-93	**Pittsburgh**	**NHL**	**42**	**3**	**13**	**16**	**29**	**0**	**0**	**1**	**28**	**10.7**	**2**	....	....	....	....	....	**11**	**2**	**1**	**3**	**2**	**0**	**0**	**0**
	Cleveland	IHL	4	4	3	7	0	....	....	....	....	....	....	....	....	....	....	....	....	....	....	....	....	....	....	....
1993-94	**Pittsburgh**	**NHL**	**84**	**30**	**34**	**64**	**24**	**2**	**0**	**6**	**130**	**23.1**	**24**	....	....	....	....	....	**6**	**1**	**0**	**1**	**2**	**0**	**0**	**0**
1994-95	ZKZ Plzen	Cze-Rep	19	10	11	21	18	....	....	....	....	....	....	....	....	....	....	....	....	....	....	....	....	....	....	....
	Pittsburgh	**NHL**	**31**	**4**	**12**	**16**	**16**	**0**	**0**	**0**	**36**	**11.1**	**0**	....	....	....	....	....	....	....	....	....	....	....	....	....
	Ottawa	**NHL**	**6**	**1**	**1**	**2**	**0**	**0**	**0**	**0**	**13**	**7.7**	**–1**	....	....	....	....	....	....	....	....	....	....	....	....	....
1995-96	**Ottawa**	**NHL**	**43**	**9**	**16**	**25**	**29**	**5**	**0**	**1**	**63**	**14.3**	**–14**	....	....	....	....	....	....	....	....	....	....	....	....	....
	NY Islanders	**NHL**	**22**	**2**	**10**	**12**	**6**	**0**	**0**	**0**	**18**	**11.1**	**–6**	....	....	....	....	....	....	....	....	....	....	....	....	....
	Florida	**NHL**	**12**	**2**	**4**	**6**	**6**	**1**	**0**	**0**	**17**	**11.8**	**1**	....	....	....	....	....	**13**	**2**	**2**	**4**	**2**	**0**	**0**	**0**
1996-97	**Florida**	**NHL**	**55**	**7**	**22**	**29**	**12**	**2**	**0**	**1**	**94**	**7.4**	**9**	....	....	....	....	....	**4**	**0**	**0**	**0**	**0**	**0**	**0**	**0**
1997-98	**Pittsburgh**	**NHL**	**75**	**19**	**23**	**42**	**28**	**4**	**3**	**4**	**117**	**16.2**	**–1**	....	....	....	....	....	**6**	**2**	**0**	**2**	**2**	**0**	**1**	**0**
	Czech-Republic	Olympics	6	1	2	3	0	....	....	....	....	....	....	....	....	....	....	....	....	....	....	....	....	....	....	....
1998-99	**Pittsburgh**	**NHL**	**80**	**35**	**48**	**83**	**26**	**5**	**4**	**4**	**177**	**19.8**	**12**	**845**	**43.6**	**75**	**59**	**23:35**	**13**	**6**	**9**	**15**	**6**	**1**	**0**	**0**
99-2000	**Pittsburgh**	**NHL**	**71**	**20**	**39**	**59**	**26**	**3**	**1**	**2**	**146**	**13.7**	**24**	**651**	**42.9**	**62**	**35**	**23:58**	**11**	**3**	**9**	**12**	**10**	**1**	**0**	**0**
2000-01	**Pittsburgh**	**NHL**	**82**	**27**	**68**	**95**	**38**	**7**	**1**	**4**	**185**	**14.6**	**19**	**331**	**43.2**	**58**	**39**	**23:01**	**18**	**5**	**8**	**13**	**8**	**3**	**0**	**2**
	NHL Totals		**603**	**159**	**290**	**449**	**240**	**29**	**9**	**23**	**1024**	**15.5**		**1827**	**43.2**	**195**	**133**	**23:30**	**82**	**21**	**29**	**50**	**32**	**5**	**1**	**2**

Played in NHL All-Star Game (1999)

Traded to **Ottawa** by **Pittsburgh** for Troy Murray and Norm Maciver, April 7, 1995. Traded to **NY Islanders** by **Ottawa** with Don Beaupre and Bryan Berard for Damian Rhodes and Wade Redden, January 23, 1996. Claimed on waivers by **Florida** from **NY Islanders**, March 15, 1996. Signed as a free agent by **Pittsburgh**, August 6, 1997.

STRUDWICK, Jason

(STRUHD-wihk, JAY-suhn)

Defense. Shoots left. 6'3", 215 lbs. Born, Edmonton, Alta., July 17, 1975. NY Islanders' 3rd choice, 63rd overall, in 1994 Entry Draft.

Season	Club	League	GP	G	A	Pts	PIM	PP	SH	GW	S	%	+/-	TF	F%	H	SB	Min	GP	G	A	Pts	PIM	PP	SH	GW
1991-92	Edmonton Legion	AAHA	35	3	8	11	67	....	....	....	....	....	....	....	....	....	....	....	....	....	....	....	....	....	....	....
1992-93	Edmonton Pats	AMHL	33	8	20	28	135	....	....	....	....	....	....	....	....	....	....	....	....	....	....	....	....	....	....	....
1993-94	Kamloops Blazers	WHL	61	6	8	14	118	....	....	....	....	....	....	....	....	....	....	....	19	0	4	4	24	....	....	....
1994-95	Kamloops Blazers	WHL	72	3	11	14	183	....	....	....	....	....	....	....	....	....	....	....	21	1	1	2	39	....	....	....
1995-96	**NY Islanders**	**NHL**	**1**	**0**	**0**	**0**	**7**	**0**	**0**	**0**	**0**	**0.0**	**0**	....	....	....	....	....	....	....	....	....	....	....	....	....
	Worcester	AHL	60	2	7	9	119	....	....	....	....	....	....	....	....	....	....	....	4	0	1	1	0	....	....	....
1996-97	Kentucky	AHL	80	1	9	10	198	....	....	....	....	....	....	....	....	....	....	....	4	0	0	0	0	....	....	....
1997-98	**NY Islanders**	**NHL**	**17**	**0**	**1**	**1**	**36**	**0**	**0**	**0**	**3**	**0.0**	**1**	....	....	....	....	....	....	....	....	....	....	....	....	....
	Kentucky	AHL	39	3	1	4	87	....	....	....	....	....	....	....	....	....	....	....	....	....	....	....	....	....	....	....
	Vancouver	**NHL**	**11**	**0**	**1**	**1**	**29**	**0**	**0**	**0**	**5**	**0.0**	**–3**	....	....	....	....	....	....	....	....	....	....	....	....	....
	Syracuse Crunch	AHL	....	....	....	....	....	....	....	....	....	....	....	....	....	....	....	....	3	0	0	0	6	....	....	....
1998-99	**Vancouver**	**NHL**	**65**	**0**	**3**	**3**	**114**	**0**	**0**	**0**	**25**	**0.0**	**–19**	**0**	**0.0**	**62**	**52**	**12:49**	....	....	....	....	....	....	....	....
99-2000	**Vancouver**	**NHL**	**63**	**1**	**3**	**4**	**64**	**0**	**0**	**0**	**18**	**5.6**	**–13**	**0**	**0.0**	**105**	**87**	**15:12**	....	....	....	....	....	....	....	....
2000-01	**Vancouver**	**NHL**	**60**	**1**	**4**	**5**	**64**	**0**	**0**	**1**	**21**	**4.8**	**16**	**0**	**0.0**	**90**	**43**	**9:59**	**2**	**0**	**0**	**0**	**0**	**0**	**0**	**0**
	NHL Totals		**217**	**2**	**12**	**14**	**314**	**0**	**0**	**1**	**72**	**2.8**		**0**	**0.0**	**257**	**182**	**12:43**	**2**	**0**	**0**	**0**	**0**	**0**	**0**	**0**

Traded to **Vancouver** by **NY Islanders** for Gino Odjick, March 23, 1998.

STUART, Brad

(STEW-ahrt, BRAD) **S.J.**

Defense. Shoots left. 6'2", 215 lbs. Born, Rocky Mountain House, Alta., November 6, 1979. San Jose's 1st choice, 3rd overall, in 1998 Entry Draft.

Season	Club	League	GP	G	A	Pts	PIM	PP	SH	GW	S	%	+/-	TF	F%	H	SB	Min	GP	G	A	Pts	PIM	PP	SH	GW
1995-96	Red Deer Chiefs	AMHL	35	12	25	37	83	....	....	....	....	....	....	....	....	....	....	....	....	....	....	....	....	....	....	....
	Regina Pats	WHL	3	0	0	0	0	....	....	....	....	....	....	....	....	....	....	....	....	....	....	....	....	....	....	....
1996-97	Regina Pats	WHL	57	7	36	43	58	....	....	....	....	....	....	....	....	....	....	....	5	0	4	4	14	....	....	....
1997-98	Regina Pats	WHL	72	20	45	65	82	....	....	....	....	....	....	....	....	....	....	....	9	3	4	7	10	....	....	....
1998-99	Regina Pats	WHL	29	10	19	29	43	....	....	....	....	....	....	....	....	....	....	....	....	....	....	....	....	....	....	....
	Calgary Hitmen	WHL	30	11	22	33	26	....	....	....	....	....	....	....	....	....	....	....	21	8	15	23	59	....	....	....
99-2000	**San Jose**	**NHL**	**82**	**10**	**26**	**36**	**32**	**5**	**1**	**3**	**133**	**7.5**	**3**	**0**	**0.0**	**123**	**57**	**20:24**	**12**	**1**	**0**	**1**	**6**	**1**	**0**	**0**
2000-01	**San Jose**	**NHL**	**77**	**5**	**18**	**23**	**56**	**1**	**0**	**2**	**119**	**4.2**	**10**	**0**	**0.0**	**160**	**70**	**20:06**	**5**	**1**	**0**	**1**	**0**	**0**	**0**	**0**
	NHL Totals		**159**	**15**	**44**	**59**	**88**	**6**	**1**	**5**	**252**	**6.0**		**0**	**0.0**	**283**	**127**	**20:15**	**17**	**2**	**0**	**2**	**6**	**1**	**0**	**0**

WHL East Second All-Star Team (1998) • WHL East First All-Star Team (1999) • Canadian Major Junior First All-Star Team (1999) • Canadian Major Junior Defenseman of the Year (1999) • NHL All-Rookie Team (2000)

STUMPEL, Jozef

(STUM-puhl, JOH-zehf) **L.A.**

Center. Shoots right. 6'3", 225 lbs. Born, Nitra, Czech., July 20, 1972. Boston's 2nd choice, 40th overall, in 1991 Entry Draft.

Season	Club	League	GP	G	A	Pts	PIM	PP	SH	GW	S	%	+/-	TF	F%	H	SB	Min	GP	G	A	Pts	PIM	PP	SH	GW
1989-90	AC Nitra	Czech-2	38	12	11	23	....	....	....	....	....	....	....	....	....	....	....	....	....	....	....	....	....	....	....	....
1990-91	AC Nitra	Czech.	49	23	22	45	14	....	....	....	....	....	....	....	....	....	....	....	....	....	....	....	....	....	....	....
1991-92	Kolner EC	DEL	33	19	18	37	35	....	....	....	....	....	....	....	....	....	....	....	4	1	1	2	0	....	....	....
	Boston	**NHL**	**4**	**1**	**0**	**1**	**0**	**0**	**0**	**0**	**3**	**33.3**	**1**	....	....	....	....	....	....	....	....	....	....	....	....	....
1992-93	**Boston**	**NHL**	**13**	**1**	**3**	**4**	**4**	**0**	**0**	**0**	**8**	**12.5**	**–3**	....	....	....	....	....	....	....	....	....	....	....	....	....
	Providence Bruins	AHL	56	31	61	92	26	....	....	....	....	....	....	....	....	....	....	....	6	4	4	8	0	....	....	....
1993-94	**Boston**	**NHL**	**59**	**8**	**15**	**23**	**14**	**0**	**0**	**1**	**62**	**12.9**	**4**	....	....	....	....	....	**13**	**1**	**7**	**8**	**4**	**0**	**0**	**0**
	Providence Bruins	AHL	17	5	12	17	4	....	....	....	....	....	....	....	....	....	....	....	....	....	....	....	....	....	....	....
1994-95	Kolner Haie	DEL	25	16	23	39	18	....	....	....	....	....	....	....	....	....	....	....	....	....	....	....	....	....	....	....
	Boston	**NHL**	**44**	**5**	**13**	**18**	**8**	**1**	**0**	**2**	**46**	**10.9**	**4**	....	....	....	....	....	**5**	**0**	**0**	**0**	**0**	**0**	**0**	**0**
1995-96	**Boston**	**NHL**	**76**	**18**	**36**	**54**	**14**	**5**	**0**	**2**	**158**	**11.4**	**–8**	....	....	....	....	....	**5**	**1**	**2**	**3**	**0**	**0**	**0**	**0**
1996-97	**Boston**	**NHL**	**78**	**21**	**55**	**76**	**14**	**6**	**0**	**1**	**168**	**12.5**	**–22**	....	....	....	....	....	....	....	....	....	....	....	....	....
1997-98	**Los Angeles**	**NHL**	**77**	**21**	**58**	**79**	**53**	**4**	**0**	**2**	**162**	**13.0**	**17**	....	....	....	....	....	**4**	**1**	**2**	**3**	**2**	**0**	**0**	**0**
1998-99	**Los Angeles**	**NHL**	**64**	**13**	**21**	**34**	**10**	**1**	**0**	**1**	**131**	**9.9**	**–18**	**1484**	**54.0**	**67**	**30**	**19:44**	....	....	....	....	....	....	....	....
99-2000	**Los Angeles**	**NHL**	**57**	**17**	**41**	**58**	**10**	**3**	**0**	**7**	**126**	**13.5**	**23**	**1088**	**50.6**	**77**	**10**	**19:16**	**4**	**0**	**4**	**4**	**8**	**0**	**0**	**0**
2000-01	Slovan Bratislava	Slovakia	9	2	4	6	16	....	....	....	....	....	....	....	....	....	....	....	....	....	....	....	....	....	....	....
	Los Angeles	**NHL**	**63**	**16**	**39**	**55**	**14**	**9**	**0**	**6**	**95**	**16.8**	**20**	**1278**	**52.7**	**70**	**21**	**19:35**	**13**	**3**	**5**	**8**	**10**	**2**	**0**	**1**
	NHL Totals		**535**	**121**	**281**	**402**	**141**	**29**	**0**	**22**	**959**	**12.6**		**3850**	**52.6**	**214**	**61**	**19:32**	**44**	**6**	**20**	**26**	**24**	**2**	**0**	**1**

Traded to **LA Kings** by **Boston** with Sandy Moger and Boston's 4th round choice (later traded to New Jersey - New Jersey selected Pierre Dagenais) in 1998 Entry Draft for Dmitri Kristich and Byron Dafoe, August 29, 1997.

STURM, Marco

(STURHM, MAHR-koh) **S.J.**

Center. Shoots left. 6', 195 lbs. Born, Dingolfing, West Germany, September 8, 1978. San Jose's 2nd choice, 21st overall, in 1996 Entry Draft.

			Regular Season																Playoffs							
Season	Club	League	GP	G	A	Pts	PIM	PP	SH	GW	S	%	+/-	TF	F%	H	SB	Min	GP	G	A	Pts	PIM	PP	SH	GW
1995-96	EV Landshut	DEL	47	12	20	32	50	....	....	....	....	....	....	....	....	....	....	....	11	1	3	4	18	....	....	....
1996-97	EV Landshut	DEL	46	16	27	43	40	....	....	....	....	....	....	....	....	....	....	....	7	1	4	5	6	....	....	....
1997-98	**San Jose**	**NHL**	**74**	**10**	**20**	**30**	**40**	**2**	**0**	**3**	**118**	**8.5**	**–2**	....	....	....	....	....	**2**	**0**	**0**	**0**	**0**	**0**	**0**	**0**
	Germany	Olympics	2	0	0	0	0	....	....	....	....	....	....	....	....	....	....	....	....	....	....	....	....	....	....	....
1998-99	**San Jose**	**NHL**	**78**	**16**	**22**	**38**	**52**	**3**	**2**	**3**	**140**	**11.4**	**7**	**576**	**45.0**	**98**	**37**	**15:23**	**6**	**2**	**2**	**4**	**4**	**0**	**0**	**1**
99-2000	**San Jose**	**NHL**	**74**	**12**	**15**	**27**	**22**	**2**	**4**	**3**	**120**	**10.0**	**4**	**183**	**45.4**	**102**	**28**	**14:07**	**12**	**1**	**3**	**4**	**6**	**0**	**0**	**0**
2000-01	**San Jose**	**NHL**	**81**	**14**	**18**	**32**	**28**	**2**	**3**	**5**	**153**	**9.2**	**9**	**517**	**40.2**	**101**	**46**	**16:06**	**6**	**0**	**2**	**2**	**0**	**0**	**0**	**0**
	NHL Totals		**307**	**52**	**75**	**127**	**142**	**9**	**9**	**14**	**531**	**9.8**		**1276**	**43.1**	**301**	**111**	**15:14**	**26**	**3**	**7**	**10**	**10**	**0**	**0**	**1**

Played in NHL All-Star Game (1999)

SUCHY, Radoslav

(soo-KHEE, RAD-oh-slav) **PHX.**

Defense. Shoots left. 6'2", 198 lbs. Born, Kezmarok, Czech., April 7, 1976.

Season	Club	League	GP	G	A	Pts	PIM	PP	SH	GW	S	%	+/-	TF	F%	H	SB	Min	GP	G	A	Pts	PIM	PP	SH	GW
1993-94	SKP Poprad	Slovak-Jr.	30	11	12	23	16	....	....	....	....	....	....	....	....	....	....	....	....	....	....	....	....	....	....	....
	SKP Poprad	Slovakia	3	0	0	0	0	....	....	....	....	....	....	....	....	....	....	....	....	....	....	....	....	....	....	....
1994-95	Sherbrooke	QMJHL	69	12	32	44	30	....	....	....	....	....	....	....	....	....	....	....	7	0	3	3	2	....	....	....
1995-96	Sherbrooke	QMJHL	68	15	53	68	68	....	....	....	....	....	....	....	....	....	....	....	7	0	3	3	2	....	....	....
1996-97	Sherbrooke	QMJHL	32	6	34	40	14	....	....	....	....	....	....	....	....	....	....	....	....	....	....	....	....	....	....	....
	Chicoutimi	QMJHL	28	5	24	29	26	....	....	....	....	....	....	....	....	....	....	....	19	6	15	21	12	....	....	....
1997-98	Las Vegas	IHL	26	1	4	5	10	....	....	....	....	....	....	....	....	....	....	....	....	....	....	....	....	....	....	....
	Springfield	AHL	41	6	15	21	16	....	....	....	....	....	....	....	....	....	....	....	4	0	1	1	2	....	....	....
1998-99	Springfield	AHL	69	4	32	36	10	....	....	....	....	....	....	....	....	....	....	....	3	0	1	1	0	....	....	....
99-2000	**Phoenix**	**NHL**	**60**	**0**	**6**	**6**	**16**	**0**	**0**	**0**	**36**	**0.0**	**2**	**0**	**0.0**	**57**	**55**	**15:09**	**5**	**0**	**1**	**1**	**0**	**0**	**0**	**0**
	Springfield	AHL	2	0	1	1	0	....	....	....	....	....	....	....	....	....	....	....	....	....	....	....	....	....	....	....
2000-01	**Phoenix**	**NHL**	**72**	**0**	**10**	**10**	**22**	**0**	**0**	**0**	**33**	**0.0**	**1**	**0**	**0.0**	**80**	**112**	**17:09**	....	....	....	....	....	....	....	....
	NHL Totals		**132**	**0**	**16**	**16**	**38**	**0**	**0**	**0**	**69**	**0.0**		**0**	**0.0**	**137**	**167**	**16:15**	**5**	**0**	**1**	**1**	**0**	**0**	**0**	**0**

QMJHL Second All-Star Team (1997) • Won George Parsons Trophy (Memorial Cup Tournament Most Sportsmanlike Player) (1997)

Signed as a free agent by **Phoenix**, September 26, 1997.

SULLIVAN, Mike

(SUH-lih-van, MIGHK) **PHX.**

Center. Shoots left. 6'2", 204 lbs. Born, Marshfield, MA, February 27, 1968. NY Rangers' 4th choice, 69th overall, in 1987 Entry Draft.

Season	Club	League	GP	G	A	Pts	PIM	PP	SH	GW	S	%	+/-	TF	F%	H	SB	Min	GP	G	A	Pts	PIM	PP	SH	GW
1985-86	Boston Prep	Hi-School	22	26	33	59	....	....	....	....	....	....	....	....	....	....	....	....	....	....	....	....	....	....	....	....
1986-87	Boston University	H-East	37	13	18	31	18	....	....	....	....	....	....	....	....	....	....	....	....	....	....	....	....	....	....	....
1987-88	Boston University	H-East	30	18	22	40	30	....	....	....	....	....	....	....	....	....	....	....	....	....	....	....	....	....	....	....
1988-89	Boston University	H-East	36	19	17	36	30	....	....	....	....	....	....	....	....	....	....	....	....	....	....	....	....	....	....	....
1989-90	Boston University	H-East	38	11	20	31	26	....	....	....	....	....	....	....	....	....	....	....	....	....	....	....	....	....	....	....
1990-91	San Diego Gulls	IHL	74	12	23	35	27	....	....	....	....	....	....	....	....	....	....	....	....	....	....	....	....	....	....	....
1991-92	**San Jose**	**NHL**	**64**	**8**	**11**	**19**	**15**	**1**	**0**	**1**	**72**	**11.1**	**–18**	....	....	....	....	....	....	....	....	....	....	....	....	....
	Kansas City	IHL	10	2	8	10	8	....	....	....	....	....	....	....	....	....	....	....	....	....	....	....	....	....	....	....
1992-93	**San Jose**	**NHL**	**81**	**6**	**8**	**14**	**30**	**0**	**2**	**0**	**95**	**6.3**	**–42**	....	....	....	....	....	....	....	....	....	....	....	....	....
1993-94	**San Jose**	**NHL**	**26**	**2**	**2**	**4**	**4**	**0**	**2**	**1**	**21**	**9.5**	**–3**	....	....	....	....	....	....	....	....	....	....	....	....	....
	Kansas City	IHL	6	3	3	6	0	....	....	....	....	....	....	....	....	....	....	....	....	....	....	....	....	....	....	....
	Calgary	**NHL**	**19**	**2**	**3**	**5**	**6**	**0**	**2**	**0**	**27**	**7.4**	**2**	....	....	....	....	....	**7**	**1**	**1**	**2**	**8**	**0**	**1**	**0**
	Saint John Flames	AHL	5	2	0	2	4	....	....	....	....	....	....	....	....	....	....	....	....	....	....	....	....	....	....	....
1994-95	**Calgary**	**NHL**	**38**	**4**	**7**	**11**	**14**	**0**	**0**	**2**	**31**	**12.9**	**–2**	....	....	....	....	....	**7**	**3**	**5**	**8**	**2**	**0**	**1**	**1**
1995-96	**Calgary**	**NHL**	**81**	**9**	**12**	**21**	**24**	**0**	**1**	**1**	**106**	**8.5**	**–6**	....	....	....	....	....	**4**	**0**	**0**	**0**	**0**	**0**	**0**	**0**
1996-97	**Calgary**	**NHL**	**67**	**5**	**6**	**11**	**10**	**0**	**3**	**2**	**64**	**7.8**	**–11**	....	....	....	....	....	....	....	....	....	....	....	....	....
1997-98	**Boston**	**NHL**	**77**	**5**	**13**	**18**	**34**	**0**	**0**	**2**	**83**	**6.0**	**–1**	....	....	....	....	....	**6**	**0**	**1**	**1**	**2**	**0**	**0**	**0**
1998-99	**Phoenix**	**NHL**	**63**	**2**	**4**	**6**	**24**	**0**	**1**	**1**	**66**	**3.0**	**–11**	**74**	**50.0**	**52**	**40**	**12:09**	**5**	**0**	**0**	**0**	**2**	**0**	**0**	**0**
99-2000	**Phoenix**	**NHL**	**79**	**5**	**10**	**15**	**10**	**0**	**2**	**1**	**59**	**8.5**	**–4**	**820**	**51.5**	**77**	**37**	**11:36**	**5**	**0**	**1**	**1**	**0**	**0**	**0**	**0**
2000-01	**Phoenix**	**NHL**	**72**	**5**	**4**	**9**	**16**	**0**	**3**	**0**	**59**	**8.5**	**–6**	**797**	**50.3**	**52**	**65**	**12:48**	....	....	....	....	....	....	....	....
	NHL Totals		**667**	**53**	**80**	**133**	**187**	**1**	**16**	**11**	**683**	**7.8**		**1691**	**50.9**	**181**	**142**	**12:10**	**34**	**4**	**8**	**12**	**14**	**0**	**2**	**1**

Rights traded to **Minnesota** by **NY Rangers** with Mark Tinordi, Paul Jerrard, the rights to Bret Barnett and LA Kings' 3rd round choice (previously acquired, Minnesota selected Murray Garbutt) in 1989 Entry Draft for Brian Lawton, Igor Liba and the rights to Eric Bennett, October 11, 1988. Signed as a free agent by **San Jose**, August 9, 1991. Claimed on waivers by **Calgary** from **San Jose**, January 6, 1994. Traded to **Boston** by **Calgary** for Boston's 7th round choice (Radek Duda) in 1998 Entry Draft, June 21, 1997. Claimed by **Nashville** from **Boston** in Expansion Draft, June 26, 1998. Traded to **Phoenix** by **Nashville** for Phoenix's 7th round choice (Kyle Kettles) in 1999 Entry Draft, June 30, 1998.

SULLIVAN, Steve

(SUH-lih-van, STEEV) **CHI.**

Right wing. Shoots right. 5'9", 160 lbs. Born, Timmins, Ont., July 6, 1974. New Jersey's 10th choice, 233rd overall, in 1994 Entry Draft.

Season	Club	League	GP	G	A	Pts	PIM	PP	SH	GW	S	%	+/-	TF	F%	H	SB	Min	GP	G	A	Pts	PIM	PP	SH	GW
1991-92	Timmins Bears	NOJHL	47	66	55	121	141	....	....	....	....	....	....	....	....	....	....	....	....	....	....	....	....	....	....	....
1992-93	Sault Ste. Marie	OHL	62	36	27	63	44	....	....	....	....	....	....	....	....	....	....	....	16	3	8	11	18	....	....	....
1993-94	Sault Ste. Marie	OHL	63	51	62	113	82	....	....	....	....	....	....	....	....	....	....	....	14	9	16	25	22	....	....	....
1994-95	Albany River Rats	AHL	75	31	50	81	124	....	....	....	....	....	....	....	....	....	....	....	14	4	7	11	10	....	....	....
1995-96	**New Jersey**	**NHL**	**16**	**5**	**4**	**9**	**8**	**2**	**0**	**1**	**23**	**21.7**	**3**	....	....	....	....	....	....	....	....	....	....	....	....	....
	Albany River Rats	AHL	53	33	42	75	127	....	....	....	....	....	....	....	....	....	....	....	4	3	0	3	6	....	....	....
1996-97	**New Jersey**	**NHL**	**33**	**8**	**14**	**22**	**14**	**2**	**0**	**2**	**63**	**12.7**	**9**	....	....	....	....	....	....	....	....	....	....	....	....	....
	Albany River Rats	AHL	15	8	7	15	16	....	....	....	....	....	....	....	....	....	....	....	....	....	....	....	....	....	....	....
	Toronto	**NHL**	**21**	**5**	**11**	**16**	**23**	**1**	**0**	**1**	**45**	**11.1**	**5**	....	....	....	....	....	....	....	....	....	....	....	....	....
1997-98	**Toronto**	**NHL**	**63**	**10**	**18**	**28**	**40**	**1**	**0**	**1**	**112**	**8.9**	**–8**	....	....	....	....	....	....	....	....	....	....	....	....	....
1998-99	**Toronto**	**NHL**	**63**	**20**	**20**	**40**	**28**	**4**	**0**	**5**	**110**	**18.2**	**12**	**685**	**44.4**	**26**	**11**	**14:12**	**13**	**3**	**3**	**6**	**14**	**2**	**0**	**0**
99-2000	**Toronto**	**NHL**	**7**	**0**	**1**	**1**	**4**	**0**	**0**	**0**	**11**	**0.0**	**–1**	**47**	**48.9**	**1**	**0**	**11:52**	....	....	....	....	....	....	....	....
	Chicago	**NHL**	**73**	**22**	**42**	**64**	**52**	**2**	**1**	**6**	**169**	**13.0**	**20**	**692**	**48.0**	**39**	**15**	**18:05**	....	....	....	....	....	....	....	....
2000-01	**Chicago**	**NHL**	**81**	**34**	**41**	**75**	**54**	**6**	**8**	**3**	**204**	**16.7**	**3**	**649**	**42.4**	**34**	**22**	**20:32**	....	....	....	....	....	....	....	....
	NHL Totals		**357**	**104**	**151**	**255**	**223**	**18**	**9**	**19**	**737**	**14.1**		**2073**	**45.1**	**100**	**48**	**17:41**	**13**	**3**	**3**	**6**	**14**	**2**	**0**	**0**

AHL First All-Star Team (1996)

Traded to **Toronto** by **New Jersey** with Jason Smith and the rights to Alyn McCauley for Doug Gilmour, Dave Ellett and New Jersey's 3rd round choice (previously acquired, New Jersey selected Andre Lakos) in 1999 Entry Draft, February 25, 1997. Claimed on waivers by **Chicago** from **Toronto**, October 23, 1999.

SUNDIN, Mats

(SUHN-deen, MATS) **TOR.**

Center/Right wing. Shoots right. 6'4", 220 lbs. Born, Bromma, Sweden, February 13, 1971. Quebec's 1st choice, 1st overall, in 1989 Entry Draft.

Season	Club	League	GP	G	A	Pts	PIM	PP	SH	GW	S	%	+/-	TF	F%	H	SB	Min	GP	G	A	Pts	PIM	PP	SH	GW
1988-89	Nacka IK	Sweden-2	25	10	8	18	18	....	....	....	....	....	....	....	....	....	....	....	....	....	....	....	....	....	....	....
1989-90	Djurgardens IF	Sweden	34	10	8	18	16	....	....	....	....	....	....	....	....	....	....	....	8	7	0	7	4	....	....	....
1990-91	**Quebec**	**NHL**	**80**	**23**	**36**	**59**	**58**	**4**	**0**	**0**	**155**	**14.8**	**–24**	....	....	....	....	....	....	....	....	....	....	....	....	....
1991-92	**Quebec**	**NHL**	**80**	**33**	**43**	**76**	**103**	**8**	**2**	**2**	**231**	**14.3**	**–19**	....	....	....	....	....	....	....	....	....	....	....	....	....
1992-93	**Quebec**	**NHL**	**80**	**47**	**67**	**114**	**96**	**13**	**4**	**9**	**215**	**21.9**	**21**	....	....	....	....	....	**6**	**3**	**1**	**4**	**6**	**1**	**0**	**0**
1993-94	**Quebec**	**NHL**	**84**	**32**	**53**	**85**	**60**	**6**	**2**	**4**	**226**	**14.2**	**1**	....	....	....	....	....	....	....	....	....	....	....	....	....
1994-95	Djurgardens IF	Sweden	12	7	2	9	14	....	....	....	....	....	....	....	....	....	....	....	....	....	....	....	....	....	....	....
	Toronto	**NHL**	**47**	**23**	**24**	**47**	**14**	**9**	**0**	**4**	**173**	**13.3**	**–5**	....	....	....	....	....	**7**	**5**	**4**	**9**	**4**	**2**	**0**	**1**
1995-96	**Toronto**	**NHL**	**76**	**33**	**50**	**83**	**46**	**7**	**6**	**7**	**301**	**11.0**	**8**	....	....	....	....	....	**6**	**3**	**1**	**4**	**4**	**2**	**0**	**1**
1996-97	**Toronto**	**NHL**	**82**	**41**	**53**	**94**	**59**	**7**	**4**	**8**	**281**	**14.6**	**6**	....	....	....	....	....	....	....	....	....	....	....	....	....
1997-98	**Toronto**	**NHL**	**82**	**33**	**41**	**74**	**49**	**9**	**1**	**5**	**219**	**15.1**	**–3**	....	....	....	....	....	....	....	....	....	....	....	....	....
	Sweden	Olympics	4	3	0	3	4	....	....	....	....	....	....	....	....	....	....	....	....	....	....	....	....	....	....	....
1998-99	**Toronto**	**NHL**	**82**	**31**	**52**	**83**	**58**	**4**	**0**	**6**	**209**	**14.8**	**22**	**1993**	**57.3**	**54**	**17**	**20:41**	**17**	**8**	**8**	**16**	**16**	**3**	**0**	**2**
99-2000	**Toronto**	**NHL**	**73**	**32**	**41**	**73**	**46**	**10**	**2**	**7**	**184**	**17.4**	**16**	**1619**	**50.8**	**48**	**33**	**20:11**	**12**	**3**	**5**	**8**	**10**	**0**	**0**	**1**
2000-01	**Toronto**	**NHL**	**82**	**28**	**46**	**74**	**76**	**9**	**0**	**6**	**226**	**12.4**	**15**	**1870**	**56.6**	**83**	**33**	**19:21**	**11**	**6**	**7**	**13**	**14**	**2**	**1**	**1**
	NHL Totals		**848**	**356**	**506**	**862**	**665**	**86**	**21**	**58**	**2420**	**14.7**		**5482**	**55.1**	**185**	**83**	**20:04**	**59**	**28**	**26**	**54**	**54**	**10**	**1**	**6**

Played in NHL All-Star Game (1996, 1997, 1998, 1999, 2000, 2001)

Traded to **Toronto** by **Quebec** with Garth Butcher, Todd Warriner and Philadelphia's 1st round choice (previously acquired by Quebec - later traded to Washington - Washington selected Nolan Baumgartner) in 1994 Entry Draft for Wendel Clark, Sylvain Lefebvre, Landon Wilson and Toronto's 1st round choice (Jeffrey Kealty) in 1994 Entry Draft, June 28, 1994.

			Regular Season																Playoffs							
Season	Club	League	GP	G	A	Pts	PIM	PP	SH	GW	S	%	+/-	TF	F%	H	SB	Min	GP	G	A	Pts	PIM	PP	SH	GW

SUNDSTROM, Niklas (SUHN-struhm, NIHK-las) S.J.

Left wing. Shoots left. 6', 190 lbs. Born, Ornskoldsvik, Sweden, June 6, 1975. NY Rangers' 1st choice, 8th overall, in 1993 Entry Draft.

Season	Club	League	GP	G	A	Pts	PIM	PP	SH	GW	S	%	+/-	TF	F%	H	SB	Min	GP	G	A	Pts	PIM	PP	SH	GW
1991-92	MoDo AIK	Sweden	9	1	3	4	0																			
1992-93	MoDo AIK	Swede-Jr.	2	3	1	4	0																			
	MoDo AIK	Sweden	40	7	11	18	18												3	0	0	0	0			
1993-94	MoDo AIK	Swede-Jr.	3	3	4	7	2																			
	MoDo AIK	Sweden	37	7	12	19	28												11	4	3	7	2			
1994-95	MoDo Hockey	Sweden	33	8	13	21	30																			
1995-96	**NY Rangers**	**NHL**	**82**	**9**	**12**	**21**	**14**	**1**	**1**	**2**	**90**	**10.0**	**2**						**11**	**4**	**3**	**7**	**4**	**1**	**0**	**0**
1996-97	**NY Rangers**	**NHL**	**82**	**24**	**28**	**52**	**20**	**5**	**1**	**4**	**132**	**18.2**	**23**						**9**	**0**	**5**	**5**	**2**	**0**	**0**	**0**
1997-98	**NY Rangers**	**NHL**	**70**	**19**	**28**	**47**	**24**	**4**	**0**	**1**	**115**	**16.5**	**0**													
	Sweden	Olympics	4	1	1	2	2																			
1998-99	**NY Rangers**	**NHL**	**81**	**13**	**30**	**43**	**20**	**1**	**2**	**3**	**89**	**14.6**	**-2**	**376**	**40.4**	**118**	**55**	**19:11**								
99-2000	**San Jose**	**NHL**	**79**	**12**	**25**	**37**	**22**	**2**	**1**	**2**	**90**	**13.3**	**9**	**10**	**50.0**	**44**	**12**	**15:10**	**12**	**0**	**2**	**2**	**2**	**0**	**0**	**0**
2000-01	**San Jose**	**NHL**	**82**	**10**	**39**	**49**	**28**	**4**	**1**	**0**	**100**	**10.0**	**10**	**26**	**30.8**	**40**	**16**	**16:44**	**6**	**0**	**3**	**3**	**2**	**0**	**0**	**0**
	NHL Totals		**476**	**87**	**162**	**249**	**128**	**17**	**6**	**12**	**616**	**14.1**		**412**	**40.0**	**202**	**83**	**17:02**	**38**	**4**	**13**	**17**	**10**	**1**	**0**	**0**

Traded to **Tampa Bay** by **NY Rangers** with Dan Cloutier and NY Rangers' 1st (Nikita Alexeev) and 3rd (later traded to San Jose - later traded to Chicago - Chicago selected Igor Radulov) round choices in 2000 Entry Draft for Chicago's 1st round choice (previously acquired, NY Rangers selected Pavel Brendl) in 1999 Entry Draft, June 26, 1999. Traded to **San Jose** by **Tampa Bay** with NY Rangers' 3rd round choice (previously acquired, later traded to Chicago - Chicago selected Igor Radulov) in 2000 Entry Draft for Bill Houlder, Andrei Zyuzin, Shawn Burr and Steve Guolla, August 4, 1999.

SUSHINSKY, Maxim (soo-SHIHN-skee, max-EEM) MIN.

Right wing. Shoots left. 5'8", 165 lbs. Born, St. Petersburg, USSR, July 1, 1974. Minnesota's 4th choice, 132nd overall, in 2000 Entry Draft.

Season	Club	League	GP	G	A	Pts	PIM	PP	SH	GW	S	%	+/-	TF	F%	H	SB	Min	GP	G	A	Pts	PIM	PP	SH	GW
1990-91	SKA Leningrad-2	USSR-3	8	1	0	1	0																			
	SKA Leningrad	USSR	4	0	1	1	0																			
1991-92	St. Petersburg-2	CIS-3	20	14	1	15	38																			
	St. Petersburg	CIS-2	45	5	3	8	16																			
1992-93	St. Petersburg	CIS	23	2	3	5	22												6	2	1	3	2			
1993-94	St. Petersburg	CIS	45	7	4	11	26																			
1994-95	St. Petersburg	CIS	52	11	11	22	57												3	1	0	1	6			
1995-96	St. Petersburg	CIS	49	21	15	36	43												2	0	0	0	0			
1996-97	Avangard Omsk	Russia	39	20	16	36	24												5	3	1	4	0			
1997-98	Avangard Omsk	Russia	20	6	11	17	6																			
1998-99	Avangard Omsk	Russia	41	15	16	31	46												5	3	1	4	10			
99-2000	Avangard Omsk	Russia	37	19	24	43	58												8	2	5	7	6			
2000-01	**Minnesota**	**NHL**	**30**	**7**	**4**	**11**	**29**	**3**	**0**	**0**	**62**	**11.3**	**-7**	**2**	**50.0**	**17**	**2**	**14:01**								
	Avangard Omsk	Russia	12	5	3	8	14												13	*9	4	13	12			
	NHL Totals		**30**	**7**	**4**	**11**	**29**	**3**	**0**	**0**	**62**	**11.3**		**2**	**50.0**	**17**	**2**	**14:01**								

• Released by **Minnesota**, January 7, 2001. Signed as a free agent by **Avangard Omsk** (Russia) with Minnesota retaining NHL rights, January 9, 2001.

SUTER, Gary (SOO-tuhr, GAIR-ee) S.J.

Defense. Shoots left. 6', 215 lbs. Born, Madison, WI, June 24, 1964. Calgary's 9th choice, 180th overall, in 1984 Entry Draft.

Season	Club	League	GP	G	A	Pts	PIM	PP	SH	GW	S	%	+/-	TF	F%	H	SB	Min	GP	G	A	Pts	PIM	PP	SH	GW
1981-82	Dubuque Saints	USHL	18	3	4	7	32																			
1982-83	Dubuque Saints	USHL	41	9	30	39	112																			
1983-84	U. of Wisconsin	WCHA	35	4	18	22	32																			
1984-85	U. of Wisconsin	WCHA	39	12	39	51	110																			
1985-86	**Calgary**	**NHL**	**80**	**18**	**50**	**68**	**141**	**9**	**0**	**4**	**195**	**9.2**	**11**						**10**	**2**	**8**	**10**	**8**	**0**	**0**	**1**
1986-87	**Calgary**	**NHL**	**68**	**9**	**39**	**48**	**70**	**4**	**0**	**0**	**152**	**5.9**	**-10**						**6**	**0**	**3**	**3**	**10**	**0**	**0**	**0**
1987-88	**Calgary**	**NHL**	**75**	**21**	**70**	**91**	**124**	**6**	**1**	**3**	**204**	**10.3**	**39**						**9**	**1**	**9**	**10**	**6**	**0**	**1**	**0**
1988-89♦	**Calgary**	**NHL**	**63**	**13**	**49**	**62**	**78**	**8**	**0**	**1**	**216**	**6.0**	**26**						**5**	**0**	**3**	**3**	**10**	**0**	**0**	**0**
1989-90	**Calgary**	**NHL**	**76**	**16**	**60**	**76**	**97**	**5**	**0**	**1**	**211**	**7.6**	**4**						**6**	**0**	**1**	**1**	**14**	**0**	**0**	**0**
1990-91	**Calgary**	**NHL**	**79**	**12**	**58**	**70**	**102**	**6**	**0**	**1**	**258**	**4.7**	**26**						**7**	**1**	**6**	**7**	**12**	**1**	**0**	**0**
1991-92	**Calgary**	**NHL**	**70**	**12**	**43**	**55**	**128**	**4**	**0**	**0**	**189**	**6.3**	**1**													
1992-93	**Calgary**	**NHL**	**81**	**23**	**58**	**81**	**112**	**10**	**1**	**2**	**263**	**8.7**	**-1**						**6**	**2**	**3**	**5**	**8**	**0**	**1**	**0**
1993-94	**Calgary**	**NHL**	**25**	**4**	**9**	**13**	**20**	**2**	**1**	**0**	**51**	**7.8**	**-3**													
	Chicago	**NHL**	**16**	**2**	**3**	**5**	**18**	**2**	**0**	**0**	**35**	**5.7**	**-9**						**6**	**3**	**2**	**5**	**6**	**2**	**0**	**0**
1994-95	**Chicago**	**NHL**	**48**	**10**	**27**	**37**	**42**	**5**	**0**	**0**	**144**	**6.9**	**14**						**12**	**2**	**5**	**7**	**10**	**1**	**0**	**0**
1995-96	**Chicago**	**NHL**	**82**	**20**	**47**	**67**	**80**	**12**	**2**	**4**	**242**	**8.3**	**3**						**10**	**3**	**3**	**6**	**8**	**2**	**0**	**1**
1996-97	**Chicago**	**NHL**	**82**	**7**	**21**	**28**	**70**	**3**	**0**	**0**	**225**	**3.1**	**-4**						**6**	**1**	**4**	**5**	**8**	**0**	**0**	**0**
1997-98	**Chicago**	**NHL**	**73**	**14**	**28**	**42**	**74**	**5**	**2**	**0**	**199**	**7.0**	**1**													
	United States	Olympics	4	0	0	0	2																			
1998-99	**San Jose**	**NHL**	**1**	**0**	**0**	**0**	**0**	**0**	**0**	**0**	**1**	**0.0**	**0**	**0**	**0.0**	**0**	**0**	**12:56**								
99-2000	**San Jose**	**NHL**	**76**	**6**	**28**	**34**	**52**	**2**	**1**	**0**	**175**	**3.4**	**7**	**0**	**0.0**	**118**	**102**	**23:30**	**12**	**2**	**5**	**7**	**12**	**1**	**0**	**1**
2000-01	**San Jose**	**NHL**	**68**	**10**	**24**	**34**	**84**	**4**	**0**	**1**	**157**	**6.4**	**8**	**2**	**50.0**	**126**	**68**	**21:27**	**1**	**0**	**0**	**0**	**0**	**0**	**0**	**0**
	NHL Totals		**1063**	**197**	**614**	**811**	**1292**	**87**	**8**	**17**	**2917**	**6.8**		**2**	**50.0**	**244**	**170**	**22:28**	**96**	**17**	**52**	**69**	**112**	**7**	**2**	**3**

NHL All-Rookie Team (1986) • Won Calder Memorial Trophy (1986) • NHL Second All-Star Team (1988) • Played in NHL All-Star Game (1986, 1988, 1989, 1991)

Traded to **Hartford** by **Calgary** with Paul Ranheim and Ted Drury for James Patrick, Zarley Zalapski and Michael Nylander, March 10, 1994. Traded to **Chicago** by **Hartford** with Randy Cunneyworth and Hartford's 3rd round choice (later traded to Vancouver - Vancouver selected Larry Courville) in 1995 Entry Draft for Frantisek Kucera and Jocelyn Lemieux, March 11, 1994. Signed as a free agent by **San Jose**, July 1, 1998. • Missed majority of 1998-99 season recovering from tricep muscle injury suffered in game vs. Dallas, October 24, 1998.

SUTTER, Ron (SUH-tuhr, RAWN)

Center. Shoots right. 6', 180 lbs. Born, Viking, Alta., December 2, 1963. Philadelphia's 1st choice, 4th overall, in 1982 Entry Draft.

Season	Club	League	GP	G	A	Pts	PIM	PP	SH	GW	S	%	+/-	TF	F%	H	SB	Min	GP	G	A	Pts	PIM	PP	SH	GW
1979-80	Red Deer Rustlers	AJHL	60	12	33	45	44												13	6	12	18	26			
1980-81	Lethbridge	WHL	72	13	32	45	152												9	2	5	7	29			
1981-82	Lethbridge	WHL	59	38	54	92	207												12	6	5	11	28			
1982-83	Lethbridge	WHL	58	35	48	83	98												20	*22	*19	*41	45			
	Philadelphia	**NHL**	**10**	**1**	**1**	**2**	**9**	**0**	**0**	**1**	**4**	**25.0**	**0**													
1983-84	**Philadelphia**	**NHL**	**79**	**19**	**32**	**51**	**101**	**5**	**3**	**3**	**145**	**13.1**	**4**						**3**	**0**	**0**	**0**	**22**	**0**	**0**	**0**
1984-85	**Philadelphia**	**NHL**	**73**	**16**	**29**	**45**	**94**	**2**	**0**	**5**	**140**	**11.4**	**13**						**19**	**4**	**8**	**12**	**28**	**0**	**0**	**1**
1985-86	**Philadelphia**	**NHL**	**75**	**18**	**42**	**60**	**159**	**0**	**0**	**4**	**145**	**12.4**	**26**						**5**	**0**	**2**	**2**	**10**	**0**	**0**	**0**
1986-87	**Philadelphia**	**NHL**	**39**	**10**	**17**	**27**	**69**	**0**	**0**	**0**	**68**	**14.7**	**10**						**16**	**1**	**7**	**8**	**12**	**0**	**0**	**0**
1987-88	**Philadelphia**	**NHL**	**69**	**8**	**25**	**33**	**146**	**1**	**0**	**0**	**107**	**7.5**	**-9**						**7**	**0**	**1**	**1**	**26**	**0**	**0**	**0**
1988-89	**Philadelphia**	**NHL**	**55**	**26**	**22**	**48**	**80**	**4**	**1**	**2**	**106**	**24.5**	**25**						**19**	**1**	**9**	**10**	**51**	**0**	**0**	**0**
1989-90	**Philadelphia**	**NHL**	**75**	**22**	**26**	**48**	**104**	**0**	**2**	**6**	**157**	**14.0**	**2**													
1990-91	**Philadelphia**	**NHL**	**80**	**17**	**28**	**45**	**92**	**2**	**0**	**1**	**149**	**11.4**	**2**													
1991-92	**St. Louis**	**NHL**	**68**	**19**	**27**	**46**	**91**	**5**	**4**	**1**	**106**	**17.9**	**9**						**6**	**1**	**3**	**4**	**8**	**1**	**0**	**0**
1992-93	**St. Louis**	**NHL**	**59**	**12**	**15**	**27**	**99**	**4**	**0**	**3**	**90**	**13.3**	**-11**													
1993-94	**St. Louis**	**NHL**	**36**	**6**	**12**	**18**	**46**	**1**	**0**	**2**	**42**	**14.3**	**-1**													
	Quebec	**NHL**	**37**	**9**	**13**	**22**	**44**	**4**	**0**	**0**	**66**	**13.6**	**3**													
1994-95	**NY Islanders**	**NHL**	**27**	**1**	**4**	**5**	**21**	**0**	**0**	**1**	**29**	**3.4**	**-8**													
1995-96	Phoenix	IHL	25	6	13	19	28																			
	Boston	**NHL**	**18**	**5**	**7**	**12**	**24**	**0**	**1**	**0**	**34**	**14.7**	**10**						**5**	**0**	**0**	**0**	**8**	**0**	**0**	**0**
1996-97	**San Jose**	**NHL**	**78**	**5**	**7**	**12**	**65**	**1**	**2**	**1**	**78**	**6.4**	**-8**													
1997-98	**San Jose**	**NHL**	**57**	**2**	**7**	**9**	**22**	**0**	**0**	**1**	**57**	**3.5**	**-2**						**6**	**1**	**0**	**1**	**14**	**0**	**0**	**0**
1998-99	**San Jose**	**NHL**	**59**	**3**	**6**	**9**	**40**	**0**	**0**	**1**	**67**	**4.5**	**-8**	**636**	**49.1**	**83**	**18**	**9:54**	**6**	**0**	**0**	**0**	**4**	**0**	**0**	**0**
99-2000	**San Jose**	**NHL**	**78**	**5**	**6**	**11**	**34**	**0**	**1**	**1**	**68**	**7.4**	**-3**	**825**	**54.8**	**94**	**31**	**9:34**	**12**	**0**	**2**	**2**	**10**	**0**	**0**	**0**
2000-01	**Calgary**	**NHL**	**21**	**1**	**3**	**4**	**12**	**0**	**0**	**0**	**16**	**6.3**	**4**	**210**	**53.8**	**17**	**12**	**11:49**								
	NHL Totals		**1093**	**205**	**329**	**534**	**1352**	**29**	**14**	**33**	**1674**	**12.2**		**1671**	**52.5**	**194**	**61**	**9:59**	**104**	**8**	**32**	**40**	**193**	**1**	**0**	**1**

Traded to **St. Louis** by **Philadelphia** with Murray Baron for Dan Quinn and Rod Brind'Amour, September 22, 1991. Traded to **Quebec** by **St. Louis** with Garth Butcher and Bob Bassen for Steve Duchesne and Denis Chasse, January 23, 1994. Traded to **NY Islanders** by **Quebec** with Quebec's 1st round choice (Brett Lindros) in 1994 Entry Draft for Uwe Krupp and NY Islanders' 1st round choice (Wade Belak) in 1994 Entry Draft, June 28, 1994. Signed as a free agent by **Boston**, March 9, 1996. Signed as a free agent by **San Jose**, October 12, 1996. Signed as a free agent by **Calgary**, February 16, 2001.

SUTTON, Andy
(SUH-tohn, AN-dee) **MIN.**

Defense. Shoots left. 6'6", 245 lbs. Born, Edmonton, Alta., March 10, 1975.

			Regular Season																Playoffs							
Season	Club	League	GP	G	A	Pts	PIM	PP	SH	GW	S	%	+/-	TF	F%	H	SB	Min	GP	G	A	Pts	PIM	PP	SH	GW
1991-92	Gananoque	OJHL-B	36	11	9	20													14	9	21	30				
1992-93	Gananoque	OJHL-B	38	14	9	23													12	16	13	29				
1993-94	St. Michael's	MTJHL	48	17	23	40	161												3	0	0	0	20			
1994-95	Michigan Tech	WCHA	19	2	1	3	42																			
1995-96	Michigan Tech	WCHA	33	2	2	4	58																			
1996-97	Michigan Tech	WCHA	32	2	7	9	73																			
1997-98	Michigan Tech	WCHA	38	16	24	40	97																			
	Kentucky	AHL	7	0	0	0	33																			
1998-99	**San Jose**	**NHL**	31	0	3	3	65	0	0	0	24	0.0	–4	0	0.0	50	14	12:58								
	Kentucky	AHL	21	5	10	15	53												5	0	0	0	23			
99-2000	**San Jose**	**NHL**	40	1	1	2	80	0	0	0	29	3.4	–5	0	0.0	93	22	12:57								
	Kentucky	AHL	3	0	1	1	0																			
2000-01	**Minnesota**	**NHL**	69	3	4	7	131	2	0	0	64	4.7	–11	3	33.3	123	49	12:55								
	NHL Totals		140	4	8	12	276	2	0	0	117	3.4		3	33.3	266	85	12:56								

WCHA Second All-Star Team (1998)

Signed as a free agent by **San Jose**, March 20, 1998. Traded to **Minnesota** by **San Jose** with San Jose's 7th round choice (Peter Bartos) in 2000 Entry Draft and 3rd round choice (later traded to Atlanta - later traded to Pittsburgh - later traded to Columbus - Columbus selected Aaron Johnson) in 2001 Entry Draft for Minnesota's 8th round choice (later traded to Calgary - Calgary selected Joe Campbell) in 2001 Entry Draft and future considerations, June 12, 2000.

SUTTON, Ken
(SUH-tohn, KEHN) **NYI**

Defense. Shoots left. 6'1", 205 lbs. Born, Edmonton, Alta., November 5, 1969. Buffalo's 4th choice, 98th overall, in 1989 Entry Draft.

			Regular Season																Playoffs							
Season	Club	League	GP	G	A	Pts	PIM	PP	SH	GW	S	%	+/-	TF	F%	H	SB	Min	GP	G	A	Pts	PIM	PP	SH	GW
1987-88	Calgary Canucks	AJHL	53	13	43	56	228																			
1988-89	Saskatoon Blades	WHL	71	22	31	53	104												8	2	5	7	12			
1989-90	Rochester	AHL	57	5	14	19	83												11	1	6	7	15			
1990-91	**Buffalo**	**NHL**	15	3	6	9	13	2	0	0	26	11.5	2						6	0	1	1	2	0	0	0
	Rochester	AHL	62	7	24	31	65												3	1	1	2	14			
1991-92	**Buffalo**	**NHL**	64	2	18	20	71	0	0	0	81	2.5	5						7	0	2	2	4	0	0	0
1992-93	**Buffalo**	**NHL**	63	8	14	22	30	1	0	2	77	10.4	–3						8	3	1	4	8	0	0	0
1993-94	**Buffalo**	**NHL**	78	4	20	24	71	1	0	0	95	4.2	–6						4	0	0	0	2	0	0	0
1994-95	**Buffalo**	**NHL**	12	1	2	3	30	0	0	1	12	8.3	–2													
	Edmonton	**NHL**	12	3	1	4	12	0	0	0	28	10.7	–1													
1995-96	**Edmonton**	**NHL**	32	0	8	8	39	0	0	0	38	0.0	–12													
	St. Louis	**NHL**	6	0	0	0	4	0	0	0	3	0.0	–1						1	0	0	0	0	0	0	0
	Worcester	AHL	32	4	16	20	60												4	0	2	2	21			
1996-97	Manitoba Moose	IHL	20	3	10	13	48																			
	Albany River Rats	AHL	61	6	13	19	79												16	4	8	12	55			
1997-98	**New Jersey**	**NHL**	13	0	0	0	6	0	0	0	5	0.0	1													
	Albany River Rats	AHL	10	0	7	7	15																			
	San Jose	**NHL**	8	0	0	0	15	0	0	0	7	0.0	–4													
1998-99	**New Jersey**	**NHL**	5	1	0	1	0	0	0	0	5	20.0	1	0	0.0	3	1	13:02								
	Albany River Rats	AHL	75	13	42	55	118												5	0	2	2	12			
99-2000♦	**New Jersey**	**NHL**	6	0	2	2	2	0	0	0	10	0.0	2	0	0.0	4	5	17:20								
	Albany River Rats	AHL	57	5	16	21	129																			
2000-01	**New Jersey**	**NHL**	53	1	7	8	37	0	0	0	35	2.9	9	0	0.0	40	71	15:44	6	0	0	0	13	0	0	0
	NHL Totals		367	23	78	101	330	4	0	3	422	5.5		0	0.0	47	77	15:40	32	3	4	7	29	0	0	0

Memorial Cup All-Star Team (1989) • AHL First All-Star Team (1999) • Won Eddie Shore Award (Top Defenseman - AHL) (1999)

Traded to **Edmonton** by **Buffalo** for Scott Pearson, April 7, 1995. Traded to **St. Louis** by **Edmonton** with Igor Kravchuk for Jeff Norton and Donald Dufresne, January 4, 1996. Traded to **New Jersey** by **St. Louis** with St. Louis' 2nd round choice (Brett Clouthier) in 1999 Entry Draft for Mike Peluso and Ricard Persson, November 26, 1996. Traded to **San Jose** by **New Jersey** with John MacLean for Doug Bodger and Dody Wood, December 7, 1997. Traded to **New Jersey** by **San Jose** for future considerations, August 26, 1998. Claimed by **Washington** from **New Jersey** in Waiver Draft, September 27, 1999. Traded to **New Jersey** by **Washington** for future considerations, October 5, 1999. Signed as a free agent by **NY Islanders**, July 5, 2001.

SVARTVADET, Per
(svahrt-VAH-deht, PAIR) **ATL.**

Center. Shoots left. 6'1", 195 lbs. Born, Solleftea, Sweden, May 17, 1975. Dallas' 5th choice, 139th overall, in 1993 Entry Draft.

			Regular Season																Playoffs							
Season	Club	League	GP	G	A	Pts	PIM	PP	SH	GW	S	%	+/-	TF	F%	H	SB	Min	GP	G	A	Pts	PIM	PP	SH	GW
1990-91	Solleftea HK	Sweden-2	5	1	0	1	0																			
1991-92	MoDo AIK	Swede-Jr.	30	17	19	36	36																			
1992-93	MoDo AIK	Swede-Jr.	14	5	10	15	18																			
	MoDo AIK	Sweden	2	0	0	0	0																			
1993-94	MoDo AIK	Swede-Jr.	12	7	12	19	6																			
	MoDo AIK	Sweden	36	2	1	3	4												11	0	0	0	6			
1994-95	MoDo Hockey	Sweden	40	6	9	15	31																			
1995-96	MoDo Hockey	Sweden	40	9	14	23	26												8	2	3	5	0			
1996-97	MoDo Hockey	Sweden	50	7	18	25	38																			
1997-98	MoDo Hockey	Sweden	46	6	12	18	28												7	3	2	5	2			
1998-99	MoDo Hockey	Sweden	50	9	23	32	30												13	3	6	9	6			
99-2000	**Atlanta**	**NHL**	38	3	4	7	6	0	0	0	36	8.3	–8	452	45.6	29	16	13:24								
	Orlando	IHL	27	4	6	10	10												5	0	1	1	0			
2000-01	**Atlanta**	**NHL**	69	10	11	21	20	0	2	1	98	10.2	–6	902	42.5	41	34	14:42								
	NHL Totals		107	13	15	28	26	0	2	1	134	9.7		1354	43.5	70	50	14:14								

Traded to **Atlanta** by **Dallas** for Ottawa's 6th round choice (previously acquired, Dallas selected Justin Cox) in 1999 Entry Draft, June 26, 1999.

SVEHLA, Robert
(SHVEH-lah, RAW-buhrt) **FLA.**

Defense. Shoots right. 6'1", 210 lbs. Born, Martin, Czech., January 2, 1969. Calgary's 4th choice, 78th overall, in 1992 Entry Draft.

			Regular Season																Playoffs							
Season	Club	League	GP	G	A	Pts	PIM	PP	SH	GW	S	%	+/-	TF	F%	H	SB	Min	GP	G	A	Pts	PIM	PP	SH	GW
1989-90	Dukla Trencin	Czech.	29	4	3	7																				
1990-91	Dukla Trencin	Czech.	52	16	9	25	62																			
1991-92	Dukla Trencin	Czech.	51	23	28	51	74																			
	Czechoslovakia	Olympics	8	2	1	3	8																			
1992-93	Malmo IF	Sweden	40	19	10	29	86												6	0	1	1	14			
1993-94	Malmo IF	Sweden	37	14	25	39	*127												10	5	1	6	23			
	Slovakia	Olympics	8	2	4	6	26																			
1994-95	Malmo IF	Sweden	32	11	13	24	83												9	2	3	5	6			
	Florida	**NHL**	5	1	1	2	0	1	0	0	6	16.7	3													
1995-96	**Florida**	**NHL**	81	8	49	57	94	7	0	0	146	5.5	3						22	0	6	6	32	0	0	0
1996-97	**Florida**	**NHL**	82	13	32	45	86	5	0	3	159	8.2	2						5	1	4	5	4	1	0	0
1997-98	**Florida**	**NHL**	79	9	34	43	113	3	0	0	144	6.3	–3													
	Slovakia	Olympics	2	0	1	1	0																			
1998-99	**Florida**	**NHL**	80	8	29	37	83	4	0	0	157	5.1	–13	2	0.0	101	92	24:45								
99-2000	**Florida**	**NHL**	82	9	40	49	64	3	0	1	143	6.3	23	1	0.0	97	169	24:33	4	0	1	1	4	0	0	0
2000-01	**Florida**	**NHL**	82	6	22	28	76	0	0	0	121	5.0	–8	1	0.0	354	130	25:34								
	NHL Totals		491	54	207	261	516	23	0	4	876	6.2		4	0.0	552	391	24:57	31	1	11	12	40	1	0	0

Played in NHL All-Star Game (1997)

Traded to **Florida** by **Calgary** with Magnus Svensson for Florida's 3rd round choice (Dmitri Vlasenkov) in 1996 Entry Draft and 4th round choice (Ryan Ready) in 1997 Entry Draft, September 29, 1994.

SVEJKOVSKY, Jaroslav
(svehzh-KOHV-skee, YAHR-oh-slav)

Right wing. Shoots right. 6'1", 193 lbs. Born, Plzen, Czech., October 1, 1976. Washington's 2nd choice, 17th overall, in 1996 Entry Draft.

			Regular Season																Playoffs							
Season	Club	League	GP	G	A	Pts	PIM	PP	SH	GW	S	%	+/-	TF	F%	H	SB	Min	GP	G	A	Pts	PIM	PP	SH	GW
1993-94	ZKZ Plzen	Cze-Rep	8	0	0	0	8																			
1994-95	ZKZ Plzen-Jr.	Cze-Rep	25	18	19	37	30																			
	SK Tabor	Cze-Rep	11	6	7	13																				
1995-96	Tri-City Americans	WHL	70	58	43	101	118												11	10	9	19	8			
1996-97	**Washington**	**NHL**	19	7	3	10	4	2	0	1	30	23.3	–1													
	Portland Pirates	AHL	54	38	28	66	56												5	2	0	2	6			
1997-98	**Washington**	**NHL**	17	4	1	5	10	2	0	1	29	13.8	–5						1	0	0	0	2	0	0	0
	Portland Pirates	AHL	16	12	7	19	16												7	1	2	3	2			

			Regular Season																Playoffs							
Season	Club	League	GP	G	A	Pts	PIM	PP	SH	GW	S	%	+/-	TF	F%	H	SB	Min	GP	G	A	Pts	PIM	PP	SH	GW
1998-99	**Washington**	**NHL**	**25**	**6**	**8**	**14**	**12**	**4**	**0**	**2**	**50**	**12.0**	**–2**	**0**	**0.0**	**40**	**6**	**13:36**								
99-2000	**Washington**	**NHL**	**23**	**1**	**2**	**3**	**2**	**1**	**0**	**0**	**18**	**5.6**	**–7**	**1**	**0.0**	**26**	**3**	**8:60**								
	Tampa Bay	**NHL**	**29**	**5**	**5**	**10**	**28**	**0**	**0**	**0**	**42**	**11.9**	**–7**	**5**	**80.0**	**27**	**9**	**12:22**								
2000-01	Detroit Vipers	IHL	2	2	2	4	2																			
	NHL Totals		**113**	**23**	**19**	**42**	**56**	**9**	**0**	**4**	**169**	**13.6**		**6**	**66.7**	**93**	**18**	**11:46**	**1**	**0**	**0**	**0**	**2**	**0**	**0**	**0**

WHL West Second All-Star Team (1996) • Won Dudley "Red" Garrett Memorial Trophy (Top Rookie - AHL) (1997)

Traded to **Tampa Bay** by **Washington** for Tampa Bay's 7th round choice (later traded to LA Kings - LA Kings selected Yevgeny Fedorov) in 2000 Entry Draft and 3rd round choice (later traded to Toronto - Toronto selected Brendan Bell) in 2001 Entry Draft, January 17, 2000. • Missed majority of 2000-01 season recovering from knee surgery, October 24, 2001.

SVOBODA, Petr

(svah-BOH-duh, PEE-tuhr) **TOR.**

Defense. Shoots right. 6'3", 200 lbs. Born, Jihlava, Czech., June 20, 1980. Toronto's 2nd choice, 35th overall, in 1998 Entry Draft.

Season	Club	League	GP	G	A	Pts	PIM	PP	SH	GW	S	%	+/-	TF	F%	H	SB	Min	GP	G	A	Pts	PIM	PP	SH	GW
1995-96	SK Jihlava-Jr.	Cze-Rep	38	4	12	16	50																			
1996-97	SK Jihlava-Jr.	Cze-Rep	29	1	3	4																				
1997-98	SK Jihlava-Jr.	Cze-Rep	12	0	2	2																				
	Havlickuv Brod-2	Cze-Rep	18	1	2	3	16																			
	Dukla Jihlava	Cze-Rep	1	0	0	0	0																			
1998-99	Dukla Jihlava	Cze-Rep	40	1	5	6	28																			
	Dukla Jihlava	EuroHL	5	1	0	1	4																			
99-2000	HC Ocelari Trinec	Cze-Rep	46	1	2	3	44												3	0	0	0	0			
2000-01	**Toronto**	**NHL**	**18**	**1**	**2**	**3**	**10**	**1**	**0**	**0**	**17**	**5.9**	**–5**	**0**	**0.0**	**46**	**23**	**0:00**								
	St. John's Leafs	AHL	38	7	7	14	48												4	0	0	0	4			
	NHL Totals		**18**	**1**	**2**	**3**	**10**	**1**	**0**	**0**	**17**	**5.9**		**0**	**0.0**	**46**	**23**									

SVOBODA, Petr

(svah-BOH-duh, PEE-tuhr) **T.B.**

Defense. Shoots left. 6'1", 198 lbs. Born, Most, Czech., February 14, 1966. Montreal's 1st choice, 5th overall, in 1984 Entry Draft.

Season	Club	League	GP	G	A	Pts	PIM	PP	SH	GW	S	%	+/-	TF	F%	H	SB	Min	GP	G	A	Pts	PIM	PP	SH	GW
1982-83	CHZ Litvinov	Czech.	4	0	0	0	2																			
1983-84	CHZ Litvinov	Czech.	18	3	1	4	20																			
1984-85	**Montreal**	**NHL**	**73**	**4**	**27**	**31**	**65**	**0**	**0**	**1**	**80**	**5.0**	**16**						**7**	**1**	**1**	**2**	**12**	**0**	**0**	**0**
1985-86♦	**Montreal**	**NHL**	**73**	**1**	**18**	**19**	**93**	**0**	**0**	**0**	**63**	**1.6**	**24**						**8**	**0**	**0**	**0**	**21**	**0**	**0**	**0**
1986-87	**Montreal**	**NHL**	**70**	**5**	**17**	**22**	**63**	**1**	**0**	**1**	**80**	**6.3**	**14**						**14**	**0**	**5**	**5**	**10**	**0**	**0**	**0**
1987-88	**Montreal**	**NHL**	**69**	**7**	**22**	**29**	**149**	**2**	**0**	**1**	**138**	**5.1**	**46**						**10**	**0**	**5**	**5**	**12**	**0**	**0**	**0**
1988-89	**Montreal**	**NHL**	**71**	**8**	**37**	**45**	**147**	**4**	**0**	**1**	**131**	**6.1**	**28**						**21**	**1**	**11**	**12**	**16**	**0**	**0**	**0**
1989-90	**Montreal**	**NHL**	**60**	**5**	**31**	**36**	**98**	**2**	**0**	**2**	**90**	**5.6**	**20**						**10**	**0**	**5**	**5**	**7**	**0**	**0**	**0**
1990-91	**Montreal**	**NHL**	**60**	**4**	**22**	**26**	**52**	**3**	**0**	**1**	**67**	**6.0**	**5**						**2**	**0**	**1**	**1**	**2**	**0**	**0**	**0**
1991-92	**Montreal**	**NHL**	**58**	**5**	**16**	**21**	**94**	**1**	**0**	**3**	**88**	**5.7**	**9**													
	Buffalo	**NHL**	**13**	**1**	**6**	**7**	**52**	**0**	**0**	**0**	**23**	**4.3**	**–8**						**7**	**1**	**4**	**5**	**6**	**0**	**1**	**0**
1992-93	**Buffalo**	**NHL**	**40**	**2**	**24**	**26**	**59**	**1**	**0**	**1**	**61**	**3.3**	**3**													
1993-94	**Buffalo**	**NHL**	**60**	**2**	**14**	**16**	**89**	**1**	**0**	**0**	**80**	**2.5**	**11**						**3**	**0**	**0**	**0**	**4**	**0**	**0**	**0**
1994-95	CHZ Litvinov	Cze-Rep	8	2	0	2	50																			
	Buffalo	**NHL**	**26**	**0**	**5**	**5**	**60**	**0**	**0**	**0**	**22**	**0.0**	**–5**													
	Philadelphia	**NHL**	**11**	**0**	**3**	**3**	**10**	**0**	**0**	**0**	**17**	**0.0**	**0**						**14**	**0**	**4**	**4**	**8**	**0**	**0**	**0**
1995-96	**Philadelphia**	**NHL**	**73**	**1**	**28**	**29**	**105**	**0**	**0**	**0**	**91**	**1.1**	**28**						**12**	**0**	**6**	**6**	**22**	**0**	**0**	**0**
1996-97	**Philadelphia**	**NHL**	**67**	**2**	**12**	**14**	**94**	**1**	**0**	**0**	**36**	**5.6**	**10**						**16**	**1**	**2**	**3**	**16**	**0**	**0**	**0**
1997-98	**Philadelphia**	**NHL**	**56**	**3**	**15**	**18**	**83**	**2**	**0**	**0**	**44**	**6.8**	**19**						**3**	**0**	**1**	**1**	**4**	**0**	**0**	**0**
	Czech-Republic	Olympics	6	1	1	2	*39																			
1998-99	**Philadelphia**	**NHL**	**25**	**4**	**2**	**6**	**28**	**1**	**1**	**1**	**37**	**10.8**	**5**	**0**	**0.0**	**13**	**24**	**20:15**								
	Tampa Bay	**NHL**	**34**	**1**	**16**	**17**	**53**	**0**	**0**	**0**	**46**	**2.2**	**–4**	**0**	**0.0**	**47**	**61**	**25:33**								
99-2000	**Tampa Bay**	**NHL**	**70**	**2**	**23**	**25**	**170**	**2**	**0**	**0**	**93**	**2.2**	**–11**	**0**	**0.0**	**65**	**124**	**23:00**								
2000-01	**Tampa Bay**	**NHL**	**19**	**1**	**3**	**4**	**41**	**0**	**0**	**0**	**16**	**6.3**	**–4**	**0**	**0.0**	**26**	**31**	**18:48**								
	NHL Totals		**1028**	**58**	**341**	**399**	**1605**	**21**	**1**	**12**	**1303**	**4.5**		**0**	**0.0**	**151**	**240**	**22:12**	**127**	**4**	**45**	**49**	**140**	**0**	**1**	**0**

Played in NHL All-Star Game (2000)

Traded to **Buffalo** by **Montreal** for Kevin Haller, March 10, 1992. Traded to **Philadelphia** by **Buffalo** for Garry Galley, April 7, 1995. Traded to **Tampa Bay** by **Philadelphia** for Karl Dykhuis, December 28, 1998. • Missed majority of 2000-01 season recovering from head injury suffered in game vs. LA Kings, December 16, 2000.

SWANSON, Brian

(SWAHN-suhn, BRIGH-uhn) **EDM.**

Center. Shoots left. 5'10", 185 lbs. Born, Eagle River, AK, March 24, 1976. San Jose's 5th choice, 115th overall, in 1994 Entry Draft.

Season	Club	League	GP	G	A	Pts	PIM	PP	SH	GW	S	%	+/-	TF	F%	H	SB	Min	GP	G	A	Pts	PIM	PP	SH	GW
1991-92	Anchorage Stars	AAHL	50	35	40	75	10																			
1992-93	Anchorage Stars	AAHL	45	40	50	90	12																			
1993-94	Omaha Lancers	USHL	47	38	42	80	40																			
1994-95	Omaha Lancers	USHL	33	14	35	49	12																			
1995-96	Colorado College	WCHA	40	26	33	59	24																			
1996-97	Colorado College	WCHA	43	19	32	51	47																			
1997-98	Colorado College	WCHA	42	18	*38	*56	26																			
1998-99	Colorado College	WCHA	42	25	*41	66	28																			
	Hartford	AHL	4	0	0	0	4																			
99-2000	Hamilton Bulldogs	AHL	69	19	40	59	18												10	2	5	7	6			
2000-01	**Edmonton**	**NHL**	**16**	**1**	**1**	**2**	**6**	**0**	**0**	**0**	**8**	**12.5**	**–1**	**150**	**44.0**	**3**	**4**	**10:55**								
	Hamilton Bulldogs	AHL	49	18	29	47	20																			
	NHL Totals		**16**	**1**	**1**	**2**	**6**	**0**	**0**	**0**	**8**	**12.5**		**150**	**44.0**	**3**	**4**	**10:55**								

USHL First All-Star Team (1994) • USHL Second Team All-Star (1995) • WCHA Second All-Star Team (1996) • WCHA First All-Star Team (1997, 1998, 1999) • NCAA West Second All-American Team (1998) • NCAA West First All-American Team (1999)

Traded to **NY Rangers** by **San Jose** with Jayson More and San Jose's 4th round choice (later traded back to San Jose - San Jose selected Adam Colagiacomo) in 1997 Entry Draft for Marty McSorley, August 20, 1996. Signed as a free agent by **Edmonton**, August 19, 1999.

SWEENEY, Don

(SWEE-nee, DAWN) **BOS.**

Defense. Shoots left. 5'10", 185 lbs. Born, St. Stephen, N.B., August 17, 1966. Boston's 8th choice, 166th overall, in 1984 Entry Draft.

Season	Club	League	GP	G	A	Pts	PIM	PP	SH	GW	S	%	+/-	TF	F%	H	SB	Min	GP	G	A	Pts	PIM	PP	SH	GW
1983-84	South St. Paul	Hi-School	22	33	26	59																				
1984-85	Harvard University	ECAC	29	3	7	10	30																			
1985-86	Harvard University	ECAC	31	4	5	9	12																			
1986-87	Harvard University	ECAC	34	7	4	11	22																			
1987-88	Harvard University	ECAC	30	6	23	29	37																			
	Maine Mariners	AHL																	6	1	3	4	0			
1988-89	**Boston**	**NHL**	**36**	**3**	**5**	**8**	**20**	**0**	**0**	**0**	**35**	**8.6**	**–6**													
	Maine Mariners	AHL	42	8	17	25	24																			
1989-90	**Boston**	**NHL**	**58**	**3**	**5**	**8**	**58**	**0**	**0**	**0**	**49**	**6.1**	**11**						**21**	**1**	**5**	**6**	**18**	**1**	**0**	**0**
	Maine Mariners	AHL	11	0	8	8	8																			
1990-91	**Boston**	**NHL**	**77**	**8**	**13**	**21**	**67**	**0**	**1**	**3**	**102**	**7.8**	**2**						**19**	**3**	**0**	**3**	**25**	**0**	**0**	**0**
1991-92	**Boston**	**NHL**	**75**	**3**	**11**	**14**	**74**	**0**	**0**	**1**	**92**	**3.3**	**–9**						**15**	**0**	**0**	**0**	**10**	**0**	**0**	**0**
1992-93	**Boston**	**NHL**	**84**	**7**	**27**	**34**	**68**	**0**	**1**	**0**	**107**	**6.5**	**34**						**4**	**0**	**0**	**0**	**4**	**0**	**0**	**0**
1993-94	**Boston**	**NHL**	**75**	**6**	**15**	**21**	**50**	**1**	**2**	**2**	**136**	**4.4**	**29**						**12**	**2**	**1**	**3**	**4**	**0**	**0**	**1**
1994-95	**Boston**	**NHL**	**47**	**3**	**19**	**22**	**24**	**1**	**0**	**2**	**102**	**2.9**	**6**						**5**	**0**	**0**	**0**	**4**	**0**	**0**	**0**
1995-96	**Boston**	**NHL**	**77**	**4**	**24**	**28**	**42**	**2**	**0**	**3**	**142**	**2.8**	**–4**						**5**	**0**	**2**	**2**	**6**	**0**	**0**	**0**
1996-97	**Boston**	**NHL**	**82**	**3**	**23**	**26**	**39**	**0**	**0**	**0**	**113**	**2.7**	**–5**													
1997-98	**Boston**	**NHL**	**59**	**1**	**15**	**16**	**24**	**0**	**0**	**0**	**55**	**1.8**	**12**													
1998-99	**Boston**	**NHL**	**81**	**2**	**10**	**12**	**64**	**0**	**0**	**0**	**79**	**2.5**	**14**	**0**	**0.0**	**205**	**85**	**19:31**	**11**	**3**	**0**	**3**	**6**	**1**	**0**	**0**
99-2000	**Boston**	**NHL**	**81**	**1**	**13**	**14**	**48**	**0**	**0**	**0**	**82**	**1.2**	**–14**	**1**	**0.0**	**301**	**84**	**21:08**								
2000-01	**Boston**	**NHL**	**72**	**2**	**10**	**12**	**26**	**1**	**0**	**1**	**60**	**3.3**	**–1**	**0**	**0.0**	**182**	**82**	**19:16**								
	NHL Totals		**904**	**46**	**190**	**236**	**604**	**5**	**4**	**12**	**1154**	**4.0**		**1**	**0.0**	**688**	**251**	**20:00**	**92**	**9**	**8**	**17**	**77**	**2**	**0**	**1**

ECAC First All-Star Team (1988) • NCAA East All-American Team (1988)

SYDOR, Darryl
(sih-DOHR, DAIR-ihl) **DAL.**

Defense. Shoots left. 6'1", 205 lbs. Born, Edmonton, Alta., May 13, 1972. Los Angeles' 1st choice, 7th overall, in 1990 Entry Draft.

			Regular Season																Playoffs							
Season	Club	League	GP	G	A	Pts	PIM	PP	SH	GW	S	%	+/-	TF	F%	H	SB	Min	GP	G	A	Pts	PIM	PP	SH	GW
1985-86	Genstar Cement	AAHA	34	20	17	37	60																			
1986-87	Genstar Cement	AAHA	36	15	20	35	60																			
1987-88	Edmonton Mets	AMHL	38	10	11	21	54																			
1988-89	Kamloops Blazers	WHL	65	12	14	26	86												15	1	4	5	19			
1989-90	Kamloops Blazers	WHL	67	29	66	95	129												17	2	9	11	28			
1990-91	Kamloops Blazers	WHL	66	27	78	105	88												12	3	*22	25	10			
1991-92	Kamloops Blazers	WHL	29	9	39	48	33												17	3	15	18	18			
	Los Angeles	NHL	18	1	5	6	22	0	0	0	18	5.6	-3													
1992-93	Los Angeles	NHL	80	6	23	29	63	0	0	1	112	5.4	-2						24	3	8	11	16	2	0	0
1993-94	Los Angeles	NHL	84	8	27	35	94	1	0	0	146	5.5	-9													
1994-95	Los Angeles	NHL	48	4	19	23	36	3	0	0	96	4.2	-2													
1995-96	Los Angeles	NHL	58	1	11	12	34	1	0	0	84	1.2	-11													
	Dallas	NHL	26	2	6	8	41	1	0	0	33	6.1	-1													
1996-97	Dallas	NHL	82	8	40	48	51	2	0	2	142	5.6	37						7	0	2	2	0	0	0	0
1997-98	Dallas	NHL	79	11	35	46	51	4	1	1	166	6.6	17						17	0	5	5	14	0	0	0
1998-99♦	Dallas	NHL	74	14	34	48	50	9	0	2	163	8.6	-1	1	100.0	83	83	21:16	23	3	9	12	16	1	0	1
99-2000	Dallas	NHL	74	8	26	34	32	5	0	1	132	6.1	6	1	0.0	85	76	23:09	23	1	6	7	6	0	0	0
2000-01	Dallas	NHL	81	10	37	47	34	8	0	1	140	7.1	5	1	0.0	72	86	21:25	10	1	3	4	0	1	0	0
	NHL Totals		704	73	263	336	508	34	1	8	1232	5.9		3	33.3	240	245	21:56	104	8	33	41	52	4	0	1

WHL West First All-Star Team (1990, 1991, 1992) • Played in NHL All-Star Game (1998, 1999)

Traded to **Dallas** by **LA Kings** with LA Kings' 5th round choice (Ryan Christie) in 1996 Entry Draft for Shane Churla and Doug Zmolek, February 17, 1996.

SYKORA, Michal
(SEE-koh-ra, MIHK-al)

Defense. Shoots left. 6'5", 225 lbs. Born, Pardubice, Czech., July 5, 1973. San Jose's 6th choice, 123rd overall, in 1992 Entry Draft.

Season	Club	League	GP	G	A	Pts	PIM	PP	SH	GW	S	%	+/-	TF	F%	H	SB	Min	GP	G	A	Pts	PIM	PP	SH	GW
1990-91	HC Tesla	Czech-Jr.	40	17	26	43	45																			
	HC Pardubice	Czech.	2	0	0	0	....																			
1991-92	Tacoma Rockets	WHL	61	13	23	36	46												4	0	2	2	2			
1992-93	Tacoma Rockets	WHL	70	23	50	73	73												7	4	8	12	2			
1993-94	San Jose	NHL	22	1	4	5	14	0	0	0	22	4.5	-4													
	Kansas City	IHL	47	5	11	16	30																			
1994-95	Kansas City	IHL	36	1	10	11	30																			
	San Jose	NHL	16	0	4	4	10	0	0	0	6	0.0	6													
1995-96	San Jose	NHL	79	4	16	20	54	1	0	0	80	5.0	-14													
1996-97	San Jose	NHL	35	2	5	7	59	1	0	0	39	5.1	0													
	Chicago	NHL	28	1	9	10	10	0	0	0	38	2.6	4						1	0	0	0	0	0	0	0
1997-98	Chicago	NHL	28	1	3	4	12	0	0	0	35	2.9	-10													
	Indianapolis Ice	IHL	6	0	0	0	4																			
	HC Pardubice	Cze-Rep	1	1	0	1	2																			
1998-99	Sparta Praha	Cze-Rep	26	4	9	13	38												8	2	0	2	....			
	Sparta Praha	EuroHL	2	2	2	4	4												2	2	2	4	0			
	Tampa Bay	NHL	10	1	2	3	0	0	0	1	24	4.2	-7	0	0.0	10	8	16:20								
99-2000	Sparta Praha	Cze-Rep	48	11	14	25	89												9	5	3	8	8			
2000-01	Philadelphia	NHL	49	5	11	16	26	1	1	1	71	7.0	9	1	0.0	45	58	16:27	6	0	1	1	0	0	0	0
	NHL Totals		267	15	54	69	185	3	1	2	315	4.8		1	0.0	55	66	16:26	7	0	1	1	0	0	0	0

WHL West First All-Star Team (1993)

Traded to **Chicago** by **San Jose** with Chris Terreri and Ulf Dahlen for Ed Belfour, January 25, 1997. Traded to **Tampa Bay** by **Chicago** for Mark Fitzpatrick and Tampa Bay's 4th round choice (later traded to Montreal - Montreal selected Chris Dyment) in 1999 Entry Draft, July 17, 1998. Signed as a free agent by **Philadelphia**, July 6, 2000.

SYKORA, Petr
(SEE-koh-ra, PEE-tuhr) **N.J.**

Right wing. Shoots left. 6', 190 lbs. Born, Plzen, Czech., November 19, 1976. New Jersey's 1st choice, 18th overall, in 1995 Entry Draft.

Season	Club	League	GP	G	A	Pts	PIM	PP	SH	GW	S	%	+/-	TF	F%	H	SB	Min	GP	G	A	Pts	PIM	PP	SH	GW
1991-92	Skoda Plzen	Czech-Jr.	30	50	50	100	....																			
1992-93	Skoda Plzen	Czech.	19	12	5	17	....																			
1993-94	Skoda Plzen	Cze-Rep	37	10	16	26	....												4	0	1	1	....			
	Cleveland	IHL	13	4	5	9	8																			
1994-95	Detroit Vipers	IHL	29	12	17	29	16																			
1995-96	New Jersey	NHL	63	18	24	42	32	8	0	3	128	14.1	7													
	Albany River Rats	AHL	5	4	1	5	0																			
1996-97	New Jersey	NHL	19	1	2	3	4	0	0	0	26	3.8	-8						2	0	0	0	2	0	0	0
	Albany River Rats	AHL	43	20	25	45	48												4	1	4	5	2			
1997-98	New Jersey	NHL	58	16	20	36	22	3	1	4	130	12.3	0						2	0	0	0	0	0	0	0
	Albany River Rats	AHL	2	4	1	5	0																			
1998-99	New Jersey	NHL	80	29	43	72	22	15	0	7	222	13.1	16	33	33.3	65	16	16:14	7	3	3	6	4	0	0	1
99-2000♦	New Jersey	NHL	79	25	43	68	26	5	1	4	222	11.3	24	47	61.7	33	22	17:06	23	9	8	17	10	1	0	3
2000-01	New Jersey	NHL	73	35	46	81	32	9	2	3	249	14.1	36	15	33.3	19	21	17:44	25	10	12	22	12	2	2	2
	NHL Totals		372	124	178	302	138	40	4	21	977	12.7		95	16.8	117	59	16:57	59	22	23	45	28	3	2	6

NHL All-Rookie Team (1996)

SYKORA, Petr
(SEE-koh-ra, PEE-tuhr) **NSH.**

Center. Shoots right. 6'3", 206 lbs. Born, Pardubice, Czech., December 21, 1978. Detroit's 2nd choice, 76th overall, in 1997 Entry Draft.

Season	Club	League	GP	G	A	Pts	PIM	PP	SH	GW	S	%	+/-	TF	F%	H	SB	Min	GP	G	A	Pts	PIM	PP	SH	GW
1994-95	HC Pardubice-Jr.	Cze-Rep	38	35	33	68	....																			
1995-96	HC Pardubice-Jr.	Cze-Rep	16	26	17	43	....																			
1996-97	HC Pardubice-Jr.	Cze-Rep	12	14	4	18	....																			
	HC Pardubice	Cze-Rep	29	1	3	4	4																			
1997-98	HC Pardubice	Cze-Rep	39	4	5	9	8												3	0	0	0	....			
1998-99	Nashville	NHL	2	0	0	0	0	0	0	0	2	0.0	-1	11	45.5	0	0	8:19								
	Milwaukee	IHL	73	14	15	29	50												2	1	1	2	0			
99-2000	Milwaukee	IHL	3	0	1	1	2																			
	HC Pardubice	Cze-Rep	36	7	13	20	49												3	0	0	0	2			
2000-01	HC Pardubice	Cze-Rep	47	26	18	44	42												7	5	3	8	6			
	NHL Totals		2	0	0	0	0	0	0	0	2	0.0		11	45.5	0	0	8:19								

Traded to **Nashville** by **Detroit** with Detroit's 3rd round choice (later traded to Edmonton - Edmonton selected Mike Comrie) and 4th round compensatory choice (Alexander Krevsun) in 1999 Entry Draft for Doug Brown, July 14, 1998.

SYLVESTER, Dean
(sihl-VEHS-tuhr, DEEN)

Right wing. Shoots right. 6'2", 210 lbs. Born, Hanson, MA, December 30, 1972.

Season	Club	League	GP	G	A	Pts	PIM	PP	SH	GW	S	%	+/-	TF	F%	H	SB	Min	GP	G	A	Pts	PIM	PP	SH	GW
1990-91	Boston College	Hi-School	18	19	13	32	....																			
1991-92	Kent State	NCAA	31	7	21	28	10																			
1992-93	Kent State	NCAA	38	33	20	53	28																			
1993-94	Kent State	NCAA	39	22	24	46	28																			
1994-95	Michigan State	CCHA	40	15	15	30	38																			
1995-96	Mobile Mysticks	ECHL	44	24	27	51	35																			
	Kansas City	IHL	36	11	10	21	15												4	0	0	0	2			
1996-97	Kansas City	IHL	77	23	22	45	47												3	1	1	2	0			
1997-98	Kansas City	IHL	77	33	20	53	63												11	5	2	7	4			
1998-99	Buffalo	NHL	1	0	0	0	0	0	0	0	1	0.0	-1	0	0.0	1	0	14:31	4	0	0	0	0	0	0	0
	Rochester	AHL	76	35	30	65	46												18	*12	5	17	8			
99-2000	Atlanta	NHL	52	16	10	26	24	1	0	2	98	16.3	-14	14	35.7	108	17	13:44								
	Orlando	IHL	16	4	3	7	43																			
2000-01	Atlanta	NHL	43	5	6	11	8	1	0	0	82	6.1	-16	15	40.0	60	19	14:04								
	Orlando	IHL	27	9	9	18	20												9	0	1	1	6			
	NHL Totals		96	21	16	37	32	2	0	2	181	11.6		29	37.9	169	36	13:54	4	0	0	0	0	0	0	0

Signed as a free agent by **Buffalo**, October 1, 1998. Traded to **Atlanta** by **Buffalo** for future considerations, June 25, 1999.

TAMER, Chris
(TAY-muhr, KRIHS) **ATL.**

Defense. Shoots left. 6'2", 205 lbs. Born, Dearborn, MI, November 17, 1970. Pittsburgh's 3rd choice, 68th overall, in 1990 Entry Draft.

			Regular Season																Playoffs							
Season	Club	League	GP	G	A	Pts	PIM	PP	SH	GW	S	%	+/-	TF	F%	H	SB	Min	GP	G	A	Pts	PIM	PP	SH	GW
1987-88	Redford Royals	NAJHL	40	10	20	30	217	....	....	....	....	....	....	....	....	....	....	....	....	....	....	....	....	....	....	....
1988-89	Redford Royals	NAJHL	31	6	13	19	79	....	....	....	....	....	....	....	....	....	....	....	....	....	....	....	....	....	....	....
1989-90	U. of Michigan	CCHA	42	2	7	9	147	....	....	....	....	....	....	....	....	....	....	....	....	....	....	....	....	....	....	....
1990-91	U. of Michigan	CCHA	45	8	19	27	130	....	....	....	....	....	....	....	....	....	....	....	....	....	....	....	....	....	....	....
1991-92	U. of Michigan	CCHA	43	4	15	19	125	....	....	....	....	....	....	....	....	....	....	....	....	....	....	....	....	....	....	....
1992-93	U. of Michigan	CCHA	39	5	18	23	113	....	....	....	....	....	....	....	....	....	....	....	....	....	....	....	....	....	....	....
1993-94	**Pittsburgh**	**NHL**	**12**	**0**	**0**	**0**	**9**	**0**	**0**	**0**	**10**	**0.0**	**3**	....	....	....	....	....	**5**	**0**	**0**	**0**	**2**	**0**	**0**	**0**
	Cleveland	IHL	53	1	2	3	160	....	....	....	....	....	....	....	....	....	....	....	....	....	....	....	....	....	....	....
1994-95	Cleveland	IHL	48	4	10	14	204	....	....	....	....	....	....	....	....	....	....	....	....	....	....	....	....	....	....	....
	Pittsburgh	**NHL**	**36**	**2**	**0**	**2**	**82**	**0**	**0**	**0**	**26**	**7.7**	**0**	....	....	....	....	....	**4**	**0**	**0**	**0**	**18**	**0**	**0**	**0**
1995-96	**Pittsburgh**	**NHL**	**70**	**4**	**10**	**14**	**153**	**0**	**0**	**1**	**75**	**5.3**	**20**	....	....	....	....	....	**18**	**0**	**7**	**7**	**24**	**0**	**0**	**0**
1996-97	**Pittsburgh**	**NHL**	**45**	**2**	**4**	**6**	**131**	**0**	**1**	**0**	**56**	**3.6**	**–25**	....	....	....	....	....	**4**	**0**	**0**	**0**	**4**	**0**	**0**	**0**
1997-98	**Pittsburgh**	**NHL**	**79**	**0**	**7**	**7**	**181**	**0**	**0**	**0**	**55**	**0.0**	**4**	....	....	....	....	....	**6**	**0**	**1**	**1**	**4**	**0**	**0**	**0**
1998-99	**Pittsburgh**	**NHL**	**11**	**0**	**0**	**0**	**32**	**0**	**0**	**0**	**2**	**0.0**	**–2**	**0**	**0.0**	**6**	**8**	**5:59**	....	....	....	....	....	....	....	....
	NY Rangers	**NHL**	**52**	**1**	**5**	**6**	**92**	**0**	**0**	**1**	**46**	**2.2**	**–12**	**0**	**0.0**	**88**	**77**	**15:25**	....	....	....	....	....	....	....	....
99-2000	**Atlanta**	**NHL**	**69**	**2**	**8**	**10**	**91**	**0**	**0**	**0**	**61**	**3.3**	**–32**	**5**	**40.0**	**129**	**102**	**18:29**	....	....	....	....	....	....	....	....
2000-01	**Atlanta**	**NHL**	**82**	**4**	**13**	**17**	**128**	**0**	**1**	**1**	**90**	**4.4**	**–1**	**1**	**0.0**	**170**	**134**	**19:42**	....	....	....	....	....	....	....	....
	NHL Totals		**456**	**15**	**47**	**62**	**899**	**0**	**2**	**3**	**421**	**3.6**		**6**	**33.3**	**393**	**321**	**17:34**	**37**	**0**	**8**	**8**	**52**	**0**	**0**	**0**

Traded to **NY Rangers** by **Pittsburgh** with Petr Nedved and Sean Pronger for Alexei Kovalev and Harry York, November 25, 1998. Claimed by **Atlanta** from **NY Rangers** in Expansion Draft, June 25, 1999.

TANABE, David
(tuh-NA-bee, DAY-vihd) **CAR.**

Defense. Shoots right. 6'1", 190 lbs. Born, Minneapolis, MN, July 19, 1980. Carolina's 1st choice, 16th overall, in 1999 Entry Draft.

Season	Club	League	GP	G	A	Pts	PIM	PP	SH	GW	S	%	+/-	TF	F%	H	SB	Min	GP	G	A	Pts	PIM	PP	SH	GW
1996-97	Hill-Murray	Hi-School	28	12	14	26	....	....	....	....	....	....	....	....	....	....	....	....	....	....	....	....	....	....	....	....
1997-98	Team USA	USDP	73	8	21	29	96	....	....	....	....	....	....	....	....	....	....	....	....	....	....	....	....	....	....	....
1998-99	U. of Wisconsin	WCHA	35	10	12	22	44	....	....	....	....	....	....	....	....	....	....	....	....	....	....	....	....	....	....	....
99-2000	**Carolina**	**NHL**	**31**	**4**	**0**	**4**	**14**	**3**	**0**	**0**	**28**	**14.3**	**–4**	**0**	**0.0**	**11**	**10**	**12:53**	....	....	....	....	....	....	....	....
	Cincinnati	IHL	32	0	13	13	14	....	....	....	....	....	....	....	....	....	....	....	11	1	4	5	6	....	....	....
2000-01	**Carolina**	**NHL**	**74**	**7**	**22**	**29**	**42**	**5**	**0**	**1**	**130**	**5.4**	**–9**	**0**	**0.0**	**52**	**50**	**17:55**	**6**	**2**	**0**	**2**	**12**	**2**	**0**	**0**
	NHL Totals		**105**	**11**	**22**	**33**	**56**	**8**	**0**	**1**	**158**	**7.0**		**0**	**0.0**	**63**	**60**	**16:26**	**6**	**2**	**0**	**2**	**12**	**2**	**0**	**0**

WCHA All-Rookie Team (1998-99)

TANGUAY, Alex
(TAN-guay, AL-ehx) **COL.**

Center. Shoots left. 6', 190 lbs. Born, Ste-Justine, Que., November 21, 1979. Colorado's 1st choice, 12th overall, in 1998 Entry Draft.

Season	Club	League	GP	G	A	Pts	PIM	PP	SH	GW	S	%	+/-	TF	F%	H	SB	Min	GP	G	A	Pts	PIM	PP	SH	GW
1994-95	Cap-d-Madelaine	QAAA	1	0	1	1	0	....	....	....	....	....	....	....	....	....	....	....	....	....	....	....	....	....	....	....
1995-96	Cap-d-Madelaine	QAAA	44	29	34	63	64	....	....	....	....	....	....	....	....	....	....	....	5	2	4	6	14	....	....	....
1996-97	Halifax	QMJHL	70	27	41	68	60	....	....	....	....	....	....	....	....	....	....	....	12	5	8	13	8	....	....	....
1997-98	Halifax	QMJHL	51	47	38	85	32	....	....	....	....	....	....	....	....	....	....	....	5	7	6	13	4	....	....	....
1998-99	Halifax	QMJHL	31	27	34	61	30	....	....	....	....	....	....	....	....	....	....	....	5	1	2	3	2	....	....	....
	Hershey Bears	AHL	5	1	2	3	2	....	....	....	....	....	....	....	....	....	....	....	5	0	2	2	0	....	....	....
99-2000	**Colorado**	**NHL**	**76**	**17**	**34**	**51**	**22**	**5**	**0**	**3**	**74**	**23.0**	**6**	**11**	**45.5**	**72**	**23**	**15:38**	**17**	**2**	**1**	**3**	**2**	**1**	**0**	**1**
2000-01♦	**Colorado**	**NHL**	**82**	**27**	**50**	**77**	**37**	**7**	**1**	**3**	**135**	**20.0**	**35**	**30**	**43.3**	**102**	**22**	**17:51**	**23**	**6**	**15**	**21**	**8**	**1**	**0**	**2**
	NHL Totals		**158**	**44**	**84**	**128**	**59**	**12**	**1**	**6**	**209**	**21.1**		**41**	**43.9**	**174**	**45**	**16:47**	**40**	**8**	**16**	**24**	**10**	**2**	**0**	**3**

TAPPER, Brad
(TA-puhr, BRAD) **ATL.**

Center. Shoots right. 6', 185 lbs. Born, Scarborough, Ont., April 28, 1978.

Season	Club	League	GP	G	A	Pts	PIM	PP	SH	GW	S	%	+/-	TF	F%	H	SB	Min	GP	G	A	Pts	PIM	PP	SH	GW
1996-97	Wexford Raiders	MTJHL	50	42	70	112	169	....	....	....	....	....	....	....	....	....	....	....	....	....	....	....	....	....	....	....
1997-98	RPI Engineers	ECAC	34	14	11	25	62	....	....	....	....	....	....	....	....	....	....	....	....	....	....	....	....	....	....	....
1998-99	RPI Engineers	ECAC	35	20	20	40	60	....	....	....	....	....	....	....	....	....	....	....	....	....	....	....	....	....	....	....
99-2000	RPI Engineers	ECAC	37	*31	20	51	81	....	....	....	....	....	....	....	....	....	....	....	....	....	....	....	....	....	....	....
2000-01	**Atlanta**	**NHL**	**16**	**2**	**3**	**5**	**6**	**0**	**0**	**0**	**21**	**9.5**	**1**	**0**	**0.0**	**11**	**2**	**12:44**	....	....	....	....	....	....	....	....
	Orlando	IHL	45	7	9	16	39	....	....	....	....	....	....	....	....	....	....	....	2	0	0	0	2	....	....	....
	NHL Totals		**16**	**2**	**3**	**5**	**6**	**0**	**0**	**0**	**21**	**9.5**		**0**	**0.0**	**11**	**2**	**12:44**	....	....	....	....	....	....	....	....

ECAC First All-Star Team (2000) • NCAA East Second All-American Team (2000)

Signed as a free agent by **Atlanta**, April 11, 2000.

TAYLOR, Chris
(TAY-lohr, KRIHS) **BUF.**

Center. Shoots left. 6'2", 195 lbs. Born, Stratford, Ont., March 6, 1972. NY Islanders' 2nd choice, 27th overall, in 1990 Entry Draft.

Season	Club	League	GP	G	A	Pts	PIM	PP	SH	GW	S	%	+/-	TF	F%	H	SB	Min	GP	G	A	Pts	PIM	PP	SH	GW
1987-88	Stratford Cullitons	OJHL-B	52	28	37	65	112	....	....	....	....	....	....	....	....	....	....	....	....	....	....	....	....	....	....	....
1988-89	London Knights	OHL	62	7	16	23	52	....	....	....	....	....	....	....	....	....	....	....	15	0	2	2	15	....	....	....
1989-90	London Knights	OHL	66	45	60	105	60	....	....	....	....	....	....	....	....	....	....	....	6	3	2	5	6	....	....	....
1990-91	London Knights	OHL	65	50	78	128	50	....	....	....	....	....	....	....	....	....	....	....	7	4	8	12	6	....	....	....
1991-92	London Knights	OHL	66	48	74	122	57	....	....	....	....	....	....	....	....	....	....	....	10	8	16	24	9	....	....	....
1992-93	Capital District	AHL	77	19	43	62	32	....	....	....	....	....	....	....	....	....	....	....	4	0	1	1	2	....	....	....
1993-94	Salt Lake City	IHL	79	21	20	41	38	....	....	....	....	....	....	....	....	....	....	....	....	....	....	....	....	....	....	....
1994-95	Denver Grizzlies	IHL	78	38	48	86	47	....	....	....	....	....	....	....	....	....	....	....	14	7	6	13	10	....	....	....
	NY Islanders	**NHL**	**10**	**0**	**3**	**3**	**2**	**0**	**0**	**0**	**13**	**0.0**	**1**	....	....	....	....	....	....	....	....	....	....	....	....	....
1995-96	**NY Islanders**	**NHL**	**11**	**0**	**1**	**1**	**2**	**0**	**0**	**0**	**4**	**0.0**	**1**	....	....	....	....	....	....	....	....	....	....	....	....	....
	Utah Grizzlies	IHL	50	18	23	41	60	....	....	....	....	....	....	....	....	....	....	....	22	5	11	16	26	....	....	....
1996-97	**NY Islanders**	**NHL**	**1**	**0**	**0**	**0**	**0**	**0**	**0**	**0**	**1**	**0.0**	**0**	....	....	....	....	....	....	....	....	....	....	....	....	....
	Utah Grizzlies	IHL	71	27	40	67	24	....	....	....	....	....	....	....	....	....	....	....	7	1	2	3	0	....	....	....
1997-98	Utah Grizzlies	IHL	79	28	56	84	66	....	....	....	....	....	....	....	....	....	....	....	4	0	2	2	6	....	....	....
1998-99	**Boston**	**NHL**	**37**	**3**	**5**	**8**	**12**	**0**	**1**	**0**	**60**	**5.0**	**–3**	**512**	**53.7**	**52**	**16**	**14:24**	....	....	....	....	....	....	....	....
	Providence Bruins	AHL	21	6	11	17	6	....	....	....	....	....	....	....	....	....	....	....	....	....	....	....	....	....	....	....
	Las Vegas	IHL	14	3	12	15	2	....	....	....	....	....	....	....	....	....	....	....	....	....	....	....	....	....	....	....
99-2000	**Buffalo**	**NHL**	**11**	**1**	**1**	**2**	**2**	**0**	**0**	**0**	**15**	**6.7**	**–2**	**125**	**45.6**	**15**	**3**	**10:54**	**2**	**0**	**0**	**0**	**2**	**0**	**0**	**0**
	Rochester	AHL	49	21	28	49	21	....	....	....	....	....	....	....	....	....	....	....	....	....	....	....	....	....	....	....
2000-01	**Buffalo**	**NHL**	**14**	**0**	**2**	**2**	**6**	**0**	**0**	**0**	**21**	**0.0**	**1**	**138**	**50.7**	**28**	**3**	**11:08**	....	....	....	....	....	....	....	....
	Rochester	AHL	45	20	24	44	25	....	....	....	....	....	....	....	....	....	....	....	....	....	....	....	....	....	....	....
	NHL Totals		**84**	**4**	**12**	**16**	**24**	**0**	**1**	**0**	**114**	**3.5**		**775**	**51.9**	**95**	**22**	**13:02**	**2**	**0**	**0**	**0**	**2**	**0**	**0**	**0**

Signed as a free agent by **LA Kings**, July 25, 1997. Signed as a free agent by **Boston**, August 5, 1998. Signed as a free agent by **Buffalo**, August 13, 1999.

TAYLOR, Tim
(TAY-lohr, TIHM) **T.B.**

Center. Shoots left. 6'1", 190 lbs. Born, Stratford, Ont., February 6, 1969. Washington's 2nd choice, 36th overall, in 1988 Entry Draft.

Season	Club	League	GP	G	A	Pts	PIM	PP	SH	GW	S	%	+/-	TF	F%	H	SB	Min	GP	G	A	Pts	PIM	PP	SH	GW
1985-86	Stratford Cullitons	OJHL-B	1	0	0	0	0	....	....	....	....	....	....	....	....	....	....	....	....	....	....	....	....	....	....	....
1986-87	Stratford Cullitons	OJHL-B	31	25	26	51	51	....	....	....	....	....	....	....	....	....	....	....	....	....	....	....	....	....	....	....
	London Knights	OHL	34	7	9	16	11	....	....	....	....	....	....	....	....	....	....	....	....	....	....	....	....	....	....	....
1987-88	London Knights	OHL	64	46	50	96	66	....	....	....	....	....	....	....	....	....	....	....	12	9	9	18	26	....	....	....
1988-89	London Knights	OHL	61	34	80	114	93	....	....	....	....	....	....	....	....	....	....	....	21	*21	25	*46	58	....	....	....
1989-90	Baltimore	AHL	79	31	36	67	124	....	....	....	....	....	....	....	....	....	....	....	9	2	2	4	13	....	....	....
1990-91	Baltimore	AHL	79	25	42	67	75	....	....	....	....	....	....	....	....	....	....	....	5	0	1	1	4	....	....	....
1991-92	Baltimore	AHL	65	9	18	27	131	....	....	....	....	....	....	....	....	....	....	....	....	....	....	....	....	....	....	....
1992-93	Baltimore	AHL	41	15	16	31	49	....	....	....	....	....	....	....	....	....	....	....	....	....	....	....	....	....	....	....
	Hamilton Canucks	AHL	36	15	22	37	37	....	....	....	....	....	....	....	....	....	....	....	....	....	....	....	....	....	....	....
1993-94	**Detroit**	**NHL**	**1**	**1**	**0**	**1**	**0**	**0**	**0**	**0**	**4**	**25.0**	**–1**	....	....	....	....	....	....	....	....	....	....	....	....	....
	Adirondack	AHL	79	36	*81	*117	86	....	....	....	....	....	....	....	....	....	....	....	12	2	10	12	12	....	....	....
1994-95	**Detroit**	**NHL**	**22**	**0**	**4**	**4**	**16**	**0**	**0**	**0**	**21**	**0.0**	**3**	....	....	....	....	....	**6**	**0**	**1**	**1**	**12**	**0**	**0**	**0**
1995-96	**Detroit**	**NHL**	**72**	**11**	**14**	**25**	**39**	**1**	**1**	**4**	**81**	**13.6**	**11**	....	....	....	....	....	**18**	**0**	**4**	**4**	**4**	**0**	**0**	**0**
1996-97♦	**Detroit**	**NHL**	**44**	**3**	**4**	**7**	**52**	**0**	**1**	**0**	**44**	**6.8**	**–6**	....	....	....	....	....	**2**	**0**	**0**	**0**	**0**	**0**	**0**	**0**
1997-98	**Boston**	**NHL**	**79**	**20**	**11**	**31**	**57**	**1**	**3**	**0**	**127**	**15.7**	**–16**	....	....	....	....	....	**6**	**0**	**0**	**0**	**10**	**0**	**0**	**0**
1998-99	**Boston**	**NHL**	**49**	**4**	**7**	**11**	**55**	**0**	**0**	**1**	**76**	**5.3**	**–10**	**834**	**58.3**	**93**	**16**	**15:56**	**12**	**0**	**3**	**3**	**8**	**0**	**0**	**0**

			Regular Season																Playoffs							
Season	Club	League	GP	G	A	Pts	PIM	PP	SH	GW	S	%	+/-	TF	F%	H	SB	Min	GP	G	A	Pts	PIM	PP	SH	GW
99-2000	NY Rangers	NHL	76	9	11	20	72	0	0	2	79	11.4	-4	1276	58.9	94	41	14:09								
2000-01	NY Rangers	NHL	38	2	5	7	16	0	0	1	34	5.9	-6	292	59.3	34	18	8:57								
	NHL Totals		381	50	56	106	307	2	5	8	466	10.7		2402	58.7	221	75	13:28	44	0	8	8	34	0	0	0

AHL First All-Star Team (1994) • Won John B. Sollenberger Trophy (Top Scorer - AHL) (1994)

Traded to **Vancouver** by **Washington** for Eric Murano, January 29, 1993. Signed as a free agent by **Detroit**, July 28, 1993. Claimed by **Boston** from **Detroit** in NHL Waiver Draft, September 28, 1997. Signed as a free agent by **NY Rangers**, July 30, 1999. • Missed majority of 2000-01 season recovering from abdominal injury suffered in game vs. Phoenix, January 4, 2001. Traded to **Tampa Bay** by **NY Rangers** for Kyle Freadrich and Nils Ekman, June 30, 2001.

TENKRAT, Petr

(TEHN-krat, PEE-tuhr) **ANA.**

Right wing. Shoots right. 5'11", 207 lbs. Born, Kladno, Czech., May 31, 1977. Anaheim's 6th choice, 230th overall, in 1999 Entry Draft.

Season	Club	League	GP	G	A	Pts	PIM	PP	SH	GW	S	%	+/-	TF	F%	H	SB	Min	GP	G	A	Pts	PIM	PP	SH	GW
1994-95	Poldi Kladno	Cze-Rep	1	0	0	0	0																			
1995-96	Poldi Kladno	Cze-Rep	20	0	4	4	4												3	0	1	1	0			
1996-97	Poldi Kladno	Cze-Rep	43	5	9	14	6												3	0	1	1	0			
1997-98	Poldi Kladno	Cze-Rep	52	9	10	19	24																			
1998-99	Velvana Kladno	Cze-Rep	50	21	14	35	32																			
99-2000	HPK Hameenlinna	Finland	32	20	9	29	31																			
	Ilves Tampere	Finland	22	15	5	20	44												3	1	1	2	14			
2000-01	Anaheim	NHL	46	5	9	14	16	0	0	2	79	6.3	-11	0	0.0	33	3	12:48								
	Cincinnati Ducks	AHL	25	9	9	18	24												4	3	2	5	0			
	NHL Totals		46	5	9	14	16	0	0	2	79	6.3		0	0.0	33	3	12:48								

TETARENKO, Joey

(teh-tar-EHN-koh, JOH-ee) **FLA.**

Right wing. Shoots right. 6'2", 212 lbs. Born, Prince Albert, Sask., March 3, 1978. Florida's 4th choice, 82nd overall, in 1996 Entry Draft.

Season	Club	League	GP	G	A	Pts	PIM	PP	SH	GW	S	%	+/-	TF	F%	H	SB	Min	GP	G	A	Pts	PIM	PP	SH	GW
1993-94	North Battleford	SMHL	36	6	13	19	75																			
1994-95	Portland	WHL	59	0	1	1	134												9	0	0	0	8			
1995-96	Portland	WHL	71	4	11	15	190												7	0	1	1	17			
1996-97	Portland	WHL	68	8	18	26	182												2	0	0	0	2			
1997-98	Portland	WHL	49	2	12	14	148												16	0	2	2	30			
1998-99	New Haven	AHL	65	4	10	14	154																			
99-2000	Louisville Panthers	AHL	57	3	11	14	136												4	0	0	0	2			
2000-01	Florida	NHL	29	3	1	4	44	0	0	0	21	14.3	-1	0	0.0	30	5	6:12								
	Louisville Panthers	AHL	29	1	4	5	74																			
	NHL Totals		29	3	1	4	44	0	0	0	21	14.3		0	0.0	30	5	6:12								

TEZIKOV, Alexei

(TEH-zih-kahf, al-EHX-ay)

Defense. Shoots left. 6'1", 208 lbs. Born, Togliatti, USSR, June 22, 1978. Buffalo's 7th choice, 115th overall, in 1996 Entry Draft.

Season	Club	League	GP	G	A	Pts	PIM	PP	SH	GW	S	%	+/-	TF	F%	H	SB	Min	GP	G	A	Pts	PIM	PP	SH	GW
1995-96	Lada Togliatti	CIS	14	0	0	0	8																			
1996-97	Lada Togliatti	Russia	7	0	0	0	4																			
	Torpedo Nizhny	Russia	5	0	2	2	2																			
1997-98	Moncton Wildcats	QMJHL	60	15	33	48	144												10	3	8	11	20			
1998-99	Moncton Wildcats	QMJHL	25	9	21	30	52																			
	Rochester	AHL	31	3	7	10	41																			
	Washington	NHL	5	0	0	0	0	0	0	0	4	0.0	-1	0	0.0	9	3	18:11								
	Cincinnati	IHL	5	0	0	0	2												3	0	0	0	10			
99-2000	Washington	NHL	23	1	1	2	2	1	0	1	18	5.6	-2	0	0.0	17	9	10:30								
	Portland Pirates	AHL	53	6	9	15	70																			
2000-01	Portland Pirates	AHL	58	7	24	31	58																			
	Cincinnati Ducks	AHL	13	2	6	8	8												4	0	1	1	0			
	NHL Totals		28	1	1	2	2	1	0	1	22	4.5		0	0.0	26	12	11:52								

QMJHL Second All-Star Team (1998)

Traded to **Washington** by **Buffalo** with Buffalo's 4th round compensatory choice (later traded to Calgary - Calgary selected Levente Szuper) in 2000 Entry Draft for Joe Juneau and Washington's 3rd round choice (Tim Preston) in 1999 Entry Draft, March 22, 1999. Traded to **Anaheim** by **Washington** with Edmonton's 4th round choice (previously acquired, Anaheim selected Brandon Rogers) in 2001 Entry Draft for Jason Marshall, March 13, 2001.

THERIEN, Chris

(TEH-ree-ehn, KRIHS) **PHI.**

Defense. Shoots left. 6'5", 235 lbs. Born, Ottawa, Ont., December 14, 1971. Philadelphia's 7th choice, 47th overall, in 1990 Entry Draft.

Season	Club	League	GP	G	A	Pts	PIM	PP	SH	GW	S	%	+/-	TF	F%	H	SB	Min	GP	G	A	Pts	PIM	PP	SH	GW
1988-89	Ottawa Jr. Sens	OCJHL	8	3	1	4	22																			
1989-90	Ottawa Jr. Sens	OCJHL	3	0	2	2	2																			
	Northwood Prep	Hi-School	31	35	37	72	54																			
1990-91	Providence	H-East	36	4	18	22	36																			
1991-92	Providence	H-East	36	16	25	41	38																			
1992-93	Providence	H-East	33	8	11	19	52																			
	Canada	Nat-Team	8	1	4	5	8																			
1993-94	Canada	Nat-Team	59	7	15	22	46																			
	Canada	Olympics	4	0	0	0	4																			
	Hershey Bears	AHL	6	0	0	0	2																			
1994-95	Hershey Bears	AHL	34	3	13	16	27																			
	Philadelphia	NHL	48	3	10	13	38	1	0	0	53	5.7	8						15	0	0	0	10	0	0	0
1995-96	Philadelphia	NHL	82	6	17	23	89	3	0	1	123	4.9	16						12	0	0	0	18	0	0	0
1996-97	Philadelphia	NHL	71	2	22	24	64	0	0	0	107	1.9	27						19	1	6	7	6	0	0	1
1997-98	Philadelphia	NHL	78	3	16	19	80	1	0	1	102	2.9	5						5	0	1	1	4	0	0	0
1998-99	Philadelphia	NHL	74	3	15	18	48	1	0	0	115	2.6	16	0	0.0	167	103	20:45	6	0	0	0	6	0	0	0
99-2000	Philadelphia	NHL	80	4	9	13	66	1	0	1	126	3.2	11	0	0.0	171	137	20:12	18	0	1	1	12	0	0	0
2000-01	Philadelphia	NHL	73	2	12	14	48	1	0	0	103	1.9	22	0	0.0	196	84	20:38	6	1	0	1	8	0	0	0
	NHL Totals		506	23	101	124	433	8	0	3	729	3.2		0	0.0	534	324	20:31	81	2	8	10	64	0	0	1

Hockey East Second All-Star Team (1993) • NHL All-Rookie Team (1995)

THOMAS, Scott

(TAW-mas, SKAWT) **L.A.**

Right wing. Shoots right. 6'2", 200 lbs. Born, Buffalo, NY, January 18, 1970. Buffalo's 2nd choice, 56th overall, in 1989 Entry Draft.

Season	Club	League	GP	G	A	Pts	PIM	PP	SH	GW	S	%	+/-	TF	F%	H	SB	Min	GP	G	A	Pts	PIM	PP	SH	GW
1987-88	Nichols High	Hi-School	16	23	39	62	62																			
1988-89	Nichols High	Hi-School	17	38	52	90																				
1989-90	Clarkson Knights	ECAC	34	19	13	32	95																			
1990-91	Clarkson Knights	ECAC	40	28	14	42	89																			
1991-92	Clarkson Knights	ECAC	29	22	20	42	57																			
	Rochester	AHL																	9	0	1	1	17			
1992-93	Buffalo	NHL	7	1	1	2	15	0	0	0	4	25.0	2													
	Rochester	AHL	65	32	27	59	38												17	8	5	13	6			
1993-94	Buffalo	NHL	32	2	2	4	8	1	0	0	26	7.7	-6													
	Rochester	AHL	11	4	5	9	0																			
1994-95	Rochester	AHL	55	21	25	46	115												5	4	0	4	4			
1995-96	Cincinnati	IHL	78	32	28	60	54												17	*13	2	15	4			
1996-97	Cincinnati	IHL	71	32	29	61	46												3	0	0	0	0			
1997-98	Detroit Vipers	IHL	44	11	16	27	18																			
	Manitoba Moose	IHL	26	12	4	16	8												3	0	1	1	2			
1998-99	Manitoba Moose	IHL	78	45	25	70	32												5	3	4	7	4			
99-2000	Long Beach	IHL	52	15	16	31	18												6	2	1	3	6			
2000-01	Los Angeles	NHL	24	3	1	4	9	0	0	0	16	18.8	0	0	0.0	32	5	8:07	12	1	0	1	4	1	0	0
	Manitoba Moose	IHL	22	9	14	23	21												3	1	2	3	0			
	NHL Totals		63	6	4	10	32	1	0	0	46	13.0		0	0.0	32	5	8:07	12	1	0	1	4	1	0	0

Signed as a free agent by **LA Kings**, July 30, 1999.

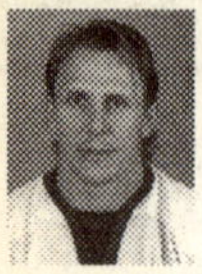

THOMAS, Steve

(TAW-mas, STEEV) **CHI.**

Right wing. Shoots left. 5'10", 185 lbs. Born, Stockport, England, July 15, 1963.

Season	Club	League	Regular Season GP	G	A	Pts	PIM	PP	SH	GW	S	%	+/-	TF	F%	H	SB	Min	Playoffs GP	G	A	Pts	PIM	PP	SH	GW
1980-81	Markham Waxers	MTJHL	42	22	25	47	76	....	....	....	....	....	....	....	....	....	....	....	....	....	....	....	....	....	....	....
	Toronto Marlies	OMJHL	1	0	0	0	0	....	....	....	....	....	....	....	....	....	....	....	....	....	....	....	....	....	....	....
1981-82	Markham Waxers	MTJHL	48	68	57	125	113	....	....	....	....	....	....	....	....	....	....	....	....	....	....	....	....	....	....	....
	Toronto Marlies	OHL	1	0	0	0	0	....	....	....	....	....	....	....	....	....	....	....	....	....	....	....	....	....	....	....
1982-83	Toronto Marlies	OHL	61	18	20	38	42	....	....	....	....	....	....	....	....	....	....	....	....	....	....	....	....	....	....	....
1983-84	Toronto Marlies	OHL	70	51	54	105	77	....	....	....	....	....	....	....	....	....	....	....	....	....	....	....	....	....	....	....
1984-85	**Toronto**	**NHL**	18	1	1	2	2	0	0	0	26	3.8	-13	....	....	....	....	....	....	....	....	....	....	....	....	....
	St. Catharines	AHL	64	42	48	90	56	....	....	....	....	....	....	....	....	....	....	....	....	....	....	....	....	....	....	....
1985-86	**Toronto**	**NHL**	65	20	37	57	36	5	0	5	197	10.2	-15	....	....	....	....	....	10	6	8	14	9	3	0	0
	St. Catharines	AHL	19	18	14	32	35	....	....	....	....	....	....	....	....	....	....	....	....	....	....	....	....	....	....	....
1986-87	**Toronto**	**NHL**	78	35	27	62	114	3	0	7	245	14.3	-3	....	....	....	....	....	13	2	3	5	13	0	0	0
1987-88	**Chicago**	**NHL**	30	13	13	26	40	5	0	3	69	18.8	1	....	....	....	....	....	3	1	2	3	6	0	0	0
1988-89	**Chicago**	**NHL**	45	21	19	40	69	8	0	0	124	16.9	-2	....	....	....	....	....	12	3	5	8	10	1	0	2
1989-90	**Chicago**	**NHL**	76	40	30	70	91	13	0	7	235	17.0	-3	....	....	....	....	....	20	7	6	13	33	1	0	3
1990-91	**Chicago**	**NHL**	69	19	35	54	129	2	0	3	192	9.9	8	....	....	....	....	....	6	1	2	3	15	0	0	0
1991-92	**Chicago**	**NHL**	11	2	6	8	26	0	0	1	35	5.7	-3	....	....	....	....	....	....	....	....	....	....	....	....	....
	NY Islanders	**NHL**	71	28	42	70	71	3	0	2	210	13.3	11	....	....	....	....	....	....	....	....	....	....	....	....	....
1992-93	**NY Islanders**	**NHL**	79	37	50	87	111	12	0	7	264	14.0	3	....	....	....	....	....	18	9	8	17	37	0	0	0
1993-94	**NY Islanders**	**NHL**	78	42	33	75	139	17	0	5	249	16.9	-9	....	....	....	....	....	4	1	0	1	8	1	0	0
1994-95	**NY Islanders**	**NHL**	47	11	15	26	60	3	0	2	133	8.3	-14	....	....	....	....	....	....	....	....	....	....	....	....	....
1995-96	**New Jersey**	**NHL**	81	26	35	61	98	6	0	6	192	13.5	-2	....	....	....	....	....	....	....	....	....	....	....	....	....
1996-97	**New Jersey**	**NHL**	57	15	19	34	46	1	0	2	124	12.1	9	....	....	....	....	....	10	1	1	2	18	0	0	0
1997-98	**New Jersey**	**NHL**	55	14	10	24	32	3	0	4	111	12.6	4	....	....	....	....	....	6	0	3	3	2	0	0	0
1998-99	**Toronto**	**NHL**	78	28	45	73	33	11	0	7	209	13.4	26	4	25.0	65	25	18:23	17	6	3	9	12	2	0	1
99-2000	**Toronto**	**NHL**	81	26	37	63	68	9	0	9	151	17.2	1	8	50.0	62	20	16:19	12	6	3	9	10	0	0	1
2000-01	**Toronto**	**NHL**	57	8	26	34	46	1	0	1	140	5.7	0	3	33.3	54	17	16:02	11	6	3	9	4	4	0	0
	NHL Totals		**1076**	**386**	**480**	**866**	**1211**	**102**	**0**	**71**	**2906**	**13.3**		**15**	**40.0**	**181**	**62**	**16:59**	**142**	**49**	**47**	**96**	**177**	**12**	**0**	**7**

AHL First All-Star Team (1985) • Won Dudley "Red" Garrett Memorial Trophy (Top Rookie - AHL) (1985)

Signed as a free agent by **Toronto,** May 12, 1984. Traded to **Chicago** by **Toronto** with Rick Vaive and Bob McGill for Al Secord and Ed Olczyk, September 3, 1987. Traded to **NY Islanders** by **Chicago** with Adam Creighton for Brent Sutter and Brad Lauer, October 25, 1991. Traded to **New Jersey** by **NY Islanders** for Claude Lemieux, October 3, 1995. Signed as a free agent by **Toronto,** July 30, 1998. Signed as a free agent by **Chicago,** July 17, 2001.

THOMPSON, Brent

(TAWM-suhn, BREHNT) **COL.**

Defense. Shoots left. 6'2", 205 lbs. Born, Calgary, Alta., January 9, 1971. Los Angeles' 1st choice, 39th overall, in 1989 Entry Draft.

Season	Club	League	Regular Season GP	G	A	Pts	PIM	PP	SH	GW	S	%	+/-	TF	F%	H	SB	Min	Playoffs GP	G	A	Pts	PIM	PP	SH	GW
1987-88	Calgary Stars	AMHL	25	0	13	13	33	....	....	....	....	....	....	....	....	....	....	....	....	....	....	....	....	....	....	....
1988-89	Medicine Hat	WHL	72	3	10	13	160	....	....	....	....	....	....	....	....	....	....	....	3	0	0	0	2	....	....	....
1989-90	Medicine Hat	WHL	68	10	35	45	167	....	....	....	....	....	....	....	....	....	....	....	3	0	1	1	14	....	....	....
1990-91	Medicine Hat	WHL	51	5	40	45	87	....	....	....	....	....	....	....	....	....	....	....	12	1	7	8	16	....	....	....
	Phoenix	IHL	....	....	....	....	....	....	....	....	....	....	....	....	....	....	....	....	4	0	1	1	6	....	....	....
1991-92	**Los Angeles**	**NHL**	27	0	5	5	89	0	0	0	18	0.0	-7	....	....	....	....	....	4	0	0	0	4	0	0	0
	Phoenix	IHL	42	4	13	17	139	....	....	....	....	....	....	....	....	....	....	....	....	....	....	....	....	....	....	....
1992-93	**Los Angeles**	**NHL**	30	0	4	4	76	0	0	0	18	0.0	-4	....	....	....	....	....	....	....	....	....	....	....	....	....
	Phoenix	IHL	22	0	5	5	112	....	....	....	....	....	....	....	....	....	....	....	....	....	....	....	....	....	....	....
1993-94	**Los Angeles**	**NHL**	24	1	0	1	81	0	0	0	9	11.1	-1	....	....	....	....	....	....	....	....	....	....	....	....	....
	Phoenix	IHL	26	1	11	12	118	....	....	....	....	....	....	....	....	....	....	....	....	....	....	....	....	....	....	....
1994-95	**Winnipeg**	**NHL**	29	0	0	0	78	0	0	0	16	0.0	-17	....	....	....	....	....	....	....	....	....	....	....	....	....
1995-96	**Winnipeg**	**NHL**	10	0	1	1	21	0	0	0	7	0.0	-2	....	....	....	....	....	....	....	....	....	....	....	....	....
	Springfield	AHL	58	2	10	12	203	....	....	....	....	....	....	....	....	....	....	....	10	1	4	5	*55	....	....	....
1996-97	**Phoenix**	**NHL**	1	0	0	0	7	0	0	0	0	0.0	-1	....	....	....	....	....	....	....	....	....	....	....	....	....
	Springfield	AHL	64	2	15	17	215	....	....	....	....	....	....	....	....	....	....	....	17	0	2	2	31	....	....	....
	Phoenix	IHL	12	0	1	1	67	....	....	....	....	....	....	....	....	....	....	....	....	....	....	....	....	....	....	....
1997-98	Hartford	AHL	77	4	15	19	308	....	....	....	....	....	....	....	....	....	....	....	15	0	4	4	25	....	....	....
1998-99	Hartford	AHL	76	3	15	18	265	....	....	....	....	....	....	....	....	....	....	....	7	0	0	0	23	....	....	....
99-2000	Louisville Panthers	AHL	67	4	22	26	311	....	....	....	....	....	....	....	....	....	....	....	3	0	0	0	11	....	....	....
2000-01	Louisville Panthers	AHL	59	1	9	10	170	....	....	....	....	....	....	....	....	....	....	....	....	....	....	....	....	....	....	....
	Hershey Bears	AHL	15	0	1	1	44	....	....	....	....	....	....	....	....	....	....	....	12	0	0	0	10	....	....	....
	NHL Totals		**121**	**1**	**10**	**11**	**352**	**0**	**0**	**0**	**68**	**1.5**		....	....	....	....	....	**4**	**0**	**0**	**0**	**4**	**0**	**0**	**0**

WHL East Second All-Star Team (1991)

Traded to **Winnipeg** by **LA Kings** with cash for the rights to Ruslan Batyrshin and Winnipeg's 2nd round choice (Marian Cisar) in 1996 Entry Draft, August 8, 1994. Transferred to **Phoenix** after **Winnipeg** franchise relocated, July 1, 1996. Signed as a free agent by **NY Rangers,** August 26, 1997. Signed as a free agent by **Florida,** July 27, 1999. Traded to **Colorado** by **Florida** for future considerations, March 3, 2001.

THOMPSON, Rocky

(TAWM-suhn, RAW-kee) **FLA.**

Right wing. Shoots right. 6'2", 205 lbs. Born, Calgary, Alta., August 8, 1977. Calgary's 3rd choice, 72nd overall, in 1995 Entry Draft.

Season	Club	League	Regular Season GP	G	A	Pts	PIM	PP	SH	GW	S	%	+/-	TF	F%	H	SB	Min	Playoffs GP	G	A	Pts	PIM	PP	SH	GW
1992-93	Spruce Grove	AAHA	65	13	50	63	295	....	....	....	....	....	....	....	....	....	....	....	....	....	....	....	....	....	....	....
1993-94	Medicine Hat	WHL	68	1	4	5	166	....	....	....	....	....	....	....	....	....	....	....	3	0	0	0	2	....	....	....
1994-95	Medicine Hat	WHL	63	1	6	7	220	....	....	....	....	....	....	....	....	....	....	....	5	0	0	0	17	....	....	....
1995-96	Medicine Hat	WHL	71	9	20	29	260	....	....	....	....	....	....	....	....	....	....	....	5	2	3	5	26	....	....	....
	Saint John Flames	AHL	4	0	0	0	33	....	....	....	....	....	....	....	....	....	....	....	....	....	....	....	....	....	....	....
1996-97	Medicine Hat	WHL	47	6	9	15	170	....	....	....	....	....	....	....	....	....	....	....	....	....	....	....	....	....	....	....
	Swift Current	WHL	22	3	5	8	90	....	....	....	....	....	....	....	....	....	....	....	10	1	2	3	22	....	....	....
1997-98	**Calgary**	**NHL**	12	0	0	0	61	0	0	0	3	0.0	0	....	....	....	....	....	....	....	....	....	....	....	....	....
	Saint John Flames	AHL	51	3	0	3	187	....	....	....	....	....	....	....	....	....	....	....	18	1	1	2	47	....	....	....
1998-99	**Calgary**	**NHL**	3	0	0	0	25	0	0	0	0	0.0	0	0	0.0	0	0	2:01	....	....	....	....	....	....	....	....
	Saint John Flames	AHL	27	2	2	4	108	....	....	....	....	....	....	....	....	....	....	....	....	....	....	....	....	....	....	....
99-2000	Saint John Flames	AHL	53	2	8	10	125	....	....	....	....	....	....	....	....	....	....	....	....	....	....	....	....	....	....	....
	Louisville Panthers	AHL	3	0	1	1	54	....	....	....	....	....	....	....	....	....	....	....	4	0	0	0	4	....	....	....
2000-01	**Florida**	**NHL**	4	0	0	0	19	0	0	0	0	0.0	0	0	0.0	4	0	1:28	....	....	....	....	....	....	....	....
	Louisville Panthers	AHL	55	3	5	8	193	....	....	....	....	....	....	....	....	....	....	....	....	....	....	....	....	....	....	....
	NHL Totals		**19**	**0**	**0**	**0**	**105**	**0**	**0**	**0**	**3**	**0.0**		**0**	**0.0**	**4**	**0**	**1:42**	....	....	....	....	....	....	....	....

Traded to **Florida** by **Calgary** for Filip Kuba, March 16, 2000.

THORNTON, Joe

(THOHRN-tuhn, JOH) **BOS.**

Center. Shoots left. 6'4", 215 lbs. Born, London, Ont., July 2, 1979. Boston's 1st choice, 1st overall, in 1997 Entry Draft.

Season	Club	League	Regular Season GP	G	A	Pts	PIM	PP	SH	GW	S	%	+/-	TF	F%	H	SB	Min	Playoffs GP	G	A	Pts	PIM	PP	SH	GW
1993-94	Elgin Elks	OMHA	67	*83	*85	*168	45	....	....	....	....	....	....	....	....	....	....	....	....	....	....	....	....	....	....	....
	St. Thomas Stars	OJHL-B	6	2	6	8	2	....	....	....	....	....	....	....	....	....	....	....	....	....	....	....	....	....	....	....
1994-95	St. Thomas Stars	OJHL-B	50	40	64	104	53	....	....	....	....	....	....	....	....	....	....	....	....	....	....	....	....	....	....	....
1995-96	Sault Ste. Marie	OHL	66	30	46	76	53	....	....	....	....	....	....	....	....	....	....	....	4	1	1	2	11	....	....	....
1996-97	Sault Ste. Marie	OHL	59	41	81	122	123	....	....	....	....	....	....	....	....	....	....	....	11	11	8	19	24	....	....	....
1997-98	**Boston**	**NHL**	55	3	4	7	19	0	0	1	33	9.1	-6	....	....	....	....	....	6	0	0	0	9	0	0	0
1998-99	**Boston**	**NHL**	81	16	25	41	69	7	0	1	128	12.5	3	1073	48.7	124	11	15:21	11	3	6	9	4	2	0	2
99-2000	**Boston**	**NHL**	81	23	37	60	82	5	0	3	171	13.5	-5	1861	49.5	134	14	21:18	....	....	....	....	....	....	....	....
2000-01	**Boston**	**NHL**	72	37	34	71	107	19	1	5	181	20.4	-4	1651	52.1	108	20	21:45	....	....	....	....	....	....	....	....
	NHL Totals		**289**	**79**	**100**	**179**	**277**	**31**	**1**	**10**	**513**	**15.4**		**4585**	**50.3**	**366**	**45**	**19:23**	**17**	**3**	**6**	**9**	**13**	**2**	**0**	**2**

Canadian Major Junior Rookie of the Year (1996) • OHL Second All-Star Team (1997)

THORNTON, Scott

(THOHRN-tuhn, SKAWT) **S.J.**

Center. Shoots left. 6'3", 220 lbs. Born, London, Ont., January 9, 1971. Toronto's 1st choice, 3rd overall, in 1989 Entry Draft.

			Regular Season																Playoffs							
Season	Club	League	GP	G	A	Pts	PIM	PP	SH	GW	S	%	+/-	TF	F%	H	SB	Min	GP	G	A	Pts	PIM	PP	SH	GW
1986-87	London Diamonds	OJHL-B	31	10	7	17	10																			
1987-88	Belleville Bulls	OHL	62	11	19	30	54												6	0	1	1	2			
1988-89	Belleville Bulls	OHL	59	28	34	62	103												5	1	1	2	6			
1989-90	Belleville Bulls	OHL	47	21	28	49	91												11	2	10	12	15			
1990-91	Belleville Bulls	OHL	3	2	1	3	2												6	0	7	7	14			
	Toronto	**NHL**	**33**	**1**	**3**	**4**	**30**	**0**	**0**	**0**	**31**	**3.2**	**-15**													
	Newmarket	AHL	5	1	0	1	4																			
1991-92	**Edmonton**	**NHL**	**15**	**0**	**1**	**1**	**43**	**0**	**0**	**0**	**11**	**0.0**	**-6**						**1**	**0**	**0**	**0**	**0**	**0**	**0**	**0**
	Cape Breton	AHL	49	9	14	23	40												5	1	0	1	8			
1992-93	**Edmonton**	**NHL**	**9**	**0**	**1**	**1**	**0**	**0**	**0**	**0**	**7**	**0.0**	**-4**													
	Cape Breton	AHL	58	23	27	50	102												16	1	2	3	35			
1993-94	**Edmonton**	**NHL**	**61**	**4**	**7**	**11**	**104**	**0**	**0**	**0**	**65**	**6.2**	**-15**													
	Cape Breton	AHL	2	1	1	2	31																			
1994-95	**Edmonton**	**NHL**	**47**	**10**	**12**	**22**	**89**	**0**	**1**	**1**	**69**	**14.5**	**-4**													
1995-96	**Edmonton**	**NHL**	**77**	**9**	**9**	**18**	**149**	**0**	**2**	**3**	**95**	**9.5**	**-25**													
1996-97	**Montreal**	**NHL**	**73**	**10**	**10**	**20**	**128**	**1**	**1**	**1**	**110**	**9.1**	**-19**						**5**	**1**	**0**	**1**	**2**	**0**	**0**	**0**
1997-98	**Montreal**	**NHL**	**67**	**6**	**9**	**15**	**158**	**1**	**0**	**1**	**51**	**11.8**	**0**						**9**	**0**	**2**	**2**	**10**	**0**	**0**	**0**
1998-99	**Montreal**	**NHL**	**47**	**7**	**4**	**11**	**87**	**1**	**0**	**1**	**56**	**12.5**	**-2**	**466**	**52.8**	**74**	**13**	**12:24**								
99-2000	**Montreal**	**NHL**	**35**	**2**	**3**	**5**	**70**	**0**	**0**	**1**	**36**	**5.6**	**-7**	**253**	**51.8**	**43**	**13**	**12:40**								
	Dallas	**NHL**	**30**	**6**	**3**	**9**	**38**	**1**	**0**	**0**	**47**	**12.8**	**-5**	**14**	**14.3**	**66**	**7**	**13:03**	**23**	**2**	**7**	**9**	**28**	**0**	**0**	**1**
2000-01	**San Jose**	**NHL**	**73**	**19**	**17**	**36**	**114**	**4**	**0**	**1**	**159**	**11.9**	**4**	**29**	**41.4**	**167**	**19**	**13:54**	**6**	**3**	**0**	**3**	**8**	**0**	**0**	**1**
	NHL Totals		**567**	**74**	**79**	**153**	**1010**	**8**	**4**	**9**	**737**	**10.0**		**762**	**51.3**	**350**	**52**	**13:09**	**44**	**6**	**9**	**15**	**48**	**0**	**0**	**2**

Traded to **Edmonton** by **Toronto** with Vincent Damphousse, Peter Ing and Luke Richardson for Grant Fuhr, Glenn Anderson and Craig Berube, September 19, 1991. Traded to **Montreal** by **Edmonton** for Andrei Kovalenko, September 6, 1996. Traded to **Dallas** by **Montreal** for Juha Lind, January 22, 2000. Signed as a free agent by **San Jose**, July 1, 2000.

TIBBETTS, Billy

(TIH-buhts, BIHL-ee) **PIT.**

Right wing. Shoots right. 6'2", 215 lbs. Born, Boston, MA, October 14, 1974.

			Regular Season																Playoffs							
Season	Club	League	GP	G	A	Pts	PIM	PP	SH	GW	S	%	+/-	TF	F%	H	SB	Min	GP	G	A	Pts	PIM	PP	SH	GW
1992-93	Boston Jr. Bruins	NEJHL	73	60	80	140	150																			
1993-94	Sioux City	USHL	7	1	4	5	27																			
	London Knights	OHL	14	6	6	12	49																			
	Tri-City Americans	WHL	9	0	2	2	39																			
1994-95	Birmingham Bulls	ECHL	2	0	1	1	18																			
1995-96	Johnstown Chiefs	ECHL	58	37	31	68	300																			
1996/00			DID NOT PLAY																							
2000-01	**Pittsburgh**	**NHL**	**29**	**1**	**2**	**3**	**79**	**0**	**0**	**0**	**16**	**6.3**	**-2**	**115**	**28.7**	**46**	**9**	**7:14**								
	Wilkes-Barre	AHL	38	14	24	38	185												12	4	6	10	55			
	NHL Totals		**29**	**1**	**2**	**3**	**79**	**0**	**0**	**0**	**16**	**6.3**		**115**	**28.7**	**46**	**9**	**7:14**								

• Missed 1996-97 through 1999-2000 seasons serving prison sentence that commenced July 12, 1996. Signed as a free agent by **Pittsburgh**, April 10, 2000.

TIKKANEN, Esa

(TEE-kuh-nehn, EHS-uh)

Left wing. Shoots left. 6'1", 190 lbs. Born, Helsinki, Finland, January 25, 1965. Edmonton's 4th choice, 82nd overall, in 1983 Entry Draft.

			Regular Season																Playoffs							
Season	Club	League	GP	G	A	Pts	PIM	PP	SH	GW	S	%	+/-	TF	F%	H	SB	Min	GP	G	A	Pts	PIM	PP	SH	GW
1981-82	Regina Blues	SJHL	59	38	37	75	216																			
	Regina Pats	WHL	2	0	0	0	0																			
1982-83	HIFK Helsinki	Finn-Jr.	30	34	31	65	*104												4	4	3	7	10			
	HIFK Helsinki	Finland																	1	0	0	0	2			
1983-84	HIFK Helsinki	Finn-Jr.	6	5	9	14	13												4	4	3	7	8			
	HIFK Helsinki	Finland	36	19	11	30	30												2	0	0	0	0			
1984-85	HIFK Helsinki	Finland	36	21	33	54	42																			
	♦ **Edmonton**	**NHL**																	**3**	**0**	**0**	**0**	**2**	**0**	**0**	**0**
1985-86	**Edmonton**	**NHL**	**35**	**7**	**6**	**13**	**28**	**0**	**0**	**2**	**44**	**15.9**	**5**						**8**	**3**	**2**	**5**	**7**	**0**	**0**	**0**
	Nova Scotia	AHL	15	4	8	12	17																			
1986-87♦	**Edmonton**	**NHL**	**76**	**34**	**44**	**78**	**120**	**7**	**0**	**6**	**126**	**27.0**	**44**						**21**	**7**	**2**	**9**	**22**	**1**	**0**	**1**
1987-88♦	**Edmonton**	**NHL**	**80**	**23**	**51**	**74**	**153**	**6**	**1**	**2**	**142**	**16.2**	**21**						**19**	**10**	**17**	**27**	**72**	**5**	**0**	**1**
1988-89	**Edmonton**	**NHL**	**67**	**31**	**47**	**78**	**92**	**6**	**8**	**4**	**151**	**20.5**	**10**						**7**	**1**	**3**	**4**	**12**	**0**	**0**	**0**
1989-90♦	**Edmonton**	**NHL**	**79**	**30**	**33**	**63**	**161**	**6**	**4**	**6**	**199**	**15.1**	**17**						**22**	**13**	**11**	**24**	**26**	**2**	**2**	**0**
1990-91	**Edmonton**	**NHL**	**79**	**27**	**42**	**69**	**85**	**3**	**2**	**6**	**235**	**11.5**	**22**						**18**	**12**	**8**	**20**	**24**	**3**	**0**	**3**
1991-92	**Edmonton**	**NHL**	**40**	**12**	**16**	**28**	**44**	**6**	**2**	**1**	**117**	**10.3**	**-8**						**16**	**5**	**3**	**8**	**8**	**1**	**0**	**1**
1992-93	**Edmonton**	**NHL**	**66**	**14**	**19**	**33**	**76**	**2**	**4**	**3**	**162**	**8.6**	**-11**													
	NY Rangers	**NHL**	**15**	**2**	**5**	**7**	**18**	**0**	**0**	**0**	**40**	**5.0**	**-13**													
1993-94♦	**NY Rangers**	**NHL**	**83**	**22**	**32**	**54**	**114**	**5**	**3**	**4**	**257**	**8.6**	**5**						**23**	**4**	**4**	**8**	**34**	**0**	**0**	**1**
1994-95	HIFK Helsinki	Finland	19	2	11	13	16																			
	St. Louis	**NHL**	**43**	**12**	**23**	**35**	**22**	**5**	**2**	**1**	**107**	**11.2**	**13**						**7**	**2**	**2**	**4**	**20**	**1**	**0**	**1**
1995-96	**St. Louis**	**NHL**	**11**	**1**	**4**	**5**	**18**	**0**	**1**	**0**	**19**	**5.3**	**1**													
	New Jersey	**NHL**	**9**	**0**	**2**	**2**	**4**	**0**	**0**	**0**	**15**	**0.0**	**-6**													
	Vancouver	**NHL**	**38**	**13**	**24**	**37**	**14**	**8**	**0**	**2**	**61**	**21.3**	**6**						**6**	**3**	**2**	**5**	**2**	**2**	**0**	**0**
1996-97	**Vancouver**	**NHL**	**62**	**12**	**15**	**27**	**66**	**4**	**1**	**2**	**103**	**11.7**	**-9**													
	NY Rangers	**NHL**	**14**	**1**	**2**	**3**	**6**	**0**	**1**	**0**	**30**	**3.3**	**0**						**15**	**9**	**3**	**12**	**26**	**3**	**1**	**3**
1997-98	**Florida**	**NHL**	**28**	**1**	**8**	**9**	**16**	**0**	**0**	**0**	**34**	**2.9**	**-7**													
	Finland	Olympics	6	1	1	2	0																			
	Washington	**NHL**	**20**	**2**	**10**	**12**	**2**	**1**	**0**	**2**	**33**	**6.1**	**-4**						**21**	**3**	**3**	**6**	**20**	**1**	**0**	**0**
1998-99	**NY Rangers**	**NHL**	**32**	**0**	**3**	**3**	**38**	**0**	**0**	**0**	**25**	**0.0**	**-5**	**312**	**47.4**	**30**	**14**	**13:38**								
99-2000	Jokerit Helsinki	Finland	43	10	13	23	85												11	1	6	7	10			
2000-01	ESC Essen	DEL	46	8	21	29	81																			
	NHL Totals		**877**	**244**	**386**	**630**	**1077**	**59**	**29**	**41**	**1900**	**12.8**		**312**	**47.4**	**30**	**14**	**13:38**	**186**	**72**	**60**	**132**	**275**	**19**	**3**	**11**

Traded to **NY Rangers** by **Edmonton** for Doug Weight, March 17, 1993. Traded to **St. Louis** by **NY Rangers** with Doug Lidster for Petr Nedved, July 24, 1994. Traded to **New Jersey** by **St. Louis** for New Jersey's 3rd round choice (later traded to Colorado - Colorado selected Ville Nieminen) in 1997 Entry Draft, November 1, 1995. Traded to **Vancouver** by **New Jersey** for Vancouver's 2nd round choice (Wes Mason) in 1996 Entry Draft, November 23, 1995. Traded to **NY Rangers** by **Vancouver** with Russ Courtnall for Sergei Nemchinov and Brian Noonan, March 8, 1997. Signed as a free agent by **Florida**, September 17, 1997. Traded to **Washington** by **Florida** for Dwayne Hay and future considerations, March 9, 1998. Signed as a free agent by **NY Rangers**, October 9, 1998. • Officially announced retirement, April 19, 2001.

TILEY, Brad

(TIHL-ee, BRAD) **PHI.**

Defense. Shoots left. 6'1", 185 lbs. Born, Markdale, Ont., July 5, 1971. Boston's 4th choice, 84th overall, in 1991 Entry Draft.

			Regular Season																Playoffs							
Season	Club	League	GP	G	A	Pts	PIM	PP	SH	GW	S	%	+/-	TF	F%	H	SB	Min	GP	G	A	Pts	PIM	PP	SH	GW
1987-88	Owen Sound	OJHL-B	45	18	25	43	69																			
1988-89	Sault Ste. Marie	OHL	50	4	11	15	31																			
1989-90	Sault Ste. Marie	OHL	66	9	32	41	47																			
1990-91	Sault Ste. Marie	OHL	66	11	55	66	29												14	4	15	19	12			
1991-92	Maine Mariners	AHL	62	7	22	29	36																			
1992-93	Phoenix	IHL	46	11	27	38	35																			
	Binghamton	AHL	26	6	10	16	19												8	0	1	1	2			
1993-94	Binghamton	AHL	29	6	10	16	6																			
	Phoenix	IHL	35	8	15	23	21																			
1994-95	Detroit Vipers	IHL	56	7	19	26	32																			
	Fort Wayne	IHL	14	1	6	7	2												3	1	2	3	0			
1995-96	Orlando	IHL	69	11	23	34	82												23	2	4	6	16			
1996-97	Phoenix	IHL	66	8	28	36	34																			
	Long Beach	IHL	3	1	0	1	2																			
1997-98	**Phoenix**	**NHL**	**1**	**0**	**0**	**0**	**0**																			
	Springfield	AHL	60	10	31	41	36												4	0	4	4	2			
1998-99	**Phoenix**	**NHL**	**8**	**0**	**0**	**0**	**0**	**0**	**0**	**0**	**1**	**0.0**	**-1**	**0**	**0.0**	**5**	**3**	**11:29**	**1**	**0**	**0**	**0**	**0**	**0**	**0**	**0**
	Springfield	AHL	69	9	35	44	14												1	0	0	0	0			
99-2000	Springfield	AHL	80	14	54	68	51												5	0	4	4	2			

			Regular Season																Playoffs							
Season	Club	League	GP	G	A	Pts	PIM	PP	SH	GW	S	%	+/-	TF	F%	H	SB	Min	GP	G	A	Pts	PIM	PP	SH	GW
2000-01	Philadelphia	NHL	2	0	0	0	0	0	0	0	1	0.0	-1	0	0.0	1	1	15:46								
	Philadelphia	AHL	56	11	19	30	10												10	1	2	3	2			
	NHL Totals		11	0	0	0	0	0	0	0	2	0.0		0	0.0	6	4	12:20	1	0	0	0	0	0	0	0

Memorial Cup All-Star Team (1991) • AHL First All-Star Team (2000) • Won Eddie Shore Award (Top Defenseman - AHL) (2000)

Signed as a free agent by **NY Rangers**, September 4, 1992. Traded to **LA Kings** by **NY Rangers** for LA Kings' 11th round choice (Jamie Butt) in 1994 Entry Draft, January 28, 1994. Signed as a free agent by **Phoenix**, September 4, 1997. Signed as a free agent by **Philadelphia**, July 14, 2000.

TIMANDER, Mattias

(tih-MAHN-duhr, MA-tee-uhs) **CBJ**

Defense. Shoots left. 6'2", 210 lbs. Born, Solleftea, Sweden, April 16, 1974. Boston's 7th choice, 208th overall, in 1992 Entry Draft.

Season	Club	League	GP	G	A	Pts	PIM	PP	SH	GW	S	%	+/-	TF	F%	H	SB	Min	GP	G	A	Pts	PIM	PP	SH	GW
1992-93	MoDo AIK	Swede-Jr.	4	0	0	0	0																			
	Husums IF	Sweden-2	27	4	9	13	22																			
	MoDo AIK	Sweden	1	0	0	0	0																			
1993-94	MoDo AIK	Swede-Jr.	3	2	2	4	10																			
	MoDo AIK	Sweden	23	2	2	4	6												11	2	0	2	10			
1994-95	MoDo Hockey	Sweden	39	8	9	17	24																			
1995-96	MoDo Hockey	Sweden	37	4	10	14	34												7	1	1	2	8			
1996-97	Boston	NHL	41	1	8	9	14	0	0	0	62	1.6	-9													
	Providence Bruins	AHL	32	3	11	14	20												10	1	1	2	12			
1997-98	Boston	NHL	23	1	1	2	6	0	0	0	17	5.9	-9													
	Providence Bruins	AHL	31	3	7	10	25																			
1998-99	Boston	NHL	22	0	6	6	10	0	0	0	22	0.0	4	0	0.0	14	13	12:54	4	1	1	2	2	0	0	0
	Providence Bruins	AHL	43	2	22	24	24																			
99-2000	Boston	NHL	60	0	8	8	22	0	0	0	39	0.0	-11	0	0.0	50	63	12:29								
	Hershey Bears	AHL	1	0	0	0	2																			
2000-01	Columbus	NHL	76	2	9	11	24	0	0	1	68	2.9	-8	2	100.0	51	129	21:02								
	NHL Totals		222	4	32	36	76	0	0	1	208	1.9		2	100.0	115	205	16:40	4	1	1	2	2	0	0	0

Selected by **Columbus** from **Boston** in Expansion Draft, June 23, 2000.

TIMONEN, Kimmo

(TEEM-oh-nehn, KEE-moh) **NSH.**

Defense. Shoots left. 5'10", 196 lbs. Born, Kuopio, Finland, March 18, 1975. Los Angeles' 11th choice, 250th overall, in 1993 Entry Draft.

Season	Club	League	GP	G	A	Pts	PIM	PP	SH	GW	S	%	+/-	TF	F%	H	SB	Min	GP	G	A	Pts	PIM	PP	SH	GW
1990-91	KalPa Kuopio	Finn-Jr.	4	0	1	1	2																			
1991-92	KalPa Kuopio	Finn-Jr.	32	7	10	17	4																			
	KalPa Kuopio	Finland	5	0	0	0	0																			
1992-93	KalPa Kuopio	Finn-Jr.	16	9	15	24	10																			
	KalPa Kuopio	Finland	33	0	2	2	4																			
1993-94	KalPa Kuopio	Finn-Jr.	5	4	7	11	0																			
	KalPa Kuopio	Finland	46	6	7	13	55																			
1994-95	TPS Turku	Finn-Jr.	1	0	0	0	0																			
	TPS Turku	Finland	45	3	4	7	10												13	0	1	1	6			
1995-96	TPS Turku	Finland	48	3	21	24	22												9	1	2	3	12			
1996-97	TPS Turku	Finland	50	10	14	24	18												12	2	7	9	8			
	TPS Turku	EuroHL	6	1	0	1	27												4	0	1	1	0			
1997-98	HIFK Helsinki	Finland	45	10	15	25	59												9	3	4	7	8			
	Finland	Olympics	6	0	1	1	2																			
1998-99	Nashville	NHL	50	4	8	12	30	1	0	0	75	5.3	-4	0	0.0	68	34	19:04								
	Milwaukee	IHL	29	2	13	15	22																			
99-2000	Nashville	NHL	51	8	25	33	26	2	1	2	97	8.2	-5	0	0.0	48	34	21:06								
2000-01	Nashville	NHL	82	12	13	25	50	6	0	3	151	7.9	-6	2	50.0	86	71	23:11								
	NHL Totals		183	24	46	70	106	9	1	5	323	7.4		2	50.0	202	139	21:29								

Traded to **Nashville** by **LA Kings** with Jan Vopat for future considerations, June 26, 1998.

TITOV, German

(TEE-tahf, GUHR-mihn) **ANA.**

Center. Shoots left. 6'1", 205 lbs. Born, Moscow, USSR, October 16, 1965. Calgary's 10th choice, 252nd overall, in 1993 Entry Draft.

Season	Club	League	GP	G	A	Pts	PIM	PP	SH	GW	S	%	+/-	TF	F%	H	SB	Min	GP	G	A	Pts	PIM	PP	SH	GW
1986-87	HK Khimik	USSR	23	1	0	1	10																			
1987-88	HK Khimik	USSR	39	6	5	11	10																			
1988-89	HK Khimik	USSR	44	10	3	13	24																			
1989-90	HK Khimik	USSR	44	6	14	20	19																			
1990-91	HK Khimik	USSR	45	13	11	24	28																			
1991-92	HK Khimik	CIS	42	18	13	31	35																			
1992-93	TPS Turku	Finland	47	25	19	44	49												12	5	12	17	10			
1993-94	Calgary	NHL	76	27	18	45	28	8	3	2	153	17.6	20						7	2	1	3	4	1	0	0
1994-95	TPS Turku	Finland	14	6	6	12	20																			
	Calgary	NHL	40	12	12	24	16	3	2	3	88	13.6	6						7	5	3	8	10	0	1	0
1995-96	Calgary	NHL	82	28	39	67	24	13	2	2	214	13.1	9						4	0	2	2	0	0	0	0
1996-97	Calgary	NHL	79	22	30	52	36	12	0	4	192	11.5	-12													
1997-98	Calgary	NHL	68	18	22	40	38	6	1	2	133	13.5	-1													
	Russia	Olympics	6	1	0	1	6																			
1998-99	Pittsburgh	NHL	72	11	45	56	34	3	1	3	113	9.7	18	41	39.0	67	50	19:31	11	3	5	8	4	0	0	0
99-2000	Pittsburgh	NHL	63	17	25	42	34	4	2	3	111	15.3	-3	102	37.3	58	26	20:20								
	Edmonton	NHL	7	0	4	4	4	0	0	0	11	0.0	2	0	0.0	5	4	13:33	5	1	1	2	0	0	0	0
2000-01	Anaheim	NHL	71	9	11	20	61	1	0	0	78	11.5	-21	226	38.9	60	25	15:53								
	NHL Totals		558	144	206	350	275	50	11	19	1093	13.2		369	38.5	190	105	18:21	34	11	12	23	18	1	1	0

Traded to **Pittsburgh** by **Calgary** with Todd Hlushko for Ken Wregget and Dave Roche, June 17, 1998. Traded to **Edmonton** by **Pittsburgh** for Josef Beranek, March 14, 2000. Signed as a free agent by **Anaheim**, July 1, 2000.

TKACHUK, Keith

(kuh-CHUK, KEETH) **ST.L.**

Left wing. Shoots left. 6'2", 225 lbs. Born, Melrose, MA, March 28, 1972. Winnipeg's 1st choice, 19th overall, in 1990 Entry Draft.

Season	Club	League	GP	G	A	Pts	PIM	PP	SH	GW	S	%	+/-	TF	F%	H	SB	Min	GP	G	A	Pts	PIM	PP	SH	GW
1988-89	Malden High	Hi-School	21	30	16	46	....																			
1989-90	Malden High	Hi-School	6	12	14	26	....																			
1990-91	Boston University	H-East	36	17	23	40	70																			
1991-92	United States	Nat-Team	45	10	10	20	141																			
	United States	Olympics	8	1	1	2	12																			
	Winnipeg	NHL	17	3	5	8	28	2	0	0	22	13.6	0						7	3	0	3	30	0	0	0
1992-93	Winnipeg	NHL	83	28	23	51	201	12	0	2	199	14.1	-13						6	4	0	4	14	1	0	0
1993-94	Winnipeg	NHL	84	41	40	81	255	22	3	3	218	18.8	-12													
1994-95	Winnipeg	NHL	48	22	29	51	152	7	2	2	129	17.1	-4													
1995-96	Winnipeg	NHL	76	50	48	98	156	20	2	6	249	20.1	11						6	1	2	3	22	0	0	0
1996-97	Phoenix	NHL	81	*52	34	86	228	9	2	7	296	17.6	-1						7	6	0	6	7	2	0	0
1997-98	Phoenix	NHL	69	40	26	66	147	11	0	8	232	17.2	9						6	3	3	6	10	0	0	0
	United States	Olympics	4	0	2	2	6																			
1998-99	Phoenix	NHL	68	36	32	68	151	11	2	7	258	14.0	22	770	47.7	102	20	20:59	7	1	3	4	13	1	0	0
99-2000	Phoenix	NHL	50	22	21	43	82	5	1	1	183	12.0	7	500	50.4	100	9	19:21	5	1	1	2	4	1	0	0
2000-01	Phoenix	NHL	64	29	42	71	108	15	0	4	230	12.6	6	646	51.9	86	18	20:11								
	St. Louis	NHL	12	6	2	8	14	2	0	1	41	14.6	-3	87	54.0	25	3	19:39	15	2	7	9	20	2	0	1
	NHL Totals		652	329	302	631	1522	116	12	41	2057	16.0		2003	50.0	313	50	20:13	59	21	16	37	120	7	0	1

NHL Second All-Star Team (1995, 1998) • Played in NHL All-Star Game (1997, 1998, 1999)

Transferred to **Phoenix** after **Winnipeg** franchise relocated, July 1, 1996. Traded to **St. Louis** by **Phoenix** for Michal Handzus, Ladislav Nagy, the rights to Jeff Taffe and St. Louis' 1st round choice in 2002 Entry Draft, March 13, 2001.

TKACZUK, Daniel
(kuh-CHUK, DAN-yehl) **ST.L.**

Center. Shoots left. 6'1", 197 lbs. Born, Toronto, Ont., June 10, 1979. Calgary's 1st choice, 6th overall, in 1997 Entry Draft.

			Regular Season																Playoffs							
Season	Club	League	GP	G	A	Pts	PIM	PP	SH	GW	S	%	+/-	TF	F%	H	SB	Min	GP	G	A	Pts	PIM	PP	SH	GW
1994-95	Mississauga Reps	MTHL	53	65	66	131	20																			
1995-96	Barrie Colts	OHL	61	22	39	61	38												7	1	2	3	8			
1996-97	Barrie Colts	OHL	62	45	48	93	49												9	7	2	9	2			
1997-98	Barrie Colts	OHL	57	35	40	75	38												6	2	3	5	8			
1998-99	Barrie Colts	OHL	58	43	62	105	58												12	7	8	15	10			
99-2000	Saint John Flames	AHL	80	25	41	66	56												3	0	0	0	0			
2000-01	**Calgary**	**NHL**	**19**	**4**	**7**	**11**	**14**	**1**	**0**	**0**	**34**	**11.8**	**1**	**197**	**43.2**	**16**	**5**	**12:14**								
	Saint John Flames	AHL	50	15	21	36	48												14	10	9	19	4			
	NHL Totals		**19**	**4**	**7**	**11**	**14**	**1**	**0**	**0**	**34**	**11.8**		**197**	**43.1**	**16**	**5**	**12:14**								

OHL First All-Star Team (1999)

Traded to **St. Louis** by **Calgary** with Fred Brathwaite, Sergei Varlamov and Calgary's 9th round choice (Grant Jacobsen) in 2001 Entry Draft for Roman Turek and St. Louis' 4th round choice (Yegor Shastin) in 2001 Entry Draft, June 23, 2001.

TOCCHET, Rick
(TAH-keht, RIHK) **PHI.**

Right wing. Shoots right. 6', 210 lbs. Born, Scarborough, Ont., April 9, 1964. Philadelphia's 5th choice, 125th overall, in 1983 Entry Draft.

			Regular Season																Playoffs							
Season	Club	League	GP	G	A	Pts	PIM	PP	SH	GW	S	%	+/-	TF	F%	H	SB	Min	GP	G	A	Pts	PIM	PP	SH	GW
1980-81	St. Michael's	MTHL	41	28	46	74																				
	St. Michael's	MTJHL	5	1	1	2	2																			
1981-82	Sault Ste. Marie	OHL	59	7	15	22	184												11	1	1	2	28			
1982-83	Sault Ste. Marie	OHL	66	32	34	66	146												16	4	13	17	67			
1983-84	Sault Ste. Marie	OHL	64	44	64	108	209												16	*22	14	*36	41			
1984-85	**Philadelphia**	**NHL**	**75**	**14**	**25**	**39**	**181**	**0**	**0**	**0**	**112**	**12.5**	**6**						**19**	**3**	**4**	**7**	**72**	**0**	**0**	**2**
1985-86	**Philadelphia**	**NHL**	**69**	**14**	**21**	**35**	**284**	**3**	**0**	**1**	**107**	**13.1**	**12**						**5**	**1**	**2**	**3**	**26**	**0**	**0**	**0**
1986-87	**Philadelphia**	**NHL**	**69**	**21**	**28**	**49**	**288**	**1**	**1**	**5**	**147**	**14.3**	**16**						**26**	**11**	**10**	**21**	**72**	**0**	**1**	**2**
1987-88	**Philadelphia**	**NHL**	**65**	**31**	**33**	**64**	**299**	**10**	**2**	**3**	**182**	**17.0**	**3**						**5**	**1**	**4**	**5**	**55**	**0**	**1**	**0**
1988-89	**Philadelphia**	**NHL**	**66**	**45**	**36**	**81**	**183**	**16**	**1**	**5**	**220**	**20.5**	**-1**						**16**	**6**	**6**	**12**	**69**	**2**	**0**	**1**
1989-90	**Philadelphia**	**NHL**	**75**	**37**	**59**	**96**	**196**	**15**	**1**	**0**	**269**	**13.8**	**4**													
1990-91	**Philadelphia**	**NHL**	**70**	**40**	**31**	**71**	**150**	**8**	**0**	**5**	**217**	**18.4**	**2**													
1991-92	**Philadelphia**	**NHL**	**42**	**13**	**16**	**29**	**102**	**4**	**0**	**1**	**107**	**12.1**	**3**													
	♦ Pittsburgh	**NHL**	**19**	**14**	**16**	**30**	**49**	**4**	**1**	**1**	**59**	**23.7**	**12**						**14**	**6**	**13**	**19**	**24**	**3**	**0**	**1**
1992-93	**Pittsburgh**	**NHL**	**80**	**48**	**61**	**109**	**252**	**20**	**4**	**5**	**240**	**20.0**	**28**						**12**	**7**	**6**	**13**	**24**	**1**	**0**	**0**
1993-94	**Pittsburgh**	**NHL**	**51**	**14**	**26**	**40**	**134**	**5**	**1**	**2**	**150**	**9.3**	**-15**						**6**	**2**	**3**	**5**	**20**	**1**	**0**	**1**
1994-95	**Los Angeles**	**NHL**	**36**	**18**	**17**	**35**	**70**	**7**	**1**	**3**	**95**	**18.9**	**-8**													
1995-96	**Los Angeles**	**NHL**	**44**	**13**	**23**	**36**	**117**	**4**	**0**	**0**	**100**	**13.0**	**3**													
	Boston	**NHL**	**27**	**16**	**8**	**24**	**64**	**6**	**0**	**3**	**85**	**18.8**	**7**						**5**	**4**	**0**	**4**	**21**	**3**	**0**	**1**
1996-97	**Boston**	**NHL**	**40**	**16**	**14**	**30**	**67**	**3**	**0**	**1**	**120**	**13.3**	**-3**													
	Washington	**NHL**	**13**	**5**	**5**	**10**	**31**	**1**	**0**	**1**	**37**	**13.5**	**0**													
1997-98	**Phoenix**	**NHL**	**68**	**26**	**19**	**45**	**157**	**8**	**0**	**6**	**161**	**16.1**	**1**						**6**	**6**	**2**	**8**	**25**	**3**	**0**	**0**
1998-99	**Phoenix**	**NHL**	**81**	**26**	**30**	**56**	**147**	**6**	**1**	**5**	**178**	**14.6**	**5**	**4**	**25.0**	**115**	**13**	**18:34**	**7**	**0**	**3**	**3**	**8**	**0**	**0**	**0**
99-2000	**Phoenix**	**NHL**	**64**	**12**	**17**	**29**	**67**	**2**	**0**	**1**	**107**	**11.2**	**-5**	**1**	**0.0**	**103**	**17**	**15:54**								
	Philadelphia	**NHL**	**16**	**3**	**3**	**6**	**23**	**2**	**0**	**0**	**23**	**13.0**	**4**	**0**	**0.0**	**26**	**3**	**14:47**	**18**	**5**	**6**	**11**	***49**	**2**	**0**	**1**
2000-01	**Philadelphia**	**NHL**	**60**	**14**	**22**	**36**	**83**	**5**	**0**	**2**	**76**	**18.4**	**10**	**1**	**0.0**	**68**	**8**	**15:20**	**6**	**0**	**1**	**1**	**6**	**0**	**0**	**0**
	NHL Totals		**1130**	**440**	**510**	**950**	**2944**	**130**	**13**	**50**	**2792**	**15.8**		**6**	**16.7**	**312**	**41**	**16:39**	**145**	**52**	**60**	**112**	**471**	**15**	**2**	**9**

Played in NHL All-Star Game (1989, 1990, 1991, 1993)

Traded to **Pittsburgh** by **Philadelphia** with Kjell Samuelsson, Ken Wregget and Philadelphia's 3rd round choice (Dave Roche) in 1993 Entry Draft for Mark Recchi, Brian Benning and LA Kings' 1st round choice (previously acquired, Philadelphia selected Jason Bowen) in 1992 Entry Draft, February 19, 1992 Traded to **LA Kings** by **Pittsburgh** with Pittsburgh's 2nd round choice (Pavel Rosa) in 1995 Entry Draft for Luc Robitaille, July 29, 1994. Traded to **Boston** by **LA Kings** for Kevin Stevens, January 25, 1996. Traded to **Washington** by **Boston** with Bill Ranford and Adam Oates for Jim Carey, Anson Carter, Jason Allison and Washington's 3rd round choice (Lee Goren) in 1997 Entry Draft, March 1, 1997. Signed as a free agent by **Phoenix**, July 23, 1997. Traded to **Philadelphia** by **Phoenix** for Mikael Renberg, March 8, 2000.

TOMS, Jeff
(TAWMS, JEHF) **NYR**

Left wing. Shoots left. 6'5", 200 lbs. Born, Swift Current, Sask., June 4, 1974. New Jersey's 10th choice, 210th overall, in 1992 Entry Draft.

			Regular Season																Playoffs							
Season	Club	League	GP	G	A	Pts	PIM	PP	SH	GW	S	%	+/-	TF	F%	H	SB	Min	GP	G	A	Pts	PIM	PP	SH	GW
1990-91	Oakville Oaks	OMHA	58	34	47	81	72																			
1991-92	Sault Ste. Marie	OHL	36	9	5	14	0												16	0	1	1	2			
1992-93	Sault Ste. Marie	OHL	59	16	23	39	20												16	4	4	8	7			
1993-94	Sault Ste. Marie	OHL	64	52	45	97	19												14	11	4	15	2			
1994-95	Atlanta Knights	IHL	40	7	8	15	10												4	0	0	0	4			
1995-96	**Tampa Bay**	**NHL**	**1**	**0**	**0**	**0**	**0**	**0**	**0**	**0**	**1**	**0.0**	**0**													
	Atlanta Knights	IHL	68	16	18	34	18												1	0	0	0	0			
1996-97	**Tampa Bay**	**NHL**	**34**	**2**	**8**	**10**	**10**	**0**	**0**	**1**	**53**	**3.8**	**2**													
	Adirondack	AHL	37	11	16	27	8												4	1	2	3	0			
1997-98	**Tampa Bay**	**NHL**	**13**	**1**	**2**	**3**	**7**	**0**	**0**	**0**	**14**	**7.1**	**-6**													
	Washington	**NHL**	**33**	**3**	**4**	**7**	**8**	**0**	**0**	**1**	**55**	**5.5**	**-11**						**1**	**0**	**0**	**0**	**0**	**0**	**0**	**0**
1998-99	**Washington**	**NHL**	**21**	**1**	**5**	**6**	**2**	**0**	**0**	**0**	**30**	**3.3**	**0**	**92**	**54.3**	**9**	**1**	**13:35**								
	Portland Pirates	AHL	20	3	7	10	8																			
99-2000	**Washington**	**NHL**	**20**	**1**	**2**	**3**	**4**	**0**	**0**	**1**	**18**	**5.6**	**-1**	**17**	**52.9**	**8**	**2**	**8:26**								
	Portland Pirates	AHL	33	16	21	37	16												4	1	1	2	2			
2000-01	**NY Islanders**	**NHL**	**39**	**2**	**4**	**6**	**10**	**0**	**0**	**0**	**37**	**5.4**	**-7**	**172**	**42.4**	**30**	**4**	**9:44**								
	Springfield	AHL	5	6	5	11	0																			
	NY Rangers	**NHL**	**15**	**1**	**1**	**2**	**0**	**0**	**0**	**0**	**12**	**8.3**	**-3**	**21**	**33.3**	**1**	**2**	**6:34**								
	Hartford	AHL	12	4	9	13	2												5	6	0	6	2			
	NHL Totals		**176**	**11**	**26**	**37**	**41**	**0**	**0**	**3**	**220**	**5.0**		**302**	**46.0**	**48**	**9**	**9:49**	**1**	**0**	**0**	**0**	**0**	**0**	**0**	**0**

Traded to **Tampa Bay** by **New Jersey** for Vancouver's 4th round choice (previously acquired by Tampa Bay - later traded to New Jersey - later traded to Calgary - Calgary selected Ryan Duthie) in 1994 Entry Draft, May 31, 1994. Claimed by on waivers by **Washington** from **Tampa Bay**, November 19, 1997. Signed as a free agent by **NY Islanders**, July 27, 2000. Claimed on waivers by **NY Rangers** from **NY Islanders**, January 13, 2001.

TRAVERSE, Patrick
(tra-VAIRZ, PAT-rihk) **MTL.**

Defense. Shoots left. 6'4", 204 lbs. Born, Montreal, Que., March 14, 1974. Ottawa's 3rd choice, 50th overall, in 1992 Entry Draft.

			Regular Season																Playoffs							
Season	Club	League	GP	G	A	Pts	PIM	PP	SH	GW	S	%	+/-	TF	F%	H	SB	Min	GP	G	A	Pts	PIM	PP	SH	GW
1990-91	Mtl-Bourassa	QAAA	42	4	19	23	10												5	0	3	3	2			
1991-92	Shawinigan	QMJHL	59	3	11	14	12												10	0	0	0	4			
1992-93	Shawinigan	QMJHL	53	5	24	29	24																			
	New Haven	AHL	2	0	0	0	2																			
	St-Jean Lynx	QMJHL	15	1	6	7	0												4	0	1	1	2			
1993-94	St-Jean Lynx	QMJHL	66	15	37	52	30												5	0	4	4	4			
	P.E.I. Senators	AHL	3	0	1	1	2																			
1994-95	P.E.I. Senators	AHL	70	5	13	18	19												7	0	2	2	0			
1995-96	**Ottawa**	**NHL**	**5**	**0**	**0**	**0**	**2**	**0**	**0**	**0**	**2**	**0.0**	**-1**													
	P.E.I. Senators	AHL	55	4	21	25	32												5	1	2	3	2			
1996-97	Worcester	AHL	24	0	4	4	23																			
	Grand Rapids	IHL	10	2	1	3	10												2	0	1	1	2			
1997-98	Hershey Bears	AHL	71	14	15	29	67												7	1	3	4	4			
1998-99	**Ottawa**	**NHL**	**46**	**1**	**9**	**10**	**22**	**0**	**0**	**0**	**35**	**2.9**	**12**	**0**	**0.0**	**41**	**42**	**14:56**								
99-2000	**Ottawa**	**NHL**	**66**	**6**	**17**	**23**	**21**	**1**	**0**	**0**	**73**	**8.2**	**17**	**0**	**0.0**	**51**	**78**	**18:43**	**6**	**0**	**0**	**0**	**2**	**0**	**0**	**0**
2000-01	**Anaheim**	**NHL**	**15**	**1**	**0**	**1**	**6**	**0**	**0**	**0**	**7**	**14.3**	**-6**	**0**	**0.0**	**15**	**12**	**17:19**								
	Boston	**NHL**	**37**	**2**	**6**	**8**	**14**	**1**	**0**	**1**	**39**	**5.1**	**4**	**0**	**0.0**	**39**	**25**	**16:38**								
	Montreal	**NHL**	**19**	**2**	**3**	**5**	**10**	**0**	**0**	**0**	**16**	**12.5**	**-8**	**0**	**0.0**	**25**	**27**	**21:36**								
	NHL Totals		**188**	**12**	**35**	**47**	**75**	**2**	**0**	**1**	**172**	**7.0**		**0**	**0.0**	**171**	**184**	**17:32**	**6**	**0**	**0**	**0**	**2**	**0**	**0**	**0**

Traded to **Anaheim** by **Ottawa** for Joel Kwiatkowski, June 12, 2000. Traded to **Boston** by **Anaheim** with Andrei Nazarov for Sami Pahlsson, November 18, 2000. Traded to **Montreal** by **Boston** for Eric Weinrich, February 21, 2001.

TREBIL, Dan

(TREH-bihl, DAN-yehl)

Defense. Shoots right. 6'3", 210 lbs. Born, Bloomington, MN, April 10, 1974. New Jersey's 7th choice, 138th overall, in 1992 Entry Draft.

			Regular Season																Playoffs							
Season	Club	League	GP	G	A	Pts	PIM	PP	SH	GW	S	%	+/-	TF	F%	H	SB	Min	GP	G	A	Pts	PIM	PP	SH	GW
1989-90	Jefferson High	Hi-School	22	3	6	9	10	....	....	....	....	....	....	....	....	....	....	....	....	....	....	....	....	....	....	....
1990-91	Jefferson High	Hi-School	23	4	12	16	8	....	....	....	....	....	....	....	....	....	....	....	....	....	....	....	....	....	....	....
1991-92	Jefferson High	Hi-School	28	7	26	33	6	....	....	....	....	....	....	....	....	....	....	....	....	....	....	....	....	....	....	....
1992-93	U. of Minnesota	WCHA	36	2	11	13	16	....	....	....	....	....	....	....	....	....	....	....	....	....	....	....	....	....	....	....
1993-94	U. of Minnesota	WCHA	42	1	21	22	24	....	....	....	....	....	....	....	....	....	....	....	....	....	....	....	....	....	....	....
1994-95	U. of Minnesota	WCHA	44	10	33	43	10	....	....	....	....	....	....	....	....	....	....	....	....	....	....	....	....	....	....	....
1995-96	U. of Minnesota	WCHA	42	11	35	46	36	....	....	....	....	....	....	....	....	....	....	....	....	....	....	....	....	....	....	....
1996-97	**Anaheim**	**NHL**	**29**	**3**	**3**	**6**	**23**	**0**	**0**	**0**	**30**	**10.0**	**5**	....	....	....	....	....	**9**	**0**	**1**	**1**	**6**	**0**	**0**	**0**
	Baltimore Bandits	AHL	49	4	20	24	38	....	....	....	....	....	....	....	....	....	....	....	....	....	....	....	....	....	....	....
1997-98	**Anaheim**	**NHL**	**21**	**0**	**1**	**1**	**2**	**0**	**0**	**0**	**11**	**0.0**	**−8**	....	....	....	....	....	....	....	....	....	....	....	....	....
	Cincinnati Ducks	AHL	32	5	15	20	21	....	....	....	....	....	....	....	....	....	....	....	....	....	....	....	....	....	....	....
1998-99	**Anaheim**	**NHL**	**6**	**0**	**0**	**0**	**0**	**0**	**0**	**0**	**1**	**0.0**	**−2**	**1**	**0.0**	**7**	**7**	**15:02**	**1**	**0**	**0**	**0**	**2**	**0**	**0**	**0**
	Cincinnati Ducks	AHL	52	6	15	21	31	....	....	....	....	....	....	....	....	....	....	....	....	....	....	....	....	....	....	....
99-2000	Cincinnati Ducks	AHL	52	7	21	28	48	....	....	....	....	....	....	....	....	....	....	....	....	....	....	....	....	....	....	....
	Pittsburgh	**NHL**	**3**	**1**	**0**	**1**	**0**	**0**	**0**	**0**	**2**	**50.0**	**2**	**0**	**0.0**	**3**	**1**	**12:33**	....	....	....	....	....	....	....	....
2000-01	**Pittsburgh**	**NHL**	**16**	**0**	**0**	**0**	**7**	**0**	**0**	**0**	**17**	**0.0**	**−1**	**0**	**0.0**	**23**	**6**	**12:59**	....	....	....	....	....	....	....	....
	Chicago Wolves	IHL	6	0	2	2	4	....	....	....	....	....	....	....	....	....	....	....	....	....	....	....	....	....	....	....
	St. Louis	**NHL**	**10**	**0**	**0**	**0**	**0**	**0**	**0**	**0**	**9**	**0.0**	**1**	**0**	**0.0**	**7**	**6**	**14:14**	....	....	....	....	....	....	....	....
	Worcester	AHL	14	2	7	9	0	....	....	....	....	....	....	....	....	....	....	....	9	0	5	5	2	....	....	....
	NHL Totals		**85**	**4**	**4**	**8**	**32**	**0**	**0**	**0**	**70**	**5.7**		**1**	**0.0**	**40**	**20**	**13:39**	**10**	**0**	**1**	**1**	**8**	**0**	**0**	**0**

WCHA Second All-Star Team (1996) • NCAA West Second All-American Team (1996)

Signed as a free agent by **Anaheim**, May 30, 1996. Traded to **Pittsburgh** by **Anaheim** for Pittsburgh's 5th round choice (Bill Cass) in 2000 Entry Draft, March 14, 2000. Signed as a free agent by **NY Islanders**, July 31, 2000. Traded to **Pittsburgh** by **NY Islanders** for Pittsburgh's 9th round choice (Roman Kuhtinov) in 2001 Entry Draft, November 14, 2000. Traded to **St. Louis** by **Pittsburgh** for Marc Bergevin, December 28, 2000.

TREMBLAY, Yannick

(TRAHM-blay, YA-nihk) **ATL.**

Defense. Shoots right. 6'2", 195 lbs. Born, Pointe-aux-Trembles, Que., November 15, 1975. Toronto's 4th choice, 145th overall, in 1995 Entry Draft.

Season	Club	League	GP	G	A	Pts	PIM	PP	SH	GW	S	%	+/-	TF	F%	H	SB	Min	GP	G	A	Pts	PIM	PP	SH	GW
1991-92	Mtl-Bourassa	QAAA	35	2	5	7	55	....	....	....	....	....	....	....	....	....	....	....	8	0	4	4	2	....	....	....
1992-93	Bourassa College	CEGEP	21	2	5	7	10	....	....	....	....	....	....	....	....	....	....	....	3	0	0	0	2	....	....	....
1993-94	St. Thomas U.	AUAA	25	2	3	5	10	....	....	....	....	....	....	....	....	....	....	....	....	....	....	....	....	....	....	....
1994-95	Beauport	QMJHL	70	10	32	42	22	....	....	....	....	....	....	....	....	....	....	....	17	6	8	14	6	....	....	....
1995-96	Beauport	QMJHL	61	12	33	45	42	....	....	....	....	....	....	....	....	....	....	....	20	3	16	19	18	....	....	....
	St. John's Leafs	AHL	3	0	1	1	0	....	....	....	....	....	....	....	....	....	....	....	....	....	....	....	....	....	....	....
1996-97	**Toronto**	**NHL**	**5**	**0**	**0**	**0**	**0**	**0**	**0**	**0**	**2**	**0.0**	**−4**	....	....	....	....	....	....	....	....	....	....	....	....	....
	St. John's Leafs	AHL	67	7	25	32	34	....	....	....	....	....	....	....	....	....	....	....	11	2	9	11	0	....	....	....
1997-98	**Toronto**	**NHL**	**38**	**2**	**4**	**6**	**6**	**1**	**0**	**0**	**45**	**4.4**	**−6**	....	....	....	....	....	....	....	....	....	....	....	....	....
	St. John's Leafs	AHL	17	3	7	10	4	....	....	....	....	....	....	....	....	....	....	....	4	0	1	1	5	....	....	....
1998-99	**Toronto**	**NHL**	**35**	**2**	**7**	**9**	**16**	**0**	**0**	**0**	**37**	**5.4**	**0**	**0**	**0.0**	**20**	**28**	**17:39**	....	....	....	....	....	....	....	....
99-2000	**Atlanta**	**NHL**	**75**	**10**	**21**	**31**	**22**	**4**	**1**	**2**	**139**	**7.2**	**−42**	**3**	**0.0**	**117**	**91**	**19:27**	....	....	....	....	....	....	....	....
2000-01	**Atlanta**	**NHL**	**46**	**4**	**8**	**12**	**30**	**1**	**0**	**1**	**102**	**3.9**	**−6**	**1**	**100.0**	**84**	**45**	**20:27**	....	....	....	....	....	....	....	....
	NHL Totals		**199**	**18**	**40**	**58**	**74**	**6**	**1**	**3**	**325**	**5.5**		**4**	**25.0**	**221**	**164**	**19:20**	....	....	....	....	....	....	....	....

Claimed by **Atlanta** from **Toronto** in Expansion Draft, June 25, 1999.

TREPANIER, Pascal

(truh-PAN-yai, PAS-kal)

Defense. Shoots right. 6', 210 lbs. Born, Gaspe, Que., September 4, 1973.

Season	Club	League	GP	G	A	Pts	PIM	PP	SH	GW	S	%	+/-	TF	F%	H	SB	Min	GP	G	A	Pts	PIM	PP	SH	GW
1989-90	Jonquiere Regents	QAAA	40	2	8	10	46	....	....	....	....	....	....	....	....	....	....	....	....	....	....	....	....	....	....	....
1990-91	Hull Olympiques	QMJHL	46	3	3	6	56	....	....	....	....	....	....	....	....	....	....	....	4	0	2	2	7	....	....	....
1991-92	Trois-Rivieres	QMJHL	53	4	18	22	125	....	....	....	....	....	....	....	....	....	....	....	15	3	5	8	21	....	....	....
1992-93	Sherbrooke	QMJHL	59	15	33	48	130	....	....	....	....	....	....	....	....	....	....	....	15	5	7	12	36	....	....	....
1993-94	Sherbrooke	QMJHL	48	16	41	57	67	....	....	....	....	....	....	....	....	....	....	....	12	1	8	9	14	....	....	....
1994-95	Dayton Bombers	ECHL	36	16	28	44	113	....	....	....	....	....	....	....	....	....	....	....	9	2	4	6	20	....	....	....
	Kalamazoo Wings	IHL	14	1	2	3	47	....	....	....	....	....	....	....	....	....	....	....	....	....	....	....	....	....	....	....
	Cornwall Aces	AHL	4	0	0	0	9	....	....	....	....	....	....	....	....	....	....	....	14	2	7	9	32	....	....	....
1995-96	Cornwall Aces	AHL	70	13	20	33	142	....	....	....	....	....	....	....	....	....	....	....	8	1	2	3	24	....	....	....
1996-97	Hershey Bears	AHL	73	14	39	53	151	....	....	....	....	....	....	....	....	....	....	....	23	6	13	19	59	....	....	....
1997-98	**Colorado**	**NHL**	**15**	**0**	**1**	**1**	**18**	**0**	**0**	**0**	**9**	**0.0**	**−2**	....	....	....	....	....	....	....	....	....	....	....	....	....
	Hershey Bears	AHL	43	13	18	31	105	....	....	....	....	....	....	....	....	....	....	....	7	4	2	6	8	....	....	....
1998-99	**Anaheim**	**NHL**	**45**	**2**	**4**	**6**	**48**	**0**	**0**	**1**	**49**	**4.1**	**0**	**1**	**0.0**	**65**	**52**	**12:42**	....	....	....	....	....	....	....	....
99-2000	**Anaheim**	**NHL**	**37**	**0**	**4**	**4**	**54**	**0**	**0**	**0**	**33**	**0.0**	**2**	**1**	**0.0**	**61**	**30**	**11:18**	....	....	....	....	....	....	....	....
2000-01	**Anaheim**	**NHL**	**57**	**6**	**4**	**10**	**73**	**3**	**0**	**0**	**86**	**7.0**	**−12**	**1**	**100.0**	**82**	**63**	**16:47**	....	....	....	....	....	....	....	....
	NHL Totals		**154**	**8**	**13**	**21**	**193**	**3**	**0**	**1**	**177**	**4.5**		**3**	**33.3**	**208**	**145**	**14:00**	....	....	....	....	....	....	....	....

AHL Second All-Star Team (1997)

Signed as a free agent by **Colorado**, August 30, 1995. Claimed by **Anaheim** from **Colorado** in NHL Waiver Draft, October 5, 1998.

TRNKA, Pavel

(truhn-KAH, PAH-vehl) **ANA.**

Defense. Shoots left. 6'2", 200 lbs. Born, Plzen, Czech., July 27, 1976. Anaheim's 5th choice, 106th overall, in 1994 Entry Draft.

Season	Club	League	GP	G	A	Pts	PIM	PP	SH	GW	S	%	+/-	TF	F%	H	SB	Min	GP	G	A	Pts	PIM	PP	SH	GW
1993-94	ZKZ Plzen	Cze-Rep	12	0	1	1		....	....	....	....	....	....	....	....	....	....	....	....	....	....	....	....	....	....	....
1994-95	Poldi Kladno	Cze-Rep	28	0	5	5	24	....	....	....	....	....	....	....	....	....	....	....	....	....	....	....	....	....	....	....
	ZKZ Plzen	Cze-Rep	6	0	0	0	0	....	....	....	....	....	....	....	....	....	....	....	....	....	....	....	....	....	....	....
1995-96	Baltimore Bandits	AHL	69	2	6	8	44	....	....	....	....	....	....	....	....	....	....	....	6	0	0	0	2	....	....	....
1996-97	Baltimore Bandits	AHL	69	6	14	20	86	....	....	....	....	....	....	....	....	....	....	....	3	0	0	0	2	....	....	....
1997-98	**Anaheim**	**NHL**	**48**	**3**	**4**	**7**	**40**	**1**	**0**	**0**	**46**	**6.5**	**−4**	....	....	....	....	....	....	....	....	....	....	....	....	....
	Cincinnati Ducks	AHL	23	3	5	8	28	....	....	....	....	....	....	....	....	....	....	....	....	....	....	....	....	....	....	....
1998-99	**Anaheim**	**NHL**	**63**	**0**	**4**	**4**	**60**	**0**	**0**	**0**	**50**	**0.0**	**−6**	**0**	**0.0**	**115**	**41**	**16:06**	**4**	**0**	**1**	**1**	**2**	**0**	**0**	**0**
99-2000	**Anaheim**	**NHL**	**57**	**2**	**15**	**17**	**34**	**0**	**0**	**0**	**54**	**3.7**	**12**	**0**	**0.0**	**152**	**48**	**19:21**	....	....	....	....	....	....	....	....
2000-01	**Anaheim**	**NHL**	**59**	**1**	**7**	**8**	**42**	**0**	**0**	**0**	**59**	**1.7**	**−12**	**0**	**0.0**	**146**	**54**	**20:07**	....	....	....	....	....	....	....	....
	NHL Totals		**227**	**6**	**30**	**36**	**176**	**1**	**0**	**0**	**209**	**2.9**		**0**	**0.0**	**413**	**143**	**18:27**	**4**	**0**	**1**	**1**	**2**	**0**	**0**	**0**

TRUDEL, Jean-Guy

(TROO-dehl, zhawn-gee) **PHX.**

Left wing. Shoots left. 5'11", 202 lbs. Born, Sudbury, Ont., October 18, 1975.

Season	Club	League	GP	G	A	Pts	PIM	PP	SH	GW	S	%	+/-	TF	F%	H	SB	Min	GP	G	A	Pts	PIM	PP	SH	GW
1991-92	Beauport	QMJHL	35	5	7	12	20	....	....	....	....	....	....	....	....	....	....	....	....	....	....	....	....	....	....	....
1992-93	Beauport	QMJHL	56	1	4	5	20	....	....	....	....	....	....	....	....	....	....	....	....	....	....	....	....	....	....	....
	Verdun College	QMJHL	10	1	0	1	0	....	....	....	....	....	....	....	....	....	....	....	2	0	0	0	5	....	....	....
1993-94			DID NOT PLAY																							
1994-95	Hull Olympiques	QMJHL	54	29	42	71	76	....	....	....	....	....	....	....	....	....	....	....	19	4	13	17	25	....	....	....
1995-96	Hull Olympiques	QMJHL	70	50	71	121	96	....	....	....	....	....	....	....	....	....	....	....	17	11	18	29	8	....	....	....
1996-97	Quad City	ColHL	5	8	7	15	4	....	....	....	....	....	....	....	....	....	....	....	....	....	....	....	....	....	....	....
	Chicago Wolves	IHL	6	1	2	3	2	....	....	....	....	....	....	....	....	....	....	....	....	....	....	....	....	....	....	....
	San Antonio	IHL	12	1	5	6	4	....	....	....	....	....	....	....	....	....	....	....	....	....	....	....	....	....	....	....
	Peoria Rivermen	ECHL	37	25	29	54	47	....	....	....	....	....	....	....	....	....	....	....	9	9	10	19	22	....	....	....
1997-98	Peoria Rivermen	ECHL	62	39	74	113	147	....	....	....	....	....	....	....	....	....	....	....	3	0	0	0	2	....	....	....
1998-99	Kansas City	IHL	76	24	25	49	66	....	....	....	....	....	....	....	....	....	....	....	3	1	0	1	0	....	....	....
99-2000	**Phoenix**	**NHL**	**1**	**0**	**0**	**0**	**0**	**0**	**0**	**0**	**0**	**0.0**	**−1**	**0**	**0.0**	**4**	**0**	**4:33**	....	....	....	....	....	....	....	....
	Springfield	AHL	72	34	39	73	80	....	....	....	....	....	....	....	....	....	....	....	3	0	1	1	4	....	....	....
2000-01	Springfield	AHL	80	34	65	99	89	....	....	....	....	....	....	....	....	....	....	....	....	....	....	....	....	....	....	....
	NHL Totals		**1**	**0**	**0**	**0**	**0**	**0**	**0**	**0**	**0**	**0.0**		**0**	**0.0**	**4**	**0**	**4:33**	....	....	....	....	....	....	....	....

AHL Second All-Star Team (2000) • AHL First All-Star Team (2001)

• Missed 1993-94 season to regain eligibility for U.S. College scholarship. Signed as a free agent by **Phoenix**, July 17, 1999.

TSYPLAKOV, Vladimir

(tsih-plah-KAHF, vla-DIH-meer)

Left wing. Shoots left. 6'1", 197 lbs. Born, Inta, USSR, April 18, 1969. Los Angeles' 4th choice, 59th overall, in 1995 Entry Draft.

			Regular Season																Playoffs							
Season	Club	League	GP	G	A	Pts	PIM	PP	SH	GW	S	%	+/-	TF	F%	H	SB	Min	GP	G	A	Pts	PIM	PP	SH	GW
1988-89	Dynamo Minsk	USSR	19	6	1	7	4	....	....	....	....	....	....	....	....	....	....	....	....	....	....	....	....	....	....	....
1989-90	Dynamo Minsk	USSR	47	11	6	17	20	....	....	....	....	....	....	....	....	....	....	....	....	....	....	....	....	....	....	....
1990-91	Dynamo Minsk	USSR	28	6	5	11	14	....	....	....	....	....	....	....	....	....	....	....	....	....	....	....	....	....	....	....
1991-92	Dynamo Minsk	CIS	29	10	9	19	16	....	....	....	....	....	....	....	....	....	....	....	....	....	....	....	....	....	....	....
1992-93	Detroit Falcons	ColHL	44	33	43	76	20	....	....	....	....	....	....	....	....	....	....	....	6	5	4	9	6	....	....	....
	Indianapolis Ice	IHL	11	6	7	13	4	....	....	....	....	....	....	....	....	....	....	....	5	1	1	2	2	....	....	....
1993-94	Fort Wayne	IHL	63	31	32	63	51	....	....	....	....	....	....	....	....	....	....	....	14	6	8	14	16	....	....	....
1994-95	Fort Wayne	IHL	79	38	40	78	39	....	....	....	....	....	....	....	....	....	....	....	4	2	4	6	2	....	....	....
1995-96	**Los Angeles**	**NHL**	**23**	**5**	**5**	**10**	**4**	**0**	**0**	**0**	**40**	**12.5**	**1**	....	....	....	....	....	....	....	....	....	....	....	....	....
	Las Vegas	IHL	9	5	6	11	4	....	....	....	....	....	....	....	....	....	....	....	....	....	....	....	....	....	....	....
1996-97	**Los Angeles**	**NHL**	**67**	**16**	**23**	**39**	**12**	**1**	**0**	**2**	**118**	**13.6**	**8**	....	....	....	....	....	....	....	....	....	....	....	....	....
1997-98	**Los Angeles**	**NHL**	**73**	**18**	**34**	**52**	**18**	**2**	**0**	**1**	**113**	**15.9**	**15**	....	....	....	....	....	**4**	**0**	**1**	**1**	**8**	**0**	**0**	**0**
	Belarus	Olympics	5	1	1	2	2	....	....	....	....	....	....	....	....	....	....	....	....	....	....	....	....	....	....	....
1998-99	**Los Angeles**	**NHL**	**69**	**11**	**12**	**23**	**32**	**0**	**2**	**2**	**111**	**9.9**	**–7**	**1**	**100.0**	**72**	**14**	**16:23**	....	....	....	....	....	....	....	....
99-2000	**Los Angeles**	**NHL**	**29**	**6**	**7**	**13**	**4**	**1**	**0**	**1**	**30**	**20.0**	**6**	**3**	**0.0**	**32**	**5**	**10:39**	....	....	....	....	....	....	....	....
	Buffalo	**NHL**	**34**	**6**	**13**	**19**	**10**	**0**	**0**	**1**	**46**	**13.0**	**17**	**0**	**0.0**	**44**	**4**	**13:41**	**5**	**0**	**1**	**1**	**4**	**0**	**0**	**0**
2000-01	**Buffalo**	**NHL**	**36**	**7**	**7**	**14**	**10**	**0**	**0**	**0**	**39**	**17.9**	**2**	**1**	**0.0**	**29**	**9**	**11:18**	**9**	**1**	**0**	**1**	**4**	**0**	**0**	**0**
	NHL Totals		**331**	**69**	**101**	**170**	**90**	**4**	**2**	**7**	**497**	**13.9**		**5**	**20.0**	**177**	**32**	**13:45**	**18**	**1**	**2**	**3**	**16**	**0**	**0**	**0**

ColHL First All-Star Team (1993)

Traded to **Buffalo** by **LA Kings** for Buffalo's 8th round choice (Dan Welch) in 2000 Entry Draft, January 24, 2000. • Missed majority of 2000-01 season recovering from knee injury suffered in game vs. Edmonton, October 13, 2000.

TUCKER, Darcy

(TUH-kuhr, DAHR-see) **TOR.**

Center. Shoots left. 5'11", 185 lbs. Born, Castor, Alta., March 15, 1975. Montreal's 8th choice, 151st overall, in 1993 Entry Draft.

Season	Club	League	GP	G	A	Pts	PIM	PP	SH	GW	S	%	+/-	TF	F%	H	SB	Min	GP	G	A	Pts	PIM	PP	SH	GW
1990-91	Red Deer Chiefs	AAHA	47	70	90	160	48	....	....	....	....	....	....	....	....	....	....	....	....	....	....	....	....	....	....	....
1991-92	Kamloops Blazers	WHL	26	3	10	13	32	....	....	....	....	....	....	....	....	....	....	....	9	0	1	1	16	....	....	....
1992-93	Kamloops Blazers	WHL	67	31	58	89	155	....	....	....	....	....	....	....	....	....	....	....	13	7	6	13	34	....	....	....
1993-94	Kamloops Blazers	WHL	66	52	88	140	143	....	....	....	....	....	....	....	....	....	....	....	19	9	*18	*27	43	....	....	....
1994-95	Kamloops Blazers	WHL	64	64	73	137	94	....	....	....	....	....	....	....	....	....	....	....	21	*16	15	*31	19	....	....	....
1995-96	**Montreal**	**NHL**	**3**	**0**	**0**	**0**	**0**	**0**	**0**	**0**	**1**	**0.0**	**–1**	....	....	....	....	....	....	....	....	....	....	....	....	....
	Fredericton	AHL	74	29	64	93	174	....	....	....	....	....	....	....	....	....	....	....	7	7	3	10	14	....	....	....
1996-97	**Montreal**	**NHL**	**73**	**7**	**13**	**20**	**110**	**1**	**0**	**3**	**62**	**11.3**	**–5**	....	....	....	....	....	**4**	**0**	**0**	**0**	**0**	**0**	**0**	**0**
1997-98	**Montreal**	**NHL**	**39**	**1**	**5**	**6**	**57**	**0**	**0**	**0**	**19**	**5.3**	**–6**	....	....	....	....	....	....	....	....	....	....	....	....	....
	Tampa Bay	**NHL**	**35**	**6**	**8**	**14**	**89**	**1**	**1**	**0**	**44**	**13.6**	**–8**	....	....	....	....	....	....	....	....	....	....	....	....	....
1998-99	**Tampa Bay**	**NHL**	**82**	**21**	**22**	**43**	**176**	**8**	**2**	**3**	**178**	**11.8**	**–34**	**1470**	**45.6**	**120**	**49**	**19:24**	....	....	....	....	....	....	....	....
99-2000	**Tampa Bay**	**NHL**	**50**	**14**	**20**	**34**	**108**	**1**	**0**	**2**	**98**	**14.3**	**–15**	**152**	**48.7**	**106**	**19**	**19:58**	....	....	....	....	....	....	....	....
	Toronto	**NHL**	**27**	**7**	**10**	**17**	**55**	**0**	**2**	**3**	**40**	**17.5**	**3**	**11**	**54.6**	**62**	**19**	**16:41**	**12**	**4**	**2**	**6**	**15**	**1**	**0**	**2**
2000-01	**Toronto**	**NHL**	**82**	**16**	**21**	**37**	**141**	**2**	**0**	**4**	**122**	**13.1**	**6**	**413**	**47.0**	**151**	**50**	**16:09**	**11**	**0**	**2**	**2**	**6**	**0**	**0**	**0**
	NHL Totals		**391**	**72**	**99**	**171**	**736**	**13**	**5**	**15**	**564**	**12.8**		**2046**	**46.1**	**439**	**137**	**18:07**	**27**	**4**	**4**	**8**	**21**	**1**	**0**	**2**

WHL West First All-Star Team (1994, 1995) • Canadian Major Junior First All-Star Team (1994) • Memorial Cup All-Star Team (1994, 1995) • Won Stafford Smythe Memorial Trophy (Memorial Cup Tournament MVP) (1994) • Won Dudley "Red" Garrett Memorial Trophy (Top Rookie - AHL) (1996)

Traded to **Tampa Bay** by **Montreal** with Stephane Richer and David Wilkie for Patrick Poulin, Mick Vukota and Igor Ulanov, January 15, 1998. Traded to **Toronto** by **Tampa Bay** with Tampa Bay's 4th round choice (Miguel Delisle) in 2000 Entry Draft and future considerations for Mike Johnson, Marek Posmyk, Toronto's 5th (Pavel Sedov) and 6th (Aaron Gionet) round choices in 2000 Entry Draft and future considerations, February 9, 2000.

TUOMAINEN, Marko

(TOO-oh-migh-nehn, MAHR-koh)

Right wing. Shoots right. 6'3", 218 lbs. Born, Kuopio, Finland, April 25, 1972. Edmonton's 10th choice, 205th overall, in 1992 Entry Draft.

Season	Club	League	GP	G	A	Pts	PIM	PP	SH	GW	S	%	+/-	TF	F%	H	SB	Min	GP	G	A	Pts	PIM	PP	SH	GW
1988-89	KalPa Kuopio	Finn-Jr.	7	6	6	12	4	....	....	....	....	....	....	....	....	....	....	....	....	....	....	....	....	....	....	....
1989-90	KalPa Kuopio	Finn-Jr.	36	13	24	37	30	....	....	....	....	....	....	....	....	....	....	....	....	....	....	....	....	....	....	....
	KalPa Kuopio	Finland	5	0	0	0	0	....	....	....	....	....	....	....	....	....	....	....	....	....	....	....	....	....	....	....
1990-91	KalPa Kuopio	Finn-Jr.	35	36	17	53	61	....	....	....	....	....	....	....	....	....	....	....	....	....	....	....	....	....	....	....
	KalPa Kuopio	Finland	30	2	1	3	2	....	....	....	....	....	....	....	....	....	....	....	8	0	0	0	6	....	....	....
1991-92	Clarkson Knights	ECAC	28	11	12	23	32	....	....	....	....	....	....	....	....	....	....	....	....	....	....	....	....	....	....	....
1992-93	Clarkson Knights	ECAC	35	25	30	55	26	....	....	....	....	....	....	....	....	....	....	....	....	....	....	....	....	....	....	....
1993-94	Clarkson Knights	ECAC	34	23	29	52	60	....	....	....	....	....	....	....	....	....	....	....	....	....	....	....	....	....	....	....
1994-95	Clarkson Knights	ECAC	37	23	38	61	34	....	....	....	....	....	....	....	....	....	....	....	....	....	....	....	....	....	....	....
	Edmonton	**NHL**	**4**	**0**	**0**	**0**	**0**	**0**	**0**	**0**	**5**	**0.0**	**0**	....	....	....	....	....	....	....	....	....	....	....	....	....
1995-96	Cape Breton	AHL	58	25	35	60	71	....	....	....	....	....	....	....	....	....	....	....	....	....	....	....	....	....	....	....
1996-97	Hamilton Bulldogs	AHL	79	31	21	52	130	....	....	....	....	....	....	....	....	....	....	....	22	7	5	12	4	....	....	....
1997-98	HIFK Helsinki	Finland	46	13	9	22	20	....	....	....	....	....	....	....	....	....	....	....	9	0	3	3	0	....	....	....
1998-99	HIFK Helsinki	Finland	48	11	17	28	*173	....	....	....	....	....	....	....	....	....	....	....	11	1	3	4	12	....	....	....
	HIFK Helsinki	EuroHL	6	0	1	1	8	....	....	....	....	....	....	....	....	....	....	....	4	3	0	3	4	....	....	....
99-2000	**Los Angeles**	**NHL**	**63**	**9**	**8**	**17**	**80**	**2**	**1**	**1**	**74**	**12.2**	**–12**	**8**	**25.0**	**69**	**9**	**11:30**	**1**	**0**	**0**	**0**	**0**	**0**	**0**	**0**
2000-01	Lowell	AHL	59	28	39	67	73	....	....	....	....	....	....	....	....	....	....	....	4	3	3	6	10	....	....	....
	Los Angeles	**NHL**	**11**	**0**	**1**	**1**	**4**	**0**	**0**	**0**	**12**	**0.0**	**1**	**1**	**100.0**	**10**	**1**	**9:22**	....	....	....	....	....	....	....	....
	NHL Totals		**78**	**9**	**9**	**18**	**84**	**2**	**1**	**1**	**91**	**9.9**		**9**	**33.3**	**79**	**10**	**11:11**	**1**	**0**	**0**	**0**	**0**	**0**	**0**	**0**

ECAC First All-Star Team (1993, 1995) • NCAA East Second All-American Team (1995)

Signed as a free agent by **LA Kings**, June 20, 1999. Signed as a free agent by **LA Kings**, January 4, 2001.

TURGEON, Pierre

(TUHR-zhaw, PEE-air) **DAL.**

Center. Shoots left. 6'1", 199 lbs. Born, Rouyn, Que., August 28, 1969. Buffalo's 1st choice, 1st overall, in 1987 Entry Draft.

Season	Club	League	GP	G	A	Pts	PIM	PP	SH	GW	S	%	+/-	TF	F%	H	SB	Min	GP	G	A	Pts	PIM	PP	SH	GW
1984-85	Mtl-Bourassa	QAAA	41	49	52	101	26	....	....	....	....	....	....	....	....	....	....	....	5	3	8	11	2	....	....	....
1985-86	Granby Bisons	QMJHL	69	47	67	114	31	....	....	....	....	....	....	....	....	....	....	....	....	....	....	....	....	....	....	....
1986-87	Granby Bisons	QMJHL	58	69	85	154	8	....	....	....	....	....	....	....	....	....	....	....	7	9	6	15	15	....	....	....
1987-88	**Buffalo**	**NHL**	**76**	**14**	**28**	**42**	**34**	**8**	**0**	**3**	**101**	**13.9**	**–8**	....	....	....	....	....	**6**	**4**	**3**	**7**	**4**	**3**	**0**	**0**
1988-89	**Buffalo**	**NHL**	**80**	**34**	**54**	**88**	**26**	**19**	**0**	**5**	**182**	**18.7**	**–2**	....	....	....	....	....	**5**	**3**	**5**	**8**	**2**	**1**	**0**	**0**
1989-90	**Buffalo**	**NHL**	**80**	**40**	**66**	**106**	**29**	**17**	**1**	**10**	**193**	**20.7**	**10**	....	....	....	....	....	**6**	**2**	**4**	**6**	**2**	**0**	**0**	**1**
1990-91	**Buffalo**	**NHL**	**78**	**32**	**47**	**79**	**26**	**13**	**2**	**3**	**174**	**18.4**	**14**	....	....	....	....	....	**6**	**3**	**1**	**4**	**6**	**1**	**0**	**0**
1991-92	**Buffalo**	**NHL**	**8**	**2**	**6**	**8**	**4**	**0**	**0**	**0**	**14**	**14.3**	**–1**	....	....	....	....	....	....	....	....	....	....	....	....	....
	NY Islanders	**NHL**	**69**	**38**	**49**	**87**	**16**	**13**	**0**	**6**	**193**	**19.7**	**8**	....	....	....	....	....	....	....	....	....	....	....	....	....
1992-93	**NY Islanders**	**NHL**	**83**	**58**	**74**	**132**	**26**	**24**	**0**	**10**	**301**	**19.3**	**–1**	....	....	....	....	....	**11**	**6**	**7**	**13**	**0**	**0**	**0**	**0**
1993 94	**NY Islanders**	**NHL**	**69**	**38**	**56**	**94**	**18**	**10**	**4**	**6**	**254**	**15.0**	**14**	....	....	....	....	....	**4**	**0**	**1**	**1**	**0**	**0**	**0**	**0**
1994-95	**NY Islanders**	**NHL**	**34**	**13**	**14**	**27**	**10**	**3**	**2**	**2**	**93**	**14.0**	**–12**	....	....	....	....	....	....	....	....	....	....	....	....	....
	Montreal	**NHL**	**15**	**11**	**9**	**20**	**4**	**2**	**0**	**2**	**67**	**16.4**	**12**	....	....	....	....	....	....	....	....	....	....	....	....	....
1995-96	**Montreal**	**NHL**	**80**	**38**	**58**	**96**	**44**	**17**	**1**	**6**	**297**	**12.8**	**19**	....	....	....	....	....	**6**	**2**	**4**	**6**	**2**	**0**	**0**	**0**
1996-97	**Montreal**	**NHL**	**9**	**1**	**10**	**11**	**2**	**0**	**0**	**0**	**22**	**4.5**	**4**	....	....	....	....	....	....	....	....	....	....	....	....	....
	St. Louis	**NHL**	**69**	**25**	**49**	**74**	**12**	**5**	**0**	**7**	**194**	**12.9**	**4**	....	....	....	....	....	**5**	**1**	**1**	**2**	**2**	**1**	**0**	**0**
1997-98	**St. Louis**	**NHL**	**60**	**22**	**46**	**68**	**24**	**6**	**0**	**4**	**140**	**15.7**	**13**	....	....	....	....	....	**10**	**4**	**4**	**8**	**2**	**2**	**0**	**0**
1998-99	**St. Louis**	**NHL**	**67**	**31**	**34**	**65**	**36**	**10**	**0**	**5**	**193**	**16.1**	**4**	**1285**	**50.0**	**16**	**24**	**19:07**	**13**	**4**	**9**	**13**	**6**	**0**	**0**	**2**
99-2000	**St. Louis**	**NHL**	**52**	**26**	**40**	**66**	**8**	**8**	**0**	**3**	**139**	**18.7**	**30**	**1016**	**53.2**	**5**	**19**	**19:13**	**7**	**0**	**7**	**7**	**0**	**0**	**0**	**0**
2000-01	**St. Louis**	**NHL**	**79**	**30**	**52**	**82**	**37**	**11**	**0**	**6**	**171**	**17.5**	**14**	**1569**	**49.7**	**9**	**22**	**18:50**	**15**	**5**	**10**	**15**	**2**	**1**	**0**	**0**
	NHL Totals		**1008**	**453**	**692**	**1145**	**356**	**166**	**10**	**78**	**2728**	**16.6**		**3870**	**50.7**	**30**	**65**	**19:02**	**94**	**34**	**56**	**90**	**28**	**9**	**0**	**3**

Won Lady Byng Memorial Trophy (1993) • Played in NHL All-Star Game (1990, 1993, 1994, 1996)

Traded to **NY Islanders** by **Buffalo** with Uwe Krupp, Benoit Hogue and Dave McLlwain for Pat LaFontaine, Randy Hillier, Randy Wood and NY Islanders' 4th round choice (Dean Melanson) in 1992 Entry Draft, October 25, 1991. Traded to **Montreal** by **NY Islanders** with Vladimir Malakhov for Kirk Muller, Mathieu Schneider and Craig Darby, April 5, 1995. Traded to **St. Louis** by **Montreal** with Rory Fitzpatrick and Craig Conroy for Murray Baron, Shayne Corson and St. Louis' 5th round choice (Gennady Razin) in 1997 Entry Draft, October 29, 1996. Signed as a free agent by **Dallas**, July 1, 2001.

TUZZOLINO, Tony
(too-zuh-LEE-noh, TOH-nee) **BOS.**

Right wing. Shoots right. 6'2", 208 lbs. Born, Buffalo, NY, October 9, 1975. Quebec's 7th choice, 113th overall, in 1994 Entry Draft.

Season	Club	League	Regular Season GP	G	A	Pts	PIM	PP	SH	GW	S	%	+/-	TF	F%	H	SB	Min	Playoffs GP	G	A	Pts	PIM	PP	SH	GW
1989-90	Amherst Knights	NYAHA	29	50	95	145	....																			
1990-91	Buffalo Regals	NAJHL	55	39	47	86	....																			
1991-92	Niagara Scenics	NAJHL	45	19	27	46	82																			
1992-93	Niagara Scenics	NAJHL	50	36	41	77	134																			
1993-94	Michigan State	CCHA	35	4	3	7	46																			
1994-95	Michigan State	CCHA	39	9	18	27	81																			
1995-96	Michigan State	CCHA	41	12	17	29	120																			
1996-97	Michigan State	CCHA	39	14	18	32	120																			
1997-98	Kentucky	AHL	35	9	14	23	83																			
	Anaheim	**NHL**	**1**	**0**	**0**	**0**	**2**	**0**	**0**	**0**	**0**	**0.0**	**–2**													
	Cincinnati Ducks	AHL	13	3	3	6	6																			
1998-99	Cincinnati Ducks	AHL	50	4	10	14	55																			
	Cleveland	IHL	15	2	4	6	22																			
99-2000	Cincinnati Ducks	AHL	15	0	3	3	8																			
	Huntington	ECHL	20	6	13	19	43																			
	Hartford	AHL	32	3	8	11	41												19	2	2	4	16			
2000-01	Hartford	AHL	47	12	23	35	136												5	0	2	2	6			
	NY Rangers	**NHL**	**6**	**0**	**0**	**0**	**5**	**0**	**0**	**0**	**3**	**0.0**	**–1**	**1**	**0.0**	**11**	**3**	**3:41**								
	NHL Totals		**7**	**0**	**0**	**0**	**7**	**0**	**0**	**0**	**3**	**0.0**		**1**	**0.0**	**11**	**3**	**3:41**								

Rights transferred to **Colorado** after **Quebec** franchise relocated, June 21, 1995. Signed as a free agent by **NY Islanders**, April 26, 1997. Traded to **Anaheim** by **NY Islanders** with Travis Green and Doug Houda for Joe Sacco, J-J Daigneault and Mark Janssens, February 6, 1998. Loaned to **Hartford** (AHL) by **Anaheim**, January 25, 2000. Signed as a free agent by **NY Rangers**, February 9, 2001. Signed as a free agent by **Boston**, July 23, 2001.

TVERDOVSKY, Oleg
(tvehr-DOHV-skee, OH-lehg) **ANA.**

Defense. Shoots left. 6'1", 204 lbs. Born, Donetsk, USSR, May 18, 1976. Anaheim's 1st choice, 2nd overall, in 1994 Entry Draft.

Season	Club	League	GP	G	A	Pts	PIM	PP	SH	GW	S	%	+/-	TF	F%	H	SB	Min	GP	G	A	Pts	PIM	PP	SH	GW
1992-93	Krylja Sovetov	CIS	21	0	1	1	6												6	0	0	0	0			
1993-94	Krylja Sovetov	CIS	46	4	10	14	22												3	1	0	1	2			
1994-95	Brandon	WHL	7	1	4	5	4																			
	Anaheim	**NHL**	**36**	**3**	**9**	**12**	**14**	**1**	**1**	**0**	**26**	**11.5**	**–6**													
1995-96	**Anaheim**	**NHL**	**51**	**7**	**15**	**22**	**35**	**2**	**0**	**0**	**84**	**8.3**	**0**													
	Winnipeg	**NHL**	**31**	**0**	**8**	**8**	**6**	**0**	**0**	**0**	**35**	**0.0**	**–7**						**6**	**0**	**1**	**1**	**0**	**0**	**0**	**0**
1996-97	**Phoenix**	**NHL**	**82**	**10**	**45**	**55**	**30**	**3**	**1**	**2**	**144**	**6.9**	**–5**						**7**	**0**	**1**	**1**	**0**	**0**	**0**	**0**
1997-98	Hamilton Bulldogs	AHL	9	8	6	14	2																			
	Phoenix	**NHL**	**46**	**7**	**12**	**19**	**12**	**4**	**0**	**1**	**83**	**8.4**	**1**						**6**	**0**	**7**	**7**	**0**	**0**	**0**	**0**
1998-99	**Phoenix**	**NHL**	**82**	**7**	**18**	**25**	**32**	**2**	**0**	**2**	**117**	**6.0**	**11**	**1**	**0.0**	**50**	**53**	**20:48**	**6**	**0**	**2**	**2**	**6**	**0**	**0**	**0**
99-2000	**Anaheim**	**NHL**	**82**	**15**	**36**	**51**	**30**	**5**	**0**	**5**	**153**	**9.8**	**5**	**1**	**0.0**	**79**	**89**	**22:46**								
2000-01	**Anaheim**	**NHL**	**82**	**14**	**39**	**53**	**32**	**8**	**0**	**3**	**188**	**7.4**	**–11**	**0**	**0.0**	**77**	**70**	**24:25**								
	NHL Totals		**492**	**63**	**182**	**245**	**191**	**25**	**2**	**13**	**830**	**7.6**		**2**	**0.0**	**206**	**212**	**22:40**	**25**	**0**	**11**	**11**	**6**	**0**	**0**	**0**

Played in NHL All-Star Game (1997)

Traded to **Winnipeg** by **Anaheim** with Chad Kilger and Anaheim's 3rd round choice (Per-Anton Lundstrom) in 1996 Entry Draft for Teemu Selanne, Marc Chouinard and Winnipeg's 4th round choice (later traded to Toronto - later traded to Montreal - Montreal selected Kim Staal) in 1996 Entry Draft, February 7, 1996. Transferred to **Phoenix** after **Winnipeg** franchise relocated, July 1, 1996. Traded to **Anaheim** by **Phoenix** for Travis Green and Anaheim's 1st round choice (Scott Kelman) in 1999 Entry Draft, June 26, 1999.

ULANOV, Igor
(yoo-LAH-nahf, EE-gohr) **NYR**

Defense. Shoots left. 6'3", 211 lbs. Born, Krasnokamsk, USSR, October 1, 1969. Winnipeg's 8th choice, 203rd overall, in 1991 Entry Draft.

Season	Club	League	GP	G	A	Pts	PIM	PP	SH	GW	S	%	+/-	TF	F%	H	SB	Min	GP	G	A	Pts	PIM	PP	SH	GW
1990-91	HK Khimik	USSR	41	2	2	4	52																			
1991-92	HK Khimik	CIS	27	1	4	5	24																			
	Winnipeg	**NHL**	**27**	**2**	**9**	**11**	**67**	**0**	**0**	**0**	**23**	**8.7**	**5**						**7**	**0**	**0**	**0**	**39**	**0**	**0**	**0**
	Moncton Hawks	AHL	3	0	1	1	16																			
1992-93	**Winnipeg**	**NHL**	**56**	**2**	**14**	**16**	**124**	**0**	**0**	**0**	**26**	**7.7**	**6**						**4**	**0**	**0**	**0**	**4**	**0**	**0**	**0**
	Moncton Hawks	AHL	9	1	3	4	26																			
	Fort Wayne	IHL	3	0	1	1	29																			
1993-94	**Winnipeg**	**NHL**	**74**	**0**	**17**	**17**	**165**	**0**	**0**	**0**	**46**	**0.0**	**–11**													
1994-95	**Winnipeg**	**NHL**	**19**	**1**	**3**	**4**	**27**	**0**	**0**	**0**	**13**	**7.7**	**–2**													
	Washington	**NHL**	**3**	**0**	**1**	**1**	**2**	**0**	**0**	**0**	**0**	**0.0**	**3**						**2**	**0**	**0**	**0**	**4**	**0**	**0**	**0**
1995-96	**Chicago**	**NHL**	**53**	**1**	**8**	**9**	**92**	**0**	**0**	**0**	**24**	**4.2**	**12**													
	Indianapolis Ice	IHL	1	0	0	0	0																			
	Tampa Bay	**NHL**	**11**	**2**	**1**	**3**	**24**	**0**	**0**	**1**	**13**	**15.4**	**–1**						**5**	**0**	**0**	**0**	**15**	**0**	**0**	**0**
1996-97	**Tampa Bay**	**NHL**	**59**	**1**	**7**	**8**	**108**	**0**	**0**	**0**	**56**	**1.8**	**2**													
1997-98	**Tampa Bay**	**NHL**	**45**	**2**	**7**	**9**	**85**	**1**	**0**	**0**	**32**	**6.3**	**–5**													
	Montreal	**NHL**	**4**	**0**	**1**	**1**	**12**	**0**	**0**	**0**	**4**	**0.0**	**–2**						**10**	**1**	**4**	**5**	**12**	**0**	**0**	**0**
1998-99	**Montreal**	**NHL**	**76**	**3**	**9**	**12**	**109**	**0**	**0**	**0**	**55**	**5.5**	**–3**	**0**	**0.0**	**136**	**163**	**17:35**								
99-2000	**Montreal**	**NHL**	**43**	**1**	**5**	**6**	**76**	**0**	**0**	**0**	**33**	**3.0**	**–11**	**0**	**0.0**	**79**	**86**	**16:33**								
	Edmonton	**NHL**	**14**	**0**	**3**	**3**	**10**	**0**	**0**	**0**	**6**	**0.0**	**–3**	**0**	**0.0**	**20**	**21**	**16:23**	**5**	**0**	**0**	**0**	**6**	**0**	**0**	**0**
2000-01	**Edmonton**	**NHL**	**67**	**3**	**20**	**23**	**90**	**1**	**0**	**0**	**74**	**4.1**	**15**	**0**	**0.0**	**106**	**172**	**23:01**	**6**	**0**	**0**	**0**	**4**	**0**	**0**	**0**
	NHL Totals		**551**	**18**	**105**	**123**	**991**	**2**	**0**	**1**	**405**	**4.4**		**0**	**0.0**	**341**	**442**	**19:06**	**39**	**1**	**4**	**5**	**84**	**0**	**0**	**0**

Traded to **Washington** by **Winnipeg** with Mike Eagles for Washington's 3rd (later traded to Dallas - Dallas selected Sergey Gusev) and 5th (Brian Elder) round choices in 1995 Entry Draft, April 7, 1995. Traded to **Chicago** by **Washington** for Chicago's 3rd round choice (Dave Weninger) in 1996 Entry Draft, October 17, 1995. Traded to **Tampa Bay** by **Chicago** with Patrick Poulin and Chicago's 2nd round choice (later traded to New Jersey - New Jersey selected Pierre Dagenais) in 1996 Entry Draft for Enrico Ciccone and Tampa Bay's 2nd round choice (Jeff Paul) in 1996 Entry Draft, March 20, 1996. Traded to **Montreal** by **Tampa Bay** with Patrick Poulin and Mick Vukota for Stephane Richer, Darcy Tucker and David Wilkie, January 15, 1998. Traded to **Edmonton** by **Montreal** with Alain Nasreddine for Christian Laflamme and Matthieu Descoteaux, March 9, 2000. Signed as a free agent by **NY Rangers**, July 20, 2001.

ULMER, Jeff
(UHL-muhr, JEHF) **OTT.**

Right wing. Shoots right. 5'11", 195 lbs. Born, Wilcox, Sask., April 27, 1977.

Season	Club	League	GP	G	A	Pts	PIM	PP	SH	GW	S	%	+/-	TF	F%	H	SB	Min	GP	G	A	Pts	PIM	PP	SH	GW
1994-95	Notre Dame	AJHL	63	25	35	60																				
1995-96	North Dakota	WCHA	29	5	3	8	26																			
1996-97	North Dakota	WCHA	26	6	11	17	16																			
1997-98	North Dakota	WCHA	32	12	12	24	44																			
1998-99	North Dakota	WCHA	38	16	20	36	46																			
99-2000	Team Canada	Nat-Team	48	14	25	39	20																			
	Houston Aeros	IHL	5	1	0	1	0												11	2	4	6	6			
2000-01	**NY Rangers**	**NHL**	**21**	**3**	**0**	**3**	**8**	**0**	**0**	**0**	**22**	**13.6**	**–6**	**16**	**31.3**	**14**	**2**	**10:23**								
	Hartford	AHL	48	11	14	25	34																			
	NHL Totals		**21**	**3**	**0**	**3**	**8**	**0**	**0**	**0**	**22**	**13.6**		**16**	**31.3**	**14**	**2**	**10:23**								

Signed as a free agent by **Houston** (IHL), March 30, 2000. Signed as a free agent by **NY Rangers**, July 27, 2000. Traded to **Ottawa** by **NY Rangers** with Jason Doig for Sean Gagnon, June 29, 2001.

USTORF, Stefan
(OOSH-tohrf, SHTEH-fuhn)

Center. Shoots left. 6', 195 lbs. Born, Kaufbeuren, West Germany, January 3, 1974. Washington's 3rd choice, 53rd overall, in 1992 Entry Draft.

Season	Club	League	GP	G	A	Pts	PIM	PP	SH	GW	S	%	+/-	TF	F%	H	SB	Min	GP	G	A	Pts	PIM	PP	SH	GW
1989-90	ESV Kaufbeuren	DEL-Jr.	8	10	11	21	8																			
1990-91	ESV Kaufbeuren	DEL-Jr.	37	33	34	67	78																			
1991-92	ESV Kaufbeuren	DEL	41	2	22	24	46												5	2	7	9	6			
1992-93	ESV Kaufbeuren	DEL	37	14	18	32	32												3	1	0	1	10			
1993-94	ESV Kaufbeuren	DEL	38	10	20	30	21												3	0	0	0	4			
	Germany	Olympics	8	1	2	3	2																			
1994-95	Portland Pirates	AHL	63	21	38	59	51												7	1	6	7	7			
1995-96	**Washington**	**NHL**	**48**	**7**	**10**	**17**	**14**	**0**	**0**	**1**	**39**	**17.9**	**8**						**5**	**0**	**0**	**0**	**0**	**0**	**0**	**0**
	Portland Pirates	AHL	8	1	4	5	6																			
1996-97	**Washington**	**NHL**	**6**	**0**	**0**	**0**	**2**	**0**	**0**	**0**	**7**	**0.0**	**–3**													
	Portland Pirates	AHL	36	7	17	24	27																			
1997-98	Berlin Capitals	DEL	45	17	23	40	54																			
	Germany	Olympics	4	0	0	0	0																			
1998-99	Las Vegas	IHL	40	11	17	28	40																			
	Detroit Vipers	IHL	14	3	7	10	11												11	4	7	11	2			

			Regular Season																Playoffs							
Season	Club	League	GP	G	A	Pts	PIM	PP	SH	GW	S	%	+/-	TF	F%	H	SB	Min	GP	G	A	Pts	PIM	PP	SH	GW
99-2000	Cincinnati	IHL	79	20	34	54	53												11	1	4	5	10			
2000-01	Cincinnati	IHL	71	19	38	57	43												5	0	6	6	4			
	NHL Totals		**54**	**7**	**10**	**17**	**16**	**0**	**0**	**1**	**46**	**15.2**							**5**	**0**	**0**	**0**	**0**	**0**	**0**	**0**

Signed as a free agent by **Cincinnati** (IHL), September 29, 1999. Signed as a free agent by **Washington**, July 13, 2000.

VAANANEN, Ossi

(VAN-ih-nehn, AW-see) **PHX.**

Defense. Shoots left. 6'4", 205 lbs. Born, Vantaa, Finland, August 18, 1980. Phoenix's 2nd choice, 43rd overall, in 1998 Entry Draft.

Season	Club	League	GP	G	A	Pts	PIM	PP	SH	GW	S	%	+/-	TF	F%	H	SB	Min	GP	G	A	Pts	PIM	PP	SH	GW
1994-95	Jokerit Helsinki-C	Finn-Jr.	23	0	1	1	10												6	0	0	0	8			
1995-96	Jokerit Helsinki-C	Finn-Jr.	12	0	0	0	10																			
	Jokerit Helsinki-B	Finn-Jr.	1	0	0	0	0												1	0	0	0	0			
1996-97	Jokerit Helsinki	Finn-Jr.	17	1	2	3	43																			
1997-98	Jokerit Helsinki	Finn-Jr.	31	0	6	6	24																			
1998-99	Jokerit Helsinki	Finn-Jr.	12	1	6	7	16																			
	Jokerit Helsinki	EuroHL	5	0	0	0	2												1	0	1	1	2			
	Jokerit Helsinki	Finland	48	0	1	1	42												3	0	1	1	2			
99-2000	Jokerit Helsinki	Finland	49	1	6	7	46												11	1	1	2	2			
2000-01	**Phoenix**	**NHL**	**81**	**4**	**12**	**16**	**90**	**0**	**0**	**2**	**69**	**5.8**	**9**	**0**	**0.0**	**190**	**79**	**19:09**								
	NHL Totals		**81**	**4**	**12**	**16**	**90**	**0**	**0**	**2**	**69**	**5.8**		**0**	**0.0**	**190**	**79**	**19:09**								

VAIC, Lubomir

(VIGHTZ, LEW-boh-MEER)

Center. Shoots left. 5'9", 178 lbs. Born, Spisska Nova Ves, Czech., March 6, 1977. Vancouver's 8th choice, 227th overall, in 1996 Entry Draft.

Season	Club	League	GP	G	A	Pts	PIM	PP	SH	GW	S	%	+/-	TF	F%	H	SB	Min	GP	G	A	Pts	PIM	PP	SH	GW
1993-94	SKP Poprad	Slovakia	28	10	6	16	10																			
1994-95	VTJ Spisska	Slovakia	19	5	4	9	2																			
1995-96	VSV Kosice	Slovakia	36	7	19	26	10												13	0	7	7				
1996-97	VSV Kosice	Slovakia	36	13	12	25													7	2	0	2				
1997-98	**Vancouver**	**NHL**	**5**	**1**	**1**	**2**	**2**	**0**	**0**	**0**	**8**	**12.5**	**-2**													
	Syracuse Crunch	AHL	50	12	15	27	22												3	0	0	0	4			
1998-99	VTJ Spisska	Slovakia	35	20	22	42	42																			
	VSV Kosice	Slovakia																	11	2	3	5	8			
99-2000	**Vancouver**	**NHL**	**4**	**0**	**0**	**0**	**0**	**0**	**0**	**0**	**2**	**0.0**	**0**	**30**	**46.7**	**4**	**0**	**7:28**								
	Syracuse Crunch	AHL	63	13	29	42	42												4	0	3	3	8			
2000-01	Eisbaren Berlin	DEL	26	1	6	7	70																			
	NHL Totals		**9**	**1**	**1**	**2**	**2**	**0**	**0**	**0**	**10**	**10.0**		**30**	**46.7**	**4**	**0**	**7:28**								

VALICEVIC, Rob

(val-IH-seh-VIK, RAWB) **L.A.**

Right wing. Shoots right. 6'1", 198 lbs. Born, Detroit, MI, January 6, 1971. NY Islanders' 6th choice, 114th overall, in 1991 Entry Draft.

Season	Club	League	GP	G	A	Pts	PIM	PP	SH	GW	S	%	+/-	TF	F%	H	SB	Min	GP	G	A	Pts	PIM	PP	SH	GW
1990-91	Det-Compuware	NAJHL	39	31	44	75	54																			
1991-92	Lake Superior	CCHA	32	8	4	12	12																			
1992-93	Lake Superior	CCHA	43	21	20	41	28																			
1993-94	Lake Superior	CCHA	45	18	20	38	46																			
1994-95	Lake Superior	CCHA	37	10	21	31	40																			
1995-96	Louisiana Gators	ECHL	60	42	20	62	85												5	2	3	5	8			
	Springfield	AHL	2	0	0	0	2																			
1996-97	Louisiana Gators	ECHL	8	7	2	9	21																			
	Houston Aeros	IHL	58	11	12	23	42												12	1	3	4	11			
1997-98	Houston Aeros	IHL	72	29	28	57	47												4	2	0	2	2			
1998-99	**Nashville**	**NHL**	**19**	**4**	**2**	**6**	**2**	**0**	**0**	**2**	**23**	**17.4**	**4**	**17**	**29.4**	**8**	**8**	**11:01**								
	Houston Aeros	IHL	57	16	33	49	62												19	7	10	17	8			
99-2000	**Nashville**	**NHL**	**80**	**14**	**11**	**25**	**21**	**2**	**1**	**3**	**113**	**12.4**	**-11**	**50**	**44.0**	**100**	**38**	**14:31**								
2000-01	**Nashville**	**NHL**	**60**	**8**	**6**	**14**	**26**	**1**	**0**	**4**	**62**	**12.9**	**-2**	**35**	**40.0**	**89**	**28**	**14:06**								
	NHL Totals		**159**	**26**	**19**	**45**	**49**	**3**	**1**	**9**	**198**	**13.1**		**102**	**40.2**	**197**	**74**	**13:56**								

Signed as a free agent by **Nashville**, May 28, 1998. Signed as a free agent by **LA Kings**, August 16, 2001.

VALK, Garry

(VAHLK, GAIR-ee) **TOR.**

Right wing. Shoots left. 6'1", 200 lbs. Born, Edmonton, Alta., November 27, 1967. Vancouver's 5th choice, 108th overall, in 1987 Entry Draft.

Season	Club	League	GP	G	A	Pts	PIM	PP	SH	GW	S	%	+/-	TF	F%	H	SB	Min	GP	G	A	Pts	PIM	PP	SH	GW
1984-85	Sherwood Park	AJHL	53	20	22	42	66																			
1985-86	Sherwood Park	AJHL	40	20	26	46	116																			
1986-87	Sherwood Park	AJHL	59	42	44	86	204																			
1987-88	North Dakota	WCHA	38	23	12	35	64																			
1988-89	North Dakota	WCHA	40	14	17	31	71																			
1989-90	North Dakota	WCHA	43	22	17	39	92																			
1990-91	**Vancouver**	**NHL**	**59**	**10**	**11**	**21**	**67**	**1**	**0**	**1**	**90**	**11.1**	**-23**						**5**	**0**	**0**	**0**	**20**	**0**	**0**	**0**
	Milwaukee	IHL	10	12	4	16	13												3	0	0	0	2			
1991-92	**Vancouver**	**NHL**	**65**	**8**	**17**	**25**	**56**	**2**	**1**	**2**	**93**	**8.6**	**3**						**4**	**0**	**0**	**0**	**5**	**0**	**0**	**0**
1992-93	**Vancouver**	**NHL**	**48**	**6**	**7**	**13**	**77**	**0**	**0**	**2**	**46**	**13.0**	**6**						**7**	**0**	**1**	**1**	**12**	**0**	**0**	**0**
	Hamilton Canucks	AHL	7	3	6	9	6																			
1993-94	**Anaheim**	**NHL**	**78**	**18**	**27**	**45**	**100**	**4**	**1**	**5**	**165**	**10.9**	**8**													
1994-95	**Anaheim**	**NHL**	**36**	**3**	**6**	**9**	**34**	**0**	**0**	**0**	**53**	**5.7**	**-4**													
1995-96	**Anaheim**	**NHL**	**79**	**12**	**12**	**24**	**125**	**1**	**1**	**2**	**108**	**11.1**	**8**													
1996-97	**Anaheim**	**NHL**	**53**	**7**	**7**	**14**	**53**	**0**	**0**	**1**	**68**	**10.3**	**-2**													
	Pittsburgh	**NHL**	**17**	**3**	**4**	**7**	**25**	**0**	**0**	**0**	**32**	**9.4**	**-6**													
1997-98	**Pittsburgh**	**NHL**	**39**	**2**	**1**	**3**	**33**	**0**	**0**	**0**	**32**	**6.3**	**-3**													
1998-99	**Toronto**	**NHL**	**77**	**8**	**21**	**29**	**53**	**1**	**0**	**0**	**93**	**8.6**	**8**	**19**	**36.8**	**99**	**20**	**13:53**	**17**	**3**	**4**	**7**	**22**	**0**	**0**	**1**
99-2000	**Toronto**	**NHL**	**73**	**10**	**14**	**24**	**44**	**0**	**1**	**1**	**91**	**11.0**	**-2**	**10**	**30.0**	**109**	**14**	**12:51**	**12**	**1**	**2**	**3**	**14**	**0**	**0**	**0**
2000-01	**Toronto**	**NHL**	**74**	**8**	**18**	**26**	**46**	**1**	**0**	**2**	**87**	**9.2**	**4**	**30**	**33.3**	**112**	**18**	**11:33**	**5**	**1**	**0**	**1**	**2**	**0**	**0**	**0**
	NHL Totals		**698**	**95**	**145**	**240**	**713**	**10**	**4**	**16**	**958**	**9.9**		**59**	**33.9**	**320**	**52**	**12:46**	**50**	**5**	**7**	**12**	**75**	**0**	**0**	**1**

Claimed by **Anaheim** from **Vancouver** in NHL Waiver Draft, October 3, 1993. Traded to **Pittsburgh** by **Anaheim** for Jean-Jacques Daigneault, February 21, 1997. Signed as a free agent by **Toronto**, October 8, 1998.

VAN ALLEN, Shaun

(VAN-AL-ehn, SHAWN) **DAL.**

Center. Shoots left. 6'1", 204 lbs. Born, Calgary, Alta., August 29, 1967. Edmonton's 5th choice, 105th overall, in 1987 Entry Draft.

Season	Club	League	GP	G	A	Pts	PIM	PP	SH	GW	S	%	+/-	TF	F%	H	SB	Min	GP	G	A	Pts	PIM	PP	SH	GW
1984-85	Swift Current	SJHL	61	12	20	32	136																			
1985-86	Saskatoon Blades	WHL	55	12	11	23	43												13	4	8	12	28			
1986-87	Saskatoon Blades	WHL	72	38	59	97	116												11	4	6	10	24			
1987-88	Milwaukee	IHL	40	14	28	42	34																			
	Nova Scotia	AHL	19	4	10	14	17												4	1	1	2	4			
1988-89	Cape Breton	AHL	76	32	42	74	81																			
1989-90	Cape Breton	AHL	61	25	44	69	83												4	0	2	2	8			
1990-91	**Edmonton**	**NHL**	**2**	**0**	**0**	**0**	**0**	**0**	**0**	**0**	**0**	**0.0**	**0**													
	Cape Breton	AHL	76	25	75	100	182												4	0	1	1	8			
1991-92	Cape Breton	AHL	77	29	*84	*113	80												5	3	7	10	14			
1992-93	**Edmonton**	**NHL**	**21**	**1**	**4**	**5**	**6**	**0**	**0**	**0**	**19**	**5.3**	**-2**													
	Cape Breton	AHL	43	14	62	76	68												15	8	9	17	18			
1993-94	**Anaheim**	**NHL**	**80**	**8**	**25**	**33**	**64**	**2**	**2**	**1**	**104**	**7.7**	**0**													
1994-95	**Anaheim**	**NHL**	**45**	**8**	**21**	**29**	**32**	**1**	**1**	**1**	**68**	**11.8**	**-4**													
1995-96	**Anaheim**	**NHL**	**49**	**8**	**17**	**25**	**41**	**0**	**0**	**2**	**78**	**10.3**	**13**													
1996-97	**Ottawa**	**NHL**	**80**	**11**	**14**	**25**	**35**	**1**	**1**	**2**	**123**	**8.9**	**-8**						**7**	**0**	**1**	**1**	**4**	**0**	**0**	**0**
1997-98	**Ottawa**	**NHL**	**80**	**4**	**15**	**19**	**48**	**0**	**0**	**0**	**104**	**3.8**	**4**						**11**	**0**	**1**	**1**	**10**	**0**	**0**	**0**
1998-99	**Ottawa**	**NHL**	**79**	**6**	**11**	**17**	**30**	**0**	**1**	**0**	**47**	**12.8**	**3**	**656**	**47.4**	**84**	**23**	**11:07**	**4**	**0**	**0**	**0**	**0**	**0**	**0**	**0**

			Regular Season																Playoffs							
Season	Club	League	GP	G	A	Pts	PIM	PP	SH	GW	S	%	+/-	TF	F%	H	SB	Min	GP	G	A	Pts	PIM	PP	SH	GW
99-2000	**Ottawa**	**NHL**	75	9	19	28	37	0	2	4	75	12.0	20	911	48.6	119	35	11:49	6	0	1	1	9	0	0	0
2000-01	**Dallas**	**NHL**	59	7	16	23	16	0	2	3	51	13.7	5	559	47.1	114	29	12:05	8	0	2	2	8	0	0	0
	NHL Totals		570	62	142	204	309	4	9	13	669	9.3		2126	47.8	317	87	11:38	36	0	5	5	31	0	0	0

AHL Second All-Star Team (1991) • AHL First All-Star Team (1992) • Won John B. Sollenberger Trophy (Top Scorer - AHL) (1992)

Signed as a free agent by **Anaheim**, July 22, 1993. Traded to **Ottawa** by **Anaheim** with Jason York for Ted Drury and the rights to Marc Moro, October 1, 1996. Signed as a free agent by **Dallas**, July 12, 2000.

VANDENBUSSCHE, Ryan (van-dehn-BUHSH, RIGH-yuhn) CHI.

Right wing. Shoots right. 6', 200 lbs. Born, Simcoe, Ont., February 28, 1973. Toronto's 9th choice, 173rd overall, in 1992 Entry Draft.

1988-89	Delhi Flames	OJHL-D	3	1	1	2	2																			
1989-90	Norwich	OJHL-C	21	12	10	22	146																			
	Tillsonburg Titans	OJHL-B	24	0	5	5	113																			
1990-91	Massena	OCJHL	10	2	3	5	46																			
	Cornwall Royals	OHL	49	3	8	11	139																			
1991-92	Cornwall Royals	OHL	61	13	15	28	232												6	0	2	2	9			
1992-93	Newmarket	OHL	30	15	12	27	161																			
	Guelph Storm	OHL	29	3	14	17	99												5	1	3	4	13			
	St. John's Leafs	AHL	1	0	0	0	0																			
1993-94	St. John's Leafs	AHL	44	4	10	14	124																			
	Springfield	AHL	9	1	2	3	29												5	0	0	0	16			
1994-95	St. John's Leafs	AHL	53	2	13	15	239												3	0	0	0	17			
1995-96	Binghamton	AHL	68	3	17	20	240												4	0	0	0	9			
1996-97	**NY Rangers**	**NHL**	11	1	0	1	30	0	0	0	4	25.0	–2													
	Binghamton	AHL	38	8	11	19	133																			
1997-98	**NY Rangers**	**NHL**	16	1	0	1	38	0	0	0	2	50.0	–2													
	Hartford	AHL	15	2	0	2	45																			
	Chicago	**NHL**	4	0	1	1	5	0	0	0	0	0.0	0													
	Indianapolis Ice	IHL	3	1	1	2	4																			
1998-99	**Chicago**	**NHL**	6	0	0	0	17	0	0	0	3	0.0	0	0	0.0	13	2	9:29								
	Indianapolis Ice	IHL	34	3	10	13	130																			
	Portland Pirates	AHL	37	4	1	5	119																			
99-2000	**Chicago**	**NHL**	52	0	1	1	143	0	0	0	19	0.0	–3	3	0.0	68	3	5:37								
2000-01	**Chicago**	**NHL**	64	2	5	7	146	0	0	0	24	8.3	–8	2	0.0	118	3	7:46								
	NHL Totals		153	4	7	11	379	0	0	0	52	7.7		5	0.0	199	8	6:56								

Signed as a free agent by **NY Rangers**, August 22, 1995. Traded to **Chicago** by **NY Rangers** for Ryan Risidore, March 24, 1998.

VAN IMPE, Darren (van-IHMP, DAIR-ehn) NYR

Defense. Shoots left. 6'1", 205 lbs. Born, Saskatoon, Sask., May 18, 1973. NY Islanders' 7th choice, 170th overall, in 1993 Entry Draft.

1989-90	Prince Albert	AMHL	32	16	31	47	100																			
	Prince Albert	WHL	1	0	1	1	0																			
1990-91	Prince Albert	WHL	70	15	45	60	57												3	1	1	2	2			
1991-92	Prince Albert	WHL	69	9	37	46	89												8	1	5	6	10			
1992-93	Red Deer Rebels	WHL	54	23	47	70	118												4	2	5	7	16			
1993-94	Red Deer Rebels	WHL	58	20	64	84	125												4	2	4	6	6			
1994-95	San Diego Gulls	IHL	76	6	17	23	74												5	0	0	0	0			
	Anaheim	**NHL**	1	0	1	1	4	0	0	0	0	0.0	0													
1995-96	**Anaheim**	**NHL**	16	1	2	3	14	0	0	1	13	7.7	8													
	Baltimore Bandits	AHL	63	11	47	58	79																			
1996-97	**Anaheim**	**NHL**	74	4	19	23	90	2	0	0	107	3.7	3						9	0	2	2	16	0	0	0
1997-98	**Anaheim**	**NHL**	19	1	3	4	4	0	0	0	21	4.8	–10													
	Boston	**NHL**	50	2	8	10	36	2	0	0	50	4.0	4						6	2	1	3	0	1	0	1
1998-99	**Boston**	**NHL**	60	5	15	20	66	4	0	0	92	5.4	–5	0	0.0	45	60	17:54	11	1	2	3	4	1	0	0
99-2000	**Boston**	**NHL**	79	5	23	28	73	4	0	0	97	5.2	–19	0	0.0	93	87	19:31								
2000-01	**Boston**	**NHL**	31	3	10	13	41	2	0	0	40	7.5	–9	0	0.0	37	33	20:11								
	NHL Totals		330	21	81	102	328	14	0	1	420	5.0		0	0.0	175	180	19:04	26	3	5	8	20	2	0	1

WHL East First All-Star Team (1993, 1994)

Traded to **Anaheim** by **NY Islanders** for Anaheim's 8th round choice (Mike Broda) in 1995 Entry Draft, August 31, 1994. Claimed on waivers by **Boston** from **Anaheim**, November 26, 1997. • Missed majority of 2000-01 season recovering from shoulder injury suffered in game vs. Detroit, December 23, 2000. Claimed on waivers by **NY Rangers** from **Boston**, August 7, 2001.

VAN RYN, Mike (VAN RIHN, MIGHK) ST.L.

Defense. Shoots right. 6'1", 190 lbs. Born, London, Ont., May 14, 1979. New Jersey's 1st choice, 26th overall, in 1998 Entry Draft.

1995-96	London Nationals	OJHL-B	44	9	14	23	24																			
1996-97	London Nationals	OJHL-B	46	14	31	45	32																			
1997-98	U. of Michigan	CCHA	38	4	14	18	44																			
1998-99	U. of Michigan	CCHA	37	10	13	23	52																			
99-2000	Sarnia Sting	OHL	61	6	35	41	34												7	0	5	5	4			
2000-01	**St. Louis**	**NHL**	1	0	0	0	0	0	0	0	1	0.0	–2	0	0.0	1	0	13:43								
	Worcester	AHL	37	3	10	13	12												7	1	1	2	2			
	NHL Totals		1	0	0	0	0	0	0	0	1	0.0		0	0.0	1	0	13:43								

OJHL-B First All-Star Team (1997)

Signed as a free agent by **St. Louis**, June 30, 2000. • Missed majority of 2000-01 season recovering from shoulder injury suffered in game vs. Phoenix, October 5, 2000.

VARADA, Vaclav (vuh-RA-da, VATS-LAV) BUF.

Right wing. Shoots left. 6', 214 lbs. Born, Vsetin, Czech., April 26, 1976. San Jose's 4th choice, 89th overall, in 1994 Entry Draft.

1993-94	HC Vitkovice	Cze-Rep	24	6	7	13	....												5	1	1	2	....			
1994-95	Tacoma Rockets	WHL	68	50	38	88	108												4	4	3	7	11			
1995-96	Kelowna Rockets	WHL	59	39	46	85	100												6	3	3	6	16			
	Buffalo	**NHL**	1	0	0	0	0	0	0	0	2	0.0	0													
	Rochester	AHL	5	3	0	3	4																			
1996-97	**Buffalo**	**NHL**	5	0	0	0	2	0	0	0	2	0.0	0													
	Rochester	AHL	53	23	25	48	81												10	1	6	7	27			
1997-98	**Buffalo**	**NHL**	27	5	6	11	15	0	0	1	27	18.5	0						15	3	4	7	18	0	0	0
	Rochester	AHL	45	30	26	56	74																			
1998-99	**Buffalo**	**NHL**	72	7	24	31	61	1	0	1	123	5.7	11	1	0.0	185	12	14:30	21	5	4	9	14	1	0	0
99-2000	HC Vitkovice	Cze-Rep	5	2	3	5	12																			
	Buffalo	**NHL**	76	10	27	37	62	0	0	0	140	7.1	12	1	0.0	150	16	14:58	5	0	0	0	8	0	0	0
2000-01	**Buffalo**	**NHL**	75	10	21	31	81	2	0	2	112	8.9	–2	2	0.0	134	25	15:57	13	0	4	4	8	0	0	0
	NHL Totals		256	32	78	110	221	3	0	4	406	7.9		4	0.0	469	53	15:09	54	8	12	20	48	1	0	0

Traded to **Buffalo** by **San Jose** with Martin Spahnel and Philadelphia's 1st (previously acquired by San Jose - later traded to Phoenix - Phoenix selected Daniel Briere) and 4th (previously acquired, Buffalo selected Mike Martone) round choices in 1996 Entry Draft for Doug Bodger, November 16, 1995.

VARIS, Petri (VAH-rihs, PEE-tree)

Left wing. Shoots left. 6'1", 200 lbs. Born, Varkaus, Finland, May 13, 1969. San Jose's 7th choice, 132nd overall, in 1993 Entry Draft.

1986-87	Karhu Kissat	Finn-Jr.	2	0	1	1	0																			
1987-88	Karhu Kissat	Finland-2	42	9	15	24	21																			
1988-89	Karhu Kissat	Finn-Jr.	7	4	5	9	10																			
	Karhu Kissat	Finland-2	44	18	19	37	26																			
1989-90	Karhu Kissat	Finland-2	42	30	24	54	44																			
1990-91	KooKoo Kouvola	Finland-2	44	20	31	51	42																			
1991-92	Assat-Pori	Finland	36	13	23	36	24																			
1992-93	Assat-Pori	Finland	46	14	35	49	42												8	2	2	4	12			
1993-94	Jokerit Helsinki	Finland	31	14	15	29	16												11	3	4	7	6			
	Finland	Olympics	5	1	1	2	2																			

			Regular Season																Playoffs							
Season	Club	League	GP	G	A	Pts	PIM	PP	SH	GW	S	%	+/-	TF	F%	H	SB	Min	GP	G	A	Pts	PIM	PP	SH	GW
1994-95	HJK Jarvanpaa	Finland-2	1	0	1	1	2																			
	Jokerit Helsinki	Finland	47	21	20	41	53												11	7	2	9	10			
1995-96	Jokerit Helsinki	Finland	50	*28	28	56	22												11	*12	7	19	6			
1996-97	Jokerit Helsinki	Finland	50	*36	23	*59	38												9	*7	4	11	14			
	Jokerit Helsinki	EuroHL	6	2	8	10	2																			
1997-98	**Chicago**	**NHL**	**1**	**0**	**0**	**0**	**0**	**0**	**0**	**0**	**0**	**0.0**	**0**													
	Indianapolis Ice	IHL	77	18	54	72	32												5	3	4	7	4			
1998-99	Kolner Haie	DEL	52	10	25	35	22												5	3	0	5	4			
99-2000	Jokerit Helsinki	Finland	53	21	25	46	42												10	0	6	6	14			
2000-01	Jokerit Helsinki	Finland	56	27	*43	*70	38												5	0	2	2	4			
	NHL Totals		**1**	**0**	**0**	**0**	**0**	**0**	**0**	**0**	**0**	**0.0**														

Rights traded to **Chicago** by **San Jose** with San Jose's 6th round choice (Jari Viuhkola) in 1998 Entry Draft for Murray Craven, July 25, 1997.

VARLAMOV, Sergei (vahr-LAHM-uhf, SAIR-gay) ST.L.

Left wing. Shoots left. 5'11", 195 lbs. Born, Kiev, USSR, July 21, 1978.

1994-95	Nelson Leafs	RMJHL	26	11	15	26	56																			
1995-96	Swift Current	WHL	55	23	21	44	65																			
1996-97	Swift Current	WHL	72	46	39	85	94												10	3	8	11	10			
	Saint John Flames	AHL	1	0	0	0	0																			
1997-98	Swift Current	WHL	72	*66	53	*119	132												12	10	5	15	28			
	Calgary	**NHL**	**1**	**0**	**0**	**0**	**0**	**0**	**0**	**0**	**0**	**0.0**	**0**													
	Saint John Flames	AHL																	3	0	0	0	0			
1998-99	Saint John Flames	AHL	76	24	33	57	66												7	0	4	4	8			
99-2000	**Calgary**	**NHL**	**7**	**3**	**0**	**3**	**0**	**0**	**0**	**1**	**11**	**27.3**	**0**	**1**	**0.0**	**4**	**1**	**10:22**								
	Saint John Flames	AHL	68	20	21	41	88												3	0	0	0	24			
2000-01	Saint John Flames	AHL	55	21	30	51	56												19	*15	8	23	10			
	NHL Totals		**8**	**3**	**0**	**3**	**0**	**0**	**0**	**1**	**11**	**27.3**		**1**	**0.0**	**4**	**1**	**10:22**								

WHL East First All-Star Team (1998) • Canadian Major Junior First All-Star Team (1998) • Canadian Major Junior Player of the Year (1998)

Signed as a free agent by **Calgary**, September 18, 1996. Traded to **St. Louis** by **Calgary** with Fred Brathwaite, Daniel Tkaczuk and Calgary's 9th round choice (Grant Jacobsen) in 2001 Entry Draft for Roman Turek and St. Louis' 4th round choice (Yegor Shastin) in 2001 Entry Draft, June 23, 2001.

VASICEK, Josef (VAHSH-ih-chehk, YOH-zehf) CAR.

Center. Shoots left. 6'4", 200 lbs. Born, Havlickuv Brod, Czech., September 12, 1980. Carolina's 4th choice, 91st overall, in 1998 Entry Draft.

1995-96	HK Brod-Jr.	Cze-Rep	36	25	25	50																				
1996-97	Slavia Praha-Jr.	Cze-Rep	37	20	40	60																				
1997-98	Slavia Praha-Jr.	Cze-Rep	34	13	20	33																				
1998-99	Sault Ste. Marie	OHL	66	21	35	56	30												5	3	0	3	10			
99-2000	Sault Ste. Marie	OHL	54	26	46	72	49												17	5	15	20	8			
2000-01	**Carolina**	**NHL**	**76**	**8**	**13**	**21**	**53**	**1**	**0**	**0**	**103**	**7.8**	**–8**	**786**	**46.6**	**69**	**8**	**11:49**	**6**	**2**	**0**	**2**	**0**	**0**	**0**	**0**
	Cincinnati	IHL																	3	0	0	0	0			
	NHL Totals		**76**	**8**	**13**	**21**	**53**	**1**	**0**	**0**	**103**	**7.8**		**786**	**46.6**	**69**	**8**	**11:49**	**6**	**2**	**0**	**2**	**0**	**0**	**0**	**0**

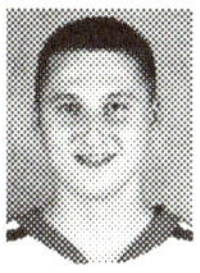

VASILIEV, Alexei (vah-SEE-lee-ehf, al-EHX-ay)

Defense. Shoots left. 6'1", 192 lbs. Born, Yaroslavl, USSR, September 1, 1977. NY Rangers' 4th choice, 110th overall, in 1995 Entry Draft.

1995-96	Torpedo Yaroslavl	CIS	40	4	7	11	4																			
1996-97	Torpedo Yaroslavl	Russia	44	2	8	10	10												9	1	1	2	8			
1997-98	Hartford	AHL	DID NOT PLAY – INJURED																							
1998-99	Hartford	AHL	75	8	19	27	24												6	0	1	1	2			
99-2000	**NY Rangers**	**NHL**	**1**	**0**	**0**	**0**	**2**	**0**	**0**	**0**	**0**	**0.0**	**–1**	**0**	**0.0**	**3**	**0**	**15:57**								
	Hartford	AHL	75	10	28	38	20												15	3	1	4	2			
2000-01	Milwaukee	IHL	69	6	12	18	20												4	0	0	0	2			
	NHL Totals		**1**	**0**	**0**	**0**	**2**	**0**	**0**	**0**	**0**	**0.0**		**0**	**0.0**	**3**	**0**									

• Missed entire 1997-98 season recovering from knee injury suffered in training camp, October, 1997. Traded to **Nashville** by **NY Rangers** for future considerations, September 25, 2000. Signed as a free agent by **Locomotiv Yaroslavl** (Russia), July 18, 2001.

VASILJEVS, Herbert (vah-SEE-lee-ehf, HUHR-buhrt) VAN.

Center. Shoots right. 5'11", 180 lbs. Born, Riga, Latvia, May 27, 1976.

1994-95	Krefelder EV	DEL	42	4	5	9	24												15	1	4	5	10			
1995-96	Guelph Storm	OHL	65	34	33	67	63												16	6	13	19	6			
1996-97	Carolina	AHL	54	13	18	31	30																			
	Port Huron	ColHL	3	3	2	5	4																			
1997-98	New Haven	AHL	76	36	30	66	60												3	1	0	1	2			
1998-99	**Florida**	**NHL**	**5**	**0**	**0**	**0**	**2**	**0**	**0**	**0**	**6**	**0.0**	**–1**	**3**	**66.7**	**0**	**0**	**11:06**								
	Kentucky	AHL	76	28	48	76	66												12	2	1	3	4			
99-2000	**Atlanta**	**NHL**	**7**	**1**	**0**	**1**	**4**	**0**	**0**	**0**	**2**	**50.0**	**–3**	**27**	**48.2**	**10**	**3**	**9:18**								
	Orlando	IHL	73	25	35	60	60												6	2	2	4	6			
2000-01	**Atlanta**	**NHL**	**21**	**4**	**5**	**9**	**14**	**2**	**0**	**1**	**41**	**9.8**	**–11**	**37**	**40.5**	**10**	**6**	**16:01**								
	Orlando	IHL	58	22	26	48	32												12	8	3	11	14			
	NHL Totals		**33**	**5**	**5**	**10**	**20**	**2**	**0**	**1**	**49**	**10.2**		**67**	**44.8**	**20**	**9**	**13:51**								

Signed as a free agent by **Florida**, October 3, 1996. Traded to **Atlanta** by **Florida** with Gord Murphy, Daniel Tjarnqvist and Ottawa's 6th round choice (previously acquired, later traded to Dallas - Dallas selected Justin Cox) in 1999 Entry Draft for Trevor Kidd, June 25, 1999. Signed as a free agent by **Vancouver**, August 11, 2001.

VASILYEV, Andrei (vah-SEE-lee-ehf, AWN-dray)

Left wing. Shoots right. 5'9", 180 lbs. Born, Voskresensk, USSR, March 30, 1972. NY Islanders' 11th choice, 248th overall, in 1992 Entry Draft.

1991-92	CSKA Moscow	CIS	28	7	2	9	2																			
1992-93	HK Khimik	CIS	34	4	8	12	20																			
1993-94	CSKA Moscow	CIS	46	17	6	23	8												3	1	0	1	0			
1994-95	Denver Grizzlies	IHL	74	28	37	65	48												13	9	4	13	22			
	NY Islanders	**NHL**	**2**	**0**	**0**	**0**	**2**	**0**	**0**	**0**	**2**	**0.0**	**0**													
1995-96	**NY Islanders**	**NHL**	**10**	**2**	**5**	**7**	**2**	**0**	**0**	**1**	**12**	**16.7**	**4**													
	Utah Grizzlies	IHL	43	26	20	46	34												22	12	4	16	18			
1996-97	**NY Islanders**	**NHL**	**3**	**0**	**0**	**0**	**2**	**0**	**0**	**0**	**1**	**0.0**	**–3**													
	Utah Grizzlies	IHL	56	16	18	34	42												7	4	1	5	0			
1997-98	Long Beach	IHL	62	33	34	67	60												17	9	4	13	14			
1998-99	**Phoenix**	**NHL**	**1**	**0**	**0**	**0**	**0**	**0**	**0**	**0**	**0**	**0.0**	**–2**	**0**	**0.0**	**0**	**0**	**1:19**								
	Las Vegas	IHL	15	3	6	9	6																			
	Grand Rapids	IHL	59	21	27	48	24																			
99-2000	Frankfurt Lions	DEL	54	26	21	47	18												5	2	1	3	30			
2000-01	Revier Lowen	DEL	33	13	10	23	8												2	0	0	0	2			
	NHL Totals		**16**	**2**	**5**	**7**	**6**	**0**	**0**	**1**	**15**	**13.3**		**0**	**0.0**	**0**	**0**	**1:19**								

Signed as a free agent by **Phoenix**, August 26, 1998.

VERBEEK, Pat (vuhr-BEEK, PAT) DET.

Right wing. Shoots right. 5'9", 192 lbs. Born, Sarnia, Ont., May 24, 1964. New Jersey's 3rd choice, 43rd overall, in 1982 Entry Draft.

1979-80	Petrolia Jets	OHA-B	41	17	24	41	85																			
1980-81	Petrolia Jets	OHA-B	42	44	44	88	155																			
1981-82	Sudbury Wolves	OHL	66	37	51	88	180																			
1982-83	Sudbury Wolves	OHL	61	40	67	107	184																			
	New Jersey	**NHL**	**6**	**3**	**2**	**5**	**8**	**0**	**0**	**0**	**12**	**25.0**	**–2**													
1983-84	**New Jersey**	**NHL**	**79**	**20**	**27**	**47**	**158**	**5**	**1**	**2**	**167**	**12.0**	**–19**													
1984-85	**New Jersey**	**NHL**	**78**	**15**	**18**	**33**	**162**	**5**	**1**	**1**	**147**	**10.2**	**–24**													

			Regular Season																Playoffs							
Season	Club	League	GP	G	A	Pts	PIM	PP	SH	GW	S	%	+/-	TF	F%	H	SB	Min	GP	G	A	Pts	PIM	PP	SH	GW
1985-86	**New Jersey**	**NHL**	**76**	**25**	**28**	**53**	**79**	**4**	**1**	**0**	**159**	**15.7**	**–24**	....	....	....	....	....	....	....	....	....	....	....	....	....
1986-87	**New Jersey**	**NHL**	**74**	**35**	**24**	**59**	**120**	**17**	**0**	**5**	**143**	**24.5**	**–23**	....	....	....	....	....	....	....	....	....	....	....	....	....
1987-88	**New Jersey**	**NHL**	**73**	**46**	**31**	**77**	**227**	**13**	**0**	**8**	**179**	**25.7**	**29**	....	....	....	....	....	**20**	**4**	**8**	**12**	**51**	**2**	**0**	**1**
1988-89	**New Jersey**	**NHL**	**77**	**26**	**21**	**47**	**189**	**9**	**0**	**1**	**175**	**14.9**	**–18**	....	....	....	....	....	....	....	....	....	....	....	....	....
1989-90	**Hartford**	**NHL**	**80**	**44**	**45**	**89**	**228**	**14**	**0**	**5**	**219**	**20.1**	**1**	....	....	....	....	....	**7**	**2**	**2**	**4**	**26**	**1**	**0**	**1**
1990-91	**Hartford**	**NHL**	**80**	**43**	**39**	**82**	**246**	**15**	**0**	**5**	**247**	**17.4**	**0**	....	....	....	....	....	**6**	**3**	**2**	**5**	**40**	**2**	**0**	**0**
1991-92	**Hartford**	**NHL**	**76**	**22**	**35**	**57**	**243**	**10**	**0**	**3**	**163**	**13.5**	**–16**	....	....	....	....	....	**7**	**0**	**2**	**2**	**12**	**0**	**0**	**0**
1992-93	**Hartford**	**NHL**	**84**	**39**	**43**	**82**	**197**	**16**	**0**	**6**	**235**	**16.6**	**–7**	....	....	....	....	....	....	....	....	....	....	....	....	....
1993-94	**Hartford**	**NHL**	**84**	**37**	**38**	**75**	**177**	**15**	**1**	**3**	**226**	**16.4**	**–15**	....	....	....	....	....	....	....	....	....	....	....	....	....
1994-95	**Hartford**	**NHL**	**29**	**7**	**11**	**18**	**53**	**3**	**0**	**0**	**75**	**9.3**	**0**	....	....	....	....	....	....	....	....	....	....	....	....	....
	NY Rangers	**NHL**	**19**	**10**	**5**	**15**	**18**	**4**	**0**	**2**	**56**	**17.9**	**–2**	....	....	....	....	....	**10**	**4**	**6**	**10**	**20**	**3**	**0**	**0**
1995-96	**NY Rangers**	**NHL**	**69**	**41**	**41**	**82**	**129**	**17**	**0**	**6**	**252**	**16.3**	**29**	....	....	....	....	....	**11**	**3**	**6**	**9**	**12**	**1**	**0**	**0**
1996-97	**Dallas**	**NHL**	**81**	**17**	**36**	**53**	**128**	**5**	**0**	**4**	**172**	**9.9**	**3**	....	....	....	....	....	**7**	**1**	**3**	**4**	**16**	**1**	**0**	**0**
1997-98	**Dallas**	**NHL**	**82**	**31**	**26**	**57**	**170**	**9**	**0**	**8**	**190**	**16.3**	**15**	....	....	....	....	....	**17**	**3**	**2**	**5**	**26**	**2**	**0**	**1**
1998-99♦	**Dallas**	**NHL**	**78**	**17**	**17**	**34**	**133**	**8**	**0**	**2**	**134**	**12.7**	**11**	**1**	**100.0**	**130**	**15**	**14:34**	**18**	**3**	**4**	**7**	**14**	**0**	**0**	**1**
99-2000	**Detroit**	**NHL**	**68**	**22**	**26**	**48**	**95**	**7**	**0**	**5**	**138**	**15.9**	**22**	**1**	**0.0**	**148**	**8**	**16:04**	**9**	**1**	**1**	**2**	**2**	**1**	**0**	**1**
2000-01	**Detroit**	**NHL**	**67**	**15**	**15**	**30**	**73**	**7**	**0**	**0**	**113**	**13.3**	**0**	**7**	**57.1**	**141**	**13**	**13:31**	**5**	**2**	**0**	**2**	**6**	**2**	**0**	**0**
	NHL Totals		**1360**	**515**	**528**	**1043**	**2833**	**183**	**4**	**66**	**3202**	**16.1**		**9**	**55.6**	**419**	**36**	**14:43**	**117**	**26**	**36**	**62**	**225**	**15**	**0**	**5**

Played in NHL All-Star Game (1991, 1996)

Traded to **Hartford** by **New Jersey** for Sylvain Turgeon, June 17, 1989. Traded to **NY Rangers** by **Hartford** for Glen Featherstone, Michael Stewart, NY Rangers' 1st round choice (Jean-Sebastien Giguere) in 1995 Entry Draft and 4th round choice (Steve Wasylko) in 1996 Entry Draft, March 23, 1995. Signed as a free agent by **Dallas**, August 21, 1996. Signed as a free agent by **Detroit**, November 11, 1999.

VIGIER, Jean-Pierre (vih-ZHAY, zhaw-pee-AIR) ATL.

Right wing. Shoots right. 6', 195 lbs. Born, Notre Dame de Lourdes, Man., September 11, 1976.

Season	Club	League	GP	G	A	Pts	PIM	PP	SH	GW	S	%	+/-	TF	F%	H	SB	Min	GP	G	A	Pts	PIM	PP	SH	GW
1995-96	Portage Terriers	MJHL	56	32	49	81	....	....	....	....	....	....	....	....	....	....	....	....	....	....	....	....	....	....	....	....
1996-97	North-Michigan	WCHA	36	10	14	24	54	....	....	....	....	....	....	....	....	....	....	....	....	....	....	....	....	....	....	....
1997-98	North-Michigan	WCHA	36	12	15	27	60	....	....	....	....	....	....	....	....	....	....	....	....	....	....	....	....	....	....	....
1998-99	North-Michigan	WCHA	42	21	18	39	80	....	....	....	....	....	....	....	....	....	....	....	....	....	....	....	....	....	....	....
99-2000	North-Michigan	CCHA	39	18	17	35	72	....	....	....	....	....	....	....	....	....	....	....	....	....	....	....	....	....	....	....
	Orlando	IHL	3	1	0	1	0	....	....	....	....	....	....	....	....	....	....	....	....	....	....	....	....	....	....	....
2000-01	**Atlanta**	**NHL**	**2**	**0**	**0**	**0**	**0**	**0**	**0**	**0**	**1**	**0.0**	**–2**	**1**	**100.0**	**0**	**1**	**9:56**	....	....	....	....	....	....	....	....
	Orlando	IHL	78	23	17	40	66	....	....	....	....	....	....	....	....	....	....	....	16	6	6	12	14	....	....	....
	NHL Totals		**2**	**0**	**0**	**0**	**0**	**0**	**0**	**0**	**1**	**0.0**		**1**	**100.0**	**0**	**1**	**9:56**	....	....	....	....	....	....	....	....

CCHA Second All-Star Team (1999) • CCHA All-Tournament Team (1999)

Signed as a free agent by **Atlanta**, April 20, 2000.

VIRTUE, Terry (VIR-too, TAIR-ee) NYR

Defense. Shoots right. 6', 207 lbs. Born, Scarborough, Ont., August 12, 1970.

Season	Club	League	GP	G	A	Pts	PIM	PP	SH	GW	S	%	+/-	TF	F%	H	SB	Min	GP	G	A	Pts	PIM	PP	SH	GW
1988-89	Hobbema Hawks	AJHL	56	6	31	37	339	....	....	....	....	....	....	....	....	....	....	....	....	....	....	....	....	....	....	....
	Victoria Cougars	WHL	8	1	1	2	13	....	....	....	....	....	....	....	....	....	....	....	....	....	....	....	....	....	....	....
1989-90	Victoria Cougars	WHL	24	1	9	10	85	....	....	....	....	....	....	....	....	....	....	....	....	....	....	....	....	....	....	....
	Tri-City Americans	WHL	34	1	10	11	82	....	....	....	....	....	....	....	....	....	....	....	6	0	0	0	30	....	....	....
1990-91	Tri-City Americans	WHL	11	1	8	9	24	....	....	....	....	....	....	....	....	....	....	....	....	....	....	....	....	....	....	....
	Portland	WHL	59	9	44	53	127	....	....	....	....	....	....	....	....	....	....	....	....	....	....	....	....	....	....	....
1991-92	Roanoke Valley	ECHL	38	4	22	26	165	....	....	....	....	....	....	....	....	....	....	....	....	....	....	....	....	....	....	....
	Louisville	ECHL	23	1	15	16	58	....	....	....	....	....	....	....	....	....	....	....	13	0	8	8	49	....	....	....
1992-93	Louisville	ECHL	28	0	17	17	84	....	....	....	....	....	....	....	....	....	....	....	....	....	....	....	....	....	....	....
	Wheeling	ECHL	31	3	15	18	86	....	....	....	....	....	....	....	....	....	....	....	16	3	5	8	18	....	....	....
1993-94	Wheeling	ECHL	34	5	28	33	61	....	....	....	....	....	....	....	....	....	....	....	6	2	2	4	4	....	....	....
	Cape Breton	AHL	26	4	6	10	10	....	....	....	....	....	....	....	....	....	....	....	5	0	0	0	17	....	....	....
1994-95	Worcester	AHL	73	14	25	39	183	....	....	....	....	....	....	....	....	....	....	....	....	....	....	....	....	....	....	....
	Atlanta Knights	IHL	1	0	0	0	2	....	....	....	....	....	....	....	....	....	....	....	....	....	....	....	....	....	....	....
1995-96	Worcester	AHL	76	7	31	38	234	....	....	....	....	....	....	....	....	....	....	....	4	0	0	0	4	....	....	....
1996-97	Worcester	AHL	80	16	26	42	220	....	....	....	....	....	....	....	....	....	....	....	5	0	4	4	8	....	....	....
1997-98	Worcester	AHL	74	8	26	34	233	....	....	....	....	....	....	....	....	....	....	....	11	1	4	5	41	....	....	....
1998-99	**Boston**	**NHL**	**4**	**0**	**0**	**0**	**0**	**0**	**0**	**0**	**2**	**0.0**	**2**	**0**	**0.0**	**4**	**2**	**9:41**	....	....	....	....	....	....	....	....
	Providence Bruins	AHL	76	8	48	56	117	....	....	....	....	....	....	....	....	....	....	....	17	2	12	14	29	....	....	....
99-2000	**NY Rangers**	**NHL**	**1**	**0**	**0**	**0**	**0**	**0**	**0**	**0**	**2**	**0.0**	**–2**	**0**	**0.0**	**3**	**1**	**12:32**	....	....	....	....	....	....	....	....
	Hartford	AHL	67	5	22	27	166	....	....	....	....	....	....	....	....	....	....	....	23	3	7	10	51	....	....	....
2000-01	Hartford	AHL	71	5	24	29	166	....	....	....	....	....	....	....	....	....	....	....	5	1	0	1	2	....	....	....
	NHL Totals		**5**	**0**	**0**	**0**	**0**	**0**	**0**	**0**	**4**	**0.0**		**0**	**0.0**	**7**	**3**	**10:15**	....	....	....	....	....	....	....	....

AHL Second All-Star Team (1999)

Signed as a free agent by **St. Louis**, January 29, 1996. Signed as a free agent by **Boston**, August 28, 1998. Signed as a free agent by **NY Rangers**, July 29, 1999.

VISHNEVSKI, Vitaly (vihsh-NEHV-skee, vih-TAL-ee) ANA.

Defense. Shoots left. 6'2", 206 lbs. Born, Kharkov, USSR, March 18, 1980. Anaheim's 1st choice, 5th overall, in 1998 Entry Draft.

Season	Club	League	GP	G	A	Pts	PIM	PP	SH	GW	S	%	+/-	TF	F%	H	SB	Min	GP	G	A	Pts	PIM	PP	SH	GW
1995-96	Torpedo Yaroslavl	Russia-2	40	4	4	8	20	....	....	....	....	....	....	....	....	....	....	....	....	....	....	....	....	....	....	....
1996-97	HC Yaroslavl-2	Russia-3	45	0	2	2	30	....	....	....	....	....	....	....	....	....	....	....	....	....	....	....	....	....	....	....
1997-98	Torpedo Yaroslavl	Russia-2	47	8	9	17	164	....	....	....	....	....	....	....	....	....	....	....	....	....	....	....	....	....	....	....
1998-99	Torpedo Yaroslavl	Russia	34	3	4	7	38	....	....	....	....	....	....	....	....	....	....	....	10	0	0	0	4	....	....	....
99-2000	**Anaheim**	**NHL**	**31**	**1**	**1**	**2**	**26**	**1**	**0**	**0**	**17**	**5.9**	**0**	**0**	**0.0**	**113**	**28**	**16:38**	....	....	....	....	....	....	....	....
	Cincinnati Ducks	AHL	35	1	3	4	45	....	....	....	....	....	....	....	....	....	....	....	....	....	....	....	....	....	....	....
2000-01	**Anaheim**	**NHL**	**76**	**1**	**10**	**11**	**99**	**0**	**0**	**0**	**49**	**2.0**	**–1**	**0**	**0.0**	**286**	**69**	**19:14**	....	....	....	....	....	....	....	....
	NHL Totals		**107**	**2**	**11**	**13**	**125**	**1**	**0**	**0**	**66**	**3.0**		**0**	**0.0**	**399**	**97**	**19:14**	....	....	....	....	....	....	....	....

VISNOVSKY, Lubomir (vihsh-NAWV-skee, LOO-boh-mihr) L.A.

Defense. Shoots left. 5'10", 183 lbs. Born, Topolcany, Czech., August 11, 1976. Los Angeles' 4th choice, 118th overall, in 2000 Entry Draft.

Season	Club	League	GP	G	A	Pts	PIM	PP	SH	GW	S	%	+/-	TF	F%	H	SB	Min	GP	G	A	Pts	PIM	PP	SH	GW
1994-95	Slovan Bratislava	Slovakia	36	11	12	23	10	....	....	....	....	....	....	....	....	....	....	....	9	1	3	4	2	....	....	....
1995-96	Slovan Bratislava	Slovakia	35	8	6	14	22	....	....	....	....	....	....	....	....	....	....	....	13	1	5	6	2	....	....	....
1996-97	Slovan Bratislava	Slovakia	44	11	12	23	....	....	....	....	....	....	....	....	....	....	....	....	2	0	1	1	....	....	....	....
	Slovan Bratislava	EuroHL	6	3	1	4	2	....	....	....	....	....	....	....	....	....	....	....	2	0	0	0	6	....	....	....
1997-98	Slovan Bratislava	Slovakia	36	7	9	16	16	....	....	....	....	....	....	....	....	....	....	....	11	2	4	6	8	....	....	....
	Slovan Bratislava	EuroHL	6	1	0	1	4	....	....	....	....	....	....	....	....	....	....	....	....	....	....	....	....	....	....	....
1998-99	Slovan Bratislava	Slovakia	40	9	10	19	31	....	....	....	....	....	....	....	....	....	....	....	10	5	5	10	0	....	....	....
	Slovan Bratislava	EuroHL	6	0	3	3	4	....	....	....	....	....	....	....	....	....	....	....	....	....	....	....	....	....	....	....
99-2000	Slovan Bratislava	Slovakia	52	21	24	45	38	....	....	....	....	....	....	....	....	....	....	....	8	5	3	8	16	....	....	....
2000-01	**Los Angeles**	**NHL**	**81**	**7**	**32**	**39**	**36**	**3**	**0**	**3**	**105**	**6.7**	**16**	**0**	**0.0**	**99**	**87**	**16:58**	**8**	**0**	**0**	**0**	**0**	**0**	**0**	**0**
	NHL Totals		**81**	**7**	**32**	**39**	**36**	**3**	**0**	**3**	**105**	**6.7**		**0**	**0.0**	**99**	**87**	**16:58**	**8**	**0**	**0**	**0**	**0**	**0**	**0**	**0**

NHL All-Rookie Team (2001)

VLASAK, Tomas (VLAH-sahk, TAW-mawsh)

Center. Shoots right. 5'10", 175 lbs. Born, Prague, Czech., February 1, 1975. Los Angeles' 6th choice, 120th overall, in 1993 Entry Draft.

Season	Club	League	GP	G	A	Pts	PIM	PP	SH	GW	S	%	+/-	TF	F%	H	SB	Min	GP	G	A	Pts	PIM	PP	SH	GW
1992-93	Slavia Praha	Czech-2	31	17	6	23	....	....	....	....	....	....	....	....	....	....	....	....	....	....	....	....	....	....	....	....
1993-94	CHZ Litvinov	Cze-Rep	41	16	11	27	0	....	....	....	....	....	....	....	....	....	....	....	4	0	1	1	0	....	....	....
1994-95	CHZ Litvinov	Cze-Rep	35	6	14	20	4	....	....	....	....	....	....	....	....	....	....	....	4	0	0	0	4	....	....	....
1995-96	CHZ Litvinov	Cze-Rep	35	10	22	32	....	....	....	....	....	....	....	....	....	....	....	....	15	5	5	10	....	....	....	....
1996-97	CHZ Litvinov	EuroHL	6	0	2	2	29	....	....	....	....	....	....	....	....	....	....	....	....	....	....	....	....	....	....	....
	CHZ Litvinov	EuroHL	6	0	2	2	29	....	....	....	....	....	....	....	....	....	....	....	2	0	2	2	0	....	....	....
	CHZ Litvinov	Cze-Rep	52	26	34	60	16	....	....	....	....	....	....	....	....	....	....	....	....	....	....	....	....	....	....	....
1997-98	CHZ Litvinov	Cze-Rep	51	22	22	44	40	....	....	....	....	....	....	....	....	....	....	....	4	1	2	3	2	....	....	....
1998-99	HPK Hameenlinna	Finland	54	28	29	57	36	....	....	....	....	....	....	....	....	....	....	....	8	2	*9	11	0	....	....	....
99-2000	HPK Hameenlinna	Finland	48	24	39	63	63	....	....	....	....	....	....	....	....	....	....	....	8	3	4	7	6	....	....	....

Season	Club	League	GP	G	A	Pts	PIM	PP	SH	GW	S	%	+/-	TF	F%	H	SB	Min	GP	G	A	Pts	PIM	PP	SH	GW
			Regular Season																Playoffs							
2000-01	**Los Angeles**	**NHL**	**10**	**1**	**3**	**4**	**2**	**0**	**0**	**0**	**15**	**6.7**	**4**	**1**	**0.0**	**5**	**0**	**11:28**								
	Lowell	AHL	5	0	1	1	5																			
	HPK Hameenlinna	Finland	27	6	12	18	10																			
	NHL Totals		**10**	**1**	**3**	**4**	**2**	**0**	**0**	**0**	**15**	**6.7**		**1**	**0.0**	**5**	**0**	**11:28**								

VOLCHKOV, Alexandre

(VOHLCH-kahf, al-ehx-AN-duhr)

Center. Shoots left. 6'2", 204 lbs. Born, Moscow, USSR, September 25, 1977. Washington's 1st choice, 4th overall, in 1996 Entry Draft.

Season	Club	League	GP	G	A	Pts	PIM	PP	SH	GW	S	%	+/-	TF	F%	H	SB	Min	GP	G	A	Pts	PIM	PP	SH	GW
1994-95	CSKA Moscow	CIS	1	0	0	0	0																			
1995-96	Barrie Colts	OHL	47	37	27	64	36												7	2	3	5	12			
1996-97	Barrie Colts	OHL	56	29	53	82	76												9	6	9	15	12			
	Portland Pirates	AHL																	4	0	0	0	0			
1997-98	Portland Pirates	AHL	34	2	5	7	20												1	0	0	0	0			
1998-99	Portland Pirates	AHL	27	3	8	11	24																			
	Cincinnati	IHL	25	1	3	4	8																			
99-2000	**Washington**	**NHL**	**3**	**0**	**0**	**0**	**0**	**0**	**0**	**0**	**1**	**0.0**	**–2**	**0**	**0.0**	**2**	**0**	**10:07**								
	Portland Pirates	AHL	35	11	15	26	47																			
	Hamilton Bulldogs	AHL	25	2	6	8	11																			
2000-01	Molot-Perm	Russia	14	2	1	3	6																			
	Vityaz Podolsk	Russia	10	1	1	2	8																			
	NHL Totals		**3**	**0**	**0**	**0**	**0**	**0**	**0**	**0**	**1**	**0.0**		**0**	**0.0**	**2**	**0**	**10:07**								

OHL Second All-Star Team (1997)

Traded to **Edmonton** by **Washington** for a Edmonton's 4th round choice (later traded to Anaheim - Anaheim selected Brandon Rogers) in 2001 Entry Draft, February 4, 2000.

VON ARX, Reto

(VAWN-ARX, RAY-toh) **CHI.**

Center. Shoots left. 5'10", 190 lbs. Born, Egerkingen, Switz., September 13, 1976. Chicago's 14th choice, 271st overall, in 2000 Entry Draft.

Season	Club	League	GP	G	A	Pts	PIM	PP	SH	GW	S	%	+/-	TF	F%	H	SB	Min	GP	G	A	Pts	PIM	PP	SH	GW
1992-93	SC Langnau	Switz-2	35	11	4	15	28												5	0	0	0	6			
1993-94	SC Langnau	Switz-3	36	35	31	66	42																			
1994-95	SC Langnau	Switz-2	36	14	9	23	72												5	1	2	3	27			
1995-96	HC Davos	Switz.	34	4	6	10	59												5	0	2	2	4			
1996-97	HC Davos	Switz.	42	10	17	27	78												6	1	3	4	4			
1997-98	HC Davos	Switz.	39	8	15	23	113												18	10	6	16	18			
1998-99	HC Davos	Switz.	45	21	20	41	76												6	4	6	10	16			
99-2000	HC Davos	Switz.	45	19	26	45	70												5	2	0	2	10			
2000-01	**Chicago**	**NHL**	**19**	**3**	**1**	**4**	**4**	**0**	**0**	**1**	**12**	**25.0**	**–4**	**94**	**42.6**	**1**	**5**	**11:26**								
	Norfolk Admirals	AHL	49	16	26	42	28												9	1	2	3	8			
	NHL Totals		**19**	**3**	**1**	**4**	**4**	**0**	**0**	**1**	**12**	**25.0**		**94**	**42.6**	**1**	**5**	**11:26**								

VOPAT, Jan

(VOH-paht, YAN)

Defense. Shoots left. 6', 205 lbs. Born, Most, Czech., March 22, 1973. Hartford's 3rd choice, 57th overall, in 1992 Entry Draft.

Season	Club	League	GP	G	A	Pts	PIM	PP	SH	GW	S	%	+/-	TF	F%	H	SB	Min	GP	G	A	Pts	PIM	PP	SH	GW
1990-91	CHZ Litvinov	Czech.	25	1	4	5	4																			
1991-92	CHZ Litvinov	Czech.	46	4	2	6	16																			
1992-93	CHZ Litvinov	Czech.	45	12	10	22																				
1993-94	CHZ Litvinov	Cze-Rep	41	9	19	28	0												4	1	1	2				
	Czech-Republic	Olympics	8	0	1	1	8																			
1994-95	CHZ Litvinov	Cze-Rep	42	7	18	25	49												4	0	2	2	2			
1995-96	**Los Angeles**	**NHL**	**11**	**1**	**4**	**5**	**4**	**0**	**0**	**0**	**13**	**7.7**	**3**													
	Phoenix	IHL	47	0	9	9	34												4	0	2	2	4			
1996-97	**Los Angeles**	**NHL**	**33**	**4**	**5**	**9**	**22**	**0**	**0**	**1**	**44**	**9.1**	**3**													
	Phoenix	IHL	4	0	6	6	6																			
1997-98	**Los Angeles**	**NHL**	**21**	**1**	**5**	**6**	**10**	**0**	**0**	**1**	**13**	**7.7**	**8**						**2**	**0**	**1**	**1**	**2**	**0**	**0**	**0**
	Utah Grizzlies	IHL	38	8	13	21	24																			
1998-99	**Nashville**	**NHL**	**55**	**5**	**6**	**11**	**28**	**0**	**0**	**0**	**46**	**10.9**	**0**	**0**	**0.0**	**98**	**70**	**18:05**								
99-2000	**Nashville**	**NHL**	**6**	**0**	**0**	**0**	**6**	**0**	**0**	**0**	**3**	**0.0**	**1**	**0**	**0.0**	**8**	**6**	**17:55**								
	Milwaukee	IHL	2	1	0	1	2																			
2000-01	HPK Hameenlinna	Finland	DID NOT PLAY																							
	NHL Totals		**126**	**11**	**20**	**31**	**70**	**0**	**0**	**2**	**119**	**9.2**		**0**	**0.0**	**106**	**76**	**18:04**	**2**	**0**	**1**	**1**	**2**	**0**	**0**	**0**

Rights traded to **LA Kings** by **Hartford** for LA Kings' 4th round choice (Ian MacNeil) in 1995 Entry Draft, May 31, 1995. Traded to **Nashville** by **LA Kings** with Kimmo Timonen for future considerations, June 26, 1998. • Missed remainder of 1999-2000 and entire 2000-01 seasons recovering from rare skin allergy, December 10, 1999.

VUJTEK, Vladimir

(VYOO-tehk, VLAD-dih-MEER)

Left wing. Shoots left. 6'1", 190 lbs. Born, Ostrava, Czech., February 17, 1972. Montreal's 5th choice, 73rd overall, in 1991 Entry Draft.

Season	Club	League	GP	G	A	Pts	PIM	PP	SH	GW	S	%	+/-	TF	F%	H	SB	Min	GP	G	A	Pts	PIM	PP	SH	GW
1988-89	TJ Vitkovice	Czech.	3	0	1	1	0																			
1989-90	TJ Vitkovice	Czech.	22	3	4	7													7	4	3	7				
1990-91	TJ Vitkovice	Czech.	26	7	4	11																				
	Tri-City Americans	WHL	37	26	18	44	74												7	2	3	5	4			
1991-92	Tri-City Americans	WHL	53	41	61	102	114																			
	Montreal	**NHL**	**2**	**0**	**0**	**0**	**0**	**0**	**0**	**0**	**1**	**0.0**	**–1**													
1992-93	**Edmonton**	**NHL**	**30**	**1**	**10**	**11**	**8**	**0**	**0**	**0**	**49**	**2.0**	**–1**													
	Cape Breton	AHL	20	10	9	19	14												1	0	0	0	0			
1993-94	**Edmonton**	**NHL**	**40**	**4**	**15**	**19**	**14**	**1**	**0**	**0**	**66**	**6.1**	**–7**													
1994-95	HC Vitkovice	Cze-Rep	18	5	7	12	51																			
	Cape Breton	AHL	30	10	11	21	30																			
	Las Vegas	IHL	1	0	0	0	0																			
1995-96	HC Vitkovice	Cze-Rep	26	6	7	13													4	1	1	2				
1996-97	Assat-Pori	Finland	50	27	31	58	48												4	1	2	3	2			
1997-98	**Tampa Bay**	**NHL**	**30**	**2**	**4**	**6**	**16**	**0**	**0**	**1**	**44**	**4.5**	**–2**													
	Adirondack	AHL	2	1	2	3	0																			
1998-99	HC Vitkovice	Cze-Rep	47	20	35	55	75																			
99-2000	**Atlanta**	**NHL**	**3**	**0**	**0**	**0**	**0**	**0**	**0**	**0**	**2**	**0.0**	**0**	**0**	**0.0**	**1**	**0**	**10:52**								
	Sparta Praha	Cze-Rep	21	12	19	31	10												8	2	3	5	10			
2000-01	Sparta Praha	Cze-Rep	38	11	18	29	28												13	3	6	9	4			
	NHL Totals		**105**	**7**	**29**	**36**	**38**	**1**	**0**	**1**	**162**	**4.3**		**0**	**0.0**	**1**	**0**	**10:52**								

WHL West First All-Star Team (1992)

Traded to **Edmonton** by **Montreal** with Shayne Corson and Brent Gilchrist for Vincent Damphousse and Edmonton's 4th round choice (Adam Wiesel) in 1993 Entry Draft, August 27, 1992. Traded to **Tampa Bay** by **Edmonton** with Edmonton's 3rd round choice (Dmitry Afanasenkov) in 1998 Entry Draft for Brantt Myhres and Toronto's 3rd round choice (previously acquired, Edmonton selected Alex Henry) in 1998 Entry Draft, July 16, 1997. • Missed majority of 1997-98 season recovering from Epstein-Barr Virus, December, 1997. Signed as a free agent by **Atlanta**, July 29, 1999. • Missed majority of 1999-2000 season recovering from facial injuries suffered in exhibition game vs. NY Rangers, September 18, 1999.

VYBORNY, David

(vih-BOHR-nee, DAY-vihd) **CBJ**

Right wing. Shoots right. 5'10", 183 lbs. Born, Jihlava, Czech., June 2, 1975. Edmonton's 3rd choice, 33rd overall, in 1993 Entry Draft.

Season	Club	League	GP	G	A	Pts	PIM	PP	SH	GW	S	%	+/-	TF	F%	H	SB	Min	GP	G	A	Pts	PIM	PP	SH	GW
1991-92	Sparta Praha	Czech.	32	6	9	15	2																			
1992-93	Sparta Praha	Czech.	52	20	24	44																				
1993-94	Sparta Praha	Cze-Rep	44	15	20	35	0												6	4	7	11	0			
1994-95	Cape Breton	AHL	76	23	38	61	30																			
1995-96	Sparta Praha	Cze-Rep	40	12	18	30													12	6	5	11				
1996-97	Sparta Praha	Cze-Rep	47	20	29	49	14												10	7	7	14	6			
1997-98	MoDo Hockey	Sweden	45	16	21	37	34												9	0	2	2	2			
1998-99	Sparta Praha	Cze-Rep	52	24	*46	*70	22												8	1	3	4				
99-2000	Sparta Praha	Cze-Rep	50	25	38	63	30												9	3	*8	*11	4			
2000-01	**Columbus**	**NHL**	**79**	**13**	**19**	**32**	**22**	**5**	**0**	**1**	**125**	**10.4**	**–9**	**36**	**44.4**	**23**	**17**	**15:25**								
	NHL Totals		**79**	**13**	**19**	**32**	**22**	**5**	**0**	**1**	**125**	**10.4**		**36**	**44.4**	**23**	**17**	**15:25**								

Signed as a free agent by **Columbus**, June 8, 2000.

			Regular Season																Playoffs							
Season	Club	League	GP	G	A	Pts	PIM	PP	SH	GW	S	%	+/-	TF	F%	H	SB	Min	GP	G	A	Pts	PIM	PP	SH	GW

VYSHEDKEVICH, Sergei

(vee-shehd-KAY-vihch, SAIR-gay)

Defense. Shoots left. 6', 195 lbs. Born, Dedovsk, USSR, January 3, 1975. New Jersey's 3rd choice, 70th overall, in 1995 Entry Draft.

Season	Club	League	GP	G	A	Pts	PIM	PP	SH	GW	S	%	+/-	TF	F%	H	SB	Min	GP	G	A	Pts	PIM	PP	SH	GW
1994-95	Dynamo Moscow	CIS	49	6	7	13	67	....	....	....	....	....	....	....	....	....	....	....	14	2	0	2	12	....	....	....
1995-96	Dynamo Moscow	CIS	49	5	4	9	12	....	....	....	....	....	....	....	....	....	....	....	13	1	1	2	6	....	....	....
1996-97	Albany River Rats	AHL	65	8	27	35	16	....	....	....	....	....	....	....	....	....	....	....	12	0	6	6	0	....	....	....
1997-98	Albany River Rats	AHL	54	12	16	28	12	....	....	....	....	....	....	....	....	....	....	....	13	0	10	10	4	....	....	....
1998-99	Albany River Rats	AHL	79	11	38	49	28	....	....	....	....	....	....	....	....	....	....	....	5	0	3	3	0	....	....	....
99-2000	**Atlanta**	**NHL**	**7**	**1**	**3**	**4**	**2**	**1**	**0**	**0**	**5**	**20.0**	**–3**	**0**	**0.0**	**14**	**8**	**23:18**	....	....	....	....	....	....	....	....
	Orlando	IHL	69	11	24	35	32	....	....	....	....	....	....	....	....	....	....	....	6	3	3	6	8	....	....	....
2000-01	**Atlanta**	**NHL**	**23**	**1**	**2**	**3**	**14**	**0**	**0**	**0**	**28**	**3.6**	**–7**	**0**	**0.0**	**19**	**24**	**20:34**	....	....	....	....	....	....	....	....
	Orlando	IHL	10	2	3	5	2	....	....	....	....	....	....	....	....	....	....	....	....	....	....	....	....	....	....	....
	Cincinnati Ducks	AHL	17	3	2	5	2	....	....	....	....	....	....	....	....	....	....	....	....	....	....	....	....	....	....	....
	NHL Totals		**30**	**2**	**5**	**7**	**16**	**1**	**0**	**0**	**33**	**6.1**		**0**	**0.0**	**33**	**32**	**21:13**	....	....	....	....	....	....	....	....

Traded to **Atlanta** by **New Jersey** for future considerations, June 25, 1999. Traded to **Anaheim** by **Atlanta** with Scott Langkow for Ladislav Kohn, February 9, 2001.

WALKER, Scott

(WAH-kuhr, SKAWT) **NSH.**

Center. Shoots right. 5'10", 196 lbs. Born, Cambridge, Ont., July 19, 1973. Vancouver's 4th choice, 124th overall, in 1993 Entry Draft.

Season	Club	League	GP	G	A	Pts	PIM	PP	SH	GW	S	%	+/-	TF	F%	H	SB	Min	GP	G	A	Pts	PIM	PP	SH	GW
1989-90	Kitchener	OJHL-B	6	0	5	5	4	....	....	....	....	....	....	....	....	....	....	....	....	....	....	....	....	....	....	....
	Cambridge Hawks	OJHL-B	27	7	22	29	87	....	....	....	....	....	....	....	....	....	....	....	....	....	....	....	....	....	....	....
1990-91	Cambridge Hawks	OJHL-B	45	10	27	37	241	....	....	....	....	....	....	....	....	....	....	....	....	....	....	....	....	....	....	....
1991-92	Owen Sound	OHL	53	7	31	38	128	....	....	....	....	....	....	....	....	....	....	....	5	0	7	7	8	....	....	....
1992-93	Owen Sound	OHL	57	23	68	91	110	....	....	....	....	....	....	....	....	....	....	....	8	1	5	6	16	....	....	....
1993-94	Hamilton Canucks	AHL	77	10	29	39	272	....	....	....	....	....	....	....	....	....	....	....	4	0	1	1	25	....	....	....
1994-95	Syracuse Crunch	AHL	74	14	38	52	334	....	....	....	....	....	....	....	....	....	....	....	....	....	....	....	....	....	....	....
	Vancouver	**NHL**	**11**	**0**	**1**	**1**	**33**	**0**	**0**	**0**	**8**	**0.0**	**0**	....	....	....	....	....	....	....	....	....	....	....	....	....
1995-96	**Vancouver**	**NHL**	**63**	**4**	**8**	**12**	**137**	**0**	**1**	**1**	**45**	**8.9**	**–7**	....	....	....	....	....	....	....	....	....	....	....	....	....
	Syracuse Crunch	AHL	15	3	12	15	52	....	....	....	....	....	....	....	....	....	....	....	16	9	8	17	39	....	....	....
1996-97	**Vancouver**	**NHL**	**64**	**3**	**15**	**18**	**132**	**0**	**0**	**0**	**55**	**5.5**	**2**	....	....	....	....	....	....	....	....	....	....	....	....	....
1997-98	**Vancouver**	**NHL**	**59**	**3**	**10**	**13**	**164**	**0**	**1**	**1**	**40**	**7.5**	**–8**	....	....	....	....	....	....	....	....	....	....	....	....	....
1998-99	**Nashville**	**NHL**	**71**	**15**	**25**	**40**	**103**	**0**	**1**	**2**	**96**	**15.6**	**0**	**265**	**48.3**	**82**	**41**	**16:21**	....	....	....	....	....	....	....	....
99-2000	**Nashville**	**NHL**	**69**	**7**	**21**	**28**	**90**	**0**	**1**	**0**	**98**	**7.1**	**–16**	**30**	**36.7**	**121**	**36**	**15:49**	....	....	....	....	....	....	....	....
2000-01	**Nashville**	**NHL**	**74**	**25**	**29**	**54**	**66**	**9**	**3**	**1**	**159**	**15.7**	**–2**	**541**	**51.4**	**92**	**10**	**19:17**	....	....	....	....	....	....	....	....
	NHL Totals		**411**	**57**	**109**	**166**	**725**	**9**	**7**	**5**	**501**	**11.4**		**836**	**49.9**	**295**	**87**	**17:12**	....	....	....	....	....	....	....	....

OHL Second All-Star Team (1993)

Claimed by **Nashville** from **Vancouver** in Expansion Draft, June 26, 1998.

WALLIN, Jesse

(WAHL-ihn, JEH-see) **DET.**

Defense. Shoots left. 6'2", 190 lbs. Born, Saskatoon, Sask., March 10, 1978. Detroit's 1st choice, 26th overall, in 1996 Entry Draft.

Season	Club	League	GP	G	A	Pts	PIM	PP	SH	GW	S	%	+/-	TF	F%	H	SB	Min	GP	G	A	Pts	PIM	PP	SH	GW
1993-94	North Battleford	SMHL	32	1	7	8	41	....	....	....	....	....	....	....	....	....	....	....	....	....	....	....	....	....	....	....
1994-95	Red Deer Rebels	WHL	72	4	20	24	72	....	....	....	....	....	....	....	....	....	....	....	....	....	....	....	....	....	....	....
1995-96	Red Deer Rebels	WHL	70	5	19	24	61	....	....	....	....	....	....	....	....	....	....	....	9	0	3	3	4	....	....	....
1996-97	Red Deer Rebels	WHL	59	6	33	39	70	....	....	....	....	....	....	....	....	....	....	....	16	1	4	5	10	....	....	....
1997-98	Red Deer Rebels	WHL	14	1	6	7	17	....	....	....	....	....	....	....	....	....	....	....	5	0	1	1	2	....	....	....
1998-99	Adirondack	AHL	76	4	12	16	34	....	....	....	....	....	....	....	....	....	....	....	3	0	2	2	2	....	....	....
99-2000	**Detroit**	**NHL**	**1**	**0**	**0**	**0**	**0**	**0**	**0**	**0**	**0**	**0.0**	**–2**	**0**	**0.0**	**2**	**1**	**19:22**	....	....	....	....	....	....	....	....
	Cincinnati Ducks	AHL	75	3	14	17	61	....	....	....	....	....	....	....	....	....	....	....	....	....	....	....	....	....	....	....
2000-01	**Detroit**	**NHL**	**1**	**0**	**0**	**0**	**2**	**0**	**0**	**0**	**1**	**0.0**	**0**	**0**	**0.0**	**1**	**1**	**3:50**	....	....	....	....	....	....	....	....
	Cincinnati Ducks	AHL	76	2	15	17	50	....	....	....	....	....	....	....	....	....	....	....	4	0	1	1	4	....	....	....
	NHL Totals		**2**	**0**	**0**	**0**	**2**	**0**	**0**	**0**	**1**	**0.0**		**0**	**0.0**	**3**	**2**	**11:36**	....	....	....	....	....	....	....	....

Canadian Major Junior Humanitarian Player of the Year (1997)

WALLIN, Niclas

(VAH-lihn, NIH-kluhs) **CAR.**

Defense. Shoots left. 6'3", 220 lbs. Born, Boden, Sweden, February 20, 1975. Carolina's 3rd choice, 97th overall, in 2000 Entry Draft.

Season	Club	League	GP	G	A	Pts	PIM	PP	SH	GW	S	%	+/-	TF	F%	H	SB	Min	GP	G	A	Pts	PIM	PP	SH	GW
1994-95	Bodens IK	Sweden-Jr.	30	2	13	15	125	....	....	....	....	....	....	....	....	....	....	....	....	....	....	....	....	....	....	....
	Bodens IK	Sweden-2	13	0	0	0	0	....	....	....	....	....	....	....	....	....	....	....	2	0	0	0	0	....	....	....
1995-96	Bodens IK	Sweden-Jr.	2	2	2	4	0	....	....	....	....	....	....	....	....	....	....	....	....	....	....	....	....	....	....	....
	Bodens IK	Sweden-2	30	2	7	9	26	....	....	....	....	....	....	....	....	....	....	....	2	0	1	1	2	....	....	....
1996-97	Brynas IF	Sweden	47	1	1	2	14	....	....	....	....	....	....	....	....	....	....	....	....	....	....	....	....	....	....	....
1997-98	Brynas IF	Sweden	44	2	3	5	57	....	....	....	....	....	....	....	....	....	....	....	3	0	1	1	4	....	....	....
1998-99	Brynas IF	Sweden	46	2	4	6	52	....	....	....	....	....	....	....	....	....	....	....	14	0	1	1	8	....	....	....
99-2000	Brynas IF	Sweden	48	7	9	16	73	....	....	....	....	....	....	....	....	....	....	....	11	2	1	3	14	....	....	....
	Brynas IF	EuroHL	5	1	1	2	10	....	....	....	....	....	....	....	....	....	....	....	....	....	....	....	....	....	....	....
2000-01	**Carolina**	**NHL**	**37**	**2**	**3**	**5**	**21**	**0**	**0**	**0**	**19**	**10.5**	**–11**	**0**	**0.0**	**51**	**45**	**14:57**	**3**	**0**	**0**	**0**	**2**	**0**	**0**	**0**
	Cincinnati	IHL	8	1	2	3	4	....	....	....	....	....	....	....	....	....	....	....	3	0	0	0	2	....	....	....
	NHL Totals		**37**	**2**	**3**	**5**	**21**	**0**	**0**	**0**	**19**	**10.5**		**0**	**0.0**	**51**	**45**	**14:57**	**3**	**0**	**0**	**0**	**2**	**0**	**0**	**0**

• Missed most of 2000-01 season recovering from shoulder injury suffered in game vs. Florida, January 12, 2001.

WALZ, Wes

(WAHLZ, WEHS) **MIN.**

Center. Shoots right. 5'10", 180 lbs. Born, Calgary, Alta., May 15, 1970. Boston's 3rd choice, 57th overall, in 1989 Entry Draft.

Season	Club	League	GP	G	A	Pts	PIM	PP	SH	GW	S	%	+/-	TF	F%	H	SB	Min	GP	G	A	Pts	PIM	PP	SH	GW
1987-88	Calgary Stars	AMHL	35	47	52	99	72	....	....	....	....	....	....	....	....	....	....	....	....	....	....	....	....	....	....	....
	Prince Albert	WHL	1	1	1	2	0	....	....	....	....	....	....	....	....	....	....	....	....	....	....	....	....	....	....	....
1988-89	Lethbridge	WHL	63	29	75	104	32	....	....	....	....	....	....	....	....	....	....	....	8	1	5	6	6	....	....	....
1989-90	Lethbridge	WHL	56	54	86	140	69	....	....	....	....	....	....	....	....	....	....	....	19	13	*24	*37	33	....	....	....
	Boston	**NHL**	**2**	**1**	**1**	**2**	**0**	**1**	**0**	**0**	**1**	**100.0**	**–1**	....	....	....	....	....	....	....	....	....	....	....	....	....
1990-91	**Boston**	**NHL**	**56**	**8**	**8**	**16**	**32**	**1**	**0**	**1**	**57**	**14.0**	**–14**	....	....	....	....	....	**2**	**0**	**0**	**0**	**0**	**0**	**0**	**0**
	Maine Mariners	AHL	20	8	12	20	19	....	....	....	....	....	....	....	....	....	....	....	2	0	0	0	21	....	....	....
1991-92	**Boston**	**NHL**	**15**	**0**	**3**	**3**	**12**	**0**	**0**	**0**	**17**	**0.0**	**–3**	....	....	....	....	....	....	....	....	....	....	....	....	....
	Maine Mariners	AHL	21	13	11	24	38	....	....	....	....	....	....	....	....	....	....	....	....	....	....	....	....	....	....	....
	Philadelphia	**NHL**	**2**	**1**	**0**	**1**	**0**	**0**	**0**	**1**	**2**	**50.0**	**1**	....	....	....	....	....	....	....	....	....	....	....	....	....
	Hershey Bears	AHL	41	13	28	41	37	....	....	....	....	....	....	....	....	....	....	....	6	1	2	3	0	....	....	....
1992-93	Hershey Bears	AHL	78	35	45	80	106	....	....	....	....	....	....	....	....	....	....	....	....	....	....	....	....	....	....	....
1993-94	**Calgary**	**NHL**	**53**	**11**	**27**	**38**	**16**	**1**	**0**	**0**	**79**	**13.9**	**20**	....	....	....	....	....	**6**	**3**	**0**	**3**	**2**	**0**	**0**	**0**
	Saint John Flames	AHL	15	6	6	12	14	....	....	....	....	....	....	....	....	....	....	....	....	....	....	....	....	....	....	....
1994-95	**Calgary**	**NHL**	**39**	**6**	**12**	**18**	**11**	**4**	**0**	**1**	**73**	**8.2**	**7**	....	....	....	....	....	**1**	**0**	**0**	**0**	**0**	**0**	**0**	**0**
1995-96	**Detroit**	**NHL**	**2**	**0**	**0**	**0**	**0**	**0**	**0**	**0**	**2**	**0.0**	**0**	....	....	....	....	....	....	....	....	....	....	....	....	....
	Adirondack	AHL	38	20	35	55	58	....	....	....	....	....	....	....	....	....	....	....	....	....	....	....	....	....	....	....
1996-97	EV Zug	Switz.	41	24	22	46	67	....	....	....	....	....	....	....	....	....	....	....	9	5	1	6	39	....	....	....
1997-98	EV Zug	Switz.	38	18	34	52	32	....	....	....	....	....	....	....	....	....	....	....	20	*16	*12	*28	18	....	....	....
	EV Zug	EuroHL	5	1	3	4	10	....	....	....	....	....	....	....	....	....	....	....	....	....	....	....	....	....	....	....
1998-99	EV Zug	Switz.	42	22	27	49	75	....	....	....	....	....	....	....	....	....	....	....	10	3	9	12	2	....	....	....
	EV Zug	EuroHL	6	7	5	12	4	....	....	....	....	....	....	....	....	....	....	....	2	0	0	0	12	....	....	....
99-2000	Long Beach	IHL	6	4	3	7	8	....	....	....	....	....	....	....	....	....	....	....	....	....	....	....	....	....	....	....
	HC Lugano	Switz.	13	7	11	18	14	....	....	....	....	....	....	....	....	....	....	....	5	3	4	7	4	....	....	....
2000-01	**Minnesota**	**NHL**	**82**	**18**	**12**	**30**	**37**	**0**	**7**	**3**	**152**	**11.8**	**–8**	**1533**	**47.2**	**51**	**105**	**16:45**	....	....	....	....	....	....	....	....
	NHL Totals		**251**	**45**	**63**	**108**	**108**	**7**	**7**	**6**	**383**	**11.7**		**1533**	**47.2**	**51**	**105**	**16:45**	**9**	**3**	**0**	**3**	**2**	**0**	**0**	**0**

WHL East First All-Star Team (1990)

Traded to **Philadelphia** by **Boston** with Garry Galley and Boston's 3rd round choice (Milos Holan) in 1993 Entry Draft for Gord Murphy, Brian Dobbin, Philadelphia's 3rd round choice (Sergei Zholtok) in 1992 Entry Draft and 4th round choice (Charles Paquette) in 1993 Entry Draft, January 2, 1992. Signed as a free agent by **Calgary**, August 26, 1993. Signed as a free agent by **Detroit**, September 6, 1995. Signed as a free agent by **Long Beach** (IHL), October 12, 1999. Signed as a free agent by **Minnesota**, June 28, 2000.

Season	Club	League	Regular Season GP	G	A	Pts	PIM	PP	SH	GW	S	%	+/-	TF	F%	H	SB	Min	Playoffs GP	G	A	Pts	PIM	PP	SH	GW

WARD, Aaron

(WOHRD, AIR-ruhn) **CAR.**

Defense. Shoots right. 6'2", 200 lbs. Born, Windsor, Ont., January 17, 1973. Winnipeg's 1st choice, 5th overall, in 1991 Entry Draft.

Season	Club	League	GP	G	A	Pts	PIM	PP	SH	GW	S	%	+/-	TF	F%	H	SB	Min	GP	G	A	Pts	PIM	PP	SH	GW
1988-89	Nepean Raiders	OCJHL	54	1	14	15	40																			
1989-90	Nepean Raiders	OCJHL	52	6	33	39	85																			
1990-91	U. of Michigan	CCHA	46	8	11	19	126																			
1991-92	U. of Michigan	CCHA	42	7	12	19	64																			
1992-93	U. of Michigan	CCHA	30	5	8	13	73																			
1993-94	**Detroit**	**NHL**	**5**	**1**	**0**	**1**	**4**	**0**	**0**	**0**	**3**	**33.3**	**2**													
	Adirondack	AHL	58	4	12	16	87												9	2	6	8	6			
1994-95	Adirondack	AHL	76	11	24	35	87												4	0	1	1	0			
	Detroit	**NHL**	**1**	**0**	**1**	**1**	**2**	**0**	**0**	**0**	**0**	**0.0**	**1**													
1995-96	Adirondack	AHL	74	5	10	15	133												3	0	0	0	6			
1996-97♦	**Detroit**	**NHL**	**49**	**2**	**5**	**7**	**52**	**0**	**0**	**0**	**40**	**5.0**	**–9**						**19**	**0**	**0**	**0**	**17**	**0**	**0**	**0**
1997-98♦	**Detroit**	**NHL**	**52**	**5**	**5**	**10**	**47**	**0**	**0**	**1**	**47**	**10.6**	**–1**													
1998-99	**Detroit**	**NHL**	**60**	**3**	**8**	**11**	**52**	**0**	**0**	**0**	**46**	**6.5**	**–5**	**0**	**0.0**	**133**	**37**	**13:55**	**8**	**0**	**1**	**1**	**8**	**0**	**0**	**0**
99-2000	**Detroit**	**NHL**	**36**	**1**	**3**	**4**	**24**	**0**	**0**	**0**	**25**	**4.0**	**–4**	**0**	**0.0**	**87**	**19**	**12:36**	**3**	**0**	**0**	**0**	**0**	**0**	**0**	**0**
2000-01	**Detroit**	**NHL**	**73**	**4**	**5**	**9**	**57**	**0**	**0**	**1**	**48**	**8.3**	**–4**	**0**	**0.0**	**191**	**70**	**16:60**								
	NHL Totals		**276**	**16**	**27**	**43**	**238**	**0**	**0**	**2**	**209**	**7.7**		**0**	**0.0**	**411**	**126**	**14:58**	**30**	**0**	**1**	**1**	**25**	**0**	**0**	**0**

Traded to **Detroit** by **Winnipeg** with Toronto's 4th round choice (previously acquired by Winnipeg - later traded to Detroit - Detroit selected John Jakopin) in 1993 Entry Draft for Paul Ysebaert and future considerations (Alan Kerr, June 18, 1993), June 11, 1993. • Missed majority of 1999-2000 season recovering from shoulder injury suffered in game vs. Vancouver, January 19, 2000. Traded to **Carolina** by **Detroit** for future considerations, July 9, 2001.

WARD, Dixon

(WOHRD, DIHX-ohn)

Right wing. Shoots right. 6', 200 lbs. Born, Leduc, Alta., September 23, 1968. Vancouver's 6th choice, 128th overall, in 1988 Entry Draft.

Season	Club	League	GP	G	A	Pts	PIM	PP	SH	GW	S	%	+/-	TF	F%	H	SB	Min	GP	G	A	Pts	PIM	PP	SH	GW
1986-87	Red Deer Rebels	AJHL	59	46	40	86	153												20	11	11	22	16			
1987-88	Red Deer Rebels	AJHL	51	60	71	131	167																			
1988-89	North Dakota	WCHA	37	8	9	17	26																			
1989-90	North Dakota	WCHA	45	35	34	69	44																			
1990-91	North Dakota	WCHA	43	34	35	69	84																			
1991-92	North Dakota	WCHA	38	33	31	64	90																			
1992-93	**Vancouver**	**NHL**	**70**	**22**	**30**	**52**	**82**	**4**	**1**	**0**	**111**	**19.8**	**34**						**9**	**2**	**3**	**5**	**0**	**2**	**0**	**0**
1993-94	**Vancouver**	**NHL**	**33**	**6**	**1**	**7**	**37**	**2**	**0**	**1**	**46**	**13.0**	**–14**													
	Los Angeles	**NHL**	**34**	**6**	**2**	**8**	**45**	**2**	**0**	**0**	**44**	**13.6**	**–8**													
1994-95	**Toronto**	**NHL**	**22**	**0**	**3**	**3**	**31**	**0**	**0**	**0**	**15**	**0.0**	**–4**													
	St. John's Leafs	AHL	6	3	3	6	19																			
	Detroit Vipers	IHL	7	3	6	9	7												5	3	0	3	7			
1995-96	**Buffalo**	**NHL**	**8**	**2**	**2**	**4**	**6**	**0**	**0**	**1**	**12**	**16.7**	**1**													
	Rochester	AHL	71	38	56	94	74												19	11	*24	*35	8			
1996-97	**Buffalo**	**NHL**	**79**	**13**	**32**	**45**	**36**	**1**	**2**	**4**	**93**	**14.0**	**17**						**12**	**2**	**3**	**5**	**6**	**0**	**0**	**1**
1997-98	**Buffalo**	**NHL**	**71**	**10**	**13**	**23**	**42**	**0**	**2**	**3**	**99**	**10.1**	**9**						**15**	**3**	**8**	**11**	**6**	**0**	**0**	**0**
1998-99	**Buffalo**	**NHL**	**78**	**20**	**24**	**44**	**44**	**2**	**1**	**4**	**101**	**19.8**	**10**	**11**	**54.5**	**45**	**49**	**15:47**	**21**	**7**	**5**	**12**	**32**	**0**	**2**	**3**
99-2000	**Buffalo**	**NHL**	**71**	**11**	**9**	**20**	**41**	**1**	**2**	**2**	**101**	**10.9**	**1**	**8**	**50.0**	**48**	**44**	**13:58**	**5**	**0**	**1**	**1**	**2**	**0**	**0**	**0**
2000-01	**Boston**	**NHL**	**63**	**5**	**13**	**18**	**65**	**0**	**0**	**0**	**88**	**5.7**	**–1**	**108**	**48.2**	**62**	**19**	**12:38**								
	NHL Totals		**529**	**95**	**129**	**224**	**429**	**12**	**8**	**15**	**710**	**13.4**		**127**	**48.8**	**155**	**112**	**14:14**	**62**	**14**	**20**	**34**	**46**	**2**	**2**	**4**

WCHA Second All-Star Team (1991, 1992) • Won Jack A. Butterfield Trophy (Playoff MVP - AHL) (1996)

Traded to **LA Kings** by **Vancouver** for Jimmy Carson, January 8, 1994. Traded to **Toronto** by **LA Kings** with Guy Leveque, Kelly Fairchild and Shayne Toporowski for Eric Lacroix, Chris Snell and Toronto's 4th round choice (Eric Belanger) in 1996 Entry Draft, October 3, 1994. Signed as a free agent by **Buffalo**, September 20, 1995. Signed as a free agent by **Boston**, November 8, 2000.

WARD, Ed

(WOHRD, EHD)

Right wing. Shoots right. 6'3", 220 lbs. Born, Edmonton, Alta., November 10, 1969. Quebec's 7th choice, 108th overall, in 1988 Entry Draft.

Season	Club	League	GP	G	A	Pts	PIM	PP	SH	GW	S	%	+/-	TF	F%	H	SB	Min	GP	G	A	Pts	PIM	PP	SH	GW
1986-87	Sherwood Park	AJHL	60	18	28	46	272																			
1987-88	North-Michigan	WCHA	25	0	2	2	40																			
1988-89	North-Michigan	WCHA	42	5	15	20	36																			
1989-90	North-Michigan	WCHA	39	5	11	16	77																			
1990-91	North-Michigan	WCHA	46	13	18	31	109																			
1991-92	Greensboro	ECHL	12	4	8	12	21																			
	Halifax Citadels	AHL	51	7	11	18	65																			
1992-93	Halifax Citadels	AHL	70	13	19	32	56																			
1993-94	**Quebec**	**NHL**	**7**	**1**	**0**	**1**	**5**	**0**	**0**	**0**	**3**	**33.3**	**0**													
	Cornwall Aces	AHL	60	12	30	42	65												12	1	3	4	14			
1994-95	Cornwall Aces	AHL	56	10	14	24	118																			
	Calgary	**NHL**	**2**	**1**	**1**	**2**	**2**	**0**	**0**	**0**	**1**	**100.0**	**–2**													
	Saint John Flames	AHL	11	4	5	9	20												5	1	0	1	10			
1995-96	**Calgary**	**NHL**	**41**	**3**	**5**	**8**	**44**	**0**	**0**	**0**	**33**	**9.1**	**–2**													
	Saint John Flames	AHL	12	1	2	3	45												16	4	4	8	27			
1996-97	**Calgary**	**NHL**	**40**	**5**	**8**	**13**	**49**	**0**	**0**	**1**	**33**	**15.2**	**–3**													
	Saint John Flames	AHL	1	0	0	0	0																			
	Detroit Vipers	IHL	31	7	6	13	45																			
1997-98	**Calgary**	**NHL**	**64**	**4**	**5**	**9**	**122**	**0**	**0**	**0**	**52**	**7.7**	**–1**													
1998-99	**Calgary**	**NHL**	**68**	**3**	**5**	**8**	**67**	**0**	**0**	**0**	**56**	**5.4**	**–4**	**6**	**33.3**	**122**	**14**	**8:02**								
99-2000	**Atlanta**	**NHL**	**44**	**5**	**1**	**6**	**44**	**0**	**2**	**0**	**51**	**9.8**	**–5**	**7**	**28.6**	**130**	**15**	**11:26**								
	Anaheim	**NHL**	**8**	**1**	**0**	**1**	**15**	**0**	**0**	**0**	**5**	**20.0**	**–2**	**0**	**0.0**	**13**	**0**	**6:56**								
2000-01	**New Jersey**	**NHL**	**4**	**0**	**1**	**1**	**6**	**0**	**0**	**0**	**4**	**0.0**	**2**	**0**	**0.0**	**2**	**0**	**4:48**								
	Albany River Rats	AHL	65	14	19	33	71																			
	NHL Totals		**278**	**23**	**26**	**49**	**354**	**0**	**2**	**1**	**238**	**9.7**		**13**	**30.8**	**267**	**29**	**9:04**								

Traded to **Calgary** by **Quebec** for Francois Groleau, March 23, 1995. Claimed by **Atlanta** from **Calgary** in Expansion Draft, June 25, 1999. Traded to **Anaheim** by **Atlanta** for Anaheim's 7th round choice (Colin Fitzrandolph) in 2001 Entry Draft, March 14, 2000. Traded to **New Jersey** by **Anaheim** for New Jersey's 7th round choice (Tony Martensson) in 2001 Entry Draft, June 12, 2000.

WARD, Jason

(WOHRD, JAY-suhn) **MTL.**

Right wing. Shoots right. 6'2", 200 lbs. Born, Chapleau, Ont., January 16, 1979. Montreal's 1st choice, 11th overall, in 1997 Entry Draft.

Season	Club	League	GP	G	A	Pts	PIM	PP	SH	GW	S	%	+/-	TF	F%	H	SB	Min	GP	G	A	Pts	PIM	PP	SH	GW
1994-95	Oshawa Legion	MTJHL	47	30	31	61	75																			
1995-96	Niagara Falls	OHL	64	15	35	50	139												10	6	4	10	23			
1996-97	Erie Otters	OHL	58	25	39	64	137												5	1	2	3	2			
1997-98	Erie Otters	OHL	21	7	9	16	42																			
	Windsor Spitfires	OHL	26	19	27	46	34																			
	Fredericton	AHL	7	1	0	1	2												1	0	0	0	2			
1998-99	Windsor Spitfires	OHL	12	8	11	19	25																			
	Plymouth Whalers	OHL	23	14	13	27	28												11	6	8	14	12			
	Fredericton	AHL																	10	4	2	6	22			
99-2000	**Montreal**	**NHL**	**32**	**2**	**1**	**3**	**10**	**1**	**0**	**0**	**24**	**8.3**	**–1**	**86**	**44.2**	**37**	**5**	**9:10**								
	Quebec Citadelles	AHL	40	14	12	26	30												3	2	1	3	4			
2000-01	**Montreal**	**NHL**	**12**	**0**	**0**	**0**	**12**	**0**	**0**	**0**	**4**	**0.0**	**3**	**2**	**50.0**	**10**	**6**	**8:16**								
	Quebec Citadelles	AHL	23	7	12	19	69																			
	NHL Totals		**44**	**2**	**1**	**3**	**22**	**1**	**0**	**0**	**28**	**7.1**		**88**	**44.3**	**47**	**11**	**8:55**								

• Missed majority of 2000-01 season recovering from knee injury suffered in game vs. Carolina, January 16, 2001.

WARD, Lance

(WAWRD, LANTS) **FLA.**

Defense. Shoots left. 6'3", 225 lbs. Born, Lloydminster, Alta., June 2, 1978. Florida's 3rd choice, 63rd overall, in 1998 Entry Draft.

Season	Club	League	GP	G	A	Pts	PIM	PP	SH	GW	S	%	+/-	TF	F%	H	SB	Min	GP	G	A	Pts	PIM	PP	SH	GW
1993-94	Lloydminister	AAHA	20	8	12	20	68																			
1994-95	Red Deer Rebels	WHL	28	0	0	0	57																			
1995-96	Red Deer Rebels	WHL	72	4	13	17	127												10	0	4	4	10			
1996-97	Red Deer Rebels	WHL	70	5	34	39	229												16	0	3	3	36			
1997-98	Red Deer Rebels	WHL	71	8	25	33	233												5	0	0	0	16			

			Regular Season																Playoffs							
Season	Club	League	GP	G	A	Pts	PIM	PP	SH	GW	S	%	+/-	TF	F%	H	SB	Min	GP	G	A	Pts	PIM	PP	SH	GW
1998-99	Miami Matadors	ECHL	6	1	0	1	12																			
	Fort Wayne	IHL	13	0	2	2	28																			
	New Haven	AHL	43	2	5	7	51																			
99-2000	Louisville Panthers	AHL	80	4	16	20	190												4	0	0	0	6			
2000-01	Florida	NHL	30	0	2	2	45	0	0	0	17	0.0	–3	0	0.0	50	21	15:50								
	Louisville Panthers	AHL	35	3	2	5	78																			
	NHL Totals		30	0	2	2	45	0	0	0	17	0.0		0	0.0	50	21	15:50								

• Re-entered NHL Entry Draft. Originally New Jersey's 1st choice, 10th overall, in 1996 Entry Draft.

WARE, Jeff

(WAIR, JEHF) **CBJ**

Defense. Shoots left. 6'4", 220 lbs. Born, Toronto, Ont., May 19, 1977. Toronto's 1st choice, 15th overall, in 1995 Entry Draft.

Season	Club	League	GP	G	A	Pts	PIM	PP	SH	GW	S	%	+/-	TF	F%	H	SB	Min	GP	G	A	Pts	PIM	PP	SH	GW
1993-94	Wexford Raiders	MTJHL	45	1	9	10	75																			
1994-95	Oshawa Generals	OHL	55	2	11	13	86												7	1	1	2	6			
1995-96	Oshawa Generals	OHL	62	4	19	23	128												5	0	1	1	8			
	St. John's Leafs	AHL	4	0	0	0	4												4	0	0	0	2			
1996-97	Oshawa Generals	OHL	24	1	10	11	38												13	0	3	3	34			
	Toronto	NHL	13	0	0	0	6	0	0	0	4	0.0	2													
1997-98	Toronto	NHL	2	0	0	0	0	0	0	0	0	0.0	1													
	St. John's Leafs	AHL	67	0	3	3	182												4	0	0	0	4			
1998-99	St. John's Leafs	AHL	55	1	4	5	130																			
	Florida	NHL	6	0	1	1	6	0	0	0	1	0.0	–6	0	0.0	13	8	15:57								
	New Haven	AHL	20	0	1	1	26																			
99-2000	Louisville Panthers	AHL	51	0	10	10	128												4	0	0	0	4			
2000-01	Syracuse Crunch	AHL	71	0	4	4	174												5	0	0	0	16			
	NHL Totals		21	0	1	1	12	0	0	0	5	0.0		0	0.0	13	8	15:57								

Traded to **Florida** by **Toronto** for David Nemirovsky, February 17, 1999. Signed as a free agent by **Columbus**, May 31, 2001.

WARRENER, Rhett

(WAHR-ihn-uhr, REHT) **BUF.**

Defense. Shoots right. 6'1", 206 lbs. Born, Shaunavon, Sask., January 27, 1976. Florida's 2nd choice, 27th overall, in 1994 Entry Draft.

Season	Club	League	GP	G	A	Pts	PIM	PP	SH	GW	S	%	+/-	TF	F%	H	SB	Min	GP	G	A	Pts	PIM	PP	SH	GW
1991-92	Saskatoon Blaze	SMHL	33	6	5	11	71																			
	Saskatoon Blades	WHL	2	0	0	0	0																			
1992-93	Saskatoon Blades	WHL	68	2	17	19	100												9	0	0	0	14			
1993-94	Saskatoon Blades	WHL	61	7	19	26	131												16	0	5	5	33			
1994-95	Saskatoon Blades	WHL	66	13	26	39	137												10	0	3	3	6			
1995-96	Florida	NHL	28	0	3	3	46	0	0	0	19	0.0	4						21	0	1	1	0	0	0	0
	Carolina	AHL	9	0	0	0	4																			
1996-97	Florida	NHL	62	4	9	13	88	1	0	1	58	6.9	20						5	0	0	0	0	0	0	0
1997-98	Florida	NHL	79	0	4	4	99	0	0	0	66	0.0	–16													
1998-99	Florida	NHL	48	0	7	7	64	0	0	0	33	0.0	–1	0	0.0	75	38	19:01								
	Buffalo	NHL	13	1	0	1	20	0	0	0	11	9.1	3	0	0.0	28	12	18:13	20	1	3	4	32	0	0	0
99-2000	Buffalo	NHL	61	0	3	3	89	0	0	0	68	0.0	18	0	0.0	131	79	19:51	5	0	0	0	2	0	0	0
2000-01	Buffalo	NHL	77	3	16	19	78	0	0	2	103	2.9	10	0	0.0	187	107	20:24	13	0	2	2	4	0	0	0
	NHL Totals		368	8	42	50	484	1	0	3	358	2.2		0	0.0	421	236	19:45	64	1	6	7	38	0	0	0

Traded to **Buffalo** by **Florida** with Florida's 5th round choice (Ryan Miller) in 1999 Entry Draft for Mike Wilson, March 23, 1999.

WARRINER, Todd

(WAHR-ihn-uhr, TAWD) **PHX.**

Left wing. Shoots left. 6'1", 200 lbs. Born, Blenheim, Ont., January 3, 1974. Quebec's 1st choice, 4th overall, in 1992 Entry Draft.

Season	Club	League	GP	G	A	Pts	PIM	PP	SH	GW	S	%	+/-	TF	F%	H	SB	Min	GP	G	A	Pts	PIM	PP	SH	GW
1988-89	Blenheim Blades	OJHL-C	10	1	4	5	0																			
1989-90	Chatham	OJHL-B	40	24	21	45	12																			
1990-91	Windsor Spitfires	OHL	57	36	28	64	26												11	5	6	11	12			
1991-92	Windsor Spitfires	OHL	50	41	41	82	64												7	5	4	9	6			
1992-93	Windsor Spitfires	OHL	23	13	21	34	29																			
	Kitchener	OHL	32	19	24	43	35												7	5	14	19	14			
1993-94	Canada	Nat-Team	50	11	20	31	33																			
	Canada	Olympics	4	1	1	2	0																			
	Kitchener	OHL																	1	0	1	1	0			
	Cornwall Aces	AHL																	10	1	4	5	4			
1994-95	St. John's Leafs	AHL	46	8	10	18	22												4	1	0	1	2			
	Toronto	NHL	5	0	0	0	0	0	0	0	1	0.0	–3													
1995-96	Toronto	NHL	57	7	8	15	26	1	0	0	79	8.9	–11						6	1	1	2	2	0	0	0
	St. John's Leafs	AHL	11	5	6	11	16																			
1996-97	Toronto	NHL	75	12	21	33	41	2	2	0	146	8.2	–3													
1997-98	Toronto	NHL	45	5	8	13	20	0	0	1	73	6.8	5													
1998-99	Toronto	NHL	53	9	10	19	28	1	0	1	96	9.4	–6	579	47.8	52	10	14:06	9	0	0	0	2	0	0	0
99-2000	Toronto	NHL	18	3	1	4	2	0	0	0	33	9.1	6	33	45.5	18	5	12:33								
	Tampa Bay	NHL	55	11	13	24	34	3	1	0	100	11.0	–14	175	52.0	72	20	16:28								
2000-01	Tampa Bay	NHL	64	10	11	21	46	3	2	1	99	10.1	–13	400	50.5	80	22	14:43								
	NHL Totals		372	57	72	129	197	10	5	3	627	9.1		1187	49.3	222	57	14:51	15	1	1	2	4	0	0	0

OHL First All-Star Team (1992)

Traded to **Toronto** by **Quebec** with Mats Sundin, Garth Butcher and Philadelphia's 1st round choice (previously acquired by Quebec - later traded to Washington - Washington selected Nolan Baumgartner) in 1994 Entry Draft for Wendel Clark, Sylvain Lefebvre, Landon Wilson and Toronto's 1st round choice (Jeffrey Kealty) in 1994 Entry Draft, June 28, 1994. Traded to **Tampa Bay** by **Toronto** for Tampa Bay's 3rd round choice (Mikael Tellqvist) in 2000 Entry Draft, November 29, 1999. Traded to **Phoenix** by **Tampa Bay** for Juha Ylonen, June 18, 2001.

WASHBURN, Steve

(WAWSH-buhrn, STEEV)

Center. Shoots left. 6'2", 198 lbs. Born, Ottawa, Ont., April 10, 1975. Florida's 5th choice, 78th overall, in 1993 Entry Draft.

Season	Club	League	GP	G	A	Pts	PIM	PP	SH	GW	S	%	+/-	TF	F%	H	SB	Min	GP	G	A	Pts	PIM	PP	SH	GW
1990-91	Gloucester	OCJHL	56	21	30	51	47																			
1991-92	Ottawa 67's	OHL	59	5	17	22	10												11	2	3	5	4			
1992-93	Ottawa 67's	OHL	66	20	38	58	54																			
1993-94	Ottawa 67's	OHL	65	30	50	80	88												17	7	16	23	10			
1994-95	Ottawa 67's	OHL	63	43	63	106	72																			
	Cincinnati	IHL	6	3	1	4	0												9	1	3	4	4			
1995-96	Florida	NHL	1	0	1	1	0	0	0	0	1	0.0	1						1	0	1	1	0	0	0	0
	Carolina	AHL	78	29	54	83	45																			
1996-97	Florida	NHL	18	3	6	9	4	1	0	0	21	14.3	2													
	Carolina	AHL	60	23	40	63	66																			
1997-98	Florida	NHL	58	11	8	19	32	4	0	2	61	18.0	–6													
	New Haven	AHL	6	3	5	8	4												3	2	0	2	15			
1998-99	Florida	NHL	4	0	0	0	4	0	0	0	0	0.0	–1	21	38.1	1	0	6:17								
	New Haven	AHL	10	4	3	7	6																			
	Vancouver	NHL	8	0	0	0	2	0	0	0	6	0.0	0	30	40.0	9	1	8:05								
	Syracuse Crunch	AHL	13	1	6	7	6																			
99-2000	Milwaukee	IHL	12	0	4	4	16																			
	Philadelphia	NHL	1	0	0	0	0	0	0	0	1	0.0	0	8	12.5	7	0	14:26								
	Philadelphia	AHL	61	19	52	71	93												5	0	2	2	8			
2000-01	EHC Kloten	Switz.	8	0	6	6	16																			
	Philadelphia	NHL	3	0	0	0	0	0	0	0	0	0.0	0	16	50.0	3	0	7:04								
	Philadelphia	AHL	46	12	16	28	52												2	0	0	0	2			
	NHL Totals		93	14	15	29	42	5	0	2	90	15.6		75	38.7	20	1	7:50	1	0	1	1	0	0	0	0

Claimed on waivers by **Vancouver** from **Florida**, February 18, 1999. Signed as a free agent by **Nashville**, August 11, 1999. Traded to **Philadelphia** by **Nashville** for future considerations, November 16, 1999. Signed as a free agent by **EHC Kloten** (Switz.), July 26, 2000. Signed as a free agent by **Philadelphia**, November 21, 2000.

WATT, Mike

(WAHT, MIGHK) **PHI.**

Left wing. Shoots left. 6'2", 212 lbs. Born, Seaforth, Ont., March 31, 1976. Edmonton's 3rd choice, 32nd overall, in 1994 Entry Draft.

			Regular Season																Playoffs							
Season	Club	League	GP	G	A	Pts	PIM	PP	SH	GW	S	%	+/-	TF	F%	H	SB	Min	GP	G	A	Pts	PIM	PP	SH	GW
1990-91	Seaforth	OJHL-D	39	15	23	38	43																			
1991-92	Stratford Cullitons	OJHL-B	40	5	21	26	103																			
1992-93	Stratford Cullitons	OJHL-B	45	20	35	55	100																			
1993-94	Stratford Cullitons	OJHL-B	48	34	34	68	165																			
1994-95	Michigan State	CCHA	39	12	6	18	64																			
1995-96	Michigan State	CCHA	37	17	22	39	60																			
1996-97	Michigan State	CCHA	39	24	17	41	109																			
1997-98	Edmonton	NHL	14	1	2	3	4	0	0	1	14	7.1	-4													
	Hamilton Bulldogs	AHL	63	24	25	49	65												9	2	2	4	8			
1998-99	NY Islanders	NHL	75	8	17	25	12	0	0	4	75	10.7	-2	180	50.6	73	29	11:15								
99-2000	NY Islanders	NHL	45	5	6	11	17	0	1	0	49	10.2	-8	81	48.2	45	17	12:02								
	Lowell	AHL	16	6	11	17	6												7	1	1	2	4			
2000-01	Milwaukee	IHL	60	20	20	40	48												5	1	2	3	6			
	Nashville	NHL	18	1	1	2	8	0	0	1	18	5.6	-2	2	50.0	22	7	11:02								
	NHL Totals		152	15	26	41	41	0	1	6	156	9.6		263	49.8	140	53	11:29								

Traded to **NY Islanders** by **Edmonton** for Eric Fichaud, June 18, 1998. Claimed on waivers by **Nashville** from **NY Islanders**, May 23, 2000. Traded to **Philadelphia** by **Nashville** for Mikhail Chernov, May 24, 2001.

WEBB, Steve

(WEHB, STEEV) **NYI**

Right wing. Shoots right. 6', 195 lbs. Born, Peterborough, Ont., April 30, 1975. Buffalo's 8th choice, 176th overall, in 1994 Entry Draft.

Season	Club	League	GP	G	A	Pts	PIM	PP	SH	GW	S	%	+/-	TF	F%	H	SB	Min	GP	G	A	Pts	PIM	PP	SH	GW
1991-92	Peterborough B's	OJHL-B	37	9	9	18	195																			
1992-93	Windsor Spitfires	OHL	63	14	25	39	184																			
1993-94	Windsor Spitfires	OHL	2	0	1	1	9																			
	Peterborough	OHL	33	6	15	21	117												6	1	1	2	20			
1994-95	Peterborough	OHL	42	8	16	24	109												11	3	3	6	22			
1995-96	Muskegon Fury	ColHL	58	18	24	42	263												5	1	2	3	22			
	Detroit Vipers	IHL	4	0	0	0	24																			
1996-97	NY Islanders	NHL	41	1	4	5	144	1	0	0	21	4.8	-10													
	Kentucky	AHL	25	6	6	12	103												2	0	0	0	19			
1997-98	NY Islanders	NHL	20	0	0	0	35	0	0	0	6	0.0	-2													
	Kentucky	AHL	37	5	13	18	139												3	0	1	1	10			
1998-99	NY Islanders	NHL	45	0	0	0	32	0	0	0	18	0.0	-10	0	0.0	64	1	4:13								
	Lowell	AHL	23	2	4	6	80																			
99-2000	NY Islanders	NHL	65	1	3	4	103	0	0	0	27	3.7	-4	1	0.0	194	12	7:00								
2000-01	NY Islanders	NHL	31	0	2	2	35	0	0	0	8	0.0	1	0	0.0	88	10	6:26								
	NHL Totals		202	2	9	11	349	1	0	0	80	2.5		1	0.0	346	23	5:59								

Signed as a free agent by **NY Islanders**, October 10, 1996. • Missed majority of 2000-01 season recovering from knee injury originally suffered in game vs. Anaheim, November 19, 2000.

WEIGHT, Doug

(WAYT, DUHG) **ST.L.**

Center. Shoots left. 5'11", 200 lbs. Born, Warren, MI, January 21, 1971. NY Rangers' 2nd choice, 34th overall, in 1990 Entry Draft.

Season	Club	League	GP	G	A	Pts	PIM	PP	SH	GW	S	%	+/-	TF	F%	H	SB	Min	GP	G	A	Pts	PIM	PP	SH	GW
1988-89	Bloomfield	NAJHL	34	26	53	79	105																			
1989-90	Lake Superior	CCHA	46	21	48	69	44																			
1990-91	Lake Superior	CCHA	42	29	46	75	86																			
	NY Rangers	NHL																	1	0	0	0	0	0	0	0
1991-92	NY Rangers	NHL	53	8	22	30	23	0	0	2	72	11.1	-3						7	2	2	4	0	1	0	0
	Binghamton	AHL	9	3	14	17	2												4	1	4	5	6			
1992-93	NY Rangers	NHL	65	15	25	40	55	3	0	1	90	16.7	4													
	Edmonton	NHL	13	2	6	8	10	0	0	0	35	5.7	-2													
1993-94	Edmonton	NHL	84	24	50	74	47	4	1	1	188	12.8	-22													
1994-95	SB Rosenheim	DEL	8	2	3	5	18																			
	Edmonton	NHL	48	7	33	40	69	1	0	1	104	6.7	-17													
1995-96	Edmonton	NHL	82	25	79	104	95	9	0	2	204	12.3	-19													
1996-97	Edmonton	NHL	80	21	61	82	80	4	0	2	235	8.9	1						12	3	8	11	8	0	0	0
1997-98	Edmonton	NHL	79	26	44	70	69	9	0	4	205	12.7	1						12	2	7	9	14	2	0	1
	United States	Olympics	4	0	2	2	2																			
1998-99	Edmonton	NHL	43	6	31	37	12	1	0	0	79	7.6	-8	853	49.5	43	16	19:51	4	1	1	2	15	0	0	0
99-2000	Edmonton	NHL	77	21	51	72	54	3	1	4	167	12.6	6	1588	50.4	76	44	20:35	5	3	2	5	4	2	0	1
2000-01	Edmonton	NHL	82	25	65	90	91	8	0	3	188	13.3	12	1514	51.3	57	45	22:08	6	1	5	6	17	0	0	0
	NHL Totals		706	180	467	647	605	42	2	20	1567	11.5		3955	50.5	176	105	21:03	47	12	25	37	58	5	0	2

CCHA First All-Star Team (1991) • NCAA West Second All-American Team (1991) • Played in NHL All-Star Game (1996, 1998, 2001)

Traded to **Edmonton** by **NY Rangers** for Esa Tikkanen, March 17, 1993. Traded to **St. Louis** by **Edmonton** with Michel Riesen for Marty Reasoner, Jochen Hecht and Jan Horacek, July 1, 2001.

WEINRICH, Eric

(WIGHN-rihk, AIR-ihk) **PHI.**

Defense. Shoots left. 6'1", 213 lbs. Born, Roanoke, VA, December 19, 1966. New Jersey's 3rd choice, 32nd overall, in 1985 Entry Draft.

Season	Club	League	GP	G	A	Pts	PIM	PP	SH	GW	S	%	+/-	TF	F%	H	SB	Min	GP	G	A	Pts	PIM	PP	SH	GW
1983-84	North Yarmouth	Hi-School	17	23	33	56																				
1984-85	North Yarmouth	Hi-School	20	6	21	27																				
1985-86	U. of Maine	H-East	34	0	14	14	26																			
1986-87	U. of Maine	H-East	41	12	32	44	59																			
1987-88	U. of Maine	H-East	8	4	7	11	22																			
	United States	Nat-Team	38	3	9	12	24																			
	United States	Olympics	3	0	0	0	0																			
1988-89	New Jersey	NHL	2	0	0	0	0	0	0	0	3	0.0	-1													
	Utica Devils	AHL	80	17	27	44	70												5	0	1	1	4			
1989-90	New Jersey	NHL	19	2	7	9	11	1	0	1	16	12.5	1						6	1	3	4	17	0	0	0
	Utica Devils	AHL	57	12	48	60	38																			
1990-91	New Jersey	NHL	76	4	34	38	48	1	0	0	96	4.2	10						7	1	2	3	6	1	0	0
1991-92	New Jersey	NHL	76	7	25	32	55	5	0	0	97	7.2	10						7	0	2	2	4	0	0	0
1992-93	Hartford	NHL	79	7	29	36	76	0	2	2	104	6.7	-11													
1993-94	Hartford	NHL	8	1	1	2	2	1	0	0	10	10.0	-5													
	Chicago	NHL	54	3	23	26	31	1	0	2	105	2.9	6						6	0	2	2	6	0	0	0
1994-95	Chicago	NHL	48	3	10	13	33	1	0	2	50	6.0	1						16	1	5	6	4	0	0	0
1995-96	Chicago	NHL	77	5	10	15	65	0	0	0	76	6.6	14						10	1	4	5	10	1	0	0
1996-97	Chicago	NHL	81	7	25	32	62	1	0	0	115	6.1	19						6	0	1	1	4	0	0	0
1997-98	Chicago	NHL	82	2	21	23	106	0	0	0	85	2.4	10													
1998-99	Chicago	NHL	14	1	3	4	12	0	0	0	24	4.2	-13	0	0.0	27	13	20:12								
	Montreal	NHL	66	6	12	18	77	4	0	1	95	6.3	-12	0	0.0	100	117	24:44								
99-2000	Montreal	NHL	77	4	25	29	39	2	0	0	120	3.3	4	0	0.0	124	152	25:21								
2000-01	Montreal	NHL	60	6	19	25	34	2	0	1	81	7.4	-1	1	100.0	77	125	24:27								
	Boston	NHL	22	1	5	6	10	0	0	1	28	3.6	-8	0	0.0	33	39	25:52								
	NHL Totals		841	59	249	308	661	20	2	10	1105	5.3		1	100.0	361	446	24:42	58	4	19	23	51	2	0	0

Hockey East First All-Star Team (1987) • NCAA East Second All-American Team (1987) • AHL First All-Star Team (1990) • Won Eddie Shore Award (Top Defenseman - AHL) (1990) • NHL All-Rookie Team (1991)

Traded to **Hartford** by **New Jersey** with Sean Burke for Bobby Holik and Hartford's 2nd round choice (Jay Pandolfo) in 1993 Entry Draft, August 28, 1992. Traded to **Chicago** by **Hartford** with Patrick Poulin for Steve Larmer and Bryan Marchment, November 2, 1993. Traded to **Montreal** by **Chicago** with Jeff Hackett, Alain Nasreddine and Tampa Bay's 4th round choice (previously acquired, Montreal selected Chris Dyment) in 1999 Entry Draft for Jocelyn Thibault, Dave Manson and Brad Brown, November 16, 1998. Traded to **Boston** by **Montreal** for Patrick Traverse, February 21, 2001. Signed as a free agent by **Philadelphia**, July 5, 2001.

WELLS, Chris
(WEHLS, KRIHS)

Center. Shoots left. 6'6", 223 lbs. Born, Calgary, Alta., November 12, 1975. Pittsburgh's 1st choice, 24th overall, in 1994 Entry Draft.

			Regular Season																Playoffs							
Season	Club	League	GP	G	A	Pts	PIM	PP	SH	GW	S	%	+/-	TF	F%	H	SB	Min	GP	G	A	Pts	PIM	PP	SH	GW
1990-91	Calgary Royals	AJHL	35	13	14	27	33																			
1991-92	Seattle T-Birds	WHL	64	13	8	21	80												11	0	0	0	15			
1992-93	Seattle T-Birds	WHL	63	18	37	55	111												5	2	3	5	4			
1993-94	Seattle T-Birds	WHL	69	30	44	74	150												9	6	5	11	23			
1994-95	Seattle T-Birds	WHL	69	45	63	108	148												3	0	1	1	4			
	Cleveland	IHL	3	0	1	1	2																			
1995-96	**Pittsburgh**	**NHL**	**54**	**2**	**2**	**4**	**59**	**0**	**1**	**0**	**25**	**8.0**	**–6**													
1996-97	Cleveland	IHL	15	4	6	10	9																			
	Florida	**NHL**	**47**	**2**	**6**	**8**	**42**	**0**	**0**	**0**	**29**	**6.9**	**5**						**3**	**0**	**0**	**0**	**0**	**0**	**0**	**0**
1997-98	**Florida**	**NHL**	**61**	**5**	**10**	**15**	**47**	**0**	**1**	**0**	**57**	**8.8**	**4**													
1998-99	**Florida**	**NHL**	**20**	**0**	**2**	**2**	**31**	**0**	**0**	**0**	**28**	**0.0**	**–4**	**231**	**40.7**	**21**	**12**	**11:52**								
	New Haven	AHL	9	3	1	4	28																			
99-2000	**Florida**	**NHL**	**13**	**0**	**0**	**0**	**14**	**0**	**0**	**0**	**5**	**0.0**	**–5**	**124**	**45.2**	**5**	**2**	**8:23**								
	Louisville Panthers	AHL	31	8	10	18	20																			
	Hartford	AHL	14	2	2	4	6												20	3	4	7	38			
2000-01	Utah Grizzlies	IHL	43	6	6	12	33																			
	NHL Totals		**195**	**9**	**20**	**29**	**193**	**0**	**2**	**0**	**144**	**6.3**		**355**	**42.3**	**26**	**14**	**10:30**	**3**	**0**	**0**	**0**	**0**	**0**	**0**	**0**

WHL West First All-Star Team (1995)

Traded to **Florida** by **Pittsburgh** for Stu Barnes and Jason Woolley, November 19, 1996. Traded to **NY Rangers** by **Florida** for future considerations, March 13, 2000. Signed as a free agent by **Dallas**, July 28, 2000.

WERENKA, Brad
(wuh-REHN-kuh, BRAD) **CGY.**

Defense. Shoots left. 6'1", 225 lbs. Born, Two Hills, Alta., February 12, 1969. Edmonton's 2nd choice, 42nd overall, in 1987 Entry Draft.

			Regular Season																Playoffs							
Season	Club	League	GP	G	A	Pts	PIM	PP	SH	GW	S	%	+/-	TF	F%	H	SB	Min	GP	G	A	Pts	PIM	PP	SH	GW
1983-84	Sherwood Park	AMHL	32	9	27	36	40																			
1984-85	Ft-Saskatchewan	AJHL	32	35	28	63	51																			
1985-86	Ft-Saskatchewan	AJHL	29	12	23	35	24																			
1986-87	North-Michigan	WCHA	30	4	4	8	35																			
1987-88	North-Michigan	WCHA	34	7	23	30	26																			
1988-89	North-Michigan	WCHA	28	7	13	20	16																			
1989-90	North-Michigan	WCHA	8	2	5	7	8																			
1990-91	North-Michigan	WCHA	47	20	43	63	36																			
1991-92	Cape Breton	AHL	66	6	21	27	95												5	0	3	3	6			
1992-93	Canada	Nat-Team	18	3	7	10	10																			
	Edmonton	**NHL**	**27**	**5**	**4**	**9**	**24**	**0**	**1**	**1**	**38**	**13.2**	**1**													
	Cape Breton	AHL	4	1	1	2	4												16	4	17	21	12			
1993-94	**Edmonton**	**NHL**	**15**	**0**	**4**	**4**	**14**	**0**	**0**	**0**	**11**	**0.0**	**–1**													
	Cape Breton	AHL	25	6	17	23	19																			
	Canada	Olympics	8	2	2	4	8																			
	Quebec	**NHL**	**11**	**0**	**7**	**7**	**8**	**0**	**0**	**0**	**17**	**0.0**	**4**													
	Cornwall Aces	AHL																	12	2	10	12	22			
1994-95	Milwaukee	IHL	80	8	45	53	161												15	3	10	13	36			
1995-96	**Chicago**	**NHL**	**9**	**0**	**0**	**0**	**8**	**0**	**0**	**0**	**2**	**0.0**	**–2**													
	Indianapolis Ice	IHL	73	15	42	57	85												5	1	3	4	8			
1996-97	Indianapolis Ice	IHL	82	20	56	76	83												4	1	4	5	6			
1997-98	**Pittsburgh**	**NHL**	**71**	**3**	**15**	**18**	**46**	**2**	**0**	**0**	**50**	**6.0**	**15**						**6**	**1**	**0**	**1**	**8**	**0**	**1**	**0**
1998-99	**Pittsburgh**	**NHL**	**81**	**6**	**18**	**24**	**93**	**1**	**0**	**4**	**77**	**7.8**	**17**	**0**	**0.0**	**115**	**120**	**21:12**	**13**	**1**	**1**	**2**	**6**	**0**	**0**	**0**
99-2000	**Pittsburgh**	**NHL**	**61**	**3**	**8**	**11**	**69**	**0**	**0**	**1**	**42**	**7.1**	**15**	**0**	**0.0**	**74**	**78**	**18:02**								
	Calgary	**NHL**	**12**	**1**	**1**	**2**	**21**	**0**	**0**	**0**	**20**	**5.0**	**–2**	**0**	**0.0**	**17**	**17**	**24:37**								
2000-01	**Calgary**	**NHL**	**33**	**1**	**4**	**5**	**16**	**0**	**0**	**0**	**23**	**4.3**	**–3**	**0**	**0.0**	**33**	**60**	**18:02**								
	NHL Totals		**320**	**19**	**61**	**80**	**299**	**3**	**1**	**6**	**280**	**6.8**		**0**	**0.0**	**239**	**275**	**19:50**	**19**	**2**	**1**	**3**	**14**	**0**	**1**	**0**

WCHA First All-Star Team (1991) • NCAA West First All-American Team (1991) • NCAA Championship All-Tournament Team (1991) • IHL First All-Star Team (1997) • Won Governors' Trophy (Top Defenseman - IHL) (1997)

Traded to **Quebec** by **Edmonton** for Steve Passmore, March 21, 1994. Signed as a free agent by **Chicago**, July 20, 1995. Signed as a free agent by **Pittsburgh**, July 31, 1997. Traded to **Calgary** by **Pittsburgh** for Tyler Moss and Rene Corbet, March 14, 2000. • Missed majority of 2000-01 season recovering from head injury suffered in game vs. Dallas, December 29, 2000.

WESLEY, Glen
(WEH-slee, GLEHN) **CAR.**

Defense. Shoots left. 6'1", 205 lbs. Born, Red Deer, Alta., October 2, 1968. Boston's 1st choice, 3rd overall, in 1987 Entry Draft.

			Regular Season																Playoffs							
Season	Club	League	GP	G	A	Pts	PIM	PP	SH	GW	S	%	+/-	TF	F%	H	SB	Min	GP	G	A	Pts	PIM	PP	SH	GW
1983-84	Red Deer Rustlers	AJHL	57	9	20	29	40																			
	Portland	WHL	3	1	2	3	0																			
1984-85	Portland	WHL	67	16	52	68	76												6	1	6	7	8			
1985-86	Portland	WHL	69	16	75	91	96												15	3	11	14	29			
1986-87	Portland	WHL	63	16	46	62	72												20	8	18	26	27			
1987-88	**Boston**	**NHL**	**79**	**7**	**30**	**37**	**69**	**1**	**2**	**0**	**158**	**4.4**	**21**						**23**	**6**	**8**	**14**	**22**	**4**	**1**	**0**
1988-89	**Boston**	**NHL**	**77**	**19**	**35**	**54**	**61**	**8**	**1**	**1**	**181**	**10.5**	**23**						**10**	**0**	**2**	**2**	**4**	**0**	**0**	**0**
1989-90	**Boston**	**NHL**	**78**	**9**	**27**	**36**	**48**	**5**	**0**	**4**	**166**	**5.4**	**6**						**21**	**2**	**6**	**8**	**36**	**0**	**0**	**1**
1990-91	**Boston**	**NHL**	**80**	**11**	**32**	**43**	**78**	**5**	**1**	**1**	**199**	**5.5**	**0**						**19**	**2**	**9**	**11**	**19**	**2**	**0**	**0**
1991-92	**Boston**	**NHL**	**78**	**9**	**37**	**46**	**54**	**4**	**0**	**1**	**211**	**4.3**	**–9**						**15**	**2**	**4**	**6**	**16**	**0**	**0**	**0**
1992-93	**Boston**	**NHL**	**64**	**8**	**25**	**33**	**47**	**4**	**1**	**0**	**183**	**4.4**	**–2**						**4**	**0**	**0**	**0**	**0**	**0**	**0**	**0**
1993-94	**Boston**	**NHL**	**81**	**14**	**44**	**58**	**64**	**6**	**1**	**1**	**265**	**5.3**	**1**						**13**	**3**	**3**	**6**	**12**	**1**	**0**	**0**
1994-95	**Hartford**	**NHL**	**48**	**2**	**14**	**16**	**50**	**1**	**0**	**1**	**125**	**1.6**	**–6**													
1995-96	**Hartford**	**NHL**	**68**	**8**	**16**	**24**	**88**	**6**	**0**	**1**	**129**	**6.2**	**–9**													
1996-97	**Hartford**	**NHL**	**68**	**6**	**26**	**32**	**40**	**3**	**1**	**0**	**126**	**4.8**	**0**													
1997-98	**Carolina**	**NHL**	**82**	**6**	**19**	**25**	**36**	**1**	**0**	**1**	**121**	**5.0**	**7**													
1998-99	**Carolina**	**NHL**	**74**	**7**	**17**	**24**	**44**	**0**	**0**	**2**	**112**	**6.3**	**14**	**1**	**0.0**	**121**	**94**	**22:31**	**6**	**0**	**0**	**0**	**2**	**0**	**0**	**0**
99-2000	**Carolina**	**NHL**	**78**	**7**	**15**	**22**	**38**	**1**	**0**	**0**	**99**	**7.1**	**–4**	**0**	**0.0**	**116**	**111**	**21:32**								
2000-01	**Carolina**	**NHL**	**71**	**5**	**16**	**21**	**42**	**3**	**0**	**0**	**92**	**5.4**	**–2**	**0**	**0.0**	**132**	**124**	**22:21**	**6**	**0**	**0**	**0**	**0**	**0**	**0**	**0**
	NHL Totals		**1026**	**118**	**353**	**471**	**759**	**48**	**7**	**13**	**2167**	**5.4**		**1**	**0.0**	**369**	**329**	**22:07**	**117**	**15**	**32**	**47**	**111**	**7**	**1**	**1**

WHL West First All-Star Team (1986, 1987) • NHL All-Rookie Team (1988) • Played in NHL All-Star Game (1989)

Traded to **Hartford** by **Boston** for Hartford/Carolina's 1st round choices in 1995 (Kyle McLaren), 1996 (Johnathan Aitken) and 1997 (Sergei Samsonov) Entry Drafts, August 26, 1994. Transferred to **Carolina** after **Hartford** franchise relocated, June 25, 1997.

WESTLUND, Tommy
(WEHST-luhnd, TOHM-mee) **CAR.**

Right wing. Shoots right. 6', 210 lbs. Born, Fors, Sweden, December 29, 1974. Carolina's 5th choice, 93rd overall, in 1998 Entry Draft.

			Regular Season																Playoffs							
Season	Club	League	GP	G	A	Pts	PIM	PP	SH	GW	S	%	+/-	TF	F%	H	SB	Min	GP	G	A	Pts	PIM	PP	SH	GW
1991-92	Avesta BK	Sweden-3	27	11	9	20	8																			
1992-93	Avesta BK	Sweden-2	32	9	5	14	32																			
1993-94	Avesta BK	Sweden-2	31	20	11	31	34																			
1994-95	Avesta BK	Sweden-2	32	17	13	30	22																			
1995-96	Brynas IF	Sweden-2	18	10	10	20	4												8	1	0	1	4			
	Brynas IF	Sweden	18	2	1	3	2																			
1996-97	Brynas IF	Sweden	50	21	13	34	16																			
1997-98	Brynas IF	Sweden	46	29	9	38	45												3	0	1	1	0			
1998-99	New Haven	AHL	50	8	18	26	31																			
99-2000	**Carolina**	**NHL**	**81**	**4**	**8**	**12**	**19**	**0**	**1**	**0**	**67**	**6.0**	**–10**	**336**	**52.7**	**86**	**25**	**10:23**								
2000-01	**Carolina**	**NHL**	**79**	**5**	**3**	**8**	**23**	**0**	**0**	**1**	**47**	**10.6**	**–9**	**340**	**50.9**	**71**	**37**	**9:22**	**6**	**0**	**0**	**0**	**17**	**0**	**0**	**0**
	NHL Totals		**160**	**9**	**11**	**20**	**42**	**0**	**1**	**1**	**114**	**7.9**		**676**	**51.8**	**157**	**62**	**9:53**	**6**	**0**	**0**	**0**	**17**	**0**	**0**	**0**

					Regular Season																	Playoffs				
Season	Club	League	GP	G	A	Pts	PIM	PP	SH	GW	S	%	+/-	TF	F%	H	SB	Min	GP	G	A	Pts	PIM	PP	SH	GW

WHITE, Brian

(WHIGHT, BRIGH-uhn) **ANA.**

Defense. Shoots right. 6'1", 195 lbs. Born, Winchester, MA, February 7, 1976. Tampa Bay's 11th choice, 268th overall, in 1994 Entry Draft.

1993-94	Arlington High	Hi-School	40	14	18	32	81	....	....	....	....	....	....	....	....	....	....	....	....	....	....	....	....	....	....	....
1994-95	U. of Maine	H-East	28	1	1	2	16	....	....	....	....	....	....	....	....	....	....	....	....	....	....	....	....	....	....	....
1995-96	U. of Maine	H-East	39	0	4	4	18	....	....	....	....	....	....	....	....	....	....	....	....	....	....	....	....	....	....	....
1996-97	U. of Maine	H-East	35	4	12	16	36	....	....	....	....	....	....	....	....	....	....	....	....	....	....	....	....	....	....	....
1997-98	U. of Maine	H-East	33	0	12	12	45	....	....	....	....	....	....	....	....	....	....	....	....	....	....	....	....	....	....	....
	Long Beach	IHL	1	0	0	0	0	....	....	....	....	....	....	....	....	....	....	....	....	....	....	....	....	....	....	....
1998-99	**Colorado**	**NHL**	**2**	**0**	**0**	**0**	**0**	**0**	**0**	**0**	**0**	**0.0**	**0**	**0**	**0.0**	**1**	**0**	**0:40**	....	....	....	....	....	....	....	....
	Hershey Bears	AHL	71	4	8	12	41	....	....	....	....	....	....	....	....	....	....	....	4	0	1	1	2	....	....	....
99-2000	Hershey Bears	AHL	79	3	19	22	78	....	....	....	....	....	....	....	....	....	....	....	14	0	3	3	21	....	....	....
2000-01	Hershey Bears	AHL	75	2	9	11	44	....	....	....	....	....	....	....	....	....	....	....	9	0	1	1	12	....	....	....
	NHL Totals		**2**	**0**	**0**	**0**	**0**	**0**	**0**	**0**	**0**	**0.0**		**0**	**0.0**	**1**	**0**	**0:40**	....	....	....	....	....	....	....	....

Signed as a free agent by **Colorado**, July 7, 1998. Signed as a free agent by **Anaheim**, August 14, 2001.

WHITE, Colin

(WHIGHT, CAWI-ihn) **N.J.**

Defense. Shoots left. 6'4", 215 lbs. Born, New Glasgow, N.S., December 12, 1977. New Jersey's 5th choice, 49th overall, in 1996 Entry Draft.

1994-95	Laval Titan	QMJHL	7	0	1	1	32	....	....	....	....	....	....	....	....	....	....	....	....	....	....	....	....	....	....	....
	Hull Olympiques	QMJHL	5	0	1	1	4	....	....	....	....	....	....	....	....	....	....	....	12	0	0	0	23	....	....	....
1995-96	Hull Olympiques	QMJHL	62	2	8	10	303	....	....	....	....	....	....	....	....	....	....	....	18	0	4	4	42	....	....	....
1996-97	Hull Olympiques	QMJHL	63	3	12	15	297	....	....	....	....	....	....	....	....	....	....	....	14	3	12	15	65	....	....	....
1997-98	Albany River Rats	AHL	76	3	13	16	235	....	....	....	....	....	....	....	....	....	....	....	13	0	0	0	55	....	....	....
1998-99	Albany River Rats	AHL	77	2	12	14	265	....	....	....	....	....	....	....	....	....	....	....	5	0	1	1	8	....	....	....
99-2000♦	**New Jersey**	**NHL**	**21**	**2**	**1**	**3**	**40**	**0**	**0**	**1**	**29**	**6.9**	**3**	**0**	**0.0**	**35**	**26**	**14:45**	**23**	**1**	**5**	**6**	**18**	**0**	**0**	**1**
	Albany River Rats	AHL	52	5	21	26	176	....	....	....	....	....	....	....	....	....	....	....	....	....	....	....	....	....	....	....
2000-01	**New Jersey**	**NHL**	**82**	**1**	**19**	**20**	**155**	**0**	**0**	**1**	**114**	**0.9**	**32**	**0**	**0.0**	**163**	**116**	**19:06**	**25**	**0**	**3**	**3**	**42**	**0**	**0**	**0**
	NHL Totals		**103**	**3**	**20**	**23**	**195**	**0**	**0**	**2**	**143**	**2.1**		**0**	**0.0**	**198**	**142**	**18:13**	**48**	**1**	**8**	**9**	**60**	**0**	**0**	**1**

NHL All-Rookie Team (2001)

WHITE, Peter

(WHIGHT, PEE-tuhr)

Center. Shoots left. 5'11", 200 lbs. Born, Montreal, Que., March 15, 1969. Edmonton's 4th choice, 92nd overall, in 1989 Entry Draft.

1984-85	Lac St-Louis	QAAA	42	16	32	48	18	....	....	....	....	....	....	....	....	....	....	....	11	4	3	7	4	....	....	....
1985-86	Lac St-Louis	QAAA	42	38	62	100	28	....	....	....	....	....	....	....	....	....	....	....	2	3	1	4	2	....	....	....
1986-87	Pembroke	OCJHL	55	20	34	54	20	....	....	....	....	....	....	....	....	....	....	....	....	....	....	....	....	....	....	....
1987-88	Pembroke	OCJHL	56	*90	*136	*226	32	....	....	....	....	....	....	....	....	....	....	....	....	....	....	....	....	....	....	....
1988-89	Michigan State	CCHA	46	20	33	53	17	....	....	....	....	....	....	....	....	....	....	....	....	....	....	....	....	....	....	....
1989-90	Michigan State	CCHA	45	22	40	62	6	....	....	....	....	....	....	....	....	....	....	....	....	....	....	....	....	....	....	....
1990-91	Michigan State	CCHA	37	7	31	38	28	....	....	....	....	....	....	....	....	....	....	....	....	....	....	....	....	....	....	....
1991-92	Michigan State	CCHA	41	26	49	75	32	....	....	....	....	....	....	....	....	....	....	....	....	....	....	....	....	....	....	....
1992-93	Cape Breton	AHL	64	12	28	40	10	....	....	....	....	....	....	....	....	....	....	....	16	3	3	6	12	....	....	....
1993-94	**Edmonton**	**NHL**	**26**	**3**	**5**	**8**	**2**	**0**	**0**	**0**	**17**	**17.6**	**1**	....	....	....	....	....	....	....	....	....	....	....	....	....
	Cape Breton	AHL	45	21	49	70	12	....	....	....	....	....	....	....	....	....	....	....	5	2	3	5	2	....	....	....
1994-95	Cape Breton	AHL	65	36	*69	*105	30	....	....	....	....	....	....	....	....	....	....	....	....	....	....	....	....	....	....	....
	Edmonton	**NHL**	**9**	**2**	**4**	**6**	**0**	**2**	**0**	**0**	**13**	**15.4**	**1**	....	....	....	....	....	....	....	....	....	....	....	....	....
1995-96	**Edmonton**	**NHL**	**26**	**5**	**3**	**8**	**0**	**1**	**0**	**0**	**34**	**14.7**	**–14**	....	....	....	....	....	....	....	....	....	....	....	....	....
	Toronto	**NHL**	**1**	**0**	**0**	**0**	**0**	**0**	**0**	**0**	**0**	**0.0**	**0**	....	....	....	....	....	....	....	....	....	....	....	....	....
	St. John's Leafs	AHL	17	6	7	13	6	....	....	....	....	....	....	....	....	....	....	....	....	....	....	....	....	....	....	....
	Atlanta Knights	IHL	36	21	20	41	4	....	....	....	....	....	....	....	....	....	....	....	3	0	3	3	2	....	....	....
1996-97	Philadelphia	AHL	80	*44	61	*105	28	....	....	....	....	....	....	....	....	....	....	....	10	6	8	14	6	....	....	....
1997-98	Philadelphia	AHL	80	27	*78	*105	28	....	....	....	....	....	....	....	....	....	....	....	20	9	9	18	6	....	....	....
1998-99	**Philadelphia**	**NHL**	**3**	**0**	**0**	**0**	**0**	**0**	**0**	**0**	**0**	**0.0**	**0**	**8**	**37.5**	**0**	**0**	**2:02**	....	....	....	....	....	....	....	....
	Philadelphia	AHL	77	31	59	90	20	....	....	....	....	....	....	....	....	....	....	....	16	4	13	17	12	....	....	....
99-2000	**Philadelphia**	**NHL**	**21**	**1**	**5**	**6**	**6**	**0**	**0**	**0**	**24**	**4.2**	**1**	**277**	**54.5**	**9**	**15**	**13:04**	**16**	**0**	**2**	**2**	**0**	**0**	**0**	**0**
	Philadelphia	AHL	62	20	41	61	38	....	....	....	....	....	....	....	....	....	....	....	....	....	....	....	....	....	....	....
2000-01	**Philadelphia**	**NHL**	**77**	**9**	**16**	**25**	**16**	**1**	**0**	**1**	**68**	**13.2**	**1**	**1038**	**54.3**	**23**	**27**	**12:56**	**3**	**0**	**0**	**0**	**0**	**0**	**0**	**0**
	NHL Totals		**163**	**20**	**33**	**53**	**24**	**4**	**0**	**1**	**156**	**12.8**		**1323**	**54.3**	**32**	**42**	**12:38**	**19**	**0**	**2**	**2**	**0**	**0**	**0**	**0**

AHL Second All-Star Team (1995, 1997) • Won John B. Sollenberger Trophy (Top Scorer - AHL) (1995, 1997, 1998)

Traded to **Toronto** by **Edmonton** with Edmonton's 4th round choice (Jason Sessa) in 1996 Entry Draft for Kent Manderville, December 4, 1995. Signed as a free agent by **Philadelphia**, August 19, 1996.

WHITE, Todd

(WHIGHT, TAWD) **OTT.**

Center. Shoots left. 5'10", 194 lbs. Born, Kanata, Ont., May 21, 1975.

1990-91	Powassan	OCJHL	38	34	38	72	118	....	....	....	....	....	....	....	....	....	....	....	....	....	....	....	....	....	....	....
1991-92	Kanata Valley	OCJHL	55	39	49	88	30	....	....	....	....	....	....	....	....	....	....	....	....	....	....	....	....	....	....	....
1992-93	Kanata Valley	OCJHL	49	51	87	138	46	....	....	....	....	....	....	....	....	....	....	....	....	....	....	....	....	....	....	....
1993-94	Clarkson Knights	ECAC	33	10	12	22	28	....	....	....	....	....	....	....	....	....	....	....	....	....	....	....	....	....	....	....
1994-95	Clarkson Knights	ECAC	34	13	16	29	44	....	....	....	....	....	....	....	....	....	....	....	....	....	....	....	....	....	....	....
1995-96	Clarkson Knights	ECAC	38	29	43	72	36	....	....	....	....	....	....	....	....	....	....	....	....	....	....	....	....	....	....	....
1996-97	Clarkson Knights	ECAC	37	*38	*36	*74	22	....	....	....	....	....	....	....	....	....	....	....	....	....	....	....	....	....	....	....
1997-98	**Chicago**	**NHL**	**7**	**1**	**0**	**1**	**2**	**0**	**0**	**0**	**3**	**33.3**	**0**	....	....	....	....	....	....	....	....	....	....	....	....	....
	Indianapolis Ice	IHL	65	46	36	82	28	....	....	....	....	....	....	....	....	....	....	....	5	2	3	5	4	....	....	....
1998-99	**Chicago**	**NHL**	**35**	**5**	**8**	**13**	**20**	**2**	**0**	**0**	**43**	**11.6**	**–1**	**452**	**46.0**	**27**	**11**	**13:39**	....	....	....	....	....	....	....	....
	Chicago Wolves	IHL	25	11	13	24	8	....	....	....	....	....	....	....	....	....	....	....	10	1	4	5	8	....	....	....
99-2000	**Chicago**	**NHL**	**1**	**0**	**0**	**0**	**0**	**0**	**0**	**0**	**0**	**0.0**	**0**	**9**	**55.6**	**2**	**0**	**13:02**	....	....	....	....	....	....	....	....
	Cleveland	IHL	42	21	30	51	32	....	....	....	....	....	....	....	....	....	....	....	....	....	....	....	....	....	....	....
	Philadelphia	**NHL**	**3**	**1**	**0**	**1**	**0**	**0**	**0**	**0**	**4**	**25.0**	**–1**	**25**	**40.0**	**1**	**1**	**10:29**	....	....	....	....	....	....	....	....
	Philadelphia	AHL	32	19	24	43	12	....	....	....	....	....	....	....	....	....	....	....	5	2	1	3	8	....	....	....
2000-01	**Ottawa**	**NHL**	**16**	**4**	**1**	**5**	**4**	**0**	**0**	**0**	**12**	**33.3**	**5**	**133**	**57.1**	**9**	**6**	**8:33**	**2**	**0**	**0**	**0**	**0**	**0**	**0**	**0**
	Grand Rapids	IHL	64	22	32	54	20	....	....	....	....	....	....	....	....	....	....	....	10	4	4	8	10	....	....	....
	NHL Totals		**62**	**11**	**9**	**20**	**26**	**2**	**0**	**0**	**62**	**17.7**		**619**	**48.3**	**39**	**18**	**11:59**	**2**	**0**	**0**	**0**	**0**	**0**	**0**	**0**

ECAC Second All-Star Team (1996) • NCAA East Second All-American Team (1996) • ECAC First All-Star Team (1997) • NCAA East First All-American Team (1997) • Won Garry F. Longman Memorial Trophy (Top Rookie - IHL) (1998)

Signed as a free agent by **Chicago**, August 27, 1997. Traded to **Philadelphia** by **Chicago** for future considerations, January 26, 2000. Signed as a free agent by **Ottawa**, July 12, 2000.

WHITFIELD, Trent

(WHIHT-feeld, TREHNT) **WSH.**

Center. Shoots left. 5'11", 200 lbs. Born, Estevan, Sask., June 17, 1977. Boston's 5th choice, 100th overall, in 1996 Entry Draft.

1993-94	Saskatoon Blaze	SMHL	36	26	22	48	42	....	....	....	....	....	....	....	....	....	....	....	....	....	....	....	....	....	....	....
	Spokane Chiefs	WHL	5	1	1	2	0	....	....	....	....	....	....	....	....	....	....	....	....	....	....	....	....	....	....	....
1994-95	Spokane Chiefs	WHL	48	8	17	25	26	....	....	....	....	....	....	....	....	....	....	....	11	7	6	13	5	....	....	....
1995-96	Spokane Chiefs	WHL	72	33	51	84	75	....	....	....	....	....	....	....	....	....	....	....	18	8	10	18	10	....	....	....
1996-97	Spokane Chiefs	WHL	58	34	42	76	74	....	....	....	....	....	....	....	....	....	....	....	9	5	7	12	10	....	....	....
1997-98	Spokane Chiefs	WHL	65	38	44	82	97	....	....	....	....	....	....	....	....	....	....	....	18	9	10	19	15	....	....	....
1998-99	Portland Pirates	AHL	50	10	8	18	20	....	....	....	....	....	....	....	....	....	....	....	....	....	....	....	....	....	....	....
	Hampton Roads	ECHL	19	13	12	25	12	....	....	....	....	....	....	....	....	....	....	....	4	2	0	2	14	....	....	....
99-2000	Portland Pirates	AHL	79	18	35	53	52	....	....	....	....	....	....	....	....	....	....	....	3	1	1	2	2	....	....	....
	Washington	**NHL**	....	....	....	....	....	....	....	....	....	....	....	....	....	....	....	....	**3**	**0**	**0**	**0**	**0**	**0**	**0**	**0**
2000-01	**Washington**	**NHL**	**61**	**2**	**4**	**6**	**35**	**0**	**0**	**0**	**47**	**4.3**	**3**	**520**	**51.9**	**70**	**24**	**9:39**	**5**	**0**	**0**	**0**	**2**	**0**	**0**	**0**
	Portland Pirates	AHL	19	9	11	20	27	....	....	....	....	....	....	....	....	....	....	....	....	....	....	....	....	....	....	....
	NHL Totals		**61**	**2**	**4**	**6**	**35**	**0**	**0**	**0**	**47**	**4.3**		**520**	**51.9**	**70**	**24**	**9:39**	**8**	**0**	**0**	**0**	**2**	**0**	**0**	**0**

WHL West First All-Star Team (1997) • WHL West Second All-Star Team (1998)

Signed as a free agent by **Washington**, September 1, 1998.

WHITNEY, Ray (WHIHT-nee, RAY) CBJ

Left wing. Shoots right. 5'10", 175 lbs. Born, Fort Saskatchewan, Alta., May 8, 1972. San Jose's 2nd choice, 23rd overall, in 1991 Entry Draft.

			Regular Season															Playoffs							
Season	Club	League	GP	G	A	Pts	PIM	PP	SH	GW	S	%	+/-	TF	F%	H	SB	Min	GP	G	A	Pts	PIM	PP	SH	GW
1987-88	Ft-Saskatchewan	AAHA	71	80	155	235	119																			
1988-89	Spokane Chiefs	WHL	71	17	33	50	16																			
1989-90	Spokane Chiefs	WHL	71	57	56	113	50												6	3	4	7	6			
1990-91	Spokane Chiefs	WHL	72	67	118	*185	36												15	13	18	*31	12			
1991-92	Kolner EC	DEL	10	3	6	9	4																			
	Canada	Nat-Team	5	1	0	1	6																			
	San Jose	**NHL**	**2**	**0**	**3**	**3**	**0**	**0**	**0**	**0**	**4**	**0.0**	**-1**													
	San Diego Gulls	IHL	63	36	54	90	12												4	0	0	0	0			
1992-93	**San Jose**	**NHL**	**26**	**4**	**6**	**10**	**4**	**1**	**0**	**0**	**24**	**16.7**	**-14**													
	Kansas City	IHL	46	20	33	53	14												12	5	7	12	2			
1993-94	**San Jose**	**NHL**	**61**	**14**	**26**	**40**	**14**	**1**	**0**	**0**	**82**	**17.1**	**2**						**14**	**0**	**4**	**4**	**8**	**0**	**0**	**0**
1994-95	**San Jose**	**NHL**	**39**	**13**	**12**	**25**	**14**	**4**	**0**	**1**	**67**	**19.4**	**-7**						**11**	**4**	**4**	**8**	**2**	**0**	**0**	**1**
1995-96	**San Jose**	**NHL**	**60**	**17**	**24**	**41**	**16**	**4**	**2**	**2**	**106**	**16.0**	**-23**													
1996-97	**San Jose**	**NHL**	**12**	**0**	**2**	**2**	**4**	**0**	**0**	**0**	**24**	**0.0**	**-6**													
	Kentucky	AHL	9	1	7	8	2																			
	Utah Grizzlies	IHL	43	13	35	48	34												7	3	1	4	6			
1997-98	**Edmonton**	**NHL**	**9**	**1**	**3**	**4**	**0**	**0**	**0**	**0**	**19**	**5.3**	**-1**													
	Florida	**NHL**	**68**	**32**	**29**	**61**	**28**	**12**	**0**	**2**	**156**	**20.5**	**10**													
1998-99	**Florida**	**NHL**	**81**	**26**	**38**	**64**	**18**	**7**	**0**	**6**	**193**	**13.5**	**-3**	**144**	**43.8**	**14**	**7**	**18:20**								
99-2000	**Florida**	**NHL**	**81**	**29**	**42**	**71**	**35**	**5**	**0**	**3**	**198**	**14.6**	**16**	**198**	**49.0**	**17**	**16**	**18:41**	**4**	**1**	**0**	**1**	**4**	**0**	**0**	**0**
2000-01	**Florida**	**NHL**	**43**	**10**	**21**	**31**	**28**	**5**	**0**	**0**	**117**	**8.5**	**-16**	**38**	**39.5**	**6**	**15**	**17:41**								
	Columbus	**NHL**	**3**	**0**	**3**	**3**	**2**	**0**	**0**	**0**	**3**	**0.0**	**-1**	**19**	**36.8**	**2**	**0**	**20:17**								
	NHL Totals		**485**	**146**	**209**	**355**	**163**	**39**	**2**	**14**	**993**	**14.7**		**399**	**45.6**	**39**	**38**	**18:22**	**29**	**5**	**8**	**13**	**14**	**0**	**0**	**1**

WHL West First All-Star Team (1991) • Memorial Cup All-Star Team (1991) • Won George Parsons Trophy (Memorial Cup Tournament Most Sportsmanlike Player) (1991) • Played in NHL All-Star Game (2000)

Signed as a free agent by **Edmonton**, October 1, 1997. Claimed on waivers by **Florida** from **Edmonton**, November 6, 1997. Traded to **Columbus** by **Florida** for Kevyn Adams and future considerations, March 13, 2001.

WIEMER, Jason (WEE-muhr, JAY-suhn) FLA.

Center. Shoots left. 6'1", 220 lbs. Born, Kimberley, B.C., April 14, 1976. Tampa Bay's 1st choice, 8th overall, in 1994 Entry Draft.

1991-92	Kimberley	RMJHL	45	33	33	66	211																			
	Portland	WHL	2	0	1	1	0																			
1992-93	Portland	WHL	68	18	34	52	159												16	7	3	10	27			
1993-94	Portland	WHL	72	45	51	96	236												10	4	4	8	32			
1994-95	Portland	WHL	16	10	14	24	63																			
	Tampa Bay	**NHL**	**36**	**1**	**4**	**5**	**44**	**0**	**0**	**0**	**10**	**10.0**	**-2**													
1995-96	**Tampa Bay**	**NHL**	**66**	**9**	**9**	**18**	**81**	**4**	**0**	**1**	**89**	**10.1**	**-9**						**6**	**1**	**0**	**1**	**28**	**1**	**0**	**0**
1996-97	**Tampa Bay**	**NHL**	**63**	**9**	**5**	**14**	**134**	**2**	**0**	**0**	**103**	**8.7**	**-13**													
	Adirondack	AHL	4	1	0	1	7																			
1997-98	**Tampa Bay**	**NHL**	**67**	**8**	**9**	**17**	**132**	**2**	**0**	**0**	**106**	**7.5**	**-9**													
	Calgary	**NHL**	**12**	**4**	**1**	**5**	**28**	**1**	**0**	**2**	**16**	**25.0**	**-1**													
1998-99	**Calgary**	**NHL**	**78**	**8**	**13**	**21**	**177**	**1**	**0**	**1**	**128**	**6.3**	**-12**	**867**	**40.9**	**171**	**20**	**13:17**								
99-2000	**Calgary**	**NHL**	**64**	**11**	**11**	**22**	**120**	**2**	**0**	**3**	**104**	**10.6**	**-10**	**955**	**47.6**	**149**	**22**	**14:41**								
2000-01	**Calgary**	**NHL**	**65**	**10**	**5**	**15**	**177**	**3**	**0**	**1**	**76**	**13.2**	**-15**	**599**	**51.1**	**143**	**28**	**13:56**								
	NHL Totals		**451**	**60**	**57**	**117**	**893**	**15**	**0**	**8**	**632**	**9.5**		**2421**	**46.1**	**463**	**70**	**13:55**	**6**	**1**	**0**	**1**	**28**	**1**	**0**	**0**

Traded to **Calgary** by **Tampa Bay** for Sandy McCarthy and Calgary's 3rd (Brad Richards) and 5th (Curtis Rich) round choices in 1998 Entry Draft, March 24, 1998. Traded to **Florida** by **Calgary** with Valeri Bure for Rob Neidermayer and Philadelphia's 2nd round choice (previously acquired, Calgary selected Andrei Medvedev) in 2001 Entry Draft, June 24, 2001.

WILKIE, David (WIHL-kee, DAY-vihd)

Defense. Shoots right. 6'3", 215 lbs. Born, Ellensburgh, WA, May 30, 1974. Montreal's 1st choice, 20th overall, in 1992 Entry Draft.

1989-90	Seattle North	PJHL	41	21	27	48	59																			
1990-91	Omaha Lancers	USHL	19	2	2	4	18																			
	Seattle T-Birds	WHL	25	1	1	2	22																			
1991-92	Kamloops Blazers	WHL	71	12	28	40	153												16	6	5	11	19			
1992-93	Kamloops Blazers	WHL	53	11	26	37	109												6	4	2	6	2			
1993-94	Kamloops Blazers	WHL	27	11	18	29	18																			
	Regina Pats	WHL	29	27	21	48	16												4	1	4	5	4			
1994-95	Fredericton	AHL	70	10	43	53	34												1	0	0	0	0			
	Montreal	**NHL**	**1**	**0**	**0**	**0**	**0**	**0**	**0**	**0**	**0**	**0.0**	**0**													
1995-96	**Montreal**	**NHL**	**24**	**1**	**5**	**6**	**10**	**1**	**0**	**0**	**39**	**2.6**	**-10**						**6**	**1**	**2**	**3**	**12**	**0**	**0**	**0**
	Fredericton	AHL	23	5	12	17	20																			
1996-97	**Montreal**	**NHL**	**61**	**6**	**9**	**15**	**63**	**3**	**0**	**0**	**65**	**9.2**	**-9**						**2**	**0**	**0**	**0**	**2**	**0**	**0**	**0**
1997-98	**Montreal**	**NHL**	**5**	**1**	**0**	**1**	**4**	**0**	**0**	**1**	**2**	**50.0**	**-1**													
	Tampa Bay	**NHL**	**29**	**1**	**5**	**6**	**17**	**0**	**0**	**0**	**46**	**2.2**	**-21**													
1998-99	**Tampa Bay**	**NHL**	**46**	**1**	**7**	**8**	**69**	**0**	**0**	**0**	**35**	**2.9**	**-19**	**0**	**0.0**	**49**	**48**	**12:18**								
	Cleveland	IHL	2	0	2	2	0																			
99-2000	Houston Aeros	IHL	57	4	24	28	71												11	1	8	9	10			
	Hartford	AHL	1	0	2	2	0																			
2000-01	**NY Rangers**	**NHL**	**1**	**0**	**0**	**0**	**2**	**0**	**0**	**0**	**1**	**0.0**	**-2**	**0**	**0.0**	**1**	**3**	**11:33**								
	Houston Aeros	IHL	49	8	11	19	29												7	1	1	2	4			
	NHL Totals		**167**	**10**	**26**	**36**	**165**	**4**	**0**	**1**	**188**	**5.3**		**0**	**0.0**	**50**	**51**	**12:17**	**8**	**1**	**2**	**3**	**14**	**0**	**0**	**0**

Traded to **Tampa Bay** by **Montreal** with Stephane Richer and Darcy Tucker for Patrick Poulin, Mick Vukota and Igor Ulanov, January 15, 1998. Signed as a free agent by **NY Rangers**, September 29, 1999. Signed as a free agent by **Augusta** (ECHL) and named Player-Assistant Coach, August 11, 2001.

WILLIAMS, Jason (WIHL-yuhms, JAY-suhn) DET.

Center. Shoots Right. 5'11", 185 lbs. Born, London, Ont., August 11, 1980.

1995-96	Mount Brydges	OJHL-D	36	31	28	59	18																			
1996-97	Peterborough	OHL	60	4	8	12	8												10	1	0	1	2			
1997-98	Peterborough	OHL	55	8	27	35	31												4	0	1	1	2			
1998-99	Peterborough	OHL	68	26	48	74	42												5	1	2	3	2			
99-2000	Peterborough	OHL	66	36	37	75	64												5	2	1	3	2			
2000-01	**Detroit**	**NHL**	**5**	**0**	**3**	**3**	**2**	**0**	**0**	**0**	**7**	**0.0**	**1**	**56**	**39.3**	**15**	**2**	**12:24**	**2**	**0**	**0**	**0**	**0**	**0**	**0**	**0**
	Cincinnati Ducks	AHL	76	24	45	69	48												1	0	0	0	2			
	NHL Totals		**5**	**0**	**3**	**3**	**2**	**0**	**0**	**0**	**7**	**0.0**		**56**	**39.3**	**15**	**2**	**12:24**	**2**	**0**	**0**	**0**	**0**	**0**	**0**	**0**

OHL Third Team All-Star (2000)

Signed as a free agent by **Detroit**, September 18, 2000.

WILLIAMS, Justin (WIHL-yuhms, JUHS-tihn) PHI.

Right wing. Shoots right. 6'1", 190 lbs. Born, Cobourg, Ont., October 4, 1981. Philadelphia's 1st choice, 28th overall, in 2000 Entry Draft.

1997-98	Cobourne Colts	OJHL-C	36	32	35	67	26																			
	Cobourg Cougars	OJHL-B	17	0	3	3	5																			
1998-99	Plymouth Whalers	OHL	47	4	8	12	28												7	1	2	3	0			
99-2000	Plymouth Whalers	OHL	68	37	46	83	46												23	*14	16	*30	10			
2000-01	**Philadelphia**	**NHL**	**63**	**12**	**13**	**25**	**22**	**0**	**0**	**0**	**99**	**12.1**	**6**	**13**	**53.9**	**20**	**18**	**12:31**								
	NHL Totals		**63**	**12**	**13**	**25**	**22**	**0**	**0**	**0**	**99**	**12.1**		**13**	**53.8**	**20**	**18**	**12:31**								

WILLIS, Shane

(WIH-lihs, SHAYN) **CAR.**

Right wing. Shoots right. 6', 185 lbs. Born, Edmonton, Alta., June 13, 1977. Carolina's 4th choice, 88th overall, in 1997 Entry Draft.

			Regular Season																Playoffs							
Season	Club	League	GP	G	A	Pts	PIM	PP	SH	GW	S	%	+/-	TF	F%	H	SB	Min	GP	G	A	Pts	PIM	PP	SH	GW
1992-93	Red Deer Raiders	AAHA	36	32	18	50	88	....	....	....	....	....	....	....	....	....	....	....	....	....	....	....	....	....	....	....
1993-94	Red Deer Chiefs	AMHL	34	40	26	66	103	....	....	....	....	....	....	....	....	....	....	....	....	....	....	....	....	....	....	....
1994-95	Prince Albert	WHL	65	24	19	43	38	....	....	....	....	....	....	....	....	....	....	....	13	3	4	7	6	....	....	....
1995-96	Prince Albert	WHL	69	41	40	81	47	....	....	....	....	....	....	....	....	....	....	....	18	11	10	21	18	....	....	....
1996-97	Prince Albert	WHL	41	34	22	56	63	....	....	....	....	....	....	....	....	....	....	....	....	....	....	....	....	....	....	....
	Lethbridge	WHL	26	22	17	39	24	....	....	....	....	....	....	....	....	....	....	....	19	13	11	24	20	....	....	....
1997-98	Lethbridge	WHL	64	58	54	112	73	....	....	....	....	....	....	....	....	....	....	....	4	2	3	5	6	....	....	....
	New Haven	AHL	1	0	1	1	2	....	....	....	....	....	....	....	....	....	....	....	....	....	....	....	....	....	....	....
1998-99	**Carolina**	**NHL**	**7**	**0**	**0**	**0**	**0**	**0**	**0**	**0**	**1**	**0.0**	**–2**	**0**	**0.0**	**4**	**2**	**2:14**	....	....	....	....	....	....	....	....
	New Haven	AHL	73	31	50	81	49	....	....	....	....	....	....	....	....	....	....	....	....	....	....	....	....	....	....	....
99-2000	**Carolina**	**NHL**	**2**	**0**	**0**	**0**	**0**	**0**	**0**	**0**	**1**	**0.0**	**–1**	**0**	**0.0**	**6**	**0**	**5:50**	....	....	....	....	....	....	....	....
	Cincinnati	IHL	80	35	25	60	64	....	....	....	....	....	....	....	....	....	....	....	11	5	3	8	8	....	....	....
2000-01	**Carolina**	**NHL**	**73**	**20**	**24**	**44**	**45**	**9**	**0**	**6**	**172**	**11.6**	**–6**	**10**	**20.0**	**117**	**16**	**15:58**	**2**	**0**	**0**	**0**	**0**	**0**	**0**	**0**
	NHL Totals		**82**	**20**	**24**	**44**	**45**	**9**	**0**	**6**	**174**	**11.5**		**10**	**20.0**	**127**	**18**	**14:33**	**2**	**0**	**0**	**0**	**0**	**0**	**0**	**0**

• Re-entered NHL Entry Draft. Originally Tampa Bay's 3rd choice, 56th overall, in 1995 Entry Draft.

WHL East First All-Star Team (1997, 1998) • AHL First All-Star Team (1999) • Won Dudley "Red" Garrett Memorial Trophy (Top Rookie - AHL) (1999) • NHL All-Rookie Team (2001)

WILLSIE, Brian

(WIHL-see, BRIGH-uhn) **COL.**

Right wing. Shoots right. 6'1", 195 lbs. Born, London, Ont., March 16, 1978. Colorado's 7th choice, 146th overall, in 1996 Entry Draft.

			Regular Season																Playoffs							
Season	Club	League	GP	G	A	Pts	PIM	PP	SH	GW	S	%	+/-	TF	F%	H	SB	Min	GP	G	A	Pts	PIM	PP	SH	GW
1993-94	Belmont Bombers	OJHL-D	13	9	5	14	14	....	....	....	....	....	....	....	....	....	....	....	....	....	....	....	....	....	....	....
1994-95	St. Thomas Stars	OJHL-B	45	35	47	82	47	....	....	....	....	....	....	....	....	....	....	....	....	....	....	....	....	....	....	....
1995-96	Guelph Storm	OHL	65	13	21	34	18	....	....	....	....	....	....	....	....	....	....	....	16	4	2	6	6	....	....	....
1996-97	Guelph Storm	OHL	64	37	31	68	37	....	....	....	....	....	....	....	....	....	....	....	18	15	4	19	10	....	....	....
1997-98	Guelph Storm	OHL	57	45	31	76	41	....	....	....	....	....	....	....	....	....	....	....	12	9	5	14	18	....	....	....
1998-99	Hershey Bears	AHL	72	19	10	29	28	....	....	....	....	....	....	....	....	....	....	....	3	1	0	1	0	....	....	....
99-2000	**Colorado**	**NHL**	**1**	**0**	**0**	**0**	**0**	**0**	**0**	**0**	**1**	**0.0**	**0**	**0**	**0.0**	**0**	**0**	**8:16**	....	....	....	....	....	....	....	....
	Hershey Bears	AHL	78	20	39	59	44	....	....	....	....	....	....	....	....	....	....	....	12	2	6	8	8	....	....	....
2000-01	Hershey Bears	AHL	48	18	23	41	20	....	....	....	....	....	....	....	....	....	....	....	12	7	2	9	14	....	....	....
	NHL Totals		**1**	**0**	**0**	**0**	**0**	**0**	**0**	**0**	**1**	**0.0**		**0**	**0.0**	**0**	**0**	**8:16**	....	....	....	....	....	....	....	....

OHL First All-Star Team (1998)

WILM, Clarke

(WIHLM, KLAHRK) **CGY.**

Center. Shoots left. 6', 202 lbs. Born, Central Butte, Sask., October 24, 1976. Calgary's 5th choice, 150th overall, in 1995 Entry Draft.

			Regular Season																Playoffs							
Season	Club	League	GP	G	A	Pts	PIM	PP	SH	GW	S	%	+/-	TF	F%	H	SB	Min	GP	G	A	Pts	PIM	PP	SH	GW
1991-92	Saskatoon Blaze	SMHL	36	18	28	46	16	....	....	....	....	....	....	....	....	....	....	....	....	....	....	....	....	....	....	....
	Saskatoon Blades	WHL	....	....	....	....	....	....	....	....	....	....	....	....	....	....	....	....	1	0	0	0	0	....	....	....
1992-93	Saskatoon Blades	WHL	69	14	19	33	71	....	....	....	....	....	....	....	....	....	....	....	9	4	2	6	13	....	....	....
1993-94	Saskatoon Blades	WHL	70	18	32	50	181	....	....	....	....	....	....	....	....	....	....	....	16	0	9	9	19	....	....	....
1994-95	Saskatoon Blades	WHL	71	20	39	59	179	....	....	....	....	....	....	....	....	....	....	....	10	6	1	7	21	....	....	....
1995-96	Saskatoon Blades	WHL	72	49	61	110	83	....	....	....	....	....	....	....	....	....	....	....	4	1	1	2	4	....	....	....
1996-97	Saint John Flames	AHL	62	9	19	28	107	....	....	....	....	....	....	....	....	....	....	....	5	2	0	2	15	....	....	....
1997-98	Saint John Flames	AHL	68	13	26	39	112	....	....	....	....	....	....	....	....	....	....	....	21	5	9	14	8	....	....	....
1998-99	**Calgary**	**NHL**	**78**	**10**	**8**	**18**	**53**	**2**	**2**	**0**	**94**	**10.6**	**11**	**609**	**40.9**	**94**	**21**	**11:32**	....	....	....	....	....	....	....	....
99-2000	**Calgary**	**NHL**	**78**	**10**	**12**	**22**	**67**	**1**	**3**	**0**	**81**	**12.3**	**–6**	**872**	**44.4**	**113**	**34**	**12:38**	....	....	....	....	....	....	....	....
2000-01	**Calgary**	**NHL**	**81**	**7**	**8**	**15**	**69**	**2**	**0**	**0**	**85**	**8.2**	**–11**	**992**	**51.9**	**111**	**54**	**14:11**	....	....	....	....	....	....	....	....
	NHL Totals		**237**	**27**	**28**	**55**	**189**	**5**	**5**	**0**	**260**	**10.4**		**2473**	**46.5**	**318**	**109**	**12:48**	....	....	....	....	....	....	....	....

WILSON, Landon

(WIHL-sohn, LAN-duhn) **PHX.**

Right wing. Shoots right. 6'3", 226 lbs. Born, St. Louis, MO, March 13, 1975. Toronto's 2nd choice, 19th overall, in 1993 Entry Draft.

			Regular Season																Playoffs							
Season	Club	League	GP	G	A	Pts	PIM	PP	SH	GW	S	%	+/-	TF	F%	H	SB	Min	GP	G	A	Pts	PIM	PP	SH	GW
1991-92	California Kings	WSJHL	38	50	42	92	135	....	....	....	....	....	....	....	....	....	....	....	....	....	....	....	....	....	....	....
1992-93	Dubuque Saints	USHL	43	29	36	65	284	....	....	....	....	....	....	....	....	....	....	....	....	....	....	....	....	....	....	....
1993-94	North Dakota	WCHA	35	18	15	33	*147	....	....	....	....	....	....	....	....	....	....	....	....	....	....	....	....	....	....	....
1994-95	North Dakota	WCHA	31	7	16	23	141	....	....	....	....	....	....	....	....	....	....	....	....	....	....	....	....	....	....	....
	Cornwall Aces	AHL	8	4	4	8	25	....	....	....	....	....	....	....	....	....	....	....	13	3	4	7	68	....	....	....
1995-96	**Colorado**	**NHL**	**7**	**1**	**0**	**1**	**6**	**0**	**0**	**0**	**6**	**16.7**	**3**	....	....	....	....	....	....	....	....	....	....	....	....	....
	Cornwall Aces	AHL	53	21	13	34	154	....	....	....	....	....	....	....	....	....	....	....	8	1	3	4	22	....	....	....
1996-97	**Colorado**	**NHL**	**9**	**1**	**2**	**3**	**23**	**0**	**0**	**0**	**7**	**14.3**	**1**	....	....	....	....	....	....	....	....	....	....	....	....	....
	Boston	**NHL**	**40**	**7**	**10**	**17**	**49**	**0**	**0**	**0**	**76**	**9.2**	**–6**	....	....	....	....	....	....	....	....	....	....	....	....	....
	Providence Bruins	AHL	2	2	1	3	2	....	....	....	....	....	....	....	....	....	....	....	10	3	4	7	16	....	....	....
1997-98	**Boston**	**NHL**	**28**	**1**	**5**	**6**	**7**	**0**	**0**	**0**	**26**	**3.8**	**3**	....	....	....	....	....	**1**	**0**	**0**	**0**	**0**	**0**	**0**	**0**
	Providence Bruins	AHL	42	18	10	28	146	....	....	....	....	....	....	....	....	....	....	....	....	....	....	....	....	....	....	....
1998-99	**Boston**	**NHL**	**22**	**3**	**3**	**6**	**17**	**0**	**0**	**0**	**32**	**9.4**	**0**	**3**	**0.0**	**59**	**2**	**10:04**	**8**	**1**	**1**	**2**	**8**	**1**	**0**	**1**
	Providence Bruins	AHL	48	31	22	53	89	....	....	....	....	....	....	....	....	....	....	....	11	7	1	8	19	....	....	....
99-2000	**Boston**	**NHL**	**40**	**1**	**3**	**4**	**18**	**0**	**0**	**0**	**67**	**1.5**	**–6**	**14**	**42.9**	**84**	**5**	**10:09**	....	....	....	....	....	....	....	....
	Providence Bruins	AHL	17	5	5	10	45	....	....	....	....	....	....	....	....	....	....	....	9	2	3	5	38	....	....	....
2000-01	**Phoenix**	**NHL**	**70**	**18**	**13**	**31**	**92**	**2**	**0**	**3**	**123**	**14.6**	**3**	**13**	**46.2**	**129**	**10**	**11:26**	....	....	....	....	....	....	....	....
	NHL Totals		**216**	**32**	**36**	**68**	**212**	**2**	**0**	**3**	**337**	**9.5**		**30**	**40.0**	**272**	**17**	**10:49**	**9**	**1**	**1**	**2**	**8**	**1**	**0**	**1**

AHL First All-Star Team (1999)

Traded to **Quebec** by **Toronto** with Wendel Clark, Sylvain Lefebvre and Toronto's 1st round choice (Jeffrey Kealty) in 1994 Entry Draft for Mats Sundin, Garth Butcher, Todd Warriner and Philadelphia's 1st round choice (previously acquired by Quebec - later traded to Washington - Washington selected Nolan Baumgartner) in 1994 Entry Draft, June 28, 1994. Transferred to **Colorado** after **Quebec** franchise relocated, June 21, 1995. Traded to **Boston** by **Colorado** with Anders Myrvold for Boston's 1st round choice (Robyn Regehr) in 1998 Entry Draft, November 22, 1996. Signed as a free agent by **Phoenix**, July 7, 2000.

WILSON, Mike

(WIHL-sohn, MIGHK) **PIT.**

Defense. Shoots left. 6'6", 212 lbs. Born, Brampton, Ont., February 26, 1975. Vancouver's 1st choice, 20th overall, in 1993 Entry Draft.

			Regular Season																Playoffs							
Season	Club	League	GP	G	A	Pts	PIM	PP	SH	GW	S	%	+/-	TF	F%	H	SB	Min	GP	G	A	Pts	PIM	PP	SH	GW
1991-92	Georgetown	OJHL-B	41	9	13	22	65	....	....	....	....	....	....	....	....	....	....	....	....	....	....	....	....	....	....	....
1992-93	Sudbury Wolves	OHL	53	6	7	13	58	....	....	....	....	....	....	....	....	....	....	....	14	1	1	2	2	....	....	....
1993-94	Sudbury Wolves	OHL	60	4	22	26	62	....	....	....	....	....	....	....	....	....	....	....	9	1	3	4	8	....	....	....
1994-95	Sudbury Wolves	OHL	64	13	34	47	46	....	....	....	....	....	....	....	....	....	....	....	18	1	8	9	10	....	....	....
1995-96	**Buffalo**	**NHL**	**58**	**4**	**8**	**12**	**41**	**1**	**0**	**1**	**52**	**7.7**	**13**	....	....	....	....	....	....	....	....	....	....	....	....	....
	Rochester	AHL	15	0	5	5	38	....	....	....	....	....	....	....	....	....	....	....	....	....	....	....	....	....	....	....
1996-97	**Buffalo**	**NHL**	**77**	**2**	**9**	**11**	**51**	**0**	**0**	**1**	**57**	**3.5**	**13**	....	....	....	....	....	**10**	**0**	**1**	**1**	**2**	**0**	**0**	**0**
1997-98	**Buffalo**	**NHL**	**66**	**4**	**4**	**8**	**48**	**0**	**0**	**1**	**52**	**7.7**	**13**	....	....	....	....	....	**15**	**0**	**1**	**1**	**13**	**0**	**0**	**0**
1998-99	Las Vegas	IHL	6	3	1	4	6	....	....	....	....	....	....	....	....	....	....	....	....	....	....	....	....	....	....	....
	Buffalo	**NHL**	**30**	**1**	**2**	**3**	**47**	**0**	**0**	**1**	**40**	**2.5**	**10**	**0**	**0.0**	**54**	**19**	**16:40**	....	....	....	....	....	....	....	....
	Florida	**NHL**	**4**	**0**	**0**	**0**	**0**	**0**	**0**	**0**	**8**	**0.0**	**2**	**0**	**0.0**	**4**	**6**	**19:23**	....	....	....	....	....	....	....	....
99-2000	**Florida**	**NHL**	**60**	**4**	**16**	**20**	**35**	**0**	**0**	**2**	**65**	**6.2**	**10**	**0**	**0.0**	**130**	**62**	**18:07**	**4**	**0**	**0**	**0**	**0**	**0**	**0**	**0**
2000-01	**Florida**	**NHL**	**19**	**0**	**1**	**1**	**25**	**0**	**0**	**0**	**26**	**0.0**	**–7**	**0**	**0.0**	**54**	**14**	**13:20**	....	....	....	....	....	....	....	....
	Louisville Panthers	AHL	4	0	2	2	5	....	....	....	....	....	....	....	....	....	....	....	....	....	....	....	....	....	....	....
	NHL Totals		**314**	**15**	**40**	**55**	**247**	**1**	**0**	**6**	**300**	**5.0**		**0**	**0.0**	**242**	**101**	**16:58**	**29**	**0**	**2**	**2**	**15**	**0**	**0**	**0**

Traded to **Buffalo** by **Vancouver** with Michael Peca and Vancouver's 1st round choice (Jay McKee) in 1995 Entry Draft for Alexander Mogilny and Buffalo's 5th round choice (Todd Norman) in 1995 Entry Draft, July 8, 1995. Traded to **Florida** by **Buffalo** for Rhett Warrener and Florida's 5th round choice (Ryan Miller) in 1999 Entry Draft, March 23, 1999. • Missed majority of 2000-01 season recovering from shoulder injury suffered in game vs. New Jersey, October 25, 2000. • Missed majority of 2000-01 season recovering from shoulder injury suffered in game vs. New Jersey, October 25, 2000. Signed as a free agent by **Pittsburgh**, July 5, 2001.

WISEMAN, Brian
(WIGHS-man, BRIGH-uhn)

Center. Shoots left. 5'8", 175 lbs. Born, Chatham, Ont., July 13, 1971. NY Rangers' 11th choice, 257th overall, in 1991 Entry Draft.

			Regular Season																Playoffs							
Season	Club	League	GP	G	A	Pts	PIM	PP	SH	GW	S	%	+/-	TF	F%	H	SB	Min	GP	G	A	Pts	PIM	PP	SH	GW
1986-87	Dresden Kings	OJHL-C	33	12	29	41	53																			
1987-88	Chatham	OJHL-B	41	26	33	59	35																			
1988-89	Chatham	OJHL-B	42	36	*71	*107	34																			
1989-90	Chatham	OJHL-B	40	*70	*77	*147	32																			
1990-91	U. of Michigan	CCHA	47	25	33	58	58																			
1991-92	U. of Michigan	CCHA	44	27	44	71	38																			
1992-93	U. of Michigan	CCHA	35	13	37	50	40																			
1993-94	U. of Michigan	CCHA	40	19	50	69	44																			
1994-95	Chicago Wolves	IHL	75	17	55	72	52												3	1	1	2	4			
1995-96	Chicago Wolves	IHL	73	33	55	88	117																			
1996-97	**Toronto**	**NHL**	**3**	**0**	**0**	**0**	**0**	**0**	**0**	**0**	**1**	**0.0**	**0**													
	St. John's Leafs	AHL	71	33	62	95	83												7	5	4	9	8			
1997-98	Houston Aeros	IHL	78	26	72	98	86												4	0	3	3	8			
1998-99	Houston Aeros	IHL	77	21	*88	*109	106												19	3	13	16	26			
99-2000	Houston Aeros	IHL	72	15	38	53	52												3	0	1	1	6			
2000-01	Houston Aeros	AHL	DID NOT PLAY – INJURED																							
	NHL Totals		**3**	**0**	**0**	**0**	**0**	**0**	**0**	**0**	**1**	**0.0**														

CCHA First All-Star Team (1994) • NCAA West First All-American Team (1994) • IHL First All-Star Team (1998, 1999) • Won Leo P. Lamoureux Memorial Trophy (Top Scorer - IHL) (1999) • Won James Gatschene Memorial Trophy (MVP - IHL) (1999)

Signed as a free agent by **Toronto**, August 14, 1996. Signed as a free agent by **Houston** (IHL), August 4, 1997. Signed as a free agent by **Toronto**, July 13, 1999. • Missed entire 2000-01 season recovering from head injury suffered during 1999-2000 IHL playoffs.

WITEHALL, Johan
(WITH-hall, YOH-han)

Left wing. Shoots left. 6'1", 198 lbs. Born, Goteborg, Sweden, January 7, 1972. NY Rangers' 8th choice, 207th overall, in 1998 Entry Draft.

Season	Club	League	GP	G	A	Pts	PIM	PP	SH	GW	S	%	+/-	TF	F%	H	SB	Min	GP	G	A	Pts	PIM	PP	SH	GW
1991-92	Hanhals IF	Sweden-2	32	23	14	37	52																			
1992-93	Hanhals IF	Sweden-2	29	12	7	19	34																			
1993-94	Hanhals IF	Sweden-2	30	13	12	25	66																			
1994-95	Hanhals IF	Sweden-3	32	*38	13	*51	44																			
1995-96	Hanhals IF	Sweden-3	36	*43	17	60	48																			
1996-97	IK Oskarshamn	Sweden-2	32	19	16	35	38																			
1997-98	Leksands IF	Sweden	42	12	4	16	34												2	0	0	0	2			
	Leksands IF	EuroHL	5	3	0	3	2																			
1998-99	**NY Rangers**	**NHL**	**4**	**0**	**0**	**0**	**0**	**0**	**0**	**0**	**1**	**0.0**	**0**	**1**	**100.0**	**5**	**0**	**4:06**								
	Hartford	AHL	62	14	15	29	56												7	1	2	3	6			
99-2000	**NY Rangers**	**NHL**	**9**	**1**	**1**	**2**	**2**	**0**	**0**	**0**	**6**	**16.7**	**0**	**1**	**0.0**	**13**	**0**	**8:26**								
	Hartford	AHL	73	17	24	41	65												17	6	7	13	10			
2000-01	**NY Rangers**	**NHL**	**15**	**0**	**3**	**3**	**8**	**0**	**0**	**0**	**16**	**0.0**	**–5**	**3**	**66.7**	**20**	**2**	**9:11**								
	Hartford	AHL	19	10	8	18	19																			
	Montreal	**NHL**	**26**	**1**	**1**	**2**	**6**	**0**	**0**	**0**	**18**	**5.6**	**0**	**3**	**66.7**	**36**	**5**	**10:17**								
	Quebec Citadelles	AHL	1	0	0	0	0												9	3	5	8	6			
	NHL Totals		**54**	**2**	**5**	**7**	**16**	**0**	**0**	**0**	**41**	**4.9**		**8**	**62.5**	**74**	**7**	**9:13**								

Claimed on waivers by **Montreal** from **NY Rangers**, January 12, 2001.

WITT, Brendan
(WITH, BREHN-duhn) **WSH.**

Defense. Shoots left. 6'1", 226 lbs. Born, Humbolt, Sask., February 20, 1975. Washington's 1st choice, 11th overall, in 1993 Entry Draft.

Season	Club	League	GP	G	A	Pts	PIM	PP	SH	GW	S	%	+/-	TF	F%	H	SB	Min	GP	G	A	Pts	PIM	PP	SH	GW
1990-91	Saskatoon Blaze	SMHL	31	5	13	18	42																			
	Seattle T-Birds	WHL																	1	0	0	0	0			
1991-92	Seattle T-Birds	WHL	67	3	9	12	212												15	1	1	2	84			
1992-93	Seattle T-Birds	WHL	70	2	26	28	239												5	1	2	3	30			
1993-94	Seattle T-Birds	WHL	56	8	31	39	235												9	3	8	11	23			
1994-95			DID NOT PLAY																							
1995-96	**Washington**	**NHL**	**48**	**2**	**3**	**5**	**85**	**0**	**0**	**1**	**44**	**4.5**	**–4**													
1996-97	**Washington**	**NHL**	**44**	**3**	**2**	**5**	**88**	**0**	**0**	**0**	**41**	**7.3**	**–20**													
	Portland Pirates	AHL	30	2	4	6	56												5	1	0	1	30			
1997-98	**Washington**	**NHL**	**64**	**1**	**7**	**8**	**112**	**0**	**0**	**0**	**68**	**1.5**	**–11**						**16**	**1**	**0**	**1**	**14**	**0**	**0**	**0**
1998-99	**Washington**	**NHL**	**54**	**2**	**5**	**7**	**87**	**0**	**0**	**0**	**51**	**3.9**	**–6**	**0**	**0.0**	**148**	**52**	**15:50**								
99-2000	**Washington**	**NHL**	**77**	**1**	**7**	**8**	**114**	**0**	**0**	**0**	**64**	**1.6**	**5**	**2**	**50.0**	**322**	**105**	**20:56**	**3**	**0**	**0**	**0**	**0**	**0**	**0**	**0**
2000-01	**Washington**	**NHL**	**72**	**3**	**3**	**6**	**101**	**0**	**0**	**0**	**87**	**3.4**	**2**	**1**	**100.0**	**207**	**103**	**20:41**	**6**	**2**	**0**	**2**	**12**	**1**	**0**	**0**
	NHL Totals		**359**	**12**	**27**	**39**	**587**	**0**	**0**	**1**	**355**	**3.4**		**3**	**66.7**	**677**	**260**	**19:29**	**25**	**3**	**0**	**3**	**26**	**1**	**0**	**0**

WHL West First All-Star Team (1993, 1994) • Canadian Major Junior First All-Star Team (1994)
• Missed entire 1994-95 season after failing to come to contract terms with **Washington**.

WOOD, Dody
(WUD, DOH-dee)

Center. Shoots left. 6', 200 lbs. Born, Chetwynd, B.C., March 18, 1972. San Jose's 4th choice, 45th overall, in 1991 Entry Draft.

Season	Club	League	GP	G	A	Pts	PIM	PP	SH	GW	S	%	+/-	TF	F%	H	SB	Min	GP	G	A	Pts	PIM	PP	SH	GW
1989-90	Fort St. John	PCJHL	44	51	73	124	270																			
	Seattle T-Birds	WHL																	5	0	0	0	2			
1990-91	Seattle T-Birds	WHL	69	28	37	65	272												6	0	1	1	2			
1991-92	Seattle T-Birds	WHL	37	13	19	32	232																			
	Swift Current	WHL	3	0	2	2	14												7	2	1	3	37			
1992-93	**San Jose**	**NHL**	**13**	**1**	**1**	**2**	**71**	**0**	**0**	**0**	**10**	**10.0**	**–5**													
	Kansas City	IHL	36	3	2	5	216												6	0	1	1	15			
1993-94	Kansas City	IHL	48	5	15	20	320																			
1994-95	Kansas City	IHL	44	5	13	18	255												21	7	10	17	87			
	San Jose	**NHL**	**9**	**1**	**1**	**2**	**29**	**0**	**0**	**0**	**5**	**20.0**	**0**													
1995-96	**San Jose**	**NHL**	**32**	**3**	**6**	**9**	**138**	**0**	**1**	**0**	**33**	**9.1**	**0**													
1996-97	**San Jose**	**NHL**	**44**	**3**	**2**	**5**	**193**	**0**	**0**	**0**	**43**	**7.0**	**–3**													
	Kansas City	IHL	6	3	6	9	35																			
1997-98	**San Jose**	**NHL**	**8**	**0**	**0**	**0**	**40**	**0**	**0**	**0**	**4**	**0.0**	**–3**													
	Kansas City	IHL	2	0	1	1	31																			
	Albany River Rats	AHL	34	4	13	17	185												13	2	0	2	55			
1998-99	Kansas City	IHL	60	11	16	27	286												3	0	1	1	25			
99-2000	Kansas City	IHL	77	13	28	41	*341																			
2000-01	Kansas City	IHL	45	9	14	23	211																			
	NHL Totals		**106**	**8**	**10**	**18**	**471**	**0**	**1**	**0**	**95**	**8.4**														

Traded to **New Jersey** by **San Jose** with Doug Bodger for John MacLean and Ken Sutton, December 7, 1997. Signed as a free agent by **Vancouver**, September 5, 2000.

WOOLLEY, Jason
(WU-lee, JAY-suhn) **BUF.**

Defense. Shoots left. 6', 200 lbs. Born, Toronto, Ont., July 27, 1969. Washington's 4th choice, 61st overall, in 1989 Entry Draft.

Season	Club	League	GP	G	A	Pts	PIM	PP	SH	GW	S	%	+/-	TF	F%	H	SB	Min	GP	G	A	Pts	PIM	PP	SH	GW
1986-87	St. Michael's	MTJHL	35	13	22	35	40																			
1987-88	St. Michael's	MTJHL	31	19	37	56	22																			
1988-89	Michigan State	CCHA	47	12	25	37	26																			
1989-90	Michigan State	CCHA	45	10	38	48	26																			
1990-91	Michigan State	CCHA	40	15	44	59	24																			
1991-92	Canada	Nat-Team	60	14	30	44	36																			
	Canada	Olympics	8	0	5	5	4																			
	Washington	**NHL**	**1**	**0**	**0**	**0**	**0**	**0**	**0**	**0**	**2**	**0.0**	**1**													
	Baltimore	AHL	15	1	10	11	6																			
1992-93	**Washington**	**NHL**	**26**	**0**	**2**	**2**	**10**	**0**	**0**	**0**	**11**	**0.0**	**3**													
	Baltimore	AHL	29	14	27	41	22												1	0	2	2	0			
1993-94	**Washington**	**NHL**	**10**	**1**	**2**	**3**	**4**	**0**	**0**	**0**	**15**	**6.7**	**2**						**4**	**1**	**0**	**1**	**4**	**0**	**0**	**1**
	Portland Pirates	AHL	41	12	29	41	14												9	2	2	4	4			
1994-95	Detroit Vipers	IHL	48	8	28	36	38																			
	Florida	**NHL**	**34**	**4**	**9**	**13**	**18**	**1**	**0**	**0**	**76**	**5.3**	**–1**													

Season	Club	League	GP	G	A	Pts	PIM	PP	SH	GW	S	%	+/-	TF	F%	H	SB	Min	GP	G	A	Pts	PIM	PP	SH	GW
			Regular Season																Playoffs							
1995-96	**Florida**	**NHL**	**52**	**6**	**28**	**34**	**32**	**3**	**0**	**0**	**98**	**6.1**	**–9**	....	....	....	....	....	**13**	**2**	**6**	**8**	**14**	**1**	**0**	**1**
1996-97	**Florida**	**NHL**	**3**	**0**	**0**	**0**	**2**	**0**	**0**	**0**	**7**	**0.0**	**1**	....	....	....	....	....	....	....	....	....	....	....	....	....
	Pittsburgh	**NHL**	**57**	**6**	**30**	**36**	**28**	**2**	**0**	**1**	**79**	**7.6**	**3**	....	....	....	....	....	**5**	**0**	**3**	**3**	**0**	**0**	**0**	**0**
1997-98	**Buffalo**	**NHL**	**71**	**9**	**26**	**35**	**35**	**3**	**0**	**2**	**129**	**7.0**	**8**	....	....	....	....	....	**15**	**2**	**9**	**11**	**12**	**1**	**0**	**1**
1998-99	**Buffalo**	**NHL**	**80**	**10**	**33**	**43**	**62**	**4**	**0**	**2**	**154**	**6.5**	**16**	**0**	**0.0**	**68**	**67**	**18:43**	**21**	**4**	**11**	**15**	**10**	**2**	**0**	**1**
99-2000	**Buffalo**	**NHL**	**74**	**8**	**25**	**33**	**52**	**2**	**0**	**2**	**113**	**7.1**	**14**	**0**	**0.0**	**43**	**57**	**17:51**	**5**	**0**	**2**	**2**	**2**	**0**	**0**	**0**
2000-01	**Buffalo**	**NHL**	**67**	**5**	**18**	**23**	**46**	**4**	**0**	**3**	**92**	**5.4**	**0**	**0**	**0.0**	**33**	**58**	**17:22**	**8**	**1**	**5**	**6**	**2**	**0**	**0**	**1**
	NHL Totals		**475**	**49**	**173**	**222**	**289**	**19**	**0**	**10**	**776**	**6.3**		**0**	**0.0**	**144**	**182**	**18:01**	**71**	**10**	**36**	**46**	**44**	**4**	**0**	**5**

CCHA First All-Star Team (1991) • NCAA West First All-American Team (1991)

Signed as a free agent by **Florida**, February 15, 1995. Traded to **Pittsburgh** by **Florida** with Stu Barnes for Chris Wells, November 19, 1996. Traded to **Buffalo** by **Pittsburgh** for Buffalo's 5th round choice (Robert Scuderi) in 1998 Entry Draft, September 24, 1997.

WORRELL, Peter

(woh-REHL, PEE-tuhr) **FLA.**

Left wing. Shoots left. 6'6", 245 lbs. Born, Pierrefonds, Que., August 18, 1977. Florida's 7th choice, 166th overall, in 1995 Entry Draft.

Season	Club	League	GP	G	A	Pts	PIM	PP	SH	GW	S	%	+/-	TF	F%	H	SB	Min	GP	G	A	Pts	PIM	PP	SH	GW
1993-94	Lac St-Louis	QAAA	1	0	0	0	0	....	....	....	....	....	....	....	....	....	....	....	1	0	0	0	0	....	....	....
1994-95	Hull Olympiques	QMJHL	56	1	8	9	243	....	....	....	....	....	....	....	....	....	....	....	21	0	1	1	91	....	....	....
1995-96	Hull Olympiques	QMJHL	63	23	36	59	464	....	....	....	....	....	....	....	....	....	....	....	18	11	8	19	81	....	....	....
1996-97	Hull Olympiques	QMJHL	62	17	46	63	437	....	....	....	....	....	....	....	....	....	....	....	14	3	13	16	83	....	....	....
1997-98	**Florida**	**NHL**	**19**	**0**	**0**	**0**	**153**	**0**	**0**	**0**	**15**	**0.0**	**–4**	....	....	....	....	....	....	....	....	....	....	....	....	....
	New Haven	AHL	50	15	12	27	309	....	....	....	....	....	....	....	....	....	....	....	1	0	1	1	6	....	....	....
1998-99	**Florida**	**NHL**	**62**	**4**	**5**	**9**	**258**	**0**	**0**	**2**	**50**	**8.0**	**0**	**0**	**0.0**	**100**	**5**	**6:15**	....	....	....	....	....	....	....	....
	New Haven	AHL	10	3	1	4	65	....	....	....	....	....	....	....	....	....	....	....	....	....	....	....	....	....	....	....
99-2000	**Florida**	**NHL**	**48**	**3**	**6**	**9**	**169**	**2**	**0**	**1**	**45**	**6.7**	**–7**	**1**	**100.0**	**141**	**12**	**8:25**	**4**	**1**	**0**	**1**	**8**	**0**	**0**	**0**
2000-01	**Florida**	**NHL**	**71**	**3**	**7**	**10**	**248**	**0**	**0**	**0**	**86**	**3.5**	**–10**	**3**	**33.3**	**221**	**15**	**9:28**	....	....	....	....	....	....	....	....
	NHL Totals		**200**	**10**	**18**	**28**	**828**	**2**	**0**	**3**	**196**	**5.1**		**4**	**50.0**	**462**	**32**	**8:05**	**4**	**1**	**0**	**1**	**8**	**0**	**0**	**0**

WOTTON, Mark

(WAH-tuhn, MAHRK) **DAL.**

Defense. Shoots left. 6'1", 195 lbs. Born, Foxwarren, Man., November 16, 1973. Vancouver's 11th choice, 237th overall, in 1992 Entry Draft.

Season	Club	League	GP	G	A	Pts	PIM	PP	SH	GW	S	%	+/-	TF	F%	H	SB	Min	GP	G	A	Pts	PIM	PP	SH	GW
1988-89	Foxwarren Blades	MAHA	60	10	30	40	70	....	....	....	....	....	....	....	....	....	....	....	....	....	....	....	....	....	....	....
1989-90	Saskatoon Blades	WHL	51	2	3	5	31	....	....	....	....	....	....	....	....	....	....	....	7	1	1	2	15	....	....	....
1990-91	Saskatoon Blades	WHL	45	4	11	15	37	....	....	....	....	....	....	....	....	....	....	....	....	....	....	....	....	....	....	....
1991-92	Saskatoon Blades	WHL	64	11	25	36	62	....	....	....	....	....	....	....	....	....	....	....	21	2	6	8	22	....	....	....
1992-93	Saskatoon Blades	WHL	71	15	51	66	90	....	....	....	....	....	....	....	....	....	....	....	9	6	5	11	18	....	....	....
1993-94	Saskatoon Blades	WHL	65	12	34	46	108	....	....	....	....	....	....	....	....	....	....	....	16	3	12	15	32	....	....	....
1994-95	Syracuse Crunch	AHL	75	12	29	41	50	....	....	....	....	....	....	....	....	....	....	....	....	....	....	....	....	....	....	....
	Vancouver	**NHL**	**1**	**0**	**0**	**0**	**0**	**0**	**0**	**0**	**2**	**0.0**	**1**	....	....	....	....	....	**5**	**0**	**0**	**0**	**4**	**0**	**0**	**0**
1995-96	Syracuse Crunch	AHL	80	10	35	45	96	....	....	....	....	....	....	....	....	....	....	....	15	1	12	13	20	....	....	....
1996-97	**Vancouver**	**NHL**	**36**	**3**	**6**	**9**	**19**	**0**	**1**	**0**	**41**	**7.3**	**8**	....	....	....	....	....	....	....	....	....	....	....	....	....
	Syracuse Crunch	AHL	27	2	8	10	25	....	....	....	....	....	....	....	....	....	....	....	2	0	0	0	4	....	....	....
1997-98	**Vancouver**	**NHL**	**5**	**0**	**0**	**0**	**6**	**0**	**0**	**0**	**3**	**0.0**	**–2**	....	....	....	....	....	....	....	....	....	....	....	....	....
	Syracuse Crunch	AHL	56	12	21	33	80	....	....	....	....	....	....	....	....	....	....	....	5	0	0	0	12	....	....	....
1998-99	Syracuse Crunch	AHL	72	4	31	35	74	....	....	....	....	....	....	....	....	....	....	....	....	....	....	....	....	....	....	....
99-2000	Michigan K-Wings	IHL	70	3	7	10	72	....	....	....	....	....	....	....	....	....	....	....	....	....	....	....	....	....	....	....
2000-01	**Dallas**	**NHL**	**1**	**0**	**0**	**0**	**0**	**0**	**0**	**0**	**0**	**0.0**	**0**	**0**	**0.0**	**0**	**2**	**13:45**	....	....	....	....	....	....	....	....
	Utah Grizzlies	IHL	63	2	2	4	64	....	....	....	....	....	....	....	....	....	....	....	....	....	....	....	....	....	....	....
	NHL Totals		**43**	**3**	**6**	**9**	**25**	**0**	**1**	**0**	**46**	**6.5**		**0**	**0.0**	**0**	**2**	**13:45**	**5**	**0**	**0**	**0**	**4**	**0**	**0**	**0**

WHL East Second All-Star Team (1994)

Signed as a free agent by **Dallas**, July 19, 1999.

WREN, Bob

(REHN, BAWB) **TOR.**

Center. Shoots left. 5'10", 185 lbs. Born, Preston, Ont., September 16, 1974. Los Angeles' 3rd choice, 94th overall, in 1993 Entry Draft.

Season	Club	League	GP	G	A	Pts	PIM	PP	SH	GW	S	%	+/-	TF	F%	H	SB	Min	GP	G	A	Pts	PIM	PP	SH	GW
1989-90	Guelph Jr. B's	OJHL-B	48	24	36	60	82	....	....	....	....	....	....	....	....	....	....	....	....	....	....	....	....	....	....	....
1990-91	Guelph Jr. B's	OJHL-B	18	17	13	30	51	....	....	....	....	....	....	....	....	....	....	....	....	....	....	....	....	....	....	....
	Kingston	OCJHL	14	10	15	25	34	....	....	....	....	....	....	....	....	....	....	....	....	....	....	....	....	....	....	....
1991-92	Detroit	OHL	62	13	36	49	58	....	....	....	....	....	....	....	....	....	....	....	7	3	4	7	19	....	....	....
1992-93	Detroit Jr. Wings	OHL	63	57	88	145	91	....	....	....	....	....	....	....	....	....	....	....	15	4	11	15	20	....	....	....
1993-94	Detroit Jr. Wings	OHL	57	45	64	109	81	....	....	....	....	....	....	....	....	....	....	....	17	12	18	30	20	....	....	....
1994-95	Springfield	AHL	61	16	15	31	118	....	....	....	....	....	....	....	....	....	....	....	....	....	....	....	....	....	....	....
	Richmond	ECHL	2	0	1	1	0	....	....	....	....	....	....	....	....	....	....	....	....	....	....	....	....	....	....	....
1995-96	Detroit Vipers	IHL	1	0	0	0	0	....	....	....	....	....	....	....	....	....	....	....	....	....	....	....	....	....	....	....
	Knoxville	ECHL	50	21	35	56	257	....	....	....	....	....	....	....	....	....	....	....	8	4	11	15	32	....	....	....
1996-97	Baltimore Bandits	AHL	72	23	36	59	97	....	....	....	....	....	....	....	....	....	....	....	3	1	1	2	0	....	....	....
1997-98	**Anaheim**	**NHL**	**3**	**0**	**0**	**0**	**0**	**0**	**0**	**0**	**4**	**0.0**	**0**	....	....	....	....	....	....	....	....	....	....	....	....	....
	Cincinnati Ducks	AHL	77	*42	58	100	151	....	....	....	....	....	....	....	....	....	....	....	....	....	....	....	....	....	....	....
1998-99	Cincinnati Ducks	AHL	73	27	43	70	102	....	....	....	....	....	....	....	....	....	....	....	3	1	2	3	8	....	....	....
99-2000	Cincinnati Ducks	AHL	57	24	38	62	61	....	....	....	....	....	....	....	....	....	....	....	....	....	....	....	....	....	....	....
2000-01	**Anaheim**	**NHL**	**1**	**0**	**0**	**0**	**0**	**0**	**0**	**0**	**0**	**0.0**	**–1**	**0**	**0.0**	**0**	**0**	**11:41**	....	....	....	....	....	....	....	....
	Cincinnati Ducks	AHL	70	20	47	67	103	....	....	....	....	....	....	....	....	....	....	....	4	4	2	6	2	....	....	....
	NHL Totals		**4**	**0**	**0**	**0**	**0**	**0**	**0**	**0**	**4**	**0.0**		**0**	**0.0**	**0**	**0**	**11:41**	....	....	....	....	....	....	....	....

OHL Second All-Star Team (1993, 1994)

Signed as a free agent by **Hartford**, September 6, 1994. Signed as a free agent by **Anaheim**, August 1, 1997. Signed as a free agent by **Toronto**, July 24, 2001.

WRIGHT, Jamie

(RIGHT, JAY-mee) **CGY.**

Left wing. Shoots left. 6', 195 lbs. Born, Kitchener, Ont., May 13, 1976. Dallas' 3rd choice, 98th overall, in 1994 Entry Draft.

Season	Club	League	GP	G	A	Pts	PIM	PP	SH	GW	S	%	+/-	TF	F%	H	SB	Min	GP	G	A	Pts	PIM	PP	SH	GW
1991-92	Elmira Kings	OJHL-B	44	17	11	28	46	....	....	....	....	....	....	....	....	....	....	....	....	....	....	....	....	....	....	....
1992-93	Elmira Kings	OJHL-B	47	22	32	54	52	....	....	....	....	....	....	....	....	....	....	....	....	....	....	....	....	....	....	....
1993-94	Guelph Storm	OHL	65	17	15	32	34	....	....	....	....	....	....	....	....	....	....	....	8	2	1	3	10	....	....	....
1994-95	Guelph Storm	OHL	65	43	39	82	36	....	....	....	....	....	....	....	....	....	....	....	14	6	8	14	6	....	....	....
1995-96	Guelph Storm	OHL	55	30	36	66	45	....	....	....	....	....	....	....	....	....	....	....	16	10	12	22	35	....	....	....
1996-97	Michigan K-Wings	IHL	60	6	8	14	34	....	....	....	....	....	....	....	....	....	....	....	1	0	0	0	0	....	....	....
1997-98	**Dallas**	**NHL**	**21**	**4**	**2**	**6**	**2**	**0**	**0**	**2**	**15**	**26.7**	**8**	....	....	....	....	....	**5**	**0**	**0**	**0**	**0**	**0**	**0**	**0**
	Michigan K-Wings	IHL	53	15	11	26	31	....	....	....	....	....	....	....	....	....	....	....	....	....	....	....	....	....	....	....
1998-99	**Dallas**	**NHL**	**11**	**0**	**0**	**0**	**0**	**0**	**0**	**0**	**10**	**0.0**	**–3**	**0**	**0.0**	**18**	**4**	**7:37**	....	....	....	....	....	....	....	....
	Michigan K-Wings	IHL	64	16	15	31	92	....	....	....	....	....	....	....	....	....	....	....	2	0	0	0	2	....	....	....
99-2000	**Dallas**	**NHL**	**23**	**1**	**4**	**5**	**16**	**0**	**0**	**0**	**15**	**6.7**	**4**	**2**	**50.0**	**53**	**5**	**9:50**	....	....	....	....	....	....	....	....
	Michigan K-Wings	IHL	49	12	4	16	64	....	....	....	....	....	....	....	....	....	....	....	....	....	....	....	....	....	....	....
2000-01	**Dallas**	**NHL**	**2**	**1**	**0**	**1**	**0**	**0**	**0**	**0**	**4**	**25.0**	**–3**	**1**	**0.0**	**3**	**1**	**10:45**	....	....	....	....	....	....	....	....
	Utah Grizzlies	IHL	74	25	27	52	126	....	....	....	....	....	....	....	....	....	....	....	....	....	....	....	....	....	....	....
	NHL Totals		**57**	**6**	**6**	**12**	**18**	**0**	**0**	**2**	**44**	**13.6**		**3**	**33.3**	**74**	**10**	**9:12**	**5**	**0**	**0**	**0**	**0**	**0**	**0**	**0**

Signed as a free agent by **Calgary**, August 2, 2001.

WRIGHT, Tyler

(RIGHT, TIGH-luhr) **CBJ**

Center. Shoots right. 6', 185 lbs. Born, Canora, Sask., April 6, 1973. Edmonton's 1st choice, 12th overall, in 1991 Entry Draft.

Season	Club	League	GP	G	A	Pts	PIM	PP	SH	GW	S	%	+/-	TF	F%	H	SB	Min	GP	G	A	Pts	PIM	PP	SH	GW
1988-89	Swift Current	SMHL	36	20	13	33	102	....	....	....	....	....	....	....	....	....	....	....	....	....	....	....	....	....	....	....
1989-90	Swift Current	WHL	67	14	18	32	119	....	....	....	....	....	....	....	....	....	....	....	4	0	0	0	12	....	....	....
1990-91	Swift Current	WHL	66	41	51	92	157	....	....	....	....	....	....	....	....	....	....	....	3	0	0	0	6	....	....	....
1991-92	Swift Current	WHL	63	36	46	82	185	....	....	....	....	....	....	....	....	....	....	....	8	2	5	7	16	....	....	....
1992-93	Swift Current	WHL	37	24	41	65	76	....	....	....	....	....	....	....	....	....	....	....	17	9	17	26	*49	....	....	....
	Edmonton	**NHL**	**7**	**1**	**1**	**2**	**19**	**0**	**0**	**0**	**7**	**14.3**	**–4**	....	....	....	....	....	....	....	....	....	....	....	....	....
1993-94	**Edmonton**	**NHL**	**5**	**0**	**0**	**0**	**4**	**0**	**0**	**0**	**2**	**0.0**	**–3**	....	....	....	....	....	....	....	....	....	....	....	....	....
	Cape Breton	AHL	65	14	27	41	160	....	....	....	....	....	....	....	....	....	....	....	5	2	0	2	11	....	....	....
1994-95	Cape Breton	AHL	70	16	15	31	184	....	....	....	....	....	....	....	....	....	....	....	....	....	....	....	....	....	....	....
	Edmonton	**NHL**	**6**	**1**	**0**	**1**	**14**	**0**	**0**	**0**	**6**	**16.7**	**1**	....	....	....	....	....	....	....	....	....	....	....	....	....

			Regular Season																Playoffs							
Season	Club	League	GP	G	A	Pts	PIM	PP	SH	GW	S	%	+/-	TF	F%	H	SB	Min	GP	G	A	Pts	PIM	PP	SH	GW
1995-96	**Edmonton**	**NHL**	**23**	**1**	**0**	**1**	**33**	**0**	**0**	**0**	**18**	**5.6**	**–7**													
	Cape Breton	AHL	31	6	12	18	158																			
1996-97	**Pittsburgh**	**NHL**	**45**	**2**	**2**	**4**	**70**	**0**	**0**	**2**	**30**	**6.7**	**–7**													
	Cleveland	IHL	10	4	3	7	34												14	4	2	6	44			
1997-98	**Pittsburgh**	**NHL**	**82**	**3**	**4**	**7**	**112**	**1**	**0**	**0**	**46**	**6.5**	**–3**						**6**	**0**	**1**	**1**	**4**	**0**	**0**	**0**
1998-99	**Pittsburgh**	**NHL**	**61**	**0**	**0**	**0**	**90**	**0**	**0**	**0**	**16**	**0.0**	**–2**	**122**	**46.7**	**57**	**3**	**3:46**	**13**	**0**	**0**	**0**	**19**	**0**	**0**	**0**
99-2000	**Pittsburgh**	**NHL**	**50**	**12**	**10**	**22**	**45**	**0**	**0**	**1**	**68**	**17.6**	**4**	**698**	**47.1**	**89**	**13**	**13:24**	**11**	**3**	**1**	**4**	**17**	**0**	**0**	**0**
	Wilkes-Barre	AHL	25	5	15	20	86																			
2000-01	**Columbus**	**NHL**	**76**	**16**	**16**	**32**	**140**	**4**	**1**	**2**	**141**	**11.3**	**–9**	**999**	**45.1**	**197**	**42**	**17:41**								
	NHL Totals		**355**	**36**	**33**	**69**	**527**	**5**	**1**	**5**	**334**	**10.8**		**1819**	**46.0**	**343**	**58**	**11:60**	**30**	**3**	**2**	**5**	**40**	**0**	**0**	**0**

Traded to **Pittsburgh** by **Edmonton** for Pittsburgh's 7th round choice (Brandon Lafrance) in 1996 Entry Draft, June 22, 1996. Selected by **Columbus** from **Pittsburgh** in Expansion Draft, June 23, 2000.

YACHMENEV, Vitali (YATCH-muh-nehv, VIH-tal-ee) NSH.

Left wing. Shoots left. 5'11", 195 lbs. Born, Chelyabinsk, USSR, January 8, 1975. Los Angeles' 3rd choice, 59th overall, in 1994 Entry Draft.

1990-91	HC Chelyabinsk	CIS-Jr.	80	88	60	148	72																			
1991-92	HC Chelyabinsk	CIS-Jr.	80	82	70	152	20																			
1992-93	HC Chelyabinsk	CIS-2	51	23	20	43	12																			
1993-94	North Bay	OHL	66	*61	52	113	18												18	13	19	32	12			
1994-95	North Bay	OHL	59	53	52	105	8												6	1	8	9	2			
	Phoenix	IHL																	4	1	0	1	0			
1995-96	**Los Angeles**	**NHL**	**80**	**19**	**34**	**53**	**16**	**6**	**1**	**2**	**133**	**14.3**	**–3**													
1996-97	**Los Angeles**	**NHL**	**65**	**10**	**22**	**32**	**10**	**2**	**0**	**2**	**97**	**10.3**	**–9**													
1997-98	**Los Angeles**	**NHL**	**4**	**0**	**1**	**1**	**4**	**0**	**0**	**0**	**4**	**0.0**	**1**													
	Long Beach	IHL	59	23	28	51	14												17	8	9	17	4			
1998-99	**Nashville**	**NHL**	**55**	**7**	**10**	**17**	**10**	**0**	**1**	**2**	**83**	**8.4**	**–10**	**0**	**0.0**	**28**	**21**	**15:06**								
	Milwaukee	IHL	16	7	6	13	0																			
99-2000	**Nashville**	**NHL**	**68**	**16**	**16**	**32**	**12**	**1**	**1**	**3**	**120**	**13.3**	**5**	**8**	**25.0**	**26**	**19**	**15:26**								
2000-01	**Nashville**	**NHL**	**78**	**15**	**19**	**34**	**10**	**4**	**1**	**4**	**123**	**12.2**	**–5**	**29**	**37.9**	**40**	**38**	**17:52**								
	NHL Totals		**350**	**67**	**102**	**169**	**62**	**13**	**4**	**13**	**560**	**12.0**		**37**	**35.1**	**94**	**78**	**16:17**								

Canadian Major Junior Rookie of the Year (1994)

Traded to **Nashville** by **LA Kings** for future considerations, July 7, 1998.

YAKE, Terry (YAYK, TAIR-ee)

Center. Shoots right. 5'11", 190 lbs. Born, New Westminster, B.C., October 22, 1968. Hartford's 3rd choice, 81st overall, in 1987 Entry Draft.

1984-85	Brandon	WHL	11	1	1	2	0																			
1985-86	Brandon	WHL	72	26	26	52	49																			
1986-87	Brandon	WHL	71	44	58	102	64																			
1987-88	Brandon	WHL	72	55	85	140	59												4	5	6	11	12			
1988-89	**Hartford**	**NHL**	**2**	**0**	**0**	**0**	**0**	**0**	**0**	**0**	**0**	**0.0**	**1**													
	Binghamton	AHL	75	39	56	95	57																			
1989-90	**Hartford**	**NHL**	**2**	**0**	**1**	**1**	**0**	**0**	**0**	**0**	**2**	**0.0**	**–1**													
	Binghamton	AHL	77	13	42	55	37																			
1990-91	**Hartford**	**NHL**	**19**	**1**	**4**	**5**	**10**	**0**	**0**	**1**	**19**	**5.3**	**–3**						**6**	**1**	**1**	**2**	**16**	**0**	**1**	**0**
	Springfield	AHL	60	35	42	77	56												15	9	9	18	10			
1991-92	**Hartford**	**NHL**	**15**	**1**	**1**	**2**	**4**	**0**	**0**	**0**	**12**	**8.3**	**–2**													
	Springfield	AHL	53	21	34	55	63												8	3	4	7	2			
1992-93	**Hartford**	**NHL**	**66**	**22**	**31**	**53**	**46**	**4**	**1**	**2**	**98**	**22.4**	**3**													
	Springfield	AHL	16	8	14	22	27																			
1993-94	**Anaheim**	**NHL**	**82**	**21**	**31**	**52**	**44**	**5**	**0**	**2**	**188**	**11.2**	**2**													
1994-95	**Toronto**	**NHL**	**19**	**3**	**2**	**5**	**2**	**1**	**0**	**2**	**26**	**11.5**	**1**													
	Denver Grizzlies	IHL	2	0	3	3	2												17	4	11	15	16			
1995-96	Milwaukee	IHL	70	32	56	88	70												5	3	6	9	4			
1996-97	Rochester	AHL	78	34	*67	101	77												10	8	8	16	2			
1997-98	**St. Louis**	**NHL**	**65**	**10**	**15**	**25**	**38**	**3**	**1**	**4**	**60**	**16.7**	**1**						**10**	**2**	**1**	**3**	**6**	**2**	**0**	**1**
1998-99	**St. Louis**	**NHL**	**60**	**9**	**18**	**27**	**34**	**3**	**0**	**4**	**59**	**15.3**	**–9**	**453**	**48.1**	**39**	**17**	**14:50**	**13**	**1**	**2**	**3**	**14**	**1**	**0**	**0**
	Worcester	AHL	24	8	11	19	26																			
99-2000	**St. Louis**	**NHL**	**26**	**4**	**9**	**13**	**22**	**2**	**0**	**2**	**26**	**15.4**	**2**	**129**	**55.8**	**18**	**8**	**13:51**								
	Washington	**NHL**	**35**	**6**	**5**	**11**	**12**	**1**	**0**	**1**	**29**	**20.7**	**2**	**219**	**51.1**	**9**	**8**	**12:36**	**3**	**0**	**0**	**0**	**0**	**0**	**0**	**0**
2000-01	**Washington**	**NHL**	**12**	**0**	**3**	**3**	**8**	**0**	**0**	**0**	**13**	**0.0**	**0**	**32**	**65.6**	**3**	**4**	**12:11**								
	Portland Pirates	AHL	55	11	38	49	47												3	0	1	1	12			
	NHL Totals		**403**	**77**	**120**	**197**	**220**	**19**	**2**	**18**	**532**	**14.5**		**833**	**50.8**	**69**	**37**	**13:49**	**32**	**4**	**4**	**8**	**36**	**3**	**1**	**1**

Claimed by **Anaheim** from **Hartford** in Expansion Draft, June 24, 1993. Traded to **Toronto** by **Anaheim** for David Sacco, September 28, 1994. Signed as a free agent by **Buffalo**, September 17, 1996. Signed as a free agent by **St. Louis**, July 24, 1997. Claimed by **Atlanta** from **St. Louis** in Expansion Draft, June 25, 1999. Claimed by **St. Louis** from **Atlanta** in Waiver Draft, September 27, 1999. Claimed on waivers by **Washington** from **St. Louis**, January 18, 2000.

YAKUSHIN, Dmitri (yah-KOO-shihn, DIH-mee-TREE) TOR.

Defense. Shoots left. 6', 200 lbs. Born, Kharkov, USSR, January 21, 1978. Toronto's 9th choice, 140th overall, in 1996 Entry Draft.

1995-96	Pembroke Kings	OCJHL	31	8	5	13	62																			
1996-97	Edmonton Ice	WHL	63	3	14	17	103																			
1997-98	Edmonton Ice	WHL	29	1	10	11	41																			
	Regina Pats	WHL	13	0	14	14	16												9	2	8	10	12			
1998-99	St. John's Leafs	AHL	71	2	6	8	65												4	0	0	0	0			
99-2000	**Toronto**	**NHL**	**2**	**0**	**0**	**0**	**2**	**0**	**0**	**0**	**1**	**0.0**	**0**	**0**	**0.0**	**3**	**1**	**10:03**								
	St. John's Leafs	AHL	64	1	13	14	106																			
2000-01	St. John's Leafs	AHL	45	2	0	0	61												1	0	0	0	0			
	NHL Totals		**2**	**0**	**0**	**0**	**2**	**0**	**0**	**0**	**1**	**0.0**		**0**	**0.0**	**3**	**1**	**10:03**								

YASHIN, Alexei (YAH-shin, al-EHX-ay) NYI

Center. Shoots right. 6'3", 225 lbs. Born, Sverdlovsk, USSR, November 5, 1973. Ottawa's 1st choice, 2nd overall, in 1992 Entry Draft.

1990-91	HC Sverdlovsk	USSR	26	2	1	3	10																			
1991-92	Dynamo Moscow	CIS	35	7	5	12	19																			
1992-93	Dynamo Moscow	CIS	27	10	12	22	18												10	7	3	10	18			
1993-94	**Ottawa**	**NHL**	**83**	**30**	**49**	**79**	**22**	**11**	**2**	**3**	**232**	**12.9**	**–49**													
1994-95	Las Vegas	IHL	24	15	20	35	32																			
	Ottawa	**NHL**	**47**	**21**	**23**	**44**	**20**	**11**	**0**	**1**	**154**	**13.6**	**–20**													
1995-96	CSKA Moscow	CIS	4	2	2	4	4																			
	Ottawa	**NHL**	**46**	**15**	**24**	**39**	**28**	**8**	**0**	**1**	**143**	**10.5**	**–15**													
1996-97	**Ottawa**	**NHL**	**82**	**35**	**40**	**75**	**44**	**10**	**0**	**5**	**291**	**12.0**	**–7**						**7**	**1**	**5**	**6**	**2**	**1**	**0**	**0**
1997-98	**Ottawa**	**NHL**	**82**	**33**	**39**	**72**	**24**	**5**	**0**	**6**	**291**	**11.3**	**6**						**11**	**5**	**3**	**8**	**8**	**3**	**0**	**2**
	Russia	Olympics	6	3	3	6	0																			
1998-99	**Ottawa**	**NHL**	**82**	**44**	**50**	**94**	**54**	**19**	**0**	**5**	**337**	**13.1**	**16**	**1428**	**41.9**	**73**	**22**	**22:05**	**4**	**0**	**0**	**0**	**10**	**0**	**0**	**0**
99-2000	**Ottawa**	**NHL**	DID NOT PLAY – SUSPENDED																							
2000-01	**Ottawa**	**NHL**	**82**	**40**	**48**	**88**	**30**	**13**	**2**	**10**	**263**	**15.2**	**10**	**1414**	**43.1**	**50**	**28**	**20:24**	**4**	**0**	**1**	**1**	**0**	**0**	**0**	**0**
	NHL Totals		**504**	**218**	**273**	**491**	**222**	**77**	**4**	**31**	**1711**	**12.7**		**2842**	**42.5**	**123**	**50**	**21:14**	**26**	**6**	**9**	**15**	**20**	**4**	**0**	**2**

NHL Second All-Star Team (1999) • Played in NHL All-Star Game (1994, 1999)

• Suspended for entire 1999-2000 season by **Ottawa** for refusing to report to team, November 9, 1999. Traded to **NY Islanders** by **Ottawa** for Bill Muckalt, Zdeno Chara and NY Islanders' 1st round choice (Jason Spezza) in 2001 Entry Draft, June 23, 2001.

			Regular Season																Playoffs							
Season	Club	League	GP	G	A	Pts	PIM	PP	SH	GW	S	%	+/-	TF	F%	H	SB	Min	GP	G	A	Pts	PIM	PP	SH	GW

YEGOROV, Alexei

(yeh-GOH-rohv, al-EHX-ay)

Right wing. Shoots left. 5'11", 185 lbs. Born, St. Petersburg, USSR, May 21, 1975. San Jose's 3rd choice, 66th overall, in 1994 Entry Draft.

Season	Club	League	GP	G	A	Pts	PIM	PP	SH	GW	S	%	+/-	TF	F%	H	SB	Min	GP	G	A	Pts	PIM	PP	SH	GW
1992-93	St. Petersburg	CIS	17	1	2	3	10												6	3	1	4	6			
1993-94	St. Petersburg	CIS	23	5	3	8	18												6	0	0	0	4			
1994-95	St. Petersburg	CIS	10	2	1	3	10																			
	Fort Worth Fire	CHL	18	4	10	14	15																			
1995-96	**San Jose**	**NHL**	**9**	**3**	**2**	**5**	**2**	**2**	**0**	**0**	**10**	**30.0**	**-5**													
	Kansas City	IHL	65	31	25	56	84												5	2	0	2	8			
1996-97	**San Jose**	**NHL**	**2**	**0**	**1**	**1**	**0**	**0**	**0**	**0**	**0**	**0.0**	**1**													
	Kentucky	AHL	75	26	32	58	59												4	0	1	1	2			
1997-98	Kentucky	AHL	79	32	52	84	56												3	2	0	2	0			
1998-99	Torpedo Yaroslavl	Russia	13	3	1	4	8																			
	St. Petersburg	Russia	25	8	8	16	30																			
99-2000	Adirondack	UHL	41	16	26	42	35																			
	Long Beach	IHL	20	4	9	13	8												6	1	0	1	2			
2000-01	Schwenningen	DEL	55	6	16	22	24																			
	NHL Totals		**11**	**3**	**3**	**6**	**2**	**2**	**0**	**0**	**10**	**30.0**														

Claimed by **Atlanta** from **San Jose** in Expansion Draft, June 25, 1999.

YELLE, Stephane

(YEHL, STEH-fan) **COL.**

Center. Shoots left. 6'1", 190 lbs. Born, Ottawa, Ont., May 9, 1974. New Jersey's 9th choice, 186th overall, in 1992 Entry Draft.

Season	Club	League	GP	G	A	Pts	PIM	PP	SH	GW	S	%	+/-	TF	F%	H	SB	Min	GP	G	A	Pts	PIM	PP	SH	GW
1990-91	Cumberland	OJHL-B	33	20	30	50	16																			
1991-92	Oshawa Generals	OHL	55	12	14	26	20												7	2	0	2	1			
1992-93	Oshawa Generals	OHL	66	24	50	74	20												10	2	4	6	4			
1993-94	Oshawa Generals	OHL	66	35	69	104	22												5	1	7	8	2			
1994-95	Cornwall Aces	AHL	40	18	15	33	22												13	7	7	14	8			
1995-96♦	**Colorado**	**NHL**	**71**	**13**	**14**	**27**	**30**	**0**	**2**	**1**	**93**	**14.0**	**15**						**22**	**1**	**4**	**5**	**8**	**0**	**1**	**0**
1996-97	**Colorado**	**NHL**	**79**	**9**	**17**	**26**	**38**	**0**	**1**	**1**	**89**	**10.1**	**1**						**12**	**1**	**6**	**7**	**2**	**0**	**0**	**0**
1997-98	**Colorado**	**NHL**	**81**	**7**	**15**	**22**	**48**	**0**	**1**	**0**	**93**	**7.5**	**-10**						**7**	**1**	**0**	**1**	**12**	**0**	**0**	**0**
1998-99	**Colorado**	**NHL**	**72**	**8**	**7**	**15**	**40**	**1**	**0**	**0**	**99**	**8.1**	**-8**	**1201**	**51.2**	**136**	**72**	**15:15**	**10**	**0**	**1**	**1**	**6**	**0**	**0**	**0**
99-2000	**Colorado**	**NHL**	**79**	**8**	**14**	**22**	**28**	**0**	**1**	**1**	**90**	**8.9**	**9**	**1294**	**52.2**	**140**	**81**	**15:51**	**17**	**1**	**2**	**3**	**4**	**0**	**0**	**0**
2000-01♦	**Colorado**	**NHL**	**50**	**4**	**10**	**14**	**20**	**0**	**1**	**0**	**54**	**7.4**	**-3**	**736**	**56.4**	**92**	**29**	**14:28**	**23**	**1**	**2**	**3**	**8**	**0**	**0**	**1**
	NHL Totals		**432**	**49**	**77**	**126**	**204**	**1**	**6**	**3**	**518**	**9.5**		**3231**	**52.8**	**368**	**182**	**15:18**	**91**	**5**	**15**	**20**	**40**	**0**	**1**	**1**

Traded to **Quebec** by **New Jersey** with New Jersey's 11th round choice (Steven Low) in 1994 Entry Draft for Quebec's 11th round choice (Mike Hanson) in 1994 Entry Draft, June 1, 1994. Transferred to **Colorado** after **Quebec** franchise relocated, June 21, 1995.

YLONEN, Juha

(YOO-lih-nehn, YOO-hah) **T.B.**

Center. Shoots left. 6'1", 189 lbs. Born, Helsinki, Finland, February 13, 1972. Winnipeg's 3rd choice, 91st overall, in 1991 Entry Draft.

Season	Club	League	GP	G	A	Pts	PIM	PP	SH	GW	S	%	+/-	TF	F%	H	SB	Min	GP	G	A	Pts	PIM	PP	SH	GW
1988-89	Kiekko Espoo	Finn-Jr.	31	9	14	23	8																			
1989-90	Kiekko Espoo	Finn-Jr.	4	1	5	6	0												5	1	5	6	0			
	Kiekko Espoo	Finland-2	38	10	17	27	12																			
1990-91	Kiekko Espoo	Finn-Jr.	5	3	1	4	2																			
	Kiekko Espoo	Finland-2	40	12	21	33	4																			
1991-92	HPK Hameenlinna	Finn-Jr.	2	1	2	3	0																			
	HPK Hameenlinna	Finland-2	9	8	14	22	0																			
	HPK Hameenlinna	Finland	43	7	11	18	8																			
1992-93	HPK Hameenlinna	Finland	48	8	18	26	22												12	3	5	8	2			
	HPK Hameenlinna	Finn-Jr.	2	2	1	3	0												1	0	0	0	0			
1993-94	Jokerit Helsinki	Finland	37	5	11	16	2												12	1	3	4	8			
1994-95	Jokerit Helsinki	Finland	50	13	15	28	10												11	3	2	5	0			
1995-96	Jokerit Helsinki	Finland	24	3	13	16	20												11	4	5	9	4			
1996-97	**Phoenix**	**NHL**	**2**	**0**	**0**	**0**	**0**	**0**	**0**	**0**	**2**	**0.0**	**0**													
	Springfield	AHL	70	20	41	61	6												17	5	*16	21	4			
1997-98	**Phoenix**	**NHL**	**55**	**1**	**11**	**12**	**10**	**0**	**1**	**0**	**60**	**1.7**	**-3**													
	Finland	Olympics	6	0	0	0	8																			
1998-99	**Phoenix**	**NHL**	**59**	**6**	**17**	**23**	**20**	**2**	**0**	**1**	**66**	**9.1**	**18**	**297**	**46.5**	**48**	**37**	**15:55**	**2**	**0**	**2**	**2**	**2**	**0**	**0**	**0**
99-2000	**Phoenix**	**NHL**	**76**	**6**	**23**	**29**	**12**	**0**	**1**	**1**	**82**	**7.3**	**-6**	**753**	**45.6**	**52**	**51**	**16:43**	**1**	**0**	**0**	**0**	**0**	**0**	**0**	**0**
2000-01	**Phoenix**	**NHL**	**69**	**9**	**14**	**23**	**38**	**0**	**1**	**1**	**72**	**12.5**	**10**	**163**	**41.1**	**42**	**36**	**14:18**								
	NHL Totals		**261**	**22**	**65**	**87**	**80**	**2**	**3**	**3**	**282**	**7.8**		**1213**	**45.2**	**142**	**124**	**15:40**	**3**	**0**	**2**	**2**	**2**	**0**	**0**	**0**

Rights transferred to **Phoenix** after **Winnipeg** franchise relocated, July 1, 1996. Traded to **Tampa Bay** by **Phoenix** for Todd Warriner, June 18, 2001.

YORK, Jason

(YOHRK, JAY-suhn) **ANA.**

Defense. Shoots right. 6'1", 200 lbs. Born, Nepean, Ont., May 20, 1970. Detroit's 6th choice, 129th overall, in 1990 Entry Draft.

Season	Club	League	GP	G	A	Pts	PIM	PP	SH	GW	S	%	+/-	TF	F%	H	SB	Min	GP	G	A	Pts	PIM	PP	SH	GW
1986-87	Smiths Falls Bears	OCJHL	46	6	13	19	86																			
1987-88	Hamilton Hawks	OHL	58	4	9	13	110																			
1988-89	Windsor Spitfires	OHL	65	19	44	63	105																			
1989-90	Windsor Spitfires	OHL	39	9	30	39	38																			
	Kitchener	OHL	25	11	25	36	17												17	3	19	22	10			
1990-91	Windsor Spitfires	OHL	66	13	80	93	40												11	3	10	13	12			
1991-92	Adirondack	AHL	49	4	20	24	32												5	0	1	1	0			
1992-93	**Detroit**	**NHL**	**2**	**0**	**0**	**0**	**0**	**0**	**0**	**0**	**1**	**0.0**	**0**													
	Adirondack	AHL	77	15	40	55	86												11	0	3	3	18			
1993-94	**Detroit**	**NHL**	**7**	**1**	**2**	**3**	**2**	**0**	**0**	**0**	**9**	**11.1**	**0**													
	Adirondack	AHL	74	10	56	66	98												12	3	11	14	22			
1994-95	**Detroit**	**NHL**	**10**	**1**	**2**	**3**	**2**	**0**	**0**	**0**	**6**	**16.7**	**0**													
	Adirondack	AHL	5	1	3	4	4																			
	Anaheim	**NHL**	**15**	**0**	**8**	**8**	**12**	**0**	**0**	**0**	**22**	**0.0**	**4**													
1995-96	**Anaheim**	**NHL**	**79**	**3**	**21**	**24**	**88**	**0**	**0**	**0**	**106**	**2.8**	**-7**													
1996-97	**Ottawa**	**NHL**	**75**	**4**	**17**	**21**	**67**	**1**	**0**	**0**	**121**	**3.3**	**-8**						**7**	**0**	**0**	**0**	**4**	**0**	**0**	**0**
1997-98	**Ottawa**	**NHL**	**73**	**3**	**13**	**16**	**62**	**0**	**0**	**0**	**109**	**2.8**	**8**						**7**	**1**	**1**	**2**	**7**	**1**	**0**	**0**
1998-99	**Ottawa**	**NHL**	**79**	**4**	**31**	**35**	**48**	**2**	**0**	**0**	**177**	**2.3**	**17**	**2**	**0.0**	**166**	**127**	**23:49**	**4**	**1**	**1**	**2**	**4**	**0**	**0**	**0**
99-2000	**Ottawa**	**NHL**	**79**	**8**	**22**	**30**	**60**	**1**	**0**	**1**	**159**	**5.0**	**-3**	**0**	**0.0**	**158**	**111**	**23:20**	**6**	**0**	**2**	**2**	**2**	**0**	**0**	**0**
2000-01	**Ottawa**	**NHL**	**74**	**6**	**16**	**22**	**72**	**3**	**0**	**2**	**133**	**4.5**	**7**	**0**	**0.0**	**167**	**101**	**23:49**	**4**	**0**	**0**	**0**	**4**	**0**	**0**	**0**
	NHL Totals		**493**	**30**	**132**	**162**	**413**	**7**	**0**	**3**	**843**	**3.6**		**2**	**0.0**	**491**	**339**	**23:39**	**28**	**2**	**4**	**6**	**21**	**1**	**0**	**0**

AHL First All-Star Team (1994)

Traded to **Anaheim** by **Detroit** with Mike Sillinger for Stu Grimson, Mark Ferner and Anaheim's 6th round choice (Magnus Nilsson) in 1996 Entry Draft, April 4, 1995. Traded to **Ottawa** by **Anaheim** with Shaun Van Allen for Ted Drury and the rights to Marc Moro, October 1, 1996. Signed as a free agent by **Anaheim**, July 3, 2001.

YORK, Mike

(YOHRK, MIGHK) **NYR**

Center. Shoots right. 5'10", 185 lbs. Born, Waterford, MI, January 3, 1978. NY Rangers' 7th choice, 136th overall, in 1997 Entry Draft.

Season	Club	League	GP	G	A	Pts	PIM	PP	SH	GW	S	%	+/-	TF	F%	H	SB	Min	GP	G	A	Pts	PIM	PP	SH	GW
1992-93	Michigan Nats	MNHL	50	45	50	95	....																			
1993-94	Det-Compuware	MNHL	85	136	140	276	....																			
1994-95	Thornhill Islanders	MTJHL	49	39	54	*93	44												11	7	6	13	0			
1995-96	Michigan State	CCHA	39	12	27	39	20																			
1996-97	Michigan State	CCHA	37	18	29	47	42																			
1997-98	Michigan State	CCHA	40	27	34	61	38																			
1998-99	Michigan State	CCHA	42	22	32	*54	41																			
	Hartford	AHL	3	2	2	4	0												6	3	1	4	0			
99-2000	**NY Rangers**	**NHL**	**82**	**26**	**24**	**50**	**18**	**8**	**0**	**4**	**177**	**14.7**	**-17**	**1131**	**48.1**	**75**	**23**	**15:50**								
2000-01	**NY Rangers**	**NHL**	**79**	**14**	**17**	**31**	**20**	**3**	**2**	**4**	**171**	**8.2**	**1**	**1098**	**46.9**	**78**	**41**	**17:45**								
	NHL Totals		**161**	**40**	**41**	**81**	**38**	**11**	**2**	**8**	**348**	**11.5**		**2229**	**23.1**	**153**	**64**	**17:45**								

MTJHL Bauer Divison Rookie of the Year (1995) • MTJHL Bauer Divison All-Star Team (1995) • CCHA Second All-Star Team (1998) • NCAA West First All-American Team (1998, 1999) • CCHA First All-Star Team (1999) • NHL All-Rookie Team (2000)

YOUNG, B.J.

(YUHNG, BEE-JAY)

Right wing. Shoots right. 5'10", 178 lbs. Born, Anchorage, AK, July 23, 1977. Detroit's 5th choice, 157th overall, in 1997 Entry Draft.

			Regular Season																Playoffs							
Season	Club	League	GP	G	A	Pts	PIM	PP	SH	GW	S	%	+/-	TF	F%	H	SB	Min	GP	G	A	Pts	PIM	PP	SH	GW
1992-93	Anchorage Stars	AAHL	50	48	60	108	94	....	....	....	....	....	....	....	....	....	....	....	....	....	....	....	....	....	....	....
1993-94	Tri-City Americans	WHL	54	19	24	43	66	....	....	....	....	....	....	....	....	....	....	....	2	1	1	2	2	....	....	....
1994-95	Tri-City Americans	WHL	30	6	3	9	39	....	....	....	....	....	....	....	....	....	....	....	....	....	....	....	....	....	....	....
	Red Deer Rebels	WHL	21	5	9	14	33	....	....	....	....	....	....	....	....	....	....	....	....	....	....	....	....	....	....	....
1995-96	Red Deer Rebels	WHL	67	49	45	94	144	....	....	....	....	....	....	....	....	....	....	....	8	4	9	13	12	....	....	....
1996-97	Red Deer Rebels	WHL	63	*58	56	114	97	....	....	....	....	....	....	....	....	....	....	....	16	8	14	22	26	....	....	....
1997-98	Adirondack	AHL	65	15	22	37	191	....	....	....	....	....	....	....	....	....	....	....	3	0	2	2	6	....	....	....
1998-99	Adirondack	AHL	58	13	17	30	150	....	....	....	....	....	....	....	....	....	....	....	3	1	0	1	6	....	....	....
99-2000	**Detroit**	**NHL**	**1**	**0**	**0**	**0**	**0**	**0**	**0**	**0**	**1**	**0.0**	**0**	**1**	**100.0**	**0**	**0**	**1:04**	....	....	....	....	....	....	....	....
	Cincinnati Ducks	AHL	71	25	26	51	147	....	....	....	....	....	....	....	....	....	....	....	....	....	....	....	....	....	....	....
2000-01	Cincinnati Ducks	AHL	42	14	22	36	111	....	....	....	....	....	....	....	....	....	....	....	....	....	....	....	....	....	....	....
	Manitoba Moose	IHL	33	8	7	15	47	....	....	....	....	....	....	....	....	....	....	....	13	4	2	6	14	....	....	....
	NHL Totals		**1**	**0**	**0**	**0**	**0**	**0**	**0**	**0**	**1**	**0.0**		**1**	**100.0**	**0**	**0**	**1:04**	....	....	....	....	....	....	....	....

WHL East First All-Star Team (1997)

YOUNG, Scott

(YUHNG, SKAWT) **ST.L.**

Right wing. Shoots right. 6'1", 200 lbs. Born, Clinton, MA, October 1, 1967. Hartford's 1st choice, 11th overall, in 1986 Entry Draft.

			Regular Season																Playoffs							
Season	Club	League	GP	G	A	Pts	PIM	PP	SH	GW	S	%	+/-	TF	F%	H	SB	Min	GP	G	A	Pts	PIM	PP	SH	GW
1984-85	St. Marks	Hi-School	23	28	41	69	....	....	....	....	....	....	....	....	....	....	....	....	....	....	....	....	....	....	....	....
1985-86	Boston University	H-East	38	16	13	29	31	....	....	....	....	....	....	....	....	....	....	....	....	....	....	....	....	....	....	....
1986-87	Boston University	H-East	33	15	21	36	24	....	....	....	....	....	....	....	....	....	....	....	....	....	....	....	....	....	....	....
1987-88	United States	Nat-Team	56	11	47	58	31	....	....	....	....	....	....	....	....	....	....	....	....	....	....	....	....	....	....	....
	United States	Olympics	6	2	6	8	4	....	....	....	....	....	....	....	....	....	....	....	....	....	....	....	....	....	....	....
	Hartford	**NHL**	**7**	**0**	**0**	**0**	**2**	**0**	**0**	**0**	**6**	**0.0**	**–6**	....	....	....	....	....	**4**	**1**	**0**	**1**	**0**	**0**	**0**	**0**
1988-89	**Hartford**	**NHL**	**76**	**19**	**40**	**59**	**27**	**6**	**0**	**2**	**203**	**9.4**	**–21**	....	....	....	....	....	**4**	**2**	**0**	**2**	**4**	**0**	**0**	**0**
1989-90	**Hartford**	**NHL**	**80**	**24**	**40**	**64**	**47**	**10**	**2**	**5**	**239**	**10.0**	**–24**	....	....	....	....	....	**7**	**2**	**0**	**2**	**2**	**0**	**0**	**0**
1990-91	**Hartford**	**NHL**	**34**	**6**	**9**	**15**	**8**	**3**	**1**	**2**	**94**	**6.4**	**–9**	....	....	....	....	....	....	....	....	....	....	....	....	....
	♦ Pittsburgh	**NHL**	**43**	**11**	**16**	**27**	**33**	**3**	**1**	**3**	**116**	**9.5**	**3**	....	....	....	....	....	**17**	**1**	**6**	**7**	**2**	**1**	**0**	**0**
1991-92	HC Bolzano	Alpenliga	15	19	11	30	14	....	....	....	....	....	....	....	....	....	....	....	....	....	....	....	....	....	....	....
	HC Bolzano	Italy	18	22	17	39	6	....	....	....	....	....	....	....	....	....	....	....	5	4	3	7	7	....	....	....
	United States	Nat-Team	10	2	4	6	21	....	....	....	....	....	....	....	....	....	....	....	....	....	....	....	....	....	....	....
	United States	Olympics	8	2	1	3	2	....	....	....	....	....	....	....	....	....	....	....	....	....	....	....	....	....	....	....
1992-93	**Quebec**	**NHL**	**82**	**30**	**30**	**60**	**20**	**9**	**6**	**5**	**225**	**13.3**	**5**	....	....	....	....	....	**6**	**4**	**1**	**5**	**0**	**0**	**0**	**2**
1993-94	**Quebec**	**NHL**	**76**	**26**	**25**	**51**	**14**	**6**	**1**	**1**	**236**	**11.0**	**–4**	....	....	....	....	....	....	....	....	....	....	....	....	....
1994-95	EV Landshut	DEL	4	6	1	7	6	....	....	....	....	....	....	....	....	....	....	....	....	....	....	....	....	....	....	....
	Frankfurt Lions	DEL	1	1	0	1	0	....	....	....	....	....	....	....	....	....	....	....	....	....	....	....	....	....	....	....
	Quebec	**NHL**	**48**	**18**	**21**	**39**	**14**	**3**	**3**	**0**	**167**	**10.8**	**9**	....	....	....	....	....	**6**	**3**	**3**	**6**	**2**	**0**	**1**	**0**
1995-96♦	**Colorado**	**NHL**	**81**	**21**	**39**	**60**	**50**	**7**	**0**	**5**	**229**	**9.2**	**2**	....	....	....	....	....	**22**	**3**	**12**	**15**	**10**	**0**	**0**	**0**
1996-97	**Colorado**	**NHL**	**72**	**18**	**19**	**37**	**14**	**7**	**0**	**0**	**164**	**11.0**	**–5**	....	....	....	....	....	**17**	**4**	**2**	**6**	**14**	**2**	**0**	**0**
1997-98	**Anaheim**	**NHL**	**73**	**13**	**20**	**33**	**22**	**4**	**2**	**1**	**187**	**7.0**	**–13**	....	....	....	....	....	....	....	....	....	....	....	....	....
1998-99	**St. Louis**	**NHL**	**75**	**24**	**28**	**52**	**27**	**8**	**0**	**4**	**205**	**11.7**	**8**	**4**	**25.0**	**51**	**18**	**15:14**	**13**	**4**	**7**	**11**	**10**	**1**	**0**	**1**
99-2000	**St. Louis**	**NHL**	**75**	**24**	**15**	**39**	**18**	**6**	**1**	**7**	**244**	**9.8**	**12**	**2**	**50.0**	**63**	**15**	**16:06**	**6**	**6**	**2**	**8**	**8**	**3**	**0**	**0**
2000-01	**St. Louis**	**NHL**	**81**	**40**	**33**	**73**	**30**	**14**	**3**	**7**	**321**	**12.5**	**15**	**4**	**25.0**	**67**	**29**	**19:18**	**15**	**6**	**7**	**13**	**2**	**0**	**2**	**3**
	NHL Totals		**903**	**274**	**335**	**609**	**326**	**86**	**20**	**42**	**2636**	**10.4**		**10**	**30.0**	**181**	**62**	**16:56**	**117**	**36**	**40**	**76**	**54**	**7**	**3**	**6**

Traded to **Pittsburgh** by **Hartford** for Rob Brown, December 21, 1990. Traded to **Quebec** by **Pittsburgh** for Bryan Fogarty, March 10, 1992. Transferred to **Colorado** after **Quebec** franchise relocated, June 21, 1995. Traded to **Anaheim** by **Colorado** for Anaheim's 3rd round choice (later traded to Florida - Florida selected Lance Ward) in 1998 Entry Draft, September 17, 1997. Signed as a free agent by **St. Louis**, July 28, 1998.

YUSHKEVICH, Dmitry

(yoosh-KAY-vihch, dih-MEE-tree) **TOR.**

Defense. Shoots right. 5'11", 208 lbs. Born, Yaroslavl, USSR, November 19, 1971. Philadelphia's 6th choice, 122nd overall, in 1991 Entry Draft.

			Regular Season																Playoffs							
Season	Club	League	GP	G	A	Pts	PIM	PP	SH	GW	S	%	+/-	TF	F%	H	SB	Min	GP	G	A	Pts	PIM	PP	SH	GW
1988-89	Torpedo Yaroslavl	USSR	23	2	1	3	8	....	....	....	....	....	....	....	....	....	....	....	....	....	....	....	....	....	....	....
1989-90	Torpedo Yaroslavl	USSR	41	2	3	5	39	....	....	....	....	....	....	....	....	....	....	....	....	....	....	....	....	....	....	....
1990-91	Torpedo Yaroslavl	USSR	41	10	4	14	22	....	....	....	....	....	....	....	....	....	....	....	....	....	....	....	....	....	....	....
1991-92	Dynamo Moscow	CIS	35	5	7	12	14	....	....	....	....	....	....	....	....	....	....	....	....	....	....	....	....	....	....	....
	Russia	Olympics	8	1	2	3	4	....	....	....	....	....	....	....	....	....	....	....	....	....	....	....	....	....	....	....
1992-93	**Philadelphia**	**NHL**	**82**	**5**	**27**	**32**	**71**	**1**	**0**	**1**	**155**	**3.2**	**12**	....	....	....	....	....	....	....	....	....	....	....	....	....
1993-94	**Philadelphia**	**NHL**	**75**	**5**	**25**	**30**	**86**	**1**	**0**	**2**	**136**	**3.7**	**–8**	....	....	....	....	....	....	....	....	....	....	....	....	....
1994-95	Torpedo Yaroslavl	CIS	10	3	4	7	8	....	....	....	....	....	....	....	....	....	....	....	....	....	....	....	....	....	....	....
	Philadelphia	**NHL**	**40**	**5**	**9**	**14**	**47**	**3**	**1**	**1**	**80**	**6.3**	**–4**	....	....	....	....	....	**15**	**1**	**5**	**6**	**12**	**0**	**0**	**0**
1995-96	**Toronto**	**NHL**	**69**	**1**	**10**	**11**	**54**	**1**	**0**	**0**	**96**	**1.0**	**–14**	....	....	....	....	....	**4**	**0**	**0**	**0**	**0**	**0**	**0**	**0**
1996-97	**Toronto**	**NHL**	**74**	**4**	**10**	**14**	**56**	**1**	**1**	**1**	**99**	**4.0**	**–24**	....	....	....	....	....	....	....	....	....	....	....	....	....
1997-98	**Toronto**	**NHL**	**72**	**0**	**12**	**12**	**78**	**0**	**0**	**0**	**92**	**0.0**	**–13**	....	....	....	....	....	....	....	....	....	....	....	....	....
	Russia	Olympics	6	0	0	0	2	....	....	....	....	....	....	....	....	....	....	....	....	....	....	....	....	....	....	....
1998-99	**Toronto**	**NHL**	**78**	**6**	**22**	**28**	**88**	**2**	**1**	**0**	**95**	**6.3**	**25**	**0**	**0.0**	**169**	**107**	**22:20**	**17**	**1**	**5**	**6**	**22**	**1**	**0**	**0**
99-2000	Torpedo Yaroslavl	Russia	7	2	3	5	2	....	....	....	....	....	....	....	....	....	....	....	....	....	....	....	....	....	....	....
	Toronto	**NHL**	**77**	**3**	**24**	**27**	**55**	**2**	**1**	**1**	**103**	**2.9**	**2**	**0**	**0.0**	**266**	**160**	**23:18**	**12**	**1**	**1**	**2**	**4**	**0**	**0**	**0**
2000-01	**Toronto**	**NHL**	**81**	**5**	**19**	**24**	**52**	**1**	**0**	**0**	**110**	**4.5**	**–2**	**0**	**0.0**	**171**	**174**	**24:14**	**11**	**0**	**4**	**4**	**12**	**0**	**0**	**0**
	NHL Totals		**648**	**34**	**158**	**192**	**587**	**12**	**4**	**6**	**966**	**3.5**		**0**	**0.0**	**606**	**441**	**23:18**	**59**	**3**	**15**	**18**	**50**	**1**	**0**	**0**

Played in NHL All-Star Game (2000)

Traded to **Toronto** by **Philadelphia** with Philadelphia's 2nd round choice (Francis Larivee) in 1996 Entry Draft for Toronto's 1st round choice (Dainius Zubrus) in 1996 Entry Draft, 2nd round choice (Jean-Marc Pelletier) in 1997 Entry Draft and LA Kings' 4th round choice (previously acquired by Toronto - later traded to LA Kings - LA Kings selected Mikael Simons) in 1996 Entry Draft, August 30, 1995.

YZERMAN, Steve

(IGH-zuhr-muhn, STEEV) **DET.**

Center. Shoots right. 5'11", 185 lbs. Born, Cranbrook, B.C., May 9, 1965. Detroit's 1st choice, 4th overall, in 1983 Entry Draft.

			Regular Season																Playoffs							
Season	Club	League	GP	G	A	Pts	PIM	PP	SH	GW	S	%	+/-	TF	F%	H	SB	Min	GP	G	A	Pts	PIM	PP	SH	GW
1980-81	Nepean Raiders	OCJHL	50	38	*54	92	44	....	....	....	....	....	....	....	....	....	....	....	....	....	....	....	....	....	....	....
1981-82	Peterborough	OHL	58	21	43	64	65	....	....	....	....	....	....	....	....	....	....	....	6	0	1	1	16	....	....	....
1982-83	Peterborough	OHL	56	42	49	91	33	....	....	....	....	....	....	....	....	....	....	....	4	1	4	5	0	....	....	....
1983-84	**Detroit**	**NHL**	**80**	**39**	**48**	**87**	**33**	**13**	**0**	**2**	**177**	**22.0**	**–17**	....	....	....	....	....	**4**	**3**	**3**	**6**	**0**	**1**	**0**	**1**
1984-85	**Detroit**	**NHL**	**80**	**30**	**59**	**89**	**58**	**9**	**0**	**3**	**231**	**13.0**	**–17**	....	....	....	....	....	**3**	**2**	**1**	**3**	**2**	**0**	**0**	**0**
1985-86	**Detroit**	**NHL**	**51**	**14**	**28**	**42**	**16**	**3**	**0**	**3**	**132**	**10.6**	**–24**	....	....	....	....	....	....	....	....	....	....	....	....	....
1986-87	**Detroit**	**NHL**	**80**	**31**	**59**	**90**	**43**	**9**	**1**	**2**	**217**	**14.3**	**–1**	....	....	....	....	....	**16**	**5**	**13**	**18**	**8**	**1**	**0**	**0**
1987-88	**Detroit**	**NHL**	**64**	**50**	**52**	**102**	**44**	**10**	**6**	**6**	**242**	**20.7**	**30**	....	....	....	....	....	**3**	**1**	**3**	**4**	**6**	**0**	**0**	**0**
1988-89	**Detroit**	**NHL**	**80**	**65**	**90**	**155**	**61**	**17**	**3**	**7**	**388**	**16.8**	**17**	....	....	....	....	....	**6**	**5**	**5**	**10**	**2**	**2**	**0**	**0**
1989-90	**Detroit**	**NHL**	**79**	**62**	**65**	**127**	**79**	**16**	**7**	**8**	**332**	**18.7**	**–6**	....	....	....	....	....	....	....	....	....	....	....	....	....
1990-91	**Detroit**	**NHL**	**80**	**51**	**57**	**108**	**34**	**12**	**6**	**4**	**326**	**15.6**	**–2**	....	....	....	....	....	**7**	**3**	**3**	**6**	**4**	**1**	**0**	**0**
1991-92	**Detroit**	**NHL**	**79**	**45**	**58**	**103**	**64**	**9**	**8**	**9**	**295**	**15.3**	**26**	....	....	....	....	....	**11**	**3**	**5**	**8**	**12**	**0**	**1**	**1**
1992-93	**Detroit**	**NHL**	**84**	**58**	**79**	**137**	**44**	**13**	**7**	**6**	**307**	**18.9**	**33**	....	....	....	....	....	**7**	**4**	**3**	**7**	**4**	**1**	**1**	**1**
1993-94	**Detroit**	**NHL**	**58**	**24**	**58**	**82**	**36**	**7**	**3**	**3**	**217**	**11.1**	**11**	....	....	....	....	....	**3**	**1**	**3**	**4**	**0**	**0**	**0**	**0**
1994-95	**Detroit**	**NHL**	**47**	**12**	**26**	**38**	**40**	**4**	**0**	**1**	**134**	**9.0**	**6**	....	....	....	....	....	**15**	**4**	**8**	**12**	**0**	**2**	**0**	**1**
1995-96	**Detroit**	**NHL**	**80**	**36**	**59**	**95**	**64**	**16**	**2**	**8**	**220**	**16.4**	**29**	....	....	....	....	....	**18**	**8**	**12**	**20**	**4**	**4**	**0**	**1**
1996-97♦	**Detroit**	**NHL**	**81**	**22**	**63**	**85**	**78**	**8**	**0**	**3**	**232**	**9.5**	**22**	....	....	....	....	....	**20**	**7**	**6**	**13**	**4**	**3**	**0**	**2**
1997-98♦	**Detroit**	**NHL**	**75**	**24**	**45**	**69**	**46**	**6**	**2**	**0**	**188**	**12.8**	**3**	....	....	....	....	....	**22**	**6**	***18**	***24**	**22**	**3**	**1**	**0**
	Canada	Olympics	6	1	1	2	10	....	....	....	....	....	....	....	....	....	....	....	....	....	....	....	....	....	....	....
1998-99	**Detroit**	**NHL**	**80**	**29**	**45**	**74**	**42**	**13**	**2**	**4**	**231**	**12.6**	**8**	**1600**	**56.9**	**46**	**58**	**21:35**	**10**	**9**	**4**	**13**	**0**	**4**	**0**	**2**
99-2000	**Detroit**	**NHL**	**78**	**35**	**44**	**79**	**34**	**15**	**2**	**6**	**234**	**15.0**	**28**	**1868**	**56.8**	**67**	**56**	**21:07**	**8**	**0**	**4**	**4**	**0**	**0**	**0**	**0**
2000-01	**Detroit**	**NHL**	**54**	**18**	**34**	**52**	**18**	**5**	**0**	**7**	**155**	**11.6**	**4**	**1197**	**59.6**	**38**	**51**	**22:14**	**1**	**0**	**0**	**0**	**0**	**0**	**0**	**0**
	NHL Totals		**1310**	**645**	**969**	**1614**	**834**	**185**	**49**	**82**	**4258**	**15.1**		**4665**	**57.5**	**151**	**165**	**21:35**	**154**	**61**	**91**	**152**	**68**	**22**	**3**	**9**

NHL All-Rookie Team (1984) • Won Lester B. Pearson Award (1989) • Won Conn Smythe Trophy (1998) • NHL First All-Star Team (2000) • Won Frank J. Selke Trophy (2000) • Played in NHL All-Star Game (1984, 1988, 1989, 1990, 1991, 1992, 1993, 1997, 2000)

ZALAPSKI, Zarley
(zah-LAP-skee, ZAHR-lee)

Defense. Shoots left. 6'1", 215 lbs. Born, Edmonton, Alta., April 22, 1968. Pittsburgh's 1st choice, 4th overall, in 1986 Entry Draft.

								Regular Season											Playoffs							
Season	Club	League	GP	G	A	Pts	PIM	PP	SH	GW	S	%	+/-	TF	F%	H	SB	Min	GP	G	A	Pts	PIM	PP	SH	GW
1984-85	Ft-Saskatchewan	AJHL	23	17	30	47	14																			
1985-86	Ft-Saskatchewan	AJHL	27	20	33	53	46																			
	Canada	Nat-Team	32	2	4	6	10																			
1986-87	Canada	Nat-Team	74	11	29	40	28																			
1987-88	Canada	Nat-Team	47	3	13	16	32																			
	Canada	Olympics	8	1	3	4	2																			
	Pittsburgh	**NHL**	**15**	**3**	**8**	**11**	**7**	**0**	**0**	**0**	**31**	**9.7**	**10**													
1988-89	**Pittsburgh**	**NHL**	**58**	**12**	**33**	**45**	**57**	**5**	**1**	**2**	**95**	**12.6**	**9**						**11**	**1**	**8**	**9**	**13**	**1**	**0**	**0**
1989-90	**Pittsburgh**	**NHL**	**51**	**6**	**25**	**31**	**37**	**5**	**0**	**2**	**85**	**7.1**	**–14**													
1990-91	**Pittsburgh**	**NHL**	**66**	**12**	**36**	**48**	**59**	**5**	**1**	**1**	**135**	**8.9**	**15**													
	Hartford	**NHL**	**11**	**3**	**3**	**6**	**6**	**3**	**0**	**0**	**21**	**14.3**	**–7**						**6**	**1**	**3**	**4**	**8**	**0**	**0**	**1**
1991-92	**Hartford**	**NHL**	**79**	**20**	**37**	**57**	**120**	**4**	**0**	**3**	**230**	**8.7**	**–7**						**7**	**2**	**3**	**5**	**6**	**0**	**0**	**0**
1992-93	**Hartford**	**NHL**	**83**	**14**	**51**	**65**	**94**	**8**	**1**	**0**	**192**	**7.3**	**–34**													
1993-94	**Hartford**	**NHL**	**56**	**7**	**30**	**37**	**56**	**0**	**0**	**0**	**121**	**5.8**	**–6**													
	Calgary	**NHL**	**13**	**3**	**7**	**10**	**18**	**1**	**0**	**1**	**35**	**8.6**	**0**						**7**	**0**	**3**	**3**	**2**	**0**	**0**	**0**
1994-95	**Calgary**	**NHL**	**48**	**4**	**24**	**28**	**46**	**1**	**0**	**1**	**76**	**5.3**	**9**						**7**	**0**	**4**	**4**	**4**	**0**	**0**	**0**
1995-96	**Calgary**	**NHL**	**80**	**12**	**17**	**29**	**115**	**5**	**0**	**1**	**145**	**8.3**	**11**						**4**	**0**	**1**	**1**	**10**	**0**	**0**	**0**
1996-97	**Calgary**	**NHL**	**2**	**0**	**0**	**0**	**0**	**0**	**0**	**0**	**7**	**0.0**	**–1**													
1997-98	**Calgary**	**NHL**	**35**	**2**	**7**	**9**	**41**	**2**	**0**	**1**	**46**	**4.3**	**–12**													
	Montreal	**NHL**	**28**	**1**	**5**	**6**	**22**	**0**	**1**	**0**	**27**	**3.7**	**–1**						**6**	**0**	**1**	**1**	**4**	**0**	**0**	**0**
1998-99	ZSC Zurich	Switz.	11	1	5	6	37												3	1	0	1	4			
99-2000	Long Beach	IHL	7	0	5	5	6																			
	Utah Grizzlies	IHL	56	4	24	28	69												5	1	1	2	4			
	Philadelphia	**NHL**	**12**	**0**	**2**	**2**	**6**	**0**	**0**	**0**	**6**	**0.0**	**0**	**0**	**0.0**	**10**	**7**	**14:12**								
2000-01	Houston Aeros	IHL	9	0	2	2	12																			
	Munich Barons	DEL	20	3	3	6	43												3	0	0	0	2			
	NHL Totals		**637**	**99**	**285**	**384**	**684**	**39**	**4**	**12**	**1252**	**7.9**		**0**	**0.0**	**10**	**7**	**14:12**	**48**	**4**	**23**	**27**	**47**	**1**	**0**	**1**

NHL All-Rookie Team (1989) • Played in NHL All-Star Game (1993)

Traded to **Hartford** by **Pittsburgh** with John Cullen and Jeff Parker for Ron Francis, Grant Jennings and Ulf Samuelsson, March 4, 1991. Traded to **Calgary** by **Hartford** with James Patrick and Michael Nylander for Gary Suter, Paul Ranheim and Ted Drury, March 10, 1994. • Missed majority of 1996-97 season recovering from knee injury suffered during practice, October 7, 1996. Traded to **Montreal** by **Calgary** with Jonas Hoglund for Valeri Bure and Montreal's 4th round choice (Shaun Sutter) in 1998 Entry Draft, February 1, 1998. Signed as a free agent by **NY Rangers**, August 31, 1998. Signed as a free agent by **Long Beach** (IHL), September 14, 1999. Signed as a free agent by **Utah** (IHL), November 5, 1999. Signed as a free agent by **Philadelphia**, February 15, 2000. • Signed as a free agent by **Munich** (DEL), January 15, 2001.

ZAMUNER, Rob
(ZAM-nuhr, RAWB) **BOS.**

Left wing. Shoots left. 6'3", 203 lbs. Born, Oakville, Ont., September 17, 1969. NY Rangers' 3rd choice, 45th overall, in 1989 Entry Draft.

								Regular Season											Playoffs							
Season	Club	League	GP	G	A	Pts	PIM	PP	SH	GW	S	%	+/-	TF	F%	H	SB	Min	GP	G	A	Pts	PIM	PP	SH	GW
1985-86	Oakville Oaks	OMHA	48	43	50	93	66																			
1986-87	Guelph Jr. B's	OJHL-B	3	6	7	13	15																			
	Guelph Platers	OHL	62	6	15	21	8																			
1987-88	Guelph Platers	OHL	58	20	41	61	18																			
1988-89	Guelph Platers	OHL	66	46	65	111	38												7	5	5	10	9			
1989-90	Flint Spirits	IHL	77	44	35	79	32												4	1	0	1	6			
1990-91	Binghamton	AHL	80	25	58	83	50												9	7	6	13	35			
1991-92	**NY Rangers**	**NHL**	**9**	**1**	**2**	**3**	**2**	**0**	**0**	**0**	**11**	**9.1**	**0**													
	Binghamton	AHL	61	19	53	72	42												11	8	9	17	8			
1992-93	**Tampa Bay**	**NHL**	**84**	**15**	**28**	**43**	**74**	**1**	**0**	**0**	**183**	**8.2**	**–25**													
1993-94	**Tampa Bay**	**NHL**	**59**	**6**	**6**	**12**	**42**	**0**	**0**	**1**	**109**	**5.5**	**–9**													
1994-95	**Tampa Bay**	**NHL**	**43**	**9**	**6**	**15**	**24**	**0**	**3**	**1**	**74**	**12.2**	**–3**													
1995-96	**Tampa Bay**	**NHL**	**72**	**15**	**20**	**35**	**62**	**0**	**3**	**4**	**152**	**9.9**	**11**						**6**	**2**	**3**	**5**	**10**	**0**	**1**	**0**
1996-97	**Tampa Bay**	**NHL**	**82**	**17**	**33**	**50**	**56**	**0**	**4**	**3**	**216**	**7.9**	**3**													
1997-98	**Tampa Bay**	**NHL**	**77**	**14**	**12**	**26**	**41**	**0**	**3**	**4**	**126**	**11.1**	**–31**													
	Canada	Olympics	6	1	0	1	8																			
1998-99	**Tampa Bay**	**NHL**	**58**	**8**	**11**	**19**	**24**	**1**	**1**	**2**	**89**	**9.0**	**–15**	**34**	**47.1**	**52**	**11**	**16:26**								
99-2000	**Ottawa**	**NHL**	**57**	**9**	**12**	**21**	**32**	**0**	**1**	**0**	**103**	**8.7**	**–6**	**29**	**37.9**	**65**	**19**	**14:56**	**6**	**2**	**0**	**2**	**2**	**0**	**0**	**1**
2000-01	**Ottawa**	**NHL**	**79**	**19**	**18**	**37**	**52**	**1**	**2**	**4**	**123**	**15.4**	**7**	**162**	**35.8**	**94**	**24**	**14:46**	**4**	**0**	**0**	**0**	**6**	**0**	**0**	**0**
	NHL Totals		**620**	**113**	**148**	**261**	**409**	**3**	**17**	**19**	**1186**	**9.5**		**225**	**37.8**	**211**	**54**	**15:19**	**16**	**4**	**3**	**7**	**18**	**0**	**1**	**1**

Signed as a free agent by **Tampa Bay**, July 13, 1992. Traded to **Ottawa** by **Tampa Bay** with a conditional 2nd round choice in 2002 Entry Draft for Andreas Johansson, June 29, 1999. Signed as a free agent by **Boston**, July 6, 2001.

ZEDNIK, Richard
(ZEHD-nihk, REE-khahrd) **MTL.**

Left wing. Shoots left. 6', 200 lbs. Born, Bystrica, Czech., January 6, 1976. Washington's 10th choice, 249th overall, in 1994 Entry Draft.

								Regular Season											Playoffs							
Season	Club	League	GP	G	A	Pts	PIM	PP	SH	GW	S	%	+/-	TF	F%	H	SB	Min	GP	G	A	Pts	PIM	PP	SH	GW
1993-94	SK Banska	Slovakia-2	25	3	6	9																				
1994-95	Portland	WHL	65	35	51	86	89												9	5	5	10	20			
1995-96	Portland	WHL	61	44	37	81	154												7	8	4	12	23			
	Washington	**NHL**	**1**	**0**	**0**	**0**	**0**	**0**	**0**	**0**	**0**	**0.0**	**0**													
	Portland Pirates	AHL	1	1	1	2	0												21	4	5	9	26			
1996-97	**Washington**	**NHL**	**11**	**2**	**1**	**3**	**4**	**1**	**0**	**0**	**21**	**9.5**	**–5**													
	Portland Pirates	AHL	56	15	20	35	70												5	1	0	1	6			
1997-98	**Washington**	**NHL**	**65**	**17**	**9**	**26**	**28**	**2**	**0**	**2**	**148**	**11.5**	**–2**						**17**	**7**	**3**	**10**	**16**	**2**	**0**	**0**
1998-99	**Washington**	**NHL**	**49**	**9**	**8**	**17**	**50**	**1**	**0**	**2**	**115**	**7.8**	**–6**	**2**	**0.0**	**81**	**9**	**15:08**								
99-2000	**Washington**	**NHL**	**69**	**19**	**16**	**35**	**54**	**1**	**0**	**2**	**179**	**10.6**	**6**	**1**	**100.0**	**155**	**27**	**15:34**	**5**	**0**	**0**	**0**	**5**	**0**	**0**	**0**
2000-01	**Washington**	**NHL**	**62**	**16**	**19**	**35**	**61**	**4**	**0**	**3**	**155**	**10.3**	**–2**	**1**	**0.0**	**112**	**23**	**15:32**								
	Montreal	**NHL**	**12**	**3**	**6**	**9**	**10**	**1**	**0**	**0**	**23**	**13.0**	**–2**	**0**	**0.0**	**13**	**7**	**18:29**								
	NHL Totals		**269**	**66**	**59**	**125**	**207**	**10**	**0**	**9**	**641**	**10.3**		**4**	**25.0**	**361**	**66**	**15:38**	**22**	**7**	**3**	**10**	**21**	**2**	**0**	**0**

WHL West Second All-Star Team (1996)

Traded to **Montreal** by **Washington** with Jan Bulis and Washington's 1st round choice (Alexander Perezhogin) in 2001 Entry Draft for Trevor Linden, Dainius Zubrus and New Jersey's 2nd round choice (previously acquired, later traded to Tampa Bay - Tampa Bay selected Andreas Holmqvist) in 2001 Entry Draft, March 13, 2001.

ZEHR, Jeff
(ZAIR, JEHF) **BOS.**

Left wing. Shoots left. 6'3", 195 lbs. Born, Woodstock, Ont., December 10, 1978. NY Islanders' 3rd choice, 31st overall, in 1997 Entry Draft.

								Regular Season											Playoffs							
Season	Club	League	GP	G	A	Pts	PIM	PP	SH	GW	S	%	+/-	TF	F%	H	SB	Min	GP	G	A	Pts	PIM	PP	SH	GW
1993-94	Tavistock Braves	OJHL-D	6	2	1	3	6																			
1994-95	Stratford Cullitons	OJHL-B	44	26	32	58	143																			
1995-96	Windsor Spitfires	OHL	56	4	21	25	103												7	0	1	1	2			
1996-97	Windsor Spitfires	OHL	57	27	32	59	196												5	2	1	3	4			
1997-98	Windsor Spitfires	OHL	20	12	18	30	67																			
	Erie Otters	OHL	32	15	24	39	91												5	0	3	3	24			
1998-99	Erie Otters	OHL	28	20	23	43	78																			
	Sarnia Sting	OHL	14	4	10	14	43												6	3	4	7	27			
99-2000	**Boston**	**NHL**	**4**	**0**	**0**	**0**	**2**	**0**	**0**	**0**	**3**	**0.0**	**–1**	**0**	**0.0**	**9**	**0**	**7:25**								
	Providence Bruins	AHL	12	3	3	6	37																			
2000-01	Greenville Growl	ECHL	23	2	1	3	76																			
	NHL Totals		**4**	**0**	**0**	**0**	**2**	**0**	**0**	**0**	**3**	**0.0**		**0**	**0.0**	**9**	**0**	**7:25**								

Signed as a free agent by **Boston**, June 21, 1999. • Missed majority of 1999-2000 and 2000-01 seasons recovering from knee injury suffered in practice, December 22, 1999.

ZELEPUKIN, Valeri
(zeh-leh-POO-kin, VAL-uhr-ee) **CHI.**

Left wing. Shoots left. 6'1", 200 lbs. Born, Voskresensk, USSR, September 17, 1968. New Jersey's 13th choice, 221st overall, in 1990 Entry Draft.

								Regular Season											Playoffs							
Season	Club	League	GP	G	A	Pts	PIM	PP	SH	GW	S	%	+/-	TF	F%	H	SB	Min	GP	G	A	Pts	PIM	PP	SH	GW
1984-85	HK Khimik	USSR	5	0	0	0	2																			
1985-86	HK Khimik	USSR	33	2	2	4	10																			
1986-87	HK Khimik	USSR	19	1	0	1	4																			
1987-88	CSKA Moscow	USSR	19	3	1	4	8																			
1988-89	CSKA Moscow	USSR	17	2	3	5	2																			
1989-90	HK Khimik	USSR	46	17	14	31	26																			
1990-91	HK Khimik	USSR	34	11	6	17	38																			

			Regular Season																Playoffs							
Season	Club	League	GP	G	A	Pts	PIM	PP	SH	GW	S	%	+/-	TF	F%	H	SB	Min	GP	G	A	Pts	PIM	PP	SH	GW
1991-92	**New Jersey**	**NHL**	**44**	**13**	**18**	**31**	**28**	**3**	**0**	**3**	**94**	**13.8**	**11**	....	....	....	....	....	**4**	**1**	**1**	**2**	**2**	**0**	**0**	**0**
	Utica Devils	AHL	22	20	9	29	8	....	....	....	....	....	....	....	....	....	....	....	....	....	....	....	....	....	....	....
1992-93	**New Jersey**	**NHL**	**78**	**23**	**41**	**64**	**70**	**5**	**1**	**2**	**174**	**13.2**	**19**	....	....	....	....	....	**5**	**0**	**2**	**2**	**0**	**0**	**0**	**0**
1993-94	**New Jersey**	**NHL**	**82**	**26**	**31**	**57**	**70**	**8**	**0**	**0**	**155**	**16.8**	**36**	....	....	....	....	....	**20**	**5**	**2**	**7**	**14**	**1**	**0**	**0**
1994-95♦	**New Jersey**	**NHL**	**4**	**1**	**2**	**3**	**6**	**0**	**0**	**0**	**6**	**16.7**	**3**	....	....	....	....	....	**18**	**1**	**2**	**3**	**12**	**0**	**0**	**1**
1995-96	**New Jersey**	**NHL**	**61**	**6**	**9**	**15**	**107**	**3**	**0**	**1**	**86**	**7.0**	**–10**	....	....	....	....	....	....	....	....	....	....	....	....	....
1996-97	**New Jersey**	**NHL**	**71**	**14**	**24**	**38**	**36**	**3**	**0**	**2**	**111**	**12.6**	**–10**	....	....	....	....	....	**8**	**3**	**2**	**5**	**2**	**1**	**0**	**1**
1997-98	**New Jersey**	**NHL**	**35**	**2**	**8**	**10**	**32**	**0**	**0**	**0**	**54**	**3.7**	**0**	....	....	....	....	....	....	....	....	....	....	....	....	....
	Edmonton	**NHL**	**33**	**2**	**10**	**12**	**57**	**0**	**0**	**0**	**47**	**4.3**	**–2**	....	....	....	....	....	**8**	**1**	**2**	**3**	**2**	**0**	**0**	**0**
	Russia	Olympics	6	1	2	3	0	....	....	....	....	....	....	....	....	....	....	....	....	....	....	....	....	....	....	....
1998-99	**Philadelphia**	**NHL**	**74**	**16**	**9**	**25**	**48**	**0**	**0**	**5**	**129**	**12.4**	**0**	**0**	**0.0**	**85**	**22**	**14:33**	**4**	**1**	**0**	**1**	**4**	**0**	**0**	**1**
99-2000	**Philadelphia**	**NHL**	**77**	**11**	**21**	**32**	**55**	**2**	**0**	**3**	**125**	**8.8**	**–3**	**0**	**0.0**	**104**	**33**	**14:37**	**18**	**1**	**2**	**3**	**12**	**1**	**0**	**0**
2000-01	**Chicago**	**NHL**	**36**	**3**	**4**	**7**	**18**	**0**	**2**	**0**	**38**	**7.9**	**–14**	**1**	**0.0**	**60**	**11**	**12:07**	....	....	....	....	....	....	....	....
	Norfolk Admirals	AHL	29	10	9	19	28	....	....	....	....	....	....	....	....	....	....	....	9	5	3	8	6	....	....	....
	NHL Totals		**595**	**117**	**177**	**294**	**527**	**24**	**3**	**16**	**1019**	**11.5**		**1**	**0.0**	**249**	**66**	**14:07**	**85**	**13**	**13**	**26**	**48**	**3**	**0**	**3**

• Missed majority of 1994-95 season recovering from eye injury suffered in practice, January 24, 1995. Traded to **Edmonton** by **New Jersey** with Bill Guerin for Jason Arnott and Bryan Muir, January 4, 1998. Traded to **Philadelphia** by **Edmonton** for Daniel Lacroix, October 5, 1998. Signed as a free agent by **Chicago**, July 18, 2000.

ZETTLER, Rob (ZEHT-luhr, RAWB) WSH.

Defense. Shoots left. 6'3", 200 lbs. Born, Sept Iles, Que., March 8, 1968. Minnesota's 5th choice, 55th overall, in 1986 Entry Draft.

1983-84	S.S. Marie Legion	NOHA	40	9	24	33	28	....	....	....	....	....	....	....	....	....	....	....	....	....	....	....	....	....	....	....
1984-85	Sault Ste. Marie	OHL	60	2	14	16	37	....	....	....	....	....	....	....	....	....	....	....	....	....	....	....	....	....	....	....
1985-86	Sault Ste. Marie	OHL	57	5	23	28	92	....	....	....	....	....	....	....	....	....	....	....	....	....	....	....	....	....	....	....
1986-87	Sault Ste. Marie	OHL	64	13	22	35	89	....	....	....	....	....	....	....	....	....	....	....	4	0	0	0	0	....	....	....
1987-88	Sault Ste. Marie	OHL	64	7	41	48	77	....	....	....	....	....	....	....	....	....	....	....	6	2	2	4	9	....	....	....
	Kalamazoo Wings	IHL	2	0	1	1	0	....	....	....	....	....	....	....	....	....	....	....	7	0	2	2	2	....	....	....
1988-89	**Minnesota**	**NHL**	**2**	**0**	**0**	**0**	**0**	**0**	**0**	**0**	**0**	**0.0**	**–1**	....	....	....	....	....	....	....	....	....	....	....	....	....
	Kalamazoo Wings	IHL	80	5	21	26	79	....	....	....	....	....	....	....	....	....	....	....	6	0	1	1	26	....	....	....
1989-90	**Minnesota**	**NHL**	**31**	**0**	**8**	**8**	**45**	**0**	**0**	**0**	**21**	**0.0**	**–7**	....	....	....	....	....	....	....	....	....	....	....	....	....
	Kalamazoo Wings	IHL	41	6	10	16	64	....	....	....	....	....	....	....	....	....	....	....	7	0	0	0	6	....	....	....
1990-91	**Minnesota**	**NHL**	**47**	**1**	**4**	**5**	**119**	**0**	**0**	**0**	**30**	**3.3**	**–10**	....	....	....	....	....	....	....	....	....	....	....	....	....
	Kalamazoo Wings	IHL	1	0	0	0	2	....	....	....	....	....	....	....	....	....	....	....	....	....	....	....	....	....	....	....
1991-92	**San Jose**	**NHL**	**74**	**1**	**8**	**9**	**99**	**0**	**0**	**0**	**72**	**1.4**	**–23**	....	....	....	....	....	....	....	....	....	....	....	....	....
1992-93	**San Jose**	**NHL**	**80**	**0**	**7**	**7**	**150**	**0**	**0**	**0**	**60**	**0.0**	**–50**	....	....	....	....	....	....	....	....	....	....	....	....	....
1993-94	**San Jose**	**NHL**	**42**	**0**	**3**	**3**	**65**	**0**	**0**	**0**	**28**	**0.0**	**–7**	....	....	....	....	....	....	....	....	....	....	....	....	....
	Philadelphia	**NHL**	**33**	**0**	**4**	**4**	**69**	**0**	**0**	**0**	**27**	**0.0**	**–19**	....	....	....	....	....	....	....	....	....	....	....	....	....
1994-95	**Philadelphia**	**NHL**	**32**	**0**	**1**	**1**	**34**	**0**	**0**	**0**	**17**	**0.0**	**–3**	....	....	....	....	....	**1**	**0**	**0**	**0**	**2**	**0**	**0**	**0**
1995-96	**Toronto**	**NHL**	**29**	**0**	**1**	**1**	**48**	**0**	**0**	**0**	**11**	**0.0**	**–1**	....	....	....	....	....	**2**	**0**	**0**	**0**	**0**	**0**	**0**	**0**
1996-97	**Toronto**	**NHL**	**48**	**2**	**12**	**14**	**51**	**0**	**0**	**0**	**31**	**6.5**	**8**	....	....	....	....	....	....	....	....	....	....	....	....	....
	Utah Grizzlies	IHL	30	0	10	10	60	....	....	....	....	....	....	....	....	....	....	....	....	....	....	....	....	....	....	....
1997-98	**Toronto**	**NHL**	**59**	**0**	**7**	**7**	**108**	**0**	**0**	**0**	**28**	**0.0**	**–8**	....	....	....	....	....	....	....	....	....	....	....	....	....
1998-99	**Nashville**	**NHL**	**2**	**0**	**0**	**0**	**2**	**0**	**0**	**0**	**0**	**0.0**	**–2**	**0**	**0.0**	**5**	**1**	**16:16**	....	....	....	....	....	....	....	....
	Utah Grizzlies	IHL	77	2	16	18	136	....	....	....	....	....	....	....	....	....	....	....	....	....	....	....	....	....	....	....
99-2000	**Washington**	**NHL**	**12**	**0**	**2**	**2**	**19**	**0**	**0**	**0**	**15**	**0.0**	**–1**	**0**	**0.0**	**15**	**18**	**15:22**	**5**	**0**	**0**	**0**	**2**	**0**	**0**	**0**
	Portland Pirates	AHL	23	2	2	4	27	....	....	....	....	....	....	....	....	....	....	....	....	....	....	....	....	....	....	....
2000-01	**Washington**	**NHL**	**29**	**0**	**4**	**4**	**55**	**0**	**0**	**0**	**17**	**0.0**	**0**	**0**	**0.0**	**44**	**19**	**12:08**	**6**	**0**	**0**	**0**	**0**	**0**	**0**	**0**
	Portland Pirates	AHL	36	1	9	10	84	....	....	....	....	....	....	....	....	....	....	....	....	....	....	....	....	....	....	....
	NHL Totals		**520**	**4**	**61**	**65**	**864**	**0**	**0**	**0**	**357**	**1.1**		**0**	**0.0**	**64**	**38**	**13:14**	**14**	**0**	**0**	**0**	**4**	**0**	**0**	**0**

Claimed by **San Jose** from **Minnesota** in Dispersal Draft, May 30, 1991. Traded to **Philadelphia** by **San Jose** for Viacheslav Butsayev, February 1, 1994. Traded to **Toronto** by **Philadelphia** for Toronto's 5th round choice (Per-Ragna Bergqvist) in 1996 Entry Draft, July 8, 1995. Claimed by **Nashville** from **Toronto** in Expansion Draft, June 26, 1998. Signed as a free agent by **Washington**, September 7, 1999. • Missed majority of 1999-2000 season recovering from head injury suffered in game vs. Albany (AHL), October 21, 1999.

ZHAMNOV, Alexei (ZHAHM-nahf, al-EHX-ay) CHI.

Center. Shoots left. 6'1", 200 lbs. Born, Moscow, USSR, October 1, 1970. Winnipeg's 5th choice, 77th overall, in 1990 Entry Draft.

1988-89	Dynamo Moscow	USSR	4	0	0	0	0	....	....	....	....	....	....	....	....	....	....	....	....	....	....	....	....	....	....	....
1989-90	Dynamo Moscow	USSR	43	11	6	17	21	....	....	....	....	....	....	....	....	....	....	....	....	....	....	....	....	....	....	....
1990-91	Dynamo Moscow	USSR	46	16	12	28	24	....	....	....	....	....	....	....	....	....	....	....	....	....	....	....	....	....	....	....
1991-92	Dynamo Moscow	CIS	39	15	21	36	28	....	....	....	....	....	....	....	....	....	....	....	....	....	....	....	....	....	....	....
	Russia	Olympics	8	0	3	3	8	....	....	....	....	....	....	....	....	....	....	....	....	....	....	....	....	....	....	....
1992-93	**Winnipeg**	**NHL**	**68**	**25**	**47**	**72**	**58**	**6**	**1**	**4**	**163**	**15.3**	**7**	....	....	....	....	....	**6**	**0**	**2**	**2**	**2**	**0**	**0**	**0**
1993-94	**Winnipeg**	**NHL**	**61**	**26**	**45**	**71**	**62**	**7**	**0**	**1**	**196**	**13.3**	**–20**	....	....	....	....	....	....	....	....	....	....	....	....	....
1994-95	**Winnipeg**	**NHL**	**48**	**30**	**35**	**65**	**20**	**9**	**0**	**4**	**155**	**19.4**	**5**	....	....	....	....	....	....	....	....	....	....	....	....	....
1995-96	**Winnipeg**	**NHL**	**58**	**22**	**37**	**59**	**65**	**5**	**0**	**2**	**199**	**11.1**	**–4**	....	....	....	....	....	**6**	**2**	**1**	**3**	**8**	**0**	**0**	**0**
1996-97	**Chicago**	**NHL**	**74**	**20**	**42**	**62**	**56**	**6**	**1**	**2**	**208**	**9.6**	**18**	....	....	....	....	....	....	....	....	....	....	....	....	....
1997-98	**Chicago**	**NHL**	**70**	**21**	**28**	**49**	**61**	**6**	**2**	**3**	**193**	**10.9**	**16**	....	....	....	....	....	....	....	....	....	....	....	....	....
	Russia	Olympics	6	2	1	3	2	....	....	....	....	....	....	....	....	....	....	....	....	....	....	....	....	....	....	....
1998-99	**Chicago**	**NHL**	**76**	**20**	**41**	**61**	**50**	**8**	**1**	**2**	**200**	**10.0**	**–10**	**1299**	**48.9**	**40**	**38**	**21:30**	....	....	....	....	....	....	....	....
99-2000	**Chicago**	**NHL**	**71**	**23**	**37**	**60**	**61**	**5**	**0**	**7**	**175**	**13.1**	**7**	**1171**	**45.8**	**28**	**43**	**22:08**	....	....	....	....	....	....	....	....
2000-01	**Chicago**	**NHL**	**63**	**13**	**36**	**49**	**40**	**3**	**1**	**3**	**117**	**11.1**	**–12**	**1486**	**48.1**	**32**	**35**	**21:15**	....	....	....	....	....	....	....	....
	NHL Totals		**589**	**200**	**348**	**548**	**473**	**55**	**6**	**28**	**1606**	**12.5**		**3956**	**47.6**	**100**	**116**	**21:39**	**12**	**2**	**3**	**5**	**10**	**0**	**0**	**0**

NHL Second All-Star Team (1995)

Traded to **Chicago** by **Phoenix** with Craig Mills and Phoenix's 1st round choice (Ty Jones) in 1997 Entry Draft for Jeremy Roenick, August 16, 1996.

ZHITNIK, Alexei (ZHIHT-nihk, al-EHX-ay) BUF.

Defense. Shoots left. 5'11", 215 lbs. Born, Kiev, USSR, October 10, 1972. Los Angeles' 3rd choice, 81st overall, in 1991 Entry Draft.

1989-90	Sokol Kiev	USSR	31	3	4	7	16	....	....	....	....	....	....	....	....	....	....	....	....	....	....	....	....	....	....	....
1990-91	Sokol Kiev	USSR	46	1	4	5	46	....	....	....	....	....	....	....	....	....	....	....	....	....	....	....	....	....	....	....
1991-92	CSKA Moscow	CIS	44	2	7	9	52	....	....	....	....	....	....	....	....	....	....	....	....	....	....	....	....	....	....	....
	Russia	Olympics	8	1	0	1	0	....	....	....	....	....	....	....	....	....	....	....	....	....	....	....	....	....	....	....
1992-93	**Los Angeles**	**NHL**	**78**	**12**	**36**	**48**	**80**	**5**	**0**	**2**	**136**	**8.8**	**–3**	....	....	....	....	....	**24**	**3**	**9**	**12**	**26**	**2**	**0**	**1**
1993-94	**Los Angeles**	**NHL**	**81**	**12**	**40**	**52**	**101**	**11**	**0**	**1**	**227**	**5.3**	**–11**	....	....	....	....	....	....	....	....	....	....	....	....	....
1994-95	**Los Angeles**	**NHL**	**11**	**2**	**5**	**7**	**27**	**2**	**0**	**0**	**33**	**6.1**	**–3**	....	....	....	....	....	....	....	....	....	....	....	....	....
	Buffalo	**NHL**	**21**	**2**	**5**	**7**	**34**	**1**	**0**	**0**	**33**	**6.1**	**–3**	....	....	....	....	....	**5**	**0**	**1**	**1**	**14**	**0**	**0**	**0**
1995-96	**Buffalo**	**NHL**	**80**	**6**	**30**	**36**	**58**	**5**	**0**	**0**	**193**	**3.1**	**–25**	....	....	....	....	....	....	....	....	....	....	....	....	....
1996-97	**Buffalo**	**NHL**	**80**	**7**	**28**	**35**	**95**	**3**	**1**	**0**	**170**	**4.1**	**10**	....	....	....	....	....	**12**	**1**	**0**	**1**	**16**	**0**	**0**	**0**
1997-98	**Buffalo**	**NHL**	**78**	**15**	**30**	**45**	**102**	**2**	**3**	**3**	**191**	**7.9**	**19**	....	....	....	....	....	**15**	**0**	**3**	**3**	**36**	**0**	**0**	**0**
	Russia	Olympics	6	0	2	2	2	....	....	....	....	....	....	....	....	....	....	....	....	....	....	....	....	....	....	....
1998-99	**Buffalo**	**NHL**	**81**	**7**	**26**	**33**	**96**	**3**	**1**	**2**	**185**	**3.8**	**–6**	**0**	**0.0**	**122**	**109**	**25:39**	**21**	**4**	**11**	**15**	***52**	**4**	**0**	**2**
99-2000	**Buffalo**	**NHL**	**74**	**2**	**11**	**13**	**95**	**1**	**0**	**0**	**139**	**1.4**	**–6**	**0**	**0.0**	**117**	**88**	**24:48**	**4**	**0**	**0**	**0**	**8**	**0**	**0**	**0**
2000-01	**Buffalo**	**NHL**	**78**	**8**	**29**	**37**	**75**	**5**	**0**	**1**	**149**	**5.4**	**–3**	**0**	**0.0**	**175**	**70**	**24:15**	**13**	**1**	**6**	**7**	**12**	**0**	**0**	**0**
	NHL Totals		**662**	**73**	**240**	**313**	**763**	**38**	**5**	**9**	**1456**	**5.0**		**0**	**0.0**	**414**	**267**	**24:55**	**94**	**9**	**30**	**39**	**164**	**6**	**0**	**3**

Played in NHL All-Star Game (1999)

Traded to **Buffalo** by **LA Kings** with Robb Stauber, Charlie Huddy and LA Kings' 5th round choice (Marian Menhart) in 1995 Entry Draft for Philippe Boucher, Denis Tsygurov and Grant Fuhr, February 14, 1995.

ZHOLTOK, Sergei (ZHOL-tok, SAIR-gay) MIN.

Center. Shoots right. 6'2", 191 lbs. Born, Riga, Latvia, February 12, 1972. Boston's 2nd choice, 55th overall, in 1992 Entry Draft.

1990-91	Dynamo Riga	USSR	39	4	0	4	16	....	....	....	....	....	....	....	....	....	....	....	....	....	....	....	....	....	....	....
1991-92	Dynamo Riga	CIS	27	6	3	9	6	....	....	....	....	....	....	....	....	....	....	....	....	....	....	....	....	....	....	....
1992-93	**Boston**	**NHL**	**1**	**0**	**1**	**1**	**0**	**0**	**0**	**0**	**2**	**0.0**	**1**	....	....	....	....	....	....	....	....	....	....	....	....	....
	Providence Bruins	AHL	64	31	35	66	57	....	....	....	....	....	....	....	....	....	....	....	6	3	5	8	4	....	....	....
1993-94	**Boston**	**NHL**	**24**	**2**	**1**	**3**	**2**	**1**	**0**	**0**	**25**	**8.0**	**–7**	....	....	....	....	....	....	....	....	....	....	....	....	....
	Providence Bruins	AHL	54	29	33	62	16	....	....	....	....	....	....	....	....	....	....	....	....	....	....	....	....	....	....	....
1994-95	Providence Bruins	AHL	78	23	35	58	42	....	....	....	....	....	....	....	....	....	....	....	13	8	5	13	6	....	....	....
1995-96	Las Vegas	IHL	82	51	50	101	30	....	....	....	....	....	....	....	....	....	....	....	15	7	13	20	6	....	....	....

			Regular Season																Playoffs							
Season	Club	League	GP	G	A	Pts	PIM	PP	SH	GW	S	%	+/-	TF	F%	H	SB	Min	GP	G	A	Pts	PIM	PP	SH	GW
1996-97	**Ottawa**	**NHL**	**57**	**12**	**16**	**28**	**19**	**5**	**0**	**0**	**96**	**12.5**	**2**	....	....	....	....	....	**7**	**1**	**1**	**2**	**0**	**1**	**0**	**0**
	Las Vegas	IHL	19	13	14	27	20	....	....	....	....	....	....	....	....	....	....	....	....	....	....	....	....	....	....	....
1997-98	**Ottawa**	**NHL**	**78**	**10**	**13**	**23**	**16**	**7**	**0**	**1**	**127**	**7.9**	**–7**	....	....	....	....	....	**11**	**0**	**2**	**2**	**0**	**0**	**0**	**0**
1998-99	**Montreal**	**NHL**	**70**	**7**	**15**	**22**	**6**	**2**	**0**	**3**	**102**	**6.9**	**–12**	**522**	**49.0**	**23**	**12**	**11:11**	....	....	....	....	....	....	....	....
	Fredericton	AHL	7	3	4	7	0	....	....	....	....	....	....	....	....	....	....	....	....	....	....	....	....	....	....	....
99-2000	**Montreal**	**NHL**	**68**	**26**	**12**	**38**	**28**	**9**	**0**	**7**	**163**	**16.0**	**2**	**914**	**48.9**	**12**	**18**	**17:17**	....	....	....	....	....	....	....	....
	Quebec Citadelles	AHL	1	0	1	1	2	....	....	....	....	....	....	....	....	....	....	....	....	....	....	....	....	....	....	....
2000-01	**Montreal**	**NHL**	**32**	**1**	**10**	**11**	**8**	**0**	**0**	**0**	**78**	**1.3**	**–15**	**318**	**52.2**	**6**	**8**	**15:38**	....	....	....	....	....	....	....	....
	Edmonton	**NHL**	**37**	**4**	**16**	**20**	**22**	**1**	**0**	**0**	**61**	**6.6**	**8**	**109**	**60.6**	**20**	**7**	**12:55**	**3**	**0**	**0**	**0**	**0**	**0**	**0**	**0**
	NHL Totals		**367**	**62**	**84**	**146**	**101**	**25**	**0**	**11**	**654**	**9.5**		**1863**	**50.2**	**61**	**45**	**14:11**	**21**	**1**	**3**	**4**	**0**	**1**	**0**	**0**

Signed as a free agent by **Ottawa**, July 10, 1996. Signed as a free agent by **Montreal**, September 9, 1998. Traded to **Edmonton** by **Montreal** for Chad Kilger, December 18, 2000. Traded to **Minnesota** by **Edmonton** for future considerations, June 29, 2001.

ZIEGLER, Thomas — T.B.

Right wing. Shoots left. 5'11", 174 lbs. Born, Zurich, Switz., June 9, 1978. Tampa Bay's 10th choice, 263rd overall, in 2000 Entry Draft.

Season	Club	League	GP	G	A	Pts	PIM	PP	SH	GW	S	%	+/-	TF	F%	H	SB	Min	GP	G	A	Pts	PIM	PP	SH	GW
1995-96	GC Zurich	Switz-2	10	0	0	0	0	....	....	....	....	....	....	....	....	....	....	....	....	....	....	....	....	....	....	....
1996-97	GC Zurich	Switz-Jr.	34	19	11	30	....	....	....	....	....	....	....	....	....	....	....	....	....	....	....	....	....	....	....	....
	GC Zurich	Switz-2	11	0	1	1	2	....	....	....	....	....	....	....	....	....	....	....	....	....	....	....	....	....	....	....
1997-98	GC Zurich	Switz-Jr.	13	9	3	12	32	....	....	....	....	....	....	....	....	....	....	....	....	....	....	....	....	....	....	....
	GC Zurich	Switz-2	25	5	4	9	22	....	....	....	....	....	....	....	....	....	....	....	....	....	....	....	....	....	....	....
	ZSC Zurich	Switz.	18	0	2	2	4	....	....	....	....	....	....	....	....	....	....	....	....	....	....	....	....	....	....	....
1998-99	Ambri-Piotta	Switz.	38	2	4	6	18	....	....	....	....	....	....	....	....	....	....	....	12	0	0	0	8	....	....	....
	HC Sierre	Switz-2	4	1	2	3	2	....	....	....	....	....	....	....	....	....	....	....	....	....	....	....	....	....	....	....
99-2000	Ambri-Piotta	Switz.	45	7	7	14	24	....	....	....	....	....	....	....	....	....	....	....	9	1	5	6	16	....	....	....
2000-01	**Tampa Bay**	**NHL**	**5**	**0**	**0**	**0**	**0**	**0**	**0**	**0**	**2**	**0.0**	**–2**	**12**	**41.7**	**2**	**0**	**4:57**	....	....	....	....	....	....	....	....
	Detroit Vipers	IHL	67	8	19	27	40	....	....	....	....	....	....	....	....	....	....	....	....	....	....	....	....	....	....	....
	NHL Totals		**5**	**0**	**0**	**0**	**0**	**0**	**0**	**0**	**2**	**0.0**		**12**	**41.7**	**2**	**0**	**4:57**	....	....	....	....	....	....	....	....

ZUBOV, Sergei (ZOO-bahf, SAIR-gay) — DAL.

Defense. Shoots right. 6'1", 200 lbs. Born, Moscow, USSR, July 22, 1970. NY Rangers' 6th choice, 85th overall, in 1990 Entry Draft.

Season	Club	League	GP	G	A	Pts	PIM	PP	SH	GW	S	%	+/-	TF	F%	H	SB	Min	GP	G	A	Pts	PIM	PP	SH	GW
1988-89	CSKA Moscow	USSR	29	1	4	5	10	....	....	....	....	....	....	....	....	....	....	....	....	....	....	....	....	....	....	....
1989-90	CSKA Moscow	USSR	48	6	2	8	16	....	....	....	....	....	....	....	....	....	....	....	....	....	....	....	....	....	....	....
1990-91	CSKA Moscow	USSR	41	6	5	11	12	....	....	....	....	....	....	....	....	....	....	....	....	....	....	....	....	....	....	....
1991-92	CSKA Moscow	CIS	44	4	7	11	8	....	....	....	....	....	....	....	....	....	....	....	....	....	....	....	....	....	....	....
	Russia	Olympics	8	0	1	1	0	....	....	....	....	....	....	....	....	....	....	....	....	....	....	....	....	....	....	....
1992-93	CSKA Moscow	CIS	1	0	1	1	0	....	....	....	....	....	....	....	....	....	....	....	....	....	....	....	....	....	....	....
	NY Rangers	**NHL**	**49**	**8**	**23**	**31**	**4**	**3**	**0**	**0**	**93**	**8.6**	**–1**	....	....	....	....	....	....	....	....	....	....	....	....	....
	Binghamton	AHL	30	7	29	36	14	....	....	....	....	....	....	....	....	....	....	....	11	5	5	10	2	....	....	....
1993-94♦	**NY Rangers**	**NHL**	**78**	**12**	**77**	**89**	**39**	**9**	**0**	**1**	**222**	**5.4**	**20**	....	....	....	....	....	**22**	**5**	**14**	**19**	**0**	**2**	**0**	**0**
	Binghamton	AHL	2	1	2	3	0	....	....	....	....	....	....	....	....	....	....	....	....	....	....	....	....	....	....	....
1994-95	**NY Rangers**	**NHL**	**38**	**10**	**26**	**36**	**18**	**6**	**0**	**0**	**116**	**8.6**	**–2**	....	....	....	....	....	**10**	**3**	**8**	**11**	**2**	**1**	**0**	**0**
1995-96	**Pittsburgh**	**NHL**	**64**	**11**	**55**	**66**	**22**	**3**	**2**	**1**	**141**	**7.8**	**28**	....	....	....	....	....	**18**	**1**	**14**	**15**	**26**	**1**	**0**	**0**
1996-97	**Dallas**	**NHL**	**78**	**13**	**30**	**43**	**24**	**1**	**0**	**3**	**133**	**9.8**	**19**	....	....	....	....	....	**7**	**0**	**3**	**3**	**2**	**0**	**0**	**0**
1997-98	**Dallas**	**NHL**	**73**	**10**	**47**	**57**	**16**	**5**	**1**	**2**	**148**	**6.8**	**16**	....	....	....	....	....	**17**	**4**	**5**	**9**	**2**	**3**	**0**	**1**
1998-99♦	**Dallas**	**NHL**	**81**	**10**	**41**	**51**	**20**	**5**	**0**	**3**	**155**	**6.5**	**9**	**0**	**0.0**	**35**	**41**	**24:14**	**23**	**1**	**12**	**13**	**4**	**0**	**0**	**0**
99-2000	**Dallas**	**NHL**	**77**	**9**	**33**	**42**	**18**	**3**	**1**	**3**	**179**	**5.0**	**–2**	**0**	**0.0**	**52**	**58**	**28:50**	**18**	**2**	**7**	**9**	**6**	**1**	**1**	**0**
2000-01	**Dallas**	**NHL**	**79**	**10**	**41**	**51**	**24**	**6**	**0**	**1**	**173**	**5.8**	**22**	**0**	**0.0**	**49**	**78**	**26:37**	**10**	**1**	**5**	**6**	**4**	**0**	**0**	**0**
	NHL Totals		**617**	**93**	**373**	**466**	**185**	**41**	**4**	**14**	**1360**	**6.8**		**0**	**0.0**	**136**	**177**	**26:31**	**125**	**17**	**68**	**85**	**46**	**8**	**1**	**1**

Played in NHL All-Star Game (1998, 1999, 2000)

Traded to **Pittsburgh** by **NY Rangers** with Petr Nedved for Luc Robitaille and Ulf Samuelsson, August 31, 1995. Traded to **Dallas** by **Pittsburgh** for Kevin Hatcher, June 22, 1996.

ZUBRUS, Dainius (ZOO-bruhs, DAYN-ihs) — WSH.

Right wing. Shoots left. 6'4", 227 lbs. Born, Elektrenai, USSR, June 16, 1978. Philadelphia's 1st choice, 15th overall, in 1996 Entry Draft.

Season	Club	League	GP	G	A	Pts	PIM	PP	SH	GW	S	%	+/-	TF	F%	H	SB	Min	GP	G	A	Pts	PIM	PP	SH	GW
1995-96	Pembroke Kings	OCJHL	28	19	13	32	73	....	....	....	....	....	....	....	....	....	....	....	....	....	....	....	....	....	....	....
	Caledon Canucks	OCJHL	7	3	7	10	2	....	....	....	....	....	....	....	....	....	....	....	17	11	12	23	4	....	....	....
1996-97	**Philadelphia**	**NHL**	**68**	**8**	**13**	**21**	**22**	**1**	**0**	**2**	**71**	**11.3**	**3**	....	....	....	....	....	**19**	**5**	**4**	**9**	**12**	**1**	**0**	**1**
1997-98	**Philadelphia**	**NHL**	**69**	**8**	**25**	**33**	**42**	**1**	**0**	**5**	**101**	**7.9**	**29**	....	....	....	....	....	**5**	**0**	**1**	**1**	**2**	**0**	**0**	**0**
1998-99	**Philadelphia**	**NHL**	**63**	**3**	**5**	**8**	**25**	**0**	**1**	**0**	**49**	**6.1**	**–5**	**29**	**51.7**	**54**	**30**	**11:00**	....	....	....	....	....	....	....	....
	Montreal	**NHL**	**17**	**3**	**5**	**8**	**4**	**0**	**0**	**1**	**31**	**9.7**	**–3**	**2**	**50.0**	**15**	**6**	**16:53**	....	....	....	....	....	....	....	....
99-2000	**Montreal**	**NHL**	**73**	**14**	**28**	**42**	**54**	**3**	**0**	**1**	**139**	**10.1**	**–1**	**212**	**39.2**	**99**	**27**	**17:37**	....	....	....	....	....	....	....	....
2000-01	**Montreal**	**NHL**	**49**	**12**	**12**	**24**	**30**	**3**	**0**	**0**	**70**	**17.1**	**–7**	**190**	**41.1**	**58**	**34**	**18:30**	....	....	....	....	....	....	....	....
	Washington	**NHL**	**12**	**1**	**1**	**2**	**7**	**1**	**0**	**0**	**13**	**7.7**	**–4**	**0**	**0.0**	**15**	**3**	**13:05**	**6**	**0**	**0**	**0**	**2**	**0**	**0**	**0**
	NHL Totals		**351**	**49**	**89**	**138**	**184**	**9**	**1**	**9**	**474**	**10.3**		**433**	**40.9**	**241**	**100**	**15:34**	**30**	**5**	**5**	**10**	**16**	**1**	**0**	**1**

Traded to **Montreal** by **Philadelphia** with Philadelphia's 2nd round choice (Matt Carkner) in 1999 Entry Draft and NY Islanders' 6th round choice (previously acquired, Montreal selected Scott Selig) in 2000 Entry Draft for Mark Recchi, March 10, 1999. Traded to **Washington by Montreal** with Trevor Linden and New Jersey's 2nd round choice (previously acquired, later traded to Tampa Bay - Tampa Bay selected Andreas Holmqvist) in 2001 Entry Draft for Richard Zednik, Jan Bulis and Washington's 1st round choice (Alexander Perezhogin) in 2001 Entry Draft, March 13, 2001.

ZYUZIN, Andrei (ZYOO-zin, AWN-dray) — T.B.

Defense. Shoots right. 6'1", 210 lbs. Born, Ufa, USSR, January 21, 1978. San Jose's 1st choice, 2nd overall, in 1996 Entry Draft.

Season	Club	League	GP	G	A	Pts	PIM	PP	SH	GW	S	%	+/-	TF	F%	H	SB	Min	GP	G	A	Pts	PIM	PP	SH	GW
1994-95	Ufa Salavat	CIS	30	3	0	3	16	....	....	....	....	....	....	....	....	....	....	....	....	....	....	....	....	....	....	....
1995-96	Ufa Salavat	CIS	41	6	3	9	24	....	....	....	....	....	....	....	....	....	....	....	....	....	....	....	....	....	....	....
1996-97	Ufa Salavat	Russia	32	7	10	17	28	....	....	....	....	....	....	....	....	....	....	....	7	1	1	2	4	....	....	....
1997-98	**San Jose**	**NHL**	**56**	**6**	**7**	**13**	**66**	**2**	**0**	**2**	**72**	**8.3**	**8**	....	....	....	....	....	**6**	**1**	**0**	**1**	**14**	**0**	**0**	**1**
	Kentucky	AHL	17	4	5	9	28	....	....	....	....	....	....	....	....	....	....	....	....	....	....	....	....	....	....	....
1998-99	**San Jose**	**NHL**	**25**	**3**	**1**	**4**	**38**	**2**	**0**	**0**	**44**	**6.8**	**5**	**0**	**0.0**	**25**	**11**	**15:56**	....	....	....	....	....	....	....	....
	Kentucky	AHL	23	2	12	14	42	....	....	....	....	....	....	....	....	....	....	....	....	....	....	....	....	....	....	....
99-2000	**Tampa Bay**	**NHL**	**34**	**2**	**9**	**11**	**33**	**0**	**0**	**0**	**47**	**4.3**	**–11**	**0**	**0.0**	**33**	**27**	**20:28**	....	....	....	....	....	....	....	....
2000-01	**Tampa Bay**	**NHL**	**64**	**4**	**16**	**20**	**76**	**2**	**1**	**1**	**92**	**4.3**	**–8**	**0**	**0.0**	**42**	**66**	**18:39**	....	....	....	....	....	....	....	....
	Detroit Vipers	IHL	2	0	1	1	0	....	....	....	....	....	....	....	....	....	....	....	....	....	....	....	....	....	....	....
	NHL Totals		**179**	**15**	**33**	**48**	**213**	**6**	**1**	**3**	**255**	**5.9**		**0**	**0.0**	**100**	**104**	**18:36**	**6**	**1**	**0**	**1**	**14**	**0**	**0**	**1**

• Suspended for remainder of 1998-99 season by **San Jose** for leaving team without permission, April 1, 1999. Traded to **Tampa Bay** by **San Jose** with Bill Houlder, Shawn Burr and Steve Guolla for Niklas Sundstrom and NY Rangers' 3rd round choice (previously acquired, later traded to Chicago - Chicago selected Igor Radulov) in 2000 Entry Draft, August 4, 1999. • Missed majority of 1999-2000 season recovering from shoulder injury suffered in game vs. NY Islanders, January 13, 2000.

Goaltenders

Jean-Sebastien Aubin · Tom Barrasso · Ed Belfour · Zac Bierk · Craig Billington · Martin Biron · Brian Boucher · Fred Brathwaite · Martin Brodeur · Sean Burke

Roman Cechmanek · Dan Cloutier · Marcel Cousineau · Byron Dafoe · Jean-Francois Damphousse · Marc Denis · Rick DiPietro · Mike Dunham · Robert Esche · Bob Essensa

Scott Fankhouser · Manny Fernandez · Eric Fichaud · Stephane Fiset · Mark Fitzpatrick · Wade Flaherty · Mike Fountain · Mathieu Garon · Jean-Sebastien Giguere · John Grahame

Jeff Hackett · Dominik Hasek · Guy Hebert · Johan Hedberg · Corey Hirsch · Milan Hnilicka · Jani Hurme · Arturs Irbe · Brent Johnson · Curtis Joseph

Nikolai Khabibulin · Trevor Kidd · Olaf Kolzig · Jean-Francois Labbe · Patrick Lalime · Marc Lamothe · Scott Langkow · Manny Legace · Neil Little · Roberto Luongo

Norm Maracle · Kirk McLean · Jamie McLennan · Alfie Michaud · Tyler Moss · Evgeni Nabokov · Chris Osgood · Rich Parent · Steve Passmore · Felix Potvin

Andrew Raycroft · Damian Rhodes · Mike Richter · Dwayne Roloson · Dominic Roussel · Patrick Roy · Tommy Salo · Philippe Sauve · Corey Schwab · Steve Shields

Mikhail Shtalenkov · Richard Shulmistra · Peter Skudra · Garth Snow · Jamie Storr · Rick Tabaracci · Robbie Tallas · Jose Theodore · Jocelyn Thibault · Andrei Trefilov

Ron Tugnutt · Roman Turek · Marty Turco · Stephen Valiquette · Mike Vernon · Tomas Vokoun · Jimmy Waite · Kevin Weekes · Kay Whitmore · Ken Wregget

2001-02 Goaltender Register

Note: The 2001-02 Goaltender Register lists every goaltender who appeared in an NHL game in the 2000-01 season, every goaltender drafted in the first five rounds of the 2001 Entry Draft, goaltenders on NHL Reserve Lists and other goaltenders.

Trades and roster changes are current as of August 20, 2001.

To calculate a goaltender's goals-against-per-game average **(Avg)**, divide goals against **(GA)** by minutes played **(Mins)** and multiply this result by **60**.

Abbreviations: Lea – league; **GP** – games played; **W** – wins; **L** – losses; **T** – ties; **GA** – goals against; **SO** – shutouts; **Avg** – goals against per game average.
♦ – member of Stanley Cup-winning team.

NHL Player Register begins on page 338.
Prospect Register begins on page 275.
League Abbreviations are listed on page 274.

AEBISCHER, David (A-bih-shuhr, DAY-vihd) COL.

Goaltender. Catches left. 6'1", 190 lbs. Born, Fribourg, Switz., February 7, 1978.
(Colorado's 7th choice, 161st overall, in 1997 Entry Draft).

			Regular Season								Playoffs						
Season	**Club**	**Lea**	**GP**	**W**	**L**	**T**	**Mins**	**GA**	**SO**	**Avg**	**GP**	**W**	**L**	**Mins**	**GA**	**SO**	**Avg**
1996-97	HC Fribourg	Switz.	10	....	....	....	577	34	0	3.53	3	1	2	184	13	0	4.24
1997-98	Chesapeake	ECHL	17	5	7	2	930	52	0	3.35	....	....	....	....	....	....	....
	Wheeling Nailers	ECHL	10	5	3	1	564	30	1	3.19	....	....	....	....	....	....	....
	Hershey Bears	AHL	2	0	0	1	79	5	0	3.76	....	....	....	....	....	....	....
	HC Fribourg	Switz.	1	1	0	0	60	1	0	1.00	4	....	....	240	17	....	4.25
1998-99	Hershey Bears	AHL	38	17	10	5	1932	79	2	2.45	3	1	2	152	6	0	2.37
99-2000	Hershey Bears	AHL	58	29	23	2	3259	180	1	3.31	14	7	6	788	40	2	3.05
2000-01♦	**Colorado**	**NHL**	**26**	**12**	**7**	**3**	**1393**	**52**	**3**	**2.24**	**1**	**0**	**0**	**1**	**0**	**0**	**0.00**
	NHL Totals		**26**	**12**	**7**	**3**	**1393**	**52**	**3**	**2.24**	**1**	**0**	**0**	**1**	**0**	**0**	**0.00**

AHONEN, Ari (ah-HOH-nuhn, AH-ree) N.J.

Goaltender. Catches left. 6'1", 185 lbs. Born, Jyvaskyla, Finland, February 6, 1981.
(New Jersey's 1st choice, 27th overall, in 1999 Entry Draft).

			Regular Season								Playoffs						
Season	**Club**	**Lea**	**GP**	**W**	**L**	**T**	**Mins**	**GA**	**SO**	**Avg**	**GP**	**W**	**L**	**Mins**	**GA**	**SO**	**Avg**
1997-98	JyP Jyvaskyla	Finn-Jr.	31	....	....	....	1853	64	....	2.09	....	....	....	....	....	....	....
1998-99	JyP Jyvaskyla	Finn-Jr.	24	....	....	....	1447	70	....	2.90	....	....	....	....	....	....	....
99-2000	HIFK Helsinki	Finland	24	11	7	1	1347	70	1	3.12	2	0	2	119	7	0	3.53
	HIFK Helsinki	EuroHL	5	4	1	0	285	15	1	3.16	....	....	....	....	....	....	....
2000-01	HIFK Helsinki	Finland	37	18	13	4	2101	97	2	2.77	5	2	3	395	9	1	1.37

ALBAN, Chad (AL-ban, CHAD) DAL.

Goaltender. Catches left. 5'9", 165 lbs. Born, Kalamazoo, MI, April 27, 1976.

			Regular Season								Playoffs						
Season	**Club**	**Lea**	**GP**	**W**	**L**	**T**	**Mins**	**GA**	**SO**	**Avg**	**GP**	**W**	**L**	**Mins**	**GA**	**SO**	**Avg**
1994-95	Michigan State	CCHA	13	8	2	0	636	29	0	2.73	....	....	....	....	....	....	....
1995-96	Michigan State	CCHA	40	26	13	1	2286	117	0	3.07	....	....	....	....	....	....	....
1996-97	Michigan State	CCHA	39	23	11	4	2272	103	3	2.72	....	....	....	....	....	....	....
1997-98	Michigan State	CCHA	40	31	4	5	2438	64	*6	*1.57	....	....	....	....	....	....	....
1998-99	Mobile Mysticks	ECHL	34	16	14	3	1960	111	1	3.40	2	0	2	119	9	0	4.54
	Houston Aeros	IHL	5	1	3	1	284	14	0	2.96	....	....	....	....	....	....	....
99-2000	Mobile Mysticks	ECHL	39	25	13	1	2334	114	0	2.93	5	2	3	299	20	0	4.01
	Utah Grizzlies	IHL	1	0	1	0	35	3	0	5.16	....	....	....	....	....	....	....
2000-01	Idaho Steelheads	WCHL	20	14	5	1	1121	56	1	3.00	10	6	4	596	33	0	3.32
	Grand Rapids	IHL	3	2	1	0	180	4	1	1.33	....	....	....	....	....	....	....
	Utah Grizzlies	IHL	11	2	4	4	597	23	0	2.31	....	....	....	....	....	....	....

Won CCHA Rookie of the Year Award (1995) • CCHA First All-Star Team (1998) • NCAA West First All-American Team (1998) • CCHA Player-of-the-Year (1998) • Scored goal in game vs. Ferris State (CCHA), February 28, 1998.

Signed as a free agent by **Dallas**, August 30, 2000.

ALLEN, Andrew (AHL-lehn, AN-droo)

Goaltender. Catches left. 6'4", 210 lbs. Born, Vankleek Hill, Ont., August 2, 1976.

			Regular Season								Playoffs						
Season	**Club**	**Lea**	**GP**	**W**	**L**	**T**	**Mins**	**GA**	**SO**	**Avg**	**GP**	**W**	**L**	**Mins**	**GA**	**SO**	**Avg**
1994-95	Hawkesbury	OCJHL	13	7	3	0	579	34	0	3.52	....	....	....	....	....	....	....
1995-96	Hawkesbury	OCJHL	39	22	10	3	2151	132	0	3.68	....	....	....	....	....	....	....
1996-97	Hawkesbury	OCJHL	40	6	22	4	2010	160	0	4.78	....	....	....	....	....	....	....
1997-98	U. of Vermont	ECAC	27	8	13	4	1474	82	0	3.34	....	....	....	....	....	....	....
1998-99	U. of Vermont	ECAC	24	8	13	2	1296	56	0	2.59	....	....	....	....	....	....	....
99-2000	U. of Vermont	ECAC	11	3	5	1	558	41	0	4.41	....	....	....	....	....	....	....
2000-01	U. of Vermont	ECAC	24	9	10	2	1340	64	1	2.87	....	....	....	....	....	....	....
	Dayton Bombers	ECAC	4	4	0	0	240	5	2	1.25	....	....	....	....	....	....	....

ECAC Academic All-Star Team (2000, 2001)

Signed as a free agent by **Florida**, August 2, 2001.

AMIDOVSKI, Bujar (am-ih-DAWV-skee, BOO-jahr) CAR.

Goaltender. Catches left. 5'11", 180 lbs. Born, Toronto, Ont., February 19, 1977.

			Regular Season								Playoffs						
Season	**Club**	**Lea**	**GP**	**W**	**L**	**T**	**Mins**	**GA**	**SO**	**Avg**	**GP**	**W**	**L**	**Mins**	**GA**	**SO**	**Avg**
1994-95	North York	MTJHL	35	....	....	....	2089	137	0	3.93	....	....	....	....	....	....	....
1995-96	Kingston	OHL	38	16	16	2	1970	136	1	4.14	4	1	2	194	11	0	3.40
1996-97	Kingston	OHL	36	11	14	1	1797	116	0	3.87	5	1	3	280	24	0	5.14
	Dayton Bombers	ECHL	3	1	1	0	90	5	0	3.31	2	0	2	118	9	0	4.56
1997-98	St. Michael's	OHL	48	12	25	7	2697	153	0	3.40	....	....	....	....	....	....	....
1998-99	Louisiana	ECHL	27	17	5	3	1525	59	3	2.32	....	....	....	....	....	....	....
	Philadelphia	AHL	2	2	0	0	120	5	0	2.50	....	....	....	....	....	....	....
	Saint John Flames	AHL	6	2	2	0	243	19	0	4.69	....	....	....	....	....	....	....
99-2000	Trenton Titans	ECHL	34	19	11	3	1979	82	2	2.49	5	2	3	254	13	1	3.07
	Philadelphia	AHL	6	3	1	0	250	8	0	1.92	....	....	....	....	....	....	....
2000-01	Cincinnati	IHL	3	0	1	0	94	6	0	3.83	....	....	....	....	....	....	....
	Florida Everblades	ECHL	30	11	8	3	1456	88	0	3.63	....	....	....	....	....	....	....

OHL First All-Star Team (1998)

Signed as a free agent by **Philadelphia**, August 15, 1999. Signed as a free agent by **Carolina**, August 21, 2000.

ANDERSSON, Andreas (AN-duhr-suhn, AN-dree-as) ANA.

Goaltender. Catches left. 6', 180 lbs. Born, Jonkoping, Sweden, April 4, 1979.
(Anaheim's 8th choice, 245th overall, in 1998 Entry Draft).

			Regular Season								Playoffs						
Season	**Club**	**Lea**	**GP**	**W**	**L**	**T**	**Mins**	**GA**	**SO**	**Avg**	**GP**	**W**	**L**	**Mins**	**GA**	**SO**	**Avg**
1997-98	HV Jonkoping	Swede-Jr.	10	....	....	....	600	31	....	3.10	....	....	....	....	....	....	....
	HV Jonkoping	Sweden	7	....	....	....	420	20	....	2.86	....	....	....	....	....	....	....
1998-99	Mora IK	Swede-Jr.	12	....	....	....	720	28	0	1.92	....	....	....	....	....	....	....
	HV Jonkoping	Sweden	12	....	....	....	633	35	0	3.32	....	....	....	....	....	....	....
99-2000	Tranas AIF	Swede-2	5	....	....	....	297	17	0	3.44	....	....	....	....	....	....	....
	HV Jonkoping	Sweden	1	....	....	....	51	5	0	5.88	....	....	....	....	....	....	....
2000-01	IF Troja Ljunby	Swede-2	19	....	....	....	1076	66	0	3.68	2	1	1	120	5	0	2.50

ANDERSSON, Craig (AN-duhr-suhn, KRAYG) CHI.

Goaltender. Catches left. 6'2", 174 lbs. Born, Park Ridge, IL, May 21, 1981.
(Chicago's 4th choice, 73rd overall, in 2001 Entry Draft).

			Regular Season								Playoffs						
Season	**Club**	**Lea**	**GP**	**W**	**L**	**T**	**Mins**	**GA**	**SO**	**Avg**	**GP**	**W**	**L**	**Mins**	**GA**	**SO**	**Avg**
1997-98	Chicago Jets	MEHL	50	....	....	....	2991	143	2	2.86	....	....	....	....	....	....	....
1998-99	Chicago Freeze	NAJHL	14	11	3	0	840	40	0	2.56	....	....	....	....	....	....	....
	Guelph Storm	OHL	21	12	5	1	1006	52	1	3.10	3	0	2	114	9	0	4.74
99-2000	Guelph Storm	OHL	38	12	17	2	1955	117	0	3.59	3	0	1	110	5	0	2.73
2000-01	Guelph Storm	OHL	59	30	19	9	3555	156	3	2.63	4	0	4	240	17	0	4.25

• Re-entered NHL Entry Draft. Originally Calgary's 3rd choice, 77th overall, in 1999 Entry Draft.

OHL First All-Star Team (2001)

ANTILA, Kristian (AN-tih-luh, KRIHS-tan) EDM.

Goaltender. Catches left. 6'3", 207 lbs. Born, Vammala, Finland, January 10, 1980.
(Edmonton's 4th choice, 113th overall, in 1998 Entry Draft).

			Regular Season								Playoffs						
Season	**Club**	**Lea**	**GP**	**W**	**L**	**T**	**Mins**	**GA**	**SO**	**Avg**	**GP**	**W**	**L**	**Mins**	**GA**	**SO**	**Avg**
1997-98	Ilves Tampere	Finn-Jr.	11	....	....	....	564	28	0	2.97	....	....	....	....	....	....	....
1998-99	Ilves Tampere	Finn-Jr.	14	....	....	....	798	35	....	2.63	....	....	....	....	....	....	....
	Ilves Tampere	Finland	5	1	2	0	207	12	0	3.48	....	....	....	....	....	....	....
99-2000	Ilves Tampere	Finland	25	4	11	4	1239	74	1	3.58	1	0	1	20	4	0	12.00
2000-01	Assat-Pori	Finland	42	9	27	7	2417	146	1	3.62	....	....	....	....	....	....	....

ASKEY, Tom (AS-kee, TAWM) BUF.

Goaltender. Catches left. 6'2", 185 lbs. Born, Kenmore, NY, October 4, 1974.
(Anaheim's 8th choice, 186th overall, in 1993 Entry Draft).

			Regular Season								Playoffs						
Season	Club	Lea	GP	W	L	T	Mins	GA	SO	Avg	GP	W	L	Mins	GA	SO	Avg
1992-93	Ohio State	CCHA	25	2	19	0	1235	125	0	6.07	....	....	....	....	....	....	....
1993-94	Ohio State	CCHA	27	3	19	4	1488	103	0	4.15	....	....	....	....	....	....	....
1994-95	Ohio State	CCHA	26	4	19	2	1387	121	0	5.23	....	....	....	....	....	....	....
1995-96	Ohio State	CCHA	26	8	11	4	1340	68	0	3.05	....	....	....	....	....	....	....
1996-97	Baltimore Bandits	AHL	40	17	18	2	2238	140	1	3.75	3	0	3	137	11	0	4.79
1997-98	**Anaheim**	**NHL**	**7**	**0**	**1**	**2**	**273**	**12**	**0**	**2.64**	....	....	....	....	....	....	....
	Cincinnati Ducks	AHL	32	10	16	4	1753	104	3	3.56	....	....	....	....	....	....	....
1998-99	Cincinnati Ducks	AHL	53	21	22	3	2893	131	3	2.72	3	0	3	178	13	0	4.38
	Anaheim	**NHL**	....	....	....	....	....	....	....	....	**1**	**0**	**1**	**30**	**2**	**0**	**4.00**
99-2000	Kansas City	IHL	13	3	5	3	658	43	0	3.92	....	....	....	....	....	....	....
	Houston Aeros	IHL	13	4	7	1	727	33	0	2.72	....	....	....	....	....	....	....
2000-01	Rochester	AHL	29	15	8	4	1671	71	1	2.55	....	....	....	....	....	....	....
	NHL Totals		**7**	**0**	**1**	**2**	**273**	**12**	**0**	**2.64**	**1**	**0**	**1**	**30**	**2**	**0**	**4.00**

CCHA Second All-Star Team (1996) • Shared Harry "Hap" Holmes Memorial Trophy (fewest goals against - AHL) with Mika Noronen (2001)

Signed as a free agent by **Rochester** AHL), September 29, 2000. Signed as a free agent by **Buffalo**, August 10, 2001.

ASPLUND, Johan (AS-pluhnd, YOH-hahn) NYR

Goaltender. Catches left. 6'1", 180 lbs. Born, Slutskar, Sweden, December 15, 1980.
(NY Rangers' 4th choice, 79th overall, in 1999 Entry Draft).

			Regular Season								Playoffs						
Season	Club	Lea	GP	W	L	T	Mins	GA	SO	Avg	GP	W	L	Mins	GA	SO	Avg
1998-99	Brynas IF	Sweden	12	....	....	....	646	32	0	2.97	....	....	....	....	....	....	....
99-2000	Mora IK	Swede-2	3	3	0	0	180	6	0	2.00	....	....	....	....	....	....	....
	Brynas IF	Sweden	10	....	....	....	622	30	0	2.89	....	....	....	....	....	....	....
2000-01	Brynas IF	Sweden	29	....	....	....	1761	79	2	2.69	3	....	....	177	11	0	3.73

AUBIN, Jean-Sebastien (OH-behn, ZHAWN-suh-BAS-tee-yeh) PIT.

Goaltender. Catches right. 5'11", 176 lbs. Born, Montreal, Que., July 17, 1977.
(Pittsburgh's 2nd choice, 76th overall, in 1995 Entry Draft).

			Regular Season								Playoffs						
Season	Club	Lea	GP	W	L	T	Mins	GA	SO	Avg	GP	W	L	Mins	GA	SO	Avg
1993-94	Montreal-Bourassa	QAAA	27	14	13	0	1524	96	1	3.74	4	1	3	222	19	0	5.14
1994-95	Sherbrooke	QMJHL	27	13	10	1	1287	73	1	3.40	3	1	2	185	11	0	3.57
1995-96	Sherbrooke	QMJHL	40	18	14	2	2140	127	0	3.57	4	1	3	238	23	0	5.55
1996-97	Laval Titan	QMJHL	11	2	6	1	532	41	0	4.62	....	....	....	....	....	....	....
	Moncton Wildcats	QMJHL	22	9	12	0	1252	67	1	3.21	....	....	....	....	....	....	....
	Sherbrooke	QMJHL	4	3	1	0	249	8	0	1.93	1	0	1	60	4	0	4.00
1997-98	Syracuse Crunch	AHL	8	2	4	1	380	26	0	4.10	....	....	....	....	....	....	....
	Dayton Bombers	ECHL	21	15	2	2	1177	59	1	3.01	3	1	1	142	4	0	1.69
1998-99	**Pittsburgh**	**NHL**	**17**	**4**	**3**	**6**	**756**	**28**	**2**	**2.22**	....	....	....	....	....	....	....
	Kansas City	IHL	13	5	7	1	751	41	0	3.28	....	....	....	....	....	....	....
99-2000	**Pittsburgh**	**NHL**	**51**	**23**	**21**	**3**	**2789**	**120**	**2**	**2.58**	....	....	....	....	....	....	....
	Wilkes-Barre	AHL	11	2	8	0	538	39	0	4.35	....	....	....	....	....	....	....
2000-01	**Pittsburgh**	**NHL**	**36**	**20**	**14**	**1**	**2050**	**107**	**0**	**3.13**	**1**	**0**	**0**	**1**	**0**	**0**	**0.00**
	NHL Totals		**104**	**47**	**38**	**10**	**5595**	**255**	**4**	**2.73**	**1**	**0**	**0**	**1**	**0**	**0**	**0.00**

AULD, Alexander (AWLD, al-ehx-AN-duhr) VAN.

Goaltender. Catches left. 6'4", 197 lbs. Born, Cold Lake, Alta., January 7, 1981.
(Florida's 2nd choice, 40th overall, in 1999 Entry Draft).

			Regular Season								Playoffs						
Season	Club	Lea	GP	W	L	T	Mins	GA	SO	Avg	GP	W	L	Mins	GA	SO	Avg
1996-97	Thunder Bay	TBMHL	35	....	....	....	2100	46	10	1.35	....	....	....	....	....	....	....
1997-98	Sturgeon Falls	NOJHA	11	4	6	0	611	46	0	4.52	....	....	....	....	....	....	....
	North Bay	OHL	6	0	4	0	206	17	0	4.95	....	....	....	....	....	....	....
1998-99	North Bay	OHL	37	9	20	1	1894	106	1	3.36	3	0	3	170	10	0	3.53
99-2000	North Bay	OHL	55	21	26	6	3047	167	2	3.29	6	2	4	374	12	0	*1.93
2000-01	North Bay	OHL	40	22	11	5	2319	98	1	2.54	4	0	4	240	15	0	3.75

Traded to **Vancouver** by **Florida** for future considerations, May 31, 2001.

AYERS, Michael (AY-uhrs, MIGH-kuhl) CHI.

Goaltender. Catches left. 5'11", 183 lbs. Born, Weymouth, MA, January 16, 1980.
(Chicago's 8th choice, 177th overall, in 2000 Entry Draft).

			Regular Season								Playoffs						
Season	Club	Lea	GP	W	L	T	Mins	GA	SO	Avg	GP	W	L	Mins	GA	SO	Avg
1998-99	Trinity Pawling	Hi-School	STATISTICS NOT AVAILABLE														
99-2000	Dubuque Saints	USHL	55	16	35	3	3188	196	0	3.69	....	....	....	....	....	....	....
2000-01	New Hampshire	H-East	4	0	0	0	26	2	0	4.68	....	....	....	....	....	....	....

BACASHIHUA, Jason (bak-ah-SHIH-hu-ah, JAY-suhn) DAL.

Goaltender. Catches left. 5'11", 167 lbs. Born, Garden City, MI, September 20, 1982.
(Dallas' 1st choice, 26th overall, in 2001 Entry Draft).

			Regular Season								Playoffs						
Season	Club	Lea	GP	W	L	T	Mins	GA	SO	Avg	GP	W	L	Mins	GA	SO	Avg
99-2000	Chicago Freeze	NAJHL	41	20	19	2	2432	118	2	2.91	2	0	2	103	12	0	6.97
2000-01	Chicago Freeze	NAJHL	39	24	14	0	2246	121	1	3.23	3	1	2	190	12	0	3.79

BACH, Ryan (BAWK, RIGH-uhn)

Goaltender. Catches left. 6'1", 185 lbs. Born, Sherwood Park, Alta., October 21, 1973.
(Detroit's 11th choice, 262nd overall, in 1992 Entry Draft).

			Regular Season								Playoffs						
Season	Club	Lea	GP	W	L	T	Mins	GA	SO	Avg	GP	W	L	Mins	GA	SO	Avg
1991-92	Notre Dame	SJHL	33	16	11	6	1062	124	0	4.00	....	....	....	....	....	....	....
1992-93	Colorado College	WCHA	4	1	1	0	239	11	0	2.76	....	....	....	....	....	....	....
1993-94	Colorado College	WCHA	30	17	7	5	1733	105	0	3.64	....	....	....	....	....	....	....
1994-95	Colorado College	WCHA	27	18	5	1	1522	83	0	3.27	....	....	....	....	....	....	....
1995-96	Colorado College	WCHA	23	*17	4	2	1390	62	2	2.68	....	....	....	....	....	....	....
1996-97	Utica Blizzard	ColHL	2	0	1	1	119	8	0	4.03	....	....	....	....	....	....	....
	Toledo Storm	ECHL	20	5	11	3	1168	74	0	3.80	....	....	....	....	....	....	....
	Adirondack	AHL	13	2	3	1	451	29	0	3.86	1	0	0	46	3	0	3.92
1997-98	Houston Aeros	IHL	43	26	9	6	2452	95	5	2.32	....	....	....	....	....	....	....
1998-99	Utah Grizzlies	IHL	4	2	1	0	197	9	0	2.74	....	....	....	....	....	....	....
	Los Angeles	**NHL**	**3**	**0**	**3**	**0**	**108**	**8**	**0**	**4.44**	....	....	....	....	....	....	....
	Long Beach	IHL	27	10	9	5	1491	74	1	2.98	3	0	2	152	7	0	2.76
99-2000	Louisville Panthers	AHL	11	4	4	1	603	33	0	3.28	....	....	....	....	....	....	....
	Wilkes-Barre	AHL	28	8	18	2	1590	100	0	3.77	....	....	....	....	....	....	....
	Kansas City	IHL	6	3	3	0	358	19	0	3.18	....	....	....	....	....	....	....
2000-01	Louisville Panthers	AHL	30	6	13	1	1297	66	1	3.05	....	....	....	....	....	....	....
	NHL Totals		**3**	**0**	**3**	**0**	**108**	**8**	**0**	**4.44**	....	....	....	....	....	....	....

WCHA First All-Star Team (1995, 1996) • NCAA West Second All-American Team (1995) • NCAA West First All-American Team (1996)

Traded to **Los Angeles** by **Detroit** for Los Angeles' 6th round choice (Per Backer) in 2000 Entry Draft, October 22, 1998. Signed as a free agent by **Florida**, July 27, 1999.

BAILEY, Scott (BAY-lee, SKAWT)

Goaltender. Catches left. 6', 195 lbs. Born, Calgary, Alta., May 2, 1972.
(Boston's 3rd choice, 112th overall, in 1992 Entry Draft).

			Regular Season								Playoffs						
Season	Club	Lea	GP	W	L	T	Mins	GA	SO	Avg	GP	W	L	Mins	GA	SO	Avg
1988-89	Calgary Flames	AMHL	STATISTICS NOT AVAILABLE														
	Moose Jaw	WHL	2	0	1	0	34	7	0	12.35	....	....	....	....	....	....	....
1989-90	Calgary Buffaloes	AJHL	17	....	....	....	991	55	1	3.33	....	....	....	....	....	....	....
1990-91	Spokane Chiefs	WHL	46	33	11	0	2537	157	*4	3.71	....	....	....	....	....	....	....
1991-92	Spokane Chiefs	WHL	65	34	23	5	3798	206	1	3.30	10	5	5	605	43	0	4.26
1992-93	Johnstown Chiefs	ECHL	36	13	15	3	1750	112	1	3.84	....	....	....	....	....	....	....
1993-94	Providence Bruins	AHL	7	2	2	2	377	24	0	3.82	....	....	....	....	....	....	....
	Charlotte	ECHL	36	22	11	3	2180	130	1	3.58	3	1	2	187	12	0	3.83
1994-95	Providence Bruins	AHL	52	25	16	9	2936	147	2	3.00	9	4	4	504	31	*2	3.69
1995-96	**Boston**	**NHL**	**11**	**5**	**1**	**2**	**571**	**31**	**0**	**3.26**	....	....	....	....	....	....	....
	Providence Bruins	AHL	37	15	19	3	2210	120	1	3.26	2	1	1	119	6	0	3.03
1996-97	**Boston**	**NHL**	**8**	**1**	**5**	**0**	**394**	**24**	**0**	**3.65**	....	....	....	....	....	....	....
	Providence Bruins	AHL	31	11	17	2	1735	112	0	3.87	7	3	4	453	23	0	3.05
1997-98	San Antonio	IHL	37	11	17	3	1898	118	1	3.73	....	....	....	....	....	....	....
1998-99	Orlando	IHL	17	5	7	0	749	36	0	2.88	....	....	....	....	....	....	....
	Birmingham Bulls	ECHL	27	16	8	2	1557	90	1	3.47	5	2	3	299	21	0	4.21
99-2000	Tappara Tampere	Finland	6	0	4	2	347	29	0	5.01	....	....	....	....	....	....	....
	Charlotte	ECHL	31	10	16	4	1735	93	2	3.22	....	....	....	....	....	....	....
	Saint John Flames	AHL	4	0	1	0	135	11	0	4.90	....	....	....	....	....	....	....
2000-01	Charlotte	ECHL	29	10	12	5	1682	89	1	3.17	3	1	2	197	10	0	3.02
	NHL Totals		**19**	**6**	**6**	**2**	**965**	**55**	**0**	**3.42**	....	....	....	....	....	....	....

Won WHL West Rookie of the Year Award (1991) • WHL West Second All-Star Team (1991, 1992)

Signed as a free agent by **Charlotte** (ECHL), December 10, 1999. Loaned to **Saint John** (AHL) by **Charlotte** (ECHL), February 6, 2000.

BALES, Mike (BAYLZ, MIGHK)

Goaltender. Catches left. 6'1", 200 lbs. Born, Prince Albert, Sask., August 6, 1971.
(Boston's 4th choice, 105th overall, in 1990 Entry Draft).

			Regular Season								Playoffs						
Season	Club	Lea	GP	W	L	T	Mins	GA	SO	Avg	GP	W	L	Mins	GA	SO	Avg
1988-89	Estevan Bruins	SJHL	44	....	....	....	2412	197	1	4.90	....	....	....	....	....	....	....
1989-90	Ohio State	CCHA	21	6	13	2	1117	95	0	5.11	....	....	....	....	....	....	....
1990-91	Ohio State	CCHA	*39	11	24	3	*2180	184	0	5.06	....	....	....	....	....	....	....
1991-92	Ohio State	CCHA	36	11	20	5	2060	180	0	5.24	....	....	....	....	....	....	....
1992-93	**Boston**	**NHL**	**1**	**0**	**0**	**0**	**25**	**1**	**0**	**2.40**	....	....	....	....	....	....	....
	Providence Bruins	AHL	44	22	17	0	2363	166	1	4.21	2	0	2	118	8	0	4.07
1993-94	Providence Bruins	AHL	33	9	15	4	1757	130	0	4.44	....	....	....	....	....	....	....
1994-95	P.E.I. Senators	AHL	45	25	16	3	2649	160	2	3.62	9	6	3	530	24	*2	2.72
	Ottawa	**NHL**	**1**	**0**	**0**	**0**	**3**	**0**	**0**	**0.00**	....	....	....	....	....	....	....
1995-96	**Ottawa**	**NHL**	**20**	**2**	**14**	**1**	**1040**	**72**	**0**	**4.15**	....	....	....	....	....	....	....
	P.E.I. Senators	AHL	2	0	2	0	118	11	0	5.58	....	....	....	....	....	....	....
1996-97	**Ottawa**	**NHL**	**1**	**0**	**1**	**0**	**52**	**4**	**0**	**4.62**	....	....	....	....	....	....	....
	Baltimore Bandits	AHL	46	13	21	8	2544	130	3	3.07	....	....	....	....	....	....	....
1997-98	Rochester	AHL	39	13	19	5	2229	127	0	3.42	....	....	....	....	....	....	....
1998-99	Michigan K-Wings	IHL	32	11	17	3	1773	96	1	3.25	....	....	....	....	....	....	....
99-2000	Michigan K-Wings	IHL	25	9	9	5	1341	56	0	2.50	....	....	....	....	....	....	....
2000-01	Utah Grizzlies	IHL	50	22	19	3	2697	111	5	2.47	....	....	....	....	....	....	....
	NHL Totals		**23**	**2**	**15**	**1**	**1120**	**77**	**0**	**4.13**	....	....	....	....	....	....	....

Signed as a free agent by **Ottawa**, July 4, 1994. Signed as a free agent by **Buffalo**, September 9, 1997. Signed as a free agent by **Dallas**, July 8, 1998. Signed as a free agent by **Bracknell** (Britain), August 13, 2001.

BARRASSO, Tom (buh-RAH-soh, TAWM) CAR.

Goaltender. Catches right. 6'3", 210 lbs. Born, Boston, MA, March 31, 1965.
(Buffalo's 1st choice, 5th overall, in 1983 Entry Draft).

			Regular Season								Playoffs						
Season	Club	Lea	GP	W	L	T	Mins	GA	SO	Avg	GP	W	L	Mins	GA	SO	Avg
1981-82	Acton-Boxboro	H.S.	23	....	....	....	1035	32	7	1.86	....	....	....	....	....	....	....
1982-83	Acton-Boxboro	H.S.	23	22	0	1	1035	17	10	0.99	....	....	....	....	....	....	....
1983-84	**Buffalo**	**NHL**	**42**	**26**	**12**	**3**	**2475**	**117**	**2**	**2.84**	**3**	**0**	**2**	**139**	**8**	**0**	**3.45**
1984-85	**Buffalo**	**NHL**	**54**	**25**	**18**	**10**	**3248**	**144**	***5**	***2.66**	**5**	**2**	**3**	**300**	**22**	**0**	**4.40**
	Rochester	AHL	5	3	1	1	267	6	1	1.35	....	....	....	....	....	....	....
1985-86	**Buffalo**	**NHL**	**60**	**29**	**24**	**5**	**3561**	**214**	**2**	**3.61**	....	....	....	....	....	....	....
1986-87	**Buffalo**	**NHL**	**46**	**17**	**23**	**2**	**2501**	**152**	**2**	**3.65**	....	....	....	....	....	....	....
1987-88	**Buffalo**	**NHL**	**54**	**25**	**18**	**8**	**3133**	**173**	**2**	**3.31**	**4**	**1**	**3**	**224**	**16**	**0**	**4.29**
1988-89	**Buffalo**	**NHL**	**10**	**2**	**7**	**0**	**545**	**45**	**0**	**4.95**	....	....	....	....	....	....	....
	Pittsburgh	**NHL**	**44**	**18**	**15**	**7**	**2406**	**162**	**0**	**4.04**	**11**	**7**	**4**	**631**	**40**	**0**	**3.80**
1989-90	**Pittsburgh**	**NHL**	**24**	**7**	**12**	**3**	**1294**	**101**	**0**	**4.68**	....	....	....	....	....	....	....
1990-91♦	**Pittsburgh**	**NHL**	**48**	**27**	**16**	**3**	**2754**	**165**	**1**	**3.59**	**20**	**12**	**7**	**1175**	**51**	***1**	***2.60**
1991-92♦	**Pittsburgh**	**NHL**	**57**	**25**	**22**	**9**	**3329**	**196**	**1**	**3.53**	***21**	***16**	**5**	***1233**	**58**	**1**	**2.82**
1992-93	**Pittsburgh**	**NHL**	**63**	***43**	**14**	**5**	**3702**	**186**	**4**	**3.01**	**12**	**7**	**5**	**722**	**35**	***2**	**2.91**
1993-94	**Pittsburgh**	**NHL**	**44**	**22**	**15**	**5**	**2482**	**139**	**2**	**3.36**	**6**	**2**	**4**	**356**	**17**	**0**	**2.87**
1994-95	**Pittsburgh**	**NHL**	**2**	**0**	**1**	**1**	**125**	**8**	**0**	**3.84**	**2**	**0**	**1**	**80**	**8**	**0**	**6.00**
1995-96	**Pittsburgh**	**NHL**	**49**	**29**	**16**	**2**	**2799**	**160**	**2**	**3.43**	**10**	**4**	**5**	**558**	**26**	**1**	**2.80**
1996-97	**Pittsburgh**	**NHL**	**5**	**0**	**5**	**0**	**270**	**26**	**0**	**5.78**	....	....	....	....	....	....	....
1997-98	**Pittsburgh**	**NHL**	**63**	**31**	**14**	**13**	**3542**	**122**	**7**	**2.07**	**6**	**2**	**4**	**376**	**17**	**0**	**2.71**
1998-99	**Pittsburgh**	**NHL**	**43**	**19**	**16**	**3**	**2306**	**98**	**4**	**2.55**	**13**	**6**	**7**	**787**	**35**	**1**	**2.67**
99-2000	**Pittsburgh**	**NHL**	**18**	**5**	**7**	**2**	**870**	**46**	**1**	**3.17**	....	....	....	....	....	....	....
	Ottawa	**NHL**	**7**	**3**	**4**	**0**	**418**	**22**	**0**	**3.16**	**6**	**2**	**4**	**372**	**16**	**0**	**2.58**
2000-01			DID NOT PLAY														
	NHL Totals		**733**	**353**	**259**	**81**	**41760**	**2276**	**35**	**3.27**	**119**	**61**	**54**	**6953**	**349**	**6**	**3.01**

NHL All-Rookie Team (1984) • NHL First All-Star Team (1984) • Won Calder Memorial Trophy (1984) • Won Vezina Trophy (1984) • NHL Second All-Star Team (1985, 1993) • Shared William Jennings Trophy with Bob Sauve (1985) • Played in NHL All-Star Game (1985)

Traded to **Pittsburgh** by **Buffalo** with Buffalo's 3rd round choice (Joe Dziedzic) in 1990 Entry Draft for Doug Bodger and Darrin Shannon, November 12, 1988. • Missed majority of 1994-95 season recovering from wrist surgery, January 20, 1995. • Missed majority of 1996-97 season recovering from shoulder injury originally suffered in game vs. Montreal, February 5, 1996. Traded to **Ottawa** by **Pittsburgh** for Ron Tugnutt and Janne Laukkanen, March 14, 2000. • Missed entire 2000-01 season for personal reasons. Signed as a free agent by **Carolina**, July 17, 2001.

BELFOUR, Ed (BEHL-fohr, EHD) DAL.

Goaltender. Catches left. 5'11", 192 lbs. Born, Carman, Man., April 21, 1965.

			Regular Season								Playoffs						
Season	Club	Lea	GP	W	L	T	Mins	GA	SO	Avg	GP	W	L	Mins	GA	SO	Avg
1983-84	Winkler Flyers	MJHL	14	....	....	....	818	68	0	5.06	....	....	....	....	....	....	....
1984-85	Winkler Flyers	MJHL	34	....	....	....	1973	145	1	4.41	7	3	4	528	41	0	4.66
1985-86	Winkler Flyers	MJHL	33	....	....	....	1943	124	1	3.83	....	....	....	....	....	....	....
1986-87	North Dakota	WCHA	34	29	4	0	2049	81	3	2.43	....	....	....	....	....	....	....
1987-88	Saginaw Hawks	IHL	61	32	25	0	*3446	183	3	3.19	9	4	5	561	33	0	3.53
1988-89	**Chicago**	**NHL**	**23**	**4**	**12**	**3**	**1148**	**74**	**0**	**3.87**	....	....	....	....	....	....	....
	Saginaw Hawks	IHL	29	12	10	0	1760	92	0	3.10	5	2	3	298	14	0	2.82
1989-90	Canada	Nt-Team	33	13	12	6	1808	93	0	3.08	....	....	....	....	....	....	....
	Chicago	**NHL**	....	....	....	....	....	....	....	....	**9**	**4**	**2**	**409**	**17**	**0**	**2.49**
1990-91	**Chicago**	**NHL**	***74**	***43**	**19**	**7**	***4127**	**170**	**4**	***2.47**	**6**	**2**	**4**	**295**	**20**	**0**	**4.07**
1991-92	**Chicago**	**NHL**	**52**	**21**	**18**	**10**	**2928**	**132**	***5**	**2.70**	**18**	**12**	**4**	**949**	**39**	**1**	***2.47**
1992-93	**Chicago**	**NHL**	***71**	**41**	**18**	**11**	***4106**	**177**	***7**	**2.59**	**4**	**0**	**4**	**249**	**13**	**0**	**3.13**
1993-94	**Chicago**	**NHL**	**70**	**37**	**24**	**6**	**3998**	**178**	***7**	**2.67**	**6**	**2**	**4**	**360**	**15**	**0**	**2.50**
1994-95	**Chicago**	**NHL**	**42**	**22**	**15**	**3**	**2450**	**93**	***5**	**2.28**	**16**	**9**	**7**	**1014**	**37**	**1**	**2.19**
1995-96	**Chicago**	**NHL**	**50**	**22**	**17**	**10**	**2956**	**135**	**1**	**2.74**	**9**	**6**	**3**	**666**	**23**	**1**	**2.07**
1996-97	**Chicago**	**NHL**	**33**	**11**	**15**	**6**	**1966**	**88**	**1**	**2.69**	....	....	....	....	....	....	....
	San Jose	**NHL**	**13**	**3**	**9**	**0**	**757**	**43**	**1**	**3.41**	....	....	....	....	....	....	....
1997-98	**Dallas**	**NHL**	**61**	**37**	**12**	**10**	**3581**	**112**	**9**	***1.88**	**17**	**10**	**7**	**1039**	**31**	**1**	***1.79**
1998-99♦	**Dallas**	**NHL**	**61**	**35**	**15**	**9**	**3536**	**117**	**5**	**1.99**	***23**	***16**	**7**	***1544**	**43**	***3**	***1.67**
99-2000	**Dallas**	**NHL**	**62**	**32**	**21**	**7**	**3620**	**127**	**4**	**2.10**	***23**	**14**	**9**	**1443**	**45**	***4**	**1.87**
2000-01	**Dallas**	**NHL**	**63**	**35**	**20**	**7**	**3687**	**144**	**8**	**2.34**	**10**	**4**	**6**	**671**	**25**	**0**	**2.24**
	NHL Totals		**675**	**343**	**215**	**89**	**38860**	**1590**	**57**	**2.45**	**141**	**79**	**57**	**8639**	**308**	**11**	**2.14**

WCHA First All-Star Team (1987) • NCAA Championship All-Tournament Team (1987) • IHL First All-Star Team (1988) • Shared Garry F. Longman Memorial Trophy (Top Rookie - IHL) with John Cullen (1988) • NHL All-Rookie Team (1991) • NHL First All-Star Team (1991, 1993) • Won Trico Goaltender Award (1991) • Won Calder Memorial Trophy (1991) • Won William M. Jennings Trophy (1991, 1993, 1995) • Won Vezina Trophy (1991, 1993) • NHL Second All-Star Team (1995) • Shared William M. Jennings Trophy with Roman Turek (1999) • Won MBNA Roger Crozier Saving Grace Award (2000) • Played in NHL All-Star Game (1992, 1993, 1996, 1998, 1999)

Signed as a free agent by **Chicago**, September 25, 1987. Traded to **San Jose** by **Chicago** for Chris Terreri, Ulf Dahlen and Michal Sykora, January 25, 1997. Signed as a free agent by **Dallas**, July 2, 1997.

BENDERA, Shane (behn-DEHR-ah, SHAYN) CBJ

Goaltender. Catches left. 6', 170 lbs. Born, St. Albert, Alta., July 13, 1982.
(Columbus' 6th choice, 169th overall, in 2000 Entry Draft).

			Regular Season								Playoffs						
Season	Club	Lea	GP	W	L	T	Mins	GA	SO	Avg	GP	W	L	Mins	GA	SO	Avg
1997-98	Edmonton KC Pats	AMHL	22	8	10	2	1284	82	0	3.84	....	....	....	....	....	....	....
	Red Deer Rebels	WHL	1	0	0	0	8	0	0	0.00	....	....	....	....	....	....	....
1998-99	Bonnyville	AJHL	20	....	....	....	956	70	0	4.38	....	....	....	....	....	....	....
	Red Deer Rebels	WHL	2	0	1	0	72	7	0	5.83	....	....	....	....	....	....	....
99-2000	Red Deer Rebels	WHL	*69	31	27	9	*4003	202	0	3.03	3	0	2	76	15	0	11.84
2000-01	Red Deer Rebels	WHL	45	32	8	2	2603	108	*5	*2.49	*22	*16	6	*1404	43	*4	1.84

WHL East Second All-Star Team (2001)

BERKHOEL, Adam (BUHRK-uhl, A-duhm) CHI.

Goaltender. Catches left. 5'11", 173 lbs. Born, St. Paul, MN, May 16, 1981.
(Chicago's 12th choice, 240th overall, in 2000 Entry Draft).

			Regular Season								Playoffs						
Season	Club	Lea	GP	W	L	T	Mins	GA	SO	Avg	GP	W	L	Mins	GA	SO	Avg
1998-99	Stillwater Ponies	H.S.					STATISTICS NOT AVAILABLE										
99-2000	Twin Cities	USHL	49	25	15	7	2848	129	0	2.72	13	7	6	797	43	0	3.24
2000-01	U. of Denver	WCHA	15	7	6	1	745	38	1	3.06	....	....	....	....	....	....	....

USHL All-Rookie Team (2000) • USHL Second All-Star Team (2000)

BIERK, Zac (BUHRK, ZAK)

Goaltender. Catches left. 6'4", 205 lbs. Born, Peterborough, Ont., September 17, 1976.
(Tampa Bay's 8th choice, 212th overall, in 1995 Entry Draft).

			Regular Season								Playoffs						
Season	Club	Lea	GP	W	L	T	Mins	GA	SO	Avg	GP	W	L	Mins	GA	SO	Avg
1993-94	Peterborough	OPJHL	4	....	....	....	205	17	0	4.98	....	....	....	....	....	....	....
	Peterborough	OHL	9	0	4	2	423	37	0	5.22	1	0	0	33	7	0	12.70
1994-95	Peterborough	OHL	35	11	15	5	1779	117	0	3.95	6	2	3	301	24	0	4.78
1995-96	Peterborough	OHL	58	31	16	6	3292	174	2	3.17	*22	*14	7	*1383	83	0	3.60
1996-97	Peterborough	OHL	49	*28	16	0	2744	151	2	3.30	11	6	5	666	35	0	3.15
1997-98	**Tampa Bay**	**NHL**	**13**	**1**	**4**	**1**	**433**	**30**	**0**	**4.16**	....	....	....	....	....	....	....
	Adirondack	AHL	12	1	6	1	557	36	0	3.87	....	....	....	....	....	....	....
1998-99	**Tampa Bay**	**NHL**	**1**	**0**	**1**	**0**	**59**	**2**	**0**	**2.03**	....	....	....	....	....	....	....
	Cleveland	IHL	27	11	12	4	1556	79	0	3.05	....	....	....	....	....	....	....
99-2000	**Tampa Bay**	**NHL**	**12**	**4**	**4**	**1**	**509**	**31**	**0**	**3.65**	....	....	....	....	....	....	....
	Detroit Vipers	IHL	15	4	8	2	846	46	1	3.26	....	....	....	....	....	....	....
2000-01	**Minnesota**	**NHL**	**1**	**0**	**1**	**0**	**60**	**6**	**0**	**6.00**	....	....	....	....	....	....	....
	Cleveland	IHL	49	24	18	5	2785	134	6	2.89	4	0	3	182	10	0	3.29
	NHL Totals		**27**	**5**	**10**	**2**	**1061**	**69**	**0**	**3.90**	....	....	....	....	....	....	....

OHL First All-Star Team (1997)

• Missed remainder of 1998-99 season recovering from Meniere's Disease which was diagnosed on March 25, 1999. Selected by **Minnesota** from **Tampa Bay** in Expansion Draft, June 23, 2000.

BILLINGTON, Craig (BIHL-lihng-TOHN, KRAYG) WSH.

Goaltender. Catches left. 5'10", 170 lbs. Born, London, Ont., September 11, 1966.
(New Jersey's 2nd choice, 23rd overall, in 1984 Entry Draft).

			Regular Season								Playoffs						
Season	Club	Lea	GP	W	L	T	Mins	GA	SO	Avg	GP	W	L	Mins	GA	SO	Avg
1982-83	London Diamonds	OJHL-B	23	....	....	....	1338	76	0	3.41	....	....	....	....	....	....	....
1983-84	Belleville Bulls	OHL	44	20	19	0	2335	162	1	4.16	1	0	0	30	3	0	6.00
1984-85	Belleville Bulls	OHL	47	26	19	0	2544	180	1	4.25	14	7	5	761	47	1	3.71
1985-86	Belleville Bulls	OHL	3	2	1	0	180	11	0	3.67	20	9	6	1133	68	0	3.60
	New Jersey	**NHL**	**18**	**4**	**9**	**1**	**901**	**77**	**0**	**5.13**	....	....	....	....	....	....	....
1986-87	**New Jersey**	**NHL**	**22**	**4**	**13**	**2**	**1114**	**89**	**0**	**4.79**	....	....	....	....	....	....	....
	Maine Mariners	AHL	20	9	8	2	1151	70	0	3.65	....	....	....	....	....	....	....
1987-88	Utica Devils	AHL	*59	22	27	8	*3404	208	1	3.67	....	....	....	....	....	....	....
1988-89	**New Jersey**	**NHL**	**3**	**1**	**1**	**0**	**140**	**11**	**0**	**4.71**	....	....	....	....	....	....	....
	Utica Devils	AHL	41	17	18	6	2432	150	2	3.70	4	1	3	220	18	0	4.91
1989-90	Utica Devils	AHL	38	20	13	1	2087	138	0	3.97	....	....	....	....	....	....	....
1990-91	Canada	Nt-Team	34	17	14	2	1879	110	2	3.51	....	....	....	....	....	....	....
1991-92	**New Jersey**	**NHL**	**26**	**13**	**7**	**1**	**1363**	**69**	**2**	**3.04**	....	....	....	....	....	....	....
1992-93	**New Jersey**	**NHL**	**42**	**21**	**16**	**4**	**2389**	**146**	**2**	**3.67**	**2**	**0**	**1**	**78**	**5**	**0**	**3.85**
1993-94	**Ottawa**	**NHL**	**63**	**11**	**41**	**4**	**3319**	**254**	**0**	**4.59**	....	....	....	....	....	....	....
1994-95	**Ottawa**	**NHL**	**9**	**0**	**6**	**2**	**472**	**32**	**0**	**4.07**	....	....	....	....	....	....	....
	Boston	**NHL**	**8**	**5**	**1**	**0**	**373**	**19**	**0**	**3.06**	**1**	**0**	**0**	**25**	**1**	**0**	**2.40**
1995-96	**Boston**	**NHL**	**27**	**10**	**13**	**3**	**1380**	**79**	**1**	**3.43**	**1**	**0**	**1**	**60**	**6**	**0**	**6.00**
1996-97	**Colorado**	**NHL**	**23**	**11**	**8**	**2**	**1200**	**53**	**1**	**2.65**	**1**	**0**	**0**	**20**	**1**	**0**	**3.00**
1997-98	**Colorado**	**NHL**	**23**	**8**	**7**	**4**	**1162**	**45**	**1**	**2.32**	**1**	**0**	**0**	**1**	**0**	**0**	**0.00**
1998-99	**Colorado**	**NHL**	**21**	**11**	**8**	**1**	**1086**	**52**	**0**	**2.87**	**1**	**0**	**0**	**9**	**1**	**0**	**6.67**
99-2000	**Washington**	**NHL**	**13**	**3**	**6**	**1**	**611**	**28**	**2**	**2.75**	**1**	**0**	**0**	**20**	**1**	**0**	**3.00**
2000-01	**Washington**	**NHL**	**12**	**3**	**5**	**2**	**660**	**27**	**0**	**2.45**	....	....	....	....	....	....	....
	NHL Totals		**310**	**105**	**141**	**27**	**16170**	**981**	**9**	**3.64**	**8**	**0**	**2**	**213**	**15**	**0**	**4.23**

OHL First All-Star Team (1985) • Played in NHL All-Star Game (1993)

Traded to **Ottawa** by **New Jersey** with Troy Mallette and New Jersey's 4th round choice (Cosmo Dupaul) in 1993 Entry Draft for Peter Sidorkiewicz and future considerations (Mike Peluso, June 26, 1993), June 20, 1993. Traded to **Boston** by **Ottawa** for NY Islanders' 8th round choice (previously acquired, Ottawa selected Ray Schultz) in 1995 Entry Draft, April 7, 1995. Signed as a free agent by **Florida**, September 5, 1996. Claimed by **Colorado** from **Florida** in NHL Waiver Draft, September 30, 1996. Traded to **Washington** by **Colorado** for future considerations, July 16, 1999.

BIRON, Martin (BIH-rohn, MAHR-tihn) BUF.

Goaltender. Catches left. 6'2", 163 lbs. Born, Lac St-Charles, Que., August 15, 1977.
(Buffalo's 2nd choice, 16th overall, in 1995 Entry Draft).

			Regular Season								Playoffs						
Season	Club	Lea	GP	W	L	T	Mins	GA	SO	Avg	GP	W	L	Mins	GA	SO	Avg
1993-94	Trois-Rivieres	QAAA	23	14	8	1	1412	80	1	3.40	2	1	1	112	7	0	3.73
1994-95	Beauport Harfangs	QMJHL	56	29	16	9	3193	132	3	*2.48	16	8	7	900	37	*4	2.47
1995-96	Beauport Harfangs	QMJHL	55	29	17	7	3201	152	1	2.85	*19	*12	7	1134	64	0	3.39
	Buffalo	**NHL**	**3**	**0**	**2**	**0**	**119**	**10**	**0**	**5.04**	....	....	....	....	....	....	....
1996-97	Beauport Harfangs	QMJHL	18	6	9	1	928	61	1	3.94	....	....	....	....	....	....	....
	Hull Olympiques	QMJHL	16	11	4	1	974	43	2	2.65	6	3	1	325	19	0	3.51
1997-98	South Carolina	ECHL	2	0	1	1	86	3	0	2.09	....	....	....	....	....	....	....
	Rochester	AHL	41	14	18	6	2312	113	*5	2.93	4	1	3	239	16	0	4.01
1998-99	**Buffalo**	**NHL**	**6**	**1**	**2**	**1**	**281**	**10**	**0**	**2.14**	....	....	....	....	....	....	....
	Rochester	AHL	52	36	13	3	3129	108	*6	*2.07	*20	12	8	1167	42	1	*2.16
99-2000	**Buffalo**	**NHL**	**41**	**19**	**18**	**2**	**2229**	**90**	**5**	**2.42**	....	....	....	....	....	....	....
	Rochester	AHL	6	6	0	0	344	12	1	2.09	....	....	....	....	....	....	....
2000-01	**Buffalo**	**NHL**	**18**	**7**	**7**	**1**	**918**	**39**	**2**	**2.55**	....	....	....	....	....	....	....
	Rochester	AHL	4	3	1	0	239	4	1	1.00	....	....	....	....	....	....	....
	NHL Totals		**68**	**27**	**29**	**4**	**3547**	**149**	**7**	**2.52**	....	....	....	....	....	....	....

Canadian Major Junior First All-Star Team (1995) • Canadian Major Junior Goaltender of the Year (1995) • AHL First All-Star Team (1999) • Shared Harry "Hap" Holmes Memorial Trophy (fewest goals against - AHL) with Tom Draper (1999) • Won Baz Bastien Memorial Trophy (Top Goaltender - AHL) (1999)

BLACKBURN, Dan (BLAK-buhrn, DAN) NYR

Goaltender. Catches left. 6', 180 lbs. Born, Montreal, Que., May 20, 1983.
(NY Rangers' 1st choice, 10th overall, in 2001 Entry Draft).

			Regular Season								Playoffs						
Season	Club	Lea	GP	W	L	T	Mins	GA	SO	Avg	GP	W	L	Mins	GA	SO	Avg
1997-98	Bow Valley	AJHL	20	9	6	1	1039	58	1	3.35	3	0	0	97	8	0	4.95
1998-99	Bow Valley	AJHL	38	7	19	6	1941	146	0	4.51	2	0	2	118	8	0	4.07
99-2000	Kootenay Ice	WHL	51	34	8	7	3004	126	3	2.52	*21	*16	5	*1272	43	2	*2.03
2000-01	Kootenay Ice	WHL	50	*33	14	2	2922	135	1	2.77	11	7	4	706	23	1	1.95

AJHL Scholastic Player of the Year (1998, 1999) • WHL East First All-Star Team (2001) • Canadian Major Junior First All-Star Team (2001) • Canadian Major Junior Goaltender of the Year (2001)

BLACKBURN, Josh (BLAK-buhrn, JAWSH) PHX.

Goaltender. Catches left. 6', 185 lbs. Born, Delrio, TX, November 13, 1978.
(Phoenix's 6th choice, 116th overall, in 1998 Entry Draft).

			Regular Season								Playoffs						
Season	Club	Lea	GP	W	L	T	Mins	GA	SO	Avg	GP	W	L	Mins	GA	SO	Avg
1996-97	Dubuque Saints	USHL	52	15	32	3	2979	185	1	3.72	....	....	....	....	....	....	....
1997-98	Dubuque Saints	USHL	28	11	15	1	1605	94	0	3.51	....	....	....	....	....	....	....
	Lincoln Stars	USHL	17	13	4	0	1004	41	1	2.45	9	4	5	522	29	0	3.33
1998-99	U. of Michigan	CCHA	*42	*25	10	6	*2398	91	3	2.28	....	....	....	....	....	....	....
99-2000	U. of Michigan	CCHA	22	14	4	4	1337	53	1	2.38	....	....	....	....	....	....	....
2000-01	U. of Michigan	CCHA	*45	26	13	5	*2647	101	5	2.29	....	....	....	....	....	....	....

CCHA Second All-Star Team (1999, 2001) • NCAA West First All-American Team (1999)

BOISCLAIR, Daniel (BWUH-klair, DAN-yehl) CAR.

Goaltender. Catches left. 6'2", 185 lbs. Born, Sept-Iles, Que., November 2, 1982.
(Carolina's 5th choice, 181st overall, in 2001 Entry Draft).

			Regular Season								Playoffs						
Season	Club	Lea	GP	W	L	T	Mins	GA	SO	Avg	GP	W	L	Mins	GA	SO	Avg
99-2000	Cape Breton	QMJHL	29	7	14	1	1421	95	0	4.01	3	0	1	86	6	0	4.21
2000-01	Cape Breton	QMJHL	47	16	23	2	2426	161	0	3.98	12	5	6	685	36	0	3.16

BOUCHER, Brian (BOO-shay, BRIGH-uhn) PHI.

Goaltender. Catches left. 6'2", 190 lbs. Born, Woonsocket, RI, January 2, 1977.
(Philadelphia's 1st choice, 22nd overall, in 1995 Entry Draft).

			Regular Season								Playoffs						
Season	Club	Lea	GP	W	L	T	Mins	GA	SO	Avg	GP	W	L	Mins	GA	SO	Avg
1993-94	Mount St. Charles	H.S.	15	*14	0	1	*504	*8	*9	*0.57	4	*4	0	*180	*6	*1	*1.20
1994-95	Wexford Raiders	MTJHL	8	....	....	....	425	23	0	3.25	....	....	....	....	....	....	....
	Tri-City Americans	WHL	35	17	11	2	1969	108	1	3.29	13	6	5	795	50	0	3.77
1995-96	Tri-City Americans	WHL	55	33	19	2	3183	181	1	3.41	11	6	5	653	37	*2	3.40
1996-97	Tri-City Americans	WHL	41	10	24	6	2458	149	1	3.64	....	....	....	....	....	....	....
1997-98	Philadelphia	AHL	34	16	12	3	1901	101	0	3.19	2	0	0	30	1	0	1.95
1998-99	Philadelphia	AHL	36	20	8	5	2061	89	2	2.59	16	9	7	947	45	0	2.85
99-2000	**Philadelphia**	**NHL**	**35**	**20**	**10**	**3**	**2038**	**65**	**4**	***1.91**	**18**	**11**	**7**	**1183**	**40**	**1**	**2.03**
	Philadelphia	AHL	1	0	0	1	65	3	0	2.77	....	....	....	....	....	....	....
2000-01	**Philadelphia**	**NHL**	**27**	**8**	**12**	**5**	**1470**	**80**	**1**	**3.27**	**1**	**0**	**0**	**37**	**3**	**0**	**4.86**
	NHL Totals		**62**	**28**	**22**	**8**	**3508**	**145**	**5**	**2.48**	**19**	**11**	**7**	**1220**	**43**	**1**	**2.11**

WHL West Second All-Star Team (1996) • WHL West First All-Star Team (1997) • NHL All-Rookie Team (2000)

BOUCHER, Nick (BOO-shay, NIHK) PIT.

Goaltender. Catches left. 5'11", 175 lbs. Born, Leduc, Alta., December 29, 1980.
(Pittsburgh's 10th choice, 280th overall, in 2000 Entry Draft).

			Regular Season								Playoffs						
Season	Club	Lea	GP	W	L	T	Mins	GA	SO	Avg	GP	W	L	Mins	GA	SO	Avg
1997-98	Cowichan Capitals	BCJHL	20	6	7	0	918	65	0	4.25	....	....	....	....	....	....	....
1998-99	Cowichan Capitals	BCJHL	10	3	5	0	464	40	0	5.17	....	....	....	....	....	....	....
	Ft-Saskatchewan	AJHL	22	11	9	2	1243	70	1	3.38	7	3	4	420	24	3	3.43
99-2000	Dartmouth	ECAC	24	8	12	3	1378	66	1	2.87	....	....	....	....	....	....	....
2000-01	Dartmouth	ECAC	*33	*16	12	4	*1966	84	1	2.56	....	....	....	....	....	....	....

BRATHWAITE, Fred (BRAYTH-wayt, FREHD) ST.L.

Goaltender. Catches left. 5'7", 175 lbs. Born, Ottawa, Ont., November 24, 1972.

			Regular Season								Playoffs						
Season	Club	Lea	GP	W	L	T	Mins	GA	SO	Avg	GP	W	L	Mins	GA	SO	Avg
1988-89	Smiths Falls Bears	COJHL	38	16	18	1	2130	187	0	5.27	....	....	....	....	....	....	....
1989-90	OrilliaTerriers	OJHL-B	15	....	....	....	782	47	0	3.61	....	....	....	....	....	....	....
	Oshawa Generals	OHL	20	11	2	1	886	43	1	2.91	10	4	2	451	22	0	*2.93
1990-91	Oshawa Generals	OHL	39	25	6	3	1986	112	1	3.38	13	*9	2	677	43	0	3.81
1991-92	Oshawa Generals	OHL	24	12	7	2	1248	81	0	3.89	....	....	....	....	....	....	....
	London Knights	OHL	23	15	6	2	1325	61	*4	2.76	10	5	5	615	36	0	3.51
1992-93	Detroit Jr. Wings	OHL	37	23	10	4	2192	134	0	3.67	15	9	6	858	48	1	3.36
1993-94	**Edmonton**	**NHL**	**19**	**3**	**10**	**3**	**982**	**58**	**0**	**3.54**	....	....	....	....	....	....	....
	Cape Breton Oilers	AHL	2	1	1	0	119	6	0	3.04	....	....	....	....	....	....	....
1994-95	**Edmonton**	**NHL**	**14**	**2**	**5**	**1**	**601**	**40**	**0**	**3.99**	....	....	....	....	....	....	....
1995-96	**Edmonton**	**NHL**	**7**	**0**	**2**	**0**	**293**	**12**	**0**	**2.46**	....	....	....	....	....	....	....
	Cape Breton Oilers	AHL	31	12	16	0	1699	110	1	3.88	....	....	....	....	....	....	....
1996-97	Manitoba Moose	IHL	58	22	22	5	2945	167	1	3.40	....	....	....	....	....	....	....
1997-98	Manitoba Moose	IHL	51	23	18	4	2736	138	1	3.03	2	0	1	72	4	0	3.30
1998-99	Canada	Nt-Team	24	6	8	3	989	47	2	2.85	....	....	....	....	....	....	....
	Calgary	**NHL**	**28**	**11**	**9**	**7**	**1663**	**68**	**1**	**2.45**	....	....	....	....	....	....	....
99-2000	**Calgary**	**NHL**	**61**	**25**	**25**	**7**	**3448**	**158**	**5**	**2.75**	....	....	....	....	....	....	....
	Saint John Flames	AHL	2	2	0	0	120	4	0	2.00	....	....	....	....	....	....	....
2000-01	**Calgary**	**NHL**	**49**	**15**	**17**	**10**	**2742**	**106**	**5**	**2.32**	....	....	....	....	....	....	....
	NHL Totals		**178**	**56**	**68**	**28**	**9729**	**442**	**11**	**2.73**	....	....	....	....	....	....	....

• Scored a goal while with Detroit (OHL), April 20, 1993. • Scored a goal while with Manitoba (IHL), November 9, 1996.

Signed as a free agent by **Edmonton**, October 6, 1993. Signed as a free agent by **Calgary**, January 6, 1999. Traded to **St. Louis** by **Calgary** with Daniel Tkaczuk, Sergei Varlamov and Calgary's 9th round choice (Grant Jacobsen) in 2001 Entry Draft for Roman Turek and St. Louis' 4th round choice (Yegor Shastin) in 2001 Entry Draft, June 23, 2001.

BROCHU, Martin (broh-SHOO, MAHR-tihn) MIN.

Goaltender. Catches left. 6', 199 lbs. Born, Anjou, Que., March 10, 1973.

			Regular Season								Playoffs						
Season	Club	Lea	GP	W	L	T	Mins	GA	SO	Avg	GP	W	L	Mins	GA	SO	Avg
1989-90	Montreal-Bourassa	QAAA	27	11	14	1	1471	103	3	4.20	3	1	2	193	10	1	3.10
1990-91	Granby Bisons	QMJHL	16	6	5	0	622	39	....	3.76	....	....	....	....	....	....	....
1991-92	Granby Bisons	QMJHL	52	15	29	2	2772	278	0	4.72	....	....	....	....	....	....	....
1992-93	Hull Olympiques	QMJHL	29	9	15	1	1453	137	0	5.66	2	0	1	69	7	0	6.07
1993-94	Fredericton	AHL	32	10	11	3	1505	76	2	3.03	....	....	....	....	....	....	....
1994-95	Fredericton	AHL	44	18	18	4	2475	145	0	3.51	....	....	....	....	....	....	....
1995-96	Fredericton	AHL	17	6	8	2	986	70	0	4.26	....	....	....	....	....	....	....
	Wheeling	ECHL	19	10	6	2	1060	51	1	2.89	....	....	....	....	....	....	....
	Portland Pirates	AHL	5	2	2	1	287	15	0	3.14	12	7	4	700	28	*2	*2.40
1996-97	Portland Pirates	AHL	55	23	17	7	2962	150	2	3.04	5	2	3	324	13	0	2.41
1997-98	Portland Pirates	AHL	37	16	14	1	1926	96	2	2.99	6	3	2	296	16	0	3.24
1998-99	**Washington**	**NHL**	**2**	**0**	**2**	**0**	**120**	**6**	**0**	**3.00**	....	....	....	....	....	....	....
	Portland Pirates	AHL	20	6	10	3	1164	57	2	2.94	....	....	....	....	....	....	....
	Utah Grizzlies	IHL	5	1	3	1	298	13	0	2.62	....	....	....	....	....	....	....
99-2000	Portland Pirates	AHL	54	32	15	6	3192	116	4	2.18	2	0	2	80	7	0	5.27
2000-01	Saint John Flames	AHL	55	27	19	5	3049	132	2	2.60	19	*14	4	1148	39	*4	2.04
	NHL Totals		**2**	**0**	**2**	**0**	**120**	**6**	**0**	**3.00**	....	....	....	....	....	....	....

AHL First All-Star Team (2000) • Won Baz Bastien Memorial Trophy (Top Goaltender - AHL) (2000) • Won Les Cunningham Award (MVP - AHL) (2000)

Signed as a free agent by **Montreal**, September 22, 1992. Traded to **Washington** by **Montreal** for future considerations, March 15, 1996. Signed as a free agent by **Calgary**, August 25, 2000. Signed as a free agent by **Minnesota**, July 17, 2001.

BRODEUR, Martin (broh-DOOR, MAHR-tihn) N.J.

Goaltender. Catches left. 6'2", 205 lbs. Born, Montreal, Que., May 6, 1972.
(New Jersey's 1st choice, 20th overall, in 1990 Entry Draft).

			Regular Season								Playoffs						
Season	Club	Lea	GP	W	L	T	Mins	GA	SO	Avg	GP	W	L	Mins	GA	SO	Avg
1988-89	Montreal-Bourassa	QAAA	27	13	12	1	1580	98	0	3.72	3	0	3	210	14	0	3.99
1989-90	St-Hyacinthe	QMJHL	42	23	13	2	2333	156	0	4.01	12	5	7	678	46	0	4.07
1990-91	St-Hyacinthe	QMJHL	52	22	24	4	2946	162	2	3.30	4	0	4	232	16	0	4.14
1991-92	St-Hyacinthe	QMJHL	48	27	16	4	2846	161	2	3.39	5	2	3	317	14	0	2.65
	New Jersey	**NHL**	**4**	**2**	**1**	**0**	**179**	**10**	**0**	**3.35**	**1**	**0**	**1**	**32**	**3**	**0**	**5.63**
1992-93	Utica Devils	AHL	32	14	13	5	1952	131	0	4.03	4	1	3	258	18	0	4.19
1993-94	**New Jersey**	**NHL**	**47**	**27**	**11**	**8**	**2625**	**105**	**3**	**2.40**	**17**	**8**	**9**	**1171**	**38**	**1**	**1.95**
1994-95♦	**New Jersey**	**NHL**	**40**	**19**	**11**	**6**	**2184**	**89**	**3**	**2.45**	***20**	***16**	**4**	***1222**	**34**	***3**	***1.67**
1995-96	**New Jersey**	**NHL**	**77**	**34**	**30**	**12**	***4433**	**173**	**6**	**2.34**	....	....	....	....	....	....	....
1996-97	**New Jersey**	**NHL**	**67**	**37**	**14**	**13**	**3838**	**120**	***10**	***1.88**	**10**	**5**	**5**	**659**	**19**	**2**	***1.73**
1997-98	**New Jersey**	**NHL**	**70**	***43**	**17**	**8**	**4128**	**130**	**10**	**1.89**	**6**	**2**	**4**	**366**	**12**	**0**	**1.97**
1998-99	**New Jersey**	**NHL**	***70**	***39**	**21**	**10**	***4239**	**162**	**4**	**2.29**	**7**	**3**	**4**	**425**	**20**	**0**	**2.82**
99-2000♦	**New Jersey**	**NHL**	**72**	***43**	**20**	**8**	**4312**	**161**	**6**	**2.24**	***23**	***16**	**7**	***1450**	**39**	**2**	***1.61**
2000-01	**New Jersey**	**NHL**	**72**	***42**	**17**	**11**	**4297**	**166**	**9**	**2.32**	***25**	**15**	**10**	***1505**	**52**	***4**	**2.07**
	NHL Totals		**519**	**286**	**142**	**76**	**30235**	**1116**	**51**	**2.21**	**109**	**65**	**44**	**6830**	**217**	**12**	**1.91**

QMJHL Second All-Star Team (1992) • NHL All-Rookie Team (1994) • Won Calder Memorial Trophy (1994) • NHL Second All-Star Team (1997, 1998) • Shared William M. Jennings Trophy with Mike Dunham (1997) • Won William M. Jennings Trophy (1998) • Played in NHL All-Star Game (1996, 1997, 1998, 1999, 2000, 2001) • Scored a goal while with New Jersey in playoffs vs. Montreal, April 17, 1997.

BRUCKLER, Bernd (BRUK-luhr, BUHRND) PHI.

Goaltender. Catches left. 6'1", 180 lbs. Born, Graz, Austria, September 26, 1981.
(Philadelphia's 4th choice, 150th overall, in 2001 Entry Draft).

			Regular Season								Playoffs						
Season	Club	Lea	GP	W	L	T	Mins	GA	SO	Avg	GP	W	L	Mins	GA	SO	Avg
1997-98	EC Graz	Austria	2	....	....	....	61	11	0	10.82	....	....	....	....	....	....	....
1998-99	Ponoka Stamps	HJHL					STATISTICS NOT AVAILABLE										
99-2000	EC Graz	Austria-Jr.					STATISTICS NOT AVAILABLE										
2000-01	Tri-City Storm	USHL	28	15	8	3	1624	67	2	2.48	7	3	4	420	....	....	....

BRUMBY, David (BRUHM-bee, DAY-vihd)

Goaltender. Catches left. 6'1", 190 lbs. Born, Victoria, B.C., May 21, 1975.
(Toronto's 6th choice, 201st overall, in 1993 Entry Draft).

			Regular Season								Playoffs						
Season	Club	Lea	GP	W	L	T	Mins	GA	SO	Avg	GP	W	L	Mins	GA	SO	Avg
1992-93	Tri-City Americans	WHL	30	13	12	0	1529	123	0	4.83	4	0	4	240	20	0	5.00
1993-94	Tri-City Americans	WHL	28	7	16	2	1518	132	0	5.22	2	1	1	120	9	0	4.50
1994-95	Tri-City Americans	WHL	15	5	6	1	851	60	0	4.23	....	....	....	....	....	....	....
	Regina Pats	WHL	4	0	3	0	230	15	0	3.91	....	....	....	....	....	....	....
	Lethbridge	WHL	19	6	11	0	1036	78	0	4.52	....	....	....	....	....	....	....
1995-96	Lethbridge	WHL	50	19	20	2	2502	133	1	3.19	4	0	3	262	14	0	3.21
1996-97	Columbus Chill	ECHL	18	9	5	2	997	68	0	4.09	1	0	0	9	0	0	0.00
	Baltimore Bandits	AHL	2	0	1	0	60	7	0	7.00	....	....	....	....	....	....	....
1997-98	Columbus Chill	ECHL	18	8	8	1	1015	46	*2	2.72	....	....	....	....	....	....	....
	Wheeling Nailers	ECHL	23	15	4	4	1348	64	*2	2.85	15	8	7	983	36	*2	2.24
	Cleveland	IHL	2	0	1	0	99	4	0	2.42	....	....	....	....	....	....	....
1998-99	Wheeling Nailers	ECHL	31	11	14	4	1741	89	0	3.07	....	....	....	....	....	....	....
	Providence Bruins	AHL	2	1	1	0	119	6	0	3.02	....	....	....	....	....	....	....
	Charlotte	ECHL	6	3	1	0	300	18	0	3.60	....	....	....	....	....	....	....
99-2000	Jackson Bandits	ECHL	*59	28	25	4	3368	167	*7	2.97	....	....	....	....	....	....	....
	Providence Bruins	AHL	1	1	0	0	61	1	0	0.98	....	....	....	....	....	....	....
2000-01	Cleveland	IHL	17	5	7	1	893	53	1	3.56	....	....	....	....	....	....	....
	Jackson Bandits	ECHL	15	6	6	3	877	47	0	3.21	1	0	1	60	5	0	5.00

Signed as a free agent by **Minnesota**, June 7, 2000.

BRYZGALOV, Ilja (breez-GAH-lahf, ihl-YUH) ANA.

Goaltender. Catches left. 6'3", 196 lbs. Born, Togliatti, USSR, June 22, 1980.
(Anaheim's 2nd choice, 44th overall, in 2000 Entry Draft).

			Regular Season								Playoffs						
Season	Club	Lea	GP	W	L	T	Mins	GA	SO	Avg	GP	W	L	Mins	GA	SO	Avg
1997-98	Lada Togliatti-2	Russia-3	8	....	....	....	480	28	....	3.50	....	....	....	....	....	....	....
1998-99	Lada Togliatti-2	Russia-4	20	....	....	....	1200	43	....	2.15	....	....	....	....	....	....	....
99-2000	Krylja Sovetov	Russia-2	9	....	....	....	500	21	....	2.52	....	....	....	....	....	....	....
	Lada Togliatti	Russia	14	....	....	....	796	18	3	1.36	7	....	....	407	10	1	1.47
2000-01	Lada Togliatti	Russia	34	....	....	....	1992	61	*8	1.84	5	....	....	249	8	0	1.93

BUDAJ, Peter (BOO-digh, PEE-tuhr) COL.

Goaltender. Catches left. 6', 200 lbs. Born, Bystrica, Czech., September 18, 1982.
(Colorado's 1st choice, 63rd overall, in 2001 Entry Draft).

			Regular Season								Playoffs						
Season	Club	Lea	GP	W	L	T	Mins	GA	SO	Avg	GP	W	L	Mins	GA	SO	Avg
99-2000	St. Michael's	OHL	34	6	18	1	1676	112	1	4.01	....	....	....	....	....	....	....
2000-01	St. Michael's	OHL	37	17	12	3	1996	95	3	2.86	11	6	4	621	26	1	2.51

BURKE, Sean (BUHRK, SHAWN) PHX.

Goaltender. Catches left. 6'4", 210 lbs. Born, Windsor, Ont., January 29, 1967.
(New Jersey's 2nd choice, 24th overall, in 1985 Entry Draft).

			Regular Season								Playoffs						
Season	Club	Lea	GP	W	L	T	Mins	GA	SO	Avg	GP	W	L	Mins	GA	SO	Avg
1983-84	St. Michael's	MTJHL	25	....	....	....	1482	120	0	4.86	....	....	....	....	....	....	....
1984-85	Toronto Marlies	OHL	49	25	21	3	2987	211	0	4.24	5	1	3	266	25	0	5.64
1985-86	Toronto Marlies	OHL	47	16	27	3	2840	233	0	4.92	4	0	4	238	24	0	6.05
1986-87	Canada	Nt-Team	42	27	13	2	2550	130	0	3.05	....	....	....	....	....	....	....
1987-88	Canada	Nt-Team	37	19	9	2	1962	92	1	2.81	....	....	....	....	....	....	....
	Canada	Olympics	4	1	2	1	238	12	0	3.02	....	....	....	....	....	....	....
	New Jersey	**NHL**	**13**	**10**	**1**	**0**	**689**	**35**	**1**	**3.05**	**17**	**9**	**8**	**1001**	**57**	***1**	**3.42**
1988-89	**New Jersey**	**NHL**	**62**	**22**	**31**	**9**	**3590**	**230**	**3**	**3.84**	....	....	....	....	....	....	....
1989-90	**New Jersey**	**NHL**	**52**	**22**	**22**	**6**	**2914**	**175**	**0**	**3.60**	**2**	**0**	**2**	**125**	**8**	**0**	**3.84**
1990-91	**New Jersey**	**NHL**	**35**	**8**	**12**	**8**	**1870**	**112**	**0**	**3.59**	....	....	....	....	....	....	....
1991-92	Canada	Nt-Team	31	18	6	4	1721	75	1	2.61	....	....	....	....	....	....	....
	Canada	Olympics	7	5	2	0	429	17	0	2.37	....	....	....	....	....	....	....
	San Diego Gulls	IHL	7	4	2	1	424	17	0	2.41	3	0	3	160	13	0	4.88
1992-93	**Hartford**	**NHL**	**50**	**16**	**27**	**3**	**2656**	**184**	**0**	**4.16**	....	....	....	....	....	....	....
1993-94	**Hartford**	**NHL**	**47**	**17**	**24**	**5**	**2750**	**137**	**2**	**2.99**	....	....	....	....	....	....	....
1994-95	**Hartford**	**NHL**	**42**	**17**	**19**	**4**	**2418**	**108**	**0**	**2.68**	....	....	....	....	....	....	....
1995-96	**Hartford**	**NHL**	**66**	**28**	**28**	**6**	**3669**	**190**	**4**	**3.11**	....	....	....	....	....	....	....
1996-97	**Hartford**	**NHL**	**51**	**22**	**22**	**6**	**2985**	**134**	**4**	**2.69**	....	....	....	....	....	....	....
1997-98	**Carolina**	**NHL**	**25**	**7**	**11**	**5**	**1415**	**66**	**1**	**2.80**	....	....	....	....	....	....	....
	Vancouver	**NHL**	**16**	**2**	**9**	**4**	**838**	**49**	**0**	**3.51**	....	....	....	....	....	....	....
	Philadelphia	**NHL**	**11**	**7**	**3**	**0**	**632**	**27**	**1**	**2.56**	**5**	**1**	**4**	**283**	**17**	**0**	**3.60**
1998-99	**Florida**	**NHL**	**59**	**21**	**24**	**14**	**3402**	**151**	**3**	**2.66**	....	....	....	....	....	....	....
99-2000	**Florida**	**NHL**	**7**	**2**	**5**	**0**	**418**	**18**	**0**	**2.58**	....	....	....	....	....	....	....
	Phoenix	**NHL**	**35**	**17**	**14**	**3**	**2074**	**88**	**3**	**2.55**	**5**	**1**	**4**	**296**	**16**	**0**	**3.24**
2000-01	**Phoenix**	**NHL**	**62**	**25**	**22**	**13**	**3644**	**138**	**4**	**2.27**	....	....	....	....	....	....	....
	NHL Totals		**633**	**243**	**274**	**86**	**35964**	**1842**	**26**	**3.07**	**29**	**11**	**18**	**1705**	**98**	**1**	**3.45**

Played in NHL All-Star Game (1989, 2001)

Traded to **Hartford** by **New Jersey** with Eric Weinrich for Bobby Holik and Hartford's 2nd round choice (Jay Pandolfo) in 1993 Entry Draft, August 28, 1992. Transferred to **Carolina** after **Hartford** franchise relocated, June 25, 1997. Traded to **Vancouver** by **Carolina** with Geoff Sanderson and Enrico Ciccone for Kirk McLean and Martin Gelinas, January 3, 1998. Traded to **Philadelphia** by **Vancouver** for Garth Snow, March 4, 1998. Signed as a free agent by **Florida**, September 12, 1998. Traded to **Phoenix** by **Florida** with Florida's 5th round choice (Nate Kiser) in 2000 Entry Draft for Mikhail Shtalenkov and Phoenix's 4th round choice (Chris Eade) in 2000 Entry Draft, November 18, 1999.

BUZAK, Mike (BOO-zehk, MIGHK)

Goaltender. Catches left. 6'3", 220 lbs. Born, Edson, Alta., February 10, 1973.
(St. Louis' 5th choice, 167th overall, in 1993 Entry Draft).

			Regular Season								Playoffs						
Season	Club	Lea	GP	W	L	T	Mins	GA	SO	Avg	GP	W	L	Mins	GA	SO	Avg
1989-90	Ft-Saskatchewan	AJHL	30	19	11	0	1731	112	0	3.88	....	....	....	....	....	....	....
1990-91	Ft-Saskatchewan	AJHL	32	22	9	1	1883	114	2	3.63	....	....	....	....	....	....	....
1991-92	Michigan State	CCHA	7	4	0	0	311	22	0	4.25	....	....	....	....	....	....	....
1992-93	Michigan State	CCHA	38	22	10	2	*2090	102	0	2.93	....	....	....	....	....	....	....
1993-94	Michigan State	CCHA	*39	21	12	5	*2297	104	2	2.72	....	....	....	....	....	....	....
1994-95	Michigan State	CCHA	31	17	10	3	1796	94	0	3.14	....	....	....	....	....	....	....
1995-96	Worcester	AHL	30	9	10	5	1672	85	0	3.05	....	....	....	....	....	....	....
1996-97	Baton Rouge	ECHL	3	0	2	0	108	7	0	3.87	....	....	....	....	....	....	....
	Worcester	AHL	19	9	4	3	972	41	1	2.53	1	0	1	58	3	0	3.06
1997-98	Long Beach	IHL	31	18	6	5	1763	58	*6	*1.97	5	0	3	215	11	0	3.06
	Tucson	WCHL	2	0	2	0	106	6	0	3.37	....	....	....	....	....	....	....
	Phoenix	WCHL	6	3	3	0	357	27	0	4.53	....	....	....	....	....	....	....
1998-99	Albany River Rats	AHL	48	22	13	3	2382	102	0	2.57	5	2	1	272	12	0	2.65
99-2000	Albany River Rats	AHL	14	3	9	2	776	41	1	3.17	....	....	....	....	....	....	....
	Augusta Lynx	ECHL	3	2	0	0	150	11	0	4.40	....	....	....	....	....	....	....
	Milwaukee	IHL	8	2	5	0	426	24	0	3.38	....	....	....	....	....	....	....
	Utah Grizzlies	IHL	4	0	1	1	168	7	0	2.50	....	....	....	....	....	....	....
2000-01	Long Beach	WCHL	42	23	12	7	2495	117	1	2.81	5	2	3	298	17	0	3.41

CCHA Second All-Star Team (1994, 1995) • Shared James Norris Memorial Trophy (fewest goals against - IHL) with Kay Whitmore (1998)

Signed as a free agent by **New Jersey**, August 14, 1998.

CARON, Sebastian (KAIR-aw, suh-BAS-tee-yeh) PIT.

Goaltender. Catches left. 6'1", 160 lbs. Born, Amqui, Que., June 25, 1980.
(Pittsburgh's 4th choice, 86th overall, in 1999 Entry Draft).

			Regular Season								Playoffs						
Season	Club	Lea	GP	W	L	T	Mins	GA	SO	Avg	GP	W	L	Mins	GA	SO	Avg
1997-98	TGV Pentagone	QAHA	17	....	....	....	762	48	1	2.84	....	....	....	....	....	....	....
1998-99	Rimouski Oceanic	QMJHL	30	13	10	3	1570	85	0	3.25	2	1	0	68	0	0	0.00
99-2000	Rimouski Oceanic	QMJHL	54	*38	11	3	3040	179	1	3.53	14	*12	2	828	50	0	3.62
2000-01	Wilkes-Barre	AHL	30	12	14	3	1746	103	4	3.54	....	....	....	....	....	....	....

Memorial Cup All-Star Team (2000) • Won Hap Emms Memorial Trophy (Memorial Cup Tournament Top Goaltender) (2000)

CASSIVI, Frederic (KASS-ih-vee, FREHD-uhr-IHK) COL.

Goaltender. Catches left. 6'4", 220 lbs. Born, Sorel, Que., June 12, 1975.
(Ottawa's 7th choice, 210th overall, in 1994 Entry Draft).

			Regular Season								Playoffs						
Season	Club	Lea	GP	W	L	T	Mins	GA	SO	Avg	GP	W	L	Mins	GA	SO	Avg
1991-92	Abitibi Forestiers	QAAA	22	5	17	0	1320	106	0	4.84	3	1	2	180	15	0	5.06
1992-93							STATISTICS NOT AVAILABLE										
1993-94	St-Hyacinthe	QMJHL	35	15	13	3	1751	127	1	4.35	....	....	....	....	....	....	....
1994-95	Halifax	QMJHL	24	9	12	1	1362	105	0	4.63	....	....	....	....	....	....	....
	St-Jean Lynx	QMJHL	19	12	6	0	1021	55	1	3.23	5	2	3	258	18	0	4.19
1995-96	Thunder Bay	ColHL	12	6	4	2	715	51	0	4.28	....	....	....	....	....	....	....
	P.E.I. Senators	AHL	41	20	14	3	2347	128	1	3.27	5	2	3	317	24	0	4.54
1996-97	Syracuse Crunch	AHL	55	23	22	8	3069	164	2	3.21	1	0	1	60	3	0	3.01
1997-98	Worcester	AHL	45	20	22	2	2593	140	1	3.24	6	3	3	326	18	0	3.31
1998-99	Cincinnati	IHL	44	21	17	2	2418	123	1	3.05	3	1	2	139	6	0	2.59
99-2000	Hershey Bears	AHL	31	14	9	3	1554	78	1	3.01	2	0	1	63	5	0	4.75
2000-01	Hershey Bears	AHL	49	17	24	3	2620	124	2	2.84	9	7	2	564	14	1	*1.49

Signed as a free agent by **Colorado**, August 17, 1999.

CECHMANEK, Roman (chehkh-MAN-ehk, ROH-muhn) PHI.

Goaltender. Catches left. 6'3", 187 lbs. Born, Gottwaldov, Czech., March 2, 1971.
(Philadelphia's 3rd choice, 171st overall, in 2000 Entry Draft).

			Regular Season								Playoffs						
Season	Club	Lea	GP	W	L	T	Mins	GA	SO	Avg	GP	W	L	Mins	GA	SO	Avg
1988-89	TJ Gottwaldov	Czech.	1	0	0	0	13	0	0	0.00	....	....	....	....	....	....	....
1989-90	TJ Zlin	Czech.	2	0	0	0	89	5	0	3.37	....	....	....	....	....	....	....
1990-91	Dukla Jihlava	Czech.	9	....	....	....	447	18	2	2.42	....	....	....	....	....	....	....
1991-92	DS Olomouc	Czech.	13	....	....	....	731	54	0	4.43	....	....	....	....	....	....	....
	ZPS Zlin	Czech.	2	0	1	0	67	8	0	7.73	....	....	....	....	....	....	....
1992-93	Banik Hodonin	Czech-2					STATISTICS NOT AVAILABLE										
1993-94	Zbojovka Vsetin-2	Cze-Rep					STATISTICS NOT AVAILABLE										
1994-95	HC Dadak Vsetin	Cze-Rep	41	....	....	....	2413	98	5	2.44	11	....	....	619	23	1	2.23
1995-96	HC Petra Vsetin	Cze-Rep	36	....	....	....	2142	77	4	2.16	13	....	....	783	17	2	1.30
1996-97	HC Petra Vsetin	Cze-Rep	48	....	....	....	2762	98	3	2.13	10	....	....	602	11	2	1.10
1997-98	HC Petra Vsetin	Cze-Rep	41	....	....	....	2306	76	....	*1.98	10	....	....	600	16	1	*1.60
1998-99	HC Slovnaft Vsetin	Cze-Rep	45	....	....	....	2696	77	5	*1.71	12	8	4	*747	23	1	1.85
99-2000	HC Slovnaft Vsetin	Cze-Rep	37	....	....	....	2141	88	0	2.47	9	5	4	545	15	3	1.65
2000-01	**Philadelphia**	**NHL**	**59**	**35**	**15**	**6**	**3431**	**115**	**10**	**2.01**	**6**	**2**	**4**	**347**	**18**	**0**	**3.11**
	Philadelphia	AHL	3	1	1	0	160	3	0	1.12	....	....	....	....	....	....	....
	NHL Totals		**59**	**35**	**15**	**6**	**3431**	**115**	**10**	**2.01**	**6**	**2**	**4**	**347**	**18**	**0**	**3.11**

NHL Second All-Star Team (2001) • Played in NHL All-Star Game (2001)

CENTOMO, Sebastien (sehn-TOH-moh, suh-BAS-tee-yeh) TOR.

Goaltender. Catches right. 6'1", 193 lbs. Born, Montreal, Que., March 26, 1981.

			Regular Season								Playoffs						
Season	Club	Lea	GP	W	L	T	Mins	GA	SO	Avg	GP	W	L	Mins	GA	SO	Avg
1997-98	Laval-Laurentides	QAAA	30	16	11	2	1696	87	0	2.86	....	....	....	....	....	....	....
1998-99	Rouyn-Noranda	QMJHL	32	14	9	4	1658	104	1	3.76	2	0	1	28	5	0	10.71
99-2000	Rouyn-Noranda	QMJHL	50	24	17	3	2758	160	1	3.48	11	6	5	695	41	0	3.54
2000-01	Rouyn-Noranda	QMJHL	46	25	14	4	2599	158	3	3.65	1	0	1	60	4	0	4.00

Signed as a free agent by **Toronto**, September 10, 1999.

CHABOT, Frederic (shah-BOH, FREHD-uhr-IHK)

Goaltender. Catches left. 5'11", 187 lbs. Born, Hebertville-Station, Que., February 12, 1968.
(New Jersey's 10th choice, 192nd overall, in 1986 Entry Draft).

			Regular Season								Playoffs						
Season	Club	Lea	GP	W	L	T	Mins	GA	SO	Avg	GP	W	L	Mins	GA	SO	Avg
1985-86	Trois-Rivieres	QAAA	34	25	9	0	2038	139	0	3.90	7	6	1	320	30	0	4.29
1986-87	Drummondville	QMJHL	62	31	29	0	3508	293	1	5.01	8	2	6	481	40	0	4.99
1987-88	Drummondville	QMJHL	58	27	24	4	3276	237	1	4.34	16	10	6	1019	56	*1	*3.30
1988-89	Moose Jaw	WHL	26	....	....	....	1385	114	....	4.94	....	....	....	....	....	....	....
	Prince Albert	WHL	28	....	....	....	1572	88	....	3.36	4	1	1	199	16	0	4.82
1989-90	Sherbrooke	AHL	2	1	1	0	119	8	0	4.03	....	....	....	....	....	....	....
	Fort Wayne	IHL	23	6	13	3	1208	87	1	4.32	....	....	....	....	....	....	....
1990-91	**Montreal**	**NHL**	**3**	**0**	**0**	**1**	**108**	**6**	**0**	**3.33**	....	....	....	....	....	....	....
	Fredericton	AHL	35	9	15	5	1800	122	0	4.07	....	....	....	....	....	....	....
1991-92	Fredericton	AHL	30	17	9	4	1761	79	2	*2.69	7	3	4	457	20	0	2.63
	Winston-Salem	ECHL	24	15	7	2	1449	71	0	*2.94	....	....	....	....	....	....	....
1992-93	**Montreal**	**NHL**	**1**	**0**	**0**	**0**	**40**	**1**	**0**	**1.50**	....	....	....	....	....	....	....
	Fredericton	AHL	45	22	17	4	2544	141	0	3.33	4	1	3	261	16	0	3.68
1993-94	**Montreal**	**NHL**	**1**	**0**	**1**	**0**	**60**	**5**	**0**	**5.00**	....	....	....	....	....	....	....
	Fredericton	AHL	3	0	1	1	143	12	0	5.03	....	....	....	....	....	....	....
	Las Vegas	IHL	2	1	1	0	110	5	0	2.72	....	....	....	....	....	....	....
	Philadelphia	**NHL**	**4**	**0**	**1**	**1**	**70**	**5**	**0**	**4.29**	....	....	....	....	....	....	....
	Hershey Bears	AHL	28	13	5	6	1464	63	2	*2.58	11	7	4	665	32	0	2.89
1994-95	Cincinnati	IHL	48	25	12	7	2622	128	1	2.93	5	3	2	326	16	0	2.94
1995-96	Cincinnati	IHL	38	23	9	4	2147	88	3	*2.46	14	9	5	854	37	1	2.60
1996-97	Houston Aeros	IHL	*72	*39	26	7	*4265	180	*7	2.53	13	8	5	777	34	*2	2.63
1997-98	**Los Angeles**	**NHL**	**12**	**3**	**3**	**2**	**554**	**29**	**0**	**3.14**	....	....	....	....	....	....	....
	Houston Aeros	IHL	22	12	7	2	1237	46	1	2.23	4	1	3	238	11	0	2.77
1998-99	**Montreal**	**NHL**	**11**	**1**	**3**	**0**	**430**	**16**	**0**	**2.23**	....	....	....	....	....	....	....
	Houston Aeros	IHL	21	16	4	1	1259	49	3	2.34	....	....	....	....	....	....	....
99-2000	Houston Aeros	IHL	*62	*36	19	7	*3695	131	4	2.13	11	6	5	658	20	*3	1.82
2000-01	Houston Aeros	IHL	47	23	16	5	2705	119	3	2.64	7	3	4	482	15	0	*1.87
	NHL Totals		**32**	**4**	**8**	**4**	**1262**	**62**	**0**	**2.95**	....	....	....	....	....	....	....

WHL East All-Star Team (1989) • Won Baz Bastien Award (Top Goaltender - AHL) (1994) • IHL Second All-Star Team (1996) • IHL First All-Star Team (1997, 2000) • Won James Gatschene Memorial Trophy (MVP - IHL) (1997) • Won James Norris Memorial Trophy (fewest goals against - IHL) (2000) • Shared James Gatschene Memorial Trophy (MVP - IHL) with Nikolai Khabibulin, (2000).

Signed as a free agent by **Montreal**, January 16, 1990. Claimed by **Tampa Bay** from **Montreal** in Expansion Draft, June 18, 1992. Traded to **Montreal** by **Tampa Bay** for Jean-Claude Bergeron, June 19, 1992. Traded to **Philadelphia** by **Montreal** for cash, February 21, 1994. Signed as a free agent by **Florida**, August 11, 1994. Signed as a free agent by **LA Kings**, September 3, 1997. Claimed by **Nashville** from **LA Kings** in Expansion Draft, June 26, 1998. Claimed on waivers by **LA Kings** from **Nashville**, July 18, 1998. Claimed by **Montreal** from **LA Kings** in NHL Waiver Draft, October 5, 1998. Selected by **Columbus** from **Montreal** in Expansion Draft, June 23, 2000.

CHARPENTIER, Sebastien (shahr-PUHNT-yay, suh-BAS-tee-yeh) WSH.

Goaltender. Catches left. 5'9", 177 lbs. Born, Drummondville, Que., April 18, 1977.
(Washington's 4th choice, 93rd overall, in 1995 Entry Draft).

			Regular Season								Playoffs						
Season	Club	Lea	GP	W	L	T	Mins	GA	SO	Avg	GP	W	L	Mins	GA	SO	Avg
1991-92	Drummondville	QAHA	14	....	....	....	840	34	2	2.42	....	....	....	....	....	....	....
1992-93	Drummondville	QAHA	20	....	....	....	1215	37	*7	*1.80	....	....	....	....	....	....	....
1993-94	Magog Selectes	QAAA	24	14	5	1	1443	75	1	3.16	....	....	....	....	....	....	....
1994-95	Laval Titan	QMJHL	41	25	12	1	2152	99	2	2.76	16	9	4	886	45	0	3.05
1995-96	Laval Titan	QMJHL	18	4	10	0	938	97	0	6.20	....	....	....	....	....	....	....
	Val-d'Or Foreurs	QMJHL	33	21	9	1	1906	87	1	2.74	13	7	5	740	45	0	3.64
1996-97	Shawinigan	QMJHL	*62	*37	17	4	*3480	177	1	3.05	4	2	1	196	13	0	3.98
1997-98	Portland Pirates	AHL	4	1	3	0	229	10	0	2.61	....	....	....	....	....	....	....
	Hampton Roads	ECHL	43	20	16	6	2388	114	0	2.86	18	*14	4	*1183	38	1	*1.93
1998-99	Quad City Mallards	UHL	6	0	0	0	4	0	0	0.00	....	....	....	....	....	....	....
	Portland Pirates	AHL	3	0	3	0	180	10	0	3.34	....	....	....	....	....	....	....
99-2000	Portland Pirates	AHL	18	10	4	3	1041	48	0	2.77	3	1	1	183	9	0	2.96
2000-01	Portland Pirates	AHL	34	16	16	1	1978	113	1	3.43	1	0	1	102	3	0	1.76

QMJHL Second All-Rookie Team (1995) • Won ECHL Playoff MVP Award (1998)

CHOUINARD, Mathieu (SHWEE-nuhr, ma-TEW) OTT.

Goaltender. Catches left. 6'1", 211 lbs. Born, Laval, Que., April 11, 1980.
(Ottawa's 2nd choice, 45th overall, in 2000 Entry Draft).

			Regular Season								Playoffs						
Season	Club	Lea	GP	W	L	T	Mins	GA	SO	Avg	GP	W	L	Mins	GA	SO	Avg
1995-96	Amos Forrestiers	QAAA	31	14	14	1	1613	114	1	4.24	1	1	2	190	11	0	3.48
1996-97	Shawinigan	QMJHL	17	4	7	1	795	51	0	3.85	4	1	3	264	15	0	3.41
1997-98	Shawinigan	QMJHL	55	*32	18	3	3055	142	2	2.79	6	2	4	348	24	0	4.14
1998-99	Shawinigan	QMJHL	56	36	16	4	3288	150	*5	2.74	6	2	4	392	27	0	4.13
99-2000	Shawinigan	QMJHL	*59	32	20	5	*3339	186	4	3.34	13	7	6	769	41	0	3.20
2000-01	Grand Rapids	IHL	28	17	7	1	1567	69	1	2.64	3	1	1	135	4	0	1.78

• Re-entered NHL Entry Draft. Originally Ottawa's 1st choice, 15th overall, in 1998 Entry Draft.

QMJHL First All-Star Team (1999)

CLEMMENSEN, Scott (KLEH-mehn-SEHN, SKAWT) N.J.

Goaltender. Catches left. 6'2", 185 lbs. Born, Des Moines, IA, July 23, 1977.
(New Jersey's 7th choice, 215th overall, in 1997 Entry Draft).

			Regular Season								Playoffs						
Season	Club	Lea	GP	W	L	T	Mins	GA	SO	Avg	GP	W	L	Mins	GA	SO	Avg
1995-96	Des Moines	USHL	20	10	7	1	1082	62	0	3.44	....	....	....	....	....	....	....
1996-97	Des Moines	USHL	36	22	9	2	2042	111	1	3.26	4	1	2	200	9	1	2.70
1997-98	Boston College	H-East	37	24	9	4	2205	102	*4	2.78	....	....	....	....	....	....	....
1998-99	Boston College	H-East	*42	26	12	4	*2507	120	1	2.87	....	....	....	....	....	....	....
99-2000	Boston College	H-East	29	19	7	0	1610	59	*5	2.20	....	....	....	....	....	....	....
2000-01	Boston College	H-East	*39	*30	7	2	*2312	82	3	2.13	....	....	....	....	....	....	....

NCAA Championship All-Tournament Team (2001)

CLOUTIER, Dan (KLOO-tyay, DAN) VAN.

Goaltender. Catches left. 6'1", 182 lbs. Born, Mont-Laurier, Que., April 22, 1976.
(NY Rangers' 1st choice, 26th overall, in 1994 Entry Draft).

			Regular Season								Playoffs						
Season	Club	Lea	GP	W	L	T	Mins	GA	SO	Avg	GP	W	L	Mins	GA	SO	Avg
1991-92	St. Thomas Stars	OJHL-B	14	....	....	....	823	80	0	5.83	....	....	....	....	....	....	....
1992-93	Timmons Bears	NOJHA	5	4	0	0	255	10	0	2.35	....	....	....	....	....	....	....
	Sault Ste. Marie	OHL	12	4	6	0	572	44	0	4.62	4	1	2	231	12	0	3.12
1993-94	Sault Ste. Marie	OHL	55	28	14	6	2934	174	*2	3.56	14	*10	4	833	52	0	3.75
1994-95	Sault Ste. Marie	OHL	45	15	26	2	2518	185	1	4.41	....	....	....	....	....	....	....
1995-96	Sault Ste. Marie	OHL	13	9	3	0	641	43	0	4.02	....	....	....	....	....	....	....
	Guelph Storm	OHL	17	12	2	2	1004	35	2	2.09	16	11	5	993	52	*2	3.14
1996-97	Binghamton	AHL	60	23	28	8	3367	199	3	3.55	4	1	3	236	13	0	3.31
1997-98	**NY Rangers**	**NHL**	**12**	**4**	**5**	**1**	**551**	**23**	**0**	**2.50**	....	....	....	....	....	....	....
	Hartford	AHL	24	12	8	3	1417	62	0	2.63	8	5	3	478	24	0	3.01
1998-99	**NY Rangers**	**NHL**	**22**	**6**	**8**	**3**	**1097**	**49**	**0**	**2.68**	....	....	....	....	....	....	....
99-2000	**Tampa Bay**	**NHL**	**52**	**9**	**30**	**3**	**2492**	**145**	**0**	**3.49**	....	....	....	....	....	....	....
2000-01	**Tampa Bay**	**NHL**	**24**	**3**	**13**	**3**	**1005**	**59**	**1**	**3.52**	....	....	....	....	....	....	....
	Detroit Vipers	IHL	1	0	1	0	59	3	0	3.05	....	....	....	....	....	....	....
	Vancouver	**NHL**	**16**	**4**	**6**	**5**	**914**	**37**	**0**	**2.43**	**2**	**0**	**2**	**117**	**9**	**0**	**4.62**
	NHL Totals		**126**	**26**	**62**	**15**	**6059**	**313**	**1**	**3.10**	**2**	**0**	**2**	**117**	**9**	**0**	**4.62**

OHL Second All-Star Team (1996)

Traded to **Tampa Bay** by **NY Rangers** with Niklas Sundstrom and NY Rangers' 1st (Nikita Alexeev) and 3rd (later traded to San Jose - later traded to Chicago - Chicago selected Igor Radulov) round choices in 2000 Entry Draft for Chicago's 1st round choice (previously acquired, NY Rangers selected Pavel Brendl) in 1999 Entry Draft, June 26, 1999. Traded to **Vancouver** by **Tampa Bay** for Adrian Aucoin and Vancouver's 2nd round choice (Alexander Polushin) in 2001 Entry Draft, February 7, 2001.

CONKLIN, Ty (KAWN-klihn, TIGH) EDM.

Goaltender. Catches left. 6', 190 lbs. Born, Anchorage, AK, March 30, 1976.

			Regular Season								Playoffs						
Season	Club	Lea	GP	W	L	T	Mins	GA	SO	Avg	GP	W	L	Mins	GA	SO	Avg
1995-96	Green Bay	USHL	30	....	....	....	1727	82	1	2.85	....	....	....	....	....	....	....
1996-97	Alaska-Anchorage	WCHA	DID NOT PLAY – FRESHMAN														
	Green Bay	USHL	30	19	7	1	1609	86	1	3.21	17	8	9	980	56	1	3.43
1997-98	New Hampshire	WCHA	DID NOT PLAY – TRANSFERRED COLLEGES														
1998-99	New Hampshire	H-East	22	18	3	1	1338	41	0	*1.84	....	....	....	....	....	....	....
99-2000	New Hampshire	H-East	*37	*22	8	6	*2194	91	2	2.49	....	....	....	....	....	....	....
2000-01	New Hampshire	H-East	34	17	12	5	2048	70	*5	*2.05	....	....	....	....	....	....	....

USHL Second All-Star Team (1996) • Left **Alaska-Anchorage** and returned to **Green Bay** (USHL), November 14, 1996. • Hockey East All-Rookie Team (1999) • Hockey East Second All-Star Team (1999) • Hockey East First All-Star Team (2000, 2001) • NCAA East Second All-American Team (2000) • First goaltender to be named captain of Univerisity of New Hampshire Wildcats since 1961, October 5, 2000. • NCAA East First All-American Team (2001) • Shared Walter Brown Award (New England's Outstanding American-born College player) with Brian Gionta, March 14, 2001.

Signed as a free agent by **Edmonton**, April 18, 2001.

COUSINEAU, Marcel (koo-ZEE-noh, MAHR-sehl) L.A.

Goaltender. Catches left. 5'9", 183 lbs. Born, Delson, Que., April 30, 1973.
(Boston's 3rd choice, 62nd overall, in 1991 Entry Draft).

			Regular Season								Playoffs						
Season	Club	Lea	GP	W	L	T	Mins	GA	SO	Avg	GP	W	L	Mins	GA	SO	Avg
1989-90	Richelieu Riverains	QAAA	27	22	5	0	1618	104	0	3.83	4	1	3	238	126	0	4.29
1990-91	Beauport	QMJHL	49	13	29	3	2739	196	1	4.29	....	....	....	....	....	....	....
1991-92	Beauport	QMJHL	*67	26	32	5	*3673	241	0	3.94	....	....	....	....	....	....	....
1992-93	Drummondville	QMJHL	60	20	32	2	3298	225	0	4.09	9	3	6	498	37	*1	4.45
1993-94	St. John's Leafs	AHL	37	13	11	9	2015	118	0	3.51	....	....	....	....	....	....	....
1994-95	St. John's Leafs	AHL	58	22	27	6	3342	171	4	3.07	3	0	3	179	9	0	3.01
1995-96	St. John's Leafs	AHL	62	21	26	13	3629	192	1	3.17	4	1	3	258	11	0	2.56
1996-97	**Toronto**	**NHL**	**13**	**3**	**5**	**1**	**566**	**31**	**1**	**3.29**	....	....	....	....	....	....	....
	St. John's Leafs	AHL	19	7	8	3	1053	58	0	3.30	11	6	5	658	28	0	2.55
1997-98	**Toronto**	**NHL**	**2**	**0**	**0**	**0**	**17**	**0**	**0**	**0.00**	....	....	....	....	....	....	....
	St. John's Leafs	AHL	57	17	25	13	3306	167	1	3.03	4	1	3	254	10	0	2.36
1998-99	**NY Islanders**	**NHL**	**6**	**0**	**4**	**0**	**293**	**14**	**0**	**2.87**	....	....	....	....	....	....	....
	Lowell	AHL	53	26	17	7	3034	139	3	2.75	3	0	3	186	13	0	4.20
99-2000	**Los Angeles**	**NHL**	**5**	**1**	**1**	**0**	**171**	**6**	**0**	**2.11**	....	....	....	....	....	....	....
	Long Beach	IHL	23	15	6	1	1328	62	0	2.80	....	....	....	....	....	....	....
2000-01	Lowell	AHL	37	15	20	2	2135	101	1	2.84	1	0	1	58	4	0	4.10
	NHL Totals		**26**	**4**	**10**	**1**	**1047**	**51**	**1**	**2.92**	....	....	....	....	....	....	....

Signed as a free agent by **Toronto**, November 13, 1993. Signed as a free agent by **NY Islanders**, July 29, 1998. Traded to **LA Kings** by **NY Islanders** with Ziggy Palffy, Brian Smolinski and New Jersey's 4th round choice (previously acquired, LA Kings selected Daniel Johansson) in 1999 Entry Draft for Olli Jokinen, Josh Green, Mathieu Biron and LA Kings' 1st round choice (Taylor Pyatt) in 1999 Entry Draft, June 20, 1999.

CRUICKSHANK, Curtis (KRUHK-shank, KUHR-tihs) WSH.

Goaltender. Catches left. 6'3", 220 lbs. Born, Ottawa, Ont., March 21, 1979.
(Washington's 3rd choice, 89th overall, in 1997 Entry Draft).

			Regular Season								Playoffs						
Season	Club	Lea	GP	W	L	T	Mins	GA	SO	Avg	GP	W	L	Mins	GA	SO	Avg
1995-96	Ottawa Jr. Sens	COJHL	24	12	4	0	....	....	0	4.27	....	....	....	....	....	....	....
1996-97	Kingston	OHL	35	13	16	1	1792	118	2	3.95	1	0	1	26	4	0	9.23
1997-98	Kingston	OHL	57	30	20	4	3166	207	2	3.92	12	5	6	702	45	0	3.85
1998-99	Kingston	OHL	16	5	9	0	835	63	1	4.53	....	....	....	....	....	....	....
	Sarnia Sting	OHL	28	18	5	1	1557	66	2	2.54	4	1	0	71	6	0	5.07
99-2000	Portland Pirates	AHL	10	4	5	1	605	30	0	2.98	....	....	....	....	....	....	....
	Hampton Roads	ECHL	7	4	3	0	375	22	0	3.52	1	0	0	12	2	0	10.23
2000-01	Portland Pirates	AHL	10	1	7	0	533	44	0	4.95	....	....	....	....	....	....	....
	Rockford IceHogs	UHL	9	3	5	1	489	29	0	3.56	....	....	....	....	....	....	....

DAFOE, Byron (day-FOH, BIGH-ruhn) BOS.

Goaltender. Catches left. 5'11", 200 lbs. Born, Sussex, England, February 25, 1971.
(Washington's 2nd choice, 35th overall, in 1989 Entry Draft).

			Regular Season								Playoffs						
Season	Club	Lea	GP	W	L	T	Mins	GA	SO	Avg	GP	W	L	Mins	GA	SO	Avg
1987-88	Juan de Fuca	BCJHL	32	....	....	....	1716	129	0	4.51	....	....	....	....	....	....	....
1988-89	Portland	WHL	59	29	24	3	3279	291	1	5.32	*18	10	8	*1091	81	*1	4.45
1989-90	Portland	WHL	40	14	21	3	2265	193	0	5.11	....	....	....	....	....	....	....
1990-91	Portland	WHL	8	1	5	1	414	41	0	5.94	....	....	....	....	....	....	....
	Prince Albert	WHL	32	13	12	4	1839	124	0	4.05	....	....	....	....	....	....	....
1991-92	Baltimore	AHL	33	12	16	4	1847	119	0	3.87	....	....	....	....	....	....	....
	New Haven	AHL	7	3	2	1	364	22	0	3.63	....	....	....	....	....	....	....
	Hampton Roads	ECHL	10	6	4	0	562	26	0	2.78	....	....	....	....	....	....	....
1992-93	**Washington**	**NHL**	**1**	**0**	**0**	**0**	**1**	**0**	**0**	**0.00**	....	....	....	....	....	....	....
	Baltimore	AHL	48	16	20	7	2617	191	1	4.38	5	2	3	241	22	0	5.48
1993-94	**Washington**	**NHL**	**5**	**2**	**2**	**0**	**230**	**13**	**0**	**3.39**	**2**	**0**	**2**	**118**	**5**	**0**	**2.54**
	Portland Pirates	AHL	47	24	16	4	2661	148	1	3.34	1	0	0	9	1	0	6.79
1994-95	**Washington**	**NHL**	**4**	**1**	**1**	**1**	**187**	**11**	**0**	**3.53**	**1**	**0**	**0**	**20**	**1**	**0**	**3.00**
	Phoenix	IHL	49	25	16	6	2743	169	2	3.70	....	....	....	....	....	....	....
	Portland Pirates	AHL	6	5	0	0	330	16	0	2.91	7	3	4	416	29	0	4.18
1995-96	**Los Angeles**	**NHL**	**47**	**14**	**24**	**8**	**2666**	**172**	**1**	**3.87**	....	....	....	....	....	....	....
1996-97	**Los Angeles**	**NHL**	**40**	**13**	**17**	**5**	**2162**	**112**	**0**	**3.11**	....	....	....	....	....	....	....
1997-98	**Boston**	**NHL**	**65**	**30**	**25**	**9**	**3693**	**138**	**6**	**2.24**	**6**	**2**	**4**	**422**	**14**	**1**	**1.99**
1998-99	**Boston**	**NHL**	**68**	**32**	**23**	**11**	**4001**	**133**	***10**	**1.99**	**12**	**6**	**6**	**768**	**26**	**2**	**2.03**
99-2000	**Boston**	**NHL**	**41**	**13**	**16**	**10**	**2307**	**114**	**3**	**2.96**	....	....	....	....	....	....	....
2000-01	**Boston**	**NHL**	**45**	**22**	**14**	**7**	**2536**	**101**	**2**	**2.39**	....	....	....	....	....	....	....
	NHL Totals		**316**	**127**	**122**	**51**	**17783**	**794**	**22**	**2.68**	**21**	**8**	**12**	**1328**	**46**	**3**	**2.08**

AHL First All-Star Team (1994) • Shared Harry "Hap" Holmes Trophy (fewest goals against - AHL) with Olaf Kolzig (1994) • NHL Second All-Star Team (1999)

Traded to **Los Angeles** by **Washington** with Dmitri Khristich for Los Angeles' 1st round choice (Alexandre Volchkov) and Dallas' 4th round choice (previously acquired, Washington selected Justin Davis) in 1996 Entry Draft, July 8, 1995. Traded to **Boston** by **Los Angeles** with Dimitri Khristich for Jozef Stumpel, Sandy Moger and Boston's 4th round choice (later traded to New Jersey - New Jersey selected Pierre Dagenais) in 1998 Entry Draft, August 29, 1997.

DAMPHOUSSE, Jean-Francois (DAHM-fooz, ZHAWN-fran-SWUH) N.J.

Goaltender. Catches left. 6', 180 lbs. Born, St-Alexis-des-Monts, Que., July 21, 1979.
(New Jersey's 1st choice, 24th overall, in 1997 Entry Draft).

			Regular Season								Playoffs						
Season	Club	Lea	GP	W	L	T	Mins	GA	SO	Avg	GP	W	L	Mins	GA	SO	Avg
1993-94	Ste-Foy AA	QAHA	18	10	1	0	1078	53	0	2.95	14	10	4	842	50	0	3.52
1994-95	Ste-Foy AA	QAHA	16	....	....	....	958	48	0	3.01	....	....	....	....	....	....	....
	Ste-Foy Governors	QAAA	2	1	0	1	120	8	0	3.84	....	....	....	....	....	....	....
1995-96	Ste-Foy Governors	QAAA	32	18	10	1	1629	83	2	3.06	....	....	....	....	....	....	....
1996-97	Moncton Wildcats	QMJHL	39	6	25	2	2063	190	0	5.53	....	....	....	....	....	....	....
1997-98	Moncton Wildcats	QMJHL	59	24	26	6	3400	174	1	3.07	10	5	5	595	28	0	2.82
1998-99	Moncton Wildcats	QMJHL	40	19	17	2	2163	121	1	3.36	4	0	4	200	12	0	3.60
	Albany River Rats	AHL	1	0	1	0	59	3	0	3.06	....	....	....	....	....	....	....
99-2000	Augusta Lynx	ECHL	14	4	7	0	676	49	0	4.35	....	....	....	....	....	....	....
	Albany River Rats	AHL	26	9	11	2	1326	62	0	2.81	2	0	1	62	4	0	3.86
2000-01	Albany River Rats	AHL	55	24	23	3	2963	141	1	2.86	....	....	....	....	....	....	....

DENIKE, Terry (deh-NIGHK, TEHR-ee) L.A.

Goaltender. Catches left. 6'2", 190 lbs. Born, Burlington, Ont., April 16, 1981.
(Los Angeles' 7th choice, 152nd overall, in 2001 Entry Draft).

			Regular Season								Playoffs						
Season	Club	Lea	GP	W	L	T	Mins	GA	SO	Avg	GP	W	L	Mins	GA	SO	Avg
99-2000	Weyburn Wings	SJHL	38	25	7	5	2171	108	2	2.99	....	....	....	....	....	....	....
2000-01	Weyburn Wings	SJHL	43	28	14	0	2528	107	*6	*2.54	17	13	4	1005	47	0	2.81

Won Harold L. Jones Trophy (Top Goaltender - SJHL) (2001) • Won Graham Christie Memorial Award (Dedication and Sportsmanship - SJHL) (2001) • SJHL Second All-Star Team (2001)

DENIS, Marc (deh-NEE, MAHRK) CBJ

Goaltender. Catches left. 6', 190 lbs. Born, Montreal, Que., August 1, 1977.
(Colorado's 1st choice, 25th overall, in 1995 Entry Draft).

			Regular Season								Playoffs						
Season	Club	Lea	GP	W	L	T	Mins	GA	SO	Avg	GP	W	L	Mins	GA	SO	Avg
1992-93	Montreal-Bourassa	QAAA	26	....	....	....	1559	74	5	2.87	....	....	....	....	....	....	....
1993-94	Trois-Rivieres	QAAA	36	10	22	3	2093	158	0	4.53	4	1	3	249	20	0	4.83
1994-95	Chicoutimi	QMJHL	32	17	9	1	1688	98	0	3.48	6	4	2	372	19	1	3.06
1995-96	Chicoutimi	QMJHL	51	23	21	4	2951	157	2	3.19	16	8	8	957	69	0	4.33
1996-97	Chicoutimi	QMJHL	41	22	15	2	2323	104	4	*2.69	*21	*11	10	*1229	70	*1	3.42
	Colorado	**NHL**	**1**	**0**	**1**	**0**	**60**	**3**	**0**	**3.00**	....	....	....	....	....	....	....
	Hershey Bears	AHL	....	....	....	....	....	....	....	....	4	1	0	56	1	0	1.08
1997-98	Hershey Bears	AHL	47	17	23	4	2588	125	1	2.90	6	3	3	346	15	0	2.59
1998-99	**Colorado**	**NHL**	**4**	**1**	**1**	**1**	**217**	**9**	**0**	**2.49**	....	....	....	....	....	....	....
	Hershey Bears	AHL	52	20	23	5	2908	137	4	2.83	3	1	1	143	7	0	2.93
99-2000	**Colorado**	**NHL**	**23**	**9**	**8**	**3**	**1203**	**51**	**3**	**2.54**	....	....	....	....	....	....	....
2000-01	**Columbus**	**NHL**	**32**	**6**	**20**	**4**	**1830**	**99**	**0**	**3.25**	....	....	....	....	....	....	....
	NHL Totals		**60**	**16**	**30**	**8**	**3310**	**162**	**3**	**2.94**	....	....	....	....	....	....	....

QMJHL First All-Star Team (1997) • Canadian Major Junior First All-Star Team (1997) • Canadian Major Junior Goaltender of the Year (1997)

Traded to **Columbus** by **Colorado** for Columbus' 2nd round choice (later traded to Carolina - Carolina selected Tomas Kurka) in 2000 Entry Draft, June 7, 2000.

DesROCHERS, Patrick (duh-RAWSH-ay, PAT-rihk) PHX.

Goaltender. Catches left. 6'4", 207 lbs. Born, Penetanguishene, Ont., October 27, 1979.
(Phoenix's 1st choice, 14th overall, in 1998 Entry Draft).

			Regular Season								Playoffs						
Season	Club	Lea	GP	W	L	T	Mins	GA	SO	Avg	GP	W	L	Mins	GA	SO	Avg
1994-95	Barrie Colts	OPJHL	26	....	....	....	3205	179	3	3.08	....	....	....	....	....	....	....
1995-96	Sarnia Sting	OHL	29	12	6	2	1265	96	0	4.55	3	0	1	71	5	0	4.23
1996-97	Sarnia Sting	OHL	50	22	17	4	2667	154	*4	3.46	11	6	5	576	42	0	4.38
1997-98	Sarnia Sting	OHL	56	26	17	11	3205	179	1	3.35	4	1	2	160	12	0	4.50
1998-99	Sarnia Sting	OHL	8	3	5	0	425	26	0	3.67	....	....	....	....	....	....	....
	Kingston	OHL	44	14	22	3	2389	177	1	4.45	5	1	4	323	21	0	3.90
99-2000	Springfield	AHL	52	21	17	7	2710	137	1	3.03	2	1	1	120	7	1	3.50
2000-01	Springfield	AHL	50	17	24	5	2807	156	0	3.33	....	....	....	....	....	....	....

DiPIETRO, Rick (dee-pee-EHT-roh, RIHK) NYI

Goaltender. Catches right. 5'11", 185 lbs. Born, Winthrop, MA, September 19, 1981.
(NY Islanders' 1st choice, 1st overall, in 2000 Entry Draft).

			Regular Season								Playoffs						
Season	Club	Lea	GP	W	L	T	Mins	GA	SO	Avg	GP	W	L	Mins	GA	SO	Avg
1997-98	Team USA	USDP	46	21	19	0	2526	131	2	3.11	....	....	....	....	....	....	....
1998-99	Team USA	USDP	46	31	11	2	2760	113	2	2.46	....	....	....	....	....	....	....
99-2000	Boston University	H-East	29	18	5	5	1790	73	2	2.45	....	....	....	....	....	....	....
2000-01	**NY Islanders**	**NHL**	**20**	**3**	**15**	**1**	**1083**	**63**	**0**	**3.49**	....	....	....	....	....	....	....
	Chicago Wolves	IHL	14	4	5	2	778	44	0	3.39	....	....	....	....	....	....	....
	NHL Totals		**20**	**3**	**15**	**1**	**1083**	**63**	**0**	**3.49**	....	....	....	....	....	....	....

Hockey East Second All-Star Team (2000)

DIVIS, Reinhard (DIH-vihs, RIGHN-hard) ST.L.

Goaltender. Catches left. 5'11", 200 lbs. Born, Vienna, Austria, July 4, 1975.
(St. Louis' 8th choice, 261st overall, in 2000 Entry Draft).

			Regular Season								Playoffs						
Season	Club	Lea	GP	W	L	T	Mins	GA	SO	Avg	GP	W	L	Mins	GA	SO	Avg
1995-96	VEU Feldkirch	Austria	37	....	....	....	2200	85	0	2.32	....	....	....	....	....	....	....
1996-97	VEU Feldkirch	Alpenliga	45	....	....	....	2738	105	0	2.30	....	....	....	....	....	....	....
	VEU Feldkirch	Austria	....	....	....	....	....	....	....	....	11	....	....	620	27	0	2.61
1997-98	VEU Feldkirch	Alpenliga	13	....	....	....	779	22	0	1.69	....	....	....	....	....	....	....
	VEU Feldkirch	Austria	27	....	....	....	1620	55	0	2.07	....	....	....	....	....	....	....
1998-99	VEU Feldkirch	Austria	15	....	....	....	900	58	0	3.86	....	....	....	....	....	....	....
99-2000	Leksands IF	Sweden	48	....	....	....	2839	160	3	3.38	....	....	....	....	....	....	....
2000-01	Leksands IF	Sweden	41	....	....	....	2451	141	3	3.45	....	....	....	....	....	....	....

DUNHAM, Mike (DUHN-uhm, MIGHK) NSH.

Goaltender. Catches left. 6'3", 200 lbs. Born, Johnson City, NY, June 1, 1972.
(New Jersey's 4th choice, 53rd overall, in 1990 Entry Draft).

			Regular Season								Playoffs						
Season	Club	Lea	GP	W	L	T	Mins	GA	SO	Avg	GP	W	L	Mins	GA	SO	Avg
1987-88	Canterbury School	H.S.	29	....	....	....	1740	69	4	2.37	....	....	....	....	....	....	....
1988-89	Canterbury School	H.S.	25	....	....	....	1500	63	2	2.52	....	....	....	....	....	....	....
1989-90	Canterbury School	H.S.	32	....	....	....	1558	68	3	1.96	....	....	....	....	....	....	....
1990-91	U. of Maine	H-East	23	14	5	2	1275	63	0	*2.96	....	....	....	....	....	....	....
1991-92	U. of Maine	H-East	7	6	0	0	382	14	1	2.20	....	....	....	....	....	....	....
	United States	Nt-Team	3	0	1	1	157	10	0	3.82	....	....	....	....	....	....	....
1992-93	U. of Maine	H-East	25	*21	1	1	1429	63	0	2.65	....	....	....	....	....	....	....
1993-94	United States	Nt-Team	33	22	9	2	1983	125	2	3.78	....	....	....	....	....	....	....
	United States	Olympics	3	0	1	2	180	15	0	5.00	....	....	....	....	....	....	....
	Albany River Rats	AHL	5	2	2	1	304	26	0	5.12	....	....	....	....	....	....	....
1994-95	Albany River Rats	AHL	35	20	7	8	2120	99	1	2.80	7	6	1	419	20	1	2.86
1995-96	Albany River Rats	AHL	44	30	10	2	2592	109	1	2.52	3	1	2	182	5	1	1.65
1996-97	**New Jersey**	**NHL**	**26**	**8**	**7**	**1**	**1013**	**43**	**2**	**2.55**	....	....	....	....	....	....	....
	Albany River Rats	AHL	3	1	1	1	184	12	0	3.91	....	....	....	....	....	....	....
1997-98	**New Jersey**	**NHL**	**15**	**5**	**5**	**3**	**773**	**29**	**1**	**2.25**	....	....	....	....	....	....	....
1998-99	**Nashville**	**NHL**	**44**	**16**	**23**	**3**	**2472**	**127**	**1**	**3.08**	....	....	....	....	....	....	....
99-2000	**Nashville**	**NHL**	**52**	**19**	**27**	**6**	**3077**	**146**	**0**	**2.85**	....	....	....	....	....	....	....
	Milwaukee	IHL	1	1	0	0	60	1	0	1.00	....	....	....	....	....	....	....
2000-01	**Nashville**	**NHL**	**48**	**21**	**21**	**4**	**2810**	**107**	**4**	**2.28**	....	....	....	....	....	....	....
	NHL Totals		**185**	**69**	**83**	**17**	**10145**	**452**	**8**	**2.67**	....	....	....	....	....	....	....

Hockey East First All-Star Team (1993) • NCAA East First All-American Team (1993) • Shared Harry "Hap" Holmes Memorial Trophy (fewest goals against - AHL) with Corey Schwab (1995) • Shared Jack A. Butterfield Trophy (Playoff MVP - AHL) with Corey Schwab (1995) • AHL Second All-Star Team (1996) • Shared William M. Jennings Trophy with Martin Brodeur (1997)

Claimed by **Nashville** from **New Jersey** in Expansion Draft, June 26, 1998.

EKLUND, Brian (EHK-luhnd, BRIGH-uhn) T.B.

Goaltender. Catches left. 6'5", 200 lbs. Born, Quincy, MA, May 24, 1980.
(Tampa Bay's 8th choice, 226th overall, in 2000 Entry Draft).

			Regular Season								Playoffs						
Season	Club	Lea	GP	W	L	T	Mins	GA	SO	Avg	GP	W	L	Mins	GA	SO	Avg
1998-99	Bishop Williams	H.S.					STATISTICS NOT AVAILABLE										
99-2000	Brown University	ECAC	12	1	6	2	569	28	1	2.95	....	....	....	....	....	....	....
2000-01	Brown University	ECAC	19	2	13	3	1084	62	0	3.43	....	....	....	....	....	....	....

ELLIOT, Jason (EHL-lee-awt, JAY-suhn) DET.

Goaltender. Catches left. 6'2", 183 lbs. Born, Inuvik, N.W.T., November 10, 1975.
(Detroit's 7th choice, 205th overall, in 1994 Entry Draft).

			Regular Season								Playoffs						
Season	Club	Lea	GP	W	L	T	Mins	GA	SO	Avg	GP	W	L	Mins	GA	SO	Avg
1993-94	Kimberley	RMJHL					STATISTICS NOT AVAILABLE										
1994-95	Cornell Big Red	ECAC	16	3	11	1	877	62	0	4.24	....	....	....	....	....	....	....
1995-96	Cornell Big Red	ECAC	19	12	2	1	971	38	2	2.35	....	....	....	....	....	....	....
1996-97	Cornell Big Red	ECAC	27	16	7	2	1475	67	0	2.73	....	....	....	....	....	....	....
1997-98	Cornell Big Red	ECAC	29	14	12	2	1683	74	2	2.64	....	....	....	....	....	....	....
1998-99	Adirondack	AHL	51	14	27	5	2710	146	2	3.23	1	0	1	59	2	0	2.04
99-2000	Manitoba Moose	IHL	43	19	12	9	1187	108	1	2.76	....	....	....	....	....	....	....
2000-01	Houston Aeros	IHL	41	19	16	3	2235	113	0	3.03	....	....	....	....	....	....	....

ECAC Second All-Star Team (1998)

ELLIS, Dan (EHL-ihs, DAN) DAL.

Goaltender. Catches left. 6', 185 lbs. Born, Saskatoon, Sask., June 19, 1980.
(Dallas' 2nd choice, 60th overall, in 2000 Entry Draft).

			Regular Season								Playoffs						
Season	Club	Lea	GP	W	L	T	Mins	GA	SO	Avg	GP	W	L	Mins	GA	SO	Avg
1998-99	Newmarket 87's	OPJHL	28	24	3	1	1670	63	3	2.25	....	....	....	....	....	....	....
99-2000	Omaha Lancers	USHL	55	*34	16	4	*3274	123	*11	*2.25	4	1	3	238	10	0	2.52
2000-01	Nebraska-Omaha	CCHA	40	21	14	3	2285	95	2	2.49	....	....	....	....	....	....	....

USHL First All-Star Team (2000) • USHL Goaltender of the Year (2000) • USHL Player of the Year (2000)

EMERY, Ray (EH-muhr-ee, RAY) OTT.

Goaltender. Catches left. 6'3", 192 lbs. Born, Cayuga, Ont., September 28, 1982.
(Ottawa's 4th choice, 99th overall, in 2001 Entry Draft).

			Regular Season								Playoffs						
Season	Club	Lea	GP	W	L	T	Mins	GA	SO	Avg	GP	W	L	Mins	GA	SO	Avg
1998-99	Dunnville Terriers	OJHL-C	22	3	19	0	1320	140	0	6.37	....	....	....	....	....	....	....
99-2000	Welland Cougars	OJHL-B	23	13	10	1	1323	62	1	2.68	....	....	....	....	....	....	....
	Sault Ste. Marie	OHL	16	9	3	0	716	36	1	3.02	15	8	7	883	33	*3	2.24
2000-01	Sault Ste. Marie	OHL	52	18	29	2	2938	174	1	3.55	....	....	....	....	....	....	....

ESCHE, Robert (EHSH, RAW-buhrt) PHX.

Goaltender. Catches left. 6'1", 200 lbs. Born, Whitesboro, NY, January 22, 1978.
(Phoenix's 5th choice, 139th overall, in 1996 Entry Draft).

			Regular Season								Playoffs						
Season	Club	Lea	GP	W	L	T	Mins	GA	SO	Avg	GP	W	L	Mins	GA	SO	Avg
1994-95	Gloucester	COJHL	20	10	6	0	1034	70	0	4.06	....	....	....	....	....	....	....
1995-96	Detroit Jr. Whalers	OHL	23	13	6	0	1219	76	1	3.74	3	0	2	105	4	0	2.29
1996-97	Detroit Jr. Whalers	OHL	58	24	28	2	3241	206	2	3.81	5	1	4	317	19	0	3.60
1997-98	Plymouth Whalers	OHL	48	29	13	4	2810	135	3	2.88	15	8	7	869	45	0	3.11
1998-99	**Phoenix**	**NHL**	**3**	**0**	**1**	**0**	**130**	**7**	**0**	**3.23**	....	....	....	....	....	....	....
	Springfield	AHL	55	24	20	6	2957	138	1	2.80	1	0	1	60	4	0	4.02
99-2000	**Phoenix**	**NHL**	**8**	**2**	**5**	**0**	**408**	**23**	**0**	**3.38**	....	....	....	....	....	....	....
	Houston Aeros	IHL	7	4	2	1	419	16	2	2.29	....	....	....	....	....	....	....
	Springfield	AHL	21	9	9	2	1207	61	2	3.03	3	1	2	180	12	0	4.01
2000-01	**Phoenix**	**NHL**	**25**	**10**	**8**	**4**	**1350**	**68**	**2**	**3.02**	....	....	....	....	....	....	....
	NHL Totals		**36**	**12**	**14**	**4**	**1888**	**98**	**2**	**3.11**	....	....	....	....	....	....	....

OHL Second All-Star Team (1998)

ESSENSA, Bob (EH-sehn-suh, BAWB) BUF.

Goaltender. Catches left. 6', 190 lbs. Born, Toronto, Ont., January 14, 1965.
(Winnipeg's 5th choice, 71st overall, in 1983 Entry Draft).

			Regular Season								Playoffs						
Season	Club	Lea	GP	W	L	T	Mins	GA	SO	Avg	GP	W	L	Mins	GA	SO	Avg
1981-82	Henry Carr	MTJHL	17	....	....	....	948	79	0	4.99	....	....	....	....	....	....	....
1982-83	Henry Carr	MTJHL	31	....	....	....	1840	98	2	3.20	....	....	....	....	....	....	....
	Markham Waxers	MTJHL	1	1	0	0	60	1	0	1.00	....	....	....	....	....	....	....
1983-84	Michigan State	CCHA	17	11	4	0	946	44	2	2.79	....	....	....	....	....	....	....
1984-85	Michigan State	CCHA	18	15	2	0	1059	29	2	1.64	....	....	....	....	....	....	....
1985-86	Michigan State	CCHA	23	17	4	1	1333	74	1	3.33	....	....	....	....	....	....	....
1986-87	Michigan State	CCHA	25	19	3	1	1383	64	2	2.78	....	....	....	....	....	....	....
1987-88	Moncton Hawks	AHL	27	7	11	1	1287	100	1	4.66	....	....	....	....	....	....	....
1988-89	**Winnipeg**	**NHL**	**20**	**6**	**8**	**3**	**1102**	**68**	**1**	**3.70**	....	....	....	....	....	....	....
	Fort Wayne	IHL	22	14	7	0	1287	70	0	3.26	....	....	....	....	....	....	....
1989-90	**Winnipeg**	**NHL**	**36**	**18**	**9**	**5**	**2035**	**107**	**1**	**3.15**	**4**	**2**	**1**	**206**	**12**	**0**	**3.50**
	Moncton Hawks	AHL	6	3	3	0	358	15	0	2.51	....	....	....	....	....	....	....
1990-91	**Winnipeg**	**NHL**	**55**	**19**	**24**	**6**	**2916**	**153**	**4**	**3.15**	....	....	....	....	....	....	....
	Moncton Hawks	AHL	2	1	0	1	125	6	0	2.88	....	....	....	....	....	....	....
1991-92	**Winnipeg**	**NHL**	**47**	**21**	**17**	**6**	**2627**	**126**	***5**	**2.88**	**1**	**0**	**0**	**33**	**3**	**0**	**5.45**
1992-93	**Winnipeg**	**NHL**	**67**	**33**	**26**	**6**	**3855**	**227**	**2**	**3.53**	**6**	**2**	**4**	**367**	**20**	**0**	**3.27**
1993-94	**Winnipeg**	**NHL**	**56**	**19**	**30**	**6**	**3136**	**201**	**1**	**3.85**	....	....	....	....	....	....	....
	Detroit	**NHL**	**13**	**4**	**7**	**2**	**778**	**34**	**1**	**2.62**	**2**	**0**	**2**	**109**	**9**	**0**	**4.95**
1994-95	San Diego Gulls	IHL	16	6	8	1	919	52	0	3.39	1	0	1	59	3	0	3.05
1995-96	Adirondack	AHL	3	1	2	0	179	11	0	3.69	....	....	....	....	....	....	....
	Fort Wayne	IHL	45	24	14	5	2529	122	1	2.89	5	2	3	299	12	0	2.41
1996-97	**Edmonton**	**NHL**	**19**	**4**	**8**	**0**	**868**	**41**	**1**	**2.83**	....	....	....	....	....	....	....
1997-98	**Edmonton**	**NHL**	**16**	**6**	**6**	**1**	**825**	**35**	**0**	**2.55**	**1**	**0**	**0**	**27**	**1**	**0**	**2.22**
1998-99	**Edmonton**	**NHL**	**39**	**12**	**14**	**6**	**2091**	**96**	**0**	**2.75**	....	....	....	....	....	....	....
99-2000	**Phoenix**	**NHL**	**30**	**13**	**10**	**3**	**1573**	**73**	**1**	**2.78**	....	....	....	....	....	....	....
2000-01	**Vancouver**	**NHL**	**39**	**18**	**12**	**3**	**2059**	**92**	**1**	**2.68**	**2**	**0**	**2**	**122**	**6**	**0**	**2.95**
	NHL Totals		**437**	**173**	**171**	**47**	**23865**	**1253**	**18**	**3.15**	**16**	**4**	**9**	**864**	**51**	**0**	**3.54**

CCHA First All-Star Team (1985) • CCHA Second All-Star Team (1986) • NHL All-Rookie Team (1990)

Traded to **Detroit** by **Winnipeg** with Sergei Bautin for Tim Cheveldae and Dallas Drake, March 8, 1994. Traded to **Edmonton** by **Detroit** for future considerations, June 14, 1996. Signed as a free agent by **Phoenix**, September 5, 1999. Signed as a free agent by **Vancouver**, July 26, 2000. Signed as a free agent by **Buffalo**, August 3, 2001.

FANKHOUSER, Scott (FANK-how-suhr, SKAWT) ATL.

Goaltender. Catches left. 6'2", 205 lbs. Born, Bismark, ND, July 1, 1975.
(St. Louis' 8th choice, 276th overall, in 1994 Entry Draft).

			Regular Season								Playoffs						
Season	Club	Lea	GP	W	L	T	Mins	GA	SO	Avg	GP	W	L	Mins	GA	SO	Avg
1993-94	Loomis-Chaffe	H.S.					STATISTICS NOT AVAILABLE										
1994-95	U. Mass-Lowell	H-East	11	4	4	1	499	37	0	4.44	....	....	....	....	....	....	....
1995-96	Melfort Mustangs	SJHL	45	31	9	4	2544	109	3	2.57	....	....	....	....	....	....	....
1996-97	U. Mass-Lowell	H-East	11	2	4	1	517	38	0	4.41	....	....	....	....	....	....	....
1997-98	U. Mass-Lowell	H-East	16	4	7	2	798	48	0	3.61	....	....	....	....	....	....	....
1998-99	U. Mass-Lowell	H-East	32	16	14	0	1729	80	1	2.78	....	....	....	....	....	....	....
99-2000	**Atlanta**	**NHL**	**16**	**2**	**11**	**2**	**920**	**49**	**0**	**3.20**	....	....	....	....	....	....	....
	Greenville Growl	ECHL	7	6	1	0	419	18	0	2.58	....	....	....	....	....	....	....
	Orlando	IHL	6	2	2	1	320	14	0	2.63	....	....	....	....	....	....	....
	Louisville Panthers	AHL	1	0	1	0	59	3	0	3.05	....	....	....	....	....	....	....
2000-01	**Atlanta**	**NHL**	**7**	**2**	**1**	**0**	**260**	**16**	**0**	**3.69**	....	....	....	....	....	....	....
	Orlando	IHL	28	13	12	3	1603	69	1	2.58	1	0	0	37	3	0	4.83
	NHL Totals		**23**	**4**	**12**	**2**	**1180**	**65**	**0**	**3.31**	....	....	....	....	....	....	....

SJHL First All-Star Team (1996) • Won SJHL Playoff MVP Award (1996) • Shared James Norris Memorial Trophy (fewest goals against - IHL) with Norm Maracle (2001)

Signed as a free agent by **Atlanta**, August 24, 1999.

FERNANDEZ, Manny (fuhr-NAN-dehz, MAN-ee) MIN.

Goaltender. Catches left. 6', 180 lbs. Born, Etobicoke, Ont., August 27, 1974.
(Quebec's 4th choice, 52nd overall, in 1992 Entry Draft).

			Regular Season								Playoffs						
Season	Club	Lea	GP	W	L	T	Mins	GA	SO	Avg	GP	W	L	Mins	GA	SO	Avg
1990-91	Lac St-Louis	QAAA	20	13	5	0	1176	69	*3	3.52	3	2	1	181	12	0	3.98
1991-92	Laval Titan	QMJHL	31	14	13	2	1593	99	1	3.73	9	3	5	468	39	0	5.00
1992-93	Laval Titan	QMJHL	43	26	14	2	2347	141	1	3.60	13	*12	1	818	42	0	3.08
1993-94	Laval Titan	QMJHL	51	29	14	1	2776	143	*5	3.09	19	14	5	1116	49	*1	*2.63
1994-95	Kalamazoo Wings	IHL	46	21	10	9	2470	115	2	2.79	14	10	2	753	34	1	2.71
	Dallas	**NHL**	**1**	**0**	**1**	**0**	**59**	**3**	**0**	**3.05**	....	....	....	....	....	....	....
1995-96	**Dallas**	**NHL**	**5**	**0**	**1**	**1**	**249**	**19**	**0**	**4.58**	....	....	....	....	....	....	....
	Michigan K-Wings	IHL	47	22	15	9	2664	133	*4	3.00	6	5	1	372	14	0	*2.26
1996-97	Michigan K-Wings	IHL	48	20	24	2	2720	142	2	3.13	4	1	3	277	15	0	3.25
1997-98	**Dallas**	**NHL**	**2**	**1**	**0**	**0**	**69**	**2**	**0**	**1.74**	**1**	**0**	**0**	**2**	**0**	**0**	**0.00**
	Michigan K-Wings	IHL	55	27	17	5	3022	139	5	2.76	2	0	2	88	7	0	4.73
1998-99	**Dallas**	**NHL**	**1**	**0**	**1**	**0**	**60**	**2**	**0**	**2.00**	....	....	....	....	....	....	....
	Houston Aeros	IHL	50	34	6	9	2949	116	2	2.36	*19	*11	8	*1126	49	1	2.61
99-2000	**Dallas**	**NHL**	**24**	**11**	**8**	**3**	**1353**	**48**	**1**	**2.13**	**1**	**0**	**0**	**17**	**1**	**0**	**3.53**
2000-01	**Minnesota**	**NHL**	**42**	**19**	**17**	**4**	**2461**	**92**	**4**	**2.24**	....	....	....	....	....	....	....
	NHL Totals		**75**	**31**	**28**	**8**	**4251**	**166**	**5**	**2.34**	**2**	**0**	**0**	**19**	**1**	**0**	**3.16**

QMJHL First All-Star Team (1994) • IHL Second All-Star Team (1995)

Rights traded to **Dallas** by **Quebec** for Tommy Sjodin and Dallas' 3rd round choice (Chris Drury) in 1994 Entry Draft, February 13, 1994. Traded to **Minnesota** by **Dallas** with Brad Lukowich for Minnesota's 3rd round choice (Joel Lundqvist) in 2000 Entry Draft and 4th round choice (later traded back to Minnesota) in 2002 Entry Draft, June 12, 2000.

FICHAUD, Eric (FEE-shoh, AIR-ihk)

Goaltender. Catches left. 5'11", 171 lbs. Born, Anjou, Que., November 4, 1975.
(Toronto's 1st choice, 16th overall, in 1994 Entry Draft).

			Regular Season								Playoffs						
Season	Club	Lea	GP	W	L	T	Mins	GA	SO	Avg	GP	W	L	Mins	GA	SO	Avg
1991-92	Montreal-Bourassa	QAAA	28	12	15	1	1678	110	0	3.95	9	5	4	567	32	0	3.39
1992-93	Chicoutimi	QMJHL	43	18	13	1	2039	149	0	4.38							
1993-94	Chicoutimi	QMJHL	*63	*37	21	3	*3493	192	4	3.30	*26	*16	10	*1560	86	*1	3.31
1994-95	Chicoutimi	QMJHL	46	21	19	4	2637	151	4	3.44	7	2	5	428	20	0	2.80
1995-96	NY Islanders	NHL	24	7	12	2	1234	68	1	3.31							
	Worcester	AHL	34	13	15	6	1989	97	1	2.93	2	1	1	127	7	0	3.30
1996-97	NY Islanders	NHL	34	9	14	4	1759	91	0	3.10							
1997-98	NY Islanders	NHL	17	3	8	3	807	40	0	2.97							
	Utah Grizzlies	IHL	1	0	0	0	40	3	0	4.45							
1998-99	Nashville	NHL	9	0	6	0	447	24	0	3.22							
	Milwaukee	IHL	8	5	2	1	480	25	0	3.13							
99-2000	Carolina	NHL	9	3	5	1	490	24	1	2.94							
	Quebec Citadelles	AHL	6	4	1	1	368	17	0	2.77	3	0	3	177	10	0	3.39
2000-01	Montreal	NHL	2	0	2	0	62	4	0	3.87							
	Quebec Citadelles	AHL	42	19	19	2	2441	127	1	3.12	2	0	1	98	3	0	1.84
	NHL Totals		95	22	47	10	4799	251	2	3.14							

Canadian Major Junior Second All-Star Team (1994) • Memorial Cup All-Star Team (1994) • Won Hap Emms Memorial Trophy (Memorial Cup Tournament Top Goaltender) (1994) • QMJHL First All-Star Team (1995)

Traded to **NY Islanders** by **Toronto** for Benoit Hogue, NY Islanders' 3rd round choice (Ryan Pepperall) in 1995 Entry Draft and 5th round choice (Brandon Sugden) in 1996 Entry Draft, April 6, 1995. Traded to **Edmonton** by **NY Islanders** for Mike Watt, June 18, 1998. Traded to **Nashville** by **Edmonton** with Drake Berehowsky and Greg de Vries for Mikhail Shtalenkov and Jim Dowd, October 1, 1998. Traded to **Carolina** by **Nashville** for Toronto's 4th round choice (previously acquired, Nashville selected Yevgeny Pavlov) in 1999 Entry Draft and future considerations, June 26, 1999. Claimed on waivers by **Montreal** from **Carolina**, February 11, 2000.

FINLEY, Brian (FIHN-lee, BRIGH-uhn) NSH.

Goaltender. Catches right. 6'3", 205 lbs. Born, Sault Ste. Marie, Ont., July 13, 1981.
(Nashville's 1st choice, 6th overall, in 1999 Entry Draft).

			Regular Season								Playoffs						
Season	Club	Lea	GP	W	L	T	Mins	GA	SO	Avg	GP	W	L	Mins	GA	SO	Avg
1996-97	Sault Ste. Marie	NOBHL	45				1943	109	3	2.38							
1997-98	Barrie Colts	OHL	41	23	14	1	2154	105	3	2.92	5	1	3	260	13	0	3.00
1998-99	Barrie Colts	OHL	52	*36	10	4	3063	136	3	2.66	5	4	1	323	15	0	2.79
99-2000	Barrie Colts	OHL	47	24	12	6	2540	130	2	3.07	*23	14	8	1353	58	1	2.57
2000-01	Barrie Colts	OHL	16	5	8	0	818	42	0	3.08							
	Brampton	OHL	11	7	3	1	631	31	0	2.95	9	5	4	503	26	1	3.10

Won NOBHL Top Goaltender Award (1997) • OHL First All-Star Team (1999)

Traded to **Brampton** by **Barrie** with Mississauga's 7th round choice (Michael Root) in 2001 OHL Midget Draft and Kitchener's 4th round choice(previously acquired) in 2002 OHL Priority Draft for David Chant, Tyler Hanchuk and Matt Grenier, January 10, 2001.

FISCHER, Kai (FIH-shuhr, KIGH) COL.

Goaltender. Catches left. 5'11", 175 lbs. Born, Forst, West Germany, March 25, 1977.
(Colorado's 8th choice, 160th overall, in 1996 Entry Draft).

			Regular Season								Playoffs						
Season	Club	Lea	GP	W	L	T	Mins	GA	SO	Avg	GP	W	L	Mins	GA	SO	Avg
1995-96	Dusseldorfer EG	DEL-Jr.	1	0	0	1	60	5	0	5.00							
1996-97	Dusseldorfer EG	DEL	2	1	0	0	125	7	0	3.36							
1997-98	REV Bremerhaven	DEB	45				2674	172	0	3.86							
1998-99	Moskitos Essen	DEB	16				896	56	0	3.75							
99-2000	Revier Lowen	DEL	17				818	55	0	4.03							
2000-01	Heilbronner EC	DEB	19				1036	55	0	3.19	1	0	1	60	7	0	7.00

FISET, Stephane (fih-SEHT, STEH-fan) L.A.

Goaltender. Catches left. 6'1", 215 lbs. Born, Montreal, Que., June 17, 1970.
(Quebec's 3rd choice, 24th overall, in 1988 Entry Draft).

			Regular Season								Playoffs						
Season	Club	Lea	GP	W	L	T	Mins	GA	SO	Avg	GP	W	L	Mins	GA	SO	Avg
1986-87	Montreal-Bourassa	QAAA	30	8	21	1	1689	155	0	5.51							
1987-88	Victoriaville Tigres	QMJHL	40	15	17	4	2221	146	1	3.94	2	0	2	163	10	0	3.68
1988-89	Victoriaville Tigres	QMJHL	43	25	14	0	2401	138	1	*3.45	12	*9	2	711	33	0	*2.78
1989-90	Quebec	NHL	6	0	5	1	342	34	0	5.96							
	Victoriaville Tigres	QMJHL	24	14	6	3	1383	63	1	*2.73	*14	7	6	*790	49	0	3.72
1990-91	Quebec	NHL	3	0	2	1	186	12	0	3.87							
	Halifax Citadels	AHL	36	10	15	8	1902	131	0	4.13							
1991-92	Quebec	NHL	23	7	10	2	1133	71	1	3.76							
	Halifax Citadels	AHL	29	8	14	6	1675	110	*3	3.94							
1992-93	Quebec	NHL	37	18	9	4	1939	110	0	3.40	1	0	0	21	1	0	2.86
	Halifax Citadels	AHL	3	2	1	0	180	11	0	3.67							
1993-94	Quebec	NHL	50	20	25	4	2798	158	2	3.39							
	Cornwall Aces	AHL	1	0	1	0	60	4	0	4.00							
1994-95	Quebec	NHL	32	17	10	3	1879	87	2	2.78	4	1	2	209	16	0	4.59
1995-96♦	Colorado	NHL	37	22	6	7	2107	103	1	2.93	1	0	0	1	0	0	0.00
1996-97	Los Angeles	NHL	44	13	24	5	2482	132	4	3.19							
1997-98	Los Angeles	NHL	60	26	25	8	3497	158	2	2.71	2	0	2	93	7	0	4.52
1998-99	Los Angeles	NHL	42	18	21	1	2403	104	3	2.60							
99-2000	Los Angeles	NHL	47	20	15	7	2592	119	1	2.75	4	0	3	200	10	0	3.00
2000-01	Los Angeles	NHL	7	3	0	1	318	19	0	3.58							
	Lowell	AHL	3	1	0	2	190	9	0	2.84							
	NHL Totals		388	164	152	44	21676	1107	16	3.06	12	1	7	524	34	0	3.89

QMJHL First All-Star Team (1989) • Canadian Major Junior Goaltender of the Year (1989)

Transferred to **Colorado** after **Quebec** franchise relocated, June 21, 1995. Traded to **LA Kings** by **Colorado** with Colorado's 1st round choice (Mathieu Biron) in 1998 Entry Draft for Eric Lacroix and Los Angeles' 1st round choice (Martin Skoula) in 1998 Entry Draft, June 20, 1996. Missed majority of 2000-01 season recovering from knee injury originally suffered in exhibition game vs. Anaheim, September 22, 2000. • Played 12 seconds of playoff game vs. Colorado, April 28, 2001.

FITZPATRICK, Mark (FIHTZ-pa-TRIHK, MAHRK)

Goaltender. Catches left. 6'2", 195 lbs. Born, Toronto, Ont., November 13, 1968.
(Los Angeles' 2nd choice, 27th overall, in 1987 Entry Draft).

			Regular Season								Playoffs						
Season	Club	Lea	GP	W	L	T	Mins	GA	SO	Avg	GP	W	L	Mins	GA	SO	Avg
1983-84	Revelstoke	BCJHL	21				1019	90	0	5.30							
1984-85	Calgary Canucks	AJHL	29	18	8	0	1631	102	*2	3.75							
	Medicine Hat	WHL	3	1	2	0	180	9	0	3.00	1	0	0	20	2	0	6.00
1985-86	Medicine Hat	WHL	41	26	6	1	2074	99	1	*2.86	*19	*11	5	*986	58	0	3.53
1986-87	Medicine Hat	WHL	50	31	11	4	2844	159	4	3.35	20	12	8	1224	71	1	3.48
1987-88	Medicine Hat	WHL	63	36	15	6	3600	194	2	3.23	16	12	4	959	52	*1	*3.25
1988-89	Los Angeles	NHL	17	6	7	3	957	64	0	4.01							
	New Haven	AHL	18	10	5	1	980	54	1	3.31							
	NY Islanders	NHL	11	3	5	2	627	41	0	3.92							
1989-90	NY Islanders	NHL	47	19	19	5	2653	150	3	3.39	4	0	2	152	13	0	5.13
1990-91	NY Islanders	NHL	2	1	1	0	120	6	0	3.00							
	Capital District	AHL	12	3	7	2	734	47	0	3.84							
1991-92	NY Islanders	NHL	30	11	13	5	1743	93	0	3.20							
	Capital District	AHL	14	6	5	1	782	39	0	2.99							
1992-93	NY Islanders	NHL	39	17	15	5	2253	130	0	3.46	3	0	1	77	4	0	3.12
	Capital District	AHL	5	1	3	1	284	18	0	3.80							
1993-94	Florida	NHL	28	12	8	6	1603	73	1	2.73							
1994-95	Florida	NHL	15	6	7	2	819	36	2	2.64							
1995-96	Florida	NHL	34	15	11	3	1786	88	0	2.96	2	0	0	60	6	0	6.00
1996-97	Florida	NHL	30	8	9	9	1680	66	0	2.36							
1997-98	Florida	NHL	12	2	7	2	640	32	1	3.00							
	Fort Wayne	IHL	2	1	1	0	119	8	0	4.03							
	Tampa Bay	NHL	34	7	24	1	1938	102	1	3.16							
1998-99	Chicago	NHL	27	6	8	6	1403	64	0	2.74							
99-2000	Carolina	NHL	3	0	2	0	107	8	0	4.49							
	Cincinnati	IHL	24	11	11	1	1379	59	4	2.57							
2000-01	Detroit Vipers	IHL	9	4	4	0	485	21	0	2.60							
	NHL Totals		329	113	136	49	18329	953	8	3.12	9	0	3	289	23	0	4.78

WHL East Second All-Star Team (1986, 1988) • Won Hap Emms Memorial Trophy (Memorial Cup Tournament Top Goaltender) (1987, 1988) • Won Bill Masterton Memorial Trophy (1992)

Traded to **NY Islanders** by **Los Angeles** with Wayne McBean and future considerations (Doug Crossman, May 23, 1989) for Kelly Hrudey, February 22, 1989. Traded to **Quebec** by **NY Islanders** with NY Islanders' 1st round choice (Adam Deadmarsh) in 1993 Entry Draft for Ron Hextall and Quebec's 1st round choice (Todd Bertuzzi) in 1993 Entry Draft, June 20, 1993. Claimed by **Florida** from **Quebec** in Expansion Draft, June 24, 1993. Traded to **Tampa Bay** by **Florida** with Jody Hull for Dino Ciccarelli and Jeff Norton, January 15, 1998. Traded to **Chicago** by **Tampa Bay** with Tampa Bay's 4th round choice (later traded to Montreal - Montreal selected Chris Dyment) in 1999 Entry Draft for Michal Sykora, July 17, 1998. Signed as a free agent by **Carolina**, August 19, 1999.

FLAHERTY, Wade (FLAY-uhr-tee, WAYD) FLA.

Goaltender. Catches left. 6', 170 lbs. Born, Terrace, B.C., January 11, 1968.
(Buffalo's 10th choice, 181st overall, in 1988 Entry Draft).

			Regular Season								Playoffs						
Season	Club	Lea	GP	W	L	T	Mins	GA	SO	Avg	GP	W	L	Mins	GA	SO	Avg
1984-85	Kelowna Wings	WHL	1	0	0	0	55	5	0	5.45							
1985-86	Seattle T-Birds	WHL	9	1	3	0	271	36	0	7.97							
	Spokane Chiefs	WHL	5	0	3	0	161	21	0	7.83							
1986-87	Nanaimo Clippers	BCJHL	15				830	53	0	3.83							
	Victoria Cougars	WHL	3	0	2	0	127	16	0	7.56							
1987-88	Victoria Cougars	WHL	36	20	15	0	2052	135	0	3.95	5	2	3	300	18	0	3.60
1988-89	Victoria Cougars	WHL	42	21	19	0	2408	180	4	4.49							
1989-90	Greensboro	ECHL	27	12	10	0	1308	96	0	4.40							
1990-91	Kansas City	IHL	*56	16	31	4	2990	224	0	4.49							
1991-92	San Jose	NHL	3	0	3	0	178	13	0	4.38							
	Kansas City	IHL	43	26	14	3	2603	140	1	3.23	1	0	0	1	0	0	0.00
1992-93	San Jose	NHL	1	0	1	0	60	5	0	5.00							
	Kansas City	IHL	*61	*34	19	7	*3642	195	2	3.21	*12	6	6	733	34	*1	2.78
1993-94	Kansas City	IHL	*60	32	19	9	*3564	202	0	3.40							
1994-95	San Jose	NHL	18	5	6	1	852	44	1	3.10	7	2	3	377	31	0	4.93
1995-96	San Jose	NHL	24	3	12	1	1137	92	0	4.85							
1996-97	San Jose	NHL	7	2	4	0	359	31	0	5.18							
	Kentucky	AHL	19	8	6	2	1032	54	1	3.14	3	1	2	200	11	0	3.30
1997-98	NY Islanders	NHL	16	4	4	3	694	23	3	1.99							
	Utah Grizzlies	IHL	24	16	5	3	1341	40	3	1.79							
1998-99	NY Islanders	NHL	20	5	11	2	1048	53	0	3.03							
	Lowell	AHL	5	1	3	1	305	16	0	3.15							
99-2000	NY Islanders	NHL	4	0	1	1	182	7	0	2.31							
2000-01	NY Islanders	NHL	20	6	10	0	1017	56	1	3.30							
	Tampa Bay	NHL	2	0	2	0	118	8	0	4.07							
	NHL Totals		115	25	54	8	5645	332	5	3.53	7	2	3	377	31	0	4.93

WHL West Second All-Star Team (1988) • Won ECHL Playoff MVP Award (1990) • Shared James Norris Memorial Trophy (fewest goals against - IHL) with Arturs Irbe (1992) • IHL Second All-Star Team (1993, 1994)

Signed as a free agent by **San Jose**, September 3, 1991. Signed as a free agent by **NY Islanders**, July 22, 1997. Traded to **Tampa Bay** by **NY Islanders** for future considerations, February 16, 2001. Signed as a free agent by **Florida**, August 2, 2001.

FOMITCHEV, Alexander (FOH-mih-chehv, al-ehx-AN-duhr) EDM.

Goaltender. Catches left. 5'10", 180 lbs. Born, Moscow, USSR, February 19, 1979.
(Edmonton's 10th choice, 231st overall, in 1997 Entry Draft).

			Regular Season								Playoffs						
Season	Club	Lea	GP	W	L	T	Mins	GA	SO	Avg	GP	W	L	Mins	GA	SO	Avg
1996-97	St. Albert	AJHL	35	17	9	0	2063	99	*4	2.88	13			737	37	1	3.07
1997-98	Calgary Hitmen	WHL	60	32	23	2	3381	168	1	2.98	*18	9	9	*1075	50	*2	2.79
1998-99	Calgary Hitmen	WHL	57	*39	10	7	3317	142	4	2.57	*21	*16	5	*1299	61	1	2.82
99-2000	Calgary Hitmen	WHL	1	1	0	0	60	5	0	5.00							
	Seattle T-birds	WHL	46	20	21	4	2685	126	3	2.82	7	4	3	420	24	0	3.43
2000-01	Tallahassee	ECHL	28	16	8	2	1628	72	2	2.65							
	Hamilton Bulldogs	AHL	6	2	2	1	316	14	0	2.66							
	Asheville Smoke	UHL	14	9	3	2	838	37	0	2.65							

WHL East First All-Star Team (1999)

FORSBERG, Jonas (FOHRZ-buhrg, YOH-nuhs)

Goaltender. Catches left. 5'10", 160 lbs. Born, Stockholm, Sweden, June 15, 1975.
(San Jose's 12th choice, 210th overall, in 1993 Entry Draft).

			Regular Season								Playoffs						
Season	Club	Lea	GP	W	L	T	Mins	GA	SO	Avg	GP	W	L	Mins	GA	SO	Avg
1992-93	Djurgardens IF	Swede-Jr.	41				2460	114	0	2.78							
1993-94	Djurgardens IF	Sweden	1	1	0	0	60	4	0	4.00							
1994-95	Djurgardens IF	Sweden	1	0	1	0	60	6	0	6.00							
1995-96	Djurgardens IF	Sweden	DID NOT PLAY – INJURED														
1996-97	IF Mangerland	Norway	16				947	76	0	4.81							
1997-98	Sodertalje SK	Sweden	23				1252	60	0	2.88							
1998-99	AIK Solna	Sweden	29				1668	81	2	2.91							
99-2000	AIK Solna	Sweden	30				1696	91	2	3.22							
2000-01	EHC Linz	Austria	44	22	13	8	2635	122	0	2.77							

FOUNTAIN, Mike (FOWN-tehn, MIGHK)

Goaltender. Catches left. 6'1", 180 lbs. Born, North York, Ont., January 26, 1972.
(Vancouver's 3rd choice, 45th overall, in 1992 Entry Draft).

			Regular Season								Playoffs						
Season	**Club**	**Lea**	**GP**	**W**	**L**	**T**	**Mins**	**GA**	**SO**	**Avg**	**GP**	**W**	**L**	**Mins**	**GA**	**SO**	**Avg**
1988-89	Huntsville	OJHL-C	22	*18	3	2	1306	82	0	3.77	....	....	....	....	....	....	....
1989-90	Chatham Maroons	OJHL-B	21	....	....	....	1249	76	0	3.65	....	....	....	....	....	....	....
1990-91	Sault Ste. Marie	OHL	7	5	2	0	380	19	0	3.00	....	....	....	....	....	....	....
	Oshawa Generals	OHL	30	17	5	1	1483	84	0	3.40	8	1	4	292	26	0	5.34
1991-92	Oshawa Generals	OHL	40	18	13	6	2260	149	1	3.96	7	3	4	429	26	0	3.64
1992-93	Canada	Nt-Team	13	7	5	1	745	37	1	2.98	....	....	....	....	....	....	....
	Hamilton Canucks	AHL	12	2	8	0	618	46	0	4.47	....	....	....	....	....	....	....
1993-94	Hamilton Canucks	AHL	*70	*34	28	6	*4005	241	*4	3.61	3	0	2	146	12	0	4.92
1994-95	Syracuse Crunch	AHL	61	25	29	7	3618	225	2	3.73	....	....	....	....	....	....	....
1995-96	Syracuse Crunch	AHL	54	21	27	3	3060	184	1	3.61	15	8	7	915	57	*2	3.74
1996-97	**Vancouver**	**NHL**	**6**	**2**	**2**	**0**	**245**	**14**	**1**	**3.43**	....	....	....	....	....	....	....
	Syracuse Crunch	AHL	25	8	14	2	1462	78	1	3.20	2	0	2	120	12	0	6.02
1997-98	**Carolina**	**NHL**	**3**	**0**	**3**	**0**	**163**	**10**	**0**	**3.68**	....	....	....	....	....	....	....
	New Haven	AHL	50	25	19	5	2922	139	3	2.85	....	....	....	....	....	....	....
1998-99	New Haven	AHL	51	23	24	3	2989	150	2	3.01	....	....	....	....	....	....	....
99-2000	**Ottawa**	**NHL**	**1**	**0**	**0**	**0**	**16**	**1**	**0**	**3.75**	....	....	....	....	....	....	....
	Grand Rapids	IHL	36	21	7	4	1851	77	3	2.50	1	0	0	20	4	0	12.00
2000-01	**Ottawa**	**NHL**	**1**	**0**	**1**	**0**	**59**	**3**	**0**	**3.05**	....	....	....	....	....	....	....
	Grand Rapids	IHL	*52	*34	10	6	*3005	104	6	2.08	8	5	3	522	21	1	2.41
	NHL Totals		**11**	**2**	**6**	**0**	**483**	**28**	**1**	**3.48**	....	....	....	....	....	....	....

OHL First All-Star Team (1992) • AHL Second All-Star Team (1994) • IHL Second All-Star Team (2001)

• Recorded shutout (3-0) in NHL debut vs. **New Jersey**, November 14, 1996. Signed as a free agent by **Carolina**, August 19, 1997. Signed as a free agent by **Ottawa**, July 30, 1999.

FRANEK, Petr (FRAH-nehk, PEE-tuhr) COL.

Goaltender. Catches left. 5'11", 185 lbs. Born, Most, Czech., April 6, 1975.
(Quebec's 10th choice, 205th overall, in 1993 Entry Draft).

			Regular Season								Playoffs						
Season	**Club**	**Lea**	**GP**	**W**	**L**	**T**	**Mins**	**GA**	**SO**	**Avg**	**GP**	**W**	**L**	**Mins**	**GA**	**SO**	**Avg**
1992-93	CHZ Litvinov	Czech.	5	....	....	....	273	15	0	3.29	....	....	....	....	....	....	....
1993-94	CHZ Litvinov	Cze-Rep	11	....	....	....	535	34	0	3.81	2	0	1	61	10	0	9.83
1994-95	CHZ Litvinov	Cze-Rep	12	....	....	....	657	47	0	4.29	1	0	0	16	0	0	0.00
1995-96	CHZ Litvinov	Cze-Rep	36	....	....	....	2096	85	3	2.43	16	....	....	948	47	1	2.97
1996-97	Hershey Bears	AHL	15	4	1	0	457	23	3	3.02	....	....	....	....	....	....	....
	Brantford Smoke	ColHL	6	4	1	0	321	14	0	2.61	....	....	....	....	....	....	....
	Quebec Rafales	IHL	6	3	3	0	357	18	0	3.02	1	0	1	40	4	0	6.00
1997-98	Hershey Bears	AHL	43	19	14	2	2169	98	2	2.71	1	0	1	60	4	0	4.00
1998-99	Utah Grizzlies	IHL	8	1	6	1	446	26	0	3.50	....	....	....	....	....	....	....
	Las Vegas	IHL	37	17	13	2	1879	107	0	3.42	....	....	....	....	....	....	....
99-2000	EHC Nurnberg	DEL	30	....	....	....	1603	73	2	2.73	....	....	....	....	....	....	....
2000-01	Karlovy Vary	Cze-Rep	44	....	....	....	2507	121	....	2.90	....	....	....	....	....	....	....

Rights transferred to **Colorado** after **Quebec** franchise relocated, June 21, 1995.

GAGE, Joaquin (GAYJ, YOH-ah-keen)

Goaltender. Catches left. 6', 200 lbs. Born, Vancouver, B.C., October 19, 1973.
(Edmonton's 6th choice, 109th overall, in 1992 Entry Draft).

			Regular Season								Playoffs						
Season	**Club**	**Lea**	**GP**	**W**	**L**	**T**	**Mins**	**GA**	**SO**	**Avg**	**GP**	**W**	**L**	**Mins**	**GA**	**SO**	**Avg**
1990-91	Bellingham	BCJHL	16	....	....	....	751	64	0	5.11	....	....	....	....	....	....	....
	Chilliwack Chiefs	BCJHL	2	1	0	0	85	11	0	7.76	....	....	....	....	....	....	....
	Portland	WHL	3	0	3	0	180	17	0	5.70	....	....	....	....	....	....	....
1991-92	Portland	WHL	63	27	30	4	3635	269	2	4.44	6	2	4	366	28	0	4.59
1992-93	Portland	WHL	38	21	16	1	2302	153	2	3.99	8	5	2	427	30	0	4.22
1993-94	Prince Albert	WHL	53	24	25	3	3041	212	1	4.18	....	....	....	....	....	....	....
1994-95	Cape Breton Oilers	AHL	54	17	28	5	3010	207	0	4.13	....	....	....	....	....	....	....
	Edmonton	**NHL**	**2**	**0**	**2**	**0**	**99**	**7**	**0**	**4.24**	....	....	....	....	....	....	....
1995-96	**Edmonton**	**NHL**	**16**	**2**	**8**	**1**	**717**	**45**	**0**	**3.77**	....	....	....	....	....	....	....
	Cape Breton Oilers	AHL	21	8	11	0	1162	80	0	4.13	....	....	....	....	....	....	....
1996-97	Hamilton Bulldogs	AHL	29	7	14	4	1558	91	0	3.50	....	....	....	....	....	....	....
	Wheeling Nailers	ECHL	3	1	0	0	120	8	0	4.00	....	....	....	....	....	....	....
1997-98	Raleigh IceCaps	ECHL	39	19	14	3	2173	116	1	3.20	....	....	....	....	....	....	....
	Syracuse Crunch	AHL	2	1	1	0	120	7	0	3.50	....	....	....	....	....	....	....
1998-99	Augusta Lynx	ECHL	5	5	0	0	300	16	0	3.20	....	....	....	....	....	....	....
	Portland Pirates	AHL	26	8	11	3	1429	69	2	2.90	....	....	....	....	....	....	....
	Providence Bruins	AHL	3	0	2	0	130	9	0	4.16	....	....	....	....	....	....	....
	Syracuse Crunch	AHL	12	2	8	2	706	46	0	3.91	....	....	....	....	....	....,	....
99-2000	Canada	Nt-Team	29	13	10	2	1530	83	0	3.25	....	....	....	....	....	....	....
	Hamilton Bulldogs	AHL	2	0	1	1	124	5	0	2.42	10	5	5	580	28	0	2.89
2000-01	**Edmonton**	**NHL**	**5**	**2**	**2**	**0**	**260**	**15**	**0**	**3.46**	....	....	....	....	....	....	....
	Hamilton Bulldogs	AHL	37	12	22	2	2129	118	0	3.33	....	....	....	....	....	....	....
	NHL Totals		**23**	**4**	**12**	**1**	**1076**	**67**	**0**	**3.74**	....	....	....	....	....	....	....

Signed as a free agent by **Hamilton** (AHL), April 7, 2000. Signed as a free agent by **Edmonton**, July 25, 2000. Signed as a free agent by **Ayr Scottish Eagles** (Britain), August 12, 2001.

GARDNER, Greg (GAHR-dih-nuhr, GREHG) CBJ

Goaltender. Catches left. 6', 190 lbs. Born, Mississauga, Ont., November 21, 1975.

			Regular Season								Playoffs						
Season	**Club**	**Lea**	**GP**	**W**	**L**	**T**	**Mins**	**GA**	**SO**	**Avg**	**GP**	**W**	**L**	**Mins**	**GA**	**SO**	**Avg**
1992-93	Caledon Canucks	MTJHL	28	....	....	....	1390	73	1	3.15	....	....	....	....	....	....	....
1993-94	Caledon Canucks	MTJHL	1	1	0	0	40	5	0	7.50	....	....	....	....	....	....	....
	Thornhill Islanders	MTJHL	31	18	11	1	1813	103	1	3.41	....	....	....	....	....	....	....
1994-95	Thornhill Islanders	MTJHL	42	....	....	....	2430	117	4	2.89	11	7	4	677	36	1	3.19
1995-96	Thornhill Islanders	MTJHL	34	....	....	....	2012	99	2	2.95	18	11	7	1095	59	0	3.23
1996-97	Niagara University	ECAC-2	17	8	5	2	939	54	0	3.45	....	....	....	....	....	....	....
1997-98	Niagara University	ECAC-2	25	12	10	3	1454	74	0	3.05	....	....	....	....	....	....	....
1998-99	Niagara University	CHA	30	15	10	3	1742	78	4	2.69	....	....	....	....	....	....	....
99-2000	Niagara University	CHA	*41	*29	8	4	*2503	64	*12	*1.53	....	....	....	....	....	....	....
2000-01	Dayton Bombers	ECHL	28	14	9	2	1600	70	2	2.62	3	1	2	181	9	0	2.96
	Syracuse Crunch	AHL	9	1	5	0	351	28	0	4.78	....	....	....	....	....	....	....

MTJHL East All-Star Team (1994, 1995) • MTJHL East Goaltender of the Year (1995, 1996) • CHA First All-Star Team (2000) • CHA Goaltender of the Year (2000) • CHA Player of the Year (2000)

Signed as a free agent by **Columbus**, May 16, 2000.

GARNER, Tyrone (GAHR-nuhr, TIGH-rohn)

Goaltender. Catches left. 6'1", 200 lbs. Born, Stoney Creek, Ont., July 27, 1978.
(NY Islanders' 4th choice, 83rd overall, in 1996 Entry Draft).

			Regular Season								Playoffs						
Season	**Club**	**Lea**	**GP**	**W**	**L**	**T**	**Mins**	**GA**	**SO**	**Avg**	**GP**	**W**	**L**	**Mins**	**GA**	**SO**	**Avg**
1994-95	Stoney Creek	OJHL-B	10	2	7	1	589	62	0	6.32	....	....	....	....	....	....	....
	Hamilton B's	OPJHL	8	....	....	....	419	28	0	4.01	....	....	....	....	....	....	....
1995-96	Oshawa Generals	OHL	32	11	15	4	1697	112	0	3.96	....	....	....	....	....	....	....
1996-97	Oshawa Generals	OHL	9	6	1	0	434	20	0	2.76	3	1	0	88	6	0	4.09
1997-98	Oshawa Generals	OHL	54	23	17	8	2946	162	1	3.30	7	3	4	450	25	0	3.33
1998-99	Oshawa Generals	OHL	44	24	15	3	2496	124	4	2.98	15	9	6	901	57	0	3.80
	Calgary	**NHL**	**3**	**0**	**2**	**0**	**139**	**12**	**0**	**5.18**	....	....	....	....	....	....	....
99-2000	Saint John Flames	AHL	19	4	8	4	940	70	0	4.47	....	....	....	....	....	....	....
	Dayton Bombers	ECHL	3	0	2	0	113	11	0	5.86	....	....	....	....	....	....	....
	Johnstown Chiefs	ECHL	17	8	6	3	971	48	0	2.97	1	0	1	59	2	0	2.03
2000-01	Johnstown Chiefs	ECHL	5	3	1	1	306	15	0	2.94	....	....	....	....	....	....	....
	Greenville Growl	ECHL	35	17	15	3	2114	99	3	2.81	....	....	....	....	....	....	....
	NHL Totals		**3**	**0**	**2**	**0**	**139**	**12**	**0**	**5.18**	....	....	....	....	....	....	....

OHL Second All-Star Team (1999)

Traded to **Calgary** by **NY Islanders** with Marty McInnis and Calgary's 6th round choice (previously acquired, Calgary selected Ilja Demidov) in 1997 Entry Draft for Robert Reichel, March 18, 1997.

GARNETT, Michael (gahr-NEHT, MIGHK-uhl) ATL.

Goaltender. Catches left. 6'1", 185 lbs. Born, Saskatoon, Sask., November 25, 1982.
(Atlanta's 2nd choice, 80th overall, in 2001 Entry Draft).

			Regular Season								Playoffs						
Season	**Club**	**Lea**	**GP**	**W**	**L**	**T**	**Mins**	**GA**	**SO**	**Avg**	**GP**	**W**	**L**	**Mins**	**GA**	**SO**	**Avg**
1997-98	Saskatoon AAA	SMHL	3	1	1	0	82	8	0	5.85	....	....	....	....	....	....	....
1998-99	Saskatoon AAA	SMHL					STATISTICS NOT AVAILABLE										
99-2000	Kindersley	SJHL	36	....	....	....	2067	140	1	3.57	....	....	....	....	....	....	....
	Red Deer Rebels	WHL	1	0	0	0	14	0	0	0.00	....	....	....	....	....	....	....
2000-01	Red Deer Rebels	WHL	21	14	5	1	1133	39	3	2.07	....	....	....	....	....	....	....
	Saskatoon Blades	WHL	28	7	17	2	1501	83	1	3.32	....	....	....	....	....	....	....

Traded to **Saskatoon** by **Red Deer** with Justin Wallin, Martin Vymazzal and future considerations for Martin Erat, Darcy Robinson and Cam Ornik, January 11, 2001.

GARON, Mathieu (gah-ROHN, MAT-yoo) MTL.

Goaltender. Catches right. 6'2", 192 lbs. Born, Chandler, Que., January 9, 1978.
(Montreal's 2nd choice, 44th overall, in 1996 Entry Draft).

			Regular Season								Playoffs						
Season	**Club**	**Lea**	**GP**	**W**	**L**	**T**	**Mins**	**GA**	**SO**	**Avg**	**GP**	**W**	**L**	**Mins**	**GA**	**SO**	**Avg**
1993-94	Jonquiere Elites	QAAA	17	0	13	0	834	88	0	6.33	....	....	....	....	....	....	....
1994-95	Jonquiere Elites	QAAA	27	13	13	1	1554	94	0	3.63	9	6	2	467	26	0	3.34
1995-96	Victoriaville Tigres	QMJHL	51	18	27	0	2709	189	1	4.19	12	7	4	676	38	1	3.39
1996-97	Victoriaville Tigres	QMJHL	53	29	18	3	3032	150	*6	2.97	6	2	4	330	23	0	4.18
1997-98	Victoriaville Tigres	QMJHL	47	27	18	2	2802	125	5	2.68	6	2	4	345	22	0	3.82
1998-99	Fredericton	AHL	40	14	22	2	2222	114	3	3.08	6	1	1	208	12	0	3.47
99-2000	Quebec Citadelles	AHL	53	17	28	3	2884	149	2	3.10	1	0	0	20	3	0	8.82
2000-01	**Montreal**	**NHL**	**11**	**4**	**5**	**1**	**589**	**24**	**2**	**2.44**	....	....	....	....	....	....	....
	Quebec Citadelles	AHL	31	16	13	1	1768	86	1	2.92	8	4	4	459	22	1	2.88
	NHL Totals		**11**	**4**	**5**	**1**	**589**	**24**	**2**	**2.44**	....	....	....	....	....	....	....

QMJHL First All-Star Team (1998) • Canadian Major Junior First All-Star Team (1998) • Canadian Major Junior Goaltender of the Year (1998)

GAUTHIER, Sean (GOH-tyay, SHAWN)

Goaltender. Catches left. 5'11", 200 lbs. Born, Sudbury, Ont., March 28, 1971.
(Winnipeg's 7th choice, 181st overall, in 1991 Entry Draft).

			Regular Season								Playoffs						
Season	**Club**	**Lea**	**GP**	**W**	**L**	**T**	**Mins**	**GA**	**SO**	**Avg**	**GP**	**W**	**L**	**Mins**	**GA**	**SO**	**Avg**
1987-88	Oakville Blades	OJHL-B	28	....	....	....	1491	110	2	4.43	....	....	....	....	....	....	....
1988-89	Kingston Raiders	OHL	37	7	18	1	1528	141	0	5.54	....	....	....	....	....	....	....
1989-90	Kingston	OHL	32	17	9	0	1602	101	0	3.78	2	0	1	76	6	0	4.74
1990-91	Kingston	OHL	59	16	36	3	3200	282	0	5.29	....	....	....	....	....	....	....
1991-92	Moncton Hawks	AHL	25	8	10	5	1415	88	1	3.73	2	0	0	26	2	0	4.62
	Fort Wayne	IHL	18	10	4	2	978	59	1	3.62	2	0	0	48	7	0	8.74
1992-93	Moncton Hawks	AHL	38	10	16	9	2196	145	0	3.96	2	0	1	75	6	0	4.80
1993-94	Moncton Hawks	AHL	13	3	5	1	616	41	0	3.99	....	....	....	....	....	....	....
	Fort Wayne	IHL	22	9	9	3	1139	66	0	3.48	....	....	....	....	....	....	....
1994-95	Fort Wayne	IHL	5	0	2	1	217	15	0	4.13	....	....	....	....	....	....	....
	Canada	Nt-Team	24	....	....	....	1326	53	0	2.40	....	....	....	....	....	....	....
1995-96	South Carolina	ECHL	49	31	11	7	2891	149	0	3.09	8	5	3	478	24	0	3.01
	St. John's Leafs	AHL	5	1	1	0	173	9	0	3.12	....	....	....	....	....	....	....
1996-97	Pensacola	ECHL	46	23	21	1	2692	168	1	3.74	12	8	4	749	44	*1	3.52
1997-98	Pensacola	ECHL	54	29	17	7	3213	194	0	3.62	*19	12	7	1180	58	1	2.95
1998-99	**San Jose**	**NHL**	**1**	**0**	**0**	**0**	**3**	**0**	**0**	**0.00**	....	....	....	....	....	....	....
	Kentucky	AHL	40	18	15	6	2376	99	1	2.50	4	0	1	130	8	0	3.68
99-2000	Louisiana	ECHL	22	12	6	3	1230	62	0	3.02	....	....	....	....	....	....	....
	Louisville Panthers	AHL	39	24	12	2	2259	102	3	2.71	4	1	3	239	14	0	3.52
2000-01	Louisville Panthers	AHL	54	11	33	4	2725	165	2	3.63	....	....	....	....	....	....	....
	NHL Totals		**1**	**0**	**0**	**0**	**3**	**0**	**0**	**0.00**	....	....	....	....	....	....	....

ECHL Second All-Star Team (1996, 1998)

Signed as a free agent by **San Jose**, July 23, 1998. Signed as a free agent by **Florida**, January 13, 2000.

GIGUERE, Jean-Sebastien (ZHEE-gair, ZHAWN-suh-BAS-tee-yeh) ANA.

Goaltender. Catches left. 6'1", 175 lbs. Born, Montreal, Que., May 16, 1977.
(Hartford's 1st choice, 13th overall, in 1995 Entry Draft).

			Regular Season								Playoffs						
Season	**Club**	**Lea**	**GP**	**W**	**L**	**T**	**Mins**	**GA**	**SO**	**Avg**	**GP**	**W**	**L**	**Mins**	**GA**	**SO**	**Avg**
1992-93	Laval Regents	QAAA	25	12	11	2	1498	76	0	3.02	11	6	5	654	38	0	3.49
1993-94	Verdun College	QMJHL	25	13	5	2	1234	66	1	3.21	....	....	....	....	....	....	....
1994-95	Halifax	QMJHL	47	14	27	5	2755	181	2	3.94	7	3	4	417	17	1	*2.45
1995-96	Halifax	QMJHL	55	26	23	2	3230	185	1	3.44	6	1	5	354	24	0	4.07
1996-97	**Hartford**	**NHL**	**8**	**1**	**4**	**0**	**394**	**24**	**0**	**3.65**	....	....	....	....	....	....	....
	Halifax	QMJHL	50	28	19	3	3014	170	2	3.38	16	9	7	954	58	0	3.65
1997-98	Saint John Flames	AHL	31	16	10	3	1758	72	2	2.46	10	5	3	536	27	0	3.02
1998-99	**Calgary**	**NHL**	**15**	**6**	**7**	**1**	**860**	**46**	**0**	**3.21**	....	....	....	....	....	....	....
	Saint John Flames	AHL	39	18	16	3	2145	123	3	3.44	7	3	2	304	21	0	4.14
99-2000	**Calgary**	**NHL**	**7**	**1**	**3**	**1**	**330**	**15**	**0**	**2.73**	....	....	....	....	....	....	....
	Saint John Flames	AHL	41	17	17	3	2243	114	0	3.05	3	0	3	178	9	0	3.03
2000-01	**Anaheim**	**NHL**	**34**	**11**	**17**	**5**	**2031**	**87**	**4**	**2.57**	....	....	....	....	....	....	....
	Cincinnati Ducks	AHL	23	12	7	2	1306	53	0	2.43	....	....	....	....	....	....	....
	NHL Totals		**64**	**19**	**31**	**7**	**3615**	**172**	**4**	**2.85**	....	....	....	....	....	....	....

QMJHL Second All-Star Team (1997) • Shared Harry "Hap" Holmes Memorial Trophy (fewest goals against - AHL) with Tyler Moss (1998)

Transferred to **Carolina** after **Hartford** franchise relocated, June 25, 1997. Traded to **Calgary** by **Carolina** with Andrew Cassels for Gary Roberts and Trevor Kidd, August 25, 1997. Traded to **Anaheim** by **Calgary** for Anaheim's 2nd round choice (later traded to Washington - Washington selected Matt Pettinger) in 2000 Entry Draft, June 10, 2000.

GOEHRING, Karl (GAIR-ihng, KAHRL) CBJ

Goaltender. Catches left. 5'7", 155 lbs. Born, Apple Valley, MN, August 23, 1978.

			Regular Season								Playoffs						
Season	Club	Lea	GP	W	L	T	Mins	GA	SO	Avg	GP	W	L	Mins	GA	SO	Avg
1996-97	Fargo-Moorhead	USHL	32	13	18	1	1909	79	*4	*2.48	5	2	3	251	15	1	3.58
1997-98	North Dakota	WCHA	27	23	3	1	1504	57	1	*2.27	....	....	....	....	....	....	....
1998-99	North Dakota	WCHA	31	22	5	2	1774	71	3	2.40	....	....	....	....	....	....	....
99-2000	North Dakota	WCHA	30	19	6	4	1747	55	*8	*1.89	....	....	....	....	....	....	....
2000-01	North Dakota	WCHA	30	16	6	6	1662	66	*3	2.38	....	....	....	....	....	....	....

WCHA First All-Star Team (1998, 2000) • NCAA West First All-American Team (1998, 2000) • WCHA Second All-Star Team (1999)

Signed as a free agent by **Columbus**, May 7, 2001.

GRAHAME, John (GRAY-ham, JAWN) BOS.

Goaltender. Catches left. 6'2", 214 lbs. Born, Denver, CO, August 31, 1975.
(Boston's 7th choice, 229th overall, in 1994 Entry Draft).

			Regular Season								Playoffs						
Season	Club	Lea	GP	W	L	T	Mins	GA	SO	Avg	GP	W	L	Mins	GA	SO	Avg
1993-94	Sioux City	USHL	20	....	....	....	1200	73	0	3.70	....	....	....	....	....	....	....
1994-95	Lake Superior	CCHA	28	16	7	3	1616	75	2	2.79	....	....	....	....	....	....	....
1995-96	Lake Superior	CCHA	29	21	4	2	1558	66	2	2.54	....	....	....	....	....	....	....
1996-97	Lake Superior	CCHA	37	19	13	4	2197	134	3	3.66	....	....	....	....	....	....	....
1997-98	Providence Bruins	AHL	55	15	31	4	3053	164	3	3.22	....	....	....	....	....	....	....
1998-99	Providence Bruins	AHL	48	*37	9	1	2771	134	3	2.90	19	*15	4	*1209	48	1	2.38
99-2000	**Boston**	**NHL**	**24**	**7**	**10**	**5**	**1344**	**55**	**2**	**2.46**	....	....	....	....	....	....	....
	Providence Bruins	AHL	27	11	13	2	1528	86	1	3.38	13	10	3	839	35	0	2.50
2000-01	**Boston**	**NHL**	**10**	**3**	**4**	**0**	**471**	**28**	**0**	**3.57**	....	....	....	....	....	....	....
	Providence Bruins	AHL	16	4	7	3	893	47	0	3.16	17	8	9	1043	46	2	2.65
	NHL Totals		**34**	**10**	**14**	**5**	**1815**	**83**	**2**	**2.74**	....	....	....	....	....	....	....

GRAHN, Carl (GRAHN, KARL) L.A.

Goaltender. Catches left. 5'11", 169 lbs. Born, Kouvola, Finland, January 8, 1981.
(Los Angeles' 11th choice, 282nd overall, in 2000 Entry Draft).

			Regular Season								Playoffs						
Season	Club	Lea	GP	W	L	T	Mins	GA	SO	Avg	GP	W	L	Mins	GA	SO	Avg
1998-99	KalPa Kuopio	Finn-Jr.	20	7	10	1	1153	63	1	3.28	....	....	....	....	....	....	....
	KalPa Kuopio	Finland	3	0	2	0	126	16	0	7.63	....	....	....	....	....	....	....
99-2000	KooKoo Kouvola	Finn-Jr.	38	....	....	....	2165	124	1	3.44	....	....	....	....	....	....	....
2000-01	KalPa Kuopio	Finn-2	39	20	15	4	2340	105	2	2.69	....	....	....	....	....	....	....

GUSTAFSON, Derek (GUHST-ahf-suhn, DEH-rihk) MIN.

Goaltender. Catches left. 5'11", 210 lbs. Born, Gresham, OR, June 21, 1979.

			Regular Season								Playoffs						
Season	Club	Lea	GP	W	L	T	Mins	GA	SO	Avg	GP	W	L	Mins	GA	SO	Avg
1995-96	Seattle Ironmen	BCAHA	16	....	....	....	913	46	0	3.02	....	....	....	....	....	....	....
1996-97	Vernon Vipers	BCJHL	23	....	....	....	1241	70	0	3.38	....	....	....	....	....	....	....
1997-98	Vernon Vipers	BCJHL	42	27	13	2	2270	144	1	3.81	6	2	1	257	13	0	3.04
1998-99	Vernon Vipers	BCJHL	42	39	3	0	2505	94	3	2.25	....	....	....	....	....	....	....
99-2000	St. Lawrence	ECAC	24	17	4	2	1475	51	2	2.07	....	....	....	....	....	....	....
2000-01	**Minnesota**	**NHL**	**4**	**1**	**3**	**0**	**239**	**10**	**0**	**2.51**	....	....	....	....	....	....	....
	Jackson Bandits	ECHL	7	4	3	0	404	15	1	2.23	....	....	....	....	....	....	....
	Cleveland	IHL	24	14	7	1	1293	59	2	2.74	2	0	1	53	5	0	5.64
	NHL Totals		**4**	**1**	**3**	**0**	**239**	**10**	**0**	**2.51**	....	....	....	....	....	....	....

BCJHL First All-Star Team (1999) • Won BCJHL Interior Top Goaltender Award (1999) • ECAC Second All-Star Team (2000) • ECAC Rookie of the Year (2000)

Signed as a free agent by **Minnesota**, June 9, 2000.

HACKETT, Jeff (HA-keht, JEHF) MTL.

Goaltender. Catches left. 6'1", 198 lbs. Born, London, Ont., June 1, 1968.
(NY Islanders' 2nd choice, 34th overall, in 1987 Entry Draft).

			Regular Season								Playoffs						
Season	Club	Lea	GP	W	L	T	Mins	GA	SO	Avg	GP	W	L	Mins	GA	SO	Avg
1984-85	London Diamonds	OJHL-B	18	....	....	....	1078	73	1	4.06	....	....	....	....	....	....	....
1985-86	London Diamonds	OJHL-B	19	....	....	....	1150	66	0	3.43	....	....	....	....	....	....	....
1986-87	Oshawa Generals	OHL	31	18	9	2	1672	85	2	3.05	15	8	7	895	40	0	2.68
1987-88	Oshawa Generals	OHL	53	30	21	2	3165	205	0	3.89	7	3	4	438	31	0	4.25
1988-89	**NY Islanders**	**NHL**	**13**	**4**	**7**	**0**	**662**	**39**	**0**	**3.53**	....	....	....	....	....	....	....
	Springfield Indians	AHL	29	12	14	2	1677	116	0	4.15	....	....	....	....	....	....	....
1989-90	Springfield Indians	AHL	54	24	25	3	3045	187	1	3.68	*17	*10	5	934	60	0	3.85
1990-91	**NY Islanders**	**NHL**	**30**	**5**	**18**	**1**	**1508**	**91**	**0**	**3.62**	....	....	....	....	....	....	....
1991-92	**San Jose**	**NHL**	**42**	**11**	**27**	**1**	**2314**	**148**	**0**	**3.84**	....	....	....	....	....	....	....
1992-93	**San Jose**	**NHL**	**36**	**2**	**30**	**1**	**2000**	**176**	**0**	**5.28**	....	....	....	....	....	....	....
1993-94	**Chicago**	**NHL**	**22**	**2**	**12**	**3**	**1084**	**62**	**0**	**3.43**	....	....	....	....	....	....	....
1994-95	**Chicago**	**NHL**	**7**	**1**	**3**	**2**	**328**	**13**	**0**	**2.38**	**2**	**0**	**0**	**26**	**1**	**0**	**2.31**
1995-96	**Chicago**	**NHL**	**35**	**18**	**11**	**4**	**2000**	**80**	**4**	**2.40**	**1**	**0**	**1**	**60**	**5**	**0**	**5.00**
1996-97	**Chicago**	**NHL**	**41**	**19**	**18**	**4**	**2473**	**89**	**2**	**2.16**	**6**	**2**	**4**	**345**	**25**	**0**	**4.35**
1997-98	**Chicago**	**NHL**	**58**	**21**	**25**	**11**	**3441**	**126**	**8**	**2.20**	....	....	....	....	....	....	....
1998-99	**Chicago**	**NHL**	**10**	**2**	**6**	**1**	**524**	**33**	**0**	**3.78**	....	....	....	....	....	....	....
	Montreal	**NHL**	**53**	**24**	**20**	**9**	**3091**	**117**	**5**	**2.27**	....	....	....	....	....	....	....
99-2000	**Montreal**	**NHL**	**56**	**23**	**25**	**7**	**3301**	**132**	**3**	**2.40**	....	....	....	....	....	....	....
2000-01	**Montreal**	**NHL**	**19**	**4**	**10**	**2**	**998**	**54**	**0**	**3.25**	....	....	....	....	....	....	....
	NHL Totals		**422**	**136**	**212**	**46**	**23724**	**1160**	**22**	**2.93**	**9**	**2**	**5**	**431**	**31**	**0**	**4.32**

Won Jack A. Butterfield Trophy (Playoff MVP - AHL) (1990)

Claimed by **San Jose** from **NY Islanders** in Expansion Draft, May 30, 1991. Traded to **Chicago** by **San Jose** for Chicago's 3rd round choice (Alexei Yegorov) in 1994 Entry Draft, July 13, 1993. Traded to **Montreal** by **Chicago** with Eric Weinrich, Alain Nasreddine and Tampa Bay's 4th round choice (previously acquired, Montreal selected Chris Dyment) in 1999 Entry Draft for Jocelyn Thibault, Dave Manson and Brad Brown, November 16, 1998.

HAMERLIK, Peter (HAHM-reh-lik, PEE-tuhr) PIT.

Goaltender. Catches left. 6'1", 183 lbs. Born, Myjava, Czech., January 2, 1982.
(Pittsburgh's 3rd choice, 84th overall, in 2000 Entry Draft).

			Regular Season								Playoffs						
Season	Club	Lea	GP	W	L	T	Mins	GA	SO	Avg	GP	W	L	Mins	GA	SO	Avg
1997-98	HK Skalica	Slovak-Jr.	49	....	....	....	2969	168	....	3.40	....	....	....	....	....	....	....
1998-99	HK Skalica	Slovakia	1	0	1	0	24	3	0	7.50	....	....	....	....	....	....	....
99-2000	HK Skalica	Slovak-Jr.	37	....	....	....	1850	121	....	3.92	....	....	....	....	....	....	....
	HK Skalica	Slovakia	7	....	....	....	286	16	....	3.36	....	....	....	....	....	....	....
2000-01	Kingston	OHL	56	21	21	8	3026	153	*4	3.03	3	0	2	131	13	0	5.95

HASEK, Dominik (HAH-shihk, DOHM-ih-NIHK) DET.

Goaltender. Catches left. 5'11", 180 lbs. Born, Pardubice, Czech., January 29, 1965.
(Chicago's 11th choice, 207th overall, in 1983 Entry Draft).

			Regular Season								Playoffs						
Season	Club	Lea	GP	W	L	T	Mins	GA	SO	Avg	GP	W	L	Mins	GA	SO	Avg
1981-82	HC Pardubice	Czech.	12	....	....	....	661	34	....	3.09	....	....	....	....	....	....	....
1982-83	HC Pardubice	Czech.	42	....	....	....	2358	105	....	2.67	....	....	....	....	....	....	....
1983-84	HC Pardubice	Czech.	40	....	....	....	2304	108	....	2.81	....	....	....	....	....	....	....
1984-85	HC Pardubice	Czech.	42	....	....	....	2419	131	....	3.25	....	....	....	....	....	....	....
1985-86	HC Pardubice	Czech.	45	....	....	....	2689	138	....	3.08	....	....	....	....	....	....	....
1986-87	HC Pardubice	Czech.	43	....	....	....	2515	103	....	2.46	....	....	....	....	....	....	....
1987-88	HC Pardubice	Czech.	31	....	....	....	1862	93	....	3.00	....	....	....	....	....	....	....
	Czechoslovakia	Olympics	5	3	2	0	217	18	1	4.98	....	....	....	....	....	....	....
1988-89	HC Pardubice	Czech.	42	....	....	....	2507	114	....	2.73	....	....	....	....	....	....	....
1989-90	Dukla Jihlava	Czech.	40	....	....	....	2251	80	....	2.13	....	....	....	....	....	....	....
1990-91	**Chicago**	**NHL**	**5**	**3**	**0**	**1**	**195**	**8**	**0**	**2.46**	**3**	**0**	**0**	**69**	**3**	**0**	**2.61**
	Indianapolis Ice	IHL	33	20	11	1	1903	80	*5	*2.52	1	1	0	60	3	0	3.00
1991-92	**Chicago**	**NHL**	**20**	**10**	**4**	**1**	**1014**	**44**	**1**	**2.60**	**3**	**0**	**2**	**158**	**8**	**0**	**3.04**
	Indianapolis Ice	IHL	20	7	10	3	1162	69	1	3.56	....	....	....	....	....	....	....
1992-93	**Buffalo**	**NHL**	**28**	**11**	**10**	**4**	**1429**	**75**	**0**	**3.15**	**1**	**1**	**0**	**45**	**1**	**0**	**1.33**
1993-94	**Buffalo**	**NHL**	**58**	**30**	**20**	**6**	**3358**	**109**	***7**	***1.95**	**7**	**3**	**4**	**484**	**13**	**2**	***1.61**
1994-95	HC Pardubice	Cze-Rep	2	1	0	1	124	6	0	2.90	....	....	....	....	....	....	....
	Buffalo	**NHL**	**41**	**19**	**14**	**7**	**2416**	**85**	***5**	***2.11**	**5**	**1**	**4**	**309**	**18**	**0**	**3.50**
1995-96	**Buffalo**	**NHL**	**59**	**22**	**30**	**6**	**3417**	**161**	**2**	**2.83**	....	....	....	....	....	....	....
1996-97	**Buffalo**	**NHL**	**67**	**37**	**20**	**10**	**4037**	**153**	**5**	**2.27**	**3**	**1**	**1**	**153**	**5**	**0**	**1.96**
1997-98	**Buffalo**	**NHL**	***72**	**33**	**23**	**13**	***4220**	**147**	***13**	**2.09**	**15**	**10**	**5**	**948**	**32**	**1**	**2.03**
	Czech-Republic	Olympics	6	*5	1	0	*369	6	*2	*0.97	....	....	....	....	....	....	....
1998-99	**Buffalo**	**NHL**	**64**	**30**	**18**	**14**	**3817**	**119**	**9**	**1.87**	**19**	**13**	**6**	**1217**	**36**	**2**	**1.77**
99-2000	**Buffalo**	**NHL**	**35**	**15**	**11**	**6**	**2066**	**76**	**3**	**2.21**	**5**	**1**	**4**	**301**	**12**	**0**	**2.39**
2000-01	**Buffalo**	**NHL**	**67**	**37**	**24**	**4**	**3904**	**137**	***11**	**2.11**	**13**	**7**	**6**	**833**	**29**	**1**	**2.09**
	NHL Totals		**516**	**247**	**174**	**72**	**29873**	**1114**	**56**	**2.24**	**74**	**37**	**32**	**4517**	**157**	**6**	**2.09**

• Played in NHL All-Star Game (1996, 1997, 1998, 1999, 2001)

Traded to **Buffalo** by **Chicago** for Stephane Beauregard and Buffalo's 4th round choice (Eric Daze) in 1993 Entry Draft, August 7, 1992. Traded to **Detroit** by **Buffalo** for Vyacheslav Kozlov, Detroit's 1st round choice in 2002 Entry Draft and future considerations, July 1, 2001.

HAUSER, Adam (HOW-suhr, A-duhm) EDM.

Goaltender. Catches left. 6'2", 195 lbs. Born, Bovey, MN, May 27, 1980.
(Edmonton's 4th choice, 81st overall, in 1999 Entry Draft).

			Regular Season								Playoffs						
Season	Club	Lea	GP	W	L	T	Mins	GA	SO	Avg	GP	W	L	Mins	GA	SO	Avg
1996-97	Greenway High	H.S.	25	....	....	....	1496	63	0	2.54	....	....	....	....	....	....	....
1997-98	Team USA	USDP	38	19	10	7	2110	94	4	2.67	....	....	....	....	....	....	....
1998-99	U. of Minnesota	WCHA	*40	14	18	8	*2350	136	3	3.47	....	....	....	....	....	....	....
99-2000	U. of Minnesota	WCHA	36	20	14	2	2114	104	1	2.95	....	....	....	....	....	....	....
2000-01	U. of Minnesota	WCHA	40	*26	12	2	2366	101	*3	2.56	....	....	....	....	....	....	....

HEALY, Glenn (HEE-lee, GLEHN)

Goaltender. Catches left. 5'9", 190 lbs. Born, Pickering, Ont., August 23, 1962.

			Regular Season								Playoffs						
Season	Club	Lea	GP	W	L	T	Mins	GA	SO	Avg	GP	W	L	Mins	GA	SO	Avg
1979-80	Pickering Panthers	MTJHL	31	....	....	....	1850	123	0	3.99	....	....	....	....	....	....	....
1980-81	Pickering Panthers	MTJHL	35	....	....	....	2080	120	1	3.46	....	....	....	....	....	....	....
1981-82	Western Michigan	CCHA	27	7	19	1	1569	116	0	4.44	....	....	....	....	....	....	....
1982-83	Western Michigan	CCHA	30	8	19	2	1732	116	0	4.01	....	....	....	....	....	....	....
1983-84	Western Michigan	CCHA	38	19	16	3	2241	146	0	3.90	....	....	....	....	....	....	....
1984-85	Western Michigan	CCHA	37	21	14	2	2171	118	0	3.26	....	....	....	....	....	....	....
1985-86	**Los Angeles**	**NHL**	**1**	**0**	**0**	**0**	**51**	**6**	**0**	**7.06**	....	....	....	....	....	....	....
	Toledo	IHL	7	....	....	....	402	28	0	4.18	....	....	....	....	....	....	....
	New Haven	AHL	43	21	15	4	2410	160	0	3.98	2	0	2	49	11	0	5.55
1986-87	New Haven	AHL	47	21	15	0	2828	173	1	3.67	7	3	4	427	19	0	2.67
1987-88	**Los Angeles**	**NHL**	**34**	**12**	**18**	**1**	**1869**	**135**	**1**	**4.33**	**4**	**1**	**3**	**240**	**20**	**0**	**5.00**
1988-89	**Los Angeles**	**NHL**	**48**	**25**	**19**	**2**	**2699**	**192**	**0**	**4.27**	**3**	**0**	**1**	**97**	**6**	**0**	**3.71**
1989-90	**NY Islanders**	**NHL**	**39**	**12**	**19**	**6**	**2197**	**128**	**2**	**3.50**	**4**	**1**	**2**	**166**	**9**	**0**	**3.25**
1990-91	**NY Islanders**	**NHL**	**53**	**18**	**24**	**9**	**2999**	**166**	**0**	**3.32**	....	....	....	....	....	....	....
1991-92	**NY Islanders**	**NHL**	**37**	**14**	**16**	**4**	**1960**	**124**	**1**	**3.80**	....	....	....	....	....	....	....
1992-93	**NY Islanders**	**NHL**	**47**	**22**	**20**	**2**	**2655**	**146**	**1**	**3.30**	**18**	**9**	**8**	**1109**	**59**	**0**	**3.19**
1993-94♦	**NY Rangers**	**NHL**	**29**	**10**	**12**	**2**	**1368**	**69**	**2**	**3.03**	**2**	**0**	**0**	**68**	**1**	**0**	**0.88**
1994-95	**NY Rangers**	**NHL**	**17**	**8**	**6**	**1**	**888**	**35**	**1**	**2.36**	**5**	**2**	**1**	**230**	**13**	**0**	**3.39**
1995-96	**NY Rangers**	**NHL**	**44**	**17**	**14**	**11**	**2564**	**124**	**2**	**2.90**	....	....	....	....	....	....	....
1996-97	**NY Rangers**	**NHL**	**23**	**5**	**12**	**4**	**1357**	**59**	**1**	**2.61**	....	....	....	....	....	....	....
1997-98	**Toronto**	**NHL**	**21**	**4**	**10**	**2**	**1068**	**53**	**0**	**2.98**	....	....	....	....	....	....	....
1998-99	**Toronto**	**NHL**	**9**	**6**	**3**	**0**	**546**	**27**	**0**	**2.97**	**1**	**0**	**0**	**20**	**0**	**0**	**0.00**
	Chicago Wolves	IHL	10	6	3	1	597	33	0	3.32	....	....	....	....	....	....	....
99-2000	**Toronto**	**NHL**	**20**	**9**	**10**	**0**	**1164**	**59**	**2**	**3.04**	....	....	....	....	....	....	....
2000-01	**Toronto**	**NHL**	**15**	**4**	**7**	**3**	**871**	**38**	**0**	**2.62**	....	....	....	....	....	....	....
	NHL Totals		**437**	**166**	**190**	**47**	**24256**	**1361**	**13**	**3.37**	**37**	**13**	**15**	**1930**	**108**	**0**	**3.36**

CCHA Second All-Star Team (1985) • NCAA West Second All-American Team (1985)

Signed as a free agent by **Los Angeles**, June 13, 1985. Signed as a free agent by **NY Islanders**, August 16, 1989. Claimed by **Anaheim** from **NY Islanders** in Expansion Draft, June 24, 1993. Claimed by **Tampa Bay** from **Anaheim** in Phase II of Expansion Draft, June 25, 1993. Traded to **NY Rangers** by **Tampa Bay** for Tampa Bay's 3rd round choice (previously acquired, Tampa Bay selected Allan Egeland) in 1993 Entry Draft, June 25, 1993. Signed as a free agent by **Toronto**, August 8, 1997.

HEBERT, Guy (ay-BAIR, GEE)

Goaltender. Catches left. 5'11", 186 lbs. Born, Troy, NY, January 7, 1967.
(St. Louis' 8th choice, 159th overall, in 1987 Entry Draft).

			Regular Season								Playoffs						
Season	Club	Lea	GP	W	L	T	Mins	GA	SO	Avg	GP	W	L	Mins	GA	SO	Avg
1985-86	Hamilton College	NCAA-2	18	4	12	2	1011	69	2	4.09	....	....	....	....	....	....	....
1986-87	Hamilton College	NCAA-2	18	12	5	0	1070	40	3	2.19	2	1	1	134	6	0	2.69
1987-88	Hamilton College	NCAA-2	9	5	3	0	510	22	1	2.58	1	0	1	60	3	0	3.00
1988-89	Hamilton College	NCAA-2	25	18	7	0	1454	62	2	2.56	2	1	1	126	4	0	1.90
1989-90	Peoria Rivermen	IHL	30	7	13	7	1706	124	1	4.36	2	0	1	76	5	0	3.95
1990-91	Peoria Rivermen	IHL	36	24	10	1	2093	100	2	2.87	8	3	4	458	32	0	4.19
1991-92	**St. Louis**	**NHL**	**13**	**5**	**5**	**1**	**738**	**36**	**0**	**2.93**	....	....	....	....	....	....	....
	Peoria Rivermen	IHL	29	20	9	0	1731	98	0	3.40	4	3	1	239	9	0	2.26
1992-93	**St. Louis**	**NHL**	**24**	**8**	**8**	**2**	**1210**	**74**	**1**	**3.67**	**1**	**0**	**0**	**2**	**0**	**0**	**0.00**
1993-94	**Anaheim**	**NHL**	**52**	**20**	**27**	**3**	**2991**	**141**	**2**	**2.83**	....	....	....	....	....	....	....
1994-95	**Anaheim**	**NHL**	**39**	**12**	**20**	**4**	**2092**	**109**	**2**	**3.13**	....	....	....	....	....	....	....
1995-96	**Anaheim**	**NHL**	**59**	**28**	**23**	**5**	**3326**	**157**	**4**	**2.83**	....	....	....	....	....	....	....
1996-97	**Anaheim**	**NHL**	**67**	**29**	**25**	**12**	**3863**	**172**	**4**	**2.67**	**9**	**4**	**4**	**534**	**18**	**1**	**2.02**
1997-98	**Anaheim**	**NHL**	**46**	**13**	**24**	**6**	**2660**	**130**	**3**	**2.93**	....	....	....	....	....	....	....
1998-99	**Anaheim**	**NHL**	**69**	**31**	**29**	**9**	**4083**	**165**	**6**	**2.42**	**4**	**0**	**3**	**208**	**15**	**0**	**4.33**
99-2000	**Anaheim**	**NHL**	**68**	**28**	**31**	**9**	**3976**	**166**	**4**	**2.51**	....	....	....	....	....	....	....
2000-01	**Anaheim**	**NHL**	**41**	**12**	**23**	**4**	**2215**	**115**	**2**	**3.12**	....	....	....	....	....	....	....
	NY Rangers	**NHL**	**13**	**5**	**7**	**1**	**735**	**42**	**0**	**3.43**	....	....	....	....	....	....	....
	NHL Totals		**491**	**191**	**222**	**56**	**27889**	**1307**	**28**	**2.81**	**14**	**4**	**7**	**744**	**33**	**1**	**2.66**

IHL Second All-Star Team (1991) • Shared James Norris Memorial Trophy (fewest goals against - IHL) with Pat Jablonski (1991) • Played in NHL All-Star Game (1997)

Claimed by **Anaheim** from **St. Louis** in Expansion Draft, June 24, 1993. Claimed on waivers by **NY Rangers** from **Anaheim**, March 7, 2001.

HEDBERG, Johan (HEHD-buhrg, YO-han) PIT.

Goaltender. Catches left. 5'11", 185 lbs. Born, Leksand, Sweden, May 5, 1973.
(Philadelphia's 8th choice, 218th overall, in 1994 Entry Draft).

			Regular Season								Playoffs						
Season	Club	Lea	GP	W	L	T	Mins	GA	SO	Avg	GP	W	L	Mins	GA	SO	Avg
1992-93	Leksands IF	Sweden	10	....	....	....	600	24	....	2.40	....	....	....	....	....	....	....
1993-94	Leksands IF	Sweden	17	....	....	....	1020	48	....	2.81	....	....	....	....	....	....	....
1994-95	Leksands IF	Sweden	17	....	....	....	986	58	....	3.53	....	....	....	....	....	....	....
1995-96	Leksands IF	Sweden	34	....	....	....	2013	95	....	2.83	4	....	....	240	13	....	3.25
1996-97	Leksands IF	Sweden	38	....	....	....	2260	95	3	2.52	8	....	....	581	18	1	1.86
1997-98	Baton Rouge	ECHL	2	1	1	0	100	7	0	4.20	....	....	....	....	....	....	....
	Detroit Vipers	IHL	16	7	2	2	726	32	1	2.64	....	....	....	....	....	....	....
	Manitoba Moose	IHL	14	8	4	1	745	32	1	2.58	2	0	2	105	6	0	3.40
1998-99	Leksands IF	Sweden	*48	....	....	....	*2940	140	0	2.86	4	....	....	255	15	0	3.53
99-2000	Kentucky	AHL	33	18	9	5	1973	88	3	2.68	5	3	2	311	10	1	1.93
2000-01	Manitoba Moose	IHL	46	23	13	7	2697	115	1	2.56	....	....	....	....	....	....	....
	Pittsburgh	NHL	9	7	1	1	545	24	0	2.64	18	9	9	1123	43	2	2.30
	NHL Totals		9	7	1	1	545	24	0	2.64	18	9	9	1123	43	2	2.30

Rights traded to **San Jose** by **Philadelphia** for San Jose's 7th round choice (Pavel Kasparik) in 1999 Entry Draft, August 6, 1998. Traded to **Pittsburgh** by **San Jose** with Bobby Dollas for Jeff Norton, March 12, 2001.

HEFFLER, Eric (HEH-fluhr, AIR-ihk) EDM.

Goaltender. Catches left. 6'3", 190 lbs. Born, Williamsville, NY, February 29, 1976.

			Regular Season								Playoffs						
Season	Club	Lea	GP	W	L	T	Mins	GA	SO	Avg	GP	W	L	Mins	GA	SO	Avg
1994-95	Oshawa Legion	MTJHL	29	....	....	....	1540	111	1	4.32	....	....	....	....	....	....	....
1995-96	St. Lawrence	ECAC	4	0	0	0	55	3	0	3.25	....	....	....	....	....	....	....
1996-97	St. Lawrence	ECAC	12	2	3	1	458	31	0	4.06	....	....	....	....	....	....	....
1997-98	St. Lawrence	ECAC	26	8	14	0	1529	73	2	2.90	....	....	....	....	....	....	....
1998-99	St. Lawrence	ECAC	*37	22	12	3	*2206	88	3	2.39	....	....	....	....	....	....	....
	Hamilton Bulldogs	AHL	2	1	1	0	119	5	0	2.52	....	....	....	....	....	....	....
99-2000	Hamilton Bulldogs	AHL	47	11	25	7	2643	138	5	3.13	....	....	....	....	....	....	....
2000-01	Hamilton Bulldogs	AHL	19	5	11	0	1037	68	0	3.93	....	....	....	....	....	....	....
	Greensboro	ECHL	15	4	10	0	821	55	0	4.02	....	....	....	....	....	....	....

ECAC First All-Star Team (1999) • ECAC Player of the Year (1999) • NCAA East First All-American Team (1999)

Signed as a free agent by **Edmonton**, April 30, 1999.

HENRY, Frederic (HEHN-ree, FREHD-uhr-IHK) N.J.

Goaltender. Catches left. 5'11", 180 lbs. Born, Cap-Rouge, Que., August 9, 1977.
(New Jersey's 10th choice, 200th overall, in 1995 Entry Draft).

			Regular Season								Playoffs						
Season	Club	Lea	GP	W	L	T	Mins	GA	SO	Avg	GP	W	L	Mins	GA	SO	Avg
1993-94	Ste-Foy Governors	QAAA	30	19	7	1	1571	76	1	2.98	6	2	4	333	15	1	....
1994-95	Granby Predateurs	QMJHL	15	8	5	0	866	47	0	3.26	6	1	2	232	21	0	5.43
1995-96	Granby Predateurs	QMJHL	28	19	5	2	1530	69	*3	2.71	12	9	2	610	21	2	*2.08
1996-97	Granby Predateurs	QMJHL	57	33	16	6	3330	162	4	2.92	5	1	4	251	17	0	4.06
	Albany River Rats	AHL	1	1	0	0	60	3	0	3.00	....	....	....	....	....	....	....
1997-98	Raleigh IceCaps	ECHL	34	13	17	2	1889	119	2	3.78	....	....	....	....	....	....	....
	Albany River Rats	AHL	4	2	0	1	199	8	0	2.41	....	....	....	....	....	....	....
1998-99	Albany River Rats	AHL	35	17	10	3	1690	84	1	2.98	....	....	....	....	....	....	....
99-2000	Albany River Rats	AHL	53	18	23	3	2732	138	1	3.03	4	2	2	236	6	1	1.52
2000-01	Albany River Rats	AHL	32	6	17	3	1651	99	1	3.60	....	....	....	....	....	....	....

HIRSCH, Corey (HUHRSH, KOHR-ee) WSH.

Goaltender. Catches left. 5'10", 175 lbs. Born, Medicine Hat, Alta., August 10, 1972.
(NY Rangers' 7th choice, 169th overall, in 1991 Entry Draft).

			Regular Season								Playoffs						
Season	Club	Lea	GP	W	L	T	Mins	GA	SO	Avg	GP	W	L	Mins	GA	SO	Avg
1987-88	Calgary Canucks	AJHL	32	22	5	0	1538	91	1	3.55	....	....	....	....	....	....	....
1988-89	Kamloops Blazers	WHL	32	11	12	2	1516	106	2	4.20	5	3	2	245	19	0	4.65
1989-90	Kamloops Blazers	WHL	*63	*48	13	0	3608	230	*3	3.82	*17	*14	3	*1043	60	0	*3.45
1990-91	Kamloops Blazers	WHL	38	26	7	1	1970	100	3	*3.05	11	5	6	623	42	0	4.04
1991-92	Kamloops Blazers	WHL	48	35	10	2	2732	124	*5	*2.72	*16	*11	5	954	35	*2	*2.20
1992-93	NY Rangers	NHL	4	1	2	1	224	14	0	3.75	....	....	....	....	....	....	....
	Binghamton	AHL	46	*35	4	5	2692	125	1	*2.79	14	7	7	831	46	0	3.32
1993-94	Canada	Nt-Team	45	24	17	3	2653	124	0	2.80	....	....	....	....	....	....	....
	Canada	Olympics	8	5	2	1	495	18	0	2.18	....	....	....	....	....	....	....
	Binghamton	AHL	10	5	4	1	610	38	0	3.73	....	....	....	....	....	....	....
1994-95	Binghamton	AHL	57	31	20	5	3371	175	0	3.11	....	....	....	....	....	....	....
1995-96	Vancouver	NHL	41	17	14	6	2338	114	1	2.93	6	2	3	338	21	0	3.73
1996-97	Vancouver	NHL	39	12	20	4	2127	116	2	3.27	....	....	....	....	....	....	....
1997-98	Vancouver	NHL	1	0	0	0	50	5	0	6.00	....	....	....	....	....	....	....
	Syracuse Crunch	AHL	60	30	22	6	3512	187	1	3.19	5	2	3	297	10	1	*2.02
1998-99	Vancouver	NHL	20	3	8	3	919	48	1	3.13	....	....	....	....	....	....	....
	Syracuse Crunch	AHL	5	2	3	0	300	14	0	2.80	....	....	....	....	....	....	....
99-2000	Milwaukee	IHL	19	9	8	1	1098	49	0	2.68	....	....	....	....	....	....	....
	Utah Grizzlies	IHL	17	9	5	1	937	42	3	2.69	2	0	2	121	4	0	1.99
2000-01	Albany River Rats	AHL	4	0	4	0	199	19	0	5.72	....	....	....	....	....	....	....
	Washington	NHL	1	1	0	0	20	0	0	0.00	....	....	....	....	....	....	....
	Cincinnati	IHL	13	11	2	0	783	28	1	2.15	....	....	....	....	....	....	....
	Portland	AHL	36	17	17	2	2142	104	1	2.91	2	0	2	118	7	0	3.55
	NHL Totals		106	34	44	14	5678	297	4	3.14	6	2	3	338	21	0	3.73

WHL West Second All-Star Team (1990) • WHL West First All-Star Team (1991, 1992) • Canadian Major Junior Goaltender of the Year (1992) • Memorial Cup All-Star Team (1992) • Won Hap Emms Memorial Trophy (Memorial Cup Tournament Top Goaltender) (1992) • AHL First All-Star Team (1993) • Won Dudley "Red" Garrett Memorial Trophy (Top Rookie - AHL) (1993) • Shared Harry "Hap" Holmes Memorial Trophy (fewest goals against - AHL) with Boris Rousson (1993) • NHL All-Rookie Team (1996)

Traded to **Vancouver** by **NY Rangers** for Nathan Lafayette, April 7, 1995. Signed as a free agent by **Nashville**, August 10, 1999. Traded to **Anaheim** by **Nashville** for future considerations, March 14, 2000. Signed as a free agent by **Washington**, October 27, 2000.

HNILICKA, Milan (huh-LEETCH-kuh, MEE-lan) ATL.

Goaltender. Catches left. 6'1", 195 lbs. Born, Kladno, Czech., June 25, 1973.
(NY Islanders' 4th choice, 70th overall, in 1991 Entry Draft).

			Regular Season								Playoffs						
Season	Club	Lea	GP	W	L	T	Mins	GA	SO	Avg	GP	W	L	Mins	GA	SO	Avg
1989-90	Poldi Kladno	Czech.	24	....	....	....	1113	70	....	3.77	....	....	....	....	....	....	....
1990-91	Poldi Kladno	Czech.	40	....	....	....	2122	98	0	2.80	....	....	....	....	....	....	....
1991-92	Poldi Kladno	Czech.	38	....	....	....	2066	128	0	3.73	....	....	....	....	....	....	....
1992-93	Swift Current	WHL	*65	*46	12	2	3679	206	2	3.36	*17	*12	5	*1017	54	*2	3.19
1993-94	Richmond	ECHL	43	18	16	5	2299	155	4	4.05	....	....	....	....	....	....	....
	Salt Lake City	IHL	8	5	1	0	378	25	0	3.97	....	....	....	....	....	....	....
1994-95	Denver Grizzlies	IHL	15	9	4	1	798	47	1	3.53	....	....	....	....	....	....	....
1995-96	Poldi Kladno	Cze-Rep	33	....	....	....	1959	93	1	2.84	8	....	....	493	24	....	2.92
1996-97	Poldi Kladno	Cze-Rep	48	....	....	....	2736	120	4	2.63	3	....	....	151	14	0	5.56
1997-98	Sparta Praha	Cze-Rep	49	....	....	....	2847	99	....	2.09	11	....	....	632	31	....	3.00
1998-99	Sparta Praha	Cze-Rep	*50	....	....	....	*2877	109	....	2.27	8	....	....	507	13	....	*1.54
99-2000	NY Rangers	NHL	2	0	1	0	86	5	0	3.49	....	....	....	....	....	....	....
	Hartford	AHL	36	22	11	0	1979	71	5	2.15	3	0	1	99	6	0	3.64
2000-01	Atlanta	NHL	36	12	19	2	1879	105	2	3.35	....	....	....	....	....	....	....
	NHL Totals		38	12	20	2	1965	110	2	3.36	....	....	....	....	....	....	....

Shared Harry "Hap" Holmes Memorial Trophy (fewest goals against - AHL) with Jean-Francois Labbe (2000)

Signed as a free agent by **NY Rangers**, July 15, 1999. Signed as a free agent by **Atlanta**, July 28, 2000.

HODSON, Jamie (HAWD-suhn, JAY-mee) TOR.

Goaltender. Catches left. 6'2", 206 lbs. Born, Brandon, Man., April 8, 1980.
(Toronto's 3rd choice, 69th overall, in 1998 Entry Draft).

			Regular Season								Playoffs						
Season	Club	Lea	GP	W	L	T	Mins	GA	SO	Avg	GP	W	L	Mins	GA	SO	Avg
1996-97	Yellowhead Chiefs	MMHL	12	....	....	....	720	58	1	4.83	....	....	....	....	....	....	....
1997-98	Brandon	WHL	20	12	2	2	964	52	2	3.24	6	5	0	337	16	0	2.85
1998-99	Brandon	WHL	43	23	12	3	2295	123	4	3.22	5	1	4	275	26	0	5.67
99-2000	Brandon	WHL	39	13	22	3	2321	130	2	3.36	....	....	....	....	....	....	....
2000-01	St. John's Leafs	AHL	4	0	2	0	137	13	0	5.71	....	....	....	....	....	....	....
	Brandon	WHL	29	9	17	1	1587	92	0	3.48	1	0	1	59	3	0	3.05

• Returned to **Brandon** (WHL) by **St. John's** (AHL), October 25, 2000.

HOLMQVIST, Johan (HOHLM-kvihst, YOH-han) NYR

Goaltender. Catches left. 6'3", 190 lbs. Born, Tolfta, Sweden, May 24, 1978.
(NY Rangers' 9th choice, 175th overall, in 1997 Entry Draft).

			Regular Season								Playoffs						
Season	Club	Lea	GP	W	L	T	Mins	GA	SO	Avg	GP	W	L	Mins	GA	SO	Avg
1996-97	Brynas IF	Sweden	2	0	0	0	80	4	0	3.00	....	....	....	....	....	....	....
1997-98	Brynas IF	Sweden	33	....	....	....	1897	82	....	2.59	3	0	3	180	14	....	4.67
1998-99	Brynas IF	Sweden	41	....	....	....	2383	111	4	2.79	*14	9	5	*855	34	0	2.39
99-2000	Brynas IF	Sweden	41	....	....	....	2402	104	4	2.60	11	....	....	671	30	1	2.68
2000-01	NY Rangers	NHL	2	0	2	0	119	10	0	5.04	....	....	....	....	....	....	....
	Hartford	AHL	43	19	14	4	2305	111	2	2.89	5	2	3	314	13	0	2.48
	NHL Totals		2	0	2	0	119	10	0	5.04	....	....	....	....	....	....	....

HURME, Jani (HOOR-meh, YAN-ee) OTT.

Goaltender. Catches left. 6', 187 lbs. Born, Turku, Finland, January 7, 1975.
(Ottawa's 2nd choice, 58th overall, in 1997 Entry Draft).

			Regular Season								Playoffs						
Season	Club	Lea	GP	W	L	T	Mins	GA	SO	Avg	GP	W	L	Mins	GA	SO	Avg
1992-93	TPS Turku	Finn-Jr.	12	....	....	....	669	47	0	4.22	1	....	....	60	0	1	0.00
1993-94	Kiekko-67 Turku	Finn-Jr.	18	....	....	....	1082	57	0	3.16	....	....	....	....	....	....	....
	Kiekko-67 Turku	Finland-2	3	....	....	....	190	7	0	2.21	....	....	....	....	....	....	....
	TPS Turku	Finland	1	....	....	....	2	0	0	0.00	....	....	....	....	....	....	....
1994-95	TPS Turku	Finn-Jr.	2	....	....	....	125	5	0	2.40	....	....	....	....	....	....	....
	Kiekko-67 Turku	Finn-Jr.	9	....	....	....	540	47	....	5.22	....	....	....	....	....	....	....
	Kiekko-67 Turku	Finland-2	19	....	....	....	1049	53	....	3.03	3	....	....	180	6	....	2.00
1995-96	TPS Turku	Finn-Jr.	13	....	....	....	777	34	1	2.63	....	....	....	....	....	....	....
	Kiekko-67 Turku	Finland-2	16	....	....	....	968	39	1	2.42	....	....	....	....	....	....	....
	TPS Turku	Finland	16	....	....	....	946	34	2	2.16	10	....	....	545	22	2	2.42
1996-97	TPS Turku	Finland	48	31	11	6	2917	101	6	2.08	12	6	6	722	39	0	3.24
1997-98	Detroit Vipers	IHL	6	2	2	2	290	20	0	4.13	....	....	....	....	....	....	....
	Indianapolis Ice	IHL	29	11	11	3	1506	83	1	3.30	3	1	0	129	10	0	4.62
1998-99	Detroit Vipers	IHL	12	7	3	1	643	26	1	2.43	....	....	....	....	....	....	....
	Cincinnati	IHL	26	14	9	2	1428	81	0	3.40	....	....	....	....	....	....	....
99-2000	Ottawa	NHL	1	1	0	0	60	2	0	2.00	....	....	....	....	....	....	....
	Grand Rapids	IHL	52	29	15	4	2948	107	4	2.18	*17	*10	7	*1028	37	1	2.16
2000-01	Ottawa	NHL	22	12	5	4	1296	54	2	2.50	....	....	....	....	....	....	....
	NHL Totals		23	13	5	4	1356	56	2	2.48	....	....	....	....	....	....	....

IHL Second All-Star Team (2000)

IRBE, Arturs (UHR-bay, AHR-tuhrs) CAR.

Goaltender. Catches left. 5'8", 190 lbs. Born, Riga, Latvia, February 2, 1967.
(Minnesota's 11th choice, 196th overall, in 1989 Entry Draft).

			Regular Season								Playoffs						
Season	Club	Lea	GP	W	L	T	Mins	GA	SO	Avg	GP	W	L	Mins	GA	SO	Avg
1986-87	Dynamo Riga	USSR	2	....	....	....	27	1	0	2.22	....	....	....	....	....	....	....
1987-88	Dynamo Riga	USSR	34	....	....	....	1870	86	4	2.69	....	....	....	....	....	....	....
1988-89	Dynamo Riga	USSR	40	....	....	....	2460	116	4	2.85	....	....	....	....	....	....	....
1989-90	Dynamo Riga	USSR	48	....	....	....	2880	115	2	2.42	....	....	....	....	....	....	....
1990-91	Dynamo Riga	USSR	46	....	....	....	2713	133	5	2.94	....	....	....	....	....	....	....
1991-92	San Jose	NHL	13	2	6	3	645	48	0	4.47	....	....	....	....	....	....	....
	Kansas City	IHL	32	24	7	1	1955	80	0	*2.46	*15	*12	3	914	44	0	*2.89
1992-93	San Jose	NHL	36	7	26	0	2074	142	1	4.11	....	....	....	....	....	....	....
	Kansas City	IHL	6	3	3	0	364	20	0	3.30	....	....	....	....	....	....	....
1993-94	San Jose	NHL	*74	30	28	16	*4412	209	3	2.84	14	7	7	806	50	0	3.72
1994-95	San Jose	NHL	38	14	19	3	2043	111	4	3.26	6	2	4	316	27	0	5.13
1995-96	San Jose	NHL	22	4	12	4	1112	85	0	4.59	....	....	....	....	....	....	....
	Kansas City	IHL	4	1	2	1	226	16	0	4.24	....	....	....	....	....	....	....
1996-97	Dallas	NHL	35	17	12	3	1965	88	3	2.69	1	0	0	13	0	0	0.00
1997-98	Vancouver	NHL	41	14	11	6	1999	91	2	2.73	....	....	....	....	....	....	....
1998-99	Carolina	NHL	62	27	20	12	3643	135	6	2.22	6	2	4	408	15	0	2.21
99-2000	Carolina	NHL	*75	34	28	9	4345	175	5	2.42	....	....	....	....	....	....	....
2000-01	Carolina	NHL	*77	37	29	9	*4406	180	6	2.45	6	2	4	360	20	0	3.33
	NHL Totals		473	186	191	65	26644	1264	30	2.85	33	13	19	1903	112	0	3.53

IHL First All-Star Team (1992) • Shared James Norris Memorial Trophy (fewest goals against - IHL) with Wade Flaherty (1992) • Played in NHL All-Star Game (1994, 1999)

Claimed by **San Jose** from **Minnesota** in Dispersal Draft, May 30, 1991. Signed as a free agent by **Dallas**, August 19, 1996. Signed as a free agent by **Vancouver**, August 25, 1997. Signed as a free agent by **Carolina**, September 14, 1998.

JABLONSKI, Pat (ja-BLAWN-skee, PAT)

Goaltender. Catches right. 6', 180 lbs. Born, Toledo, OH, June 20, 1967.
(St. Louis' 6th choice, 138th overall, in 1985 Entry Draft).

			Regular Season								Playoffs						
Season	Club	Lea	GP	W	L	T	Mins	GA	SO	Avg	GP	W	L	Mins	GA	SO	Avg
1984-85	Det-Compuware	NAJHL	29	....	....	....	1483	95	0	3.84	....	....	....	....	....	....	....
1985-86	Windsor Spitfires	OHL	29	6	16	4	1600	119	1	4.46	6	0	3	263	20	0	4.56
1986-87	Windsor Spitfires	OHL	41	22	14	2	2328	128	*3	3.30	12	8	4	710	38	0	3.21
1987-88	Peoria Rivermen	IHL	5	2	2	1	285	17	0	3.58	....	....	....	....	....	....	....
	Windsor Spitfires	OHL	18	14	3	0	994	48	2	2.90	9	*8	0	537	28	0	3.13
1988-89	Peoria Rivermen	IHL	35	11	20	0	2051	163	1	4.77	3	0	2	130	13	0	6.00
1989-90	**St. Louis**	**NHL**	**4**	**0**	**3**	**0**	**208**	**17**	**0**	**4.90**	....	....	....	....	....	....	....
	Peoria Rivermen	IHL	36	14	17	4	2023	165	0	4.89	4	1	3	223	19	0	5.11
1990-91	**St. Louis**	**NHL**	**8**	**2**	**3**	**3**	**492**	**25**	**0**	**3.05**	**3**	**0**	**0**	**90**	**5**	**0**	**3.33**
	Peoria Rivermen	IHL	29	23	3	2	1738	87	0	3.00	10	7	2	532	23	0	2.59
1991-92	**St. Louis**	**NHL**	**10**	**3**	**6**	**0**	**468**	**38**	**0**	**4.87**	....	....	....	....	....	....	....
	Peoria Rivermen	IHL	8	6	1	1	493	29	1	3.53	....	....	....	....	....	....	....
1992-93	**Tampa Bay**	**NHL**	**43**	**8**	**24**	**4**	**2268**	**150**	**1**	**3.97**	....	....	....	....	....	....	....
1993-94	**Tampa Bay**	**NHL**	**15**	**5**	**6**	**3**	**834**	**54**	**0**	**3.88**	....	....	....	....	....	....	....
	St. John's Leafs	AHL	16	12	3	1	962	49	1	3.05	11	6	5	676	36	0	3.19
1994-95	Chicago Wolves	IHL	4	0	4	0	216	17	0	4.71	....	....	....	....	....	....	....
	Houston Aeros	IHL	3	1	1	1	179	9	0	3.01	....	....	....	....	....	....	....
1995-96	**St. Louis**	**NHL**	**1**	**0**	**0**	**0**	**8**	**1**	**0**	**7.50**	....	....	....	....	....	....	....
	Montreal	**NHL**	**23**	**5**	**9**	**6**	**1264**	**62**	**0**	**2.94**	**1**	**0**	**0**	**49**	**1**	**0**	**1.22**
1996-97	**Montreal**	**NHL**	**17**	**4**	**6**	**2**	**754**	**50**	**0**	**3.98**	....	....	....	....	....	....	....
	Phoenix	**NHL**	**2**	**0**	**1**	**0**	**59**	**2**	**0**	**2.03**	....	....	....	....	....	....	....
1997-98	**Carolina**	**NHL**	**5**	**1**	**4**	**0**	**279**	**14**	**0**	**3.01**	....	....	....	....	....	....	....
	Cleveland	IHL	34	13	13	6	1950	98	0	3.01	....	....	....	....	....	....	....
	Quebec Rafales	IHL	7	3	3	0	368	21	0	3.42	....	....	....	....	....	....	....
1998-99	Chicago Wolves	IHL	36	22	7	7	2119	106	1	3.00	3	2	1	185	11	0	3.57
99-2000	Vastra Frolunda	Sweden	27	....	....	....	1624	65	4	2.40	5	....	....	298	18	0	3.62
2000-01	Vastra Frolunda	Sweden	22	....	....	....	1328	64	1	2.89	1	....	....	40	3	0	4.50
	NHL Totals		**128**	**28**	**62**	**18**	**6634**	**413**	**1**	**3.74**	**4**	**0**	**0**	**139**	**6**	**0**	**2.59**

Shared James Norris Memorial Trophy (fewest goals against - IHL) with Guy Hebert (1991)

Traded to **Tampa Bay** by **St. Louis** with Steve Tuttle, Darin Kimble and Rob Robinson for future considerations, June 19, 1992. Traded to **Toronto** by **Tampa Bay** for cash, February 21, 1994. Claimed by **St. Louis** from **Toronto** in NHL Waiver Draft, October 2, 1995. Traded to **Montreal** by **St. Louis** for J.J. Daigneault, November 7, 1995. Traded to **Phoenix** by **Montreal** for Steve Cheredaryk, March 18, 1997. Signed as a free agent by **Carolina**, August 12, 1997.

JOHNSON, Brent (JAWN-suhn, BREHNT) ST.L.

Goaltender. Catches left. 6'2", 200 lbs. Born, Farmington, MI, March 12, 1977.
(Colorado's 5th choice, 129th overall, in 1995 Entry Draft).

			Regular Season								Playoffs						
Season	Club	Lea	GP	W	L	T	Mins	GA	SO	Avg	GP	W	L	Mins	GA	SO	Avg
1993-94	Det-Compuware	MTJHL	18	....	....	....	1024	49	1	3.52	....	....	....	....	....	....	....
1994-95	Owen Sound	OHL	18	3	9	1	904	75	0	4.98	....	....	....	....	....	....	....
1995-96	Owen Sound	OHL	58	24	28	1	3211	243	1	4.54	6	2	4	371	29	0	4.69
1996-97	Owen Sound	OHL	50	20	28	1	2798	201	1	4.31	4	0	4	253	24	0	5.69
1997-98	Worcester	AHL	42	14	15	7	2240	119	0	3.19	6	3	2	332	19	0	3.43
1998-99	**St. Louis**	**NHL**	**6**	**3**	**2**	**0**	**286**	**10**	**0**	**2.10**	....	....	....	....	....	....	....
	Worcester	AHL	49	22	22	4	2925	146	2	2.99	4	1	3	238	12	0	3.02
99-2000	Worcester	AHL	58	24	27	5	3319	161	3	2.91	9	4	5	561	23	1	2.46
2000-01	**St. Louis**	**NHL**	**31**	**19**	**9**	**2**	**1744**	**63**	**4**	**2.17**	**2**	**0**	**1**	**62**	**2**	**0**	**1.94**
	NHL Totals		**37**	**22**	**11**	**2**	**2030**	**73**	**4**	**2.16**	**2**	**0**	**1**	**62**	**2**	**0**	**1.94**

Traded to **St. Louis** by **Colorado** for San Jose's 3rd round choice (previously acquired, Colorado selected Rick Berry) in 1997 Entry Draft, May 30, 1997.

JOKELA, Antti (YOH-keh-luh, AHN-tee) CAR.

Goaltender. Catches left. 5'11", 165 lbs. Born, Rauma, Finland, May 7, 1981.
(Carolina's 8th choice, 237th overall, in 1999 Entry Draft).

			Regular Season								Playoffs						
Season	Club	Lea	GP	W	L	T	Mins	GA	SO	Avg	GP	W	L	Mins	GA	SO	Avg
1998-99	Lukko Rauma-B	Finn-Jr.	8	....	....	....	480	26	0	3.25	....	....	....	....	....	....	....
	Lukko Rauma	Finn-Jr.	18	....	....	....	1038	66	1	3.81	....	....	....	....	....	....	....
99-2000	Lukko Rauma	Finn-Jr.	21	....	....	....	1196	71	0	3.56	....	....	....	....	....	....	....
2000-01	Jaa-Kothat	Finn-Jr.	42	20	20	2	2520	100	4	2.38	....	....	....	....	....	....	....
	Lukko Rauma	Finland	1	0	0	0	19	2	0	6.32	....	....	....	....	....	....	....

JOSEPH, Curtis (JOH-sehf, KUR-tihs) TOR.

Goaltender. Catches left. 5'11", 190 lbs. Born, Keswick, Ont., April 29, 1967.

			Regular Season								Playoffs						
Season	Club	Lea	GP	W	L	T	Mins	GA	SO	Avg	GP	W	L	Mins	GA	SO	Avg
1984-85	King City Dukes	OJHL-B	18	....	....	....	947	76	0	4.82	....	....	....	....	....	....	....
	Newmarket Flyers	OPJHL	2	1	1	0	120	16	0	8.00	....	....	....	....	....	....	....
1985-86	Richmond Hill	OPJHL	33	12	18	0	1716	156	1	5.45	....	....	....	....	....	....	....
1986-87	Richmond Hill	OPJHL	30	14	7	6	1764	128	1	4.35	....	....	....	....	....	....	....
1987-88	Notre Dame	SJHL	36	25	4	7	2174	94	1	2.59	....	....	....	....	....	....	....
1988-89	U. of Wisconsin	WCHA	38	21	11	5	2267	94	1	2.49	....	....	....	....	....	....	....
1989-90	Peoria Rivermen	IHL	23	10	8	2	1241	80	0	3.87	....	....	....	....	....	....	....
	St. Louis	**NHL**	**15**	**9**	**5**	**1**	**852**	**48**	**0**	**3.38**	**6**	**4**	**1**	**327**	**18**	**0**	**3.30**
1990-91	**St. Louis**	**NHL**	**30**	**16**	**10**	**2**	**1710**	**89**	**0**	**3.12**	....	....	....	....	....	....	....
1991-92	**St. Louis**	**NHL**	**60**	**27**	**20**	**10**	**3494**	**175**	**2**	**3.01**	**6**	**2**	**4**	**379**	**23**	**0**	**3.64**
1992-93	**St. Louis**	**NHL**	**68**	**29**	**28**	**9**	**3890**	**196**	**1**	**3.02**	**11**	**7**	**4**	**715**	**27**	***2**	**2.27**
1993-94	**St. Louis**	**NHL**	**71**	**36**	**23**	**11**	**4127**	**213**	**1**	**3.10**	**4**	**0**	**4**	**246**	**15**	**0**	**3.66**
1994-95	**St. Louis**	**NHL**	**36**	**20**	**10**	**1**	**1914**	**89**	**1**	**2.79**	**7**	**3**	**3**	**392**	**24**	**0**	**3.67**
1995-96	Las Vegas	IHL	15	12	2	1	874	29	1	1.99	....	....	....	....	....	....	....
	Edmonton	**NHL**	**34**	**15**	**16**	**2**	**1936**	**111**	**0**	**3.44**	....	....	....	....	....	....	....
1996-97	**Edmonton**	**NHL**	**72**	**32**	**29**	**9**	**4100**	**200**	**6**	**2.93**	**12**	**5**	**7**	**767**	**36**	**2**	**2.82**
1997-98	**Edmonton**	**NHL**	**71**	**29**	**31**	**9**	**4132**	**181**	**8**	**2.63**	**12**	**5**	**7**	**716**	**23**	**3**	**1.93**
1998-99	**Toronto**	**NHL**	**67**	**35**	**24**	**7**	**4001**	**171**	**3**	**2.56**	**17**	**9**	**8**	**1011**	**41**	**1**	**2.43**
99-2000	**Toronto**	**NHL**	**63**	**36**	**20**	**7**	**3801**	**158**	**4**	**2.49**	**12**	**6**	**6**	**729**	**25**	**1**	**2.06**
2000-01	**Toronto**	**NHL**	**68**	**33**	**27**	**8**	**4100**	**163**	**6**	**2.39**	**11**	**7**	**4**	**685**	**24**	**3**	**2.10**
	NHL Totals		**655**	**317**	**243**	**76**	**38057**	**1794**	**32**	**2.83**	**98**	**48**	**48**	**5967**	**256**	**12**	**2.57**

WCHA First All-Star Team (1989) • NCAA West Second All-American Team (1989) • Won King Clancy Memorial Trophy (2000) • Played in NHL All-Star Game (1994, 2000)

Signed as a free agent by **St. Louis**, June 16, 1989. Traded to **Edmonton** by **St. Louis** with the rights to Michael Grier for St. Louis' 1st round choices (previously acquired) in 1996 (Marty Reasoner) and 1997 (later traded to LA Kings - LA Kings selected Matt Zultek) Entry Drafts, August 4, 1995. Signed as a free agent by **Toronto**, July 15, 1998.

KALTIAINEN, Matti (KAL-tee-AY-nehn, MAT-tee) BOS.

Goaltender. Catches left. 6'2", 216 lbs. Born, Espoo, Finland, April 30, 1982.
(Boston's 3rd choice, 111th overall, in 2001 Entry Draft).

			Regular Season								Playoffs						
Season	Club	Lea	GP	W	L	T	Mins	GA	SO	Avg	GP	W	L	Mins	GA	SO	Avg
1998-99	Blues Espoo	Finn-Jr.	4	....	....	....	258	10	0	2.33	....	....	....	....	....	....	....
99-2000	Blues Espoo	Finn-Jr.	23	....	....	....	1337	56	0	2.51	4	2	2	244	15	0	3.93
2000-01	Blues Espoo	Finn-Jr.	25	....	....	....	1500	65	0	2.60	....	....	....	....	....	....	....

KHABIBULIN, Nikolai (khah-bee-BOO-lihn, NIH-koh-ligh) T.B.

Goaltender. Catches left. 6'1", 195 lbs. Born, Sverdlovsk, USSR, January 13, 1973.
(Winnipeg's 8th choice, 204th overall, in 1992 Entry Draft).

			Regular Season								Playoffs						
Season	Club	Lea	GP	W	L	T	Mins	GA	SO	Avg	GP	W	L	Mins	GA	SO	Avg
1991-92	CSKA Moscow	CIS	2	0	0	0	34	2	0	3.52	....	....	....	....	....	....	....
1992-93	CSKA Moscow	CIS	13	....	....	....	491	27	....	3.29	....	....	....	....	....	....	....
1993-94	CSKA Moscow	CIS	46	....	....	....	2625	116	....	2.65	3	....	....	193	11	....	3.42
	Russian Pens	IHL	12	2	7	2	639	47	0	4.41	....	....	....	....	....	....	....
1994-95	Springfield	AHL	23	9	9	3	1240	80	0	3.87	....	....	....	....	....	....	....
	Winnipeg	**NHL**	**26**	**8**	**9**	**4**	**1339**	**76**	**0**	**3.41**	....	....	....	....	....	....	....
1995-96	**Winnipeg**	**NHL**	**53**	**26**	**20**	**3**	**2914**	**152**	**2**	**3.13**	**6**	**2**	**4**	**359**	**19**	**0**	**3.18**
1996-97	**Phoenix**	**NHL**	**72**	**30**	**33**	**6**	**4091**	**193**	**7**	**2.83**	**7**	**3**	**4**	**426**	**15**	**1**	**2.11**
1997-98	**Phoenix**	**NHL**	**70**	**30**	**28**	**10**	**4026**	**184**	**4**	**2.74**	**4**	**2**	**1**	**185**	**13**	**0**	**4.22**
1998-99	**Phoenix**	**NHL**	**63**	**32**	**23**	**7**	**3657**	**130**	**8**	**2.13**	**7**	**3**	**4**	**449**	**18**	**0**	**2.41**
99-2000	Long Beach	IHL	33	21	11	1	1936	59	5	*1.83	5	2	3	321	15	0	2.81
2000-01	**Tampa Bay**	**NHL**	**2**	**1**	**1**	**0**	**123**	**6**	**0**	**2.93**	....	....	....	....	....	....	....
	NHL Totals		**286**	**127**	**114**	**30**	**16150**	**741**	**21**	**2.75**	**24**	**10**	**13**	**1419**	**65**	**1**	**2.75**

Shared James Gatschene Memorial Trophy (MVP - IHL) with Frederic Chabot (2000) • Played in NHL All-Star Game (1998, 1999)

Transferred to **Phoenix** after **Winnipeg** franchise relocated, July 1, 1996. • Missed entire 1999-2000 NHL season and majority of 2000-01 season after failing to come to contract terms with **Phoenix**. Signed as a free agent by **Long Beach** (IHL) with **Phoenix** retaining NHL rights, January 14, 2000. Traded to **Tampa Bay** by **Phoenix** with Stan Neckar for Mike Johnson, Paul Mara, Ruslan Zainullin and NY Islanders' 2nd round choice (previously acquired, Phoenix selected Matthew Spiller) in 2001 Entry Draft, March 5, 2001.

KHLOPTONOV, Denis (khloh-POHT-nahv, DEH-nihs) FLA.

Goaltender. Catches left. 6'4", 198 lbs. Born, Moscow, USSR, January 27, 1978.
(Florida's 8th choice, 209th overall, in 1996 Entry Draft).

			Regular Season								Playoffs						
Season	Club	Lea	GP	W	L	T	Mins	GA	SO	Avg	GP	W	L	Mins	GA	SO	Avg
1996-97	CSKA Moscow	Russia	21	....	....	....	1260	42	0	2.00	....	....	....	....	....	....	....
1997-98	CSKA Moscow	Russia	20	....	....	....	987	58	....	3.53	....	....	....	....	....	....	....
1998-99	Muskegon	UHL	37	21	8	2	1950	98	1	3.02	4	1	1	166	9	0	3.25
99-2000	CSKA Moscow	Russia	10	....	....	....	540	22	1	2.44	2	....	....	119	7	0	3.53
2000-01	CSKA Moscow	Russia	14	....	....	....	753	26	1	2.07	....	....	....	....	....	....	....

KIDD, Trevor (KIHD, TREH-vohr) FLA.

Goaltender. Catches left. 6'2", 190 lbs. Born, Dugald, Man., March 29, 1972.
(Calgary's 1st choice, 11th overall, in 1990 Entry Draft).

			Regular Season								Playoffs						
Season	Club	Lea	GP	W	L	T	Mins	GA	SO	Avg	GP	W	L	Mins	GA	SO	Avg
1987-88	Eastman Selects	MAHA	14	....	....	....	840	66	0	4.72	....	....	....	....	....	....	....
1988-89	Brandon	WHL	32	11	13	1	1509	102	0	4.06	....	....	....	....	....	....	....
1989-90	Brandon	WHL	*63	24	32	2	*3676	254	2	4.15	....	....	....	....	....	....	....
1990-91	Brandon	WHL	30	10	19	1	1730	117	0	4.06	....	....	....	....	....	....	....
	Spokane Chiefs	WHL	14	8	3	0	749	44	0	3.52	15	*14	1	926	32	2	*2.07
1991-92	Canada	Nt-Team	28	18	4	4	1349	79	2	3.51	....	....	....	....	....	....	....
	Canada	Olympics	1	1	0	0	60	0	1	0.00	....	....	....	....	....	....	....
	Calgary	**NHL**	**2**	**1**	**1**	**0**	**120**	**8**	**0**	**4.00**	....	....	....	....	....	....	....
1992-93	Salt Lake City	IHL	29	10	16	1	1696	111	1	3.93	....	....	....	....	....	....	....
1993-94	**Calgary**	**NHL**	**31**	**13**	**7**	**6**	**1614**	**85**	**0**	**3.16**	....	....	....	....	....	....	....
1994-95	**Calgary**	**NHL**	***43**	**22**	**14**	**6**	***2463**	**107**	**3**	**2.61**	**7**	**3**	**4**	**434**	**26**	**1**	**3.59**
1995-96	**Calgary**	**NHL**	**47**	**15**	**21**	**8**	**2570**	**119**	**3**	**2.78**	**2**	**0**	**1**	**83**	**9**	**0**	**6.51**
1996-97	**Calgary**	**NHL**	**55**	**21**	**23**	**6**	**2979**	**141**	**4**	**2.84**	....	....	....	....	....	....	....
1997-98	**Carolina**	**NHL**	**47**	**21**	**21**	**3**	**2685**	**97**	**3**	**2.17**	....	....	....	....	....	....	....
1998-99	**Carolina**	**NHL**	**25**	**7**	**10**	**6**	**1358**	**61**	**2**	**2.70**	....	....	....	....	....	....	....
99-2000	**Florida**	**NHL**	**28**	**14**	**11**	**2**	**1574**	**69**	**1**	**2.63**	....	....	....	....	....	....	....
	Louisville Panthers	AHL	1	0	1	0	60	5	0	5.04	....	....	....	....	....	....	....
2000-01	**Florida**	**NHL**	**42**	**10**	**23**	**6**	**2354**	**130**	**1**	**3.31**	....	....	....	....	....	....	....
	NHL Totals		**320**	**124**	**131**	**43**	**17717**	**817**	**17**	**2.77**	**9**	**3**	**5**	**517**	**35**	**1**	**4.06**

WHL East First All-Star Team (1990) • Canadian Major Junior Goaltender of the Year (1990)

Traded to **Carolina** by **Calgary** with Gary Roberts for Andrew Cassels and Jean-Sebastien Giguere, August 25, 1997. Claimed by **Atlanta** from **Carolina** in Expansion Draft, June 25, 1999. Traded to **Florida** by **Atlanta** for Gord Murphy, Herbert Vasiljevs, Daniel Tjarnqvist and Ottawa's 6th round choice (previously acquired, later traded to Dallas - Dallas selected Justin Cox) in 1999 Entry Draft, June 25, 1999.

KIELKUCKI, Marc (keel-KOO-kee, MAHRK) S.J.

Goaltender. Catches left. 6'4", 195 lbs. Born, Brooklyn Park, MN, June 5, 1979.

			Regular Season								Playoffs						
Season	Club	Lea	GP	W	L	T	Mins	GA	SO	Avg	GP	W	L	Mins	GA	SO	Avg
1996-97	Champlin Park	Hi-School					STATISTICS NOT AVAILABLE										
1997-98	Air Force Falcons	CHA	5	0	1	0	148	17	0	6.89	....	....	....	....	....	....	....
1998-99	Air Force Falcons	CHA	33	14	15	2	1729	96	5	3.33	....	....	....	....	....	....	....
99-2000	Air Force Falcons	CHA	37	18	16	2	2007	102	3	3.05	....	....	....	....	....	....	....
2000-01	Air Force Falcons	CHA	*35	*14	16	4	*2024	96	2	2.85	....	....	....	....	....	....	....

CHA Player of the Year (2001) • CHA First All-Star Team (2001)

Signed as a free agent by **San Jose**, July 5, 2001.

KIPRUSOFF, Miikka (KIHP-ruh-sohf, MEE-kah) S.J.

Goaltender. Catches left. 6'2", 190 lbs. Born, Turku, Finland, October 26, 1976.
(San Jose's 5th choice, 116th overall, in 1995 Entry Draft).

			Regular Season								Playoffs						
Season	Club	Lea	GP	W	L	T	Mins	GA	SO	Avg	GP	W	L	Mins	GA	SO	Avg
1994-95	TPS Turku	Finn-Jr.	31	....	....	....	1896	92	....	2.91	....	....	....	....	....	....	....
	TPS Turku	Finland	4	....	....	....	240	12	0	3.00	2	....	....	120	7	....	3.50
1995-96	TPS Turku	Finn-Jr.	3	....	....	....	180	9	....	3.00	....	....	....	....	....	....	....
	Kiekko-67 Turku	Finland-2	5	....	....	....	300	7	....	1.40	....	....	....	....	....	....	....
	TPS Turku	Finland	12	....	....	....	550	38	0	4.14	3	....	....	114	4	....	2.11
1996-97	AIK Solna	Sweden	42	....	....	....	2466	104	3	2.53	7	....	....	420	23	0	3.28
1997-98	AIK Solna	Sweden	42	....	....	....	2457	110	....	2.69	....	....	....	....	....	....	....
1998-99	TPS Turku	Finland	39	*26	6	6	2259	70	4	1.86	10	*9	1	580	15	*3	*1.55
99-2000	Kentucky	AHL	47	23	19	4	2759	114	3	2.48	5	1	3	239	13	0	3.27
2000-01	**San Jose**	**NHL**	**5**	**2**	**1**	**0**	**154**	**5**	**0**	**1.95**	**3**	**1**	**1**	**149**	**5**	**0**	**2.01**
	Kentucky	AHL	36	19	9	6	2038	76	2	2.24	....	....	....	....	....	....	....
	NHL Totals		**5**	**2**	**1**	**0**	**154**	**5**	**0**	**1.95**	**3**	**1**	**1**	**149**	**5**	**0**	**2.01**

KOCHAN, Dieter (KAH-kuhn, DEE-tuhr) T.B.

Goaltender. Catches left. 6'1", 180 lbs. Born, Saskatoon, Sask., May 11, 1974.
(Vancouver's 3rd choice, 98th overall, in 1993 Entry Draft).

			Regular Season								Playoffs						
Season	**Club**	**Lea**	**GP**	**W**	**L**	**T**	**Mins**	**GA**	**SO**	**Avg**	**GP**	**W**	**L**	**Mins**	**GA**	**SO**	**Avg**
1991-92	Sioux City	USHL	23	7	10	0	1131	100	0	5.31	....	....	....	....	....	....	....
1992-93	Kelowna Spartans	BCJHL	44	34	8	0	2582	137	1	3.18	15	12	3	927	48	1	3.10
1993-94	North-Michigan	WCHA	20	9	7	0	985	57	2	3.47	....	....	....	....	....	....	....
1994-95	North-Michigan	WCHA	29	8	17	3	1512	107	0	4.25	....	....	....	....	....	....	....
1995-96	North-Michigan	WCHA	31	7	21	2	1627	123	0	4.54	....	....	....	....	....	....	....
1996-97	North-Michigan	WCHA	26	8	15	2	1528	99	0	3.89	....	....	....	....	....	....	....
1997-98	Louisville	ECHL	18	7	9	2	980	61	1	3.73	....	....	....	....	....	....	....
1998-99	Binghamton	UHL	40	18	16	5	2322	115	2	2.97	4	1	2	208	9	0	2.60
99-2000	Binghamton	UHL	43	29	11	3	2544	110	4	2.59	....	....	....	....	....	....	....
	Orlando	IHL	4	4	0	0	240	4	1	1.00	....	....	....	....	....	....	....
	Springfield	AHL	2	1	1	0	120	5	1	2.50	....	....	....	....	....	....	....
	Tampa Bay	**NHL**	**5**	**1**	**4**	**0**	**238**	**17**	**0**	**4.29**	....	....	....	....	....	....	....
	Grand Rapids	IHL	2	1	0	1	93	1	0	0.64	....	....	....	....	....	....	....
2000-01	**Tampa Bay**	**NHL**	**10**	**0**	**3**	**0**	**314**	**18**	**0**	**3.44**	....	....	....	....	....	....	....
	Detroit Vipers	IHL	49	13	28	3	2606	154	0	3.55	....	....	....	....	....	....	....
	NHL Totals		**15**	**1**	**7**	**0**	**552**	**35**	**0**	**3.80**	....	....	....	....	....	....	....

UHL Second All-Star Team (2000) • Scored a goal vs. Winston-Salem (ECHL), January 5, 1998.

Signed as a free agent by **Tampa Bay**, March 27, 2000.

KOLZIG, Olaf (KOHL-zihg, OH-lahf) WSH.

Goaltender. Catches left. 6'3", 225 lbs. Born, Johannesburg, South Africa, April 9, 1970.
(Washington's 1st choice, 19th overall, in 1989 Entry Draft).

			Regular Season								Playoffs						
Season	**Club**	**Lea**	**GP**	**W**	**L**	**T**	**Mins**	**GA**	**SO**	**Avg**	**GP**	**W**	**L**	**Mins**	**GA**	**SO**	**Avg**
1986-87	Abbottsford Pilots	BCAHA	17	5	9	0	857	81	0	3.65	....	....	....	....	....	....	....
1987-88	New Westminster	WHL	15	6	5	0	650	48	1	4.43	3	0	3	149	11	0	4.43
1988-89	Tri-City Americans	WHL	30	16	10	2	1671	97	1	*3.48	....	....	....	....	....	....	....
1989-90	**Washington**	**NHL**	**2**	**0**	**2**	**0**	**120**	**12**	**0**	**6.00**	....	....	....	....	....	....	....
	Tri-City Americans	WHL	48	27	27	3	2504	250	1	4.38	6	4	0	318	27	0	5.09
1990-91	Baltimore	AHL	26	10	12	1	1367	72	0	3.16	....	....	....	....	....	....	....
	Hampton Roads	ECHL	21	11	9	1	1248	71	2	3.41	3	1	2	180	14	0	4.66
1991-92	Baltimore	AHL	28	5	17	2	1503	105	1	4.19	....	....	....	....	....	....	....
	Hampton Roads	ECHL	14	11	3	0	847	41	0	2.90	....	....	....	....	....	....	....
1992-93	**Washington**	**NHL**	**1**	**0**	**0**	**0**	**20**	**2**	**0**	**6.00**	....	....	....	....	....	....	....
	Rochester	AHL	49	25	16	4	2737	168	0	3.68	*17	9	8	*1040	61	0	3.52
1993-94	**Washington**	**NHL**	**7**	**0**	**3**	**0**	**224**	**20**	**0**	**5.36**	....	....	....	....	....	....	....
	Portland Pirates	AHL	29	16	8	5	1725	88	3	3.06	17	*12	5	1035	44	0	*2.55
1994-95	**Washington**	**NHL**	**14**	**2**	**8**	**2**	**724**	**30**	**0**	**2.49**	**2**	**1**	**0**	**44**	**1**	**0**	**1.36**
	Portland Pirates	AHL	2	1	0	1	125	3	0	1.44	....	....	....	....	....	....	....
1995-96	**Washington**	**NHL**	**18**	**4**	**8**	**2**	**897**	**46**	**0**	**3.08**	**5**	**2**	**3**	**341**	**11**	**0**	***1.94**
	Portland Pirates	AHL	5	5	0	0	300	7	1	1.40	....	....	....	....	....	....	....
1996-97	**Washington**	**NHL**	**29**	**8**	**15**	**4**	**1645**	**71**	**2**	**2.59**	....	....	....	....	....	....	....
1997-98	**Washington**	**NHL**	**64**	**33**	**18**	**10**	**3788**	**139**	**5**	**2.20**	**21**	**12**	**9**	**1351**	**44**	***4**	**1.95**
	Germany	Olympics	2	2	0	0	120	2	1	1.00	....	....	....	....	....	....	....
1998-99	**Washington**	**NHL**	**64**	**26**	**31**	**3**	**3586**	**154**	**4**	**2.58**	....	....	....	....	....	....	....
99-2000	**Washington**	**NHL**	**73**	**41**	**20**	**11**	***4371**	**163**	**5**	**2.24**	**5**	**1**	**4**	**284**	**16**	**0**	**3.38**
2000-01	**Washington**	**NHL**	**72**	**37**	**26**	**8**	**4279**	**177**	**5**	**2.48**	**6**	**2**	**4**	**375**	**14**	**1**	**2.24**
	NHL Totals		**344**	**151**	**131**	**40**	**19654**	**814**	**21**	**2.48**	**39**	**18**	**20**	**2395**	**86**	**5**	**2.15**

WHL West Second All-Star Team (1989) • Shared Harry "Hap" Holmes Trophy (fewest goals against - AHL) with Byron Dafoe (1994) • Won Jack Butterfield Trophy (Playoff MVP - AHL) (1994) • NHL First All-Star Team (2000) • Won Vezina Trophy (2000) • Played in NHL All-Star Game (1998, 2000)

• Scored a goal while with Tri-City (WHL), November 29, 1989.

KONSTANTINOV, Evgeny (kohn-stahn-TEE-nahf, EHV-jeh-nee) T.B.

Goaltender. Catches left. 6', 176 lbs. Born, Kazan, USSR, March 29, 1981.
(Tampa Bay's 2nd choice, 67th overall, in 1999 Entry Draft).

			Regular Season								Playoffs						
Season	**Club**	**Lea**	**GP**	**W**	**L**	**T**	**Mins**	**GA**	**SO**	**Avg**	**GP**	**W**	**L**	**Mins**	**GA**	**SO**	**Avg**
1997-98	Ak Bars Kazan-2	Russia-3	34	....	....	....	2040	129	....	3.79	....	....	....	....	....	....	....
1998-99	Ak Bars Kazan-2	Russia-4	17	....	....	....	1020	38	....	2.24	....	....	....	....	....	....	....
99-2000	Ak Bars Kazan	Russia	2	....	....	....	59	5	0	5.08	....	....	....	....	....	....	....
2000-01	Detroit Vipers	IHL	27	4	15	2	1197	85	0	4.26	....	....	....	....	....	....	....
	Louisiana	ECHL	8	4	4	0	458	21	0	2.75	12	5	6	637	32	0	3.01

• Played 24 seconds of game vs. **Colorado**, December 18, 2000.

KOSTUR, Matus (KAW-stuhr, ma-TOOSH) N.J.

Goaltender. Catches left. 6'2", 185 lbs. Born, Banska Bystrica, Czech., March 28, 1980.
(New Jersey's 10th choice, 164th overall, in 2000 Entry Draft).

			Regular Season								Playoffs						
Season	**Club**	**Lea**	**GP**	**W**	**L**	**T**	**Mins**	**GA**	**SO**	**Avg**	**GP**	**W**	**L**	**Mins**	**GA**	**SO**	**Avg**
1997-98	Banska Bystrica	Slovak-Jr.	36	....	....	....	2152	120	0	3.35	....	....	....	....	....	....	....
1998-99	Banska Bystrica	Slovakia	3	....	....	....	133	9	0	4.06	....	....	....	....	....	....	....
99-2000	HKm Zvolen	Slovak-2	10	....	....	....	538	32	0	3.57	....	....	....	....	....	....	....
	HKm Zvolen	Slovakia	20	....	....	....	768	36	0	2.81	2	0	0	41	3	0	4.39
2000-01	HC Nitra	Slovak-2	20	18	1	1	1132	24	4	1.53	....	....	....	....	....	....	....
	HKm Zvolen	Slovakia	3	....	....	....	110	11	0	6.00	....	....	....	....	....	....	....

KOTYK, Seamus (koh-TIHK, SHAY-muhs) S.J.

Goaltender. Catches left. 5'11", 187 lbs. Born, London, Ont., October 7, 1980.
(Boston's 5th choice, 147th overall, in 1999 Entry Draft).

			Regular Season								Playoffs						
Season	**Club**	**Lea**	**GP**	**W**	**L**	**T**	**Mins**	**GA**	**SO**	**Avg**	**GP**	**W**	**L**	**Mins**	**GA**	**SO**	**Avg**
1996-97	Stratford Cullitons	OJHL-B	28	....	....	....	1615	105	0	3.82	....	....	....	....	....	....	....
1997-98	Ottawa 67's	OHL	31	13	5	5	1422	63	4	2.66	7	3	2	332	11	0	1.99
1998-99	Ottawa 67's	OHL	41	26	7	4	2314	92	5	2.39	5	3	2	338	13	0	*2.31
99-2000	Ottawa 67's	OHL	26	12	6	2	1241	65	1	3.14	....	....	....	....	....	....	....
2000-01	Ottawa 67's	OHL	55	24	20	7	3087	141	2	2.74	*20	*16	4	*1157	46	*3	2.39

Signed as a free agent by **San Jose**, July 23, 2001.

KOWALSKI, Craig (koh-WAHL-skee, KRAYG) CAR.

Goaltender. Catches left. 5'9", 190 lbs. Born, Warren, MI, January 15, 1981.
(Carolina's 6th choice, 235th overall, in 2000 Entry Draft).

			Regular Season								Playoffs						
Season	**Club**	**Lea**	**GP**	**W**	**L**	**T**	**Mins**	**GA**	**SO**	**Avg**	**GP**	**W**	**L**	**Mins**	**GA**	**SO**	**Avg**
1998-99	Det-Compuware	NAJHL	42	*34	7	6	2733	96	3	*2.10	7	*7	0	420	13	1	*1.86
99-2000	Det-Compuware	NAJHL	49	33	12	3	2850	113	4	2.38	5	2	3	334	13	0	2.34
2000-01	Northern Michigan	CCHA	19	7	8	4	1078	49	1	2.73	....	....	....	....	....	....	....

NAJHL First All-Star Team (1998, 1999) • Won NAJHL Goaltender of the Year Award (1999)

KRAHN, Brent (KRAWN, BREHNT) CGY.

Goaltender. Catches left. 6'4", 200 lbs. Born, Winnipeg, Man., April 2, 1982.
(Calgary's 1st choice, 9th overall, in 2000 Entry Draft).

			Regular Season								Playoffs						
Season	**Club**	**Lea**	**GP**	**W**	**L**	**T**	**Mins**	**GA**	**SO**	**Avg**	**GP**	**W**	**L**	**Mins**	**GA**	**SO**	**Avg**
1997-98	Pembina Valley	MMHL	22	20	0	1	1265	40	3	1.90	2	2	0	120	2	1	1.00
1998-99	Pembina Valley	MMHL	13	10	3	0	770	30	2	2.34	....	....	....	....	....	....	....
99-2000	Calgary Hitmen	WHL	39	33	6	0	2315	92	4	2.38	5	2	2	266	13	0	2.93
2000-01	Calgary Hitmen	WHL	37	22	10	3	2087	104	1	2.99	....	....	....	....	....	....	....

KULIKOV, Vladimir (kuhl-ee-KAHF, vla-DIH-meer) TOR.

Goaltender. Catches left. 5'11", 170 lbs. Born, Moscow, USSR, May 28, 1981.
(Toronto's 7th choice, 211th overall, in 1999 Entry Draft).

			Regular Season								Playoffs						
Season	**Club**	**Lea**	**GP**	**W**	**L**	**T**	**Mins**	**GA**	**SO**	**Avg**	**GP**	**W**	**L**	**Mins**	**GA**	**SO**	**Avg**
1997-98	Meadville Bulldogs	H.S.	40	32	6	2	2400	72	2	1.79	....	....	....	....	....	....	....
1998-99	HC Moscow	Russia-2	14	....	....	....	848	39	....	2.76	9	....	....	540	21	0	2.33
99-2000	Kesklinna HK	Estonia					STATISTICS NOT AVAILABLE										
2000-01	Memphis	CHL	8	2	2	1	335	25	0	4.48	....	....	....	....	....	....	....

LABARBERA, Jason (lah-BAR-buhr-uh, JAY-suhn) NYR

Goaltender. Catches left. 6'2", 205 lbs. Born, Prince George, B.C., January 18, 1980.
(NY Rangers' 3rd choice, 66th overall, in 1998 Entry Draft).

			Regular Season								Playoffs						
Season	**Club**	**Lea**	**GP**	**W**	**L**	**T**	**Mins**	**GA**	**SO**	**Avg**	**GP**	**W**	**L**	**Mins**	**GA**	**SO**	**Avg**
1995-96	Prince George	BCAHA	31	....	....	....	1860	83	0	2.68	....	....	....	....	....	....	....
1996-97	Tri-City Americans	WHL	2	1	0	0	63	4	0	3.81	....	....	....	....	....	....	....
	Portland	WHL	9	5	1	1	443	18	0	2.44	....	....	....	....	....	....	....
1997-98	Portland	WHL	23	18	4	0	1305	72	1	3.31	....	....	....	....	....	....	....
1998-99	Portland	WHL	51	18	23	9	2991	170	4	3.41	4	0	4	252	19	0	4.52
99-2000	Portland	WHL	34	8	24	2	2005	123	1	3.68	....	....	....	....	....	....	....
	Spokane Chiefs	WHL	21	12	6	2	1146	50	0	2.62	9	6	1	435	18	1	2.48
2000-01	**NY Rangers**	**NHL**	**1**	**0**	**0**	**0**	**10**	**0**	**0**	**0.00**	....	....	....	....	....	....	....
	Hartford	AHL	4	1	1	0	156	12	0	4.61	....	....	....	....	....	....	....
	Charlotte	ECHL	35	18	10	7	2100	112	1	3.20	2	1	1	143	5	0	2.09
	NHL Totals		**1**	**0**	**0**	**0**	**10**	**0**	**0**	**0.00**	....	....	....	....	....	....	....

LABBE, Jean-Francois (lah-BAY, ZHAWN-fran-SWUH) CBJ

Goaltender. Catches left. 5'10", 172 lbs. Born, Sherbrooke, Que., June 15, 1972.

			Regular Season								Playoffs						
Season	**Club**	**Lea**	**GP**	**W**	**L**	**T**	**Mins**	**GA**	**SO**	**Avg**	**GP**	**W**	**L**	**Mins**	**GA**	**SO**	**Avg**
1988-89	Montreal L'est	QAAA	29	*22	7	0	1764	94	1	3.20	5	1	4	333	19	0	3.42
1989-90	Trois-Rivieres	QMJHL	28	13	10	0	1499	106	1	4.24	3	1	1	132	8	0	3.64
1990-91	Trois-Rivieres	QMJHL	54	*35	14	0	2870	158	5	3.30	5	1	4	230	19	0	4.96
1991-92	Trois-Rivieres	QMJHL	48	*31	13	3	2749	142	1	3.10	*15	*10	3	791	33	*1	*2.50
1992-93	Hull Olympiques	QMJHL	46	26	18	2	2701	156	2	3.46	10	6	3	518	24	*1	*2.78
1993-94	Thunder Bay	ColHL	52	*35	11	4	*2900	150	*2	*3.10	8	7	1	493	18	*2	*2.19
	P.E.I. Senators	AHL	7	4	3	0	389	22	0	3.39	....	....	....	....	....	....	....
1994-95	P.E.I. Senators	AHL	32	13	14	3	1817	94	2	3.10	....	....	....	....	....	....	....
1995-96	Cornwall Aces	AHL	55	25	21	5	2972	144	3	2.91	8	3	5	471	21	1	2.68
1996-97	Hershey Bears	AHL	66	*34	22	9	3811	160	*6	*2.52	*23	*14	8	*1364	59	1	2.60
1997-98	Hamilton Bulldogs	AHL	52	24	17	11	3138	149	2	2.85	7	3	4	413	20	0	2.90
1998-99	Hartford	AHL	*59	28	26	3	*3392	182	2	3.22	7	3	4	447	22	0	2.95
99-2000	**NY Rangers**	**NHL**	**1**	**0**	**1**	**0**	**60**	**3**	**0**	**3.00**	....	....	....	....	....	....	....
	Hartford	AHL	49	27	13	7	2853	120	1	2.52	*22	*15	7	*1320	48	3	2.18
2000-01	Hartford	AHL	8	4	2	1	394	20	0	3.04	....	....	....	....	....	....	....
	Syracuse Crunch	AHL	37	15	15	5	2201	105	2	2.86	5	2	3	323	18	0	3.34
	NHL Totals		**1**	**0**	**1**	**0**	**60**	**3**	**0**	**3.00**	....	....	....	....	....	....	....

QMJHL First All-Star Team (1992) • ColHL First All-Star Team (1994) • Won ColHL Rookie of the Year Award (1994) • Won ColHL Outstanding Goaltender Award (1994) • Won ColHL Playoff MVP Award (1994) • AHL First All-Star Team (1997) • Won Harry "Hap" Holmes Memorial Trophy (fewest goals against - AHL) (1997) • Won Baz Bastien Memorial Trophy (Top Goaltender - AHL) (1997) • Won Les Cunningham Award (MVP - AHL) (1997) • Shared Harry "Hap" Holmes Memorial Trophy (fewest goals against - AHL) with Milan Hnilicka (2000) • Scored a goal while with Hartford (AHL) vs. Quebec (AHL), February 5, 2000.

Signed as a free agent by **Ottawa**, May 12, 1994. Traded to **Colorado** by **Ottawa** for future considerations, September 20, 1995. Signed as a free agent by **Edmonton**, September 2, 1997. Signed as a free agent by **NY Rangers**, July 30, 1998. Traded to **Columbus** by **NY Rangers** for Bert Robertsson, November 9, 2000.

LAJEUNESSE, Simon (lah-ZHUH-nehs, SIGH-mohn) OTT.

Goaltender. Catches left. 6', 175 lbs. Born, Quebec City, Que., January 22, 1981.
(Ottawa's 2nd choice, 48th overall, in 1999 Entry Draft).

			Regular Season								Playoffs						
Season	**Club**	**Lea**	**GP**	**W**	**L**	**T**	**Mins**	**GA**	**SO**	**Avg**	**GP**	**W**	**L**	**Mins**	**GA**	**SO**	**Avg**
1996-97	Cap-de-Madelaine	QAAA	23	15	5	1	1300	89	0	4.11	4	1	3	240	26	0	4.72
1997-98	Moncton Alpines	QMJHL	19	5	6	3	925	51	1	3.31	2	0	0	1	0	0	0.00
1998-99	Moncton Wildcats	QMJHL	36	18	9	3	1993	98	1	2.95	1	0	0	43	2	0	2.79
99-2000	Moncton Wildcats	QMJHL	55	31	15	1	2922	127	6	2.61	16	9	6	910	56	1	3.69
2000-01	Acadie-Bathurst	QMJHL	36	10	19	2	1879	121	1	3.86	....	....	....	....	....	....	....
	Val-d'Or Foreurs	QMJHL	21	16	3	1	1159	54	1	2.80	14	8	4	760	52	0	4.10

QMJHL First All-Star Team (2000)

Traded to **Val d'Or** by **Acadie-Bathurst** with Acadie-Bathurst's 4th round choice (Mathieu Curadeau) in 2001 QMJHL Midget Draft for Antoine Bergeron, J-F Laniel, Eric Labelle and future considerations, January 7, 2001.

LALIME, Patrick (lah-LEEM, PAT-rihk) OTT.

Goaltender. Catches left. 6'3", 185 lbs. Born, St-Bonaventure, Que., July 7, 1974.
(Pittsburgh's 6th choice, 156th overall, in 1993 Entry Draft).

			Regular Season								Playoffs						
Season	**Club**	**Lea**	**GP**	**W**	**L**	**T**	**Mins**	**GA**	**SO**	**Avg**	**GP**	**W**	**L**	**Mins**	**GA**	**SO**	**Avg**
1990-91	D'abitibi Forestiers	QAAA	26	9	17	0	1595	151	0	5.81	....	....	....	....	....	....	....
1991-92	Shawinigan	QMJHL	6	....	....	....	272	25	0	5.50	....	....	....	....	....	....	....
1992-93	Shawinigan	QMJHL	44	10	24	4	2467	192	0	4.67	....	....	....	....	....	....	....
1993-94	Shawinigan	QMJHL	48	22	20	0	2733	192	1	4.22	5	1	3	223	25	0	6.73
1994-95	Hampton Roads	ECHL	26	15	7	3	1470	82	2	3.35	....	....	....	....	....	....	....
	Cleveland	IHL	23	7	10	4	1230	91	0	4.44	....	....	....	....	....	....	....
1995-96	Cleveland	IHL	41	20	12	7	2314	149	0	3.86	....	....	....	....	....	....	....
1996-97	**Pittsburgh**	**NHL**	**39**	**21**	**12**	**2**	**2058**	**101**	**3**	**2.94**	....	....	....	....	....	....	....
	Cleveland	IHL	14	6	6	2	834	45	1	3.24	....	....	....	....	....	....	....
1997-98	Grand Rapids	IHL	31	10	10	9	1749	76	2	2.61	1	0	1	77	4	0	3.11
1998-99	Kansas City	IHL	*66	*39	20	4	*3789	190	2	3.01	3	1	2	179	6	1	2.01
99-2000	**Ottawa**	**NHL**	**38**	**19**	**14**	**3**	**2038**	**79**	**3**	**2.33**	....	....	....	....	....	....	....
2000-01	**Ottawa**	**NHL**	**60**	**36**	**19**	**5**	**3607**	**141**	**7**	**2.35**	**4**	**0**	**4**	**251**	**10**	**0**	**2.39**
	NHL Totals		**137**	**76**	**45**	**10**	**7703**	**321**	**13**	**2.50**	**4**	**0**	**4**	**251**	**10**	**0**	**2.39**

NHL All-Rookie Team (1997) • IHL First All-Star Team (1999)

Rights traded to **Anaheim** by **Pittsburgh** for Sean Pronger, March 24, 1998. Traded to **Ottawa** by **Anaheim** for Ted Donato and the rights to Antti-Jussi Niemi, June 18, 1999.

LAMOTHE, Marc (luh-MAWTH, MAHRK)

Goaltender. Catches left. 6'2", 210 lbs. Born, New Liskeard, Ont., February 27, 1974.
(Montreal's 6th choice, 92nd overall, in 1992 Entry Draft).

			Regular Season								Playoffs						
Season	**Club**	**Lea**	**GP**	**W**	**L**	**T**	**Mins**	**GA**	**SO**	**Avg**	**GP**	**W**	**L**	**Mins**	**GA**	**SO**	**Avg**
1990-91	Ottawa Jr. Sens	OCJHL	25	13	7	0	1220	82	1	4.03	....	....	....	....	....	....	....
1991-92	Kingston	OHL	42	10	25	2	2378	189	1	4.77	....	....	....	....	....	....	....
1992-93	Kingston	OHL	45	23	12	6	2489	162	1	3.91	15	8	5	753	48	1	3.82
1993-94	Kingston	OHL	48	23	20	5	2828	177	*2	3.76	6	2	2	224	12	0	3.21
1994-95	Fredericton	AHL	9	2	5	0	428	32	0	4.48	....	....	....	....	....	....	....
	Wheeling	ECHL	13	9	2	1	737	38	0	3.10	....	....	....	....	....	....	....
1995-96	Fredericton	AHL	23	5	9	3	1166	73	1	3.76	3	1	2	161	9	0	3.36
1996-97	Indianapolis Ice	IHL	38	20	14	4	2271	100	1	2.64	1	0	0	20	1	0	3.00
1997-98	Indianapolis Ice	IHL	31	18	10	2	1772	72	3	2.44	4	1	3	177	10	0	3.38
1998-99	Indianapolis Ice	IHL	32	9	16	6	1823	115	1	3.78	6	3	3	338	10	*2	1.78
99-2000	**Chicago**	**NHL**	**2**	**1**	**1**	**0**	**116**	**10**	**0**	**5.17**	....	....	....	....	....	....	....
	Cleveland	IHL	44	19	18	4	2455	112	2	2.74	4	2	2	325	12	0	2.21
2000-01	Syracuse Crunch	AHL	42	17	15	7	2323	112	2	2.89	....	....	....	....	....	....	....
	NHL Totals		**2**	**1**	**1**	**0**	**116**	**10**	**0**	**5.17**	....	....	....	....	....	....	....

Signed as a free agent by **Chicago**, September 26, 1996.

LANGKOW, Scott (LAING-kow, SKAWT)

Goaltender. Catches left. 5'11", 190 lbs. Born, Sherwood Park, Alta., April 21, 1975.
(Winnipeg's 2nd choice, 31st overall, in 1993 Entry Draft).

			Regular Season								Playoffs						
Season	**Club**	**Lea**	**GP**	**W**	**L**	**T**	**Mins**	**GA**	**SO**	**Avg**	**GP**	**W**	**L**	**Mins**	**GA**	**SO**	**Avg**
1990-91	Sherwood Park	AMHL	32	....	....	....	1920	128	0	4.00	....	....	....	....	....	....	....
1991-92	Abbotsford Pilots	PIJHL					STATISTICS NOT AVAILABLE										
	Portland	WHL	1	0	0	0	33	2	0	3.46	....	....	....	....	....	....	....
1992-93	Portland	WHL	34	24	8	2	2064	119	2	3.46	9	6	3	535	31	0	3.48
1993-94	Portland	WHL	39	27	9	1	2302	121	2	3.15	10	6	4	600	34	0	3.40
1994-95	Portland	WHL	63	20	36	5	*3638	240	1	3.96	8	3	5	510	30	0	3.53
1995-96	**Winnipeg**	**NHL**	**1**	**0**	**0**	**0**	**6**	**0**	**0**	**0.00**	....	....	....	....	....	....	....
	Springfield	AHL	39	18	15	6	2329	116	3	2.99	7	4	2	393	23	0	3.51
1996-97	Springfield	AHL	33	15	9	7	1929	85	0	2.64	....	....	....	....	....	....	....
1997-98	**Phoenix**	**NHL**	**3**	**0**	**1**	**1**	**137**	**10**	**0**	**4.38**	....	....	....	....	....	....	....
	Springfield	AHL	51	30	13	5	2874	128	3	2.67	4	1	3	216	14	0	3.88
1998-99	**Phoenix**	**NHL**	**1**	**0**	**0**	**0**	**35**	**3**	**0**	**5.14**	....	....	....	....	....	....	....
	Las Vegas	IHL	27	7	14	2	1402	97	1	4.15	....	....	....	....	....	....	....
	Utah Grizzlies	IHL	21	10	9	2	1227	59	1	2.89	....	....	....	....	....	....	....
99-2000	**Atlanta**	**NHL**	**15**	**3**	**11**	**0**	**765**	**55**	**0**	**4.31**	....	....	....	....	....	....	....
	Orlando	IHL	27	14	8	2	1487	57	4	2.30	6	2	3	381	16	0	2.52
2000-01	Orlando	IHL	4	1	1	1	187	9	0	2.88	....	....	....	....	....	....	....
	Mobile Mysticks	ECHL	6	2	4	0	358	23	0	3.86	....	....	....	....	....	....	....
	Cincinnati Ducks	AHL	15	6	4	4	838	44	1	3.15	3	1	1	142	7	0	2.95
	NHL Totals		**20**	**3**	**12**	**1**	**943**	**68**	**0**	**4.33**	....	....	....	....	....	....	....

WHL West Second All-Star Team (1994, 1995) • Shared Harry "Hap" Holmes Memorial Trophy (fewest goals against - AHL) with Manny Legace (1996) • AHL First All-Star Team (1998) • Won Baz Bastien Memorial Trophy (Top Goaltender - AHL) (1998)

Transferred to **Phoenix** after **Winnipeg** franchise relocated, July 1, 1996. Traded to **Atlanta** by **Phoenix** for future considerations, June 25, 1999. Traded to **Anaheim** by **Atlanta** with Sergei Vyshedkevich for Ladislav Kohn, February 9, 2001.

LANICEK, Michal (LAN-ih-CHEHK, MIHK-uhl) T.B.

Goaltender. Catches left. 6'1", 172 lbs. Born, Benesov, Czech., July 6, 1981.
(Tampa Bay's 6th choice, 148th overall, in 1999 Entry Draft).

			Regular Season								Playoffs						
Season	**Club**	**Lea**	**GP**	**W**	**L**	**T**	**Mins**	**GA**	**SO**	**Avg**	**GP**	**W**	**L**	**Mins**	**GA**	**SO**	**Avg**
1996-97	Slavia Praha-Jr.	Cze-Rep	22	....	....	....	1260	42	....	2.00	....	....	....	....	....	....	....
1997-98	Slavia Praha-Jr.	Cze-Rep	39	....	....	....	2162	75	....	2.08	....	....	....	....	....	....	....
1998-99	Slavia Praha-Jr.	Cze-Rep	43	....	....	....	2412	87	....	2.16	....	....	....	....	....	....	....
99-2000	Slavia Praha-Jr.	Cze-Rep	18	....	....	....	1020	35	1	2.06	6	....	....	328	7	0	1.28
	HC Bili Liberec-2	Cze-Rep	4	....	....	....	109	11	0	6.06	....	....	....	....	....	....	....
	Berouni Medvedi-2	Cze-Rep	7	....	....	....	365	12	0	1.97	1	0	1	70	4	0	3.43
2000-01	HC Beroun-2	Cze-Rep	17	....	....	....	958	39	0	2.44	4	1	3	247	14	0	3.40

LAROCQUE, Michel (lah-RAWK, mih-SHEHL)

Goaltender. Catches left. 5'11", 200 lbs. Born, Lahr, West Germany, October 3, 1976.
(San Jose's 5th choice, 137th overall, in 1996 Entry Draft).

			Regular Season								Playoffs						
Season	**Club**	**Lea**	**GP**	**W**	**L**	**T**	**Mins**	**GA**	**SO**	**Avg**	**GP**	**W**	**L**	**Mins**	**GA**	**SO**	**Avg**
1995-96	Boston University	H-East	14	10	1	1	735	42	0	3.43	....	....	....	....	....	....	....
1996-97	Boston University	H-East	24	16	4	4	1466	58	0	*2.37	....	....	....	....	....	....	....
1997-98	Boston University	H-East	24	17	4	1	1370	50	1	2.19	....	....	....	....	....	....	....
1998-99	Boston University	H-East	35	14	18	3	2072	117	0	3.39	....	....	....	....	....	....	....
99-2000	Cleveland	IHL	1	0	0	1	60	2	0	2.00	....	....	....	....	....	....	....
	Wilkes-Barre	AHL	13	5	6	1	727	34	0	2.81	....	....	....	....	....	....	....
	Saint John Flames	AHL	4	2	1	1	243	8	0	1.98	....	....	....	....	....	....	....
	Greensboro	ECHL	4	1	3	0	229	20	0	5.24	....	....	....	....	....	....	....
2000-01	**Chicago**	**NHL**	**3**	**0**	**2**	**0**	**152**	**9**	**0**	**3.55**	....	....	....	....	....	....	....
	Norfolk Admirals	AHL	35	13	17	4	2087	96	2	2.76	5	2	3	304	13	0	2.57
	NHL Totals		**3**	**0**	**2**	**0**	**152**	**9**	**0**	**3.55**	....	....	....	....	....	....	....

Hockey East Second All-Star Team (1998) • Hockey East First All-Star Team (1999) • NCAA East Second All-American Team (1999)

Traded to **Chicago** by **San Jose** for Chicago's 5th round choice (Michael Pinc) in 2000 Entry Draft, August 23, 1999.

LASAK, Jan (LA-shak, YAN) NSH.

Goaltender. Catches left. 6'1", 204 lbs. Born, Zvolen, Czech., April 10, 1979.
(Nashville's 6th choice, 65th overall, in 1999 Entry Draft).

			Regular Season								Playoffs						
Season	**Club**	**Lea**	**GP**	**W**	**L**	**T**	**Mins**	**GA**	**SO**	**Avg**	**GP**	**W**	**L**	**Mins**	**GA**	**SO**	**Avg**
1996-97	HKm Zvolen-Jr.	Slovakia	49	....	....	....	2940	111	....	2.27	....	....	....	....	....	....	....
1997-98	HKm Zvolen-Jr.	Slovakia	48	....	....	....	2881	119	....	2.48	....	....	....	....	....	....	....
	HK Zilina-2	Slovakia	4	....	....	....	208	12	....	3.46	....	....	....	....	....	....	....
1998-99	HKm Zvolen-Jr.	Slovakia	43	....	....	....	2580	91	....	2.12	....	....	....	....	....	....	....
	HKm Zvolen	Slovakia	8	....	....	....	387	29	....	4.50	....	....	....	....	....	....	....
99-2000	Hampton Roads	ECHL	*59	*36	17	4	*3409	145	0	2.55	10	5	5	610	28	1	2.75
2000-01	Milwaukee	IHL	43	23	17	2	2439	106	1	2.61	3	0	1	60	5	0	4.97

ECHL First All-Star Team (2000) • Won ECHL Rookie of the Year Award (2000) • Won ECHL Top Goaltender Award (2000).

LECLAIRE, Pascal (lah-CLAIR, pas-CAL) CBJ

Goaltender. Catches left. 6'1", 185 lbs. Born, Repentigny, Que., November 7, 1982.
(Columbus' 1st choice, 8th overall, in 2001 Entry Draft).

			Regular Season								Playoffs						
Season	**Club**	**Lea**	**GP**	**W**	**L**	**T**	**Mins**	**GA**	**SO**	**Avg**	**GP**	**W**	**L**	**Mins**	**GA**	**SO**	**Avg**
1997-98	Cap-de-Madelaine	QAAA	26	6	17	3	1580	127	0	4.90	....	....	....	....	....	....	....
1998-99	Halifax	QMJHL	33	19	11	1	1828	96	2	3.15	1	0	0	17	2	0	7.06
99-2000	Halifax	QMJHL	31	16	8	4	1729	103	1	3.57	5	1	2	198	12	0	3.65
2000-01	Halifax	QMJHL	35	14	16	5	2111	126	1	3.58	2	0	2	109	10	0	5.49

LEGACE, Manny (LEH-gah-see, MAN-nee) DET.

Goaltender. Catches left. 5'9", 162 lbs. Born, Toronto, Ont., February 4, 1973.
(Hartford's 5th choice, 188th overall, in 1993 Entry Draft).

			Regular Season								Playoffs						
Season	**Club**	**Lea**	**GP**	**W**	**L**	**T**	**Mins**	**GA**	**SO**	**Avg**	**GP**	**W**	**L**	**Mins**	**GA**	**SO**	**Avg**
1987-88	Alliston Hornets	OJHL-C	16	7	9	0	960	83	0	5.17	....	....	....	....	....	....	....
1988-89	Vaughan Raiders	MTJHL	23	....	....	....	1303	92	1	4.24	....	....	....	....	....	....	....
1989-90	Vaughan Raiders	MTJHL	21	8	11	1	1180	89	1	4.53	....	....	....	....	....	....	....
	Thornhill T-Birds	MTJHL	8	3	3	2	480	30	0	3.75	....	....	....	....	....	....	....
1990-91	Niagara Falls	OHL	30	13	11	2	1515	107	0	4.24	4	1	1	119	10	0	5.04
1991-92	Niagara Falls	OHL	43	21	16	3	2384	143	0	3.60	14	8	5	791	56	0	4.25
1992-93	Niagara Falls	OHL	48	22	19	3	2630	171	0	3.90	4	0	4	240	18	0	4.50
1993-94	Canada	Nt-Team	16	8	6	0	859	36	2	2.51	....	....	....	....	....	....	....
1994-95	Springfield	AHL	39	12	17	6	2169	128	2	3.54	....	....	....	....	....	....	....
1995-96	Springfield	AHL	37	20	12	4	2196	83	*5	*2.27	4	1	3	220	18	0	4.91
1996-97	Springfield	AHL	36	17	14	5	2119	107	1	3.03	12	9	3	745	25	*2	2.01
	Richmond	ECHL	3	2	1	0	157	8	0	3.05	....	....	....	....	....	....	....
1997-98	Springfield	AHL	6	4	2	0	345	16	0	2.78	....	....	....	....	....	....	....
	Las Vegas	IHL	41	18	16	4	2106	111	1	3.16	4	1	3	237	16	0	4.05
1998-99	**Los Angeles**	**NHL**	**17**	**2**	**9**	**2**	**899**	**39**	**0**	**2.60**	....	....	....	....	....	....	....
	Long Beach	IHL	33	22	8	1	1796	67	2	2.24	6	4	2	338	9	0	*1.60
99-2000	**Detroit**	**NHL**	**4**	**4**	**0**	**0**	**240**	**11**	**0**	**2.75**	....	....	....	....	....	....	....
	Manitoba Moose	IHL	42	17	18	5	2409	104	2	2.59	2	0	2	141	7	0	2.97
2000-01	**Detroit**	**NHL**	**39**	**24**	**5**	**5**	**2136**	**73**	**2**	**2.05**	....	....	....	....	....	....	....
	NHL Totals		**60**	**30**	**14**	**7**	**3275**	**123**	**2**	**2.25**	....	....	....	....	....	....	....

OHL First All-Star Team (1993) • AHL First All-Star Team (1996) • Shared Harry "Hap" Holmes Memorial Trophy (fewest goals against - AHL) with Scott Langkow (1996) • Won Baz Bastien Memorial Trophy (Top Goaltender - AHL) (1996)

Rights transferred to **Carolina** after **Hartford** franchise relocated, June 25, 1997. Traded to **LA Kings** by **Carolina** for future considerations, July 31, 1998. Signed as a free agent by **Detroit**, August 9, 1999. Claimed on waivers by **Vancouver** from **Detroit**, September 30, 1999. Claimed on waivers by **Detroit** from **Vancouver**, October 13, 1999.

LEHTO, Mika (leh-TOH, MEE-kuh) PIT.

Goaltender. Catches left. 5'11", 172 lbs. Born, Vammala, Finland, April 12, 1979.
(Pittsburgh's 8th choice, 224th overall, in 1998 Entry Draft).

			Regular Season								Playoffs						
Season	**Club**	**Lea**	**GP**	**W**	**L**	**T**	**Mins**	**GA**	**SO**	**Avg**	**GP**	**W**	**L**	**Mins**	**GA**	**SO**	**Avg**
1997-98	Assat-Pori	Finn-Jr.	36	....	....	....	2160	103	2	2.86	....	....	....	....	....	....	....
	Assat-Pori	Finland	1	0	0	0	35	1	0	1.71	1	0	0	17	0	0	0.00
1998-99	Assat-Pori	Finn-Jr.	20	....	....	....	1202	68	....	3.39	....	....	....	....	....	....	....
	Assat-Pori	Finland	15	4	6	1	773	38	1	2.95	....	....	....	....	....	....	....
99-2000	Assat-Pori	Finland	23	4	11	3	1099	87	0	4.75	....	....	....	....	....	....	....
2000-01	JyP Jyvaskyla	Finland	41	12	20	8	2384	126	1	3.17	....	....	....	....	....	....	....

LEIGHTON, Michael (LAY-tohn, MIGH-kuhl) CHI.

Goaltender. Catches left. 6'2", 175 lbs. Born, Petrolia, Ont., May 19, 1981.
(Chicago's 5th choice, 165th overall, in 1999 Entry Draft).

			Regular Season								Playoffs						
Season	**Club**	**Lea**	**GP**	**W**	**L**	**T**	**Mins**	**GA**	**SO**	**Avg**	**GP**	**W**	**L**	**Mins**	**GA**	**SO**	**Avg**
1997-98	Petrolia Jets	OJHL-B	30	....	....	....	1583	87	2	3.30	....	....	....	....	....	....	....
1998-99	Windsor Spitfires	OHL	28	4	17	2	1389	112	0	4.84	3	0	1	80	10	0	7.50
99-2000	Windsor Spitfires	OHL	42	17	17	2	2272	118	1	3.12	12	5	6	616	32	0	3.12
2000-01	Windsor Spitfires	OHL	54	32	13	5	3035	138	2	2.73	9	4	5	519	27	1	3.12

LINDSAY, Evan (LIHND-say, EH-vihn) MTL.

Goaltender. Catches left. 6'2", 195 lbs. Born, Calgary, Alta., May 15, 1979.
(Montreal's 4th choice, 107th overall, in 1999 Entry Draft).

			Regular Season								Playoffs						
Season	**Club**	**Lea**	**GP**	**W**	**L**	**T**	**Mins**	**GA**	**SO**	**Avg**	**GP**	**W**	**L**	**Mins**	**GA**	**SO**	**Avg**
1995-96	Olds Grizzlys	AJHL	11	4	5	0	....	....	0	3.64	....	....	....	....	....	....	....
1996-97	Prince Albert	WHL	44	20	17	6	2651	153	1	3.46	4	0	4	240	16	0	4.00
1997-98	Prince Albert	WHL	52	14	30	4	3005	193	1	3.85	....	....	....	....	....	....	....
1998-99	Prince Albert	WHL	56	34	16	5	3334	158	1	2.84	14	9	5	780	43	1	3.31
99-2000	Prince Albert	WHL	54	17	30	5	3061	175	1	3.43	6	2	4	359	24	0	4.01
2000-01	Tallahassee	ECHL	17	8	7	2	1017	50	0	2.95	....	....	....	....	....	....	....
	Quebec Citadelles	AHL	1	0	0	0	2	0	0	0.00	....	....	....	....	....	....	....

• Re-entered NHL Entry Draft. Originally Calgary's 2nd choice, 32nd overall, in 1997 Entry Draft.

WHL East Second All-Star Team (1998, 1999)

LITTLE, Neil (LIHTL, NEEL) PHI.

Goaltender. Catches left. 6'1", 193 lbs. Born, Medicine Hat, Alta., December 18, 1971.
(Philadelphia's 10th choice, 226th overall, in 1991 Entry Draft).

			Regular Season								Playoffs						
Season	**Club**	**Lea**	**GP**	**W**	**L**	**T**	**Mins**	**GA**	**SO**	**Avg**	**GP**	**W**	**L**	**Mins**	**GA**	**SO**	**Avg**
1989-90	Estevan Bruins	SJHL	46	21	19	4	2707	150	1	3.32	....	....	....	....	....	....	....
1990-91	RPI Engineers	ECAC	18	9	8	0	1032	71	0	4.13	....	....	....	....	....	....	....
1991-92	RPI Engineers	ECAC	28	11	11	3	1532	96	0	3.76	....	....	....	....	....	....	....
1992-93	RPI Engineers	ECAC	*31	*19	9	3	*1801	88	0	2.93	....	....	....	....	....	....	....
1993-94	RPI Engineers	ECAC	27	16	7	4	1570	88	0	3.36	....	....	....	....	....	....	....
	Hershey Bears	AHL	1	0	0	0	18	1	0	3.33	....	....	....	....	....	....	....
1994-95	Hershey Bears	AHL	19	5	7	3	919	60	0	3.91	....	....	....	....	....	....	....
	Johnstown Chiefs	ECHL	16	7	6	1	897	55	0	3.68	3	0	2	145	11	0	4.55
1995-96	Hershey Bears	AHL	48	21	18	6	2680	149	0	3.34	1	0	1	60	4	0	4.02
1996-97	Philadelphia	AHL	54	31	12	7	3007	145	0	2.89	10	6	4	620	20	1	*1.94
1997-98	Philadelphia	AHL	51	*31	11	7	2960	145	0	2.94	*20	*15	5	*1193	48	*3	2.41
1998-99	Grand Rapids	IHL	50	18	21	5	2740	144	3	3.15	....	....	....	....	....	....	....
99-2000	Philadelphia	AHL	51	26	18	2	2830	143	1	3.03	5	2	3	298	15	0	3.02
2000-01	Philadelphia	AHL	*58	22	27	4	3117	148	2	2.85	10	5	5	631	23	1	2.19

ECAC First All-Star Team (1993) • NCAA East Second All-American Team (1993)

LIV, Stefan (LIHV, STEH-fuhn) DET.

Goaltender. Catches left. 6', 172 lbs. Born, Jonkoping, Sweden, December 21, 1980.
(Detroit's 3rd choice, 102nd overall, in 2000 Entry Draft).

			Regular Season								Playoffs						
Season	**Club**	**Lea**	**GP**	**W**	**L**	**T**	**Mins**	**GA**	**SO**	**Avg**	**GP**	**W**	**L**	**Mins**	**GA**	**SO**	**Avg**
1997-98	HV-Jonkoping	Swede-Jr.	17	....	....	....	1020	47	....	2.76	....	....	....	....	....	....	....
1998-99	HV-Jonkoping	Sweden					DID NOT PLAY – SPARE GOALTENDER										
99-2000	HV-Jonkoping	Swede-Jr.	10	....	....	....	600	17	2	1.70	....	....	....	....	....	....	....
	Tranas AIF	Swede-2	9	....	....	....	541	20	0	2.17	....	....	....	....	....	....	....
	HV-Jonkoping	Sweden	12	....	....	....	716	24	1	2.01	3	....	....	178	12	0	4.04
2000-01	HV Jonkoping	Sweden	*46	....	....	....	*2752	127	4	2.77	....	....	....	....	....	....	....

LUNDQVIST, Henrik (LUHND-kvihst, HEHN-rihk) NYR

Goaltender. Catches left. 5'11", 167 lbs. Born, Are, Sweden, March 2, 1982.
(NY Rangers' 7th choice, 205th overall, in 2000 Entry Draft).

			Regular Season								Playoffs						
Season	**Club**	**Lea**	**GP**	**W**	**L**	**T**	**Mins**	**GA**	**SO**	**Avg**	**GP**	**W**	**L**	**Mins**	**GA**	**SO**	**Avg**
1998-99	Vastra Frolunda	Swede-Jr.	35	....	....	....	2100	95	0	2.73	....	....	....	....	....	....	....
99-2000	Vastra Frolunda	Swede-Jr.	30	....	....	....	1726	73	0	2.54	5	4	1	300	7	2	1.40
2000-01	Vastra Frolunda-B	Swede-Jr.	2	....	....	....	120	5	0	2.50	3	2	1	182	5	0	1.62
	Vastra Frolunda	Swede-Jr.	19	....	....	....	1140	50	2	2.64	....	....	....	....	....	....	....
	Molndal IF	Swede-2	7	....	....	....	420	29	0	4.22	....	....	....	....	....	....	....
	Vastra Frolunda	Sweden	4	....	....	....	190	11	0	3.47	....	....	....	....	....	....	....

LUONGO, Roberto (loo-WAHN-goh, ROH-buhr-TOH) FLA.

Goaltender. Catches left. 6'3", 198 lbs. Born, Montreal, Que., April 4, 1979.
(NY Islanders' 1st choice, 4th overall, in 1997 Entry Draft).

			Regular Season								Playoffs						
Season	**Club**	**Lea**	**GP**	**W**	**L**	**T**	**Mins**	**GA**	**SO**	**Avg**	**GP**	**W**	**L**	**Mins**	**GA**	**SO**	**Avg**
1994-95	Montreal-Bourassa	QAAA	25	10	14	0	94	1465	0	3.85	....	....	....	....	....	....	....
1995-96	Val-d'Or Foreurs	QMJHL	23	6	11	4	1201	74	0	3.70	3	0	1	68	5	0	4.41
1996-97	Val-d'Or Foreurs	QMJHL	60	32	22	2	3305	171	2	3.10	13	8	5	777	44	0	3.40
1997-98	Val-d'Or Foreurs	QMJHL	54	27	20	5	3046	157	*7	3.09	*17	*14	3	*1019	37	*2	*2.18
1998-99	Val-d'Or Foreurs	QMJHL	21	6	10	2	1176	77	1	3.93	....	....	....	....	....	....	....
	Acadie-Bathurst	QMJHL	22	14	7	1	1340	74	0	3.31	*23	*16	6	*1400	64	0	2.74
99-2000	**NY Islanders**	**NHL**	**24**	**7**	**14**	**1**	**1292**	**70**	**1**	**3.25**	....	....	....	....	....	....	....
	Lowell	AHL	26	10	12	4	1517	74	1	2.93	6	3	3	359	18	0	3.01
2000-01	**Florida**	**NHL**	**47**	**12**	**24**	**7**	**2628**	**107**	**5**	**2.44**	....	....	....	....	....	....	....
	Louisville Panthers	AHL	3	1	2	0	178	10	0	3.38	....	....	....	....	....	....	....
	NHL Totals		**71**	**19**	**38**	**8**	**3920**	**177**	**6**	**2.71**	....	....	....	....	....	....	....

Traded to **Florida** by **NY Islanders** with Olli Jokinen for Mark Parrish and Oleg Kvasha, June 24, 2000.

MacINTYRE, Drew (MAK-ihn-TIGHR, DROO) DET.

Goaltender. Catches left. 6', 173 lbs. Born, Charlottetown, PEI, June 24, 1983.
(Detroit's 2nd choice, 121st overall, in 2001 Entry Draft).

			Regular Season								Playoffs						
Season	**Club**	**Lea**	**GP**	**W**	**L**	**T**	**Mins**	**GA**	**SO**	**Avg**	**GP**	**W**	**L**	**Mins**	**GA**	**SO**	**Avg**
1998-99	Trenton Sting	OPJHL	20	....	....	....	1173	71	2	3.63	....	....	....	....	....	....	....
99-2000	Sherbrooke	QMJHL	24	10	7	2	1253	67	0	3.21	....	....	....	....	....	....	....
2000-01	Sherbrooke	QMJHL	48	17	22	3	2552	139	4	3.27	4	0	4	238	19	0	4.78

MAGLIARDITI, Marc (mag-lee-ahr-DIH-tee, MAHRK)

Goaltender. Catches left. 6', 180 lbs. Born, Niagara Falls, NY, July 9, 1976.
(Chicago's 6th choice, 146th overall, in 1995 Entry Draft).

			Regular Season								Playoffs						
Season	**Club**	**Lea**	**GP**	**W**	**L**	**T**	**Mins**	**GA**	**SO**	**Avg**	**GP**	**W**	**L**	**Mins**	**GA**	**SO**	**Avg**
1994-95	Des Moines	USHL	29	21	2	4	1727	82	0	2.85	8	7	1	490	24	0	2.94
1995-96	Western Michigan	CCHA	36	23	11	2	2110	91	5	2.59	....	....	....	....	....	....	....
1996-97	Spokane Chiefs	WHL	29	12	13	1	1456	74	0	3.05	....	....	....	....	....	....	....
	Red Deer Rebels	WHL	13	8	3	0	653	41	0	3.77	16	9	7	945	54	0	3.43
1997-98	Indianapolis Ice	IHL	3	1	2	0	179	10	0	3.35	....	....	....	....	....	....	....
	Columbus Chill	ECHL	28	13	11	3	1644	86	2	3.14	....	....	....	....	....	....	....
	Detroit Vipers	IHL	10	5	4	0	512	30	0	3.51	....	....	....	....	....	....	....
	Fort Wayne	IHL	2	0	1	1	119	6	0	3.01	....	....	....	....	....	....	....
1998-99	Florida Everblades	ECHL	47	*32	10	3	2746	104	5	2.27	5	3	2	332	14	1	2.53
99-2000	Cincinnati	IHL	14	5	6	2	752	35	1	2.79	....	....	....	....	....	....	....
	Florida Everblades	ECHL	33	22	9	0	1794	69	3	2.31	4	1	2	209	12	0	3.44
2000-01	Cincinnati	IHL	17	6	6	3	893	48	0	3.22	....	....	....	....	....	....	....
	Florida Everblades	ECHL	26	16	6	2	1445	65	1	2.70	5	2	3	309	15	0	2.89

USHL First All-Star Team (1995) • CCHA All-Rookie Team (1996) • CCHA First All-Star Team (1996) • ECHL Second All-Star Team (1999)

Signed as a free agent by **Carolina**, September 14, 1999.

MALEK, Roman (MAHL-ehk, ROH-muhn) PHI.

Goaltender. Catches left. 5'11", 161 lbs. Born, Prague, Czech., September 25, 1977.
(Philadelphia's 5th choice, 158th overall, in 2001 Entry Draft).

			Regular Season								Playoffs						
Season	**Club**	**Lea**	**GP**	**W**	**L**	**T**	**Mins**	**GA**	**SO**	**Avg**	**GP**	**W**	**L**	**Mins**	**GA**	**SO**	**Avg**
1998-99	HC Slavia Praha	Cze-Rep.	18	....	....	....	830	51	....	3.69	....	....	....	....	....	....	....
99-2000	HC Slavia Praha	Cze-Rep.	25	....	....	....	1342	59	....	2.64	....	....	....	....	....	....	....
2000-01	HC Slavia Praha	Cze-Rep.	46	....	....	....	2550	100	....	2.35	11	....	....	665	28	....	2.53

MARACLE, Norm (MAHR-ah-kuhl, NOHRM) ATL.

Goaltender. Catches left. 5'9", 190 lbs. Born, Belleville, Ont., October 2, 1974.
(Detroit's 6th choice, 126th overall, in 1993 Entry Draft).

			Regular Season								Playoffs						
Season	**Club**	**Lea**	**GP**	**W**	**L**	**T**	**Mins**	**GA**	**SO**	**Avg**	**GP**	**W**	**L**	**Mins**	**GA**	**SO**	**Avg**
1990-91	Calgary Stars	AMHL	29	....	....	....	1740	99	0	3.43	....	....	....	....	....	....	....
1991-92	Saskatoon Blades	WHL	29	13	6	3	1529	87	1	3.41	15	9	5	860	37	0	3.38
1992-93	Saskatoon Blades	WHL	53	27	18	3	1939	160	1	3.27	9	4	5	569	33	0	3.48
1993-94	Saskatoon Blades	WHL	56	*41	13	1	3219	148	2	2.76	16	*11	5	940	48	*1	3.06
1994-95	Adirondack	AHL	39	12	15	2	1997	119	0	3.57	....	....	....	....	....	....	....
1995-96	Adirondack	AHL	54	24	18	6	2949	135	2	2.75	1	0	1	30	4	0	8.11
1996-97	Adirondack	AHL	*68	*34	22	9	*3843	173	5	2.70	4	1	3	192	10	1	3.13
1997-98	**Detroit**	**NHL**	**4**	**2**	**0**	**1**	**178**	**6**	**0**	**2.02**	....	....	....	....	....	....	....
	Adirondack	AHL	*66	27	29	8	*3709	190	1	3.07	3	0	3	180	10	0	3.33
1998-99	**Detroit**	**NHL**	**16**	**6**	**5**	**2**	**821**	**31**	**0**	**2.27**	**2**	**0**	**0**	**58**	**3**	**0**	**3.10**
	Adirondack	AHL	6	3	3	0	359	18	0	3.01	....	....	....	....	....	....	....
99-2000	**Atlanta**	**NHL**	**32**	**4**	**19**	**2**	**1618**	**94**	**1**	**3.49**	....	....	....	....	....	....	....
2000-01	**Atlanta**	**NHL**	**13**	**2**	**8**	**3**	**753**	**43**	**0**	**3.43**	....	....	....	....	....	....	....
	Orlando	IHL	51	33	13	3	2963	100	*8	*2.02	*16	*12	4	*1003	37	1	2.21
	NHL Totals		**65**	**14**	**32**	**8**	**3370**	**174**	**1**	**3.10**	**2**	**0**	**0**	**58**	**3**	**0**	**3.10**

Won Warwick Trophy (MVP - AMHL) (1991) • WHL East Second All-Star Team (1993) • WHL East First All-Star Team (1994) • Canadian Major Junior First All-Star Team (1994) • Canadian Major Junior Goaltender of the Year (1994) • AHL Second All-Star Team (1997, 1998) • IHL First All-Star Team (2001) • Shared James Norris Memorial Trophy (fewest goals against - IHL) with Scott Fankhouser (2001) • Won James Gatschene Memorial Trophy (MVP - IHL) (2001) • Won "Bud" Poile Trophy (Playoff MVP - IHL) (2001)

Claimed by **Atlanta** from **Detroit** in Expansion Draft, June 25, 1999.

MARKKANEN, Jussi (MAHR-kah-nehn, YOO-see) EDM.

Goaltender. Catches left. 5'11", 183 lbs. Born, Imatra, Finland, May 8, 1975.
(Edmonton's 5th choice, 133rd overall, in 2001 Entry Draft).

			Regular Season								Playoffs						
Season	**Club**	**Lea**	**GP**	**W**	**L**	**T**	**Mins**	**GA**	**SO**	**Avg**	**GP**	**W**	**L**	**Mins**	**GA**	**SO**	**Avg**
1991-92	Sai-Lappeenranta	Finn-Jr.	2	....	....	....	120	11	0	5.50	....	....	....	....	....	....	....
1992-93	Sai-Lappeenranta	Finn-Jr.	7	....	....	....	367	28	....	4.58	....	....	....	....	....	....	....
	Sai-Lappeenranta	Finland-2	16	....	....	....	798	60	....	4.51	....	....	....	....	....	....	....
1993-94	Sai-Lappeenranta	Finland-2	30	....	....	....	1726	97	....	3.37	....	....	....	....	....	....	....
1994-95	Sai-Lappeenranta	Finland-2	43	....	....	....	2493	122	....	2.94	3	....	....	179	5	....	1.68
1995-96	Tappara Tampere	Finn-Jr.	5	....	....	....	298	21	....	4.23	....	....	....	....	....	....	....
	Tappara Tampere	Finland	23	11	8	2	1238	59	1	2.86	....	....	....	....	....	....	....
1996-97	Sai-Lappeenranta	Finland	41	9	24	7	2340	132	0	3.38	....	....	....	....	....	....	....
1997-98	Sai-Lappeenranta	Finland	48	21	20	5	2870	138	4	2.89	3	0	3	164	11	0	4.02
1998-99	Sai-Lappeenranta	Finland	48	21	19	4	2633	105	4	2.39	7	3	3	366	21	0	3.44
99-2000	Sai-Lappeenranta	Finland	48	4	23	9	2794	150	2	3.22	....	....	....	....	....	....	....
2000-01	Tappara Tampere	Finland	52	*30	17	5	3076	107	*9	2.09	*10	7	3	*608	18	1	1.78

MARSTERS, Nathan (MAHR-stuhrs, NAY-thuhn) L.A.

Goaltender. Catches left. 6'4", 190 lbs. Born, Burlington, Ont., January 20, 1980.
(Los Angeles' 5th choice, 165th overall, in 2000 Entry Draft).

			Regular Season								Playoffs						
Season	**Club**	**Lea**	**GP**	**W**	**L**	**T**	**Mins**	**GA**	**SO**	**Avg**	**GP**	**W**	**L**	**Mins**	**GA**	**SO**	**Avg**
1997-98	Bramalea Blues	OPJHL	12	....	....	....	539	25	2	2.78	....	....	....	....	....	....	....
1998-99	Chilliwack Chiefs	BCJHL	9	6	2	0	478	29	0	3.65	....	....	....	....	....	....	....
99-2000	Bramalea Blues	OPJHL	27	....	....	....	1668	98	2	3.53	....	....	....	....	....	....	....
	Chilliwack Chiefs	BCJHL	15	9	6	0	825	63	0	4.58	20	15	5	1187	62	0	3.13
2000-01	RPI Engineers	ECAC	28	14	13	1	1631	64	*4	2.35	....	....	....	....	....	....	....

MASON, Chris (MAY-sohn, KRIHS) NSH.

Goaltender. Catches left. 6', 195 lbs. Born, Red Deer, Alta., April 20, 1976.
(New Jersey's 7th choice, 122nd overall, in 1995 Entry Draft).

			Regular Season								Playoffs						
Season	**Club**	**Lea**	**GP**	**W**	**L**	**T**	**Mins**	**GA**	**SO**	**Avg**	**GP**	**W**	**L**	**Mins**	**GA**	**SO**	**Avg**
1992-93	Red Deer Chiefs	AMHL	20	....	....	....	1280	76	0	3.35	....	....	....	....	....	....	....
1993-94	Victoria Cougars	WHL	5	1	4	0	237	27	0	6.84	....	....	....	....	....	....	....
1994-95	Prince George	WHL	44	8	30	1	2288	192	1	5.03	....	....	....	....	....	....	....
1995-96	Prince George	WHL	59	16	37	1	3289	236	1	4.31	....	....	....	....	....	....	....
1996-97	Prince George	WHL	50	19	24	4	2851	172	2	3.62	15	9	6	938	44	*1	2.81
1997-98	Cincinnati Ducks	AHL	47	13	19	7	2368	136	0	3.45	....	....	....	....	....	....	....
1998-99	**Nashville**	**NHL**	**3**	**0**	**0**	**0**	**69**	**6**	**0**	**5.22**	....	....	....	....	....	....	....
	Milwaukee	IHL	34	15	12	6	1901	92	1	2.90	....	....	....	....	....	....	....
99-2000	Milwaukee	IHL	53	20	21	8	2952	137	2	2.78	3	1	2	252	11	0	2.62
2000-01	**Nashville**	**NHL**	**1**	**0**	**1**	**0**	**59**	**2**	**0**	**2.03**	....	....	....	....	....	....	....
	Milwaukee	IHL	37	17	14	5	2226	87	5	2.35	4	1	3	239	12	0	3.02
	NHL Totals		**4**	**0**	**1**	**0**	**128**	**8**	**0**	**3.75**	....	....	....	....	....	....	....

Signed as a free agent by **Anaheim**, June 27, 1997. Traded to **Nashville** by **Anaheim** with Marc Moro for Dominic Roussel, October 5, 1998.

MAUND, Jeff (MAHND, JEHF) BOS.

Goaltender. Catches left. 6', 174 lbs. Born, Belleville, Ont., April 8, 1976.

			Regular Season								Playoffs						
Season	**Club**	**Lea**	**GP**	**W**	**L**	**T**	**Mins**	**GA**	**SO**	**Avg**	**GP**	**W**	**L**	**Mins**	**GA**	**SO**	**Avg**
1993-94	Caledon Canucks	MTJHL	28	18	4	1	1410	77	0	3.28	....	....	....	....	....	....	....
1994-95	Richmond Hill	MTJHL	37	....	....	....	1976	154	0	4.68	....	....	....	....	....	....	....
1995-96	Shelburne Hornets	MTJHL	11	....	....	....	538	49	1	5.46	....	....	....	....	....	....	....
	Brampton Caps	OPJHL	19	....	....	....	1052	54	1	3.08	....	....	....	....	....	....	....
1996-97	Aurora Tigers	MTJHL	30	....	....	....	1731	72	5	2.50	....	....	....	....	....	....	....
1997-98	Ohio State	CCHA	32	22	8	0	1858	73	4	2.36	....	....	....	....	....	....	....
1998-99	Ohio State	CCHA	38	20	14	4	2283	89	3	2.34	....	....	....	....	....	....	....
99-2000	Florida Everblades	ECHL	37	26	6	1	2055	89	3	2.60	2	1	1	89	4	0	2.69
2000-01	Norfolk Admirals	AHL	42	20	12	7	2385	94	3	2.36	4	2	2	259	13	0	3.01

CCHA First All-Star Team (1999) • NCAA West Second All-American Team (1999)

Signed as a free agent by **Chicago**, April 14, 1999. Signed as a free agent by **Boston**, July 23, 2001.

McLEAN, Kirk (muh-KLAYN, KUHRK)

Goaltender. Catches left. 6', 180 lbs. Born, Willowdale, Ont., June 26, 1966.
(New Jersey's 6th choice, 107th overall, in 1984 Entry Draft).

			Regular Season								Playoffs						
Season	**Club**	**Lea**	**GP**	**W**	**L**	**T**	**Mins**	**GA**	**SO**	**Avg**	**GP**	**W**	**L**	**Mins**	**GA**	**SO**	**Avg**
1982-83	Don Mills Flyers	MTHL	26	....	....	....	1575	52	0	2.01	....	....	....	....	....	....	....
1983-84	Oshawa Generals	OHL	17	5	9	0	940	67	0	4.28	....	....	....	....	....	....	....
1984-85	Oshawa Generals	OHL	47	23	17	2	2581	143	1	*3.32	5	1	3	271	21	0	4.65
1985-86	Oshawa Generals	OHL	51	24	21	2	2830	169	1	3.58	4	1	2	201	18	0	5.37
	New Jersey	**NHL**	**2**	**1**	**1**	**0**	**111**	**11**	**0**	**5.95**	....	....	....	....	....	....	....
1986-87	**New Jersey**	**NHL**	**4**	**1**	**1**	**0**	**160**	**10**	**0**	**3.75**	....	....	....	....	....	....	....
	Maine Mariners	AHL	45	15	23	4	2606	140	1	3.22	....	....	....	....	....	....	....
1987-88	**Vancouver**	**NHL**	**41**	**11**	**27**	**3**	**2380**	**147**	**1**	**3.71**	....	....	....	....	....	....	....
1988-89	**Vancouver**	**NHL**	**42**	**20**	**17**	**3**	**2477**	**127**	**4**	**3.08**	**5**	**2**	**3**	**302**	**18**	**0**	**3.58**
1989-90	**Vancouver**	**NHL**	***63**	**21**	**30**	**10**	***3739**	**216**	**0**	**3.47**	....	....	....	....	....	....	....
1990-91	**Vancouver**	**NHL**	**41**	**10**	**22**	**3**	**1969**	**131**	**0**	**3.99**	**2**	**1**	**1**	**123**	**7**	**0**	**3.41**
1991-92	**Vancouver**	**NHL**	**65**	***38**	**17**	**9**	**3852**	**176**	***5**	**2.74**	**13**	**6**	**7**	**785**	**33**	***2**	**2.52**
1992-93	**Vancouver**	**NHL**	**54**	**28**	**21**	**5**	**3261**	**184**	**3**	**3.39**	**12**	**6**	**6**	**754**	**42**	**0**	**3.34**
1993-94	**Vancouver**	**NHL**	**52**	**23**	**26**	**3**	**3128**	**156**	**3**	**2.99**	***24**	**15**	**9**	***1544**	**59**	***4**	**2.29**
1994-95	**Vancouver**	**NHL**	**40**	**18**	**12**	**10**	**2374**	**109**	**1**	**2.75**	**11**	**4**	**7**	**660**	**36**	**0**	**3.27**
1995-96	**Vancouver**	**NHL**	**45**	**15**	**21**	**9**	**2645**	**156**	**2**	**3.54**	**1**	**0**	**1**	**21**	**3**	**0**	**8.57**
1996-97	**Vancouver**	**NHL**	**44**	**21**	**18**	**3**	**2581**	**138**	**0**	**3.21**	....	....	....	....	....	....	....
1997-98	**Vancouver**	**NHL**	**29**	**6**	**17**	**4**	**1583**	**97**	**1**	**3.68**	....	....	....	....	....	....	....
	Carolina	**NHL**	**8**	**4**	**2**	**0**	**401**	**22**	**0**	**3.29**	....	....	....	....	....	....	....
	Florida	**NHL**	**7**	**4**	**2**	**1**	**406**	**22**	**0**	**3.25**	....	....	....	....	....	....	....
1998-99	**Florida**	**NHL**	**30**	**9**	**10**	**4**	**1597**	**73**	**2**	**2.74**	....	....	....	....	....	....	....
99-2000	**NY Rangers**	**NHL**	**22**	**7**	**8**	**4**	**1206**	**58**	**0**	**2.89**	....	....	....	....	....	....	....
2000-01	**NY Rangers**	**NHL**	**23**	**8**	**10**	**1**	**1220**	**71**	**0**	**3.49**	....	....	....	....	....	....	....
	NHL Totals		**612**	**245**	**262**	**72**	**35090**	**1904**	**22**	**3.26**	**68**	**34**	**34**	**4189**	**198**	**6**	**2.84**

NHL Second All-Star Team (1992) • Played in NHL All-Star Game (1990, 1992)

Traded to **Vancouver** by **New Jersey** with Greg Adams and New Jersey's 2nd round choice (Leif Rohlin) in 1988 Entry Draft for Patrik Sundstrom and Vancouver's 2nd (Jeff Christian) and 4th (Matt Ruchty) round choices in 1988 Entry Draft, September 15, 1987. Traded to **Carolina** by **Vancouver** with Martin Gelinas for Sean Burke, Geoff Sanderson and Enrico Ciccone, January 3, 1998. Traded to **Florida** by **Carolina** for Ray Sheppard, March 24, 1998. Signed as a free agent by **NY Rangers**, July 20, 1999.

McLENNAN, Jamie (muh-KLEH-nuhn, JAY-mee) MIN.

Goaltender. Catches left. 6', 190 lbs. Born, Edmonton, Alta., June 30, 1971.
(NY Islanders' 3rd choice, 48th overall, in 1991 Entry Draft).

			Regular Season								Playoffs						
Season	Club	Lea	GP	W	L	T	Mins	GA	SO	Avg	GP	W	L	Mins	GA	SO	Avg
1987-88	St. Albert Royals	AMHL	21	....	....	....	1224	80	0	3.92	....	....	....	....	....	....	....
1988-89	Spokane Chiefs	WHL	11	....	....	....	578	63	0	6.54	....	....	....	....	....	....	....
	Lethbridge	WHL	7	....	....	....	368	22	0	3.59	....	....	....	....	....	....	....
1989-90	Lethbridge	WHL	34	20	4	2	1690	110	1	3.91	13	6	5	677	44	0	3.90
1990-91	Lethbridge	WHL	56	32	18	4	3230	205	0	3.81	*16	8	8	*970	56	0	3.46
1991-92	Capital District	AHL	18	4	10	2	952	60	1	3.78	....	....	....	....	....	....	....
	Richmond	ECHL	32	16	12	2	1837	114	0	3.72	....	....	....	....	....	....	....
1992-93	Capital District	AHL	38	17	14	6	2171	117	1	3.23	1	0	1	20	5	0	15.00
1993-94	**NY Islanders**	**NHL**	**22**	**8**	**7**	**6**	**1287**	**61**	**0**	**2.84**	**2**	**0**	**1**	**82**	**6**	**0**	**4.39**
	Salt Lake City	IHL	24	8	12	2	1320	80	0	3.64	....	....	....	....	....	....	....
1994-95	**NY Islanders**	**NHL**	**21**	**6**	**11**	**2**	**1185**	**67**	**0**	**3.39**	....	....	....	....	....	....	....
	Denver Grizzlies	IHL	4	3	0	1	239	12	0	3.00	11	8	2	640	23	1	*2.15
1995-96	**NY Islanders**	**NHL**	**13**	**3**	**9**	**1**	**636**	**39**	**0**	**3.68**	....	....	....	....	....	....	....
	Utah Grizzlies	IHL	14	9	2	2	728	29	0	2.39	....	....	....	....	....	....	....
	Worcester	AHL	22	14	7	1	1216	57	0	2.81	2	0	2	119	8	0	4.04
1996-97	Worcester	AHL	39	18	13	4	2152	100	2	2.79	4	2	2	262	16	0	3.67
1997-98	**St. Louis**	**NHL**	**30**	**16**	**8**	**2**	**1658**	**60**	**2**	**2.17**	**1**	**0**	**0**	**14**	**1**	**0**	**4.29**
1998-99	**St. Louis**	**NHL**	**33**	**13**	**14**	**4**	**1763**	**70**	**3**	**2.38**	**1**	**0**	**1**	**37**	**0**	**0**	**0.00**
99-2000	**St. Louis**	**NHL**	**19**	**9**	**5**	**2**	**1009**	**33**	**2**	**1.96**	....	....	....	....	....	....	....
2000-01	**Minnesota**	**NHL**	**38**	**5**	**23**	**9**	**2230**	**98**	**2**	**2.64**	....	....	....	....	....	....	....
	NHL Totals		**176**	**60**	**77**	**26**	**9768**	**428**	**9**	**2.63**	**4**	**0**	**2**	**133**	**7**	**0**	**3.16**

WHL East First All-Star Team (1991) • Won Bill Masterton Memorial Trophy (1998)

Signed as a free agent by **St. Louis**, July 15, 1996. Selected by **Minnesota** from **St. Louis** in Expansion Draft, June 23, 2000.

MEDVEDEV, Andrei (mehd-VEH-dehv, AN-dray) CGY.

Goaltender. Catches left. 6', 211 lbs. Born, Moscow, USSR, April 1, 1983.
(Calgary's 3rd choice, 56th overall, in 2001 Entry Draft).

			Regular Season								Playoffs						
Season	Club	Lea	GP	W	L	T	Mins	GA	SO	Avg	GP	W	L	Mins	GA	SO	Avg
1998-99	Kryjla Sovetov	Russia	2	....	....	....	80	2	1	1.50	....	....	....	....	....	....	....
99-2000	Kryjla Sovetov	Russia-2	STATISTICS NOT AVAILABLE														
2000-01	Kryjla Sovetov	Russia-2	11	....	....	....	208	8	0	2.31	....	....	....	....	....	....	....

MEYER, Scott (MIGH-uhr, SKAWT) NYR

Goaltender. Catches left. 6', 185 lbs. Born, White Bear Lake, MN, April 10, 1976.

			Regular Season								Playoffs						
Season	Club	Lea	GP	W	L	T	Mins	GA	SO	Avg	GP	W	L	Mins	GA	SO	Avg
1995-96	Fargo-Moorhead	USHL	27	....	....	....	1620	82	1	3.04	....	....	....	....	....	....	....
1996-97	St. Cloud State	WCHA	1	0	0	0	29	1	0	2.07	....	....	....	....	....	....	....
1997-98	St. Cloud State	WCHA	2	0	1	0	75	4	0	3.21	....	....	....	....	....	....	....
1998-99	St. Cloud State	WCHA	9	2	5	1	464	23	0	2.97	....	....	....	....	....	....	....
99-2000	St. Cloud State	WCHA	32	20	8	3	1922	76	7	2.37	....	....	....	....	....	....	....
2000-01	St. Cloud State	WCHA	36	25	8	1	2096	78	2	2.23	....	....	....	....	....	....	....

WCHA Second All-Star Team (2000) • WCHA First All-Star Team (2001) • NCAA West Second All-American Team (2001)

Signed as a free agent by **NY Rangers**, July 5, 2001.

MICHAUD, Alfie (mee-SHOH, AL-fee) VAN.

Goaltender. Catches left. 5'10", 177 lbs. Born, Selkirk, Man., November 6, 1976.

			Regular Season								Playoffs						
Season	Club	Lea	GP	W	L	T	Mins	GA	SO	Avg	GP	W	L	Mins	GA	SO	Avg
1995-96	Lebret Eagles	SJHL	44	....	....	....	2547	121	2	2.85	....	....	....	....	....	....	....
1996-97	U. of Maine	H-East	29	*17	8	1	1515	78	1	3.09	....	....	....	....	....	....	....
1997-98	U. of Maine	H-East	32	15	12	4	1794	94	2	3.14	....	....	....	....	....	....	....
1998-99	U. of Maine	H-East	37	*28	6	3	2147	83	3	2.32	....	....	....	....	....	....	....
99-2000	**Vancouver**	**NHL**	**2**	**0**	**1**	**0**	**69**	**5**	**0**	**4.35**	....	....	....	....	....	....	....
	Syracuse Crunch	AHL	38	10	17	5	2052	132	0	3.86	....	....	....	....	....	....	....
2000-01	Kansas City	IHL	32	14	14	2	1778	93	1	3.14	....	....	....	....	....	....	....
	NHL Totals		**2**	**0**	**1**	**0**	**69**	**5**	**0**	**4.35**	....	....	....	....	....	....	....

NCAA Championship All-Tournament Team (1999) • NCAA Championship Tournament MVP (1999)

Signed as a free agent by **Vancouver**, July 12, 1999.

MILLER, Ryan (MIHL-luhr, RIGH-uhn) BUF.

Goaltender. Catches left. 6'1", 150 lbs. Born, East Lansing, MI, July 17, 1980.
(Buffalo's 7th choice, 138th overall, in 1999 Entry Draft).

			Regular Season								Playoffs						
Season	Club	Lea	GP	W	L	T	Mins	GA	SO	Avg	GP	W	L	Mins	GA	SO	Avg
1997-98	Soo Indians	NAJHL	31	17	13	0	1804	72	1	2.39	6	2	4	311	10	0	1.93
1998-99	Soo Indians	NAJHL	47	31	14	1	2711	104	8	2.30	4	2	2	218	10	1	2.76
99-2000	Michigan State	CCHA	26	16	5	3	1525	39	*8	*1.53	....	....	....	....	....	....	....
2000-01	Michigan State	CCHA	40	*31	5	4	2447	54	*10	*1.32	....	....	....	....	....	....	....

CCHA Second All-Star Team (2000) • CCHA First All-Star Team (2001) • NCAA West First All-American Team (2001) • Won Hobey Baker Memorial Award (Top U.S. Collegiate Player) (2001)

MINARD, Mike (mih-NAHRD, MIGHK) TOR.

Goaltender. Catches left. 6'3", 205 lbs. Born, Owen Sound, Ont., November 1, 1976.
(Edmonton's 4th choice, 83rd overall, in 1995 Entry Draft).

			Regular Season								Playoffs						
Season	Club	Lea	GP	W	L	T	Mins	GA	SO	Avg	GP	W	L	Mins	GA	SO	Avg
1992-93	St. Marys Lincolns	OJHL-B	23	....	....	....	1374	162	0	3.10	....	....	....	....	....	....	....
1993-94	St. Mary's Lincolns	OJHL-B	31	*25	5	0	1710	78	1	*2.74	....	....	....	....	....	....	....
1994-95	Chilliwack Chiefs	BCJHL	40	....	....	....	2330	136	0	3.50	....	....	....	....	....	....	....
1995-96	Barrie Colts	OHL	1	0	1	0	52	8	0	9.23	....	....	....	....	....	....	....
	Detroit Whalers	OHL	42	25	10	4	2314	128	2	3.32	17	9	6	922	55	1	3.58
1996-97	Hamilton Bulldogs	AHL	3	1	1	0	100	7	0	4.20	....	....	....	....	....	....	....
	Wheeling Nailers	ECHL	23	3	7	1	899	69	0	4.60	3	0	2	148	16	0	6.47
1997-98	Hamilton Bulldogs	AHL	2	1	0	0	80	2	0	1.50	....	....	....	....	....	....	....
	Brantford Smoke	UHL	2	1	1	0	74	7	0	5.63	....	....	....	....	....	....	....
	New Orleans	ECHL	11	6	2	0	429	30	0	4.19	....	....	....	....	....	....	....
	Milwaukee	IHL	8	2	2	0	362	19	0	3.15	....	....	....	....	....	....	....
1998-99	Dayton Bombers	ECHL	15	8	5	2	788	42	1	3.20	....	....	....	....	....	....	....
	Milwaukee	IHL	10	3	5	0	531	27	0	3.05	....	....	....	....	....	....	....
	Hamilton Bulldogs	AHL	11	8	3	0	645	30	1	2.79	1	0	0	20	0	0	0.00
99-2000	**Edmonton**	**NHL**	**1**	**1**	**0**	**0**	**60**	**3**	**0**	**3.00**	....	....	....	....	....	....	....
	Hamilton Bulldogs	AHL	38	16	12	5	1987	102	0	3.08	1	0	0	23	0	0	0.00
2000-01	St. John's Leafs	AHL	43	23	10	4	2252	91	1	2.42	4	1	3	252	15	0	3.57
	NHL Totals		**1**	**1**	**0**	**0**	**60**	**3**	**0**	**3.00**	....	....	....	....	....	....	....

Signed as a free agent by **Toronto**, March 16, 2001.

MOLNAR, Aaron (MOHL-nahr, AIR-ruhn) COL.

Goaltender. Catches left. 6'1", 165 lbs. Born, London, Ont., October 8, 1981.
(Colorado's 11th choice, 221st overall, in 2000 Entry Draft).

			Regular Season								Playoffs						
Season	Club	Lea	GP	W	L	T	Mins	GA	SO	Avg	GP	W	L	Mins	GA	SO	Avg
1997-98	St. Thomas Stars	OJHL-B	32	19	5	2	1656	109	0	3.95	....	....	....	....	....	....	....
1998-99	St. Thomas Stars	OJHL-B	33	....	....	....	1879	122	1	3.90	....	....	....	....	....	....	....
99-2000	Plymouth Whalers	OHL	11	3	6	1	576	31	0	3.23	....	....	....	....	....	....	....
	London Knights	OHL	17	4	10	1	858	61	0	4.12	....	....	....	....	....	....	....
2000-01	London Knights	OHL	*68	26	37	5	*3925	245	1	3.75	5	1	4	285	19	0	4.00

MORRISON, Michael (MOHR-rihs-ohn, MIGH-kuhl) EDM.

Goaltender. Catches right. 6'3", 194 lbs. Born, Medford, MA, July 11, 1979.
(Edmonton's 8th choice, 186th overall, in 1998 Entry Draft).

			Regular Season								Playoffs						
Season	Club	Lea	GP	W	L	T	Mins	GA	SO	Avg	GP	W	L	Mins	GA	SO	Avg
1997-98	Exeter Academy	H.S.	27	15	11	2	1632	64	1	2.35	....	....	....	....	....	....	....
1998-99	U. of Maine	H-East	11	3	0	1	347	10	1	1.73	....	....	....	....	....	....	....
99-2000	U. of Maine	H-East	12	7	2	1	608	27	1	2.67	....	....	....	....	....	....	....
2000-01	U. of Maine	H-East	10	2	3	3	490	16	1	1.96	....	....	....	....	....	....	....

MOSS, Tyler (MAWS, TIGH-luhr) CAR.

Goaltender. Catches right. 6', 185 lbs. Born, Ottawa, Ont., June 29, 1975.
(Tampa Bay's 2nd choice, 29th overall, in 1993 Entry Draft).

			Regular Season								Playoffs						
Season	Club	Lea	GP	W	L	T	Mins	GA	SO	Avg	GP	W	L	Mins	GA	SO	Avg
1991-92	Nepean Raiders	OCJHL	26	7	12	1	1335	109	0	4.90	....	....	....	....	....	....	....
1992-93	Kingston	OHL	31	13	7	5	1537	97	0	3.79	6	1	2	228	19	0	5.00
1993-94	Kingston	OHL	13	6	4	3	795	42	1	3.17	3	0	2	136	8	0	3.53
1994-95	Kingston	OHL	*57	33	17	5	*3249	164	1	3.03	6	2	4	333	27	0	4.86
1995-96	Atlanta Knights	IHL	40	11	19	4	2030	138	1	4.08	3	0	3	213	11	0	3.10
1996-97	Adirondack	AHL	11	1	5	2	507	42	1	4.97	....	....	....	....	....	....	....
	Grand Rapids	IHL	15	5	6	1	715	35	0	2.94	....	....	....	....	....	....	....
	Muskegon Fury	ColHL	2	1	1	0	119	5	0	2.51	....	....	....	....	....	....	....
	Saint John Flames	AHL	9	6	1	1	534	17	0	1.91	5	2	3	242	15	0	3.72
1997-98	**Calgary**	**NHL**	**6**	**2**	**3**	**1**	**367**	**20**	**0**	**3.27**	....	....	....	....	....	....	....
	Saint John Flames	AHL	39	19	10	7	2194	91	0	2.49	15	8	5	761	37	0	2.91
1998-99	**Calgary**	**NHL**	**11**	**3**	**7**	**0**	**550**	**23**	**0**	**2.51**	....	....	....	....	....	....	....
	Saint John Flames	AHL	9	2	5	1	475	25	0	3.16	....	....	....	....	....	....	....
	Orlando	IHL	9	6	2	1	515	21	1	2.45	17	10	7	1017	53	0	3.13
99-2000	Kansas City	IHL	36	18	12	5	2116	105	3	2.98	....	....	....	....	....	....	....
	Wilkes-Barre	AHL	4	1	1	1	188	11	0	3.52	....	....	....	....	....	....	....
2000-01	**Carolina**	**NHL**	**12**	**1**	**6**	**0**	**557**	**37**	**0**	**3.99**	....	....	....	....	....	....	....
	Cincinnati	IHL	9	5	3	1	506	24	2	2.85	....	....	....	....	....	....	....
	NHL Totals		**29**	**6**	**16**	**1**	**1474**	**80**	**0**	**3.26**	....	....	....	....	....	....	....

OHL First All-Star Team (1995) • Shared Harry "Hap" Holmes Memorial Trophy (fewest goals against - AHL) with Jean-Sebastien Giguere (1998)

Traded to **Calgary** by **Tampa Bay** for Jamie Huscroft, March 18, 1997. Traded to **Pittsburgh** by **Calgary** with Rene Corbet for Brad Werenka, March 14, 2000. Signed as a free agent by **Carolina**, August 9, 2000.

MUNRO, Adam (MUHN-roh, A-duhm) CHI.

Goaltender. Catches left. 6'1", 194 lbs. Born, St. George, Ont., November 12, 1982.
(Chicago's 1st choice, 29th overall, in 2001 Entry Draft).

			Regular Season								Playoffs						
Season	Club	Lea	GP	W	L	T	Mins	GA	SO	Avg	GP	W	L	Mins	GA	SO	Avg
1997-98	Brantford Classics	OMHA	15	13	2	0	660	20	*4	*1.36	....	....	....	....	....	....	....
1998-99	Bowmanville	OPJHL	14	....	....	....	816	50	0	3.68	....	....	....	....	....	....	....
	Erie Otters	OHL	1	0	0	0	1	0	0	0.00	....	....	....	....	....	....	....
99-2000	Bowmanville	OPJHL	2	2	0	0	125	5	0	2.40	....	....	....	....	....	....	....
	Erie Otters	OHL	22	8	7	1	948	48	1	3.04	1	0	0	5	1	0	12.00
2000-01	Erie Otters	OHL	41	26	6	6	2283	88	*4	2.31	10	6	2	509	27	1	3.18

MURPHY, Dan (MUHR-fee, DAN) PHI.

Goaltender. Catches left. 6'2", 191 lbs. Born, Nanaimo, B.C., May 6, 1974.

			Regular Season								Playoffs						
Season	Club	Lea	GP	W	L	T	Mins	GA	SO	Avg	GP	W	L	Mins	GA	SO	Avg
1993-94	Nanaimo Clippers	BCJHL	36	....	....	....	2123	190	0	5.31	....	....	....	....	....	....	....
1994-95	Clarkson Knights	ECAC	*37	*23	9	4	*2157	118	0	3.28	....	....	....	....	....	....	....
1995-96	Clarkson Knights	ECAC	*38	25	10	3	2230	100	0	2.69	....	....	....	....	....	....	....
1996-97	Clarkson Knights	ECAC	*37	*27	9	0	*2162	84	*4	2.33	....	....	....	....	....	....	....
1997-98	Clarkson Knights	ECAC	23	10	9	2	1266	48	2	2.27	....	....	....	....	....	....	....
1998-99	Worcester IceCats	AHL	8	2	4	1	410	26	0	3.81	....	....	....	....	....	....	....
	Peoria Rivermen	ECHL	29	16	10	2	1672	92	0	3.30	3	1	2	180	11	0	3.67
99-2000	Quebec Citadelles	AHL	33	16	9	1	1573	62	3	2.37	....	....	....	....	....	....	....
	Philadelphia	AHL	5	1	4	0	258	17	0	3.95	....	....	....	....	....	....	....
2000-01	Philadelphia	AHL	2	0	2	0	80	9	0	6.75	....	....	....	....	....	....	....
	Springfield Falcons	AHL	16	4	7	2	824	51	0	3.71	....	....	....	....	....	....	....
	Trenton Titans	ECHL	15	7	7	1	862	33	2	2.30	3	1	0	154	8	0	3.08

ECAC All-Rookie Team (1995) • ECAC Second All-Star Team (1996) • NCAA East Second All-American Team (1996, 1997)

Signed as a free agent by **Philadelphia**, March 21, 2000.

MUZZATTI, Jason (moo-ZAH-tee, JAY-suhn)

Goaltender. Catches left. 6'2", 210 lbs. Born, Toronto, Ont., February 3, 1970.
(Calgary's 1st choice, 21st overall, in 1988 Entry Draft).

			Regular Season								Playoffs						
Season	**Club**	**Lea**	**GP**	**W**	**L**	**T**	**Mins**	**GA**	**SO**	**Avg**	**GP**	**W**	**L**	**Mins**	**GA**	**SO**	**Avg**
1985-86	St. Michael's	MTJHL	11	6	3	0	517	48	0	5.57	....	....	....	....	....	....	....
1986-87	St. Michael's	MTJHL	20	10	5	2	1054	69	1	3.93	....	....	....	....	....	....	....
1987-88	Michigan State	CCHA	33	19	9	3	1915	109	0	3.41	....	....	....	....	....	....	....
1988-89	Michigan State	CCHA	42	32	9	1	2515	127	3	*3.03	....	....	....	....	....	....	....
1989-90	Michigan State	CCHA	33	*24	6	0	1976	99	0	3.01	....	....	....	....	....	....	....
1990-91	Michigan State	CCHA	22	8	10	2	1204	75	1	3.74	....	....	....	....	....	....	....
1991-92	Salt Lake City	IHL	52	24	22	5	3033	167	2	3.30	4	1	3	247	18	0	4.37
1992-93	Canada	Nt-Team	16	6	9	0	880	53	0	3.84	....	....	....	....	....	....	....
	Indianapolis Ice	IHL	12	5	6	1	707	48	0	4.07	....	....	....	....	....	....	....
	Salt Lake City	IHL	13	5	6	1	747	52	0	4.18	....	....	....	....	....	....	....
1993-94	**Calgary**	**NHL**	**1**	**0**	**1**	**0**	**60**	**8**	**0**	**8.00**	....	....	....	....	....	....	....
	Saint John Flames	AHL	51	26	21	3	2939	183	2	3.74	7	3	4	415	19	0	2.75
1994-95	**Calgary**	**NHL**	**1**	**0**	**0**	**0**	**10**	**0**	**0**	**0.00**	....	....	....	....	....	....	....
	Saint John Flames	AHL	31	10	14	4	1741	101	2	3.48	....	....	....	....	....	....	....
1995-96	**Hartford**	**NHL**	**22**	**4**	**8**	**3**	**1013**	**49**	**1**	**2.90**	....	....	....	....	....	....	....
	Springfield	AHL	5	4	0	1	300	12	1	2.40	....	....	....	....	....	....	....
1996-97	**Hartford**	**NHL**	**31**	**9**	**13**	**5**	**1591**	**91**	**0**	**3.43**	....	....	....	....	....	....	....
1997-98	**NY Rangers**	**NHL**	**6**	**0**	**3**	**2**	**313**	**17**	**0**	**3.26**	....	....	....	....	....	....	....
	Hartford	AHL	17	11	5	1	999	57	0	3.42	....	....	....	....	....	....	....
	San Jose	**NHL**	**1**	**0**	**0**	**0**	**27**	**2**	**0**	**4.44**	....	....	....	....	....	....	....
	Kentucky	AHL	7	2	3	2	430	25	0	3.49	3	0	3	153	13	0	5.07
1998-99	Eisbaren Berlin	DEL	4	....	....	....	240	12	0	3.00	3	0	3	166	14	0	5.06
99-2000	Tappara Tampere	Finland	41	26	9	5	2479	94	5	2.28	4	1	3	252	14	0	3.33
2000-01	Augsburger EV	DEL	43	....	....	....	2391	143	1	3.59	....	....	....	....	....	....	....
	NHL Totals		**62**	**13**	**25**	**10**	**3014**	**167**	**1**	**3.32**	....	....	....	....	....	....	....

CCHA Second All-Star Team (1988) • CCHA First All-Star Team (1990) • NCAA West Second All-American Team (1990)

Claimed on waivers by **Hartford** from **Calgary**, October 6, 1995. Transferred to **Carolina** after **Hartford** franchise relocated, June 25, 1997. Traded to **NY Rangers** by **Carolina** for NY Rangers' 4th round choice (Tommy Westlund) in 1998 Entry Draft, August 8, 1997. Traded to **San Jose** by **NY Rangers** for Rich Brennan, March 24, 1998. • Missed majority of 1998-99 season recovering from heart surgery, September 1998.

NABOKOV, Evgeni (na-BAW-kahv, ehv-GEH-nee) S.J.

Goaltender. Catches left. 6', 200 lbs. Born, Ust-Kamenogorsk, USSR, July 25, 1975.
(San Jose's 9th choice, 219th overall, in 1994 Entry Draft).

			Regular Season								Playoffs						
Season	**Club**	**Lea**	**GP**	**W**	**L**	**T**	**Mins**	**GA**	**SO**	**Avg**	**GP**	**W**	**L**	**Mins**	**GA**	**SO**	**Avg**
1992-93	Ust-Kamenogorsk	CIS	4	1	0	0	109	5	0	2.75	....	....	....	....	....	....	....
1993-94	Ust-Kamenogorsk	CIS	11	....	....	....	539	29	0	3.22	....	....	....	....	....	....	....
1994-95	Dynamo Moscow	CIS	24	....	....	....	1265	40	....	1.89	....	....	....	....	....	....	....
1995-96	Dynamo Moscow	CIS	39	....	....	....	2008	67	5	2.00	6	....	....	298	7	....	1.41
1996-97	Dynamo Moscow	Russia	27	....	....	....	1588	56	2	2.11	4	....	....	255	12	0	2.82
1997-98	Kentucky	AHL	33	10	21	2	1866	122	0	3.92	1	0	0	23	1	0	2.59
1998-99	Kentucky	AHL	43	26	14	1	2429	106	5	2.62	11	6	5	599	30	*2	3.00
99-2000	**San Jose**	**NHL**	**11**	**2**	**2**	**1**	**414**	**15**	**1**	**2.17**	**1**	**0**	**0**	**20**	**0**	**0**	**0.00**
	Cleveland	IHL	20	12	4	3	1164	52	0	2.68	....	....	....	....	....	....	....
	Kentucky	AHL	2	1	1	0	120	3	1	1.50	....	....	....	....	....	....	....
2000-01	**San Jose**	**NHL**	**66**	**32**	**21**	**7**	**3700**	**135**	**6**	**2.19**	**4**	**1**	**3**	**218**	**10**	**1**	**2.75**
	NHL Totals		**77**	**34**	**23**	**8**	**4114**	**150**	**7**	**2.19**	**5**	**1**	**3**	**238**	**10**	**1**	**2.52**

NHL All-Rookie Team (2001) • Won Calder Memorial Trophy (2001) • Played in NHL All-Star Game (2001)

NAUMENKO, Gregg (naw-MEHN-koh, GREHG) ANA.

Goaltender. Catches left. 6'1", 201 lbs. Born, Chicago, IL, March 30, 1977.

			Regular Season								Playoffs						
Season	**Club**	**Lea**	**GP**	**W**	**L**	**T**	**Mins**	**GA**	**SO**	**Avg**	**GP**	**W**	**L**	**Mins**	**GA**	**SO**	**Avg**
1995-96	North Iowa	USHL	27	15	12	0	1649	103	1	3.75	4	1	3	239	15	0	3.77
1996-97	North Iowa	USHL	25	11	11	1	1342	85	1	3.80	6	3	2	284	19	0	4.01
1997-98	North Iowa	USHL	38	23	11	3	2171	80	3	2.21	5	4	1	299	11	0	2.21
1998-99	Alaska-Anchorage	WCHA	29	11	13	5	1691	65	1	*2.31	....	....	....	....	....	....	....
99-2000	Cincinnati Ducks	AHL	50	17	25	7	2877	143	2	2.98	....	....	....	....	....	....	....
2000-01	**Anaheim**	**NHL**	**2**	**0**	**1**	**0**	**70**	**7**	**0**	**6.00**	....	....	....	....	....	....	....
	Cincinnati Ducks	AHL	39	20	12	3	2079	101	2	2.91	2	0	2	123	10	0	4.90
	NHL Totals		**2**	**0**	**1**	**0**	**70**	**7**	**0**	**6.00**	....	....	....	....	....	....	....

WCHA First All-Star Team (1999)

Signed as a free agent by **Anaheim**, March 31, 1999.

NIITTYMAKI, Antero (NEE-too-mah-kee, AN-tehr-oh) PHI.

Goaltender. Catches left. 6', 176 lbs. Born, Turku, Finland, June 18, 1980.
(Philadelphia's 7th choice, 168th overall, in 1998 Entry Draft).

			Regular Season								Playoffs						
Season	**Club**	**Lea**	**GP**	**W**	**L**	**T**	**Mins**	**GA**	**SO**	**Avg**	**GP**	**W**	**L**	**Mins**	**GA**	**SO**	**Avg**
1998-99	TPS Turku	Finn-Jr.	35	....	....	....	2095	60	0	1.72	....	....	....	....	....	....	....
99-2000	TPS Turku	Finn-Jr.	1	1	0	0	60	1	0	1.00	....	....	....	....	....	....	....
	TPS Turku	Finland	32	23	6	2	1899	68	3	2.15	8	6	1	453	13	0	1.72
2000-01	TPS Turku	Finland	21	10	6	1	1112	46	2	2.48	....	....	....	....	....	....	....

NISSINEN, Tuomas (NIHS-ih-nehn, too-OH-muhs) ST.L.

Goaltender. Catches left. 6'1", 176 lbs. Born, Kuopio, Finland, July 17, 1983.
(St. Louis' 2nd choice, 89th overall, in 2001 Entry Draft).

			Regular Season								Playoffs						
Season	**Club**	**Lea**	**GP**	**W**	**L**	**T**	**Mins**	**GA**	**SO**	**Avg**	**GP**	**W**	**L**	**Mins**	**GA**	**SO**	**Avg**
2000-01	Kalpa Kuopio	Finn-Jr.	40	....	....	....	2327	125	....	3.22	....	....	....	....			

NORONEN, Mika (NOH-rah-nehn, MEE-kah) BUF.

Goaltender. Catches left. 6'1", 206 lbs. Born, Tampere, Finland, June 17, 1979.
(Buffalo's 1st choice, 21st overall, in 1997 Entry Draft).

			Regular Season								Playoffs						
Season	**Club**	**Lea**	**GP**	**W**	**L**	**T**	**Mins**	**GA**	**SO**	**Avg**	**GP**	**W**	**L**	**Mins**	**GA**	**SO**	**Avg**
1995-96	Tappara Tampere	Finn-Jr.	16	....	....	....	962	37	2	2.31	....	....	....	....	....	....	....
1996-97	Tappara Tampere	Finland	5	1	3	0	215	17	0	4.73	....	....	....	....	....	....	....
1997-98	Tappara Tampere	Finland	37	14	12	3	1704	83	1	2.92	4	1	2	196	12	0	3.67
1998-99	Tappara Tampere	Finland	43	18	20	5	2494	135	2	3.25	....	....	....	....	....	....	....
99-2000	Rochester	AHL	54	*33	13	4	3089	112	*6	*2.18	21	13	8	1235	37	*6	*1.80
2000-01	**Buffalo**	**NHL**	**2**	**2**	**0**	**0**	**108**	**5**	**0**	**2.78**	....	....	....	....	....	....	....
	Rochester	AHL	47	26	15	5	2753	100	4	2.18	4	1	3	250	11	0	2.64
	NHL Totals		**2**	**2**	**0**	**0**	**108**	**5**	**0**	**2.78**	....	....	....	....	....	....	....

AHL Second All-Star Team (2000, 2001) • Won Dudley "Red" Garrett Memorial Trophy (Top Rookie - AHL) (2000) • Shared Harry "Hap" Holmes Memorial Trophy (fewest goals against - AHL) with Tom Askey (2001)

NURMINEN, Pasi (NUR-mih-nehn, PAS-ee) ATL.

Goaltender. Catches left. 5'10", 189 lbs. Born, Lahti, Finland, December 17, 1975.
(Atlanta's 6th choice, 189th overall, in 2001 Entry Draft).

			Regular Season								Playoffs						
Season	**Club**	**Lea**	**GP**	**W**	**L**	**T**	**Mins**	**GA**	**SO**	**Avg**	**GP**	**W**	**L**	**Mins**	**GA**	**SO**	**Avg**
1993-94	Reipas Lahti	Finn-Jr.	14	....	....	....	847	58	0	4.11	....	....	....	....	....	....	....
	Reipas Lahti	Finland	1	....	....	....	30	2	0	4.00	....	....	....	....	....	....	....
1994-95	Reipas Lahti	Finn-Jr.	9	....	....	....	542	22	....	2.44	....	....	....	....	....	....	....
	Reipas Lahti	Finland-2	9	....	....	....	423	44	0	6.24	....	....	....	....	....	....	....
1995-96	Kettera Imatra	Finland-2	38	....	....	....	2204	146	0	3.97	....	....	....	....	....	....	....
1996-97	Pelicans Lahti	Finland-2	30	....	....	....	1726	69	0	2.40	3	....	....	204	8	....	2.35
1997-98	Pelicans Lahti	Finland-2	35	....	....	....	3044	59	....	1.73	3	....	....	180	4	....	1.33
1998-99	HPK Hameenlinna	Finland	48	24	17	6	2810	127	2	2.71	7	3	4	425	24	1	3.39
99-2000	Jokerit Helsinki	Finland	48	24	15	8	2770	104	6	2.25	11	7	4	719	22	2	1.84
2000-01	Jokerit Helsinki	Finland	52	30	13	7	2971	107	5	2.16	5	2	3	308	11	1	2.14

OSAER, Phil (OH-shar, FIHL) ST.L.

Goaltender. Catches left. 6'1", 186 lbs. Born, Dearborn, MI, February 10, 1980.
(St. Louis' 6th choice, 203rd overall, in 1999 Entry Draft).

			Regular Season								Playoffs						
Season	**Club**	**Lea**	**GP**	**W**	**L**	**T**	**Mins**	**GA**	**SO**	**Avg**	**GP**	**W**	**L**	**Mins**	**GA**	**SO**	**Avg**
1997-98	Waterloo Hawks	USHL	36	12	20	2	2094	107	2	3.07	5	1	4	295	17	0	3.46
1998-99	Ferris State	CCHA	9	2	2	1	399	10	0	1.51	....	....	....	....	....	....	....
99-2000	Ferris State	CCHA	25	13	8	2	1350	49	3	2.18	....	....	....	....	....	....	....
2000-01	Ferris State	CCHA	25	9	12	3	1449	57	3	2.36	....	....	....	....	....	....	....

CCHA Second All-Star Team (2001)

OSGOOD, Chris (AWS-gud, KRIHS) DET.

Goaltender. Catches left. 5'10", 175 lbs. Born, Peace River, Alta., November 26, 1972.
(Detroit's 3rd choice, 54th overall, in 1991 Entry Draft).

			Regular Season								Playoffs						
Season	**Club**	**Lea**	**GP**	**W**	**L**	**T**	**Mins**	**GA**	**SO**	**Avg**	**GP**	**W**	**L**	**Mins**	**GA**	**SO**	**Avg**
1988-89	Medicine Hat	AMHL	26	....	....	....	1441	88	0	3.66	....	....	....	....	....	....	....
1989-90	Medicine Hat	WHL	57	24	28	2	3094	228	0	4.42	3	0	3	173	17	0	5.91
1990-91	Medicine Hat	WHL	46	23	18	3	2630	173	2	3.95	12	7	5	712	42	0	3.54
1991-92	Medicine Hat	WHL	15	10	3	0	819	44	0	3.22	....	....	....	....	....	....	....
	Brandon	WHL	16	3	10	1	890	60	1	4.04	....	....	....	....	....	....	....
	Seattle T-Birds	WHL	21	12	7	1	1217	65	1	3.20	15	9	6	904	51	0	3.38
1992-93	Adirondack	AHL	45	19	19	4	2438	159	0	3.91	1	0	1	59	2	0	2.03
1993-94	**Detroit**	**NHL**	**41**	**23**	**8**	**5**	**2206**	**105**	**2**	**2.86**	**6**	**3**	**2**	**307**	**12**	**1**	**2.35**
	Adirondack	AHL	4	3	1	0	239	13	0	3.26	....	....	....	....	....	....	....
1994-95	**Detroit**	**NHL**	**19**	**14**	**5**	**0**	**1087**	**41**	**1**	**2.26**	**2**	**0**	**0**	**68**	**2**	**0**	**1.76**
	Adirondack	AHL	2	1	1	0	120	6	0	3.00	....	....	....	....	....	....	....
1995-96	**Detroit**	**NHL**	**50**	***39**	**6**	**5**	**2933**	**106**	**5**	**2.17**	**15**	**8**	**7**	**936**	**33**	**2**	**2.12**
1996-97♦	**Detroit**	**NHL**	**47**	**23**	**13**	**9**	**2769**	**106**	**6**	**2.30**	**2**	**0**	**0**	**47**	**2**	**0**	**2.55**
1997-98♦	**Detroit**	**NHL**	**64**	**33**	**20**	**11**	**3807**	**140**	**6**	**2.21**	***22**	***16**	**6**	***1361**	**48**	**2**	**2.12**
1998-99	**Detroit**	**NHL**	**63**	**34**	**25**	**4**	**3691**	**149**	**3**	**2.42**	**6**	**4**	**2**	**358**	**14**	**1**	**2.35**
99-2000	**Detroit**	**NHL**	**53**	**30**	**14**	**8**	**3148**	**126**	**6**	**2.40**	**9**	**5**	**4**	**547**	**18**	**2**	**1.97**
2000-01	**Detroit**	**NHL**	**52**	**25**	**19**	**4**	**2834**	**127**	**1**	**2.69**	**6**	**2**	**4**	**365**	**15**	**1**	**2.47**
	NHL Totals		**389**	**221**	**110**	**46**	**22475**	**900**	**30**	**2.40**	**68**	**38**	**25**	**3989**	**144**	**9**	**2.17**

WHL East Second All-Star Team (1991) • NHL Second All-Star Team (1996) • Shared William M. Jennings Trophy with Mike Vernon (1996) • Played in NHL All-Star Game (1996, 1997, 1998)

• Scored a goal while with Medicine Hat (WHL), January 3, 1991. • Scored a goal while with Detroit vs. Hartford, March 6, 1996.

OUELLET, Maxime (OO-leht, MAX-eem) PHI.

Goaltender. Catches left. 6'2", 195 lbs. Born, Beauport, Que., June 17, 1981.
(Philadelphia's 1st choice, 22nd overall, in 1999 Entry Draft).

			Regular Season								Playoffs						
Season	**Club**	**Lea**	**GP**	**W**	**L**	**T**	**Mins**	**GA**	**SO**	**Avg**	**GP**	**W**	**L**	**Mins**	**GA**	**SO**	**Avg**
1996-97	Ste-Foy Governors	QAAA	29	16	8	0	1470	81	0	2.75	9	4	5	555	31	0	3.37
1997-98	Quebec Remparts	QMJHL	24	12	7	1	1188	66	0	3.33	7	3	1	305	16	0	3.15
1998-99	Quebec Remparts	QMJHL	*59	*40	12	6	*3447	155	3	*2.70	13	6	7	803	41	*1	3.06
99-2000	Quebec Remparts	QMJHL	53	31	16	4	2984	133	2	2.67	11	7	4	638	28	*2	*2.63
2000-01	**Philadelphia**	**NHL**	**2**	**0**	**1**	**0**	**76**	**3**	**0**	**2.37**	....	....	....	....	....	....	....
	Philadelphia	AHL	2	1	0	0	86	4	0	2.78	....	....	....	....	....	....	....
	Rouyn-Noranda	QMJHL	25	18	6	1	1471	65	3	2.65	8	4	4	490	25	0	3.06
	NHL Totals		**2**	**0**	**1**	**0**	**76**	**3**	**0**	**2.37**	....	....	....	....	....	....	....

QMJHL Second All-Star Team (1999, 2000, 2001) • Won Jacques Plante Trophy (fewest goals against - QMJHL) (1999)

• Returned to **Rouyn-Noranda** (QMJHL) by **Philadelphia**, October 27, 2000.

PARENT, Rich (PEH-ruhn, RIHCH)

Goaltender. Catches left. 6'3", 195 lbs. Born, Montreal, Que., January 12, 1973.

			Regular Season								Playoffs						
Season	**Club**	**Lea**	**GP**	**W**	**L**	**T**	**Mins**	**GA**	**SO**	**Avg**	**GP**	**W**	**L**	**Mins**	**GA**	**SO**	**Avg**
1991-92	Fort McMurray	AJHL	23	....	....	....	1363	90	0	3.96	9	....	....	519	30	*1	3.47
	Vernon Lakers	BCJHL	2	0	1	0	52	5	0	5.77	....	....	....	....	....	....	....
1992-93	Spokane Chiefs	WHL	36	12	14	2	1767	129	2	4.38	1	0	0	5	0	0	0.00
1993-94	Fort McMurray	AJHL	29	....	....	....	1712	91	1	3.19	....	....	....	....	....	....	....
1994-95	Muskegon Fury	ColHL	35	17	11	3	1867	112	1	3.60	13	7	3	725	47	1	3.89
1995-96	Muskegon Fury	ColHL	36	23	7	4	2087	85	2	2.44	....	....	....	....	....	....	....
	Rochester	AHL	2	0	1	0	90	6	0	4.02	....	....	....	....	....	....	....
	Detroit Vipers	IHL	19	16	0	1	1040	48	2	2.77	7	3	3	363	22	0	3.64
1996-97	Detroit Vipers	IHL	53	31	13	4	2815	104	4	2.22	15	8	3	786	21	1	*1.60
1997-98	**St. Louis**	**NHL**	**1**	**0**	**0**	**0**	**12**	**0**	**0**	**0.00**	....	....	....	....	....	....	....
	Manitoba Moose	IHL	26	8	12	2	1334	69	3	3.10	....	....	....	....	....	....	....
	Detroit Vipers	IHL	7	4	0	3	417	15	0	2.15	5	1	0	157	6	0	2.29
1998-99	**St. Louis**	**NHL**	**10**	**4**	**3**	**1**	**519**	**22**	**1**	**2.54**	....	....	....	....	....	....	....
	Worcester	AHL	20	8	8	2	1100	56	1	3.05	....	....	....	....	....	....	....
99-2000	Utah Grizzlies	IHL	27	17	7	3	1571	58	1	2.21	....	....	....	....	....	....	....
	Tampa Bay	**NHL**	**14**	**2**	**7**	**1**	**698**	**43**	**0**	**3.70**	....	....	....	....	....	....	....
	Detroit Vipers	IHL	10	3	5	1	539	23	1	2.56	....	....	....	....	....	....	....
2000-01	**Pittsburgh**	**NHL**	**7**	**1**	**1**	**3**	**332**	**17**	**0**	**3.07**	....	....	....	....	....	....	....
	Wilkes-Barre	AHL	35	17	12	5	2043	80	2	2.35	*21	13	8	*1347	58	1	2.58
	NHL Totals		**32**	**7**	**11**	**5**	**1561**	**82**	**1**	**3.15**	....	....	....	....	....	....	....

ColHL First All-Star Team (1996) • Won ColHL Outstanding Goaltender Award (1996) • Shared James Norris Memorial Trophy (fewest goals against - IHL) with Jeff Reese (1997)

Signed as a free agent by **St. Louis**, July 31, 1997. Traded to **Tampa Bay** by **St. Louis** with Chris McAlpine for Stephane Richer, January 13, 2000. Traded to **Ottawa** by **Tampa Bay** for Ottawa's 7th round choice (later traded to NY Islanders - later traded to Buffalo - Buffalo selected Paul Gaustad) in 2000 Entry Draft, June 4, 2000. Signed as a free agent by **Pittsburgh**, September 20, 2000.

PARLEY, Davis (PAHR-lee, DAY-vihs) FLA.

Goaltender. Catches left. 6'2", 178 lbs. Born, Grenfell, Sask., September 4, 1982.
(Florida's 5th choice, 120th overall, in 2000 Entry Draft).

			Regular Season								Playoffs						
Season	**Club**	**Lea**	**GP**	**W**	**L**	**T**	**Mins**	**GA**	**SO**	**Avg**	**GP**	**W**	**L**	**Mins**	**GA**	**SO**	**Avg**
1998-99	Campbell River	VIJHL	23	....	....	....	1380	43	4	1.87	....	....	....	....	....	....	....
99-2000	Kamloops Blazers	WHL	26	8	15	2	1497	80	2	3.21	1	0	0	37	3	0	4.86
2000-01	Kamloops Blazers	WHL	52	27	16	3	2948	170	1	3.46	3	0	3	154	13	0	5.06

PASSMORE, Steve (PAS-mohr, STEEV) CHI.

Goaltender. Catches left. 5'9", 165 lbs. Born, Thunder Bay, Ont., January 29, 1973.
(Quebec's 10th choice, 196th overall, in 1992 Entry Draft).

			Regular Season								Playoffs						
Season	**Club**	**Lea**	**GP**	**W**	**L**	**T**	**Mins**	**GA**	**SO**	**Avg**	**GP**	**W**	**L**	**Mins**	**GA**	**SO**	**Avg**
1988-89	Tri-City Americans	WHL	1	0	1	0	60	6	0	6.00	....	....	....	....	....	....	....
1989-90	West Island Deltas	BCAHA	STATISTICS NOT AVAILABLE														
	Tri-City Americans	WHL	4	....	....	....	215	17	0	4.74	....	....	....	....	....	....	....
1990-91	Victoria Cougars	WHL	35	3	25	1	1838	190	0	6.20	....	....	....	....	....	....	....
1991-92	Victoria Cougars	WHL	*71	15	50	5	*4228	347	0	4.92	....	....	....	....	....	....	....
1992-93	Victoria Cougars	WHL	43	14	24	2	2402	150	1	3.75	....	....	....	....	....	....	....
	Kamloops Blazers	WHL	25	19	6	0	1479	69	1	2.80	7	4	2	401	22	1	3.29
1993-94	Kamloops Blazers	WHL	36	22	9	2	1927	88	1	*2.74	*18	*11	7	*1099	60	0	3.28
1994-95	Cape Breton Oilers	AHL	25	8	13	3	1455	93	0	3.83	....	....	....	....	....	....	....
1995-96	Cape Breton Oilers	AHL	2	1	0	0	90	2	0	1.33	....	....	....	....	....	....	....
1996-97	Hamilton Bulldogs	AHL	27	12	12	3	1568	70	1	2.68	22	12	10	1325	61	*2	2.76
	Raleigh IceCaps	ECHL	2	1	1	0	118	13	0	6.56	....	....	....	....	....	....	....
1997-98	Hamilton Bulldogs	AHL	27	11	10	6	1655	87	2	3.15	3	0	2	132	14	0	6.33
	San Antonio	IHL	14	3	8	2	736	56	0	4.56	....	....	....	....	....	....	....
1998-99	**Edmonton**	**NHL**	**6**	**1**	**4**	**1**	**362**	**17**	**0**	**2.82**	....	....	....	....	....	....	....
	Hamilton Bulldogs	AHL	54	24	21	7	3148	117	4	2.23	11	5	6	680	31	0	2.74
99-2000	**Chicago**	**NHL**	**24**	**7**	**12**	**3**	**1388**	**63**	**1**	**2.72**	....	....	....	....	....	....	....
	Cleveland	IHL	2	1	0	1	120	3	1	1.50	....	....	....	....	....	....	....
2000-01	**Los Angeles**	**NHL**	**14**	**3**	**8**	**1**	**718**	**37**	**1**	**3.09**	....	....	....	....	....	....	....
	Lowell	AHL	6	2	4	0	334	24	0	4.32	....	....	....	....	....	....	....
	Chicago	**NHL**	**6**	**0**	**4**	**1**	**340**	**14**	**0**	**2.47**	....	....	....	....	....	....	....
	Chicago Wolves	IHL	6	2	2	2	340	22	0	3.88	....	....	....	....	....	....	....
	NHL Totals		**50**	**11**	**28**	**6**	**2808**	**131**	**2**	**2.80**	....	....	....	....	....	....	....

WHL West First All-Star Team (1993, 1994) • Won Fred Hunt Memorial Trophy (Sportsmanship - AHL) (1997) • AHL Second All-Star Team (1999)

Traded to **Edmonton** by **Quebec** for Brad Werenka, March 21, 1994. • Missed majority of the 1995-96 season recovering from blood disorder, October, 1995. Signed as a free agent by **Chicago**, July 8, 1999. Traded to **LA Kings** by **Chicago** for LA Kings' 4th round choice (Olli Malmivaara) in 2000 Entry Draft, May 1, 2000. Traded to **Chicago** by **LA Kings** for Chicago's 8th round choice (Mike Gabinet) in 2001 Entry Draft, February 28, 2001.

PATZOLD, Dimitri (PATZ-ohld, dih-MEE-tree) S.J.

Goaltender. Catches left. 6', 183 lbs. Born, Ust-Kamenogorsk, USSR, February 3, 1983.
(San Jose's 3rd choice, 107th overall, in 2001 Entry Draft).

			Regular Season								Playoffs						
Season	**Club**	**Lea**	**GP**	**W**	**L**	**T**	**Mins**	**GA**	**SO**	**Avg**	**GP**	**W**	**L**	**Mins**	**GA**	**SO**	**Avg**
99-2000	Kolner Haie	DEL-Jr.	38	....	....	....	2131	73	0	2.06	....	....	....	....	....	....	....
	Kolner Haie-2	DEB-4	16	....	....	....	896	58	0	3.88	....	....	....	....	....	....	....
2000-01	Kolner Haie-2	DEB-4	6	....	....	....	359	17	0	2.84	....	....	....	....	....	....	....
	TSV Erding Jets	DEB	24	....	....	....	1378	89	0	3.88	....	....	....	....	....	....	....

PELLETIER, Jean-Marc (PEHL-tyay, ZHAWN-MAHRK) CAR.

Goaltender. Catches left. 6'3", 200 lbs. Born, Atlanta, GA, March 4, 1978.
(Philadelphia's 1st choice, 30th overall, in 1997 Entry Draft).

			Regular Season								Playoffs						
Season	**Club**	**Lea**	**GP**	**W**	**L**	**T**	**Mins**	**GA**	**SO**	**Avg**	**GP**	**W**	**L**	**Mins**	**GA**	**SO**	**Avg**
1993-94	Richelieu Riverains	QAAA	24	14	8	2	1440	91	0	3.79	2	1	0	104	11	0	6.32
1994-95	Richelieu Riverains	QAAA	21	15	6	0	1260	71	0	3.36	2	1	1	153	11	0	4.32
1995-96	Cornell Big Red	ECAC	5	1	2	0	179	15	0	5.03	....	....	....	....	....	....	....
1996-97	Cornell Big Red	ECAC	11	5	2	3	679	28	1	2.47	....	....	....	....	....	....	....
1997-98	Rimouski Oceanic	QMJHL	34	17	11	3	1913	118	0	3.70	16	11	3	895	51	1	3.42
1998-99	**Philadelphia**	**NHL**	**1**	**0**	**1**	**0**	**60**	**5**	**0**	**5.00**	....	....	....	....	....	....	....
	Philadelphia	AHl	47	25	16	4	2636	122	2	2.78	1	0	0	27	0	0	0.00
99-2000	Philadelphia	AHL	24	14	10	0	1405	58	3	2.48	....	....	....	....	....	....	....
	Cincinnati	IHL	22	14	4	2	1278	52	2	2.44	3	1	1	160	8	1	3.00
2000-01	Cincinnati	IHL	39	18	14	5	2261	119	2	3.16	5	1	4	318	15	0	2.83
	NHL Totals		**1**	**0**	**1**	**0**	**60**	**5**	**0**	**5.00**	....	....	....	....	....	....	....

Traded to **Carolina** by **Philadelphia** with Rod Brind'Amour and Philadelphia's 2nd round choice (later traded to Colorado - Colorado selected Argis Saviels) in 2000 Entry Draft for Keith Primeau and Carolina's 5th round choice (later traded to NY Islanders - NY Islanders selected Kristofer Ottosson) in 2000 Entry Draft, January 23, 2000.

PENKO, Jure (PEHN-koh, YOO-ree) NSH.

Goaltender. Catches left. 6'1", 188 lbs. Born, Ljublijuna, Yugoslavia, April 6, 1981.
(Nashville's 10th choice, 203rd overall, in 2000 Entry Draft).

			Regular Season								Playoffs						
Season	**Club**	**Lea**	**GP**	**W**	**L**	**T**	**Mins**	**GA**	**SO**	**Avg**	**GP**	**W**	**L**	**Mins**	**GA**	**SO**	**Avg**
1998-99	Leamington	OJHL-B	20	17	3	0	1129	45	3	2.89	12	7	4	691	32	1	2.52
99-2000	Green Bay	USHL	40	25	12	3	2416	113	1	2.81	14	10	4	900	32	1	2.13
	Arkansas Blades	ECHL	2	0	1	0	95	8	0	5.05	....	....	....	....	....	....	....
2000-01	Green Bay	USHL	46	28	8	10	2711	108	4	2.39	4	1	3	238	9	1	2.27

PETRUK, Randy (PEHT-ruhk, RAN-dee) CAR.

Goaltender. Catches right. 5'9", 175 lbs. Born, Cranbrook, B.C., April 23, 1978.
(Colorado's 5th choice, 107th overall, in 1996 Entry Draft).

			Regular Season								Playoffs						
Season	**Club**	**Lea**	**GP**	**W**	**L**	**T**	**Mins**	**GA**	**SO**	**Avg**	**GP**	**W**	**L**	**Mins**	**GA**	**SO**	**Avg**
1993-94	Cranbrook Colts	RMJHL	21	....	....	....	1158	89	0	4.61	....	....	....	....	....	....	....
1994-95	Kamloops Blazers	WHL	27	16	3	4	1462	71	1	2.91	7	5	2	423	19	0	2.70
1995-96	Kamloops Blazers	WHL	52	34	15	1	3071	181	1	3.54	16	9	6	990	58	0	3.52
1996-97	Kamloops Blazers	WHL	*60	25	28	5	*3475	210	0	3.63	....	....	....	....	....	....	....
1997-98	Kamloops Blazers	WHL	57	31	21	1	3097	157	3	3.04	7	3	4	425	21	0	2.96
1998-99	Florida Everblades	ECHL	25	13	10	2	1441	66	1	2.75	1	0	1	60	5	0	5.00
	New Haven	AHL	1	0	0	1	65	3	0	2.77	....	....	....	....	....	....	....
99-2000	Florida Everblades	ECHL	6	5	0	1	339	19	0	3.36	....	....	....	....	....	....	....
	Cincinnati	IHL	26	13	9	3	1436	84	2	3.51	9	4	5	551	27	1	2.94
2000-01	Cincinnati	IHL	8	4	3	0	420	23	1	3.29	....	....	....	....	....	....	....
	Florida Everblades	ECHL	13	5	7	1	742	41	0	3.31	....	....	....	....	....	....	....

WHL West Second All-Star Team (1998)

Traded to **Carolina** by **Colorado** for Carolina's 5th round choice (William Magnuson) in 1999 Entry Draft, June 1, 1998.

POLUKEYEV, Alexander (pawl-oo-KAY-ehv, al-ehx-AN-duhr) T.B.

Goaltender. Catches left. 6'3", 187 lbs. Born, Leningrad, USSR, January 7, 1981.
(Tampa Bay's 9th choice, 233rd overall, in 2000 Entry Draft).

			Regular Season								Playoffs						
Season	**Club**	**Lea**	**GP**	**W**	**L**	**T**	**Mins**	**GA**	**SO**	**Avg**	**GP**	**W**	**L**	**Mins**	**GA**	**SO**	**Avg**
1997-98	St. Petersburg-2	Russia-3	10	....	....	....	600	39	....	3.90	....	....	....	....	....	....	....
1998-99	St. Petersburg-3	Russia-4	1	1	0	0	60	1	0	1.00	....	....	....	....	....	....	....
99-2000	St. Petersburg	Russia-Jr.	18	....	....	....	1080	85	....	4.72	....	....	....	....	....	....	....
2000-01	St. Petersburg	Russia	5	0	4	0	264	20	0	4.55	....	....	....	....	....	....	....

POTVIN, Felix (PAHT-vihn, FEEL-ihx) L.A.

Goaltender. Catches left. 6'1", 190 lbs. Born, Anjou, Que., June 23, 1971.
(Toronto's 2nd choice, 31st overall, in 1990 Entry Draft).

			Regular Season								Playoffs						
Season	**Club**	**Lea**	**GP**	**W**	**L**	**T**	**Mins**	**GA**	**SO**	**Avg**	**GP**	**W**	**L**	**Mins**	**GA**	**SO**	**Avg**
1987-88	Montreal-Bourassa	QAAA	27	15	7	3	1585	103	3	3.90	6	2	4	341	20	0	3.51
1988-89	Chicoutimi	QMJHL	*65	25	31	1	*3489	271	*2	4.66	....	....	....	....	....	....	....
1989-90	Chicoutimi	QMJHL	*62	*31	26	2	*3478	231	*2	3.99	....	....	....	....	....	....	....
1990-91	Chicoutimi	QMJHL	54	33	15	4	3216	145	*6	*2.70	*16	*11	5	*992	46	0	*2.78
1991-92	**Toronto**	**NHL**	**4**	**0**	**2**	**1**	**210**	**8**	**0**	**2.29**	....	....	....	....	....	....	....
	St. John's Leafs	AHL	35	18	10	6	2070	101	2	2.93	11	7	4	642	41	0	3.83
1992-93	**Toronto**	**NHL**	**48**	**25**	**15**	**7**	**2781**	**116**	**2**	***2.50**	***21**	**11**	**10**	***1308**	**62**	**1**	**2.84**
	St. John's Leafs	AHL	5	3	0	2	309	18	0	3.50	....	....	....	....	....	....	....
1993-94	**Toronto**	**NHL**	**66**	**34**	**22**	**9**	**3883**	**187**	**3**	**2.89**	**18**	**9**	**9**	**1124**	**46**	**3**	**2.46**
1994-95	**Toronto**	**NHL**	**36**	**15**	**13**	**7**	**2144**	**104**	**0**	**2.91**	**7**	**3**	**4**	**424**	**20**	**1**	**2.83**
1995-96	**Toronto**	**NHL**	**69**	**30**	**26**	**11**	**4009**	**192**	**2**	**2.87**	**6**	**2**	**4**	**350**	**19**	**0**	**3.26**
1996-97	**Toronto**	**NHL**	***74**	**27**	**36**	**7**	***4271**	**224**	**0**	**3.15**	....	....	....	....	....	....	....
1997-98	**Toronto**	**NHL**	**67**	**26**	**33**	**7**	**3864**	**176**	**5**	**2.73**	....	....	....	....	....	....	....
1998-99	**Toronto**	**NHL**	**5**	**3**	**2**	**0**	**299**	**19**	**0**	**3.81**	....	....	....	....	....	....	....
	NY Islanders	**NHL**	**11**	**2**	**7**	**1**	**606**	**37**	**0**	**3.66**	....	....	....	....	....	....	....
99-2000	**NY Islanders**	**NHL**	**22**	**5**	**14**	**3**	**1273**	**68**	**1**	**3.21**	....	....	....	....	....	....	....
	Vancouver	**NHL**	**34**	**12**	**13**	**7**	**1966**	**85**	**0**	**2.59**	....	....	....	....	....	....	....
2000-01	**Vancouver**	**NHL**	**35**	**14**	**17**	**3**	**2006**	**103**	**1**	**3.08**	....	....	....	....	....	....	....
	Los Angeles	**NHL**	**23**	**13**	**5**	**5**	**1410**	**46**	**5**	**1.96**	**13**	**7**	**6**	**812**	**33**	**2**	**2.44**
	NHL Totals		**494**	**206**	**205**	**68**	**28722**	**1365**	**19**	**2.85**	**65**	**32**	**33**	**4018**	**180**	**7**	**2.69**

QMJHL Second All-Star Team (1990) • QMJHL First All-Star Team (1991) • Canadian Major Junior Goaltender of the Year (1991) • Memorial Cup All-Star Team (1991) • Won Hap Emms Memorial Trophy (Memorial Cup Tournament Top Goaltender) (1991) • AHL First All-Star Team (1992) • Won Dudley "Red" Garrett Memorial Trophy (Top Rookie - AHL) (1992) • Won Baz Bastien Memorial Trophy (Top Goaltender - AHL) (1992) • NHL All-Rookie Team (1993) • Played in NHL All-Star Game (1994, 1996)

Traded to **NY Islanders** by **Toronto** with Toronto's 6th round choice (later traded to Tampa Bay - Tampa Bay selected Fedor Fedorov) in 1999 Entry Draft for Bryan Berard and NY Islanders' 6th round choice (Jan Sochor) in 1999 Entry Draft, January 9, 1999. Traded to **Vancouver** by **NY Islanders** with NY Islanders' compensatory 2nd (later traded to New Jersey - New Jersey selected Teemu Laine) and 3rd (Thatcher Bell) round choices in 2000 Entry Draft for Kevin Weekes, Dave Scatchard and Bill Muckalt, December 19, 1999. Traded to **LA Kings** by **Vancouver** for future considerations, February 15, 2001.

PRUSEK, Martin (PREW-sehk, MAHR-tihn) OTT.

Goaltender. Catches left. 6'1", 163 lbs. Born, Ostrava, Czech., December 11, 1975.
(Ottawa's 6th choice, 164th overall, in 1999 Entry Draft).

			Regular Season								Playoffs						
Season	**Club**	**Lea**	**GP**	**W**	**L**	**T**	**Mins**	**GA**	**SO**	**Avg**	**GP**	**W**	**L**	**Mins**	**GA**	**SO**	**Avg**
1994-95	HC Vitkovice	Cze-Rep	5	....	....	....	232	18	....	4.65	....	....	....	....	....	....	....
1995-96	HC Vitkovice	Cze-Rep	40	....	....	....	2336	113	1	2.90	4	....	....	250	10	1	2.40
1996-97	HC Vitkovice	Cze-Rep	49	....	....	....	2841	109	8	2.30	9	....	....	546	19	1	2.08
1997-98	HC Vitkovice	Cze-Rep	50	....	....	....	2901	129	....	2.67	9	....	....	529	26	....	3.00
1998-99	HC Vitkovice	Cze-Rep	37	....	....	....	1905	85	....	2.68	4	....	....	250	12	....	2.88
99-2000	HC Vitkovice	Cze-Rep	50	....	....	....	2647	132	....	2.99	....	....	....	....	....	....	....
2000-01	HC Vitkovice	Cze-Rep	30	....	....	....	1679	64	....	2.29	9	....	....	460	25	....	3.26

PUURULA, Joni (pu-u-ROO-luh, YOHN-ee) MTL.

Goaltender. Catches left. 5'11", 180 lbs. Born, Kokkola, Finland, August 4, 1982.
(Montreal's 10th choice, 243rd overall, in 2000 Entry Draft).

			Regular Season								Playoffs						
Season	**Club**	**Lea**	**GP**	**W**	**L**	**T**	**Mins**	**GA**	**SO**	**Avg**	**GP**	**W**	**L**	**Mins**	**GA**	**SO**	**Avg**
1998-99	Junkkarit Kalajoki	Finland-2	12	....	....	....	782	37	0	2.84	....	....	....	....	....	....	....
99-2000	Hermes Kokkola	Finland-2	23	8	12	2	1251	81	1	3.88	....	....	....	....	....	....	....
2000-01	FPS Fossa	Finland-2	39	....	....	....	2263	142	1	3.76	....	....	....	....	....	....	....
	FPS Fossa	Finn-Jr.	....	....	....	....	....	....	....	....	4	1	3	240	8	0	2.00

RACINE, Jean-Francois (RAY-seen, ZHAWN-fran-SWUH) TOR.

Goaltender. Catches left. 6'3", 183 lbs. Born, St-Hyacinthe, Que., April 27, 1982.
(Toronto's 4th choice, 90th overall, in 2000 Entry Draft).

			Regular Season								Playoffs						
Season	**Club**	**Lea**	**GP**	**W**	**L**	**T**	**Mins**	**GA**	**SO**	**Avg**	**GP**	**W**	**L**	**Mins**	**GA**	**SO**	**Avg**
1998-99	Magog Selectes	QAAA	36	19	12	1	2160	107	3	2.98	11	5	6	656	37	0	3.39
99-2000	Moncton Wildcats	QMJHL	10	3	3	1	410	28	0	4.10	....	....	....	....	....	....	....
	Drummondville	QMJHL	20	14	6	0	1152	63	1	3.28	3	0	0	65	5	0	4.60
2000-01	Drummondville	QMJHL	61	27	26	3	3362	189	4	3.37	5	2	3	303	20	0	3.97

RAYCROFT, Andrew (RAY-krawft, AN-droo) BOS.

Goaltender. Catches left. 6', 174 lbs. Born, Belleville, Ont., May 4, 1980.
(Boston's 4th choice, 135th overall, in 1998 Entry Draft).

			Regular Season								Playoffs						
Season	**Club**	**Lea**	**GP**	**W**	**L**	**T**	**Mins**	**GA**	**SO**	**Avg**	**GP**	**W**	**L**	**Mins**	**GA**	**SO**	**Avg**
1996-97	Wellington Dukes	MTJHL	27	....	....	....	1402	92	0	3.94	....	....	....	....	....	....	....
1997-98	Sudbury Wolves	OHL	33	8	16	5	1802	125	0	4.16	2	0	1	89	8	0	5.39
1998-99	Sudbury Wolves	OHL	45	17	22	5	2528	173	1	4.11	3	0	2	96	13	0	8.13
99-2000	Kingston	OHL	*61	33	20	5	3340	191	0	3.43	5	1	4	300	21	0	4.20
2000-01	**Boston**	**NHL**	**15**	**4**	**6**	**0**	**649**	**32**	**0**	**2.96**	....	....	....	....	....	....	....
	Providence Bruins	AHL	26	8	14	4	1459	82	1	3.37	....	....	....	....	....	....	....
	NHL Totals		**15**	**4**	**6**	**0**	**649**	**32**	**0**	**2.96**	....	....	....	....	....	....	....

OHL First All-Star Team (2000) • Canadian Major Junior First All-Star Team (2000) • Canadian Major Junior Goaltender of the Year (2000)

RHODES, Damian (ROHDZ, DAY-mee-uhn) ATL.

Goaltender. Catches left. 5'11", 195 lbs. Born, St. Paul, MN, May 28, 1969.
(Toronto's 6th choice, 112th overall, in 1987 Entry Draft).

			Regular Season								Playoffs						
Season	Club	Lea	GP	W	L	T	Mins	GA	SO	Avg	GP	W	L	Mins	GA	SO	Avg
1985-86	Richfield High	H.S.	16	....	....	....	720	56	0	3.50	....	....	....	....	....	....	....
1986-87	Richfield High	H.S.	19	....	....	....	673	51	1	4.55	....	....	....	....	....	....	....
1987-88	Michigan Tech	WCHA	29	16	10	1	1625	114	0	4.20	....	....	....	....	....	....	....
1988-89	Michigan Tech	WCHA	37	15	22	0	2216	163	0	4.41	....	....	....	....	....	....	....
1989-90	Michigan Tech	WCHA	25	6	17	0	1358	119	0	6.26	....	....	....	....	....	....	....
1990-91	**Toronto**	**NHL**	**1**	**1**	**0**	**0**	**60**	**1**	**0**	**1.00**	....	....	....	....	....	....	....
	Newmarket Saints	AHL	38	8	24	3	2154	144	1	4.01	....	....	....	....	....	....	....
1991-92	St. John's Leafs	AHL	43	20	16	5	2454	148	0	3.62	6	4	1	331	16	0	2.90
1992-93	St. John's Leafs	AHL	*52	27	16	8	*3074	184	1	3.59	9	4	5	538	37	0	4.13
1993-94	**Toronto**	**NHL**	**22**	**9**	**7**	**3**	**1213**	**53**	**0**	**2.62**	**1**	**0**	**0**	**1**	**0**	**0**	**0.00**
1994-95	**Toronto**	**NHL**	**13**	**6**	**6**	**1**	**760**	**34**	**0**	**2.68**	....	....	....	....	....	....	....
1995-96	**Toronto**	**NHL**	**11**	**4**	**5**	**1**	**624**	**29**	**0**	**2.79**	....	....	....	....	....	....	....
	Ottawa	**NHL**	**36**	**10**	**22**	**4**	**2123**	**98**	**2**	**2.77**	....	....	....	....	....	....	....
1996-97	**Ottawa**	**NHL**	**50**	**14**	**20**	**14**	**2934**	**133**	**1**	**2.72**	....	....	....	....	....	....	....
1997-98	**Ottawa**	**NHL**	**50**	**19**	**19**	**7**	**2743**	**107**	**5**	**2.34**	**10**	**5**	**5**	**590**	**21**	**0**	**2.14**
1998-99	**Ottawa**	**NHL**	**45**	**22**	**13**	**7**	**2480**	**101**	**3**	**2.44**	**2**	**0**	**2**	**150**	**6**	**0**	**2.40**
99-2000	**Atlanta**	**NHL**	**28**	**5**	**19**	**3**	**1561**	**101**	**1**	**3.88**	....	....	....	....	....	....	....
2000-01	**Atlanta**	**NHL**	**38**	**7**	**19**	**7**	**2072**	**116**	**0**	**3.36**	....	....	....	....	....	....	....
	NHL Totals		**294**	**97**	**130**	**47**	**16570**	**773**	**12**	**2.80**	**13**	**5**	**7**	**741**	**27**	**0**	**2.19**

• Credited with scoring a goal while with Michigan Tech (WCHA), January 21, 1989. • Played 10 seconds of playoff game vs. San Jose, May 6, 1994. • Credited with scoring a goal while with Ottawa vs. New Jersey, January 2, 1999.

Traded to **NY Islanders** by **Toronto** with Ken Belanger for future considerations (Kirk Muller and Don Beaupre, January 23, 1996), January 23, 1996. Traded to **Ottawa** by **NY Islanders** with Wade Redden for Don Beaupre, Martin Straka and Bryan Berard, January 23, 1996. Traded to **Atlanta** by **Ottawa** for future considerations, June 18, 1999.

RICHTER, Mike (RIHK-tuhr, MIGHK) NYR

Goaltender. Catches left. 5'11", 185 lbs. Born, Abington, PA, September 22, 1966.
(NY Rangers' 2nd choice, 28th overall, in 1985 Entry Draft).

			Regular Season								Playoffs						
Season	Club	Lea	GP	W	L	T	Mins	GA	SO	Avg	GP	W	L	Mins	GA	SO	Avg
1983-84	Philadelphia	NEJHL	36	23	10	3	2160	94	0	2.61	....	....	....	....	....	....	....
1984-85	Northwood Prep	H.S.	24	....	....	....	1374	52	2	2.27	....	....	....	....	....	....	....
1985-86	U. of Wisconsin	WCHA	24	14	9	0	1394	92	1	3.96	....	....	....	....	....	....	....
1986-87	U. of Wisconsin	WCHA	36	19	16	1	2136	126	0	3.54	....	....	....	....	....	....	....
1987-88	United States	Nt-Team	29	17	7	2	1559	86	0	3.31	....	....	....	....	....	....	....
	United States	Olympics	4	2	2	0	230	15	0	3.91	....	....	....	....	....	....	....
	Colorado Rangers	IHL	22	16	5	0	1298	68	1	3.14	10	5	3	536	35	0	3.92
1988-89	Denver Rangers	IHL	*57	23	26	0	3031	217	1	4.30	4	0	4	210	21	0	6.00
	NY Rangers	**NHL**	....	....	....	....	....	....	....	....	**1**	**0**	**1**	**58**	**4**	**0**	**4.14**
1989-90	**NY Rangers**	**NHL**	**23**	**12**	**5**	**5**	**1320**	**66**	**0**	**3.00**	**6**	**3**	**2**	**330**	**19**	**0**	**3.45**
	Flint Spirits	IHL	13	7	4	2	782	49	0	3.76	....	....	....	....	....	....	....
1990-91	**NY Rangers**	**NHL**	**45**	**21**	**13**	**7**	**2596**	**135**	**0**	**3.12**	**6**	**2**	**4**	**313**	**14**	***1**	**2.68**
1991-92	**NY Rangers**	**NHL**	**41**	**23**	**12**	**2**	**2298**	**119**	**3**	**3.11**	**7**	**4**	**2**	**412**	**24**	**1**	**3.50**
1992-93	**NY Rangers**	**NHL**	**38**	**13**	**19**	**3**	**2105**	**134**	**1**	**3.82**	....	....	....	....	....	....	....
	Binghamton	AHL	5	4	0	1	305	6	0	1.18	....	....	....	....	....	....	....
1993-94♦	**NY Rangers**	**NHL**	**68**	***42**	**12**	**6**	**3710**	**159**	**5**	**2.57**	**23**	***16**	**7**	**1417**	**49**	***4**	**2.07**
1994-95	**NY Rangers**	**NHL**	**35**	**14**	**17**	**2**	**1993**	**97**	**2**	**2.92**	**7**	**2**	**5**	**384**	**23**	**0**	**3.59**
1995-96	**NY Rangers**	**NHL**	**41**	**24**	**13**	**3**	**2396**	**107**	**3**	**2.68**	**11**	**5**	**6**	**661**	**36**	**0**	**3.27**
1996-97	**NY Rangers**	**NHL**	**61**	**33**	**22**	**6**	**3598**	**161**	**4**	**2.68**	**15**	**9**	**6**	**939**	**33**	***3**	**2.11**
1997-98	**NY Rangers**	**NHL**	***72**	**21**	**31**	**15**	**4143**	**184**	**0**	**2.66**	....	....	....	....	....	....	....
	United States	Olympics	4	1	3	0	237	14	0	3.55	....	....	....	....	....	....	....
1998-99	**NY Rangers**	**NHL**	**68**	**27**	**30**	**8**	**3878**	**170**	**4**	**2.63**	....	....	....	....	....	....	....
99-2000	**NY Rangers**	**NHL**	**61**	**22**	**31**	**8**	**3622**	**173**	**0**	**2.87**	....	....	....	....	....	....	....
2000-01	**NY Rangers**	**NHL**	**45**	**20**	**21**	**3**	**2635**	**144**	**0**	**3.28**	....	....	....	....	....	....	....
	NHL Totals		**598**	**272**	**226**	**68**	**34294**	**1649**	**22**	**2.89**	**76**	**41**	**33**	**4514**	**202**	**9**	**2.68**

WCHA Second All-Star Team (1987) • Played in NHL All-Star Game (1992, 1994, 2000)

Claimed by **Nashville** from **NY Rangers** in Expansion Draft, June 26, 1998. Signed as a free agent by **NY Rangers**, July 15, 1998.

ROLOSON, Dwayne (ROH-loh-suhn, DWAYN) MIN.

Goaltender. Catches left. 6'1", 178 lbs. Born, Simcoe, Ont., October 12, 1969.

			Regular Season								Playoffs						
Season	Club	Lea	GP	W	L	T	Mins	GA	SO	Avg	GP	W	L	Mins	GA	SO	Avg
1984-85	Simcoe Penguins	OJHL-C	3	....	....	....	100	21	0	12.60	....	....	....	....	....	....	....
1985-86	Simcoe Rams	OJHL-C	1	....	....	....	60	6	0	6.00	....	....	....	....	....	....	....
1986-87	Norwich Merchants	OJHL-C	19	....	....	....	1091	55	0	*3.03	....	....	....	....	....	....	....
1987-88	Belleville Bobcats	OJHL-B	21	9	6	1	1070	60	*2	3.36	....	....	....	....	....	....	....
1988-89	Thorold Hawks	OJHL-B	27	15	6	4	1490	82	0	3.30	....	....	....	....	....	....	....
1989-90	Thorold Hawks	OJHL-B	30	18	8	1	1683	108	0	3.85	....	....	....	....	....	....	....
1990-91	U. Mass-Lowell	H-East	15	5	9	0	823	63	0	4.59	....	....	....	....	....	....	....
1991-92	U. Mass-Lowell	H-East	12	3	8	0	660	52	0	4.73	....	....	....	....	....	....	....
1992-93	U. Mass-Lowell	H-East	*39	20	17	2	*2342	150	0	3.84	....	....	....	....	....	....	....
1993-94	U. Mass-Lowell	H-East	*40	*23	10	7	*2305	106	0	2.76	....	....	....	....	....	....	....
1994-95	Saint John Flames	AHL	46	16	21	8	2734	156	1	3.42	5	1	4	298	13	0	2.61
1995-96	Saint John Flames	AHL	67	*33	22	11	4026	190	1	2.83	16	10	6	1027	49	1	2.86
1996-97	**Calgary**	**NHL**	**31**	**9**	**14**	**3**	**1618**	**78**	**1**	**2.89**	....	....	....	....	....	....	....
	Saint John Flames	AHL	8	6	2	0	481	22	1	2.75	....	....	....	....	....	....	....
1997-98	**Calgary**	**NHL**	**39**	**11**	**16**	**8**	**2205**	**110**	**0**	**2.99**	....	....	....	....	....	....	....
	Saint John Flames	AHL	4	3	0	1	245	8	0	1.96	....	....	....	....	....	....	....
1998-99	**Buffalo**	**NHL**	**18**	**6**	**8**	**2**	**911**	**42**	**1**	**2.77**	**4**	**1**	**1**	**139**	**10**	**0**	**4.32**
	Rochester	AHL	2	2	0	0	120	4	0	2.00	....	....	....	....	....	....	....
99-2000	**Buffalo**	**NHL**	**14**	**1**	**7**	**3**	**677**	**32**	**0**	**2.84**	....	....	....	....	....	....	....
2000-01	Worcester	AHL	52	*32	15	5	*3127	113	*6	*2.17	11	6	5	697	23	1	1.98
	NHL Totals		**102**	**27**	**45**	**16**	**5411**	**262**	**2**	**2.91**	**4**	**1**	**1**	**139**	**10**	**0**	**4.32**

Hockey East First All-Star Team (1994) • NCAA East First All-Ameircan Team (1994) • AHL First All-Star Team (2001) • Won Baz Bastien Memorial Trophy (Top Goaltender - AHL) (2001)

Signed as a free agent by **Calgary**, July 4, 1994. Signed as a free agent by **Buffalo**, July 15, 1998. Selected by **Columbus** from **Buffalo** in Expansion Draft, June 23, 2000. Signed as a free agent by **St. Louis**, July 14, 2000. Signed as a free agent by **Minnesota**, July 2, 2001.

ROUSSEAU, Ghyslain (roo-SOH, zhihz-LEH) BUF.

Goaltender. Catches left. 6'1", 160 lbs. Born, Black Lake, Que., February 6, 1982.
(Buffalo's 3rd choice, 111th overall, in 2000 Entry Draft).

			Regular Season								Playoffs						
Season	Club	Lea	GP	W	L	T	Mins	GA	SO	Avg	GP	W	L	Mins	GA	SO	Avg
1998-99	Levis Commanders	QAAA	24	2	17	1	1176	112	0	5.71	....	....	....	....	....	....	....
99-2000	Baie-Comeau	QMJHL	46	19	15	1	2301	147	0	3.83	1	0	0	1	0	0	0.00
2000-01	Baie-Comeau	QMJHL	29	9	10	4	1445	86	1	3.57	1	0	1	47	3	0	3.88

ROUSSEL, Dominic (roo-SEHL, DOHM-ih-NIHK)

Goaltender. Catches left. 6'1", 200 lbs. Born, Hull, Que., February 22, 1970.
(Philadelphia's 4th choice, 63rd overall, in 1988 Entry Draft).

			Regular Season								Playoffs						
Season	Club	Lea	GP	W	L	T	Mins	GA	SO	Avg	GP	W	L	Mins	GA	SO	Avg
1986-87	Lac St-Louis	QAAA	24	7	12	3	804	112	1	5.10	2	0	2	134	7	0	3.13
1987-88	Trois-Rivieres	QMJHL	51	18	25	4	2905	251	0	5.18	....	....	....	....	....	....	....
1988-89	Shawinigan	QMJHL	46	24	15	2	2555	171	0	4.02	10	6	4	638	36	0	3.39
1989-90	Shawinigan	QMJHL	37	20	14	1	1985	133	0	4.02	2	1	1	120	12	0	6.00
1990-91	Hershey Bears	AHL	45	20	14	7	2507	151	1	3.61	7	3	4	366	21	0	3.44
1991-92	**Philadelphia**	**NHL**	**17**	**7**	**8**	**2**	**922**	**40**	**1**	**2.60**	....	....	....	....	....	....	....
	Hershey Bears	AHL	35	15	11	6	2040	121	1	3.56	....	....	....	....	....	....	....
1992-93	**Philadelphia**	**NHL**	**34**	**13**	**11**	**5**	**1769**	**111**	**1**	**3.76**	....	....	....	....	....	....	....
	Hershey Bears	AHL	6	0	3	3	372	23	0	3.71	....	....	....	....	....	....	....
1993-94	**Philadelphia**	**NHL**	**60**	**29**	**20**	**5**	**3285**	**183**	**1**	**3.34**	....	....	....	....	....	....	....
1994-95	**Philadelphia**	**NHL**	**19**	**11**	**7**	**0**	**1075**	**42**	**1**	**2.34**	**1**	**0**	**0**	**23**	**0**	**0**	**0.00**
	Hershey Bears	AHL	1	0	1	0	59	5	0	5.07	....	....	....	....	....	....	....
1995-96	**Philadelphia**	**NHL**	**9**	**2**	**3**	**2**	**456**	**22**	**1**	**2.89**	....	....	....	....	....	....	....
	Hershey Bears	AHL	12	4	4	3	690	32	0	2.78	....	....	....	....	....	....	....
	Winnipeg	**NHL**	**7**	**2**	**2**	**0**	**285**	**16**	**0**	**3.37**	....	....	....	....	....	....	....
1996-97	Philadelphia	AHL	36	18	9	3	1852	82	2	2.66	1	0	0	26	3	0	6.93
1997-98	Canada	Nt-Team	41	25	12	1	2307	86	5	2.24	....	....	....	....	....	....	....
	SB Rosenheim	DEL	2	0	2	0	120	12	0	6.00	....	....	....	....	....	....	....
1998-99	**Anaheim**	**NHL**	**18**	**4**	**5**	**4**	**884**	**37**	**1**	**2.51**	....	....	....	....	....	....	....
99-2000	**Anaheim**	**NHL**	**20**	**6**	**5**	**3**	**988**	**52**	**1**	**3.16**	....	....	....	....	....	....	....
2000-01	**Anaheim**	**NHL**	**13**	**2**	**5**	**2**	**653**	**31**	**0**	**2.85**	....	....	....	....	....	....	....
	Edmonton	**NHL**	**8**	**1**	**4**	**0**	**348**	**21**	**0**	**3.62**	....	....	....	....	....	....	....
	NHL Totals		**205**	**77**	**70**	**23**	**10665**	**555**	**7**	**3.12**	**1**	**0**	**0**	**23**	**0**	**0**	**0.00**

Traded to **Winnipeg** by **Philadelphia** for Tim Cheveldae and Winnipeg's 3rd round choice (Chester Gallant) in 1996 Entry Draft, February 27, 1996. Signed as a free agent by **Philadelphia**, July 3, 1996. Traded to **Nashville** by **Philadelphia** with Jeff Staples for Nashville's 7th round choice (Cam Ondrik) in 1998 Entry Draft, June 26, 1998. Traded to **Anaheim** by **Nashville** for Chris Mason and Marc Moro, October 5, 1998. Claimed on waivers by **Edmonton** from **Anaheim**, January 10, 2001.

ROY, Patrick (WAH, PAT-rihk) COL.

Goaltender. Catches left. 6'2", 185 lbs. Born, Quebec City, Que., October 5, 1965.
(Montreal's 4th choice, 51st overall, in 1984 Entry Draft).

			Regular Season								Playoffs						
Season	Club	Lea	GP	W	L	T	Mins	GA	SO	Avg	GP	W	L	Mins	GA	SO	Avg
1981-82	Ste-Foy Governors	QAAA	40	*27	3	10	2400	156	*3	*2.63	2	2	0	114	2	*1	1.05
1982-83	Granby Bisons	QMJHL	54	13	35	1	2808	293	0	6.26	....	....	....	....	....	....	....
1983-84	Granby Bisons	QMJHL	61	29	29	1	3585	265	0	4.44	4	0	4	244	22	0	5.41
1984-85	Granby Bisons	QMJHL	44	16	25	1	2463	228	0	5.55	....	....	....	....	....	....	....
	Montreal	**NHL**	**1**	**1**	**0**	**0**	**20**	**0**	**0**	**0.00**	....	....	....	....	....	....	....
	Sherbrooke	AHL	1	1	0	0	60	4	0	4.00	13	10	3	*769	37	0	*2.89
1985-86♦	**Montreal**	**NHL**	**47**	**23**	**18**	**3**	**2651**	**148**	**1**	**3.35**	**20**	***15**	**5**	**1218**	**39**	***1**	**1.92**
1986-87	**Montreal**	**NHL**	**46**	**22**	**16**	**6**	**2686**	**131**	**1**	**2.93**	**6**	**4**	**2**	**330**	**22**	**0**	**4.00**
1987-88	**Montreal**	**NHL**	**45**	**23**	**12**	**9**	**2586**	**125**	**3**	**2.90**	**8**	**3**	**4**	**430**	**24**	**0**	**3.35**
1988-89	**Montreal**	**NHL**	**48**	**33**	**5**	**6**	**2744**	**113**	**4**	***2.47**	**19**	**13**	**6**	**1206**	**42**	**2**	***2.09**
1989-90	**Montreal**	**NHL**	**54**	***31**	**16**	**5**	**3173**	**134**	**3**	**2.53**	**11**	**5**	**6**	**641**	**26**	**1**	**2.43**
1990-91	**Montreal**	**NHL**	**48**	**25**	**15**	**6**	**2835**	**128**	**1**	**2.71**	**13**	**7**	**5**	**785**	**40**	**0**	**3.06**
1991-92	**Montreal**	**NHL**	**67**	**36**	**22**	**8**	**3935**	**155**	***5**	***2.36**	**11**	**4**	**7**	**686**	**30**	**1**	**2.62**
1992-93♦	**Montreal**	**NHL**	**62**	**31**	**25**	**5**	**3595**	**192**	**2**	**3.20**	**20**	***16**	**4**	**1293**	**46**	**0**	***2.13**
1993-94	**Montreal**	**NHL**	**68**	**35**	**17**	**11**	**3867**	**161**	***7**	**2.50**	**6**	**3**	**3**	**375**	**16**	**0**	**2.56**
1994-95	**Montreal**	**NHL**	**43**	**17**	**20**	**6**	**2566**	**127**	**1**	**2.97**	....	....	....	....	....	....	....
1995-96	**Montreal**	**NHL**	**22**	**12**	**9**	**1**	**1260**	**62**	**1**	**2.95**	....	....	....	....	....	....	....
♦	**Colorado**	**NHL**	**39**	**22**	**15**	**1**	**2305**	**103**	**1**	**2.68**	***22**	***16**	**6**	***1454**	**51**	***3**	**2.10**
1996-97	**Colorado**	**NHL**	**62**	***38**	**15**	**7**	**3698**	**143**	**7**	**2.32**	**17**	**10**	**7**	**1034**	**38**	***3**	**2.21**
1997-98	**Colorado**	**NHL**	**65**	**31**	**19**	**13**	**3835**	**153**	**4**	**2.39**	**7**	**3**	**4**	**430**	**18**	**0**	**2.51**
	Canada	Olympics	6	4	2	0	*369	9	1	1.46	....	....	....	....	....	....	....
1998-99	**Colorado**	**NHL**	**61**	**32**	**19**	**8**	**3648**	**139**	**5**	**2.29**	**19**	**11**	**8**	**1173**	**52**	**1**	**2.66**
99-2000	**Colorado**	**NHL**	**63**	**32**	**21**	**8**	**3704**	**141**	**2**	**2.28**	**17**	**11**	**6**	**1039**	**31**	**3**	**1.79**
2000-01♦	**Colorado**	**NHL**	**62**	**40**	**13**	**7**	**3585**	**132**	**4**	**2.21**	**23**	***16**	**7**	**1451**	**41**	***4**	***1.70**
	NHL Totals		**903**	***484**	**277**	**110**	**52693**	**2287**	**52**	**2.60**	***219**	***137**	**80**	**13545**	**516**	***19**	**2.29**

NHL All-Rookie Team (1986) • Won Conn Smythe Trophy (1986, 1993, 2001) • Shared William Jennings Trophy with Brian Hayward (1987, 1988, 1989) • NHL Second All-Star Team (1988, 1991) • NHL First All-Star Team (1989, 1990, 1992) • Won Trico Goaltending Award (1989, 1990) • Won Vezina Trophy (1989, 1990, 1992) • Won William M. Jennings Trophy (1992) • Played in NHL All-Star Game (1988, 1990, 1991, 1992, 1993, 1994, 1997, 1998, 2001)

Traded to **Colorado** by **Montreal** with Mike Keane for Andrei Kovalenko, Martin Rucinsky and Jocelyn Thibault, December 6, 1995.

RUDKOWSKY, Cody (RUHD-kow-SKEE, KOH-dee) ST.L.

Goaltender. Catches left. 6'1", 206 lbs. Born, Willingdon, Alta., July 21, 1978.

			Regular Season								Playoffs						
Season	Club	Lea	GP	W	L	T	Mins	GA	SO	Avg	GP	W	L	Mins	GA	SO	Avg
1995-96	Langley Thunder	BCJHL	23	....	....	....	1172	73	1	3.73	....	....	....	....	....	....	....
	Seattle T-Birds	WHL	2	0	0	0	21	3	0	8.57	....	....	....	....	....	....	....
1996-97	Seattle T-Birds	WHL	40	19	16	1	2162	124	0	3.44	1	1	0	30	0	0	0.00
1997-98	Seattle T-Birds	WHL	53	20	22	3	2805	176	1	3.74	5	1	4	278	18	0	3.88
1998-99	Seattle T-Birds	WHL	64	34	17	10	3665	177	*7	2.90	11	5	6	637	31	1	2.92
99-2000	Worcester	AHL	28	9	7	6	1405	75	0	3.20	....	....	....	....	....	....	....
	Peoria Rivermen	ECHL	10	6	4	0	599	32	0	3.20	2	1	1	119	6	0	3.02
2000-01	Worcester	AHL	25	13	8	3	1477	66	3	2.68	....	....	....	....	....	....	....

WHL West First All-Star Team (1999) • Canadian Major Junior First All-Star Team (1999) • Canadian Major Junior Goaltender of the Year (1999)

Signed as a free agent by **St. Louis**, March 25, 1999.

SABOURIN, Dany (SA-boo-rihn, DAN-ee) CGY.

Goaltender. Catches left. 6'2", 182 lbs. Born, Val d'Or, Que., September 2, 1980.
(Calgary's 5th choice, 108th overall, in 1998 Entry Draft).

			Regular Season								Playoffs						
Season	Club	Lea	GP	W	L	T	Mins	GA	SO	Avg	GP	W	L	Mins	GA	SO	Avg
1996-97	Amos Forestiers	QAAA	24	6	16	0	1440	107	0	4.48	....	....	....	....	....	....	....
1997-98	Sherbrooke	QMJHL	37	15	15	2	1906	128	1	4.03	....	....	....	....	....	....	....
1998-99	Sherbrooke	QMJHL	30	8	13	2	1477	102	1	4.14	1	0	1	49	2	0	2.45
	Saint John Flames	AHL	....	....	....	....	....	....	....	....	1	0	1	57	4	0	4.19
99-2000	Sherbrooke	QMJHL	55	25	22	5	3067	181	1	3.54	5	1	4	324	18	0	3.33
2000-01	Saint John Flames	AHL	1	1	0	0	40	0	0	0.00	....	....	....	....	....	....	....
	Johnstown Chiefs	ECHL	19	4	9	1	903	56	0	3.72	1	0	0	40	2	0	3.00

SALFICKY, Dusan (sal-FITZ-kee, DOO-shahn) NYI

Goaltender. Catches left. 6'1", 185 lbs. Born, Chrudim, Czech., March 28, 1972.
(NY Islanders' 2nd choice, 132nd overall, in 2001 Entry Draft).

			Regular Season								Playoffs						
Season	Club	Lea	GP	W	L	T	Mins	GA	SO	Avg	GP	W	L	Mins	GA	SO	Avg
1990-91	Tri-City Americans	WHL	2	1	1	0	119	11	0	5.55	....	....	....	....	....	....	....
	Tesla Pardubice	Czech.	18	....	....	....	1000	60	....	3.60	....	....	....	....	....	....	....
1991-92	Tesla Pardubice	Czech-Jr.					STATISTICS NOT AVAILABLE										
1992-93	VTJ Tabor	Czech-2					STATISTICS NOT AVAILABLE										
1993-94	HC Pardubice	Cze-Rep	1	0	0	1	59	0	1	0.00	....	....	....	....	....	....	....
1994-95	HC Pardubice	Cze-Rep	10	....	....	....	548	23	1	2.52	3	....	....	185	12	0	3.89
1995-96	HC Pardubice	Cze-Rep	8	....	....	....	315	22	0	4.19	....	....	....	....	....	....	....
1996-97	HC Pardubice	Cze-Rep	21	....	....	....	1180	48	0	2.44	3	....	....	134	12	0	5.37
1997-98	HCK Plzen	Cze-Rep	50	....	....	....	2939	134	0	2.75	5	2	3	310	14	0	2.71
1998-99	HCK Plzen	Cze-Rep	44	....	....	....	2506	100	0	2.39	5	2	3	233	14	0	3.32
99-2000	HCK Plzen	Cze-Rep	52	....	....	....	3061	108	3	2.12	7	....	....	415	15	....	2.17
2000-01	HCK Plzen	Cze-Rep	52	....	....	....	3014	132	0	2.63	....	....	....	....	....	....	....

SALO, Tommy (SAH-loh,TAW-mee) EDM.

Goaltender. Catches left. 5'11", 173 lbs. Born, Surahammar, Sweden, February 1, 1971.
(NY Islanders' 5th choice, 118th overall, in 1993 Entry Draft).

			Regular Season								Playoffs						
Season	Club	Lea	GP	W	L	T	Mins	GA	SO	Avg	GP	W	L	Mins	GA	SO	Avg
1990-91	Vasteras IK	Sweden	2	....	....	....	100	11	0	6.60	....	....	....	....	....	....	....
1991-92	Vasteras IK	Swede-Jr.					STATISTICS NOT AVAILABLE										
1992-93	Vasteras IK	Sweden	24	....	....	....	1431	59	2	2.47	2	....	....	120	6	0	3.00
1993-94	Vasteras IK	Sweden	32	....	....	....	1896	106	0	3.35	....	....	....	....	....	....	....
	Sweden	Olympics	6	5	1	0	370	13	1	2.11	....	....	....	....	....	....	....
1994-95	Denver Grizzlies	IHL	*65	*45	14	4	*3810	165	*3	*2.60	8	7	0	390	20	0	3.07
	NY Islanders	**NHL**	**6**	**1**	**5**	**0**	**358**	**18**	**0**	**3.02**	....	....	....	....	....	....	....
1995-96	**NY Islanders**	**NHL**	**10**	**1**	**7**	**1**	**523**	**35**	**0**	**4.02**	....	....	....	....	....	....	....
	Utah Grizzlies	IHL	45	28	15	2	2695	119	*4	2.65	22	*15	7	1342	51	*3	2.28
1996-97	**NY Islanders**	**NHL**	**58**	**20**	**27**	**8**	**3208**	**151**	**5**	**2.82**	....	....	....	....	....	....	....
1997-98	**NY Islanders**	**NHL**	**62**	**23**	**29**	**5**	**3461**	**152**	**4**	**2.64**	....	....	....	....	....	....	....
	Sweden	Olympics	4	2	2	0	238	9	0	2.27	....	....	....	....	....	....	....
1998-99	**NY Islanders**	**NHL**	**51**	**17**	**26**	**7**	**3018**	**132**	**5**	**2.62**	....	....	....	....	....	....	....
	Edmonton	**NHL**	**13**	**8**	**2**	**2**	**700**	**27**	**0**	**2.31**	**4**	**0**	**4**	**296**	**11**	**0**	**2.23**
99-2000	**Edmonton**	**NHL**	**70**	**27**	**28**	**13**	**4164**	**162**	**2**	**2.33**	**5**	**1**	**4**	**297**	**14**	**0**	**2.83**
2000-01	**Edmonton**	**NHL**	**73**	**36**	**25**	**12**	**4364**	**179**	**8**	**2.46**	**6**	**2**	**4**	**406**	**15**	**0**	**2.22**
	NHL Totals		**343**	**133**	**149**	**48**	**19796**	**856**	**24**	**2.59**	**15**	**3**	**12**	**999**	**40**	**0**	**2.40**

IHL First All-Star Team (1995) • Won Garry F. Longman Memorial Trophy (Top Rookie - IHL) (1995) • Won James Norris Memorial Trophy (fewest goals against - IHL) (1995) • Won James Gatschene Memorial Trophy (MVP - IHL) (1995) • Shared James Norris Memorial Trophy (fewest goals against in IHL) with Mark McArthur (1996) • Won "Bud" Poile Trophy (Playoff MVP - IHL) (1996) • Played in NHL All-Star Game (2000)

Traded to **Edmonton** by **NY Islanders** for Mats Lindgren and Edmonton's 8th round choice (Radek Martinek) in 1999 Entry Draft, March 20, 1999.

SAUVE, Philippe (SOH-vay, FIHL-ihp) COL.

Goaltender. Catches left. 6', 180 lbs. Born, Buffalo, NY, February 27, 1980.
(Colorado's 6th choice, 38th overall, in 1998 Entry Draft).

			Regular Season								Playoffs						
Season	Club	Lea	GP	W	L	T	Mins	GA	SO	Avg	GP	W	L	Mins	GA	SO	Avg
1995-96	Laval-Laurentides	QAAA	25	9	10	0	1184	87	1	4.11	15	7	8	900	54	0	3.58
1996-97	Rimouski Oceanic	QMJHL	26	11	9	2	1334	84	0	3.78	1	0	0	14	3	0	12.90
1997-98	Rimouski Oceanic	QMJHL	40	23	16	0	2326	131	1	3.38	7	0	5	262	33	0	7.55
1998-99	Rimouski Oceanic	QMJHL	44	16	19	4	2401	155	0	3.87	11	6	4	595	30	*1	3.03
99-2000	Drummondville	QMJHL	28	12	12	2	1526	106	0	4.17	....	....	....	....	....	....	....
	Hull Olympiques	QMJHL	17	9	7	1	992	57	0	3.45	12	6	6	735	47	0	3.84
2000-01	Hershey Bears	AHL	42	17	18	1	2182	100	3	2.75	3	0	3	218	10	0	2.75

Canadian Major Junior Humanitarian Player of the Year (1999)

SCHAEFER, Nolan (SHAY-fuhr, NOH-luhn) S.J.

Goaltender. Catches left. 6'1", 175 lbs. Born, Yellow Grass, Sask., January 15, 1980.
(San Jose's 4th choice, 166th overall, in 2000 Entry Draft).

			Regular Season								Playoffs						
Season	Club	Lea	GP	W	L	T	Mins	GA	SO	Avg	GP	W	L	Mins	GA	SO	Avg
1996-97	Yorkton Mallers	SMHL	36	....	....	....	1854	132	0	4.27	....	....	....	....	....	....	....
1997-98	Yorkton Mallers	SMHL	5	....	....	....	239	17	0	4.25	....	....	....	....	....	....	....
	Nipawin Hawks	SJHL	21	12	4	3	1080	42	*3	*2.33	....	....	....	....	....	....	....
1998-99	Nipawin Hawks	SJHL					DID NOT PLAY – INJURED										
99-2000	Providence	H-East	14	6	5	1	778	42	0	3.24	....	....	....	....	....	....	....
2000-01	Providence	H-East	25	15	8	2	1529	63	3	2.47	....	....	....	....	....	....	....

SJHL All-Rookie Team (1998) • Hockey East Second All-Star Team (2001) • NCAA East Second All-American Team (2001)

SCHWAB, Corey (SHWAHB, KOHR-ree)

Goaltender. Catches left. 6', 180 lbs. Born, North Battleford, Sask., November 4, 1970.
(New Jersey's 12th choice, 200th overall, in 1990 Entry Draft).

			Regular Season								Playoffs						
Season	Club	Lea	GP	W	L	T	Mins	GA	SO	Avg	GP	W	L	Mins	GA	SO	Avg
1988-89	Seattle T-Birds	WHL	10	2	2	0	386	31	0	4.82	....	....	....	....	....	....	....
1989-90	Seattle T-Birds	WHL	27	15	2	1	1150	69	1	3.60	3	0	0	49	2	0	2.45
1990-91	Seattle T-Birds	WHL	*58	32	18	3	*3289	224	0	4.09	6	1	5	382	25	0	3.93
1991-92	Utica Devils	AHL	24	9	12	1	1322	95	0	4.31	....	....	....	....	....	....	....
	Cincinnati	ECHL	8	6	0	1	450	31	0	4.13	9	6	3	540	29	0	3.22
1992-93	Utica Devils	AHL	40	18	16	5	2387	169	*2	4.25	1	0	1	59	6	0	6.10
	Cincinnati	IHL	3	1	2	0	185	17	0	5.51	....	....	....	....	....	....	....
1993-94	Albany River Rats	AHL	51	27	21	3	3058	184	0	3.61	5	1	4	298	20	0	4.02
1994-95	Albany River Rats	AHL	45	25	10	9	2711	117	3	*2.59	7	6	1	425	19	0	2.68
1995-96	**New Jersey**	**NHL**	**10**	**0**	**3**	**0**	**331**	**12**	**0**	**2.18**	....	....	....	....	....	....	....
	Albany River Rats	AHL	5	3	2	0	299	13	0	2.61	....	....	....	....	....	....	....
1996-97	**Tampa Bay**	**NHL**	**31**	**11**	**12**	**1**	**1462**	**74**	**2**	**3.04**	....	....	....	....	....	....	....
1997-98	**Tampa Bay**	**NHL**	**16**	**2**	**9**	**1**	**821**	**40**	**1**	**2.92**	....	....	....	....	....	....	....
1998-99	**Tampa Bay**	**NHL**	**40**	**8**	**25**	**3**	**2146**	**126**	**0**	**3.52**	....	....	....	....	....	....	....
	Cleveland	IHL	8	1	6	1	477	31	0	3.90	....	....	....	....	....	....	....
99-2000	Orlando	IHL	16	9	4	2	868	31	1	2.14	....	....	....	....	....	....	....
	Vancouver	**NHL**	**6**	**2**	**1**	**1**	**269**	**16**	**0**	**3.57**	....	....	....	....	....	....	....
	Syracuse Crunch	AHL	12	7	5	0	720	42	0	3.50	4	1	3	246	11	1	2.69
2000-01	Kansas City	IHL	50	22	24	1	2866	150	2	3.14	....	....	....	....	....	....	....
	NHL Totals		**103**	**23**	**50**	**6**	**5029**	**268**	**3**	**3.20**	....	....	....	....	....	....	....

AHL Second All-Star Team (1995) • Shared Harry "Hap" Holmes Memorial Trophy (fewest goals against - AHL) with Mike Dunham (1995) • Shared Jack A. Butterfield Trophy (Playoff MVP - AHL) with Mike Dunham (1995)

Traded to **Tampa Bay** by **New Jersey** for Jeff Reese, Chicago's 2nd round choice (previously acquired, New Jersey selected Pierre Dagenais) in 1996 Entry Draft and Tampa Bay's 8th round choice (Jason Bertsch) in 1996 Entry Draft, June 22, 1996. Claimed by **Atlanta** from **Tampa Bay** in Expansion Draft, June 25, 1999. Traded to **Vancouver** by **Atlanta** for Vancouver's 4th round choice (Carl Mallette) in 2000 Entry Draft, October 29, 1999.

SCOTT, Travis (SKAWT, TRA-vihs) L.A.

Goaltender. Catches left. 6'2", 185 lbs. Born, Kanata, Ont., September 14, 1975.

			Regular Season								Playoffs						
Season	Club	Lea	GP	W	L	T	Mins	GA	SO	Avg	GP	W	L	Mins	GA	SO	Avg
1991-92	Nepean Raiders	COJHL	19	14	5	0	1065	71	1	4.00	....	....	....	....	....	....	....
1992-93	Nepean Raiders	COJHL	36	19	10	2	1968	133	0	4.05	....	....	....	....	....	....	....
1993-94	Windsor Spitfires	OHL	45	20	18	0	2312	158	1	4.10	4	0	4	240	16	0	4.00
1994-95	Windsor Spitfires	OHL	48	26	14	3	2644	147	3	3.34	3	0	1	94	6	1	3.83
1995-96	Oshawa Generals	OHL	31	15	9	4	1763	78	3	2.65	5	1	4	315	23	0	4.38
1996-97	Baton Rouge	ECHL	10	5	2	1	501	22	0	2.63	....	....	....	....	....	....	....
	Worcester	AHL	29	14	10	1	1482	75	1	3.04	....	....	....	....	....	....	....
1997-98	Baton Rouge	ECHL	36	14	11	6	1949	96	1	2.96	....	....	....	....	....	....	....
1998-99	Mississippi	ECHL	44	22	12	5	2337	112	1	2.88	*18	*14	4	*1252	42	3	2.01
99-2000	Lowell	AHL	46	15	23	3	2595	126	3	2.91	1	0	1	60	2	0	2.01
2000-01	**Los Angeles**	**NHL**	**1**	**0**	**0**	**0**	**25**	**3**	**0**	**7.20**	....	....	....	....	....	....	....
	Lowell	AHL	34	16	15	1	1977	83	2	2.52	4	1	2	209	7	1	2.01
	NHL Totals		**1**	**0**	**0**	**0**	**25**	**3**	**0**	**7.20**	....	....	....	....	....	....	....

Won ECHL Playoff MVP Award (1999)

Signed as a free agent by **St. Louis**, December 30, 1996. Signed as a free agent by **LA Kings**, February 18, 2000.

SHIELDS, Steve (SHEELDS, STEEV) ANA.

Goaltender. Catches left. 6'3", 215 lbs. Born, Toronto, Ont., July 19, 1972.
(Buffalo's 5th choice, 101st overall, in 1991 Entry Draft).

			Regular Season								Playoffs						
Season	Club	Lea	GP	W	L	T	Mins	GA	SO	Avg	GP	W	L	Mins	GA	SO	Avg
1989-90	St. Marys Lincolns	OJHL-B	26	....	....	....	1512	121	0	4.80	....	....	....	....	....	....	....
1990-91	U. of Michigan	CCHA	37	26	6	3	1963	106	0	3.24	....	....	....	....	....	....	....
1991-92	U. of Michigan	CCHA	*37	*27	7	2	*2090	99	1	2.84	....	....	....	....	....	....	....
1992-93	U. of Michigan	CCHA	*39	*30	6	2	2027	75	2	*2.22	....	....	....	....	....	....	....
1993-94	U. of Michigan	CCHA	36	*28	6	1	1961	87	0	2.66	....	....	....	....	....	....	....
1994-95	Rochester	AHL	13	3	8	0	673	53	0	4.72	1	0	0	20	3	0	9.00
	South Carolina	ECHL	21	11	5	2	1158	52	2	2.69	3	0	2	144	11	0	4.58
1995-96	**Buffalo**	**NHL**	**2**	**1**	**0**	**0**	**75**	**4**	**0**	**3.20**	....	....	....	....	....	....	....
	Rochester	AHL	43	20	17	2	2357	140	1	3.56	*19	*15	3	*1127	47	1	2.50
1996-97	**Buffalo**	**NHL**	**13**	**3**	**8**	**2**	**789**	**39**	**0**	**2.97**	**10**	**4**	**6**	**570**	**26**	**1**	**2.74**
	Rochester	AHL	23	14	6	2	1331	60	1	2.70	....	....	....	....	....	....	....
1997-98	**Buffalo**	**NHL**	**16**	**3**	**6**	**4**	**785**	**37**	**0**	**2.83**	....	....	....	....	....	....	....
	Rochester	AHL	1	0	1	0	59	3	0	3.04	....	....	....	....	....	....	....
1998-99	**San Jose**	**NHL**	**37**	**15**	**11**	**8**	**2162**	**80**	**4**	**2.22**	**1**	**0**	**1**	**60**	**6**	**0**	**6.00**
99-2000	**San Jose**	**NHL**	**67**	**27**	**30**	**8**	**3797**	**162**	**4**	**2.56**	**12**	**5**	**7**	**696**	**36**	**0**	**3.10**
2000-01	**San Jose**	**NHL**	**21**	**6**	**8**	**5**	**1135**	**47**	**2**	**2.48**	....	....	....	....	....	....	....
	NHL Totals		**156**	**55**	**63**	**27**	**8743**	**369**	**10**	**2.53**	**23**	**9**	**14**	**1326**	**68**	**1**	**3.08**

CCHA First All-Star Team (1993, 1994) • NCAA West Second All-American Team (1993, 1994)

Traded to **San Jose** by **Buffalo** with Buffalo's 4th round choice (Miroslav Zalesak) in 1998 Entry Draft for Kay Whitmore, Colorado's 2nd round choice (previously acquired, Buffalo selected Jaroslav Kristek) in 1998 Entry Draft and San Jose's 5th round choice (later traded to Columbus - Columbus selected Tyler Kolarik) in 2000 Entry Draft, June 18, 1998. Traded to **Anaheim** by **San Jose** with Jeff Friesen and future considerations for Teemu Selanne, March 5, 2001.

SHTALENKOV, Mikhail (shtuh-LEHN-kahf, mihk-HAIL)

Goaltender. Catches left. 6'2", 185 lbs. Born, Moscow, USSR, October 20, 1965.
(Anaheim's 5th choice, 108th overall, in 1993 Entry Draft).

			Regular Season								Playoffs						
Season	Club	Lea	GP	W	L	T	Mins	GA	SO	Avg	GP	W	L	Mins	GA	SO	Avg
1986-87	Dynamo Moscow	USSR	17				893	36	1	2.41							
1987-88	Dynamo Moscow	USSR	25				1302	72	1	3.31							
1988-89	Dynamo Moscow	USSR	4				80	3	0	2.25							
1989-90	Dynamo Moscow	USSR	6				20	1	0	3.00							
1990-91	Dynamo Moscow	USSR	31				1568	56	2	2.14							
1991-92	Dynamo Moscow	CIS	27				1268	45	1	2.12							
	Russia	Olympics	8	*7	1	0	440	12	1	1.64							
1992-93	Milwaukee	IHL	47	26	14	5	2669	135	2	3.03	3	1	2	209	11	0	3.16
1993-94	**Anaheim**	**NHL**	**10**	**3**	**4**	**1**	**543**	**24**	**0**	**2.65**							
	San Diego Gulls	IHL	28	15	11	2	1616	93	0	3.45							
1994-95	**Anaheim**	**NHL**	**18**	**4**	**7**	**1**	**810**	**49**	**0**	**3.63**							
1995-96	**Anaheim**	**NHL**	**30**	**7**	**16**	**3**	**1637**	**85**	**0**	**3.12**							
1996-97	**Anaheim**	**NHL**	**24**	**7**	**8**	**1**	**1079**	**52**	**2**	**2.89**	**4**	**0**	**3**	**211**	**10**	**0**	**2.84**
1997-98	**Anaheim**	**NHL**	**40**	**13**	**18**	**5**	**2049**	**110**	**1**	**3.22**							
	Russia	Olympics	5	4	1	0	290	8	0	1.65							
1998-99	**Edmonton**	**NHL**	**34**	**12**	**17**	**3**	**1819**	**81**	**3**	**2.67**							
	Phoenix	**NHL**	**4**	**1**	**2**	**1**	**243**	**9**	**0**	**2.22**							
99-2000	**Phoenix**	**NHL**	**15**	**7**	**6**	**2**	**904**	**36**	**2**	**2.39**							
	Florida	**NHL**	**15**	**8**	**4**	**2**	**882**	**34**	**0**	**2.31**							
2000-01	Dynamo Moscow	Russia	25				1446	47	6	1.95							
	NHL Totals		**190**	**62**	**82**	**19**	**9966**	**480**	**8**	**2.89**	**4**	**0**	**3**	**211**	**10**	**0**	**2.84**

USSR Rookie of the Year (1987) • Won Garry F. Longman Memorial Trophy (Top Rookie - IHL) (1993)

Claimed by **Nashville** from **Anaheim** in Expansion Draft, June 26, 1998. Traded to **Edmonton** by **Nashville** with Jim Dowd for Eric Fichaud, Drake Berehowsky and Greg de Vries, October 1, 1998. Traded to **Phoenix** by **Edmonton** for Phoenix's 5th round choice (later traded to Nashville - Nashville selected Matt Koalska) in 2000 Entry Draft, March 11, 1999. Traded to **Florida** by **Phoenix** with Phoenix's 4th round choice (Chris Eade) in 2000 Entry Draft for Sean Burke and Florida's 5th round choice (Nate Kiser) in 2000 Entry Draft, November 18, 1999.

SHULMISTRA, Richard (shuhl-MIHS-trah, RIH-chahrd)

Goaltender. Catches right. 6'2", 185 lbs. Born, Sudbury, Ont., April 1, 1971.
(Quebec's 1st choice, 4th overall, in 1992 Supplemental Draft).

			Regular Season								Playoffs						
Season	Club	Lea	GP	W	L	T	Mins	GA	SO	Avg	GP	W	L	Mins	GA	SO	Avg
1988-89	St. Michael's	OJHL-B	12	10	2	0	715	29	*1	2.43							
1989-90	Thunder Bay	TBJHL	37				2090	131	0	3.76							
1990-91	U. of Miami-Ohio	CCHA	20	2	12	2	920	80	0	5.21							
1991-92	U. of Miami-Ohio	CCHA	19	3	5	2	850	67	0	4.72							
1992-93	U. of Miami-Ohio	CCHA	33	22	6	4	1949	88	1	2.71							
1993-94	U. of Miami-Ohio	CCHA	27	13	12	1	1521	74	0	2.92							
1994-95	Cornwall Aces	AHL	20	4	9	2	937	58	0	3.71	8	4	3	446	22	0	2.95
1995-96	Cornwall Aces	AHL	36	9	18	2	1844	100	0	3.25	1	0	0	9	1	0	6.76
1996-97	Albany River Rats	AHL	23	5	9	2	1062	43	2	2.43	2	1	0	77	2	0	1.56
1997-98	Fort Wayne	IHL	11	3	8	0	656	34	1	3.11							
	New Jersey	**NHL**	**1**	**0**	**1**	**0**	**62**	**2**	**0**	**1.94**							
	Albany River Rats	AHL	35	20	8	4	2022	78	2	*2.31	13	8	3	696	32	1	2.76
1998-99	Manitoba Moose	IHL	44	25	11	7	2469	117	2	2.84							
	Albany River Rats	AHL	12	6	4	0	596	34	0	3.42	2	0	2	64	3	0	2.82
99-2000	**Florida**	**NHL**	**1**	**1**	**0**	**0**	**60**	**1**	**0**	**1.00**							
	Louisville Panthers	AHL	27	12	11	2	1447	80	2	3.32							
	Orlando	IHL	9	5	1	3	520	16	1	1.85	1	0	1	30	3	0	5.90
2000-01	Louisville Panthers	AHL	1	0	1	0	60	4	0	4.00							
	Kansas City Blades	IHL	4	1	3	0	239	13	0	3.26							
	Florida Everblades	ECHL	2	2	0	0	130	7	0	3.23							
	Chicago Wolves	IHL	29	20	8	0	1616	51	4	1.89	10	7	3	591	20	*2	2.03
	NHL Totals		**2**	**1**	**1**	**0**	**122**	**3**	**0**	**1.48**							

CCHA Second All-Star Team (1993) • AHL Second All-Star Team (1998)

Rights transferred to **Colorado** after **Quebec** franchise relocated, June 21, 1995. Signed as a free agent by **New Jersey**, December 31, 1997. Signed as a free agent by **Florida**, July 27, 1999.

SKUDRA, Peter (SKOO-druh, PEE-tuhr)

Goaltender. Catches left. 6'1", 189 lbs. Born, Riga, USSR, April 24, 1973.

			Regular Season								Playoffs						
Season	Club	Lea	GP	W	L	T	Mins	GA	SO	Avg	GP	W	L	Mins	GA	SO	Avg
1992-93	Pardaugava Riga	CIS	27				1498	74		2.96	1			60	5	0	5.00
1993-94	Pardaugava Riga	CIS	14				783	42		3.22	1			55	4	0	4.36
1994-95	Greensboro	ECHL	33	13	9	5	1612	113	0	4.20	6	2	2	341	28	0	4.92
	Memphis	CHL	2	0	1	0	60	8	0	6.01							
1995-96	Erie Panthers	ECHL	12	3	8	1	681	47	0	4.14							
	Johnstown Chiefs	ECHL	30	12	11	4	1657	98	0	3.55							
1996-97	Hamilton Bulldogs	AHL	32	8	16	2	1615	101	0	3.75							
	Johnstown Chiefs	ECHL	4	2	1	1	200	11	0	3.30							
1997-98	**Pittsburgh**	**NHL**	**17**	**6**	**4**	**3**	**851**	**26**	**0**	**1.83**							
	Houston Aeros	IHL	9	5	3	1	499	23	0	2.77							
	Kansas City	IHL	13	10	3	0	775	37	0	2.86	8	4	4	512	20	1	*2.34
1998-99	**Pittsburgh**	**NHL**	**37**	**15**	**11**	**5**	**1914**	**89**	**3**	**2.79**							
99-2000	**Pittsburgh**	**NHL**	**20**	**5**	**7**	**3**	**922**	**48**	**1**	**3.12**	**1**	**0**	**0**	**20**	**1**	**0**	**3.00**
2000-01	**Buffalo**	**NHL**	**1**	**0**	**0**	**0**	**0**	**0**	**0**	**0.00**							
	Rochester	AHL	2	2	0	0	120	5	0	2.50							
	Boston	**NHL**	**25**	**6**	**12**	**1**	**1116**	**62**	**0**	**3.33**							
	Providence Bruins	AHL	3	3	0	0	180	5	0	1.67							
	NHL Totals		**100**	**32**	**34**	**12**	**4803**	**225**	**4**	**2.81**	**1**	**0**	**0**	**20**	**1**	**0**	**3.00**

Signed as a free agent by **Pittsburgh**, September 25, 1997. Signed as a free agent by **Boston**, October 3, 2000. Claimed on waivers by **Buffalo** from **Boston**, October 6, 2000. Claimed on waivers by **Boston** from **Buffalo**, November 14, 2000.

SMID, Zdenek (SHMIHD, zuh-DEHN-ehk) ATL.

Goaltender. Catches left. 5'10", 172 lbs. Born, Plzen, Czech., February 3, 1980.
(Atlanta's 7th choice, 168th overall, in 2000 Entry Draft).

			Regular Season								Playoffs						
Season	Club	Lea	GP	W	L	T	Mins	GA	SO	Avg	GP	W	L	Mins	GA	SO	Avg
1996-97	HC Plzen-Jr.	Cze-Rep	23				1304	48		2.21							
1997-98	HC Plzen-Jr.	Cze-Rep	30				1601	91		3.41							
1998-99	Karlovy Vary	Cze-Rep	3				160	11		4.13							
99-2000	Karlovy Vary-Jr.	Cze-Rep	24				1409	54		2.30	2			86	9		6.28
	Karlovy Vary	Cze-Rep	14				650	41	0	3.78	3			150	8		3.20
2000-01	Karlovy Vary	Cze-Rep	12				630	34		3.24							

SMITH, Mike (SMIHTH, MIGHK) DAL.

Goaltender. Catches left. 6'3", 189 lbs. Born, Kingston, Ont., March 22, 1982.
(Dallas' 5th choice, 161st overall, in 2001 Entry Draft).

			Regular Season								Playoffs						
Season	Club	Lea	GP	W	L	T	Mins	GA	SO	Avg	GP	W	L	Mins	GA	SO	Avg
1998-99	Kingston	OPJHL	16				906	53	0	3.51							
99-2000	Kingston	OHL	15	4	5	0	666	42	0	3.78							
2000-01	Kingston	OHL	3	0	0	2	136	8	0	3.53							
	Sudbury Wolves	OHL	43	22	13	7	2571	108	3	2.52	12	7	5	735	26	2	*2.12

Traded to **Sudbury** by **Kingston** for Sudbury's 10th round choice in 2002 OHL Midget Draft, October 25, 2000.

SNEE, Brandon (SNEE, BRAN-duhn) NYR

Goaltender. Catches left. 6'1", 195 lbs. Born, Philadelphia, PA, June 10, 1980.
(NY Rangers' 5th choice, 143rd overall, in 2000 Entry Draft).

			Regular Season								Playoffs						
Season	Club	Lea	GP	W	L	T	Mins	GA	SO	Avg	GP	W	L	Mins	GA	SO	Avg
1997-98	The Hill School	H.S.	22				1320	43	0	2.02							
1998-99	Union College	ECAC	19	1	12	3	1011	59	1	3.50							
99-2000	Union College	ECAC	*31	8	22	1	1765	114	0	3.87							
2000-01	Union College	ECAC	*33	12	17	4	1849	96	1	3.11							

SNOW, Garth (SNOH, GAHRTH) NYI

Goaltender. Catches left. 6'3", 200 lbs. Born, Wrentham, MA, July 28, 1969.
(Quebec's 6th choice, 114th overall, in 1987 Entry Draft).

			Regular Season								Playoffs						
Season	Club	Lea	GP	W	L	T	Mins	GA	SO	Avg	GP	W	L	Mins	GA	SO	Avg
1986-87	Mount St. Charles	H.S.	30				1795	53	10	1.77							
1987-88	Stratford Cullitons	OJHL-B	30	20	6	0	1642	93	2	3.40							
1988-89	U. of Maine	H-East	5	2	2	0	241	14	1	3.49							
1989-90	U. of Maine	H-East	DID NOT PLAY – ACADEMICALLY INELIGIBLE														
1990-91	U. of Maine	H-East	25	*18	4	0	1290	64	2	2.98							
1991-92	U. of Maine	H-East	31	*25	4	2	1792	73	*2	*2.44							
1992-93	U. of Maine	H-East	23	*21	0	1	1210	42	1	*2.08							
1993-94	United States	Nt-Team	23	13	5	3	1324	71	1	3.22							
	United States	Olympics	5	1	3	1	299	17	0	3.41							
	Quebec	**NHL**	**5**	**3**	**2**	**0**	**279**	**16**	**0**	**3.44**							
	Cornwall Aces	AHL	16	6	5	3	927	51	0	3.30	13	8	5	790	42	0	3.19
1994-95	Cornwall Aces	AHL	*62	*32	20	7	*3558	162	3	2.73	8	4	3	402	14	*2	*2.09
	Quebec	**NHL**	**2**	**1**	**1**	**0**	**119**	**11**	**0**	**5.55**	**1**	**0**	**0**	**9**	**1**	**0**	**6.67**
1995-96	**Philadelphia**	**NHL**	**26**	**12**	**8**	**4**	**1437**	**69**	**0**	**2.88**	**1**	**0**	**0**	**1**	**0**	**0**	**0.00**
1996-97	**Philadelphia**	**NHL**	**35**	**14**	**8**	**8**	**1884**	**79**	**2**	**2.52**	**12**	**8**	**4**	**699**	**33**	**0**	**2.83**
1997-98	**Philadelphia**	**NHL**	**29**	**14**	**9**	**4**	**1651**	**67**	**1**	**2.43**							
	Vancouver	**NHL**	**12**	**3**	**6**	**0**	**504**	**26**	**0**	**3.10**							
1998-99	**Vancouver**	**NHL**	**65**	**20**	**31**	**8**	**3501**	**171**	**6**	**2.93**							
99-2000	**Vancouver**	**NHL**	**32**	**10**	**15**	**3**	**1712**	**76**	**0**	**2.66**							
2000-01	**Pittsburgh**	**NHL**	**35**	**14**	**15**	**4**	**2032**	**101**	**3**	**2.98**							
	Wilkes-Barre	AHL	3	2	1	0	178	7	0	2.36							
	NHL Totals		**241**	**91**	**95**	**31**	**13119**	**616**	**12**	**2.82**	**14**	**8**	**4**	**709**	**34**	**0**	**2.88**

Hockey East Second All-Star Team (1992, 1993) • NCAA Championship All-Tournament Team (1993)

Transferred to **Colorado** after **Quebec** franchise relocated, June 21, 1995. Traded to **Philadelphia** by **Colorado** for Philadelphia's 3rd (later traded to Washington - Washington selected Shawn McNeil) and 6th (Kai Fischer) round choices in 1996 Entry Draft, July 12, 1995. Traded to **Vancouver** by **Philadelphia** for Sean Burke, March 4, 1998. Signed as a free agent by **Pittsburgh**, October 10, 2000. Signed as a free agent by **NY Islanders**, July 14, 2001.

STANA, Ratislav (STAN-ah, RAH-tih-slahv) WSH.

Goaltender. Catches left. 6'2", 161 lbs. Born, Kosice, Czech., January 10, 1980.
(Washington's 8th choice, 193rd overall, in 1998 Entry Draft).

			Regular Season								Playoffs						
Season	Club	Lea	GP	W	L	T	Mins	GA	SO	Avg	GP	W	L	Mins	GA	SO	Avg
1997-98	HC Kosice	Slovak-Jr.	32				1920	56	2	1.75							
1998-99	Moose Jaw	WHL	36	21	14	1	2131	123	2	3.46	9	4	5	544	30	0	3.31
99-2000	Moose Jaw	WHL	14	4	9	0	730	48	0	3.95							
	Calgary Hitmen	WHL	16	13	2	1	971	37	1	2.29	9	7	2	526	21	1	2.40
2000-01	Richmond	ECHL	38	15	16	2	2111	90	1	2.56	3	1	2	178	7	1	2.34

ST-GERMAIN, David (SAN-zhur-meh, DAH-vee) NYI

Goaltender. Catches left. 5'11", 172 lbs. Born, Charles-Lemoye, Que., March 18, 1980.

			Regular Season								Playoffs						
Season	Club	Lea	GP	W	L	T	Mins	GA	SO	Avg	GP	W	L	Mins	GA	SO	Avg
1996-97	Richileau Elites	QAHA	35				2133	113	2	3.18							
1997-98	Val d'Or Foreurs	QMJHL	18	6	4	2	893	51	0	3.42	2	0	2	119	9	0	4.53
1998-99	Val d'Or Foreurs	QMJHL	16	7	7	1	833	68	0	4.90							
	Cape Breton	QMJHL	35	10	23	1	1959	127	1	3.89	5	1	4	299	19	0	3.81
99-2000	Cape Breton	QMJHL	36	10	23	2	1986	147	0	4.44							
	Baie-Comeau	QMJHL	23	10	11	2	1287	77	2	3.59	6	2	4	361	21	0	3.49
2000-01	Baie-Comeau	QMJHL	53	32	13	4	2913	169	3	3.48	11	6	4	683	29	1	2.55

Signed as a free agent by **NY Islanders**, December 12, 2000.

STORR, Jamie (STOHR, JAY-mee) L.A.

Goaltender. Catches left. 6'2", 195 lbs. Born, Brampton, Ont., December 28, 1975.
(Los Angeles' 1st choice, 7th overall, in 1994 Entry Draft).

			Regular Season								Playoffs						
Season	Club	Lea	GP	W	L	T	Mins	GA	SO	Avg	GP	W	L	Mins	GA	SO	Avg
1990-91	Brampton Caps	MTJHL	24				1145	91	0	4.77	15			885	60	0	4.07
1991-92	Owen Sound	OHL	34	11	16	1	1732	128	0	4.43	5	1	4	299	28	0	5.62
1992-93	Owen Sound	OHL	41	20	17	3	2362	180	0	4.57	8	4	4	454	35	0	4.63
1993-94	Owen Sound	OHL	35	21	11	1	2004	120	1	3.59	9	4	5	547	44	0	4.83
1994-95	Owen Sound	OHL	17	5	9	2	977	64	0	3.93							
	Los Angeles	**NHL**	**5**	**1**	**3**	**1**	**263**	**17**	**0**	**3.88**							
	Windsor Spitfires	OHL	4	3	1	0	241	8	1	1.99	10	6	3	520	34	1	3.92
1995-96	**Los Angeles**	**NHL**	**5**	**3**	**1**	**0**	**262**	**12**	**0**	**2.75**							
	Phoenix	IHL	48	22	20	4	2711	139	2	3.08	2	1	1	118	4	1	2.03
1996-97	**Los Angeles**	**NHL**	**5**	**2**	**1**	**1**	**265**	**11**	**0**	**2.49**							
	Phoenix	IHL	44	16	22	4	2441	147	0	3.61							
1997-98	**Los Angeles**	**NHL**	**17**	**9**	**5**	**1**	**920**	**34**	**2**	**2.22**	**3**	**0**	**2**	**145**	**9**	**0**	**3.72**
	Long Beach	IHL	11	7	2	1	629	31	0	2.96							
1998-99	**Los Angeles**	**NHL**	**28**	**12**	**12**	**2**	**1525**	**61**	**4**	**2.40**							
99-2000	**Los Angeles**	**NHL**	**42**	**18**	**15**	**5**	**2206**	**93**	**1**	**2.53**	**1**	**0**	**1**	**36**	**2**	**0**	**3.33**
2000-01	**Los Angeles**	**NHL**	**45**	**19**	**18**	**6**	**2498**	**114**	**4**	**2.74**							
	NHL Totals		**147**	**64**	**55**	**16**	**7939**	**342**	**11**	**2.58**	**4**	**0**	**3**	**181**	**11**	**0**	**3.65**

OHL First All-Star Team (1994) • NHL All-Rookie Team (1998, 1999)

SWANSON, Kevin (SWAHN-suhn, KEH-vihn) VAN.

Goaltender. Catches left. 5'10", 170 lbs. Born, Calgary, Alta., April 18, 1980.
(Vancouver's 6th choice, 189th overall, in 1999 Entry Draft).

			Regular Season								Playoffs						
Season	Club	Lea	GP	W	L	T	Mins	GA	SO	Avg	GP	W	L	Mins	GA	SO	Avg
1996-97	Red Deer Chiefs	AMHL	20	....	....	....	1284	94	0	4.39	....	....	....	....	....	....	....
1997-98	Prince George	WHL	28	14	11	1	1532	93	0	3.64	....	....	....	....	....	....	....
1998-99	Prince George	WHL	4	1	2	0	180	10	0	3.33	....	....	....	....	....	....	....
	Kelowna Rockets	WHL	50	18	23	3	2507	144	2	3.45	6	2	4	355	14	0	2.37
99-2000	Kelowna Rockets	WHL	68	25	40	3	3943	194	*7	2.95	5	1	4	297	16	0	3.23
2000-01	Kelowna Rockets	WHL	49	27	16	5	2854	148	0	3.11	6	2	4	361	17	1	2.83

WHL West First All-Star Team (2000) • WHL West Second All-Star Team (2001)

SZUPER, Levente (SHOO-puhr, leh-VEHN-teh) CGY.

Goaltender. Catches left. 5'11", 180 lbs. Born, Budapest, Hungary, June 11, 1980.
(Calgary's 4th choice, 116th overall, in 2000 Entry Draft).

			Regular Season								Playoffs						
Season	Club	Lea	GP	W	L	T	Mins	GA	SO	Avg	GP	W	L	Mins	GA	SO	Avg
1996-97	TC Budapest-Jr.	Hungary	10	....	....	....	600	9	....	0.90	....	....	....	....	....	....	....
	TC Budapest	Hungary	30	....	....	....	1660	74	3	2.67	....	....	....	....	....	....	....
1997-98	Krefelder EV	DEL-Jr.	40	....	....	....	2300	103	3	2.69	....	....	....	....	....	....	....
1998-99	Ottawa 67's	OHL	32	22	6	3	1800	70	4	2.33	4	2	2	241	11	*1	2.74
99-2000	Ottawa 67's	OHL	53	31	15	2	2862	122	*5	2.56	11	6	5	680	35	1	3.09
2000-01	Saint John Flames	AHL	34	16	10	2	1750	73	2	2.50	1	1	0	36	0	0	0.00

TABARACCI, Rick (tab-uh-RA-chee, RIHK) DAL.

Goaltender. Catches left. 6'1", 190 lbs. Born, Toronto, Ont., January 2, 1969.
(Pittsburgh's 2nd choice, 26th overall, in 1987 Entry Draft).

			Regular Season								Playoffs						
Season	Club	Lea	GP	W	L	T	Mins	GA	SO	Avg	GP	W	L	Mins	GA	SO	Avg
1985-86	Markham Waxers	MTJHL	40	19	11	6	2176	188	1	5.18	....	....	....	....	....	....	....
1986-87	Cornwall Royals	OHL	*59	23	32	3	*3347	290	1	5.20	5	1	4	303	26	0	3.17
1987-88	Cornwall Royals	OHL	58	*33	18	6	3448	200	*3	3.48	11	5	6	642	37	0	3.46
	Muskegon	IHL	....	....	....	....	....	....	....	....	1	0	0	13	1	0	4.62
1988-89	**Pittsburgh**	**NHL**	**1**	**0**	**0**	**0**	**33**	**4**	**0**	**7.27**	....	....	....	....	....	....	....
	Cornwall Royals	OHL	50	24	20	5	2974	210	1	4.24	18	10	8	1080	65	*1	3.61
1989-90	Moncton Hawks	AHL	27	10	15	2	1580	107	2	4.06	....	....	....	....	....	....	....
	Fort Wayne	IHL	22	8	9	1	1064	73	0	4.12	3	1	2	159	19	0	7.17
1990-91	**Winnipeg**	**NHL**	**24**	**4**	**9**	**4**	**1093**	**71**	**1**	**3.90**	....	....	....	....	....	....	....
	Moncton Hawks	AHL	11	4	5	2	645	41	0	3.81	....	....	....	....	....	....	....
1991-92	**Winnipeg**	**NHL**	**18**	**6**	**7**	**3**	**966**	**52**	**0**	**3.23**	**7**	**3**	**4**	**387**	**26**	**0**	**4.03**
	Moncton Hawks	AHL	23	10	11	1	1313	80	0	3.66	....	....	....	....	....	....	....
1992-93	**Winnipeg**	**NHL**	**19**	**5**	**10**	**0**	**959**	**70**	**0**	**4.38**	....	....	....	....	....	....	....
	Moncton Hawks	AHL	5	2	1	2	290	18	0	3.72	....	....	....	....	....	....	....
	Washington	**NHL**	**6**	**3**	**2**	**0**	**343**	**10**	**2**	**1.75**	**4**	**1**	**3**	**304**	**14**	**0**	**2.76**
1993-94	**Washington**	**NHL**	**32**	**13**	**14**	**2**	**1770**	**91**	**2**	**3.08**	**2**	**0**	**2**	**111**	**6**	**0**	**3.24**
	Portland Pirates	AHL	3	3	0	0	176	8	0	2.72	....	....	....	....	....	....	....
1994-95	**Washington**	**NHL**	**8**	**1**	**3**	**2**	**394**	**16**	**0**	**2.44**	....	....	....	....	....	....	....
	Chicago Wolves	IHL	2	1	1	0	119	9	0	4.51	....	....	....	....	....	....	....
	Calgary	**NHL**	**5**	**2**	**0**	**1**	**202**	**5**	**0**	**1.49**	**1**	**0**	**0**	**19**	**0**	**0**	**0.00**
1995-96	**Calgary**	**NHL**	**43**	**19**	**16**	**3**	**2391**	**117**	**3**	**2.94**	**3**	**0**	**3**	**204**	**7**	**0**	**2.06**
1996-97	**Calgary**	**NHL**	**7**	**2**	**4**	**0**	**361**	**14**	**1**	**2.33**	....	....	....	....	....	....	....
	Tampa Bay	**NHL**	**55**	**20**	**25**	**6**	**3012**	**138**	**4**	**2.75**	....	....	....	....	....	....	....
1997-98	**Calgary**	**NHL**	**42**	**13**	**22**	**6**	**2419**	**116**	**0**	**2.88**	....	....	....	....	....	....	....
1998-99	**Washington**	**NHL**	**23**	**4**	**12**	**3**	**1193**	**50**	**2**	**2.51**	....	....	....	....	....	....	....
99-2000	**Atlanta**	**NHL**	**1**	**0**	**1**	**0**	**59**	**4**	**0**	**4.07**	....	....	....	....	....	....	....
	Cleveland	IHL	10	5	5	0	568	28	0	2.96	....	....	....	....	....	....	....
	Orlando	IHL	21	11	6	4	1231	53	1	2.58	....	....	....	....	....	....	....
	Colorado	**NHL**	**2**	**1**	**0**	**0**	**60**	**2**	**0**	**2.00**	....	....	....	....	....	....	....
	Utah Grizzlies	IHL	11	4	4	3	626	24	1	2.30	3	1	2	179	7	0	2.34
2000-01	Utah Grizzlies	IHL	30	14	13	1	1648	67	1	2.44	....	....	....	....	....	....	....
	NHL Totals		**286**	**93**	**125**	**30**	**15255**	**760**	**15**	**2.99**	**17**	**4**	**12**	**1025**	**53**	**0**	**3.10**

OHL First All-Star Team (1988) • OHL Second All-Star Team (1989)

Traded to **Winnipeg** by **Pittsburgh** with Randy Cunneyworth and Dave McLlwain for Jim Kyte, Andrew McBain and Randy Gilhen, June 17, 1989. Traded to **Washington** by **Winnipeg** for Jim Hrivnak and Washington's 2nd round choice (Alexei Budayev) in 1993 Entry Draft, March 22, 1993. Traded to **Calgary** by **Washington** for Calgary's 5th round choice (Joel Cort) in 1995 Entry Draft, April 7, 1995. Traded to **Tampa Bay** by **Calgary** for Aaron Gavey, November 19, 1996. Traded to **Calgary** by **Tampa Bay** for Calgary's 4th round choice (Eric Beaudoin) in 1998 Entry Draft, June 21, 1997. Traded to **Washington** by **Calgary** for future considerations, August 7, 1998. Signed as a free agent by **Atlanta**, November 3, 1999. Traded to **Colorado** by **Atlanta** for Shean Donovan, December 8, 1999. Selected by **Columbus** from **Colorado** in Expansion Draft, June 23, 2000. Signed as a free agent by **Dallas**, July 12, 2000.

TALLAS, Robbie (TAL-as, RAW-bee) PIT.

Goaltender. Catches left. 6', 170 lbs. Born, Edmonton, Alta., March 20, 1973.

			Regular Season								Playoffs						
Season	Club	Lea	GP	W	L	T	Mins	GA	SO	Avg	GP	W	L	Mins	GA	SO	Avg
1990-91	Penticton	BCJHL	37	....	....	....	2055	196	0	5.72	....	....	....	....	....	....	....
1991-92	Seattle T-Birds	WHL	14	4	7	0	708	52	0	4.41	....	....	....	....	....	....	....
	South Surrey	BCJHL	19	6	12	0	1043	112	1	6.44	....	....	....	....	....	....	....
1992-93	Seattle T-Birds	WHL	58	24	23	3	3151	194	2	3.69	5	1	4	333	18	0	3.24
1993-94	Seattle T-Birds	WHL	51	23	21	3	2849	188	0	3.96	9	5	4	567	40	0	4.23
1994-95	Charlotte	ECHL	36	21	9	3	2011	114	0	3.40	....	....	....	....	....	....	....
	Providence Bruins	AHL	2	1	0	0	82	4	1	2.90	....	....	....	....	....	....	....
1995-96	**Boston**	**NHL**	**1**	**1**	**0**	**0**	**60**	**3**	**0**	**3.00**	....	....	....	....	....	....	....
	Providence Bruins	AHL	37	12	16	7	2136	117	1	3.29	2	0	2	135	9	0	4.01
1996-97	**Boston**	**NHL**	**28**	**8**	**12**	**1**	**1244**	**69**	**1**	**3.33**	....	....	....	....	....	....	....
	Providence Bruins	AHL	24	9	14	1	1424	83	0	3.50	....	....	....	....	....	....	....
1997-98	**Boston**	**NHL**	**14**	**6**	**3**	**3**	**788**	**24**	**1**	**1.83**	....	....	....	....	....	....	....
	Providence Bruins	AHL	10	1	8	1	575	39	0	4.07	....	....	....	....	....	....	....
1998-99	**Boston**	**NHL**	**17**	**7**	**7**	**2**	**987**	**43**	**1**	**2.61**	....	....	....	....	....	....	....
99-2000	**Boston**	**NHL**	**27**	**4**	**13**	**4**	**1363**	**72**	**0**	**3.17**	....	....	....	....	....	....	....
2000-01	**Chicago**	**NHL**	**12**	**2**	**7**	**0**	**627**	**35**	**0**	**3.35**	....	....	....	....	....	....	....
	Chicago Wolves	IHL	3	0	1	0	87	6	0	4.13	....	....	....	....	....	....	....
	Norfolk Admirals	AHL	6	2	2	2	333	12	0	2.16	....	....	....	....	....	....	....
	NHL Totals		**99**	**28**	**42**	**10**	**5069**	**246**	**3**	**2.91**	....	....	....	....	....	....	....

Signed as a free agent by **Boston**, September 13, 1995. Signed as a free agent by **Chicago**, July 31, 2000. Signed as a free agent by **Pittsburgh**, August 14, 2001.

TARASOV, Vadim (ta-RA-sahf, va-DEEM) MTL.

Goaltender. Catches left. 5'11", 187 lbs. Born, Ust-Kamenogorsk, USSR, December 31, 1976.
(Montreal's 9th choice, 196th overall, in 1999 Entry Draft).

			Regular Season								Playoffs						
Season	Club	Lea	GP	W	L	T	Mins	GA	SO	Avg	GP	W	L	Mins	GA	SO	Avg
1995-96	HC Novokuznetsk	CIS	26	....	....	....	1355	60	1	2.66	....	....	....	....	....	....	....
1996-97	HC Novokuznetsk	Russia	34	....	....	....	1971	87	0	2.65	....	....	....	....	....	....	....
1997-98	HC Novokuznetsk	Russia	23	....	....	....	1364	61	2	2.68	....	....	....	....	....	....	....
1998-99	HC Novokuznetsk	Russia	*41	....	....	....	*2346	56	*8	1.43	6	....	....	349	16	0	2.75
99-2000	HC Novokuznetsk	Russia	28	....	....	....	1583	66	1	2.50	14	....	....	791	26	1	1.97
2000-01	HC Novokuznetsk	Russia	33	....	....	....	1960	69	4	2.11	....	....	....	....	....	....	....

TELLQVIST, Mikael (TEHL-kvihst, mih-KIGH-ehl) TOR.

Goaltender. Catches left. 5'11", 185 lbs. Born, Sundbyberg, Sweden, September 19, 1979.
(Toronto's 3rd choice, 70th overall, in 2000 Entry Draft).

			Regular Season								Playoffs						
Season	Club	Lea	GP	W	L	T	Mins	GA	SO	Avg	GP	W	L	Mins	GA	SO	Avg
1997-98	Djurgardens IF	Swede-Jr.	23	....	....	....	1380	55	....	2.39	2	0	2	120	8	0	4.00
1998-99	Djurgardens IF	Sweden	3	....	....	....	124	8	0	3.87	4	....	....	240	11	0	2.75
99-2000	Djurgardens IF	Sweden	30	....	....	....	1909	66	2	2.07	13	....	....	814	21	3	1.55
2000-01	Djurgardens IF	Sweden	43	....	....	....	2622	91	*5	*2.08	*16	....	....	*1006	45	*1	2.68

TERRERI, Chris (tuh-RAIR-ee, KRIHS)

Goaltender. Catches left. 5'9", 170 lbs. Born, Providence, RI, November 15, 1964.
(New Jersey's 3rd choice, 87th overall, in 1983 Entry Draft).

			Regular Season								Playoffs						
Season	Club	Lea	GP	W	L	T	Mins	GA	SO	Avg	GP	W	L	Mins	GA	SO	Avg
1982-83	Providence	ECAC	11	7	1	0	528	17	2	1.93	....	....	....	....	....	....	....
1983-84	Providence	ECAC	10	4	2	0	391	20	0	3.07	....	....	....	....	....	....	....
1984-85	Providence	H-East	33	15	13	5	1956	116	1	3.35	....	....	....	....	....	....	....
1985-86	Providence	H-East	22	6	16	0	1320	84	0	3.74	....	....	....	....	....	....	....
1986-87	**New Jersey**	**NHL**	**7**	**0**	**3**	**1**	**286**	**21**	**0**	**4.41**	....	....	....	....	....	....	....
	Maine Mariners	AHL	14	4	9	1	765	57	0	4.47	....	....	....	....	....	....	....
1987-88	Utica Devils	AHL	7	5	1	0	399	18	0	2.71	....	....	....	....	....	....	....
	United States	Nt-Team	26	17	7	2	1430	81	0	3.40	....	....	....	....	....	....	....
	United States	Olympics	3	1	1	0	127	14	0	6.58	....	....	....	....	....	....	....
1988-89	**New Jersey**	**NHL**	**8**	**0**	**4**	**2**	**402**	**18**	**0**	**2.69**	....	....	....	....	....	....	....
	Utica Devils	AHL	39	20	15	3	2314	132	0	3.42	2	0	1	80	6	0	4.50
1989-90	**New Jersey**	**NHL**	**35**	**15**	**12**	**3**	**1931**	**110**	**0**	**3.42**	**4**	**2**	**2**	**238**	**13**	**0**	**3.28**
1990-91	**New Jersey**	**NHL**	**53**	**24**	**21**	**7**	**2970**	**144**	**1**	**2.91**	**7**	**3**	**4**	**428**	**21**	**0**	**2.94**
1991-92	**New Jersey**	**NHL**	**54**	**22**	**22**	**10**	**3186**	**169**	**1**	**3.18**	**7**	**3**	**3**	**386**	**23**	**0**	**3.58**
1992-93	**New Jersey**	**NHL**	**48**	**19**	**21**	**3**	**2672**	**151**	**2**	**3.39**	**4**	**1**	**3**	**219**	**17**	**0**	**4.66**
1993-94	**New Jersey**	**NHL**	**44**	**20**	**11**	**4**	**2340**	**106**	**2**	**2.72**	**4**	**3**	**0**	**200**	**9**	**0**	**2.70**
1994-95 ♦	**New Jersey**	**NHL**	**15**	**3**	**7**	**2**	**734**	**31**	**0**	**2.53**	**1**	**0**	**0**	**8**	**0**	**0**	**0.00**
1995-96	**New Jersey**	**NHL**	**4**	**3**	**0**	**0**	**210**	**9**	**0**	**2.57**	....	....	....	....	....	....	....
	San Jose	**NHL**	**46**	**13**	**29**	**1**	**2516**	**155**	**0**	**3.70**	....	....	....	....	....	....	....
1996-97	**San Jose**	**NHL**	**22**	**6**	**10**	**3**	**1200**	**55**	**0**	**2.75**	....	....	....	....	....	....	....
	Chicago	**NHL**	**7**	**4**	**1**	**2**	**429**	**19**	**0**	**2.66**	**2**	**0**	**0**	**44**	**3**	**0**	**4.09**
1997-98	**Chicago**	**NHL**	**21**	**8**	**10**	**2**	**1222**	**49**	**2**	**2.41**	....	....	....	....	....	....	....
	Indianapolis Ice	IHL	3	2	0	1	180	3	1	1.00	....	....	....	....	....	....	....
1998-99	**New Jersey**	**NHL**	**12**	**8**	**3**	**1**	**726**	**30**	**1**	**2.48**	....	....	....	....	....	....	....
99-2000 ♦	**New Jersey**	**NHL**	**12**	**2**	**9**	**0**	**649**	**37**	**0**	**3.42**	....	....	....	....	....	....	....
2000-01	**New Jersey**	**NHL**	**10**	**2**	**5**	**1**	**453**	**21**	**0**	**2.78**	....	....	....	....	....	....	....
	NY Islanders	**NHL**	**8**	**2**	**4**	**1**	**443**	**18**	**0**	**2.44**	....	....	....	....	....	....	....
	NHL Totals		**406**	**151**	**172**	**43**	**22369**	**1143**	**9**	**3.07**	**29**	**12**	**12**	**1523**	**86**	**0**	**3.39**

Hockey East First All-Star Team (1985) • NCAA East First All-American Team (1985) • NCAA Championship All-Tournament Team (1985) • NCAA Championship Tournament MVP (1985)

Traded to **San Jose** by **New Jersey** for San Jose's 2nd round choice (later traded to Pittsburgh - Pittsburgh selected Pavel Skrbek) in 1996 Entry Draft, November 15, 1995. Traded to **Chicago** by **San Jose** with Ulf Dahlen and Michal Sykora for Ed Belfour, January 25, 1997. Traded to **New Jersey** by **Chicago** for New Jersey's 2nd round choice (Stepan Mokhov) in 1999 Entry Draft, August 25, 1998. Selected by **Minnesota** from **New Jersey** in Expansion Draft, June 23, 2000. Traded to **New Jersey** by **Minnesota** with Minnesota's 9th round choice (later traded to Tampa Bay - Tampa Bay selected Thomas Ziegler) in 2000 Entry Draft for Brad Bombardir, June 23, 2000. Traded to **NY Islanders** by **New Jersey** with New Jersey's 9th round choice (Juha-Pekka Ketola) in 2001 Entry Draft for John Vanbiesbrouck, March 12, 2001. • Officially announced retirement and named Assistant Coach of **Albany** (AHL), August 4, 2001.

THEODORE, Jose (TEE-uh-dohr, joh-SAY) MTL.

Goaltender. Catches right. 5'11", 182 lbs. Born, Laval, Que., September 13, 1976.
(Montreal's 2nd choice, 44th overall, in 1994 Entry Draft).

			Regular Season								Playoffs						
Season	Club	Lea	GP	W	L	T	Mins	GA	SO	Avg	GP	W	L	Mins	GA	SO	Avg
1990-91	Richelieu Regents	QAHA	42	....	....	....	2520	80	0	1.90	....	....	....	....	....	....	....
1991-92	Richelieu Riverains	QAAA	24	9	13	2	1440	96	0	3.99	5	2	3	295	26	0	5.28
1992-93	St-Jean Lynx	QMJHL	34	12	16	2	1776	112	0	3.78	3	0	2	175	11	0	3.77
1993-94	St-Jean Lynx	QMJHL	57	20	29	6	3225	194	0	3.61	5	1	4	296	18	0	3.65
1994-95	Hull Olympiques	QMJHL	*58	*32	22	2	*3348	193	5	3.46	*21	*15	6	*1263	59	*1	2.80
	Fredericton	AHL	....	....	....	....	....	....	....	....	1	0	1	60	3	0	3.00
1995-96	**Montreal**	**NHL**	**1**	**0**	**0**	**0**	**9**	**1**	**0**	**6.67**	....	....	....	....	....	....	....
	Hull Olympiques	QMJHL	48	33	11	2	2807	158	0	3.38	5	2	3	299	20	0	4.01
1996-97	**Montreal**	**NHL**	**16**	**5**	**6**	**2**	**821**	**53**	**0**	**3.87**	**2**	**1**	**1**	**168**	**7**	**0**	**2.50**
	Fredericton	AHL	26	12	12	0	1469	87	0	3.55	....	....	....	....	....	....	....
1997-98	Fredericton	AHL	53	20	23	8	3053	145	2	2.85	4	1	3	237	13	0	3.28
	Montreal	**NHL**	....	....	....	....	....	....	....	....	**3**	**0**	**1**	**120**	**1**	**0**	**0.50**
1998-99	**Montreal**	**NHL**	**18**	**4**	**12**	**0**	**913**	**50**	**1**	**3.29**	....	....	....	....	....	....	....
	Fredericton	AHL	27	12	13	2	1609	77	2	2.87	13	8	5	694	35	1	3.03
99-2000	**Montreal**	**NHL**	**30**	**12**	**13**	**2**	**1655**	**58**	**5**	**2.10**	....	....	....	....	....	....	....
2000-01	**Montreal**	**NHL**	**59**	**20**	**29**	**5**	**3298**	**141**	**2**	**2.57**	....	....	....	....	....	....	....
	Quebec Citadelles	AHL	3	3	0	0	180	9	0	3.00	....	....	....	....	....	....	....
	NHL Totals		**124**	**41**	**60**	**9**	**6696**	**303**	**8**	**2.72**	**5**	**1**	**2**	**288**	**8**	**0**	**1.67**

QMJHL Second All-Star Team (1995, 1996) • Scored a goal while with Montreal vs. NY Islanders, January 2, 2001.

THIBAULT, Jocelyn (tee-BOW, JAW-seh-lihn) CHI.

Goaltender. Catches left. 5'11", 170 lbs. Born, Montreal, Que., January 12, 1975.
(Quebec's 1st choice, 10th overall, in 1993 Entry Draft).

			Regular Season								Playoffs						
Season	Club	Lea	GP	W	L	T	Mins	GA	SO	Avg	GP	W	L	Mins	GA	SO	Avg
1990-91	Laval Regents	QAAA	20	14	5	0	1178	78	1	3.94	5	2	3	300	20	0	4.00
1991-92	Trois-Rivieres	QMJHL	30	14	7	1	1496	77	0	3.09	3	1	1	110	4	0	2.19
1992-93	Sherbrooke	QMJHL	56	34	14	5	3190	159	3	2.99	15	9	6	882	57	0	3.87
1993-94	**Quebec**	**NHL**	**29**	**8**	**13**	**3**	**1504**	**83**	**0**	**3.31**	....	....	....	....	....	....	....
	Cornwall Aces	AHL	4	4	0	0	240	9	1	2.25	....	....	....	....	....	....	....
1994-95	Sherbrooke	QMJHL	13	6	6	1	776	38	1	2.94	....	....	....	....	....	....	....
	Quebec	**NHL**	**18**	**12**	**2**	**2**	**898**	**35**	**1**	**2.34**	**3**	**1**	**2**	**148**	**8**	**0**	**3.24**
1995-96	**Colorado**	**NHL**	**10**	**3**	**4**	**2**	**558**	**28**	**0**	**3.01**	....	....	....	....	....	....	....
	Montreal	**NHL**	**40**	**23**	**13**	**3**	**2334**	**110**	**3**	**2.83**	**6**	**2**	**4**	**311**	**18**	**0**	**3.47**
1996-97	**Montreal**	**NHL**	**61**	**22**	**24**	**11**	**3397**	**164**	**1**	**2.90**	**3**	**0**	**3**	**179**	**13**	**0**	**4.36**
1997-98	**Montreal**	**NHL**	**47**	**19**	**15**	**8**	**2652**	**109**	**2**	**2.47**	**2**	**0**	**0**	**43**	**4**	**0**	**5.58**
1998-99	**Montreal**	**NHL**	**10**	**3**	**4**	**2**	**529**	**23**	**1**	**2.61**	....	....	....	....	....	....	....
	Chicago	**NHL**	**52**	**21**	**26**	**5**	**3014**	**136**	**4**	**2.71**	....	....	....	....	....	....	....
99-2000	**Chicago**	**NHL**	**60**	**25**	**26**	**7**	**3438**	**158**	**3**	**2.76**	....	....	....	....	....	....	....
2000-01	**Chicago**	**NHL**	**66**	**27**	**32**	**7**	**3844**	**180**	**6**	**2.81**	....	....	....	....	....	....	....
	NHL Totals		**393**	**163**	**159**	**50**	**22168**	**1026**	**21**	**2.78**	**14**	**3**	**9**	**681**	**43**	**0**	**3.79**

QMJHL First All-Star Team (1993) • Canadian Major Junior First All-Star Team (1993) • Canadian Major Junior Goaltender of the Year (1993)

Transferred to **Colorado** after **Quebec** franchise relocated, June 21, 1995. Traded to **Montreal** by **Colorado** with Andrei Kovalenko and Martin Rucinsky for Patrick Roy and Mike Keane, December 6, 1995. Traded to **Chicago** by **Montreal** with Dave Manson and Brad Brown for Jeff Hackett, Eric Weinrich, Alain Nasreddine and Tampa Bay's 4th round choice (previously acquired, Montreal selected Chris Dyment) in 1999 Entry Draft, November 16, 1998.

THOMPSON, Billy (TAWMP-suhn, BIHL-lee) FLA.

Goaltender. Catches left. 6'3", 188 lbs. Born, Saskatoon, Sask., September 24, 1982.
(Florida's 7th choice, 136th overall, in 2001 Entry Draft).

			Regular Season								Playoffs						
Season	Club	Lea	GP	W	L	T	Mins	GA	SO	Avg	GP	W	L	Mins	GA	SO	Avg
1997-98	Saskatoon AAA	SMHL	23	14	5	3	1336	65	2	2.92	....	....	....	....	....	....	....
1998-99	Lebret Eagles	SJHL					STATISTICS NOT AVAILABLE										
99-2000	Estevan Bruins	SJHL	31	....	....	....	1763	132	1	4.49	5	1	3	328	17	0	3.11
	Prince George	WHL	1	0	1	0	60	5	0	5.00	....	....	....	....	....	....	....
2000-01	Prince George	WHL	57	24	24	3	3185	178	1	3.35	6	2	4	324	22	0	4.07

TOSKALA, Vesa (TAWS-kah-lah, VEH-sa) S.J.

Goaltender. Catches left. 5'10", 190 lbs. Born, Tampere, Finland, May 20, 1977.
(San Jose's 4th choice, 90th overall, in 1995 Entry Draft).

			Regular Season								Playoffs						
Season	Club	Lea	GP	W	L	T	Mins	GA	SO	Avg	GP	W	L	Mins	GA	SO	Avg
1993-94	Ilves Tampere-2	Finn-Jr.					STATISTICS NOT AVAILABLE										
1994-95	Ilves Tampere	Finn-Jr.	17	....	....	....	956	36	....	2.26	....	....	....	....	....	....	....
1995-96	Ilves Tampere	Finn-Jr.	3	....	....	....	180	3	....	1.00	....	....	....	....	....	....	....
	KooVee Tampere	Finland-2	2	....	....	....	119	5	....	2.51	....	....	....	....	....	....	....
	Ilves Tampere	Finland	37	....	....	....	2073	109	1	3.16	2	....	....	78	11	....	8.49
1996-97	Ilves Tampere	Finland	40	22	12	5	2270	108	0	2.85	8	3	5	479	29	0	3.63
1997-98	Ilves Tampere	Finland	43	*26	13	3	2555	118	1	2.77	*9	6	3	519	18	1	2.08
1998-99	Ilves Tampere	Finland	33	21	12	0	1966	70	*5	2.14	4	1	3	248	14	0	3.39
99-2000	Farjestads BK	Sweden	44	....	....	....	2652	118	3	2.67	7	....	....	439	19	0	2.60
2000-01	Kentucky	AHL	44	22	13	5	2466	114	2	2.77	3	0	3	197	8	0	2.43

TREFILOV, Andrei (TREH-fee-lahf, AWN-dray) CGY.

Goaltender. Catches left. 6', 190 lbs. Born, Kirovo-Chepetsk, USSR, August 31, 1969.
(Calgary's 14th choice, 261st overall, in 1991 Entry Draft).

			Regular Season								Playoffs						
Season	Club	Lea	GP	W	L	T	Mins	GA	SO	Avg	GP	W	L	Mins	GA	SO	Avg
1990-91	Dynamo Moscow	USSR	20	....	....	....	1070	36	0	2.01	....	....	....	....	....	....	....
1991-92	Dynamo Moscow	CIS	28	....	....	....	1326	35	0	1.58	....	....	....	....	....	....	....
	Russia	Olympics	4	0	0	0	39	2	0	3.08	....	....	....	....	....	....	....
1992-93	**Calgary**	**NHL**	**1**	**0**	**0**	**1**	**65**	**5**	**0**	**4.62**	....	....	....	....	....	....	....
	Salt Lake City	IHL	44	23	17	3	2536	135	0	3.19	....	....	....	....	....	....	....
1993-94	**Calgary**	**NHL**	**11**	**3**	**4**	**2**	**623**	**26**	**2**	**2.50**	....	....	....	....	....	....	....
	Saint John Flames	AHL	28	10	10	7	1629	93	0	3.42	....	....	....	....	....	....	....
1994-95	**Calgary**	**NHL**	**6**	**0**	**3**	**0**	**236**	**16**	**0**	**4.07**	....	....	....	....	....	....	....
	Saint John Flames	AHL	7	1	5	1	383	20	0	3.13	....	....	....	....	....	....	....
1995-96	**Buffalo**	**NHL**	**22**	**8**	**8**	**1**	**1094**	**64**	**0**	**3.51**	....	....	....	....	....	....	....
	Rochester	AHL	5	4	1	0	299	13	0	2.61	....	....	....	....	....	....	....
1996-97	**Buffalo**	**NHL**	**3**	**0**	**2**	**0**	**159**	**10**	**0**	**3.77**	**1**	**0**	**0**	**5**	**0**	**0**	**0.00**
1997-98	Rochester	AHL	3	1	0	1	138	6	0	2.60	....	....	....	....	....	....	....
	Chicago	**NHL**	**6**	**1**	**4**	**0**	**299**	**17**	**0**	**3.41**	....	....	....	....	....	....	....
	Indianapolis Ice	IHL	1	0	1	0	59	3	0	3.03	....	....	....	....	....	....	....
	Russia	Olympics	2	1	0	0	69	4	0	3.45	....	....	....	....	....	....	....
1998-99	AK Bars Kazan	Russia	3	....	....	....	160	7	1	2.63	....	....	....	....	....	....	....
	Chicago	**NHL**	**1**	**0**	**1**	**0**	**25**	**4**	**0**	**9.60**	....	....	....	....	....	....	....
	Indianapolis Ice	IHL	18	9	6	2	986	39	0	2.37	....	....	....	....	....	....	....
	Calgary	**NHL**	**4**	**0**	**3**	**0**	**162**	**11**	**0**	**4.07**	....	....	....	....	....	....	....
	Detroit Vipers	IHL	27	17	8	2	1613	53	3	1.97	10	6	4	647	22	0	2.04
99-2000	Chicago Wolves	IHL	37	21	9	3	2060	81	3	2.36	9	7	1	489	11	1	*1.35
2000-01	Dusseldorfer EG	DEL	50	....	....	....	2864	120	2	2.51	....	....	....	....	....	....	....
	NHL Totals		**54**	**12**	**25**	**4**	**2663**	**153**	**2**	**3.45**	**1**	**0**	**0**	**5**	**0**	**0**	**0.00**

IHL Second All-Star Team (1999) • Shared James Norris Memorial Trophy (fewest goals against - IHL) with Kevin Weekes (1999) • Won "Bud" Poile Trophy (Playoff MVP - IHL) (2000)

Signed as a free agent by **Buffalo**, July 11, 1995. Traded to **Chicago** by **Buffalo** for future considerations, November 12, 1997. Traded to **Calgary** by **Chicago** for future considerations, December 29, 1998.

TUGNUTT, Ron (TUHG-nuht, RAWN) CBJ

Goaltender. Catches left. 5'11", 160 lbs. Born, Scarborough, Ont., October 22, 1967.
(Quebec's 4th choice, 81st overall, in 1986 Entry Draft).

			Regular Season								Playoffs						
Season	Club	Lea	GP	W	L	T	Mins	GA	SO	Avg	GP	W	L	Mins	GA	SO	Avg
1983-84	Toronto Nationals	MTHL	34	....	....	....	1690	91	3	2.67	....	....	....	....	....	....	....
	Weston Dukes	MTJHL	1	0	0	0	20	2	0	6.00	....	....	....	....	....	....	....
1984-85	Peterborough	OHL	18	7	4	2	938	59	0	3.77	....	....	....	....	....	....	....
1985-86	Peterborough	OHL	26	18	7	0	1543	74	1	2.88	3	2	0	133	6	0	2.71
1986-87	Peterborough	OHL	31	21	7	2	1891	88	2	*2.79	6	3	3	374	21	1	3.37
1987-88	**Quebec**	**NHL**	**6**	**2**	**3**	**0**	**284**	**16**	**0**	**3.38**	....	....	....	....	....	....	....
	Fredericton	AHL	34	20	9	4	1964	118	1	3.60	4	1	2	204	11	0	3.24
1988-89	**Quebec**	**NHL**	**26**	**10**	**10**	**3**	**1367**	**82**	**0**	**3.60**	....	....	....	....	....	....	....
	Halifax Citadels	AHL	24	14	7	2	1368	79	1	3.46	....	....	....	....	....	....	....
1989-90	**Quebec**	**NHL**	**35**	**5**	**24**	**3**	**1978**	**152**	**0**	**4.61**	....	....	....	....	....	....	....
	Halifax Citadels	AHL	6	1	5	0	366	23	0	3.77	....	....	....	....	....	....	....
1990-91	**Quebec**	**NHL**	**56**	**12**	**29**	**10**	**3144**	**212**	**0**	**4.05**	....	....	....	....	....	....	....
	Halifax Citadels	AHL	2	0	1	0	100	8	0	4.80	....	....	....	....	....	....	....
1991-92	**Quebec**	**NHL**	**30**	**6**	**17**	**3**	**1583**	**106**	**1**	**4.02**	....	....	....	....	....	....	....
	Halifax Citadels	AHL	8	3	3	1	447	30	0	4.03	....	....	....	....	....	....	....
	Edmonton	**NHL**	**3**	**1**	**1**	**0**	**124**	**10**	**0**	**4.84**	**2**	**0**	**0**	**60**	**3**	**0**	**3.00**
1992-93	**Edmonton**	**NHL**	**26**	**9**	**12**	**2**	**1338**	**93**	**0**	**4.17**	....	....	....	....	....	....	....
1993-94	**Anaheim**	**NHL**	**28**	**10**	**15**	**1**	**1520**	**76**	**1**	**3.00**	....	....	....	....	....	....	....
	Montreal	**NHL**	**8**	**2**	**3**	**1**	**378**	**24**	**0**	**3.81**	**1**	**0**	**1**	**59**	**5**	**0**	**5.08**
1994-95	**Montreal**	**NHL**	**7**	**1**	**3**	**1**	**346**	**18**	**0**	**3.12**	....	....	....	....	....	....	....
1995-96	Portland Pirates	AHL	58	21	23	6	3068	171	2	3.34	13	7	6	782	36	1	2.76
1996-97	**Ottawa**	**NHL**	**37**	**17**	**15**	**1**	**1991**	**93**	**3**	**2.80**	**7**	**3**	**4**	**425**	**14**	**1**	**1.98**
1997-98	**Ottawa**	**NHL**	**42**	**15**	**14**	**8**	**2236**	**84**	**3**	**2.25**	**2**	**0**	**1**	**74**	**6**	**0**	**4.86**
1998-99	**Ottawa**	**NHL**	**43**	**22**	**10**	**8**	**2508**	**75**	**3**	***1.79**	**2**	**0**	**2**	**118**	**6**	**0**	**3.05**
99-2000	**Ottawa**	**NHL**	**44**	**18**	**12**	**8**	**2435**	**103**	**4**	**2.54**	....	....	....	....	....	....	....
	Pittsburgh	**NHL**	**7**	**4**	**2**	**0**	**374**	**15**	**0**	**2.41**	**11**	**6**	**5**	**746**	**22**	**2**	**1.77**
2000-01	**Columbus**	**NHL**	**53**	**22**	**25**	**5**	**3129**	**127**	**4**	**2.44**	....	....	....	....	....	....	....
	NHL Totals		**451**	**156**	**195**	**54**	**24735**	**1286**	**19**	**3.12**	**25**	**9**	**13**	**1482**	**56**	**3**	**2.27**

OHL First All-Star Team (1987) • Played in NHL All-Star Game (1999)

Traded to **Edmonton** by **Quebec** with Brad Zavisha for Martin Rucinsky, March 10, 1992. Claimed by **Anaheim** from **Edmonton** in Expansion Draft, June 24, 1993. Traded to **Montreal** by **Anaheim** for Stephan Lebeau, February 20, 1994. Signed as a free agent by **Washington**, September 25, 1995. Signed as a free agent by **Ottawa**, August 14, 1996. Traded to **Pittsburgh** by **Ottawa** with Janne Laukkanen for Tom Barrasso, March 14, 2000. Signed as a free agent by **Columbus**, July 4, 2000.

TURCO, Marty (TUHR-koh, MAHR-tee) DAL.

Goaltender. Catches left. 5'11", 183 lbs. Born, Sault Ste. Marie, Ont., August 13, 1975.
(Dallas' 4th choice, 124th overall, in 1994 Entry Draft).

			Regular Season								Playoffs						
Season	Club	Lea	GP	W	L	T	Mins	GA	SO	Avg	GP	W	L	Mins	GA	SO	Avg
1993-94	Cambridge Hawks	OJHL-B	34	19	10	3	1973	114	0	3.47	....	....	....	....	....	....	....
1994-95	U. of Michigan	CCHA	37	*27	7	1	2063	95	1	2.76	....	....	....	....	....	....	....
1995-96	U. of Michigan	CCHA	*42	*34	7	1	*2335	84	*5	*2.16	....	....	....	....	....	....	....
1996-97	U. of Michigan	CCHA	*41	*33	4	4	*2296	87	*4	*2.27	....	....	....	....	....	....	....
1997-98	U. of Michigan	CCHA	*45	*33	10	1	*2640	95	4	2.16	....	....	....	....	....	....	....
1998-99	Michigan K-Wings	IHL	54	24	17	10	3127	136	1	2.61	5	2	3	300	14	0	2.80
99-2000	Michigan K-Wings	IHL	60	23	27	*7	3399	139	*7	2.45	....	....	....	....	....	....	....
2000-01	**Dallas**	**NHL**	**26**	**13**	**6**	**1**	**1266**	**40**	**3**	***1.90**	....	....	....	....	....	....	....
	NHL Totals		**26**	**13**	**6**	**1**	**1266**	**40**	**3**	**1.90**	....	....	....	....	....	....	....

NCAA Championship All-Tournament Team (1996, 1998) • CCHA First All-Star Team (1997) • NCAA West First All-American Team (1997) • CCHA Second All-Star Team (1998) • NCAA Championship Tournament MVP (1998) • Won Garry F. Longman Memorial Trophy (Top Rookie - IHL) (1999) • Won MBNA Roger Crozier Saving Grace Award (2001)

TUREK, Roman (TOOR-ehk, ROH-muhn) CGY.

Goaltender. Catches right. 6'3", 215 lbs. Born, Strakonice, Czech., May 21, 1970.
(Minnesota's 6th choice, 113th overall, in 1990 Entry Draft).

			Regular Season								Playoffs						
Season	Club	Lea	GP	W	L	T	Mins	GA	SO	Avg	GP	W	L	Mins	GA	SO	Avg
1990-91	MC Budejovice	Czech.	26	....	....	....	1244	98	0	4.70	....	....	....	....	....	....	....
1991-92	MC Budejovice	Czech-2					STATISTICS NOT AVAILABLE										
1992-93	MC Budejovice	Czech.	43	....	....	....	2555	121	....	2.84	....	....	....	....	....	....	....
1993-94	MC Budejovice	Cze-Rep	44	....	....	....	2584	111	....	2.51	3	....	....	180	12	0	4.00
	Czech-Republic	Olympics	2	2	0	0	120	3	0	1.50	....	....	....	....	....	....	....
1994-95	MC Budejovice	Cze-Rep	44	....	....	....	2587	119	....	2.76	9	....	....	498	25	....	3.01
1995-96	EHC Nurnberg	DEL	48	....	....	....	2787	154	....	3.31	5	....	....	338	14	....	2.48
1996-97	**Dallas**	**NHL**	**6**	**3**	**1**	**0**	**263**	**9**	**0**	**2.05**	....	....	....	....	....	....	....
	Michigan K-Wings	IHL	29	8	13	4	1555	77	0	2.97	....	....	....	....	....	....	....
1997-98	**Dallas**	**NHL**	**23**	**11**	**10**	**1**	**1324**	**49**	**1**	**2.22**	....	....	....	....	....	....	....
	Michigan K-Wings	IHL	2	1	1	0	119	5	0	2.51	....	....	....	....	....	....	....
1998-99 ◆	**Dallas**	**NHL**	**26**	**16**	**3**	**3**	**1382**	**48**	**1**	**2.08**	....	....	....	....	....	....	....
99-2000	**St. Louis**	**NHL**	**67**	**42**	**15**	**9**	**3960**	**129**	***7**	**1.95**	**7**	**3**	**4**	**415**	**19**	**0**	**2.75**
2000-01	**St. Louis**	**NHL**	**54**	**24**	**18**	**10**	**3232**	**123**	**6**	**2.28**	**14**	**9**	**5**	**908**	**31**	**0**	**2.05**
	NHL Totals		**176**	**96**	**47**	**23**	**10161**	**358**	**15**	**2.11**	**21**	**12**	**9**	**1323**	**50**	**0**	**2.27**

Shared William M. Jennings Trophy with Ed Belfour (1999) • NHL Second All-Star Team (2000) • Won William M. Jennings Trophy (2000) • Played in NHL All-Star Game (2000)

Rights transferred to **Dallas** after **Minnesota** franchise relocated, June 9, 1993. Traded to **St. Louis** by **Dallas** for St. Louis' compensatory 2nd round choice (Dan Jancevski) in 1999 Entry Draft, June 20, 1999. Traded to **Calgary** by **St. Louis** with St. Louis' 4th round choice (Yegor Shastin) in 2001 Entry Draft for Fred Brathwaite, Daniel Tkaczuk, Sergei Varlamov and Calgary's 9th round choice (Grant Jacobsen) in 2001 Entry Draft, June 23, 2001.

UNDERHILL, Matt (UHN-duhr-HIHL, MAT) CGY.

Goaltender. Catches left. 6'2", 195 lbs. Born, Merrill, B.C., September 16, 1979.
(Calgary's 8th choice, 170th overall, in 1999 Entry Draft).

			Regular Season								Playoffs						
Season	Club	Lea	GP	W	L	T	Mins	GA	SO	Avg	GP	W	L	Mins	GA	SO	Avg
1997-98	Notre Dame	SJHL	43	18	22	3	2573	132	2	3.07	....	....	....	....	....	....	....
1998-99	Cornell Big Red	ECAC	25	7	10	4	1320	65	1	2.95	....	....	....	....	....	....	....
99-2000	Cornell Big Red	ECAC	18	8	7	1	912	44	1	2.89	....	....	....	....	....	....	....
2000-01	Cornell Big Red	ECAC	25	13	8	3	1504	47	1	1.88	....	....	....	....	....	....	....

VALIQUETTE, Stephen (val-ih-KEHT, STEEV-uhn) NYI

Goaltender. Catches left. 6'5", 190 lbs. Born, Etobicoke, Ont., August 20, 1977.
(Los Angeles' 8th choice, 190th overall, in 1996 Entry Draft).

			Regular Season								Playoffs						
Season	Club	Lea	GP	W	L	T	Mins	GA	SO	Avg	GP	W	L	Mins	GA	SO	Avg
1993-94	Burlington	OPJHL	30	....	....	....	1663	112	1	4.04	....	....	....	....	....	....	....
1994-95	Rayside Balfour	NOJHA	2	0	2	0	89	12	0	8.09	....	....	....	....	....	....	....
	Smiths Falls Bears	OCJHL	21	10	8	3	1275	75	0	3.53	....	....	....	....	....	....	....
	Sudbury Wolves	OHL	4	2	0	0	138	6	0	2.61	....	....	....	....	....	....	....
1995-96	Sudbury Wolves	OHL	39	13	16	2	1887	123	0	3.91	....	....	....	....	....	....	....
1996-97	Sudbury Wolves	OHL	*61	21	29	7	3311	232	1	4.20	....	....	....	....	....	....	....
	Dayton Bombers	ECHL	3	1	0	0	89	6	0	4.03	2	1	1	118	5	0	2.54
1997-98	Sudbury Wolves	OHL	14	5	7	1	807	50	0	3.72	....	....	....	....	....	....	....
	Erie Otters	OHL	28	16	7	3	1525	65	3	2.56	7	3	4	467	15	1	1.93
1998-99	Hampton Roads	ECHL	31	18	7	3	1713	84	1	2.94	2	0	1	60	7	0	7.00
	Lowell	AHL	1	0	1	0	59	3	0	3.05	....	....	....	....	....	....	....
99-2000	**NY Islanders**	**NHL**	**6**	**2**	**0**	**0**	**193**	**6**	**0**	**1.87**	....	....	....	....	....	....	....
	Lowell	AHL	14	8	5	0	727	36	0	2.97	....	....	....	....	....	....	....
	Providence Bruins	AHL	1	1	0	0	60	3	0	3.00	....	....	....	....	....	....	....
	Trenton Titans	ECHL	12	5	6	1	692	36	1	3.12	....	....	....	....	....	....	....
2000-01	Springfield	AHL	20	7	10	1	1066	54	0	3.04	....	....	....	....	....	....	....
	NHL Totals		**6**	**2**	**0**	**0**	**193**	**6**	**0**	**1.87**	....	....	....	....	....	....	....

Signed as a free agent by **NY Islanders**, August 18, 1998.

VANBIESBROUCK, John (van-BEES-bruhk, JAWN)

Goaltender. Catches left. 5'8", 176 lbs. Born, Detroit, MI, September 4, 1963.
(NY Rangers' 5th choice, 72nd overall, in 1981 Entry Draft).

			Regular Season								Playoffs						
Season	Club	Lea	GP	W	L	T	Mins	GA	SO	Avg	GP	W	L	Mins	GA	SO	Avg
1979-80	Bishop Gallagher	H.S.					STATISTICS NOT AVAILABLE										
1980-81	Sault Ste. Marie	OMJHL	56	31	16	1	2941	203	0	4.14	11	3	3	457	24	1	3.15
1981-82	Sault Ste. Marie	OHL	31	12	12	2	1686	102	0	3.62	7	1	4	276	20	0	4.35
	NY Rangers	**NHL**	**1**	**1**	**0**	**0**	**60**	**1**	**0**	**1.00**	....	....	....	....	....	....	....
1982-83	Sault Ste. Marie	OHL	*62	39	21	1	3471	209	0	3.61	16	7	6	944	56	*1	3.56
1983-84	**NY Rangers**	**NHL**	**3**	**2**	**1**	**0**	**180**	**10**	**0**	**3.33**	**1**	**0**	**0**	**1**	**0**	**0**	**0.00**
	Tulsa Oilers	CHL	37	20	13	2	2153	124	*3	3.46	4	4	0	240	10	0	*2.50
1984-85	**NY Rangers**	**NHL**	**42**	**12**	**24**	**3**	**2358**	**166**	**1**	**4.22**	**1**	**0**	**0**	**20**	**0**	**0**	**0.00**
1985-86	**NY Rangers**	**NHL**	**61**	***31**	**21**	**5**	**3326**	**184**	**3**	**3.32**	**16**	**8**	**8**	**899**	**49**	***1**	**3.27**
1986-87	**NY Rangers**	**NHL**	**50**	**18**	**20**	**5**	**2656**	**161**	**0**	**3.64**	**4**	**1**	**3**	**195**	**11**	**1**	**3.38**
1987-88	**NY Rangers**	**NHL**	**56**	**27**	**22**	**7**	**3319**	**187**	**2**	**3.38**	....	....	....	....	....	....	....
1988-89	**NY Rangers**	**NHL**	**56**	**28**	**21**	**4**	**3207**	**197**	**0**	**3.69**	**2**	**0**	**1**	**107**	**6**	**0**	**3.36**
1989-90	**NY Rangers**	**NHL**	**47**	**19**	**19**	**7**	**2734**	**154**	**1**	**3.38**	**6**	**2**	**3**	**298**	**15**	**0**	**3.02**
1990-91	**NY Rangers**	**NHL**	**40**	**15**	**18**	**6**	**2257**	**126**	**3**	**3.35**	**1**	**0**	**0**	**52**	**1**	**0**	**1.15**
1991-92	**NY Rangers**	**NHL**	**45**	**27**	**13**	**3**	**2526**	**120**	**2**	**2.85**	**7**	**2**	**5**	**368**	**23**	**0**	**3.75**
1992-93	**NY Rangers**	**NHL**	**48**	**20**	**18**	**7**	**2757**	**152**	**4**	**3.31**	....	....	....	....	....	....	....
1993-94	**Florida**	**NHL**	**57**	**21**	**25**	**11**	**3440**	**145**	**1**	**2.53**	....	....	....	....	....	....	....
1994-95	**Florida**	**NHL**	**37**	**14**	**15**	**4**	**2087**	**86**	**4**	**2.47**	....	....	....	....	....	....	....
1995-96	**Florida**	**NHL**	**57**	**26**	**20**	**7**	**3178**	**142**	**2**	**2.68**	***22**	**12**	**10**	**1332**	**50**	**1**	**2.25**
1996-97	**Florida**	**NHL**	**57**	**27**	**19**	**10**	**3347**	**128**	**2**	**2.29**	**5**	**1**	**4**	**328**	**13**	**1**	**2.38**
1997-98	**Florida**	**NHL**	**60**	**18**	**29**	**11**	**3451**	**165**	**4**	**2.87**	....	....	....	....	....	....	....
	United States	Olympics	1	0	0	0	1	0	0	0.00	....	....	....	....	....	....	....
1998-99	**Philadelphia**	**NHL**	**62**	**27**	**18**	**15**	**3712**	**135**	**6**	**2.18**	**6**	**2**	**4**	**369**	**9**	**1**	**1.46**
99-2000	**Philadelphia**	**NHL**	**50**	**25**	**15**	**9**	**2950**	**108**	**3**	**2.20**	....	....	....	....	....	....	....
2000-01	**NY Islanders**	**NHL**	**44**	**10**	**25**	**5**	**2390**	**120**	**1**	**3.01**	....	....	....	....	....	....	....
	New Jersey	**NHL**	**4**	**4**	**0**	**0**	**240**	**6**	**1**	**1.50**	....	....	....	....	....	....	....
	NHL Totals		**877**	**372**	**343**	**119**	**50175**	**2493**	**40**	**2.98**	**71**	**28**	**38**	**3969**	**177**	**5**	**2.68**

OHL Second All-Star Team (1983) • CHL First All-Star Team (1984) • Shared Terry Sawchuk Trophy (fewest goals against - CHL) with Ron Scott (1984) • Shared Tommy Ivan Trophy (MVP - CHL) with Bruce Affleck (1984) • NHL First All-Star Team (1986) • Won Vezina Trophy (1986) • NHL Second All-Star Team (1994) • Played in NHL All-Star Game (1994, 1996, 1997)

Traded to **Vancouver** by **NY Rangers** for future considerations (Doug Lidster, June 25, 1993), June 20, 1993. Claimed by **Florida** from **Vancouver** in Expansion Draft, June 24, 1993. Signed as a free agent by **Philadelphia**, July 16, 1998. Traded to **NY Islanders** by **Philadelphia** for NY Islanders' 4th round choice (later traded to Nashville - Nashville selected Jordin Tootoo) in 2001 Entry Draft, June 25, 2000. Traded to **New Jersey** by **NY Islanders** for Chris Terreri and New Jersey's 9th round choice (Juha-Pekka Ketola) in 2001 Entry Draft, March 12, 2001. • Officially announced retirement, June 10, 2001.

VERNON, Mike (VUHR-nuhn, MIGHK) CGY.

Goaltender. Catches left. 5'9", 180 lbs. Born, Calgary, Alta., February 24, 1963.
(Calgary's 2nd choice, 56th overall, in 1981 Entry Draft).

			Regular Season								Playoffs						
Season	Club	Lea	GP	W	L	T	Mins	GA	SO	Avg	GP	W	L	Mins	GA	SO	Avg
1979-80	Calgary Canucks	AJHL	31	21	7	0	1796	88	0	2.95	7	3	4	399	22	0	3.30
1980-81	Calgary Wranglers	WHL	59	33	17	1	3154	198	1	3.77	22	14	8	1271	82	1	3.87
1981-82	Calgary Wranglers	WHL	42	22	14	2	2329	143	3	3.68	9	5	4	527	30	0	3.42
	Oklahoma City	CHL	....	....	....	....	....	....	....	....	1	0	1	70	4	0	3.43
1982-83	Calgary Wranglers	WHL	50	29	18	2	2856	155	*3	*3.26	16	9	7	925	60	0	3.89
	Calgary	**NHL**	**2**	**0**	**2**	**0**	**100**	**11**	**0**	**6.59**	....	....	....	....	....	....	....
1983-84	**Calgary**	**NHL**	**1**	**0**	**1**	**0**	**11**	**4**	**0**	**22.22**	....	....	....	....	....	....	....
	Colorado Flames	CHL	46	30	13	2	2648	148	1	*3.35	6	2	4	347	21	0	3.63
1984-85	Moncton Flames	AHL	41	10	20	4	2050	134	0	3.92	....	....	....	....	....	....	....
1985-86	**Calgary**	**NHL**	**18**	**9**	**3**	**3**	**921**	**52**	**1**	**3.39**	***21**	**12**	***9**	***1229**	**60**	**0**	**2.93**
	Moncton Flames	AHL	6	3	1	2	374	21	0	3.37	....	....	....	....	....	....	....
	Salt Lake City	IHL	10	6	4	0	600	34	1	3.40	....	....	....	....	....	....	....
1986-87	**Calgary**	**NHL**	**54**	**30**	**21**	**1**	**2957**	**178**	**1**	**3.61**	**5**	**2**	**3**	**263**	**16**	**0**	**3.65**
1987-88	**Calgary**	**NHL**	**64**	**39**	**16**	**7**	**3565**	**210**	**1**	**3.53**	**9**	**4**	**4**	**515**	**34**	**0**	**3.96**
1988-89 ♦	**Calgary**	**NHL**	**52**	***37**	**6**	**5**	**2938**	**130**	**0**	**2.65**	***22**	***16**	**5**	***1381**	**52**	***3**	**2.26**
1989-90	**Calgary**	**NHL**	**47**	**23**	**14**	**9**	**2795**	**146**	**0**	**3.13**	**6**	**2**	**3**	**342**	**19**	**0**	**3.33**
1990-91	**Calgary**	**NHL**	**54**	**31**	**19**	**3**	**3121**	**172**	**1**	**3.31**	**7**	**3**	**4**	**427**	**21**	**0**	**2.95**
1991-92	**Calgary**	**NHL**	**63**	**24**	**30**	**9**	**3640**	**217**	**0**	**3.58**	....	....	....	....	....	....	....
1992-93	**Calgary**	**NHL**	**64**	**29**	**26**	**9**	**3732**	**203**	**2**	**3.26**	**4**	**1**	**1**	**150**	**15**	**0**	**6.00**
1993-94	**Calgary**	**NHL**	**48**	**26**	**17**	**5**	**2798**	**131**	**3**	**2.81**	**7**	**3**	**4**	**466**	**23**	**0**	**2.96**
1994-95	**Detroit**	**NHL**	**30**	**19**	**6**	**4**	**1807**	**76**	**1**	**2.52**	**18**	**12**	**6**	**1063**	**41**	**1**	**2.31**
1995-96	**Detroit**	**NHL**	**32**	**21**	**7**	**2**	**1855**	**70**	**3**	**2.26**	**4**	**2**	**2**	**243**	**11**	**0**	**2.72**
1996-97 ♦	**Detroit**	**NHL**	**33**	**13**	**11**	**8**	**1952**	**79**	**0**	**2.43**	***20**	***16**	**4**	***1229**	**36**	**1**	**1.76**
1997-98	**San Jose**	**NHL**	**62**	**30**	**22**	**8**	**3564**	**146**	**5**	**2.46**	**6**	**2**	**4**	**348**	**14**	**1**	**2.41**
1998-99	**San Jose**	**NHL**	**49**	**16**	**22**	**10**	**2831**	**107**	**4**	**2.27**	**5**	**2**	**3**	**321**	**13**	**0**	**2.43**
99-2000	**San Jose**	**NHL**	**15**	**6**	**5**	**1**	**772**	**32**	**0**	**2.49**	....	....	....	....	....	....	....
	Florida	**NHL**	**34**	**18**	**13**	**2**	**2019**	**83**	**1**	**2.47**	**4**	**0**	**4**	**237**	**12**	**0**	**3.04**
2000-01	**Calgary**	**NHL**	**41**	**12**	**23**	**5**	**2246**	**121**	**3**	**3.23**	....	....	....	....	....	....	....
	NHL Totals		**763**	**383**	**264**	**91**	**43624**	**2168**	**26**	**2.98**	**138**	**77**	**56**	**8214**	**367**	**6**	**2.68**

WHL First All-Star Team (1982, 1983) • Won Hap Emms Memorial Trophy (Memorial Cup Tournament Top Goaltender) (1983) • CHL Second All-Star Team (1984) • NHL Second All-Star Team (1989) • Shared William M. Jennings Trophy with Chris Osgood (1996) • Won Conn Smythe Trophy (1997) • Played in NHL All-Star Game (1988, 1989, 1990, 1991, 1993)

Traded to **Detroit** by **Calgary** for Steve Chiasson, June 29, 1994. Traded to **San Jose** by **Detroit** with Detroit's 5th round choice (later traded back to Detroit - Detroit selected Andrei Maximenko) in 1999 Entry Draft for San Jose's 2nd round choice (later traded to St. Louis - St. Louis selected Maxim Linnik) in 1998 Entry Draft and San Jose's 2nd round choice (later traded to Tampa Bay - Tampa Bay selected Sheldon Keefe) in 1999 Entry Draft, August 18, 1997. Traded to **Florida** by **San Jose** with San Jose's 3rd round choice (Sean O'Connor) in 2000 Entry Draft for Radek Dvorak, December 30, 1999. Selected by **Minnesota** from **Florida** in Expansion Draft, June 23, 2000. Traded to **Calgary** by **Minnesota** for the rights to Dan Cavanaugh and Calgary's 8th round choice (Jake Riddle) in 2001 Entry Draft, June 23, 2000.

VOKOUN, Tomas (voh-KOHN, TAW-mas) NSH.

Goaltender. Catches right. 6', 195 lbs. Born, Karlovy Vary, Czech., July 2, 1976.
(Montreal's 11th choice, 226th overall, in 1994 Entry Draft).

			Regular Season								Playoffs						
Season	Club	Lea	GP	W	L	T	Mins	GA	SO	Avg	GP	W	L	Mins	GA	SO	Avg
1993-94	Poldi Kladno	Cze-Rep	1	0	0	0	20	2	0	6.01	....	....	....	....	....	....	....
1994-95	Poldi Kladno	Cze-Rep	26	....	....	....	1368	70	....	3.07	5	....	....	240	19	....	4.75
1995-96	Wheeling	ECHL	35	20	10	2	1912	117	0	3.67	7	4	3	436	19	0	2.61
	Fredericton	AHL	....	....	....	....	....	....	....	....	1	0	1	59	4	0	4.09
1996-97	**Montreal**	**NHL**	**1**	**0**	**0**	**0**	**20**	**4**	**0**	**12.00**	....	....	....	....	....	....	....
	Fredericton	AHL	47	12	26	7	2645	154	2	3.49	....	....	....	....	....	....	....
1997-98	Fredericton	AHL	31	13	13	2	1735	90	0	3.11	....	....	....	....	....	....	....
1998-99	**Nashville**	**NHL**	**37**	**12**	**18**	**4**	**1954**	**96**	**1**	**2.95**	....	....	....	....	....	....	....
	Milwaukee	IHL	9	3	2	4	539	22	1	2.45	2	0	2	149	8	0	3.22
99-2000	**Nashville**	**NHL**	**33**	**9**	**20**	**1**	**1879**	**87**	**1**	**2.78**	....	....	....	....	....	....	....
	Milwaukee	IHL	7	5	2	0	364	17	0	2.80	....	....	....	....	....	....	....
2000-01	**Nashville**	**NHL**	**37**	**13**	**17**	**5**	**2088**	**85**	**2**	**2.44**	....	....	....	....	....	....	....
	NHL Totals		**108**	**34**	**55**	**10**	**5941**	**272**	**4**	**2.75**	....	....	....	....	....	....	....

Claimed by **Nashville** from **Montreal** in Expansion Draft, June 26, 1998.

VOLKOV, Alexei (VOHL-kawf, al-EHX-ay) L.A.

Goaltender. Catches left. 6'1", 195 lbs. Born, Yekaterinburg, USSR, March 15, 1980.
(Los Angeles' 3rd choice, 76th overall, in 1998 Entry Draft).

			Regular Season								Playoffs						
Season	Club	Lea	GP	W	L	T	Mins	GA	SO	Avg	GP	W	L	Mins	GA	SO	Avg
1995-96	SKA Yekaterinburg	Russia-2	42	....	....	....	2520	78	....	1.87	....	....	....	....	....	....	....
1996-97	Krylja Sovetov	Russia-Jr.	8	....	....	....	48	9	....	1.25	....	....	....	....	....	....	....
	Yekaterinburg-2	Russia-3	34	....	....	....	2040	66	....	1.94	....	....	....	....	....	....	....
1997-98	Krylja Sovetov-2	Russia-3	27	....	....	....	1620	72	....	2.67	....	....	....	....	....	....	....
1998-99	Halifax	QMJHL	39	25	9	3	2332	105	2	2.70	5	1	4	282	21	0	4.47
99-2000	Halifax	QMJHL	40	23	13	2	2222	124	1	3.35	8	3	4	417	29	0	4.18
2000-01	Lowell	AHL	5	1	1	0	202	16	0	4.75	....	....	....	....	....	....	....
	New Orleans	ECHL	29	12	9	5	1577	81	1	3.08	....	....	....	....	....	....	....

WAITE, Jimmy
(WAYT, JIHM-ee) **TOR.**

Goaltender. Catches left. 6'1", 180 lbs. Born, Sherbrooke, Que., April 15, 1969.
(Chicago's 1st choice, 8th overall, in 1987 Entry Draft).

			Regular Season								Playoffs						
Season	Club	Lea	GP	W	L	T	Mins	GA	SO	Avg	GP	W	L	Mins	GA	SO	Avg
1984-85	Cantons de l'Est	QAAA	10	6	4	0	598	52	0	5.22	3	2	1	143	15	0	6.29
1985-86	Cantons de l'Est	QAAA	27	11	15	1	1644	143	0	5.22	2	0	2	100	11	0	6.60
1986-87	Chicoutimi	QMJHL	50	23	17	3	2569	209	2	4.48	11	4	6	576	54	1	5.63
1987-88	Chicoutimi	QMJHL	36	17	16	1	2000	150	0	4.50	4	1	2	222	17	0	4.59
1988-89	**Chicago**	**NHL**	**11**	**0**	**7**	**1**	**494**	**43**	**0**	**5.22**	....	....	....	....	....	....	....
	Saginaw Hawks	IHL	5	3	1	0	304	10	0	1.97	....	....	....	....	....	....	....
1989-90	**Chicago**	**NHL**	**4**	**2**	**0**	**0**	**183**	**14**	**0**	**4.59**	....	....	....	....	....	....	....
	Indianapolis Ice	IHL	54	*34	14	5	*3207	135	*5	*2.53	*10	*9	1	*602	19	*1	*1.89
1990-91	**Chicago**	**NHL**	**1**	**1**	**0**	**0**	**60**	**2**	**0**	**2.00**	....	....	....	....	....	....	....
	Indianapolis Ice	IHL	49	*26	18	4	2888	167	3	3.47	6	2	4	369	20	0	3.25
1991-92	**Chicago**	**NHL**	**17**	**4**	**7**	**4**	**877**	**54**	**0**	**3.69**	....	....	....	....	....	....	....
	Indianapolis Ice	IHL	13	4	7	1	702	53	0	4.53	....	....	....	....	....	....	....
	Hershey Bears	AHL	11	6	4	1	631	44	0	4.18	6	2	4	360	19	0	3.17
1992-93	**Chicago**	**NHL**	**20**	**6**	**7**	**1**	**996**	**49**	**2**	**2.95**	....	....	....	....	....	....	....
1993-94	**San Jose**	**NHL**	**15**	**3**	**7**	**0**	**697**	**50**	**0**	**4.30**	**2**	**0**	**0**	**40**	**3**	**0**	**4.50**
1994-95	**Chicago**	**NHL**	**2**	**1**	**1**	**0**	**119**	**5**	**0**	**2.52**	....	....	....	....	....	....	....
	Indianapolis Ice	IHL	4	2	1	1	239	13	0	3.25	....	....	....	....	....	....	....
1995-96	**Chicago**	**NHL**	**1**	**0**	**0**	**0**	**31**	**0**	**0**	**0.00**	....	....	....	....	....	....	....
	Indianapolis Ice	IHL	56	28	18	6	3157	179	0	3.40	5	2	3	298	15	1	3.02
1996-97	**Chicago**	**NHL**	**2**	**0**	**1**	**1**	**105**	**7**	**0**	**4.00**	....	....	....	....	....	....	....
	Indianapolis Ice	IHL	41	22	15	4	2450	112	4	2.74	4	1	3	222	13	0	3.51
1997-98	**Phoenix**	**NHL**	**17**	**5**	**6**	**1**	**793**	**28**	**1**	**2.12**	**4**	**0**	**3**	**171**	**11**	**0**	**3.86**
1998-99	**Phoenix**	**NHL**	**16**	**6**	**5**	**4**	**898**	**41**	**1**	**2.74**	....	....	....	....	....	....	....
	Springfield Falcons	AHL	8	3	4	1	483	19	0	2.36	2	0	2	118	6	0	3.05
	Utah Grizzlies	IHL	11	6	3	2	622	30	0	2.89	....	....	....	....	....	....	....
99-2000	St. John's Leafs	AHL	*62	20	37	4	*3461	176	6	3.05	....	....	....	....	....	....	....
2000-01	St. John's Leafs	AHL	43	12	25	4	2445	132	1	3.24	....	....	....	....	....	....	....
	NHL Totals		**106**	**28**	**41**	**12**	**5253**	**293**	**4**	**3.35**	**6**	**0**	**3**	**211**	**14**	**0**	**3.98**

QMJHL Second All-Star Team (1987) • IHL First All-Star Team (1990) • Won James Norris Memorial Trophy (fewest goals against - IHL) (1990)

Traded to **San Jose** by **Chicago** for future considerations (Neil Wilkinson, July 9, 1993), June 18, 1993. Traded to **Chicago** by **San Jose** for Chicago's 4th round choice (later traded to NY Rangers - NY Rangers selected Tomi Kallarsson) in 1997 Entry Draft, February 5, 1995. Claimed by **Phoenix** from **Chicago** in NHL Waiver Draft, September 28, 1997. Signed as a free agent by **Toronto**, August 19, 1999.

WANDLER, Bryce
(WAND-luhr, BRIGHS) **NYR**

Goaltender. Catches left. 6', 180 lbs. Born, Lacombe, Alta., February 25, 1979.

			Regular Season								Playoffs						
Season	Club	Lea	GP	W	L	T	Mins	GA	SO	Avg	GP	W	L	Mins	GA	SO	Avg
1996-97	Kamloops Blazers	WHL	1	0	0	0	34	3	0	5.29	....	....	....	....	....	....	....
	Edmonton Ice	WHL	19	2	11	1	936	84	0	5.38	....	....	....	....	....	....	....
1997-98	Edmonton Ice	WHL	47	12	27	4	2576	180	1	4.19	....	....	....	....	....	....	....
1998-99	Swift Current	WHL	51	23	20	4	2882	123	3	2.56	6	2	4	364	17	1	2.80
99-2000	Swift Current	WHL	56	*37	15	2	3255	112	6	*2.06	10	5	5	597	29	0	2.91
2000-01	New Haven	UHL	26	10	13	1	1429	71	0	2.98	2	0	1	71	6	0	5.04
	Hartford	AHL	1	0	0	0	29	1	0	2.04	....	....	....	....	....	....	....
	Charlotte	ECHL	4	2	2	0	240	18	0	4.50	....	....	....	....	....	....	....

Signed as a free agent by **NY Rangers**, March 15, 2000.

WARD, Blake
(WOHRD, BLAYK) **COL.**

Goaltender. Catches left. 6'3", 200 lbs. Born, Lloydminster, Alta., January 18, 1982.
(Colorado's 14th choice, 285th overall, in 2000 Entry Draft).

			Regular Season								Playoffs						
Season	Club	Lea	GP	W	L	T	Mins	GA	SO	Avg	GP	W	L	Mins	GA	SO	Avg
1997-98	Lloydminster	SAHA	35	....	....	....	2100	106	1	2.90	....	....	....	....	....	....	....
1998-99	Tri-City Americans	WHL	21	5	5	2	844	34	0	2.42	1	0	0	20	1	0	3.00
99-2000	Tri-City Americans	WHL	37	14	12	2	1853	111	1	3.59	4	0	3	187	12	0	3.85
2000-01	Tri-City Americans	WHL	8	2	3	3	470	30	0	3.83	....	....	....	....	....	....	....
	Lethbridge	WHL	30	10	15	3	1676	79	2	2.83	4	1	3	238	20	0	5.04

Traded to **Lethbridge** by **Tri-City** for future considerations, October 25, 2000.

WEEKES, Kevin
(WEEKS, KEH-vihn) **T.B.**

Goaltender. Catches left. 6', 195 lbs. Born, Toronto, Ont., April 4, 1975.
(Florida's 2nd choice, 41st overall, in 1993 Entry Draft).

			Regular Season								Playoffs						
Season	Club	Lea	GP	W	L	T	Mins	GA	SO	Avg	GP	W	L	Mins	GA	SO	Avg
1990-91	Toronto Wings	MTHL	STATISTICS NOT AVAILABLE														
	St. Michael's	MTJHL	1	0	0	0	41	1	0	1.46	....	....	....	....	....	....	....
1991-92	Toronto Wings	MTHL	35	....	....	....	1575	68	4	1.94	....	....	....	....	....	....	....
	St. Michael's	MTJHL	2	0	1	1	127	11	0	5.20	4	1	2	214	15	1	4.21
1992-93	Owen Sound	OHL	29	9	12	5	1645	143	0	5.22	1	0	0	26	5	0	11.50
1993-94	Owen Sound	OHL	34	13	19	1	1974	158	0	4.80	....	....	....	....	....	....	....
1994-95	Ottawa 67's	OHL	41	13	23	4	2266	153	1	4.05	....	....	....	....	....	....	....
1995-96	Carolina	AHL	60	24	25	8	3404	229	2	4.04	....	....	....	....	....	....	....
1996-97	Carolina	AHL	51	17	28	4	2899	172	1	3.56	....	....	....	....	....	....	....
1997-98	**Florida**	**NHL**	**11**	**0**	**5**	**1**	**485**	**32**	**0**	**3.96**	....	....	....	....	....	....	....
	Fort Wayne	IHL	12	9	2	1	719	34	1	2.84	....	....	....	....	....	....	....
1998-99	Detroit Vipers	IHL	33	19	5	7	1857	64	*4	*2.07	....	....	....	....	....	....	....
	Vancouver	**NHL**	**11**	**0**	**8**	**1**	**532**	**34**	**0**	**3.83**	....	....	....	....	....	....	....
99-2000	**Vancouver**	**NHL**	**20**	**6**	**7**	**4**	**987**	**47**	**1**	**2.86**	....	....	....	....	....	....	....
	NY Islanders	**NHL**	**36**	**10**	**20**	**4**	**2026**	**115**	**1**	**3.41**	....	....	....	....	....	....	....
2000-01	**Tampa Bay**	**NHL**	**61**	**20**	**33**	**3**	**3378**	**177**	**4**	**3.14**	....	....	....	....	....	....	....
	NHL Totals		**139**	**36**	**73**	**13**	**7408**	**405**	**6**	**3.28**	....	....	....	....	....	....	....

Shared James Norris Memorial Trophy (fewest goals against - IHL) with Andrei Trefilov (1999)

Traded to **Vancouver** by **Florida** with Ed Jovanovski, Dave Gagner, Mike Brown and Florida's 1st round choice (Nathan Smith) in 2000 Entry Draft for Pavel Bure, Bret Hedican, Brad Ference and Vancouver's 3rd round choice (Robert Fried) in 2000 Entry Draft, January 17, 1999. Traded to **NY Islanders** by **Vancouver** with Dave Scatchard and Bill Muckalt for Felix Potvin and NY Islanders' compensatory 2nd (later traded to New Jersey - New Jersey selected Teemu Laine) and 3rd (Thatcher Bell) round choices in 2000 Entry Draft, December 19, 1999. Traded to **Tampa Bay** by **NY Islanders** with the rights to Kristian Kudroc and NY Islanders' 2nd round choice (later traded to Phoenix - Phoenix selected Matthew Spiller) in 2001 Entry Draft for Tampa Bay's 1st round choice (Raffi Torres) in 2000 Entry Draft, Calgary's 4th round choice (previously acquired, NY Islanders selected Vladimir Gorbunov) in 2000 Entry Draft and NY Islanders' 7th round choice (previously acquired, NY Islanders selected Ryan Caldwell) in 2000 Entry Draft, June 24, 2000.

WHITMORE, Kay
(WHIHT-mohr, KAY) **CGY.**

Goaltender. Catches left. 5'11", 175 lbs. Born, Sudbury, Ont., April 10, 1967.
(Hartford's 2nd choice, 26th overall, in 1985 Entry Draft).

			Regular Season								Playoffs						
Season	Club	Lea	GP	W	L	T	Mins	GA	SO	Avg	GP	W	L	Mins	GA	SO	Avg
1982-83	Sudbury Legion	NOJHA	43	....	....	....	2580	108	4	2.51	....	....	....	....	....	....	....
1983-84	Peterborough	OHL	29	17	8	0	1471	110	0	4.49	....	....	....	....	....	....	....
1984-85	Peterborough	OHL	*53	*35	16	2	*3077	172	*2	3.35	17	10	4	1020	58	0	3.41
1985-86	Peterborough	OHL	41	27	12	2	2467	114	*3	*2.77	14	8	5	837	40	0	2.87
1986-87	Peterborough	OHL	36	14	17	5	2159	118	1	3.28	7	3	3	366	17	1	2.79
1987-88	Binghamton	AHL	38	17	15	4	2137	121	*3	3.40	2	0	2	118	10	0	5.08
1988-89	**Hartford**	**NHL**	**3**	**2**	**1**	**0**	**180**	**10**	**0**	**3.33**	**2**	**0**	**2**	**135**	**10**	**0**	**4.44**
	Binghamton	AHL	*56	21	29	4	*3200	241	1	4.52	....	....	....	....	....	....	....
1989-90	**Hartford**	**NHL**	**9**	**4**	**2**	**1**	**442**	**26**	**0**	**3.53**	....	....	....	....	....	....	....
	Binghamton	AHL	24	3	19	2	1386	109	0	4.72	....	....	....	....	....	....	....
1990-91	**Hartford**	**NHL**	**18**	**3**	**9**	**3**	**850**	**52**	**0**	**3.67**	....	....	....	....	....	....	....
	Springfield	AHL	33	22	9	1	1916	98	1	3.07	*15	*11	4	*926	37	0	*2.40
1991-92	**Hartford**	**NHL**	**45**	**14**	**21**	**6**	**2567**	**155**	**3**	**3.62**	**1**	**0**	**0**	**19**	**1**	**0**	**3.16**
1992-93	**Vancouver**	**NHL**	**31**	**18**	**8**	**4**	**1817**	**94**	**1**	**3.10**	....	....	....	....	....	....	....
1993-94	**Vancouver**	**NHL**	**32**	**18**	**14**	**0**	**1921**	**113**	**0**	**3.53**	....	....	....	....	....	....	....
1994-95	**Vancouver**	**NHL**	**11**	**0**	**6**	**2**	**558**	**37**	**0**	**3.98**	**1**	**0**	**0**	**20**	**2**	**0**	**6.00**
1995-96	Detroit Vipers	IHL	10	3	5	0	501	33	0	3.95	....	....	....	....	....	....	....
	Los Angeles	IHL	30	10	9	7	1563	99	1	3.80	....	....	....	....	....	....	....
	Syracuse Crunch	AHL	11	6	4	1	663	37	0	3.35	....	....	....	....	....	....	....
	Binghamton	AHL	....	....	....	....	....	....	....	....	2	0	2	127	9	0	4.27
1996-97	Sodertalje SK	Sweden	25	....	....	....	1320	85	0	3.86	....	....	....	....	....	....	....
1997-98	Long Beach	IHL	46	28	12	3	2516	109	3	2.60	14	9	5	838	43	0	3.08
1998-99	Milwaukee	IHL	23	10	6	4	1304	64	0	2.94	....	....	....	....	....	....	....
	Hartford	AHL	18	8	8	2	1080	47	0	2.61	....	....	....	....	....	....	....
99-2000	Providence Bruins	AHL	43	17	19	3	2393	127	1	3.18	1	0	1	59	2	0	2.04
2000-01	**Boston**	**NHL**	**5**	**1**	**2**	**0**	**203**	**18**	**0**	**5.32**	....	....	....	....	....	....	....
	Providence Bruins	AHL	26	13	8	2	1460	65	2	2.67	....	....	....	....	....	....	....
	NHL Totals		**154**	**60**	**63**	**16**	**8538**	**505**	**4**	**3.55**	**4**	**0**	**2**	**174**	**13**	**0**	**4.48**

OHL First All-Star Team (1986) • Won Jack A. Butterfield Trophy (Playoff MVP - AHL) (1991) • Shared James Norris Memorial Trophy (fewest goals against - IHL) with Mike Buzak (1998)

Traded to **Vancouver** by **Hartford** for Corrie D'Alessio and cash, October 1, 1992. Traded to **NY Rangers** by **Vancouver** for Joe Kocur, March 20, 1996. Signed as a free agent by **San Jose**, September 10, 1997. Traded to **Buffalo** by **San Jose** with Colorado's 2nd round choice (previously acquired, Buffalo selected Jaroslav Kristek) in 1998 Entry Draft and San Jose's 5th round choice (later traded to Columbus - Columbus selected Tyler Kolarik) in 2000 Entry Draft for Steve Shields and Buffalo's 4th round choice (Miroslav Zalesak) in 1998 Entry Draft, June 18, 1998. Signed as a free agent by **NY Rangers**, August 17, 1998. Signed as a free agent by **Boston**, August 25, 1999. Traded to **Edmonton** by **Boston** for Mike Matteucci, December 28, 1999. Traded to **Boston** by **Edmonton** for future considerations, July 20, 2000. Signed as a free agent by **Calgary**, July 9, 2001.

WREGGET, Ken
(REHG-eht, KEHN)

Goaltender. Catches left. 6'1", 201 lbs. Born, Brandon, Man., March 25, 1964.
(Toronto's 4th choice, 45th overall, in 1982 Entry Draft).

			Regular Season								Playoffs						
Season	Club	Lea	GP	W	L	T	Mins	GA	SO	Avg	GP	W	L	Mins	GA	SO	Avg
1981-82	Lethbridge	WHL	36	19	12	0	1713	118	0	4.13	3	2	0	84	3	0	2.14
1982-83	Lethbridge	WHL	48	26	17	1	2696	157	1	3.49	*20	14	5	*1154	58	*1	*3.02
1983-84	**Toronto**	**NHL**	**3**	**1**	**1**	**1**	**165**	**14**	**0**	**5.09**	....	....	....	....	....	....	....
	Lethbridge	WHL	53	32	20	0	3053	161	0	*3.16	4	1	3	210	18	0	5.14
1984-85	**Toronto**	**NHL**	**23**	**2**	**15**	**3**	**1278**	**103**	**0**	**4.84**	....	....	....	....	....	....	....
	St. Catharines	AHL	12	2	8	1	688	48	0	4.19	....	....	....	....	....	....	....
1985-86	**Toronto**	**NHL**	**30**	**9**	**13**	**4**	**1566**	**113**	**0**	**4.33**	**10**	**6**	**4**	**607**	**32**	***1**	**3.16**
	St. Catharines	AHL	18	8	9	0	1058	78	1	4.42	....	....	....	....	....	....	....
1986-87	**Toronto**	**NHL**	**56**	**22**	**28**	**3**	**3026**	**200**	**0**	**3.97**	**13**	**7**	**6**	**761**	**29**	**1**	**2.29**
1987-88	**Toronto**	**NHL**	**56**	**12**	**35**	**4**	**3000**	**222**	**2**	**4.44**	**2**	**0**	**1**	**108**	**11**	**0**	**6.11**
1988-89	**Toronto**	**NHL**	**32**	**9**	**20**	**2**	**1888**	**139**	**0**	**4.42**	....	....	....	....	....	....	....
	Philadelphia	**NHL**	**3**	**1**	**1**	**0**	**130**	**13**	**0**	**6.00**	**5**	**2**	**2**	**268**	**10**	**0**	**2.24**
1989-90	**Philadelphia**	**NHL**	**51**	**22**	**24**	**3**	**2961**	**169**	**0**	**3.42**	....	....	....	....	....	....	....
1990-91	**Philadelphia**	**NHL**	**30**	**10**	**14**	**3**	**1484**	**88**	**0**	**3.56**	....	....	....	....	....	....	....
1991-92	**Philadelphia**	**NHL**	**23**	**9**	**8**	**3**	**1259**	**75**	**0**	**3.57**	....	....	....	....	....	....	....
♦	**Pittsburgh**	**NHL**	**9**	**5**	**3**	**0**	**448**	**31**	**0**	**4.15**	**1**	**0**	**0**	**40**	**4**	**0**	**6.00**
1992-93	**Pittsburgh**	**NHL**	**25**	**13**	**7**	**2**	**1368**	**78**	**0**	**3.42**	....	....	....	....	....	....	....
1993-94	**Pittsburgh**	**NHL**	**42**	**21**	**12**	**7**	**2456**	**138**	**1**	**3.37**	....	....	....	....	....	....	....
1994-95	**Pittsburgh**	**NHL**	**38**	***25**	**9**	**2**	**2208**	**118**	**0**	**3.21**	**11**	**5**	**6**	**661**	**33**	**1**	**3.00**
1995-96	**Pittsburgh**	**NHL**	**37**	**20**	**13**	**2**	**2132**	**115**	**3**	**3.24**	**9**	**7**	**2**	**599**	**23**	**0**	**2.30**
1996-97	**Pittsburgh**	**NHL**	**46**	**17**	**17**	**6**	**2514**	**136**	**2**	**3.25**	**5**	**1**	**4**	**297**	**18**	**0**	**3.64**
1997-98	**Pittsburgh**	**NHL**	**15**	**3**	**6**	**2**	**611**	**28**	**0**	**2.75**	....	....	....	....	....	....	....
1998-99	**Calgary**	**NHL**	**27**	**10**	**12**	**4**	**1590**	**67**	**1**	**2.53**	....	....	....	....	....	....	....
99-2000	**Detroit**	**NHL**	**29**	**14**	**10**	**2**	**1579**	**70**	**0**	**2.66**	....	....	....	....	....	....	....
2000-01	Manitoba Moose	IHL	30	11	13	4	1601	72	2	2.70	12	6	5	774	30	0	2.33
	NHL Totals		**575**	**225**	**248**	**53**	**31663**	**1917**	**9**	**3.63**	**56**	**28**	**25**	**3341**	**160**	**3**	**2.87**

WHL East First All-Star Team (1984)

Traded to **Philadelphia** by **Toronto** for Philadelphia's 1st round choice (Rob Pearson) and Calgary's 1st round choice (previously acquired, Toronto selected Steve Bancroft) in 1989 Entry Draft, March 6, 1989. Traded to **Pittsburgh** by **Philadelphia** with Rick Tocchet, Kjell Samuelsson and Philadelphia's 3rd round choice (Dave Roche) in 1993 Entry Draft for Mark Recchi, Brian Benning and Los Angeles' 1st round choice (previously acquired, Philadelphia selected Jason Bowen) in 1992 Entry Draft, February 19, 1992. Traded to **Calgary** by **Pittsburgh** with Dave Roche for German Titov and Todd Hlushko, June 17, 1998. Signed as a free agent by **Detroit**, July 23, 1999.

YEATS, Matthew
(YAYTS, MAT-thew) **L.A.**

Goaltender. Catches left. 5'11", 165 lbs. Born, Montreal, Que., April 6, 1979.
(Los Angeles' 9th choice, 248th overall, in 1998 Entry Draft).

			Regular Season								Playoffs						
Season	Club	Lea	GP	W	L	T	Mins	GA	SO	Avg	GP	W	L	Mins	GA	SO	Avg
1995-96	Lethbridge	WHL	1	0	0	0	20	3	0	9.00	....	....	....	....	....	....	....
1996-97	Olds Grizzlys	AJHL	32	....	....	....	1678	95	1	3.41	....	....	....	....	....	....	....
1997-98	Olds Grizzlys	AJHL	26	12	12	1	1498	96	0	3.85	....	....	....	....	....	....	....
1998-99	U. of Maine	H-East	DID NOT PLAY – ACADEMICALLY INELIGIBLE														
99-2000	U. of Maine	H-East	32	20	6	4	1821	79	0	2.60	....	....	....	....	....	....	....
2000-01	U. of Maine	H-East	33	18	9	4	1897	76	2	2.40	....	....	....	....	....	....	....

• Ruled ineligible to play 1998-99 season by NCAA due to appearance with **Lethbridge** (WHL) in 1995-96.

YEREMEYEV, Vitali (yehr-eh-MAY-ehv, VIH-tal-ee) NYR

Goaltender. Catches left. 5'10", 167 lbs. Born, Ust-Kamenogorsk, USSR, September 23, 1975.
(NY Rangers' 11th choice, 209th overall, in 1994 Entry Draft).

			Regular Season								Playoffs						
Season	Club	Lea	GP	W	L	T	Mins	GA	SO	Avg	GP	W	L	Mins	GA	SO	Avg
1993-94	Ust-Kamenogorsk	CIS	19	....	....	....	1015	38	....	2.24	....	....	....	....	....	....	....
1994-95	CSKA Moscow	CIS	49	....	....	....	2733	97	....	2.13	2	....	....	120	8	....	4.00
1995-96	CSKA Moscow	CIS	25	....	....	....	1339	37	5	1.66	3	....	....	179	7	....	2.34
1996-97	CSKA Moscow	Russia	14	....	....	....	635	35	0	3.31	1	....	....	59	3	0	3.05
1997-98	Torpedo Yaroslavl	Russia	17	....	....	....	979	19	3	*1.16	....	....	....	....	....	....	....
	Kazakhstan	Olympics	*7	1	3	1	292	28	0	5.76	....	....	....	....	....	....	....
1998-99	HC Moscow	Russia-2	19	....	....	....	1100	33	....	1.80	....	....	....	....	....	....	....
99-2000	Dynamo Moscow	Russia	26	....	....	....	1564	32	*7	*1.23	*17	....	....	*1039	22	*4	*1.27
2000-01	**NY Rangers**	**NHL**	**4**	**0**	**4**	**0**	**212**	**16**	**0**	**4.53**	....	....	....	....	....	....	....
	Hartford	AHL	36	16	15	3	1977	98	2	2.97	....	....	....	....	....	....	....
	Charlotte	ECHL	5	3	2	0	298	21	0	4.23	....	....	....	....	....	....	....
	NHL Totals		**4**	**0**	**4**	**0**	**212**	**16**	**0**	**4.53**	....	....	....	....	....	....	....

AHL All-Rookie Team (2001)

YOUNG, Wendell (YUHNG, WEHN-dawl)

Goaltender. Catches left. 5'9", 181 lbs. Born, Halifax, N.S., August 1, 1963.
(Vancouver's 3rd choice, 73rd overall, in 1981 Entry Draft).

			Regular Season								Playoffs						
Season	Club	Lea	GP	W	L	T	Mins	GA	SO	Avg	GP	W	L	Mins	GA	SO	Avg
1979-80	Cole Harbour Colts	MJrHL	25	....	....	....	1446	94	0	3.90	....	....	....	....	....	....	....
1980-81	Kitchener Rangers	OMJHL	42	19	15	0	2215	164	1	4.44	14	9	1	800	42	*1	3.15
1981-82	Kitchener Rangers	OHL	*60	*38	17	2	*3470	195	1	3.37	15	12	1	900	35	*1	*2.33
1982-83	Kitchener Rangers	OHL	61	*41	19	0	*3611	231	1	3.84	12	6	5	720	43	0	3.58
1983-84	Fredericton	AHL	11	7	3	0	569	39	1	4.11	....	....	....	....	....	....	....
	Milwaukee	IHL	6	4	1	1	339	17	0	3.01	....	....	....	....	....	....	....
	Salt Lake City	CHL	20	11	6	0	1094	80	0	4.39	4	0	2	122	11	0	5.42
1984-85	Fredericton	AHL	22	7	11	3	1242	83	0	4.01	....	....	....	....	....	....	....
1985-86	**Vancouver**	**NHL**	**22**	**4**	**9**	**3**	**1023**	**61**	**0**	**3.58**	**1**	**0**	**1**	**60**	**5**	**0**	**5.00**
	Fredericton	AHL	24	12	8	4	1457	78	0	3.21	....	....	....	....	....	....	....
1986-87	**Vancouver**	**NHL**	**8**	**1**	**6**	**1**	**420**	**35**	**0**	**5.00**	....	....	....	....	....	....	....
	Fredericton	AHL	30	11	16	0	1676	118	0	4.22	....	....	....	....	....	....	....
1987-88	**Philadelphia**	**NHL**	**6**	**3**	**2**	**0**	**320**	**20**	**0**	**3.75**	....	....	....	....	....	....	....
	Hershey Bears	AHL	51	*33	15	1	2922	135	1	2.77	12	*12	0	*767	28	*1	*2.19
1988-89	**Pittsburgh**	**NHL**	**22**	**12**	**9**	**0**	**1150**	**92**	**0**	**4.80**	**1**	**0**	**0**	**39**	**1**	**0**	**1.54**
	Muskegon	IHL	2	1	0	1	125	7	0	3.36	....	....	....	....	....	....	....
1989-90	**Pittsburgh**	**NHL**	**43**	**16**	**20**	**3**	**2318**	**161**	**1**	**4.17**	....	....	....	....	....	....	....
1990-91◆	**Pittsburgh**	**NHL**	**18**	**4**	**6**	**2**	**773**	**52**	**0**	**4.04**	....	....	....	....	....	....	....
1991-92◆	**Pittsburgh**	**NHL**	**18**	**7**	**6**	**0**	**838**	**53**	**0**	**3.79**	....	....	....	....	....	....	....
1992-93	**Tampa Bay**	**NHL**	**31**	**7**	**19**	**2**	**1591**	**97**	**0**	**3.66**	....	....	....	....	....	....	....
	Atlanta Knights	IHL	3	3	0	0	183	8	0	2.62	....	....	....	....	....	....	....
1993-94	**Tampa Bay**	**NHL**	**9**	**2**	**3**	**1**	**480**	**20**	**1**	**2.50**	....	....	....	....	....	....	....
	Atlanta Knights	IHL	2	2	0	0	120	6	0	3.00	....	....	....	....	....	....	....
1994-95	Chicago Wolves	IHL	37	14	11	7	1882	112	0	3.57	....	....	....	....	....	....	....
	Pittsburgh	**NHL**	**10**	**3**	**6**	**0**	**497**	**27**	**0**	**3.26**	....	....	....	....	....	....	....
1995-96	Chicago Wolves	IHL	61	30	20	6	3285	199	1	3.63	9	4	5	540	30	0	3.33
1996-97	Chicago Wolves	IHL	52	25	21	4	2931	170	1	3.48	4	1	3	256	13	0	3.04
1997-98	Chicago Wolves	IHL	51	31	14	3	2912	149	2	3.07	9	5	3	515	24	1	2.79
1998-99	Chicago Wolves	IHL	35	20	10	4	2047	84	3	2.46	7	4	3	421	19	1	2.71
99-2000	Chicago Wolves	IHL	48	32	12	4	2781	128	6	2.76	9	5	3	488	27	0	3.32
2000-01	Chicago Wolves	IHL	38	17	16	3	2074	109	3	3.15	7	2	4	373	21	0	3.38
	NHL Totals		**187**	**59**	**86**	**12**	**9410**	**618**	**2**	**3.94**	**2**	**0**	**1**	**99**	**6**	**0**	**3.64**

AHL First All-Star Team (1988) • Won Baz Bastien Memorial Trophy (Top Goaltender - AHL) (1988)
• Won Jack Butterfield Trophy (Playoff MVP - AHL) (1988)

Traded to **Philadelphia** by **Vancouver** with Vancouver's 3rd round choice (Kimbi Daniels) in 1990 Entry Draft for Darren Jensen and Daryl Stanley, August 31, 1987. Traded to **Pittsburgh** by **Philadelphia** with Philadelphia's 7th round choice (Mika Valila) in 1990 Entry Draft for Pittsburgh's 3rd round choice (Chris Therien) in 1990 Entry Draft, Steptember 1, 1988. Claimed by **Tampa Bay** from **Pittsburgh** in Expansion Draft, June 18, 1992. Traded to **Pittsburgh** by **Tampa Bay** for future considerations, February 16, 1995.

• Only goaltender in hockey history to win Memorial Cup (1982); Calder Cup (1988); Stanley Cup (1991, 1992) and Turner Cup (1998, 2000).

ZEPP, Rob (ZEHP, RAWB) CAR.

Goaltender. Catches left. 6'1", 181 lbs. Born, Scarborough, Ont., September 7, 1981.
(Carolina's 4th choice, 110th overall, in 2001 Entry Draft).

			Regular Season								Playoffs						
Season	Club	Lea	GP	W	L	T	Mins	GA	SO	Avg	GP	W	L	Mins	GA	SO	Avg
1997-98	Newmarket 87's	OPJHL	3	....	....	....	181	13	0	4.31	....	....	....	....	....	....	....
1998-99	Plymouth Whalers	OHL	31	19	3	4	1662	76	3	2.74	3	1	0	100	10	0	6.00
99-2000	Plymouth Whalers	OHL	53	*36	11	3	3005	119	3	*2.38	*23	*15	8	*1374	52	2	2.27
2000-01	Plymouth Whalers	OHL	55	*34	18	3	3246	122	*4	*2.26	19	14	5	1139	51	2	2.69

• Re-entered NHL Entry Draft. Originally Atlanta's 5th choice, 99th overall, in 1999 Entry Draft.

OHL Second All-Star Team (2000, 2001)

Retired NHL Player Index

Abbreviations: Teams/Cities: – **Ana.** – Anaheim; **Atl.** – Atlanta; **Bos.** – Boston; **Bro.** – Brooklyn; **Buf.** – Buffalo; **Cal.** – California; **Cgy.** – Calgary; **Cle.** – Cleveland; **Col.** – Colorado; **Dal.** – Dallas; **Det.** – Detroit; **Edm.** – Edmonton; **Fla.** – Florida; **Ham.** – Hamilton; **Hfd.** – Hartford; **K.C.** – Kansas City; **L.A.** – Los Angeles; **Min.** – Minnesota; **Mtl.** – Montreal; **Mtl. M.** – Montreal Maroons; **Mtl. W.** – Montreal Wanderers; **N.J.** – New Jersey; **NYA** – NY Americans; **NYI** – NY Islanders; **NYR** – New York Rangers; – **Oak.** – Oakland; **Ott.** – Ottawa; – **Phi.** – Philadelphia; **Phx.** – Phoenix; **Pit.** – Pittsburgh; **Que.** – Quebec; **St. L.** – St. Louis; **S.J.** – San Jose; **T.B.** – Tampa Bay; **Tor.** – Toronto; **Van.** – Vancouver; **Wpg.** – Winnipeg; **Wsh.** – Washington

Total seasons are rounded off to the nearest full season. **A** – assists; **G** – goals; **GP** – games played; **PIM** – penalties in minutes; **TP** – total points.
● – deceased. Assists not recorded during 1917-18 season ‡ – Remains active in other leagues.

			Regular Schedule					Playoffs					NHL	First	Last
Name	NHL Teams	NHL Seasons	GP	G	A	TP	PIM	GP	G	A	TP	PIM	Cup Wins	NHL Season	NHL Season
A															
Abbott, Reg	Mtl.	1	3	0	0	0	0	....	....	....	....	....	....	1952-53	1952-53
● Abel, Clarence	NYR, Chi.	8	333	19	18	37	359	38	1	1	2	58	2	1926-27	1933-34
Abel, Gerry	Det.	1	1	0	0	0	0	....	....	....	....	....	....	1966-67	1966-67
● Abel, Sid	Det., Chi.	14	612	189	283	472	376	97	28	30	58	79	3	1938-39	1953-54
Abgrall, Dennis	L.A.	1	13	0	2	2	4	....	....	....	....	....	....	1975-76	1975-76
Abrahamsson, Thommy	Hfd.	1	32	6	11	17	16	....	....	....	....	....	....	1980-81	1980-81
Achtymichuk, Gene	Mtl., Det.	4	32	3	5	8	2	....	....	....	....	....	....	1951-52	1958-59
Acomb, Doug	Tor.	1	2	0	1	1	0	....	....	....	....	....	....	1969-70	1969-70
Acton, Keith	Mtl., Min., Edm., Phi., Wsh., NYI	15	1023	226	358	584	1172	66	12	21	33	88	1	1979-80	1993-94
Adam, Douglas	NYR	1	4	0	1	1	0	....	....	....	....	....	....	1949-50	1949-50
Adam, Russ	Tor.	1	8	1	2	3	11	....	....	....	....	....	....	1982-83	1982-83
Adams, Greg	Phi., Hfd., Wsh., Edm., Van., Que., Det.	10	545	84	143	227	1173	43	2	11	13	153	....	1980-81	1989-90
● Adams, Jack	Tor., Ott.	7	173	83	32	115	366	10	1	0	1	13	2	1917-18	1926-27
Adams, John	Mtl.	1	42	6	12	18	11	3	0	0	0	0	....	1940-41	1940-41
● Adams, Stew	Chi., Tor.	4	95	9	26	35	60	11	3	3	6	14	....	1929-30	1932-33
Adduono, Rick	Bos., Atl.	2	4	0	0	0	2	....	....	....	....	....	....	1975-76	1979-80
Affleck, Bruce	St.L., Van., NYI	7	280	14	66	80	86	8	0	0	0	0	....	1974-75	1983-84
Agnew, Jim	Van., Hfd.	6	81	0	1	1	257	4	0	0	0	6	....	1986-87	1992-93
Ahern, Fred	Cal., Cle., Col.	4	146	31	30	61	130	2	0	1	1	2	....	1974-75	1977-78
Ahlin, Tony	Chi.	1	1	0	0	0	0	....	....	....	....	....	....	1937-38	1937-38
‡ Ahola, Peter	L.A., Pit., S.J., Cgy.	3	123	10	17	27	137	6	0	0	0	2	....	1991-92	1993-94
Ahrens, Chris	Min.	6	52	0	3	3	84	1	0	0	0	0	....	1972-73	1977-78
Ailsby, Lloyd	NYR	1	3	0	0	0	2	....	....	....	....	....	....	1951-52	1951-52
Aitken, Brad	Pit., Edm.	2	14	1	3	4	25	....	....	....	....	....	....	1987-88	1990-91
‡ Aivazoff, Micah	Det., Edm., NYI	3	92	4	6	10	46	....	....	....	....	....	....	1993-94	1995-96
● Albright, Clint	NYR	1	59	14	5	19	19	....	....	....	....	....	....	1948-49	1948-49
Aldcorn, Gary	Tor., Det., Bos.	5	226	41	56	97	78	6	1	2	3	4	....	1956-57	1960-61
Alexander, Claire	Tor., Van.	4	155	18	47	65	36	16	2	4	6	4	....	1974-75	1977-78
● Alexandre, Art	Mtl.C.	2	11	0	2	2	8	4	0	0	0	0	....	1931-32	1932-33
Allan, Jeff	Cle.	1	4	0	0	0	2	....	....	....	....	....	....	1977-78	1977-78
‡ Allen, Chris	Fla.	2	2	0	0	0	2	....	....	....	....	....	....	1997-98	1998-99
Allen, George	NYR, Chi., Mtl.	8	339	82	115	197	179	41	9	10	19	32	....	1938-39	1946-47
Allen, Keith	Det.	2	28	0	4	4	8	5	0	0	0	0	1	1953-54	1954-55
‡ Allen, Peter	Pit.	1	8	0	0	0	8	....	....	....	....	....	....	1995-96	1995-96
● Allen, Vivian	NYA	1	6	0	1	1	0	....	....	....	....	....	....	1940-41	1940-41
Alley, Steve	Hfd.	2	15	3	3	6	11	3	0	1	1	0	....	1979-80	1980-81
Allison, Dave	Mtl.	1	3	0	0	0	12	....	....	....	....	....	....	1983-84	1983-84
Allison, Mike	NYR, Tor., L.A.	10	499	102	166	268	630	82	9	17	26	135	....	1980-81	1989-90
Allison, Ray	Hfd., Phi.	7	238	64	93	157	223	12	2	3	5	20	....	1979-80	1986-87
● Allum, Bill	NYR	1	1	0	1	1	0	....	....	....	....	....	....	1940-41	1940-41
● Amadio, Dave	Det., L.A.	3	125	5	11	16	163	16	1	2	3	18	....	1957-58	1968-69
‡ Ambroziak, Peter	Buf.	1	12	0	1	1	0	....	....	....	....	....	....	1994-95	1994-95
Amodeo, Mike	Wpg.	1	19	0	0	0	2	....	....	....	....	....	....	1979-80	1979-80
● Anderson, Bill	Bos.	1	....	....	....	....	....	1	0	0	0	0	....	1942-43	1942-43
Anderson, Dale	Det.	1	13	0	0	0	6	2	0	0	0	0	....	1956-57	1956-57
Anderson, Doug	Mtl.	1	....	....	....	....	....	2	0	0	0	0	1	1952-53	1952-53
Anderson, Earl	Det., Bos.	3	109	19	19	38	22	5	0	1	1	0	....	1974-75	1976-77
Anderson, Glenn	Edm., Tor., NYR, St.L.	16	1129	498	601	1099	1120	225	93	121	214	442	6	1980-81	1995-96
Anderson, Jim	L.A.	1	7	1	2	3	2	....	....	....	....	....	....	1967-68	1967-68
Anderson, John	Tor., Que., Hfd.	12	814	282	349	631	263	37	9	18	27	2	....	1977-78	1988-89
Anderson, Murray	Wsh.	1	40	0	1	1	68	....	....	....	....	....	....	1974-75	1974-75
Anderson, Perry	St.L., N.J., S.J.	10	400	50	59	109	1051	36	2	1	3	161	....	1981-82	1991-92
Anderson, Ron	Det., L.A., St.L., Buf.	5	251	28	30	58	146	5	0	0	0	4	....	1967-68	1971-72
Anderson, Ron	Wsh.	1	28	9	7	16	8	....	....	....	....	....	....	1974-75	1974-75
Anderson, Russ	Pit., Hfd., L.A.	9	519	22	99	121	1086	10	0	3	3	28	....	1976-77	1984-85
‡ Anderson, Shawn	Buf., Que., Wsh., Phi.	8	255	11	51	62	117	19	1	1	2	16	....	1986-87	1994-95
● Anderson, Tom	Det., NYA, Bro.	8	319	62	127	189	180	16	2	7	9	8	....	1934-35	1941-42
‡ Andersson, Erik	Cgy.	1	12	2	1	3	8	....	....	....	....	....	....	1997-98	1997-98
Andersson, Kent-Erik	Min., NYR	7	456	72	103	175	78	50	4	11	15	4	....	1977-78	1983-84
Andersson, Peter	Wsh., Que.	3	172	10	41	51	81	7	0	2	2	2	....	1983-84	1985-86
‡ Andersson, Peter	NYR, Fla.	2	47	6	13	19	20	....	....	....	....	....	....	1992-93	1993-94
Andrascik, Steve	NYR	1	....	....	....	....	....	1	0	0	0	0	....	1971-72	1971-72
Andrea, Paul	NYR, Pit., Cal., Buf.	4	150	31	49	80	10	....	....	....	....	....	....	1965-66	1970-71
● Andrews, Lloyd	Tor.	4	53	8	5	13	10	2	0	0	0	0	1	1921-22	1924-25
‡ Andrievski, Alexander	Chi.	1	1	0	0	0	0	....	....	....	....	....	....	1992-93	1992-93
Andruff, Ron	Mtl., Col.	5	153	19	36	55	54	2	0	0	0	0	....	1974-75	1978-79
Angotti, Lou	NYR, Chi., Phi., Pit., St.L.	10	653	103	186	289	228	65	8	8	16	17	....	1964-65	1973-74
Anholt, Darrel	Chi.	1	1	0	0	0	0	....	....	....	....	....	....	1983-84	1983-84
Anslow, Hub	NYR	1	2	0	0	0	0	....	....	....	....	....	....	1947-48	1947-48
Antonovich, Mike	Min., Hfd., N.J.	5	87	10	15	25	37	....	....	....	....	....	....	1975-76	1983-84
Antoski, Shawn	Van., Phi., Pit., Ana.	8	183	3	5	8	599	36	1	3	4	74	....	1990-91	1997-98
● Apps, Syl	Tor.	10	423	201	231	432	56	69	25	29	54	8	3	1936-37	1947-48
Apps, Syl Jr.	NYR, Pit., L.A.	10	727	183	423	606	311	23	5	5	10	23	....	1970-71	1979-80
Arbour, Al	Det., Chi., Tor., St.L.	16	626	12	58	70	617	86	1	8	9	92	4	1953-54	1970-71
● Arbour, Amos	Mtl.C., Ham., Tor.	6	113	52	20	72	77	....	....	....	....	....	....	1918-19	1923-24
● Arbour, Jack	Det., Tor.	2	47	5	1	6	56	....	....	....	....	....	....	1926-27	1928-29
Arbour, John	Bos., Pit., Van., St.L.	5	106	1	9	10	149	5	0	0	0	0	....	1965-66	1971-72
● Arbour, Ty	Pit., Chi.	5	207	28	28	56	112	11	2	0	2	6	....	1926-27	1930-31
Archambault, Michel	Chi.	1	3	0	0	0	0	....	....	....	....	....	....	1976-77	1976-77
Archibald, Dave	Min., NYR, Ott., NYI	8	323	57	67	124	139	5	0	1	1	0	....	1987-88	1996-97
Archibald, Jim	Min.	3	16	1	2	3	45	....	....	....	....	....	....	1984-85	1986-87
Areshenkoff, Ron	Edm.	1	4	0	0	0	0	....	....	....	....	....	....	1979-80	1979-80
Armstrong, Bill	Phi.	1	1	0	1	1	0	....	....	....	....	....	....	1990-91	1990-91
● Armstrong, Bob	Bos.	12	542	13	86	99	671	42	1	7	8	28	....	1950-51	1961-62
Armstrong, George	Tor.	21	1187	296	417	713	721	110	26	34	60	52	4	1949-50	1970-71
Armstrong, Murray	Tor., NYA, Bro., Det.	8	270	67	121	188	72	30	4	6	10	2	....	1937-38	1945-46
● Armstrong, Norm	Tor.	1	7	1	1	2	2	....	....	....	....	....	....	1962-63	1962-63
Armstrong, Tim	Tor.	1	11	1	0	1	6	....	....	....	....	....	....	1988-89	1988-89
Arnason, Chuck	Mtl., Atl., Pit., K.C., Col., Cle., Min., Wsh.	8	401	109	90	199	122	9	2	4	6	4	....	1971-72	1978-79
Arniel, Scott	Wpg., Buf., Bos.	11	730	149	189	338	599	34	3	3	6	39	....	1981-82	1991-92
Arthur, Fred	Hfd., Phi.	3	80	1	8	9	49	4	0	0	0	2	....	1980-81	1982-83
Arundel, John	Tor.	1	3	0	0	0	9	....	....	....	....	....	....	1949-50	1949-50
● Ashbee, Barry	Bos., Phi.	5	284	15	70	85	291	17	0	4	4	22	1	1965-66	1973-74
● Ashby, Don	Tor., Col., Edm.	6	188	40	56	96	40	12	1	0	1	4	....	1975-76	1980-81
Ashton, Brent	Van., Col., N.J., Min., Que., Det., Wpg., Bos., Cgy.	14	998	284	345	629	635	85	24	25	49	70	....	1979-80	1992-93
Ashworth, Frank	Chi.	1	18	5	4	9	2	....	....	....	....	....	....	1946-47	1946-47
Asmundson, Oscar	NYR, Det., St.L., NYA, Mtl.C.	5	111	11	23	34	30	9	0	2	2	4	1	1932-33	1937-38
Astley, Mark	Buf.	3	75	4	19	23	92	2	0	0	0	0	....	1993-94	1995-96
● Atanas, Walt	NYR	1	49	13	8	21	40	....	....	....	....	....	....	1944-45	1944-45
Atkinson, Steve	Bos., Buf., Wsh.	6	302	60	51	111	104	1	0	0	0	0	....	1968-69	1974-75
Attwell, Bob	Col.	2	22	1	5	6	0	....	....	....	....	....	....	1979-80	1980-81

Greg Adams

Jim Agnew

John Anderson

Lou Angotti

Bill Baker

Bob Bassen

Barry Beck

Frank Bialowas

Name	NHL Teams	NHL Seasons	Regular Schedule					Playoffs					NHL Cup Wins	First NHL Season	Last NHL Season
			GP	G	A	TP	PIM	GP	G	A	TP	PIM			
Attwell, Ron	St.L., NYR	1	22	1	7	8	8	....	....	....	....	....	....	1967-68	1967-68
Aubin, Norm	Tor.	2	69	18	13	31	30	1	0	0	0	0	....	1981-82	1982-83
Aubry, Pierre	Que., Det.	5	202	24	26	50	133	20	1	1	2	32	....	1980-81	1984-85
Aubuchon, Ossie	Bos., NYR	2	50	20	12	32	4	6	1	0	1	0	....	1942-43	1943-44
Auge, Les	Col.	1	6	0	3	3	4	....	....	....	....	....	....	1980-81	1980-81
• Aurie, Larry	Det.	12	489	147	129	276	279	24	6	9	15	10	2	1927-28	1938-39
Awrey, Don	Bos., St.L., Mtl., Pit., NYR, Col.	16	979	31	158	189	1065	71	0	18	18	150	3	1963-64	1978-79
• Ayres, Vern	NYA, Mtl., St.L., NYR	6	211	6	11	17	350	....	....	....	....	....	....	1930-31	1935-36
B															
Babando, Pete	Bos., Det., Chi., NYR	6	351	86	73	159	194	17	3	3	6	6	1	1947-48	1952-53
Babcock, Bobby	Wsh.	2	2	0	0	0	2	....	....	....	....	....	....	1990-91	1992-93
Babe, Warren	Min.	3	21	2	5	7	23	2	0	0	0	0	....	1987-88	1990-91
Babin, Mitch	St.L.	1	8	0	0	0	0	....	....	....	....	....	....	1975-76	1975-76
Baby, John	Cle., Min.	2	26	2	8	10	26	....	....	....	....	....	....	1977-78	1978-79
Babych, Dave	Wpg., Hfd., Van., Phi., L.A.	19	1195	142	581	723	970	114	21	41	62	113	....	1980-81	1998-99
Babych, Wayne	St.L., Pit., Que., Hfd.	9	519	192	246	438	498	41	7	9	16	24	....	1978-79	1986-87
‡ Baca, Jergus	Hfd.	2	10	0	2	2	14	....	....	....	....	....	....	1990-91	1991-92
Backman, Mike	NYR	3	18	1	6	7	18	10	2	2	4	2	....	1981-82	1983-84
• Backor, Pete	Tor.	1	36	4	5	9	6	....	....	....	....	....	1	1944-45	1944-45
Backstrom, Ralph	Mtl., L.A., Chi.	17	1032	278	361	639	386	116	27	32	59	68	6	1956-57	1972-73
• Bailey, Ace	Tor.	8	313	111	82	193	472	21	3	4	7	12	1	1926-27	1933-34
Bailey, Bob	Tor., Det., Chi.	5	150	15	21	36	207	15	0	4	4	22	....	1953-54	1957-58
Bailey, Garnet	Bos., Det., St.L., Wsh.	10	568	107	171	278	633	15	2	4	6	28	2	1968-69	1977-78
Bailey, Reid	Phi., Tor., Hfd.	4	40	1	3	4	105	16	0	2	2	25	....	1980-81	1983-84
Baillargeon, Joel	Wpg., Que.	3	20	0	2	2	31	....	....	....	....	....	....	1986-87	1988-89
Baird, Ken	Cal.	1	10	0	2	2	15	....	....	....	....	....	....	1971-72	1971-72
Baker, Bill	Mtl., Col., St.L., NYR	3	143	7	25	32	175	6	0	0	0	0	....	1980-81	1982-83
Baker, Jamie	Que., Ott., S.J., Tor.	10	404	71	79	150	271	25	5	4	9	42	....	1989-90	1998-99
Bakovic, Peter	Van.	1	10	2	0	2	48	....	....	....	....	....	....	1987-88	1987-88
Balderis, Helmut	Min.	1	26	3	6	9	2	....	....	....	....	....	....	1989-90	1989-90
Baldwin, Doug	Tor., Det., Chi.	3	24	0	1	1	8	....	....	....	....	....	....	1945-46	1947-48
Balfour, Earl	Tor., Chi.	7	288	30	22	52	78	26	0	3	3	4	1	1951-52	1960-61
• Balfour, Murray	Mtl., Chi., Bos.	8	306	67	90	157	393	40	9	10	19	45	1	1956-57	1964-65
Ball, Terry	Phi., Buf.	4	74	7	19	26	26	....	....	....	....	....	....	1967-68	1971-72
Balon, Dave	NYR, Mtl., Min., Van.	14	776	192	222	414	607	78	14	21	35	109	2	1959-60	1972-73
Baltimore, Bryon	Edm.	1	2	0	0	0	4	....	....	....	....	....	....	1979-80	1979-80
Baluik, Stan	Bos.	1	7	0	0	0	2	....	....	....	....	....	....	1959-60	1959-60
Bandura, Jeff	NYR	1	2	0	1	1	0	....	....	....	....	....	....	1980-81	1980-81
Banks, Darren	Bos.	2	20	2	2	4	73	....	....	....	....	....	....	1992-93	1993-94
‡ Barahona, Ralph	Bos.	2	6	2	2	4	0	....	....	....	....	....	....	1990-91	1991-92
Barbe, Andy	Tor.	1	1	0	0	0	2	....	....	....	....	....	....	1950-51	1950-51
Barber, Bill	Phi.	12	903	420	463	883	623	129	53	55	108	109	2	1972-73	1983-84
Barber, Don	Min., Wpg., Que., S.J.	4	115	25	32	57	64	11	4	4	8	10	....	1988-89	1991-92
• Barilko, Bill	Tor.	5	252	26	36	62	456	47	5	7	12	104	4	1946-47	1950-51
Barkley, Doug	Chi., Det.	6	253	24	80	104	382	30	0	9	9	63	....	1957-58	1965-66
Barlow, Bob	Min.	2	77	16	17	33	10	6	2	2	4	6	....	1969-70	1970-71
Barnes, Blair	L.A.	1	1	0	0	0	0	....	....	....	....	....	....	1982-83	1982-83
Barnes, Norm	Phi., Hfd.	5	156	6	38	44	178	12	0	0	0	8	....	1976-77	1981-82
Baron, Normand	Mtl., St.L.	2	27	2	0	2	51	3	0	0	0	22	....	1983-84	1985-86
Barr, Dave	Bos., NYR, St.L., Hfd., Det., N.J., Dal.	13	614	128	204	332	520	71	12	10	22	70	....	1981-82	1993-94
Barrault, Doug	Min., Fla.	2	4	0	0	0	2	....	....	....	....	....	....	1992-93	1993-94
Barrett, Fred	Min., L.A.	13	745	25	123	148	671	44	0	2	2	60	....	1970-71	1983-84
Barrett, John	Det., Wsh., Min.	8	488	20	77	97	604	16	2	2	4	50	....	1980-81	1987-88
Barrie, Doug	Pit., Buf., L.A.	3	158	10	42	52	268	....	....	....	....	....	....	1968-69	1971-72
Barry, Ed	Bos.	1	19	1	3	4	2	....	....	....	....	....	....	1946-47	1946-47
• Barry, Marty	NYA, Bos., Det., Mtl.	12	509	195	192	387	231	43	15	18	33	34	2	1927-28	1939-40
Barry, Ray	Bos.	1	18	1	2	3	6	....	....	....	....	....	....	1951-52	1951-52
Bartel, Robin	Cgy., Van.	2	41	0	1	1	14	6	0	0	0	16	....	1985-86	1986-87
Bartlett, Jim	Mtl., NYR, Bos.	5	191	34	23	57	273	2	0	0	0	0	....	1954-55	1960-61
• Barton, Cliff	Pit., Phi., NYR	3	85	10	9	19	22	....	....	....	....	....	....	1929-30	1939-40
Bassen, Bob	NYI, Chi., St.L., Que., Dal., Cgy.	15	765	88	144	232	1004	93	9	15	24	134	....	1985-86	1999-00
Bathe, Frank	Det., Phi.	9	224	3	28	31	542	27	1	3	4	42	....	1974-75	1983-84
Bathgate, Andy	NYR, Tor., Det., Pit.	17	1069	349	624	973	624	54	21	14	35	76	1	1952-53	1970-71
Bathgate, Frank	NYR	1	2	0	0	0	2	....	....	....	....	....	....	1952-53	1952-53
• Batters, Jeff	St.L.	2	16	0	0	0	28	....	....	....	....	....	....	1993-94	1994-95
‡ Batyrshin, Ruslan	L.A.	1	2	0	0	0	6	....	....	....	....	....	....	1995-96	1995-96
• Bauer, Bobby	Bos.	9	327	123	137	260	36	48	11	8	19	6	2	1936-37	1951-52
Baumgartner, Ken	L.A., NYI, Tor., Ana., Bos.	12	696	13	41	54	2244	51	1	2	3	106	....	1987-88	1998-99
Baumgartner, Mike	K.C.	1	17	0	0	0	0	....	....	....	....	....	....	1974-75	1974-75
Baun, Bob	Tor., Oak., Det.	17	964	37	187	224	1493	96	3	12	15	171	4	1956-57	1972-73
‡ Bautin, Sergei	Wpg., Det., S.J.	3	132	5	25	30	176	6	0	0	0	2	....	1992-93	1995-96
Bawa, Robin	Wsh., Van., S.J., Ana.	4	61	6	1	7	60	1	0	0	0	0	....	1989-90	1993-94
Baxter, Paul	Que., Pit., Cgy.	8	472	48	121	169	1564	40	0	5	5	162	....	1979-80	1986-87
Beadle, Sandy	Wpg.	1	6	1	0	1	2	....	....	....	....	....	....	1980-81	1980-81
Beaton, Frank	NYR	2	25	1	1	2	43	....	....	....	....	....	....	1978-79	1979-80
• Beattie, Red	Bos., Det., NYA	9	334	62	85	147	137	24	4	2	6	8	....	1930-31	1938-39
Beaudin, Norm	St.L., Min.	2	25	1	2	3	4	....	....	....	....	....	....	1967-68	1970-71
Beaudoin, Serge	Atl.	1	3	0	0	0	0	....	....	....	....	....	....	1979-80	1979-80
Beaudoin, Yves	Wsh.	3	11	0	0	0	5	....	....	....	....	....	....	1985-86	1987-88
Beck, Barry	Col., NYR, L.A.	10	615	104	251	355	1016	51	10	23	33	77	....	1977-78	1989-90
Beckett, Bob	Bos.	4	68	7	6	13	18	....	....	....	....	....	....	1956-57	1963-64
Bedard, James	Chi.	2	22	1	1	2	8	....	....	....	....	....	....	1949-50	1950-51
‡ Beddoes, Clayton	Bos.	2	60	2	8	10	57	....	....	....	....	....	....	1995-96	1996-97
Bednarski, John	NYR, Edm.	4	100	2	18	20	114	1	0	0	0	17	....	1974-75	1979-80
Beers, Bob	Bos., T.B., Edm., NYI	8	258	28	79	107	225	21	1	1	2	22	....	1989-90	1996-97
Beers, Eddy	Cgy., St.L.	5	250	94	116	210	256	41	7	10	17	47	....	1981-82	1985-86
• Behling, Dick	Det.	2	5	1	0	1	2	....	....	....	....	....	....	1940-41	1942-43
Beisler, Frank	NYA	2	2	0	0	0	0	....	....	....	....	....	....	1936-37	1939-40
Belanger, Alain	Tor.	1	9	0	1	1	6	....	....	....	....	....	....	1977-78	1977-78
Belanger, Roger	Pit.	1	44	3	5	8	32	....	....	....	....	....	....	1984-85	1984-85
Belisle, Danny	NYR	1	4	2	0	2	0	....	....	....	....	....	....	1960-61	1960-61
Beliveau, Jean	Mtl.	20	1125	507	712	1219	1029	162	79	97	176	211	10	1950-51	1970-71
• Bell, Billy	Mtl., Mtl.C., Ott.	6	72	4	2	6	14	5	0	0	0	0	1	1917-18	1923-24
Bell, Bruce	Que., St.L., NYR, Edm.	5	209	12	64	76	113	34	3	5	8	41	....	1984-85	1989-90
Bell, Harry	NYR	1	1	0	1	1	0	....	....	....	....	....	....	1946-47	1946-47
Bell, Joe	NYR	2	62	8	9	17	18	....	....	....	....	....	....	1942-43	1946-47
Belland, Neil	Van., Pit.	6	109	13	32	45	54	21	2	9	11	23	....	1981-82	1986-87
• Bellefeuille, Pete	Tor., Det.	4	92	26	4	30	58	....	....	....	....	....	....	1925-26	1929-30
• Bellemer, Andy	Mtl.M.	1	15	0	0	0	0	....	....	....	....	....	....	1932-33	1932-33
Bellows, Brian	Min., Mtl., T.B., Ana., Wsh.	17	1188	485	537	1022	718	143	51	71	122	143	1	1982-83	1998-99
• Bend, Lin	NYR	1	8	3	1	4	2	....	....	....	....	....	....	1942-43	1942-43
Bennett, Adam	Chi., Edm.	3	69	3	8	11	69	....	....	....	....	....	....	1991-92	1993-94
Bennett, Bill	Bos., Hfd.	2	31	4	7	11	65	....	....	....	....	....	....	1978-79	1979-80
Bennett, Curt	St.L., NYR, Atl.	10	580	152	182	334	347	21	1	1	2	57	....	1970-71	1979-80
Bennett, Frank	Det.	1	7	0	1	1	2	....	....	....	....	....	....	1943-44	1943-44
Bennett, Harvey	Pit., Wsh., Phi., Min., St.L.	5	268	44	46	90	347	4	0	0	0	2	....	1974-75	1978-79
• Bennett, Max	Mtl.C.	1	1	0	0	0	0	....	....	....	....	....	....	1935-36	1935-36
Bennett, Rick	NYR	3	15	1	1	2	13	....	....	....	....	....	....	1989-90	1991-92
Benning, Brian	St.L., L.A., Phi., Edm., Fla.	11	568	63	233	296	963	48	3	20	23	74	....	1984-85	1994-95
Benning, Jim	Tor., Van.	9	605	52	191	243	461	7	1	1	2	2	....	1981-82	1989-90
• Benoit, Joe	Mtl.	5	185	75	69	144	94	11	6	3	9	11	1	1940-41	1946-47
Benson, Bill	NYA, Bro.	2	67	11	25	36	35	....	....	....	....	....	....	1940-41	1941-42
• Benson, Bobby	Bos.	1	8	0	1	1	4	....	....	....	....	....	....	1924-25	1924-25
• Bentley, Doug	Chi., NYR	13	566	219	324	543	217	23	9	8	17	12	....	1939-40	1953-54
• Bentley, Max	Chi., Tor., NYR	12	646	245	299	544	179	51	18	27	45	14	3	1940-41	1953-54
Bentley, Reggie	Chi.	1	11	1	2	3	2	....	....	....	....	....	....	1942-43	1942-43
Beraldo, Paul	Bos.	2	10	0	0	0	4	....	....	....	....	....	....	1987-88	1988-89
Berard, Bryan	NYI, Tor.	4	290	34	124	158	235	17	1	8	9	8	....	1996-97	1999-00
Berenson, Red	Mtl., NYR, St.L., Det.	17	987	261	397	658	305	85	23	14	37	49	1	1961-62	1977-78
Berezan, Perry	Cgy., Min., S.J.	9	378	61	75	136	279	31	4	7	11	34	....	1984-85	1992-93
Berg, Bill	NYI, Tor., NYR, Ott.	10	546	55	67	122	488	61	3	4	7	34	....	1988-89	1998-99
• Bergdinon, Fred	Bos.	1	2	0	0	0	0	....	....	....	....	....	....	1925-26	1925-26
Bergen, Todd	Phi.	1	14	11	5	16	4	17	4	9	13	8	....	1984-85	1984-85
Berger, Mike	Min.	2	30	3	1	4	67	....	....	....	....	....	....	1987-88	1988-89

			Regular Schedule					Playoffs							
Name	NHL Teams	NHL Seasons	GP	G	A	TP	PIM	GP	G	A	TP	PIM	NHL Cup Wins	First NHL Season	Last NHL Season
Bergeron, Michel	Det., NYI, Wsh.	5	229	80	58	138	165	....	....	....	....	....	....	1974-75	1978-79
Bergeron, Yves	Pit.	2	3	0	0	0	0	....	....	....	....	....	....	1974-75	1976-77
Bergkvist, Stefan	Pit.	2	7	0	0	0	9	4	0	0	0	2	....	1995-96	1996-97
Bergland, Tim	Wsh., T.B.	5	182	17	26	43	75	26	2	2	4	22	....	1989-90	1993-94
Bergloff, Bob	Min.	1	2	0	0	0	5	....	....	....	....	....	....	1982-83	1982-83
Berglund, Bo	Que., Min., Phi.	3	130	28	39	67	40	9	2	0	2	6	....	1983-84	1985-86
• Bergman, Gary	Det., Min., K.C.	12	838	68	299	367	1249	21	0	5	5	20	....	1964-65	1975-76
Bergman, Thommie	Det.	6	246	21	44	65	243	7	0	2	2	2	....	1972-73	1979-80
Bergqvist, Jonas	Cgy.	1	22	2	5	7	10	....	....	....	....	....	....	1989-90	1989-90
• Berlinquette, Louis	Mtl.C., Mtl.M., Pit.	8	193	45	33	78	129	11	0	4	4	9	....	1917-18	1925-26
Bernier, Serge	Phi., L.A., Que.	7	302	78	119	197	234	5	1	1	2	0	....	1968-69	1980-81
Berry, Bob	Mtl., L.A.	8	541	159	191	350	344	26	2	6	8	6	....	1968-69	1976-77
Berry, Brad	Wpg., Min., Dal.	8	241	4	28	32	323	13	0	1	1	16	....	1985-86	1993-94
Berry, Doug	Col.	2	121	10	33	43	25	....	....	....	....	....	....	1979-80	1980-81
Berry, Fred	Det.	1	3	0	0	0	0	....	....	....	....	....	....	1976-77	1976-77
Berry, Ken	Edm., Van.	4	55	8	10	18	30	....	....	....	....	....	....	1981-82	1988-89
• Besler, Phil	Bos., Chi., Det.	2	30	1	4	5	18	....	....	....	....	....	....	1935-36	1938-39
• Bessone, Pete	Det.	1	6	0	1	1	6	....	....	....	....	....	....	1937-38	1937-38
Bethel, John	Wpg.	1	17	0	2	2	4	....	....	....	....	....	....	1979-80	1979-80
‡ Bets, Maxim	Ana.	1	3	0	0	0	0	....	....	....	....	....	....	1993-94	1993-94
Bettio, Sam	Bos.	1	44	9	12	21	32	....	....	....	....	....	....	1949-50	1949-50
Beukeboom, Jeff	Edm., NYR	14	804	30	129	159	1890	99	3	16	19	197	4	1985-86	1998-99
Beverley, Nick	Bos., Pit., NYR, Min., L.A., Col.	11	502	18	94	112	156	7	0	1	1	0	....	1966-67	1979-80
Bialowas, Dwight	Atl., Min.	4	164	11	46	57	46	....	....	....	....	....	....	1973-74	1976-77
Bialowas, Frank	Tor.	1	3	0	0	0	12	....	....	....	....	....	....	1993-94	1993-94
Bianchin, Wayne	Pit., Edm.	7	276	68	41	109	137	3	0	1	1	6	....	1973-74	1979-80
Bidner, Todd	Wsh.	1	12	2	1	3	7	....	....	....	....	....	....	1981-82	1981-82
Biggs, Don	Min., Phi.	2	12	2	0	2	8	....	....	....	....	....	....	1984-85	1989-90
Bignell, Larry	Pit.	2	20	0	3	3	2	3	0	0	0	2	....	1973-74	1974-75
Bilodeau, Gilles	Que.	1	9	0	1	1	25	....	....	....	....	....	....	1979-80	1979-80
• Bionda, Jack	Tor., Bos.	4	93	3	9	12	113	11	0	1	1	14	....	1955-56	1958-59
Bissett, Tom	Det.	1	5	0	0	0	0	....	....	....	....	....	....	1990-91	1990-91
Bjugstad, Scott	Min., Pit., L.A.	9	317	76	68	144	144	9	0	1	1	2	....	1983-84	1991-92
Black, Stephen	Det., Chi.	2	113	11	20	31	77	13	0	0	0	13	1	1949-50	1950-51
Blackburn, Bob	NYR, Pit.	3	135	8	12	20	105	6	0	0	0	4	....	1968-69	1970-71
Blackburn, Don	Bos., Phi., NYR, NYI, Min.	6	185	23	44	67	87	12	3	0	3	10	....	1962-63	1972-73
Blade, Hank	Chi.	2	24	2	3	5	2	....	....	....	....	....	....	1946-47	1947-48
Bladon, Tom	Phi., Pit., Edm., Wpg., Det.	9	610	73	197	270	392	86	8	29	37	70	2	1972-73	1980-81
• Blaine, Garry	Mtl.	1	1	0	0	0	0	....	....	....	....	....	....	1954-55	1954-55
• Blair, Andy	Tor., Chi.	9	402	74	86	160	323	38	6	6	12	32	1	1928-29	1936-37
Blair, Chuck	Tor.	1	1	0	0	0	0	....	....	....	....	....	....	1948-49	1948-49
Blair, Dusty	Tor.	1	2	0	0	0	0	....	....	....	....	....	....	1950-51	1950-51
Blaisdell, Mike	Det., NYR, Pit., Tor.	9	343	70	84	154	166	6	1	2	3	10	....	1980-81	1988-89
Blake, Bob	Bos.	1	12	0	0	0	0	....	....	....	....	....	....	1935-36	1935-36
• Blake, Mickey	Mtl.M., St.L., Tor.	3	10	1	1	2	4	....	....	....	....	....	....	1932-33	1935-36
• Blake, Toe	Mtl.M., Mtl.C., Mtl.	14	577	235	292	527	272	58	25	37	62	23	3	1934-35	1947-48
Blight, Rick	Van., L.A.	7	326	96	125	221	170	5	0	5	5	2	....	1975-76	1982-83
• Blinco, Russ	Mtl.M., Chi.	6	268	59	66	125	24	19	3	3	6	4	1	1933-34	1938-39
Block, Ken	Van.	1	1	0	0	0	0	....	....	....	....	....	....	1970-71	1970-71
Bloemberg, Jeff	NYR	4	43	3	6	9	25	7	0	3	3	5	....	1988-89	1991-92
Blomqvist, Timo	Wsh., N.J.	5	243	4	53	57	293	13	0	0	0	24	....	1981-82	1986-87
Blomsten, Arto	Wpg., L.A.	3	25	0	4	4	8	....	....	....	....	....	....	1993-94	1995-96
Bloom, Mike	Wsh., Det.	3	201	30	47	77	215	....	....	....	....	....	....	1974-75	1976-77
Blum, John	Edm., Bos., Wsh., Det.	8	250	7	34	41	610	20	0	2	2	27	....	1982-83	1989-90
Bodak, Bob	Cgy., Hfd.	2	4	0	0	0	29	....	....	....	....	....	....	1987-88	1989-90
Boddy, Gregg	Van.	5	273	23	44	67	263	3	0	0	0	0	....	1971-72	1975-76
Bodger, Doug	Pit., Buf., S.J., N.J., L.A., Van.	16	1071	106	422	528	1007	47	6	18	24	25	....	1984-85	1999-00
Bodnar, Gus	Tor., Chi., Bos.	12	667	142	254	396	207	32	4	3	7	10	2	1943-44	1954-55
Boehm, Ron	Oak.	1	16	2	1	3	10	....	....	....	....	....	....	1967-68	1967-68
• Boesch, Garth	Tor.	4	197	9	28	37	205	34	2	5	7	18	3	1946-47	1949-50
Boh, Rick	Min.	1	8	2	1	3	4	....	....	....	....	....	....	1987-88	1987-88
Boileau, Marc	Det.	1	54	5	6	11	8	....	....	....	....	....	....	1961-62	1961-62
Boileau, Rene	NYA	1	7	0	0	0	0	....	....	....	....	....	....	1925-26	1925-26
Boimistruck, Fred	Tor.	2	83	4	14	18	45	....	....	....	....	....	....	1981-82	1982-83
Boisvert, Serge	Tor., Mtl.	5	46	5	7	12	8	23	3	7	10	4	1	1982-83	1987-88
Boivin, Claude	Phi., Ott.	4	132	12	19	31	364	....	....	....	....	....	....	1991-92	1994-95
Boivin, Leo	Tor., Bos., Det., Pit., Min.	19	1150	72	250	322	1192	54	3	10	13	59	....	1951-52	1969-70
Boland, Mike	Phi.	1	2	0	0	0	0	....	....	....	....	....	....	1974-75	1974-75
Boland, Mike J.	K.C., Buf.	2	23	1	2	3	29	3	1	0	1	2	....	1974-75	1978-79
Boldirev, Ivan	Bos., Cal., Chi., Atl., Van., Det.	15	1052	361	505	866	507	48	13	20	33	14	....	1970-71	1984-85
Bolduc, Danny	Det., Cgy.	3	102	22	19	41	33	1	0	0	0	0	....	1978-79	1983-84
Bolduc, Michel	Que.	2	10	0	0	0	6	....	....	....	....	....	....	1981-82	1982-83
• Boll, Buzz	Tor., NYA, Bro., Bos.	12	437	133	130	263	148	31	7	3	10	13	....	1932-33	1943-44
Bolonchuk, Larry	Van., Wsh.	4	74	3	9	12	97	....	....	....	....	....	....	1972-73	1977-78
• Bolton, Hugh	Tor.	8	235	10	51	61	221	17	0	5	5	14	1	1949-50	1956-57
Bonar, Dan	L.A.	3	170	25	39	64	208	14	3	4	7	22	....	1980-81	1982-83
Bonin, Marcel	Det., Bos., Mtl.	9	454	97	175	272	336	50	11	14	25	51	4	1952-53	1961-62
Bonsignore, Jason	Edm., T.B.	4	79	3	13	16	34	....	....	....	....	....	....	1994-95	1998-99
Boo, Jim	Min.	1	6	0	0	0	22	....	....	....	....	....	....	1977-78	1977-78
Boone, Buddy	Bos.	2	34	5	3	8	28	22	2	1	3	25	....	1956-57	1957-58
Boothman, George	Tor.	2	58	17	19	36	18	5	2	1	3	2	....	1942-43	1943-44
Bordeleau, Christian	Mtl., St.L., Chi.	4	205	38	65	103	82	19	4	7	11	17	1	1968-69	1971-72
Bordeleau, J.P.	Chi.	10	519	97	126	223	143	48	3	6	9	12	....	1969-70	1979-80
Bordeleau, Paulin	Van.	3	183	33	56	89	47	5	2	1	3	0	....	1973-74	1975-76
Borotsik, Jack	St.L.	1	1	0	0	0	0	....	....	....	....	....	....	1974-75	1974-75
‡ Borsato, Luciano	Wpg.	5	203	35	55	90	113	7	1	0	1	4	....	1990-91	1994-95
Borschevsky, Nikolai	Tor., Cgy., Dal.	4	162	49	73	122	44	31	4	9	13	4	....	1992-93	1995-96
Boschman, Laurie	Tor., Edm., Wpg., N.J., Ott.	14	1009	229	348	577	2265	57	8	13	21	140	....	1979-80	1992-93
Bossy, Mike	NYI	10	752	573	553	1126	210	129	85	75	160	38	4	1977-78	1986-87
Bostrom, Helge	Chi.	4	96	3	3	6	58	13	0	0	0	16	....	1929-30	1932-33
Botell, Mark	Phi.	1	32	4	10	14	31	....	....	....	....	....	....	1981-82	1981-82
Bothwell, Tim	NYR, St.L., Hfd.	11	502	28	93	121	382	49	0	3	3	56	....	1978-79	1988-89
Botting, Cam	Atl.	1	2	0	1	1	0	....	....	....	....	....	....	1975-76	1975-76
Boucha, Henry	Det., Min., K.C., Col.	6	247	53	49	102	157	....	....	....	....	....	....	1971-72	1976-77
Bouchard, Butch	Mtl.	15	785	49	144	193	863	113	11	21	32	121	4	1941-42	1955-56
Bouchard, Dick	NYR	1	1	0	0	0	0	....	....	....	....	....	....	1954-55	1954-55
• Bouchard, Edmond	Mtl.C., Ham., NYA, Pit.	8	211	19	21	40	117	....	....	....	....	....	....	1921-22	1928-29
Bouchard, Pierre	Mtl., Wsh.	12	595	24	82	106	433	76	3	10	13	56	5	1970-71	1981-82
• Boucher, Billy	Mtl.C., Bos., NYA	7	213	93	38	131	409	14	3	0	3	17	1	1921-22	1927-28
• Boucher, Bobby	Mtl.C.	1	11	1	0	1	0	2	0	0	0	0	1	1923-24	1923-24
• Boucher, Clarence	NYA	2	47	2	2	4	133	....	....	....	....	....	....	1926-27	1927-28
• Boucher, Frank	Ott., NYR	14	557	160	263	423	119	55	16	20	36	12	2	1921-22	1943-44
• Boucher, Georges	Ott., Mtl.M., Chi.	15	449	117	87	204	838	28	5	3	8	88	4	1917-18	1931-32
Boudreau, Bruce	Tor., Chi.	8	141	28	42	70	46	9	2	0	2	0	....	1976-77	1985-86
Boudrias, Andre	Mtl., Min., Chi., St.L., Van.	12	662	151	340	491	216	34	6	10	16	12	....	1963-64	1975-76
Boughner, Barry	Oak., Cal.	2	20	0	0	0	11	....	....	....	....	....	....	1969-70	1970-71
Bourbonnais, Dan	Hfd.	2	59	3	25	28	11	....	....	....	....	....	....	1981-82	1983-84
Bourbonnais, Rick	St.L.	3	71	9	15	24	29	4	0	1	1	0	....	1975-76	1977-78
• Bourcier, Conrad	Mtl.C.	1	6	0	0	0	0	....	....	....	....	....	....	1935-36	1935-36
Bourcier, Jean	Mtl.C.	1	9	0	1	1	0	....	....	....	....	....	....	1935-36	1935-36
• Bourgeault, Leo	Tor., NYR, Ott., Mtl.C.	8	307	24	20	44	269	24	1	1	2	18	1	1926-27	1934-35
Bourgeois, Charlie	Cgy., St.L., Hfd.	7	290	16	54	70	788	40	2	3	5	194	....	1981-82	1987-88
Bourne, Bob	NYI, L.A.	14	964	258	324	582	605	139	40	56	96	108	4	1974-75	1987-88
Bourque, Phil	Pit., NYR, Ott.	12	477	88	111	199	516	56	13	12	25	107	2	1983-84	1995-96
Boutette, Pat	Tor., Hfd., Pit.	10	756	171	282	453	1354	46	10	14	24	109	....	1975-76	1984-85
Boutilier, Paul	NYI, Bos., Min., NYR, Wpg.	8	288	27	83	110	358	41	1	9	10	45	1	1981-82	1988-89
‡ Bowen, Jason	Phi., Edm.	6	77	2	6	8	109	....	....	....	....	....	....	1992-93	1997-98
Bowman, Kirk	Chi.	3	88	11	17	28	19	7	1	0	1	0	....	1976-77	1978-79
• Bowman, Ralph	Ott., St.L., Det.	7	274	8	17	25	260	22	2	2	4	6	2	1933-34	1939-40
Bownass, Jack	Mtl., NYR	4	80	3	8	11	58	....	....	....	....	....	....	1957-58	1961-62
Bowness, Rick	Atl., Det., St.L., Wpg.	7	173	18	37	55	191	5	0	0	0	2	....	1975-76	1981-82
• Boyd, Bill	NYR, NYA	4	138	15	7	22	72	10	0	0	0	4	1	1926-27	1929-30
Boyd, Irvin	Bos., Det.	4	96	10	10	20	30	5	0	1	1	4	....	1931-32	1943-44
Boyd, Randy	Pit., Chi., NYI, Van.	8	257	20	67	87	328	13	0	2	2	26	....	1981-82	1988-89
Boyer, Wally	Tor., Chi., Oak., Pit.	7	365	54	105	159	163	15	1	3	4	0	....	1965-66	1971-72
‡ Boyer, Zac	Dal.	2	3	0	0	0	0	2	0	0	0	0	....	1994-95	1995-96

Todd Bidner

Doug Bodger

Jason Bonsignore

Frank Boucher

Charles Bourgeois

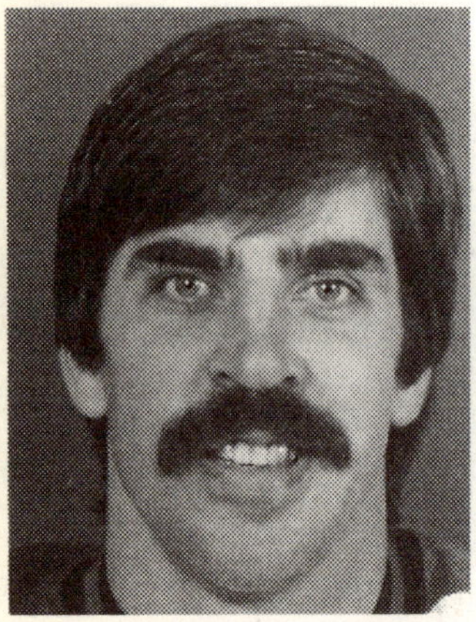

Mel Bridgman

Punch Broadbent

Jack Brownschidle

			Regular Schedule					Playoffs					NHL	First	Last
Name	NHL Teams	NHL Seasons	GP	G	A	TP	PIM	GP	G	A	TP	PIM	Cup Wins	NHL Season	NHL Season
Boyko, Darren	Wpg.	1	1	0	0	0	0	....	....	....	....	....	....	1988-89	1988-89
Bozek, Steve	L.A., Cgy., St.L., Van., S.J.	11	641	164	167	331	309	58	12	11	23	69	....	1981-82	1991-92
‡ Bozon, Philippe	St.L.	4	144	16	25	41	101	19	2	0	2	31	....	1991-92	1994-95
• Brackenborough, John	Bos.	1	7	0	0	0	0	....	....	....	....	....	....	1925-26	1925-26
Brackenbury, Curt	Que., Edm., St.L.	4	141	9	17	26	226	2	0	0	0	0	....	1979-80	1982-83
Bradley, Bart	Bos.	1	1	0	0	0	0	....	....	....	....	....	....	1949-50	1949-50
Bradley, Brian	Cgy., Van., Tor., T.B.	13	651	182	321	503	528	13	3	7	10	16	....	1985-86	1997-98
Bradley, Lyle	Cal., Cle.	2	6	1	0	1	2	....	....	....	....	....	....	1973-74	1976-77
‡ Brady, Neil	N.J., Ott., Dal.	5	89	9	22	31	95	....	....	....	....	....	....	1989-90	1993-94
Bragnalo, Rick	Wsh.	4	145	15	35	50	46	....	....	....	....	....	....	1975-76	1978-79
• Branigan, Andy	NYA, Bro.	2	27	1	2	3	31	....	....	....	....	....	....	1940-41	1941-42
Brasar, Per-Olov	Min., Van.	5	348	64	142	206	33	13	1	2	3	0	....	1977-78	1981-82
• Brayshaw, Russ	Chi.	1	43	5	9	14	24	....	....	....	....	....	....	1944-45	1944-45
Breault, Francois	L.A.	3	27	2	4	6	42	....	....	....	....	....	....	1990-91	1992-93
Breitenbach, Ken	Buf.	3	68	1	13	14	49	8	0	1	1	4	....	1975-76	1978-79
Brennan, Dan	L.A.	2	8	0	1	1	9	....	....	....	....	....	....	1983-84	1985-86
Brennan, Doug	NYR	3	123	9	7	16	152	16	1	0	1	21	1	1931-32	1933-34
Brennan, Tom	Bos.	2	12	2	2	4	2	....	....	....	....	....	....	1943-44	1944-45
Brenneman, John	Chi., NYR, Tor., Det., Oak.	5	152	21	19	40	46	....	....	....	....	....	1	1964-65	1968-69
Bretto, Joe	Chi.	1	3	0	0	0	4	....	....	....	....	....	....	1944-45	1944-45
Brewer, Carl	Tor., Det., St.L.	12	604	25	198	223	1037	72	3	17	20	146	3	1957-58	1979-80
Brickley, Andy	Phi., Pit., N.J., Bos., Wpg.	11	385	82	140	222	81	17	1	4	5	4	....	1982-83	1993-94
• Briden, Archie	Bos., Det., Pit.	2	71	9	5	14	56	....	....	....	....	....	....	1926-27	1929-30
Bridgman, Mel	Phi., Cgy., N.J., Det., Van.	14	977	252	449	701	1625	125	28	39	67	298	....	1975-76	1988-89
• Briere, Michel	Pit.	1	76	12	32	44	20	10	5	3	8	17	....	1969-70	1969-70
Brindley, Doug	Tor.	1	3	0	0	0	0	....	....	....	....	....	....	1970-71	1970-71
• Brink, Milt	Chi.	1	5	0	0	0	0	....	....	....	....	....	....	1936-37	1936-37
Brisson, Gerry	Mtl.	1	4	0	2	2	4	....	....	....	....	....	....	1962-63	1962-63
Britz, Greg	Tor., Hfd.	3	8	0	0	0	4	....	....	....	....	....	....	1983-84	1986-87
• Broadbent, Punch	Ott., Mtl.M., NYA	11	303	121	51	172	564	23	4	5	9	50	4	1918-19	1928-29
‡ Brochu, Stephane	NYR	1	1	0	0	0	0	....	....	....	....	....	....	1988-89	1988-89
Broden, Connie	Mtl.	3	6	2	1	3	2	7	0	1	1	0	2	1955-56	1957-58
Brooke, Bob	NYR, Min., N.J.	7	447	69	97	166	520	34	9	9	18	59	....	1983-84	1989-90
Brooks, Gord	St.L., Wsh.	3	70	7	18	25	37	....	....	....	....	....	....	1971-72	1974-75
• Brophy, Bernie	Mtl.M., Det.	3	62	4	4	8	25	2	0	0	0	2	1	1925-26	1929-30
Brossart, Willie	Phi., Tor., Wsh.	6	129	1	14	15	88	1	0	0	0	0	....	1970-71	1975-76
Broten, Aaron	Col., N.J., Min., Que., Tor., Wpg.	12	748	186	329	515	441	34	7	18	25	40	....	1980-81	1991-92
Broten, Neal	Min., Dal., N.J., L.A.	17	1099	289	634	923	569	135	35	63	98	77	1	1980-81	1996-97
Broten, Paul	NYR, Dal., St.L.	7	322	46	55	101	264	38	4	6	10	18	....	1989-90	1995-96
• Brown, Adam	Det., Chi., Bos.	10	391	104	113	217	378	26	2	4	6	14	1	1941-42	1951-52
Brown, Arnie	Tor., NYR, Det., NYI, Atl.	12	681	44	141	185	738	22	0	6	6	23	....	1961-62	1973-74
‡ Brown, Cam	Van.	1	1	0	0	0	7	....	....	....	....	....	....	1990-91	1990-91
• Brown, Connie	Det.	5	73	15	24	39	12	14	2	3	5	0	1	1938-39	1942-43
Brown, Dave	Phi., Edm., S.J.	14	729	45	52	97	1789	80	2	3	5	209	1	1982-83	1995-96
• Brown, Fred	Mtl.M.	1	19	1	0	1	0	9	0	0	0	0	....	1927-28	1927-28
Brown, George	Mtl.C.	3	79	6	22	28	34	7	0	0	0	2	....	1936-37	1938-39
• Brown, Gerry	Det.	2	23	4	5	9	2	12	2	1	3	4	....	1941-42	1945-46
‡ Brown, Greg	Buf., Pit., Wpg.	4	94	4	14	18	86	6	0	1	1	4	....	1990-91	1994-95
Brown, Harold	NYR	1	13	2	1	3	2	....	....	....	....	....	....	1945-46	1945-46
Brown, Jeff	Que., St.L., Van., Hfd., Car., Tor., Wsh.	13	747	154	430	584	498	87	20	45	65	59	....	1985-86	1997-98
Brown, Jim	L.A.	1	3	0	1	1	5	....	....	....	....	....	....	1982-83	1982-83
Brown, Keith	Chi., Fla.	16	876	68	274	342	916	103	4	32	36	184	....	1979-80	1994-95
Brown, Larry	NYR, Det., Phi., L.A.	9	455	7	53	60	180	35	0	4	4	10	....	1969-70	1977-78
• Brown, Stan	NYR, Det.	2	48	8	2	10	18	2	0	0	0	0	....	1926-27	1927-28
Brown, Wayne	Bos.	1	....	....	....	....	....	4	0	0	0	2	....	1953-54	1953-54
• Browne, Cecil	Chi.	1	13	2	0	2	4	....	....	....	....	....	....	1927-28	1927-28
Brownschidle, Jack	St.L., Hfd.	9	494	39	162	201	151	26	0	5	5	18	....	1977-78	1985-86
Brownschidle, Jeff	Hfd.	2	7	0	1	1	2	....	....	....	....	....	....	1981-82	1982-83
Brubaker, Jeff	Hfd., Mtl., Cgy., Tor., Edm., NYR, Det.	8	178	16	9	25	512	2	0	0	0	27	....	1979-80	1988-89
Bruce, David	Van., St.L., S.J.	8	234	48	39	87	338	3	0	0	0	2	....	1985-86	1993-94
• Bruce, Gordie	Bos.	3	28	4	9	13	13	7	2	3	5	4	....	1940-41	1945-46
• Bruce, Morley	Ott.	4	71	8	3	11	27	3	0	0	0	2	2	1917-18	1921-22
Brumwell, Murray	Min., N.J.	7	128	12	31	43	70	2	0	0	0	2	....	1980-81	1987-88
Bruneteau, Eddie	Det.	7	180	40	42	82	35	31	7	6	13	0	....	1940-41	1948-49
• Bruneteau, Mud	Det.	11	411	139	138	277	80	77	23	14	37	22	3	1935-36	1945-46
• Brydge, Bill	Tor., Det., NYA	9	368	26	52	78	506	2	0	0	0	4	....	1926-27	1935-36
Brydges, Paul	Buf.	1	15	2	2	4	6	....	....	....	....	....	....	1986-87	1986-87
• Brydson, Glenn	Mtl.M., St.L., NYR, Chi.	8	299	56	79	135	203	11	0	0	0	8	....	1930-31	1937-38
• Brydson, Gord	Tor.	1	8	2	0	2	8	....	....	....	....	....	....	1929-30	1929-30
Bubla, Jiri	Van.	5	256	17	101	118	202	6	0	0	0	7	....	1981-82	1985-86
• Buchanan, Al	Tor.	2	4	0	1	1	2	....	....	....	....	....	....	1948-49	1949-50
Buchanan, Bucky	NYR	1	2	0	0	0	0	....	....	....	....	....	....	1948-49	1948-49
Buchanan, Jeff	Col.	1	6	0	0	0	6	....	....	....	....	....	....	1998-99	1998-99
Buchanan, Mike	Chi.	1	1	0	0	0	0	....	....	....	....	....	....	1951-52	1951-52
Buchanan, Ron	Bos., St.L.	2	5	0	0	0	0	....	....	....	....	....	....	1966-67	1969-70
Bucyk, John	Det., Bos.	23	1540	556	813	1369	497	124	41	62	103	42	2	1955-56	1977-78
Bucyk, Randy	Mtl., Cgy.	2	19	4	2	6	8	2	0	0	0	0	....	1985-86	1987-88
Buhr, Doug	K.C.	1	6	0	2	2	4	....	....	....	....	....	....	1974-75	1974-75
Bukovich, Tony	Det.	2	17	7	3	10	6	6	0	1	1	0	....	1943-44	1944-45
‡ Bullard, Mike	Pit., Cgy., St.L., Phi., Tor.	11	727	329	345	674	703	40	11	18	29	44	....	1980-81	1991-92
• Buller, Hy	Det., NYR	5	188	22	58	80	215	....	....	....	....	....	....	1943-44	1953-54
Bulley, Ted	Chi., Wsh., Pit.	8	414	101	113	214	704	29	5	5	10	24	....	1976-77	1983-84
Burakovsky, Robert	Ott.	1	23	2	3	5	6	....	....	....	....	....	....	1993-94	1993-94
• Burch, Billy	Ham., NYA, Bos., Chi.	11	390	137	61	198	255	2	0	0	0	0	....	1922-23	1932-33
• Burchell, Fred	Mtl.	2	4	0	0	0	2	....	....	....	....	....	....	1950-51	1953-54
Burdon, Glen	K.C.	1	11	0	2	2	0	....	....	....	....	....	....	1974-75	1974-75
Burega, Bill	Tor.	1	4	0	1	1	4	....	....	....	....	....	....	1955-56	1955-56
• Burke, Eddie	Bos., NYA	4	106	29	20	49	55	....	....	....	....	....	....	1931-32	1934-35
• Burke, Marty	Mtl.C., Pit., Ott., Chi.	11	494	19	47	66	560	31	2	4	6	44	2	1927-28	1937-38
• Burmeister, Roy	NYA	3	67	4	3	7	2	....	....	....	....	....	....	1929-30	1931-32
Burnett, Kelly	NYR	1	3	1	0	1	0	....	....	....	....	....	....	1952-53	1952-53
• Burns, Bobby	Chi.	3	20	1	0	1	8	....	....	....	....	....	....	1927-28	1929-30
Burns, Charlie	Det., Bos., Oak., Pit., Min.	11	749	106	198	304	252	31	5	4	9	6	....	1958-59	1972-73
Burns, Gary	NYR	2	11	2	2	4	18	5	0	0	0	2	....	1980-81	1981-82
• Burns, Norm	NYR	1	11	0	4	4	2	....	....	....	....	....	....	1941-42	1941-42
Burns, Robin	Pit., K.C.	5	190	31	38	69	139	....	....	....	....	....	....	1970-71	1975-76
Burr, Shawn	Det., T.B., S.J.	16	878	181	259	440	1069	91	16	19	35	95	....	1984-85	1999-00
Burridge, Randy	Bos., Wsh., L.A., Buf.	13	706	199	251	450	458	107	18	34	52	103	....	1985-86	1997-98
Burrows, Dave	Pit., Tor.	10	724	29	135	164	373	29	1	5	6	25	....	1971-72	1980-81
• Burry, Bert	Ott.	1	4	0	0	0	0	....	....	....	....	....	....	1932-33	1932-33
Burton, Cummy	Det.	3	43	0	2	2	21	3	0	0	0	0	....	1955-56	1958-59
Burton, Nelson	Wsh.	2	8	1	0	1	21	....	....	....	....	....	....	1977-78	1978-79
• Bush, Eddie	Det.	2	26	4	6	10	40	11	1	6	7	23	....	1938-39	1941-42
Buskas, Rod	Pit., Van., L.A., Chi.	11	556	19	63	82	1294	18	0	3	3	45	....	1982-83	1992-93
Busniuk, Mike	Phi.	2	143	3	23	26	297	25	2	5	7	34	....	1979-80	1980-81
Busniuk, Ron	Buf.	2	6	0	3	3	13	....	....	....	....	....	....	1972-73	1973-74
• Buswell, Walt	Det., Mtl.C., Mtl.	8	368	10	40	50	164	24	2	1	3	10	....	1932-33	1939-40
Butcher, Garth	Van., St.L., Que., Tor.	14	897	48	158	206	2302	50	6	5	11	122	....	1981-82	1994-95
Butler, Dick	Chi.	1	7	2	0	2	0	....	....	....	....	....	....	1947-48	1947-48
Butler, Jerry	NYR, St.L., Tor., Van., Wpg.	11	641	99	120	219	515	48	3	3	6	79	....	1972-73	1982-83
Butters, Bill	Min.	2	72	1	4	5	77	....	....	....	....	....	....	1977-78	1978-79
Buttrey, Gord	Chi.	1	10	0	0	0	0	....	....	....	....	....	....	1943-44	1943-44
Buynak, Gord	St.L.	1	4	0	0	0	2	....	....	....	....	....	....	1974-75	1974-75
‡ Byakin, Ilja	Edm., S.J.	2	57	8	25	33	44	....	....	....	....	....	....	1993-94	1994-95
Byce, John	Bos.	3	21	2	3	5	6	8	2	0	2	2	....	1989-90	1991-92
Byers, Gord	Bos.	1	1	0	1	1	0	....	....	....	....	....	....	1949-50	1949-50
Byers, Jerry	Min., Atl., NYR	4	43	3	4	7	15	....	....	....	....	....	....	1972-73	1977-78
Byers, Lyndon	Bos., S.J.	10	279	28	43	71	1081	37	2	2	4	96	....	1983-84	1992-93
Byers, Mike	Tor., Phi., L.A., Buf.	4	166	42	34	76	39	4	0	1	1	0	....	1967-68	1971-72
Byram, Shawn	NYI, Chi.	2	5	0	0	0	14	....	....	....	....	....	....	1990-91	1991-92

C

• Caffery, Jack	Tor., Bos.	3	57	3	2	5	22	10	1	0	1	4	....	1954-55	1957-58
Caffery, Terry	Chi., Min.	2	14	0	0	0	0	1	0	0	0	0	....	1969-70	1970-71
• Cahan, Larry	Tor., NYR, Oak., L.A.	13	666	38	92	130	700	29	1	1	2	38	....	1954-55	1970-71

			Regular Schedule					Playoffs							
Name	**NHL Teams**	**NHL Seasons**	**GP**	**G**	**A**	**TP**	**PIM**	**GP**	**G**	**A**	**TP**	**PIM**	**NHL Cup Wins**	**First NHL Season**	**Last NHL Season**
● Cahill, Charles	Bos.	2	32	0	1	1	4	....	....	....	....	....	....	1925-26	1926-27
● Cain, Francis	Mtl.M., Tor.	2	61	4	0	4	35	....	....	....	....	....	....	1924-25	1925-26
● Cain, Herb	Mtl.M., Mtl.C., Bos.	13	570	206	194	400	178	67	16	13	29	13	2	1933-34	1945-46
Cairns, Don	K.C., Col.	2	9	0	1	1	2	....	....	....	....	....	....	1975-76	1976-77
Calder, Eric	Wsh.	2	2	0	0	0	0	....	....	....	....	....	....	1981-82	1982-83
● Calladine, Norm	Bos.	3	63	19	29	48	8	....	....	....	....	....	....	1942-43	1944-45
Callander, Drew	Phi., Van.	4	39	6	2	8	7	....	....	....	....	....	....	1976-77	1979-80
Callander, Jock	Pit., T.B.	5	109	22	29	51	116	22	3	8	11	12	1	1987-88	1992-93
Callighen, Brett	Edm.	3	160	56	89	145	132	14	4	6	10	8	....	1979-80	1981-82
Callighen, Patsy	NYR	1	36	0	0	0	32	9	0	0	0	0	1	1927-28	1927-28
‡ Camazzola, James	Chi.	2	3	0	0	0	0	....	....	....	....	....	....	1983-84	1986-87
Camazzola, Tony	Wsh.	1	3	0	0	0	4	....	....	....	....	....	....	1981-82	1981-82
Cameron, Al	Det., Wpg.	6	282	11	44	55	356	7	0	1	1	2	....	1975-76	1980-81
● Cameron, Billy	Mtl.C., NYA	2	39	0	0	0	2	2	0	0	0	0	1	1923-24	1925-26
Cameron, Craig	Det., St.L., Min., NYI	9	552	87	65	152	196	27	3	1	4	17	....	1966-67	1975-76
Cameron, Dave	Col., N.J.	3	168	25	28	53	238	....	....	....	....	....	....	1981-82	1983-84
● Cameron, Harry	Tor., Ott., Mtl.C.	6	128	88	51	139	189	11	5	4	9	16	2	1917-18	1922-23
● Cameron, Scotty	NYR	1	35	8	11	19	0	....	....	....	....	....	....	1942-43	1942-43
Campbell, Bryan	L.A., Chi.	5	260	35	71	106	74	22	3	4	7	2	....	1967-68	1971-72
Campbell, Colin	Pit., Col., Edm., Van., Det.	11	636	25	103	128	1292	45	4	10	14	181	....	1974-75	1984-85
● Campbell, Dave	Mtl.C.	1	2	0	0	0	0	....	....	....	....	....	....	1920-21	1920-21
Campbell, Don	Chi.	1	17	1	3	4	8	....	....	....	....	....	....	1943-44	1943-44
● Campbell, Earl	Ott., NYA	3	76	6	3	9	14	1	0	0	0	6	....	1923-24	1925-26
Campbell, Scott	Wpg., St.L.	3	80	4	21	25	243	....	....	....	....	....	....	1979-80	1981-82
Campbell, Wade	Wpg., Bos.	6	213	9	27	36	305	10	0	0	0	20	....	1982-83	1987-88
Campeau, Tod	Mtl.	3	42	5	9	14	16	1	0	0	0	0	....	1943-44	1948-49
Campedelli, Dom	Mtl.	1	2	0	0	0	0	....	....	....	....	....	....	1985-86	1985-86
Capuano, Dave	Pit., Van., T.B., S.J.	4	104	17	38	55	56	6	1	1	2	5	....	1989-90	1993-94
Capuano, Jack	Tor., Van., Bos.	3	6	0	0	0	0	....	....	....	....	....	....	1989-90	1991-92
Carbol, Leo	Chi.	1	6	0	1	1	4	....	....	....	....	....	....	1942-43	1942-43
Carbonneau, Guy	Mtl., St.L., Dal.	19	1318	260	403	663	820	231	38	55	93	161	3	1980-81	1999-00
Cardin, Claude	St.L.	1	1	0	0	0	0	....	....	....	....	....	....	1967-68	1967-68
Cardwell, Steve	Pit.	3	53	9	11	20	35	4	0	0	0	2	....	1970-71	1972-73
● Carey, George	Que., Ham., Tor.	5	72	21	12	33	20	....	....	....	....	....	....	1919-20	1923-24
Carkner, Terry	NYR, Que., Phi., Det., Fla.	13	858	42	188	230	1588	54	1	9	10	48	....	1986-87	1998-99
Carleton, Wayne	Tor., Bos., Cal.	7	278	55	73	128	172	18	2	4	6	14	1	1965-66	1971-72
Carlin, Brian	L.A.	1	5	1	0	1	0	....	....	....	....	....	....	1971-72	1971-72
Carlson, Jack	Min., St.L.	6	236	30	15	45	417	25	1	2	3	72	....	1978-79	1986-87
Carlson, Kent	Mtl., St.L., Wsh.	5	113	7	11	18	148	8	0	0	0	13	....	1983-84	1988-89
Carlson, Steve	L.A.	1	52	9	12	21	23	4	1	1	2	7	....	1979-80	1979-80
‡ Carlsson, Anders	N.J.	3	104	7	26	33	34	3	1	0	1	2	....	1986-87	1988-89
Carlyle, Randy	Tor., Pit., Wpg.	17	1055	148	499	647	1400	69	9	24	33	120	....	1976-77	1992-93
‡ Carnback, Patrik	Mtl., Ana.	4	154	24	38	62	122	....	....	....	....	....	....	1992-93	1995-96
● Caron, Alain	Oak., Mtl.	2	60	9	13	22	18	....	....	....	....	....	....	1967-68	1968-69
Carpenter, Bob	Wsh., NYR, L.A., Bos., N.J.	18	1178	320	408	728	919	140	21	38	59	136	1	1981-82	1998-99
● Carpenter, Ed	Que., Ham.	2	45	10	5	15	41	....	....	....	....	....	....	1919-20	1920-21
Carr, Gene	St.L., NYR, L.A., Pit., Atl.	8	465	79	136	215	365	35	5	8	13	66	....	1971-72	1978-79
Carr, Lorne	NYR, NYA, Tor.	13	580	204	222	426	132	53	10	9	19	13	2	1933-34	1945-46
Carr, Red	Tor.	1	5	0	1	1	2	....	....	....	....	....	....	1943-44	1943-44
Carriere, Larry	Buf., Atl., Van., L.A., Tor.	7	367	16	74	90	462	27	0	3	3	42	....	1972-73	1979-80
● Carrigan, Gene	NYR, Det., St.L.	3	37	2	1	3	13	4	0	0	0	0	....	1930-31	1934-35
Carroll, Billy	NYI, Edm., Det.	7	322	30	54	84	113	71	6	12	18	18	4	1980-81	1986-87
● Carroll, George	Mtl.M., Bos.	1	16	0	0	0	11	....	....	....	....	....	....	1924-25	1924-25
Carroll, Greg	Wsh., Det., Hfd.	2	131	20	34	54	44	....	....	....	....	....	....	1978-79	1979-80
Carruthers, Dwight	Det., Phi.	2	2	0	0	0	0	....	....	....	....	....	....	1965-66	1967-68
● Carse, Bill	NYR, Chi.	4	124	28	43	71	38	13	3	2	5	0	....	1938-39	1941-42
● Carse, Bob	Chi., Mtl.	5	167	32	55	87	52	10	0	2	2	2	....	1939-40	1947-48
● Carson, Bill	Tor., Bos.	4	159	54	24	78	156	11	3	0	3	14	1	1926-27	1929-30
● Carson, Frank	Mtl.M., NYA, Det.	7	248	42	48	90	166	27	0	2	2	9	1	1925-26	1933-34
● Carson, Gerry	Mtl.C., NYR, Mtl.M.	6	261	12	11	23	205	22	0	0	0	12	1	1928-29	1936-37
Carson, Jimmy	L.A., Edm., Det., Van., Hfd.	10	626	275	286	561	254	55	17	15	32	22	....	1986-87	1995-96
Carson, Lindsay	Phi., Hfd.	7	373	66	80	146	524	49	4	10	14	56	....	1981-82	1987-88
Carter, Billy	Mtl., Bos.	3	16	0	0	0	6	....	....	....	....	....	....	1957-58	1961-62
Carter, John	Bos., S.J.	8	244	40	50	90	201	31	7	5	12	51	....	1985-86	1992-93
Carter, Ron	Edm.	1	2	0	0	0	0	....	....	....	....	....	....	1979-80	1979-80
● Carveth, Joe	Det., Bos., Mtl.	11	504	150	189	339	81	69	21	16	37	28	2	1940-41	1950-51
Cashman, Wayne	Bos.	17	1027	277	516	793	1041	145	31	57	88	250	2	1964-65	1982-83
‡ Casselman, Mike	Fla.	1	3	0	0	0	0	....	....	....	....	....	....	1995-96	1995-96
Cassidy, Bruce	Chi.	6	36	4	13	17	10	1	0	0	0	0	....	1983-84	1989-90
Cassidy, Tom	Pit.	1	26	3	4	7	15	....	....	....	....	....	....	1977-78	1977-78
Cassolato, Tony	Wsh.	3	23	1	6	7	4	....	....	....	....	....	....	1979-80	1981-82
Caufield, Jay	NYR, Min., Pit.	7	208	5	8	13	759	17	0	0	0	42	2	1986-87	1992-93
‡ Cavallini, Gino	Cgy., St.L., Que.	9	593	114	159	273	507	74	14	19	33	66	....	1984-85	1992-93
Cavallini, Paul	Wsh., St.L., Dal.	10	564	56	177	233	750	69	8	27	35	114	....	1986-87	1995-96
Ceresino, Ray	Tor.	1	12	1	1	2	2	....	....	....	....	....	....	1948-49	1948-49
Cernik, Frantisek	Det.	1	49	5	4	9	13	....	....	....	....	....	....	1984-85	1984-85
‡ Chabot, John	Mtl., Pit., Det.	8	508	84	228	312	85	33	6	20	26	2	....	1983-84	1990-91
● Chad, John	Chi.	3	80	15	22	37	29	10	0	1	1	2	....	1939-40	1945-46
● Chalmers, Chick	NYR	1	1	0	0	0	0	....	....	....	....	....	....	1953-54	1953-54
Chalupa, Milan	Det.	1	14	0	5	5	6	....	....	....	....	....	....	1984-85	1984-85
● Chamberlain, Murph	Tor., Mtl., Bro., Bos.	12	510	100	175	275	769	66	14	17	31	96	2	1937-38	1948-49
Chambers, Shawn	Min., Wsh., T.B., N.J., Dal.	13	625	50	185	235	364	94	7	26	33	72	2	1987-88	1999-00
Champagne, Andre	Tor.	1	2	0	0	0	0	....	....	....	....	....	....	1962-63	1962-63
‡ Chapdelaine, Rene	L.A.	3	32	0	2	2	32	....	....	....	....	....	....	1990-91	1992-93
● Chapman, Art	Bos., NYA	10	438	62	176	238	140	26	1	5	6	9	....	1930-31	1939-40
Chapman, Blair	Pit., St.L.	7	402	106	125	231	158	25	4	6	10	15	....	1976-77	1982-83
‡ Chapman, Brian	Hfd.	1	3	0	0	0	29	....	....	....	....	....	....	1990-91	1990-91
‡ Charbonneau, Jose	Mtl., Van.	4	71	9	13	22	67	11	1	0	1	8	....	1987-88	1994-95
Charbonneau, Stephane	Que.	1	2	0	0	0	0	....	....	....	....	....	....	1991-92	1991-92
Charlebois, Bob	Min.	1	7	1	0	1	0	....	....	....	....	....	....	1967-68	1967-68
Charlesworth, Todd	Pit., NYR	6	93	3	9	12	47	....	....	....	....	....	....	1983-84	1989-90
Charron, Guy	Mtl., Det., K.C., Wsh.	12	734	221	309	530	146	....	....	....	....	....	....	1969-70	1980-81
Chartier, Dave	Wpg.	1	1	0	0	0	0	....	....	....	....	....	....	1980-81	1980-81
Chartraw, Rick	Mtl., L.A., NYR, Edm.	10	420	28	64	92	399	75	7	9	16	80	4	1974-75	1983-84
Chase, Kelly	St.L., Hfd., Tor.	11	458	17	36	53	2017	27	1	1	2	100	....	1989-90	1999-00
Chasse, Denis	St.L., Wsh., Wpg., Ott.	4	132	11	14	25	292	7	1	7	8	23	....	1993-94	1996-97
Check, Lude	Det., Chi.	2	27	6	2	8	4	....	....	....	....	....	....	1943-44	1944-45
Chernoff, Mike	Min.	1	1	0	0	0	0	....	....	....	....	....	....	1968-69	1968-69
Chernomaz, Rich	Col., N.J., Cgy.	7	51	9	7	16	18	....	....	....	....	....	....	1981-82	1991-92
Cherry, Dick	Bos., Phi.	3	145	12	10	22	45	4	1	0	1	4	....	1956-57	1969-70
Cherry, Don	Bos.	1	....	....	....	....	....	1	0	0	0	0	....	1954-55	1954-55
‡ Chervyakov, Denis	Bos.	1	2	0	0	0	2	....	....	....	....	....	....	1992-93	1992-93
● Chevrefils, Real	Bos., Det.	8	387	104	97	201	185	30	5	4	9	20	....	1951-52	1958-59
● Chiasson, Steve	Det., Cgy., Hfd., Car.	13	751	93	305	398	1107	63	16	19	35	119	....	1986-87	1998-99
‡ Chibirev, Igor	Hfd.	2	45	7	12	19	2	....	....	....	....	....	....	1993-94	1994-95
Chicoine, Dan	Cle., Min.	3	31	1	2	3	12	1	0	0	0	0	....	1977-78	1979-80
Chinnick, Rick	Min.	2	4	0	2	2	0	....	....	....	....	....	....	1973-74	1974-75
Chipperfield, Ron	Edm., Que.	2	83	22	24	46	34	....	....	....	....	....	....	1979-80	1980-81
Chisholm, Art	Bos.	1	3	0	0	0	0	....	....	....	....	....	....	1960-61	1960-61
Chisholm, Colin	Min.	1	1	0	0	0	0	....	....	....	....	....	....	1986-87	1986-87
● Chisholm, Lex	Tor.	2	54	10	8	18	19	3	1	0	1	0	....	1939-40	1940-41
Chorney, Marc	Pit., L.A.	4	210	8	27	35	209	7	0	1	1	2	....	1980-81	1983-84
● Chouinard, Gene	Ott.	1	8	0	0	0	0	....	....	....	....	....	....	1927-28	1927-28
Chouinard, Guy	Atl., Cgy., St.L.	10	578	205	370	575	120	46	9	28	37	12	....	1974-75	1983-84
Christian, Dave	Wpg., Wsh., Bos., St.L., Chi.	15	1009	340	433	773	284	102	32	25	57	27	....	1979-80	1993-94
Christie, Mike	Cal., Cle., Col., Van.	7	412	15	101	116	550	2	0	0	0	0	....	1974-75	1980-81
Christoff, Steve	Min., Cgy., L.A.	5	248	77	64	141	108	35	16	12	28	25	....	1979-80	1983-84
Chrystal, Bob	NYR	2	132	11	14	25	112	....	....	....	....	....	....	1953-54	1954-55
● Church, Jack	Tor., Bro., Bos.	5	130	4	19	23	154	25	1	1	2	18	....	1938-39	1945-46
Churla, Shane	Hfd., Cgy., Min., Dal., L.A., NYR	11	488	26	45	71	2301	78	5	7	12	282	....	1986-87	1996-97
Chychrun, Jeff	Phi., L.A., Pit., Edm.	8	262	3	22	25	744	19	0	2	2	65	1	1986-87	1993-94
Chynoweth, Dean	NYI, Bos.	9	241	4	18	22	667	6	0	0	0	26	....	1988-89	1997-98
‡ Chyzowski, Dave	NYI, Chi.	6	126	15	16	31	144	2	0	0	0	0	....	1989-90	1996-97
‡ Ciavaglia, Peter	Buf.	2	5	0	0	0	0	....	....	....	....	....	....	1991-92	1992-93
Ciccarelli, Dino	Min., Wsh., Det., T.B., Fla.	19	1232	608	592	1200	1425	141	73	45	118	211	....	1980-81	1998-99
Cichocki, Chris	Det., N.J.	4	68	11	12	23	27	....	....	....	....	....	....	1985-86	1988-89

Jock Callender

Guy Carboneau

Shawn Chambers

Kelly Chase

Dit Clapper

Wendel Clark

Pete Conacher

Geoff Courtnall

			Regular Schedule					Playoffs					NHL	First	Last
Name	NHL Teams	NHL Seasons	GP	G	A	TP	PIM	GP	G	A	TP	PIM	Cup Wins	NHL Season	NHL Season
• Ciesla, Hank	Chi., NYR	4	269	26	51	77	87	6	0	2	2	0	....	1955-56	1958-59
‡ Cimellaro, Tony	Ott.	1	2	0	0	0	0	....	....	....	....	....	....	1992-93	1992-93
‡ Cimetta, Rob	Bos., Tor.	4	103	16	16	32	66	1	0	0	0	15	....	1988-89	1991-92
Cirella, Joe	Col., N.J., Que., NYR, Fla., Ott.	15	828	64	211	275	1446	38	0	13	13	98	....	1981-82	1995-96
‡ Cirone, Jason	Wpg.	1	3	0	0	0	2	....	....	....	....	....	....	1991-92	1991-92
Clackson, Kim	Pit., Que.	2	106	0	8	8	370	8	0	0	0	70	....	1979-80	1980-81
• Clancy, King	Ott., Tor.	16	592	136	147	283	914	55	8	8	16	92	3	1921-22	1936-37
Clancy, Terry	Oak., Tor.	4	93	6	6	12	39	....	....	....	....	....	....	1967-68	1972-73
• Clapper, Dit	Bos.	20	833	228	246	474	462	82	13	17	30	50	3	1927-28	1946-47
Clark, Dan	NYR	1	4	0	1	1	6	....	....	....	....	....	....	1978-79	1978-79
Clark, Dean	Edm.	1	1	0	0	0	0	....	....	....	....	....	....	1983-84	1983-84
Clark, Gordie	Bos.	2	8	0	1	1	0	1	0	0	0	0	....	1974-75	1975-76
• Clark, Nobby	Bos.	1	5	0	0	0	0	....	....	....	....	....	....	1927-28	1927-28
Clark, Wendel	Tor., Que., NYI, T.B., Det., Chi.	15	793	330	234	564	1690	95	37	32	69	201	....	1985-86	1999-00
Clarke, Bobby	Phi.	15	1144	358	852	1210	1453	136	42	77	119	152	2	1969-70	1983-84
• Cleghorn, Odie	Mtl.C., Pit.	10	181	95	34	129	142	12	7	1	8	2	1	1918-19	1927-28
• Cleghorn, Sprague	Ott., Tor., Mtl.C., Bos.	10	259	83	55	138	538	21	4	2	6	28	2	1918-19	1927-28
Clement, Bill	Phi., Wsh., Atl., Cgy.	11	719	148	208	356	383	50	5	3	8	26	2	1971-72	1981-82
Cline, Bruce	NYR	1	30	2	3	5	10	....	....	....	....	....	....	1956-57	1956-57
Clippingdale, Steve	L.A., Wsh.	2	19	1	2	3	9	1	0	0	0	0	....	1976-77	1979-80
Cloutier, Real	Que., Buf.	6	317	146	198	344	119	25	7	5	12	20	....	1979-80	1984-85
Cloutier, Rejean	Det.	2	5	0	2	2	2	....	....	....	....	....	....	1979-80	1981-82
Cloutier, Roland	Det., Que.	3	34	8	9	17	2	....	....	....	....	....	....	1977-78	1979-80
• Clune, Wally	Mtl.	1	5	0	0	0	6	....	....	....	....	....	....	1955-56	1955-56
Coalter, Gary	Cal., K.C.	2	34	2	4	6	2	....	....	....	....	....	....	1973-74	1974-75
Coates, Steve	Det.	1	5	1	0	1	24	....	....	....	....	....	....	1976-77	1976-77
Cochrane, Glen	Phi., Van., Chi., Edm.	10	411	17	72	89	1556	18	1	1	2	31	....	1978-79	1988-89
Coflin, Hugh	Chi.	1	31	0	3	3	33	....	....	....	....	....	....	1950-51	1950-51
Cole, Danton	Wpg., T.B., N.J., NYI, Chi.	7	318	58	60	118	125	1	0	0	0	0	1	1989-90	1995-96
Colley, Tom	Min.	1	1	0	0	0	2	....	....	....	....	....	....	1974-75	1974-75
Collings, Norm	Mtl.C.	1	1	0	1	1	0	....	....	....	....	....	....	1934-35	1934-35
Collins, Bill	Min., Mtl., Det., St.L., NYR, Phi., Wsh.	11	768	157	154	311	415	18	3	5	8	12	....	1967-68	1977-78
Collins, Gary	Tor.	1	....	....	....	....	....	2	0	0	0	0	....	1958-59	1958-59
Collyard, Bob	St.L.	1	10	1	3	4	4	....	....	....	....	....	....	1973-74	1973-74
• Colman, Michael	S.J.	1	15	0	1	1	32	....	....	....	....	....	....	1991-92	1991-92
Colville, Mac	NYR	9	353	71	104	175	130	40	9	10	19	14	1	1935-36	1946-47
• Colville, Neil	NYR	12	464	99	166	265	213	46	7	19	26	32	1	1935-36	1948-49
Colwill, Les	NYR	1	69	7	6	13	16	....	....	....	....	....	....	1958-59	1958-59
Comeau, Rey	Mtl., Atl., Col.	9	564	98	141	239	175	9	2	1	3	8	....	1971-72	1979-80
Conacher, Brian	Tor., Det.	5	155	28	28	56	84	12	3	2	5	21	1	1961-62	1971-72
• Conacher, Charlie	Tor., Det., NYA	12	459	225	173	398	523	49	17	18	35	49	1	1929-30	1940-41
Conacher, Jim	Det., Chi., NYR	8	328	85	117	202	91	19	5	2	7	4	....	1945-46	1952-53
• Conacher, Lionel	Pit., NYA, Mtl.M., Chi.	12	498	80	105	185	882	35	2	2	4	34	2	1925-26	1936-37
Conacher, Pat	NYR, Edm., N.J., L.A., Cgy., NYI	13	521	63	76	139	235	66	11	10	21	40	1	1979-80	1995-96
Conacher, Pete	Chi., NYR, Tor.	6	229	47	39	86	57	7	0	0	0	0	....	1951-52	1957-58
• Conacher, Roy	Bos., Det., Chi.	11	490	226	200	426	90	42	15	15	30	14	2	1938-39	1951-52
• Conn, Red	NYA	2	96	9	28	37	22	....	....	....	....	....	....	1933-34	1934-35
Conn, Rob	Chi., Buf.	2	30	2	5	7	20	....	....	....	....	....	....	1991-92	1995-96
• Connelly, Bert	NYR, Chi.	3	87	13	15	28	37	14	1	0	1	0	1	1934-35	1937-38
Connelly, Wayne	Mtl., Bos., Min., Det., St.L., Van.	10	543	133	174	307	156	24	11	7	18	4	....	1960-61	1971-72
Connor, Cam	Mtl., Edm., NYR	5	89	9	22	31	256	20	5	0	5	6	1	1978-79	1982-83
• Connor, Harry	Bos., NYA, Ott.	4	134	16	5	21	149	10	0	0	0	2	....	1927-28	1930-31
• Connors, Bob	NYA, Det.	3	78	17	10	27	110	2	0	0	0	10	....	1926-27	1929-30
‡ Conroy, Al	Phi.	3	114	9	14	23	156	....	....	....	....	....	....	1991-92	1993-94
Contini, Joe	Col., Min.	3	68	17	21	38	34	2	0	0	0	0	....	1977-78	1980-81
‡ Convery, Brandon	Tor., Van., L.A.	4	72	9	19	28	36	5	0	0	0	2	....	1995-96	1998-99
• Convey, Eddie	NYA	3	36	1	1	2	33	....	....	....	....	....	....	1930-31	1932-33
• Cook, Bill	NYR	11	474	229	138	367	386	46	13	11	24	68	2	1926-27	1936-37
• Cook, Bob	Van., Det., NYI, Min.	4	72	13	9	22	22	....	....	....	....	....	....	1970-71	1974-75
• Cook, Bud	Bos., Ott., St.L.	3	50	5	4	9	22	....	....	....	....	....	....	1931-32	1934-35
• Cook, Bun	NYR, Bos.	11	473	158	144	302	444	46	15	3	18	50	2	1926-27	1936-37
• Cook, Lloyd	Bos.	1	4	1	0	1	0	....	....	....	....	....	....	1924-25	1924-25
• Cook, Tom	Chi., Mtl.M.	9	349	77	98	175	184	24	2	4	6	19	1	1929-30	1937-38
• Cooper, Carson	Bos., Mtl.C., Det.	8	294	110	57	167	111	7	0	0	0	2	....	1924-25	1931-32
Cooper, Ed	Col.	2	49	8	7	15	46	....	....	....	....	....	....	1980-81	1981-82
• Cooper, Hal	NYR	1	8	0	0	0	2	....	....	....	....	....	....	1944-45	1944-45
• Cooper, Joe	NYR, Chi.	11	420	30	66	96	442	35	3	5	8	58	....	1935-36	1946-47
Copp, Bob	Tor.	2	40	3	9	12	26	....	....	....	....	....	....	1942-43	1950-51
• Corbeau, Bert	Mtl.C., Ham., Tor.	10	258	63	49	112	629	9	2	2	4	38	....	1917-18	1926-27
Corbett, Mike	L.A.	1	....	....	....	....	....	2	0	1	1	2	....	1967-68	1967-68
Corcoran, Norm	Bos., Det., Chi.	4	29	1	3	4	21	4	0	0	0	6	....	1949-50	1955-56
• Cormier, Roger	Mtl.C.	1	1	0	0	0	0	....	....	....	....	....	....	1925-26	1925-26
Cornforth, Mark	Bos.	1	6	0	0	0	4	....	....	....	....	....	....	1995-96	1995-96
Corrigan, Chuck	Tor., NYA	2	19	2	2	4	2	....	....	....	....	....	....	1937-38	1940-41
Corrigan, Mike	L.A., Van., Pit.	10	594	152	195	347	698	17	2	3	5	20	....	1967-68	1977-78
• Corriveau, Andre	Mtl.	1	3	0	1	1	0	....	....	....	....	....	....	1953-54	1953-54
‡ Corriveau, Yvon	Wsh., Hfd., S.J.	9	280	48	40	88	310	29	5	7	12	50	....	1985-86	1993-94
Cory, Ross	Wpg.	2	51	2	10	12	41	....	....	....	....	....	....	1979-80	1980-81
Cossette, Jacques	Pit.	3	64	8	6	14	29	3	0	1	1	4	....	1975-76	1978-79
Costello, Les	Tor.	3	15	2	3	5	11	6	2	2	4	2	1	1947-48	1949-50
Costello, Murray	Chi., Bos., Det.	4	162	13	19	32	54	5	0	0	0	2	....	1953-54	1956-57
Costello, Rich	Tor.	2	12	2	2	4	2	....	....	....	....	....	....	1983-84	1985-86
• Cotch, Charlie	Ham., Tor.	1	12	1	0	1	0	....	....	....	....	....	....	1924-25	1924-25
Cote, Alain	Que.	10	696	103	190	293	383	67	9	15	24	44	....	1979-80	1988-89
‡ Cote, Alain	Bos., Wsh., Mtl., T.B., Que.	9	119	2	18	20	124	11	0	2	2	26	....	1985-86	1993-94
Cote, Ray	Edm.	3	15	0	0	0	4	14	3	2	5	0	....	1982-83	1984-85
• Cotton, Baldy	Pit., Tor., NYA	12	503	101	103	204	419	43	4	9	13	46	1	1925-26	1936-37
• Coughlin, Jack	Tor., Que., Mtl.C., Ham.	3	19	2	0	2	3	....	....	....	....	....	1	1917-18	1920-21
Coulis, Tim	Wsh., Min.	4	47	4	5	9	138	3	1	0	1	2	....	1979-80	1985-86
Coulson, D'arcy	Phi.	1	28	0	0	0	103	....	....	....	....	....	....	1930-31	1930-31
• Coulter, Art	Chi., NYR	11	465	30	82	112	543	49	4	5	9	61	2	1931-32	1941-42
Coulter, Neal	NYI	3	26	5	5	10	11	....	....	....	....	....	....	1985-86	1987-88
Cournoyer, Yvan	Mtl.	16	968	428	435	863	255	147	64	63	127	47	10	1963-64	1978-79
Courteau, Yves	Cgy., Hfd.	3	22	2	5	7	4	1	0	0	0	0	....	1984-85	1986-87
Courtenay, Ed	S.J.	2	44	7	13	20	10	....	....	....	....	....	....	1991-92	1992-93
Courtnall, Geoff	Bos., Edm., Wsh., St.L., Van.	17	1048	367	432	799	1465	156	39	70	109	262	1	1983-84	1999-00
Courtnall, Russ	Tor., Mtl., Min., Dal., Van., NYR, L.A.	16	1029	297	447	744	557	129	39	44	83	83	....	1983-84	1998-99
• Coutu, Billy	Mtl.C., Ham., Bos.	10	244	33	21	54	478	19	1	1	2	35	1	1917-18	1926-27
• Couture, Gerry	Det., Mtl., Chi.	10	385	86	70	156	89	45	9	7	16	4	1	1944-45	1953-54
• Couture, Rosie	Chi., Mtl.C.	8	309	48	56	104	184	23	1	5	6	15	1	1928-29	1935-36
‡ Couturier, Sylvain	L.A.	3	33	4	5	9	4	....	....	....	....	....	....	1988-89	1991-92
Cowick, Bruce	Phi., Wsh., St.L.	3	70	5	6	11	43	8	0	0	0	9	1	1973-74	1975-76
‡ Cowie, Rob	L.A.	2	78	7	12	19	52	....	....	....	....	....	....	1994-95	1995-96
• Cowley, Bill	St.L., Bos.	13	549	195	353	548	143	64	12	34	46	22	2	1934-35	1946-47
• Cox, Danny	Tor., Ott., Det., NYR	8	319	47	49	96	128	10	0	1	1	6	....	1926-27	1933-34
‡ Coxe, Craig	Van., Cgy., St.L., S.J.	8	235	14	31	45	713	5	1	0	1	18	....	1984-85	1991-92
‡ Craighead, John	Tor.	1	5	0	0	0	10	....	....	....	....	....	....	1996-97	1996-97
‡ Craigwell, Dale	S.J.	3	98	11	18	29	28	....	....	....	....	....	....	1991-92	1993-94
Crashley, Bart	Det., K.C., L.A.	6	140	7	36	43	50	....	....	....	....	....	....	1965-66	1975-76
Craven, Murray	Det., Phi., Hfd., Van., Chi., S.J.	18	1071	266	493	759	524	118	27	43	70	64	....	1982-83	1999-00
Crawford, Bob	St.L., Hfd., NYR, Wsh.	7	246	71	71	142	72	11	0	1	1	8	....	1979-80	1986-87
Crawford, Bobby	Col., Det.	2	16	1	3	4	6	....	....	....	....	....	....	1980-81	1982-83
• Crawford, Jack	Bos.	13	548	38	140	178	202	66	3	13	16	36	2	1937-38	1949-50
Crawford, Lou	Bos.	2	26	2	1	3	29	1	0	0	0	0	....	1989-90	1991-92
Crawford, Marc	Van.	6	176	19	31	50	229	20	1	2	3	44	....	1981-82	1986-87
• Crawford, Rusty	Ott., Tor.	2	38	10	8	18	117	2	2	1	3	9	1	1917-18	1918-19
Creighton, Adam	Buf., Chi., NYI, T.B., St.L.	14	708	187	216	403	1077	61	11	14	25	137	....	1983-84	1996-97
Creighton, Dave	Bos., Tor., Chi., NYR	12	616	140	174	314	223	51	11	13	24	20	....	1948-49	1959-60
• Creighton, Jimmy	Det.	1	11	1	0	1	2	....	....	....	....	....	....	1930-31	1930-31
Cressman, Dave	Min.	2	85	6	8	14	37	....	....	....	....	....	....	1974-75	1975-76
Cressman, Glen	Mtl.	1	4	0	0	0	2	....	....	....	....	....	....	1956-57	1956-57
Crisp, Terry	Bos., St.L., NYI, Phi.	11	536	67	134	201	135	110	15	28	43	40	2	1965-66	1976-77
Cristofoli, Ed	Mtl.	1	9	0	1	1	4	....	....	....	....	....	....	1989-90	1989-90
• Croghan, Maurice	Mtl.M.	1	16	0	0	0	4	....	....	....	....	....	....	1937-38	1937-38
Crombeen, Mike	Cle., St.L., Hfd.	8	475	55	68	123	218	27	6	2	8	32	....	1977-78	1984-85
Cronin, Shawn	Wsh., Wpg., Phi., S.J.	7	292	3	18	21	877	32	1	0	1	38	....	1988-89	1994-95

			Regular Schedule					Playoffs							
Name	NHL Teams	NHL Seasons	GP	G	A	TP	PIM	GP	G	A	TP	PIM	NHL Cup Wins	First NHL Season	Last NHL Season
• Crossett, Stan	Phi.	1	21	0	0	0	10	....	....	....	....	....	....	1930-31	1930-31
Crossman, Doug	Chi., Phi., L.A., NYI, Hfd., Det., T.B., St.L.	14	914	105	359	464	534	97	12	39	51	105	....	1980-81	1993-94
Croteau, Gary	L.A., Det., Cal., K.C., Col.	12	684	144	175	319	143	11	3	2	5	8	....	1968-69	1979-80
Crowder, Bruce	Bos., Pit.	4	243	47	51	98	156	31	8	4	12	41	....	1981-82	1984-85
Crowder, Keith	Bos., L.A.	10	662	223	271	494	1354	85	14	22	36	218	....	1980-81	1989-90
Crowder, Troy	N.J., Det., L.A., Van.	7	150	9	7	16	433	4	0	0	0	22	....	1987-88	1996-97
‡ Crowley, Ted	Hfd., Col., NYI	2	34	2	4	6	12	....	....	....	....	....	....	1993-94	1998-99
Crozier, Joe	Tor.	1	5	0	3	3	2	....	....	....	....	....	....	1959-60	1959-60
• Crutchfield, Nels	Mtl.C.	1	41	5	5	10	20	2	0	1	1	22	....	1934-35	1934-35
Culhane, Jim	Hfd.	1	6	0	1	1	4	....	....	....	....	....	....	1989-90	1989-90
Cullen, Barry	Tor., Det.	5	219	32	52	84	111	6	0	0	0	2	....	1955-56	1959-60
Cullen, Brian	Tor., NYR	7	326	56	100	156	92	19	3	0	3	2	....	1954-55	1960-61
Cullen, John	Pit., Hfd., Tor., T.B.	11	621	187	363	550	898	53	12	22	34	58	....	1988-89	1998-99
Cullen, Ray	NYR, Det., Min., Van.	6	313	92	123	215	120	20	3	10	13	2	....	1965-66	1970-71
Cummins, Barry	Cal.	1	36	1	2	3	39	....	....	....	....	....	....	1973-74	1973-74
Cunneyworth, Randy	Buf., Pit., Wpg., Hfd., Chi., Ott.	16	866	189	225	414	1280	45	7	7	14	61	....	1980-81	1998-99
Cunningham, Bob	NYR	2	4	0	1	1	0	....	....	....	....	....	....	1960-61	1961-62
Cunningham, Jim	Phi.	1	1	0	0	0	4	....	....	....	....	....	....	1977-78	1977-78
• Cunningham, Les	NYA, Chi.	2	60	7	19	26	21	1	0	0	0	0	....	1936-37	1939-40
Cupolo, Bill	Bos.	1	47	11	13	24	10	7	1	2	3	0	....	1944-45	1944-45
Curran, Brian	Bos., NYI, Tor., Buf., Wsh.	10	381	7	33	40	1461	24	0	1	1	122	....	1983-84	1993-94
‡ Currie, Dan	Edm., L.A.	4	22	2	1	3	4	....	....	....	....	....	....	1990-91	1993-94
Currie, Glen	Wsh., L.A.	8	326	39	79	118	100	12	1	3	4	4	....	1979-80	1987-88
Currie, Hugh	Mtl.	1	1	0	0	0	0	....	....	....	....	....	....	1950-51	1950-51
Currie, Tony	St.L., Van., Hfd.	8	290	92	119	211	83	16	4	12	16	14	....	1977-78	1984-85
Curry, Floyd	Mtl.	11	601	105	99	204	147	91	23	17	40	38	4	1947-48	1957-58
Curtale, Tony	Cgy.	1	2	0	0	0	0	....	....	....	....	....	....	1980-81	1980-81
Curtis, Paul	Mtl., L.A., St.L.	4	185	3	34	37	161	5	0	0	0	2	....	1969-70	1972-73
Cushenan, Ian	Chi., Mtl., NYR, Det.	5	129	3	11	14	134	....	....	....	....	....	1	1956-57	1963-64
Cusson, Jean	Oak.	1	2	0	0	0	0	....	....	....	....	....	....	1967-68	1967-68
Cyr, Denis	Cgy., Chi., St.L.	6	193	41	43	84	36	4	0	0	0	0	....	1980-81	1985-86
Cyr, Paul	Buf., NYR, Hfd.	9	470	101	140	241	623	24	4	6	10	31	....	1982-83	1991-92

D

Dahlin, Kjell	Mtl.	3	166	57	59	116	10	35	6	11	17	6	1	1985-86	1987-88
Dahlquist, Chris	Pit., Min., Cgy., Ott.	11	532	19	71	90	488	39	4	7	11	30	....	1985-86	1995-96
• Dahlstrom, Cully	Chi.	8	342	88	118	206	58	29	6	8	14	4	1	1937-38	1944-45
Daigle, Alain	Chi.	6	389	56	50	106	122	17	0	1	1	0	....	1974-75	1979-80
‡ Daigle, Alexandre	Ott., Phi., T.B., NYR	7	459	100	141	241	152	12	0	2	2	2	....	1993-94	1999-00
Dailey, Bob	Van., Phi.	9	561	94	231	325	814	63	12	34	46	105	....	1973-74	1981-82
• Daley, Frank	Det.	1	5	0	0	0	0	2	0	0	0	0	....	1928-29	1928-29
Daley, Pat	Wpg.	2	12	1	0	1	13	....	....	....	....	....	....	1979-80	1980-81
Dalgarno, Brad	NYI	10	321	49	71	120	332	27	2	4	6	37	....	1985-86	1995-96
Dallman, Marty	Tor.	2	6	0	1	1	0	....	....	....	....	....	....	1987-88	1988-89
Dallman, Rod	NYI, Phi.	4	6	1	0	1	26	1	0	1	1	0	....	1987-88	1991-92
Dame, Bunny	Mtl.	1	34	2	5	7	4	....	....	....	....	....	....	1941-42	1941-42
Damore, Hank	NYR	1	4	1	0	1	2	....	....	....	....	....	....	1943-44	1943-44
‡ Daniels, Kimbi	Phi.	2	27	1	2	3	4	....	....	....	....	....	....	1990-91	1991-92
Daniels, Scott	Hfd., Phi., N.J.	6	149	8	12	20	667	1	0	0	0	0	....	1992-93	1998-99
Daoust, Dan	Mtl., Tor.	8	522	87	167	254	544	32	7	5	12	83	....	1982-83	1989-90
Dark, Michael	St.L.	2	43	5	6	11	14	....	....	....	....	....	....	1986-87	1987-88
• Darragh, Harold	Pit., Phi., Bos., Tor.	8	308	68	49	117	50	16	1	3	4	4	1	1925-26	1932-33
• Darragh, Jack	Ott.	6	121	66	46	112	113	11	3	0	3	9	3	1917-18	1923-24
David, Richard	Que.	3	31	4	4	8	10	1	0	0	0	0	....	1979-80	1982-83
• Davidson, Bob	Tor.	12	491	94	160	254	398	79	5	17	22	76	2	1934-35	1945-46
• Davidson, Gord	NYR	2	51	3	6	9	8	....	....	....	....	....	....	1942-43	1943-44
• Davie, Bob	Bos.	3	41	0	1	1	25	....	....	....	....	....	....	1933-34	1935-36
Davies, Buck	NYR	1	....	....	....	....	....	1	0	0	0	0	....	1947-48	1947-48
• Davis, Bob	Det.	1	3	0	0	0	0	....	....	....	....	....	....	1932-33	1932-33
Davis, Kim	Pit., Tor.	4	36	5	7	12	51	4	0	0	0	0	....	1977-78	1980-81
Davis, Lorne	Mtl., Chi., Det., Bos.	6	95	8	12	20	20	18	3	1	4	10	1	1951-52	1959-60
Davis, Mal	Det., Buf.	6	100	31	22	53	34	7	1	0	1	0	....	1978-79	1985-86
• Davison, Murray	Bos.	1	1	0	0	0	0	....	....	....	....	....	....	1965-66	1965-66
‡ Davydov, Evgeny	Wpg., Fla., Ott.	4	155	40	39	79	120	11	2	2	4	2	....	1991-92	1994-95
Dawes, Bobby	Tor., Mtl.	4	32	2	7	9	6	10	0	0	0	2	1	1946-47	1950-51
• Day, Hap	Tor., NYA	14	581	86	116	202	601	53	4	7	11	56	1	1924-25	1937-38
Day, Joe	Hfd., NYI	3	72	1	10	11	87	....	....	....	....	....	....	1991-92	1993-94
Dea, Billy	NYR, Det., Chi., Pit.	8	397	67	54	121	44	11	2	1	3	6	....	1953-54	1970-71
• Deacon, Don	Det.	3	30	6	4	10	6	2	2	1	3	0	....	1936-37	1939-40
Deadmarsh, Butch	Buf., Atl., K.C.	5	137	12	5	17	155	4	0	0	0	17	....	1970-71	1974-75
Dean, Barry	Col., Phi.	3	165	25	56	81	146	....	....	....	....	....	....	1976-77	1978-79
Debenedet, Nelson	Det., Pit.	2	46	10	4	14	13	....	....	....	....	....	....	1973-74	1974-75
DeBlois, Lucien	NYR, Col., Wpg., Mtl., Que., Tor.	15	993	249	276	525	814	52	7	6	13	38	1	1977-78	1991-92
Debol, Dave	Hfd.	2	92	26	26	52	4	3	0	0	0	0	....	1979-80	1980-81
Defazio, Dean	Pit.	1	22	0	2	2	28	....	....	....	....	....	....	1983-84	1983-84
DeGray, Dale	Cgy., Tor., L.A., Buf.	5	153	18	47	65	195	13	1	3	4	28	....	1985-86	1989-90
• Delmonte, Armand	Bos.	1	1	0	0	0	0	....	....	....	....	....	....	1945-46	1945-46
Delorme, Gilbert	Mtl., St.L., Que., Det., Pit.	9	541	31	92	123	520	56	1	9	10	56	....	1981-82	1989-90
Delorme, Ron	Col., Van.	9	524	83	83	166	667	25	1	2	3	59	....	1976-77	1984-85
Delory, Val	NYR	1	1	0	0	0	0	....	....	....	....	....	....	1948-49	1948-49
Delparte, Guy	Col.	1	48	1	8	9	18	....	....	....	....	....	....	1976-77	1976-77
Delvecchio, Alex	Det.	24	1549	456	825	1281	383	121	35	69	104	29	3	1950-51	1973-74
DeMarco, Ab Jr.	NYR, St.L., Pit., Van., L.A., Bos.	9	344	44	80	124	75	25	1	2	3	17	....	1969-70	1978-79
• DeMarco, Ab Sr.	Chi., Tor., Bos., NYR	7	209	72	93	165	53	11	3	0	3	2	....	1938-39	1946-47
• Demers, Tony	Mtl.C., Mtl., NYR	6	83	20	22	42	23	2	0	0	0	0	....	1937-38	1943-44
Denis, Jean-Paul	NYR	2	10	0	2	2	2	....	....	....	....	....	....	1946-47	1949-50
Denis, Lulu	Mtl.	2	3	0	1	1	0	....	....	....	....	....	....	1949-50	1950-51
• Denneny, Corb	Tor., Ham., Chi.	9	176	103	42	145	148	6	1	0	1	4	2	1917-18	1927-28
• Denneny, Cy	Ott., Bos.	12	328	248	85	333	301	25	16	2	18	17	5	1917-18	1928-29
Dennis, Norm	St.L.	4	12	3	0	3	11	5	0	0	0	2	....	1968-69	1971-72
• Denoird, Gerry	Tor.	1	17	0	1	1	0	....	....	....	....	....	....	1922-23	1922-23
DePalma, Larry	Min., S.J., Pit.	7	148	21	20	41	408	3	0	0	0	6	....	1985-86	1993-94
Derlago, Bill	Van., Tor., Bos., Wpg., Que.	9	555	189	227	416	247	13	5	0	5	8	....	1978-79	1986-87
• Desaulniers, Gerard	Mtl.	3	8	0	2	2	4	....	....	....	....	....	....	1950-51	1953-54
• Desilets, Joffre	Mtl.C., Chi.	5	192	37	45	82	57	7	1	0	1	7	....	1935-36	1939-40
Desjardins, Martin	Mtl.	1	8	0	2	2	2	....	....	....	....	....	....	1989-90	1989-90
• Desjardins, Vic	Chi., NYR	2	87	6	15	21	27	16	0	0	0	0	....	1930-31	1931-32
Deslauriers, Jacques	Mtl.	1	2	0	0	0	0	....	....	....	....	....	....	1955-56	1955-56
Devine, Kevin	NYI	1	2	0	1	1	8	....	....	....	....	....	....	1982-83	1982-83
• Dewar, Tom	NYR	1	9	0	2	2	4	....	....	....	....	....	....	1943-44	1943-44
Dewsbury, Al	Det., Chi.	9	347	30	78	108	365	14	1	5	6	16	1	1946-47	1955-56
Deziel, Michel	Buf.	1	....	....	....	....	....	1	0	0	0	0	....	1974-75	1974-75
Dheere, Marcel	Mtl.	1	11	1	2	3	2	5	0	0	0	6	....	1942-43	1942-43
‡ Di Pietro, Paul	Mtl., Tor., L.A.	6	192	31	49	80	96	31	11	10	21	10	1	1991-92	1996-97
Diachuk, Edward	Det.	1	12	0	0	0	19	....	....	....	....	....	....	1960-61	1960-61
Dick, Harry	Chi.	1	12	0	1	1	12	....	....	....	....	....	....	1946-47	1946-47
Dickens, Ernie	Tor., Chi.	6	278	12	44	56	98	13	0	0	0	4	1	1941-42	1950-51
Dickenson, Herb	NYR	2	48	18	17	35	10	....	....	....	....	....	....	1951-52	1952-53
Dietrich, Don	Chi., N.J.	2	28	0	7	7	10	....	....	....	....	....	....	1983-84	1985-86
• Dill, Bob	NYR	2	76	15	15	30	135	....	....	....	....	....	....	1943-44	1944-45
• Dillabough, Bob	Det., Bos., Pit., Oak.	9	283	32	54	86	76	17	3	0	3	0	....	1961-62	1969-70
• Dillon, Cecil	NYR, Det.	10	453	167	131	298	105	43	14	9	23	14	1	1930-31	1939-40
Dillon, Gary	Col.	1	13	1	1	2	29	....	....	....	....	....	....	1980-81	1980-81
Dillon, Wayne	NYR, Wpg.	4	229	43	66	109	60	3	0	1	1	0	....	1975-76	1979-80
Dineen, Bill	Det., Chi.	5	323	51	44	95	122	37	1	1	2	18	2	1953-54	1957-58
Dineen, Gary	Min.	1	4	0	1	1	0	....	....	....	....	....	....	1968-69	1968-69
‡ Dineen, Gord	NYI, Min., Pit., Ott.	13	528	16	90	106	695	40	1	7	8	68	....	1982-83	1994-95
Dineen, Peter	L.A., Det.	2	13	0	2	2	13	....	....	....	....	....	....	1986-87	1989-90
• Dinsmore, Dinny	Mtl.M.	4	100	6	2	8	50	8	1	0	1	2	1	1924-25	1929-30
Dionne, Marcel	Det., L.A., NYR	18	1348	731	1040	1771	600	49	21	24	45	17	....	1971-72	1988-89
Dirk, Robert	St.L., Van., Chi., Ana., Mtl.	9	402	13	29	42	786	39	0	1	1	56	....	1987-88	1995-96
‡ Djoos, Per	Det., NYR	3	82	2	31	33	58	....	....	....	....	....	....	1990-91	1992-93
Doak, Gary	Det., Bos., Van., NYR	16	789	23	107	130	908	78	2	4	6	121	1	1965-66	1980-81
Dobbin, Brian	Phi., Bos.	5	63	7	8	15	61	2	0	0	0	17	....	1986-87	1991-92

Murray Craven

Randy Cunneyworth

Alexandre Daigle

Brad Dalgarno

Wayne Dillon

Dick Duff

Mike Eagles

Dave Ellett

Name	NHL Teams	NHL Seasons	Regular Schedule GP	G	A	TP	PIM	Playoffs GP	G	A	TP	PIM	NHL Cup Wins	First NHL Season	Last NHL Season
Dobson, Jim	Min., Col., Que.	4	12	0	0	0	6	....	....	....	....	....	....	1979-80	1983-84
• Doherty, Fred	Mtl.C.	1	1	0	0	0	0	....	....	....	....	....	....	1918-19	1918-19
Donaldson, Gary	Chi.	1	1	0	0	0	0	....	....	....	....	....	....	1973-74	1973-74
Donatelli, Clark	Min., Bos.	2	35	3	4	7	39	2	0	0	0	0	....	1989-90	1991-92
• Donnelly, Babe	Mtl.M.	1	34	0	1	1	14	2	0	0	0	0	....	1926-27	1926-27
Donnelly, Dave	Bos., Chi., Edm.	5	137	15	24	39	150	5	0	0	0	0	....	1983-84	1987-88
‡ Donnelly, Gord	Que., Wpg., Buf., Dal.	12	554	28	41	69	2069	26	0	2	2	61	....	1983-84	1994-95
Donnelly, Mike	NYR, Buf., L.A., Dal., NYI	11	465	114	121	235	255	47	12	12	24	30	....	1986-87	1996-97
• Doran, John	NYA, Det., Mtl.	5	98	5	10	15	110	3	0	0	0	0	....	1933-34	1939-40
Doran, Lloyd	Det.	1	24	3	2	5	10	....	....	....	....	....	....	1946-47	1946-47
• Doraty, Ken	Chi., Tor., Det.	5	103	15	26	41	24	15	7	2	9	2	....	1926-27	1937-38
Dore, Andre	NYR, St.L., Que.	7	257	14	81	95	261	23	1	2	3	32	....	1978-79	1984-85
Dore, Daniel	Que.	2	17	2	3	5	59	....	....	....	....	....	....	1989-90	1990-91
Dorey, Jim	Tor., NYR	4	232	25	74	99	553	11	0	2	2	40	....	1968-69	1971-72
Dorion, Dan	N.J.	2	4	1	1	2	2	....	....	....	....	....	....	1985-86	1987-88
Dornhoefer, Gary	Bos., Phi.	14	787	214	328	542	1291	80	17	19	36	203	2	1963-64	1977-78
Dorohoy, Eddie	Mtl.	1	16	0	0	0	6	....	....	....	....	....	....	1948-49	1948-49
Douglas, Jordy	Hfd., Min., Wpg.	6	268	76	62	138	160	6	0	0	0	4	....	1979-80	1984-85
Douglas, Kent	Tor., Oak., Det.	7	428	33	115	148	631	19	1	3	4	33	3	1962-63	1968-69
Douglas, Les	Det.	4	52	6	12	18	8	10	3	2	5	2	1	1940-41	1946-47
‡ Douris, Peter	Wpg., Bos., Ana., Dal.	11	321	54	67	121	80	27	3	5	8	14	....	1985-86	1997-98
• Downie, Dave	Tor.	1	11	0	1	1	2	....	....	....	....	....	....	1932-33	1932-33
‡ Doyon, Mario	Chi., Que.	3	28	3	4	7	16	....	....	....	....	....	....	1988-89	1990-91
• Draper, Bruce	Tor.	1	1	0	0	0	0	....	....	....	....	....	....	1962-63	1962-63
• Drillon, Gordie	Tor., Mtl.	7	311	155	139	294	56	50	26	15	41	10	1	1936-37	1942-43
Driscoll, Peter	Edm.	2	60	3	8	11	97	3	0	0	0	0	....	1979-80	1980-81
Driver, Bruce	N.J., NYR	15	922	96	390	486	670	108	10	40	50	64	1	1983-84	1997-98
Drolet, Rene	Phi., Det.	2	2	0	0	0	0	....	....	....	....	....	....	1971-72	1974-75
‡ Droppa, Ivan	Chi.	2	19	0	1	1	14	....	....	....	....	....	....	1993-94	1995-96
• Drouillard, Clarence	Det.	1	10	0	1	1	0	....	....	....	....	....	....	1937-38	1937-38
Drouin, Jude	Mtl., Min., NYI, Wpg.	12	666	151	305	456	346	72	27	41	68	33	....	1968-69	1980-81
‡ Drouin, P.C.	Bos.	1	3	0	0	0	0	....	....	....	....	....	....	1996-97	1996-97
• Drouin, Polly	Mtl.C., Mtl.	7	160	23	50	73	80	5	0	1	1	5	....	1934-35	1940-41
‡ Druce, John	Wsh., Wpg., L.A., Phi.	10	531	113	126	239	347	53	17	6	23	38	....	1988-89	1997-98
• Drummond, Jim	NYR	1	2	0	0	0	0	....	....	....	....	....	....	1944-45	1944-45
• Drury, Herb	Pit., Phi.	6	213	24	13	37	203	4	1	1	2	0	....	1925-26	1930-31
Dube, Gilles	Mtl., Det.	2	12	1	2	3	2	2	0	0	0	0	1	1949-50	1953-54
Dube, Norm	K.C.	2	57	8	10	18	54	....	....	....	....	....	....	1974-75	1975-76
Duberman, Justin	Pit.	1	4	0	0	0	0	....	....	....	....	....	....	1993-94	1993-94
Duchesne, Gaetan	Wsh., Que., Min., S.J., Fla.	14	1028	179	254	433	617	84	14	13	27	97	....	1981-82	1994-95
Dudley, Rick	Buf., Wpg.	6	309	75	99	174	292	25	7	2	9	69	....	1972-73	1980-81
Duff, Dick	Tor., NYR, Mtl., L.A., Buf.	18	1030	283	289	572	743	114	30	49	79	78	6	1954-55	1971-72
Dufour, Luc	Bos., Que., St.L.	3	167	23	21	44	199	18	1	0	1	32	....	1982-83	1984-85
Dufour, Marc	NYR, L.A.	3	14	1	0	1	2	....	....	....	....	....	....	1963-64	1968-69
Dufresne, Donald	Mtl., T.B., L.A., St.L., Edm.	9	268	6	36	42	258	34	1	3	4	47	1	1988-89	1996-97
• Duggan, John	Ott.	1	27	0	0	0	0	2	0	0	0	0	....	1925-26	1925-26
Duggan, Ken	Min.	1	1	0	0	0	0	....	....	....	....	....	....	1987-88	1987-88
Duguay, Ron	NYR, Det., Pit., L.A.	12	864	274	346	620	582	89	31	22	53	118	....	1977-78	1988-89
• Duguid, Lorne	Mtl.M., Det., Bos.	6	135	9	15	24	57	4	1	0	1	6	....	1931-32	1936-37
• Dukowski, Duke	Chi., NYA, NYR	5	200	16	30	46	172	6	0	0	0	6	....	1926-27	1933-34
Dumart, Woody	Bos.	16	772	211	218	429	99	88	12	15	27	23	2	1935-36	1953-54
Dunbar, Dale	Van., Bos.	2	2	0	0	0	2	....	....	....	....	....	....	1985-86	1988-89
• Duncan, Art	Det., Tor.	5	156	18	16	34	225	5	0	0	0	4	....	1926-27	1930-31
Duncan, Iain	Wpg.	4	127	34	55	89	149	11	0	3	3	6	....	1986-87	1990-91
Duncanson, Craig	L.A., Wpg., NYR	7	38	5	4	9	61	....	....	....	....	....	....	1985-86	1992-93
Dundas, Rocky	Tor.	1	5	0	0	0	14	....	....	....	....	....	....	1989-90	1989-90
• Dunlap, Frank	Tor.	1	15	0	1	1	2	....	....	....	....	....	....	1943-44	1943-44
Dunlop, Blake	Min., Phi., St.L., Det.	11	550	130	274	404	172	40	4	10	14	18	....	1973-74	1983-84
Dunn, Dave	Van., Tor.	3	184	14	41	55	313	10	1	1	2	41	....	1973-74	1975-76
Dunn, Richie	Buf., Cgy., Hfd.	12	483	36	140	176	314	36	3	15	18	24	....	1977-78	1988-89
Dupere, Denis	Tor., Wsh., St.L., K.C., Col.	8	421	80	99	179	66	16	1	0	1	0	....	1970-71	1977-78
Dupont, Andre	NYR, St.L., Phi., Que.	13	800	59	185	244	1986	140	14	18	32	352	2	1970-71	1982-83
Dupont, Jerome	Chi., Tor.	6	214	7	29	36	468	20	0	2	2	56	....	1981-82	1986-87
Dupont, Norm	Mtl., Wpg., Hfd.	5	256	55	85	140	52	13	4	2	6	0	....	1979-80	1983-84
• Dupre, Yanick	Phi.	3	35	2	0	2	16	....	....	....	....	....	....	1991-92	1995-96
Durbano, Steve	St.L., Pit., K.C., Col.	6	220	13	60	73	1127	5	0	2	2	8	....	1972-73	1978-79
Duris, Vitezslav	Tor.	2	89	3	20	23	62	3	0	1	1	2	....	1980-81	1982-83
Dussault, Norm	Mtl.	4	206	31	62	93	47	7	3	1	4	0	....	1947-48	1950-51
• Dutton, Red	Mtl.M., NYA	10	449	29	67	96	871	18	1	0	1	33	....	1926-27	1935-36
Dvorak, Miroslav	Phi.	3	193	11	74	85	51	18	0	2	2	6	....	1982-83	1984-85
Dwyer, Mike	Col., Cgy.	4	31	2	6	8	25	1	1	0	1	0	....	1978-79	1981-82
• Dyck, Henry	NYR	1	1	0	0	0	0	....	....	....	....	....	....	1943-44	1943-44
• Dye, Babe	Tor., Ham., Chi., NYA	11	271	201	47	248	221	10	2	0	2	11	1	1919-20	1930-31
Dykstra, Steve	Buf., Edm., Pit., Hfd.	5	217	8	32	40	545	1	0	0	0	2	....	1985-86	1989-90
Dyte, Jack	Chi.	1	27	1	0	1	31	....	....	....	....	....	....	1943-44	1943-44
Dziedzic, Joe	Pit., Phx.	3	130	14	14	28	131	21	1	3	4	23	....	1995-96	1998-99
E															
‡ Eagles, Mike	Que., Chi., Wpg., Wsh.	16	853	74	122	196	928	44	2	6	8	34	....	1982-83	1999-00
Eakin, Bruce	Cgy., Det.	4	13	2	2	4	4	....	....	....	....	....	....	1981-82	1985-86
Eatough, Jeff	Buf.	1	1	0	0	0	0	....	....	....	....	....	....	1981-82	1981-82
Eaves, Mike	Min., Cgy.	8	324	83	143	226	80	43	7	10	17	14	....	1978-79	1985-86
Eaves, Murray	Wpg., Det.	8	57	4	13	17	9	4	0	1	1	2	....	1980-81	1989-90
Ecclestone, Tim	St.L., Det., Tor., Atl.	11	692	126	233	359	344	48	6	11	17	76	....	1967-68	1977-78
Edberg, Rolf	Wsh.	3	184	45	58	103	24	....	....	....	....	....	....	1978-79	1980-81
• Eddolls, Frank	Mtl., NYR, Chi.	9	317	23	43	66	114	31	0	2	2	10	1	1944-45	1954-55
Edestrand, Darryl	St.L., Phi., Pit., Bos., L.A.	10	455	34	90	124	404	42	3	9	12	57	....	1967-68	1978-79
Edmundson, Garry	Mtl., Tor.	3	43	4	6	10	49	11	0	1	1	8	....	1951-52	1960-61
Edur, Tom	Col., Pit.	2	158	17	70	87	67	....	....	....	....	....	....	1976-77	1977-78
Egan, Pat	NYA, Bro., Det., Bos., NYR	11	554	77	153	230	776	46	9	4	13	48	....	1939-40	1950-51
‡ Egeland, Allan	T.B.	3	17	0	0	0	16	....	....	....	....	....	....	1995-96	1997-98
Egers, Jack	NYR, St.L., Wsh.	7	284	64	69	133	154	32	5	6	11	32	....	1969-70	1975-76
Ehman, Gerry	Bos., Det., Tor., Oak., Cal.	9	429	96	118	214	100	41	10	10	20	12	1	1957-58	1970-71
‡ Eisenhut, Neil	Van., Cgy.	2	16	1	3	4	21	....	....	....	....	....	....	1993-94	1994-95
Eklund, Per-Erik	Phi., Dal.	9	594	120	335	455	109	66	10	36	46	8	....	1985-86	1993-94
Eldebrink, Anders	Van., Que.	2	55	3	11	14	29	14	0	0	0	10	....	1981-82	1982-83
Elik, Bo	Det.	1	3	0	0	0	0	....	....	....	....	....	....	1962-63	1962-63
‡ Elik, Todd	L.A., Min., Edm., S.J., St.L., Bos.	8	448	110	219	329	453	52	15	27	42	48	....	1989-90	1996-97
‡ Ellett, Dave	Wpg., Tor., N.J., Bos., St.L.	16	1129	153	415	568	985	116	11	46	57	87	....	1984-85	1999-00
• Elliott, Fred	Ott.	1	43	2	0	2	6	....	....	....	....	....	....	1928-29	1928-29
Ellis, Ron	Tor.	16	1034	332	308	640	207	70	18	8	26	20	1	1963-64	1980-81
Eloranta, Kari	Cgy., St.L.	5	267	13	103	116	155	26	1	7	8	19	....	1981-82	1986-87
Elynuik, Pat	Wpg., Wsh., T.B., Ott.	9	506	154	188	342	459	20	6	9	15	25	....	1987-88	1995-96
Emberg, Eddie	Mtl.	1	....	....	....	....	....	2	1	0	1	0	....	1944-45	1944-45
Emmons, Gary	S.J.	1	3	1	0	1	0	....	....	....	....	....	....	1993-94	1993-94
• Emms, Hap	Mtl.M., NYA, Det., Bos.	10	320	36	53	89	311	14	0	0	0	12	....	1926-27	1937-38
Endean, Craig	Wpg.	1	2	0	1	1	0	....	....	....	....	....	....	1986-87	1986-87
Engblom, Brian	Mtl., Wsh., L.A., Buf., Cgy.	11	659	29	177	206	599	48	3	9	12	43	3	1976-77	1986-87
Engele, Jerry	Min.	3	100	2	13	15	162	2	0	1	1	0	....	1975-76	1977-78
English, John	L.A.	1	3	1	3	4	4	1	0	0	0	0	....	1987-88	1987-88
Ennis, Jim	Edm.	1	5	1	0	1	10	....	....	....	....	....	....	1987-88	1987-88
Erickson, Aut	Bos., Chi., Tor., Oak.	7	226	7	24	31	182	7	0	0	0	2	1	1959-60	1969-70
Erickson, Bryan	Wsh., L.A., Pit., Wpg.	9	351	80	125	205	141	14	3	4	7	7	....	1983-84	1993-94
Erickson, Grant	Bos., Min.	2	6	1	0	1	0	....	....	....	....	....	....	1968-69	1969-70
Eriksson, Peter	Edm.	1	20	3	3	6	24	....	....	....	....	....	....	1989-90	1989-90
Eriksson, Roland	Min., Van.	3	193	48	95	143	26	2	1	0	1	0	....	1976-77	1978-79
Eriksson, Thomas	Phi.	5	208	22	76	98	107	19	0	3	3	12	....	1980-81	1985-86
Erixon, Jan	NYR	10	556	57	159	216	167	58	7	7	14	16	....	1983-84	1992-93
Errey, Bob	Pit., Buf., S.J., Det., Dal., NYR	15	895	170	212	382	1005	99	13	16	29	109	2	1983-84	1997-98
‡ Esau, Len	Tor., Que., Cgy., Edm.	4	27	0	10	10	24	....	....	....	....	....	....	1991-92	1994-95
Esposito, Phil	Chi., Bos., NYR	18	1282	717	873	1590	910	130	61	76	137	138	2	1963-64	1980-81
• Evans, Chris	Tor., Buf., St.L., Det., K.C.	5	241	19	42	61	143	12	1	1	2	8	....	1969-70	1974-75
Evans, Daryl	L.A., Wsh., Tor.	6	113	22	30	52	25	11	5	8	13	12	....	1981-82	1986-87
Evans, Doug	St.L., Wpg., Phi.	8	355	48	87	135	502	22	3	4	7	38	....	1985-86	1992-93
• Evans, Jack	NYR, Chi.	14	752	19	80	99	989	56	2	2	4	97	1	1948-49	1962-63

Name	NHL Teams	NHL Seasons	Regular Schedule GP	G	A	TP	PIM	Playoffs GP	G	A	TP	PIM	NHL Cup Wins	First NHL Season	Last NHL Season
Evans, John Paul	Phi.	3	103	14	25	39	34	1	0	0	0	0	....	1978-79	1982-83
‡ Evans, Kevin	Min., S.J.	2	9	0	1	1	44	....	....	....	....	....	....	1990-91	1991-92
Evans, Paul	Tor.	2	11	1	1	2	21	2	0	0	0	0	....	1976-77	1977-78
Evans, Shawn	St.L., NYI	2	9	1	0	1	2	....	....	....	....	....	....	1985-86	1989-90
● Evans, Stewart	Det., Mtl.M., Mtl.C.	8	367	28	49	77	425	26	0	0	0	20	1	1930-31	1938-39
Evason, Dean	Wsh., Hfd., S.J., Dal., Cgy.	13	803	139	233	372	1002	55	9	20	29	132	....	1983-84	1995-96
Ewen, Todd	St.L., Mtl., Ana., S.J.	11	518	36	40	76	1911	26	0	0	0	87	1	1986-87	1996-97
Ezinicki, Bill	Tor., Bos., NYR	9	368	79	105	184	713	40	5	8	13	87	3	1944-45	1954-55

F

Name	NHL Teams	NHL Seasons	Regular Schedule GP	G	A	TP	PIM	Playoffs GP	G	A	TP	PIM	NHL Cup Wins	First NHL Season	Last NHL Season
Fahey, Trevor	NYR	1	1	0	0	0	0	....	....	....	....	....	....	1964-65	1964-65
Fairbairn, Bill	NYR, Min., St.L.	11	658	162	261	423	173	54	13	22	35	42	....	1968-69	1978-79
Falkenberg, Bob	Det.	5	54	1	5	6	26	....	....	....	....	....	....	1966-67	1971-72
Farrant, Walt	Chi.	1	1	0	0	0	0	....	....	....	....	....	....	1943-44	1943-44
Farrish, Dave	NYR, Que., Tor.	7	430	17	110	127	440	14	0	2	2	24	....	1976-77	1983-84
Fashoway, Gordie	Chi.	1	13	3	2	5	14	....	....	....	....	....	....	1950-51	1950-51
Faubert, Mario	Pit.	7	231	21	90	111	292	10	2	2	4	6	....	1974-75	1981-82
Faulkner, Alex	Tor., Det.	3	101	15	17	32	15	12	5	0	5	2	....	1961-62	1963-64
Fauss, Ted	Tor.	2	28	0	2	2	15	....	....	....	....	....	....	1986-87	1987-88
‡ Faust, Andre	Phi.	2	47	10	7	17	14	....	....	....	....	....	....	1992-93	1993-94
Feamster, Dave	Chi.	4	169	13	24	37	154	33	3	5	8	61	....	1981-82	1984-85
‡ Featherstone, Glen	St.L., Bos., NYR, Hfd., Cgy.	9	384	19	61	80	939	28	0	2	2	103	....	1988-89	1996-97
Featherstone, Tony	Oak., Cal., Min.	3	130	17	21	38	65	2	0	0	0	0	....	1969-70	1973-74
Federko, Bernie	St.L., Det.	14	1000	369	761	1130	487	91	35	66	101	83	....	1976-77	1989-90
‡ Fedotov, Anatoli	Wpg., Ana.	2	4	0	2	2	0	....	....	....	....	....	....	1992-93	1993-94
‡ Fedyk, Brent	Det., Phi., Dal., NYR	10	470	97	112	209	308	16	3	2	5	12	....	1987-88	1998-99
‡ Felix, Chris	Wsh.	4	35	1	12	13	10	2	0	1	1	0	....	1987-88	1990-91
‡ Felsner, Denny	St.L.	4	18	1	4	5	6	10	2	3	5	2	....	1991-92	1994-95
Feltrin, Tony	Pit., NYR	4	48	3	3	6	65	....	....	....	....	....	....	1980-81	1985-86
Fenton, Paul	Hfd., NYR, L.A., Wpg., Tor., Cgy., S.J.	8	411	100	83	183	198	17	4	1	5	27	....	1984-85	1991-92
Fenyves, David	Buf., Phi.	9	206	3	32	35	119	11	0	0	0	9	....	1982-83	1990-91
Fergus, Tom	Bos., Tor., Van.	12	726	235	346	581	499	65	21	17	38	48	....	1981-82	1992-93
Ferguson, George	Tor., Pit., Min.	12	797	160	238	398	431	86	14	23	37	44	....	1972-73	1983-84
Ferguson, John	Mtl.	8	500	145	158	303	1214	85	20	18	38	260	5	1963-64	1970-71
Ferguson, Lorne	Bos., Det., Chi.	8	422	82	80	162	193	31	6	3	9	24	....	1949-50	1958-59
Ferguson, Norm	Oak., Cal.	4	279	73	66	139	72	10	1	4	5	7	....	1968-69	1971-72
‡ Ferner, Mark	Buf., Wsh., Ana., Det.	6	91	3	10	13	51	....	....	....	....	....	....	1986-87	1994-95
Fetisov, Viacheslav	N.J., Det.	9	546	36	192	228	656	116	2	26	28	147	2	1989-90	1997-98
Fidler, Mike	Cle., Min., Hfd., Chi.	7	271	84	97	181	124	....	....	....	....	....	....	1976-77	1982-83
● Field, Wilf	NYA, Bro., Mtl., Chi.	6	219	17	25	42	151	2	0	0	0	2	....	1936-37	1944-45
Fielder, Guyle	Chi., Det., Bos.	4	9	0	0	0	2	6	0	0	0	2	....	1950-51	1957-58
‡ Filimonov, Dmitri	Ott.	1	30	1	4	5	18	....	....	....	....	....	....	1993-94	1993-94
Fillion, Bob	Mtl.	7	327	42	61	103	84	33	7	4	11	10	2	1943-44	1949-50
● Fillion, Marcel	Bos.	1	1	0	0	0	0	....	....	....	....	....	....	1944-45	1944-45
● Filmore, Tommy	Det., NYA, Bos.	4	117	15	12	27	33	....	....	....	....	....	....	1930-31	1933-34
● Finkbeiner, Lloyd	NYA	1	2	0	0	0	0	....	....	....	....	....	....	1940-41	1940-41
Finn, Steven	Que., T.B., L.A.	12	725	34	78	112	1724	23	0	4	4	39	....	1985-86	1996-97
Finney, Sid	Chi.	3	59	10	7	17	4	7	0	2	2	0	....	1951-52	1953-54
● Finnigan, Ed	St.L., Bos.	2	15	1	1	2	2	....	....	....	....	....	....	1934-35	1935-36
● Finnigan, Frank	Ott., Tor., St.L.	14	553	115	88	203	407	38	6	9	15	22	2	1923-24	1936-37
Fiorentino, Peter	NYR	1	1	0	0	0	0	....	....	....	....	....	....	1991-92	1991-92
Fischer, Ron	Buf.	2	18	0	7	7	6	....	....	....	....	....	....	1981-82	1982-83
● Fisher, Alvin	Tor.	1	9	1	0	1	4	....	....	....	....	....	....	1924-25	1924-25
‡ Fisher, Craig	Phi., Wpg., Fla.	4	12	0	0	0	2	....	....	....	....	....	....	1989-90	1996-97
Fisher, Dunc	NYR, Bos., Det.	7	275	45	70	115	104	21	4	4	8	14	....	1947-48	1958-59
Fisher, Joe	Det.	4	65	8	12	20	13	12	2	1	3	6	1	1939-40	1942-43
Fitchner, Bob	Que.	2	78	12	20	32	59	3	0	0	0	10	....	1979-80	1980-81
‡ Fitzgerald, Rusty	Pit.	2	25	2	2	4	12	5	0	0	0	4	....	1994-95	1995-96
Fitzpatrick, Ross	Phi.	4	20	5	2	7	0	....	....	....	....	....	....	1982-83	1985-86
Fitzpatrick, Sandy	NYR, Min.	2	22	3	6	9	8	12	0	0	0	0	....	1964-65	1967-68
Flaman, Fern	Bos., Tor.	17	910	34	174	208	1370	63	4	8	12	93	1	1944-45	1960-61
Flatley, Pat	NYI, NYR	14	780	170	340	510	686	70	18	15	33	75	....	1983-84	1996-97
Fleming, Gerry	Mtl.	2	11	0	0	0	42	....	....	....	....	....	....	1993-94	1994-95
Fleming, Reggie	Mtl., Chi., Bos., NYR, Phi., Buf.	12	749	108	132	240	1468	50	3	6	9	106	1	1959-60	1970-71
Flesch, John	Min., Pit., Col.	4	124	18	23	41	117	....	....	....	....	....	....	1974-75	1979-80
Fletcher, Steven	Mtl., Wpg.	2	3	0	0	0	5	1	0	0	0	5	....	1987-88	1988-89
● Flett, Bill	L.A., Phi., Tor., Atl., Edm.	11	689	202	215	417	501	52	7	16	23	42	1	1967-68	1979-80
Flichel, Todd	Wpg.	3	6	0	1	1	4	....	....	....	....	....	....	1987-88	1989-90
Flockhart, Rob	Van., Min.	5	55	2	5	7	14	1	1	0	1	2	....	1976-77	1980-81
Flockhart, Ron	Phi., Pit., Mtl., St.L., Bos.	9	453	145	183	328	208	19	4	6	10	14	....	1980-81	1988-89
Floyd, Larry	N.J.	2	12	2	3	5	9	....	....	....	....	....	....	1982-83	1983-84
‡ Fogarty, Bryan	Que., Pit., Mtl.	6	156	22	52	74	119	....	....	....	....	....	....	1989-90	1994-95
Fogolin, Lee Jr.	Buf., Edm.	13	924	44	195	239	1318	108	5	19	24	173	2	1974-75	1986-87
Fogolin, Lee Sr.	Det., Chi.	9	427	10	48	58	575	28	0	2	2	30	1	1947-48	1955-56
Folco, Peter	Van.	1	2	0	0	0	0	....	....	....	....	....	....	1973-74	1973-74
Foley, Gerry	Tor., NYR, L.A.	4	142	9	14	23	99	9	0	1	1	2	....	1954-55	1968-69
Foley, Rick	Chi., Phi., Det.	3	67	11	26	37	180	4	0	1	1	4	....	1970-71	1973-74
Foligno, Mike	Det., Buf., Tor., Fla.	15	1018	355	372	727	2049	57	15	17	32	185	....	1979-80	1993-94
Folk, Bill	Det.	2	12	0	0	0	4	....	....	....	....	....	....	1951-52	1952-53
Fontaine, Len	Det.	2	46	8	11	19	10	....	....	....	....	....	....	1972-73	1973-74
Fontas, Jon	Min.	2	2	0	0	0	0	....	....	....	....	....	....	1979-80	1980-81
Fonteyne, Val	Det., NYR, Pit.	13	820	75	154	229	26	59	3	10	13	8	....	1959-60	1971-72
Fontinato, Lou	NYR, Mtl.	9	535	26	78	104	1247	21	0	2	2	42	....	1954-55	1962-63
Forbes, Dave	Bos., Wsh.	6	363	64	64	128	341	45	1	4	5	13	....	1973-74	1978-79
Forbes, Mike	Bos., Edm.	3	50	1	11	12	41	....	....	....	....	....	....	1977-78	1981-82
Forey, Connie	St.L.	1	4	0	0	0	2	....	....	....	....	....	....	1973-74	1973-74
● Forsey, Jack	Tor.	1	19	7	9	16	10	3	0	1	1	0	....	1942-43	1942-43
● Forslund, Gus	Ott.	1	48	4	9	13	2	....	....	....	....	....	....	1932-33	1932-33
‡ Forslund, Tomas	Cgy.	2	44	5	11	16	12	....	....	....	....	....	....	1991-92	1992-93
Forsyth, Alex	Wsh.	1	1	0	0	0	0	....	....	....	....	....	....	1976-77	1976-77
Fortier, Dave	Tor., NYI, Van.	4	205	8	21	29	335	20	0	2	2	33	....	1972-73	1976-77
‡ Fortier, Marc	Que., Ott., L.A.	6	212	42	60	102	135	....	....	....	....	....	....	1987-88	1992-93
Fortin, Ray	St.L.	3	92	2	6	8	33	6	0	0	0	8	....	1967-68	1969-70
‡ Foster, Corey	N.J., Phi., Pit., NYI	4	45	5	6	11	24	3	0	0	0	4	....	1988-89	1996-97
Foster, Dwight	Bos., Col., N.J., Det.	10	541	111	163	274	420	35	5	12	17	4	....	1977-78	1986-87
Foster, Herb	NYR	2	6	1	0	1	5	....	....	....	....	....	....	1940-41	1947-48
● Foster, Yip	NYR, Bos., Det.	4	83	3	2	5	32	....	....	....	....	....	....	1929-30	1934-35
Fotiu, Nick	NYR, Hfd., Cgy., Phi., Edm.	13	646	60	77	137	1362	38	0	4	4	67	....	1976-77	1988-89
● Fowler, Jimmy	Tor.	3	135	18	29	47	39	18	0	3	3	2	....	1936-37	1938-39
Fowler, Tom	Chi.	1	24	0	1	1	18	....	....	....	....	....	....	1946-47	1946-47
Fox, Greg	Atl., Chi., Pit.	8	494	14	92	106	637	44	1	9	10	67	....	1977-78	1984-85
Fox, Jim	L.A.	9	578	186	293	479	143	22	4	8	12	0	....	1980-81	1989-90
● Foyston, Frank	Det.	2	64	17	7	24	32	....	....	....	....	....	....	1926-27	1927-28
Frampton, Bob	Mtl.	1	2	0	0	0	0	3	0	0	0	0	....	1949-50	1949-50
Franceschetti, Lou	Wsh., Tor., Buf.	10	459	59	81	140	747	44	3	2	5	111	....	1981-82	1991-92
Francis, Bobby	Det.	1	14	2	0	2	0	....	....	....	....	....	....	1982-83	1982-83
● Fraser, Archie	NYR	1	3	0	1	1	0	....	....	....	....	....	....	1943-44	1943-44
● Fraser, Charles	Ham.	1	1	0	0	0	0	....	....	....	....	....	....	1923-24	1923-24
Fraser, Curt	Van., Chi., Min.	12	704	193	240	433	1306	65	15	18	33	198	....	1978-79	1989-90
● Fraser, Gord	Chi., Det., Mtl.C., Pit., Phi.	5	144	24	12	36	224	2	1	0	1	6	....	1926-27	1930-31
Fraser, Harvey	Chi.	1	21	5	4	9	0	....	....	....	....	....	....	1944-45	1944-45
‡ Fraser, Iain	NYI, Que., Dal., Edm., Wpg., S.J.	5	94	23	23	46	31	4	0	0	0	0	....	1992-93	1996-97
Fraser, Scott	Mtl., Edm., NYR	3	72	16	15	31	24	11	1	1	2	0	....	1995-96	1998-99
Frawley, Dan	Chi., Pit.	6	273	37	40	77	674	1	0	0	0	0	....	1983-84	1988-89
● Fredrickson, Frank	Det., Bos., Pit.	5	161	39	34	73	206	10	2	3	5	24	....	1926-27	1930-31
‡ Freer, Mark	Phi., Ott., Cgy.	7	124	16	23	39	61	....	....	....	....	....	....	1986-87	1993-94
● Frew, Irv	Mtl.M., St.L., Mtl.C.	3	96	2	5	7	146	4	0	0	0	6	....	1933-34	1935-36
Friday, Tim	Det.	1	23	0	3	3	6	....	....	....	....	....	....	1985-86	1985-86
Fridgen, Dan	Hfd.	2	13	2	3	5	2	....	....	....	....	....	....	1981-82	1982-83
Friest, Ron	Min.	3	64	7	7	14	191	6	1	0	1	7	....	1980-81	1982-83
Frig, Len	Chi., Cal., Cle., St.L.	7	311	13	51	64	479	14	2	1	3	0	....	1972-73	1979-80
Frost, Harry	Bos.	1	4	0	0	0	0	1	0	0	0	0	1	1938-39	1938-39
Frycer, Miroslav	Que., Tor., Det., Edm.	8	415	147	183	330	486	17	3	8	11	16	....	1981-82	1988-89
Fryday, Bob	Mtl.	2	5	1	0	1	0	....	....	....	....	....	....	1949-50	1951-52
Ftorek, Robbie	Det., Que., NYR	8	334	77	150	227	262	19	9	6	15	28	....	1972-73	1984-85

Brent Fedyk

Tom Fergus

Fern Flamin

Jim Fox

Name	NHL Teams	NHL Seasons	Regular Schedule GP	G	A	TP	PIM	Playoffs GP	G	A	TP	PIM	NHL Cup Wins	First NHL Season	Last NHL Season
Fullan, Larry	Wsh.	1	4	1	0	1	0	....	....	....	....	....	....	1974-75	1974-75
Fusco, Mark	Hfd.	2	80	3	12	15	42	....	....	....	....	....	....	1983-84	1984-85

G

Name	NHL Teams	NHL Seasons	Regular Schedule GP	G	A	TP	PIM	Playoffs GP	G	A	TP	PIM	NHL Cup Wins	First NHL Season	Last NHL Season
Gadsby, Bill	Chi., NYR, Det.	20	1248	130	438	568	1539	67	4	23	27	92	....	1946-47	1965-66
‡ Gaetz, Link	Min., S.J.	3	65	6	8	14	412	....	....	....	....	....	....	1988-89	1991-92
Gage, Jody	Det., Buf.	6	68	14	15	29	26	....	....	....	....	....	....	1980-81	1991-92
• Gagne, Art	Mtl.C., Bos., Ott., Det.	6	228	67	33	100	257	11	2	1	3	20	....	1926-27	1931-32
Gagne, Paul	Col., N.J., Tor., NYI	8	390	110	101	211	127	....	....	....	....	....	....	1980-81	1989-90
Gagne, Pierre	Bos.	1	2	0	0	0	0	....	....	....	....	....	....	1959-60	1959-60
Gagner, Dave	NYR, Min., Dal., Tor., Cgy., Fla., Van.	15	946	318	401	719	1018	57	22	26	48	64	....	1984-85	1998-99
Gagnon, Germaine	Mtl., NYI, Chi., K.C.	5	259	40	101	141	72	19	2	3	5	2	....	1971-72	1975-76
• Gagnon, Johnny	Mtl.C., Bos., Mtl., NYA	10	454	120	141	261	295	32	12	12	24	37	1	1930-31	1939-40
Gainey, Bob	Mtl.	16	1160	239	262	501	585	182	25	48	73	151	5	1973-74	1988-89
• Gainor, Norm	Bos., NYR, Ott., Mtl.M.	7	246	51	56	107	129	22	2	1	3	14	2	1927-28	1934-35
‡ Galarneau, Michel	Hfd.	3	78	7	10	17	34	....	....	....	....	....	....	1980-81	1982-83
• Galbraith, Percy	Bos., Ott.	8	347	29	31	60	224	31	4	7	11	24	1	1926-27	1933-34
• Gallagher, John	Mtl.M., Det., NYA	7	205	14	19	33	153	24	2	3	5	27	1	1930-31	1938-39
Gallant, Gerard	Det., T.B.	11	615	211	269	480	1674	58	18	21	39	178	....	1984-85	1994-95
Gallimore, Jamie	Min.	1	2	0	0	0	0	....	....	....	....	....	....	1977-78	1977-78
• Gallinger, Don	Bos.	5	222	65	88	153	89	23	5	5	10	19	....	1942-43	1947-48
Gamble, Dick	Mtl., Chi., Tor.	8	195	41	41	82	66	14	1	2	3	4	1	1950-51	1966-67
Gambucci, Gary	Min.	2	51	2	7	9	9	....	....	....	....	....	....	1971-72	1973-74
Ganchar, Perry	St.L., Mtl., Pit.	4	42	3	7	10	36	7	3	1	4	0	....	1983-84	1988-89
Gans, Dave	L.A.	2	6	0	0	0	2	....	....	....	....	....	....	1982-83	1985-86
• Gardiner, Herb	Mtl.C., Chi.	3	108	10	9	19	52	9	0	1	1	16	....	1926-27	1928-29
Gardner, Bill	Chi., Hfd.	9	380	73	115	188	68	45	3	8	11	17	....	1980-81	1988-89
Gardner, Cal	NYR, Tor., Chi., Bos.	12	696	154	238	392	517	61	7	10	17	20	2	1945-46	1956-57
Gardner, Dave	Mtl., St.L., Cal., Cle., Phi.	7	350	75	115	190	41	....	....	....	....	....	....	1972-73	1979-80
Gardner, Paul	Col., Tor., Pit., Wsh., Buf.	10	447	201	201	402	207	16	2	6	8	14	....	1976-77	1985-86
Gare, Danny	Buf., Det., Edm.	13	827	354	331	685	1285	64	25	21	46	195	....	1974-75	1986-87
Gariepy, Ray	Bos., Tor.	2	36	1	6	7	43	....	....	....	....	....	....	1953-54	1955-56
• Garland, Scott	Tor., L.A.	3	91	13	24	37	115	7	1	2	3	35	....	1975-76	1978-79
Garner, Rob	Pit.	1	1	0	0	0	0	....	....	....	....	....	....	1982-83	1982-83
• Garrett, Red	NYR	1	23	1	1	2	18	....	....	....	....	....	....	1942-43	1942-43
Gartner, Mike	Wsh., Min., NYR, Tor., Phx.	19	1432	708	627	1335	1159	122	43	50	93	125	....	1979-80	1997-98
• Gassoff, Bob	St.L.	4	245	11	47	58	866	9	0	1	1	16	....	1973-74	1976-77
Gassoff, Brad	Van.	4	122	19	17	36	163	3	0	0	0	0	....	1975-76	1978-79
Gatzos, Steve	Pit.	4	89	15	20	35	83	1	0	0	0	0	....	1981-82	1984-85
Gaudreau, Rob	S.J., Ott.	4	231	51	54	105	69	14	2	0	2	0	....	1992-93	1995-96
Gaudreault, Armand	Bos.	1	44	15	9	24	27	7	0	2	2	8	....	1944-45	1944-45
• Gaudreault, Leo	Mtl.C.	3	67	8	4	12	30	....	....	....	....	....	....	1927-28	1932-33
Gaulin, Jean-Marc	Que.	4	26	4	3	7	8	1	0	0	0	0	....	1982-83	1985-86
Gaume, Dallas	Hfd.	1	4	1	1	2	0	....	....	....	....	....	....	1988-89	1988-89
• Gauthier, Art	Mtl.C.	1	13	0	0	0	0	1	0	0	0	0	....	1926-27	1926-27
‡ Gauthier, Daniel	Chi.	1	5	0	0	0	0	....	....	....	....	....	....	1994-95	1994-95
• Gauthier, Fern	NYR, Mtl., Det.	6	229	46	50	96	35	22	5	1	6	7	....	1943-44	1948-49
Gauthier, Jean	Mtl., Phi., Bos.	10	166	6	29	35	150	14	1	3	4	22	1	1960-61	1969-70
Gauthier, Luc	Mtl.	1	3	0	0	0	2	....	....	....	....	....	....	1990-91	1990-91
Gauvreau, Jocelyn	Mtl.	1	2	0	0	0	0	....	....	....	....	....	....	1983-84	1983-84
Gavin, Stew	Tor., Hfd., Min.	13	768	130	155	285	584	66	14	20	34	75	....	1980-81	1992-93
Geale, Bob	Pit.	1	1	0	0	0	2	....	....	....	....	....	....	1984-85	1984-85
• Gee, George	Chi., Det.	9	551	135	183	318	345	41	6	13	19	32	1	1945-46	1953-54
Geldart, Gary	Min.	1	4	0	0	0	5	....	....	....	....	....	....	1970-71	1970-71
Gendron, Jean-Guy	NYR, Bos., Mtl., Phi.	14	863	182	201	383	701	42	7	4	11	47	....	1955-56	1971-72
‡ Gendron, Martin	Wsh., Chi.	3	30	4	2	6	10	....	....	....	....	....	....	1994-95	1997-98
Geoffrion, Bernie	Mtl., NYR	16	883	393	429	822	689	132	58	60	118	88	6	1950-51	1967-68
Geoffrion, Danny	Mtl., Wpg.	3	111	20	32	52	99	2	0	0	0	7	....	1979-80	1981-82
• Geran, Gerry	Mtl., Bos.	2	37	5	1	6	6	....	....	....	....	....	....	1917-18	1925-26
• Gerard, Eddie	Ott.	6	128	50	48	98	108	16	4	0	4	61	3	1917-18	1922-23
Germain, Eric	L.A.	1	4	0	1	1	13	1	0	0	0	4	....	1987-88	1987-88
Getliffe, Ray	Bos., Mtl.	10	393	136	137	273	250	45	9	10	19	30	2	1935-36	1944-45
Giallonardo, Mario	Col.	2	23	0	3	3	6	....	....	....	....	....	....	1979-80	1980-81
Gibbs, Barry	Bos., Min., Atl., St.L., L.A.	13	797	58	224	282	945	36	4	2	6	67	....	1967-68	1979-80
Gibson, Don	Van.	1	14	0	3	3	20	....	....	....	....	....	....	1990-91	1990-91
Gibson, Doug	Bos., Wsh.	3	63	9	19	28	0	1	0	0	0	0	....	1973-74	1977-78
Gibson, John	L.A., Tor., Wpg.	3	48	0	2	2	120	....	....	....	....	....	....	1980-81	1983-84
Giesebrecht, Gus	Det.	4	135	27	51	78	13	17	2	3	5	0	....	1938-39	1941-42
Giffin, Lee	Pit.	2	27	1	3	4	9	....	....	....	....	....	....	1986-87	1987-88
Gilbert, Ed	K.C., Pit.	3	166	21	31	52	22	....	....	....	....	....	....	1974-75	1976-77
Gilbert, Greg	NYI, Chi., NYR, St.L.	15	837	150	228	378	576	133	17	33	50	162	3	1981-82	1995-96
Gilbert, Jeannot	Bos.	2	9	0	1	1	4	....	....	....	....	....	....	1962-63	1964-65
Gilbert, Rod	NYR	18	1065	406	615	1021	508	79	34	33	67	43	....	1960-61	1977-78
Gilbertson, Stan	Cal., St.L., Wsh., Pit.	6	428	85	89	174	148	3	1	1	2	2	....	1971-72	1976-77
Giles, Curt	Min., NYR, St.L.	14	895	43	199	242	733	103	6	16	22	118	....	1979-80	1992-93
Gilhen, Randy	Hfd., Wpg., Pit., L.A., NYR, T.B., Fla.	11	457	55	60	115	314	33	3	2	5	26	1	1982-83	1995-96
Gillen, Don	Phi., Hfd.	2	35	2	4	6	22	....	....	....	....	....	....	1979-80	1981-82
• Gillie, Farrand	Det.	1	1	0	0	0	0	....	....	....	....	....	....	1928-29	1928-29
Gillies, Clark	NYI, Buf.	14	958	319	378	697	1023	164	47	47	94	287	4	1974-75	1987-88
Gillis, Jere	Van., NYR, Que., Buf., Phi.	9	386	78	95	173	230	19	4	7	11	9	....	1977-78	1986-87
Gillis, Mike	Col., Bos.	6	246	33	43	76	186	27	2	5	7	10	....	1978-79	1983-84
Gillis, Paul	Que., Chi., Hfd.	11	624	88	154	242	1498	42	3	14	17	156	....	1982-83	1992-93
Gingras, Gaston	Mtl., Tor., St.L.	10	476	61	174	235	161	52	6	18	24	20	1	1979-80	1988-89
Girard, Bob	Cal., Cle., Wsh.	5	305	45	69	114	140	....	....	....	....	....	....	1975-76	1979-80
Girard, Kenny	Tor.	3	7	0	1	1	2	....	....	....	....	....	....	1956-57	1959-60
• Giroux, Art	Mtl.C., Bos., Det.	3	54	6	4	10	14	2	0	0	0	0	....	1932-33	1935-36
Giroux, Larry	St.L., K.C., Det., Hfd.	7	274	15	74	89	333	5	0	0	0	4	....	1973-74	1979-80
Giroux, Pierre	L.A.	1	6	1	0	1	17	....	....	....	....	....	....	1982-83	1982-83
Gladney, Bob	L.A., Pit.	2	14	1	5	6	4	....	....	....	....	....	....	1982-83	1983-84
Gladu, Jean-Paul	Bos.	1	40	6	14	20	2	7	2	2	4	0	....	1944-45	1944-45
Glennie, Brian	Tor., L.A.	10	572	14	100	114	621	32	0	1	1	66	....	1969-70	1978-79
Glennon, Matt	Bos.	1	3	0	0	0	2	....	....	....	....	....	....	1991-92	1991-92
Gloeckner, Lorry	Det.	1	13	0	2	2	6	....	....	....	....	....	....	1978-79	1978-79
Gloor, Dan	Van.	1	2	0	0	0	0	....	....	....	....	....	....	1973-74	1973-74
• Glover, Fred	Det., Chi.	5	92	13	11	24	62	8	0	0	0	0	1	1948-49	1952-53
Glover, Howie	Chi., Det., NYR, Mtl.	5	144	29	17	46	101	11	1	2	3	2	....	1958-59	1968-69
Glynn, Brian	Cgy., Min., Edm., Ott., Van., Hfd.	10	431	25	79	104	410	57	6	10	16	40	....	1987-88	1996-97
Godden, Ernie	Tor.	1	5	1	1	2	6	....	....	....	....	....	....	1981-82	1981-82
• Godfrey, Warren	Bos., Det.	16	786	32	125	157	752	52	1	4	5	42	....	1952-53	1967-68
Godin, Eddy	Wsh.	2	27	3	6	9	12	....	....	....	....	....	....	1977-78	1978-79
• Godin, Sam	Ott., Mtl.C.	3	83	4	3	7	36	....	....	....	....	....	....	1927-28	1933-34
‡ Godynyuk, Alexander	Tor., Cgy., Fla., Hfd.	7	223	10	39	49	224	....	....	....	....	....	....	1990-91	1996-97
Goegan, Pete	Det., NYR, Min.	11	383	19	67	86	365	33	1	3	4	61	....	1957-58	1967-68
Goertz, Dave	Pit.	1	2	0	0	0	2	....	....	....	....	....	....	1987-88	1987-88
• Goldham, Bob	Tor., Chi., Det.	12	650	28	143	171	400	66	3	14	17	53	5	1941-42	1955-56
• Goldsworthy, Bill	Bos., Min., NYR	14	771	283	258	541	793	40	18	19	37	30	....	1964-65	1977-78
• Goldsworthy, Leroy	NYR, Det., Chi., Mtl.C., Bos., NYA	10	336	66	57	123	79	24	1	0	1	4	1	1928-29	1938-39
Goldup, Glenn	Mtl., L.A.	9	291	52	67	119	303	16	4	3	7	22	....	1973-74	1981-82
Goldup, Hank	Tor., NYR	6	202	63	80	143	97	26	5	1	6	6	1	1939-40	1945-46
• Gooden, Bill	NYR	2	53	9	11	20	15	....	....	....	....	....	....	1942-43	1943-44
Goodenough, Larry	Phi., Van.	6	242	22	77	99	179	22	3	15	18	10	1	1974-75	1979-80
• Goodfellow, Ebbie	Det.	14	557	134	190	324	511	45	8	8	16	65	3	1929-30	1942-43
‡ Gordiouk, Viktor	Buf.	2	26	3	8	11	0	....	....	....	....	....	....	1992-93	1994-95
Gordon, Fred	Det., Bos.	2	81	8	7	15	68	2	0	0	0	0	....	1926-27	1927-28
Gordon, Jackie	NYR	3	36	3	10	13	0	9	1	1	2	7	....	1948-49	1950-51
‡ Gordon, Robb	Van.	1	4	0	0	0	2	....	....	....	....	....	....	1998-99	1998-99
Gorence, Tom	Phi., Edm.	6	303	58	53	111	89	37	9	6	15	47	....	1978-79	1983-84
Goring, Butch	L.A., NYI, Bos.	16	1107	375	513	888	102	134	38	50	88	32	4	1969-70	1984-85
Gorman, Dave	Atl.	1	3	0	0	0	0	....	....	....	....	....	....	1979-80	1979-80
• Gorman, Ed	Ott., Tor.	4	111	14	6	20	108	8	0	0	0	2	1	1924-25	1927-28
Gosselin, Benoit	NYR	1	7	0	0	0	33	....	....	....	....	....	....	1977-78	1977-78
Gosselin, Guy	Wpg.	1	5	0	0	0	6	....	....	....	....	....	....	1987-88	1987-88
Gotaas, Steve	Pit., Min.	3	49	6	9	15	53	3	0	1	1	5	....	1987-88	1990-91
• Gottselig, Johnny	Chi.	16	589	176	195	371	203	43	13	13	26	18	2	1928-29	1944-45
Gould, Bobby	Atl., Cgy., Wsh., Bos.	11	697	145	159	304	572	78	15	13	28	58	....	1979-80	1989-90

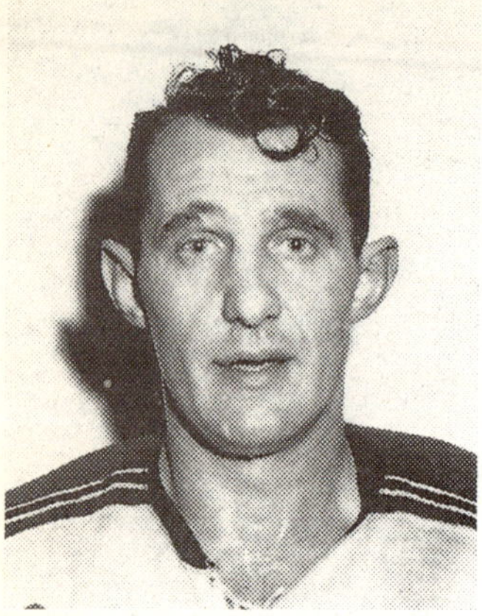
Bill Gadsby

Fern Gauthier

Rod Gilbert

Brian Glynn

			Regular Schedule					Playoffs							
Name	NHL Teams	NHL Seasons	GP	G	A	TP	PIM	GP	G	A	TP	PIM	NHL Cup Wins	First NHL Season	Last NHL Season
Gould, John	Buf., Van., Atl.	9	504	131	138	269	112	14	3	2	5	4	....	1971-72	1979-80
Gould, Larry	Van.	1	2	0	0	0	0	....	....	....	....	....	....	1973-74	1973-74
Goulet, Michel	Que., Chi.	15	1089	548	604	1152	825	92	39	39	78	110	....	1979-80	1993-94
Goupille, Red	Mtl.C., Mtl.	8	222	12	28	40	256	8	2	0	2	6	....	1935-36	1942-43
‡ Govedaris, Chris	Hfd., Tor.	4	45	4	6	10	24	4	0	0	0	2	....	1989-90	1993-94
Goyer, Gerry	Chi.	1	40	1	2	3	4	3	0	0	0	2	....	1967-68	1967-68
Goyette, Phil	Mtl., NYR, St.L., Buf.	16	941	207	467	674	131	94	17	29	46	26	4	1956-57	1971-72
Graboski, Tony	Mtl.	3	66	6	10	16	24	3	0	0	0	6	....	1940-41	1942-43
● Gracie, Bob	Tor., Bos., NYA, Mtl.M., Mtl.C., Chi.	9	379	82	109	191	205	33	4	7	11	4	2	1930-31	1938-39
Gradin, Thomas	Van., Bos.	9	677	209	384	593	298	42	17	25	42	20	....	1978-79	1986-87
Graham, Dirk	Min., Chi.	12	772	219	270	489	917	90	17	27	44	92	....	1983-84	1994-95
● Graham, Leth	Ott., Ham.	6	27	3	0	3	0	1	0	0	0	0	1	1920-21	1925-26
Graham, Pat	Pit., Tor.	3	103	11	17	28	136	4	0	0	0	2	....	1981-82	1983-84
Graham, Rod	Bos.	1	14	2	1	3	7	....	....	....	....	....	....	1974-75	1974-75
● Graham, Teddy	Chi., Mtl.M., Det., St.L., Bos., NYA	9	346	14	25	39	300	24	3	1	4	30	....	1927-28	1936-37
Grant, Danny	Mtl., Min., Det., L.A.	13	736	263	273	536	239	43	10	14	24	19	1	1965-66	1978-79
Gratton, Dan	L.A.	1	7	1	0	1	5	....	....	....	....	....	....	1987-88	1987-88
Gratton, Norm	NYR, Atl., Buf., Min.	5	201	39	44	83	64	6	0	1	1	2	....	1971-72	1975-76
Gravelle, Leo	Mtl., Det.	5	223	44	34	78	42	17	4	1	5	2	....	1946-47	1950-51
Graves, Hilliard	Cal., Atl., Van., Wpg.	9	556	118	163	281	209	2	0	0	0	0	....	1970-71	1979-80
Graves, Steve	Edm.	3	35	5	4	9	10	....	....	....	....	....	....	1983-84	1987-88
● Gray, Alex	NYR, Tor.	2	50	7	0	7	32	13	1	0	1	0	1	1927-28	1928-29
Gray, Terry	Bos., Mtl., L.A., St.L.	6	147	26	28	54	64	35	5	5	10	22	....	1961-62	1970-71
● Green, Red	Ham., NYA, Bos., Det.	6	195	59	26	85	290	1	0	0	0	0	1	1923-24	1928-29
Green, Rick	Wsh., Mtl., Det., NYI	15	845	43	220	263	588	100	3	16	19	73	1	1976-77	1991-92
● Green, Shorty	Ham., NYA	4	103	33	20	53	151	....	....	....	....	....	....	1923-24	1926-27
Green, Ted	Bos.	11	620	48	206	254	1029	31	4	8	12	54	1	1960-61	1971-72
‡ Greenlaw, Jeff	Wsh., Fla.	6	57	3	6	9	108	2	0	0	0	21	....	1986-87	1993-94
Gregg, Randy	Edm., Van.	10	474	41	152	193	333	137	13	38	51	127	5	1981-82	1991-92
Greig, Bruce	Cal.	2	9	0	1	1	46	....	....	....	....	....	....	1973-74	1974-75
Grenier, Lucien	Mtl., L.A.	4	151	14	14	28	18	2	0	0	0	0	1	1968-69	1971-72
Grenier, Richard	NYI	1	10	1	1	2	2	....	....	....	....	....	....	1972-73	1972-73
Greschner, Ron	NYR	16	982	179	431	610	1226	84	17	32	49	106	....	1974-75	1989-90
‡ Gretzky, Brent	T.B.	2	13	1	3	4	2	....	....	....	....	....	....	1993-94	1994-95
Gretzky, Wayne	Edm., L.A., St.L., NYR	20	1487	894	1963	2857	577	208	122	260	382	66	4	1979-80	1998-99
Grieve, Brent	NYI, Edm., Chi., L.A.	4	97	20	16	36	87	....	....	....	....	....	....	1993-94	1996-97
Grigor, George	Chi.	1	2	1	0	1	0	1	0	0	0	0	....	1943-44	1943-44
Grisdale, John	Tor., Van.	6	250	4	39	43	346	10	0	1	1	15	....	1972-73	1978-79
‡ Gronman, Tuomas	Chi., Pit.	2	38	1	3	4	38	1	0	0	0	0	....	1996-97	1997-98
Gronsdahl, Lloyd	Bos.	1	10	1	2	3	0	....	....	....	....	....	....	1941-42	1941-42
Gronstrand, Jari	Min., NYR, Que., NYI	5	185	8	26	34	135	3	0	0	0	4	....	1986-87	1990-91
Gross, Lloyd	Tor., NYA, Bos., Det.	3	62	11	5	16	20	1	0	0	0	0	....	1926-27	1934-35
● Grosso, Don	Det., Chi., Bos.	9	336	87	117	204	90	48	15	14	29	63	1	1938-39	1946-47
Grosvenor, Len	Ott., NYA, Mtl.C.	6	149	9	11	20	78	4	0	0	0	2	....	1927-28	1932-33
Groulx, Wayne	Que.	1	1	0	0	0	0	....	....	....	....	....	....	1984-85	1984-85
Gruen, Danny	Det., Col.	3	49	9	13	22	19	....	....	....	....	....	....	1972-73	1976-77
Gruhl, Scott	L.A., Pit.	3	20	3	3	6	6	....	....	....	....	....	....	1981-82	1987-88
Gryp, Bob	Bos., Wsh.	3	74	11	13	24	33	....	....	....	....	....	....	1973-74	1975-76
‡ Guay, Francois	Buf.	1	1	0	0	0	0	....	....	....	....	....	....	1989-90	1989-90
Guay, Paul	Phi., L.A., Bos., NYI	7	117	11	23	34	92	9	0	1	1	12	....	1983-84	1990-91
‡ Guerard, Daniel	Ott.	1	2	0	0	0	0	....	....	....	....	....	....	1994-95	1994-95
Guerard, Stephane	Que.	2	34	0	0	0	40	....	....	....	....	....	....	1987-88	1989-90
Guevremont, Jocelyn	Van., Buf., NYR	9	571	84	223	307	319	40	4	17	21	18	....	1971-72	1979-80
Guidolin, Aldo	NYR	4	182	9	15	24	117	....	....	....	....	....	....	1952-53	1955-56
Guidolin, Bep	Bos., Det., Chi.	9	519	107	171	278	606	24	5	7	12	35	....	1942-43	1951-52
Guindon, Bobby	Wpg.	1	6	0	1	1	0	....	....	....	....	....	....	1979-80	1979-80
Gustafsson, Bengt-Ake	Wsh.	9	629	196	359	555	196	32	9	19	28	16	....	1979-80	1988-89
‡ Gustafsson, Per	Fla., Tor., Ott.	2	89	8	27	35	38	1	0	0	0	0	....	1996-97	1997-98
Gustavsson, Peter	Col.	1	2	0	0	0	0	....	....	....	....	....	....	1981-82	1981-82
Guy, Kevan	Cgy., Van.	6	156	5	20	25	138	5	0	1	1	23	....	1986-87	1991-92

H

Name	NHL Teams	NHL Seasons	GP	G	A	TP	PIM	GP	G	A	TP	PIM	NHL Cup Wins	First NHL Season	Last NHL Season
Haanpaa, Ari	NYI	3	60	6	11	17	37	6	0	0	0	10	....	1985-86	1987-88
‡ Haas, David	Edm., Cgy.	2	7	2	1	3	7	....	....	....	....	....	....	1990-91	1993-94
Habscheid, Marc	Edm., Min., Det., Cgy.	11	345	72	91	163	171	12	1	3	4	13	....	1981-82	1991-92
‡ Hachborn, Len	Phi., L.A.	3	102	20	39	59	29	7	0	3	3	7	....	1983-84	1985-86
Haddon, Lloyd	Det.	1	8	0	0	0	2	1	0	0	0	0	....	1959-60	1959-60
Hadfield, Vic	NYR, Pit.	16	1002	323	389	712	1154	73	27	21	48	117	....	1961-62	1976-77
● Haggarty, Jim	Mtl.	1	5	1	1	2	0	3	2	1	3	0	....	1941-42	1941-42
● Hagglund, Roger	Que.	1	3	0	0	0	0	....	....	....	....	....	....	1984-85	1984-85
Hagman, Matti	Bos., Edm.	4	237	56	89	145	36	20	5	2	7	6	....	1976-77	1981-82
Haidy, Gord	Det.	1	....	....	....	....	....	1	0	0	0	0	1	1949-50	1949-50
Hajdu, Richard	Buf.	2	5	0	0	0	4	....	....	....	....	....	....	1985-86	1986-87
Hajt, Bill	Buf.	14	854	42	202	244	433	80	2	16	18	70	....	1973-74	1986-87
Hakansson, Anders	Min., Pit., L.A.	5	330	52	46	98	141	6	0	0	0	2	....	1981-82	1985-86
● Halderson, Harold	Det., Tor.	1	44	3	2	5	65	....	....	....	....	....	....	1926-27	1926-27
Hale, Larry	Phi.	4	196	5	37	42	90	8	0	0	0	12	....	1968-69	1971-72
Haley, Len	Det.	2	30	2	2	4	14	6	1	3	4	6	....	1959-60	1960-61
‡ Halkidis, Bob	Buf., L.A., Tor., Det., T.B., NYI	11	256	8	32	40	825	20	0	1	1	51	....	1984-85	1995-96
● Hall, Bob	NYA	1	8	0	0	0	0	....	....	....	....	....	....	1925-26	1925-26
Hall, Del	Cal.	3	9	2	0	2	2	....	....	....	....	....	....	1971-72	1973-74
● Hall, Joe	Mtl.C.	2	38	15	8	23	189	7	0	1	1	29	....	1917-18	1918-19
Hall, Murray	Chi., Det., Min., Van.	9	164	35	48	83	46	6	0	0	0	0	....	1961-62	1971-72
Hall, Taylor	Van., Bos.	5	41	7	9	16	29	....	....	....	....	....	....	1983-84	1987-88
Hall, Wayne	NYR	1	4	0	0	0	0	....	....	....	....	....	....	1960-61	1960-61
● Halliday, Milt	Ott.	3	67	1	0	1	4	6	0	0	0	0	1	1926-27	1928-29
Hallin, Mats	NYI, Min.	5	152	17	14	31	193	15	1	0	1	13	1	1982-83	1986-87
‡ Halverson, Trevor	Wsh.	1	17	0	4	4	28	....	....	....	....	....	....	1998-99	1998-99
Halward, Doug	Bos., L.A., Van., Det., Edm.	14	653	69	224	293	774	47	7	10	17	113	....	1975-76	1988-89
Hamel, Gilles	Buf., Wpg., L.A.	9	519	127	147	274	276	27	4	5	9	10	....	1980-81	1988-89
● Hamel, Herb	Tor.	1	2	0	0	0	4	....	....	....	....	....	....	1930-31	1930-31
Hamel, Jean	St.L., Det., Que., Mtl.	12	699	26	95	121	766	33	0	2	2	44	....	1972-73	1983-84
● Hamill, Red	Bos., Chi.	12	419	128	94	222	160	24	1	2	3	20	1	1937-38	1950-51
Hamilton, Al	NYR, Buf., Edm.	7	257	10	78	88	258	7	0	0	0	2	....	1965-66	1979-80
Hamilton, Chuck	Mtl., St.L.	2	4	0	2	2	2	....	....	....	....	....	....	1961-62	1972-73
● Hamilton, Jack	Tor.	3	102	28	32	60	20	11	2	1	3	0	....	1942-43	1945-46
Hamilton, Jim	Pit.	8	95	14	18	32	28	6	3	0	3	0	....	1977-78	1984-85
● Hamilton, Reg	Tor., Chi.	12	424	21	87	108	412	64	3	8	11	46	2	1935-36	1946-47
Hammarstrom, Inge	Tor., St.L.	6	427	116	123	239	86	13	2	3	5	4	....	1973-74	1978-79
Hammond, Ken	L.A., Edm., NYR, Tor., Bos., S.J., Van., Ott.	8	193	18	29	47	290	15	0	0	0	24	....	1984-85	1992-93
Hampson, Gord	Cgy.	1	4	0	0	0	5	....	....	....	....	....	....	1982-83	1982-83
Hampson, Ted	Tor., NYR, Det., Oak., Cal., Min.	12	676	108	245	353	94	35	7	10	17	2	....	1959-60	1971-72
Hampton, Rick	Cal., Cle., L.A.	6	337	59	113	172	147	2	0	0	0	0	....	1974-75	1979-80
‡ Hamr, Radek	Ott.	2	11	0	0	0	0	....	....	....	....	....	....	1992-93	1993-94
Hamway, Mark	NYI	3	53	5	13	18	9	1	0	0	0	0	....	1984-85	1986-87
‡ Handy, Ron	NYI, St.L.	2	14	0	3	3	0	....	....	....	....	....	....	1984-85	1987-88
Hangsleben, Al	Hfd., Wsh., L.A.	3	185	21	48	69	396	....	....	....	....	....	....	1979-80	1981-82
Hankinson, Ben	N.J., T.B.	3	43	3	3	6	45	2	1	0	1	4	....	1992-93	1994-95
Hanna, John	NYR, Mtl., Phi.	5	198	6	26	32	206	....	....	....	....	....	....	1958-59	1967-68
Hannan, Dave	Pit., Edm., Tor., Buf., Col., Ott.	16	841	114	191	305	942	63	6	7	13	46	2	1981-82	1996-97
● Hannigan, Gord	Tor.	4	161	29	31	60	117	9	2	0	2	8	....	1952-53	1955-56
Hannigan, Pat	Tor., NYR, Phi.	5	182	30	39	69	116	11	1	2	3	11	....	1959-60	1968-69
Hannigan, Ray	Tor.	1	3	0	0	0	2	....	....	....	....	....	....	1948-49	1948-49
Hansen, Richie	NYI, St.L.	4	20	2	8	10	4	....	....	....	....	....	....	1976-77	1981-82
Hanson, Dave	Det., Min.	2	33	1	1	2	65	....	....	....	....	....	....	1978-79	1979-80
● Hanson, Emil	Det.	1	7	0	0	0	6	....	....	....	....	....	....	1932-33	1932-33
Hanson, Keith	Cgy.	1	25	0	2	2	77	....	....	....	....	....	....	1983-84	1983-84
● Hanson, Oscar	Chi.	1	8	0	0	0	0	....	....	....	....	....	....	1937-38	1937-38
Harbaruk, Nick	Pit., St.L.	5	364	45	75	120	273	14	3	1	4	20	....	1969-70	1973-74
Harding, Jeff	Phi.	2	15	0	0	0	47	....	....	....	....	....	....	1988-89	1989-90
Hardy, Joe	Oak., Cal.	2	63	9	14	23	51	4	0	0	0	0	....	1969-70	1970-71
Hardy, Mark	L.A., NYR, Min.	15	915	62	306	368	1293	67	5	16	21	158	....	1979-80	1993-94
Hargreaves, Jim	Van.	2	66	1	7	8	105	....	....	....	....	....	....	1970-71	1972-73
‡ Harkins, Todd	Cgy., Hfd.	3	48	3	3	6	78	....	....	....	....	....	....	1991-92	1993-94

Jeff Greenlaw

Wayne Gretzky

Marc Habscheid

Anders Hakansson

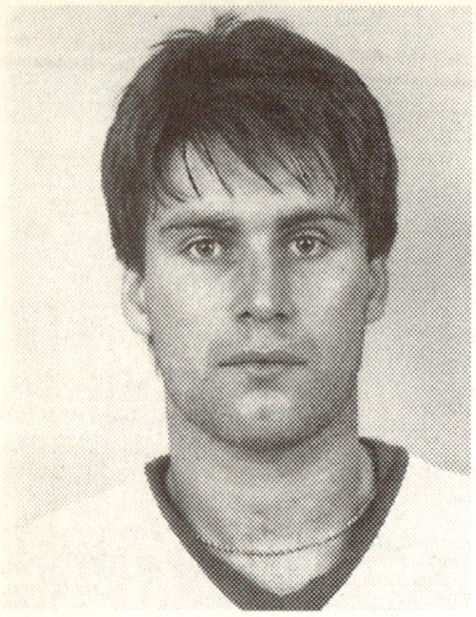

Mats Hallin

Trevor Halverson

Doug Harvey

Red Hay

			Regular Schedule					Playoffs							
Name	NHL Teams	NHL Seasons	GP	G	A	TP	PIM	GP	G	A	TP	PIM	NHL Cup Wins	First NHL Season	Last NHL Season
Harlow, Scott	St.L.	1	1	0	1	1	0	....	....	....	....	....	....	1987-88	1987-88
Harmon, Glen	Mtl.	9	452	50	96	146	334	53	5	10	15	37	2	1942-43	1950-51
Harms, John	Chi.	2	44	5	5	10	21	4	3	0	3	2	....	1943-44	1944-45
● Harnott, Walter	Bos.	1	6	0	0	0	2	....	....	....	....	....	....	1933-34	1933-34
Harper, Terry	Mtl., L.A., Det., St.L., Col.	19	1066	35	221	256	1362	112	4	13	17	140	5	1962-63	1980-81
Harrer, Tim	Cgy.	1	3	0	0	0	2	....	....	....	....	....	....	1982-83	1982-83
● Harrington, Hago	Bos., Mtl.C.	3	72	9	3	12	15	4	1	0	1	2	....	1925-26	1932-33
Harris, Billy	Tor., Det., Oak., Pit.	13	769	126	219	345	205	62	8	10	18	30	3	1955-56	1968-69
Harris, Billy	NYI, L.A., Tor.	12	897	231	327	558	394	71	19	19	38	48	....	1972-73	1983-84
Harris, Duke	Min., Tor.	1	26	1	4	5	4	....	....	....	....	....	....	1967-68	1967-68
● Harris, Henry	Bos.	1	32	2	4	6	20	....	....	....	....	....	....	1930-31	1930-31
Harris, Hugh	Buf.	1	60	12	26	38	17	3	0	0	0	0	....	1972-73	1972-73
Harris, Ron	Det., Oak., Atl., NYR	11	476	20	91	111	474	28	4	3	7	33	....	1962-63	1975-76
● Harris, Smokey	Bos.	1	6	3	1	4	8	....	....	....	....	....	....	1924-25	1924-25
Harris, Ted	Mtl., Min., Det., St.L., Phi.	12	788	30	168	198	1000	100	1	22	23	230	5	1963-64	1974-75
Harrison, Ed	Bos., NYR	4	194	27	24	51	53	9	1	0	1	2	....	1947-48	1950-51
Harrison, Jim	Bos., Tor., Chi., Edm.	8	324	67	86	153	435	13	1	1	2	43	....	1968-69	1979-80
Hart, Gerry	Det., NYI, Que., St.L.	15	730	29	150	179	1240	78	3	12	15	175	....	1968-69	1982-83
● Hart, Gizzy	Det., Mtl.C.	3	104	6	8	14	12	8	0	1	1	0	....	1926-27	1932-33
Hartman, Mike	Buf., Wpg., T.B., NYR	9	397	43	35	78	1388	21	0	0	0	106	1	1986-87	1994-95
Hartsburg, Craig	Min.	10	570	98	315	413	818	61	15	27	42	70	....	1979-80	1988-89
Harvey, Buster	Min., Atl., K.C., Det.	7	407	90	118	208	131	14	0	2	2	8	....	1970-71	1976-77
● Harvey, Doug	Mtl., NYR, Det., St.L.	20	1113	88	452	540	1216	137	8	64	72	152	6	1947-48	1968-69
Harvey, Hugh	K.C.	2	18	1	1	2	4	....	....	....	....	....	....	1974-75	1975-76
Hassard, Bob	Tor., Chi.	5	126	9	28	37	22	....	....	....	....	....	1	1949-50	1954-55
Hatoum, Ed	Det., Van.	3	47	3	6	9	25	....	....	....	....	....	....	1968-69	1970-71
Hawerchuk, Dale	Wpg., Buf., St.L., Phi.	16	1188	518	891	1409	730	97	30	69	99	67	....	1981-82	1996-97
‡ Hawkins, Todd	Van., Tor.	3	10	0	0	0	15	....	....	....	....	....	....	1988-89	1991-92
Haworth, Alan	Buf., Wsh., Que.	8	524	189	211	400	425	42	12	16	28	28	....	1980-81	1987-88
Haworth, Gord	NYR	1	2	0	1	1	0	....	....	....	....	....	....	1952-53	1952-53
Hawryliw, Neil	NYI	1	1	0	0	0	0	....	....	....	....	....	....	1981-82	1981-82
Hay, Bill	Chi.	8	506	113	273	386	244	67	15	21	36	62	1	1959-60	1966-67
● Hay, George	Chi., Det.	7	239	74	60	134	84	8	2	3	5	2	....	1926-27	1933-34
Hay, Jim	Det.	3	75	1	5	6	22	9	1	0	1	2	1	1952-53	1954-55
Hayek, Peter	Min.	1	1	0	0	0	0	....	....	....	....	....	....	1981-82	1981-82
Hayes, Chris	Bos.	1	....	....	....	....	....	1	0	0	0	0	1	1971-72	1971-72
● Haynes, Paul	Mtl.M., Bos., Mtl.C., Mtl.	11	391	61	134	195	164	24	2	8	10	13	....	1930-31	1940-41
‡ Hayward, Rick	L.A.	1	4	0	0	0	5	....	....	....	....	....	....	1990-91	1990-91
Hazlett, Steve	Van.	1	1	0	0	0	0	....	....	....	....	....	....	1979-80	1979-80
Head, Galen	Det.	1	1	0	0	0	0	....	....	....	....	....	....	1967-68	1967-68
● Headley, Fern	Bos., Mtl.C.	1	30	1	3	4	10	1	0	0	0	0	....	1924-25	1924-25
Healey, Rich	Det.	1	1	0	0	0	2	....	....	....	....	....	....	1960-61	1960-61
‡ Heaphy, Shawn	Cgy.	1	1	0	0	0	0	....	....	....	....	....	....	1992-93	1992-93
Heaslip, Mark	NYR, L.A.	3	117	10	19	29	110	5	0	0	0	2	....	1976-77	1978-79
Heath, Randy	NYR	2	13	2	4	6	15	....	....	....	....	....	....	1984-85	1985-86
Hebenton, Andy	NYR, Bos.	9	630	189	202	391	83	22	6	5	11	8	....	1955-56	1963-64
Hedberg, Anders	NYR	7	465	172	225	397	144	58	22	24	46	31	....	1978-79	1984-85
● Heffernan, Frank	Tor.	1	19	0	1	1	10	....	....	....	....	....	....	1919-20	1919-20
Heffernan, Gerry	Mtl.	3	83	33	35	68	27	11	3	3	6	8	1	1941-42	1943-44
Heidt, Michael	L.A.	1	6	0	1	1	7	....	....	....	....	....	....	1983-84	1983-84
● Heindl, Bill	Min., NYR	3	18	2	1	3	0	....	....	....	....	....	....	1970-71	1972-73
Heinrich, Lionel	Bos.	1	35	1	1	2	33	....	....	....	....	....	....	1955-56	1955-56
Heiskala, Earl	Phi.	3	127	13	11	24	294	....	....	....	....	....	....	1968-69	1970-71
Helander, Peter	L.A.	1	7	0	1	1	0	....	....	....	....	....	....	1982-83	1982-83
● Heller, Ott	NYR	15	647	55	176	231	465	61	6	8	14	61	2	1931-32	1945-46
Helman, Harry	Ott.	3	44	1	0	1	7	2	0	0	0	0	1	1922-23	1924-25
‡ Helminen, Raimo	NYR, Min., NYI	3	117	13	46	59	16	2	0	0	0	0	....	1985-86	1988-89
● Hemmerling, Tony	NYA	2	22	3	3	6	4						....	1935-36	1936-37
Henderson, Archie	Wsh., Min., Hfd.	3	23	3	1	4	92	....	....	....	....	....	....	1980-81	1982-83
Henderson, Murray	Bos.	8	405	24	62	86	305	41	2	3	5	23	....	1944-45	1951-52
Henderson, Paul	Det., Tor., Atl.	13	707	236	241	477	304	56	11	14	25	28	....	1962-63	1979-80
Hendrickson, John	Det.	3	5	0	0	0	4	....	....	....	....	....	....	1957-58	1961-62
Henning, Lorne	NYI	9	544	73	111	184	102	81	7	7	14	8	2	1972-73	1980-81
● Henry, Camille	NYR, Chi., St.L.	14	727	279	249	528	88	47	6	12	18	7	....	1953-54	1969-70
Hepple, Alan	N.J.	3	3	0	0	0	7	....	....	....	....	....	....	1983-84	1985-86
● Herbert, Jimmy	Bos., Tor., Det.	6	206	83	31	114	253	9	3	0	3	10	....	1924-25	1929-30
Herchenratter, Art	Det.	1	10	1	2	3	2	....	....	....	....	....	....	1940-41	1940-41
Hergerts, Fred	NYA	2	20	2	4	6	2	....	....	....	....	....	....	1934-35	1935-36
Hergesheimer, Phil	Chi., Bos.	4	125	21	41	62	19	6	0	0	0	2	....	1939-40	1942-43
Hergesheimer, Wally	NYR, Chi.	7	351	114	85	199	106	5	1	0	1	0	....	1951-52	1958-59
● Heron, Red	Tor., Bro., Mtl.	4	106	21	19	40	38	21	2	2	4	6	....	1938-39	1941-42
Heroux, Yves	Que.	1	1	0	0	0	0	....	....	....	....	....	....	1986-87	1986-87
‡ Herter, Jason	NYI	1	1	0	1	1	0	....	....	....	....	....	....	1995-96	1995-96
Hervey, Matt	Wpg., Bos., T.B.	3	35	0	5	5	97	5	0	0	0	6	....	1988-89	1992-93
Hess, Bob	St.L., Buf., Hfd.	8	329	27	95	122	178	4	1	1	2	2	....	1974-75	1983-84
● Heximer, Obs	NYR, Bos., NYA	3	84	13	7	20	16	5	0	0	0	2	....	1929-30	1934-35
● Hextall, Bryan	NYR	11	449	187	175	362	227	37	8	9	17	19	1	1936-37	1947-48
Hextall, Bryan Jr.	NYR, Pit., Atl., Det., Min.	8	549	99	161	260	738	18	0	4	4	59	....	1962-63	1975-76
Hextall, Dennis	NYR, L.A., Cal., Min., Det., Wsh.	13	681	153	350	503	1398	22	3	3	6	45	....	1967-68	1979-80
Heyliger, Vic	Chi.	2	33	2	3	5	2	....	....	....	....	....	....	1937-38	1943-44
Hicke, Bill	Mtl., NYR, Oak., Cal., Pit.	14	729	168	234	402	395	42	3	10	13	41	2	1958-59	1971-72
Hicke, Ernie	Cal., Atl., NYI, Min., L.A.	8	520	132	140	272	407	2	1	0	1	0	....	1970-71	1977-78
Hickey, Greg	NYR	1	1	0	0	0	0	....	....	....	....	....	....	1977-78	1977-78
Hickey, Pat	NYR, Col., Tor., Que., St.L.	10	646	192	212	404	351	55	5	11	16	37	....	1975-76	1984-85
Hicks, Doug	Min., Chi., Edm., Wsh.	9	561	37	131	168	442	18	2	1	3	15	....	1974-75	1982-83
Hicks, Glenn	Det.	2	108	6	12	18	127	....	....	....	....	....	....	1979-80	1980-81
● Hicks, Henry	Mtl.M., Det.	3	96	7	2	9	72	....	....	....	....	....	....	1928-29	1930-31
Hicks, Wayne	Chi., Bos., Mtl., Phi., Pit.	5	115	13	23	36	22	2	0	1	1	2	1	1959-60	1967-68
Hidi, Andre	Wsh.	2	7	2	1	3	9	2	0	0	0	0	....	1983-84	1984-85
Hiemer, Uli	N.J.	3	143	19	54	73	176	....	....	....	....	....	....	1984-85	1986-87
Higgins, Paul	Tor.	2	25	0	0	0	152	1	0	0	0	0	....	1981-82	1982-83
Higgins, Tim	Chi., N.J., Det.	11	706	154	198	352	719	65	5	8	13	77	....	1978-79	1988-89
Hildebrand, Ike	NYR, Chi.	2	41	7	11	18	16	....	....	....	....	....	....	1953-54	1954-55
Hill, Al	Phi.	8	221	40	55	95	227	51	8	11	19	43	....	1976-77	1987-88
Hill, Brian	Hfd.	1	19	1	1	2	4	....	....	....	....	....	....	1979-80	1979-80
● Hill, Mel	Bos., Bro., Tor.	9	324	89	109	198	128	43	12	7	19	18	3	1937-38	1945-46
Hiller, Dutch	NYR, Det., Bos., Mtl.	9	383	91	113	204	163	48	9	8	17	21	2	1937-38	1945-46
‡ Hiller, Jim	L.A., Det., NYR	2	63	8	12	20	116	2	0	0	0	4	....	1992-93	1993-94
Hillier, Randy	Bos., Pit., NYI, Buf.	11	543	16	110	126	906	28	0	2	2	93	1	1981-82	1991-92
Hillman, Floyd	Bos.	1	6	0	0	0	10	....	....	....	....	....	....	1956-57	1956-57
Hillman, Larry	Det., Bos., Tor., Min., Mtl., Phi., L.A., Buf.	19	790	36	196	232	579	74	2	9	11	30	6	1954-55	1972-73
● Hillman, Wayne	Chi., NYR, Min., Phi.	13	691	18	86	104	534	28	0	3	3	19	1	1960-61	1972-73
Hilworth, John	Det.	3	57	1	1	2	89	....	....	....	....	....	....	1977-78	1979-80
● Himes, Normie	NYA	9	402	106	113	219	127	2	0	0	0	0	....	1926-27	1934-35
Hindmarch, Dave	Cgy.	4	99	21	17	38	25	10	0	0	0	6	....	1980-81	1983-84
Hinse, Andre	Tor.	1	4	0	0	0	0	....	....	....	....	....	....	1967-68	1967-68
Hinton, Dan	Chi.	1	14	0	0	0	16	....	....	....	....	....	....	1976-77	1976-77
Hirsch, Tom	Min.	3	31	1	7	8	30	12	0	0	0	6	....	1983-84	1987-88
● Hirschfeld, Bert	Mtl.	2	33	1	4	5	2	5	1	0	1	0	....	1949-50	1950-51
Hislop, Jamie	Que., Cgy.	5	345	75	103	178	86	28	3	2	5	11	....	1979-80	1983-84
● Hitchman, Lionel	Ott., Bos.	12	417	28	34	62	523	35	3	1	4	73	2	1922-23	1933-34
Hlinka, Ivan	Van.	2	137	42	81	123	28	16	3	10	13	8	....	1981-82	1982-83
Hodge, Ken	Chi., Bos., NYR	14	881	328	472	800	779	97	34	47	81	120	2	1964-65	1977-78
Hodge, Ken	Min., Bos., T.B.	4	142	39	48	87	32	15	4	6	10	6	....	1988-89	1992-93
‡ Hodgson, Dan	Tor., Van.	4	114	29	45	74	64	....	....	....	....	....	....	1985-86	1988-89
Hodgson, Rick	Hfd.	1	6	0	0	0	6	1	0	0	0	0	....	1979-80	1979-80
Hodgson, Ted	Bos.	1	4	0	0	0	0	....	....	....	....	....	....	1966-67	1966-67
Hoekstra, Cec	Mtl.	1	4	0	0	0	0	....	....	....	....	....	....	1959-60	1959-60
Hoekstra, Ed	Phi.	1	70	15	21	36	6	7	0	1	1	0	....	1967-68	1967-68
Hoene, Phil	L.A.	3	37	2	4	6	22	....	....	....	....	....	....	1972-73	1974-75
Hoffinger, Val	Chi.	2	28	0	1	1	30	....	....	....	....	....	....	1927-28	1928-29
Hoffman, Mike	Hfd.	3	9	1	3	4	2	....	....	....	....	....	....	1982-83	1985-86
Hoffmeyer, Bob	Chi., Phi., N.J.	6	198	14	52	66	325	3	0	1	1	25	....	1977-78	1984-85
Hofford, Jim	Buf., L.A.	3	18	0	0	0	47	....	....	....	....	....	....	1985-86	1988-89
Hogaboam, Bill	Atl., Det., Min.	8	332	80	109	189	100	2	0	0	0	0	....	1972-73	1979-80

			Regular Schedule					Playoffs					NHL	First	Last
Name	NHL Teams	NHL Seasons	GP	G	A	TP	PIM	GP	G	A	TP	PIM	Cup Wins	NHL Season	NHL Season
Hoganson, Dale	L.A., Mtl., Que.	7	343	13	77	90	186	11	0	3	3	12	....	1969-70	1981-82
‡ Holan, Milos	Phi., Ana.	3	49	5	11	16	42	....	....	....	....	....	....	1993-94	1995-96
Holbrook, Terry	Min.	2	43	3	6	9	4	6	0	0	0	0	....	1972-73	1973-74
Holland, Jerry	NYR	2	37	8	4	12	6	....	....	....	....	....	....	1974-75	1975-76
• Hollett, Flash	Tor., Ott., Bos., Det.	13	562	132	181	313	358	79	8	26	34	38	2	1933-34	1945-46
• Hollingworth, Gord	Chi., Det.	4	163	4	14	18	201	3	0	0	0	2	....	1954-55	1957-58
Holloway, Bruce	Van.	1	2	0	0	0	0	....	....	....	....	....	....	1984-85	1984-85
• Holmes, Bill	Mtl.C., NYA	3	52	6	4	10	35	....	....	....	....	....	....	1925-26	1929-30
Holmes, Chuck	Det.	2	23	1	3	4	10	....	....	....	....	....	....	1958-59	1961-62
Holmes, Lou	Chi.	2	59	1	4	5	6	2	0	0	0	2	....	1931-32	1932-33
Holmes, Warren	L.A.	3	45	8	18	26	7	....	....	....	....	....	....	1981-82	1983-84
Holmgren, Paul	Phi., Min.	10	527	144	179	323	1684	82	19	32	51	195	....	1975-76	1984-85
• Holota, John	Det.	2	15	2	0	2	0	....	....	....	....	....	....	1942-43	1945-46
Holst, Greg	NYR	3	11	0	0	0	0	....	....	....	....	....	....	1975-76	1977-78
Holt, Gary	Cal., Cle., St.L.	5	101	13	11	24	133	....	....	....	....	....	....	1973-74	1977-78
Holt, Randy	Chi., Cle., Van., L.A., Cgy., Wsh., Phi.	10	395	4	37	41	1438	21	2	3	5	83	....	1974-75	1983-84
• Holway, Albert	Tor., Mtl.M., Pit.	5	112	7	2	9	48	6	0	0	0	0	1	1923-24	1928-29
Homenuke, Ron	Van.	1	1	0	0	0	0	....	....	....	....	....	....	1972-73	1972-73
Hoover, Ron	Bos., St.L.	3	18	4	0	4	31	8	0	0	0	18	....	1989-90	1991-92
Hopkins, Dean	L.A., Edm., Que.	6	223	23	51	74	306	18	1	5	6	29	....	1979-80	1988-89
Hopkins, Larry	Tor., Wpg.	4	60	13	16	29	26	6	0	0	0	2	....	1977-78	1982-83
Horacek, Tony	Phi., Chi.	5	154	10	19	29	316	2	1	0	1	2	....	1989-90	1994-95
‡ Horava, Miloslav	NYR	3	80	5	17	22	38	2	0	1	1	0	....	1988-89	1990-91
Horbul, Doug	K.C.	1	4	1	0	1	2	....	....	....	....	....	....	1974-75	1974-75
Hordy, Mike	NYI	2	11	0	0	0	7	....	....	....	....	....	....	1978-79	1979-80
Horeck, Pete	Chi., Det., Bos.	8	426	106	118	224	340	34	6	8	14	43	....	1944-45	1951-52
• Horne, George	Mtl.M., Tor.	3	54	9	3	12	34	4	0	0	0	4	1	1925-26	1928-29
Horner, Red	Tor.	12	490	42	110	152	1254	71	7	10	17	170	1	1928-29	1939-40
• Hornung, Larry	St.L.	2	48	2	9	11	10	11	0	2	2	2	....	1970-71	1971-72
• Horton, Tim	Tor., NYR, Pit., Buf.	24	1446	115	403	518	1611	126	11	39	50	183	4	1949-50	1973-74
Horvath, Bronco	NYR, Mtl., Bos., Chi., Tor., Min.	9	434	141	185	326	319	36	12	9	21	18	....	1955-56	1967-68
Hospodar, Ed	NYR, Hfd., Phi., Min., Buf.	9	450	17	51	68	1314	44	4	1	5	208	....	1979-80	1987-88
‡ Hostak, Martin	Phi.	2	55	3	11	14	24	....	....	....	....	....	....	1990-91	1991-92
Hotham, Greg	Tor., Pit.	6	230	15	74	89	139	5	0	3	3	6	....	1979-80	1984-85
Houck, Paul	Min.	3	16	1	2	3	2	....	....	....	....	....	....	1985-86	1987-88
Houde, Claude	K.C.	2	59	3	6	9	40	....	....	....	....	....	....	1974-75	1975-76
Hough, Mike	Que., Fla., NYI	13	707	100	156	256	675	42	5	5	10	38	....	1986-87	1998-99
Houle, Rejean	Mtl.	11	635	161	247	408	395	90	14	34	48	66	5	1969-70	1982-83
Houston, Ken	Atl., Cgy., Wsh., L.A.	9	570	161	167	328	624	35	10	9	19	66	....	1975-76	1983-84
Howard, Jack	Tor.	1	2	0	0	0	0	....	....	....	....	....	....	1936-37	1936-37
Howatt, Garry	NYI, Hfd., N.J.	12	720	112	156	268	1836	87	12	14	26	289	2	1972-73	1983-84
Howe, Gordie	Det., Hfd.	26	1767	801	1049	1850	1685	157	68	92	160	220	4	1946-47	1979-80
Howe, Mark	Hfd., Phi., Det.	16	929	197	545	742	455	101	10	51	61	34	....	1979-80	1994-95
Howe, Marty	Hfd., Bos.	6	197	2	29	31	99	15	1	2	3	9	....	1979-80	1984-85
• Howe, Syd	Ott., Phi., Tor., St.L., Det.	17	698	237	291	528	212	70	17	27	44	10	3	1929-30	1945-46
Howe, Vic	NYR	3	33	3	4	7	10	....	....	....	....	....	....	1950-51	1954-55
Howell, Harry	NYR, Oak., Cal., L.A.	21	1411	94	324	418	1298	38	3	3	6	32	....	1952-53	1972-73
• Howell, Ron	NYR	2	4	0	0	0	0	....	....	....	....	....	....	1954-55	1955-56
Howse, Don	L.A.	1	33	2	5	7	6	2	0	0	0	0	....	1979-80	1979-80
Howson, Scott	NYI	2	18	5	3	8	4	....	....	....	....	....	....	1984-85	1985-86
Hoyda, Dave	Phi., Wpg.	4	132	6	17	23	299	12	0	0	0	17	....	1977-78	1980-81
Hrdina, Jiri	Cgy., Pit.	5	250	45	85	130	92	46	2	5	7	24	3	1987-88	1991-92
Hrechkosy, Dave	Cal., St.L.	4	140	42	24	66	41	3	1	0	1	2	....	1973-74	1976-77
Hrycuik, Jim	Wsh.	1	21	5	5	10	12	....	....	....	....	....	....	1974-75	1974-75
Hrymnak, Steve	Chi., Det.	2	18	2	1	3	4	2	0	0	0	0	....	1951-52	1952-53
Hrynewich, Tim	Pit.	2	55	6	8	14	82	....	....	....	....	....	....	1982-83	1983-84
Huard, Rolly	Tor.	1	1	1	0	1	0	....	....	....	....	....	....	1930-31	1930-31
Huber, Willie	Det., NYR, Van., Phi.	10	655	104	217	321	950	33	5	5	10	35	....	1978-79	1987-88
Hubick, Greg	Tor., Van.	2	77	6	9	15	10	....	....	....	....	....	....	1975-76	1979-80
Huck, Fran	Mtl., St.L.	3	94	24	30	54	38	11	3	4	7	2	....	1969-70	1972-73
Hucul, Fred	Chi., St.L.	5	164	11	30	41	113	6	1	0	1	10	....	1950-51	1967-68
Huddy, Charlie	Edm., L.A., Buf., St.L.	17	1017	99	354	453	785	183	19	66	85	135	5	1980-81	1996-97
Hudson, Dave	NYI, K.C., Col.	6	409	59	124	183	89	2	1	1	2	0	....	1972-73	1977-78
Hudson, Lex	Pit.	1	2	0	0	0	0	2	0	0	0	0	....	1978-79	1978-79
Hudson, Mike	Chi., Edm., NYR, Pit., Tor., St.L., Phx.	9	416	49	87	136	414	49	4	10	14	64	1	1988-89	1996-97
Hudson, Ron	Det.	2	33	5	2	7	2	....	....	....	....	....	....	1937-38	1939-40
Huffman, Kerry	Phi., Que., Ott.	10	401	37	108	145	361	11	0	0	0	2	....	1986-87	1995-96
Huggins, Al	Mtl.M.	1	20	1	1	2	2	....	....	....	....	....	....	1930-31	1930-31
Hughes, Albert	NYA	2	60	6	8	14	22	....	....	....	....	....	....	1930-31	1931-32
Hughes, Brent	L.A., Phi., St.L., Det., K.C.	8	435	15	117	132	440	22	1	3	4	53	....	1967-68	1974-75
Hughes, Brent	Wpg., Bos., Buf., NYI	8	357	41	39	80	831	29	4	1	5	53	....	1988-89	1996-97
Hughes, Frank	Cal.	1	5	0	0	0	0	....	....	....	....	....	....	1971-72	1971-72
Hughes, Howie	L.A.	3	168	25	32	57	30	14	2	0	2	2	....	1967-68	1969-70
Hughes, Jack	Col.	2	46	2	5	7	104	....	....	....	....	....	....	1980-81	1981-82
Hughes, James	Det.	1	40	0	1	1	48	....	....	....	....	....	....	1929-30	1929-30
Hughes, John	Van., Edm., NYR	2	70	2	14	16	211	7	0	1	1	16	....	1979-80	1980-81
Hughes, Pat	Mtl., Pit., Edm., Buf., St.L., Hfd.	10	573	130	128	258	646	71	8	25	33	77	3	1977-78	1986-87
Hughes, Ryan	Bos.	1	3	0	0	0	0	....	....	....	....	....	....	1995-96	1995-96
Hull, Bobby	Chi., Wpg., Hfd.	16	1063	610	560	1170	640	119	62	67	129	102	1	1957-58	1979-80
Hull, Dennis	Chi., Det.	14	959	303	351	654	261	104	33	34	67	30	....	1964-65	1977-78
• Hunt, Fred	NYA, NYR	2	59	15	14	29	6	....	....	....	....	....	....	1940-41	1944-45
Hunter, Dale	Que., Wsh., Col.	19	1407	323	697	1020	3565	186	42	76	118	729	....	1980-81	1998-99
Hunter, Dave	Edm., Pit., Wpg.	10	746	133	190	323	918	105	16	24	40	211	3	1979-80	1988-89
Hunter, Mark	Mtl., St.L., Cgy., Hfd., Wsh.	12	628	213	171	384	1426	79	18	20	38	230	1	1981-82	1992-93
Hunter, Tim	Cgy., Que., Van., S.J.	16	815	62	76	138	3146	132	5	7	12	426	1	1981-82	1996-97
Huras, Larry	NYR	1	2	0	0	0	0	....	....	....	....	....	....	1976-77	1976-77
Hurlburt, Bob	Van.	1	1	0	0	0	2	....	....	....	....	....	....	1974-75	1974-75
Hurley, Paul	Bos.	1	1	0	1	1	0	....	....	....	....	....	....	1968-69	1968-69
Hurst, Ron	Tor.	2	64	9	7	16	70	3	0	2	2	4	....	1955-56	1956-57
‡ Huska, Ryan	Chi.	1	1	0	0	0	0	....	....	....	....	....	....	1997-98	1997-98
Huston, Ron	Cal.	2	79	15	31	46	8	....	....	....	....	....	....	1973-74	1974-75
Hutchinson, Ron	NYR	1	9	0	0	0	0	....	....	....	....	....	....	1960-61	1960-61
Hutchison, Dave	L.A., Tor., Chi., N.J.	10	584	19	97	116	1550	48	2	12	14	149	....	1974-75	1983-84
• Hutton, Bill	Bos., Ott., Phi.	2	64	3	2	5	8	2	0	0	0	0	....	1929-30	1930-31
• Hyland, Harry	Mtl., Ott.	1	17	14	2	16	65	....	....	....	....	....	....	1917-18	1917-18
Hynes, Dave	Bos.	2	22	4	0	4	2	....	....	....	....	....	....	1973-74	1974-75
‡ Hynes, Gord	Bos., Phi.	2	52	3	9	12	22	12	1	2	3	6	....	1991-92	1992-93

I

Iafrate, Al	Tor., Wsh., Bos., S.J.	12	799	152	311	463	1301	71	19	16	35	77	....	1984-85	1997-98
‡ Ihnacak, Miroslav	Tor., Det.	3	56	8	9	17	39	1	0	0	0	0	....	1985-86	1988-89
Ihnacak, Peter	Tor.	8	417	102	165	267	175	28	4	10	14	25	....	1982-83	1989-90
Imlach, Brent	Tor.	2	3	0	0	0	0	....	....	....	....	....	....	1965-66	1966-67
Ingarfield, Earl	NYR, Pit., Oak., Cal.	13	746	179	226	405	239	21	9	8	17	10	....	1958-59	1970-71
Ingarfield, Earl Jr.	Atl., Cgy., Det.	2	39	4	4	8	22	2	0	1	1	0	....	1979-80	1980-81
Inglis, Billy	L.A., Buf.	3	36	1	3	4	4	11	1	2	3	4	....	1967-68	1970-71
• Ingoldsby, Johnny	Tor.	2	29	5	1	6	15	....	....	....	....	....	....	1942-43	1943-44
Ingram, Frank	Chi.	3	101	24	16	40	69	11	0	1	1	2	....	1929-30	1931-32
• Ingram, John J.	Bos.	1	1	0	0	0	0	....	....	....	....	....	....	1924-25	1924-25
Ingram, Ron	Chi., Det., NYR	4	114	5	15	20	81	2	0	0	0	0	....	1956-57	1964-65
‡ Intranuovo, Ralph	Edm., Tor.	3	22	2	4	6	4	....	....	....	....	....	....	1994-95	1996-97
• Irvin, Dick	Chi.	3	94	29	23	52	78	2	2	0	2	4	....	1926-27	1928-29
Irvine, Ted	Bos., L.A., NYR, St.L.	11	724	154	177	331	657	83	16	24	40	115	....	1963-64	1976-77
Irwin, Ivan	Mtl., NYR	5	155	2	27	29	214	5	0	0	0	8	....	1952-53	1957-58
Isaksson, Ulf	L.A.	1	50	7	15	22	10	....	....	....	....	....	....	1982-83	1982-83
Issel, Kim	Edm.	1	4	0	0	0	0	....	....	....	....	....	....	1988-89	1988-89

J

• Jackson, Art	Tor., Bos., NYA	11	468	123	178	301	144	52	8	12	20	29	2	1934-35	1944-45
• Jackson, Busher	Tor., NYA, Bos.	15	633	241	234	475	437	71	18	12	30	53	1	1929-30	1943-44
Jackson, Don	Min., Edm., NYR	10	311	16	52	68	640	53	4	5	9	147	2	1977-78	1986-87
• Jackson, Harold	Chi., Det.	8	219	17	34	51	208	31	1	2	3	33	2	1936-37	1946-47
Jackson, Jack	Chi.	1	48	2	5	7	38	....	....	....	....	....	....	1946-47	1946-47
Jackson, Jeff	Tor., NYR, Que., Chi.	8	263	38	48	86	313	6	1	1	2	16	....	1984-85	1991-92

Wally Hergesheimer

Gordie Howe

Bobby Hull

Dick Irvin

Ed Johnstone

Aurel Joliat

Stan Jonathan

Kevin Kaminski

			Regular Schedule					Playoffs							
Name	NHL Teams	NHL Seasons	GP	G	A	TP	PIM	GP	G	A	TP	PIM	NHL Cup Wins	First NHL Season	Last NHL Season
Jackson, Jim	Cgy., Buf.	4	112	17	30	47	20	14	3	2	5	6	....	1982-83	1987-88
● Jackson, Lloyd	NYA	1	14	1	1	2	0	....	....	....	....	....	....	1936-37	1936-37
● Jackson, Stan	Tor., Bos., Ott.	5	86	9	6	15	75	....	....	....	....	....	1	1921-22	1926-27
Jackson, Walter	NYA, Bos.	4	84	16	11	27	18	....	....	....	....	....	....	1932-33	1935-36
● Jacobs, Paul	Tor.	1	1	0	0	0	0	....	....	....	....	....	....	1918-19	1918-19
Jacobs, Tim	Cal.	1	46	0	10	10	35	....	....	....	....	....	....	1975-76	1975-76
Jalo, Risto	Edm.	1	3	0	3	3	0	....	....	....	....	....	....	1985-86	1985-86
Jalonen, Kari	Cgy., Edm.	2	37	9	6	15	4	5	1	0	1	0	....	1982-83	1983-84
James, Gerry	Tor.	5	149	14	26	40	257	15	1	0	1	8	....	1954-55	1959-60
James, Val	Buf., Tor.	2	11	0	0	0	30	....	....	....	....	....	....	1981-82	1986-87
Jamieson, Jim	NYR	1	1	0	1	1	0	....	....	....	....	....	....	1943-44	1943-44
Jankowski, Lou	Det., Chi.	4	127	19	18	37	15	1	0	0	0	0	....	1950-51	1954-55
Janney, Craig	Bos., St.L., S.J., Wpg., Phx., T.B., NYI	12	760	188	563	751	170	120	24	86	110	53	....	1987-88	1998-99
‡ Jantunen, Marko	Cgy.	1	3	0	0	0	0	....	....	....	....	....	....	1996-97	1996-97
Jarrett, Doug	Chi., NYR	13	775	38	182	220	631	99	7	16	23	82	....	1964-65	1976-77
Jarrett, Gary	Tor., Det., Oak., Cal.	7	341	72	92	164	131	11	3	1	4	9	....	1960-61	1971-72
Jarry, Pierre	NYR, Tor., Det., Min.	7	344	88	117	205	142	5	0	1	1	0	....	1971-72	1977-78
Jarvenpaa, Hannu	Wpg.	3	114	11	26	37	83	....	....	....	....	....	....	1986-87	1988-89
Jarvi, Iiro	Que.	2	116	18	43	61	58	....	....	....	....	....	....	1988-89	1989-90
Jarvis, Doug	Mtl., Wsh., Hfd.	13	964	139	264	403	263	105	14	27	41	42	4	1975-76	1987-88
● Jarvis, James	Pit., Phi., Tor.	3	112	17	15	32	62	....	....	....	....	....	....	1929-30	1936-37
Jarvis, Wes	Wsh., Min., L.A., Tor.	9	237	31	55	86	98	2	0	0	0	2	....	1979-80	1987-88
Javanainen, Arto	Pit.	1	14	4	1	5	2	....	....	....	....	....	....	1984-85	1984-85
Jay, Bob	L.A.	1	3	0	1	1	0	....	....	....	....	....	....	1993-94	1993-94
Jeffrey, Larry	Det., Tor., NYR	8	368	39	62	101	293	38	4	10	14	42	1	1961-62	1968-69
Jelinek, Tomas	Ott.	1	49	7	6	13	52	....	....	....	....	....	....	1992-93	1992-93
Jenkins, Dean	L.A.	1	5	0	0	0	2	....	....	....	....	....	....	1983-84	1983-84
Jenkins, Roger	Chi., Tor., Mtl.C., Bos., Mtl.M., NYA	8	325	15	39	54	253	25	1	7	8	12	2	1930-31	1938-39
Jennings, Bill	Det., Bos.	5	108	32	33	65	45	20	4	4	8	6	....	1940-41	1944-45
Jennings, Grant	Wsh., Hfd., Pit., Tor., Buf.	9	389	14	43	57	804	54	2	1	3	68	2	1987-88	1995-96
Jensen, Chris	NYR, Phi.	6	74	9	12	21	27	....	....	....	....	....	....	1985-86	1991-92
Jensen, David	Min.	3	18	0	2	2	11	....	....	....	....	....	....	1983-84	1985-86
Jensen, David	Hfd., Wsh.	4	69	9	13	22	22	11	0	0	0	2	....	1984-85	1987-88
Jensen, Steve	Min., L.A.	7	438	113	107	220	318	12	0	3	3	9	....	1975-76	1981-82
● Jeremiah, Ed	NYA, Bos.	1	15	0	1	1	0	....	....	....	....	....	....	1931-32	1931-32
Jerrard, Paul	Min.	1	5	0	0	0	4	....	....	....	....	....	....	1988-89	1988-89
● Jerwa, Frank	Bos., St.L.	4	81	11	16	27	53	....	....	....	....	....	....	1931-32	1934-35
● Jerwa, Joe	NYR, Bos., NYA	7	234	29	58	87	309	17	2	3	5	16	....	1930-31	1938-39
Jirik, Jaroslav	St.L.	1	3	0	0	0	0	....	....	....	....	....	....	1969-70	1969-70
● Joanette, Rosario	Mtl.	1	2	0	1	1	4	....	....	....	....	....	....	1944-45	1944-45
Jodzio, Rick	Col., Cle.	1	70	2	8	10	71	....	....	....	....	....	....	1977-78	1977-78
Johannesen, Glenn	NYI	1	2	0	0	0	0	....	....	....	....	....	....	1985-86	1985-86
Johannson, John	N.J.	1	5	0	0	0	0	....	....	....	....	....	....	1983-84	1983-84
Johansen, Bill	Tor.	1	1	0	0	0	0	....	....	....	....	....	....	1949-50	1949-50
Johansen, Trevor	Tor., Col., L.A.	5	286	11	46	57	282	13	0	3	3	21	....	1977-78	1981-82
Johansson, Bjorn	Cle.	2	15	1	1	2	10	....	....	....	....	....	....	1976-77	1977-78
‡ Johansson, Roger	Cgy., Chi.	4	161	9	34	43	163	5	0	1	1	2	....	1989-90	1994-95
Johns, Don	NYR, Mtl., Min.	6	153	2	21	23	76	....	....	....	....	....	....	1960-61	1967-68
Johnson, Al	Mtl., Det.	4	105	21	28	49	30	11	2	2	4	6	....	1956-57	1962-63
Johnson, Brian	Det.	1	3	0	0	0	5	....	....	....	....	....	....	1983-84	1983-84
● Johnson, Ching	NYR, NYA	12	436	38	48	86	808	61	5	2	7	161	2	1926-27	1937-38
● Johnson, Danny	Tor., Van., Det.	3	121	18	19	37	24	....	....	....	....	....	....	1969-70	1971-72
Johnson, Earl	Det.	1	1	0	0	0	0	....	....	....	....	....	....	1953-54	1953-54
Johnson, Jim	NYR, Phi., L.A.	8	302	75	111	186	73	7	0	2	2	2	....	1964-65	1971-72
Johnson, Jim	Pit., Min., Dal., Wsh., Phx.	13	829	29	166	195	1197	51	1	11	12	132	....	1985-86	1997-98
Johnson, Mark	Pit., Min., Hfd., St.L., N.J.	11	669	203	305	508	260	37	16	12	28	10	....	1979-80	1989-90
Johnson, Norm	Bos., Chi.	3	61	5	20	25	41	14	4	0	4	6	....	1957-58	1959-60
Johnson, Terry	Que., St.L., Cgy., Tor.	9	285	3	24	27	580	38	0	4	4	118	....	1979-80	1987-88
Johnson, Tom	Mtl., Bos.	17	978	51	213	264	960	111	8	15	23	109	6	1947-48	1964-65
● Johnson, Virgil	Chi.	3	75	1	11	12	27	19	0	3	3	4	1	1937-38	1944-45
Johnston, Bernie	Hfd.	2	57	12	24	36	16	3	0	1	1	0	....	1979-80	1980-81
Johnston, George	Chi.	4	58	20	12	32	2	....	....	....	....	....	....	1941-42	1946-47
‡ Johnston, Greg	Bos., Tor.	9	187	26	29	55	124	22	2	1	3	12	....	1983-84	1991-92
Johnston, Jay	Wsh.	2	8	0	0	0	13	....	....	....	....	....	....	1980-81	1981-82
Johnston, Joey	Min., Cal., Chi.	6	331	85	106	191	320	....	....	....	....	....	....	1968-69	1975-76
Johnston, Larry	L.A., Det., K.C., Col.	7	320	9	64	73	580	....	....	....	....	....	....	1967-68	1976-77
Johnston, Marshall	Min., Cal.	7	251	14	52	66	58	6	0	0	0	2	....	1967-68	1973-74
Johnston, Randy	NYI	1	4	0	0	0	4	....	....	....	....	....	....	1979-80	1979-80
Johnstone, Eddie	NYR, Det.	10	426	122	136	258	375	55	13	10	23	83	....	1975-76	1986-87
Johnstone, Ross	Tor.	2	42	5	4	9	14	3	0	0	0	0	1	1943-44	1944-45
● Joliat, Aurel	Mtl.C.	16	655	270	190	460	771	46	9	13	22	66	3	1922-23	1937-38
● Joliat, Rene	Mtl.C.	1	1	0	0	0	0	....	....	....	....	....	....	1924-25	1924-25
Joly, Greg	Wsh., Det.	9	365	21	76	97	250	5	0	0	0	8	....	1974-75	1982-83
Joly, Yvan	Mtl.	3	2	0	0	0	0	1	0	0	0	0	....	1979-80	1982-83
Jonathan, Stan	Bos., Pit.	8	411	91	110	201	751	63	8	4	12	137	....	1975-76	1982-83
Jones, Bob	NYR	1	2	0	0	0	0	....	....	....	....	....	....	1968-69	1968-69
Jones, Brad	Wpg., L.A., Phi.	6	148	25	31	56	122	9	1	1	2	2	....	1986-87	1991-92
Jones, Buck	Det., Tor.	4	50	2	2	4	36	12	0	1	1	18	....	1938-39	1942-43
Jones, Jim	Cal.	1	2	0	0	0	0	....	....	....	....	....	....	1971-72	1971-72
Jones, Jimmy	Tor.	3	148	13	18	31	68	19	1	5	6	11	....	1977-78	1979-80
Jones, Ron	Bos., Pit., Wsh.	5	54	1	4	5	31	....	....	....	....	....	....	1971-72	1975-76
Jonsson, Tomas	NYI, Edm.	8	552	85	259	344	482	80	11	26	37	97	2	1981-82	1988-89
Joseph, Tony	Wpg.	1	2	1	0	1	0	....	....	....	....	....	....	1988-89	1988-89
Joyal, Eddie	Det., Tor., L.A., Phi.	9	466	128	134	262	103	50	11	8	19	18	....	1962-63	1971-72
‡ Joyce, Bob	Bos., Wsh., Wpg.	6	158	34	49	83	90	46	15	9	24	29	....	1987-88	1992-93
Joyce, Duane	Dal.	1	3	0	0	0	0	....	....	....	....	....	....	1993-94	1993-94
Juckes, Bing	NYR	2	16	2	1	3	6	....	....	....	....	....	....	1947-48	1949-50
‡ Juhlin, Patrik	Phi.	2	56	7	6	13	23	13	1	0	1	2	....	1994-95	1995-96
Julien, Claude	Que.	2	14	0	1	1	25	....	....	....	....	....	....	1984-85	1985-86
‡ Junker, Steve	NYI	2	5	0	0	0	0	3	0	1	1	0	....	1992-93	1993-94
Jutila, Timo	Buf.	1	10	1	5	6	13	....	....	....	....	....	....	1984-85	1984-85
Juzda, Bill	NYR, Tor.	9	398	14	54	68	398	42	0	3	3	46	2	1940-41	1951-52

K

Kabel, Bob	NYR	2	48	5	13	18	34	....	....	....	....	....	....	1959-60	1960-61
Kachowski, Mark	Pit.	3	64	6	5	11	209	....	....	....	....	....	....	1987-88	1989-90
Kachur, Ed	Chi.	2	96	10	14	24	35	....	....	....	....	....	....	1956-57	1957-58
Kaese, Trent	Buf.	1	1	0	0	0	0	....	....	....	....	....	....	1988-89	1988-89
Kaiser, Vern	Mtl.	1	50	7	5	12	33	2	0	0	0	0	....	1950-51	1950-51
● Kalbfleish, Walter	Ott., St.L., NYA, Bos.	4	36	0	4	4	32	5	0	0	0	2	....	1933-34	1936-37
● Kaleta, Alex	Chi., NYR	7	387	92	121	213	190	17	1	6	7	2	....	1941-42	1950-51
Kallur, Anders	NYI	6	383	101	110	211	149	78	12	23	35	32	4	1979-80	1984-85
‡ Kaminski, Kevin	Min., Que., Wsh.	7	139	3	10	13	528	8	0	0	0	52	....	1988-89	1996-97
● Kaminsky, Max	Ott., Bos., St.L., Mtl.M.	4	130	22	34	56	38	4	0	0	0	0	....	1933-34	1936-37
Kaminsky, Yan	Wpg., NYI	2	26	3	2	5	4	2	0	0	0	4	....	1993-94	1994-95
● Kampman, Rudolph	Tor.	5	189	14	30	44	287	47	1	4	5	38	1	1937-38	1941-42
Kane, Francis	Det.	1	2	0	0	0	0	....	....	....	....	....	....	1943-44	1943-44
Kannegiesser, Gord	St.L.	2	23	0	1	1	15	....	....	....	....	....	....	1967-68	1971-72
Kannegiesser, Sheldon	Pit., NYR, L.A., Van.	8	366	14	67	81	292	18	0	2	2	10	....	1970-71	1977-78
‡ Karabin, Ladislav	Pit.	1	9	0	0	0	2	....	....	....	....	....	....	1993-94	1993-94
‡ Karamnov, Vitali	St.L.	3	92	12	20	32	65	2	0	0	0	2	....	1992-93	1994-95
‡ Karjalainen, Kyosti	L.A.	1	28	1	8	9	12	3	0	1	1	2	....	1991-92	1991-92
Karlander, Al	Det.	4	212	36	56	92	70	4	0	1	1	0	....	1969-70	1972-73
‡ Karpov, Valeri	Ana.	3	76	14	15	29	32	....	....	....	....	....	....	1994-95	1996-97
Kasatonov, Alexei	N.J., Ana., St.L., Bos.	7	383	38	122	160	326	33	4	7	11	40	....	1989-90	1995-96
Kasper, Steve	Bos., L.A., Phi., T.B.	13	821	177	291	468	554	94	20	28	48	82	....	1980-81	1992-93
Kastelic, Ed	Wsh., Hfd.	7	220	11	10	21	719	8	1	0	1	32	....	1985-86	1991-92
Kaszycki, Mike	NYI, Wsh., Tor.	5	226	42	80	122	108	19	2	6	8	10	....	1977-78	1982-83
● Kea, Ed	Atl., St.L.	10	583	30	145	175	508	32	2	4	6	39	....	1973-74	1982-83
Kearns, Dennis	Van.	10	677	31	290	321	386	11	1	2	3	8	....	1971-72	1980-81
● Keating, Jack	Det.	2	11	3	0	3	4	....	....	....	....	....	....	1938-39	1939-40
● Keating, John	NYA	2	35	5	5	10	17	....	....	....	....	....	....	1931-32	1932-33
Keating, Mike	NYR	1	1	0	0	0	0	....	....	....	....	....	....	1977-78	1977-78
● Keats, Duke	Bos., Det., Chi.	3	82	30	19	49	113	....	....	....	....	....	....	1926-27	1928-29
‡ Keczmer, Dan	Min., Hfd., Cgy., Dal., Nsh.	10	235	8	38	46	212	12	0	1	1	8	....	1990-91	1999-00

Name	NHL Teams	NHL Seasons	Regular Schedule GP	G	A	TP	PIM	Playoffs GP	G	A	TP	PIM	NHL Cup Wins	First NHL Season	Last NHL Season
• Keeling, Butch	Tor., NYR	12	525	157	63	220	331	47	11	11	22	34	1	1926-27	1937-38
Keenan, Larry	Tor., St.L., Buf., Phi.	6	233	38	64	102	28	46	15	16	31	12	....	1961-62	1971-72
Kehoe, Rick	Tor., Pit.	14	906	371	396	767	120	39	4	17	21	4	....	1971-72	1984-85
Kekalainen, Jarmo	Bos., Ott.	3	55	5	8	13	28	....	....	....	....	....	....	1989-90	1993-94
Keller, Ralph	NYR	1	3	1	0	1	6	....	....	....	....	....	....	1962-63	1962-63
Kellgren, Christer	Col.	1	5	0	0	0	0	....	....	....	....	....	....	1981-82	1981-82
Kelly, Bob	Phi., Wsh.	12	837	154	208	362	1454	101	9	14	23	172	2	1970-71	1981-82
Kelly, Bob	St.L., Pit., Chi.	6	425	87	109	196	687	23	6	3	9	40	....	1973-74	1978-79
Kelly, Dave	Det.	1	16	2	0	2	4	....	....	....	....	....	....	1976-77	1976-77
Kelly, John Paul	L.A.	7	400	54	70	124	366	18	1	1	2	41	....	1979-80	1985-86
Kelly, Pete	St.L., Det., NYA, Bro.	7	177	21	38	59	68	19	3	1	4	2	2	1934-35	1941-42
Kelly, Red	Det., Tor.	20	1316	281	542	823	327	164	33	59	92	51	8	1947-48	1966-67
• Kelly, Regis	Tor., Chi., Bro.	8	288	74	53	127	105	38	7	6	13	10	....	1934-35	1941-42
• Kemp, Kevin	Hfd.	1	3	0	0	0	4	....	....	....	....	....	....	1980-81	1980-81
Kemp, Stan	Tor.	1	1	0	0	0	2	....	....	....	....	....	....	1948-49	1948-49
• Kendall, Bill	Chi., Tor.	5	131	16	10	26	28	6	0	0	0	0	1	1933-34	1937-38
Kennedy, Dean	L.A., NYR, Buf., Wpg., Edm.	12	717	26	108	134	1118	36	1	7	8	59	....	1982-83	1994-95
Kennedy, Forbes	Chi., Det., Bos., Phi., Tor.	11	603	70	108	178	988	12	2	4	6	64	....	1956-57	1968-69
Kennedy, Sheldon	Det., Cgy., Bos.	8	310	49	58	107	233	24	6	4	10	20	....	1989-90	1996-97
Kennedy, Ted	Tor.	14	696	231	329	560	432	78	29	31	60	32	5	1942-43	1956-57
• Kenny, Ernest	NYR, Chi.	2	10	0	0	0	18	....	....	....	....	....	....	1930-31	1934-35
Keon, Dave	Tor., Hfd.	18	1296	396	590	986	117	92	32	36	68	6	4	1960-61	1981-82
‡ Kerch, Alexander	Edm.	1	5	0	0	0	2	....	....	....	....	....	....	1993-94	1993-94
Kerr, Alan	NYI, Det., Wpg.	9	391	72	94	166	826	38	5	4	9	70	....	1984-85	1992-93
Kerr, Reg	Cle., Chi., Edm.	6	263	66	94	160	169	7	1	0	1	7	....	1977-78	1983-84
Kerr, Tim	Phi., NYR, Hfd.	13	655	370	304	674	596	81	40	31	71	58	....	1980-81	1992-93
Kessell, Rick	Pit., Cal.	5	135	4	24	28	6	....	....	....	....	....	....	1969-70	1973-74
Ketola, Veli-Pekka	Col.	1	44	9	5	14	4	....	....	....	....	....	....	1981-82	1981-82
Ketter, Kerry	Atl.	1	41	0	2	2	58	....	....	....	....	....	....	1972-73	1972-73
‡ Kharin, Sergei	Wpg.	1	7	2	3	5	2	....	....	....	....	....	....	1990-91	1990-91
Khmylev, Yuri	Buf., St.L.	5	263	64	88	152	133	26	8	6	14	24	....	1992-93	1996-97
Kidd, Ian	Van.	2	20	4	7	11	25	....	....	....	....	....	....	1987-88	1988-89
Kiessling, Udo	Min.	1	1	0	0	0	2	....	....	....	....	....	....	1981-82	1981-82
Kilrea, Brian	Det., L.A.	2	26	3	5	8	12	....	....	....	....	....	....	1957-58	1967-68
• Kilrea, Hec	Ott., Det., Tor.	15	633	167	129	296	438	48	8	7	15	18	3	1925-26	1939-40
• Kilrea, Ken	Det.	5	91	16	23	39	8	15	2	2	4	4	....	1938-39	1943-44
Kilrea, Wally	Ott., Phi., NYA, Mtl.M., Det.	9	329	35	58	93	87	25	2	4	6	6	2	1929-30	1937-38
‡ Kimble, Darin	Que., St.L., Bos., Chi.	7	311	23	20	43	1082	23	0	0	0	52	....	1988-89	1994-95
Kindrachuk, Orest	Phi., Pit., Wsh.	10	508	118	261	379	648	76	20	20	40	53	2	1972-73	1981-82
King, Frank	Mtl.	1	10	1	0	1	2	....	....	....	....	....	....	1950-51	1950-51
‡ King, Steven	NYR, Ana.	3	67	17	8	25	75	....	....	....	....	....	....	1992-93	1995-96
King, Wayne	Cal.	3	73	5	18	23	34	....	....	....	....	....	....	1973-74	1975-76
‡ Kinnear, Geordie	Atl.	1	4	0	0	0	13	....	....	....	....	....	....	1999-00	1999-00
Kinsella, Brian	Wsh.	2	10	0	1	1	0	....	....	....	....	....	....	1975-76	1976-77
• Kinsella, Ray	Ott.	1	14	0	0	0	0	....	....	....	....	....	....	1930-31	1930-31
‡ Kiprusoff, Marko	Mtl.	1	24	0	4	4	8	....	....	....	....	....	....	1995-96	1995-96
• Kirk, Bobby	NYR	1	39	4	8	12	14	....	....	....	....	....	....	1937-38	1937-38
Kirkpatrick, Bob	NYR	1	49	12	12	24	6	....	....	....	....	....	....	1942-43	1942-43
Kirton, Mark	Tor., Det., Van.	6	266	57	56	113	121	4	1	2	3	7	....	1979-80	1984-85
Kisio, Kelly	Det., NYR, S.J., Cgy.	13	761	229	429	658	768	39	6	15	21	52	....	1982-83	1994-95
Kitchen, Bill	Mtl., Tor.	4	41	1	4	5	40	3	0	1	1	0	....	1981-82	1984-85
• Kitchen, Hobie	Mtl.M., Det.	2	47	5	4	9	58	....	....	....	....	....	1	1925-26	1926-27
Kitchen, Mike	Col., N.J.	8	474	12	62	74	370	2	0	0	0	2	....	1976-77	1983-84
Klassen, Ralph	Cal., Cle., Col., St.L.	9	497	52	93	145	120	26	4	2	6	12	....	1975-76	1983-84
• Klein, Lloyd	Bos., NYA	8	164	30	24	54	68	5	0	0	0	2	1	1928-29	1937-38
Kleinendorst, Scot	NYR, Hfd., Wsh.	8	281	12	46	58	452	26	2	7	9	40	....	1982-83	1989-90
Klima, Petr	Det., Edm., T.B., L.A., Pit.	13	786	313	260	573	671	95	28	24	52	83	1	1985-86	1998-99
‡ Klimovich, Sergei	Chi.	1	1	0	0	0	2	....	....	....	....	....	....	1996-97	1996-97
Klingbeil, Ike	Chi.	1	5	1	2	3	2	....	....	....	....	....	....	1936-37	1936-37
Klukay, Joe	Tor., Bos.	11	566	109	127	236	189	71	13	10	23	23	4	1942-43	1955-56
Kluzak, Gord	Bos.	7	299	25	98	123	543	46	6	13	19	129	....	1982-83	1990-91
Knibbs, Bill	Bos.	1	53	7	10	17	4	....	....	....	....	....	....	1964-65	1964-65
‡ Knipscheer, Fred	Bos., St.L.	3	28	6	3	9	18	16	2	1	3	6	....	1993-94	1995-96
• Knott, Nick	Bro.	1	14	3	1	4	9	....	....	....	....	....	....	1941-42	1941-42
Knox, Paul	Tor.	1	1	0	0	0	0	....	....	....	....	....	....	1954-55	1954-55
‡ Kocur, Joe	Det., NYR, Van.	15	820	80	82	162	2519	118	10	12	22	231	3	1984-85	1998-99
‡ Kolesar, Mark	Tor.	2	28	2	2	4	14	3	1	0	1	2	....	1995-96	1996-97
Kolstad, Dean	Min., S.J.	3	40	1	7	8	69	....	....	....	....	....	....	1988-89	1992-93
Komadoski, Neil	L.A., St.L.	8	502	16	76	92	632	23	0	2	2	47	....	1972-73	1979-80
Konik, George	Pit.	1	52	7	8	15	26	....	....	....	....	....	....	1967-68	1967-68
Konroyd, Steve	Cgy., NYI, Chi., Hfd., Det., Ott.	15	895	41	195	236	863	97	10	15	25	99	....	1980-81	1994-95
Konstantinov, Vladimir	Det.	6	446	47	128	175	838	82	5	14	19	107	1	1991-92	1996-97
Kontos, Chris	NYR, Pit., L.A., T.B.	8	230	54	69	123	103	20	11	0	11	12	....	1982-83	1992-93
• Kopak, Russ	Bos.	1	24	7	9	16	0	....	....	....	....	....	....	1943-44	1943-44
Korab, Jerry	Chi., Van., Buf., L.A.	15	975	114	341	455	1629	93	8	18	26	201	....	1970-71	1984-85
Kordic, Dan	Phi.	6	197	4	8	12	584	12	1	0	1	22	....	1991-92	1998-99
• Kordic, John	Mtl., Tor., Wsh., Que.	7	244	17	18	35	997	41	4	3	7	131	1	1985-86	1991-92
Korn, Jim	Det., Tor., Buf., N.J., Cgy.	10	597	66	122	188	1801	16	1	2	3	109	....	1979-80	1989-90
Korney, Mike	Det., NYR	4	77	9	10	19	59	....	....	....	....	....	....	1973-74	1978-79
Koroll, Cliff	Chi.	11	814	208	254	462	376	85	19	29	48	67	....	1969-70	1979-80
Kortko, Roger	NYI	2	79	7	17	24	28	10	0	3	3	17	....	1984-85	1985-86
Kostynski, Doug	Bos.	2	15	3	1	4	4	....	....	....	....	....	....	1983-84	1984-85
Kotanen, Dick	NYR	1	1	0	0	0	0	....	....	....	....	....	....	1950-51	1950-51
Kotsopoulos, Chris	NYR, Hfd., Tor., Det.	10	479	44	109	153	827	31	1	3	4	91	....	1980-81	1989-90
Kowal, Joe	Buf.	2	22	0	5	5	13	2	0	0	0	0	....	1976-77	1977-78
Kozak, Don	L.A., Van.	7	437	96	86	182	480	29	7	2	9	69	....	1972-73	1978-79
Kozak, Les	Tor.	1	12	1	0	1	2	....	....	....	....	....	....	1961-62	1961-62
• Kraftcheck, Stephen	Bos., NYR, Tor.	4	157	11	18	29	83	6	0	0	0	7	....	1950-51	1958-59
Krake, Skip	Bos., L.A., Buf.	7	249	23	40	63	182	10	1	0	1	17	....	1963-64	1970-71
‡ Kravets, Mikhail	S.J.	2	2	0	0	0	0	....	....	....	....	....	....	1991-92	1992-93
Krentz, Dale	Det.	3	30	5	3	8	9	2	0	0	0	0	....	1986-87	1988-89
• Krol, Joe	NYR, Bro.	3	26	10	4	14	8	....	....	....	....	....	....	1936-37	1941-42
Kromm, Rich	Cgy., NYI	9	372	70	103	173	138	36	2	6	8	22	....	1983-84	1992-93
Krook, Kevin	Col.	1	3	0	0	0	2	....	....	....	....	....	....	1978-79	1978-79
‡ Kroupa, Vlastimil	S.J., N.J.	5	105	4	19	23	66	20	1	2	3	25	....	1993-94	1997-98
Krulicki, Jim	NYR, Det.	1	41	0	3	3	6	....	....	....	....	....	....	1970-71	1970-71
‡ Krupp, Uwe	Buf., NYI, Que., Col., Det.	13	717	69	211	280	642	79	6	23	29	84	1	1986-87	1998-99
Kruppke, Gord	Det.	3	23	0	0	0	32	....	....	....	....	....	....	1990-91	1993-94
Krushelnyski, Mike	Bos., Edm., L.A., Tor., Det.	14	897	241	328	569	699	139	29	43	72	106	3	1981-82	1994-95
Krutov, Vladimir	Van.	1	61	11	23	34	20	....	....	....	....	....	....	1989-90	1989-90
Krygier, Todd	Hfd., Wsh., Ana.	9	543	100	143	243	533	48	10	7	17	40	....	1989-90	1997-98
Kryskow, Dave	Chi., Wsh., Det., Atl.	4	231	33	56	89	174	12	2	0	2	4	....	1972-73	1975-76
Kryzanowski, Ed	Bos., Chi.	5	237	15	22	37	65	18	0	1	1	4	....	1948-49	1952-53
‡ Kudashov, Alexei	Tor.	1	25	1	0	1	4	....	....	....	....	....	....	1993-94	1993-94
Kudelski, Bob	L.A., Ott., Fla.	9	442	139	102	241	218	22	4	4	8	4	....	1987-88	1995-96
• Kuhn, Gord	NYA	1	12	1	1	2	4	....	....	....	....	....	....	1932-33	1932-33
Kukulowicz, Aggie	NYR	2	4	1	0	1	0	....	....	....	....	....	....	1952-53	1953-54
‡ Kulak, Stu	Van., Edm., NYR, Que., Wpg.	4	90	8	4	12	130	3	0	0	0	2	....	1982-83	1988-89
Kullman, Arnie	Bos.	2	13	0	1	1	11	....	....	....	....	....	....	1947-48	1949-50
• Kullman, Eddie	NYR	6	343	56	70	126	298	6	1	0	1	2	....	1947-48	1953-54
Kumpel, Mark	Que., Det., Wpg.	6	288	38	46	84	113	39	6	4	10	14	....	1984-85	1990-91
• Kuntz, Alan	NYR	2	45	10	12	22	12	6	1	0	1	2	....	1941-42	1945-46
Kuntz, Murray	St.L.	1	7	1	2	3	0	....	....	....	....	....	....	1974-75	1974-75
Kurri, Jari	Edm., L.A., NYR, Ana., Col.	17	1251	601	797	1398	545	200	106	127	233	123	5	1980-81	1997-98
Kurtenbach, Orland	NYR, Bos., Tor., Van.	13	639	119	213	332	628	19	2	4	6	70	....	1960-61	1973-74
Kurvers, Tom	Mtl., Buf., N.J., Tor., Van., NYI, Ana.	11	659	93	328	421	350	57	8	22	30	68	1	1984-85	1994-95
Kuryluk, Merv	Chi.	1	....	....	....	....	....	2	0	0	0	0	....	1961-62	1961-62
Kushner, Dale	NYI, Phi.	3	84	10	13	23	215	....	....	....	....	....	....	1989-90	1991-92
Kuzyk, Ken	Cle.	2	41	5	9	14	8	....	....	....	....	....	....	1976-77	1977-78
‡ Kvartalnov, Dmitri	Bos.	2	112	42	49	91	26	4	0	0	0	0	....	1992-93	1993-94
Kwong, Larry	NYR	1	1	0	0	0	0	....	....	....	....	....	....	1947-48	1947-48
• Kyle, Bill	NYR	2	3	0	3	3	0	....	....	....	....	....	....	1949-50	1950-51
• Kyle, Gus	NYR, Bos.	3	203	6	20	26	362	14	1	2	3	34	....	1949-50	1951-52
‡ Kyllonen, Markku	Wpg.	1	9	0	2	2	2	....	....	....	....	....	....	1988-89	1988-89
Kypreos, Nick	Wsh., Hfd., NYR, Tor.	8	442	46	44	90	1210	34	1	3	4	65	1	1989-90	1996-97
Kyte, Jim	Wpg., Pit., Cgy., Ott., S.J.	13	598	17	49	66	1342	42	0	6	6	94	....	1982-83	1995-96

Sheldon Kennedy

Todd Krygier

Tom Kurvers

Dale Kushner

Elmer Lach

Nathan Lafayette

Garry Lariviere

Jeff Lazaro

			Regular Schedule					Playoffs					NHL	First	Last
Name	NHL Teams	NHL Seasons	GP	G	A	TP	PIM	GP	G	A	TP	PIM	Cup Wins	NHL Season	NHL Season
L															
Labadie, Mike	NYR	1	3	0	0	0	0	....	....	....	....	....	....	1952-53	1952-53
Labatte, Neil	St.L.	2	26	0	2	2	19	....	....	....	....	....	....	1978-79	1981-82
L'Abbe, Moe	Chi.	1	5	0	1	1	0	....	....	....	....	....	....	1972-73	1972-73
‡ Labelle, Marc	Dal.	1	9	0	0	0	46	....	....	....	....	....	....	1996-97	1996-97
Labine, Leo	Bos., Det.	11	643	128	193	321	730	60	12	11	23	82	....	1951-52	1961-62
Labossiere, Gord	NYR, L.A., Min.	6	215	44	62	106	75	10	2	3	5	28	....	1963-64	1971-72
Labovitch, Max	NYR	1	5	0	0	0	4	....	....	....	....	....	....	1943-44	1943-44
Labraaten, Dan	Det., Cgy.	4	268	71	73	144	47	8	1	0	1	4	....	1978-79	1981-82
Labre, Yvon	Pit., Wsh.	9	371	14	87	101	788	....	....	....	....	....	....	1970-71	1980-81
Labrie, Guy	Bos., NYR	2	42	4	9	13	16	....	....	....	....	....	....	1943-44	1944-45
Lach, Elmer	Mtl.	14	664	215	408	623	478	76	19	45	64	36	3	1940-41	1953-54
Lachance, Michel	Col.	1	21	0	4	4	22	....	....	....	....	....	....	1978-79	1978-79
Lacombe, Francois	Oak., Buf., Que.	4	78	2	17	19	54	3	1	0	1	0	....	1968-69	1979-80
Lacombe, Normand	Buf., Edm., Phi.	7	319	53	62	115	196	26	5	1	6	49	1	1984-85	1990-91
Lacroix, Andre	Phi., Chi., Hfd.	6	325	79	119	198	44	16	2	5	7	0	....	1967-68	1979-80
Lacroix, Pierre	Que., Hfd.	4	274	24	108	132	197	8	0	2	2	10	....	1979-80	1982-83
Ladouceur, Randy	Det., Hfd., Ana.	14	930	30	126	156	1322	40	5	8	13	59	....	1982-83	1995-96
‡ LaFayette, Nathan	St.L., Van., NYR, L.A.	6	187	17	20	37	103	32	2	7	9	8	....	1993-94	1998-99
Lafleur, Guy	Mtl., NYR, Que.	17	1126	560	793	1353	399	128	58	76	134	67	5	1971-72	1990-91
• Lafleur, Roland	Mtl.C.	1	1	0	0	0	0	....	....	....	....	....	....	1924-25	1924-25
LaFontaine, Pat	NYI, Buf., NYR	15	865	468	545	1013	552	69	26	36	62	36	....	1983-84	1997-98
Laforce, Ernie	Mtl.	1	1	0	0	0	0	....	....	....	....	....	....	1942-43	1942-43
LaForest, Bob	L.A.	1	5	1	0	1	2	....	....	....	....	....	....	1983-84	1983-84
Laforge, Claude	Mtl., Det., Phi.	8	193	24	33	57	82	5	1	2	3	15	....	1957-58	1968-69
‡ Laforge, Marc	Hfd., Edm.	2	14	0	0	0	64	....	....	....	....	....	....	1989-90	1993-94
Laframboise, Pete	Cal., Wsh., Pit.	4	227	33	55	88	70	9	1	0	1	0	....	1971-72	1974-75
Lafrance, Adie	Mtl.C.	1	3	0	0	0	2	2	0	0	0	0	....	1933-34	1933-34
• Lafrance, Leo	Mtl.C., Chi.	2	33	2	0	2	6	....	....	....	....	....	....	1926-27	1927-28
‡ Lafreniere, Jason	Que., NYR, T.B.	5	146	34	53	87	22	15	1	5	6	19	....	1986-87	1993-94
Lafreniere, Roger	Det., St.L.	2	13	0	0	0	4	....	....	....	....	....	....	1962-63	1972-73
Lagace, Jean-Guy	Pit., Buf., K.C.	6	197	9	39	48	251	....	....	....	....	....	....	1968-69	1975-76
Laidlaw, Tom	NYR, L.A.	10	705	25	139	164	717	69	4	17	21	78	....	1980-81	1989-90
Laird, Robbie	Min.	1	1	0	0	0	0	....	....	....	....	....	....	1979-80	1979-80
Lajeunesse, Serge	Det., Phi.	5	103	1	4	5	103	....	....	....	....	....	....	1970-71	1974-75
Lalande, Hec	Chi., Det.	4	151	21	39	60	120	....	....	....	....	....	....	1953-54	1957-58
Lalonde, Bobby	Van., Atl., Bos., Cgy.	11	641	124	210	334	298	16	4	2	6	6	....	1971-72	1981-82
• Lalonde, Newsy	Mtl.C., NYA	6	99	124	41	165	183	7	15	24	19	23	....	1917-18	1926-27
Lalonde, Ron	Pit., Wsh.	7	397	45	78	123	106	....	....	....	....	....	....	1972-73	1978-79
Lalor, Mike	Mtl., St.L., Wsh., Wpg., S.J., Dal.	12	687	17	88	105	677	92	5	10	15	167	1	1985-86	1996-97
• Lamb, Joe	Mtl.M., Ott., NYA, Bos., Mtl.C., St.L., Det.	11	443	108	101	209	601	18	1	1	2	51	....	1927-28	1937-38
‡ Lamb, Mark	Cgy., Det., Edm., Ott., Phi., Mtl.	11	403	46	100	146	291	70	7	19	26	51	1	1985-86	1995-96
‡ Lambert, Dan	Que.	2	29	6	9	15	22	....	....	....	....	....	....	1990-91	1991-92
‡ Lambert, Lane	Det., NYR, Que.	6	283	58	66	124	521	17	2	4	6	40	....	1983-84	1988-89
Lambert, Yvon	Mtl., Buf.	10	683	206	273	479	340	90	27	22	49	67	4	1972-73	1981-82
Lamby, Dick	St.L.	3	22	0	5	5	22	....	....	....	....	....	....	1978-79	1980-81
• Lamirande, Jean-Paul	NYR, Mtl.	4	49	5	5	10	26	8	0	0	0	4	....	1946-47	1954-55
Lammens, Hank	Ott.	1	27	1	2	3	22	....	....	....	....	....	....	1993-94	1993-94
• Lamoureux, Leo	Mtl.	6	235	19	79	98	175	28	1	6	7	16	2	1941-42	1946-47
Lamoureux, Mitch	Pit., Phi.	3	73	11	9	20	59	....	....	....	....	....	....	1983-84	1987-88
Lampman, Mike	St.L., Van., Wsh.	4	96	17	20	37	34	....	....	....	....	....	....	1972-73	1976-77
Lancien, Jack	NYR	4	63	1	5	6	35	6	0	1	1	2	....	1946-47	1950-51
Landon, Larry	Mtl., Tor.	2	9	0	0	0	2	....	....	....	....	....	....	1983-84	1984-85
Lane, Gord	Wsh., NYI	10	539	19	94	113	1228	75	3	14	17	214	4	1975-76	1984-85
• Lane, Myles	NYR, Bos.	3	71	4	1	5	41	11	0	0	0	0	1	1928-29	1933-34
Langdon, Steve	Bos.	3	7	0	1	1	2	4	0	0	0	0	....	1974-75	1977-78
Langelle, Pete	Tor.	4	136	22	51	73	11	41	5	9	14	4	1	1938-39	1941-42
Langevin, Chris	Buf.	2	22	3	1	4	22	....	....	....	....	....	....	1983-84	1985-86
Langevin, Dave	NYI, Min., L.A.	8	513	12	107	119	530	87	2	17	19	106	4	1979-80	1986-87
Langlais, Alain	Min.	2	25	4	4	8	10	....	....	....	....	....	....	1973-74	1974-75
Langlois, Albert	Mtl., NYR, Det., Bos.	9	497	21	91	112	488	53	1	5	6	50	3	1957-58	1965-66
• Langlois, Charlie	Ham., NYA, Pit., Mtl.C.	4	151	22	5	27	189	2	0	0	0	0	....	1924-25	1927-28
Langway, Rod	Mtl., Wsh.	15	994	51	278	329	849	104	5	22	27	97	1	1978-79	1992-93
‡ Lank, Jeff	Phi.	1	2	0	0	0	2	....	....	....	....	....	....	1999-00	1999-00
Lanthier, Jean-Marc	Van.	4	105	16	16	32	29	....	....	....	....	....	....	1983-84	1987-88
Lanyon, Ted	Pit.	1	5	0	0	0	4	....	....	....	....	....	....	1967-68	1967-68
Lanz, Rick	Van., Tor., Chi.	10	569	65	221	286	448	28	3	8	11	35	....	1980-81	1991-92
‡ Laperriere, Daniel	St.L., Ott.	4	48	2	5	7	27	....	....	....	....	....	....	1992-93	1995-96
Laperriere, Jacques	Mtl.	12	691	40	242	282	674	88	9	22	31	101	6	1962-63	1973-74
Lapointe, Guy	Mtl., St.L., Bos.	16	884	171	451	622	893	123	26	44	70	138	6	1968-69	1983-84
• Lapointe, Rick	Det., Phi., St.L., Que., L.A.	11	664	44	176	220	831	46	2	7	9	64	....	1975-76	1985-86
Lappin, Peter	Min., S.J.	2	7	0	0	0	2	....	....	....	....	....	....	1989-90	1991-92
Laprade, Edgar	NYR	10	500	108	172	280	42	18	4	9	13	4	....	1945-46	1954-55
LaPrairie, Benjamin	Chi.	1	7	0	0	0	0	....	....	....	....	....	....	1936-37	1936-37
Lariviere, Garry	Que., Edm.	4	219	6	57	63	167	14	0	5	5	8	....	1979-80	1982-83
Larmer, Jeff	Col., N.J., Chi.	5	158	37	51	88	57	5	1	0	1	2	....	1981-82	1985-86
Larmer, Steve	Chi., NYR	15	1006	441	571	1012	532	140	56	75	131	89	1	1980-81	1994-95
• Larochelle, Wildor	Mtl.C., Chi.	12	474	92	74	166	211	34	6	4	10	24	2	1925-26	1936-37
Larocque, Denis	L.A.	1	8	0	1	1	18	....	....	....	....	....	....	1987-88	1987-88
• Larose, Bonner	Bos.	1	6	0	0	0	0	....	....	....	....	....	....	1925-26	1925-26
Larose, Claude	Mtl., Min., St.L.	16	943	226	257	483	887	97	14	18	32	143	5	1962-63	1977-78
Larose, Claude	NYR	2	25	4	7	11	2	2	0	0	0	0	....	1979-80	1981-82
‡ Larose, Guy	Wpg., Tor., Cgy., Bos.	6	70	10	9	19	63	4	0	0	0	0	....	1988-89	1994-95
Larouche, Pierre	Pit., Mtl., Hfd., NYR	14	812	395	427	822	237	64	20	34	54	16	2	1974-75	1987-88
Larson, Norm	NYA, Bro., NYR	3	89	25	18	43	12	....	....	....	....	....	....	1940-41	1946-47
Larson, Reed	Det., Bos., Edm., NYI, Min., Buf.	14	904	222	463	685	1391	32	4	7	11	63	....	1976-77	1989-90
Larter, Tyler	Wsh.	1	1	0	0	0	0	....	....	....	....	....	....	1989-90	1989-90
Latal, Jiri	Phi.	3	92	12	36	48	24	....	....	....	....	....	....	1989-90	1991-92
Latos, James	NYR	1	1	0	0	0	0	....	....	....	....	....	....	1988-89	1988-89
Latreille, Phil	NYR	1	4	0	0	0	2	....	....	....	....	....	....	1960-61	1960-61
Latta, David	Que.	4	36	4	8	12	4	....	....	....	....	....	....	1985-86	1990-91
Lauder, Martin	Bos.	1	3	0	0	0	2	....	....	....	....	....	....	1927-28	1927-28
Lauen, Mike	Wpg.	1	4	0	1	1	0	....	....	....	....	....	....	1983-84	1983-84
Laughlin, Craig	Mtl., Wsh., L.A., Tor.	8	549	136	205	341	364	33	6	6	12	20	....	1981-82	1988-89
Laughton, Mike	Oak., Cal.	4	189	39	48	87	101	11	2	4	6	0	....	1967-68	1970-71
Laurence, Don	Atl., St.L.	2	79	15	22	37	14	....	....	....	....	....	....	1978-79	1979-80
LaVallee, Kevin	Cgy., L.A., St.L., Pit.	7	366	110	125	235	85	32	5	8	13	21	....	1980-81	1986-87
LaVarre, Mark	Chi.	3	78	9	16	25	58	1	0	0	0	2	....	1985-86	1987-88
Lavender, Brian	St.L., NYI, Det., Cal.	4	184	16	26	42	174	3	0	0	0	2	....	1971-72	1974-75
‡ Lavigne, Eric	L.A.	1	1	0	0	0	0	....	....	....	....	....	....	1994-95	1994-95
• Laviolette, Jack	Mtl.C.	1	18	2	1	3	6	2	0	0	0	0	....	1917-18	1917-18
Laviolette, Peter	NYR	1	12	0	0	0	6	....	....	....	....	....	....	1988-89	1988-89
‡ Lavoie, Dominic	St.L., Ott., Bos., L.A.	6	38	5	8	13	32	....	....	....	....	....	....	1988-89	1993-94
Lawless, Paul	Hfd., Phi., Van., Tor.	7	239	49	77	126	54	3	0	2	2	2	....	1982-83	1989-90
Lawson, Danny	Det., Min., Buf.	5	219	28	29	57	61	16	0	1	1	2	....	1967-68	1971-72
Lawton, Brian	Min., NYR, Hfd., Que., Bos., S.J.	9	483	112	154	266	401	11	1	1	2	12	....	1983-84	1992-93
Laxdal, Derek	Tor., NYI	6	67	12	7	19	88	1	0	2	2	2	....	1984-85	1990-91
• Laycoe, Hal	NYR, Mtl., Bos.	11	531	25	77	102	292	40	2	5	7	39	....	1945-46	1955-56
‡ Lazaro, Jeff	Bos., Ott.	3	102	14	23	37	114	28	3	3	6	32	....	1990-91	1992-93
Leach, Jamie	Pit., Hfd., Fla.	5	81	11	9	20	12	....	....	....	....	....	1	1989-90	1993-94
Leach, Larry	Bos.	3	126	13	29	42	91	7	1	1	2	8	....	1958-59	1961-62
Leach, Reggie	Bos., Cal., Phi., Det.	13	934	381	285	666	387	94	47	22	69	22	1	1970-71	1982-83
Leavins, Jim	Det., NYR	2	41	2	12	14	30	....	....	....	....	....	....	1985-86	1986-87
‡ Lebeau, Stephan	Mtl., Ana.	7	373	118	159	277	105	30	9	7	16	12	1	1988-89	1994-95
LeBlanc, Fern	Det.	3	34	5	6	11	0	....	....	....	....	....	....	1976-77	1978-79
LeBlanc, J.P.	Chi., Det.	5	153	14	30	44	87	2	0	0	0	0	....	1968-69	1978-79
LeBlanc, John	Van., Edm., Wpg.	7	83	26	13	39	28	1	0	0	0	0	....	1986-87	1994-95
LeBrun, Al	NYR	2	6	0	2	2	4	....	....	....	....	....	....	1960-61	1965-66
Lecaine, Bill	Pit.	1	4	0	0	0	0	....	....	....	....	....	....	1968-69	1968-69
Leclair, Jackie	Mtl.	3	160	20	40	60	56	20	6	1	7	6	2	1954-55	1956-57
Leclerc, Rene	Det.	2	87	10	11	21	105	....	....	....	....	....	....	1968-69	1970-71
Lecuyer, Doug	Chi., Wpg., Pit.	4	126	11	31	42	178	7	4	0	4	15	....	1978-79	1982-83
Ledingham, Walt	Chi., NYI	3	15	0	2	2	4	....	....	....	....	....	....	1972-73	1976-77
• LeDuc, Albert	Mtl.C., Ott., NYR	10	383	57	35	92	614	28	5	6	11	32	2	1925-26	1934-35
LeDuc, Rich	Bos., Que.	4	130	28	38	66	69	5	0	0	0	9	....	1972-73	1980-81

Name	NHL Teams	NHL Seasons	Regular Schedule					Playoffs					NHL Cup Wins	First NHL Season	Last NHL Season
			GP	G	A	TP	PIM	GP	G	A	TP	PIM			
• Lee, Bobby	Mtl.	1	1	0	0	0	0	....	....	....	....	....	....	1942-43	1942-43
Lee, Edward	Que.	1	2	0	0	0	5	....	....	....	....	....	....	1984-85	1984-85
Lee, Peter	Pit.	6	431	114	131	245	257	19	0	8	8	4	....	1977-78	1982-83
Leeman, Gary	Tor., Cgy., Mtl., Van., St.L.	14	667	199	267	466	531	36	8	16	24	36	1	1982-83	1996-97
‡ Lefebvre, Patrice	Wsh.	1	3	0	0	0	2	....	....	....	....	....	....	1998-99	1998-99
• Lefley, Bryan	NYI, K.C., Col.	5	228	7	29	36	101	2	0	0	0	0	....	1972-73	1977-78
Lefley, Chuck	Mtl., St.L.	9	407	128	164	292	137	29	5	8	13	10	2	1970-71	1980-81
• Leger, Roger	NYR, Mtl.	5	187	18	53	71	71	20	0	7	7	14	....	1943-44	1949-50
Legge, Barry	Que., Wpg.	3	107	1	11	12	144	....	....	....	....	....	....	1979-80	1981-82
Legge, Randy	NYR	1	12	0	2	2	2	....	....	....	....	....	....	1972-73	1972-73
Lehman, Tommy	Bos., Edm.	3	36	5	5	10	16	....	....	....	....	....	....	1987-88	1989-90
Lehto, Petteri	Pit.	1	6	0	0	0	4	....	....	....	....	....	....	1984-85	1984-85
Lehtonen, Antero	Wsh.	1	65	9	12	21	14	....	....	....	....	....	....	1979-80	1979-80
Lehvonen, Henri	K.C.	1	4	0	0	0	0	....	....	....	....	....	....	1974-75	1974-75
Leier, Edward	Chi.	2	16	2	1	3	2	....	....	....	....	....	....	1949-50	1950-51
Leinonen, Mikko	NYR, Wsh.	4	162	31	78	109	71	20	2	11	13	28	....	1981-82	1984-85
Leiter, Bobby	Bos., Pit., Atl.	10	447	98	126	224	144	8	3	0	3	2	....	1962-63	1975-76
Leiter, Ken	NYI, Min.	5	143	14	36	50	62	15	0	6	6	8	....	1984-85	1989-90
Lemaire, Jacques	Mtl.	12	853	366	469	835	217	145	61	78	139	63	8	1967-68	1978-79
‡ Lemay, Moe	Van., Edm., Bos., Wpg.	8	317	72	94	166	442	28	6	3	9	55	1	1981-82	1988-89
Lemelin, Roger	K.C., Col.	4	36	1	2	3	27	....	....	....	....	....	....	1974-75	1977-78
Lemieux, Alain	St.L., Que., Pit.	6	119	28	44	72	38	19	4	6	10	0	....	1981-82	1986-87
Lemieux, Bob	Oak.	1	19	0	1	1	12	....	....	....	....	....	....	1967-68	1967-68
Lemieux, Jacques	L.A.	3	19	0	4	4	8	1	0	0	0	0	....	1967-68	1969-70
Lemieux, Jean	Atl., Wsh.	5	204	23	63	86	39	3	1	1	2	0	....	1973-74	1977-78
Lemieux, Jocelyn	St.L., Mtl., Chi., Hfd., N.J., Cgy., Phx.	12	598	80	84	164	740	60	5	10	15	88	....	1986-87	1997-98
• Lemieux, Real	Det., L.A., NYR, Buf.	8	456	51	104	155	262	18	2	4	6	10	....	1966-67	1973-74
Lemieux, Rich	Van., K.C., Atl.	5	274	39	82	121	132	2	0	0	0	0	....	1971-72	1975-76
Lenardon, Tim	N.J., Van.	2	15	2	1	3	4	....	....	....	....	....	....	1986-87	1989-90
• Lepine, Hec	Mtl.C.	1	33	5	2	7	2	....	....	....	....	....	....	1925-26	1925-26
• Lepine, Pit	Mtl.C.	13	526	143	98	241	392	41	7	5	12	26	2	1925-26	1937-38
Leroux, Gaston	Mtl.C.	1	2	0	0	0	0	....	....	....	....	....	....	1935-36	1935-36
Lesieur, Art	Mtl.C., Chi.	4	100	4	2	6	50	14	0	0	0	4	1	1928-29	1935-36
Lessard, Rick	Cgy., S.J.	3	15	0	4	4	18	....	....	....	....	....	....	1988-89	1991-92
Lesuk, Bill	Bos., Phi., L.A., Wsh., Wpg.	8	388	44	63	107	368	9	1	0	1	12	1	1968-69	1979-80
• Leswick, Jack	Chi.	1	37	1	7	8	16	....	....	....	....	....	1	1933-34	1933-34
Leswick, Pete	NYA, Bos.	2	3	1	0	1	0	....	....	....	....	....	....	1936-37	1944-45
• Leswick, Tony	NYR, Det., Chi.	12	740	165	159	324	900	59	13	10	23	91	3	1945-46	1957-58
Levandoski, Joe	NYR	1	8	1	1	2	0	....	....	....	....	....	....	1946-47	1946-47
Leveille, Normand	Bos.	2	75	17	25	42	49	....	....	....	....	....	....	1981-82	1982-83
Leveque, Guy	L.A.	2	17	2	2	4	21	....	....	....	....	....	....	1992-93	1993-94
Lever, Don	Van., Atl., Cgy., Col., N.J., Buf.	15	1020	313	367	680	593	30	7	10	17	26	....	1972-73	1986-87
Levie, Craig	Wpg., Min., St.L., Van.	6	183	22	53	75	177	16	2	3	5	32	....	1981-82	1986-87
‡ Levins, Scott	Wpg., Fla., Ott., Phx.	5	124	13	20	33	316	....	....	....	....	....	....	1992-93	1997-98
• Levinsky, Alex	Tor., NYR, Chi.	9	367	19	49	68	307	37	2	1	3	26	2	1930-31	1938-39
Levo, Tapio	Col., N.J.	2	107	16	53	69	36	....	....	....	....	....	....	1981-82	1982-83
Lewicki, Danny	Tor., NYR, Chi.	9	461	105	135	240	177	28	0	4	4	8	1	1950-51	1958-59
Lewis, Dale	NYR	1	8	0	0	0	0	....	....	....	....	....	....	1975-76	1975-76
Lewis, Dave	NYI, L.A., N.J., Det.	15	1008	36	187	223	953	91	1	20	21	143	....	1973-74	1987-88
Lewis, Doug	Mtl.	1	3	0	0	0	0	....	....	....	....	....	....	1946-47	1946-47
• Lewis, Herbie	Det.	11	483	148	161	309	248	38	13	10	23	6	2	1928-29	1938-39
Ley, Rick	Tor., Hfd.	6	310	12	72	84	528	14	0	2	2	20	....	1968-69	1980-81
‡ Liba, Igor	NYR, L.A.	1	37	7	18	25	36	2	0	0	0	2	....	1988-89	1988-89
Libby, Jeff	NYI	1	1	0	0	0	0	....	....	....	....	....	....	1997-98	1997-98
Libett, Nick	Det., Pit.	14	982	237	268	505	472	16	6	2	8	2	....	1967-68	1980-81
Licari, Tony	Det.	1	9	0	1	1	0	....	....	....	....	....	....	1946-47	1946-47
Liddington, Bob	Tor.	1	11	0	1	1	2	....	....	....	....	....	....	1970-71	1970-71
Lidster, Doug	Van., NYR, St.L., Dal.	16	897	75	268	343	679	80	6	15	21	64	1	1983-84	1998-99
‡ Lilley, John	Ana.	3	23	3	8	11	13	....	....	....	....	....	....	1993-94	1995-96
‡ Lindberg, Chris	Cgy., Que.	3	116	17	25	42	47	2	0	1	1	2	....	1991-92	1993-94
‡ Lindbom, Johan	NYR	1	38	1	3	4	28	....	....	....	....	....	....	1997-98	1997-98
Linden, Jamie	Fla.	1	4	0	0	0	17	....	....	....	....	....	....	1994-95	1994-95
Lindgren, Lars	Van., Min.	6	394	25	113	138	325	40	5	6	11	20	....	1978-79	1983-84
‡ Lindholm, Mikael	L.A.	1	18	2	2	4	2	....	....	....	....	....	....	1989-90	1989-90
Lindros, Brett	NYI	2	51	2	5	7	147	....	....	....	....	....	....	1994-95	1995-96
Lindsay, Ted	Det., Chi.	17	1068	379	472	851	1808	133	47	49	96	194	4	1944-45	1964-65
Lindstrom, Willy	Wpg., Edm., Pit.	8	582	161	162	323	200	57	14	18	32	24	2	1979-80	1986-87
Linseman, Ken	Phi., Edm., Bos., Tor.	14	860	256	551	807	1727	113	43	77	120	325	1	1978-79	1991-92
‡ Lipuma, Chris	T.B., S.J.	5	72	0	9	9	146	....	....	....	....	....	....	1992-93	1996-97
Liscombe, Carl	Det.	9	373	137	140	277	117	59	22	19	41	20	1	1937-38	1945-46
Litzenberger, Ed	Mtl., Chi., Det., Tor.	12	618	178	238	416	283	40	5	13	18	34	4	1952-53	1963-64
‡ Loach, Lonnie	Ott., L.A., Ana.	2	56	10	13	23	29	1	0	0	0	0	....	1992-93	1993-94
• Locas, Jacques	Mtl.	2	59	7	8	15	66	....	....	....	....	....	....	1947-48	1948-49
Lochead, Bill	Det., Col., NYR	6	330	69	62	131	180	7	3	0	3	6	....	1974-75	1979-80
• Locking, Norm	Chi.	2	48	2	6	8	26	....	....	....	....	....	....	1934-35	1935-36
‡ Loewen, Darcy	Buf., Ott.	5	135	4	8	12	211	....	....	....	....	....	....	1989-90	1993-94
Lofthouse, Mark	Wsh., Det.	6	181	42	38	80	73	....	....	....	....	....	....	1977-78	1982-83
Logan, Dave	Chi., Van.	6	218	5	29	34	470	12	0	0	0	10	....	1975-76	1980-81
Logan, Robert	Buf., L.A.	3	42	10	5	15	0	....	....	....	....	....	....	1986-87	1988-89
Loiselle, Claude	Det., N.J., Que., Tor., NYI	13	616	92	117	209	1149	41	4	11	15	60	....	1981-82	1993-94
Lomakin, Andrei	Phi., Fla.	4	215	42	62	104	92	....	....	....	....	....	....	1991-92	1994-95
‡ Loney, Brian	Van.	1	12	2	3	5	6	....	....	....	....	....	....	1995-96	1995-96
Loney, Troy	Pit., Ana., NYI, NYR	12	624	87	110	197	1091	67	8	14	22	97	2	1983-84	1994-95
Long, Barry	L.A., Det., Wpg.	5	280	11	68	79	250	5	0	1	1	18	....	1972-73	1981-82
• Long, Stanley	Mtl.	1	....	....	....	....	....	3	0	0	0	0	....	1951-52	1951-52
Lonsberry, Ross	Bos., L.A., Phi., Pit.	15	968	256	310	566	806	100	21	25	46	87	2	1966-67	1980-81
Loob, Hakan	Cgy.	6	450	193	236	429	189	73	26	28	54	16	1	1983-84	1988-89
Loob, Peter	Que.	1	8	1	2	3	0	....	....	....	....	....	....	1984-85	1984-85
Lorentz, Jim	Bos., St.L., NYR, Buf.	10	659	161	238	399	208	54	12	10	22	30	1	1968-69	1977-78
Lorimer, Bob	NYI, Col., N.J.	10	529	22	90	112	431	49	3	10	13	83	2	1976-77	1985-86
• Lorrain, Rod	Mtl.C., Mtl.	6	179	28	39	67	30	11	0	3	3	0	....	1935-36	1941-42
• Loughlin, Clem	Det., Chi.	3	101	8	6	14	77	....	....	....	....	....	....	1926-27	1928-29
• Loughlin, Wilf	Tor.	1	14	0	0	0	2	....	....	....	....	....	....	1923-24	1923-24
Lovsin, Ken	Wsh.	1	1	0	0	0	0	....	....	....	....	....	....	1990-91	1990-91
Lowdermilk, Dwayne	Wsh.	1	2	0	1	1	2	....	....	....	....	....	....	1980-81	1980-81
Lowe, Darren	Pit.	1	8	1	2	3	0	....	....	....	....	....	....	1983-84	1983-84
Lowe, Kevin	Edm., NYR	19	1254	84	347	431	1498	214	10	48	58	192	6	1979-80	1997-98
Lowe, Odie	NYR	1	4	1	1	2	0	....	....	....	....	....	....	1949-50	1949-50
• Lowe, Ross	Bos., Mtl.	3	77	6	8	14	82	2	0	0	0	0	....	1949-50	1951-52
• Lowrey, Ed	Ott., Ham.	3	27	2	2	4	6	....	....	....	....	....	....	1917-18	1920-21
• Lowrey, Fred	Mtl.M., Pit.	2	53	1	1	2	10	2	0	0	0	....	....	1924-25	1925-26
• Lowrey, Gerry	Tor., Pit., Phi., Chi., Ott.	6	211	48	48	96	148	2	1	0	1	2	....	1927-28	1932-33
Lucas, Danny	Phi.	1	6	1	0	1	0	....	....	....	....	....	....	1978-79	1978-79
Lucas, Dave	Det.	1	1	0	0	0	0	....	....	....	....	....	....	1962-63	1962-63
Luce, Don	NYR, Det., Buf., L.A., Tor.	13	894	225	329	554	364	71	17	22	39	52	....	1969-70	1981-82
Ludvig, Jan	N.J., Buf.	7	314	54	87	141	418	....	....	....	....	....	....	1982-83	1988-89
Ludwig, Craig	Mtl., NYI, Min., Dal.	17	1256	38	184	222	1437	177	4	25	29	244	2	1982-83	1998-99
Ludzik, Steve	Chi., Buf.	9	424	46	93	139	333	44	4	8	12	70	....	1981-82	1989-90
‡ Luhning, Warren	NYI, Dal.	3	29	0	1	1	21	....	....	....	....	....	....	1997-98	1999-00
Lukowich, Bernie	Pit., St.L.	2	79	13	15	28	34	2	0	0	0	0	....	1973-74	1974-75
Lukowich, Morris	Wpg., Bos., L.A.	8	582	199	219	418	584	11	0	2	2	24	....	1979-80	1986-87
Luksa, Charlie	Hfd.	1	8	0	1	1	4	....	....	....	....	....	....	1979-80	1979-80
Lumley, Dave	Mtl., Edm., Hfd.	9	437	98	160	258	680	61	6	8	14	131	2	1978-79	1986-87
Lund, Pentti	Bos., NYR	7	259	44	55	99	40	19	7	5	12	0	....	1946-47	1952-53
Lundberg, Brian	Pit.	1	1	0	0	0	2	....	....	....	....	....	....	1982-83	1982-83
Lunde, Len	Det., Chi., Min., Van.	8	321	39	83	122	75	20	3	2	5	2	....	1958-59	1970-71
Lundholm, Bengt	Wpg.	5	275	48	95	143	72	14	3	4	7	14	....	1981-82	1985-86
Lundrigan, Joe	Tor., Wsh.	2	52	2	8	10	22	....	....	....	....	....	....	1972-73	1974-75
Lundstrom, Tord	Det.	1	11	1	1	2	0	....	....	....	....	....	....	1973-74	1973-74
Lundy, Pat	Det., Chi.	5	150	37	32	69	31	16	2	2	4	2	....	1945-46	1950-51
‡ Luongo, Chris	Det., Ott., NYI	5	218	8	23	31	176	....	....	....	....	....	....	1990-91	1995-96
Lupien, Gilles	Mtl., Pit., Hfd.	5	226	5	25	30	416	25	0	0	0	21	2	1977-78	1981-82
Lupul, Gary	Van.	7	293	70	75	145	243	25	4	7	11	11	....	1979-80	1985-86
Lyle, George	Det., Hfd.	4	99	24	38	62	51	....	....	....	....	....	....	1979-80	1982-83
Lynch, Jack	Pit., Det., Wsh.	7	382	24	106	130	336	....	....	....	....	....	....	1972-73	1978-79
Lynn, Vic	NYR, Det., Mtl., Tor., Bos., Chi.	11	327	49	76	125	274	47	7	10	17	46	3	1942-43	1953-54

Tommy Lehman

Danny Lewicki

Nick Libett

Ed Litzenberger

Paul MacLean

Al Macneil

Mikko Makela

Joe Malone

			Regular Schedule					Playoffs					NHL	First	Last
Name	NHL Teams	NHL Seasons	GP	G	A	TP	PIM	GP	G	A	TP	PIM	Cup Wins	NHL Season	NHL Season
Lyon, Steve	Pit.	1	3	0	0	0	2	....	....	....	....	....	....	1976-77	1976-77
Lyons, Ron	Bos., Phi.	1	36	2	4	6	27	5	0	0	0	0	....	1930-31	1930-31
Lysiak, Tom	Atl., Chi.	13	919	292	551	843	567	76	25	38	63	49	....	1973-74	1985-86

M

MacAdam, Al	Phi., Cal., Cle., Min., Van.	12	864	240	351	591	509	64	20	24	44	21	1	1973-74	1984-85
MacDermid, Paul	Hfd., Wpg., Wsh., Que.	14	690	116	142	258	1303	43	5	11	16	116	....	1981-82	1994-95
MacDonald, Blair	Edm., Van.	4	219	91	100	191	65	11	0	6	6	2	....	1979-80	1982-83
MacDonald, Brett	Van.	1	1	0	0	0	0	....	....	....	....	....	....	1987-88	1987-88
‡ MacDonald, Doug	Buf.	3	11	1	0	1	2	....	....	....	....	....	....	1992-93	1994-95
MacDonald, Kevin	Ott.	1	1	0	0	0	2	....	....	....	....	....	....	1993-94	1993-94
• MacDonald, Kilby	NYR	4	151	36	34	70	47	15	1	2	3	4	1	1939-40	1944-45
MacDonald, Lowell	Det., L.A., Pit.	13	506	180	210	390	92	30	11	11	22	12	....	1961-62	1977-78
MacDonald, Parker	Tor., NYR, Det., Bos., Min.	14	676	144	179	323	253	75	14	14	28	20	....	1952-53	1968-69
MacDougall, Kim	Min.	1	1	0	0	0	0	....	....	....	....	....	....	1974-75	1974-75
MacEachern, Shane	St.L.	1	1	0	0	0	0	....	....	....	....	....	....	1987-88	1987-88
Macey, Hub	NYR, Mtl.	3	30	6	9	15	0	8	0	0	0	0	....	1941-42	1946-47
MacGregor, Bruce	Det., NYR	14	893	213	257	470	217	107	19	28	47	44	....	1960-61	1973-74
MacGregor, Randy	Hfd.	1	2	1	1	2	2	....	....	....	....	....	....	1981-82	1981-82
MacGuigan, Garth	NYI	2	5	0	1	1	2	....	....	....	....	....	....	1979-80	1983-84
MacIntosh, Ian	NYR	1	4	0	0	0	4	....	....	....	....	....	....	1952-53	1952-53
MacIver, Don	Wpg.	1	6	0	0	0	2	....	....	....	....	....	....	1979-80	1979-80
Maciver, Norm	NYR, Hfd., Edm., Ott., Pit., Wpg., Phx.	12	500	55	230	285	350	56	3	11	14	32	....	1986-87	1997-98
MacKasey, Blair	Tor.	1	1	0	0	0	2	....	....	....	....	....	....	1976-77	1976-77
MacKay, Calum	Det., Mtl.	8	237	50	55	105	214	38	5	13	18	20	1	1946-47	1954-55
MacKay, Dave	Chi.	1	29	3	0	3	26	5	0	1	1	2	....	1940-41	1940-41
• MacKay, Mickey	Chi., Pit., Bos.	4	147	44	19	63	79	11	0	0	0	6	1	1926-27	1929-30
• MacKay, Murdo	Mtl.	4	19	0	3	3	0	15	1	2	3	0	....	1945-46	1948-49
MacKell, Fleming	Tor., Bos.	13	665	149	220	369	562	80	22	41	63	75	2	1947-48	1959-60
• MacKell, Jack	Ott.	2	45	4	2	6	59	2	0	0	0	0	2	1919-20	1920-21
MacKenzie, Barry	Min.	1	6	0	1	1	6	....	....	....	....	....	....	1968-69	1968-69
• MacKenzie, Bill	Chi., Mtl.M., NYR, Mtl.C.	7	264	15	14	29	145	21	1	1	2	11	1	1932-33	1939-40
‡ Mackey, David	Chi., Min., St.L.	6	126	8	12	20	305	3	0	0	0	2	....	1987-88	1993-94
• Mackey, Reg	NYR	1	34	0	0	0	16	1	0	0	0	0	....	1926-27	1926-27
• Mackie, Howie	Det.	2	20	1	0	1	4	8	0	0	0	0	1	1936-37	1937-38
MacKinnon, Paul	Wsh.	5	147	5	23	28	91	....	....	....	....	....	....	1979-80	1983-84
MacLean, Paul	St.L., Wpg., Det.	11	719	324	349	673	968	53	21	14	35	110	....	1980-81	1990-91
MacLeish, Rick	Phi., Hfd., Pit., Det.	14	846	349	410	759	434	114	54	53	107	38	2	1970-71	1983-84
MacLellan, Brian	L.A., NYR, Min., Cgy., Det.	10	606	172	241	413	551	47	5	9	14	42	1	1982-83	1991-92
‡ MacLeod, Pat	Min., S.J., Dal.	4	53	5	13	18	14	....	....	....	....	....	....	1990-91	1995-96
MacMillan, Billy	Tor., Atl., NYI	7	446	74	77	151	184	53	6	6	12	40	....	1970-71	1976-77
MacMillan, Bob	NYR, St.L., Atl., Cgy., Col., N.J., Chi.	11	753	228	349	577	260	31	8	11	19	16	....	1974-75	1984-85
MacMillan, John	Tor., Det.	5	104	5	10	15	32	12	0	1	1	2	2	1960-61	1964-65
MacNeil, Al	Tor., Mtl., Chi., NYR, Pit.	11	524	17	75	92	617	37	0	4	4	67	....	1955-56	1967-68
MacNeil, Bernie	St.L.	1	4	0	0	0	0	....	....	....	....	....	....	1973-74	1973-74
Macoun, Jamie	Cgy., Tor., Det.	16	1128	76	282	358	1208	159	10	32	42	169	2	1982-83	1998-99
• MacPherson, Bud	Mtl.	7	259	5	33	38	233	29	0	3	3	21	1	1948-49	1956-57
• MacSweyn, Ralph	Phi.	5	47	0	5	5	10	8	0	0	0	6	....	1967-68	1971-72
MacTavish, Craig	Bos., Edm., NYR, Phi., St.L.	17	1093	213	267	480	891	193	20	38	58	218	4	1979-80	1996-97
MacWILLIAM, Mike	NYI	1	6	0	0	0	14	....	....	....	....	....	....	1995-96	1995-96
Madigan, Connie	St.L.	1	20	0	3	3	25	5	0	0	0	4	....	1972-73	1972-73
Madill, Jeff	N.J.	1	14	4	0	4	46	7	0	2	2	8	....	1990-91	1990-91
Magee, Dean	Min.	1	7	0	0	0	4	....	....	....	....	....	....	1977-78	1977-78
Maggs, Daryl	Chi., Cal., Tor.	3	135	14	19	33	54	4	0	0	0	0	....	1971-72	1979-80
Magnan, Marc	Tor.	1	4	0	1	1	5	....	....	....	....	....	....	1982-83	1982-83
Magnuson, Keith	Chi.	11	589	14	125	139	1442	68	3	9	12	164	....	1969-70	1979-80
Maguire, Kevin	Tor., Buf., Phi.	6	260	29	30	59	782	11	0	0	0	86	....	1986-87	1991-92
Mahaffy, John	Mtl., NYR	3	37	11	25	36	4	1	0	1	1	0	....	1942-43	1944-45
Mahovlich, Frank	Tor., Det., Mtl.	18	1181	533	570	1103	1056	137	51	67	118	163	6	1956-57	1973-74
Mahovlich, Pete	Det., Mtl., Pit.	16	884	288	485	773	916	88	30	42	72	134	4	1965-66	1980-81
‡ Mailhot, Jacques	Que.	1	5	0	0	0	33	....	....	....	....	....	....	1988-89	1988-89
Mailley, Frank	Mtl.	1	1	0	0	0	0	....	....	....	....	....	....	1942-43	1942-43
Mair, Jim	Phi., NYI, Van.	5	76	4	15	19	49	3	1	2	3	4	....	1970-71	1974-75
• Majeau, Fern	Mtl.	2	56	22	24	46	43	1	0	0	0	0	1	1943-44	1944-45
Major, Bruce	Que.	1	4	0	0	0	0	....	....	....	....	....	....	1990-91	1990-91
‡ Major, Mark	Det.	1	2	0	0	0	5	....	....	....	....	....	....	1996-97	1996-97
Makarov, Sergei	Cgy., S.J., Dal.	7	424	134	250	384	317	34	12	11	23	8	....	1989-90	1996-97
Makela, Mikko	NYI, L.A., Buf., Bos.	7	423	118	147	265	139	18	3	8	11	14	....	1985-86	1994-95
Maki, Chico	Chi.	15	841	143	292	435	345	113	17	36	53	43	1	1960-61	1975-76
• Maki, Wayne	Chi., St.L., Van.	6	246	57	79	136	184	2	1	0	1	2	....	1967-68	1972-73
Makkonen, Kari	Edm.	1	9	2	2	4	0	....	....	....	....	....	....	1979-80	1979-80
‡ Maley, David	Mtl., N.J., Edm., S.J., NYI	9	466	43	81	124	1043	46	5	5	10	111	1	1985-86	1993-94
Malinowski, Merlin	Col., N.J., Hfd.	5	282	54	111	165	121	....	....	....	....	....	....	1978-79	1982-83
Mallette, Troy	NYR, Edm., N.J., Ott., Bos., T.B.	9	456	51	68	119	1226	15	2	2	4	99	....	1989-90	1997-98
Malone, Cliff	Mtl.	1	3	0	0	0	0	....	....	....	....	....	....	1951-52	1951-52
Malone, Greg	Pit., Hfd., Que.	11	704	191	310	501	661	20	3	5	8	32	....	1976-77	1986-87
• Malone, Joe	Mtl.C., Que., Ham.	7	126	143	32	175	57	9	6	0	6	3	1	1917-18	1923-24
Maloney, Dan	Chi., L.A., Det., Tor.	11	737	192	259	451	1489	40	4	7	11	35	....	1970-71	1981-82
Maloney, Dave	NYR, Buf.	11	657	71	246	317	1154	49	7	17	24	91	....	1974-75	1984-85
Maloney, Don	NYR, Hfd., NYI	13	765	214	350	564	815	94	22	35	57	101	....	1978-79	1990-91
Maloney, Phil	Bos., Tor., Chi.	5	158	28	43	71	16	6	0	0	0	0	....	1949-50	1959-60
Maluta, Ray	Bos.	2	25	2	3	5	6	2	0	0	0	0	....	1975-76	1976-77
Manastersky, Tom	Mtl.	1	6	0	0	0	11	....	....	....	....	....	....	1950-51	1950-51
Mancuso, Gus	Mtl.C., Mtl., NYR	4	42	7	9	16	17	....	....	....	....	....	....	1937-38	1942-43
Mandich, Dan	Min.	4	111	5	11	16	303	7	0	0	0	2	....	1982-83	1985-86
Manery, Kris	Cle., Min., Van., Wpg.	4	250	63	64	127	91	....	....	....	....	....	....	1977-78	1980-81
Manery, Randy	Det., Atl., L.A.	10	582	50	206	256	415	13	0	2	2	12	....	1970-71	1979-80
Mann, Jack	NYR	2	9	3	4	7	0	....	....	....	....	....	....	1943-44	1944-45
Mann, Jimmy	Wpg., Que., Pit.	8	293	10	20	30	895	22	0	0	0	89	....	1979-80	1987-88
Mann, Ken	Det.	1	1	0	0	0	0	....	....	....	....	....	....	1975-76	1975-76
• Mann, Norm	Tor.	3	31	0	3	3	4	2	0	0	0	0	....	1935-36	1940-41
• Manners, Rennison	Pit., Phi.	2	37	3	2	5	14	....	....	....	....	....	....	1929-30	1930-31
Manno, Bob	Van., Tor., Det.	8	371	41	131	172	274	17	2	4	6	12	....	1976-77	1984-85
Manson, Ray	Bos., NYR	2	2	0	1	1	0	....	....	....	....	....	....	1947-48	1948-49
• Mantha, Georges	Mtl.C., Mtl.	13	488	89	102	191	148	36	6	2	8	24	2	1928-29	1940-41
Mantha, Moe	Wpg., Pit., Edm., Min., Phi.	12	656	81	289	370	501	17	5	10	15	18	....	1980-81	1991-92
• Mantha, Sylvio	Mtl.C., Bos.	14	542	63	78	141	671	39	5	5	10	64	3	1923-24	1936-37
• Maracle, Bud	NYR	1	11	1	3	4	4	4	0	0	0	0	....	1930-31	1930-31
Marcetta, Milan	Tor., Min.	3	54	7	15	22	10	17	7	7	14	4	1	1966-67	1968-69
March, Mush	Chi.	17	759	153	230	383	540	45	12	15	27	41	2	1928-29	1944-45
Marchinko, Brian	Tor., NYI	4	47	2	6	8	0	....	....	....	....	....	....	1970-71	1973-74
Marcinyshyn, Dave	N.J., Que., NYR	3	16	0	1	1	49	....	....	....	....	....	....	1990-91	1992-93
Marcon, Lou	Det.	3	60	0	4	4	42	....	....	....	....	....	....	1958-59	1962-63
Marcotte, Don	Bos.	15	868	230	254	484	317	132	34	27	61	81	2	1965-66	1981-82
Marini, Hector	NYI, N.J.	5	154	27	46	73	246	10	3	6	9	14	2	1978-79	1983-84
‡ Marinucci, Chris	NYI, L.A.	2	13	1	4	5	2	....	....	....	....	....	....	1994-95	1996-97
• Mario, Frank	Bos.	2	53	9	19	28	24	....	....	....	....	....	....	1941-42	1944-45
• Mariucci, John	Chi.	5	223	11	34	45	308	12	0	3	3	26	....	1940-41	1947-48
Mark, Gordon	N.J., Edm.	4	85	3	10	13	187	....	....	....	....	....	....	1986-87	1994-95
Markell, John	Wpg., St.L., Min.	4	55	11	10	21	36	....	....	....	....	....	....	1979-80	1984-85
• Marker, Gus	Det., Mtl.M., Tor., Bro.	10	322	64	69	133	133	46	5	7	12	36	1	1932-33	1941-42
Markham, Ray	NYR	1	14	1	1	2	21	7	1	0	1	24	....	1979-80	1979-80
• Markle, Jack	Tor.	1	8	0	1	1	0	....	....	....	....	....	....	1935-36	1935-36
• Marks, Jack	Mtl., Tor., Que.	2	7	0	0	0	4	....	....	....	....	....	1	1917-18	1919-20
Marks, John	Chi.	10	657	112	163	275	330	57	5	9	14	60	....	1972-73	1981-82
Markwart, Nevin	Bos., Cgy.	8	309	41	68	109	794	19	1	0	1	33	....	1983-84	1991-92
‡ Marois, Daniel	Tor., NYI, Bos., Dal.	8	350	117	93	210	419	19	3	3	6	28	....	1987-88	1995-96
Marois, Mario	NYR, Van., Que., Wpg., St.L.	15	955	76	357	433	1746	100	4	34	38	182	....	1977-78	1991-92
Marotte, Gilles	Bos., Chi., L.A., NYR, St.L.	12	808	56	265	321	919	29	3	3	6	26	....	1965-66	1976-77
Marquess, Mark	Bos.	1	27	5	4	9	6	4	0	0	0	0	....	1946-47	1946-47
Marsh, Brad	Atl., Cgy., Phi., Tor., Det., Ott.	15	1086	23	175	198	1241	97	6	18	24	124	....	1978-79	1992-93
Marsh, Gary	Det., Tor.	2	7	1	3	4	4	....	....	....	....	....	....	1967-68	1968-69
Marsh, Peter	Wpg., Chi.	5	278	48	71	119	224	26	1	5	6	33	....	1979-80	1983-84
Marshall, Bert	Det., Oak., Cal., NYR, NYI	14	868	17	181	198	926	72	4	22	26	99	....	1965-66	1978-79
Marshall, Don	Mtl., NYR, Buf., Tor.	19	1176	265	324	589	127	94	8	15	23	14	5	1951-52	1971-72

Name	NHL Teams	NHL Seasons	Regular Schedule GP	G	A	TP	PIM	Playoffs GP	G	A	TP	PIM	NHL Cup Wins	First NHL Season	Last NHL Season
Marshall, Paul	Pit., Tor., Hfd.	4	95	15	18	33	17	1	0	0	0	0	....	1979-80	1982-83
Marshall, Willie	Tor.	4	33	1	5	6	2	....	....	....	....	....	....	1952-53	1958-59
Marson, Mike	Wsh., L.A.	6	196	24	24	48	233	....	....	....	....	....	....	1974-75	1979-80
● Martin, Clare	Bos., Det., Chi., NYR	6	237	12	28	40	78	27	0	2	2	6	1	1941-42	1951-52
‡ Martin, Craig	Wpg., Fla.	2	21	0	1	1	24	....	....	....	....	....	....	1994-95	1996-97
Martin, Frank	Bos., Chi.	6	282	11	46	57	122	10	0	2	2	2	....	1952-53	1957-58
Martin, Grant	Van., Wsh.	4	44	0	4	4	55	1	1	0	1	2	....	1983-84	1986-87
Martin, Jack	Tor.	1	1	0	0	0	0	....	....	....	....	....	....	1960-61	1960-61
‡ Martin, Matt	Tor.	4	76	0	5	5	71	....	....	....	....	....	....	1993-94	1996-97
Martin, Pit	Det., Bos., Chi., Van.	17	1101	324	485	809	609	100	27	31	58	56	....	1961-62	1978-79
Martin, Rick	Buf., L.A.	11	685	384	317	701	477	63	24	29	53	74	....	1971-72	1981-82
● Martin, Ron	NYA	2	94	13	16	29	36	....	....	....	....	....	....	1932-33	1933-34
Martin, Terry	Buf., Que., Tor., Edm., Min.	10	479	104	101	205	202	21	4	2	6	26	....	1975-76	1984-85
Martin, Tom	Tor.	1	3	1	0	1	0	....	....	....	....	....	....	1967-68	1967-68
Martin, Tom	Wpg., Hfd., Min.	6	92	12	11	23	249	4	0	0	0	6	....	1984-85	1989-90
Martineau, Don	Atl., Min., Det.	4	90	6	10	16	63	....	....	....	....	....	....	1973-74	1976-77
‡ Martini, Darcy	Edm.	1	2	0	0	0	0	....	....	....	....	....	....	1993-94	1993-94
Martinson, Steve	Det., Mtl., Min.	4	49	2	1	3	244	1	0	0	0	10	....	1987-88	1991-92
Maruk, Dennis	Cal., Cle., Min., Wsh.	14	888	356	522	878	761	34	14	22	36	26	....	1975-76	1988-89
Masnick, Paul	Mtl., Chi., Tor.	6	232	18	41	59	139	33	4	5	9	27	1	1950-51	1957-58
● Mason, Charley	NYR, NYA, Det., Chi.	4	95	7	18	25	44	4	0	1	1	0	....	1934-35	1938-39
● Massecar, George	NYA	3	100	12	11	23	46	....	....	....	....	....	....	1929-30	1931-32
Masters, Jamie	St.L.	3	33	1	13	14	2	2	0	0	0	0	....	1975-76	1978-79
● Masterton, Bill	Min.	1	38	4	8	12	4	....	....	....	....	....	....	1967-68	1967-68
Mathers, Frank	Tor.	3	23	1	3	4	4	....	....	....	....	....	....	1948-49	1951-52
Mathiasen, Dwight	Pit.	3	33	1	7	8	18	....	....	....	....	....	....	1985-86	1987-88
Mathieson, Jim	Wsh.	1	2	0	0	0	4	....	....	....	....	....	....	1989-90	1989-90
● Matte, Joe	Tor., Ham., Bos., Mtl.C.	4	68	17	15	32	54	....	....	....	....	....	....	1919-20	1925-26
● Matte, Joe	Det., Chi.	2	24	0	3	3	8	....	....	....	....	....	....	1929-30	1942-43
Mattiussi, Dick	Pit., Oak., Cal.	4	200	8	31	39	124	8	0	1	1	6	....	1967-68	1970-71
● Matz, Johnny	Mtl.C.	1	30	2	3	5	0	1	0	0	0	0	....	1924-25	1924-25
Maxner, Wayne	Bos.	2	62	8	9	17	48	....	....	....	....	....	....	1964-65	1965-66
Maxwell, Brad	Min., Que., Tor., Van., NYR	10	612	98	270	368	1292	79	12	49	61	178	....	1977-78	1986-87
Maxwell, Bryan	Min., St.L., Wpg., Pit.	8	331	18	77	95	745	15	1	1	2	86	....	1977-78	1984-85
Maxwell, Kevin	Min., Col., N.J.	3	66	6	15	21	61	16	3	4	7	24	....	1980-81	1983-84
Maxwell, Wally	Tor.	1	2	0	0	0	0	....	....	....	....	....	....	1952-53	1952-53
May, Alan	Bos., Edm., Wsh., Dal., Cgy.	8	393	31	45	76	1348	40	1	2	3	80	....	1987-88	1994-95
‡ Mayer, Derek	Ott.	1	17	2	2	4	8	....	....	....	....	....	....	1993-94	1993-94
Mayer, Jim	NYR	1	4	0	0	0	0	....	....	....	....	....	....	1979-80	1979-80
Mayer, Pat	Pit.	1	1	0	0	0	4	....	....	....	....	....	....	1987-88	1987-88
Mayer, Shep	Tor.	1	12	1	2	3	4	....	....	....	....	....	....	1942-43	1942-43
● Mazur, Eddie	Mtl., Chi.	6	107	8	20	28	120	25	4	5	9	22	1	1950-51	1956-57
‡ Mazur, Jay	Van.	4	47	11	7	18	20	6	0	1	1	8	....	1988-89	1991-92
McAdam, Gary	Buf., Pit., Det., Cgy., Wsh., N.J., Tor.	11	534	96	132	228	243	30	6	5	11	16	....	1975-76	1985-86
● McAdam, Sam	NYR	1	5	0	0	0	0	....	....	....	....	....	....	1930-31	1930-31
● McAndrew, Hazen	Bro.	1	7	0	1	1	6	....	....	....	....	....	....	1941-42	1941-42
McAneeley, Ted	Cal.	3	158	8	35	43	141	....	....	....	....	....	....	1972-73	1974-75
McAtee, Jud	Det.	3	46	15	13	28	6	14	2	1	3	0	....	1942-43	1944-45
McAtee, Norm	Bos.	1	13	0	1	1	0	....	....	....	....	....	....	1946-47	1946-47
● McAvoy, George	Mtl.	1	....	....	....	....	....	4	0	0	0	0	....	1954-55	1954-55
McBain, Andrew	Wpg., Pit., Van., Ott.	11	608	129	172	301	633	24	5	7	12	39	....	1983-84	1993-94
‡ McBain, Jason	Hfd.	2	9	0	0	0	0	....	....	....	....	....	....	1995-96	1996-97
McBean, Wayne	L.A., NYI, Wpg.	6	211	10	39	49	168	2	1	1	2	0	....	1987-88	1993-94
McBride, Cliff	Mtl.M., Tor.	2	2	0	0	0	0	....	....	....	....	....	....	1928-29	1929-30
McBurney, Jim	Chi.	1	1	0	1	1	0	....	....	....	....	....	....	1952-53	1952-53
● McCabe, Stan	Det., Mtl.M.	4	78	9	4	13	49	....	....	....	....	....	....	1929-30	1933-34
● McCaffrey, Bert	Tor., Pit., Mtl.C.	7	260	43	30	73	202	8	2	1	3	10	1	1924-25	1930-31
McCahill, John	Col.	1	1	0	0	0	0	....	....	....	....	....	....	1977-78	1977-78
McCaig, Doug	Det., Chi.	7	263	8	21	29	255	7	0	1	1	10	....	1941-42	1950-51
● McCallum, Dunc	NYR, Pit.	5	187	14	35	49	230	10	1	2	3	12	....	1965-66	1970-71
● McCalmon, Eddie	Chi., Phi.	2	39	5	0	5	14	....	....	....	....	....	....	1927-28	1930-31
McCann, Rick	Det.	6	43	1	4	5	6	....	....	....	....	....	....	1967-68	1974-75
McCarthy, Dan	NYR	1	5	4	0	4	4	....	....	....	....	....	....	1980-81	1980-81
McCarthy, Kevin	Phi., Van., Pit.	10	537	67	191	258	527	21	2	3	5	20	....	1977-78	1986-87
● McCarthy, Thomas	Que., Ham.	2	35	22	7	29	10	....	....	....	....	....	....	1919-20	1920-21
McCarthy, Tom	Det., Bos.	4	60	8	9	17	8	....	....	....	....	....	....	1956-57	1960-61
McCarthy, Tom	Min., Bos.	9	460	178	221	399	330	68	12	26	38	67	....	1979-80	1987-88
● McCartney, Walt	Mtl.C.	1	2	0	0	0	0	....	....	....	....	....	....	1932-33	1932-33
McCaskill, Ted	Min.	1	4	0	2	2	0	....	....	....	....	....	....	1967-68	1967-68
McClanahan, Rob	Buf., Hfd., NYR	5	224	38	63	101	126	34	4	12	16	31	....	1979-80	1983-84
‡ McCleary, Trent	Ott., Bos., Mtl.	4	192	8	15	23	134	....	....	....	....	....	....	1995-96	1999-00
McClelland, Kevin	Pit., Edm., Det., Tor., Wpg.	12	588	68	112	180	1672	98	11	18	29	281	4	1981-82	1993-94
McCord, Bob	Bos., Det., Min., St.L.	7	316	10	58	68	262	14	2	5	7	10	....	1963-64	1972-73
McCord, Dennis	Van.	1	3	0	0	0	6	....	....	....	....	....	....	1973-74	1973-74
McCormack, John	Tor., Mtl., Chi.	8	311	25	49	74	35	22	1	1	2	0	2	1947-48	1954-55
‡ McCosh, Shawn	L.A., NYR	2	9	1	0	1	6	....	....	....	....	....	....	1991-92	1994-95
McCourt, Dale	Det., Buf., Tor.	7	532	194	284	478	124	21	9	7	16	6	....	1977-78	1983-84
McCreary, Bill Jr.	Tor.	1	12	1	0	1	4	....	....	....	....	....	....	1980-81	1980-81
McCreary, Bill Sr.	NYR, Det., Mtl., St.L.	8	309	53	62	115	108	48	6	16	22	14	....	1953-54	1970-71
McCreary, Keith	Mtl., Pit., Atl.	10	532	131	112	243	294	16	0	4	4	6	....	1961-62	1974-75
● McCreedy, Johnny	Tor.	2	64	17	12	29	25	21	4	3	7	16	2	1941-42	1944-45
McCrimmon, Brad	Bos., Phi., Cgy., Det., Hfd., Phx.	18	1222	81	322	403	1416	116	11	18	29	176	1	1979-80	1996-97
McCrimmon, Jim	St.L.	1	2	0	0	0	0	....	....	....	....	....	....	1974-75	1974-75
McCulley, Bob	Mtl.C.	1	1	0	0	0	0	....	....	....	....	....	....	1934-35	1934-35
● McCurry, Duke	Pit.	4	148	21	11	32	119	4	0	2	2	4	....	1925-26	1928-29
McCutcheon, Brian	Det.	3	37	3	1	4	7	....	....	....	....	....	....	1974-75	1976-77
McCutcheon, Darwin	Tor.	1	1	0	0	0	2	....	....	....	....	....	....	1981-82	1981-82
McDill, Jeff	Chi.	1	1	0	0	0	0	....	....	....	....	....	....	1976-77	1976-77
McDonagh, Bill	NYR	1	4	0	0	0	2	....	....	....	....	....	....	1949-50	1949-50
McDonald, Ab	Mtl., Chi., Bos., Det., Pit., St.L.	15	762	182	248	430	200	84	21	29	50	42	4	1957-58	1971-72
McDonald, Brian	Chi., Buf.	2	12	0	0	0	29	8	0	0	0	2	....	1967-68	1970-71
● McDonald, Bucko	Det., Tor., NYR	11	446	35	88	123	206	50	6	1	7	24	3	1934-35	1944-45
McDonald, Butch	Det., Chi.	2	66	8	20	28	2	5	0	2	2	10	....	1939-40	1944-45
McDonald, Gerry	Hfd.	2	8	0	0	0	4	....	....	....	....	....	....	1981-82	1983-84
● McDonald, Jack	Mtl., Mtl.C., Que., Tor.	5	69	26	14	40	30	7	1	1	2	3	....	1917-18	1921-22
McDonald, Jack	NYR	1	43	10	9	19	6	....	....	....	....	....	....	1943-44	1943-44
McDonald, Lanny	Tor., Col., Cgy.	16	1111	500	506	1006	899	117	44	40	84	120	1	1973-74	1988-89
McDonald, Robert	NYR	1	1	0	0	0	0	....	....	....	....	....	....	1943-44	1943-44
McDonald, Terry	K.C.	1	8	0	1	1	6	....	....	....	....	....	....	1975-76	1975-76
McDonnell, Joe	Van., Pit.	3	50	2	10	12	34	....	....	....	....	....	....	1981-82	1985-86
● McDonnell, Moylan	Ham.	1	22	1	2	3	2	....	....	....	....	....		1920-21	1920-21
McDonough, Al	L.A., Pit., Atl., Det.	5	237	73	88	161	73	8	0	1	1	2	....	1970-71	1977-78
McDonough, Hubie	L.A., NYI, S.J.	5	195	40	26	66	67	5	1	0	1	4	....	1988-89	1992-93
McDougal, Mike	NYR, Hfd.	4	61	8	10	18	43	....	....	....	....	....	....	1978-79	1982-83
‡ McDougall, Bill	Det., Edm., T.B.	3	28	5	5	10	12	1	0	0	0	0	....	1990-91	1993-94
McElmury, Jim	Min., K.C., Col.	5	180	14	47	61	49	....	....	....	....	....	....	1972-73	1977-78
McEwen, Mike	NYR, Col., NYI, L.A., Wsh., Det., Hfd.	12	716	108	296	404	460	78	12	36	48	48	3	1976-77	1987-88
McFadden, Jim	Det., Chi.	8	412	100	126	226	89	49	10	9	19	30	1	1946-47	1953-54
McFadyen, Don	Chi.	4	179	12	33	45	77	11	2	2	4	5	1	1932-33	1935-36
McFall, Dan	Wpg.	2	9	0	1	1	0	....	....	....	....	....	....	1984-85	1985-86
● McFarlane, Gord	Chi.	1	2	0	0	0	0	....	....	....	....	....	....	1926-27	1926-27
‡ McGeough, Jim	Wsh., Pit.	4	57	7	10	17	32	....	....	....	....	....	....	1981-82	1986-87
● McGibbon, Irv	Mtl.	1	1	0	0	0	2	....	....	....	....	....	....	1942-43	1942-43
McGill, Bob	Tor., Chi., S.J., Det., NYI, Hfd.	13	705	17	55	72	1766	49	0	0	0	88	....	1981-82	1993-94
● McGill, Jack	Mtl.C.	3	134	27	10	37	71	3	2	0	2	0	....	1934-35	1936-37
● McGill, Jack	Bos.	4	97	23	36	59	42	27	7	4	11	17	....	1941-42	1946-47
McGill, Ryan	Chi., Phi., Edm.	4	151	4	15	19	391	....	....	....	....	....	....	1991-92	1994-95
McGregor, Sandy	NYR	1	2	0	0	0	2	....	....	....	....	....	....	1963-64	1963-64
● McGuire, Mickey	Pit.	2	36	3	0	3	6	....	....	....	....	....	....	1926-27	1927-28
McHugh, Mike	Min., S.J.	4	20	1	0	1	16	....	....	....	....	....	....	1988-89	1991-92
McIlhargey, Jack	Phi., Van., Hfd.	8	393	11	36	47	1102	27	0	3	3	68	....	1974-75	1981-82
● McInenly, Bert	Det., NYA, Ott., Bos.	6	166	19	15	34	144	4	0	0	0	2	....	1930-31	1935-36
McIntosh, Bruce	Min.	1	2	0	0	0	0	....	....	....	....	....	....	1972-73	1972-73
McIntosh, Paul	Buf.	2	48	0	2	2	66	2	0	0	0	7	....	1974-75	1975-76
● McIntyre, Jack	Bos., Chi., Det.	11	499	109	102	211	173	29	7	6	13	4	....	1949-50	1959-60
McIntyre, John	Tor., L.A., NYR, Van.	6	351	24	54	78	516	44	0	6	6	54	....	1989-90	1994-95

Nevin Markwart

Brad Marsh

Gilles Marotte

Gary McAdam

Hubie McDonough

Walt McKechnie

Jim McKenny

Howie Meeker

			Regular Schedule					Playoffs							
Name	**NHL Teams**	**NHL Seasons**	**GP**	**G**	**A**	**TP**	**PIM**	**GP**	**G**	**A**	**TP**	**PIM**	**NHL Cup Wins**	**First NHL Season**	**Last NHL Season**
McIntyre, Larry	Tor.	2	41	0	3	3	26	....	....	....	....	....	....	1969-70	1972-73
McKay, Doug	Det.	1	....	....	....	....	....	1	0	0	0	0	1	1949-50	1949-50
McKay, Ray	Chi., Buf., Cal.	6	140	2	16	18	102	....	....	....	....	....	....	1968-69	1973-74
McKay, Scott	Ana.	1	1	0	0	0	0	....	....	....	....	....	....	1993-94	1993-94
McKechnie, Walt	Min., Cal., Bos., Det., Wsh., Cle., Tor., Col.	16	955	214	392	606	469	15	7	5	12	7	....	1967-68	1982-83
McKee, Mike	Que.	1	48	3	12	15	41	....	....	....	....	....	....	1993-94	1993-94
McKegney, Ian	Chi.	1	3	0	0	0	2	....	....	....	....	....	....	1976-77	1976-77
McKegney, Tony	Buf., Que., Min., NYR, St.L., Det., Chi.	13	912	320	319	639	517	79	24	23	47	56	....	1978-79	1990-91
McKendry, Alex	NYI, Cgy.	4	46	3	6	9	21	6	2	2	4	0	1	1977-78	1980-81
McKenna, Sean	Buf., L.A., Tor.	9	414	82	80	162	181	15	1	2	3	2	....	1981-82	1989-90
McKenney, Don	Bos., NYR, Tor., Det., St.L.	13	798	237	345	582	211	58	18	29	47	10	1	1954-55	1967-68
McKenny, Jim	Tor., Min.	14	604	82	247	329	294	37	7	9	16	10	....	1965-66	1978-79
McKenzie, Brian	Pit.	1	6	1	1	2	4	....	....	....	....	....	....	1971-72	1971-72
McKenzie, John	Chi., Det., NYR, Bos.	12	691	206	268	474	917	69	15	32	47	133	2	1958-59	1971-72
‡ McKim, Andrew	Bos., Det.	3	38	1	4	5	6	....	....	....	....	....	....	1992-93	1994-95
• McKinnon, Alex	Ham., NYA, Chi.	5	193	19	11	30	237	....	....	....	....	....	....	1924-25	1928-29
• McKinnon, John	Mtl.C., Pit., Phi.	6	208	28	11	39	224	2	0	0	0	4	....	1925-26	1930-31
McLean, Don	Wsh.	1	9	0	0	0	6	....	....	....	....	....	....	1975-76	1975-76
• McLean, Fred	Que., Ham.	2	8	0	0	0	2	....	....	....	....	....	....	1919-20	1920-21
McLean, Jack	Tor.	3	67	14	24	38	76	13	2	2	4	8	1	1942-43	1944-45
‡ McLean, Jeff	S.J.	1	6	1	0	1	0	....	....	....	....	....	....	1993-94	1993-94
• McLellan, John	Tor.	1	2	0	0	0	0	....	....	....	....	....	....	1951-52	1951-52
McLellan, Scott	Bos.	1	2	0	0	0	0	....	....	....	....	....	....	1982-83	1982-83
McLellan, Todd	NYI	1	5	1	1	2	0	....	....	....	....	....	....	1987-88	1987-88
• McLenahan, Rollie	Det.	1	9	2	1	3	10	2	0	0	0	0	....	1945-46	1945-46
McLeod, Al	Det.	1	26	2	2	4	24	....	....	....	....	....	....	1973-74	1973-74
McLeod, Jackie	NYR	5	106	14	23	37	12	7	0	0	0	0	....	1949-50	1954-55
‡ McLlwain, Dave	Pit., Wpg., Buf., NYI, Tor., Ott.	10	501	100	107	207	292	20	0	2	2	2	....	1987-88	1996-97
• McMahon, Mike	Mtl., Bos.	3	57	7	18	25	102	13	1	2	3	30	1	1942-43	1945-46
McMahon, Mike	NYR, Min., Chi., Det., Pit., Buf.	8	224	15	68	83	171	14	3	7	10	4	....	1963-64	1971-72
McManama, Bob	Pit.	3	99	11	25	36	28	8	0	1	1	6	....	1973-74	1975-76
• McManus, Sammy	Mtl.M., Bos.	2	26	0	1	1	8	1	0	0	0	0	1	1934-35	1936-37
McMurchy, Tom	Chi., Edm.	4	55	8	4	12	65	....	....	....	....	....	....	1983-84	1987-88
McNab, Max	Det.	4	128	16	19	35	24	25	1	0	1	4	1	1947-48	1950-51
McNab, Peter	Buf., Bos., Van., N.J.	14	954	363	450	813	179	107	40	42	82	20	....	1973-74	1986-87
• McNabney, Sid	Mtl.	1	....	....	....	....	....	5	0	1	1	2	....	1950-51	1950-51
• McNamara, Howard	Mtl.C.	1	10	1	0	1	4	....	....	....	....	....	....	1919-20	1919-20
• McNaughton, George	Que.	1	1	0	0	0	0	....	....	....	....	....	....	1919-20	1919-20
McNeill, Billy	Det.	6	257	21	46	67	142	4	1	1	2	4	....	1956-57	1963-64
‡ McNeill, Mike	Chi., Que.	2	63	5	11	16	18	....	....	....	....	....	....	1990-91	1991-92
McNeill, Stu	Det.	3	10	1	1	2	2	....	....	....	....	....	....	1957-58	1959-60
McPhee, George	NYR, N.J.	7	115	24	25	49	257	29	5	3	8	69	....	1982-83	1988-89
McPhee, Mike	Mtl., Min., Dal.	11	744	200	199	399	661	134	28	27	55	193	1	1983-84	1993-94
McRae, Basil	Que., Tor., Det., Min., T.B., St.L., Chi.	16	576	53	83	136	2457	78	8	4	12	349	....	1981-82	1996-97
McRae, Chris	Tor., Det.	3	21	1	0	1	122	....	....	....	....	....	....	1987-88	1989-90
McRae, Ken	Que., Tor.	7	137	14	21	35	364	6	0	0	0	4	....	1987-88	1993-94
McReavy, Pat	Bos., Det.	4	55	5	10	15	4	22	3	3	6	9	1	1938-39	1941-42
McReynolds, Brian	Wpg., NYR, L.A.	3	30	1	5	6	8	....	....	....	....	....	....	1989-90	1993-94
McSheffrey, Bryan	Van., Buf.	3	90	13	7	20	44	....	....	....	....	....	....	1972-73	1974-75
‡ McSween, Don	Buf., Ana.	5	47	3	10	13	55	....	....	....	....	....	....	1987-88	1995-96
McTaggart, Jim	Wsh.	2	71	3	10	13	205	....	....	....	....	....	....	1980-81	1981-82
‡ McTavish, Dale	Cgy.	1	9	1	2	3	2	....	....	....	....	....	....	1996-97	1996-97
McTavish, Gord	St.L., Wpg.	2	11	1	3	4	2	....	....	....	....	....	....	1978-79	1979-80
• McVeigh, Charley	Chi., NYA	9	397	84	88	172	138	4	0	0	0	2	....	1926-27	1934-35
• McVicar, Jack	Mtl.M.	2	88	2	4	6	63	6	0	0	0	2	....	1930-31	1931-32
Meagher, Rick	Mtl., Hfd., N.J., St.L.	12	691	144	165	309	383	62	8	7	15	41	....	1979-80	1990-91
Meehan, Gerry	Tor., Phi., Buf., Van., Atl., Wsh.	10	670	180	243	423	111	10	0	1	1	0	....	1968-69	1978-79
Meeke, Brent	Cal., Cle.	5	75	9	22	31	8	....	....	....	....	....	....	1972-73	1976-77
Meeker, Howie	Tor.	8	346	83	102	185	329	42	6	9	15	50	4	1946-47	1953-54
Meeker, Mike	Pit.	1	4	0	0	0	5	....	....	....	....	....	....	1978-79	1978-79
• Meeking, Harry	Tor., Det., Bos.	3	64	18	12	30	66	9	3	0	3	6	....	1917-18	1926-27
Meger, Paul	Mtl.	6	212	39	52	91	118	35	3	8	11	16	1	1949-50	1954-55
Meighan, Ron	Min., Pit.	2	48	3	7	10	18	....	....	....	....	....	....	1981-82	1982-83
Meissner, Barrie	Min.	2	6	0	1	1	4	....	....	....	....	....	....	1967-68	1968-69
Meissner, Dick	Bos., NYR	5	171	11	15	26	37	....	....	....	....	....	....	1959-60	1964-65
Melametsa, Anssi	Wpg.	1	27	0	3	3	2	....	....	....	....	....	....	1985-86	1985-86
Melin, Roger	Min.	2	3	0	0	0	0	....	....	....	....	....	....	1980-81	1981-82
Mellor, Tom	Det.	2	26	2	4	6	25	....	....	....	....	....	....	1973-74	1974-75
• Melnyk, Gerry	Det., Chi., St.L.	6	269	39	77	116	34	53	6	6	12	6	....	1955-56	1967-68
Melnyk, Larry	Bos., Edm., NYR, Van.	10	432	11	63	74	686	66	2	9	11	127	2	1980-81	1989-90
Melrose, Barry	Wpg., Tor., Det.	6	300	10	23	33	728	7	0	2	2	38	....	1979-80	1985-86
Menard, Hillary	Chi.	1	1	0	0	0	0	....	....	....	....	....	....	1953-54	1953-54
Menard, Howie	Det., L.A., Chi., Oak.	4	151	23	42	65	87	19	3	7	10	36	....	1963-64	1969-70
Mercredi, Vic	Atl.	1	2	0	0	0	0	....	....	....	....	....	....	1974-75	1974-75
Meredith, Greg	Cgy.	2	38	6	4	10	8	5	3	1	4	4	....	1980-81	1982-83
Merkosky, Glenn	Hfd., N.J., Det.	5	66	5	12	17	22	....	....	....	....	....	....	1981-82	1989-90
• Meronek, Bill	Mtl.	2	19	5	8	13	0	1	0	0	0	0	....	1939-40	1942-43
Merrick, Wayne	St.L., Cal., Cle., NYI	12	774	191	265	456	303	102	19	30	49	30	4	1972-73	1983-84
• Merrill, Horace	Ott.	2	8	0	0	0	3	....	....	....	....	....	1	1917-18	1919-20
‡ Mertzig, Jan	NYR	1	23	0	2	2	8	....	....	....	....	....	....	1998-99	1998-99
Messier, Joby	NYR	3	25	0	4	4	24	....	....	....	....	....	....	1992-93	1994-95
Messier, Mitch	Min.	4	20	0	2	2	11	....	....	....	....	....	....	1987-88	1990-91
Messier, Paul	Col.	1	9	0	0	0	4	....	....	....	....	....	....	1978-79	1978-79
‡ Metcalfe, Scott	Edm., Buf.	3	19	1	2	3	18	....	....	....	....	....	....	1987-88	1989-90
Metz, Don	Tor.	9	172	20	35	55	42	42	7	8	15	12	5	1938-39	1948-49
• Metz, Nick	Tor.	12	518	131	119	250	149	76	19	20	39	31	4	1934-35	1947-48
Michaluk, Art	Chi.	1	5	0	0	0	0	....	....	....	....	....	....	1947-48	1947-48
Michaluk, John	Chi.	1	1	0	0	0	0	....	....	....	....	....	....	1950-51	1950-51
Michayluk, Dave	Phi., Pit.	3	14	2	6	8	8	7	1	1	2	0	1	1981-82	1991-92
Micheletti, Joe	St.L., Col.	3	158	11	60	71	114	11	1	11	12	10	....	1979-80	1981-82
Micheletti, Pat	Min.	1	12	2	0	2	8	....	....	....	....	....	....	1987-88	1987-88
• Mickey, Larry	Chi., NYR, Tor., Mtl., L.A., Phi., Buf.	11	292	39	53	92	160	9	1	0	1	10	....	1964-65	1974-75
Mickoski, Nick	NYR, Chi., Det., Bos.	13	703	158	185	343	319	18	1	6	7	6	....	1947-48	1959-60
Middendorf, Max	Que., Edm.	4	13	2	4	6	6	....	....	....	....	....	....	1986-87	1990-91
Middleton, Rick	NYR, Bos.	14	1005	448	540	988	157	114	45	55	100	19	....	1974-75	1987-88
‡ Miehm, Kevin	St.L.	2	22	1	4	5	8	2	0	1	1	0	....	1992-93	1993-94
Migay, Rudy	Tor.	10	418	59	92	151	293	15	1	0	1	20	....	1949-50	1959-60
Mikita, Stan	Chi.	22	1394	541	926	1467	1270	155	59	91	150	169	1	1958-59	1979-80
Mikkelson, Bill	L.A., NYI, Wsh.	4	147	4	18	22	105	....	....	....	....	....	....	1971-72	1976-77
Mikol, Jim	Tor., NYR	2	34	1	4	5	8	....	....	....	....	....	....	1962-63	1964-65
‡ Mikulchik, Oleg	Wpg., Ana.	3	37	0	3	3	33	....	....	....	....	....	....	1993-94	1995-96
Milbury, Mike	Bos.	12	754	49	189	238	1552	86	4	24	28	219	....	1975-76	1986-87
• Milks, Hib	Pit., Phi., NYR, Ott.	8	317	87	41	128	179	11	0	0	0	2	....	1925-26	1932-33
Millar, Hugh	Det.	1	4	0	0	0	0	1	0	0	0	0	....	1946-47	1946-47
‡ Millar, Mike	Hfd., Wsh., Bos., Tor.	5	78	18	18	36	12	....	....	....	....	....	....	1986-87	1990-91
‡ Millen, Corey	NYR, L.A., N.J., Dal., Cgy.	8	335	90	119	209	236	47	5	7	12	22	....	1989-90	1996-97
• Miller, Bill	Mtl.M., Mtl.C.	3	95	7	3	10	16	12	0	0	0	0	1	1934-35	1936-37
Miller, Bob	Bos., Col., L.A.	6	404	75	119	194	220	36	4	7	11	27	....	1977-78	1984-85
‡ Miller, Brad	Buf., Ott., Cgy.	6	82	1	5	6	321	....	....	....	....	....	....	1988-89	1993-94
• Miller, Earl	Chi., Tor.	5	109	19	14	33	124	10	1	0	1	6	1	1927-28	1931-32
Miller, Jack	Chi.	2	17	0	0	0	4	....	....	....	....	....	....	1949-50	1950-51
‡ Miller, Jason	N.J.	3	6	0	0	0	0	....	....	....	....	....	....	1990-91	1992-93
Miller, Jay	Bos., L.A.	7	446	40	44	84	1723	48	2	3	5	243	....	1985-86	1991-92
Miller, Kelly	NYR, Wsh.	15	1057	181	282	463	512	119	20	34	54	65	....	1984-85	1998-99
Miller, Paul	Col.	1	3	0	3	3	0	....	....	....	....	....	....	1981-82	1981-82
Miller, Perry	Det.	4	217	10	51	61	387	....	....	....	....	....	....	1977-78	1980-81
Miller, Tom	Det., NYI	4	118	16	25	41	34	....	....	....	....	....	....	1970-71	1974-75
Miller, Warren	NYR, Hfd.	4	262	40	50	90	137	6	1	0	1	0	....	1979-80	1982-83
‡ Miner, John	Edm.	1	14	2	3	5	16	....	....	....	....	....	....	1987-88	1987-88
Minor, Gerry	Van.	5	140	11	21	32	173	12	1	3	4	25	....	1979-80	1983-84
Miszuk, John	Det., Chi., Phi., Min.	6	237	7	39	46	232	19	0	3	3	19	....	1963-64	1969-70
Mitchell, Bill	Det.	1	1	0	0	0	0	....	....	....	....	....	....	1963-64	1963-64
• Mitchell, Herb	Bos.	2	44	6	0	6	36	....	....	....	....	....	....	1924-25	1925-26
‡ Mitchell, Jeff	Dal.	1	7	0	0	0	7	....	....	....	....	....	....	1997-98	1997-98
Mitchell, Red	Chi.	3	83	4	5	9	67	....	....	....	....	....	....	1941-42	1944-45

				Regular Schedule					Playoffs							
	Name	NHL Teams	NHL Seasons	GP	G	A	TP	PIM	GP	G	A	TP	PIM	NHL Cup Wins	First NHL Season	Last NHL Season
‡	Mitchell, Roy	Min.	1	3	0	0	0	0	....	....	....	....	....	....	1992-93	1992-93
•	Moe, Bill	NYR	5	261	11	42	53	163	1	0	0	0	0	....	1944-45	1948-49
	Moffat, Lyle	Tor., Wpg.	3	97	12	16	28	51	....	....	....	....	....	....	1972-73	1979-80
•	Moffat, Ron	Det.	3	37	1	1	2	8	7	0	0	0	0	....	1932-33	1934-35
	Moher, Mike	N.J.	1	9	0	1	1	28	....	....	....	....	....	....	1982-83	1982-83
	Mohns, Doug	Bos., Chi., Min., Atl., Wsh.	22	1390	248	462	710	1250	94	14	36	50	122	....	1953-54	1974-75
	Mohns, Lloyd	NYR	1	1	0	0	0	0	....	....	....	....	....	....	1943-44	1943-44
	Mokosak, Carl	Cgy., L.A., Phi., Pit., Bos.	6	83	11	15	26	170	1	0	0	0	0	....	1981-82	1988-89
	Mokosak, John	Det.	2	41	0	2	2	96	....	....	....	....	....	....	1988-89	1989-90
	Molin, Lars	Van.	3	172	33	65	98	37	19	2	9	11	7	....	1981-82	1983-84
	Moller, Mike	Buf., Edm.	7	134	15	28	43	41	3	0	1	1	0	....	1980-81	1986-87
	Moller, Randy	Que., NYR, Buf., Fla.	14	815	45	180	225	1692	78	6	16	22	197	....	1981-82	1994-95
	Molloy, Mitch	Buf.	1	2	0	0	0	10	....	....	....	....	....	....	1989-90	1989-90
	Molyneaux, Larry	NYR	2	45	0	1	1	20	10	0	0	0	8	....	1937-38	1938-39
‡	Momesso, Sergio	Mtl., St.L., Van., Tor., NYR	13	710	152	193	345	1557	119	18	26	44	311	....	1983-84	1996-97
	Monahan, Garry	Mtl., Det., L.A., Tor., Van.	12	748	116	169	285	484	22	3	1	4	13	....	1967-68	1978-79
	Monahan, Hartland	Cal., NYR, Wsh., Pit., L.A., St.L.	7	334	61	80	141	163	6	0	0	0	4	....	1973-74	1980-81
•	Mondou, Armand	Mtl.C., Mtl.	12	386	47	71	118	99	32	3	5	8	12	2	1928-29	1939-40
	Mondou, Pierre	Mtl.	9	548	194	262	456	179	69	17	28	45	26	3	1976-77	1984-85
‡	Mongeau, Michel	St.L., T.B.	4	54	6	19	25	10	2	0	1	1	0	....	1989-90	1992-93
	Mongrain, Bob	Buf., L.A.	6	81	13	14	27	14	11	1	2	3	2	....	1979-80	1985-86
	Monteith, Hank	Det.	3	77	5	12	17	6	4	0	0	0	0	....	1968-69	1970-71
	Moore, Dickie	Mtl., Tor., St.L.	14	719	261	347	608	652	135	46	64	110	122	6	1951-52	1967-68
•	Moran, Amby	Mtl.C., Chi.	2	35	1	1	2	24	....	....	....	....	....	....	1926-27	1927-28
‡	More, Jay	NYR, Min., S.J., Phx., Chi., Nsh.	10	406	18	54	72	702	31	0	6	6	45	....	1988-89	1998-99
•	Morenz, Howie	Mtl.C., Chi., NYR	14	550	271	201	472	546	39	13	9	22	58	3	1923-24	1936-37
	Moretto, Angelo	Cle.	1	5	1	2	3	2	....	....	....	....	....	....	1976-77	1976-77
•	Morin, Pete	Mtl.	1	31	10	12	22	7	1	0	0	0	0	....	1941-42	1941-42
•	Morin, Stephane	Que., Van.	5	90	16	39	55	52	....	....	....	....	....	....	1989-90	1993-94
•	Morris, Bernie	Bos.	1	6	1	0	1	0	....	....	....	....	....	....	1924-25	1924-25
	Morris, Jon	N.J., S.J., Bos.	6	103	16	33	49	47	11	1	7	8	25	....	1988-89	1993-94
•	Morris, Moe	Tor., NYR	4	135	13	29	42	58	18	4	2	6	16	1	1943-44	1948-49
	Morrison, Dave	L.A., Van.	4	39	3	3	6	4	....	....	....	....	....	....	1980-81	1984-85
	Morrison, Don	Det., Chi.	3	112	18	28	46	12	3	0	1	1	0	....	1947-48	1950-51
	Morrison, Doug	Bos.	4	23	7	3	10	15	....	....	....	....	....	....	1979-80	1984-85
	Morrison, Gary	Phi.	3	43	1	15	16	70	5	0	1	1	2	....	1979-80	1981-82
	Morrison, George	St.L.	2	115	17	21	38	13	3	0	0	0	0	....	1970-71	1971-72
	Morrison, Jim	Bos., Tor., Det., NYR, Pit.	12	704	40	160	200	542	36	0	12	12	38	....	1951-52	1970-71
•	Morrison, John	NYA	1	18	0	0	0	0	....	....	....	....	....	....	1925-26	1925-26
	Morrison, Kevin	Col.	1	41	4	11	15	23	....	....	....	....	....	....	1979-80	1979-80
	Morrison, Lew	Phi., Atl., Wsh., Pit.	9	564	39	52	91	107	17	0	0	0	2	....	1969-70	1977-78
	Morrison, Mark	NYR	2	10	1	1	2	0	....	....	....	....	....	....	1981-82	1983-84
•	Morrison, Rod	Det.	1	34	8	7	15	4	3	0	0	0	0	....	1947-48	1947-48
	Morrow, Ken	NYI	10	550	17	88	105	309	127	11	22	33	97	4	1979-80	1988-89
‡	Morrow, Scott	Cgy.	1	4	0	0	0	0	....	....	....	....	....	....	1994-95	1994-95
	Morton, Dean	Det.	1	1	1	0	1	2	....	....	....	....	....	....	1989-90	1989-90
	Mortson, Gus	Tor., Chi., Det.	13	797	46	152	198	1380	54	5	8	13	68	4	1946-47	1958-59
	Mosdell, Kenny	Bro., Mtl., Chi.	16	693	141	168	309	475	80	16	13	29	48	4	1941-42	1958-59
•	Mosienko, Bill	Chi.	14	711	258	282	540	121	22	10	4	14	15	....	1941-42	1954-55
	Mott, Morris	Cal.	3	199	18	32	50	49	....	....	....	....	....	....	1972-73	1974-75
•	Motter, Alex	Bos., Det.	8	255	39	64	103	135	41	3	9	12	41	1	1934-35	1942-43
	Moxey, Jim	Cal., Cle., L.A.	3	127	22	27	49	59	....	....	....	....	....	....	1974-75	1976-77
	Mulhern, Richard	Atl., L.A., Tor., Wpg.	6	303	27	93	120	217	7	0	3	3	5	....	1975-76	1980-81
‡	Mulhern, Ryan	Wsh.	1	3	0	0	0	0	....	....	....	....	....	....	1997-98	1997-98
	Mullen, Brian	Wpg., NYR, S.J., NYI	11	832	260	362	622	414	62	12	18	30	30	....	1982-83	1992-93
	Mullen, Joe	St.L., Cgy., Pit., Bos.	17	1062	502	561	1063	241	143	60	46	106	42	3	1979-80	1996-97
	Muloin, Wayne	Det., Oak., Cal., Min.	3	147	3	21	24	93	11	0	0	0	2	....	1963-64	1970-71
	Mulvenna, Glenn	Pit., Phi.	2	2	0	0	0	4	....	....	....	....	....	....	1991-92	1992-93
	Mulvey, Grant	Chi., N.J.	10	586	149	135	284	816	42	10	5	15	70	....	1974-75	1983-84
	Mulvey, Paul	Wsh., Pit., L.A.	4	225	30	51	81	613	....	....	....	....	....	....	1978-79	1981-82
•	Mummery, Harry	Tor., Que., Mtl.C., Ham.	6	106	33	19	52	226	2	1	1	2	17	1	1917-18	1922-23
	Muni, Craig	Tor., Edm., Chi., Buf., Wpg., Pit., Dal.	16	819	28	119	147	775	113	0	17	17	108	3	1981-82	1997-98
•	Munro, Dunc	Mtl.M., Mtl.C.	8	239	28	18	46	172	21	2	2	4	18	1	1924-25	1931-32
•	Munro, Gerry	Mtl.M., Tor.	2	34	1	0	1	37	....	....	....	....	....	....	1924-25	1925-26
	Murdoch, Bob	Mtl., L.A., Atl., Cgy.	12	757	60	218	278	764	69	4	18	22	92	2	1970-71	1981-82
	Murdoch, Bob	Cal., Cle., St.L.	4	260	72	85	157	127	....	....	....	....	....	....	1975-76	1978-79
	Murdoch, Don	NYR, Edm., Det.	6	320	121	117	238	155	24	10	8	18	16	....	1976-77	1981-82
•	Murdoch, Murray	NYR	11	508	84	108	192	197	55	9	12	21	28	2	1926-27	1936-37
	Murphy, Brian	Det.	1	1	0	0	0	0	....	....	....	....	....	....	1974-75	1974-75
	Murphy, Mike	St.L., NYR, L.A.	12	831	238	318	556	514	66	13	23	36	54	....	1971-72	1982-83
‡	Murphy, Rob	Van., Ott., L.A.	7	125	9	12	21	152	4	0	0	0	2	....	1987-88	1993-94
	Murphy, Ron	NYR, Chi., Det., Bos.	18	889	205	274	479	460	53	7	8	15	26	1	1952-53	1969-70
	Murray, Allan	NYA	7	271	5	9	14	163	14	0	0	0	10	....	1933-34	1939-40
	Murray, Bob	Atl., Van.	4	194	6	16	22	98	10	1	1	2	15	....	1973-74	1976-77
	Murray, Bob	Chi.	15	1008	132	382	514	873	112	19	37	56	106	....	1975-76	1989-90
	Murray, Jim	L.A.	1	30	0	2	2	14	....	....	....	....	....	....	1967-68	1967-68
	Murray, Ken	Tor., NYI, Det., K.C.	5	106	1	10	11	135	....	....	....	....	....	....	1969-70	1975-76
•	Murray, Leo	Mtl.C.	1	6	0	0	0	2	....	....	....	....	....	....	1932-33	1932-33
‡	Murray, Mike	Phi.	1	1	0	0	0	0	....	....	....	....	....	....	1987-88	1987-88
	Murray, Pat	Phi.	2	25	3	1	4	15	....	....	....	....	....	....	1990-91	1991-92
	Murray, Randy	Tor.	1	3	0	0	0	2	....	....	....	....	....	....	1969-70	1969-70
	Murray, Terry	Cal., Phi., Det., Wsh.	8	302	4	76	80	199	18	2	2	4	10	....	1972-73	1981-82
	Murray, Troy	Chi., Wpg., Ott., Pit., Col.	15	915	230	354	584	875	113	17	26	43	145	1	1981-82	1995-96
	Murzyn, Dana	Hfd., Cgy., Van.	14	838	52	152	204	1571	82	9	10	19	166	1	1985-86	1998-99
	Myers, Hap	Buf.	1	13	0	0	0	6	....	....	....	....	....	....	1970-71	1970-71
	Myles, Vic	NYR	1	45	6	9	15	57	....	....	....	....	....	....	1942-43	1942-43

N

				Regular Schedule					Playoffs							
	Name	NHL Teams	NHL Seasons	GP	G	A	TP	PIM	GP	G	A	TP	PIM	NHL Cup Wins	First NHL Season	Last NHL Season
	Nachbaur, Don	Hfd., Edm., Phi.	8	223	23	46	69	465	11	1	1	2	24	....	1980-81	1989-90
	Nahrgang, Jim	Det.	3	57	5	12	17	34	....	....	....	....	....	....	1974-75	1976-77
	Nanne, Lou	Min.	11	635	68	157	225	356	32	4	10	14	8	....	1967-68	1977-78
	Nantais, Rich	Min.	3	63	5	4	9	79	....	....	....	....	....	....	1974-75	1976-77
	Napier, Mark	Mtl., Min., Edm., Buf.	11	767	235	306	541	157	82	18	24	42	11	2	1978-79	1988-89
	Naslund, Mats	Mtl., Bos.	9	651	251	383	634	111	102	35	57	92	33	1	1982-83	1994-95
	Nattrass, Ralph	Chi.	4	223	18	38	56	308	....	....	....	....	....	....	1946-47	1949-50
	Nattress, Ric	Mtl., St.L., Cgy., Tor., Phi.	11	536	29	135	164	377	67	5	10	15	60	1	1982-83	1992-93
	Natyshak, Mike	Que.	1	4	0	0	0	0	....	....	....	....	....	....	1987-88	1987-88
‡	Neaton, Pat	Pit.	1	9	1	1	2	12	....	....	....	....	....	....	1993-94	1993-94
	Nechayev, Viktor	L.A.	1	3	1	0	1	0	....	....	....	....	....	....	1982-83	1982-83
	Nedomansky, Vaclav	Det., NYR, St.L.	6	421	122	156	278	88	7	3	5	8	0	....	1977-78	1982-83
‡	Nedved, Zdenek	Tor.	3	31	4	6	10	14	....	....	....	....	....	....	1994-95	1996-97
	Needham, Mike	Pit., Dal.	3	86	9	5	14	16	14	2	0	2	4	1	1991-92	1993-94
	Neely, Bob	Tor., Col.	5	283	39	59	98	266	26	5	7	12	15	....	1973-74	1977-78
	Neely, Cam	Van., Bos.	13	726	395	299	694	1241	93	57	32	89	168	....	1983-84	1995-96
	Neilson, Jim	NYR, Cal., Cle.	16	1023	69	299	368	904	65	1	17	18	61	....	1962-63	1977-78
	Nelson, Gordie	Tor.	1	3	0	0	0	11	....	....	....	....	....	....	1969-70	1969-70
‡	Nelson, Todd	Pit., Wsh.	2	3	1	0	1	2	4	0	0	0	0	....	1991-92	1993-94
	Nemeth, Steve	NYR	1	12	2	0	2	2	....	....	....	....	....	....	1987-88	1987-88
	Nesterenko, Eric	Tor., Chi.	21	1219	250	324	574	1273	124	13	24	37	127	1	1951-52	1971-72
	Nethery, Lance	NYR, Edm.	2	41	11	14	25	14	14	5	3	8	9	....	1980-81	1981-82
	Neufeld, Ray	Hfd., Wpg., Bos.	11	595	157	200	357	816	28	8	6	14	55	....	1979-80	1989-90
•	Neville, Mike	Tor., NYA	3	65	5	5	10	14	2	0	0	0	0	....	1924-25	1930-31
	Nevin, Bob	Tor., NYR, Min., L.A.	18	1128	307	419	726	211	84	16	18	34	24	2	1957-58	1975-76
	Newberry, John	Mtl., Hfd.	4	22	0	4	4	6	2	0	0	0	0	....	1982-83	1985-86
	Newell, Rick	Det.	2	6	0	0	0	0	....	....	....	....	....	....	1972-73	1973-74
	Newman, Dan	NYR, Mtl., Edm.	4	126	17	24	41	63	3	0	0	0	4	....	1976-77	1979-80
•	Newman, John	Det.	1	8	1	1	2	0	....	....	....	....	....	....	1930-31	1930-31
	Nicholls, Bernie	L.A., NYR, Edm., N.J., Chi., S.J.	18	1127	475	734	1209	1292	118	42	72	114	164	....	1981-82	1998-99
	Nicholson, Al	Bos.	2	19	0	1	1	4	....	....	....	....	....	....	1955-56	1956-57
•	Nicholson, Ed	Det.	1	1	0	0	0	0	....	....	....	....	....	....	1947-48	1947-48
•	Nicholson, Hickey	Chi.	1	2	1	0	1	0	....	....	....	....	....	....	1937-38	1937-38
	Nicholson, Neil	Oak., NYI	4	39	3	1	4	23	2	0	0	0	0	....	1969-70	1977-78
	Nicholson, Paul	Wsh.	3	62	4	8	12	18	....	....	....	....	....	....	1974-75	1976-77
	Nicolson, Graeme	Bos., Col., NYR	3	52	2	7	9	60	....	....	....	....	....	....	1978-79	1982-83
‡	Nieckar, Barry	Hfd., Cgy., Ana.	4	8	0	0	0	21	....	....	....	....	....	....	1992-93	1997-98

Sergio Momesso

Jay More

Jim Neilson

Lee Norwood

Bob Nystrom

Ed Olczyk

Mark Osborne

Jim Pappin

			Regular Schedule					Playoffs					NHL	First	Last
Name	NHL Teams	NHL Seasons	GP	G	A	TP	PIM	GP	G	A	TP	PIM	Cup Wins	NHL Season	NHL Season
Niekamp, Jim	Det.	2	29	0	2	2	37	....	....	....	....	....	....	1970-71	1971-72
Nielsen, Kirk	Bos.	1	6	0	0	0	0	....	....	....	....	....	....	1997-98	1997-98
‡ Nienhuis, Kraig	Bos.	3	87	20	16	36	39	2	0	0	0	14	....	1985-86	1987-88
● Nighbor, Frank	Ott., Tor.	13	349	139	98	237	249	20	4	9	13	13	4	1917-18	1929-30
Nigro, Frank	Tor.	2	68	8	18	26	39	3	0	0	0	2	....	1982-83	1983-84
‡ Nikulin, Igor	Ana.	1	....	....	....	....	....	1	0	0	0	0	....	1996-97	1996-97
Nilan, Chris	Mtl., NYR, Bos.	13	688	110	115	225	3043	111	8	9	17	541	1	1979-80	1991-92
Nill, Jim	St.L., Van., Bos., Wpg., Det.	9	524	58	87	145	854	59	10	5	15	203	....	1981-82	1989-90
Nilsson, Kent	Atl., Cgy., Min., Edm.	9	553	264	422	686	116	59	11	41	52	14	1	1979-80	1994-95
Nilsson, Ulf	NYR	4	170	57	112	169	85	25	8	14	22	27	....	1978-79	1982-83
Nistico, Lou	Col.	1	3	0	0	0	0	....	....	....	....	....	....	1977-78	1977-78
● Noble, Reg	Tor., Mtl.M., Det.	16	510	168	106	274	916	18	2	2	4	33	3	1917-18	1932-33
Noel, Claude	Wsh.	1	7	0	0	0	0	....	....	....	....	....	....	1979-80	1979-80
● Nolan, Paddy	Tor.	1	2	0	0	0	0	....	....	....	....	....	....	1921-22	1921-22
Nolan, Ted	Det., Pit.	3	78	6	16	22	105	....	....	....	....	....	....	1981-82	1985-86
Nolet, Simon	Phi., K.C., Pit., Col.	10	562	150	182	332	187	34	6	3	9	8	1	1967-68	1976-77
‡ Nordmark, Robert	St.L., Van.	4	236	13	70	83	254	7	3	2	5	8	....	1987-88	1990-91
Noris, Joe	Pit., St.L., Buf.	3	55	2	5	7	22	....	....	....	....	....	....	1971-72	1973-74
‡ Norris, Dwayne	Que., Ana.	3	20	2	4	6	8	....	....	....	....	....	....	1993-94	1995-96
Norrish, Rod	Min.	2	21	3	3	6	2	....	....	....	....	....	....	1973-74	1974-75
● Northcott, Baldy	Mtl.M., Chi.	11	446	133	112	245	273	31	8	5	13	14	1	1928-29	1938-39
Norwich, Craig	Wpg., St.L., Col.	2	104	17	58	75	60	....	....	....	....	....	....	1979-80	1980-81
Norwood, Lee	Que., Wsh., St.L., Det., N.J., Hfd., Cgy.	12	503	58	153	211	1099	65	6	22	28	171	....	1980-81	1993-94
Novy, Milan	Wsh.	1	73	18	30	48	16	2	0	0	0	0	....	1982-83	1982-83
Nowak, Hank	Pit., Det., Bos.	4	180	26	29	55	161	13	1	0	1	8	....	1973-74	1976-77
Nykoluk, Mike	Tor.	1	32	3	1	4	20	....	....	....	....	....	....	1956-57	1956-57
Nylund, Gary	Tor., Chi., NYI	11	608	32	139	171	1235	24	0	6	6	63	....	1982-83	1992-93
● Nyrop, Bill	Mtl., Min.	4	207	12	51	63	101	35	1	7	8	22	3	1975-76	1981-82
Nystrom, Bob	NYI	14	900	235	278	513	1248	157	39	44	83	236	4	1972-73	1985-86

O

Name	NHL Teams	NHL Seasons	GP	G	A	TP	PIM	GP	G	A	TP	PIM	NHL Cup Wins	First NHL Season	Last NHL Season
● Oatman, Russell	Det., Mtl.M., NYR	3	120	20	9	29	100	15	1	0	1	18	....	1926-27	1928-29
O'Brien, Dennis	Min., Col., Cle., Bos.	10	592	31	91	122	1017	34	1	2	3	101	....	1970-71	1979-80
O'Brien, Ellard	Bos.	1	2	0	0	0	0	....	....	....	....	....	....	1955-56	1955-56
O'Callahan, Jack	Chi., N.J.	7	389	27	104	131	541	32	4	11	15	41	....	1982-83	1988-89
O'Connell, Mike	Chi., Bos., Det.	13	860	105	334	439	605	82	8	24	32	64	....	1977-78	1989-90
● O'Connor, Buddy	Mtl., NYR	10	509	140	257	397	34	53	15	21	36	6	2	1941-42	1950-51
O'Connor, Myles	N.J., Ana.	4	43	3	4	7	69	....	....	....	....	....	....	1990-91	1993-94
Oddleifson, Chris	Bos., Van.	9	524	95	191	286	464	14	1	6	7	8	....	1972-73	1980-81
Odelein, Selmar	Edm.	3	18	0	2	2	35	....	....	....	....	....	....	1985-86	1988-89
O'Donnell, Fred	Bos.	2	115	15	11	26	98	5	0	1	1	5	....	1972-73	1973-74
O'Donoghue, Don	Oak., Cal.	3	125	18	17	35	35	3	0	0	0	0	....	1969-70	1971-72
Odrowski, Gerry	Det., Oak., St.L.	6	309	12	19	31	111	30	0	1	1	16	....	1960-61	1971-72
O'Dwyer, Bill	L.A., Bos.	5	120	9	13	22	108	10	0	0	0	2	....	1983-84	1989-90
O'Flaherty, Gerry	Tor., Van., Atl.	8	438	99	95	194	168	7	2	2	4	6	....	1971-72	1978-79
O'Flaherty, Peanuts	NYA, Bro.	2	21	5	1	6	0	....	....	....	....	....	....	1940-41	1941-42
Ogilvie, Brian	Chi., St.L.	6	90	15	21	36	29	....	....	....	....	....	....	1972-73	1978-79
● O'Grady, George	Mtl.	1	4	0	0	0	0	....	....	....	....	....	....	1917-18	1917-18
Ogrodnick, John	Det., Que., NYR	14	928	402	425	827	260	41	18	8	26	6	....	1979-80	1992-93
‡ Ojanen, Janne	N.J.	4	98	21	23	44	28	3	0	2	2	0	....	1988-89	1992-93
Okerlund, Todd	NYI	1	4	0	0	0	2	....	....	....	....	....	....	1987-88	1987-88
Oksiuta, Roman	Edm., Van., Ana., Pit.	4	153	46	41	87	100	10	2	3	5	0	....	1993-94	1996-97
‡ Olczyk, Ed	Chi., Tor., Wpg., NYR, L.A., Pit.	16	1031	342	452	794	874	57	19	15	34	57	1	1984-85	1999-00
● Oliver, Harry	Bos., NYA	11	463	127	85	212	147	35	10	6	16	24	1	1926-27	1936-37
Oliver, Murray	Det., Bos., Tor., Min.	17	1127	274	454	728	320	35	9	16	25	10	....	1957-58	1974-75
Olmstead, Bert	Chi., Mtl., Tor.	14	848	181	421	602	884	115	16	43	59	101	5	1948-49	1961-62
‡ Olsen, Darryl	Cgy.	1	1	0	0	0	0	....	....	....	....	....	....	1991-92	1991-92
Olson, Dennis	Det.	1	4	0	0	0	0	....	....	....	....	....	....	1957-58	1957-58
‡ Olsson, Christer	St.L., Ott.	2	56	4	12	16	24	3	0	0	0	0	....	1995-96	1996-97
● O'Neil, Jim	Bos., Mtl.	6	156	6	30	36	109	9	1	1	2	13	....	1933-34	1941-42
O'Neil, Paul	Van., Bos.	2	6	0	0	0	0	....	....	....	....	....	....	1973-74	1975-76
● O'Neill, Tom	Tor.	2	66	10	12	22	53	4	0	0	0	6	1	1943-44	1944-45
Orban, Bill	Chi., Min.	3	114	8	15	23	67	3	0	0	0	0	....	1967-68	1969-70
O'Ree, Willie	Bos.	2	45	4	10	14	26	....	....	....	....	....	....	1957-58	1960-61
O'Regan, Tom	Pit.	3	61	5	12	17	10	....	....	....	....	....	....	1983-84	1985-86
O'Reilly, Terry	Bos.	14	891	204	402	606	2095	108	25	42	67	335	....	1971-72	1984-85
Orlando, Gates	Buf.	3	98	18	26	44	51	5	0	4	4	14	....	1984-85	1986-87
● Orlando, Jimmy	Det.	6	199	6	25	31	375	36	0	9	9	105	1	1936-37	1942-43
Orleski, Dave	Mtl.	2	2	0	0	0	0	....	....	....	....	....	....	1980-81	1981-82
● Orr, Bobby	Bos., Chi.	12	657	270	645	915	953	74	26	66	92	107	2	1966-67	1978-79
‡ Osborne, Keith	St.L., T.B.	2	16	1	3	4	16	....	....	....	....	....	....	1989-90	1992-93
Osborne, Mark	Det., NYR, Tor., Wpg.	14	919	212	319	531	1152	87	12	16	28	141	....	1981-82	1994-95
Osburn, Randy	Tor., Phi.	2	27	0	2	2	0	....	....	....	....	....	....	1972-73	1974-75
O'Shea, Danny	Min., Chi., St.L.	5	369	64	115	179	265	39	3	7	10	61	....	1968-69	1972-73
O'Shea, Kevin	Buf., St.L.	3	134	13	18	31	85	12	2	1	3	10	....	1970-71	1972-73
Osiecki, Mark	Cgy., Ott., Wpg., Min.	2	93	3	11	14	43	....	....	....	....	....	....	1991-92	1992-93
Otevrel, Jaroslav	S.J.	2	16	3	4	7	2	....	....	....	....	....	....	1992-93	1993-94
Otto, Joel	Cgy., Phi.	14	943	195	313	508	1934	122	27	47	74	207	1	1984-85	1997-98
Ouellette, Eddie	Chi.	1	43	3	2	5	11	1	0	0	0	0	....	1935-36	1935-36
Ouellette, Gerry	Bos.	1	34	5	4	9	0	....	....	....	....	....	....	1960-61	1960-61
Owchar, Dennis	Pit., Col.	6	288	30	85	115	200	10	1	1	2	8	....	1974-75	1979-80
● Owen, George	Bos.	5	183	44	33	77	151	21	2	5	7	25	1	1928-29	1932-33

P

Name	NHL Teams	NHL Seasons	GP	G	A	TP	PIM	GP	G	A	TP	PIM	NHL Cup Wins	First NHL Season	Last NHL Season
Pachal, Clayton	Bos., Col.	3	35	2	3	5	95	....	....	....	....	....	....	1976-77	1978-79
Paddock, John	Wsh., Phi., Que.	5	87	8	14	22	86	5	2	0	2	0	....	1975-76	1982-83
‡ Paek, Jim	Pit., L.A., Ott.	5	217	5	29	34	155	27	1	4	5	8	2	1990-91	1994-95
Paiement, Rosaire	Phi., Van.	5	190	48	52	100	343	3	3	0	3	0	....	1967-68	1971-72
Paiement, Wilf	K.C., Col., Tor., Que., NYR, Buf., Pit.	14	946	356	458	814	1757	69	18	17	35	185	....	1974-75	1987-88
Palangio, Pete	Mtl.C., Det., Chi.	5	71	13	10	23	28	7	0	0	0	0	1	1926-27	1937-38
Palazzari, Aldo	Bos., NYR	1	35	8	3	11	4	....	....	....	....	....	....	1943-44	1943-44
Palazzari, Doug	St.L.	4	108	18	20	38	23	2	0	0	0	0	....	1974-75	1978-79
Palmer, Brad	Min., Bos.	3	168	32	38	70	58	29	9	5	14	16	....	1980-81	1982-83
Palmer, Rob	Chi.	3	16	0	3	3	2	....	....	....	....	....	....	1973-74	1975-76
Palmer, Robert	L.A., N.J.	7	320	9	101	110	115	8	1	2	3	6	....	1977-78	1983-84
● Panagabko, Ed	Bos.	2	29	0	3	3	38	....	....	....	....	....	....	1955-56	1956-57
‡ Panteleev, Grigori	Bos., NYI	4	54	8	6	14	12	....	....	....	....	....	....	1992-93	1995-96
● Papike, Joe	Chi.	3	20	3	3	6	4	5	0	2	2	0	....	1940-41	1944-45
Pappin, Jim	Tor., Chi., Cal., Cle.	14	767	278	295	573	667	92	33	34	67	101	2	1963-64	1976-77
Paradise, Bob	Min., Atl., Pit., Wsh.	8	368	8	54	62	393	12	0	1	1	19	....	1971-72	1978-79
Pargeter, George	Mtl.	1	4	0	0	0	0	....	....	....	....	....	....	1946-47	1946-47
Parise, Jean-Paul	Bos., Tor., Min., NYI, Cle.	14	890	238	356	594	706	86	27	31	58	87	....	1965-66	1978-79
Parizeau, Michel	St.L., Phi.	1	58	3	14	17	18	....	....	....	....	....	....	1971-72	1971-72
Park, Brad	NYR, Bos., Det.	17	1113	213	683	896	1429	161	35	90	125	217	....	1968-69	1984-85
Parker, Jeff	Buf., Hfd.	5	141	16	19	35	163	5	0	0	0	26	....	1986-87	1990-91
● Parkes, Ernie	Mtl.M.	1	17	0	0	0	2	....	....	....	....	....	....	1924-25	1924-25
‡ Parks, Greg	NYI	3	23	1	2	3	6	2	0	0	0	0	....	1990-91	1992-93
● Parsons, George	Tor.	3	78	12	13	25	20	7	3	2	5	11	....	1936-37	1938-39
● Pasek, Dusan	Min.	1	48	4	10	14	30	2	1	0	1	0	....	1988-89	1988-89
Pasin, Dave	Bos., L.A.	2	76	18	19	37	50	3	0	1	1	0	....	1985-86	1988-89
Paslawski, Greg	Mtl., St.L., Wpg., Buf., Que., Phi., Cgy.	11	650	187	185	372	169	60	19	13	32	25	....	1983-84	1993-94
Paterson, Joe	Det., Phi., L.A., NYR	9	291	19	37	56	829	22	3	4	7	77	....	1980-81	1988-89
Paterson, Mark	Hfd.	4	29	3	3	6	33	....	....	....	....	....	....	1982-83	1985-86
Paterson, Rick	Chi.	9	430	50	43	93	136	61	7	10	17	51	....	1978-79	1986-87
Patey, Doug	Wsh.	3	45	4	2	6	8	....	....	....	....	....	....	1976-77	1978-79
Patey, Larry	Cal., St.L., NYR	12	717	153	163	316	631	40	8	10	18	57	....	1973-74	1984-85
Patrick, Craig	Cal., St.L., K.C., Wsh.	8	401	72	91	163	61	2	0	1	1	0	....	1971-72	1978-79
Patrick, Glenn	St.L., Cal., Cle.	4	38	2	3	5	72	....	....	....	....	....	....	1973-74	1976-77
● Patrick, Lester	NYR	1	1	0	0	0	2	....	....	....	....	....	....	1926-27	1926-27
● Patrick, Lynn	NYR	10	455	145	190	335	240	44	10	6	16	22	1	1934-35	1945-46
● Patrick, Muzz	NYR	5	166	5	26	31	133	25	4	0	4	34	1	1937-38	1945-46
Patrick, Steve	Buf., NYR, Que.	6	250	40	68	108	242	12	0	1	1	12	....	1980-81	1985-86
Patterson, Colin	Cgy., Buf.	10	504	96	109	205	239	85	12	17	29	57	1	1983-84	1992-93
Patterson, Dennis	K.C., Phi.	3	138	6	22	28	67	....	....	....	....	....	....	1974-75	1979-80

			Regular Schedule					Playoffs					NHL	First	Last
Name	NHL Teams	NHL Seasons	GP	G	A	TP	PIM	GP	G	A	TP	PIM	Cup Wins	NHL Season	NHL Season
• Patterson, George	Tor., Mtl.C., NYA, Bos., Det., St.L.	9	284	51	27	78	218	3	0	0	0	2	....	1926-27	1934-35
• Paul, Butch	Det.	1	3	0	0	0	0	....	....	....	....	....	....	1964-65	1964-65
• Paulhus, Rollie	Mtl.C.	1	33	0	0	0	0	....	....	....	....	....	....	1925-26	1925-26
Pavelich, Mark	NYR, Min., S.J.	7	355	137	192	329	340	23	7	17	24	14	....	1981-82	1991-92
Pavelich, Marty	Det.	10	634	93	159	252	454	91	13	15	28	74	4	1947-48	1956-57
Pavese, Jim	St.L., NYR, Det., Hfd.	8	328	13	44	57	689	34	0	6	6	81	....	1981-82	1988-89
• Payer, Evariste	Mtl.C.	1	1	0	0	0	0	....	....	....	....	....	....	1917-18	1917-18
‡ Payne, Davis	Bos.	2	22	0	1	1	14	....	....	....	....	....	....	1995-96	1996-97
Payne, Steve	Min.	10	613	228	238	466	435	71	35	35	70	60	....	1978-79	1987-88
Paynter, Kent	Chi., Wsh., Wpg., Ott.	7	37	1	3	4	69	4	0	0	0	10	....	1987-88	1993-94
Peake, Pat	Wsh.	5	134	28	41	69	105	13	2	2	4	20	....	1993-94	1997-98
• Pearson, Mel	NYR, Pit.	5	38	2	6	8	25	....	....	....	....	....	....	1959-60	1967-68
Pearson, Rob	Tor., Wsh., St.L.	6	269	56	54	110	645	33	4	2	6	94	....	1991-92	1996-97
Pedersen, Allen	Bos., Min., Hfd.	8	428	5	36	41	487	64	0	0	0	91	....	1986-87	1993-94
Pederson, Barry	Bos., Van., Pit., Hfd.	12	701	238	416	654	472	34	22	30	52	25	1	1980-81	1991-92
‡ Pederson, Mark	Mtl., Phi., S.J., Det.	5	169	35	50	85	77	2	0	0	0	0	....	1989-90	1993-94
‡ Pederson, Tom	S.J., Tor.	5	240	20	49	69	142	24	1	11	12	10	....	1992-93	1996-97
• Peer, Bert	Det.	1	1	0	0	0	0	....	....	....	....	....	....	1939-40	1939-40
Peirson, Johnny	Bos.	11	545	153	173	326	315	49	10	16	26	26	....	1946-47	1957-58
Pelensky, Perry	Chi.	1	4	0	0	0	5	....	....	....	....	....	....	1983-84	1983-84
Pelletier, Roger	Phi.	1	1	0	0	0	0	....	....	....	....	....	....	1967-68	1967-68
Peloffy, Andre	Wsh.	1	9	0	0	0	0	....	....	....	....	....	....	1974-75	1974-75
Peluso, Mike	Chi., Ott., N.J., St.L., Cgy.	9	458	38	52	90	1951	62	3	4	7	107	1	1989-90	1997-98
Pelyk, Mike	Tor.	9	441	26	88	114	566	40	0	3	3	41	....	1967-68	1977-78
Penney, Chad	Ott.	1	3	0	0	0	2	....	....	....	....	....	....	1993-94	1993-94
Pennington, Cliff	Mtl., Bos.	3	101	17	42	59	6	....	....	....	....	....	....	1960-61	1962-63
Peplinski, Jim	Cgy.	11	711	161	263	424	1467	99	15	31	46	382	1	1980-81	1994-95
Perlini, Fred	Tor.	2	8	2	3	5	0	....	....	....	....	....	....	1981-82	1983-84
Perreault, Fern	NYR	2	3	0	0	0	0	....	....	....	....	....	....	1947-48	1949-50
Perreault, Gilbert	Buf.	17	1191	512	814	1326	500	90	33	70	103	44	....	1970-71	1986-87
Perry, Brian	Oak., Buf.	3	96	16	29	45	24	8	1	1	2	4	....	1968-69	1970-71
Persson, Stefan	NYI	9	622	52	317	369	574	102	7	50	57	69	4	1977-78	1985-86
Pesut, George	Cal.	2	92	3	22	25	130	....	....	....	....	....	....	1974-75	1975-76
• Peters, Frank	NYR	1	43	0	0	0	59	4	0	0	0	2	....	1930-31	1930-31
Peters, Garry	Mtl., NYR, Phi., Bos.	8	311	34	34	68	261	9	2	2	4	31	1	1964-65	1971-72
Peters, Jimmy Jr.	Det., L.A.	9	309	37	36	73	48	11	0	2	2	2	....	1964-65	1974-75
Peters, Jimmy Sr.	Mtl., Bos., Det., Chi.	9	574	125	150	275	186	60	5	9	14	22	3	1945-46	1953-54
Peters, Steve	Col.	1	2	0	1	1	0	....	....	....	....	....	....	1979-80	1979-80
Peterson, Brent	Det., Buf., Van., Hfd.	11	620	72	141	213	484	31	4	4	8	65	....	1978-79	1988-89
‡ Petit, Michel	Van., NYR, Que., Tor., Cgy., L.A., T.B., Edm., Phi., Phx.	16	827	90	238	328	1839	19	0	2	2	61	....	1982-83	1997-98
‡ Petrenko, Sergei	Buf.	1	14	0	4	4	0	....	....	....	....	....	....	1993-94	1993-94
Pettersson, Jorgen	St.L., Hfd., Wsh.	6	435	174	192	366	117	44	15	12	27	4	....	1980-81	1985-86
• Pettinger, Eric	Bos., Tor., Ott.	3	98	7	12	19	83	4	1	0	1	8	....	1928-29	1930-31
• Pettinger, Gord	NYR, Det., Bos.	8	292	42	74	116	77	47	4	5	9	11	4	1932-33	1939-40
Phair, Lyle	L.A.	3	48	6	7	13	12	1	0	0	0	0	....	1985-86	1987-88
Phillipoff, Harold	Atl., Chi.	3	141	26	57	83	267	6	0	2	2	9	....	1977-78	1979-80
• Phillips, Batt	Mtl.M.	1	27	1	1	2	6	4	0	0	0	2	....	1929-30	1929-30
Phillips, Charlie	Mtl.	1	17	0	0	0	6	....	....	....	....	....	....	1942-43	1942-43
• Phillips, Merlyn	Mtl.M., NYA	8	302	52	31	83	232	24	5	1	6	19	1	1925-26	1932-33
Picard, Noel	Mtl., St.L., Atl.	7	335	12	63	75	616	50	2	11	13	167	1	1964-65	1972-73
Picard, Robert	Wsh., Tor., Mtl., Wpg., Que., Det.	13	899	104	319	423	1025	36	5	15	20	39	....	1977-78	1989-90
Picard, Roger	St.L.	1	15	2	2	4	21	....	....	....	....	....	....	1967-68	1967-68
Pichette, Dave	Que., St.L., N.J., NYR	7	322	41	140	181	348	28	3	7	10	54	....	1980-81	1987-88
Picketts, Hal	NYA	1	48	3	1	4	32	....	....	....	....	....	....	1933-34	1933-34
Pidhirny, Harry	Bos.	1	2	0	0	0	0	....	....	....	....	....	....	1957-58	1957-58
Pierce, Randy	Col., N.J., Hfd.	8	277	62	76	138	223	2	0	0	0	0	....	1977-78	1984-85
Pike, Alf	NYR	6	234	42	77	119	145	21	4	2	6	12	1	1939-40	1946-47
Pilote, Pierre	Chi., Tor.	14	890	80	418	498	1251	86	8	53	61	102	1	1955-56	1968-69
Pinder, Gerry	Chi., Cal.	3	223	55	69	124	135	17	0	4	4	6	....	1969-70	1971-72
Pirus, Alex	Min., Det.	4	159	30	28	58	94	2	0	1	1	2	....	1976-77	1979-80
• Pitre, Didier	Mtl.C.	6	127	64	34	98	84	9	2	4	6	16	....	1917-18	1922-23
Pivonka, Michal	Wsh.	13	825	181	418	599	478	95	19	36	55	86	....	1986-87	1998-99
• Plager, Barclay	St.L.	10	614	44	187	231	1115	68	3	20	23	182	....	1967-68	1976-77
Plager, Bill	Min., St.L., Atl.	9	263	4	34	38	294	31	0	2	2	26	....	1967-68	1975-76
Plager, Bob	NYR, St.L.	14	644	20	126	146	802	74	2	17	19	195	....	1964-65	1977-78
Plamondon, Gerry	Mtl.	5	74	7	13	20	10	11	5	2	7	2	1	1945-46	1950-51
Plante, Cam	Tor.	1	2	0	0	0	0	....	....	....	....	....	....	1984-85	1984-85
Plante, Pierre	Phi., St.L., Chi., NYR, Que.	9	599	125	172	297	599	33	2	6	8	51	....	1971-72	1979-80
Plantery, Mark	Wpg.	1	25	1	5	6	14	....	....	....	....	....	....	1980-81	1980-81
‡ Plavsic, Adrien	St.L., Van., T.B., Ana.	8	214	16	56	72	161	13	1	7	8	4	....	1989-90	1996-97
• Plaxton, Hugh	Mtl.M.	1	15	1	2	3	4	....	....	....	....	....	....	1932-33	1932-33
Playfair, Jim	Edm., Chi.	3	21	2	4	6	51	....	....	....	....	....	....	1983-84	1988-89
Playfair, Larry	Buf., L.A.	12	688	26	94	120	1812	43	0	6	6	111	....	1978-79	1989-90
Pleau, Larry	Mtl.	3	94	9	15	24	27	4	0	0	0	0	....	1969-70	1971-72
• Pletsch, Charles	Ham.	1	1	0	0	0	0	....	....	....	....	....	....	1920-21	1920-21
Plett, Willi	Atl., Cgy., Min., Bos.	13	834	222	215	437	2572	83	24	22	46	466	....	1975-76	1987-88
Plumb, Rob	Det.	2	14	3	2	5	2	....	....	....	....	....	....	1977-78	1978-79
Plumb, Ron	Hfd.	1	26	3	4	7	14	....	....	....	....	....	....	1979-80	1979-80
Pocza, Harvie	Wsh.	2	3	0	0	0	2	....	....	....	....	....	....	1979-80	1981-82
Poddubny, Walt	Edm., Tor., NYR, Que., N.J.	11	468	184	238	422	454	19	7	2	9	12	....	1981-82	1991-92
‡ Podloski, Ray	Bos.	1	8	0	1	1	17	....	....	....	....	....	....	1988-89	1988-89
Podolsky, Nels	Det.	1	1	0	0	0	0	7	0	0	0	4	....	1948-49	1948-49
Poeta, Tony	Chi.	1	1	0	0	0	0	....	....	....	....	....	....	1951-52	1951-52
Poile, Bud	Tor., Chi., Det., NYR, Bos.	7	311	107	122	229	91	23	4	5	9	8	1	1942-43	1949-50
Poile, Don	Det.	2	66	7	9	16	12	4	0	0	0	0	....	1954-55	1957-58
Poirier, Gordie	Mtl.	1	10	0	0	0	0	....	....	....	....	....	....	1939-40	1939-40
Polanic, Tom	Min.	2	19	0	2	2	53	5	1	1	2	4	....	1969-70	1970-71
• Polich, John	NYR	2	3	0	1	1	0	....	....	....	....	....	....	1939-40	1940-41
Polich, Mike	Mtl., Min.	5	226	24	29	53	57	23	2	1	3	2	1	1976-77	1980-81
Polis, Greg	Pit., St.L., NYR, Wsh.	10	615	174	169	343	391	7	0	2	2	6	....	1970-71	1979-80
Poliziani, Dan	Bos.	1	1	0	0	0	0	3	0	0	0	0	....	1958-59	1958-59
Polonich, Dennis	Det.	8	390	59	82	141	1242	7	1	0	1	19	....	1974-75	1982-83
Pooley, Paul	Wpg.	2	15	0	3	3	0	....	....	....	....	....	....	1984-85	1985-86
Popein, Larry	NYR, Oak.	8	449	80	141	221	162	16	1	4	5	6	....	1954-55	1967-68
Popiel, Poul	Bos., L.A., Det., Van., Edm.	7	224	13	41	54	210	4	1	0	1	4	....	1965-66	1979-80
• Portland, Jack	Mtl.C., Bos., Chi., Mtl.	10	381	15	56	71	323	33	1	3	4	25	1	1933-34	1942-43
Porvari, Jukka	Col., N.J.	2	39	3	9	12	4	....	....	....	....	....	....	1981-82	1982-83
Posa, Victor	Chi.	1	2	0	0	0	2	....	....	....	....	....	....	1985-86	1985-86
Posavad, Mike	St.L.	2	8	0	0	0	0	....	....	....	....	....	....	1985-86	1986-87
‡ Potomski, Barry	L.A., S.J.	3	68	6	5	11	227	....	....	....	....	....	....	1995-96	1997-98
Potvin, Denis	NYI	15	1060	310	742	1052	1356	185	56	108	164	253	4	1973-74	1987-88
Potvin, Jean	L.A., Phi., NYI, Cle., Min.	11	613	63	224	287	478	39	2	9	11	17	1	1970-71	1980-81
Potvin, Marc	Det., L.A., Hfd., Bos.	6	121	3	5	8	456	13	0	1	1	50	....	1990-91	1995-96
‡ Poudrier, Daniel	Que.	3	25	1	5	6	10	....	....	....	....	....	....	1985-86	1987-88
Poulin, Daniel	Min.	1	3	1	1	2	2	....	....	....	....	....	....	1981-82	1981-82
Poulin, Dave	Phi., Bos., Wsh.	13	724	205	325	530	482	129	31	42	73	132	....	1982-83	1994-95
Pouzar, Jaroslav	Edm.	4	186	34	48	82	135	29	6	4	10	16	3	1982-83	1986-87
Powell, Ray	Chi.	1	31	7	15	22	2	....	....	....	....	....	....	1950-51	1950-51
Powis, Geoff	Chi.	1	2	0	0	0	0	....	....	....	....	....	....	1967-68	1967-68
Powis, Lynn	Chi., K.C.	2	130	19	33	52	25	1	0	0	0	0	....	1973-74	1974-75
Prajsler, Petr	L.A., Bos.	4	46	3	10	13	51	4	0	0	0	0	....	1987-88	1991-92
• Pratt, Babe	NYR, Tor., Bos.	12	517	83	209	292	463	63	12	17	29	90	2	1935-36	1946-47
Pratt, Jack	Bos.	2	37	2	0	2	42	4	0	0	0	0	....	1930-31	1931-32
Pratt, Kelly	Pit.	1	22	0	6	6	15	....	....	....	....	....	....	1974-75	1974-75
Pratt, Tracy	Oak., Pit., Buf., Van., Col., Tor.	10	580	17	97	114	1026	25	0	1	1	62	....	1967-68	1976-77
Prentice, Dean	NYR, Bos., Det., Pit., Min.	22	1378	391	469	860	484	54	13	17	30	38	....	1952-53	1973-74
Prentice, Eric	Tor.	1	5	0	0	0	4	....	....	....	....	....	....	1943-44	1943-44
Presley, Wayne	Chi., S.J., Buf., NYR, Tor.	12	684	155	147	302	953	83	26	17	43	142	....	1984-85	1995-96
Preston, Rich	Chi., N.J.	8	580	127	164	291	348	47	4	18	22	56	....	1979-80	1986-87
Preston, Yves	Phi.	2	28	7	3	10	4	....	....	....	....	....	....	1978-79	1980-81
Priakin, Sergei	Cgy.	3	46	3	8	11	2	1	0	0	0	0	....	1988-89	1990-91
Price, Jack	Chi.	3	57	4	6	10	24	4	0	0	0	0	....	1951-52	1953-54
Price, Noel	Tor., NYR, Det., Mtl., Pit., L.A., Atl.	14	499	14	114	128	333	12	0	1	1	8	1	1957-58	1975-76
Price, Pat	NYI, Edm., Pit., Que., NYR, Min.	13	726	43	218	261	1456	74	2	10	12	195	....	1975-76	1987-88
Price, Tom	Cal., Cle., Pit.	5	29	0	2	2	12	....	....	....	....	....	....	1974-75	1978-79

J.P. Parise

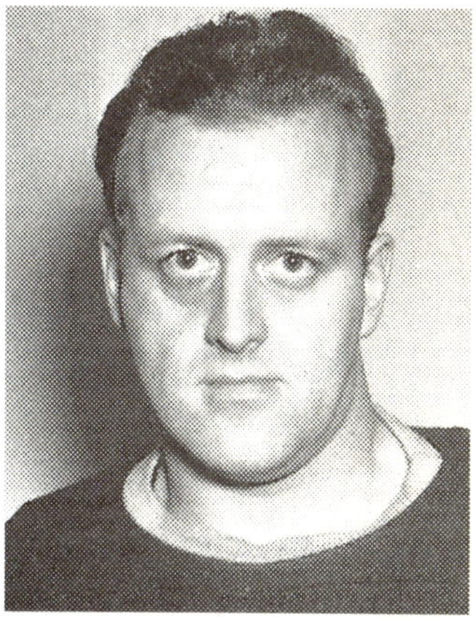
Lynn Patrick

Michal Pivonka

Sergei Priakin

Brian Propp

John Quilty

Jean Ratelle

Henri Richard

			Regular Schedule					Playoffs							
Name	NHL Teams	NHL Seasons	GP	G	A	TP	PIM	GP	G	A	TP	PIM	NHL Cup Wins	First NHL Season	Last NHL Season
‡ Priestlay, Ken	Buf., Pit.	6	168	27	34	61	63	14	0	0	0	21	1	1986-87	1991-92
• Primeau, Joe	Tor.	9	310	66	177	243	105	38	5	18	23	12	1	1927-28	1935-36
Primeau, Kevin	Van.	1	2	0	0	0	4	....	....	....	....	....	....	1980-81	1980-81
• Pringle, Ellie	NYA	1	6	0	0	0	0	....	....	....	....	....	....	1930-31	1930-31
• Prodgers, Goldie	Tor., Ham.	6	111	63	29	92	39	....	....	....	....	....	....	1919-20	1924-25
‡ Prokhorov, Vitali	St.L.	3	83	19	11	30	35	4	0	0	0	0	....	1992-93	1994-95
Prokopec, Mike	Chi.	2	15	0	0	0	11	....	....	....	....	....	....	1995-96	1996-97
Pronovost, Andre	Mtl., Bos., Det., Min.	10	556	94	104	198	408	70	11	11	22	58	4	1956-57	1967-68
Pronovost, Jean	Pit., Atl., Wsh.	14	998	391	383	774	413	35	11	9	20	14	....	1968-69	1981-82
Pronovost, Marcel	Det., Tor.	21	1206	88	257	345	851	134	8	23	31	104	5	1949-50	1969-70
Propp, Brian	Phi., Bos., Min., Hfd.	15	1016	425	579	1004	830	160	64	84	148	151	....	1979-80	1993-94
‡ Proulx, Christian	Mtl.	1	7	1	2	3	20	....	....	....	....	....	....	1993-94	1993-94
• Provost, Claude	Mtl.	15	1005	254	335	589	469	126	25	38	63	86	9	1955-56	1969-70
Pryor, Chris	Min., NYI	6	82	1	4	5	122	....	....	....	....	....	....	1984-85	1989-90
Prystai, Metro	Chi., Det.	11	674	151	179	330	231	43	12	14	26	8	2	1947-48	1957-58
• Pudas, Al	Tor.	1	4	0	0	0	0	....	....	....	....	....	....	1926-27	1926-27
Pulford, Bob	Tor., L.A.	16	1079	281	362	643	792	89	25	26	51	126	4	1956-57	1971-72
Pulkkinen, Dave	NYI	1	2	0	0	0	0	....	....	....	....	....	....	1972-73	1972-73
• Purpur, Fido	St.L., Chi., Det.	5	144	25	35	60	46	16	1	2	3	4	....	1934-35	1944-45
‡ Purves, John	Wsh.	1	7	1	0	1	0	....	....	....	....	....	....	1990-91	1990-91
• Pusie, Jean	Mtl.C., NYR, Bos.	5	61	1	4	5	28	7	0	0	0	0	1	1930-31	1935-36
Pyatt, Nelson	Det., Wsh., Col.	7	296	71	63	134	69	....	....	....	....	....	....	1973-74	1979-80
Q															
• Quackenbush, Bill	Det., Bos.	14	774	62	222	284	95	80	2	19	21	8	....	1942-43	1955-56
Quackenbush, Max	Bos., Chi.	2	61	4	7	11	30	6	0	0	0	4	....	1950-51	1951-52
Quenneville, Joel	Tor., Col., N.J., Hfd., Wsh.	13	803	54	136	190	705	32	0	8	8	22	....	1978-79	1990-91
• Quenneville, Leo	NYR	1	25	0	3	3	10	3	0	0	0	0	....	1929-30	1929-30
• Quilty, John	Mtl., Bos.	4	125	36	34	70	81	13	3	5	8	9	....	1940-41	1947-48
Quinn, Dan	Cgy., Pit., Van., St.L., Phi., Min., Ott., L.A.	14	805	266	419	685	533	65	22	26	48	62	....	1983-84	1996-97
Quinn, Pat	Tor., Van., Atl.	9	606	18	113	131	950	11	0	1	1	21	....	1968-69	1976-77
‡ Quinney, Ken	Que.	3	59	7	13	20	23	....	....	....	....	....	....	1986-87	1990-91
‡ Quintin, Jean-Francois	S.J.	2	22	5	5	10	4	....	....	....	....	....	....	1991-92	1992-93
R															
‡ Racine, Yves	Det., Phi., Mtl., S.J., Cgy., T.B.	9	508	37	194	231	439	25	5	4	9	37	....	1989-90	1997-98
• Radley, Yip	NYA, Mtl.M.	2	18	0	1	1	13	....	....	....	....	....	....	1930-31	1936-37
Raglan, Herb	St.L., Que., T.B., Ott.	9	343	33	56	89	775	32	3	6	9	50	....	1985-86	1993-94
Raglan, Rags	Det., Chi.	3	100	4	9	13	52	3	0	0	0	0	....	1950-51	1952-53
Raleigh, Don	NYR	10	535	101	219	320	96	18	6	5	11	6	....	1943-44	1955-56
Ramage, Rob	Col., St.L., Cgy., Tor., Min., T.B., Mtl., Phi.	15	1044	139	425	564	2226	84	8	42	50	218	2	1979-80	1993-94
• Ramsay, Beattie	Tor.	1	43	0	2	2	10	....	....	....	....	....	....	1927-28	1927-28
Ramsay, Craig	Buf.	14	1070	252	420	672	201	89	17	31	48	27	....	1971-72	1984-85
Ramsay, Les	Chi.	1	11	2	2	4	2	....	....	....	....	....	....	1944-45	1944-45
Ramsey, Mike	Buf., Pit., Det.	18	1070	79	266	345	1012	115	8	29	37	176	....	1979-80	1996-97
Ramsey, Wayne	Buf.	1	2	0	0	0	0	....	....	....	....	....	....	1977-78	1977-78
• Randall, Ken	Tor., Ham., NYA	10	218	68	50	118	533	6	2	1	3	27	2	1917-18	1926-27
Ranieri, George	Bos.	1	2	0	0	0	0	....	....	....	....	....	....	1956-57	1956-57
Ratelle, Jean	NYR, Bos.	21	1281	491	776	1267	276	123	32	66	98	24	....	1960-61	1980-81
Rathwell, Jake	Bos.	1	1	0	0	0	0	....	....	....	....	....	....	1974-75	1974-75
‡ Ratushny, Dan	Van.	1	1	0	1	1	2	....	....	....	....	....	....	1992-93	1992-93
Rausse, Errol	Wsh.	3	31	7	3	10	0	....	....	....	....	....	....	1979-80	1981-82
Rautakallio, Pekka	Atl., Cgy.	3	235	33	121	154	122	23	2	5	7	8	....	1979-80	1981-82
Ravlich, Matt	Bos., Chi., Det., L.A.	10	410	12	78	90	364	24	1	5	6	16	....	1962-63	1972-73
• Raymond, Armand	Mtl.C., Mtl.	2	22	0	2	2	10	....	....	....	....	....	....	1937-38	1939-40
• Raymond, Paul	Mtl.C.	4	76	2	3	5	6	5	0	0	0	2	....	1932-33	1938-39
Read, Mel	NYR	1	1	0	0	0	0	....	....	....	....	....	....	1946-47	1946-47
Reardon, Ken	Mtl.	7	341	26	96	122	604	31	2	5	7	62	1	1940-41	1949-50
• Reardon, Terry	Bos., Mtl.	7	193	47	53	100	73	30	8	10	18	12	1	1938-39	1946-47
Reaume, Marc	Tor., Det., Mtl., Van.	9	344	8	43	51	273	21	0	2	2	8	....	1954-55	1970-71
Reay, Billy	Det., Mtl.	10	479	105	162	267	202	63	13	16	29	43	2	1943-44	1952-53
Redahl, Gord	Bos.	1	18	0	1	1	2	....	....	....	....	....	....	1958-59	1958-59
• Redding, George	Bos.	2	55	3	2	5	23	....	....	....	....	....	....	1924-25	1925-26
Redmond, Craig	L.A., Edm.	5	191	16	68	84	134	3	1	0	1	2	....	1984-85	1988-89
Redmond, Dick	Min., Cal., Chi., St.L., Atl., Bos.	13	771	133	312	445	504	66	9	22	31	27	....	1969-70	1981-82
Redmond, Keith	L.A.	1	12	1	0	1	20	....	....	....	....	....	....	1993-94	1993-94
Redmond, Mickey	Mtl., Det.	9	538	233	195	428	219	16	2	3	5	2	2	1967-68	1975-76
Reeds, Mark	St.L., Hfd.	8	365	45	114	159	135	53	8	9	17	23	....	1981-82	1988-89
• Regan, Bill	NYR, NYA	3	67	3	2	5	67	8	0	0	0	2	....	1929-30	1932-33
Regan, Larry	Bos., Tor.	5	280	41	95	136	71	42	7	14	21	18	....	1956-57	1960-61
Regier, Darcy	Cle., NYI	3	26	0	2	2	35	....	....	....	....	....	....	1977-78	1983-84
Reibel, Earl	Det., Chi., Bos.	6	409	84	161	245	75	39	6	14	20	4	2	1953-54	1958-59
• Reid, Dave	Tor.	3	7	0	0	0	0	....	....	....	....	....	....	1952-53	1955-56
Reid, Gerry	Det.	1	....	....	....	....	....	2	0	0	0	2	....	1948-49	1948-49
Reid, Gord	NYA	1	1	0	0	0	2	....	....	....	....	....	....	1936-37	1936-37
• Reid, Reg	Tor.	2	39	1	0	1	4	2	0	0	0	0	....	1924-25	1925-26
Reid, Tom	Chi., Min.	11	701	17	113	130	654	42	1	13	14	49	....	1967-68	1977-78
Reierson, Dave	Cgy.	1	2	0	0	0	2	....	....	....	....	....	....	1988-89	1988-89
Reigle, Ed	Bos.	1	17	0	2	2	25	....	....	....	....	....	....	1950-51	1950-51
Reinhart, Paul	Atl., Cgy., Van.	11	648	133	426	559	277	83	23	54	77	42	....	1979-80	1989-90
• Reinikka, Ollie	NYR	1	16	0	0	0	0	....	....	....	....	....	....	1926-27	1926-27
Reise Jr., Leo	Chi., Det., NYR	9	494	28	81	109	399	52	8	5	13	68	2	1945-46	1953-54
• Reise Sr., Leo	Ham., NYA, NYR	8	241	43	43	86	187	6	0	0	0	16	....	1920-21	1929-30
Renaud, Mark	Hfd., Buf.	5	152	6	50	56	86	....	....	....	....	....	....	1979-80	1983-84
‡ Reynolds, Bobby	Tor.	1	7	1	1	2	0	....	....	....	....	....	....	1989-90	1989-90
Ribble, Pat	Atl., Chi., Tor., Wsh., Cgy.	8	349	19	60	79	365	8	0	1	1	12	....	1975-76	1982-83
Rice, Steven	NYR, Edm., Hfd., Car.	8	329	64	61	125	275	2	2	1	3	6	....	1990-91	1997-98
Richard, Henri	Mtl.	20	1256	358	688	1046	928	180	49	80	129	181	11	1955-56	1974-75
Richard, Jacques	Atl., Buf., Que.	10	556	160	187	347	307	35	5	5	10	34	....	1972-73	1982-83
‡ Richard, Jean-Marc	Que.	2	5	2	1	3	2	....	....	....	....	....	....	1987-88	1989-90
• Richard, Maurice	Mtl.	18	978	544	421	965	1285	133	82	44	126	188	8	1942-43	1959-60
‡ Richard, Mike	Wsh.	2	7	0	2	2	0	....	....	....	....	....	....	1987-88	1989-90
‡ Richards, Todd	Hfd.	2	8	0	4	4	4	11	0	3	3	6	....	1990-91	1991-92
Richardson, Dave	NYR, Chi., Det.	4	45	3	2	5	27	....	....	....	....	....	....	1963-64	1967-68
Richardson, Glen	Van.	1	24	3	6	9	19	....	....	....	....	....	....	1975-76	1975-76
Richardson, Ken	St.L.	3	49	8	13	21	16	....	....	....	....	....	....	1974-75	1978-79
Richer, Bob	Buf.	1	3	0	0	0	0	....	....	....	....	....	....	1972-73	1972-73
‡ Richer, Stephane	T.B., Bos., Fla.	3	27	1	5	6	20	3	0	0	0	0	....	1992-93	1994-95
Richmond, Steve	NYR, Det., N.J., L.A.	5	159	4	23	27	514	4	0	0	0	12	....	1983-84	1988-89
Richter, Dave	Min., Phi., Van., St.L.	9	365	9	40	49	1030	22	1	0	1	80	....	1981-82	1989-90
Ridley, Mike	NYR, Wsh., Tor., Van.	12	866	292	466	758	424	104	28	50	78	70	....	1985-86	1996-97
Riley, Bill	Wsh., Wpg.	5	139	31	30	61	320	....	....	....	....	....	....	1974-75	1979-80
Riley, Jack	Det., Mtl.C., Bos.	4	104	10	22	32	8	4	0	3	3	0	....	1932-33	1935-36
• Riley, Jim	Chi., Det.	1	9	0	2	2	14	....	....	....	....	....	....	1926-27	1926-27
Riopelle, Rip	Mtl.	3	169	27	16	43	73	8	1	1	2	2	....	1947-48	1949-50
Rioux, Gerry	Wpg.	1	8	0	0	0	6	....	....	....	....	....	....	1979-80	1979-80
‡ Rioux, Pierre	Cgy.	1	14	1	2	3	4	....	....	....	....	....	....	1982-83	1982-83
• Ripley, Vic	Chi., Bos., NYR, St.L.	7	278	51	49	100	173	20	4	1	5	10	....	1928-29	1934-35
Risebrough, Doug	Mtl., Cgy.	13	740	185	286	471	1542	124	21	37	58	238	4	1974-75	1986-87
Rissling, Gary	Wsh., Pit.	7	221	23	30	53	1008	5	0	1	1	4	....	1978-79	1984-85
Ritchie, Bob	Phi., Det.	2	29	8	4	12	10	....	....	....	....	....	....	1976-77	1977-78
• Ritchie, Dave	Mtl., Ott., Tor., Que., Mtl.C.	6	58	15	6	21	50	1	0	0	0	0	....	1917-18	1925-26
Ritson, Alex	NYR	1	1	0	0	0	0	....	....	....	....	....	....	1944-45	1944-45
Rittinger, Alan	Bos.	1	19	3	7	10	0	....	....	....	....	....	....	1943-44	1943-44
Rivard, Bob	Pit.	1	27	5	12	17	4	....	....	....	....	....	....	1967-68	1967-68
• Rivers, Gus	Mtl.C.	3	88	4	5	9	12	16	2	0	2	2	2	1929-30	1931-32
Rivers, Shawn	T.B.	1	4	0	2	2	2	....	....	....	....	....	....	1992-93	1992-93
Rivers, Wayne	Det., Bos., St.L., NYR	7	108	15	30	45	94	....	....	....	....	....	....	1961-62	1968-69
Rizzuto, Garth	Van.	1	37	3	4	7	16	....	....	....	....	....	....	1970-71	1970-71
• Roach, Mickey	Tor., Ham., NYA	8	211	77	34	111	54	....	....	....	....	....	....	1919-20	1926-27
‡ Roberge, Mario	Mtl.	5	112	7	7	14	314	15	0	0	0	24	1	1990-91	1994-95
‡ Roberge, Serge	Que.	1	9	0	0	0	24	....	....	....	....	....	....	1990-91	1990-91

			Regular Schedule					Playoffs					NHL	First	Last
Name	NHL Teams	NHL Seasons	GP	G	A	TP	PIM	GP	G	A	TP	PIM	Cup Wins	NHL Season	NHL Season
Robert, Claude	Mtl.	1	23	1	0	1	9	....	....	....	....	....	....	1950-51	1950-51
Robert, Rene	Tor., Pit., Buf., Col.	12	744	284	418	702	597	50	22	19	41	73	....	1970-71	1981-82
Roberto, Phil	Mtl., St.L., Det., K.C., Col., Cle.	8	385	75	106	181	464	31	9	8	17	69	1	1969-70	1976-77
‡ Roberts, David	St.L., Edm., Van.	5	125	20	33	53	85	9	0	0	0	16	....	1993-94	1997-98
Roberts, Doug	Det., Oak., Cal., Bos.	10	419	43	104	147	342	16	2	3	5	46	....	1965-66	1974-75
Roberts, Gordie	Hfd., Min., Phi., St.L., Pit., Bos.	15	1097	61	359	420	1582	153	10	47	57	273	2	1979-80	1993-94
Roberts, Jim	Min.	3	106	17	23	40	33	2	0	0	0	0	....	1976-77	1978-79
Roberts, Jimmy	Mtl., St.L.	15	1006	126	194	320	621	153	20	16	36	160	5	1963-64	1977-78
● Robertson, Fred	Tor., Det.	2	34	1	0	1	35	7	0	0	0	0	1	1931-32	1933-34
Robertson, Geordie	Buf.	1	5	1	2	3	7	....	....	....	....	....	....	1982-83	1982-83
Robertson, George	Mtl.	2	31	2	5	7	6	....	....	....	....	....	....	1947-48	1948-49
Robertson, Torrie	Wsh., Hfd., Det.	10	442	49	99	148	1751	22	2	1	3	90	....	1980-81	1989-90
Robidoux, Florent	Chi.	3	52	7	4	11	75	....	....	....	....	....	....	1980-81	1983-84
Robinson, Doug	Chi., NYR, L.A.	7	239	44	67	111	34	11	4	3	7	0	....	1963-64	1970-71
● Robinson, Earl	Mtl.M., Chi., Mtl.	11	417	83	98	181	133	25	5	4	9	0	1	1928-29	1939-40
Robinson, Larry	Mtl., L.A.	20	1384	208	750	958	793	227	28	116	144	211	6	1972-73	1991-92
Robinson, Moe	Mtl.	1	1	0	0	0	0	....	....	....	....	....	....	1979-80	1979-80
Robinson, Rob	St.L.	1	22	0	1	1	8	....	....	....	....	....	....	1991-92	1991-92
Robinson, Scott	Min.	1	1	0	0	0	2	....	....	....	....	....	....	1989-90	1989-90
Robitaille, Mike	NYR, Det., Buf., Van.	8	382	23	105	128	280	13	0	1	1	4	....	1969-70	1976-77
● Roche, Des	Mtl.M., Ott., St.L., Mtl.C., Det.	4	113	20	18	38	44	....	....	....	....	....	....	1930-31	1934-35
● Roche, Earl	Mtl.M., Bos., Ott., St.L., Det.	4	147	25	27	52	48	2	0	0	0	0	....	1930-31	1934-35
Roche, Ernie	Mtl.	1	4	0	0	0	2	....	....	....	....	....	....	1950-51	1950-51
Rochefort, Dave	Det.	1	1	0	0	0	0	....	....	....	....	....	....	1966-67	1966-67
Rochefort, Leon	NYR, Mtl., Phi., L.A., Det., Atl., Van.	15	617	121	147	268	93	39	4	4	8	16	2	1960-61	1975-76
Rochefort, Normand	Que., NYR, T.B.	13	598	39	119	158	570	69	7	5	12	82	....	1980-81	1993-94
● Rockburn, Harvey	Det., Ott.	3	94	4	2	6	254	....	....	....	....	....	....	1929-30	1932-33
● Rodden, Eddie	Chi., Tor., Bos., NYR	4	97	6	14	20	60	2	0	1	1	0	....	1926-27	1930-31
Rogers, John	Min.	2	14	2	4	6	0	....	....	....	....	....	....	1973-74	1974-75
Rogers, Mike	Hfd., NYR, Edm.	7	484	202	317	519	184	17	1	13	14	6	....	1979-80	1985-86
Rohlicek, Jeff	Van.	2	9	0	0	0	8	....	....	....	....	....	....	1987-88	1988-89
‡ Rohlin, Leif	Van.	2	96	8	24	32	40	5	0	0	0	0	....	1995-96	1996-97
Rolfe, Dale	Bos., L.A., Det., NYR	9	509	25	125	150	556	71	5	24	29	89	....	1959-60	1974-75
Romanchych, Larry	Chi., Atl.	6	298	68	97	165	102	7	2	2	4	4	....	1970-71	1976-77
‡ Romaniuk, Russell	Wpg., Phi.	5	102	13	14	27	63	2	0	0	0	0	....	1991-92	1995-96
Rombough, Doug	Buf., NYI, Min.	4	150	24	27	51	80	....	....	....	....	....	....	1972-73	1975-76
● Romnes, Doc	Chi., Tor., NYA	10	360	68	136	204	42	45	7	18	25	4	2	1930-31	1939-40
Ronan, Ed	Mtl., Wpg., Buf.	6	182	13	23	36	101	27	4	3	7	16	1	1991-92	1996-97
● Ronan, Skene	Ott.	1	11	0	0	0	6	....	....	....	....	....	....	1918-19	1918-19
Ronson, Len	NYR, Oak.	2	18	2	1	3	10	....	....	....	....	....	....	1960-61	1968-69
Ronty, Paul	Bos., NYR, Mtl.	8	488	101	211	312	103	21	1	7	8	6	....	1947-48	1954-55
Rooney, Steve	Mtl., Wpg., N.J.	5	154	15	13	28	496	25	3	2	5	86	1	1984-85	1988-89
Root, Bill	Mtl., Tor., St.L., Phi.	6	247	11	23	34	180	22	1	2	3	25	....	1982-83	1987-88
● Ross, Art	Mtl.	1	3	1	0	1	12	....	....	....	....	....	....	1917-18	1917-18
Ross, Jim	NYR	2	62	2	11	13	29	....	....	....	....	....	....	1951-52	1952-53
Rossignol, Roly	Det., Mtl.	3	14	3	5	8	6	1	0	0	0	2	....	1943-44	1945-46
Rota, Darcy	Chi., Atl., Van.	11	794	256	239	495	973	60	14	7	21	147	....	1973-74	1983-84
Rota, Randy	Mtl., L.A., K.C., Col.	5	212	38	39	77	60	5	0	1	1	0	....	1972-73	1976-77
● Rothschild, Sam	Mtl.M., Pit., NYA	4	100	8	6	14	25	6	0	0	0	0	1	1924-25	1927-28
● Roulston, Rolly	Det.	3	24	0	6	6	10	....	....	....	....	....	1	1935-36	1937-38
Roulston, Tom	Edm., Pit.	5	195	47	49	96	74	21	2	2	4	2	....	1980-81	1985-86
Roupe, Magnus	Phi.	2	40	3	5	8	42	....	....	....	....	....	....	1987-88	1988-89
‡ Rouse, Bob	Min., Wsh., Tor., Det., S.J.	17	1061	37	181	218	1559	136	7	21	28	198	2	1983-84	1999-00
Rousseau, Bobby	Mtl., Min., NYR	15	942	245	458	703	359	128	27	57	84	69	4	1960-61	1974-75
Rousseau, Guy	Mtl.	2	4	0	1	1	0	....	....	....	....	....	....	1954-55	1956-57
Rousseau, Roland	Mtl.	1	2	0	0	0	0	....	....	....	....	....	....	1952-53	1952-53
‡ Routhier, Jean-Marc	Que.	1	8	0	0	0	9	....	....	....	....	....	....	1989-90	1989-90
● Rowe, Bobby	Bos.	1	4	1	0	1	0	....	....	....	....	....	....	1924-25	1924-25
Rowe, Mike	Pit.	3	11	0	0	0	11	....	....	....	....	....	....	1984-85	1986-87
Rowe, Ron	NYR	1	5	1	0	1	0	....	....	....	....	....	....	1947-48	1947-48
Rowe, Tom	Wsh., Hfd., Det.	7	357	85	100	185	615	3	2	0	2	0	....	1976-77	1982-83
‡ Roy, Jean-Yves	NYR, Ott., Bos.	4	61	12	16	28	26	....	....	....	....	....	....	1994-95	1997-98
‡ Roy, Stephane	Min.	1	12	1	0	1	0	....	....	....	....	....	....	1987-88	1987-88
Rozzini, Gino	Bos.	1	31	5	10	15	20	6	1	2	3	6	....	1944-45	1944-45
Rucinski, Mike	Chi.	2	1	0	0	0	0	2	0	0	0	0	....	1987-88	1988-89
Ruelle, Bernie	Det.	1	2	1	0	1	0	....	....	....	....	....	....	1943-44	1943-44
‡ Ruff, Jason	St.L., T.B.	2	14	3	3	6	10	....	....	....	....	....	....	1992-93	1993-94
Ruff, Lindy	Buf., NYR	12	691	105	195	300	1264	52	11	13	24	193	....	1979-80	1990-91
Ruhnke, Kent	Bos.	1	2	0	1	1	0	....	....	....	....	....	....	1975-76	1975-76
Rundqvist, Thomas	Mtl.	1	2	0	1	1	0	....	....	....	....	....	....	1984-85	1984-85
● Runge, Paul	Bos., Mtl.M., Mtl.C.	7	140	18	22	40	57	7	0	0	0	6	....	1930-31	1937-38
Ruotsalainen, Reijo	NYR, Edm., N.J.	7	446	107	237	344	180	86	15	32	47	44	2	1981-82	1989-90
Rupp, Duane	NYR, Tor., Min., Pit.	10	374	24	93	117	220	10	2	2	4	8	....	1962-63	1972-73
Ruskowski, Terry	Chi., L.A., Pit., Min.	10	630	113	313	426	1354	21	1	6	7	86	....	1979-80	1988-89
Russell, Cam	Chi., Col.	10	396	9	21	30	872	44	0	5	5	16	....	1989-90	1998-99
● Russell, Church	NYR	3	90	20	16	36	12	....	....	....	....	....	....	1945-46	1947-48
Russell, Phil	Chi., Atl., Cgy., N.J., Buf.	15	1016	99	325	424	2038	73	4	22	26	202	....	1972-73	1986-87
Ruuttu, Christian	Buf., Chi., Van.	9	621	134	298	432	714	42	4	9	13	49	....	1986-87	1994-95
‡ Ruzicka, Vladimir	Edm., Bos., Ott.	5	233	82	85	167	129	30	4	14	18	2	....	1989-90	1993-94
Rychel, Warren	Chi., L.A., Tor., Col., Ana.	9	406	38	39	77	1422	70	8	13	21	121	1	1988-89	1998-99
‡ Rymsha, Andy	Que.	1	6	0	0	0	23	....	....	....	....	....	....	1991-92	1991-92

S

Saarinen, Simo	NYR	1	8	0	0	0	0	....	....	....	....	....	....	1984-85	1984-85
Sabol, Shaun	Phi.	1	2	0	0	0	0	....	....	....	....	....	....	1989-90	1989-90
Sabourin, Bob	Tor.	1	1	0	0	0	2	....	....	....	....	....	....	1951-52	1951-52
Sabourin, Gary	St.L., Tor., Cal., Cle.	10	627	169	188	357	397	62	19	11	30	58	....	1967-68	1976-77
Sabourin, Ken	Cgy., Wsh.	4	74	2	8	10	201	12	0	0	0	34	....	1988-89	1991-92
Sacco, David	Tor., Ana.	3	35	5	13	18	22	....	....	....	....	....	....	1993-94	1995-96
Sacharuk, Larry	NYR, St.L.	5	151	29	33	62	42	2	1	1	2	2	....	1972-73	1976-77
Saganiuk, Rocky	Tor., Pit.	6	259	57	65	122	201	6	1	0	1	15	....	1978-79	1983-84
Saleski, Don	Phi., Col.	9	543	128	125	253	629	82	13	17	30	131	2	1971-72	1979-80
Salming, Borje	Tor., Det.	17	1148	150	637	787	1344	81	12	37	49	91	....	1973-74	1989-90
Salovaara, Barry	Det.	2	90	2	13	15	70	....	....	....	....	....	....	1974-75	1975-76
Salvian, Dave	NYI	1	....	....	....	....	....	1	0	1	1	2	....	1976-77	1976-77
Samis, Phil	Tor.	2	2	0	0	0	0	5	0	1	1	2	1	1947-48	1949-50
Sampson, Gary	Wsh.	4	105	13	22	35	25	12	1	0	1	0	....	1983-84	1986-87
Samuelsson, Kjell	NYR, Phi., Pit., T.B.	14	813	48	138	186	1225	123	4	20	24	178	1	1985-86	1998-99
‡ Samuelsson, Ulf	Hfd., Pit., NYR, Det., Phi.	16	1080	57	275	332	2453	132	7	27	34	272	2	1984-85	1999-00
Sandelin, Scott	Mtl., Phi., Min.	4	25	0	4	4	7	....	....	....	....	....	....	1986-87	1991-92
Sanderson, Derek	Bos., NYR, St.L., Van., Pit.	13	598	202	250	452	911	56	18	12	30	187	2	1965-66	1977-78
Sandford, Ed	Bos., Det., Chi.	9	502	106	145	251	355	42	13	11	24	27	....	1947-48	1955-56
Sandlak, Jim	Van., Hfd.	11	549	110	119	229	821	33	7	10	17	30	....	1985-86	1995-96
● Sands, Charlie	Tor., Bos., Mtl., NYR	12	427	99	109	208	58	34	6	6	12	4	1	1932-33	1943-44
Sanipass, Everett	Chi., Que.	5	164	25	34	59	358	5	2	0	2	4	....	1986-87	1990-91
Sargent, Gary	L.A., Min.	8	402	61	161	222	273	20	5	7	12	8	....	1975-76	1982-83
Sarner, Craig	Bos.	1	7	0	0	0	0	....	....	....	....	....	....	1974-75	1974-75
Sarrazin, Dick	Phi.	3	100	20	35	55	22	4	0	0	0	0	....	1968-69	1971-72
Saskamoose, Fred	Chi.	1	11	0	0	0	6	....	....	....	....	....	....	1953-54	1953-54
Sasser, Grant	Pit.	1	3	0	0	0	0	....	....	....	....	....	....	1983-84	1983-84
Sather, Glen	Bos., Pit., NYR, St.L., Mtl., Min.	10	658	80	113	193	724	72	1	5	6	86	....	1966-67	1975-76
Saunders, Bernie	Que.	2	10	0	1	1	8	....	....	....	....	....	....	1979-80	1980-81
Saunders, David	Van.	1	56	7	13	20	10	....	....	....	....	....	....	1987-88	1987-88
Saunders, Ted	Ott.	1	18	1	3	4	4	....	....	....	....	....	....	1933-34	1933-34
Sauve, Jean-Francois	Buf., Que.	7	290	65	138	203	114	36	9	12	21	10	....	1980-81	1986-87
‡ Savage, Joel	Buf.	1	3	0	1	1	0	....	....	....	....	....	....	1990-91	1990-91
● Savage, Tony	Bos., Mtl.C.	1	49	1	5	6	6	2	0	0	0	0	....	1934-35	1934-35
Savard, Andre	Bos., Buf., Que.	12	790	211	271	482	411	85	13	18	31	77	....	1973-74	1984-85
Savard, Denis	Chi., Mtl., T.B.	17	1196	473	865	1338	1336	169	66	109	175	256	1	1980-81	1996-97
Savard, Jean	Chi., Hfd.	3	43	7	12	19	29	....	....	....	....	....	....	1977-78	1979-80
Savard, Serge	Mtl., Wpg.	17	1040	106	333	439	592	130	19	49	68	88	8	1966-67	1982-83
‡ Savoia, Ryan	Pit.	1	3	0	0	0	0	....	....	....	....	....	....	1998-99	1998-99
Scamurra, Peter	Wsh.	4	132	8	25	33	59	....	....	....	....	....	....	1975-76	1979-80
Sceviour, Darin	Chi.	1	1	0	0	0	0	....	....	....	....	....	....	1986-87	1986-87
Schaeffer, Butch	Chi.	1	5	0	0	0	6	....	....	....	....	....	....	1936-37	1936-37

Stephane Richer

Bob Rouse

Cam Russell

Ulf Samuelsson

Anatoli Semenov

Bruce Shoebottom

Brian Skrudland

Harold Snepsts

Name	NHL Teams	NHL Seasons	Regular Schedule					Playoffs					NHL Cup Wins	First NHL Season	Last NHL Season
			GP	G	A	TP	PIM	GP	G	A	TP	PIM			
Schamehorn, Kevin	Det., L.A.	3	10	0	0	0	17	....	....	....	....	....	....	1976-77	1980-81
Schella, John	Van.	2	115	2	18	20	224	....	....	....	....	....	....	1970-71	1971-72
Scherza, Chuck	Bos., NYR	2	36	6	6	12	35	....	....	....	....	....	....	1943-44	1944-45
Schinkel, Ken	NYR, Pit.	12	636	127	198	325	163	19	7	2	9	4	....	1959-60	1972-73
‡ Schlegel, Brad	Wsh., Cgy.	3	48	1	8	9	10	7	0	1	1	2	....	1991-92	1993-94
Schliebener, Andy	Van.	3	84	2	11	13	74	6	0	0	0	0	....	1981-82	1984-85
Schmautz, Bobby	Chi., Van., Bos., Edm., Col.	13	764	271	286	557	988	84	28	33	61	92	....	1967-68	1980-81
Schmautz, Cliff	Buf., Phi.	1	56	13	19	32	33	....	....	....	....	....	....	1970-71	1970-71
● Schmidt, Clarence	Bos.	1	7	1	0	1	2	....	....	....	....	....	....	1943-44	1943-44
Schmidt, Jackie	Bos.	1	45	6	7	13	6	5	0	0	0	0	....	1942-43	1942-43
Schmidt, Milt	Bos.	16	776	229	346	575	466	86	24	25	49	60	2	1936-37	1954-55
Schmidt, Norm	Pit.	4	125	23	33	56	73	....	....	....	....	....	....	1983-84	1987-88
Schmidt, Otto	Bos.	1	2	0	0	0	0	....	....	....	....	....	....	1943-44	1943-44
● Schnarr, Werner	Bos.	2	26	0	0	0	0	....	....	....	....	....	....	1924-25	1925-26
‡ Schneider, Andy	Ott.	1	10	0	0	0	15	....	....	....	....	....	....	1993-94	1993-94
Schock, Danny	Bos., Phi.	2	20	1	2	3	0	1	0	0	0	0	1	1969-70	1970-71
Schock, Ron	Bos., St.L., Pit., Buf.	15	909	166	351	517	260	55	4	16	20	29	....	1963-64	1977-78
Schoenfeld, Jim	Buf., Det., Bos.	13	719	51	204	255	1132	75	3	13	16	151	....	1972-73	1984-85
Schofield, Dwight	Det., Mtl., St.L., Wsh., Pit., Wpg.	7	211	8	22	30	631	9	0	0	0	55	....	1976-77	1987-88
‡ Schreiber, Wally	Min.	2	41	8	10	18	12	....	....	....	....	....	....	1987-88	1988-89
● Schriner, Sweeney	NYA, Tor.	11	484	201	204	405	148	59	18	11	29	54	2	1934-35	1945-46
Schulte, Paxton	Que., Cgy.	2	2	0	0	0	4	....	....	....	....	....	....	1993-94	1996-97
Schultz, Dave	Phi., L.A., Pit., Buf.	9	535	79	121	200	2294	73	8	12	20	412	2	1971-72	1979-80
Schurman, Maynard	Hfd.	1	7	0	0	0	0	....	....	....	....	....	....	1979-80	1979-80
Schutt, Rod	Mtl., Pit., Tor.	8	286	77	92	169	177	22	8	6	14	26	....	1977-78	1985-86
Scissons, Scott	NYI	3	2	0	0	0	0	1	0	0	0	0	....	1990-91	1993-94
Sclisizzi, Enio	Det., Chi.	6	81	12	11	23	26	13	0	0	0	6	....	1946-47	1952-53
● Scott, Ganton	Tor., Ham., Mtl.M.	3	57	1	1	2	0	....	....	....	....	....	....	1922-23	1924-25
● Scott, Laurie	NYA, NYR	2	62	6	3	9	28	....	....	....	....	....	....	1926-27	1927-28
Scremin, Claudio	S.J.	2	17	0	1	1	29	....	....	....	....	....	....	1991-92	1992-93
Scruton, Howard	L.A.	1	4	0	4	4	9	....	....	....	....	....	....	1982-83	1982-83
Seabrooke, Glen	Phi.	3	19	1	6	7	4	....	....	....	....	....	....	1986-87	1988-89
Secord, Al	Bos., Chi., Tor., Phi.	12	766	273	222	495	2093	102	21	34	55	382	....	1978-79	1989-90
Sedlbauer, Ron	Van., Chi., Tor.	7	430	143	86	229	210	19	1	3	4	27	....	1974-75	1980-81
Seftel, Steve	Wsh.	1	4	0	0	0	2	....	....	....	....	....	....	1990-91	1990-91
Seguin, Dan	Min., Van.	2	37	2	6	8	50	....	....	....	....	....	....	1970-71	1973-74
Seguin, Steve	L.A.	1	5	0	0	0	9	....	....	....	....	....	....	1984-85	1984-85
● Seibert, Earl	NYR, Chi., Det.	15	645	89	187	276	746	66	11	8	19	76	2	1931-32	1945-46
Seiling, Ric	Buf., Det.	10	738	179	208	387	573	62	14	14	28	36	....	1977-78	1986-87
Seiling, Rod	Tor., NYR, Wsh., St.L., Atl.	17	979	62	269	331	601	77	4	8	12	55	....	1962-63	1978-79
‡ Sejba, Jiri	Buf.	1	11	0	2	2	8	....	....	....	....	....	....	1990-91	1990-91
Selby, Brit	Tor., Phi., St.L.	8	350	55	62	117	163	16	1	1	2	8	....	1964-65	1971-72
Self, Steve	Wsh.	1	3	0	0	0	0	....	....	....	....	....	....	1976-77	1976-77
Selwood, Brad	Tor., L.A.	3	163	7	40	47	153	6	0	0	0	4	....	1970-71	1979-80
‡ Semak, Alexander	N.J., T.B., NYI, Van.	6	289	83	91	174	187	8	1	1	2	0	....	1991-92	1996-97
Semchuk, Brandy	L.A.	1	1	0	0	0	2	....	....	....	....	....	....	1992-93	1992-93
Semenko, Dave	Edm., Hfd., Tor.	9	575	65	88	153	1175	73	6	6	12	208	2	1979-80	1987-88
Semenov, Anatoli	Edm., T.B., Van., Ana., Phi., Buf.	8	362	68	126	194	122	49	9	13	22	12	....	1989-90	1996-97
Senick, George	NYR	1	13	2	3	5	8	....	....	....	....	....	....	1952-53	1952-53
Seppa, Jyrki	Wpg.	1	13	0	2	2	6	....	....	....	....	....	....	1983-84	1983-84
Serafini, Ron	Cal.	1	2	0	0	0	2	....	....	....	....	....	....	1973-74	1973-74
Serowik, Jeff	Tor., Bos., Pit.	3	28	0	6	6	16	....	....	....	....	....	....	1990-91	1998-99
Servinis, George	Min.	1	5	0	0	0	0	....	....	....	....	....	....	1987-88	1987-88
‡ Sevcik, Jaroslav	Que.	1	13	0	2	2	2	....	....	....	....	....	....	1989-90	1989-90
Shack, Eddie	NYR, Tor., Bos., L.A., Buf., Pit.	17	1047	239	226	465	1437	74	6	7	13	151	4	1958-59	1974-75
● Shack, Joe	NYR	2	70	9	27	36	20	....	....	....	....	....	....	1942-43	1944-45
‡ Shafranov, Konstantin	St.L.	1	5	2	1	3	0	....	....	....	....	....	....	1996-97	1996-97
Shakes, Paul	Cal.	1	21	0	4	4	12	....	....	....	....	....	....	1973-74	1973-74
‡ Shaldybin, Yevgeny	Bos.	1	3	1	0	1	0	....	....	....	....	....	....	1996-97	1996-97
Shanahan, Sean	Mtl., Col., Bos.	3	40	1	3	4	47	....	....	....	....	....	....	1975-76	1977-78
Shand, Dave	Atl., Tor., Wsh.	8	421	19	84	103	544	26	1	2	3	83	....	1976-77	1984-85
‡ Shank, Daniel	Det., Hfd.	3	77	13	14	27	175	5	0	0	0	22	....	1989-90	1991-92
Shannon, Chuck	NYA	1	4	0	0	0	2	....	....	....	....	....	....	1939-40	1939-40
Shannon, Darrin	Buf., Wpg., Phx.	10	506	87	163	250	344	45	7	10	17	38	....	1988-89	1997-98
● Shannon, Gerry	Ott., St.L., Bos., Mtl.M.	5	180	23	29	52	80	9	0	1	1	2	....	1933-34	1937-38
‡ Sharples, Jeff	Det.	3	105	14	35	49	70	7	0	3	3	6	....	1986-87	1988-89
Sharpley, Glen	Min., Chi.	6	389	117	161	278	199	27	7	11	18	24	....	1976-77	1981-82
Shaunessy, Scott	Que.	2	7	0	0	0	23	....	....	....	....	....	....	1986-87	1988-89
Shaw, Brad	Hfd., Ott., Wsh., St.L.	11	377	22	137	159	208	23	4	8	12	6	....	1985-86	1998-99
Shaw, David	Que., NYR, Edm., Min., Bos., T.B.	16	769	41	153	194	906	45	3	9	12	81	....	1982-83	1997-98
● Shay, Norm	Bos., Tor.	2	53	5	3	8	34	....	....	....	....	....	....	1924-25	1925-26
● Shea, Pat	Chi.	1	10	1	0	1	0	....	....	....	....	....	....	1931-32	1931-32
Shedden, Doug	Pit., Det., Que., Tor.	8	416	139	186	325	176	....	....	....	....	....	....	1981-82	1990-91
Sheehan, Bobby	Mtl., Cal., Chi., Det., NYR, Col., L.A.	9	310	48	63	111	40	25	4	3	7	8	1	1969-70	1981-82
Sheehy, Neil	Cgy., Hfd., Wsh.	9	379	18	47	65	1311	54	0	3	3	241	....	1983-84	1991-92
Sheehy, Tim	Det., Hfd.	2	27	2	1	3	0	....	....	....	....	....	....	1977-78	1979-80
Shelton, Doug	Chi.	1	5	0	1	1	2	....	....	....	....	....	....	1967-68	1967-68
● Sheppard, Frank	Det.	1	8	1	1	2	0	....	....	....	....	....	....	1927-28	1927-28
Sheppard, Gregg	Bos., Pit.	10	657	205	293	498	243	82	32	40	72	31	....	1972-73	1981-82
● Sheppard, Johnny	Det., NYA, Bos., Chi.	8	308	68	58	126	224	10	0	0	0	0	1	1926-27	1933-34
● Sherf, John	Det.	5	19	0	0	0	8	8	0	1	1	2	1	1935-36	1943-44
● Shero, Fred	NYR	3	145	6	14	20	137	13	0	2	2	8	....	1947-48	1949-50
Sherritt, Gordon	Det.	1	8	0	0	0	12	....	....	....	....	....	....	1943-44	1943-44
‡ Sherven, Gord	Edm., Min., Hfd.	5	97	13	22	35	33	3	0	0	0	0	....	1983-84	1987-88
‡ Shevalier, Jeff	L.A., T.B.	3	32	5	9	14	8	....	....	....	....	....	....	1994-95	1999-00
● Shewchuck, Jack	Bos.	6	187	9	19	28	160	20	0	1	1	19	1	1938-39	1944-45
Shibicky, Alex	NYR	8	324	110	91	201	161	39	12	12	24	12	1	1935-36	1945-46
● Shields, Al	Ott., Phi., NYA, Mtl.M., Bos.	11	459	42	46	88	637	17	0	1	1	14	1	1927-28	1937-38
Shill, Bill	Bos.	3	79	21	13	34	18	7	1	2	3	2	....	1942-43	1946-47
● Shill, Jack	Tor., Bos., NYA, Chi.	6	160	15	20	35	70	25	1	6	7	23	1	1933-34	1938-39
Shinske, Rick	Cle., St.L.	3	63	5	16	21	10	....	....	....	....	....	....	1976-77	1978-79
Shires, Jim	Det., St.L., Pit.	3	56	3	6	9	32	....	....	....	....	....	....	1970-71	1972-73
Shmyr, Paul	Chi., Cal., Min., Hfd.	7	343	13	72	85	528	34	3	3	6	44	....	1968-69	1981-82
Shoebottom, Bruce	Bos.	4	35	1	4	5	53	14	1	2	3	77	....	1987-88	1990-91
● Shore, Eddie	Bos., NYA	14	550	105	179	284	1047	55	6	13	19	181	2	1926-27	1939-40
● Shore, Hamby	Ott.	1	18	3	8	11	51	....	....	....	....	....	....	1917-18	1917-18
Short, Steve	L.A., Det.	2	6	0	0	0	2	....	....	....	....	....	....	1977-78	1978-79
‡ Shuchuk, Gary	Det., L.A.	5	142	13	26	39	70	20	2	2	4	12	....	1990-91	1995-96
‡ Shudra, Ron	Edm.	1	10	0	5	5	6	....	....	....	....	....	....	1987-88	1987-88
Shutt, Steve	Mtl., L.A.	13	930	424	393	817	410	99	50	48	98	65	5	1972-73	1984-85
● Siebert, Babe	Mtl.M., NYR, Bos., Mtl.C.	14	592	140	156	296	982	49	7	5	12	62	2	1925-26	1938-39
Silk, Dave	NYR, Bos., Det., Wpg.	7	249	54	59	113	271	13	2	4	6	13	....	1979-80	1985-86
Siltala, Mike	Wsh., NYR	3	7	1	0	1	2	....	....	....	....	....	....	1981-82	1987-88
Siltanen, Risto	Edm., Hfd., Que.	8	562	90	265	355	266	32	6	12	18	30	....	1979-80	1986-87
Sim, Trevor	Edm.	1	3	0	1	1	2	....	....	....	....	....	....	1989-90	1989-90
Simard, Martin	Cgy., T.B.	3	44	1	5	6	183	....	....	....	....	....	....	1990-91	1992-93
Simmer, Charlie	Cal., Cle., L.A., Bos., Pit.	14	712	342	369	711	544	24	9	9	18	32	....	1974-75	1987-88
Simmons, Al	Cal., Bos.	3	11	0	1	1	21	1	0	0	0	0	....	1971-72	1975-76
● Simon, Cully	Det., Chi.	3	130	4	11	15	121	14	1	0	1	6	1	1942-43	1944-45
‡ Simon, Jason	NYI, Phx.	2	5	0	0	0	34	....	....	....	....	....	....	1993-94	1996-97
Simon, Thain	Det.	1	3	0	0	0	0	....	....	....	....	....	....	1946-47	1946-47
‡ Simon, Todd	Buf.	1	15	0	1	1	0	5	1	0	1	0	....	1993-94	1993-94
Simonetti, Frank	Bos.	4	115	5	8	13	76	12	0	1	1	8	....	1984-85	1987-88
Simpson, Bobby	Atl., St.L., Pit.	5	175	35	29	64	98	6	0	1	1	2	....	1976-77	1982-83
● Simpson, Cliff	Det.	2	6	0	1	1	0	2	0	0	0	2	....	1946-47	1947-48
Simpson, Craig	Pit., Edm., Buf.	10	634	247	250	497	659	67	36	32	68	56	2	1985-86	1994-95
● Simpson, Joe	NYA	6	228	21	19	40	156	2	0	0	0	0	....	1925-26	1930-31
Sims, Al	Bos., Hfd., L.A.	10	475	49	116	165	286	41	0	2	2	14	....	1973-74	1982-83
Sinclair, Reg	NYR, Det.	3	208	49	43	92	139	3	1	0	1	0	....	1950-51	1952-53
● Singbush, Alex	Mtl.	1	32	0	5	5	15	3	0	0	0	4	....	1940-41	1940-41
Sinisalo, Ilkka	Phi., Min., L.A.	11	582	204	222	426	208	68	21	11	32	6	....	1981-82	1991-92
Siren, Ville	Pit., Min.	5	290	14	68	82	276	7	0	0	0	6	....	1985-86	1989-90
Sirois, Bob	Phi., Wsh.	6	286	92	120	212	42	....	....	....	....	....	....	1974-75	1979-80
Sittler, Darryl	Tor., Phi., Det.	15	1096	484	637	1121	948	76	29	45	74	137	....	1970-71	1984-85
● Sjoberg, Lars-Erik	Wpg.	1	79	7	27	34	48	....	....	....	....	....	....	1979-80	1979-80
‡ Sjodin, Tommy	Min., Dal., Que.	2	106	8	40	48	52	....	....	....	....	....	....	1992-93	1993-94

			Regular Schedule					Playoffs							
Name	NHL Teams	NHL Seasons	GP	G	A	TP	PIM	GP	G	A	TP	PIM	NHL Cup Wins	First NHL Season	Last NHL Season
• Skaare, Bjorn	Det.	1	1	0	0	0	0	....	....	....	....	....	....	1978-79	1978-79
Skarda, Randy	St.L.	2	26	0	5	5	11	....	....	....	....	....	....	1989-90	1991-92
• Skilton, Raymie	Mtl.	1	1	0	0	0	0	....	....	....	....	....	....	1917-18	1917-18
• Skinner, Alf	Tor., Bos., Mtl.M., Pit.	4	71	26	10	36	87	2	0	1	1	9	1	1917-18	1925-26
Skinner, Larry	Col.	4	47	10	12	22	8	2	0	0	0	0	....	1976-77	1979-80
Skov, Glen	Det., Chi., Mtl.	12	650	106	136	242	413	53	7	7	14	48	3	1949-50	1960-61
Skriko, Petri	Van., Bos., Wpg., S.J.	9	541	183	222	405	246	28	5	9	14	4	....	1984-85	1992-93
‡ Skrudland, Brian	Mtl., Cgy., Fla., NYR, Dal.	15	881	124	219	343	1107	164	15	46	61	323	2	1985-86	1999-00
Sleaver, John	Chi.	2	13	1	0	1	6	....	....	....	....	....	....	1953-54	1956-57
Sleigher, Louis	Que., Bos.	6	194	46	53	99	146	17	1	1	2	64	....	1979-80	1985-86
Sloan, Tod	Tor., Chi.	13	745	220	262	482	831	47	9	12	21	47	2	1947-48	1960-61
• Slobodian, Peter	NYA	1	41	3	2	5	54	....	....	....	....	....	....	1940-41	1940-41
• Slowinski, Eddie	NYR	6	291	58	74	132	63	16	2	6	8	6	....	1947-48	1952-53
Sly, Darryl	Tor., Min., Van.	4	79	1	2	3	20	....	....	....	....	....	....	1965-66	1970-71
Smail, Doug	Wpg., Min., Que., Ott.	13	845	210	249	459	602	42	9	2	11	49	....	1980-81	1992-93
Smart, Alex	Mtl.	1	8	5	2	7	0	....	....	....	....	....	....	1942-43	1942-43
Smedsmo, Dale	Tor.	1	4	0	0	0	0	....	....	....	....	....	....	1972-73	1972-73
Smillie, Don	Bos.	1	12	2	2	4	4	....	....	....	....	....	....	1933-34	1933-34
• Smith, Alex	Ott., Det., Bos., NYA	11	443	41	50	91	645	19	0	2	2	28	1	1924-25	1934-35
• Smith, Art	Tor., Ott.	4	144	15	10	25	249	4	1	1	2	8	....	1927-28	1930-31
Smith, Barry	Bos., Col.	3	114	7	7	14	10	....	....	....	....	....	....	1975-76	1980-81
Smith, Bobby	Min., Mtl.	15	1077	357	679	1036	917	184	64	96	160	245	1	1978-79	1992-93
Smith, Brad	Van., Atl., Cgy., Det., Tor.	9	222	28	34	62	591	20	3	3	6	49	....	1978-79	1986-87
Smith, Brian	Det.	3	61	2	8	10	12	5	0	0	0	0	....	1957-58	1960-61
• Smith, Brian	L.A., Min.	2	67	10	10	20	33	7	0	0	0	0	....	1967-68	1968-69
• Smith, Carl	Det.	1	7	1	1	2	2	....	....	....	....	....	....	1943-44	1943-44
Smith, Clint	NYR, Chi.	11	483	161	236	397	24	42	10	14	24	2	1	1936-37	1946-47
Smith, Dallas	Bos., NYR	16	890	55	252	307	959	86	3	29	32	128	2	1959-60	1977-78
Smith, Dennis	Wsh., L.A.	2	8	0	0	0	4	....	....	....	....	....	....	1989-90	1990-91
Smith, Derek	Buf., Det.	8	335	78	116	194	60	30	9	14	23	13	....	1975-76	1982-83
‡ Smith, Derrick	Phi., Min., Dal.	10	537	82	92	174	373	82	14	11	25	79	....	1984-85	1993-94
• Smith, Des	Mtl.M., Mtl.C., Chi., Bos.	5	196	22	25	47	236	25	1	4	5	18	1	1937-38	1941-42
• Smith, Don	Mtl.C.	1	12	1	0	1	6	....	....	....	....	....	....	1919-20	1919-20
Smith, Don	NYR	1	11	1	1	2	0	1	0	0	0	0	....	1949-50	1949-50
Smith, Doug	L.A., Buf., Edm., Van., Pit.	9	535	115	138	253	624	18	4	2	6	21	....	1981-82	1989-90
Smith, Floyd	Bos., NYR, Det., Tor., Buf.	13	616	129	178	307	207	48	12	11	23	16	....	1954-55	1971-72
Smith, Geoff	Edm., Fla., NYR	10	462	18	73	91	282	13	0	1	1	8	1	1989-90	1998-99
Smith, Glen	Chi.	1	2	0	0	0	0	....	....	....	....	....	....	1950-51	1950-51
• Smith, Glenn	Tor.	1	9	0	0	0	0	....	....	....	....	....	....	1921-22	1921-22
Smith, Gord	Wsh., Wpg.	6	299	9	30	39	284	....	....	....	....	....	....	1974-75	1979-80
Smith, Greg	Cal., Cle., Min., Det., Wsh.	13	829	56	232	288	1110	63	4	7	11	106	....	1975-76	1987-88
• Smith, Hooley	Ott., Mtl.M., Bos., NYA	17	715	200	225	425	1013	54	11	8	19	109	2	1924-25	1940-41
• Smith, Ken	Bos.	7	331	78	93	171	49	30	8	13	21	6	....	1944-45	1950-51
Smith, Nakina	Det.	1	10	1	2	3	0	....	....	....	....	....	....	1943-44	1943-44
Smith, Randy	Min.	2	3	0	0	0	0	....	....	....	....	....	....	1985-86	1986-87
Smith, Rick	Bos., Cal., St.L., Det., Wsh.	11	687	52	167	219	560	78	3	23	26	73	1	1968-69	1980-81
• Smith, Rodger	Pit., Phi.	6	210	20	4	24	172	4	3	0	3	0	....	1925-26	1930-31
Smith, Ron	NYI	1	11	1	1	2	14	....	....	....	....	....	....	1972-73	1972-73
Smith, Sid	Tor.	12	601	186	183	369	94	44	17	10	27	2	3	1946-47	1957-58
Smith, Stan	NYR	2	9	2	1	3	0	1	0	0	0	0	1	1939-40	1940-41
Smith, Steve	Phi., Phialdelphia, Buf.	6	18	0	1	1	15	....	....	....	....	....	....	1981-82	1988-89
Smith, Stu	Mtl.	2	4	2	2	4	2	1	0	0	0	0	....	1940-41	1941-42
Smith, Stu	Hfd.	4	77	2	10	12	95	....	....	....	....	....	....	1979-80	1982-83
• Smith, Tommy	Que.	1	10	0	1	1	11	....	....	....	....	....	....	1919-20	1919-20
Smith, Vern	NYI	1	1	0	0	0	0	....	....	....	....	....	....	1984-85	1984-85
Smith, Wayne	Chi.	1	2	1	1	2	2	1	0	0	0	0	....	1966-67	1966-67
Smrke, John	St.L., Que.	3	103	11	17	28	33	....	....	....	....	....	....	1977-78	1979-80
• Smrke, Stan	Mtl.	2	9	0	3	3	0	....	....	....	....	....	....	1956-57	1957-58
Smyl, Stan	Van.	13	896	262	411	673	1556	41	16	17	33	64	....	1978-79	1990-91
• Smylie, Rod	Tor., Ott.	6	74	4	2	6	12	4	0	0	0	2	1	1920-21	1925-26
Smyth, Greg	Phi., Que., Cgy., Fla., Tor., Chi.	10	229	4	16	20	783	12	0	0	0	40	....	1986-87	1996-97
Smyth, Kevin	Hfd.	3	58	6	8	14	31	....	....	....	....	....	....	1993-94	1995-96
‡ Snell, Chris	Tor., L.A.	2	34	2	7	9	24	....	....	....	....	....	....	1993-94	1994-95
Snell, Ron	Pit.	2	7	3	2	5	6	....	....	....	....	....	....	1968-69	1969-70
Snell, Ted	Pit., K.C., Det.	2	104	7	18	25	22	....	....	....	....	....	....	1973-74	1974-75
Snepsts, Harold	Van., Min., Det., St.L.	17	1033	38	195	233	2009	93	1	14	15	231	....	1974-75	1990-91
Snow, Sandy	Det.	1	3	0	0	0	2	....	....	....	....	....	....	1968-69	1968-69
Snuggerud, Dave	Buf., S.J., Phi.	4	265	30	54	84	127	12	1	3	4	6	....	1989-90	1992-93
Sobchuk, Dennis	Det., Que.	2	35	5	6	11	2	....	....	....	....	....	....	1979-80	1982-83
• Sobchuk, Gene	Van.	1	1	0	0	0	0	....	....	....	....	....	....	1973-74	1973-74
Solheim, Ken	Chi., Min., Det., Edm.	5	135	19	20	39	34	3	1	1	2	2	....	1980-81	1985-86
Solinger, Bob	Tor., Det.	5	99	10	11	21	19	....	....	....	....	....	....	1951-52	1959-60
• Somers, Art	Chi., NYR	6	222	33	56	89	189	30	1	5	6	20	1	1929-30	1934-35
Sommer, Roy	Edm.	1	3	1	0	1	7	....	....	....	....	....	....	1980-81	1980-81
Songin, Tom	Bos.	3	43	5	5	10	22	....	....	....	....	....	....	1978-79	1980-81
Sonmor, Glen	NYR	2	28	2	0	2	21	....	....	....	....	....	....	1953-54	1954-55
• Sorrell, John	Det., NYA	11	490	127	119	246	100	42	12	15	27	10	2	1930-31	1940-41
• Sparrow, Emory	Bos.	1	8	0	0	0	4	....	....	....	....	....	....	1924-25	1924-25
Speck, Fred	Det., Van.	3	28	1	2	3	2	....	....	....	....	....	....	1968-69	1971-72
• Speer, Bill	Pit., Bos.	4	130	5	20	25	79	8	1	0	1	4	1	1967-68	1970-71
Speers, Ted	Det.	1	4	1	1	2	0	....	....	....	....	....	....	1985-86	1985-86
• Spence, Gordon	Tor.	1	3	0	0	0	0	....	....	....	....	....	....	1925-26	1925-26
• Spencer, Brian	Tor., NYI, Buf., Pit.	10	553	80	143	223	634	37	1	5	6	29	....	1969-70	1978-79
Spencer, Irv	NYR, Bos., Det.	8	230	12	38	50	127	16	0	0	0	8	....	1959-60	1967-68
• Speyer, Chris	Tor., NYA	3	14	0	0	0	0	....	....	....	....	....	....	1923-24	1933-34
‡ Spring, Corey	T.B.	2	16	1	1	2	12	....	....	....	....	....	....	1997-98	1998-99
Spring, Don	Wpg.	4	259	1	54	55	80	6	0	0	0	10	....	1980-81	1983-84
Spring, Frank	Bos., St.L., Cal., Cle.	5	61	14	20	34	12	....	....	....	....	....	....	1969-70	1976-77
• Spring, Jesse	Ham., Pit., Tor., NYA	6	133	11	4	15	74	2	0	2	2	2	....	1923-24	1929-30
Spruce, Andy	Van., Col.	3	172	31	42	73	111	2	0	2	2	0	....	1976-77	1978-79
‡ Srsen, Tomas	Edm.	1	2	0	0	0	0	....	....	....	....	....	....	1990-91	1990-91
‡ St. Amour, Martin	Ott.	1	1	0	0	0	2	....	....	....	....	....	....	1992-93	1992-93
St. Laurent, Andre	NYI, Det., L.A., Pit.	11	644	129	187	316	749	59	8	12	20	48	....	1973-74	1983-84
St. Laurent, Dollard	Mtl., Chi.	12	652	29	133	162	496	92	2	22	24	87	5	1950-51	1961-62
St. Marseille, Frank	St.L., L.A.	10	707	140	285	425	242	88	20	25	45	18	....	1967-68	1976-77
St. Sauveur, Claude	Atl.	1	79	24	24	48	23	2	0	0	0	0	....	1975-76	1975-76
Stackhouse, Ron	Cal., Det., Pit.	12	889	87	372	459	824	32	5	8	13	38	....	1970-71	1981-82
• Stackhouse, Ted	Tor.	1	13	0	0	0	2	1	0	0	0	0	1	1921-22	1921-22
• Stahan, Butch	Mtl.	1	....	....	....	....	....	3	0	1	1	2	....	1944-45	1944-45
‡ Stajduhar, Nick	Edm.	1	2	0	0	0	4	....	....	....	....	....	....	1995-96	1995-96
Staley, Al	NYR	1	1	0	1	1	0	....	....	....	....	....	....	1948-49	1948-49
Stamler, Lorne	L.A., Tor., Wpg.	4	116	14	11	25	16	....	....	....	....	....	....	1976-77	1979-80
Standing, George	Min.	1	2	0	0	0	0	....	....	....	....	....	....	1967-68	1967-68
Stanfield, Fred	Chi., Bos., Min., Buf.	14	914	211	405	616	134	106	21	35	56	10	2	1964-65	1977-78
Stanfield, Jack	Chi.	1	....	....	....	....	....	1	0	0	0	0	....	1965-66	1965-66
Stanfield, Jim	L.A.	3	7	0	1	1	0	....	....	....	....	....	....	1969-70	1971-72
Stankiewicz, Ed	Det.	2	6	0	0	0	2	....	....	....	....	....	....	1953-54	1955-56
Stankiewicz, Myron	St.L., Phi.	1	35	0	7	7	36	1	0	0	0	0	....	1968-69	1968-69
Stanley, Allan	NYR, Chi., Bos., Tor., Phi.	21	1244	100	333	433	792	109	7	36	43	80	4	1948-49	1968-69
• Stanley, Barney	Chi.	1	1	0	0	0	0	....	....	....	....	....	....	1927-28	1927-28
Stanley, Daryl	Phi., Van.	6	189	8	17	25	408	17	0	0	0	30	....	1983-84	1989-90
Stanowski, Wally	Tor., NYR	10	428	23	88	111	160	60	3	14	17	13	4	1939-40	1950-51
‡ Stanton, Paul	Pit., Bos., NYI	5	295	14	49	63	262	44	2	10	12	66	2	1990-91	1994-95
Stapleton, Brian	Wsh.	1	1	0	0	0	0	....	....	....	....	....	....	1975-76	1975-76
Stapleton, Pat	Bos., Chi.	10	635	43	294	337	353	65	10	39	49	38	....	1961-62	1972-73
Starikov, Sergei	N.J.	1	16	0	1	1	8	....	....	....	....	....	....	1989-90	1989-90
• Starr, Harold	Ott., Mtl.M., Mtl.C., NYR	7	205	6	5	11	186	15	1	0	1	4	....	1929-30	1935-36
Starr, Wilf	NYA, Det.	4	87	8	6	14	25	7	0	2	2	2	....	1932-33	1935-36
Stasiuk, Vic	Chi., Det., Bos.	14	745	183	254	437	669	69	16	18	34	40	3	1949-50	1962-63
Stastny, Anton	Que.	9	650	252	384	636	150	66	20	32	52	31	....	1980-81	1988-89
Stastny, Marian	Que., Tor.	5	322	121	173	294	110	32	5	17	22	7	....	1981-82	1985-86
Stastny, Peter	Que., N.J., St.L.	15	977	450	789	1239	824	93	33	72	105	123	....	1980-81	1994-95
Staszak, Ray	Det.	1	4	0	1	1	7	....	....	....	....	....	....	1985-86	1985-86
• Steele, Frank	Det.	1	1	0	0	0	0	....	....	....	....	....	....	1930-31	1930-31
Steen, Anders	Wpg.	1	42	5	11	16	22	....	....	....	....	....	....	1980-81	1980-81
Steen, Thomas	Wpg.	14	950	264	553	817	753	56	12	32	44	62	....	1981-82	1994-95

Ron Stern

Darryl Sutter

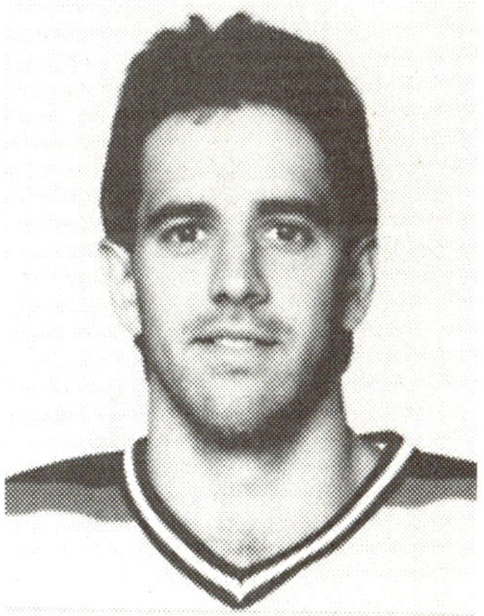

Peter Taglianetti

Jean Guy Talbot

Dale Tallon

Errol Thompson

Jari Torkki

Mick Vukota

			Regular Schedule					Playoffs							
Name	NHL Teams	NHL Seasons	GP	G	A	TP	PIM	GP	G	A	TP	PIM	NHL Cup Wins	First NHL Season	Last NHL Season
Stefaniw, Morris	Atl.	1	13	1	1	2	2	....	....	....	....	....	....	1972-73	1972-73
Stefanski, Bud	NYR	1	1	0	0	0	0	....	....	....	....	....	....	1977-78	1977-78
Stemkowski, Pete	Tor., Det., NYR, L.A.	15	967	206	349	555	866	83	25	29	54	136	1	1963-64	1977-78
Stenlund, Vern	Cle.	1	4	0	0	0	0	....	....	....	....	....	....	1976-77	1976-77
Stephenson, Bob	Hfd., Tor.	1	18	2	3	5	4	....	....	....	....	....	....	1979-80	1979-80
Stern, Ron	Van., Cgy., S.J.	12	638	75	86	161	2077	43	7	7	14	119	....	1987-88	1999-00
Sterner, Ulf	NYR	1	4	0	0	0	0	....	....	....	....	....	....	1964-65	1964-65
Stevens, John	Phi., Hfd.	5	53	0	10	10	48	....	....	....	....	....	....	1986-87	1993-94
‡ Stevens, Mike	Van., Bos., NYI, Tor.	4	23	1	4	5	29	....	....	....	....	....	....	1984-85	1989-90
• Stevens, Phil	Mtl., Mtl.C., Bos.	3	25	1	0	1	3	....	....	....	....	....	....	1917-18	1925-26
‡ Stevenson, Shayne	Bos., T.B.	3	27	0	2	2	35	....	....	....	....	....	....	1990-91	1992-93
Stewart, Allan	N.J., Bos.	6	64	6	4	10	243	....	....	....	....	....	....	1985-86	1991-92
Stewart, Bill	Buf., St.L., Tor., Min.	8	261	7	64	71	424	13	1	3	4	11	....	1977-78	1985-86
Stewart, Blair	Det., Wsh., Que.	7	229	34	44	78	326	....	....	....	....	....	....	1973-74	1979-80
Stewart, Bob	Bos., Cal., Cle., St.L., Pit.	9	575	27	101	128	809	5	1	1	2	2	....	1971-72	1979-80
Stewart, Gaye	Tor., Chi., Det., NYR, Mtl.	11	502	185	159	344	274	25	2	9	11	16	2	1941-42	1953-54
• Stewart, Jack	Det., Chi.	12	565	31	84	115	765	80	5	14	19	143	2	1938-39	1951-52
Stewart, John	Pit., Atl., Cal.	5	258	58	60	118	158	4	0	0	0	10	....	1970-71	1974-75
Stewart, John	Que.	1	2	0	0	0	0	....	....	....	....	....	....	1979-80	1979-80
• Stewart, Ken	Chi.	1	6	1	1	2	2	....	....	....	....	....	....	1941-42	1941-42
• Stewart, Nels	Mtl.M., Bos., NYA	15	650	324	191	515	953	50	9	12	21	47	1	1925-26	1939-40
Stewart, Paul	Que.	1	21	2	0	2	74	....	....	....	....	....	....	1979-80	1979-80
Stewart, Ralph	Van., NYI	7	252	57	73	130	28	19	4	4	8	2	....	1970-71	1977-78
Stewart, Ron	Tor., Bos., St.L., NYR, Van., NYI	21	1353	276	253	529	560	119	14	21	35	60	3	1952-53	1972-73
Stewart, Ryan	Wpg.	1	3	1	0	1	0	....	....	....	....	....	....	1985-86	1985-86
Stienburg, Trevor	Que.	4	71	8	4	12	161	1	0	0	0	0	....	1985-86	1988-89
Stiles, Tony	Cgy.	1	30	2	7	9	20	....	....	....	....	....	....	1983-84	1983-84
Stoddard, Jack	NYR	2	80	16	15	31	31	....	....	....	....	....	....	1951-52	1952-53
‡ Stojanov, Alek	Van., Pit.	3	107	2	5	7	222	14	0	0	0	21	....	1994-95	1996-97
Stoltz, Roland	Wsh.	1	14	2	2	4	14	....	....	....	....	....	....	1981-82	1981-82
Stone, Steve	Van.	1	2	0	0	0	0	....	....	....	....	....	....	1973-74	1973-74
Storm, Jim	Hfd., Dal.	3	84	7	15	22	44	....	....	....	....	....	....	1993-94	1995-96
Stothers, Mike	Phi., Tor.	4	30	0	2	2	65	5	0	0	0	11	....	1984-85	1987-88
Stoughton, Blaine	Pit., Tor., Hfd., NYR	8	526	258	191	449	204	8	4	2	6	2	....	1973-74	1983-84
Stoyanovich, Steve	Hfd.	1	23	3	5	8	11	....	....	....	....	....	....	1983-84	1983-84
• Strain, Neil	NYR	1	52	11	13	24	12	....	....	....	....	....	....	1952-53	1952-53
Strate, Gord	Det.	3	61	0	0	0	34	....	....	....	....	....	....	1956-57	1958-59
Stratton, Art	NYR, Det., Chi., Pit., Phi.	4	95	18	33	51	24	5	0	0	0	0	....	1959-60	1967-68
Strobel, Art	NYR	1	7	0	0	0	0	....	....	....	....	....	....	1943-44	1943-44
Strong, Ken	Tor.	3	15	2	2	4	6	....	....	....	....	....	....	1982-83	1984-85
Struch, David	Cgy.	1	4	0	0	0	4	....	....	....	....	....	....	1993-94	1993-94
‡ Strueby, Todd	Edm.	3	5	0	1	1	2	....	....	....	....	....	....	1981-82	1983-84
• Stuart, Billy	Tor., Bos.	7	195	30	20	50	151	12	1	1	2	6	1	1920-21	1926-27
Stumpf, Bob	St.L., Pit.	1	10	1	1	2	20	....	....	....	....	....	....	1974-75	1974-75
Sturgeon, Peter	Col.	2	6	0	1	1	2	....	....	....	....	....	....	1979-80	1980-81
Suikkanen, Kai	Buf.	2	2	0	0	0	0	....	....	....	....	....	....	1981-82	1982-83
Sulliman, Doug	NYR, Hfd., N.J., Phi.	11	631	160	168	328	175	16	1	3	4	2	....	1979-80	1989-90
Sullivan, Barry	Det.	1	1	0	0	0	0	....	....	....	....	....	....	1947-48	1947-48
Sullivan, Bob	Hfd.	1	62	18	19	37	18	....	....	....	....	....	....	1982-83	1982-83
Sullivan, Brian	N.J.	1	2	0	1	1	0	....	....	....	....	....	....	1992-93	1992-93
Sullivan, Frank	Tor., Chi.	4	8	0	0	0	2	....	....	....	....	....	....	1949-50	1955-56
Sullivan, Peter	Wpg.	2	126	28	54	82	40	....	....	....	....	....	....	1979-80	1980-81
Sullivan, Red	Bos., Chi., NYR	11	557	107	239	346	441	18	1	2	3	6	....	1949-50	1960-61
Summanen, Raimo	Edm., Van.	5	151	36	40	76	35	10	2	5	7	0	....	1983-84	1987-88
• Summerhill, Bill	Mtl.C., Mtl., Bro.	4	72	14	17	31	70	3	0	0	0	2	....	1937-38	1941-42
‡ Sundblad, Niklas	Cgy.	1	2	0	0	0	0	....	....	....	....	....	....	1995-96	1995-96
‡ Sundin, Ronnie	NYR	1	1	0	0	0	0	....	....	....	....	....	....	1997-98	1997-98
Sundstrom, Patrik	Van., N.J.	10	679	219	369	588	349	37	9	17	26	25	....	1982-83	1991-92
Sundstrom, Peter	NYR, Wsh., N.J.	6	338	61	83	144	120	23	3	3	6	8	....	1983-84	1989-90
• Suomi, Al	Chi.	1	5	0	0	0	0	....	....	....	....	....	....	1936-37	1936-37
Sutherland, Bill	Mtl., Phi., Tor., St.L., Det.	6	250	70	58	128	99	14	2	4	6	0	....	1962-63	1971-72
• Sutherland, Max	Bos.	1	2	0	0	0	0	....	....	....	....	....	....	1931-32	1931-32
Sutter, Brent	NYI, Chi.	18	1111	363	466	829	1054	144	30	44	74	164	2	1980-81	1997-98
Sutter, Brian	St.L.	12	779	303	333	636	1786	65	21	21	42	249	....	1976-77	1987-88
Sutter, Darryl	Chi.	8	406	161	118	279	288	51	24	19	43	26	....	1979-80	1986-87
Sutter, Duane	NYI, Chi.	11	731	139	203	342	1333	161	26	32	58	405	4	1979-80	1989-90
Sutter, Rich	Pit., Phi., Van., St.L., Chi., T.B., Tor.	13	874	149	166	315	1411	78	13	5	18	133	....	1982-83	1994-95
Suzor, Mark	Phi., Col.	2	64	4	16	20	60	....	....	....	....	....	....	1976-77	1977-78
Svensson, Leif	Wsh.	2	121	6	40	46	49	....	....	....	....	....	....	1978-79	1979-80
‡ Svensson, Magnus	Fla.	2	46	4	14	18	31	....	....	....	....	....	....	1994-95	1995-96
Swain, Garry	Pit.	1	9	1	1	2	0	....	....	....	....	....	....	1968-69	1968-69
Swarbrick, George	Oak., Pit., Phi.	4	132	17	25	42	173	....	....	....	....	....	....	1967-68	1970-71
• Sweeney, Bill	NYR	1	4	1	0	1	0	....	....	....	....	....	....	1959-60	1959-60
‡ Sweeney, Bob	Bos., Buf., NYI, Cgy.	10	639	125	163	288	799	103	15	18	33	197	....	1986-87	1995-96
Sweeney, Tim	Cgy., Bos., Ana., NYR	8	291	55	83	138	123	4	0	0	0	2	....	1990-91	1997-98
Sykes, Bob	Tor.	1	2	0	0	0	0	....	....	....	....	....	....	1974-75	1974-75
Sykes, Phil	L.A., Wpg.	10	456	79	85	164	519	26	0	3	3	29	....	1982-83	1991-92
Szura, Joe	Oak.	2	90	10	15	25	30	7	2	3	5	2	....	1967-68	1968-69

T

Taft, John	Det.	1	15	0	2	2	4	....	....	....	....	....	....	1978-79	1978-79
Taglianetti, Peter	Wpg., Min., Pit., T.B.	11	451	18	74	92	1106	53	2	8	10	103	2	1984-85	1994-95
Talafous, Dean	Atl., Min., NYR	8	497	104	154	258	163	21	4	7	11	11	....	1974-75	1981-82
Talakoski, Ron	NYR	2	9	0	1	1	33	....	....	....	....	....	....	1986-87	1987-88
Talbot, Jean-Guy	Mtl., Min., Det., St.L., Buf.	17	1056	43	242	285	1006	150	4	26	30	142	7	1954-55	1970-71
Tallon, Dale	Van., Chi., Pit.	10	642	98	238	336	568	33	2	10	12	45	....	1970-71	1979-80
Tambellini, Steve	NYI, Col., N.J., Cgy., Van.	10	553	160	150	310	105	2	0	1	1	0	1	1978-79	1987-88
‡ Tancill, Chris	Hfd., Det., Dal., S.J.	8	134	17	32	49	54	11	1	1	2	8	....	1990-91	1997-98
Tanguay, Christian	Que.	1	2	0	0	0	0	....	....	....	....	....	....	1981-82	1981-82
Tannahill, Don	Van.	2	111	30	33	63	25	....	....	....	....	....	....	1972-73	1973-74
Tanti, Tony	Chi., Van., Pit., Buf.	11	697	287	273	560	661	30	3	12	15	27	....	1981-82	1991-92
Tardif, Marc	Mtl., Que.	8	517	194	207	401	443	62	13	15	28	75	2	1969-70	1982-83
‡ Tardif, Patrice	St.L., L.A.	2	65	7	11	18	78	....	....	....	....	....	....	1994-95	1995-96
Tatarinov, Mikhail	Wsh., Que., Bos.	4	161	21	48	69	184	....	....	....	....	....	....	1990-91	1993-94
Tatchell, Spence	NYR	1	1	0	0	0	0	....	....	....	....	....	....	1942-43	1942-43
• Taylor, Billy	Tor., Det., Bos., NYR	7	323	87	180	267	120	33	6	18	24	13	1	1939-40	1947-48
• Taylor, Bob	Bos.	1	8	0	0	0	6	....	....	....	....	....	....	1929-30	1929-30
Taylor, Dave	L.A.	17	1111	431	638	1069	1589	92	26	33	59	145	....	1977-78	1993-94
Taylor, Harry	Tor., Chi.	3	66	5	10	15	30	1	0	0	0	0	1	1946-47	1951-52
Taylor, Mark	Phi., Pit., Wsh.	5	209	42	68	110	73	6	0	0	0	0	....	1981-82	1985-86
• Taylor, Ralph	Chi., NYR	3	99	4	1	5	169	4	0	0	0	10	....	1927-28	1929-30
Taylor, Ted	NYR, Det., Min., Van.	6	166	23	35	58	181	....	....	....	....	....	....	1964-65	1971-72
Taylor Jr., Billy	NYR	1	2	0	0	0	0	....	....	....	....	....	....	1964-65	1964-65
Teal, Jeff	Mtl.	1	6	0	1	1	0	....	....	....	....	....	....	1984-85	1984-85
Teal, Skip	Bos.	1	1	0	0	0	0	....	....	....	....	....	....	1954-55	1954-55
Teal, Vic	NYI	1	1	0	0	0	0	....	....	....	....	....	....	1973-74	1973-74
Tebbutt, Greg	Que., Pit.	2	26	0	3	3	35	....	....	....	....	....	....	1979-80	1983-84
Tepper, Stephen	Chi.	1	1	0	0	0	0	....	....	....	....	....	....	1992-93	1992-93
Terbenche, Paul	Chi., Buf.	5	189	5	26	31	28	12	0	0	0	0	....	1967-68	1973-74
Terrion, Greg	L.A., Tor.	8	561	93	150	243	339	35	2	9	11	41	....	1980-81	1987-88
Terry, Bill	Min.	1	5	0	0	0	0	....	....	....	....	....	....	1987-88	1987-88
• Tertyshny, Dmitri	Phi.	1	62	2	8	10	30	1	0	0	0	0	....	1998-99	1998-99
Tessier, Orval	Mtl., Bos.	3	59	5	7	12	6	....	....	....	....	....	....	1954-55	1960-61
Theberge, Greg	Wsh.	5	153	15	63	78	73	4	0	1	1	0	....	1979-80	1983-84
Thelin, Mats	Bos.	3	163	8	19	27	107	5	0	0	0	6	....	1984-85	1986-87
Thelven, Michael	Bos.	5	207	20	80	100	217	34	4	10	14	34	....	1985-86	1989-90
Therrien, Gaston	Que.	3	22	0	8	8	12	9	0	1	1	4	....	1980-81	1982-83
‡ Thibaudeau, Gilles	Mtl., NYI, Tor.	5	119	25	37	62	40	8	3	3	6	2	....	1986-87	1990-91
Thibeault, Lorrain	Det., Mtl.	2	5	0	2	2	2	....	....	....	....	....	....	1944-45	1945-46
Thiffault, Leo	Min.	1	....	....	....	....	....	5	0	0	0	0	....	1967-68	1967-68
Thomas, Cy	Chi., Tor.	1	14	2	2	4	12	....	....	....	....	....	....	1947-48	1947-48
Thomas, Reg	Que.	1	39	9	7	16	6	....	....	....	....	....	....	1979-80	1979-80
Thomlinson, Dave	St.L., Bos., L.A.	5	42	1	3	4	50	9	3	1	4	4	....	1989-90	1994-95
Thompson, Cliff	Bos.	2	13	0	1	1	2	....	....	....	....	....	....	1941-42	1948-49
Thompson, Errol	Tor., Det., Pit.	10	599	208	185	393	184	34	7	5	12	11	....	1970-71	1980-81

Name	NHL Teams	NHL Seasons	Regular Schedule GP	G	A	TP	PIM	Playoffs GP	G	A	TP	PIM	NHL Cup Wins	First NHL Season	Last NHL Season
● Thompson, Ken	Mtl.	1	1	0	0	0	0	....	....	....	....	....	....	1917-18	1917-18
● Thompson, Paul	NYR, Chi.	13	582	153	179	332	336	48	11	11	22	54	3	1926-27	1938-39
● Thoms, Bill	Tor., Chi., Bos.	13	548	135	206	341	154	44	6	10	16	6	....	1932-33	1944-45
● Thomson, Bill	Det.	2	9	2	2	4	0	2	0	0	0	0	....	1938-39	1943-44
Thomson, Floyd	St.L.	8	411	56	97	153	341	10	0	2	2	6	....	1971-72	1979-80
Thomson, Jim	Wsh., Hfd., N.J., L.A., Ott., Ana.	7	115	4	3	7	416	1	0	0	0	0	....	1986-87	1993-94
● Thomson, Jimmy	Tor., Chi.	13	787	19	215	234	920	63	2	13	15	135	4	1945-46	1957-58
● Thomson, Rhys	Mtl., Tor.	2	25	0	2	2	38	....	....	....	....	....	....	1939-40	1942-43
Thornbury, Tom	Pit.	1	14	1	8	9	16	....	....	....	....	....	....	1983-84	1983-84
● Thorsteinson, Joe	NYA	1	4	0	0	0	0	....	....	....	....	....	....	1932-33	1932-33
● Thurier, Fred	NYA, Bro., NYR	3	80	25	27	52	18	....	....	....	....	....	....	1940-41	1944-45
Thurlby, Tom	Oak.	1	20	1	1	2	4	....	....	....	....	....	....	1967-68	1967-68
Thyer, Mario	Min.	1	5	0	0	0	0	1	0	0	0	2	....	1989-90	1989-90
Tichy, Milan	Chi., NYI	3	23	0	5	5	40	....	....	....	....	....	....	1992-93	1995-96
Tidey, Alex	Buf., Edm.	3	9	0	0	0	8	2	0	0	0	0	....	1976-77	1979-80
‡ Tilley, Tom	St.L.	4	174	4	38	42	89	14	1	3	4	19	....	1988-89	1993-94
● Timgren, Ray	Tor., Chi.	6	251	14	44	58	70	30	3	9	12	6	2	1948-49	1954-55
Tinordi, Mark	NYR, Min., Dal., Wsh.	12	663	52	148	200	1514	70	7	11	18	165	....	1987-88	1998-99
Tippett, Dave	Hfd., Wsh., Pit., Phi.	11	721	93	169	262	317	62	6	16	22	34	....	1983-84	1993-94
Titanic, Morris	Buf.	2	19	0	0	0	0	....	....	....	....	....	....	1974-75	1975-76
Tkaczuk, Walt	NYR	14	945	227	451	678	556	93	19	32	51	119	....	1967-68	1980-81
Toal, Mike	Edm.	1	3	0	0	0	0	....	....	....	....	....	....	1979-80	1979-80
Todd, Kevin	N.J., Edm., Chi., L.A., Ana.	9	383	70	133	203	225	12	3	2	5	16	....	1988-89	1997-98
Tomalty, Glenn	Wpg.	1	1	0	0	0	0	....	....	....	....	....	....	1979-80	1979-80
Tomlak, Mike	Hfd.	4	141	15	22	37	103	10	0	1	1	4	....	1989-90	1993-94
‡ Tomlinson, Dave	Tor., Wpg., Fla.	4	42	1	3	4	28	....	....	....	....	....	....	1991-92	1994-95
Tomlinson, Kirk	Min.	1	1	0	0	0	0	....	....	....	....	....	....	1987-88	1987-88
Tomson, Jack	NYA	3	15	1	1	2	0	2	0	0	0	0	....	1938-39	1940-41
Tonelli, John	NYI, Cgy., L.A., Chi., Que.	14	1028	325	511	836	911	172	40	75	115	200	4	1978-79	1991-92
Tookey, Tim	Wsh., Que., Pit., Phi., L.A.	7	106	22	36	58	71	10	1	3	4	2	....	1980-81	1988-89
Toomey, Sean	Min.	1	1	0	0	0	0	....	....	....	....	....	....	1986-87	1986-87
‡ Toporowski, Shayne	Tor.	1	3	0	0	0	7	....	....	....	....	....	....	1996-97	1996-97
Toppazzini, Jerry	Bos., Chi., Det.	12	783	163	244	407	436	40	13	9	22	13	....	1952-53	1963-64
● Toppazzini, Zellio	Bos., NYR, Chi.	5	123	21	22	43	49	2	0	0	0	0	....	1948-49	1956-57
‡ Torgaev, Pavel	Cgy., T.B.	2	55	6	14	20	20	1	0	0	0	0	....	1995-96	1999-00
‡ Torkki, Jari	Chi.	1	4	1	0	1	0	....	....	....	....	....	....	1988-89	1988-89
‡ Tormanen, Antti	Ott.	1	50	7	8	15	28	....	....	....	....	....	....	1995-96	1995-96
● Touhey, Bill	Mtl.M., Ott., Bos.	7	280	65	40	105	107	2	1	0	1	0	....	1927-28	1933-34
● Toupin, Jacques	Chi.	1	8	1	2	3	0	4	0	0	0	0	....	1943-44	1943-44
● Townsend, Art	Chi.	1	5	0	0	0	0	....	....	....	....	....	....	1926-27	1926-27
Townshend, Graeme	Bos., NYI, Ott.	5	45	3	7	10	28	....	....	....	....	....	....	1989-90	1993-94
Trader, Larry	Det., St.L., Mtl.	4	91	5	13	18	74	3	0	0	0	0	....	1982-83	1987-88
● Trainor, Wes	NYR	1	17	1	2	3	6	....	....	....	....	....	....	1948-49	1948-49
● Trapp, Bob	Chi.	2	82	4	4	8	129	2	0	0	0	4	....	1926-27	1927-28
Trapp, Doug	Buf.	1	2	0	0	0	0	....	....	....	....	....	....	1986-87	1986-87
● Traub, Percy	Chi., Det.	3	130	3	3	6	217	4	0	0	0	6	....	1926-27	1928-29
Tredway, Brock	L.A.	1	....	....	....	....	....	1	0	0	0	0	....	1981-82	1981-82
Tremblay, Brent	Wsh.	2	10	1	0	1	6	....	....	....	....	....	....	1978-79	1979-80
Tremblay, Gilles	Mtl.	9	509	168	162	330	161	48	9	14	23	4	3	1960-61	1968-69
● Tremblay, J.C.	Mtl.	13	794	57	306	363	204	108	14	51	65	58	5	1959-60	1971-72
Tremblay, Marcel	Mtl.C.	1	10	0	2	2	0	....	....	....	....	....	....	1938-39	1938-39
Tremblay, Mario	Mtl.	12	852	258	326	584	1043	101	20	29	49	187	5	1974-75	1985-86
● Tremblay, Nil	Mtl.	2	3	0	1	1	0	2	0	0	0	0	....	1944-45	1945-46
Trimper, Tim	Chi., Wpg., Min.	6	190	30	36	66	153	2	0	0	0	2	....	1979-80	1984-85
Trottier, Bryan	NYI, Pit.	18	1279	524	901	1425	912	221	71	113	184	277	6	1975-76	1993-94
● Trottier, Dave	Mtl.M., Det.	11	446	121	113	234	517	31	4	3	7	39	1	1928-29	1938-39
Trottier, Guy	NYR, Tor.	3	115	28	17	45	37	9	1	0	1	16	....	1968-69	1971-72
Trottier, Rocky	N.J.	2	38	6	4	10	2	....	....	....	....	....	....	1983-84	1984-85
● Trudel, Lou	Chi., Mtl.C., Mtl.	8	306	49	69	118	122	24	1	3	4	4	2	1933-34	1940-41
Trudell, Rene	NYR	3	129	24	28	52	72	5	0	0	0	2	....	1945-46	1947-48
‡ Tsulygin, Nikolai	Ana.	1	22	0	1	1	8	....	....	....	....	....	....	1996-97	1996-97
‡ Tsygurov, Denis	Buf., L.A.	3	51	1	5	6	45	....	....	....	....	....	....	1993-94	1995-96
‡ Tucker, John	Buf., Wsh., NYI, T.B.	12	656	177	259	436	285	31	10	18	28	24	....	1983-84	1995-96
● Tudin, Connie	Mtl.	1	4	0	1	1	4	....	....	....	....	....	....	1941-42	1941-42
Tudor, Rob	Van., St.L.	3	28	4	4	8	19	3	0	0	0	0	....	1978-79	1982-83
Tuer, Allan	L.A., Min., Hfd.	4	57	1	1	2	208	....	....	....	....	....	....	1985-86	1989-90
Turcotte, Alfie	Mtl., Wpg., Wsh.	7	112	17	29	46	49	5	0	0	0	0	....	1983-84	1990-91
‡ Turgeon, Sylvain	Hfd., N.J., Mtl., Ott.	12	669	269	226	495	691	36	4	7	11	22	....	1983-84	1994-95
Turlick, Gord	Bos.	1	2	0	0	0	2	....	....	....	....	....	....	1959-60	1959-60
Turnbull, Ian	Tor., L.A., Pit.	10	628	123	317	440	736	55	13	32	45	94	....	1973-74	1982-83
Turnbull, Perry	St.L., Mtl., Wpg.	9	608	188	163	351	1245	34	6	7	13	86	....	1979-80	1987-88
Turnbull, Randy	Cgy.	1	1	0	0	0	2	....	....	....	....	....	....	1981-82	1981-82
Turner, Bob	Mtl., Chi.	8	478	19	51	70	307	68	1	4	5	44	5	1955-56	1962-63
Turner, Brad	NYI	1	3	0	0	0	0	....	....	....	....	....	....	1991-92	1991-92
Turner, Dean	NYR, Col., L.A.	4	35	1	0	1	59	....	....	....	....	....	....	1978-79	1982-83
● Tustin, Norm	NYR	1	18	2	4	6	0	....	....	....	....	....	....	1941-42	1941-42
Tuten, Aut	Chi.	2	39	4	8	12	48	....	....	....	....	....	....	1941-42	1942-43
‡ Tutt, Brian	Wsh.	1	7	1	0	1	2	....	....	....	....	....	....	1989-90	1989-90
Tuttle, Steve	St.L.	3	144	28	28	56	12	17	1	6	7	2	....	1988-89	1990-91

U V

Name	NHL Teams	NHL Seasons	Regular Schedule GP	G	A	TP	PIM	Playoffs GP	G	A	TP	PIM	NHL Cup Wins	First NHL Season	Last NHL Season
Ubriaco, Gene	Pit., Oak., Chi.	3	177	39	35	74	50	11	2	0	2	4	....	1967-68	1969-70
Ullman, Norm	Det., Tor.	20	1410	490	739	1229	712	106	30	53	83	67	....	1955-56	1974-75
Unger, Garry	Tor., Det., St.L., Atl., L.A., Edm.	16	1105	413	391	804	1075	52	12	18	30	105	....	1967-68	1982-83
Vachon, Nick	NYI	1	1	0	0	0	0	....	....	....	....	....	....	1996-97	1996-97
Vadnais, Carol	Mtl., Oak., Cal., Bos., NYR, N.J.	17	1087	169	418	587	1813	106	10	40	50	185	2	1966-67	1982-83
Vail, Eric	Atl., Cgy., Det.	9	591	216	260	476	281	20	5	6	11	6	....	1973-74	1981-82
● Vail, Sparky	NYR	2	50	4	1	5	18	10	0	0	0	2	....	1928-29	1929-30
Vaive, Rick	Van., Tor., Chi., Buf.	13	876	441	347	788	1445	54	27	16	43	111	....	1979-80	1991-92
Valentine, Chris	Wsh.	3	105	43	52	95	127	2	0	0	0	4	....	1981-82	1983-84
Valiquette, Jack	Tor., Col.	7	350	84	134	218	79	23	3	6	9	4	....	1974-75	1980-81
‡ Vallis, Lindsay	Mtl.	1	1	0	0	0	0	....	....	....	....	....	....	1993-94	1993-94
Van Boxmeer, John	Mtl., Col., Buf., Que.	11	588	84	274	358	465	38	5	15	20	37	1	1973-74	1983-84
Van Dorp, Wayne	Edm., Pit., Chi., Que.	6	125	12	12	24	565	27	0	1	1	42	....	1986-87	1991-92
‡ Van Drunen, David	Ott.	1	1	0	0	0	0	....	....	....	....	....	....	1999-00	1999-00
Van Impe, Ed	Chi., Phi., Pit.	11	700	27	126	153	1025	66	1	12	13	131	2	1966-67	1976-77
‡ Varvio, Jarkko	Dal.	2	13	3	4	7	4	....	....	....	....	....	....	1993-94	1994-95
‡ Vasilevski, Alexander	St.L.	2	4	0	0	0	2	....	....	....	....	....	....	1995-96	1996-97
Vaske, Dennis	NYI, Bos.	9	235	5	41	46	253	22	0	7	7	16	....	1990-91	1998-99
● Vasko, Moose	Chi., Min.	13	786	34	166	200	719	78	2	7	9	73	1	1956-57	1969-70
Vasko, Rick	Det.	3	31	3	7	10	29	....	....	....	....	....	....	1977-78	1980-81
Vautour, Yvon	NYI, Col., N.J., Que.	6	204	26	33	59	401	....	....	....	....	....	....	1979-80	1984-85
Vaydik, Greg	Chi.	1	5	0	0	0	0	....	....	....	....	....	....	1976-77	1976-77
Veitch, Darren	Wsh., Det., Tor.	10	511	48	209	257	296	33	4	11	15	33	....	1980-81	1990-91
Velischek, Randy	Min., N.J., Que.	10	509	21	76	97	401	44	2	5	7	32	....	1982-83	1991-92
Vellucci, Mike	Hfd.	1	2	0	0	0	11	....	....	....	....	....	....	1987-88	1987-88
Venasky, Vic	L.A.	7	430	61	101	162	66	21	1	5	6	12	....	1972-73	1978-79
Veneruzzo, Gary	St.L.	2	7	1	1	2	0	9	0	2	2	2	....	1967-68	1971-72
Vermette, Mark	Que.	4	67	5	13	18	33	....	....	....	....	....	....	1988-89	1991-92
‡ Verret, Claude	Buf.	2	14	2	5	7	2	....	....	....	....	....	....	1983-84	1984-85
Verstraete, Leigh	Tor.	3	8	0	1	1	14	....	....	....	....	....	....	1982-83	1987-88
Ververgaert, Dennis	Van., Phi., Wsh.	8	583	176	216	392	247	8	1	2	3	6	....	1973-74	1980-81
Vesey, Jim	St.L., Bos.	3	15	1	2	3	7	....	....	....	....	....	....	1988-89	1991-92
Veysey, Sid	Van.	1	1	0	0	0	0	....	....	....	....	....	....	1977-78	1977-78
‡ Vial, Dennis	NYR, Det., Ott.	8	242	4	15	19	794	....	....	....	....	....	....	1990-91	1997-98
Vickers, Steve	NYR	10	698	246	340	586	330	68	24	25	49	58	....	1972-73	1981-82
Vigneault, Alain	St.L.	2	42	2	5	7	82	4	0	1	1	26	....	1981-82	1982-83
‡ Viitakoski, Vesa	Cgy.	3	23	2	4	6	8	....	....	....	....	....	....	1993-94	1995-96
‡ Vilgrain, Claude	Van., N.J., Phi.	5	89	21	32	53	78	11	1	1	2	17	....	1987-88	1993-94
Vincelette, Dan	Chi., Que.	6	193	20	22	42	351	12	0	0	0	4	....	1986-87	1991-92
Vipond, Pete	Cal.	1	3	0	0	0	0	....	....	....	....	....	....	1972-73	1972-73
Virta, Hannu	Buf.	5	245	25	101	126	66	17	1	3	4	6	....	1981-82	1985-86
‡ Visheau, Mark	Wpg., L.A.	2	29	1	3	4	107	....	....	....	....	....	....	1993-94	1998-99
‡ Vitolinsh, Harijs	Wpg.	1	8	0	0	0	4	....	....	....	....	....	....	1993-94	1993-94
‡ Viveiros, Emanuel	Min.	3	29	1	11	12	6	....	....	....	....	....	....	1985-86	1987-88

Harry Watson

Joe Watson

Wally Weir

Brian Wilks

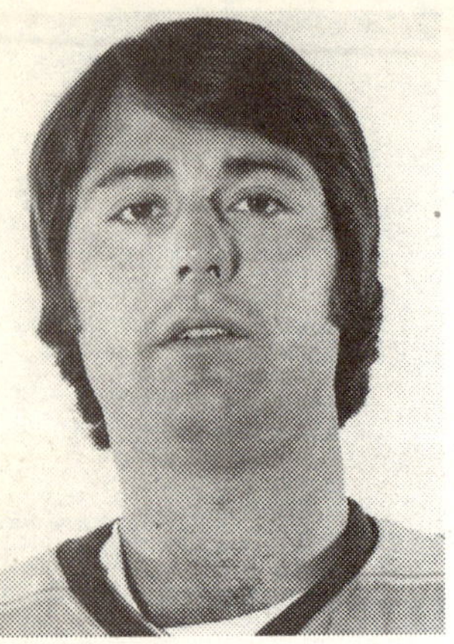
Tommy Williams

Murray Wilson

Ken Yaremchuk

C.J. Young

			Regular Schedule					Playoffs					NHL	First	Last
Name	NHL Teams	NHL Seasons	GP	G	A	TP	PIM	GP	G	A	TP	PIM	Cup Wins	NHL Season	NHL Season
● Vokes, Ed	Chi.	1	5	0	0	0	0	....	....	....	....	....	....	1930-31	1930-31
Volcan, Mickey	Hfd., Cgy.	4	162	8	33	41	146	....	....	....	....	....	....	1980-81	1983-84
Volek, David	NYI	6	396	95	154	249	201	15	5	5	10	2	....	1988-89	1993-94
Volmar, Doug	Det., L.A.	4	62	13	8	21	26	2	1	0	1	0	....	1969-70	1972-73
‡ Von Stefenelli, Phil	Bos., Ott.	2	33	0	5	5	23	....	....	....	....	....	....	1995-96	1996-97
‡ Vopat, Roman	St.L., L.A., Chi., Phi.	4	133	6	14	20	253	....	....	....	....	....	....	1995-96	1998-99
‡ Vorobiev, Vladimir	NYR, Edm.	3	33	9	7	16	14	1	0	0	0	0	....	1996-97	1998-99
● Voss, Carl	Tor., NYR, Det., Ott., St.L., NYA, Mtl.M., Chi.	8	261	34	70	104	50	24	5	3	8	0	1	1926-27	1937-38
Vukota, Mick	NYI, T.B., Mtl.	11	574	17	29	46	2071	23	0	0	0	73	....	1987-88	1997-98
Vyazmikin, Igor	Edm.	1	4	1	0	1	0	....	....	....	....	....	....	1990-91	1990-91

W

Waddell, Don	L.A.	1	1	0	0	0	0	....	....	....	....	....	....	1980-81	1980-81
● Waite, Frank	NYR	1	17	1	3	4	4	....	....	....	....	....	....	1930-31	1930-31
Walker, Gord	NYR, L.A.	4	31	3	4	7	23	....	....	....	....	....	....	1986-87	1989-90
Walker, Howard	Wsh., Cgy.	3	83	2	13	15	133	....	....	....	....	....	....	1980-81	1982-83
● Walker, Jack	Det.	2	80	5	8	13	18	....	....	....	....	....	....	1926-27	1927-28
Walker, Kurt	Tor.	3	71	4	5	9	142	16	0	0	0	34	....	1975-76	1977-78
Walker, Russ	L.A.	2	17	1	0	1	41	....	....	....	....	....	....	1976-77	1977-78
Wall, Bob	Det., L.A., St.L.	8	322	30	55	85	155	22	0	3	3	2	....	1964-65	1971-72
Wallin, Peter	NYR	2	52	3	14	17	14	14	2	6	8	6	....	1980-81	1981-82
Walsh, Jim	Buf.	1	4	0	1	1	4	....	....	....	....	....	....	1981-82	1981-82
Walsh, Mike	NYI	2	14	2	0	2	4	....	....	....	....	....	....	1987-88	1988-89
Walter, Ryan	Wsh., Mtl., Van.	15	1003	264	382	646	946	113	16	35	51	62	1	1978-79	1992-93
● Walton, Bobby	Mtl.	1	4	0	0	0	0	....	....	....	....	....	....	1943-44	1943-44
Walton, Mike	Tor., Bos., Van., St.L., Chi.	12	588	201	247	448	357	47	14	10	24	45	2	1965-66	1978-79
Wappel, Gord	Atl., Cgy.	3	20	1	1	2	10	2	0	0	0	4	....	1979-80	1981-82
Ward, Don	Chi., Bos.	2	34	0	1	1	16	....	....	....	....	....	....	1957-58	1959-60
● Ward, Jimmy	Mtl.M., Mtl.C.	12	527	147	127	274	455	36	4	4	8	26	1	1927-28	1938-39
Ward, Joe	Col.	1	4	0	0	0	2	....	....	....	....	....	....	1980-81	1980-81
Ward, Ron	Tor., Van.	2	89	2	5	7	6	....	....	....	....	....	....	1969-70	1971-72
Ware, Michael	Edm.	2	5	0	1	1	15	....	....	....	....	....	....	1988-89	1989-90
● Wares, Eddie	NYR, Det., Chi.	9	321	60	102	162	161	45	5	7	12	34	1	1936-37	1946-47
Warner, Bob	Tor.	2	10	1	1	2	4	4	0	0	0	0	....	1975-76	1976-77
Warner, Jim	Hfd.	1	32	0	3	3	10	....	....	....	....	....	....	1979-80	1979-80
Warwick, Bill	NYR	2	14	3	3	6	16	....	....	....	....	....	....	1942-43	1943-44
● Warwick, Grant	NYR, Bos., Mtl.	9	395	147	142	289	220	16	2	4	6	6	....	1941-42	1949-50
● Wasnie, Nick	Chi., Mtl.C., NYA, Ott., St.L.	7	248	57	34	91	176	20	6	3	9	20	2	1927-28	1934-35
Watson, Bill	Chi.	4	115	23	36	59	12	6	0	2	2	0	....	1985-86	1988-89
Watson, Bryan	Mtl., Det., Oak., Pit., St.L., Wsh.	16	878	17	135	152	2212	32	2	0	2	70	....	1963-64	1978-79
Watson, Dave	Col.	2	18	0	1	1	10	....	....	....	....	....	....	1979-80	1980-81
Watson, Harry	Bro., Det., Tor., Chi.	14	809	236	207	443	150	62	16	9	25	27	5	1941-42	1956-57
Watson, Jim	Det., Buf.	8	221	4	19	23	345	....	....	....	....	....	....	1963-64	1971-72
Watson, Jimmy	Phi.	10	613	38	148	186	492	101	5	34	39	89	2	1972-73	1981-82
Watson, Joe	Bos., Phi., Col.	14	835	38	178	216	447	84	3	12	15	82	2	1964-65	1978-79
● Watson, Phil	NYR, Mtl.	13	590	144	265	409	532	54	10	25	35	67	2	1935-36	1947-48
Watters, Tim	Wpg., L.A.	14	741	26	151	177	1289	82	1	5	6	115	....	1981-82	1994-95
Watts, Brian	Det.	1	4	0	0	0	0	....	....	....	....	....	....	1975-76	1975-76
● Webster, Aubrey	Phi., Mtl.M.	2	5	0	0	0	0	....	....	....	....	....	....	1930-31	1934-35
● Webster, Don	Tor.	1	27	7	6	13	28	5	0	0	0	12	....	1943-44	1943-44
Webster, John	NYR	1	14	0	0	0	4	....	....	....	....	....	....	1949-50	1949-50
Webster, Tom	Bos., Det., Cal.	5	102	33	42	75	61	1	0	0	0	0	....	1968-69	1979-80
● Weiland, Cooney	Bos., Ott., Det.	11	509	173	160	333	147	45	12	10	22	12	2	1928-29	1938-39
Weir, Stan	Cal., Tor., Edm., Col., Det.	10	642	139	207	346	183	37	6	5	11	4	....	1972-73	1982-83
Weir, Wally	Que., Hfd., Pit.	6	320	21	45	66	625	23	0	1	1	96	....	1979-80	1984-85
● Wellington, Alex	Que.	1	1	0	0	0	0	....	....	....	....	....	....	1919-20	1919-20
Wells, Jay	L.A., Phi., Buf., NYR, St.L., T.B.	18	1098	47	216	263	2359	114	3	14	17	213	1	1979-80	1996-97
Wensink, John	St.L., Bos., Que., Col., N.J.	8	403	70	68	138	840	43	2	6	8	86	....	1973-74	1982-83
● Wentworth, Cy	Chi., Mtl.M., Mtl.C., Mtl.	13	575	39	68	107	355	35	5	6	11	20	1	1927-28	1939-40
‡ Wesenberg, Brian	Phi.	1	1	0	0	0	5	....	....	....	....	....	....	1998-99	1998-99
Wesley, Blake	Phi., Hfd., Que., Tor.	7	298	18	46	64	486	19	2	2	4	30	....	1979-80	1985-86
Westfall, Ed	Bos., NYI	18	1220	231	394	625	544	95	22	37	59	41	2	1961-62	1978-79
Wharram, Kenny	Chi.	14	766	252	281	533	222	80	16	27	43	38	1	1951-52	1968-69
Wharton, Len	NYR	1	1	0	0	0	0	....	....	....	....	....	....	1944-45	1944-45
‡ Wheeldon, Simon	NYR, Wpg.	3	15	0	2	2	10	....	....	....	....	....	....	1987-88	1990-91
● Wheldon, Don	St.L.	1	2	0	0	0	0	....	....	....	....	....	....	1974-75	1974-75
Whelton, Bill	Wpg.	1	2	0	0	0	0	....	....	....	....	....	....	1980-81	1980-81
Whistle, Rob	NYR, St.L.	2	51	7	5	12	16	4	0	0	0	2	....	1985-86	1987-88
White, Bill	L.A., Chi.	9	604	50	215	265	495	91	7	32	39	76	....	1967-68	1975-76
White, Moe	Mtl.	1	4	0	1	1	2	....	....	....	....	....	....	1945-46	1945-46
● White, Sherman	NYR	2	4	0	2	2	0	....	....	....	....	....	....	1946-47	1949-50
● White, Tex	Pit., NYA, Phi.	6	203	33	12	45	141	4	0	0	0	4	....	1925-26	1930-31
White, Tony	Wsh., Min.	5	164	37	28	65	104	....	....	....	....	....	....	1974-75	1979-80
Whitelaw, Bob	Det.	2	32	0	2	2	2	8	0	0	0	0	....	1940-41	1941-42
Whitlock, Bob	Min.	1	1	0	0	0	0	....	....	....	....	....	....	1969-70	1969-70
‡ Whyte, Sean	L.A.	2	21	0	2	2	12	....	....	....	....	....	....	1991-92	1992-93
● Wickenheiser, Doug	Mtl., St.L., Van., NYR, Wsh.	10	556	111	165	276	286	41	4	7	11	18	....	1980-81	1989-90
● Widing, Juha	NYR, L.A., Cle.	8	575	144	226	370	208	8	1	2	3	2	....	1969-70	1976-77
‡ Widmer, Jason	NYI, S.J.	3	7	0	1	1	7	....	....	....	....	....	....	1994-95	1996-97
● Wiebe, Art	Chi.	11	414	14	27	41	201	31	1	3	4	10	1	1932-33	1943-44
Wiemer, Jim	Buf., NYR, Edm., L.A., Bos.	11	325	29	72	101	378	62	5	8	13	63	....	1982-83	1993-94
● Wilcox, Archie	Mtl.M., Bos., St.L.	6	208	8	14	22	158	12	1	0	1	8	....	1929-30	1934-35
Wilcox, Barry	Van.	2	33	3	2	5	15	....	....	....	....	....	....	1972-73	1974-75
Wilder, Arch	Det.	1	18	0	2	2	2	....	....	....	....	....	....	1940-41	1940-41
Wiley, Jim	Pit., Van.	5	63	4	10	14	8	....	....	....	....	....	....	1972-73	1976-77
Wilkie, Bob	Det., Phi.	2	18	2	5	7	10	....	....	....	....	....	....	1990-91	1993-94
Wilkins, Barry	Bos., Van., Pit.	9	418	27	125	152	663	6	0	1	1	4	....	1966-67	1975-76
● Wilkinson, John	Bos.	1	9	0	0	0	6	....	....	....	....	....	....	1943-44	1943-44
Wilkinson, Neil	Min., S.J., Chi., Wpg., Pit.	10	460	16	67	83	813	53	3	6	9	41	....	1989-90	1998-99
Wilks, Brian	L.A.	4	48	4	8	12	27	....	....	....	....	....	....	1984-85	1988-89
Willard, Rod	Tor.	1	1	0	0	0	0	....	....	....	....	....	....	1982-83	1982-83
● Williams, Burr	Det., St.L., Bos.	3	19	0	1	1	28	7	0	0	0	8	....	1933-34	1936-37
Williams, Butch	St.L., Cal.	3	108	14	35	49	131	....	....	....	....	....	....	1973-74	1975-76
Williams, Darryl	L.A.	1	2	0	0	0	10	....	....	....	....	....	....	1992-93	1992-93
Williams, David	S.J., Ana.	4	173	11	53	64	157	....	....	....	....	....	....	1991-92	1994-95
Williams, Fred	Det.	1	44	2	5	7	10	....	....	....	....	....	....	1976-77	1976-77
Williams, Gord	Phi.	2	2	0	0	0	2	....	....	....	....	....	....	1981-82	1982-83
Williams, Sean	Chi.	1	2	0	0	0	4	....	....	....	....	....	....	1991-92	1991-92
Williams, Tiger	Tor., Van., Det., L.A., Hfd.	14	962	241	272	513	3966	83	12	23	35	455	....	1974-75	1987-88
Williams, Tom	NYR, L.A.	8	397	115	138	253	73	29	8	7	15	4	....	1971-72	1978-79
● Williams, Tommy	Bos., Min., Cal., Wsh.	13	663	161	269	430	177	10	2	5	7	2	....	1961-62	1975-76
Willson, Don	Mtl.C.	2	22	2	7	9	0	3	0	0	0	0	....	1937-38	1938-39
Wilson, Behn	Phi., Chi.	9	601	98	260	358	1480	67	12	29	41	190	....	1978-79	1987-88
● Wilson, Bert	NYR, St.L., L.A., Cgy.	8	478	37	44	81	646	21	0	2	2	42	....	1973-74	1980-81
Wilson, Bob	Chi.	1	1	0	0	0	0	....	....	....	....	....	....	1953-54	1953-54
Wilson, Carey	Cgy., Hfd., NYR	10	552	169	258	427	314	52	11	13	24	14	....	1983-84	1992-93
● Wilson, Cully	Tor., Mtl.C., Ham., Chi.	5	127	59	28	87	243	2	1	0	1	6	....	1919-20	1926-27
Wilson, Doug	Chi., S.J.	16	1024	237	590	827	830	95	19	61	80	88	....	1977-78	1992-93
Wilson, Gord	Bos.	1	....	....	....	....	....	2	0	0	0	0	....	1954-55	1954-55
Wilson, Hub	NYA	1	2	0	0	0	0	....	....	....	....	....	....	1931-32	1931-32
Wilson, Jerry	Mtl.	1	3	0	0	0	2	....	....	....	....	....	....	1956-57	1956-57
Wilson, Johnny	Det., Chi., Tor., NYR	13	688	161	171	332	190	66	14	13	27	11	4	1949-50	1961-62
● Wilson, Larry	Det., Chi.	6	152	21	48	69	75	4	0	0	0	0	1	1949-50	1955-56
Wilson, Mitch	N.J., Pit.	2	26	2	3	5	104	....	....	....	....	....	....	1984-85	1986-87
Wilson, Murray	Mtl., L.A.	7	386	94	95	189	162	53	5	14	19	32	4	1972-73	1978-79
Wilson, Rick	Mtl., St.L., Det.	4	239	6	26	32	165	3	0	0	0	0	....	1973-74	1976-77
Wilson, Rik	St.L., Cgy., Chi.	6	251	25	65	90	220	22	0	4	4	23	....	1981-82	1987-88
Wilson, Roger	Chi.	1	7	0	2	2	6	....	....	....	....	....	....	1974-75	1974-75
Wilson, Ron	Tor., Min.	7	177	26	67	93	68	20	4	13	17	8	....	1977-78	1987-88
Wilson, Ron	Wpg., St.L., Mtl.	14	832	110	216	326	415	63	10	12	22	64	....	1979-80	1993-94
Wilson, Wally	Bos.	1	53	11	8	19	18	1	0	0	0	0	....	1947-48	1947-48
Wing, Murray	Det.	1	1	0	1	1	0	....	....	....	....	....	....	1973-74	1973-74
‡ Winnes, Chris	Bos., Phi.	4	33	1	6	7	6	1	0	0	0	0	....	1990-91	1993-94
● Wiseman, Eddie	Det., NYA, Bos.	10	456	115	165	280	136	43	10	10	20	16	1	1932-33	1941-42

			Regular Schedule					Playoffs							
Name	NHL Teams	NHL Seasons	GP	G	A	TP	PIM	GP	G	A	TP	PIM	NHL Cup Wins	First NHL Season	Last NHL Season
Wiste, Jim	Chi., Van.	3	52	1	10	11	8	....	....	....	....	....	....	1968-69	1970-71
Witherspoon, Jim	L.A.	1	2	0	0	0	2	....	....	....	....	....	....	1975-76	1975-76
Witiuk, Steve	Chi.	1	33	3	8	11	14	....	....	....	....	....	....	1951-52	1951-52
Woit, Benny	Det., Chi.	7	334	7	26	33	170	41	2	6	8	18	3	1950-51	1956-57
Wojciechowski, Steve	Det.	2	54	19	20	39	17	6	0	1	1	0	....	1944-45	1946-47
Wolanin, Craig	N.J., Que., Col., T.B., Tor.	13	695	40	133	173	894	35	4	6	10	67	1	1985-86	1997-98
Wolf, Bennett	Pit.	3	30	0	1	1	133	....	....	....	....	....	....	1980-81	1982-83
Wong, Mike	Det.	1	22	1	1	2	12	....	....	....	....	....	....	1975-76	1975-76
Wood, Randy	NYI, Buf., Tor., Dal.	11	741	175	159	334	603	51	8	9	17	40	....	1986-87	1996-97
Wood, Robert	NYR	1	1	0	0	0	0	....	....	....	....	....	....	1950-51	1950-51
Woodley, Dan	Van.	1	5	2	0	2	17	....	....	....	....	....	....	1987-88	1987-88
Woods, Paul	Det.	7	501	72	124	196	276	7	0	5	5	4	....	1977-78	1983-84
‡ Wortman, Kevin	Cgy.	1	5	0	0	0	2	....	....	....	....	....	....	1993-94	1993-94
• Woytowich, Bob	Bos., Min., Pit., L.A.	8	503	32	126	158	352	24	1	3	4	20	....	1964-65	1971-72
Wright, John	Van., St.L., K.C.	3	127	16	36	52	67	....	....	....	....	....	....	1972-73	1974-75
Wright, Keith	Phi.	1	1	0	0	0	0	....	....	....	....	....	....	1967-68	1967-68
Wright, Larry	Phi., Cal., Det.	5	106	4	8	12	19	....	....	....	....	....	....	1971-72	1977-78
Wycherley, Ralph	NYA, Bro.	2	28	4	7	11	6	....	....	....	....	....	....	1940-41	1941-42
• Wylie, Bill	NYR	1	1	0	0	0	0	....	....	....	....	....	....	1950-51	1950-51
Wylie, Duane	Chi.	2	14	3	3	6	2	....	....	....	....	....	....	1974-75	1976-77
Wyrozub, Randy	Buf.	4	100	8	10	18	10	....	....	....	....	....	....	1970-71	1973-74

Y Z

• Yackel, Ken	Bos.	1	6	0	0	0	2	2	0	0	0	2	....	1958-59	1958-59
Yaremchuk, Gary	Tor.	4	34	1	4	5	28	....	....	....	....	....	....	1981-82	1984-85
Yaremchuk, Ken	Chi., Tor.	6	235	36	56	92	106	31	6	8	14	49	....	1983-84	1988-89
Yates, Ross	Hfd.	1	7	1	1	2	4	....	....	....	....	....	....	1983-84	1983-84
Yawney, Trent	Chi., Cgy., St.L.	12	593	27	102	129	783	60	9	17	26	81	....	1987-88	1998-99
York, Harry	St.L., NYR, Pit., Van.	4	244	29	46	75	99	5	0	0	0	2	....	1996-97	1999-00
Young, Brian	Chi.	1	8	0	2	2	6	....	....	....	....	....	....	1980-81	1980-81
Young, C.J.	Cgy., Bos.	1	43	7	7	14	32	....	....	....	....	....	....	1992-93	1992-93
• Young, Doug	Det., Mtl.	10	388	35	45	80	303	28	1	5	6	16	2	1931-32	1940-41
• Young, Howie	Det., Chi., Van.	8	336	12	62	74	851	19	2	4	6	46	....	1960-61	1970-71
Young, Tim	Min., Wpg., Phi.	10	628	195	341	536	438	36	7	24	31	27	....	1975-76	1984-85
Young, Warren	Min., Pit., Det.	7	236	72	77	149	472	....	....	....	....	....	....	1981-82	1987-88
Younghans, Tom	Min., NYR	6	429	44	41	85	373	24	2	1	3	21	....	1976-77	1981-82
‡ Ysebaert, Paul	N.J., Det., Wpg., Chi., T.B.	11	532	149	187	336	217	30	4	3	7	20	....	1988-89	1998-99
‡ Zabransky, Libor	St.L.	2	40	1	6	7	50	....	....	....	....	....	....	1996-97	1997-98
Zaharko, Miles	Atl., Chi.	4	129	5	32	37	84	3	0	0	0	0	....	1977-78	1981-82
Zaine, Rod	Pit., Buf.	2	61	10	6	16	25	....	....	....	....	....	....	1970-71	1971-72
Zanussi, Joe	NYR, Bos., St.L.	3	87	1	13	14	46	4	0	1	1	2	....	1974-75	1976-77
Zanussi, Ron	Min., Tor.	5	299	52	83	135	373	17	0	4	4	17	....	1977-78	1981-82
Zavisha, Brad	Edm.	1	2	0	0	0	0	....	....	....	....	....	....	1993-94	1993-94
Zeidel, Larry	Det., Chi., Phi.	5	158	3	16	19	198	12	0	1	1	12	1	1951-52	1968-69
Zemlak, Richard	Que., Min., Pit., Cgy.	5	132	2	12	14	587	1	0	0	0	10	....	1986-87	1991-92
Zeniuk, Ed	Det.	1	2	0	0	0	0	....	....	....	....	....	....	1954-55	1954-55
Zent, Jason	Ott., Phi.	3	27	3	3	6	13	....	....	....	....	....	....	1996-97	1998-99
Zetterstrom, Lars	Van.	1	14	0	1	1	2	....	....	....	....	....	....	1978-79	1978-79
Zezel, Peter	Phi., St.L., Wsh., Tor., Dal., N.J., Van.	15	873	219	389	608	435	131	25	39	64	83	....	1984-85	1998-99
‡ Zmolek, Doug	S.J., Dal., L.A., Chi.	8	467	11	53	64	905	14	0	1	1	16	....	1992-93	1999-00
Zoborosky, Marty	Chi.	1	1	0	0	0	2	....	....	....	....	....	....	1944-45	1944-45
Zombo, Rick	Det., St.L., Bos.	12	652	24	130	154	728	60	1	11	12	127	....	1984-85	1995-96
Zuke, Mike	St.L., Hfd.	8	455	86	196	282	220	26	6	6	12	12	....	1978-79	1985-86
Zunich, Rudy	Det.	1	2	0	0	0	2	....	....	....	....	....	....	1943-44	1943-44

Tom Younghans

Jason Zent

Retired Players, Goaltenders and Coaches Research Project

Throughout the Retired Players and Retired Goaltenders sections of this book, you will notice many players with a bullet (•) by their names. These players, according to our records, are deceased. The editors recognize that our information on the death dates of NHLers is incomplete. If you have documented information on the passing of any player not marked with a bullet (•) in this edition, we would like to hear from you. We also welcome information on deceased NHL head coaches. Please send this information to:

Retired Player Research Project
c/o NHL Publishing
194 Dovercourt Road
Toronto, Ontario
M6J 3C8 Canada
Fax: 416/531-3939

Many thanks to the following contributors in 2000-01:

Patricia Barry, Ed Calhoun, Paul R. Carroll, Jr., Bob Duff, Peter Fillman, Ernie Fitzsimmons, Mel Foster, Glen Goodhand, Bob Gregoire, Michelle G. Keller, Christopher MacDonald, Gordon Mills, Joseph Nieforth, John Paton, Gary J. Pearce, Ed Sweeney, Marie Woodruff.

Gerry Cheevers

Grant Fuhr

Jacques Plante

Roger Crozier

Harry Lumley

Daren Puppa

John Davidson

Gilles Meloche

Bill Ranford

Jake Forbes

Darren Pang

Lorne Worsley

Retired NHL Goaltender Index

Abbreviations: Teams/Cities: – **Ana.** – Anaheim; **Atl.** – Atlanta; **Bos.** – Boston; **Bro.** – Brooklyn; **Buf.** – Buffalo; **Cal.** – California; **Cgy.** – Calgary; **Cle.** – Cleveland; **Col.** – Colorado; **Dal.** – Dallas; **Det.** – Detroit; **Edm.** – Edmonton; **Fla.** – Florida; **Ham.** – Hamilton; **Hfd.** – Hartford; **K.C.** – Kansas City; **L.A.** – Los Angeles; **Min.** – Minnesota; **Mtl.** – Montreal; **Mtl. M.** – Montreal Maroons; **Mtl. W.** – Montreal Wanderers; **N.J.** – New Jersey; **NYA** – NY Americans; **NYI** – NY Islanders; **NYR** – New York Rangers; – **Oak.** – Oakland; **Ott.** – Ottawa; – **Phi.** – Philadelphia; **Phx.** – Phoenix; **Pit.** – Pittsburgh; **Que.** – Quebec; **St. L.** – St. Louis; **S.J.** – San Jose; **T.B.** – Tampa Bay; **Tor.** – Toronto; **Van.** – Vancouver; **Wpg.** – Winnipeg; **Wsh.** – Washington

Avg. – goals against per 60 minutes played; **GA** – goals agains; **GP** – games played; **Mins** – minutes played; **SO** – shutouts.
• – deceased. § – Forward, defenseman or coach who appeared in goal. For complete career, see Retired Player Index. ‡ – Remains active in other leagues.

			Regular Schedule								Playoffs										
Name	NHL Teams	NHL Seasons	GP	W	L	T	Mins	GA	SO	Avg	GP	W	L	T	Mins	GA	SO	Avg	NHL Cup Wins	First NHL Season	Last NHL Season
Abbott, George	Bos.	1	1	0	1	0	60	7	0	7.00	....	....	....	....	....	....	....	....		1943-44	1943-44
Adams, John	Bos., Wsh.	2	22	9	10	1	1180	85	1	4.32	....	....	....	....	....	....	....	....		1972-73	1974-75
Aiken, Don	Mtl.	1	1	0	1	0	34	6	0	10.59	....	....	....	....	....	....	....	....		1957-58	1957-58
• Aitkenhead, Andy	NYR	3	106	47	43	16	6570	257	11	2.35	10	6	2	2	608	15	3	1.48	1	1932-33	1934-35
Almas, Red	Det., Chi.	3	3	0	2	1	180	13	0	4.33	5	1	3	....	263	13	0	2.97		1946-47	1952-53
• Anderson, Lorne	NYR	1	3	1	2	0	180	18	0	6.00	....	....	....	....	....	....	....	....		1951-52	1951-52
Astrom, Hardy	NYR, Col.	3	83	17	44	12	4456	278	0	3.74	....	....	....	....	....	....	....	....		1977-78	1980-81
Baker, Steve	NYR	4	57	20	20	11	3081	190	3	3.70	14	7	7	....	826	55	0	4.00		1979-80	1982-83
Bannerman, Murray	Van., Chi.	8	289	116	125	33	16470	1051	8	3.83	40	20	18	....	2322	165	0	4.26		1977-78	1986-87
Baron, Marco	Bos., L.A., Edm.	6	86	34	38	9	4822	292	1	3.63	1	0	1	....	20	3	0	9.00		1979-80	1984-85
Bassen, Hank	Chi., Det., Pit.	9	156	46	66	31	8759	434	5	2.97	5	1	3	....	274	11	0	2.41		1954-55	1967-68
• Bastien, Baz	Tor.	1	5	0	4	1	300	20	0	4.00	....	....	....	....	....	....	....	....		1945-46	1945-46
Bauman, Gary	Mtl., Min.	3	35	6	18	6	1718	102	0	3.56	....	....	....	....	....	....	....	....		1966-67	1968-69
Beaupre, Don	Min., Wsh., Ott., Tor.	17	667	268	277	75	37396	2151	17	3.45	72	33	31	....	3943	220	3	3.35		1980-81	1996-97
Beauregard, Stephane	Wpg., Phi.	5	90	19	39	11	4402	268	2	3.65	4	1	3	....	238	12	0	3.03		1989-90	1993-94
Bedard, Jim	Wsh.	2	73	17	40	13	4232	278	1	3.94	....	....	....	....	....	....	....	....		1977-78	1978-79
Behrend, Marc	Wpg.	3	39	12	19	3	1991	160	1	4.82	7	1	3	0	312	19	0	3.65		1983-84	1985-86
Belanger, Yves	St.L., Atl., Bos.	6	78	29	33	6	4134	259	2	3.76	....	....	....	....	....	....	....	....		1974-75	1979-80
Belhumeur, Michel	Phi., Wsh.	3	65	9	36	7	3306	254	0	4.61	1	0	0	....	10	1	0	6.00		1972-73	1975-76
• Bell, Gordie	Tor., NYR	2	8	3	5	0	480	31	0	3.88	2	1	1	....	120	9	0	4.50		1945-46	1955-56
• Benedict, Clint	Ott., Mtl.M.	13	362	190	143	28	22367	863	58	2.32	28	12	11	3	1707	53	9	1.86	4	1917-18	1929-30
Bennett, Harvey	Bos.	1	25	10	12	2	1470	103	0	4.20	....	....	....	....	....	....	....	....		1944-45	1944-45
Bergeron, Jean-Claude	Mtl., T.B., L.A.	6	72	21	33	7	3772	232	1	3.69	....	....	....	....	....	....	....	....		1990-91	1996-97
Bernhardt, Tim	Cgy., Tor.	4	67	17	36	7	3748	267	0	4.27	....	....	....	....	....	....	....	....		1982-83	1986-87
‡ Berthiaume, Daniel	Wpg., Min., L.A., Bos., Ott.	9	215	81	90	21	11662	714	5	3.67	14	5	9	....	807	50	0	3.72		1985-86	1993-94
Bester, Allan	Tor., Det., Dal.	10	219	73	99	17	11773	786	7	4.01	11	2	6	....	508	37	0	4.37		1983-84	1995-96
• Beveridge, Bill	Det., Ott., St.L., Mtl.M., NYR	9	297	87	166	42	18375	879	18	2.87	5	2	3	....	300	11	0	2.20		1929-30	1942-43
• Bibeault, Paul	Mtl., Tor., Bos., Chi.	7	214	81	107	25	12890	785	10	3.65	20	6	14	....	1237	71	2	3.44		1940-41	1946-47
Binette, Andre	Mtl.	1	1	1	0	0	60	4	0	4.00	....	....	....	....	....	....	....	....		1954-55	1954-55
Binkley, Les	Pit.	5	196	58	94	34	11046	575	11	3.12	7	5	2	....	428	15	0	2.10		1967-68	1971-72
Bittner, Richard	Bos.	1	1	0	0	1	60	3	0	3.00	....	....	....	....	....	....	....	....		1949-50	1949-50
Blake, Mike	L.A.	3	40	13	15	5	2117	150	0	4.25	....	....	....	....	....	....	....	....		1981-82	1983-84
Blue, John	Bos., Buf.	3	46	16	18	7	2521	126	1	3.00	2	0	1	....	96	5	0	3.13		1992-93	1995-96
Boisvert, Gilles	Det.	1	3	0	3	0	180	9	0	3.00	....	....	....	....	....	....	....	....		1959-60	1959-60
Bouchard, Dan	Atl., Cgy., Que., Wpg.	14	655	286	232	113	37919	2061	27	3.26	43	13	30	....	2549	147	1	3.46		1972-73	1985-86
• Bourque, Claude	Mtl., Det.	2	62	16	38	8	3830	193	4	3.02	3	1	2	....	188	8	1	2.55		1938-39	1939-40
Boutin, Rollie	Wsh.	3	22	7	10	1	1137	75	0	3.96	....	....	....	....	....	....	....	....		1978-79	1980-81
Bouvrette, Lionel	NYR	1	1	0	1	0	60	6	0	6.00	....	....	....	....	....	....	....	....		1942-43	1942-43
Bower, Johnny	NYR, Tor.	15	552	250	195	90	32016	1340	37	2.51	74	35	34	....	4378	180	5	2.47	4	1953-54	1969-70
§ • Branigan, Andy			1	0	0	0	7	0	0	0.00	....	....	....	....	....	....	....	....			
• Brimsek, Frank	Bos., Chi.	10	514	252	182	80	31210	1404	40	2.70	68	32	36	....	4395	186	2	2.54	2	1938-39	1949-50
• Broda, Turk	Tor.	14	629	302	224	101	38167	1609	62	2.53	101	60	39	....	6389	211	13	1.98	5	1936-37	1951-52
Broderick, Ken	Min., Bos.	3	27	11	12	1	1464	74	1	3.03	....	....	....	....	....	....	....	....		1969-70	1974-75
Broderick, Len	Mtl.	1	1	1	0	0	60	2	0	2.00	....	....	....	....	....	....	....	....		1957-58	1957-58
Brodeur, Richard	NYI, Van., Hfd.	9	385	131	175	62	21968	1410	6	3.85	33	13	20	....	2009	111	1	3.32		1979-80	1987-88
Bromley, Gary	Buf., Van.	6	136	54	44	28	7427	425	7	3.43	7	2	5	....	360	25	0	4.17		1973-74	1980-81
• Brooks, Art	Tor.	1	4	2	2	0	220	23	0	6.27	....	....	....	....	....	....	....	....		1917-18	1917-18
Brooks, Ross	Bos.	3	54	37	7	6	3047	134	4	2.64	1	0	0	....	20	3	0	9.00		1972-73	1974-75
• Brophy, Frank	Que.	1	21	3	18	0	1249	148	0	7.11	....	....	....	....	....	....	....	....		1919-20	1919-20
Brown, Andy	Det., Pit.	3	62	22	26	9	3373	213	1	3.79	....	....	....	....	....	....	....	....		1971-72	1973-74
Brown, Ken	Chi.	1	1	0	0	0	18	1	0	3.33	....	....	....	....	....	....	....	....		1970-71	1970-71
‡ Brunetta, Mario	Que.	3	40	12	17	1	1967	128	0	3.90	....	....	....	....	....	....	....	....		1987-88	1989-90
Bullock, Bruce	Van.	3	16	3	9	3	927	74	0	4.79	....	....	....	....	....	....	....	....		1972-73	1976-77
Buzinski, Steve	NYR	1	9	2	6	1	560	55	0	5.89	....	....	....	....	....	....	....	....		1942-43	1942-43
Caley, Don	St.L.	1	1	0	0	0	30	3	0	6.00	....	....	....	....	....	....	....	....		1967-68	1967-68
Caprice, Frank	Van.	6	102	31	46	11	5589	391	1	4.20	....	....	....	....	....	....	....	....		1982-83	1987-88
Carey, Jim	Wsh., Bos., St.L.	5	172	79	65	16	9668	416	16	2.58	10	2	5	....	455	35	0	4.62		1994-95	1998-99
Caron, Jacques	L.A., St.L., Van.	5	72	24	29	11	3846	211	2	3.29	12	4	7	....	639	34	0	3.19		1967-68	1973-74
Carter, Lyle	Cal.	1	15	4	7	0	721	50	0	4.16	....	....	....	....	....	....	....	....		1971-72	1971-72
Casey, Jon	Min., Bos., St.L.	12	425	170	157	55	23255	1246	16	3.21	66	32	31	....	3743	192	3	3.08		1983-84	1996-97
• Chabot, Lorne	NYR, Tor., Mtl.C., Chi., Mtl.M., NYA	11	411	201	148	62	25307	860	73	2.04	37	13	17	6	2498	64	5	1.54	2	1926-27	1936-37
Chadwick, Ed	Tor., Bos.	6	184	57	92	35	11040	541	14	2.94	....	....	....	....	....	....	....	....		1955-56	1961-62
Champoux, Bob	Det., Cal.	2	17	2	11	3	923	80	0	5.20	1	1	0	....	55	4	0	4.36		1963-64	1973-74
Cheevers, Gerry	Tor., Bos.	13	418	230	102	74	24394	1174	26	2.89	88	53	34	....	5396	242	8	2.69	2	1961-62	1979-80
Cheveldae, Tim	Det., Wpg., Bos.	9	340	149	136	37	19172	1116	10	3.49	25	9	15	....	1418	71	2	3.00		1988-89	1996-97
Chevrier, Alain	N.J., Wpg., Chi., Pit., Det.	6	234	91	100	14	12202	845	2	4.16	16	9	7	....	1013	44	0	2.61		1985-86	1990-91
§ • Clancy, King			2	0	0	0	3	1	0	20.00	....	....	....	....	....	....	....	....			
§ • Cleghorn, Odie			1	1	0	0	60	2	0	2.00	....	....	....	....	....	....	....	....			
§ • Cleghorn, Sprague			2	0	0	0	5	0	0	0.00	....	....	....	....	....	....	....	....			
Clifford, Chris	Chi.	2	2	0	0	0	24	0	0	0.00	....	....	....	....	....	....	....	....		1984-85	1988-89
Cloutier, Jacques	Buf., Chi., Que.	12	255	82	102	24	12826	778	3	3.64	8	1	5	....	413	18	1	2.62		1981-82	1993-94
Colvin, Les	Bos.	1	1	0	1	0	60	4	0	4.00	....	....	....	....	....	....	....	....		1948-49	1948-49
§ • Conacher, Charlie			4	0	0	0	10	0	0	0.00	....	....	....	....	....	....	....	....			
• Connell, Alex	Ott., Det., NYA, Mtl.M.	12	417	193	156	67	26050	830	81	1.91	21	8	5	8	1309	26	4	1.19	2	1924-25	1936-37
Corsi, Jim	Edm.	1	26	8	14	3	1366	83	0	3.65	....	....	....	....	....	....	....	....		1979 80	1979-80
Courteau, Maurice	Bos.	1	6	2	4	0	360	33	0	5.50	....	....	....	....	....	....	....	....		1943-44	1943-44
‡ Cowley, Wayne	Edm.	1	1	0	1	0	57	3	0	3.16	....	....	....	....	....	....	....	....		1993-94	1993-94
Cox, Abbie	Mtl.M., NYA, Det., Mtl.C.	3	5	1	1	2	263	11	0	2.51	....	....	....	....	....	....	....	....		1929-30	1935-36
Craig, Jim	Atl., Bos., Min.	3	30	11	10	7	1588	100	0	3.78	....	....	....	....	....	....	....	....		1979-80	1983-84
Crha, Jiri	Tor.	2	69	28	27	11	3942	261	0	3.97	5	0	4	....	186	21	0	6.77		1979-80	1980-81
• Crozier, Roger	Det., Buf., Wsh.	14	518	206	197	70	28567	1446	30	3.04	32	14	16	....	1789	82	1	2.75		1963-64	1976-77
• Cude, Wilf	Phi., Bos., Chi., Mtl.C., Det., Mtl.	10	282	100	132	49	17586	798	24	2.72	19	7	11	1	1257	51	1	2.43		1930-31	1940-41
Cutts, Don	Edm.	1	6	1	2	1	269	16	0	3.57	....	....	....	....	....	....	....	....		1979-80	1979-80
• Cyr, Claude	Mtl.	1	1	0	0	0	20	1	0	3.00	....	....	....	....	....	....	....	....		1958-59	1958-59
Dadswell, Doug	Cgy.	2	27	8	8	3	1346	99	0	4.41	....	....	....	....	....	....	....	....		1986-87	1987-88
D'Alessio, Corrie	Hfd.	1	1	0	0	0	11	0	0	0.00	....	....	....	....	....	....	....	....		1992-93	1992-93
Daley, Joe	Pit., Buf., Det.	4	105	34	44	19	5836	326	3	3.35	....	....	....	....	....	....	....	....		1968-69	1971-72
Damore, Nick	Bos.	1	1	1	0	0	60	3	0	3.00	....	....	....	....	....	....	....	....		1941-42	1941-42
D'Amour, Marc	Cgy., Phi.	2	16	2	4	2	579	32	0	3.32	....	....	....	....	....	....	....	....		1985-86	1988-89
Daskalakis, Cleon	Bos.	3	12	3	4	1	506	41	0	4.86	....	....	....	....	....	....	....	....		1984-85	1986-87
Davidson, John	St.L., NYR	10	301	123	124	39	17109	1004	7	3.52	31	16	14	....	1862	77	1	2.48		1973-74	1982-83
Decourcy, Bob	NYR	1	1	0	1	0	29	6	0	12.41	....	....	....	....	....	....	....	....		1947-48	1947-48
Defelice, Norm	Bos.	1	10	3	5	2	600	30	0	3.00	....	....	....	....	....	....	....	....		1956-57	1956-57
DeJordy, Denis	Chi., L.A., Mtl., Det.	12	316	124	128	51	17798	929	15	3.13	18	6	9	....	946	55	0	3.49	1	1960-61	1973-74
DelGuidice, Matt	Bos.	2	11	2	5	1	434	28	0	3.87	....	....	....	....	....	....	....	....		1990-91	1991-92
‡ DeRouville, Philippe	Pit.	2	3	1	2	0	171	9	0	3.16	....	....	....	....	....	....	....	....		1994-95	1996-97
Desjardins, Gerry	L.A., Chi., NYI, Buf.	10	331	122	153	44	19014	1042	12	3.29	35	15	15	....	1874	108	0	3.46		1968-69	1977-78
• Dickie, Bill	Chi.	1	1	1	0	0	60	3	0	3.00	....	....	....	....	....	....	....	....		1941-42	1941-42

Name	NHL Teams	NHL Seasons	Regular Schedule GP	W	L	T	Mins	GA	SO	Avg	Playoffs GP	W	L	T	Mins	GA	SO	Avg	NHL Cup Wins	First NHL Season	Last NHL Season
Dion, Connie	Det.	2	38	23	11	4	2280	119	1	3.13	5	1	4	....	300	17	0	3.40		1943-44	1944-45
Dion, Michel	Que., Wpg., Pit.	6	227	60	118	32	12695	898	2	4.24	5	2	3	....	304	22	0	4.34		1979-80	1984-85
Dolson, Dolly	Det.	3	93	35	41	17	5820	192	16	1.98	2	0	2	0	120	7	0	3.50		1928-29	1930-31
‡ Dopson, Rob	Pit.	1	2	0	0	0	45	3	0	4.00	....	....	....	....	....	....	....	....		1993-94	1993-94
Dowie, Bruce	Tor.	1	2	0	1	0	72	4	0	3.33	....	....	....	....	....	....	....	....		1983-84	1983-84
‡ Draper, Tom	Wpg., Buf., NYI	6	53	19	23	5	2807	173	1	3.70	7	3	4	....	433	19	1	2.63		1988-89	1995-96
Dryden, Dave	NYR, Chi., Buf., Edm.	9	203	66	76	31	10424	555	9	3.19	3	0	2	....	133	9	0	4.06		1961-62	1979-80
Dryden, Ken	Mtl.	8	397	258	57	74	23352	870	46	2.24	112	80	32	....	6846	274	10	2.40	6	1970-71	1978-79
‡ Duffus, Parris	Phx.	1	1	0	0	0	29	1	0	2.07	....	....	....	....	....	....	....	....		1996-97	1996-97
Dumas, Michel	Chi.	3	8	2	1	2	362	24	0	3.98	1	0	0	....	19	1	0	3.16		1974-75	1976-77
Dupuis, Bob	Edm.	1	1	0	1	0	60	4	0	4.00	....	....	....	....	....	....	....	....		1979-80	1979-80
• Durnan, Bill	Mtl.	7	383	208	112	62	22945	901	34	2.36	45	27	18	....	2871	99	2	2.07	2	1943-44	1949-50
Dyck, Ed	Van.	3	49	8	28	5	2453	178	1	4.35	....	....	....	....	....	....	....	....		1971-72	1973-74
Edwards, Don	Buf., Cgy., Tor.	10	459	208	155	74	26181	1449	16	3.32	42	16	21	....	2302	132	1	3.44		1976-77	1985-86
Edwards, Gary	St.L., L.A., Cle., Min., Edm., Pit.	13	286	88	125	51	16002	973	10	3.65	11	5	4	....	537	34	0	3.80		1968-69	1981-82
Edwards, Marv	Pit., Tor., Cal.	4	61	15	34	7	3467	218	2	3.77	....	....	....	....	....	....	....	....		1968-69	1973-74
• Edwards, Roy	Det., Pit.	7	236	97	88	38	13109	637	12	2.92	4	0	3	....	206	11	0	3.20		1967-68	1973-74
Eliot, Darren	L.A., Det., Buf.	5	89	25	41	12	4931	377	1	4.59	1	0	0	....	40	7	0	10.50		1984-85	1988-89
Ellacott, Ken	Van.	1	12	2	3	4	555	41	0	4.43	....	....	....	....	....	....	....	....		1982-83	1982-83
‡ Erickson, Chad	N.J.	1	2	1	1	0	120	9	0	4.50	....	....	....	....	....	....	....	....		1991-92	1991-92
Esposito, Tony	Mtl., Chi.	16	886	423	306	151	52585	2563	76	2.92	99	45	53	....	6017	308	6	3.07	1	1968-69	1983-84
• Evans, Claude	Mtl., Bos.	2	5	1	2	1	260	16	0	3.69	....	....	....	....	....	....	....	....		1954-55	1957-58
Exelby, Randy	Mtl., Edm.	2	2	0	1	0	63	5	0	4.76	....	....	....	....	....	....	....	....		1988-89	1989-90
Farr, Rocky	Buf.	3	19	2	6	3	722	42	0	3.49	....	....	....	....	....	....	....	....		1972-73	1974-75
Favell, Doug	Phi., Tor., Col.	12	373	123	153	69	20771	1096	18	3.17	21	6	15	....	1270	66	1	3.12		1967-68	1978-79
• Forbes, Jake	Tor., Ham., NYA, Phi.	13	210	85	114	11	12922	594	19	2.76	2	0	2	0	120	7	0	3.50		1919-20	1932-33
Ford, Brian	Que., Pit.	2	11	3	7	0	580	61	0	6.31	....	....	....	....	....	....	....	....		1983-84	1984-85
Foster, Norm	Bos., Edm.	2	13	7	4	0	623	34	0	3.27	....	....	....	....	....	....	....	....		1990-91	1991-92
Fowler, Hec	Bos.	1	7	1	6	0	409	42	0	6.16	....	....	....	....	....	....	....	....		1924-25	1924-25
Francis, Emile	Chi., NYR	6	95	31	52	11	5660	355	1	3.76	....	....	....	....	....	....	....	....		1946-47	1951-52
• Franks, Jim	Det., NYR, Bos.	4	42	12	23	7	2520	181	1	4.31	1	0	1	....	30	2	0	4.00	1	1936-37	1943-44
Frederick, Ray	Chi.	1	5	0	4	1	300	22	0	4.40	....	....	....	....	....	....	....	....		1954-55	1954-55
Friesen, Karl	N.J.	1	4	0	2	1	130	16	0	7.38	....	....	....	....	....	....	....	....		1986-87	1986-87
Froese, Bob	Phi., NYR	8	242	128	72	20	13451	694	13	3.10	18	3	9	....	830	55	0	3.98		1982-83	1989-90
Fuhr, Grant	Edm., Tor., Buf., L.A., St.L., Cgy.	19	868	403	295	114	48945	2756	25	3.38	150	92	50	....	8834	430	6	2.92	5	1981-82	1999-00
Gagnon, David	Det.	1	2	0	1	0	35	6	0	10.29	....	....	....	....	....	....	....	....		1990-91	1990-91
• Gamble, Bruce	NYR, Bos., Tor., Phi.	10	327	110	150	46	18442	988	22	3.21	5	0	4	....	206	25	0	7.28	1	1958-59	1971-72
Gamble, Troy	Van.	4	72	22	29	9	3804	229	1	3.61	4	1	3	....	249	16	0	3.86		1986-87	1991-92
Gardiner, Bert	NYR, Mtl., Chi., Bos.	6	144	49	68	27	8760	554	4	3.79	9	4	5	....	647	20	0	1.85		1935-36	1943-44
• Gardiner, Charlie	Chi.	7	316	112	152	52	19687	664	42	2.02	21	12	6	3	1472	35	5	1.43	1	1927-28	1933-34
Gardner, George	Det., Van.	5	66	16	30	6	3313	207	0	3.75	....	....	....	....	....	....	....	....		1965-66	1971-72
Garrett, John	Hfd., Que., Van.	6	207	68	91	37	11763	837	1	4.27	9	4	3	....	461	33	0	4.30		1979-80	1984-85
Gatherum, Dave	Det.	1	3	2	0	1	180	3	1	1.00	....	....	....	....	....	....	....	....	1	1953-54	1953-54
Gauthier, Paul	Mtl.C.	1	1	0	0	1	70	2	0	1.71	....	....	....	....	....	....	....	....		1937-38	1937-38
• Gelineau, Jack	Bos., Chi.	4	143	46	64	33	8580	447	7	3.13	4	1	2	....	260	7	1	1.62		1948-49	1953-54
Giacomin, Ed	NYR, Det.	13	610	289	208	97	35693	1675	54	2.82	65	29	35	....	3838	180	1	2.81		1965-66	1977-78
Gilbert, Gilles	Min., Bos., Det.	14	416	192	143	60	23677	1290	18	3.27	32	17	15	....	1919	97	3	3.03		1969-70	1982-83
Gill, Andre	Bos.	1	5	3	2	0	270	13	1	2.89	....	....	....	....	....	....	....	....		1967-68	1967-68
• Goodman, Paul	Chi.	3	52	23	20	9	3240	117	6	2.17	3	0	3	....	187	10	0	3.21	1	1937-38	1940-41
Gordon, Scott	Que.	2	23	2	16	0	1082	101	0	5.60	....	....	....	....	....	....	....	....		1989-90	1990-91
Gosselin, Mario	Que., L.A., Hfd.	9	241	91	107	14	12857	801	6	3.74	32	16	15	....	1816	99	0	3.27		1983-84	1993-94
‡ Goverde, David	L.A.	3	5	1	4	0	278	29	0	6.26	....	....	....	....	....	....	....	....		1991-92	1993-94
Grahame, Ron	Bos., L.A., Que.	4	114	50	43	15	6472	409	5	3.79	4	2	1	....	202	7	0	2.08		1977-78	1980-81
• Grant, Benny	Tor., NYA, Bos.	6	50	17	26	4	2990	187	4	3.75	....	....	....	....	....	....	....	....		1928-29	1943-44
Grant, Doug	Det., St.L.	7	77	27	34	8	4199	280	2	4.00	....	....	....	....	....	....	....	....		1973-74	1979-80
Gratton, Gilles	St.L., NYR	2	47	13	18	9	2299	154	0	4.02	....	....	....	....	....	....	....	....		1975-76	1976-77
Gray, Gerry	Det., NYI	2	8	1	5	1	440	35	0	4.77	....	....	....	....	....	....	....	....		1970-71	1972-73
Gray, Harrison	Det.	1	1	0	1	0	40	5	0	7.50	....	....	....	....	....	....	....	....		1963-64	1963-64
Greenlay, Mike	Edm.	1	2	0	0	0	20	4	0	12.00	....	....	....	....	....	....	....	....		1989-90	1989-90
Guenette, Steve	Pit., Cgy.	5	35	19	16	0	1958	122	1	3.74	....	....	....	....	....	....	....	....		1986-87	1990-91
• Hainsworth, George	Mtl.C., Tor.	11	465	246	145	74	29087	937	94	1.93	52	22	25	5	3486	112	8	1.93	2	1926-27	1936-37
Hall, Glenn	Det., Chi., St.L.	19	906	407	326	163	53484	2222	84	2.49	115	49	65	....	6899	320	6	2.78	2	1951-52	1970-71
Hamel, Pierre	Tor., Wpg.	4	69	13	41	7	3766	276	0	4.40	....	....	....	....	....	....	....	....		1974-75	1980-81
Hanlon, Glen	Van., St.L., NYR, Det.	14	477	167	202	61	26037	1561	13	3.60	35	11	15	....	1756	92	4	3.14		1977-78	1990-91
Harrison, Paul	Min., Tor., Pit., Buf.	7	109	28	59	9	5806	408	2	4.22	4	0	1	....	157	9	0	3.44		1975-76	1981-82
Hayward, Brian	Wpg., Mtl., Min., S.J.	11	357	143	156	37	20025	1242	8	3.72	37	11	18	....	1803	104	0	3.46		1982-83	1992-93
Head, Don	Bos.	1	38	9	26	3	2280	158	2	4.16	....	....	....	....	....	....	....	....		1961-62	1961-62
• Hebert, Sammy	Tor., Ott.	2	4	2	1	0	200	19	0	5.70	....	....	....	....	....	....	....	....	1	1917-18	1923-24
Heinz, Rick	St.L., Van.	5	49	14	19	5	2356	159	2	4.05	1	0	0	....	8	1	0	7.50		1980-81	1984-85
Henderson, John	Bos.	2	46	15	15	15	2688	113	5	2.52	2	0	2	....	120	8	0	4.00		1954-55	1955-56
• Henry, Gord	Bos.	4	3	1	2	0	180	5	1	1.67	5	0	4	....	283	21	0	4.45		1948-49	1952-53
Henry, Jim	NYR, Chi., Bos.	9	406	161	173	70	24355	1166	27	2.87	29	11	18	....	1741	81	2	2.79		1941-42	1954-55
Herron, Denis	Pit., K.C., Mtl.	14	462	146	203	76	25608	1579	10	3.70	15	5	10	....	901	50	0	3.33		1972-73	1985-86
Hextall, Ron	Phi., Que., NYI	13	608	296	214	69	34750	1723	23	2.97	93	47	43	....	5456	276	2	3.04		1986-87	1998-99
Highton, Hec	Chi.	1	24	10	14	0	1440	108	0	4.50	....	....	....	....	....	....	....	....		1943-44	1943-44
§ • Himes, Normie			2	0	1	0	79	3	0	2.28	....	....	....	....	....	....	....	....			
Hodge, Charlie	Mtl., Oak., Van.	14	358	151	124	61	20593	925	24	2.70	16	7	8	....	804	32	2	2.39	5	1954-55	1970-71
Hodson, Kevin	Det., T.B.	5	64	17	15	9	2627	122	4	2.79	1	0	0	....	1	0	0	0.00	2	1995-96	1999-00
Hoffort, Bruce	Phi.	2	9	4	0	3	368	22	0	3.59	....	....	....	....	....	....	....	....		1989-90	1990-91
Hoganson, Paul	Pit.	1	2	0	1	0	57	7	0	7.37	....	....	....	....	....	....	....	....		1970-71	1970-71
Hogosta, Goran	NYI, Que.	2	22	5	12	3	1208	83	1	4.12	....	....	....	....	....	....	....	....		1977-78	1979-80
Holden, Mark	Mtl., Wpg.	4	8	2	2	1	372	25	0	4.03	....	....	....	....	....	....	....	....		1981-82	1984-85
Holland, Ken	Hfd., Det.	2	4	0	2	1	206	17	0	4.95	....	....	....	....	....	....	....	....		1980-81	1983-84
Holland, Robbie	Pit.	2	44	11	22	9	2513	171	1	4.08	....	....	....	....	....	....	....	....		1979-80	1980-81
• Holmes, Hap	Tor., Det.	4	103	39	54	10	6510	264	17	2.43	2	1	1	0	120	7	0	3.50	1	1917-18	1927-28
§ Horner, Red			1	0	0	0	1	1	0	60.00	....	....	....	....	....	....	....	....			
‡ Hrivnak, Jim	Wsh., Wpg., St.L.	5	85	34	30	3	4217	262	0	3.73	....	....	....	....	....	....	....	....		1989-90	1993-94
Hrudey, Kelly	NYI, L.A., S.J.	15	677	271	265	88	38084	2174	17	3.43	85	36	46	....	5163	283	0	3.29		1983-84	1997-98
Ing, Peter	Tor., Edm., Det.	4	74	20	37	9	3941	266	1	4.05	....	....	....	....	....	....	....	....		1989-90	1993-94
Inness, Gary	Pit., Phi., Wsh.	7	162	58	61	27	8710	494	2	3.40	9	5	4	....	540	24	0	2.67		1973-74	1980-81
Ireland, Randy	Buf.	1	2	0	0	0	30	3	0	6.00	....	....	....	....	....	....	....	....		1978-79	1978-79
Irons, Robbie	St.L.	1	1	0	0	0	3	0	0	0.00	....	....	....	....	....	....	....	....		1968-69	1968-69
• Ironstone, Joe	Ott., NYA, Tor.	3	2	0	0	1	110	3	1	1.64	....	....	....	....	....	....	....	....		1924-25	1927-28
Jackson, Doug	Chi.	1	6	2	3	1	360	42	0	7.00	....	....	....	....	....	....	....	....		1947-48	1947-48
Jackson, Percy	Bos., NYA, NYR	4	7	1	3	1	392	26	0	3.98	....	....	....	....	....	....	....	....		1931-32	1935-36
‡ Jaks, Pauli	L.A.	1	1	0	0	0	40	2	0	3.00	....	....	....	....	....	....	....	....		1994-95	1994-95
Janaszak, Steve	Min., Col.	2	3	0	1	1	160	15	0	5.63	....	....	....	....	....	....	....	....		1979-80	1981-82
Janecyk, Bob	Chi., L.A.	6	110	43	47	13	6250	432	2	4.15	3	0	3	....	184	10	0	3.26		1983-84	1988-89
§ Jenkins, Roger			1	0	1	0	30	7	0	14.00	....	....	....	....	....	....	....	....			
Jensen, Al	Det., Wsh., L.A.	7	179	95	53	18	9974	557	8	3.35	12	5	5	....	598	32	0	3.21		1980-81	1986-87
Jensen, Darren	Phi.	2	30	15	10	1	1496	95	2	3.81	....	....	....	....	....	....	....	....		1984-85	1985-86
Johnson, Bob	St.L., Pit.	2	24	9	9	1	1059	66	0	3.74	....	....	....	....	....	....	....	....		1972-73	1974-75
Johnston, Eddie	Bos., Tor., St.L., Chi.	16	592	234	257	80	34216	1852	32	3.25	18	7	10	....	1023	57	1	3.34	2	1962-63	1977-78
Junkin, Joe	Bos.	1	1	0	0	0	8	0	0	0.00	....	....	....	....	....	....	....	....		1968-69	1968-69
Kaarela, Jari	Col.	1	5	2	2	0	220	22	0	6.00	....	....	....	....	....	....	....	....		1980-81	1980-81
Kamppuri, Hannu	N.J.	1	13	1	10	1	645	54	0	5.02	....	....	....	....	....	....	....	....		1984-85	1984-85
• Karakas, Mike	Chi., Mtl.	8	336	114	169	53	20616	1002	28	2.92	23	11	12	0	1434	72	3	3.01	1	1935-36	1945-46
Keans, Doug	L.A., Bos.	9	210	96	64	26	11388	666	4	3.51	9	2	6	....	432	34	0	4.72		1979-80	1987-88
Keenan, Don	Bos.	1	1	0	1	0	60	4	0	4.00	....	....	....	....	....	....	....	....		1958-59	1958-59
• Kerr, Dave	Mtl.M., NYA, NYR	11	427	203	148	75	26639	954	51	2.15	40	18	19	3	2616	76	8	1.74	1	1930-31	1940-41

Name	NHL Teams	NHL Seasons	Regular Schedule GP	W	L	T	Mins	GA	SO	Avg	Playoffs GP	W	L	T	Mins	GA	SO	Avg	NHL Cup Wins	First NHL Season	Last NHL Season
King, Scott	Det.	2	2	0	0	0	61	3	0	2.95	....	....	....	....	....	....	....	....		1990-91	1991-92
Kleisinger, Terry	NYR	1	4	0	2	0	191	14	0	4.40	....	....	....	....	....	....	....	....		1985-86	1985-86
Klymkiw, Julian	NYR	1	1	0	0	0	19	2	0	6.32	....	....	....	....	....	....	....	....		1958-59	1958-59
Knickle, Rick	L.A.	2	14	7	6	0	706	44	0	3.74	....	....	....	....	....	....	....	....		1992-93	1993-94
Kuntar, Les	Mtl.	1	6	2	2	0	302	16	0	3.18	....	....	....	....	....	....	....	....		1993-94	1993-94
Kurt, Gary	Cal.	1	16	1	7	5	838	60	0	4.30	....	....	....	....	....	....	....	....		1971-72	1971-72
‡ Labrecque, Patrick	Mtl.	1	2	0	1	0	98	7	0	4.29	....	....	....	....	....	....	....	....		1995-96	1995-96
Lacher, Blaine	Bos.	2	47	22	16	4	2636	123	4	2.80	5	1	4	....	283	12	0	2.54		1994-95	1995-96
• Lacroix, Frenchy	Mtl.C.	2	5	1	4	0	280	16	0	3.43	....	....	....	....	....	....	....	....		1925-26	1926-27
LaFerriere, Rick	Col.	1	1	0	0	0	20	1	0	3.00	....	....	....	....	....	....	....	....		1981-82	1981-82
LaForest, Mark	Det., Phi., Tor., Ott.	6	103	25	54	4	5032	354	2	4.22	2	1	0	....	48	1	0	1.25		1985-86	1993-94
• Larocque, Michel	Mtl., Tor., Phi., St.L.	11	312	160	89	45	17615	978	17	3.33	14	6	6	....	759	37	1	2.92	4	1973-74	1983-84
Laskowski, Gary	L.A.	2	59	19	27	5	2942	228	0	4.65	....	....	....	....	....	....	....	....		1982-83	1983-84
Laxton, Gord	Pit.	4	17	4	9	0	800	74	0	5.55	....	....	....	....	....	....	....	....		1975-76	1978-79
LeBlanc, Ray	Chi.	1	1	1	0	0	60	1	0	1.00	....	....	....	....	....	....	....	....		1991-92	1991-92
§ • LeDuc, Albert			1	0	0	0	2	1	0	30.00	....	....	....	....	....	....	....	....			
Legris, Claude	Det.	2	4	0	1	1	91	4	0	2.64	....	....	....	....	....	....	....	....		1980-81	1981-82
• Lehman, Hugh	Chi.	2	48	20	24	4	3047	136	6	2.68	2	0	1	1	120	10	0	5.00		1926-27	1927-28
Lemelin, Reggie	Atl., Cgy., Bos.	15	507	236	162	63	28006	1613	12	3.46	59	23	25	....	3119	186	2	3.58		1978-79	1992-93
Lenarduzzi, Mike	Hfd.	2	4	1	1	1	189	10	0	3.17	....	....	....	....	....	....	....	....		1992-93	1993-94
Lessard, Mario	L.A.	6	240	92	97	39	13529	843	9	3.74	20	6	12	....	1136	83	0	4.38		1978-79	1983-84
Levasseur, Jean-Louis	Min.	1	1	0	1	0	60	7	0	7.00	....	....	....	....	....	....	....	....		1979-80	1979-80
§ • Levinsky, Alex			1	0	0	0	1	1	0	60.00	....	....	....	....	....	....	....	....			
• Lindbergh, Pelle	Phi.	5	157	87	49	15	9150	503	7	3.30	23	12	10	....	1214	63	3	3.11		1981-82	1985-86
• Lindsay, Bert	Mtl., Tor.	2	20	6	14	0	1238	118	0	5.72	....	....	....	....	....	....	....	....		1917-18	1918-19
Littman, David	Buf., T.B.	3	3	0	2	0	141	14	0	5.96	....	....	....	....	....	....	....	....		1990-91	1992-93
Liut, Mike	St.L., Hfd., Wsh.	13	664	294	271	74	38215	2221	25	3.49	67	29	32	....	3814	215	2	3.38		1979-80	1991-92
Lockett, Ken	Van.	2	55	13	15	8	2348	131	2	3.35	1	0	1	....	60	6	0	6.00		1974-75	1975-76
• Lockhart, Howard	Tor., Que., Ham., Bos.	5	59	16	41	0	3413	287	1	5.05	....	....	....	....	....	....	....	....		1919-20	1924-25
LoPresti, Pete	Min., Edm.	6	175	43	102	20	9858	668	5	4.07	2	0	2	....	77	6	0	4.68		1974-75	1980-81
• LoPresti, Sam	Chi.	2	74	30	38	6	4530	236	4	3.13	8	3	5	....	530	17	1	1.92		1940-41	1941-42
‡ Lorenz, Danny	NYI	3	8	1	5	0	357	25	0	4.20	....	....	....	....	....	....	....	....		1990-91	1992-93
Loustel, Ron	Wpg.	1	1	0	1	0	60	10	0	10.00	....	....	....	....	....	....	....	....		1980-81	1980-81
Low, Ron	Tor., Wsh., Det., Que., Edm., N.J.	11	382	102	203	38	20502	1463	4	4.28	7	1	6	....	452	29	0	3.85		1972-73	1984-85
Lozinski, Larry	Det.	1	30	6	11	7	1459	105	0	4.32	....	....	....	....	....	....	....	....		1980-81	1980-81
• Lumley, Harry	Det., NYR, Chi., Tor., Bos.	16	803	330	329	142	48044	2206	71	2.75	76	29	47	....	4778	198	7	2.49	1	1943-44	1959-60
MacKenzie, Shawn	N.J.	1	4	0	1	0	130	15	0	6.92	....	....	....	....	....	....	....	....		1982-83	1982-83
Madeley, Darrin	Ott.	3	39	4	23	5	1928	140	0	4.36	....	....	....	....	....	....	....	....		1992-93	1994-95
Malarchuk, Clint	Que., Wsh., Buf.	10	338	141	130	45	19030	1100	12	3.47	15	2	9	0	781	56	0	4.30		1981-82	1991-92
Maneluk, George	NYI	1	4	1	1	0	140	15	0	6.43	....	....	....	....	....	....	....	....		1990-91	1990-91
Maniago, Cesare	Tor., Mtl., NYR, Min., Van.	15	568	189	259	96	32570	1773	30	3.27	36	15	21	....	2245	100	3	2.67		1960-61	1977-78
Marois, Jean	Tor., Chi.	2	3	1	2	0	180	15	0	5.00	....	....	....	....	....	....	....	....		1943-44	1953-54
Martin, Seth	St.L.	1	30	8	10	7	1552	67	1	2.59	2	0	0	....	73	5	0	4.11		1967-68	1967-68
Mason, Bob	Wsh., Chi., Que., Van.	8	145	55	65	16	7988	500	1	3.76	5	2	3	....	369	12	1	1.95		1983-84	1990-91
Mattsson, Markus	Wpg., Min., L.A.	4	92	21	46	14	5007	343	6	4.11	....	....	....	....	....	....	....	....		1979-80	1983-84
May, Darrell	St.L.	2	6	1	5	0	364	31	0	5.11	....	....	....	....	....	....	....	....		1985-86	1987-88
Mayer, Gilles	Tor.	4	9	2	6	1	540	24	0	2.67	....	....	....	....	....	....	....	....		1949-50	1955-56
McAuley, Ken	NYR	2	96	17	64	15	5740	537	1	5.61	....	....	....	....	....	....	....	....		1943-44	1944-45
McCartan, Jack	NYR	2	12	2	7	3	680	42	1	3.71	....	....	....	....	....	....	....	....		1959-60	1960-61
• McCool, Frank	Tor.	2	72	34	31	7	4320	242	4	3.36	13	8	5	....	807	30	4	2.23	1	1944-45	1945-46
McDuffe, Peter	St.L., NYR, K.C., Det.	5	57	11	36	6	3207	218	0	4.08	1	0	1	....	60	7	0	7.00		1971-72	1975-76
McGrattan, Tom	Det.	1	1	0	0	0	8	1	0	7.50	....	....	....	....	....	....	....	....		1947-48	1947-48
McKay, Ross	Hfd.	1	1	0	0	0	35	3	0	5.14	....	....	....	....	....	....	....	....		1990-91	1990-91
McKenzie, Bill	Det., K.C., Col.	6	91	18	49	13	4776	326	2	4.10	....	....	....	....	....	....	....	....		1973-74	1979-80
McKichan, Steve	Van.	1	1	0	0	0	20	2	0	6.00	....	....	....	....	....	....	....	....		1990-91	1990-91
McLachlan, Murray	Tor.	1	2	0	1	0	25	4	0	9.60	....	....	....	....	....	....	....	....		1970-71	1970-71
McLelland, Dave	Van.	1	2	1	1	0	120	10	0	5.00	....	....	....	....	....	....	....	....		1972-73	1972-73
McLeod, Don	Det., Phi.	2	18	3	10	1	879	74	0	5.05	....	....	....	....	....	....	....	....		1970-71	1971-72
McLeod, Jim	St.L.	1	16	6	6	4	880	44	0	3.00	....	....	....	....	....	....	....	....		1971-72	1971-72
McNamara, Gerry	Tor.	2	7	2	2	1	323	14	0	2.60	....	....	....	....	....	....	....	....		1960-61	1969-70
McNeil, Gerry	Mtl.	8	276	119	105	52	16535	649	28	2.36	35	17	18	....	2284	72	5	1.89	3	1947-48	1957-58
McRae, Gord	Tor.	5	71	30	22	10	3799	221	1	3.49	8	2	5	....	454	22	0	2.91		1972-73	1977-78
Melanson, Rollie	NYI, Min., L.A., N.J., Mtl.	11	291	129	106	33	16452	995	6	3.63	23	4	9	....	801	59	0	4.42	3	1980-81	1991-92
Meloche, Gilles	Chi., Cal., Cle., Min., Pit.	18	788	270	351	131	45401	2756	20	3.64	45	21	19	....	2464	143	2	3.48		1970-71	1987-88
Micalef, Corrado	Det.	5	113	26	59	15	5794	409	2	4.24	3	0	0	....	49	8	0	9.80		1981-82	1985-86
Middlebrook, Lindsay	Wpg., Min., N.J., Edm.	4	37	3	23	6	1845	152	0	4.94	....	....	....	....	....	....	....	....		1979-80	1982-83
• Millar, Al	Bos.	1	6	1	4	1	360	25	0	4.17	....	....	....	....	....	....	....	....		1957-58	1957-58
Millen, Greg	Pit., Hfd., St.L., Que., Chi., Det.	14	604	215	284	89	35377	2281	17	3.87	59	27	29	....	3383	193	0	3.42		1978-79	1991-92
• Miller, Joe	NYA, NYR, Pit., Phi.	4	127	24	87	16	7871	383	16	2.92	3	2	1	0	180	3	1	1.00	1	1927-28	1930-31
Mio, Eddie	Edm., NYR, Det.	7	192	64	73	30	10428	705	4	4.06	17	9	7	....	986	63	0	3.83		1979-80	1985-86
• Mitchell, Ivan	Tor.	3	22	10	9	0	1190	88	0	4.44	....	....	....	....	....	....	....	....	1	1919-20	1921-22
Moffat, Mike	Bos.	3	19	7	7	2	979	70	0	4.29	11	6	5	....	663	38	0	3.44		1981-82	1983-84
Moog, Andy	Edm., Bos., Dal., Mtl.	18	713	372	209	88	40151	2097	28	3.13	132	68	57	....	7452	377	4	3.04	3	1980-81	1997-98
Moore, Alfie	NYA, Chi., Det.	4	21	7	14	0	1290	81	1	3.77	3	1	2	....	180	7	0	2.33	1	1936-37	1939-40
Moore, Robbie	Phi., Wsh.	2	6	3	1	1	257	8	2	1.87	5	3	2	....	268	18	0	4.03		1978-79	1982-83
Morissette, Jean-Guy	Mtl.	1	1	0	1	0	36	4	0	6.67	....	....	....	....	....	....	....	....		1963-64	1963-64
• Mowers, Johnny	Det.	4	152	65	61	26	9350	399	15	2.56	32	19	13	....	2000	85	2	2.55	1	1940-41	1946-47
Mrazek, Jerome	Phi.	1	1	0	0	0	6	1	0	10.00	....	....	....	....	....	....	....	....		1975-76	1975-76
§ • Mummery, Harry			4	2	1	0	192	20	0	6.25	....	....	....	....	....	....	....	....			
§ • Munro, Dunc			1	0	0	0	2	0	0	0.00	....	....	....	....	....	....	....	....			
• Murphy, Hal	Mtl.	1	1	1	0	0	60	4	0	4.00	....	....	....	....	....	....	....	....		1952-53	1952-53
• Murray, Mickey	Mtl.C.	1	1	0	1	0	60	4	0	4.00	....	....	....	....	....	....	....	....		1929-30	1929-30
‡ Myllys, Jarmo	Min., S.J.	4	39	4	27	1	1846	161	0	5.23	....	....	....	....	....	....	....	....		1988-89	1991-92
Mylnikov, Sergei	Que.	1	10	1	7	2	568	47	0	4.96	....	....	....	....	....	....	....	....		1989-90	1989-90
Myre, Phil	Mtl., Atl., St.L., Phi., Col., Buf.	14	439	149	198	76	25220	1482	14	3.53	12	6	5	....	747	41	1	3.29	1	1969-70	1982-83
Newton, Cam	Pit.	2	16	4	7	1	814	51	0	3.76	....	....	....	....	....	....	....	....		1970-71	1972-73
Norris, Jack	Bos., Chi., L.A.	4	58	20	25	4	3119	202	2	3.89	....	....	....	....	....	....	....	....		1964-65	1970-71
Oleschuk, Bill	K.C., Col.	4	55	7	28	10	2835	188	1	3.98	....	....	....	....	....	....	....	....		1975-76	1979-80
• Olesevich, Dan	NYR	1	1	0	0	1	29	2	0	4.14	....	....	....	....	....	....	....	....		1961-62	1961-62
‡ O'Neill, Mike	Wpg., Ana.	4	21	0	9	2	855	61	0	4.28	....	....	....	....	....	....	....	....		1991-92	1996-97
Ouimet, Ted	St.L.	1	1	0	1	0	60	2	0	2.00	....	....	....	....	....	....	....	....		1968-69	1968-69
Pageau, Paul	L.A.	1	1	0	1	0	60	8	0	8.00	....	....	....	....	....	....	....	....		1980-81	1980-81
Paille, Marcel	NYR	7	107	32	52	22	6342	362	2	3.42	....	....	....	....	....	....	....	....		1957-58	1964-65
Palmateer, Mike	Tor., Wsh.	8	356	149	138	52	20131	1183	17	3.53	29	12	17	....	1765	89	2	3.03		1976-77	1983-84
Pang, Darren	Chi.	3	81	27	35	7	4252	287	0	4.05	6	1	3	....	250	18	0	4.32		1984-85	1988-89
Parent, Bernie	Bos., Phi., Tor.	13	608	271	198	121	35136	1493	54	2.55	71	38	33	....	4302	174	6	2.43	2	1965-66	1978-79
Parent, Bob	Tor.	2	3	0	2	0	160	15	0	5.63	....	....	....	....	....	....	....	....		1981-82	1982-83
Parro, Dave	Wsh.	4	77	21	36	10	4015	274	2	4.09	....	....	....	....	....	....	....	....		1980-81	1983-84
§ • Patrick, Lester			....	....	....	....	....	....	....	....	1	1	0	0	46	1	0	1.30	1		
Peeters, Pete	Phi., Bos., Wsh.	13	489	246	155	51	27699	1424	21	3.08	71	35	35	....	4200	232	2	3.31		1978-79	1990-91
Pelletier, Marcel	Chi., NYR	2	8	1	6	0	395	32	0	4.86	....	....	....	....	....	....	....	....		1950-51	1962-63
Penney, Steve	Mtl., Wpg.	5	91	35	38	12	5194	313	1	3.62	27	15	12	....	1604	72	4	2.69		1983-84	1987-88
• Perreault, Bob	Mtl., Det., Bos.	3	31	8	16	7	1827	103	3	3.38	....	....	....	....	....	....	....	....		1955-56	1962-63
Pettie, Jim	Bos.	3	21	9	7	2	1157	71	1	3.68	....	....	....	....	....	....	....	....		1976-77	1978-79
Pietrangelo, Frank	Pit., Hfd.	7	141	46	59	6	7141	490	1	4.12	12	7	5	....	713	34	1	2.86	1	1987-88	1993-94
• Plante, Jacques	Mtl., NYR, St.L., Tor., Bos.	18	837	435	247	145	49493	1964	82	2.38	112	71	36	....	6651	237	14	2.14	6	1952-53	1972-73
Plasse, Michel	St.L., Mtl., K.C., Pit., Col., Que.	11	299	92	136	54	16760	1058	2	3.79	4	1	2	....	195	9	1	2.77	1	1970-71	1981-82
§ • Plaxton, Hugh			1	0	1	0	57	5	0	5.26	....	....	....	....	....	....	....	....			
Pronovost, Claude	Bos., Mtl.	2	3	1	1	0	120	7	1	3.50	....	....	....	....	....	....	....	....		1955-56	1958-59
Puppa, Daren	Buf., Tor., T.B.	15	429	179	161	54	23819	1204	19	3.03	16	4	9	....	786	51	0	3.89		1985-86	1999-00
Pusey, Chris	Det.	1	1	0	0	0	40	3	0	4.50	....	....	....	....	....	....	....	....		1985-86	1985-86

Name	NHL Teams	NHL Seasons	Regular Schedule GP	W	L	T	Mins	GA	SO	Avg	Playoffs GP	W	L	T	Mins	GA	SO	Avg	NHL Cup Wins	First NHL Season	Last NHL Season
‡ Racicot, Andre	Mtl.	5	68	26	23	8	3357	196	2	3.50	4	0	1	....	31	4	0	7.74	1	1989-90	1993-94
‡ Racine, Bruce	St.L.	1	11	0	3	0	230	12	0	3.13	1	0	0	....	1	0	0	0.00		1995-96	1995-96
‡ Ram, Jamie	NYR	1	1	0	0	0	27	0	0	0.00	....	....	....	....	....	....	....	....		1995-96	1995-96
Ranford, Bill	Bos., Edm., Wsh., T.B., Det.	15	647	240	279	76	35936	2042	15	3.41	53	28	25	....	3110	159	4	3.07	2	1985-86	1999-00
Raymond, Alain	Wsh.	1	1	0	1	0	40	2	0	3.00	....	....	....	....	....	....	....	....		1987-88	1987-88
Rayner, Chuck	NYA, Bro., NYR	10	424	138	208	77	25491	1294	25	3.05	18	9	9	....	1135	46	1	2.43		1940-41	1952-53
Reaugh, Daryl	Edm., Hfd.	3	27	8	9	1	1246	72	1	3.47	....	....	....	....	....	....	....	....		1984-85	1990-91
‡ Reddick, Pokey	Wpg., Edm., Fla.	6	132	46	58	16	7162	443	0	3.71	4	0	2	....	168	10	0	3.57	1	1986-87	1993-94
• Redding, George	Bos.	1	1	0	0	0	11	1	0	5.45	....	....	....	....	....	....	....	....		1924-25	1924-25
Redquest, Greg	Pit.	1	1	0	0	0	13	3	0	13.85	....	....	....	....	....	....	....	....		1977-78	1977-78
Reece, Dave	Bos.	1	14	7	5	2	777	43	2	3.32	....	....	....	....	....	....	....	....		1975-76	1975-76
Reese, Jeff	Tor., Cgy., Hfd., T.B., N.J.	11	174	53	65	17	8667	529	5	3.66	11	3	5	....	515	35	0	4.08		1987-88	1998-99
Resch, Chico	NYI, Col., N.J., Phi.	14	571	231	224	82	32279	1761	26	3.27	41	17	17	....	2044	85	2	2.50	1	1973-74	1986-87
• Rheaume, Herb	Mtl.C.	1	31	10	20	1	1889	92	0	2.92	....	....	....	....	....	....	....	....		1925-26	1925-26
Ricci, Nick	Pit.	4	19	7	12	0	1087	79	0	4.36	....	....	....	....	....	....	....	....		1979-80	1982-83
Richardson, Terry	Det., St.L.	5	20	3	11	0	906	85	0	5.63	....	....	....	....	....	....	....	....		1973-74	1978-79
Ridley, Curt	NYR, Van., Tor.	6	104	27	47	16	5498	355	1	3.87	2	0	2	....	120	8	0	4.00		1974-75	1980-81
‡ Riendeau, Vincent	Mtl., St.L., Det., Bos.	8	184	85	65	20	10423	573	5	3.30	25	11	12	....	1277	71	1	3.34		1987-88	1994-95
Riggin, Dennis	Det.	2	18	6	10	2	999	52	1	3.12	....	....	....	....	....	....	....	....		1959-60	1962-63
Riggin, Pat	Atl., Cgy., Wsh., Bos., Pit.	9	350	153	120	52	19872	1135	11	3.43	25	8	13	....	1336	72	0	3.23		1979-80	1987-88
Ring, Bob	Bos.	1	1	0	0	0	33	4	0	7.27	....	....	....	....	....	....	....	....		1965-66	1965-66
Rivard, Fern	Min.	4	55	9	26	11	2865	190	2	3.98	....	....	....	....	....	....	....	....		1968-69	1974-75
• Roach, John Ross	Tor., NYR, Det.	14	492	219	204	68	30444	1246	58	2.46	29	12	14	3	1901	60	7	1.89	1	1921-22	1934-35
• Roberts, Moe	Bos., NYA, Chi.	4	10	3	5	0	501	31	0	3.71	....	....	....	....	....	....	....	....		1925-26	1951-52
• Robertson, Earl	Det., NYA, Bro.	6	190	60	95	34	11820	575	16	2.92	15	7	7	....	995	29	2	1.75	1	1936-37	1941-42
• Rollins, Al	Tor., Chi., NYR	9	430	141	205	83	25723	1192	28	2.78	13	6	7	....	755	30	0	2.38	1	1949-50	1959-60
Romano, Roberto	Pit., Bos.	6	126	46	63	8	7111	471	4	3.97	....	....	....	....	....	....	....	....		1982-83	1993-94
‡ Rosati, Mike	Wsh.	1	1	1	0	0	28	0	0	0.00	....	....	....	....	....	....	....	....		1998-99	1998-99
Rupp, Pat	Det.	1	1	0	1	0	60	4	0	4.00	....	....	....	....	....	....	....	....		1963-64	1963-64
Rutherford, Jim	Det., Pit., Tor., L.A.	13	457	151	227	59	25895	1576	14	3.65	8	2	5	....	440	28	0	3.82		1970-71	1982-83
Rutledge, Wayne	L.A.	3	82	28	37	9	4325	241	2	3.34	8	2	4	....	378	20	0	3.17		1967-68	1969-70
St. Croix, Rick	Phi., Tor.	8	130	49	54	18	7295	451	2	3.71	11	4	6	....	562	29	1	3.10		1977-78	1984-85
St. Laurent, Sam	N.J., Det.	5	34	7	12	4	1572	92	1	3.51	1	0	0	....	10	1	0	6.00		1985-86	1989-90
§ • Sands, Charlie			1	0	0	0	25	5	0	12.00	....	....	....	....	....	....	....	....			
Sands, Mike	Min.	2	6	0	5	0	302	26	0	5.17	....	....	....	....	....	....	....	....		1984-85	1986-87
Sarjeant, Geoff	St.L., S.J.	2	8	1	2	1	291	20	0	4.12	....	....	....	....	....	....	....	....		1994-95	1995-96
Sauve, Bob	Buf., Det., Chi., N.J.	13	420	182	154	54	23711	1377	8	3.48	34	15	16	....	1850	95	4	3.08		1976-77	1988-89
• Sawchuk, Terry	Det., Bos., Tor., L.A., NYR	21	971	447	330	172	57194	2389	103	2.51	106	54	48	....	6290	266	12	2.54	4	1949-50	1969-70
• Schaefer, Joe	NYR	2	2	0	2	0	86	8	0	5.58	....	....	....	....	....	....	....	....		1959-60	1960-61
‡ Schafer, Paxton	Bos.	1	3	0	0	0	77	6	0	4.68	....	....	....	....	....	....	....	....		1996-97	1996-97
Scott, Ron	NYR, L.A.	5	28	8	13	4	1450	91	0	3.77	1	0	0	....	32	4	0	7.50		1983-84	1989-90
Sevigny, Richard	Mtl., Que.	9	176	80	54	20	9485	507	5	3.21	4	0	3	....	208	13	0	3.75	1	1978-79	1986-87
Sharples, Scott	Cgy.	1	1	0	0	1	65	4	0	3.69	....	....	....	....	....	....	....	....		1991-92	1991-92
§ • Shields, Al			2	0	0	0	41	9	0	13.17	....	....	....	....	....	....	....	....			
Sidorkiewicz, Peter	Hfd., Ott., N.J.	8	246	79	128	27	13884	832	8	3.60	15	5	10	....	912	55	0	3.62		1987-88	1997-98
Simmons, Don	Bos., Tor., NYR	11	248	101	100	41	14495	698	20	2.89	24	13	11	....	1436	62	3	2.59	3	1956-57	1968-69
Simmons, Gary	Cal., Cle., L.A.	4	107	30	57	15	6162	366	5	3.56	1	0	0	....	20	1	0	3.00		1974-75	1977-78
Skidmore, Paul	St.L.	1	2	1	1	0	120	6	0	3.00	....	....	....	....	....	....	....	....		1981-82	1981-82
Skorodenski, Warren	Chi., Edm.	5	35	12	11	4	1732	100	2	3.46	2	0	0	....	33	6	0	10.91		1981-82	1987-88
Smith, Al	Tor., Pit., Det., Buf., Hfd., Col.	10	233	74	99	36	12752	735	10	3.46	6	1	4	....	317	21	0	3.97		1965-66	1980-81
Smith, Billy	L.A., NYI	18	680	305	233	105	38431	2031	22	3.17	132	88	36	....	7645	348	5	2.73	4	1971-72	1988-89
Smith, Gary	Tor., Oak., Cal., Chi., Van.,																				
Min., Wsh., Wpg.	14	532	173	261	7429619			1675	26	3.39	20	5	13	....	1153	62	1	3.23	1965-66		
1979-80																					
• Smith, Normie	Mtl.M., Det.	8	199	81	83	35	12357	479	17	2.33	12	9	2	0	820	18	3	1.32	2	1931-32	1944-45
Sneddon, Bob	Cal.	1	5	0	2	0	225	21	0	5.60	....	....	....	....	....	....	....	....		1970-71	1970-71
‡ Soderstrom, Tommy	Phi., NYI	5	156	45	69	19	8189	496	10	3.63	....	....	....	....	....	....	....	....		1992-93	1996-97
Soetaert, Doug	NYR, Wpg., Mtl.	12	284	110	104	42	15583	1030	6	3.97	5	1	2	....	180	14	0	4.67	1	1975-76	1986-87
‡ Soucy, Christian	Chi.	1	1	0	0	0	3	0	0	0.00	....	....	....	....	....	....	....	....		1993-94	1993-94
• Spooner, Red	Pit.	1	1	0	1	0	60	6	0	6.00	....	....	....	....	....	....	....	....		1929-30	1929-30
§ • Spring, Jesse			1	0	0	0	2	0	0	0.00	....	....	....	....	....	....	....	....			
Staniowski, Ed	St.L., Wpg., Hfd.	10	219	67	104	21	12075	818	2	4.06	8	1	6	....	428	28	0	3.93		1975-76	1984-85
§ • Starr, Harold			1	0	0	0	3	0	0	0.00	....	....	....	....	....	....	....	....			
Stauber, Robb	L.A., Buf.	4	62	21	23	9	3295	209	1	3.81	4	3	1	....	240	16	0	4.00		1989-90	1994-95
Stefan, Greg	Det.	9	299	115	127	30	16333	1068	5	3.92	30	12	17	....	1681	99	1	3.53		1981-82	1989-90
Stein, Phil	Tor.	1	1	0	0	1	70	2	0	1.71	....	....	....	....	....	....	....	....		1939-40	1939-40
Stephenson, Wayne	St.L., Phi., Wsh.	10	328	146	103	49	18343	937	14	3.06	26	11	12	....	1522	79	2	3.11	1	1971-72	1980-81
Stevenson, Doug	Chi., NYR	3	8	2	6	0	480	39	0	4.88	....	....	....	....	....	....	....	....		1942-43	1945-46
Stewart, Charles	Bos.	3	77	30	41	5	4742	194	10	2.45	....	....	....	....	....	....	....	....		1924-25	1926-27
Stewart, Jim	Bos.	1	1	0	1	0	20	5	0	15.00	....	....	....	....	....	....	....	....		1979-80	1979-80
• Stuart, Herb	Det.	1	3	1	2	0	180	5	0	1.67	....	....	....	....	....	....	....	....		1926-27	1926-27
Sylvestri, Don	Bos.	1	3	0	0	2	102	6	0	3.53	....	....	....	....	....	....	....	....		1984-85	1984-85
Takko, Kari	Min., Edm.	6	142	37	71	14	7317	475	1	3.90	4	0	1	....	109	7	0	3.85		1985-86	1990-91
Tanner, John	Que.	3	21	2	11	5	1084	65	1	3.60	....	....	....	....	....	....	....	....		1989-90	1991-92
Tataryn, Dave	NYR	1	2	1	1	0	80	10	0	7.50	....	....	....	....	....	....	....	....		1976-77	1976-77
Taylor, Bobby	Phi., Pit.	5	46	15	17	6	2268	155	0	4.10	....	....	....	....	....	....	....	....	1	1971-72	1975-76
• Teno, Harvey	Det.	1	5	2	3	0	300	15	0	3.00	....	....	....	....	....	....	....	....		1938-39	1938-39
Thomas, Wayne	Mtl., Tor., NYR	9	243	103	93	34	13768	766	10	3.34	15	6	8	....	849	50	1	3.53		1972-73	1980-81
• Thompson, Tiny	Bos., Det.	12	553	284	194	75	34175	1183	81	2.08	44	20	24	0	2974	93	7	1.88	1	1928-29	1939-40
§ Toppazzini, Jerry			1	0	0	0	1	0	0	0.00	....	....	....	....	....	....	....	....			
‡ Torchia, Mike	Dal.	1	6	3	2	1	327	18	0	3.30	....	....	....	....	....	....	....	....		1994-95	1994-95
Tremblay, Vincent	Tor., Pit.	5	58	12	26	8	2785	223	1	4.80	....	....	....	....	....	....	....	....		1979-80	1983-84
Tucker, Ted	Cal.	1	5	1	1	1	177	10	0	3.39	....	....	....	....	....	....	....	....		1973-74	1973-74
• Turner, Joe	Det.	1	1	0	0	1	70	3	0	2.57	....	....	....	....	....	....	....	....		1941-42	1941-42
Vachon, Rogie	Mtl., L.A., Det., Bos.	16	795	355	291	127	46298	2310	51	2.99	48	23	23	....	2876	133	2	2.77	3	1966-67	1981-82
Veisor, Mike	Chi., Hfd., Wpg.	10	139	41	62	26	7806	532	5	4.09	4	0	2	....	180	15	0	5.00		1973-74	1983-84
• Vezina, Georges	Mtl.C.	9	190	103	81	5	11592	633	13	3.28	13	9	4	1	780	36	2	2.77	1	1917-18	1925-26
Villemure, Gilles	NYR, Chi.	10	205	100	64	29	11581	542	13	2.81	14	5	5	....	656	32	0	2.93		1963-64	1976-77
Wakaluk, Darcy	Buf., Min., Dal., Phx.	8	191	67	75	21	9756	524	9	3.22	8	4	2	....	364	18	0	2.97		1988-89	1996-97
Wakely, Ernie	Mtl., St.L.	5	113	41	42	17	6244	290	8	2.79	10	2	6	....	509	37	1	4.36		1962-63	1971-72
• Walsh, Flat	Mtl.M., NYA	7	108	48	43	16	6641	256	12	2.31	8	2	4	2	570	16	2	1.68		1926-27	1932-33
Wamsley, Rick	Mtl., St.L., Cgy., Tor.	13	407	204	131	46	23123	1287	12	3.34	27	7	18	....	1397	81	0	3.48	1	1980-81	1992-93
Watt, Jim	St.L.	1	1	0	0	0	20	2	0	6.00	....	....	....	....	....	....	....	....		1973-74	1973-74
Weeks, Steve	NYR, Hfd., Van., NYI, L.A., Ott.	13	290	111	119	33	15879	989	5	3.74	12	3	5	....	486	27	0	3.33		1980-81	1992-93
Wetzel, Carl	Det., Min.	2	7	1	3	1	301	22	0	4.39	....	....	....	....	....	....	....	....		1964-65	1967-68
‡ Wilkinson, Derek	T.B.	4	22	3	12	3	933	57	0	3.67	....	....	....	....	....	....	....	....		1995-96	1998-99
Willis, Jordan	Dal.	1	1	0	1	0	19	1	0	3.16	....	....	....	....	....	....	....	....		1995-96	1995-96
Wilson, Dunc	Phi., Van., Tor., NYR, Pit.	10	287	80	150	33	15851	988	8	3.74	....	....	....	....	....	....	....	....		1969-70	1978-79
Wilson, Lefty	Det., Tor., Bos.	3	3	0	0	1	81	1	0	0.74	....	....	....	....	....	....	....	....		1953-54	1957-58
• Winkler, Hal	NYR, Bos.	2	75	35	26	14	4739	126	21	1.60	10	2	3	5	640	18	2	1.69		1926-27	1927-28
Wolfe, Bernie	Wsh.	4	120	20	61	21	6104	424	1	4.17	....	....	....	....	....	....	....	....		1975-76	1978-79
Wood, Alex	NYA	1	1	0	1	0	70	3	0	2.57	....	....	....	....	....	....	....	....		1936-37	1936-37
Worsley, Gump	NYR, Mtl., Min.	21	861	335	352	150	50183	2407	43	2.88	70	40	26	....	4084	189	5	2.78	4	1952-53	1973-74
• Worters, Roy	Pit., NYA, Mtl.C.	12	484	171	229	83	30175	1143	67	2.27	11	3	6	2	690	24	3	2.09		1925-26	1936-37
Worthy, Chris	Oak., Cal.	3	26	5	10	4	1326	98	0	4.43	....	....	....	....	....	....	....	....		1968-69	1970-71
§ • Young, Doug			1	0	0	0	21	1	0	2.86	....	....	....	....	....	....	....	....			
Zanier, Mike	Edm.	1	3	1	1	1	185	12	0	3.89	....	....	....	....	....	....	....	....		1984-85	1984-85

2000-01 NHL Player Transactions

(listed in chronological order)

September, 2000

29 – **NHL Waiver Draft**

Pos.	Player	Claimed By	Claimed From
LW	**Zdeno Ciger**	Minnesota	Nashville
C	**Jason Podollan**	Tampa Bay	Los Angeles
LW	**Andreas Johansson**	NY Rangers	Calgary
LW	**Sylvain Blouin**	Minnesota	Montreal
RW	**Jeff Odgers**	Atlanta	Minnesota

October, 2000

2 – Toronto trades **Alexander Karpovtsev** and a 4th round pick in 2001 (**Vladimir Gusev**) to Chicago for **Bryan McCabe**.

5 – Chicago trades **Michal Grosek** and **Brad Brown** to NY Rangers for future considerations.

29 – Toronto trades **Gerald Diduck** to Dallas for future considerations.

November, 2000

6 – Atlanta trades **Geordie Kinnear** to New Jersey for future considerations.

6 – Chicago trades **Anders Eriksson** to Florida for **Jaroslav Spacek**.

9 – NY Rangers trade **J-F Labbe** to Columbus for **Bert Robertsson**.

14 – NY Islanders trade **Dan Trebil** to Pittsburgh for a 9th round pick in 2001 (**Roman Kukhtinov**).

15 – Boston trades the rights to **Anson Carter**, a 2nd round pick in 2001 (**Doug Lynch**) and conditional pick in 2003 to Edmonton for **Bill Guerin**. Edmonton also has the option to exchange 1st round picks in 2001 or 2002 (Edmonton exercised this option in 2001 and selected **Ales Hemsky**. Boston selected **Shaone Morrisonn**).

18 – Boston trades **Sami Pahlsson** to Anaheim for **Patrick Traverse** and **Andrei Nazarov**.

29 – Washington trades **Mike Peluso** and future considerations to St. Louis for **Derek Bekar** and future considerations.

December, 2000

5 – Boston trades **Sean Pronger** to NY Islanders for future considerations.

7 – Philadelphia trades **Gino Odjick** to Montreal for **P.J. Stock** and Montreal's 6th round pick in 2001 (**Denis Seidenberg**).

11 – Toronto trades **Dmitri Khristich** to Washington for Tampa Bay's 3rd round pick in 2001 (previously acquired, **Brendan Bell**).

17 – Florida trades **Eric Boguniecki** to St. Louis for **Andrei Podkonicky**.

18 – Montreal trades **Sergei Zholtok** to Edmonton for **Chad Kilger**.

28 – NY Islanders trade **Mike Stapleton** to Vancouver for a 9th round pick in 2001 (later traded).

28 – Colorado trades Alexei Gusarov to NY Rangers for a 5th round pick in 2001 (**Frantisek Skaladny**).

28 – Pittsburgh trades **Dan Trebil** to St. Louis for **Marc Bergevin**.

28 – Detroit trades **Yan Golubovsky** to Florida for **Igor Larionov**.

January, 2001

3 – Los Angeles trades **Jason Blake** to NY Islanders for a conditional pick in 2002.

4 – Tampa Bay trades **Steve Martins** to NY Islanders for future considerations.

11 – Washington trades **Craig Berube** to NY Islanders for Vancouver's 9th round pick in 2001 (previously acquired, **Robert Muller**).

12 – Nashville trades **Rory Fitzpatrick** to Edmonton for future considerations.

13 – Minnesota trades **Steve McKenna** to Pittsburgh for **Roman Simicek**.

14 – Pittsburgh trades **John Slaney** to Philadelphia for **Kevin Stevens**.

14 – Columbus trades **Krzysztof Oliwa** to Pittsburgh for a 6th round pick in 2001 (**Artem Vostrikov**).

14 – Pittsburgh trades **Jiri Slegr** to Atlanta for San Jose's 3rd round pick in 2001 (previously acquired and later traded).

20 – Ottawa trades **Vaclav Prospal** to Florida for an optional pick in 2002.

23 – Tampa Bay trades **Bryan Muir** to Colorado for an 8th round pick in 2001 (**Dmitri Bezrukov**).

February, 2001

1 – Pittsburgh trades **Matthew Barnaby** to Tampa Bay for **Wayne Primeau**.

1 – Nashville trades **Brantt Myhres** to Washington for future considerations.

5 – NY Rangers trade **John MacLean** to Dallas for future considerations.

7 – Tampa Bay trades **Dan Cloutier** to Vancouver for **Adrian Aucoin** and Vancouver's 2nd round pick in 2001 (**Alexander Polushkin**).

9 – Anaheim trades **Ladislav Kohn** to Atlanta for **Scott Langkow** and **Sergei Vyshedkevich**.

9 – Florida trades **Scott Mellanby** to St. Louis for the rights to **David Morisset** and a conditional pick.

13 – Boston trades the rights to **Matt Zultek** to Philadelphia for Philadelphia's 9th round pick in 2001 (**Marcel Rodman**).

15 – Vancouver trades **Felix Potvin** to Los Angeles for a conditional pick in 2002.

16 – NY Islanders trade **Wade Flaherty** to Tampa Bay for a conditional pick in 2002.

20 – Toronto trades **Konstantin Kalmikov** to Tampa Bay for **Maxim Galanov**.

21 – Montreal trades **Eric Weinrich** to Boston for **Patrick Traverse**.

21 – Los Angeles trades **Rob Blake** and **Steve Reinprecht** to Colorado for **Adam Deadmarsh**, **Aaron Miller**, Colorado's 1st round pick in 2001 (**David Steckel**) and a conditional pick. In addition, Los Angeles has the choice of selecting one player from a list of Colorado prospects. Los Angeles selected **Jared Aulin**.

23 – Los Angeles trades **Bob Corkum** to New Jersey for future considerations (**Steve Kelly**, February 27).

27 – New Jersey trades **Steve Kelly** to Los Angeles to complete **Bob Corkum** transaction (February 23).

28 – Los Angeles trades **Steve Passmore** to Chicago for an 8th round pick in 2001 (**Mike Gabinet**).

March, 2001

1 – NY Rangers trade **Eric Lacroix** to Ottawa for **Colin Forbes**.

1 – Minnesota trades **Scott Pellerin** to Carolina for **Askhat Rakhmatullin**, a 3rd round pick in 2001 (later traded) and a conditional pick in 2002.

3 – Florida trades **Brent Thompson** to Colorado for **future considerations**.

3 – Washington trades **Remi Royer** to Florida for **David Emma**.

4 – Minnesota trades **Sean O'Donnell** to New Jersey for **Willie Mitchell** and a conditional pick in 2002.

5 – NY Rangers trade **Alexei Gusarov** to St. Louis for **Peter Smrek**.

5 – Anaheim trades **Teemu Selanne** to San Jose for **Jeff Friesen**, **Steve Shields** and a conditional pick in 2003.

5 – Phoenix trades **Stanislav Neckar** and the rights to **Nikolai Khabibulin** to Tampa Bay for **Paul Mara**, **Mike Johnson**, **Ruslan Zainullin** and NY Islanders' 2nd round pick in 2001 (previously acquired, **Matthew Spiller**).

6 – Calgary trades **Bill Lindsay** to San Jose for Minnesota's 8th round pick in 2001 (previously acquired, **Joe Campbell**).

7 – Nashville trades **Ryan Tobler** to NY Rangers for **Bert Robertsson**.

9 – Nashville trades **Drake Berehowsky** to Vancouver for Atlanta's 2nd round pick in 2001 (previously acquired, **Timofei Shishkanov**).

12 – NY Islanders trade **John Vanbiesbrouck** to New Jersey for **Chris Terreri** and a 9th round pick in 2001 (**Juha-Pekka Ketola**).

12 – San Jose trades **Johan Hedberg** and **Bobby Dollas** to Pittsburgh for **Jeff Norton**.

13 – Anaheim trades **Jason Marshall** to Washington for **Alexei Tezikov** and Edmonton's 4th round pick in 2001 (previously acquired, **Brandon Rogers**).

13 – Atlanta trades **Donald Audette** to Buffalo for the rights to **Kamil Piros** and Buffalo's 4th round pick in 2001 (later traded).

13 – Calgary trades **Cory Stillman** to St. Louis for **Craig Conroy** and St. Louis' 7th round pick in 2001 (**David Moss**).

13 – Chicago trades **Dean McAmmond** to Philadelphia for Philadelphia's 3rd round pick in 2001 (later traded).

13 – Columbus trades **Frantisek Kucera** to Pittsburgh for Pittsburgh's 6th round pick in 2001 (**Artem Vostrikov**).

13 – Columbus trades **Kevyn Adams** and a 4th round pick in 2001 (**Michael Woodford**) to Florida for **Ray Whitney**.

13 – Columbus trades **Steve Heinze** to Buffalo for Buffalo's 3rd round pick in 2001 (**Per Mars**).

13 – Edmonton trades **Dan LaCouture** to Pittsburgh for **Sven Butenschon**.

13 – Florida trades **Todd Simpson** to Phoenix for a 2nd round pick in 2001 (later traded).

13 – Florida trades **Mike Sillinger** to Ottawa for the return of a conditional pick in 2002. The pick had been acquired from Florida in a previous transaction.

13 – Los Angeles trades **Aki Berg** to Toronto for **Adam Mair** and Toronto's 2nd round pick in 2001 (**Mike Cammalleri**).

13 – Minnesota trades **Curtis Leschyshyn** to Ottawa for Ottawa's 3rd round pick in 2001 (**Stephane Veilleux**) and a conditional pick in 2002.

13 – Washington trades **Richard Zednik**, **Jan Bulis** and Washington's 1st round pick in 2001 (**Alexander Perezhogin**) to Montreal for **Trevor Linden**, **Dainius Zubrus** and New Jersey's 2nd round pick in 2001 (previously acquired and later traded).

13 – Ottawa trades **John Emmons** to Tampa Bay for **Craig Millar**.

13 – Philadelphia trades **Dean Melanson** to Washington for **Matthew Herr**.

13 – Phoenix trades **Keith Tkachuk** to St. Louis for **Michal Handzus**, **Ladislav Nagy**, the rights to **Jeff Taffe** and a 1st round pick in 2002.

13 – Tampa Bay trades **Grant Ledyard** to Dallas for Dallas' 7th round pick in 2001 (**Jeremy Van Hoof**).

May, 2001

24 – Philadelphia trades **Mikhail Chernov** to Nashville for **Mike Watt**.

31 – Florida trades the rights to **Alexander Auld** to Vancouver for future considerations .

June, 2001

12 – Toronto trades **Danny Markov** to Phoenix for **Travis Green**, **Craig Mills** and the rights to **Robert Reichel.**

15 – Phoenix trades **Joe Juneau** to Montreal for a conditional pick in 2004.

18 – Tampa Bay trades **Todd Warriner** to Phoenix for **Juha Ylonen**.

19 – Phoenix trades **Keith Carney** to Anaheim for Calgary's 2nd round pick in 2001 (previously acquired and later traded).

22 – Phoenix trades the rights to **Mikael Renberg** to Toronto for **Sergei Berezin**.

22 – NY Islanders trade **Mathieu Biron** and their 2nd round pick in 2002 to Tampa Bay for **Alexander Kharitonov and** the rights to **Adrian Aucoin**.

23 – Ottawa trades **Alexei Yashin** to NY Islanders for the Islanders' 1st round pick in 2001 (**Jason Spezza**), **Zdeno Chara** and **Bill Muckalt**.

23 – Toronto trades **Igor Korolev** to Chicago for Philadelphia's 3rd round pick in 2001 (previously acquired, **Nicholas Corbeil**).

23 – Montreal trades a 4th round pick in 2001 (**Brent MacLellan**) to Chicago for **Stephane Quintal**.

23 – Calgary trades a 1st round pick in 2001 (**Fredrik Sjostrom**) to Phoenix for a 1st round pick (**Chuck Kobasew**) and a return of Calgary's 2nd round pick in 2001 (previously acquired, **Andrei Taratukhin**).

23 – Florida trades the rights to **Jiri Dopita** to Philadelphia for Philadelphia's 2nd round pick in 2001 (later traded).

23 – Philadelphia trades a 1st round pick in 2001 (**Tim Gleason**) to Ottawa for a 1st round pick (**Jeff Woywitka**) and 7th round pick (**David Printz**) in 2001 and Tampa Bay's 2nd round pick in 2002 (previously acquired).

23 – New Jersey trades St. Louis' 1st round pick in 2001 (previously acquired, **Lukas Krajicek**) to Florida for Phoenix's 2nd round pick in 2001 (previously acquired, **Igor Prohanka**) and Vancouver's 2nd round compensatory pick in 2001 (previously acquired, **Thomas Pihlman**).

23 – Calgary trades **Valeri Bure** and **Jason Wiemer** to Florida in exchange for **Rob Niedermayer** and Philadelphia's 2nd round pick in 2001 (previously acquired, **Andrei Medvedev**).

23 – Calgary trades **Fred Brathwaite**, **Daniel Tkaczuk**, **Sergei Varlamov** and a 9th round pick in 2001 (**Grant Jacobsen**) to St. Louis in exchange for Roman Turek and a 4th round pick in 2001 (**Yegor Shastin**).

23 – Ottawa trades a 2nd round pick in 2001 (**Victor Uchevatov**) to New Jersey for a 3rd round compensatory pick in 2001 (**Neil Komadoski**) and a 3rd round pick in 2001 (later traded).

23 – Washington trades New Jersey's 2nd round pick in 2001 (previously acquired, **Andreas Holmqvist**) to Tampa Bay in exchange for NY Islanders 2nd round pick in 2002 (previously acquired).

23 – NY Islanders trades a 3rd round pick in 2001 (**Tomas Malec**) to Florida in exchange for a 4th round pick in 2001 (**Cory Stillman**) and a 3rd round pick in 2002.

23 – Minnesota trades Carolina's 3rd round pick (previously acquired, **Garth Murray**) and a 5th round pick in 2001 (**Shawn Collymore**) to the NY Rangers in exchange for a 3rd round pick in 2001 (**Chris Heid**).

23 – New Jersey returns Phoenix's 3rd round pick in 2001 (previously acquired, **Beat Forster**) in exchange for Phoenix's 4th round pick in 2001 (later traded) and a 3rd round pick in 2002.

23 – Phoenix trades **Jyrki Lumme** to Dallas in exchange for **Tyler Bouck**.

23 – Ottawa trades New Jersey's 3rd round pick in 2001 (previously acquired, **Evgeni Artukhin**) to Tampa Bay in exchange for a 4th round pick (**Ray Emery**) and Buffalo's 7th round pick (previously acquired, **Jan Platil**) in 2001.

23 – Calgary trades **Chris St. Croix** to NY Rangers for **Burke Henry**.

24 – Atlanta trades an 8th round pick in 2001 (**Leonid Zhvachin**) to the NY Rangers for **Jeff Dessner**.

24 – New Jersey trades Phoenix's 4th round pick in 2001 (previously acquired, **Milan Gajic**) and a 7th round pick in 2002 to Atlanta for Atlanta's 3rd round pick in 2002.

24 – Philadelphia trades NY Islanders' 4th round pick in 2001 (previously acquired, **Jordin Tootoo**) to Nashville for Nashville's picks in the 4th round (later traded), 5th round (**Jussi Timonen**) and 7th round (**Thierry Douville**) in 2001.

24 – Chicago trades a 4th round pick in 2001 (**Christian Ehrhoff**) to San Jose for San Jose's picks in the 4th round (**Aleksey Zotkin**), 6th round (**Petr Puncochar**) and 7th round (**Oleg Minakov**) in 2001.

24 – Calgary trades the rights to **Paul Manning** to Columbus for Buffalo's 5th round pick in 2001 (previously acquired, later traded).

24 – Philadelphia trades Nashville's 4th round pick in 2001 (previously acquired, **Rob Zepp**) to Carolina for Carolina's 3rd round pick in 2002.
24 – Dallas trades **Richard Jackman** to Boston for **Cameron Mann**.
24 – Philadelphia trades picks in the 4th round (**Aaron Lobb**), 5th round (compensatory, **Paul Lynch**) and 7th round (**Dennis Packard**) in 2001 to Tampa Bay for Tampa Bay's 3rd round pick in 2002.
24 – Atlanta trades Buffalo's 4th round pick in 2001 (previously acquired, **Igor Valeyev**) to St. Louis for **Lubos Bartecko**.
24 – Carolina trades a 5th round pick (**Mikko Viitanen**) in 2001 to Colorado for **Chris Dingman**.
24 – San Jose trades a picks in the 5th round (**Michal Vondrka**), 8th round (compensatory, **Calle Aslund**) and 9th round (**Ryan Jorde**) in 2001 to Buffalo for Montreal's 5th round pick in 2001 (previously acquired, **Tomas Plihal**).
24 – Tampa Bay trades Toronto's 5th round pick in 2001 (previously acquired, **Terry Denike**) to Los Angeles for Los Angeles' 6th round pick (later traded) and Buffalo's 6th round pick (previously acquired, **Art Femenella**) in 2001.
24 – Detroit trades a 5th round pick (**Yuri Trubachev**) and 7th round pick (later traded) in 2001 to Calgary for Buffalo's 5th round pick in 2001 (previously acquired, **Andreas Jamtin**).
24 – Tampa Bay trades Los Angeles' 6th round pick in 2001 (previously acquired, **Scott Horvath**) to Colorado for **Nolan Pratt**.
24 – Montreal trades an 8th round pick in 2001 (**Neil Petruic**) to Ottawa for **Andreas Dackell**.
24 – Philadelphia trades **Dean McAmmond** to Calgary for Calgary's 4th round pick in 2002.
24 – Calgary trades Detroit's 7th round pick in 2001(previously acquired, **Pontus Petterstrom**) to NY Rangers for NY Rangers' 7th round pick in 2002.
24 – Philadelphia trades an 8th round pick in 2001 (**Jean-Francois Soucy**) and a 9th round pick in 2002 to Tampa Bay for Tampa Bay's 7th round pick in 2002.
24 – Colorado trades a 9th round pick in 2001 (**Henrik Bergfors**) to Tampa Bay for Tampa Bay's 9th round pick in 2002.
24 – Buffalo trades the rights to **Michael Peca** to NY Islanders for **Tim Connolly** and **Taylor Pyatt**.
28 – NY Rangers trade **Jason Doig** and **Jeff Ulmer** to Ottawa for **Sean Gagnon** and a conditional pick in 2002.
29 – Edmonton trades **Sergei Zholtok** to Minnesota for a conditional pick in 2002.
29 – Florida trades **Dave Duerden** to NY Rangers for future considerations.
29 – NY Rangers trade **Rich Pilon** to San Jose for a conditional pick in 2002.
30 – NY Rangers trade **Tim Taylor** to Tampa Bay for **Kyle Freadrich** and **Nisse Ekman**.

July, 2001

1 – Buffalo trades **Dominik Hasek** to Detroit for **Vyacheslav Kozlov**, Detroit's 1st round pick in 2002 and a conditional pick in 2003.
1 – Edmonton trades **Doug Weight** and **Michel Riesen** to St. Louis for **Jochen Hecht**, **Marty Reasoner** and **Jan Horacek**.
2 – Philadelphia trades **Daymond Langkow** to Phoenix for optional picks in 2002 or 2003.
2 – Atlanta trades **Denny Lambert** and a 9th round pick in 2002 to Anaheim for an 8th round pick in 2002.
9 – Detroit trades **Aaron Ward** to Carolina for a 2nd round pick in 2002 or 2003.
10 – Tampa Bay trades **Ryan Johnson** and a 6th round pick in 2003 to Florida for **Vaclav Prospal**.
11 – Pittsburgh trades **Jaromir Jagr** and **Frantisek Kucera** to Washington for **Kris Beech**, **Ross Lupaschuk** and **Michal Sivek**.
31 – Philadelphia trades **Andy Delmore** to Nashville for a 3rd round pick in 2002.

August, 2001

20 – Philadelphia trades the rights to **Eric Lindros** and a conditional 1st round pick in 2003 to NY Rangers for **Pavel Brendl**, **Jan Hlavac**, **Kim Johnsson** and a 3rd round pick in 2003.

Trades and free agent signings that occurred after August 20, 2001 are listed on page 274.

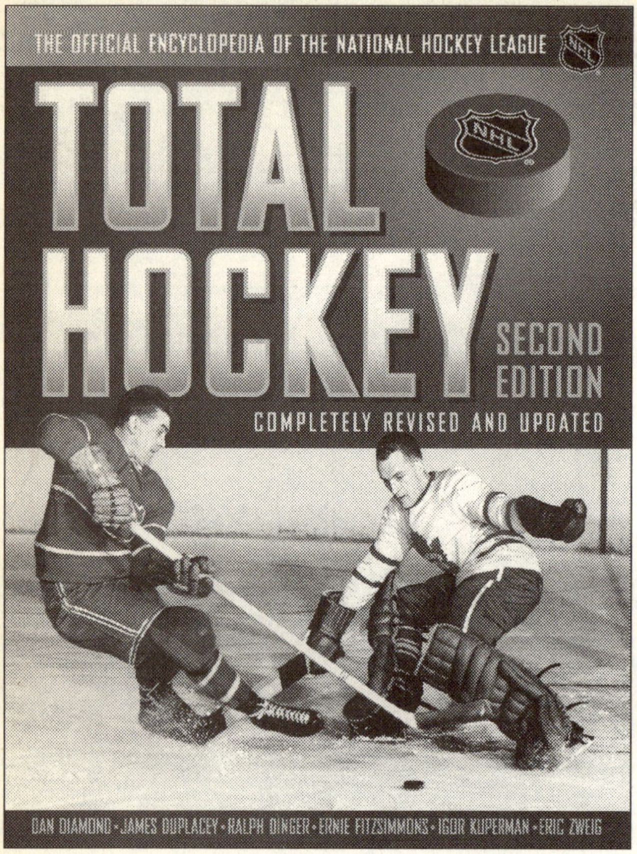
THE OFFICIAL ENCYCLOPEDIA OF THE NATIONAL HOCKEY LEAGUE
NHL
TOTAL HOCKEY
SECOND EDITION
COMPLETELY REVISED AND UPDATED
DAN DIAMOND • JAMES DUPLACEY • RALPH DINGER • ERNIE FITZSIMMONS • IGOR KUPERMAN • ERIC ZWEIG